American Places
DICTIONARY

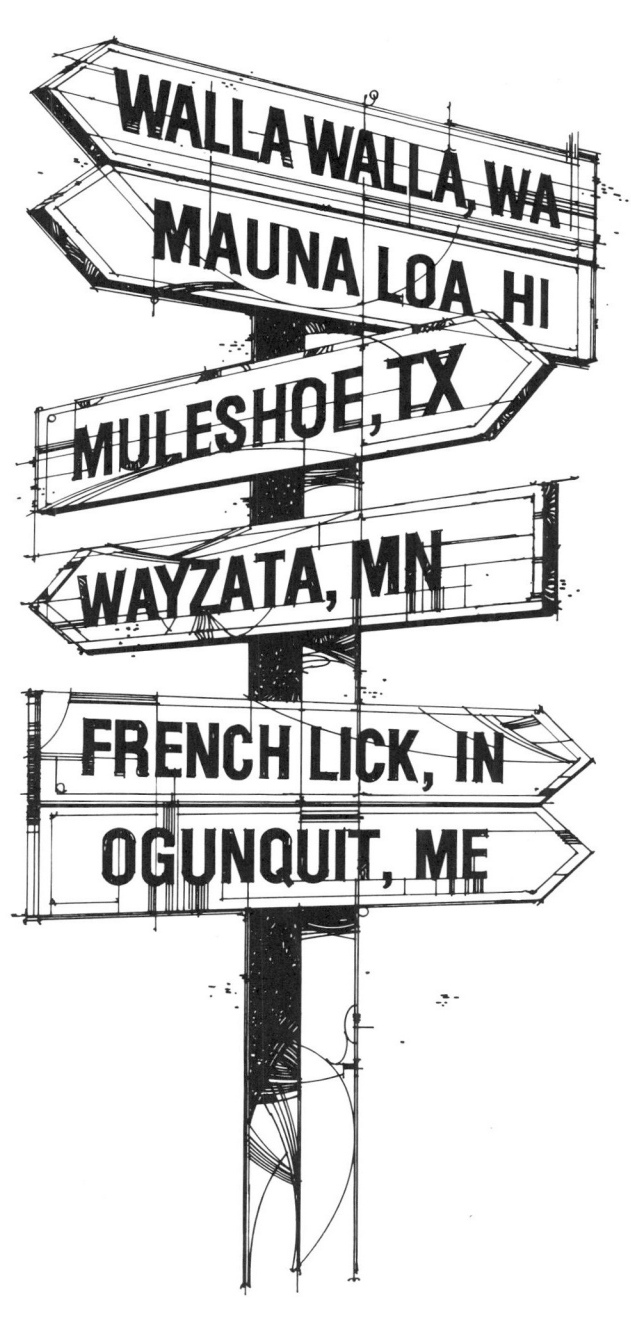

American Places Dictionary

A Guide to 45,000 Populated Places, Natural Features, and Other Places in the United States

Covering States, Counties, Cities, Towns, Townships, Villages, and Boroughs, as well as Indian Reservations, Military Bases, and Major Geographical Features, the Entries Providing Description, Precise Location, and Name Origin Information, and Supplemented by Maps & Indexes

in Four Volumes

Volume Four: West, Appendix, and Index

Alaska	Kansas	Oregon
Arizona	Montana	South Dakota
California	Nebraska	Utah
Colorado	Nevada	Washington
Hawaii	New Mexico	Wyoming
Idaho	North Dakota	

Appendix A: American Indian Reservations
Appendix B: Major U.S. Military Installations
Appendix C: Major U.S. Geographic Features

Index: Including entries for Volumes One through Four and the Appendices

SAN DIEGO PUBLIC LIBRARY
LA JOLLA BRANCH

Edited by

Frank R. Abate

Omnigraphics, Inc.
Penobscot Building • Detroit, Michigan 48226

Editorial Staff

Frank R. Abate, *Editor*
Jacquelyn S. Goodwin, Katherine M. Isaacs, and Elizabeth J. Jewell, *Associate Editors*
Margaret Mary Missar, *Research*
Terri Finkeldey and Christine Kelley, *Editorial Assistants*

Additional Editorial Services provided by Sachem Publishing Associates, Inc., Guilford, CT
Data Processing and Typesetting: Weimer Graphics, Indianapolis, IN

Omnigraphics, Inc.

Eric Berger, *Vice President, Production*
Laurie Lanzen Harris, *Editorial Director*
Peter E. Ruffner, *Vice President, Administration*
James A. Sellgren, *Vice President, Operations & Finance*

Frederick G. Ruffner, Jr., *Publisher*

Copyright © 1994 Omnigraphics, Inc.

Library of Congress Cataloging-in-Publication Data

American places dictionary : a guide to 45,000 populated places, natural features, and other places in the United States . . . in four volumes / Frank R. Abate, editor.
    p.   cm.
    Includes indexes.
    Contents: v. 1. Northeast — v. 2. South — v. 3. Midwest — v. 4. West. Appendices & index.
    ISBN 1-55888-747-4 (lib. bdg. : alk. paper : set). — ISBN 1-55888-146-8 (lib. bdg. : alk. paper : v. 1). — ISBN 1-55888-147-6 (lib. bdg. : alk. paper : v. 2). — ISBN 1-55888-148-4 (lib. bdg. : alk. paper : v. 3). — ISBN 1-55888-149-2 (lib. bdg. : alk. paper : v. 4)
    1. United States—Gazetteers.   I. Abate, Frank R.
E154.A48   1994
917.3′003—dc20
                                                      93-12306
                                                         CIP

Grateful acknowledgment is made to Dr. Kelsie Harder for permission to use the name origin information from his book, *Illustrated Dictionary of Place Names: United States and Canada* (copyright © 1974 by Kelsie Harder).

The information in this publication was compiled from sources considered reliable. While every possible effort has been made to ensure reliability, the publisher will not assume liability for damages caused by inaccuracies in the data, and makes no warranty, express or implied, on the accuracy of the information contained herein.

This book is printed on acid-free paper meeting the ANSI Z38.48 Standard. The infinity symbol that appears above indicates that the paper in this book meets that standard.

Printed in the United States of America

Contents

Volume Four: West

Foreword vii

Introduction & How to Use This Book xv
    Organization of Entries by County xv
    Coverage xvi
    Contents of the Four Volumes xviii
    Entry Presentation and Information in *APD* xix
    Name Origin Information xxii
    Hierarchy of Government in the United States xxv

Editor's Miscellany:
    American Places and American Names—Curiosities and Peculiarities xxxiii

Bibliography xli

American Places Dictionary-West:
    Alaska 3
    Arizona 31
    California 51
    Colorado 125
    Hawaii 167
    Idaho 181
    Kansas 209
    Montana 339
    Nebraska 369
    Nevada 449
    New Mexico 461
    North Dakota 487
    Oregon 583
    South Dakota 617
    Utah 703
    Washington 729
    Wyoming 767

American Places Dictionary-Appendices:
    Appendix A: Indian Reservations 785
    Appendix B: Major U.S. Military Installations 815
    Appendix C: Major U.S. Geographic Features 831

Index:
    Entries from Volumes One through Four and Appendices 901

(Statewide Index at the end of each state section)

Foreword:

Patterns and Practices in the Naming of American Places

Place names in the United States reflect the attitudes, ambitions, and desires of the namers, who themselves were uprooted from their homes in other countries or from their former homes in eastern states as they moved westward across the North American continent. That they found the land occupied already is also reflected in the Amerindian-derived names (names used by Native Americans) that dot the landscape. The southwestern areas—Texas, New Mexico, Arizona, and California—were settled by Spaniards, who also assigned names as did their English-speaking counterparts who were moving west. Primarily, however, the names now existing came from European languages, the namers being of European descent who sought new living conditions, more freedom, and more space to live out their dreams. From their point of view, they had a new land to settle and, hence, names to give. George R. Stewart, in his *Names on the Land,* wrote that "the names lay thickly over the land, and the Americans spoke them, great and little, easily and carelessly—Virginia, Susquehanna, Rio Grande, Deadman Creek, Sugarloaf Hill, Detroit, Wall Street—not thinking how they came to be."

And they did come to be. A good instance of the way naming occurred comes from the story of how **Hope**, county seat of Hempstead County, Arkansas, received its name. The name also is indicative of how names somehow interact historically, alluding to other names and other places. Hope appears to be an abstract name, symbolizing the thoughts of desire and expectation, placing faith in the future, all in all a good name. Established in 1874, the Arkansas city of Hope was named not necessarily in allegorical anticipation but for Hope Loughborough, daughter of James Loughborough, a director of the Cairo and Fulton Railroad. This is simple enough and a standard naming method, that of giving to a place the name of a loved one, such as a wife, daughter, sometimes a son, and many such names exist in the United States. But the former county seat of Hempstead County, **Washington**, named for George Washington, was called the "birthplace of Texas," because Stephen F. Austin resided there and held court before he went to Texas. James Bowie also lived in Washington, Arkansas, before he, too, went to Texas. Before leaving Bowie engaged a certain James Black to craft a special knife for him.

The citizens of Washington, however, would not cooperate with the railway officials, who took their revenge by building Hope and bypassing Washington. Hope became the county seat and the boyhood home of U.S. President Bill Clinton, while Washington became another hamlet. Intertwined here, with many meaningful connotations, are names that have become important for places. Hope is second only to **Union** as the abstract name most often used in the United States. **Austin** became the name for the capital of Texas and a county. Bowie went to his destiny at the Alamo, as well as being remembered for his Bowie knife and also by a county name in Texas.

Sometimes the bizarre occurs. **California**, the county seat of Moniteau County, Missouri, was to be established in 1834 as **Boonesborough**, for Daniel Boone, the frontiersman. But another **Boonesborough** existed in Missouri, so the name was not approved by postal officials, who often forced the alteration or wholesale change of place names before they could be made official. A man happened along who offered a jug of whiskey if the people would name the town for him. The offer was accepted. His name was California Wilson. An extreme case, no doubt, but indeed many honorific names were bestowed by town officials in recognition of the owner or purveyor of the land on which the town was first platted. **Lovewell**, Kansas, for instance, was named for Thomas Lovewell, who gave land for the railroad, a church, and a school. **Chardon**, Ohio, was named for Peter Chardon Brooks, who donated the site. Thomas Bell granted the land that became **Bellville**, Texas. **Phil Campbell**, Alabama, was named for the man who built a depot and railroad spur to the town in exchange for its being given his name.

Occasionally, town leaders will name the place for a wealthy person in hope of obtaining favors (money included). For instance, **Vanderbilt**, Tennessee, was named for Cornelius Vanderbilt, in the hope that this would persuade him and his family to live there during summer months. Vanderbilt chose Asheville, North Carolina, for that purpose, whereupon **Vanderbilt**, Tennessee, changed its name to **Ervin**, honoring Dr. J. N. Ervin, who had donated land for the courthouse. All along, the post office had been called **Erwin**, for Jesse B. Erwin, the first county-court clerk. When the town was incorporated, **Erwin** was made official, the excuse being that it was close enough to **Ervin**.

A close examination of the names in *American Places Dictionary* will reveal many patterns. It will also reveal psychological aspects of the minds of the namers and give insight into the character of the historical period in which the patterns occur. In the colonial years, from the time settlers began to arrive from Europe in the 17th century to the end of the Revolutionary War in 1783, place names indicated three distinct patterns: descriptive, those based on English royalty, and English transfer names. Also, a few religious names appeared (**Bethel**, **Canaan**, **Providence**), but the three larger patterns dominated.

The descriptive names always reflect the point of view of the namer, for what is now **Trout Brook** could just as easily have been **Birch Brook**. Descriptive names were attached especially to features, seldom to habitation places, unless a community developed around a feature, usually a spring or other watercourse, such as **Big Spring** and **Deep River**. The descriptive names were merely identifiers, serving the purpose of immediacy; some were actually translated from an Amerindian name.

English royalty names contributed many of the major names in the original colonies: **New York** (state and city) and **Albany** for James, Duke of York and Albany, later King James II of England; **Brunswick**, for one of the titles of the British royal house of Hanover; **Buckingham**, in reference to the title of George Villiers and later of his son; **Elizabeth** (New Jersey) for the wife of Sir George Carteret; **Cape Ann** (Massachusetts) for the wife of James I; **Annapolis** (Maryland) and **Anne Arundel County** (Virginia) for Anne Arundell, daughter of Lord Thomas Arundell of Wardour and wife of Cecilius Calvert, Lord Baltimore; **North Carolina**, **South Carolina**, **Cape Charles** (Virginia), **Charles River** (Massachusetts), **Charles City** (Virginia), and **Charles City County** (Virginia), for Charles I; **Charleston** and **Charleston County** (South Carolina) are named for Charles II. Such a list could go on for pages.

English county and town names used during these years show both nostalgia for the former homes of colonists and also the desire to perpetuate the names. Among the more well known transfers are **New England**, **Chester** (Connecticut, Massachusetts, Pennsylvania, and throughout the United States; at least forty other municipalities are named **Chester**), **Durham** (Connecticut, New Hampshire, New York, North Carolina, and nine other states), **Winchester** (Connecticut, Massachusetts, New Hampshire, Virginia, and twelve other states), **Kent** (Connecticut, Delaware, Florida, Maryland, New York, Rhode Island, and nine other states), **Norfolk** (Connecticut, Massachusetts, New York, Virginia, and three other states), **Dover** (Delaware, New Hampshire, New Jersey, North Carolina, Pennsylvania, and twenty other states), **New London** (Connecticut, New Hampshire, North Carolina, Pennsylvania, and six other states), **Plymouth** (Connecticut, Massachusetts, New Hampshire, Pennsylvania, Virginia, and seventeen other states), **Cumberland** (Maryland, Pennsylvania, Rhode Island, and seven other states), **Portland** (Connecticut, New York, Pennsylvania, and thirteen other states), **Essex** (Connecticut, Massachusetts, New York, and five other states), and **Bristol** (Connecticut, New York, New Hampshire, Rhode Island, and sixteen other states).

Other English place name transfers are not so well known, but still were quite popular. Examples include **Farmington** (Connecticut, Delaware, New Hampshire, New York, North Carolina, Pennsylvania, and sixteen other states), **Enfield** (Connecticut, New Hampshire, New York, North Carolina, and Illinois), **Glastonbury** (Connecticut), **Newington** (Connecticut, Georgia, and New Hampshire), **Torrington** (Connecticut), **Litchfield** (Connecticut, New York, New Hampshire, and seven other states), **Haddam** (Connecticut), **Killingworth** (from **Kenilworth**; Connecticut), **Guilford** (Connecticut, New York, and nine other states), **Derby** (Connecticut and three other states), and many more. **Brentford** (South Dakota) shows that the practice continued beyond colonial times. In some cases, particularly as Americans moved westward, the names were actually given in honor of the American town the pioneers had left behind, rather than for the original English name.

After the Revolutionary War, places began to be named for war heroes and leaders. This occurred especially in the new states being formed west of the Appalachian Mountains and were influenced strongly by the fervor of patriotism that swept through the former colonies. County names especially reflect this commemorative movement, with the major leaders all being so honored: (George) **Washington** (31 counties), (Benjamin) **Franklin** (23 counties), (Thomas) **Jefferson** (25 counties), (General Nathanael) **Greene** (17 counties), (Alexander) **Hamilton** (eight counties), (German-born French soldier Johann, Baron de Kalb, who fought with the Americans during the war) **DeKalb** (ten counties), (Patrick) **Henry** (ten counties), (James) **Madison** (20 counties), (General Richard) **Montgomery** (16 counties), (General Francis "The Swamp Fox") **Marion** (17 counties), (General Daniel) **Morgan** (9 counties), (Polish soldier Count Casimir, who also fought with the Americans) **Pulaski** (7 counties), (General Israel) **Putnam** (9 counties), and (General "Mad Anthony") **Wayne** (16 counties). The Marquis de **LaFayette**, French statesman and aide to Washington, is commemorated in 17 U.S. counties, and a host of cities and towns, some using only the **Fayette** portion of his name.

Names of other heroes from the American Revolution, now obscure, dot the maps of states: (soldier Anthony) **Bledsoe** (Tennessee), (Kentucky soldier and statesman John) **Adair** (Louisiana, Kentucky, Missouri), (Major General Ethan) **Allen** (Ohio), (soldier and U.S. Senator John) **Armstrong** (Pennsylvania), (soldier Nicholas) **Herkimer** (New York), (Sergeant William) **Jasper** (8 counties), (soldier and U.S. Representative Joseph) **McDowell** (North Carolina), (General Hugh)

Mercer (six counties), (soldier John) **Newton** (Georgia, Indiana), (one of the captors of British spy John Andre, soldier John) **Paulding** (Georgia, Oklahoma), (General Thomas) **Person** (North Carolina), and (soldier and U.S. Representative Andrew) **Pickins** (Alabama, Georgia, South Carolina) are examples.

Signers of the Declaration of Independence were among the most commemorated: (John) **Adams** (eight counties), (Carter) **Braxton** (Virginia), (Charles) **Carroll** (11 counties), (Benjamin) **Franklin** (23 counties), (Button) **Gwinnett** and (Lyman) **Hall** (Georgia), (John) **Hancock** (10 counties), (Benjamin) **Harrison** (West Virginia), (Samuel) **Huntington** (Indiana), (Thomas) **Jefferson** (25 counties), (Richard Henry) **Lee** (Georgia, Illinois), (Thomas) **McKean** (Pennsylvania), (Robert Hunter) **Morris** (New Jersey), (Thomas) **Nelson** (Virginia, Kentucky), (Benjamin) **Rush** (Indiana), (George) **Walton** (Georgia), and (George) **Wythe** (Virginia).

The same was true after the War of 1812, with counties being named for leaders and heroes, including (Andrew) **Jackson** (21 counties); (John) **Coffee** (Alabama, Tennessee); (Stephen F.) **Decatur** (five counties); (Oliver Hazard) **Perry** (10 counties); (Thomas) **McDonough** and (William, who also fought in the Black Hawk War of 1832) **McHenry** (Illinois); (James) **Lawrence** (11 counties); (Alexander) **Macomb** (Michigan); (Virgil) **McCracken,** (James) **Meade,** and (Alney) **McLean** (Kentucky); (William) **Moore** (Tennessee); and (Zebulon) **Pike** (10 counties).

In the so-called Military Tract of upstate New York, as noted by George R. Stewart in *Names on the Land*, many names from Greco-Roman history and culture were given by the state land commissioners. Though they themselves probably were not steeped in the classics, perhaps the influence of a name already assigned, **Seneca Lake** (itself of Amerindian origin, not classical, but converted into a classical name from Mohegan—with a Dutch spelling—**Sinneken**, or **Sinnegar**, or **Sennicky**), started the trend. Along with nearby **Troy, Seneca** seems to have been the catalyst to the naming of 23 townships on classical or literary models: **Lysander, Hannibal, Cato, Camillus, Cicero, Manlius, Marcellus, Aurelius, Romulus, Scipio, Sempronius, Tully, Fabius, Ovid, Homer, Solon, Hector, Ulysses, Virgil,** and **Cincinnatus**. After exhausting their store of classical names, they added the English literary greats, improvising with **Milton, Locke,** and **Dryden**. Once the precedent was set in New York, the custom of using classical or literary names became common and a pattern throughout the United States.

The use of suffixes in places has continued from the time of **Jamestown** to the present: **Elizabethtown, Youngstown,** and **Austintown,** plus the many **-towns** that were shortened to **-ton** (**Charles Town** to **Charleston**). The suffixes **-boro, -burg(h), -ville, -field,** and **-polis** yielded, among hundreds of others, **Hatboro** (Pennsylvania), **Pittsburgh** (Pennsylvania and elsewhere), **Bloomfield** (Illinois and elsewhere), and **Annapolis** (Maryland).

As befits a new country with a strong religious base, biblical names became common between the Revolutionary War and the Civil War, including **Bethel** (possibly the most popular biblical name), **Shiloh, Bethlehem, Corinth, Dothan, Ephrata, Jerusalem, Joseph, Mary, Salem, Zion,** and **Zoar**, along with many names assigned by the Church of Latter-Day Saints in Utah. In parts of the country already settled by Spanish speakers, the names of saints prevailed, many such names having been given by Spanish explorers for the saint's day, or day of naming: **San Luis Obispo, Santa Rosa, San Francisco, San Diego, San Gabriel, San Bernardino, San Juan, San Rafael,** and **Santa Barbara**, as well as many others in the western states. In Florida, **Saint Augustine** survives from the Spanish colonial era there, the oldest continuously inhabited settlement in the United States.

In the middle states and in Louisiana and in areas bordering Quebec in Canada, French names of saints survive, among them **St. Bernard Parish** (Louisiana), **Lake St. Catherine** (Vermont), **St. Croix County** (Wisconsin), **Ste. Genevieve County** (Missouri), and, probably the most famous French-derived name, **St. Lawrence River** (anglicized from **St. Laurent**), given originally to a harbor by explorer Jacques Cartier on the saint's day, August 10, 1535, and then spread to the gulf, the river, and places along the river. But not much direct use of honorific saints' names occurred after the Revolutionary War, except humorously or facetiously. Some that are apparently saint's names actually have a more mundane explanation, such as **St. John** (Kansas) for John Pierce St. John, a prohibitionist; **St. James** (Missouri), probably for Thomas James, founder; and **St. George** (South Carolina), for James George, first settler.

The coming of the railroads in the mid-nineteenth century and the resulting explosion of new settlements dictated the need for many, many names, spread hastily and almost indiscriminately across the United States. The name origins of many of these towns are opaque, forgotten or buried in stored files of long discontinued railway offices. Railway officials, clerks, engineers, even some company presidents were entrusted with the practical necessity of naming stations along a line. Perhaps rough guidelines existed, but generally the namer was left to his or her devices, and these included names of superiors, female friends, male friends, family members, names from back East, foreign names, spelling deviations, back formations, blends, and personal whim. A few examples include **Mitchell** (Indiana), for a chief surveyor; **Conroe** (Texas), for a sawmill owner; **Crete** (Illinois) and **Corfu** (Washington), for the Mediterranean islands; **Creston** (Louisiana), for the highest point along the line; **Cressona** (Pennsylvania), for John Champman Cresson, president of a railroad; and **Depot** (Oregon), when inspiration ends.

After the Civil War **Lincoln** became the most popular name in the United States, commemorating the martyred president, although the giving of this honorific for Abraham Lincoln was far less common in the South. But **Lincoln**, for Benjamin Lincoln, commander of the American forces in the South during the Revolutionary War, does occur in southern states and several southern counties have his name. The continuing popularity of **Lincoln** is such that it still surpasses **Washington** as the name most often given to places needing a name, especially housing developments.

Names commemorating state and local politicians (legislators, state officials, and governors) represent a naming pattern of sizeable proportions. These names perpetuate the memory of the authors of bills, of friends in state legislatures, of those courted for political favors, and of self-aggrandizing legislators. A representative selection includes **Alexander County** (North Carolina), **Allen County** and **Anderson County** (Kansas), **Ashville** (Alabama), **Casey** and **Menard** (Illinois), **Morgan** (Utah), **Rabun** (Georgia), **Miller County** (Missouri), and **Pitkin** (Colorado).

Place names in the twentieth century generally were given by land developers and realtors, who are not apt to follow traditional patterns. Rather, they name to impress potential customers, the name somehow appealing to nostalgia, to Amerindian themes, to prestige, to love of nature, to snobbery, or to what is aesthetically pleasing. The names are self-consciously selected, sometimes invented. Examples of these types of names (typically with British connotations) would include **Cambridge Estates**, **Berkeley Grove**, **Essex Homes**, **Strathmore Village**, and **Brentwood-in-the-**

Pines. Nature names include **Tanglewood**, **Woodland Acres**, **Oak Manor**, **Seaside Shores**, **Sunset Hills**, **Cedar Farms**, and **Beechwood Lawns**. Amerindian names have strong appeal, but not necessarily to the Amerindians. Still, **Connetquot Park, Haccabauk Park, St. Regis Homes**, and **Winnesunk Gardens** indicate that such names have prestige value. Land development names strove to avoid the coarse, vulgar, or deviant; as a result, they have an innocence or blandness about them. This new wave of promotional naming has largely supplanted such older, unprepossessing examples as **Hog Hollow, Skunk Creek, Duck Pond.** Similarly, ethnic names that could possibly intimidate have given way to carefully sanitized ones.

Some influence in assigning place names was wielded by the U.S. Post Office Department, and also by the U.S. Board on Geographic Names, an interdepartmental agency composed of federal government officials. In the latter part of the nineteenth century, postal officials decided that names of places should be short, yielding the likes of **Ink** (Missouri), **Fry** (Texas), **Ono** and **Igo** (California), **Roy** (New Mexico), and **Ely** (Nevada). Some "original" names were changed by postal officials, either because the same name was already in use in the same state or out of bureaucratic propriety. One postal regulation stipulated that for "names consisting of more than one word, it is desirable to combine them into one word," resulting in **Mountpleasant, Boilingsprings, Bigprairie, Bigflat, Beaverdam, Bearcreek, Bonaire, Musselshell, Warmsprings, Plentywood, Forestgrove, Coscob, Glenlyon**, and **Polebridge**. Many have been changed back to two words, but many still exist unchanged. Apostrophes, with few exceptions—**Martha's Vineyard, D'hanis, O'brien**, and **O'Fallon**—have been eliminated through official guidelines. On the whole, however, the U.S. Board on Geographic Names has, at least in recent years, approved local preferences on names.

Names deriving from Amerindian languages have been popular since the earliest days of European settlement. The Amerindians had their own names (sometimes many, designating different locales along a single river) for geographical features, and many of these were used by the invaders, especially river names, such as **Potomac, Rappahanock, Susquehanna, Connecticut, Mohawk, Pomperaug, Naugatuck, Mystic**, and **Willimantic**. The names changed as they were filtered through the pronunciation and spellings of the English, French, or Dutch settlers, and were used without any consciousness of original meaning. Only later did an interest in the etymology of the place names develop, but by then the original meaning and pronunciation had been lost in so many instances that origins were either guessed at or romanticized. Still, the influence of Amerindian names led to several states having Amerindian-derived names, including two in the colonies—**Connecticut** and **Massachusetts**. The reasons why settlers retained and accepted Amerindian names are complicated. A practical reason was that the names were already there. Also, during the late eighteenth and early nineteenth centuries, Enlightenment and Romantic thinkers tended to idealize the Amerindians as "noble savages," symbolizing the goodness of natural life.

On the other hand, some Europeans looked upon the Amerindians as enemies and savages whose names should not be used for places. This attitude is shown in such states as Kentucky, which has few Amerindian-derived names. Whatever the reasons, the Europeans retained or gave Amerindian names to thousands of places, including the state name, **Indiana**. Such names as **Rockaway, Cherokee, Chickasaw, Apache, Ute, Creek, Iroquois, Minnewashka, Cathlamet, Catoctin, Edisto, Erie, Guyandot, Hassayampa, Manitou**, and **Winnebago** may only resemble the original names, but stand at least as commemoratives of the many Amerindian groups in the United States, all now woven into the country's fabric of names.

The geographical names in the United States have an unsurpassed variety. The ethnic mix of peoples has produced names not only from the four main linguistic sources (Amerindian, English, Spanish, and French) but also from the languages of immigrants who have settled throughout the fifty states. Germans, Swedes, Italians, Hungarians, Dutch, Russians, Polynesians, Japanese, Chinese, Czechs, Slovaks, Greeks, Norwegians, Danes, Hindus, and Middle Easterners have contributed to the named places, and their legacy appears on the pages of *American Places Dictionary*. Above all, the wonder is the assimilation of these names into acceptance in an expanse of land so varied and with peoples of such different national backgrounds. In this rich mix of names is the culture of a nation, its history, psychology, folklore, and perhaps its destiny.

Kelsie B. Harder
State University of
New York at Potsdam

October 1993

Introduction & How to Use This Book

American Places Dictionary (APD) provides comprehensive coverage of places throughout the United States that are the subject of frequent inquiry. Included among the 45,000 entries are:

Political Entities

- States

- Counties and County Equivalents

- Legally Incorporated Places: e.g., cities; towns in New England; etc.

- Unincorporated Places: e.g., townships and villages in some states; Census Designated Places (CDPs) in certain states; etc.

American Indian Reservations

Major U.S. Military Installations

Major U.S. Geographic Features: mountains and ranges, rivers, natural landmarks, etc.

This Introduction will first discuss the overall organization and contents of *APD*; then explain the entry presentation and information given at the state, county, and place levels; and finally touch on two major areas covered in *APD*: name origin information and the variety of government structures in the United States.

Organization of Entries by County

Each volume of *APD* covers the states of one region of the country, with each state presented alphabetically in its own section. In each state section entries appear *alphabetically by county*. This organization brings together entries that are closely related.

Unique Arrangement by County

There are few, if any, major reference books that present material by county. The county-by-county organization of APD was deliberately chosen to meet the needs of the many users who are interested in the local context. Within a county the places tend to be closely linked historically, culturally, and economically. The county-by-county organization of APD provides 3,141 county profiles covering the entire United States. This allows quick comparison and cross-study at the county level, and brings out clearly the interrelationship of entries. Thus population, land and water area, population density, historical background, and name origins can be easily compared. In metropolitan areas, suburbs and other communities are listed with their near neighbors.

State Indexes and National Index

For those needing alphabetical access to the populated places in a state, or all the populated places (and other entries) in the United States, both state indexes and a national index are provided. *State indexes*, including all places and counties listed alphabetically, are at the end of each state section. Volume Four contains a *national index*, covering all places and counties in the entire United States.

Coverage

Populated Places

Volumes One through Four of *APD* offer comprehensive coverage of populated places in the United States that have a functioning government, as well as many other inhabited places. No population limit or other arbitrary cutoff was applied to limit the coverage of *APD*. Every city, town or township, borough, or village was included—no matter its size—if it had legal, incorporated status. In addition, thousands of unincorporated townships and other places also have entries. Such places are common in many states and, despite their lack of formal legal status, residents of them often say they are "from...." Our editorial goal in *APD* was to cover U.S. populated places as comprehensively as possible while still giving a substantial amount of reliable data in each entry.

In some states selecting entries for comprehensive coverage presented difficulties, particularly for areas in the western U.S., where many vast tracts of inhabited land have no incorporated places. The editors of *APD* relied on baseline data from the U.S. Bureau of the Census, one of whose many tasks it is to keep track of all the inhabited places in the U.S. that have a functioning government and many less formally defined places that do not. As it is the purpose of the decennial censuses conducted by the Bureau to count all the inhabitants of the U.S., no inhabited area can be overlooked. Unincorporated places and districts must be given some status and name for purposes of the Census.

Another problem confronted the editors when it was discovered that some widely known places, such as La Jolla and Hollywood, California, were not incorporated cities and therefore had no census data from which to create an entry. For the fifty or so best-known of these unincorporated places, the editors placed a cross-reference in the county listing for the place, directing the reader to the incorporated place where data covering it was included. These unincorporated places also appear in the state and national indexes, with cross-references to the relevant entries.

Other Places and Features

In addition, other U.S. places that merit particular attention—American Indian reservations, major military installations, and major geographic features (see list of types below)—are each covered in separate Appendices in Volume Four. As many of these places are so vast that they cover all or parts of several counties, entering them in the state entries of Volumes One through

Four would have been impracticable. Stilltext, many of these places have important historical and cultural links to the populated places covered in Volumes One through Four, and are often referred to in the name origin or other information for populated places in *APD*. In addition, the American Indian reservations and military installations are themselves populated places.

Appendix A: American Indian Reservations

Appendix A of Volume Four has entries for each of the more than 300 American Indian reservations throughout the United States.

Appendix B: Military Installations

Appendix B of Volume Four has entries for more than 100 major U.S. military installations in the United States. In addition to the basic information given for each, the entries also note which facilities are scheduled to be affected by the 1993 recommendations of the Base Closure Commission.

Appendix C: Major Geographic Features

Appendix C of Volume Four has entries for more than 600 major geographic features across the United States. These include natural features on both land and water. In addition, some sizable features of human construction, such as dams and reservoirs, are also included. Many of these features are frequently referred to in written works, have historical significance, or are popular tourist spots. We have not included national parks as such, although some natural features found within national parks (e.g., Old Faithful, the geyser) do have entries.

The following types of major features are covered:

bays	deserts	oceans	seas
beaches	gaps	passes	sounds
canals	glaciers	peninsulas	trails
capes	gorges	plains	valleys
canyons	gulfs	plateaus	volcanoes
caves	islands	regions	waterfalls
currents	lakes	reservoirs	
dams	mountain ranges and peaks	rivers	

Contents of the Four Volumes

The complete *APD* is a four-volume set, organized as follows:

Volume One-Northeast:
    Connecticut
    Delaware
    District of Columbia (also in Vol. Two)
    Maine
    Maryland
    Massachusetts
    New Hampshire
    New Jersey
    New York
    Pennsylvania
    Rhode Island
    Vermont

Volume Two-South:
    Alabama
    Arkansas
    District of Columbia (also in Vol. One)
    Florida
    Georgia
    Kentucky
    Louisiana
    Mississippi
    North Carolina
    Oklahoma
    South Carolina
    Tennessee
    Texas
    Virginia
    West Virginia

Volume Three-Midwest:
    Illinois
    Indiana
    Iowa
    Michigan
    Minnesota
    Missouri
    Ohio
    Wisconsin

Volume Four-West:
    Alaska
    Arizona
    California
    Colorado
    Hawaii
    Idaho
    Kansas
    Montana
    Nebraska
    Nevada
    New Mexico
    North Dakota
    Oregon
    South Dakota
    Utah
    Washington
    Wyoming

Appendices & Index
Appendix A: American Indian Reservations
Appendix B: Major U.S. Military Installations
Appendix C: Major U.S. Geographic Features

Index: Including entries for Volumes One through Four and the Appendices

American Places Dictionary   xix ☐ Introduction

Entry Presentation and Information in *APD*

Entries for States

In each regional volume the states appear in alphabetic order, each in its own section. There is a section for each of the 50 states, plus a section for Washington, D.C., which appears in both Volume One (Northeast) and Volume Two (South).

Each state section opens with the state seal, followed by a one-page map showing the state and county boundaries and the names of neighboring states or provinces. Each map includes latitude and longitude references in the margins and a scale of miles and kilometers.

Opposite the map page is the state entry information and introductory information. Entries at the state level include the following basic information:

Population: in 1990 and 1980; 1990 rank among the 50 states; percent change from 1980 to 1990; projections for 1995 and 2000 (data from the U.S. Bureau of the Census).

Area: for land and water, in square miles; rank among the 50 states (data from the U.S. Bureau of the Census).

Coastline: number of miles of coastline, as applicable, as reported by the state and other sources.

Elevation: highest and lowest points (data from U.S. Geological Survey and other sources).
State capital: with county
Largest city: with population
Second largest city: with population
Largest county: with population

Housing: number of units, number occupied, percentage vacant (data from the U.S. Bureau of the Census).

Distribution of population by race and Hispanic origin: percentages for White, Black, Hispanic (may be of any race), Native American, Asian and Pacific islander, Other (data from the U.S. Bureau of the Census).

Admission date: with order of admission.

Location: descriptive, noting bordering states, provinces, and bodies of water.

Name Origin: concise account of state name origin.

State Symbols or Emblems: as given by state authorities.

State motto and nickname(s): as given by state authorities.

Telephone Area code(s): with indication of where used if multiple.

Time Zone(s): with indication of where used if multiple.

Abbreviations: both official postal and traditional.

Part of (region): the region or regions that the state is generally considered to be part of.

Following this standard presentation of basic data is a brief introductory essay. Generally, these essays follow a standard outline and include information on local government (counties and municipalities), settlement history and early development, and later history through the twentieth century. They close with a discussion of the state's boundaries, including any peculiarities or disputes with other states.

The state introduction closes with a list of all the counties and, for those states that have them, a list of all multi-county places. The multi-county places are municipalities or census designated places (CDPs) whose area lies within more than one county. Typically, multi-county places have a large portion in one county, with a smaller portion in a second county, often without any population residing there. For each multi-county place the population of the entire place and of each county portion is given. For further discussion of the multi-county places in the United States, see under "Counties" in the discussion below on **Hierarchy of Government in the United States**.

Entries for Counties or County Equivalents

Following the state introduction, each county appears alphabetically, followed by the populated places that are in that county. Each county has an entry that gives the following basic information:

Name
County Seat: with ZIP code
Population (1990 Census; 1980 Census)
Population density (per square mile)
Land area and water area (square miles)
Area code
Descriptive location
Background and establishment
Name origin

Entries for Places below the County Level

In compiling material for the populated places below the county level, which comprise the bulk of the entries in *APD*, the editorial policy was to include as much information as could be reliably reported for each data element in the entry. At minimum, entries in *APD* provide the following for each incorporated populated place below the county level:

Name
Status: city, town, township, etc.

Population (1990 Census)
Land area and water area (square miles)
Latitude and longitude
Population density (per square mile)
Area code (given with county entry)

For some unincorporated places, only name and some 1990 census data are given.

For larger places, particularly for those with a population above 10,000, the amount of data provided is greater, and normally also includes:

ZIP code
Population (1980 Census)

Aside from the statistical data, many entries also include:

Other Information: location, founder, dates of incorporation, etc.
Name Origin: as available; date of naming and previous names given whenever possible.

A typical "full" entry for a municipality in *APD* looks like this:

> **Worcester** City
> **ZIP:** 01601   **Lat:** 42-16-10 N **Long:** 71-48-32 W
> **Pop:** 169,759 (1990); 161,799 (1980)   **Pop Density:** 4514.9
> **Land:** 37.6 sq. mi.; **Water:** 1.0 sq. mi.   **Elev:** 480 ft.
> In central MA, 15 mi. west of Boston. Second largest city in MA: settled 1673; incorporated as town 1722; as city 1848. Diverse industrial city: machinery and machine tools, fabricated metals, printed materials, and chemicals, plastics, and abrasives.
> **Name origin:** Either for the town of Worcester or for Worcestershire, the county in England in which it is located.

The various elements of an entry may be explained as follows:

Name: the full legal name for the place, or the common name for unincorporated places. In some cases the popular form of the name is given.

Status: (to the right of the name) the legal status of the incorporated place—e.g., City, Town, Township, Village, Borough—according to local use. The types of incorporated places in the state are discussed in each state introduction under the heading *Municipalities*. In the case of unincorporated places, status may be given as "populated place" if official or legal status could not be verified. Certain unincorporated places for which the U.S. Bureau of the Census reports population figures and other data, known as Census Designated Places, are identified as "CDP". *U.S. military installations with resident population* are identified as "Military Facility".

Population (1990 Census): the population reported by the U.S. Bureau of the Census for the decennial census of April 1, 1990. (1980 Census): the population reported by the U.S. Bureau of the Census for the decennial census of April 1, 1980, as corrected, for comparison with 1990. If the populated place is new since 1980 (or its boundaries changed between the 1980 and the 1990 censuses), 1980 data is not given.

Land area and water area (square miles): as provided by the U.S. Bureau of the Census.

Latitude and longitude: in degrees, minutes, and seconds; as provided by the U.S. Bureau of the Census.

Population density (per square mile): calculated by dividing the 1990 population by the land area in square miles.

Telephone Area code (given with county entry).

ZIP code: as reported by the U.S. Postal Service.

Other information: for state capitals, larger cities, county seats, commercial and industrial centers, and municipalities of historic or cultural significance, descriptive location and other background information are also provided. As often as possible, when reliable information could be obtained, incorporation dates of municipalities are also provided.

Name origin: given when reliable information could be obtained and verified.

Data given in *APD* for population (1990, 1980; 1995 and 2000 projections for states), for housing and population distribution (for states), and for latitude and longitude is from published reports or data files provided by the U.S. Bureau of the Census.

Land and water area measurement are from data files provided by the U.S. Bureau of the Census. The Bureau calculates area measurements by computer based on information from the TIGER geographic data base.

Water area measurements include all water, unlike previous Census measurements, which included only inland water. As a result, total water area reported, especially for coastal states, has increased from previous Census figures. Water area measurements from the 1990 Census include inland, coastal, Great Lakes (including Lake St. Clair), and territorial water (from the 3-mile limit to the shoreline or base lines that delimit inland and coastal waters).

Name Origin Information

This element of entry information was the greatest challenge to compile and remains an unfinished (perhaps never to be finished) task. Sources for the data are variable in quality and reliability, and are often very difficult to obtain. Many tend to deal with names within a state, county, or region, and it is typically difficult to acquire books or locally published material regarding name origins. Aside from the initial problem of acquiring or accessing any good source material, the information provided in the sources was often found to be incomplete, conflicting, or lacking in credibility.

"Onomastic Fact"

We have attempted to present *the reason a particular name was given to a place*, what Prof. Kelsie Harder (see "Foreword") has termed the "onomastic fact." Whenever possible, we have also indicated who gave the name and the date it was bestowed. Former names for a place, if known, are also indicated.

Occasionally the onomastic fact is easy to determine, well documented, and well known. More often the determination requires a study of history and biography, a sense for the settlement pattern within a state or region, and an understanding of the tenor of the times in which the naming was done. Some sensitivity for language and knowledge of naming practices also proves useful. For most of the name origins, we have relied upon Kelsie Harder's *Illustrated Dictionary of Place Names: United States and Canada* (1976).

What we have *not* done is to trace the etymology in terms of the linguistic roots of the names themselves. Such work is certainly legitimate and important, often fascinating, but is beyond the requirements of determining onomastic fact. We have been content with determining and presenting, as often as possible, when and why a place was named.

Borrowed Names

If the name was borrowed from another U.S. place, the entry indicates this. The onomastic fact for the eponymous place, if known, is given under its entry. If the place is not an entry in *APD* (e.g., a small river whose name is used for a populated place), we have attempted to give the onomastic fact, if known, within the name origin information for the populated place.

The editorial policy for name origins in *APD* was to present as much material as we could reliably offer, but to say nothing if reliable information could not be obtained. We were able to give such information for all states, counties, and a majority of the larger cities, as well as many smaller places, perhaps 10,000 entries overall. Thus many entries in *APD* lack name origin data. We hope that this feature can be augmented in subsequent editions of the book. We encourage users who have such information on a place, county, region, or state to notify the publisher. Please mail correspondence to:

> Editor, *American Places Dictionary*
> Omnigraphics, Inc.
> Penobscot Bldg.
> Detroit, MI 48226

Variability by Region

For some states name origin material is abundant and well researched. This generally reflects the interests of a local expert, or a set of experts over the years, who had access to good historical sources and who devoted prodigious amounts of research time and scholarly effort to producing publications of quality, knowing that their audience would likely be a small, albeit devoted one. For the names of counties and municipalities, the New England states have perhaps the best coverage of any single region, perhaps reflecting the relative simplicity or lack of complications for the names (many are of English origin), the existence of good historical records, and the geographic compactness of the region and its states. Other states have been blessed by the scholarship of particular researchers, so that the name origins and other information for places in Kentucky, Oregon, and California are generally better documented and widely available, thanks to the efforts of Robert Rennick, Lewis McArthur (father and son), and Erwin Gudde, to name but a notable few.

"American Indian" Names

This is an area fraught with controversy, even regarding the question of how to refer to these names. While recent developments have led some to favor such terms as *Amerindian* or *Native American* to refer to these names and the languages from which they originate, *APD* uses the more traditional forms *Indian* or *American Indian* when speaking in general of such names, or, whenever possible, notes a specific language or people.

Putting aside the issue of style, more critical to understanding the origin of names is the fact that American Indian languages have been less well documented and studied. Several reasons may be cited for this, including the fact that these languages were rarely recorded in writing by native speakers, so that records for them, if they exist, are generally sparse and very often second-hand, in the form of observations by Europeans or Americans. As a result, place names of American Indian origin generally have come down to us as if through a filter.

Another factor results from cultural differences regarding the use of names. As a rule, American Indian naming practices differed greatly from the tradition of the European cultures. Whereas the European explorers and settlers made a great issue of naming features and places and dutifully recording everything—as evidence of a claim, for convenience of future reference, and out of pride—it seems that American Indian cultures did not follow and in fact may have been opposed to the practice of systematically assigning names to particular places. Additionally, Indian naming seems to have been more localized, so that a river, for example, may have been referred to in several if not many ways along its entire course, each "name" reflecting local experience.

As Lewis L. McArthur notes in his Introduction to *Oregon Geographic Names,* Sixth Edition:

A good deal of nonsense has been written about the meaning of Indian names. The late Lewis A. McArthur knew many Indians. They eked out a living amidst hard circumstances and it seems improbable that Oregon Indians ever made up geographic names because of "moonlight filtering through trees," "sunshine dancing on the water," "rose petals floating on water" and "water rippling over pebbles." Competent researchers have found that most Indian names were based on much more practical and everyday matters.

What often can be said about an American place name is that it originates from an earlier Indian name or term. Beyond that the situation becomes much murkier. It has been the practice of *APD* to avoid speculation about names of American Indian origin. We have on occasion reported what is believed about certain names, but maintain that it is perilous to assert the original meaning of many American Indian names.

Hierarchy of Government in the United States

The organization of *APD* into state sections, county groupings, and entries for the individual places themselves repeats the pattern of government administration of the entire country below the federal level. This hierarchy of government starts at the state level, and at each level the entire territory of the United States is included in some administrative entity. Thus the "mosaic of governments" is complete at the state, county, and place levels. The primary reason for this bit of bureaucratic thoroughness is to ensure that all the U.S. population is included in each decennial census at every level, allowing for statistical integrity and (technically) equitable distribution of federal benefits at each level.

States

Most people are quite familiar with the state government level—50 states, plus the District of Columbia. This is the top level covered by *APD*, which has entries for each of these 51 entities.

Four of the states refer to themselves as commonwealths: Kentucky, Massachusetts, Pennsylvania, and Virginia.

There are no entries in *APD* for Puerto Rico or any territories or possessions of the United States.

Counties and County Equivalents

Below the state level are the counties or county equivalents, of which there are 3,141 in the entire United States. This total includes the District of Columbia government as a state and a county equivalent. If one considers Washington, D.C., also as a city, then the nation's capital is the only place that functions technically at all three government levels.

States without Counties or with County Equivalents

In certain states the county level of government is somewhat different from the "normal" pattern, as outlined for each state listed below.

In Louisiana, the parishes provide the equivalent of county government in other states.

In Connecticut and Rhode Island, county government has actually been abolished, but county boundaries still are used administratively, and counties are still recognized popularly.

In Maryland, the city of Baltimore is independent and serves as a county equivalent.

In Virginia, 41 independent cities serve as county equivalents; there are also 95 counties.

In Missouri, the city of St. Louis is an independent city and serves as a county equivalent.

In Nevada, Carson City is an independent city and serves as a county equivalent.

In Alaska there are no counties as such. Areas with some concentration of population are called boroughs and do provide government administration. Most of the territory of the state is included in large tracts called census areas, which have been designated by the U.S. Bureau of the Census.

In Hawaii alone among the states, all local government is at the county level. There are no incorporated municipalities. The four main islands—Oahu, Hawaii, Kauai, and Maui—are essentially each treated as counties. The island of Oahu and most of the smaller Hawaiian Islands are all governed by the consolidated government called the City and County of Honolulu. Also, a small part of Molokai Island is administered by the state Department of Health as Kalawao County, and is occupied by patients with Hansen's disease, or leprosy. This is the site of the noted leper colony ministered to by Father Joseph Damien (1840–89).

Two other variations on the standard county pattern, city-county consolidations and multi-county places, lead to the discussion of municipalities and other sub-county entities.

City-County Consolidations

A number of cities have consolidated their government with the county, and the two are largely functionally equivalent. These city-county consolidations are:

Anchorage, AK (city consolidated with Anchorage Borough)

Juneau, AK (city consolidated with Juneau Borough)

Sitka, AK (city consolidated with Sitka Borough)

San Francisco, CA (city consolidated with San Francisco County)

Denver, CO (city consolidated with Denver County)

Jacksonville, FL (city consolidated with Duval County, but the municipalities of Atlantic Beach, Baldwin, Jacksonville Beach, and Neptune Beach remain as separate entities in the county)

Columbus, GA (city consolidated with Muscogee County; Bibb City also consolidated with the county, but is a separate entity)

Honolulu, HI (city and county consolidated as the City and County of Honolulu)

Indianapolis, IN (city government consolidated with Marion County; the four suburbs of Beech Grove, Lawrence, Southport, and Speedway maintain independent status, and 13 other suburbs have quasi-independent status)

Lexington, KY (city consolidated with Fayette County as Lexington Fayette Urban County)

Baton Rouge, LA (city consolidated with East Baton Rouge Parish, but not coextensive)

Houma, LA (city consolidated with Terrebonne Parish, but not coextensive)

New Orleans, LA (city consolidated with Orleans Parish)

Nantucket, MA (town coextensive with Nantucket County; the whole of Nantucket Island)

Suffolk County, MA (government consolidated with city of Boston, but not coextensive)

Anaconda, MT (consolidated with Deer Lodge County as Anaconda-Deer Lodge County)

Butte, MT (consolidated with Silver Bow County as Butte-Silver Bow; Walkerville remains a separate municipality)

Yellowstone National Park, MT (administered by the National Park Service, but considered as a county equivalent)

Philadelphia, PA (city consolidated with Philadelphia County)

Lynchburg, TN (consolidated with Moore County as Lynchburg, Moore County)

Nashville, TN (city consolidated with Davidson County; six suburban cities continue as separate municipalities for certain purposes)

Multi-County Places

As noted above, a number of municipalities in the United States cover an area that is in more than one county. Typically, multi-county places have a large portion in one county, with a smaller portion in a second county, often without any population residing in the second county. The total number of multi-county places in the United States is 923, broken down as follows:

2-county places: 855
3-county places: 60
4-county places: 5*
5-county places: 3**

 * Broomfield, CO; Allentown, GA; Barrington Hills, IL; Kansas City, MO; High Point, NC
** New York, NY (its five boroughs are county equivalents); Oklahoma City, OK; Dallas, TX

Municipalities and Other Sub-county Entities

Owing to the diverse and varied settlement of the United States (and to the diverse and varied nature of its settlers), no two states treat their sub-county populated places in exactly the same way administratively. In different regions of the nation, government below the county level is represented by cities, towns, villages, townships, boroughs, and other administrative entities.

In the western and southern states particularly many populated areas are not administered by any government below the county level. These places are not cities or towns, but often have established popular names, even if they lack legal boundaries.

Taken as a whole, the variety of local governments and other populated districts reflects the long and varied history of settlement in the United States. But the situation also means a complicated burden for the federal agencies, such as the U.S. Bureau of the Census, that have to deal with this patchwork of local administration or, in some cases, lack thereof. Two common problems encountered at the sub-county level are discussed here to illustrate the kinds of unexpected peculiarities that arise in compiling entries for these places.

"Same Name, Same County" (Entries with Asterisks)

Frequently in *APD* there will be two entries for places in a single county, that will have the same name. This may seem puzzling, but reflects the fact that, in many states, local government or administrative units may overlap or divide certain functions. In states where land was surveyed into townships prior to much of the subsequent settlement, the township pattern was established before incorporated places were in existence or even necessary. As townships became settled, centers of population desired corporate status and legal standing as a government. Depending on the state, the incorporated place might be called a town, village, borough, or city. Frequently, places that were incorporated as towns would develop and grow to the point where they would want to become cities, often gaining thereby a greater amount of autonomy under state law. But as the incorporated places—cities, towns, villages, or whatever—became established, the original township pattern usually remained. Very often, the incorporated area might be only part (the most densely settled part) of a township. Also very often, the township name was adopted by the new incorporated place. The result usually is two places with the same name in the same county. Examples include Chevy Chase, MD; Farmington, NH; Grosse Pointe, MI; Green Bay, WI.

Our policy for this situation has been to retain both places if they are recognized by the state as incorporated. Naturally, they will come together alphabetically as entries within their county. One of the two entries, normally the one of lesser administrative function (and often smaller population), will appear second and be marked with an asterisk.

The Differing Use of *Borough* in Five States

One example of variation among the states can be seen in the use of the term *borough* in conjunction with other terms for municipalities in five states. Each has populated places called boroughs, but they differ greatly in function and relationship to other administrative units.

Alaska: the 16 boroughs are actually county equivalents; three are governmentally consolidated with cities (Anchorage, Juneau, Sitka).

Connecticut: the 11 boroughs are incorporated places; but are actually part of a town and not entirely independent. The borough of Naugatuck is coextensive with the town of the same name.

New Jersey: the 252 boroughs function as municipalities. New Jersey's cities, towns, townships, and villages are other types of municipalities.

New York: the five boroughs that make up New York City—Manhattan, Brooklyn, the Bronx, Queens, and Staten Island—function as parts of the city and county equivalents. Manhattan is coextensive with New York County, Brooklyn is coextensive with Kings County, and Staten Island is coextensive with Richmond County. Borough and county names are the same for the Bronx and Queens.

Pennsylvania: the 966 boroughs function as municipalities, along with 55 cities and one town. Pennsylvania also has 1,549 townships, which are similar in character to townships in New England (see below).

In *APD* we have attempted to present as much sub-county administrative detail as possible for populated places. As a result, many places that might normally be thought of as a single city or town may have two (or more) entries in *APD*. In the introductions for the individual states some of the nature of each state's municipalities is noted.

In the following paragraphs we shall attempt to suggest something of the complexity of the local administrative hierarchy that must be taken into account in any comprehensive treatment of U.S. populated places nationwide.

Minor Civil Divisions (MCDs) in 28 States

In 28 states the sub-county entities are functioning local governments or other sub-county administrative entities, broadly referred to as minor civil divisions (MCDs). In these states the U.S. Bureau of the Census tracks population totals within these established local boundaries. The names and relationships of the sub-county populated places in these 28 states varies regionally and from state to state.

In the Northeast (the six New England states, New York, New Jersey, and Pennsylvania), counties are generally divided into towns or townships. Typically, these are much more important administratively than the counties (hence, the vestigial counties of Connecticut and Rhode Island, noted above). Towns in the Northeast are typically incorporated, legal entities, and in most of these states there are very few areas that lie outside the boundaries of some town or township (except for some incorporated cities). In northern New England some sparsely inhabited or uninhabited districts provide sub-county boundaries. These areas are called plantations, gores, grants, unorganized territory (in northern Maine), or locations and purchases (in New Hampshire).

In the six Great Lakes states (Ohio, Michigan, Indiana, Illinois, Wisconsin, and Minnesota) and six other central states (Iowa, Kansas, Missouri, Nebraska, North Dakota, and South Dakota) the division into townships (called *towns* in Wisconsin) is the typical pattern. Compared to the Northeast, however, the townships in most of these states are generally of considerably less administrative importance than the counties. The towns or townships of the central states may or may not be incorporated, and less often have the authority to levy taxes or otherwise carry on the governmental functions of their counterparts in the Northeast. The exception is Wisconsin, where the towns function in a manner very similar to New England towns.

In North Carolina and Arkansas townships and unorganized territories provide sub-county boundaries where there are no incorporated places such as cities.

In some so-called "MCD states," the Census Bureau tracks population within the boundaries of other existing administrative districts, which vary in designation by state; these are listed as "Populated Places" in *APD*.

Census County Divisions (CCDs) in 21 States

In 21 states the U.S. Bureau of the Census, in cooperation with state and local officials, has established statistical entities below the county level for states that do not have MCDs or where MCDs are not adequate for reporting sub-county statistics. These statistical entities are called Census County Divisions (CCDs). The 21 "CCD states" are primarily in the South and the West, where, except for the incorporated places, much of the area below the county level is unincorporated. CCDs were created solely for statistical purposes, and are not normally used or referred to by the resident population. They have no legal functions and are not units of government. CCDs do have names, however, based on a place, county, or well-known local name. The Census County Divisions exist to maintain statistical integrity—and a complete "mosaic" at the sub-county level.

The 21 CCD states are as follows:

Alabama	Georgia	New Mexico	Utah
Arizona	Hawaii	Oklahoma	Washington
California	Idaho	Oregon	Wyoming
Colorado	Kentucky	South Carolina	
Delaware	Montana	Tennessee	
Florida	Nevada	Texas	

Census Subareas in Alaska

In Alaska the Census Bureau and the state delineated census subareas as statistical subdivisions of the county equivalent boroughs and census areas.

Census Designated Places (CDPs)

Another statistical entity used by the Census Bureau is called the Census Designated Place (CDP). CDPs, delineated in 49 states, are densely settled concentrations of population that are identifiable by name, but are not legally incorporated places. Like CCDs, their names are generally reflective of local usage, but they have no legal status.

In *APD* we have included entries for CDPs where they provide additional detail and do not cause potential confusion because of close similarity of the CDP name with an actual municipality within the same county. One state in which they are particularly noticeable is Hawaii, where there are no legally incorporated places besides the City and County of Honolulu. All other populated places in Hawaii that are entries are based on CDPs.

Conclusion

The melting pot that has become the United States of America reveals itself in many facets of our culture, not the least of which are historical settlement patterns, the place names given to settlements, and the diverse systems of organization and administration. As we delve deeper into why the United States, or the individual states, were set up as they were, we see more and more diversity. Establishing order in the midst of the state-by-state variation, as the Bureau of the Census has done with minor civil divisions and census county divisions (and census areas in Alaska), is a necessary task of government.

✶ ✶ ✶ ✶ ✶

Acknowledgments

The compilation of *American Places Dictionary* would not have been possible without the vision, inspiration, and diligence of many individuals and organizations. Foremost among all those who had a role in the work is Fred Ruffner, publisher and president of Omnigraphics, Inc., who conceived of the project originally and whose support for it was unwavering despite unforeseen delays and setbacks. Other key personnel at Omnigraphics included Laurie Harris, editorial director; Jim Sellgren, operations; Jane Steele, promotion; and Eric Berger, production manager. The concern for quality that they exhibited, as well as their patience with the editor, are much appreciated.

Assisting the editorial process in all its details was Chuck Lacy of Weimer Graphics, Indianapolis, Indiana, who met the formidable challenge of the data processing and typesetting with exceptional skill and efficiency. Mr. Lacy helped conceive and implement the procedures to process, consolidate, sort, and typeset a massive body of data. The quality and efficiency of his work were never compromised by the demands imposed by editorial and publishing specifications.

We also wish to recognize the assistance provided by a number of specialists in federal agencies, including especially, at the Bureau of the Census, Marie Pees, of the Population Division; Don Hirschfeld (retired) and Joel Miller, of the Geography Division; and, at the National Institute of Standards and Technology, Henry Tom. These highly skilled, dedicated, and profoundly knowledgeable professionals promptly and ably responded to our many inquiries into the vagaries of U.S. populated places. Their work, and that of others like them in various federal agencies, is indispensable to the creation of place name reference tools.

Officials in state and local government nationwide, far too numerous to mention, assisted throughout the editorial process, sometimes answering single, focused inquiries, often sending enormously important publications and other data from their files. This state-specific information was vital to our work, especially given the complexity and variation across the United States in the way government and administration function below the federal level.

While the invaluable contributions of each of the individuals mentioned cannot be overemphasized, we must add that the responsibility for any errors or omissions in *American Places Dictionary* rests solely with the editor.

We encourage users of this dictionary to send suggestions on how the work might be improved, expanded, or made more accessible in subsequent editions.

> Editor, *American Places Dictionary*
> Omnigraphics, Inc.
> Penobscot Bldg.
> Detroit, MI, 48226

> Frank R. Abate
> *Editor*

Old Saybrook, Connecticut
April 1994

Editor's Miscellany:

American Places and American Names—
Curiosities and Peculiarities

In the course of compiling and editing *American Places Dictionary* the editorial staff came upon many fascinating tidbits and facts about the United States. Collectively, this grab-bag of trivia, history, odd names, and other surprises lacks a coherent theme, and while the material seemed inappropriate for the Introduction, we could not resist the opportunity to present what we found. Hence, this brief miscellany, a collection of unrelated details that we felt should not go unrecorded.

This brief list reveals the variety of items included here and serves as a handy summary:

I. Early U.S. Capitals
II. Geopolitical Peculiarities
III. Unusual Official State Symbols
IV. Historical Development and Changes in Counties
V. Some Out-of-the-Ordinary Place Names
VI. First Name/Last Name Places

I. Early U.S. Capitals

In the earliest years of U.S. history there was no permanent federal capital. This situation lasted from the signing of the Declaration of Independence in 1776 until 1800, when the federal government settled into the newly established Washington, D.C. The different meeting places of the Continental Congress, the Congress of the Confederation (authorized under the Articles of Confederation), and later the U.S. Congress (under the U.S. Constitution, from March 4, 1789) in these years, a total of eight different cities in four states, are listed below, with the span of first and last meeting dates in each place:

Philadelphia:	September 5, 1774 to December 12, 1776
Baltimore:	December 20, 1776 to March 4, 1777
Philadelphia:	March 5, 1777 to September 18, 1777
Lancaster, PA:	September 27, 1777 (one day only)
York, PA:	September 30, 1777 to June 27, 1778
Philadelphia:	July 2, 1778 to June 21, 1783
Princeton, NJ:	June 30, 1783 to November 4, 1783
Annapolis, MD:	November 26, 1783 to June 3, 1784
Trenton, NJ:	November 1, 1784 to December 24, 1784

New York City: January 11, 1785 to August 12, 1790
Philadelphia: December 6, 1790 to May 14, 1800

II. Geopolitical Peculiarities

The following section describes a number of instances of geopolitical peculiarities across the U.S. Some of these unusual or unique border patterns are rather obvious on a map of the United States, while others are quite hard to find except on very detailed maps. Several different kinds of situations are described, some affecting several states and others peculiar to a single state.

Panhandles and Other Border Extensions

The following states have panhandles or border extensions of some sort. A panhandle is generally defined as a projecting, relatively narrow strip of land that is surrounded by the territory of other states or a water boundary, but is not a peninsula.

Alabama	Missouri
Alaska	New Mexico
Florida	Oklahoma
Idaho	Pennsylvania
Maryland	Texas
Mississippi	West Virginia

Two "classic" panhandles are those of Oklahoma and Florida, projecting as long narrow strips to the west in each case, and truly resembling panhandles when viewed on a map. The panhandle of **Oklahoma** was ceded to the U.S. by Texas before Texas was admitted to the Union. It was part of Oklahoma Territory by 1890, called the Public Land Strip, sometimes referred to as "No Man's Land." **Florida's** panhandle, the area west of the Apalachicola River, was part of the original Spanish province that extended west to the Mississippi River. When Spain ceded Florida to Great Britain in 1763, the territory was divided into West Florida and East Florida along the river. West Florida was later reduced in extent as western portions to the Mississippi River became part of Louisiana, Mississippi, and Alabama.

The other commonly referred to panhandle, that of **Texas**, was created when the state sold a portion of its original northwest territory to the federal government in 1850. The new boundary lines of northwest Texas were set by survey, and left a distinctive broad panhandle that projects northward.

The panhandle of **Alaska**, extending southeast from the 141st meridian, is a remnant of the boundaries established by Great Britain and Russia in a convention of 1825. The territory, including this panhandle, was purchased by the United States from Russia in 1867, and the United States consistently maintained claim to the region despite objection over the years from Canada. The dispute was settled by an international tribunal in 1903.

West Virginia is the only state to have two panhandles, one extending north between Ohio and Pennsylvania near Wheeling, the other east, bordering Virginia to the south and Maryland to the north.

Western **Maryland**, from Hagerstown west, extends like a panhandle between West Virginia and Pennsylvania. In addition, Maryland is also cut by Chesapeake Bay, so that to the east there is a portion on the Delmarva Peninsula (see below) that is separated from the rest of the state. This region of the state is called the Eastern Shore.

Missouri has a distinctive portion at its southeast corner that is called the "bootheel" because of its shape. It lies below the line of 36 degrees, 30 minutes north latitude that marks the rest of Missouri's southern border. The eastern border of the bootheel is the Mississippi River, and the western the St. Francis River. This portion became a part of Missouri on its admission to statehood. Prominent landowner J. Hardeman Walker, founder of Caruthersville, an important town in the region, was influential in having this addition become part of the state.

The panhandle of **Idaho** is the result of a reduction to the original Idaho territory prior to statehood in 1890. This narrow area, lying between Idaho's western border with Washington and the Bitterroot Range of the Rockies, was left when land to the east of the Bitterroot Range was made part of the Territory of Montana in 1864.

The extreme southwestern corner of **New Mexico**, extending below its long southern boundary with Texas at 32 degrees north latitude, was an addition made to the original territory of 1850. The land was acquired from Mexico in the Gadsden Purchase of 1853, negotiated for the United States by James Gadsden, who wanted to ensure a good route for a southern railroad to the Pacific. The bulk of the Gadsden Purchase became part of the Territory of Arizona (1863) along its southern border with Mexico.

While they are not truly panhandles, Pennsylvania, Alabama, and Mississippi each have narrow projections that give the states access to water. The "Erie Triangle" of **Pennsylvania**, once a part of New York but ceded to the federal government in 1781, was purchased from the U.S. by Pennsylvania on March 3, 1792, to give the state a broader land access to Lake Erie. The purchase price was $151,640.25, and the deed was signed by George Washington. **Alabama** and **Mississippi** each have projections to the Gulf of Mexico that are a part of what was once called West Florida, originally part of the Spanish province of Florida. The land, to the west of the Perdido River, was occupied by the United States in 1812, and eventually was added to the territories of Alabama and Mississippi.

The Four Corners: Utah, Colorado, New Mexico, Arizona

One corner of each of these four states, each of which has very regular, straight borders, meets at a point referred to as the Four Corners. The point is the intersection of 37 degrees north latitude and 109 degrees, 2 minutes west longitude. The longitude is exactly 32 degrees west of Washington, D.C. The spot is marked by a prominent boundary monument, and is the only point in the U.S. common to four states.

Portions of Land Separated from the Rest of the State along Rivers

In a number of places, particularly along major rivers such as the Mississippi and Missouri, small portions of certain states are separated from the rest of the state owing to changes over the years in the course of the rivers. Natural events such as floods and earthquakes bring about these changes in river channels. The situation arises when two states have fixed their border along the channel of a river. Whenever the river changes course, an area of land that was once on one side of the river is left on the other. There are many such places along the southern course of the Mississippi River to the Gulf of Mexico, affecting, on the eastern banks, Kentucky, Tennessee, and Mississippi, and on the western banks Missouri, Arkansas, and Louisiana.

Kentucky–Missouri–Tennessee at New Madrid

A small portion of extreme southwestern Kentucky lies isolated from the rest of the state along the course of the Mississippi River near New Madrid, Missouri. This is the result of a change in the course of the river caused by the noted earthquake of 1811, whose epicenter was at New Madrid. From this part of Kentucky one can cross by land into Tennessee or by river to Missouri, but must pass through one of these two states to get to the rest of Kentucky.

Iowa–Nebraska at Omaha

A small portion of Iowa is separated from the rest of the state near Omaha, Nebraska. The border between the states is the Missouri River. When the river changed course in 1877, moving to its present channel, it isolated a portion of what had been on the eastern bank, also leaving a small lake, Carter Lake, as a remnant of the former channel. This small portion on the western bank of the Missouri is still part of Iowa.

Delmarva Peninsula

This peninsula extends between Chesapeake Bay to the west and Delaware Bay and the Atlantic Ocean to the east. It is divided among three states, Delaware, Maryland, and Virginia, hence the name, a combination of the first syllables of the first two states with the standard abbreviation letters for Virginia. The extreme southern portion of the peninsula has been a part of Virginia since colonial days, although it is totally separated from the rest of the state. The exact border with Maryland was a source of controversy from colonial times until 1972, when both states finally agreed on a well-defined boundary.

Going *South* from the United States into Canada—Detroit to Windsor

Owing to the natural course of the Detroit River, which forms the international boundary between southeastern Michigan and the Canadian province of Ontario, travelers crossing the border from Detroit into Canada, using either the Ambassador Bridge or the Detroit-Windsor tunnel under the river, are actually going nearly due south. Excepting in Alaska, this is the only instance of a major border crossing between the two countries where one travels south to reach Canada.

The Notch in the Connecticut–Massachusetts Border

The generally straight west-east border line between Connecticut and Massachusetts is broken by a notch north of Hartford, Connecticut. The Massachusetts town of Southwick extends into this notch; hence it is sometimes referred to as the "Southwick jog." In Connecticut it is sometimes referred to as the "Suffield gap," as it lies between the towns of Suffield and Granby. The area within the notch became part of Massachusetts in 1803 by ruling of a survey commission formed by both states. The commission determined that Massachusetts had lost territory owing to errors in the previous surveys that had set the straight-line border between the states. The notch was intended to compensate Massachusetts with an area equivalent to that lost.

Arc-of-a-Circle Border between Delaware and Pennsylvania

Most of Delaware's short northern border with Pennsylvania is the arc of a circle, the center of which is some 12 miles to the south at New Castle, Delaware. This unusual boundary line was fixed by a survey authorized in 1701 by William Penn. It is the only instance of such a border shape in the United States.

Michigan's Upper Peninsula

A portion of the state of Michigan shares a border with Wisconsin but is not connected to the rest of the state. Michigan's Upper Peninsula separates Lake Michigan from Lake Superior and extends to the Canadian province of Ontario at Sault Ste. Marie and to the Lower Peninsula of the state at the Straits of Mackinac and the entrance to Lake Huron. It was not a part of the original Michigan Territory organized in 1805, but was added as part of an extension of Michigan Territory in 1818. Wisconsin Territory was created in 1836 from the western portion of this extension, but the Upper Peninsula was retained by Michigan upon its admission to statehood in 1837. Subsequent disputes over the exact border line with Wisconsin raged for many years, finally being settled in 1948 after U.S. Supreme Court intervention and approval of the U.S. Congress.

Portion of Minnesota North of the 49th Parallel—The "Northwest Angle"

Minnesota's Lake of the Woods County includes an area of about 124 square miles, called the Northwest Angle, that is non-contiguous with the rest of the state. This area can only be reached from the rest of Minnesota by boat or by traveling through or over part of Canada (Manitoba or Ontario). Excepting Alaska, it is the northernmost tract of the United States, wholly above the forty-ninth parallel. This area became part of the United States because inaccurate maps were used during treaty negotiations with the British in 1783 and 1818. In 1917 the International Joint Commission between the United States and Canada described the situation as a "politico-geographical curiosity of a boundary."

Portion of New Hampshire North of the Forty-Fifth Parallel—Pittsburg, N.H.

This small portion of northern New Hampshire extends north of 45 degrees north latitude, which is the general line for the international boundary between the Canadian province of Quebec and the U.S. states of New York and Vermont. The area above the forty-fifth parallel was disputed for many years by New Hampshire and Canada. In 1829 the settlers in the region organized an independent republic known as the Indian Stream Territory. This government was in effect until New Hampshire took control in 1835. The area is now the town of Pittsburg, N.H., the largest town (in area) in the state, population 901 (in 1990).

III. Unusual Official State Symbols (by state)

Each state introduction provides a complete list of official state symbols. Some of the more unusual ones are listed here.

Alaska
  sport: dog mushing (sled-dog racing)
Arizona
  neckwear: bola tie
Connecticut
  hero: Nathan Hale
  ship: Nautilus (first nuclear submarine)
Idaho
  horse: Appaloosa
Maryland
  sport: jousting
Massachusetts
  bean: baked navy bean (Boston baked beans)
  cat: tabby
  heroine: Deborah Samson
  horse: Morgan
  muffin: corn
Michigan
  soil: Kalkaska soil series
Minnesota
  muffin: blueberry
Missouri
  musical instrument: fiddle
New Mexico
  cookie: biscochito
  vegetables: frijol (pinto bean) and chile (pepper)
Ohio
  rock song: "Hang On Sloopy"
Pennsylvania
  flagship: Niagara (U.S. Brig)
Vermont
  horse: Morgan
Wisconsin
  dog: American water spaniel
  soil: Antigo silt loam

IV. Historical Development and Changes in Counties

The counties of the U.S. today appear fairly stable and unchanging. In fact, from the 1950 Census through 1993 the total number of counties in the U.S. increased only from 3,112 to 3,143, a net gain of 31, or about one percent. But this apparent stability does not reflect the historical development and increase in counties over the decades from the founding of the nation, especially in the states east of the Rockies. The story is an exceedingly complicated one geographically, as large areas were broken up to form new, more compact entities. The number of counties in a state proliferated as the state was settled by pioneers or by residents seeking open land or new horizons. Very often, as previously unsettled territory was reached, it became inconvenient for the residents to make the journey to the county seat to register births, deaths, and marriages, or to file a suit or make a claim in court. In agricultural, pre-industrial America, any day away from the livestock on the farm was a serious inconvenience, and more than a day nearly impossible to arrange or too costly to bear. The farmers' need to be within a day's ride of the county seat was frequently the reason for the formation of new counties, with county seats nearer the newer settlers.

V. Some Out-of-the-Ordinary Place Names

The following list is highly selective, and reflects only a sampling of what struck us as most noteworthy.

Aubbeenaubbee, IN
Bee Branch, MO
Beisizl, ND
Coffee Springs, AL
Correctionville, IA
Dismal, NC
Dog Ear, SD
Dry Prong, LA
East and West Chillisquaque, PA
East Loony, MO
Fair Play, MO
Farr West, UT
Flippin, AR
Funks Grove, IL

Gun Barrel City, TX
Haymow, NE
Humansville, MO
Kaaawa, HI
Magnetic Springs, OH
Mule Barn, OK
Nanty-Glo, PA
New Diggins, WI
Nodaway, IA
Oil Trough, AR
Omphghent, IL

One Road, SD
Oolagah, OK
Pecan Gap, TX
Pe Ell, WA
Quewhiffle, NC
Roasting Ear, AR
Skedee, OK
Sleepy Eye, MN
Snee Oosh, WA
Sni-A-Bar, MO
Snow Shoe, PA

Sopchoppy, FL
Sublimity, OR
Teec Nos Pos, AZ
Tightwad, MO
Turnback, MO
Tywappity, MO
Uncertain, TX
Weeki Wachee, FL
What Cheer, IA
White Eyes, OH

VI. First Name/Last Name Municipalities (by state)

The pattern of the following place names suggests a person's name, and in some cases that is clearly behind the origin of the name. In any case, these are distinctive.

Alabama:
  Phil Campbell
Arkansas:
  Ben Lomond
  Lou Norris
  Reed Keathly
  Joe Burleson
California:
  Ben Lomond
Florida:
  Mary Esther
  Anna Maria
  Jan Phyl Village

Georgia:
  Warner Robins
Indiana:
  Dick Johnson
Louisiana:
  Jean Lafitte
Missouri:
  Jim Henry
Oklahoma:
  John Day
  Gene Autry
Pennsylvania:
  Jim Thorpe

  Henry Clay
  Glen Campbell
Texas:
  Robert Lee
  Tom Bean
  Seth Ward
  George West
Virginia:
  Jack Jonett
  Samuel Miller
  Patrick Henry
West Virginia:
  Jane Lew

Selected Bibliography

In addition to the sources listed below, the editors consulted various printed sources issued by state and local governments, government assoications, etc., including "blue books" or state government manuals, state and municipal directories, and informational brochures.

The *Flying the Colors* series, published by Clements Research II of Dallas, TX (published from 1987 to 1991) was also consulted for the following states: AL, AZ, CA, CT, FL, GA, IL, IN, IA, KS, KY, MA, MI, MO, NH, NJ, NY, NC, PA, SC, TX, VA, WA, WI.

Abate, Frank R., ed. *Omni Gazetteer of the United States of America*, 11 vols. Detroit: Omnigraphics, 1991.

Adams, James N., compiler, and Keller, William E. *Illinois Place Names*. Springfield: Illinois State Historical Society, 1989.

Andriot, Jay, compiler. *Township Atlas of the United States*. McLean, VA: Documents Index, 1991.

Baker, Ronald L., and Carmony, Marvin. *Indiana Place Names*. Bloomington: Indiana University Press, 1975.

Barnes, Will C. *Arizona Place Names*. Tucson: University of Arizona Press, 1988.

Beck, Warren A., and Haase, Ynez D. *Historical Atlas of California*. Norman: University of Oklahoma Press, 1974.

—. *Historical Atlas of New Mexico*. Norman: University of Oklahoma Press, 1969.

Bentley, Elizabeth Petty. *County Courthouse Book*. Baltimore: Genealogical Publishing Co., 1990.

Bloid, John T. *Gazetteer of the State of Michigan*. New York: Arno Press, 1975 (reprint).

Bloodworth, Bertha E. and Morris, Alton C. *Places in the Sun*. Gainesville: University Presses of Florida, 1978.

Boone, Lalia. *Idaho Place Names: A Geographical Dictionary*. Moscow, ID: University of Idaho Press, 1988.

Browning, Peter. *Place Names of the Sierra Nevada, from Abbot to Zumwalt*.

—. *Yosemite Place Names: The Historic Background of Geographic Names in Yosemite National Park*. Lafayette, CA: Great West Books, 1988.

Carlson, Helen S. *Nevada Place Names: A Geographical Dictionary*. Reno: University of Nevada Press, 1974.

Cheney, Roberta Carkeek. *Names on the Face of Montana: The Story of Montana's Place Names*. Missoula, MT: Mountain Press, 1983.

Chernow, Barbara A., and Vallasi, George A., eds. *Columbia Encyclopedia*, 5th ed. New York: Columbia University Press, 1993.

Confederation of American Indians, compilers. *Indian Reservations: A State and Federal Handbook*. Jefferson, NC: McFarland, 1986.

Coulet du Gard, Rene, and Western, Dominique C. *Handbook of American Counties, Parishes and Independent Cities.* Newark, DE: Editions des Deux Mondes, 1981.

Dean, Ernie. *Arkansas Place Names.* Branson, MO: Ozarks Mountaineer, 1986.

Espenshade, A. Howry. *Pennsylvania Place Names.* Harrisburg: Evangelical Press, 1925.

Evinger, William R. *Directory of Military Bases in the U.S.* Phoenix, AZ: Oryx Press, 1991.

Fitzpatrick, Lilian L. *Nebraska Place Names.* Lincoln: University of Nebraska Press, 1960.

Foscue, Virginia O. *Place Names in Alabama.* Tuscaloosa: University of Alabama Press, 1989.

Fullerton, Ralph O. *Place Names of Tennessee.* Nashville: Tennessee Division of Geology, 1974.

Gannett, Henry. *Geographic Dictionary of Connecticut and Rhode Island.* Baltimore: Genealogical Publishing, 1978 (reprint).

—. *Origin of Certain Place Names in the United States*, 2nd ed. Williamstown, MA: Corner House, 1978 (reprint).

Gard, Robert, and Sorden, L.G. *Romance of Wisconsin Placenames.* Minocqua, WI: Heartland Press, 1988.

Gudde, Erwin G. *California Place Names: The Origin and Etymology of Current Geographical Names.* Berkeley: University of California Press, 1949.

Hagemann, James. *Heritage of Virginia: The Story of Place Names in the Old Dominion.* West Chester, PA: Whitford Press, 1986.

Halverson, F. Douglas, compiler. *County Histories of the United States Giving Present Name, Date Formed, Parent County, and County Seat.* (unpublished manuscript, n.d.)

Hanson, Gerald T., and Moneyhon, Carl H. *Historical Atlas of Arkansas.* Norman: University of Oklahoma Press, 1989.

Harder, Kelsie B., ed. *Illustrated Dictionary of Place Names, United States and Canada.* New York: Facts On File, 1985.

Harris, William H., and Levey, Judith S., eds. *New Columbia Encyclopedia.* New York: Columbia University Press, 1975.

Hart, James D. *Companion to California.* New York: Oxford University Press, 1978.

Heck, L.W.; Wraight, A.J.; Orth, D.J.; Carter, J.R.; Van Winkle, L.G.; and Hazen, Janet. *Delaware Place Names.* Geological Survey and Coast & Geodetic Survey, 1966.

Hitchman, Robert. *Place Names of Washington.* Washington State Historical Society, 1985.

Hunt, Elmer Munson. *New Hampshire Town Names and Whence They Came.* Peterborough, NH: Noone House, 1970.

Indian Service Population and Labor Force Estimates. U.S. Dept. of the Interior, Bureau of Indian Affairs (report), 1991.

Kaminkow, Marion J. *Maryland A to Z: A Topographical Dictionary.* Baltimore: Magna Carta Book Co., 1985.

Kane, Joseph Nathan. *American Counties,* 4th ed. Metuchen, NJ: Scarecrow Press, 1983.

Kenny, Hamill. *Placenames of Maryland: Their Origin and Meaning.* Baltimore: Museum and Library of Maryland History, Maryland Historical Society, 1984.

Krakow, Kenneth K. *Georgia Place-Names.* Macon, GA: Winship Press, 1975.

Lekisch, Barbara. *Tahoe Place Names: The Origin and History of Names in the Lake Tahoe Basin.* Lafayette, CA: Great West Books, 1988.

McArthur, Lewis A. *Oregon Geographic Names*, 6th ed. Oregon Historical Society Press, 1992.

McCoy, Sondra Van Meter, and Hults, Jan. *1001 Kansas Place Names.* University Press of Kansas, 1989.

Morris, Allen. *Florida Place Names.* Coral Gables: University of Miami, 1974.

Morris, John W.; Goins, Charles R.; and McReynolds, Edwin C. *Historical Atlas of Oklahoma.* Norman: University of Oklahoma Press, 1969.

National Gazetteer of the United States of America, United States Concise. U.S. Geological Survey in cooperation with U.S. Board on Geographic Names, 1990.

Neuffer, Claude Henry. *Names in South Carolina: Vols. I-XII, 1954-1965.* University of South Carolina, 1967.

Neuffer, Claude and Irene. *Correct Mispronunciations of Some South Carolina Names.* Columbia: University of South Carolina, 1983.

Origin of New Jersey Place Names. Reprinted by NJ Public Library Commission, Trenton, 1945.

Orth, Donald J. *Dictionary of Alaska Place Names.* U.S. Geological Survey, Dept. of the Interior, 1967.

Paisano, Edna; Greendeer-Lee, Joan; Cowles, June; and Carroll, Debbie. *American Indian and Alaska Native Areas.* Population Division, Bureau of Census, 1990.

Palmer, T.S., ed. *Place Names of the Death Valley Region in California and Nevada.* Morongo Valley, CA: Sagebrush Press, 1980.

Palmetto Place Names. South Carolina Education Association, n.d.

Payne, Roger L. *Place Names of the Outer Banks.* Washington, NC: Thomas A. Williams, 1985.

Pearce, T.M., ed. *New Mexico Place Names: A Geographical Dictionary.* University of New Mexico Press, 1965.

Perkey, Elton A. *Perkey's Nebraska Place Names.* Lincoln: Nebraska State Historical Society, 1982.

Phillips, James W. *Washington State Place Names.* Seattle: University of Washington Press, 1971.

Powell William S. *North Carolina Gazetteer: A Dictionary of Tar Heel Places.* Chapel Hill: University of North Carolina Press, 1968.

Pukui, Mary Kawena, and Elbert, Samuel H. *Hawaiian Dictionary: Hawaiian-English, English-Hawaiian*, rev. ed. Honolulu: University of Hawaii Press, 1986.

Pukui, Mary Kawena; Elbert, Samuel H.; and Mookini, Esther T. *Place Names of Hawaii.* Honolulu: University of Hawaii Press, 1974.

Quimby, Myron J. *Scratch Ankle, U.S.A.: American Place Names and their Derivation.* New York: A.S. Barnes, 1969.

Rafferty, Milton D. *Historical Atlas of Missouri.* Norman: University of Oklahoma Press, 1982.

Ramsey, Robert L. *Our Storehouse of Missouri Place Names.* Columbia: University of Missouri Press, 1973.

Read, William A. *Florida Place-names of Indian Origin and Seminole Personal Names.* Baton Rouge: Louisiana State University, 1934.

Rennick, Robert M. *Kentucky Place Names.* University Press of Kentucky, 1984.

Rippley, La Verne J., and Schmeissner, Rainer H. *German Place Names in Minnesota (Deutsche Ortsnamen in Minnesota).* Northfield, MN: St. Olaf College, 1989.

Romig, Walter. *Michigan Place Names: The History of the Founding and the Naming of More than Five Thousand Past and Present Michigan Communities.* Detroit: Wayne State University Press, 1986.

Rydjord, John. *Indian Place-Names: Their Origin, Evolution, and Meanings, Collected in Kansas from the Siouan, Algonquian, Shoshonean, Caddoan, Iroquoian, and Other Tongues.* Norman: University of Oklahoma Press, 1968.

—. *Kansas Place-Names.* Norman: University of Oklahoma Press, 1972.

Savela, Judith A., ed. *Michigan Municipalities.* Sterling Heights Public Library, MI, 1989.

Scott, James W., and De Lorme, Roland L. *Historical Atlas of Washington.* Norman: University of Oklahoma Press, 1988.

Seltzer, Leon E., ed. *Columbia Lippincott Gazetteer of the World.* New York: Columbia University Press, 1952.

Shirk, George H. *Oklahoma Place Names*, 2nd ed. Norman: University of Oklahoma Press, 1965.

Sixth Report of the United States Geographic Board, 1890 to 1932. U.S. Government Printing Office; reprinted by Gale Research, 1967.

Sneve, Virginia Driving Hawk, ed. *South Dakota Geographic Names.* Sioux Falls, SD: Brevet Press, 1973.

Snyder, John P. *The Story of New Jersey's Civil Boundaries, 1606-1968.* Trenton: Bureau of Geology and Topography, 1969.

Socolofsky, Homer E., and Self, Huber. *Historical Atlas of Kansas*, 2nd ed. Norman: University of Oklahoma Press, 1972.

Stephens, A. Ray, and Holmes, William M. *Historical Atlas of Texas.* Norman: University of Oklahoma Press, 1989.

Stewart, George R. *American Place-Names: A Concise and Selective Dictionary for the Continental United States of America.* New York: Oxford University Press, 1970.

—. *Names on the Land: A Historical Account of Place-Naming in the United States.* Boston: Houghton Mifflin, 1967.

Swift, Esther Munroe. *Vermont Place-Names.* Brattleboro: Stephen Greene Press, 1977.

Tarpley, Fred. *1001 Texas Place Names.* Austin: University of Texas Press, 1980.

—. *Place Names of Northeast Texas.* Commerce, TX: East Texas State University, 1969.

Tilden, Freeman; revised and expanded by Paul Schullery. *National Parks: The Classic Book on the National Parks, National Monuments, & Historic Sites.* New York: Alfred A. Knopf, 1986.

Upham, Warren. *Minnesota Geographic Names: Their Origin and Historic Significance.* St. Paul: Minnesota Historical Society, 1969.

Urbanek, Mae. *Wyoming Place Names.* Missoula, MT: Mountain Press, 1988.

Van Cott, John W. *Utah Place Names: A Comprehensive Guide to the Origins of Geographic Names.* Salt Lake City: University of Utah Press, 1990.

Van Zandt, Franklin K. *Boundaries of the United States and the Several States.* Geological Survey, U.S. Dept. of the Interior, 1976.

Vermont Year Book. Chester, VT: The National Survey, 1992.

Vogel, Virgil J. *Indian Names in Michigan.* Ann Arbor: University of Michigan Press, 1986.

—. *Iowa Place Names of Indian Origin.* Iowa City: University of Iowa Press, 1983.

Walker, Henry P., and Bufkin, Don. *Historical Atlas of Arizona.* Norman: University of Oklahoma Press, 1979.

Warmsley, Arthur J. *Connecticut Post Offices and Postmarks.* Portland, CT (private publication), 1977.

Webster's New Geographical Dictionary. Springfield, MA: Merriam-Webster, 1988.

Worldmark Encyclopedia of the States, 2nd ed. New York: John Wiley & Sons, 1986.

Who Was Who in America: Historical Volume 1607-1896, rev. ed. Chicago: Marquis Who's Who, 1967

Wick, Doulgas A. *North Dakota Place Names.* Hedemarken Collectibles, 1988.

Alaska

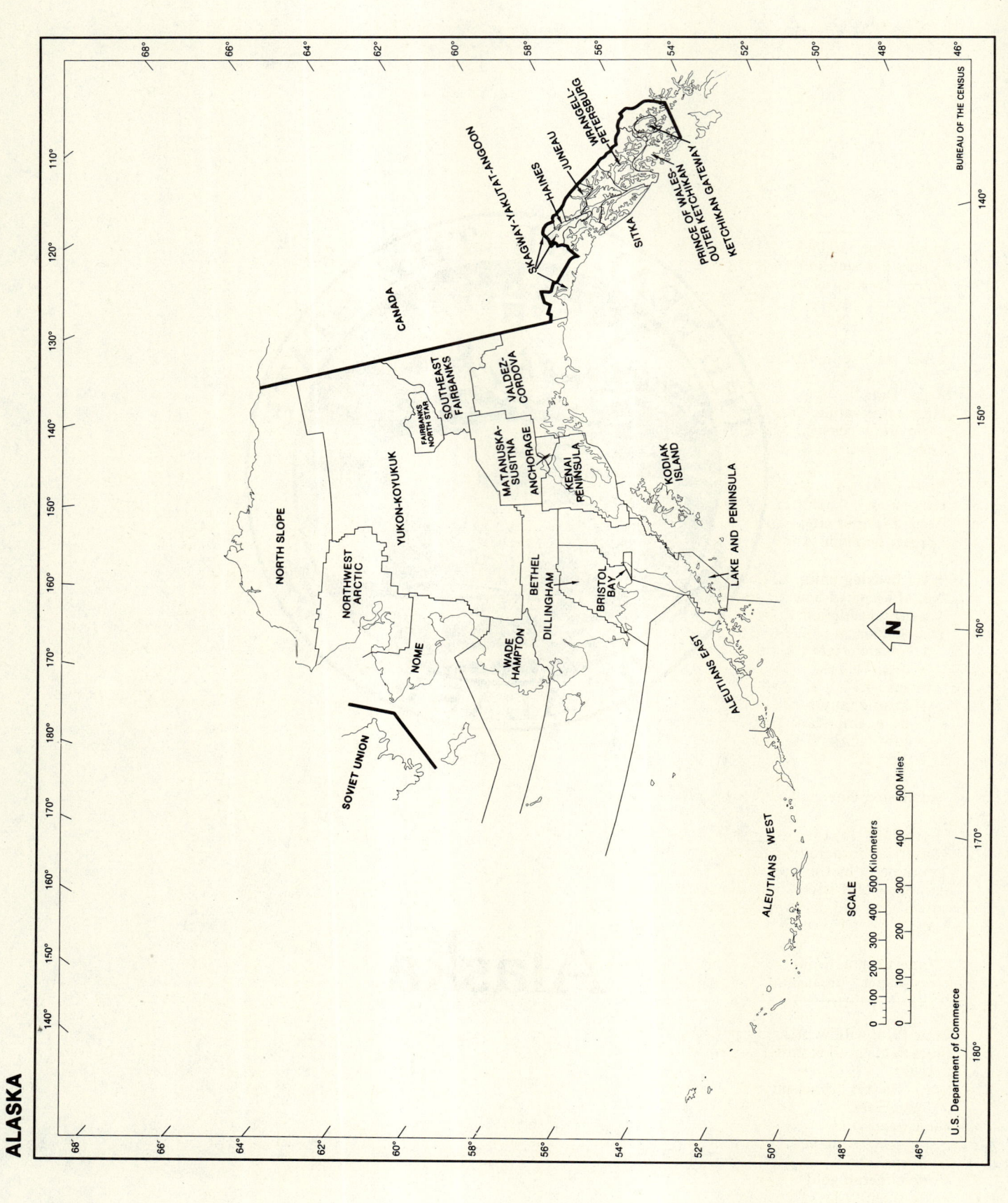

Alaska

Population: 550,043 (1990); 401,851 (1980)
Population rank (1990): 49
Percent population change (1980–1990): 36.9
Population projection: 609,000 (1995); 655,000 (2000)

Area: total: 656,424 sq. mi.; 570,374 sq. mi. land, 86,051 sq. mi. water
Area rank: 1
Highest elevation: 20,320 ft., Mt. McKinley (Yukon-Koyukuk census area; highest point in U.S.)
Lowest point: sea level

State capital: Juneau (Juneau Borough)
Largest city: Anchorage (226,338)
Second largest city: Fairbanks (30,843)
Largest borough: Anchorage Borough (226,338)

Total housing units: 232,608
No. of occupied housing units: 188,915
Vacant housing units (%): 18.8
Distribution of population by race and Hispanic origin (%):
  White: 75.5
  Black: 4.1
  Hispanic (any race): 3.2
  Native American: 15.6
  Asian/Pacific: 3.6
  Other: 1.2

Admission date: January 3, 1959 (49th state).

Location: In the northwestern corner of North America, bordered on the north by the Beaufort Sea, on the east by the Canadian Yukon Territory and the province of British Columbia, on the south by the Gulf of Alaska, and on the west by the Chukchi and Bering seas.

Name Origin: From the Aleut word *alakshak*, meaning 'peninsula,' 'great land,' or 'mainland.'

State bird: willow ptarmigan *(Lagopus lagopus)*
State fish: chinook (king) salmon *(Oncorhynchus tshawytscha)*
State flower: forget-me-not *(Myosotis sylvatica* or *M. scorpioides)*
State gem: jade
State marine mammal: bowhead whale *(Balaena mysticetus)*
State mineral: gold
State song: "Alaska's Flag"
State sport: dogteam racing (mushing)
State tree: Sitka spruce *(Picea sitchensis)*

State motto: North to the Future
State nickname: Last Frontier

Area code: 907
Time zone: Alaska Standard Time
Abbreviations: AK (postal); Ala. (traditional)
Part of (region): Pacific Coast

Local Government

Counties

Alaska has no counties as such; the state has 16 organized boroughs (as of September 22, 1992), each governed by an assembly of from 5 to 11 members. These boroughs cover most of the populated area. The rest of the state is unorganized, although the U.S. Bureau of the Census has designated 11 "census areas" for classifying the population outside the boroughs.

Municipalities

There are 44 cities, governed by elected mayors and councils. Three cities, Juneau, Sitka, and Anchorage, are considered unified municipalities and have consolidated city and borough functions.

Settlement History and Early Development

Between 10,000 and 40,000 years ago, Alaska's first inhabitants arrived via a land bridge from Siberia. Those settlers were the ancestors of the Eskimo, Aleut, and Indian (including Tlingit, Haida, Tsimshian, and Athabaskan) groups that lived in Alaska when the first white explorers, Russians led by Vitus Bering, landed in 1741. Russian hunters and fur traders established settlements on Kodiak Island, and, after battles with the Tlingit Indians in 1802 and 1804, at New Archangel (present-day Sitka) on the mainland.

Following the decline of the fur trade and the Crimean War (1853–56), Russia agreed to sell Alaska to the United States for $7,200,000, or about 2 cents per acre. The purchase was arranged by Secretary of State William H. Seward in 1867. Seward was severely criticized at the time by some, who dubbed Alaska "Seward's Folly" or "Seward's Icebox" because they thought the land was worthless frozen tundra. Alaska was administered by various federal government departments until given a code of laws and federal court in 1884.

The Gold Rush

In 1896, gold was discovered in the Canadian Klondike district of the Yukon, bringing thousands of prospectors through Alaska. When gold was also discovered near Nome in 1899, more people were attracted to Alaska. In addition to the gold mines, copper mines and fish canneries were established. In 1906 Alaskans elected a non-voting representative to Congress. Attention was focused on Alaska by the Ballinger-Pinchot Affair in 1910, a dispute over national forest lands being turned over to a private syndicate. In 1912, Alaska was established as a U.S. territory.

World War II
Recognizing the military importance of Alaska as a route to East Asia, the U.S. government constructed military bases and, in 1942, the Alaska Highway. Two of Alaska's islands, Attu and Kiska, were briefly occupied by the Japanese in 1942–43.

Statehood
Alaska was voted into the Union in 1958 and officially became the 49th state on Jan. 3, 1959. During the next decade, the new state established a ferry system and faced two disasters: a March 1964 earthquake near Anchorage that was the biggest ever recorded in North America and a 1967 flood in Fairbanks.

The discovery of oil in Prudhoe Bay in 1968 led to the construction of the 800-mile Alaskan Pipeline from Prudhoe Bay to Valdez and increased prosperity for Alaska, although that diminished in the 1980s with falling oil prices. Two congressional acts caused some dissention: the Alaska Native Claims Settlement Act in 1971 gave land to Alaska's Eskimos and Indians and the Alaska National Interest Lands Conservation Act of 1980 set aside 104 million acres of land. Tensions exist between whites and Alaskan Indians and Eskimos, as well as between groups favoring development versus those who favor conservation.

On March 24, 1989, the *Exxon Valdez* struck a reef and spilled 10 million gallons of oil into Prince William Sound. This disaster caused great damage to the ecosystem of the area; relief efforts were undertaken to preserve wildlife endangered by the oil spill. Despite this incident, dwindling oil production at Prudhoe Bay has led some to consider oil exploration at the Arctic National Wildlife Refuge.

State Boundaries
The long eastern boundary between Alaska and Canada was described in conventions between Russia and Great Britain in 1825 and 1827. Alaska's southern boundary was established at latitude 54° 40' by Russian treaties with the United States in 1824 and Canada in 1825. A dispute between the U.S. and Canada regarding Alaska's southeastern border, which followed the discovery of gold in the Yukon, was settled in favor of the United States by an international commission in 1903.

Alaska Boroughs and Census Areas

- Aleutians East
- Aleutians West Census Area
- Anchorage
- Bethel Census Area
- Bristol Bay
- Denali
- Dillingham Census Area
- Fairbanks North Star
- Haines
- Juneau
- Kenai Peninsula
- Ketchikan Gateway
- Kodiak Island
- Lake and Peninsula
- Matanuska-Susitna
- Nome Census Area
- North Slope
- Northwest Arctic
- Prince of Wales-Outer Ketchikan Census Area
- Sitka
- Skagway-Hoonah-Angoon Census Area
- Southeast Fairbanks Census Area
- Valdez-Cordova Census Area
- Wade Hampton Census Area
- Wrangell-Petersburg Census Area
- Yakutat
- Yukon-Koyukuk Census Area

Multi-County Places

The following Alaska place is in more than one county. Given here is the total population and the names of the counties it is in.

Newtok, pop. 207; Bethel Census Area (207), Wade Hampton Census Area (0)

Aleutians East Borough
Chief Town: Sand Point (ZIP: 99661)

Pop: 2,464 (1990); 1,643 (1980) **Pop Density:** 0.4
Land: 6984.7 sq. mi.; **Water:** 8027.0 sq. mi. **Area Code:** 907

In southwestern AK, extending south and west from the Alaska Peninsula as far west as Akutan Island; bounded on south and east by Pacific Ocean, on north by Bering Sea. Established Oct 23, 1987 from the eastern portion of the former Aleutian Islands Census Area and the southwestern portion of the Dillingham Census Area.

Name origin: Adjective form of *Aleut*, the natives of the Aleutian Islands.

Akutan City
ZIP: 99553 **Lat:** 54-08-10 N **Long:** 165-47-09 W
Pop: 589 (1990); 169 (1980) **Pop Density:** 43.3
Land: 13.6 sq. mi.; **Water:** 4.6 sq. mi.

On a chain of islands that extend 1700 mi. from the Alaskan Peninsula.
Name origin: From Aleut term meaning 'mistake.'

Cold Bay City
ZIP: 99571 **Lat:** 55-13-30 N **Long:** 162-44-19 W
Pop: 148 (1990) **Pop Density:** 2.6
Land: 58.0 sq. mi.; **Water:** 21.9 sq. mi.

False Pass CDP
ZIP: 99583 **Lat:** 54-50-27 N **Long:** 163-26-12 W
Pop: 68 (1990) **Pop Density:** 4.6
Land: 14.8 sq. mi.; **Water:** 2.4 sq. mi.

King Cove City
ZIP: 99612 **Lat:** 55-03-30 N **Long:** 162-17-59 W
Pop: 451 (1990); 460 (1980) **Pop Density:** 155.5
Land: 2.9 sq. mi.; **Water:** 2.0 sq. mi.

At the southwestern end of the Aleutian Peninsula.
Name origin: Possibly for an early settler.

Nelson Lagoon CDP
Lat: 55-55-14 N **Long:** 161-11-20 W
Pop: 83 (1990) **Pop Density:** 0.3
Land: 245.1 sq. mi.; **Water:** 196.6 sq. mi.

Sand Point City
ZIP: 99661 **Lat:** 55-19-10 N **Long:** 160-29-28 W
Pop: 878 (1990); 625 (1980) **Pop Density:** 114.0
Land: 7.7 sq. mi.; **Water:** 0.7 sq. mi.

On the southwestern end of the Alaska Peninsula.
Name origin: For the low, flat, sandy spit nearby.

Aleutians West Census Area
Chief Town: Adak Station (ZIP: 98791)

Pop: 9,478 (1990); 6,125 (1980) **Pop Density:** 2.2
Land: 4402.1 sq. mi.; **Water:** 9712.6 sq. mi. **Area Code:** 907

Southwest of Alaska Peninsula, from the Andreanof Islands in east to the Near Islands in west; bounded on north by Bering Sea and on south and east by Pacific Ocean.

Name origin: Adjective form of *Aleut*, the natives of the Aleutian Islands. Originally called the *Aleutian Islands Census Area*; name officially changed Jan 1, 1990.

Adak Station Military Facility
ZIP: 98791 **Lat:** 51-50-34 N **Long:** 176-38-25 W
Pop: 4,633 (1990) **Pop Density:** 37.9
Land: 122.3 sq. mi.; **Water:** 4.9 sq. mi.

Amchitka CDP
Lat: 51-34-01 N **Long:** 78-52-38 W
Pop: 25 (1990) **Pop Density:** 0.2
Land: 115.8 sq. mi.; **Water:** 161.2 sq. mi.

Atka City
Lat: 52-14-31 N **Long:** 174-12-18 W
Pop: 73 (1990) **Pop Density:** 7.9
Land: 9.2 sq. mi.; **Water:** 27.0 sq. mi.

Nikolski CDP
Lat: 52-57-40 N **Long:** 168-49-19 W
Pop: 35 (1990) **Pop Density:** 0.4
Land: 88.4 sq. mi.; **Water:** 116.0 sq. mi.

St. George City
Lat: 56-36-53 N **Long:** 169-35-40 W
Pop: 138 (1990) **Pop Density:** 4.0
Land: 34.9 sq. mi.; **Water:** 26.6 sq. mi.

St. Paul City
Lat: 57-12-37 N **Long:** 170-13-08 W
Pop: 763 (1990); 551 (1980) **Pop Density:** 18.9
Land: 40.4 sq. mi.; **Water:** 255.2 sq. mi.

Part of the Pribilof Islands southwest of the southwestern coast of AK in the Bering Sea.
Name origin: For the apostle.

Unalaska City
ZIP: 99685 **Lat:** 53-56-04 N **Long:** 166-30-37 W
Pop: 3,089 (1990); 1,322 (1980) **Pop Density:** 29.6
Land: 104.3 sq. mi.; **Water:** 111.4 sq. mi.

One of the Aleutian Islands at the western end of the Alaskan Peninsula in southwestern AK.
Name origin: An Aleut name of disputed meaning.

Anchorage Borough and City
Chief Town: Anchorage (ZIP: 99501)

Pop: 226,338 (1990); 174,431 (1980)
Land: 1697.6 sq. mi.; **Water:** 263.9 sq. mi.
Lat: 61-10-42 N **Long:** 149-11-11 W
Pop Density: 133.3
Area Code: 907
Elev: 101 ft.

On the south-central coast of AK, at the head of Cook Inlet, 470 mi. south of Fairbanks. Founded 1914. Borough and city were consolidated as the municipality of Anchorage; includes Glen Alps and Girdwood.

Name origin: For Knik Anchorage, a settlement just offshore. This was named for a Tanaina village spelled *Kinik* and *Kinnick* 'fire.' Previously called *Ship Creek* and *Woodrow*.

Bethel Census Area
Chief Town: Bethel (ZIP: 99559)

Pop: 13,656 (1990); 10,999 (1980)
Land: 41087.4 sq. mi.; **Water:** 4867.2 sq. mi.
Pop Density: 0.3
Area Code: 907

In southwestern AK with coastal area on Bering Sea. Established from the former *Kuskokwim Division*.

Name origin: For the city.

Akiachak — City
ZIP: 99551 **Lat:** 60-52-18 N **Long:** 161-24-12 W
Pop: 481 (1990); 438 (1980) **Pop Density:** 50.1
Land: 9.6 sq. mi.; **Water:** 1.9 sq. mi.

Akiak — City
ZIP: 99552 **Lat:** 60-53-08 N **Long:** 161-11-32 W
Pop: 285 (1990); 198 (1980) **Pop Density:** 150.0
Land: 1.9 sq. mi.; **Water:** 1.0 sq. mi.
Name origin: From an Inuit term meaning 'crossing over place.'

Aniak — City
ZIP: 99557 **Lat:** 61-34-50 N **Long:** 159-32-20 W
Pop: 540 (1990); 341 (1980) **Pop Density:** 114.9
Land: 4.7 sq. mi.; **Water:** 1.4 sq. mi. **Elev:** 84 ft.
Name origin: For the nearby river.

Atmautluak — City
ZIP: 99559 **Lat:** 60-51-15 N **Long:** 162-16-08 W
Pop: 258 (1990); 219 (1980) **Pop Density:** 151.8
Land: 1.7 sq. mi.; **Water:** 0.0 sq. mi.

Bethel — City
ZIP: 99559 **Lat:** 60-46-05 N **Long:** 161-46-19 W
Pop: 4,674 (1990); 3,576 (1980) **Pop Density:** 105.5
Land: 44.3 sq. mi.; **Water:** 5.8 sq. mi.

In western AK near the mouth of the Kuskokwim River.

Chefornak — City
ZIP: 99561 **Lat:** 60-09-13 N **Long:** 164-12-37 W
Pop: 320 (1990); 230 (1980) **Pop Density:** 10.0
Land: 32.1 sq. mi.; **Water:** 4.1 sq. mi.

Chuathbaluk — City
Lat: 61-34-23 N **Long:** 159-12-59 W
Pop: 97 (1990); 105 (1980) **Pop Density:** 23.1
Land: 4.2 sq. mi.; **Water:** 2.1 sq. mi.

Crooked Creek — CDP
ZIP: 99575 **Lat:** 61-52-36 N **Long:** 158-04-40 W
Pop: 106 (1990); 108 (1980) **Pop Density:** 2.6
Land: 40.3 sq. mi.; **Water:** 3.3 sq. mi.

Eek — City
ZIP: 99578 **Lat:** 60-13-08 N **Long:** 162-01-35 W
Pop: 254 (1990); 228 (1980) **Pop Density:** 254.0
Land: 1.0 sq. mi.; **Water:** 0.1 sq. mi.
Name origin: For the Eek River on which it is located; meaning of name is unknown.

Goodnews Bay — City
ZIP: 99589 **Lat:** 59-06-35 N **Long:** 161-33-55 W
Pop: 241 (1990); 168 (1980) **Pop Density:** 75.3
Land: 3.2 sq. mi.; **Water:** 2.0 sq. mi.
Name origin: From Russian referring to unknown good news that arrived here in 1818.

Kasigluk — City
ZIP: 99609 **Lat:** 60-53-20 N **Long:** 162-32-44 W
Pop: 425 (1990) **Pop Density:** 22.5
Land: 18.9 sq. mi.; **Water:** 0.4 sq. mi.

Kipnuk — CDP
ZIP: 99614 **Lat:** 59-55-23 N **Long:** 164-06-03 W
Pop: 470 (1990); 371 (1980) **Pop Density:** 15.9
Land: 29.5 sq. mi.; **Water:** 0.7 sq. mi.

Kongiganak — CDP
Lat: 59-55-26 N **Long:** 162-51-06 W
Pop: 294 (1990); 239 (1980) **Pop Density:** 25.8
Land: 11.4 sq. mi.; **Water:** 0.8 sq. mi.

Kwethluk — City
ZIP: 99621 **Lat:** 60-46-18 N **Long:** 161-23-18 W
Pop: 558 (1990); 454 (1980) **Pop Density:** 54.7
Land: 10.2 sq. mi.; **Water:** 1.9 sq. mi.
Name origin: From an Inuit term meaning 'bad river.'

Kwigillingok — CDP
ZIP: 99622 Lat: 59-50-09 N Long: 163-06-49 W
Pop: 278 (1990); 354 (1980) Pop Density: 17.7
Land: 15.7 sq. mi.; Water: 5.0 sq. mi.

Lime Village — CDP
Lat: 61-25-58 N Long: 155-28-21 W
Pop: 42 (1990); 48 (1980) Pop Density: 0.8
Land: 53.4 sq. mi.; Water: 0.0 sq. mi.

Lower Kalskag — City
ZIP: 99626 Lat: 61-31-07 N Long: 160-20-59 W
Pop: 291 (1990); 246 (1980) Pop Density: 223.8
Land: 1.3 sq. mi.; Water: 0.4 sq. mi.

Mekoryuk — City
ZIP: 99630 Lat: 60-21-56 N Long: 166-17-00 W
Pop: 177 (1990); 160 (1980) Pop Density: 23.9
Land: 7.4 sq. mi.; Water: 0.0 sq. mi.

Napakiak — City
ZIP: 99634 Lat: 60-40-36 N Long: 161-58-43 W
Pop: 318 (1990); 262 (1980) Pop Density: 48.9
Land: 6.5 sq. mi.; Water: 0.1 sq. mi.
Name origin: From the Inuit term meaning 'wood people.'

Napaskiak — City
ZIP: 99559 Lat: 60-39-49 N Long: 161-44-17 W
Pop: 328 (1990); 244 (1980) Pop Density: 74.5
Land: 4.4 sq. mi.; Water: 0.3 sq. mi.
Name origin: Variation of the Inuit term for 'wood people.'

Newtok — City
ZIP: 99559 Lat: 60-56-12 N Long: 164-38-04 W
Pop: 207 (1990); 131 (1980) Pop Density: 43.1
Land: 4.8 sq. mi.; Water: 1.3 sq. mi.
Part of the town is also in Wade Hampton Census Area.

Nightmute — City
ZIP: 99690 Lat: 60-26-53 N Long: 164-48-14 W
Pop: 153 (1990); 119 (1980) Pop Density: 1.6
Land: 97.2 sq. mi.; Water: 4.6 sq. mi.

Nunapitchuk — City
ZIP: 99641 Lat: 60-52-44 N Long: 162-27-08 W
Pop: 378 (1990) Pop Density: 49.7
Land: 7.6 sq. mi.; Water: 0.3 sq. mi.

Oscarville — CDP
Lat: 60-41-47 N Long: 161-45-33 W
Pop: 57 (1990); 56 (1980) Pop Density: 38.0
Land: 1.5 sq. mi.; Water: 0.6 sq. mi.

Platinum — City
ZIP: 99651 Lat: 58-58-26 N Long: 161-43-30 W
Pop: 64 (1990); 55 (1980) Pop Density: 1.4
Land: 44.6 sq. mi.; Water: 0.0 sq. mi.
Name origin: For the discovery of platinum here in 1927.

Quinhagak — City
ZIP: 99655 Lat: 59-44-21 N Long: 161-52-20 W
Pop: 501 (1990); 412 (1980) Pop Density: 102.2
Land: 4.9 sq. mi.; Water: 0.0 sq. mi.
Name origin: From an Inuit term possibly meaning 'newly formed river,' a reference to the constantly changing channel of the Kanektok River on which the town is located.

Red Devil — CDP
ZIP: 99656 Lat: 61-47-25 N Long: 157-20-52 W
Pop: 53 (1990); 39 (1980) Pop Density: 2.3
Land: 23.5 sq. mi.; Water: 1.9 sq. mi.

Sleetmute — CDP
ZIP: 99668 Lat: 61-43-16 N Long: 157-11-00 W
Pop: 106 (1990); 107 (1980) Pop Density: 3.8
Land: 27.6 sq. mi.; Water: 2.0 sq. mi.

Stony River — CDP
Lat: 61-47-35 N Long: 156-34-50 W
Pop: 51 (1990); 62 (1980) Pop Density: 3.0
Land: 17.1 sq. mi.; Water: 3.2 sq. mi.

Toksook Bay — City
Lat: 60-29-35 N Long: 165-05-39 W
Pop: 420 (1990); 333 (1980) Pop Density: 13.0
Land: 32.2 sq. mi.; Water: 40.6 sq. mi.

Tuluksak — City
ZIP: 99679 Lat: 61-06-56 N Long: 160-56-21 W
Pop: 358 (1990); 236 (1980) Pop Density: 111.9
Land: 3.2 sq. mi.; Water: 1.0 sq. mi.

Tuntutuliak — CDP
Lat: 60-19-34 N Long: 162-44-26 W
Pop: 300 (1990); 216 (1980) Pop Density: 11.2
Land: 26.9 sq. mi.; Water: 0.3 sq. mi.

Tununak — City
ZIP: 99681 Lat: 60-34-44 N Long: 165-14-41 W
Pop: 316 (1990); 298 (1980) Pop Density: 73.5
Land: 4.3 sq. mi.; Water: 0.0 sq. mi.

Upper Kalskag — City
Lat: 61-32-20 N Long: 160-19-44 W
Pop: 172 (1990); 129 (1980) Pop Density: 45.3
Land: 3.8 sq. mi.; Water: 0.4 sq. mi.

ALASKA, Bristol Bay Borough   American Places Dictionary

Bristol Bay Borough
Chief Town: Naknek (ZIP: 99633)

Pop: 1,410 (1990); 1,094 (1980)   **Pop Density:** 2.7
Land: 519.2 sq. mi.; **Water:** 398.4 sq. mi.   **Area Code:** 907

In southwestern AK at head of Kvichak Bay, an inlet of the Bering Sea, west of Katmai National Park.

Name origin: For the bay, named in 1778 by Capt. James Cook (1728–79) for the Earl of Bristol (England). Formerly the *Bristol Bay Borough Division*.

King Salmon CDP
ZIP: 99613   **Lat:** 58-44-34 N **Long:** 156-32-40 W
Pop: 696 (1990); 545 (1980)   **Pop Density:** 3.2
Land: 219.3 sq. mi.; **Water:** 18.5 sq. mi.

South Naknek CDP
ZIP: 99670   **Lat:** 58-41-06 N **Long:** 156-58-49 W
Pop: 136 (1990); 145 (1980)   **Pop Density:** 1.4
Land: 95.5 sq. mi.; **Water:** 16.5 sq. mi.

Naknek CDP
ZIP: 99633   **Lat:** 58-45-38 N **Long:** 156-54-06 W
Pop: 575 (1990); 318 (1980)   **Pop Density:** 8.0
Land: 72.1 sq. mi.; **Water:** 17.0 sq. mi.

Denali Borough
Chief Town: Cantwell (ZIP: 99744)

Pop: 1,992 (1990)
Area Code: 907

In south-central AK, southwest of Fairbanks. Includes Denali National Park, where Mount McKinley, the highest point in North America, is located. Established Dec 28, 1990, primarily from the Yukon-Koyukuk Census Area and a small part of the Southeast Fairbanks Census Area. Exact figures for land and water area in Denali borough have not yet been determined, but the land area is approximately 12,000 sq. mi.

Name origin: The Tanana Indian name for Mount McKinley, meaning 'the great one' or 'the high one.'

Dillingham Census Area
Chief Town: Dillingham (ZIP: 99576)

Pop: 4,012 (1990); 3,232 (1980)   **Pop Density:** 0.2
Land: 18466.9 sq. mi.; **Water:** 2146.2 sq. mi.   **Area Code:** 907

In southwestern AK, along Bristol Bay, northwest of Katmai National Park. Has been reduced in area as portions have been separated off to create new boroughs and census areas.

Name origin: For the city.

Aleknagik City
ZIP: 99555   **Lat:** 59-17-07 N **Long:** 158-37-44 W
Pop: 185 (1990); 154 (1980)   **Pop Density:** 15.0
Land: 12.3 sq. mi.; **Water:** 6.8 sq. mi.

Dillingham City
ZIP: 99576   **Lat:** 59-03-43 N **Long:** 158-31-40 W
Pop: 2,017 (1990); 1,563 (1980)   **Pop Density:** 61.7
Land: 32.7 sq. mi.; **Water:** 2.1 sq. mi.   **Elev:** 85 ft.
Name origin: For VT Sen. William Dillingham, who toured AK in 1903.

Clarks Point City
ZIP: 99569   **Lat:** 58-50-44 N **Long:** 158-30-56 W
Pop: 60 (1990); 79 (1980)   **Pop Density:** 15.8
Land: 3.8 sq. mi.; **Water:** 1.5 sq. mi.

Ekwok City
ZIP: 99580   **Lat:** 59-21-36 N **Long:** 157-28-45 W
Pop: 77 (1990); 77 (1980)   **Pop Density:** 3.9
Land: 19.7 sq. mi.; **Water:** 1.3 sq. mi.

American Places Dictionary   ALASKA, Fairbanks North Star Borough

Koliganek   CDP
Lat: 59-44-10 N   Long: 157-15-58 W
Pop: 181 (1990); 117 (1980)   Pop Density: 1.9
Land: 97.1 sq. mi.; Water: 0.0 sq. mi.

Manokotak   City
ZIP: 99628   Lat: 59-00-34 N   Long: 158-59-22 W
Pop: 385 (1990); 294 (1980)   Pop Density: 11.0
Land: 34.9 sq. mi.; Water: 0.7 sq. mi.

New Stuyahok   City
ZIP: 99636   Lat: 59-28-23 N   Long: 157-15-43 W
Pop: 391 (1990); 331 (1980)   Pop Density: 11.5
Land: 33.9 sq. mi.; Water: 1.7 sq. mi.

Togiak   City
ZIP: 99678   Lat: 58-56-09 N   Long: 160-34-36 W
Pop: 613 (1990); 470 (1980)   Pop Density: 13.7
Land: 44.8 sq. mi.; Water: 126.8 sq. mi.
Name origin: For the nearby Togiak River, itself named from an Inuit tribal term for the Togiaga people.

Twin Hills   CDP
Lat: 59-04-46 N   Long: 160-12-36 W
Pop: 66 (1990); 70 (1980)   Pop Density: 2.1
Land: 31.0 sq. mi.; Water: 0.8 sq. mi.

Fairbanks North Star Borough
Chief Town: Fairbanks (ZIP: 99707)

Pop: 77,720 (1990); 53,983 (1980)   Pop Density: 10.6
Land: 7362.4 sq. mi.; Water: 81.2 sq. mi.   Area Code: 907
In east-central AK.
Name origin: Formerly called the *Fairbanks Division*, for the city.

College   CDP
ZIP: 99701   Lat: 64-52-10 N   Long: 147-49-24 W
Pop: 11,249 (1990); 4,043 (1980)   Pop Density: 707.5
Land: 15.9 sq. mi.; Water: 0.4 sq. mi.
Site of the University of Alaska.

Eielson Air Force Base   Military Facility
ZIP: 99702   Lat: 64-40-32 N   Long: 147-05-28 W
Pop: 5,251 (1990); 5,232 (1980)   Pop Density: 426.9
Land: 12.3 sq. mi.; Water: 0.9 sq. mi.

Ester   CDP
ZIP: 99725   Lat: 64-51-40 N   Long: 148-01-28 W
Pop: 147 (1990); 149 (1980)   Pop Density: 98.0
Land: 1.5 sq. mi.; Water: 0.0 sq. mi.

Fairbanks   City
ZIP: 99701   Lat: 64-50-13 N   Long: 147-38-56 W
Pop: 30,843 (1990); 22,645 (1980)   Pop Density: 985.4
Land: 31.3 sq. mi.; Water: 0.8 sq. mi.   Elev: 440 ft.
In east-central AK at the junction of the Tanana and Chena rivers. Founded 1901.
Name origin: For U.S. Sen. Charles W. Fairbanks (1852–1918).

Fox   CDP
Lat: 64-57-38 N   Long: 147-37-16 W
Pop: 275 (1990); 123 (1980)   Pop Density: 15.6
Land: 17.6 sq. mi.; Water: 0.0 sq. mi.

Harding Lake   CDP
Lat: 64-25-18 N   Long: 146-51-02 W
Pop: 27 (1990); 38 (1980)   Pop Density: 7.7
Land: 3.5 sq. mi.; Water: 3.8 sq. mi.

Moose Creek   CDP
Lat: 64-42-49 N   Long: 147-09-54 W
Pop: 610 (1990); 510 (1980)   Pop Density: 381.3
Land: 1.6 sq. mi.; Water: 0.1 sq. mi.

North Pole   City
ZIP: 99705   Lat: 64-45-11 N   Long: 147-21-21 W
Pop: 1,456 (1990); 724 (1980)   Pop Density: 355.1
Land: 4.1 sq. mi.; Water: 0.0 sq. mi.
Incorporated 1953.
Name origin: For promotional reasons upon incorporation.

Pleasant Valley   CDP
Lat: 64-52-52 N   Long: 146-52-06 W
Pop: 401 (1990)   Pop Density: 18.5
Land: 21.7 sq. mi.; Water: 0.0 sq. mi.

Salcha   CDP
Lat: 64-28-09 N   Long: 146-56-29 W
Pop: 354 (1990); 319 (1980)   Pop Density: 11.5
Land: 30.7 sq. mi.; Water: 0.7 sq. mi.

Two Rivers   CDP
Lat: 64-52-15 N   Long: 147-05-24 W
Pop: 453 (1990); 359 (1980)   Pop Density: 36.0
Land: 12.6 sq. mi.; Water: 0.0 sq. mi.

Haines Borough
Chief Town: Haines (ZIP: 99827)

Pop: 2,117 (1990); 1,680 (1980) **Pop Density:** 0.9
Land: 2357.0 sq. mi.; **Water:** 397.1 sq. mi. **Area Code:** 907

In AK, panhandle, northeastern (inner) portion of Alexander Archipelago, north of Juneau, bordering the province of British Colombia, Canada, to the east.
Name origin: For the city.

Covenant Life CDP
Lat: 59-25-02 N Long: 136-01-30 W
Pop: 47 (1990) **Pop Density:** 3.1
Land: 15.3 sq. mi.; **Water:** 0.4 sq. mi.

Haines City
ZIP: 99827 Lat: 59-14-24 N Long: 135-26-25 W
Pop: 1,238 (1990); 993 (1980) **Pop Density:** 442.1
Land: 2.8 sq. mi.; **Water:** 0.4 sq. mi. **Elev:** 66 ft.
Name origin: Settled 1881. For Presbyterian official, Mrs. Francina Haines.

Lutak CDP
Lat: 59-20-27 N Long: 135-33-55 W
Pop: 45 (1990) **Pop Density:** 0.7
Land: 65.9 sq. mi.; **Water:** 8.9 sq. mi.

Mosquito Lake CDP
Lat: 59-31-45 N Long: 136-05-27 W
Pop: 80 (1990) **Pop Density:** 0.7
Land: 116.4 sq. mi.; **Water:** 0.4 sq. mi.

Juneau Borough and City
Chief Town: Juneau (ZIP: 99801)

Pop: 26,751 (1990); 19,528 (1980) **Pop Density:** 10.3
Land: 2593.6 sq. mi.; **Water:** 487.6 sq. mi. **Area Code:** 907
Lat: 58-23-18 N **Long:** 134-08-00 W

In panhandle, southeastern AK on the Gastineau Channel, 90 mi. northeast of Sitka. State capital and largest city in the U.S. (by area). Founded 1880; designated to replace Sitka as capital in 1900, but the move to Juneau did not take place until 1906. Major industries: fishing, lumbering, tourism. Borough and city were consolidated in 1970; includes Douglas.
Name origin: For miner Joseph Juneau (1826–99), who discovered gold here in 1880. Formerly *Harrisburg*.

Kenai Peninsula Borough
Chief Town: Soldotna (ZIP: 99669)

Pop: 40,802 (1990); 25,282 (1980) **Pop Density:** 2.5
Land: 16078.9 sq. mi.; **Water:** 5585.4 sq. mi. **Area Code:** 907

In south-central AK, bounded on west by Cook Inlet, on east by the Gulf of Alaska, inlets of the Pacific. Established by combining the former divisions of *Kenai-Cook Inlet* and *Seward*.
Name origin: For a local Indian tribe; meaning of name unknown.

Anchor Point CDP
ZIP: 99556 Lat: 59-46-14 N Long: 151-48-47 W
Pop: 866 (1990); 226 (1980) **Pop Density:** 42.2
Land: 20.5 sq. mi.; **Water:** 4.2 sq. mi.

Clam Gulch CDP
ZIP: 99568 Lat: 60-13-28 N Long: 151-24-07 W
Pop: 79 (1990); 50 (1980) **Pop Density:** 14.9
Land: 5.3 sq. mi.; **Water:** 5.1 sq. mi.

Cohoe CDP
Lat: 60-19-00 N Long: 151-33-51 W
Pop: 508 (1990) **Pop Density:** 18.5
Land: 27.4 sq. mi.; **Water:** 122.2 sq. mi.

Cooper Landing CDP
ZIP: 99572 Lat: 60-29-27 N Long: 149-47-32 W
Pop: 243 (1990); 116 (1980) **Pop Density:** 4.4
Land: 54.8 sq. mi.; **Water:** 5.0 sq. mi.

Crown Point CDP
Lat: 60-25-21 N Long: 149-20-15 W
Pop: 62 (1990) **Pop Density:** 9.8
Land: 6.3 sq. mi.; **Water:** 0.3 sq. mi.

English Bay CDP
Lat: 59-20-48 N Long: 151-54-12 W
Pop: 158 (1990); 124 (1980) **Pop Density:** 20.8
Land: 7.6 sq. mi.; **Water:** 1.6 sq. mi.

ALASKA, Kenai Peninsula Borough

Fox River CDP
Lat: 59-51-29 N Long: 150-57-29 W
Pop: 382 (1990) Pop Density: 4.4
Land: 85.9 sq. mi.; Water: 4.6 sq. mi.

Frit Creek CDP
Lat: 59-44-09 N Long: 151-17-43 W
Pop: 1,426 (1990); 302 (1980) Pop Density: 23.3
Land: 61.3 sq. mi.; Water: 23.6 sq. mi.

Halibut Cove CDP
Lat: 59-35-13 N Long: 151-14-15 W
Pop: 78 (1990); 47 (1980) Pop Density: 10.8
Land: 7.2 sq. mi.; Water: 4.6 sq. mi.

Happy Valley CDP
Lat: 59-56-50 N Long: 151-43-55 W
Pop: 309 (1990) Pop Density: 9.2
Land: 33.6 sq. mi.; Water: 40.4 sq. mi.

Homer City
ZIP: 99603 Lat: 59-38-07 N Long: 151-31-19 W
Pop: 3,660 (1990); 2,209 (1980) Pop Density: 335.8
Land: 10.9 sq. mi.; Water: 15.8 sq. mi.
In southern AK southwest of Seward. Founded 1896.
Name origin: For gold prospector Homer Pennock.

Hope CDP
ZIP: 99605 Lat: 60-53-49 N Long: 149-37-53 W
Pop: 161 (1990); 103 (1980) Pop Density: 3.3
Land: 48.4 sq. mi.; Water: 15.8 sq. mi.

Jakolof Bay CDP
Lat: 59-26-48 N Long: 151-30-37 W
Pop: 28 (1990); 36 (1980) Pop Density: 1.4
Land: 20.2 sq. mi.; Water: 6.5 sq. mi.

Kachemak City
ZIP: 99603 Lat: 59-40-26 N Long: 151-25-51 W
Pop: 365 (1990); 403 (1980) Pop Density: 202.8
Land: 1.8 sq. mi.; Water: 0.0 sq. mi.
Name origin: From Aleut term meaning 'high cliff bay.'

Kalifonsky CDP
Lat: 60-24-36 N Long: 151-16-47 W
Pop: 285 (1990); 92 (1980) Pop Density: 26.6
Land: 10.7 sq. mi.; Water: 2.5 sq. mi.

Kasilof CDP
ZIP: 99610 Lat: 60-19-58 N Long: 151-13-47 W
Pop: 383 (1990); 201 (1980) Pop Density: 33.6
Land: 11.4 sq. mi.; Water: 0.6 sq. mi.

Kenai City
ZIP: 99611 Lat: 60-33-13 N Long: 151-12-26 W
Pop: 6,327 (1990); 4,324 (1980) Pop Density: 241.5
Land: 26.2 sq. mi.; Water: 5.4 sq. mi.
In south-central AK on the west coast of the Kenai Peninsula.
Name origin: An abbreviated version of *Kenaiowkotana*, a term for non-Inuit people.

Moose Pass CDP
ZIP: 99631 Lat: 60-28-02 N Long: 149-23-18 W
Pop: 81 (1990); 76 (1980) Pop Density: 10.1
Land: 8.0 sq. mi.; Water: 0.9 sq. mi.

Nikiski CDP
Lat: 60-43-30 N Long: 151-22-57 W
Pop: 2,743 (1990); 1,109 (1980) Pop Density: 97.6
Land: 28.1 sq. mi.; Water: 90.1 sq. mi.

Nikolaevsk CDP
Lat: 59-49-56 N Long: 151-35-21 W
Pop: 371 (1990) Pop Density: 9.1
Land: 40.7 sq. mi.; Water: 0.0 sq. mi.

Ninilchik CDP
ZIP: 99639 Lat: 60-04-24 N Long: 151-37-52 W
Pop: 456 (1990); 341 (1980) Pop Density: 11.9
Land: 38.2 sq. mi.; Water: 36.5 sq. mi.

Port Graham CDP
Lat: 59-20-54 N Long: 151-50-14 W
Pop: 166 (1990); 161 (1980) Pop Density: 28.1
Land: 5.9 sq. mi.; Water: 1.3 sq. mi.

Primrose CDP
Lat: 60-22-41 N Long: 149-19-22 W
Pop: 63 (1990) Pop Density: 3.9
Land: 16.1 sq. mi.; Water: 2.2 sq. mi.

Ridgeway CDP
Lat: 60-31-55 N Long: 151-05-06 W
Pop: 2,018 (1990) Pop Density: 92.6
Land: 21.8 sq. mi.; Water: 1.1 sq. mi.

Salamatof CDP
Lat: 60-36-57 N Long: 151-20-14 W
Pop: 999 (1990); 334 (1980) Pop Density: 123.3
Land: 8.1 sq. mi.; Water: 9.5 sq. mi.

Seldovia City
ZIP: 99663 Lat: 59-26-20 N Long: 151-42-32 W
Pop: 316 (1990); 479 (1980) Pop Density: 1053.3
Land: 0.3 sq. mi.; Water: 0.1 sq. mi.
Name origin: From Russian *Seldovoy* 'herring bay.'

Seward City
ZIP: 99664 Lat: 60-06-48 N Long: 149-23-34 W
Pop: 2,699 (1990); 1,843 (1980) Pop Density: 175.3
Land: 15.4 sq. mi.; Water: 7.2 sq. mi. Elev: 55 ft.
Name origin: For Sec. of State William Seward (1801–72), who led the effort to purchase AK from the Russians in 1867.

Soldotna City
ZIP: 99669 Lat: 60-29-14 N Long: 151-03-51 W
Pop: 3,482 (1990); 2,320 (1980) Pop Density: 504.6
Land: 6.9 sq. mi.; Water: 0.5 sq. mi. Elev: 88 ft.
Name origin: For Soldotna Creek, itself named either from a derivation of Russian *soldat* 'soldier' or an Indian term meaning 'stream fork.'

Sterling CDP
ZIP: 99672 Lat: 60-30-54 N Long: 150-47-49 W
Pop: 3,802 (1990); 919 (1980) Pop Density: 44.6
Land: 85.3 sq. mi.; Water: 2.8 sq. mi.

Tyonek CDP
ZIP: 99682 Lat: 61-04-01 N Long: 151-12-54 W
Pop: 154 (1990); 239 (1980) Pop Density: 6.9
Land: 22.3 sq. mi.; Water: 3.3 sq. mi.

Ketchikan Gateway Borough
Chief Town: Ketchikan (ZIP: 99901)

Pop: 13,828 (1990); 11,316 (1980)   **Pop Density:** 11.3
Land: 1219.6 sq. mi.; **Water:** 523.9 sq. mi.   **Area Code:** 907
In AK panhandle, southern Alexander Archipelago, east of Prince of Wales Island.
Name origin: For the city, which is in the southernmost portion of AK. Formerly called *Ketchican Division*.

Ketchikan — City
ZIP: 99901   **Lat:** 55-21-09 N   **Long:** 131-39-34 W
Pop: 8,263 (1990); 7,198 (1980)   **Pop Density:** 2754.3
Land: 3.0 sq. mi.; **Water:** 0.8 sq. mi.
In southeastern AK on the southwestern coast of Revillagigedo Island.
Name origin: From the Tlingit term meaning 'eagle wing river.'

Saxman — City
Lat: 55-19-28 N   **Long:** 131-35-31 W
Pop: 369 (1990); 273 (1980)   **Pop Density:** 615.0
Land: 0.6 sq. mi.; **Water:** 0.0 sq. mi.
Name origin: For 1880s schoolteacher Samuel Saxman.

Kodiak Island Borough
Chief Town: Kodiak (ZIP: 99615)

Pop: 13,309 (1990); 9,939 (1980)   **Pop Density:** 2.1
Land: 6462.6 sq. mi.; **Water:** 5383.3 sq. mi.   **Area Code:** 907
Off southern coast of AK, east of the Alaska Peninsula in the Gulf of Alaska.
Name origin: For the island. Formerly called *Kodiak Division*.

Akhiok — City
ZIP: 99615   **Lat:** 56-58-38 N   **Long:** 154-13-03 W
Pop: 77 (1990); 105 (1980)   **Pop Density:** 10.5
Land: 7.3 sq. mi.; **Water:** 2.0 sq. mi.
Off the coast of south-central AK on Kodiak Island.
Name origin: For an Inuit village.

Chiniak — CDP
Lat: 57-37-54 N   **Long:** 152-10-57 W
Pop: 69 (1990)   **Pop Density:** 1.7
Land: 39.9 sq. mi.; **Water:** 74.4 sq. mi.

Karluk — CDP
ZIP: 99608   **Lat:** 57-35-09 N   **Long:** 154-23-43 W
Pop: 71 (1990); 96 (1980)   **Pop Density:** 1.5
Land: 46.5 sq. mi.; **Water:** 20.6 sq. mi.

Kodiak — City
ZIP: 99615   **Lat:** 57-47-54 N   **Long:** 152-24-08 W
Pop: 6,365 (1990); 4,756 (1980)   **Pop Density:** 1989.1
Land: 3.2 sq. mi.; **Water:** 1.3 sq. mi.
In southern AK on an island in the Gulf of Alaska, east of the northern end of the Alaskan Peninsula.
Name origin: From the Inuit word meaning 'island.'

Kodiak Station — Military Facility
Lat: 57-45-46 N   **Long:** 152-31-36 W
Pop: 2,025 (1990); 1,370 (1980)   **Pop Density:** 88.0
Land: 23.0 sq. mi.; **Water:** 7.3 sq. mi.

Larsen Bay — City
ZIP: 99624   **Lat:** 57-33-31 N   **Long:** 154-01-11 W
Pop: 147 (1990); 168 (1980)   **Pop Density:** 28.3
Land: 5.2 sq. mi.; **Water:** 2.3 sq. mi.   **Elev:** 12 ft.
Off the coast of south-central AK, on the western coast of Kodiak Island.
Name origin: For Peter Larsen, a professionial hunter who worked in the area around 1900.

Old Harbor — City
ZIP: 99643   **Lat:** 57-14-42 N   **Long:** 153-22-24 W
Pop: 284 (1990); 340 (1980)   **Pop Density:** 13.9
Land: 20.4 sq. mi.; **Water:** 6.0 sq. mi.
Off the coast of south-central AK on Kodiak Island.

Ouzinkie — City
ZIP: 99644   **Lat:** 57-56-06 N   **Long:** 152-27-29 W
Pop: 209 (1990); 173 (1980)   **Pop Density:** 37.3
Land: 5.6 sq. mi.; **Water:** 1.5 sq. mi.
Name origin: From Russian *uzenkiy* meaning 'very narrow,' a reference to Narrow Strait upon which the town is located.

Port Lions — City
ZIP: 99550   **Lat:** 57-53-26 N   **Long:** 152-51-32 W
Pop: 222 (1990); 215 (1980)   **Pop Density:** 33.6
Land: 6.6 sq. mi.; **Water:** 2.8 sq. mi.
Off the coast of south-central AK on Kodiak Island.
Name origin: For the Lions Club that helped rebuild the former town of Afognak after it was destroyed in the 1964 earthquake.

Womens Bay — CDP
Lat: 57-40-56 N   **Long:** 152-40-07 W
Pop: 620 (1990)   **Pop Density:** 13.8
Land: 44.9 sq. mi.; **Water:** 0.1 sq. mi.

American Places Dictionary   ALASKA, Lake and Peninsula Borough

Lake and Peninsula Borough
Chief Town: Nondalton (ZIP: 99640)

Pop: 1,668 (1990); 1,384 (1980)   **Pop Density:** 0.1
Land: 23632.3 sq. mi.; **Water:** 5375.9 sq. mi.   **Area Code:** 907

In southwestern AK, including most of the upper Alaska Peninsula. Established April 24, 1989 from eastern portions of the Dillingham Census Area plus the Alaska Peninsula.

Name origin: For Iliamna Lake and the Alaska Peninsula.

Chignik   City
ZIP: 99564   **Lat:** 56-18-05 N   **Long:** 158-24-56 W
Pop: 188 (1990)   **Pop Density:** 16.1
Land: 11.7 sq. mi.; **Water:** 4.1 sq. mi.

Chignik Lagoon   CDP
ZIP: 99565   **Lat:** 56-17-02 N   **Long:** 158-30-40 W
Pop: 53 (1990)   **Pop Density:** 4.3
Land: 12.3 sq. mi.; **Water:** 0.0 sq. mi.

Chignik Lake   CDP
Lat: 56-15-22 N   **Long:** 158-46-19 W
Pop: 133 (1990)   **Pop Density:** 7.2
Land: 18.4 sq. mi.; **Water:** 3.8 sq. mi.

Egegik   CDP
ZIP: 99579   **Lat:** 58-13-43 N   **Long:** 157-23-33 W
Pop: 122 (1990)   **Pop Density:** 2.3
Land: 53.9 sq. mi.; **Water:** 22.5 sq. mi.

Igiugig   CDP
Lat: 59-20-06 N   **Long:** 155-54-25 W
Pop: 33 (1990)   **Pop Density:** 1.2
Land: 27.3 sq. mi.; **Water:** 20.8 sq. mi.

Iliamna   CDP
Lat: 59-46-30 N   **Long:** 154-52-03 W
Pop: 94 (1990)   **Pop Density:** 4.3
Land: 22.1 sq. mi.; **Water:** 2.4 sq. mi.

Ivanof Bay   CDP
Lat: 55-57-39 N   **Long:** 159-29-22 W
Pop: 35 (1990)   **Pop Density:** 3.2
Land: 11.1 sq. mi.; **Water:** 1.1 sq. mi.

Kokhanok   CDP
Lat: 59-24-27 N   **Long:** 154-44-39 W
Pop: 152 (1990)   **Pop Density:** 7.0
Land: 21.7 sq. mi.; **Water:** 7.8 sq. mi.

Levelock   CDP
ZIP: 99625   **Lat:** 59-06-30 N   **Long:** 156-53-06 W
Pop: 105 (1990)   **Pop Density:** 3.7
Land: 28.2 sq. mi.; **Water:** 4.5 sq. mi.

Newhalen   City
Lat: 59-44-03 N   **Long:** 154-52-48 W
Pop: 160 (1990); 87 (1980)   **Pop Density:** 26.7
Land: 6.0 sq. mi.; **Water:** 2.2 sq. mi.

Nondalton   City
ZIP: 99640   **Lat:** 59-59-25 N   **Long:** 154-51-11 W
Pop: 178 (1990); 173 (1980)   **Pop Density:** 21.4
Land: 8.3 sq. mi.; **Water:** 0.5 sq. mi.

Pedro Bay   CDP
Lat: 59-47-25 N   **Long:** 154-08-11 W
Pop: 42 (1990)   **Pop Density:** 2.3
Land: 18.2 sq. mi.; **Water:** 8.5 sq. mi.

Perryville   CDP
ZIP: 99648   **Lat:** 55-57-31 N   **Long:** 159-13-33 W
Pop: 108 (1990)   **Pop Density:** 2.9
Land: 37.1 sq. mi.; **Water:** 8.3 sq. mi.

Pilot Point   CDP
ZIP: 99649   **Lat:** 57-37-09 N   **Long:** 157-27-32 W
Pop: 53 (1990)   **Pop Density:** 0.8
Land: 66.7 sq. mi.; **Water:** 16.5 sq. mi.

Port Alsworth   CDP
ZIP: 99653   **Lat:** 60-12-34 N   **Long:** 154-18-14 W
Pop: 55 (1990)   **Pop Density:** 2.6
Land: 21.0 sq. mi.; **Water:** 6.9 sq. mi.

Port Heiden   City
Lat: 56-57-18 N   **Long:** 158-35-16 W
Pop: 119 (1990); 92 (1980)   **Pop Density:** 2.3
Land: 51.1 sq. mi.; **Water:** 0.7 sq. mi.

Matanuska-Susitna Borough
Chief Town: Palmer (ZIP: 99645)

Pop: 39,683 (1990); 17,816 (1980)
Land: 24693.6 sq. mi.; **Water:** 538.8 sq. mi.
Pop Density: 1.6
Area Code: 907

In south-central AK, north of Anchorage.

Name origin: For the Metanuska River, derived from Russian 'for copper river people,' variously spelled *Matanooski, Mednofski, Miduuski*; and the Susitna River, from Tanaina Indian meaning 'sandy river'; also spelled *Sushitna, Sushit, Sutschitna, Sustchino*.

Big Lake   CDP
Lat: 61-31-17 N   Long: 149-57-15 W
Pop: 1,477 (1990); 410 (1980)   **Pop Density:** 11.1
Land: 133.2 sq. mi.; **Water:** 13.0 sq. mi.

Butte   CDP
Lat: 61-32-32 N   Long: 149-03-06 W
Pop: 2,039 (1990)   **Pop Density:** 41.9
Land: 48.7 sq. mi.; **Water:** 3.9 sq. mi.

Chase   CDP
Lat: 62-26-56 N   Long: 150-06-06 W
Pop: 38 (1990)   **Pop Density:** 1.1
Land: 36.1 sq. mi.; **Water:** 1.0 sq. mi.

Chickaloon   CDP
Lat: 61-47-42 N   Long: 148-28-49 W
Pop: 145 (1990)   **Pop Density:** 3.1
Land: 47.0 sq. mi.; **Water:** 0.5 sq. mi.

Houston   City
ZIP: 99694   Lat: 61-37-26 N   Long: 149-46-51 W
Pop: 697 (1990); 370 (1980)   **Pop Density:** 29.4
Land: 23.7 sq. mi.; **Water:** 1.1 sq. mi.   **Elev:** 241 ft.
Founded 1917.
Name origin: For U. S. Congressman, William C. Houston.

Knik   CDP
Lat: 61-27-11 N   Long: 149-44-29 W
Pop: 272 (1990)   **Pop Density:** 28.0
Land: 9.7 sq. mi.; **Water:** 9.6 sq. mi.

Lazy Mountain   CDP
Lat: 61-37-34 N   Long: 148-56-44 W
Pop: 838 (1990)   **Pop Density:** 20.3
Land: 41.3 sq. mi.; **Water:** 1.4 sq. mi.

Meadow Lakes   CDP
Lat: 61-37-28 N   Long: 149-36-04 W
Pop: 2,374 (1990)   **Pop Density:** 44.1
Land: 53.8 sq. mi.; **Water:** 2.9 sq. mi.

Palmer   City
ZIP: 99645   Lat: 61-35-56 N   Long: 149-06-35 W
Pop: 2,866 (1990); 2,141 (1980)   **Pop Density:** 774.6
Land: 3.7 sq. mi.; **Water:** 0.0 sq. mi.   **Elev:** 239 ft.
In southeastern AK, 5 mi. northeast of Matanuska.
Name origin: For George Palmer, a local trader here in 1880.

Skwentna   CDP
ZIP: 99667   Lat: 61-59-24 N   Long: 151-23-52 W
Pop: 85 (1990)   **Pop Density:** 0.2
Land: 398.6 sq. mi.; **Water:** 6.8 sq. mi.

Sutton   CDP
ZIP: 99674   Lat: 61-43-02 N   Long: 148-52-52 W
Pop: 308 (1990); 182 (1980)   **Pop Density:** 48.1
Land: 6.4 sq. mi.; **Water:** 0.2 sq. mi.

Talkeetna   CDP
ZIP: 99676   Lat: 62-20-12 N   Long: 150-05-33 W
Pop: 250 (1990); 264 (1980)   **Pop Density:** 92.6
Land: 2.7 sq. mi.; **Water:** 0.3 sq. mi.

Trapper Creek   CDP
Lat: 62-14-29 N   Long: 150-24-56 W
Pop: 296 (1990)   **Pop Density:** 1.4
Land: 215.5 sq. mi.; **Water:** 3.3 sq. mi.

Wasilla   City
ZIP: 99687   Lat: 61-34-48 N   Long: 149-27-41 W
Pop: 4,028 (1990); 1,559 (1980)   **Pop Density:** 359.6
Land: 11.2 sq. mi.; **Water:** 0.6 sq. mi.   **Elev:** 333 ft.
Founded 1916.
Name origin: For nearby Wasilla Creek, itself named for a Knik Indian chief.

Willow   CDP
ZIP: 99683   Lat: 61-44-26 N   Long: 150-03-22 W
Pop: 285 (1990); 139 (1980)   **Pop Density:** 21.0
Land: 13.6 sq. mi.; **Water:** 0.9 sq. mi.

Nome Census Area
Chief Town: Nome (ZIP: 99762)

Pop: 8,288 (1990); 6,537 (1980)
Land: 23012.5 sq. mi.; **Water:** 5263.6 sq. mi.
In west-central AK, including much of Seward Peninsula.
Name origin: For the city.

Pop Density: 0.4
Area Code: 907

Brevig Mission — City
ZIP: 99785　　Lat: 65-20-06 N　**Long:** 166-28-51 W
Pop: 198 (1990); 138 (1980)　　**Pop Density:** 47.1
Land: 4.2 sq. mi.; **Water:** 0.0 sq. mi.
Name origin: For Presbyterian missionary T. L. Brevig.

Diomede — City
ZIP: 99762　　**Lat:** 65-46-28 N　**Long:** 168-54-55 W
Pop: 178 (1990); 139 (1980)　　**Pop Density:** 93.7
Land: 1.9 sq. mi.; **Water:** 3.7 sq. mi.
Name origin: Named by Russian explorer Vitus Bering for Diomede Islands after Saint Diomede.

Elim — City
ZIP: 99739　　**Lat:** 64-37-17 N　**Long:** 162-15-37 W
Pop: 264 (1990); 211 (1980)　　**Pop Density:** 114.8
Land: 2.3 sq. mi.; **Water:** 0.0 sq. mi.
In northwestern AK.

Gambell — City
ZIP: 99742　　**Lat:** 63-46-35 N　**Long:** 171-42-06 W
Pop: 525 (1990); 445 (1980)　　**Pop Density:** 47.3
Land: 11.1 sq. mi.; **Water:** 19.2 sq. mi.
Name origin: For Mr. and Mrs. Vene C. Gambell, Presbyterian missionaries who lived here in the 1890s.

Golovin — City
Lat: 64-34-44 N　**Long:** 162-59-27 W
Pop: 127 (1990); 87 (1980)　　**Pop Density:** 33.4
Land: 3.8 sq. mi.; **Water:** 0.0 sq. mi.
In western AK on the southern coast of the Seward Peninsula.
Name origin: Named in 1821 for the nearby bay off Norton Sound, which was named for a Russian brig.

Koyuk — City
ZIP: 99753　　**Lat:** 64-55-58 N　**Long:** 161-08-54 W
Pop: 231 (1990); 188 (1980)　　**Pop Density:** 51.3
Land: 4.5 sq. mi.; **Water:** 0.0 sq. mi.

Nome — City
ZIP: 99762　　**Lat:** 64-30-33 N　**Long:** 165-24-54 W
Pop: 3,500 (1990); 2,301 (1980)　　**Pop Density:** 253.6
Land: 13.8 sq. mi.; **Water:** 9.1 sq. mi.
In western AK on the south side of Seward Peninsula, 14 mi. west of Cape Nome and approximately 100 mi. east of the Bering Strait. Gold mining, tourism, and building.
Name origin: For nearby Cape Nome, whose name is generally attributed to a misreading by a mapmaker. A chart of the area said *? name*, which the mapmaker recorded as *C. Nome* or *Cape Nome*. Originally known as *Anvil City*.

Port Clarence — Military Facility
Lat: 65-03-58 N　**Long:** 166-49-28 W
Pop: 26 (1990); 29 (1980)　　**Pop Density:** 0.7
Land: 35.5 sq. mi.; **Water:** 42.3 sq. mi.

St. Michael — City
Lat: 63-28-39 N　**Long:** 162-06-32 W
Pop: 295 (1990); 239 (1980)　　**Pop Density:** 13.9
Land: 21.2 sq. mi.; **Water:** 6.1 sq. mi.
Name origin: Named in 1831 for the name saint of Russian explorer Mikhail Tebenkov.

Savoonga — City
ZIP: 99769　　**Lat:** 63-40-47 N　**Long:** 170-28-15 W
Pop: 519 (1990); 491 (1980)　　**Pop Density:** 71.1
Land: 7.3 sq. mi.; **Water:** 0.0 sq. mi.

Shaktoolik — City
ZIP: 99771　　**Lat:** 64-21-50 N　**Long:** 161-12-15 W
Pop: 178 (1990); 164 (1980)　　**Pop Density:** 111.3
Land: 1.6 sq. mi.; **Water:** 0.0 sq. mi.

Shishmaref — City
ZIP: 99772　　**Lat:** 66-15-02 N　**Long:** 166-07-10 W
Pop: 456 (1990); 394 (1980)　　**Pop Density:** 162.9
Land: 2.8 sq. mi.; **Water:** 4.5 sq. mi.
Name origin: For a nearby inlet, itself named for an 1816 Russian explorer.

Stebbins — City
ZIP: 99671　　**Lat:** 63-28-42 N　**Long:** 162-13-38 W
Pop: 400 (1990); 331 (1980)　　**Pop Density:** 11.2
Land: 35.8 sq. mi.; **Water:** 1.8 sq. mi.

Teller — City
ZIP: 99778　　**Lat:** 65-15-21 N　**Long:** 166-21-46 W
Pop: 151 (1990); 212 (1980)　　**Pop Density:** 503.3
Land: 0.3 sq. mi.; **Water:** 0.2 sq. mi.
Name origin: For U. S. Sen. Henry Teller from CO.

Unalakleet — City
ZIP: 99684　　**Lat:** 63-53-04 N　**Long:** 160-47-23 W
Pop: 714 (1990); 623 (1980)　　**Pop Density:** 246.2
Land: 2.9 sq. mi.; **Water:** 2.3 sq. mi.
Name origin: For the nearby Unalakleet River, itself named from the Inuit term meaning 'the southernmost one.'

Wales — City
ZIP: 99783　　**Lat:** 65-36-33 N　**Long:** 168-04-47 W
Pop: 161 (1990); 133 (1980)　　**Pop Density:** 67.1
Land: 2.4 sq. mi.; **Water:** 0.0 sq. mi.
Name origin: For the nearby cape which was named in 1778 by Capt. Cook for the Prince of Wales.

White Mountain — City
ZIP: 99784　　**Lat:** 64-41-00 N　**Long:** 163-25-10 W
Pop: 180 (1990); 125 (1980)　　**Pop Density:** 69.2
Land: 2.6 sq. mi.; **Water:** 0.3 sq. mi.
Name origin: For the mountain, itself so named for the massive white limestone outcroppings on its eastern slope.

North Slope Borough
Chief Town: Barrow (ZIP: 99723)

Pop: 5,979 (1990); 4,199 (1980) **Pop Density:** 0.1
Land: 87860.4 sq. mi.; **Water:** 5962.6 sq. mi. **Area Code:** 907
Across northernmost AK from Pt. Hope in west to border of Yukon province, Canada in east; bounded on the north by the Arctic Ocean and Beaufort Sea.
Name origin: Formerly called *Barrow-North Slope Division*.

Anaktuvuk Pass — City
ZIP: 99721 **Lat:** 68-06-57 N **Long:** 151-40-46 W
Pop: 259 (1990); 203 (1980) **Pop Density:** 18.6
Land: 13.9 sq. mi.; **Water:** 0.1 sq. mi.
Name origin: For the Anaktuvuk River, which flows through it.

Atqasuk — City
ZIP: 99791 **Lat:** 70-27-56 N **Long:** 157-24-31 W
Pop: 216 (1990) **Pop Density:** 5.2
Land: 41.2 sq. mi.; **Water:** 3.5 sq. mi.

Barrow — City
ZIP: 99723 **Lat:** 71-16-05 N **Long:** 156-48-22 W
Pop: 3,469 (1990); 2,267 (1980) **Pop Density:** 184.5
Land: 18.8 sq. mi.; **Water:** 2.2 sq. mi.
Approximately 10 mi. south of Barrow Point, the most northerly point of AK.
Name origin: For secretary of the British Admiralty, Sir John Barrow (1764–1848), who supported Arctic exploration.

Deadhorse — CDP
Lat: 70-12-20 N **Long:** 148-30-41 W
Pop: 26 (1990); 64 (1980) **Pop Density:** 0.9
Land: 28.6 sq. mi.; **Water:** 2.5 sq. mi.

Kaktovik — City
ZIP: 99747 **Lat:** 70-02-57 N **Long:** 143-38-13 W
Pop: 224 (1990); 165 (1980) **Pop Density:** 280.0
Land: 0.8 sq. mi.; **Water:** 0.2 sq. mi.
Name origin: From the Inuit term meaning 'place to fish.'

Nuiqsut — City
Lat: 70-11-29 N **Long:** 150-59-40 W
Pop: 354 (1990); 208 (1980) **Pop Density:** 42.7
Land: 8.3 sq. mi.; **Water:** 0.0 sq. mi.

Point Hope — City
ZIP: 99766 **Lat:** 68-18-40 N **Long:** 166-43-37 W
Pop: 639 (1990); 464 (1980) **Pop Density:** 114.1
Land: 5.6 sq. mi.; **Water:** 0.1 sq. mi.
Name origin: For Sir William J. Hope, from a well-known family of seamen.

Point Lay — CDP
Lat: 69-42-40 N **Long:** 163-00-32 W
Pop: 139 (1990); 68 (1980) **Pop Density:** 8.0
Land: 17.4 sq. mi.; **Water:** 33.1 sq. mi.

Prudhoe Bay — CDP
Lat: 70-17-02 N **Long:** 148-22-34 W
Pop: 47 (1990); 50 (1980) **Pop Density:** 1.4
Land: 34.7 sq. mi.; **Water:** 12.1 sq. mi.

Wainwright — City
ZIP: 99782 **Lat:** 70-35-59 N **Long:** 160-04-17 W
Pop: 492 (1990); 405 (1980) **Pop Density:** 120.0
Land: 4.1 sq. mi.; **Water:** 11.7 sq. mi.
Name origin: Named for the adjacent inlet, itself named by British explorer Capt. Frederick Beechey (1796–1865) for expedition astronomer Lt. John Wainwright.

Northwest Arctic Borough
Chief Town: Kotzebue (ZIP: 99752)

Pop: 6,113 (1990); 4,831 (1980) **Pop Density:** 0.2
Land: 35862.4 sq. mi.; **Water:** 4798.5 sq. mi. **Area Code:** 907
On northwestern coast of AK on Kotzebue Sound, north of Nome. Known as the Kobak Census Area until change to borough status on Jun 2, 1986.
Name origin: For its location.

Ambler — City
ZIP: 99786 **Lat:** 67-04-36 N **Long:** 157-55-05 W
Pop: 311 (1990); 192 (1980) **Pop Density:** 26.8
Land: 11.6 sq. mi.; **Water:** 1.5 sq. mi.
Name origin: For Arctic explorer Dr. James Ambler, who died while exploring the Arctic in 1881.

Buckland — City
ZIP: 99727 **Lat:** 65-58-51 N **Long:** 161-07-54 W
Pop: 318 (1990); 177 (1980) **Pop Density:** 227.1
Land: 1.4 sq. mi.; **Water:** 0.0 sq. mi.
Name origin: For the river on which it is located, which was named by Capt. Frederick Beechey (1796–1865) of the British Royal Navy for an Oxford University professor of geology.

Deering — City
ZIP: 99736 **Lat:** 66-04-24 N **Long:** 162-43-54 W
Pop: 157 (1990); 150 (1980) **Pop Density:** 29.6
Land: 5.3 sq. mi.; **Water:** 0.0 sq. mi.
Name origin: For the schooner *Abbie Deering* that sailed the area's waters at the turn of the century.

Kiana
City
ZIP: 99749　**Lat:** 66-58-12 N　**Long:** 160-27-29 W
Pop: 385 (1990); 345 (1980)　**Pop Density:** 1283.3
Land: 0.3 sq. mi.; **Water:** 0.0 sq. mi.

Kivalina
City
ZIP: 99750　**Lat:** 67-43-20 N　**Long:** 164-31-59 W
Pop: 317 (1990); 241 (1980)　**Pop Density:** 176.1
Land: 1.8 sq. mi.; **Water:** 3.2 sq. mi.　**Elev:** 8 ft.

Kobuk
City
ZIP: 99751　**Lat:** 66-54-16 N　**Long:** 156-53-46 W
Pop: 69 (1990); 62 (1980)　**Pop Density:** 4.2
Land: 16.4 sq. mi.; **Water:** 0.7 sq. mi.
Name origin: For the Kobuk River, from the Inuit term for 'big river.'

Kotzebue
City
ZIP: 99752　**Lat:** 66-53-16 N　**Long:** 162-32-07 W
Pop: 2,751 (1990); 2,090 (1980)　**Pop Density:** 102.3
Land: 26.9 sq. mi.; **Water:** 17.5 sq. mi.　**Elev:** 9 ft.
In northwestern AK, at the tip of the Baldwin Peninsula.
Name origin: For Russian explorer Otto von Kotzebue (1787–1846), who sailed through this area in 1815.

Noatak
CDP
ZIP: 99761　**Lat:** 67-34-58 N　**Long:** 163-00-18 W
Pop: 333 (1990)　**Pop Density:** 18.8
Land: 17.7 sq. mi.; **Water:** 3.8 sq. mi.

Noorvik
City
ZIP: 99763　**Lat:** 66-49-43 N　**Long:** 161-02-33 W
Pop: 531 (1990); 492 (1980)　**Pop Density:** 590.0
Land: 0.9 sq. mi.; **Water:** 0.4 sq. mi.　**Elev:** 82 ft.

Selawik
City
ZIP: 99770　**Lat:** 66-36-11 N　**Long:** 160-01-30 W
Pop: 596 (1990); 535 (1980)　**Pop Density:** 205.5
Land: 2.9 sq. mi.; **Water:** 1.1 sq. mi.
Name origin: For the nearby Selawik River; meaning of the name is unknown.

Shungnak
City
ZIP: 99773　**Lat:** 66-52-33 N　**Long:** 157-09-20 W
Pop: 223 (1990); 202 (1980)　**Pop Density:** 26.2
Land: 8.5 sq. mi.; **Water:** 1.2 sq. mi.
Name origin: For the Shungnak River, itself named from the Inuit term meaning 'jade,' which is found in its headwaters.

Prince of Wales-Outer Ketchikan Census Area
Chief Town: Metlakatla (ZIP: 99926)

Pop: 6,278 (1990); 3,822 (1980)　**Pop Density:** 0.9
Land: 7324.5 sq. mi.; **Water:** 5241.9 sq. mi.　**Area Code:** 907
In AK panhandle, southern outer portion of Alexander Archipelago, including Prince of Wales Island. Established by combining the former divisions of *Prince of Wales* and *Outer Ketchikan*.
Name origin: For the Prince of Wales Archipelago and nearby Ketchikan.

Annette
CDP
Lat: 55-02-31 N　**Long:** 131-35-08 W
Pop: 43 (1990); 139 (1980)　**Pop Density:** 3.2
Land: 13.5 sq. mi.; **Water:** 10.8 sq. mi.

Coffman Cove
City
Lat: 56-00-29 N　**Long:** 132-50-20 W
Pop: 186 (1990); 193 (1980)　**Pop Density:** 16.0
Land: 11.6 sq. mi.; **Water:** 3.6 sq. mi.

Craig
City
ZIP: 99921　**Lat:** 55-28-58 N　**Long:** 133-07-23 W
Pop: 1,260 (1990); 527 (1980)　**Pop Density:** 213.6
Land: 5.9 sq. mi.; **Water:** 2.6 sq. mi.　**Elev:** 3326 ft.
Name origin: For cannery owner Craig Miller.

Dora Bay
CDP
Lat: 55-11-20 N　**Long:** 132-17-42 W
Pop: 57 (1990)　**Pop Density:** 2.3
Land: 24.9 sq. mi.; **Water:** 9.3 sq. mi.

Edna Bay
CDP
Lat: 55-57-14 N　**Long:** 133-39-02 W
Pop: 86 (1990)　**Pop Density:** 3.2
Land: 26.9 sq. mi.; **Water:** 9.5 sq. mi.

Hollis
CDP
Lat: 55-33-24 N　**Long:** 132-38-10 W
Pop: 111 (1990)　**Pop Density:** 2.3
Land: 47.7 sq. mi.; **Water:** 13.4 sq. mi.

Hydaburg
City
ZIP: 99922　**Lat:** 55-12-32 N　**Long:** 132-49-02 W
Pop: 384 (1990); 298 (1980)　**Pop Density:** 768.0
Land: 0.5 sq. mi.; **Water:** 0.0 sq. mi.
Established 1911.
Name origin: For the Haida Indians, who migrated from British Columbia; with a spelling variation.

Hyder
CDP
ZIP: 99923　**Lat:** 55-58-49 N　**Long:** 130-03-31 W
Pop: 99 (1990); 77 (1980)　**Pop Density:** 6.5
Land: 15.2 sq. mi.; **Water:** 1.3 sq. mi.

Kasaan
City
Lat: 55-32-48 N　**Long:** 132-24-14 W
Pop: 54 (1990); 25 (1980)　**Pop Density:** 10.2
Land: 5.3 sq. mi.; **Water:** 0.0 sq. mi.
Name origin: From the Tlingit term meaning 'pretty village.'

ALASKA, Prince of Wales-Outer Ketchikan Census Area

Klawock City
ZIP: 99925 **Lat:** 55-33-13 N **Long:** 133-05-27 W
Pop: 722 (1990); 318 (1980) **Pop Density:** 2406.7
Land: 0.3 sq. mi.; **Water:** 0.3 sq. mi.

Labouchere Bay CDP
Lat: 56-17-46 N **Long:** 133-37-56 W
Pop: 149 (1990) **Pop Density:** 24.0
Land: 6.2 sq. mi.; **Water:** 5.5 sq. mi.

Long Island CDP
Lat: 54-55-01 N **Long:** 132-40-45 W
Pop: 198 (1990) **Pop Density:** 6.6
Land: 29.9 sq. mi.; **Water:** 35.9 sq. mi.

Metlakatla CDP
ZIP: 99926 **Lat:** 55-07-28 N **Long:** 131-34-50 W
Pop: 1,407 (1990); 1,056 (1980) **Pop Density:** 180.4
Land: 7.8 sq. mi.; **Water:** 4.8 sq. mi.

Meyers Chuck CDP
Lat: 55-42-53 N **Long:** 132-13-22 W
Pop: 37 (1990); 50 (1980) **Pop Density:** 4.6
Land: 8.1 sq. mi.; **Water:** 2.5 sq. mi.

Naukati Bay CDP
Lat: 55-52-25 N **Long:** 133-11-05 W
Pop: 93 (1990) **Pop Density:** 14.3
Land: 6.5 sq. mi.; **Water:** 3.8 sq. mi.

Point Baker CDP
ZIP: 99927 **Lat:** 56-21-16 N **Long:** 133-37-25 W
Pop: 39 (1990); 90 (1980) **Pop Density:** 48.8
Land: 0.8 sq. mi.; **Water:** 1.2 sq. mi.

Polk Inlet CDP
Lat: 55-20-58 N **Long:** 132-32-45 W
Pop: 135 (1990) **Pop Density:** 10.1
Land: 13.4 sq. mi.; **Water:** 1.8 sq. mi.

Port Alice CDP
Lat: 55-49-35 N **Long:** 133-36-10 W
Pop: 30 (1990) **Pop Density:** 2.6
Land: 11.6 sq. mi.; **Water:** 6.6 sq. mi.

Port Protection CDP
Lat: 56-19-01 N **Long:** 133-35-53 W
Pop: 62 (1990) **Pop Density:** 34.4
Land: 1.8 sq. mi.; **Water:** 1.3 sq. mi.

Thorne Bay City
Lat: 55-39-33 N **Long:** 132-31-28 W
Pop: 569 (1990); 320 (1980) **Pop Density:** 30.3
Land: 18.8 sq. mi.; **Water:** 5.2 sq. mi.

Whale Pass CDP
Lat: 56-06-11 N **Long:** 133-10-21 W
Pop: 75 (1990) **Pop Density:** 2.1
Land: 35.4 sq. mi.; **Water:** 6.8 sq. mi.

Sitka Borough and City
Chief Town: Sitka (ZIP: 99835)

Pop: 8,588 (1990); 7,803 (1980) **Pop Density:** 3.0
Land: 2881.5 sq. mi.; **Water:** 1968.3 sq. mi. **Area Code:** 907
Lat: 57-12-50 N **Long:** 135-26-48 W

In AK panhandle, western (outer) portion of the central Alexander Archipelago, southwest of Juneau. City center on the west coast of Baranof Island, 930 mi. north of Seattle, WA.

Name origin: From Tlingit term for 'by the sea' or 'on Shi,' the Tlingit name for Baranof Island.

Skagway-Hoonah-Angoon Census Area
Chief Town: Skagway (ZIP: 99840)

Pop: 4,385 (1990); 3,478 (1980) **Pop Density:** 0.3
Land: 12880.6 sq. mi.; **Water:** 4619.6 sq. mi. **Area Code:** 907

In AK panhandle, north of the Alexander Archipelago. Originally established by combining former divisions of Skagway-Yakutat and Angoon; renamed Sep 22, 1992 upon formation of Yakutat Borough. Census population figures shown above apply to census area of 1990 and 1980, which included Yakutat.

Name origin: For the towns that define its northern, western and eastern extent.

Angoon City
ZIP: 99820 **Lat:** 57-28-42 N **Long:** 134-31-12 W
Pop: 638 (1990); 465 (1980) **Pop Density:** 27.7
Land: 23.0 sq. mi.; **Water:** 14.1 sq. mi.

Cube Cove CDP
Lat: 57-56-06 N **Long:** 134-42-40 W
Pop: 156 (1990) **Pop Density:** 13.4
Land: 11.6 sq. mi.; **Water:** 5.4 sq. mi.

Elfin Cove CDP
ZIP: 99825 **Lat:** 58-11-10 N **Long:** 136-20-12 W
Pop: 57 (1990); 28 (1980) **Pop Density:** 5.0
Land: 11.4 sq. mi.; **Water:** 10.9 sq. mi.

Freshwater Bay CDP
Lat: 57-53-29 N **Long:** 135-04-45 W
Pop: 68 (1990) **Pop Density:** 2.3
Land: 30.2 sq. mi.; **Water:** 23.0 sq. mi.

Game Creek CDP
Lat: 58-03-24 N **Long:** 135-30-28 W
Pop: 61 (1990) **Pop Density:** 13.3
Land: 4.6 sq. mi.; **Water:** 3.0 sq. mi.

Gustavus CDP
ZIP: 99826 **Lat:** 58-24-21 N **Long:** 135-48-03 W
Pop: 258 (1990); 98 (1980) **Pop Density:** 6.8
Land: 37.9 sq. mi.; **Water:** 17.8 sq. mi.

Hobart Bay CDP
Lat: 57-27-56 N **Long:** 133-21-11 W
Pop: 187 (1990) **Pop Density:** 2.6
Land: 71.5 sq. mi.; **Water:** 15.8 sq. mi.

Hoonah City
ZIP: 99829 **Lat:** 58-06-41 N **Long:** 135-25-11 W
Pop: 795 (1990); 680 (1980) **Pop Density:** 611.5
Land: 1.3 sq. mi.; **Water:** 0.1 sq. mi.

Klukwan CDP
Lat: 59-24-13 N **Long:** 135-53-04 W
Pop: 129 (1990); 135 (1980) **Pop Density:** 67.9
Land: 1.9 sq. mi.; **Water:** 0.0 sq. mi.

Pelican City
ZIP: 99832 **Lat:** 57-57-11 N **Long:** 136-12-35 W
Pop: 222 (1990); 180 (1980) **Pop Density:** 444.0
Land: 0.5 sq. mi.; **Water:** 0.1 sq. mi.

Skagway City
ZIP: 99840 **Lat:** 59-31-13 N **Long:** 135-20-08 W
Pop: 692 (1990); 768 (1980) **Pop Density:** 1.5
Land: 454.7 sq. mi.; **Water:** 11.1 sq. mi.

Tenakee Springs City
ZIP: 99841 **Lat:** 57-46-42 N **Long:** 135-08-21 W
Pop: 94 (1990); 138 (1980) **Pop Density:** 8.0
Land: 11.7 sq. mi.; **Water:** 5.0 sq. mi.

Whitestone Logging Camp CDP
Lat: 58-04-16 N **Long:** 135-25-47 W
Pop: 164 (1990) **Pop Density:** 20.0
Land: 8.2 sq. mi.; **Water:** 1.7 sq. mi.

Southeast Fairbanks Census Area
Chief Town: Delta Junction (ZIP: 99737)

Pop: 5,913 (1990); 5,676 (1980) **Pop Density:** 0.2
Land: 25994.1 sq. mi.; **Water:** 241.3 sq. mi. **Area Code:** 907

In east-central AK, southeast of Fairbanks, bordering the Yukon Territory of Canada to the east. Includes portion of former *Upper Yukon Division*. A small portion of the census area was removed to establish Denali Borough on Dec. 28, 1990.

Name origin: For its location.

Alcan CDP
Lat: 62-43-22 N **Long:** 141-11-17 W
Pop: 27 (1990) **Pop Density:** 0.2
Land: 153.9 sq. mi.; **Water:** 0.7 sq. mi.

Big Delta CDP
Lat: 64-08-23 N **Long:** 145-45-43 W
Pop: 400 (1990); 285 (1980) **Pop Density:** 21.5
Land: 18.6 sq. mi.; **Water:** 1.5 sq. mi.

Delta Junction City
ZIP: 99737 **Lat:** 64-03-49 N **Long:** 145-42-29 W
Pop: 652 (1990); 945 (1980) **Pop Density:** 42.3
Land: 15.4 sq. mi.; **Water:** 0.0 sq. mi.
In central AK on the Delta River.
Name origin: For its location at the junction of two highways.

Dot Lake CDP
Lat: 63-37-44 N **Long:** 144-05-42 W
Pop: 70 (1990); 67 (1980) **Pop Density:** 1.9
Land: 36.9 sq. mi.; **Water:** 0.0 sq. mi.

Dry Creek CDP
Lat: 63-39-12 N **Long:** 144-39-55 W
Pop: 106 (1990) **Pop Density:** 22.6
Land: 4.7 sq. mi.; **Water:** 0.0 sq. mi.

Eagle City
ZIP: 99738 **Lat:** 64-46-41 N **Long:** 141-12-02 W
Pop: 168 (1990); 110 (1980) **Pop Density:** 120.0
Land: 1.4 sq. mi.; **Water:** 0.0 sq. mi.
Settled 1898.
Name origin: For the many American eagles nesting in the area.

Eagle Village CDP
Lat: 64-47-25 N **Long:** 141-06-32 W
Pop: 35 (1990); 54 (1980) **Pop Density:** 1.0
Land: 33.8 sq. mi.; **Water:** 2.7 sq. mi.

Fort Greely Military Facility
Lat: 63-57-31 N **Long:** 145-45-21 W
Pop: 1,147 (1990); 1,635 (1980) **Pop Density:** 44.8
Land: 25.6 sq. mi.; **Water:** 1.6 sq. mi.

Healy Lake CDP
Lat: 63-58-37 N **Long:** 144-43-26 W
Pop: 47 (1990); 33 (1980) **Pop Density:** 0.3
Land: 159.3 sq. mi.; **Water:** 12.4 sq. mi.

Northway CDP
ZIP: 99764 **Lat:** 62-55-58 N **Long:** 141-52-29 W
Pop: 123 (1990); 73 (1980) **Pop Density:** 6.9
Land: 17.8 sq. mi.; **Water:** 2.0 sq. mi.

Northway Junction CDP
Lat: 63-00-07 N **Long:** 141-46-38 W
Pop: 88 (1990) **Pop Density:** 21.5
Land: 4.1 sq. mi.; **Water:** 0.0 sq. mi.

ALASKA, Southeast Fairbanks Census Area

Northway Village CDP
Lat: 62-58-38 N Long: 141-54-12 W
Pop: 113 (1990) Pop Density: 26.9
Land: 4.2 sq. mi.; Water: 0.4 sq. mi.

Tanacross CDP
Lat: 63-20-20 N Long: 143-25-57 W
Pop: 106 (1990); 117 (1980) Pop Density: 1.4
Land: 78.4 sq. mi.; Water: 1.0 sq. mi.

Tetlin CDP
Lat: 63-03-52 N Long: 142-26-20 W
Pop: 87 (1990); 107 (1980) Pop Density: 0.6
Land: 152.9 sq. mi.; Water: 16.3 sq. mi.

Tok CDP
Lat: 63-18-01 N Long: 143-02-19 W
Pop: 935 (1990); 589 (1980) Pop Density: 7.0
Land: 133.0 sq. mi.; Water: 0.0 sq. mi.

Valdez-Cordova Census Area
Chief Town: Valdez (ZIP: 99686)

Pop: 9,952 (1990); 8,348 (1980) Pop Density: 0.3
Land: 36945.3 sq. mi.; Water: 6570.3 sq. mi. Area Code: 907

In southeastern AK, bounded on east by Yukon Territory of Canada and on south by the Gulf of Alaska. Established by combining the former divisions of *Cordova-McCarthy* and *Valdez-Chitina-Whittier* with part of *Southeast Fairbanks Division*.
Name origin: For the city of Valdez.

Chenega CDP
Lat: 60-06-17 N Long: 147-56-37 W
Pop: 94 (1990) Pop Density: 3.3
Land: 28.8 sq. mi.; Water: 25.4 sq. mi.

Chistochina CDP
Lat: 62-33-51 N Long: 144-41-13 W
Pop: 60 (1990); 55 (1980) Pop Density: 3.6
Land: 16.9 sq. mi.; Water: 0.0 sq. mi.

Chitina CDP
ZIP: 99566 Lat: 61-31-29 N Long: 144-29-20 W
Pop: 49 (1990); 42 (1980) Pop Density: 1.7
Land: 28.6 sq. mi.; Water: 1.4 sq. mi.

Copper Center CDP
ZIP: 99573 Lat: 61-58-50 N Long: 145-21-04 W
Pop: 449 (1990); 213 (1980) Pop Density: 21.1
Land: 21.3 sq. mi.; Water: 0.4 sq. mi.

Copperville CDP
Lat: 62-02-38 N Long: 145-25-14 W
Pop: 163 (1990) Pop Density: 50.9
Land: 3.2 sq. mi.; Water: 0.5 sq. mi.

Cordova City
ZIP: 99574 Lat: 60-32-51 N Long: 145-44-51 W
Pop: 2,110 (1990); 1,879 (1980) Pop Density: 458.7
Land: 4.6 sq. mi.; Water: 2.0 sq. mi.
In southeastern AK on the southeastern corner of Prince William Sound. Founded 1906.
Name origin: Named in 1790 by Spanish explorer Salvador Fidalgo for the Spanish city.

Eyak CDP
Lat: 60-31-42 N Long: 145-35-33 W
Pop: 172 (1990); 47 (1980) Pop Density: 13.1
Land: 13.1 sq. mi.; Water: 0.9 sq. mi.

Gakona CDP
ZIP: 99586 Lat: 62-17-33 N Long: 145-18-34 W
Pop: 25 (1990); 87 (1980) Pop Density: 20.8
Land: 1.2 sq. mi.; Water: 0.0 sq. mi.

Glennallen CDP
ZIP: 99588 Lat: 62-05-05 N Long: 145-36-12 W
Pop: 451 (1990); 511 (1980) Pop Density: 24.0
Land: 18.8 sq. mi.; Water: 0.0 sq. mi.

Gulkana CDP
ZIP: 99586 Lat: 62-15-09 N Long: 145-23-56 W
Pop: 103 (1990); 104 (1980) Pop Density: 8.6
Land: 12.0 sq. mi.; Water: 0.0 sq. mi.

Kenny Lake CDP
Lat: 61-43-09 N Long: 144-56-53 W
Pop: 423 (1990) Pop Density: 3.8
Land: 111.1 sq. mi.; Water: 1.2 sq. mi.

McCarthy CDP
Lat: 61-25-23 N Long: 142-53-52 W
Pop: 25 (1990) Pop Density: 0.2
Land: 101.4 sq. mi.; Water: 1.3 sq. mi.

Mendeltna CDP
Lat: 62-03-58 N Long: 146-26-59 W
Pop: 37 (1990) Pop Density: 0.5
Land: 67.3 sq. mi.; Water: 1.3 sq. mi.

Mentasta Lake CDP
Lat: 62-51-06 N Long: 143-45-39 W
Pop: 96 (1990); 59 (1980) Pop Density: 1.2
Land: 78.4 sq. mi.; Water: 1.9 sq. mi.

Paxson CDP
Lat: 63-05-23 N Long: 145-36-46 W
Pop: 30 (1990); 30 (1980) Pop Density: 0.6
Land: 50.7 sq. mi.; Water: 5.5 sq. mi.

Slana CDP
Lat: 62-42-05 N Long: 143-59-38 W
Pop: 63 (1990); 49 (1980) Pop Density: 3.6
Land: 17.3 sq. mi.; Water: 0.4 sq. mi.

Tatitlek CDP
Lat: 60-53-01 N Long: 146-40-39 W
Pop: 119 (1990); 68 (1980) Pop Density: 21.3
Land: 5.6 sq. mi.; Water: 2.7 sq. mi.

ALASKA, Wade Hampton Census Area

Tonsina
CDP
Lat: 61-38-08 N **Long:** 145-09-26 W
Pop: 38 (1990); 135 (1980) **Pop Density:** 1.7
Land: 22.2 sq. mi.; **Water:** 0.0 sq. mi.

Valdez
City
ZIP: 99686 **Lat:** 61-05-00 N **Long:** 146-18-08 W
Pop: 4,068 (1990); 3,079 (1980) **Pop Density:** 18.6
Land: 218.8 sq. mi.; **Water:** 54.6 sq. mi. **Elev:** ft.
In southern AK east of Anchorage, on the northeastern shore of Prince William Sound.
Name origin: For the celebrated Spanish naval officer Antonio Valdes y Basan, who organized the exploration of the area in 1791; with a spelling variation.

Whittier
City
Lat: 60-47-36 N **Long:** 148-39-05 W
Pop: 243 (1990); 198 (1980) **Pop Density:** 20.4
Land: 11.9 sq. mi.; **Water:** 6.6 sq. mi.
Founded during World War II.
Name origin: For poet John Greenleaf Whittier (1807–92).

Wade Hampton Census Area
Chief Town: Mountain Village (ZIP: 99632)

Pop: 5,791 (1990); 4,665 (1980) **Pop Density:** 0.3
Land: 17124.1 sq. mi.; **Water:** 2556.0 sq. mi. **Area Code:** 907
On central-western coast of AK, north of Bethel.

Alakanuk
City
ZIP: 99554 **Lat:** 62-40-32 N **Long:** 164-38-36 W
Pop: 544 (1990); 522 (1980) **Pop Density:** 15.7
Land: 34.7 sq. mi.; **Water:** 6.0 sq. mi.
Name origin: From the Inuit term meaning 'wrong way' or 'mistakes.'

Chevak
City
ZIP: 99563 **Lat:** 61-32-00 N **Long:** 165-35-29 W
Pop: 598 (1990); 466 (1980) **Pop Density:** 398.7
Land: 1.5 sq. mi.; **Water:** 0.0 sq. mi.
Name origin: From a term meaning 'connecting slough.'

Emmonak
City
ZIP: 99581 **Lat:** 62-46-42 N **Long:** 164-32-13 W
Pop: 642 (1990); 567 (1980) **Pop Density:** 103.5
Land: 6.2 sq. mi.; **Water:** 0.8 sq. mi.

Hooper Bay
City
ZIP: 99604 **Lat:** 61-32-23 N **Long:** 166-06-10 W
Pop: 845 (1990); 627 (1980) **Pop Density:** 99.4
Land: 8.5 sq. mi.; **Water:** 0.0 sq. mi. **Elev:** 35 ft.
Name origin: For American Capt. Calvin Hooper.

Kotlik
City
ZIP: 99620 **Lat:** 63-02-02 N **Long:** 163-33-16 W
Pop: 461 (1990); 293 (1980) **Pop Density:** 131.7
Land: 3.5 sq. mi.; **Water:** 1.0 sq. mi. **Elev:** 7 ft.
Name origin: From the Inuit term meaning 'breeches.'

Marshall
City
Lat: 61-52-31 N **Long:** 162-03-36 W
Pop: 273 (1990); 262 (1980) **Pop Density:** 60.7
Land: 4.5 sq. mi.; **Water:** 0.0 sq. mi.

Mountain Village
City
ZIP: 99632 **Lat:** 62-05-16 N **Long:** 163-43-00 W
Pop: 674 (1990); 583 (1980) **Pop Density:** 156.7
Land: 4.3 sq. mi.; **Water:** 1.3 sq. mi.
Name origin: For its descriptive connotations.

Newtok
City
ZIP: 99559 **Lat:** 60-58-15 N **Long:** 164-39-07 W
Pop: 0 (1990)
Land: 2.4 sq. mi.; **Water:** 0.0 sq. mi.
Part of the town is also in Bethel Census Area.

Pilot Station
City
ZIP: 99650 **Lat:** 61-56-29 N **Long:** 162-52-33 W
Pop: 463 (1990); 325 (1980) **Pop Density:** 308.7
Land: 1.5 sq. mi.; **Water:** 0.5 sq. mi.
Name origin: For its use as a landmark by early Yukon River boat pilots.

Pitkas Point
CDP
Lat: 62-01-52 N **Long:** 163-16-11 W
Pop: 135 (1990); 88 (1980) **Pop Density:** 135.0
Land: 1.0 sq. mi.; **Water:** 1.5 sq. mi.

Russian Mission
City
ZIP: 99657 **Lat:** 61-47-40 N **Long:** 161-21-13 W
Pop: 246 (1990); 169 (1980) **Pop Density:** 48.2
Land: 5.1 sq. mi.; **Water:** 0.5 sq. mi.
Founded 1837.
Name origin: For the Russian Orthodox church here.

St. Mary's
City
Lat: 62-02-45 N **Long:** 163-14-46 W
Pop: 441 (1990); 382 (1980) **Pop Density:** 10.6
Land: 41.8 sq. mi.; **Water:** 5.7 sq. mi.
Name origin: For an early church.

Scammon Bay
City
ZIP: 99662 **Lat:** 61-50-42 N **Long:** 165-34-55 W
Pop: 343 (1990); 250 (1980) **Pop Density:** 490.0
Land: 0.7 sq. mi.; **Water:** 0.1 sq. mi.
Name origin: For Capt. Charles Scammon, who helped chart the area in 1865.

Sheldon Point
City
Lat: 62-31-00 N **Long:** 164-53-34 W
Pop: 109 (1990); 103 (1980) **Pop Density:** 8.3
Land: 13.2 sq. mi.; **Water:** 5.2 sq. mi.
Name origin: For an early settler and salt miller named Sheldon.

Wrangell-Petersburg Census Area
Chief Town: Petersburg (ZIP: 99833)

Pop: 7,042 (1990); 6,167 (1980)
Land: 5808.5 sq. mi.; **Water:** 3165.2 sq. mi.
Pop Density: 1.2
Area Code: 907

In AK panhandle in central-eastern Alexander Archipelago, south of Juneau.
Name origin: For the two chief cities.

Kake — City
ZIP: 99830 **Lat:** 56-58-06 N **Long:** 133-55-29 W
Pop: 700 (1990); 555 (1980) **Pop Density:** 87.5
Land: 8.0 sq. mi.; **Water:** 5.8 sq. mi.
Name origin: For a once-warlike Kake tribe of Tlingit Indians who lived in the area.

Kupreanof — City
ZIP: 99833 **Lat:** 56-48-32 N **Long:** 132-59-06 W
Pop: 23 (1990); 47 (1980) **Pop Density:** 3.7
Land: 6.2 sq. mi.; **Water:** 2.2 sq. mi.
In southeastern AK, southeast of Juneau.
Name origin: For Capt. Ivan Kupreanof, who served as governor of Russian America in 1835.

Petersburg — City
ZIP: 99833 **Lat:** 56-46-26 N **Long:** 132-51-41 W
Pop: 3,207 (1990); 2,821 (1980) **Pop Density:** 73.9
Land: 43.4 sq. mi.; **Water:** 5.3 sq. mi.
In southeastern AK, 35 mi. north northwest of Wrangell.
Name origin: For Peter Buschmann, who founded a cannery here in 1897.

Port Alexander — City
ZIP: 99836 **Lat:** 56-13-05 N **Long:** 134-37-51 W
Pop: 119 (1990); 86 (1980) **Pop Density:** 36.1
Land: 3.3 sq. mi.; **Water:** 11.7 sq. mi.
Name origin: For Alexander A. Andreevich, governor of Russian America (1799–1818).

Rowan Bay — CDP
Lat: 56-39-14 N **Long:** 134-15-04 W
Pop: 133 (1990) **Pop Density:** 4.1
Land: 32.1 sq. mi.; **Water:** 11.9 sq. mi.

St. John Harbor — CDP
Lat: 56-26-22 N **Long:** 132-57-48 W
Pop: 69 (1990) **Pop Density:** 15.3
Land: 4.5 sq. mi.; **Water:** 5.7 sq. mi.

Wrangell — City
ZIP: 99929 **Lat:** 56-21-41 N **Long:** 132-16-17 W
Pop: 2,479 (1990); 2,184 (1980) **Pop Density:** 42.1
Land: 58.9 sq. mi.; **Water:** 33.7 sq. mi.
In southeastern AK on the northern tip of Wrangell Island, northeast of Prince of Wales Island, south of the mouth of the Sitkine River.
Name origin: For Baron Ferdinand Wrangell, governor of Russian America (1830–35).

Yakutat Census Area
Chief Town: Yakutat (ZIP: 99689)

Pop: 534 (1990); 449 (1980)
Land: 2.9 sq. mi.; **Water:** 4.7 sq. mi.
Lat: 59-33-27N **Long:** 139-45-43W
Pop Density: 184.1
Area Code: 907

In AK panhandle, north of the Alexander Archipelago. Established Sep 22, 1992 from the former Skagway-Yakutat-Angoon Census Area (now Skagway-Hoonah-Angoon Census Area).
Name origin: Probably for Yakutat Bay, from the name of a Tlingit Indian village; meaning of name unknown.

Yukon-Koyukuk Census Area
Chief Town: Fort Yukon (ZIP: 99740)

Pop: 8,478 (1990); 7,873 (1980)
Land: 157121.0 sq. mi.; **Water:** 1874.7 sq. mi.
Pop Density: 0.1
Area Code: 907

Spanning much of central AK to the border with Yukon Territory of Canada. Established from portions of former divisions of *Kuskokwim* and *Upper Yukon*. Some territory was removed from the census area to establish Denali Borough on Dec. 28, 1990.

Name origin: For the Yukon and Koyukuk rivers.

Allakaket — City
ZIP: 99720 Lat: 66-32-42 N Long: 152-43-59 W
Pop: 170 (1990); 163 (1980) Pop Density: 38.6
Land: 4.4 sq. mi.; Water: 0.7 sq. mi.
Name origin: From an Indian term meaning 'mouth of the Alatna River.'

Anderson — City
Lat: 64-18-23 N Long: 149-09-34 W
Pop: 628 (1990); 517 (1980) Pop Density: 13.3
Land: 47.2 sq. mi.; Water: 0.4 sq. mi.
Name origin: For founder Arthur Anderson.

Anvik — City
ZIP: 99558 Lat: 62-39-19 N Long: 160-12-29 W
Pop: 82 (1990); 114 (1980) Pop Density: 7.3
Land: 11.2 sq. mi.; Water: 2.6 sq. mi.
Name origin: For the Anvik River, on which the town is located. From an Indian term possibly meaning 'going out place.'

Arctic Village — CDP
ZIP: 99722 Lat: 68-07-30 N Long: 145-31-36 W
Pop: 96 (1990); 111 (1980) Pop Density: 1.4
Land: 67.1 sq. mi.; Water: 5.1 sq. mi.

Beaver — CDP
ZIP: 99724 Lat: 66-20-03 N Long: 147-18-52 W
Pop: 103 (1990); 66 (1980) Pop Density: 5.4
Land: 19.2 sq. mi.; Water: 4.3 sq. mi.

Bettles — City
Lat: 66-53-11 N Long: 151-35-39 W
Pop: 36 (1990) Pop Density: 24.0
Land: 1.5 sq. mi.; Water: 0.0 sq. mi.

Birch Creek — CDP
Lat: 66-14-43 N Long: 145-49-48 W
Pop: 42 (1990); 32 (1980) Pop Density: 4.2
Land: 10.1 sq. mi.; Water: 0.3 sq. mi.

Cantwell — CDP
ZIP: 99729 Lat: 63-22-17 N Long: 148-55-12 W
Pop: 147 (1990); 89 (1980) Pop Density: 3.4
Land: 43.7 sq. mi.; Water: 0.1 sq. mi.

Central — CDP
ZIP: 99730 Lat: 65-33-20 N Long: 144-51-28 W
Pop: 52 (1990); 36 (1980) Pop Density: 1.0
Land: 54.4 sq. mi.; Water: 0.0 sq. mi.

Chalkyitsik — CDP
Lat: 66-38-16 N Long: 143-45-18 W
Pop: 90 (1990); 100 (1980) Pop Density: 45.0
Land: 2.0 sq. mi.; Water: 0.4 sq. mi.

Circle — CDP
ZIP: 99733 Lat: 65-49-28 N Long: 144-04-57 W
Pop: 73 (1990); 81 (1980) Pop Density: 15.9
Land: 4.6 sq. mi.; Water: 1.1 sq. mi.

Circle Hot Springs Station — CDP
Lat: 65-28-13 N Long: 144-41-20 W
Pop: 29 (1990) Pop Density: 0.5
Land: 53.3 sq. mi.; Water: 1.0 sq. mi.

Evansville — CDP
Lat: 66-52-42 N Long: 151-27-34 W
Pop: 33 (1990); 94 (1980) Pop Density: 0.7
Land: 44.6 sq. mi.; Water: 0.6 sq. mi.

Ferry — CDP
Lat: 63-55-40 N Long: 149-07-48 W
Pop: 56 (1990) Pop Density: 0.6
Land: 86.9 sq. mi.; Water: 0.0 sq. mi.

Fort Yukon — City
ZIP: 99740 Lat: 66-33-53 N Long: 145-15-42 W
Pop: 580 (1990); 619 (1980) Pop Density: 85.3
Land: 6.8 sq. mi.; Water: 0.4 sq. mi. Elev: 447 ft.
Name origin: For its location on the Yukon River.

Galena — City
ZIP: 99741 Lat: 64-44-26 N Long: 156-49-11 W
Pop: 833 (1990); 765 (1980) Pop Density: 50.5
Land: 16.5 sq. mi.; Water: 6.4 sq. mi.
Name origin: For the deposits of lead ore, or galena, mined here.

Grayling — City
ZIP: 99590 Lat: 62-53-58 N Long: 160-06-26 W
Pop: 208 (1990); 209 (1980) Pop Density: 19.4
Land: 10.7 sq. mi.; Water: 0.0 sq. mi.
Name origin: For the freshwater stream game fish.

Healy — CDP
ZIP: 99743 Lat: 63-48-41 N Long: 149-00-07 W
Pop: 487 (1990); 334 (1980) Pop Density: 10.9
Land: 44.7 sq. mi.; Water: 0.2 sq. mi.

Holy Cross — City
ZIP: 99602 Lat: 62-10-52 N Long: 159-47-57 W
Pop: 277 (1990); 241 (1980) Pop Density: 8.8
Land: 31.3 sq. mi.; Water: 6.1 sq. mi.
Name origin: For the Jesuit mission founded here in 1886.

Hughes — City
ZIP: 99745 Lat: 66-02-13 N Long: 154-16-03 W
Pop: 54 (1990); 73 (1980) Pop Density: 21.6
Land: 2.5 sq. mi.; Water: 0.0 sq. mi. Elev: 289 ft.
Name origin: For NY Gov. Charles Evans Hughes (1862–1948).

Huslia City
ZIP: 99746　　　　Lat: 65-41-23 N　Long: 156-17-31 W
Pop: 207 (1990); 188 (1980)　　Pop Density: 13.4
Land: 15.5 sq. mi.; Water: 0.6 sq. mi.

Kaltag City
ZIP: 99748　　　　Lat: 64-20-19 N　Long: 158-41-10 W
Pop: 240 (1990); 247 (1980)　　Pop Density: 11.0
Land: 21.9 sq. mi.; Water: 5.0 sq. mi.
Name origin: From the term for a species of salmon.

Koyukuk City
ZIP: 99754　　　　Lat: 64-54-48 N　Long: 157-39-02 W
Pop: 126 (1990); 98 (1980)　　Pop Density: 21.0
Land: 6.0 sq. mi.; Water: 0.2 sq. mi.

Lake Minchumina CDP
ZIP: 99757　　　　Lat: 63-52-27 N　Long: 152-24-46 W
Pop: 32 (1990)　　Pop Density: 0.4
Land: 73.1 sq. mi.; Water: 22.4 sq. mi.

Lignite CDP
　　　　Lat: 63-53-25 N　Long: 149-02-47 W
Pop: 99 (1990)　　Pop Density: 1.7
Land: 58.2 sq. mi.; Water: 0.0 sq. mi.

McGrath City
ZIP: 99627　　　　Lat: 62-57-15 N　Long: 155-34-32 W
Pop: 528 (1990); 355 (1980)　　Pop Density: 14.0
Land: 37.6 sq. mi.; Water: 4.6 sq. mi.　　Elev: 33 ft.
Name origin: For Peter McGrath, a fur trader and deputy marshall in the area in 1900.

McKinley Park CDP
　　　　Lat: 63-41-47 N　Long: 148-57-17 W
Pop: 171 (1990); 32 (1980)　　Pop Density: 2.4
Land: 72.2 sq. mi.; Water: 0.4 sq. mi.

Manley Hot Springs CDP
ZIP: 99756　　　　Lat: 64-59-08 N　Long: 150-38-11 W
Pop: 96 (1990); 61 (1980)　　Pop Density: 1.6
Land: 58.5 sq. mi.; Water: 3.3 sq. mi.

Minto CDP
ZIP: 99758　　　　Lat: 65-01-34 N　Long: 149-31-46 W
Pop: 218 (1990); 153 (1980)　　Pop Density: 1.3
Land: 162.9 sq. mi.; Water: 3.9 sq. mi.

Nenana City
ZIP: 99760　　　　Lat: 64-32-38 N　Long: 149-05-12 W
Pop: 393 (1990); 470 (1980)　　Pop Density: 71.5
Land: 5.5 sq. mi.; Water: 0.0 sq. mi.
Name origin: From an unknown Indian term, possibly including -na, meaning 'river.'

Nikolai City
ZIP: 99691　　　　Lat: 62-59-42 N　Long: 154-23-26 W
Pop: 109 (1990); 91 (1980)　　Pop Density: 22.2
Land: 4.9 sq. mi.; Water: 0.0 sq. mi.
Name origin: For an early Russian explorer.

Nulato City
ZIP: 99765　　　　Lat: 64-42-27 N　Long: 158-13-24 W
Pop: 359 (1990); 350 (1980)　　Pop Density: 7.7
Land: 46.5 sq. mi.; Water: 6.5 sq. mi.
Name origin: Possibly an Indian term for 'place where the salmon come.'

Rampart CDP
　　　　Lat: 65-23-01 N　Long: 150-00-40 W
Pop: 68 (1990); 50 (1980)　　Pop Density: 0.3
Land: 233.3 sq. mi.; Water: 8.4 sq. mi.

Ruby City
ZIP: 99768　　　　Lat: 64-43-03 N　Long: 155-31-14 W
Pop: 170 (1990); 197 (1980)　　Pop Density: 23.0
Land: 7.4 sq. mi.; Water: 0.0 sq. mi.
Name origin: For nearby Ruby Creek.

Shageluk City
ZIP: 99665　　　　Lat: 62-40-06 N　Long: 159-33-54 W
Pop: 139 (1990); 131 (1980)　　Pop Density: 14.5
Land: 9.6 sq. mi.; Water: 1.2 sq. mi.
Name origin: From an Ingalik term applied by the Russians to the Innoko River, on which the village is located; meaning unknown.

Stevens Village CDP
ZIP: 99774　　　　Lat: 65-59-56 N　Long: 149-03-16 W
Pop: 102 (1990); 96 (1980)　　Pop Density: 11.7
Land: 8.7 sq. mi.; Water: 2.9 sq. mi.

Takotna CDP
　　　　Lat: 62-59-34 N　Long: 156-10-18 W
Pop: 38 (1990); 48 (1980)　　Pop Density: 2.6
Land: 14.5 sq. mi.; Water: 0.0 sq. mi.

Tanana City
ZIP: 99777　　　　Lat: 65-09-21 N　Long: 152-06-06 W
Pop: 345 (1990); 388 (1980)　　Pop Density: 20.4
Land: 16.9 sq. mi.; Water: 4.6 sq. mi.
In central AK near the confluence of the Tanana and Yukon rivers.
Name origin: From an Indian name meaning 'mountain river.'

Venetie CDP
ZIP: 99781　　　　Lat: 67-00-52 N　Long: 146-23-52 W
Pop: 182 (1990); 132 (1980)　　Pop Density: 13.8
Land: 13.2 sq. mi.; Water: 1.2 sq. mi.

American Places Dictionary   ALASKA

Index to Places and Counties in Alaska

Adak Station (Aleutians West Census Area) Military Facility 5
Akhiok (Kodiak Island Borough) City *12*
Akiachak (Bethel Census Area) City *6*
Akiak (Bethel Census Area) City *6*
Akutan (Aleutians East Borough) City . *5*
Alakanuk (Wade Hampton Census Area) City *21*
Alcan (Southeast Fairbanks Census Area) CDP *19*
Aleknagik (Dillingham Census Area) City *8*
Aleutians East Borough *5*
Aleutians West Census Area *5*
Allakaket (Yukon-Koyukuk Census Area) City *23*
Ambler (Northwest Arctic Borough) City *16*
Amchitka (Aleutians West Census Area) CDP *5*
Anaktuvuk Pass (North Slope Borough) City *16*
Anchorage Borough and City *6*
Anchor Point (Kenai Peninsula Borough) CDP *10*
Anderson (Yukon-Koyukuk Census Area) City *23*
Angoon (Skagway-Hoonah-Angoon Census Area) City *18*
Aniak (Bethel Census Area) City *6*
Annette (Prince of Wales-Outer Ketchikan Census Area) CDP *17*
Anvik (Yukon-Koyukuk Census Area) City *23*
Arctic Village (Yukon-Koyukuk Census Area) CDP *23*
Atka (Aleutians West Census Area) City *5*
Atmautluak (Bethel Census Area) City . *6*
Atqasuk (North Slope Borough) City .. *16*
Barrow (North Slope Borough) City ... *16*
Beaver (Yukon-Koyukuk Census Area) CDP *23*
Bethel (Bethel Census Area) City *6*
Bethel Census Area *6*
Bettles (Yukon-Koyukuk Census Area) City *23*
Big Delta (Southeast Fairbanks Census Area) CDP *19*
Big Lake (Matanuska-Susitna Borough) CDP *14*
Birch Creek (Yukon-Koyukuk Census Area) CDP *23*
Brevig Mission (Nome Census Area) City *15*
Bristol Bay Borough *8*
Buckland (Northwest Arctic Borough) City *16*
Butte (Matanuska-Susitna Borough) CDP *14*
Cantwell (Yukon-Koyukuk Census Area) CDP *23*
Central (Yukon-Koyukuk Census Area) CDP *23*
Chalkyitsik (Yukon-Koyukuk Census Area) CDP *23*
Chase (Matanuska-Susitna Borough) CDP *14*
Chefornak (Bethel Census Area) City ... *6*

Chenega (Valdez-Cordova Census Area) CDP *20*
Chevak (Wade Hampton Census Area) City *21*
Chickaloon (Matanuska-Susitna Borough) CDP *14*
Chignik (Lake and Peninsula Borough) City *13*
Chignik Lagoon (Lake and Peninsula Borough) CDP *13*
Chignik Lake (Lake and Peninsula Borough) CDP *13*
Chiniak (Kodiak Island Borough) CDP *12*
Chistochina (Valdez-Cordova Census Area) CDP *20*
Chitina (Valdez-Cordova Census Area) CDP *20*
Chuathbaluk (Bethel Census Area) City *6*
Circle (Yukon-Koyukuk Census Area) CDP *23*
Circle Hot Springs Station (Yukon-Koyukuk Census Area) CDP *23*
Clam Gulch (Kenai Peninsula Borough) CDP *10*
Clarks Point (Dillingham Census Area) City *8*
Coffman Cove (Prince of Wales-Outer Ketchikan Census Area) City *17*
Cohoe (Kenai Peninsula Borough) CDP *10*
Cold Bay (Aleutians East Borough) City *5*
College (Fairbanks North Star Borough) CDP *9*
Cooper Landing (Kenai Peninsula Borough) CDP *10*
Copper Center (Valdez-Cordova Census Area) CDP *20*
Copperville (Valdez-Cordova Census Area) CDP *20*
Cordova (Valdez-Cordova Census Area) City *20*
Covenant Life (Haines Borough) CDP *10*
Craig (Prince of Wales-Outer Ketchikan Census Area) City *17*
Crooked Creek (Bethel Census Area) CDP *6*
Crown Point (Kenai Peninsula Borough) CDP *10*
Cube Cove (Skagway-Hoonah-Angoon Census Area) CDP *18*
Deadhorse (North Slope Borough) CDP *16*
Deering (Northwest Arctic Borough) City *16*
Delta Junction (Southeast Fairbanks Census Area) City *19*
Denali Borough *8*
Dillingham (Dillingham Census Area) City *8*
Dillingham Census Area *8*
Diomede (Nome Census Area) City ... *15*
Dora Bay (Prince of Wales-Outer Ketchikan Census Area) CDP *17*
Dot Lake (Southeast Fairbanks Census Area) CDP *19*

Dry Creek (Southeast Fairbanks Census Area) CDP *19*
Eagle (Southeast Fairbanks Census Area) City *19*
Eagle Village (Southeast Fairbanks Census Area) CDP *19*
Edna Bay (Prince of Wales-Outer Ketchikan Census Area) CDP *17*
Eek (Bethel Census Area) City *6*
Egegik (Lake and Peninsula Borough) CDP *13*
Eielson Air Force Base (Fairbanks North Star Borough) Military Facility *9*
Ekwok (Dillingham Census Area) City . *8*
Elfin Cove (Skagway-Hoonah-Angoon Census Area) CDP *18*
Elim (Nome Census Area) City *15*
Emmonak (Wade Hampton Census Area) City *21*
English Bay (Kenai Peninsula Borough) CDP *10*
Ester (Fairbanks North Star Borough) CDP *9*
Evansville (Yukon-Koyukuk Census Area) CDP *23*
Eyak (Valdez-Cordova Census Area) CDP *20*
Fairbanks (Fairbanks North Star Borough) City *9*
Fairbanks North Star Borough *9*
False Pass (Aleutians East Borough) CDP *5*
Ferry (Yukon-Koyukuk Census Area) CDP *23*
Fort Greely (Southeast Fairbanks Census Area) Military Facility *19*
Fort Yukon (Yukon-Koyukuk Census Area) City *23*
Fox (Fairbanks North Star Borough) CDP *9*
Fox River (Kenai Peninsula Borough) CDP *11*
Freshwater Bay (Skagway-Hoonah-Angoon Census Area) CDP *18*
Frit Creek (Kenai Peninsula Borough) CDP *11*
Gakona (Valdez-Cordova Census Area) CDP *20*
Galena (Yukon-Koyukuk Census Area) City *23*
Gambell (Nome Census Area) City *15*
Game Creek (Skagway-Hoonah-Angoon Census Area) CDP *19*
Glennallen (Valdez-Cordova Census Area) CDP *20*
Golovin (Nome Census Area) City *15*
Goodnews Bay (Bethel Census Area) City *6*
Grayling (Yukon-Koyukuk Census Area) City *23*
Gulkana (Valdez-Cordova Census Area) CDP *20*
Gustavus (Skagway-Hoonah-Angoon Census Area) CDP *19*
Haines (Haines Borough) City *10*
Haines Borough *10*
Halibut Cove (Kenai Peninsula Borough) CDP *11*

ALASKA

Happy Valley (Kenai Peninsula Borough) CDP *11*
Harding Lake (Fairbanks North Star Borough) CDP *9*
Healy (Yukon-Koyukuk Census Area) CDP *23*
Healy Lake (Southeast Fairbanks Census Area) CDP *19*
Hobart Bay (Skagway-Hoonah-Angoon Census Area) CDP *19*
Hollis (Prince of Wales-Outer Ketchikan Census Area) CDP *17*
Holy Cross (Yukon-Koyukuk Census Area) City *23*
Homer (Kenai Peninsula Borough) City *11*
Hoonah (Skagway-Hoonah-Angoon Census Area) City *19*
Hooper Bay (Wade Hampton Census Area) City *21*
Hope (Kenai Peninsula Borough) CDP *11*
Houston (Matanuska-Susitna Borough) City *14*
Hughes (Yukon-Koyukuk Census Area) City *23*
Huslia (Yukon-Koyukuk Census Area) City *24*
Hydaburg (Prince of Wales-Outer Ketchikan Census Area) City *17*
Hyder (Prince of Wales-Outer Ketchikan Census Area) CDP *17*
Igiugig (Lake and Peninsula Borough) CDP *13*
Iliamna (Lake and Peninsula Borough) CDP *13*
Ivanof Bay (Lake and Peninsula Borough) CDP *13*
Jakolof Bay (Kenai Peninsula Borough) CDP *11*
Juneau Borough and City *10*
Kachemak (Kenai Peninsula Borough) City *11*
Kake (Wrangell-Petersburg Census Area) City *22*
Kaktovik (North Slope Borough) City *16*
Kalifonsky (Kenai Peninsula Borough) CDP *11*
Kaltag (Yukon-Koyukuk Census Area) City *24*
Karluk (Kodiak Island Borough) CDP *12*
Kasaan (Prince of Wales-Outer Ketchikan Census Area) City *17*
Kasigluk (Bethel Census Area) City *6*
Kasilof (Kenai Peninsula Borough) CDP *11*
Kenai (Kenai Peninsula Borough) City *11*
Kenai Peninsula Borough *10*
Kenny Lake (Valdez-Cordova Census Area) CDP *20*
Ketchikan (Ketchikan Gateway Borough) City *12*
Ketchikan Gateway Borough *12*
Kiana (Northwest Arctic Borough) City *17*
King Cove (Aleutians East Borough) City *5*
King Salmon (Bristol Bay Borough) CDP *8*
Kipnuk (Bethel Census Area) CDP *6*
Kivalina (Northwest Arctic Borough) City *17*

Klawock (Prince of Wales-Outer Ketchikan Census Area) City *18*
Klukwan (Skagway-Hoonah-Angoon Census Area) CDP *19*
Knik (Matanuska-Susitna Borough) CDP *14*
Kobuk (Northwest Arctic Borough) City *17*
Kodiak (Kodiak Island Borough) City *12*
Kodiak Island Borough *12*
Kodiak Station (Kodiak Island Borough) Military Facility *12*
Kokhanok (Lake and Peninsula Borough) CDP *13*
Koliganek (Dillingham Census Area) CDP *9*
Konginganak (Bethel Census Area) CDP *6*
Kotlik (Wade Hampton Census Area) City *21*
Kotzebue (Northwest Arctic Borough) City *17*
Koyuk (Nome Census Area) City *15*
Koyukuk (Yukon-Koyukuk Census Area) City *24*
Kupreanof (Wrangell-Petersburg Census Area) City *22*
Kwethluk (Bethel Census Area) City *6*
Kwigillingok (Bethel Census Area) CDP *7*
Labouchere Bay (Prince of Wales-Outer Ketchikan Census Area) CDP *18*
Lake and Peninsula Borough *13*
Lake Minchumina (Yukon-Koyukuk Census Area) CDP *24*
Larsen Bay (Kodiak Island Borough) City *12*
Lazy Mountain (Matanuska-Susitna Borough) CDP *14*
Levelock (Lake and Peninsula Borough) CDP *13*
Lignite (Yukon-Koyukuk Census Area) CDP *24*
Lime Village (Bethel Census Area) CDP *7*
Long Island (Prince of Wales-Outer Ketchikan Census Area) CDP *18*
Lower Kalskag (Bethel Census Area) City *7*
Lutak (Haines Borough) CDP *10*
Manley Hot Springs (Yukon-Koyukuk Census Area) CDP *24*
Manokotak (Dillingham Census Area) City *9*
Marshall (Wade Hampton Census Area) City *21*
Matanuska-Susitna Borough *14*
McCarthy (Valdez-Cordova Census Area) CDP *20*
McGrath (Yukon-Koyukuk Census Area) City *24*
McKinley Park (Yukon-Koyukuk Census Area) CDP *24*
Meadow Lakes (Matanuska-Susitna Borough) CDP *14*
Mekoryuk (Bethel Census Area) City *7*
Mendeltna (Valdez-Cordova Census Area) CDP *20*
Mentasta Lake (Valdez-Cordova Census Area) CDP *20*
Metlakatla (Prince of Wales-Outer Ketchikan Census Area) CDP *18*
Meyers Chuck (Prince of Wales-Outer Ketchikan Census Area) CDP .. *18*

Minto (Yukon-Koyukuk Census Area) CDP *24*
Moose Creek (Fairbanks North Star Borough) CDP *9*
Moose Pass (Kenai Peninsula Borough) CDP *11*
Mosquito Lake (Haines Borough) CDP *10*
Mountain Village (Wade Hampton Census Area) City *21*
Naknek (Bristol Bay Borough) CDP *8*
Napakiak (Bethel Census Area) City *7*
Napaskiak (Bethel Census Area) City *7*
Naukati Bay (Prince of Wales-Outer Ketchikan Census Area) CDP *18*
Nelson Lagoon (Aleutians East Borough) CDP *5*
Nenana (Yukon-Koyukuk Census Area) City *24*
Newhalen (Lake and Peninsula Borough) City *13*
New Stuyahok (Dillingham Census Area) City *9*
Newtok (Bethel Census Area) City *7*
Newtok (Wade Hampton Census Area) City *21*
Nightmute (Bethel Census Area) City *7*
Nikiski (Kenai Peninsula Borough) CDP *11*
Nikolaevsk (Kenai Peninsula Borough) CDP *11*
Nikolai (Yukon-Koyukuk Census Area) City *24*
Nikolski (Aleutians West Census Area) CDP *5*
Ninilchik (Kenai Peninsula Borough) CDP *11*
Noatak (Northwest Arctic Borough) CDP *17*
Nome (Nome Census Area) City *15*
Nome Census Area *15*
Nondalton (Lake and Peninsula Borough) City *13*
Noorvik (Northwest Arctic Borough) City *17*
North Pole (Fairbanks North Star Borough) City *9*
North Slope Borough *16*
Northway (Southeast Fairbanks Census Area) CDP *19*
Northway Junction (Southeast Fairbanks Census Area) CDP *19*
Northway Village (Southeast Fairbanks Census Area) CDP *20*
Northwest Arctic Borough *16*
Nuiqsut (North Slope Borough) City *16*
Nulato (Yukon-Koyukuk Census Area) City *24*
Nunapitchuk (Bethel Census Area) City *7*
Old Harbor (Kodiak Island Borough) City *12*
Oscarville (Bethel Census Area) CDP *7*
Ouzinkie (Kodiak Island Borough) City *12*
Palmer (Matanuska-Susitna Borough) City *14*
Paxson (Valdez-Cordova Census Area) CDP *20*
Pedro Bay (Lake and Peninsula Borough) CDP *13*
Pelican (Skagway-Hoonah-Angoon Census Area) City *19*
Perryville (Lake and Peninsula Borough) CDP *13*

Petersburg (Wrangell-Petersburg Census Area) City 22
Pilot Point (Lake and Peninsula Borough) CDP 13
Pilot Station (Wade Hampton Census Area) City 21
Pitkas Point (Wade Hampton Census Area) CDP 21
Platinum (Bethel Census Area) City 7
Pleasant Valley (Fairbanks North Star Borough) CDP 9
Point Baker (Prince of Wales-Outer Ketchikan Census Area) CDP 18
Point Hope (North Slope Borough) City 16
Point Lay (North Slope Borough) CDP 16
Polk Inlet (Prince of Wales-Outer Ketchikan Census Area) CDP 18
Port Alexander (Wrangell-Petersburg Census Area) City 22
Port Alice (Prince of Wales-Outer Ketchikan Census Area) CDP 18
Port Alsworth (Lake and Peninsula Borough) CDP 13
Port Clarence (Nome Census Area) Military Facility 15
Port Graham (Kenai Peninsula Borough) CDP 11
Port Heiden (Lake and Peninsula Borough) City 13
Port Lions (Kodiak Island Borough) City 12
Port Protection (Prince of Wales-Outer Ketchikan Census Area) CDP 18
Primrose (Kenai Peninsula Borough) CDP 11
Prince of Wales-Outer Ketchikan Census Area 17
Prudhoe Bay (North Slope Borough) CDP 16
Quinhagak (Bethel Census Area) City ..7
Rampart (Yukon-Koyukuk Census Area) CDP 24
Red Devil (Bethel Census Area) CDP ..7
Ridgeway (Kenai Peninsula Borough) CDP 11
Rowan Bay (Wrangell-Petersburg Census Area) CDP 22
Ruby (Yukon-Koyukuk Census Area) City 24
Russian Mission (Wade Hampton Census Area) City 21
St. George (Aleutians West Census Area) City 5
St. John Harbor (Wrangell-Petersburg Census Area) CDP 22
St. Mary's (Wade Hampton Census Area) City 21
St. Michael (Nome Census Area) City 15

St. Paul (Aleutians West Census Area) City 5
Salamatof (Kenai Peninsula Borough) CDP 11
Salcha (Fairbanks North Star Borough) CDP 9
Sand Point (Aleutians East Borough) City 5
Savoonga (Nome Census Area) City ... 15
Saxman (Ketchikan Gateway Borough) City 12
Scammon Bay (Wade Hampton Census Area) City 21
Selawik (Northwest Arctic Borough) City 17
Seldovia (Kenai Peninsula Borough) City 11
Seward (Kenai Peninsula Borough) City 11
Shageluk (Yukon-Koyukuk Census Area) City 24
Shaktoolik (Nome Census Area) City . 15
Sheldon Point (Wade Hampton Census Area) City 21
Shishmaref (Nome Census Area) City 15
Shungnak (Northwest Arctic Borough) City 17
Sitka Borough and City 18
Skagway (Skagway-Hoonah-Angoon Census Area) City 19
Skagway-Hoonah-Angoon Census Area 18
Skwentna (Matanuska-Susitna Borough) CDP 14
Slana (Valdez-Cordova Census Area) CDP 20
Sleetmute (Bethel Census Area) CDP ... 7
Soldotna (Kenai Peninsula Borough) City 11
Southeast Fairbanks Census Area 19
South Naknek (Bristol Bay Borough) CDP 8
Stebbins (Nome Census Area) City 15
Sterling (Kenai Peninsula Borough) CDP 11
Stevens Village (Yukon-Koyukuk Census Area) CDP 24
Stony River (Bethel Census Area) CDP 7
Sutton (Matanuska-Susitna Borough) CDP 14
Takotna (Yukon-Koyukuk Census Area) CDP 24
Talkeetna (Matanuska-Susitna Borough) CDP 14
Tanacross (Southeast Fairbanks Census Area) CDP 20
Tanana (Yukon-Koyukuk Census Area) City 24
Tatitlek (Valdez-Cordova Census Area) CDP 20

Teller (Nome Census Area) City 15
Tenakee Springs (Skagway-Hoonah-Angoon Census Area) City 19
Tetlin (Southeast Fairbanks Census Area) CDP 20
Thorne Bay (Prince of Wales-Outer Ketchikan Census Area) City 18
Togiak (Dillingham Census Area) City . 9
Tok (Southeast Fairbanks Census Area) CDP 20
Toksook Bay (Bethel Census Area) City 7
Tonsina (Valdez-Cordova Census Area) CDP 21
Trapper Creek (Matanuska-Susitna Borough) CDP 14
Tuluksak (Bethel Census Area) City 7
Tuntutuliak (Bethel Census Area) CDP 7
Tununak (Bethel Census Area) City 7
Twin Hills (Dillingham Census Area) CDP 9
Two Rivers (Fairbanks North Star Borough) CDP 9
Tyonek (Kenai Peninsula Borough) CDP 11
Unalakleet (Nome Census Area) City . 15
Unalaska (Aleutians West Census Area) City 5
Upper Kalskag (Bethel Census Area) City 7
Valdez (Valdez-Cordova Census Area) City 21
Valdez-Cordova Census Area 20
Venetie (Yukon-Koyukuk Census Area) CDP 24
Wade Hampton Census Area 21
Wainwright (North Slope Borough) City 16
Wales (Nome Census Area) City 15
Wasilla (Matanuska-Susitna Borough) City 14
Whale Pass (Prince of Wales-Outer Ketchikan Census Area) CDP 18
White Mountain (Nome Census Area) City 15
Whitestone Logging Camp (Skagway-Hoonah-Angoon Census Area) CDP 19
Whittier (Valdez-Cordova Census Area) City 21
Willow (Matanuska-Susitna Borough) CDP 14
Womens Bay (Kodiak Island Borough) CDP 12
Wrangell (Wrangell-Petersburg Census Area) City 22
Wrangell-Petersburg Census Area 22
Yakutat Census Area 22
Yukon-Koyukuk Census Area 23

Arizona

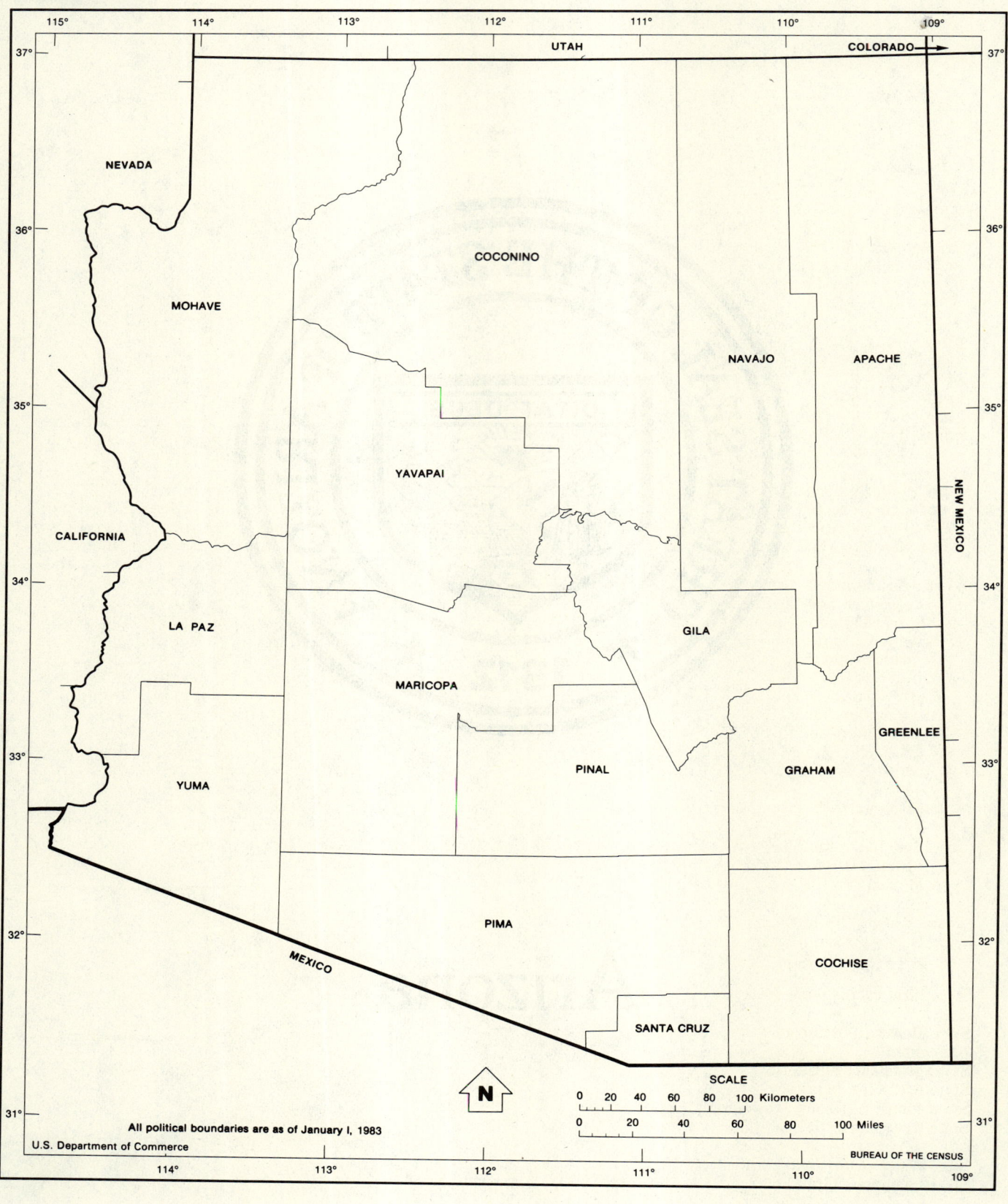

Arizona

Population: 3,665,228 (1990); 2,718,215 (1980)
Population rank (1990): 24
Percent population change (1980–1990): 34.8
Population projection: 4,097,000 (1995); 4,457,000 (2000)

Area: total: 114,006 sq. mi.; 113,642 sq. mi. land, 364 sq. mi. water
Area rank: 6
Highest elevation: 12,633 ft., Humphreys Peak (Coconino County)
Lowest point: 70 ft., along the Colorado River (Yuma County)

State capital: Phoenix (Maricopa County)
Largest city: Phoenix (983,403)
Second largest city: Tuscon (405,390)
Largest county: Maricopa (2,122,101)

Total housing units: 1,659,430
No. of occupied housing units: 1,368,843
Vacant housing units (%): 17.5
Distribution of population by race and Hispanic origin (%):
White: 80.8
Black: 3.0
Hispanic (any race): 18.8
Native American: 5.6
Asian/Pacific: 1.5
Other: 9.1

Admission date: February 14, 1912 (48th state).

Location: In the southwestern United States, bordering California, Nevada, Utah, Colorado, New Mexico, and Mexico.

Name Origin: From the Pima or Papago Indian word *arizonac*, which may mean 'place of small springs.'

State bird: cactus wren *(Campylorhynchus brunneicapillus)*
State flower: blossom of the saguaro cactus *(Carnegiea gigantea)*
State gemstone: turquoise
State neckwear: bola tie
State songs: "Arizona March Song" and "Arizona"
State tree: paloverde *(Cercidium floridum)*

State motto: *Ditat Deus* (Latin 'God Enriches')
State nickname: Grand Canyon State

Area code: 602
Time zone: Mountain
Abbreviations: AZ (postal); Ariz. (traditional)

Part of (region): Mountain; Southwest; Far West

Local Government

Counties

Arizona has 15 counties, each governed by three or five elected supervisors. Arizona also has 22 Indian reservations, each with an elected tribal council or board.

Municipalities

Arizona has 40 incorporated cities and 42 incorporated towns. Other areas are administered at the county level.

Settlement History and Early Development

What is now Arizona was first inhabited more than 12,000 years ago. By about 1,000 B.C. there were several distinct groups living in Arizona: the Anasazi (ancestors of the Pueblo Indians), the Hohokam (ancestors of the Papago and Pima Indians), and the Mogollon tribes. Not long before Spanish explorers came to Arizona, Apache and Navajo Indians moved into the area from the plains.

The first white man known to enter Arizona was Marcos de Niza, a Franciscan priest, who traveled through the San Pedro Valley in 1539 searching for the Seven Cities of Cibola, legendary centers of great wealth. In 1540 Francisco Vásquez de Coronado visited Hopi and Zuni villages in search of the fabled cities and their treasure. Spanish missionaries soon entered the region; starting in 1692, Father Eusebio Kino traveled as far north as the site of present-day Fairbank and founded 24 missions. In 1736 silver was discovered near a Pima village southwest of present-day Nogales. Despite resistance from the Indians, the Spanish established a fort at Tubac in 1752 and a fort at Tucson in 1776.

When Mexico became independent of Spain in 1821, Arizona was part of the Mexican province of Sonora. It was occupied by U.S. forces at the start of the Mexican-American War in 1846 and ceded to the U.S. at the end of the war by the Treaty of Guadalupe Hidalgo in 1848.

The Arizona Territory

In 1850 most of present-day Arizona became part of the newly organized New Mexico Territory. During the 1850s settlers unsuccessfully petitioned Congress to recognize Arizona as a territory. In the early 1860s Arizonans chose a delegate to the Confederacy, which sent troops in 1862 to occupy the area of present-day Arizona and New Mexico. Confederate troops were defeated by Union forces, making the 1863 creation of the Confederate Territory of Arizona a moot point. Still, the U.S. Congress responded to the Confederate action by creating the Arizona Territory in late 1863.

Kit Carson led a successful campaign against Arizona's Navajo in 1864, but the Apache Indians, under such leaders as Cochise and Geronimo, continued to fight the whites until Geronimo's surrender in 1886. Despite the hazards posed by the Indians, settlers were drawn to Arizona by farming (made possible by irrigation); ranching; mining of gold, silver, and copper; and the arrival of the Southern Pacific Railroad from California in 1877. Phoenix was established in 1868.

Statehood

President William Howard Taft refused to approve the admission of Arizona as a state because of a provision in the state constitution for the recall of judges. Arizona obligingly removed the provision for as long as it took to become a state, then promptly rewrote the state constitution to re-institute it. Arizona became the 48th state on February 14, 1912. The first governor, George W.P. Hunt, served seven terms and was a strong supporter of the development of dams and irrigation systems. Between 1911 and 1936 the construction of the Theodore Roosevelt Dam on the Salt River, Coolidge Dam on the Gila River, Bartlett Dam on the Verde River, and Hoover Dam on the Colorado River contributed irrigation water to the state.

Business and Industry

Arizona's climate attracted new residents who moved to the state for their health, as well as winter vacationers. Tourists were also attracted by scenic wonders such as the Grand Canyon, the Painted Desert, and the Petrified Forest.

World War I brought economic prosperity in the livestock, agriculture, and copper industries, but there were also serious strikes by miners. During the 1920s and 1930s Arizona shared the nation's economic woes, but during these years both copper and agricultural production increased, so that even during the Great Depression of the 1930s the state's population grew. World War II brought prosperity to the state as Arizona again supplied cattle, copper, cotton, and agricultural products. Many air force bases were established in Arizona, as were camps for displaced Japanese-Americans. In the 1950s Arizona continued to grow. The widespread use of air conditioning meant that it was much more comfortable to live in the state. Many of the new inhabitants were retired people.

In 1948 the state constitution was changed to allow the state's large Indian population to vote.

Throughout the 1950s and 1960s the state gradually shifted toward an economy based more on manufacturing than agriculture. The production of electrical and electronic equipment, transportation equipment, and metal products are among the most important industries. Tourism continued to be a major economic factor.

Between 1950 and 1980, Arizona's population grew rapidly, almost quadrupling. As the population has grown, water resources have been increasingly strained. In 1963 the U.S. Supreme Court gave Arizona a right to water from the Colorado River. In 1974 construction began on the Central Arizona Project, which draws water from the Colorado River to supply Arizona.

Congress attempted to resolve a dispute over land ownership between the Navajo and Hopi Indians by giving each tribe half of a northern Arizona reservation area in 1974. The tribes had been using the area jointly; this decision meant that many people had to relocate because Navajo were living on land that had been given to the Hopi and vice versa.

In 1981 Arizona judge Sandra Day O'Connor became the first woman appointed to the U.S. Supreme Court.

State Boundaries

The Treaty of Guadalupe Hidalgo in 1848 established the Arizona-Mexico border at the Gila River. The territory south of the Gila River was added to Arizona by the Gadsden Purchase in 1853, when the present U.S.-Mexican border was established. Arizona was organized as a territory separate from New Mexico in 1863 with its present boundaries, except for the western boundary with Nevada, which was determined in 1866.

Arizona Counties

Apache	Gila	La Paz	Navajo	Santa Cruz
Cochise	Graham	Maricopa	Pima	Yavapai
Coconino	Greenlee	Mohave	Pinal	Yuma

Multi-County Places

The following Arizona places are in more than one county. Given here is the total population for each multi-county place, and the names of the counties it is in.

Apache Junction, pop. 18,100; Pinal (17,931), Maricopa (169)
Hayden, pop. 909; Gila (909), Pinal (0)
McNary, pop. 355; Apache (202), Navajo (153)
Peridot, pop. 957; Graham (697), Gila (260)
Sedona, pop. 7,720; Yavapai (5,336), Coconino (2,384)

Apache County
County Seat: Saint Johns (ZIP: 85936)

Pop: 61,591 (1990); 52,108 (1980) **Pop Density:** 5.5
Land: 11205.7 sq. mi.; **Water:** 13.5 sq. mi. **Area Code:** 602
On eastern border of AZ; organized Feb 14, 1879 (prior to statehood) from Mohave County.
Name origin: For the Apache Indian tribe, of Athapascan linguistic stock, who inhabited the land for centuries. The name is variously said to mean 'man,' 'battles,' or 'enemy.'

Chinle CDP
ZIP: 86503 **Lat:** 36-09-06 N **Long:** 109-34-48 W
Pop: 5,059 (1990); 2,815 (1980) **Pop Density:** 302.9
Land: 16.7 sq. mi.; **Water:** 0.0 sq. mi.

Dennehotso CDP
Lat: 36-49-17 N **Long:** 109-53-01 W
Pop: 616 (1990) **Pop Density:** 67.7
Land: 9.1 sq. mi.; **Water:** 0.0 sq. mi.

Eagar Town
ZIP: 85925 **Lat:** 34-06-17 N **Long:** 109-17-31 W
Pop: 4,025 (1990); 2,791 (1980) **Pop Density:** 394.6
Land: 10.2 sq. mi.; **Water:** 0.0 sq. mi.
In the northeastern corner of AZ.

Fort Defiance CDP
Lat: 35-44-37 N **Long:** 109-03-59 W
Pop: 4,489 (1990); 3,431 (1980) **Pop Density:** 831.3
Land: 5.4 sq. mi.; **Water:** 0.0 sq. mi.

Ganado CDP
Lat: 35-42-27 N **Long:** 109-33-07 W
Pop: 1,257 (1990) **Pop Density:** 163.2
Land: 7.7 sq. mi.; **Water:** 0.0 sq. mi.

Lukachukai CDP
Lat: 36-24-00 N **Long:** 109-15-24 W
Pop: 113 (1990); 1,049 (1980) **Pop Density:** 37.7
Land: 3.0 sq. mi.; **Water:** 0.0 sq. mi.

McNary CDP
Lat: 34-05-44 N **Long:** 109-51-01 W
Pop: 202 (1990); 318 (1980) **Pop Density:** 54.6
Land: 3.7 sq. mi.; **Water:** 0.1 sq. mi.
Part of the town is in Navajo county.

Many Farms CDP
Lat: 36-21-00 N **Long:** 109-37-06 W
Pop: 1,294 (1990); 1,364 (1980) **Pop Density:** 157.8
Land: 8.2 sq. mi.; **Water:** 0.0 sq. mi.

Rough Rock CDP
Lat: 36-24-34 N **Long:** 109-52-03 W
Pop: 523 (1990) **Pop Density:** 44.3
Land: 11.8 sq. mi.; **Water:** 0.0 sq. mi.

St. Johns City
ZIP: 85936 **Lat:** 34-30-35 N **Long:** 109-22-36 W
Pop: 3,294 (1990); 3,368 (1980) **Pop Density:** 499.1
Land: 6.6 sq. mi.; **Water:** 0.0 sq. mi. **Elev:** 5686 ft.
Name origin: Anglicized form of San Juan, named either for its first woman resident, Maria San Juan Baca de Padilla, or for the annual feast of San Juan (June 24). Previously known as El Vadito, Spanish 'little crossing,' for its location at the crossing of the Little Colorado River.

St. Michaels CDP
Lat: 35-39-42 N **Long:** 109-05-37 W
Pop: 1,119 (1990) **Pop Density:** 294.5
Land: 3.8 sq. mi.; **Water:** 0.0 sq. mi.

Sawmill CDP
Lat: 35-53-30 N **Long:** 109-09-12 W
Pop: 507 (1990) **Pop Density:** 85.9
Land: 5.9 sq. mi.; **Water:** 0.0 sq. mi.

Springerville Town
ZIP: 85938 **Lat:** 34-09-21 N **Long:** 109-17-47 W
Pop: 1,802 (1990); 1,452 (1980) **Pop Density:** 156.7
Land: 11.5 sq. mi.; **Water:** 0.1 sq. mi. **Elev:** 6968 ft.
Name origin: For Harry Springer, who opened a general store here in 1875. Previously called Springer's Store.

Teec Nos Pos CDP
Lat: 36-55-44 N **Long:** 109-04-55 W
Pop: 317 (1990) **Pop Density:** 22.3
Land: 14.2 sq. mi.; **Water:** 0.0 sq. mi.

Tsaile CDP
Lat: 36-18-13 N **Long:** 109-12-52 W
Pop: 1,043 (1990) **Pop Density:** 173.8
Land: 6.0 sq. mi.; **Water:** 0.0 sq. mi.

Window Rock CDP
ZIP: 86515 **Lat:** 35-40-15 N **Long:** 109-03-51 W
Pop: 3,306 (1990); 2,230 (1980) **Pop Density:** 635.8
Land: 5.2 sq. mi.; **Water:** 0.0 sq. mi.

Cochise County
County Seat: Bisbee (ZIP: 85603)

Pop: 97,624 (1990); 85,686 (1980)   **Pop Density:** 15.8
Land: 6170.0 sq. mi.; **Water:** 49.3 sq. mi.   **Area Code:** 602

In southeastern corner of AZ; organized Feb 1, 1881 (prior to statehood) from Pima County.

Name origin: For the famous Chiricahua Apache chief (c. 1812–74), who conducted raids against the U.S. after brutal treatment by U.S. Army officers and surrendered in 1871.

Benson — Town
ZIP: 85602   **Lat:** 31-57-43 N   **Long:** 110-18-11 W
Pop: 3,824 (1990); 4,190 (1980)   **Pop Density:** 449.9
Land: 8.5 sq. mi.; **Water:** 0.0 sq. mi.

Founded 1880 as the railroad town for Tombstone.

Bisbee — City
ZIP: 85603   **Lat:** 31-24-16 N   **Long:** 109-55-02 W
Pop: 6,288 (1990); 7,154 (1980)   **Pop Density:** 1310.0
Land: 4.8 sq. mi.; **Water:** 0.0 sq. mi.

In southeastern AZ, 60 mi. east of Nogales.

Douglas — City
ZIP: 85607   **Lat:** 31-20-33 N   **Long:** 109-31-41 W
Pop: 12,822 (1990); 13,058 (1980)   **Pop Density:** 2728.1
Land: 4.7 sq. mi.; **Water:** 0.0 sq. mi.   **Elev:** 4004 ft.

In southern AZ on the Mexican border. Founded 1901 at a place known as Black Water, site of a dirty but much-used water hole.

Name origin: For Dr. James Stewart Douglas (1837–1918).

Huachuca City — Town
ZIP: 85616   **Lat:** 31-37-55 N   **Long:** 110-20-27 W
Pop: 1,782 (1990); 1,661 (1980)   **Pop Density:** 636.4
Land: 2.8 sq. mi.; **Water:** 0.0 sq. mi.

In the southeastern corner of AZ, southeast of Tucson.

Name origin: Probably for the nearby Huachuca Mountains, from the Chiricahua-Apache term meaning 'thunder.'

Pirtleville — CDP
ZIP: 85626   **Lat:** 31-21-41 N   **Long:** 109-34-00 W
Pop: 1,364 (1990)   **Pop Density:** 682.0
Land: 2.0 sq. mi.; **Water:** 0.0 sq. mi.

St. David — CDP
Lat: 31-54-00 N   **Long:** 110-13-45 W
Pop: 1,468 (1990)   **Pop Density:** 299.6
Land: 4.9 sq. mi.; **Water:** 0.0 sq. mi.

Sierra Vista — City
ZIP: 85635   **Lat:** 31-33-54 N   **Long:** 110-19-20 W
Pop: 32,983 (1990); 24,937 (1980)   **Pop Density:** 231.6
Land: 142.4 sq. mi.; **Water:** 0.0 sq. mi.

In southeastern AZ, 50 mi. southeast of Tucson.

Name origin: Named by its citizens in 1955, descriptively and promotionally, from the Spanish for 'mountain view.' Previously called Garden Canyon, for the canyon gardens that supplied produce for nearby Fort Huachuca, and Fry, for homesteader Oliver Fry.

Sierra Vista Southeast — CDP
Lat: 31-27-38 N   **Long:** 110-13-02 W
Pop: 9,237 (1990)   **Pop Density:** 80.9
Land: 114.2 sq. mi.; **Water:** 0.0 sq. mi.

Tombstone — City
ZIP: 85638   **Lat:** 31-43-02 N   **Long:** 110-03-43 W
Pop: 1,220 (1990); 1,632 (1980)   **Pop Density:** 283.7
Land: 4.3 sq. mi.; **Water:** 0.0 sq. mi.

In southeastern corner of AZ, southeast of Tucson.

Name origin: Named by prospector Ed Schieffelin when he hit his first strike here Feb 1870. He had been warned by the soldiers that in his search for silver in Apache country all he would find would be his own tombstone.

Whetstone — CDP
Lat: 31-42-06 N   **Long:** 110-20-26 W
Pop: 1,289 (1990)   **Pop Density:** 102.3
Land: 12.6 sq. mi.; **Water:** 0.0 sq. mi.

Willcox — City
Lat: 32-15-02 N   **Long:** 109-50-06 W
Pop: 3,122 (1990); 3,243 (1980)   **Pop Density:** 538.3
Land: 5.8 sq. mi.; **Water:** 0.1 sq. mi.   **Elev:** 4167 ft.

Name origin: Probably for Gen. Orlando B. Willcox, commander of the Dept. of AZ, who was on board the first train to come through here and who was given an ovation. Previously called Maley for James H. Mahley, a rancher who gave the right-of-way to the railroad.

Coconino County
County Seat: Flagstaff (ZIP: 86001)

Pop: 96,591 (1990); 75,008 (1980)　　　　**Pop Density:** 5.2
Land: 18619.1 sq. mi.; **Water:** 43.4 sq. mi.　　**Area Code:** 602

In north-central AZ; organized Feb 19, 1891 (prior to statehood) from Yavapai County.

Name origin: Possibly from the Hopi Indian name, *Kohnina*, for the Havasupai tribe that inhabits the Grand Canyon region, which is within the county. Or derived from a Havasupai word meaning 'little water.'

Cameron　　　　　　　　　　　　　　CDP
　　　　　　　　Lat: 35-50-53 N　Long: 111-25-54 W
Pop: 493 (1990)　　　　　　　**Pop Density:** 38.2
Land: 12.9 sq. mi.; **Water:** 0.0 sq. mi.

Flagstaff　　　　　　　　　　　　　　City
ZIP: 86004　　　　Lat: 35-11-20 N　Long: 111-37-11 W
Pop: 45,857 (1990); 34,743 (1980)　**Pop Density:** 725.6
Land: 63.2 sq. mi.; **Water:** 0.0 sq. mi.

In northern AZ, 65 mi. northeast of Prescott. County seat since 1891. Settled 1876; incorporated 1928. Health resort. Site of Northern Arizona Univ. and Lowell Observatory.

Name origin: Probably for a lone pine in an open valley that was spotted by a scouting party or early settler F. F. McMillen; it was stripped of its branches to serve as the staff for an American flag.

Fredonia　　　　　　　　　　　　　　Town
ZIP: 86022　　　　Lat: 36-57-53 N　Long: 112-31-07 W
Pop: 1,207 (1990); 1,040 (1980)　**Pop Density:** 236.7
Land: 5.1 sq. mi.; **Water:** 0.0 sq. mi.

Founded by Mormons.

Name origin: A combination of *free* and *donia* 'woman' signifying the hoped for freedom from prosecution for polygamy sought by its founders. Previously called Hardscrabble.

Grand Canyon Village　　　　　　　　CDP
　　　　　　　　Lat: 36-02-47 N　Long: 112-09-12 W
Pop: 1,499 (1990)　　　　　　**Pop Density:** 111.9
Land: 13.4 sq. mi.; **Water:** 0.0 sq. mi.

Kachina Village　　　　　　　　　　　CDP
　　　　　　　　Lat: 35-05-49 N　Long: 111-41-30 W
Pop: 1,711 (1990)　　　　　　**Pop Density:** 1425.8
Land: 1.2 sq. mi.; **Water:** 0.0 sq. mi.

Kaibito　　　　　　　　　　　　　　　CDP
　　　　　　　　Lat: 36-35-20 N　Long: 111-06-37 W
Pop: 641 (1990)　　　　　　　**Pop Density:** 40.1
Land: 16.0 sq. mi.; **Water:** 0.0 sq. mi.

Leupp　　　　　　　　　　　　　　　CDP
　　　　　　　　Lat: 35-17-43 N　Long: 111-00-02 W
Pop: 857 (1990)　　　　　　　**Pop Density:** 65.4
Land: 13.1 sq. mi.; **Water:** 0.0 sq. mi.

Moenkopi　　　　　　　　　　　　　CDP
　　　　　　　　Lat: 36-06-39 N　Long: 111-13-19 W
Pop: 924 (1990)　　　　　　　**Pop Density:** 462.0
Land: 2.0 sq. mi.; **Water:** 0.0 sq. mi.

Page　　　　　　　　　　　　　　　　City
ZIP: 86036　　　　Lat: 36-54-15 N　Long: 111-27-28 W
Pop: 6,598 (1990); 4,907 (1980)　**Pop Density:** 397.5
Land: 16.6 sq. mi.; **Water:** 0.0 sq. mi.

In north-central AZ, just south of the UT border. Community began in 1957 as a home for construction workers for Glen Canyon Dam.

Name origin: For John Chatfield Page, the commissioner of reclamation (1937–43).

Sedona　　　　　　　　　　　　　　　City
　　　　　　　　Lat: 34-51-22 N　Long: 111-45-53 W
Pop: 2,384 (1990); 1,778 (1980)　**Pop Density:** 372.5
Land: 6.4 sq. mi.; **Water:** 0.0 sq. mi.

Part of the town is in Yavapai County.

Supai　　　　　　　　　　　　　　　CDP
　　　　　　　　Lat: 36-13-26 N　Long: 112-41-35 W
Pop: 423 (1990)　　　　　　　**Pop Density:** 248.8
Land: 1.7 sq. mi.; **Water:** 0.0 sq. mi.

Tuba City　　　　　　　　　　　　　CDP
ZIP: 86045　　　　Lat: 36-07-29 N　Long: 111-14-32 W
Pop: 7,323 (1990); 5,045 (1980)　**Pop Density:** 671.8
Land: 10.9 sq. mi.; **Water:** 0.0 sq. mi.

Williams　　　　　　　　　　　　　　City
ZIP: 86046　　　　Lat: 35-15-52 N　Long: 112-10-22 W
Pop: 2,532 (1990); 2,266 (1980)　**Pop Density:** 88.2
Land: 28.7 sq. mi.; **Water:** 0.3 sq. mi.

Name origin: For its location at the base of Bill Williams Mountain.

Gila County
County Seat: Globe (ZIP: 85501)

Pop: 40,216 (1990); 37,080 (1980)   **Pop Density:** 8.4
Land: 4768.1 sq. mi.; **Water:** 28.0 sq. mi.   **Area Code:** 602

In east-central AZ, east of Phoenix; organized Feb 8, 1881 (prior to statehood) from Maricopa and Pinal counties.

Name origin: For the Gila River, which forms part of the county's southern boundary. Some sources suggest the name may refer to the Gila monster.

Canyon Day   CDP
Lat: 33-46-53 N   Long: 110-01-34 W
Pop: 857 (1990)   **Pop Density:** 225.5
Land: 3.8 sq. mi.; **Water:** 0.0 sq. mi.

Central Heights-Midland City   CDP
Lat: 33-24-18 N   Long: 110-48-43 W
Pop: 2,969 (1990); 2,791 (1980)   **Pop Density:** 1349.5
Land: 2.2 sq. mi.; **Water:** 0.0 sq. mi.

Claypool   CDP
ZIP: 85532   Lat: 33-24-24 N   Long: 110-50-24 W
Pop: 1,942 (1990); 2,362 (1980)   **Pop Density:** 1387.1
Land: 1.4 sq. mi.; **Water:** 0.0 sq. mi.

Globe   City
ZIP: 85501   Lat: 33-22-58 N   Long: 110-45-15 W
Pop: 6,062 (1990); 6,886 (1980)   **Pop Density:** 730.4
Land: 8.3 sq. mi.; **Water:** 0.0 sq. mi.   **Elev:** 3509 ft.

In east-central AZ, 70 mi. east of Phoenix.

Name origin: For the nearby Globe Mine, so named, possibly, by silver prospectors, for the site's immense size; or by cavalry men, for a perfectly round boulder discovered here.

Hayden   Town
ZIP: 85235   Lat: 32-59-59 N   Long: 110-46-51 W
Pop: 909 (1990); 1,205 (1980)   **Pop Density:** 757.5
Land: 1.2 sq. mi.; **Water:** 0.0 sq. mi.

Part of the town is also in Pinal County.

Miami   Town
ZIP: 85539   Lat: 33-23-39 N   Long: 110-52-19 W
Pop: 2,018 (1990); 2,716 (1980)   **Pop Density:** 2018.0
Land: 1.0 sq. mi.; **Water:** 0.0 sq. mi.   **Elev:** 3411 ft.

Name origin: For the nearby Miami Mine and Miami Wash, a creek so named by a group from Miami, OH, who built a custom mill there.

Payson   Town
ZIP: 85541   Lat: 34-14-33 N   Long: 111-19-37 W
Pop: 8,377 (1990); 5,068 (1980)   **Pop Density:** 644.4
Land: 13.0 sq. mi.; **Water:** 0.0 sq. mi.   **Elev:** 4887 ft.

In east-central AZ, northeast of Phoenix. Founded 1882.

Name origin: Named for Sen. Louis Edward Payson when the post office was established. Previously called Green Valley but founded as Union Park.

Peridot   CDP
ZIP: 85542   Lat: 33-18-00 N   Long: 110-27-40 W
Pop: 260 (1990)   **Pop Density:** 92.9
Land: 2.8 sq. mi.; **Water:** 0.0 sq. mi.

Part of the town is in Graham County.

San Carlos   CDP
ZIP: 85550   Lat: 33-20-55 N   Long: 110-27-54 W
Pop: 2,918 (1990); 2,668 (1980)   **Pop Density:** 327.9
Land: 8.9 sq. mi.; **Water:** 0.0 sq. mi.

Winkelman   Town
ZIP: 85292   Lat: 32-59-20 N   Long: 110-46-10 W
Pop: 676 (1990); 1,060 (1980)   **Pop Density:** 2253.3
Land: 0.3 sq. mi.; **Water:** 0.0 sq. mi.

Name origin: For Peter Winkelman, who owned a ranch nearby.

Graham County
County Seat: Safford (ZIP: 85546)

Pop: 26,554 (1990); 22,862 (1980)   **Pop Density:** 5.7
Land: 4629.6 sq. mi.; **Water:** 11.8 sq. mi.   **Area Code:** 602

In southeastern AZ, northeast of Tucson; organized Mar 10, 1881 (prior to statehood) from Apache and Pima counties.

Name origin: For its most prominent feature, Mount Graham, in the Pinaleno Mountains; elevation 10,720 ft.

Bylas   CDP
ZIP: 85530   Lat: 33-07-50 N   Long: 110-06-36 W
Pop: 1,219 (1990); 1,175 (1980)   **Pop Density:** 297.3
Land: 4.1 sq. mi.; **Water:** 0.0 sq. mi.

Peridot   CDP
Lat: 33-18-15 N   Long: 110-26-45 W
Pop: 697 (1990)   **Pop Density:** 303.0
Land: 2.3 sq. mi.; **Water:** 0.0 sq. mi.

Part of the town is in Gila County.

Pima
Town
ZIP: 85543 **Lat:** 32-53-17 N **Long:** 109-49-59 W
Pop: 1,725 (1990); 1,599 (1980) **Pop Density:** 663.5
Land: 2.6 sq. mi.; **Water:** 0.0 sq. mi.
In southeastern AZ, northeast of Tucson. Founded 1879 by Mormons.
Name origin: Named for the Pima Indians when the post office was established. Previously called Smithville for Mormon leader Jesse N. Smith.

Safford
City
ZIP: 85546 **Lat:** 32-49-52 N **Long:** 109-41-53 W
Pop: 7,359 (1990); 7,010 (1980) **Pop Density:** 1036.5
Land: 7.1 sq. mi.; **Water:** 0.0 sq. mi.
Settled 1874 by farmers.
Name origin: For Gov. Anson Pacely Killen Safford, who had recently visited the valley.

Swift Trail Junction
CDP
Lat: 32-43-56 N **Long:** 109-42-53 W
Pop: 1,203 (1990) **Pop Density:** 273.4
Land: 4.4 sq. mi.; **Water:** 0.0 sq. mi.

Thatcher
Town
ZIP: 85552 **Lat:** 32-50-18 N **Long:** 109-45-32 W
Pop: 3,763 (1990); 3,374 (1980) **Pop Density:** 1175.9
Land: 3.2 sq. mi.; **Water:** 0.0 sq. mi.
Name origin: For the Mormon apostle Moses Thatcher, who visited it Christmas 1882.

Greenlee County
County Seat: Clifton (ZIP: 85533)

Pop: 8,008 (1990); 11,406 (1980) **Pop Density:** 4.3
Land: 1847.1 sq. mi.; **Water:** 1.4 sq. mi. **Area Code:** 602
On southeastern border of AZ; organized Mar 10, 1909 (prior to statehood) from Graham County.
Name origin: For Mason Greenlee (1835–1903), a Virginian who settled in the area in the 1870s.

Clifton
Town
ZIP: 85533 **Lat:** 33-01-24 N **Long:** 109-17-25 W
Pop: 2,840 (1990); 4,245 (1980) **Pop Density:** 190.6
Land: 14.9 sq. mi.; **Water:** 0.1 sq. mi. **Elev:** 3468 ft.
In northeastern AZ, 110 mi. northeast of Tucson. Copper-mining town.
Name origin: For its location in the midst of towering cliffs. Originally called Cliff Town.

Duncan
Town
ZIP: 85534 **Lat:** 32-44-10 N **Long:** 109-05-30 W
Pop: 662 (1990); 603 (1980) **Pop Density:** 254.6
Land: 2.6 sq. mi.; **Water:** 0.0 sq. mi. **Elev:** 3759 ft.
Name origin: For either Duncan Smith, who sold his land to the Arizona Copper Company at the coming of the railroad in 1883, or the Duncan brothers, who settled here and were killed by Apaches c. 1885.

Morenci
CDP
ZIP: 85540 **Lat:** 33-03-10 N **Long:** 109-19-46 W
Pop: 1,799 (1990); 2,736 (1980) **Pop Density:** 2248.8
Land: 0.8 sq. mi.; **Water:** 0.0 sq. mi.

La Paz County
County Seat: Parker (ZIP: 85344)

Pop: 13,844 (1990); 12,557 (1980) **Pop Density:** 3.1
Land: 4499.6 sq. mi.; **Water:** 14.1 sq. mi. **Area Code:** 602
On western border of AZ, west of Phoenix; organized Jan 1, 1983 from Yuma County.
Name origin: For the once-prominent AZ city of La Paz, an important gold-mining center in the 1860s that eventually was abandoned. Gold had been discovered near the site on Jan 12, 1862, the Feast of Our Lady of Peace, Spanish *Nuestra Señora de la Paz*.

Bluewater
CDP
Lat: 34-10-06 N **Long:** 114-15-50 W
Pop: 505 (1990) **Pop Density:** 240.5
Land: 2.1 sq. mi.; **Water:** 0.3 sq. mi.

Ehrenberg
CDP
ZIP: 85328 **Lat:** 33-37-22 N **Long:** 114-29-38 W
Pop: 1,226 (1990) **Pop Density:** 147.7
Land: 8.3 sq. mi.; **Water:** 0.2 sq. mi.

American Places Dictionary — ARIZONA, Maricopa County

Parker
Town
ZIP: 85344 **Lat:** 34-01-18 N **Long:** 114-13-51 W
Pop: 2,897 (1990); 2,542 (1980) **Pop Density:** 131.7
Land: 22.0 sq. mi.; **Water:** 0.0 sq. mi. **Elev:** 1642 ft.
In southwestern AZ within the Colorado River Indian Reservation on the CA border.
Name origin: For Gen. Eli Parker, commissioner of Indian affairs.

Parker Strip
CDP
Lat: 34-15-27 N **Long:** 114-08-31 W
Pop: 1,646 (1990) **Pop Density:** 245.7
Land: 6.7 sq. mi.; **Water:** 1.3 sq. mi.

Poston
CDP
Lat: 33-57-32 N **Long:** 114-24-54 W
Pop: 480 (1990) **Pop Density:** 67.6
Land: 7.1 sq. mi.; **Water:** 0.0 sq. mi.

Quartzsite
Town
Lat: 33-40-01 N **Long:** 114-12-53 W
Pop: 1,876 (1990) **Pop Density:** 51.7
Land: 36.3 sq. mi.; **Water:** 0.0 sq. mi.

Maricopa County
County Seat: Phoenix (ZIP: 85003)

Pop: 2,122,100 (1990); 1,509,180 (1980) **Pop Density:** 230.6
Land: 9204.0 sq. mi.; **Water:** 20.8 sq. mi. **Area Code:** 602
In south-central AZ; organized Feb 14, 1871 (prior to statehood) from Yavapai and Yuma counties.
Name origin: From the name of an Indian tribe of Yuman linguistic stock. The name may be a variant of the Spanish *mariposa*, or 'butterfly,' as the Spanish found the tribe wearing bright paints. The tribe called itself *Pipatsje*, 'people.'

Apache Junction
City
Lat: 33-25-08 N **Long:** 111-34-51 W
Pop: 169 (1990); 9,935 (1980) **Pop Density:** 3380.0
Land: 0.05 sq. mi.; **Water:** 0.0 sq. mi.
Part of the town is in Pinal County.

Avondale
City
ZIP: 85323 **Lat:** 33-25-12 N **Long:** 112-19-26 W
Pop: 16,169 (1990); 8,168 (1980) **Pop Density:** 731.6
Land: 22.1 sq. mi.; **Water:** 0.1 sq. mi.
In southwestern AZ, west of Phoenix.
Name origin: For nearby Avondale Ranch.

Buckeye
Town
ZIP: 85326 **Lat:** 33-24-45 N **Long:** 112-35-07 W
Pop: 5,038 (1990); 3,434 (1980) **Pop Density:** 269.4
Land: 18.7 sq. mi.; **Water:** 0.0 sq. mi.
In southwest-central AZ, 30 mi. west of Phoenix. Incorporated 1931.
Name origin: Unofficially named by early founders Thomas Newton Clanton and M. M. Jackson, from the nickname for OH, their home state. Previously called Sydney, but so many people still used the name "Buckeye" that the town was incorporated under that name.

Carefree
Town
ZIP: 85377 **Lat:** 33-49-20 N **Long:** 111-55-06 W
Pop: 1,666 (1990) **Pop Density:** 187.2
Land: 8.9 sq. mi.; **Water:** 0.0 sq. mi. **Elev:** 2389 ft.

Cave Creek
Town
ZIP: 85331 **Lat:** 33-49-34 N **Long:** 111-57-54 W
Pop: 2,925 (1990); 1,589 (1980) **Pop Density:** 117.9
Land: 24.8 sq. mi.; **Water:** 0.0 sq. mi.

Chandler
City
ZIP: 85225 **Lat:** 33-17-41 N **Long:** 111-52-00 W
Pop: 90,533 (1990); 29,673 (1980) **Pop Density:** 1902.0
Land: 47.6 sq. mi.; **Water:** 0.1 sq. mi. **Elev:** 1213 ft.
In southern AZ, 15 mi. southeast of Phoenix.
Name origin: For Alexander John Chandler (1859–1950), who came to AZ in 1887 as the territory's first veterinary surgeon.

El Mirage
Town
ZIP: 85335 **Lat:** 33-35-28 N **Long:** 112-19-26 W
Pop: 5,001 (1990); 4,307 (1980) **Pop Density:** 515.6
Land: 9.7 sq. mi.; **Water:** 0.0 sq. mi.
In southwestern AZ, 5 mi. northwest of Phoenix.

Fountain Hills
Town
ZIP: 85269 **Lat:** 33-36-19 N **Long:** 111-44-28 W
Pop: 10,030 (1990); 2,771 (1980) **Pop Density:** 600.6
Land: 16.7 sq. mi.; **Water:** 0.1 sq. mi.

Gila Bend
Town
ZIP: 85337 **Lat:** 32-57-05 N **Long:** 112-41-05 W
Pop: 1,747 (1990); 1,585 (1980) **Pop Density:** 196.3
Land: 8.9 sq. mi.; **Water:** 0.0 sq. mi.
Name origin: For its original location at the 90-degree 'Great Bend' in the Gila River. Early visitors called the place Big Bend.

Gilbert
Town
ZIP: 85234 **Lat:** 33-19-55 N **Long:** 111-45-51 W
Pop: 29,188 (1990); 5,717 (1980) **Pop Density:** 1077.0
Land: 27.1 sq. mi.; **Water:** 0.3 sq. mi.
In southern AZ, 18 mi. southeast of Phoenix.
Name origin: For Robert Gilbert, who donated land on which the railroad station and town were built.

Glendale — City
ZIP: 85301 **Lat:** 33-35-02 N **Long:** 112-12-05 W
Pop: 148,134 (1990); 97,172 (1980) **Pop Density:** 2837.8
Land: 52.2 sq. mi.; **Water:** 0.1 sq. mi.

In southwest-central AZ, 10 mi. northwest of Phoenix. Established 1892 by the New England Land Company.
Name origin: For its location.

Goodyear — Town
ZIP: 85338 **Lat:** 33-20-49 N **Long:** 112-24-40 W
Pop: 6,258 (1990); 2,747 (1980) **Pop Density:** 54.4
Land: 115.0 sq. mi.; **Water:** 0.0 sq. mi.

Built on land purchased by the Goodyear Tire and Rubber Company to produce Egyptian cotton.
Name origin: For the tire company. Previously called Egypt, after the cotton.

Guadalupe — Town
ZIP: 85283 **Lat:** 33-21-56 N **Long:** 111-57-42 W
Pop: 5,458 (1990); 4,506 (1980) **Pop Density:** 7797.1
Land: 0.7 sq. mi.; **Water:** 0.0 sq. mi.

Established by Yaqui Indians, who fled Mexico to avoid the persecution of Porfirio Díaz (1830–1915).
Name origin: For the Virgin of Guadalupe, patron saint of Mexico.

Komatke — CDP
Lat: 33-18-22 N **Long:** 112-10-41 W
Pop: 1,116 (1990) **Pop Density:** 214.6
Land: 5.2 sq. mi.; **Water:** 0.0 sq. mi.

Litchfield Park — City
ZIP: 85340 **Lat:** 33-30-09 N **Long:** 112-21-31 W
Pop: 3,303 (1990) **Pop Density:** 1139.0
Land: 2.9 sq. mi.; **Water:** 0.0 sq. mi.

Luke Air Force Base — Military Facility
Lat: 33-31-59 N **Long:** 112-22-14 W
Pop: 4,371 (1990); 3,515 (1980) **Pop Density:** 1181.4
Land: 3.7 sq. mi.; **Water:** 0.0 sq. mi.

Mesa — City
ZIP: 85201 **Lat:** 33-25-03 N **Long:** 111-44-25 W
Pop: 288,091 (1990); 152,404 (1980) **Pop Density:** 2652.8
Land: 108.6 sq. mi.; **Water:** 0.2 sq. mi. **Elev:** 1234 ft.

In southwestern AZ, 15 mi. east of Phoenix. Founded 1878 by Mormons.
Name origin: From the Spanish term meaning 'table'; descriptive of a high, flat, tableland with sharply eroded sides.

Paradise Valley — Town
ZIP: 85253 **Lat:** 33-32-21 N **Long:** 111-57-16 W
Pop: 11,671 (1990); 11,085 (1980) **Pop Density:** 767.8
Land: 15.2 sq. mi.; **Water:** 0.0 sq. mi.

In southwestern AZ, 9 mi. northeast of Phoenix.
Name origin: Promotionally named by Rio Verde Canal Company, which arrived in the spring of 1899 and found the valley covered with flowers.

Peoria — City
ZIP: 85345 **Lat:** 33-41-18 N **Long:** 112-14-40 W
Pop: 50,618 (1990); 12,171 (1980) **Pop Density:** 823.1
Land: 61.5 sq. mi.; **Water:** 0.0 sq. mi.

In southwest-central AZ, 14 mi. northwest of Phoenix.
Name origin: Probably named either by early settler Chauncey Clark or by town planners D. S. Brown and J. B. Greenhut, all of whom came from Peoria, IL.

Phoenix — City
ZIP: 85026 **Lat:** 33-32-33 N **Long:** 112-04-17 W
Pop: 983,403 (1990); 789,704 (1980) **Pop Density:** 2342.0
Land: 419.9 sq. mi.; **Water:** 0.2 sq. mi.

In southwest-central AZ in the Salt River Valley. State capital since 1912 and largest city. Settled 1870; incorporated as city 1881. Territorial capital 1889. Major resort center; manufacture of computers and electronic equipment. Luke Air Force Base and Williams Air Force Base are nearby.
Name origin: For the mythological bird that is supposed to rise from the ashes of its funeral pyre and live again, thus a symbol of hope or immortality; the city was built on the remains of an Indian city.

Queen Creek — Town
ZIP: 85242 **Lat:** 33-14-29 N **Long:** 111-38-35 W
Pop: 2,667 (1990) **Pop Density:** 244.7
Land: 10.9 sq. mi.; **Water:** 0.0 sq. mi.

Scottsdale — City
ZIP: 85251 **Lat:** 33-41-09 N **Long:** 111-52-13 W
Pop: 130,069 (1990); 88,622 (1980) **Pop Density:** 705.4
Land: 184.4 sq. mi.; **Water:** 0.2 sq. mi.

In central AZ, a residential suburb of Phoenix.
Name origin: For Maj. Winfield Scott (1837–1910), an army chaplain and homesteader who came here in 1881.

Sun City — CDP
ZIP: 85351 **Lat:** 33-36-58 N **Long:** 112-16-54 W
Pop: 38,126 (1990); 40,505 (1980) **Pop Density:** 2593.6
Land: 14.7 sq. mi.; **Water:** 0.1 sq. mi.

Sun City West — CDP
ZIP: 85375 **Lat:** 33-39-55 N **Long:** 112-21-14 W
Pop: 15,997 (1990); 3,772 (1980) **Pop Density:** 1738.8
Land: 9.2 sq. mi.; **Water:** 0.0 sq. mi.

Sun Lakes — CDP
ZIP: 85224 **Lat:** 33-13-00 N **Long:** 111-52-12 W
Pop: 6,578 (1990) **Pop Density:** 1265.0
Land: 5.2 sq. mi.; **Water:** 0.0 sq. mi.

Surprise — Town
ZIP: 85374 **Lat:** 33-39-50 N **Long:** 112-28-06 W
Pop: 7,122 (1990); 3,723 (1980) **Pop Density:** 114.3
Land: 62.3 sq. mi.; **Water:** 0.0 sq. mi. **Elev:** 1178 ft.

In southwest-central AZ, a northwestern suburb of Phoenix.
Name origin: For a well here that hit water at 40 ft., a "surprise" since most wells in the area don't hit water until 100-300 ft.

Tempe — City
ZIP: 85282 **Lat:** 33-23-18 N **Long:** 111-55-50 W
Pop: 141,865 (1990); 106,919 (1980) **Pop Density:** 3591.5
Land: 39.5 sq. mi.; **Water:** 0.1 sq. mi.

In southwest-central AZ on the Salt River, 10 mi. northeast of Phoenix. Site of Arizona State Univ.
Name origin: For its similarity to the landscape of the Vale of Tempe in Greek mythology. Formerly called Butte City and Hayden's Butte, for its founder, Charles Trumbull Hayden.

Tolleson — City
ZIP: 85353 **Lat:** 33-26-55 N **Long:** 112-15-17 W
Pop: 4,434 (1990); 4,433 (1980) **Pop Density:** 886.8
Land: 5.0 sq. mi.; **Water:** 0.0 sq. mi.

Name origin: Named in 1912 for W. G. Tolleson.

Wickenburg   Town
Lat: 33-57-59 N   **Long:** 112-45-15 W
Pop: 4,515 (1990); 3,535 (1980)   **Pop Density:** 410.5
Land: 11.0 sq. mi.; **Water:** 0.0 sq. mi.   **Elev:** 2903 ft.

In southwest-central AZ, northwest of Phoenix.

Name origin: For Henry Wickenburg, who fled Austria for selling coal instead of turning it over to the state; he came to AZ in 1862 and built a ranch in the area that later became known by his name.

Youngtown   Town
ZIP: 85363   **Lat:** 33-35-13 N   **Long:** 112-18-10 W
Pop: 2,542 (1990); 2,254 (1980)   **Pop Density:** 1955.4
Land: 1.3 sq. mi.; **Water:** 0.0 sq. mi.

Established 1955 as a retirement village.

Name origin: Euphemistically named.

Mohave County
County Seat: Kingman (ZIP: 86401)

Pop: 93,497 (1990); 55,865 (1980)   **Pop Density:** 7.0
Land: 13312.4 sq. mi.; **Water:** 158.1 sq. mi.   **Area Code:** 602

On western border of AZ; original county; organized Dec 21, 1864 (prior to statehood); in 1871 annexed Pah-Ute County, which had been organized in 1865.

Name origin: For a tribe of Yuman linguistic stock, who inhabited both the CA and AZ sides of the Colorado River. Name means 'three mountains' and refers to the Needles, the three pointed mountain peaks at the center of tribal activities. Also spelled *Mojave*.

Bullhead City   City
ZIP: 86430   **Lat:** 35-06-51 N   **Long:** 114-33-30 W
Pop: 21,951 (1990); 10,364 (1980)   **Pop Density:** 509.3
Land: 43.1 sq. mi.; **Water:** 0.7 sq. mi.

Colorado City   Town
Lat: 36-58-51 N   **Long:** 112-58-57 W
Pop: 2,426 (1990)   **Pop Density:** 231.0
Land: 10.5 sq. mi.; **Water:** 0.0 sq. mi.

Desert Hills   CDP
Lat: 34-33-14 N   **Long:** 114-22-18 W
Pop: 1,700 (1990)   **Pop Density:** 361.7
Land: 4.7 sq. mi.; **Water:** 0.0 sq. mi.

Dolan Springs   CDP
Lat: 35-36-16 N   **Long:** 114-15-59 W
Pop: 1,090 (1990)   **Pop Density:** 38.4
Land: 28.4 sq. mi.; **Water:** 0.0 sq. mi.

Golden Valley   CDP
Lat: 35-13-23 N   **Long:** 114-13-19 W
Pop: 2,619 (1990)   **Pop Density:** 93.5
Land: 28.0 sq. mi.; **Water:** 0.0 sq. mi.

Kingman   City
ZIP: 86401   **Lat:** 35-12-25 N   **Long:** 114-01-55 W
Pop: 12,722 (1990); 9,257 (1980)   **Pop Density:** 611.6
Land: 20.8 sq. mi.; **Water:** 0.0 sq. mi.   **Elev:** 3341 ft.

In northwestern AZ, 65 mi. southeast of Boulder Dam.

Name origin: For Lewis Kingman, a railroad engineer who chose the location in the 1880s.

Lake Havasu City   City
ZIP: 86403   **Lat:** 34-30-10 N   **Long:** 114-18-51 W
Pop: 24,363 (1990); 15,909 (1980)   **Pop Density:** 566.6
Land: 43.0 sq. mi.; **Water:** 0.0 sq. mi.

In northwestern AZ on the CA border, 140 mi. northwest of Phoenix.

Mohave Valley   CDP
ZIP: 86440   **Lat:** 34-55-59 N   **Long:** 114-35-16 W
Pop: 6,962 (1990)   **Pop Density:** 153.0
Land: 45.5 sq. mi.; **Water:** 0.2 sq. mi.

New Kingman-Butler   CDP
Lat: 35-15-36 N   **Long:** 114-01-47 W
Pop: 11,627 (1990)   **Pop Density:** 807.4
Land: 14.4 sq. mi.; **Water:** 0.0 sq. mi.

Peach Springs   CDP
ZIP: 86434   **Lat:** 35-31-38 N   **Long:** 113-25-47 W
Pop: 787 (1990)   **Pop Density:** 238.5
Land: 3.3 sq. mi.; **Water:** 0.0 sq. mi.

Willow Valley   CDP
Lat: 34-54-43 N   **Long:** 114-36-20 W
Pop: 355 (1990)   **Pop Density:** 355.0
Land: 1.0 sq. mi.; **Water:** 0.0 sq. mi.

ARIZONA, Navajo County *American Places Dictionary*

Navajo County
County Seat: Holbrook (ZIP: 86025)

Pop: 77,658 (1990); 67,629 (1980) **Pop Density:** 7.8
Land: 9953.8 sq. mi.; **Water:** 6.4 sq. mi. **Area Code:** 602
In northeastern AZ, east of Flagstaff; organized Mar 21, 1895 (prior to statehood).
Name origin: For the Navajo Indian tribe. Site of the Navajo National Monument.

Cibecue   CDP
                      Lat: 34-01-46 N Long: 110-28-55 W
Pop: 1,254 (1990)   **Pop Density:** 209.0
Land: 6.0 sq. mi.; **Water:** 0.0 sq. mi.

East Fork   CDP
                      Lat: 33-48-23 N Long: 109-55-53 W
Pop: 752 (1990)   **Pop Density:** 250.7
Land: 3.0 sq. mi.; **Water:** 0.0 sq. mi.

Greasewood   CDP
                      Lat: 35-31-40 N Long: 109-51-36 W
Pop: 196 (1990)   **Pop Density:** 38.4
Land: 5.1 sq. mi.; **Water:** 0.0 sq. mi.

Heber-Overgaard   CDP
                      Lat: 34-24-50 N Long: 110-34-07 W
Pop: 1,581 (1990)   **Pop Density:** 236.0
Land: 6.7 sq. mi.; **Water:** 0.0 sq. mi.

Holbrook   City
ZIP: 86025   Lat: 34-54-46 N Long: 110-09-18 W
Pop: 4,686 (1990); 5,785 (1980) **Pop Density:** 768.2
Land: 6.1 sq. mi.; **Water:** 0.0 sq. mi.   **Elev:** 5083 ft.
Name origin: Named in 1882 for H. R. Holbrook, first chief engineer of the Atlantic and Pacific railroad.

Hotevilla   CDP
                      Lat: 35-55-25 N Long: 110-39-27 W
Pop: 869 (1990)   **Pop Density:** 76.2
Land: 11.4 sq. mi.; **Water:** 0.0 sq. mi.

Kayenta   CDP
                      Lat: 36-43-04 N Long: 110-15-09 W
Pop: 4,372 (1990); 3,343 (1980) **Pop Density:** 397.5
Land: 11.0 sq. mi.; **Water:** 0.0 sq. mi.

Keams Canyon   CDP
                      Lat: 35-48-57 N Long: 110-12-32 W
Pop: 393 (1990)   **Pop Density:** 42.3
Land: 9.3 sq. mi.; **Water:** 0.0 sq. mi.

Kykotsmovi Village   CDP
                      Lat: 35-52-27 N Long: 110-37-21 W
Pop: 773 (1990)   **Pop Density:** 72.2
Land: 10.7 sq. mi.; **Water:** 0.0 sq. mi.

McNary   CDP
                      Lat: 34-05-08 N Long: 109-51-48 W
Pop: 153 (1990); 1,002 (1980)   **Pop Density:** 191.3
Land: 0.8 sq. mi.; **Water:** 0.0 sq. mi.
Part of the town is in Apache County.

Pinetop-Lakeside   Town
                      Lat: 34-08-53 N Long: 109-57-58 W
Pop: 2,422 (1990)   **Pop Density:** 216.3
Land: 11.2 sq. mi.; **Water:** 0.1 sq. mi.

Pinon   CDP
ZIP: 86510   Lat: 36-06-02 N Long: 110-13-16 W
Pop: 468 (1990)   **Pop Density:** 73.1
Land: 6.4 sq. mi.; **Water:** 0.0 sq. mi.

Polacca   CDP
                      Lat: 35-50-08 N Long: 110-21-56 W
Pop: 1,108 (1990)   **Pop Density:** 117.9
Land: 9.4 sq. mi.; **Water:** 0.0 sq. mi.

Second Mesa   CDP
                      Lat: 35-49-03 N Long: 110-30-12 W
Pop: 929 (1990)   **Pop Density:** 35.5
Land: 26.2 sq. mi.; **Water:** 0.0 sq. mi.

Shongopovi   CDP
                      Lat: 35-49-05 N Long: 110-32-02 W
Pop: 730 (1990)   **Pop Density:** 486.7
Land: 1.5 sq. mi.; **Water:** 0.0 sq. mi.

Shonto   CDP
                      Lat: 36-35-16 N Long: 110-39-15 W
Pop: 710 (1990)   **Pop Density:** 182.1
Land: 3.9 sq. mi.; **Water:** 0.0 sq. mi.

Show Low   City
ZIP: 85901   Lat: 34-14-14 N Long: 110-02-39 W
Pop: 5,019 (1990); 4,298 (1980) **Pop Density:** 182.5
Land: 27.5 sq. mi.; **Water:** 0.1 sq. mi.   **Elev:** 6347 ft.
In northeastern AZ, northeast of Phoenix.
Name origin: According to legend, a game of seven-up was played to dissolve the partnership between two AZ pioneers with the townsite as the stake. Marion Clark said, "If you show low, you win." Corydon Cooley won.

Snowflake   Town
ZIP: 85937   Lat: 34-31-19 N Long: 110-05-03 W
Pop: 3,679 (1990); 3,510 (1980) **Pop Density:** 123.9
Land: 29.7 sq. mi.; **Water:** 0.1 sq. mi.
Name origin: For rancher William J. Flake, and Erastus Snow, who settled in the area in 1878.

Taylor   Town
ZIP: 85939   Lat: 34-26-59 N Long: 110-06-41 W
Pop: 2,418 (1990); 1,915 (1980) **Pop Density:** 102.0
Land: 23.7 sq. mi.; **Water:** 0.1 sq. mi.
Name origin: For John Taylor (1808–87), president of the Church of Latter-Day Saints. Originally called Walker, but that name conflicted with another AZ town of the same name.

Whiteriver   CDP
                      Lat: 33-50-20 N Long: 109-57-41 W
Pop: 3,775 (1990); 2,256 (1980) **Pop Density:** 343.2
Land: 11.0 sq. mi.; **Water:** 0.0 sq. mi.

Winslow
City
ZIP: 86047   **Lat:** 35-01-40 N   **Long:** 110-42-24 W
Pop: 8,190 (1990); 7,921 (1980)   **Pop Density:** 694.1
Land: 11.8 sq. mi.; **Water:** 0.0 sq. mi.

In northeastern AZ, 60 mi. east of Flagstaff. First established as a terminal for the Atlantic & Pacific Railroad.
Name origin: For either prospector Tom Winslow or Gen. Edward Winslow, president of the associated St. Louis & San Francisco Railroad.

Pima County
County Seat: Tucson (ZIP: 85701)

Pop: 666,880 (1990); 531,443 (1980)   **Pop Density:** 72.6
Land: 9187.0 sq. mi.; **Water:** 2.4 sq. mi.   **Area Code:** 602

On south-central border of AZ; original county; organized Dec 15, 1864 (prior to statehood).
Name origin: For the Pima Indian tribe, who inhabited the Gila and Salt River valleys of AZ. *Pima* was the name given the tribe by the Spanish; it means 'no' or 'I don't know,' the response the Spanish received to their questions and mistook for the tribe's name.

Ajo
CDP
ZIP: 85321   **Lat:** 32-23-14 N   **Long:** 112-52-06 W
Pop: 2,919 (1990); 5,189 (1980)   **Pop Density:** 540.6
Land: 5.4 sq. mi.; **Water:** 0.0 sq. mi.

Avra Valley
CDP
Lat: 32-26-16 N   **Long:** 111-18-52 W
Pop: 3,403 (1990)   **Pop Density:** 73.3
Land: 46.4 sq. mi.; **Water:** 0.0 sq. mi.

Catalina
CDP
Lat: 32-28-36 N   **Long:** 110-54-00 W
Pop: 4,864 (1990); 2,749 (1980)   **Pop Density:** 349.9
Land: 13.9 sq. mi.; **Water:** 0.0 sq. mi.

Flowing Wells
CDP
Lat: 32-17-37 N   **Long:** 111-00-32 W
Pop: 14,013 (1990)   **Pop Density:** 4003.7
Land: 3.5 sq. mi.; **Water:** 0.0 sq. mi.

Green Valley
CDP
ZIP: 85614   **Lat:** 31-50-54 N   **Long:** 111-00-35 W
Pop: 13,231 (1990); 7,999 (1980)   **Pop Density:** 596.0
Land: 22.2 sq. mi.; **Water:** 0.0 sq. mi.

Marana
Town
ZIP: 85653   **Lat:** 32-24-51 N   **Long:** 111-10-21 W
Pop: 2,187 (1990); 1,674 (1980)   **Pop Density:** 41.5
Land: 52.7 sq. mi.; **Water:** 0.8 sq. mi.

In southern AZ, a northwestern suburb of Tucson. Located in a valley once noted for its thick growth of mesquite and other desert plants.
Name origin: From Spanish 'tangle' or 'impassable' because of briars and brambles.

Oro Valley
Town
ZIP: 85704   **Lat:** 32-25-29 N   **Long:** 110-57-52 W
Pop: 6,670 (1990); 1,489 (1980)   **Pop Density:** 281.4
Land: 23.7 sq. mi.; **Water:** 0.0 sq. mi.   **Elev:** 2520 ft.
Name origin: From Spanish 'gold.'

Picture Rocks
CDP
Lat: 32-20-44 N   **Long:** 111-14-44 W
Pop: 4,026 (1990)   **Pop Density:** 73.3
Land: 54.9 sq. mi.; **Water:** 0.1 sq. mi.

Pisinemo
CDP
Lat: 32-02-16 N   **Long:** 112-19-13 W
Pop: 341 (1990)   **Pop Density:** 200.6
Land: 1.7 sq. mi.; **Water:** 0.0 sq. mi.

Santa Rosa
CDP
Lat: 32-20-05 N   **Long:** 112-02-43 W
Pop: 493 (1990)   **Pop Density:** 86.5
Land: 5.7 sq. mi.; **Water:** 0.0 sq. mi.

Sells
CDP
ZIP: 85634   **Lat:** 31-55-06 N   **Long:** 111-52-35 W
Pop: 2,750 (1990); 1,864 (1980)   **Pop Density:** 292.6
Land: 9.4 sq. mi.; **Water:** 0.0 sq. mi.

South Tucson
City
ZIP: 85713   **Lat:** 32-11-45 N   **Long:** 110-58-05 W
Pop: 5,093 (1990); 6,554 (1980)   **Pop Density:** 5093.0
Land: 1.0 sq. mi.; **Water:** 0.0 sq. mi.

In southern AZ, a suburb of Tucson.

Three Points
CDP
Lat: 32-04-03 N   **Long:** 111-16-42 W
Pop: 2,175 (1990)   **Pop Density:** 44.7
Land: 48.7 sq. mi.; **Water:** 0.0 sq. mi.

Tucson
City
ZIP: 85726   **Lat:** 32-11-44 N   **Long:** 110-53-30 W
Pop: 405,390 (1990); 330,537 (1980)   **Pop Density:** 2593.7
Land: 156.3 sq. mi.; **Water:** 0.4 sq. mi.

In southern AZ on the Santa Cruz River, 105 mi. southeast of Phoenix. Tourist and health resort; commercial and research center of the Southwest. Site of Univ. of Arizona and San Xavier Mission, called the "White Dove of the Desert."
Name origin: Spanish rendering of the Papago Indian name *Chuk Shon* 'black base,' for nearby Sentinel Mountain.

Tucson Estates
CDP
Lat: 32-11-22 N   **Long:** 111-05-02 W
Pop: 2,662 (1990); 2,814 (1980)   **Pop Density:** 1774.7
Land: 1.5 sq. mi.; **Water:** 0.0 sq. mi.

Valencia West
CDP
Lat: 32-08-06 N   **Long:** 111-06-24 W
Pop: 3,277 (1990)   **Pop Density:** 292.6
Land: 11.2 sq. mi.; **Water:** 0.0 sq. mi.

ARIZONA, Pinal County   *American Places Dictionary*

Pinal County
County Seat: Florence (ZIP: 85232)

Pop: 116,379 (1990); 90,918 (1980)   **Pop Density:** 21.7
Land: 5370.0 sq. mi.; **Water:** 4.5 sq. mi.   **Area Code:** 602

In south-central AZ, southeast of Phoenix; organized Feb 1, 1875 (prior to statehood) from Pima County.

Name origin: Probably for the Pinal tribe of the Apaches, or for an Apache chief. Name means 'deer' in Apache; in Spanish it means 'pine' or possibly 'the Apaches who live in the pines.' Pine groves and deer can be found on nearby mountains.

Ak-Chin Village   CDP
Lat: 33-01-41 N   Long: 112-05-13 W
Pop: 353 (1990)   **Pop Density:** 33.3
Land: 10.6 sq. mi.; **Water:** 0.0 sq. mi.

Apache Junction   City
ZIP: 85220   Lat: 33-24-18 N   Long: 111-32-49 W
Pop: 17,931 (1990); 9,935 (1980)   **Pop Density:** 1093.4
Land: 16.4 sq. mi.; **Water:** 0.0 sq. mi.   **Elev:** 1719 ft.

In southern AZ, 30 mi. east of Phoenix. Part of the city is in Maricopa County.

Name origin: For Apache Trail, which begins at the east end of city.

Arizona City   CDP
Lat: 32-45-02 N   Long: 111-40-11 W
Pop: 1,940 (1990)   **Pop Density:** 318.0
Land: 6.1 sq. mi.; **Water:** 0.1 sq. mi.

Blackwater   CDP
Lat: 33-01-50 N   Long: 111-36-54 W
Pop: 400 (1990)   **Pop Density:** 60.6
Land: 6.6 sq. mi.; **Water:** 0.0 sq. mi.

Casa Grande   City
ZIP: 85222   Lat: 32-53-32 N   Long: 111-44-09 W
Pop: 19,082 (1990); 14,971 (1980)   **Pop Density:** 875.3
Land: 21.8 sq. mi.; **Water:** 0.0 sq. mi.

In southwest-central AZ, 45 mi. southeast of Phoenix. Site of Casa Grande National Monument.

Name origin: Named by the railroad after the nearby Casa Grande (Spanish 'big house') ruins.

Chuichu   CDP
Lat: 32-44-41 N   Long: 111-47-50 W
Pop: 330 (1990)   **Pop Density:** 132.0
Land: 2.5 sq. mi.; **Water:** 0.0 sq. mi.

Coolidge   City
ZIP: 85228   Lat: 32-58-56 N   Long: 111-31-39 W
Pop: 6,927 (1990); 6,851 (1980)   **Pop Density:** 1443.1
Land: 4.8 sq. mi.; **Water:** 0.0 sq. mi.

Name origin: For Coolidge Dam, itself named for Calvin Coolidge (1872–1933), thirtieth U.S. president.

Dudleyville   CDP
Lat: 32-54-51 N   Long: 110-44-01 W
Pop: 1,356 (1990); 1,205 (1980)   **Pop Density:** 196.5
Land: 6.9 sq. mi.; **Water:** 0.0 sq. mi.

Eloy   City
ZIP: 85231   Lat: 32-44-42 N   Long: 111-36-23 W
Pop: 7,211 (1990); 6,240 (1980)   **Pop Density:** 104.1
Land: 69.3 sq. mi.; **Water:** 0.0 sq. mi.

Established c. 1920.

Name origin: For the traditional name of the site.

Florence   Town
ZIP: 85232   Lat: 33-02-15 N   Long: 111-22-26 W
Pop: 7,510 (1990); 3,391 (1980)   **Pop Density:** 1294.8
Land: 5.8 sq. mi.; **Water:** 0.0 sq. mi.   **Elev:** 1490 ft.

In southern AZ, 50 mi. southeast of Phoenix.

Name origin: Named 1868 by Gov. Richard McCormick for his sister Florence.

Hayden   Town
ZIP: 85235   Lat: 32-59-17 N   Long: 110-47-07 W
Pop: 0 (1990)
Land: 0.01 sq. mi.; **Water:** 0.0 sq. mi.

Part of the town is also in Gila County.

Name origin: For Charles Hayden of Hayden, Stone and Company, which operated area mines.

Kearny   Town
ZIP: 85237   Lat: 33-03-22 N   Long: 110-54-21 W
Pop: 2,262 (1990); 2,646 (1980)   **Pop Density:** 807.9
Land: 2.8 sq. mi.; **Water:** 0.0 sq. mi.

In southern AZ, between Phoenix and Tucson. Founded 1958 by Kennecott Copper Company.

Name origin: For Gen. Philip Kearny (1814–62), who explored the Gila River area (1849–50).

Mammoth   Town
ZIP: 85618   Lat: 32-43-17 N   Long: 110-38-36 W
Pop: 1,845 (1990); 1,906 (1980)   **Pop Density:** 1845.0
Land: 1.0 sq. mi.; **Water:** 0.0 sq. mi.

In southern AZ, northeast of Tucson. Town developed around a stamp mill that worked ores from a gold mine.

Name origin: For nearby Mammoth Mine.

Oracle   CDP
ZIP: 85623   Lat: 32-37-07 N   Long: 110-47-03 W
Pop: 3,043 (1990); 2,484 (1980)   **Pop Density:** 317.0
Land: 9.6 sq. mi.; **Water:** 0.0 sq. mi.

Sacaton   CDP
Lat: 33-04-55 N   Long: 111-44-45 W
Pop: 1,452 (1990)   **Pop Density:** 968.0
Land: 1.5 sq. mi.; **Water:** 0.0 sq. mi.

San Manuel   CDP
ZIP: 85631   Lat: 32-36-50 N   Long: 110-38-10 W
Pop: 4,009 (1990); 5,443 (1980)   **Pop Density:** 191.8
Land: 20.9 sq. mi.; **Water:** 0.0 sq. mi.

Santan   CDP
Lat: 33-08-43 N   Long: 111-48-05 W
Pop: 330 (1990)   **Pop Density:** 50.0
Land: 6.6 sq. mi.; **Water:** 0.0 sq. mi.

Superior   Town
ZIP: 85273   **Lat:** 33-17-09 N   **Long:** 111-06-34 W
Pop: 3,468 (1990); 4,600 (1980)   **Pop Density:** 1926.7
Land: 1.8 sq. mi.; **Water:** 0.0 sq. mi.   **Elev:** 2830 ft.
In southern AZ, southeast of Phoenix. Laid out c. 1910.
Name origin: For the Arizona and Lake Superior Mining Company, which operated silver mines in the area. Previously called Barnes.

Santa Cruz County
County Seat: Nogales (ZIP: 85628)

Pop: 29,676 (1990); 20,459 (1980)   **Pop Density:** 24.0
Land: 1237.7 sq. mi.; **Water:** 0.5 sq. mi.   **Area Code:** 602
On south-central border of AZ; organized Mar 15, 1899 (prior to statehood) from Pima County.
Name origin: For the Santa Cruz River, which flows through the county. From the Spanish meaning 'holy cross.'

Nogales   City
ZIP: 85621   **Lat:** 31-21-49 N   **Long:** 110-55-57 W
Pop: 19,489 (1990); 15,683 (1980)   **Pop Density:** 937.0
Land: 20.8 sq. mi.; **Water:** 0.0 sq. mi.
In southern AZ adjacent to Nogales, Mexico, 60 mi. south of Tucson. Incorporated 1893. Site of Spanish mission (1687).
Name origin: From Spanish 'walnut trees,' which once lined the nearby creek.

Patagonia   Town
ZIP: 85624   **Lat:** 31-32-35 N   **Long:** 110-44-56 W
Pop: 888 (1990); 980 (1980)   **Pop Density:** 740.0
Land: 1.2 sq. mi.; **Water:** 0.0 sq. mi.   **Elev:** 4057 ft.
In southern AZ, south of Tucson.
Name origin: Named by townspeople for the nearby Patagonia Mountains, against oil baron and rancher Rollen Richardson's proposal to name it Rollen.

Rio Rico East   CDP
    Lat: 31-28-47 N   **Long:** 110-58-32 W
Pop: 1,407 (1990)   **Pop Density:** 781.7
Land: 1.8 sq. mi.; **Water:** 0.0 sq. mi.

Yavapai County
County Seat: Prescott (ZIP: 86301)

Pop: 107,714 (1990); 68,145 (1980)   **Pop Density:** 13.3
Land: 8123.5 sq. mi.; **Water:** 4.8 sq. mi.   **Area Code:** 602
In central AZ, north of Phoenix; original county; organized Dec 21, 1860 (prior to statehood).
Name origin: For a tribe of Yuman linguistic stock who lived in western AZ. Name has been variously explained. Most probable is 'sun people,' from *enyaeva* 'sun'; *pai* 'people'. Other theories include 'hill country' from *yava* 'hill'; Spanish *pais* 'country'; and 'crooked-mouth (surly) people.'

Bagdad   CDP
ZIP: 86321   **Lat:** 34-34-40 N   **Long:** 113-10-25 W
Pop: 1,858 (1990); 2,331 (1980)   **Pop Density:** 244.5
Land: 7.6 sq. mi.; **Water:** 0.0 sq. mi.

Big Park   CDP
    Lat: 34-46-48 N   **Long:** 111-45-42 W
Pop: 3,024 (1990)   **Pop Density:** 657.4
Land: 4.6 sq. mi.; **Water:** 0.0 sq. mi.

Black Canyon City   CDP
ZIP: 85324   **Lat:** 34-03-44 N   **Long:** 112-06-33 W
Pop: 1,811 (1990)   **Pop Density:** 90.6
Land: 20.0 sq. mi.; **Water:** 0.0 sq. mi.

Camp Verde   Town
ZIP: 86322   **Lat:** 34-34-10 N   **Long:** 111-51-22 W
Pop: 6,243 (1990)   **Pop Density:** 146.5
Land: 42.6 sq. mi.; **Water:** 0.0 sq. mi.

Chino Valley   Town
ZIP: 86323   **Lat:** 34-45-47 N   **Long:** 112-27-16 W
Pop: 4,837 (1990); 2,858 (1980)   **Pop Density:** 260.1
Land: 18.6 sq. mi.; **Water:** 0.0 sq. mi.
Name origin: From Mexican Spanish meaning 'grama grass,' which grows abundantly in the valley.

ARIZONA, Yavapai County *American Places Dictionary*

Clarkdale — Town
ZIP: 86324 Lat: 34-45-34 N Long: 112-03-23 W
Pop: 2,144 (1990); 1,512 (1980) Pop Density: 376.1
Land: 5.7 sq. mi.; Water: 0.0 sq. mi. Elev: 3545 ft.
Name origin: For William A. Clark, a MT senator who bought a mining interest here and established a smelter.

Cornville — CDP
ZIP: 86325 Lat: 34-43-18 N Long: 111-54-28 W
Pop: 2,089 (1990) Pop Density: 267.8
Land: 7.8 sq. mi.; Water: 0.0 sq. mi.

Cottonwood — Town
ZIP: 86326 Lat: 34-44-04 N Long: 112-01-27 W
Pop: 5,918 (1990); 4,550 (1980) Pop Density: 1116.6
Land: 5.3 sq. mi.; Water: 0.0 sq. mi. Elev: 3314 ft.
In central AZ, 15 mi. southwest of Flagstaff.
Name origin: For a once-present circle of 16 large cottonwood trees nearby.

Dewey-Humboldt — CDP
Lat: 34-31-57 N Long: 112-15-06 W
Pop: 3,640 (1990) Pop Density: 145.6
Land: 25.0 sq. mi.; Water: 0.0 sq. mi.

Jerome — Town
ZIP: 86331 Lat: 34-44-48 N Long: 112-06-22 W
Pop: 403 (1990); 420 (1980) Pop Density: 575.7
Land: 0.7 sq. mi.; Water: 0.0 sq. mi.
In central AZ north of Phoenix. A mining town that grew up around nearby copper mines.
Name origin: For one of its founders, Eugene Jerome.

Lake Montezuma — CDP
Lat: 34-38-21 N Long: 111-47-43 W
Pop: 1,841 (1990) Pop Density: 153.4
Land: 12.0 sq. mi.; Water: 0.0 sq. mi.

Prescott — City
ZIP: 86301 Lat: 34-34-33 N Long: 112-26-56 W
Pop: 26,455 (1990); 19,865 (1980) Pop Density: 816.5
Land: 32.4 sq. mi.; Water: 0.2 sq. mi. Elev: 5368 ft.
In central AZ, 80 mi. northwest of Phoenix. Established 1864.
Name origin: For historian William Hickling Prescott (1796–1859), for his books on Aztecs and Incas.

Prescott Valley — Town
ZIP: 86314 Lat: 34-36-29 N Long: 112-19-17 W
Pop: 8,858 (1990); 2,284 (1980) Pop Density: 536.8
Land: 16.5 sq. mi.; Water: 0.0 sq. mi.

Sedona — City
ZIP: 86336 Lat: 34-51-34 N Long: 111-48-36 W
Pop: 5,336 (1990); 3,590 (1980) Pop Density: 401.2
Land: 13.3 sq. mi.; Water: 0.0 sq. mi.
Part of the city is in Coconino County.

Yuma County
County Seat: Yuma (ZIP: 85364)

Pop: 106,895 (1990); 76,205 (1980) Pop Density: 19.4
Land: 5514.4 sq. mi.; Water: 4.9 sq. mi. Area Code: 602
In southwestern corner of AZ; original county; organized Dec 21, 1864 (prior to statehood).
Name origin: For the Yuma Indian tribe, who lived principally along the Colorado River. The name, given to the tribe by the Spanish, may mean 'son of the captain' or may come from the Spanish *umo* 'smoke.'

Fortuna Foothills — CDP
Lat: 32-39-27 N Long: 114-24-39 W
Pop: 7,737 (1990) Pop Density: 163.6
Land: 47.3 sq. mi.; Water: 0.0 sq. mi.

San Luis — Town
ZIP: 85349 Lat: 32-29-32 N Long: 114-46-40 W
Pop: 4,212 (1990); 1,946 (1980) Pop Density: 2106.0
Land: 2.0 sq. mi.; Water: 0.0 sq. mi.
In the southwestern corner of AZ on the Mexico border.

Somerton — Town
ZIP: 85350 Lat: 32-35-49 N Long: 114-42-34 W
Pop: 5,282 (1990); 3,969 (1980) Pop Density: 6602.5
Land: 0.8 sq. mi.; Water: 0.0 sq. mi.
In southwestern corner of AZ, south of Yuma.
Name origin: Named by Capt. A. D. Yocum for his hometown in IN.

Wellton — Town
ZIP: 85356 Lat: 32-40-22 N Long: 114-08-21 W
Pop: 1,066 (1990); 911 (1980) Pop Density: 969.1
Land: 1.1 sq. mi.; Water: 0.0 sq. mi.
Name origin: For the wells sunk here to supply water for trains coming through region.

Yuma — City
ZIP: 85364 Lat: 32-40-38 N Long: 114-37-12 W
Pop: 54,923 (1990); 42,481 (1980) Pop Density: 2507.9
Land: 21.9 sq. mi.; Water: 0.1 sq. mi.
In the southwestern corner of AZ on the Colorado River, 18 mi. north of the Mexican border. Incorporated 1871.
Name origin: Perhaps from the Indian title *yah-mayo* meaning 'son of the captain'; early Spanish missionairies may have mistakenly applied the name *yuma* to the entire tribe. Originally called Colorado City.

Index to Places and Counties in Arizona

Ajo (Pima) CDP *43*
Ak-Chin Village (Pinal) CDP *44*
Apache County *34*
Apache Junction (Maricopa) City *39*
Apache Junction (Pinal) City *44*
Arizona City (Pinal) CDP *44*
Avondale (Maricopa) City *39*
Avra Valley (Pima) CDP *43*
Bagdad (Yavapai) CDP *45*
Benson (Cochise) Town *35*
Big Park (Yavapai) CDP *45*
Bisbee (Cochise) City *35*
Black Canyon City (Yavapai) CDP *45*
Blackwater (Pinal) CDP *44*
Bluewater (La Paz) CDP *38*
Buckeye (Maricopa) Town *39*
Bullhead City (Mohave) City *41*
Bylas (Graham) CDP *37*
Cameron (Coconino) CDP *36*
Camp Verde (Yavapai) Town *45*
Canyon Day (Gila) CDP *37*
Carefree (Maricopa) Town *39*
Casa Grande (Pinal) City *44*
Catalina (Pima) CDP *43*
Cave Creek (Maricopa) Town *39*
Central Heights-Midland City (Gila)
 CDP *37*
Chandler (Maricopa) City *39*
Chinle (Apache) CDP *34*
Chino Valley (Yavapai) Town *45*
Chuichu (Pinal) CDP *44*
Cibecue (Navajo) CDP *42*
Clarkdale (Yavapai) Town *46*
Claypool (Gila) CDP *37*
Clifton (Greenlee) Town *38*
Cochise County *35*
Coconino County *36*
Colorado City (Mohave) Town *41*
Coolidge (Pinal) City *44*
Cornville (Yavapai) CDP *46*
Cottonwood (Yavapai) Town *46*
Dennehotso (Apache) CDP *34*
Desert Hills (Mohave) CDP *41*
Dewey-Humboldt (Yavapai) CDP *46*
Dolan Springs (Mohave) CDP *41*
Douglas (Cochise) City *35*
Dudleyville (Pinal) CDP *44*
Duncan (Greenlee) Town *38*
Eagar (Apache) Town *34*
East Fork (Navajo) CDP *42*
Ehrenberg (La Paz) CDP *38*
El Mirage (Maricopa) Town *39*
Eloy (Pinal) City *44*
Flagstaff (Coconino) City *36*
Florence (Pinal) Town *44*
Flowing Wells (Pima) CDP *43*
Fort Defiance (Apache) CDP *34*
Fortuna Foothills (Yuma) CDP *46*
Fountain Hills (Maricopa) Town *39*
Fredonia (Coconino) Town *36*
Ganado (Apache) CDP *34*
Gila Bend (Maricopa) Town *39*
Gila County *37*
Gilbert (Maricopa) Town *39*
Glendale (Maricopa) City *40*
Globe (Gila) City *37*
Golden Valley (Mohave) CDP *41*

Goodyear (Maricopa) Town *40*
Graham County *37*
Grand Canyon Village (Coconino)
 CDP *36*
Greasewood (Navajo) CDP *42*
Greenlee County *38*
Green Valley (Pima) CDP *43*
Guadalupe (Maricopa) Town *40*
Hayden (Gila) Town *37*
Hayden (Pinal) Town *44*
Heber-Overgaard (Navajo) CDP *42*
Holbrook (Navajo) City *42*
Hotevilla (Navajo) CDP *42*
Huachuca City (Cochise) Town *35*
Jerome (Yavapai) Town *46*
Kachina Village (Coconino) CDP *36*
Kaibito (Coconino) CDP *36*
Kayenta (Navajo) CDP *42*
Keams Canyon (Navajo) CDP *42*
Kearny (Pinal) Town *44*
Kingman (Mohave) City *41*
Komatke (Maricopa) CDP *40*
Kykotsmovi Village (Navajo) CDP *42*
Lake Havasu City (Mohave) City *41*
Lake Montezuma (Yavapai) CDP *46*
La Paz County *38*
Leupp (Coconino) CDP *36*
Litchfield Park (Maricopa) City *40*
Lukachukai (Apache) CDP *34*
Luke Air Force Base (Maricopa) Military Facility *40*
Mammoth (Pinal) Town *44*
Many Farms (Apache) CDP *34*
Marana (Pima) Town *43*
Maricopa County *39*
McNary (Apache) CDP *34*
McNary (Navajo) CDP *42*
Mesa (Maricopa) City *40*
Miami (Gila) Town *37*
Moenkopi (Coconino) CDP *36*
Mohave County *41*
Mohave Valley (Mohave) CDP *41*
Morenci (Greenlee) CDP *38*
Navajo County *42*
New Kingman-Butler (Mohave) CDP. *41*
Nogales (Santa Cruz) City *45*
Oracle (Pinal) CDP *44*
Oro Valley (Pima) Town *43*
Page (Coconino) City *36*
Paradise Valley (Maricopa) Town *40*
Parker (La Paz) Town *39*
Parker Strip (La Paz) CDP *39*
Patagonia (Santa Cruz) Town *45*
Payson (Gila) Town *37*
Peach Springs (Mohave) CDP *41*
Peoria (Maricopa) City *40*
Peridot (Gila) CDP *37*
Peridot (Graham) CDP *37*
Phoenix (Maricopa) City *40*
Picture Rocks (Pima) CDP *43*
Pima (Graham) Town *38*
Pima County *43*
Pinal County *44*
Pinetop-Lakeside (Navajo) Town *42*
Pinon (Navajo) CDP *42*
Pirtleville (Cochise) CDP *35*
Pisinemo (Pima) CDP *43*

Polacca (Navajo) CDP *42*
Poston (La Paz) CDP *39*
Prescott (Yavapai) City *46*
Prescott Valley (Yavapai) Town *46*
Quartzsite (La Paz) Town *39*
Queen Creek (Maricopa) Town *40*
Rio Rico East (Santa Cruz) CDP *45*
Rough Rock (Apache) CDP *34*
Sacaton (Pinal) CDP *44*
Safford (Graham) City *38*
St. David (Cochise) CDP *35*
St. Johns (Apache) City *34*
St. Michaels (Apache) CDP *34*
San Carlos (Gila) CDP *37*
San Luis (Yuma) Town *46*
San Manuel (Pinal) CDP *44*
Santa Cruz County *45*
Santan (Pinal) CDP *44*
Santa Rosa (Pima) CDP *43*
Sawmill (Apache) CDP *34*
Scottsdale (Maricopa) City *40*
Second Mesa (Navajo) CDP *42*
Sedona (Coconino) City *36*
Sedona (Yavapai) City *46*
Sells (Pima) CDP *43*
Shongopovi (Navajo) CDP *42*
Shonto (Navajo) CDP *42*
Show Low (Navajo) City *42*
Sierra Vista (Cochise) City *35*
Sierra Vista Southeast (Cochise) CDP *35*
Snowflake (Navajo) Town *42*
Somerton (Yuma) Town *46*
South Tucson (Pima) City *43*
Springerville (Apache) Town *34*
Sun City (Maricopa) CDP *40*
Sun City West (Maricopa) CDP *40*
Sun Lakes (Maricopa) CDP *40*
Supai (Coconino) CDP *36*
Superior (Pinal) Town *45*
Surprise (Maricopa) Town *40*
Swift Trail Junction (Graham) CDP ... *38*
Taylor (Navajo) Town *42*
Teec Nos Pos (Apache) CDP *34*
Tempe (Maricopa) City *40*
Thatcher (Graham) Town *38*
Three Points (Pima) CDP *43*
Tolleson (Maricopa) City *40*
Tombstone (Cochise) City *35*
Tsaile (Apache) CDP *34*
Tuba City (Coconino) CDP *36*
Tucson (Pima) City *43*
Tucson Estates (Pima) CDP *43*
Valencia West (Pima) CDP *43*
Wellton (Yuma) Town *46*
Whetstone (Cochise) CDP *35*
Whiteriver (Navajo) CDP *42*
Wickenburg (Maricopa) Town *41*
Willcox (Cochise) City *35*
Williams (Coconino) City *36*
Willow Valley (Mohave) CDP *41*
Window Rock (Apache) CDP *34*
Winkelman (Gila) Town *37*
Winslow (Navajo) City *43*
Yavapai County *45*
Youngtown (Maricopa) Town *41*
Yuma (Yuma) City *46*
Yuma County *46*

California

California

Population: 29,760,021 (1990); 23,667,902 (1980)
Population rank (1990): 1
Percent population change (1980–1990): 25.7
Population projection: 31,780,000 (1995); 33,981,000 (2000)

Area: total 163,707 sq. mi.; 155,973 sq. mi. land, 7,734 sq. mi. water. Coastline 780 mi.
Area rank: 3
Highest elevation: 14,494 ft., Mount Whitney (Tulare County)
Lowest point: -282 ft., Death Valley (Inyo County)

State capital: Sacramento (Sacramento County)
Largest city: Los Angeles (3,485,398)
Second largest city: San Diego (1,110,549)
Largest county: Los Angeles (8,863,164)

Total housing units: 11,182,882
No. of occupied housing units: 10,381,206
Vacant housing units (%): 7.2
Distribution of population by race and Hispanic origin (%):
White: 69.0
Black: 7.4
Hispanic (any race): 25.8
Native American: 0.8
Asian/Pacific: 9.6
Other: 13.2

Admission date: September 9, 1850 (31st state).

Location: On the Pacific coast of the United States, bordering Mexico, Oregon, Nevada, and Arizona.

Name Origin: As Spanish explorers moved north from Baja (Lower) California, the Mexican peninsula to the south, they named the land above the peninsula Alta 'upper' California. The name was originally that of a treasure island in a Spanish romance, *Las sergas de esplandian* (1510), by Ordóñez de Montalvo.

State animal: California grizzly bear *(Ursus (arctos) horribilis)*
State bird: California valley quail *(Callipepla californica)*
State fish: South Fork golden trout
State fossil: California saber-toothed cat *(Smilodon californicus)*
State flower: Golden poppy *(Eschscholtzia californica)*
State insect: California dog-face butterfly (flying pansy)
State marine mammal: California gray whale *(Eschrichtius robustus)*
State mineral: native gold
State reptile: California desert tortoise
State rock: serpentine

State song: "I Love You, California"
State tree: California redwood *(Sequoia sempervirens)*

State motto: *Eureka* (Greek 'I Have Found It')
State nickname: The Golden State

Area codes: 209 (Fresno), 213 (Los Angeles), 310 (Long Beach), 408 (San Jose), 415 (San Francisco), 510 (Oakland), 619 (San Diego), 707 (Santa Rosa), 714 (Orange), 805 (Santa Barbara), 818 (Pasadena), 916 (Sacramento)
Time zone: Pacific
Abbreviations: CA (postal); Cal., Calif. (traditional)
Part of (region): Far West; Pacific Coast

Local Government

Counties

California has 58 counties, of which 11 have adopted home-rule.

Municipalities

There are 431 incorporated cities. The city and county of San Francisco are coterminous, and their governments have been combined since 1856. Much of the state is unincorporated territory.

Settlement History and Early Development

Historians have estimated that before the arrival of Spanish explorers in the last half of the eighteenth century, between 150,000 and 300,000 Indians lived in California. Among the better known tribes were the Hupa, Pomo, Miwok, Modoc, Yurok, Yuma, Mohave, Mono, and Maidu. There were roughly 135 spoken dialects in 20 linguistic families. This diversity of languages, plus their separation by deserts and high mountains, prevented their presenting a unified front against European colonization; but they were also more peaceful than many of the tribes on the East coast and were quite friendly to newcomers.

Spanish exploration and settlement of California began in 1542, when Juan Rodríguez, a Portuguese explorer employed by Spain, sailed into San Diego Bay. In 1579, English sea captain Sir Francis Drake sailed the California coast during his circumnavigation of the globe. He claimed it for England and named the land New Albion, alluding to the literary name for England. More Spanish explorations quickly followed, and in 1602 Sebastián Vizcaíno urged the king of Spain to colonize the land. Beginning in 1697 the Spanish established missions and settled in Baja (Lower) California, the peninsula to the south of present-day California that is now part of Mexico. Gaspar de Portolá, governor of Baja California, established military forts at San Diego and Monterey. The first Franciscan mission was established by Fr. Junípero Serra near present-day San Diego in 1769. By 1776 Spanish settlers from New Spain (Mexico) had established a military fort and a mission in what is now San Francisco.

In 1812 Russian fur traders from Alaska expanded south and established Fort Ross on the northern California coast. This was a factor leading to the promulgation of the Monroe Doctrine of 1823, in which the U.S. proclaimed that North and South America could not be settled by Europeans. The Russians finally left in 1840.

Mexico won its independence from Spain in 1821, and in 1822 California ceased being governed by Spain and became a province of Mexico. The province set up its own legislature, but Mexico sent a series of governors, which angered the Californians, and their continued opposition weakened Mexico's control of the area.

American Settlement

The first organized group of American settlers arrived in California in 1841, rapidly followed by many others. In May 1846 the Mexican-American War began. The following month a group of American settlers, not knowing war had been declared, took over Mexico's northern headquarters in Sonoma and raised the flag of the California Republic, which bore a single star and a grizzly bear. On January 13, 1847 California came under U.S. rule, and by the treaty of Guadalupe Hidalgo of February 2, 1848, which ended the war, Mexico ceded Alta (Upper) California (including the islands off the southwestern coast), the Territory of New Mexico (including Arizona), and Texas to the U.S. for $15,000,000.

The Gold Rush of 1849

In January 1848 James W. Marshall discovered the "Mother Lode" of gold at Sutter's Mill on a branch of the American River, northeast of Sacramento in Placer County. President James Polk mentioned this discovery during his state of the union address on December 5, 1848 and thereby began the Gold Rush of 1849. The "Forty-Niners," as they were called, flocked in from all parts of the world; California's population grew from 20,000 to 225,000 in just three years.

Statehood

The first California constitution was ratified November 13, 1849, and on September 9, 1850, California became the 31st state. Through the efforts of Stephen A. Douglas it was made a free state even though much of its territory was south of the boundary set by the Missouri Compromise. After the Civil War settlers flocked to California for the high wages and inexpensive land. Many Chinese laborers were brought to California to work on the railroads; a transcontinental line that linked Sacramento with the eastern U.S. was completed in 1869.

During the 1870s California experienced a depression but by the 1880s a land boom occurred as thousands moved to California, bringing prosperity to agriculture and industry. Despite the devastation of the 1906 San Francisco earthquake, the city was soon rebuilt.

During the early years of the twentieth century, new water sources for irrigation benefited farming, oil and natural gas resources were developed, and the motion picture industry became firmly identified with Hollywood. In 1914 the sea route to the East was considerably shortened by the completion of the Panama Canal, giving California additional access to the heavily populated markets of the eastern states.

California continued to prosper during World War I and after. During the 1930s California's water and power supplies were greatly improved by the construction of Hoover Dam on the Colorado River. During the Great Depression thousands of people moved to California seeking better opportunities, but the state's economy did not really improve until World War II, with the production of airplanes, ships, and weapons. During the war years thousands of Japanese-Americans were moved from their California homes to detention camps.

After the war California's population continued to grow, creating continuing challenges for the state in such areas as highways, air quality, and water supplies. By 1963 estimated census figures showed that California had surpassed New York as the most populous state. California also experienced the widespread racial problems of the 1960s, most notably in the 1965 Watts riots.

California became established (and still functions) as a national trendsetter in everything from law to popular culture. Hollywood produced movies, television, and other entertainment; popular music was influenced heavily by the "California sound" from Los Angeles and San Francisco; fashions in clothing, hairstyles, and language originated in California; and California's state and urban centers set trends in social legislation, environmental regulations, and human relations. The sheer physical size, complexity, topographical variety, and huge populations and economy (considered as a separate nation, California would rank tenth in the world in economic output) make it a bellwether for America.

In the 1970s military cutbacks affected California's economy. In what was dubbed a "taxpayer's revolt," citizens approved a measure (known as Proposition 13) to cut property taxes. The economy rebounded in the 1980s with increased military spending and the growth of California's electronics industry, which led to a section of northern California being called "Silicon Valley" for its concentration of computer-related industries.

A drop in petroleum prices in the mid-1980s and military spending cutbacks in the early 1990s adversely affected California's economy. Additionally, many citizens of the state have been increasingly concerned about the influx of immigrants into the state and the cost of providing services for them.

State Boundaries

California's southern boundary was set by the treaty of Guadalupe Hidalgo and runs from mid-channel of the Colorado River westward to the Pacific Ocean, and extending three miles into it. This is also the international boundary between the United States and Mexico that extends 12 nautical miles into the Pacific Ocean and the

American Places Dictionary   CALIFORNIA

Gulf of Mexico, in accordance with a treaty of November 23, 1970. The California-Oregon border was resurveyed in 1927; the official California-Nevada border was set in 1873; and on March 12, 1963, California and Arizona fixed their border in such a way that the continually shifting bed of the Colorado River would not affect it.

California Counties

Alameda	Imperial	Modoc	San Diego	Solano
Alpine	Inyo	Mono	San Francisco	Sonoma
Amador	Kern	Monterey	San Joaquin	Stanislaus
Butte	Kings	Napa	San Luis Obispo	Sutter
Calaveras	Lake	Nevada		Tehama
Colusa	Lassen	Orange	San Mateo	Trinity
Contra Costa	Los Angeles	Placer	Santa Barbara	Tulare
Del Norte	Madera	Plumas	Santa Clara	Tuolumne
El Dorado	Marin	Riverside	Santa Cruz	Ventura
Fresno	Mariposa	Sacramento	Shasta	Yolo
Glenn	Mendocino	San Benito	Sierra	Yuba
Humboldt	Merced	San Bernardino	Siskiyou	

Multi-County Places

The following California place is in more than one county. Given here is the total population and the names of the counties it is in.

Aromas, pop. 2,275; San Benito (1,149), Monterey (1,126)

CALIFORNIA, Alameda County   *American Places Dictionary*

> ## Alameda County
> ### County Seat: Oakland (ZIP: 94612)
>
> **Pop:** 1,279,180 (1990); 1,105,380 (1980)   **Pop Density:** 1734.5
> **Land:** 737.5 sq. mi.; **Water:** 83.8 sq. mi.   **Area Code:** 415
> Along San Francisco Bay E of San Francisco; organized in Mar. 25, 1853 from Contra Costa and Santa Clara counties.
> **Name origin:** From Spanish 'grove of poplar trees.'

Alameda   City
ZIP: 94501   **Lat:** 37-45-09 N **Long:** 122-16-33 W
Pop: 76,459 (1990); 63,852 (1980)   **Pop Density:** 7145.7
Land: 10.7 sq. mi.; **Water:** 12.2 sq. mi.   **Elev:** 30 ft.

In central-western CA, 5 mi. east of San Francisco on an island near the eastern shore of San Francisco Bay. Incorporated Apr 19, 1854.
Name origin: Possibly for Alameda Creek, which runs through it; from Spanish 'grove of poplar trees.'

Albany   City
ZIP: 94706   **Lat:** 37-53-26 N **Long:** 122-19-37 W
Pop: 16,327 (1990); 15,130 (1980)   **Pop Density:** 9604.1
Land: 1.7 sq. mi.; **Water:** 3.8 sq. mi.

In central-western CA, 4 mi. north of Oakland on San Francisco Bay. Incorporated as Ocean View Sep 22, 1908; name changed 1909.
Name origin: For Albany, NY, the birthplace of Frank J. Roberts, the town's first mayor.

Ashland   CDP
ZIP: 94541   **Lat:** 37-41-40 N **Long:** 122-06-55 W
Pop: 16,590 (1990); 13,893 (1980)   **Pop Density:** 8731.6
Land: 1.9 sq. mi.; **Water:** 0.0 sq. mi.

Berkeley   City
ZIP: 94704   **Lat:** 37-52-02 N **Long:** 122-17-50 W
Pop: 102,724 (1990); 103,328 (1980) **Pop Density:** 9783.2
Land: 10.5 sq. mi.; **Water:** 7.2 sq. mi.

In central-western CA, 3 mi. north of Oakland. Founded 1853; incorporated Apr 4, 1878.
Name origin: Named in 1866 by Frederick Billings, a trustee of the University of California (centered here), for Bishop George Berkeley (1685–1753), who in 1728 wrote the famous line: "Westward the course of empire takes its way."

Castro Valley   CDP
ZIP: 94546   **Lat:** 37-42-39 N **Long:** 122-03-40 W
Pop: 48,619 (1990); 44,011 (1980)   **Pop Density:** 3655.6
Land: 13.3 sq. mi.; **Water:** 0.1 sq. mi.

Cherryland   CDP
ZIP: 94541   **Lat:** 37-40-45 N **Long:** 122-06-08 W
Pop: 11,088 (1990); 9,425 (1980)   **Pop Density:** 9240.0
Land: 1.2 sq. mi.; **Water:** 0.0 sq. mi.

Dublin   City
ZIP: 94568   **Lat:** 37-42-57 N **Long:** 121-54-35 W
Pop: 23,229 (1990); 13,496 (1980)   **Pop Density:** 2701.0
Land: 8.6 sq. mi.; **Water:** 0.0 sq. mi.

In central-western CA, 20 mi. southeast of Oakland. Incorporated Feb 1, 1982.
Name origin: Named by James W. Dougherty of TN, who called the southern part of the town Dublin because so many Irish lived there. Previously called Dougherty's Station.

Emeryville   City
ZIP: 94608   **Lat:** 37-50-20 N **Long:** 122-17-57 W
Pop: 5,740 (1990); 3,714 (1980)   **Pop Density:** 4783.3
Land: 1.2 sq. mi.; **Water:** 0.7 sq. mi.

In western CA on San Francisco Bay. Incorporated Dec 8, 1896.

Fairview   CDP
ZIP: 94542   **Lat:** 37-40-43 N **Long:** 122-02-40 W
Pop: 9,045 (1990)   **Pop Density:** 1845.9
Land: 4.9 sq. mi.; **Water:** 0.0 sq. mi.

Fremont   City
ZIP: 94537   **Lat:** 37-31-42 N **Long:** 121-59-49 W
Pop: 173,339 (1990); 131,945 (1980) **Pop Density:** 2251.2
Land: 77.0 sq. mi.; **Water:** 10.4 sq. mi.

In western CA, southeast of Oakland. The towns of Centerville, Niles, Irvington, Mission San Jose, and Warm Springs united to form this city; incorporated January 24, 1956.
Name origin: Named by the Incorporation Committee for John C. Frémont (1813–90), soldier and explorer, and U.S. senator from CA (1850–51).

Hayward   City
ZIP: 94544   **Lat:** 37-37-39 N **Long:** 122-06-16 W
Pop: 111,498 (1990); 93,585 (1980) **Pop Density:** 2563.2
Land: 43.5 sq. mi.; **Water:** 18.7 sq. mi.   **Elev:** 111 ft.

In central-western CA, 5 mi. east of San Francisco Bay at the base of Walpert Ridge. Incorporated Mar 11, 1876; an industrial and residential city, and important East Bay transportation center.
Name origin: For William Hayward, a local hotel owner.

Livermore   City
ZIP: 94550   **Lat:** 37-41-30 N **Long:** 121-45-49 W
Pop: 56,741 (1990); 48,349 (1980)   **Pop Density:** 2894.9
Land: 19.6 sq. mi.; **Water:** 0.0 sq. mi.   **Elev:** 486 ft.

In central-western CA, 22 mi. east of San Francisco Bay. Founded 1864; incorporated Apr 1, 1876. A center for vineyards and wine-making.
Name origin: For Robert Livermore (1799–1858), English sailor who jumped ship and around whose rancho the town grew up. Previously called Laddville for Alphonso S. Ladd, who built the first building, then Nottingham for Livermore's home town in England; name changed in 1869.

Newark   City
ZIP: 94560   **Lat:** 37-31-09 N **Long:** 122-01-49 W
Pop: 37,861 (1990); 32,126 (1980)   **Pop Density:** 2704.4
Land: 14.0 sq. mi.; **Water:** 0.0 sq. mi.   **Elev:** 16 ft.

In central-western CA, southeast of San Francisco. Incorporated Sep 22, 1955.
Name origin: For the Southern Pacific station named in 1876 for the former NJ home of A. E. Davis and his brother.

Oakland   City
ZIP: 94617 **Lat:** 37-46-17 N **Long:** 122-13-28 W
Pop: 372,242 (1990); 339,337 (1980) **Pop Density:** 6635.3
Land: 56.1 sq. mi.; **Water:** 22.1 sq. mi. **Elev:** 42 ft.
In central-western CA on San Francisco Bay, east of San Francisco. Settled 1820; incorporated May 4, 1852.
Name origin: Named by Horace W. Carpentier for the numerous evergreen oaks.

Piedmont   City
ZIP: 94611 **Lat:** 37-49-22 N **Long:** 122-13-44 W
Pop: 10,602 (1990); 10,498 (1980) **Pop Density:** 6236.5
Land: 1.7 sq. mi.; **Water:** 0.0 sq. mi.
In central-western CA, 6 mi. east of San Francisco Bay; a suburb of Oakland. Incorporated Jan 31, 1907.
Name origin: From French or Italian 'at the foot of the mountain.'

Pleasanton   City
ZIP: 94566 **Lat:** 37-40-20 N **Long:** 121-53-20 W
Pop: 50,553 (1990); 35,160 (1980) **Pop Density:** 3120.6
Land: 16.2 sq. mi.; **Water:** 0.0 sq. mi. **Elev:** 352 ft.
In central-western CA, southeast of Oakland. Incorporated Jun 18, 1894.
Name origin: Named by John W. Kottinger in 1867 for Mexican War Gen. Alfred Pleasonton, an Austrian pioneer. Misspelled through clerical error.

San Leandro   City
ZIP: 94577 **Lat:** 37-42-16 N **Long:** 122-09-38 W
Pop: 68,223 (1990); 63,952 (1980) **Pop Density:** 5207.9
Land: 13.1 sq. mi.; **Water:** 2.4 sq. mi.
In central-western CA, 15 mi. southeast of Oakland. Incorporated Mar 21, 1872.
Name origin: For San Leandro Creek, named for St. Leander, 6th century archbishop of Seville.

San Lorenzo   CDP
ZIP: 94580 **Lat:** 37-40-30 N **Long:** 122-07-48 W
Pop: 19,987 (1990); 20,545 (1980) **Pop Density:** 8327.9
Land: 2.4 sq. mi.; **Water:** 0.0 sq. mi.

Union City   City
ZIP: 94587 **Lat:** 37-36-05 N **Long:** 122-00-57 W
Pop: 53,762 (1990); 39,406 (1980) **Pop Density:** 2859.7
Land: 18.8 sq. mi.; **Water:** 0.0 sq. mi. **Elev:** 59 ft.
In central-western CA, southeast of Oakland. Incorporated Jan 26, 1959.
Name origin: Named in 1851 for the American union of states.

Alpine County
County Seat: Markleeville (ZIP: 96120)

Pop: 1,113 (1990); 1,097 (1980) **Pop Density:** 1.5
Land: 738.7 sq. mi.; **Water:** 4.6 sq. mi. **Area Code:** 916
In NE CA on Nevada border, E of Sacramento; organized Mar 16, 1864 from Calaveras, Amador, El Dorado, and Mono counties.
Name origin: For the mountainous terrain of the Sierra Nevada.

Amador County
County Seat: Jackson (ZIP: 95642)

Pop: 30,039 (1990); 19,314 (1980) **Pop Density:** 50.7
Land: 592.6 sq. mi.; **Water:** 11.7 sq. mi. **Area Code:** 209
In NE CA, due E of Sacramento; organized May 11, 1854 from Calaveras County.
Name origin: For José María Amador, a construction foreman at the San Jose Mission, miner, and early landowner.

Amador City   City
Lat: 38-25-06 N **Long:** 120-49-23 W
Pop: 196 (1990); 136 (1980) **Pop Density:** 653.3
Land: 0.3 sq. mi.; **Water:** 0.0 sq. mi.
In east-central CA, southeast of Sacramento; incorporated Jun 2, 1915.
Name origin: For José María Amador, a Mexican soldier who established a mining settlement on the nearby creek in 1848.

Ione   City
ZIP: 95640 **Lat:** 38-21-34 N **Long:** 120-56-28 W
Pop: 6,516 (1990); 2,207 (1980) **Pop Density:** 1357.5
Land: 4.8 sq. mi.; **Water:** 0.0 sq. mi.
Incorporated Mar 23, 1953.
Name origin: Origin of name is uncertain: possibly for a heroine in one of the novels by English author Edward Bulwer–Lytton (1803–73); for Ione, IL; or for a variation of "I own."

Jackson   City
ZIP: 95642 **Lat:** 38-21-01 N **Long:** 120-46-24 W
Pop: 3,545 (1990); 2,331 (1980) **Pop Density:** 1143.5
Land: 3.1 sq. mi.; **Water:** 0.0 sq. mi.
In central CA. Incorporated Dec 5, 1905.
Name origin: For "Col." Alden M. Jackson, a lawyer from New England who settled many miners' quarrels out of court.

CALIFORNIA, Amador County

Plymouth — City
ZIP: 95669   Lat: 38-28-42 N   Long: 120-50-41 W
Pop: 811 (1990); 699 (1980)   Pop Density: 901.1
Land: 0.9 sq. mi.; Water: 0.0 sq. mi.   Elev: 1086 ft.
In central CA, east of Sacramento. Incorporated Feb 8, 1917.
Name origin: For the nearby Plymouth Mines, active since 1850. Formerly a goldmining camp called Puckerviller or Pokerville.

Sutter Creek — City
ZIP: 95685   Lat: 38-23-26 N   Long: 120-48-12 W
Pop: 1,835 (1990); 1,705 (1980)   Pop Density: 1223.3
Land: 1.5 sq. mi.; Water: 0.0 sq. mi.   Elev: 1198 ft.
In east-central CA, southeast of Sacramento. Founded 1854; incorporated Feb 11, 1913.
Name origin: For the nearby creek, named for Sutter's mining camp here 1849.

Butte County
County Seat: Oroville (ZIP: 95965)

Pop: 182,120 (1990); 143,851 (1980)   Pop Density: 111.1
Land: 1639.6 sq. mi.; Water: 37.6 sq. mi.   Area Code: 916
In N central CA; original county; organized Feb 18, 1850 (prior to statehood).
Name origin: For the Sutter Buttes of the Sacramento Valley, or the Butte River, which flows through the county.

Biggs — City
ZIP: 95917   Lat: 39-24-50 N   Long: 121-42-33 W
Pop: 1,581 (1990); 1,413 (1980)   Pop Density: 3162.0
Land: 0.5 sq. mi.; Water: 0.0 sq. mi.   Elev: 94 ft.
Incorporated Jun 26, 1903.
Name origin: For the California and Oregon Railroad station, named in 1870 for Major Marion Biggs, the first rancher to ship grain from here.

Chico — City
ZIP: 95926   Lat: 39-45-13 N   Long: 121-48-24 W
Pop: 40,079 (1990); 26,716 (1980)   Pop Density: 1789.2
Land: 22.4 sq. mi.; Water: 0.0 sq. mi.
In northern CA, 81 mi. northwest of Sacramento. Incorporated Jan 8, 1872.
Name origin: For nearby Chico Creek, from Spanish 'little.'

Concow — CDP
Lat: 39-44-45 N   Long: 121-29-37 W
Pop: 1,392 (1990)   Pop Density: 20.7
Land: 67.2 sq. mi.; Water: 0.8 sq. mi.

Durham — CDP
ZIP: 95938   Lat: 39-35-58 N   Long: 121-49-39 W
Pop: 4,784 (1990)   Pop Density: 34.6
Land: 138.2 sq. mi.; Water: 0.6 sq. mi.

Gridley — City
ZIP: 95948   Lat: 39-21-51 N   Long: 121-41-42 W
Pop: 4,631 (1990); 3,982 (1980)   Pop Density: 3307.9
Land: 1.4 sq. mi.; Water: 0.0 sq. mi.   Elev: 91 ft.
In northern CA, 55 mi. north of Sacramento. Incorporated Nov 23, 1905.
Name origin: Named in 1870 by the Southern Pacific Railroad for George W. Gridley, owner of the land on which town was built.

Magalia — CDP
ZIP: 95954   Lat: 39-49-39 N   Long: 121-36-38 W
Pop: 8,987 (1990)   Pop Density: 558.2
Land: 16.1 sq. mi.; Water: 0.0 sq. mi.

Oroville — City
ZIP: 95965   Lat: 39-30-05 N   Long: 121-33-57 W
Pop: 11,960 (1990); 8,683 (1980)   Pop Density: 1107.4
Land: 10.8 sq. mi.; Water: 0.0 sq. mi.   Elev: 174 ft.
In northern CA on the Feather River, 65 mi. north of Sacramento. Settled 1849; incorporated Jan 3, 1906.
Name origin: Coined from Spanish *oro* 'gold' plus French *ville* 'city.' Originally called Ophir City; changed to present name in 1855.

Oroville East — CDP
Lat: 39-30-48 N   Long: 121-28-38 W
Pop: 8,462 (1990)   Pop Density: 401.0
Land: 21.1 sq. mi.; Water: 3.1 sq. mi.

Palermo — CDP
ZIP: 95968   Lat: 39-26-11 N   Long: 121-31-49 W
Pop: 5,260 (1990); 2,572 (1980)   Pop Density: 133.2
Land: 39.5 sq. mi.; Water: 0.0 sq. mi.

Paradise — City
ZIP: 95969   Lat: 39-45-23 N   Long: 121-36-15 W
Pop: 25,408 (1990); 22,571 (1980)   Pop Density: 1366.0
Land: 18.6 sq. mi.; Water: 0.0 sq. mi.   Elev: 1708 ft.
In north-central CA, northeast of Chico. Founded 1879; incorporated Nov 27, 1979.
Name origin: Name spelled Paradice in 1900, which might support the story that it was named for the Pair o' Dice Saloon; or possibly just a misspelling of the present name.

South Oroville — CDP
ZIP: 95965   Lat: 39-28-57 N   Long: 121-31-57 W
Pop: 7,463 (1990); 7,246 (1980)   Pop Density: 1658.4
Land: 4.5 sq. mi.; Water: 0.0 sq. mi.

Thermalito — CDP
ZIP: 95965   Lat: 39-29-28 N   Long: 121-36-28 W
Pop: 5,646 (1990); 4,961 (1980)   Pop Density: 437.7
Land: 12.9 sq. mi.; Water: 0.1 sq. mi.

Calaveras County
County Seat: San Andreas (ZIP: 95249)

Pop: 31,998 (1990); 20,710 (1980) **Pop Density:** 31.4
Land: 1020.2 sq. mi.; **Water:** 16.7 sq. mi. **Area Code:** 209

In NE CA, SE of Sacramento; original county; organized Feb 18, 1850 (prior to statehood).

Name origin: For the Calaveras River, which flows through the county, from the Spanish 'skulls,' so named because skulls were found on the river's banks in the 1830s.

Angels — City
Lat: 38-04-32 N Long: 120-32-52 W
Pop: 2,409 (1990); 2,302 (1980) **Pop Density:** 1147.1
Land: 2.1 sq. mi.; **Water:** 0.0 sq. mi.
Incorporated Jan 24, 1912

Arnold — CDP
ZIP: 95223 Lat: 38-13-55 N Long: 120-22-10 W
Pop: 3,788 (1990); 2,385 (1980) **Pop Density:** 196.3
Land: 19.3 sq. mi.; **Water:** 0.1 sq. mi.

Murphys — CDP
ZIP: 95247 Lat: 38-09-07 N Long: 120-27-39 W
Pop: 1,517 (1990); 1,183 (1980) **Pop Density:** 322.8
Land: 4.7 sq. mi.; **Water:** 0.0 sq. mi.
In north-central CA, northeast of Stockton.
Name origin: For John and Daniel Murphy, brothers who were the first to discover gold here in 1849.

San Andreas — CDP
ZIP: 95249 Lat: 38-11-21 N Long: 120-40-28 W
Pop: 2,115 (1990); 1,912 (1980) **Pop Density:** 293.8
Land: 7.2 sq. mi.; **Water:** 0.0 sq. mi.
In east-central CA, northeast of Stockton. Settled 1848/49.
Name origin: For San Andreas Gulch, named for St. Andrew.

Colusa County
County Seat: Colusa (ZIP: 95932)

Pop: 16,275 (1990); 12,791 (1980) **Pop Density:** 14.1
Land: 1150.8 sq. mi.; **Water:** 5.5 sq. mi. **Area Code:** 916

In N CA, NW of Sacramento; original county; organized Feb 18, 1850 (prior to statehood).

Name origin: From the name of a former village of the Patwin Indians; earlier spelled *Colusi*.

Arbuckle — CDP
ZIP: 95912 Lat: 39-00-58 N Long: 122-03-38 W
Pop: 1,912 (1990); 1,306 (1980) **Pop Density:** 1365.7
Land: 1.4 sq. mi.; **Water:** 0.0 sq. mi.

Colusa — City
ZIP: 95932 Lat: 39-12-21 N Long: 122-00-40 W
Pop: 4,934 (1990); 4,075 (1980) **Pop Density:** 3289.3
Land: 1.5 sq. mi.; **Water:** 0.0 sq. mi. **Elev:** 61 ft.
Incorporated Jun 16, 1868.
Name origin: Originally called Salmon Bend, then Colusi, a variant of the Indian name *Coru*.

Williams — City
ZIP: 95987 Lat: 39-09-16 N Long: 122-08-12 W
Pop: 2,297 (1990); 1,655 (1980) **Pop Density:** 546.9
Land: 4.2 sq. mi.; **Water:** 0.0 sq. mi. **Elev:** 801 ft.
In north-central CA, west of Yuba City. Laid out 1876; incorporated May 10, 1920.
Name origin: For W.H. Williams, who platted the town.

CALIFORNIA, Contra Costa County   *American Places Dictionary*

Contra Costa County
County Seat: Martinez (ZIP: 94553)

Pop: 803,732 (1990); 656,331 (1980)   **Pop Density:** 1115.9
Land: 720.3 sq. mi.; **Water:** 81.9 sq. mi.   **Area Code:** 415
On San Pablo Bay, E of San Francisco; original county; organized Feb 18, 1850 (prior to statehood).
Name origin: From Spanish 'opposite coast' designating the coast opposite Marin County, north of San Francisco.

Alamo   CDP
ZIP: 94507   **Lat:** 37-51-25 N   **Long:** 121-59-55 W
Pop: 12,277 (1990); 8,505 (1980)   **Pop Density:** 656.5
Land: 18.7 sq. mi.; **Water:** 0.0 sq. mi.

Antioch   City
ZIP: 94509   **Lat:** 37-59-19 N   **Long:** 121-47-56 W
Pop: 62,195 (1990); 42,683 (1980)   **Pop Density:** 3173.2
Land: 19.6 sq. mi.; **Water:** 0.7 sq. mi.
In western CA, 20 mi. northeast of Oakland, on the San Joaquin River, near the mouth of the Sacramento River. Founded 1849; incorporated Feb 6, 1872.
Name origin: Originally called Smith's Landing for the first settlers, twin brothers J. H. and W. W. Smith. Name changed to that of the biblical city in Syria on Jul 4, 1851.

Bayview-Montalvin   CDP
Lat: 38-00-05 N   **Long:** 122-19-21 W
Pop: 3,988 (1990)   **Pop Density:** 6646.7
Land: 0.6 sq. mi.; **Water:** 0.0 sq. mi.

Bethel Island   CDP
Lat: 38-01-55 N   **Long:** 121-38-48 W
Pop: 2,115 (1990); 1,774 (1980)   **Pop Density:** 414.7
Land: 5.1 sq. mi.; **Water:** 0.2 sq. mi.

Blackhawk   CDP
Lat: 37-49-05 N   **Long:** 121-54-26 W
Pop: 6,199 (1990)   **Pop Density:** 681.2
Land: 9.1 sq. mi.; **Water:** 0.0 sq. mi.

Brentwood   City
ZIP: 94513   **Lat:** 37-56-01 N   **Long:** 121-42-31 W
Pop: 7,563 (1990); 4,434 (1980)   **Pop Density:** 1512.6
Land: 5.0 sq. mi.; **Water:** 0.0 sq. mi.   **Elev:** 79 ft.
In central-western CA, 38 mi. east of San Francisco. Founded 1878; incorporated Jan 21, 1948.
Name origin: For Brentwood in Essex, England, the ancestral home of John Marsh, who had owned Rancho Los Meganos on which the present town was built.

Clayton   City
ZIP: 94517   **Lat:** 37-56-27 N   **Long:** 121-55-44 W
Pop: 7,317 (1990); 4,325 (1980)   **Pop Density:** 1876.2
Land: 3.9 sq. mi.; **Water:** 0.0 sq. mi.   **Elev:** 394 ft.
Founded 1861; incorporated Mar 18, 1964.
Name origin: For Joel Clayton, an early settler.

Concord   City
ZIP: 94520   **Lat:** 37-58-23 N   **Long:** 121-59-59 W
Pop: 111,348 (1990); 103,763 (1980)   **Pop Density:** 3774.5
Land: 29.5 sq. mi.; **Water:** 0.0 sq. mi.
In west-central CA, 15 mi. northeast of Berkeley. Founded 1862; incorporated Feb 9, 1905.
Name origin: For the town in MA. Originally called Todos Santos 'All Saints,' by founder Salvio Pacheco in 1834.

Crockett   CDP
ZIP: 94525   **Lat:** 38-03-03 N   **Long:** 122-13-09 W
Pop: 3,228 (1990)   **Pop Density:** 2017.5
Land: 1.6 sq. mi.; **Water:** 0.4 sq. mi.

Danville   Town
ZIP: 94526   **Lat:** 37-48-51 N   **Long:** 121-58-16 W
Pop: 31,306 (1990); 26,446 (1980)   **Pop Density:** 1768.7
Land: 17.7 sq. mi.; **Water:** 0.0 sq. mi.   **Elev:** 368 ft.
In central-western CA, 17 mi. east of Oakland. Incorporated Jul 1, 1982.
Name origin: Named in 1867 for Danville, KY, the hometown of a relative of Daniel Inman, owner of the land who settled here in 1858.

Discovery Bay   CDP
ZIP: 94514   **Lat:** 37-54-31 N   **Long:** 121-35-42 W
Pop: 5,351 (1990); 1,326 (1980)   **Pop Density:** 798.7
Land: 6.7 sq. mi.; **Water:** 0.8 sq. mi.

East Richmond Heights   CDP
Lat: 37-56-42 N   **Long:** 122-18-45 W
Pop: 3,266 (1990)   **Pop Density:** 5443.3
Land: 0.6 sq. mi.; **Water:** 0.0 sq. mi.

El Cerrito   City
ZIP: 94530   **Lat:** 37-55-13 N   **Long:** 122-18-07 W
Pop: 22,869 (1990); 22,731 (1980)   **Pop Density:** 6352.5
Land: 3.6 sq. mi.; **Water:** 0.0 sq. mi.   **Elev:** 66 ft.
In central-western CA, on San Francisco Bay, 5 mi. north of Oakland. Incorporated Aug 23, 1917.
Name origin: From Spanish 'little hill.' Originally known as County Line; later as Rust for William R. Rust, first postmaster.

El Sobrante   CDP
ZIP: 94803   **Lat:** 37-58-35 N   **Long:** 122-17-33 W
Pop: 9,852 (1990); 10,535 (1980)   **Pop Density:** 2985.5
Land: 3.3 sq. mi.; **Water:** 0.0 sq. mi.

Hercules   City
ZIP: 94547   **Lat:** 38-01-13 N   **Long:** 122-17-48 W
Pop: 16,829 (1990); 5,963 (1980)   **Pop Density:** 3059.8
Land: 5.5 sq. mi.; **Water:** 11.8 sq. mi.
In western CA, 10 mi. north of Berkeley overlooking San Pablo Bay. Incorporated Dec 15, 1900.
Name origin: For the Hercules Powder Co., established 1869 to manufacture dynamite for the gold mines.

Kensington   CDP
Lat: 37-54-29 N   **Long:** 122-16-38 W
Pop: 4,974 (1990); 5,342 (1980)   **Pop Density:** 4521.8
Land: 1.1 sq. mi.; **Water:** 0.0 sq. mi.

Lafayette — City
ZIP: 94549 **Lat:** 37-53-37 N **Long:** 122-07-04 W
Pop: 23,501 (1990); 20,837 (1980) **Pop Density:** 1546.1
Land: 15.2 sq. mi.; **Water:** 0.2 sq. mi. **Elev:** 302 ft.

In central-western CA, 20 mi. northeast of San Francisco in the San Ramon Valley. Incorporated Jul 29, 1968.

Name origin: Named in 1853 by Benjamin Shreve, store owner, for the Marquis de Lafayette (1757–1834), French general who fought with the Americans in the Revolutionary War.

Martinez — City
ZIP: 94553 **Lat:** 38-00-02 N **Long:** 122-06-52 W
Pop: 31,808 (1990); 22,582 (1980) **Pop Density:** 2840.0
Land: 11.2 sq. mi.; **Water:** 1.2 sq. mi. **Elev:** 23 ft.

In central-western CA on Carquinez Strait, 17 mi. northeast of Oakland. Founded 1849; incorporated Apr 1, 1876. Home town of baseball great Joe DiMaggio and naturalist and explorer John Muir (1838–1914). Varied industry: oil refineries, canning plants, and fishing port.

Name origin: For Ignacio Martinez, commandant of the San Francisco Presidio (1822–27), on whose Rancho El Pinole the town was laid out.

Moraga Town — City
ZIP: 94556 **Lat:** 37-50-37 N **Long:** 122-07-24 W
Pop: 15,852 (1990); 15,014 (1980) **Pop Density:** 1704.5
Land: 9.3 sq. mi.; **Water:** 0.0 sq. mi.

In central-western CA, 10 mi. east of Oakland. Founded c. 1886; incorporated Nov 12, 1974.

Name origin: For Moraga Valley, named for Joaquin Moraga (1793–1855), who in 1835 was co-grantee of the rancho containing the valley.

Oakley — CDP
ZIP: 94561 **Lat:** 37-59-11 N **Long:** 121-42-57 W
Pop: 18,374 (1990); 2,816 (1980) **Pop Density:** 1331.4
Land: 13.8 sq. mi.; **Water:** 0.0 sq. mi.

Orinda — City
ZIP: 94563 **Lat:** 37-52-51 N **Long:** 122-10-38 W
Pop: 16,642 (1990); 16,825 (1980) **Pop Density:** 1320.8
Land: 12.6 sq. mi.; **Water:** 0.0 sq. mi.

In central-western CA, northeast of Oakland. Incorporated Jul 1, 1985.

Name origin: For Orinda Park, the estate of Theodore Wagner, U.S. Surveyor General for CA (1880).

Pacheco — CDP
Lat: 37-59-15 N **Long:** 122-03-44 W
Pop: 3,325 (1990) **Pop Density:** 2216.7
Land: 1.5 sq. mi.; **Water:** 0.0 sq. mi.

Pinole — City
ZIP: 94564 **Lat:** 38-00-43 N **Long:** 122-18-55 W
Pop: 17,460 (1990); 14,253 (1980) **Pop Density:** 3423.5
Land: 5.1 sq. mi.; **Water:** 8.1 sq. mi. **Elev:** 21 ft.

In central-western CA, 16 mi. north of Oakland on San Pablo Bay. Incorporated Jun 25, 1903.

Name origin: For an Indian camp named by Mexican soldiers when they were given corn meal. From Aztec *pinolli* designating ground and parched or toasted grain or seeds.

Pittsburg — City
ZIP: 94565 **Lat:** 38-01-05 N **Long:** 121-53-22 W
Pop: 47,564 (1990); 33,465 (1980) **Pop Density:** 4363.7
Land: 10.9 sq. mi.; **Water:** 1.0 sq. mi.

In central-western CA near the mouth of the Sacramento River, 16 mi. northeast of Oakland. Founded 1835; incorporated Jun 25, 1903.

Name origin: For the industrial city in PA, a reference to the coal deposits. Originally named City of New York of the Pacific because of its size.

Pleasant Hill — City
ZIP: 94523 **Lat:** 37-57-13 N **Long:** 122-04-27 W
Pop: 31,585 (1990); 25,547 (1980) **Pop Density:** 4644.9
Land: 6.8 sq. mi.; **Water:** 0.0 sq. mi.

In central-western CA in the Intermont Basins, 15 mi. northeast of Oakland. Incorporated Nov 14, 1961.

Richmond — City
ZIP: 94802 **Lat:** 37-57-04 N **Long:** 122-21-39 W
Pop: 87,425 (1990); 74,676 (1980) **Pop Density:** 2943.6
Land: 29.7 sq. mi.; **Water:** 22.6 sq. mi.

In central-western CA on the eastern shore of San Francisco Bay, 8 mi. northwest of Oakland. Founded 1899; incorporated Aug 7, 1905.

Name origin: For Richmond Point, probably named for one of the various U.S. places so named.

Rodeo — CDP
ZIP: 94547 **Lat:** 38-02-43 N **Long:** 122-14-15 W
Pop: 7,589 (1990); 8,286 (1980) **Pop Density:** 1011.9
Land: 7.5 sq. mi.; **Water:** 1.8 sq. mi.

San Pablo — City
ZIP: 94806 **Lat:** 37-57-43 N **Long:** 122-20-33 W
Pop: 25,158 (1990); 19,750 (1980) **Pop Density:** 9676.2
Land: 2.6 sq. mi.; **Water:** 0.0 sq. mi.

In central-western CA, northeast of San Francisco. Incorporated Apr 27, 1948.

Name origin: For the point on the eastern shore of San Pablo Strait, named for St. Paul the Evangelist.

San Ramon — City
ZIP: 94583 **Lat:** 37-45-26 N **Long:** 121-57-03 W
Pop: 35,303 (1990); 22,356 (1980) **Pop Density:** 3096.8
Land: 11.4 sq. mi.; **Water:** 0.0 sq. mi.

In central-western CA, 19 mi. southeast of Oakland. Incorporated Jul 1, 1983.

Name origin: For Ramon Creek, named for a sheepherder; *san* was added to make the name conform to other similar ones. Originally named Lynchville, and nicknamed Limerick because most of the settlers were Irish.

Tara Hills — CDP
Lat: 37-59-36 N **Long:** 122-19-02 W
Pop: 4,998 (1990); 9,471 (1980) **Pop Density:** 6247.5
Land: 0.8 sq. mi.; **Water:** 0.0 sq. mi.

Vine Hill — CDP
Lat: 38-00-57 N **Long:** 122-05-29 W
Pop: 3,214 (1990); 6,129 (1980) **Pop Density:** 868.6
Land: 3.7 sq. mi.; **Water:** 0.0 sq. mi.

Walnut Creek — City
ZIP: 94596 **Lat:** 37-54-07 N **Long:** 122-02-27 W
Pop: 60,569 (1990); 54,033 (1980) **Pop Density:** 3138.3
Land: 19.3 sq. mi.; **Water:** 0.0 sq. mi.

In central-western CA, northeast of Oakland. Established c. 1860; incorporated Oct 21, 1914.

West Pittsburg — CDP
ZIP: 94565 **Lat:** 38-02-17 N **Long:** 121-58-26 W
Pop: 17,453 (1990); 8,773 (1980) **Pop Density:** 1745.3
Land: 10.0 sq. mi.; **Water:** 1.4 sq. mi.

CALIFORNIA, Del Norte County — *American Places Dictionary*

Del Norte County
County Seat: Crescent City (ZIP: 95531)

Pop: 23,460 (1990); 18,217 (1980)　　**Pop Density:** 23.3
Land: 1007.9 sq. mi.; **Water:** 221.9 sq. mi.　　**Area Code:** 707
In NW corner of CA; organized Mar 2, 1857 from Klamath County.
Name origin: Spanish 'of the North,' for the county's position in the state.

Crescent City — City
ZIP: 95531　　Lat: 41-45-14 N　Long: 124-11-52 W
Pop: 4,380 (1990); 3,075 (1980)　　**Pop Density:** 3369.2
Land: 1.3 sq. mi.; **Water:** 0.3 sq. mi.　　**Elev:** 44 ft.
Incorporated Apr 13, 1854.
Name origin: For its crescent-shaped bay. Formerly called Paragon Bay.

Crescent City North — CDP
Lat: 41-45-49 N　Long: 124-12-50 W
Pop: 3,853 (1990); 2,846 (1980)　　**Pop Density:** 1926.5
Land: 2.0 sq. mi.; **Water:** 0.0 sq. mi.

Klamath — CDP
ZIP: 95548　　Lat: 41-31-21 N　Long: 123-59-47 W
Pop: 827 (1990)　　**Pop Density:** 66.2
Land: 12.5 sq. mi.; **Water:** 0.0 sq. mi.

El Dorado County
County Seat: Placerville (ZIP: 95667)

Pop: 125,995 (1990); 85,812 (1980)　　**Pop Density:** 73.6
Land: 1711.5 sq. mi.; **Water:** 79.8 sq. mi.　　**Area Code:** 916
In NE CA, E of Sacramento; original county; organized Feb 18, 1850 (prior to statehood).
Name origin: From Spanish 'the gilded' or 'the golden,' originally applied to a legendary chief and city sought by the early Spanish explorers; here the name refers to gold discovered in the area in 1848.

Cameron Park — CDP
ZIP: 95682　　Lat: 38-40-54 N　Long: 120-59-13 W
Pop: 11,897 (1990); 5,607 (1980)　　**Pop Density:** 1830.3
Land: 6.5 sq. mi.; **Water:** 0.1 sq. mi.

Diamond Springs — CDP
ZIP: 95619　　Lat: 38-41-09 N　Long: 120-49-17 W
Pop: 2,872 (1990); 2,287 (1980)　　**Pop Density:** 870.3
Land: 3.3 sq. mi.; **Water:** 0.0 sq. mi.

El Dorado Hills — CDP
ZIP: 95630　　Lat: 38-41-09 N　Long: 121-04-51 W
Pop: 6,395 (1990)　　**Pop Density:** 743.6
Land: 8.6 sq. mi.; **Water:** 0.0 sq. mi.

Placerville — City
ZIP: 95643　　Lat: 38-43-48 N　Long: 120-47-44 W
Pop: 8,355 (1990); 6,739 (1980)　　**Pop Density:** 1547.2
Land: 5.4 sq. mi.; **Water:** 0.0 sq. mi.　　**Elev:** 1866 ft.
In east-central CA, northeast of Sacramento. Settled 1848; incorporated May 13, 1854.
Name origin: For the abundance of rich placering holes. Originally called Dry Diggings; name changed 1850.

Pollock Pines — CDP
ZIP: 95726　　Lat: 38-45-07 N　Long: 120-34-14 W
Pop: 4,291 (1990); 1,941 (1980)　　**Pop Density:** 825.2
Land: 5.2 sq. mi.; **Water:** 0.0 sq. mi.

Shingle Springs — CDP
ZIP: 95682　　Lat: 38-40-14 N　Long: 120-56-22 W
Pop: 2,049 (1990); 1,268 (1980)　　**Pop Density:** 499.8
Land: 4.1 sq. mi.; **Water:** 0.0 sq. mi.

South Lake Tahoe — City
ZIP: 96151　　Lat: 38-56-21 N　Long: 119-58-52 W
Pop: 21,586 (1990); 20,681 (1980)　　**Pop Density:** 2137.2
Land: 10.1 sq. mi.; **Water:** 6.4 sq. mi.
In northeastern CA, 74 mi. northeast of Sacramento on the CA-NV border at the south end of Lake Tahoe. Incorporated Nov 30, 1965.

Fresno County
County Seat: Fresno (ZIP: 93721)

Pop: 667,490 (1990); 514,621 (1980)　　**Pop Density:** 111.9
Land: 5963.2 sq. mi.; **Water:** 54.7 sq. mi.　　**Area Code:** 209
In C CA; organized Apr 19, 1856 from Mariposa and Merced counties.
Name origin: From Spanish 'ash (tree)'; name originally applied to the river, for the ash trees that grew near it.

Auberry　　CDP
ZIP: 93602　　**Lat:** 37-04-40 N **Long:** 119-29-37 W
Pop: 1,866 (1990)　　**Pop Density:** 98.2
Land: 19.0 sq. mi.; **Water:** 0.1 sq. mi.

Caruthers　　CDP
ZIP: 93609　　**Lat:** 36-32-30 N **Long:** 119-50-30 W
Pop: 1,603 (1990); 1,514 (1980)　　**Pop Density:** 801.5
Land: 2.0 sq. mi.; **Water:** 0.0 sq. mi.

Clovis　　City
ZIP: 93612　　**Lat:** 36-49-10 N **Long:** 119-41-45 W
Pop: 50,323 (1990); 33,021 (1980)　　**Pop Density:** 3519.1
Land: 14.3 sq. mi.; **Water:** 0.0 sq. mi.

In south-central CA, 8 mi. northeast of Fresno. Incorporated Feb 27, 1912.
Name origin: For Clovis Cole, through whose land the Southern Pacific Railroad built a branch line in 1889.

Coalinga　　City
ZIP: 93210　　**Lat:** 36-08-32 N **Long:** 120-21-16 W
Pop: 8,212 (1990); 6,593 (1980)　　**Pop Density:** 2649.0
Land: 3.1 sq. mi.; **Water:** 0.0 sq. mi.　　**Elev:** 667 ft.
Incorporated Apr 3, 1906.
Name origin: Named by a Southern Pacific railroad official for the lignite deposits tapped here in 1888 and touted as great coal deposits. Originally known as Coaling Station; later shortened and *a* added for euphony.

Del Rey　　CDP
ZIP: 93616　　**Lat:** 36-39-27 N **Long:** 119-35-45 W
Pop: 1,150 (1990); 1,126 (1980)　　**Pop Density:** 958.3
Land: 1.2 sq. mi.; **Water:** 0.0 sq. mi.

Easton　　CDP
Lat: 36-39-06 N **Long:** 119-47-19 W
Pop: 1,877 (1990); 1,710 (1980)　　**Pop Density:** 625.7
Land: 3.0 sq. mi.; **Water:** 0.0 sq. mi.

Firebaugh　　City
ZIP: 93622　　**Lat:** 36-50-57 N **Long:** 120-26-56 W
Pop: 4,429 (1990); 3,740 (1980)　　**Pop Density:** 1581.8
Land: 2.8 sq. mi.; **Water:** 0.1 sq. mi.　　**Elev:** 151 ft.
In central CA, 35 mi. west-northwest of Fresno, on Mendota Canal and the San Joaquin River. Established 1854; incorporated Sep 17, 1914.
Name origin: For Firebaugh's Ferry, which crossed the San Joaquin River, and was run by A.D. Fierbaugh; the misspelling was allowed to stand.

Fowler　　City
ZIP: 93625　　**Lat:** 36-37-28 N **Long:** 119-40-20 W
Pop: 3,208 (1990); 2,496 (1980)　　**Pop Density:** 1604.0
Land: 2.0 sq. mi.; **Water:** 0.0 sq. mi.
In south-central CA, 10 mi. southeast of Fresno. Incorporated Jun 15, 1908.
Name origin: For Thomas Fowler, state senator from Fresno (1869–72; 1877–78).

Fresno　　City
ZIP: 93706　　**Lat:** 36-46-50 N **Long:** 119-47-34 W
Pop: 354,202 (1990); 217,491 (1980)　　**Pop Density:** 3574.2
Land: 99.1 sq. mi.; **Water:** 0.3 sq. mi.　　**Elev:** 296 ft.
In central CA, east of Monterey in the San Joaquin Valley. Founded 1872; incorporated Oct 12, 1885.
Name origin: From Spanish 'ash tree' for the abundance of Oregon ash *Fraxinus oregona* found here.

Huron　　Town
ZIP: 93234　　**Lat:** 36-12-12 N **Long:** 120-05-43 W
Pop: 4,766 (1990); 2,768 (1980)　　**Pop Density:** 2978.8
Land: 1.6 sq. mi.; **Water:** 0.0 sq. mi.　　**Elev:** 368 ft.
Incorporated May 3, 1951.
Name origin: For the railroad station, named for the Huron Indians.

Kerman　　City
ZIP: 93630　　**Lat:** 36-43-27 N **Long:** 120-03-39 W
Pop: 5,448 (1990); 4,002 (1980)　　**Pop Density:** 3026.7
Land: 1.8 sq. mi.; **Water:** 0.0 sq. mi.
In south-central CA, 14 mi. west of Fresno. Established 1906; incorporated Jul 2, 1946.
Name origin: Coined from the first three letters of the founders' surnames: W.G. *Ker*ckhoff and Jacob *Man*sar.

Kingsburg　　City
ZIP: 93631　　**Lat:** 36-31-10 N **Long:** 119-33-17 W
Pop: 7,205 (1990); 5,115 (1980)　　**Pop Density:** 3431.0
Land: 2.1 sq. mi.; **Water:** 0.0 sq. mi.　　**Elev:** 297 ft.
Incorporated May 19, 1908.
Name origin: For the nearby Kings River, itself named by Spanish explorers who reached the river on Jan 6, 1806, the feast of the Three Kings or Magi. Originally called Kings River Switch, Drapersville, and Wheatville; present name adopted 1875.

Laton　　CDP
ZIP: 93242　　**Lat:** 36-26-02 N **Long:** 119-41-19 W
Pop: 1,415 (1990); 1,100 (1980)　　**Pop Density:** 1010.7
Land: 1.4 sq. mi.; **Water:** 0.0 sq. mi.

CALIFORNIA, Fresno County

Mendota — City
ZIP: 93640 **Lat:** 36-45-27 N **Long:** 120-22-44 W
Pop: 6,821 (1990); 5,038 (1980) **Pop Density:** 4012.4
Land: 1.7 sq. mi.; **Water:** 0.0 sq. mi.

In south-central CA, 34 mi. west of Fresno. Incorporated Jun 17, 1942.
Name origin: For the railroad station, possibly named for the home town of some early settlers.

Orange Cove — City
ZIP: 93646 **Lat:** 36-37-20 N **Long:** 119-19-02 W
Pop: 5,604 (1990); 4,026 (1980) **Pop Density:** 3736.0
Land: 1.5 sq. mi.; **Water:** 0.0 sq. mi. **Elev:** 425 ft.

In south-central CA in a cove in the Sierra foothills where citrus fruit flourishes. Incorporated Jan 20, 1948.
Name origin: For the Orosi Orange Lands Company.

Parlier — City
ZIP: 93648 **Lat:** 36-36-30 N **Long:** 119-32-17 W
Pop: 7,938 (1990); 2,902 (1980) **Pop Density:** 5670.0
Land: 1.4 sq. mi.; **Water:** 0.0 sq. mi.

In south-central CA, southeast of Fresno. Incorporated Nov 14, 1921.
Name origin: For I.N. Parlier, early settler and first postmaster (1898).

Reedley — City
ZIP: 93654 **Lat:** 36-36-01 N **Long:** 119-26-53 W
Pop: 15,791 (1990); 11,071 (1980) **Pop Density:** 4049.0
Land: 3.9 sq. mi.; **Water:** 0.1 sq. mi.

In central CA, 19 mi. southeast of Fresno.
Name origin: For Thomas L. Reed, a veteran of the famed march to the sea with the forces of, Gen. William Tecumseh Sherman (1820–91) who in 1888 gave half of his holdings to the city. The suffix was added when he objected to the use of his name.

Riverdale — CDP
ZIP: 93656 **Lat:** 36-25-50 N **Long:** 119-51-57 W
Pop: 1,980 (1990); 1,866 (1980) **Pop Density:** 495.0
Land: 4.0 sq. mi.; **Water:** 0.0 sq. mi.

Sanger — City
ZIP: 93657 **Lat:** 36-42-00 N **Long:** 119-33-11 W
Pop: 16,839 (1990); 12,542 (1980) **Pop Density:** 3660.7
Land: 4.6 sq. mi.; **Water:** 0.0 sq. mi. **Elev:** 363 ft.

In central CA, 15 mi. southeast of Fresno. Incorporated May 25, 1911. Site of the famous General Grant tree, a giant sequoia over 4,000 years old.
Name origin: For Joseph Sanger, Jr. (?–1899), official of the Pacific Improvement Co.

San Joaquin — City
ZIP: 93660 **Lat:** 36-36-24 N **Long:** 120-11-12 W
Pop: 2,311 (1990); 1,930 (1980) **Pop Density:** 2311.0
Land: 1.0 sq. mi.; **Water:** 0.0 sq. mi. **Elev:** 170 ft.

In west-central CA on the San Joaquin River, southwest of Fresno. Incorporated Feb 14, 1920.
Name origin: For the river, itself named for St. Joachim, believed by many to be the father of the Virgin Mary.

Selma — City
ZIP: 93662 **Lat:** 36-34-27 N **Long:** 119-36-55 W
Pop: 14,757 (1990); 10,942 (1980) **Pop Density:** 3883.4
Land: 3.8 sq. mi.; **Water:** 0.0 sq. mi.

In central CA, 15 mi. southeast of Fresno. Established 1880; incorporated Mar 15, 1893.
Name origin: Name origin uncertain: either for the daughter of Max Gruenberg, at the request of Leland Stanford, or for Selma Michelson Kingsbury, wife of a Central Pacific Railroad official.

Squaw Valley — CDP
Lat: 36-41-47 N **Long:** 119-11-39 W
Pop: 2,161 (1990) **Pop Density:** 38.1
Land: 56.7 sq. mi.; **Water:** 0.1 sq. mi.

Glenn County
County Seat: Willows (ZIP: 95988)

Pop: 24,798 (1990); 21,350 (1980) **Pop Density:** 18.9
Land: 1314.9 sq. mi.; **Water:** 12.4 sq. mi. **Area Code:** 916
In NW CA; organized Mar 11, 1891 from Colusa County.
Name origin: For Dr. Hugh James Glenn (1824–83), the most important wheat-grower in California during the latter half of the 1800s.

Hamilton City — CDP
Lat: 39-44-32 N **Long:** 122-00-41 W
Pop: 1,811 (1990); 1,337 (1980) **Pop Density:** 6036.7
Land: 0.3 sq. mi.; **Water:** 0.0 sq. mi.

Orland — City
ZIP: 95963 **Lat:** 39-44-44 N **Long:** 122-11-14 W
Pop: 5,052 (1990); 4,031 (1980) **Pop Density:** 2296.4
Land: 2.2 sq. mi.; **Water:** 0.0 sq. mi.

In north-central CA, west of Chico. Incorporated Nov 11, 1909.
Name origin: For the railroad station, itself named for the English birthplace of a settler.

Willows — City
ZIP: 95988 **Lat:** 39-30-57 N **Long:** 122-11-56 W
Pop: 5,988 (1990); 4,777 (1980) **Pop Density:** 2303.1
Land: 2.6 sq. mi.; **Water:** 0.0 sq. mi.

In north-central CA, southwest of Chico. Laid out 1876; incorporated Jan 16, 1886.
Name origin: For its willow-framed pond, the one watering place south of Stony Creek. Called Willow till 1917.

Humboldt County
County Seat: Eureka (ZIP: 95501)

Pop: 119,118 (1990); 108,525 (1980) **Pop Density:** 33.3
Land: 3572.8 sq. mi.; **Water:** 479.7 sq. mi. **Area Code:** 707
On NW coast of CA; organized Mar 12, 1853 from Trinity County, and in 1874 annexed part of Klamath County.
Name origin: For Humboldt Bay, which was named for German naturalist and traveler, [Friedrich Heinrich] Alexander von Humboldt (1769–1859).

Arcata   City
ZIP: 95521 **Lat:** 40-52-04 N **Long:** 124-04-51 W
Pop: 15,197 (1990); 12,849 (1980) **Pop Density:** 1876.2
Land: 8.1 sq. mi.; **Water:** 1.9 sq. mi. **Elev:** 33 ft.
In northwestern CA, on Arcata Bay, 6 mi. north of Eureka. Founded 1850; incorporated Feb 2, 1858.
Name origin: From an Indian term of unknown meaning. Called Uniontown until 1860.

Bayview   CDP
Lat: 40-45-53 N **Long:** 124-10-33 W
Pop: 1,318 (1990) **Pop Density:** 1882.9
Land: 0.7 sq. mi.; **Water:** 0.0 sq. mi.

Blue Lake   City
ZIP: 95525 **Lat:** 40-52-48 N **Long:** 123-59-29 W
Pop: 1,235 (1990); 1,201 (1980) **Pop Density:** 2058.3
Land: 0.6 sq. mi.; **Water:** 0.0 sq. mi.
Incorporated Apr 23, 1910.

Cutten   CDP
Lat: 40-46-02 N **Long:** 124-08-31 W
Pop: 1,516 (1990); 2,375 (1980) **Pop Density:** 1166.2
Land: 1.3 sq. mi.; **Water:** 0.0 sq. mi.

Eureka   City
ZIP: 95501 **Lat:** 40-47-43 N **Long:** 124-09-20 W
Pop: 27,025 (1990); 24,153 (1980) **Pop Density:** 2844.7
Land: 9.5 sq. mi.; **Water:** 5.0 sq. mi. **Elev:** 44 ft.
In northwestern CA on Humboldt Bay, 83 mi. south of the OR border. Settled 1850; incorporated Apr 18, 1856.
Name origin: Greek for 'I have found it,' attributed to James Ryan, who surveyed the first town lots. Name also became the state motto.

Ferndale   City
ZIP: 95536 **Lat:** 40-34-46 N **Long:** 124-15-38 W
Pop: 1,331 (1990); 1,367 (1980) **Pop Density:** 1331.0
Land: 1.0 sq. mi.; **Water:** 0.0 sq. mi. **Elev:** 50 ft.
In northwestern CA, south of Eureka. Founded 1870; incorporated Aug 28, 1893.

Fortuna   City
ZIP: 95540 **Lat:** 40-35-08 N **Long:** 124-08-22 W
Pop: 8,788 (1990); 7,591 (1980) **Pop Density:** 1830.8
Land: 4.8 sq. mi.; **Water:** 0.0 sq. mi. **Elev:** 61 ft.
In northwestern CA, 14 mi. south of Eureka. Settled late 1870s; incorporated Feb 20, 1906.
Name origin: Named Fortune by town founder, a Rev. Gardiner, who believed it to be an ideal place to live; the last letter was later changed for the sake of euphony. Previously called Springville and Slide for a landslide.

Humboldt Hill   CDP
Lat: 40-43-34 N **Long:** 124-11-18 W
Pop: 2,865 (1990) **Pop Density:** 698.8
Land: 4.1 sq. mi.; **Water:** 0.0 sq. mi.

Hydesville   CDP
ZIP: 95547 **Lat:** 40-32-55 N **Long:** 124-05-13 W
Pop: 1,131 (1990) **Pop Density:** 195.0
Land: 5.8 sq. mi.; **Water:** 0.0 sq. mi.

McKinleyville   CDP
ZIP: 95521 **Lat:** 40-57-11 N **Long:** 124-06-56 W
Pop: 10,749 (1990); 7,772 (1980) **Pop Density:** 639.8
Land: 16.8 sq. mi.; **Water:** 7.4 sq. mi.

Myrtletown   CDP
Lat: 40-47-20 N **Long:** 124-07-44 W
Pop: 4,413 (1990); 3,959 (1980) **Pop Density:** 2322.6
Land: 1.9 sq. mi.; **Water:** 0.0 sq. mi.

Pine Hills   CDP
Lat: 40-44-00 N **Long:** 124-09-04 W
Pop: 2,947 (1990) **Pop Density:** 288.9
Land: 10.2 sq. mi.; **Water:** 0.0 sq. mi.

Redway   CDP
ZIP: 95560 **Lat:** 40-07-03 N **Long:** 123-49-09 W
Pop: 1,212 (1990); 1,094 (1980) **Pop Density:** 1010.0
Land: 1.2 sq. mi.; **Water:** 0.0 sq. mi.

Rio Dell   City
ZIP: 95562 **Lat:** 40-30-02 N **Long:** 124-06-22 W
Pop: 3,012 (1990); 2,687 (1980) **Pop Density:** 1673.3
Land: 1.8 sq. mi.; **Water:** 0.1 sq. mi. **Elev:** 126 ft.
In northwestern CA on the Eel River, south of Eureka. Incorporated Feb 23, 1965.
Name origin: Named in 1890 when the post office was established, from Spanish 'river.' Originally called Eagle Prairie.

Trinidad   City
ZIP: 95570 **Lat:** 41-03-27 N **Long:** 124-08-31 W
Pop: 362 (1990); 379 (1980) **Pop Density:** 724.0
Land: 0.5 sq. mi.; **Water:** 0.2 sq. mi.
On the northwestern coast of CA, north of Eureka. Incorporated Nov 7, 1870.
Name origin: For the bay, which was discovered on 'Trinity' Sunday 1775.

Westhaven-Moonstone   CDP
Lat: 41-02-31 N **Long:** 124-06-10 W
Pop: 1,109 (1990) **Pop Density:** 136.9
Land: 8.1 sq. mi.; **Water:** 0.0 sq. mi.

Willow Creek   CDP
ZIP: 95573 **Lat:** 40-52-55 N **Long:** 123-39-55 W
Pop: 1,576 (1990) **Pop Density:** 7.6
Land: 206.5 sq. mi.; **Water:** 0.2 sq. mi.

CALIFORNIA, Imperial County

Imperial County
County Seat: El Centro (ZIP: 92243)

Pop: 109,303 (1990); 92,110 (1980) **Pop Density:** 26.2
Land: 4175.0 sq. mi.; **Water:** 307.0 sq. mi. **Area Code:** 619
In SE CA on border with Baja California; organized Aug 15, 1907 from San Diego County.
Name origin: For the Imperial Valley, itself named for the Imperial Land Company that was organized to colonize the southern Colorado Desert.

Brawley City
ZIP: 92227 **Lat:** 32-58-47 N **Long:** 115-32-00 W
Pop: 18,923 (1990); 14,946 (1980) **Pop Density:** 3784.6
Land: 5.0 sq. mi.; **Water:** 0.0 sq. mi.
In southeastern CA, in Imperial Valley, 15 mi. south of the Salton Sea. Founded 1902; incorporated Apr 6, 1908.
Name origin: J. H. Braly, owner of the property, objected to the use of his name for the town. A. H. Heber, general manager of the Imperial Land Co., which laid out the town, suggested Brawley, the name of one of his friends.

Calexico City
ZIP: 92232 **Lat:** 32-40-42 N **Long:** 115-30-02 W
Pop: 18,633 (1990); 14,412 (1980) **Pop Density:** 4544.6
Land: 4.1 sq. mi.; **Water:** 0.0 sq. mi. **Elev:** 2 ft.
On central southern border of CA, across from Mexicali, Mexico. Founded 1908; incorporated Apr 16, 1908.
Name origin: A coinage from *Cal*ifornia and M*exico*.

Calipatria City
ZIP: 92233 **Lat:** 33-07-38 N **Long:** 115-31-03 W
Pop: 2,690 (1990); 2,636 (1980) **Pop Density:** 1494.4
Land: 1.8 sq. mi.; **Water:** 0.0 sq. mi. **Elev:** 184 ft.
Incorporated Feb 28, 1919.
Name origin: A coinage of *Cal*ifornia plus the Latin root *patria* 'fatherland.'

El Centro City
ZIP: 92244 **Lat:** 32-47-13 N **Long:** 115-33-33 W
Pop: 31,384 (1990); 23,996 (1980) **Pop Density:** 5061.9
Land: 6.2 sq. mi.; **Water:** 0.0 sq. mi.
In south-central CA in Imperial Valley, north of Calexico near the Mexican border. Settled 1906; incorporated Apr 16, 1908.
Name origin: From Spanish 'the center' in reference to its location near the center of Imperial Valley. Previously called Cabarker for C. A. Barker, a friend of W. F. Holt, owner of the land on which town was developed.

Heber CDP
ZIP: 92249 **Lat:** 32-44-02 N **Long:** 115-31-12 W
Pop: 2,566 (1990); 2,221 (1980) **Pop Density:** 1710.7
Land: 1.5 sq. mi.; **Water:** 0.0 sq. mi.

Holtville City
ZIP: 92250 **Lat:** 32-48-49 N **Long:** 115-22-38 W
Pop: 4,820 (1990); 4,399 (1980) **Pop Density:** 4381.8
Land: 1.1 sq. mi.; **Water:** 0.0 sq. mi.
In southern CA, 14 mi. northeast of Mexicali, Mexico. Established 1903; incorporated Jul 1, 1908.
Name origin: For founder W.F. Holt, president of Holton Power Co. and an organizer of the Imperial Valley irrigation project (1899).

Imperial Town
ZIP: 92251 **Lat:** 32-50-25 N **Long:** 115-34-15 W
Pop: 4,113 (1990); 3,451 (1980) **Pop Density:** 1713.7
Land: 2.4 sq. mi.; **Water:** 0.0 sq. mi. **Elev:** 60 ft.
Incorporated Jul 12, 1904.
Name origin: For the Imperial Land Co., a subsidiary of the California Development Co., an enterprise established in the early 1900s to obtain land.

Niland CDP
ZIP: 92257 **Lat:** 33-14-18 N **Long:** 115-30-47 W
Pop: 1,183 (1990) **Pop Density:** 2957.5
Land: 0.4 sq. mi.; **Water:** 0.0 sq. mi.

Seeley CDP
Lat: 32-47-20 N **Long:** 115-40-48 W
Pop: 1,228 (1990); 1,058 (1980) **Pop Density:** 1023.3
Land: 1.2 sq. mi.; **Water:** 0.0 sq. mi.

Westmorland City
ZIP: 92281 **Lat:** 33-02-12 N **Long:** 115-37-17 W
Pop: 1,380 (1990); 1,590 (1980) **Pop Density:** 3450.0
Land: 0.4 sq. mi.; **Water:** 0.0 sq. mi. **Elev:** 159 ft.
In southeastern CA, south of the Salton Sea. Incorporated Jun 30, 1934.
Name origin: Locals say the developers named it not for the English county but to call attention to "more land to the west" in Irrigation District No. 8.

Inyo County
County Seat: Independence (ZIP: 93526)

Pop: 18,281 (1990); 17,895 (1980)   **Pop Density:** 1.8
Land: 10192.1 sq. mi.; **Water:** 35.7 sq. mi.   **Area Code:** 619
On E border of CA, E of Fresno; organized Mar 22, 1866 from Tulare County.
Name origin: For the Inyo Mountains, from an Indian name said to mean 'where the great spirit dwells.'

Big Pine   CDP
ZIP: 93513   **Lat:** 37-09-55 N   **Long:** 118-17-43 W
Pop: 1,158 (1990); 469 (1980)   **Pop Density:** 482.5
Land: 2.4 sq. mi.; **Water:** 0.0 sq. mi.

Bishop   City
ZIP: 93514   **Lat:** 37-22-03 N   **Long:** 118-23-48 W
Pop: 3,475 (1990); 3,333 (1980)   **Pop Density:** 1930.6
Land: 1.8 sq. mi.; **Water:** 0.0 sq. mi.   **Elev:** 4147 ft.
In central-eastern CA, in Owens River valley, 35 mi. west of the NV border. Incorporated May 6, 1903.
Name origin: For Samuel A. Bishop of VA, a cattleman who drove the first herd into Owens Valley in 1861.

Dixon Lane-Meadow Creek   CDP
Lat: 37-23-14 N   **Long:** 118-24-44 W
Pop: 2,561 (1990)   **Pop Density:** 753.2
Land: 3.4 sq. mi.; **Water:** 0.0 sq. mi.

Independence   City
ZIP: 93526
Pop: 1,000 (1990)
Elev: 3923 ft.

Lone Pine   CDP
ZIP: 93545   **Lat:** 36-34-29 N   **Long:** 118-05-02 W
Pop: 1,818 (1990); 1,684 (1980)   **Pop Density:** 97.7
Land: 18.6 sq. mi.; **Water:** 0.1 sq. mi.

West Bishop   CDP
Lat: 37-21-39 N   **Long:** 118-27-14 W
Pop: 2,908 (1990)   **Pop Density:** 334.3
Land: 8.7 sq. mi.; **Water:** 0.0 sq. mi.

Kern County
County Seat: Bakersfield (ZIP: 93301)

Pop: 543,477 (1990); 403,089 (1980)   **Pop Density:** 66.8
Land: 8141.6 sq. mi.; **Water:** 20.4 sq. mi.   **Area Code:** 805
In SW CA, N of Los Angeles; organized Apr 2, 1866 from Los Angeles and Tulare counties.
Name origin: For the Kern River, which was named in 1845 by explorer John C. Frémont (1813–90) for Edward M. Kern, the topographer and artist for the expedition.

Arvin   City
ZIP: 93203   **Lat:** 35-12-01 N   **Long:** 118-50-01 W
Pop: 9,286 (1990); 6,863 (1980)   **Pop Density:** 2995.5
Land: 3.1 sq. mi.; **Water:** 0.0 sq. mi.   **Elev:** 445 ft.
In southern CA, 16 mi. southeast of Bakersfield. Established 1910; incorporated Dec 21, 1960.
Name origin: For Arvin Richardson, first storekeeper in the colony.

Bakersfield   City
ZIP: 93302   **Lat:** 35-21-27 N   **Long:** 119-00-16 W
Pop: 174,820 (1990); 105,611 (1980)   **Pop Density:** 1904.4
Land: 91.8 sq. mi.; **Water:** 1.3 sq. mi.   **Elev:** 408 ft.
In southern CA, northwest of Los Angeles, on the Kern River. Incorporated Jan 11, 1898.
Name origin: For Col. Thomas Baker, who tried to develop a waterway from Kern Lake to San Francisco Bay in the early 1860s, and whose corral here was known as Baker's field.

Bear Valley Springs   CDP
Lat: 35-09-33 N   **Long:** 118-37-39 W
Pop: 1,593 (1990)   **Pop Density:** 312.4
Land: 5.1 sq. mi.; **Water:** 0.0 sq. mi.

Bodfish   CDP
ZIP: 93205   **Lat:** 35-34-57 N   **Long:** 118-28-58 W
Pop: 1,283 (1990); 1,379 (1980)   **Pop Density:** 237.6
Land: 5.4 sq. mi.; **Water:** 0.0 sq. mi.

Boron   CDP
Lat: 35-00-17 N   **Long:** 117-39-01 W
Pop: 2,101 (1990); 2,040 (1980)   **Pop Density:** 724.5
Land: 2.9 sq. mi.; **Water:** 0.0 sq. mi.

Buttonwillow   CDP
ZIP: 93206   **Lat:** 35-24-06 N   **Long:** 119-28-11 W
Pop: 1,301 (1990); 1,350 (1980)   **Pop Density:** 1084.2
Land: 1.2 sq. mi.; **Water:** 0.0 sq. mi.

California City   City
ZIP: 93505   **Lat:** 35-11-21 N   **Long:** 117-48-41 W
Pop: 5,955 (1990); 2,743 (1980)   **Pop Density:** 32.3
Land: 184.6 sq. mi.; **Water:** 0.1 sq. mi.
Incorporated Dec 10, 1965.

CALIFORNIA, Kern County

Delano — City
ZIP: 93215 **Lat:** 35-45-53 N **Long:** 119-15-01 W
Pop: 22,762 (1990); 16,491 (1980) **Pop Density:** 2677.9
Land: 8.5 sq. mi.; **Water:** 0.1 sq. mi. **Elev:** 316 ft.
In south-central CA, 28 mi. northwest of Bakersfield. Incorporated Apr 13, 1915.
Name origin: For Columbus Delano (1809–96), U.S. Secretary of the Interior when the town was founded.

Edwards Air Force Base — Military Facility
ZIP: 93523 **Lat:** 34-54-34 N **Long:** 117-56-04 W
Pop: 7,423 (1990); 8,554 (1980) **Pop Density:** 498.2
Land: 14.9 sq. mi.; **Water:** 0.0 sq. mi.

Ford City — CDP
Lat: 35-09-59 N **Long:** 119-27-30 W
Pop: 3,781 (1990); 3,392 (1980) **Pop Density:** 2520.7
Land: 1.5 sq. mi.; **Water:** 0.0 sq. mi.

Frazier Park — CDP
Lat: 34-49-19 N **Long:** 118-56-43 W
Pop: 2,201 (1990); 1,444 (1980) **Pop Density:** 2000.9
Land: 1.1 sq. mi.; **Water:** 0.0 sq. mi.

Golden Hills — CDP
Lat: 35-08-32 N **Long:** 118-29-21 W
Pop: 5,423 (1990) **Pop Density:** 1291.2
Land: 4.2 sq. mi.; **Water:** 0.0 sq. mi.

Greenacres — CDP
ZIP: 93308 **Lat:** 35-23-00 N **Long:** 119-07-32 W
Pop: 7,379 (1990); 5,381 (1980) **Pop Density:** 1844.8
Land: 4.0 sq. mi.; **Water:** 0.0 sq. mi.

Kernville — CDP
ZIP: 93238 **Lat:** 35-45-41 N **Long:** 118-25-48 W
Pop: 1,656 (1990); 1,660 (1980) **Pop Density:** 162.4
Land: 10.2 sq. mi.; **Water:** 0.0 sq. mi.

Lake Isabella — CDP
ZIP: 93240 **Lat:** 35-36-54 N **Long:** 118-27-56 W
Pop: 3,323 (1990); 3,428 (1980) **Pop Density:** 420.6
Land: 7.9 sq. mi.; **Water:** 0.0 sq. mi.

Lamont — CDP
ZIP: 93241 **Lat:** 35-15-50 N **Long:** 118-54-50 W
Pop: 11,517 (1990); 9,616 (1980) **Pop Density:** 2503.7
Land: 4.6 sq. mi.; **Water:** 0.0 sq. mi.

Lost Hills — CDP
ZIP: 93249 **Lat:** 35-37-24 N **Long:** 119-41-36 W
Pop: 1,212 (1990) **Pop Density:** 2020.0
Land: 0.6 sq. mi.; **Water:** 0.0 sq. mi.

McFarland — City
ZIP: 93250 **Lat:** 35-40-44 N **Long:** 119-14-08 W
Pop: 7,005 (1990); 5,151 (1980) **Pop Density:** 3335.7
Land: 2.1 sq. mi.; **Water:** 0.0 sq. mi. **Elev:** 350 ft.
In southern CA, 23 mi. north of Bakersfield. Incorporated Jul 18, 1957.
Name origin: Named in 1908 for J.B. McFarland, one of the town's founders.

Maricopa — City
ZIP: 93252 **Lat:** 35-03-34 N **Long:** 119-24-05 W
Pop: 1,193 (1990); 946 (1980) **Pop Density:** 1704.3
Land: 0.7 sq. mi.; **Water:** 0.0 sq. mi. **Elev:** 854 ft.
In southwestern CA, southeast of Bakersfield. Incorporated Jul 25, 1911.
Name origin: For the terminus of the Southern Pacific Railroad's 1904 extension from Sunset. Sunset Valley had earlier been named Maricopa, evidently a transferred name from AZ for the Maricopa Indians on the Gila River there.

Mojave — CDP
Lat: 35-03-07 N **Long:** 118-10-47 W
Pop: 3,763 (1990); 2,886 (1980) **Pop Density:** 278.7
Land: 13.5 sq. mi.; **Water:** 0.0 sq. mi.

Mountain Mesa — CDP
Lat: 35-37-38 N **Long:** 118-24-21 W
Pop: 1,153 (1990) **Pop Density:** 1153.0
Land: 1.0 sq. mi.; **Water:** 0.0 sq. mi.

North Edwards — CDP
Lat: 35-01-08 N **Long:** 117-49-48 W
Pop: 1,259 (1990); 1,107 (1980) **Pop Density:** 292.8
Land: 4.3 sq. mi.; **Water:** 0.0 sq. mi.

Oildale — CDP
ZIP: 93308 **Lat:** 35-25-24 N **Long:** 119-01-40 W
Pop: 26,553 (1990); 23,382 (1980) **Pop Density:** 4425.5
Land: 6.0 sq. mi.; **Water:** 0.0 sq. mi.

Ridgecrest — City
ZIP: 93555 **Lat:** 35-37-51 N **Long:** 117-39-39 W
Pop: 27,725 (1990); 15,929 (1980) **Pop Density:** 1332.9
Land: 20.8 sq. mi.; **Water:** 0.3 sq. mi. **Elev:** 2289 ft.
In south-central CA, northeast of Bakersfield. Incorporated Nov 29, 1963.

Rosamond — CDP
ZIP: 93560 **Lat:** 34-51-36 N **Long:** 118-11-58 W
Pop: 7,430 (1990); 2,869 (1980) **Pop Density:** 367.8
Land: 20.2 sq. mi.; **Water:** 0.0 sq. mi.

Rosedale — CDP
Lat: 35-23-40 N **Long:** 119-12-12 W
Pop: 4,673 (1990) **Pop Density:** 122.7
Land: 38.1 sq. mi.; **Water:** 0.0 sq. mi.

Shafter — City
ZIP: 93263 **Lat:** 35-30-04 N **Long:** 119-16-21 W
Pop: 8,409 (1990); 7,010 (1980) **Pop Density:** 4425.8
Land: 1.9 sq. mi.; **Water:** 0.0 sq. mi.
In southwestern CA, 17 mi. northwest of Bakersfield. Incorporated Jan 20, 1938.
Name origin: For Gen. William "Pecos Bill" Shafter (1835–1906), commander of U.S. forces in Cuba during the Spanish-American War.

South Lake — CDP
Lat: 35-38-00 N **Long:** 118-21-20 W
Pop: 1,059 (1990) **Pop Density:** 220.6
Land: 4.8 sq. mi.; **Water:** 0.0 sq. mi.

South Taft — CDP
Lat: 35-07-37 N **Long:** 119-27-17 W
Pop: 2,170 (1990); 2,073 (1980) **Pop Density:** 1550.0
Land: 1.4 sq. mi.; **Water:** 0.0 sq. mi.

Taft — City
ZIP: 93268 **Lat:** 35-08-32 N **Long:** 119-27-17 W
Pop: 5,902 (1990); 5,316 (1980) **Pop Density:** 1639.4
Land: 3.6 sq. mi.; **Water:** 0.0 sq. mi.
In southwestern CA, 28 mi. southwest of Bakersfield. Established 1909; incorporated Nov 7, 1910.
Name origin: For newly elected William H. Taft (1857–1930), twenty-seventh U.S. president.

Taft Heights
CDP
Lat: 35-07-51 N **Long:** 119-28-24 W
Pop: 2,050 (1990); 2,111 (1980) **Pop Density:** 3416.7
Land: 0.6 sq. mi.; **Water:** 0.0 sq. mi.

Tehachapi
City
ZIP: 93561 **Lat:** 35-08-05 N **Long:** 118-26-25 W
Pop: 5,791 (1990); 4,126 (1980) **Pop Density:** 981.5
Land: 5.9 sq. mi.; **Water:** 0.0 sq. mi. **Elev:** 3973 ft.

In southwestern CA, southeast of Bakersfield. Incorporated Aug 13, 1909.

Name origin: For the nearby creek, itself named by a Pacific Railroad survey from a Yokuts Indian placename meaning 'frozen.'

Wasco
City
ZIP: 93280 **Lat:** 35-35-37 N **Long:** 119-20-27 W
Pop: 12,412 (1990); 9,613 (1980) **Pop Density:** 3878.8
Land: 3.2 sq. mi.; **Water:** 0.0 sq. mi.

In southwestern CA, northwest of Bakersfield. Incorporated Dec 22, 1945.

Name origin: For the Santa Fe station, named by settler William Bonham for his home county in OR. Originally called Dewey for the victorious admiral of the Spanish-American War.

Weedpatch
CDP
Lat: 35-14-13 N **Long:** 118-54-46 W
Pop: 1,892 (1990); 1,553 (1980) **Pop Density:** 652.4
Land: 2.9 sq. mi.; **Water:** 0.0 sq. mi.

Wofford Heights
CDP
ZIP: 93285 **Lat:** 35-42-45 N **Long:** 118-28-21 W
Pop: 2,270 (1990); 2,112 (1980) **Pop Density:** 391.4
Land: 5.8 sq. mi.; **Water:** 0.0 sq. mi.

Kings County
County Seat: Hanford (ZIP: 93230)

Pop: 101,469 (1990); 73,738 (1980) **Pop Density:** 73.0
Land: 1389.5 sq. mi.; **Water:** 2.1 sq. mi. **Area Code:** 209

In central CA, S of Fresno; organized Mar 22, 1893 from Tulare County.

Name origin: For the Kings River, which flows through the county, itself from Spanish *Rio de los Santos Reyes* 'River of the Holy Kings,' for the Biblical figures known in English as the Three Wise Men or Magi; river discovered on Jan 6, 1806, their feast day.

Armona
CDP
ZIP: 93202 **Lat:** 36-19-04 N **Long:** 119-42-21 W
Pop: 3,122 (1990); 2,644 (1980) **Pop Density:** 1643.2
Land: 1.9 sq. mi.; **Water:** 0.0 sq. mi.

Avenal
City
ZIP: 93204 **Lat:** 36-01-46 N **Long:** 120-06-52 W
Pop: 9,770 (1990); 4,137 (1980) **Pop Density:** 511.5
Land: 19.1 sq. mi.; **Water:** 0.0 sq. mi.

In southwest-central CA; incorporated Sep 11, 1979.

Name origin: For Avenal Creek, which runs through it; Spanish 'oat field.'

Corcoran
City
ZIP: 93212 **Lat:** 36-04-54 N **Long:** 119-33-35 W
Pop: 13,364 (1990); 6,454 (1980) **Pop Density:** 2344.6
Land: 5.7 sq. mi.; **Water:** 0.0 sq. mi. **Elev:** 207 ft.

In southwest-central CA, south of Fresno. Incorporated Aug 11, 1914.

Name origin: For a civil engineer of the Santa Fe Railroad.

Hanford
City
ZIP: 93230 **Lat:** 36-19-30 N **Long:** 119-38-48 W
Pop: 30,897 (1990); 20,958 (1980) **Pop Density:** 2686.7
Land: 11.5 sq. mi.; **Water:** 0.0 sq. mi.

In southwest-central CA, 30 mi. south of Fresno on the western edge of Kaweah Delta. Settled 1871; incorporated Aug 12, 1891.

Name origin: Named in 1877 for James Hanford, treasurer of the Central Pacific Railroad.

Home Garden
CDP
Lat: 36-18-11 N **Long:** 119-38-06 W
Pop: 1,549 (1990); 1,495 (1980) **Pop Density:** 2581.7
Land: 0.6 sq. mi.; **Water:** 0.0 sq. mi.

Kettleman City
CDP
ZIP: 93239 **Lat:** 36-00-31 N **Long:** 119-57-42 W
Pop: 1,411 (1990); 1,051 (1980) **Pop Density:** 7055.0
Land: 0.2 sq. mi.; **Water:** 0.0 sq. mi.

Lemoore
City
ZIP: 93245 **Lat:** 36-17-55 N **Long:** 119-47-14 W
Pop: 13,622 (1990); 8,832 (1980) **Pop Density:** 2389.8
Land: 5.7 sq. mi.; **Water:** 0.0 sq. mi.

In central CA, 28 mi. south of Fresno. Incorporated Aug 4, 1900.

Name origin: Coined from the name of the founder, Dr. Lovern Lee Moore. Previously named Latache.

Lemoore Station
Military Facility
Lat: 36-15-51 N **Long:** 119-54-13 W
Pop: 0 (1990); 5,888 (1980)
Land: 4.2 sq. mi.; **Water:** 0.0 sq. mi.

CALIFORNIA, Lake County *American Places Dictionary*

Lake County
County Seat: Lakeport (ZIP: 95453)

Pop: 50,631 (1990); 36,366 (1980) **Pop Density:** 40.2
Land: 1258.5 sq. mi.; **Water:** 71.1 sq. mi. **Area Code:** 707
In NW CA, N of San Francisco; organized May 20, 1861 from Napa County.
Name origin: For Clear Lake, the principal feature of the county.

Clearlake — City
ZIP: 95422 Lat: 38-57-29 N Long: 122-37-53 W
Pop: 11,804 (1990) Pop Density: 1146.0
Land: 10.3 sq. mi.; Water: 0.3 sq. mi.
In western CA, west of Yuba City; incorporated Nov 14, 1908.

Clearlake Oaks — CDP
ZIP: 95423 Lat: 39-01-21 N Long: 122-39-54 W
Pop: 2,419 (1990); 1,610 (1980) Pop Density: 834.1
Land: 2.9 sq. mi.; Water: 0.1 sq. mi.

Cobb — CDP
ZIP: 95426 Lat: 38-50-16 N Long: 122-43-26 W
Pop: 1,477 (1990) Pop Density: 301.4
Land: 4.9 sq. mi.; Water: 0.0 sq. mi.

Hidden Valley Lake — CDP
Lat: 38-48-30 N Long: 122-31-02 W
Pop: 1,961 (1990) Pop Density: 179.9
Land: 10.9 sq. mi.; Water: 0.1 sq. mi.

Kelseyville — CDP
ZIP: 95451 Lat: 38-57-29 N Long: 122-49-28 W
Pop: 2,861 (1990); 1,567 (1980) Pop Density: 596.0
Land: 4.8 sq. mi.; Water: 0.0 sq. mi.

Lakeport — City
ZIP: 95453 Lat: 39-02-32 N Long: 122-55-11 W
Pop: 4,390 (1990); 3,675 (1980) Pop Density: 1829.2
Land: 2.4 sq. mi.; Water: 0.1 sq. mi. Elev: 1343 ft.
In northwest-central CA, 18 mi. southeast of Ukiah on Clear Lake. Incorporated Apr 30, 1888.

Lower Lake — CDP
ZIP: 95457 Lat: 38-54-40 N Long: 122-36-36 W
Pop: 1,217 (1990); 1,043 (1980) Pop Density: 312.1
Land: 3.9 sq. mi.; Water: 0.1 sq. mi.

Lucerne — CDP
ZIP: 95458 Lat: 39-05-39 N Long: 122-48-35 W
Pop: 2,011 (1990); 1,767 (1980) Pop Density: 529.2
Land: 3.8 sq. mi.; Water: 6.2 sq. mi.
In northern CA, 48 mi. north of Santa Rosa on Clear Lake. Established Jul 2, 1926.
Name origin: For the lake in Switzerland.

Nice — CDP
ZIP: 95464 Lat: 39-07-31 N Long: 122-51-01 W
Pop: 2,126 (1990) Pop Density: 1012.4
Land: 2.1 sq. mi.; Water: 0.0 sq. mi.

Lassen County
County Seat: Susanville (ZIP: 96130)

Pop: 27,598 (1990); 21,661 (1980) **Pop Density:** 6.1
Land: 4557.5 sq. mi.; **Water:** 163.1 sq. mi. **Area Code:** 916
In NE CA; organized Apr 1, 1864 from Plumas and Shasta counties.
Name origin: For Peter Lassen (1793–1895), a Danish-born pioneer.

Susanville — City
ZIP: 96130 Lat: 40-24-39 N Long: 120-39-02 W
Pop: 7,279 (1990); 6,520 (1980) Pop Density: 2599.6
Land: 2.8 sq. mi.; Water: 0.0 sq. mi. Elev: 4258 ft.
In northeastern CA, east of Lassen Volcanic National Park. Incorporated Aug 24, 1900.
Name origin: Named in 1857 by pioneer Isaac Roop for his daughter Susan. Originally called Rooptown.

Westwood — CDP
ZIP: 96137 Lat: 40-18-11 N Long: 121-00-14 W
Pop: 2,017 (1990); 2,081 (1980) Pop Density: 353.9
Land: 5.7 sq. mi.; Water: 0.0 sq. mi.

Los Angeles County
County Seat: Los Angeles (ZIP: 90012)

Pop: 8,863,160 (1990); 7,477,240 (1980)   **Pop Density:** 2183.1
Land: 4060.0 sq. mi.; **Water:** 692.3 sq. mi.   **Area Code:** 213
On SW coast of CA; original county; organized Feb 18, 1850 (prior to statehood).
Name origin: For the city.

Acton   CDP
ZIP: 93510   **Lat:** 34-28-58 N   **Long:** 118-10-56 W
Pop: 1,471 (1990)   **Pop Density:** 319.8
Land: 4.6 sq. mi.; **Water:** 0.0 sq. mi.

Agoura Hills   City
ZIP: 91301   **Lat:** 34-09-03 N   **Long:** 118-45-35 W
Pop: 20,390 (1990)   **Pop Density:** 2486.6
Land: 8.2 sq. mi.; **Water:** 0.0 sq. mi.
In southwestern CA, 55 mi. west of Pasadena. Incorporated Dec. 8, 1982.
Name origin: Probably for Agoure, the name of a local ranching family, with a spelling variation.

Alhambra   City
ZIP: 91802   **Lat:** 34-05-02 N   **Long:** 118-08-04 W
Pop: 82,106 (1990); 64,767 (1980)   **Pop Density:** 10803.4
Land: 7.6 sq. mi.; **Water:** 0.0 sq. mi.
In southwestern CA, 5 mi. east of Los Angeles; incorporated Jul 11, 1903.
Name origin: Arabic 'the red,' an allusion to the color of the bricks used to construct the original Alhambra palace and citadel in Granada, Spain.

Alondra Park   CDP
ZIP: 90249   **Lat:** 33-53-22 N   **Long:** 118-19-47 W
Pop: 12,215 (1990); 12,096 (1980)   **Pop Density:** 7634.4
Land: 1.6 sq. mi.; **Water:** 0.0 sq. mi.

Altadena   CDP
ZIP: 91001   **Lat:** 34-11-32 N   **Long:** 118-08-04 W
Pop: 42,658 (1990); 40,510 (1980)   **Pop Density:** 4903.2
Land: 8.7 sq. mi.; **Water:** 0.0 sq. mi.

Arcadia   City
ZIP: 91006   **Lat:** 34-07-55 N   **Long:** 118-02-08 W
Pop: 48,290 (1990); 45,993 (1980)   **Pop Density:** 4430.3
Land: 10.9 sq. mi.; **Water:** 0.2 sq. mi.   **Elev:** 485 ft.
In southwestern CA, 12 mi. northeast of Los Angeles. Founded 1888; incorporated Aug 5, 1903.
Name origin: Named by Herman A. Unruh, of the San Gabriel Valley Railroad, for the district in ancient Greece.

Artesia   City
ZIP: 90701   **Lat:** 33-52-01 N   **Long:** 118-04-47 W
Pop: 15,464 (1990); 14,301 (1980)   **Pop Density:** 9665.0
Land: 1.6 sq. mi.; **Water:** 0.0 sq. mi.
In southwestern CA, 8 mi. northeast of Long Beach. Established c. 1870; incorporated May 29, 1959.
Name origin: Named by the Artesia Co., which drilled artesian wells and established the town.

Avalon   City
ZIP: 90704   **Lat:** 33-20-34 N   **Long:** 118-19-38 W
Pop: 2,918 (1990); 2,022 (1980)   **Pop Density:** 2431.7
Land: 1.2 sq. mi.; **Water:** 0.2 sq. mi.
Off the southwestern coast of CA, at the eastern end of Santa Catalina Island. Founded 1887; incorporated Jun 26, 1913.
Name origin: For the legendary elysium of King Arthur, a sort of Celtic paradise.

Avocado Heights   CDP
ZIP: 91746   **Lat:** 34-02-18 N   **Long:** 118-00-05 W
Pop: 14,232 (1990); 11,721 (1980)   **Pop Density:** 5271.1
Land: 2.7 sq. mi.; **Water:** 0.1 sq. mi.

Azusa   City
ZIP: 91702   **Lat:** 34-08-17 N   **Long:** 117-54-44 W
Pop: 41,333 (1990); 29,380 (1980)   **Pop Density:** 4592.6
Land: 9.0 sq. mi.; **Water:** 0.0 sq. mi.   **Elev:** 612 ft.
In southwestern CA, 18 mi. east-northeast of Los Angeles. Settled 1887 as a citrus center; incorporated Dec 29, 1898.
Name origin: For the Azusa Grant. Name is a corruption of an Indian word, *azuncsabit* meaning 'skunk hill.'

Baldwin Park   City
ZIP: 91706   **Lat:** 34-04-58 N   **Long:** 117-58-14 W
Pop: 69,330 (1990); 50,554 (1980)   **Pop Density:** 10504.5
Land: 6.6 sq. mi.; **Water:** 0.1 sq. mi.   **Elev:** 374 ft.
In southwestern CA, northeast of Los Angeles. Incorporated Jan 25, 1956.
Name origin: Named in 1912 for E. J. "Lucky" Baldwin (1825–1910), a spectacular 1890s financier on whose former estate, Puente de San Gabriel, the city was built.

Bel Air *See* Los Angeles

Bell   City
ZIP: 90201   **Lat:** 33-58-46 N   **Long:** 118-10-41 W
Pop: 34,365 (1990); 25,450 (1980)   **Pop Density:** 13217.3
Land: 2.6 sq. mi.; **Water:** 0.2 sq. mi.
In southwestern CA, 4 mi. south of Los Angeles. Founded 1898; incorporated Nov 7, 1927.
Name origin: For the town founders, A. and J. G. Bell.

Bellflower   City
ZIP: 90706   **Lat:** 33-53-17 N   **Long:** 118-07-35 W
Pop: 61,815 (1990); 53,441 (1980)   **Pop Density:** 10133.6
Land: 6.1 sq. mi.; **Water:** 0.0 sq. mi.   **Elev:** 71 ft.
In southern CA, 12 mi. north of Long Beach. Incorporated Sep 3, 1957.
Name origin: For an orchard of bellflower apples on the ranch on which the town was laid out. Originally named Somerset.

CALIFORNIA, Los Angeles County American Places Dictionary

Bell Gardens City
ZIP: 90201 Lat: 33-58-02 N Long: 118-09-09 W
Pop: 42,355 (1990); 34,117 (1980) Pop Density: 16942.0
Land: 2.5 sq. mi.; Water: 0.0 sq. mi.
In southwestern CA, 15 mi. north of Long Beach. Established in 1930s; incorporated Aug 1, 1961.
Name origin: When the vegetable tracts developed by Japanese gardeners were subdivided in 1930, the area was named for them and for nearby Bell.

Beverly Hills City
ZIP: 90210 Lat: 34-04-45 N Long: 118-24-04 W
Pop: 31,971 (1990); 32,646 (1980) Pop Density: 5608.9
Land: 5.7 sq. mi.; Water: 0.0 sq. mi. Elev: 225 ft.
In southwestern CA, 16 mi. southwest of downtown Los Angeles and entirely surrounded by that city. An exclusive residential city, the site of early movie stars' mansions; founded 1906; incorporated Jan 28, 1914.
Name origin: Named by Burton E. Green, president of the Rodeo Land and Water Co. for Beverly Farms, MA, suggested by a newspaper account of a vacation by President William Howard Taft (1857–1930).

Bradbury City
ZIP: 91010 Lat: 34-09-08 N Long: 117-58-06 W
Pop: 829 (1990); 846 (1980) Pop Density: 487.6
Land: 1.7 sq. mi.; Water: 0.0 sq. mi.
Incorporated Jul 26, 1957.
Name origin: For L.L. Bradbury, owner of the property at the turn of the century.

Burbank City
ZIP: 91505 Lat: 34-11-28 N Long: 118-19-32 W
Pop: 93,643 (1990); 84,625 (1980) Pop Density: 5412.9
Land: 17.3 sq. mi.; Water: 0.0 sq. mi. Elev: 598 ft.
In southwestern CA, 10 mi. northwest of Los Angeles. Founded in 1887; incorporated Jul 8, 1911.
Name origin: For one of the subdividers of the Providencia Rancho, Dr. David Burbank (c. 1821–?), a Los Angeles dentist.

Canoga Park See **Los Angeles**

Carson City
ZIP: 90745 Lat: 33-50-10 N Long: 118-15-28 W
Pop: 83,995 (1990); 81,221 (1980) Pop Density: 4467.8
Land: 18.8 sq. mi.; Water: 0.1 sq. mi.
In southwestern CA, 15 mi. northwest of Long Beach. Incorporated Feb 20, 1968.
Name origin: Probably for Kit (Christopher) Carson (1809–68), trapper, frontier guide, and Indian agent.

Century City See **Los Angeles**

Cerritos City
ZIP: 90703 Lat: 33-52-03 N Long: 118-04-06 W
Pop: 53,240 (1990); 53,020 (1980) Pop Density: 6190.7
Land: 8.6 sq. mi.; Water: 0.3 sq. mi.
In southwestern CA, 27 mi. southeast of Los Angeles. Incorporated Apr 24, 1956.
Name origin: From Spanish 'hillocks.' Railroad name was Dairy Valley; changed to present name in 1956.

Charter Oak CDP
ZIP: 91724 Lat: 34-06-08 N Long: 117-51-13 W
Pop: 8,858 (1990) Pop Density: 9842.2
Land: 0.9 sq. mi.; Water: 0.0 sq. mi.

Citrus CDP
ZIP: 91702 Lat: 34-06-53 N Long: 117-53-27 W
Pop: 9,481 (1990); 12,450 (1980) Pop Density: 10534.4
Land: 0.9 sq. mi.; Water: 0.0 sq. mi.

Claremont City
ZIP: 91711 Lat: 34-07-18 N Long: 117-42-56 W
Pop: 32,503 (1990); 31,028 (1980) Pop Density: 2954.8
Land: 11.0 sq. mi.; Water: 0.2 sq. mi. Elev: 1169 ft.
In southwestern CA, 27 mi. east of Los Angeles. Platted 1887; incorporated Oct 3, 1907.
Name origin: For Claremont, NH, home of the director of a development company.

Commerce City
ZIP: 90040 Lat: 33-59-43 N Long: 118-09-00 W
Pop: 12,135 (1990); 10,509 (1980) Pop Density: 1866.9
Land: 6.5 sq. mi.; Water: 0.0 sq. mi.
In southwestern CA, 34 mi. north of Long Beach. Incorporated Jan 28, 1960.
Name origin: Named in the hope that the town would develop into a thriving business community.

Compton City
ZIP: 90221 Lat: 33-53-33 N Long: 118-13-35 W
Pop: 90,454 (1990); 81,350 (1980) Pop Density: 8868.0
Land: 10.2 sq. mi.; Water: 0.1 sq. mi. Elev: 66 ft.
In southwestern CA, 12 mi. south of Los Angeles. Incorporated May 11, 1888.
Name origin: For the railroad station, named in 1869 for Griffith D. Compton (1820–1905), founder of both a Methodist temperance colony and the University of Southern CA.

Covina City
ZIP: 91722 Lat: 34-05-24 N Long: 117-52-51 W
Pop: 43,207 (1990); 32,746 (1980) Pop Density: 6261.9
Land: 6.9 sq. mi.; Water: 0.0 sq. mi. Elev: 546 ft.
In southwestern CA, 18 mi. east of Los Angeles. Incorporated Aug 14, 1901.
Name origin: Locally said to mean 'place of vines'; name was given to a subdivision of La Puente Rancho in the late 1880s.

Cudahy City
ZIP: 90201 Lat: 33-57-51 N Long: 118-10-54 W
Pop: 22,817 (1990); 18,275 (1980) Pop Density: 20742.7
Land: 1.1 sq. mi.; Water: 0.0 sq. mi. Elev: 121 ft.
In southwestern CA, 20 mi. southeast of Los Angeles. Incorporated Nov 10, 1960.
Name origin: Either for Patrick Cudahy, merchant and meat-packing industrialist, or Cudahy, WI.

Culver City City
ZIP: 90230 Lat: 34-00-20 N Long: 118-23-46 W
Pop: 38,793 (1990); 38,139 (1980) Pop Density: 7606.5
Land: 5.1 sq. mi.; Water: 0.0 sq. mi. Elev: 94 ft.
In southwestern CA, 20 mi. southwest of Los Angeles. Incorporated Sep 17, 1917.
Name origin: Named for Harry H. Culver, who came from NE in 1914 and acquired and subdivided part of the Ballona land grant.

Del Aire CDP
ZIP: 90250 Lat: 33-54-57 N Long: 118-22-07 W
Pop: 8,040 (1990) Pop Density: 8040.0
Land: 1.0 sq. mi.; Water: 0.0 sq. mi.

Desert View Highlands CDP
Lat: 34-35-23 N Long: 118-09-09 W
Pop: 2,154 (1990); 2,175 (1980) Pop Density: 4308.0
Land: 0.5 sq. mi.; Water: 0.0 sq. mi.

Diamond Bar City
ZIP: 91765 Lat: 33-59-57 N Long: 117-48-51 W
Pop: 53,672 (1990); 28,045 (1980) Pop Density: 3554.4
Land: 15.1 sq. mi.; Water: 0.0 sq. mi.

In southwestern CA, southeast of San Bernardino. Incorporated Apr 18, 1989.

Name origin: Probably for the discovery of diamonds or diamond-like quartz crystals.

Downey City
ZIP: 90241 Lat: 33-56-17 N Long: 118-07-47 W
Pop: 91,444 (1990); 82,602 (1980) Pop Density: 7374.5
Land: 12.4 sq. mi.; Water: 0.2 sq. mi. Elev: 119 ft.

In southwestern CA, 10 mi. southeast of Los Angeles. Incorporated Dec 17, 1956.

Name origin: For John Gately Downey (1827–94), governor of CA (1860–62) and divider of the land on which the town was built.

Duarte City
ZIP: 91010 Lat: 34-09-28 N Long: 117-57-11 W
Pop: 20,688 (1990); 16,766 (1980) Pop Density: 2873.3
Land: 7.2 sq. mi.; Water: 0.0 sq. mi. Elev: 510 ft.

In southwestern CA, 22 mi. east of Pasadena. Incorporated Aug 22, 1957.

Name origin: For Andres Duarte, the original ranchero of the region, who settled on his Rancho Azusas in 1841.

East Compton CDP
ZIP: 90221 Lat: 33-53-53 N Long: 118-11-39 W
Pop: 7,967 (1990); 6,435 (1980) Pop Density: 15934.0
Land: 0.5 sq. mi.; Water: 0.0 sq. mi.

East La Mirada CDP
ZIP: 90638 Lat: 33-55-27 N Long: 117-59-17 W
Pop: 9,367 (1990); 9,688 (1980) Pop Density: 8515.5
Land: 1.1 sq. mi.; Water: 0.0 sq. mi.

East Los Angeles CDP
ZIP: 90022 Lat: 34-01-57 N Long: 118-10-06 W
Pop: 126,379 (1990); 109,594 (1980) Pop Density: 16850.5
Land: 7.5 sq. mi.; Water: 0.0 sq. mi.

In southwestern CA, part of Los Angeles.

East Pasadena CDP
ZIP: 91107 Lat: 34-08-17 N Long: 118-04-36 W
Pop: 5,910 (1990) Pop Density: 4546.2
Land: 1.3 sq. mi.; Water: 0.0 sq. mi.

East San Gabriel CDP
Lat: 34-07-11 N Long: 118-04-46 W
Pop: 12,736 (1990) Pop Density: 8490.7
Land: 1.5 sq. mi.; Water: 0.0 sq. mi.

El Monte City
ZIP: 91731 Lat: 34-04-29 N Long: 118-01-40 W
Pop: 106,209 (1990); 79,494 (1980) Pop Density: 11179.9
Land: 9.5 sq. mi.; Water: 0.1 sq. mi. Elev: 283 ft.

In southwestern CA, 12 mi. east of Los Angeles. Settled 1852; incorporated Nov 18, 1912.

Name origin: From Spanish 'thicket,' referring to a dense growth of willows.

El Segundo City
ZIP: 90245 Lat: 33-54-38 N Long: 118-25-29 W
Pop: 15,223 (1990); 13,752 (1980) Pop Density: 2767.8
Land: 5.5 sq. mi.; Water: 5.3 sq. mi.

In southwestern CA, 14 mi. southwest of Los Angeles near Santa Monica Bay. Incorporated Jan 18, 1917.

Name origin: Named in 1911 by Col. Pheem of the Standard Oil Co., from Spanish 'the second,' referring to their second refinery in the state.

Encino *See* Los Angeles

Florence-Graham CDP
ZIP: 90001 Lat: 33-58-01 N Long: 118-14-39 W
Pop: 57,147 (1990); 48,662 (1980) Pop Density: 15874.2
Land: 3.6 sq. mi.; Water: 0.0 sq. mi.

Gardena City
ZIP: 90247 Lat: 33-53-36 N Long: 118-18-17 W
Pop: 49,847 (1990); 45,165 (1980) Pop Density: 9405.1
Land: 5.3 sq. mi.; Water: 0.0 sq. mi.

In southwestern CA, a southern suburb of Los Angeles. Incorporated Sep 11, 1930.

Name origin: Named in 1880 with a poetic version of 'garden,' for the fertile land.

Glendale City
ZIP: 91209 Lat: 34-10-36 N Long: 118-15-11 W
Pop: 180,038 (1990); 139,060 (1980) Pop Density: 5883.6
Land: 30.6 sq. mi.; Water: 0.0 sq. mi.

In southwestern CA, 6 mi. north of Los Angeles at the Coastal Plain entrance of the San Fernando Valley. Founded 1880; incorporated Feb 16, 1906.

Name origin: Originally known as Riverdale, then Mason; present name adopted c. 1890.

Glendora City
ZIP: 91740 Lat: 34-08-45 N Long: 117-50-38 W
Pop: 47,828 (1990); 38,500 (1980) Pop Density: 2452.7
Land: 19.5 sq. mi.; Water: 0.1 sq. mi. Elev: 776 ft.

In southwestern CA, 22 mi. east-northeast of Los Angeles. Incorporated Nov 13, 1911.

Name origin: Name coined in 1887 by Chicago manufacturer, George Whitcomb, from *glen* and Le*dora*, his wife's name.

Hacienda Heights CDP
ZIP: 91745 Lat: 33-59-44 N Long: 117-58-16 W
Pop: 52,354 (1990); 49,422 (1980) Pop Density: 4716.6
Land: 11.1 sq. mi.; Water: 0.0 sq. mi.

Hawaiian Gardens City
ZIP: 90716 Lat: 33-49-49 N Long: 118-04-18 W
Pop: 13,639 (1990); 10,548 (1980) Pop Density: 15154.4
Land: 0.9 sq. mi.; Water: 0.0 sq. mi. Elev: 29 ft.

In southwestern CA, 19 mi. southeast of Los Angeles. Incorporated Apr 9, 1964.

Hawthorne City
ZIP: 90250 Lat: 33-54-52 N Long: 118-20-49 W
Pop: 71,349 (1990); 56,437 (1980) Pop Density: 12093.1
Land: 5.9 sq. mi.; Water: 0.0 sq. mi. Elev: 69 ft.

In southwestern CA, 12 mi. southwest of Los Angeles. Incorporated Jul 12, 1922.

Name origin: For American novelist Nathaniel Hawthorne (1804–64) by Mrs. Laurine H. Woolwine, daughter of H.D. Harding, one of the town founders.

CALIFORNIA, Los Angeles County

Hermosa Beach — City
ZIP: 90254 Lat: 33-51-06 N Long: 118-25-21 W
Pop: 18,219 (1990); 18,070 (1980) Pop Density: 13013.6
Land: 1.4 sq. mi.; Water: 4.5 sq. mi. Elev: 15 ft.
On the southwestern coast of CA, 15 mi. south of Los Angeles, between Manhattan and Redondo beaches. Incorporated Jan 14, 1907.
Name origin: Named by the Hermosa Beach Land and Water Co. in 1901; from Spanish 'beautiful.'

Hidden Hills — City
Lat: 34-10-03 N Long: 118-39-35 W
Pop: 1,729 (1990); 1,760 (1980) Pop Density: 1080.6
Land: 1.6 sq. mi.; Water: 0.0 sq. mi.
In southwestern CA, northeast of Malibu. Incorporated Oct 19, 1961.

Hollywood See Los Angeles

Huntington Park — City
ZIP: 90255 Lat: 33-58-49 N Long: 118-12-54 W
Pop: 56,065 (1990); 45,932 (1980) Pop Density: 18085.5
Land: 3.1 sq. mi.; Water: 0.0 sq. mi.
In southwestern CA, 4 mi. south of Los Angeles. Incorporated Sep 1, 1906.

Industry — City
Lat: 34-00-48 N Long: 117-55-17 W
Pop: 631 (1990); 412 (1980) Pop Density: 54.4
Land: 11.6 sq. mi.; Water: 0.2 sq. mi. Elev: 329 ft.

Inglewood — City
ZIP: 90301 Lat: 33-57-21 N Long: 118-20-37 W
Pop: 109,602 (1990); 94,162 (1980) Pop Density: 11913.3
Land: 9.2 sq. mi.; Water: 0.0 sq. mi.
In southwestern CA, 9 mi. southwest of Los Angeles. Founded 1873; incorporated Feb 14, 1908. Noted for its sports center, the Forum, and for Hollywood Park, the thoroughbred horse racing track.
Name origin: For the Canadian home town of its founder, Daniel Freeman.

Irwindale — City
ZIP: 91706 Lat: 34-06-42 N Long: 117-58-03 W
Pop: 1,050 (1990); 1,030 (1980) Pop Density: 112.9
Land: 9.3 sq. mi.; Water: 0.2 sq. mi. Elev: 467 ft.
In southwestern CA, 26 mi. north of Santa Ana. Incorporated Aug 6, 1957.
Name origin: For a local citrus grower.

La Cañada Flintridge — City
ZIP: 91011 Lat: 34-12-37 N Long: 118-12-01 W
Pop: 19,378 (1990); 20,153 (1980) Pop Density: 2227.4
Land: 8.7 sq. mi.; Water: 0.0 sq. mi.
In southwestern CA northwest of Pasadena. Flintridge incorporated Dec 8, 1976 with La Cañada.
Name origin: From Spanish *la cañada* 'valley' or 'glen'; Flintridge for Frank P. Flint (1862–1929), U.S. senator from CA (1905–11), who subdivided part of Rancho la Cañada in 1920.

La Crescenta-Montrose — CDP
ZIP: 91214 Lat: 34-14-01 N Long: 118-14-06 W
Pop: 16,968 (1990); 16,531 (1980) Pop Density: 4990.6
Land: 3.4 sq. mi.; Water: 0.0 sq. mi.

Ladera Heights — CDP
ZIP: 90045 Lat: 33-59-38 N Long: 118-22-28 W
Pop: 6,316 (1990); 6,647 (1980) Pop Density: 2870.9
Land: 2.2 sq. mi.; Water: 0.0 sq. mi.

La Habra Heights — City
ZIP: 90631 Lat: 33-57-43 N Long: 117-57-01 W
Pop: 6,226 (1990); 4,786 (1980) Pop Density: 972.8
Land: 6.4 sq. mi.; Water: 0.0 sq. mi.
Incorporated Dec 4, 1978.

Lake Los Angeles — CDP
ZIP: 93550 Lat: 34-36-42 N Long: 117-49-36 W
Pop: 7,977 (1990) Pop Density: 1628.0
Land: 4.9 sq. mi.; Water: 0.1 sq. mi.

Lakewood — City
ZIP: 90714 Lat: 33-50-55 N Long: 118-07-19 W
Pop: 73,557 (1990); 74,511 (1980) Pop Density: 7825.2
Land: 9.4 sq. mi.; Water: 0.1 sq. mi.
In southwestern CA, northeast of Long Beach near Bouton Lake. Laid out 1934; incorporated Apr 16, 1954.

La Mirada — City
ZIP: 90638 Lat: 33-54-07 N Long: 118-00-31 W
Pop: 40,452 (1990); 40,986 (1980) Pop Density: 5120.5
Land: 7.9 sq. mi.; Water: 0.0 sq. mi. Elev: 181 ft.
In southwestern CA, 17 mi. southeast of Los Angeles. Incorporated Mar 23, 1960.
Name origin: For the Santa Fe station; from Spanish 'the glance.'

Lancaster — City
ZIP: 93534 Lat: 34-41-35 N Long: 118-10-35 W
Pop: 97,291 (1990); 48,027 (1980) Pop Density: 1095.6
Land: 88.8 sq. mi.; Water: 0.1 sq. mi. Elev: 2355 ft.
In south-central CA, in the Mojave Desert. Founded 1877 by settlers from PA; incorporated Nov 22, 1977. A major agricultural shipping center.
Name origin: Origin of the name is uncertain: possibly for a railroad official, or for Lancaster, PA.

La Puente — City
ZIP: 91744 Lat: 34-01-56 N Long: 117-57-08 W
Pop: 36,955 (1990); 30,882 (1980) Pop Density: 10558.6
Land: 3.5 sq. mi.; Water: 0.0 sq. mi.
In southwestern CA, northeast of Long Beach. Incorporated Aug 1, 1956.
Name origin: For the railroad station named from Spanish 'the bridge,' because the Portola expedition of 1769 had to build a bridge to cross the nearby San Jose Creek.

La Verne — City
ZIP: 91750 Lat: 34-07-05 N Long: 117-46-15 W
Pop: 30,897 (1990); 23,508 (1980) Pop Density: 3961.2
Land: 7.8 sq. mi.; Water: 0.1 sq. mi.
In southwestern CA, 24 mi. east of Los Angeles. Incorporated Aug 20, 1906.
Name origin: Named in 1916 for La Verne Heights, a nearby subdivision named for the promoter. Originally called Lordsburg, for I.W. Lord, who laid out the town.

Lawndale — City
ZIP: 90260 **Lat:** 33-53-18 N **Long:** 118-21-09 W
Pop: 27,331 (1990); 23,460 (1980) **Pop Density:** 13665.5
Land: 2.0 sq. mi.; **Water:** 0.0 sq. mi. **Elev:** 55 ft.

In southwestern CA, 12 mi. northwest of Long Beach. Incorporated Dec 28, 1959.

Name origin: For a station of the Northwestern Pacific Railroad.

Lennox — CDP
ZIP: 90304 **Lat:** 33-56-23 N **Long:** 118-21-27 W
Pop: 22,757 (1990); 18,445 (1980) **Pop Density:** 18964.2
Land: 1.2 sq. mi.; **Water:** 0.0 sq. mi.

Littlerock — CDP
ZIP: 93543 **Lat:** 34-31-30 N **Long:** 117-59-05 W
Pop: 1,320 (1990) **Pop Density:** 880.0
Land: 1.5 sq. mi.; **Water:** 0.0 sq. mi.

Lomita — City
ZIP: 90717 **Lat:** 33-47-36 N **Long:** 118-19-02 W
Pop: 19,382 (1990); 18,807 (1980) **Pop Density:** 10201.1
Land: 1.9 sq. mi.; **Water:** 0.0 sq. mi.

In southwestern CA, 7 mi. west of Long Beach. Incorporated Jan 30, 1964.

Name origin: Mexican-Spanish diminutive of *loma*, 'long, low hill.'

Long Beach — City
ZIP: 90801 **Lat:** 33-47-20 N **Long:** 118-09-35 W
Pop: 429,433 (1990); 361,498 (1980) **Pop Density:** 8588.7
Land: 50.0 sq. mi.; **Water:** 15.4 sq. mi. **Elev:** 29 ft.

On the southwestern coast of CA, 19 mi. south of Los Angeles on San Pedro Bay. Incorporated Dec 13, 1897. A seaside resort and industrial center (oil, shipping, and manufacturing).

Name origin: Originally named Willmore City for W.E. Willmore, who subdivided the area. In 1887 the Long Beach Land and Water Co. acquired the city's interests and renamed it.

Los Angeles — City
ZIP: 90086 **Lat:** 34-06-43 N **Long:** 118-24-40 W
Pop: 3,485,398 (1990); 2,968,528 (1980)
Pop Density: 7426.8
Land: 469.3 sq. mi.; **Water:** 29.1 sq. mi. **Elev:** 330 ft.

In southwestern CA. Founded 1781 by monks of the San Gabriel mission; incorporated Apr 4, 1850. The county forms the Los Angeles metropolitan area. The city is the industrial, financial, and trade center of the western U.S.; the largest manufacturing center in the U.S.; and the major TV and film center. Site of the University of California. Includes the following unincorporated places: Bel Air, Canoga Park, Century City, Encino, Hollywood, Pacific Palisades, Sepulveda, Sherman Oaks, Studio City, Tarzana, Van Nuys, Watts.

Name origin: From the name given to the river by Spanish Franciscan monk Fr. Juan Crespi of the Portolá expedition. The name honors Our Lady of the Angels of the Porciuncula, Spanish *El Pueblo do la Reina Nuestra Señora de los Angeles de Porciuncula*, given to the river because the expedition camped on its banks on the feast day, Aug 1, 1769. The Porciuncula chapel in Assisi, Italy, is the cradle of the Franciscan order. The official pronunciation, announced Sep 12, 1952, by a jury appointed by the mayor, is "laws ANN jeh les."

Lynwood — City
ZIP: 90262 **Lat:** 33-55-25 N **Long:** 118-12-05 W
Pop: 61,945 (1990); 48,289 (1980) **Pop Density:** 12641.8
Land: 4.9 sq. mi.; **Water:** 0.0 sq. mi.

In southwestern CA, 7 mi. south of Los Angeles. Incorporated Jul 16, 1921.

Name origin: Named for Lynn Wood Sessions, wife of a local dairy owner.

Manhattan Beach — City
ZIP: 90266 **Lat:** 33-53-42 N **Long:** 118-25-16 W
Pop: 32,063 (1990); 31,542 (1980) **Pop Density:** 8221.3
Land: 3.9 sq. mi.; **Water:** 6.4 sq. mi.

On the southwestern coast of CA, 12 mi. south of Los Angeles. Incorporated Dec 7, 1912.

Name origin: Named by founder Stewart Merrill for Manhattan, NY. Formerly called Shore Acres.

Marina del Rey — CDP
ZIP: 90292 **Lat:** 33-58-49 N **Long:** 118-27-03 W
Pop: 7,431 (1990); 8,065 (1980) **Pop Density:** 8256.7
Land: 0.9 sq. mi.; **Water:** 0.6 sq. mi.

Mayflower Village — CDP
Lat: 34-06-53 N **Long:** 118-00-32 W
Pop: 4,978 (1990); 5,017 (1980) **Pop Density:** 7111.4
Land: 0.7 sq. mi.; **Water:** 0.0 sq. mi.

Maywood — City
ZIP: 90270 **Lat:** 33-59-20 N **Long:** 118-11-15 W
Pop: 27,850 (1990); 21,810 (1980) **Pop Density:** 23208.3
Land: 1.2 sq. mi.; **Water:** 0.0 sq. mi.

In southwestern CA, 4 mi. southeast of Los Angeles. Incorporated Sep 2, 1924.

Monrovia — City
ZIP: 91016 **Lat:** 34-09-48 N **Long:** 117-59-25 W
Pop: 35,761 (1990); 30,531 (1980) **Pop Density:** 2668.7
Land: 13.4 sq. mi.; **Water:** 0.1 sq. mi.

In southwestern CA, 14 mi. east-northeast of Los Angeles. Incorporated Dec 15, 1887.

Name origin: For William N. Monroe (1841–1925), a railroad construction engineer who, with his associates, laid out the town in 1886 on 60 acres of ranchos Santa Anita and Azusa de Duarte.

Montebello — City
ZIP: 90640 **Lat:** 34-00-55 N **Long:** 118-06-35 W
Pop: 59,564 (1990); 52,929 (1980) **Pop Density:** 7176.4
Land: 8.3 sq. mi.; **Water:** 0.1 sq. mi.

In southwestern CA, 8 mi. southeast of Los Angeles. Incorporated Oct 16, 1920.

Name origin: Town originally called Newmark for Harris Newmark, who, in 1887, bought part of the Repetto Ranch called Montebello, Italian for 'beautiful mountain.' Name was changed on incorporation.

Monterey Park — City
ZIP: 91754 **Lat:** 34-02-48 N **Long:** 118-07-50 W
Pop: 60,738 (1990); 54,338 (1980) **Pop Density:** 7991.8
Land: 7.6 sq. mi.; **Water:** 0.0 sq. mi. **Elev:** 381 ft.

In southwestern CA, 8 mi. east of Los Angeles. Incorporated May 29, 1916.

Name origin: For Monterey Pass to the west (now called Coyote Pass). Previously called Ramona Acres.

North El Monte
CDP
Lat: 34-06-10 N Long: 118-01-24 W
Pop: 3,384 (1990) **Pop Density:** 8460.0
Land: 0.4 sq. mi.; **Water:** 0.0 sq. mi.

Norwalk
City
ZIP: 90650 Lat: 33-54-24 N Long: 118-04-56 W
Pop: 94,279 (1990); 84,901 (1980) **Pop Density:** 9620.3
Land: 9.8 sq. mi.; **Water:** 0.1 sq. mi.
In southwestern CA, southeast of Los Angeles. Settled by Atwood and Gilbert Sproul 1877; incorporated Aug 26, 1957.
Name origin: Originally named Corvallis, the former OR home town of the original settlers; renamed on the establishment of the post office in 1879 for the former CT home of other settlers.

Pacific Palisades *See* Los Angeles

Palmdale
City
ZIP: 93550 Lat: 34-36-19 N Long: 118-05-10 W
Pop: 68,842 (1990); 12,277 (1980) **Pop Density:** 887.1
Land: 77.6 sq. mi.; **Water:** 0.1 sq. mi. **Elev:** 2659 ft.
In southwestern CA, south of Lancaster. Founded 1886 by German Lutherans; incorporated Aug 24, 1962.
Name origin: For the Joshua tree, sometimes called the yucca palm. Originally called Palmenthal; name changed Aug 13, 1890.

Palmdale East
CDP
Lat: 34-34-54 N Long: 118-04-18 W
Pop: 3,052 (1990); 2,920 (1980) **Pop Density:** 6104.0
Land: 0.5 sq. mi.; **Water:** 0.0 sq. mi.

Palos Verdes Estates
City
ZIP: 90274 Lat: 33-47-15 N Long: 118-23-46 W
Pop: 13,512 (1990); 14,376 (1980) **Pop Density:** 2815.0
Land: 4.8 sq. mi.; **Water:** 0.0 sq. mi. **Elev:** 217 ft.
In southwestern CA, 18 mi. south of Los Angeles. Founded 1922; incorporated Dec 20, 1939.
Name origin: For Cañada de los Palos Verdes, from Spanish 'valley of green trees,' now known as Bixby Slough.

Paramount
City
ZIP: 90723 Lat: 33-53-43 N Long: 118-09-50 W
Pop: 47,669 (1990); 36,407 (1980) **Pop Density:** 10142.3
Land: 4.7 sq. mi.; **Water:** 0.1 sq. mi. **Elev:** 67 ft.
In southwestern CA, 13 mi. southeast of Los Angeles. Settled 1866; incorporated Jan 30, 1957.
Name origin: Named in 1948 at the merger of Hynes and Clearwater cities for Paramount Boulevard, the main thoroughfare, itself named for the movie company.

Pasadena
City
ZIP: 91109 Lat: 34-09-38 N Long: 118-08-19 W
Pop: 131,591 (1990); 118,072 (1980) **Pop Density:** 5721.3
Land: 23.0 sq. mi.; **Water:** 0.2 sq. mi. **Elev:** 865 ft.
In southwestern CA in the foothills of the Sierra Madre Mountains, 7 mi. northeast of Los Angeles. Founded 1874; incorporated Jun 19, 1886. Site of the New Year's Day Tournament of Roses Parade and the Rose Bowl football game.
Name origin: Believed to be from Ojibway Indian 'crown of the valley.'

Pico Rivera
City
ZIP: 90660 Lat: 33-59-23 N Long: 118-05-17 W
Pop: 59,177 (1990); 53,387 (1980) **Pop Density:** 7397.1
Land: 8.0 sq. mi.; **Water:** 0.4 sq. mi. **Elev:** 161 ft.
In southwestern CA, 17 mi. southeast of Los Angeles. Incorporated Jan 29, 1958.
Name origin: Chosen at the incorporation of two towns, *Pico*, named for Po Pico, governor of Mexican CA, and *Rivera* 'brook, stream,' referring to the San Gabriel River and Rio Hondo, between which the town is located.

Point Dume
CDP
Lat: 34-00-52 N Long: 118-48-06 W
Pop: 2,809 (1990); 2,438 (1980) **Pop Density:** 1652.4
Land: 1.7 sq. mi.; **Water:** 0.0 sq. mi.

Pomona
City
ZIP: 91768 Lat: 34-03-32 N Long: 117-45-41 W
Pop: 131,723 (1990); 92,742 (1980) **Pop Density:** 5777.3
Land: 22.8 sq. mi.; **Water:** 0.0 sq. mi.
In southwestern CA, 14 mi. east of Los Angeles. Established 1875; incorporated Jan 6, 1888.
Name origin: For the ancient Roman goddess of orchards and gardens; named by nurseryman Solomon Gates.

Quartz Hill
CDP
ZIP: 93536 Lat: 34-39-07 N Long: 118-12-53 W
Pop: 9,626 (1990); 5,522 (1980) **Pop Density:** 2468.2
Land: 3.9 sq. mi.; **Water:** 0.0 sq. mi.

Rancho Palos Verdes
City
ZIP: 90717 Lat: 33-45-29 N Long: 118-21-46 W
Pop: 41,659 (1990); 36,577 (1980) **Pop Density:** 3040.8
Land: 13.7 sq. mi.; **Water:** 0.0 sq. mi.
On the southwestern coast of CA, 11 mi. west of Long Beach. Incorporated Sep 7, 1973.
Name origin: Spanish 'ranch of the green trees.'

Redondo Beach
City
ZIP: 90277 Lat: 33-51-23 N Long: 118-22-34 W
Pop: 60,167 (1990); 57,102 (1980) **Pop Density:** 9550.3
Land: 6.3 sq. mi.; **Water:** 0.1 sq. mi. **Elev:** 59 ft.
On the southwestern coast of CA, 16 mi. south of Los Angeles. Founded 1881; incorporated Apr 29, 1892.
Name origin: From Spanish 'round' from the adjacent Rancho Sausal Redondo, 'round willow grove.'

Rolling Hills
City
Lat: 33-45-42 N Long: 118-20-30 W
Pop: 1,871 (1990); 2,049 (1980) **Pop Density:** 603.5
Land: 3.1 sq. mi.; **Water:** 0.0 sq. mi.
In southwestern CA, south of Los Angeles. Incorporated Jan 24, 1957.

Rolling Hills Estates
City
ZIP: 90274 Lat: 33-46-57 N Long: 118-21-07 W
Pop: 7,789 (1990); 7,701 (1980) **Pop Density:** 2225.4
Land: 3.5 sq. mi.; **Water:** 0.0 sq. mi.
In southwestern CA, south of Los Angeles. Incorporated Sep 18, 1957.

Rosemead
City
ZIP: 91770 Lat: 34-04-07 N Long: 118-04-54 W
Pop: 51,638 (1990); 42,604 (1980) **Pop Density:** 10125.1
Land: 5.1 sq. mi.; **Water:** 0.0 sq. mi.
In southwestern CA, 11 mi. east of Los Angeles. Incorporated Aug 4, 1959.
Name origin: Named in the 1870s for the famous horse farm

on Leonard J. Rose's Sunny Slope estate; a combination of his name and *meadow*, which was later shortened to *mead*.

Rowland Heights CDP
ZIP: 91748 **Lat:** 33-58-47 N **Long:** 117-53-29 W
Pop: 42,647 (1990); 28,252 (1980) **Pop Density:** 5200.9
Land: 8.2 sq. mi.; **Water:** 0.0 sq. mi.

San Dimas City
ZIP: 91773 **Lat:** 34-06-32 N **Long:** 117-48-25 W
Pop: 32,397 (1990); 24,014 (1980) **Pop Density:** 2090.1
Land: 15.5 sq. mi.; **Water:** 0.1 sq. mi. **Elev:** 952 ft.

In southwestern CA, 25 mi. east of Los Angeles. Incorporated Aug 4, 1960.

Name origin: Spanish for St. Dismas, the name given to the penitent thief crucified with Christ. Previously named Mud Springs.

San Fernando City
ZIP: 91341 **Lat:** 34-17-22 N **Long:** 118-26-05 W
Pop: 22,580 (1990); 17,731 (1980) **Pop Density:** 9408.3
Land: 2.4 sq. mi.; **Water:** 0.0 sq. mi. **Elev:** 1061 ft.

In southwestern CA, 20 mi. northwest of Los Angeles. Mission founded Sep 8, 1797; incorporated Aug 31, 1911.

Name origin: For the mission, which was named for Ferdinand III (1200–52), King of Castile and Leon, later canonized.

San Gabriel City
ZIP: 91776 **Lat:** 34-05-40 N **Long:** 118-05-51 W
Pop: 37,120 (1990); 30,072 (1980) **Pop Density:** 9053.7
Land: 4.1 sq. mi.; **Water:** 0.0 sq. mi.

In southwestern CA, 7 mi. northeast of Los Angeles. Incorporated Apr 24, 1913.

Name origin: For the mission named for Gabriel the archangel.

San Marino City
ZIP: 91108 **Lat:** 34-07-21 N **Long:** 118-06-43 W
Pop: 12,959 (1990); 13,307 (1980) **Pop Density:** 3410.3
Land: 3.8 sq. mi.; **Water:** 0.0 sq. mi. **Elev:** 566 ft.

In southwestern CA, 10 mi. northeast of Los Angeles. Incorporated Apr 25, 1913.

Name origin: For James de Barth Shorb's estate, named for his birthplace in Emmitsburg, MD. The estate is now the site of the Huntington Library and Art Gallery.

Santa Clarita City
ZIP: 91380 **Lat:** 34-24-48 N **Long:** 118-30-36 W
Pop: 110,642 (1990) **Pop Density:** 2731.9
Land: 40.5 sq. mi.; **Water:** 0.0 sq. mi.

In southwestern CA, northwest of Los Angeles, 1 mi. south of Saugus, near the Santa Clara River. Incorporated Dec 15, 1987.

Name origin: Diminutive for St. Clare of Assisi.

Santa Fe Springs City
ZIP: 90670 **Lat:** 33-56-00 N **Long:** 118-03-41 W
Pop: 15,520 (1990); 14,520 (1980) **Pop Density:** 1783.9
Land: 8.7 sq. mi.; **Water:** 0.1 sq. mi.

In southwestern CA, east of Los Angeles. Incorporated May 15, 1957.

Name origin: From Spanish 'holy faith,' applied to mineral springs purchased by the Santa Fe Railroad from J.E. Fulton.

Santa Monica City
ZIP: 90401 **Lat:** 34-00-48 N **Long:** 118-29-35 W
Pop: 86,905 (1990); 88,314 (1980) **Pop Density:** 10470.5
Land: 8.3 sq. mi.; **Water:** 7.6 sq. mi. **Elev:** 101 ft.

In southwestern CA, on the bay of the same name, 15 mi. west of the center of Los Angeles. Settled 1875; incorporated Nov 30, 1886.

Name origin: Probably for the mountains, named for the mother of St. Augustine.

Sepulveda *See* Los Angeles

Sherman Oaks *See* Los Angeles

Sierra Madre City
ZIP: 91024 **Lat:** 34-10-07 N **Long:** 118-02-57 W
Pop: 10,762 (1990); 10,837 (1980) **Pop Density:** 3587.3
Land: 3.0 sq. mi.; **Water:** 0.0 sq. mi.

In southwestern CA, 12 mi. northeast of Los Angeles, near Pasadena. Incorporated Feb 2, 1907.

Name origin: From Spanish for 'mother range,' referring to the mountain range.

Signal Hill City
ZIP: 90806 **Lat:** 33-48-12 N **Long:** 118-10-02 W
Pop: 8,371 (1990); 5,734 (1980) **Pop Density:** 3805.0
Land: 2.2 sq. mi.; **Water:** 0.0 sq. mi.

On the southwestern coast of CA, north of Long Beach. Incorporated Apr 22, 1924.

Name origin: Named in 1889 when its 300-ft. elevation became the signal point of the coast survey, as it had once served the Indians and Spanish. Previously known as Los Cerritos from Spanish 'little hills.'

South El Monte City
ZIP: 91733 **Lat:** 34-02-55 N **Long:** 118-02-51 W
Pop: 20,850 (1990); 16,623 (1980) **Pop Density:** 7189.7
Land: 2.9 sq. mi.; **Water:** 0.0 sq. mi.

In southwestern CA, 10 mi. southeast of Los Angeles. Incorporated Jul 30, 1958.

South Gate City
ZIP: 90280 **Lat:** 33-56-38 N **Long:** 118-11-30 W
Pop: 86,284 (1990); 66,784 (1980) **Pop Density:** 11660.0
Land: 7.4 sq. mi.; **Water:** 0.1 sq. mi. **Elev:** 111 ft.

In southwestern CA, 7 mi. southeast of Los Angeles between Watts and Downey. Founded 1918; incorporated Jan 20, 1923.

Name origin: For the South Gate Gardens on the Cudahy Ranch.

South Pasadena City
ZIP: 91030 **Lat:** 34-06-40 N **Long:** 118-09-25 W
Pop: 23,936 (1990); 22,681 (1980) **Pop Density:** 7040.0
Land: 3.4 sq. mi.; **Water:** 0.0 sq. mi.

In southwestern CA, 4 mi. northeast of Los Angeles. Incorporated Mar 2, 1888.

South San Gabriel CDP
ZIP: 91770 **Lat:** 34-02-55 N **Long:** 118-05-46 W
Pop: 7,700 (1990); 5,421 (1980) **Pop Density:** 9625.0
Land: 0.8 sq. mi.; **Water:** 0.0 sq. mi.

South San Jose Hills CDP
ZIP: 91744 **Lat:** 34-00-46 N **Long:** 117-54-13 W
Pop: 17,814 (1990); 16,049 (1980) **Pop Density:** 12724.3
Land: 1.4 sq. mi.; **Water:** 0.0 sq. mi.

CALIFORNIA, Los Angeles County

South Whittier CDP
ZIP: 90605 Lat: 33-55-58 N Long: 118-01-46 W
Pop: 49,514 (1990); 43,815 (1980) Pop Density: 9169.3
Land: 5.4 sq. mi.; Water: 0.0 sq. mi.

Studio City *See* **Los Angeles**

Tarzana *See* **Los Angeles**

Temple City City
ZIP: 91780 Lat: 34-06-09 N Long: 118-03-25 W
Pop: 31,100 (1990); 28,972 (1980) Pop Density: 7775.0
Land: 4.0 sq. mi.; Water: 0.0 sq. mi.
In southwestern CA, 12 mi. east of Los Angeles. Incorporated May 25, 1960.
Name origin: Named in 1923 for Walter P. Temple (?–1938), town founder.

Torrance City
ZIP: 90510 Lat: 33-50-05 N Long: 118-20-25 W
Pop: 133,107 (1990); 129,881 (1980) Pop Density: 6493.0
Land: 20.5 sq. mi.; Water: 0.0 sq. mi. Elev: 84 ft.
In southwestern CA, northwest of Long Beach. Founded 1911; incorporated May 12, 1921.
Name origin: For Jared S. Torrance, townsite owner.

Valinda CDP
ZIP: 91744 Lat: 34-02-21 N Long: 117-55-45 W
Pop: 18,735 (1990); 18,700 (1980) Pop Density: 9367.5
Land: 2.0 sq. mi.; Water: 0.0 sq. mi.

Val Verde CDP
Lat: 34-26-43 N Long: 118-39-20 W
Pop: 1,689 (1990) Pop Density: 5630.0
Land: 0.3 sq. mi.; Water: 0.0 sq. mi.

Van Nuys *See* **Los Angeles**

Vernon City
ZIP: 90058 Lat: 34-00-04 N Long: 118-12-36 W
Pop: 152 (1990); 90 (1980) Pop Density: 31.0
Land: 4.9 sq. mi.; Water: 0.1 sq. mi.
In southwestern CA, about 10 mi. southwest of Los Angeles. Incorporated Sep 22, 1905.
Name origin: An abbreviated form of Vernondale, the post office and railroad station names, in honor of Capt. George R. Vernon, Civil War officer and local settler.

View Park-Windsor Hills CDP
ZIP: 90043 Lat: 33-59-46 N Long: 118-20-55 W
Pop: 11,769 (1990); 12,101 (1980) Pop Density: 6538.3
Land: 1.8 sq. mi.; Water: 0.0 sq. mi.

Vincent CDP
Lat: 34-05-54 N Long: 117-55-24 W
Pop: 13,713 (1990) Pop Density: 9142.0
Land: 1.5 sq. mi.; Water: 0.0 sq. mi.

Walnut City
ZIP: 91789 Lat: 34-01-44 N Long: 117-51-26 W
Pop: 29,105 (1990); 12,478 (1980) Pop Density: 3270.2
Land: 8.9 sq. mi.; Water: 0.0 sq. mi. Elev: 569 ft.
In southwestern CA, 18 mi. southeast of Los Angeles. Incorporated Jan 19, 1959.
Name origin: For the Southern Pacific station originally called Lemon, which was changed to the present name in 1912 probably because "lemon" began to be used in the slang sense of something not good.

American Places Dictionary

Walnut Park CDP
ZIP: 90255 Lat: 33-58-06 N Long: 118-13-09 W
Pop: 14,722 (1990); 11,811 (1980) Pop Density: 21031.4
Land: 0.7 sq. mi.; Water: 0.0 sq. mi.

Watts *See* **Los Angeles**

West Athens CDP
ZIP: 90247 Lat: 33-55-24 N Long: 118-18-08 W
Pop: 8,859 (1990) Pop Density: 6814.6
Land: 1.3 sq. mi.; Water: 0.0 sq. mi.

West Carson CDP
ZIP: 90502 Lat: 33-49-17 N Long: 118-17-29 W
Pop: 20,143 (1990); 17,997 (1980) Pop Density: 8757.8
Land: 2.3 sq. mi.; Water: 0.0 sq. mi.

West Compton CDP
ZIP: 90220 Lat: 33-53-38 N Long: 118-16-10 W
Pop: 5,451 (1990); 5,907 (1980) Pop Density: 3406.9
Land: 1.6 sq. mi.; Water: 0.0 sq. mi.

West Covina City
ZIP: 91790 Lat: 34-03-15 N Long: 117-54-35 W
Pop: 96,086 (1990); 80,292 (1980) Pop Density: 5931.2
Land: 16.2 sq. mi.; Water: 0.0 sq. mi. Elev: 381 ft.
In southwestern CA in the San Gabriel Valley, 23 mi. west of Los Angeles. Incorporated Feb 17, 1923.

West Hollywood City
ZIP: 90069 Lat: 34-05-16 N Long: 118-22-16 W
Pop: 36,118 (1990); 35,703 (1980) Pop Density: 19009.5
Land: 1.9 sq. mi.; Water: 0.0 sq. mi.
In southwestern CA, north of Los Angeles.

Westlake Village City
ZIP: 91361 Lat: 34-08-09 N Long: 118-49-16 W
Pop: 7,455 (1990) Pop Density: 1433.7
Land: 5.2 sq. mi.; Water: 0.5 sq. mi.
In southwestern CA, 3 mi. southeast of Thousand Oaks. Incorporated Dec 11, 1981.

Westmont CDP
ZIP: 90044 Lat: 33-56-29 N Long: 118-18-05 W
Pop: 31,044 (1990); 27,916 (1980) Pop Density: 16338.9
Land: 1.9 sq. mi.; Water: 0.0 sq. mi.

West Puente Valley CDP
ZIP: 91744 Lat: 34-03-06 N Long: 117-58-02 W
Pop: 20,254 (1990); 20,445 (1980) Pop Density: 11252.2
Land: 1.8 sq. mi.; Water: 0.0 sq. mi.

West Whittier-Los Nietos CDP
ZIP: 90606 Lat: 33-58-40 N Long: 118-04-03 W
Pop: 24,164 (1990); 21,001 (1980) Pop Density: 9293.8
Land: 2.6 sq. mi.; Water: 0.1 sq. mi.

Whittier City
ZIP: 90605 Lat: 33-57-59 N Long: 118-01-18 W
Pop: 77,671 (1990); 68,558 (1980) Pop Density: 6213.7
Land: 12.5 sq. mi.; Water: 0.0 sq. mi. Elev: 365 ft.
In southwestern CA, 11 mi. southeast of Los Angeles. Founded 1881 by Quakers; incorporated Feb 25, 1898.
Name origin: For poet John Greenleaf Whittier (1807–92), a Quaker.

Willowbrook CDP
ZIP: 90222 Lat: 33-55-01 N Long: 118-15-14 W
Pop: 32,772 (1990); 30,845 (1980) Pop Density: 8857.3
Land: 3.7 sq. mi.; Water: 0.0 sq. mi.

American Places Dictionary   CALIFORNIA, Marin County

Madera County
County Seat: Madera (ZIP: 93637)

Pop: 88,090 (1990); 63,116 (1980)   **Pop Density:** 41.2
Land: 2138.4 sq. mi.; **Water:** 15.0 sq. mi.   **Area Code:** 209
In central CA, N of Fresno; organized Mar 11, 1893 from Fresno County.
Name origin: Spanish for 'lumber' because the town around which the county developed was a lumbering center.

Bonadelle Ranchos-Madera Ranchos   CDP
ZIP: 93637   **Lat:** 36-57-35 N   **Long:** 119-53-44 W
Pop: 5,705 (1990); 2,836 (1980)   **Pop Density:** 523.4
Land: 10.9 sq. mi.; **Water:** 0.0 sq. mi.

Chowchilla   City
ZIP: 93610   **Lat:** 37-06-55 N   **Long:** 120-15-23 W
Pop: 5,930 (1990); 5,122 (1980)   **Pop Density:** 2044.8
Land: 2.9 sq. mi.; **Water:** 0.0 sq. mi.   **Elev:** 240 ft.
Incorporated Feb 7, 1923.
Name origin: For the nearby Chowchilla River, named for the Chauciles Indian tribe that lived on its banks.

Madera   City
ZIP: 93638   **Lat:** 36-58-03 N   **Long:** 120-04-36 W
Pop: 29,281 (1990); 21,732 (1980)   **Pop Density:** 2842.8
Land: 10.3 sq. mi.; **Water:** 0.0 sq. mi.   **Elev:** 275 ft.
In central CA, 21 mi. northwest of Fresno. Founded 1876; incorporated Mar 27, 1907.
Name origin: From Spanish 'wood' or 'timber.' Name given by the California Lumber Co. to the town at the terminus of the water flume connecting the company to the railroad.

Madera Acres   CDP
ZIP: 93637   **Lat:** 37-01-09 N   **Long:** 120-03-57 W
Pop: 5,245 (1990); 2,173 (1980)   **Pop Density:** 440.8
Land: 11.9 sq. mi.; **Water:** 0.0 sq. mi.

Oakhurst   CDP
ZIP: 93644   **Lat:** 37-19-59 N   **Long:** 119-38-49 W
Pop: 2,602 (1990); 1,959 (1980)   **Pop Density:** 441.0
Land: 5.9 sq. mi.; **Water:** 0.0 sq. mi.

Parksdale   CDP
Lat: 36-56-49 N   **Long:** 120-01-18 W
Pop: 1,911 (1990); 1,267 (1980)   **Pop Density:** 1061.7
Land: 1.8 sq. mi.; **Water:** 0.0 sq. mi.

Parkwood   CDP
Lat: 36-55-36 N   **Long:** 120-02-36 W
Pop: 1,659 (1990); 1,146 (1980)   **Pop Density:** 1382.5
Land: 1.2 sq. mi.; **Water:** 0.0 sq. mi.

Yosemite Lakes   CDP
Lat: 37-11-27 N   **Long:** 119-46-18 W
Pop: 2,367 (1990)   **Pop Density:** 113.3
Land: 20.9 sq. mi.; **Water:** 0.1 sq. mi.

Marin County
County Seat: San Rafael (ZIP: 94903)

Pop: 230,096 (1990); 222,592 (1980)   **Pop Density:** 442.7
Land: 519.8 sq. mi.; **Water:** 308.4 sq. mi.   **Area Code:** 415
Located on N coast of California, N of San Francisco; organized in 1850
Name origin: Two main theories: 1) From the old Spanish name of San Rafael Bay, *Bahía de Nuestra Señora del Rosario la Marinera*, 'Bay of Our Lady of the Rosary, Mariner's Patron'; this name was given in 1775 by the surveyor Ayala. 2) For the name of a mythical Indian leader, transliterated to Marin; also applied to the islands in San Rafael Bay.

Belvedere   City
ZIP: 94920   **Lat:** 37-52-17 N   **Long:** 122-28-07 W
Pop: 2,147 (1990); 2,401 (1980)   **Pop Density:** 4294.0
Land: 0.5 sq. mi.; **Water:** 1.9 sq. mi.
In central-western CA on San Francisco Bay. Founded 1890 by the Belvedere Club of San Francisco; incorporated Dec 24, 1896.
Name origin: From Italian 'beautiful view.'

Bolinas   CDP
ZIP: 94924   **Lat:** 37-54-20 N   **Long:** 122-41-49 W
Pop: 1,098 (1990); 1,225 (1980)   **Pop Density:** 784.3
Land: 1.4 sq. mi.; **Water:** 0.0 sq. mi.

Corte Madera   Town
ZIP: 94925   **Lat:** 37-55-25 N   **Long:** 122-30-26 W
Pop: 8,272 (1990); 8,074 (1980)   **Pop Density:** 2585.0
Land: 3.2 sq. mi.; **Water:** 1.2 sq. mi.   **Elev:** 27 ft.
In central-western CA, near the junction of San Pablo and San Francisco bays. Incorporated Jun 10, 1916.
Name origin: Spanish for 'place where lumber or timber is cut'; first applied to Corte de Madera del Presidio land grant (1834), owned by John Reed, whose sawmill here was the Bay area's most important lumber source.

CALIFORNIA, Marin County

Fairfax — Town
ZIP: 94930 Lat: 37-59-19 N Long: 122-35-37 W
Pop: 6,931 (1990); 7,391 (1980) Pop Density: 3300.5
Land: 2.1 sq. mi.; Water: 0.0 sq. mi. Elev: 120 ft.
In central-western CA, 15 mi. northwest of San Francisco. Incorporated Mar 2, 1931.
Name origin: For Charles Snowden Fairfax of VA, popularly called Lord Fairfax, who went to CA in the Gold Rush and settled with his bride in an elaborate home on the site of the present town.

Inverness — CDP
ZIP: 94937 Lat: 38-05-06 N Long: 122-50-27 W
Pop: 1,422 (1990) Pop Density: 245.2
Land: 5.8 sq. mi.; Water: 0.4 sq. mi.

Kentfield — CDP
ZIP: 94904 Lat: 37-57-01 N Long: 122-32-50 W
Pop: 6,030 (1990) Pop Density: 2512.5
Land: 2.4 sq. mi.; Water: 0.0 sq. mi.

Lagunitas-Forest Knolls — CDP
Lat: 38-00-54 N Long: 122-41-15 W
Pop: 1,821 (1990); 1,465 (1980) Pop Density: 387.4
Land: 4.7 sq. mi.; Water: 0.0 sq. mi.

Larkspur — City
ZIP: 94939 Lat: 37-56-28 N Long: 122-31-44 W
Pop: 11,070 (1990); 11,064 (1980) Pop Density: 3571.0
Land: 3.1 sq. mi.; Water: 0.1 sq. mi. Elev: 43 ft.
In central-western CA, about 10 mi. northwest of San Francisco in the basin of Corte Madera Creek. Founded 1887; incorporated Mar 1, 1908.
Name origin: For the profusion of blue larkspur flowers that grew in the area.

Lucas Valley-Marinwood — CDP
ZIP: 94903 Lat: 38-02-06 N Long: 122-33-55 W
Pop: 5,982 (1990); 6,409 (1980) Pop Density: 1616.8
Land: 3.7 sq. mi.; Water: 0.0 sq. mi.

Mill Valley — City
ZIP: 94941 Lat: 37-54-28 N Long: 122-32-27 W
Pop: 13,038 (1990); 12,967 (1980) Pop Density: 2774.0
Land: 4.7 sq. mi.; Water: 0.1 sq. mi.
In central-western CA, 10 mi. northwest of San Francisco. Incorporated Sep 4, 1900.
Name origin: For a sawmill in the valley operated for years by John Reed.

Novato — City
ZIP: 94947 Lat: 38-05-31 N Long: 122-33-24 W
Pop: 47,585 (1990); 43,916 (1980) Pop Density: 1724.1
Land: 27.6 sq. mi.; Water: 0.5 sq. mi. Elev: 18 ft.
In central-western CA, north of San Francisco. Incorporated Jan 20, 1960.
Name origin: For Cañada de Novato, Spanish 'Novato valley', probably the Spanish name of a chief of the Hookoeko Indians, who was baptized in the name of St. Novatus.

Ross — Town
ZIP: 94957 Lat: 37-57-42 N Long: 122-33-38 W
Pop: 2,123 (1990); 2,801 (1980) Pop Density: 1326.9
Land: 1.6 sq. mi.; Water: 0.0 sq. mi. Elev: 23 ft.
In central-western CA, north of San Francisco. Incorporated Aug 21, 1908.
Name origin: For James Ross, landowner.

San Anselmo — Town
ZIP: 94960 Lat: 37-58-57 N Long: 122-34-07 W
Pop: 11,743 (1990); 12,067 (1980) Pop Density: 4193.9
Land: 2.8 sq. mi.; Water: 0.0 sq. mi. Elev: 45 ft.
In central-western CA, 14 mi. northwest of San Francisco. Incorporated Apr 9, 1907.
Name origin: For the railroad station named for Cañada de Anselmo, probably for an Indian baptized Anselmo; *San* added later.

San Rafael — City
ZIP: 94915 Lat: 37-58-51 N Long: 122-30-21 W
Pop: 48,404 (1990); 44,700 (1980) Pop Density: 2915.9
Land: 16.6 sq. mi.; Water: 5.8 sq. mi.
In central-western CA, 12 mi. northwest of San Francisco. Incorporated Feb 18, 1874.
Name origin: For a mission named for St. Raphael the Archangel, founded as a branch of Mission Dolores.

Santa Venetia — CDP
Lat: 38-00-32 N Long: 122-30-13 W
Pop: 3,362 (1990) Pop Density: 1681.0
Land: 2.0 sq. mi.; Water: 0.0 sq. mi.

Sausalito — City
ZIP: 94965 Lat: 37-51-27 N Long: 122-29-29 W
Pop: 7,152 (1990); 7,338 (1980) Pop Density: 3764.2
Land: 1.9 sq. mi.; Water: 0.4 sq. mi. Elev: 14 ft.
In central-western CA on San Francisco Bay north of the Golden Gate Bridge. Incorporated Sep 4, 1893.
Name origin: From Spanish 'little willow grove,' name of the land grant of the first settler, William A. Richardson.

Strawberry — CDP
Lat: 37-53-49 N Long: 122-30-27 W
Pop: 4,377 (1990) Pop Density: 3366.9
Land: 1.3 sq. mi.; Water: 0.0 sq. mi.

Tamalpais-Homestead Valley — CDP
ZIP: 94941 Lat: 37-53-18 N Long: 122-32-20 W
Pop: 9,601 (1990); 8,511 (1980) Pop Density: 3310.7
Land: 2.9 sq. mi.; Water: 0.0 sq. mi.

Tiburon — City
ZIP: 94920 Lat: 37-53-12 N Long: 122-27-24 W
Pop: 7,532 (1990); 6,685 (1980) Pop Density: 1711.8
Land: 4.4 sq. mi.; Water: 8.7 sq. mi.
In central-western CA, 7 mi. north of San Francisco on the bay. Incorporated Jun 23, 1964.
Name origin: For Tiburon Point from Spanish 'shark.'

Woodacre — CDP
ZIP: 94973 Lat: 38-00-20 N Long: 122-38-04 W
Pop: 1,478 (1990); 1,300 (1980) Pop Density: 821.1
Land: 1.8 sq. mi.; Water: 0.0 sq. mi.

Mariposa County
County Seat: Mariposa (ZIP: 95338)

Pop: 14,302 (1990); 11,108 (1980)   **Pop Density:** 9.9
Land: 1451.2 sq. mi.; **Water:** 11.7 sq. mi.   **Area Code:** 209

In central CA, E of San Francisco; original county; organized Feb 18, 1850 (prior to statehood).

Name origin: Spanish 'butterfly,' a name originally applied to an area in the county in which butterflies were numerous.

Bootjack   CDP
Lat: 37-28-10 N   Long: 119-52-59 W
Pop: 1,295 (1990)   **Pop Density:** 71.9
Land: 18.0 sq. mi.; **Water:** 0.0 sq. mi.

Mariposa   CDP
ZIP: 95338   Lat: 37-29-18 N   Long: 119-57-59 W
Pop: 1,152 (1990); 1,150 (1980)   **Pop Density:** 360.0
Land: 3.2 sq. mi.; **Water:** 0.0 sq. mi.

In central CA, northeast of Merced. Settled 1849.

Name origin: For Mariposa Creek, from Spanish for 'butterfly,' so-named for the large numbers found there every morning and evening.

Mendocino County
County Seat: Ukiah (ZIP: 95482)

Pop: 80,345 (1990); 66,738 (1980)   **Pop Density:** 22.9
Land: 3509.3 sq. mi.; **Water:** 369.2 sq. mi.   **Area Code:** 707

On N coast of California; original county; organized Feb 18, 1850 (prior to statehood).

Name origin: For Cabo (Cape) Mendocino, which early records indicate was named for Antonio de Mendoza (c. 1485–1552), viceroy of New Spain in 1542, or Lorenzo Suarez de Mendoza, viceroy of New Spain (1580–83). Name merely means someone from Mendoza.

Covelo   CDP
ZIP: 95428   Lat: 39-48-00 N   Long: 123-14-51 W
Pop: 1,057 (1990); 1,448 (1980)   **Pop Density:** 148.9
Land: 7.1 sq. mi.; **Water:** 0.0 sq. mi.

Fort Bragg   City
ZIP: 95437   Lat: 39-26-32 N   Long: 123-48-10 W
Pop: 6,078 (1990); 5,019 (1980)   **Pop Density:** 2251.1
Land: 2.7 sq. mi.; **Water:** 0.0 sq. mi.

On the west coast of CA, southwest of Chico. Founded 1885; incorporated Aug 5, 1889.

Name origin: For the military post established 1857 by Lt. H.G. Gibson, named for Lt. Col. Braxton Bragg (1817–76), Mexican War veteran and later a Confederate general.

Laytonville   CDP
ZIP: 95417   Lat: 39-40-28 N   Long: 123-29-42 W
Pop: 1,133 (1990); 1,096 (1980)   **Pop Density:** 226.6
Land: 5.0 sq. mi.; **Water:** 0.1 sq. mi.

Point Arena   City
ZIP: 95468   Lat: 38-54-41 N   Long: 123-41-26 W
Pop: 407 (1990); 425 (1980)   **Pop Density:** 290.7
Land: 1.4 sq. mi.; **Water:** 0.0 sq. mi.

On the northwestern coast of CA, north of San Francisco. Incorporated Jul 11, 1908.

Name origin: For the nearby cape; originally called Punta Arenas from Spanish 'sandy point.'

Ukiah   City
ZIP: 95482   Lat: 39-08-43 N   Long: 123-12-31 W
Pop: 14,599 (1990); 12,035 (1980)   **Pop Density:** 3106.2
Land: 4.7 sq. mi.; **Water:** 0.0 sq. mi.   **Elev:** 639 ft.

In western CA, 54 mi. northwest of Santa Rosa. Incorporated Mar 8, 1876.

Name origin: For Ukiah Valley, itself named probably from Central Pomo Indian *yo* 'deep' and *kaia* 'valley.'

Willits   City
ZIP: 95429   Lat: 39-24-18 N   Long: 123-20-52 W
Pop: 5,027 (1990); 4,008 (1980)   **Pop Density:** 1795.4
Land: 2.8 sq. mi.; **Water:** 0.0 sq. mi.   **Elev:** 1364 ft.

In northwestern CA, northwest of Santa Rosa. Incorporated Dec 19, 1888.

Name origin: For Hiram Willits, who settled here in 1857.

CALIFORNIA, Merced County *American Places Dictionary*

Merced County
County Seat: Merced (ZIP: 95340)

Pop: 178,403 (1990); 134,558 (1980) **Pop Density:** 92.5
Land: 1928.9 sq. mi.; **Water:** 43.1 sq. mi. **Area Code:** 209
In central CA, SE of San Francisco; organized Apr 19, 1855 from Mariposa County.
Name origin: Spanish 'mercy', from the original Spanish name of Lake Merced, *Nuestra Señora de la Merced* 'Our Lady of Mercy.'

Atwater City
ZIP: 95301 **Lat:** 37-21-11 N **Long:** 120-36-00 W
Pop: 22,282 (1990); 17,530 (1980) **Pop Density:** 4285.0
Land: 5.2 sq. mi.; **Water:** 0.0 sq. mi. **Elev:** 151 ft.
In western CA, 9 mi. northwest of Merced. Founded 1888 by the Merced Land and Fruit Co; incorporated Aug 16, 1922.
Name origin: For the railroad station named for the property's owner, Marshall D. Atwater, a well-known wheat rancher.

Delhi CDP
ZIP: 95315 **Lat:** 37-26-02 N **Long:** 120-46-36 W
Pop: 3,280 (1990); 2,832 (1980) **Pop Density:** 1726.3
Land: 1.9 sq. mi.; **Water:** 0.0 sq. mi.

Dos Palos City
ZIP: 93620 **Lat:** 36-59-11 N **Long:** 120-38-12 W
Pop: 4,196 (1990); 3,121 (1980) **Pop Density:** 2997.1
Land: 1.4 sq. mi.; **Water:** 0.0 sq. mi. **Elev:** 116 ft.
Incorporated Mar 4, 1935.
Name origin: For the railroad station; from Spanish 'two trees.'

Gustine City
ZIP: 95322 **Lat:** 37-15-09 N **Long:** 120-59-35 W
Pop: 3,931 (1990); 3,142 (1980) **Pop Density:** 2807.9
Land: 1.4 sq. mi.; **Water:** 0.0 sq. mi.
Laid out in 1890s; incorporated Nov 11, 1915.
Name origin: For cattle baron and town founder Henry Miller's daughter, Augustine, who was killed when thrown from a horse.

Hilmar-Irwin CDP
Lat: 37-24-20 N **Long:** 120-51-02 W
Pop: 3,392 (1990); 1,706 (1980) **Pop Density:** 942.2
Land: 3.6 sq. mi.; **Water:** 0.0 sq. mi.

Le Grand CDP
ZIP: 95333 **Lat:** 37-13-08 N **Long:** 120-15-37 W
Pop: 1,205 (1990) **Pop Density:** 334.7
Land: 3.6 sq. mi.; **Water:** 0.0 sq. mi.

Livingston City
ZIP: 95334 **Lat:** 37-23-16 N **Long:** 120-43-17 W
Pop: 7,317 (1990); 5,326 (1980) **Pop Density:** 3851.1
Land: 1.9 sq. mi.; **Water:** 0.0 sq. mi.
Incorporated Sep 11, 1922.
Name origin: For the railroad station named for David Livingstone (1813–73), Scottish explorer. Originally called Cressey for a land owner.

Los Baños City
ZIP: 93635 **Lat:** 37-03-51 N **Long:** 120-50-07 W
Pop: 14,519 (1990); 10,341 (1980) **Pop Density:** 2074.1
Land: 7.0 sq. mi.; **Water:** 0.2 sq. mi. **Elev:** 120 ft.
In central CA, southwest of Merced. Incorporated May 8, 1907.
Name origin: Named in 1874 for Los Baños Creek, from Spanish 'the baths,' for the pools near its source. Originally known as Kreyenhagen's, for an early settler.

Merced City
ZIP: 95342 **Lat:** 37-17-46 N **Long:** 120-29-03 W
Pop: 56,216 (1990); 36,423 (1980) **Pop Density:** 3491.7
Land: 16.1 sq. mi.; **Water:** 0.0 sq. mi.
In west-central CA, 54 mi. northwest of Fresno. Incorporated Apr 1, 1889. The principal rail and motor gateway to Yosemite National Park.
Name origin: For the Merced River, named in 1806 by a Spanish expedition *Nuestra Señora de la Merced* 'Our Lady of Mercy.'

Planada CDP
Lat: 37-17-17 N **Long:** 120-19-23 W
Pop: 3,531 (1990); 2,406 (1980) **Pop Density:** 1681.4
Land: 2.1 sq. mi.; **Water:** 0.0 sq. mi.

South Dos Palos CDP
Lat: 36-58-16 N **Long:** 120-38-53 W
Pop: 1,214 (1990) **Pop Density:** 809.3
Land: 1.5 sq. mi.; **Water:** 0.0 sq. mi.

Winton CDP
ZIP: 95388 **Lat:** 37-23-07 N **Long:** 120-36-58 W
Pop: 7,559 (1990); 4,995 (1980) **Pop Density:** 2606.6
Land: 2.9 sq. mi.; **Water:** 0.0 sq. mi.

Modoc County
County Seat: Alturas (ZIP: 96101)

Pop: 9,678 (1990); 8,610 (1980)   **Pop Density:** 2.5
Land: 3944.4 sq. mi.; **Water:** 259.3 sq. mi.   **Area Code:** 916
In NE CA; organized Feb 17, 1874 from Siskiyou County.
Name origin: For the Modoc Indian tribe, who had been subdued in the Modoc War of 1872–73. The name, derived from *moatokni,* means 'southerners.'

Alturas   City
ZIP: 96101   **Lat:** 41-29-29 N   **Long:** 120-32-43 W
Pop: 3,231 (1990); 3,025 (1980)   **Pop Density:** 1468.6
Land: 2.2 sq. mi.; **Water:** 0.0 sq. mi.   **Elev:** 4366 ft.
Settled 1869; incorporated Sep 16, 1901.
Name origin: From Spanish 'heights.' Originally called Dorris' Bridge for Presley Dorris, who built a bridge across the Pit River. Later called Dorrisville; changed to present name Jun 1, 1876.

Mono County
County Seat: Bridgeport (ZIP: 93517)

Pop: 9,956 (1990); 8,577 (1980)   **Pop Density:** 3.3
Land: 3044.5 sq. mi.; **Water:** 87.4 sq. mi.   **Area Code:** 619
On W central border of CA and NV; organized Apr 24, 1861 from Calaveras and Fresno counties.
Name origin: For Mono Lake; the lake's name is probably a Spanish-influenced shortened form of a Shoshonean tribal name, *monache* or *monachi* 'fly people'; their staple food was the pupae of a fly.

Bridgeport   CDP
Pop: 0 (1990)
In central-eastern CA, northeast of Yosemite National Park. County seat since 1864.

Mammoth Lakes   Town
ZIP: 93546   **Lat:** 37-37-40 N   **Long:** 118-59-24 W
Pop: 4,785 (1990); 3,929 (1980)   **Pop Density:** 194.5
Land: 24.6 sq. mi.; **Water:** 0.4 sq. mi.
In central-eastern CA, northeast of Fresno. Incorporated Aug 20, 1984.
Name origin: From Mammoth City, a big boom town that flourished briefly after the organization of the Mammoth Lakes Recreation Area.

Monterey County
County Seat: Salinas (ZIP: 93902)

Pop: 355,660 (1990); 290,444 (1980)   **Pop Density:** 107.1
Land: 3321.9 sq. mi.; **Water:** 449.2 sq. mi.   **Area Code:** 408
On central coast of CA; original county; organized Feb 18, 1850 (prior to statehood).
Name origin: For Monterey Bay.

Aromas   CDP
ZIP: 95004   **Lat:** 36-52-27 N   **Long:** 121-39-09 W
Pop: 1,126 (1990)   **Pop Density:** 536.2
Land: 2.1 sq. mi.; **Water:** 0.0 sq. mi.
Part of the town is in San Benito County.

Carmel-by-the-Sea   City
ZIP: 93921   **Lat:** 36-33-12 N   **Long:** 121-55-15 W
Pop: 4,239 (1990); 4,707 (1980)   **Pop Density:** 3853.6
Land: 1.1 sq. mi.; **Water:** 0.0 sq. mi.
In central coastal CA, south of Santa Cruz. Incorporated Oct 31, 1916.
Name origin: For its bay and river, both named Rio del Carmelo by Spanish explorer Sebastián Vizcaíno (1550?–1616) in Jan 1603, for the three Carmelite friars with the expedition.

Carmel Valley Village   CDP
ZIP: 93924   **Lat:** 36-29-10 N   **Long:** 121-43-22 W
Pop: 4,407 (1990); 4,013 (1980)   **Pop Density:** 223.7
Land: 19.7 sq. mi.; **Water:** 0.0 sq. mi.

Castroville   CDP
ZIP: 95012   **Lat:** 36-45-50 N   **Long:** 121-45-06 W
Pop: 5,272 (1990); 4,396 (1980)   **Pop Density:** 5272.0
Land: 1.0 sq. mi.; **Water:** 0.0 sq. mi.

CALIFORNIA, Monterey County

Del Monte Forest   CDP
ZIP: 93953   Lat: 36-35-10 N   Long: 121-56-46 W
Pop: 5,069 (1990)   Pop Density: 625.8
Land: 8.1 sq. mi.; Water: 2.6 sq. mi.

Del Rey Oaks   City
ZIP: 93940   Lat: 36-35-34 N   Long: 121-50-14 W
Pop: 1,661 (1990); 1,557 (1980)   Pop Density: 3322.0
Land: 0.5 sq. mi.; Water: 0.0 sq. mi.
Incorporated Sep 3, 1953.

Elkhorn   CDP
Lat: 36-48-39 N   Long: 121-43-02 W
Pop: 1,458 (1990)   Pop Density: 297.6
Land: 4.9 sq. mi.; Water: 0.0 sq. mi.

Gonzales   City
ZIP: 93926   Lat: 36-30-23 N   Long: 121-26-33 W
Pop: 4,660 (1990); 2,891 (1980)   Pop Density: 4236.4
Land: 1.1 sq. mi.; Water: 0.0 sq. mi.
Incorporated Jan 14, 1947.
Name origin: Named in 1873 either for Teodoro Gonzales because the railroad station was built on his extensive grant, or for his sons, Alfredo and Mariano, who were prominently associated with the Monterey and Salinas Railroad.

Greenfield   City
ZIP: 93927   Lat: 36-19-18 N   Long: 121-14-32 W
Pop: 7,464 (1990); 4,181 (1980)   Pop Density: 6785.5
Land: 1.1 sq. mi.; Water: 0.0 sq. mi.
In western CA, 32 mi. southeast of Salinas. Laid out 1902–05 on Arroyo Seco Rancho; incorporated Jan 7, 1947.
Name origin: For its surrounding alfalfa fields, which are green year-round. Originally called Clarke City for John S. Clarke, a principal Home Extension officer.

King City   City
ZIP: 93930   Lat: 36-12-46 N   Long: 121-07-41 W
Pop: 7,634 (1990); 5,495 (1980)   Pop Density: 2726.4
Land: 2.8 sq. mi.; Water: 0.1 sq. mi.   Elev: 330 ft.
In central-western CA, 58 mi. southeast of Salinas, on the Salinas River. Established 1886; incorporated Feb 9, 1911.
Name origin: For C.H. King, who laid out the town on his Rancho San Lorenzo in 1886.

Las Lomas   CDP
Lat: 36-52-07 N   Long: 121-43-51 W
Pop: 2,127 (1990); 1,740 (1980)   Pop Density: 1933.6
Land: 1.1 sq. mi.; Water: 0.0 sq. mi.

Marina   City
ZIP: 93933   Lat: 36-40-57 N   Long: 121-47-26 W
Pop: 26,436 (1990); 20,647 (1980)   Pop Density: 3038.6
Land: 8.7 sq. mi.; Water: 0.9 sq. mi.
On the west-central coast of CA, 5 mi. north of Monterey. Incorporated Nov 13, 1975.
Name origin: From Spanish 'shore' or 'seacoast.'

Monterey   City
ZIP: 93940   Lat: 36-36-04 N   Long: 121-52-54 W
Pop: 31,954 (1990); 27,558 (1980)   Pop Density: 3804.0
Land: 8.4 sq. mi.; Water: 3.3 sq. mi.
On the western coast of CA, at the southern end of Monterey Bay. Established 1770 as the first Spanish military post in CA; incorporated Jun 14, 1850.
Name origin: For the bay, named in honor of the Conde of Monterey (Gaspar de Acevedo y Zúñiga, c. 1560–1606), viceroy of New Spain.

Pacific Grove   City
ZIP: 93950   Lat: 36-37-22 N   Long: 121-55-30 W
Pop: 16,117 (1990); 15,755 (1980)   Pop Density: 5756.1
Land: 2.8 sq. mi.; Water: 1.1 sq. mi.
On the central-western coast of CA, at the southern end of Monterey Bay. Founded 1874; incorporated Jul 16, 1889.

Pajaro   CDP
Lat: 36-54-00 N   Long: 121-44-27 W
Pop: 3,332 (1990); 1,426 (1980)   Pop Density: 3332.0
Land: 1.0 sq. mi.; Water: 0.0 sq. mi.

Prunedale   CDP
ZIP: 93907   Lat: 36-47-59 N   Long: 121-39-22 W
Pop: 7,393 (1990)   Pop Density: 717.8
Land: 10.3 sq. mi.; Water: 0.0 sq. mi.

Salinas   City
ZIP: 93907   Lat: 36-41-05 N   Long: 121-38-06 W
Pop: 108,777 (1990); 80,479 (1980)   Pop Density: 5848.2
Land: 18.6 sq. mi.; Water: 0.0 sq. mi.   Elev: 53 ft.
In central-western CA on Monterey Bay, 45 mi. southeast of San Jose. Settled 1856; incorporated Mar 4, 1874. A market and processing center; birthplace of John Steinbeck (1902–68).
Name origin: For the Salinas River, Spanish for the 'salt marshes' at its mouth.

Sand City   City
ZIP: 93955   Lat: 36-38-55 N   Long: 121-50-40 W
Pop: 192 (1990); 182 (1980)   Pop Density: 91.4
Land: 2.1 sq. mi.; Water: 6.3 sq. mi.
On the central-western coast of CA, south of Monterey. Incorporated May 31, 1960.

Seaside   City
ZIP: 93955   Lat: 36-37-17 N   Long: 121-49-06 W
Pop: 38,901 (1990); 36,567 (1980)   Pop Density: 4420.6
Land: 8.8 sq. mi.; Water: 0.1 sq. mi.
On the central-western coast of CA, 4 mi. north of Monterey. Laid out 1888; incorporated Oct 13, 1954.
Name origin: Named East Monterey by Dr. J.L.D. Roberts; name changed 1890.

Soledad   City
ZIP: 93960   Lat: 36-25-48 N   Long: 121-19-21 W
Pop: 7,146 (1990); 5,928 (1980)   Pop Density: 3970.0
Land: 1.8 sq. mi.; Water: 0.0 sq. mi.
In southwest-central CA, 35 mi. southeast of Monterey. Incorporated Mar 9, 1921.
Name origin: Spanish 'solitude,' applied by the expedition led by Gaspar de Portolá (c. 1723–c. 1784) because it sounded like the name of an Indian they had met.

Napa County
County Seat: Napa (ZIP: 94559)

Pop: 110,765 (1990); 99,199 (1980)   **Pop Density:** 146.9
Land: 753.9 sq. mi.; **Water:** 34.5 sq. mi.   **Area Code:** 707
In NW CA, N of San Francisco; original county; organized Feb 18, 1850 (prior to statehood). World-famous wine-making area.
Name origin: For the valley, whose name is possibly that of an Indian tribe that formerly inhabited the area.

American Canyon   CDP
ZIP: 94589   **Lat:** 38-10-23 N   **Long:** 122-15-40 W
Pop: 7,706 (1990); 5,712 (1980)   **Pop Density:** 2082.7
Land: 3.7 sq. mi.; **Water:** 0.0 sq. mi.

Angwin   CDP
ZIP: 94508   **Lat:** 38-34-39 N   **Long:** 122-26-52 W
Pop: 3,503 (1990); 3,526 (1980)   **Pop Density:** 714.9
Land: 4.9 sq. mi.; **Water:** 0.0 sq. mi.

Calistoga   City
ZIP: 94515   **Lat:** 38-34-53 N   **Long:** 122-34-53 W
Pop: 4,468 (1990); 3,879 (1980)   **Pop Density:** 1718.5
Land: 2.6 sq. mi.; **Water:** 0.0 sq. mi.   **Elev:** 362 ft.
Incorporated Jan 6, 1886.
Name origin: Named through a spoonerism by its founder, Samuel Brannan, who instead of saying "I'll make this place the Saratoga of California," instead said "I'll make this place the Calistoga of Sarafornia.".

Deer Park   CDP
Lat: 38-31-57 N   **Long:** 122-28-07 W
Pop: 1,825 (1990)   **Pop Density:** 320.2
Land: 5.7 sq. mi.; **Water:** 0.0 sq. mi.

Napa   City
ZIP: 94558   **Lat:** 38-17-52 N   **Long:** 122-17-59 W
Pop: 61,842 (1990); 50,879 (1980)   **Pop Density:** 3554.1
Land: 17.4 sq. mi.; **Water:** 0.1 sq. mi.   **Elev:** 17 ft.
In central-western CA, 33 mi. north of Oakland. Settled 1847/48; incorporated Mar 23, 1872.
Name origin: Meaning of name is uncertain: possibly the name of an Indian tribe that once lived here; or 'grizzly bear,' or from Indian *napo* 'house.'

St. Helena   City
Lat: 38-30-16 N   **Long:** 122-27-56 W
Pop: 4,990 (1990); 4,898 (1980)   **Pop Density:** 1039.6
Land: 4.8 sq. mi.; **Water:** 0.0 sq. mi.   **Elev:** 257 ft.
In west-central CA, west of Sacramento. Incorporated Mar 24, 1876.
Name origin: For Mount St. Helena; reason for the name is unclear.

Yountville   Town
ZIP: 94599   **Lat:** 38-23-28 N   **Long:** 122-22-04 W
Pop: 3,259 (1990); 2,893 (1980)   **Pop Density:** 2036.9
Land: 1.6 sq. mi.; **Water:** 0.0 sq. mi.   **Elev:** 97 ft.
In central-western CA, southeast of Santa Rosa. Incorporated Feb 4, 1965.
Name origin: For George C. Yount of NC, who came to CA with the Wolfskill party in 1831, and in 1836 was grantee of Rancho Caymus, on which the town is situated. Formerly called Sebastopol.

Nevada County
County Seat: Nevada City (ZIP: 95959)

Pop: 78,510 (1990); 51,645 (1980)   **Pop Density:** 82.0
Land: 957.7 sq. mi.; **Water:** 16.9 sq. mi.   **Area Code:** 916
On NE border of CA and NV; organized Apr 25, 1851 from Yuba County.
Name origin: For Nevada City, named for the Sierra Nevada range, from the Spanish words meaning 'snow-covered mountain range.'

Alta Sierra   CDP
ZIP: 95949   **Lat:** 39-07-22 N   **Long:** 121-03-09 W
Pop: 5,709 (1990); 2,168 (1980)   **Pop Density:** 679.6
Land: 8.4 sq. mi.; **Water:** 0.0 sq. mi.

Glenshire-Devonshire   CDP
Lat: 39-21-01 N   **Long:** 120-05-15 W
Pop: 2,133 (1990)   **Pop Density:** 205.1
Land: 10.4 sq. mi.; **Water:** 0.0 sq. mi.

Grass Valley   City
ZIP: 95945   **Lat:** 39-13-17 N   **Long:** 121-03-24 W
Pop: 9,048 (1990); 6,697 (1980)   **Pop Density:** 2585.1
Land: 3.5 sq. mi.; **Water:** 0.0 sq. mi.   **Elev:** 2411 ft.
In eastern CA, 45 mi. west of Lake Tahoe. Established 1850; incorporated Mar 5, 1855.
Name origin: For the valley, itself named in 1849 by immigrants who found plenty of forage for their half-starved cattle. Previously called Centerville.

CALIFORNIA, Nevada County

Lake of the Pines CDP
Lat: 39-02-19 N **Long:** 121-03-37 W
Pop: 3,890 (1990) **Pop Density:** 2593.3
Land: 1.5 sq. mi.; **Water:** 0.3 sq. mi.

Nevada City City
ZIP: 95959 **Lat:** 39-15-37 N **Long:** 121-01-16 W
Pop: 2,855 (1990); 2,431 (1980) **Pop Density:** 1502.6
Land: 1.9 sq. mi.; **Water:** 0.0 sq. mi.
In eastern CA, 45 mi. west of Lake Tahoe. Incorporated Apr 19, 1856.
Name origin: From Spanish 'snow-covered,' probably referring to the nearby Sierra Nevada range. In 1849 it was a major mining town called Deer Creek Dry Diggings; also called Caldwell's Upper Store as against the "lower store" down the creek.

Penn Valley CDP
Lat: 39-11-46 N **Long:** 121-11-23 W
Pop: 1,242 (1990); 1,032 (1980) **Pop Density:** 591.4
Land: 2.1 sq. mi.; **Water:** 0.0 sq. mi.

Truckee CDP
Lat: 39-19-34 N **Long:** 120-12-08 W
Pop: 3,484 (1990); 2,389 (1980) **Pop Density:** 580.7
Land: 6.0 sq. mi.; **Water:** 0.0 sq. mi.
In northeastern CA, north of Lake Tahoe.
Name origin: For the river that runs through it, itself named for an Indian who piloted part of the Stevens party to it. Originally called Coburn Station for the local saloon owner.

Orange County
County Seat: Santa Ana (ZIP: 92701)

Pop: 2,410,560 (1990); 1,932,920 (1980) **Pop Density:** 3052.6
Land: 789.7 sq. mi.; **Water:** 158.2 sq. mi. **Area Code:** 714
On SW coast of CA, S of Los Angeles; organized Mar 11, 1889 from Los Angeles County.
Name origin: For local orange groves.

Aliso Viejo CDP
Lat: 33-34-03 N **Long:** 117-43-31 W
Pop: 7,612 (1990) **Pop Density:** 776.7
Land: 9.8 sq. mi.; **Water:** 0.0 sq. mi.

Anaheim City
ZIP: 92803 **Lat:** 33-50-20 N **Long:** 117-52-20 W
Pop: 266,406 (1990); 219,494 (1980) **Pop Density:** 6013.7
Land: 44.3 sq. mi.; **Water:** 1.5 sq. mi. **Elev:** 160 ft.
In southwestern CA, 16 mi. east of Long Beach. Founded 1857 by 50 German families; incorporated Mar 18, 1876. Site of Disneyland.
Name origin: For the Santa Ana River, which runs through it, plus German suffix *heim* 'home.'

Brea City
ZIP: 92621 **Lat:** 33-55-24 N **Long:** 117-52-01 W
Pop: 32,873 (1990); 27,913 (1980) **Pop Density:** 3287.3
Land: 10.0 sq. mi.; **Water:** 0.2 sq. mi.
In southwestern CA, 22 mi. northeast of Long Beach. Incorporated Feb 23, 1917.
Name origin: For a rancho called Cañada de la Brea 'valley of pitch (tar)' for the asphalt beds here.

Buena Park City
ZIP: 90622 **Lat:** 33-51-27 N **Long:** 118-00-11 W
Pop: 68,784 (1990); 64,165 (1980) **Pop Density:** 6489.1
Land: 10.6 sq. mi.; **Water:** 0.0 sq. mi. **Elev:** 74 ft.
In southwestern CA, 5 mi. west of Anaheim. Founded 1887; incorporated Jan 27, 1953.
Name origin: From Spanish 'good.'

Costa Mesa City
ZIP: 92628 **Lat:** 33-40-00 N **Long:** 117-54-45 W
Pop: 96,357 (1990); 82,562 (1980) **Pop Density:** 6176.7
Land: 15.6 sq. mi.; **Water:** 0.0 sq. mi. **Elev:** 101 ft.
In southwestern CA, 7 mi. southwest of Santa Ana. Incorporated Jun 29, 1953.
Name origin: An Americanized combination of two Spanish words, *costa* 'coast' and *mesa* 'tableland.' Originally called Harper.

Coto De Caza CDP
Lat: 33-36-14 N **Long:** 117-35-09 W
Pop: 2,853 (1990) **Pop Density:** 279.7
Land: 10.2 sq. mi.; **Water:** 0.0 sq. mi.

Cypress City
ZIP: 90630 **Lat:** 33-48-58 N **Long:** 118-02-16 W
Pop: 42,655 (1990); 40,738 (1980) **Pop Density:** 6462.9
Land: 6.6 sq. mi.; **Water:** 0.0 sq. mi. **Elev:** 36 ft.
In southwestern CA, 8 mi. northeast of Long Beach. Incorporated Jul 24, 1956.
Name origin: For the preponderance of cypress trees (Cupressaceae), the evergreen conifer.

Dana Point City
ZIP: 92624 **Lat:** 33-27-25 N **Long:** 117-41-46 W
Pop: 31,896 (1990); 10,602 (1980) **Pop Density:** 4832.7
Land: 6.6 sq. mi.; **Water:** 29.8 sq. mi.
On the southwestern coast of CA, on a headland between Laguna Beach and San Clemente. Incorporated Jan 1, 1989.
Name origin: For Richard Henry Dana (1815–82), author of *Two Years Before the Mast* (1840), who swung over a cliff here on halyards to dislodge some cowhides.

El Toro CDP
ZIP: 92630 **Lat:** 33-38-49 N **Long:** 117-40-57 W
Pop: 62,685 (1990); 25,300 (1980) **Pop Density:** 5312.3
Land: 11.8 sq. mi.; **Water:** 0.1 sq. mi.

CALIFORNIA, Orange County

El Toro Station
Military Facility
ZIP: 92709 **Lat:** 33-40-45 N **Long:** 117-43-06 W
Pop: 6,869 (1990); 7,632 (1980) **Pop Density:** 1144.8
Land: 6.0 sq. mi.; **Water:** 0.0 sq. mi.

Fountain Valley
City
ZIP: 92708 **Lat:** 33-42-39 N **Long:** 117-57-01 W
Pop: 53,691 (1990); 55,080 (1980) **Pop Density:** 6032.7
Land: 8.9 sq. mi.; **Water:** 0.1 sq. mi.

In southwestern CA, 28 mi. southeast of Los Angeles. Incorporated Jun 13, 1957.

Name origin: For artesian wells that once were located under the city.

Fullerton
City
ZIP: 92634 **Lat:** 33-53-05 N **Long:** 117-55-40 W
Pop: 114,144 (1990); 102,246 (1980) **Pop Density:** 5164.9
Land: 22.1 sq. mi.; **Water:** 0.0 sq. mi.

In southwestern CA, 17 mi. northeast of Long Beach. Founded 1887; incorporated Feb 15, 1904.

Name origin: For George H. Fullerton, the Santa Fe railroad representative who arranged to route the railroad through the site.

Garden Grove
City
ZIP: 92642 **Lat:** 33-46-43 N **Long:** 117-57-33 W
Pop: 143,050 (1990); 123,307 (1980) **Pop Density:** 7991.6
Land: 17.9 sq. mi.; **Water:** 0.0 sq. mi.

In southwestern CA, southeast of Los Angeles. Incorporated Jun 18, 1956.

Name origin: Once a farming settlement among citrus groves until the period after WW II when it boomed fantastically and developed mile after mile of tract housing.

Huntington Beach
City
ZIP: 92647 **Lat:** 33-41-30 N **Long:** 118-00-29 W
Pop: 181,519 (1990); 170,505 (1980) **Pop Density:** 6875.7
Land: 26.4 sq. mi.; **Water:** 5.2 sq. mi. **Elev:** 28 ft.

On the southwestern coast of CA, 15 mi. south of Long Beach. Incorporated Feb 17, 1909. A residential, industrial (oil drilling), and agricultural (sugar beets) city.

Name origin: For Henry E. Huntington (1850–1927), influential promoter of electric railroads. Originally called Pacific Beach.

Irvine
City
ZIP: 92713 **Lat:** 33-39-43 N **Long:** 117-47-44 W
Pop: 110,330 (1990); 62,134 (1980) **Pop Density:** 2608.3
Land: 42.3 sq. mi.; **Water:** 0.3 sq. mi.

In southwestern CA, 23 mi. southeast of Long Beach. Incorporated Dec 28, 1971. Site of a campus of the Univ of CA; mainly residential, but many aerospace, chemical, and electronics companies there.

Name origin: For James Irvine of San Francisco, who owned the land the town was built on. In 1899 a post office was named Myford for his son; changed 1914.

Laguna Beach
City
ZIP: 92607 **Lat:** 33-32-23 N **Long:** 117-45-38 W
Pop: 23,170 (1990); 17,858 (1980) **Pop Density:** 2663.2
Land: 8.7 sq. mi.; **Water:** 0.9 sq. mi.

On the southwestern coast of CA, an oceanside resort city 27 mi. southeast of Long Beach. Incorporated Jun 29, 1927.

Name origin: For Laguna Canyon, from Spanish 'lake.'

Laguna Hills
CDP
ZIP: 92653 **Lat:** 33-35-59 N **Long:** 117-42-39 W
Pop: 46,731 (1990); 33,600 (1980) **Pop Density:** 4326.9
Land: 10.8 sq. mi.; **Water:** 0.1 sq. mi.

Laguna Niguel
City
ZIP: 92677 **Lat:** 33-31-35 N **Long:** 117-42-15 W
Pop: 44,400 (1990); 12,237 (1980) **Pop Density:** 3020.4
Land: 14.7 sq. mi.; **Water:** 0.1 sq. mi.

In southwestern CA, 4 mi. east of Long Beach. Incorporated Dec 1, 1989.

Name origin: For Laguna Canyon and nearby Niguel Hill, from Indian *niguili*, meaning unknown.

La Habra
City
ZIP: 90631 **Lat:** 33-55-38 N **Long:** 117-57-02 W
Pop: 51,266 (1990); 45,232 (1980) **Pop Density:** 7022.7
Land: 7.3 sq. mi.; **Water:** 0.0 sq. mi. **Elev:** 298 ft.

In southwestern CA, 8 mi. from Fullerton and 19 mi. northeast of Long Beach. Incorporated Jan 20, 1925.

Name origin: From Spanish 'gorge' or 'pass through the mountains,' referring to the pass through the Puente Hills used by the 1769 expedition led by Gaspar de Portolá (c. 1723–c. 1784).

La Palma
City
ZIP: 90623 **Lat:** 33-51-03 N **Long:** 118-02-19 W
Pop: 15,392 (1990); 15,399 (1980) **Pop Density:** 8551.1
Land: 1.8 sq. mi.; **Water:** 0.0 sq. mi. **Elev:** 44 ft.

In southwestern CA, 18 mi. southeast of Los Angeles. Incorporated Oct 26, 1955.

Name origin: From Spanish 'the palm,' referring to the trees.

Los Alamitos
City
ZIP: 90720 **Lat:** 33-47-54 N **Long:** 118-03-29 W
Pop: 11,676 (1990); 11,529 (1980) **Pop Density:** 2919.0
Land: 4.0 sq. mi.; **Water:** 0.0 sq. mi. **Elev:** 22 ft.

In southwestern CA, 9 mi. northeast of Long Beach. Incorporated Mar 1, 1960.

Name origin: For the Rancho los Alamitos, Spanish 'little poplars' or 'little cottonwood [trees].'

Mission Viejo
City
ZIP: 92691 **Lat:** 33-36-44 N **Long:** 117-39-05 W
Pop: 72,820 (1990); 50,666 (1980) **Pop Density:** 4161.1
Land: 17.5 sq. mi.; **Water:** 0.4 sq. mi.

Newport Beach
City
ZIP: 92658 **Lat:** 33-36-50 N **Long:** 117-54-33 W
Pop: 66,643 (1990); 62,556 (1980) **Pop Density:** 4760.2
Land: 14.0 sq. mi.; **Water:** 10.4 sq. mi.

On the southwestern coast of CA, 18 mi. south of Long Beach. Established Feb 16, 1904; incorporated Sep 1, 1906.

Name origin: Named in 1873 by the McFadden brothers of DE for their steamer *Newport*; *Beach* was added in 1904.

Orange
City
ZIP: 92613 **Lat:** 33-48-18 N **Long:** 117-49-26 W
Pop: 110,658 (1990); 91,450 (1980) **Pop Density:** 4749.3
Land: 23.3 sq. mi.; **Water:** 0.4 sq. mi. **Elev:** 187 ft.

In southwestern CA, 21 mi. east of Long Beach. Founded 1868; incorporated Apr 6, 1888.

Name origin: Named in 1875 either for the developing orange culture in the district, or possibly brought from the East. Andrew Glassell, a town founder, came from VA, which has an Orange County. Previously called Richland.

Placentia — City
ZIP: 92670 **Lat:** 33-52-53 N **Long:** 117-51-17 W
Pop: 41,259 (1990); 35,041 (1980) **Pop Density:** 6251.4
Land: 6.6 sq. mi.; **Water:** 0.0 sq. mi.

In southwestern CA, 19 mi. northeast of Long Beach. Incorporated Dec 2, 1926.

Name origin: For the school district named in June 1884 by Sarah Jane McFadden, probably for the town and bay in Newfoundland.

Portola Hills — CDP
Lat: 33-41-01 N **Long:** 117-37-55 W
Pop: 2,677 (1990) **Pop Density:** 1487.2
Land: 1.8 sq. mi.; **Water:** 0.0 sq. mi.

Rancho Santa Margarita — CDP
ZIP: 92688 **Lat:** 33-38-26 N **Long:** 117-36-07 W
Pop: 11,390 (1990) **Pop Density:** 2711.9
Land: 4.2 sq. mi.; **Water:** 0.0 sq. mi.

Rossmoor — CDP
ZIP: 90740 **Lat:** 33-47-22 N **Long:** 118-04-44 W
Pop: 9,893 (1990); 10,457 (1980) **Pop Density:** 6183.1
Land: 1.6 sq. mi.; **Water:** 0.0 sq. mi.

San Clemente — City
ZIP: 92674 **Lat:** 33-26-49 N **Long:** 117-36-39 W
Pop: 41,100 (1990); 27,325 (1980) **Pop Density:** 2348.6
Land: 17.5 sq. mi.; **Water:** 0.7 sq. mi.

On the southwestern coast of CA, 55 mi. southeast of Los Angeles. Founded 1925; incorporated Feb 28, 1928.

Name origin: For Saint Clement, the third pope, and also the name of an island 60 miles offshore. A large estate here was the "western White House" during Richard Nixon's presidency.

San Juan Capistrano — City
ZIP: 92690 **Lat:** 33-30-05 N **Long:** 117-39-09 W
Pop: 26,183 (1990); 18,959 (1980) **Pop Density:** 1843.9
Land: 14.2 sq. mi.; **Water:** 0.1 sq. mi.

In southwestern CA, 50 mi. south of Los Angeles. Founded 1776; incorporated Apr 19, 1961.

Name origin: For the valley now known as San Luis Rey Valley; originally named for St. John of Capistrano (1385–1456), a 14th century Italian theologian who fought against the Turks to defend Vienna.

Santa Ana — City
ZIP: 92799 **Lat:** 33-44-11 N **Long:** 117-52-55 W
Pop: 293,742 (1990); 204,023 (1980) **Pop Density:** 10839.2
Land: 27.1 sq. mi.; **Water:** 0.3 sq. mi. **Elev:** 110 ft.

In southwestern CA, 20 mi. east of Long Beach. Founded 1869; incorporated Jul 12, 1886.

Name origin: For St. Anne, believed to be the name of the mother of the Virgin Mary.

Seal Beach — City
ZIP: 90740 **Lat:** 33-45-30 N **Long:** 118-04-32 W
Pop: 25,098 (1990); 25,975 (1980) **Pop Density:** 2145.1
Land: 11.7 sq. mi.; **Water:** 1.5 sq. mi.

On the southwestern coast of CA on San Pedro Bay, 7 mi. south of Long Beach. Incorporated Oct 27, 1915.

Name origin: Named by Philip A. Stanton for the seals that float offshore. Previously called Bay City.

Stanton — City
ZIP: 90680 **Lat:** 33-48-01 N **Long:** 117-59-27 W
Pop: 30,491 (1990); 23,723 (1980) **Pop Density:** 9835.8
Land: 3.1 sq. mi.; **Water:** 0.0 sq. mi.

In southwestern CA, 12 mi. northeast of Long Beach. Established 1912; incorporated Jun 4, 1956.

Name origin: For Philip A. Stanton, town founder and Republican assemblyman from Los Angeles (1903–09).

Trabuco Highlands — CDP
Lat: 33-36-53 N **Long:** 117-33-55 W
Pop: 3,191 (1990) **Pop Density:** 559.8
Land: 5.7 sq. mi.; **Water:** 0.0 sq. mi.

Tustin — City
ZIP: 92680 **Lat:** 33-43-48 N **Long:** 117-48-39 W
Pop: 50,689 (1990); 32,248 (1980) **Pop Density:** 4485.8
Land: 11.3 sq. mi.; **Water:** 0.0 sq. mi.

In southwestern CA, 20 mi. east of Long Beach. Incorporated Sep 21, 1927.

Name origin: For Columbus Tustin (1826–83), founder and first postmaster.

Tustin Foothills — CDP
ZIP: 92680 **Lat:** 33-45-52 N **Long:** 117-47-34 W
Pop: 24,358 (1990); 26,174 (1980) **Pop Density:** 3635.5
Land: 6.7 sq. mi.; **Water:** 0.0 sq. mi.

Villa Park — City
ZIP: 92667 **Lat:** 33-49-06 N **Long:** 117-48-37 W
Pop: 6,299 (1990); 7,137 (1980) **Pop Density:** 2999.5
Land: 2.1 sq. mi.; **Water:** 0.0 sq. mi.

In southwestern CA, northeast of Long Beach. Incorporated Jan 11, 1962.

Name origin: Originally called Mountain View; name changed in 1890 when the post office was established.

Westminster — City
ZIP: 92683 **Lat:** 33-45-05 N **Long:** 117-59-34 W
Pop: 78,118 (1990); 71,133 (1980) **Pop Density:** 7811.8
Land: 10.0 sq. mi.; **Water:** 0.0 sq. mi. **Elev:** 35 ft.

In southwestern CA, southeast of Long Beach. Incorporated Mar 27, 1957.

Name origin: Named c. 1870 by the Rev. L.P. Weber, who founded a colony here for those sympathetic to the ideals laid down in the Westminster Assembly of Presbyterians (1643–49).

Yorba Linda — City
ZIP: 92686 **Lat:** 33-53-19 N **Long:** 117-45-58 W
Pop: 52,422 (1990); 28,254 (1980) **Pop Density:** 2995.5
Land: 17.5 sq. mi.; **Water:** 0.5 sq. mi. **Elev:** 397 ft.

In southwestern CA, 24 mi. southeast of Los Angeles. Incorporated Nov 1, 1967.

Name origin: A coined name from *Yorba*, one of the oldest families in southern CA, plus *linda* from nearby Olinda.

Placer County
County Seat: Auburn (ZIP: 95603)

Pop: 172,796 (1990); 117,247 (1980) **Pop Density:** 123.0
Land: 1404.4 sq. mi.; **Water:** 95.8 sq. mi. **Area Code:** 916
On NE border of CA and NV; county organized 1851 from Yuba and Sutter counties.
Name origin: For the many placer deposits in the county's territory.

Auburn City
ZIP: 95603 **Lat:** 38-53-31 N **Long:** 121-04-33 W
Pop: 10,592 (1990); 7,540 (1980) **Pop Density:** 1736.4
Land: 6.1 sq. mi.; **Water:** 0.0 sq. mi.
In north-central CA, 36 mi. northeast of Sacramento. Founded 1848; incorporated May 2, 1888.
Name origin: For Auburn, NY, home of some early settlers.

Colfax City
ZIP: 95713 **Lat:** 39-05-42 N **Long:** 120-57-11 W
Pop: 1,306 (1990); 981 (1980) **Pop Density:** 1004.6
Land: 1.3 sq. mi.; **Water:** 0.0 sq. mi.
Incorporated Feb 23, 1910.
Name origin: For the railroad station named for Schuyler Colfax (1823–85), U.S. Speaker of the House and later U.S. vice president, who visited CA in 1865.

Dollar Point CDP
Lat: 39-11-23 N **Long:** 120-06-30 W
Pop: 1,449 (1990) **Pop Density:** 905.6
Land: 1.6 sq. mi.; **Water:** 0.0 sq. mi.

Foresthill CDP
ZIP: 95631 **Lat:** 38-59-57 N **Long:** 120-49-55 W
Pop: 1,409 (1990); 1,304 (1980) **Pop Density:** 128.1
Land: 11.0 sq. mi.; **Water:** 0.0 sq. mi.

Kings Beach CDP
Lat: 39-14-53 N **Long:** 120-01-03 W
Pop: 2,796 (1990); 1,942 (1980) **Pop Density:** 822.4
Land: 3.4 sq. mi.; **Water:** 0.0 sq. mi.

Lincoln City
ZIP: 95648 **Lat:** 38-53-57 N **Long:** 121-18-59 W
Pop: 7,248 (1990); 4,132 (1980) **Pop Density:** 1115.1
Land: 6.5 sq. mi.; **Water:** 0.0 sq. mi. **Elev:** 164 ft.
In central CA, 25 mi. northeast of Sacramento. Laid out 1859; incorporated Aug 7, 1890.
Name origin: For C. Lincoln Wilson, town founder.

Loomis Town
ZIP: 95650 **Lat:** 38-48-34 N **Long:** 121-11-39 W
Pop: 5,705 (1990); 1,284 (1980) **Pop Density:** 781.5
Land: 7.3 sq. mi.; **Water:** 0.0 sq. mi. **Elev:** 399 ft.
Incorporated Dec 17, 1984.
Name origin: Named for Jim Loomis, an agent for the Southern Pacific Railroad. Originally known as Pino and Pine.

Meadow Vista CDP
ZIP: 95722 **Lat:** 39-00-14 N **Long:** 121-01-50 W
Pop: 3,067 (1990); 2,683 (1980) **Pop Density:** 557.6
Land: 5.5 sq. mi.; **Water:** 0.2 sq. mi.

North Auburn CDP
ZIP: 95603 **Lat:** 38-55-52 N **Long:** 121-04-50 W
Pop: 10,301 (1990); 7,619 (1980) **Pop Density:** 1337.8
Land: 7.7 sq. mi.; **Water:** 0.0 sq. mi.

Rocklin City
ZIP: 95677 **Lat:** 38-48-08 N **Long:** 121-14-24 W
Pop: 19,033 (1990); 7,344 (1980) **Pop Density:** 1510.6
Land: 12.6 sq. mi.; **Water:** 0.0 sq. mi. **Elev:** 248 ft.
In eastern CA, 16 mi. northeast of Sacramento. Incorporated Feb 24, 1893.
Name origin: For the railroad station; its name suggested by nearby quarries.

Roseville City
ZIP: 95678 **Lat:** 38-45-35 N **Long:** 121-17-37 W
Pop: 44,685 (1990); 24,347 (1980) **Pop Density:** 1494.5
Land: 29.9 sq. mi.; **Water:** 0.0 sq. mi.
In central CA, 19 mi. northeast of Sacramento. Incorporated Apr 10, 1909.
Name origin: For the railroad station, named possibly for the roses found there, or for its pleasant sound.

Sunnyside-Tahoe City CDP
Lat: 39-08-51 N **Long:** 120-09-49 W
Pop: 1,643 (1990); 1,836 (1980) **Pop Density:** 483.2
Land: 3.4 sq. mi.; **Water:** 0.0 sq. mi.

Tahoe Vista CDP
Lat: 39-14-52 N **Long:** 120-03-13 W
Pop: 1,144 (1990) **Pop Density:** 423.7
Land: 2.7 sq. mi.; **Water:** 0.0 sq. mi.

CALIFORNIA, Plumas County — American Places Dictionary

Plumas County
County Seat: Quincy-East Quincy (ZIP: 95971)

Pop: 19,739 (1990); 17,340 (1980)   **Pop Density:** 7.7
Land: 2554.0 sq. mi.; **Water:** 59.8 sq. mi.   **Area Code:** 916
On NE border of CA and NV; organized Mar 18, 1854, from Butte County.
Name origin: Spanish 'feathers,' for the Feather River, once known as *Río de las Plumas*. Named by John A. Sutter, first settler in the Sacramento Valley, for the quantities of feathers found all around it with which the Indians decorated themselves and made blankets.

Chester   CDP
ZIP: 96020   **Lat:** 40-18-01 N   **Long:** 121-13-59 W
Pop: 2,082 (1990); 1,756 (1980)   **Pop Density:** 289.2
Land: 7.2 sq. mi.; **Water:** 0.1 sq. mi.

In northeastern CA, northeast of Chico. Established 1910; incorporated May 16, 1946.
Name origin: For Gaspar de Portolá, 18th-century Mexican explorer.

Greenville   CDP
ZIP: 95947   **Lat:** 40-08-08 N   **Long:** 120-56-16 W
Pop: 1,396 (1990); 1,537 (1980)   **Pop Density:** 170.2
Land: 8.2 sq. mi.; **Water:** 0.0 sq. mi.

Quincy-East Quincy   CDP
ZIP: 95971   **Lat:** 39-55-24 N   **Long:** 120-55-25 W
Pop: 4,271 (1990); 4,451 (1980)   **Pop Density:** 273.8
Land: 15.6 sq. mi.; **Water:** 0.0 sq. mi.

Portola   City
ZIP: 96122   **Lat:** 39-48-17 N   **Long:** 120-28-03 W
Pop: 2,193 (1990); 1,885 (1980)   **Pop Density:** 1096.5
Land: 2.0 sq. mi.; **Water:** 0.0 sq. mi.   **Elev:** ft.

Riverside County
County Seat: Riverside (ZIP: 92502)

Pop: 1,170,410 (1990); 663,199 (1980)   **Pop Density:** 162.4
Land: 7208.1 sq. mi.; **Water:** 95.7 sq. mi.   **Area Code:** 714
In S CA; organized Mar 11, 1893, from San Bernardino and San Diego counties.
Name origin: For the city.

Banning   City
ZIP: 92220   **Lat:** 33-56-14 N   **Long:** 116-53-31 W
Pop: 20,570 (1990); 14,020 (1980)   **Pop Density:** 1117.9
Land: 18.4 sq. mi.; **Water:** 0.0 sq. mi.

In southeastern CA, 23 mi. southeast of San Bernardino. Incorporated Feb 6, 1913.
Name origin: For Phineas Banning (?–1885), a stagecoach operator and transportation promoter who laid out the town.

Beaumont   City
ZIP: 92223   **Lat:** 33-55-54 N   **Long:** 116-58-42 W
Pop: 9,685 (1990); 6,818 (1980)   **Pop Density:** 1291.3
Land: 7.5 sq. mi.; **Water:** 0.0 sq. mi.

In south-central CA, southeast of Riverside. Incorporated Nov 18, 1912.
Name origin: From French 'beautiful mountain.' Originally called Edgar Station; changed to Summit in 1875; to San Gorgonio in 1884; to present name in 1887.

Bermuda Dunes   CDP
Lat: 33-44-33 N   **Long:** 116-17-18 W
Pop: 4,571 (1990)   **Pop Density:** 1269.7
Land: 3.6 sq. mi.; **Water:** 0.0 sq. mi.

Blythe   City
ZIP: 92226   **Lat:** 33-36-33 N   **Long:** 114-35-24 W
Pop: 8,428 (1990); 6,805 (1980)   **Pop Density:** 2217.9
Land: 3.8 sq. mi.; **Water:** 0.0 sq. mi.

In southeastern CA, near the Colorado River in Palo Verde valley. Founded 1908; incorporated Jul 21, 1916.
Name origin: For Thomas H. Blythe of San Francisco, a promoter of irrigation in the 1870s.

Cabazon   CDP
ZIP: 92230   **Lat:** 33-54-41 N   **Long:** 116-46-18 W
Pop: 1,588 (1990)   **Pop Density:** 441.1
Land: 3.6 sq. mi.; **Water:** 0.0 sq. mi.

Calimesa   CDP
ZIP: 92320   **Lat:** 33-59-45 N   **Long:** 117-02-42 W
Pop: 4,647 (1990)   **Pop Density:** 1858.8
Land: 2.5 sq. mi.; **Water:** 0.0 sq. mi.

Canyon Lake   CDP
ZIP: 92587   **Lat:** 33-41-00 N   **Long:** 117-15-12 W
Pop: 7,938 (1990); 2,039 (1980)   **Pop Density:** 3175.2
Land: 2.5 sq. mi.; **Water:** 0.3 sq. mi.

Cathedral City — City
ZIP: 92234 **Lat:** 33-49-50 N **Long:** 116-27-48 W
Pop: 30,085 (1990); 4,130 (1980) **Pop Density:** 1591.8
Land: 18.9 sq. mi.; **Water:** 0.0 sq. mi.

In south-central CA, 5 mi. southeast of Palm Springs. Incorporated Nov 16, 1981.

Name origin: For nearby Cathedral Canyon, whose rock formations are said to resemble a cathedral.

Cherry Valley — CDP
ZIP: 92223 **Lat:** 33-58-20 N **Long:** 116-57-55 W
Pop: 5,945 (1990); 5,012 (1980) **Pop Density:** 540.5
Land: 11.0 sq. mi.; **Water:** 0.0 sq. mi.

Coachella — City
ZIP: 92236 **Lat:** 33-40-51 N **Long:** 116-09-08 W
Pop: 16,896 (1990); 9,129 (1980) **Pop Density:** 840.6
Land: 20.1 sq. mi.; **Water:** 0.0 sq. mi. **Elev:** 71 ft.

In southeastern CA, 80 mi. northeast of San Diego in the Coachella Valley. Incorporated Dec 13, 1946.

Name origin: For the Coachella Valley, until c. 1900 called Cahuilla for the Indian tribe living there. Also called Salton Sea Sink and Conchilla Valley (for shells found there). The present name is an apparent misreading but was made official in 1909.

Corona — City
ZIP: 91720 **Lat:** 33-52-04 N **Long:** 117-34-10 W
Pop: 76,095 (1990); 37,791 (1980) **Pop Density:** 2670.0
Land: 28.5 sq. mi.; **Water:** 0.0 sq. mi. **Elev:** 678 ft.

In south-central CA, 11 mi. southwest of San Bernardino.

Name origin: From Latin 'wreath' or 'circle' because the city has a circular drive around it. Previously called South Riverside and Circle City.

Desert Hot Springs — City
ZIP: 92240 **Lat:** 33-57-32 N **Long:** 116-30-00 W
Pop: 11,668 (1990); 5,941 (1980) **Pop Density:** 1143.9
Land: 10.2 sq. mi.; **Water:** 0.0 sq. mi.

In southeastern CA, 7 mi. north of Palm Springs. Incorporated Sep 24, 1963.

East Blythe — CDP
Lat: 33-36-42 N **Long:** 114-34-38 W
Pop: 1,511 (1990); 1,660 (1980) **Pop Density:** 629.6
Land: 2.4 sq. mi.; **Water:** 0.0 sq. mi.

East Hemet — CDP
ZIP: 92544 **Lat:** 33-44-23 N **Long:** 116-56-16 W
Pop: 17,611 (1990); 14,712 (1980) **Pop Density:** 4295.4
Land: 4.1 sq. mi.; **Water:** 0.0 sq. mi.

El Cerrito — CDP
Lat: 33-50-24 N **Long:** 117-31-18 W
Pop: 4,490 (1990) **Pop Density:** 1360.6
Land: 3.3 sq. mi.; **Water:** 0.2 sq. mi.

Glen Avon — CDP
ZIP: 92509 **Lat:** 34-01-02 N **Long:** 117-29-15 W
Pop: 12,663 (1990); 8,444 (1980) **Pop Density:** 1711.2
Land: 7.4 sq. mi.; **Water:** 0.0 sq. mi.

Hemet — City
ZIP: 92546 **Lat:** 33-43-53 N **Long:** 116-59-51 W
Pop: 36,094 (1990); 22,531 (1980) **Pop Density:** 2050.8
Land: 17.6 sq. mi.; **Water:** 0.0 sq. mi. **Elev:** 1596 ft.

In southeastern CA, 31 mi. southeast of San Bernardino in the San Jacinto Basin west of San Bernardino National Forest. Founded 1898; incorporated Jan 20, 1910.

Name origin: Origin of name is unknown: it may be the Luiseno Shoshonean Indian name for the nearby valley, or possibly the Swedish word *hemmet*, 'in the home.'

Highgrove — CDP
Lat: 34-00-52 N **Long:** 117-19-40 W
Pop: 3,175 (1990) **Pop Density:** 2886.4
Land: 1.1 sq. mi.; **Water:** 0.0 sq. mi.

Home Gardens — CDP
ZIP: 91720 **Lat:** 33-52-51 N **Long:** 117-30-47 W
Pop: 7,780 (1990); 5,783 (1980) **Pop Density:** 7072.7
Land: 1.1 sq. mi.; **Water:** 0.0 sq. mi.

Homeland — CDP
ZIP: 92548 **Lat:** 33-44-54 N **Long:** 117-06-30 W
Pop: 3,312 (1990); 2,616 (1980) **Pop Density:** 1142.1
Land: 2.9 sq. mi.; **Water:** 0.0 sq. mi.

Idyllwild-Pine Cove — CDP
Lat: 33-44-50 N **Long:** 116-43-23 W
Pop: 2,853 (1990); 2,959 (1980) **Pop Density:** 209.8
Land: 13.6 sq. mi.; **Water:** 0.0 sq. mi.

Indian Wells — City
ZIP: 92210 **Lat:** 33-42-19 N **Long:** 116-20-26 W
Pop: 2,647 (1990); 1,394 (1980) **Pop Density:** 197.5
Land: 13.4 sq. mi.; **Water:** 0.0 sq. mi.

Incorporated Jul 14, 1967.

Indio — City
ZIP: 92202 **Lat:** 33-43-11 N **Long:** 116-13-43 W
Pop: 36,793 (1990); 21,611 (1980) **Pop Density:** 2164.3
Land: 17.0 sq. mi.; **Water:** 0.0 sq. mi. **Elev:** 14 ft.

In south-central CA, 62 miles southeast of San Bernardino. Founded 1876; incorporated May 16, 1930.

Name origin: From Spanish 'Indian,' referring to the former large Indian population when it was a construction camp for the Southern Pacific railroad.

Lake Elsinore — City
ZIP: 92531 **Lat:** 33-40-08 N **Long:** 117-19-17 W
Pop: 18,285 (1990); 5,982 (1980) **Pop Density:** 781.4
Land: 23.4 sq. mi.; **Water:** 6.6 sq. mi. **Elev:** 1306 ft.

In southern CA, on the northeastern shore of Lake Elsinore, 28 mi. south of San Bernardino. Incorporated Apr 20, 1888.

Name origin: For the Danish castle made famous in Shakespeare's *Hamlet*.

Lakeland Village — CDP
ZIP: 92530 **Lat:** 33-38-17 N **Long:** 117-20-41 W
Pop: 5,159 (1990); 2,796 (1980) **Pop Density:** 2579.5
Land: 2.0 sq. mi.; **Water:** 0.1 sq. mi.

Lakeview — CDP
ZIP: 92353 **Lat:** 33-49-41 N **Long:** 117-07-25 W
Pop: 1,448 (1990) **Pop Density:** 452.5
Land: 3.2 sq. mi.; **Water:** 0.0 sq. mi.

La Quinta — City
ZIP: 92253 **Lat:** 33-40-16 N **Long:** 116-17-32 W
Pop: 11,215 (1990); 3,328 (1980) **Pop Density:** 459.6
Land: 24.4 sq. mi.; **Water:** 0.2 sq. mi.

Incorporated May 1, 1982.

Name origin: For La Quinta Hotel, around which the town grew up; from Spanish 'country estate.'

CALIFORNIA, Riverside County

March Air Force Base — Military Facility
ZIP: 92508 **Lat:** 33-53-28 N **Long:** 117-15-49 W
Pop: 5,523 (1990); 3,607 (1980) **Pop Density:** 905.4
Land: 6.1 sq. mi.; **Water:** 0.0 sq. mi.

Mecca — CDP
Lat: 33-34-33 N **Long:** 116-04-18 W
Pop: 1,966 (1990); 1,698 (1980) **Pop Density:** 1512.3
Land: 1.3 sq. mi.; **Water:** 0.0 sq. mi.

Mira Loma — CDP
ZIP: 91752 **Lat:** 33-59-04 N **Long:** 117-30-45 W
Pop: 15,786 (1990); 8,707 (1980) **Pop Density:** 2466.6
Land: 6.4 sq. mi.; **Water:** 0.1 sq. mi.

Moreno Valley — City
ZIP: 92552 **Lat:** 33-55-34 N **Long:** 117-12-37 W
Pop: 118,779 (1990) **Pop Density:** 2419.1
Land: 49.1 sq. mi.; **Water:** 0.2 sq. mi.
In southwestern CA, 13 mi. southeast of Riverside. Incorporated Dec 3, 1984.
Name origin: From Spanish 'brown,' substituted when F.E. Brown, a town founder, refused to have his name used.

Murrieta — City
Lat: 33-33-34 N **Long:** 117-12-34 W
Pop: 1,628 (1990) **Pop Density:** 581.4
Land: 2.8 sq. mi.; **Water:** 0.0 sq. mi.
In southwestern CA, northeast of Oceanside. Incorporated Jul 1, 1991.
Name origin: For John Murrieta, ranch owner and bookkeeper in the sheriff's office.

Murrieta Hot Springs — CDP
Lat: 33-33-54 N **Long:** 117-09-02 W
Pop: 1,938 (1990); 1,091 (1980) **Pop Density:** 1020.0
Land: 1.9 sq. mi.; **Water:** 0.0 sq. mi.

Norco — City
ZIP: 91760 **Lat:** 33-55-31 N **Long:** 117-33-04 W
Pop: 23,302 (1990); 19,732 (1980) **Pop Density:** 1700.9
Land: 13.7 sq. mi.; **Water:** 0.2 sq. mi. **Elev:** 640 ft.
In southeastern CA, 45 mi. west of Palm Springs.
Name origin: Name was coined in 1922 from *No*rth *Co*rona Land Co. by Rex B. Clark.

Nuevo — CDP
ZIP: 92567 **Lat:** 33-48-24 N **Long:** 117-08-13 W
Pop: 3,010 (1990); 1,628 (1980) **Pop Density:** 567.9
Land: 5.3 sq. mi.; **Water:** 0.0 sq. mi.

Palm Desert — City
ZIP: 92261 **Lat:** 33-43-59 N **Long:** 116-22-31 W
Pop: 23,252 (1990); 11,801 (1980) **Pop Density:** 1217.4
Land: 19.1 sq. mi.; **Water:** 0.0 sq. mi. **Elev:** 243 ft.
In southeastern CA, southeast of Palm Springs. Incorporated Nov 26, 1973.
Name origin: For its location on an alluvial fan near Palm Springs.

Palm Desert Country — CDP
Lat: 33-44-26 N **Long:** 116-18-52 W
Pop: 5,626 (1990) **Pop Density:** 2250.4
Land: 2.5 sq. mi.; **Water:** 0.0 sq. mi.

Palm Springs — City
ZIP: 92263 **Lat:** 33-46-32 N **Long:** 116-31-43 W
Pop: 40,181 (1990); 32,359 (1980) **Pop Density:** 525.2
Land: 76.5 sq. mi.; **Water:** 0.7 sq. mi. **Elev:** 466 ft.
In south-central CA, southeast of Riverside. Incorporated Apr 20, 1938.
Name origin: Originally named Palmetto Spring, Big Palm Spring, and Agua Caliente from Spanish 'hot water' for the hot springs; present name chosen c. 1890.

Pedley — CDP
ZIP: 92509 **Lat:** 33-58-36 N **Long:** 117-28-14 W
Pop: 8,869 (1990) **Pop Density:** 1739.0
Land: 5.1 sq. mi.; **Water:** 0.1 sq. mi.

Perris — City
ZIP: 92572 **Lat:** 33-47-34 N **Long:** 117-13-23 W
Pop: 21,460 (1990); 6,827 (1980) **Pop Density:** 722.6
Land: 29.7 sq. mi.; **Water:** 0.2 sq. mi. **Elev:** 1457 ft.
In southwestern CA, 36 mi. west of Palm Springs. Incorporated May 26, 1911.
Name origin: Laid out and named for Fred T. Perris, one of the founders and chief engineer of California Southern Railroad.

Quail Valley — CDP
Lat: 33-42-19 N **Long:** 117-15-07 W
Pop: 1,937 (1990) **Pop Density:** 968.5
Land: 2.0 sq. mi.; **Water:** 0.1 sq. mi.

Rancho Mirage — City
ZIP: 92270 **Lat:** 33-45-28 N **Long:** 116-25-32 W
Pop: 9,778 (1990); 6,281 (1980) **Pop Density:** 416.1
Land: 23.5 sq. mi.; **Water:** 0.0 sq. mi.
In south-central CA, a suburb south of Palm Springs. Incorporated Aug 3, 1973.

Riverside — City
ZIP: 92502 **Lat:** 33-56-25 N **Long:** 117-23-50 W
Pop: 226,505 (1990); 170,591 (1980) **Pop Density:** 2915.1
Land: 77.7 sq. mi.; **Water:** 0.3 sq. mi.
In southwestern CA, 9 mi. southwest of San Bernardino. Settled 1870; incorporated Oct 11, 1883.
Name origin: For its location on the upper canal of the Santa Ana River.

Romoland — CDP
Lat: 33-44-40 N **Long:** 117-10-18 W
Pop: 2,319 (1990); 1,349 (1980) **Pop Density:** 702.7
Land: 3.3 sq. mi.; **Water:** 0.0 sq. mi.

Rubidoux — CDP
ZIP: 92509 **Lat:** 33-59-43 N **Long:** 117-25-16 W
Pop: 24,367 (1990); 16,763 (1980) **Pop Density:** 2677.7
Land: 9.1 sq. mi.; **Water:** 0.1 sq. mi.

San Jacinto — City
ZIP: 92581 **Lat:** 33-47-33 N **Long:** 116-57-51 W
Pop: 16,210 (1990); 7,098 (1980) **Pop Density:** 1529.2
Land: 10.6 sq. mi.; **Water:** 0.3 sq. mi. **Elev:** 1567 ft.
In southwestern CA, 24 mi. west of Palm Springs. Incorporated Apr 20, 1888.
Name origin: For a cattle ranch named for St. Hyacinth, a Dominican friar.

Sedco Hills — CDP
Lat: 33-38-24 N **Long:** 117-16-57 W
Pop: 3,008 (1990); 2,678 (1980) **Pop Density:** 1769.4
Land: 1.7 sq. mi.; **Water:** 0.0 sq. mi.

Sun City
ZIP: 92586   **Lat:** 33-42-46 N   **Long:** 117-12-09 W   CDP
Pop: 14,930 (1990); 8,460 (1980)   **Pop Density:** 1843.2
Land: 8.1 sq. mi.; **Water:** 0.0 sq. mi.

Sunnyslope
CDP
Lat: 34-01-08 N   **Long:** 117-25-21 W
Pop: 3,766 (1990)   **Pop Density:** 2690.0
Land: 1.4 sq. mi.; **Water:** 0.0 sq. mi.

Temecula
City
ZIP: 92589   **Lat:** 33-30-09 N   **Long:** 117-07-43 W
Pop: 27,099 (1990); 1,783 (1980)   **Pop Density:** 1026.5
Land: 26.4 sq. mi.; **Water:** 0.1 sq. mi.
In southwestern CA, northeast of Oceanside. Incorporated Dec 1, 1989.
Name origin: For a rancho, from a Luiseno Indian name *temeko*, meaning unknown.

Thousand Palms
CDP
ZIP: 92276   **Lat:** 33-49-18 N   **Long:** 116-23-08 W
Pop: 4,122 (1990); 1,718 (1980)   **Pop Density:** 1030.5
Land: 4.0 sq. mi.; **Water:** 0.0 sq. mi.

Valle Vista
CDP
ZIP: 92544   **Lat:** 33-45-02 N   **Long:** 116-53-45 W
Pop: 8,751 (1990); 5,474 (1980)   **Pop Density:** 2500.3
Land: 3.5 sq. mi.; **Water:** 0.2 sq. mi.

Wildomar
CDP
ZIP: 92595   **Lat:** 33-36-34 N   **Long:** 117-15-05 W
Pop: 10,411 (1990)   **Pop Density:** 846.4
Land: 12.3 sq. mi.; **Water:** 0.0 sq. mi.

Winchester
CDP
ZIP: 92596   **Lat:** 33-42-32 N   **Long:** 117-04-50 W
Pop: 1,689 (1990)   **Pop Density:** 344.7
Land: 4.9 sq. mi.; **Water:** 0.0 sq. mi.

Woodcrest
CDP
ZIP: 92504   **Lat:** 33-53-09 N   **Long:** 117-21-43 W
Pop: 7,796 (1990)   **Pop Density:** 749.6
Land: 10.4 sq. mi.; **Water:** 0.0 sq. mi.

Sacramento County
County Seat: Sacramento (ZIP: 95814)

Pop: 1,041,220 (1990); 783,381 (1980)   **Pop Density:** 1078.2
Land: 965.7 sq. mi.; **Water:** 30.0 sq. mi.   **Area Code:** 916
In N central CA; original county; organized Feb 18, 1850 (prior to statehood).
Name origin: For the Sacramento River.

Arden-Arcade
CDP
ZIP: 95821   **Lat:** 38-36-03 N   **Long:** 121-22-36 W
Pop: 92,040 (1990); 87,570 (1980)   **Pop Density:** 4869.8
Land: 18.9 sq. mi.; **Water:** 0.1 sq. mi.

Carmichael
CDP
ZIP: 95608   **Lat:** 38-38-02 N   **Long:** 121-19-07 W
Pop: 48,702 (1990); 43,108 (1980)   **Pop Density:** 4509.4
Land: 10.8 sq. mi.; **Water:** 0.1 sq. mi.

Citrus Heights
CDP
ZIP: 95621   **Lat:** 38-41-29 N   **Long:** 121-17-12 W
Pop: 107,439 (1990); 85,911 (1980)   **Pop Density:** 5509.7
Land: 19.5 sq. mi.; **Water:** 0.0 sq. mi.

Elk Grove
CDP
ZIP: 95624   **Lat:** 38-24-02 N   **Long:** 121-22-02 W
Pop: 17,483 (1990); 10,959 (1980)   **Pop Density:** 4482.8
Land: 3.9 sq. mi.; **Water:** 0.0 sq. mi.

Fair Oaks
CDP
ZIP: 95628   **Lat:** 38-38-54 N   **Long:** 121-14-49 W
Pop: 26,867 (1990); 22,602 (1980)   **Pop Density:** 2713.8
Land: 9.9 sq. mi.; **Water:** 0.4 sq. mi.

Florin
CDP
ZIP: 95828   **Lat:** 38-29-26 N   **Long:** 121-24-15 W
Pop: 24,330 (1990); 16,523 (1980)   **Pop Density:** 4344.6
Land: 5.6 sq. mi.; **Water:** 0.0 sq. mi.

Folsom
City
ZIP: 95630   **Lat:** 38-40-36 N   **Long:** 121-08-46 W
Pop: 29,802 (1990); 11,003 (1980)   **Pop Density:** 1392.6
Land: 21.4 sq. mi.; **Water:** 2.2 sq. mi.   **Elev:** 218 ft.
In north-central CA, 19 mi. northeast of Sacramento. Incorporated Apr 20, 1946.
Name origin: For Capt. Joseph L. Folsom (?–1855), assistant quartermaster of Stevenson's New York Volunteers, who purchased William A. Leidesdorff's 35,000-acre estate on the American River on which the town was laid out. Formerly called Negro Bar for the black goldminers who dug here.

Foothill Farms
CDP
ZIP: 95841   **Lat:** 38-40-39 N   **Long:** 121-20-48 W
Pop: 17,135 (1990); 13,700 (1980)   **Pop Density:** 7450.0
Land: 2.3 sq. mi.; **Water:** 0.0 sq. mi.

Galt
City
ZIP: 95632   **Lat:** 38-16-07 N   **Long:** 121-18-04 W
Pop: 8,889 (1990); 5,514 (1980)   **Pop Density:** 1587.3
Land: 5.6 sq. mi.; **Water:** 0.0 sq. mi.   **Elev:** 47 ft.
Incorporated Aug 16, 1946.
Name origin: Named in 1869 by John McFarland, an early settler, for his former home in Galt, Ontario, Canada.

Isleton
City
ZIP: 95641   **Lat:** 38-09-41 N   **Long:** 121-36-15 W
Pop: 833 (1990); 914 (1980)   **Pop Density:** 2082.5
Land: 0.4 sq. mi.; **Water:** 0.1 sq. mi.   **Elev:** 5 ft.
In central CA, at the confluence of the Sacramento and San Joaquin rivers. Founded 1874; incorporated May 14, 1923.
Name origin: For its location on Andrus Island.

CALIFORNIA, Sacramento County

Laguna
CDP
Lat: 38-25-16 N **Long:** 121-25-21 W
Pop: 9,828 (1990) **Pop Density:** 1786.9
Land: 5.5 sq. mi.; **Water:** 0.0 sq. mi.

La Riviera
CDP
ZIP: 95826 **Lat:** 38-34-00 N **Long:** 121-21-20 W
Pop: 10,986 (1990); 10,906 (1980) **Pop Density:** 6103.3
Land: 1.8 sq. mi.; **Water:** 0.2 sq. mi.

Mather Air Force Base
Military Facility
Lat: 38-32-54 N **Long:** 121-16-37 W
Pop: 4,885 (1990); 5,245 (1980) **Pop Density:** 508.9
Land: 9.6 sq. mi.; **Water:** 0.0 sq. mi.

North Highlands
CDP
ZIP: 95660 **Lat:** 38-40-03 N **Long:** 121-22-49 W
Pop: 42,105 (1990); 37,825 (1980) **Pop Density:** 3289.5
Land: 12.8 sq. mi.; **Water:** 0.0 sq. mi.

Orangevale
CDP
ZIP: 95662 **Lat:** 38-41-17 N **Long:** 121-13-02 W
Pop: 26,266 (1990); 20,585 (1980) **Pop Density:** 2626.6
Land: 10.0 sq. mi.; **Water:** 0.1 sq. mi.

Parkway-South Sacramento
CDP
ZIP: 95823 **Lat:** 38-30-30 N **Long:** 121-27-07 W
Pop: 31,903 (1990); 26,815 (1980) **Pop Density:** 6646.5
Land: 4.8 sq. mi.; **Water:** 0.0 sq. mi.

Rancho Cordova
CDP
ZIP: 95670 **Lat:** 38-35-43 N **Long:** 121-18-00 W
Pop: 48,731 (1990); 42,881 (1980) **Pop Density:** 4777.5
Land: 10.2 sq. mi.; **Water:** 0.3 sq. mi.

Rancho Murieta
CDP
Lat: 38-31-13 N **Long:** 121-03-36 W
Pop: 2,336 (1990) **Pop Density:** 265.5
Land: 8.8 sq. mi.; **Water:** 0.0 sq. mi.

Rio Linda
CDP
ZIP: 95673 **Lat:** 38-41-15 N **Long:** 121-27-29 W
Pop: 9,481 (1990); 7,359 (1980) **Pop Density:** 1723.8
Land: 5.5 sq. mi.; **Water:** 0.0 sq. mi.

Rosemont
CDP
ZIP: 95826 **Lat:** 38-32-49 N **Long:** 121-21-02 W
Pop: 22,851 (1990); 18,888 (1980) **Pop Density:** 5859.2
Land: 3.9 sq. mi.; **Water:** 0.0 sq. mi.

Sacramento
City
ZIP: 95814 **Lat:** 38-34-00 N **Long:** 121-28-02 W
Pop: 369,365 (1990); 275,741 (1980) **Pop Density:** 3835.6
Land: 96.3 sq. mi.; **Water:** 2.2 sq. mi.

In north-central CA on the Sacramento River, 70 mi. northeast of San Francisco. Settled by John A. Sutter 1839; incorporated Feb 27, 1850; state capital since 1854. A major transportation center; major industry is food processing.

Name origin: For the river, from Spanish 'sacrament' (Holy Communion). Previously called New or Nueva Helvetia, the ancient name of Switzerland, Sutter's former home.

Wilton
CDP
ZIP: 95693 **Lat:** 38-25-08 N **Long:** 121-12-27 W
Pop: 3,858 (1990) **Pop Density:** 130.3
Land: 29.6 sq. mi.; **Water:** 0.0 sq. mi.

San Benito County
County Seat: Hollister (ZIP: 95023)

Pop: 36,697 (1990); 25,005 (1980) **Pop Density:** 26.4
Land: 1389.1 sq. mi.; **Water:** 1.7 sq. mi. **Area Code:** 408
In W central CA, east of Monterey; organized Feb 12, 1874 from Monterey County.
Name origin: For San Benito, 'Saint Benedict,' the original name of San Juan Creek.

Aromas
CDP
Lat: 36-52-32 N **Long:** 121-37-51 W
Pop: 1,149 (1990) **Pop Density:** 441.9
Land: 2.6 sq. mi.; **Water:** 0.0 sq. mi.
Part of the town is in Monterey County.

Hollister
City
ZIP: 95023 **Lat:** 36-51-19 N **Long:** 121-23-56 W
Pop: 19,212 (1990); 11,488 (1980) **Pop Density:** 3430.7
Land: 5.6 sq. mi.; **Water:** 0.0 sq. mi.
In central-western CA, southeast of San Jose. Established 1868; incorporated Mar 26, 1872.

Name origin: For Col. W.W. Hollister, who had driven the first flock of sheep across the continent and acquired the San Justo grant on which the new town was established.

San Juan Bautista
City
ZIP: 95045 **Lat:** 36-50-45 N **Long:** 121-32-13 W
Pop: 1,570 (1990); 1,276 (1980) **Pop Density:** 2242.9
Land: 0.7 sq. mi.; **Water:** 0.0 sq. mi.

In west-central CA, northeast of Salinas. Incorporated May 4, 1896.
Name origin: For the mission named for St. John the Baptist.

San Bernardino County
County Seat: San Bernardino (ZIP: 92415)

Pop: 1,418,380 (1990); 895,016 (1980) **Pop Density:** 70.7
Land: 20061.8 sq. mi.; **Water:** 44.6 sq. mi. **Area Code:** 714

In SE CA, east of Los Angeles; organized in 1853 from Los Angeles County. Largest county in the U.S. in land area, 20,062 sq. mi.
Name origin: Named for the city, Spanish 'Saint Bernard [of Siena].'

Adelanto — City
ZIP: 92301 **Lat:** 34-34-10 N **Long:** 117-26-12 W
Pop: 8,517 (1990); 2,164 (1980) **Pop Density:** 230.8
Land: 36.9 sq. mi.; **Water:** 0.0 sq. mi.

In southeastern CA, northeast of Los Angeles. Founded 1917; incorporated Dec 22, 1970.
Name origin: Spanish for 'progress' or 'advance.'

Apple Valley — Town
ZIP: 92307 **Lat:** 34-31-45 N **Long:** 117-12-50 W
Pop: 46,079 (1990); 14,305 (1980) **Pop Density:** 685.7
Land: 67.2 sq. mi.; **Water:** 0.0 sq. mi.

Barstow — City
ZIP: 92312 **Lat:** 34-52-39 N **Long:** 117-03-57 W
Pop: 21,472 (1990); 17,690 (1980) **Pop Density:** 937.6
Land: 22.9 sq. mi.; **Water:** 0.0 sq. mi. **Elev:** 2106 ft.

In southwestern CA, at the foot of the Calico Mts., 51 mi. north of San Bernardino. Incorporated Sep 30, 1947.
Name origin: Originally called Fishpond, then Waterman Junction in honor of the governor, who owned a silver mine nearby. Name changed in 1886 by the Santa Fe Railroad for its president, William Barstow Strong.

Big Bear City — CDP
ZIP: 92314 **Lat:** 34-15-58 N **Long:** 116-50-43 W
Pop: 4,920 (1990) **Pop Density:** 1405.7
Land: 3.5 sq. mi.; **Water:** 0.0 sq. mi.

Big Bear Lake — City
ZIP: 92315 **Lat:** 34-14-37 N **Long:** 116-53-40 W
Pop: 5,351 (1990) **Pop Density:** 863.1
Land: 6.2 sq. mi.; **Water:** 0.2 sq. mi.

In southwestern CA, northeast of San Bernardino, built around the 7-mi. long reservoir created in 1884. Incorporated Nov 24, 1980.
Name origin: For Old Bear Valley Dam, which was built to create the lake.

Big River — CDP
Lat: 34-08-24 N **Long:** 114-21-37 W
Pop: 705 (1990) **Pop Density:** 67.1
Land: 10.5 sq. mi.; **Water:** 0.5 sq. mi.

Bloomington — CDP
ZIP: 92316 **Lat:** 34-03-34 N **Long:** 117-23-52 W
Pop: 15,116 (1990); 12,781 (1980) **Pop Density:** 2651.9
Land: 5.7 sq. mi.; **Water:** 0.0 sq. mi.

Bluewater — CDP
Lat: 34-10-28 N **Long:** 114-16-14 W
Pop: 261 (1990) **Pop Density:** 200.8
Land: 1.3 sq. mi.; **Water:** 0.5 sq. mi.

Chino — City
ZIP: 91710 **Lat:** 34-00-24 N **Long:** 117-41-09 W
Pop: 59,682 (1990); 40,165 (1980) **Pop Density:** 3510.7
Land: 17.0 sq. mi.; **Water:** 0.0 sq. mi.

In southwestern CA, 20 mi. west of San Bernardino. Founded 1887; incorporated Feb 28, 1910.
Name origin: For the Santa Ana del Chino land grant on which the settlement was laid out. From Spanish for persons of mixed blood.

Chino Hills — CDP
Lat: 33-58-29 N **Long:** 117-44-55 W
Pop: 27,608 (1990) **Pop Density:** 1781.2
Land: 15.5 sq. mi.; **Water:** 0.0 sq. mi.

Colton — City
ZIP: 92324 **Lat:** 34-03-28 N **Long:** 117-19-19 W
Pop: 40,213 (1990); 21,310 (1980) **Pop Density:** 2852.0
Land: 14.1 sq. mi.; **Water:** 0.5 sq. mi. **Elev:** 1000 ft.

In south-central CA, 4 mi. south of San Bernardino. Incorporated Jul 11, 1887.
Name origin: For David D. Colton, financial director of the Central Pacific railroad.

Crestline — CDP
ZIP: 92325 **Lat:** 34-14-48 N **Long:** 117-17-44 W
Pop: 8,594 (1990); 6,715 (1980) **Pop Density:** 788.4
Land: 10.9 sq. mi.; **Water:** 0.1 sq. mi.

Fontana — City
ZIP: 92334 **Lat:** 34-05-51 N **Long:** 117-27-26 W
Pop: 87,535 (1990); 36,804 (1980) **Pop Density:** 2458.8
Land: 35.6 sq. mi.; **Water:** 0.0 sq. mi. **Elev:** 1232 ft.

In southern CA, 8 mi. west of San Bernardino. Incorporated Jun 25, 1952.
Name origin: Named in 1913 for the Fontana Development Co., which may be a family name or the Spanish word meaning 'fountain.' Previously called Rosena.

George Air Force Base — Military Facility
ZIP: 92394 **Lat:** 34-34-54 N **Long:** 117-21-59 W
Pop: 5,085 (1990); 7,061 (1980) **Pop Density:** 1816.1
Land: 2.8 sq. mi.; **Water:** 0.0 sq. mi.

Grand Terrace — City
ZIP: 92324 **Lat:** 34-01-50 N **Long:** 117-18-52 W
Pop: 10,946 (1990); 8,498 (1980) **Pop Density:** 3127.4
Land: 3.5 sq. mi.; **Water:** 0.0 sq. mi.

In southeastern CA, 6 mi. south of San Bernardino. Incorporated Nov 30, 1978.
Name origin: Originally called Black Point, for pioneer James Black. Changed in 1905 by real estate promoters.

CALIFORNIA, San Bernardino County

Hesperia — City
ZIP: 92345 Lat: 34-25-08 N Long: 117-18-08 W
Pop: 50,418 (1990); 13,540 (1980) Pop Density: 1043.9
Land: 48.3 sq. mi.; Water: 0.1 sq. mi.
In southwestern CA, north of San Bernardino. Incorporated Jul 1, 1988.
Name origin: For the railroad station, possibly named for Hesperia, MI. Name used by Greek and Roman poets in the sense of "the Western Land."

Highland — City
ZIP: 92346 Lat: 34-07-02 N Long: 117-11-20 W
Pop: 34,439 (1990) Pop Density: 2532.3
Land: 13.6 sq. mi.; Water: 0.2 sq. mi.

Joshua Tree — CDP
ZIP: 92252 Lat: 34-07-37 N Long: 116-19-03 W
Pop: 3,898 (1990); 2,083 (1980) Pop Density: 639.0
Land: 6.1 sq. mi.; Water: 0.0 sq. mi.

Lake Arrowhead — CDP
ZIP: 92317 Lat: 34-15-44 N Long: 117-11-18 W
Pop: 6,539 (1990); 6,272 (1980) Pop Density: 568.6
Land: 11.5 sq. mi.; Water: 1.2 sq. mi.

Lenwood — CDP
Lat: 34-53-08 N Long: 117-06-12 W
Pop: 3,190 (1990); 2,974 (1980) Pop Density: 1226.9
Land: 2.6 sq. mi.; Water: 0.0 sq. mi.

Loma Linda — City
ZIP: 92354 Lat: 34-02-38 N Long: 117-14-56 W
Pop: 17,400 (1990); 10,694 (1980) Pop Density: 2485.7
Land: 7.0 sq. mi.; Water: 0.0 sq. mi.
In southwestern CA, 4 mi. south of San Bernardino. Incorporated Sep 29, 1970.
Name origin: For the railroad station; from Spanish 'pretty hill.' Previously called Mound Station and Mound City.

Los Serranos — CDP
ZIP: 91709 Lat: 33-58-25 N Long: 117-42-11 W
Pop: 7,099 (1990) Pop Density: 4175.9
Land: 1.7 sq. mi.; Water: 0.0 sq. mi.

Mentone — CDP
ZIP: 92359 Lat: 34-03-46 N Long: 117-07-21 W
Pop: 5,675 (1990) Pop Density: 1621.4
Land: 3.5 sq. mi.; Water: 0.0 sq. mi.

Montclair — City
ZIP: 91763 Lat: 34-04-22 N Long: 117-41-47 W
Pop: 28,434 (1990); 22,628 (1980) Pop Density: 5686.8
Land: 5.0 sq. mi.; Water: 0.0 sq. mi. Elev: 1060 ft.
In southwestern CA, 20 mi. west of San Bernardino. Incorporated Apr 25, 1956.
Name origin: From French 'clear [view of the] mountain.'

Morongo Valley — CDP
ZIP: 92256 Lat: 34-03-49 N Long: 116-35-30 W
Pop: 1,544 (1990); 1,137 (1980) Pop Density: 200.5
Land: 7.7 sq. mi.; Water: 0.0 sq. mi.

Mountain View Acres — CDP
Lat: 34-29-48 N Long: 117-20-52 W
Pop: 2,469 (1990); 1,686 (1980) Pop Density: 1371.7
Land: 1.8 sq. mi.; Water: 0.0 sq. mi.

Muscoy — CDP
ZIP: 92405 Lat: 34-09-08 N Long: 117-20-44 W
Pop: 7,541 (1990); 6,188 (1980) Pop Density: 2600.3
Land: 2.9 sq. mi.; Water: 0.1 sq. mi.

Nebo Center — Military Facility
Lat: 34-52-17 N Long: 116-57-20 W
Pop: 1,459 (1990); 1,749 (1980) Pop Density: 486.3
Land: 3.0 sq. mi.; Water: 0.0 sq. mi.

Needles — City
ZIP: 92363 Lat: 34-48-50 N Long: 114-36-47 W
Pop: 5,191 (1990); 4,120 (1980) Pop Density: 174.2
Land: 29.8 sq. mi.; Water: 0.4 sq. mi. Elev: 488 ft.
In southeastern CA, 12 mi. south of the junction of CA, NV, and AZ, on the Colorado River in the Mojave Desert near Hoover Dam. Founded Feb 1883; incorporated Oct 30, 1913.
Name origin: For the nearby needlelike peaks in AZ.

Ontario — City
ZIP: 91761 Lat: 34-03-15 N Long: 117-36-20 W
Pop: 133,179 (1990); 88,820 (1980) Pop Density: 3628.9
Land: 36.7 sq. mi.; Water: 0.1 sq. mi. Elev: 988 ft.
In southwestern CA, 21 mi. west of San Bernardino. Incorporated Dec 10, 1896.
Name origin: For Ontario, Canada, former home of George B. Chaffee, town founder.

Rancho Cucamonga — City
ZIP: 91739 Lat: 34-07-25 N Long: 117-34-12 W
Pop: 101,409 (1990); 55,250 (1980) Pop Density: 2682.8
Land: 37.8 sq. mi.; Water: 0.0 sq. mi.
In southwestern CA, 45 mi. west of Los Angeles. Incorporated Nov 30, 1977.
Name origin: For the land grant around whose winery the town developed. A Shoshonean name meaning 'sandy place.'

Redlands — City
ZIP: 92373 Lat: 34-03-28 N Long: 117-10-15 W
Pop: 60,394 (1990); 43,619 (1980) Pop Density: 2485.3
Land: 24.3 sq. mi.; Water: 0.3 sq. mi.
In southeastern CA, 7 mi. southeast of San Bernardino. Settled 1887; incorporated Dec 3, 1888.

Rialto — City
ZIP: 92376 Lat: 34-06-48 N Long: 117-23-13 W
Pop: 72,388 (1990); 37,862 (1980) Pop Density: 3414.5
Land: 21.2 sq. mi.; Water: 0.0 sq. mi.
In southwestern CA, 5 mi. west of San Bernardino. Incorporated Nov 17, 1911.
Name origin: For the contraction of Latin *Rivus Altus*, 'high river,' the grand canal of Venice, which had become synonymous with 'place of business.' Named by a group of Methodists from Halstead, KS.

Running Springs — CDP
Lat: 34-12-35 N Long: 117-06-48 W
Pop: 4,195 (1990) Pop Density: 1048.8
Land: 4.0 sq. mi.; Water: 0.0 sq. mi.

San Antonio Heights — CDP
Lat: 34-09-15 N Long: 117-39-30 W
Pop: 2,935 (1990) Pop Density: 2096.4
Land: 1.4 sq. mi.; Water: 0.0 sq. mi.

San Bernardino — City
ZIP: 92402 Lat: 34-08-23 N Long: 117-17-32 W
Pop: 164,164 (1990); 118,794 (1980) Pop Density: 2979.4
Land: 55.1 sq. mi.; Water: 0.4 sq. mi.
In southeastern CA, 54 mi. east of Los Angeles. Founded 1851; incorporated Aug 10, 1886. A citrus-packing center.

Name origin: For St. Bernard of Siena, Italy, a great Franciscan preacher of the fifteenth century.

Searles Valley — CDP
Lat: 35-46-03 N **Long:** 117-24-10 W
Pop: 2,740 (1990); 3,439 (1980) **Pop Density:** 234.2
Land: 11.7 sq. mi.; **Water:** 0.0 sq. mi.

Twentynine Palms — City
ZIP: 92277 **Lat:** 34-08-22 N **Long:** 116-03-56 W
Pop: 11,821 (1990); 7,465 (1980) **Pop Density:** 218.5
Land: 54.1 sq. mi.; **Water:** 0.0 sq. mi.

In south-central CA, northeast of Palm Springs. Incorporated Nov 23, 1987.

Twentynine Palms Base — Military Facility
ZIP: 92278 **Lat:** 34-13-41 N **Long:** 116-03-20 W
Pop: 10,606 (1990); 7,079 (1980) **Pop Density:** 7575.7
Land: 1.4 sq. mi.; **Water:** 0.0 sq. mi.

Upland — City
ZIP: 91786 **Lat:** 34-07-07 N **Long:** 117-39-27 W
Pop: 63,374 (1990); 47,647 (1980) **Pop Density:** 4197.0
Land: 15.1 sq. mi.; **Water:** 0.0 sq. mi.

In southeastern CA, in the foothills of the San Gabriel Mountains, 35 mi. east of Los Angeles. Incorporated May 15, 1906.
Name origin: So named in 1902 because it was slightly more elevated than Ontario to the south. Originally called Magnolia Villa.

Victorville — City
ZIP: 92393 **Lat:** 34-31-22 N **Long:** 117-19-53 W
Pop: 40,674 (1990); 14,220 (1980) **Pop Density:** 973.1
Land: 41.8 sq. mi.; **Water:** 0.0 sq. mi. **Elev:** 2715 ft.

In southwestern CA, north of San Bernardino. Incorporated Sep 21, 1962.
Name origin: For the station, named Victor in 1885 for J.N. Victor, construction superintendent of the California Southern Railroad; name changed 1901.

Wrightwood — CDP
ZIP: 92397 **Lat:** 34-21-33 N **Long:** 117-37-49 W
Pop: 3,308 (1990); 2,511 (1980) **Pop Density:** 1503.6
Land: 2.2 sq. mi.; **Water:** 0.0 sq. mi.

Yucaipa — City
ZIP: 92399 **Lat:** 34-01-58 N **Long:** 117-02-40 W
Pop: 32,824 (1990); 23,345 (1980) **Pop Density:** 1238.6
Land: 26.5 sq. mi.; **Water:** 0.0 sq. mi.

In southwestern CA, northeast of Riverside. Incorporated Nov 27, 1989.
Name origin: For Yucaipa Creek, from the Guachama (Serrano Shoshonean) Indian dialect 'wet or marshy land.'

Yucca Valley — CDP
ZIP: 92286 **Lat:** 34-06-40 N **Long:** 116-25-42 W
Pop: 13,701 (1990); 8,294 (1980) **Pop Density:** 985.7
Land: 13.9 sq. mi.; **Water:** 0.0 sq. mi.

San Diego County
County Seat: San Diego (ZIP: 92101)

Pop: 2,498,020 (1990); 1,861,850 (1980) **Pop Density:** 594.1
Land: 4204.5 sq. mi.; **Water:** 321.4 sq. mi. **Area Code:** 619

In SW CA on border with Baja California; original county; organized Feb 18, 1850 (prior to statehood).
Name origin: For the bay, named for San Diego de Alcala de Henares (Saint Didacus), Spanish Franciscan saint of the 15th century.

Alpine — CDP
ZIP: 91901 **Lat:** 32-50-34 N **Long:** 116-45-40 W
Pop: 9,695 (1990); 5,368 (1980) **Pop Density:** 371.5
Land: 26.1 sq. mi.; **Water:** 0.0 sq. mi.

Bonita — CDP
ZIP: 91902 **Lat:** 32-40-02 N **Long:** 117-01-47 W
Pop: 12,542 (1990); 6,257 (1980) **Pop Density:** 2559.6
Land: 4.9 sq. mi.; **Water:** 0.2 sq. mi.

Bonsall — CDP
ZIP: 92003 **Lat:** 33-16-58 N **Long:** 117-13-11 W
Pop: 1,881 (1990) **Pop Density:** 482.3
Land: 3.9 sq. mi.; **Water:** 0.1 sq. mi.

Borrego Springs — CDP
ZIP: 92004 **Lat:** 33-14-19 N **Long:** 116-21-16 W
Pop: 2,244 (1990); 1,405 (1980) **Pop Density:** 52.8
Land: 42.5 sq. mi.; **Water:** 0.0 sq. mi.

Bostonia — CDP
ZIP: 92021 **Lat:** 32-49-11 N **Long:** 116-56-44 W
Pop: 13,670 (1990) **Pop Density:** 6835.0
Land: 2.0 sq. mi.; **Water:** 0.0 sq. mi.

Camp Pendleton North — Military Facility
ZIP: 92055 **Lat:** 33-18-50 N **Long:** 117-18-52 W
Pop: 10,373 (1990); 2,065 (1980) **Pop Density:** 1152.6
Land: 9.0 sq. mi.; **Water:** 0.2 sq. mi.

Camp Pendleton South — Military Facility
ZIP: 92055 **Lat:** 33-13-59 N **Long:** 117-22-24 W
Pop: 11,299 (1990); 7,952 (1980) **Pop Density:** 2973.4
Land: 3.8 sq. mi.; **Water:** 0.1 sq. mi.

Carlsbad — City
ZIP: 92008 **Lat:** 33-07-25 N **Long:** 117-17-09 W
Pop: 63,126 (1990); 35,490 (1980) **Pop Density:** 1674.4
Land: 37.7 sq. mi.; **Water:** 3.2 sq. mi.

In southwestern CA, 28 mi. northwest of San Diego. Incorporated Jul 16, 1952.
Name origin: Named in 1886 by Gerhard Schutte for Karlsbad in Bohemia because the mineral waters found in the two places are similar in composition; spelling was anglicized later.

Casa de Oro-Mount Helix — CDP
ZIP: 91977 **Lat:** 32-45-55 N **Long:** 116-56-17 W
Pop: 30,727 (1990); 19,651 (1980) **Pop Density:** 2381.9
Land: 12.9 sq. mi.; **Water:** 0.0 sq. mi.

Chula Vista — City
ZIP: 91910 **Lat:** 32-37-42 N **Long:** 117-02-41 W
Pop: 135,163 (1990); 83,927 (1980) **Pop Density:** 4660.8
Land: 29.0 sq. mi.; **Water:** 1.8 sq. mi.
In southwestern CA, 8 mi. south of San Diego; incorporated Oct 26, 1911.
Name origin: Name derived in 1880 from Mexican-Spanish *chula* 'pretty,' plus Spanish *vista* 'view.'

Coronado — City
ZIP: 92118 **Lat:** 32-37-50 N **Long:** 117-10-25 W
Pop: 26,540 (1990); 18,790 (1980) **Pop Density:** 3446.8
Land: 7.7 sq. mi.; **Water:** 24.9 sq. mi.
In southwestern CA, opposite San Diego on San Diego Bay. Incorporated Dec 11, 1890.
Name origin: From Spanish 'crowned,' for Los Coronados, nearby islands, which were named for four brothers, known as the Cuatro Coronados, who were martyred in the time of Diocletian.

Del Mar — City
ZIP: 92014 **Lat:** 32-57-53 N **Long:** 117-15-44 W
Pop: 4,860 (1990); 5,017 (1980) **Pop Density:** 2700.0
Land: 1.8 sq. mi.; **Water:** 0.1 sq. mi.
Founded 1884 by Col. S. Taylor of OK; incorporated Jul 15, 1959.
Name origin: Name suggested because the town site was near the setting of the poem, "The Fight of Paso del Mar," by Bayard Taylor (1825–78).

El Cajon — City
ZIP: 92020 **Lat:** 32-48-08 N **Long:** 116-57-39 W
Pop: 88,693 (1990); 73,892 (1980) **Pop Density:** 6159.2
Land: 14.4 sq. mi.; **Water:** 0.0 sq. mi. **Elev:** 435 ft.
In southwestern CA, east of San Diego. Settled 1869; incorporated Nov 12, 1912.
Name origin: Spanish 'the big box,' because the city is boxed in by hills.

Encinitas — City
ZIP: 92024 **Lat:** 33-02-51 N **Long:** 117-15-45 W
Pop: 55,386 (1990); 10,796 (1980) **Pop Density:** 3094.2
Land: 17.9 sq. mi.; **Water:** 0.5 sq. mi.
On the southwestern coast of CA, south of Oceanside. Settled 1881; incorporated Oct 1, 1986.
Name origin: For the valley and creek named Cañada de los Encinos 'valley of the little live oaks' by the 1769 expedition led by Gaspar de Portolá (c. 1723–c 1784).

Escondido — City
ZIP: 92025 **Lat:** 33-08-11 N **Long:** 117-04-16 W
Pop: 108,635 (1990); 64,355 (1980) **Pop Density:** 3051.5
Land: 35.6 sq. mi.; **Water:** 0.2 sq. mi. **Elev:** 684 ft.
In southwestern CA, 28 mi. north of San Diego. Incorporated Oct 8, 1888.
Name origin: For nearby Escondido Creek; from Spanish 'hidden.'

Fallbrook — CDP
ZIP: 92028 **Lat:** 33-22-06 N **Long:** 117-14-15 W
Pop: 22,095 (1990); 14,041 (1980) **Pop Density:** 2027.1
Land: 10.9 sq. mi.; **Water:** 0.0 sq. mi.

Granite Hills — CDP
Lat: 32-48-10 N **Long:** 116-54-13 W
Pop: 3,157 (1990) **Pop Density:** 1052.3
Land: 3.0 sq. mi.; **Water:** 0.0 sq. mi.

Harbison Canyon — CDP
Lat: 32-49-09 N **Long:** 116-49-46 W
Pop: 2,122 (1990) **Pop Density:** 353.7
Land: 6.0 sq. mi.; **Water:** 0.0 sq. mi.

Hidden Meadows — CDP
Lat: 33-13-30 N **Long:** 117-06-42 W
Pop: 2,371 (1990) **Pop Density:** 370.5
Land: 6.4 sq. mi.; **Water:** 0.0 sq. mi.

Imperial Beach — City
ZIP: 91932 **Lat:** 32-34-12 N **Long:** 117-07-06 W
Pop: 26,512 (1990); 22,689 (1980) **Pop Density:** 6165.6
Land: 4.3 sq. mi.; **Water:** 0.3 sq. mi.
In southwestern CA, on San Diego Bay near the Mexican border. Founded 1910; incorporated Jul 18, 1956.
Name origin: Named in 1906 by E.W. Peterson, with the hope that Imperial Valley residents would build summer homes here. Originally called South San Diego.

Jamul — CDP
ZIP: 91935 **Lat:** 32-43-12 N **Long:** 116-53-19 W
Pop: 2,258 (1990); 1,826 (1980) **Pop Density:** 364.2
Land: 6.2 sq. mi.; **Water:** 0.0 sq. mi.

Julian — CDP
ZIP: 92036 **Lat:** 33-04-23 N **Long:** 116-35-14 W
Pop: 1,284 (1990); 1,320 (1980) **Pop Density:** 162.5
Land: 7.9 sq. mi.; **Water:** 0.0 sq. mi.

La Jolla *See* San Diego

Lake San Marcos — CDP
Lat: 33-07-08 N **Long:** 117-12-32 W
Pop: 3,802 (1990) **Pop Density:** 2112.2
Land: 1.8 sq. mi.; **Water:** 0.2 sq. mi.

Lakeside — CDP
ZIP: 92040 **Lat:** 32-50-56 N **Long:** 116-54-35 W
Pop: 39,412 (1990); 23,921 (1980) **Pop Density:** 2919.4
Land: 13.5 sq. mi.; **Water:** 0.5 sq. mi.

La Mesa — City
ZIP: 91941 **Lat:** 32-46-10 N **Long:** 117-01-07 W
Pop: 52,931 (1990); 50,308 (1980) **Pop Density:** 5753.4
Land: 9.2 sq. mi.; **Water:** 0.0 sq. mi.
In southwestern CA, 8 mi. northeast of San Diego. Incorporated Feb 16, 1912.
Name origin: From Spanish 'the tableland.' Originally La Mesa Heights, then La Mesa Springs.

Lemon Grove — City
ZIP: 91945 **Lat:** 32-44-00 N **Long:** 117-01-58 W
Pop: 23,984 (1990); 20,780 (1980) **Pop Density:** 6311.6
Land: 3.8 sq. mi.; **Water:** 0.0 sq. mi.
In southwestern CA, 8 mi. east of San Diego. Incorporated Jul 1, 1977.
Name origin: Named by the Allison brothers, who were convinced the area was perfect for lemon cultivation.

National City — City
ZIP: 91950 **Lat:** 32-39-57 N **Long:** 117-05-54 W
Pop: 54,249 (1990); 48,772 (1980) **Pop Density:** 7138.0
Land: 7.6 sq. mi.; **Water:** 1.7 sq. mi.
In southwestern CA, 5 mi. south of San Diego on the bay. Incorporated Sep 17, 1887.
Name origin: Named in 1868 for the Rancho de la Nacion on which the town was laid out; from Spanish 'the nation,' in celebration of Mexican independence.

Oceanside — City
ZIP: 92054 **Lat:** 33-13-30 N **Long:** 117-18-37 W
Pop: 128,398 (1990); 76,698 (1980) **Pop Density:** 3154.7
Land: 40.7 sq. mi.; **Water:** 0.8 sq. mi. **Elev:** 47 ft.

On the southwestern coast of CA, on the Gulf of Santa Catalina 45 mi. north of San Diego. Established 1883; incorporated Jul 3, 1888.

Name origin: Named by J.C. Hayes.

Pine Valley — CDP
ZIP: 91962 **Lat:** 32-51-19 N **Long:** 116-30-04 W
Pop: 1,297 (1990) **Pop Density:** 182.7
Land: 7.1 sq. mi.; **Water:** 0.0 sq. mi.

Poway — City
ZIP: 92064 **Lat:** 32-59-07 N **Long:** 117-01-04 W
Pop: 43,516 (1990); 32,263 (1980) **Pop Density:** 1107.3
Land: 39.3 sq. mi.; **Water:** 0.1 sq. mi.

In southwestern CA, 19 mi. north of San Diego. Incorporated Dec 1, 1980.

Name origin: From Rancho Paguay, a Spanish term supposedly meaning 'it is finished' or 'at the end of the valley.'

Rainbow — CDP
Lat: 33-24-18 N **Long:** 117-08-50 W
Pop: 2,006 (1990); 1,092 (1980) **Pop Density:** 124.6
Land: 16.1 sq. mi.; **Water:** 0.0 sq. mi.

Ramona — CDP
ZIP: 92065 **Lat:** 33-02-10 N **Long:** 116-52-12 W
Pop: 13,040 (1990); 8,173 (1980) **Pop Density:** 1253.8
Land: 10.4 sq. mi.; **Water:** 0.0 sq. mi.

Rancho San Diego — CDP
ZIP: 91941 **Lat:** 32-44-50 N **Long:** 116-56-04 W
Pop: 6,977 (1990) **Pop Density:** 1661.2
Land: 4.2 sq. mi.; **Water:** 0.2 sq. mi.

San Diego — City
ZIP: 92138 **Lat:** 32-48-53 N **Long:** 117-08-08 W
Pop: 1,110,549 (1990); 875,538 (1980) **Pop Density:** 3427.6
Land: 324.0 sq. mi.; **Water:** 47.9 sq. mi.

On the southwestern coast of CA, 10 mi. north of the Mexican border, on San Diego Bay. First visited in 1539 by Father Marcos; a mission established Jul 16, 1769, by Fr. Junipero Serra; incorporated Mar 27, 1850; new charter granted 1872. Home of major army and navy bases; site of the world-class San Diego Zoo and Botanical Gardens, campuses of Univ of CA and CA State Univ. Includes La Jolla. The original Mexican pueblo is now Old Town.

Name origin: For the bay, named for San Diego de Alcala de Henares (St. Didacus), Spanish Franciscan saint of the 15th century.

San Diego Country Estates — CDP
ZIP: 92065 **Lat:** 33-00-23 N **Long:** 116-46-58 W
Pop: 6,874 (1990) **Pop Density:** 446.4
Land: 15.4 sq. mi.; **Water:** 0.0 sq. mi.

San Marcos — City
ZIP: 92069 **Lat:** 33-08-11 N **Long:** 117-10-23 W
Pop: 38,974 (1990); 17,479 (1980) **Pop Density:** 1679.9
Land: 23.2 sq. mi.; **Water:** 0.0 sq. mi.

In southwestern CA, 21 mi. north of San Diego. Incorporated Jan 28, 1963.

Name origin: For San Marcos Valley, named for St. Mark the Evangelist.

Santee — City
ZIP: 92071 **Lat:** 32-51-18 N **Long:** 116-58-57 W
Pop: 52,902 (1990); 47,080 (1980) **Pop Density:** 3327.2
Land: 15.9 sq. mi.; **Water:** 0.2 sq. mi.

In southwestern CA, 15 mi. northeast of San Diego. Incorporated Dec 1, 1980.

Name origin: For Milton Santee, the first postmaster. Previously called Fanita, for Mrs. Fanita McCoon, and Cowles.

Solana Beach — City
ZIP: 92075 **Lat:** 32-59-45 N **Long:** 117-15-21 W
Pop: 12,962 (1990); 13,047 (1980) **Pop Density:** 3703.4
Land: 3.5 sq. mi.; **Water:** 0.1 sq. mi.

In southwestern CA, north of San Diego. Platted 1923; incorporated Jul 1, 1986.

Name origin: From Spanish 'sunny spot.'

Spring Valley — CDP
ZIP: 91977 **Lat:** 32-43-15 N **Long:** 116-59-19 W
Pop: 55,331 (1990); 40,191 (1980) **Pop Density:** 4535.3
Land: 12.2 sq. mi.; **Water:** 0.7 sq. mi.

Valley Center — CDP
ZIP: 92082 **Lat:** 33-13-02 N **Long:** 117-00-39 W
Pop: 1,711 (1990); 1,242 (1980) **Pop Density:** 201.3
Land: 8.5 sq. mi.; **Water:** 0.0 sq. mi.

Vista — City
ZIP: 92083 **Lat:** 33-11-19 N **Long:** 117-14-17 W
Pop: 71,872 (1990); 35,834 (1980) **Pop Density:** 4015.2
Land: 17.9 sq. mi.; **Water:** 0.0 sq. mi.

In southwestern CA, northeast of San Diego. Incorporated Jan 28, 1963.

Name origin: From Spanish 'view.'

San Francisco County
County Seat: San Francisco (ZIP: 94102)

Pop: 723,959 (1990); 678,974 (1980) **Pop Density:** 15502.1
Land: 46.7 sq. mi.; **Water:** 185.2 sq. mi. **Area Code:** 415
On N coast of CA; original county; organized Feb 18, 1850 (prior to statehood).
Name origin: For the bay, named for St. Francis of Assisi (c. 1181–1226).

San Francisco — City
ZIP: 94142 **Lat:** 37-47-35 N **Long:** 122-33-17 W
Pop: 723,959 (1990); 678,974 (1980) **Pop Density:** 15502.3
Land: 46.7 sq. mi.; **Water:** 185.2 sq. mi. **Elev:** 63 ft.

On a peninsula on the central-western coast of CA, bordered on the east by San Francisco Bay and on the north by Golden Gate. City and county are coterminus. Settled Oct 8/9, 1776, by Fr. Junipero Serra; incorporated Feb 18, 1850. A major seaport; commercial, financial, and industrial center; tourist and cultural center; site of many colleges and universities; army, navy, and marine bases.

Name origin: For the mission named *la mision de Nuestro Serafico Padre San Francisco de Asis a la Laguna de los Dolores* 'Mission of our seraphic father, St. Francis of Assisi at the Lake of Sorrows,' later known as Mission Dolores. Previously called Yerba Buena.

San Joaquin County
County Seat: Stockton (ZIP: 95202)

Pop: 480,628 (1990); 347,342 (1980) **Pop Density:** 343.4
Land: 1399.4 sq. mi.; **Water:** 26.9 sq. mi. **Area Code:** 209
In N central CA, E of San Francisco; original county; organized Feb 18, 1850 (prior to statehood).
Name origin: For the river, named for Saint Joachim, father of the Virgin Mary.

August — CDP
ZIP: 95201 **Lat:** 37-58-44 N **Long:** 121-15-39 W
Pop: 6,376 (1990); 5,445 (1980) **Pop Density:** 4904.6
Land: 1.3 sq. mi.; **Water:** 0.0 sq. mi.

Country Club — CDP
ZIP: 95204 **Lat:** 37-58-08 N **Long:** 121-20-22 W
Pop: 9,325 (1990); 9,585 (1980) **Pop Density:** 4907.9
Land: 1.9 sq. mi.; **Water:** 0.1 sq. mi.

Escalon — City
ZIP: 95320 **Lat:** 37-47-22 N **Long:** 120-59-46 W
Pop: 4,437 (1990); 3,127 (1980) **Pop Density:** 2610.0
Land: 1.7 sq. mi.; **Water:** 0.0 sq. mi.

In central CA, between Stockton and Modesto. Laid out 1895/96; incorporated Mar 12, 1957.
Name origin: From Spanish 'step of a stair,' named by James W. Jones, town founder, who liked the sound of the word gotten from a book at a local library.

French Camp — CDP
ZIP: 95231 **Lat:** 37-52-58 N **Long:** 121-16-43 W
Pop: 3,018 (1990) **Pop Density:** 973.5
Land: 3.1 sq. mi.; **Water:** 0.0 sq. mi.

In north-central CA, south of Stockton. Established 1832 by La Framboise as the southernmost regular campsite of Hudson Bay Co. trappers.
Name origin: Anglicized version of the Spanish name for the camp *campo de los franceses*, also applied to a land grant.

Garden Acres — CDP
ZIP: 95205 **Lat:** 37-57-50 N **Long:** 121-13-41 W
Pop: 8,547 (1990); 7,361 (1980) **Pop Density:** 3287.3
Land: 2.6 sq. mi.; **Water:** 0.0 sq. mi.

Lathrop — City
ZIP: 95330 **Lat:** 37-49-15 N **Long:** 121-16-35 W
Pop: 6,841 (1990); 3,717 (1980) **Pop Density:** 1052.5
Land: 6.5 sq. mi.; **Water:** 0.0 sq. mi.

In central-western CA, south of Stockton. Laid out 1887; incorporated Jul 1, 1989.
Name origin: Named by Leland Stanford for Charles Lathrop, his brother-in-law.

Lincoln Village — CDP
Lat: 38-00-15 N **Long:** 121-20-00 W
Pop: 4,236 (1990); 6,476 (1980) **Pop Density:** 6051.4
Land: 0.7 sq. mi.; **Water:** 0.0 sq. mi.

Linden — CDP
ZIP: 95236 **Lat:** 38-01-07 N **Long:** 121-05-59 W
Pop: 1,339 (1990) **Pop Density:** 178.5
Land: 7.5 sq. mi.; **Water:** 0.0 sq. mi.

Lockeford — CDP
ZIP: 95237 **Lat:** 38-09-05 N **Long:** 121-09-19 W
Pop: 2,722 (1990); 1,852 (1980) **Pop Density:** 353.5
Land: 7.7 sq. mi.; **Water:** 0.0 sq. mi.

Lodi — City
ZIP: 95240 **Lat:** 38-07-23 N **Long:** 121-17-39 W
Pop: 51,874 (1990); 35,221 (1980) **Pop Density:** 4893.8
Land: 10.6 sq. mi.; **Water:** 0.1 sq. mi. **Elev:** 51 ft.

In central CA, 11 mi. north of Stockton. Incorporated Dec 6, 1906.
Name origin: Named in 1874 for the railroad station, itself probably named either for the first spectacular victory at Lodi, Italy by Napoleon (1769–1821); or for the famous racehorse of the 1870s.

Manteca — City
ZIP: 95336　　Lat: 37-48-08 N　Long: 121-13-24 W
Pop: 40,773 (1990); 24,925 (1980)　　Pop Density: 4633.3
Land: 8.8 sq. mi.; Water: 0.0 sq. mi.

In central CA, 9 mi. south of Stockton; incorporated Jun 5, 1918.
Name origin: For the Southern Pacific Railroad station named for a local creamery; from Spanish 'lard.'

Morada — CDP
Lat: 38-02-19 N　Long: 121-14-40 W
Pop: 3,570 (1990)　　Pop Density: 1190.0
Land: 3.0 sq. mi.; Water: 0.0 sq. mi.

Ripon — Town
ZIP: 95366　　Lat: 37-44-06 N　Long: 121-07-35 W
Pop: 7,455 (1990); 3,509 (1980)　　Pop Density: 2662.5
Land: 2.8 sq. mi.; Water: 0.1 sq. mi.　　Elev: 62 ft.

In central CA, southeast of Stockton. Incorporated Nov 27, 1945.
Name origin: For the former home in WI of Applias Crook, the town's first postmaster. Formerly Stanislaus City.

Stockton — City
ZIP: 95208　　Lat: 37-58-11 N　Long: 121-18-24 W
Pop: 210,943 (1990); 148,283 (1980)　　Pop Density: 4010.3
Land: 52.6 sq. mi.; Water: 0.9 sq. mi.

In central-western CA, 50 mi. east of Oakland. Founded 1847 by noted pioneer, Charles M. Weber, who bought out his partner William Gulnac's interests in a 50,000 acre tract of land here for $60; incorporated Jul 23, 1850.
Name origin: For Commodore Robert Field Stockton (1795–1866), naval officer who took possession of CA (1847) for the U.S. Originally named Tuleburg.

Tracy — City
ZIP: 95376　　Lat: 37-44-13 N　Long: 121-25-54 W
Pop: 33,558 (1990); 18,428 (1980)　　Pop Density: 3495.6
Land: 9.6 sq. mi.; Water: 0.0 sq. mi.　　Elev: 48 ft.

In central CA, 19 mi. southwest of Stockton. Incorporated Jul 22, 1910.
Name origin: For the railroad station named for Lathrop J. Tracy, a Southern Pacific official.

Woodbridge — CDP
ZIP: 95258　　Lat: 38-09-48 N　Long: 121-19-02 W
Pop: 3,456 (1990); 1,672 (1980)　　Pop Density: 785.5
Land: 4.4 sq. mi.; Water: 0.1 sq. mi.

San Luis Obispo County
County Seat: San Luis Obispo (ZIP: 93401)

Pop: 217,162 (1990); 155,435 (1980)　　Pop Density: 65.7
Land: 3304.5 sq. mi.; Water: 311.2 sq. mi.　　Area Code: 805

On central coast of CA; original county; organized Feb 18, 1850 (prior to statehood).
Name origin: For the mission, named for St. Louis, Bishop of Toulouse, son of King Charles II of Naples and Sicily.

Arroyo Grande — City
ZIP: 93420　　Lat: 35-07-31 N　Long: 120-35-00 W
Pop: 14,378 (1990); 11,290 (1980)　　Pop Density: 2522.5
Land: 5.7 sq. mi.; Water: 0.0 sq. mi.

In southwestern CA, 13 mi. south of San Luis Obispo. Incorporated Jul 10, 1911.
Name origin: Spanish 'large watercourse.'

Atascadero — City
ZIP: 93422　　Lat: 35-29-07 N　Long: 120-41-16 W
Pop: 23,138 (1990); 16,232 (1980)　　Pop Density: 914.5
Land: 25.3 sq. mi.; Water: 0.0 sq. mi.

In southwestern CA, 14 mi. north of San Luis Obispo. Founded 1886; incorporated Jul 2, 1979.
Name origin: From the name of the provisional land grant, from Spanish 'miry place.'

Baywood-Los Osos — CDP
ZIP: 93402　　Lat: 35-18-52 N　Long: 120-50-21 W
Pop: 14,377 (1990); 10,933 (1980)　　Pop Density: 1891.7
Land: 7.6 sq. mi.; Water: 0.0 sq. mi.

Cambria — CDP
ZIP: 93428　　Lat: 35-32-47 N　Long: 121-04-47 W
Pop: 5,382 (1990); 3,061 (1980)　　Pop Density: 727.3
Land: 7.4 sq. mi.; Water: 0.0 sq. mi.

Cayucos — CDP
ZIP: 93430　　Lat: 35-26-16 N　Long: 120-53-05 W
Pop: 2,960 (1990); 2,301 (1980)　　Pop Density: 986.7
Land: 3.0 sq. mi.; Water: 0.4 sq. mi.

El Paso de Robles (Paso Robles) — City
ZIP: 93446　　Lat: 35-37-56 N　Long: 120-39-51 W
Pop: 18,583 (1990); 9,163 (1980)　　Pop Density: 1407.8
Land: 13.2 sq. mi.; Water: 0.0 sq. mi.

Grover City — City
ZIP: 93433　　Lat: 35-07-15 N　Long: 120-37-06 W
Pop: 11,656 (1990); 8,827 (1980)　　Pop Density: 5067.8
Land: 2.3 sq. mi.; Water: 0.0 sq. mi.

On the central western coast of CA, south of San Luis Obispo. Incorporated Dec 21, 1959.
Name origin: Named Grover in 1892 for Henry Grover; renamed 1937.

Lake Nacimiento — CDP
Lat: 35-43-42 N　Long: 120-52-42 W
Pop: 1,556 (1990)　　Pop Density: 778.0
Land: 2.0 sq. mi.; Water: 0.0 sq. mi.

CALIFORNIA, San Luis Obispo County

Morro Bay — City
ZIP: 93442 Lat: 35-22-02 N Long: 120-51-58 W
Pop: 9,664 (1990); 9,064 (1980) Pop Density: 1894.9
Land: 5.1 sq. mi.; Water: 5.2 sq. mi.
On the central western coast of CA, on Morro Bay. Incorporated Jul 17, 1964.
Name origin: For the bay, from the Spanish geographical term for the 'crown-shaped rock' at the entrance.

Nipomo — CDP
ZIP: 93444 Lat: 35-01-56 N Long: 120-28-58 W
Pop: 7,109 (1990); 5,247 (1980) Pop Density: 1077.1
Land: 6.6 sq. mi.; Water: 0.0 sq. mi.

Oceano — CDP
ZIP: 93445 Lat: 35-06-06 N Long: 120-36-31 W
Pop: 6,169 (1990); 4,478 (1980) Pop Density: 4112.7
Land: 1.5 sq. mi.; Water: 0.0 sq. mi.

Pismo Beach — City
ZIP: 93449 Lat: 35-08-09 N Long: 120-40-37 W
Pop: 7,669 (1990); 5,364 (1980) Pop Density: 2191.1
Land: 3.5 sq. mi.; Water: 9.8 sq. mi.
In southwestern CA, northwest of Santa Maria. Founded 1891; incorporated Apr 25, 1946.
Name origin: From its location on the Pismo land grant; *beach* was added after 1904. From the Chumash Indian word meaning 'tar.'

San Luis Obispo — City
ZIP: 93401 Lat: 35-16-22 N Long: 120-39-53 W
Pop: 41,958 (1990); 34,252 (1980) Pop Density: 4511.6
Land: 9.3 sq. mi.; Water: 0.2 sq. mi. Elev: 234 ft.
In southwestern CA, west of Bakersfield. Founded Aug 1850; incorporated Feb 19, 1856.
Name origin: For the mission, named for St. Louis, Bishop of Toulouse (1274–97), son of the King of Naples and Sicily. Indian name was Tixlini.

San Miguel — CDP
ZIP: 93451 Lat: 35-45-06 N Long: 120-41-32 W
Pop: 1,123 (1990) Pop Density: 1247.8
Land: 0.9 sq. mi.; Water: 0.0 sq. mi.

Templeton — CDP
ZIP: 93465 Lat: 35-33-13 N Long: 120-42-30 W
Pop: 2,887 (1990) Pop Density: 1031.1
Land: 2.8 sq. mi.; Water: 0.0 sq. mi.

San Mateo County
County Seat: Redwood City (ZIP: 94063)

Pop: 649,623 (1990); 587,329 (1980) Pop Density: 1446.5
Land: 449.1 sq. mi.; Water: 292.0 sq. mi. Area Code: 415
On N central coast of CA, S of San Francisco; organized Apr 19, 1856 from San Francisco County.
Name origin: For the creek, named for St. Matthew the Apostle.

Atherton — City
ZIP: 94027 Lat: 37-27-16 N Long: 122-12-08 W
Pop: 7,163 (1990); 7,797 (1980) Pop Density: 1461.8
Land: 4.9 sq. mi.; Water: 0.0 sq. mi.
In central-western CA, 22 mi. southeast of San Francisco. Incorporated Sep 12, 1923.
Name origin: For Faxon D. Atherton, father-in-law of novelist Gertrude Atherton (1857–1948).

Belmont — City
ZIP: 94002 Lat: 37-30-54 N Long: 122-17-42 W
Pop: 24,127 (1990); 24,505 (1980) Pop Density: 5361.6
Land: 4.5 sq. mi.; Water: 0.0 sq. mi.
In central-western CA, 20 mi. south of San Francisco; incorporated Oct 29, 1926.
Name origin: From French 'beautiful mountain,' a variant of *beaumont*.

Brisbane — City
ZIP: 94005 Lat: 37-41-21 N Long: 122-23-59 W
Pop: 2,952 (1990); 2,969 (1980) Pop Density: 894.5
Land: 3.3 sq. mi.; Water: 0.1 sq. mi.
In central-western CA, 5 mi. south of San Francisco, on San Francisco Bay. Founded 1908; incorporated Nov 27, 1961.
Name origin: For journalist Arthur Brisbane (1864–1936), so-named in 1931 by promoter Arthur Annis from Brisbane, Australia. Originally named Visitacion City but changed to avoid confusion with Visitacion Valley.

Broadmoor — CDP
Lat: 37-41-30 N Long: 122-28-46 W
Pop: 3,739 (1990) Pop Density: 9347.5
Land: 0.4 sq. mi.; Water: 0.0 sq. mi.

Burlingame — City
ZIP: 94010 Lat: 37-35-25 N Long: 122-21-45 W
Pop: 26,801 (1990); 26,173 (1980) Pop Density: 6232.8
Land: 4.3 sq. mi.; Water: 1.7 sq. mi.
In central-western CA, 12 mi. south of San Francisco on San Francisco Bay. Incorporated Jun 6, 1908.
Name origin: Named in 1868 by William C. Ralston for his friend, Anson C. Burlingame (1822–70), then U.S. Minister to China.

Colma — Town
Lat: 37-40-25 N Long: 122-27-12 W
Pop: 1,103 (1990); 395 (1980) Pop Density: 580.5
Land: 1.9 sq. mi.; Water: 0.0 sq. mi.
In central-western CA, just south of San Francisco. Incorporated Aug 5, 1924.
Name origin: Origin of name not known. Previously called Schoolhouse Station.

Daly City — City
ZIP: 94015 **Lat:** 37-41-13 N **Long:** 122-28-02 W
Pop: 92,311 (1990); 78,519 (1980) **Pop Density:** 12308.1
Land: 7.5 sq. mi.; **Water:** 0.0 sq. mi.

In central-western CA, 5 mi. south of San Francisco. Incorporated Mar 22, 1911.

Name origin: For John Daly, a dairyman in the district since the 1850s and owner of a ranch where people found refuge after the San Francisco earthquake (1906).

East Palo Alto — City
ZIP: 94303 **Lat:** 37-27-57 N **Long:** 122-07-55 W
Pop: 23,451 (1990); 18,191 (1980) **Pop Density:** 9380.4
Land: 2.5 sq. mi.; **Water:** 0.0 sq. mi.

In central-western CA, northeast of Palo Alto. Incorporated Jan 1, 1983.

El Granada — CDP
ZIP: 94018 **Lat:** 37-30-34 N **Long:** 122-27-59 W
Pop: 4,426 (1990); 3,582 (1980) **Pop Density:** 903.3
Land: 4.9 sq. mi.; **Water:** 0.0 sq. mi.

Emerald Lake Hills — CDP
Lat: 37-27-52 N **Long:** 122-16-00 W
Pop: 3,328 (1990) **Pop Density:** 2773.3
Land: 1.2 sq. mi.; **Water:** 0.0 sq. mi.

Foster City — City
ZIP: 94404 **Lat:** 37-33-49 N **Long:** 122-14-40 W
Pop: 28,176 (1990); 23,287 (1980) **Pop Density:** 7414.7
Land: 3.8 sq. mi.; **Water:** 16.2 sq. mi.

In central-western CA, 18 mi. south of San Francisco. Established 1965; incorporated Apr 27, 1971.

Name origin: For T. Jack Foster, who deeded a large parcel of real estate to the county.

Half Moon Bay — City
ZIP: 94019 **Lat:** 37-28-12 N **Long:** 122-26-12 W
Pop: 8,886 (1990); 7,282 (1980) **Pop Density:** 1367.1
Land: 6.5 sq. mi.; **Water:** 0.0 sq. mi. **Elev:** 69 ft.

In western CA, on Half Moon Bay inlet. Established 1867; incorporated Jul 15, 1959.

Name origin: For the bay, itself named for its crescent shape. Formerly called Spanish Town.

Highlands — CDP
Lat: 37-31-11 N **Long:** 122-20-34 W
Pop: 2,644 (1990) **Pop Density:** 2203.3
Land: 1.2 sq. mi.; **Water:** 0.0 sq. mi.

Hillsborough — Town
ZIP: 94010 **Lat:** 37-33-27 N **Long:** 122-21-22 W
Pop: 10,667 (1990); 10,372 (1980) **Pop Density:** 1720.5
Land: 6.2 sq. mi.; **Water:** 0.0 sq. mi.

In central-western CA, 10 mi. south of San Francisco, west of Burlingame in an oak woodland. Founded and incorporated May 5, 1910.

Name origin: Exclusive residential community founded by Henry T. Scott in 1910 and named after Hillsboro, NH, ancestral home of W.D.M. Howard, former owner of the site.

Menlo Park — City
ZIP: 94025 **Lat:** 37-28-47 N **Long:** 122-08-38 W
Pop: 28,040 (1990); 26,438 (1980) **Pop Density:** 2776.2
Land: 10.1 sq. mi.; **Water:** 7.3 sq. mi.

In central-western CA, 23 mi. southeast of San Francisco. Settled 1861; incorporated Nov 23, 1927.

Name origin: For the railroad station named in August 1854 by D.J. Oliver and D.C. McGlynn, brothers-in-law from Menlough, County Galway, Ireland, who erected an arched gate at the joint entrance to their ranches with the inscription *Menlo Park*.

Millbrae — City
ZIP: 94030 **Lat:** 37-35-56 N **Long:** 122-24-03 W
Pop: 20,412 (1990); 20,058 (1980) **Pop Density:** 6378.8
Land: 3.2 sq. mi.; **Water:** 0.0 sq. mi.

In western CA, northwest of San Mateo. Incorporated Jan 14, 1948.

Name origin: For the estate of Darius O. Mills, a leading banker and promoter from San Francisco and NY. The name was coined from his last name and *brae* Scottish 'hill slope.'

Montara — CDP
ZIP: 94037 **Lat:** 37-32-43 N **Long:** 122-29-49 W
Pop: 2,552 (1990); 1,972 (1980) **Pop Density:** 654.4
Land: 3.9 sq. mi.; **Water:** 0.0 sq. mi.

Moss Beach — CDP
ZIP: 94038 **Lat:** 37-31-18 N **Long:** 122-30-20 W
Pop: 3,002 (1990); 1,868 (1980) **Pop Density:** 1305.2
Land: 2.3 sq. mi.; **Water:** 0.0 sq. mi.

North Fair Oaks — CDP
ZIP: 94025 **Lat:** 37-28-28 N **Long:** 122-12-06 W
Pop: 13,912 (1990); 10,308 (1980) **Pop Density:** 11593.3
Land: 1.2 sq. mi.; **Water:** 0.0 sq. mi.

Pacifica — City
ZIP: 94044 **Lat:** 37-36-40 N **Long:** 122-28-34 W
Pop: 37,670 (1990); 36,866 (1980) **Pop Density:** 2989.7
Land: 12.6 sq. mi.; **Water:** 0.0 sq. mi. **Elev:** 76 ft.

On the western coast of CA, south of San Francisco. Created Oct 29, 1957, by joining nine communities; incorporated Nov 22, 1957.

Portola Valley — City
Lat: 37-22-18 N **Long:** 122-13-06 W
Pop: 4,194 (1990); 3,939 (1980) **Pop Density:** 455.9
Land: 9.2 sq. mi.; **Water:** 0.0 sq. mi.

In central-western CA, northeast of San Jose. Incorporated Jul 14, 1964.

Redwood City — City
ZIP: 94063 **Lat:** 37-30-59 N **Long:** 122-12-21 W
Pop: 66,072 (1990); 54,951 (1980) **Pop Density:** 3477.5
Land: 19.0 sq. mi.; **Water:** 15.1 sq. mi. **Elev:** 15 ft.

In central-western CA, 19 mi. southeast of San Francisco. Platted 1854; incorporated May 11, 1867. Site of Marine World.

Name origin: For the large-scale lumbering industry based on the abundant redwood trees. Previously called Mezesville for an early settler.

San Bruno — City
ZIP: 94066 **Lat:** 37-37-29 N **Long:** 122-25-40 W
Pop: 38,961 (1990); 35,417 (1980) **Pop Density:** 6087.7
Land: 6.4 sq. mi.; **Water:** 0.0 sq. mi. **Elev:** 16 ft.

In central-western CA, 15 mi. south of San Francisco. Incorporated Dec 23, 1914.

Name origin: Named by Lt. Bruno Hecate, naval officer to the king of Spain, for his patron saint, Bruno (c. 1030–1101), founder of the Carthusian monastic order.

CALIFORNIA, San Mateo County   *American Places Dictionary*

San Carlos   City
ZIP: 94070   **Lat:** 37-29-51 N   **Long:** 122-16-02 W
Pop: 26,167 (1990); 24,710 (1980)   **Pop Density:** 4672.7
Land: 5.6 sq. mi.; **Water:** 0.0 sq. mi.   **Elev:** 76 ft.
In central-western CA, 16 mi. southeast of San Francisco. Incorporated Jul 8, 1925.
Name origin: Named in 1887 by founder "Capt." N.T. Smith because it was believed that the 1769 expedition led by Gaspar de Portolá (c. 1723–c. 1784) first saw San Francisco Bay on Nov 4, 1769, the feast day of St. Charles (San Carlos) of Borromeo.

San Mateo   City
ZIP: 94402   **Lat:** 37-33-40 N   **Long:** 122-18-43 W
Pop: 85,486 (1990); 77,640 (1980)   **Pop Density:** 7007.0
Land: 12.2 sq. mi.; **Water:** 3.7 sq. mi.
In central-western CA, 18 mi. south of San Francisco. Platted 1863; incorporated Sep 4, 1894.
Name origin: For Arroyo de San Mateo, named for St. Matthew the Apostle.

South San Francisco   City
ZIP: 94080   **Lat:** 37-39-31 N   **Long:** 122-18-30 W
Pop: 54,312 (1990); 49,393 (1980)   **Pop Density:** 6034.7
Land: 9.0 sq. mi.; **Water:** 20.7 sq. mi.   **Elev:** 19 ft.
In central-western CA, 8 mi. south of San Francisco. Incorporated Sep 19, 1908.
Name origin: Previously called Baden for the railroad station.

West Menlo Park   CDP
Lat: 37-26-01 N   **Long:** 122-12-06 W
Pop: 3,959 (1990)   **Pop Density:** 6598.3
Land: 0.6 sq. mi.; **Water:** 0.0 sq. mi.

Woodside   Town
ZIP: 94062   **Lat:** 37-25-29 N   **Long:** 122-15-33 W
Pop: 5,035 (1990); 5,291 (1980)   **Pop Density:** 430.3
Land: 11.7 sq. mi.; **Water:** 0.0 sq. mi.
In central-northern CA, west of Palo Alto. Incorporated Nov 16, 1956.
Name origin: Named in 1849 for a lumber camp.

Santa Barbara County
County Seat: Santa Barbara (ZIP: 93101)

Pop: 369,608 (1990); 298,694 (1980)   **Pop Density:** 135.0
Land: 2738.5 sq. mi.; **Water:** 1051.1 sq. mi.   **Area Code:** 805
On S coast of CA, northwest of Los Angeles; original county; organized Feb 18, 1850 (prior to statehood).
Name origin: For the channel named for St. Barbara.

Buellton   CDP
ZIP: 93427   **Lat:** 34-37-33 N   **Long:** 120-12-04 W
Pop: 3,506 (1990); 2,364 (1980)   **Pop Density:** 762.2
Land: 4.6 sq. mi.; **Water:** 0.0 sq. mi.

Carpinteria   City
ZIP: 93013   **Lat:** 34-23-16 N   **Long:** 119-30-47 W
Pop: 13,747 (1990); 10,835 (1980)   **Pop Density:** 5091.5
Land: 2.7 sq. mi.; **Water:** 4.6 sq. mi.   **Elev:** 14 ft.
On the southwestern coast of CA, 10 mi. south of Santa Barbara. Incorporated Sep 28, 1965.
Name origin: From Spanish 'carpenter shop,' so named by Fr. Crespi, a member of the 1769 expedition led by Gaspar de Portolá (c. 1723–c. 1784) because he found Indians building a canoe here.

Guadalupe   City
ZIP: 93434   **Lat:** 34-57-48 N   **Long:** 120-34-28 W
Pop: 5,479 (1990); 3,629 (1980)   **Pop Density:** 6087.8
Land: 0.9 sq. mi.; **Water:** 0.0 sq. mi.   **Elev:** 85 ft.
In southwestern CA, 50 mi. northwest of Santa Barbara. Incorporated Aug 2, 1946.
Name origin: For the Guadalupe Rancho on which the town was built, itself named for the Virgin of Guadalupe, patron saint of Mexico.

Isla Vista   CDP
ZIP: 93117   **Lat:** 34-24-57 N   **Long:** 119-51-24 W
Pop: 20,395 (1990)   **Pop Density:** 9711.9
Land: 2.1 sq. mi.; **Water:** 0.1 sq. mi.

Lompoc   City
ZIP: 93436   **Lat:** 34-39-38 N   **Long:** 120-28-10 W
Pop: 37,649 (1990); 26,267 (1980)   **Pop Density:** 3361.5
Land: 11.2 sq. mi.; **Water:** 0.0 sq. mi.   **Elev:** 104 ft.
In southwestern CA, 45 mi. west-northwest of Santa Barbara. Founded 1874; incorporated Aug 13, 1888. Noted for vast fields of flowers grown for seed, and its Flower Festival; site of Vandenberg Air Force Base.
Name origin: A Chumash Indian placename of uncertain meaning.

Mission Hills   CDP
Lat: 34-41-09 N   **Long:** 120-26-09 W
Pop: 3,112 (1990); 2,797 (1980)   **Pop Density:** 2593.3
Land: 1.2 sq. mi.; **Water:** 0.0 sq. mi.

Santa Barbara   City
ZIP: 93102   **Lat:** 34-25-42 N   **Long:** 119-43-18 W
Pop: 85,571 (1990); 74,414 (1980)   **Pop Density:** 4527.6
Land: 18.9 sq. mi.; **Water:** 0.7 sq. mi.
On the southwestern coast of CA, 81 mi. northwest of Los Angeles. Founded 1782 on land called Yamnonalit by the Indians; incorporated Apr 9, 1850.
Name origin: For the Santa Barbara Channel, which was named for St. Barbara, virgin martyr.

Santa Maria   City
ZIP: 93454   **Lat:** 34-56-13 N   **Long:** 120-26-12 W
Pop: 61,284 (1990); 39,685 (1980)   **Pop Density:** 3563.0
Land: 17.2 sq. mi.; **Water:** 0.4 sq. mi.   **Elev:** 216 ft.
In southwestern CA, north of Lompoc. Incorporated Sep 12, 1905.
Name origin: For a land grant, also called Tepusquet, named

for a St. Mary but probably not the Virgin because she was referred to as *Nuestra Señora*.

Santa Ynez — CDP
ZIP: 93460 Lat: 34-36-28 N Long: 120-06-10 W
Pop: 4,200 (1990); 3,335 (1980) Pop Density: 538.5
Land: 7.8 sq. mi.; Water: 0.0 sq. mi.

In southwestern CA, northwest of Santa Barbara. Founded 1804.
Name origin: For St. Agnes, one of the four great virgin martyrs of the early church.

Solvang — City
ZIP: 93463 Lat: 34-35-32 N Long: 120-08-21 W
Pop: 4,741 (1990); 3,091 (1980) Pop Density: 1896.4
Land: 2.5 sq. mi.; Water: 0.0 sq. mi.

In southwestern CA, northwest of Santa Barbara. Founded 1911 by the Danish-American Corp., headed by professors of the Danish College in Des Moines, IA; incorporated May 1, 1985.
Name origin: From Danish 'sun meadow.'

Vandenberg Air Force Base — Military Facility
ZIP: 93437 Lat: 34-44-57 N Long: 120-31-02 W
Pop: 9,846 (1990); 5,839 (1980) Pop Density: 445.5
Land: 22.1 sq. mi.; Water: 0.1 sq. mi.

Vandenberg Village — CDP
ZIP: 93436 Lat: 34-42-40 N Long: 120-27-45 W
Pop: 5,971 (1990) Pop Density: 1148.3
Land: 5.2 sq. mi.; Water: 0.0 sq. mi.

Santa Clara County
County Seat: San Jose (ZIP: 95113)

Pop: 1,497,580 (1990); 1,295,070 (1980) Pop Density: 1159.8
Land: 1291.2 sq. mi.; Water: 13.3 sq. mi. Area Code: 408

In W central CA, north of Monterey; original county; organized Feb 18, 1850 (prior to statehood).
Name origin: For the river named for St. Clare of Assisi.

Burbank — CDP
Lat: 37-18-59 N Long: 121-55-54 W
Pop: 4,902 (1990) Pop Density: 7002.9
Land: 0.7 sq. mi.; Water: 0.0 sq. mi.

Cambrian Park — CDP
Lat: 37-15-20 N Long: 121-55-40 W
Pop: 2,998 (1990) Pop Density: 4996.7
Land: 0.6 sq. mi.; Water: 0.0 sq. mi.

Campbell — City
ZIP: 95008 Lat: 37-16-43 N Long: 121-57-12 W
Pop: 36,048 (1990); 26,843 (1980) Pop Density: 6437.1
Land: 5.6 sq. mi.; Water: 0.1 sq. mi. Elev: 196 ft.

In western CA, 5 mi. southwest of San Jose. Founded 1885; incorporated Mar 28, 1952.
Name origin: For Campbell Creek, which runs through it, itself named for William Campbell, who established a sawmill here in 1848 and a stage station in 1852. The creek is now called Saratoga Creek.

Cupertino — City
ZIP: 95014 Lat: 37-18-51 N Long: 122-02-50 W
Pop: 40,263 (1990); 34,297 (1980) Pop Density: 3909.0
Land: 10.3 sq. mi.; Water: 0.0 sq. mi. Elev: 236 ft.

In central-western CA, 7 mi. west of San Jose. Incorporated Oct 10, 1955.
Name origin: For Arroyo de San Jose Cupertino, named in honor of the seventeenth-century Italian saint. The arroyo is now called Stevens Creek, but the post office preserves the old name.

East Foothills — CDP
Lat: 37-22-52 N Long: 121-48-59 W
Pop: 14,898 (1990) Pop Density: 4805.8
Land: 3.1 sq. mi.; Water: 0.0 sq. mi.

Gilroy — City
ZIP: 95020 Lat: 37-00-36 N Long: 121-34-41 W
Pop: 31,487 (1990); 21,641 (1980) Pop Density: 3057.0
Land: 10.3 sq. mi.; Water: 0.0 sq. mi. Elev: 200 ft.

In western CA, 30 mi. southeast of San Jose in the lower Santa Clara Valley. The "Garlic Capital of the World"; incorporated Mar 12, 1870.
Name origin: For John Gilroy (1794–1869), a Scots sailor who arrived in CA in 1814, settled in the Santa Clara Valley, and in 1833 came into possession of the land where the city is located.

Lexington Hills — CDP
Lat: 37-09-53 N Long: 121-58-18 W
Pop: 2,064 (1990) Pop Density: 308.1
Land: 6.7 sq. mi.; Water: 0.0 sq. mi.

Los Altos — City
ZIP: 94022 Lat: 37-22-09 N Long: 122-05-43 W
Pop: 26,303 (1990); 25,769 (1980) Pop Density: 4109.8
Land: 6.4 sq. mi.; Water: 0.0 sq. mi.

In central-western CA, southeast of Palo Alto. Established 1908; incorporated Dec 1, 1952.
Name origin: From Spanish 'the heights,' for its location in the hills overlooking San Francisco Bay.

Los Altos Hills — Town
ZIP: 94022 Lat: 37-22-04 N Long: 122-08-21 W
Pop: 7,514 (1990); 7,421 (1980) Pop Density: 894.5
Land: 8.4 sq. mi.; Water: 0.0 sq. mi.

Incorporated Jan 27, 1956.

Los Gatos
Town
ZIP: 95030　　　Lat: 37-13-50 N　Long: 121-57-35 W
Pop: 27,357 (1990); 26,906 (1980)　　Pop Density: 2630.5
Land: 10.4 sq. mi.; Water: 0.1 sq. mi.

In western CA, 7 mi. southwest of San Jose. Incorporated Aug 10, 1887.

Name origin: From Spanish 'little corner of the cats,' the name of the former Rancho Rinconada de los Gatos, around which the town grew.

Loyola
CDP
　　　　　　　　Lat: 37-21-05 N　Long: 122-05-58 W
Pop: 3,076 (1990)　　　　Pop Density: 2197.1
Land: 1.4 sq. mi.; Water: 0.0 sq. mi.

Milpitas
City
ZIP: 95035　　　Lat: 37-26-04 N　Long: 121-53-31 W
Pop: 50,686 (1990); 37,820 (1980)　　Pop Density: 3672.9
Land: 13.8 sq. mi.; Water: 0.1 sq. mi.

In central-western CA near Penitencia Creek, south of Palo Alto. Founded c. 1850; incorporated Jan 26, 1954.

Name origin: For the Milpitas land granted (1835) to Maximo Martinez; from Spanish 'little corn field.'

Monte Sereno
City
ZIP: 95030　　　Lat: 37-14-17 N　Long: 121-59-18 W
Pop: 3,287 (1990); 3,434 (1980)　　Pop Density: 2054.4
Land: 1.6 sq. mi.; Water: 0.0 sq. mi.　　　Elev: 503 ft.

In central-western CA, 10 mi. southwest of San Jose. Incorporated May 14, 1957.

Name origin: From Spanish 'serene mountain.'

Morgan Hill
City
ZIP: 95037　　　Lat: 37-07-49 N　Long: 121-38-22 W
Pop: 23,928 (1990); 17,060 (1980)　　Pop Density: 2278.9
Land: 10.5 sq. mi.; Water: 0.0 sq. mi.

In west-central CA, 17 mi. southeast of San Jose. Incorporated Nov 10, 1906.

Name origin: Named in 1892 for Morgan Hill –1914), on whose ranch the settlement developed.

Mountain View
City
ZIP: 94041　　　Lat: 37-24-07 N　Long: 122-04-39 W
Pop: 67,460 (1990); 58,655 (1980)　　Pop Density: 5621.7
Land: 12.0 sq. mi.; Water: 0.2 sq. mi.　　　Elev: 97 ft.

In central-western CA, 10 mi. northwest of San Jose. Settled 1852; incorporated Nov 7, 1902.

Name origin: For its view of the Santa Cruz Mountains, Mt. Diablo, and Mt. Hamilton.

Palo Alto
City
ZIP: 94303　　　Lat: 37-23-57 N　Long: 122-08-21 W
Pop: 55,900 (1990); 55,225 (1980)　　Pop Density: 2358.6
Land: 23.7 sq. mi.; Water: 2.0 sq. mi.　　　Elev: 23 ft.

In central-western CA, 16 mi. northwest of San Jose. Founded 1891; incorporated Apr 23, 1894. Home of Stanford University.

Name origin: Named by Palau, a member of the 1774 expedition led by Juan Bautista de Anza (1735–c. 1788); from Spanish 'tall tree,' referring to a redwood used as a landmark by travelers.

Rancho Rinconada
CDP
　　　　　　　　Lat: 37-18-53 N　Long: 122-00-06 W
Pop: 4,206 (1990)　　　　Pop Density: 8412.0
Land: 0.5 sq. mi.; Water: 0.0 sq. mi.

San Jose
City
ZIP: 95113　　　Lat: 37-18-14 N　Long: 121-50-59 W
Pop: 782,248 (1990); 629,400 (1980)　　Pop Density: 4566.5
Land: 171.3 sq. mi.; Water: 3.3 sq. mi.　　　Elev: 87 ft.

In central-western CA, 38 mi. southeast of San Francisco on the Guadalupe River. Founded Nov 29, 1777; first state capital (1849–52); incorporated Mar 27, 1850. Oldest civic municipality in CA.

Name origin: For St. Joseph, husband of the Virgin Mary and patron saint of CA. Spanish name was *el Pueblo de San Jose de Guadalupe*.

San Martin
CDP
ZIP: 95046　　　Lat: 37-05-05 N　Long: 121-36-22 W
Pop: 1,713 (1990); 1,731 (1980)　　Pop Density: 856.5
Land: 2.0 sq. mi.; Water: 0.0 sq. mi.

Santa Clara
City
ZIP: 95050　　　Lat: 37-21-54 N　Long: 121-58-00 W
Pop: 93,613 (1990); 87,700 (1980)　　Pop Density: 5115.5
Land: 18.3 sq. mi.; Water: 0.0 sq. mi.　　　Elev: 88 ft.

In central-western CA, 5 mi. northwest of San Jose. Settled 1777; incorporated Jul 5, 1852.

Name origin: For the mission named for St. Clare of Assisi (1194–1253), founder of the Poor Clares, the sister order of the Franciscans.

Saratoga
City
ZIP: 95070　　　Lat: 37-16-04 N　Long: 122-01-22 W
Pop: 28,061 (1990); 29,261 (1980)　　Pop Density: 2338.4
Land: 12.0 sq. mi.; Water: 0.0 sq. mi.

In central-western CA, 8 mi. southwest of San Jose in the Santa Cruz Mts. Founded 1851; incorporated Oct 15, 1956.

Name origin: For the waters of the nearby Pacific Congress Spring, which resemble those of Congress Spring at Saratoga, NY. Originally called McCarthysville, for Martin McCarthy, a local miller.

Stanford
CDP
ZIP: 94305　　　Lat: 37-25-26 N　Long: 122-09-53 W
Pop: 18,097 (1990); 11,045 (1980)　　Pop Density: 6463.2
Land: 2.8 sq. mi.; Water: 0.0 sq. mi.

Sunnyvale
City
ZIP: 94086　　　Lat: 37-23-08 N　Long: 122-01-31 W
Pop: 117,229 (1990); 106,618 (1980)　　Pop Density: 5352.9
Land: 21.9 sq. mi.; Water: 0.7 sq. mi.

In central-western CA, 8 mi. northwest of San Jose. Settled 1849 by Martin Murphy; incorporated Dec 24, 1912.

Santa Cruz County
County Seat: Santa Cruz (ZIP: 95060)

Pop: 229,734 (1990); 188,141 (1980) **Pop Density:** 515.3
Land: 445.8 sq. mi.; **Water:** 161.9 sq. mi. **Area Code:** 408
On S central coast of CA; original county; organized Feb 18, 1850 (prior to statehood).
Name origin: Spanish 'holy cross,' a common Spanish placename. Originally named *Branciforte* for the viceroy, but changed Apr 6, 1850.

Aptos CDP
ZIP: 95003 **Lat:** 36-59-30 N **Long:** 121-53-58 W
Pop: 9,061 (1990); 7,039 (1980) **Pop Density:** 1118.6
Land: 8.1 sq. mi.; **Water:** 0.0 sq. mi.
In central-western CA east of Santa Cruz. Founded 1831. Site of Cabrillo College.
Name origin: A Spanish rendering of an Indian word meaning 'meeting of two streams,' referring to Valencia and Aptos creeks.

Aptos Hills-Larkin Valley CDP
Lat: 36-57-39 N **Long:** 121-49-48 W
Pop: 2,205 (1990) **Pop Density:** 237.1
Land: 9.3 sq. mi.; **Water:** 0.0 sq. mi.

Ben Lomond CDP
ZIP: 95005 **Lat:** 37-06-12 N **Long:** 122-05-04 W
Pop: 7,884 (1990); 7,238 (1980) **Pop Density:** 563.1
Land: 14.0 sq. mi.; **Water:** 0.2 sq. mi.
In central-western CA in the Santa Cruz Mountains, northwest of Santa Cruz. Founded 1872.
Name origin: For the mountain in Scotland at Loch Lomond; from Scottish *ben* 'mountain.'

Boulder Creek CDP
ZIP: 95006 **Lat:** 37-08-15 N **Long:** 122-07-40 W
Pop: 6,725 (1990); 5,662 (1980) **Pop Density:** 551.2
Land: 12.2 sq. mi.; **Water:** 0.0 sq. mi.
In central-western CA, northwest of Santa Cruz. Established c. 1870.
Name origin: Originally called Lorenzo.

Capitola City
ZIP: 95010 **Lat:** 36-58-33 N **Long:** 121-57-10 W
Pop: 10,171 (1990); 9,095 (1980) **Pop Density:** 6356.9
Land: 1.6 sq. mi.; **Water:** 0.1 sq. mi.
In western CA, 4 mi. east of Santa Cruz. Incorporated Jan 11, 1949.
Name origin: For the resort village, Camp Capitola, developed in 1876 by F. A. Hihn.

Corralitos CDP
Lat: 36-59-47 N **Long:** 121-47-55 W
Pop: 2,513 (1990) **Pop Density:** 288.9
Land: 8.7 sq. mi.; **Water:** 0.0 sq. mi.

Day Valley CDP
Lat: 37-02-09 N **Long:** 121-51-40 W
Pop: 2,842 (1990) **Pop Density:** 167.2
Land: 17.0 sq. mi.; **Water:** 0.0 sq. mi.

Felton CDP
ZIP: 95018 **Lat:** 37-02-33 N **Long:** 122-04-19 W
Pop: 5,350 (1990); 4,564 (1980) **Pop Density:** 891.7
Land: 6.0 sq. mi.; **Water:** 0.0 sq. mi.
In central-western CA, northwest of Santa Cruz.
Name origin: Named in 1878 by George Treat for Charles Felton, state assemblyman.

Freedom CDP
ZIP: 95019 **Lat:** 36-56-24 N **Long:** 121-47-21 W
Pop: 8,361 (1990); 6,416 (1980) **Pop Density:** 5225.6
Land: 1.6 sq. mi.; **Water:** 0.0 sq. mi.

Interlaken CDP
Lat: 36-57-04 N **Long:** 121-43-58 W
Pop: 6,404 (1990) **Pop Density:** 681.3
Land: 9.4 sq. mi.; **Water:** 0.6 sq. mi.

Live Oak CDP
ZIP: 95062 **Lat:** 36-59-01 N **Long:** 121-58-46 W
Pop: 15,212 (1990); 11,482 (1980) **Pop Density:** 4609.7
Land: 3.3 sq. mi.; **Water:** 0.0 sq. mi.

Opal Cliffs CDP
ZIP: 95062 **Lat:** 36-57-18 N **Long:** 121-58-29 W
Pop: 5,940 (1990); 5,041 (1980) **Pop Density:** 7425.0
Land: 0.8 sq. mi.; **Water:** 1.2 sq. mi.

Rio del Mar CDP
ZIP: 95003 **Lat:** 36-57-28 N **Long:** 121-53-01 W
Pop: 8,919 (1990); 7,067 (1980) **Pop Density:** 2973.0
Land: 3.0 sq. mi.; **Water:** 1.6 sq. mi.

Santa Cruz City
ZIP: 95060 **Lat:** 36-58-23 N **Long:** 122-02-08 W
Pop: 49,040 (1990); 41,483 (1980) **Pop Density:** 3687.2
Land: 13.3 sq. mi.; **Water:** 3.1 sq. mi.
On the central-western coast of CA, 28 mi. south of San Jose. Founded 1791; incorporated Mar 31, 1866.
Name origin: From Spanish 'holy cross.'

Scotts Valley City
ZIP: 95066 **Lat:** 37-03-22 N **Long:** 122-00-28 W
Pop: 8,615 (1990); 6,891 (1980) **Pop Density:** 1914.4
Land: 4.5 sq. mi.; **Water:** 0.0 sq. mi. **Elev:** 570 ft.
In west-central CA, north of Santa Cruz. Incorporated Aug 2, 1966.
Name origin: For Hiram Daniel Scott, a sailor who bought Rancho San Agustin in 1852.

CALIFORNIA, Santa Cruz County   American Places Dictionary

Soquel   CDP
ZIP: 95073   **Lat:** 36-59-37 N **Long:** 121-56-48 W
Pop: 9,188 (1990); 6,212 (1980)   **Pop Density:** 1997.4
Land: 4.6 sq. mi.; **Water:** 0.0 sq. mi.
In central-western CA, northeast of Santa Cruz.
Name origin: For a land grant named for a Shoshonean village.

Twin Lakes   CDP
ZIP: 95060   **Lat:** 36-57-40 N **Long:** 121-59-27 W
Pop: 5,379 (1990); 4,502 (1980)   **Pop Density:** 7684.3
Land: 0.7 sq. mi.; **Water:** 0.5 sq. mi.

Watsonville   City
ZIP: 95076   **Lat:** 36-55-09 N **Long:** 121-46-06 W
Pop: 31,099 (1990); 23,662 (1980)   **Pop Density:** 5271.0
Land: 5.9 sq. mi.; **Water:** 0.1 sq. mi.
In central-western CA near Monterey Bay, south of Santa Cruz. Established 1854; incorporated Mar 30, 1868.
Name origin: For Judge John H. Watson, landowner.

Shasta County
County Seat: Redding (ZIP: 96001)

Pop: 147,036 (1990); 115,613 (1980)   **Pop Density:** 38.8
Land: 3785.7 sq. mi.; **Water:** 62.0 sq. mi.   **Area Code:** 916
In N central CA, north of Chico; original county; organized Feb 18, 1850 (prior to statehood).
Name origin: For the Indian tribe of Hokan linguistic stock; the original meaning is uncertain. Also spelled *Sasty*, *Sastise*, *Chasty*, *Chasta*.

Anderson   City
ZIP: 96007   **Lat:** 40-26-59 N **Long:** 122-17-39 W
Pop: 8,299 (1990); 7,381 (1980)   **Pop Density:** 1360.5
Land: 6.1 sq. mi.; **Water:** 0.2 sq. mi.   **Elev:** 430 ft.
In north-central CA, 10 mi. south of Redding. Founded 1872; incorporated Jan 16, 1956.
Name origin: For Elias Anderson, who granted a right of way to the California and Oregon Railroad.

Burney   CDP
ZIP: 96013   **Lat:** 40-53-03 N **Long:** 121-40-07 W
Pop: 3,423 (1990); 3,187 (1980)   **Pop Density:** 658.3
Land: 5.2 sq. mi.; **Water:** 0.0 sq. mi.

Central Valley   CDP
ZIP: 96019   **Lat:** 40-40-46 N **Long:** 122-22-29 W
Pop: 4,340 (1990); 3,424 (1980)   **Pop Density:** 1400.0
Land: 3.1 sq. mi.; **Water:** 0.0 sq. mi.

Cottonwood   CDP
ZIP: 96022   **Lat:** 40-23-25 N **Long:** 122-16-47 W
Pop: 1,747 (1990); 1,553 (1980)   **Pop Density:** 1588.2
Land: 1.1 sq. mi.; **Water:** 0.0 sq. mi.

Redding   City
ZIP: 96049   **Lat:** 40-34-20 N **Long:** 122-21-53 W
Pop: 66,462 (1990); 42,103 (1980)   **Pop Density:** 1298.1
Land: 51.2 sq. mi.; **Water:** 1.1 sq. mi.   **Elev:** 557 ft.
In north-central CA on the Sacramento River, 65 mi. northwest of Chico. Incorporated Oct 4, 1887.
Name origin: A town was laid out south of the present city and called Latona then changed to Reading for Pierson B. Reading, county pioneer. The present town was laid out in 1872 by B.B. Redding, a land agent for the Central Pacific Railroad, and named for him.

Sierra County
County Seat: Downieville (ZIP: 95936)

Pop: 3,318 (1990); 3,073 (1980)   **Pop Density:** 3.5
Land: 953.4 sq. mi.; **Water:** 8.6 sq. mi.   **Area Code:** 916
On NE border of CA with NV; organized Apr 16, 1852 from Yuba County.
Name origin: Spanish 'mountain range,' for its location in the northern part of the Sierra Nevada.

Downieville   CDP
ZIP: 95936
Pop: 950 (1990)
    Elev: 2899 ft.
In northeastern CA, southeast of Chico. County seat. Settled 1849.
Name origin: For "Major" William Downie, a Scots miner. Originally called The Forks (of the Yuba River).

Loyalton   City
ZIP: 96118   **Lat:** 39-40-35 N **Long:** 120-14-36 W
Pop: 931 (1990); 1,030 (1980)   **Pop Density:** 3103.3
Land: 0.3 sq. mi.; **Water:** 0.0 sq. mi.   **Elev:** 4936 ft.
Incorporated Sep 21, 1901; a lumbering center.
Name origin: For the strong Union sentiment here in 1863. Previously known as Smith's Neck, possibly for the Smith Mining Co.

Siskiyou County
County Seat: Yreka (ZIP: 96097)

Pop: 43,531 (1990); 39,732 (1980)　　**Pop Density:** 6.9
Land: 6287.3 sq. mi.; **Water:** 60.6 sq. mi.　　**Area Code:** 916

In N central CA on OR border; organized Mar 22, 1852, from Klamath and Shasta counties, and in 1874 annexed part of Klamath County. Site of Mt. Shasta, 14,162 ft.

Name origin: Possibly Chinook from Cree for 'bob-tailed horse,' or French *six cailloux* 'six boulders.'

Dorris　　City
ZIP: 96023　　**Lat:** 41-57-54 N **Long:** 121-55-11 W
Pop: 892 (1990); 836 (1980)　　**Pop Density:** 1274.3
Land: 0.7 sq. mi.; **Water:** 0.0 sq. mi.　　**Elev:** 4240 ft.
Incorporated Dec 23, 1908.
Name origin: Named by the Southern Pacific Railroad in 1907 for brothers Presley A. and Carlos J. Dorris, stock raisers in Little Shasta in the 1860s.

Dunsmuir　　City
ZIP: 96025　　**Lat:** 41-14-00 N **Long:** 122-16-11 W
Pop: 2,129 (1990); 2,253 (1980)　　**Pop Density:** 1120.5
Land: 1.9 sq. mi.; **Water:** 0.0 sq. mi.　　**Elev:** 2289 ft.
Incorporated Aug 7, 1909.

Etna　　City
ZIP: 96027　　**Lat:** 41-27-33 N **Long:** 122-53-34 W
Pop: 835 (1990); 754 (1980)　　**Pop Density:** 1043.8
Land: 0.8 sq. mi.; **Water:** 0.0 sq. mi.　　**Elev:** 2929 ft.
Incorporated Mar 13, 1878.
Name origin: For the nearby Aetna flour mill located here in the 1850s; spelling changed by statute in 1874. Originally called Rough and Ready.

Fort Jones　　City
ZIP: 96032　　**Lat:** 41-36-25 N **Long:** 122-50-23 W
Pop: 639 (1990); 544 (1980)　　**Pop Density:** 1278.0
Land: 0.5 sq. mi.; **Water:** 0.0 sq. mi.　　**Elev:** 2747 ft.
Incorporated Mar 16, 1872.
Name origin: For the U.S. Army fort named for Col. Roger Jones. Formerly known as Wheelock, Scottsburg, and Ottitiewa.

McCloud　　CDP
ZIP: 96057　　**Lat:** 41-15-17 N **Long:** 122-08-06 W
Pop: 1,555 (1990); 1,656 (1980)　　**Pop Density:** 622.0
Land: 2.5 sq. mi.; **Water:** 0.1 sq. mi.

Montague　　City
ZIP: 96064　　**Lat:** 41-43-38 N **Long:** 122-31-46 W
Pop: 1,415 (1990); 1,285 (1980)　　**Pop Density:** 832.4
Land: 1.7 sq. mi.; **Water:** 0.0 sq. mi.　　**Elev:** 2538 ft.
In north-central CA on the Shasta River, north of Redding. Incorporated Jan 25, 1909; important campsite on the CA-OR trail prior to 1850.
Name origin: For the railroad station, itself named for S.S. Montague, chief engineer of the Central Pacific Railroad.

Mount Shasta　　City
ZIP: 96067　　**Lat:** 41-19-20 N **Long:** 122-18-52 W
Pop: 3,460 (1990); 2,837 (1980)　　**Pop Density:** 935.1
Land: 3.7 sq. mi.; **Water:** 0.0 sq. mi.　　**Elev:** 3554 ft.
In north-central CA, near the base of Mt. Shasta within Shasta National Forest. Founded 1850; incorporated May 31, 1905.

Tulelake　　City
ZIP: 96134　　**Lat:** 41-57-14 N **Long:** 121-28-29 W
Pop: 1,010 (1990); 783 (1980)　　**Pop Density:** 2525.0
Land: 0.4 sq. mi.; **Water:** 0.0 sq. mi.
Incorporated Mar 1, 1937.

Weed　　City
ZIP: 96094　　**Lat:** 41-24-59 N **Long:** 122-22-42 W
Pop: 3,062 (1990); 2,879 (1980)　　**Pop Density:** 765.5
Land: 4.0 sq. mi.; **Water:** 0.0 sq. mi.　　**Elev:** 3466 ft.
In central-northern CA, north of Redding. Incorporated Jan 25, 1961.
Name origin: For Abner Weed, who founded a lumber company here and was state senator (1907–09).

Yreka　　City
ZIP: 96097　　**Lat:** 41-43-44 N **Long:** 122-37-53 W
Pop: 6,948 (1990); 5,916 (1980)　　**Pop Density:** 772.0
Land: 9.0 sq. mi.; **Water:** 0.1 sq. mi.
In north-central CA. Incorporated Apr 21, 1857.
Name origin: Derived from the Shasta Indian name *Wyekah* for Mount Shasta, possibly meaning 'north mountain.' Formerly called Thompson's Dry Diggings and Shasta Butte City; name changed to the present one Mar 22, 1852.

Solano County
County Seat: Fairfield (ZIP: 94533)

Pop: 340,421 (1990); 235,203 (1980) **Pop Density:** 411.1
Land: 828.2 sq. mi.; **Water:** 78.7 sq. mi. **Area Code:** 707

In N central CA, NE of San Francisco; original county; organized Feb 18, 1850 (prior to statehood).

Name origin: For St. Francis Solano and for Sem-yeto, a chief of the Soscol and Suisun Indians, who had accepted the Christian name of the saint at his baptism.

Benicia City
ZIP: 94510 **Lat:** 38-04-18 N **Long:** 122-09-14 W
Pop: 24,437 (1990); 15,376 (1980) **Pop Density:** 1909.1
Land: 12.8 sq. mi.; **Water:** 1.2 sq. mi. **Elev:** 33 ft.

In central-western CA, 17 mi. northeast of Oakland, on the north shore of Carquinez Strait. Founded 1848; capital of CA 1853–54; incorporated Mar 27, 1850.

Name origin: For the second name of the wife of Mariano G. Vallejo, a town founder. Previously called Santa Francisca.

Dixon City
ZIP: 95620 **Lat:** 38-26-40 N **Long:** 121-49-25 W
Pop: 10,401 (1990); 7,541 (1980) **Pop Density:** 2737.1
Land: 3.8 sq. mi.; **Water:** 0.1 sq. mi.

In central-western CA, 19 mi. southwest of Sacramento. Incorporated Mar 30, 1878.

Name origin: Named in 1870 for Thomas Dickson, who gave 10 acres for the townsite. Present spelling adopted by the Post Office Dept. through clerical error.

Fairfield City
ZIP: 94533 **Lat:** 38-15-08 N **Long:** 122-02-29 W
Pop: 77,211 (1990); 58,099 (1980) **Pop Density:** 2150.7
Land: 35.9 sq. mi.; **Water:** 0.0 sq. mi.

In central CA, 40 mi. southwest of Sacramento in the Vaca Valley. Incorporated Dec 12, 1903.

Name origin: For Fairfield, CT, former home of Robert H. Waterman (1808–84), a famous clipper ship captain who lived here and donated the land for the city.

Rio Vista City
ZIP: 94571 **Lat:** 38-09-54 N **Long:** 121-41-40 W
Pop: 3,316 (1990); 3,142 (1980) **Pop Density:** 1842.2
Land: 1.8 sq. mi.; **Water:** 0.2 sq. mi. **Elev:** 22 ft.

In west-central CA, 26 mi. northwest of Stockton on the Sacramento River. Founded 1857 by Col. N.H. David; incorporated Jan 6, 1894.

Name origin: Originally called Brazos del Rio because it was near the three 'arms' of the Sacramento River; given present name in 1860. The town was destroyed by a flood on Jan 9, 1862; it was rebuilt at the present site and at first called New Rio Vista.

Suisun City City
ZIP: 94585 **Lat:** 38-14-44 N **Long:** 122-00-35 W
Pop: 22,686 (1990); 11,087 (1980) **Pop Density:** 6301.7
Land: 3.6 sq. mi.; **Water:** 0.0 sq. mi.

In central-western CA, 35 mi. southwest of Sacramento. Incorporated Oct 9, 1868.

Name origin: For Suisun Bay, named for an Indian tribe living on the north shore; meaning of the name is unknown.

Vacaville City
ZIP: 95687 **Lat:** 38-21-44 N **Long:** 121-57-57 W
Pop: 71,479 (1990); 43,367 (1980) **Pop Density:** 3162.8
Land: 22.6 sq. mi.; **Water:** 0.0 sq. mi. **Elev:** 179 ft.

In central CA, 32 mi. southwest of Sacramento. Founded 1852; incorporated Aug 9, 1892.

Name origin: For the Vaca family, who came to the area in 1841. Juan Manuel Vaca was co-grantee of the land on which the town lies.

Vallejo City
ZIP: 94590 **Lat:** 38-06-26 N **Long:** 122-15-51 W
Pop: 109,199 (1990); 80,303 (1980) **Pop Density:** 3615.9
Land: 30.2 sq. mi.; **Water:** 18.6 sq. mi.

In central CA, 18 mi. north of Oakland on San Pablo Bay. Founded 1850; state capital 1851 and 1852; incorporated Mar 30, 1868.

Name origin: For founder Mariano Vallejo on whose rancho the town was laid out.

Sonoma County
County Seat: Santa Rosa (ZIP: 95406)

Pop: 388,222 (1990); 299,681 (1980) **Pop Density:** 246.3
Land: 1576.2 sq. mi.; **Water:** 192.1 sq. mi.   **Area Code:** 707
On NW coast of CA, north of San Francisco; original county; organized Feb 18, 1850 (prior to statehood).

Name origin: For the city, named for a Wintun Indian group that lived in the Sacramento Valley. The name means 'nose' but the reason is unknown; possibly referring to the shape of a peak. A fanciful interpretation is 'valley of the moon.'

Bodega Bay CDP
ZIP: 94923 **Lat:** 38-19-22 N **Long:** 123-01-47 W
Pop: 1,127 (1990) **Pop Density:** 142.7
Land: 7.9 sq. mi.; **Water:** 0.0 sq. mi.

Boyes Hot Springs CDP
ZIP: 95416 **Lat:** 38-18-46 N **Long:** 122-29-06 W
Pop: 5,973 (1990); 4,177 (1980) **Pop Density:** 4594.6
Land: 1.3 sq. mi.; **Water:** 0.0 sq. mi.

Cloverdale City
ZIP: 95425 **Lat:** 38-47-58 N **Long:** 123-01-02 W
Pop: 4,924 (1990); 3,989 (1980) **Pop Density:** 2140.9
Land: 2.3 sq. mi.; **Water:** 0.0 sq. mi. **Elev:** 316 ft.
Established Aug 15, 1857; incorporated Feb 28, 1872.

Name origin: For the fodder grown here; originally called Markleville, for R. B. Markle, former owner of the land.

Cotati City
ZIP: 94931 **Lat:** 38-19-40 N **Long:** 122-42-34 W
Pop: 5,714 (1990); 3,346 (1980) **Pop Density:** 3174.4
Land: 1.8 sq. mi.; **Water:** 0.0 sq. mi.
Incorporated Jul 6, 1963.

Name origin: From *Kotati*, the name of an Indian rancheria; present spelling was applied to a land grant in 1844.

Eldridge CDP
ZIP: 95431 **Lat:** 38-20-06 N **Long:** 122-30-24 W
Pop: 1,144 (1990) **Pop Density:** 1906.7
Land: 0.6 sq. mi.; **Water:** 0.0 sq. mi.

El Verano CDP
ZIP: 95433 **Lat:** 38-17-51 N **Long:** 122-29-21 W
Pop: 3,498 (1990); 2,384 (1980) **Pop Density:** 3180.0
Land: 1.1 sq. mi.; **Water:** 0.0 sq. mi.

Fetters Hot Springs-Agua Caliente CDP
Lat: 38-19-20 N **Long:** 122-28-47 W
Pop: 2,024 (1990); 1,675 (1980) **Pop Density:** 2024.0
Land: 1.0 sq. mi.; **Water:** 0.0 sq. mi.

Forestville CDP
ZIP: 95436 **Lat:** 38-28-52 N **Long:** 122-53-18 W
Pop: 2,443 (1990) **Pop Density:** 595.9
Land: 4.1 sq. mi.; **Water:** 0.0 sq. mi.

Glen Ellen CDP
ZIP: 95442 **Lat:** 38-21-20 N **Long:** 122-32-18 W
Pop: 1,191 (1990); 1,014 (1980) **Pop Density:** 496.2
Land: 2.4 sq. mi.; **Water:** 0.0 sq. mi.

Graton CDP
ZIP: 95444 **Lat:** 38-26-15 N **Long:** 122-51-54 W
Pop: 1,409 (1990); 324 (1980) **Pop Density:** 880.6
Land: 1.6 sq. mi.; **Water:** 0.0 sq. mi.

Guerneville CDP
Lat: 38-30-29 N **Long:** 122-59-05 W
Pop: 1,966 (1990); 1,525 (1980) **Pop Density:** 756.2
Land: 2.6 sq. mi.; **Water:** 0.1 sq. mi.
In central-western CA, northwest of Santa Rosa.

Name origin: For George E. Guerne, town founder.

Healdsburg City
ZIP: 95448 **Lat:** 38-37-06 N **Long:** 122-51-45 W
Pop: 9,469 (1990); 7,217 (1980) **Pop Density:** 2785.0
Land: 3.4 sq. mi.; **Water:** 0.0 sq. mi. **Elev:** 106 ft.
In western CA, 14 mi. north-northwest of Santa Rosa. Founded 1852; incorporated Feb 20, 1867.

Name origin: For Harmon G. Heald, who had had a trading post here since 1846 and had built the town's first store in 1852.

Larkfield-Wikiup CDP
Lat: 38-30-48 N **Long:** 122-45-08 W
Pop: 6,779 (1990) **Pop Density:** 1506.4
Land: 4.5 sq. mi.; **Water:** 0.0 sq. mi.

Monte Rio CDP
ZIP: 95462 **Lat:** 38-27-54 N **Long:** 123-00-44 W
Pop: 1,058 (1990); 1,137 (1980) **Pop Density:** 705.3
Land: 1.5 sq. mi.; **Water:** 0.1 sq. mi.

Occidental CDP
ZIP: 95465 **Lat:** 38-23-43 N **Long:** 122-56-16 W
Pop: 1,300 (1990) **Pop Density:** 250.0
Land: 5.2 sq. mi.; **Water:** 0.0 sq. mi.

Petaluma City
ZIP: 94952 **Lat:** 38-14-28 N **Long:** 122-37-31 W
Pop: 43,184 (1990); 33,834 (1980) **Pop Density:** 3510.9
Land: 12.3 sq. mi.; **Water:** 0.1 sq. mi. **Elev:** 12 ft.
In western CA on the Petaluma River, 15 mi. south of Santa Rosa. Founded 1851; incorporated Apr 12, 1858.

Name origin: For a land grant of the same name, part of which was used for the city. Possibly from Miwok Indian *peta* 'flat' and *luma* 'back,' referring to a hill; or for an Indian tribe of that name.

Rohnert Park City
ZIP: 94928 **Lat:** 38-20-51 N **Long:** 122-41-51 W
Pop: 36,326 (1990); 22,965 (1980) **Pop Density:** 5675.9
Land: 6.4 sq. mi.; **Water:** 0.0 sq. mi.
In central-western CA, 5 mi. south of Santa Rosa. Incorporated Aug 27, 1962.

Name origin: For the Waldo Rohnert Seed Farm located here.

Roseland CDP
ZIP: 95407 **Lat:** 38-25-17 N **Long:** 122-43-29 W
Pop: 8,779 (1990); 7,915 (1980) **Pop Density:** 6270.7
Land: 1.4 sq. mi.; **Water:** 0.0 sq. mi.

CALIFORNIA, Sonoma County

Santa Rosa — City
ZIP: 95402 Lat: 38-26-54 N Long: 122-42-02 W
Pop: 113,313 (1990); 82,658 (1980) Pop Density: 3362.4
Land: 33.7 sq. mi.; Water: 0.2 sq. mi.
In central-western CA, 50 mi. northwest of San Francisco. Incorporated Mar 16, 1868. Site of the house and gardens of horticulturist Luther Burbank (1849–1926).
Name origin: For St. Rose of Lima (1586–1617).

Sebastopol — City
ZIP: 95472 Lat: 38-23-57 N Long: 122-49-33 W
Pop: 7,004 (1990); 5,595 (1980) Pop Density: 3891.1
Land: 1.8 sq. mi.; Water: 0.0 sq. mi. Elev: 78 ft.
In central-western CA, 7 mi. southwest of Santa Rosa. Incorporated Jun 13, 1902.
Name origin: For the Russian port held in siege during the Crimean War.

Sonoma — City
ZIP: 95476 Lat: 38-17-25 N Long: 122-27-33 W
Pop: 8,121 (1990); 6,054 (1980) Pop Density: 3383.7
Land: 2.4 sq. mi.; Water: 0.0 sq. mi. Elev: 84 ft.
In central-western CA, 13 mi. southeast of Santa Rosa. Incorporated Sep 3, 1883.
Name origin: For the Mission San Francisco Solano, commonly called Sonoma Mission from the Wintun Indian term for 'nose.' Reason for the name is unclear: possibly for an Indian chief with a prominent one, or for a nose-shaped feature in the mountains. Name originally spelled Zanoma.

South Santa Rosa — CDP
Lat: 38-24-17 N Long: 122-43-35 W
Pop: 4,128 (1990) Pop Density: 509.6
Land: 8.1 sq. mi.; Water: 0.0 sq. mi.

Temelec — CDP
Lat: 38-15-22 N Long: 122-30-12 W
Pop: 1,594 (1990) Pop Density: 937.6
Land: 1.7 sq. mi.; Water: 0.0 sq. mi.

Windsor — CDP
ZIP: 95492 Lat: 38-32-44 N Long: 122-47-52 W
Pop: 13,371 (1990) Pop Density: 1364.4
Land: 9.8 sq. mi.; Water: 0.0 sq. mi.

Stanislaus County
County Seat: Modesto (ZIP: 95354)

Pop: 370,522 (1990); 265,900 (1980) Pop Density: 247.9
Land: 1494.6 sq. mi.; Water: 20.2 sq. mi. Area Code: 209
In central CA, E of San Francisco; organized Apr 1, 1854, from Tuolumne County.
Name origin: For the Stanislaus River, the baptismal name of an Indian leader who fought bravely there. John C. Frémont (1813–90) used the anglicization of Spanish *Estanislao*.

Ceres — City
ZIP: 95307 Lat: 37-35-57 N Long: 120-57-22 W
Pop: 26,314 (1990); 13,281 (1980) Pop Density: 4698.9
Land: 5.6 sq. mi.; Water: 0.0 sq. mi.
In central CA, 5 mi. southeast of Modesto. Incorporated Feb 25, 1918.
Name origin: Named by early settler Elma Carter in 1874 for the ancient Greek goddess of agriculture.

Denair — CDP
ZIP: 95316 Lat: 37-31-46 N Long: 120-48-00 W
Pop: 3,693 (1990); 2,892 (1980) Pop Density: 1846.5
Land: 2.0 sq. mi.; Water: 0.0 sq. mi.

Hughson — City
ZIP: 95326 Lat: 37-36-03 N Long: 120-52-00 W
Pop: 3,259 (1990); 2,943 (1980) Pop Density: 3621.1
Land: 0.9 sq. mi.; Water: 0.0 sq. mi.
Laid out 1907; incorporated Dec 9, 1972.
Name origin: For Hiram Hughson, owner of the land.

Keyes — CDP
Lat: 37-33-51 N Long: 120-55-02 W
Pop: 2,878 (1990) Pop Density: 2213.8
Land: 1.3 sq. mi.; Water: 0.0 sq. mi.

Modesto — City
ZIP: 95350 Lat: 37-39-35 N Long: 120-59-38 W
Pop: 164,730 (1990); 106,963 (1980) Pop Density: 5454.6
Land: 30.2 sq. mi.; Water: 0.2 sq. mi. Elev: 87 ft.
In central CA on the Tuolumne River, 24 mi. southeast of Stockton. Founded 1870; incorporated Aug 6, 1884.
Name origin: Named by the Central Pacific Railroad for San Francisco banker William C. Ralston, who declined the honor, an act that led to the present name, which is Spanish for 'modest.'

Newman — City
ZIP: 95360 Lat: 37-18-54 N Long: 121-01-17 W
Pop: 4,151 (1990); 2,785 (1980) Pop Density: 3459.2
Land: 1.2 sq. mi.; Water: 0.0 sq. mi. Elev: 91 ft.
In central CA, 28 mi. south of Modesto, between the CA Aqueduct and the San Joaquin River. Incorporated Jun 10, 1908.
Name origin: For Simon Newman, local merchant who donated the land for the Southern Pacific Railroad's right of way.

Oakdale — City
ZIP: 95361 **Lat:** 37-46-05 N **Long:** 120-51-06 W
Pop: 11,961 (1990); 8,474 (1980) **Pop Density:** 2990.3
Land: 4.0 sq. mi.; **Water:** 0.0 sq. mi. **Elev:** 155 ft.

In central CA, 22 mi. southeast of Stockton. Established 1871; incorporated Nov 24, 1906.

Name origin: Named in 1871 when the Copperopolis and Visalia Railroad reached here.

Patterson — City
ZIP: 95363 **Lat:** 37-28-27 N **Long:** 121-07-39 W
Pop: 8,626 (1990); 3,908 (1980) **Pop Density:** 5074.1
Land: 1.7 sq. mi.; **Water:** 0.0 sq. mi. **Elev:** 97 ft.

In central CA, 12 mi. southwest of Modesto, between the California Aqueduct and the San Joaquin River. Laid out 1910; incorporated Dec 18, 1919.

Name origin: Named by Thomas J. Patterson, a Fresno banker and town founder, for his uncle, John D. Patterson, who had bought the land.

Riverbank — City
ZIP: 95367 **Lat:** 37-43-58 N **Long:** 120-56-42 W
Pop: 8,547 (1990); 5,695 (1980) **Pop Density:** 5027.6
Land: 1.7 sq. mi.; **Water:** 0.1 sq. mi.

In central CA on the Stanislaus River, 7 mi. north of Modesto. Established 1911; incorporated Aug 23, 1922.

Name origin: For the new terminal of the Santa Fe railroad.

Salida — CDP
ZIP: 95368 **Lat:** 37-42-30 N **Long:** 121-05-05 W
Pop: 4,499 (1990) **Pop Density:** 882.2
Land: 5.1 sq. mi.; **Water:** 0.0 sq. mi.

Turlock — City
ZIP: 95380 **Lat:** 37-30-17 N **Long:** 120-51-01 W
Pop: 42,198 (1990); 26,287 (1980) **Pop Density:** 4395.6
Land: 9.6 sq. mi.; **Water:** 0.0 sq. mi. **Elev:** 101 ft.

In central CA, 38 mi. southeast of Stockton. Incorporated Feb 15, 1908.

Name origin: For Turlough, County Mayo, Ireland, suggested by John W. Mitchell, owner of the property the station was on, and who declined to have his name used.

Waterford — City
ZIP: 95386 **Lat:** 37-38-43 N **Long:** 120-45-52 W
Pop: 4,771 (1990); 2,683 (1980) **Pop Density:** 3407.9
Land: 1.4 sq. mi.; **Water:** 0.0 sq. mi.

In central CA, southeast of Stockton. Incorporated Nov 7, 1969.

Name origin: For the railroad station, named for a much-used ford across the Tuolumne River.

Sutter County
County Seat: Yuba City (ZIP: 95991)

Pop: 64,415 (1990); 52,246 (1980) **Pop Density:** 106.9
Land: 602.7 sq. mi.; **Water:** 6.2 sq. mi. **Area Code:** 916

In N central CA, NW of Sacramento; original county; organized Feb 18, 1850 (prior to statehood).

Name origin: For Sutter's Creek, named for John Augustus Sutter (Johann August Suter 1803–80), on whose property gold was discovered in 1848, the beginning of the California Gold Rush.

Live Oak — City
ZIP: 95953 **Lat:** 39-16-24 N **Long:** 121-39-40 W
Pop: 4,320 (1990); 3,103 (1980) **Pop Density:** 3323.1
Land: 1.3 sq. mi.; **Water:** 0.0 sq. mi. **Elev:** 75 ft.

Incorporated Jan 22, 1947.

Name origin: Named in 1874 for the area's native evergreen oaks, of which there are several species.

South Yuba City — CDP
ZIP: 95991 **Lat:** 39-06-59 N **Long:** 121-38-16 W
Pop: 8,816 (1990); 7,530 (1980) **Pop Density:** 3265.2
Land: 2.7 sq. mi.; **Water:** 0.0 sq. mi.

Sutter — CDP
ZIP: 95982 **Lat:** 39-09-33 N **Long:** 121-44-46 W
Pop: 2,606 (1990); 2,225 (1980) **Pop Density:** 1184.5
Land: 2.2 sq. mi.; **Water:** 0.0 sq. mi.

Tierra Buena — CDP
Lat: 39-09-31 N **Long:** 121-40-03 W
Pop: 2,878 (1990); 2,374 (1980) **Pop Density:** 1151.2
Land: 2.5 sq. mi.; **Water:** 0.0 sq. mi.

Yuba City — City
ZIP: 95991 **Lat:** 39-08-07 N **Long:** 121-37-21 W
Pop: 27,437 (1990); 18,736 (1980) **Pop Density:** 3976.4
Land: 6.9 sq. mi.; **Water:** 0.2 sq. mi.

In northern CA on the Feather River, 40 mi. north of Sacramento. Incorporated Jan 23, 1908.

Name origin: For the Yuba River, itself named by John Augustus Sutter (1803–80) for the Maidu Indian village near the confluence of the Yuba and Feather rivers.

CALIFORNIA, Tehama County   American Places Dictionary

Tehama County
County Seat: Red Bluff (ZIP: 96080)

Pop: 49,625 (1990); 38,888 (1980) **Pop Density:** 16.8
Land: 2951.0 sq. mi.; **Water:** 11.3 sq. mi. **Area Code:** 916

In N central CA, north of Chico; organized Apr 9, 1856 from Butte, Colusa, and Shasta counties.

Name origin: For the city, origin and meaning uncertain. It is almost certainly Indian, though an Arabian generic *tihama* 'hot lowlands' is frequently found in Arabic placenames. The Indian parallel term may also mean 'lowlands' or 'shallow,' as in a ford of a river.

Corning   City
ZIP: 96021 **Lat:** 39-55-34 N **Long:** 122-10-55 W
Pop: 5,870 (1990); 4,745 (1980) **Pop Density:** 2024.1
Land: 2.9 sq. mi.; **Water:** 0.0 sq. mi. **Elev:** 272 ft.
Incorporated Aug 6, 1907.
Name origin: For John Corning, an official of the Central Pacific Railroad.

Gerber-Las Flores   CDP
Lat: 40-03-41 N **Long:** 122-08-57 W
Pop: 1,143 (1990) **Pop Density:** 879.2
Land: 1.3 sq. mi.; **Water:** 0.0 sq. mi.

Los Molinos   CDP
ZIP: 96055 **Lat:** 40-01-39 N **Long:** 122-05-49 W
Pop: 1,709 (1990); 1,241 (1980) **Pop Density:** 776.8
Land: 2.2 sq. mi.; **Water:** 0.0 sq. mi.

Red Bluff   City
ZIP: 96075 **Lat:** 40-10-25 N **Long:** 122-14-25 W
Pop: 12,363 (1990); 9,490 (1980) **Pop Density:** 1693.6
Land: 7.3 sq. mi.; **Water:** 0.1 sq. mi. **Elev:** 309 ft.

In north-central CA on the Sacramento River, south of Redding. Incorporated Mar 31, 1876.

Name origin: Originally named Leodocia, then Covertsburg; present name adopted in 1854.

Tehama   City
ZIP: 96090 **Lat:** 40-01-23 N **Long:** 122-07-25 W
Pop: 401 (1990); 365 (1980) **Pop Density:** 501.3
Land: 0.8 sq. mi.; **Water:** 0.0 sq. mi.

In north-central CA, northwest of Chico. Incorporated Jul 5, 1906.

Name origin: Origin of the name is unclear; possibly the name of an Indian tribe, or, since the town founders were carpenters, from Mexican-Spanish *tejamanil* 'shingle.'

Trinity County
County Seat: Weaverville (ZIP: 96093)

Pop: 13,063 (1990); 11,858 (1980) **Pop Density:** 4.1
Land: 3178.9 sq. mi.; **Water:** 28.9 sq. mi. **Area Code:** 916

In NW CA, west of Redding; original county; organized Feb 18, 1850 (prior to statehood).

Name origin: For the Trinity River, named by Pierson B. Reading in 1845, who believed it entered Trinidad Bay. (Trinity is the English version of the Spanish Trinidad.)

Hayfork   CDP
ZIP: 96041 **Lat:** 40-34-25 N **Long:** 123-07-30 W
Pop: 2,605 (1990); 1,788 (1980) **Pop Density:** 16.7
Land: 156.2 sq. mi.; **Water:** 0.1 sq. mi.

Lewiston   CDP
ZIP: 96052 **Lat:** 40-41-57 N **Long:** 122-48-07 W
Pop: 1,187 (1990) **Pop Density:** 34.5
Land: 34.4 sq. mi.; **Water:** 0.0 sq. mi.

Weaverville   CDP
ZIP: 96093 **Lat:** 40-46-07 N **Long:** 122-56-55 W
Pop: 3,370 (1990); 2,787 (1980) **Pop Density:** 95.2
Land: 35.4 sq. mi.; **Water:** 0.0 sq. mi.

Tulare County
County Seat: Visalia (ZIP: 93291)

Pop: 311,921 (1990); 245,738 (1980)   **Pop Density:** 64.7
Land: 4824.3 sq. mi.; **Water:** 15.1 sq. mi.   **Area Code:** 209
In central CA, southeast of Fresno; organized Apr 20, 1852, from Mariposa County.
Name origin: For Tulare Lake, Mexican-Spanish 'rush' or 'reed,' perhaps originally from Aztec *tullin* or *tollin*, 'cattail' or 'bulrush.'

Cutler   CDP
ZIP: 93615   **Lat:** 36-31-36 N   **Long:** 119-17-13 W
Pop: 4,450 (1990); 3,149 (1980)   **Pop Density:** 5562.5
Land: 0.8 sq. mi.; **Water:** 0.0 sq. mi.

Dinuba   City
ZIP: 93618   **Lat:** 36-32-44 N   **Long:** 119-23-14 W
Pop: 12,743 (1990); 9,907 (1980)   **Pop Density:** 4719.6
Land: 2.7 sq. mi.; **Water:** 0.0 sq. mi.
In south-central CA, 24 mi. southeast of Fresno. Incorporated Jan 6, 1906.
Name origin: Named by the construction engineer when the branch line was built in 1887–88. Origin of the name is uncertain but probably for the Greek battleground. Originally named Sibleyville.

Earlimart   CDP
ZIP: 93219   **Lat:** 35-52-51 N   **Long:** 119-16-13 W
Pop: 5,881 (1990); 4,578 (1980)   **Pop Density:** 2940.5
Land: 2.0 sq. mi.; **Water:** 0.0 sq. mi.

East Porterville   CDP
ZIP: 93257   **Lat:** 36-03-26 N   **Long:** 118-58-28 W
Pop: 5,790 (1990); 5,218 (1980)   **Pop Density:** 1809.4
Land: 3.2 sq. mi.; **Water:** 0.0 sq. mi.

Exeter   City
ZIP: 93221   **Lat:** 36-17-40 N   **Long:** 119-08-34 W
Pop: 7,276 (1990); 5,606 (1980)   **Pop Density:** 3638.0
Land: 2.0 sq. mi.; **Water:** 0.0 sq. mi.   **Elev:** 386 ft.
In south-central CA, 45 mi. southeast of Fresno. Founded 1880; incorporated Mar 2, 1911.
Name origin: For Exeter, England, the former home of D.W. Parkhurst of the Pacific Improvement Co.

Farmersville   City
ZIP: 93223   **Lat:** 36-18-14 N   **Long:** 119-12-24 W
Pop: 6,235 (1990); 5,544 (1980)   **Pop Density:** 3667.6
Land: 1.7 sq. mi.; **Water:** 0.0 sq. mi.   **Elev:** 360 ft.
Established 1870; incorporated Oct 5, 1960.

Ivanhoe   CDP
ZIP: 93235   **Lat:** 36-23-21 N   **Long:** 119-13-07 W
Pop: 3,293 (1990); 2,684 (1980)   **Pop Density:** 1646.5
Land: 2.0 sq. mi.; **Water:** 0.0 sq. mi.

Lindsay   City
ZIP: 93247   **Lat:** 36-12-22 N   **Long:** 119-05-19 W
Pop: 8,338 (1990); 6,936 (1980)   **Pop Density:** 3474.2
Land: 2.4 sq. mi.; **Water:** 0.0 sq. mi.   **Elev:** 383 ft.
In south-central CA, 52 mi. southeast of Fresno. Founded 1888; incorporated Mar 5, 1910.
Name origin: Named by Capt. A.J. Hutchinson, town founder, in honor of his wife whose maiden name was Lindsay.

London   CDP
ZIP: 93618   **Lat:** 36-28-51 N   **Long:** 119-26-34 W
Pop: 1,638 (1990); 1,257 (1980)   **Pop Density:** 2730.0
Land: 0.6 sq. mi.; **Water:** 0.0 sq. mi.

Orosi   CDP
ZIP: 93647   **Lat:** 36-32-32 N   **Long:** 119-17-16 W
Pop: 5,486 (1990); 4,076 (1980)   **Pop Density:** 2194.4
Land: 2.5 sq. mi.; **Water:** 0.0 sq. mi.

Pixley   CDP
ZIP: 93256   **Lat:** 35-58-22 N   **Long:** 119-17-13 W
Pop: 2,457 (1990); 2,488 (1980)   **Pop Density:** 792.6
Land: 3.1 sq. mi.; **Water:** 0.0 sq. mi.

Poplar-Cotton Center   CDP
Lat: 36-03-24 N   **Long:** 119-08-47 W
Pop: 1,901 (1990); 1,289 (1980)   **Pop Density:** 1728.2
Land: 1.1 sq. mi.; **Water:** 0.0 sq. mi.

Porterville   City
ZIP: 93257   **Lat:** 36-03-52 N   **Long:** 119-01-37 W
Pop: 29,563 (1990); 19,707 (1980)   **Pop Density:** 2639.6
Land: 11.2 sq. mi.; **Water:** 0.0 sq. mi.   **Elev:** 459 ft.
In south-central CA, 44 mi. north of Bakersfield. Laid out 1864; incorporated May 7, 1902.
Name origin: For Royal Porter Putnam, who operated a stage depot known as Porter's Station; originally spelled Portersville.

Richgrove   CDP
Lat: 35-47-48 N   **Long:** 119-06-20 W
Pop: 1,899 (1990); 1,398 (1980)   **Pop Density:** 3798.0
Land: 0.5 sq. mi.; **Water:** 0.0 sq. mi.

Strathmore   CDP
ZIP: 93267   **Lat:** 36-08-39 N   **Long:** 119-03-34 W
Pop: 2,353 (1990); 1,955 (1980)   **Pop Density:** 1680.7
Land: 1.4 sq. mi.; **Water:** 0.0 sq. mi.

Terra Bella   CDP
ZIP: 93270   **Lat:** 35-57-35 N   **Long:** 119-02-16 W
Pop: 2,740 (1990); 1,807 (1980)   **Pop Density:** 1611.8
Land: 1.7 sq. mi.; **Water:** 0.0 sq. mi.

Tipton   CDP
ZIP: 93272   **Lat:** 36-03-29 N   **Long:** 119-18-42 W
Pop: 1,383 (1990); 1,185 (1980)   **Pop Density:** 1383.0
Land: 1.0 sq. mi.; **Water:** 0.0 sq. mi.

Tulare   City
ZIP: 93274   **Lat:** 36-11-42 N   **Long:** 119-20-35 W
Pop: 33,249 (1990); 22,530 (1980)   **Pop Density:** 2341.5
Land: 14.2 sq. mi.; **Water:** 0.1 sq. mi.   **Elev:** 288 ft.
In south-central CA, 42 mi. southeast of Fresno. Founded 1872; incorporated Apr 12, 1888.
Name origin: For the railroad station, named for Lake Tulare; from Mexican-Spanish "rush" or "reed."

CALIFORNIA, Tulare County   *American Places Dictionary*

Visalia — City
ZIP: 93277 **Lat:** 36-19-31 N **Long:** 119-19-14 W
Pop: 75,636 (1990); 49,729 (1980) **Pop Density:** 3218.6
Land: 23.5 sq. mi.; **Water:** 0.0 sq. mi. **Elev:** 331 ft.
In central CA, 37 mi. southeast of Fresno. Founded 1852 by Nathaniel Vise; incorporated Feb 27, 1874.
Name origin: For Visalia, KY, which was named for the family of Nathaniel Vise.

Woodlake — City
ZIP: 93286 **Lat:** 36-24-45 N **Long:** 119-05-50 W
Pop: 5,678 (1990); 4,343 (1980) **Pop Density:** 2988.4
Land: 1.9 sq. mi.; **Water:** 0.5 sq. mi.
In south-central CA, east of Visalia. Incorporated Sep 23, 1941.

Woodville — CDP
Lat: 36-05-25 N **Long:** 119-12-11 W
Pop: 1,557 (1990); 1,507 (1980) **Pop Density:** 353.9
Land: 4.4 sq. mi.; **Water:** 0.0 sq. mi.

Tuolumne County
County Seat: Sonora (ZIP: 95370)

Pop: 48,456 (1990); 33,928 (1980) **Pop Density:** 21.7
Land: 2235.6 sq. mi.; **Water:** 38.9 sq. mi. **Area Code:** 209
In E central CA, east of Stockton; original county; organized Feb 18, 1850 (prior to statehood).
Name origin: For the Tuolumne River, named for either the Central Miwok or Yokut Indians, of Penutian linguistic stock. Name is believed to be a corruption of Indian *talmalamne* 'cluster of stone wigwams': they lived in caves or recesses in the rocks. Variously spelled *Taulamne*, *Tahualamne*, and *Tavalames*.

Columbia — CDP
ZIP: 95310 **Lat:** 38-01-36 N **Long:** 120-24-06 W
Pop: 1,799 (1990) **Pop Density:** 438.8
Land: 4.1 sq. mi.; **Water:** 0.0 sq. mi.

East Sonora — CDP
Lat: 37-58-49 N **Long:** 120-20-21 W
Pop: 1,675 (1990) **Pop Density:** 620.4
Land: 2.7 sq. mi.; **Water:** 0.0 sq. mi.

Groveland-Big Oak Flat — CDP
Lat: 37-50-43 N **Long:** 120-11-47 W
Pop: 2,753 (1990) **Pop Density:** 126.3
Land: 21.8 sq. mi.; **Water:** 0.3 sq. mi.

Jamestown — CDP
ZIP: 95327 **Lat:** 37-57-26 N **Long:** 120-24-49 W
Pop: 2,178 (1990); 2,206 (1980) **Pop Density:** 751.0
Land: 2.9 sq. mi.; **Water:** 0.0 sq. mi.

Mi-Wuk Village — CDP
Lat: 38-03-28 N **Long:** 120-10-34 W
Pop: 1,175 (1990) **Pop Density:** 345.6
Land: 3.4 sq. mi.; **Water:** 0.0 sq. mi.

Mono Vista — CDP
Lat: 38-00-41 N **Long:** 120-16-10 W
Pop: 2,599 (1990); 1,154 (1980) **Pop Density:** 866.3
Land: 3.0 sq. mi.; **Water:** 0.0 sq. mi.

Phoenix Lake-Cedar Ridge — CDP
Lat: 38-01-23 N **Long:** 120-18-02 W
Pop: 3,569 (1990) **Pop Density:** 356.9
Land: 10.0 sq. mi.; **Water:** 0.1 sq. mi.

Sonora — City
ZIP: 95370 **Lat:** 37-59-00 N **Long:** 120-22-53 W
Pop: 4,153 (1990); 3,247 (1980) **Pop Density:** 1730.4
Land: 2.4 sq. mi.; **Water:** 0.0 sq. mi.
In east-central CA, east of Stockton. Incorporated May 1, 1851.
Name origin: For Sonora, Mexico, the former home of the miners who established the camp. Originally called Sonorian Camp. Name changed to Stewart in 1850; changed to present one Apr 18, 1850.

Soulsbyville — CDP
ZIP: 95372 **Lat:** 37-59-33 N **Long:** 120-15-35 W
Pop: 1,732 (1990) **Pop Density:** 577.3
Land: 3.0 sq. mi.; **Water:** 0.0 sq. mi.

Tuolumne City — CDP
Lat: 37-57-46 N **Long:** 120-14-25 W
Pop: 1,686 (1990); 1,708 (1980) **Pop Density:** 648.5
Land: 2.6 sq. mi.; **Water:** 0.0 sq. mi.

Twain Harte — CDP
ZIP: 95383 **Lat:** 38-02-25 N **Long:** 120-13-57 W
Pop: 2,170 (1990); 1,369 (1980) **Pop Density:** 586.5
Land: 3.7 sq. mi.; **Water:** 0.0 sq. mi.

Ventura County
County Seat: Ventura (ZIP: 93009)

Pop: 669,016 (1990); 529,174 (1980)   **Pop Density:** 362.4
Land: 1845.9 sq. mi.; **Water:** 362.4 sq. mi.   **Area Code:** 805
On S coast of CA, N of Los Angeles; organized Mar 22, 1873 from Santa Barbara County.
Name origin: For the city, abbreviation of Spanish *San Buenaventura* 'St Bonaventure.'

Camarillo — City
ZIP: 93010   **Lat:** 34-13-21 N **Long:** 119-01-45 W
Pop: 52,303 (1990); 37,797 (1980)   **Pop Density:** 2842.6
Land: 18.4 sq. mi.; **Water:** 0.0 sq. mi.

In southwestern CA, 37 mi. southeast of Santa Barbara. Incorporated Oct 22, 1944.
Name origin: For the railroad station, named for Juan Camarillo (?–1880), a local rancher.

Casa Conejo — CDP
Lat: 34-11-00 N **Long:** 118-56-32 W
Pop: 3,286 (1990)   **Pop Density:** 6572.0
Land: 0.5 sq. mi.; **Water:** 0.0 sq. mi.

Channel Islands Beach — CDP
Lat: 34-09-28 N **Long:** 119-13-19 W
Pop: 3,317 (1990)   **Pop Density:** 8292.5
Land: 0.4 sq. mi.; **Water:** 0.0 sq. mi.

El Rio — CDP
ZIP: 93030   **Lat:** 34-14-33 N **Long:** 119-09-31 W
Pop: 6,419 (1990); 5,674 (1980)   **Pop Density:** 4011.9
Land: 1.6 sq. mi.; **Water:** 0.0 sq. mi.

Fillmore — City
ZIP: 93015   **Lat:** 34-24-00 N **Long:** 118-55-06 W
Pop: 11,992 (1990); 9,602 (1980)   **Pop Density:** 4612.3
Land: 2.6 sq. mi.; **Water:** 0.0 sq. mi.   **Elev:** 469 ft.

In southwestern CA, 43 mi. west-northwest of Los Angeles at the mouth of Sespe Canyon. Incorporated Jul 10, 1914.
Name origin: Named in 1887 for J.A. Filmore, general superintendent of the Southern Pacific Railroad.

Meiners Oaks — CDP
Lat: 34-27-01 N **Long:** 119-16-19 W
Pop: 3,329 (1990); 9,512 (1980)   **Pop Density:** 2377.9
Land: 1.4 sq. mi.; **Water:** 0.0 sq. mi.

Mira Monte — CDP
ZIP: 93023   **Lat:** 34-25-40 N **Long:** 119-16-58 W
Pop: 7,744 (1990)   **Pop Density:** 1800.9
Land: 4.3 sq. mi.; **Water:** 0.0 sq. mi.

Moorpark — City
ZIP: 93021   **Lat:** 34-17-06 N **Long:** 118-52-39 W
Pop: 25,494 (1990); 4,030 (1980)   **Pop Density:** 2072.7
Land: 12.3 sq. mi.; **Water:** 0.3 sq. mi.   **Elev:** 513 ft.

In southwestern CA, 40 mi. northwest of Los Angeles. Founded c. 1900; incorporated Jul 1, 1983.
Name origin: For the Moorpark apricot, the English variety grown in the area.

Oak Park — CDP
Lat: 34-10-17 N **Long:** 118-45-19 W
Pop: 2,412 (1990)   **Pop Density:** 8040.0
Land: 0.3 sq. mi.; **Water:** 0.0 sq. mi.

Oak View — CDP
ZIP: 93022   **Lat:** 34-23-58 N **Long:** 119-17-43 W
Pop: 3,606 (1990); 4,671 (1980)   **Pop Density:** 2253.8
Land: 1.6 sq. mi.; **Water:** 0.0 sq. mi.

Ojai — City
ZIP: 93023   **Lat:** 34-26-56 N **Long:** 119-14-44 W
Pop: 7,613 (1990); 6,816 (1980)   **Pop Density:** 1730.2
Land: 4.4 sq. mi.; **Water:** 0.0 sq. mi.   **Elev:** 746 ft.

In southwestern CA, 23 mi. east of Santa Barbara in the Ojai Valley of the Sierra Madre Range.
Name origin: For the valley, from the Chumash Indian term *a'hwai* 'moon.' Town was originally named Nordhoff for Charles Nordhoff (1830–1901), who had written enthusiastically about the valley; name changed 1916.

Oxnard — City
ZIP: 93030   **Lat:** 34-11-50 N **Long:** 119-12-49 W
Pop: 142,216 (1990); 108,195 (1980)   **Pop Density:** 5828.5
Land: 24.4 sq. mi.; **Water:** 11.1 sq. mi.   **Elev:** 52 ft.

In southwestern CA, 51 mi. northwest of Los Angeles. Incorporated Jun 30, 1903.
Name origin: For the railroad station, named in 1900 for Henry T. Oxnard, local owner of a beet sugar refinery.

Piru — CDP
Lat: 34-24-26 N **Long:** 118-47-55 W
Pop: 1,157 (1990); 1,284 (1980)   **Pop Density:** 428.5
Land: 2.7 sq. mi.; **Water:** 0.0 sq. mi.

Port Hueneme — City
ZIP: 93041   **Lat:** 34-09-43 N **Long:** 119-12-12 W
Pop: 20,319 (1990); 17,803 (1980)   **Pop Density:** 4618.0
Land: 4.4 sq. mi.; **Water:** 0.2 sq. mi.   **Elev:** 12 ft.

On the southern coast of CA on the Santa Barbara Channel, south of Oxnard. Incorporated Mar 24, 1948.
Name origin: For Hueneme Point, which was named for a Chumash Indian village. In 1870 spelled Wynema; changed in 1874; *port* added in 1940.

San Buenaventura (Ventura) — City
ZIP: 93001   **Lat:** 34-15-57 N **Long:** 119-15-30 W
Pop: 92,575 (1990); 73,774 (1980)   **Pop Density:** 4515.9
Land: 20.5 sq. mi.; **Water:** 11.6 sq. mi.

In southwestern CA on the Santa Barbara Channel, 23 mi. southeast of Santa Barbara. Founded 1782; incorporated Mar 10, 1866.
Name origin: For the mission named for St. Bonaventure, a Franciscan saint of the 13th century. The post office is named Ventura.

CALIFORNIA, Ventura County

Santa Paula — City
ZIP: 93060 Lat: 34-21-08 N Long: 119-04-09 W
Pop: 25,062 (1990); 20,658 (1980) Pop Density: 5448.3
Land: 4.6 sq. mi.; Water: 0.0 sq. mi. Elev: 274 ft.

In southwestern CA, northeast of Oxnard. Laid out and named 1872; incorporated Apr 22, 1902.

Name origin: For Rancho Santa Paula, probably named for the noble Roman matron and disciple of St. Jerome.

Simi Valley — City
ZIP: 93065 Lat: 34-15-46 N Long: 118-45-04 W
Pop: 100,217 (1990); 77,500 (1980) Pop Density: 3036.9
Land: 33.0 sq. mi.; Water: 0.3 sq. mi.

In southwestern CA, 28 mi. northwest of Los Angeles. Incorporated Oct 10, 1969.

Name origin: From Chumash Indian *shimiyi* 'village' or 'settlement.' Post office established 1889 as Simiopolis; changed Jul 15, 1889.

Thousand Oaks — City
ZIP: 91359 Lat: 34-11-33 N Long: 118-52-03 W
Pop: 104,352 (1990); 77,072 (1980) Pop Density: 2103.9
Land: 49.6 sq. mi.; Water: 0.1 sq. mi.

In southwestern CA, 30 mi. northwest of Los Angeles. Incorporated Oct 7, 1984.

Yolo County
County Seat: Woodland (ZIP: 95695)

Pop: 141,092 (1990); 113,374 (1980) Pop Density: 139.4
Land: 1012.4 sq. mi.; Water: 10.4 sq. mi. Area Code: 916

In N central CA, NE of San Francisco; original county; organized Feb 18, 1850 (prior to statehood).

Name origin: For a subtribe of Patwin Indians, of Wintun linguistic stock; meaning of name unclear. Possibly a corruption of *Yoloy* 'place abounding with rushes,' or *Yodoi* a Patwin village, or for a chief named *Yodo*. There was also a captain of a ranch who was named Yolo.

Davis — City
ZIP: 95616 Lat: 38-33-17 N Long: 121-44-09 W
Pop: 46,209 (1990); 36,640 (1980) Pop Density: 5501.1
Land: 8.4 sq. mi.; Water: 0.0 sq. mi. Elev: 50 ft.

In north-central CA, 14 mi. west of Sacramento. Incorporated Mar 28, 1917.

Name origin: For Jerome C. Davis (1822–81), a large landholder and rancher.

Esparto — CDP
Lat: 38-41-37 N Long: 122-01-16 W
Pop: 1,487 (1990); 1,303 (1980) Pop Density: 1858.8
Land: 0.8 sq. mi.; Water: 0.0 sq. mi.

West Sacramento — City
ZIP: 95605 Lat: 38-33-24 N Long: 121-32-52 W
Pop: 28,898 (1990); 10,875 (1980) Pop Density: 1376.1
Land: 21.0 sq. mi.; Water: 1.9 sq. mi.

Winters — City
ZIP: 95694 Lat: 38-31-55 N Long: 121-58-48 W
Pop: 4,639 (1990); 2,652 (1980) Pop Density: 2017.0
Land: 2.3 sq. mi.; Water: 0.0 sq. mi. Elev: 135 ft.

In north-central CA, west of Sacramento. Incorporated Feb 19,. 1898.

Name origin: For Theodore W. Winters, who donated half the land for the town.

Woodland — City
ZIP: 95695 Lat: 38-40-37 N Long: 121-45-59 W
Pop: 39,802 (1990); 30,235 (1980) Pop Density: 4326.3
Land: 9.2 sq. mi.; Water: 0.0 sq. mi. Elev: 65 ft.

In north-central CA, 14 mi. northwest of Sacramento. Founded 1855; incorporated Feb 22, 1871.

Name origin: Named in 1859 for the grove of huge oaks in which the town stood.

Yuba County
County Seat: Marysville (ZIP: 95901)

Pop: 58,228 (1990); 49,733 (1980)   **Pop Density:** 92.4
Land: 630.5 sq. mi.; **Water:** 13.1 sq. mi.   **Area Code:** 916

In N central CA, N of Sacramento; original county; organized Feb 18, 1850 (prior to statehood).

Name origin: For the Yuba River, the name of which came from a Maidu Indian village and tribal name. Also spelled *Yubu*, *Yupu*, *Jubu*.

Beale Air Force Base — Military Facility
ZIP: 95903   **Lat:** 39-06-49 N **Long:** 121-21-40 W
Pop: 6,912 (1990); 6,329 (1980)   **Pop Density:** 634.1
Land: 10.9 sq. mi.; **Water:** 0.0 sq. mi.

Challenge-Brownsville — CDP
Lat: 39-27-41 N **Long:** 121-15-32 W
Pop: 1,096 (1990)   **Pop Density:** 113.0
Land: 9.7 sq. mi.; **Water:** 0.0 sq. mi.

Linda — CDP
ZIP: 95901   **Lat:** 39-07-22 N **Long:** 121-33-16 W
Pop: 13,033 (1990); 10,225 (1980)   **Pop Density:** 2247.1
Land: 5.8 sq. mi.; **Water:** 0.0 sq. mi.

Loma Rica — CDP
Lat: 39-19-07 N **Long:** 121-24-01 W
Pop: 1,852 (1990)   **Pop Density:** 100.7
Land: 18.4 sq. mi.; **Water:** 0.0 sq. mi.

Marysville — City
ZIP: 95901   **Lat:** 39-09-05 N **Long:** 121-34-56 W
Pop: 12,324 (1990); 9,898 (1980)   **Pop Density:** 3521.1
Land: 3.5 sq. mi.; **Water:** 0.1 sq. mi.   **Elev:** 63 ft.

In north-central CA, 43 mi. north of Sacramento. Laid out 1849; incorporated Feb 5, 1851.

Name origin: Named by Charles Covillaud, town founder, for his wife, Mary (1831–67), a survivor of the Donner party (1846–47).

Olivehurst — CDP
ZIP: 95961   **Lat:** 39-05-03 N **Long:** 121-32-51 W
Pop: 9,738 (1990); 8,929 (1980)   **Pop Density:** 2782.3
Land: 3.5 sq. mi.; **Water:** 0.0 sq. mi.

Wheatland — City
ZIP: 95692   **Lat:** 39-00-46 N **Long:** 121-25-36 W
Pop: 1,631 (1990); 1,474 (1980)   **Pop Density:** 2038.8
Land: 0.8 sq. mi.; **Water:** 0.0 sq. mi.   **Elev:** 87 ft.

In central CA, north of Sacramento. Incorporated Apr 12, 1874.

CALIFORNIA

Index to Places and Counties in California

Acton (Los Angeles) CDP 69
Adelanto (San Bernardino) City 93
Agoura Hills (Los Angeles) City 69
Alameda (Alameda) City 54
Alameda County 54
Alamo (Contra Costa) CDP 58
Albany (Alameda) City 54
Alhambra (Los Angeles) City 69
Aliso Viejo (Orange) CDP 84
Alondra Park (Los Angeles) CDP 69
Alpine (San Diego) CDP 95
Alpine County 55
Altadena (Los Angeles) CDP 69
Alta Sierra (Nevada) CDP 83
Alturas (Modoc) City 81
Amador City (Amador) City 55
Amador County 55
American Canyon (Napa) CDP 83
Anaheim (Orange) City 84
Anderson (Shasta) City 106
Angels (Calaveras) City 57
Angwin (Napa) CDP 83
Antioch (Contra Costa) City 58
Apple Valley (San Bernardino) Town .93
Aptos (Santa Cruz) CDP 105
Aptos Hills-Larkin Valley (Santa Cruz)
  CDP 105
Arbuckle (Colusa) CDP 57
Arcadia (Los Angeles) City 69
Arcata (Humboldt) City 63
Arden-Arcade (Sacramento) CDP 91
Armona (Kings) CDP 67
Arnold (Calaveras) CDP 57
Aromas (Monterey) CDP 81
Aromas (San Benito) CDP 92
Arroyo Grande (San Luis Obispo)
  City 99
Artesia (Los Angeles) City 69
Arvin (Kern) City 65
Ashland (Alameda) CDP 54
Atascadero (San Luis Obispo) City 99
Atherton (San Mateo) City 100
Atwater (Merced) City 80
Auberry (Fresno) CDP 61
Auburn (Placer) City 87
August (San Joaquin) CDP 98
Avalon (Los Angeles) City 69
Avenal (Kings) City 67
Avocado Heights (Los Angeles) CDP .69
Azusa (Los Angeles) City 69
Bakersfield (Kern) City 65
Baldwin Park (Los Angeles) City 69
Banning (Riverside) City 88
Barstow (San Bernardino) City 93
Bayview (Humboldt) CDP 63
Bayview-Montalvin (Contra Costa)
  CDP 58
Baywood-Los Osos (San Luis Obispo)
  CDP 99
Beale Air Force Base (Yuba) Military
  Facility 117
Bear Valley Springs (Kern) CDP 65
Beaumont (Riverside) City 88
Bel Air *See* **Los Angeles**
  (Los Angeles) 69
Bell (Los Angeles) City 69
Bellflower (Los Angeles) City 69
Bell Gardens (Los Angeles) City 70
Belmont (San Mateo) City 100
Belvedere (Marin) City 77

Benicia (Solano) City 108
Ben Lomond (Santa Cruz) CDP 105
Berkeley (Alameda) City 54
Bermuda Dunes (Riverside) CDP 88
Bethel Island (Contra Costa) CDP 58
Beverly Hills (Los Angeles) City 70
Big Bear City (San Bernardino) CDP .93
Big Bear Lake (San Bernardino) City. 93
Biggs (Butte) City 56
Big Pine (Inyo) CDP 65
Big River (San Bernardino) CDP 93
Bishop (Inyo) City 65
Blackhawk (Contra Costa) CDP 58
Bloomington (San Bernardino) CDP ..93
Blue Lake (Humboldt) City 63
Bluewater (San Bernardino) CDP 93
Blythe (Riverside) City 88
Bodega Bay (Sonoma) CDP 109
Bodfish (Kern) CDP 65
Bolinas (Marin) CDP 77
Bonadelle Ranchos-Madera Ranchos
  (Madera) CDP 77
Bonita (San Diego) CDP 95
Bonsall (San Diego) CDP 95
Bootjack (Mariposa) CDP 79
Boron (Kern) CDP 65
Borrego Springs (San Diego) CDP 95
Bostonia (San Diego) CDP 95
Boulder Creek (Santa Cruz) CDP 105
Boyes Hot Springs (Sonoma) CDP ...109
Bradbury (Los Angeles) City 70
Brawley (Imperial) City 64
Brea (Orange) City 84
Brentwood (Contra Costa) City 58
Bridgeport (Mono) CDP 81
Brisbane (San Mateo) City 100
Broadmoor (San Mateo) CDP 100
Buellton (Santa Barbara) CDP 102
Buena Park (Orange) City 84
Burbank (Los Angeles) City 70
Burbank (Santa Clara) CDP 103
Burlingame (San Mateo) City 100
Burney (Shasta) CDP 106
Butte County 56
Buttonwillow (Kern) CDP 65
Cabazon (Riverside) CDP 88
Calaveras County 57
Calexico (Imperial) City 64
California City (Kern) City 65
Calimesa (Riverside) CDP 88
Calipatria (Imperial) City 64
Calistoga (Napa) City 83
Camarillo (Ventura) City 115
Cambria (San Luis Obispo) CDP 99
Cambrian Park (Santa Clara) CDP ...103
Cameron Park (El Dorado) CDP 60
Campbell (Santa Clara) City 103
Camp Pendleton North (San Diego)
  Military Facility 95
Camp Pendleton South (San Diego)
  Military Facility 95
Canoga Park *See* **Los Angeles** **(Los
  Angeles)** 70
Canyon Lake (Riverside) CDP 88
Capitola (Santa Cruz) City 105
Carlsbad (San Diego) City 95
Carmel-by-the-Sea (Monterey) City 81
Carmel Valley Village (Monterey)
  CDP 81
Carmichael (Sacramento) CDP 91

Carpinteria (Santa Barbara) City 102
Carson (Los Angeles) City 70
Caruthers (Fresno) CDP 61
Casa Conejo (Ventura) CDP 115
Casa de Oro-Mount Helix (San Diego)
  CDP 95
Castro Valley (Alameda) CDP 54
Castroville (Monterey) CDP 81
Cathedral City (Riverside) City 89
Cayucos (San Luis Obispo) CDP 99
Central Valley (Shasta) CDP 106
Century City *See* **Los Angeles** (Los
  Angeles) 70
Ceres (Stanislaus) City 110
Cerritos (Los Angeles) City 70
Challenge-Brownsville (Yuba) CDP ..117
Channel Islands Beach (Ventura)
  CDP 115
Charter Oak (Los Angeles) CDP 70
Cherryland (Alameda) CDP 54
Cherry Valley (Riverside) CDP 89
Chester (Plumas) CDP 88
Chico (Butte) City 56
Chino (San Bernardino) City 93
Chino Hills (San Bernardino) CDP 93
Chowchilla (Madera) City 77
Chula Vista (San Diego) City 96
Citrus (Los Angeles) CDP 70
Citrus Heights (Sacramento) CDP 91
Claremont (Los Angeles) City 70
Clayton (Contra Costa) City 58
Clearlake (Lake) City 68
Clearlake Oaks (Lake) CDP 68
Cloverdale (Sonoma) City 109
Clovis (Fresno) City 61
Coachella (Riverside) City 89
Coalinga (Fresno) City 61
Cobb (Lake) CDP 68
Colfax (Placer) City 87
Colma (San Mateo) Town 100
Colton (San Bernardino) City 93
Columbia (Tuolumne) CDP 114
Colusa (Colusa) City 57
Colusa County 57
Commerce (Los Angeles) City 70
Compton (Los Angeles) City 70
Concord (Contra Costa) City 58
Concow (Butte) CDP 56
Contra Costa County 58
Corcoran (Kings) City 67
Corning (Tehama) City 112
Corona (Riverside) City 89
Coronado (San Diego) City 96
Corralitos (Santa Cruz) CDP 105
Corte Madera (Marin) Town 77
Costa Mesa (Orange) City 84
Cotati (Sonoma) City 109
Coto De Caza (Orange) CDP 84
Cottonwood (Shasta) CDP 106
Country Club (San Joaquin) CDP 98
Covelo (Mendocino) CDP 79
Covina (Los Angeles) City 70
Crescent City (Del Norte) City 60
Crescent City North (Del Norte)
  CDP 60
Crestline (San Bernardino) CDP 93
Crockett (Contra Costa) CDP 58
Cudahy (Los Angeles) City 70
Culver City (Los Angeles) City 70
Cupertino (Santa Clara) City 103

Cutler (Tulare) CDP 113	Emerald Lake Hills (San Mateo) CDP 101	Hacienda Heights (Los Angeles) CDP 71
Cutten (Humboldt) CDP 63	Emeryville (Alameda) City 54	Half Moon Bay (San Mateo) City.....101
Cypress (Orange) City 84	Encinitas (San Diego) City 96	Hamilton City (Glenn) CDP 62
Daly City (San Mateo) City 101	Encino See **Los Angeles** (Los Angeles)...........71	Hanford (Kings) City 67
Dana Point (Orange) City 84	Escalon (San Joaquin) City 98	Harbison Canyon (San Diego) CDP ...96
Danville (Contra Costa) Town 58	Escondido (San Diego) City 96	Hawaiian Gardens (Los Angeles) City 71
Davis (Yolo) City 116	Esparto (Yolo) CDP 116	Hawthorne (Los Angeles) City 71
Day Valley (Santa Cruz) CDP 105	Etna (Siskiyou) City 107	Hayfork (Trinity) CDP 112
Deer Park (Napa) CDP 83	Eureka (Humboldt) City 63	Hayward (Alameda) City 54
Del Aire (Los Angeles) CDP 70	Exeter (Tulare) City 113	Healdsburg (Sonoma) City 109
Delano (Kern) City 66	Fairfax (Marin) Town 78	Heber (Imperial) CDP 64
Delhi (Merced) CDP 80	Fairfield (Solano) City 108	Hemet (Riverside) City 89
Del Mar (San Diego) City 96	Fair Oaks (Sacramento) CDP 91	Hercules (Contra Costa) City 58
Del Monte Forest (Monterey) CDP 82	Fairview (Alameda) CDP 54	Hermosa Beach (Los Angeles) City 72
Del Norte County 60	Fallbrook (San Diego) CDP 96	Hesperia (San Bernardino) City 94
Del Rey (Fresno) CDP 61	Farmersville (Tulare) City 113	Hidden Hills (Los Angeles) City 72
Del Rey Oaks (Monterey) City 82	Felton (Santa Cruz) CDP 105	Hidden Meadows (San Diego) CDP ...96
Denair (Stanislaus) CDP 110	Ferndale (Humboldt) City 63	Hidden Valley Lake (Lake) CDP 68
Desert Hot Springs (Riverside) City...89	Fetters Hot Springs-Agua Caliente (Sonoma) CDP 109	Highgrove (Riverside) CDP 89
Desert View Highlands (Los Angeles) CDP 71	Fillmore (Ventura) City 115	Highland (San Bernardino) City 94
Diamond Bar (Los Angeles) City 71	Firebaugh (Fresno) City 61	Highlands (San Mateo) CDP 101
Diamond Springs (El Dorado) CDP ...60	Florence-Graham (Los Angeles) CDP.71	Hillsborough (San Mateo) Town 101
Dinuba (Tulare) City 113	Florin (Sacramento) CDP 91	Hilmar-Irwin (Merced) CDP 80
Discovery Bay (Contra Costa) CDP 58	Folsom (Sacramento) City 91	Hollister (San Benito) City 92
Dixon (Solano) City 108	Fontana (San Bernardino) City 93	Hollywood See **Los Angeles** (Los Angeles)...........72
Dixon Lane-Meadow Creek (Inyo) CDP 65	Foothill Farms (Sacramento) CDP 91	Holtville (Imperial) City 64
Dollar Point (Placer) CDP 87	Ford City (Kern) CDP 66	Home Garden (Kings) CDP 67
Dorris (Siskiyou) City 107	Foresthill (Placer) CDP 87	Home Gardens (Riverside) CDP 89
Dos Palos (Merced) City 80	Forestville (Sonoma) CDP 109	Homeland (Riverside) CDP 89
Downey (Los Angeles) City 71	Fort Bragg (Mendocino) City 79	Hughson (Stanislaus) City 110
Downieville (Sierra) CDP 106	Fort Jones (Siskiyou) City 107	**Humboldt County** 63
Duarte (Los Angeles) City 71	Fortuna (Humboldt) City 63	Humboldt Hill (Humboldt) CDP 63
Dublin (Alameda) City 54	Foster City (San Mateo) City 101	Huntington Beach (Orange) City 85
Dunsmuir (Siskiyou) City 107	Fountain Valley (Orange) City 85	Huntington Park (Los Angeles) City...72
Durham (Butte) CDP 56	Fowler (Fresno) City 61	Huron (Fresno) Town 61
Earlimart (Tulare) CDP 113	Frazier Park (Kern) CDP 66	Hydesville (Humboldt) CDP 63
East Blythe (Riverside) CDP 89	Freedom (Santa Cruz) CDP 105	Idyllwild-Pine Cove (Riverside) CDP.89
East Compton (Los Angeles) CDP 71	Fremont (Alameda) City 54	Imperial (Imperial) Town 64
East Foothills (Santa Clara) CDP 103	French Camp (San Joaquin) CDP 98	Imperial Beach (San Diego) City 96
East Hemet (Riverside) CDP 89	Fresno (Fresno) City 61	**Imperial County** 64
East La Mirada (Los Angeles) CDP....71	**Fresno County** 61	Independence (Inyo) City 65
East Los Angeles (Los Angeles) CDP .71	Fullerton (Orange) City 85	Indian Wells (Riverside) City 89
Easton (Fresno) CDP 61	Galt (Sacramento) City 91	Indio (Riverside) City 89
East Palo Alto (San Mateo) City 101	Gardena (Los Angeles) City 71	Industry (Los Angeles) City 72
East Pasadena (Los Angeles) CDP 71	Garden Acres (San Joaquin) CDP 98	Inglewood (Los Angeles) City 72
East Porterville (Tulare) CDP 113	Garden Grove (Orange) City 85	Interlaken (Santa Cruz) CDP 105
East Richmond Heights (Contra Costa) CDP 58	George Air Force Base (San Bernardino) Military Facility 93	Inverness (Marin) CDP 78
East San Gabriel (Los Angeles) CDP..71	Gerber-Las Flores (Tehama) CDP 112	**Inyo County** 65
East Sonora (Tuolumne) CDP 114	Gilroy (Santa Clara) City 103	Ione (Amador) City 55
Edwards Air Force Base (Kern) Military Facility 66	Glen Avon (Riverside) CDP 89	Irvine (Orange) City 85
El Cajon (San Diego) City 96	Glendale (Los Angeles) City 71	Irwindale (Los Angeles) City 72
El Centro (Imperial) City 64	Glendora (Los Angeles) City 71	Isla Vista (Santa Barbara) CDP 102
El Cerrito (Contra Costa) City 58	Glen Ellen (Sonoma) CDP 109	Isleton (Sacramento) City 91
El Cerrito (Riverside) CDP 89	**Glenn County** 62	Ivanhoe (Tulare) CDP 113
El Dorado County 60	Glenshire-Devonshire (Nevada) CDP.83	Jackson (Amador) City 55
El Dorado Hills (El Dorado) CDP 60	Golden Hills (Kern) CDP 66	Jamestown (Tuolumne) CDP 114
Eldridge (Sonoma) CDP 109	Gonzales (Monterey) City 82	Jamul (San Diego) CDP 96
El Granada (San Mateo) CDP 101	Grand Terrace (San Bernardino) City 93	Joshua Tree (San Bernardino) CDP....94
Elk Grove (Sacramento) CDP 91	Granite Hills (San Diego) CDP 96	Julian (San Diego) CDP 96
Elkhorn (Monterey) CDP 82	Grass Valley (Nevada) City 83	Kelseyville (Lake) CDP 68
El Monte (Los Angeles) City 71	Graton (Sonoma) CDP 109	Kensington (Contra Costa) CDP 58
El Paso de Robles (Paso Robles) (San Luis Obispo) City 99	Greenacres (Kern) CDP 66	Kentfield (Marin) CDP 78
El Rio (Ventura) CDP 115	Greenfield (Monterey) City 82	Kerman (Fresno) City 61
El Segundo (Los Angeles) City 71	Greenville (Plumas) CDP 88	**Kern County** 65
El Sobrante (Contra Costa) CDP 58	Gridley (Butte) City 56	Kernville (Kern) CDP 66
El Toro (Orange) CDP 84	Groveland-Big Oak Flat (Tuolumne) CDP 114	Kettleman City (Kings) CDP 67
El Toro Station (Orange) Military Facility 85	Grover City (San Luis Obispo) City...99	Keyes (Stanislaus) CDP 110
El Verano (Sonoma) CDP 109	Guadalupe (Santa Barbara) City 102	King City (Monterey) City 82
	Guerneville (Sonoma) CDP 109	Kings Beach (Placer) CDP 87
	Gustine (Merced) City 80	Kingsburg (Fresno) City 61
		Kings County 67
		Klamath (Del Norte) CDP 60
		La Cañada Flintridge (Los Angeles) City 72

CALIFORNIA

La Crescenta-Montrose (Los Angeles) CDP 72
Ladera Heights (Los Angeles) CDP 72
Lafayette (Contra Costa) City 59
Laguna (Sacramento) CDP 92
Laguna Beach (Orange) City 85
Laguna Hills (Orange) CDP 85
Laguna Niguel (Orange) City 85
Lagunitas-Forest Knolls (Marin) CDP 78
La Habra (Orange) City 85
La Habra Heights (Los Angeles) City . 72
La Jolla See **San Diego** (San Diego) ... 96
Lake Arrowhead (San Bernardino) CDP 94
Lake County 68
Lake Elsinore (Riverside) City 89
Lake Isabella (Kern) CDP 66
Lakeland Village (Riverside) CDP 89
Lake Los Angeles (Los Angeles) CDP . 72
Lake Nacimiento (San Luis Obispo) CDP 99
Lake of the Pines (Nevada) CDP 84
Lakeport (Lake) City 68
Lake San Marcos (San Diego) CDP 96
Lakeside (San Diego) CDP 96
Lakeview (Riverside) CDP 89
Lakewood (Los Angeles) City 72
La Mesa (San Diego) City 96
La Mirada (Los Angeles) City 72
Lamont (Kern) CDP 66
Lancaster (Los Angeles) City 72
La Palma (Orange) City 85
La Puente (Los Angeles) City 72
La Quinta (Riverside) City 89
La Riviera (Sacramento) CDP 92
Larkfield-Wikiup (Sonoma) CDP 109
Larkspur (Marin) City 78
Las Lomas (Monterey) CDP 82
Lassen County 68
Lathrop (San Joaquin) City 98
Laton (Fresno) CDP 61
La Verne (Los Angeles) City 72
Lawndale (Los Angeles) City 73
Laytonville (Mendocino) CDP 79
Le Grand (Merced) CDP 80
Lemon Grove (San Diego) City 96
Lemoore (Kings) City 67
Lemoore Station (Kings) Military Facility 67
Lennox (Los Angeles) CDP 73
Lenwood (San Bernardino) CDP 94
Lewiston (Trinity) CDP 112
Lexington Hills (Santa Clara) CDP .. 103
Lincoln (Placer) City 87
Lincoln Village (San Joaquin) CDP.... 98
Linda (Yuba) CDP 117
Linden (San Joaquin) CDP 98
Lindsay (Tulare) City 113
Littlerock (Los Angeles) CDP 73
Live Oak (Santa Cruz) CDP 105
Live Oak (Sutter) City 111
Livermore (Alameda) City 54
Livingston (Merced) City 80
Lockeford (San Joaquin) CDP 98
Lodi (San Joaquin) City 98
Loma Linda (San Bernardino) City 94
Loma Rica (Yuba) CDP 117
Lomita (Los Angeles) City 73
Lompoc (Santa Barbara) City 102
London (Tulare) CDP 113
Lone Pine (Inyo) CDP 65
Long Beach (Los Angeles) City 73
Loomis (Placer) Town 87
Los Alamitos (Orange) City 85
Los Altos (Santa Clara) City 103

Los Altos Hills (Santa Clara) Town .. 103
Los Angeles (Los Angeles) City 73
Los Angeles County 69
Los Baños (Merced) City 80
Los Gatos (Santa Clara) Town 104
Los Molinos (Tehama) CDP 112
Los Serranos (San Bernardino) CDP .. 94
Lost Hills (Kern) CDP 66
Lower Lake (Lake) CDP 68
Loyalton (Sierra) City 106
Loyola (Santa Clara) CDP 104
Lucas Valley-Marinwood (Marin) CDP 78
Lucerne (Lake) CDP 68
Lynwood (Los Angeles) City 73
Madera (Madera) City 77
Madera Acres (Madera) CDP 77
Madera County 77
Magalia (Butte) CDP 56
Mammoth Lakes (Mono) Town 81
Manhattan Beach (Los Angeles) City . 73
Manteca (San Joaquin) City 99
March Air Force Base (Riverside) Military Facility 90
Maricopa (Kern) City 66
Marina (Monterey) City 82
Marina del Rey (Los Angeles) CDP.... 73
Marin County 77
Mariposa (Mariposa) CDP 79
Mariposa County 79
Martinez (Contra Costa) City 59
Marysville (Yuba) City 117
Mather Air Force Base (Sacramento) Military Facility 92
Mayflower Village (Los Angeles) CDP 73
Maywood (Los Angeles) City 73
McCloud (Siskiyou) CDP 107
McFarland (Kern) City 66
McKinleyville (Humboldt) CDP 63
Meadow Vista (Placer) CDP 87
Mecca (Riverside) CDP 90
Meiners Oaks (Ventura) CDP 115
Mendocino County 79
Mendota (Fresno) City 62
Menlo Park (San Mateo) City 101
Mentone (San Bernardino) CDP 94
Merced (Merced) City 80
Merced County 80
Millbrae (San Mateo) City 101
Mill Valley (Marin) City 78
Milpitas (Santa Clara) City 104
Mira Loma (Riverside) CDP 90
Mira Monte (Ventura) CDP 115
Mission Hills (Santa Barbara) CDP .. 102
Mission Viejo (Orange) City 85
Mi-Wuk Village (Tuolumne) CDP 114
Modesto (Stanislaus) City 110
Modoc County 81
Mojave (Kern) CDP 66
Mono County 81
Mono Vista (Tuolumne) CDP 114
Monrovia (Los Angeles) City 73
Montague (Siskiyou) City 107
Montara (San Mateo) CDP 101
Montclair (San Bernardino) City 94
Montebello (Los Angeles) City 73
Monterey (Monterey) City 82
Monterey County 81
Monterey Park (Los Angeles) City 73
Monte Rio (Sonoma) CDP 109
Monte Sereno (Santa Clara) City 104
Moorpark (Ventura) City 115
Morada (San Joaquin) CDP 99
Moraga Town (Contra Costa) City 59

Moreno Valley (Riverside) City 90
Morgan Hill (Santa Clara) City 104
Morongo Valley (San Bernardino) CDP 94
Morro Bay (San Luis Obispo) City ... 100
Moss Beach (San Mateo) CDP 101
Mountain Mesa (Kern) CDP 66
Mountain View (Santa Clara) City ... 104
Mountain View Acres (San Bernardino) CDP 94
Mount Shasta (Siskiyou) City 107
Murphys (Calaveras) CDP 57
Murrieta (Riverside) City 90
Murrieta Hot Springs (Riverside) CDP 90
Muscoy (San Bernardino) CDP 94
Myrtletown (Humboldt) CDP 63
Napa (Napa) City 83
Napa County 83
National City (San Diego) City 96
Nebo Center (San Bernardino) Military Facility 94
Needles (San Bernardino) City 94
Nevada City (Nevada) City 84
Nevada County 83
Newark (Alameda) City 54
Newman (Stanislaus) City 110
Newport Beach (Orange) City 85
Nice (Lake) CDP 68
Niland (Imperial) CDP 64
Nipomo (San Luis Obispo) CDP 100
Norco (Riverside) City 90
North Auburn (Placer) CDP 87
North Edwards (Kern) CDP 66
North El Monte (Los Angeles) CDP ... 74
North Fair Oaks (San Mateo) CDP .. 101
North Highlands (Sacramento) CDP .. 92
Norwalk (Los Angeles) City 74
Novato (Marin) City 78
Nuevo (Riverside) CDP 90
Oakdale (Stanislaus) City 111
Oakhurst (Madera) CDP 77
Oakland (Alameda) City 55
Oakley (Contra Costa) CDP 59
Oak Park (Ventura) CDP 115
Oak View (Ventura) CDP 115
Occidental (Sonoma) CDP 109
Oceano (San Luis Obispo) CDP 100
Oceanside (San Diego) City 97
Oildale (Kern) CDP 66
Ojai (Ventura) City 115
Olivehurst (Yuba) CDP 117
Ontario (San Bernardino) City 94
Opal Cliffs (Santa Cruz) CDP 105
Orange (Orange) City 85
Orange County 84
Orange Cove (Fresno) City 62
Orangevale (Sacramento) CDP 92
Orinda (Contra Costa) City 59
Orland (Glenn) City 62
Orosi (Tulare) CDP 113
Oroville (Butte) City 56
Oroville East (Butte) CDP 56
Oxnard (Ventura) City 115
Pacheco (Contra Costa) CDP 59
Pacifica (San Mateo) City 101
Pacific Grove (Monterey) City 82
Pacific Palisades See **Los Angeles** (Los Angeles) 74
Pajaro (Monterey) CDP 82
Palermo (Butte) CDP 56
Palmdale (Los Angeles) City 74
Palmdale East (Los Angeles) CDP 74
Palm Desert (Riverside) City 90

CALIFORNIA

Palm Desert Country (Riverside) CDP 90
Palm Springs (Riverside) City 90
Palo Alto (Santa Clara) City 104
Palos Verdes Estates (Los Angeles) City 74
Paradise (Butte) City 56
Paramount (Los Angeles) City 74
Parksdale (Madera) CDP 77
Parkway-South Sacramento (Sacramento) CDP 92
Parkwood (Madera) CDP 77
Parlier (Fresno) City 62
Pasadena (Los Angeles) City 74
Patterson (Stanislaus) City 111
Pedley (Riverside) CDP 90
Penn Valley (Nevada) CDP 84
Perris (Riverside) City 90
Petaluma (Sonoma) City 109
Phoenix Lake-Cedar Ridge (Tuolumne) CDP 114
Pico Rivera (Los Angeles) City 74
Piedmont (Alameda) City 55
Pine Hills (Humboldt) CDP 63
Pine Valley (San Diego) CDP 97
Pinole (Contra Costa) City 59
Piru (Ventura) CDP 115
Pismo Beach (San Luis Obispo) City 100
Pittsburg (Contra Costa) City 59
Pixley (Tulare) CDP 113
Placentia (Orange) City 86
Placer County 87
Placerville (El Dorado) City 60
Planada (Merced) CDP 80
Pleasant Hill (Contra Costa) City 59
Pleasanton (Alameda) City 55
Plumas County 88
Plymouth (Amador) City 56
Point Arena (Mendocino) City 79
Point Dume (Los Angeles) CDP 74
Pollock Pines (El Dorado) CDP 60
Pomona (Los Angeles) City 74
Poplar-Cotton Center (Tulare) CDP .113
Porterville (Tulare) City 113
Port Hueneme (Ventura) City 115
Portola (Plumas) City 88
Portola Hills (Orange) CDP 86
Portola Valley (San Mateo) City 101
Poway (San Diego) City 97
Prunedale (Monterey) CDP 82
Quail Valley (Riverside) CDP 90
Quartz Hill (Los Angeles) CDP 74
Quincy-East Quincy (Plumas) CDP 88
Rainbow (San Diego) CDP 97
Ramona (San Diego) CDP 97
Rancho Cordova (Sacramento) CDP .. 92
Rancho Cucamonga (San Bernardino) City 94
Rancho Mirage (Riverside) City 90
Rancho Murieta (Sacramento) CDP ... 92
Rancho Palos Verdes (Los Angeles) City 74
Rancho Rinconada (Santa Clara) CDP 104
Rancho San Diego (San Diego) CDP .97
Rancho Santa Margarita (Orange) CDP 86
Red Bluff (Tehama) City 112
Redding (Shasta) City 106
Redlands (San Bernardino) City 94
Redondo Beach (Los Angeles) City 74
Redway (Humboldt) CDP 63
Redwood City (San Mateo) City 101
Reedley (Fresno) City 62

Rialto (San Bernardino) City 94
Richgrove (Tulare) CDP 113
Richmond (Contra Costa) City 59
Ridgecrest (Kern) City 66
Rio Dell (Humboldt) City 63
Rio del Mar (Santa Cruz) CDP 105
Rio Linda (Sacramento) CDP 92
Rio Vista (Solano) City 108
Ripon (San Joaquin) Town 99
Riverbank (Stanislaus) City 111
Riverdale (Fresno) CDP 62
Riverside (Riverside) City 90
Riverside County 88
Rocklin (Placer) City 87
Rodeo (Contra Costa) CDP 59
Rohnert Park (Sonoma) City 109
Rolling Hills (Los Angeles) City 74
Rolling Hills Estates (Los Angeles) City 74
Romoland (Riverside) CDP 90
Rosamond (Kern) CDP 66
Rosedale (Kern) CDP 66
Roseland (Sonoma) CDP 109
Rosemead (Los Angeles) City 74
Rosemont (Sacramento) CDP 92
Roseville (Placer) City 87
Ross (Marin) Town 78
Rossmoor (Orange) CDP 86
Rowland Heights (Los Angeles) CDP .75
Rubidoux (Riverside) CDP 90
Running Springs (San Bernardino) CDP 94
Sacramento (Sacramento) City............ 92
Sacramento County 91
St. Helena (Napa) City 83
Salida (Stanislaus) CDP 111
Salinas (Monterey) City 82
San Andreas (Calaveras) CDP 57
San Anselmo (Marin) Town 78
San Antonio Heights (San Bernardino) CDP 94
San Benito County 92
San Bernardino (San Bernardino) City 94
San Bernardino County 93
San Bruno (San Mateo) City 101
San Buenaventura (Ventura) (Ventura) City 115
San Carlos (San Mateo) City 102
San Clemente (Orange) City 86
Sand City (Monterey) City 82
San Diego (San Diego) City 97
San Diego Country Estates (San Diego) CDP 97
San Diego County 95
San Dimas (Los Angeles) City 75
San Fernando (Los Angeles) City 75
San Francisco (San Francisco) City 98
San Francisco County 98
San Gabriel (Los Angeles) City 75
Sanger (Fresno) City 62
San Jacinto (Riverside) City 90
San Joaquin (Fresno) City 62
San Joaquin County 98
San Jose (Santa Clara) City 104
San Juan Bautista (San Benito) City .. 92
San Juan Capistrano (Orange) City 86
San Leandro (Alameda) City 55
San Lorenzo (Alameda) CDP 55
San Luis Obispo (San Luis Obispo) City 100
San Luis Obispo County 99
San Marcos (San Diego) City 97
San Marino (Los Angeles) City 75
San Martin (Santa Clara) CDP 104

San Mateo (San Mateo) City 102
San Mateo County 100
San Miguel (San Luis Obispo) CDP .100
San Pablo (Contra Costa) City 59
San Rafael (Marin) City 78
San Ramon (Contra Costa) City 59
Santa Ana (Orange) City 86
Santa Barbara (Santa Barbara) City ..102
Santa Barbara County 102
Santa Clara (Santa Clara) City 104
Santa Clara County 103
Santa Clarita (Los Angeles) City 75
Santa Cruz (Santa Cruz) City 105
Santa Cruz County 105
Santa Fe Springs (Los Angeles) City ...75
Santa Maria (Santa Barbara) City 102
Santa Monica (Los Angeles) City 75
Santa Paula (Ventura) City 116
Santa Rosa (Sonoma) City 110
Santa Venetia (Marin) CDP 78
Santa Ynez (Santa Barbara) CDP 103
Santee (San Diego) City 97
Saratoga (Santa Clara) City 104
Sausalito (Marin) City 78
Scotts Valley (Santa Cruz) City 105
Seal Beach (Orange) City 86
Searles Valley (San Bernardino) CDP .95
Seaside (Monterey) City 82
Sebastopol (Sonoma) City 110
Sedco Hills (Riverside) CDP 90
Seeley (Imperial) CDP 64
Selma (Fresno) City 62
Sepulveda See **Los Angeles** (Los Angeles) 75
Shafter (Kern) City 66
Shasta County 106
Sherman Oaks See **Los Angeles** (Los Angeles) 75
Shingle Springs (El Dorado) CDP 60
Sierra County 106
Sierra Madre (Los Angeles) City 75
Signal Hill (Los Angeles) City 75
Simi Valley (Ventura) City 116
Siskiyou County 107
Solana Beach (San Diego) City 97
Solano County 108
Soledad (Monterey) City 82
Solvang (Santa Barbara) City 103
Sonoma (Sonoma) City 110
Sonoma County 109
Sonora (Tuolumne) City 114
Soquel (Santa Cruz) CDP 106
Soulsbyville (Tuolumne) CDP 114
South Dos Palos (Merced) CDP 80
South El Monte (Los Angeles) City 75
South Gate (Los Angeles) City 75
South Lake (Kern) CDP 66
South Lake Tahoe (El Dorado) City 60
South Oroville (Butte) CDP 56
South Pasadena (Los Angeles) City 75
South San Francisco (San Mateo) City 102
South San Gabriel (Los Angeles) CDP 75
South San Jose Hills (Los Angeles) CDP 75
South Santa Rosa (Sonoma) CDP 110
South Taft (Kern) CDP 66
South Whittier (Los Angeles) CDP 76
South Yuba City (Sutter) CDP 111
Spring Valley (San Diego) CDP 97
Squaw Valley (Fresno) CDP 62
Stanford (Santa Clara) CDP 104
Stanislaus County 110
Stanton (Orange) City 86

CALIFORNIA

Stockton (San Joaquin) City *99*
Strathmore (Tulare) CDP *113*
Strawberry (Marin) CDP *78*
Studio City *See* **Los Angeles** (Los Angeles)... *76*
Suisun City (Solano) City *108*
Sun City (Riverside) CDP *91*
Sunnyside-Tahoe City (Placer) CDP ... *87*
Sunnyslope (Riverside) CDP *91*
Sunnyvale (Santa Clara) City *104*
Susanville (Lassen) City *68*
Sutter (Sutter) CDP *111*
Sutter County *111*
Sutter Creek (Amador) City *56*
Taft (Kern) City *66*
Taft Heights (Kern) CDP *67*
Tahoe Vista (Placer) CDP *87*
Tamalpais-Homestead Valley (Marin) CDP *78*
Tara Hills (Contra Costa) CDP *59*
Tarzana *See* **Los Angeles** (Los Angeles)... *76*
Tehachapi (Kern) City *67*
Tehama (Tehama) City *112*
Tehama County *112*
Temecula (Riverside) City *91*
Temelec (Sonoma) CDP *110*
Temple City (Los Angeles) City *76*
Templeton (San Luis Obispo) CDP .. *100*
Terra Bella (Tulare) CDP *113*
Thermalito (Butte) CDP *56*
Thousand Oaks (Ventura) City *116*
Thousand Palms (Riverside) CDP *91*
Tiburon (Marin) City *78*
Tierra Buena (Sutter) CDP *111*
Tipton (Tulare) CDP *113*
Torrance (Los Angeles) City *76*
Trabuco Highlands (Orange) CDP *86*
Tracy (San Joaquin) City *99*
Trinidad (Humboldt) City *63*
Trinity County *112*
Truckee (Nevada) CDP *84*
Tulare (Tulare) City *113*
Tulare County *113*
Tulelake (Siskiyou) City *107*
Tuolumne City (Tuolumne) CDP *114*
Tuolumne County *114*
Turlock (Stanislaus) City *111*

Tustin (Orange) City *86*
Tustin Foothills (Orange) CDP *86*
Twain Harte (Tuolumne) CDP *114*
Twentynine Palms (San Bernardino) City *95*
Twentynine Palms Base (San Bernardino) Military Facility *95*
Twin Lakes (Santa Cruz) CDP *106*
Ukiah (Mendocino) City *79*
Union City (Alameda) City *55*
Upland (San Bernardino) City *95*
Vacaville (Solano) City *108*
Valinda (Los Angeles) CDP *76*
Vallejo (Solano) City *108*
Valle Vista (Riverside) CDP *91*
Valley Center (San Diego) CDP *97*
Val Verde (Los Angeles) CDP *76*
Vandenberg Air Force Base (Santa Barbara) Military Facility *103*
Vandenberg Village (Santa Barbara) CDP *103*
Van Nuys *See* **Los Angeles** (Los Angeles)... *76*
Ventura County *115*
Vernon (Los Angeles) City *76*
Victorville (San Bernardino) City *95*
View Park-Windsor Hills (Los Angeles) CDP *76*
Villa Park (Orange) City *86*
Vincent (Los Angeles) CDP *76*
Vine Hill (Contra Costa) CDP *59*
Visalia (Tulare) City *114*
Vista (San Diego) City *97*
Walnut (Los Angeles) City *76*
Walnut Creek (Contra Costa) City *59*
Walnut Park (Los Angeles) CDP *76*
Wasco (Kern) City *67*
Waterford (Stanislaus) City *111*
Watsonville (Santa Cruz) City *106*
Watts *See* **Los Angeles** (Los Angeles).. *76*
Weaverville (Trinity) CDP *112*
Weed (Siskiyou) City *107*
Weedpatch (Kern) CDP *67*
West Athens (Los Angeles) CDP *76*
West Bishop (Inyo) CDP *65*
West Carson (Los Angeles) CDP *76*
West Compton (Los Angeles) CDP *76*

American Places Dictionary

West Covina (Los Angeles) City *76*
Westhaven-Moonstone (Humboldt) CDP *63*
West Hollywood (Los Angeles) City ... *76*
Westlake Village (Los Angeles) City ... *76*
West Menlo Park (San Mateo) CDP. *102*
Westminster (Orange) City *86*
Westmont (Los Angeles) CDP *76*
Westmorland (Imperial) City *64*
West Pittsburg (Contra Costa) CDP ... *59*
West Puente Valley (Los Angeles) CDP *76*
West Sacramento (Yolo) City *116*
West Whittier-Los Nietos (Los Angeles) CDP *76*
Westwood (Lassen) CDP *68*
Wheatland (Yuba) City *117*
Whittier (Los Angeles) City *76*
Wildomar (Riverside) CDP *91*
Williams (Colusa) City *57*
Willits (Mendocino) City *79*
Willowbrook (Los Angeles) CDP *76*
Willow Creek (Humboldt) CDP *63*
Willows (Glenn) City *62*
Wilton (Sacramento) CDP *92*
Winchester (Riverside) CDP *91*
Windsor (Sonoma) CDP *110*
Winters (Yolo) City *116*
Winton (Merced) CDP *80*
Wofford Heights (Kern) CDP *67*
Woodacre (Marin) CDP *78*
Woodbridge (San Joaquin) CDP *99*
Woodcrest (Riverside) CDP *91*
Woodlake (Tulare) City *114*
Woodland (Yolo) City *116*
Woodside (San Mateo) Town *102*
Woodville (Tulare) CDP *114*
Wrightwood (San Bernardino) CDP ... *95*
Yolo County *116*
Yorba Linda (Orange) City *86*
Yosemite Lakes (Madera) CDP *77*
Yountville (Napa) Town *83*
Yreka (Siskiyou) City *107*
Yuba City (Sutter) City *111*
Yuba County *117*
Yucaipa (San Bernardino) City *95*
Yucca Valley (San Bernardino) CDP .. *95*

Colorado

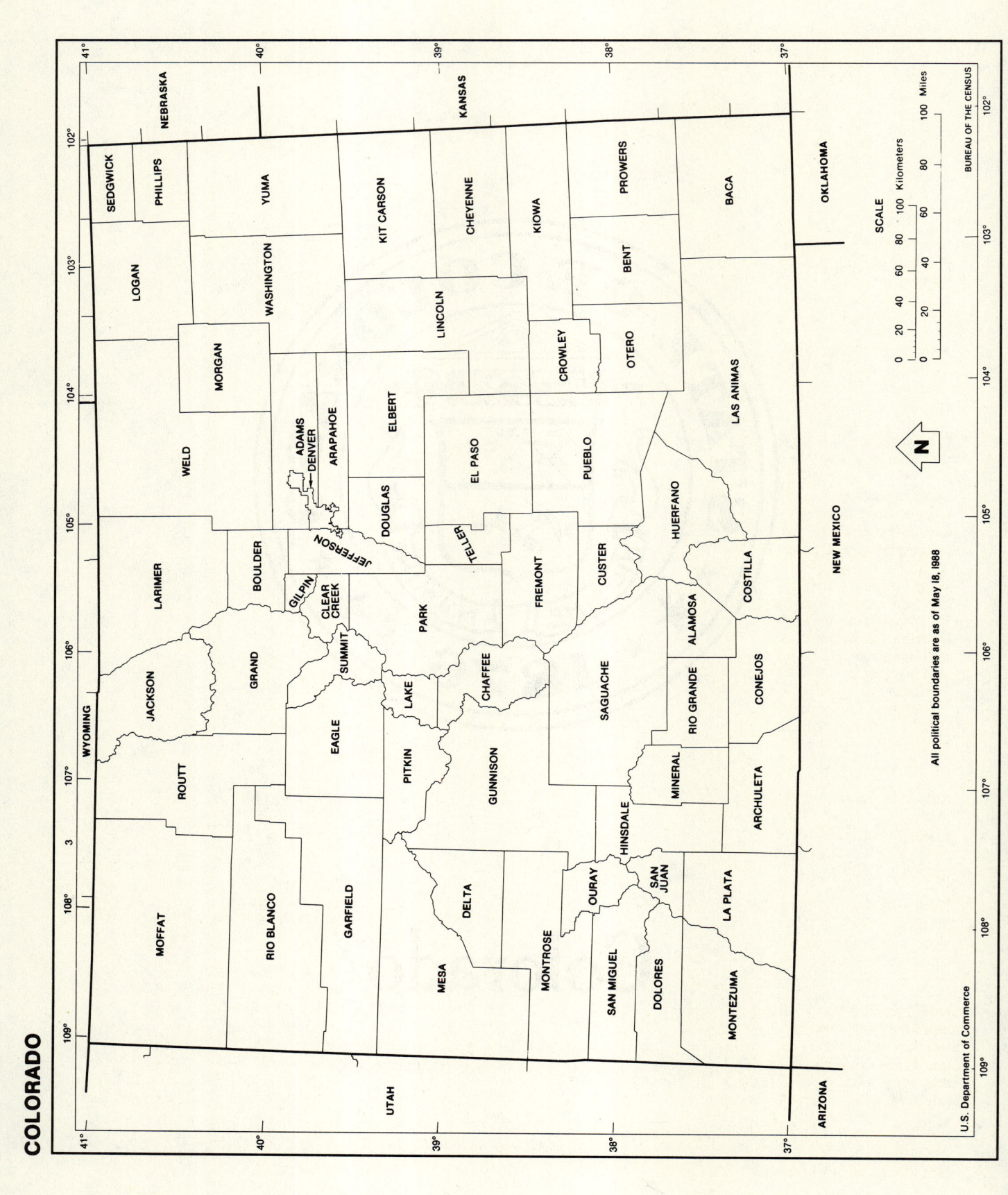

Colorado

Population: 3,294,394 (1990); 2,889,964 (1980)
Population rank (1990): 26
Percent population change (1980–1990): 14.0
Population projection: 3,460,000 (1995); 3,548,000 (2000)

Area: total: 104,100 sq. mi.; 103,730 sq. mi. land, 371 sq. mi. water
Area rank: 8
Highest elevation: 14,433 ft., Mount Elbert (Lake County)
Lowest point: 3,350 ft., along the Arkansas River (Prowers County)

State capital: Denver (Denver County)
Largest city: Denver (467,610)
Second largest city: Colorado Springs (281,140)
Largest county: Denver (467,610)

Total housing units: 1,477,349
No. of occupied housing units: 1,282,489
Vacant housing units (%): 13.2
Distribution of population by race and Hispanic origin (%):
White: 88.2
Black: 4.0
Hispanic (any race): 12.9
Native American: 0.8
Asian/Pacific: 1.8
Other: 5.1

Admission date: August 1, 1876 (38th state).

Location: In the west-central United States, bordering New Mexico, Oklahoma, Kansas, Nebraska, Wyoming, and Utah.

Name Origin: For the Colorado River, which originates within the state. Its name is the Spanish word meaning 'red' or 'reddish brown,' referring to the color of the water.

State animal: bighorn sheep (*Ovis canadensis*)
State bird: lark bunting (*Calamospiza melanocorys*)
State flower: columbine (*Aquilegia caerula*)
State gem: aquamarine
State song: "Where the Columbines Grow"
State tree: blue spruce (*Picea pungens*)

State motto: *Nil sine Numine* (Latin 'Nothing without Providence')
State nickname: Centennial State

Area codes: 303 (north and southwest, including Denver), 719 (southeast)

Time zone: Mountain
Abbreviations: CO (postal); Colo. (traditional)
Part of (region): Rocky Mountain states

Local Government

Counties

Colorado's 63 counties are each governed by an elected board of commissioners.

Municipalities

Colorado has 267 cities and towns. Colorado's municipalities have increasingly chosen home rule and most have council-manager systems of government.

Settlement History and Early Development

Present-day Colorado's earliest inhabitants may have been hunters who occupied the land more than 20,000 years ago. The Basket Makers, a tribe that practiced agriculture and lived in pit houses, inhabited the area about 2,000 years ago. About 1,000 years ago Pueblo Indians lived in Colorado and constructed elaborate cliffside apartment houses before they migrated south. By the time of white exploration, the territory that became Colorado was inhabited by Cheyenne, Arapaho, Comanche, Kiowa, and Pawnee Indians on the plains and Ute Indians in the mountain valleys.

The Spanish explorer Juan de Oñate may have traveled through southeastern Colorado in 1601. In 1706 Juan de Uribarri claimed the area then called New Mexico, including what is now southwestern Colorado, for Spain. In 1776 Padre Francisco Escalante visited the region of the Delores and Gunnison rivers. France claimed the part of Colorado east of the Rockies as part of the Louisiana Territory, which passed from the French to the Spanish in 1763 and from the Spanish back to the French in 1800. The French sold the area to the U.S. as part of the Louisiana Purchase in 1803.

In order to determine the boundary between its new land and Spanish New Mexico, the U.S. government sent Zebulon Pike to explore the area in 1806. Pike and his group reached Pueblo and attempted without success to scale the peak that bears his name. It was not until 1819 that the U.S. and Spain agreed on the Arkansas River and the Continental Divide as boundaries. In 1821 the Spanish-held territory became part of the newly independent Mexico.

Fur traders and scouts were among the few who ventured into eastern Colorado during the next decades. The first permanent American settlement was Bent's Fort in 1833. Between 1842 and 1853, John C. Frémont led five expeditions into the area, traveling along the South Platte

River in his first expedition and crossing the Rockies several times in later expeditions. Meanwhile, the U.S. acquired southern and western Colorado from Mexico in the Treaty of Guadalupe Hidalgo in 1848, at the end of the Mexican-American War.

Discovery of Gold

In 1858 the discovery of gold at Cherry Creek (present-day Denver) drew many prospectors into the territory. The slogan "Pikes Peak or Bust" was used by the prospectors as they made the arduous journey to Colorado. The reports about gold at Cherry Creek had been exaggerated, but later strikes led to the establishment of a string of mining towns, including Golden, Boulder, and Colorado City. In 1861 Congress organized the Colorado Territory, with the same boundaries as those of the present state. Colorado sided with the Union during the Civil War.

Indian Wars

The 1860s saw serious conflicts between army forces and Indians in Colorado. Most of the Indians were finally defeated in battles at Beecher Island (1868) and Summit Spring (1869). Many Indians were moved to reservations in what is now Oklahoma by the mid-1870s.

Statehood

Colorado's bid for statehood was vetoed in 1866 by Democratic President Andrew Johnson, who was facing an impeachment trial and feared the addition of two more Republicans to the Senate. Colorado became the 38th state on August 1, 1876, under President Grant.

Business and Industry

Throughout the 1870s and 1880s, settlers were attracted by silver strikes, coal mines, farming, and the budding tourist industry. Resorts and spas were opened near the state's mineral springs. The 1890s were generally a time of economic woe, however, as silver prices dropped when the federal government adopted the gold standard in 1893 and a drought forced many farmers to abandon their land. However, a major gold strike at Cripple Creek in 1891 helped, as did the opening of the Denver Mint in 1906.

During the early years of the twentieth century farmers returned to Colorado's land, using dry-land farming techniques and irrigation to good effect. The development of good roads and the automobile made tourism more popular and indirectly spurred the state's growing oil industry. The state was prosperous during World War I, but during the 1920s and 1930s both agriculture and mining declined. Farming suffered from drought and huge dust storms. The state's population fell during the Great Depression of the 1930s. World War II brought prosperity to Colorado, and after the war Colorado was chosen as the site of both the North American Air Defense Command (NORAD) and the U.S. Air Force Academy in Colorado Springs. A host of defense-related industries also contributed to Colorado's economy. In the 1970s Colorado developed as a center of energy-related development, as utility companies planned to develop Colorado's coal, natural gas, and oil.

State Boundaries

The boundaries of the state of Colorado were set when the area was organized as the Territory of Colorado in 1861 from parts of the Utah, New Mexico, Kansas, and Nebraska territories.

Colorado Counties

Adams	Custer	Hinsdale	Mineral	Rio Blanco
Alamosa	Delta	Huerfano	Moffat	Rio Grande
Arapahoe	Denver	Jackson	Montezuma	Routt
Archuleta	Dolores	Jefferson	Montrose	Saguache
Baca	Douglas	Kiowa	Morgan	San Juan
Bent	Eagle	Kit Carson	Otero	San Miguel
Boulder	Elbert	Lake	Ouray	Sedgwick
Chaffee	El Paso	La Plata	Park	Summit
Cheyenne	Fremont	Larimer	Phillips	Teller
Clear Creek	Garfield	Las Animas	Pitkin	Washington
Conejos	Gilpin	Lincoln	Prowers	Weld
Costilla	Grand	Logan	Pueblo	Yuma
Crowley	Gunnison	Mesa		

Multi-County Places

The following Colorado places are in more than one county. Given here is the total population for each multi-county place, and the names of the counties it is in.

Arvada, pop. 89,235; Jefferson (86,888), Adams (2,347)
Aurora, pop. 222,103; Arapahoe (194,352), Adams (27,747), Douglas (4)
Basalt, pop. 1,128; Eagle (1,002), Pitkin (126)
Bow Mar, pop. 854; Arapahoe (613), Jefferson (241)
Brighton, pop. 14,203; Adams (14,186), Weld (17)
Broomfield, pop. 24,638; Boulder (16,390), Adams (6,722), Jefferson (1,522), Weld (4)
Center, pop. 1,963; Saguache (1,959), Rio Grande (4)
Columbine, pop. 23,969; Jefferson (22,397), Arapahoe (1,572)
Erie, pop. 1,258; Weld (1,244), Boulder (14)
Green Mountain Falls, pop. 663; El Paso (634), Teller (29)
Littleton, pop. 33,685; Arapahoe (33,577), Douglas (108)
Northglenn, pop. 27,195; Adams (27,195), Weld (0)
Superior, pop. 255; Boulder (255), Jefferson (0)
Westminster, pop. 74,625; Adams (41,639), Jefferson (32,986)

COLORADO, Adams County

> ### Adams County
> **County Seat: Brighton (ZIP: 80601)**
>
> **Pop:** 265,038 (1990); 245,944 (1980) **Pop Density:** 222.3
> **Land:** 1192.0 sq. mi.; **Water:** 5.8 sq. mi. **Area Code:** 303
>
> In east-central CO, east of Denver; organized Apr 15, 1901 from Arapahoe County; annexed part of Denver County in 1909.
>
> **Name origin:** For Alva Adams (1850–1922), statesman and governor (1887–89; 1897–99; 1905).

Arvada City
ZIP: 80001 **Lat:** 39-48-40 N **Long:** 105-02-57 W
Pop: 2,347 (1990); 1,229 (1980) **Pop Density:** 4694.0
Land: 0.5 sq. mi.; **Water:** 0.0 sq. mi.

In central CO, west of Denver. Part of the town is also in Jefferson County.
Name origin: For Hiram Arvada Hoskins, brother-in-law of the wife of founder B.F. Wadsworth. Previously known as Ralston Point and Ralston Station.

Aurora City
ZIP: 80017 **Lat:** 39-45-13 N **Long:** 104-40-52 W
Pop: 27,747 (1990); 29,193 (1980) **Pop Density:** 518.6
Land: 53.5 sq. mi.; **Water:** 0.0 sq. mi.

In northeast-central CO, 5 mi. east of Denver. Part of the town is also in Arapahoe and Douglas Counties. The county line runs down the middle of the town's main street.
Name origin: Named by the town fathers, from Latin 'dawn.' Originally named Fletcher, for Donald Fletcher, a town promoter.

Bennett Town
ZIP: 80102 **Lat:** 39-45-18 N **Long:** 104-25-24 W
Pop: 1,757 (1990); 942 (1980) **Pop Density:** 1098.1
Land: 1.6 sq. mi.; **Water:** 0.0 sq. mi. **Elev:** 5483 ft.

Name origin: In honor of H.P. Bennett, an early Denver postmaster. Previously called Kiowa for the nearby creek, named for the Indian tribe.

Brighton City
ZIP: 80601 **Lat:** 39-57-28 N **Long:** 104-47-41 W
Pop: 14,186 (1990); 12,773 (1980) **Pop Density:** 971.6
Land: 14.6 sq. mi.; **Water:** 0.0 sq. mi. **Elev:** 4983 ft.

In northeast-central CO, 17 mi. northeast of Denver. Founded 1889; incorporated as city 1922. Part of the town is also in Weld County.
Name origin: Named by the wife of the original surveyor for her hometown in MA.

Broomfield City
ZIP: 80020 **Lat:** 39-57-27 N **Long:** 105-02-08 W
Pop: 6,722 (1990); 5,467 (1980) **Pop Density:** 672.2
Land: 10.0 sq. mi.; **Water:** 0.0 sq. mi. **Elev:** 5400 ft.

Part of the town is also in Boulder and Jefferson counties.

Commerce City City
ZIP: 80022 **Lat:** 39-52-03 N **Long:** 104-52-06 W
Pop: 16,466 (1990); 16,234 (1980) **Pop Density:** 823.3
Land: 20.0 sq. mi.; **Water:** 0.0 sq. mi. **Elev:** 5166 ft.

In northeast-central CO, northeast of Denver. Founded in the early 1900s.
Name origin: The city was industrial from its beginning.

Derby CDP
ZIP: 80022 **Lat:** 39-50-22 N **Long:** 104-55-05 W
Pop: 6,043 (1990); 8,578 (1980) **Pop Density:** 3357.2
Land: 1.8 sq. mi.; **Water:** 0.0 sq. mi.

Federal Heights City
ZIP: 80221 **Lat:** 39-51-54 N **Long:** 105-00-57 W
Pop: 9,342 (1990); 7,838 (1980) **Pop Density:** 5190.0
Land: 1.8 sq. mi.; **Water:** 0.0 sq. mi. **Elev:** 5520 ft.

Name origin: For its location on Federal Boulevard, a major north-south thoroughfare in western Denver.

Northglenn City
ZIP: 80233 **Lat:** 39-53-50 N **Long:** 104-58-52 W
Pop: 27,195 (1990); 29,847 (1980) **Pop Density:** 4249.2
Land: 6.4 sq. mi.; **Water:** 0.1 sq. mi. **Elev:** 5450 ft.

In northeast-central CO, a northern suburb of Denver. Part of the town is also in Weld County.
Name origin: For its descriptive connotations.

Sherrelwood CDP
ZIP: 80221 **Lat:** 39-50-15 N **Long:** 105-00-03 W
Pop: 16,636 (1990); 17,629 (1980) **Pop Density:** 6654.4
Land: 2.5 sq. mi.; **Water:** 0.0 sq. mi.

Thornton City
ZIP: 80229 **Lat:** 39-53-31 N **Long:** 104-57-18 W
Pop: 55,031 (1990); 42,054 (1980) **Pop Density:** 2658.5
Land: 20.7 sq. mi.; **Water:** 0.3 sq. mi. **Elev:** 5342 ft.

In northeast-central CO, north of Denver. Established 1952; incorporated 1956.
Name origin: For Dan Thornton, governor of CO when the town was established..

Welby CDP
ZIP: 80229 **Lat:** 39-50-17 N **Long:** 104-57-52 W
Pop: 10,218 (1990); 9,668 (1980) **Pop Density:** 2688.9
Land: 3.8 sq. mi.; **Water:** 0.0 sq. mi.

Westminster City
ZIP: 80030 **Lat:** 39-53-09 N **Long:** 105-01-35 W
Pop: 41,639 (1990); 32,046 (1980) **Pop Density:** 2703.8
Land: 15.4 sq. mi.; **Water:** 0.1 sq. mi. **Elev:** 5300 ft.

In northeast-central CO, northwest of Denver. Part of the town is also in Jefferson County.
Name origin: Named in 1891 by Stanford White, who founded a Presbyterian college of the same name.

Westminster East CDP
ZIP: 80221 **Lat:** 39-49-21 N **Long:** 105-00-13 W
Pop: 5,197 (1990); 6,002 (1980) **Pop Density:** 3057.1
Land: 1.7 sq. mi.; **Water:** 0.0 sq. mi.

Alamosa County
County Seat: Alamosa (ZIP: 81101)

Pop: 13,617 (1990); 11,799 (1980)   **Pop Density:** 18.8
Land: 722.8 sq. mi.; **Water:** 0.8 sq. mi.   **Area Code:** 719
In south-central CO, southwest of Pueblo; organized Mar 8, 1913 from Costilla County.
Name origin: Spanish 'cottonwood trees.'

Alamosa   *City*
ZIP: 81101   **Lat:** 37-28-07 N   **Long:** 105-52-23 W
Pop: 7,579 (1990); 6,830 (1980)   **Pop Density:** 2165.4
Land: 3.5 sq. mi.; **Water:** 0.0 sq. mi.   **Elev:** 7544 ft.
Founded by former gov. A.C. Hunt, president of the Denver & Rio Grande construction Co.
Name origin: From Spanish 'cottonwood grove.'

Alamosa East   *CDP*
Lat: 37-28-37 N   **Long:** 105-50-33 W
Pop: 1,389 (1990); 1,175 (1980)   **Pop Density:** 365.5
Land: 3.8 sq. mi.; **Water:** 0.0 sq. mi.

Hooper   *Town*
ZIP: 81136   **Lat:** 37-44-44 N   **Long:** 105-52-39 W
Pop: 112 (1990); 71 (1980)   **Pop Density:** 373.3
Land: 0.3 sq. mi.; **Water:** 0.0 sq. mi.
Name origin: For Maj. S. Hooper, passenger agent for the Denver and Rio Grande Railroad.

Arapahoe County
County Seat: Littleton (ZIP: 80120)

Pop: 391,511 (1990); 293,300 (1980)   **Pop Density:** 487.5
Land: 803.2 sq. mi.; **Water:** 2.3 sq. mi.   **Area Code:** 303
In east-central CO, south of Denver; original county, organized Nov 1, 1861 (prior to statehood).
Name origin: For a tribe of Algonquian linguistic stock. Name is probably Pawnee *tirapihu* 'trader.' Also suggested, but not documented, 'blue-sky men' and 'cloud men.'

Aurora   *City*
ZIP: 80017   **Lat:** 39-40-29 N   **Long:** 104-45-43 W
Pop: 194,352 (1990); 129,395 (1980)   **Pop Density:** 2482.1
Land: 78.3 sq. mi.; **Water:** 0.2 sq. mi.
Part of the town is also in Adams and Douglas Counties.

Bow Mar   *Town*
Lat: 39-37-27 N   **Long:** 105-02-58 W
Pop: 613 (1990); 690 (1980)   **Pop Density:** 1532.5
Land: 0.4 sq. mi.; **Water:** 0.1 sq. mi.   **Elev:** 5515 ft.
Part of the town is also in Jefferson County.

Byers   *CDP*
ZIP: 80103   **Lat:** 39-42-37 N   **Long:** 104-13-29 W
Pop: 1,065 (1990)   **Pop Density:** 247.7
Land: 4.3 sq. mi.; **Water:** 0.0 sq. mi.

Castlewood   *CDP*
ZIP: 80120   **Lat:** 39-35-05 N   **Long:** 104-54-01 W
Pop: 24,392 (1990); 16,413 (1980)   **Pop Density:** 3871.7
Land: 6.3 sq. mi.; **Water:** 0.0 sq. mi.

Cherry Hills Village   *City*
ZIP: 80110   **Lat:** 39-38-14 N   **Long:** 104-56-48 W
Pop: 5,245 (1990); 5,127 (1980)   **Pop Density:** 846.0
Land: 6.2 sq. mi.; **Water:** 0.1 sq. mi.   **Elev:** 5395 ft.
Name origin: For now vanished cherry orchards.

Columbine   *CDP*
Lat: 39-35-39 N   **Long:** 105-02-56 W
Pop: 1,572 (1990); 1,801 (1980)   **Pop Density:** 2245.7
Land: 0.7 sq. mi.; **Water:** 0.0 sq. mi.

Columbine Valley   *Town*
Lat: 39-35-53 N   **Long:** 105-02-01 W
Pop: 1,071 (1990); 923 (1980)   **Pop Density:** 1071.0
Land: 1.0 sq. mi.; **Water:** 0.0 sq. mi.   **Elev:** 5350 ft.
Part of the town is in Jefferson County.

Deer Trail   *Town*
ZIP: 80105   **Lat:** 39-37-00 N   **Long:** 104-02-30 W
Pop: 476 (1990); 463 (1980)   **Pop Density:** 528.9
Land: 0.9 sq. mi.; **Water:** 0.0 sq. mi.
Name origin: Named by frontiersman Oliver P. Wiggins for a nearby deer trail.

Englewood   *City*
ZIP: 80110   **Lat:** 39-38-50 N   **Long:** 104-59-37 W
Pop: 29,387 (1990); 30,021 (1980)   **Pop Density:** 4521.1
Land: 6.5 sq. mi.; **Water:** 0.1 sq. mi.   **Elev:** 5369 ft.
In northeast-central CO, 6 mi. south of Denver.
Name origin: Named by incorporating citizens after a similarly named city near Chicago. Previously called Fisks's Gardens and Orchard Place.

COLORADO, Arapahoe County — American Places Dictionary

Glendale
City
Lat: 39-42-14 N **Long:** 104-56-04 W
Pop: 2,453 (1990); 2,496 (1980) **Pop Density:** 4906.0
Land: 0.5 sq. mi.; **Water:** 0.0 sq. mi. **Elev:** 5350 ft.
In northeast-central CO; a suburb of Denver.
Name origin: For its descriptive connotations.

Greenwood Village
City
ZIP: 80111 **Lat:** 39-36-55 N **Long:** 104-54-53 W
Pop: 7,589 (1990); 5,729 (1980) **Pop Density:** 985.6
Land: 7.7 sq. mi.; **Water:** 0.0 sq. mi. **Elev:** 5450 ft.
Name origin: For its once wooded countryside.

Littleton
City
ZIP: 80120 **Lat:** 39-35-40 N **Long:** 105-00-51 W
Pop: 33,577 (1990); 28,503 (1980) **Pop Density:** 2775.0
Land: 12.1 sq. mi.; **Water:** 0.4 sq. mi.
In northwest-central CO, a suburb 10 mi. south of Denver. County seat. Established 1872; incorporated 1890. Part of the town is also in Douglas County.
Name origin: Named for the founder, civil engineer Richard Little (1829–99), who came to CO in 1860.

Sheridan
City
ZIP: 80110 **Lat:** 39-38-56 N **Long:** 105-01-01 W
Pop: 4,976 (1990); 5,377 (1980) **Pop Density:** 2261.8
Land: 2.2 sq. mi.; **Water:** 0.0 sq. mi. **Elev:** 5320 ft.
Name origin: For Gen. Philip Sheridan (1831–88), Union hero of the Civil War.

Southglenn
CDP
ZIP: 80122 **Lat:** 39-35-14 N **Long:** 104-57-07 W
Pop: 43,087 (1990); 37,787 (1980) **Pop Density:** 4352.2
Land: 9.9 sq. mi.; **Water:** 0.0 sq. mi.

Archuleta County
County Seat: Pagosa Springs (ZIP: 81147)

Pop: 5,345 (1990); 3,664 (1980) **Pop Density:** 4.0
Land: 1349.4 sq. mi.; **Water:** 5.3 sq. mi. **Area Code:** 303
On southern border, east of Durango; organized Apr 14, 1885 from Conejos County.
Name origin: For Antonio D. Archuleta, a CO legislator.

Pagosa Springs
Town
ZIP: 81147 **Lat:** 37-16-12 N **Long:** 107-01-05 W
Pop: 1,207 (1990); 1,331 (1980) **Pop Density:** 524.8
Land: 2.3 sq. mi.; **Water:** 0.0 sq. mi. **Elev:** 7105 ft.
Name origin: From a Ute term for 'healing waters.'

Baca County
County Seat: Springfield (ZIP: 81073)

Pop: 4,556 (1990); 5,419 (1980) **Pop Density:** 1.8
Land: 2555.9 sq. mi.; **Water:** 1.4 sq. mi. **Area Code:** 719
On southeastern border of CO; organized Apr. 16, 1889 from Las Animas County.
Name origin: For an early pioneer family from Trinidad, CO.

Campo
Town
ZIP: 81029 **Lat:** 37-06-16 N **Long:** 102-34-40 W
Pop: 121 (1990); 185 (1980) **Pop Density:** 1210.0
Land: 0.1 sq. mi.; **Water:** 0.0 sq. mi. **Elev:** 4340 ft.
Name origin: From Spanish 'field.'

Pritchett
Town
ZIP: 81064 **Lat:** 37-22-12 N **Long:** 102-51-31 W
Pop: 153 (1990); 183 (1980) **Pop Density:** 765.0
Land: 0.2 sq. mi.; **Water:** 0.0 sq. mi. **Elev:** 4830 ft.
A terminus for the Atchison, Topeka and Santa Fe Railway.
Name origin: For Henry Pritchett, a director of the Atchison, Topeka & Santa Fe Railway.

Springfield
Town
ZIP: 81073 **Lat:** 37-24-23 N **Long:** 102-37-00 W
Pop: 1,475 (1990); 1,657 (1980) **Pop Density:** 1843.8
Land: 0.8 sq. mi.; **Water:** 0.0 sq. mi. **Elev:** 4365 ft.
Name origin: Named by original landowner Andrew Harrison, for his former hometown, Springfield, MO.

Two Buttes
Town
ZIP: 81084 **Lat:** 37-33-37 N **Long:** 102-23-45 W
Pop: 63 (1990); 84 (1980) **Pop Density:** 315.0
Land: 0.2 sq. mi.; **Water:** 0.0 sq. mi.

Vilas — Town
ZIP: 81087 Lat: 37-22-26 N Long: 102-26-47 W
Pop: 105 (1990); 118 (1980) Pop Density: 1050.0
Land: 0.1 sq. mi.; Water: 0.0 sq. mi. Elev: 4160 ft.
Name origin: For William F. Vilas, U.S. Postmaster General, Secretary of the Interior, and U.S. senator from WI (1891–97).

Walsh — Town
ZIP: 81090 Lat: 37-23-07 N Long: 102-16-46 W
Pop: 692 (1990); 884 (1980) Pop Density: 1384.0
Land: 0.5 sq. mi.; Water: 0.0 sq. mi. Elev: 3955 ft.
Name origin: For a retired railroad agent.

Bent County
County Seat: Las Animas (ZIP: 81054)

Pop: 5,048 (1990); 5,945 (1980) Pop Density: 3.3
Land: 1514.0 sq. mi.; Water: 27.2 sq. mi. Area Code: 303
In southeastern CO, southwest of Pueblo; organized Feb 11, 1870, from Greenwood County (prior to statehood), which was organized in 1874 and abolished in 1878 by being divided between Bent and Elbert counties.
Name origin: For Bent's Fort on the north bank of the Arkansas River and for the Bent brothers who built it, or for one of the brothers, William Bent (1809–69), early settler, fur trader, and Indian agent.

Las Animas — City
ZIP: 81054 Lat: 38-04-00 N Long: 103-13-31 W
Pop: 2,481 (1990); 2,818 (1980) Pop Density: 1908.5
Land: 1.3 sq. mi.; Water: 0.0 sq. mi. Elev: 3893 ft.
Name origin: For the Purgatoire River, French form of the Spanish word *purgatorio* and derived from the name *Rio de las animas perdidas en purgatorio* 'river of lost souls in purgatory.'

Boulder County
County Seat: Boulder (ZIP: 80306)

Pop: 225,339 (1990); 189,625 (1980) Pop Density: 303.5
Land: 742.5 sq. mi.; Water: 8.9 sq. mi. Area Code: 303
In north-central CO, northwest of Denver; original county, organized Nov 1, 1861 (prior to statehood).
Name origin: For Boulder City and Boulder Creek, themselves named for the huge rock formations in the area.

Boulder — City
ZIP: 80302 Lat: 40-01-36 N Long: 105-15-03 W
Pop: 83,312 (1990); 76,685 (1980) Pop Density: 3686.4
Land: 22.6 sq. mi.; Water: 1.0 sq. mi. Elev: 5344 ft.
In north-central CO, 25 mi. northwest of Denver. Settled 1858; incorporated 1871. Home of the University of Colorado.
Name origin: For the profusion of boulders in the area.

Broomfield — City
ZIP: 80020 Lat: 39-55-43 N Long: 105-05-29 W
Pop: 16,390 (1990); 14,514 (1980) Pop Density: 1974.7
Land: 8.3 sq. mi.; Water: 0.0 sq. mi. Elev: 5400 ft.
Part of the town is also in Adams, Jefferson and Weld counties.

Erie — Town
ZIP: 80516 Lat: 40-02-16 N Long: 105-03-56 W
Pop: 14 (1990); 23 (1980) Pop Density: 10.8
Land: 1.3 sq. mi.; Water: 0.0 sq. mi.
Part of the town is also in Weld County.

Gunbarrel — CDP
ZIP: 80501 Lat: 40-03-55 N Long: 105-10-16 W
Pop: 9,388 (1990); 4,181 (1980) Pop Density: 1539.0
Land: 6.1 sq. mi.; Water: 0.0 sq. mi.

Jamestown — Town
ZIP: 80455 Lat: 40-06-58 N Long: 105-23-22 W
Pop: 251 (1990); 223 (1980) Pop Density: 358.6
Land: 0.7 sq. mi.; Water: 0.0 sq. mi.
Name origin: Named by postal officials. Originally known as Jimtown.

Lafayette — City
ZIP: 80026 Lat: 39-59-39 N Long: 105-05-52 W
Pop: 14,548 (1990); 8,985 (1980) Pop Density: 2108.4
Land: 6.9 sq. mi.; Water: 0.1 sq. mi. Elev: 5236 ft.
In north-central CO, 17 mi. north-northwest of Denver.
Name origin: For either the original owner Lafayette Miller, or the Marquis de Lafayette (1757–1834), French officer who fought with the Americans during the Revolutionary War.

COLORADO, Boulder County

Longmont
City
ZIP: 80501 **Lat:** 40-10-22 N **Long:** 105-06-42 W
Pop: 51,555 (1990); 42,942 (1980) **Pop Density:** 3935.5
Land: 13.1 sq. mi.; **Water:** 0.0 sq. mi.
In north-central CO, 30 mi. north of Denver. Founded 1870.
Name origin: For the highest peak in Rocky Mountain National Park, which was named for the famous engineer-explorer, Maj. Stephen H. Long (1784–1864).

Louisville
City
ZIP: 80027 **Lat:** 39-58-06 N **Long:** 105-08-22 W
Pop: 12,361 (1990); 5,593 (1980) **Pop Density:** 1605.3
Land: 7.7 sq. mi.; **Water:** 0.0 sq. mi. **Elev:** 5337 ft.
In north-central CO, a northwestern suburb of Denver.
Name origin: For an early settler, Louis Nawatny, who discovered coal on his land and started a settlement.

Lyons
Town
Lat: 40-13-22 N **Long:** 105-16-06 W
Pop: 1,227 (1990); 1,137 (1980) **Pop Density:** 1227.0
Land: 1.0 sq. mi.; **Water:** 0.0 sq. mi.
Name origin: For Mrs. Carrie Lyons, a pioneer newspaper editor.

Nederland
Town
ZIP: 80466 **Lat:** 39-57-45 N **Long:** 105-30-19 W
Pop: 1,099 (1990); 1,212 (1980) **Pop Density:** 785.0
Land: 1.4 sq. mi.; **Water:** 0.1 sq. mi. **Elev:** 8233 ft.
Name origin: Named in 1877 by Dutch owners of nearby Caribou silver mines; meaning 'lowland.'

Niwot
CDP
Lat: 40-05-44 N **Long:** 105-09-20 W
Pop: 2,666 (1990) **Pop Density:** 650.2
Land: 4.1 sq. mi.; **Water:** 0.0 sq. mi.

Superior
Town
ZIP: 80027 **Lat:** 39-55-45 N **Long:** 105-09-17 W
Pop: 255 (1990); 208 (1980) **Pop Density:** 79.7
Land: 3.2 sq. mi.; **Water:** 0.0 sq. mi. **Elev:** 5490 ft.
Part of the town is also in Jefferson County.

Ward
Town
ZIP: 80481 **Lat:** 40-04-20 N **Long:** 105-30-40 W
Pop: 159 (1990); 129 (1980) **Pop Density:** 265.0
Land: 0.6 sq. mi.; **Water:** 0.0 sq. mi.
Name origin: For Calvin Ward, who discovered the gold-bearing 'Ward Seam' in 1860.

Chaffee County
County Seat: Salida (ZIP: 81201)

Pop: 12,684 (1990); 13,227 (1980) **Pop Density:** 12.5
Land: 1013.5 sq. mi.; **Water:** 1.6 sq. mi. **Area Code:** 719
In central CO; organized as Lake County Nov 1, 1861 (prior to statehood); name changed Feb 10, 1879.
Name origin: For Jerome Bounty Chaffee (1825–86), CO territorial legislator and U.S. senator (1876–79); one of the founders of Denver.

Buena Vista
Town
Lat: 38-49-57 N **Long:** 106-08-28 W
Pop: 1,752 (1990); 2,075 (1980) **Pop Density:** 515.3
Land: 3.4 sq. mi.; **Water:** 0.0 sq. mi. **Elev:** 7955 ft.
Name origin: From Spanish 'good view.'

Poncha Springs
Town
Lat: 38-30-50 N **Long:** 106-04-26 W
Pop: 244 (1990); 321 (1980) **Pop Density:** 221.8
Land: 1.1 sq. mi.; **Water:** 0.0 sq. mi. **Elev:** 7465 ft.
Name origin: For nearby Poncha Pass and the area's famous mineral springs.

Salida
City
ZIP: 81201 **Lat:** 38-31-57 N **Long:** 105-59-59 W
Pop: 4,737 (1990); 4,870 (1980) **Pop Density:** 2153.2
Land: 2.2 sq. mi.; **Water:** 0.0 sq. mi.
Name origin: From Spanish 'exit,' 'outlet,' or 'departure'; no reason given for the choice.

Cheyenne County
County Seat: Cheyenne Wells (ZIP: 80810)

Pop: 2,397 (1990); 2,153 (1980)   **Pop Density:** 1.3
Land: 1781.5 sq. mi.; **Water:** 0.0 sq. mi.   **Area Code:** 719

On central-eastern border of CO, east of Colorado Springs; organized Mar 25, 1889 from Bent and Elbert counties.

Name origin: For the Dakota Indian tribe of Algonquian linguistic stock; name means 'red talkers.'

Cheyenne Wells — Town
ZIP: 80810   **Lat:** 38-49-09 N **Long:** 102-21-02 W
Pop: 1,128 (1990); 950 (1980)   **Pop Density:** 1128.0
Land: 1.0 sq. mi.; **Water:** 0.0 sq. mi.

Name origin: For the several wells at the old town site, and for the Indian tribe then living in the area.

Kit Carson — Town
ZIP: 80825   **Lat:** 38-45-47 N **Long:** 102-47-44 W
Pop: 305 (1990); 278 (1980)   **Pop Density:** 508.3
Land: 0.6 sq. mi.; **Water:** 0.0 sq. mi.

Name origin: For the famous Western scout and explorer Christopher "Kit" Carson (1809–68).

Clear Creek County
County Seat: Georgetown (ZIP: 80444)

Pop: 7,619 (1990); 7,308 (1980)   **Pop Density:** 19.3
Land: 395.5 sq. mi.; **Water:** 1.0 sq. mi.   **Area Code:** 303

In north-central CO, west of Denver; original county, organized Nov 1, 1861 (prior to statehood).

Name origin: For the name of a stream in the county, which was originally called Vasquez Fork, but present name adopted by 1860.

Empire — Town
ZIP: 80438   **Lat:** 39-45-34 N **Long:** 105-40-57 W
Pop: 401 (1990); 423 (1980)   **Pop Density:** 1336.7
Land: 0.3 sq. mi.; **Water:** 0.0 sq. mi.   **Elev:** 8614 ft.

Name origin: Named by the four original settlers for the nickname for NY.

Idaho Springs — City
ZIP: 80452   **Lat:** 39-44-27 N **Long:** 105-30-42 W
Pop: 1,834 (1990); 2,077 (1980)   **Pop Density:** 2292.5
Land: 0.8 sq. mi.; **Water:** 0.0 sq. mi.   **Elev:** 7524 ft.
Founded 1859.

Name origin: Politician George M. Willing claimed the name came from an Indian term *idahow*, which is given various meanings. Possibly 'gem of the mountains,' 'light on the mountains,' or 'sunup.'

Georgetown — Town
ZIP: 80444   **Lat:** 39-42-54 N **Long:** 105-41-45 W
Pop: 891 (1990); 830 (1980)   **Pop Density:** 1272.9
Land: 0.7 sq. mi.; **Water:** 0.0 sq. mi.   **Elev:** 8512 ft.

Name origin: For miner George Griffith, who, with his brother David, discovered gold in the region.

Silver Plume — Town
ZIP: 80476   **Lat:** 39-41-45 N **Long:** 105-43-36 W
Pop: 134 (1990); 140 (1980)   **Pop Density:** 670.0
Land: 0.2 sq. mi.; **Water:** 0.0 sq. mi.

Name origin: For the plumelike streaks of silver in the local silver ores.

Conejos County
County Seat: Conejos (ZIP: 81129)

Pop: 7,453 (1990); 7,794 (1980) **Pop Density:** 5.8
Land: 1287.3 sq. mi.; **Water:** 3.7 sq. mi. **Area Code:** 719

On central southern border, east of Durango; original county, organized as Guadalupe County Nov 1, 1861 (prior to statehood); name changed Nov 7, 1861.

Name origin: For the river (which runs through the county) and town called Conejos, from the Spanish meaning 'rabbits,' for the local abundance of the animals.

Antonito — Town
ZIP: 81120 **Lat:** 37-04-35 N **Long:** 106-00-36 W
Pop: 875 (1990); 1,103 (1980) **Pop Density:** 2187.5
Land: 0.4 sq. mi.; **Water:** 0.0 sq. mi.

Name origin: Named by railroad officials for the nearby San Antonio Mountains and San Antonio River. From Spanish 'little Anthony.'

Conejos — Town
ZIP: 81129
Pop: 100 (1990)

Elev: 7901 ft.

La Jara — Town
ZIP: 81140 **Lat:** 37-16-27 N **Long:** 105-57-34 W
Pop: 725 (1990); 858 (1980) **Pop Density:** 2416.7
Land: 0.3 sq. mi.; **Water:** 0.0 sq. mi. **Elev:** 7602 ft.

Name origin: From Spanish for 'rock rose,' but used by the locals to refer to brush undergrowth along river banks.

Manassa — Town
Lat: 37-10-22 N **Long:** 105-56-09 W
Pop: 988 (1990); 945 (1980) **Pop Density:** 1097.8
Land: 0.9 sq. mi.; **Water:** 0.0 sq. mi. **Elev:** 7683 ft.

Settled by Mormon colonists.

Name origin: For Manassa, eldest son of the biblical Joseph. Home of heavyweight boxing champion, Jack "Manassa Mauler" Dempsey (1895–1983).

Romeo — Town
ZIP: 81148 **Lat:** 37-10-17 N **Long:** 105-59-09 W
Pop: 341 (1990); 308 (1980) **Pop Density:** 1705.0
Land: 0.2 sq. mi.; **Water:** 0.0 sq. mi. **Elev:** 7735 ft.

Name origin: Named changed from Romero by the post office because there was another town with this name in the state.

Sanford — Town
ZIP: 81151 **Lat:** 37-15-26 N **Long:** 105-54-00 W
Pop: 750 (1990); 687 (1980) **Pop Density:** 535.7
Land: 1.4 sq. mi.; **Water:** 0.0 sq. mi. **Elev:** 7603 ft.

Started as a Mormon settlement in 1881.

Name origin: For Silas Sanford Smith, first president of the Mormon San Luis Stake.

Costilla County
County Seat: San Luis (ZIP: 81151)

Pop: 3,190 (1990); 3,071 (1980) **Pop Density:** 2.6
Land: 1227.2 sq. mi.; **Water:** 3.3 sq. mi. **Area Code:** 719

On central southern border of CO, southwest of Pueblo; original county, organized Nov 1, 1861 (prior to statehood).

Name origin: Probably for Costilla Creek, which runs through the county; Spanish 'rib' or 'furring timber'; or possibly for a local family of this name.

Blanca — Town
ZIP: 81123 **Lat:** 37-26-19 N **Long:** 105-30-43 W
Pop: 272 (1990); 252 (1980) **Pop Density:** 151.1
Land: 1.8 sq. mi.; **Water:** 0.0 sq. mi.

Name origin: For its location at the foot of Mt. Blanca, from Spanish 'white.'

San Luis — Town
ZIP: 81152 **Lat:** 37-12-03 N **Long:** 105-25-24 W
Pop: 800 (1990); 842 (1980) **Pop Density:** 1600.0
Land: 0.5 sq. mi.; **Water:** 0.0 sq. mi. **Elev:** 7965 ft.

Known as the oldest town in CO.

Name origin: From Spanish 'St. Louis.'

Crowley County
County Seat: Ordway (ZIP: 81063)

Pop: 3,946 (1990); 2,988 (1980)   **Pop Density:** 5.0
Land: 789.0 sq. mi.; **Water:** 11.3 sq. mi.   **Area Code:** 719

In southeastern CO, east of Pueblo; organized May 29, 1911 from Otero County.
Name origin: For John H. Crowley (1849–?), state senator from Otero County when Crowley County was formed.

Crowley   Town
ZIP: 81033   **Lat:** 38-11-36 N   **Long:** 103-51-30 W
Pop: 225 (1990); 192 (1980)   **Pop Density:** 750.0
Land: 0.3 sq. mi.; **Water:** 0.0 sq. mi.   **Elev:** 4347 ft.
Name origin: For John H. Crowley (1849–?), a local CO state senator.

Olney Springs   Town
ZIP: 81062   **Lat:** 38-10-02 N   **Long:** 103-56-38 W
Pop: 340 (1990); 253 (1980)   **Pop Density:** 1700.0
Land: 0.2 sq. mi.; **Water:** 0.0 sq. mi.   **Elev:** 4370 ft.
Name origin: For a Missouri and Pacific Railroad representative at the time the track was laid.

Ordway   Town
ZIP: 81063   **Lat:** 38-13-15 N   **Long:** 103-45-24 W
Pop: 1,025 (1990); 1,135 (1980)   **Pop Density:** 1281.3
Land: 0.8 sq. mi.; **Water:** 0.0 sq. mi.   **Elev:** 4312 ft.
Name origin: For original settler and land company organizer, George Ordway.

Sugar City   Town
ZIP: 81076   **Lat:** 38-13-58 N   **Long:** 103-39-47 W
Pop: 252 (1990); 306 (1980)   **Pop Density:** 630.0
Land: 0.4 sq. mi.; **Water:** 0.0 sq. mi.   **Elev:** 4300 ft.
Name origin: The town was founded by employees of the National Sugar Co., who built a factory in the rich sugar-beet growing area.

Custer County
County Seat: Westcliffe (ZIP: 81252)

Pop: 1,926 (1990); 1,528 (1980)   **Pop Density:** 2.6
Land: 738.9 sq. mi.; **Water:** 1.0 sq. mi.   **Area Code:** 719

In south-central CO, southwest of Pueblo; organized Mar 9, 1877 from Fremont County.
Name origin: For Gen. George Armstrong Custer (1839–76), U.S. soldier and Indian fighter.

Silver Cliff   Town
ZIP: 81249   **Lat:** 38-07-02 N   **Long:** 105-24-16 W
Pop: 322 (1990); 280 (1980)   **Pop Density:** 20.6
Land: 15.6 sq. mi.; **Water:** 0.0 sq. mi.   **Elev:** 7980 ft.
Name origin: For the low, black-stained cliff, indicative of the rich silver deposits found nearby.

Westcliffe   Town
ZIP: 81252   **Lat:** 38-07-58 N   **Long:** 105-27-54 W
Pop: 312 (1990); 324 (1980)   **Pop Density:** 283.6
Land: 1.1 sq. mi.; **Water:** 0.0 sq. mi.   **Elev:** 7888 ft.
Name origin: Named by Dr. W.A. Bell for his birthplace, Westcliff-on-the-Sea, England.

Delta County
County Seat: Delta (ZIP: 81416)

Pop: 20,980 (1990); 21,225 (1980)   **Pop Density:** 18.4
Land: 1142.2 sq. mi.; **Water:** 6.4 sq. mi.   **Area Code:** 303

In west-central CO, southeast of Grand Junction; organized Feb 11, 1883 from Gunnison County.
Name origin: For the city, named for its location on the delta of the Uncompahgre River.

Cedaredge   Town
ZIP: 81413   **Lat:** 38-53-55 N   **Long:** 107-55-34 W
Pop: 1,380 (1990); 1,184 (1980)   **Pop Density:** 1061.5
Land: 1.3 sq. mi.; **Water:** 0.0 sq. mi.   **Elev:** 6264 ft.
Name origin: For either a nearby belt of cedar trees at the edge of Grand Mesa, or for its location on the site of "Cedar Edge," the ranch of Henry Kohler.

Crawford   Town
ZIP: 81415   **Lat:** 38-42-18 N   **Long:** 107-36-31 W
Pop: 221 (1990); 268 (1980)   **Pop Density:** 1105.0
Land: 0.2 sq. mi.; **Water:** 0.0 sq. mi.   **Elev:** 6520 ft.
Name origin: For George Crawford, former governor of KS and frontier capitalist and speculator.

Delta
City
ZIP: 81416 **Lat:** 38-44-41 N **Long:** 108-04-25 W
Pop: 3,789 (1990); 3,931 (1980) **Pop Density:** 1353.2
Land: 2.8 sq. mi.; **Water:** 0.2 sq. mi. **Elev:** 4953 ft.
Name origin: For its location on the delta at the mouth of the Uncompahgre River. Formerly called Uncompahgre.

Hotchkiss
Town
ZIP: 81419 **Lat:** 38-48-03 N **Long:** 107-43-04 W
Pop: 744 (1990); 849 (1980) **Pop Density:** 1062.9
Land: 0.7 sq. mi.; **Water:** 0.0 sq. mi. **Elev:** 5351 ft.
Name origin: For early settler Enos Hotchkiss.

Orchard City
Town
ZIP: 81410 **Lat:** 38-48-53 N **Long:** 107-57-49 W
Pop: 2,218 (1990); 1,914 (1980) **Pop Density:** 194.6
Land: 11.4 sq. mi.; **Water:** 0.0 sq. mi. **Elev:** 5040 ft.
Name origin: For its descriptive connotations.

Paonia
Town
ZIP: 81428 **Lat:** 38-52-10 N **Long:** 107-35-22 W
Pop: 1,403 (1990); 1,425 (1980) **Pop Density:** 1753.8
Land: 0.8 sq. mi.; **Water:** 0.0 sq. mi. **Elev:** 5645 ft.
Name origin: Altered slightly by the U.S. Post Office from its original name, Peony, for the common flower, genus Peaonia.

Denver County
County Seat: Denver (ZIP: 80216)

Pop: 467,610 (1990); 492,686 (1980) **Pop Density:** 3050.3
Land: 153.3 sq. mi.; **Water:** 1.6 sq. mi. **Area Code:** 303
In north-central CO; organized Mar 18, 1901 from Adams County. The city and county are coterminous.
Name origin: For Gen. James William Denver (1817–92), CA legislator, commissioner of Indian affairs, and governor of KS Territory (1857–58).

Denver
City
ZIP: 80202 **Lat:** 39-46-04 N **Long:** 104-52-21 W
Pop: 467,610 (1990); 492,686 (1980) **Pop Density:** 3050.3
Land: 153.3 sq. mi.; **Water:** 1.6 sq. mi. **Elev:** 5280 ft.
In northeast-central CO on the South Platte River. Founded 1858; incorporated as a city 1861; state capital 1867. Nicknamed the "Mile-High City" for its location 5,280 ft. above sea level in the Rocky Mountains. National and regional headquarters for more federal agencies than any other U.S. city; diverse manufacturing (food processing; defense, high-technology, and transportation equipment); site of Denver Union Stockyards.
Name origin: Named in 1860 by KS settlers for their former governor, James W. Denver (1817–92). Previously called Auraria and Denver City.

Dolores County
County Seat: Dove Creek (ZIP: 81324)

Pop: 1,504 (1990); 1,658 (1980) **Pop Density:** 1.4
Land: 1067.0 sq. mi.; **Water:** 1.1 sq. mi. **Area Code:** 303
On southwestern border of CO, south of Grand Junction; organized Feb 19, 1881 from Ouray County.
Name origin: For the Dolores River, which runs through it; from Spanish *Río de Nuestra Señora de los Dolores*, 'River of Our Lady of Sorrows.'

Dove Creek
Town
ZIP: 81324 **Lat:** 37-45-57 N **Long:** 108-54-18 W
Pop: 643 (1990); 826 (1980) **Pop Density:** 1286.0
Land: 0.5 sq. mi.; **Water:** 0.0 sq. mi. **Elev:** 6840 ft.
Name origin: For the nearby creek, named by early pioneers for the flocks of doves in the vicinity.

Rico
Town
ZIP: 81332 **Lat:** 37-41-16 N **Long:** 108-01-51 W
Pop: 92 (1990); 76 (1980) **Pop Density:** 115.0
Land: 0.8 sq. mi.; **Water:** 0.0 sq. mi. **Elev:** 8827 ft.
Name origin: From Spanish 'rich,' a reference to the rich silver ore found in the district.

Douglas County
County Seat: Castle Rock (ZIP: 80104)

Pop: 60,391 (1990); 25,153 (1980)   **Pop Density:** 71.9
Land: 840.2 sq. mi.; **Water:** 2.6 sq. mi.   **Area Code:** 303
In central CO, between Denver and Colorado Springs; original county, organized Nov 1, 1861 (prior to statehood).
Name origin: For Stephen Arnold Douglas (1813–61), U.S. orator and statesman.

Aurora — City
Lat: 39-33-31 N   Long: 104-45-29 W
Pop: 4 (1990); 158,588 (1980)   **Pop Density:** 5.0
Land: 0.8 sq. mi.; **Water:** 0.0 sq. mi.

Castle Rock — Town
ZIP: 80104   Lat: 39-22-43 N   Long: 104-51-04 W
Pop: 8,708 (1990); 3,921 (1980)   **Pop Density:** 281.8
Land: 30.9 sq. mi.; **Water:** 0.0 sq. mi.
Name origin: Named by botanist Dr. Edwin James for a nearby castellated rock.

Gateway — CDP
Lat: 39-32-57 N   Long: 104-54-19 W
Pop: 7,510 (1990)   **Pop Density:** 1417.0
Land: 5.3 sq. mi.; **Water:** 0.0 sq. mi.

Highlands Ranch — CDP
ZIP: 80126   Lat: 39-33-14 N   Long: 104-58-08 W
Pop: 10,181 (1990)   **Pop Density:** 2121.0
Land: 4.8 sq. mi.; **Water:** 0.0 sq. mi.

Larkspur — Town
ZIP: 80118   Lat: 39-10-53 N   Long: 104-53-45 W
Pop: 232 (1990); 141 (1980)   **Pop Density:** 52.7
Land: 4.4 sq. mi.; **Water:** 0.0 sq. mi.
Name origin: For its descriptive connotations.

Littleton — City
ZIP: 80120-27   Lat: 39-33-51 N   Long: 105-01-17 W
Pop: 108 (1990); 128 (1980)   **Pop Density:** 540.0
Land: 0.2 sq. mi.; **Water:** 0.0 sq. mi.
Part of the town is also in Arapahoe County.

Parker — Town
ZIP: 80134   Lat: 39-30-34 N   Long: 104-45-49 W
Pop: 5,450 (1990)   **Pop Density:** 412.9
Land: 13.2 sq. mi.; **Water:** 0.0 sq. mi.

The Pinery — CDP
Lat: 39-27-18 N   Long: 104-44-02 W
Pop: 4,885 (1990)   **Pop Density:** 888.2
Land: 5.5 sq. mi.; **Water:** 0.0 sq. mi.

Eagle County
County Seat: Eagle (ZIP: 81631)

Pop: 21,928 (1990); 13,320 (1980)   **Pop Density:** 13.0
Land: 1688.0 sq. mi.; **Water:** 3.9 sq. mi.   **Area Code:** 303
In west-central CO, west of Denver; organized Feb 11, 1883, from Summit County.
Name origin: For the Eagle River, which flows through the county; the river was named for the bird.

Avon — Town
ZIP: 81620   Lat: 39-39-08 N   Long: 106-31-58 W
Pop: 1,798 (1990); 640 (1980)   **Pop Density:** 359.6
Land: 5.0 sq. mi.; **Water:** 0.0 sq. mi.
Name origin: Named by an early English settler for England's famous Avon River.

Basalt — Town
ZIP: 81621   Lat: 39-22-10 N   Long: 107-01-39 W
Pop: 1,002 (1990); 529 (1980)   **Pop Density:** 2505.0
Land: 0.4 sq. mi.; **Water:** 0.0 sq. mi.   **Elev:** 6620 ft.
Part of the town is also in Pitkin County.
Name origin: For nearby Basalt Peak.

Eagle — Town
ZIP: 81631   Lat: 39-39-20 N   Long: 106-49-31 W
Pop: 1,580 (1990); 950 (1980)   **Pop Density:** 1755.6
Land: 0.9 sq. mi.; **Water:** 0.0 sq. mi.   **Elev:** 6600 ft.
Name origin: For the Eagle River, which traverses the county and on which the town is located. Formerly called by the railroad by its Spanish name, Rio Aguila.

Eagle-Vail — CDP
Lat: 39-37-19 N   Long: 106-29-20 W
Pop: 1,922 (1990)   **Pop Density:** 3203.3
Land: 0.6 sq. mi.; **Water:** 0.0 sq. mi.

El Jebel — CDP
Lat: 39-23-59 N   Long: 107-05-20 W
Pop: 2,605 (1990)   **Pop Density:** 457.0
Land: 5.7 sq. mi.; **Water:** 0.0 sq. mi.

Gypsum — Town
ZIP: 81637   Lat: 39-38-36 N   Long: 106-56-51 W
Pop: 1,750 (1990); 743 (1980)   **Pop Density:** 921.1
Land: 1.9 sq. mi.; **Water:** 0.0 sq. mi.   **Elev:** 6320 ft.
Name origin: For large gypsum deposits in the area.

Minturn — Town
ZIP: 81645   Lat: 39-35-03 N   Long: 106-25-33 W
Pop: 1,066 (1990); 1,060 (1980)   **Pop Density:** 761.4
Land: 1.4 sq. mi.; **Water:** 0.0 sq. mi.
Name origin: For Denver and Rio Grande railroad roadmaster Thomas Minturn.

COLORADO, Eagle County

Red Cliff — Town
ZIP: 81649   Lat: 39-30-30 N   Long: 106-22-10 W
Pop: 297 (1990); 409 (1980)   Pop Density: 1485.0
Land: 0.2 sq. mi.; Water: 0.0 sq. mi.
Name origin: For the nearby quartzite cliffs, which shine red in the sun.

Vail — Town
ZIP: 81657   Lat: 39-38-22 N   Long: 106-21-27 W
Pop: 3,659 (1990); 2,261 (1980)   Pop Density: 778.5
Land: 4.7 sq. mi.; Water: 0.0 sq. mi.
Name origin: For Charles D. Vail, CO state highway engineer in the 1930s.

Elbert County
County Seat: Kiowa (ZIP: 80117)

Pop: 9,646 (1990); 6,850 (1980)   Pop Density: 5.2
Land: 1850.9 sq. mi.; Water: 0.1 sq. mi.   Area Code: 303
In east-central CO, southeast of Denver; organized Feb 2, 1874, from Douglas and Greenwood counties (prior to statehood), the latter of which was organized in 1874 and abolished in 1878 by being divided between Bent and Elbert counties.
Name origin: For Samuel H. Elbert (1833–1907), CO territorial governor (1873–74) and chief justice of CO Supreme Court (1880–83).

Elizabeth — Town
ZIP: 80107   Lat: 39-21-36 N   Long: 104-35-58 W
Pop: 818 (1990); 789 (1980)   Pop Density: 1636.0
Land: 0.5 sq. mi.; Water: 0.0 sq. mi.   Elev: 6448 ft.
Name origin: Named by Gov. John Evans for his sister-in-law, Elizabeth Gray Kimbark Hubbard.

Ponderosa Park — CDP
Lat: 39-23-50 N   Long: 104-38-07 W
Pop: 1,640 (1990)   Pop Density: 110.1
Land: 14.9 sq. mi.; Water: 0.0 sq. mi.

Kiowa — Town
ZIP: 80117   Lat: 39-20-42 N   Long: 104-27-39 W
Pop: 275 (1990); 206 (1980)   Pop Density: 687.5
Land: 0.4 sq. mi.; Water: 0.0 sq. mi.   Elev: 6363 ft.
Name origin: For the Kiowa Indians.

Simla — Town
ZIP: 80835   Lat: 39-08-26 N   Long: 104-04-51 W
Pop: 481 (1990); 494 (1980)   Pop Density: 962.0
Land: 0.5 sq. mi.; Water: 0.0 sq. mi.   Elev: 6030 ft.
Name origin: For an early railroad siding.

El Paso County
County Seat: Colorado Springs (ZIP: 80903)

Pop: 397,014 (1990); 309,424 (1980)   Pop Density: 186.7
Land: 2126.7 sq. mi.; Water: 3.0 sq. mi.   Area Code: 719
In central CO, south of Denver; original county, organized Nov 1, 1861 (prior to statehood).
Name origin: Spanish 'the pass' [through the mountains], referring to Ute Pass, west of Colorado Springs.

Air Force Academy — Military Facility
ZIP: 80840   Lat: 38-59-25 N   Long: 104-51-36 W
Pop: 9,062 (1990); 8,655 (1980)   Pop Density: 906.2
Land: 10.0 sq. mi.; Water: 0.0 sq. mi.

Cascade-Chipita Park — CDP
Lat: 38-57-06 N   Long: 105-00-09 W
Pop: 1,479 (1990)   Pop Density: 109.6
Land: 13.5 sq. mi.; Water: 0.0 sq. mi.

Black Forest — CDP
ZIP: 80908   Lat: 39-02-46 N   Long: 104-40-05 W
Pop: 8,143 (1990); 3,372 (1980)   Pop Density: 63.8
Land: 127.6 sq. mi.; Water: 0.1 sq. mi.

Cimarron Hills — CDP
ZIP: 80906   Lat: 38-51-30 N   Long: 104-41-54 W
Pop: 11,160 (1990); 6,597 (1980)   Pop Density: 1860.0
Land: 6.0 sq. mi.; Water: 0.0 sq. mi.

Calhan — Town
ZIP: 80808   Lat: 39-02-03 N   Long: 104-17-57 W
Pop: 562 (1990); 541 (1980)   Pop Density: 802.9
Land: 0.7 sq. mi.; Water: 0.0 sq. mi.   Elev: 6558 ft.
Name origin: For a Mr. Calahan, the contractor who built the local section of the Chicago, Rock Island, and Pacific Railroad. Name shortened to present form by the railroad.

Colorado Springs — City
ZIP: 80901   Lat: 38-51-47 N   Long: 104-45-35 W
Pop: 281,140 (1990); 215,105 (1980)   Pop Density: 1534.6
Land: 183.2 sq. mi.; Water: 0.4 sq. mi.   Elev: 6008 ft.
In east-central CO at the foot of Pikes Peak. Founded 1871; incorporated as a city 1878. Tourist and recreation center; lies 6,035 ft. above sea level in the Rocky Mountains. Site of

the U.S. Olympic Training Center; U.S. Air Force Academy is just north of city.
Name origin: For the numerous mineral springs in the area.

Fort Carson
Military Facility
ZIP: 80913 Lat: 38-44-31 N Long: 104-46-55 W
Pop: 11,309 (1990); 13,219 (1980) Pop Density: 1203.1
Land: 9.4 sq. mi.; Water: 0.0 sq. mi.

Fountain
City
ZIP: 80817 Lat: 38-40-00 N Long: 104-41-35 W
Pop: 9,984 (1990); 8,324 (1980) Pop Density: 708.1
Land: 14.1 sq. mi.; Water: 0.0 sq. mi. Elev: 5546 ft.
In east-central CO, 10 mi. south-southeast of Colorado Springs.
Name origin: For the creek that flows through the city, named for the bubbling springs at its head.

Gleneagle
CDP
Lat: 39-02-42 N Long: 104-49-25 W
Pop: 1,661 (1990) Pop Density: 1107.3
Land: 1.5 sq. mi.; Water: 0.0 sq. mi.

Green Mountain Falls
Town
Lat: 38-56-02 N Long: 105-01-04 W
Pop: 634 (1990); 589 (1980) Pop Density: 905.7
Land: 0.7 sq. mi.; Water: 0.0 sq. mi.
Part of the town is also in Teller County.
Name origin: For nearby waterfalls on Green Mountain.

Manitou Springs
City
ZIP: 80829 Lat: 38-51-25 N Long: 104-54-39 W
Pop: 4,535 (1990); 4,475 (1980) Pop Density: 1511.7
Land: 3.0 sq. mi.; Water: 0.0 sq. mi. Elev: 6320 ft.
Name origin: From the Algonquian term meaning 'spirit.'

Monument
Town
ZIP: 80132 Lat: 39-04-12 N Long: 104-51-25 W
Pop: 1,020 (1990); 690 (1980) Pop Density: 248.8
Land: 4.1 sq. mi.; Water: 0.0 sq. mi. Elev: 6961 ft.
Name origin: For a large rock formation west of the town.

Palmer Lake
Town
ZIP: 80133 Lat: 39-07-00 N Long: 104-54-21 W
Pop: 1,480 (1990); 1,130 (1980) Pop Density: 493.3
Land: 3.0 sq. mi.; Water: 0.0 sq. mi.
Name origin: For Gen. William Palmer of Denver & Rio Grande Railroad fame.

Ramah
Town
ZIP: 80832 Lat: 39-07-18 N Long: 104-09-59 W
Pop: 94 (1990); 119 (1980) Pop Density: 470.0
Land: 0.2 sq. mi.; Water: 0.0 sq. mi.

Security-Widefield
CDP
ZIP: 80911 Lat: 38-44-38 N Long: 104-42-41 W
Pop: 23,822 (1990); 18,768 (1980) Pop Density: 1609.6
Land: 14.8 sq. mi.; Water: 0.5 sq. mi.

Stratmoor
CDP
ZIP: 80906 Lat: 38-46-26 N Long: 104-46-44 W
Pop: 5,854 (1990); 5,519 (1980) Pop Density: 2018.6
Land: 2.9 sq. mi.; Water: 0.0 sq. mi.

Woodmoor
CDP
Lat: 39-06-05 N Long: 104-50-48 W
Pop: 3,858 (1990); 1,490 (1980) Pop Density: 632.5
Land: 6.1 sq. mi.; Water: 0.0 sq. mi.

Fremont County
County Seat: Canon City (ZIP: 81212)

Pop: 32,273 (1990); 28,676 (1980) Pop Density: 21.1
Land: 1533.0 sq. mi.; Water: 1.0 sq. mi. Area Code: 719
In central CO, southwest of Colorado Springs; original county, organized Nov 1, 1861 (prior to statehood).
Name origin: For John Charles Frémont (1813–90), soldier and explorer who led five expeditions to the West, U.S. senator from CA (1850–51), and governor of the AZ Territory (1878–81).

Brookside
Town
Lat: 38-24-48 N Long: 105-11-29 W
Pop: 183 (1990); 178 (1980) Pop Density: 457.5
Land: 0.4 sq. mi.; Water: 0.0 sq. mi.

Canon City
City
ZIP: 81212 Lat: 38-26-28 N Long: 105-14-03 W
Pop: 12,687 (1990); 13,037 (1980) Pop Density: 1605.9
Land: 7.9 sq. mi.; Water: 0.0 sq. mi. Elev: 5332 ft.
In south-central CO on the Arkansas River, 34 mi. southwest of Colorado Springs. Settled 1859.
Name origin: For its location near the Grand Canyon of the Arkansas River.

Coal Creek
Town
Lat: 38-21-34 N Long: 105-08-42 W
Pop: 157 (1990); 190 (1980) Pop Density: 224.3
Land: 0.7 sq. mi.; Water: 0.0 sq. mi.
Name origin: For the nearby creek, named for the coal seams running along its sides.

Florence
City
ZIP: 81226 Lat: 38-23-06 N Long: 105-06-58 W
Pop: 2,990 (1990); 2,987 (1980) Pop Density: 1495.0
Land: 2.0 sq. mi.; Water: 0.0 sq. mi. Elev: 5191 ft.
Name origin: For the daughter of prominent town father and oil businessman James McCandless. Originally called Frazerville, for "Uncle Joe" Frazer, who developed coal mines nearby.

COLORADO, Fremont County   American Places Dictionary

Lincoln Park CDP
Lat: 38-25-32 N Long: 105-12-47 W
Pop: 3,728 (1990); 3,426 (1980)   Pop Density: 981.1
Land: 3.8 sq. mi.; **Water:** 0.0 sq. mi.

Penrose CDP
ZIP: 81240   Lat: 38-25-52 N Long: 105-00-45 W
Pop: 2,235 (1990)   Pop Density: 248.3
Land: 9.0 sq. mi.; **Water:** 0.0 sq. mi.

Prospect Heights Town
ZIP: 81212   Lat: 38-25-33 N Long: 105-14-08 W
Pop: 19 (1990); 34 (1980)
Land: 0.0 sq. mi.; **Water:** 0.0 sq. mi.

Rockvale Town
ZIP: 81244   Lat: 38-22-08 N Long: 105-09-47 W
Pop: 321 (1990); 338 (1980)   Pop Density: 642.0
Land: 0.5 sq. mi.; **Water:** 0.0 sq. mi.
Name origin: For a town in MD.

Williamsburg Town
ZIP: 81226   Lat: 38-22-52 N Long: 105-10-29 W
Pop: 253 (1990); 72 (1980)   Pop Density: 84.3
Land: 3.0 sq. mi.; **Water:** 0.0 sq. mi.
Name origin: For John Williams, who founded the Williamsburg Mine in the early 1880s.

Garfield County
County Seat: Glenwood Springs (ZIP: 81601)

Pop: 29,974 (1990); 22,514 (1980)   **Pop Density:** 10.2
Land: 2947.5 sq. mi.; **Water:** 8.6 sq. mi.   **Area Code:** 303
On central-western border of CO, north of Grand Junction; organized Feb 10, 1883 from Summit County.
Name origin: For James Abram Garfield (1831–81), twentieth U.S. president.

Battlement Mesa CDP
Lat: 39-26-29 N Long: 108-01-28 W
Pop: 1,477 (1990)   Pop Density: 182.3
Land: 8.1 sq. mi.; **Water:** 0.3 sq. mi.

Carbondale Town
ZIP: 81623   Lat: 39-23-50 N Long: 107-12-50 W
Pop: 3,004 (1990); 2,084 (1980)   Pop Density: 1767.1
Land: 1.7 sq. mi.; **Water:** 0.0 sq. mi.   Elev: 6170 ft.
Name origin: Named by an original town father, John Mankin, for his home town in PA.

Glenwood Springs City
ZIP: 81601   Lat: 39-32-41 N Long: 107-19-48 W
Pop: 6,561 (1990); 4,637 (1980)   Pop Density: 1426.3
Land: 4.6 sq. mi.; **Water:** 0.0 sq. mi.   Elev: 5763 ft.
Name origin: For Glenwood, IA, and the town's mineral springs.

New Castle Town
ZIP: 81647   Lat: 39-35-07 N Long: 107-31-50 W
Pop: 679 (1990); 563 (1980)   Pop Density: 377.2
Land: 1.8 sq. mi.; **Water:** 0.0 sq. mi.
Name origin: For the famous English mining center, after the discovery of large coal deposits.

Parachute Town
ZIP: 81635   Lat: 39-26-44 N Long: 108-03-18 W
Pop: 658 (1990); 338 (1980)   Pop Density: 548.3
Land: 1.2 sq. mi.; **Water:** 0.0 sq. mi.   Elev: 5090 ft.

Rifle City
ZIP: 81650   Lat: 39-32-21 N Long: 107-46-39 W
Pop: 4,636 (1990); 3,215 (1980)   Pop Density: 1188.7
Land: 3.9 sq. mi.; **Water:** 0.0 sq. mi.   Elev: 5345 ft.
Name origin: For Rifle Creek, so named after a soldier in a surveying party found a lost gun on its bank.

Silt Town
ZIP: 81652   Lat: 39-32-58 N Long: 107-39-13 W
Pop: 1,095 (1990); 923 (1980)   Pop Density: 2190.0
Land: 0.5 sq. mi.; **Water:** 0.0 sq. mi.
Name origin: Descriptive of the local soil.

American Places Dictionary   COLORADO, Grand County

Gilpin County
County Seat: Central City (ZIP: 80427)

Pop: 3,070 (1990); 2,441 (1980)   **Pop Density:** 20.5
Land: 149.9 sq. mi.; **Water:** 0.4 sq. mi.   **Area Code:** 303
In central CO, west of Denver; original county; organized Nov 1, 1861 (prior to statehood).
Name origin: For Col. William Gilpin (1822–94), first territorial governor of CO (1861–62).

Black Hawk   Town
ZIP: 80422   **Lat:** 39-48-01 N   **Long:** 105-29-28 W
Pop: 227 (1990); 232 (1980)   **Pop Density:** 151.3
Land: 1.5 sq. mi.; **Water:** 0.0 sq. mi.   **Elev:** 8056 ft.
Name origin: For an early mining company, which brought in a quartz mill named for the famous Indian chief.

Central City   City
ZIP: 80427   **Lat:** 39-47-59 N   **Long:** 105-30-44 W
Pop: 335 (1990); 329 (1980)   **Pop Density:** 372.2
Land: 0.9 sq. mi.; **Water:** 0.0 sq. mi.   **Elev:** 8496 ft.
Name origin: A trading town named for its central location amid the surrounding mining camps.

Grand County
County Seat: Hot Sulphur Springs (ZIP: 80451)

Pop: 7,966 (1990); 7,475 (1980)   **Pop Density:** 4.3
Land: 1849.8 sq. mi.; **Water:** 19.9 sq. mi.   **Area Code:** 303
In north-central CO, west of Boulder; organized Feb 2, 1874 (prior to statehood) from Summit County.
Name origin: For Grand Lake and the Grand River; the latter was renamed the Colorado.

Fraser   Town
ZIP: 80442   **Lat:** 39-56-13 N   **Long:** 105-47-40 W
Pop: 575 (1990); 470 (1980)   **Pop Density:** 410.7
Land: 1.4 sq. mi.; **Water:** 0.0 sq. mi.   **Elev:** 8574 ft.
Name origin: For the Fraser River, which flows through the town. Originally spelling was Frazier, for Reuben Frazier, an early settler. Post office changed the name to its present form.

Granby   Town
ZIP: 80446   **Lat:** 40-05-18 N   **Long:** 105-56-14 W
Pop: 966 (1990); 963 (1980)   **Pop Density:** 1380.0
Land: 0.7 sq. mi.; **Water:** 0.0 sq. mi.   **Elev:** 7939 ft.
Name origin: Probably for attorney Granby Hillyer, who helped found the town.

Grand Lake   Town
ZIP: 80447   **Lat:** 40-15-04 N   **Long:** 105-49-16 W
Pop: 259 (1990); 382 (1980)   **Pop Density:** 287.8
Land: 0.9 sq. mi.; **Water:** 0.0 sq. mi.
Name origin: For nearby Grand Lake, the largest natural freshwater lake in CO.

Hot Sulphur Springs   Town
ZIP: 80451   **Lat:** 40-04-25 N   **Long:** 106-05-56 W
Pop: 347 (1990); 405 (1980)   **Pop Density:** 495.7
Land: 0.7 sq. mi.; **Water:** 0.0 sq. mi.   **Elev:** 7680 ft.
Name origin: For its descriptive connotations.

Kremmling   Town
ZIP: 80459   **Lat:** 40-03-23 N   **Long:** 106-22-34 W
Pop: 1,166 (1990); 1,296 (1980)   **Pop Density:** 896.9
Land: 1.3 sq. mi.; **Water:** 0.0 sq. mi.   **Elev:** 7362 ft.
Name origin: For Kare Kremmling, whose general-merchandise store was the town's beginning.

Winter Park   Town
ZIP: 80482   **Lat:** 39-53-12 N   **Long:** 105-46-45 W
Pop: 528 (1990); 480 (1980)   **Pop Density:** 67.7
Land: 7.8 sq. mi.; **Water:** 0.0 sq. mi.   **Elev:** 9040 ft.
Name origin: For the superb winter sports in the area. Previously called West Portal.

Gunnison County
County Seat: Gunnison (ZIP: 81230)

Pop: 10,273 (1990); 10,689 (1980)   **Pop Density:** 3.2
Land: 3239.0 sq. mi.; **Water:** 20.9 sq. mi.   **Area Code:** 303
In west-central CO, west of Colorado Springs; organized Mar 9, 1877, from Lake County.
Name origin: For John William Gunnison (1812–53), killed by Indians while surveying for a proposed railroad.

Crested Butte — Town
Lat: 38-52-12 N **Long:** 106-58-59 W
Pop: 878 (1990); 959 (1980)   **Pop Density:** 2195.0
Land: 0.4 sq. mi.; **Water:** 0.0 sq. mi.   **Elev:** 8908 ft.
Name origin: For a nearby mountain top, which resembles a cock's comb.

Gunnison — City
ZIP: 81230   **Lat:** 38-32-40 N **Long:** 106-55-37 W
Pop: 4,636 (1990); 5,785 (1980)   **Pop Density:** 1448.8
Land: 3.2 sq. mi.; **Water:** 0.0 sq. mi.   **Elev:** 7703 ft.
In west-central CO, southwest of Colorado Springs.
Name origin: For Capt. J. W. Gunnison, who surveyed the area in 1853 in search of a railroad route to the west.

Marble — Town
Lat: 39-04-17 N **Long:** 107-11-18 W
Pop: 64 (1990); 30 (1980)   **Pop Density:** 213.3
Land: 0.3 sq. mi.; **Water:** 0.0 sq. mi.   **Elev:** 7960 ft.

Mount Crested Butte — Town
ZIP: 81225   **Lat:** 38-54-28 N **Long:** 106-57-58 W
Pop: 264 (1990); 272 (1980)   **Pop Density:** 176.0
Land: 1.5 sq. mi.; **Water:** 0.0 sq. mi.
Name origin: For a nearby mountain that resembles a cock's comb.

Pitkin — Town
ZIP: 81241   **Lat:** 38-36-29 N **Long:** 106-30-58 W
Pop: 53 (1990); 59 (1980)   **Pop Density:** 176.7
Land: 0.3 sq. mi.; **Water:** 0.0 sq. mi.   **Elev:** 9241 ft.
Name origin: For Gov. F.W. Pitkin. Previously called Quartzville.

Hinsdale County
County Seat: Lake City (ZIP: 81235)

Pop: 467 (1990); 408 (1980)   **Pop Density:** 0.4
Land: 1117.8 sq. mi.; **Water:** 5.5 sq. mi.   **Area Code:** 303
In southwest CO, northeast of Durango; organized Feb 10, 1874, from Conejos and Summit counties (prior to statehood).
Name origin: For George A. Hinsdale, a former lieutenant governor of the state.

Lake City — Town
ZIP: 81235   **Lat:** 38-01-44 N **Long:** 107-18-37 W
Pop: 223 (1990); 206 (1980)   **Pop Density:** 278.8
Land: 0.8 sq. mi.; **Water:** 0.0 sq. mi.   **Elev:** 8658 ft.
Name origin: For Lake San Cristobal, one of the largest natural lakes in CO.

Huerfano County
County Seat: Walsenburg (ZIP: 81089)

Pop: 6,009 (1990); 6,440 (1980)   **Pop Density:** 3.8
Land: 1591.0 sq. mi.; **Water:** 2.4 sq. mi.   **Area Code:** 719
In south-central CO, south of Pueblo; original county, organized Nov 1, 1861 (prior to statehood).
Name origin: For the Huerfano River, Spanish 'orphan,' referring to an isolated butte in the river.

La Veta — Town
ZIP: 81055   **Lat:** 37-30-36 N   **Long:** 105-00-26 W
Pop: 726 (1990); 611 (1980)   **Pop Density:** 660.0
Land: 1.1 sq. mi.; **Water:** 0.0 sq. mi.   **Elev:** 7013 ft.
Name origin: From Spanish 'vein,' referring to the many dikes radiating from nearby West Spanish Mountain.

Walsenburg — City
ZIP: 81089   **Lat:** 37-37-36 N   **Long:** 104-46-37 W
Pop: 3,300 (1990); 3,945 (1980)   **Pop Density:** 1434.8
Land: 2.3 sq. mi.; **Water:** 0.0 sq. mi.   **Elev:** 6182 ft.
Name origin: For merchant Fred Walsen, around whose general store the town developed.

Jackson County
County Seat: Walden (ZIP: 80480)

Pop: 1,605 (1990); 1,863 (1980)   **Pop Density:** 1.0
Land: 1613.3 sq. mi.; **Water:** 7.7 sq. mi.   **Area Code:** 303
On central northern border of CO, west of Ft. Collins; organized May 5, 1909 from Larimer County.
Name origin: For Andrew Jackson (1767–1845), seventh U.S. president.

Walden — Town
ZIP: 80480   **Lat:** 40-43-50 N   **Long:** 106-16-51 W
Pop: 890 (1990); 947 (1980)   **Pop Density:** 2966.7
Land: 0.3 sq. mi.; **Water:** 0.0 sq. mi.   **Elev:** 8099 ft.
Name origin: For one-time postmaster Mark D. Walden.

Jefferson County
County Seat: Golden (ZIP: 80401)

Pop: 438,430 (1990); 371,753 (1980)   **Pop Density:** 567.7
Land: 772.2 sq. mi.; **Water:** 6.0 sq. mi.   **Area Code:** 303
In central CO, west of Denver; original county, organized Nov 1, 1861 (prior to statehood).
Name origin: From Jefferson Territory, the extra-legal government that preceded CO Territory. Named in honor of Thomas Jefferson (1743–1826), U.S. patriot and statesman; third U.S. president.

Applewood — CDP
ZIP: 80401   **Lat:** 39-44-50 N   **Long:** 105-09-44 W
Pop: 11,069 (1990); 319 (1980)   **Pop Density:** 1516.3
Land: 7.3 sq. mi.; **Water:** 0.0 sq. mi.

Arvada — City
ZIP: 80004   **Lat:** 39-49-16 N   **Long:** 105-06-31 W
Pop: 86,888 (1990); 83,347 (1980)   **Pop Density:** 4022.6
Land: 21.6 sq. mi.; **Water:** 0.2 sq. mi.
Part of the town is also in Adams County.

Bow Mar — Town
Lat: 39-37-33 N   **Long:** 105-03-12 W
Pop: 241 (1990); 240 (1980)   **Pop Density:** 803.3
Land: 0.3 sq. mi.; **Water:** 0.0 sq. mi.   **Elev:** 5515 ft.
Part of the town is also in Arapahoe County.
Name origin: For its location between Bowles and Marston lakes.

COLORADO, Jefferson County

Broomfield — City
ZIP: 80020-21 Lat: 39-53-49 N Long: 105-07-41 W
Pop: 1,522 (1990); 749 (1980) Pop Density: 543.6
Land: 2.8 sq. mi.; Water: 0.3 sq. mi. Elev: 5400 ft.
In northeast-central CO, 11 mi. north-northwest of Denver. Part of the town is also in Adams, Boulder and Weld counties.
Name origin: Named by railroad officials for a nearby field of broom corn. Previously called Zang's Spur for Philip Zang, a businessman and brewer who bred Percheron horses nearby.

Columbine — CDP
ZIP: 80123 Lat: 39-35-12 N Long: 105-04-15 W
Pop: 22,397 (1990); 21,609 (1980) Pop Density: 3929.3
Land: 5.7 sq. mi.; Water: 0.1 sq. mi.
Part of the town is in Arapahoe County.

Edgewater — City
ZIP: 80214 Lat: 39-45-01 N Long: 105-03-45 W
Pop: 4,613 (1990); 4,766 (1980) Pop Density: 6590.0
Land: 0.7 sq. mi.; Water: 0.0 sq. mi. Elev: 5353 ft.
Name origin: For the city's location on the shore of Sloan's Lake.

Evergreen — CDP
ZIP: 80439 Lat: 39-38-01 N Long: 105-20-32 W
Pop: 7,582 (1990); 6,376 (1980) Pop Density: 729.0
Land: 10.4 sq. mi.; Water: 0.1 sq. mi.

Genesee — CDP
Lat: 39-41-08 N Long: 105-16-19 W
Pop: 2,737 (1990) Pop Density: 414.7
Land: 6.6 sq. mi.; Water: 0.0 sq. mi.

Golden — City
ZIP: 80401 Lat: 39-44-19 N Long: 105-12-55 W
Pop: 13,116 (1990); 12,237 (1980) Pop Density: 1748.8
Land: 7.5 sq. mi.; Water: 0.0 sq. mi. Elev: 5674 ft.
In central CO, 11 mi. west of Denver. Founded 1859; capital of CO Territory 1862–67.
Name origin: For early settler, Thomas L. Golden.

Ken Caryl — CDP
ZIP: 80123 Lat: 39-34-33 N Long: 105-06-42 W
Pop: 24,391 (1990); 10,661 (1980) Pop Density: 2540.7
Land: 9.6 sq. mi.; Water: 0.0 sq. mi.

Lakeside — Town
Lat: 39-46-43 N Long: 105-03-26 W
Pop: 11 (1990); 19 (1980) Pop Density: 55.0
Land: 0.2 sq. mi.; Water: 0.1 sq. mi.

Lakewood — City
ZIP: 80215 Lat: 39-41-42 N Long: 105-06-48 W
Pop: 126,481 (1990); 113,808 (1980) Pop Density: 3100.0
Land: 40.8 sq. mi.; Water: 0.8 sq. mi. Elev: 5450 ft.
In central CO, west of Denver.
Name origin: Originally an agricultural area with many orchards and small lakes.

Morrison — Town
ZIP: 80465 Lat: 39-39-16 N Long: 105-10-56 W
Pop: 465 (1990); 478 (1980) Pop Density: 422.7
Land: 1.1 sq. mi.; Water: 0.0 sq. mi.
Name origin: For early pioneer George Morrison.

Mountain View — Town
Lat: 39-46-32 N Long: 105-03-20 W
Pop: 550 (1990); 584 (1980) Pop Density: 5500.0
Land: 0.1 sq. mi.; Water: 0.0 sq. mi. Elev: 5379 ft.

Superior — Town
Lat: 39-54-44 N Long: 105-10-26 W
Pop: 0 (1990)
Land: 0.4 sq. mi.; Water: 0.0 sq. mi.
Part of the town is also in Boulder County.

Westminster — City
ZIP: 80030 Lat: 39-52-39 N Long: 105-05-35 W
Pop: 32,986 (1990); 18,165 (1980) Pop Density: 2893.5
Land: 11.4 sq. mi.; Water: 0.1 sq. mi. Elev: 5300 ft.
Part of the town is also in Adams County.

Wheat Ridge — City
ZIP: 80033 Lat: 39-46-24 N Long: 105-05-54 W
Pop: 29,419 (1990); 30,293 (1980) Pop Density: 3305.5
Land: 8.9 sq. mi.; Water: 0.0 sq. mi. Elev: 5410 ft.
In central CO, west-northwest of Denver.
Name origin: Named by state Sen. Henry Lee for the rich wheat growing area surrounding it.

Kiowa County
County Seat: Eads (ZIP: 81036)

Pop: 1,688 (1990); 1,936 (1980) Pop Density: 1.0
Land: 1771.1 sq. mi.; Water: 14.8 sq. mi. Area Code: 303
On southeastern border of CO, east of Pueblo; organized Apr 11, 1889, from Bent County.
Name origin: For the Indian tribe of Tanoan linguistic stock; name means 'principal people.'

Eads — Town
ZIP: 81036 Lat: 38-28-53 N Long: 102-46-46 W
Pop: 780 (1990); 878 (1980) Pop Density: 1560.0
Land: 0.5 sq. mi.; Water: 0.0 sq. mi. Elev: 4213 ft.
Name origin: For engineer James B. Eads, who built the Eads Bridge across the Mississippi River at St. Louis.

Haswell — Town
ZIP: 81045 Lat: 38-27-10 N Long: 103-09-50 W
Pop: 62 (1990); 126 (1980) Pop Density: 77.5
Land: 0.8 sq. mi.; Water: 0.0 sq. mi.
Name origin: Named by railroad financier Jay Gould's daughter. The source of her choice is not known.

Sheridan Lake — Town
ZIP: 81071 **Lat:** 38-27-57 N **Long:** 102-17-36 W
Pop: 95 (1990); 87 (1980) **Pop Density:** 316.7
Land: 0.3 sq. mi.; **Water:** 0.0 sq. mi. **Elev:** 4083 ft.

Kit Carson County
County Seat: Burlington (ZIP: 80807)

Pop: 7,140 (1990); 7,599 (1980) **Pop Density:** 3.3
Land: 2161.0 sq. mi.; **Water:** 0.7 sq. mi. **Area Code:** 719
On central eastern border of CO; organized Apr 11, 1889 from Elbert County.
Name origin: For Christopher (Kit) Carson (1809–68), frontiersman, guide, and Indian agent.

Bethune — Town
ZIP: 80805 **Lat:** 39-18-12 N **Long:** 102-25-22 W
Pop: 173 (1990); 149 (1980) **Pop Density:** 865.0
Land: 0.2 sq. mi.; **Water:** 0.0 sq. mi.
Founded during World War I.
Name origin: For a town in France, possibly where some local men fought.

Burlington — City
ZIP: 80807 **Lat:** 39-18-19 N **Long:** 102-16-19 W
Pop: 2,941 (1990); 3,107 (1980) **Pop Density:** 1730.0
Land: 1.7 sq. mi.; **Water:** 0.0 sq. mi.
Name origin: For Burlington, KS, former home of early settlers.

Flagler — Town
ZIP: 80815 **Lat:** 39-17-38 N **Long:** 103-03-55 W
Pop: 564 (1990); 550 (1980) **Pop Density:** 1128.0
Land: 0.5 sq. mi.; **Water:** 0.0 sq. mi.
Name origin: For Henry M. Flagler, a millionaire railroad man who extended the railroad through the area.

Seibert — Town
ZIP: 80834 **Lat:** 39-17-53 N **Long:** 102-52-06 W
Pop: 181 (1990); 180 (1980) **Pop Density:** 603.3
Land: 0.3 sq. mi.; **Water:** 0.0 sq. mi.
Name origin: For Henry Seibert, an official of the Rock Island Railroad, which came through the town in 1888.

Stratton — Town
ZIP: 80836 **Lat:** 39-18-10 N **Long:** 102-36-13 W
Pop: 649 (1990); 705 (1980) **Pop Density:** 1298.0
Land: 0.5 sq. mi.; **Water:** 0.0 sq. mi. **Elev:** 4414 ft.
Name origin: For Winfield Scott Stratton, a carpenter who became a mining magnate in the Cripple Creek Strikes.

Vona — Town
ZIP: 80861 **Lat:** 39-18-09 N **Long:** 102-44-37 W
Pop: 104 (1990); 94 (1980) **Pop Density:** 520.0
Land: 0.2 sq. mi.; **Water:** 0.0 sq. mi.
Name origin: Named by attorney and town promoter Pearl King for his niece.

Lake County
County Seat: Leadville (ZIP: 80461)

Pop: 6,007 (1990); 8,830 (1980) **Pop Density:** 15.9
Land: 376.9 sq. mi.; **Water:** 7.0 sq. mi. **Area Code:** 719
In central CO, southwest of Denver; original county, organized Nov 1, 1861 (prior to statehood); name changed from Carbonate Feb 10, 1879.
Name origin: For the Twin Lakes, a major feature of the county.

Leadville — City
Lat: 39-14-48 N **Long:** 106-17-37 W
Pop: 2,629 (1990); 3,879 (1980) **Pop Density:** 2390.0
Land: 1.1 sq. mi.; **Water:** 0.0 sq. mi. **Elev:** 10152 ft.
Name origin: For the large amounts of silver-bearing lead ores in the area.

Leadville North — CDP
Lat: 39-15-36 N **Long:** 106-18-39 W
Pop: 1,757 (1990); 1,851 (1980) **Pop Density:** 675.8
Land: 2.6 sq. mi.; **Water:** 0.0 sq. mi.

La Plata County
County Seat: Durango (ZIP: 81301)

Pop: 32,284 (1990); 27,195 (1980) **Pop Density:** 19.1
Land: 1692.3 sq. mi.; **Water:** 7.7 sq. mi. **Area Code:** 303

On southwestern border of CO; organized Feb 10, 1874, from Conejos and Lake counties (prior to statehood).

Name origin: For La Plata River, which runs through the county; from Spanish 'silver,' for the mines in the area.

Bayfield — Town
ZIP: 81122 **Lat:** 37-14-03 N **Long:** 107-35-41 W
Pop: 1,090 (1990); 724 (1980) **Pop Density:** 1362.5
Land: 0.8 sq. mi.; **Water:** 0.0 sq. mi. **Elev:** 6892 ft.
Name origin: For W. A. Bay, who first laid it out.

Durango — City
ZIP: 81301 **Lat:** 37-17-09 N **Long:** 107-52-09 W
Pop: 12,430 (1990); 11,649 (1980) **Pop Density:** 2644.7
Land: 4.7 sq. mi.; **Water:** 0.0 sq. mi. **Elev:** 6523 ft.
In southwestern CO, 20 mi. north of the NM border. Settled 1880.
Name origin: Named by former territorial governor, A.C. Hunt, for Durango, Mexico.

Ignacio — Town
ZIP: 81137 **Lat:** 37-07-00 N **Long:** 107-38-03 W
Pop: 720 (1990); 667 (1980) **Pop Density:** 3600.0
Land: 0.2 sq. mi.; **Water:** 0.0 sq. mi.
Name origin: For a Ute chief; the town's land was purchased from the tribe in 1910.

Larimer County
County Seat: Fort Collins (ZIP: 80522)

Pop: 186,136 (1990); 149,184 (1980) **Pop Density:** 71.6
Land: 2601.4 sq. mi.; **Water:** 32.6 sq. mi. **Area Code:** 303

On central northern border of CO; original county, organized Nov 1, 1861 (prior to statehood).

Name origin: For Gen. William Larimer, a founder of Denver and prominent early settler.

Berthoud — Town
ZIP: 80513 **Lat:** 40-18-20 N **Long:** 105-04-52 W
Pop: 2,990 (1990); 2,362 (1980) **Pop Density:** 2491.7
Land: 1.2 sq. mi.; **Water:** 0.0 sq. mi.
Name origin: For Capt. Edward Berthoud, the chief civil engineer of the Colorado Central Railroad, and discoverer of Berthoud Pass.

Campion — CDP
Lat: 40-20-40 N **Long:** 105-05-41 W
Pop: 1,692 (1990) **Pop Density:** 445.3
Land: 3.8 sq. mi.; **Water:** 0.0 sq. mi.

Estes Park — Town
ZIP: 80517 **Lat:** 40-22-19 N **Long:** 105-31-15 W
Pop: 3,184 (1990); 2,703 (1980) **Pop Density:** 624.3
Land: 5.1 sq. mi.; **Water:** 0.1 sq. mi. **Elev:** 7522 ft.
Settled by Joel Estes in 1859.
Name origin: For its first permanent settler.

Fort Collins — City
ZIP: 80521 **Lat:** 40-33-19 N **Long:** 105-04-06 W
Pop: 87,758 (1990); 65,092 (1980) **Pop Density:** 2130.0
Land: 41.2 sq. mi.; **Water:** 0.5 sq. mi. **Elev:** 5003 ft.
In northern CO, 41 mi. north-northeast of Boulder. Founded 1864; incorporated 1879. Site of Colorado State University.
Name origin: For Col. W. O. Collins (1809–80), commander at Fort Laramie.

Loveland — City
ZIP: 80538 **Lat:** 40-25-06 N **Long:** 105-04-18 W
Pop: 37,352 (1990); 30,215 (1980) **Pop Density:** 1745.4
Land: 21.4 sq. mi.; **Water:** 0.9 sq. mi. **Elev:** 4982 ft.
In northern CO, 10 mi. south of Fort Collins. Founded 1877.
Name origin: For W.A.H. Loveland, a prominent CO railroad man and state politican.

Timnath — Town
ZIP: 80547 **Lat:** 40-31-45 N **Long:** 104-58-59 W
Pop: 190 (1990); 185 (1980) **Pop Density:** 950.0
Land: 0.2 sq. mi.; **Water:** 0.0 sq. mi. **Elev:** 4867 ft.
Name origin: Named by a Presbyterian minister for an Old Testament city supposedly visited by Samson.

American Places Dictionary   COLORADO, Lincoln County

Wellington   Town
ZIP: 80549   **Lat:** 40-42-10 N   **Long:** 105-00-06 W
Pop: 1,340 (1990); 1,215 (1980)   **Pop Density:** 1675.0
Land: 0.8 sq. mi.; **Water:** 0.0 sq. mi.
Name origin: For a former railroad employee.

Las Animas County
County Seat: Trinidad (ZIP: 81082)

Pop: 13,765 (1990); 14,897 (1980)   **Pop Density:** 2.9
Land: 4773.0 sq. mi.; **Water:** 2.8 sq. mi.   **Area Code:** 719

On southeastern border of CO, south of Pueblo; organized Feb 9, 1866 from Huerfano County (prior to statehood).

Name origin: From part of the original name of the Purgatoire River, which runs through the county, *El Río de las Animas Perdidas en Purgatorio*, Spanish 'river of souls lost in Purgatory,' in memory of people killed at the river by Indians c. 1595 who died without absolution. Shortened to El Purgatorio; then to its present form by French trappers; also known by Americanized *Picketwire*.

Aguilar   Town
ZIP: 81020   **Lat:** 37-24-14 N   **Long:** 104-39-15 W
Pop: 520 (1990); 624 (1980)   **Pop Density:** 1300.0
Land: 0.4 sq. mi.; **Water:** 0.0 sq. mi.
In southeastern CO, south of Pueblo.
Name origin: For prominent pioneer Jose Ramon Aguilar.

Branson   Town
ZIP: 81027   **Lat:** 37-00-52 N   **Long:** 103-52-44 W
Pop: 58 (1990); 73 (1980)   **Pop Density:** 82.9
Land: 0.7 sq. mi.; **Water:** 0.0 sq. mi.   **Elev:** 6299 ft.
Name origin: Named by and for an early pioneer, Al Branson.

Cokedale   Town
ZIP: 81032   **Lat:** 37-08-36 N   **Long:** 104-37-17 W
Pop: 116 (1990); 90 (1980)   **Pop Density:** 580.0
Land: 0.2 sq. mi.; **Water:** 0.0 sq. mi.
Name origin: For the coke ovens used to process local coal.

Kim   Town
ZIP: 81049   **Lat:** 37-14-46 N   **Long:** 103-21-06 W
Pop: 76 (1990); 100 (1980)   **Pop Density:** 253.3
Land: 0.3 sq. mi.; **Water:** 0.0 sq. mi.   **Elev:** 5686 ft.
Name origin: Named by early settlers for the famous boy hero, Kim, of the 1901 novel of the same name by Rudyard Kipling (1865–1936).

Starkville   Town
ZIP: 81074   **Lat:** 37-07-02 N   **Long:** 104-31-26 W
Pop: 104 (1990); 127 (1980)   **Pop Density:** 1040.0
Land: 0.1 sq. mi.; **Water:** 0.0 sq. mi.
Name origin: For H. G. Stark, who operated the first coal mine in the town.

Trinidad   City
ZIP: 81082   **Lat:** 37-10-06 N   **Long:** 104-30-20 W
Pop: 8,580 (1990); 9,663 (1980)   **Pop Density:** 1995.3
Land: 4.3 sq. mi.; **Water:** 0.0 sq. mi.
Founded 1859.
Name origin: From Spanish 'Trinity.' Shortened from Santisima Trinidad 'most holy Trinity.'

Lincoln County
County Seat: Hugo (ZIP: 80821)

Pop: 4,529 (1990); 4,663 (1980)   **Pop Density:** 1.8
Land: 2586.3 sq. mi.; **Water:** 0.3 sq. mi.   **Area Code:** 719

In east-central CO, east of Colorado Springs; organized Apr 11, 1889, from Bent and Elbert counties.

Name origin: For Abraham Lincoln (1809–65), sixteenth U.S. president.

Arriba   Town
ZIP: 80804   **Lat:** 39-17-01 N   **Long:** 103-16-24 W
Pop: 220 (1990); 236 (1980)   **Pop Density:** 440.0
Land: 0.5 sq. mi.; **Water:** 0.0 sq. mi.
Name origin: From Spanish 'above,' referring to its altitude in comparison with other towns in the area.

Genoa   Town
ZIP: 80818   **Lat:** 39-16-42 N   **Long:** 103-29-57 W
Pop: 167 (1990); 165 (1980)   **Pop Density:** 556.7
Land: 0.3 sq. mi.; **Water:** 0.0 sq. mi.   **Elev:** 5594 ft.
Name origin: For Genoa, Italy.

COLORADO, Lincoln County
American Places Dictionary

Hugo Town
ZIP: 80821 **Lat:** 39-08-03 N **Long:** 103-28-01 W
Pop: 660 (1990); 776 (1980) **Pop Density:** 1100.0
Land: 0.6 sq. mi.; **Water:** 0.0 sq. mi.
Name origin: For either pioneer Richard Hugo or French novelist Victor Hugo (1802-85).

Limon Town
ZIP: 80828 **Lat:** 39-15-57 N **Long:** 103-41-22 W
Pop: 1,831 (1990); 1,805 (1980) **Pop Density:** 1077.1
Land: 1.7 sq. mi.; **Water:** 0.0 sq. mi. **Elev:** 5365 ft.
Name origin: For a foreman of the Rock Island Railroad camp.

Logan County
County Seat: Sterling (ZIP: 80751)

Pop: 17,567 (1990); 19,800 (1980) **Pop Density:** 9.6
Land: 1838.6 sq. mi.; **Water:** 6.3 sq. mi. **Area Code:** 303
On northeastern border of CO, northeast of Greeley; organized Feb 25, 1887 from Weld County.
Name origin: For Gen. John Alexander Logan (1826-86), officer in the Mexican-American War and Civil War; U.S. senator from IL (1871-77; 1879-86).

Crook Town
ZIP: 80726 **Lat:** 40-51-29 N **Long:** 102-48-03 W
Pop: 148 (1990); 177 (1980) **Pop Density:** 1480.0
Land: 0.1 sq. mi.; **Water:** 0.0 sq. mi. **Elev:** 3711 ft.
Name origin: Named by the Union Pacific Railroad for Gen. George Crook (1829-90), army officer who captured Apache chief Geronimo (1829-1909).

Fleming Town
ZIP: 80728 **Lat:** 40-40-52 N **Long:** 102-50-23 W
Pop: 344 (1990); 388 (1980) **Pop Density:** 860.0
Land: 0.4 sq. mi.; **Water:** 0.0 sq. mi. **Elev:** 4240 ft.
Laid out 1889.
Name origin: For H.B. Fleming, a representative of the Lincoln Land Co., who laid out the town.

Iliff Town
ZIP: 80736 **Lat:** 40-45-28 N **Long:** 103-03-55 W
Pop: 174 (1990); 218 (1980) **Pop Density:** 580.0
Land: 0.3 sq. mi.; **Water:** 0.0 sq. mi. **Elev:** 3837 ft.
Name origin: For early CO cattle king John Iliff, whose ranch occupied the town site.

Merino Town
ZIP: 80741 **Lat:** 40-29-03 N **Long:** 103-21-12 W
Pop: 238 (1990); 255 (1980) **Pop Density:** 2380.0
Land: 0.1 sq. mi.; **Water:** 0.0 sq. mi. **Elev:** 4035 ft.
Name origin: Named in 1882 for huge flocks of merino sheep raised in the area. Originally known as Buffalo.

Peetz Town
ZIP: 80747 **Lat:** 40-57-41 N **Long:** 103-06-51 W
Pop: 179 (1990); 220 (1980) **Pop Density:** 895.0
Land: 0.2 sq. mi.; **Water:** 0.0 sq. mi. **Elev:** 4432 ft.
Name origin: For Peter Peetz, a pioneer homesteader.

Sterling City
ZIP: 80751 **Lat:** 40-37-35 N **Long:** 103-11-56 W
Pop: 10,362 (1990); 11,385 (1980) **Pop Density:** 1918.9
Land: 5.4 sq. mi.; **Water:** 0.0 sq. mi. **Elev:** 3939 ft.
In northeastern CO on the South Platte River, 40 mi. northeast of Fort Morgan.
Name origin: Named by railroad surveyor David Leavitt for his ranch, which was named for his former home in IL.

Mesa County
County Seat: Grand Junction (ZIP: 81502)

Pop: 93,145 (1990); 81,530 (1980) **Pop Density:** 28.0
Land: 3327.9 sq. mi.; **Water:** 13.4 sq. mi. **Area Code:** 303
On central western border of CO; organized Feb 14, 1883 from Gunnison County.
Name origin: Spanish 'table,' for the high, flat tablelands with sharply eroded sides common to the area.

Clifton CDP
ZIP: 81520 **Lat:** 39-04-30 N **Long:** 108-27-48 W
Pop: 12,671 (1990); 5,223 (1980) **Pop Density:** 1836.4
Land: 6.9 sq. mi.; **Water:** 0.1 sq. mi.

Collbran Town
ZIP: 81624 **Lat:** 39-14-21 N **Long:** 107-57-31 W
Pop: 228 (1990); 344 (1980) **Pop Density:** 1140.0
Land: 0.2 sq. mi.; **Water:** 0.0 sq. mi. **Elev:** 5987 ft.
Name origin: For an early local railroad man. Formerly named Hawhurst.

De Beque Town
ZIP: 81630 **Lat:** 39-19-57 N **Long:** 108-12-49 W
Pop: 257 (1990); 279 (1980) **Pop Density:** 856.7
Land: 0.3 sq. mi.; **Water:** 0.0 sq. mi. **Elev:** 4954 ft.
Name origin: For Dr. Wallace A.E. de Beque, a physician who settled in the area in 1883.

Fruita
Town
ZIP: 81521 **Lat:** 39-09-23 N **Long:** 108-43-38 W
Pop: 4,045 (1990); 2,810 (1980) **Pop Density:** 986.6
Land: 4.1 sq. mi.; **Water:** 0.1 sq. mi.
Name origin: Named by agriculturalist William Pabot to advertise the region's horticultural possibilities.

Fruitvale
CDP
ZIP: 81504 **Lat:** 39-05-35 N **Long:** 108-28-42 W
Pop: 5,222 (1990) **Pop Density:** 1631.9
Land: 3.2 sq. mi.; **Water:** 0.0 sq. mi.

Grand Junction
City
ZIP: 81501 **Lat:** 39-05-14 N **Long:** 108-33-10 W
Pop: 29,034 (1990); 27,956 (1980) **Pop Density:** 1961.8
Land: 14.8 sq. mi.; **Water:** 0.1 sq. mi. **Elev:** 4597 ft.
In western CO at the confluence of the Gunnison and Grand (Colorado) rivers. Incorporated 1881.
Name origin: For its descriptive connotations.

Orchard Mesa
CDP
ZIP: 81501 **Lat:** 39-02-01 N **Long:** 108-31-20 W
Pop: 5,977 (1990); 191 (1980) **Pop Density:** 1067.3
Land: 5.6 sq. mi.; **Water:** 0.2 sq. mi.

Palisade
Town
ZIP: 81526 **Lat:** 39-06-26 N **Long:** 108-21-28 W
Pop: 1,871 (1990); 1,551 (1980) **Pop Density:** 2338.8
Land: 0.8 sq. mi.; **Water:** 0.0 sq. mi.
Name origin: For the high perpendicular bluffs edging the valley to the north.

Redlands
CDP
ZIP: 81503 **Lat:** 39-05-06 N **Long:** 108-39-02 W
Pop: 9,355 (1990) **Pop Density:** 484.7
Land: 19.3 sq. mi.; **Water:** 0.7 sq. mi.

Mineral County
County Seat: Creede (ZIP: 81130)

Pop: 558 (1990); 804 (1980) **Pop Density:** 0.6
Land: 875.8 sq. mi.; **Water:** 2.0 sq. mi. **Area Code:** 719
In south-central CO, northeast of Durango; organized Mar 27, 1893, from Saguache and Rio Grande counties.
Name origin: For the rich mineral resources of the area.

Creede
Town
ZIP: 81130 **Lat:** 37-51-02 N **Long:** 106-55-35 W
Pop: 362 (1990); 610 (1980) **Pop Density:** 905.0
Land: 0.4 sq. mi.; **Water:** 0.0 sq. mi. **Elev:** 8838 ft.
Name origin: For miner Nicolas Creede, who made important mineral discoveries resulting in an almost overnight population explosion to 10,000.

Moffat County
County Seat: Craig (ZIP: 81625)

Pop: 11,357 (1990); 13,133 (1980) **Pop Density:** 2.4
Land: 4742.5 sq. mi.; **Water:** 8.7 sq. mi. **Area Code:** 303
On northwestern border of CO; organized Feb 27, 1911, from Routt County.
Name origin: For David Halliday Moffat (1839–1911), president of the Rio Grande Railroad (1884–91).

Craig
City
ZIP: 81625 **Lat:** 40-31-00 N **Long:** 107-33-12 W
Pop: 8,091 (1990); 8,133 (1980) **Pop Density:** 1685.6
Land: 4.8 sq. mi.; **Water:** 0.0 sq. mi. **Elev:** 6186 ft.
In the northwestern corner of CO.
Name origin: For the Rev. Bayard Craig, the town's developer.

Dinosaur
Town
ZIP: 81610 **Lat:** 40-14-29 N **Long:** 109-00-28 W
Pop: 324 (1990); 313 (1980) **Pop Density:** 462.9
Land: 0.7 sq. mi.; **Water:** 0.0 sq. mi. **Elev:** 5858 ft.
Name origin: First called Artesia, the town's present name refelcts its proximity to Dinosaur National Monument.

Montezuma County
County Seat: Cortez (ZIP: 81321)

Pop: 18,672 (1990); 16,510 (1980) **Pop Density:** 9.2
Land: 2036.9 sq. mi.; **Water:** 3.1 sq. mi. **Area Code:** 303
On southwesternmost border of CO; organized Apr 16, 1889, from La Plata County. The corners of four states, CO, AZ, NM, and UT, meet at this point, the only place in the U.S. where this occurs.
Name origin: For Montezuma (1479?–1520), Aztec Indian emperor of Mexico who was conquered by Hernán Cortez (1485–1547).

Cortez City
ZIP: 81321   Lat: 37-21-05 N Long: 108-34-38 W
Pop: 7,284 (1990); 7,095 (1980)   **Pop Density:** 1348.9
Land: 5.4 sq. mi.; **Water:** 0.0 sq. mi.   **Elev:** 6201 ft.
In the southwestern corner of CO.
Name origin: For the Spanish conqueror of Mexico.

Dolores Town
ZIP: 81323   Lat: 37-28-28 N Long: 108-29-51 W
Pop: 866 (1990); 802 (1980)   **Pop Density:** 1443.3
Land: 0.6 sq. mi.; **Water:** 0.0 sq. mi.   **Elev:** 6936 ft.
Name origin: For the Dolores River, which flows through the town.

Mancos Town
ZIP: 81328   Lat: 37-20-47 N Long: 108-17-36 W
Pop: 842 (1990); 870 (1980)   **Pop Density:** 1403.3
Land: 0.6 sq. mi.; **Water:** 0.0 sq. mi.   **Elev:** 7030 ft.
Name origin: For the Mancos River, which flows through the southern part of the county, itself named from Spanish 'one-handed,' 'faulty,' or 'crippled.'

Towaoc CDP
Lat: 37-12-35 N Long: 108-43-37 W
Pop: 700 (1990)   **Pop Density:** 200.0
Land: 3.5 sq. mi.; **Water:** 0.0 sq. mi.

Montrose County
County Seat: Montrose (ZIP: 81402)

Pop: 24,423 (1990); 24,352 (1980)   **Pop Density:** 10.9
Land: 2240.7 sq. mi.; **Water:** 2.0 sq. mi.   **Area Code:** 303
On central western border of CO, south of Grand Junction; organized Feb 11, 1883 from Gunnison County.
Name origin: For the city, named for *The Legend of Montrose*, by Sir Walter Scott (1771–1832), for the similarity of the surrounding country; also possibly an allusion to Montrose, Scotland.

Montrose City
ZIP: 81401   Lat: 38-28-45 N Long: 107-52-16 W
Pop: 8,854 (1990); 8,722 (1980)   **Pop Density:** 1526.6
Land: 5.8 sq. mi.; **Water:** 0.0 sq. mi.   **Elev:** 5806 ft.
Name origin: Named by pioneer Joe Selie for Sir Walter Scott's *The Legend of Montrose*.

Naturita Town
ZIP: 81422   Lat: 38-13-08 N Long: 108-34-04 W
Pop: 434 (1990); 819 (1980)   **Pop Density:** 620.0
Land: 0.7 sq. mi.; **Water:** 0.0 sq. mi.   **Elev:** 5431 ft.
Name origin: Named by early settler Rockwood Blake, from Spanish 'close to nature.'

Nucla Town
ZIP: 81424   Lat: 38-16-00 N Long: 108-32-58 W
Pop: 656 (1990); 1,027 (1980)   **Pop Density:** 937.1
Land: 0.7 sq. mi.; **Water:** 0.0 sq. mi.   **Elev:** 5823 ft.
Established 1904 by the CO Cooperative Co. as a socialist colony; incorporated 1915.
Name origin: A corruption of *nucleus* 'center,' chosen with the hope that their form of government would spread over the country and their town would be the center of the movement.

Olathe Town
ZIP: 81425   Lat: 38-36-20 N Long: 107-58-54 W
Pop: 1,263 (1990); 1,262 (1980)   **Pop Density:** 1263.0
Land: 1.0 sq. mi.; **Water:** 0.0 sq. mi.   **Elev:** 5356 ft.
Name origin: Named by early settlers for their former home in KS.

Morgan County
County Seat: Fort Morgan (ZIP: 80701)

Pop: 21,939 (1990); 22,513 (1980) **Pop Density:** 17.1
Land: 1285.5 sq. mi.; **Water:** 8.5 sq. mi. **Area Code:** 303
In northeastern CO, east of Boulder; organized Feb 19, 1889, from Weld County.
Name origin: For Fort Morgan, named for Col. Christopher Anthony Morgan (1825?–66), an army officer and inspector general of the Department of Missouri.

Brush — City
ZIP: 80723 **Lat:** 40-15-24 N **Long:** 103-37-56 W
Pop: 4,165 (1990); 4,082 (1980) **Pop Density:** 1735.4
Land: 2.4 sq. mi.; **Water:** 0.0 sq. mi. **Elev:** 4231 ft.
Name origin: Named by and for an early cattleman, Jared L. Brush.

Fort Morgan — City
ZIP: 80701 **Lat:** 40-15-54 N **Long:** 103-47-40 W
Pop: 9,068 (1990); 8,768 (1980) **Pop Density:** 2108.8
Land: 4.3 sq. mi.; **Water:** 0.1 sq. mi.
Established 1884, incorporated as a city 1887.
Name origin: For Civil War officer, Col. Christopher A. Morgan. The former military post was called Camp Tyler; renamed Fort Wardwell in 1865, and given present name in 1866.

Hillrose — Town
ZIP: 80733 **Lat:** 40-19-28 N **Long:** 103-31-19 W
Pop: 169 (1990); 213 (1980) **Pop Density:** 845.0
Land: 0.2 sq. mi.; **Water:** 0.0 sq. mi.
In northeastern CO. Settled by Burlington Railroad.
Name origin: Named by original landowner Kate Emerson by reversing her sister's name: Rose Hill.

Log Lane Village — Town
ZIP: 80701 **Lat:** 40-16-12 N **Long:** 103-49-42 W
Pop: 667 (1990); 709 (1980) **Pop Density:** 2223.3
Land: 0.3 sq. mi.; **Water:** 0.0 sq. mi.
Established 1955.
Name origin: Every building in the town was of log construction.

Wiggins — Town
ZIP: 80654 **Lat:** 40-13-49 N **Long:** 104-04-23 W
Pop: 499 (1990); 531 (1980) **Pop Density:** 998.0
Land: 0.5 sq. mi.; **Water:** 0.0 sq. mi. **Elev:** 4550 ft.
Name origin: For Maj. Oliver P. Wiggins, a Canadian employee of the Hudson Bay Company, who accompanied Fremont on one of his expeditons.

Otero County
County Seat: La Junta (ZIP: 81050)

Pop: 20,185 (1990); 22,567 (1980) **Pop Density:** 16.0
Land: 1262.9 sq. mi.; **Water:** 6.9 sq. mi. **Area Code:** 719
In southeastern CO, southeast of Pueblo; organized Mar 25, 1889, from Bent County.
Name origin: For Miguel Antonio Otero (1859–1944), NM territorial governor (1896–1906).

Cheraw — Town
Lat: 38-06-28 N **Long:** 103-30-38 W
Pop: 265 (1990); 233 (1980) **Pop Density:** 1325.0
Land: 0.2 sq. mi.; **Water:** 0.0 sq. mi. **Elev:** 4130 ft.
Name origin: For the nearby lake, itself believed to be named for the Cheraw Indians.

Fowler — Town
ZIP: 81039 **Lat:** 38-07-42 N **Long:** 104-01-28 W
Pop: 1,154 (1990); 1,227 (1980) **Pop Density:** 2885.0
Land: 0.4 sq. mi.; **Water:** 0.0 sq. mi. **Elev:** 4341 ft.
Platted 1887.
Name origin: For Professor O.S. Fowler, a phrenologist. Previously known as South Side, Oxford Siding, and Sibley.

La Junta — City
ZIP: 81050 **Lat:** 37-58-49 N **Long:** 103-32-39 W
Pop: 7,637 (1990); 8,338 (1980) **Pop Density:** 2937.3
Land: 2.6 sq. mi.; **Water:** 0.0 sq. mi.
Name origin: From Spanish referring to the 'junction' of the Santa Fe and Kansas Pacific railroads.

Manzanola — Town
ZIP: 81058 **Lat:** 38-06-31 N **Long:** 103-51-58 W
Pop: 437 (1990); 459 (1980) **Pop Density:** 1456.7
Land: 0.3 sq. mi.; **Water:** 0.0 sq. mi. **Elev:** 4252 ft.

Rocky Ford — City
ZIP: 81067 **Lat:** 38-02-59 N **Long:** 103-43-18 W
Pop: 4,162 (1990); 4,804 (1980) **Pop Density:** 2601.3
Land: 1.6 sq. mi.; **Water:** 0.0 sq. mi. **Elev:** 4178 ft.
Name origin: For a nearby ford of the Arkansas River.

COLORADO, Otero County   American Places Dictionary

Swink
ZIP: 81077   **Lat:** 38-00-49 N   **Long:** 103-37-38 W   Town
Pop: 584 (1990); 668 (1980)   **Pop Density:** 1946.7
Land: 0.3 sq. mi.; **Water:** 0.0 sq. mi.   **Elev:** 4118 ft.
Name origin: For state sen. George Swink, who also farmed in the area.

Ouray County
County Seat: Ouray (ZIP: 81427)

Pop: 2,295 (1990); 1,925 (1980)   **Pop Density:** 4.2
Land: 542.1 sq. mi.; **Water:** 0.2 sq. mi.   **Area Code:** 303

In southwestern CO, north of Durango; organized as Uncompahgre County Jan 18, 1877, from San Juan County; name changed Mar 2, 1883.

Name origin: For the Ute Indian chief Ouray (1820–80), possibly 'the arrow.' He was chief of Uncompahgre Utes and signed a treaty with U.S. in 1863 as 'U-ray' or 'Arrow'; signed one in 1868 'U-re,' and later that year 'Ouray.'

Ouray
ZIP: 81427   **Lat:** 38-01-33 N   **Long:** 107-40-18 W   City
Pop: 644 (1990); 684 (1980)   **Pop Density:** 805.0
Land: 0.8 sq. mi.; **Water:** 0.0 sq. mi.   **Elev:** 7811 ft.
Name origin: For the famous Ute Indian chief Ouray (1820–80).

Ridgway
ZIP: 81432   **Lat:** 38-09-20 N   **Long:** 107-45-07 W   Town
Pop: 423 (1990); 369 (1980)   **Pop Density:** 235.0
Land: 1.8 sq. mi.; **Water:** 0.0 sq. mi.
Name origin: For R. M. Ridgway, one-time superintendent of the Denver and Rio Grande Railroad's Mountain division.

Park County
County Seat: Fairplay (ZIP: 80440)

Pop: 7,174 (1990); 5,333 (1980)   **Pop Density:** 3.3
Land: 2200.8 sq. mi.; **Water:** 10.0 sq. mi.   **Area Code:** 303

In central CO, west of Colorado Springs; original county, organized Nov 1, 1861 (prior to statehood).

Name origin: For the large mountain valley known as the "South Park."

Alma
ZIP: 80420   **Lat:** 39-17-08 N   **Long:** 106-03-52 W   Town
Pop: 148 (1990); 132 (1980)   **Pop Density:** 493.3
Land: 0.3 sq. mi.; **Water:** 0.0 sq. mi.   **Elev:** 10353 ft.
Name origin: Origin is in dispute: either for the daughter of an early settler; the wife of Abner Graves, who operated the Alma Mine; or Alma James, wife of the first merchant.

Fairplay
Lat: 39-13-25 N   **Long:** 105-59-56 W   Town
Pop: 387 (1990); 421 (1980)   **Pop Density:** 483.8
Land: 0.8 sq. mi.; **Water:** 0.0 sq. mi.
Name origin: Named by early miners who discovered rich ore deposits here after having been denied good locations in a nearby area.

Phillips County
County Seat: Holyoke (ZIP: 80734)

Pop: 4,189 (1990); 4,542 (1980)   **Pop Density:** 6.1
Land: 687.7 sq. mi.; **Water:** 0.1 sq. mi.   **Area Code:** 303
On northeastern border of CO; organized Mar 27, 1889, from Logan County.
Name origin: For R. O. Phillips, an official in the Lincoln Land Company, which organized many of the towns in eastern CO.

Haxtun — Town
ZIP: 80731   **Lat:** 40-38-33 N **Long:** 102-37-43 W
Pop: 952 (1990); 1,014 (1980)   **Pop Density:** 1904.0
Land: 0.5 sq. mi.; **Water:** 0.0 sq. mi.   **Elev:** 4039 ft.
Name origin: For one of the contractors who helped build the Burlington railroad here in 1888.

Holyoke — Town
ZIP: 80734   **Lat:** 40-35-05 N **Long:** 102-18-13 W
Pop: 1,931 (1990); 2,092 (1980)   **Pop Density:** 1135.9
Land: 1.7 sq. mi.; **Water:** 0.0 sq. mi.   **Elev:** 3736 ft.
Name origin: For Holyoke, MA.

Paoli — Town
ZIP: 80746   **Lat:** 40-36-43 N **Long:** 102-28-20 W
Pop: 29 (1990); 81 (1980)   **Pop Density:** 96.7
Land: 0.3 sq. mi.; **Water:** 0.0 sq. mi.   **Elev:** 3898 ft.
Name origin: For the town in PA.

Pitkin County
County Seat: Aspen (ZIP: 81611)

Pop: 12,661 (1990); 10,338 (1980)   **Pop Density:** 13.0
Land: 970.5 sq. mi.; **Water:** 2.8 sq. mi.   **Area Code:** 303
In west-central CO, west of Leadville; organized Feb 23, 1881, from Gunnison County.
Name origin: For Frederick Walker Pitkin (1837–86), governor of CO (1879–83).

Aspen — City
ZIP: 81611   **Lat:** 39-11-40 N **Long:** 106-49-36 W
Pop: 5,049 (1990); 3,678 (1980)   **Pop Density:** 2524.5
Land: 2.0 sq. mi.; **Water:** 0.0 sq. mi.   **Elev:** 7907 ft.
Name origin: Named by early surveyor B. Clark Wheeler for the many aspen groves in the area.

Basalt — Town
Lat: 39-21-51 N **Long:** 107-01-40 W
Pop: 126 (1990)   **Pop Density:** 630.0
Land: 0.2 sq. mi.; **Water:** 0.0 sq. mi.   **Elev:** 6620 ft.
Part of the town is also in Eagle County.

Snowmass Village — Town
ZIP: 81615   **Lat:** 39-11-43 N **Long:** 106-56-19 W
Pop: 1,449 (1990); 999 (1980)   **Pop Density:** 88.4
Land: 16.4 sq. mi.; **Water:** 0.0 sq. mi.
Name origin: From nearby Snowmass Creek, itself named for Snowmass Mountain.

Prowers County
County Seat: Lamar (ZIP: 81052)

Pop: 13,347 (1990); 13,070 (1980)   **Pop Density:** 8.1
Land: 1640.5 sq. mi.; **Water:** 4.0 sq. mi.   **Area Code:** 719
On southeastern border of CO; organized Apr 11, 1889, from Bent County.
Name origin: For John Wesley Prowers (1839–84), a member of CO General Assembly who married Amanche, daughter of a Cheyenne chief, and worked with Indian agent Col. William Bent.

Granada — Town
ZIP: 81041   **Lat:** 38-03-49 N **Long:** 102-18-37 W
Pop: 513 (1990); 557 (1980)   **Pop Density:** 732.9
Land: 0.7 sq. mi.; **Water:** 0.0 sq. mi.   **Elev:** 3484 ft.
Name origin: For the town's original location on Granada Creek, itself probably named for the city and former kingdom in Spain.

COLORADO, Prowers County   *American Places Dictionary*

Hartman — Town
ZIP: 81043 **Lat:** 38-07-15 N **Long:** 102-13-05 W
Pop: 108 (1990); 122 (1980) **Pop Density:** 360.0
Land: 0.3 sq. mi.; **Water:** 0.0 sq. mi. **Elev:** 3600 ft.
Name origin: Named by the Santa Fe Railroad for one of its former company superintendents.

Holly — Town
ZIP: 81028 **Lat:** 38-03-20 N **Long:** 102-07-26 W
Pop: 877 (1990); 969 (1980) **Pop Density:** 1252.9
Land: 0.7 sq. mi.; **Water:** 0.0 sq. mi. **Elev:** 3387 ft.
Name origin: For pioneer rancher Hiram Holly, who owned a large ranch in the area.

Lamar — City
ZIP: 81052 **Lat:** 38-04-48 N **Long:** 102-37-03 W
Pop: 8,343 (1990); 7,713 (1980) **Pop Density:** 2034.9
Land: 4.1 sq. mi.; **Water:** 0.0 sq. mi. **Elev:** 3622 ft.
Established 1886; incorporated 1886.
Name origin: For then U.S. Secretary of the Interior, L. C. Lamar.

Wiley — Town
ZIP: 81092 **Lat:** 38-09-21 N **Long:** 102-43-07 W
Pop: 406 (1990); 425 (1980) **Pop Density:** 2030.0
Land: 0.2 sq. mi.; **Water:** 0.0 sq. mi.
Name origin: For W.M. Wiley, one of the community's founders.

Pueblo County
County Seat: Pueblo (ZIP: 81003)

Pop: 123,051 (1990); 125,972 (1980) **Pop Density:** 51.5
Land: 2388.8 sq. mi.; **Water:** 9.0 sq. mi. **Area Code:** 719
In south-central CO; original county, organized Nov 1, 1861, (prior to statehood).
Name origin: For the city, from Spanish 'town.'

Boone — Town
ZIP: 81025 **Lat:** 38-15-00 N **Long:** 104-15-20 W
Pop: 341 (1990); 431 (1980) **Pop Density:** 852.5
Land: 0.4 sq. mi.; **Water:** 0.0 sq. mi. **Elev:** 4476 ft.
Name origin: Named by a descendant of Daniel Boone.

Colorado City — CDP
Lat: 37-56-38 N **Long:** 104-50-46 W
Pop: 1,149 (1990) **Pop Density:** 32.6
Land: 35.2 sq. mi.; **Water:** 0.1 sq. mi.

Pueblo — City
ZIP: 81001 **Lat:** 38-16-24 N **Long:** 104-37-15 W
Pop: 98,640 (1990); 101,686 (1980) **Pop Density:** 2747.6
Land: 35.9 sq. mi.; **Water:** 0.3 sq. mi. **Elev:** 4662 ft.
In southeast-central CO, 40 mi. south-southeast of Colorado Springs. Founded 1858 by gold miners; incorporated as a town 1870, as a city 1873.
Name origin: From Spanish 'town.' Originally known as Independence, former home of some early settlers.

Pueblo West — CDP
Lat: 38-20-59 N **Long:** 104-43-19 W
Pop: 4,386 (1990) **Pop Density:** 57.9
Land: 75.7 sq. mi.; **Water:** 0.0 sq. mi.

Rye — Town
ZIP: 81069 **Lat:** 37-55-18 N **Long:** 104-55-51 W
Pop: 168 (1990); 232 (1980) **Pop Density:** 1680.0
Land: 0.1 sq. mi.; **Water:** 0.0 sq. mi.
Name origin: For the abundant grain surrounding the town. Previously called Table Mountain.

Rio Blanco County
County Seat: Meeker (ZIP: 81641)

Pop: 5,972 (1990); 6,255 (1980) **Pop Density:** 1.9
Land: 3221.2 sq. mi.; **Water:** 1.9 sq. mi. **Area Code:** 303
On northwestern border of CO, north of Grand Junction; organized Mar 25, 1889, from Garfield County.
Name origin: Spanish name for the White River, which flows through the county; possibly referring to the white caps of the rapids; probably translated from the Ute name.

Meeker — Town
ZIP: 81641 **Lat:** 40-03-16 N **Long:** 107-53-23 W
Pop: 2,098 (1990); 2,356 (1980) **Pop Density:** 699.3
Land: 3.0 sq. mi.; **Water:** 0.0 sq. mi. **Elev:** 6239 ft.
Name origin: For Indian agent Nathan Meeker, murdered by Ute Indians November 1879.

Rangely — Town
ZIP: 81648 **Lat:** 40-05-15 N **Long:** 108-46-42 W
Pop: 2,278 (1990); 2,113 (1980) **Pop Density:** 569.5
Land: 4.0 sq. mi.; **Water:** 0.0 sq. mi. **Elev:** 5230 ft.
Name origin: Named by original settler, D. B. Case, for Rangely, MA.

Rio Grande County
County Seat: Del Norte (ZIP: 81132)

Pop: 10,770 (1990); 10,511 (1980)   **Pop Density:** 11.8
Land: 912.6 sq. mi.; **Water:** 0.5 sq. mi.   **Area Code:** 719
In south-central CO; organized Feb 10, 1874, from Conejos County.
Name origin: For the Rio Grande, which flows through the county; shortened from Spanish *Rio Grande del Norte* 'Great River of the North.'

Center — Town
ZIP: 81125   **Lat:** 37-44-42 N   **Long:** 106-06-17 W
Pop: 4 (1990); 1,630 (1980)   **Pop Density:** 40.0
Land: 0.1 sq. mi.; **Water:** 0.0 sq. mi.   **Elev:** 7645 ft.
Part of the town is also in Saguache County.

Del Norte — Town
ZIP: 81132   **Lat:** 37-40-41 N   **Long:** 106-21-07 W
Pop: 1,674 (1990); 1,709 (1980)   **Pop Density:** 1860.0
Land: 0.9 sq. mi.; **Water:** 0.0 sq. mi.
Name origin: Named by gold miners; a shortened form of the Spanish *Rio Grande del Norte* 'great river of the north,' the present Rio Grande, which flows through the town.

Monte Vista — City
ZIP: 81144   **Lat:** 37-34-42 N   **Long:** 106-08-39 W
Pop: 4,324 (1990); 3,902 (1980)   **Pop Density:** 2702.5
Land: 1.6 sq. mi.; **Water:** 0.1 sq. mi.   **Elev:** 7663 ft.
Founded 1886.
Name origin: From Spanish 'mountain view.'

Routt County
County Seat: Steamboat Springs (ZIP: 80477)

Pop: 14,088 (1990); 13,404 (1980)   **Pop Density:** 6.0
Land: 2361.8 sq. mi.; **Water:** 6.4 sq. mi.   **Area Code:** 303
On central northern border of CO; organized Jan 29, 1877, from Grand County.
Name origin: For John Long Routt (1826–1907), last territorial governor (1876–79) and first CO state governor (1891–93).

Hayden — Town
ZIP: 81639   **Lat:** 40-29-17 N   **Long:** 107-15-37 W
Pop: 1,444 (1990); 1,720 (1980)   **Pop Density:** 1031.4
Land: 1.4 sq. mi.; **Water:** 0.0 sq. mi.   **Elev:** 6337 ft.
Name origin: Named by the first settlers for Ferdinand Hayden, then head of the U.S. Geological Survey.

Oak Creek — Town
ZIP: 80467   **Lat:** 40-16-28 N   **Long:** 106-57-25 W
Pop: 673 (1990); 929 (1980)   **Pop Density:** 2243.3
Land: 0.3 sq. mi.; **Water:** 0.0 sq. mi.   **Elev:** 7414 ft.
Name origin: Named by and for the Oak Creek Land and Mining Company.

Steamboat Springs — City
ZIP: 80487   **Lat:** 40-28-40 N   **Long:** 106-49-15 W
Pop: 6,695 (1990); 5,098 (1980)   **Pop Density:** 743.9
Land: 9.0 sq. mi.; **Water:** 0.0 sq. mi.   **Elev:** 6728 ft.
In northwestern CO, west of Fort Collins.
Name origin: For an old springs, now destroyed, that emitted a puffing sound, which reminded the early settlers of the sound of large river steamers.

Yampa — Town
ZIP: 80483   **Lat:** 40-09-11 N   **Long:** 106-54-26 W
Pop: 317 (1990); 472 (1980)   **Pop Density:** 1585.0
Land: 0.2 sq. mi.; **Water:** 0.0 sq. mi.   **Elev:** 7890 ft.

Saguache County
County Seat: Saguache (ZIP: 81149)

Pop: 4,619 (1990); 3,935 (1980)   **Pop Density:** 1.5
Land: 3168.7 sq. mi.; **Water:** 1.8 sq. mi.   **Area Code:** 719
In south-central CO, west of Pueblo; organized Dec 29, 1866, from Costilla County (prior to statehood).
Name origin: For Saguache Creek, which flows through the county; from a Ute Indian word meaning 'blue earth,' or 'water at the blue earth.'

Bonanza City — Town
ZIP: 81155   **Lat:** 38-17-38 N **Long:** 106-08-29 W
Pop: 16 (1990); 8 (1980)   **Pop Density:** 40.0
Land: 0.4 sq. mi.; **Water:** 0.0 sq. mi.

Center — Town
Lat: 37-45-10 N **Long:** 106-06-40 W
Pop: 1,959 (1990); 1,630 (1980)   **Pop Density:** 2798.6
Land: 0.7 sq. mi.; **Water:** 0.0 sq. mi.   **Elev:** 7645 ft.
Part of the town is also in Rio Grande County.
Name origin: Named by pioneers to designate the town's location in the center of the San Luis Valley.

Crestone — Town
ZIP: 81131   **Lat:** 37-59-41 N **Long:** 105-41-50 W
Pop: 39 (1990); 54 (1980)   **Pop Density:** 130.0
Land: 0.3 sq. mi.; **Water:** 0.0 sq. mi.
Name origin: From a loose translation of the Spanish word for 'cock's comb.'

Moffat — Town
ZIP: 81143   **Lat:** 38-00-06 N **Long:** 105-54-15 W
Pop: 99 (1990); 105 (1980)   **Pop Density:** 70.7
Land: 1.4 sq. mi.; **Water:** 0.0 sq. mi.   **Elev:** 7561 ft.
Name origin: Named by town founders for David Moffat, president of the Denver and Rio Grande railroad.

Saguache — Town
ZIP: 81149   **Lat:** 38-05-10 N **Long:** 106-08-27 W
Pop: 584 (1990); 656 (1980)   **Pop Density:** 1460.0
Land: 0.4 sq. mi.; **Water:** 0.0 sq. mi.   **Elev:** 7694 ft.
Name origin: An anglicization of a Ute term meaning 'blue earth.'

San Juan County
County Seat: Silverton (ZIP: 81433)

Pop: 745 (1990); 833 (1980)   **Pop Density:** 1.9
Land: 387.4 sq. mi.; **Water:** 0.9 sq. mi.   **Area Code:** 303
In southwestern CO, north of Durango; organized 1876, from La Plata County.
Name origin: Spanish St. John (the Baptist). Name was given by early Spanish explorers to the river, the mountain range, and then the whole region.

Silverton — Town
ZIP: 81433   **Lat:** 37-48-39 N **Long:** 107-39-50 W
Pop: 716 (1990); 794 (1980)   **Pop Density:** 895.0
Land: 0.8 sq. mi.; **Water:** 0.0 sq. mi.   **Elev:** 9305 ft.
Name origin: For the rich silver mining in the area. Previously called Baker's Park.

San Miguel County
County Seat: Telluride (ZIP: 81435)

Pop: 3,653 (1990); 3,192 (1980) **Pop Density:** 2.8
Land: 1286.6 sq. mi.; **Water:** 2.0 sq. mi. **Area Code:** 303

On southwestern border of CO; organized Nov 1, 1861, from Ouray County (prior to statehood).

Name origin: For the river, which flows through the county; Spanish for St. Michael (the Archangel).

Norwood — Town
ZIP: 81423 **Lat:** 38-07-49 N **Long:** 108-17-29 W
Pop: 429 (1990); 478 (1980) **Pop Density:** 2145.0
Land: 0.2 sq. mi.; **Water:** 0.0 sq. mi. **Elev:** 7006 ft.
Name origin: For a town in MO.

Ophir — Town
ZIP: 81426 **Lat:** 37-51-24 N **Long:** 107-49-44 W
Pop: 69 (1990); 38 (1980) **Pop Density:** 690.0
Land: 0.1 sq. mi.; **Water:** 0.0 sq. mi.
Name origin: For the biblical gold mines of King Solomon.

Sawpit — Town
ZIP: 81430 **Lat:** 37-59-41 N **Long:** 107-59-59 W
Pop: 36 (1990); 41 (1980) **Pop Density:** 1200.0
Land: 0.03 sq. mi.; **Water:** 0.0 sq. mi.
Name origin: For the town's early industry.

Telluride — Town
ZIP: 81435 **Lat:** 37-56-19 N **Long:** 107-48-44 W
Pop: 1,309 (1990); 1,047 (1980) **Pop Density:** 1870.0
Land: 0.7 sq. mi.; **Water:** 0.0 sq. mi.
Name origin: For the tellurium ore deposits found in the area.

Sedgwick County
County Seat: Julesburg (ZIP: 80737)

Pop: 2,690 (1990); 3,266 (1980) **Pop Density:** 4.9
Land: 548.3 sq. mi.; **Water:** 1.4 sq. mi. **Area Code:** 303

On northeasternmost border of CO; organized Apr 9, 1889, from Logan County.

Name origin: For Fort Sedgwick, named for Maj. Gen. John Sedgwick (1813–64), Indian fighter and Union officer in the Civil War.

Julesburg — Town
ZIP: 80737 **Lat:** 40-59-12 N **Long:** 102-15-52 W
Pop: 1,295 (1990); 1,528 (1980) **Pop Density:** 996.2
Land: 1.3 sq. mi.; **Water:** 0.0 sq. mi. **Elev:** 3477 ft.
Name origin: For Jules Beni, who originally owned the ranch and trading post here.

Ovid — Town
ZIP: 80744 **Lat:** 40-57-35 N **Long:** 102-23-17 W
Pop: 349 (1990); 439 (1980) **Pop Density:** 1745.0
Land: 0.2 sq. mi.; **Water:** 0.0 sq. mi. **Elev:** 3521 ft.
Name origin: For Newton Ovid, a local bachelor.

Sedgwick — Town
ZIP: 80749 **Lat:** 40-56-05 N **Long:** 102-31-29 W
Pop: 183 (1990); 258 (1980) **Pop Density:** 610.0
Land: 0.3 sq. mi.; **Water:** 0.0 sq. mi.
Name origin: For old Fort Sedgwick, itself named for Maj. Gen. John Sedgwick, Indian fighter and Union officer killed in the Civil War.

COLORADO, Summit County

Summit County
County Seat: Breckenridge (ZIP: 80424)

Pop: 12,881 (1990); 8,848 (1980) **Pop Density:** 21.2
Land: 608.2 sq. mi.; **Water:** 11.1 sq. mi. **Area Code:** 303
In central CO west of Denver; original county, organized 1861, (prior to statehood).
Name origin: For the mountainous terrain of the county; part of its southeastern border follows the Continental Divide.

Blue River Town
Lat: 39-25-57 N Long: 106-02-11 W
Pop: 440 (1990); 230 (1980) **Pop Density:** 200.0
Land: 2.2 sq. mi.; **Water:** 0.1 sq. mi.
Name origin: For the Blue River, which traverses the county.

Breckenridge Town
ZIP: 80424 Lat: 39-30-26 N Long: 106-02-50 W
Pop: 1,285 (1990); 818 (1980) **Pop Density:** 298.8
Land: 4.3 sq. mi.; **Water:** 0.0 sq. mi. **Elev:** 9602 ft.
Founded and named in 1859.
Name origin: For John Cabell Breckinridge (1821–75), U.S. vice president (1857–61). Because he later supported the Confederate cause, the Unionist citizens petitioned Congress for a name change, thus the first *i* was changed to the present spelling.

Dillon Town
ZIP: 80435 Lat: 39-37-29 N Long: 106-02-20 W
Pop: 553 (1990); 337 (1980) **Pop Density:** 553.0
Land: 1.0 sq. mi.; **Water:** 0.2 sq. mi.
Name origin: Named by explorers for gold miner Tom Dillon, who first discovered the area.

Frisco Town
ZIP: 80443 Lat: 39-34-44 N Long: 106-05-45 W
Pop: 1,601 (1990); 1,221 (1980) **Pop Density:** 1334.2
Land: 1.2 sq. mi.; **Water:** 0.0 sq. mi.
Name origin: Named by the first settler, H.A. Recen, possibly for San Francisco's nickname.

Montezuma Town
Lat: 39-34-52 N Long: 105-52-06 W
Pop: 60 (1990) **Pop Density:** 600.0
Land: 0.1 sq. mi.; **Water:** 0.0 sq. mi.

Silverthorne Town
ZIP: 80498 Lat: 39-39-05 N Long: 106-04-53 W
Pop: 1,768 (1990); 989 (1980) **Pop Density:** 589.3
Land: 3.0 sq. mi.; **Water:** 0.0 sq. mi.
Name origin: For Marshall Silverton, who ran a famous hotel in the town.

Teller County
County Seat: Cripple Creek (ZIP: 80813)

Pop: 12,468 (1990); 8,034 (1980) **Pop Density:** 22.4
Land: 557.1 sq. mi.; **Water:** 1.9 sq. mi. **Area Code:** 719
In central CO, west of Colorado Springs; organized Mar 23, 1899, from El Paso and Fremont Counties.
Name origin: For Henry Moore Teller (1830–1914), U.S. senator from CO (1876–82; 1885–1909), and U.S. secretary of the interior (1882–85).

Cripple Creek City
ZIP: 80813 Lat: 38-44-46 N Long: 105-10-43 W
Pop: 584 (1990); 655 (1980) **Pop Density:** 584.0
Land: 1.0 sq. mi.; **Water:** 0.0 sq. mi. **Elev:** 9508 ft.
Name origin: For a stream named by early cowboys who found the banks were so steep that the cows often broke their legs going down after water. Previously called *Pisgah Park*.

Green Mountain Falls Town
Lat: 38-56-02 N Long: 105-01-48 W
Pop: 29 (1990); 18 (1980) **Pop Density:** 290.0
Land: 0.1 sq. mi.; **Water:** 0.0 sq. mi.
Part of the town is also in El Paso County.

Victor City
ZIP: 80860 Lat: 38-42-30 N Long: 105-08-26 W
Pop: 258 (1990); 265 (1980) **Pop Density:** 860.0
Land: 0.3 sq. mi.; **Water:** 0.0 sq. mi. **Elev:** 9695 ft.
Name origin: For the rich, gold-producing Victor Mine.

Woodland Park City
ZIP: 80863 Lat: 38-59-42 N Long: 105-03-06 W
Pop: 4,610 (1990); 2,634 (1980) **Pop Density:** 1152.5
Land: 4.0 sq. mi.; **Water:** 0.0 sq. mi. **Elev:** 8437 ft.

Washington County
County Seat: Akron (ZIP: 80720)

Pop: 4,812 (1990); 5,304 (1980)   **Pop Density:** 1.9
Land: 2521.2 sq. mi.; **Water:** 3.1 sq. mi.   **Area Code:** 303
In northeastern CO, east of Denver; organized Feb 9, 1887, from Weld County.
Name origin: For George Washington (1732–1799), American patriot and first U.S. president.

Akron   Town
ZIP: 80720   **Lat:** 40-09-45 N **Long:** 103-12-42 W
Pop: 1,599 (1990); 1,716 (1980)   **Pop Density:** 1230.0
Land: 1.3 sq. mi.; **Water:** 0.0 sq. mi.   **Elev:** 4661 ft.
Name origin: For the hometown in OH of an early railroad official's wife.

Otis   Town
ZIP: 80743   **Lat:** 40-08-58 N **Long:** 102-57-41 W
Pop: 451 (1990); 534 (1980)   **Pop Density:** 1127.5
Land: 0.4 sq. mi.; **Water:** 0.0 sq. mi.   **Elev:** 4335 ft.
Name origin: Probably for an official connected with the Chicago, Burlington and Quincy Railroad, which came through the area.

Weld County
County Seat: Greeley (ZIP: 80631)

Pop: 131,821 (1990); 123,438 (1980)   **Pop Density:** 33.0
Land: 3992.8 sq. mi.; **Water:** 29.0 sq. mi.   **Area Code:** 303
On central northern border of CO, east of Fort Collins; original county, organized Nov 1, 1861, (prior to statehood).
Name origin: For Lewis Ledyard Weld, first Secretary of the CO Territory.

Ault   Town
ZIP: 80610   **Lat:** 40-35-02 N **Long:** 104-43-59 W
Pop: 1,107 (1990); 1,056 (1980)   **Pop Density:** 1581.4
Land: 0.7 sq. mi.; **Water:** 0.0 sq. mi.   **Elev:** 4939 ft.
Name origin: For pioneer miller Alexander Ault, who bought the entire local grain crop for many years before grain storage facilities were available.

Brighton   City
ZIP: 80601   **Lat:** 40-00-10 N **Long:** 104-48-26 W
Pop: 17 (1990)   **Pop Density:** 56.7
Land: 0.3 sq. mi.; **Water:** 0.0 sq. mi.   **Elev:** 4983 ft.
Part of the town is also in Adams County.

Broomfield   City
Lat: 40-00-22 N **Long:** 104-58-12 W
Pop: 4 (1990)   **Pop Density:** 3.6
Land: 1.1 sq. mi.; **Water:** 0.0 sq. mi.
Part of the town is also in Boulder, Adams, and Jefferson counties.

Dacono   Town
ZIP: 80514   **Lat:** 40-04-32 N **Long:** 104-56-34 W
Pop: 2,228 (1990); 2,321 (1980)   **Pop Density:** 1310.6
Land: 1.7 sq. mi.; **Water:** 0.0 sq. mi.
Name origin: Named by founding coal miner, C.L. Baum, for his wife Daisy, and her friends Cora Van Voorhies and Nona Brooks. Along with Firestone and Frederick, it is one of the "tri-cities."

Eaton   Town
ZIP: 80615   **Lat:** 40-31-29 N **Long:** 104-42-35 W
Pop: 1,959 (1990); 1,932 (1980)   **Pop Density:** 2176.7
Land: 0.9 sq. mi.; **Water:** 0.0 sq. mi.   **Elev:** 4839 ft.
Name origin: For Benjamin Eaton, fourth governor of CO.

Erie   Town
ZIP: 80516   **Lat:** 40-01-43 N **Long:** 105-02-28 W
Pop: 1,244 (1990); 1,231 (1980)   **Pop Density:** 518.3
Land: 2.4 sq. mi.; **Water:** 0.0 sq. mi.
Part of the town is also in Boulder County.
Name origin: Named by early coal miners for a mining town in PA.

Evans   City
ZIP: 80620   **Lat:** 40-22-40 N **Long:** 104-41-48 W
Pop: 5,877 (1990); 5,063 (1980)   **Pop Density:** 2176.7
Land: 2.7 sq. mi.; **Water:** 0.0 sq. mi.   **Elev:** 4650 ft.
Name origin: For CO's second territorial governor, John Evans.

Firestone   Town
ZIP: 80520   **Lat:** 40-07-15 N **Long:** 104-56-02 W
Pop: 1,358 (1990); 1,204 (1980)   **Pop Density:** 1234.5
Land: 1.1 sq. mi.; **Water:** 0.0 sq. mi.
Founded by the Denslow Coal and Land Co.
Name origin: For original landowner, Jacob Firestone.

Fort Lupton   City
ZIP: 80621   **Lat:** 40-05-06 N **Long:** 104-48-18 W
Pop: 5,159 (1990); 4,251 (1980)   **Pop Density:** 1779.0
Land: 2.9 sq. mi.; **Water:** 0.0 sq. mi.
Name origin: For Lancaster P. Lupton, a former Army lieutenant who established a trading post in the area.

Frederick   Town
ZIP: 80530   **Lat:** 40-06-17 N **Long:** 104-56-32 W
Pop: 988 (1990); 855 (1980)   **Pop Density:** 318.7
Land: 3.1 sq. mi.; **Water:** 0.1 sq. mi.   **Elev:** 4980 ft.
Name origin: For the town's original landowner, Frederic A. Clark. Town founded by Mary M. Clark, Maude Clark Reynolds, and Mary Clark Steele.

COLORADO, Weld County

Garden City — Town
Lat: 40-23-38 N **Long:** 104-41-19 W
Pop: 199 (1990); 85 (1980) **Pop Density:** 1990.0
Land: 0.1 sq. mi.; **Water:** 0.0 sq. mi.
Name origin: For the official slogan of nearby Greeley, CO: "Garden City of the West."

Gilcrest — Town
ZIP: 80623 **Lat:** 40-16-57 N **Long:** 104-46-55 W
Pop: 1,084 (1990); 1,025 (1980) **Pop Density:** 1548.6
Land: 0.7 sq. mi.; **Water:** 0.0 sq. mi. **Elev** 4751 ft.
Name origin: Named by banker W. K. Gilcrest, who bought up large parts of the town and established a bank, in honor of his father.

Greeley — City
ZIP: 80631 **Lat:** 40-25-16 N **Long:** 104-44-37 W
Pop: 60,536 (1990); 53,006 (1980) **Pop Density:** 2131.5
Land: 28.4 sq. mi.; **Water:** 0.1 sq. mi. **Elev** 4664 ft.
Incorporated 1885.
Name origin: For famous newspaper editor Horace Greeley (1811–72), who helped found the first settlement.

Grover — Town
ZIP: 80729 **Lat:** 40-52-09 N **Long:** 104-13-32 W
Pop: 135 (1990); 158 (1980) **Pop Density:** 270.0
Land: 0.5 sq. mi.; **Water:** 0.0 sq. mi. **Elev** 5070 ft.
Name origin: For the maiden name of pioneer settler Mrs. Neal Donovan.

Hudson — Town
ZIP: 80642 **Lat:** 40-04-15 N **Long:** 104-38-34 W
Pop: 918 (1990); 698 (1980) **Pop Density:** 2295.0
Land: 0.4 sq. mi.; **Water:** 0.0 sq. mi. **Elev** 5000 ft.
Name origin: Named by the Hudson Land Company, which developed the town.

Johnstown — Town
ZIP: 80534 **Lat:** 40-20-07 N **Long:** 104-54-41 W
Pop: 1,579 (1990); 1,535 (1980) **Pop Density:** 3947.5
Land: 0.4 sq. mi.; **Water:** 0.0 sq. mi. **Elev** 4818 ft.
Founded by Harvey Parish.
Name origin: Named by the founder for his son John.

Keenesburg — Town
ZIP: 80643 **Lat:** 40-06-31 N **Long:** 104-31-06 W
Pop: 570 (1990); 541 (1980) **Pop Density:** 1140.0
Land: 0.5 sq. mi.; **Water:** 0.0 sq. mi. **Elev** 4958 ft.
Name origin: Named in 1907 for an early rancher.

Keota — Town
Lat: 40-42-14 N **Long:** 104-04-25 W
Pop: 5 (1990); 4 (1980) **Pop Density:** 25.0
Land: 0.2 sq. mi.; **Water:** 0.0 sq. mi. **Elev** 4961 ft.

Kersey — Town
ZIP: 80644 **Lat:** 40-23-09 N **Long:** 104-33-35 W
Pop: 980 (1990); 913 (1980) **Pop Density:** 3266.7
Land: 0.3 sq. mi.; **Water:** 0.0 sq. mi.
Name origin: Named in 1896 by Union Pacific roadmaster John Painter for his mother's maiden name.

La Salle — Town
ZIP: 80645 **Lat:** 40-20-52 N **Long:** 104-42-16 W
Pop: 1,783 (1990); 1,929 (1980) **Pop Density:** 2547.1
Land: 0.7 sq. mi.; **Water:** 0.0 sq. mi. **Elev** 4676 ft.
Name origin: For the seventeenth-century French explorer who discovered the Mississippi River.

Lochbuie — Town
Lat: 40-00-27 N **Long:** 104-43-12 W
Pop: 1,168 (1990); 895 (1980) **Pop Density:** 1946.7
Land: 0.6 sq. mi.; **Water:** 0.0 sq. mi.
Name origin: For the ancestral home of one of the town's organizers, located in the Lochbuie area on the Isle of Mull in Scotland.

Mead — Town
ZIP: 80542 **Lat:** 40-14-03 N **Long:** 104-59-16 W
Pop: 456 (1990); 356 (1980) **Pop Density:** 456.0
Land: 1.0 sq. mi.; **Water:** 0.1 sq. mi. **Elev** 5001 ft.

Milliken — Town
ZIP: 80543 **Lat:** 40-18-59 N **Long:** 104-51-09 W
Pop: 1,605 (1990); 1,506 (1980) **Pop Density:** 334.4
Land: 4.8 sq. mi.; **Water:** 0.0 sq. mi.
Name origin: For John D. Milliken, prominent businessman and railroad president.

Northglenn — City
Lat: 40-00-25 N **Long:** 104-57-18 W
Pop: 0 (1990); 29,847 (1980)
Land: 0.6 sq. mi.; **Water:** 0.0 sq. mi.
Part of the town is also in Adams County.

Nunn — Town
ZIP: 80648 **Lat:** 40-42-14 N **Long:** 104-46-49 W
Pop: 324 (1990); 295 (1980) **Pop Density:** 324.0
Land: 1.0 sq. mi.; **Water:** 0.0 sq. mi. **Elev** 5185 ft.
Name origin: For homesteader Tom Nunn, who prevented a serious train wreck by flagging a train after he discovered a burning bridge.

Pierce — Town
ZIP: 80650 **Lat:** 40-37-58 N **Long:** 104-45-16 W
Pop: 823 (1990); 878 (1980) **Pop Density:** 1371.7
Land: 0.6 sq. mi.; **Water:** 0.0 sq. mi. **Elev** 5039 ft.
Name origin: For Gen. John Pierce, former surveyor general of CO, and president of the Denver Pacific Railroad.

Platteville — Town
ZIP: 80651 **Lat:** 40-13-00 N **Long:** 104-49-19 W
Pop: 1,515 (1990); 1,662 (1980) **Pop Density:** 1683.3
Land: 0.9 sq. mi.; **Water:** 0.0 sq. mi. **Elev** 4825 ft.
Name origin: For its location on the east bank of the Platte River.

Raymer — Town
ZIP: 80742 **Lat:** 40-36-26 N **Long:** 103-50-37 W
Pop: 98 (1990); 80 (1980) **Pop Density:** 140.0
Land: 0.7 sq. mi.; **Water:** 0.0 sq. mi.
Name origin: Named by the Lincoln Land Company for George Raymer, an assistant engineer on the Burlington and Missouri Railroad.

Severance — Town
ZIP: 80546 **Lat:** 40-31-20 N **Long:** 104-50-58 W
Pop: 106 (1990); 102 (1980) **Pop Density:** 530.0
Land: 0.2 sq. mi.; **Water:** 0.0 sq. mi. **Elev** 4886 ft.
Name origin: For Dave Severance, who managed to sell 160 acres to a development company for $325.00 per acre, an astronomical price at that time.

Windsor — Town
ZIP: 80550 **Lat:** 40-29-06 N **Long:** 104-54-23 W
Pop: 5,062 (1990); 4,277 (1980) **Pop Density:** 1077.0
Land: 4.7 sq. mi.; **Water:** 0.3 sq. mi.
Name origin: For the Rev. A.S. Windsor, a Methodist circuit rider.

Yuma County
County Seat: Wray (ZIP: 80758)

Pop: 8,954 (1990); 9,682 (1980) **Pop Density:** 3.8
Land: 2366.1 sq. mi.; **Water:** 3.1 sq. mi. **Area Code:** 303

On eastern border of CO, east of Denver; organized Mar 15, 1889, from Washington County.

Name origin: For the Yuma Indian tribe. The name, given to the tribe by the Spanish, may mean 'children of the sun' or may come from the Spanish *umo* 'smoke.'

Eckley — Town
ZIP: 80727 **Lat:** 40-06-43 N **Long:** 102-29-17 W
Pop: 211 (1990); 262 (1980) **Pop Density:** 422.0
Land: 0.5 sq. mi.; **Water:** 0.0 sq. mi. **Elev:** 3894 ft.

Wray — City
ZIP: 80758 **Lat:** 40-04-45 N **Long:** 102-13-33 W
Pop: 1,998 (1990); 2,131 (1980) **Pop Density:** 689.0
Land: 2.9 sq. mi.; **Water:** 0.0 sq. mi. **Elev:** 3522 ft.

Yuma — City
ZIP: 80759 **Lat:** 40-07-26 N **Long:** 102-43-26 W
Pop: 2,719 (1990); 2,824 (1980) **Pop Density:** 1182.2
Land: 2.3 sq. mi.; **Water:** 0.0 sq. mi.
Name origin: For the Yuma Indian tribe. The name, given to the tribe by the Spanish, may mean 'children of the sun' or may come from the Spanish *umo* 'smoke.'

COLORADO
American Places Dictionary

Index to Places and Counties in Colorado

Adams County *128*
Aguilar (Las Animas) Town *147*
Air Force Academy (El Paso) Military
  Facility *138*
Akron (Washington) Town *159*
Alamosa (Alamosa) City *129*
Alamosa County *129*
Alamosa East (Alamosa) CDP *129*
Alma (Park) Town *152*
Antonito (Conejos) Town *134*
Applewood (Jefferson) CDP *143*
Arapahoe County *129*
Archuleta County *130*
Arriba (Lincoln) Town *147*
Arvada (Adams) City *128*
Arvada (Jefferson) City *143*
Aspen (Pitkin) City *153*
Ault (Weld) Town *159*
Aurora (Adams) City *128*
Aurora (Arapahoe) City *129*
Aurora (Douglas) City *137*
Avon (Eagle) Town *137*
Baca County *130*
Basalt (Eagle) Town *137*
Basalt (Pitkin) Town *153*
Battlement Mesa (Garfield) CDP *140*
Bayfield (La Plata) Town *146*
Bennett (Adams) Town *128*
Bent County *131*
Berthoud (Larimer) Town *146*
Bethune (Kit Carson) Town *145*
Black Forest (El Paso) CDP *138*
Black Hawk (Gilpin) Town *141*
Blanca (Costilla) Town *134*
Blue River (Summit) Town *158*
Bonanza City (Saguache) Town *156*
Boone (Pueblo) Town *154*
Boulder (Boulder) City *131*
Boulder County *131*
Bow Mar (Arapahoe) Town *129*
Bow Mar (Jefferson) Town *143*
Branson (Las Animas) Town *147*
Breckenridge (Summit) Town *158*
Brighton (Adams) City *128*
Brighton (Weld) City *159*
Brookside (Fremont) Town *139*
Broomfield (Adams) City *128*
Broomfield (Boulder) City *131*
Broomfield (Jefferson) City *144*
Broomfield (Weld) City *159*
Brush (Morgan) City *151*
Buena Vista (Chaffee) Town *132*
Burlington (Kit Carson) City *145*
Byers (Arapahoe) CDP *129*
Calhan (El Paso) Town *138*
Campion (Larimer) CDP *146*
Campo (Baca) Town *130*
Canon City (Fremont) City *139*
Carbondale (Garfield) Town *140*
Cascade-Chipita Park (El Paso)
  CDP *138*
Castle Rock (Douglas) Town *137*
Castlewood (Arapahoe) CDP *129*
Cedaredge (Delta) Town *135*
Center (Rio Grande) Town *155*
Center (Saguache) Town *156*
Central City (Gilpin) City *141*
Chaffee County *132*
Cheraw (Otero) Town *151*
Cherry Hills Village (Arapahoe) City *129*

Cheyenne County *133*
Cheyenne Wells (Cheyenne) Town *133*
Cimarron Hills (El Paso) CDP *138*
Clear Creek County *133*
Clifton (Mesa) CDP *148*
Coal Creek (Fremont) Town *139*
Cokedale (Las Animas) Town *147*
Collbran (Mesa) Town *148*
Colorado City (Pueblo) CDP *154*
Colorado Springs (El Paso) City *138*
Columbine (Arapahoe) CDP *129*
Columbine (Jefferson) CDP *144*
Columbine Valley (Arapahoe) Town . *129*
Commerce City (Adams) City *128*
Conejos (Conejos) Town *134*
Conejos County *134*
Cortez (Montezuma) City *150*
Costilla County *134*
Craig (Moffat) City *149*
Crawford (Delta) Town *135*
Creede (Mineral) Town *149*
Crested Butte (Gunnison) Town *142*
Crestone (Saguache) Town *156*
Cripple Creek (Teller) City *158*
Crook (Logan) Town *148*
Crowley (Crowley) Town *135*
Crowley County *135*
Custer County *135*
Dacono (Weld) Town *159*
De Beque (Mesa) Town *148*
Deer Trail (Arapahoe) Town *129*
Del Norte (Rio Grande) Town *155*
Delta (Delta) City *136*
Delta County *135*
Denver (Denver) City *136*
Denver County *136*
Derby (Adams) CDP *128*
Dillon (Summit) Town *158*
Dinosaur (Moffat) Town *149*
Dolores (Montezuma) Town *150*
Dolores County *136*
Douglas County *137*
Dove Creek (Dolores) Town *136*
Durango (La Plata) City *146*
Eads (Kiowa) Town *144*
Eagle (Eagle) Town *137*
Eagle County *137*
Eagle-Vail (Eagle) CDP *137*
Eaton (Weld) Town *159*
Eckley (Yuma) Town *161*
Edgewater (Jefferson) City *144*
Elbert County *138*
Elizabeth (Elbert) Town *138*
El Jebel (Eagle) CDP *137*
El Paso County *138*
Empire (Clear Creek) Town *133*
Englewood (Arapahoe) City *129*
Erie (Boulder) Town *131*
Erie (Weld) Town *159*
Estes Park (Larimer) Town *146*
Evans (Weld) City *159*
Evergreen (Jefferson) CDP *144*
Fairplay (Park) Town *152*
Federal Heights (Adams) City *128*
Firestone (Weld) Town *159*
Flagler (Kit Carson) Town *145*
Fleming (Logan) Town *148*
Florence (Fremont) City *139*
Fort Carson (El Paso) Military
  Facility *139*

Fort Collins (Larimer) City *146*
Fort Lupton (Weld) City *159*
Fort Morgan (Morgan) City *151*
Fountain (El Paso) City *139*
Fowler (Otero) Town *151*
Fraser (Grand) Town *141*
Frederick (Weld) Town *159*
Fremont County *139*
Frisco (Summit) Town *158*
Fruita (Mesa) Town *149*
Fruitvale (Mesa) CDP *149*
Garden City (Weld) Town *160*
Garfield County *140*
Gateway (Douglas) CDP *137*
Genesee (Jefferson) CDP *144*
Genoa (Lincoln) Town *147*
Georgetown (Clear Creek) Town *133*
Gilcrest (Weld) Town *160*
Gilpin County *141*
Glendale (Arapahoe) City *130*
Gleneagle (El Paso) CDP *139*
Glenwood Springs (Garfield) City *140*
Golden (Jefferson) City *144*
Granada (Prowers) Town *153*
Granby (Grand) Town *141*
Grand County *141*
Grand Junction (Mesa) City *149*
Grand Lake (Grand) Town *141*
Greeley (Weld) City *160*
Green Mountain Falls (El Paso)
  Town *139*
Green Mountain Falls (Teller) Town *158*
Greenwood Village (Arapahoe) City . *130*
Grover (Weld) Town *160*
Gunbarrel (Boulder) CDP *131*
Gunnison (Gunnison) City *142*
Gunnison County *142*
Gypsum (Eagle) Town *137*
Hartman (Prowers) Town *154*
Haswell (Kiowa) Town *144*
Haxtun (Phillips) Town *153*
Hayden (Routt) Town *155*
Highlands Ranch (Douglas) CDP *137*
Hillrose (Morgan) Town *151*
Hinsdale County *142*
Holly (Prowers) Town *154*
Holyoke (Phillips) Town *153*
Hooper (Alamosa) Town *129*
Hotchkiss (Delta) Town *136*
Hot Sulphur Springs (Grand) Town .. *141*
Hudson (Weld) Town *160*
Huerfano County *143*
Hugo (Lincoln) Town *148*
Idaho Springs (Clear Creek) City *133*
Ignacio (La Plata) Town *146*
Iliff (Logan) Town *148*
Jackson County *143*
Jamestown (Boulder) Town *131*
Jefferson County *143*
Johnstown (Weld) Town *160*
Julesburg (Sedgwick) Town *157*
Keenesburg (Weld) Town *160*
Ken Caryl (Jefferson) CDP *144*
Keota (Weld) Town *160*
Kersey (Weld) Town *160*
Kim (Las Animas) Town *147*
Kiowa (Elbert) Town *138*
Kiowa County *144*
Kit Carson (Cheyenne) Town *133*
Kit Carson County *145*

American Places Dictionary   COLORADO

Kremmling (Grand) Town *141*
Lafayette (Boulder) City *131*
La Jara (Conejos) Town *134*
La Junta (Otero) City *151*
Lake City (Hinsdale) Town *142*
Lake County *145*
Lakeside (Jefferson) Town *144*
Lakewood (Jefferson) City *144*
Lamar (Prowers) City *154*
La Plata County *146*
Larimer County *146*
Larkspur (Douglas) Town *137*
La Salle (Weld) Town *160*
Las Animas (Bent) City *131*
Las Animas County *147*
La Veta (Huerfano) Town *143*
Leadville (Lake) City *145*
Leadville North (Lake) CDP *145*
Limon (Lincoln) Town *148*
Lincoln County *147*
Lincoln Park (Fremont) CDP *140*
Littleton (Arapahoe) City *130*
Littleton (Douglas) City *137*
Lochbuie (Weld) Town *160*
Logan County *148*
Log Lane Village (Morgan) Town *151*
Longmont (Boulder) City *132*
Louisville (Boulder) City *132*
Loveland (Larimer) City *146*
Lyons (Boulder) Town *132*
Manassa (Conejos) Town *134*
Mancos (Montezuma) Town *150*
Manitou Springs (El Paso) City *139*
Manzanola (Otero) Town *151*
Marble (Gunnison) Town *142*
Mead (Weld) Town *160*
Meeker (Rio Blanco) Town *154*
Merino (Logan) Town *148*
Mesa County *148*
Milliken (Weld) Town *160*
Mineral County *149*
Minturn (Eagle) Town *137*
Moffat (Saguache) Town *156*
Moffat County *149*
Monte Vista (Rio Grande) City *155*
Montezuma (Summit) Town *158*
Montezuma County *150*
Montrose (Montrose) City *150*
Montrose County *150*
Monument (El Paso) Town *139*
Morgan County *151*
Morrison (Jefferson) Town *144*
Mountain View (Jefferson) Town *144*
Mount Crested Butte (Gunnison)
   Town *142*
Naturita (Montrose) Town *150*
Nederland (Boulder) Town *132*
New Castle (Garfield) Town *140*
Niwot (Boulder) CDP *132*
Northglenn (Adams) City *128*
Northglenn (Weld) City *160*
Norwood (San Miguel) Town *157*

Nucla (Montrose) Town *150*
Nunn (Weld) Town *160*
Oak Creek (Routt) Town *155*
Olathe (Montrose) Town *150*
Olney Springs (Crowley) Town *135*
Ophir (San Miguel) Town *157*
Orchard City (Delta) Town *136*
Orchard Mesa (Mesa) CDP *149*
Ordway (Crowley) Town *135*
Otero County *151*
Otis (Washington) Town *159*
Ouray (Ouray) City *152*
Ouray County *152*
Ovid (Sedgwick) Town *157*
Pagosa Springs (Archuleta) Town *130*
Palisade (Mesa) Town *149*
Palmer Lake (El Paso) Town *139*
Paoli (Phillips) Town *153*
Paonia (Delta) Town *136*
Parachute (Garfield) Town *140*
Park County *152*
Parker (Douglas) Town *137*
Peetz (Logan) Town *148*
Penrose (Fremont) CDP *140*
Phillips County *153*
Pierce (Weld) Town *160*
The Pinery (Douglas) CDP *137*
Pitkin (Gunnison) Town *142*
Pitkin County *153*
Platteville (Weld) Town *160*
Poncha Springs (Chaffee) Town *132*
Ponderosa Park (Elbert) CDP *138*
Pritchett (Baca) Town *130*
Prospect Heights (Fremont) Town *140*
Prowers County *153*
Pueblo (Pueblo) City *154*
Pueblo County *154*
Pueblo West (Pueblo) CDP *154*
Ramah (El Paso) Town *139*
Rangely (Rio Blanco) Town *154*
Raymer (Weld) Town *160*
Red Cliff (Eagle) Town *138*
Redlands (Mesa) CDP *149*
Rico (Dolores) Town *136*
Ridgway (Ouray) Town *152*
Rifle (Garfield) City *140*
Rio Blanco County *154*
Rio Grande County *155*
Rockvale (Fremont) Town *140*
Rocky Ford (Otero) City *151*
Romeo (Conejos) Town *134*
Routt County *155*
Rye (Pueblo) Town *154*
Saguache (Saguache) Town *156*
Saguache County *156*
Salida (Chaffee) City *132*
Sanford (Conejos) Town *134*
San Juan County *156*
San Luis (Costilla) Town *134*
San Miguel County *157*
Sawpit (San Miguel) Town *157*
Security-Widefield (El Paso) CDP *139*

Sedgwick (Sedgwick) Town *157*
Sedgwick County *157*
Seibert (Kit Carson) Town *145*
Severance (Weld) Town *160*
Sheridan (Arapahoe) City *130*
Sheridan Lake (Kiowa) Town *145*
Sherrelwood (Adams) CDP *128*
Silt (Garfield) Town *140*
Silver Cliff (Custer) Town *135*
Silver Plume (Clear Creek) Town *133*
Silverthorne (Summit) Town *158*
Silverton (San Juan) Town *156*
Simla (Elbert) Town *138*
Snowmass Village (Pitkin) Town *153*
Southglenn (Arapahoe) CDP *130*
Springfield (Baca) Town *130*
Starkville (Las Animas) Town *147*
Steamboat Springs (Routt) City *155*
Sterling (Logan) City *148*
Stratmoor (El Paso) CDP *139*
Stratton (Kit Carson) Town *145*
Sugar City (Crowley) Town *135*
Summit County *158*
Superior (Boulder) Town *132*
Superior (Jefferson) Town *144*
Swink (Otero) Town *152*
Teller County *158*
Telluride (San Miguel) Town *157*
Thornton (Adams) City *128*
Timnath (Larimer) Town *146*
Towaoc (Montezuma) CDP *150*
Trinidad (Las Animas) City *147*
Two Buttes (Baca) Town *130*
Vail (Eagle) Town *138*
Victor (Teller) City *158*
Vilas (Baca) Town *131*
Vona (Kit Carson) Town *145*
Walden (Jackson) Town *143*
Walsenburg (Huerfano) City *143*
Walsh (Baca) Town *131*
Ward (Boulder) Town *132*
Washington County *159*
Welby (Adams) CDP *128*
Weld County *159*
Wellington (Larimer) Town *147*
Westcliffe (Custer) Town *135*
Westminster (Adams) City *128*
Westminster (Jefferson) City *144*
Westminster East (Adams) CDP *128*
Wheat Ridge (Jefferson) City *144*
Wiggins (Morgan) Town *151*
Wiley (Prowers) Town *154*
Williamsburg (Fremont) Town *140*
Windsor (Weld) Town *161*
Winter Park (Grand) Town *141*
Woodland Park (Teller) City *158*
Woodmoor (El Paso) CDP *139*
Wray (Yuma) City *161*
Yampa (Routt) Town *155*
Yuma (Yuma) City *161*
Yuma County *161*

163

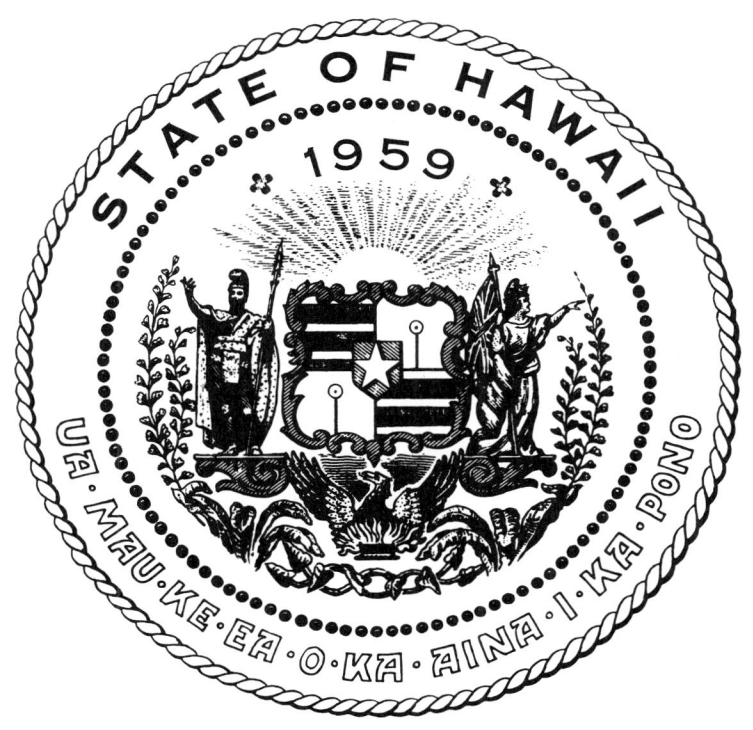

Hawaii

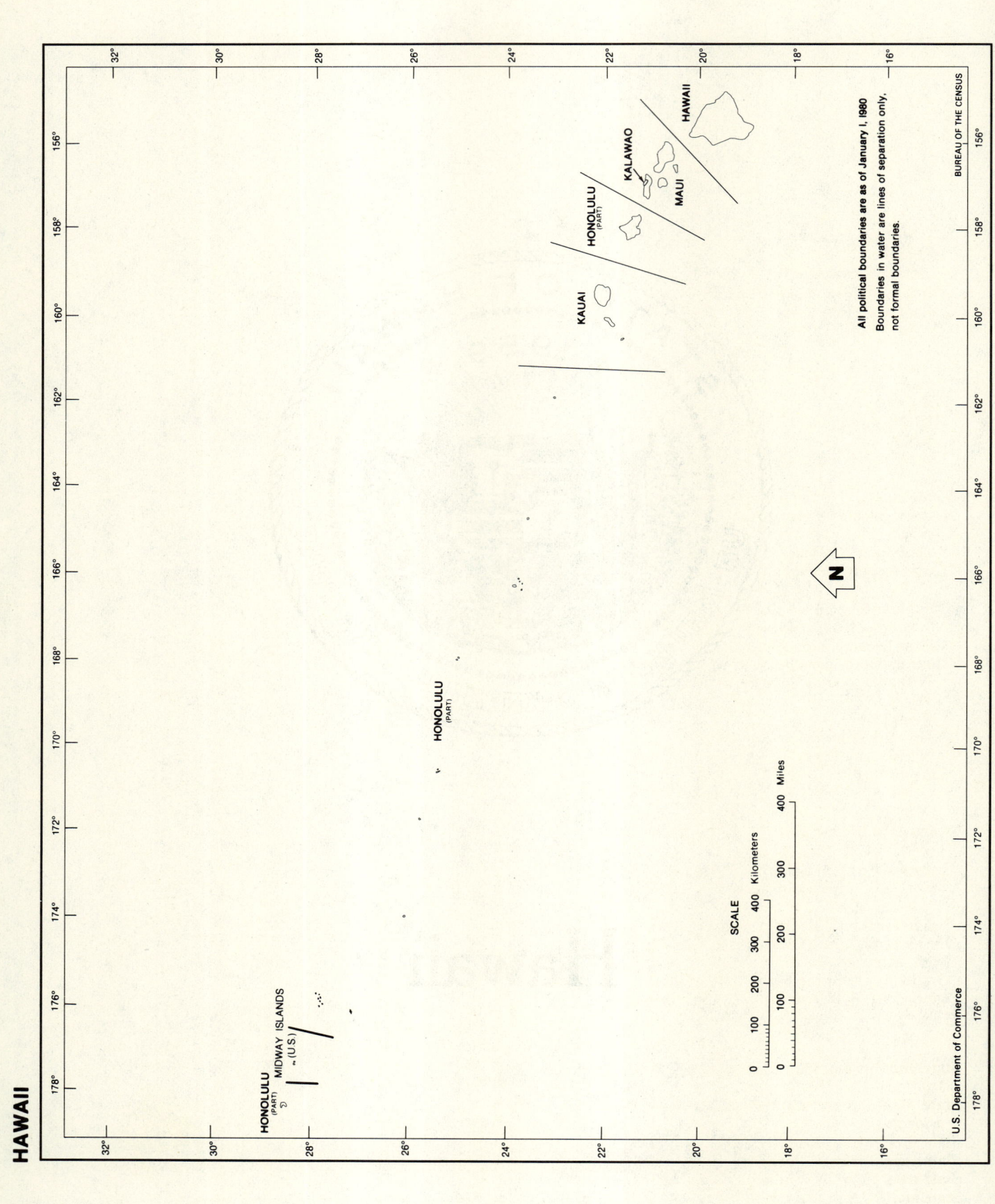

Hawaii

Population: 1,108,229 (1990); 964,691 (1980)
Population rank (1990): 41
Percent population change (1980–1990): 14.9
Population projection: 1,253,000 (1995); 1,368,000 (2000)

Area: total: 10,932 sq. mi.; 6,423 sq. mi. land, 4,508 sq. mi. water
Area rank: 43
Highest elevation: 13,796 ft., Mauna Kea (Hawaii County)
Lowest point: sea level

State capital: Honolulu (Honolulu County)
Largest populated place: Honolulu CDP Census designated place (365,272)
Second largest populated place: Hilo CDP (37,808)
Largest county: Honolulu (836,231)

Total housing units: 389,810
No. of occupied housing units: 356,267
Vacant housing units (%): 8.6
Distribution of population by race and Hispanic origin (%):
  White: 33.4
  Black: 2.5
  Hispanic (any race): 7.3
  Native American: 0.5
  Asian/Pacific: 61.8
  Other: 1.9

Admission date: August 21, 1959 (50th state).

Location: In the middle of the North Pacific Ocean, about 2,400 miles southwest of the U.S. mainland.

Name Origin: Unknown; possibly from *Hawaii-Loa*, the name of the traditional discoverer of the islands, or from *Hawaiki*, the traditional Polynesia homeland. Originally called the *Sandwich Islands* (for the Earl of Sandwich) by British explorer Capt. James Cook.

State bird: nene or Hawaiian goose *(Nesochen sandvicensis)*
State fish: humuhumunukunukuapuaa *(Rhinecantus aculeatus)*
State flower: pua aloalo (Hibiscus; *rosa-sinensis*)
State song: "Hawaii Ponoi"
State tree: kukui or candlenut *(Aleurites moluccana)*
State motto: *Ua mau ke ea o ka aina i ka pono* (Hawaiian 'The Life of the Land Is Perpetuated in Righteousness')
State nicknames: Aloha State; Paradise of the Pacific

Area code: 808
Time zone: Hawaii-Aleutian Standard Time (2 hours earlier than Pacific Standard Time)
Abbreviations: HI (postal); Haw. (traditional)

Local Government

Counties

Hawaii has four counties with governments: Hawaii, Maui, Honolulu (the island of Oahu and the smaller Hawaiian islands), and Kauai. Each has an elected mayor and council. A fifth county, Kalawao, is on the Kalanpapa Peninsula on the northern coast of the island of Molokai. It is the site of a colony for victims of leprosy or Hansen's disease (Fr. Joseph Damien de Veuster worked here, 1873–1889) and is administered by the state department of health.

The county is the main unit of local government in Hawaii.

Municipalities

The City and County of Honolulu is a single government entity and is the only incorporated municipality in Hawaii. Honolulu district consists of the city proper, but has no separate government. Other population centers are recognized as census designated places (CDPs) by the U.S. Bureau of the Census.

Settlement History and Early Development

Hawaii's earliest inhabitants were Polynesians who sailed from other Pacific islands about 2,000 years ago. Another group arrived from Tahiti about 800 years ago and dominated the earlier settlers. Although it is possible that Spanish, Dutch, or Japanese ships may have stopped in Hawaii during the 1500s, the earliest documented white exploration was by British Captain James Cook in January 1778. Cook was at first hailed as a god by the natives, but was killed the next year during a dispute between his men and the Hawaiians.

Many other ships followed to trade with the Hawaiians. Unfortunately, Europeans also brought diseases from other parts of the world that killed many native Hawaiians during the late eighteenth and early nineteenth centuries.

Kamehameha Dynasty

In a war that lasted from 1782 to 1792, a local chief, Kamehameha, gained control of the island of Hawaii. By 1795 he also controlled the other main islands except for Kauai and Niihau, which finally accepted his rule in 1810. King Kamehameha and later kings prospered from the trade of sandalwood to China. Hawaii became a supply port for whaling ships from the early to the mid-1800s. A sugar plantation began operating in 1835 on Kauai. Although pineapples may have been planted as early as 1813, they were not grown commercially until the 1880s.

When Kamehameha I's son, Liholiho, became king after his father's death in 1819, he took the name Kamehameha II. He abolished the local religion. The next year, Protestant missionaries arrived and converted many Hawaiians to Christianity. When Roman Catholic missionaries arrived in 1827, they met with resistance from Hawaiian chiefs, who forced the Catholics to leave in 1830. Roman Catholic converts were imprisoned, but a French blockade of Honolulu in 1839 forced the Hawaiians to release them and guarantee religious freedom to Catholics.

The Kingdom of Hawaii

The reign of Kamehameha III (younger brother of the previous king), which began in 1824, saw the establishment of public schools, the first newspapers, and Honolulu as the capital of the kingdom. Hawaii adopted its first constitution in 1840, and in 1842 the United States recognized the Kingdom of Hawaii as an independent government. In 1848 a law called the Great Mahele (division) provided that the land in the islands, which had formerly belonged exclusively to the king, would be divided among King Kamehameha III and his chiefs, who returned most of it to the government. Then the Hawaiian people were allowed to claim land or buy homesteads.

During the second half of the nineteenth century Hawaii attracted immigrants from a variety of backgrounds: Chinese, Polynesian, Japanese, Portuguese, Filipino, Korean, and Puerto Rican. Many of these people came to work on the sugar cane plantations.

The "Merry Monarch," King Kalakaua, reigned from 1874 to 1891. His reign was marked by political dissension between the king and the legislature and dissatisfaction with the monarchy on the part of the large sugar cane planters. However, Kalakaua is remembered for bringing back many of the old Hawaiian customs, such as the traditional Polynesian music and the hula dance. The grass skirt that is often associated with Hawaii was brought to the islands from Samoa during this period. Under Kalakaua sugar cane continued to be a vital crop, and the pineapple industry began after plants were shipped to Hawaii from Jamaica around 1885. In 1887 King Kalakaua granted the U.S. exclusive rights to use Pearl Harbor as a naval base.

The Republic of Hawaii

When Kalakaua died in 1891, his sister Liliuokalani became queen. When she tried to increase the power of the monarchy she was overthrown in 1893 by a coalition of nine Americans, two Britons, and two Germans, aided by a landing force of American marines and sailors. Following the bloodless coup, the Republic of Hawaii was formed in 1894 with Sanford B. Dole as president. The new government was largely controlled by American business executives.

In 1898 sugar cane planters influenced the U.S. to annex Hawaii as a possession (thus giving the planters more favorable trading terms). In 1900 the islands became a U.S. territory. Just before World War I, the U.S. began building its naval base at Pearl Harbor. Army camps were established on Oahu. After World War I a statehood movement began but met with little success.

World War II

On December 7, 1941, Japanese carrier-based planes attacked the U.S. naval base at Pearl Harbor and the airfields on Oahu. The attack precipitated the U.S. declaration of war against Japan and its ally, Nazi Germany. Hawaii was the headquarters for the U.S. campaign against Japan. Despite fears on the part of the U.S. government of disloyalty, thousands of Hawaiians of every background fought bravely for the U.S. side.

Statehood

The loyalty of Hawaiians in World War II and in the Korean War helped in the long campaign for statehood. The first bill for statehood had been introduced in the U.S. Congress in 1919. Hawaii finally became the 50th U.S. state on August 21, 1959.

From the 1960s until the present, tourism has been a major part of Hawaii's economy. Heavy industry is represented by an oil refinery, steel mill, and cement plants. The growth and processing of sugar cane and pineapples are important industries, as is aquaculture, the commercial growth of fish, oysters, and shrimp.

State Boundaries

When Hawaii became a state in 1959, its borders were the same as those established for the territory in 1900, with the exception of the islands of Palmyra, Midway, Johnston, and Sand, and of the Kingman Reef, which were not included within the state's boundaries.

Hawaii Counties

Hawaii
Honolulu
Kalawao
Kauai
Maui

American Places Dictionary HAWAII, Hawaii County

> ## Hawaii County
> **County Seat: Hilo (ZIP: 96720)**
>
> **Pop:** 120,317 (1990); 92,053 (1980) **Pop Density:** 29.9
> **Land:** 4028.2 sq. mi.; **Water:** 1058.7 sq. mi. **Area Code:** 808
>
> Southernmost of the Islands, bordered on the north by Alenuihaha Channel; county is coextensive with the island. Established 1905 (prior to statehood).
>
> **Name origin:** In Hawaii the name has no meaning, but in the rest of Polynesia it is the name of the underworld or of the ancestral home. Sometimes translated as 'beyond the doors of death.' Called the "Big Island."

Captain Cook CDP
ZIP: 96704 **Lat:** 19-30-03 N **Long:** 155-54-12 W
Pop: 2,595 (1990); 2,008 (1980) **Pop Density:** 212.7
Land: 12.2 sq. mi.; **Water:** 0.0 sq. mi. **Elev:** 1320 ft.

In the west-central part of the island of Hawaii.

Name origin: For English navigator and explorer, Capt. James Cook (1728–79), who was the first known European to reach the Hawaiian Islands, which he named the Sandwich Islands for the Earl of Sandwich, Britain's chief naval minister.

Halaula CDP
ZIP: 96755 **Lat:** 20-13-55 N **Long:** 155-47-00 W
Pop: 496 (1990) **Pop Density:** 183.7
Land: 2.7 sq. mi.; **Water:** 0.3 sq. mi.

On the northern tip of the island of Hawaii.

Name origin: From Hawaiian term for the red pandanus plant.

Hawaiian Beaches CDP
Lat: 19-32-34 N **Long:** 154-54-56 W
Pop: 2,846 (1990) **Pop Density:** 112.0
Land: 25.4 sq. mi.; **Water:** 0.1 sq. mi.

Hawaiian Ocean View CDP
Lat: 19-04-07 N **Long:** 155-45-53 W
Pop: 969 (1990) **Pop Density:** 9.5
Land: 102.0 sq. mi.; **Water:** 4.5 sq. mi.

Hawaiian Paradise Park CDP
Lat: 19-35-35 N **Long:** 154-58-23 W
Pop: 3,389 (1990) **Pop Density:** 150.6
Land: 22.5 sq. mi.; **Water:** 0.5 sq. mi.

Hawi CDP
ZIP: 96719 **Lat:** 20-14-34 N **Long:** 155-50-03 W
Pop: 924 (1990); 795 (1980) **Pop Density:** 770.0
Land: 1.2 sq. mi.; **Water:** 0.0 sq. mi. **Elev:** 600 ft.

On the northern tip of the island of Hawaii.

Hilo CDP
ZIP: 96720 **Lat:** 19-41-46 N **Long:** 155-05-15 W
Pop: 37,808 (1990); 35,269 (1980) **Pop Density:** 696.3
Land: 54.3 sq. mi.; **Water:** 4.2 sq. mi. **Elev:** 38 ft.

On the east-central coast of the island of Hawaii.

Name origin: For either the first night of the new moon or for a Polynesian navigator.

Holualoa CDP
ZIP: 96725 **Lat:** 19-38-09 N **Long:** 155-55-45 W
Pop: 3,834 (1990); 1,243 (1980) **Pop Density:** 271.9
Land: 14.1 sq. mi.; **Water:** 0.6 sq. mi. **Elev:** 1372 ft.

In the west-central part of the island of Hawaii, south of Kailua Kona.

Name origin: From Hawaiian term meaning 'long sled course.'

Honalo CDP
Lat: 19-34-14 N **Long:** 155-54-27 W
Pop: 1,926 (1990) **Pop Density:** 65.7
Land: 29.3 sq. mi.; **Water:** 0.0 sq. mi.

In the west-central part of the island of Hawaii, south of Kailua Kona.

Honaunau-Napoopoo CDP
Lat: 19-27-09 N **Long:** 155-52-51 W
Pop: 2,373 (1990) **Pop Density:** 62.4
Land: 38.0 sq. mi.; **Water:** 2.2 sq. mi.

Honokaa CDP
ZIP: 96727 **Lat:** 20-04-37 N **Long:** 155-28-02 W
Pop: 2,186 (1990); 1,936 (1980) **Pop Density:** 1681.5
Land: 1.3 sq. mi.; **Water:** 0.0 sq. mi. **Elev:** 1114 ft.

On the northeastern coast of the island of Hawaii.

Name origin: From Hawaiian term meaning 'rolling (as stones) bay.'

Honomu CDP
ZIP: 96728 **Lat:** 19-52-21 N **Long:** 155-06-53 W
Pop: 532 (1990); 559 (1980) **Pop Density:** 1064.0
Land: 0.5 sq. mi.; **Water:** 0.0 sq. mi. **Elev:** 300 ft.

On the eastern coast of the island of Hawaii, north of Hilo.

Name origin: From Hawaiian term meaning 'silent bay.'

Kahaluu-Keauhou CDP
Lat: 19-34-31 N **Long:** 155-57-37 W
Pop: 1,990 (1990) **Pop Density:** 337.3
Land: 5.9 sq. mi.; **Water:** 1.7 sq. mi.

Kailua CDP
ZIP: 96740 **Lat:** 19-39-51 N **Long:** 155-57-50 W
Pop: 9,126 (1990); 4,751 (1980) **Pop Density:** 261.5
Land: 34.9 sq. mi.; **Water:** 4.6 sq. mi.

Kalaoa CDP
Lat: 19-43-32 N **Long:** 156-01-06 W
Pop: 4,490 (1990) **Pop Density:** 122.3
Land: 36.7 sq. mi.; **Water:** 4.2 sq. mi.

Kapaau
CDP
ZIP: 96755 **Lat:** 20-13-50 N **Long:** 155-48-39 W
Pop: 1,083 (1990); 612 (1980) **Pop Density:** 492.3
Land: 2.2 sq. mi.; **Water:** 0.0 sq. mi. **Elev:** 481 ft.
On northeastern tip of the island of Hawaii.
Name origin: From Hawaiian 'elevated portion of an ancient place of worship.'

Keaau
CDP
ZIP: 96749 **Lat:** 19-37-09 N **Long:** 155-02-22 W
Pop: 1,584 (1990); 775 (1980) **Pop Density:** 633.6
Land: 2.5 sq. mi.; **Water:** 0.0 sq. mi. **Elev:** 359 ft.
In east-central Hawaii.

Kealakekua
CDP
ZIP: 96750 **Lat:** 19-32-24 N **Long:** 155-52-56 W
Pop: 1,453 (1990); 1,033 (1980) **Pop Density:** 193.7
Land: 7.5 sq. mi.; **Water:** 0.0 sq. mi. **Elev:** 1571 ft.
On the west-central coast of the island of Hawaii.
Name origin: From Hawaiian term meaning 'pathway (of) the god.'

Kukuihaele
CDP
ZIP: 96727 **Lat:** 20-07-31 N **Long:** 155-34-14 W
Pop: 316 (1990); 332 (1980) **Pop Density:** 185.9
Land: 1.7 sq. mi.; **Water:** 0.3 sq. mi. **Elev:** 30 ft.
On the northeastern coast of the island of Hawaii.
Name origin: From Hawaiian term meaning 'traveling light' for the night marchers seen here.

Kurtistown
CDP
ZIP: 96760 **Lat:** 19-35-20 N **Long:** 155-04-15 W
Pop: 910 (1990) **Pop Density:** 178.4
Land: 5.1 sq. mi.; **Water:** 0.0 sq. mi. **Elev:** 651 ft.
Name origin: For A.G. Curtis, a pioneer with the Olaa Sugar Company when it began operations in 1902.

Laupahoehoe
CDP
ZIP: 96764 **Lat:** 19-58-42 N **Long:** 155-14-24 W
Pop: 508 (1990); 500 (1980) **Pop Density:** 241.9
Land: 2.1 sq. mi.; **Water:** 0.2 sq. mi. **Elev:** 380 ft.
On the northeastern coast of the island of Hawaii.
Name origin: From Hawaiian term meaning 'smooth lava flat.'

Mountain View
CDP
ZIP: 96771 **Lat:** 19-31-14 N **Long:** 155-08-57 W
Pop: 3,075 (1990); 540 (1980) **Pop Density:** 36.7
Land: 83.8 sq. mi.; **Water:** 0.0 sq. mi. **Elev:** 1398 ft.
In the east-central part of the island of Hawaii.

Naalehu
CDP
ZIP: 96772 **Lat:** 19-04-37 N **Long:** 155-34-31 W
Pop: 1,027 (1990); 1,168 (1980) **Pop Density:** 466.8
Land: 2.2 sq. mi.; **Water:** 0.0 sq. mi. **Elev:** 674 ft.
On the southeastern coast of the island of Hawaii.
Name origin: From Hawaiian term meaning 'the volcanic ashes.'

Paauilo
CDP
ZIP: 96776 **Lat:** 20-02-36 N **Long:** 155-22-18 W
Pop: 620 (1990); 755 (1980) **Pop Density:** 563.6
Land: 1.1 sq. mi.; **Water:** 0.0 sq. mi. **Elev:** 766 ft.
On the northeastern coast of the island of Hawaii.

Pahala
CDP
ZIP: 96777 **Lat:** 19-12-11 N **Long:** 155-28-56 W
Pop: 1,520 (1990); 1,619 (1980) **Pop Density:** 1900.0
Land: 0.8 sq. mi.; **Water:** 0.0 sq. mi. **Elev:** 900 ft.
In the southeastern part of the island of Hawaii.
Name origin: From Hawaiian term meaning 'cultivation by burning mulch.'

Pahoa
CDP
ZIP: 96778 **Lat:** 19-29-55 N **Long:** 154-56-55 W
Pop: 1,027 (1990); 1,038 (1980) **Pop Density:** 446.5
Land: 2.3 sq. mi.; **Water:** 0.0 sq. mi. **Elev:** 655 ft.
In the east-central part of the island of Hawaii.
Name origin: From Hawaiian term meaning 'daggers.'

Papaikou
CDP
ZIP: 96781 **Lat:** 19-47-38 N **Long:** 155-05-47 W
Pop: 1,634 (1990); 1,567 (1980) **Pop Density:** 1089.3
Land: 1.5 sq. mi.; **Water:** 0.6 sq. mi. **Elev:** 200 ft.
On the east-central coast of the island of Hawaii, north of Hilo.
Name origin: From Hawaiian term meaning 'hut (in a) grove,' because a chief had a shelter here.

Paukaa
CDP
ZIP: 96720 **Lat:** 19-45-51 N **Long:** 155-05-54 W
Pop: 495 (1990); 544 (1980) **Pop Density:** 1237.5
Land: 0.4 sq. mi.; **Water:** 0.1 sq. mi. **Elev:** 155 ft.
On the east-central coast of the island of Hawaii, north of Hilo.

Pepeekeo
CDP
ZIP: 96783 **Lat:** 19-50-04 N **Long:** 155-06-31 W
Pop: 1,813 (1990) **Pop Density:** 1648.2
Land: 1.1 sq. mi.; **Water:** 0.0 sq. mi. **Elev:** 487 ft.
On the east-central coast of the island of Hawaii, north of Hilo.
Name origin: From Hawaiian term meaning 'the food crushed,' as by warriors in battle.

Puako
CDP
ZIP: 96743 **Lat:** 19-56-41 N **Long:** 155-52-15 W
Pop: 397 (1990) **Pop Density:** 38.5
Land: 10.3 sq. mi.; **Water:** 5.5 sq. mi.
In the north-central part of the island of Hawaii, southwest of Honokaa.
Name origin: From Hawaiian term meaning 'sugarcane blossom.'

Volcano
CDP
ZIP: 96785 **Lat:** 19-29-51 N **Long:** 155-14-14 W
Pop: 1,516 (1990) **Pop Density:** 26.7
Land: 56.7 sq. mi.; **Water:** 0.0 sq. mi. **Elev:** 3723 ft.
In the east-central part of the island of Hawaii, northeast of Hawaii National Park.

Waikoloa Village
CDP
ZIP: 96743 **Lat:** 19-55-56 N **Long:** 155-49-39 W
Pop: 2,248 (1990) **Pop Density:** 117.7
Land: 19.1 sq. mi.; **Water:** 0.0 sq. mi.
In the northeastern part of the island of Hawaii.
Name origin: From Hawaiian term meaning 'duck water' or, possibly, from *waiko-loa*, which is the name of a wind.

Waimea   CDP
ZIP: 96743   **Lat:** 20-00-59 N   **Long:** 155-38-11 W
Pop: 5,972 (1990); 1,179 (1980)   **Pop Density:** 154.3
Land: 38.7 sq. mi.; **Water:** 0.1 sq. mi.   **Elev:** 2669 ft.
In the north-central part of the island of Hawaii.
Name origin: From Hawaiian term meaning 'reddish water,' referring to erosion of red soil.

Wainaku   CDP
ZIP: 96720   **Lat:** 19-44-50 N   **Long:** 155-06-03 W
Pop: 1,243 (1990); 1,045 (1980)   **Pop Density:** 956.2
Land: 1.3 sq. mi.; **Water:** 0.1 sq. mi.
On the east-central coast of the island of Hawaii, north of Hilo.
Name origin: From Hawaiian term meaning 'pushing water.'

Honolulu County
County Seat: Honolulu (ZIP: 96801)

Pop: 836,231 (1990); 762,565 (1980)   **Pop Density:** 1393.3
Land: 600.2 sq. mi.; **Water:** 1526.8 sq. mi.   **Area Code:** 808

Between the islands of Kauai and Molokai; bordered on west by Kauai Channel and on southeast by Kaiwi Channel. Established 1905 (prior to statehood); legally the City and County of Honolulu with one municipal government; includes the islands of Oahu and small ones northwest of Kauai. About 80% of the state's population lives in Honolulu County.

Name origin: From two Polynesian words, *hono* 'fair haven' and *lulu* 'calm' or 'quiet,' referring to Mamala Bay, into which Pearl Harbor opens.

Ahuimanu   CDP
ZIP: 96744   **Lat:** 21-26-28 N   **Long:** 157-50-11 W
Pop: 8,387 (1990); 6,238 (1980)   **Pop Density:** 4659.4
Land: 1.8 sq. mi.; **Water:** 0.0 sq. mi.
In southeastern Oahu, 6 mi. northwest of Kaneohe.
Name origin: From Hawaiian term meaning 'bird cluster,' possibly because birds from nearby Moku-manu were caught here and tied together in bunches.

Aiea   CDP
ZIP: 96701   **Lat:** 21-23-18 N   **Long:** 157-55-40 W
Pop: 8,906 (1990); 32,879 (1980)   **Pop Density:** 5566.3
Land: 1.6 sq. mi.; **Water:** 0.1 sq. mi.
In southern Oahu, 5 mi. northwest of Honolulu.
Name origin: For the Nothocestrum tree.

Aliamanu   Military Facility
ZIP: 96818   **Lat:** 21-21-53 N   **Long:** 157-54-51 W
Pop: 8,835 (1990)   **Pop Density:** 12621.4
Land: 0.7 sq. mi.; **Water:** 0.0 sq. mi.

Barbers Point Housing   CDP
ZIP: 96862   **Lat:** 21-19-28 N   **Long:** 158-04-59 W
Pop: 2,218 (1990); 1,373 (1980)   **Pop Density:** 7393.3
Land: 0.3 sq. mi.; **Water:** 0.0 sq. mi.
On the southwestern coast of Oahu.
Name origin: For Capt. Henry Barber (d. 1796), who was shipwrecked on a coral shoal here.

Ewa Beach   CDP
ZIP: 96706   **Lat:** 21-18-58 N   **Long:** 158-00-42 W
Pop: 14,315 (1990); 14,369 (1980)   **Pop Density:** 10225.0
Land: 1.4 sq. mi.; **Water:** 0.4 sq. mi.
On the southern coast of Oahu, west of Honolulu.
Name origin: From Hawaiian term meaning 'crooked.'

Ewa Gentry   CDP
    Lat: 21-20-38 N   **Long:** 158-01-50 W
Pop: 1,992 (1990)   **Pop Density:** 6640.0
Land: 0.3 sq. mi.; **Water:** 0.0 sq. mi.

Ewa Villages   CDP
    Lat: 21-20-43 N   **Long:** 158-02-27 W
Pop: 3,780 (1990); 2,637 (1980)   **Pop Density:** 3780.0
Land: 1.0 sq. mi.; **Water:** 0.0 sq. mi.

Fort Shafter   CDP
ZIP: 96819   **Lat:** 21-21-12 N   **Long:** 157-52-27 W
Pop: 2,952 (1990)   **Pop Density:** 1341.8
Land: 2.2 sq. mi.; **Water:** 0.0 sq. mi.
On the southern coast of Oahu, part of Honolulu.
Name origin: For Civil War hero, Maj. Gen. William R. Shafter (1835–1906).

Halawa   CDP
ZIP: 96701   **Lat:** 21-22-46 N   **Long:** 157-55-17 W
Pop: 13,408 (1990)   **Pop Density:** 5829.6
Land: 2.3 sq. mi.; **Water:** 0.0 sq. mi.

Haleiwa   CDP
ZIP: 96712   **Lat:** 21-35-43 N   **Long:** 158-06-31 W
Pop: 2,442 (1990); 2,412 (1980)   **Pop Density:** 1356.7
Land: 1.8 sq. mi.; **Water:** 0.7 sq. mi.   **Elev:** 20 ft.
On the upper northwestern coast of Oahu.
Name origin: From Hawaiian term meaning 'house of [the] frigate bird,' which is a bird much admired for its beauty.

Hauula   CDP
ZIP: 96717   **Lat:** 21-35-26 N   **Long:** 157-55-23 W
Pop: 3,479 (1990); 2,997 (1980)   **Pop Density:** 579.8
Land: 6.0 sq. mi.; **Water:** 0.8 sq. mi.   **Elev:** 20 ft.
On the northeastern coast of Oahu, south of Kahuku.
Name origin: From Hawaiian term meaning 'red hau tree.'

Heeia   CDP
ZIP: 96744   **Lat:** 21-25-40 N   **Long:** 157-49-01 W
Pop: 5,010 (1990); 5,432 (1980)   **Pop Density:** 2505.0
Land: 2.0 sq. mi.; **Water:** 0.3 sq. mi.
On the east-central coast of Oahu, north of Kaneohe.

Hickam Housing   CDP
ZIP: 96818   **Lat:** 21-20-28 N **Long:** 157-57-40 W
Pop: 6,553 (1990); 4,425 (1980)   **Pop Density:** 5460.8
Land: 1.2 sq. mi.; **Water:** 0.3 sq. mi.
On the southern coast of Oahu, on the eastern shore of Pearl Harbor.
Name origin: For Lt. Col. Horace M. Hickam of the U.S. Air Force, who was killed in an airplane accident at Fort Crockett, TX, in 1934.

Honolulu   City
ZIP: 96820   **Lat:** 21-19-02 N **Long:** 157-48-15 W
Pop: 365,272 (1990); 365,048 (1980)   **Pop Density:** 4411.5
Land: 82.8 sq. mi.; **Water:** 19.4 sq. mi.   **Elev:** 18 ft.
On the southern coast of Oahu. Established as a city 1816. State capital since 1820; largest city, and chief port of HI. Official name "City and County of Honolulu." Technically, Honolulu is the entire island of Oahu, but in practice, only the urban area on the southeastern coast is so called. Nicknamed "Crossroads of the Pacific." Major industries include tourism and military bases; diverse manufacturing: food processing (pineapple and sugar cane), cement, clothing.
Name origin: From Hawaiian term meaning 'protected bay.'

Iroquois Point   CDP
ZIP: 96706   **Lat:** 21-19-31 N **Long:** 157-58-52 W
Pop: 4,188 (1990); 3,915 (1980)   **Pop Density:** 8376.0
Land: 0.5 sq. mi.; **Water:** 0.1 sq. mi.
On the southern coast of Oahu, on the western shore of Pearl Harbor.
Name origin: For the Iroquois Indians of NY.

Kaaawa   CDP
ZIP: 96730   **Lat:** 21-33-26 N **Long:** 157-51-25 W
Pop: 1,138 (1990); 959 (1980)   **Pop Density:** 1896.7
Land: 0.6 sq. mi.; **Water:** 0.5 sq. mi.
On the east-central coast of Oahu, south of Kahana Bay.
Name origin: From Hawaiian term meaning 'the wrasse fish.'

Kahaluu   CDP
ZIP: 96744   **Lat:** 21-27-43 N **Long:** 157-50-05 W
Pop: 3,068 (1990); 2,925 (1980)   **Pop Density:** 2556.7
Land: 1.2 sq. mi.; **Water:** 1.1 sq. mi.
On the eastern coast of Oahu.
Name origin: From Hawaiian term meaning 'diving place.'

Kahuku   CDP
ZIP: 96731   **Lat:** 21-40-56 N **Long:** 157-56-46 W
Pop: 2,063 (1990); 935 (1980)   **Pop Density:** 2063.0
Land: 1.0 sq. mi.; **Water:** 1.3 sq. mi.   **Elev:** 20 ft.
On the northeastern coast of Oahu.
Name origin: From Hawaiian term meaning 'the projection.'

Kailua   CDP
ZIP: 96734   **Lat:** 21-24-05 N **Long:** 157-44-18 W
Pop: 36,818 (1990); 35,812 (1980)   **Pop Density:** 5578.5
Land: 6.6 sq. mi.; **Water:** 2.9 sq. mi.
In southeastern Oahu, south of Kaneohe Bay.
Name origin: From Hawaiian term meaning 'two seas.'

Kaneohe   CDP
ZIP: 96744   **Lat:** 21-24-39 N **Long:** 157-47-32 W
Pop: 35,448 (1990); 29,919 (1980)   **Pop Density:** 5370.9
Land: 6.6 sq. mi.; **Water:** 1.9 sq. mi.   **Elev:** 40 ft.
In southeastern Oahu near Kaneohe Bay.
Name origin: From Hawaiian term meaning 'bamboo husband'; one account claims a wife compared her husband's cruelty to the cutting edge of a bamboo knife.

Kaneohe Station   Military Facility
ZIP: 96863   **Lat:** 21-27-00 N **Long:** 157-45-05 W
Pop: 11,662 (1990); 11,615 (1980)   **Pop Density:** 2650.5
Land: 4.4 sq. mi.; **Water:** 1.4 sq. mi.

Kawela Bay   CDP
Lat: 21-42-11 N **Long:** 158-00-35 W
Pop: 366 (1990)   **Pop Density:** 610.0
Land: 0.6 sq. mi.; **Water:** 1.4 sq. mi.

Laie   CDP
ZIP: 96762   **Lat:** 21-38-56 N **Long:** 157-55-31 W
Pop: 5,577 (1990); 4,643 (1980)   **Pop Density:** 4290.0
Land: 1.3 sq. mi.; **Water:** 0.9 sq. mi.   **Elev:** 20 ft.
On the northeastern coast of Oahu.
Name origin: For a sacred princess.

Maili   CDP
ZIP: 96792   **Lat:** 21-25-07 N **Long:** 158-10-49 W
Pop: 6,059 (1990); 5,026 (1980)   **Pop Density:** 6059.0
Land: 1.0 sq. mi.; **Water:** 1.1 sq. mi.
On the west-central coast of Oahu, 2 mi. south of Lualualei.
Name origin: From Hawaiian term meaning 'pebbly,' referring to the beach.

Makaha   CDP
ZIP: 96792   **Lat:** 21-28-05 N **Long:** 158-12-54 W
Pop: 7,990 (1990); 6,582 (1980)   **Pop Density:** 3473.9
Land: 2.3 sq. mi.; **Water:** 2.9 sq. mi.
On the west-central coast of Oahu.
Name origin: From Hawaiian term meaning 'fierce,' for the robberies that took place in ancient times.

Makaha Valley   CDP
Lat: 21-28-56 N **Long:** 158-12-13 W
Pop: 1,012 (1990)   **Pop Density:** 920.0
Land: 1.1 sq. mi.; **Water:** 0.0 sq. mi.

Makakilo City   CDP
ZIP: 96706   **Lat:** 21-21-30 N **Long:** 158-05-18 W
Pop: 9,828 (1990); 7,691 (1980)   **Pop Density:** 3389.0
Land: 2.9 sq. mi.; **Water:** 0.0 sq. mi.
In southwestern Oahu, west of Ewa.
Name origin: From Hawaiian term meaning 'observing eyes.'

Maunawili   CDP
ZIP: 96734   **Lat:** 21-22-20 N **Long:** 157-45-56 W
Pop: 4,847 (1990); 5,239 (1980)   **Pop Density:** 1384.9
Land: 3.5 sq. mi.; **Water:** 0.0 sq. mi.
In southeastern Oahu, southwest of Kailua.
Name origin: From Hawaiian term meaning 'twisted mountain.'

Mililani Town   CDP
ZIP: 96789   **Lat:** 21-26-56 N **Long:** 158-01-05 W
Pop: 29,359 (1990); 21,365 (1980)   **Pop Density:** 7527.9
Land: 3.9 sq. mi.; **Water:** 0.0 sq. mi.
In southern Oahu, on the western bank of West Loch, 1 mi. south of Waipio Acres.
Name origin: From Hawaiian term meaning 'beloved place (of) chiefs.'

Mokuleia — CDP
ZIP: 96791　　Lat: 21-34-55 N Long: 158-10-43 W
Pop: 1,776 (1990); 11,615 (1980)　　Pop Density: 888.0
Land: 2.0 sq. mi.; Water: 3.1 sq. mi.
On the northwestern coast of Oahu, west of Waialua.
Name origin: From Hawaiian term meaning 'isle (of) abundance.'

Nanakuli — CDP
ZIP: 96792　　Lat: 21-23-30 N Long: 158-09-23 W
Pop: 9,575 (1990); 8,185 (1980)　　Pop Density: 3830.0
Land: 2.5 sq. mi.; Water: 3.2 sq. mi.　　Elev: 20 ft.
On the southwestern coast of Oahu.
Name origin: From Hawaiian term meaning either 'look at knee,' for the tattooed knee of the priest Kaopulupulu, or 'look deaf,' because people did not have enough food to offer passersby so they just looked at them and pretended to be deaf.

Pearl City — CDP
ZIP: 96782　　Lat: 21-24-16 N Long: 157-58-08 W
Pop: 30,993 (1990); 42,575 (1980)　　Pop Density: 6198.6
Land: 5.0 sq. mi.; Water: 0.8 sq. mi.
In southern Oahu, 11 mi. northwest of Honolulu.
Name origin: For the pearl oysters that used to be found here.

Punaluu — CDP
ZIP: 96717　　Lat: 21-35-33 N Long: 157-53-47 W
Pop: 672 (1990)　　Pop Density: 840.0
Land: 0.8 sq. mi.; Water: 0.4 sq. mi.
On the southeastern coast of the island of Hawaii, south of Pahala.
Name origin: From Hawaiian term meaning 'coral dived for.'

Pupukea — CDP
ZIP: 96712　　Lat: 21-39-51 N Long: 158-03-12 W
Pop: 4,111 (1990)　　Pop Density: 1209.1
Land: 3.4 sq. mi.; Water: 2.7 sq. mi.
In northwestern Oahu, near Haleiwa.
Name origin: From Hawaiian term meaning 'white shell.'

Schofield Barracks — CDP
ZIP: 96786　　Lat: 21-29-46 N Long: 158-03-52 W
Pop: 19,597 (1990); 18,851 (1980)　　Pop Density: 7258.1
Land: 2.7 sq. mi.; Water: 0.0 sq. mi.
In central Oahu, southwest of Wahiawa.
Name origin: For Lt. Gen. John M. Schofield (1831–1906), U.S. secretary of war under seventeenth Pres. Andrew Johnson (1808–75).

Village Park — CDP
　　Lat: 21-23-53 N Long: 158-01-48 W
Pop: 7,407 (1990); 18,851 (1980)　　Pop Density: 7407.0
Land: 1.0 sq. mi.; Water: 0.0 sq. mi.

Wahiawa — CDP
ZIP: 96786　　Lat: 21-30-10 N Long: 158-01-19 W
Pop: 17,386 (1990); 16,911 (1980)　　Pop Density: 8279.0
Land: 2.1 sq. mi.; Water: 0.3 sq. mi.　　Elev: 900 ft.
In central Oahu, northeast of Schofield Barracks.
Name origin: From Hawaiian term meaning 'milkfish place.'

Waialua — CDP
ZIP: 96791　　Lat: 21-34-39 N Long: 158-07-42 W
Pop: 3,943 (1990); 4,051 (1980)　　Pop Density: 3285.8
Land: 1.2 sq. mi.; Water: 0.2 sq. mi.　　Elev: 35 ft.
On the northwestern coast of Oahu.
Name origin: From Hawaiian terms *wai* 'fresh water,' 'stream,' or 'river'; *a* 'one'; and *lua* 'pit,' 'crater,' or 'hole.'

Waianae — CDP
ZIP: 96792　　Lat: 21-26-57 N Long: 158-11-02 W
Pop: 8,758 (1990); 7,941 (1980)　　Pop Density: 2575.9
Land: 3.4 sq. mi.; Water: 1.7 sq. mi.
In west-central Oahu, 3 mi. southeast of Makaha.
Name origin: From Hawaiian term meaning 'mullet water.'

Waikane — CDP
ZIP: 96744　　Lat: 21-30-04 N Long: 157-52-30 W
Pop: 717 (1990)　　Pop Density: 105.4
Land: 6.8 sq. mi.; Water: 0.4 sq. mi.
In east-central Oahu, near Kaneohe.
Name origin: From Hawaiian term meaning 'Kane's water' for Kane, a Hawaiian god.

Waimalu — CDP
ZIP: 96701　　Lat: 21-24-16 N Long: 157-56-35 W
Pop: 29,967 (1990)　　Pop Density: 5079.2
Land: 5.9 sq. mi.; Water: 0.2 sq. mi.
In south-central Oahu, 1 mi. northwest of Aiea.
Name origin: From Hawaiian term meaning 'sheltered water.'

Waimanalo — CDP
ZIP: 96795　　Lat: 21-20-51 N Long: 157-43-29 W
Pop: 3,508 (1990); 3,562 (1980)　　Pop Density: 8770.0
Land: 0.4 sq. mi.; Water: 0.0 sq. mi.　　Elev: 30 ft.
In southeastern Oahu.
Name origin: From Hawaiian term meaning 'potable water.'

Waimanalo Beach — CDP
ZIP: 96795　　Lat: 21-19-47 N Long: 157-41-24 W
Pop: 4,185 (1990); 4,161 (1980)　　Pop Density: 2615.6
Land: 1.6 sq. mi.; Water: 1.4 sq. mi.

Waipahu — CDP
ZIP: 96797　　Lat: 21-23-26 N Long: 158-00-45 W
Pop: 31,435 (1990); 29,139 (1980)　　Pop Density: 12090.4
Land: 2.6 sq. mi.; Water: 0.1 sq. mi.　　Elev: 20 ft.
In south-central Oahu, northwest of Pearl Harbor.
Name origin: From Hawaiian term meaning 'bursting water,' referring to water that bursts forth from underground, as a geyser.

Waipio — CDP
　　Lat: 21-25-05 N Long: 158-00-02 W
Pop: 11,812 (1990)　　Pop Density: 9843.3
Land: 1.2 sq. mi.; Water: 0.0 sq. mi.

Waipio Acres — CDP
ZIP: 96786　　Lat: 21-28-26 N Long: 158-01-12 W
Pop: 5,304 (1990); 4,091 (1980)　　Pop Density: 5304.0
Land: 1.0 sq. mi.; Water: 0.0 sq. mi.
In south-central Oahu, on northern Waipio Peninsula, south of Waipahu.
Name origin: From Hawaiian term meaning 'curved water,' for the shape of the lochs surrounding the peninsula.

HAWAII, Honolulu County

Wheeler Air Force Base CDP
ZIP: 96854 **Lat:** 21-28-55 N **Long:** 158-02-29 W
Pop: 2,600 (1990) **Pop Density:** 1130.4
Land: 2.3 sq. mi.; **Water:** 0.0 sq. mi.
In central Oahu, next to Schofield Barracks.
Name origin: For Sheldon H. Wheeler, a major in the U.S. Air Force, who was killed in a plane crash in 1921.

Whitmore Village CDP
ZIP: 96786 **Lat:** 21-30-51 N **Long:** 158-01-44 W
Pop: 3,373 (1990); 2,318 (1980) **Pop Density:** 3747.8
Land: 0.9 sq. mi.; **Water:** 0.0 sq. mi. **Elev:** 1002 ft.
In central Oahu, near Schofield Barracks; a Dole Company plantation village.

Kalawao County

Pop: 130 (1990) **Pop Density:** 9.8
Land: 13.2 sq. mi.; **Water:** 39.1 sq. mi. **Area Code:** 808
On the island of Molokai, southeast of the island of Oahu. Established 1905 (prior to statehood); has no county government and for statistical purposes is considered as one of the judicial districts of Maui County. Site of a colony for victims of leprosy or Hansen's disease; administered by the state department of health.
Name origin: From the Polynesian meaning 'mountain area.'

Kauai County
County Seat: Lihue (ZIP: 96766)

Pop: 51,177 (1990); 39,082 (1980) **Pop Density:** 82.2
Land: 622.5 sq. mi.; **Water:** 644.0 sq. mi. **Area Code:** 808
Westernmost of the Islands; county includes Kauai and Niihau islands; bordered on east by Kauai Channel. Established 1905 (prior to statehood).
Name origin: From the Polynesian meaning 'drying place.'

Anahola CDP
ZIP: 96703 **Lat:** 22-08-49 N **Long:** 159-19-04 W
Pop: 1,181 (1990); 915 (1980) **Pop Density:** 310.8
Land: 3.8 sq. mi.; **Water:** 0.2 sq. mi. **Elev:** 20 ft.
On the northeastern coast of Kauai.

Eleele CDP
ZIP: 96705 **Lat:** 21-54-37 N **Long:** 159-35-03 W
Pop: 1,489 (1990); 580 (1980) **Pop Density:** 1861.3
Land: 0.8 sq. mi.; **Water:** 0.2 sq. mi. **Elev:** 40 ft.
On the southern coast of Kauai.
Name origin: From Hawaiian term meaning 'black.'

Hanalei CDP
ZIP: 96714, 96722 **Lat:** 22-12-32 N **Long:** 159-30-06 W
Pop: 461 (1990); 483 (1980) **Pop Density:** 768.3
Land: 0.6 sq. mi.; **Water:** 0.2 sq. mi. **Elev:** 13 ft.
Name origin: From Hawaiian term meaning 'crescent bay.'

Hanamaulu CDP
ZIP: 96715 **Lat:** 21-59-53 N **Long:** 159-21-08 W
Pop: 3,611 (1990); 3,227 (1980) **Pop Density:** 3282.7
Land: 1.1 sq. mi.; **Water:** 0.2 sq. mi. **Elev:** 188 ft.
On the eastern coast of Kauai.
Name origin: From Hawaiian term meaning 'tired (as from walking) bay.'

Hanapepe CDP
ZIP: 96716 **Lat:** 21-54-58 N **Long:** 159-35-25 W
Pop: 1,395 (1990); 1,417 (1980) **Pop Density:** 1550.0
Land: 0.9 sq. mi.; **Water:** 0.1 sq. mi. **Elev:** 40 ft.
In southwestern Kauai.
Name origin: From Hawaiian term meaning 'crushed bay' (because of landslides).

Kalaheo CDP
ZIP: 96741 **Lat:** 21-55-14 N **Long:** 159-31-36 W
Pop: 3,592 (1990); 2,500 (1980) **Pop Density:** 1238.6
Land: 2.9 sq. mi.; **Water:** 0.1 sq. mi. **Elev:** 700 ft.
In southwestern Kauai, east of Hanapepe.
Name origin: From Hawaiian term meaning 'the proud day.'

Kalihiwai CDP
ZIP: 96754 **Lat:** 22-13-09 N **Long:** 159-25-17 W
Pop: 435 (1990) **Pop Density:** 69.0
Land: 6.3 sq. mi.; **Water:** 1.1 sq. mi.

Kapaa CDP
ZIP: 96746 **Lat:** 22-05-50 N **Long:** 159-21-14 W
Pop: 8,149 (1990); 4,467 (1980) **Pop Density:** 831.5
Land: 9.8 sq. mi.; **Water:** 0.2 sq. mi. **Elev:** 20 ft.
On the eastern coast of Kauai.
Name origin: From Hawaiian term meaning 'the solid' or 'the closing'.

Kaumakani   CDP
ZIP: 96747 **Lat:** 21-55-19 N **Long:** 159-37-41 W
Pop: 803 (1990); 888 (1980) **Pop Density:** 803.0
Land: 1.0 sq. mi.; **Water:** 0.1 sq. mi. **Elev:** 196 ft.
On the southwestern coast of Kauai.
Name origin: From Hawaiian term meaning 'place [in] wind.'

Kekaha   CDP
ZIP: 96752 **Lat:** 21-58-20 N **Long:** 159-43-04 W
Pop: 3,506 (1990); 3,260 (1980) **Pop Density:** 3506.0
Land: 1.0 sq. mi.; **Water:** 0.2 sq. mi.
On the west-central coast of Kauai.
Name origin: From Hawaiian term meaning 'the place.'

Kilauea   CDP
ZIP: 96754 **Lat:** 22-12-39 N **Long:** 159-24-34 W
Pop: 1,685 (1990); 895 (1980) **Pop Density:** 1123.3
Land: 1.5 sq. mi.; **Water:** 0.0 sq. mi.
On the northern coast of Kauai.
Name origin: From Hawaiian term meaning 'spewing; much spreading,' in reference to volcanic eruptions.

Koloa   CDP
ZIP: 96756 **Lat:** 21-54-24 N **Long:** 159-27-51 W
Pop: 1,791 (1990); 1,457 (1980) **Pop Density:** 1492.5
Land: 1.2 sq. mi.; **Water:** 0.0 sq. mi. **Elev:** 200 ft.
Name origin: According to legend, for a steep rock called "Paliokoloa."

Lawai   CDP
ZIP: 96765 **Lat:** 21-55-29 N **Long:** 159-30-17 W
Pop: 1,787 (1990) **Pop Density:** 470.3
Land: 3.8 sq. mi.; **Water:** 0.1 sq. mi.
In southern Kauai.

Lihue   CDP
ZIP: 96766 **Lat:** 21-58-30 N **Long:** 159-21-15 W
Pop: 5,536 (1990); 4,000 (1980) **Pop Density:** 878.7
Land: 6.3 sq. mi.; **Water:** 0.8 sq. mi. **Elev:** 206 ft.
In southeastern Kauai.
Name origin: From Hawaiian term meaning 'cold chill.'

Omao   CDP
ZIP: 96756 **Lat:** 21-55-30 N **Long:** 159-29-10 W
Pop: 1,142 (1990) **Pop Density:** 951.7
Land: 1.2 sq. mi.; **Water:** 0.0 sq. mi. **Elev:** 514 ft.
In southern Kauai.
Name origin: From Hawaiian term meaning 'green.'

Pakala Village   CDP
Lat: 21-56-42 N **Long:** 159-38-55 W
Pop: 565 (1990) **Pop Density:** 245.7
Land: 2.3 sq. mi.; **Water:** 0.3 sq. mi.
On the southwestern coast of Kauai, near Makawele.
Name origin: From Hawaiian term meaning 'the sun shines.'

Poipu   CDP
ZIP: 96756 **Lat:** 21-52-53 N **Long:** 159-27-44 W
Pop: 975 (1990); 685 (1980) **Pop Density:** 390.0
Land: 2.5 sq. mi.; **Water:** 0.3 sq. mi.
On the southern tip of Kauai.
Name origin: From Hawaiian term meaning 'completely overcast' or 'crashing,' as waves.

Princeville   CDP
ZIP: 96722 **Lat:** 22-13-24 N **Long:** 159-29-07 W
Pop: 1,244 (1990); 500 (1980) **Pop Density:** 592.4
Land: 2.1 sq. mi.; **Water:** 0.3 sq. mi.
On the northern coast of Kauai, near Hanalei.
Name origin: For the 1860 visit by King Kamehameha IV (1834–63), Queen Emma, and their son, the prince Ka Haku o Hawaii, to Robert Crichton Wyllie's sugar plantation here.

Puhi   CDP
ZIP: 96766 **Lat:** 21-58-07 N **Long:** 159-23-58 W
Pop: 1,210 (1990); 991 (1980) **Pop Density:** 3025.0
Land: 0.4 sq. mi.; **Water:** 0.0 sq. mi. **Elev:** 340 ft.
In southeastern Kauai.
Name origin: From Hawaiian term meaning 'blow.'

Wailua   CDP
ZIP: 96746 **Lat:** 22-03-28 N **Long:** 159-20-26 W
Pop: 2,018 (1990); 1,587 (1980) **Pop Density:** 1552.3
Land: 1.3 sq. mi.; **Water:** 0.1 sq. mi.
On the eastern coast of Kauai, southwest of Kapaa.
Name origin: From Hawaiian term meaning 'two waters,' referring to the branching of the north and south forks of the Wailua River.

Wailua Homesteads   CDP
Lat: 22-03-56 N **Long:** 159-22-46 W
Pop: 3,870 (1990) **Pop Density:** 552.9
Land: 7.0 sq. mi.; **Water:** 0.1 sq. mi.

Waimea   CDP
ZIP: 96796 **Lat:** 21-57-43 N **Long:** 159-40-29 W
Pop: 1,840 (1990); 1,569 (1980) **Pop Density:** 1840.0
Land: 1.0 sq. mi.; **Water:** 0.2 sq. mi. **Elev:** 9 ft.
On the southwestern coast of Kauai.

Maui County
County Seat: Wailuku (ZIP: 96793)

Pop: 100,374 (1990); 70,991 (1980)
Land: 1159.3 sq. mi.; **Water:** 1239.6 sq. mi.
Pop Density: 86.6
Area Code: 808

Separated from Hawaii County to the southeast by Alenuihaha Channel and from Honolulu to the northwest by Kaiwi Channel. Established 1905 (prior to statehood). Includes Molokai, Lanai, Kahoolawe, and Maui islands.
Name origin: A Polynesian demigod.

Haiku-Pauwela   CDP
Lat: 20-55-16 N **Long:** 156-18-15 W
Pop: 4,509 (1990); 619 (1980) **Pop Density:** 285.4
Land: 15.8 sq. mi.; **Water:** 2.2 sq. mi.

Haliimaile   CDP
ZIP: 96787 **Lat:** 20-52-34 N **Long:** 156-20-53 W
Pop: 841 (1990); 741 (1980) **Pop Density:** 494.7
Land: 1.7 sq. mi.; **Water:** 0.0 sq. mi. **Elev:** 1073 ft.
Name origin: From Hawaiian term meaning 'strewn vines.'

Hana   CDP
ZIP: 96713 **Lat:** 20-46-12 N **Long:** 155-59-39 W
Pop: 683 (1990); 643 (1980) **Pop Density:** 310.5
Land: 2.2 sq. mi.; **Water:** 1.3 sq. mi. **Elev:** 98 ft.

Kaanapali   CDP
ZIP: 96761 **Lat:** 20-56-00 N **Long:** 156-41-00 W
Pop: 579 (1990); 541 (1980) **Pop Density:** 118.2
Land: 4.9 sq. mi.; **Water:** 0.9 sq. mi.
On the northwestern coast of Maui, north of Lahaina.
Name origin: From Hawaiian term meaning 'Kaana cliff.'

Kahului   CDP
ZIP: 96732 **Lat:** 20-52-25 N **Long:** 156-27-33 W
Pop: 16,889 (1990); 12,978 (1980) **Pop Density:** 1111.1
Land: 15.2 sq. mi.; **Water:** 1.2 sq. mi.
On the northern coast of Maui.
Name origin: From Hawaiian term meaning 'the winning.'

Kapalua   CDP
Lat: 20-59-58 N **Long:** 156-39-29 W
Pop: 408 (1990) **Pop Density:** 240.0
Land: 1.7 sq. mi.; **Water:** 0.6 sq. mi.

Kaunakakai   CDP
ZIP: 96748 **Lat:** 21-05-18 N **Long:** 157-00-45 W
Pop: 2,658 (1990); 2,231 (1980) **Pop Density:** 1329.0
Land: 2.0 sq. mi.; **Water:** 1.1 sq. mi. **Elev:** 52 ft.
On the southern coast of Molokai.
Name origin: From Hawaiian term meaning 'beach landing.'

Kihei   CDP
ZIP: 96753 **Lat:** 20-45-49 N **Long:** 156-27-11 W
Pop: 11,107 (1990); 5,644 (1980) **Pop Density:** 1088.9
Land: 10.2 sq. mi.; **Water:** 1.7 sq. mi.
On the west-central coast of Maui.
Name origin: Hawaiian term meaning 'cape,' or 'cloak.'

Kualapuu   CDP
ZIP: 96757 **Lat:** 21-09-35 N **Long:** 157-03-30 W
Pop: 1,661 (1990); 502 (1980) **Pop Density:** 54.5
Land: 30.5 sq. mi.; **Water:** 0.2 sq. mi. **Elev:** 878 ft.
In central Molokai.
Name origin: From Hawaiian term meaning 'hill overturned.'

Lahaina   CDP
ZIP: 96761 **Lat:** 20-53-28 N **Long:** 156-40-27 W
Pop: 9,073 (1990); 6,095 (1980) **Pop Density:** 1564.3
Land: 5.8 sq. mi.; **Water:** 1.2 sq. mi. **Elev:** 9 ft.
On the northwestern coast of Maui.
Name origin: From Hawaiian term meaning 'cruel sun,' supposedly referring to droughts.

Lanai City   CDP
ZIP: 96763 **Lat:** 20-49-57 N **Long:** 156-55-35 W
Pop: 2,400 (1990); 2,092 (1980) **Pop Density:** 666.7
Land: 3.6 sq. mi.; **Water:** 0.0 sq. mi. **Elev:** 1624 ft.
In central Lanai.
Name origin: From Hawaiian term meaning, possibly, 'day (of) conquest.'

Maalaea   CDP
ZIP: 96793 **Lat:** 20-47-59 N **Long:** 156-29-39 W
Pop: 443 (1990) **Pop Density:** 92.3
Land: 4.8 sq. mi.; **Water:** 2.9 sq. mi.
On the west-central coast of Maui.
Name origin: From, perhaps, a contraction of Hawaiian term *makaalaea* 'ocherous earth beginning.'

Makawao   CDP
ZIP: 96768 **Lat:** 20-51-27 N **Long:** 156-19-30 W
Pop: 5,405 (1990); 2,900 (1980) **Pop Density:** 1150.0
Land: 4.7 sq. mi.; **Water:** 0.0 sq. mi.
In east-central Maui.
Name origin: From Hawaiian term meaning 'forest beginning.'

Maunaloa   CDP
ZIP: 96770 **Lat:** 21-08-11 N **Long:** 157-12-49 W
Pop: 405 (1990); 633 (1980) **Pop Density:** 2025.0
Land: 0.2 sq. mi.; **Water:** 0.0 sq. mi.
In west-central Molokai.
Name origin: From Hawaiian term meaning 'long mountain.'

Napili-Honokowai   CDP
Lat: 20-58-17 N **Long:** 156-40-10 W
Pop: 4,332 (1990); 2,446 (1980) **Pop Density:** 734.2
Land: 5.9 sq. mi.; **Water:** 0.8 sq. mi.

Paia   CDP
ZIP: 96779 **Lat:** 20-54-42 N **Long:** 156-22-15 W
Pop: 2,091 (1990) **Pop Density:** 342.8
Land: 6.1 sq. mi.; **Water:** 0.7 sq. mi. **Elev:** 295 ft.
Near the northern coast of Maui.
Name origin: From Hawaiian term meaning 'noisy.'

Pukalani
CDP
ZIP: 96788 **Lat:** 20-50-12 N **Long:** 156-20-27 W
Pop: 5,879 (1990); 3,950 (1980) **Pop Density:** 1336.1
Land: 4.4 sq. mi.; **Water:** 0.0 sq. mi. **Elev:** 1622 ft.
In north-central Maui.
Name origin: From Hawaiian term meaning 'heavenly gate' or, possibly, from term *puukalani* 'hill (of) the heavens.'

Waihee-Waiehue
CDP
Lat: 20-55-34 N **Long:** 156-30-34 W
Pop: 4,004 (1990); 413 (1980) **Pop Density:** 931.2
Land: 4.3 sq. mi.; **Water:** 1.0 sq. mi.

Waikapu
CDP
ZIP: 96793 **Lat:** 20-50-22 N **Long:** 156-32-01 W
Pop: 729 (1990); 698 (1980) **Pop Density:** 66.3
Land: 11.0 sq. mi.; **Water:** 0.0 sq. mi.
In northwestern Maui, southwest of Puunene.
Name origin: From Hawaiian term meaning 'water (of) the conch.'

Wailea-Makena
CDP
Lat: 20-39-55 N **Long:** 156-25-59 W
Pop: 3,799 (1990); 1,124 (1980) **Pop Density:** 168.1
Land: 22.6 sq. mi.; **Water:** 4.2 sq. mi.

Wailuku
CDP
ZIP: 96793 **Lat:** 20-53-18 N **Long:** 156-30-24 W
Pop: 10,688 (1990); 10,260 (1980) **Pop Density:** 2095.7
Land: 5.1 sq. mi.; **Water:** 0.4 sq. mi. **Elev:** 331 ft.
In central Maui.
Name origin: From Hawaiian term meaning 'water (of) destruction.'

Index to Places and Counties in Hawaii

Ahuimanu (Honolulu) CDP *171*
Aiea (Honolulu) CDP *171*
Aliamanu (Honolulu) Military Facility *171*
Anahola (Kauai) CDP *174*
Barbers Point Housing (Honolulu) CDP *171*
Captain Cook (Hawaii) CDP *169*
Eleele (Kauai) CDP *174*
Ewa Beach (Honolulu) CDP *171*
Ewa Gentry (Honolulu) CDP *171*
Ewa Villages (Honolulu) CDP *171*
Fort Shafter (Honolulu) CDP *171*
Haiku-Pauwela (Maui) CDP *176*
Halaula (Hawaii) CDP *169*
Halawa (Honolulu) CDP *171*
Haleiwa (Honolulu) CDP *171*
Haliimaile (Maui) CDP *176*
Hana (Maui) CDP *176*
Hanalei (Kauai) CDP *174*
Hanamaulu (Kauai) CDP *174*
Hanapepe (Kauai) CDP *174*
Hauula (Honolulu) CDP *171*
Hawaiian Beaches (Hawaii) CDP *169*
Hawaiian Ocean View (Hawaii) CDP *169*
Hawaiian Paradise Park (Hawaii) CDP *169*
Hawaii County *169*
Hawi (Hawaii) CDP *169*
Heeia (Honolulu) CDP *171*
Hickam Housing (Honolulu) CDP *172*
Hilo (Hawaii) CDP *169*
Holualoa (Hawaii) CDP *169*
Honalo (Hawaii) CDP *169*
Honaunau-Napoopoo (Hawaii) CDP *169*
Honokaa (Hawaii) CDP *169*
Honolulu (Honolulu) City *172*
Honolulu County *171*
Honomu (Hawaii) CDP *169*
Iroquois Point (Honolulu) CDP *172*
Kaaawa (Honolulu) CDP *172*
Kaanapali (Maui) CDP *176*
Kahaluu (Honolulu) CDP *172*
Kahaluu-Keauhou (Hawaii) CDP *169*
Kahuku (Honolulu) CDP *172*
Kahului (Maui) CDP *176*
Kailua (Hawaii) CDP *169*
Kailua (Honolulu) CDP *172*
Kalaheo (Kauai) CDP *174*
Kalaoa (Hawaii) CDP *169*
Kalawao County *174*
Kalihiwai (Kauai) CDP *174*
Kaneohe (Honolulu) CDP *172*
Kaneohe Station (Honolulu) Military Facility *172*
Kapaa (Kauai) CDP *174*
Kapaau (Hawaii) CDP *170*
Kapalua (Maui) CDP *176*
Kauai County *174*
Kaumakani (Kauai) CDP *175*
Kaunakakai (Maui) CDP *176*
Kawela Bay (Honolulu) CDP *172*
Keaau (Hawaii) CDP *170*
Kealakekua (Hawaii) CDP *170*
Kekaha (Kauai) CDP *175*
Kihei (Maui) CDP *176*
Kilauea (Kauai) CDP *175*
Koloa (Kauai) CDP *175*
Kualapuu (Maui) CDP *176*
Kukuihaele (Hawaii) CDP *170*
Kurtistown (Hawaii) CDP *170*
Lahaina (Maui) CDP *176*
Laie (Honolulu) CDP *172*
Lanai City (Maui) CDP *176*
Laupahoehoe (Hawaii) CDP *170*
Lawai (Kauai) CDP *175*
Lihue (Kauai) CDP *175*
Maalaea (Maui) CDP *176*
Maili (Honolulu) CDP *172*
Makaha (Honolulu) CDP *172*
Makaha Valley (Honolulu) CDP *172*
Makakilo City (Honolulu) CDP *172*
Makawao (Maui) CDP *176*
Maui County *176*
Maunaloa (Maui) CDP *176*
Maunawili (Honolulu) CDP *172*
Mililani Town (Honolulu) CDP *172*
Mokuleia (Honolulu) CDP *173*
Mountain View (Hawaii) CDP *170*
Naalehu (Hawaii) CDP *170*
Nanakuli (Honolulu) CDP *173*
Napili-Honokowai (Maui) CDP *176*
Omao (Kauai) CDP *175*
Paauilo (Hawaii) CDP *170*
Pahala (Hawaii) CDP *170*
Pahoa (Hawaii) CDP *170*
Paia (Maui) CDP *176*
Pakala Village (Kauai) CDP *175*
Papaikou (Hawaii) CDP *170*
Paukaa (Hawaii) CDP *170*
Pearl City (Honolulu) CDP *173*
Pepeekeo (Hawaii) CDP *170*
Poipu (Kauai) CDP *175*
Princeville (Kauai) CDP *175*
Puako (Hawaii) CDP *170*
Puhi (Kauai) CDP *175*
Pukalani (Maui) CDP *177*
Punaluu (Honolulu) CDP *173*
Pupukea (Honolulu) CDP *173*
Schofield Barracks (Honolulu) CDP *173*
Village Park (Honolulu) CDP *173*
Volcano (Hawaii) CDP *170*
Wahiawa (Honolulu) CDP *173*
Waialua (Honolulu) CDP *173*
Waianae (Honolulu) CDP *173*
Waihee-Waiehue (Maui) CDP *177*
Waikane (Honolulu) CDP *173*
Waikapu (Maui) CDP *177*
Waikoloa Village (Hawaii) CDP *170*
Wailea-Makena (Maui) CDP *177*
Wailua (Kauai) CDP *175*
Wailua Homesteads (Kauai) CDP *175*
Wailuku (Maui) CDP *177*
Waimalu (Honolulu) CDP *173*
Waimanalo (Honolulu) CDP *173*
Waimanalo Beach (Honolulu) CDP .. *173*
Waimea (Hawaii) CDP *171*
Waimea (Kauai) CDP *175*
Wainaku (Hawaii) CDP *171*
Waipahu (Honolulu) CDP *173*
Waipio (Honolulu) CDP *173*
Waipio Acres (Honolulu) CDP *173*
Wheeler Air Force Base (Honolulu) CDP *174*
Whitmore Village (Honolulu) CDP .. *174*

Idaho

IDAHO

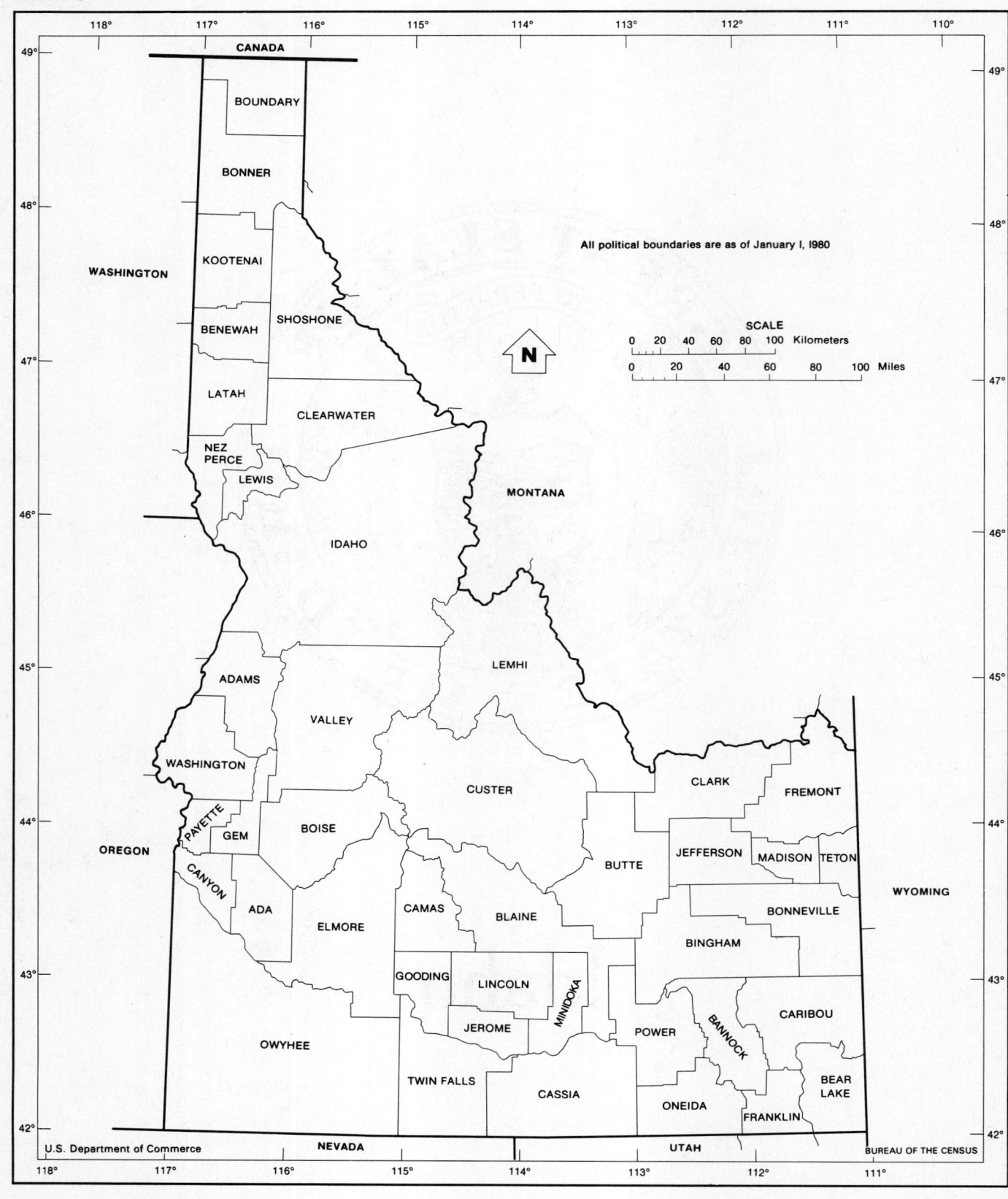

Idaho

Population: 1,006,749 (1990); 943,935 (1980)
Population rank (1990): 42
Percent population change (1980–1990): 6.7
Population projection: 1,036,000 (1995); 1,056,000 (2000)

Area: total: 83,574 sq. mi.; 82,751 sq. mi. land, 823 sq. mi. water
Area rank: 14
Highest elevation: 12,662 ft., Borah Peak (Custer County)
Lowest point: 710 ft., Snake River at Lewiston (Nez Perce County)

State capital: Boise (Ada County)
Largest city: Boise City (125,738)
Second largest city: Pocatello City (46,080)
Largest county: Ada (205,775)

Total housing units: 413,327
No. of occupied housing units: 360,723
Vacant housing units (%): 12.7
Distribution of population by race and Hispanic origin (%):
 White: 94.4
 Black: 0.3
 Hispanic (any race): 5.3
 Native American: 1.4
 Asian/Pacific: 0.9
 Other: 3.0

Admission date: July 3, 1890 (43rd state).

Location: In the northwestern United States, bordering Montana, Wyoming, Utah, Nevada, Oregon, Washington, and the Canadian province of British Columbia.

Name Origin: Idaho is apparently a coined word, and was applied to Idaho Springs and Idaho County prior to being used for Idaho Territory in 1863. The name has no origin in any known Indian language, but there is at least one documented theory: it may have been coined by lobbyist-politician George M. Willing, who claimed the name came from an Indian word *idahow*, which is thought to mean 'gem of the mountains'; this interpretation has a great many adherents.

State bird: mountain bluebird *(Sialia currucoides)*
State fish: cutthroat trout *(Salmo clarki)*
State flower: syringa *(Philadelphus lewisii)*
State folkdance: square dance
State fossil: Hagerman horse *(Equus simplicidens)*
State gem: star garnet
State horse: Appaloosa
State song: "Here We Have Idaho"

State tree: western white pine *(Pinus strobus)*
State motto: *Esto perpetua* (Latin 'May it endure forever')
State nickname: Gem State; Light on the Mountain

Area code: 208
Time zone: Mountain
Abbreviations: ID (postal); Ida. (traditional)
Part of (region): Rocky Mountain

Local Government

Counties

Idaho has 44 counties, each governed by three elected commissioners.

Municipalities

Idaho has 198 incorporated cities, most of which have an elected mayor and a council of four to six members.

Settlement History and Early Development

Prehistoric people settled in the area that is now Idaho more than 10,000 years ago. The Indian tribes living in the region in the nineteenth century included the Shoshone, Coeur d'Alene, Pend d'Oreille, Kutenai, Bannock, Paiute, and Nez Perce. The land that forms present-day Idaho was part of the Oregon Country claimed by the U.S., Great Britain, France, and Spain. The Nez Perce greeted the Lewis and Clark expedition in 1805 when they entered the Idaho region and helped them go on to reach the Columbia River and ultimately the Pacific.

Within a few years fur trappers followed; missionaries came in the 1830s. The Oregon Trail opened in 1842, but few travelers along the route stopped to settle in the area that would become Idaho. In 1846 Idaho's land became part of the U.S. through the Oregon Treaty with Great Britain; Idaho was included in the Territory of Oregon organized in 1848. In 1853 the northern part of the present state was included in the Territory of Washington. Southern Idaho remained part of Oregon until Oregon became a state in 1859, at which time southern Idaho joined the northern section as part of Washington Territory.

Idaho's first settlement, Franklin, was established by Mormon farmers from Utah in 1860. In 1860 gold was discovered in northern Idaho, and the resulting gold rush increased the population sufficiently so that Idaho was organized as a territory in 1863. Boise became the capital the next year. The next decade saw the beginning of telegraph service, the linking of Franklin with the transcontinental railroad, and the first newspaper in the territory. The white population continued to grow, leading to conflict with the Indians in the late 1870s. The Nez Perce War ended with the surrender of Chief Joseph in 1877. In

1878 the Bannock Indians rebelled, but the rebellion could not hold together after Chief Buffalo Horn was killed. Idaho's Indians were ultimately confined to reservations.

Statehood

After the discovery of lead (1880) and silver (1884) in Idaho, the territory's population again grew rapidly. Idaho became the 43rd U.S. state on July 3, 1890. The early years of statehood were tumultuous, as Mormons and non-Mormons contended for political supremacy, and violent labor disputes occurred in the mining areas, both between miners and mine owners and between union and non-union miners. In 1905 Idaho's former governor, Frank Steunenberg, was murdered. A member of a mining union confessed to the crime (he was later sentenced to life imprisonment) and implicated union leaders. The union leaders, led by William "Big Bill" Haywood, were defended by Clarence Darrow. Haywood and one man were acquitted and charges against the third defendant were dropped.

Business and Commerce

At the turn of the century irrigation projects were helping agriculture become an important industry. After prospering in World War I, the state encountered the economic troubles of the 1920s and the Great Depression of the 1930s; World War II restored prosperity. In 1949 the Atomic Energy Commission built the National Reactor Testing Station near Idaho Falls, which in 1951 generated electricity from nuclear power for the first time. Idaho's population grew rapidly during the 1970s, but recently further expansion of industry in Idaho has sometimes been at odds with conservation efforts in the state.

Idaho potatoes are nationally renowned and remain the primary cash crop; Idaho ranks first among states in potato production. Other crops such as wheat, barley, sugar beets, and beans, as well as timber, are also a vital part of the state's economy.

State Boundaries

The Territory of Idaho was formed in 1863 from parts of the Washington, Dakota, and Nebraska territories. Sections of the territory were taken when Montana Territory was formed in 1864 and when Wyoming Territory was formed in 1868, leaving Idaho with its present boundaries.

Idaho Counties

Ada	Bonneville	Custer	Kootenai	Owyhee
Adams	Boundary	Elmore	Latah	Payette
Bannock	Butte	Franklin	Lemhi	Power
Bear Lake	Camas	Fremont	Lewis	Shoshone
Benewah	Canyon	Gem	Lincoln	Teton
Bingham	Caribou	Gooding	Madison	Twin Falls
Blaine	Cassia	Idaho	Minidoka	Valley
Boise	Clark	Jefferson	Nez Perce	Washington
Bonner	Clearwater	Jerome	Oneida	

Multi-County Places

The following Idaho places are in more than one county. Given here is the total population for each multi-county place, and the names of the counties it is in.

Burley, pop. 8,702; Cassia (8,420), Minidoka (282)
Fort Hall, pop. 2,681; Bannock (1,370), Bingham (1,311)
Kamiah, pop. 1,157; Lewis (1,154), Idaho (3)
Pocatello, pop. 46,080; Bannock (46,027), Power (53)
Ririe, pop. 596; Jefferson (522), Bonneville (74)

Ada County
County Seat: Boise (ZIP: 83701)

Pop: 205,775 (1990); 173,125 (1980)   **Pop Density:** 195.0
Land: 1055.0 sq. mi.; **Water:** 5.3 sq. mi.   **Area Code:** 208

In southwestern ID; organized Dec 22, 1864 (prior to statehood) from Boise County.

Name origin: For Ada Riggs (1863–?), the first white child born in Boise, daughter of H.C. Riggs.

Boise   City
ZIP: 83707   **Lat:** 43-36-23 N   **Long:** 116-13-33 W
Pop: 125,738 (1990); 102,249 (1980)   **Pop Density:** 2727.5
Land: 46.1 sq. mi.; **Water:** 0.2 sq. mi.

In southwestern ID, northwest of Twin Falls. Founded and platted Jul 1863. State capital and largest city. Manufacturing city: computer microchips, food processing, forest products, mobile homes, laminated beams. U.S. center for the Basques.

Name origin: For the Boise River, from French *Rivière Boisière* 'wooded river.'

Eagle   City
ZIP: 83616   **Lat:** 43-41-36 N   **Long:** 116-21-17 W
Pop: 3,327 (1990); 2,620 (1980)   **Pop Density:** 665.4
Land: 5.0 sq. mi.; **Water:** 0.0 sq. mi.

Name origin: For the many eagles that nested in the area.

Garden City   City
ZIP: 83704   **Lat:** 43-38-54 N   **Long:** 116-16-01 W
Pop: 6,369 (1990); 4,571 (1980)   **Pop Density:** 1930.0
Land: 3.3 sq. mi.; **Water:** 0.0 sq. mi.

Kuna   City
ZIP: 83634   **Lat:** 43-29-24 N   **Long:** 116-25-02 W
Pop: 1,955 (1990); 1,767 (1980)   **Pop Density:** 1221.9
Land: 1.6 sq. mi.; **Water:** 0.0 sq. mi.

Meridian   City
ZIP: 83642   **Lat:** 43-36-40 N   **Long:** 116-23-58 W
Pop: 9,596 (1990); 6,658 (1980)   **Pop Density:** 1370.9
Land: 7.0 sq. mi.; **Water:** 0.0 sq. mi.

In southwestern ID, a western suburb of Boise.

Name origin: For the Meridian Lodge, named for the base meridian of the Boise survey.

Adams County
County Seat: Council (ZIP: 83612)

Pop: 3,254 (1990); 3,347 (1980)   **Pop Density:** 2.4
Land: 1364.7 sq. mi.; **Water:** 5.4 sq. mi.   **Area Code:** 208

On the central western border of ID, north of Boise; organized Mar 3, 1911 from Washington County.

Name origin: For John Adams (1735–1826), second U.S. president.

Council   City
ZIP: 83612   **Lat:** 44-43-44 N   **Long:** 116-26-06 W
Pop: 831 (1990); 917 (1980)   **Pop Density:** 1187.1
Land: 0.7 sq. mi.; **Water:** 0.0 sq. mi.   **Elev:** 2953 ft.

Name origin: For the Indian councils held here for many years.

New Meadows   City
ZIP: 83654   **Lat:** 44-58-14 N   **Long:** 116-17-03 W
Pop: 534 (1990); 576 (1980)   **Pop Density:** 1068.0
Land: 0.5 sq. mi.; **Water:** 0.0 sq. mi.   **Elev:** 3868 ft.

Bannock County
County Seat: Pocatello (ZIP: 83205)

Pop: 66,026 (1990); 65,421 (1980) **Pop Density:** 59.3
Land: 1113.2 sq. mi.; **Water:** 34.3 sq. mi. **Area Code:** 208
In southeastern ID; organized Mar 6, 1893 from Bingham County.

Name origin: For the Bannack Indians whose name in Shoshonean means 'hair in backward motion,' for their habit of wearing a lock of hair tossed back over their heads. Early settlers spelled the name 'Bannock,' with an 'o' instead of an 'a.'

Arimo — City
ZIP: 83214 **Lat:** 42-33-34 N **Long:** 112-10-14 W
Pop: 311 (1990); 338 (1980) **Pop Density:** 777.5
Land: 0.4 sq. mi.; Water: 0.0 sq. mi.

Chubbuck — City
ZIP: 83202 **Lat:** 42-55-20 N **Long:** 112-27-53 W
Pop: 7,791 (1990); 7,052 (1980) **Pop Density:** 2360.9
Land: 3.3 sq. mi.; Water: 0.0 sq. mi.

Name origin: For train conductor Earl Chubbuck. Previously called Beet Dump.

Downey — City
ZIP: 83234 **Lat:** 42-25-45 N **Long:** 112-07-22 W
Pop: 626 (1990); 645 (1980) **Pop Density:** 626.0
Land: 1.0 sq. mi.; Water: 0.0 sq. mi.

Fort Hall — CDP
Lat: 42-59-22 N **Long:** 112-26-56 W
Pop: 1,370 (1990) **Pop Density:** 51.9
Land: 26.4 sq. mi.; Water: 0.0 sq. mi.
Part of the town is also in Bingham County.

Inkom — City
ZIP: 83245 **Lat:** 42-47-48 N **Long:** 112-14-52 W
Pop: 769 (1990); 830 (1980) **Pop Density:** 1281.7
Land: 0.6 sq. mi.; Water: 0.0 sq. mi.

Lava Hot Springs — City
ZIP: 83246 **Lat:** 42-37-12 N **Long:** 112-00-34 W
Pop: 420 (1990); 467 (1980) **Pop Density:** 600.0
Land: 0.7 sq. mi.; Water: 0.0 sq. mi.

Name origin: For its descriptive connotations.

McCammon — City
ZIP: 83250 **Lat:** 42-38-49 N **Long:** 112-11-32 W
Pop: 722 (1990); 770 (1980) **Pop Density:** 555.4
Land: 1.3 sq. mi.; Water: 0.0 sq. mi.

Pocatello — City
ZIP: 83201 **Lat:** 42-52-06 N **Long:** 112-26-19 W
Pop: 46,027 (1990); 46,340 (1980) **Pop Density:** 2054.8
Land: 22.4 sq. mi.; Water: 0.0 sq. mi.

In southeastern ID, 58 mi. north of the UT border and 68 mi. west of the WY border. Founded 1882; incorporated as a city 1893. Transportation gateway to the Pacific Northwest; surrounded by rich farmland; marketplace and shipping point for livestock and crops. Diverse manufacturing: cement, dairy products, elemental phosphorus. Part of the town is also in Power County.

Name origin: For a Bannock Indian chief whose name means 'the wayward.'

Bear Lake County
County Seat: Paris (ZIP: 83261)

Pop: 6,084 (1990); 6,931 (1980) **Pop Density:** 6.3
Land: 971.4 sq. mi.; **Water:** 78.1 sq. mi. **Area Code:** 208
On the southeastern border of ID, southeast of Pocatello; organized Jan 5, 1875 from Oneida County.

Name origin: For Bear Lake, which lies half in ID and half in UT.

Bloomington — City
ZIP: 83223 **Lat:** 42-11-27 N **Long:** 111-24-17 W
Pop: 197 (1990); 212 (1980) **Pop Density:** 218.9
Land: 0.9 sq. mi.; Water: 0.0 sq. mi. **Elev:** 5969 ft.

Name origin: For the efforts of the settlers who soon had the new colony blooming.

Georgetown — City
ZIP: 83239 **Lat:** 42-28-39 N **Long:** 111-21-54 W
Pop: 558 (1990); 544 (1980) **Pop Density:** 797.1
Land: 0.7 sq. mi.; Water: 0.0 sq. mi.

Montpelier — City
ZIP: 83254 **Lat:** 42-19-23 N **Long:** 111-18-03 W
Pop: 2,656 (1990); 3,107 (1980) **Pop Density:** 1475.6
Land: 1.8 sq. mi.; Water: 0.0 sq. mi.

Paris — City
ZIP: 83261 **Lat:** 42-13-39 N **Long:** 111-24-05 W
Pop: 581 (1990); 707 (1980) **Pop Density:** 166.0
Land: 3.5 sq. mi.; Water: 0.0 sq. mi. **Elev:** 5968 ft.
In southeastern ID.

Name origin: For Frederick Perris, who platted the townsite; with a spelling variation.

St. Charles — City
ZIP: 83272 **Lat:** 42-06-45 N **Long:** 111-23-21 W
Pop: 189 (1990); 211 (1980) **Pop Density:** 315.0
Land: 0.6 sq. mi.; Water: 0.0 sq. mi. **Elev:** 5944 ft.

American Places Dictionary   IDAHO, Bingham County

Benewah County
County Seat: Saint Maries (ZIP: 83861)

Pop: 7,937 (1990); 8,292 (1980)   **Pop Density:** 10.2
Land: 776.0 sq. mi.; **Water:** 8.0 sq. mi.   **Area Code:** 208

On the western border of ID, southeast of Spokane, WA; organized Jan 23, 1915 from Kootenai County.
Name origin: For Benewah, a chief of the Coeur d'Alene Indian tribe.

Chatcolet   City
Lat: 47-21-14 N **Long:** 116-45-08 W
Pop: 72 (1990); 181 (1980)   **Pop Density:** 8.1
Land: 8.9 sq. mi.; **Water:** 3.7 sq. mi.   **Elev:** 2136 ft.
Incorporated Jul 2, 1947.
Name origin: For Lake Chatcolet at the southern end of Coeur d'Alene Lake. Name is believed to be a Coeur d'Alene Indian term for 'place where animals are trapped.'

Plummer   City
ZIP: 83851   **Lat:** 47-19-46 N **Long:** 116-53-02 W
Pop: 804 (1990); 634 (1980)   **Pop Density:** 730.9
Land: 1.1 sq. mi.; **Water:** 0.0 sq. mi.   **Elev:** 2722 ft.
Incorporated 1967.

St. Maries   City
ZIP: 83861   **Lat:** 47-18-53 N **Long:** 116-34-14 W
Pop: 2,442 (1990); 2,794 (1980)   **Pop Density:** 2220.0
Land: 1.1 sq. mi.; **Water:** 0.0 sq. mi.
In northwestern ID, southeast of Coeur d'Alene. Incorporated 1913.
Name origin: For the mother of Jesus.

Tensed   City
ZIP: 83870   **Lat:** 47-09-34 N **Long:** 116-55-24 W
Pop: 90 (1990); 113 (1980)   **Pop Density:** 450.0
Land: 0.2 sq. mi.; **Water:** 0.0 sq. mi.   **Elev:** 2557 ft.
Incorporated 1946.

Bingham County
County Seat: Blackfoot (ZIP: 83221)

Pop: 37,583 (1990); 36,489 (1980)   **Pop Density:** 17.9
Land: 2094.8 sq. mi.; **Water:** 25.5 sq. mi.   **Area Code:** 208

In southeastern ID, south of Idaho Falls; organized Jan 13, 1885 (prior to statehood) from Oneida County.
Name origin: By ID Territorial Governor William M. Bunn for his friend Henry Harrison Bingham (1841–1912), U.S. representative from PA (1879–1912) and a former Union officer who was awarded the Congressional Medal of Honor in 1864.

Aberdeen   City
ZIP: 83210   **Lat:** 42-56-40 N **Long:** 112-50-13 W
Pop: 1,406 (1990); 1,528 (1980)   **Pop Density:** 1406.0
Land: 1.0 sq. mi.; **Water:** 0.0 sq. mi.
Incorporated 1941.
Name origin: For the city in Scotland.

Atomic City   City
Lat: 43-26-39 N **Long:** 112-48-45 W
Pop: 25 (1990); 34 (1980)   **Pop Density:** 250.0
Land: 0.1 sq. mi.; **Water:** 0.0 sq. mi.
Incorporated Aug 4, 1950.
Name origin: For its location near the nuclear engineering site. Name changed from Midway in 1949.

Basalt   City
ZIP: 83218   **Lat:** 43-18-51 N **Long:** 112-09-54 W
Pop: 407 (1990); 414 (1980)   **Pop Density:** 1356.7
Land: 0.3 sq. mi.; **Water:** 0.0 sq. mi.
Incorporated Apr 11, 1906.
Name origin: For local mineral deposits.

Blackfoot   City
ZIP: 83221   **Lat:** 43-11-38 N **Long:** 112-20-41 W
Pop: 9,646 (1990); 10,065 (1980)   **Pop Density:** 1820.0
Land: 5.3 sq. mi.; **Water:** 0.3 sq. mi.
In southeastern ID, 23 mi. north of Pocatello. Incorporated May 25, 1906.
Name origin: For the Indian tribe.

Firth   City
ZIP: 83236   **Lat:** 43-18-20 N **Long:** 112-10-59 W
Pop: 429 (1990); 460 (1980)   **Pop Density:** 2145.0
Land: 0.2 sq. mi.; **Water:** 0.0 sq. mi.
Name origin: For Lorenzo Firth, who gave land for the railroad station, section house, and water tank.

Fort Hall   CDP
Lat: 43-02-24 N **Long:** 112-26-54 W
Pop: 1,311 (1990)   **Pop Density:** 89.2
Land: 14.7 sq. mi.; **Water:** 0.0 sq. mi.
Part of the town is also in Bannock County.

IDAHO, Bingham County   American Places Dictionary

Shelley   City
ZIP: 83274   **Lat:** 43-22-48 N **Long:** 112-07-23 W
Pop: 3,536 (1990); 3,300 (1980)   **Pop Density:** 2946.7
Land: 1.2 sq. mi.; **Water:** 0.0 sq. mi.
In southeastern ID, south of Idaho Falls. Incorporated 1921.
Name origin: For John F. Shelley, Mormon bishop and early settler.

Blaine County
County Seat: Hailey (ZIP: 83333)

Pop: 13,552 (1990); 9,841 (1980)   **Pop Density:** 5.1
Land: 2644.9 sq. mi.; **Water:** 16.2 sq. mi.   **Area Code:** 208
In south-central ID, west of Pocatello; organized Mar 5, 1895 from Alturas County, which was organized in 1864 and abolished in 1895, and from Logan County, which was organized in 1889 and abolished in 1895.
Name origin: For James Gillespie Blaine (1830–93), U.S. representative from ME (1863–76), U.S. senator (1876–81), and U.S. secretary of state (1881; 1889–92).

Bellevue   City
ZIP: 83313   **Lat:** 43-27-57 N **Long:** 114-15-26 W
Pop: 1,275 (1990); 1,016 (1980)   **Pop Density:** 1159.1
Land: 1.1 sq. mi.; **Water:** 0.0 sq. mi.   **Elev:** 5190 ft.
Name origin: From French 'beautiful view.'

Hailey   City
ZIP: 83333   **Lat:** 43-30-41 N **Long:** 114-17-56 W
Pop: 3,687 (1990); 2,109 (1980)   **Pop Density:** 1474.8
Land: 2.5 sq. mi.; **Water:** 0.0 sq. mi.
Name origin: For landowner Bill Hailey.

Ketchum   City
ZIP: 83340   **Lat:** 43-41-19 N **Long:** 114-22-30 W
Pop: 2,523 (1990); 2,200 (1980)   **Pop Density:** 970.4
Land: 2.6 sq. mi.; **Water:** 0.0 sq. mi.
In south-central ID, north of Twin Falls. Established 1880 as Leadville.
Name origin: To avoid confusion with other Leadvilles in the state, the town was renamed in 1881 for David Ketchum, the first settler.

Sun Valley   City
ZIP: 83353   **Lat:** 43-40-53 N **Long:** 114-19-42 W
Pop: 938 (1990); 545 (1980)   **Pop Density:** 97.7
Land: 9.6 sq. mi.; **Water:** 0.0 sq. mi.

Boise County
County Seat: Idaho City (ZIP: 83631)

Pop: 3,509 (1990); 2,999 (1980)   **Pop Density:** 1.8
Land: 1902.5 sq. mi.; **Water:** 4.3 sq. mi.   **Area Code:** 208
In west-central ID, northeast of Boise; original county, established Feb 4, 1864.
Name origin: For the Boise River, which forms part of its eastern border, from French *boise* 'woods.'

Crouch   City
                        Lat: 44-06-55 N **Long:** 115-58-17 W
Pop: 75 (1990); 69 (1980)   **Pop Density:** 250.0
Land: 0.3 sq. mi.; **Water:** 0.0 sq. mi.

Horseshoe Bend   City
ZIP: 83629   **Lat:** 43-54-46 N **Long:** 116-11-40 W
Pop: 643 (1990); 700 (1980)   **Pop Density:** 1071.7
Land: 0.6 sq. mi.; **Water:** 0.0 sq. mi.
Name origin: For the bend in the Payette River, on which the town is located.

Idaho City   City
ZIP: 83631   **Lat:** 43-50-32 N **Long:** 115-51-03 W
Pop: 322 (1990); 300 (1980)   **Pop Density:** 644.0
Land: 0.5 sq. mi.; **Water:** 0.0 sq. mi.   **Elev:** 3906 ft.
In west-central ID, northeast of Boise. Founded in 1862. Formerly called West Bannock.
Name origin: For the state.

Placerville   City
ZIP: 83666   **Lat:** 43-56-34 N **Long:** 115-56-41 W
Pop: 14 (1990); 20 (1980)   **Pop Density:** 14.0
Land: 1.0 sq. mi.; **Water:** 0.0 sq. mi.

Bonner County
County Seat: Sandpoint (ZIP: 83864)

Pop: 26,622 (1990); 24,163 (1980)   **Pop Density:** 15.3
Land: 1737.6 sq. mi.; **Water:** 182.0 sq. mi.   **Area Code:** 208

In the north of the ID panhandle, northeast of Spokane, WA; organized Feb 21, 1907 from Kootenai County.

Name origin: For Edwin L. Bonner, an early settler of northern ID who operated a ferry on the Kootenai River.

Clark Fork   City
ZIP: 83811   **Lat:** 48-08-52 N   **Long:** 116-10-36 W
Pop: 448 (1990); 449 (1980)   **Pop Density:** 448.0
Land: 1.0 sq. mi.; **Water:** 0.0 sq. mi.
Name origin: For Clark Fork River, itself named for the explorer George Rogers Clark (1752–1818).

Dover   City
Lat: 48-15-13 N   **Long:** 116-36-01 W
Pop: 294 (1990)   **Pop Density:** 226.2
Land: 1.3 sq. mi.; **Water:** 0.0 sq. mi.

East Hope   City
ZIP: 83836   **Lat:** 48-14-30 N   **Long:** 116-17-28 W
Pop: 215 (1990); 258 (1980)   **Pop Density:** 430.0
Land: 0.5 sq. mi.; **Water:** 0.1 sq. mi.
Name origin: For its location in relation to the town of Hope.

Hope   City
ZIP: 83836   **Lat:** 48-14-52 N   **Long:** 116-18-23 W
Pop: 99 (1990); 106 (1980)   **Pop Density:** 247.5
Land: 0.4 sq. mi.; **Water:** 0.0 sq. mi.
Name origin: Expresses the aspirations of the town's settlers.

Kootenai   City
ZIP: 83840   **Lat:** 48-18-38 N   **Long:** 116-31-03 W
Pop: 327 (1990); 280 (1980)   **Pop Density:** 1090.0
Land: 0.3 sq. mi.; **Water:** 0.0 sq. mi.
Name origin: For the Kootenai Indians, their name meaning 'water people.'

Oldtown   City
ZIP: 83822   **Lat:** 48-10-56 N   **Long:** 117-02-02 W
Pop: 151 (1990); 257 (1980)   **Pop Density:** 755.0
Land: 0.2 sq. mi.; **Water:** 0.0 sq. mi.

Ponderay   City
ZIP: 83852   **Lat:** 48-18-04 N   **Long:** 116-32-22 W
Pop: 449 (1990); 399 (1980)   **Pop Density:** 280.6
Land: 1.6 sq. mi.; **Water:** 0.1 sq. mi.

Priest River   City
ZIP: 83822   **Lat:** 48-11-06 N   **Long:** 116-54-36 W
Pop: 1,560 (1990); 1,639 (1980)   **Pop Density:** 1114.3
Land: 1.4 sq. mi.; **Water:** 0.0 sq. mi.

Sandpoint   City
ZIP: 83864   **Lat:** 48-16-47 N   **Long:** 116-33-29 W
Pop: 5,203 (1990); 4,460 (1980)   **Pop Density:** 1334.1
Land: 3.9 sq. mi.; **Water:** 0.8 sq. mi.

Bonneville County
County Seat: Idaho Falls (ZIP: 83402)

Pop: 72,207 (1990); 65,980 (1980)   **Pop Density:** 38.6
Land: 1868.6 sq. mi.; **Water:** 32.2 sq. mi.   **Area Code:** 208

On the southeastern border of ID, northeast of Pocatello; organized Feb 7, 1911 from Bingham County.

Name origin: For Benjamin Louis Eulalie de Bonneville (1796–1878), French-born officer in the Mexican-American War and explorer of California and the Rocky Mountains region (1831–31); immortalized in the *Adventures of Captain Bonneville* (1837) by Washington Irving (1783–1859).

Ammon   City
ZIP: 83401   **Lat:** 43-28-46 N   **Long:** 111-58-05 W
Pop: 5,002 (1990); 4,669 (1980)   **Pop Density:** 2273.6
Land: 2.2 sq. mi.; **Water:** 0.0 sq. mi.
Name origin: For a leader in the Book of Mormon.

Idaho Falls   City
ZIP: 83402   **Lat:** 43-29-34 N   **Long:** 112-02-05 W
Pop: 43,929 (1990); 39,739 (1980)   **Pop Density:** 3029.6
Land: 14.5 sq. mi.; **Water:** 0.3 sq. mi.
In southeastern ID on the Snake River, 50 mi. north-northwest of Pocatello.
Name origin: For the local falls. Previously called Taylors Ferry, Taylors Bridge, Andersons Bridge, and Eagle Rock. Changed to present name in 1891

Iona   City
ZIP: 83427   **Lat:** 43-31-42 N   **Long:** 111-55-39 W
Pop: 1,049 (1990); 1,072 (1980)   **Pop Density:** 2098.0
Land: 0.5 sq. mi.; **Water:** 0.0 sq. mi.
Incorporated 1886.
Name origin: For the wife of a settler.

Irwin   City
ZIP: 83428   **Lat:** 43-23-51 N   **Long:** 111-15-54 W
Pop: 108 (1990); 113 (1980)   **Pop Density:** 83.1
Land: 1.3 sq. mi.; **Water:** 0.0 sq. mi.

IDAHO, Bonneville County

Ririe
City
ZIP: 83443 **Lat:** 43-37-37 N **Long:** 111-46-27 W
Pop: 74 (1990); 60 (1980)
Land: 0.0 sq. mi.; **Water:** 0.0 sq. mi.
Part of the town is also in Jefferson County.

Swan Valley
City
ZIP: 83449 **Lat:** 43-26-23 N **Long:** 111-18-54 W
Pop: 141 (1990); 135 (1980) **Pop Density:** 15.2
Land: 9.3 sq. mi.; **Water:** 0.0 sq. mi. **Elev:** 5276 ft.

Ucon
City
ZIP: 83454 **Lat:** 43-35-38 N **Long:** 111-57-19 W
Pop: 895 (1990); 833 (1980) **Pop Density:** 1491.7
Land: 0.6 sq. mi.; **Water:** 0.0 sq. mi.

Boundary County
County Seat: Bonners Ferry (ZIP: 83805)

Pop: 8,332 (1990); 7,289 (1980) **Pop Density:** 6.6
Land: 1268.8 sq. mi.; **Water:** 9.4 sq. mi. **Area Code:** 208

On the northern boundary of the ID panhandle; organized Jan 23, 1915 from Kootenai and Bonner counties.

Name origin: Because it borders Canada on the north, MT on the east, and WA on the west.

Bonners Ferry
City
ZIP: 83805 **Lat:** 48-41-29 N **Long:** 116-18-54 W
Pop: 2,193 (1990); 1,906 (1980) **Pop Density:** 1154.2
Land: 1.9 sq. mi.; **Water:** 0.1 sq. mi.
Name origin: For Edwin Bonner, a ferry operator on the Kootenai River.

Moyie Springs
City
ZIP: 83845 **Lat:** 48-43-29 N **Long:** 116-11-33 W
Pop: 415 (1990); 386 (1980) **Pop Density:** 259.4
Land: 1.6 sq. mi.; **Water:** 0.0 sq. mi.
Name origin: For local springs, named for a quartz.

Butte County
County Seat: Arco (ZIP: 83213)

Pop: 2,918 (1990); 3,342 (1980) **Pop Density:** 1.3
Land: 2232.9 sq. mi.; **Water:** 0.7 sq. mi. **Area Code:** 208

In east-central ID, west of Idaho Falls; organized Feb 6, 1917 from Bingham, Blaine, and Jefferson counties.

Name origin: For the landmark buttes rising from the Snake River plains.

Arco
City
ZIP: 83213 **Lat:** 43-38-02 N **Long:** 113-17-59 W
Pop: 1,016 (1990); 1,241 (1980) **Pop Density:** 1128.9
Land: 0.9 sq. mi.; **Water:** 0.0 sq. mi.
Incorporated Nov 24, 1909.
Name origin: For Arco Smith, a stagecoach operator.

Butte City
City
Lat: 43-36-23 N **Long:** 113-14-18 W
Pop: 59 (1990); 93 (1980) **Pop Density:** 295.0
Land: 0.2 sq. mi.; **Water:** 0.0 sq. mi.
Incorporated Apr 9, 1951.
Name origin: For its descriptive connotations.

Moore
City
ZIP: 83255 **Lat:** 43-44-02 N **Long:** 113-21-57 W
Pop: 190 (1990); 210 (1980) **Pop Density:** 633.3
Land: 0.3 sq. mi.; **Water:** 0.0 sq. mi.
Incorporated 1958.

Camas County
County Seat: Fairfield (ZIP: 83327)

Pop: 727 (1990); 818 (1980)   **Pop Density:** 0.7
Land: 1075.0 sq. mi.; **Water:** 4.1 sq. mi.   **Area Code:** 208
In south-central ID, east of Boise; organized Feb 6, 1917 from Blaine County.
Name origin: From the Chinook name for the camas, an edible root of the lily family.

Fairfield   City
ZIP: 83322   **Lat:** 43-20-45 N **Long:** 114-47-31 W
Pop: 371 (1990); 404 (1980)   **Pop Density:** 1236.7
Land: 0.3 sq. mi.; **Water:** 0.0 sq. mi.
Name origin: For its descriptive connotations.

Canyon County
County Seat: Caldwell (ZIP: 83605)

Pop: 90,076 (1990); 83,756 (1980)   **Pop Density:** 152.7
Land: 589.8 sq. mi.; **Water:** 13.8 sq. mi.   **Area Code:** 208
On the southwestern border of ID, west of Boise; established Mar 7, 1891 from Ada County.
Name origin: Either for the canyon of the Boise River near Caldwell, or the Snake River canyon, which forms a county boundary.

Caldwell   City
ZIP: 83605   **Lat:** 43-39-30 N **Long:** 116-40-29 W
Pop: 18,400 (1990); 17,699 (1980)   **Pop Density:** 2067.4
Land: 8.9 sq. mi.; **Water:** 0.0 sq. mi.
In southwestern ID, 25 mi. west of Boise.
Name origin: For early settler Alexander Caldwell (1830–1917) U.S. senator from KS.

Greenleaf   City
ZIP: 83626   **Lat:** 43-40-20 N **Long:** 116-49-13 W
Pop: 648 (1990); 663 (1980)   **Pop Density:** 925.7
Land: 0.7 sq. mi.; **Water:** 0.0 sq. mi.
Name origin: For the Quaker poet, John Greenleaf Whittier (1807–92).

Melba   City
ZIP: 83641   **Lat:** 43-22-26 N **Long:** 116-31-46 W
Pop: 252 (1990); 276 (1980)   **Pop Density:** 840.0
Land: 0.3 sq. mi.; **Water:** 0.0 sq. mi.

Middleton   City
ZIP: 83644   **Lat:** 43-42-27 N **Long:** 116-37-26 W
Pop: 1,851 (1990); 1,901 (1980)   **Pop Density:** 1423.8
Land: 1.3 sq. mi.; **Water:** 0.0 sq. mi.   **Elev:** 2398 ft.
In southwestern ID, a western suburb of Boise.
Name origin: For its location halfway between Boise and Keeneys Ferry, near the confluence of the Boise and Snake rivers, a prominent stopping place on the Oregon Trail.

Nampa   City
ZIP: 83651   **Lat:** 43-34-47 N **Long:** 116-33-50 W
Pop: 28,365 (1990); 25,112 (1980)   **Pop Density:** 2626.4
Land: 10.8 sq. mi.; **Water:** 0.0 sq. mi.
In southwestern ID, 18 mi. west of Boise. Founded 1886.
Name origin: For a renegade Shoshoni chief whose name means 'Big Foot.'

Notus   City
ZIP: 83656   **Lat:** 43-43-32 N **Long:** 116-47-59 W
Pop: 380 (1990); 437 (1980)   **Pop Density:** 1266.7
Land: 0.3 sq. mi.; **Water:** 0.0 sq. mi.

Parma   City
ZIP: 83660   **Lat:** 43-47-07 N **Long:** 116-56-25 W
Pop: 1,597 (1990); 1,820 (1980)   **Pop Density:** 1774.4
Land: 0.9 sq. mi.; **Water:** 0.0 sq. mi.

Wilder   City
ZIP: 83676   **Lat:** 43-40-35 N **Long:** 116-54-28 W
Pop: 1,232 (1990); 1,260 (1980)   **Pop Density:** 4106.7
Land: 0.3 sq. mi.; **Water:** 0.0 sq. mi.

IDAHO, Caribou County

Caribou County
County Seat: Soda Springs (ZIP: 83276)

Pop: 6,963 (1990); 8,695 (1980)　　　　**Pop Density:** 3.9
Land: 1766.1 sq. mi.; **Water:** 32.6 sq. mi.　　**Area Code:** 208

On the southeastern border of ID, east of Pocatello; organized Feb 11, 1919 from Bannock and Oneida counties.

Name origin: For "Caribou (Cariboo)" Fairchild, active in mining in ID; nickname acquired in the Cariboo mine fields of British Columbia, Canada.

Bancroft　　　　　　　　　　　　　　City
ZIP: 83217　　　**Lat:** 42-43-12 N **Long:** 111-52-56 W
Pop: 393 (1990); 505 (1980)　　**Pop Density:** 561.4
Land: 0.7 sq. mi.; **Water:** 0.0 sq. mi.

Name origin: For William H. Bancroft, vice president of the Oregon Short Line Railroad.

Grace　　　　　　　　　　　　　　　City
　　　　　　　　　Lat: 42-34-34 N **Long:** 111-43-48 W
Pop: 973 (1990); 1,216 (1980)　　**Pop Density:** 973.0
Land: 1.0 sq. mi.; **Water:** 0.0 sq. mi.

Name origin: For the wife of D.W. Standrod, a government agent in Blackfoot.

Soda Springs　　　　　　　　　　　City
ZIP: 83276　　　**Lat:** 42-39-30 N **Long:** 111-35-07 W
Pop: 3,111 (1990); 4,051 (1980)　　**Pop Density:** 691.3
Land: 4.5 sq. mi.; **Water:** 0.0 sq. mi.

Cassia County
County Seat: Burley (ZIP: 83318)

Pop: 19,532 (1990); 19,427 (1980)　　**Pop Density:** 7.6
Land: 2566.6 sq. mi.; **Water:** 13.9 sq. mi.　　**Area Code:** 208

On the central southern border of ID, east of Twin Falls; organized Feb 20, 1879 (prior to statehood) from Oneida County.

Name origin: For Cassia Creek (spelled *Cassier* in 1879), named either from French *cajeaux* 'raft,' or for James John Cazier, member of the Mormon Battalion and a colorful wagon train leader. Locals also believe it is for the cassia plant.

Albion　　　　　　　　　　　　　　City
ZIP: 83311　　　**Lat:** 42-24-39 N **Long:** 113-34-48 W
Pop: 305 (1990); 286 (1980)　　**Pop Density:** 762.5
Land: 0.4 sq. mi.; **Water:** 0.0 sq. mi.

Name origin: For the literary name for England.

Burley　　　　　　　　　　　　　　City
ZIP: 83318　　　**Lat:** 42-32-10 N **Long:** 113-47-16 W
Pop: 8,420 (1990); 8,525 (1980)　　**Pop Density:** 2631.3
Land: 3.2 sq. mi.; **Water:** 0.1 sq. mi.　　**Elev:** 4165 ft.

In southern ID, 38 mi. east of Twin Falls. Part of the town is also in Minidoka County.

Name origin: For Union Pacific Railroad official David Burley.

Declo　　　　　　　　　　　　　　City
ZIP: 83323　　　**Lat:** 42-31-09 N **Long:** 113-37-41 W
Pop: 279 (1990); 276 (1980)　　**Pop Density:** 930.0
Land: 0.3 sq. mi.; **Water:** 0.0 sq. mi.

Malta　　　　　　　　　　　　　　　City
ZIP: 83342　　　**Lat:** 42-18-27 N **Long:** 113-22-10 W
Pop: 171 (1990); 196 (1980)　　**Pop Density:** 122.1
Land: 1.4 sq. mi.; **Water:** 0.0 sq. mi.

Name origin: For the island in the Mediterranean Sea.

Oakley　　　　　　　　　　　　　　City
ZIP: 83346　　　**Lat:** 42-14-32 N **Long:** 113-52-48 W
Pop: 635 (1990); 663 (1980)　　**Pop Density:** 158.8
Land: 4.0 sq. mi.; **Water:** 0.0 sq. mi.

Name origin: For Thomas Oakley, stage station operator.

Clark County
County Seat: Dubois (ZIP: 83423)

Pop: 762 (1990); 798 (1980)   **Pop Density:** 0.4
Land: 1764.7 sq. mi.; **Water:** 0.6 sq. mi.   **Area Code:** 208

On lower northern border of ID, north of Idaho Falls; organized Feb 1, 1919 from Fremont County.

Name origin: For Sam K. Clark, an early settler on Medicine Lodge Creek, and first state senator from the county.

Dubois   City
ZIP: 83423   **Lat:** 44-10-24 N   **Long:** 112-13-45 W
Pop: 420 (1990); 413 (1980)   **Pop Density:** 190.9
Land: 2.2 sq. mi.; **Water:** 0.0 sq. mi.   **Elev:** 5145 ft.
Name origin: For Fred T. DuBois, a U.S. senator from ID (1891–97; 1901–07).

Spencer   City
ZIP: 83446   **Lat:** 44-22-50 N   **Long:** 112-11-10 W
Pop: 11 (1990); 29 (1980)   **Pop Density:** 10.0
Land: 1.1 sq. mi.; **Water:** 0.0 sq. mi.

Clearwater County
County Seat: Orofino (ZIP: 83544)

Pop: 8,505 (1990); 10,390 (1980)   **Pop Density:** 3.5
Land: 2461.6 sq. mi.; **Water:** 26.7 sq. mi.   **Area Code:** 208

On the eastern border of the ID panhandle, east of Lewiston; organized Feb 27, 1911 from Nez Perce County.

Name origin: For the Clearwater River, itself named for the translation of the Nez Perce descriptive name.

Elk River   City
ZIP: 83827   **Lat:** 46-46-56 N   **Long:** 116-10-49 W
Pop: 149 (1990); 265 (1980)   **Pop Density:** 1490.0
Land: 0.1 sq. mi.; **Water:** 0.0 sq. mi.
Incorporated Oct 15, 1910.
Name origin: For once being the site of large elk herds.

Orofino   City
ZIP: 83544   **Lat:** 46-29-18 N   **Long:** 116-15-28 W
Pop: 2,868 (1990); 3,711 (1980)   **Pop Density:** 1195.0
Land: 2.4 sq. mi.; **Water:** 0.1 sq. mi.
In northeastern ID, east of Lewiston. Incorporated 1927.
Name origin: From the Spanish meaning 'fine gold,' referring to the gold mining in the area.

Pierce   City
ZIP: 83546   **Lat:** 46-29-33 N   **Long:** 115-47-54 W
Pop: 746 (1990); 1,060 (1980)   **Pop Density:** 932.5
Land: 0.8 sq. mi.; **Water:** 0.0 sq. mi.
In northeastern ID, east of Lewiston. Incorporated 1935.

Weippe   City
ZIP: 83553   **Lat:** 46-22-41 N   **Long:** 115-56-19 W
Pop: 532 (1990); 828 (1980)   **Pop Density:** 1330.0
Land: 0.4 sq. mi.; **Water:** 0.0 sq. mi.

Custer County
County Seat: Challis (ZIP: 83226)

Pop: 4,133 (1990); 3,385 (1980)   **Pop Density:** 0.8
Land: 4925.6 sq. mi.; **Water:** 11.3 sq. mi.   **Area Code:** 208
In central ID; organized Jan 8, 1881 (prior to statehood) from Alturas and Lemhi counties.
Name origin: For the General Custer mine, named for Gen. George Armstrong Custer (1839–76), U.S. officer and Indian fighter.

Challis   City
ZIP: 83226   **Lat:** 44-30-27 N   **Long:** 114-13-26 W
Pop: 1,073 (1990); 758 (1980)   **Pop Density:** 825.4
Land: 1.3 sq. mi.; **Water:** 0.0 sq. mi.   **Elev:** 5288 ft.
Incorporated Oct, 1981.
Name origin: For founder A. P. Challis.

Clayton   City
ZIP: 83227   **Lat:** 44-15-32 N   **Long:** 114-23-54 W
Pop: 26 (1990); 43 (1980)   **Pop Density:** 2600.0
Land: 0.01 sq. mi.; **Water:** 0.0 sq. mi.
Incorporated Jan 1, 1961.
Name origin: For Clayton Smith, proprietor of a house of ill-repute during the mining rush.

Lost River   City
Lat: 43-43-18 N   **Long:** 113-32-38 W
Pop: 29 (1990); 28 (1980)   **Pop Density:** 3.3
Land: 8.7 sq. mi.; **Water:** 0.0 sq. mi.
Name origin: For the Big Lost River, which runs through the southern part of the county.

Mackay   City
ZIP: 83251   **Lat:** 43-54-43 N   **Long:** 113-36-39 W
Pop: 574 (1990); 541 (1980)   **Pop Density:** 637.8
Land: 0.9 sq. mi.; **Water:** 0.0 sq. mi.

Stanley   City
ZIP: 83278   **Lat:** 44-12-56 N   **Long:** 114-56-13 W
Pop: 71 (1990); 99 (1980)   **Pop Density:** 118.3
Land: 0.6 sq. mi.; **Water:** 0.0 sq. mi.
Incorporated 1947.

Elmore County
County Seat: Mountain Home (ZIP: 83647)

Pop: 21,205 (1990); 21,565 (1980)   **Pop Density:** 6.9
Land: 3077.8 sq. mi.; **Water:** 22.9 sq. mi.   **Area Code:** 208
In southwestern ID, east of Boise; organized Feb 7, 1889 (prior to statehood) from Alturas County.
Name origin: For the Ida Elmore Quartz Mine, largest producer of gold and silver during the 1860s.

Glenns Ferry   City
ZIP: 83623   **Lat:** 42-57-14 N   **Long:** 115-17-59 W
Pop: 1,304 (1990); 1,374 (1980)   **Pop Density:** 931.4
Land: 1.4 sq. mi.; **Water:** 0.0 sq. mi.   **Elev:** 2560 ft.
In southwest-central ID, southeast of Boise on the Snake River.
Name origin: For an early ferryman.

Mountain Home   City
ZIP: 83647   **Lat:** 43-08-18 N   **Long:** 115-41-19 W
Pop: 7,913 (1990); 7,540 (1980)   **Pop Density:** 2198.1
Land: 3.6 sq. mi.; **Water:** 0.0 sq. mi.   **Elev:** 3143 ft.
In southwest-central ID, southeast of Boise.
Name origin: For its descriptive connotations.

Mountain Home Air Force Base   Military Facility
ZIP: 83648   **Lat:** 43-02-58 N   **Long:** 115-51-55 W
Pop: 5,936 (1990); 6,403 (1980)   **Pop Density:** 599.6
Land: 9.9 sq. mi.; **Water:** 0.0 sq. mi.

Franklin County
County Seat: Preston (ZIP: 83262)

Pop: 9,232 (1990); 8,895 (1980)   **Pop Density:** 13.9
Land: 665.5 sq. mi.; **Water:** 2.9 sq. mi.   **Area Code:** 208

On the southern border of ID, southeast of Pocatello; organized Jan 30, 1913 from Oneida County.

Name origin: For the first settlement in ID, named for Franklin Dewey Richards (1821–99), a Mormon apostle.

Clifton — City
ZIP: 83228   **Lat:** 42-11-15 N   **Long:** 112-00-18 W
Pop: 228 (1990); 208 (1980)   **Pop Density:** 99.1
Land: 2.3 sq. mi.; **Water:** 0.0 sq. mi.
Name origin: For a high cleft in rocks nearby.

Dayton — City
ZIP: 83232   **Lat:** 42-06-46 N   **Long:** 111-58-35 W
Pop: 357 (1990); 368 (1980)   **Pop Density:** 55.8
Land: 6.4 sq. mi.; **Water:** 0.0 sq. mi.   **Elev:** 4772 ft.
Name origin: For Johnathon Dayton, Revolutionary War general.

Franklin — City
ZIP: 83237   **Lat:** 42-00-58 N   **Long:** 111-48-08 W
Pop: 478 (1990); 423 (1980)   **Pop Density:** 597.5
Land: 0.8 sq. mi.; **Water:** 0.0 sq. mi.   **Elev:** 4504 ft.
Incorporated Aug 1, 1967.

Oxford — City
ZIP: 83263   **Lat:** 42-15-35 N   **Long:** 112-00-59 W
Pop: 44 (1990); 66 (1980)   **Pop Density:** 146.7
Land: 0.3 sq. mi.; **Water:** 0.0 sq. mi.   **Elev:** 4798 ft.
Name origin: For Oxford Creek, itself named when hunters found oxen tracks at the ford.

Preston — City
ZIP: 83263   **Lat:** 42-05-50 N   **Long:** 111-52-28 W
Pop: 3,710 (1990); 3,759 (1980)   **Pop Density:** 674.5
Land: 5.5 sq. mi.; **Water:** 0.0 sq. mi.

Weston — City
ZIP: 83286   **Lat:** 42-02-18 N   **Long:** 111-58-37 W
Pop: 390 (1990); 310 (1980)   **Pop Density:** 195.0
Land: 2.0 sq. mi.; **Water:** 0.0 sq. mi.   **Elev:** 4743 ft.

Fremont County
County Seat: Saint Anthony (ZIP: 83445)

Pop: 10,937 (1990); 10,813 (1980)   **Pop Density:** 5.9
Land: 1866.8 sq. mi.; **Water:** 28.8 sq. mi.   **Area Code:** 208

On the lower northeastern border of ID, northeast of Idaho Falls; organized Mar 4, 1893 from Bingham County.

Name origin: For John Charles Frémont (1813–90), soldier and explorer who led five expeditions to the West, U.S. senator from CA (1850–51), and governor of the AZ Territory (1878–81).

Ashton — City
Lat: 44-04-24 N   **Long:** 111-26-54 W
Pop: 1,114 (1990); 1,219 (1980)   **Pop Density:** 2228.0
Land: 0.5 sq. mi.; **Water:** 0.0 sq. mi.   **Elev:** 5260 ft.
Incorporated 1906.
Name origin: For Walter Ashton, a construction engineer on the railroad.

Drummond — City
ZIP: 83420   **Lat:** 43-59-55 N   **Long:** 111-20-29 W
Pop: 37 (1990); 25 (1980)   **Pop Density:** 370.0
Land: 0.1 sq. mi.; **Water:** 0.0 sq. mi.   **Elev:** 5607 ft.

Island Park — City
Lat: 44-33-24 N   **Long:** 111-20-13 W
Pop: 159 (1990); 154 (1980)   **Pop Density:** 25.6
Land: 6.2 sq. mi.; **Water:** 1.2 sq. mi.
Name origin: For islands of timber on the nearby sagebrush plain.

Newdale — City
ZIP: 83436   **Lat:** 43-53-09 N   **Long:** 111-36-14 W
Pop: 377 (1990); 329 (1980)   **Pop Density:** 1885.0
Land: 0.2 sq. mi.; **Water:** 0.0 sq. mi.

Parker — City
ZIP: 83438   **Lat:** 43-57-30 N   **Long:** 111-45-30 W
Pop: 288 (1990); 262 (1980)   **Pop Density:** 720.0
Land: 0.4 sq. mi.; **Water:** 0.0 sq. mi.

St. Anthony — City
ZIP: 83445   **Lat:** 43-57-58 N   **Long:** 111-41-01 W
Pop: 3,010 (1990); 3,212 (1980)   **Pop Density:** 2508.3
Land: 1.2 sq. mi.; **Water:** 0.0 sq. mi.

Teton — City
ZIP: 83451   **Lat:** 43-53-15 N   **Long:** 111-40-06 W
Pop: 570 (1990); 559 (1980)   **Pop Density:** 1140.0
Land: 0.5 sq. mi.; **Water:** 0.0 sq. mi.   **Elev:** 4949 ft.

IDAHO, Fremont County

Warm River City
ZIP: 83420 **Lat:** 44-07-10 N **Long:** 111-19-21 W
Pop: 9 (1990); 2 (1980) **Pop Density:** 18.0
Land: 0.5 sq. mi.; **Water:** 0.0 sq. mi.

Gem County
County Seat: Emmett (ZIP: 83617)

Pop: 11,844 (1990); 11,972 (1980) **Pop Density:** 21.1
Land: 562.6 sq. mi.; **Water:** 3.2 sq. mi. **Area Code:** 208
In southwestern ID, north of Boise; organized Mar 19, 1915 from Boise and Canyon counties.
Name origin: For the state nickname, "Gem State," from the supposed Indian meaning of *Idaho* 'Gem of the Mountain.'

Emmett City
ZIP: 83617 **Lat:** 43-52-26 N **Long:** 116-29-38 W
Pop: 4,601 (1990); 4,605 (1980) **Pop Density:** 3286.4
Land: 1.4 sq. mi.; **Water:** 0.0 sq. mi.
In southwestern ID, northwest of Boise.
Name origin: For Emmett Cahalan, first European child born in the area. Shortened from Emmettsville in 1885.

Gooding County
County Seat: Gooding (ZIP: 83330)

Pop: 11,633 (1990); 11,874 (1980) **Pop Density:** 15.9
Land: 730.8 sq. mi.; **Water:** 3.0 sq. mi. **Area Code:** 208
In south-central ID, northwest of Twin Falls; organized Jan 28, 1913 from Lincoln County.
Name origin: For Frank Robert Gooding (1859–1928), governor of Idaho (1905–08) and U.S. senator (1921–28).

Bliss City
ZIP: 83314 **Lat:** 42-55-34 N **Long:** 114-56-56 W
Pop: 185 (1990); 208 (1980) **Pop Density:** 370.0
Land: 0.5 sq. mi.; **Water:** 0.0 sq. mi. **Elev:** 3262 ft.
Name origin: For David B. Bliss, early settler, whose wife was instrumental in having the first school district created.

Gooding City
ZIP: 83330 **Lat:** 42-56-17 N **Long:** 114-42-45 W
Pop: 2,820 (1990); 2,949 (1980) **Pop Density:** 2169.2
Land: 1.3 sq. mi.; **Water:** 0.0 sq. mi. **Elev:** 3573 ft.

Hagerman City
ZIP: 83332 **Lat:** 42-49-01 N **Long:** 114-53-47 W
Pop: 600 (1990); 602 (1980) **Pop Density:** 2000.0
Land: 0.3 sq. mi.; **Water:** 0.0 sq. mi. **Elev:** 2959 ft.

Wendell City
ZIP: 83355 **Lat:** 42-46-33 N **Long:** 114-42-06 W
Pop: 1,963 (1990); 1,974 (1980) **Pop Density:** 1784.5
Land: 1.1 sq. mi.; **Water:** 0.0 sq. mi.

Idaho County
County Seat: Grangeville (ZIP: 83530)

Pop: 13,783 (1990); 14,769 (1980)   **Pop Density:** 1.6
Land: 8485.2 sq. mi.; **Water:** 17.6 sq. mi.   **Area Code:** 208

At the southern base of the ID panhandle, east and south of Lewiston; original county; organized Feb 4, 1864 (prior to statehood). Originally established in 1861 as the third county of WA Territory, now in ID.

Name origin: For the steamer *Idaho*, launched Jun 9, 1860 on the Columbia River to serve miners in the gold rush.

Cottonwood   City
ZIP: 83522   **Lat:** 46-03-01 N   **Long:** 116-20-52 W
Pop: 822 (1990); 941 (1980)   **Pop Density:** 1027.5
Land: 0.8 sq. mi.; **Water:** 0.0 sq. mi.
Name origin: For the local cottonwood trees.

Ferdinand   City
ZIP: 83526   **Lat:** 46-09-10 N   **Long:** 116-23-22 W
Pop: 135 (1990); 144 (1980)   **Pop Density:** 1350.0
Land: 0.1 sq. mi.; **Water:** 0.0 sq. mi.

Grangeville   City
ZIP: 83530   **Lat:** 45-55-33 N   **Long:** 116-07-14 W
Pop: 3,226 (1990); 3,666 (1980)   **Pop Density:** 2481.5
Land: 1.3 sq. mi.; **Water:** 0.0 sq. mi.
Name origin: For the local Grange, a farmers' organization.

Kamiah   City
Lat: 46-12-54 N   **Long:** 116-00-46 W
Pop: 3 (1990); 1,478 (1980)   **Pop Density:** 150.0
Land: 0.02 sq. mi.; **Water:** 0.0 sq. mi.
Part of the town is also in Lewis County.

Kooskia   City
ZIP: 83539   **Lat:** 46-08-21 N   **Long:** 115-58-19 W
Pop: 692 (1990); 784 (1980)   **Pop Density:** 988.6
Land: 0.7 sq. mi.; **Water:** 0.0 sq. mi.
In north-central ID, southeast of Lewiston, at the confluence of the Clearwater River with its Middle Fork.
Name origin: From Indian term of uncertain meaning, but possibly 'where the waters join.'.

Riggins   City
ZIP: 83549   **Lat:** 45-25-19 N   **Long:** 116-18-53 W
Pop: 443 (1990); 527 (1980)   **Pop Density:** 1476.7
Land: 0.3 sq. mi.; **Water:** 0.0 sq. mi.   **Elev:** 1800 ft.

Stites   City
ZIP: 83552   **Lat:** 46-05-32 N   **Long:** 115-58-32 W
Pop: 204 (1990); 253 (1980)   **Pop Density:** 2040.0
Land: 0.1 sq. mi.; **Water:** 0.0 sq. mi.

White Bird   City
ZIP: 83554   **Lat:** 45-45-46 N   **Long:** 116-17-56 W
Pop: 108 (1990); 154 (1980)   **Pop Density:** 1080.0
Land: 0.1 sq. mi.; **Water:** 0.0 sq. mi.

Jefferson County
County Seat: Rigby (ZIP: 83442)

Pop: 16,543 (1990); 15,304 (1980)   **Pop Density:** 15.1
Land: 1095.1 sq. mi.; **Water:** 10.5 sq. mi.   **Area Code:** 208

In southeastern ID, north of Idaho Falls; organized Feb 18, 1913 from Fremont County.

Name origin: For Thomas Jefferson (1743–1826), U.S. patriot and statesman; third U.S. president.

Hamer   City
ZIP: 83425   **Lat:** 43-55-32 N   **Long:** 112-12-13 W
Pop: 79 (1990); 93 (1980)   **Pop Density:** 395.0
Land: 0.2 sq. mi.; **Water:** 0.0 sq. mi.   **Elev:** 4814 ft.

Lewisville   City
ZIP: 83431   **Lat:** 43-41-41 N   **Long:** 112-00-50 W
Pop: 471 (1990); 502 (1980)   **Pop Density:** 785.0
Land: 0.6 sq. mi.; **Water:** 0.0 sq. mi.
Name origin: For explorer Meriwether Lewis (1774–1809).

Menan   City
ZIP: 83434   **Lat:** 43-43-19 N   **Long:** 111-59-38 W
Pop: 601 (1990); 605 (1980)   **Pop Density:** 667.8
Land: 0.9 sq. mi.; **Water:** 0.0 sq. mi.

Mud Lake   City
ZIP: 83450   **Lat:** 43-50-33 N   **Long:** 112-28-44 W
Pop: 179 (1990); 243 (1980)   **Pop Density:** 895.0
Land: 0.2 sq. mi.; **Water:** 0.0 sq. mi.

Rigby   City
ZIP: 83442   **Lat:** 43-40-26 N   **Long:** 111-54-55 W
Pop: 2,681 (1990); 2,624 (1980)   **Pop Density:** 2978.9
Land: 0.9 sq. mi.; **Water:** 0.0 sq. mi.

Ririe   City
ZIP: 83443   **Lat:** 43-37-52 N   **Long:** 111-46-24 W
Pop: 522 (1990); 495 (1980)   **Pop Density:** 2610.0
Land: 0.2 sq. mi.; **Water:** 0.0 sq. mi.
Part of the town is also in Bonneville County.

IDAHO, Jefferson County   *American Places Dictionary*

Roberts   City
ZIP: 83444   **Lat:** 43-43-14 N **Long:** 112-07-36 W
Pop: 557 (1990); 466 (1980)   **Pop Density:** 1856.7
Land: 0.3 sq. mi.; **Water:** 0.0 sq. mi.

Jerome County
County Seat: Jerome (ZIP: 83338)

Pop: 15,138 (1990); 14,840 (1980)   **Pop Density:** 25.2
Land: 599.9 sq. mi.; **Water:** 2.0 sq. mi.   **Area Code:** 208

In south-central ID, north of Twin Falls; organized Feb 18, 1919 from Gooding and Lincoln counties.

Name origin: Either for Jerome Hill, a principal figure in the Twin Falls North Side Irrigation Project (1905), or Jerome Kuhn, his son-in-law, or for Jerome Kuhn, Jr., his grandson. All were major figures in the growth of the county.

Eden   City
ZIP: 83325   **Lat:** 42-36-18 N **Long:** 114-12-31 W
Pop: 314 (1990); 355 (1980)   **Pop Density:** 1046.7
Land: 0.3 sq. mi.; **Water:** 0.0 sq. mi.
Name origin: For the Biblical garden.

Hazelton   City
ZIP: 83335   **Lat:** 42-35-41 N **Long:** 114-08-03 W
Pop: 394 (1990); 496 (1980)   **Pop Density:** 1313.3
Land: 0.3 sq. mi.; **Water:** 0.0 sq. mi.
In southern ID.
Name origin: For Hazel Barlow, daughter of the town founder.

Jerome   City
ZIP: 83338   **Lat:** 42-43-32 N **Long:** 114-30-56 W
Pop: 6,529 (1990); 6,891 (1980)   **Pop Density:** 3109.0
Land: 2.1 sq. mi.; **Water:** 0.0 sq. mi.
In southern ID, 14 mi. north of Twin Falls. Incorporated 1909.
Name origin: Either for Jerome Hill, a principal figure in the Twin Falls North Side Irrigation Project (1905), or Jerome Kuhn, his son-in-law, or for Jerome Kuhn, Jr., his grandson. All were major figures in the growth of the county.

Kootenai County
County Seat: Coeur d'Alene (ZIP: 83814)

Pop: 69,795 (1990); 59,770 (1980)   **Pop Density:** 56.1
Land: 1245.2 sq. mi.; **Water:** 70.6 sq. mi.   **Area Code:** 208

On the western border of the ID panhandle, east of Spokane, WA; original county; organized Dec 22, 1864 (prior to statehood).

Name origin: For the Kootenai (or Kutenai) Indian tribe, whose name means 'water people.'

Athol   City
ZIP: 83801   **Lat:** 47-56-42 N **Long:** 116-42-23 W
Pop: 346 (1990); 312 (1980)   **Pop Density:** 432.5
Land: 0.8 sq. mi.; **Water:** 0.0 sq. mi.   **Elev:** 2391 ft.

Coeur d'Alene   City
ZIP: 83814   **Lat:** 47-41-52 N **Long:** 116-47-05 W
Pop: 24,563 (1990); 19,913 (1980)   **Pop Density:** 2317.3
Land: 10.6 sq. mi.; **Water:** 0.4 sq. mi.   **Elev:** 2187 ft.
In northern ID, 32 mi. east of Spokane, WA.
Name origin: From the French name for a Skitswish Indian tribe meaning 'heart of awl' or 'needle-hearted,' for the shrewd trading ability of the Indians.

Dalton Gardens   City
                        Lat: 47-44-00 N **Long:** 116-46-00 W
Pop: 1,951 (1990); 1,795 (1980)   **Pop Density:** 812.9
Land: 2.4 sq. mi.; **Water:** 0.0 sq. mi.

Fernan Lake Village   City
                        Lat: 47-40-23 N **Long:** 116-44-49 W
Pop: 170 (1990); 178 (1980)   **Pop Density:** 1700.0
Land: 0.1 sq. mi.; **Water:** 0.0 sq. mi.
Name origin: For an early pioneer, who also gave the lake his name.

Harrison   City
ZIP: 83833   **Lat:** 47-27-08 N **Long:** 116-46-49 W
Pop: 226 (1990); 260 (1980)   **Pop Density:** 565.0
Land: 0.4 sq. mi.; **Water:** 0.1 sq. mi.

Hauser   City
ZIP: 83854   **Lat:** 47-46-10 N **Long:** 117-00-42 W
Pop: 380 (1990); 305 (1980)   **Pop Density:** 475.0
Land: 0.8 sq. mi.; **Water:** 0.0 sq. mi.

American Places Dictionary   IDAHO, Latah County

Hayden — City
ZIP: 83835   **Lat:** 47-45-36 N **Long:** 116-47-18 W
Pop: 3,744 (1990); 2,586 (1980)   **Pop Density:** 960.0
Land: 3.9 sq. mi.; **Water:** 0.0 sq. mi.

Name origin: Possibly for eminent geologist Ferdinand Vandiver Hayden.

Hayden Lake — City
ZIP: 83835   **Lat:** 47-45-56 N **Long:** 116-45-10 W
Pop: 338 (1990); 273 (1980)   **Pop Density:** 845.0
Land: 0.4 sq. mi.; **Water:** 0.0 sq. mi.

Name origin: For Matt Heyden, who won the right to name the lake and town in a game of seven-up; with a spelling variation.

Huetter — City
Lat: 47-42-13 N **Long:** 116-50-52 W
Pop: 82 (1990); 65 (1980)   **Pop Density:** 8200.0
Land: 0.01 sq. mi.; **Water:** 0.0 sq. mi.

Post Falls — City
ZIP: 83854   **Lat:** 47-42-44 N **Long:** 116-56-40 W
Pop: 7,349 (1990); 5,736 (1980)   **Pop Density:** 1267.1
Land: 5.8 sq. mi.; **Water:** 0.1 sq. mi.

In northern ID, east of Spokane, WA, on the Upper Falls of the Spokane River.

Name origin: For the falls created by Frederick Post when he dammed the three channels of the river to power his lumber mill.

Rathdrum — City
ZIP: 83858   **Lat:** 47-48-41 N **Long:** 116-53-19 W
Pop: 2,000 (1990); 1,369 (1980)   **Pop Density:** 1428.6
Land: 1.4 sq. mi.; **Water:** 0.0 sq. mi.

Spirit Lake — City
ZIP: 83869   **Lat:** 47-58-04 N **Long:** 116-52-10 W
Pop: 790 (1990); 834 (1980)   **Pop Density:** 790.0
Land: 1.0 sq. mi.; **Water:** 0.0 sq. mi.

State Line — City
ZIP: 83854   **Lat:** 47-42-22 N **Long:** 117-02-06 W
Pop: 26 (1990); 26 (1980)   **Pop Density:** 260.0
Land: 0.1 sq. mi.; **Water:** 0.0 sq. mi.

Worley — City
ZIP: 83876   **Lat:** 47-24-04 N **Long:** 116-55-06 W
Pop: 182 (1990); 206 (1980)   **Pop Density:** 910.0
Land: 0.2 sq. mi.; **Water:** 0.0 sq. mi.

Latah County
County Seat: Moscow (ZIP: 83843)

Pop: 30,617 (1990); 28,749 (1980)   **Pop Density:** 28.4
Land: 1076.7 sq. mi.; **Water:** 0.2 sq. mi.   **Area Code:** 208

On the western border of the ID panhandle, north of Lewiston; organized May 14, 1888 (prior to statehood) from Kootenai County.

Name origin: For Latah Creek from a combination of two Nez Perce words, *lakah* 'place of the pines,' and *tah-ol* 'pestle.' The Indians found stones there to grind camas roots and shade in which to work.

Bovill — City
ZIP: 83806   **Lat:** 46-51-29 N **Long:** 116-23-35 W
Pop: 256 (1990); 289 (1980)   **Pop Density:** 1280.0
Land: 0.2 sq. mi.; **Water:** 0.0 sq. mi.

Name origin: For Hugh Bovill, founder and first postmaster.

Deary — City
ZIP: 83823   **Lat:** 46-48-02 N **Long:** 116-33-23 W
Pop: 529 (1990); 539 (1980)   **Pop Density:** 881.7
Land: 0.6 sq. mi.; **Water:** 0.0 sq. mi.

Name origin: For William Deary, early settler who directed the construction of the lumber mill and town in 1906. Formerly called Anderson.

Genesee — City
ZIP: 83832   **Lat:** 46-33-04 N **Long:** 116-55-40 W
Pop: 725 (1990); 791 (1980)   **Pop Density:** 1208.3
Land: 0.6 sq. mi.; **Water:** 0.0 sq. mi.   **Elev:** 2675 ft.

Name origin: From an Iroquoian term meaning 'beautiful valley.'

Juliaetta — City
ZIP: 83535   **Lat:** 46-34-28 N **Long:** 116-42-28 W
Pop: 488 (1990); 522 (1980)   **Pop Density:** 697.1
Land: 0.7 sq. mi.; **Water:** 0.0 sq. mi.

Name origin: For the daughters of Charles Snyder, the first postmaster.

Kendrick — City
ZIP: 83537   **Lat:** 46-36-50 N **Long:** 116-39-07 W
Pop: 325 (1990); 395 (1980)   **Pop Density:** 812.5
Land: 0.4 sq. mi.; **Water:** 0.0 sq. mi.

Moscow — City
ZIP: 83843   **Lat:** 46-43-47 N **Long:** 116-59-48 W
Pop: 18,519 (1990); 16,513 (1980)   **Pop Density:** 3858.1
Land: 4.8 sq. mi.; **Water:** 0.0 sq. mi.   **Elev:** 2583 ft.

In northwestern ID on the WA border, 25 mi. north of Lewiston.

Name origin: For Moscow, PA, and Moscow, IA, first home towns of S.M. Neff, who filled out the post office applications.

IDAHO, Latah County — American Places Dictionary

Onaway City
Lat: 46-55-43 N Long: 116-53-17 W
Pop: 203 (1990); 254 (1980) Pop Density: 2030.0
Land: 0.1 sq. mi.; Water: 0.0 sq. mi.
Name origin: For Onaway, NY, former home of some early settlers.

Potlatch City
ZIP: 83855 Lat: 46-55-23 N Long: 116-53-52 W
Pop: 790 (1990); 819 (1980) Pop Density: 2633.3
Land: 0.3 sq. mi.; Water: 0.0 sq. mi.
In northwestern ID, northeast of Lewiston. Incorporated 1952.
Name origin: From Chinook jargon for a ceremonial gathering of Indian tribes held each spring, during which gifts were exchanged in the spirit of good fellowship.

Troy City
ZIP: 83871 Lat: 46-44-19 N Long: 116-46-04 W
Pop: 699 (1990); 820 (1980) Pop Density: 1398.0
Land: 0.5 sq. mi.; Water: 0.0 sq. mi.
Incorporated 1892.

Lemhi County
County Seat: Salmon (ZIP: 83467)

Pop: 6,899 (1990); 7,460 (1980) Pop Density: 1.5
Land: 4564.3 sq. mi.; Water: 5.3 sq. mi. Area Code: 208
On the central eastern border of ID; organized Mar 3, 1869 (prior to statehood) from Idaho County.
Name origin: For Fort Lemhi, a Mormon mission on the Salmon River, named for a character in the Book of Mormon.

Leadore City
ZIP: 83464 Lat: 44-40-47 N Long: 113-21-23 W
Pop: 74 (1990); 114 (1980) Pop Density: 246.7
Land: 0.3 sq. mi.; Water: 0.0 sq. mi.
Name origin: For the metal mined in the area.

Salmon City
ZIP: 83467 Lat: 45-10-40 N Long: 113-53-54 W
Pop: 2,941 (1990); 3,308 (1980) Pop Density: 1730.0
Land: 1.7 sq. mi.; Water: 0.1 sq. mi.

Lewis County
County Seat: Nezperce (ZIP: 83543)

Pop: 3,516 (1990); 4,118 (1980) Pop Density: 7.3
Land: 479.1 sq. mi.; Water: 0.8 sq. mi. Area Code: 208
In central-western ID, southeast of Lewiston; organized Mar 3, 1911 from Nez Perce County.
Name origin: For Meriwether Lewis (1774–1809), co-leader of the Lewis and Clark expedition (1804-06).

Craigmont City
ZIP: 83523 Lat: 46-14-34 N Long: 116-28-16 W
Pop: 542 (1990); 617 (1980) Pop Density: 774.3
Land: 0.7 sq. mi.; Water: 0.0 sq. mi.
Name origin: For Craig Mountain, itself named for William Craig, first permanent European settler in the state.

Kamiah City
ZIP: 83536 Lat: 46-13-36 N Long: 116-01-39 W
Pop: 1,154 (1990); 1,478 (1980) Pop Density: 1049.1
Land: 1.1 sq. mi.; Water: 0.1 sq. mi.
Part of the town is also in Idaho County.

Nezperce City
ZIP: 83543 Lat: 46-14-00 N Long: 116-14-19 W
Pop: 453 (1990); 517 (1980) Pop Density: 1132.5
Land: 0.4 sq. mi.; Water: 0.0 sq. mi. Elev: ft.
Name origin: The French name for the Chopunnish Indian tribe. Meaning is literally 'pierced nose,' but might be more descriptively translated as 'mashed' or 'flattened nose.'

Reubens City
ZIP: 83548 Lat: 46-19-19 N Long: 116-32-27 W
Pop: 46 (1990); 87 (1980) Pop Density: 153.3
Land: 0.3 sq. mi.; Water: 0.0 sq. mi. Elev: 3514 ft.

Winchester City
ZIP: 83555 Lat: 46-14-27 N Long: 116-37-20 W
Pop: 262 (1990); 343 (1980) Pop Density: 1310.0
Land: 0.2 sq. mi.; Water: 0.0 sq. mi. Elev: 3968 ft.

Lincoln County
County Seat: Shoshone (ZIP: 83352)

Pop: 3,308 (1990); 3,436 (1980)   **Pop Density:** 2.7
Land: 1205.6 sq. mi.; **Water:** 0.3 sq. mi.   **Area Code:** 208
In south-central ID, north of Twin Falls; organized Mar 18, 1895 from Blaine County.
Name origin: For Abraham Lincoln (1809–65), sixteenth U.S. president.

Dietrich — City
ZIP: 83324   **Lat:** 42-54-49 N   **Long:** 114-15-50 W
Pop: 127 (1990); 101 (1980)   **Pop Density:** 635.0
Land: 0.2 sq. mi.; **Water:** 0.0 sq. mi.

Richfield — City
ZIP: 83349   **Lat:** 43-03-08 N   **Long:** 114-09-18 W
Pop: 383 (1990); 357 (1980)   **Pop Density:** 638.3
Land: 0.6 sq. mi.; **Water:** 0.0 sq. mi.

Shoshone — City
ZIP: 83324   **Lat:** 42-56-10 N   **Long:** 114-24-16 W
Pop: 1,249 (1990); 1,242 (1980)   **Pop Density:** 1561.3
Land: 0.8 sq. mi.; **Water:** 0.0 sq. mi.
Name origin: For the Indian tribe.

Madison County
County Seat: Rexburg (ZIP: 83440)

Pop: 23,674 (1990); 19,480 (1980)   **Pop Density:** 50.2
Land: 471.6 sq. mi.; **Water:** 1.8 sq. mi.   **Area Code:** 208
In southeastern ID, northeast of Idaho Falls; organized Feb 18, 1913 from Fremont County.
Name origin: For James Madison (1751–1836), fourth U.S. president.

Rexburg — City
ZIP: 83440   **Lat:** 43-49-30 N   **Long:** 111-47-14 W
Pop: 14,302 (1990); 11,559 (1980)   **Pop Density:** 3405.2
Land: 4.2 sq. mi.; **Water:** 0.1 sq. mi.   **Elev:** 4865 ft.
In eastern ID, 25 mi. northeast of Idaho Falls. Settled 1883.
Name origin: For Morman leader Thomas E. Ricks, from the Latin root of his surname plus *burg* 'city.'

Sugar City — City
ZIP: 83448   **Lat:** 43-52-20 N   **Long:** 111-44-47 W
Pop: 1,275 (1990); 1,022 (1980)   **Pop Density:** 2550.0
Land: 0.5 sq. mi.; **Water:** 0.0 sq. mi.

Minidoka County
County Seat: Rupert (ZIP: 83350)

Pop: 19,361 (1990); 19,718 (1980)   **Pop Density:** 25.5
Land: 759.7 sq. mi.; **Water:** 3.4 sq. mi.   **Area Code:** 208
In south-central ID, west of Pocatello; organized Jan 28, 1913 from Lincoln County.
Name origin: For the first settlement, a railroad siding, from Shoshonean 'broad expanse,' descriptive of the Snake River plain in this area.

Acequia — City
ZIP: 83350   **Lat:** 42-40-06 N   **Long:** 113-35-44 W
Pop: 106 (1990); 100 (1980)   **Pop Density:** 1060.0
Land: 0.1 sq. mi.; **Water:** 0.0 sq. mi.

Burley — City
ZIP: 83318   **Lat:** 42-33-33 N   **Long:** 113-47-32 W
Pop: 282 (1990); 236 (1980)   **Pop Density:** 940.0
Land: 0.3 sq. mi.; **Water:** 0.1 sq. mi.   **Elev:** 4165 ft.
In southern ID, 38 mi. east of Twin Falls. Part of the town is also in Cassia County.
Name origin: For Union Pacific Railroad official David Burley.

Heyburn — City
ZIP: 83336   **Lat:** 42-33-20 N   **Long:** 113-45-39 W
Pop: 2,714 (1990); 2,889 (1980)   **Pop Density:** 1938.6
Land: 1.4 sq. mi.; **Water:** 0.0 sq. mi.

Minidoka — City
Lat: 42-45-14 N   **Long:** 113-29-20 W
Pop: 67 (1990); 101 (1980)   **Pop Density:** 670.0
Land: 0.1 sq. mi.; **Water:** 0.0 sq. mi.   **Elev:** 4286 ft.
Name origin: From the Shoshoni Indian term meaning 'broad expanse.'

IDAHO, Minidoka County

Paul City
ZIP: 83347 Lat: 42-36-23 N Long: 113-46-56 W
Pop: 901 (1990); 940 (1980) Pop Density: 3003.3
Land: 0.3 sq. mi.; Water: 0.0 sq. mi.

Rupert City
ZIP: 83350 Lat: 42-37-05 N Long: 113-40-25 W
Pop: 5,455 (1990); 5,476 (1980) Pop Density: 3030.6
Land: 1.8 sq. mi.; Water: 0.0 sq. mi. Elev: 4158 ft.

Nez Perce County
County Seat: Lewiston (ZIP: 83501)

Pop: 33,754 (1990); 33,220 (1980) Pop Density: 39.8
Land: 849.1 sq. mi.; Water: 7.3 sq. mi. Area Code: 208

On the western border of the ID panhandle; original county; organized Feb 4, 1864 (prior to statehood). It was previously established by WA Territory in 1861.

Name origin: From the French name, 'pierced nose,' for an Indian tribe that called itself *Chopunnish*. The French term might be better translated as 'mashed' or 'flattened nose.'

Culdesac City
ZIP: 83524 Lat: 46-22-29 N Long: 116-40-09 W
Pop: 280 (1990); 261 (1980) Pop Density: 1400.0
Land: 0.2 sq. mi.; Water: 0.0 sq. mi.
Name origin: For its descriptive connotations.

Lapwai City
ZIP: 83540 Lat: 46-24-17 N Long: 116-48-12 W
Pop: 932 (1990); 1,043 (1980) Pop Density: 1165.0
Land: 0.8 sq. mi.; Water: 0.0 sq. mi.
Name origin: From an Indian term of uncertain meaning.

Lewiston City
ZIP: 83501 Lat: 46-23-34 N Long: 116-59-31 W
Pop: 28,082 (1990); 27,986 (1980) Pop Density: 1712.3
Land: 16.4 sq. mi.; Water: 0.7 sq. mi.
In western ID at the confluence of the Clearwater and Snake rivers, 95 mi. south-southeast of Spokane, WA. Incorporated as first town in Idaho Territory in 1861 and first capital of the territory in 1863.
Name origin: For Meriwether Lewis (1774–1809), of the Lewis and Clark expedition (1804–06).

Peck City
ZIP: 83545 Lat: 46-28-25 N Long: 116-25-26 W
Pop: 160 (1990); 209 (1980) Pop Density: 533.3
Land: 0.3 sq. mi.; Water: 0.0 sq. mi.

Oneida County
County Seat: Malad City (ZIP: 83252)

Pop: 3,492 (1990); 3,258 (1980) Pop Density: 2.9
Land: 1200.4 sq. mi.; Water: 1.3 sq. mi. Area Code: 208

On the southern border of ID, south of Pocatello; original county; organized Jan 22, 1864 (prior to statehood).

Name origin: For Lake Oneida, NY, former home of early settlers, itself named for one of the Five Nations of the Iroquois. Name means 'stone people,' perhaps for their bravery.

Malad City City
ZIP: 83252 Lat: 42-11-22 N Long: 112-14-56 W
Pop: 1,946 (1990); 1,915 (1980) Pop Density: 1216.3
Land: 1.6 sq. mi.; Water: 0.0 sq. mi.
Name origin: For the Malad River, on which it is located.

American Places Dictionary   IDAHO, Power County

Owyhee County
County Seat: Murphy (ZIP: 83650)

Pop: 8,392 (1990); 8,272 (1980)   **Pop Density:** 1.1
Land: 7678.4 sq. mi.; **Water:** 18.7 sq. mi.   **Area Code:** 208

On the southwestern border of ID, south of Boise; original county; organized Dec 31, 1863 (prior to statehood).

Name origin: For the Owyhee River, itself named for a corrupt spelling of Hawaii, in honor of three Hawaiians (Owyhee) who were hired to trade with the Indians; they disappeared and were presumed to have been killed.

Grand View   City
ZIP: 83624   **Lat:** 42-59-00 N   **Long:** 116-05-24 W
Pop: 330 (1990); 366 (1980)   **Pop Density:** 660.0
Land: 0.5 sq. mi.; **Water:** 0.0 sq. mi.

Homedale   City
ZIP: 83628   **Lat:** 43-37-05 N   **Long:** 116-56-09 W
Pop: 1,963 (1990); 2,078 (1980)   **Pop Density:** 2181.1
Land: 0.9 sq. mi.; **Water:** 0.0 sq. mi.

Marsing   City
ZIP: 83639   **Lat:** 43-32-44 N   **Long:** 116-48-24 W
Pop: 798 (1990); 786 (1980)   **Pop Density:** 1596.0
Land: 0.5 sq. mi.; **Water:** 0.0 sq. mi.

In southwestern ID, west of Boise. Incorporated 1961.

Name origin: For Earl Q. and Mark Marsing, pioneer settlers.

Payette County
County Seat: Payette (ZIP: 83661)

Pop: 16,434 (1990); 15,825 (1980)   **Pop Density:** 40.3
Land: 407.5 sq. mi.; **Water:** 2.7 sq. mi.   **Area Code:** 208

On western border of ID, northeast of Boise; organized Feb 28, 1917 from Canyon County.

Name origin: For the Payette River, which runs diagonally through the county; named for Francis Payette, Canadian fur trapper and explorer.

Fruitland   City
ZIP: 83619   **Lat:** 44-01-04 N   **Long:** 116-55-12 W
Pop: 2,400 (1990); 2,559 (1980)   **Pop Density:** 2000.0
Land: 1.2 sq. mi.; **Water:** 0.0 sq. mi.

New Plymouth   City
ZIP: 83655   **Lat:** 43-58-14 N   **Long:** 116-49-04 W
Pop: 1,313 (1990); 1,186 (1980)   **Pop Density:** 2188.3
Land: 0.6 sq. mi.; **Water:** 0.0 sq. mi.
Name origin: For Plymouth, MA.

Payette   City
ZIP: 83661   **Lat:** 44-04-37 N   **Long:** 116-55-44 W
Pop: 5,592 (1990); 5,448 (1980)   **Pop Density:** 2541.8
Land: 2.2 sq. mi.; **Water:** 0.0 sq. mi.

Power County
County Seat: American Falls (ZIP: 83211)

Pop: 7,086 (1990); 6,844 (1980)   **Pop Density:** 5.0
Land: 1405.7 sq. mi.; **Water:** 37.0 sq. mi.   **Area Code:** 208

In southeastern ID, east of Pocatello; organized Jan 30, 1913 from Bingham, Cassia, Oneida, and Blaine counties.

Name origin: For the American Falls Canal and Power Company.

American Falls   City
ZIP: 83211   **Lat:** 42-46-55 N   **Long:** 112-51-13 W
Pop: 3,757 (1990); 3,626 (1980)   **Pop Density:** 2504.7
Land: 1.5 sq. mi.; **Water:** 0.0 sq. mi.

Arbon Valley   CDP
                 Lat: 42-53-02 N   **Long:** 112-35-52 W
Pop: 613 (1990)   **Pop Density:** 17.7
Land: 34.6 sq. mi.; **Water:** 0.1 sq. mi.

IDAHO, Power County • American Places Dictionary

Pocatello City
ZIP: 83201 Lat: 42-54-20 N Long: 112-35-33 W
Pop: 53 (1990) Pop Density: 10.2
Land: 5.2 sq. mi.; Water: 0.0 sq. mi.
In southeastern ID, 58 mi. north of the UT border and 68 mi. west of the WY border. Founded 1882; incorporated as a city 1893. Transportation gateway to the Pacific Northwest; surrounded by rich farmland; marketplace and shipping point for livestock and crops. Diverse manufacturing: cement, dairy products, elemental phosphorus. Part of the town is also in Bannock County.
Name origin: For a Bannock Indian chief whose name means 'the wayward.'

Rockland City
ZIP: 83271 Lat: 42-34-24 N Long: 112-52-27 W
Pop: 264 (1990); 283 (1980) Pop Density: 880.0
Land: 0.3 sq. mi.; Water: 0.0 sq. mi.

Shoshone County
County Seat: Wallace (ZIP: 83873)

Pop: 13,931 (1990); 19,226 (1980) Pop Density: 5.3
Land: 2634.0 sq. mi.; Water: 1.6 sq. mi. Area Code: 208
On the eastern border of the ID panhandle, northeast of Lewiston. The first organized unit of government in ID, it was originally created in 1858 as part of WA Territory, effective in 1861; reorganized Feb 4, 1864 (prior to statehood).
Name origin: For the Shonone, one of the major Indian tribes of the northern Rocky Mountain region.

Kellogg City
ZIP: 83837 Lat: 47-32-21 N Long: 116-08-06 W
Pop: 2,591 (1990); 3,417 (1980) Pop Density: 1363.7
Land: 1.9 sq. mi.; Water: 0.0 sq. mi.
Name origin: For Noah Kellogg, who discovered a mine in the area.

Mullan City
ZIP: 83846 Lat: 47-28-08 N Long: 115-47-38 W
Pop: 821 (1990); 1,269 (1980) Pop Density: 1026.3
Land: 0.8 sq. mi.; Water: 0.0 sq. mi. Elev: 3277 ft.

Osburn City
ZIP: 83849 Lat: 47-30-21 N Long: 115-59-58 W
Pop: 1,579 (1990); 2,220 (1980) Pop Density: 1214.6
Land: 1.3 sq. mi.; Water: 0.0 sq. mi.

Pinehurst City
ZIP: 83850 Lat: 47-32-08 N Long: 116-14-00 W
Pop: 1,722 (1990); 2,183 (1980) Pop Density: 1565.5
Land: 1.1 sq. mi.; Water: 0.0 sq. mi.

Smelterville City
ZIP: 83868 Lat: 47-32-32 N Long: 116-10-35 W
Pop: 464 (1990); 776 (1980) Pop Density: 1546.7
Land: 0.3 sq. mi.; Water: 0.0 sq. mi.

Wallace City
ZIP: 83873 Lat: 47-28-22 N Long: 115-55-20 W
Pop: 1,010 (1990); 1,736 (1980) Pop Density: 1122.2
Land: 0.9 sq. mi.; Water: 0.0 sq. mi. Elev: 2744 ft.

Wardner City
ZIP: 83837 Lat: 47-31-13 N Long: 116-08-02 W
Pop: 246 (1990); 423 (1980) Pop Density: 273.3
Land: 0.9 sq. mi.; Water: 0.0 sq. mi.

Teton County
County Seat: Driggs (ZIP: 83422)

Pop: 3,439 (1990); 2,897 (1980) Pop Density: 7.6
Land: 450.4 sq. mi.; Water: 0.2 sq. mi. Area Code: 208
On the eastern border of ID, northeast of Idaho Falls; organized Jan 26, 1915 from Madison County.
Name origin: For the Teton Mountains.

Driggs City
ZIP: 83422 Lat: 43-43-31 N Long: 111-06-25 W
Pop: 846 (1990); 727 (1980) Pop Density: 846.0
Land: 1.0 sq. mi.; Water: 0.0 sq. mi. Elev: 6116 ft.
In eastern ID, northeast of Idaho Falls. Incorporated Nov 1, 1916.
Name origin: For the Driggs family, which composed a large part of the local Mormon settlement.

Tetonia City
ZIP: 83424 Lat: 43-48-57 N Long: 111-09-31 W
Pop: 132 (1990); 191 (1980) Pop Density: 264.0
Land: 0.5 sq. mi.; Water: 0.0 sq. mi.

Victor City
ZIP: 83455 Lat: 43-36-13 N Long: 111-06-47 W
Pop: 292 (1990); 323 (1980) Pop Density: 584.0
Land: 0.5 sq. mi.; Water: 0.0 sq. mi.

Twin Falls County
County Seat: Twin Falls (ZIP: 83303)

Pop: 53,580 (1990); 52,927 (1980)　　**Pop Density:** 27.8
Land: 1925.1 sq. mi.; **Water:** 3.4 sq. mi.　　**Area Code:** 208
On the central southern border of ID; organized Feb 21, 1907 from Cassia County.
Name origin: For the falls on the Snake River.

Buhl　　City
ZIP: 83316　　**Lat:** 42-35-54 N **Long:** 114-45-38 W
Pop: 3,516 (1990); 3,629 (1980)　　**Pop Density:** 2511.4
Land: 1.4 sq. mi.; **Water:** 0.0 sq. mi.
Name origin: For Frank Buhl, who helped found a large irrigation project in the area.

Castleford　　City
ZIP: 83321　　**Lat:** 42-31-16 N **Long:** 114-52-15 W
Pop: 179 (1990); 191 (1980)　　**Pop Density:** 1790.0
Land: 0.1 sq. mi.; **Water:** 0.0 sq. mi.　　**Elev:** 3866 ft.
Name origin: For an early crossing on Salmon Falls Creek near a local rock formation resembling a castle.

Filer　　City
ZIP: 83328　　**Lat:** 42-34-08 N **Long:** 114-36-32 W
Pop: 1,511 (1990); 1,645 (1980)　　**Pop Density:** 2518.3
Land: 0.6 sq. mi.; **Water:** 0.0 sq. mi.　　**Elev:** 3756 ft.
Name origin: For Walter Filer, general manager of the Twin Falls Canal Co.

Hansen　　City
ZIP: 83334　　**Lat:** 42-31-52 N **Long:** 114-18-02 W
Pop: 848 (1990); 1,078 (1980)　　**Pop Density:** 2120.0
Land: 0.4 sq. mi.; **Water:** 0.0 sq. mi.

Hollister　　City
Lat: 42-21-13 N **Long:** 114-35-14 W
Pop: 144 (1990); 167 (1980)　　**Pop Density:** 144.0
Land: 1.0 sq. mi.; **Water:** 0.0 sq. mi.

Kimberly　　City
ZIP: 83341　　**Lat:** 42-32-03 N **Long:** 114-21-52 W
Pop: 2,367 (1990); 2,307 (1980)　　**Pop Density:** 2958.8
Land: 0.8 sq. mi.; **Water:** 0.0 sq. mi.

Murtaugh　　City
ZIP: 83344　　**Lat:** 42-29-30 N **Long:** 114-09-36 W
Pop: 134 (1990); 114 (1980)　　**Pop Density:** 1340.0
Land: 0.1 sq. mi.; **Water:** 0.0 sq. mi.　　**Elev:** 4082 ft.

Twin Falls　　City
ZIP: 83301　　**Lat:** 42-33-41 N **Long:** 114-27-46 W
Pop: 27,591 (1990); 26,209 (1980)　　**Pop Density:** 2627.7
Land: 10.5 sq. mi.; **Water:** 0.0 sq. mi.
In southern ID, 108 mi. west of Pocatello. Founded 1904; incorporated 1907.
Name origin: For its location near the Twin Falls on the Snake River.

Valley County
County Seat: Cascade (ZIP: 83611)

Pop: 6,109 (1990); 5,604 (1980)　　**Pop Density:** 1.7
Land: 3678.2 sq. mi.; **Water:** 55.7 sq. mi.　　**Area Code:** 208
In west-central ID; organized Feb 26, 1917.
Name origin: For Long Valley.

Cascade　　City
ZIP: 83611　　**Lat:** 44-30-46 N **Long:** 116-02-26 W
Pop: 877 (1990); 945 (1980)　　**Pop Density:** 282.9
Land: 3.1 sq. mi.; **Water:** 0.5 sq. mi.
Name origin: For Cascade Falls on the north fork of the Payette River, now almost obscured by Cascade Reservoir.

Donnelly　　City
ZIP: 83615　　**Lat:** 44-43-49 N **Long:** 116-04-33 W
Pop: 135 (1990); 139 (1980)　　**Pop Density:** 675.0
Land: 0.2 sq. mi.; **Water:** 0.0 sq. mi.

McCall　　City
Lat: 44-54-48 N **Long:** 116-06-27 W
Pop: 2,005 (1990); 2,188 (1980)　　**Pop Density:** 466.3
Land: 4.3 sq. mi.; **Water:** 0.6 sq. mi.

Washington County
County Seat: Weiser (ZIP: 83672)

Pop: 8,550 (1990); 8,803 (1980) **Pop Density:** 5.9
Land: 1456.4 sq. mi.; **Water:** 17.2 sq. mi. **Area Code:** 208
On the central western border of ID, north of Caldwell; organized Feb 20, 1879 (prior to statehood) from Boise County.
Name origin: For George Washington (1732–99), American patriot and first U.S. president.

Cambridge City
　　　　　　　　Lat: 44-34-21 N **Long:** 116-40-33 W
Pop: 374 (1990); 428 (1980) **Pop Density:** 1246.7
Land: 0.3 sq. mi.; **Water:** 0.0 sq. mi. **Elev:** 2651 ft.
Name origin: For the city in MA.

Midvale City
ZIP: 83645 **Lat:** 44-28-14 N **Long:** 116-43-59 W
Pop: 110 (1990); 205 (1980) **Pop Density:** 275.0
Land: 0.4 sq. mi.; **Water:** 0.0 sq. mi.

Weiser City
ZIP: 83672 **Lat:** 44-15-03 N **Long:** 116-58-00 W
Pop: 4,571 (1990); 4,771 (1980) **Pop Density:** 1987.4
Land: 2.3 sq. mi.; **Water:** 0.0 sq. mi.

Index to Places and Counties in Idaho

Aberdeen (Bingham) City *185*
Acequia (Minidoka) City *199*
Ada County *183*
Adams County *183*
Albion (Cassia) City *190*
American Falls (Power) City *201*
Ammon (Bonneville) City *187*
Arbon Valley (Power) CDP *201*
Arco (Butte) City *188*
Arimo (Bannock) City *184*
Ashton (Fremont) City *193*
Athol (Kootenai) City *196*
Atomic City (Bingham) City *185*
Bancroft (Caribou) City *190*
Bannock County *184*
Basalt (Bingham) City *185*
Bear Lake County *184*
Bellevue (Blaine) City *186*
Benewah County *185*
Bingham County *185*
Blackfoot (Bingham) City *185*
Blaine County *186*
Bliss (Gooding) City *194*
Bloomington (Bear Lake) City *184*
Boise (Ada) City *183*
Boise County *186*
Bonner County *187*
Bonners Ferry (Boundary) City *188*
Bonneville County *187*
Boundary County *188*
Bovill (Latah) City *197*
Buhl (Twin Falls) City *203*
Burley (Cassia) City *190*
Burley (Minidoka) City *199*
Butte City (Butte) City *188*
Butte County *188*
Caldwell (Canyon) City *189*
Camas County *189*
Cambridge (Washington) City *204*
Canyon County *189*
Caribou County *190*
Cascade (Valley) City *203*
Cassia County *190*
Castleford (Twin Falls) City *203*
Challis (Custer) City *192*
Chatcolet (Benewah) City *185*
Chubbuck (Bannock) City *184*
Clark County *191*
Clark Fork (Bonner) City *187*
Clayton (Custer) City *192*
Clearwater County *191*
Clifton (Franklin) City *193*
Coeur d'Alene (Kootenai) City *196*
Cottonwood (Idaho) City *195*
Council (Adams) City *183*
Craigmont (Lewis) City *198*
Crouch (Boise) City *186*
Culdesac (Nez Perce) City *200*
Custer County *192*
Dalton Gardens (Kootenai) City *196*
Dayton (Franklin) City *193*
Deary (Latah) City *197*
Declo (Cassia) City *190*
Dietrich (Lincoln) City *199*
Donnelly (Valley) City *203*
Dover (Bonner) City *187*
Downey (Bannock) City *184*
Driggs (Teton) City *202*
Drummond (Fremont) City *193*
Dubois (Clark) City *191*

Eagle (Ada) City *183*
East Hope (Bonner) City *187*
Eden (Jerome) City *196*
Elk River (Clearwater) City *191*
Elmore County *192*
Emmett (Gem) City *194*
Fairfield (Camas) City *189*
Ferdinand (Idaho) City *195*
Fernan Lake Village (Kootenai) City *196*
Filer (Twin Falls) City *203*
Firth (Bingham) City *185*
Fort Hall (Bannock) CDP *184*
Fort Hall (Bingham) CDP *185*
Franklin (Franklin) City *193*
Franklin County *193*
Fremont County *193*
Fruitland (Payette) City *201*
Garden City (Ada) City *183*
Gem County *194*
Genesee (Latah) City *197*
Georgetown (Bear Lake) City *184*
Glenns Ferry (Elmore) City *192*
Gooding (Gooding) City *194*
Gooding County *194*
Grace (Caribou) City *190*
Grand View (Owyhee) City *201*
Grangeville (Idaho) City *195*
Greenleaf (Canyon) City *189*
Hagerman (Gooding) City *194*
Hailey (Blaine) City *186*
Hamer (Jefferson) City *195*
Hansen (Twin Falls) City *203*
Harrison (Kootenai) City *196*
Hauser (Kootenai) City *196*
Hayden (Kootenai) City *197*
Hayden Lake (Kootenai) City *197*
Hazelton (Jerome) City *196*
Heyburn (Minidoka) City *199*
Hollister (Twin Falls) City *203*
Homedale (Owyhee) City *201*
Hope (Bonner) City *187*
Horseshoe Bend (Boise) City *186*
Huetter (Kootenai) City *197*
Idaho City (Boise) City *186*
Idaho County *195*
Idaho Falls (Bonneville) City *187*
Inkom (Bannock) City *184*
Iona (Bonneville) City *187*
Irwin (Bonneville) City *187*
Island Park (Fremont) City *193*
Jefferson County *195*
Jerome (Jerome) City *196*
Jerome County *196*
Juliaetta (Latah) City *197*
Kamiah (Idaho) City *195*
Kamiah (Lewis) City *198*
Kellogg (Shoshone) City *202*
Kendrick (Latah) City *197*
Ketchum (Blaine) City *186*
Kimberly (Twin Falls) City *203*
Kooskia (Idaho) City *195*
Kootenai (Bonner) City *187*
Kootenai County *196*
Kuna (Ada) City *183*
Lapwai (Nez Perce) City *200*
Latah County *197*
Lava Hot Springs (Bannock) City *184*
Leadore (Lemhi) City *198*
Lemhi County *198*
Lewis County *198*

Lewiston (Nez Perce) City *200*
Lewisville (Jefferson) City *195*
Lincoln County *199*
Lost River (Custer) City *192*
Mackay (Custer) City *192*
Madison County *199*
Malad City (Oneida) City *200*
Malta (Cassia) City *190*
Marsing (Owyhee) City *201*
McCall (Valley) City *203*
McCammon (Bannock) City *184*
Melba (Canyon) City *189*
Menan (Jefferson) City *195*
Meridian (Ada) City *183*
Middleton (Canyon) City *189*
Midvale (Washington) City *204*
Minidoka (Minidoka) City *199*
Minidoka County *199*
Montpelier (Bear Lake) City *184*
Moore (Butte) City *188*
Moscow (Latah) City *197*
Mountain Home (Elmore) City *192*
Mountain Home Air Force Base (Elmore) Military Facility *192*
Moyie Springs (Boundary) City *188*
Mud Lake (Jefferson) City *195*
Mullan (Shoshone) City *202*
Murtaugh (Twin Falls) City *203*
Nampa (Canyon) City *189*
Newdale (Fremont) City *193*
New Meadows (Adams) City *183*
New Plymouth (Payette) City *201*
Nezperce (Lewis) City *198*
Nez Perce County *200*
Notus (Canyon) City *189*
Oakley (Cassia) City *190*
Oldtown (Bonner) City *187*
Onaway (Latah) City *198*
Oneida County *200*
Orofino (Clearwater) City *191*
Osburn (Shoshone) City *202*
Owyhee County *201*
Oxford (Franklin) City *193*
Paris (Bear Lake) City *184*
Parker (Fremont) City *193*
Parma (Canyon) City *189*
Paul (Minidoka) City *200*
Payette (Payette) City *201*
Payette County *201*
Peck (Nez Perce) City *200*
Pierce (Clearwater) City *191*
Pinehurst (Shoshone) City *202*
Placerville (Boise) City *186*
Plummer (Benewah) City *185*
Pocatello (Bannock) City *184*
Pocatello (Power) City *202*
Ponderay (Bonner) City *187*
Post Falls (Kootenai) City *197*
Potlatch (Latah) City *198*
Power County *201*
Preston (Franklin) City *193*
Priest River (Bonner) City *187*
Rathdrum (Kootenai) City *197*
Reubens (Lewis) City *198*
Rexburg (Madison) City *199*
Richfield (Lincoln) City *199*
Rigby (Jefferson) City *195*
Riggins (Idaho) City *195*
Ririe (Bonneville) City *188*
Ririe (Jefferson) City *195*

IDAHO

Roberts (Jefferson) City *196*
Rockland (Power) City *202*
Rupert (Minidoka) City...................... *200*
St. Anthony (Fremont) City *193*
St. Charles (Bear Lake) City.............. *184*
St. Maries (Benewah) City................. *185*
Salmon (Lemhi) City *198*
Sandpoint (Bonner) City *187*
Shelley (Bingham) City..................... *186*
Shoshone (Lincoln) City.................... *199*
Shoshone County................................*202*
Smelterville (Shoshone) City *202*
Soda Springs (Caribou) City *190*
Spencer (Clark) City *191*
Spirit Lake (Kootenai) City............... *197*

Stanley (Custer) City *192*
State Line (Kootenai) City *197*
Stites (Idaho) City............................. *195*
Sugar City (Madison) City *199*
Sun Valley (Blaine) City *186*
Swan Valley (Bonneville) City.......... *188*
Tensed (Benewah) City..................... *185*
Teton (Fremont) City *193*
Teton County *202*
Tetonia (Teton) City *202*
Troy (Latah) City............................... *198*
Twin Falls (Twin Falls) City.............. *203*
Twin Falls County *203*
Ucon (Bonneville) City..................... *188*

Valley County *203*
Victor (Teton) City *202*
Wallace (Shoshone) City *202*
Wardner (Shoshone) City *202*
Warm River (Fremont) City............. *194*
Washington County *204*
Weippe (Clearwater) City *191*
Weiser (Washington) City................. *204*
Wendell (Gooding) City.................... *194*
Weston (Franklin) City..................... *193*
White Bird (Idaho) City *195*
Wilder (Canyon) City *189*
Winchester (Lewis) City *198*
Worley (Kootenai) City *197*

Kansas

KANSAS

Kansas

Population: 2,477,574 (1990); 2,363,679 (1980)
Population rank (1990): 32
Percent population change (1980–1990): 4.8
Population projection: 2,574,000 (1995); 2,613,000 (2000)

Area: total: 82,282 sq. mi.; 81,823 sq. mi. land, 459 sq. mi. water
Area rank: 15
Highest elevation: 4,039 ft., Mount Sunflower (Sherman County)
Lowest point: 680 ft., along the Verdigris River (Montgomery County)

State capital: Topeka
Largest city: Wichita (304,011)
Second largest city: Kansas City (149,767)
Largest county: Sedgwick (403,662)

Total housing units: 1,044,112
No. of occupied housing units: 944,726
Vacant housing units (%): 9.5
Distribution of population by race and Hispanic origin (%):
  White: 90.1
  Black: 5.8
  Hispanic (any race): 3.8
  Native American: 0.9
  Asian/Pacific: 1.3
  Other: 2.0

Admission date: January 29, 1861 (34th state).

Location: In the central United States, bordering Oklahoma, Colorado, Nebraska, and Missouri.

Name Origin: For the Kansas River, which flows through the northeastern part of the state into the Missouri at Kansas City. The river is named for the Kansa Indians, who lived in the region during French exploration. This name is said to mean 'people of the south wind.' The final -s represents a plural of the French name.

State animal: American buffalo or bison *(Bison bison)*
State bird: western meadowlark *(Sturnella neglecta)*
State flower: sunflower *(Helianthus annuus)*
State insect: honeybee *(Apis mellifera)*
State march: "The Kansas March"
State song: "Home on the Range"
State tree: cottonwood *(Populus deltoides)*
State motto: *Ad Astra per Aspera* (Latin 'To the Stars Through Difficulties')
State nicknames: Sunflower State, Wheat State, Breadbasket of America, Jayhawk State

Area codes: 316 (south), 913 (north)
Time zones: Central, with a small portion in the Mountain zone
Abbreviations: KS (postal); Kan., Kans. (traditional)
Part of (region): Plains States; Midwest

Local Government

Counties

Kansas has 105 counties, each governed by three elected council members.

Municipalities

Kansas has 627 incorporated cities, most of which are governed by an elected mayor and council. There are also 1,355 townships into which the counties are divided, reflective of early land surveys.

Settlement History and Early Development

The area that is now Kansas was first inhabited by prehistoric people more than 10,000 years ago. When Europeans first explored the area, they found Wichita, Pawnee, Kansa, and Osage Indians living there. Around 1800 nomadic tribes such as the Cheyenne, Arapaho, Comanche, and Kiowa also settled in Kansas.

The Spanish explorer Francisco Coronado entered Kansas in 1541, seeking fabled golden treasures in a land called Quivira. Another Spanish expedition was led into the Plains by Juan de Oñate in 1601. Most of the land of present-day Kansas was within the vast Louisiana territory claimed by France, ceded to Spain in 1762, returned to France in 1800, and sold by France to the U.S. under the terms of the Louisiana Purchase in 1803. A small part of the state, in the southwest, became part of the U.S. after the Mexican-American War (1846–48).

During the 1700s French trappers and traders had established contacts with the Indians, but the French did not settle in Kansas. The American expedition of Lewis and Clark (1804–06) explored the land along the Missouri River. Later expeditions, under Zebulon Pike (1806) and Stephen Long (1819), explored the plains from east to west and concluded that the area would make poor farming land. Kansas was used from 1825 to 1842 to relocate eastern Indian tribes, who were supposed to settle and farm the land. They were often joined by missionaries eager to convert them to Christianity.

The Sante Fe Trail, which ran through Kansas, was opened in the early 1820s. During the next several decades, thousands of settlers passed through Kansas on their way to California and Oregon. A series of forts was built to protect travelers: Fort Leavenworth in 1827, Fort Scott in 1842, and Fort Riley in 1853.

KANSAS

The Kansas Territory was created by the Kansas-Nebraska Act of 1854, which established the western border at the Rocky Mountains. Congress had "solved" the problem of creating new territories without facing the issue of slavery by decreeing that each prospective state would decide the question for itself by popular sovereignty. The Kansas Territory earned the nickname "Bleeding Kansas" from the disputes that arose over whether the state was to allow slavery or not. When the town of Lawrence was sacked by proslavery forces in 1856, abolitionist John Brown retaliated by murdering five proslavery settlers. In 1858 several antislavery settlers were killed at the Marais des Cygnes massacre. Kansas ultimately entered the Union as a free state.

Statehood and the Civil War

Kansas became the 34th U.S. state on January 29, 1861. Topeka was named as the capital and the western boundary was moved from the Rockies to its present location just west of the 102nd parallel. More than two-thirds of adult male Kansans served in the Union forces during the Civil War, although little action took place in Kansas itself.

After the Civil War settlement increased and conflict with the Indians followed. After 1878 most of the Plains Indians were removed to reservations in present-day Oklahoma. By this time most of the buffalo had disappeared from the plains as a result of massive overhunting.

Business and Commerce

The Union Pacific and Sante Fe railroads both crossed Kansas and spurred settlement. The railroads also served as the destination for the great Texas cattle drives along the Chisholm Trail and the Western Trail, which brought prosperity to such Kansas towns as Abilene, Ellsworth, Wichita, and Dodge City. From the end of the Civil War to the mid 1880s the era of the Wild West and its legendary characters, including Bat Masterson, Wyatt Earp, Doc Holliday, and Wild Bill Hickock, made Kansas a part of American legend.

In the 1870s Russian Mennonite immigrants brought a strain of hardy winter wheat to Kansas that transformed the state's agriculture and made it the "breadbasket" of America. The state adopted female suffrage in 1887 and the prohibition of alcohol from 1880 to 1948.

Falling agricultural prices after World War I, the Great Depression of the 1930s, and the drought and Dust Bowl in western Kansas all contributed to economic difficulties in Kansas that only abated with improved weather conditions and World War II's demands for Kansas's agricultural products. Industry, including aircraft production, grew, as did the production of oil, natural gas, coal, and gypsum. Since World War II, agriculture (largely mechanized) and livestock raising, along with related food processing businesses, have formed the basis of Kansas's economy.

State Boundaries

Kansas was organized as a territory in 1854 from what was then a part of the Missouri Territory. Its current boundaries were established at the time it became a state in 1861.

Kansas Counties

Allen	Doniphan	Jackson	Morris	Saline
Anderson	Douglas	Jefferson	Morton	Scott
Atchison	Edwards	Jewell	Nemaha	Sedgwick
Barber	Elk	Johnson	Neosho	Seward
Barton	Ellis	Kearny	Ness	Shawnee
Bourbon	Ellsworth	Kingman	Norton	Sheridan
Brown	Finney	Kiowa	Osage	Sherman
Butler	Ford	Labette	Osborne	Smith
Chase	Franklin	Lane	Ottawa	Stafford
Chautauqua	Geary	Leavenworth	Pawnee	Stanton
Cherokee	Gove	Lincoln	Phillips	Stevens
Cheyenne	Graham	Linn	Pottawatomie	Sumner
Clark	Grant	Logan	Pratt	Thomas
Clay	Gray	Lyon	Rawlins	Trego
Cloud	Greeley	McPherson	Reno	Wabaunsee
Coffey	Greenwood	Marion	Republic	Wallace
Comanche	Hamilton	Marshall	Rice	Washington
Cowley	Harper	Meade	Riley	Wichita
Crawford	Harvey	Miami	Rooks	Wilson
Decatur	Haskell	Mitchell	Rush	Woodson
Dickinson	Hodgeman	Montgomery	Russell	Wyandotte

Multi-County Places

The following Kansas places are in more than one county. Given here is the total population for each multi-county place, and the names of the counties it is in.

Bonner Springs, pop. 6,413; Wyandotte (6,410), Johnson (3)
Clayton, pop. 91; Norton (77), Decatur (14)
Clifton, pop. 561; Washington (334), Clay (227)
Fort Riley North, pop. 12,848; Riley (12,165), Geary (683)
Geuda Springs, pop. 219; Sumner (185), Cowley (34)
Herington, pop. 2,685; Dickinson (2,685), Morris (0)
Lake Quivira, pop. 983; Johnson (943), Wyandotte (40)
Manhattan, pop. 37,712; Riley (37,569), Pottawatomie (143)
Mulvane, pop. 4,674; Sedgwick (3,466), Sumner (1,208)
Oakley, pop. 2,045; Logan (1,987), Thomas (58)
Sabetha, pop. 2,341; Nemaha (2,335), Brown (6)
St. Marys, pop. 1,791; Pottawatomie (1,791), Wabaunsee (0)
Sedgwick, pop. 1,438; Harvey (1,306), Sedgwick (132)
Simpson, pop. 107; Mitchell (107), Cloud (0)
Spring Hill, pop. 2,191; Johnson (2,084), Miami (107)
Vining, pop. 55; Clay (35), Washington (20)
Willard, pop. 110; Shawnee (110), Wabaunsee (0)

Allen County
County Seat: Iola (ZIP: 66749)

Pop: 14,638 (1990); 15,654 (1980)　　**Pop Density:** 29.1
Land: 503.1 sq. mi.; **Water:** 2.2 sq. mi.　　**Area Code:** 316
In southeastern KS, southeast of Emporia; original county; organized Aug 30, 1855 (prior to statehood).
Name origin: For William Allen (1803–79), U.S. senator from OH (1837–49) and governor (1874–76).

Bassett — City
ZIP: 66749　　**Lat:** 37-54-24 N **Long:** 95-24-25 W
Pop: 20 (1990); 31 (1980)　　**Pop Density:** 200.0
Land: 0.1 sq. mi.; **Water:** 0.0 sq. mi.　　**Elev:** 965 ft.
Incorporated Nov 2, 1903.

Carlyle — Township
Lat: 37-59-50 N **Long:** 95-22-46 W
Pop: 278 (1990); 279 (1980)　　**Pop Density:** 9.3
Land: 30.0 sq. mi.; **Water:** 0.0 sq. mi.

Cottage Grove — Township
Lat: 37-45-16 N **Long:** 95-21-05 W
Pop: 292 (1990); 305 (1980)　　**Pop Density:** 7.9
Land: 37.0 sq. mi.; **Water:** 0.2 sq. mi.

Deer Creek — Township
Lat: 37-59-41 N **Long:** 95-16-52 W
Pop: 128 (1990); 142 (1980)　　**Pop Density:** 3.5
Land: 36.2 sq. mi.; **Water:** 0.0 sq. mi.

Elm — Township
Lat: 37-54-23 N **Long:** 95-17-51 W
Pop: 1,188 (1990); 1,326 (1980)　　**Pop Density:** 25.1
Land: 47.4 sq. mi.; **Water:** 0.2 sq. mi.

Elsmore — City
ZIP: 66732　　**Lat:** 37-47-39 N **Long:** 95-08-57 W
Pop: 91 (1990); 104 (1980)　　**Pop Density:** 455.0
Land: 0.2 sq. mi.; **Water:** 0.0 sq. mi.　　**Elev:** 1050 ft.
Incorporated May 4, 1909. Not coextensive with the town of the same name.
Name origin: Originally for the castle in Shakespeare's *Hamlet*, but a misspelling changed Elsinore to Elsmore and was allowed to stand.

*Elsmore — Township
ZIP: 66732　　**Lat:** 37-47-23 N **Long:** 95-09-32 W
Pop: 490 (1990); 535 (1980)　　**Pop Density:** 7.7
Land: 63.8 sq. mi.; **Water:** 0.0 sq. mi.

Gas — City
ZIP: 66742　　**Lat:** 37-55-21 N **Long:** 95-20-40 W
Pop: 505 (1990); 543 (1980)　　**Pop Density:** 721.4
Land: 0.7 sq. mi.; **Water:** 0.0 sq. mi.　　**Elev:** 1020 ft.
Incorporated Aug 1, 1901.
Name origin: For the area's natural gas deposits.

Geneva — Township
Lat: 37-59-46 N **Long:** 95-28-01 W
Pop: 155 (1990); 163 (1980)　　**Pop Density:** 5.2
Land: 29.9 sq. mi.; **Water:** 0.3 sq. mi.

Humboldt — City
ZIP: 66748　　**Lat:** 37-48-41 N **Long:** 95-26-13 W
Pop: 2,178 (1990); 2,230 (1980)　　**Pop Density:** 1555.7
Land: 1.4 sq. mi.; **Water:** 0.0 sq. mi.　　**Elev:** 970 ft.
Incorporated Apr 1870. Not coextensive with the town of the same name.
Name origin: For German naturalist and explorer, Alexander Von Humboldt (1769–1859).

*Humboldt — Township
ZIP: 66748　　**Lat:** 37-49-32 N **Long:** 95-24-50 W
Pop: 261 (1990); 279 (1980)　　**Pop Density:** 10.4
Land: 25.0 sq. mi.; **Water:** 0.2 sq. mi.

Iola — City
ZIP: 66749　　**Lat:** 37-55-41 N **Long:** 95-24-03 W
Pop: 6,351 (1990); 6,938 (1980)　　**Pop Density:** 1814.6
Land: 3.5 sq. mi.; **Water:** 0.0 sq. mi.　　**Elev:** 965 ft.
In southeastern KS, 15 mi. north of Chanute. Incorporated Feb 28, 1870.
Name origin: For an early settler, Iola Colburn.

*Iola — Township
ZIP: 66749　　**Lat:** 37-54-37 N **Long:** 95-27-05 W
Pop: 937 (1990); 902 (1980)　　**Pop Density:** 21.3
Land: 44.0 sq. mi.; **Water:** 0.7 sq. mi.

La Harpe — City
ZIP: 66751　　**Lat:** 37-54-59 N **Long:** 95-18-06 W
Pop: 650 (1990); 687 (1980)　　**Pop Density:** 722.2
Land: 0.9 sq. mi.; **Water:** 0.0 sq. mi.　　**Elev:** 1040 ft.
Incorporated Feb 1905.
Name origin: For 18th-century explorer, Bernard de la Harpe.

Logan — Township
Lat: 37-47-17 N **Long:** 95-29-28 W
Pop: 237 (1990); 263 (1980)　　**Pop Density:** 7.4
Land: 32.1 sq. mi.; **Water:** 0.2 sq. mi.

Marmaton — Township
Lat: 37-53-59 N **Long:** 95-09-22 W
Pop: 899 (1990); 956 (1980)　　**Pop Density:** 16.1
Land: 55.8 sq. mi.; **Water:** 0.1 sq. mi.

Mildred — City
Lat: 38-01-29 N **Long:** 95-10-25 W
Pop: 46 (1990); 64 (1980)　　**Pop Density:** 230.0
Land: 0.2 sq. mi.; **Water:** 0.0 sq. mi.　　**Elev:** 1064 ft.
Incorporated May 6, 1912.
Name origin: For Mildred, the daughter of businessman J.W. Wagner.

Moran
City
ZIP: 66755 **Lat:** 37-54-58 N **Long:** 95-10-13 W
Pop: 551 (1990); 643 (1980) **Pop Density:** 1377.5
Land: 0.4 sq. mi.; **Water:** 0.0 sq. mi. **Elev:** 1110 ft.
Incorporated Aug 1881.

Osage
Township
Lat: 37-59-18 N **Long:** 95-08-56 W
Pop: 315 (1990); 347 (1980) **Pop Density:** 6.6
Land: 48.0 sq. mi.; **Water:** 0.2 sq. mi.

Salem
Township
Lat: 37-49-08 N **Long:** 95-18-18 W
Pop: 279 (1990); 302 (1980) **Pop Density:** 5.8
Land: 47.9 sq. mi.; **Water:** 0.0 sq. mi.

Savonburg
City
ZIP: 66772 **Lat:** 37-44-56 N **Long:** 95-08-30 W
Pop: 93 (1990); 113 (1980) **Pop Density:** 465.0
Land: 0.2 sq. mi.; **Water:** 0.0 sq. mi. **Elev:** 950 ft.
Incorporated Jan 13, 1902.

Anderson County
County Seat: Garnett (ZIP: 66032)

Pop: 7,803 (1990); 8,749 (1980) **Pop Density:** 13.4
Land: 583.0 sq. mi.; **Water:** 1.4 sq. mi. **Area Code:** 913
In eastern KS, southeast of Emporia; original county; organized Aug 25, 1855 (prior to statehood).
Name origin: For Joseph C. Anderson, a member of the first KS territorial legislature.

Colony
City
ZIP: 66015 **Lat:** 38-04-14 N **Long:** 95-21-43 W
Pop: 447 (1990); 474 (1980) **Pop Density:** 894.0
Land: 0.5 sq. mi.; **Water:** 0.0 sq. mi. **Elev:** 1130 ft.
Incorporated Feb 4, 1886.
Name origin: For its settlement as a colony by pioneers from OH.

Garnett
City
ZIP: 66032 **Lat:** 38-17-01 N **Long:** 95-14-18 W
Pop: 3,210 (1990); 3,310 (1980) **Pop Density:** 1070.0
Land: 3.0 sq. mi.; **Water:** 0.1 sq. mi. **Elev:** 1049 ft.
Incorporated Oct 7, 1861.
Name origin: For W.A. Garnett, wealthy local businessman.

Greeley
City
ZIP: 66033 **Lat:** 38-22-02 N **Long:** 95-07-37 W
Pop: 339 (1990); 405 (1980) **Pop Density:** 847.5
Land: 0.4 sq. mi.; **Water:** 0.0 sq. mi. **Elev:** 880 ft.
Incorporated Jun 20, 1881.
Name origin: For 19th-century newspaper publisher Horace Greeley (1811–72).

Harris
City
Lat: 38-19-09 N **Long:** 95-26-18 W
Pop: 39 (1990); 80 (1980) **Pop Density:** 390.0
Land: 0.1 sq. mi.; **Water:** 0.0 sq. mi. **Elev:** 995 ft.
Incorporated Mar 4, 1929.

Indian Creek
Township
Lat: 38-05-56 N **Long:** 95-27-37 W
Pop: 149 (1990); 175 (1980) **Pop Density:** 3.1
Land: 48.4 sq. mi.; **Water:** 0.0 sq. mi.

Jackson
Township
Lat: 38-17-45 N **Long:** 95-18-48 W
Pop: 375 (1990); 433 (1980) **Pop Density:** 11.0
Land: 34.1 sq. mi.; **Water:** 0.0 sq. mi.

Kincaid
City
ZIP: 66039 **Lat:** 38-04-53 N **Long:** 95-09-16 W
Pop: 170 (1990); 192 (1980) **Pop Density:** 340.0
Land: 0.5 sq. mi.; **Water:** 0.0 sq. mi. **Elev:** 1045 ft.
Incorporated Apr 6, 1886.
Name origin: For a railroad promoter.

Lincoln
Township
Lat: 38-12-40 N **Long:** 95-08-47 W
Pop: 167 (1990); 239 (1980) **Pop Density:** 3.4
Land: 49.3 sq. mi.; **Water:** 0.1 sq. mi.

Lone Elm
City
Lat: 38-04-46 N **Long:** 95-14-32 W
Pop: 32 (1990); 55 (1980) **Pop Density:** 320.0
Land: 0.1 sq. mi.; **Water:** 0.0 sq. mi. **Elev:** 1100 ft.
Incorporated Apr 12, 1924. Not coextensive with the town of the same name.

*Lone Elm
Township
Lat: 38-05-17 N **Long:** 95-14-29 W
Pop: 211 (1990); 269 (1980) **Pop Density:** 4.6
Land: 46.2 sq. mi.; **Water:** 0.1 sq. mi.

Monroe
Township
Lat: 38-18-16 N **Long:** 95-12-08 W
Pop: 374 (1990); 495 (1980) **Pop Density:** 13.1
Land: 28.6 sq. mi.; **Water:** 0.0 sq. mi.

North Rich
Township
Lat: 38-08-48 N **Long:** 95-07-46 W
Pop: 98 (1990); 103 (1980) **Pop Density:** 4.1
Land: 23.9 sq. mi.; **Water:** 0.0 sq. mi.

Ozark
Township
Lat: 38-04-48 N **Long:** 95-21-16 W
Pop: 595 (1990); 661 (1980) **Pop Density:** 16.6
Land: 35.9 sq. mi.; **Water:** 0.0 sq. mi.

Putnam
Township
Lat: 38-22-07 N **Long:** 95-15-57 W
Pop: 282 (1990); 284 (1980) **Pop Density:** 8.4
Land: 33.7 sq. mi.; **Water:** 0.0 sq. mi.

KANSAS, Anderson County

Reeder
Township
Lat: 38-19-13 N Long: 95-26-04 W
Pop: 406 (1990); 523 (1980) **Pop Density:** 5.6
Land: 72.3 sq. mi.; **Water:** 0.3 sq. mi.

Rich
Township
Lat: 38-04-43 N Long: 95-07-59 W
Pop: 343 (1990); 369 (1980) **Pop Density:** 11.4
Land: 30.1 sq. mi.; **Water:** 0.1 sq. mi.

Union
Township
Lat: 38-18-30 N Long: 95-06-30 W
Pop: 175 (1990); 189 (1980) **Pop Density:** 5.8
Land: 30.2 sq. mi.; **Water:** 0.1 sq. mi.

Walker
Township
Lat: 38-21-39 N Long: 95-06-42 W
Pop: 496 (1990); 591 (1980) **Pop Density:** 33.1
Land: 15.0 sq. mi.; **Water:** 0.1 sq. mi.

Washington
Township
Lat: 38-13-36 N Long: 95-17-36 W
Pop: 267 (1990); 298 (1980) **Pop Density:** 7.4
Land: 35.9 sq. mi.; **Water:** 0.1 sq. mi.

Welda
Township
ZIP: 66091 Lat: 38-09-43 N Long: 95-19-15 W
Pop: 286 (1990); 330 (1980) **Pop Density:** 6.4
Land: 44.7 sq. mi.; **Water:** 0.1 sq. mi.

Westphalia
City
ZIP: 66093 Lat: 38-10-56 N Long: 95-29-25 W
Pop: 152 (1990); 204 (1980) **Pop Density:** 760.0
Land: 0.2 sq. mi.; **Water:** 0.0 sq. mi. **Elev:** 1100 ft.
Incorporated Apr 1920. Not coextensive with the town of the same name.
Name origin: Named by German settlers for Westphalia, a state in Germany.

*Westphalia
Township
ZIP: 66093 Lat: 38-12-29 N Long: 95-27-00 W
Pop: 369 (1990); 480 (1980) **Pop Density:** 7.2
Land: 51.6 sq. mi.; **Water:** 0.2 sq. mi.

Atchison County
County Seat: Atchison (ZIP: 66002)

Pop: 16,932 (1990); 18,397 (1980) **Pop Density:** 39.2
Land: 432.4 sq. mi.; **Water:** 2.7 sq. mi. **Area Code:** 913
On northeastern border of KS, northwest of Kansas City; original county; organized Aug 25, 1855 (prior to statehood).
Name origin: For the town of Atchison, which was named for David Rice Atchison (1807–86), MO statesman and U.S. senator (1843–55).

Atchison
City
ZIP: 66002 Lat: 39-33-41 N Long: 95-08-00 W
Pop: 10,656 (1990); 11,407 (1980) **Pop Density:** 1639.4
Land: 6.5 sq. mi.; **Water:** 0.4 sq. mi. **Elev:** 950 ft.
In northeastern KS on the Missouri River, 20 mi. north of Leavenworth. Incorporated Aug 10, 1855.
Name origin: For David Rice Atchison (1807–86), U.S. senator from MO.

Benton
Township
Lat: 39-29-37 N Long: 95-24-13 W
Pop: 1,047 (1990); 1,173 (1980) **Pop Density:** 17.4
Land: 60.2 sq. mi.; **Water:** 0.2 sq. mi.

Center
Township
Lat: 39-29-17 N Long: 95-17-00 W
Pop: 645 (1990); 692 (1980) **Pop Density:** 12.1
Land: 53.5 sq. mi.; **Water:** 0.1 sq. mi.

Effingham
City
ZIP: 66023 Lat: 39-31-20 N Long: 95-23-53 W
Pop: 540 (1990); 634 (1980) **Pop Density:** 1080.0
Land: 0.5 sq. mi.; **Water:** 0.0 sq. mi. **Elev:** 1138 ft.
Incorporated Jul 8, 1890.
Name origin: For railroad promoter Effingham Nichols.

Grasshopper
Township
Lat: 39-36-04 N Long: 95-29-12 W
Pop: 631 (1990); 744 (1980) **Pop Density:** 9.6
Land: 65.6 sq. mi.; **Water:** 0.3 sq. mi.

Huron
City
ZIP: 66038 Lat: 39-39-01 N Long: 95-20-54 W
Pop: 75 (1990); 107 (1980) **Pop Density:** 93.8
Land: 0.8 sq. mi.; **Water:** 0.0 sq. mi. **Elev:** 1160 ft.
Incorporated Jul 1, 1890.
Name origin: For the Huron Indian tribe.

Kapioma
Township
Lat: 39-29-05 N Long: 95-31-07 W
Pop: 256 (1990); 339 (1980) **Pop Density:** 5.4
Land: 47.5 sq. mi.; **Water:** 0.0 sq. mi.

Lancaster
City
ZIP: 66041 Lat: 39-34-18 N Long: 95-18-12 W
Pop: 299 (1990); 274 (1980) **Pop Density:** 1495.0
Land: 0.2 sq. mi.; **Water:** 0.0 sq. mi. **Elev:** 1150 ft.
Incorporated 1900. Not coextensive with the town of the same name.
Name origin: For Lancaster, England.

*Lancaster
Township
ZIP: 66041 Lat: 39-35-56 N Long: 95-18-37 W
Pop: 890 (1990); 878 (1980) **Pop Density:** 14.7
Land: 60.4 sq. mi.; **Water:** 0.2 sq. mi.

Mount Pleasant
Township
Lat: 39-28-25 N Long: 95-11-00 W
Pop: 685 (1990); 778 (1980) **Pop Density:** 14.4
Land: 47.7 sq. mi.; **Water:** 0.0 sq. mi.

Muscotah
City
ZIP: 66058 **Lat:** 39-33-11 N **Long:** 95-31-13 W
Pop: 194 (1990); 248 (1980) **Pop Density:** 646.7
Land: 0.3 sq. mi.; **Water:** 0.0 sq. mi. **Elev:** 964 ft.
Incorporated 1880.
Name origin: From Indian term meaning 'beautiful prairie.'

Shannon
Township
Lat: 39-35-24 N **Long:** 95-09-33 W
Pop: 1,483 (1990); 1,867 (1980) **Pop Density:** 27.2
Land: 54.6 sq. mi.; **Water:** 0.6 sq. mi.

Walnut
Township
Lat: 39-28-06 N **Long:** 95-03-53 W
Pop: 639 (1990); 519 (1980) **Pop Density:** 17.6
Land: 36.3 sq. mi.; **Water:** 0.9 sq. mi.

Barber County
County Seat: Medicine Lodge (ZIP: 67104)

Pop: 5,874 (1990); 6,548 (1980) **Pop Density:** 5.2
Land: 1134.2 sq. mi.; **Water:** 2.1 sq. mi. **Area Code:** 316
On the central-southern border of KS, southwest of Wichita; organized as Barbour County Feb 26, 1867 from Harper County; spelling changed Mar 1, 1883.
Name origin: As a memorial to Thomas W. Barber (?–1855), a Free State martyr, murdered near Lawrence, KS.

Aetna
Township
Lat: 37-05-22 N **Long:** 98-54-19 W
Pop: 24 (1990); 37 (1980) **Pop Density:** 0.2
Land: 122.9 sq. mi.; **Water:** 0.2 sq. mi.

Deerhead
Township
Lat: 37-14-13 N **Long:** 98-55-25 W
Pop: 15 (1990); 30 (1980) **Pop Density:** 0.2
Land: 63.6 sq. mi.; **Water:** 0.0 sq. mi.

Eagle
Township
Lat: 37-11-49 N **Long:** 98-45-13 W
Pop: 46 (1990); 97 (1980) **Pop Density:** 0.4
Land: 111.8 sq. mi.; **Water:** 0.0 sq. mi.

Elm Mills
Township
Lat: 37-25-34 N **Long:** 98-39-57 W
Pop: 124 (1990); 100 (1980) **Pop Density:** 2.1
Land: 59.7 sq. mi.; **Water:** 0.2 sq. mi.

Elwood
Township
Lat: 37-03-59 N **Long:** 98-42-51 W
Pop: 284 (1990); 446 (1980) **Pop Density:** 2.8
Land: 100.2 sq. mi.; **Water:** 0.2 sq. mi.

Hardtner
City
ZIP: 67057 **Lat:** 37-00-51 N **Long:** 98-38-54 W
Pop: 198 (1990); 336 (1980) **Pop Density:** 660.0
Land: 0.3 sq. mi.; **Water:** 0.0 sq. mi. **Elev:** 1420 ft.
Incorporated Aug 10, 1911.

Hazelton
City
ZIP: 67061 **Lat:** 37-05-17 N **Long:** 98-24-04 W
Pop: 128 (1990); 143 (1980) **Pop Density:** 213.3
Land: 0.6 sq. mi.; **Water:** 0.0 sq. mi. **Elev:** 1360 ft.
Incorporated 1887. Not coextensive with the town of the same name.
Name origin: For the Rev. J.W. Hazelton, founder of the town site.

*Hazelton
Township
ZIP: 67061 **Lat:** 37-07-24 N **Long:** 98-24-08 W
Pop: 201 (1990); 251 (1980) **Pop Density:** 2.7
Land: 73.1 sq. mi.; **Water:** 0.2 sq. mi.

Isabel
City
ZIP: 67065 **Lat:** 37-28-03 N **Long:** 98-33-04 W
Pop: 104 (1990); 137 (1980) **Pop Density:** 346.7
Land: 0.3 sq. mi.; **Water:** 0.0 sq. mi. **Elev:** 1850 ft.
Incorporated Oct 6, 1909.
Name origin: For the infant daughter of the surveyor who laid out the town.

Kiowa
City
ZIP: 67070 **Lat:** 37-01-02 N **Long:** 98-29-03 W
Pop: 1,160 (1990); 1,409 (1980) **Pop Density:** 1054.5
Land: 1.1 sq. mi.; **Water:** 0.0 sq. mi. **Elev:** 1330 ft.
Incorporated Apr 27, 1885. Not coextensive with the town of the same name.
Name origin: For the Kiowa Indians.

*Kiowa
Township
ZIP: 67070 **Lat:** 37-01-13 N **Long:** 98-29-44 W
Pop: 1,255 (1990); 1,532 (1980) **Pop Density:** 26.2
Land: 47.9 sq. mi.; **Water:** 0.2 sq. mi.

Lake City
Township
ZIP: 67071 **Lat:** 37-19-35 N **Long:** 98-47-47 W
Pop: 97 (1990); 94 (1980) **Pop Density:** 2.3
Land: 42.0 sq. mi.; **Water:** 0.1 sq. mi.

McAdoo
Township
Lat: 37-25-24 N **Long:** 98-48-38 W
Pop: 29 (1990); 32 (1980) **Pop Density:** 0.8
Land: 35.8 sq. mi.; **Water:** 0.1 sq. mi.

Medicine Lodge
City
ZIP: 67104 **Lat:** 37-17-09 N **Long:** 98-34-49 W
Pop: 2,453 (1990); 2,384 (1980) **Pop Density:** 1886.9
Land: 1.3 sq. mi.; **Water:** 0.0 sq. mi. **Elev:** 1510 ft.
Incorporated 1879. Not coextensive with the town of the same name.
Name origin: For the fact that the Kiowa Indians believed the Medicine River protected their green woodland along its banks.

KANSAS, Barber County

*Medicine Lodge Township
ZIP: 67104 Lat: 37-17-31 N Long: 98-33-15 W
Pop: 2,838 (1990); 2,810 (1980) Pop Density: 23.8
Land: 119.4 sq. mi.; Water: 0.4 sq. mi.

Mingona Township
Lat: 37-19-09 N Long: 98-41-42 W
Pop: 51 (1990); 89 (1980) Pop Density: 1.0
Land: 53.5 sq. mi.; Water: 0.1 sq. mi.

Moore Township
Lat: 37-05-25 N Long: 98-32-38 W
Pop: 40 (1990); 45 (1980) Pop Density: 0.9
Land: 45.8 sq. mi.; Water: 0.1 sq. mi.

Nippawalla Township
Lat: 37-10-03 N Long: 98-32-27 W
Pop: 44 (1990); 51 (1980) Pop Density: 0.8
Land: 54.2 sq. mi.; Water: 0.1 sq. mi.

Ridge Township
Lat: 37-20-18 N Long: 98-24-06 W
Pop: 26 (1990); 41 (1980) Pop Density: 0.7
Land: 36.1 sq. mi.; Water: 0.0 sq. mi.

Sharon City
ZIP: 67138 Lat: 37-14-59 N Long: 98-25-05 W
Pop: 256 (1990); 283 (1980) Pop Density: 853.3
Land: 0.3 sq. mi.; Water: 0.0 sq. mi. Elev: 1464 ft.
Incorporated Dec 24, 1885. Not coextensive with the town of the same name.
Name origin: For the biblical plain of Sharon.

*Sharon Township
ZIP: 67138 Lat: 37-15-03 N Long: 98-24-12 W
Pop: 440 (1990); 486 (1980) Pop Density: 12.0
Land: 36.7 sq. mi.; Water: 0.0 sq. mi.

Sun City City
ZIP: 67143 Lat: 37-22-42 N Long: 98-54-59 W
Pop: 88 (1990); 85 (1980) Pop Density: 880.0
Land: 0.1 sq. mi.; Water: 0.0 sq. mi. Elev: 1676 ft.
Incorporated Dec 10, 1919. Not coextensive with the town of the same name.

*Sun City Township
ZIP: 67143 Lat: 37-20-25 N Long: 98-55-30 W
Pop: 127 (1990); 131 (1980) Pop Density: 2.6
Land: 48.0 sq. mi.; Water: 0.0 sq. mi.

Turkey Creek Township
Lat: 37-25-42 N Long: 98-56-22 W
Pop: 35 (1990); 45 (1980) Pop Density: 0.7
Land: 47.4 sq. mi.; Water: 0.1 sq. mi.

Valley Township
Lat: 37-25-46 N Long: 98-30-57 W
Pop: 198 (1990); 231 (1980) Pop Density: 5.5
Land: 36.2 sq. mi.; Water: 0.0 sq. mi.

Barton County
County Seat: Great Bend (ZIP: 67530)

Pop: 29,382 (1990); 31,343 (1980) Pop Density: 32.9
Land: 894.0 sq. mi.; Water: 6.5 sq. mi. Area Code: 316
In central KS, southwest of Salina; organized Feb 26, 1867 from Ellsworth County.
Name origin: For Clara Barton (1821–1912), Civil War nurse and first president (1881) of the American Red Cross. The only KS county named for a woman.

Albert City
ZIP: 67511 Lat: 38-27-16 N Long: 99-00-42 W
Pop: 229 (1990); 236 (1980) Pop Density: 1145.0
Land: 0.2 sq. mi.; Water: 0.0 sq. mi. Elev: 1915 ft.
Incorporated Nov 9, 1929.
Name origin: For its first storekeeper, Albert Kreisinger.

Albion Township
Lat: 38-33-51 N Long: 98-52-07 W
Pop: 61 (1990); 90 (1980) Pop Density: 1.7
Land: 36.2 sq. mi.; Water: 0.0 sq. mi.

Beaver Township
Lat: 38-39-40 N Long: 98-38-41 W
Pop: 122 (1990); 185 (1980) Pop Density: 3.3
Land: 36.7 sq. mi.; Water: 0.0 sq. mi.

Buffalo Township
Lat: 38-23-28 N Long: 98-52-05 W
Pop: 587 (1990); 529 (1980) Pop Density: 17.4
Land: 33.8 sq. mi.; Water: 0.0 sq. mi.

Cheyenne Township
Lat: 38-31-20 N Long: 98-39-11 W
Pop: 281 (1990); 316 (1980) Pop Density: 4.2
Land: 67.3 sq. mi.; Water: 4.9 sq. mi.

Claflin City
ZIP: 67525 Lat: 38-31-26 N Long: 98-32-12 W
Pop: 678 (1990); 764 (1980) Pop Density: 2260.0
Land: 0.3 sq. mi.; Water: 0.0 sq. mi. Elev: 1810 ft.
Incorporated Jul 18, 1901.
Name origin: For the maiden name of the town founder's wife.

Clarence Township
Lat: 38-23-36 N Long: 98-58-08 W
Pop: 145 (1990); 163 (1980) Pop Density: 4.0
Land: 35.9 sq. mi.; Water: 0.0 sq. mi.

Cleveland Township
Lat: 38-39-11 N Long: 98-32-00 W
Pop: 79 (1990); 91 (1980) Pop Density: 2.2
Land: 36.2 sq. mi.; Water: 0.0 sq. mi.

Comanche
Township
Lat: 38-17-50 N **Long:** 98-35-58 W
Pop: 500 (1990); 362 (1980) **Pop Density:** 7.8
Land: 64.5 sq. mi.; **Water:** 0.1 sq. mi.

Ellinwood
City
ZIP: 67526 **Lat:** 38-21-22 N **Long:** 98-34-55 W
Pop: 2,329 (1990); 2,508 (1980) **Pop Density:** 2117.3
Land: 1.1 sq. mi.; **Water:** 0.0 sq. mi. **Elev:** 1800 ft.
Incorporated Apr 23, 1878.
Name origin: For a Santa Fe Railroad contractor.

Eureka
Township
Lat: 38-28-39 N **Long:** 98-52-02 W
Pop: 149 (1990); 147 (1980) **Pop Density:** 4.1
Land: 36.0 sq. mi.; **Water:** 0.1 sq. mi.

Fairview
Township
Lat: 38-39-02 N **Long:** 98-58-26 W
Pop: 125 (1990); 156 (1980) **Pop Density:** 3.5
Land: 36.1 sq. mi.; **Water:** 0.0 sq. mi.

Galatia
City
Lat: 38-38-29 N **Long:** 98-57-25 W
Pop: 47 (1990); 69 (1980) **Pop Density:** 117.5
Land: 0.4 sq. mi.; **Water:** 0.0 sq. mi. **Elev:** 1995 ft.
Incorporated Jan 3, 1921.

Grant
Township
Lat: 38-33-48 N **Long:** 98-58-35 W
Pop: 80 (1990); 119 (1980) **Pop Density:** 2.2
Land: 35.7 sq. mi.; **Water:** 0.0 sq. mi.

Great Bend
City
ZIP: 67530 **Lat:** 38-21-38 N **Long:** 98-48-31 W
Pop: 15,427 (1990); 16,608 (1980) **Pop Density:** 1590.4
Land: 9.7 sq. mi.; **Water:** 0.1 sq. mi. **Elev:** 1849 ft.
In central KS on the Arkansas River, 53 mi. west-northwest of Hutchinson. Incorporated 1872.
Name origin: For its location on the north bank of the great bend in the Arkansas River.

*Great Bend
Township
ZIP: 67530 **Lat:** 38-23-37 N **Long:** 98-43-47 W
Pop: 1,976 (1990); 1,918 (1980) **Pop Density:** 48.4
Land: 40.8 sq. mi.; **Water:** 0.2 sq. mi.

Hoisington
City
ZIP: 67544 **Lat:** 38-31-06 N **Long:** 98-46-41 W
Pop: 3,182 (1990); 3,678 (1980) **Pop Density:** 2892.7
Land: 1.1 sq. mi.; **Water:** 0.0 sq. mi. **Elev:** 1845 ft.
In central KS, north of Great Bend. Incorporated Nov 11, 1886.
Name origin: For early settler, Andrew J. Hoisington.

Independent
Township
Lat: 38-33-59 N **Long:** 98-32-13 W
Pop: 890 (1990); 914 (1980) **Pop Density:** 24.8
Land: 35.9 sq. mi.; **Water:** 0.0 sq. mi.

Lakin
Township
Lat: 38-23-09 N **Long:** 98-33-58 W
Pop: 313 (1990); 346 (1980) **Pop Density:** 4.7
Land: 66.5 sq. mi.; **Water:** 0.2 sq. mi.

Liberty
Township
Lat: 38-18-02 N **Long:** 98-52-00 W
Pop: 382 (1990); 316 (1980) **Pop Density:** 11.2
Land: 34.1 sq. mi.; **Water:** 0.1 sq. mi.

Logan
Township
Lat: 38-28-49 N **Long:** 98-32-05 W
Pop: 155 (1990); 195 (1980) **Pop Density:** 4.3
Land: 35.8 sq. mi.; **Water:** 0.0 sq. mi.

North Homestead
Township
Lat: 38-33-52 N **Long:** 98-45-01 W
Pop: 124 (1990); 133 (1980) **Pop Density:** 3.5
Land: 35.7 sq. mi.; **Water:** 0.0 sq. mi.

Olmitz
City
ZIP: 67564 **Lat:** 38-30-59 N **Long:** 98-56-13 W
Pop: 130 (1990); 140 (1980) **Pop Density:** 650.0
Land: 0.2 sq. mi.; **Water:** 0.0 sq. mi. **Elev:** 2010 ft.
Incorporated Apr 3, 1920.
Name origin: For Olmitz in eastern Bohemia, former home of early settlers.

Pawnee Rock
City
ZIP: 67567 **Lat:** 38-15-54 N **Long:** 98-58-56 W
Pop: 367 (1990); 409 (1980) **Pop Density:** 1223.3
Land: 0.3 sq. mi.; **Water:** 0.0 sq. mi.
Incorporated May 2, 1887. Not coextensive with the town of the same name.
Name origin: For the site of a battle between the Pawnees and the Comanches.

*Pawnee Rock
Township
ZIP: 67567 **Lat:** 38-18-19 N **Long:** 98-58-38 W
Pop: 515 (1990); 536 (1980) **Pop Density:** 14.4
Land: 35.7 sq. mi.; **Water:** 0.0 sq. mi.

South Bend
Township
Lat: 38-18-42 N **Long:** 98-44-48 W
Pop: 805 (1990); 750 (1980) **Pop Density:** 22.2
Land: 36.2 sq. mi.; **Water:** 0.1 sq. mi.

South Homestead
Township
Lat: 38-28-47 N **Long:** 98-45-19 W
Pop: 390 (1990); 480 (1980) **Pop Density:** 11.2
Land: 34.7 sq. mi.; **Water:** 0.4 sq. mi.

Susank
City
ZIP: 67580 **Lat:** 38-38-25 N **Long:** 98-46-28 W
Pop: 61 (1990); 52 (1980) **Pop Density:** 610.0
Land: 0.1 sq. mi.; **Water:** 0.0 sq. mi. **Elev:** 1970 ft.
Incorporated May 7, 1940.

Union
Township
Lat: 38-39-04 N **Long:** 98-45-17 W
Pop: 137 (1990); 161 (1980) **Pop Density:** 3.8
Land: 36.2 sq. mi.; **Water:** 0.1 sq. mi.

Walnut
Township
Lat: 38-28-29 N **Long:** 98-58-50 W
Pop: 544 (1990); 556 (1980) **Pop Density:** 15.2
Land: 35.9 sq. mi.; **Water:** 0.0 sq. mi.

Wheatland
Township
Lat: 38-39-20 N **Long:** 98-52-09 W
Pop: 84 (1990); 86 (1980) **Pop Density:** 2.3
Land: 36.2 sq. mi.; **Water:** 0.0 sq. mi.

KANSAS, Bourbon County   *American Places Dictionary*

Bourbon County
County Seat: Fort Scott (ZIP: 66701)

Pop: 14,966 (1990); 15,969 (1980)　　　　　**Pop Density:** 23.5
Land: 637.1 sq. mi.; **Water:** 1.7 sq. mi.　　**Area Code:** 316
On the southeastern border of KS; original county; organized Aug 25, 1855 (prior to statehood).
Name origin: For Bourbon County, KY, former home of Samuel A. Williams, a member of the first KS legislature.

Bronson　　　　　　　　　　　　　City
ZIP: 66716　　**Lat:** 37-53-45 N **Long:** 95-04-20 W
Pop: 343 (1990); 414 (1980)　　**Pop Density:** 857.5
Land: 0.4 sq. mi.; **Water:** 0.0 sq. mi.　　**Elev:** 1065 ft.
Name origin: For Fort Scott attorney Ira Bronson.

Drywood　　　　　　　　　　　Township
Lat: 37-42-35 N **Long:** 94-41-24 W
Pop: 399 (1990); 406 (1980)　　**Pop Density:** 8.6
Land: 46.5 sq. mi.; **Water:** 0.1 sq. mi.

Fort Scott　　　　　　　　　　　　City
ZIP: 66701　　**Lat:** 37-49-48 N **Long:** 94-42-09 W
Pop: 8,362 (1990); 8,893 (1980)　　**Pop Density:** 1672.4
Land: 5.0 sq. mi.; **Water:** 0.0 sq. mi.　　**Elev:** 846 ft.
In southeastern KS, 85 mi. south of Kansas City. Incorporated Feb 27, 1860.
Name origin: For Gen. Winfield Scott (1786–1866), commander of the Union armies at the beginning of the Civil War.

Franklin　　　　　　　　　　　Township
Lat: 37-58-17 N **Long:** 95-01-18 W
Pop: 227 (1990); 324 (1980)　　**Pop Density:** 3.2
Land: 71.5 sq. mi.; **Water:** 0.1 sq. mi.

Freedom　　　　　　　　　　　Township
Lat: 37-58-37 N **Long:** 94-45-39 W
Pop: 404 (1990); 490 (1980)　　**Pop Density:** 9.2
Land: 43.7 sq. mi.; **Water:** 0.1 sq. mi.

Fulton　　　　　　　　　　　　　City
ZIP: 66738　　**Lat:** 38-00-35 N **Long:** 94-43-08 W
Pop: 191 (1990); 194 (1980)　　**Pop Density:** 955.0
Land: 0.2 sq. mi.; **Water:** 0.0 sq. mi.　　**Elev:** 850 ft.
Incorporated Jun 10, 1884.
Name origin: For Capt. J.R. Fulton, who donated the land for the railroad station.

Mapleton　　　　　　　　　　　　City
ZIP: 66754　　**Lat:** 38-00-55 N **Long:** 94-52-57 W
Pop: 96 (1990); 121 (1980)　　**Pop Density:** 192.0
Land: 0.5 sq. mi.; **Water:** 0.0 sq. mi.　　**Elev:** 878 ft.
Incorporated May 6, 1905.
Name origin: For a beloved maple tree in the area.

Marion　　　　　　　　　　　Township
Lat: 37-50-16 N **Long:** 94-59-04 W
Pop: 1,147 (1990); 1,301 (1980)　　**Pop Density:** 11.5
Land: 100.1 sq. mi.; **Water:** 0.2 sq. mi.

Marmaton　　　　　　　　　　　Township
Lat: 37-49-13 N **Long:** 94-49-53 W
Pop: 744 (1990); 751 (1980)　　**Pop Density:** 13.3
Land: 56.0 sq. mi.; **Water:** 0.1 sq. mi.

Mill Creek　　　　　　　　　　　Township
Lat: 37-54-44 N **Long:** 94-49-56 W
Pop: 480 (1990); 528 (1980)　　**Pop Density:** 9.2
Land: 52.4 sq. mi.; **Water:** 0.2 sq. mi.

Osage　　　　　　　　　　　Township
Lat: 37-58-18 N **Long:** 94-40-01 W
Pop: 371 (1990); 374 (1980)　　**Pop Density:** 7.7
Land: 48.3 sq. mi.; **Water:** 0.1 sq. mi.

Pawnee　　　　　　　　　　　Township
Lat: 37-43-09 N **Long:** 94-49-32 W
Pop: 279 (1990); 333 (1980)　　**Pop Density:** 5.7
Land: 48.6 sq. mi.; **Water:** 0.2 sq. mi.

Redfield　　　　　　　　　　　　City
ZIP: 66769　　**Lat:** 37-50-10 N **Long:** 94-52-55 W
Pop: 143 (1990); 185 (1980)　　**Pop Density:** 1430.0
Land: 0.1 sq. mi.; **Water:** 0.0 sq. mi.　　**Elev:** 853 ft.
Incorporated Jun 9, 1905.

Scott　　　　　　　　　　　Township
Lat: 37-49-40 N **Long:** 94-40-41 W
Pop: 2,158 (1990); 2,090 (1980)　　**Pop Density:** 31.0
Land: 69.7 sq. mi.; **Water:** 0.7 sq. mi.

Timberhill　　　　　　　　　　Township
Lat: 37-59-57 N **Long:** 94-52-26 W
Pop: 242 (1990); 302 (1980)　　**Pop Density:** 6.7
Land: 35.9 sq. mi.; **Water:** 0.0 sq. mi.

Uniontown　　　　　　　　　　　　City
ZIP: 66779　　**Lat:** 37-50-50 N **Long:** 94-58-33 W
Pop: 290 (1990); 371 (1980)　　**Pop Density:** 1450.0
Land: 0.2 sq. mi.; **Water:** 0.0 sq. mi.　　**Elev:** 895 ft.
Incorporated Jul 1895.
Name origin: For its being a bastion of anti-slavery 'free state' sentiment.

Walnut　　　　　　　　　　　Township
Lat: 37-43-06 N **Long:** 94-59-45 W
Pop: 153 (1990); 177 (1980)　　**Pop Density:** 2.6
Land: 59.4 sq. mi.; **Water:** 0.1 sq. mi.

Brown County
County Seat: Hiawatha (ZIP: 66434)

Pop: 11,128 (1990); 11,955 (1980)   **Pop Density:** 19.5
Land: 570.7 sq. mi.; **Water:** 1.5 sq. mi.   **Area Code:** 913
On the northeastern border of KS, west of St. Joseph; original county; organized Aug 30, 1855 (prior to statehood).
Name origin: For either Orville H. Browne, a member of the 1855 KS territorial legislature, or for Albert Gallatin Browne (1813–80), governor of MS (1844–48). The *e* was dropped in 1857 when the county was named.

Everest — City
ZIP: 66424   **Lat:** 39-40-36 N   **Long:** 95-25-30 W
Pop: 310 (1990); 331 (1980)   **Pop Density:** 1033.3
Land: 0.3 sq. mi.; **Water:** 0.0 sq. mi.   **Elev:** 1150 ft.
Incorporated Jun 4, 1882.
Name origin: For Union Pacific Railroad attorney, Col. Aaron Everest.

Fairview — City
ZIP: 66425   **Lat:** 39-50-23 N   **Long:** 95-43-37 W
Pop: 306 (1990); 258 (1980)   **Pop Density:** 1020.0
Land: 0.3 sq. mi.; **Water:** 0.0 sq. mi.   **Elev:** 1230 ft.
Incorporated 1886.
Name origin: For its descriptive connotations.

Hamlin — City
Lat: 39-54-55 N   **Long:** 95-37-37 W
Pop: 50 (1990); 80 (1980)   **Pop Density:** 500.0
Land: 0.1 sq. mi.; **Water:** 0.0 sq. mi.   **Elev:** 1000 ft.
Incorporated May 1889. Not coextensive with the town of the same name.

*Hamlin — Township
Lat: 39-57-00 N   **Long:** 95-36-39 W
Pop: 387 (1990); 419 (1980)   **Pop Density:** 9.5
Land: 40.8 sq. mi.; **Water:** 0.1 sq. mi.

Hiawatha — City
ZIP: 66434   **Lat:** 39-51-09 N   **Long:** 95-32-16 W
Pop: 3,603 (1990); 3,702 (1980)   **Pop Density:** 1801.5
Land: 2.0 sq. mi.; **Water:** 0.0 sq. mi.   **Elev:** 1136 ft.
Incorporated 1859.
Name origin: For the fictional Indian Hiawatha, made popular by the poem by Henry Wadsworth Longfellow (1807–82).

*Hiawatha — Township
ZIP: 66434   **Lat:** 39-50-32 N   **Long:** 95-32-02 W
Pop: 681 (1990); 859 (1980)   **Pop Density:** 10.7
Land: 63.7 sq. mi.; **Water:** 0.1 sq. mi.

Horton — City
ZIP: 66439   **Lat:** 39-39-42 N   **Long:** 95-31-56 W
Pop: 1,885 (1990); 2,130 (1980)   **Pop Density:** 1178.1
Land: 1.6 sq. mi.; **Water:** 0.0 sq. mi.   **Elev:** 1082 ft.
Incorporated Sep 10, 1887.
Name origin: For KS Supreme Court judge, Albert Horton.

Irving — Township
Lat: 39-55-50 N   **Long:** 95-23-27 W
Pop: 315 (1990); 298 (1980)   **Pop Density:** 5.9
Land: 53.0 sq. mi.; **Water:** 0.0 sq. mi.

Mission — Township
Lat: 39-43-31 N   **Long:** 95-32-13 W
Pop: 671 (1990); 764 (1980)   **Pop Density:** 7.9
Land: 84.6 sq. mi.; **Water:** 0.6 sq. mi.

Morrill — City
ZIP: 66515   **Lat:** 39-55-44 N   **Long:** 95-41-39 W
Pop: 299 (1990); 336 (1980)   **Pop Density:** 1495.0
Land: 0.2 sq. mi.; **Water:** 0.0 sq. mi.   **Elev:** 1091 ft.
Incorporated 1886. Not coextensive with the town of the same name.
Name origin: For Gov. E.N. Morrill, who served in 1894.

*Morrill — Township
ZIP: 66515   **Lat:** 39-56-42 N   **Long:** 95-43-59 W
Pop: 587 (1990); 644 (1980)   **Pop Density:** 14.1
Land: 41.5 sq. mi.; **Water:** 0.1 sq. mi.

Padonia — Township
Lat: 39-57-10 N   **Long:** 95-29-59 W
Pop: 311 (1990); 339 (1980)   **Pop Density:** 7.5
Land: 41.3 sq. mi.; **Water:** 0.1 sq. mi.

Powhattan — City
ZIP: 66527   **Lat:** 39-45-43 N   **Long:** 95-38-00 W
Pop: 111 (1990); 95 (1980)   **Pop Density:** 1110.0
Land: 0.1 sq. mi.; **Water:** 0.0 sq. mi.   **Elev:** 1203 ft.
Incorporated Apr 13, 1887. Not coextensive with the town of the same name.
Name origin: For Indian Chief Powhatan (1550?–1618), the father of Pochahontas.

*Powhattan — Township
ZIP: 66527   **Lat:** 39-43-57 N   **Long:** 95-42-14 W
Pop: 913 (1990); 875 (1980)   **Pop Density:** 10.2
Land: 89.8 sq. mi.; **Water:** 0.1 sq. mi.

Reserve — City
ZIP: 66434   **Lat:** 39-58-38 N   **Long:** 95-33-55 W
Pop: 108 (1990); 105 (1980)   **Pop Density:** 1080.0
Land: 0.1 sq. mi.; **Water:** 0.0 sq. mi.   **Elev:** 908 ft.
Incorporated Apr 28, 1913.

Robinson — City
ZIP: 66532   **Lat:** 39-48-53 N   **Long:** 95-24-39 W
Pop: 268 (1990); 324 (1980)   **Pop Density:** 1340.0
Land: 0.2 sq. mi.; **Water:** 0.0 sq. mi.   **Elev:** 955 ft.
Incorporated Apr 1879. Not coextensive with the town of the same name.
Name origin: For Charles Robinson, the first governor of KS.

*Robinson — Township
ZIP: 66532   **Lat:** 39-48-48 N   **Long:** 95-23-46 W
Pop: 532 (1990); 589 (1980)   **Pop Density:** 11.9
Land: 44.8 sq. mi.; **Water:** 0.1 sq. mi.

Sabetha
City
Lat: 39-54-19 N Long: 95-46-38 W
Pop: 6 (1990); 9 (1980) **Pop Density:** 15.0
Land: 0.4 sq. mi.; **Water:** 0.0 sq. mi. **Elev:** 1318 ft.
Incorporated Jul 28, 1874. Part of the town is also in Nemaha County.
Name origin: Possibly for the sabbath.

Walnut
Township
Lat: 39-50-48 N Long: 95-42-16 W
Pop: 712 (1990); 729 (1980) **Pop Density:** 11.4
Land: 62.3 sq. mi.; **Water:** 0.3 sq. mi.

Washington
Township
Lat: 39-42-26 N Long: 95-23-54 W
Pop: 525 (1990); 598 (1980) **Pop Density:** 11.7
Land: 44.9 sq. mi.; **Water:** 0.1 sq. mi.

Willis
City
ZIP: 66435 Lat: 39-43-21 N Long: 95-30-18 W
Pop: 86 (1990); 85 (1980) **Pop Density:** 430.0
Land: 0.2 sq. mi.; **Water:** 0.0 sq. mi. **Elev:** 1165 ft.
Incorporated Mar 1893.
Name origin: For a state legislator, Martin Willis.

Butler County
County Seat: El Dorado (ZIP: 67042)

Pop: 50,580 (1990); 44,782 (1980) **Pop Density:** 35.4
Land: 1428.2 sq. mi.; **Water:** 18.3 sq. mi. **Area Code:** 316
In east-central KS, east of Wichita; original county, organized Aug 25, 1855 (prior to statehood).
Name origin: For Andrew Pickens Butler (1796–1857), SC legislator, jurist, and U.S. senator (1846–57).

Andover
City
ZIP: 67002 Lat: 37-41-28 N Long: 97-08-21 W
Pop: 4,047 (1990); 2,801 (1980) **Pop Density:** 1124.2
Land: 3.6 sq. mi.; **Water:** 0.0 sq. mi. **Elev:** 1350 ft.
Incorporated Feb 4, 1957.
Name origin: For Andover, MA.

Augusta
City
ZIP: 67010 Lat: 37-41-32 N Long: 96-58-30 W
Pop: 7,876 (1990); 6,968 (1980) **Pop Density:** 2812.9
Land: 2.8 sq. mi.; **Water:** 0.3 sq. mi. **Elev:** 1260 ft.
In southern KS, 20 mi. east of Wichita. Incorporated Feb 8, 1871.
Name origin: For Augusta Boynton, wife of founder C.N. James.

*Augusta
Township
ZIP: 67010 Lat: 37-41-42 N Long: 96-59-19 W
Pop: 1,077 (1990); 1,074 (1980) **Pop Density:** 33.0
Land: 32.6 sq. mi.; **Water:** 0.2 sq. mi.

Benton
City
ZIP: 67017 Lat: 37-47-19 N Long: 97-06-29 W
Pop: 669 (1990); 609 (1980) **Pop Density:** 1672.5
Land: 0.4 sq. mi.; **Water:** 0.0 sq. mi. **Elev:** 1375 ft.
Incorporated Jan 6, 1909. Not coextensive with the town of the same name.
Name origin: For KS legislator, Thomas Benton Murdock.

*Benton
Township
ZIP: 67017 Lat: 37-46-59 N Long: 97-06-10 W
Pop: 1,747 (1990); 1,404 (1980) **Pop Density:** 48.4
Land: 36.1 sq. mi.; **Water:** 0.0 sq. mi.

Bloomington
Township
Lat: 37-36-33 N Long: 96-53-03 W
Pop: 386 (1990); 316 (1980) **Pop Density:** 10.7
Land: 36.0 sq. mi.; **Water:** 0.0 sq. mi.

Bruno
Township
Lat: 37-41-20 N Long: 97-06-09 W
Pop: 7,143 (1990); 5,394 (1980) **Pop Density:** 199.0
Land: 35.9 sq. mi.; **Water:** 0.1 sq. mi.

Cassoday
City
ZIP: 66842 Lat: 38-02-19 N Long: 96-38-12 W
Pop: 95 (1990); 122 (1980) **Pop Density:** 316.7
Land: 0.3 sq. mi.; **Water:** 0.0 sq. mi. **Elev:** 1470 ft.
Incorporated Apr 4, 1960.
Name origin: For John B. Cassoday, a chief justice of the WI Supreme Court, under whom a railroad lawyer studied.

Chelsea
Township
Lat: 37-55-28 N Long: 96-40-01 W
Pop: 144 (1990); 99 (1980) **Pop Density:** 1.4
Land: 100.9 sq. mi.; **Water:** 6.4 sq. mi.

Clay
Township
Lat: 37-31-07 N Long: 96-46-11 W
Pop: 83 (1990); 112 (1980) **Pop Density:** 2.3
Land: 36.4 sq. mi.; **Water:** 0.1 sq. mi.

Clifford
Township
Lat: 38-02-32 N Long: 96-58-29 W
Pop: 255 (1990); 260 (1980) **Pop Density:** 6.1
Land: 41.7 sq. mi.; **Water:** 0.1 sq. mi.

Douglass
City
ZIP: 67039 Lat: 37-31-04 N Long: 97-00-41 W
Pop: 1,722 (1990); 1,450 (1980) **Pop Density:** 2152.5
Land: 0.8 sq. mi.; **Water:** 0.0 sq. mi. **Elev:** 1205 ft.
Incorporated Nov 25, 1879. Not coextensive with the town of the same name.
Name origin: For NY settler Capt. Joseph Douglass.

*Douglass
Township
ZIP: 67039 Lat: 37-31-10 N Long: 96-59-23 W
Pop: 2,116 (1990); 1,834 (1980) **Pop Density:** 58.9
Land: 35.9 sq. mi.; **Water:** 0.1 sq. mi.

Elbing — City
ZIP: 67041 **Lat:** 38-03-14 N **Long:** 97-07-36 W
Pop: 184 (1990); 175 (1980) **Pop Density:** 920.0
Land: 0.2 sq. mi.; **Water:** 0.0 sq. mi. **Elev:** 1440 ft.
Incorporated Jul 1919.
Name origin: Named by Mennonite settlers for Elbing, Germany.

El Dorado — City
ZIP: 67042 **Lat:** 37-49-15 N **Long:** 96-51-28 W
Pop: 11,504 (1990); 11,551 (1980) **Pop Density:** 1917.3
Land: 6.0 sq. mi.; **Water:** 0.1 sq. mi. **Elev:** 1344 ft.
In southern KS, 28 mi. east-northeast of Wichita. Incorporated Mar 30, 1870.
Name origin: For the mythical city of gold that brought Spanish explorers to the region in the 16th century.

*El Dorado — Township
ZIP: 67042 **Lat:** 37-48-17 N **Long:** 96-52-31 W
Pop: 1,347 (1990); 1,415 (1980) **Pop Density:** 24.8
Land: 54.3 sq. mi.; **Water:** 0.8 sq. mi.

Fairmount — Township
Lat: 38-02-34 N **Long:** 97-05-52 W
Pop: 422 (1990); 464 (1980) **Pop Density:** 11.6
Land: 36.4 sq. mi.; **Water:** 0.1 sq. mi.

Fairview — Township
Lat: 37-52-15 N **Long:** 96-59-44 W
Pop: 437 (1990); 384 (1980) **Pop Density:** 12.2
Land: 35.7 sq. mi.; **Water:** 0.0 sq. mi.

Glencoe — Township
Lat: 37-41-28 N **Long:** 96-36-55 W
Pop: 230 (1990); 254 (1980) **Pop Density:** 3.7
Land: 62.2 sq. mi.; **Water:** 0.4 sq. mi.

Hickory — Township
Lat: 37-36-30 N **Long:** 96-37-42 W
Pop: 85 (1990); 101 (1980) **Pop Density:** 1.4
Land: 62.5 sq. mi.; **Water:** 0.4 sq. mi.

Latham — City
ZIP: 67072 **Lat:** 37-32-06 N **Long:** 96-38-29 W
Pop: 160 (1990); 148 (1980) **Pop Density:** 800.0
Land: 0.2 sq. mi.; **Water:** 0.0 sq. mi. **Elev:** 1470 ft.
Incorporated 1902.
Name origin: For railroad commissioner Latham Young.

Leon — City
ZIP: 67074 **Lat:** 37-41-17 N **Long:** 96-47-00 W
Pop: 707 (1990); 667 (1980) **Pop Density:** 1414.0
Land: 0.5 sq. mi.; **Water:** 0.0 sq. mi. **Elev:** 1350 ft.
Incorporated 1880.
Name origin: For Leon, IA.

Lincoln — Township
Lat: 37-58-58 N **Long:** 96-51-24 W
Pop: 275 (1990); 273 (1980) **Pop Density:** 2.8
Land: 99.3 sq. mi.; **Water:** 0.6 sq. mi.

Little Walnut — Township
Lat: 37-41-41 N **Long:** 96-46-14 W
Pop: 968 (1990); 880 (1980) **Pop Density:** 26.7
Land: 36.2 sq. mi.; **Water:** 0.2 sq. mi.

Logan — Township
Lat: 37-36-29 N **Long:** 96-47-19 W
Pop: 144 (1990); 96 (1980) **Pop Density:** 4.0
Land: 36.2 sq. mi.; **Water:** 0.1 sq. mi.

Milton — Township
Lat: 37-57-23 N **Long:** 97-05-35 W
Pop: 1,100 (1990); 1,093 (1980) **Pop Density:** 30.3
Land: 36.3 sq. mi.; **Water:** 0.1 sq. mi.

Murdock — Township
Lat: 37-52-34 N **Long:** 97-06-20 W
Pop: 376 (1990); 276 (1980) **Pop Density:** 10.4
Land: 36.0 sq. mi.; **Water:** 0.0 sq. mi.

Pleasant — Township
Lat: 37-35-58 N **Long:** 97-05-21 W
Pop: 4,058 (1990); 2,938 (1980) **Pop Density:** 112.4
Land: 36.1 sq. mi.; **Water:** 0.0 sq. mi.

Plum Grove — Township
Lat: 37-56-57 N **Long:** 96-58-58 W
Pop: 645 (1990); 763 (1980) **Pop Density:** 18.1
Land: 35.6 sq. mi.; **Water:** 0.2 sq. mi.

Potwin — City
ZIP: 67123 **Lat:** 37-56-19 N **Long:** 97-01-07 W
Pop: 448 (1990); 563 (1980) **Pop Density:** 2240.0
Land: 0.2 sq. mi.; **Water:** 0.0 sq. mi. **Elev:** 1340 ft.
Incorporated Jan 8, 1907.

Prospect — Township
Lat: 37-48-37 N **Long:** 96-42-59 W
Pop: 1,117 (1990); 986 (1980) **Pop Density:** 14.3
Land: 78.3 sq. mi.; **Water:** 6.1 sq. mi. **Elev:** 1380 ft.

Richland — Township
Lat: 37-30-43 N **Long:** 97-05-23 W
Pop: 1,540 (1990); 963 (1980) **Pop Density:** 42.4
Land: 36.3 sq. mi.; **Water:** 0.0 sq. mi.

Rock Creek — Township
Lat: 37-31-18 N **Long:** 96-53-01 W
Pop: 272 (1990); 228 (1980) **Pop Density:** 7.5
Land: 36.1 sq. mi.; **Water:** 0.0 sq. mi.

Rosalia — Township
ZIP: 67132 **Lat:** 37-46-46 N **Long:** 96-37-20 W
Pop: 545 (1990); 525 (1980) **Pop Density:** 8.7
Land: 62.6 sq. mi.; **Water:** 0.4 sq. mi.

Rose Hill — City
ZIP: 67133 **Lat:** 37-33-58 N **Long:** 97-07-55 W
Pop: 2,399 (1990); 1,557 (1980) **Pop Density:** 1999.2
Land: 1.2 sq. mi.; **Water:** 0.0 sq. mi. **Elev:** 1240 ft.
Incorporated Feb 7, 1955.
Name origin: Probably for the many wild roses growing nearby.

Spring — Township
Lat: 37-41-35 N **Long:** 96-52-50 W
Pop: 1,374 (1990); 1,055 (1980) **Pop Density:** 38.0
Land: 36.2 sq. mi.; **Water:** 0.0 sq. mi.

Sycamore — Township
Lat: 38-01-42 N **Long:** 96-39-25 W
Pop: 351 (1990); 330 (1980) **Pop Density:** 3.1
Land: 113.8 sq. mi.; **Water:** 0.9 sq. mi.

KANSAS, Butler County

Towanda
City
ZIP: 67144 Lat: 37-47-48 N Long: 96-59-49 W
Pop: 1,289 (1990); 1,332 (1980) Pop Density: 2578.0
Land: 0.5 sq. mi.; Water: 0.0 sq. mi. Elev: 1300 ft.
Incorporated 1905. Not coextensive with the town of the same name.
Name origin: From an Iroquois term possibly brought by early settlers from NY or PA.

*Towanda
Township
ZIP: 67144 Lat: 37-47-05 N Long: 96-59-03 W
Pop: 2,160 (1990); 2,040 (1980) Pop Density: 60.0
Land: 36.0 sq. mi.; Water: 0.0 sq. mi.

Union
Township
Lat: 37-31-10 N Long: 96-36-43 W
Pop: 210 (1990); 205 (1980) Pop Density: 3.4
Land: 62.1 sq. mi.; Water: 0.5 sq. mi.

Walnut
Township
Lat: 37-36-03 N Long: 96-59-29 W
Pop: 593 (1990); 501 (1980) Pop Density: 16.7
Land: 35.6 sq. mi.; Water: 0.3 sq. mi.

Whitewater
City
ZIP: 67154 Lat: 37-57-47 N Long: 97-08-48 W
Pop: 683 (1990); 751 (1980) Pop Density: 2276.7
Land: 0.3 sq. mi.; Water: 0.0 sq. mi. Elev: 1370 ft.
Incorporated Apr 9, 1890.
Name origin: For the Whitewater River, which traverses the county and whose color is caused by white limestone.

Chase County
County Seat: Cottonwood Falls (ZIP: 66845)

Pop: 3,021 (1990); 3,309 (1980) Pop Density: 3.9
Land: 775.9 sq. mi.; Water: 2.1 sq. mi. Area Code: 316
In east-central KS, west of Emporia; organized Feb 11, 1859 (prior to statehood) from Butler County.
Name origin: For Salmon Portland Chase (1808–73), U.S. senator from OH (1849–53), governor of OH (1855–59), and chief justice of the U.S. Supreme Court (1864–73).

Bazaar
Township
Lat: 38-15-59 N Long: 96-30-17 W
Pop: 93 (1990); 95 (1980) Pop Density: 0.8
Land: 112.9 sq. mi.; Water: 0.2 sq. mi.

Cedar
Township
Lat: 38-09-16 N Long: 96-47-10 W
Pop: 113 (1990); 167 (1980) Pop Density: 2.1
Land: 54.8 sq. mi.; Water: 0.1 sq. mi.

Cedar Point
City
ZIP: 66843 Lat: 38-15-35 N Long: 96-49-18 W
Pop: 39 (1990); 66 (1980) Pop Density: 390.0
Land: 0.1 sq. mi.; Water: 0.0 sq. mi. Elev: 1250 ft.
Incorporated Aug 1912.

Cottonwood
Township
Lat: 38-17-19 N Long: 96-45-01 W
Pop: 200 (1990); 235 (1980) Pop Density: 2.5
Land: 80.6 sq. mi.; Water: 0.2 sq. mi.

Cottonwood Falls
City
ZIP: 66845 Lat: 38-22-08 N Long: 96-32-33 W
Pop: 889 (1990); 954 (1980) Pop Density: 1481.7
Land: 0.6 sq. mi.; Water: 0.0 sq. mi. Elev: 1175 ft.
Incorporated Oct 1872.
Name origin: For the distinctive cottonwood trees and for the falls on the Cottonwood River.

Diamond Creek
Township
Lat: 38-26-10 N Long: 96-42-33 W
Pop: 277 (1990); 311 (1980) Pop Density: 1.9
Land: 144.1 sq. mi.; Water: 0.3 sq. mi.

Elmdale
City
ZIP: 66850 Lat: 38-22-22 N Long: 96-38-44 W
Pop: 83 (1990); 109 (1980) Pop Density: 415.0
Land: 0.2 sq. mi.; Water: 0.0 sq. mi. Elev: 1200 ft.
Incorporated 1900.
Name origin: For its descriptive connotations.

Falls
Township
Lat: 38-20-21 N Long: 96-32-46 W
Pop: 1,081 (1990); 1,125 (1980) Pop Density: 21.4
Land: 50.5 sq. mi.; Water: 0.2 sq. mi.

Homestead
Township
Lat: 38-09-33 N Long: 96-41-47 W
Pop: 65 (1990); 108 (1980) Pop Density: 1.2
Land: 54.5 sq. mi.; Water: 0.1 sq. mi.

Matfield
Township
Lat: 38-08-56 N Long: 96-29-48 W
Pop: 143 (1990); 175 (1980) Pop Density: 1.2
Land: 122.1 sq. mi.; Water: 0.4 sq. mi.

Matfield Green
City
ZIP: 66862 Lat: 38-09-31 N Long: 96-33-48 W
Pop: 33 (1990); 71 (1980) Pop Density: 165.0
Land: 0.2 sq. mi.; Water: 0.0 sq. mi. Elev: 1430 ft.
Incorporated Mar 4, 1924.

Strong
Township
Lat: 38-27-14 N Long: 96-31-35 W
Pop: 774 (1990); 797 (1980) Pop Density: 11.6
Land: 66.6 sq. mi.; Water: 0.2 sq. mi.

American Places Dictionary   KANSAS, Chautauqua County

Strong City   City
ZIP: 66869   **Lat:** 38-23-44 N   **Long:** 96-32-11 W
Pop: 617 (1990); 675 (1980)   **Pop Density:** 1234.0
Land: 0.5 sq. mi.; **Water:** 0.0 sq. mi.
Incorporated Feb 5, 1880.
Name origin: For William B. Strong, president of the Santa Fe Railroad.

Toledo   Township
Lat: 38-24-46 N   **Long:** 96-24-34 W
Pop: 275 (1990); 296 (1980)   **Pop Density:** 3.1
Land: 89.8 sq. mi.; **Water:** 0.4 sq. mi.

Chautauqua County
County Seat: Sedan (ZIP: 67361)

Pop: 4,407 (1990); 5,016 (1980)   **Pop Density:** 6.9
Land: 641.7 sq. mi.; **Water:** 3.1 sq. mi.   **Area Code:** 316

On the southern border of KS, west of Joplin, MO; organized Mar 3, 1875 (prior to statehood) from Howard County, which was organized in 1855 (named Godfrey and changed to Seward in 1867) and abolished at the time of its division into Chautauqua and Elk counties.
Name origin: For Chautauqua County, NY, former home of many settlers.

Belleville   Township
Lat: 37-03-08 N   **Long:** 96-09-14 W
Pop: 689 (1990); 810 (1980)   **Pop Density:** 11.5
Land: 59.7 sq. mi.; **Water:** 0.1 sq. mi.

Caneyville   Township
Lat: 37-15-25 N   **Long:** 96-27-26 W
Pop: 80 (1990); 88 (1980)   **Pop Density:** 1.7
Land: 48.4 sq. mi.; **Water:** 0.2 sq. mi.

Cedar Vale   City
ZIP: 67024   **Lat:** 37-06-22 N   **Long:** 96-30-02 W
Pop: 760 (1990); 848 (1980)   **Pop Density:** 1085.7
Land: 0.7 sq. mi.; **Water:** 0.0 sq. mi.   **Elev:** 949 ft.
Incorporated Apr 26, 1884.

Center   Township
Lat: 37-14-30 N   **Long:** 96-19-15 W
Pop: 104 (1990); 105 (1980)   **Pop Density:** 1.7
Land: 62.6 sq. mi.; **Water:** 0.5 sq. mi.

Chautauqua   City
ZIP: 67334   **Lat:** 37-01-25 N   **Long:** 96-10-36 W
Pop: 132 (1990); 156 (1980)   **Pop Density:** 330.0
Land: 0.4 sq. mi.; **Water:** 0.0 sq. mi.   **Elev:** 903 ft.
Incorporated Feb 6, 1882.
Name origin: For Chatauqua County, NY

Elgin   City
Lat: 37-00-05 N   **Long:** 96-16-49 W
Pop: 118 (1990); 139 (1980)   **Pop Density:** 590.0
Land: 0.2 sq. mi.; **Water:** 0.0 sq. mi.   **Elev:** 784 ft.
Incorporated Aug 4, 1919.

Harrison   Township
Lat: 37-02-50 N   **Long:** 96-27-35 W
Pop: 124 (1990); 158 (1980)   **Pop Density:** 2.2
Land: 55.5 sq. mi.; **Water:** 0.1 sq. mi.

Hendricks   Township
Lat: 37-03-11 N   **Long:** 96-18-05 W
Pop: 179 (1990); 241 (1980)   **Pop Density:** 3.3
Land: 54.4 sq. mi.; **Water:** 0.0 sq. mi.

Jefferson   Township
Lat: 37-08-59 N   **Long:** 96-27-43 W
Pop: 875 (1990); 955 (1980)   **Pop Density:** 18.0
Land: 48.5 sq. mi.; **Water:** 0.2 sq. mi.

Lafayette   Township
Lat: 37-14-41 N   **Long:** 96-09-15 W
Pop: 72 (1990); 86 (1980)   **Pop Density:** 1.2
Land: 59.4 sq. mi.; **Water:** 0.8 sq. mi.

Little Caney   Township
Lat: 37-02-45 N   **Long:** 96-01-42 W
Pop: 265 (1990); 298 (1980)   **Pop Density:** 5.9
Land: 45.1 sq. mi.; **Water:** 0.1 sq. mi.

Niotaze   City
ZIP: 67355   **Lat:** 37-04-02 N   **Long:** 96-00-50 W
Pop: 99 (1990); 104 (1980)   **Pop Density:** 247.5
Land: 0.4 sq. mi.; **Water:** 0.0 sq. mi.   **Elev:** 765 ft.
Incorporated Jan 5, 1910.
Name origin: For Niota, IL.

Peru   City
ZIP: 67360   **Lat:** 37-04-52 N   **Long:** 96-05-45 W
Pop: 206 (1990); 286 (1980)   **Pop Density:** 515.0
Land: 0.4 sq. mi.; **Water:** 0.0 sq. mi.   **Elev:** 784 ft.
Incorporated 1904.
Name origin: For Peru, IL.

Salt Creek   Township
Lat: 37-14-43 N   **Long:** 96-01-40 W
Pop: 109 (1990); 139 (1980)   **Pop Density:** 2.2
Land: 49.0 sq. mi.; **Water:** 0.2 sq. mi.

Sedan   City
ZIP: 67361   **Lat:** 37-07-38 N   **Long:** 96-11-04 W
Pop: 1,306 (1990); 1,579 (1980)   **Pop Density:** 1632.5
Land: 0.8 sq. mi.; **Water:** 0.0 sq. mi.   **Elev:** 862 ft.
Incorporated Mar 16, 1876.
Name origin: For the city of Sedan in France, site of the final battle in the Franco-Prussian War.

*Sedan   Township
ZIP: 67361   **Lat:** 37-08-56 N   **Long:** 96-10-05 W
Pop: 1,676 (1990); 1,878 (1980)   **Pop Density:** 33.9
Land: 49.5 sq. mi.; **Water:** 0.3 sq. mi.

KANSAS, Chautauqua County   American Places Dictionary

Summit   Township
                  Lat: 37-09-23 N   **Long:** 96-19-30 W
Pop: 107 (1990); 126 (1980)   **Pop Density:** 1.7
Land: 62.7 sq. mi.; **Water:** 0.2 sq. mi.

Washington   Township
                  Lat: 37-09-09 N   **Long:** 96-01-19 W
Pop: 127 (1990); 132 (1980)   **Pop Density:** 2.7
Land: 46.8 sq. mi.; **Water:** 0.3 sq. mi.

Cherokee County
County Seat: Columbus (ZIP: 66725)

Pop: 21,374 (1990); 22,304 (1980)   **Pop Density:** 36.4
Land: 587.2 sq. mi.; **Water:** 3.8 sq. mi.   **Area Code:** 316

On the southeastern border of KS, west of Joplin, MO; organized as McGee County Feb 18, 1860 (prior to statehood) from unorganized territory; name changed 1866.

Name origin: For the Indian tribe of Iroquoian linguistic stock. Name may derive from Creek *tciloki* 'people of a different speech.' Originally for A.M. McGee, a noted proslavery leader.

Baxter Springs   City
ZIP: 66713   **Lat:** 37-01-15 N   **Long:** 94-44-14 W
Pop: 4,351 (1990); 4,730 (1980)   **Pop Density:** 1611.5
Land: 2.7 sq. mi.; **Water:** 0.0 sq. mi.

In the southeastern corner of KS; incorporated 1868.

Name origin: For squatter John L. Baxter, who was killed in a land dispute.

Cherokee   Township
                  Lat: 37-18-06 N   **Long:** 94-45-32 W
Pop: 342 (1990); 374 (1980)   **Pop Density:** 15.4
Land: 22.2 sq. mi.; **Water:** 0.0 sq. mi.

Columbus   City
ZIP: 66725   **Lat:** 37-10-13 N   **Long:** 94-50-39 W
Pop: 3,268 (1990); 3,426 (1980)   **Pop Density:** 1720.0
Land: 1.9 sq. mi.; **Water:** 0.0 sq. mi.   **Elev:** 910 ft.

In the southeastern corner of KS; incorporated 1871.

Name origin: For Christopher Columbus (1451–1506), discoverer of America.

Crawford   Township
                  Lat: 37-09-38 N   **Long:** 94-46-14 W
Pop: 550 (1990); 559 (1980)   **Pop Density:** 15.1
Land: 36.4 sq. mi.; **Water:** 0.1 sq. mi.

Galena   City
ZIP: 66739   **Lat:** 37-04-30 N   **Long:** 94-38-07 W
Pop: 3,308 (1990); 3,587 (1980)   **Pop Density:** 735.1
Land: 4.5 sq. mi.; **Water:** 0.0 sq. mi.   **Elev:** 941 ft.

In the southeastern corner of KS; incorporated Jun 19, 1877.

Name origin: For Galena, IL.

Garden   Township
                  Lat: 37-02-29 N   **Long:** 94-40-41 W
Pop: 2,703 (1990); 2,462 (1980)   **Pop Density:** 92.9
Land: 29.1 sq. mi.; **Water:** 0.9 sq. mi.

Lola   Township
                  Lat: 37-09-38 N   **Long:** 95-00-31 W
Pop: 357 (1990); 390 (1980)   **Pop Density:** 8.0
Land: 44.5 sq. mi.; **Water:** 0.2 sq. mi.

Lowell   Township
ZIP: 66713   **Lat:** 37-06-10 N   **Long:** 94-40-22 W
Pop: 564 (1990); 547 (1980)   **Pop Density:** 43.7
Land: 12.9 sq. mi.; **Water:** 0.4 sq. mi.

Lyon   Township
                  Lat: 37-03-25 N   **Long:** 94-53-42 W
Pop: 527 (1990); 669 (1980)   **Pop Density:** 10.5
Land: 50.1 sq. mi.; **Water:** 0.0 sq. mi.

Mineral   Township
                  Lat: 37-15-22 N   **Long:** 94-47-07 W
Pop: 239 (1990); 291 (1980)   **Pop Density:** 7.8
Land: 30.6 sq. mi.; **Water:** 0.0 sq. mi.

Incorporated 1907.

Neosho   Township
                  Lat: 37-03-46 N   **Long:** 95-00-31 W
Pop: 281 (1990); 349 (1980)   **Pop Density:** 4.6
Land: 60.6 sq. mi.; **Water:** 0.7 sq. mi.

Pleasant View   Township
                  Lat: 37-16-14 N   **Long:** 94-39-44 W
Pop: 508 (1990); 576 (1980)   **Pop Density:** 9.7
Land: 52.4 sq. mi.; **Water:** 0.1 sq. mi.

Roseland   City
ZIP: 66773   **Lat:** 37-16-45 N   **Long:** 94-51-04 W
Pop: 98 (1990); 119 (1980)   **Pop Density:** 245.0
Land: 0.4 sq. mi.; **Water:** 0.0 sq. mi.   **Elev:** 925 ft.

Incorporated Apr 3, 1906.

Ross   Township
                  Lat: 37-16-26 N   **Long:** 94-52-44 W
Pop: 847 (1990); 921 (1980)   **Pop Density:** 15.7
Land: 54.0 sq. mi.; **Water:** 0.4 sq. mi.

Salamanca   Township
                  Lat: 37-09-51 N   **Long:** 94-53-00 W
Pop: 575 (1990); 559 (1980)   **Pop Density:** 16.5
Land: 34.9 sq. mi.; **Water:** 0.0 sq. mi.

Scammon   City
ZIP: 66773   **Lat:** 37-16-41 N   **Long:** 94-49-19 W
Pop: 466 (1990); 501 (1980)   **Pop Density:** 776.7
Land: 0.6 sq. mi.; **Water:** 0.0 sq. mi.   **Elev:** 900 ft.

In the southeastern corner of KS; incorporated Jul 5, 1888.

Name origin: For the four pioneer Scammon brothers.

Shawnee   Township
                  Lat: 37-10-02 N   **Long:** 94-40-23 W
Pop: 478 (1990); 480 (1980)   **Pop Density:** 13.7
Land: 34.8 sq. mi.; **Water:** 0.2 sq. mi.

Sheridan
Township
Lat: 37-16-35 N Long: 95-00-14 W
Pop: 246 (1990); 302 (1980)   Pop Density: 3.7
Land: 66.6 sq. mi.; Water: 0.5 sq. mi.

Spring Valley
Township
Lat: 37-03-45 N Long: 94-46-18 W
Pop: 1,034 (1990); 876 (1980) Pop Density: 21.9
Land: 47.3 sq. mi.; Water: 0.2 sq. mi.

Treece
City
ZIP: 66778   Lat: 37-00-00 N Long: 94-50-36 W
Pop: 172 (1990); 194 (1980) Pop Density: 1720.0
Land: 0.1 sq. mi.; Water: 0.0 sq. mi.   Elev: 840 ft.
Incorporated 1918.

Weir
City
ZIP: 66781   Lat: 37-18-34 N Long: 94-46-32 W
Pop: 730 (1990); 705 (1980) Pop Density: 730.0
Land: 1.0 sq. mi.; Water: 0.0 sq. mi.   Elev: 920 ft.
In the southeastern corner of KS; incorporated Sep 18, 1875.
Name origin: For a local water project.

West Mineral
City
ZIP: 66782   Lat: 37-17-00 N Long: 94-55-37 W
Pop: 226 (1990); 229 (1980) Pop Density: 753.3
Land: 0.3 sq. mi.; Water: 0.0 sq. mi.   Elev: 900 ft.
In the southeastern corner of KS.
Name origin: For the numerous minerals, including coal, found nearby.

Cheyenne County
County Seat: Saint Francis (ZIP: 67756)

Pop: 3,243 (1990); 3,678 (1980)   Pop Density: 3.2
Land: 1019.9 sq. mi.; Water: 1.0 sq. mi.   Area Code: 913
On northwestern border of KS; organized Mar 20, 1873 from Kirwin Land District.
Name origin: For the Cheyenne Indians, a Dakota tribe of Algonquian linguistic stock; name means 'red talkers.'

Benkelman
Township
Lat: 39-38-52 N Long: 101-55-31 W
Pop: 55 (1990); 77 (1980)   Pop Density: 0.8
Land: 71.9 sq. mi.; Water: 0.0 sq. mi.

Bird City
City
ZIP: 67731   Lat: 39-44-59 N Long: 101-31-53 W
Pop: 467 (1990); 546 (1980) Pop Density: 212.3
Land: 2.2 sq. mi.; Water: 0.0 sq. mi.   Elev: 3460 ft.
Incorporated 1885. Not coextensive with the town of the same name.

*Bird City
Township
ZIP: 67731   Lat: 39-46-13 N Long: 101-31-03 W
Pop: 794 (1990); 947 (1980) Pop Density: 2.3
Land: 341.4 sq. mi.; Water: 0.1 sq. mi.

Calhoun
Township
Lat: 39-55-31 N Long: 101-40-42 W
Pop: 61 (1990); 88 (1980)   Pop Density: 0.7
Land: 89.3 sq. mi.; Water: 0.6 sq. mi.

Cherry Creek
Township
Lat: 39-47-03 N Long: 101-57-11 W
Pop: 117 (1990); 114 (1980) Pop Density: 1.9
Land: 60.3 sq. mi.; Water: 0.0 sq. mi.

Cleveland Run
Township
Lat: 39-55-21 N Long: 101-48-35 W
Pop: 80 (1990); 82 (1980)   Pop Density: 1.1
Land: 71.9 sq. mi.; Water: 0.1 sq. mi.

Jaqua
Township
Lat: 39-39-30 N Long: 102-01-02 W
Pop: 60 (1990); 75 (1980)   Pop Density: 1.3
Land: 47.9 sq. mi.; Water: 0.0 sq. mi.

Orlando
Township
Lat: 39-47-14 N Long: 101-41-30 W
Pop: 66 (1990); 91 (1980)   Pop Density: 1.8
Land: 35.9 sq. mi.; Water: 0.0 sq. mi.

St. Francis
City
ZIP: 67756   Lat: 39-46-17 N Long: 101-48-00 W
Pop: 1,495 (1990); 1,610 (1980) Pop Density: 1868.8
Land: 0.8 sq. mi.; Water: 0.0 sq. mi.   Elev: 3320 ft.
In the northwestern corner of KS; incorporated May 1903.
Name origin: For the 13th-century Italian saint, Francis of Assisi.

Wano
Township
Lat: 39-46-09 N Long: 101-50-50 W
Pop: 2,010 (1990); 2,204 (1980) Pop Density: 6.7
Land: 301.3 sq. mi.; Water: 0.2 sq. mi.

Clark County
County Seat: Ashland (ZIP: 67831)

Pop: 2,418 (1990); 2,599 (1980)   **Pop Density:** 2.5
Land: 974.7 sq. mi.; **Water:** 2.5 sq. mi.   **Area Code:** 316
On the central southern border of KS, south of Dodge City; first established Feb 16, 1867; abolished in 1883; recreated in 1885.
Name origin: For Capt. Charles F. Clarke (?–1862), Union officer in the Civil War. The *e* was dropped in naming the county.

Appleton   Township
Lat: 37-23-27 N   **Long:** 99-54-45 W
Pop: 875 (1990); 908 (1980)   **Pop Density:** 3.6
Land: 243.2 sq. mi.; **Water:** 0.7 sq. mi.

Ashland   City
ZIP: 67831   **Lat:** 37-11-12 N   **Long:** 99-46-07 W
Pop: 1,032 (1990); 1,096 (1980)   **Pop Density:** 607.1
Land: 1.7 sq. mi.; **Water:** 0.0 sq. mi.   **Elev:** 1979 ft.
Incorporated Apr 12, 1886.
Name origin: For the KY home of U.S. Senator Henry Clay (1777–1852).

Center   Township
Lat: 37-08-49 N   **Long:** 99-49-25 W
Pop: 1,146 (1990); 1,238 (1980)   **Pop Density:** 5.6
Land: 203.9 sq. mi.; **Water:** 0.6 sq. mi.

Englewood   City
ZIP: 67840   **Lat:** 37-02-22 N   **Long:** 99-59-07 W
Pop: 96 (1990); 111 (1980)   **Pop Density:** 96.0
Land: 1.0 sq. mi.; **Water:** 0.0 sq. mi.   **Elev:** 1970 ft.
Incorporated Oct 30, 1885. Not coextensive with the town of the same name.
Name origin: For Englewood, IL.

*Englewood   Township
ZIP: 67840   **Lat:** 37-08-24 N   **Long:** 99-59-45 W
Pop: 148 (1990); 197 (1980)   **Pop Density:** 0.7
Land: 206.8 sq. mi.; **Water:** 0.1 sq. mi.

Lexington   Township
Lat: 37-18-31 N   **Long:** 99-38-08 W
Pop: 63 (1990); 84 (1980)   **Pop Density:** 0.7
Land: 89.5 sq. mi.; **Water:** 0.2 sq. mi.

Liberty   Township
Lat: 37-25-19 N   **Long:** 99-38-53 W
Pop: 61 (1990); 42 (1980)   **Pop Density:** 1.0
Land: 59.8 sq. mi.; **Water:** 0.0 sq. mi.

Minneola   City
ZIP: 67865   **Lat:** 37-26-33 N   **Long:** 100-00-45 W
Pop: 705 (1990); 712 (1980)   **Pop Density:** 1762.5
Land: 0.4 sq. mi.; **Water:** 0.0 sq. mi.   **Elev:** 2548 ft.
Incorporated 1909.
Name origin: From a combination of the first names of Minnie Davis and Ola Watson.

Sitka   Township
Lat: 37-07-03 N   **Long:** 99-37-52 W
Pop: 125 (1990); 130 (1980)   **Pop Density:** 0.7
Land: 171.5 sq. mi.; **Water:** 0.8 sq. mi.

Clay County
County Seat: Clay Center (ZIP: 67432)

Pop: 9,158 (1990); 9,802 (1980)   **Pop Density:** 14.2
Land: 643.9 sq. mi.; **Water:** 11.6 sq. mi.   **Area Code:** 913
In north-central KS, west of Manhattan; original county, organized Feb 27, 1857 (prior to statehood).
Name origin: For Henry Clay (1777–1852), U.S. senator from KY, known as the "Great Pacificator" for his advocacy of compromise to avert national crises.

Athelstane   Township
Lat: 39-11-03 N   **Long:** 97-12-07 W
Pop: 158 (1990); 194 (1980)   **Pop Density:** 4.4
Land: 36.1 sq. mi.; **Water:** 0.0 sq. mi.

Blaine   Township
Lat: 39-20-37 N   **Long:** 97-11-09 W
Pop: 298 (1990); 293 (1980)   **Pop Density:** 6.7
Land: 44.6 sq. mi.; **Water:** 0.4 sq. mi.

Bloom   Township
Lat: 39-26-41 N   **Long:** 97-17-22 W
Pop: 98 (1990); 122 (1980)   **Pop Density:** 2.5
Land: 38.9 sq. mi.; **Water:** 0.2 sq. mi.

Chapman   Township
Lat: 39-10-27 N   **Long:** 97-19-03 W
Pop: 188 (1990); 264 (1980)   **Pop Density:** 5.2
Land: 35.9 sq. mi.; **Water:** 0.0 sq. mi.

Clay Center — City
ZIP: 67432   **Lat:** 39-22-47 N   **Long:** 97-07-22 W
Pop: 4,613 (1990); 4,948 (1980)   **Pop Density:** 2005.7
Land: 2.3 sq. mi.; **Water:** 0.0 sq. mi.   **Elev:** 1201 ft.
In northeast-central KS, northwest of Manhattan. Incorporated 1880.
Name origin: For KY statesman Henry Clay (1777–1852).

*Clay Center — Township
ZIP: 67432   **Lat:** 39-22-48 N   **Long:** 97-06-37 W
Pop: 398 (1990); 383 (1980)   **Pop Density:** 10.6
Land: 37.6 sq. mi.; **Water:** 0.5 sq. mi.

Clifton — City
Lat: 39-33-55 N   **Long:** 97-16-44 W
Pop: 227 (1990); 324 (1980)   **Pop Density:** 1135.0
Land: 0.2 sq. mi.; **Water:** 0.0 sq. mi.   **Elev:** 1302 ft.
Incorporated May 21, 1884. Part of the town is also in Washington County.
Name origin: For a well-liked government surveyor.

Exeter — Township
Lat: 39-16-07 N   **Long:** 97-11-51 W
Pop: 94 (1990); 115 (1980)   **Pop Density:** 2.6
Land: 36.2 sq. mi.; **Water:** 0.0 sq. mi.

Five Creeks — Township
Lat: 39-21-12 N   **Long:** 97-18-38 W
Pop: 160 (1990); 171 (1980)   **Pop Density:** 3.8
Land: 42.0 sq. mi.; **Water:** 0.0 sq. mi.

Garfield — Township
Lat: 39-31-28 N   **Long:** 97-07-36 W
Pop: 134 (1990); 159 (1980)   **Pop Density:** 3.8
Land: 35.2 sq. mi.; **Water:** 0.0 sq. mi.

Gill — Township
Lat: 39-11-02 N   **Long:** 97-05-59 W
Pop: 161 (1990); 150 (1980)   **Pop Density:** 5.3
Land: 30.1 sq. mi.; **Water:** 0.0 sq. mi.

Goshen — Township
Lat: 39-31-20 N   **Long:** 97-01-00 W
Pop: 80 (1990); 110 (1980)   **Pop Density:** 2.3
Land: 35.2 sq. mi.; **Water:** 0.0 sq. mi.

Grant — Township
Lat: 39-17-38 N   **Long:** 96-59-37 W
Pop: 116 (1990); 144 (1980)   **Pop Density:** 4.0
Land: 28.7 sq. mi.; **Water:** 5.0 sq. mi.

Green — City
ZIP: 67447   **Lat:** 39-25-48 N   **Long:** 96-59-59 W
Pop: 150 (1990); 155 (1980)   **Pop Density:** 750.0
Land: 0.2 sq. mi.; **Water:** 0.0 sq. mi.   **Elev:** 1383 ft.
Incorporated 1908.

Hayes — Township
Lat: 39-26-12 N   **Long:** 97-05-21 W
Pop: 261 (1990); 221 (1980)   **Pop Density:** 7.3
Land: 35.8 sq. mi.; **Water:** 0.0 sq. mi.

Highland — Township
Lat: 39-24-47 N   **Long:** 96-59-59 W
Pop: 340 (1990); 376 (1980)   **Pop Density:** 9.6
Land: 35.3 sq. mi.; **Water:** 0.0 sq. mi.

Longford — City
ZIP: 67458   **Lat:** 39-10-21 N   **Long:** 97-19-41 W
Pop: 68 (1990); 109 (1980)   **Pop Density:** 340.0
Land: 0.2 sq. mi.; **Water:** 0.0 sq. mi.   **Elev:** 1350 ft.
Incorporated Nov 7, 1910.
Name origin: For Longford, Ireland.

Morganville — City
ZIP: 67468   **Lat:** 39-27-58 N   **Long:** 97-12-11 W
Pop: 181 (1990); 261 (1980)   **Pop Density:** 603.3
Land: 0.3 sq. mi.; **Water:** 0.0 sq. mi.   **Elev:** 1233 ft.
Incorporated 1886.

Mulberry — Township
Lat: 39-31-23 N   **Long:** 97-18-40 W
Pop: 402 (1990); 501 (1980)   **Pop Density:** 10.7
Land: 37.5 sq. mi.; **Water:** 0.8 sq. mi.

Oak Hill — City
Lat: 39-14-47 N   **Long:** 97-20-36 W
Pop: 13 (1990); 35 (1980)   **Pop Density:** 260.0
Land: 0.05 sq. mi.; **Water:** 0.0 sq. mi.   **Elev:** 1280 ft.
Incorporated May 6, 1925.
Name origin: For its descriptive connotation.

Oakland — Township
Lat: 39-14-56 N   **Long:** 97-18-54 W
Pop: 96 (1990); 108 (1980)   **Pop Density:** 2.7
Land: 35.9 sq. mi.; **Water:** 0.0 sq. mi.

Republican — Township
Lat: 39-11-02 N   **Long:** 97-00-42 W
Pop: 1,055 (1990); 971 (1980)   **Pop Density:** 37.4
Land: 28.2 sq. mi.; **Water:** 4.0 sq. mi.

Sherman — Township
Lat: 39-30-04 N   **Long:** 97-12-14 W
Pop: 347 (1990); 394 (1980)   **Pop Density:** 10.5
Land: 33.0 sq. mi.; **Water:** 0.3 sq. mi.

Union — Township
Lat: 39-15-59 N   **Long:** 97-06-00 W
Pop: 159 (1990); 178 (1980)   **Pop Density:** 4.5
Land: 35.5 sq. mi.; **Water:** 0.1 sq. mi.

Vining — City
Lat: 39-33-54 N   **Long:** 97-17-38 W
Pop: 35 (1990); 55 (1980)   **Pop Density:** 350.0
Land: 0.1 sq. mi.; **Water:** 0.0 sq. mi.   **Elev:** 1280 ft.
Incorporated Feb 9, 1885. Part of the town is also in Washington County.

Wakefield — City
ZIP: 67487   **Lat:** 39-13-00 N   **Long:** 97-01-04 W
Pop: 900 (1990); 803 (1980)   **Pop Density:** 1800.0
Land: 0.5 sq. mi.; **Water:** 0.0 sq. mi.   **Elev:** 1148 ft.
Incorporated Jun 14, 1887.
Name origin: For Wakefield, England.

Cloud County
County Seat: Concordia (ZIP: 66901)

Pop: 11,023 (1990); 12,494 (1980)
Land: 715.7 sq. mi.; **Water:** 2.8 sq. mi.
Pop Density: 15.4
Area Code: 913

In north-central KS, north of Salina; organized as Shirley County Feb 27, 1860 (prior to statehood) from unorganized territory; name changed Feb 26, 1867.

Name origin: Named by John B. Rupe, a county representative, for William F. Cloud, an officer in the Kansas Volunteers. Originally named as a joke for Jane Shirley, "a notorious Leavenworth prostitute" known "to all the boys."

Arion
Township
Lat: 39-28-54 N **Long:** 97-45-31 W
Pop: 107 (1990); 137 (1980) **Pop Density:** 3.0
Land: 36.2 sq. mi.; **Water:** 0.0 sq. mi.

Aurora
City
ZIP: 67417 **Lat:** 39-27-05 N **Long:** 97-31-48 W
Pop: 101 (1990); 130 (1980) **Pop Density:** 1010.0
Land: 0.1 sq. mi.; **Water:** 0.0 sq. mi. **Elev:** 1476 ft.
Incorporated Jun 9, 1910. Not coextensive with the town of the same name.
Name origin: For the Roman goddess of dawn.

*Aurora
Township
ZIP: 67417 **Lat:** 39-26-22 N **Long:** 97-32-13 W
Pop: 195 (1990); 230 (1980) **Pop Density:** 5.4
Land: 36.2 sq. mi.; **Water:** 0.0 sq. mi.

Buffalo
Township
Lat: 39-34-39 N **Long:** 97-46-18 W
Pop: 159 (1990); 152 (1980) **Pop Density:** 3.7
Land: 43.2 sq. mi.; **Water:** 0.2 sq. mi.

Center
Township
Lat: 39-27-32 N **Long:** 97-38-42 W
Pop: 218 (1990); 196 (1980) **Pop Density:** 4.0
Land: 54.3 sq. mi.; **Water:** 0.0 sq. mi.

Clyde
City
ZIP: 66938 **Lat:** 39-35-30 N **Long:** 97-24-02 W
Pop: 793 (1990); 909 (1980) **Pop Density:** 1132.9
Land: 0.7 sq. mi.; **Water:** 0.0 sq. mi. **Elev:** 1300 ft.
Incorporated 1869.

Colfax
Township
Lat: 39-26-06 N **Long:** 97-25-17 W
Pop: 69 (1990); 95 (1980) **Pop Density:** 1.9
Land: 35.8 sq. mi.; **Water:** 0.0 sq. mi.

Concordia
City
ZIP: 66901 **Lat:** 39-33-54 N **Long:** 97-39-16 W
Pop: 6,167 (1990); 6,847 (1980) **Pop Density:** 1989.4
Land: 3.1 sq. mi.; **Water:** 0.0 sq. mi. **Elev:** 1369 ft.
In northern KS, 50 mi. north of Salina. Incorporated 1872.
Name origin: For the agreement between the town's founders.

Elk
Township
Lat: 39-36-57 N **Long:** 97-25-04 W
Pop: 906 (1990); 1,055 (1980) **Pop Density:** 32.5
Land: 27.9 sq. mi.; **Water:** 0.3 sq. mi.

Glasco
City
ZIP: 67445 **Lat:** 39-21-38 N **Long:** 97-50-11 W
Pop: 556 (1990); 710 (1980) **Pop Density:** 1853.3
Land: 0.3 sq. mi.; **Water:** 0.0 sq. mi. **Elev:** 1320 ft.
Incorporated Apr 14, 1886.
Name origin: Named by Scottish settlers for Glasgow, Scotland.

Grant
Township
Lat: 39-36-36 N **Long:** 97-52-33 W
Pop: 430 (1990); 551 (1980) **Pop Density:** 12.1
Land: 35.4 sq. mi.; **Water:** 0.6 sq. mi.

Jamestown
City
ZIP: 66948 **Lat:** 39-36-00 N **Long:** 97-51-41 W
Pop: 325 (1990); 440 (1980) **Pop Density:** 1083.3
Land: 0.3 sq. mi.; **Water:** 0.0 sq. mi. **Elev:** 1411 ft.
Incorporated Jun 1883.
Name origin: For railroad vice president James Pomeroy.

Lawrence
Township
Lat: 39-36-39 N **Long:** 97-32-07 W
Pop: 169 (1990); 230 (1980) **Pop Density:** 4.7
Land: 36.0 sq. mi.; **Water:** 0.4 sq. mi.

Lincoln
Township
Lat: 39-33-11 N **Long:** 97-38-39 W
Pop: 421 (1990); 356 (1980) **Pop Density:** 17.6
Land: 23.9 sq. mi.; **Water:** 0.3 sq. mi.

Lyon
Township
Lat: 39-22-19 N **Long:** 97-45-49 W
Pop: 126 (1990); 148 (1980) **Pop Density:** 2.3
Land: 54.7 sq. mi.; **Water:** 0.0 sq. mi.

Meredith
Township
Lat: 39-21-01 N **Long:** 97-38-51 W
Pop: 85 (1990); 104 (1980) **Pop Density:** 2.3
Land: 36.2 sq. mi.; **Water:** 0.0 sq. mi.

Miltonvale
City
ZIP: 67466 **Lat:** 39-21-02 N **Long:** 97-27-10 W
Pop: 484 (1990); 588 (1980) **Pop Density:** 691.4
Land: 0.7 sq. mi.; **Water:** 0.0 sq. mi. **Elev:** 1373 ft.
Incorporated Oct 24, 1883.

Nelson
Township
Lat: 39-31-26 N **Long:** 97-31-51 W
Pop: 161 (1990); 172 (1980) **Pop Density:** 4.6
Land: 35.2 sq. mi.; **Water:** 0.0 sq. mi.

Oakland
Township
Lat: 39-20-54 N **Long:** 97-31-58 W
Pop: 57 (1990); 70 (1980) **Pop Density:** 1.6
Land: 36.1 sq. mi.; **Water:** 0.1 sq. mi.

Shirley
Township
Lat: 39-31-54 N **Long:** 97-26-03 W
Pop: 189 (1990); 226 (1980) **Pop Density:** 4.4
Land: 42.5 sq. mi.; **Water:** 0.3 sq. mi.

Sibley
Township
Lat: 39-37-35 N **Long:** 97-40-28 W
Pop: 205 (1990); 239 (1980) **Pop Density:** 5.8
Land: 35.4 sq. mi.; **Water:** 0.5 sq. mi.

Simpson
City
Lat: 39-23-00 N **Long:** 97-55-42 W
Pop: 0 (1990); 1 (1980)
Land: 0.01 sq. mi.; **Water:** 0.0 sq. mi. **Elev:** 1337 ft.
Incorporated Apr 3, 1907. Part of the town is also in Mitchell County.
Name origin: For Alfred Simpson, who donated land for the town site.

Solomon
Township
Lat: 39-22-24 N **Long:** 97-52-39 W
Pop: 663 (1990); 855 (1980) **Pop Density:** 12.2
Land: 54.4 sq. mi.; **Water:** 0.0 sq. mi.

Starr
Township
Lat: 39-20-50 N **Long:** 97-25-33 W
Pop: 620 (1990); 757 (1980) **Pop Density:** 17.5
Land: 35.5 sq. mi.; **Water:** 0.1 sq. mi.

Summit
Township
Lat: 39-30-11 N **Long:** 97-51-57 W
Pop: 76 (1990); 74 (1980) **Pop Density:** 1.4
Land: 53.7 sq. mi.; **Water:** 0.0 sq. mi.

Coffey County
County Seat: Burlington (ZIP: 66839)

Pop: 8,404 (1990); 9,370 (1980) **Pop Density:** 13.3
Land: 630.3 sq. mi.; **Water:** 24.4 sq. mi. **Area Code:** 316
In eastern KS, east of Emporia; organized Aug 25, 1855 (prior to statehood) from Kiowa County.
Name origin: For Col. Asbury M. Coffey, a Confederate officer and settler from MO; first known white man in KS; served as a member of the Bogus Legislature in 1855.

Avon
Township
Lat: 38-10-01 N **Long:** 95-35-15 W
Pop: 185 (1990); 275 (1980) **Pop Density:** 6.0
Land: 30.9 sq. mi.; **Water:** 0.1 sq. mi.

Burlington
City
ZIP: 66839 **Lat:** 38-11-39 N **Long:** 95-44-37 W
Pop: 2,735 (1990); 2,901 (1980) **Pop Density:** 1519.4
Land: 1.8 sq. mi.; **Water:** 0.0 sq. mi. **Elev:** 1037 ft.
Incorporated 1870.
Name origin: For Burlington, IA.

*Burlington
Township
ZIP: 66839 **Lat:** 38-10-22 N **Long:** 95-45-50 W
Pop: 313 (1990); 363 (1980) **Pop Density:** 10.0
Land: 31.4 sq. mi.; **Water:** 0.1 sq. mi.

Gridley
City
ZIP: 66852 **Lat:** 38-05-50 N **Long:** 95-53-00 W
Pop: 356 (1990); 404 (1980) **Pop Density:** 1186.7
Land: 0.3 sq. mi.; **Water:** 0.0 sq. mi. **Elev:** 1130 ft.
Incorporated 1910.
Name origin: For land promoter Walter Gridley.

Hampden
Township
Lat: 38-11-46 N **Long:** 95-42-13 W
Pop: 82 (1990); 105 (1980) **Pop Density:** 3.8
Land: 21.7 sq. mi.; **Water:** 7.8 sq. mi.

Key West
Township
Lat: 38-23-23 N **Long:** 95-44-26 W
Pop: 198 (1990); 225 (1980) **Pop Density:** 4.2
Land: 47.6 sq. mi.; **Water:** 0.3 sq. mi.

Lebo
City
ZIP: 66856 **Lat:** 38-24-49 N **Long:** 95-51-22 W
Pop: 835 (1990); 966 (1980) **Pop Density:** 1043.8
Land: 0.8 sq. mi.; **Water:** 0.0 sq. mi. **Elev:** 1157 ft.
Incorporated Oct 6, 1886.
Name origin: For nearby Lebo Creek, itself named for Joe Lebo, who lived on it.

Le Roy
City
ZIP: 66857 **Lat:** 38-05-09 N **Long:** 95-37-58 W
Pop: 568 (1990); 701 (1980) **Pop Density:** 710.0
Land: 0.8 sq. mi.; **Water:** 0.0 sq. mi. **Elev:** 1007 ft.
Incorporated Jul 1900. Not coextensive with the town of the same name.
Name origin: For Le Roy, IL.

*Le Roy
Township
ZIP: 66857 **Lat:** 38-05-18 N **Long:** 95-38-19 W
Pop: 648 (1990); 792 (1980) **Pop Density:** 30.9
Land: 21.0 sq. mi.; **Water:** 0.1 sq. mi.

Liberty
Township
Lat: 38-06-13 N **Long:** 95-53-17 W
Pop: 638 (1990); 723 (1980) **Pop Density:** 8.9
Land: 72.0 sq. mi.; **Water:** 0.4 sq. mi.

Lincoln
Township
Lat: 38-21-31 N **Long:** 95-52-45 W
Pop: 1,134 (1990); 1,205 (1980) **Pop Density:** 16.2
Land: 70.0 sq. mi.; **Water:** 1.1 sq. mi.

Neosho
Township
Lat: 38-05-06 N **Long:** 95-43-59 W
Pop: 144 (1990); 173 (1980) **Pop Density:** 3.0
Land: 48.0 sq. mi.; **Water:** 0.2 sq. mi.

New Strawn
City
Lat: 38-15-40 N **Long:** 95-44-28 W
Pop: 428 (1990); 457 (1980) **Pop Density:** 535.0
Land: 0.8 sq. mi.; **Water:** 0.0 sq. mi. **Elev:** 1100 ft.
Incorporated May 18, 1970.

Ottumwa
Township
ZIP: 66839 **Lat:** 38-18-07 N **Long:** 95-44-28 W
Pop: 676 (1990); 742 (1980) **Pop Density:** 14.4
Land: 47.1 sq. mi.; **Water:** 5.8 sq. mi.

Pleasant
Township
Lat: 38-13-48 N **Long:** 95-52-50 W
Pop: 238 (1990); 270 (1980) **Pop Density:** 3.9
Land: 61.0 sq. mi.; **Water:** 7.1 sq. mi.

Pottawatomie
Township
Lat: 38-18-12 N **Long:** 95-35-18 W
Pop: 212 (1990); 239 (1980) **Pop Density:** 3.9
Land: 54.2 sq. mi.; **Water:** 0.3 sq. mi.

Rock Creek
Township
Lat: 38-23-24 N **Long:** 95-35-26 W
Pop: 900 (1990); 1,000 (1980) **Pop Density:** 16.6
Land: 54.1 sq. mi.; **Water:** 0.3 sq. mi.

Spring Creek
Township
Lat: 38-05-21 N **Long:** 95-33-50 W
Pop: 147 (1990); 160 (1980) **Pop Density:** 4.2
Land: 34.7 sq. mi.; **Water:** 0.3 sq. mi.

Star
Township
Lat: 38-13-38 N **Long:** 95-35-23 W
Pop: 154 (1990); 197 (1980) **Pop Density:** 4.4
Land: 34.7 sq. mi.; **Water:** 0.4 sq. mi.

Waverly
City
ZIP: 66871 **Lat:** 38-23-50 N **Long:** 95-36-11 W
Pop: 618 (1990); 671 (1980) **Pop Density:** 882.9
Land: 0.7 sq. mi.; **Water:** 0.0 sq. mi. **Elev:** 1131 ft.
Incorporated 1886.
Name origin: For the chief character in the novel *Waverley* by Sir Walter Scott (1771–1832).

Comanche County
County Seat: Coldwater (ZIP: 67029)

Pop: 2,313 (1990); 2,554 (1980) **Pop Density:** 2.9
Land: 788.4 sq. mi.; **Water:** 1.4 sq. mi. **Area Code:** 316
On the central southern border of KS, southeast of Dodge City; organized Feb 26, 1875 from Kiowa County.
Name origin: For the Indian tribe of Shoshonean linguistic stock; the meaning of the name is unknown.

Avilla
Township
Lat: 37-04-45 N **Long:** 99-18-23 W
Pop: 106 (1990); 111 (1980) **Pop Density:** 0.9
Land: 119.2 sq. mi.; **Water:** 0.2 sq. mi.

Coldwater
City
ZIP: 67029 **Lat:** 37-15-28 N **Long:** 99-20-12 W
Pop: 939 (1990); 989 (1980) **Pop Density:** 347.8
Land: 2.7 sq. mi.; **Water:** 0.3 sq. mi. **Elev:** 2112 ft.
Incorporated 1884. Not coextensive with the town of the same name.
Name origin: For a local spring's cool, sparkling water.

*Coldwater
Township
ZIP: 67029 **Lat:** 37-11-51 N **Long:** 99-12-39 W
Pop: 1,223 (1990); 1,359 (1980) **Pop Density:** 2.9
Land: 424.2 sq. mi.; **Water:** 0.7 sq. mi.

Powell
Township
Lat: 37-20-10 N **Long:** 99-07-03 W
Pop: 120 (1990); 156 (1980) **Pop Density:** 1.7
Land: 71.9 sq. mi.; **Water:** 0.0 sq. mi.

Protection
City
ZIP: 67127 **Lat:** 37-12-00 N **Long:** 99-28-49 W
Pop: 625 (1990); 684 (1980) **Pop Density:** 625.0
Land: 1.0 sq. mi.; **Water:** 0.0 sq. mi. **Elev:** 1850 ft.
Incorporated Jan 13, 1908. Not coextensive with the town of the same name.

*Protection
Township
ZIP: 67127 **Lat:** 37-11-05 N **Long:** 99-29-05 W
Pop: 864 (1990); 928 (1980) **Pop Density:** 5.0
Land: 173.1 sq. mi.; **Water:** 0.5 sq. mi.

Wilmore
City
ZIP: 67155 **Lat:** 37-20-09 N **Long:** 99-12-33 W
Pop: 78 (1990); 97 (1980) **Pop Density:** 390.0
Land: 0.2 sq. mi.; **Water:** 0.0 sq. mi. **Elev:** 2022 ft.
Incorporated Apr 5, 1920.

Cowley County
County Seat: Winfield (ZIP: 67156)

Pop: 36,915 (1990); 36,824 (1980)   **Pop Density:** 32.8
Land: 1126.3 sq. mi.; **Water:** 6.3 sq. mi.   **Area Code:** 316
On the southern border of KS, southeast of Wichita; organized Feb 13, 1867.
Name origin: For Lt. Matthew Cowley (?–1864), a Union officer.

Arkansas City — City
ZIP: 67005   **Lat:** 37-04-07 N **Long:** 97-02-26 W
Pop: 12,762 (1990); 13,201 (1980)   **Pop Density:** 1724.6
Land: 7.4 sq. mi.; **Water:** 0.0 sq. mi.   **Elev:** 1100 ft.
In southern KS at the confluence of the Arkansas and Walnut rivers, 50 mi. south of Wichita. Incorporated Sep 18, 1884.
Name origin: For the Arkansas Indians.

Atlanta — City
ZIP: 67008   **Lat:** 37-26-10 N **Long:** 96-46-01 W
Pop: 232 (1990); 256 (1980)   **Pop Density:** 464.0
Land: 0.5 sq. mi.; **Water:** 0.0 sq. mi.   **Elev:** 1433 ft.
Incorporated Jan 6, 1903.

Beaver — Township
Lat: 37-10-15 N **Long:** 97-05-48 W
Pop: 244 (1990); 225 (1980)   **Pop Density:** 6.9
Land: 35.6 sq. mi.; **Water:** 0.7 sq. mi.

Bolton — Township
Lat: 37-02-28 N **Long:** 97-04-13 W
Pop: 1,961 (1990); 1,681 (1980)   **Pop Density:** 37.3
Land: 52.6 sq. mi.; **Water:** 0.8 sq. mi.

Burden — City
ZIP: 67019   **Lat:** 37-18-47 N **Long:** 96-45-18 W
Pop: 518 (1990); 518 (1980)   **Pop Density:** 1036.0
Land: 0.5 sq. mi.; **Water:** 0.0 sq. mi.   **Elev:** 1383 ft.
Incorporated Feb 6, 1883.

Cambridge — City
ZIP: 67023   **Lat:** 37-19-02 N **Long:** 96-40-00 W
Pop: 74 (1990); 113 (1980)   **Pop Density:** 370.0
Land: 0.2 sq. mi.; **Water:** 0.0 sq. mi.   **Elev:** 1252 ft.
Incorporated Dec 7, 1916.
Name origin: For Cambridge, England.

Cedar — Township
Lat: 37-04-14 N **Long:** 96-35-18 W
Pop: 46 (1990); 78 (1980)   **Pop Density:** 1.0
Land: 46.0 sq. mi.; **Water:** 0.2 sq. mi.

Creswell — Township
Lat: 37-05-19 N **Long:** 97-01-03 W
Pop: 2,414 (1990); 2,290 (1980)   **Pop Density:** 64.2
Land: 37.6 sq. mi.; **Water:** 0.8 sq. mi.

Dexter — City
ZIP: 67038   **Lat:** 37-10-45 N **Long:** 96-42-56 W
Pop: 320 (1990); 366 (1980)   **Pop Density:** 1066.7
Land: 0.3 sq. mi.; **Water:** 0.0 sq. mi.   **Elev:** 1208 ft.
Incorporated 1884. Not coextensive with the town of the same name.
Name origin: For a famous racehorse.

*Dexter — Township
ZIP: 67038   **Lat:** 37-11-34 N **Long:** 96-40-48 W
Pop: 549 (1990); 570 (1980)   **Pop Density:** 7.7
Land: 71.3 sq. mi.; **Water:** 0.1 sq. mi.

Fairview — Township
Lat: 37-20-39 N **Long:** 96-59-09 W
Pop: 217 (1990); 226 (1980)   **Pop Density:** 6.0
Land: 35.9 sq. mi.; **Water:** 0.1 sq. mi.

Geuda Springs — City
Lat: 37-06-36 N **Long:** 97-08-46 W
Pop: 34 (1990); 15 (1980)   **Pop Density:** 170.0
Land: 0.2 sq. mi.; **Water:** 0.0 sq. mi.   **Elev:** 1120 ft.
Incorporated Apr 1884. Part of the town is also in Sumner County.
Name origin: For nearby 'healing springs.'

Grant — Township
Lat: 37-03-48 N **Long:** 96-41-02 W
Pop: 58 (1990); 93 (1980)   **Pop Density:** 1.3
Land: 44.8 sq. mi.; **Water:** 0.0 sq. mi.

Harvey — Township
Lat: 37-25-45 N **Long:** 96-37-00 W
Pop: 109 (1990); 118 (1980)   **Pop Density:** 1.7
Land: 62.7 sq. mi.; **Water:** 0.2 sq. mi.

Liberty — Township
Lat: 37-10-06 N **Long:** 96-50-16 W
Pop: 160 (1990); 199 (1980)   **Pop Density:** 3.3
Land: 48.0 sq. mi.; **Water:** 0.0 sq. mi.

Maple — Township
Lat: 37-26-00 N **Long:** 97-05-40 W
Pop: 588 (1990); 473 (1980)   **Pop Density:** 16.8
Land: 35.1 sq. mi.; **Water:** 0.0 sq. mi.

Ninnescah — Township
Lat: 37-20-39 N **Long:** 97-05-39 W
Pop: 1,126 (1990); 1,142 (1980)   **Pop Density:** 31.5
Land: 35.8 sq. mi.; **Water:** 0.0 sq. mi.

Omnia — Township
Lat: 37-25-56 N **Long:** 96-46-08 W
Pop: 320 (1990); 358 (1980)   **Pop Density:** 8.9
Land: 36.1 sq. mi.; **Water:** 0.1 sq. mi.

Otter — Township
Lat: 37-10-39 N **Long:** 96-33-58 W
Pop: 45 (1990); 73 (1980)   **Pop Density:** 0.9
Land: 52.0 sq. mi.; **Water:** 0.4 sq. mi.

Pleasant Valley — Township
Lat: 37-09-24 N **Long:** 96-58-52 W
Pop: 830 (1990); 1,027 (1980)   **Pop Density:** 18.1
Land: 45.8 sq. mi.; **Water:** 0.0 sq. mi.

Richland — Township
Lat: 37-25-32 N **Long:** 96-52-48 W
Pop: 184 (1990); 170 (1980)   **Pop Density:** 4.4
Land: 41.8 sq. mi.; **Water:** 0.0 sq. mi.

Rock Creek
Township
Lat: 37-25-57 N Long: 96-59-25 W
Pop: 209 (1990); 233 (1980) Pop Density: 5.9
Land: 35.4 sq. mi.; Water: 0.2 sq. mi.

Salem
Township
Lat: 37-20-08 N Long: 96-53-18 W
Pop: 298 (1990); 273 (1980) Pop Density: 11.7
Land: 25.5 sq. mi.; Water: 0.1 sq. mi.

Sheridan
Township
Lat: 37-15-56 N Long: 96-45-40 W
Pop: 160 (1990); 144 (1980) Pop Density: 4.5
Land: 35.8 sq. mi.; Water: 0.0 sq. mi.

Silver Creek
Township
Lat: 37-20-31 N Long: 96-45-58 W
Pop: 698 (1990); 707 (1980) Pop Density: 19.3
Land: 36.1 sq. mi.; Water: 0.1 sq. mi.

Silverdale
Township
ZIP: 67005 Lat: 37-03-42 N Long: 96-52-29 W
Pop: 359 (1990); 376 (1980) Pop Density: 6.8
Land: 52.6 sq. mi.; Water: 0.2 sq. mi.

Spring Creek
Township
Lat: 37-03-37 N Long: 96-46-39 W
Pop: 78 (1990); 89 (1980) Pop Density: 1.8
Land: 44.5 sq. mi.; Water: 0.1 sq. mi.

Tisdale
Township
Lat: 37-15-28 N Long: 96-52-02 W
Pop: 299 (1990); 305 (1980) Pop Density: 9.9
Land: 30.1 sq. mi.; Water: 0.0 sq. mi.

Udall
City
ZIP: 67146 Lat: 37-23-13 N Long: 97-07-02 W
Pop: 824 (1990); 891 (1980) Pop Density: 2060.0
Land: 0.4 sq. mi.; Water: 0.0 sq. mi. Elev: 1267 ft.

Vernon
Township
Lat: 37-15-24 N Long: 97-05-16 W
Pop: 513 (1990); 709 (1980) Pop Density: 13.0
Land: 39.4 sq. mi.; Water: 0.3 sq. mi.

Walnut
Township
Lat: 37-15-24 N Long: 96-57-40 W
Pop: 550 (1990); 1,105 (1980) Pop Density: 15.9
Land: 34.5 sq. mi.; Water: 0.0 sq. mi.

Windsor
Township
Lat: 37-19-23 N Long: 96-37-19 W
Pop: 207 (1990); 223 (1980) Pop Density: 2.2
Land: 93.7 sq. mi.; Water: 0.2 sq. mi.

Winfield
City
ZIP: 67156 Lat: 37-16-06 N Long: 96-58-06 W
Pop: 11,931 (1990); 10,736 (1980) Pop Density: 1147.2
Land: 10.4 sq. mi.; Water: 1.7 sq. mi. Elev: 1127 ft.
In southern KS, 12 mi. north of Arkansas City. Incorporated 1872.
Name origin: For U.S. Army officer Winfield Scott (1786–1866).

Crawford County
County Seat: Girard (ZIP: 66743)

Pop: 35,568 (1990); 37,916 (1980) Pop Density: 60.0
Land: 593.0 sq. mi.; Water: 2.1 sq. mi. Area Code: 316
On the southeastern border of KS; organized Feb 13, 1867 from Bourbon and Cherokee counties.
Name origin: For Col. Samuel J. Crawford (1835–1913), Union army officer and governor of KS (1865–68); he resigned to command a force to fight Indians.

Arcadia
City
ZIP: 66711 Lat: 37-38-28 N Long: 94-37-27 W
Pop: 338 (1990); 460 (1980) Pop Density: 845.0
Land: 0.4 sq. mi.; Water: 0.0 sq. mi. Elev: 830 ft.
Incorporated Feb 1, 1886.
Name origin: For the fertile region in ancient Greece.

Arma
City
ZIP: 66712 Lat: 37-32-33 N Long: 94-42-00 W
Pop: 1,542 (1990); 1,676 (1980) Pop Density: 1542.0
Land: 1.0 sq. mi.; Water: 0.0 sq. mi. Elev: 1003 ft.
Incorporated Jun 9, 1909.
Name origin: Originally named Rust, but changed to present name upon incorporation for W.F. Armacost, who owned most of the surrounding land.

Baker
Township
Lat: 37-23-32 N Long: 94-41-08 W
Pop: 3,350 (1990); 3,330 (1980) Pop Density: 56.4
Land: 59.4 sq. mi.; Water: 0.0 sq. mi.

Cherokee
City
ZIP: 66724 Lat: 37-20-41 N Long: 94-49-16 W
Pop: 651 (1990); 775 (1980) Pop Density: 930.0
Land: 0.7 sq. mi.; Water: 0.0 sq. mi. Elev: 949 ft.
Incorporated Feb 25, 1874.
Name origin: For the Indian tribe.

Crawford
Township
Lat: 37-30-23 N Long: 94-51-37 W
Pop: 723 (1990); 761 (1980) Pop Density: 11.7
Land: 61.6 sq. mi.; Water: 0.1 sq. mi.

Frontenac
City
ZIP: 66762 Lat: 37-27-22 N Long: 94-41-46 W
Pop: 2,588 (1990); 2,586 (1980) Pop Density: 761.2
Land: 3.4 sq. mi.; Water: 0.0 sq. mi. Elev: 950 ft.
Incorporated 1895.
Name origin: For Louis de Buade, Comte de Frontenac (1622–98), French general and governor of New France (Canada).

Girard
City
ZIP: 66743   Lat: 37-30-36 N   Long: 94-50-31 W
Pop: 2,794 (1990); 2,888 (1980)   Pop Density: 1470.5
Land: 1.9 sq. mi.; Water: 0.0 sq. mi.   Elev: 986 ft.
Incorporated Nov 10, 1869.
Name origin: For an early French trader, Michael Girard.

Grant
Township
Lat: 37-30-22 N   Long: 95-00-58 W
Pop: 267 (1990); 368 (1980)   Pop Density: 4.8
Land: 56.0 sq. mi.; Water: 0.3 sq. mi.

Hepler
City
ZIP: 66746   Lat: 37-39-42 N   Long: 94-58-11 W
Pop: 150 (1990); 165 (1980)   Pop Density: 187.5
Land: 0.8 sq. mi.; Water: 0.0 sq. mi.   Elev: 1000 ft.
Incorporated Apr 11, 1887.

Lincoln
Township
Lat: 37-37-20 N   Long: 94-41-40 W
Pop: 803 (1990); 1,048 (1980)   Pop Density: 11.5
Land: 69.9 sq. mi.; Water: 0.2 sq. mi.

McCune
City
ZIP: 66753   Lat: 37-21-13 N   Long: 95-01-08 W
Pop: 462 (1990); 528 (1980)   Pop Density: 1540.0
Land: 0.3 sq. mi.; Water: 0.0 sq. mi.
Incorporated Oct 1881.

Mulberry
City
ZIP: 66756   Lat: 37-33-21 N   Long: 94-37-23 W
Pop: 555 (1990); 647 (1980)   Pop Density: 1110.0
Land: 0.5 sq. mi.; Water: 0.0 sq. mi.   Elev: 950 ft.
Incorporated Aug 2, 1902.
Name origin: For the mulberry trees, which grew wild in the area.

Osage
Township
Lat: 37-23-48 N   Long: 95-01-38 W
Pop: 793 (1990); 853 (1980)   Pop Density: 14.6
Land: 54.4 sq. mi.; Water: 0.2 sq. mi.

Pittsburg
City
ZIP: 66762   Lat: 37-24-48 N   Long: 94-41-58 W
Pop: 17,775 (1990); 18,770 (1980)   Pop Density: 1777.5
Land: 10.0 sq. mi.; Water: 0.0 sq. mi.   Elev: 944 ft.
In southeastern KS, 30 mi. south of Fort Scott. Incorporated Jun 1, 1880.
Name origin: For Pittsburgh, PA.

Sheridan
Township
Lat: 37-24-00 N   Long: 94-51-39 W
Pop: 1,397 (1990); 1,619 (1980)   Pop Density: 17.6
Land: 79.6 sq. mi.; Water: 0.2 sq. mi.

Sherman
Township
Lat: 37-37-23 N   Long: 94-51-34 W
Pop: 519 (1990); 549 (1980)   Pop Density: 7.2
Land: 72.3 sq. mi.; Water: 0.3 sq. mi.

Walnut
City
ZIP: 66780   Lat: 37-36-01 N   Long: 95-04-28 W
Pop: 214 (1990); 308 (1980)   Pop Density: 214.0
Land: 1.0 sq. mi.; Water: 0.0 sq. mi.   Elev: 930 ft.
In corporated Mar 10, 1874. Not coextensive with the town of the same name.
Name origin: For the many walnut trees once found nearby.

*Walnut
Township
ZIP: 66780   Lat: 37-36-57 N   Long: 95-00-54 W
Pop: 612 (1990); 843 (1980)   Pop Density: 9.6
Land: 64.0 sq. mi.; Water: 0.2 sq. mi.

Washington
Township
Lat: 37-30-22 N   Long: 94-41-43 W
Pop: 3,392 (1990); 3,654 (1980)   Pop Density: 56.5
Land: 60.0 sq. mi.; Water: 0.6 sq. mi.

Decatur County
County Seat: Oberlin (ZIP: 67749)

Pop: 4,021 (1990); 4,509 (1980)   Pop Density: 4.5
Land: 893.6 sq. mi.; Water: 0.6 sq. mi.   Area Code: 913
On the northwestern border of KS; organized Mar 6, 1873 from Norton County.
Name origin: For Stephen F. Decatur (1779–1820), U.S. naval officer during the War of 1812 and in actions against the Barbary pirates near Tripoli, who said, ". . . may she always be in the right; but our country, right or wrong."

Allison
Township
Lat: 39-37-17 N   Long: 100-13-56 W
Pop: 47 (1990); 67 (1980)   Pop Density: 1.3
Land: 35.8 sq. mi.; Water: 0.0 sq. mi.

Altory
Township
Lat: 39-47-12 N   Long: 100-20-33 W
Pop: 34 (1990); 36 (1980)   Pop Density: 0.9
Land: 35.8 sq. mi.; Water: 0.0 sq. mi.

Bassettville
Township
Lat: 39-42-22 N   Long: 100-40-56 W
Pop: 52 (1990); 53 (1980)   Pop Density: 1.5
Land: 35.8 sq. mi.; Water: 0.0 sq. mi.

Beaver
Township
Lat: 39-57-36 N   Long: 100-34-41 W
Pop: 85 (1990); 105 (1980)   Pop Density: 2.4
Land: 35.7 sq. mi.; Water: 0.0 sq. mi.

Center
Township
Lat: 39-47-05 N   Long: 100-27-36 W
Pop: 61 (1990); 63 (1980)   Pop Density: 1.7
Land: 35.8 sq. mi.; Water: 0.0 sq. mi.

KANSAS, Decatur County

Clayton
City
Lat: 39-44-06 N Long: 100-10-50 W
Pop: 14 (1990); 9 (1980) Pop Density: 140.0
Land: 0.1 sq. mi.; Water: 0.0 sq. mi. Elev: 2450 ft.
Incorporated Feb 4, 1907. Part of the town is also in Norton County.
Name origin: For the clay on the roads in the area.

Cook
Township
Lat: 39-36-24 N Long: 100-41-31 W
Pop: 51 (1990); 55 (1980) Pop Density: 1.4
Land: 35.9 sq. mi.; Water: 0.0 sq. mi.

Custer
Township
Lat: 39-41-51 N Long: 100-27-36 W
Pop: 41 (1990); 48 (1980) Pop Density: 1.1
Land: 35.8 sq. mi.; Water: 0.0 sq. mi.

Dresden
City
ZIP: 67635 Lat: 39-37-17 N Long: 100-25-10 W
Pop: 73 (1990); 84 (1980) Pop Density: 81.1
Land: 0.9 sq. mi.; Water: 0.0 sq. mi. Elev: 2729 ft.
Incorporated Sep 6, 1920. Not coextensive with the town of the same name.
Name origin: For Dresden, Germany.

*Dresden
Township
ZIP: 67635 Lat: 39-37-13 N Long: 100-27-17 W
Pop: 188 (1990); 200 (1980) Pop Density: 5.3
Land: 35.7 sq. mi.; Water: 0.0 sq. mi.

Finley
Township
Lat: 39-57-42 N Long: 100-41-18 W
Pop: 58 (1990); 91 (1980) Pop Density: 1.6
Land: 35.7 sq. mi.; Water: 0.0 sq. mi.

Garfield
Township
Lat: 39-47-14 N Long: 100-14-02 W
Pop: 42 (1990); 46 (1980) Pop Density: 1.2
Land: 35.6 sq. mi.; Water: 0.0 sq. mi.

Grant
Township
Lat: 39-57-35 N Long: 100-14-09 W
Pop: 28 (1990); 45 (1980) Pop Density: 0.8
Land: 35.6 sq. mi.; Water: 0.0 sq. mi.

Harlan
Township
Lat: 39-57-36 N Long: 100-20-44 W
Pop: 52 (1990); 75 (1980) Pop Density: 1.5
Land: 35.6 sq. mi.; Water: 0.0 sq. mi.

Jennings
City
ZIP: 67643 Lat: 39-40-48 N Long: 100-17-36 W
Pop: 188 (1990); 194 (1980) Pop Density: 626.7
Land: 0.3 sq. mi.; Water: 0.0 sq. mi. Elev: 2500 ft.
Incorporated Oct 4, 1906.

*Jennings
Township
ZIP: 67643 Lat: 39-41-58 N Long: 100-20-46 W
Pop: 227 (1990); 248 (1980) Pop Density: 6.3
Land: 35.8 sq. mi.; Water: 0.1 sq. mi.

Liberty
Township
Lat: 39-52-22 N Long: 100-34-04 W
Pop: 59 (1990); 62 (1980) Pop Density: 1.7
Land: 35.2 sq. mi.; Water: 0.0 sq. mi.

Lincoln
Township
Lat: 39-52-12 N Long: 100-14-11 W
Pop: 234 (1990); 268 (1980) Pop Density: 6.6
Land: 35.6 sq. mi.; Water: 0.0 sq. mi.

Logan
Township
Lat: 39-52-16 N Long: 100-41-00 W
Pop: 59 (1990); 65 (1980) Pop Density: 1.6
Land: 35.8 sq. mi.; Water: 0.0 sq. mi.

Lyon
Township
Lat: 39-36-52 N Long: 100-21-06 W
Pop: 37 (1990); 34 (1980) Pop Density: 1.0
Land: 35.9 sq. mi.; Water: 0.0 sq. mi.

Norcatur
City
ZIP: 67653 Lat: 39-50-04 N Long: 100-11-16 W
Pop: 198 (1990); 226 (1980) Pop Density: 198.0
Land: 1.0 sq. mi.; Water: 0.0 sq. mi. Elev: 2700 ft.
Incorporated Oct 10, 1901.
Name origin: For its location on the border between *Nor*ton and De*catur* counties.

Oberlin
City
ZIP: 67749 Lat: 39-49-23 N Long: 100-31-49 W
Pop: 2,197 (1990); 2,387 (1980) Pop Density: 1156.3
Land: 1.9 sq. mi.; Water: 0.0 sq. mi. Elev: 2562 ft.
Incorporated Jun 15, 1885.
Name origin: For Oberlin, OH.

*Oberlin
Township
ZIP: 67749 Lat: 39-47-16 N Long: 100-34-20 W
Pop: 129 (1990); 101 (1980) Pop Density: 3.8
Land: 34.2 sq. mi.; Water: 0.0 sq. mi.

Olive
Township
Lat: 39-52-24 N Long: 100-27-38 W
Pop: 80 (1990); 109 (1980) Pop Density: 2.3
Land: 35.4 sq. mi.; Water: 0.2 sq. mi.

Pleasant Valley
Township
Lat: 39-41-53 N Long: 100-13-57 W
Pop: 73 (1990); 82 (1980) Pop Density: 2.0
Land: 35.8 sq. mi.; Water: 0.0 sq. mi.

Prairie Dog
Township
Lat: 39-36-08 N Long: 100-34-29 W
Pop: 48 (1990); 72 (1980) Pop Density: 1.3
Land: 35.8 sq. mi.; Water: 0.0 sq. mi.

Roosevelt
Township
Lat: 39-52-50 N Long: 100-20-20 W
Pop: 28 (1990); 42 (1980) Pop Density: 0.8
Land: 36.0 sq. mi.; Water: 0.0 sq. mi.

Sappa
Township
Lat: 39-47-01 N Long: 100-41-09 W
Pop: 47 (1990); 55 (1980) Pop Density: 1.3
Land: 36.0 sq. mi.; Water: 0.0 sq. mi.

Sherman
Township
Lat: 39-57-29 N Long: 100-27-33 W
Pop: 35 (1990); 58 (1980) Pop Density: 1.0
Land: 35.6 sq. mi.; Water: 0.0 sq. mi.

Summit
Township
Lat: 39-41-26 N Long: 100-34-35 W
Pop: 29 (1990); 42 (1980) Pop Density: 0.8
Land: 35.8 sq. mi.; Water: 0.0 sq. mi.

Dickinson County
County Seat: Abilene (ZIP: 67410)

Pop: 18,958 (1990); 20,175 (1980) **Pop Density:** 22.3
Land: 848.4 sq. mi.; **Water:** 4.2 sq. mi. **Area Code:** 913
In central KS, east of Salina; original county; organized Feb 20, 1855 (prior to statehood).
Name origin: For Daniel Stevens Dickinson (1800–66), U.S. senator from NY (1844–51).

Abilene — City
ZIP: 67410 **Lat:** 38-55-11 N **Long:** 97-13-19 W
Pop: 6,242 (1990); 6,572 (1980) **Pop Density:** 1733.9
Land: 3.6 sq. mi.; **Water:** 0.0 sq. mi. **Elev:** 1153 ft.
In east-central KS, east of Salina. Incorporated Sep 3, 1869.
Name origin: For the Roman city in ancient Syria.

Banner — Township
Lat: 38-39-16 N **Long:** 97-12-35 W
Pop: 145 (1990); 159 (1980) **Pop Density:** 4.1
Land: 35.5 sq. mi.; **Water:** 0.2 sq. mi.

Buckeye — Township
Lat: 39-00-09 N **Long:** 97-12-12 W
Pop: 403 (1990); 411 (1980) **Pop Density:** 11.1
Land: 36.2 sq. mi.; **Water:** 0.1 sq. mi.

Carlton — City
ZIP: 67429 **Lat:** 38-41-12 N **Long:** 97-17-37 W
Pop: 39 (1990); 49 (1980) **Pop Density:** 195.0
Land: 0.2 sq. mi.; **Water:** 0.0 sq. mi. **Elev:** 1310 ft.
Incorporated Apr 2, 1929.

Center — Township
Lat: 38-54-45 N **Long:** 97-05-38 W
Pop: 1,286 (1990); 1,298 (1980) **Pop Density:** 36.3
Land: 35.4 sq. mi.; **Water:** 0.8 sq. mi.

Chapman — City
ZIP: 67431 **Lat:** 38-58-18 N **Long:** 97-01-14 W
Pop: 1,264 (1990); 1,255 (1980) **Pop Density:** 2528.0
Land: 0.5 sq. mi.; **Water:** 0.0 sq. mi. **Elev:** 1113 ft.
Incorporated Sep 1883.

Cheever — Township
Lat: 39-05-17 N **Long:** 97-12-06 W
Pop: 140 (1990); 149 (1980) **Pop Density:** 3.9
Land: 35.9 sq. mi.; **Water:** 0.0 sq. mi.

Enterprise — City
ZIP: 67441 **Lat:** 38-54-06 N **Long:** 97-06-58 W
Pop: 865 (1990); 839 (1980) **Pop Density:** 1235.7
Land: 0.7 sq. mi.; **Water:** 0.0 sq. mi. **Elev:** 1137 ft.
Incorporated Feb 19, 1878.
Name origin: For its commercial ambitions. Originally called Hoffman's Mills.

Flora — Township
Lat: 39-05-25 N **Long:** 97-19-03 W
Pop: 203 (1990); 243 (1980) **Pop Density:** 5.6
Land: 36.0 sq. mi.; **Water:** 0.0 sq. mi.

Fragrant Hill — Township
Lat: 39-05-20 N **Long:** 97-00-24 W
Pop: 222 (1990); 239 (1980) **Pop Density:** 7.4
Land: 29.8 sq. mi.; **Water:** 0.1 sq. mi.

Garfield — Township
Lat: 38-49-38 N **Long:** 97-19-04 W
Pop: 170 (1990); 183 (1980) **Pop Density:** 4.7
Land: 36.3 sq. mi.; **Water:** 0.0 sq. mi.

Grant — Township
Lat: 38-54-46 N **Long:** 97-12-04 W
Pop: 888 (1990); 1,037 (1980) **Pop Density:** 27.4
Land: 32.4 sq. mi.; **Water:** 0.5 sq. mi.

Hayes — Township
Lat: 39-00-20 N **Long:** 97-05-45 W
Pop: 206 (1990); 233 (1980) **Pop Density:** 6.9
Land: 30.0 sq. mi.; **Water:** 0.0 sq. mi.

Herington — City
ZIP: 67449 **Lat:** 38-40-23 N **Long:** 96-56-46 W
Pop: 2,685 (1990); 2,930 (1980) **Pop Density:** 1278.6
Land: 2.1 sq. mi.; **Water:** 0.0 sq. mi. **Elev:** 1350 ft.
Incorporated Apr 11, 1887. Part of the town is also in Morris County.
Name origin: For pioneer rancher Monroe Herington.

Holland — Township
Lat: 38-38-54 N **Long:** 97-18-38 W
Pop: 121 (1990); 144 (1980) **Pop Density:** 3.4
Land: 36.1 sq. mi.; **Water:** 0.1 sq. mi.

Hope — City
ZIP: 67451 **Lat:** 38-41-27 N **Long:** 97-04-30 W
Pop: 404 (1990); 468 (1980) **Pop Density:** 808.0
Land: 0.5 sq. mi.; **Water:** 0.0 sq. mi. **Elev:** 1400 ft.
Incorporated Sep 1886. Not coextensive with the town of the same name.
Name origin: For Hope, a Dutch community in MI.

*Hope — Township
ZIP: 67451 **Lat:** 38-39-15 N **Long:** 97-05-50 W
Pop: 580 (1990); 659 (1980) **Pop Density:** 16.3
Land: 35.5 sq. mi.; **Water:** 0.2 sq. mi.

Jefferson — Township
Lat: 38-44-20 N **Long:** 97-12-15 W
Pop: 196 (1990); 224 (1980) **Pop Density:** 5.4
Land: 36.2 sq. mi.; **Water:** 0.2 sq. mi.

Liberty — Township
Lat: 38-49-50 N **Long:** 96-58-23 W
Pop: 384 (1990); 424 (1980) **Pop Density:** 8.8
Land: 43.8 sq. mi.; **Water:** 0.0 sq. mi.

Lincoln — Township
Lat: 38-54-14 N **Long:** 97-18-55 W
Pop: 1,472 (1990); 1,618 (1980) **Pop Density:** 41.0
Land: 35.9 sq. mi.; **Water:** 0.7 sq. mi.

KANSAS, Dickinson County   *American Places Dictionary*

Logan Township
Lat: 38-50-03 N   Long: 97-05-27 W
Pop: 205 (1990); 246 (1980)   Pop Density: 5.7
Land: 36.1 sq. mi.; Water: 0.1 sq. mi.

Lyon Township
Lat: 38-38-52 N   Long: 96-59-16 W
Pop: 256 (1990); 269 (1980)   Pop Density: 7.7
Land: 33.3 sq. mi.; Water: 0.3 sq. mi.

Manchester City
ZIP: 67463   Lat: 39-05-29 N   Long: 97-19-13 W
Pop: 80 (1990); 98 (1980)   Pop Density: 266.7
Land: 0.3 sq. mi.; Water: 0.0 sq. mi.   Elev: 1295 ft.
Incorporated Jan 1907.
Name origin: For Manchester, England.

Newbern Township
Lat: 38-49-42 N   Long: 97-12-23 W
Pop: 346 (1990); 320 (1980)   Pop Density: 9.5
Land: 36.4 sq. mi.; Water: 0.0 sq. mi.

Noble Township
Lat: 39-00-08 N   Long: 97-00-13 W
Pop: 1,773 (1990); 1,719 (1980)   Pop Density: 55.8
Land: 31.8 sq. mi.; Water: 0.4 sq. mi.

Ridge Township
Lat: 38-44-01 N   Long: 97-05-25 W
Pop: 162 (1990); 177 (1980)   Pop Density: 4.5
Land: 36.2 sq. mi.; Water: 0.2 sq. mi.

Rinehart Township
Lat: 38-55-09 N   Long: 96-58-39 W
Pop: 195 (1990); 208 (1980)   Pop Density: 5.4
Land: 35.8 sq. mi.; Water: 0.1 sq. mi.

Sherman Township
Lat: 39-05-05 N   Long: 97-06-09 W
Pop: 148 (1990); 140 (1980)   Pop Density: 4.9
Land: 30.0 sq. mi.; Water: 0.0 sq. mi.

Solomon City
ZIP: 67480   Lat: 38-55-10 N   Long: 97-22-17 W
Pop: 939 (1990); 1,018 (1980)   Pop Density: 1565.0
Land: 0.6 sq. mi.; Water: 0.0 sq. mi.   Elev: 1180 ft.
Incorporated Oct 1871.

Union Township
Lat: 38-44-25 N   Long: 96-58-53 W
Pop: 189 (1990); 212 (1980)   Pop Density: 5.2
Land: 36.1 sq. mi.; Water: 0.1 sq. mi.

Wheatland Township
Lat: 38-44-26 N   Long: 97-19-01 W
Pop: 141 (1990); 161 (1980)   Pop Density: 3.9
Land: 36.0 sq. mi.; Water: 0.1 sq. mi.

Willowdale Township
Lat: 39-00-02 N   Long: 97-18-40 W
Pop: 200 (1990); 200 (1980)   Pop Density: 5.6
Land: 36.0 sq. mi.; Water: 0.0 sq. mi.

Woodbine City
ZIP: 67492   Lat: 38-47-43 N   Long: 96-57-34 W
Pop: 186 (1990); 172 (1980)   Pop Density: 1860.0
Land: 0.1 sq. mi.; Water: 0.0 sq. mi.   Elev: 1250 ft.
Incorporated Apr 12, 1909.
Name origin: For the woodbine, an ornamental shrub, which grew abundantly in the area.

Doniphan County
County Seat: Troy (ZIP: 66087)

Pop: 8,134 (1990); 9,268 (1980)   Pop Density: 20.7
Land: 392.2 sq. mi.; Water: 4.9 sq. mi.   Area Code: 913
On the northeastern border of KS, west of St. Joseph, MO; original county; organized Aug 25, 1855 (prior to statehood).
Name origin: For Alexander William Doniphan (1808–87), MO legislator and officer in the Mexican War.

Burr Oak Township
Lat: 39-51-16 N   Long: 94-58-18 W
Pop: 236 (1990); 232 (1980)   Pop Density: 7.5
Land: 31.3 sq. mi.; Water: 0.9 sq. mi.

Center Township
Lat: 39-48-18 N   Long: 95-05-38 W
Pop: 1,719 (1990); 1,944 (1980)   Pop Density: 27.5
Land: 62.5 sq. mi.; Water: 0.8 sq. mi.

Denton City
ZIP: 66017   Lat: 39-43-53 N   Long: 95-16-11 W
Pop: 166 (1990); 156 (1980)   Pop Density: 1660.0
Land: 0.1 sq. mi.; Water: 0.0 sq. mi.   Elev: 1078 ft.
Incorporated 1896.
Name origin: For its first settlers, the four Denton brothers from England.

Elwood City
ZIP: 66024   Lat: 39-45-14 N   Long: 94-52-44 W
Pop: 1,079 (1990); 1,275 (1980)   Pop Density: 539.5
Land: 2.0 sq. mi.; Water: 0.0 sq. mi.   Elev: 813 ft.
In the northeastern corner of KS; incorporated Mar 26, 1878.
Name origin: For town reorganizer, J.B. Elwood. Originally called Rose.

Highland City
ZIP: 66035   Lat: 39-51-36 N   Long: 95-15-55 W
Pop: 942 (1990); 954 (1980)   Pop Density: 1884.0
Land: 0.5 sq. mi.; Water: 0.0 sq. mi.   Elev: 1051 ft.
Incorporated 1857.
Name origin: Named by William Sugg, of Highland, IL, with the hope of attracting Swiss settlers from the IL town to KS.

Independence
Township
Lat: 39-41-55 N **Long:** 95-10-16 W
Pop: 334 (1990); 347 (1980) **Pop Density:** 9.0
Land: 37.0 sq. mi.; **Water:** 0.0 sq. mi.

Iowa
Township
Lat: 39-53-48 N **Long:** 95-15-36 W
Pop: 1,748 (1990); 1,843 (1980) **Pop Density:** 20.9
Land: 83.5 sq. mi.; **Water:** 0.9 sq. mi.

Leona
City
Lat: 39-47-08 N **Long:** 95-19-18 W
Pop: 39 (1990); 73 (1980) **Pop Density:** 390.0
Land: 0.1 sq. mi.; **Water:** 0.0 sq. mi. **Elev:** 950 ft.
In the northeastern corner of KS; incorporated Apr 1934.
Name origin: For Leona Shock, the first child born in the community.

Marion
Township
Lat: 39-43-22 N **Long:** 95-00-09 W
Pop: 226 (1990); 264 (1980) **Pop Density:** 12.9
Land: 17.5 sq. mi.; **Water:** 0.5 sq. mi.

Severance
City
ZIP: 66081 **Lat:** 39-46-00 N **Long:** 95-14-55 W
Pop: 98 (1990); 134 (1980) **Pop Density:** 980.0
Land: 0.1 sq. mi.; **Water:** 0.0 sq. mi. **Elev:** 912 ft.
Incorporated Apr 1877.

Troy
City
ZIP: 66087 **Lat:** 39-47-10 N **Long:** 95-05-18 W
Pop: 1,073 (1990); 1,240 (1980) **Pop Density:** 1788.3
Land: 0.6 sq. mi.; **Water:** 0.0 sq. mi. **Elev:** 1099 ft.
In the northeastern corner of KS; incorporated 1860.
Name origin: For Troy, the city of Greek mythology.

Union
Township
Lat: 39-41-55 N **Long:** 95-17-32 W
Pop: 378 (1990); 390 (1980) **Pop Density:** 10.5
Land: 36.1 sq. mi.; **Water:** 0.0 sq. mi.

Washington
Township
Lat: 39-46-35 N **Long:** 94-56-28 W
Pop: 2,825 (1990); 3,459 (1980) **Pop Density:** 86.4
Land: 32.7 sq. mi.; **Water:** 1.5 sq. mi.

Wathena
City
ZIP: 66090 **Lat:** 39-45-51 N **Long:** 94-56-56 W
Pop: 1,160 (1990); 1,418 (1980) **Pop Density:** 828.6
Land: 1.4 sq. mi.; **Water:** 0.0 sq. mi. **Elev:** 823 ft.
In the northeastern corner of KS; incorporated 1874.
Name origin: For a Kickapoo Indian chief.

Wayne
Township
Lat: 39-40-55 N **Long:** 95-04-55 W
Pop: 241 (1990); 265 (1980) **Pop Density:** 6.8
Land: 35.6 sq. mi.; **Water:** 0.3 sq. mi.

White Cloud
City
ZIP: 66094 **Lat:** 39-58-27 N **Long:** 95-17-50 W
Pop: 255 (1990); 234 (1980) **Pop Density:** 364.3
Land: 0.7 sq. mi.; **Water:** 0.0 sq. mi. **Elev:** 888 ft.
In the northeastern corner of KS; incorporated Mar 5, 1862.
Name origin: For White Cloud (Waubeshiek, c. 1794–c. 1841), an Iowa Indian chief.

Wolf River
Township
Lat: 39-47-29 N **Long:** 95-15-09 W
Pop: 427 (1990); 524 (1980) **Pop Density:** 7.6
Land: 56.0 sq. mi.; **Water:** 0.0 sq. mi.

Douglas County
County Seat: Lawrence (ZIP: 66044)

Pop: 81,798 (1990); 67,640 (1980) **Pop Density:** 179.0
Land: 457.0 sq. mi.; **Water:** 17.5 sq. mi. **Area Code:** 913
In eastern KS, east of Topeka; original county; organized Aug 25, 1855 (prior to statehood).
Name origin: For Stephen Arnold Douglas (1813–61), U.S. orator and statesman.

Baldwin City
City
ZIP: 66006 **Lat:** 38-46-35 N **Long:** 95-11-06 W
Pop: 2,961 (1990); 2,829 (1980) **Pop Density:** 1974.0
Land: 1.5 sq. mi.; **Water:** 0.0 sq. mi. **Elev:** 1050 ft.
Incorporated Sep 27, 1870.
Name origin: For John Baldwin, an OH educator and builder.

Clinton
Township
Lat: 38-54-18 N **Long:** 95-24-19 W
Pop: 354 (1990); 275 (1980) **Pop Density:** 11.1
Land: 31.9 sq. mi.; **Water:** 9.9 sq. mi.

Eudora
City
ZIP: 66025 **Lat:** 38-56-17 N **Long:** 95-05-56 W
Pop: 3,006 (1990); 2,934 (1980) **Pop Density:** 2004.0
Land: 1.5 sq. mi.; **Water:** 0.0 sq. mi. **Elev:** 880 ft.
Incorporated Feb 8, 1859. Not coextensive with the town of the same name.
Name origin: For the English form of the name of a Shawnee Indian woman.

*Eudora
Township
ZIP: 66025 **Lat:** 38-54-44 N **Long:** 95-06-51 W
Pop: 4,011 (1990); 3,821 (1980) **Pop Density:** 81.0
Land: 49.5 sq. mi.; **Water:** 0.7 sq. mi.

Grant
Township
Lat: 39-00-57 N **Long:** 95-13-19 W
Pop: 440 (1990); 430 (1980) **Pop Density:** 26.7
Land: 16.5 sq. mi.; **Water:** 0.0 sq. mi.

KANSAS, Douglas County

Kanwaka
Township
Lat: 38-58-15 N Long: 95-24-38 W
Pop: 1,017 (1990); 704 (1980) **Pop Density:** 22.9
Land: 44.5 sq. mi.; **Water:** 3.2 sq. mi.

Lawrence
City
ZIP: 66044 Lat: 38-57-46 N Long: 95-15-19 W
Pop: 65,608 (1990); 52,738 (1980) **Pop Density:** 2865.0
Land: 22.9 sq. mi.; **Water:** 0.6 sq. mi. **Elev:** 850 ft.
In eastern KS on the Kansas River, 25 mi. east of Topeka. Founded 1854; incorporated Feb 20, 1858. Site of the University of Kansas.
Name origin: For town promoter, Amos Lawrence. Previously called Wakarusa.

Lecompton
City
ZIP: 66050 Lat: 39-02-42 N Long: 95-23-31 W
Pop: 619 (1990); 576 (1980) **Pop Density:** 687.8
Land: 0.9 sq. mi.; **Water:** 0.1 sq. mi. **Elev:** 950 ft.
Incorporated 1855. Not coextensive with the town of the same name.
Name origin: For pioneer judge Samuel Lecompte.

*Lecompton
Township
ZIP: 66050 Lat: 39-01-38 N Long: 95-24-50 W
Pop: 1,501 (1990); 1,250 (1980) **Pop Density:** 43.3
Land: 34.7 sq. mi.; **Water:** 0.9 sq. mi.

Marion
Township
Lat: 38-48-11 N Long: 95-25-43 W
Pop: 662 (1990); 600 (1980) **Pop Density:** 9.2
Land: 71.6 sq. mi.; **Water:** 0.4 sq. mi.

Palmyra
Township
Lat: 38-48-13 N Long: 95-09-17 W
Pop: 4,736 (1990); 4,471 (1980) **Pop Density:** 57.8
Land: 81.9 sq. mi.; **Water:** 0.7 sq. mi.

Wakarusa
Township
Lat: 38-55-43 N Long: 95-14-50 W
Pop: 2,158 (1990); 2,246 (1980) **Pop Density:** 43.8
Land: 49.3 sq. mi.; **Water:** 0.9 sq. mi.

Willow Springs
Township
Lat: 38-48-24 N Long: 95-17-30 W
Pop: 1,311 (1990); 1,105 (1980) **Pop Density:** 24.1
Land: 54.3 sq. mi.; **Water:** 0.3 sq. mi.

Edwards County
County Seat: Kinsley (ZIP: 67547)

Pop: 3,787 (1990); 4,271 (1980) **Pop Density:** 6.1
Land: 622.1 sq. mi.; **Water:** 0.1 sq. mi. **Area Code:** 316
In south-central KS, northeast of Dodge City; organized Mar 7, 1874 from Kiowa County.
Name origin: For W. C. and R. E. Edwards, prominent early KS settlers.

Belpre
City
ZIP: 67519 Lat: 37-57-03 N Long: 99-05-57 W
Pop: 116 (1990); 154 (1980) **Pop Density:** 290.0
Land: 0.4 sq. mi.; **Water:** 0.0 sq. mi. **Elev:** 2090 ft.
Incorporated Mar 22, 1906. Not coextensive with the town of the same name.
Name origin: For Belpre, OH.

*Belpre
Township
ZIP: 67519 Lat: 37-57-22 N Long: 99-06-05 W
Pop: 221 (1990); 277 (1980) **Pop Density:** 4.1
Land: 54.2 sq. mi.; **Water:** 0.0 sq. mi.

Franklin
Township
Lat: 37-48-55 N Long: 99-11-11 W
Pop: 109 (1990); 137 (1980) **Pop Density:** 1.5
Land: 73.6 sq. mi.; **Water:** 0.0 sq. mi.

Jackson
Township
Lat: 38-00-05 N Long: 99-31-19 W
Pop: 111 (1990); 118 (1980) **Pop Density:** 1.5
Land: 72.4 sq. mi.; **Water:** 0.0 sq. mi.

Kinsley
City
ZIP: 67547 Lat: 37-55-20 N Long: 99-24-40 W
Pop: 1,875 (1990); 2,074 (1980) **Pop Density:** 1442.3
Land: 1.3 sq. mi.; **Water:** 0.0 sq. mi. **Elev:** 2170 ft.
Incorporated Nov 12, 1878.
Name origin: For New England settler E.W. Kinsley.

*Kinsley
Township
ZIP: 67547 Lat: 37-56-26 N Long: 99-23-58 W
Pop: 191 (1990); 201 (1980) **Pop Density:** 4.1
Land: 46.8 sq. mi.; **Water:** 0.0 sq. mi.

Lewis
City
ZIP: 67552 Lat: 37-56-13 N Long: 99-15-15 W
Pop: 451 (1990); 551 (1980) **Pop Density:** 1503.3
Land: 0.3 sq. mi.; **Water:** 0.0 sq. mi. **Elev:** 2140 ft.
Incorporated Jan 5, 1906.
Name origin: For M.M. Lewis, editor of the *Valley Republican*.

Lincoln
Township
Lat: 37-49-23 N Long: 99-04-24 W
Pop: 164 (1990); 174 (1980) **Pop Density:** 2.2
Land: 74.5 sq. mi.; **Water:** 0.0 sq. mi.

Logan
Township
Lat: 38-03-05 N Long: 99-23-45 W
Pop: 55 (1990); 62 (1980) **Pop Density:** 1.5
Land: 35.9 sq. mi.; **Water:** 0.0 sq. mi.

North Brown
Township
Lat: 37-51-41 N Long: 99-20-26 W
Pop: 104 (1990); 97 (1980) **Pop Density:** 1.6
Land: 63.1 sq. mi.; **Water:** 0.0 sq. mi.

Offerle
City
ZIP: 67563   **Lat:** 37-53-27 N   **Long:** 99-33-37 W
Pop: 228 (1990); 244 (1980)   **Pop Density:** 760.0
Land: 0.3 sq. mi.; **Water:** 0.0 sq. mi.   **Elev:** 2270 ft.
Incorporated May 1, 1917.
Name origin: For Laurence Offerle, who surveyed the townsite.

South Brown
Township
Lat: 37-46-12 N   **Long:** 99-22-03 W
Pop: 100 (1990); 110 (1980)   **Pop Density:** 1.0
Land: 97.0 sq. mi.; **Water:** 0.0 sq. mi.

Trenton
Township
Lat: 37-50-49 N   **Long:** 99-31-31 W
Pop: 297 (1990); 333 (1980)   **Pop Density:** 5.6
Land: 52.6 sq. mi.; **Water:** 0.0 sq. mi.

Wayne
Township
Lat: 37-56-57 N   **Long:** 99-16-03 W
Pop: 560 (1990); 688 (1980)   **Pop Density:** 11.0
Land: 50.9 sq. mi.; **Water:** 0.0 sq. mi.

Elk County
County Seat: Howard (ZIP: 67349)

Pop: 3,327 (1990); 3,918 (1980)   **Pop Density:** 5.1
Land: 647.9 sq. mi.; **Water:** 2.6 sq. mi.   **Area Code:** 316

In southeastern KS, southeast of Wichita; organized Mar 3, 1875 from Howard County, which was organized in 1855 (named Godfrey and changed to Seward in 1867) and abolished at the time of its division into Chautauqua and Elk counties.
Name origin: For the large North American deer, the elk or wapiti.

Elk Falls
City
ZIP: 67345   **Lat:** 37-22-26 N   **Long:** 96-11-32 W
Pop: 122 (1990); 151 (1980)   **Pop Density:** 135.6
Land: 0.9 sq. mi.; **Water:** 0.0 sq. mi.   **Elev:** 938 ft.
Incorporated Mar 31, 1887. Not coextensive with the town of the same name.
Name origin: For the nearby falls on the Elk River.

*Elk Falls
Township
ZIP: 67345   **Lat:** 37-21-46 N   **Long:** 96-12-35 W
Pop: 206 (1990); 261 (1980)   **Pop Density:** 3.5
Land: 58.6 sq. mi.; **Water:** 0.1 sq. mi.

Greenfield
Township
Lat: 37-21-39 N   **Long:** 96-27-17 W
Pop: 340 (1990); 423 (1980)   **Pop Density:** 5.1
Land: 66.1 sq. mi.; **Water:** 0.4 sq. mi.

Grenola
City
ZIP: 67346   **Lat:** 37-21-02 N   **Long:** 96-26-53 W
Pop: 256 (1990); 335 (1980)   **Pop Density:** 512.0
Land: 0.5 sq. mi.; **Water:** 0.0 sq. mi.   **Elev:** 1117 ft.
Incorporated Aug 7, 1880.

Howard
City
ZIP: 67349   **Lat:** 37-28-10 N   **Long:** 96-15-45 W
Pop: 815 (1990); 965 (1980)   **Pop Density:** 1164.3
Land: 0.7 sq. mi.; **Water:** 0.0 sq. mi.   **Elev:** 1040 ft.
Incorporated Nov 1887. Not coextensive with the town of the same name.
Name origin: For Gen. O.O. Howard, head of the Civil War-era Freedman's Bureau.

*Howard
Township
ZIP: 67349   **Lat:** 37-27-55 N   **Long:** 96-13-29 W
Pop: 1,012 (1990); 1,163 (1980)   **Pop Density:** 15.8
Land: 64.2 sq. mi.; **Water:** 0.6 sq. mi.

Liberty
Township
Lat: 37-33-17 N   **Long:** 96-02-37 W
Pop: 132 (1990); 132 (1980)   **Pop Density:** 2.2
Land: 59.5 sq. mi.; **Water:** 0.1 sq. mi.

Longton
City
ZIP: 67352   **Lat:** 37-22-38 N   **Long:** 96-04-57 W
Pop: 389 (1990); 396 (1980)   **Pop Density:** 324.2
Land: 1.2 sq. mi.; **Water:** 0.0 sq. mi.   **Elev:** 918 ft.
Not coextensive with the town of the same name.
Name origin: For Longton, England.

*Longton
Township
ZIP: 67352   **Lat:** 37-22-08 N   **Long:** 96-05-49 W
Pop: 481 (1990); 506 (1980)   **Pop Density:** 10.7
Land: 44.8 sq. mi.; **Water:** 0.0 sq. mi.

Moline
City
ZIP: 67353   **Lat:** 37-21-49 N   **Long:** 96-18-06 W
Pop: 473 (1990); 553 (1980)   **Pop Density:** 1576.7
Land: 0.3 sq. mi.; **Water:** 0.0 sq. mi.   **Elev:** 1055 ft.
Incorporated Oct 27, 1886.
Name origin: For Moline, IL.

Oak Valley
Township
Lat: 37-22-03 N   **Long:** 96-00-46 W
Pop: 132 (1990); 136 (1980)   **Pop Density:** 2.9
Land: 44.8 sq. mi.; **Water:** 0.1 sq. mi.

Painterhood
Township
Lat: 37-28-11 N   **Long:** 96-03-16 W
Pop: 80 (1990); 94 (1980)   **Pop Density:** 1.3
Land: 59.5 sq. mi.; **Water:** 0.2 sq. mi.

Paw Paw
Township
Lat: 37-34-03 N   **Long:** 96-13-29 W
Pop: 149 (1990); 191 (1980)   **Pop Density:** 2.7
Land: 54.3 sq. mi.; **Water:** 0.1 sq. mi.

Union Center
Township
Lat: 37-31-00 N   **Long:** 96-24-56 W
Pop: 114 (1990); 199 (1980)   **Pop Density:** 0.8
Land: 143.3 sq. mi.; **Water:** 0.7 sq. mi.

Wildcat
Township
Lat: 37-22-11 N   **Long:** 96-20-08 W
Pop: 681 (1990); 813 (1980)   **Pop Density:** 12.9
Land: 52.7 sq. mi.; **Water:** 0.2 sq. mi.

Ellis County
County Seat: Hays (ZIP: 67601)

Pop: 26,004 (1990); 26,098 (1980) **Pop Density:** 28.9
Land: 900.0 sq. mi.; **Water:** 0.5 sq. mi. **Area Code:** 913
In central KS, west of Salina; organized Feb 26, 1867 from unorganized territory.
Name origin: For George Ellis (?–1864) KS infantryman killed during the Civil War.

Big Creek — Township
Lat: 38-52-05 N Long: 99-21-51 W
Pop: 2,494 (1990); 3,336 (1980) **Pop Density:** 25.2
Land: 98.8 sq. mi.; **Water:** 0.0 sq. mi.

Buckeye — Township
Lat: 39-02-39 N Long: 99-19-25 W
Pop: 280 (1990); 315 (1980) **Pop Density:** 2.1
Land: 136.0 sq. mi.; **Water:** 0.1 sq. mi.

Catherine — Township
Lat: 39-01-24 N Long: 99-11-42 W
Pop: 289 (1990); 292 (1980) **Pop Density:** 3.6
Land: 80.4 sq. mi.; **Water:** 0.0 sq. mi.

Ellis — City
ZIP: 67637 Lat: 38-56-10 N Long: 99-33-31 W
Pop: 1,814 (1990); 2,062 (1980) **Pop Density:** 1511.7
Land: 1.2 sq. mi.; **Water:** 0.0 sq. mi. **Elev:** 2117 ft.
Incorporated Jan 31, 1888. Not coextensive with the town of the same name.

*Ellis — Township
ZIP: 67637 Lat: 38-59-38 N Long: 99-30-38 W
Pop: 384 (1990); 482 (1980) **Pop Density:** 2.2
Land: 176.5 sq. mi.; **Water:** 0.0 sq. mi.

Freedom — Township
Lat: 38-43-47 N Long: 99-07-34 W
Pop: 123 (1990); 208 (1980) **Pop Density:** 2.7
Land: 45.1 sq. mi.; **Water:** 0.0 sq. mi.

Hays — City
ZIP: 67601 Lat: 38-52-41 N Long: 99-19-07 W
Pop: 17,767 (1990); 16,301 (1980) **Pop Density:** 2961.2
Land: 6.0 sq. mi.; **Water:** 0.0 sq. mi. **Elev:** 2010 ft.
In central KS, 48 mi. northeast of Great Bend. Incorporated May 18, 1885.
Name origin: For Fort Hays, which was named for Gen. Alexander Hays (d. 1864).

Herzog — Township
Lat: 38-58-25 N Long: 99-05-32 W
Pop: 901 (1990); 972 (1980) **Pop Density:** 7.2
Land: 125.6 sq. mi.; **Water:** 0.2 sq. mi.

Lookout — Township
Lat: 38-45-25 N Long: 99-27-13 W
Pop: 534 (1990); 591 (1980) **Pop Density:** 4.4
Land: 122.5 sq. mi.; **Water:** 0.1 sq. mi.

Schoenchen — City
ZIP: 67667 Lat: 38-42-47 N Long: 99-19-49 W
Pop: 128 (1990); 209 (1980) **Pop Density:** 1280.0
Land: 0.1 sq. mi.; **Water:** 0.0 sq. mi. **Elev:** 1936 ft.
Incorporated Sep 1935.
Name origin: For the town in Russia settled by Germans; from German meaning 'little beautiful one.'

Victoria — City
ZIP: 67671 Lat: 38-51-12 N Long: 99-08-49 W
Pop: 1,157 (1990); 1,328 (1980) **Pop Density:** 2314.0
Land: 0.5 sq. mi.; **Water:** 0.0 sq. mi. **Elev:** 1940 ft.
Incorporated Apr 12, 1913.
Name origin: For Britain's Queen Victoria (1819–1901).

*Victoria — Township
ZIP: 67671 Lat: 38-48-49 N Long: 99-07-22 W
Pop: 976 (1990); 1,060 (1980) **Pop Density:** 18.1
Land: 53.8 sq. mi.; **Water:** 0.0 sq. mi.

Wheatland — Township
Lat: 38-45-51 N Long: 99-15-50 W
Pop: 442 (1990); 479 (1980) **Pop Density:** 8.2
Land: 54.1 sq. mi.; **Water:** 0.0 sq. mi.

Ellsworth County
County Seat: Ellsworth (ZIP: 67439)

Pop: 6,586 (1990); 6,640 (1980)   **Pop Density:** 9.2
Land: 715.9 sq. mi.; **Water:** 7.5 sq. mi.   **Area Code:** 913
In central KS, west of Salina; organized Feb 26, 1867 from Saline County.
Name origin: For Lt. Allen Ellsworth, an officer in the Iowa Cavalry, who commanded the fort later named for him.

Ash Creek   Township
Lat: 38-39-36 N   **Long:** 98-12-21 W
Pop: 66 (1990); 76 (1980)   **Pop Density:** 1.8
Land: 35.8 sq. mi.; **Water:** 0.2 sq. mi.

Black Wolf   Township
Lat: 38-44-16 N   **Long:** 98-19-14 W
Pop: 99 (1990); 99 (1980)   **Pop Density:** 2.7
Land: 36.3 sq. mi.; **Water:** 0.0 sq. mi.

Carneiro   Township
Lat: 38-44-11 N   **Long:** 97-59-00 W
Pop: 53 (1990); 65 (1980)   **Pop Density:** 1.5
Land: 36.1 sq. mi.; **Water:** 0.1 sq. mi.

Clear Creek   Township
Lat: 38-44-18 N   **Long:** 98-05-33 W
Pop: 104 (1990); 110 (1980)   **Pop Density:** 2.9
Land: 36.3 sq. mi.; **Water:** 0.1 sq. mi.

Columbia   Township
Lat: 38-49-33 N   **Long:** 98-18-39 W
Pop: 74 (1990); 92 (1980)   **Pop Density:** 2.0
Land: 36.3 sq. mi.; **Water:** 0.0 sq. mi.

Ellsworth   City
ZIP: 67439   **Lat:** 38-44-08 N   **Long:** 98-13-41 W
Pop: 2,294 (1990); 2,465 (1980)   **Pop Density:** 1207.4
Land: 1.9 sq. mi.; **Water:** 0.0 sq. mi.   **Elev:** 1550 ft.
Incorporated 1868.
Name origin: For Civil War lieutenant, Allen Ellsworth.

*Ellsworth   Township
ZIP: 67439   **Lat:** 38-44-15 N   **Long:** 98-12-29 W
Pop: 1,425 (1990); 979 (1980)   **Pop Density:** 41.5
Land: 34.3 sq. mi.; **Water:** 0.1 sq. mi.

Empire   Township
Lat: 38-39-14 N   **Long:** 98-02-13 W
Pop: 78 (1990); 78 (1980)   **Pop Density:** 1.2
Land: 66.2 sq. mi.; **Water:** 5.6 sq. mi.

Garfield   Township
Lat: 38-50-01 N   **Long:** 98-05-42 W
Pop: 44 (1990); 44 (1980)   **Pop Density:** 1.2
Land: 35.7 sq. mi.; **Water:** 0.1 sq. mi.

Green Garden   Township
Lat: 38-33-55 N   **Long:** 98-18-45 W
Pop: 235 (1990); 250 (1980)   **Pop Density:** 6.5
Land: 36.4 sq. mi.; **Water:** 0.1 sq. mi.

Holyrood   City
ZIP: 67450   **Lat:** 38-35-14 N   **Long:** 98-24-42 W
Pop: 492 (1990); 567 (1980)   **Pop Density:** 1230.0
Land: 0.4 sq. mi.; **Water:** 0.0 sq. mi.   **Elev:** 1805 ft.
Incorporated Jul 1901.
Name origin: For Holyrood Abbey in Scotland.

Kanopolis   City
ZIP: 67454   **Lat:** 38-42-30 N   **Long:** 98-09-24 W
Pop: 605 (1990); 729 (1980)   **Pop Density:** 504.2
Land: 1.2 sq. mi.; **Water:** 0.0 sq. mi.   **Elev:** 1574 ft.
Incorporated Jan 6, 1887.
Name origin: A combination of Greek *polis* 'city' and the first syllable of *Kan*sas, with an *o* added for euphony.

Langley   Township
Lat: 38-33-29 N   **Long:** 97-58-32 W
Pop: 80 (1990); 81 (1980)   **Pop Density:** 2.3
Land: 35.5 sq. mi.; **Water:** 0.7 sq. mi.

Lincoln   Township
Lat: 38-39-12 N   **Long:** 98-18-59 W
Pop: 43 (1990); 38 (1980)   **Pop Density:** 1.2
Land: 36.7 sq. mi.; **Water:** 0.1 sq. mi.

Lorraine   City
ZIP: 67459   **Lat:** 38-34-10 N   **Long:** 98-19-01 W
Pop: 147 (1990); 157 (1980)   **Pop Density:** 735.0
Land: 0.2 sq. mi.; **Water:** 0.0 sq. mi.   **Elev:** 1781 ft.
Incorporated Jun 13, 1923.
Name origin: For Lorraine Stanley, daughter of a railroad official.

Mulberry   Township
Lat: 38-49-41 N   **Long:** 97-59-05 W
Pop: 35 (1990); 36 (1980)   **Pop Density:** 1.0
Land: 35.9 sq. mi.; **Water:** 0.1 sq. mi.

Noble   Township
Lat: 38-44-50 N   **Long:** 98-25-32 W
Pop: 93 (1990); 103 (1980)   **Pop Density:** 2.6
Land: 35.7 sq. mi.; **Water:** 0.0 sq. mi.

Palacky   Township
Lat: 38-39-04 N   **Long:** 98-25-34 W
Pop: 67 (1990); 66 (1980)   **Pop Density:** 1.8
Land: 36.4 sq. mi.; **Water:** 0.0 sq. mi.

Sherman   Township
Lat: 38-49-42 N   **Long:** 98-12-24 W
Pop: 94 (1990); 103 (1980)   **Pop Density:** 2.6
Land: 36.4 sq. mi.; **Water:** 0.1 sq. mi.

Thomas   Township
Lat: 38-33-52 N   **Long:** 98-12-07 W
Pop: 67 (1990); 78 (1980)   **Pop Density:** 1.9
Land: 36.1 sq. mi.; **Water:** 0.1 sq. mi.

Trivoli   Township
Lat: 38-33-28 N   **Long:** 98-05-42 W
Pop: 53 (1990); 80 (1980)   **Pop Density:** 1.5
Land: 36.0 sq. mi.; **Water:** 0.1 sq. mi.

KANSAS, Ellsworth County

Valley Township
Lat: 38-33-55 N Long: 98-25-27 W
Pop: 611 (1990); 700 (1980) **Pop Density:** 17.0
Land: 35.9 sq. mi.; **Water:** 0.1 sq. mi.

Wilson City
ZIP: 67490 Lat: 38-49-32 N Long: 98-28-27 W
Pop: 834 (1990); 978 (1980) **Pop Density:** 1668.0
Land: 0.5 sq. mi.; **Water:** 0.0 sq. mi. **Elev:** 1689 ft.
Incorporated Mar 3, 1883. Not coextensive with the town of the same name.
Name origin: For Isaac Wilson, town founder.

*Wilson Township
ZIP: 67490 Lat: 38-49-30 N Long: 98-25-53 W
Pop: 971 (1990); 1,097 (1980) **Pop Density:** 27.0
Land: 35.9 sq. mi.; **Water:** 0.0 sq. mi.

Finney County
County Seat: Garden City (ZIP: 67846)

Pop: 33,070 (1990); 23,825 (1980) **Pop Density:** 25.4
Land: 1300.2 sq. mi.; **Water:** 2.5 sq. mi. **Area Code:** 316

In southwestern KS, northwest of Dodge City; organized as Sequoyah County Mar 6, 1873 from Arapahoe and Foote counties; name changed Feb 21, 1883; Garfield County was annexed to Finney County in 1893.
Name origin: For David W. Finney, lieutenant governor of KS (1861–65) and KS legislator.

Garden City City
ZIP: 67846 Lat: 37-58-37 N Long: 100-51-46 W
Pop: 24,097 (1990); 18,256 (1980) **Pop Density:** 3256.4
Land: 7.4 sq. mi.; **Water:** 0.0 sq. mi. **Elev:** 2839 ft.
In western KS on the Arkansas River, northwest of Dodge City. Incorporated Jan 13, 1883.
Name origin: For its descriptive connotations.

*Garden City Township
ZIP: 67846 Lat: 37-59-52 N Long: 100-51-05 W
Pop: 5,368 (1990); 2,724 (1980) **Pop Density:** 42.2
Land: 127.3 sq. mi.; **Water:** 0.1 sq. mi.

Garfield Township
Lat: 38-08-13 N Long: 100-26-45 W
Pop: 326 (1990); 342 (1980) **Pop Density:** 0.8
Land: 430.8 sq. mi.; **Water:** 0.4 sq. mi.

Holcomb City
ZIP: 67851 Lat: 37-59-24 N Long: 100-59-17 W
Pop: 1,400 (1990); 816 (1980) **Pop Density:** 1555.6
Land: 0.9 sq. mi.; **Water:** 0.0 sq. mi. **Elev:** 2885 ft.
Incorporated May 1, 1961.
Name origin: For a local farmer.

Ivanhoe Township
Lat: 37-48-07 N Long: 100-54-33 W
Pop: 370 (1990); 298 (1980) **Pop Density:** 2.6
Land: 142.0 sq. mi.; **Water:** 0.0 sq. mi.

Pierceville Township
Lat: 37-55-00 N Long: 100-42-40 W
Pop: 495 (1990); 422 (1980) **Pop Density:** 3.4
Land: 145.9 sq. mi.; **Water:** 0.0 sq. mi.

Pleasant Valley Township
Lat: 38-10-39 N Long: 100-46-25 W
Pop: 124 (1990); 118 (1980) **Pop Density:** 0.9
Land: 143.3 sq. mi.; **Water:** 0.0 sq. mi.

Sherlock Township
Lat: 37-57-53 N Long: 101-02-01 W
Pop: 2,060 (1990); 1,436 (1980) **Pop Density:** 12.9
Land: 160.2 sq. mi.; **Water:** 1.8 sq. mi.

Terry Township
Lat: 38-10-14 N Long: 100-59-18 W
Pop: 230 (1990); 229 (1980) **Pop Density:** 1.6
Land: 143.3 sq. mi.; **Water:** 0.2 sq. mi.

Ford County
County Seat: Dodge City (ZIP: 67801)

Pop: 27,463 (1990); 24,315 (1980) **Pop Density:** 25.0
Land: 1098.6 sq. mi.; **Water:** 0.8 sq. mi. **Area Code:** 316
In southwestern KS, southeast of Garden City; organized Feb 26, 1867 from unorganized territory.
Name origin: For James Hobart Ford (?–1867), an officer in the Second Colorado cavalry during the Civil War.

Bloom Township
Lat: 37-30-47 N Long: 99-54-58 W
Pop: 134 (1990); 132 (1980) **Pop Density:** 2.4
Land: 55.4 sq. mi.; **Water:** 0.0 sq. mi.

Bucklin City
ZIP: 67834 Lat: 37-32-56 N Long: 99-38-04 W
Pop: 710 (1990); 786 (1980) **Pop Density:** 1183.3
Land: 0.6 sq. mi.; **Water:** 0.0 sq. mi. **Elev:** 2412 ft.
Incorporated Apr 20, 1909. Not coextensive with the town of the same name.

*Bucklin Township
ZIP: 67834 Lat: 37-36-07 N Long: 99-36-51 W
Pop: 848 (1990); 943 (1980) **Pop Density:** 7.7
Land: 110.1 sq. mi.; **Water:** 0.0 sq. mi.

Concord Township
Lat: 37-36-24 N Long: 100-06-38 W
Pop: 115 (1990); 99 (1980) **Pop Density:** 1.6
Land: 72.3 sq. mi.; **Water:** 0.1 sq. mi.

Dodge Township
Lat: 37-47-15 N Long: 100-02-43 W
Pop: 674 (1990); 884 (1980) **Pop Density:** 24.4
Land: 27.6 sq. mi.; **Water:** 0.1 sq. mi.

Dodge City City
ZIP: 67801 Lat: 37-45-31 N Long: 100-00-55 W
Pop: 21,129 (1990); 18,001 (1980) **Pop Density:** 1746.2
Land: 12.1 sq. mi.; **Water:** 0.1 sq. mi. **Elev:** 2550 ft.
In southern KS on the Arkansas River, 120 mi. east of the CO border. Incorporated Nov 2, 1875.
Name origin: For U.S. Army colonel Richard Dodge (1827–95). Previously called Buffalo City.

Enterprise Township
Lat: 37-39-04 N Long: 99-56-36 W
Pop: 736 (1990); 633 (1980) **Pop Density:** 10.9
Land: 67.4 sq. mi.; **Water:** 0.1 sq. mi.

Fairview Township
Lat: 37-44-04 N Long: 100-09-52 W
Pop: 309 (1990); 320 (1980) **Pop Density:** 4.3
Land: 72.7 sq. mi.; **Water:** 0.0 sq. mi.

Ford City
ZIP: 67842 Lat: 37-38-13 N Long: 99-45-14 W
Pop: 247 (1990); 272 (1980) **Pop Density:** 617.5
Land: 0.4 sq. mi.; **Water:** 0.0 sq. mi. **Elev:** 2406 ft.
Incorporated Nov 1887. Not coextensive with the town of the same name.
Name origin: For the county.

*Ford Township
ZIP: 67842 Lat: 37-36-48 N Long: 99-47-32 W
Pop: 403 (1990); 424 (1980) **Pop Density:** 4.2
Land: 96.3 sq. mi.; **Water:** 0.0 sq. mi.

Grandview Township
Lat: 37-49-30 N Long: 99-56-17 W
Pop: 759 (1990); 783 (1980) **Pop Density:** 8.7
Land: 87.3 sq. mi.; **Water:** 0.2 sq. mi.

Richland Township
Lat: 37-41-31 N Long: 100-03-01 W
Pop: 673 (1990); 319 (1980) **Pop Density:** 17.7
Land: 38.1 sq. mi.; **Water:** 0.1 sq. mi.

Royal Township
Lat: 37-52-17 N Long: 100-07-27 W
Pop: 106 (1990); 107 (1980) **Pop Density:** 1.5
Land: 71.6 sq. mi.; **Water:** 0.0 sq. mi.

Sodville Township
Lat: 37-30-42 N Long: 99-44-42 W
Pop: 124 (1990); 129 (1980) **Pop Density:** 2.2
Land: 55.9 sq. mi.; **Water:** 0.0 sq. mi.

Spearville City
ZIP: 67876 Lat: 37-50-52 N Long: 99-45-15 W
Pop: 716 (1990); 693 (1980) **Pop Density:** 1193.3
Land: 0.6 sq. mi.; **Water:** 0.0 sq. mi. **Elev:** 2460 ft.
Incorporated May 1885. Not coextensive with the town of the same name.
Name origin: For Boston financier Alden Spear, who had interests in the Santa Fe Railroad.

*Spearville Township
ZIP: 67876 Lat: 37-46-57 N Long: 99-46-38 W
Pop: 1,151 (1990); 1,172 (1980) **Pop Density:** 6.2
Land: 185.0 sq. mi.; **Water:** 0.1 sq. mi.

Wheatland Township
Lat: 37-48-58 N Long: 99-37-20 W
Pop: 210 (1990); 235 (1980) **Pop Density:** 2.8
Land: 74.4 sq. mi.; **Water:** 0.0 sq. mi.

Wilburn Township
Lat: 37-30-58 N Long: 100-06-37 W
Pop: 92 (1990); 134 (1980) **Pop Density:** 1.3
Land: 72.3 sq. mi.; **Water:** 0.0 sq. mi.

Franklin County
County Seat: Ottawa (ZIP: 66067)

Pop: 21,994 (1990); 22,062 (1980)   **Pop Density:** 38.3
Land: 573.9 sq. mi.; **Water:** 2.8 sq. mi.   **Area Code:** 913

In eastern KS, southwest of Olathe; original county; organized Aug 25, 1855 (prior to statehood).

Name origin: For Benjamin Franklin (1706–90), U.S. patriot, diplomat, and statesman.

Appanoose   Township
Lat: 38-41-41 N   Long: 95-27-08 W
Pop: 263 (1990); 257 (1980)   **Pop Density:** 8.8
Land: 29.9 sq. mi.; **Water:** 0.0 sq. mi.

Centropolis   Township
Lat: 38-41-06 N   Long: 95-21-28 W
Pop: 822 (1990); 758 (1980)   **Pop Density:** 20.2
Land: 40.7 sq. mi.; **Water:** 0.1 sq. mi.

Cutler   Township
Lat: 38-30-36 N   Long: 95-07-59 W
Pop: 669 (1990); 714 (1980)   **Pop Density:** 15.7
Land: 42.7 sq. mi.; **Water:** 0.3 sq. mi.

Franklin   Township
Lat: 38-41-35 N   Long: 95-06-49 W
Pop: 2,178 (1990); 2,219 (1980)   **Pop Density:** 61.7
Land: 35.3 sq. mi.; **Water:** 0.2 sq. mi.

Greenwood   Township
Lat: 38-33-39 N   Long: 95-26-34 W
Pop: 366 (1990); 347 (1980)   **Pop Density:** 12.0
Land: 30.4 sq. mi.; **Water:** 0.0 sq. mi.

Harrison   Township
Lat: 38-33-44 N   Long: 95-13-34 W
Pop: 402 (1990); 420 (1980)   **Pop Density:** 14.6
Land: 27.5 sq. mi.; **Water:** 0.2 sq. mi.

Hayes   Township
Lat: 38-41-59 N   Long: 95-13-47 W
Pop: 362 (1990); 314 (1980)   **Pop Density:** 12.2
Land: 29.7 sq. mi.; **Water:** 0.1 sq. mi.

Homewood   Township
Lat: 38-30-32 N   Long: 95-23-15 W
Pop: 412 (1990); 411 (1980)   **Pop Density:** 13.7
Land: 30.0 sq. mi.; **Water:** 0.1 sq. mi.

Lane   City
ZIP: 66042   Lat: 38-26-24 N   Long: 95-04-51 W
Pop: 247 (1990); 249 (1980)   **Pop Density:** 1235.0
Land: 0.2 sq. mi.; **Water:** 0.0 sq. mi.   **Elev:** 910 ft.
Incorporated Feb 18, 1908.
Name origin: For James Lane, first U.S. senator from KS.

Lincoln   Township
Lat: 38-33-54 N   Long: 95-19-29 W
Pop: 902 (1990); 475 (1980)   **Pop Density:** 29.7
Land: 30.4 sq. mi.; **Water:** 0.1 sq. mi.

Ohio   Township
Lat: 38-28-36 N   Long: 95-16-47 W
Pop: 650 (1990); 621 (1980)   **Pop Density:** 15.6
Land: 41.6 sq. mi.; **Water:** 0.4 sq. mi.

Ottawa   City
ZIP: 66067   Lat: 38-36-32 N   Long: 95-15-58 W
Pop: 10,667 (1990); 11,016 (1980)   **Pop Density:** 1641.1
Land: 6.5 sq. mi.; **Water:** 0.0 sq. mi.   **Elev:** 901 ft.
In eastern KS, 35 mi. southeast of Topeka. Incorporated Jun 18, 1866.
Name origin: For the Ottawa Indian tribe.

*Ottawa   Township
ZIP: 66067   Lat: 38-38-37 N   Long: 95-16-17 W
Pop: 792 (1990); 923 (1980)   **Pop Density:** 18.5
Land: 42.9 sq. mi.; **Water:** 0.1 sq. mi.

Peoria   Township
Lat: 38-36-26 N   Long: 95-07-19 W
Pop: 526 (1990); 514 (1980)   **Pop Density:** 14.8
Land: 35.6 sq. mi.; **Water:** 0.1 sq. mi.

Pomona   City
ZIP: 66076   Lat: 38-36-39 N   Long: 95-27-06 W
Pop: 835 (1990); 868 (1980)   **Pop Density:** 1043.8
Land: 0.8 sq. mi.; **Water:** 0.0 sq. mi.   **Elev:** 965 ft.
Incorporated Jan 1885. Not coextensive with the town of the same name.
Name origin: Named by town founder John H. Whetstone for his apple orchard, from French *pomme*.

*Pomona   Township
ZIP: 66076   Lat: 38-37-35 N   Long: 95-27-43 W
Pop: 1,051 (1990); 1,080 (1980)   **Pop Density:** 50.0
Land: 21.0 sq. mi.; **Water:** 0.1 sq. mi.

Pottawatomie   Township
Lat: 38-26-17 N   Long: 95-07-31 W
Pop: 582 (1990); 561 (1980)   **Pop Density:** 15.0
Land: 38.8 sq. mi.; **Water:** 0.2 sq. mi.

Princeton   City
ZIP: 66078   Lat: 38-29-19 N   Long: 95-16-20 W
Pop: 275 (1990); 244 (1980)   **Pop Density:** 916.7
Land: 0.3 sq. mi.; **Water:** 0.0 sq. mi.   **Elev:** 966 ft.
Incorporated Apr 4, 1921.
Name origin: For Princeton, IL.

Rantoul   City
ZIP: 66079   Lat: 38-32-54 N   Long: 95-06-00 W
Pop: 200 (1990); 212 (1980)   **Pop Density:** 2000.0
Land: 0.1 sq. mi.; **Water:** 0.0 sq. mi.   **Elev:** 892 ft.
Incorporated Sep 2, 1913.
Name origin: For U.S. Sen. Rantoul from MA.

Richmond — City
ZIP: 66080 **Lat:** 38-24-04 N **Long:** 95-15-14 W
Pop: 528 (1990); 510 (1980) **Pop Density:** 1760.0
Land: 0.3 sq. mi.; **Water:** 0.0 sq. mi. **Elev:** 1010 ft.
Incorporated Aug 18, 1910. Not coextensive with the town of the same name.
Name origin: For pioneer landowner, John Richmond, who donated 40 acres to the railroad right-of-way.

*Richmond — Township
ZIP: 66080 **Lat:** 38-24-54 N **Long:** 95-15-45 W
Pop: 833 (1990); 780 (1980) **Pop Density:** 23.8
Land: 35.0 sq. mi.; **Water:** 0.2 sq. mi.

Wellsville — City
ZIP: 66092 **Lat:** 38-43-02 N **Long:** 95-04-51 W
Pop: 1,563 (1990); 1,612 (1980) **Pop Density:** 2232.9
Land: 0.7 sq. mi.; **Water:** 0.0 sq. mi. **Elev:** 1039 ft.
Incorporated Jun 19, 1884.

Williamsburg — City
ZIP: 66095 **Lat:** 38-28-48 N **Long:** 95-27-56 W
Pop: 261 (1990); 362 (1980) **Pop Density:** 870.0
Land: 0.3 sq. mi.; **Water:** 0.0 sq. mi. **Elev:** 1138 ft.
Not coextensive with the town of the same name.
Name origin: For local farmer, William Scofield.

*Williamsburg — Township
ZIP: 66095 **Lat:** 38-26-29 N **Long:** 95-26-18 W
Pop: 517 (1990); 652 (1980) **Pop Density:** 9.2
Land: 55.9 sq. mi.; **Water:** 0.5 sq. mi.

Geary County
County Seat: Junction City (ZIP: 66441)

Pop: 30,453 (1990); 29,852 (1980) **Pop Density:** 79.2
Land: 384.3 sq. mi.; **Water:** 19.7 sq. mi. **Area Code:** 913

In east-central KS, south of Manhattan; organized as Davis County Aug 30, 1855 from Riley county; name changed Mar 7, 1889.

Name origin: For John White Geary (1819–73), territorial governor of KS (1856–57) and governor of PA (1867–73). Originally named by the pro-Southern legislature for Jefferson Davis, U.S. secretary of war (1853–57) and later president of the Confederacy.

Blakely — Township
Lat: 38-54-21 N **Long:** 96-45-26 W
Pop: 107 (1990); 94 (1980) **Pop Density:** 3.0
Land: 35.8 sq. mi.; **Water:** 0.0 sq. mi.

Camp Forsyth — Military Facility
Lat: 39-03-48 N **Long:** 96-49-27 W
Pop: 1,967 (1990); 2,054 (1980) **Pop Density:** 855.2
Land: 2.3 sq. mi.; **Water:** 0.1 sq. mi.

Fort Riley-Camp Whiteside — Military Facility
Lat: 39-05-05 N **Long:** 96-46-15 W
Pop: 112 (1990); 34 (1980) **Pop Density:** 160.0
Land: 0.7 sq. mi.; **Water:** 0.0 sq. mi.

Fort Riley North — Military Facility
Lat: 39-05-12 N **Long:** 96-48-52 W
Pop: 683 (1990); 1,656 (1980) **Pop Density:** 6830.0
Land: 0.1 sq. mi.; **Water:** 0.0 sq. mi.
Part of the town is also in Riley county.

Grandview Plaza — City
ZIP: 66441 **Lat:** 39-01-55 N **Long:** 96-47-38 W
Pop: 1,233 (1990); 1,189 (1980) **Pop Density:** 1541.3
Land: 0.8 sq. mi.; **Water:** 0.0 sq. mi. **Elev:** 1100 ft.
Incorporated Mar 4, 1963.

Jackson — Township
Lat: 39-00-59 N **Long:** 96-32-48 W
Pop: 84 (1990); 100 (1980) **Pop Density:** 2.1
Land: 40.3 sq. mi.; **Water:** 0.0 sq. mi.

Jefferson — Township
Lat: 39-00-58 N **Long:** 96-45-05 W
Pop: 1,749 (1990); 1,740 (1980) **Pop Density:** 36.5
Land: 47.9 sq. mi.; **Water:** 0.8 sq. mi.

Junction City — City
ZIP: 66441 **Lat:** 39-01-42 N **Long:** 96-50-31 W
Pop: 20,604 (1990); 19,305 (1980) **Pop Density:** 3030.0
Land: 6.8 sq. mi.; **Water:** 0.0 sq. mi. **Elev:** 1107 ft.
In northeastern KS at the confluence of the Republican and Smokey Hill rivers, 18 mi. southwest of Manhattan. Incorporated Feb 8, 1859.
Name origin: For the river junction.

Liberty — Township
Lat: 38-54-52 N **Long:** 96-36-06 W
Pop: 246 (1990); 286 (1980) **Pop Density:** 3.7
Land: 65.9 sq. mi.; **Water:** 0.0 sq. mi.

Lyon — Township
Lat: 38-55-16 N **Long:** 96-52-05 W
Pop: 301 (1990); 272 (1980) **Pop Density:** 6.9
Land: 43.5 sq. mi.; **Water:** 0.5 sq. mi.

Milford — City
ZIP: 66514 **Lat:** 39-10-27 N **Long:** 96-54-44 W
Pop: 384 (1990); 465 (1980) **Pop Density:** 1920.0
Land: 0.2 sq. mi.; **Water:** 0.0 sq. mi. **Elev:** 1194 ft.
Incorporated Apr 30, 1920. Not coextensive with the town of the same name.
Name origin: Possibly for a mill located on a ford of the Republican River.

*Milford — Township
ZIP: 66514 **Lat:** 39-09-55 N **Long:** 96-54-07 W
Pop: 1,445 (1990); 1,285 (1980) **Pop Density:** 37.2
Land: 38.8 sq. mi.; **Water:** 10.6 sq. mi.

KANSAS, Geary County   American Places Dictionary

Smoky Hill Township
Lat: 39-02-45 N Long: 96-53-24 W
Pop: 5,758 (1990); 6,625 (1980)   Pop Density: 99.8
Land: 57.7 sq. mi.; Water: 7.7 sq. mi.   Elev: 1120 ft.

Wingfield Township
Lat: 39-00-30 N Long: 96-39-11 W
Pop: 159 (1990); 145 (1980)   Pop Density: 3.3
Land: 47.6 sq. mi.; Water: 0.0 sq. mi.

Gove County
County Seat: Gove (ZIP: 67736)

Pop: 3,231 (1990); 3,726 (1980)   **Pop Density:** 3.0
Land: 1071.5 sq. mi.; **Water:** 0.1 sq. mi.   **Area Code:** 913
In west-central KS, west of Hays; organized Mar 3, 1868 from Rooks County.
Name origin: For Capt. Grenville L. Gove (?–1864), Union army officer from KS.

Baker Township
Lat: 39-00-06 N Long: 100-12-49 W
Pop: 1,344 (1990); 1,400 (1980)   Pop Density: 10.7
Land: 125.1 sq. mi.; Water: 0.0 sq. mi.

Gaeland Township
Lat: 38-56-06 N Long: 100-43-55 W
Pop: 55 (1990); 80 (1980)   Pop Density: 0.7
Land: 80.4 sq. mi.; Water: 0.0 sq. mi.

Gove Township
ZIP: 67736   Lat: 38-57-19 N Long: 100-31-42 W
Pop: 230 (1990); 293 (1980)   Pop Density: 2.0
Land: 116.3 sq. mi.; Water: 0.0 sq. mi.

Gove City City
Lat: 38-57-34 N Long: 100-29-22 W
Pop: 103 (1990); 148 (1980)   Pop Density: 257.5
Land: 0.4 sq. mi.; Water: 0.0 sq. mi.
Incorporated 1886.
Name origin: For Civil War officer Grenville Cove.

Grainfield City
ZIP: 67737   Lat: 39-06-50 N Long: 100-28-07 W
Pop: 357 (1990); 417 (1980)   Pop Density: 892.5
Land: 0.4 sq. mi.; Water: 0.0 sq. mi.   Elev: 2813 ft.
Incorporated Apr 12, 1887. Not coextensive with the town of the same name.
Name origin: For the area's rich grain production.

***Grainfield** Township
ZIP: 67737   Lat: 39-03-34 N Long: 100-29-08 W
Pop: 467 (1990); 585 (1980)   Pop Density: 6.6
Land: 71.2 sq. mi.; Water: 0.0 sq. mi.

Grinnell City
ZIP: 67738   Lat: 39-07-33 N Long: 100-37-50 W
Pop: 348 (1990); 410 (1980)   Pop Density: 696.0
Land: 0.5 sq. mi.; Water: 0.0 sq. mi.   Elev: 2910 ft.
Incorporated 1917. Not coextensive with the town of the same name.
Name origin: For Josiah Grinnell, who also founded Grinnell, IA.

***Grinnell** Township
ZIP: 67738   Lat: 39-03-42 N Long: 100-41-29 W
Pop: 557 (1990); 678 (1980)   Pop Density: 4.5
Land: 123.5 sq. mi.; Water: 0.0 sq. mi.

Jerome Township
Lat: 38-47-07 N Long: 100-29-00 W
Pop: 149 (1990); 154 (1980)   Pop Density: 1.0
Land: 143.0 sq. mi.; Water: 0.0 sq. mi.

Larrabee Township
Lat: 38-46-50 N Long: 100-16-00 W
Pop: 93 (1990); 102 (1980)   Pop Density: 0.6
Land: 143.4 sq. mi.; Water: 0.0 sq. mi.

Lewis Township
Lat: 38-47-41 N Long: 100-42-43 W
Pop: 20 (1990); 26 (1980)   Pop Density: 0.1
Land: 143.7 sq. mi.; Water: 0.0 sq. mi.

Park City
ZIP: 67751   Lat: 39-06-44 N Long: 100-21-41 W
Pop: 150 (1990); 183 (1980)   Pop Density: 500.0
Land: 0.3 sq. mi.; Water: 0.0 sq. mi.   Elev: 2750 ft.
Incorporated Feb 13, 1950.
Name origin: For its parklike setting.

Payne Township
Lat: 38-59-45 N Long: 100-20-37 W
Pop: 316 (1990); 408 (1980)   Pop Density: 2.5
Land: 125.1 sq. mi.; Water: 0.0 sq. mi.

Quinter City
ZIP: 67752   Lat: 39-03-59 N Long: 100-14-01 W
Pop: 945 (1990); 951 (1980)   Pop Density: 945.0
Land: 1.0 sq. mi.; Water: 0.0 sq. mi.   Elev: 2677 ft.
Incorporated Oct 12, 1909.

Graham County
County Seat: Hill City (ZIP: 67642)

Pop: 3,543 (1990); 3,995 (1980) **Pop Density:** 3.9
Land: 898.3 sq. mi.; **Water:** 0.4 sq. mi. **Area Code:** 913
In north-central KS, northwest of Hays; organized Feb 26, 1867 from Rooks County.
Name origin: For Capt. John L. Graham (?–1863), a KS infantry officer killed at Chickamauga.

Allodium Township
Lat: 39-29-55 N **Long:** 100-05-28 W
Pop: 64 (1990); 102 (1980) **Pop Density:** 0.9
Land: 67.4 sq. mi.; **Water:** 0.0 sq. mi.

Bogue City
ZIP: 67625 **Lat:** 39-21-34 N **Long:** 99-41-16 W
Pop: 150 (1990); 197 (1980) **Pop Density:** 500.0
Land: 0.3 sq. mi.; **Water:** 0.0 sq. mi. **Elev:** 2050 ft.
Incorporated Mar 21, 1935.
Name origin: To honor the railroad engineer named Bogue, who drove the first Union Pacific train through the town.

Bryant Township
Lat: 39-11-49 N **Long:** 100-04-27 W
Pop: 162 (1990); 231 (1980) **Pop Density:** 1.8
Land: 90.0 sq. mi.; **Water:** 0.0 sq. mi.

Gettysburg Township
Lat: 39-23-31 N **Long:** 100-01-19 W
Pop: 103 (1990); 110 (1980) **Pop Density:** 1.2
Land: 87.7 sq. mi.; **Water:** 0.0 sq. mi.

Graham Township
Lat: 39-30-10 N **Long:** 99-48-32 W
Pop: 60 (1990); 76 (1980) **Pop Density:** 0.8
Land: 71.8 sq. mi.; **Water:** 0.0 sq. mi.

Happy Township
Lat: 39-11-33 N **Long:** 99-52-46 W
Pop: 86 (1990); 108 (1980) **Pop Density:** 1.0
Land: 90.1 sq. mi.; **Water:** 0.0 sq. mi.

Hill City City
ZIP: 67642 **Lat:** 39-21-58 N **Long:** 99-50-47 W
Pop: 1,835 (1990); 2,028 (1980) **Pop Density:** 2038.9
Land: 0.9 sq. mi.; **Water:** 0.0 sq. mi. **Elev:** 2190 ft.
Incorporated 1888. Not coextensive with the town of the same name.
Name origin: For original landowner, W.R. Hill.

*Hill City Township
ZIP: 67642 **Lat:** 39-23-47 N **Long:** 99-48-47 W
Pop: 2,025 (1990); 2,205 (1980) **Pop Density:** 47.0
Land: 43.1 sq. mi.; **Water:** 0.1 sq. mi.

Indiana Township
Lat: 39-29-59 N **Long:** 99-56-51 W
Pop: 42 (1990); 65 (1980) **Pop Density:** 0.6
Land: 67.0 sq. mi.; **Water:** 0.0 sq. mi.

Millbrook Township
Lat: 39-18-48 N **Long:** 99-52-39 W
Pop: 179 (1990); 215 (1980) **Pop Density:** 2.9
Land: 61.6 sq. mi.; **Water:** 0.0 sq. mi.

Morlan Township
Lat: 39-12-40 N **Long:** 99-42-06 W
Pop: 113 (1990); 112 (1980) **Pop Density:** 1.0
Land: 110.6 sq. mi.; **Water:** 0.1 sq. mi.

Morland City
ZIP: 67650 **Lat:** 39-20-55 N **Long:** 100-04-27 W
Pop: 234 (1990); 223 (1980) **Pop Density:** 468.0
Land: 0.5 sq. mi.; **Water:** 0.0 sq. mi. **Elev:** 2310 ft.
Incorporated Jul 30, 1906.

Nicodemus Township
Lat: 39-23-54 N **Long:** 99-40-01 W
Pop: 66 (1990); 81 (1980) **Pop Density:** 2.0
Land: 32.3 sq. mi.; **Water:** 0.0 sq. mi.

Pioneer Township
Lat: 39-30-30 N **Long:** 99-40-28 W
Pop: 45 (1990); 67 (1980) **Pop Density:** 0.7
Land: 62.1 sq. mi.; **Water:** 0.0 sq. mi.

Solomon Township
Lat: 39-19-00 N **Long:** 100-04-42 W
Pop: 293 (1990); 317 (1980) **Pop Density:** 4.8
Land: 61.4 sq. mi.; **Water:** 0.0 sq. mi.

Wildhorse Township
Lat: 39-20-07 N **Long:** 99-41-33 W
Pop: 305 (1990); 306 (1980) **Pop Density:** 5.7
Land: 53.1 sq. mi.; **Water:** 0.0 sq. mi.

Grant County
County Seat: Ulysses (ZIP: 67880)

Pop: 7,159 (1990); 6,977 (1980) **Pop Density:** 12.5
Land: 574.9 sq. mi.; **Water:** 0.2 sq. mi. **Area Code:** 316
In southwestern KS; organized Mar 6, 1873 from Finney and Kearny counties.
Name origin: For Ulysses Simpson Grant (1822–85), Civil War general and eighteenth U.S. president.

Lincoln — Township
Lat: 37-33-46 N Long: 101-18-33 W
Pop: 6,226 (1990); 5,832 (1980) **Pop Density:** 43.3
Land: 143.8 sq. mi.; **Water:** 0.1 sq. mi.

Sherman — Township
Lat: 37-39-48 N Long: 101-18-30 W
Pop: 534 (1990); 536 (1980) **Pop Density:** 2.5
Land: 215.7 sq. mi.; **Water:** 0.0 sq. mi.

Sullivan — Township
Lat: 37-27-27 N Long: 101-18-09 W
Pop: 399 (1990); 609 (1980) **Pop Density:** 1.9
Land: 215.4 sq. mi.; **Water:** 0.0 sq. mi.

Ulysses — City
ZIP: 67880 Lat: 37-34-44 N Long: 101-21-20 W
Pop: 5,474 (1990); 4,653 (1980) **Pop Density:** 2105.4
Land: 2.6 sq. mi.; **Water:** 0.0 sq. mi. **Elev:** 3057 ft.
Incorporated Jan 24, 1921.
Name origin: The Latin name for the Odysseus, hero of Greek mythology; first name of Ulysses S. Grant, Civil War general and U.S. President, for whom county was named.

Gray County
County Seat: Cimarron (ZIP: 67835)

Pop: 5,396 (1990); 5,138 (1980) **Pop Density:** 6.2
Land: 868.9 sq. mi.; **Water:** 0.4 sq. mi. **Area Code:** 316
In southwestern KS, west of Dodge City; organized Mar 5, 1887 from Finney and Ford counties.
Name origin: For Alfred Gray, teacher, lawyer, and secretary of the KS Board of Agriculture (1873–80).

Cimarron — City
ZIP: 67835 Lat: 37-48-29 N Long: 100-20-44 W
Pop: 1,626 (1990); 1,491 (1980) **Pop Density:** 2032.5
Land: 0.8 sq. mi.; **Water:** 0.0 sq. mi. **Elev:** 2627 ft.
Incorporated 1885.
Name origin: For its location near the Cimarron Crossing of the Santa Fe Trail. From Spanish meaning 'wild.'

*Cimarron — Township
ZIP: 67835 Lat: 37-48-16 N Long: 100-19-47 W
Pop: 2,125 (1990); 1,937 (1980) **Pop Density:** 21.6
Land: 98.3 sq. mi.; **Water:** 0.0 sq. mi.

Copeland — City
ZIP: 67837 Lat: 37-32-24 N Long: 100-37-42 W
Pop: 290 (1990); 323 (1980) **Pop Density:** 966.7
Land: 0.3 sq. mi.; **Water:** 0.0 sq. mi. **Elev:** 2821 ft.
Incorporated Mar 3, 1927. Not coextensive with the town of the same name.
Name origin: For E. L. Copeland, one-time secretary-treasurer of the Santa Fe Railroad.

*Copeland — Township
ZIP: 67837 Lat: 37-35-05 N Long: 100-35-35 W
Pop: 536 (1990); 574 (1980) **Pop Density:** 5.9
Land: 90.1 sq. mi.; **Water:** 0.1 sq. mi.

East Hess — Township
Lat: 37-35-56 N Long: 100-16-37 W
Pop: 373 (1990); 396 (1980) **Pop Density:** 3.4
Land: 108.4 sq. mi.; **Water:** 0.0 sq. mi.

Ensign — City
ZIP: 67841 Lat: 37-39-12 N Long: 100-13-56 W
Pop: 192 (1990); 209 (1980) **Pop Density:** 640.0
Land: 0.3 sq. mi.; **Water:** 0.0 sq. mi. **Elev:** 2719 ft.
Incorporated Apr 1, 1929.
Name origin: For founder G.L. Ensign.

Foote — Township
Lat: 37-55-43 N Long: 100-19-38 W
Pop: 124 (1990); 152 (1980) **Pop Density:** 1.0
Land: 119.7 sq. mi.; **Water:** 0.0 sq. mi.

Ingalls — City
ZIP: 67853 Lat: 37-49-40 N Long: 100-27-08 W
Pop: 301 (1990); 274 (1980) **Pop Density:** 1003.3
Land: 0.3 sq. mi.; **Water:** 0.0 sq. mi. **Elev:** 2680 ft.
Incorporated Apr 1, 1929. Not coextensive with the town of the same name.
Name origin: For KS senator, John J. Ingalls.

*Ingalls — Township
ZIP: 67853 Lat: 37-46-23 N Long: 100-33-04 W
Pop: 611 (1990); 595 (1980) **Pop Density:** 4.5
Land: 134.7 sq. mi.; **Water:** 0.0 sq. mi.

Logan
Township
Lat: 37-55-19 N **Long:** 100-32-45 W
Pop: 196 (1990); 197 (1980) **Pop Density:** 1.6
Land: 119.3 sq. mi.; **Water:** 0.1 sq. mi.

Montezuma
City
ZIP: 67867 **Lat:** 37-35-47 N **Long:** 100-26-30 W
Pop: 838 (1990); 730 (1980) **Pop Density:** 1197.1
Land: 0.7 sq. mi.; **Water:** 0.0 sq. mi. **Elev:** 2785 ft.
Incorporated Jan 25, 1917. Not coextensive with the town of the same name.
Name origin: For Montezuma, an Aztec Indian ruler.

*Montezuma
Township
ZIP: 67867 **Lat:** 37-35-45 N **Long:** 100-26-03 W
Pop: 1,431 (1990); 1,287 (1980) **Pop Density:** 7.2
Land: 198.5 sq. mi.; **Water:** 0.1 sq. mi.

Greeley County
County Seat: Tribune (ZIP: 67879)

Pop: 1,774 (1990); 1,845 (1980) **Pop Density:** 2.3
Land: 778.1 sq. mi.; **Water:** 0.0 sq. mi. **Area Code:** 316
On the central western border of KS; established Mar 6, 1873.
Name origin: For Horace Greeley (1811–72), editor of the *New York Tribune* and champion of westward expansion.

Colony
Township
Lat: 38-28-35 N **Long:** 101-55-40 W
Pop: 203 (1990); 235 (1980) **Pop Density:** 0.6
Land: 354.8 sq. mi.; **Water:** 0.0 sq. mi.

Harrison
Township
Lat: 38-22-17 N **Long:** 101-42-19 W
Pop: 134 (1990); 185 (1980) **Pop Density:** 0.7
Land: 197.1 sq. mi.; **Water:** 0.0 sq. mi.

Horace
City
Lat: 38-28-36 N **Long:** 101-47-25 W
Pop: 168 (1990); 137 (1980) **Pop Density:** 840.0
Land: 0.2 sq. mi.; **Water:** 0.0 sq. mi. **Elev:** 3643 ft.
Incorporated Oct 3, 1887.
Name origin: For the first name of Horace Greeley (1811–72), for whom the county is named.

Tribune
City
ZIP: 67879 **Lat:** 38-28-16 N **Long:** 101-45-14 W
Pop: 918 (1990); 955 (1980) **Pop Density:** 1530.0
Land: 0.6 sq. mi.; **Water:** 0.0 sq. mi. **Elev:** 3616 ft.
Incorporated Feb 8, 1888.
Name origin: For the *New York Tribune*, the newspaper Horace Greeley edited.

*Tribune
Township
ZIP: 67879 **Lat:** 38-34-58 N **Long:** 101-41-28 W
Pop: 1,437 (1990); 1,425 (1980) **Pop Density:** 6.4
Land: 226.1 sq. mi.; **Water:** 0.0 sq. mi.

Greenwood County
County Seat: Eureka (ZIP: 67045)

Pop: 7,847 (1990); 8,764 (1980) **Pop Density:** 6.9
Land: 1139.8 sq. mi.; **Water:** 12.8 sq. mi. **Area Code:** 316
In southeastern KS, east of Wichita; original county; organized Aug 25, 1855 (prior to statehood).
Name origin: For Alfred Burton Greenwood (1811–89), U.S. representative from AR (1853–59).

Bachelor
Township
Lat: 37-50-29 N **Long:** 96-11-34 W
Pop: 236 (1990); 195 (1980) **Pop Density:** 3.9
Land: 59.8 sq. mi.; **Water:** 0.4 sq. mi.

Climax
City
ZIP: 67027 **Lat:** 37-43-09 N **Long:** 96-13-24 W
Pop: 57 (1990); 81 (1980) **Pop Density:** 570.0
Land: 0.1 sq. mi.; **Water:** 0.0 sq. mi. **Elev:** 1040 ft.
Incorporated Dec 3, 1923.

Eureka
City
ZIP: 67045 **Lat:** 37-49-21 N **Long:** 96-17-18 W
Pop: 2,974 (1990); 3,425 (1980) **Pop Density:** 1565.3
Land: 1.9 sq. mi.; **Water:** 0.0 sq. mi. **Elev:** 1084 ft.
Incorporated May 2, 1870. Not coextensive with the town of the same name.
Name origin: From the Greek term meaning 'I have found it.'

*Eureka
Township
ZIP: 67045   Lat: 37-50-05 N   Long: 96-18-38 W
Pop: 481 (1990); 369 (1980)   Pop Density: 8.3
Land: 57.7 sq. mi.; Water: 0.9 sq. mi.

Fall River
City
ZIP: 67047   Lat: 37-36-30 N   Long: 96-01-42 W
Pop: 113 (1990); 173 (1980)   Pop Density: 565.0
Land: 0.2 sq. mi.; Water: 0.0 sq. mi.   Elev: 930 ft.
Incorporated Nov 1879.

Name origin: For the river, on whose banks the town is located.

*Fall River
Township
ZIP: 67047   Lat: 37-43-23 N   Long: 96-11-50 W
Pop: 214 (1990); 239 (1980)   Pop Density: 3.6
Land: 59.6 sq. mi.; Water: 0.7 sq. mi.

Hamilton
City
ZIP: 66853   Lat: 37-58-52 N   Long: 96-09-49 W
Pop: 301 (1990); 363 (1980)   Pop Density: 1003.3
Land: 0.3 sq. mi.; Water: 0.0 sq. mi.   Elev: 1098 ft.
Incorporated Oct 9, 1903.

Name origin: For Alexander Hamilton (1757–1804), first U.S. secretary of the treasury.

Janesville
Township
Lat: 37-59-14 N   Long: 96-11-48 W
Pop: 600 (1990); 665 (1980)   Pop Density: 4.2
Land: 143.2 sq. mi.; Water: 0.9 sq. mi.

Lane
Township
Lat: 37-58-37 N   Long: 96-00-42 W
Pop: 153 (1990); 238 (1980)   Pop Density: 2.9
Land: 53.4 sq. mi.; Water: 0.3 sq. mi.

Madison
City
ZIP: 66860   Lat: 38-07-58 N   Long: 96-08-13 W
Pop: 845 (1990); 1,099 (1980)   Pop Density: 1408.3
Land: 0.6 sq. mi.; Water: 0.0 sq. mi.   Elev: 1100 ft.
Incorporated Feb 16, 1885. Not coextensive with the town of the same name.

Name origin: For James Madison (1751–1836), fourth U.S. president.

*Madison
Township
ZIP: 66860   Lat: 38-06-54 N   Long: 96-12-44 W
Pop: 1,222 (1990); 1,431 (1980)   Pop Density: 9.9
Land: 123.6 sq. mi.; Water: 1.1 sq. mi.

Otter Creek
Township
Lat: 37-41-00 N   Long: 96-24-47 W
Pop: 184 (1990); 238 (1980)   Pop Density: 1.6
Land: 112.2 sq. mi.; Water: 0.6 sq. mi.

Pleasant Grove
Township
Lat: 37-46-10 N   Long: 96-02-37 W
Pop: 51 (1990); 66 (1980)   Pop Density: 0.9
Land: 58.1 sq. mi.; Water: 0.9 sq. mi.

Quincy
Township
Lat: 37-52-00 N   Long: 96-02-57 W
Pop: 177 (1990); 195 (1980)   Pop Density: 3.0
Land: 60.0 sq. mi.; Water: 0.2 sq. mi.

Salem
Township
Lat: 38-00-57 N   Long: 96-25-39 W
Pop: 29 (1990); 48 (1980)   Pop Density: 0.3
Land: 89.9 sq. mi.; Water: 0.8 sq. mi.

Salt Springs
Township
Lat: 37-39-55 N   Long: 96-02-22 W
Pop: 395 (1990); 388 (1980)   Pop Density: 5.6
Land: 70.4 sq. mi.; Water: 3.8 sq. mi.

Severy
City
ZIP: 67137   Lat: 37-37-17 N   Long: 96-13-38 W
Pop: 357 (1990); 447 (1980)   Pop Density: 714.0
Land: 0.5 sq. mi.; Water: 0.0 sq. mi.   Elev: 1120 ft.
Incorporated 1883.

Name origin: For a director of the Santa Fe Railroad.

Shell Rock
Township
Lat: 38-06-04 N   Long: 96-01-00 W
Pop: 208 (1990); 238 (1980)   Pop Density: 4.0
Land: 52.6 sq. mi.; Water: 0.5 sq. mi.

South Salem
Township
Lat: 37-53-42 N   Long: 96-25-44 W
Pop: 129 (1990); 137 (1980)   Pop Density: 1.5
Land: 86.6 sq. mi.; Water: 1.0 sq. mi.

Spring Creek
Township
Lat: 37-47-25 N   Long: 96-26-19 W
Pop: 137 (1990); 122 (1980)   Pop Density: 2.5
Land: 53.8 sq. mi.; Water: 0.5 sq. mi.

Twin Grove
Township
Lat: 37-38-14 N   Long: 96-13-46 W
Pop: 657 (1990); 770 (1980)   Pop Density: 11.5
Land: 57.1 sq. mi.; Water: 0.3 sq. mi.

Virgil
City
ZIP: 66870   Lat: 37-58-50 N   Long: 96-00-38 W
Pop: 91 (1990); 169 (1980)   Pop Density: 151.7
Land: 0.6 sq. mi.; Water: 0.0 sq. mi.   Elev: 1000 ft.
Incorporated Feb 6, 1922.

Name origin: For the Roman poet (70–19 B.C.).

Hamilton County
County Seat: Syracuse (ZIP: 67878)

Pop: 2,388 (1990); 2,514 (1980)   **Pop Density:** 2.4
Land: 996.5 sq. mi.; **Water:** 1.1 sq. mi.   **Area Code:** 316
On the western border of KS, west of Garden City; organized Mar 20, 1873 from unorganized territory.
Name origin: For Alexander Hamilton (1757–1804), first U.S. secretary of the treasury (1789–95).

Bear Creek   Township
Lat: 37-49-17 N   Long: 101-54-40 W
Pop: 60 (1990); 81 (1980)   **Pop Density:** 0.3
Land: 174.4 sq. mi.; **Water:** 0.3 sq. mi.

Coolidge   City
ZIP: 67836   Lat: 38-02-27 N   Long: 102-00-26 W
Pop: 90 (1990); 82 (1980)   **Pop Density:** 180.0
Land: 0.5 sq. mi.; **Water:** 0.0 sq. mi.   **Elev:** 3355 ft.
Incorporated Mar 3, 1886. Not coextensive with the town of the same name.
Name origin: For Santa Fe Railroad president T. J. Coolidge.

*Coolidge   Township
Lat: 38-02-45 N   Long: 101-58-54 W
Pop: 144 (1990); 182 (1980)   **Pop Density:** 1.3
Land: 114.8 sq. mi.; **Water:** 0.4 sq. mi.

Kendall   Township
ZIP: 67857   Lat: 38-02-00 N   Long: 101-35-33 W
Pop: 86 (1990); 103 (1980)   **Pop Density:** 1.0
Land: 90.4 sq. mi.; **Water:** 0.0 sq. mi.

Lamont   Township
Lat: 37-49-06 N   Long: 101-39-45 W
Pop: 91 (1990); 108 (1980)   **Pop Density:** 0.6
Land: 164.4 sq. mi.; **Water:** 0.0 sq. mi.

Liberty   Township
Lat: 38-06-36 N   Long: 101-43-10 W
Pop: 30 (1990); 32 (1980)   **Pop Density:** 0.3
Land: 99.1 sq. mi.; **Water:** 0.0 sq. mi.

Medway   Township
Lat: 38-01-34 N   Long: 101-51-44 W
Pop: 38 (1990); 39 (1980)   **Pop Density:** 0.4
Land: 107.9 sq. mi.; **Water:** 0.3 sq. mi.

Richland   Township
Lat: 38-13-34 N   Long: 101-47-21 W
Pop: 28 (1990); 40 (1980)   **Pop Density:** 0.2
Land: 164.4 sq. mi.; **Water:** 0.0 sq. mi.

Syracuse   City
ZIP: 67878   Lat: 37-58-52 N   Long: 101-45-05 W
Pop: 1,606 (1990); 1,654 (1980)   **Pop Density:** 1338.3
Land: 1.2 sq. mi.; **Water:** 0.0 sq. mi.   **Elev:** 3233 ft.
Incorporated Jan 25, 1887.
Name origin: For the ancient Greek city.

*Syracuse   Township
ZIP: 67878   Lat: 37-58-46 N   Long: 101-43-49 W
Pop: 1,911 (1990); 1,929 (1980)   **Pop Density:** 23.6
Land: 81.1 sq. mi.; **Water:** 0.0 sq. mi.

Harper County
County Seat: Anthony (ZIP: 67003)

Pop: 7,124 (1990); 7,778 (1980)   **Pop Density:** 8.9
Land: 801.5 sq. mi.; **Water:** 1.5 sq. mi.   **Area Code:** 316
On the central southern border of KS, southwest of Wichita; established Feb 26, 1867 from Kingman County.
Name origin: For Sgt. Marion Harper (?–1863), soldier in the Kansas cavalry killed in the Civil War.

Anthony   City
ZIP: 67003   Lat: 37-09-13 N   Long: 98-01-44 W
Pop: 2,516 (1990); 2,661 (1980)   **Pop Density:** 1677.3
Land: 1.5 sq. mi.; **Water:** 0.0 sq. mi.   **Elev:** 1350 ft.
In southern KS, southwest of Wichita. Incorporated 1879.
Name origin: For Gov. George Tobey Anthony because he located the county seat here.

Attica   City
ZIP: 67009   Lat: 37-14-32 N   Long: 98-13-33 W
Pop: 716 (1990); 730 (1980)   **Pop Density:** 1193.3
Land: 0.6 sq. mi.; **Water:** 0.0 sq. mi.   **Elev:** 1453 ft.
Incorporated Feb 16, 1885.
Name origin: For an ancient Greek province, with connotations of 'great culture.'

Bluff City   City
ZIP: 67018   Lat: 37-04-32 N   Long: 97-52-30 W
Pop: 69 (1990); 95 (1980)   **Pop Density:** 138.0
Land: 0.5 sq. mi.; **Water:** 0.0 sq. mi.   **Elev:** 1240 ft.
Incorporated Aug 1, 1887.

Danville
City
ZIP: 67036 **Lat:** 37-17-08 N **Long:** 97-53-27 W
Pop: 56 (1990); 71 (1980) **Pop Density:** 560.0
Land: 0.1 sq. mi.; **Water:** 0.0 sq. mi. **Elev:** 1346 ft.
Incorporated Nov. 1927.

Freeport
City
ZIP: 67049 **Lat:** 37-11-55 N **Long:** 97-51-14 W
Pop: 8 (1990); 12 (1980) **Pop Density:** 40.0
Land: 0.2 sq. mi.; **Water:** 0.0 sq. mi. **Elev:** 1333 ft.
Incorporated Aug 12, 1887.

Harper
City
ZIP: 67058 **Lat:** 37-17-06 N **Long:** 98-01-34 W
Pop: 1,735 (1990); 1,823 (1980) **Pop Density:** 1334.6
Land: 1.3 sq. mi.; **Water:** 0.0 sq. mi. **Elev:** 1421 ft.
Incorporated Jun 1880.
Name origin: For Sgt. Marion Harper (?–1863), killed in the Civil War.

Township No. 1
Township
Lat: 37-16-32 N **Long:** 98-14-06 W
Pop: 1,125 (1990); 1,206 (1980) **Pop Density:** 6.2
Land: 180.8 sq. mi.; **Water:** 0.2 sq. mi.

Township No. 2
Township
Lat: 37-04-22 N **Long:** 98-14-20 W
Pop: 189 (1990); 270 (1980) **Pop Density:** 1.3
Land: 140.3 sq. mi.; **Water:** 0.3 sq. mi.

Township No. 3
Township
Lat: 37-06-42 N **Long:** 98-02-13 W
Pop: 414 (1990); 554 (1980) **Pop Density:** 2.8
Land: 147.8 sq. mi.; **Water:** 0.7 sq. mi.

Township No. 4
Township
Lat: 37-05-49 N **Long:** 97-52-23 W
Pop: 268 (1990); 318 (1980) **Pop Density:** 2.3
Land: 114.7 sq. mi.; **Water:** 0.1 sq. mi.

Township No. 5
Township
Lat: 37-14-49 N **Long:** 97-57-26 W
Pop: 499 (1990); 551 (1980) **Pop Density:** 4.7
Land: 106.9 sq. mi.; **Water:** 0.2 sq. mi.

Township No. 6
Township
Lat: 37-20-27 N **Long:** 97-57-50 W
Pop: 378 (1990); 395 (1980) **Pop Density:** 3.5
Land: 108.2 sq. mi.; **Water:** 0.1 sq. mi.

Waldron
City
ZIP: 67150 **Lat:** 37-00-02 N **Long:** 98-10-58 W
Pop: 19 (1990); 29 (1980) **Pop Density:** 63.3
Land: 0.3 sq. mi.; **Water:** 0.0 sq. mi. **Elev:** 1246 ft.
Incorporated Sep 1908.

Harvey County
County Seat: Newton (ZIP: 67114)

Pop: 31,028 (1990); 30,531 (1980) **Pop Density:** 57.5
Land: 539.4 sq. mi.; **Water:** 1.1 sq. mi. **Area Code:** 316
In central KS, east of Hutchinson; organized Feb 29, 1872 from McPherson, Butler, and Sedgwick counties.
Name origin: For Capt. James Madison Harvey (1833–94), governor of KS (1869–73) and U.S. senator (1874–77).

Alta
Township
Lat: 38-07-40 N **Long:** 97-38-42 W
Pop: 243 (1990); 242 (1980) **Pop Density:** 6.8
Land: 35.9 sq. mi.; **Water:** 0.2 sq. mi.

Burrton
City
ZIP: 67020 **Lat:** 38-01-21 N **Long:** 97-40-19 W
Pop: 866 (1990); 976 (1980) **Pop Density:** 1443.3
Land: 0.6 sq. mi.; **Water:** 0.0 sq. mi. **Elev:** 1453 ft.
Incorporated Sep 2, 1878. Not coextensive with the town of the same name.
Name origin: For I.T. Burr, vice president of the Atchison, Topeka, and Santa Fe Railroad.

*Burrton
Township
ZIP: 67020 **Lat:** 38-02-26 N **Long:** 97-39-22 W
Pop: 1,149 (1990); 1,211 (1980) **Pop Density:** 31.9
Land: 36.0 sq. mi.; **Water:** 0.0 sq. mi.

Darlington
Township
Lat: 37-57-26 N **Long:** 97-19-08 W
Pop: 471 (1990); 527 (1980) **Pop Density:** 13.2
Land: 35.6 sq. mi.; **Water:** 0.0 sq. mi.

Emma
Township
Lat: 38-07-49 N **Long:** 97-25-33 W
Pop: 3,612 (1990); 3,618 (1980) **Pop Density:** 100.1
Land: 36.1 sq. mi.; **Water:** 0.0 sq. mi.

Garden
Township
Lat: 38-07-43 N **Long:** 97-32-12 W
Pop: 301 (1990); 296 (1980) **Pop Density:** 8.3
Land: 36.1 sq. mi.; **Water:** 0.0 sq. mi.

Halstead
City
ZIP: 67056 **Lat:** 38-00-03 N **Long:** 97-30-33 W
Pop: 2,015 (1990); 1,994 (1980) **Pop Density:** 1831.8
Land: 1.1 sq. mi.; **Water:** 0.0 sq. mi. **Elev:** 1400 ft.
Incorporated Mar 12, 1877.
Name origin: For Civil War newspaper correspondent Murat Halstead.

*Halstead
Township
ZIP: 67056 **Lat:** 38-02-33 N **Long:** 97-32-16 W
Pop: 390 (1990); 378 (1980) **Pop Density:** 11.0
Land: 35.5 sq. mi.; **Water:** 0.0 sq. mi.

Hesston
City
ZIP: 67062 **Lat:** 38-08-23 N **Long:** 97-25-39 W
Pop: 3,012 (1990); 3,013 (1980) **Pop Density:** 1255.0
Land: 2.4 sq. mi.; **Water:** 0.0 sq. mi. **Elev:** 1476 ft.
Incorporated May 12, 1921.
Name origin: For founder Abraham Hess.

Highland
Township
Lat: 38-07-55 N **Long:** 97-19-06 W
Pop: 408 (1990); 386 (1980) **Pop Density:** 11.5
Land: 35.4 sq. mi.; **Water:** 0.1 sq. mi.

Lake
Township
Lat: 37-57-32 N **Long:** 97-39-05 W
Pop: 191 (1990); 219 (1980) **Pop Density:** 5.4
Land: 35.7 sq. mi.; **Water:** 0.4 sq. mi.

Lakin
Township
Lat: 37-57-18 N **Long:** 97-32-18 W
Pop: 327 (1990); 346 (1980) **Pop Density:** 9.2
Land: 35.6 sq. mi.; **Water:** 0.0 sq. mi.

Macon
Township
Lat: 38-02-40 N **Long:** 97-25-29 W
Pop: 819 (1990); 632 (1980) **Pop Density:** 22.8
Land: 35.9 sq. mi.; **Water:** 0.0 sq. mi.

Newton
City
ZIP: 67114 **Lat:** 38-02-39 N **Long:** 97-20-30 W
Pop: 16,700 (1990); 16,332 (1980) **Pop Density:** 2113.9
Land: 7.9 sq. mi.; **Water:** 0.0 sq. mi. **Elev:** 1448 ft.
In southeast-central KS, 35 mi. east of Hutchinson. Incorporated Feb 22, 1872.
Name origin: For Newton, MA.

*Newton
Township
ZIP: 67114 **Lat:** 38-02-33 N **Long:** 97-18-30 W
Pop: 1,694 (1990); 1,708 (1980) **Pop Density:** 61.4
Land: 27.6 sq. mi.; **Water:** 0.0 sq. mi.

North Newton
City
ZIP: 67117 **Lat:** 38-04-25 N **Long:** 97-20-45 W
Pop: 1,262 (1990); 1,222 (1980) **Pop Density:** 2103.3
Land: 0.6 sq. mi.; **Water:** 0.0 sq. mi. **Elev:** 1440 ft.
Incorporated Sep 20, 1938.

Pleasant
Township
Lat: 38-02-48 N **Long:** 97-12-17 W
Pop: 389 (1990); 323 (1980) **Pop Density:** 10.8
Land: 36.1 sq. mi.; **Water:** 0.3 sq. mi.

Richland
Township
Lat: 37-57-39 N **Long:** 97-12-00 W
Pop: 200 (1990); 211 (1980) **Pop Density:** 5.5
Land: 36.3 sq. mi.; **Water:** 0.1 sq. mi.

Sedgwick
City
ZIP: 67135 **Lat:** 37-55-03 N **Long:** 97-25-34 W
Pop: 1,306 (1990); 1,343 (1980) **Pop Density:** 1632.5
Land: 0.8 sq. mi.; **Water:** 0.0 sq. mi.
Incorporated 1872. Part of the town is also in Sedgwick County.
Name origin: For Civil War hero, Gen. John Sedgwick (1813–64).

*Sedgwick
Township
ZIP: 67135 **Lat:** 37-57-38 N **Long:** 97-25-51 W
Pop: 1,701 (1990); 1,682 (1980) **Pop Density:** 47.1
Land: 36.1 sq. mi.; **Water:** 0.0 sq. mi. **Elev:** 1379 ft.

Walton
City
ZIP: 67151 **Lat:** 38-07-05 N **Long:** 97-15-21 W
Pop: 226 (1990); 269 (1980) **Pop Density:** 1130.0
Land: 0.2 sq. mi.; **Water:** 0.0 sq. mi. **Elev:** 1537 ft.
Incorporated Apr 12, 1886. Not coextensive with the town of the same name.
Name origin: For a Santa Fe Railroad stockholder.

*Walton
Township
ZIP: 67151 **Lat:** 38-07-59 N **Long:** 97-12-49 W
Pop: 418 (1990); 426 (1980) **Pop Density:** 11.4
Land: 36.7 sq. mi.; **Water:** 0.0 sq. mi.

Haskell County
County Seat: Sublette (ZIP: 67877)

Pop: 3,886 (1990); 3,814 (1980) **Pop Density:** 6.7
Land: 577.4 sq. mi.; **Water:** 0.4 sq. mi. **Area Code:** 316
In southwestern KS; organized Mar 23, 1887 from Finney County.
Name origin: For Dudley Chase Haskell (1842–83), KS legislator and U.S. representative (1877–83).

Dudley
Township
Lat: 37-33-30 N **Long:** 101-00-44 W
Pop: 1,522 (1990); 1,541 (1980) **Pop Density:** 7.9
Land: 192.7 sq. mi.; **Water:** 0.1 sq. mi.

Haskell
Township
Lat: 37-33-51 N **Long:** 100-52-17 W
Pop: 1,825 (1990); 1,721 (1980) **Pop Density:** 9.5
Land: 192.4 sq. mi.; **Water:** 0.1 sq. mi.

Lockport
Township
Lat: 37-33-40 N **Long:** 100-43-35 W
Pop: 539 (1990); 552 (1980) **Pop Density:** 2.8
Land: 192.3 sq. mi.; **Water:** 0.2 sq. mi.

Satanta
City
ZIP: 67870 **Lat:** 37-26-09 N **Long:** 100-59-16 W
Pop: 1,073 (1990); 1,117 (1980) **Pop Density:** 2146.0
Land: 0.5 sq. mi.; **Water:** 0.0 sq. mi. **Elev:** 2956 ft.
Incorporated Jun 6, 1929.
Name origin: For a Kiowa Indian chief whose name means 'white bear.'

Sublette
City
ZIP: 67877 **Lat:** 37-28-46 N **Long:** 100-50-47 W
Pop: 1,378 (1990); 1,293 (1980) **Pop Density:** 1722.5
Land: 0.8 sq. mi.; **Water:** 0.0 sq. mi. **Elev:** 2918 ft.
Incorporated Apr 2, 1923.
Name origin: For pioneer William L. Sublette.

Hodgeman County
County Seat: Jetmore (ZIP: 67854)

Pop: 2,177 (1990); 2,269 (1980) **Pop Density:** 2.5
Land: 860.0 sq. mi.; **Water:** 0.3 sq. mi. **Area Code:** 316

In southwest-central KS, north of Dodge City; organized Mar 6, 1873 from Indian lands.

Name origin: For Capt. Amos Hodgman (?–1863), Civil War officer. The *e* was mistakenly inserted when the county was named.

Benton — Township
Lat: 38-02-39 N **Long:** 100-10-16 W
Pop: 42 (1990); 47 (1980) **Pop Density:** 1.2
Land: 35.8 sq. mi.; **Water:** 0.0 sq. mi.

Center — Township
Lat: 38-05-14 N **Long:** 99-53-57 W
Pop: 1,053 (1990); 1,098 (1980) **Pop Density:** 7.3
Land: 144.3 sq. mi.; **Water:** 0.1 sq. mi.

Hallet — Township
Lat: 38-04-59 N **Long:** 100-03-35 W
Pop: 41 (1990); 69 (1980) **Pop Density:** 0.6
Land: 70.3 sq. mi.; **Water:** 0.0 sq. mi.

Hanston — City
ZIP: 67849 **Lat:** 38-07-22 N **Long:** 99-42-43 W
Pop: 326 (1990); 257 (1980) **Pop Density:** 1086.7
Land: 0.3 sq. mi.; **Water:** 0.0 sq. mi. **Elev:** 2160 ft.
Incorporated Aug 21, 1929.
Name origin: For townsite owner Benjamin Hann.

Jetmore — City
ZIP: 67854 **Lat:** 38-04-59 N **Long:** 99-53-34 W
Pop: 850 (1990); 862 (1980) **Pop Density:** 850.0
Land: 1.0 sq. mi.; **Water:** 0.0 sq. mi. **Elev:** 2307 ft.
Incorporated Apr 16, 1887.
Name origin: For Col. Abraham Jetmore, a director of the Kansas Freedman's Relief Association.

Marena — Township
Lat: 38-10-26 N **Long:** 99-40-43 W
Pop: 542 (1990); 500 (1980) **Pop Density:** 3.8
Land: 144.1 sq. mi.; **Water:** 0.1 sq. mi.

North Roscoe — Township
Lat: 38-11-08 N **Long:** 100-07-57 W
Pop: 73 (1990); 76 (1980) **Pop Density:** 0.7
Land: 106.4 sq. mi.; **Water:** 0.1 sq. mi.

Sawlog — Township
Lat: 37-57-05 N **Long:** 99-53-45 W
Pop: 100 (1990); 124 (1980) **Pop Density:** 1.4
Land: 72.1 sq. mi.; **Water:** 0.0 sq. mi.

South Roscoe — Township
Lat: 37-57-51 N **Long:** 100-07-19 W
Pop: 107 (1990); 99 (1980) **Pop Density:** 1.5
Land: 71.3 sq. mi.; **Water:** 0.0 sq. mi.

Sterling — Township
Lat: 38-00-13 N **Long:** 99-41-01 W
Pop: 153 (1990); 163 (1980) **Pop Density:** 1.1
Land: 144.2 sq. mi.; **Water:** 0.0 sq. mi.

Valley — Township
Lat: 38-13-09 N **Long:** 99-54-01 W
Pop: 66 (1990); 93 (1980) **Pop Density:** 0.9
Land: 71.4 sq. mi.; **Water:** 0.0 sq. mi.

Jackson County
County Seat: Holton (ZIP: 66436)

Pop: 11,525 (1990); 11,644 (1980) **Pop Density:** 17.5
Land: 656.9 sq. mi.; **Water:** 1.0 sq. mi. **Area Code:** 913

In northeastern KS, north of Topeka; organized as Calhoun County Aug 30, 1855 (prior to statehood); name changed Feb 11, 1859.

Name origin: For Andrew Jackson (1767–1845), seventh U.S. president. Originally for John C. Calhoun (1782–1850), U.S. senator from SC.

Adrian — Township
Lat: 39-20-51 N **Long:** 95-59-45 W
Pop: 114 (1990); 125 (1980) **Pop Density:** 3.8
Land: 29.8 sq. mi.; **Water:** 0.1 sq. mi.

Banner — Township
Lat: 39-26-04 N **Long:** 95-50-24 W
Pop: 312 (1990); 329 (1980) **Pop Density:** 8.7
Land: 36.0 sq. mi.; **Water:** 0.1 sq. mi.

Cedar — Township
Lat: 39-21-23 N **Long:** 95-39-34 W
Pop: 1,132 (1990); 1,164 (1980) **Pop Density:** 28.4
Land: 39.9 sq. mi.; **Water:** 0.0 sq. mi.

Circleville — City
ZIP: 66416 **Lat:** 39-30-32 N **Long:** 95-51-19 W
Pop: 153 (1990); 164 (1980) **Pop Density:** 765.0
Land: 0.2 sq. mi.; **Water:** 0.0 sq. mi. **Elev:** 1103 ft.
Incorporated 1901.
Name origin: For Circleville, OH.

Delia
City
ZIP: 66418 **Lat:** 39-14-21 N **Long:** 95-57-51 W
Pop: 172 (1990); 181 (1980) **Pop Density:** 1720.0
Land: 0.1 sq. mi.; **Water:** 0.0 sq. mi. **Elev:** 975 ft.
Incorporated Nov 4, 1918.
Name origin: For pioneer Delia Cunningham.

Denison
City
ZIP: 66419 **Lat:** 39-23-35 N **Long:** 95-37-41 W
Pop: 225 (1990); 231 (1980) **Pop Density:** 2250.0
Land: 0.1 sq. mi.; **Water:** 0.0 sq. mi. **Elev:** 1050 ft.
Incorporated Jan 11, 1904.
Name origin: For Denison, OH.

Douglas
Township
Lat: 39-15-29 N **Long:** 95-40-45 W
Pop: 1,812 (1990); 1,711 (1980) **Pop Density:** 28.0
Land: 64.8 sq. mi.; **Water:** 0.0 sq. mi.

Franklin
Township
Lat: 39-26-03 N **Long:** 95-44-14 W
Pop: 634 (1990); 600 (1980) **Pop Density:** 19.0
Land: 33.4 sq. mi.; **Water:** 0.1 sq. mi.

Garfield
Township
Lat: 39-26-07 N **Long:** 95-37-46 W
Pop: 604 (1990); 600 (1980) **Pop Density:** 17.9
Land: 33.8 sq. mi.; **Water:** 0.2 sq. mi.

Grant
Township
Lat: 39-26-17 N **Long:** 95-58-01 W
Pop: 183 (1990); 211 (1980) **Pop Density:** 4.4
Land: 42.0 sq. mi.; **Water:** 0.0 sq. mi.

Holton
City
ZIP: 66436 **Lat:** 39-28-13 N **Long:** 95-43-50 W
Pop: 3,196 (1990); 3,132 (1980) **Pop Density:** 1389.6
Land: 2.3 sq. mi.; **Water:** 0.1 sq. mi. **Elev:** 1095 ft.
Incorporated Jul 30, 1870.
Name origin: For banker Edward Holton.

Hoyt
City
ZIP: 66440 **Lat:** 39-14-58 N **Long:** 95-42-23 W
Pop: 489 (1990); 536 (1980) **Pop Density:** 1222.5
Land: 0.4 sq. mi.; **Water:** 0.0 sq. mi. **Elev:** 1150 ft.
Incorporated Apr 1909.
Name origin: For lawyer George Hoyt, who defended John Brown (1800–59) against treason.

Jefferson
Township
Lat: 39-31-18 N **Long:** 95-50-58 W
Pop: 466 (1990); 517 (1980) **Pop Density:** 12.8
Land: 36.4 sq. mi.; **Water:** 0.0 sq. mi.

Liberty
Township
Lat: 39-31-29 N **Long:** 95-44-29 W
Pop: 410 (1990); 416 (1980) **Pop Density:** 11.5
Land: 35.5 sq. mi.; **Water:** 0.1 sq. mi.

Lincoln
Township
Lat: 39-19-40 N **Long:** 95-50-25 W
Pop: 892 (1990); 756 (1980) **Pop Density:** 9.1
Land: 98.3 sq. mi.; **Water:** 0.0 sq. mi.

Mayetta
City
ZIP: 66509 **Lat:** 39-20-19 N **Long:** 95-43-17 W
Pop: 267 (1990); 287 (1980) **Pop Density:** 2670.0
Land: 0.1 sq. mi.; **Water:** 0.0 sq. mi. **Elev:** 1200 ft.
Incorporated Oct 1902.

Netawaka
City
ZIP: 66516 **Lat:** 39-36-11 N **Long:** 95-43-06 W
Pop: 167 (1990); 218 (1980) **Pop Density:** 167.0
Land: 1.0 sq. mi.; **Water:** 0.0 sq. mi. **Elev:** 1150 ft.
Incorporated Jul 1, 1884. Not coextensive with the town of the same name.
Name origin: From a Potawatomi term meaning 'grand view.'

*Netawaka
Township
ZIP: 66516 **Lat:** 39-36-25 N **Long:** 95-44-03 W
Pop: 371 (1990); 474 (1980) **Pop Density:** 10.3
Land: 36.0 sq. mi.; **Water:** 0.0 sq. mi.

Soldier
City
ZIP: 66540 **Lat:** 39-32-16 N **Long:** 95-57-52 W
Pop: 135 (1990); 165 (1980) **Pop Density:** 675.0
Land: 0.2 sq. mi.; **Water:** 0.0 sq. mi. **Elev:** 1225 ft.
Incorporated Apr 13, 1869.
Name origin: For the township, itself named for Big Soldier Creek, so named by the Indians for all the U.S. soldiers who traversed the areas.

*Soldier
Township
ZIP: 66540 **Lat:** 39-31-22 N **Long:** 95-58-25 W
Pop: 395 (1990); 493 (1980) **Pop Density:** 9.3
Land: 42.6 sq. mi.; **Water:** 0.1 sq. mi.

Straight Creek
Township
Lat: 39-31-24 N **Long:** 95-37-40 W
Pop: 181 (1990); 193 (1980) **Pop Density:** 4.9
Land: 36.6 sq. mi.; **Water:** 0.1 sq. mi.

Washington
Township
Lat: 39-15-05 N **Long:** 95-56-16 W
Pop: 443 (1990); 453 (1980) **Pop Density:** 8.3
Land: 53.6 sq. mi.; **Water:** 0.1 sq. mi.

Whiting
City
ZIP: 66552 **Lat:** 39-35-19 N **Long:** 95-36-41 W
Pop: 213 (1990); 270 (1980) **Pop Density:** 213.0
Land: 1.0 sq. mi.; **Water:** 0.0 sq. mi. **Elev:** 1113 ft.
Incorporated Apr 27, 1888. Not coextensive with the town of the same name.
Name origin: For the maiden name of KS Sen. Promeroy's wife.

*Whiting
Township
ZIP: 66552 **Lat:** 39-36-29 N **Long:** 95-36-56 W
Pop: 380 (1990); 470 (1980) **Pop Density:** 10.6
Land: 36.0 sq. mi.; **Water:** 0.0 sq. mi.

Jefferson County
County Seat: Oskaloosa (ZIP: 66066)

Pop: 15,905 (1990); 15,207 (1980) **Pop Density:** 29.7
Land: 536.2 sq. mi.; **Water:** 20.8 sq. mi. **Area Code:** 913
In northeastern KS, east of Topeka; original county; organized Aug 25, 1855 (prior to statehood).

Name origin: For Thomas Jefferson (1743–1826), U.S. patriot and statesman; third U.S. president.

Delaware — Township
Lat: 39-21-07 N Long: 95-29-02 W
Pop: 2,000 (1990); 1,981 (1980) **Pop Density:** 22.6
Land: 88.5 sq. mi.; **Water:** 0.1 sq. mi.

Fairview — Township
Lat: 39-10-41 N Long: 95-25-45 W
Pop: 995 (1990); 669 (1980) **Pop Density:** 36.7
Land: 27.1 sq. mi.; **Water:** 7.7 sq. mi.

Jefferson No. 10 — Township
Lat: 39-19-52 N Long: 95-15-58 W
Pop: 1,191 (1990); 1,241 (1980) **Pop Density:** 20.5
Land: 58.1 sq. mi.; **Water:** 0.1 sq. mi.

Kaw — Township
Lat: 39-05-41 N Long: 95-32-01 W
Pop: 1,356 (1990); 1,301 (1980) **Pop Density:** 41.1
Land: 33.0 sq. mi.; **Water:** 0.6 sq. mi.

Kentucky — Township
Lat: 39-05-57 N Long: 95-25-07 W
Pop: 1,443 (1990); 1,453 (1980) **Pop Density:** 40.0
Land: 36.1 sq. mi.; **Water:** 5.5 sq. mi.

McLouth — City
Lat: 39-11-43 N Long: 95-12-30 W
Pop: 719 (1990); 700 (1980) **Pop Density:** 1438.0
Land: 0.5 sq. mi.; **Water:** 0.0 sq. mi. **Elev:** 1180 ft.

Meriden — City
ZIP: 66512 Lat: 39-11-24 N Long: 95-33-58 W
Pop: 622 (1990); 707 (1980) **Pop Density:** 1555.0
Land: 0.4 sq. mi.; **Water:** 0.0 sq. mi. **Elev:** 970 ft.
Incorporated Aug 15, 1891.

Name origin: For Meriden, NH, the former home of pioneer Newell Colby.

Norton — Township
Lat: 39-23-30 N Long: 95-18-32 W
Pop: 934 (1990); 1,016 (1980) **Pop Density:** 24.0
Land: 38.9 sq. mi.; **Water:** 0.1 sq. mi.

Nortonville — City
ZIP: 66060 Lat: 39-24-57 N Long: 95-19-52 W
Pop: 643 (1990); 692 (1980) **Pop Density:** 1607.5
Land: 0.4 sq. mi.; **Water:** 0.0 sq. mi. **Elev:** 1163 ft.
Incorporated Jul 12, 1884.

Name origin: For T.L. Norton, Jr., roadmaster for the Santa Fe Railroad.

Oskaloosa — City
ZIP: 66066 Lat: 39-12-57 N Long: 95-18-48 W
Pop: 1,074 (1990); 1,092 (1980) **Pop Density:** 1193.3
Land: 0.9 sq. mi.; **Water:** 0.0 sq. mi. **Elev:** 1123 ft.
Incorporated Aug 27, 1869. Not coextensive with the town of the same name.

Name origin: From a Creek or Seminole Indian term meaning 'black water.'

*Oskaloosa — Township
ZIP: 66066 Lat: 39-13-00 N Long: 95-18-43 W
Pop: 1,832 (1990); 1,776 (1980) **Pop Density:** 31.9
Land: 57.5 sq. mi.; **Water:** 0.1 sq. mi.

Ozawkie — City
ZIP: 66070 Lat: 39-14-09 N Long: 95-28-02 W
Pop: 403 (1990); 472 (1980) **Pop Density:** 1343.3
Land: 0.3 sq. mi.; **Water:** 0.0 sq. mi. **Elev:** 1000 ft.
Incorporated Sep 15, 1967. Not coextensive with the town of the same name.

Name origin: For Sac Indian Chief Ozawkie, whose name means 'yellow earth.'

*Ozawkie — Township
ZIP: 66070 Lat: 39-15-23 N Long: 95-25-48 W
Pop: 1,128 (1990); 950 (1980) **Pop Density:** 30.2
Land: 37.3 sq. mi.; **Water:** 5.4 sq. mi.

Perry — City
ZIP: 66073 Lat: 39-04-23 N Long: 95-23-14 W
Pop: 881 (1990); 907 (1980) **Pop Density:** 1101.3
Land: 0.8 sq. mi.; **Water:** 0.0 sq. mi. **Elev:** 850 ft.
Incorporated Mar 3, 1871.

Rock Creek — Township
Lat: 39-13-32 N Long: 95-32-35 W
Pop: 2,299 (1990); 2,234 (1980) **Pop Density:** 42.4
Land: 54.2 sq. mi.; **Water:** 0.5 sq. mi.

Rural — Township
Lat: 39-05-49 N Long: 95-18-36 W
Pop: 588 (1990); 588 (1980) **Pop Density:** 18.5
Land: 31.8 sq. mi.; **Water:** 0.4 sq. mi.

Sarcoxie — Township
Lat: 39-05-46 N Long: 95-13-45 W
Pop: 755 (1990); 644 (1980) **Pop Density:** 24.4
Land: 30.9 sq. mi.; **Water:** 0.1 sq. mi.

Union — Township
Lat: 39-12-59 N Long: 95-13-27 W
Pop: 1,384 (1990); 1,354 (1980) **Pop Density:** 32.4
Land: 42.7 sq. mi.; **Water:** 0.1 sq. mi.

American Places Dictionary — KANSAS, Jewell County

Valley Falls — City
ZIP: 66088   **Lat:** 39-20-28 N   **Long:** 95-27-37 W
Pop: 1,253 (1990); 1,189 (1980)   **Pop Density:** 1790.0
Land: 0.7 sq. mi.; **Water:** 0.0 sq. mi.   **Elev:** 950 ft.
Incorporated May 17, 1869.
Name origin: Originally called Grasshopper Falls. After the grasshopper plague of 1874, it was given its present name.

Winchester — City
ZIP: 66097   **Lat:** 39-19-17 N   **Long:** 95-16-04 W
Pop: 613 (1990); 570 (1980)   **Pop Density:** 3065.0
Land: 0.2 sq. mi.; **Water:** 0.0 sq. mi.   **Elev:** 1190 ft.
Incorporated Mar 1903.
Name origin: For Winchester, England.

Jewell County
County Seat: Mankato (ZIP: 66956)

Pop: 4,251 (1990); 5,241 (1980)   **Pop Density:** 4.7
Land: 909.2 sq. mi.; **Water:** 5.3 sq. mi.   **Area Code:** 913
On central northern border of KS; organized Feb 26, 1867 from Mitchell County.
Name origin: For Lt. Col. Lewis R. Jewell (?–1862), officer in the Kansas cavalry killed during the Civil War.

Allen — Township
Lat: 39-36-45 N   **Long:** 97-59-47 W
Pop: 58 (1990); 68 (1980)   **Pop Density:** 1.7
Land: 34.8 sq. mi.; **Water:** 0.0 sq. mi.

Athens — Township
Lat: 39-36-43 N   **Long:** 98-19-37 W
Pop: 91 (1990); 105 (1980)   **Pop Density:** 2.3
Land: 39.5 sq. mi.; **Water:** 0.0 sq. mi.

Browns Creek — Township
Lat: 39-36-43 N   **Long:** 98-12-53 W
Pop: 74 (1990); 71 (1980)   **Pop Density:** 2.1
Land: 36.0 sq. mi.; **Water:** 0.0 sq. mi.

Buffalo — Township
Lat: 39-41-41 N   **Long:** 98-06-15 W
Pop: 652 (1990); 723 (1980)   **Pop Density:** 16.1
Land: 40.6 sq. mi.; **Water:** 0.0 sq. mi.

Burr Oak — City
ZIP: 66936   **Lat:** 39-52-13 N   **Long:** 98-18-14 W
Pop: 278 (1990); 366 (1980)   **Pop Density:** 347.5
Land: 0.8 sq. mi.; **Water:** 0.0 sq. mi.   **Elev:** 1662 ft.
Incorporated May 15, 1880. Not coextensive with the town of the same name.
Name origin: For the abundant bur oaks in the area.

*Burr Oak — Township
ZIP: 66936   **Lat:** 39-52-13 N   **Long:** 98-19-45 W
Pop: 349 (1990); 473 (1980)   **Pop Density:** 8.9
Land: 39.4 sq. mi.; **Water:** 0.0 sq. mi.

Calvin — Township
Lat: 39-42-18 N   **Long:** 98-12-49 W
Pop: 57 (1990); 73 (1980)   **Pop Density:** 1.8
Land: 31.4 sq. mi.; **Water:** 0.0 sq. mi.

Center — Township
Lat: 39-47-09 N   **Long:** 98-12-46 W
Pop: 1,173 (1990); 1,366 (1980)   **Pop Density:** 32.8
Land: 35.8 sq. mi.; **Water:** 0.0 sq. mi.

Erving — Township
Lat: 39-36-41 N   **Long:** 98-26-55 W
Pop: 67 (1990); 86 (1980)   **Pop Density:** 1.9
Land: 35.9 sq. mi.; **Water:** 0.0 sq. mi.

Esbon — City
ZIP: 66941   **Lat:** 39-49-18 N   **Long:** 98-26-00 W
Pop: 167 (1990); 234 (1980)   **Pop Density:** 556.7
Land: 0.3 sq. mi.; **Water:** 0.0 sq. mi.   **Elev:** 1848 ft.
Incorporated Sep 22, 1904. Not coextensive with the town of the same name.

*Esbon — Township
ZIP: 66941   **Lat:** 39-47-04 N   **Long:** 98-26-59 W
Pop: 231 (1990); 358 (1980)   **Pop Density:** 6.5
Land: 35.8 sq. mi.; **Water:** 0.0 sq. mi.

Formoso — City
ZIP: 66942   **Lat:** 39-46-45 N   **Long:** 97-59-36 W
Pop: 128 (1990); 166 (1980)   **Pop Density:** 426.7
Land: 0.3 sq. mi.; **Water:** 0.0 sq. mi.   **Elev:** 1527 ft.
Incorporated Jun 1, 1882.
Name origin: For the Formoso Town Company, which platted the town. From Portuguese meaning 'beautiful isle.'

Grant — Township
Lat: 39-46-58 N   **Long:** 97-59-27 W
Pop: 223 (1990); 280 (1980)   **Pop Density:** 6.2
Land: 35.7 sq. mi.; **Water:** 0.0 sq. mi.

Harrison — Township
Lat: 39-57-04 N   **Long:** 98-12-40 W
Pop: 60 (1990); 71 (1980)   **Pop Density:** 1.7
Land: 35.8 sq. mi.; **Water:** 0.0 sq. mi.

Highland — Township
Lat: 39-57-49 N   **Long:** 98-26-41 W
Pop: 66 (1990); 67 (1980)   **Pop Density:** 1.8
Land: 35.9 sq. mi.; **Water:** 0.0 sq. mi.

Holmwood — Township
Lat: 39-52-13 N   **Long:** 98-12-31 W
Pop: 67 (1990); 71 (1980)   **Pop Density:** 1.9
Land: 35.7 sq. mi.; **Water:** 0.0 sq. mi.

Ionia — Township
Lat: 39-42-08 N   **Long:** 98-19-48 W
Pop: 106 (1990); 153 (1980)   **Pop Density:** 2.7
Land: 39.5 sq. mi.; **Water:** 0.0 sq. mi.

Jackson — Township
Lat: 39-57-24 N   **Long:** 97-59-14 W
Pop: 154 (1990); 191 (1980)   **Pop Density:** 4.4
Land: 35.4 sq. mi.; **Water:** 0.3 sq. mi.

KANSAS, Jewell County

Jewell
City
ZIP: 66949 Lat: 39-40-18 N Long: 98-09-04 W
Pop: 529 (1990); 589 (1980) Pop Density: 1322.5
Land: 0.4 sq. mi.; Water: 0.0 sq. mi. Elev: 1550 ft.
Incorporated Aug 9, 1880.
Name origin: For Lt. Col. Lewis R. Jewell (?–1862), who was killed in the Civil War.

Limestone
Township
Lat: 39-46-58 N Long: 98-19-45 W
Pop: 87 (1990); 103 (1980) Pop Density: 2.2
Land: 39.4 sq. mi.; Water: 0.0 sq. mi.

Mankato
City
ZIP: 66956 Lat: 39-47-14 N Long: 98-12-27 W
Pop: 1,037 (1990); 1,205 (1980) Pop Density: 1037.0
Land: 1.0 sq. mi.; Water: 0.0 sq. mi. Elev: 1776 ft.
Incorporated Apr 22, 1880.
Name origin: From a Sioux Indian term meaning 'blue earth.'

Montana
Township
Lat: 39-57-56 N Long: 98-06-27 W
Pop: 96 (1990); 118 (1980) Pop Density: 2.6
Land: 36.4 sq. mi.; Water: 0.0 sq. mi.

Odessa
Township
Lat: 39-42-17 N Long: 98-26-49 W
Pop: 44 (1990); 74 (1980) Pop Density: 1.2
Land: 35.9 sq. mi.; Water: 0.0 sq. mi.

Prairie
Township
Lat: 39-36-29 N Long: 98-06-09 W
Pop: 190 (1990); 250 (1980) Pop Density: 5.1
Land: 37.0 sq. mi.; Water: 0.0 sq. mi.

Randall
City
ZIP: 66963 Lat: 39-38-29 N Long: 98-02-42 W
Pop: 96 (1990); 154 (1980) Pop Density: 480.0
Land: 0.2 sq. mi.; Water: 0.0 sq. mi. Elev: 1457 ft.
Incorporated Apr 13, 1887.
Name origin: For original landowner, Edward Randall.

Richland
Township
Lat: 39-52-25 N Long: 98-06-23 W
Pop: 42 (1990); 39 (1980) Pop Density: 1.3
Land: 32.2 sq. mi.; Water: 3.6 sq. mi.

Sinclair
Township
Lat: 39-52-09 N Long: 97-59-06 W
Pop: 78 (1990); 111 (1980) Pop Density: 2.3
Land: 34.3 sq. mi.; Water: 1.0 sq. mi.

Vicksburg
Township
Lat: 39-41-44 N Long: 97-59-28 W
Pop: 42 (1990); 60 (1980) Pop Density: 1.2
Land: 35.8 sq. mi.; Water: 0.0 sq. mi.

Walnut
Township
Lat: 39-57-15 N Long: 98-20-08 W
Pop: 86 (1990); 113 (1980) Pop Density: 2.2
Land: 39.4 sq. mi.; Water: 0.0 sq. mi.

Washington
Township
Lat: 39-47-13 N Long: 98-05-47 W
Pop: 76 (1990); 115 (1980) Pop Density: 2.1
Land: 35.8 sq. mi.; Water: 0.0 sq. mi.

Webber
City
ZIP: 66970 Lat: 39-56-03 N Long: 98-02-09 W
Pop: 39 (1990); 53 (1980) Pop Density: 390.0
Land: 0.1 sq. mi.; Water: 0.0 sq. mi. Elev: 1670 ft.
Incorporated Feb 27, 1925.

White Mound
Township
Lat: 39-52-04 N Long: 98-26-58 W
Pop: 82 (1990); 102 (1980) Pop Density: 2.3
Land: 35.7 sq. mi.; Water: 0.0 sq. mi.

Johnson County
County Seat: Olathe (ZIP: 66061)

Pop: 355,054 (1990); 270,269 (1980) Pop Density: 744.7
Land: 476.8 sq. mi.; Water: 3.4 sq. mi. Area Code: 913
On eastern border of KS, south of Kansas City; original county, organized Aug 25, 1855 (prior to statehood).
Name origin: For the Rev. Thomas Johnson (1802–65), assassinated missionary to the Shawnee Indians (1829–58).

Aubry
Township
Lat: 38-46-43 N Long: 94-41-03 W
Pop: 4,294 (1990); 2,989 (1980) Pop Density: 86.7
Land: 49.5 sq. mi.; Water: 0.2 sq. mi. Elev: 1067 ft.
Part of the town is also in Wyandotte County.

Bonner Springs
City
Lat: 39-03-32 N Long: 94-51-26 W
Pop: 3 (1990); 6,266 (1980) Pop Density: 6.0
Land: 0.5 sq. mi.; Water: 0.1 sq. mi.
In northeastern KS, 15 mi. west of Kansas City. Incorporated Nov 8, 1898. Part of the town is also in Wyandotte County.
Name origin: For Robert Bonner, editor of the *New York City Ledger*, and for the local natural springs.

Countryside
City
Lat: 39-00-57 N Long: 94-39-18 W
Pop: 312 (1990); 346 (1980) Pop Density: 3120.0
Land: 0.1 sq. mi.; Water: 0.0 sq. mi. Elev: 1000 ft.
Incorporated Jul 2, 1951.

De Soto   City
ZIP: 66018 **Lat:** 38-58-24 N **Long:** 94-57-07 W
Pop: 2,291 (1990); 2,061 (1980) **Pop Density:** 381.8
Land: 6.0 sq. mi.; **Water:** 0.0 sq. mi. **Elev:** 842 ft.
Incorporated 1898.
Name origin: For the Spanish explorer Hernando de Soto (c. 1500–42).

Edgerton   City
ZIP: 66021 **Lat:** 38-45-47 N **Long:** 95-00-45 W
Pop: 1,244 (1990); 1,214 (1980) **Pop Density:** 1777.1
Land: 0.7 sq. mi.; **Water:** 0.0 sq. mi. **Elev:** 1000 ft.
Incorporated Jun 4, 1883.
Name origin: For the chief engineer of the Santa Fe Railroad.

Fairway   City
ZIP: 66205 **Lat:** 39-01-30 N **Long:** 94-37-43 W
Pop: 4,173 (1990); 4,619 (1980) **Pop Density:** 3793.6
Land: 1.1 sq. mi.; **Water:** 0.0 sq. mi. **Elev:** 950 ft.
Incorporated May 21, 1949.
Name origin: For its descriptive connotations.

Gardner   City
ZIP: 66030 **Lat:** 38-48-44 N **Long:** 94-55-33 W
Pop: 3,191 (1990); 2,392 (1980) **Pop Density:** 1100.3
Land: 2.9 sq. mi.; **Water:** 0.0 sq. mi. **Elev:** 1160 ft.
Incorporated Jan 8, 1887.
Name origin: For O.B. Gardner, a member of the local town company and a justice of the peace.

*Gardner   Township
ZIP: 66030 **Lat:** 38-48-11 N **Long:** 94-55-04 W
Pop: 2,888 (1990); 2,595 (1980) **Pop Density:** 68.8
Land: 42.0 sq. mi.; **Water:** 0.2 sq. mi.

Lake Quivira   City
Lat: 39-02-06 N **Long:** 94-46-02 W
Pop: 943 (1990); 1,029 (1980) **Pop Density:** 943.0
Land: 1.0 sq. mi.; **Water:** 0.2 sq. mi.
Incorporated Jul 1971. Part of the town is also in Wyandotte County.
Name origin: For Quivira, a legendary land of treasure, which the 16th-century Spanish believed could be found in central North America.

Leawood   City
ZIP: 66206 **Lat:** 38-54-25 N **Long:** 94-37-30 W
Pop: 19,693 (1990); 13,360 (1980) **Pop Density:** 1312.9
Land: 15.0 sq. mi.; **Water:** 0.0 sq. mi. **Elev:** 850 ft.
In eastern KS, a southern suburb of Kansas City. Incorporated Nov 30, 1948.
Name origin: For retired policeman Oscar G. Lea.

Lenexa   City
ZIP: 66215 **Lat:** 38-57-48 N **Long:** 94-47-18 W
Pop: 34,034 (1990); 18,639 (1980) **Pop Density:** 1173.6
Land: 29.0 sq. mi.; **Water:** 0.2 sq. mi. **Elev:** 860 ft.
In eastern KS, a southwestern suburb of Kansas City. Incorporated May 4, 1907.
Name origin: For Lenexa, wife of Blackhoof, a Shawnee Indian chief.

Lexington   Township
Lat: 38-55-27 N **Long:** 94-59-04 W
Pop: 1,876 (1990); 1,978 (1980) **Pop Density:** 32.7
Land: 57.4 sq. mi.; **Water:** 0.9 sq. mi.

McCamish   Township
Lat: 38-48-05 N **Long:** 95-00-36 W
Pop: 857 (1990); 922 (1980) **Pop Density:** 19.5
Land: 44.0 sq. mi.; **Water:** 0.1 sq. mi.

Merriam   City
ZIP: 66203 **Lat:** 39-01-09 N **Long:** 94-41-30 W
Pop: 11,821 (1990); 10,794 (1980) **Pop Density:** 2749.1
Land: 4.3 sq. mi.; **Water:** 0.0 sq. mi. **Elev:** 1000 ft.
In eastern KS, a suburb of Kansas City. Incorporated Oct 23, 1950.
Name origin: For the man who secured the railroad route for the town, or for local official G.F. Merriam.

Mission   City
ZIP: 66205 **Lat:** 39-01-36 N **Long:** 94-39-24 W
Pop: 9,504 (1990); 8,643 (1980) **Pop Density:** 3655.4
Land: 2.6 sq. mi.; **Water:** 0.0 sq. mi. **Elev:** 1000 ft.
Incorporated Jul 2, 1951.
Name origin: For the Shawnee Methodist Mission established here in 1829 by the Rev. Thomas Johnson.

Mission Hills   City
Lat: 39-00-48 N **Long:** 94-36-58 W
Pop: 3,446 (1990); 3,904 (1980) **Pop Density:** 1723.0
Land: 2.0 sq. mi.; **Water:** 0.0 sq. mi. **Elev:** 950 ft.
Incorporated Jun 10, 1949.
Name origin: For the Shawnee Methodist Mission established here in the 1830s by the Rev. Thomas Johnson.

Mission Woods   City
ZIP: 66205 **Lat:** 39-01-59 N **Long:** 94-36-45 W
Pop: 182 (1990); 213 (1980) **Pop Density:** 1820.0
Land: 0.1 sq. mi.; **Water:** 0.0 sq. mi. **Elev:** 900 ft.
Incorporated Jul 22, 1949.
Name origin: For the Shawnee Methodist Mission established here in the 1830s by the Rev. Thomas Johnson.

Monticello   Township
Lat: 38-57-41 N **Long:** 94-51-10 W
Pop: 134 (1990); 2,813 (1980) **Pop Density:** 23.9
Land: 5.6 sq. mi.; **Water:** 0.0 sq. mi. **Elev:** 1016 ft.

Olathe   City
ZIP: 66061 **Lat:** 38-53-12 N **Long:** 94-48-52 W
Pop: 63,352 (1990); 37,258 (1980) **Pop Density:** 1497.7
Land: 42.3 sq. mi.; **Water:** 0.3 sq. mi. **Elev:** 1040 ft.
In eastern KS, 20 mi. southwest of Kansas City. Incorporated Apr 1870.
Name origin: From a Shawnee Indian term meaning 'beautiful.'

*Olathe   Township
Lat: 38-51-33 N **Long:** 94-50-58 W
Pop: 1,931 (1990); 1,564 (1980) **Pop Density:** 69.0
Land: 28.0 sq. mi.; **Water:** 0.0 sq. mi.

Overland Park   City
ZIP: 66204 **Lat:** 38-54-52 N **Long:** 94-41-05 W
Pop: 111,790 (1990); 81,784 (1980) **Pop Density:** 2007.0
Land: 55.7 sq. mi.; **Water:** 0.1 sq. mi. **Elev:** 1000 ft.
In eastern KS, south of Kansas City. Incorporated May 20, 1960.
Name origin: For its location on a ridge that gave a panoramic view of the overland trail.

KANSAS, Johnson County

Oxford
Township
Lat: 38-49-57 N **Long:** 94-40-53 W
Pop: 1,925 (1990); 2,491 (1980) **Pop Density:** 275.0
Land: 7.0 sq. mi.; **Water:** 0.1 sq. mi.

Prairie Village
City
ZIP: 66208 **Lat:** 38-59-12 N **Long:** 94-38-09 W
Pop: 23,186 (1990); 24,657 (1980) **Pop Density:** 3739.7
Land: 6.2 sq. mi.; **Water:** 0.0 sq. mi. **Elev:** 1050 ft.
In northeastern KS, south of Kansas City. Incorporated Feb 19, 1951.
Name origin: For its descriptive connotations.

Roeland Park
City
ZIP: 66203 **Lat:** 39-02-09 N **Long:** 94-38-14 W
Pop: 7,706 (1990); 7,962 (1980) **Pop Density:** 4816.3
Land: 1.6 sq. mi.; **Water:** 0.0 sq. mi. **Elev:** 930 ft.
In northeastern KS, south of Kansas City. Incorporated Jul 2, 1951.
Name origin: For the Roe family, which donated land for the town site.

Shawnee
City
ZIP: 66203 **Lat:** 39-00-54 N **Long:** 94-48-16 W
Pop: 37,993 (1990); 29,653 (1980) **Pop Density:** 908.9
Land: 41.8 sq. mi.; **Water:** 0.8 sq. mi. **Elev:** 1000 ft.
In eastern KS, a southern suburb of Kansas City. Incorporated Jun 7, 1922.
Name origin: For the Shawnee Indians.

*Shawnee
Township
Lat: 39-01-45 N **Long:** 94-47-43 W
Pop: 106 (1990); 620 (1980) **Pop Density:** 1060.0
Land: 0.1 sq. mi.; **Water:** 0.0 sq. mi.

Spring Hill
City
ZIP: 66083 **Lat:** 38-45-28 N **Long:** 94-49-15 W
Pop: 2,084 (1990); 1,963 (1980) **Pop Density:** 906.1
Land: 2.3 sq. mi.; **Water:** 0.1 sq. mi. **Elev:** 1050 ft.
Incorporated 1885. Part of the town is also in Miami County.
Name origin: For Spring Hill, AL.

*Spring Hill
Township
ZIP: 66083 **Lat:** 38-46-34 N **Long:** 94-48-54 W
Pop: 1,940 (1990); 1,586 (1980) **Pop Density:** 70.5
Land: 27.5 sq. mi.; **Water:** 0.1 sq. mi.

Westwood
City
ZIP: 66205 **Lat:** 39-02-23 N **Long:** 94-36-54 W
Pop: 1,772 (1990); 1,783 (1980) **Pop Density:** 4430.0
Land: 0.4 sq. mi.; **Water:** 0.0 sq. mi. **Elev:** 900 ft.
Incorporated Jun 7, 1949.
Name origin: Descriptively named by early settlers.

Westwood Hills
City
ZIP: 66205 **Lat:** 39-02-20 N **Long:** 94-36-38 W
Pop: 383 (1990); 437 (1980) **Pop Density:** 3830.0
Land: 0.1 sq. mi.; **Water:** 0.0 sq. mi. **Elev:** 900 ft.
Incorporated Jun 6, 1949.

Kearny County
County Seat: Lakin (ZIP: 67860)

Pop: 4,027 (1990); 3,435 (1980) **Pop Density:** 4.6
Land: 870.0 sq. mi.; **Water:** 1.5 sq. mi. **Area Code:** 316
In southwestern KS, west of Garden City; organized Mar 6, 1873 from Finney County.
Name origin: For Gen. Philip Kearny (1814–62), hero of the Mexican-American War and Civil War.

Deerfield
City
ZIP: 67838 **Lat:** 37-58-53 N **Long:** 101-07-57 W
Pop: 677 (1990); 538 (1980) **Pop Density:** 1692.5
Land: 0.4 sq. mi.; **Water:** 0.0 sq. mi. **Elev:** 2947 ft.
Incorporated 1907. Not coextensive with the town of the same name.
Name origin: For the many deer in the area when the settlers arrived.

*Deerfield
Township
ZIP: 67838 **Lat:** 38-01-18 N **Long:** 101-09-29 W
Pop: 954 (1990); 713 (1980) **Pop Density:** 21.1
Land: 45.2 sq. mi.; **Water:** 1.3 sq. mi.

East Hibbard
Township
Lat: 38-09-58 N **Long:** 101-13-00 W
Pop: 123 (1990); 152 (1980) **Pop Density:** 0.8
Land: 155.6 sq. mi.; **Water:** 0.0 sq. mi.

Hartland
Township
Lat: 37-58-50 N **Long:** 101-25-36 W
Pop: 123 (1990); 126 (1980) **Pop Density:** 0.8
Land: 149.7 sq. mi.; **Water:** 0.0 sq. mi.

Kendall
Township
Lat: 37-49-08 N **Long:** 101-19-59 W
Pop: 133 (1990); 109 (1980) **Pop Density:** 0.7
Land: 190.8 sq. mi.; **Water:** 0.0 sq. mi.

Lakin
City
ZIP: 67860 **Lat:** 37-56-24 N **Long:** 101-15-29 W
Pop: 2,060 (1990); 1,823 (1980) **Pop Density:** 2288.9
Land: 0.9 sq. mi.; **Water:** 0.0 sq. mi. **Elev:** 3001 ft.
Incorporated 1888. Not coextensive with the town of the same name.
Name origin: For David Lakin, a Santa Fe Railroad board member in the 1860s.

*Lakin
Township
ZIP: 67860 **Lat:** 37-59-42 N **Long:** 101-16-18 W
Pop: 2,392 (1990); 2,078 (1980) **Pop Density:** 37.8
Land: 63.2 sq. mi.; **Water:** 0.1 sq. mi.

Southside
Township
Lat: 37-54-04 N **Long:** 101-11-06 W
Pop: 233 (1990); 190 (1980) **Pop Density:** 2.1
Land: 110.2 sq. mi.; **Water:** 0.1 sq. mi.

West Hibbard
Township
Lat: 38-10-09 N **Long:** 101-25-21 W
Pop: 69 (1990); 67 (1980) **Pop Density:** 0.4
Land: 155.4 sq. mi.; **Water:** 0.0 sq. mi.

Kingman County
County Seat: Kingman (ZIP: 67068)

Pop: 8,292 (1990); 8,960 (1980) **Pop Density:** 9.6
Land: 863.7 sq. mi.; **Water:** 3.0 sq. mi. **Area Code:** 316
In south-central KS, west of Wichita; established Feb 29, 1872 from unorganized territory.
Name origin: For Samuel Austin Kingman (1822–?), KY legislator and Chief Justice of the KS Supreme Court (1866–77).

Allen
Township
Lat: 37-31-14 N **Long:** 97-52-17 W
Pop: 123 (1990); 114 (1980) **Pop Density:** 3.4
Land: 36.4 sq. mi.; **Water:** 0.3 sq. mi.

Belmont
Township
Lat: 37-30-51 N **Long:** 98-11-36 W
Pop: 105 (1990); 134 (1980) **Pop Density:** 2.9
Land: 36.7 sq. mi.; **Water:** 0.0 sq. mi.

Bennett
Township
Lat: 37-25-52 N **Long:** 97-51-52 W
Pop: 617 (1990); 647 (1980) **Pop Density:** 16.9
Land: 36.5 sq. mi.; **Water:** 0.0 sq. mi.

Canton
Township
Lat: 37-26-10 N **Long:** 97-57-57 W
Pop: 88 (1990); 111 (1980) **Pop Density:** 2.4
Land: 36.3 sq. mi.; **Water:** 0.0 sq. mi.

Chikaskia
Township
Lat: 37-25-59 N **Long:** 98-11-52 W
Pop: 169 (1990); 168 (1980) **Pop Density:** 4.7
Land: 36.2 sq. mi.; **Water:** 0.0 sq. mi.

Cunningham
City
ZIP: 67035 **Lat:** 37-38-41 N **Long:** 98-25-55 W
Pop: 535 (1990); 540 (1980) **Pop Density:** 1337.5
Land: 0.4 sq. mi.; **Water:** 0.0 sq. mi. **Elev:** 1705 ft.
Incorporated Jul 8, 1908.
Name origin: For J.D. Cunningham, town promoter. Originally called Ninnescah.

Dale
Township
Lat: 37-36-12 N **Long:** 97-58-20 W
Pop: 197 (1990); 217 (1980) **Pop Density:** 5.6
Land: 35.1 sq. mi.; **Water:** 0.3 sq. mi.

Dresden
Township
Lat: 37-41-28 N **Long:** 98-24-20 W
Pop: 359 (1990); 402 (1980) **Pop Density:** 9.9
Land: 36.1 sq. mi.; **Water:** 0.1 sq. mi.

Eagle
Township
Lat: 37-31-03 N **Long:** 97-58-20 W
Pop: 125 (1990); 159 (1980) **Pop Density:** 3.4
Land: 36.3 sq. mi.; **Water:** 0.0 sq. mi.

Eureka
Township
Lat: 37-41-25 N **Long:** 98-18-11 W
Pop: 138 (1990); 147 (1980) **Pop Density:** 3.9
Land: 35.8 sq. mi.; **Water:** 0.2 sq. mi.

Evan
Township
Lat: 37-41-24 N **Long:** 97-51-38 W
Pop: 441 (1990); 425 (1980) **Pop Density:** 12.6
Land: 35.1 sq. mi.; **Water:** 1.3 sq. mi.

Galesburg
Township
Lat: 37-41-33 N **Long:** 97-58-24 W
Pop: 205 (1990); 259 (1980) **Pop Density:** 5.8
Land: 35.4 sq. mi.; **Water:** 0.1 sq. mi.

Hoosier
Township
Lat: 37-41-07 N **Long:** 98-11-41 W
Pop: 170 (1990); 185 (1980) **Pop Density:** 4.7
Land: 36.1 sq. mi.; **Water:** 0.0 sq. mi.

Kingman
City
ZIP: 67068 **Lat:** 37-38-49 N **Long:** 98-06-48 W
Pop: 3,196 (1990); 3,563 (1980) **Pop Density:** 1031.0
Land: 3.1 sq. mi.; **Water:** 0.0 sq. mi. **Elev:** 1550 ft.
Incorporated Aug 14, 1883.
Name origin: For Samuel Austin Kingman (1822–?), who served as Chief Justice of the state's Supreme Court.

*Kingman
Township
ZIP: 67068 **Lat:** 37-30-35 N **Long:** 98-24-49 W
Pop: 164 (1990); 184 (1980) **Pop Density:** 4.6
Land: 36.0 sq. mi.; **Water:** 0.0 sq. mi.

Liberty
Township
Lat: 37-25-39 N **Long:** 98-24-34 W
Pop: 220 (1990); 220 (1980) **Pop Density:** 6.1
Land: 36.3 sq. mi.; **Water:** 0.0 sq. mi.

Nashville
City
ZIP: 67112 **Lat:** 37-26-18 N **Long:** 98-25-20 W
Pop: 118 (1990); 127 (1980) **Pop Density:** 590.0
Land: 0.2 sq. mi.; **Water:** 0.0 sq. mi. **Elev:** 1740 ft.
Incorporated Aug 10, 1913.
Name origin: For Nashville, TN.

Ninnescah
Township
Lat: 37-36-22 N **Long:** 98-08-01 W
Pop: 256 (1990); 258 (1980) **Pop Density:** 3.7
Land: 69.7 sq. mi.; **Water:** 0.2 sq. mi.

Norwich
City
ZIP: 67118 **Lat:** 37-27-24 N **Long:** 97-50-43 W
Pop: 455 (1990); 476 (1980) **Pop Density:** 1137.5
Land: 0.4 sq. mi.; **Water:** 0.0 sq. mi. **Elev:** 1490 ft.
Incorporated Oct 6, 1886.
Name origin: For Norwich, England.

KANSAS, Kingman County

Penalosa
City
Lat: 37-42-56 N Long: 98-19-11 W
Pop: 21 (1990); 31 (1980)   Pop Density: 210.0
Land: 0.1 sq. mi.; Water: 0.0 sq. mi.   Elev: 1725 ft.
Incorporated Jan 1, 1929.
Name origin: For Don Diego Penalosa Berdugo, an early governor of Spanish NM.

Peters
Township
Lat: 37-31-05 N Long: 98-17-57 W
Pop: 174 (1990); 229 (1980)   Pop Density: 4.8
Land: 36.0 sq. mi.; Water: 0.0 sq. mi.

Richland
Township
Lat: 37-30-53 N Long: 98-04-56 W
Pop: 94 (1990); 139 (1980)   Pop Density: 2.6
Land: 36.5 sq. mi.; Water: 0.1 sq. mi.

Rochester
Township
Lat: 37-26-01 N Long: 98-17-55 W
Pop: 200 (1990); 248 (1980)   Pop Density: 5.5
Land: 36.2 sq. mi.; Water: 0.0 sq. mi.

Rural
Township
Lat: 37-35-38 N Long: 98-24-21 W
Pop: 377 (1990); 374 (1980)   Pop Density: 10.4
Land: 36.2 sq. mi.; Water: 0.0 sq. mi.

Spivey
City
ZIP: 67142   Lat: 37-26-53 N Long: 98-09-53 W
Pop: 88 (1990); 83 (1980)   Pop Density: 176.0
Land: 0.5 sq. mi.; Water: 0.0 sq. mi.   Elev: 1510 ft.
Incorporated Jul 8, 1887.
Name origin: For a director of the Santa Fe Railroad.

Union
Township
Lat: 37-36-11 N Long: 98-18-09 W
Pop: 98 (1990); 123 (1980)   Pop Density: 2.7
Land: 36.1 sq. mi.; Water: 0.1 sq. mi.

Valley
Township
Lat: 37-25-42 N Long: 98-04-50 W
Pop: 127 (1990); 130 (1980)   Pop Density: 3.5
Land: 36.2 sq. mi.; Water: 0.1 sq. mi.

Vinita
Township
Lat: 37-36-12 N Long: 97-52-01 W
Pop: 190 (1990); 208 (1980)   Pop Density: 5.4
Land: 35.1 sq. mi.; Water: 0.2 sq. mi.

White
Township
Lat: 37-41-30 N Long: 98-04-47 W
Pop: 459 (1990); 316 (1980)   Pop Density: 13.5
Land: 34.1 sq. mi.; Water: 0.0 sq. mi.

Zenda
City
ZIP: 67159   Lat: 37-26-41 N Long: 98-16-55 W
Pop: 96 (1990); 146 (1980)   Pop Density: 480.0
Land: 0.2 sq. mi.; Water: 0.0 sq. mi.   Elev: 1663 ft.
Incorporated Jun 3, 1913.
Name origin: For the novel *The Prisoner of Zenda* (1894) by Anthony Hope Hawkins (1863–1933).

Kiowa County
County Seat: Greensburg (ZIP: 67054)

Pop: 3,660 (1990); 4,046 (1980)   Pop Density: 5.1
Land: 722.4 sq. mi.; Water: 0.2 sq. mi.   Area Code: 316

In south-central KS, southeast of Dodge City; established Feb 26, 1867 from Comanche and Edwards counties, abolished in 1875, and recreated in 1886 from Comanche and Edwards counties.

Name origin: For the Indian tribe of Tanoan linguistic stock; name means 'principal people.'

East Kiowa
Pop. Place
Lat: 37-32-19 N Long: 99-10-15 W
Pop: 535 (1990); 579 (1980)   Pop Density: 1.4
Land: 376.1 sq. mi.; Water: 0.2 sq. mi.

Greensburg
City
ZIP: 67054   Lat: 37-36-19 N Long: 99-17-30 W
Pop: 1,792 (1990); 1,885 (1980)   Pop Density: 1194.7
Land: 1.5 sq. mi.; Water: 0.0 sq. mi.   Elev: 2235 ft.
Incorporated Jun 18, 1886.
Name origin: For a pioneer stage line owner.

Haviland
City
ZIP: 67059   Lat: 37-37-03 N Long: 99-06-18 W
Pop: 624 (1990); 770 (1980)   Pop Density: 1248.0
Land: 0.5 sq. mi.; Water: 0.0 sq. mi.   Elev: 2150 ft.
Incorporated Apr 12, 1906.
Name origin: For Quaker Laura Haviland.

Mullinville
City
ZIP: 67109   Lat: 37-35-16 N Long: 99-28-28 W
Pop: 289 (1990); 339 (1980)   Pop Density: 481.7
Land: 0.6 sq. mi.; Water: 0.0 sq. mi.   Elev: 2330 ft.
Incorporated 1911.
Name origin: For founder Judge Mullin.

West Kiowa
Pop. Place
Lat: 37-35-13 N Long: 99-25-04 W
Pop: 420 (1990); 473 (1980)   Pop Density: 1.2
Land: 343.7 sq. mi.; Water: 0.1 sq. mi.

Labette County
County Seat: Oswego (ZIP: 67356)

Pop: 23,693 (1990); 25,682 (1980) **Pop Density:** 36.5
Land: 648.9 sq. mi.; **Water:** 4.5 sq. mi. **Area Code:** 316
On the southeastern border of KS, west of Joplin, MO; organized Feb 7, 1867 from Neosho County.

Name origin: For the creek, which runs through the county, named La Bette, possibly for a Pierre Labette who lived near the mouth of the stream. An 1836 map names it *La Bête*, French 'the beast.'

Altamont — City
ZIP: 67330 Lat: 37-11-29 N Long: 95-17-40 W
Pop: 1,048 (1990); 1,054 (1980) Pop Density: 1048.0
Land: 1.0 sq. mi.; Water: 0.0 sq. mi. Elev: 910 ft.
Incorporated Sep 29, 1879.
Name origin: For Altamont, IL.

Bartlett — City
ZIP: 67332 Lat: 37-03-17 N Long: 95-12-40 W
Pop: 107 (1990); 163 (1980) Pop Density: 1070.0
Land: 0.1 sq. mi.; Water: 0.0 sq. mi. Elev: 890 ft.
Incorporated Dec 1906.
Name origin: Named by railroad officials for farmer A.G. Bartlett, who donated land for the railroad station.

Canada — Township
Lat: 37-06-44 N Long: 95-27-01 W
Pop: 253 (1990); 281 (1980) Pop Density: 6.3
Land: 39.9 sq. mi.; Water: 0.1 sq. mi.

Chetopa — City
ZIP: 67336 Lat: 37-02-10 N Long: 95-05-35 W
Pop: 1,357 (1990); 1,751 (1980) Pop Density: 1130.8
Land: 1.2 sq. mi.; Water: 0.0 sq. mi. Elev: 824 ft.
Incorporated Mar 30, 1868.
Name origin: For the Osage chief who lived nearby.

Edna — City
ZIP: 67342 Lat: 37-03-30 N Long: 95-21-29 W
Pop: 438 (1990); 537 (1980) Pop Density: 1460.0
Land: 0.3 sq. mi.; Water: 0.0 sq. mi. Elev: 979 ft.
Incorporated Jul 3, 1892.

Elm Grove — Township
Lat: 37-03-40 N Long: 95-19-10 W
Pop: 817 (1990); 947 (1980) Pop Density: 16.3
Land: 50.1 sq. mi.; Water: 0.1 sq. mi.

Fairview — Township
Lat: 37-10-19 N Long: 95-12-29 W
Pop: 234 (1990); 281 (1980) Pop Density: 6.4
Land: 36.3 sq. mi.; Water: 0.0 sq. mi.

Hackberry — Township
Lat: 37-03-37 N Long: 95-12-45 W
Pop: 385 (1990); 466 (1980) Pop Density: 7.6
Land: 50.8 sq. mi.; Water: 0.0 sq. mi.

Howard — Township
Lat: 37-02-04 N Long: 95-27-00 W
Pop: 354 (1990); 388 (1980) Pop Density: 8.3
Land: 42.9 sq. mi.; Water: 0.1 sq. mi.

Labette — City
ZIP: 67356 Lat: 37-13-49 N Long: 95-11-00 W
Pop: 74 (1990); 123 (1980) Pop Density: 370.0
Land: 0.2 sq. mi.; Water: 0.0 sq. mi. Elev: 965 ft.
Incorporated Aug 4, 1919.

*Labette — Township
ZIP: 67356 Lat: 37-15-01 N Long: 95-19-24 W
Pop: 384 (1990); 323 (1980) Pop Density: 10.5
Land: 36.4 sq. mi.; Water: 0.1 sq. mi.

Liberty — Township
Lat: 37-15-19 N Long: 95-12-40 W
Pop: 409 (1990); 485 (1980) Pop Density: 11.2
Land: 36.6 sq. mi.; Water: 0.0 sq. mi.

Montana — Township
Lat: 37-15-01 N Long: 95-06-46 W
Pop: 233 (1990); 240 (1980) Pop Density: 8.6
Land: 27.2 sq. mi.; Water: 0.5 sq. mi.

Mound Valley — City
ZIP: 67354 Lat: 37-12-25 N Long: 95-24-14 W
Pop: 405 (1990); 381 (1980) Pop Density: 578.6
Land: 0.7 sq. mi.; Water: 0.0 sq. mi. Elev: 830 ft.
Incorporated Jul 10, 1878. Not coextensive with the town of the same name.
Name origin: For a row of mound-like hills in La Bette County.

*Mound Valley — Township
ZIP: 67354 Lat: 37-12-32 N Long: 95-26-45 W
Pop: 807 (1990); 862 (1980) Pop Density: 12.6
Land: 64.2 sq. mi.; Water: 0.1 sq. mi.

Mount Pleasant — Township
Lat: 37-09-54 N Long: 95-19-10 W
Pop: 1,336 (1990); 1,342 (1980) Pop Density: 37.0
Land: 36.1 sq. mi.; Water: 0.1 sq. mi.

Neosho — Township
Lat: 37-20-34 N Long: 95-06-47 W
Pop: 213 (1990); 199 (1980) Pop Density: 7.9
Land: 27.1 sq. mi.; Water: 0.7 sq. mi.

North — Township
Lat: 37-20-33 N Long: 95-12-19 W
Pop: 638 (1990); 618 (1980) Pop Density: 19.0
Land: 33.5 sq. mi.; Water: 0.1 sq. mi.

Osage — Township
Lat: 37-19-14 N Long: 95-26-54 W
Pop: 675 (1990); 689 (1980) Pop Density: 10.9
Land: 62.1 sq. mi.; Water: 1.8 sq. mi.

Oswego — City
ZIP: 67356 **Lat:** 37-10-03 N **Long:** 95-06-42 W
Pop: 1,870 (1990); 2,218 (1980) **Pop Density:** 850.0
Land: 2.2 sq. mi.; **Water:** 0.0 sq. mi. **Elev:** 900 ft.
Incorporated Feb 8, 1870.
Name origin: For a NY State Iroquois Indian tribe.

*Oswego — Township
ZIP: 67356 **Lat:** 37-09-32 N **Long:** 95-07-04 W
Pop: 375 (1990); 326 (1980) **Pop Density:** 14.8
Land: 25.3 sq. mi.; **Water:** 0.4 sq. mi.

Parsons — City
ZIP: 67357 **Lat:** 37-20-20 N **Long:** 95-16-04 W
Pop: 11,924 (1990); 12,898 (1980) **Pop Density:** 1863.1
Land: 6.4 sq. mi.; **Water:** 0.0 sq. mi. **Elev:** 907 ft.
In southeastern KS, 35 mi. west of Pittsburg. Incorporated Mar 8, 1871.
Name origin: For New York Railroad promoter Judge Levi Parsons, who brought the railroad to the area.

Richland — Township
Lat: 37-03-45 N **Long:** 95-07-07 W
Pop: 393 (1990); 372 (1980) **Pop Density:** 10.4
Land: 37.7 sq. mi.; **Water:** 0.2 sq. mi.

Walton — Township
Lat: 37-20-22 N **Long:** 95-19-23 W
Pop: 1,036 (1990); 996 (1980) **Pop Density:** 31.3
Land: 33.1 sq. mi.; **Water:** 0.1 sq. mi.

Lane County
County Seat: Dighton (ZIP: 67839)

Pop: 2,375 (1990); 2,472 (1980) **Pop Density:** 3.3
Land: 717.3 sq. mi.; **Water:** 0.2 sq. mi. **Area Code:** 316
In west-central KS, northeast of Garden City; organized Mar 6, 1873 from Finney County.
Name origin: For Col. James Henry Lane (1814–66), officer in the Mexican-American War, U.S. representative from IN (1853–55), and first U.S. senator from KS (1861–66).

Alamota — Township
ZIP: 67830 **Lat:** 38-28-28 N **Long:** 100-19-10 W
Pop: 75 (1990); 102 (1980) **Pop Density:** 0.9
Land: 79.8 sq. mi.; **Water:** 0.0 sq. mi.

Blaine — Township
Lat: 38-24-34 N **Long:** 100-37-15 W
Pop: 124 (1990); 138 (1980) **Pop Density:** 0.8
Land: 159.1 sq. mi.; **Water:** 0.0 sq. mi.

Cheyenne — Township
Lat: 38-38-08 N **Long:** 100-37-13 W
Pop: 352 (1990); 333 (1980) **Pop Density:** 4.5
Land: 78.7 sq. mi.; **Water:** 0.0 sq. mi.

Cleveland — Township
Lat: 38-19-54 N **Long:** 100-27-36 W
Pop: 39 (1990); 45 (1980) **Pop Density:** 0.5
Land: 80.3 sq. mi.; **Water:** 0.0 sq. mi.

Dighton — City
ZIP: 67839 **Lat:** 38-28-53 N **Long:** 100-27-56 W
Pop: 1,361 (1990); 1,390 (1980) **Pop Density:** 1512.2
Land: 0.9 sq. mi.; **Water:** 0.0 sq. mi. **Elev:** 2765 ft.
Incorporated Jan 4, 1887. Not coextensive with the town of the same name.
Name origin: For surveyor Richard Dighton.

*Dighton — Township
ZIP: 67839 **Lat:** 38-28-53 N **Long:** 100-28-01 W
Pop: 1,565 (1990); 1,577 (1980) **Pop Density:** 19.7
Land: 79.6 sq. mi.; **Water:** 0.0 sq. mi.

Spring Creek — Township
Lat: 38-19-40 N **Long:** 100-19-12 W
Pop: 62 (1990); 95 (1980) **Pop Density:** 0.8
Land: 80.1 sq. mi.; **Water:** 0.0 sq. mi.

White Rock — Township
Lat: 38-37-48 N **Long:** 100-18-46 W
Pop: 50 (1990); 46 (1980) **Pop Density:** 0.6
Land: 80.1 sq. mi.; **Water:** 0.0 sq. mi.

Wilson — Township
Lat: 38-38-04 N **Long:** 100-27-33 W
Pop: 108 (1990); 136 (1980) **Pop Density:** 1.4
Land: 79.5 sq. mi.; **Water:** 0.2 sq. mi.

Leavenworth County
County Seat: Leavenworth (ZIP: 66048)

Pop: 64,371 (1990); 54,809 (1980) **Pop Density:** 138.9
Land: 463.3 sq. mi.; **Water:** 5.1 sq. mi. **Area Code:** 913
On the northeastern border of KS, north of Kansas City; original county; organized Aug 25, 1855 (prior to statehood).
Name origin: For Fort Leavenworth, the state's first fort, named for Gen. Henry Leavenworth (1783–1834), officer in the War of 1812 who later fought the Indians.

Alexandria Township
Lat: 39-15-34 N **Long:** 95-07-21 W
Pop: 655 (1990); 629 (1980) **Pop Density:** 13.7
Land: 47.7 sq. mi.; **Water:** 0.3 sq. mi.

Basehor City
ZIP: 66007 **Lat:** 39-07-37 N **Long:** 94-55-44 W
Pop: 1,591 (1990); 1,483 (1980) **Pop Density:** 568.2
Land: 2.8 sq. mi.; **Water:** 0.0 sq. mi. **Elev:** 984 ft.
Incorporated Jun 20, 1965.

Delaware Township
Lat: 39-13-53 N **Long:** 94-53-30 W
Pop: 1,056 (1990); 6,031 (1980) **Pop Density:** 43.1
Land: 24.5 sq. mi.; **Water:** 1.0 sq. mi.

Easton City
ZIP: 66020 **Lat:** 39-20-43 N **Long:** 95-06-58 W
Pop: 405 (1990); 460 (1980) **Pop Density:** 4050.0
Land: 0.1 sq. mi.; **Water:** 0.0 sq. mi. **Elev:** 903 ft.
Incorporated 1903. Not coextensive with the town of the same name.
Name origin: For Easton, PA.

*Easton Township
ZIP: 66020 **Lat:** 39-21-57 N **Long:** 95-07-26 W
Pop: 1,290 (1990); 1,178 (1980) **Pop Density:** 30.6
Land: 42.2 sq. mi.; **Water:** 0.0 sq. mi.

Fairmount Township
Lat: 39-07-53 N **Long:** 94-56-19 W
Pop: 3,909 (1990); 3,121 (1980) **Pop Density:** 99.2
Land: 39.4 sq. mi.; **Water:** 0.2 sq. mi.

High Prairie Township
Lat: 39-15-41 N **Long:** 95-00-41 W
Pop: 1,470 (1990); 1,312 (1980) **Pop Density:** 30.8
Land: 47.7 sq. mi.; **Water:** 0.1 sq. mi.

Kickapoo Township
Lat: 39-22-03 N **Long:** 95-00-23 W
Pop: 1,511 (1990); 1,394 (1980) **Pop Density:** 34.2
Land: 44.2 sq. mi.; **Water:** 1.1 sq. mi.

Lansing City
ZIP: 66043 **Lat:** 39-14-53 N **Long:** 94-53-14 W
Pop: 7,120 (1990); 5,307 (1980) **Pop Density:** 837.6
Land: 8.5 sq. mi.; **Water:** 0.1 sq. mi. **Elev:** 794 ft.
Incorporated Jun 22, 1959.
Name origin: For founder James W. Lansing.

Leavenworth City
ZIP: 66048 **Lat:** 39-19-28 N **Long:** 94-55-23 W
Pop: 38,495 (1990); 33,656 (1980) **Pop Density:** 1695.8
Land: 22.7 sq. mi.; **Water:** 0.0 sq. mi. **Elev:** 900 ft.
In northeastern KS on the Missouri River, 22 mi. northwest of Kansas City. Settled and incorporated 1854.
Name origin: For Gen. Henry Leavenworth (1783–1834). Previously called New Town.

Linwood City
ZIP: 66052 **Lat:** 38-59-59 N **Long:** 95-02-04 W
Pop: 409 (1990); 343 (1980) **Pop Density:** 1022.5
Land: 0.4 sq. mi.; **Water:** 0.0 sq. mi. **Elev:** 800 ft.
Incorporated 1895.
Name origin: For the local linden trees.

Reno Township
Lat: 39-01-21 N **Long:** 95-07-48 W
Pop: 944 (1990); 764 (1980) **Pop Density:** 22.0
Land: 42.9 sq. mi.; **Water:** 0.7 sq. mi. **Elev:** 853 ft.

Sherman Township
Lat: 39-00-49 N **Long:** 94-59-34 W
Pop: 2,036 (1990); 1,772 (1980) **Pop Density:** 49.1
Land: 41.5 sq. mi.; **Water:** 1.0 sq. mi.

Stranger Township
Lat: 39-07-40 N **Long:** 95-01-55 W
Pop: 1,828 (1990); 1,438 (1980) **Pop Density:** 37.4
Land: 48.9 sq. mi.; **Water:** 0.1 sq. mi.

Tonganoxie City
ZIP: 66086 **Lat:** 39-06-38 N **Long:** 95-05-02 W
Pop: 2,347 (1990); 1,864 (1980) **Pop Density:** 1066.8
Land: 2.2 sq. mi.; **Water:** 0.0 sq. mi. **Elev:** 853 ft.
Incorporated 1871.
Name origin: For a Delaware Indian chief.

*Tonganoxie Township
ZIP: 66086 **Lat:** 39-08-07 N **Long:** 95-07-53 W
Pop: 4,057 (1990); 3,514 (1980) **Pop Density:** 76.5
Land: 53.0 sq. mi.; **Water:** 0.4 sq. mi.

KANSAS, Lincoln County   American Places Dictionary

Lincoln County
County Seat: Lincoln (ZIP: 67455)

Pop: 3,653 (1990); 4,145 (1980)   **Pop Density:** 5.1
Land: 718.9 sq. mi.; **Water:** 1.1 sq. mi.   **Area Code:** 913
In north-central KS, northwest of Salina; organized Feb 26, 1867 from Ellsworth County.
Name origin: For Abraham Lincoln (1809–65), sixteenth U.S. president.

Barnard   City
ZIP: 67418   **Lat:** 39-11-22 N **Long:** 98-02-38 W
Pop: 129 (1990); 163 (1980)   **Pop Density:** 645.0
Land: 0.2 sq. mi.; **Water:** 0.0 sq. mi.   **Elev:** 1310 ft.
Incorporated Apr 6, 1905.
Name origin: For railroad man J. F. Barnard.

Battle Creek   Township
          Lat: 39-10-46 N **Long:** 98-12-51 W
Pop: 57 (1990); 70 (1980)   **Pop Density:** 1.6
Land: 35.9 sq. mi.; **Water:** 0.1 sq. mi.

Beaver   Township
          Lat: 39-05-36 N **Long:** 98-06-33 W
Pop: 437 (1990); 505 (1980)   **Pop Density:** 12.2
Land: 35.9 sq. mi.; **Water:** 0.0 sq. mi.

Beverly   City
ZIP: 67423   **Lat:** 39-00-49 N **Long:** 97-58-32 W
Pop: 131 (1990); 171 (1980)   **Pop Density:** 655.0
Land: 0.2 sq. mi.; **Water:** 0.0 sq. mi.   **Elev:** 1322 ft.
Incorporated Oct 29, 1904.
Name origin: For Beverly, MA.

Cedron   Township
          Lat: 39-10-34 N **Long:** 98-25-56 W
Pop: 49 (1990); 67 (1980)   **Pop Density:** 1.3
Land: 36.3 sq. mi.; **Water:** 0.0 sq. mi.

Colorado   Township
          Lat: 39-00-21 N **Long:** 97-58-34 W
Pop: 275 (1990); 290 (1980)   **Pop Density:** 7.6
Land: 36.0 sq. mi.; **Water:** 0.0 sq. mi.

Elkhorn   Township
          Lat: 39-00-09 N **Long:** 98-05-50 W
Pop: 997 (1990); 1,123 (1980)   **Pop Density:** 27.8
Land: 35.9 sq. mi.; **Water:** 0.0 sq. mi.

Franklin   Township
          Lat: 38-54-43 N **Long:** 98-05-50 W
Pop: 99 (1990); 105 (1980)   **Pop Density:** 2.7
Land: 36.1 sq. mi.; **Water:** 0.1 sq. mi.

Golden Belt   Township
          Lat: 38-54-48 N **Long:** 98-19-16 W
Pop: 79 (1990); 78 (1980)   **Pop Density:** 2.2
Land: 36.1 sq. mi.; **Water:** 0.0 sq. mi.

Grant   Township
          Lat: 39-05-20 N **Long:** 98-18-57 W
Pop: 79 (1990); 95 (1980)   **Pop Density:** 2.2
Land: 36.3 sq. mi.; **Water:** 0.0 sq. mi.

Hanover   Township
          Lat: 39-05-27 N **Long:** 98-26-05 W
Pop: 37 (1990); 50 (1980)   **Pop Density:** 1.0
Land: 36.0 sq. mi.; **Water:** 0.0 sq. mi.

Highland   Township
          Lat: 38-54-27 N **Long:** 98-26-01 W
Pop: 50 (1990); 59 (1980)   **Pop Density:** 1.4
Land: 35.6 sq. mi.; **Water:** 0.2 sq. mi.

Indiana   Township
          Lat: 38-59-50 N **Long:** 98-12-23 W
Pop: 208 (1990); 263 (1980)   **Pop Density:** 5.8
Land: 35.7 sq. mi.; **Water:** 0.0 sq. mi.

Lincoln   City
          Lat: 39-02-33 N **Long:** 98-08-53 W
Pop: 1,381 (1990); 1,599 (1980)   **Pop Density:** 1381.0
Land: 1.0 sq. mi.; **Water:** 0.0 sq. mi.
Incorporated 1879.
Name origin: For Abraham Lincoln (1809–65), sixteenth U.S. president.

Logan   Township
          Lat: 39-05-20 N **Long:** 97-59-03 W
Pop: 59 (1990); 70 (1980)   **Pop Density:** 1.7
Land: 35.7 sq. mi.; **Water:** 0.1 sq. mi.

Madison   Township
          Lat: 38-54-39 N **Long:** 97-59-00 W
Pop: 114 (1990); 107 (1980)   **Pop Density:** 3.2
Land: 35.7 sq. mi.; **Water:** 0.1 sq. mi.

Marion   Township
          Lat: 39-05-24 N **Long:** 98-12-15 W
Pop: 112 (1990); 123 (1980)   **Pop Density:** 3.2
Land: 35.5 sq. mi.; **Water:** 0.0 sq. mi.

Orange   Township
          Lat: 39-10-52 N **Long:** 98-19-43 W
Pop: 105 (1990); 96 (1980)   **Pop Density:** 2.9
Land: 36.1 sq. mi.; **Water:** 0.1 sq. mi.

Pleasant   Township
          Lat: 39-00-27 N **Long:** 98-25-56 W
Pop: 467 (1990); 549 (1980)   **Pop Density:** 13.0
Land: 36.0 sq. mi.; **Water:** 0.0 sq. mi.

Salt Creek   Township
          Lat: 39-10-28 N **Long:** 97-59-24 W
Pop: 76 (1990); 99 (1980)   **Pop Density:** 2.1
Land: 35.8 sq. mi.; **Water:** 0.0 sq. mi.

Scott   Township
          Lat: 39-10-30 N **Long:** 98-05-51 W
Pop: 169 (1990); 205 (1980)   **Pop Density:** 4.7
Land: 36.1 sq. mi.; **Water:** 0.0 sq. mi.

Sylvan Grove   City
ZIP: 67481   **Lat:** 39-00-46 N **Long:** 98-23-36 W
Pop: 321 (1990); 376 (1980)   **Pop Density:** 802.5
Land: 0.4 sq. mi.; **Water:** 0.0 sq. mi.   **Elev:** 1445 ft.
Incorporated Oct 5, 1899.
Name origin: For its descriptive connotations.

Valley
Township
Lat: 38-54-48 N **Long:** 98-12-34 W
Pop: 74 (1990); 67 (1980) **Pop Density:** 2.1
Land: 35.9 sq. mi.; **Water:** 0.1 sq. mi.

Vesper
Township
Lat: 39-00-13 N **Long:** 98-18-56 W
Pop: 110 (1990); 124 (1980) **Pop Density:** 3.0
Land: 36.6 sq. mi.; **Water:** 0.0 sq. mi.

Linn County
County Seat: Mound City (ZIP: 66056)

Pop: 8,254 (1990); 8,234 (1980) **Pop Density:** 13.8
Land: 598.8 sq. mi.; **Water:** 7.6 sq. mi. **Area Code:** 913
On the eastern border of KS, south of Kansas City; original county; organized Aug 25, 1855 (prior to statehood).
Name origin: For Lewis Fields Linn (1795–1843), U.S. senator from MO (1833–43).

Blue Mound
City
ZIP: 66010 **Lat:** 38-05-21 N **Long:** 95-00-33 W
Pop: 251 (1990); 319 (1980) **Pop Density:** 418.3
Land: 0.6 sq. mi.; **Water:** 0.0 sq. mi. **Elev:** 1040 ft.
Incorporated Nov 14, 1884. Not coextensive with the town of the same name.
Name origin: For a local Indian feature.

*Blue Mound
Township
ZIP: 66010 **Lat:** 38-05-43 N **Long:** 95-00-18 W
Pop: 484 (1990); 584 (1980) **Pop Density:** 7.7
Land: 62.7 sq. mi.; **Water:** 0.1 sq. mi.

Centerville
Township
ZIP: 66014 **Lat:** 38-12-46 N **Long:** 94-59-04 W
Pop: 381 (1990); 448 (1980) **Pop Density:** 4.8
Land: 79.5 sq. mi.; **Water:** 0.1 sq. mi.

La Cygne
City
ZIP: 66040 **Lat:** 38-20-48 N **Long:** 94-45-40 W
Pop: 1,066 (1990); 1,025 (1980) **Pop Density:** 888.3
Land: 1.2 sq. mi.; **Water:** 0.0 sq. mi. **Elev:** 828 ft.
Incorporated Jan 14, 1870.
Name origin: From the Marais des Cygnes River, on which the town is located. From a French translation of an Osage Indian name meaning 'marsh of swans.'

Liberty
Township
Lat: 38-19-50 N **Long:** 94-59-26 W
Pop: 830 (1990); 813 (1980) **Pop Density:** 12.9
Land: 64.2 sq. mi.; **Water:** 0.1 sq. mi.

Lincoln
Township
Lat: 38-20-48 N **Long:** 94-41-45 W
Pop: 1,607 (1990); 1,491 (1980) **Pop Density:** 33.2
Land: 48.4 sq. mi.; **Water:** 4.1 sq. mi.

Mound City
City
ZIP: 66056 **Lat:** 38-08-37 N **Long:** 94-49-20 W
Pop: 789 (1990); 755 (1980) **Pop Density:** 657.5
Land: 1.2 sq. mi.; **Water:** 0.0 sq. mi. **Elev:** 875 ft.
Incorporated Jun 20, 1871. Not coextensive with the town of the same name.
Name origin: For nearby Indian mounds.

*Mound City
Township
ZIP: 66056 **Lat:** 38-06-45 N **Long:** 94-50-59 W
Pop: 1,194 (1990); 1,104 (1980) **Pop Density:** 24.0
Land: 49.7 sq. mi.; **Water:** 0.1 sq. mi.

Paris
Township
Lat: 38-12-27 N **Long:** 94-49-08 W
Pop: 450 (1990); 425 (1980) **Pop Density:** 7.0
Land: 64.6 sq. mi.; **Water:** 0.1 sq. mi.

Parker
City
ZIP: 66072 **Lat:** 38-19-43 N **Long:** 94-59-25 W
Pop: 256 (1990); 270 (1980) **Pop Density:** 1280.0
Land: 0.2 sq. mi.; **Water:** 0.0 sq. mi. **Elev:** 1005 ft.
Incorporated Jul 1897.

Pleasanton
City
ZIP: 66075 **Lat:** 38-10-30 N **Long:** 94-42-46 W
Pop: 1,231 (1990); 1,303 (1980) **Pop Density:** 1367.8
Land: 0.9 sq. mi.; **Water:** 0.0 sq. mi. **Elev:** 861 ft.
Incorporated Oct 9, 1869.
Name origin: For Gen. Alfred Pleasanton, who served in KS in the 1850s.

Potosi
Township
Lat: 38-10-30 N **Long:** 94-41-26 W
Pop: 1,886 (1990); 1,940 (1980) **Pop Density:** 33.8
Land: 55.8 sq. mi.; **Water:** 0.3 sq. mi.

Prescott
City
ZIP: 66767 **Lat:** 38-03-46 N **Long:** 94-41-45 W
Pop: 301 (1990); 319 (1980) **Pop Density:** 1505.0
Land: 0.2 sq. mi.; **Water:** 0.0 sq. mi. **Elev:** 880 ft.
Incorporated 1870.
Name origin: For C.H. Prescott, an auditor for the Fort Scott and Gulf Railroad.

Scott
Township
Lat: 38-19-57 N **Long:** 94-50-32 W
Pop: 549 (1990); 464 (1980) **Pop Density:** 8.7
Land: 62.8 sq. mi.; **Water:** 0.5 sq. mi.

Sheridan
Township
Lat: 38-04-37 N **Long:** 94-40-51 W
Pop: 535 (1990); 552 (1980) **Pop Density:** 12.0
Land: 44.7 sq. mi.; **Water:** 0.1 sq. mi.

Stanton
Township
Lat: 38-03-59 N **Long:** 94-50-27 W
Pop: 174 (1990); 176 (1980) **Pop Density:** 5.8
Land: 30.0 sq. mi.; **Water:** 0.0 sq. mi.

Valley
Township
Lat: 38-15-48 N **Long:** 94-40-40 W
Pop: 164 (1990); 237 (1980) **Pop Density:** 4.5
Land: 36.4 sq. mi.; **Water:** 2.3 sq. mi.

KANSAS, Logan County

Logan County
County Seat: Oakley (ZIP: 67748)

Pop: 3,081 (1990); 3,478 (1980)   **Pop Density:** 2.9
Land: 1073.1 sq. mi.; **Water:** 0.1 sq. mi.   **Area Code:** 913

In western KS, northwest of Garden City; organized as St. John County Mar 4, 1881 from Wallace County; name changed Feb 24, 1887.

Name origin: For Gen. John Alexander Logan (1826–86), officer in the Mexican-American War and Civil War; U.S. senator from IL (1871–77; 1879–86).

Augustine   Township
Lat: 38-44-13 N   Long: 101-22-52 W
Pop: 32 (1990); 28 (1980)   **Pop Density:** 0.4
Land: 72.3 sq. mi.; **Water:** 0.0 sq. mi.

Elkader   Township
Lat: 38-52-25 N   Long: 100-53-24 W
Pop: 24 (1990); 36 (1980)   **Pop Density:** 0.2
Land: 107.5 sq. mi.; **Water:** 0.0 sq. mi.

Lees   Township
Lat: 38-44-37 N   Long: 100-56-06 W
Pop: 37 (1990); 37 (1980)   **Pop Density:** 0.5
Land: 71.5 sq. mi.; **Water:** 0.0 sq. mi.

Logansport   Township
Lat: 38-52-04 N   Long: 101-03-24 W
Pop: 5 (1990); 12 (1980)   **Pop Density:** 0.0
Land: 107.2 sq. mi.; **Water:** 0.0 sq. mi.

McAllaster   Township
Lat: 39-02-52 N   Long: 101-24-17 W
Pop: 31 (1990); 40 (1980)   **Pop Density:** 0.3
Land: 106.4 sq. mi.; **Water:** 0.0 sq. mi.

Monument   Township
ZIP: 67747   Lat: 39-02-35 N   Long: 101-04-01 W
Pop: 159 (1990); 184 (1980)   **Pop Density:** 1.5
Land: 106.6 sq. mi.; **Water:** 0.0 sq. mi.

Oakley   City
ZIP: 67748   Lat: 39-07-33 N   Long: 100-51-14 W
Pop: 1,987 (1990); 2,268 (1980)   **Pop Density:** 1528.5
Land: 1.3 sq. mi.; **Water:** 0.0 sq. mi.   **Elev:** 350 ft.

Incorporated Oct 15, 1887. Part of the town is also in Thomas County.

Name origin: For Miss Eliza Oakley. Originally called Carlyle.

*Oakley   Township
ZIP: 67748   Lat: 39-03-13 N   Long: 100-53-47 W
Pop: 2,285 (1990); 2,558 (1980)   **Pop Density:** 21.3
Land: 107.3 sq. mi.; **Water:** 0.0 sq. mi.

Paxton   Township
Lat: 38-44-53 N   Long: 101-08-08 W
Pop: 43 (1990); 33 (1980)   **Pop Density:** 0.6
Land: 71.8 sq. mi.; **Water:** 0.0 sq. mi.

Russell Springs   City
ZIP: 67755   Lat: 38-54-44 N   Long: 101-10-31 W
Pop: 29 (1990); 56 (1980)   **Pop Density:** 41.4
Land: 0.7 sq. mi.; **Water:** 0.0 sq. mi.   **Elev:** 2964 ft.

Incorporated 1888. Not coextensive with the town of the same name.

*Russell Springs   Township
ZIP: 67755   Lat: 38-52-25 N   Long: 101-12-47 W
Pop: 88 (1990); 112 (1980)   **Pop Density:** 0.8
Land: 107.6 sq. mi.; **Water:** 0.0 sq. mi.

Western   Township
Lat: 38-52-04 N   Long: 101-23-52 W
Pop: 49 (1990); 58 (1980)   **Pop Density:** 0.5
Land: 107.6 sq. mi.; **Water:** 0.0 sq. mi.

Winona   City
ZIP: 67764   Lat: 39-03-41 N   Long: 101-14-40 W
Pop: 194 (1990); 258 (1980)   **Pop Density:** 646.7
Land: 0.3 sq. mi.; **Water:** 0.0 sq. mi.   **Elev:** 3329 ft.

Incorporated Jul 15, 1920. Not coextensive with the town of the same name.

Name origin: For Wenonah in then poem *The Song of Hiawatha* (1855) by Henry Wadsworth Longfellow (1807–82), with a spelling variation.

*Winona   Township
ZIP: 67764   Lat: 39-02-54 N   Long: 101-13-47 W
Pop: 328 (1990); 380 (1980)   **Pop Density:** 3.1
Land: 107.1 sq. mi.; **Water:** 0.0 sq. mi.

American Places Dictionary   KANSAS, Lyon County

Lyon County
County Seat: Emporia (ZIP: 66801)

Pop: 34,732 (1990); 35,108 (1980)   **Pop Density:** 40.8
Land: 851.0 sq. mi.; **Water:** 4.2 sq. mi.   **Area Code:** 316

In east-central KS, northeast of Wichita; established as Breckinridge County Feb 17, 1857 (prior to statehood) from Madison County (which was abolished at the time it was divided between Lyon and Greenwood counties); name changed Feb 5, 1862.

Name origin: For Gen. Nathaniel Lyon (1818–61), Union commander in the Civil War who helped preserve MO for the Union when it seemed likely to join the Confederacy.

Admire   City
ZIP: 66830   **Lat:** 38-38-28 N   **Long:** 96-06-10 W
Pop: 147 (1990); 158 (1980)   **Pop Density:** 490.0
Land: 0.3 sq. mi.; **Water:** 0.0 sq. mi.   **Elev:** 1230 ft.
Incorporated Jul 3, 1916.
Name origin: For its founder, Capt. Jacob V. Admire.

Agnes City   Township
Lat: 38-40-39 N   **Long:** 96-14-25 W
Pop: 492 (1990); 507 (1980)   **Pop Density:** 4.6
Land: 107.7 sq. mi.; **Water:** 0.2 sq. mi.

Allen   City
ZIP: 66833   **Lat:** 38-39-19 N   **Long:** 96-10-06 W
Pop: 191 (1990); 205 (1980)   **Pop Density:** 636.7
Land: 0.3 sq. mi.; **Water:** 0.0 sq. mi.   **Elev:** 1320 ft.
Incorporated Jan 19, 1909.
Name origin: For Allen McGee of the family prominent in business and political circles in Kansas City, MO during the 1850s.

Americus   City
ZIP: 66835   **Lat:** 38-30-23 N   **Long:** 96-15-39 W
Pop: 891 (1990); 915 (1980)   **Pop Density:** 810.0
Land: 1.1 sq. mi.; **Water:** 0.0 sq. mi.   **Elev:** 1160 ft.
Incorporated Sep 29, 1884. Not coextensive with the town of the same name.
Name origin: For the Latin version of the name of the explorer Amerigo Vespucci.

*Americus   Township
ZIP: 66835   **Lat:** 38-31-42 N   **Long:** 96-16-58 W
Pop: 1,491 (1990); 1,591 (1980)   **Pop Density:** 17.1
Land: 87.0 sq. mi.; **Water:** 0.3 sq. mi.

Bushong   City
ZIP: 66833   **Lat:** 38-38-33 N   **Long:** 96-15-26 W
Pop: 57 (1990); 62 (1980)   **Pop Density:** 285.0
Land: 0.2 sq. mi.; **Water:** 0.0 sq. mi.   **Elev:** 1383 ft.
Incorporated Aug 21, 1923.

Center   Township
Lat: 38-14-41 N   **Long:** 96-14-48 W
Pop: 1,156 (1990); 1,135 (1980)   **Pop Density:** 9.7
Land: 118.9 sq. mi.; **Water:** 1.0 sq. mi.

Elmendaro   Township
Lat: 38-14-29 N   **Long:** 96-02-43 W
Pop: 1,006 (1990); 1,035 (1980)   **Pop Density:** 10.2
Land: 99.1 sq. mi.; **Water:** 0.3 sq. mi.

Emporia   City
ZIP: 66801   **Lat:** 38-24-41 N   **Long:** 96-11-35 W
Pop: 25,512 (1990); 25,287 (1980)   **Pop Density:** 2773.0
Land: 9.2 sq. mi.; **Water:** 0.1 sq. mi.   **Elev:** 1150 ft.
In eastern KS, 52 mi. southwest of Topeka. Founded 1856; incorporated 1870. Not coextensive with the town of the same name.
Name origin: For its market town origins.

*Emporia   Township
ZIP: 66801   **Lat:** 38-22-13 N   **Long:** 96-10-20 W
Pop: 1,293 (1990); 1,244 (1980)   **Pop Density:** 23.2
Land: 55.8 sq. mi.; **Water:** 0.7 sq. mi.

Fremont   Township
Lat: 38-31-15 N   **Long:** 96-09-08 W
Pop: 905 (1990); 988 (1980)   **Pop Density:** 12.7
Land: 71.0 sq. mi.; **Water:** 0.2 sq. mi.

Hartford   City
ZIP: 66854   **Lat:** 38-18-28 N   **Long:** 95-57-24 W
Pop: 541 (1990); 551 (1980)   **Pop Density:** 1352.5
Land: 0.4 sq. mi.; **Water:** 0.0 sq. mi.   **Elev:** 1085 ft.
Incorporated Mar 12, 1884.
Name origin: For Hartford, CT, former home of early settlers.

Ivy   Township
Lat: 38-38-34 N   **Long:** 96-05-01 W
Pop: 253 (1990); 275 (1980)   **Pop Density:** 7.4
Land: 34.0 sq. mi.; **Water:** 0.0 sq. mi.

Jackson   Township
Lat: 38-23-41 N   **Long:** 96-01-28 W
Pop: 865 (1990); 1,013 (1980)   **Pop Density:** 9.9
Land: 87.6 sq. mi.; **Water:** 0.5 sq. mi.

Neosho Rapids   City
ZIP: 66864   **Lat:** 38-22-07 N   **Long:** 95-59-29 W
Pop: 235 (1990); 289 (1980)   **Pop Density:** 470.0
Land: 0.5 sq. mi.; **Water:** 0.0 sq. mi.   **Elev:** 1090 ft.
Incorporated Oct 1923.
Name origin: For the rapids on the Neosho River.

Olpe   City
ZIP: 66865   **Lat:** 38-15-43 N   **Long:** 96-10-01 W
Pop: 431 (1990); 477 (1980)   **Pop Density:** 1436.7
Land: 0.3 sq. mi.; **Water:** 0.0 sq. mi.   **Elev:** 1200 ft.
Incorporated Jan 7, 1905.
Name origin: For Olpe, Germany.

Pike   Township
Lat: 38-23-08 N   **Long:** 96-17-53 W
Pop: 912 (1990); 1,212 (1980)   **Pop Density:** 16.9
Land: 53.9 sq. mi.; **Water:** 0.2 sq. mi.

KANSAS, Lyon County   American Places Dictionary

Reading City
ZIP: 66868 Lat: 38-31-08 N Long: 95-57-26 W
Pop: 264 (1990); 244 (1980) Pop Density: 1320.0
Land: 0.2 sq. mi.; Water: 0.0 sq. mi. Elev: 1080 ft.
Incorporated Sep 1881. Not coextensive with the town of the same name.
Name origin: For the Reading Iron Works in Reading, PA.

*Reading Township
ZIP: 66868 Lat: 38-32-26 N Long: 96-01-40 W
Pop: 553 (1990); 499 (1980) Pop Density: 8.2
Land: 67.5 sq. mi.; Water: 0.5 sq. mi.

Waterloo Township
Lat: 38-41-11 N Long: 96-01-00 W
Pop: 294 (1990); 322 (1980) Pop Density: 4.9
Land: 59.4 sq. mi.; Water: 0.2 sq. mi.

Marion County
County Seat: Marion (ZIP: 66861)

Pop: 12,888 (1990); 13,522 (1980) Pop Density: 13.7
Land: 943.2 sq. mi.; Water: 10.4 sq. mi. Area Code: 316
In central KS, north of Wichita; established Aug 25, 1855 (prior to statehood) from Chase County.
Name origin: For Gen. Francis Marion (c. 1732–95), SC soldier and legislator, known as "The Swamp Fox" for his tactics during the Revolutionary War.

Blaine Township
Lat: 38-33-58 N Long: 97-12-24 W
Pop: 211 (1990); 214 (1980) Pop Density: 5.9
Land: 35.8 sq. mi.; Water: 0.1 sq. mi.

Burns City
ZIP: 66840 Lat: 38-05-23 N Long: 96-53-15 W
Pop: 226 (1990); 224 (1980) Pop Density: 565.0
Land: 0.4 sq. mi.; Water: 0.0 sq. mi. Elev: 1504 ft.
Incorporated Oct 7, 1905.
Name origin: For a Santa Fe Railroad official.

Catlin Township
Lat: 38-13-09 N Long: 97-05-54 W
Pop: 194 (1990); 230 (1980) Pop Density: 5.4
Land: 36.0 sq. mi.; Water: 0.0 sq. mi.

Center Township
Lat: 38-20-56 N Long: 96-59-09 W
Pop: 494 (1990); 421 (1980) Pop Density: 9.9
Land: 49.9 sq. mi.; Water: 0.1 sq. mi.

Clark Township
Lat: 38-28-25 N Long: 97-05-28 W
Pop: 177 (1990); 217 (1980) Pop Density: 5.0
Land: 35.7 sq. mi.; Water: 0.2 sq. mi.

Clear Creek Township
Lat: 38-28-37 N Long: 96-56-49 W
Pop: 562 (1990); 668 (1980) Pop Density: 7.4
Land: 75.6 sq. mi.; Water: 0.0 sq. mi.

Colfax Township
Lat: 38-33-56 N Long: 97-05-47 W
Pop: 237 (1990); 273 (1980) Pop Density: 6.6
Land: 35.9 sq. mi.; Water: 0.0 sq. mi.

Doyle Township
Lat: 38-13-29 N Long: 96-53-45 W
Pop: 70 (1990); 95 (1980) Pop Density: 1.9
Land: 37.7 sq. mi.; Water: 0.0 sq. mi.

Durham City
ZIP: 67438 Lat: 38-29-06 N Long: 97-13-37 W
Pop: 119 (1990); 130 (1980) Pop Density: 595.0
Land: 0.2 sq. mi.; Water: 0.0 sq. mi. Elev: 1396 ft.
Incorporated May 5, 1906.
Name origin: For Durham County, England.

Durham Park Township
Lat: 38-28-36 N Long: 97-12-12 W
Pop: 258 (1990); 282 (1980) Pop Density: 7.4
Land: 34.9 sq. mi.; Water: 1.0 sq. mi.

East Branch Township
Lat: 38-12-40 N Long: 97-12-47 W
Pop: 198 (1990); 202 (1980) Pop Density: 5.6
Land: 35.4 sq. mi.; Water: 0.0 sq. mi.

Fairplay Township
Lat: 38-13-44 N Long: 96-59-21 W
Pop: 122 (1990); 162 (1980) Pop Density: 2.7
Land: 45.0 sq. mi.; Water: 0.0 sq. mi.

Florence City
ZIP: 66851 Lat: 38-14-34 N Long: 96-55-44 W
Pop: 636 (1990); 729 (1980) Pop Density: 795.0
Land: 0.8 sq. mi.; Water: 0.0 sq. mi. Elev: 1280 ft.
Incorporated Jun 8, 1872.
Name origin: For Florence, Italy.

Gale Township
Lat: 38-23-31 N Long: 97-05-33 W
Pop: 239 (1990); 243 (1980) Pop Density: 9.2
Land: 26.0 sq. mi.; Water: 8.1 sq. mi.

Goessel City
ZIP: 67053 Lat: 38-14-47 N Long: 97-20-43 W
Pop: 506 (1990); 421 (1980) Pop Density: 2530.0
Land: 0.2 sq. mi.; Water: 0.0 sq. mi. Elev: 1533 ft.
Incorporated Mar 10, 1952.
Name origin: For a sea captain named Goessel, who brought many of the area's Mennonite settlers across the Atlantic.

Grant Township
Lat: 38-21-46 N Long: 96-52-29 W
Pop: 136 (1990); 159 (1980) Pop Density: 2.0
Land: 67.1 sq. mi.; Water: 0.1 sq. mi.

Hillsboro — City
ZIP: 67063 **Lat:** 38-21-04 N **Long:** 97-12-07 W
Pop: 2,704 (1990); 2,717 (1980) **Pop Density:** 1590.6
Land: 1.7 sq. mi.; **Water:** 0.0 sq. mi. **Elev:** 1454 ft.
Incorporated Jun 24, 1884.
Name origin: For pioneer landowner, John Hill.

Lehigh — City
ZIP: 67073 **Lat:** 38-22-29 N **Long:** 97-18-08 W
Pop: 180 (1990); 189 (1980) **Pop Density:** 600.0
Land: 0.3 sq. mi.; **Water:** 0.0 sq. mi. **Elev:** 1529 ft.
Incorporated Jan 8, 1901. Not coextensive with the town of the same name.

*Lehigh — Township
ZIP: 67073 **Lat:** 38-23-27 N **Long:** 97-19-00 W
Pop: 311 (1990); 334 (1980) **Pop Density:** 8.6
Land: 36.1 sq. mi.; **Water:** 0.0 sq. mi.

Liberty — Township
Lat: 38-18-23 N **Long:** 97-12-12 W
Pop: 305 (1990); 297 (1980) **Pop Density:** 8.6
Land: 35.5 sq. mi.; **Water:** 0.0 sq. mi.

Lincolnville — City
ZIP: 66858 **Lat:** 38-29-38 N **Long:** 96-57-40 W
Pop: 197 (1990); 235 (1980) **Pop Density:** 985.0
Land: 0.2 sq. mi.; **Water:** 0.0 sq. mi. **Elev:** 1420 ft.
Incorporated Apr 20, 1910.
Name origin: For Abraham Lincoln (1809–65), sixteenth U.S. president.

Logan — Township
Lat: 38-33-45 N **Long:** 97-19-00 W
Pop: 117 (1990); 147 (1980) **Pop Density:** 3.2
Land: 36.1 sq. mi.; **Water:** 0.0 sq. mi.

Lost Springs — City
ZIP: 66859 **Lat:** 38-33-59 N **Long:** 96-57-53 W
Pop: 106 (1990); 94 (1980) **Pop Density:** 530.0
Land: 0.2 sq. mi.; **Water:** 0.0 sq. mi. **Elev:** 1490 ft.
Incorporated Oct 14, 1904. Not coextensive with the town of the same name.
Name origin: For the tendency of the local springs to go dry part of the year.

*Lost Springs — Township
ZIP: 66859 **Lat:** 38-34-17 N **Long:** 96-58-55 W
Pop: 241 (1990); 316 (1980) **Pop Density:** 6.7
Land: 35.9 sq. mi.; **Water:** 0.0 sq. mi.

Marion — City
ZIP: 66861 **Lat:** 38-20-56 N **Long:** 97-00-56 W
Pop: 1,906 (1990); 1,951 (1980) **Pop Density:** 1121.2
Land: 1.7 sq. mi.; **Water:** 0.0 sq. mi. **Elev:** 1307 ft.
Incorporated Aug 17, 1875.
Name origin: For Revolutionary War hero, Gen. Francis Marion (c. 1732–95), known as the "Swamp Fox" for his daring exploits.

Menno — Township
Lat: 38-18-14 N **Long:** 97-18-56 W
Pop: 307 (1990); 297 (1980) **Pop Density:** 8.5
Land: 36.0 sq. mi.; **Water:** 0.0 sq. mi.

Milton — Township
Lat: 38-07-53 N **Long:** 96-53-08 W
Pop: 325 (1990); 339 (1980) **Pop Density:** 10.8
Land: 30.0 sq. mi.; **Water:** 0.0 sq. mi.

Moore — Township
Lat: 38-28-45 N **Long:** 97-18-56 W
Pop: 69 (1990); 94 (1980) **Pop Density:** 1.9
Land: 36.0 sq. mi.; **Water:** 0.0 sq. mi.

Peabody — City
ZIP: 66866 **Lat:** 38-10-07 N **Long:** 97-06-24 W
Pop: 1,349 (1990); 1,474 (1980) **Pop Density:** 1124.2
Land: 1.2 sq. mi.; **Water:** 0.0 sq. mi. **Elev:** 1361 ft.
Name origin: For Boston philanthropist F.H. Peabody, a Santa Fe Railroad director.

*Peabody — Township
ZIP: 66866 **Lat:** 38-08-07 N **Long:** 97-05-57 W
Pop: 1,535 (1990); 1,671 (1980) **Pop Density:** 42.1
Land: 36.5 sq. mi.; **Water:** 0.1 sq. mi.

Ramona — City
ZIP: 67475 **Lat:** 38-35-50 N **Long:** 97-03-48 W
Pop: 106 (1990); 116 (1980) **Pop Density:** 353.3
Land: 0.3 sq. mi.; **Water:** 0.0 sq. mi. **Elev:** 1433 ft.
Incorporated Jan 11, 1910.
Name origin: For a popular novel.

Risley — Township
Lat: 38-23-26 N **Long:** 97-12-23 W
Pop: 227 (1990); 233 (1980) **Pop Density:** 6.6
Land: 34.5 sq. mi.; **Water:** 0.5 sq. mi.

Summit — Township
Lat: 38-07-47 N **Long:** 96-59-14 W
Pop: 90 (1990); 104 (1980) **Pop Density:** 2.5
Land: 35.7 sq. mi.; **Water:** 0.2 sq. mi.

Tampa — City
ZIP: 67483 **Lat:** 38-32-49 N **Long:** 97-09-14 W
Pop: 113 (1990); 113 (1980) **Pop Density:** 565.0
Land: 0.2 sq. mi.; **Water:** 0.0 sq. mi. **Elev:** 1424 ft.
Incorporated Jul 6, 1908.

West Branch — Township
Lat: 38-12-55 N **Long:** 97-18-42 W
Pop: 973 (1990); 869 (1980) **Pop Density:** 27.3
Land: 35.6 sq. mi.; **Water:** 0.0 sq. mi.

Wilson — Township
Lat: 38-18-08 N **Long:** 97-05-34 W
Pop: 244 (1990); 258 (1980) **Pop Density:** 6.8
Land: 36.1 sq. mi.; **Water:** 0.0 sq. mi.

Marshall County
County Seat: Marysville (ZIP: 66508)

Pop: 11,705 (1990); 12,787 (1980)
Land: 902.6 sq. mi.; **Water:** 1.8 sq. mi.
Pop Density: 13.0
Area Code: 913

On the northern border of KS, north of Manhattan; original county; organized Aug 25, 1855 (prior to statehood).

Name origin: For Francis J. Marshall, local businessman and member of the first KS territorial legislature. County seat was named for his wife.

Axtell — City
ZIP: 66403   **Lat:** 39-52-18 N   **Long:** 96-15-25 W
Pop: 432 (1990); 470 (1980)   **Pop Density:** 864.0
Land: 0.5 sq. mi.; **Water:** 0.0 sq. mi.   **Elev:** 1368 ft.
Incorporated 1886.
Name origin: For railroad official Jesse Axtell.

Balderson — Township
Lat: 39-57-22 N   **Long:** 96-31-40 W
Pop: 120 (1990); 154 (1980)   **Pop Density:** 3.2
Land: 37.7 sq. mi.; **Water:** 0.0 sq. mi.

Beattie — City
ZIP: 66406   **Lat:** 39-51-45 N   **Long:** 96-25-03 W
Pop: 221 (1990); 316 (1980)   **Pop Density:** 1105.0
Land: 0.2 sq. mi.; **Water:** 0.0 sq. mi.   **Elev:** 1330 ft.
Incorporated Oct 14, 1884.
Name origin: For Mayor A. Beattie, chief city official of St. Joseph, MO.

Bigelow — Township
Lat: 39-36-26 N   **Long:** 96-31-44 W
Pop: 93 (1990); 113 (1980)   **Pop Density:** 2.5
Land: 37.4 sq. mi.; **Water:** 0.4 sq. mi.

Blue Rapids — City
ZIP: 66411   **Lat:** 39-40-42 N   **Long:** 96-39-34 W
Pop: 1,131 (1990); 1,280 (1980)   **Pop Density:** 538.6
Land: 2.1 sq. mi.; **Water:** 0.0 sq. mi.   **Elev:** 1158 ft.
Incorporated 1872.
Name origin: For the rapids in the Blue River, near which the town is located.

*Blue Rapids — Township
ZIP: 66411   **Lat:** 39-36-38 N   **Long:** 96-37-59 W
Pop: 93 (1990); 113 (1980)   **Pop Density:** 2.6
Land: 35.8 sq. mi.; **Water:** 0.1 sq. mi.

Blue Rapids City — Township
Lat: 39-41-21 N   **Long:** 96-38-26 W
Pop: 1,233 (1990); 1,389 (1980)   **Pop Density:** 34.6
Land: 35.6 sq. mi.; **Water:** 0.4 sq. mi.

Center — Township
Lat: 39-46-42 N   **Long:** 96-31-45 W
Pop: 174 (1990); 164 (1980)   **Pop Density:** 4.6
Land: 37.7 sq. mi.; **Water:** 0.0 sq. mi.

Clear Fork — Township
Lat: 39-36-10 N   **Long:** 96-24-25 W
Pop: 49 (1990); 52 (1980)   **Pop Density:** 1.4
Land: 36.0 sq. mi.; **Water:** 0.0 sq. mi.

Cleveland — Township
Lat: 39-36-37 N   **Long:** 96-17-46 W
Pop: 98 (1990); 117 (1980)   **Pop Density:** 2.8
Land: 35.6 sq. mi.; **Water:** 0.3 sq. mi.

Cottage Hill — Township
Lat: 39-36-32 N   **Long:** 96-44-50 W
Pop: 138 (1990); 166 (1980)   **Pop Density:** 3.8
Land: 36.0 sq. mi.; **Water:** 0.0 sq. mi.

Elm Creek — Township
Lat: 39-46-57 N   **Long:** 96-37-51 W
Pop: 204 (1990); 229 (1980)   **Pop Density:** 5.7
Land: 35.9 sq. mi.; **Water:** 0.0 sq. mi.

Frankfort — City
ZIP: 66427   **Lat:** 39-42-13 N   **Long:** 96-25-03 W
Pop: 927 (1990); 1,038 (1980)   **Pop Density:** 927.0
Land: 1.0 sq. mi.; **Water:** 0.0 sq. mi.   **Elev:** 1150 ft.
In northeastern KS; incorporated Jul 24, 1875.
Name origin: For Frankfort, Germany.

Franklin — Township
Lat: 39-51-47 N   **Long:** 96-31-44 W
Pop: 362 (1990); 332 (1980)   **Pop Density:** 9.6
Land: 37.7 sq. mi.; **Water:** 0.0 sq. mi.

Guittard — Township
Lat: 39-51-43 N   **Long:** 96-24-29 W
Pop: 458 (1990); 505 (1980)   **Pop Density:** 12.8
Land: 35.8 sq. mi.; **Water:** 0.0 sq. mi.

Herkimer — Township
Lat: 39-57-26 N   **Long:** 96-45-00 W
Pop: 270 (1990); 318 (1980)   **Pop Density:** 7.6
Land: 35.7 sq. mi.; **Water:** 0.0 sq. mi.

Lincoln — Township
Lat: 39-47-05 N   **Long:** 96-17-39 W
Pop: 140 (1990); 181 (1980)   **Pop Density:** 3.9
Land: 35.5 sq. mi.; **Water:** 0.1 sq. mi.

Logan — Township
Lat: 39-52-41 N   **Long:** 96-44-24 W
Pop: 347 (1990); 357 (1980)   **Pop Density:** 9.7
Land: 35.9 sq. mi.; **Water:** 0.0 sq. mi.

Marysville — City
ZIP: 66508   **Lat:** 39-50-47 N   **Long:** 96-38-32 W
Pop: 3,359 (1990); 3,670 (1980)   **Pop Density:** 1767.9
Land: 1.9 sq. mi.; **Water:** 0.0 sq. mi.   **Elev:** 1202 ft.
Incorporated Feb 2, 1861.
Name origin: For Mary Williams, the wife of its founder.

*Marysville — Township
ZIP: 66508   **Lat:** 39-52-12 N   **Long:** 96-38-01 W
Pop: 541 (1990); 524 (1980)   **Pop Density:** 16.1
Land: 33.7 sq. mi.; **Water:** 0.0 sq. mi.

Murray — Township
Lat: 39-52-32 N   **Long:** 96-17-11 W
Pop: 669 (1990); 737 (1980)   **Pop Density:** 18.8
Land: 35.6 sq. mi.; **Water:** 0.0 sq. mi.

Noble
Township
Lat: 39-41-58 N **Long:** 96-17-54 W
Pop: 276 (1990); 302 (1980) **Pop Density:** 7.8
Land: 35.5 sq. mi.; **Water:** 0.3 sq. mi.

Oketo
City
ZIP: 66518 **Lat:** 39-57-46 N **Long:** 96-35-54 W
Pop: 116 (1990); 130 (1980) **Pop Density:** 1160.0
Land: 0.1 sq. mi.; **Water:** 0.0 sq. mi. **Elev:** 1178 ft.
Incorporated Oct 15, 1887. Not coextensive with the town of the same name.
Name origin: From an abbreviated form of *Arkaketah*, the name of a 19th-century Oto Indian chief.

*Oketo
Township
ZIP: 66518 **Lat:** 39-57-35 N **Long:** 96-37-52 W
Pop: 318 (1990); 316 (1980) **Pop Density:** 9.0
Land: 35.3 sq. mi.; **Water:** 0.0 sq. mi.

Richland
Township
Lat: 39-57-32 N **Long:** 96-24-25 W
Pop: 226 (1990); 247 (1980) **Pop Density:** 6.3
Land: 35.7 sq. mi.; **Water:** 0.0 sq. mi.

Rock
Township
Lat: 39-46-55 N **Long:** 96-24-09 W
Pop: 119 (1990); 151 (1980) **Pop Density:** 3.3
Land: 35.7 sq. mi.; **Water:** 0.0 sq. mi.

St. Bridget
Township
Lat: 39-57-36 N **Long:** 96-18-01 W
Pop: 206 (1990); 252 (1980) **Pop Density:** 5.8
Land: 35.5 sq. mi.; **Water:** 0.0 sq. mi.

Summerfield
City
ZIP: 66541 **Lat:** 39-59-47 N **Long:** 96-20-56 W
Pop: 169 (1990); 225 (1980) **Pop Density:** 563.3
Land: 0.3 sq. mi.; **Water:** 0.0 sq. mi. **Elev:** 1511 ft.
Incorporated Oct 18, 1889.
Name origin: For a local railroad official, Elias Summerfield.

Vermillion
City
ZIP: 66544 **Lat:** 39-43-04 N **Long:** 96-15-53 W
Pop: 113 (1990); 191 (1980) **Pop Density:** 376.7
Land: 0.3 sq. mi.; **Water:** 0.0 sq. mi. **Elev:** 1240 ft.
Incorporated Apr 11, 1899.
Name origin: For the Vermillion River, which was named for its red sandstone bottom.

*Vermillion
Township
ZIP: 66544 **Lat:** 39-41-43 N **Long:** 96-24-14 W
Pop: 1,101 (1990); 1,218 (1980) **Pop Density:** 30.7
Land: 35.9 sq. mi.; **Water:** 0.0 sq. mi.

Walnut
Township
Lat: 39-47-15 N **Long:** 96-45-07 W
Pop: 177 (1990); 183 (1980) **Pop Density:** 4.9
Land: 35.9 sq. mi.; **Water:** 0.0 sq. mi.

Waterville
City
ZIP: 66548 **Lat:** 39-41-30 N **Long:** 96-44-53 W
Pop: 601 (1990); 694 (1980) **Pop Density:** 1502.5
Land: 0.4 sq. mi.; **Water:** 0.0 sq. mi. **Elev:** 1176 ft.
Incorporated Jul 30, 1870. Not coextensive with the town of the same name.
Name origin: For Waterville, NY.

*Waterville
Township
ZIP: 66548 **Lat:** 39-41-44 N **Long:** 96-45-06 W
Pop: 801 (1990); 842 (1980) **Pop Density:** 22.3
Land: 35.9 sq. mi.; **Water:** 0.0 sq. mi.

Wells
Township
Lat: 39-41-47 N **Long:** 96-31-44 W
Pop: 133 (1990); 155 (1980) **Pop Density:** 3.5
Land: 37.8 sq. mi.; **Water:** 0.0 sq. mi.

McPherson County
County Seat: McPherson (ZIP: 67460)

Pop: 27,268 (1990); 26,855 (1980) **Pop Density:** 30.3
Land: 899.8 sq. mi.; **Water:** 1.5 sq. mi. **Area Code:** 316
In central KS, north of Hutchinson; organized Feb 26, 1867 from unorganized territory.
Name origin: For Gen. James Birdseye McPherson (1828–64), commander of the Union Army of the Tennessee during the Civil War.

Battle Hill
Township
Lat: 38-28-32 N **Long:** 97-25-32 W
Pop: 106 (1990); 120 (1980) **Pop Density:** 3.0
Land: 35.9 sq. mi.; **Water:** 0.1 sq. mi.

Bonaville
Township
Lat: 38-34-09 N **Long:** 97-32-25 W
Pop: 68 (1990); 49 (1980) **Pop Density:** 1.9
Land: 35.9 sq. mi.; **Water:** 0.1 sq. mi.

Canton
City
ZIP: 67428 **Lat:** 38-23-10 N **Long:** 97-25-47 W
Pop: 794 (1990); 926 (1980) **Pop Density:** 1588.0
Land: 0.5 sq. mi.; **Water:** 0.0 sq. mi. **Elev:** 590 ft.
Incorporated Aug 1880. Not coextensive with the town of the same name.
Name origin: For Canton, OH.

*Canton
Township
ZIP: 67428 **Lat:** 38-23-28 N **Long:** 97-25-36 W
Pop: 1,050 (1990); 1,187 (1980) **Pop Density:** 29.2
Land: 35.9 sq. mi.; **Water:** 0.0 sq. mi.

Castle
Township
Lat: 38-23-03 N Long: 97-52-10 W
Pop: 231 (1990); 250 (1980)   **Pop Density:** 6.4
Land: 36.1 sq. mi.; **Water:** 0.0 sq. mi.

Delmore
Township
Lat: 38-28-26 N Long: 97-32-26 W
Pop: 145 (1990); 131 (1980)   **Pop Density:** 4.0
Land: 35.9 sq. mi.; **Water:** 0.1 sq. mi.

Empire
Township
Lat: 38-23-13 N Long: 97-32-12 W
Pop: 1,151 (1990); 1,079 (1980)   **Pop Density:** 31.9
Land: 36.1 sq. mi.; **Water:** 0.0 sq. mi.

Galva
City
ZIP: 67443   **Lat:** 38-22-55 N **Long:** 97-32-16 W
Pop: 651 (1990); 651 (1980)   **Pop Density:** 1627.5
Land: 0.4 sq. mi.; **Water:** 0.0 sq. mi.   **Elev:** 1546 ft.
Incorporated Aug 1887.
Name origin: Named by Swedish pioneers for Galva, Sweden.

Groveland
Township
Lat: 38-18-15 N Long: 97-45-33 W
Pop: 209 (1990); 239 (1980)   **Pop Density:** 5.8
Land: 36.2 sq. mi.; **Water:** 0.0 sq. mi.

Gypsum Creek
Township
Lat: 38-33-54 N Long: 97-25-42 W
Pop: 189 (1990); 223 (1980)   **Pop Density:** 5.3
Land: 36.0 sq. mi.; **Water:** 0.0 sq. mi.

Harper
Township
Lat: 38-28-47 N Long: 97-45-25 W
Pop: 147 (1990); 167 (1980)   **Pop Density:** 4.1
Land: 35.8 sq. mi.; **Water:** 0.1 sq. mi.

Hayes
Township
Lat: 38-17-57 N Long: 97-51-59 W
Pop: 270 (1990); 287 (1980)   **Pop Density:** 7.5
Land: 36.2 sq. mi.; **Water:** 0.0 sq. mi.

Inman
City
ZIP: 67546   **Lat:** 38-13-44 N **Long:** 97-46-25 W
Pop: 1,035 (1990); 947 (1980)   **Pop Density:** 2070.0
Land: 0.5 sq. mi.; **Water:** 0.0 sq. mi.   **Elev:** 1527 ft.
Incorporated Apr 12, 1894.
Name origin: For Col. Henry Inman.

Jackson
Township
Lat: 38-23-28 N Long: 97-45-24 W
Pop: 173 (1990); 290 (1980)   **Pop Density:** 4.8
Land: 35.9 sq. mi.; **Water:** 0.2 sq. mi.

King City
Township
Lat: 38-18-16 N Long: 97-38-58 W
Pop: 448 (1990); 404 (1980)   **Pop Density:** 12.4
Land: 36.1 sq. mi.; **Water:** 0.0 sq. mi.

Lindsborg
City
ZIP: 67456   **Lat:** 38-34-27 N **Long:** 97-40-29 W
Pop: 3,076 (1990); 3,155 (1980)   **Pop Density:** 2197.1
Land: 1.4 sq. mi.; **Water:** 0.0 sq. mi.   **Elev:** 1333 ft.
Incorporated Jul 1879.
Name origin: For the Swedish surname Lind, common in the area, plus *borg* 'city, town.'

Little Valley
Township
Lat: 38-13-06 N Long: 97-51-59 W
Pop: 451 (1990); 472 (1980)   **Pop Density:** 12.5
Land: 36.0 sq. mi.; **Water:** 0.0 sq. mi.

Lone Tree
Township
Lat: 38-17-48 N Long: 97-32-05 W
Pop: 457 (1990); 422 (1980)   **Pop Density:** 12.6
Land: 36.3 sq. mi.; **Water:** 0.0 sq. mi.

McPherson
City
ZIP: 67460   **Lat:** 38-22-18 N **Long:** 97-39-42 W
Pop: 12,422 (1990); 11,753 (1980)   **Pop Density:** 2435.7
Land: 5.1 sq. mi.; **Water:** 0.0 sq. mi.   **Elev:** 1504 ft.
In central KS, 27 mi. northeast of Hutchinson. Incorporated Mar 4, 1874.
Name origin: For early Scottish pioneer James Birdsey McPherson (1828–64).

*McPherson
Township
ZIP: 67460   **Lat:** 38-23-55 N **Long:** 97-38-49 W
Pop: 697 (1990); 607 (1980)   **Pop Density:** 22.6
Land: 30.8 sq. mi.; **Water:** 0.1 sq. mi.

Marquette
City
ZIP: 67464   **Lat:** 38-33-13 N **Long:** 97-50-02 W
Pop: 593 (1990); 639 (1980)   **Pop Density:** 1482.5
Land: 0.4 sq. mi.; **Water:** 0.0 sq. mi.   **Elev:** 1385 ft.
Incorporated May 1874. Not coextensive with the town of the same name.
Name origin: For Pierre Marquette, French explorer who traveled down the Mississippi River in the late 1600s.

*Marquette
Township
ZIP: 67464   **Lat:** 38-33-45 N **Long:** 97-52-29 W
Pop: 760 (1990); 877 (1980)   **Pop Density:** 21.1
Land: 36.0 sq. mi.; **Water:** 0.1 sq. mi.

Meridian
Township
Lat: 38-13-05 N Long: 97-25-25 W
Pop: 315 (1990); 346 (1980)   **Pop Density:** 8.7
Land: 36.2 sq. mi.; **Water:** 0.0 sq. mi.

Mound
Township
Lat: 38-13-02 N Long: 97-32-16 W
Pop: 1,992 (1990); 1,888 (1980)   **Pop Density:** 55.5
Land: 35.9 sq. mi.; **Water:** 0.1 sq. mi.

Moundridge
City
ZIP: 67107   **Lat:** 38-12-06 N **Long:** 97-30-56 W
Pop: 1,531 (1990); 1,453 (1980)   **Pop Density:** 1913.8
Land: 0.8 sq. mi.; **Water:** 0.0 sq. mi.   **Elev:** 1490 ft.
Incorporated Apr 15, 1887.
Name origin: For a small hill above Black Kettle Creek.

New Gottland
Township
Lat: 38-28-45 N Long: 97-38-48 W
Pop: 293 (1990); 269 (1980)   **Pop Density:** 8.2
Land: 35.9 sq. mi.; **Water:** 0.1 sq. mi.

Smoky Hill
Township
Lat: 38-33-50 N Long: 97-38-43 W
Pop: 244 (1990); 297 (1980)   **Pop Density:** 7.1
Land: 34.6 sq. mi.; **Water:** 0.0 sq. mi.

South Sharps Creek
Township
Lat: 38-28-40 N Long: 97-52-16 W
Pop: 100 (1990); 124 (1980)   **Pop Density:** 2.8
Land: 36.1 sq. mi.; **Water:** 0.1 sq. mi.

American Places Dictionary KANSAS, Meade County

Spring Valley Township
Lat: 38-18-08 N Long: 97-25-39 W
Pop: 390 (1990); 437 (1980) **Pop Density:** 10.8
Land: 36.1 sq. mi.; **Water:** 0.0 sq. mi.

Superior Township
Lat: 38-12-54 N Long: 97-45-40 W
Pop: 1,412 (1990); 1,318 (1980) **Pop Density:** 39.7
Land: 35.6 sq. mi.; **Water:** 0.3 sq. mi.

Turkey Creek Township
Lat: 38-12-48 N Long: 97-38-35 W
Pop: 273 (1990); 288 (1980) **Pop Density:** 7.6
Land: 35.8 sq. mi.; **Water:** 0.0 sq. mi.

Union Township
Lat: 38-34-08 N Long: 97-45-34 W
Pop: 199 (1990); 176 (1980) **Pop Density:** 5.5
Land: 36.0 sq. mi.; **Water:** 0.1 sq. mi.

Windom City
ZIP: 67491 Lat: 38-23-03 N Long: 97-54-36 W
Pop: 136 (1990); 160 (1980) **Pop Density:** 680.0
Land: 0.2 sq. mi.; **Water:** 0.0 sq. mi. **Elev:** 1950 ft.
Incorporated May 18, 1885.
Name origin: For William Windom, U.S. senator from MN.

Meade County
County Seat: Meade (ZIP: 67864)

Pop: 4,247 (1990); 4,788 (1980) **Pop Density:** 4.3
Land: 978.5 sq. mi.; **Water:** 1.2 sq. mi. **Area Code:** 316
On the southern border of KS, southwest of Dodge City; organized Jan 8, 1873 from unorganized territory.
Name origin: For Gen. George Gordon Meade (1815–72), officer in the Mexican-American War and Civil War; commander of the Union army that defeated Gen. Robert E. Lee (1807–70) at Gettysburg.

Cimarron Township
Lat: 37-04-26 N Long: 100-31-57 W
Pop: 98 (1990); 89 (1980) **Pop Density:** 0.8
Land: 117.0 sq. mi.; **Water:** 0.7 sq. mi.

Crooked Creek Township
Lat: 37-24-41 N Long: 100-19-28 W
Pop: 83 (1990); 79 (1980) **Pop Density:** 1.5
Land: 54.3 sq. mi.; **Water:** 0.0 sq. mi.

Fowler City
ZIP: 67844 Lat: 37-22-59 N Long: 100-11-44 W
Pop: 571 (1990); 592 (1980) **Pop Density:** 1142.0
Land: 0.5 sq. mi.; **Water:** 0.0 sq. mi. **Elev:** 2481 ft.
Incorporated May 1908. Not coextensive with the town of the same name.

*Fowler Township
ZIP: 67844 Lat: 37-23-31 N Long: 100-11-16 W
Pop: 737 (1990); 794 (1980) **Pop Density:** 7.0
Land: 104.7 sq. mi.; **Water:** 0.0 sq. mi.

Logan Township
Lat: 37-14-27 N Long: 100-11-00 W
Pop: 100 (1990); 149 (1980) **Pop Density:** 0.9
Land: 109.8 sq. mi.; **Water:** 0.0 sq. mi.

Meade City
ZIP: 67864 Lat: 37-17-06 N Long: 100-20-15 W
Pop: 1,526 (1990); 1,777 (1980) **Pop Density:** 1695.6
Land: 0.9 sq. mi.; **Water:** 0.0 sq. mi. **Elev:** 2497 ft.
Incorporated Oct 21, 1885.
Name origin: For Civil War general George Meade (1815–72).

Meade Center Township
Lat: 37-15-00 N Long: 100-20-46 W
Pop: 1,822 (1990); 2,058 (1980) **Pop Density:** 16.9
Land: 107.9 sq. mi.; **Water:** 0.2 sq. mi.

Mertilla Township
Lat: 37-24-07 N Long: 100-30-21 W
Pop: 211 (1990); 236 (1980) **Pop Density:** 1.4
Land: 150.4 sq. mi.; **Water:** 0.0 sq. mi.

Odee Township
Lat: 37-04-45 N Long: 100-20-54 W
Pop: 44 (1990); 79 (1980) **Pop Density:** 0.5
Land: 95.0 sq. mi.; **Water:** 0.1 sq. mi.

Plains City City
ZIP: 67869 Lat: 37-15-49 N Long: 100-35-23 W
Pop: 957 (1990); 1,044 (1980) **Pop Density:** 957.0
Land: 1.0 sq. mi.; **Water:** 0.0 sq. mi. **Elev:** 2760 ft.

Sand Creek Township
Lat: 37-04-52 N Long: 100-10-51 W
Pop: 44 (1990); 76 (1980) **Pop Density:** 0.4
Land: 105.1 sq. mi.; **Water:** 0.0 sq. mi.

West Plains Township
Lat: 37-14-31 N Long: 100-32-34 W
Pop: 1,108 (1990); 1,228 (1980) **Pop Density:** 8.3
Land: 134.3 sq. mi.; **Water:** 0.2 sq. mi.
In southwestern KS; incorporated Jan 1908.
Name origin: For its location on the plains.

KANSAS, Miami County   *American Places Dictionary*

> ## Miami County
> **County Seat: Paola (ZIP: 66071)**
>
> **Pop:** 23,466 (1990); 21,618 (1980)   **Pop Density:** 40.7
> **Land:** 576.8 sq. mi.; **Water:** 13.4 sq. mi.   **Area Code:** 913
>
> On the eastern border of KS, south of Olathe; organized as Lykins County Aug 25, 1855 (prior to statehood); name changed Jun 3, 1861.
>
> **Name origin:** For the Miami Indians, an Algonquin tribe. Origin of name uncertain: probably from Ojibway *oumaumeg* 'people of the peninsula' or from Delaware *we-mi-a-mik* 'all friends.'

Fontana   City
ZIP: 66026   **Lat:** 38-25-33 N **Long:** 94-50-16 W
Pop: 131 (1990); 173 (1980)   **Pop Density:** 655.0
Land: 0.2 sq. mi.; **Water:** 0.0 sq. mi.   **Elev:** 930 ft.
Incorporated Feb 25, 1889.
Name origin: For a nearby spring. Originally called Old Fountain.

Louisburg   City
ZIP: 66053   **Lat:** 38-37-25 N **Long:** 94-40-58 W
Pop: 1,964 (1990); 1,744 (1980)   **Pop Density:** 1091.1
Land: 1.8 sq. mi.; **Water:** 0.1 sq. mi.   **Elev:** 1075 ft.
Incorporated Nov 3, 1882.
Name origin: For the Bourbon kings of France.

Marysville   Township
                         Lat: 38-40-12 N **Long:** 94-51-33 W
Pop: 1,862 (1990); 1,593 (1980)   **Pop Density:** 36.8
Land: 50.6 sq. mi.; **Water:** 4.6 sq. mi.

Miami   Township
                         Lat: 38-27-16 N **Long:** 94-44-34 W
Pop: 427 (1990); 415 (1980)   **Pop Density:** 8.8
Land: 48.5 sq. mi.; **Water:** 0.3 sq. mi.

Middle Creek   Township
                         Lat: 38-33-54 N **Long:** 94-42-08 W
Pop: 1,224 (1990); 1,002 (1980)   **Pop Density:** 20.8
Land: 58.9 sq. mi.; **Water:** 0.5 sq. mi.

Mound   Township
                         Lat: 38-24-57 N **Long:** 94-59-46 W
Pop: 563 (1990); 508 (1980)   **Pop Density:** 17.5
Land: 32.2 sq. mi.; **Water:** 0.0 sq. mi.

Osage   Township
                         Lat: 38-25-57 N **Long:** 94-51-49 W
Pop: 576 (1990); 592 (1980)   **Pop Density:** 14.1
Land: 40.9 sq. mi.; **Water:** 0.2 sq. mi.

Osawatomie   City
ZIP: 66064   **Lat:** 38-30-08 N **Long:** 94-57-03 W
Pop: 4,590 (1990); 4,459 (1980)   **Pop Density:** 1700.0
Land: 2.7 sq. mi.; **Water:** 0.0 sq. mi.   **Elev:** 865 ft.
Incorporated Oct 1, 1883.
Name origin: From a combination of *Osa*ge River and Potta*watomie* Creek.

*Osawatomie   Township
ZIP: 66064   **Lat:** 38-28-37 N **Long:** 94-59-56 W
Pop: 734 (1990); 697 (1980)   **Pop Density:** 21.0
Land: 35.0 sq. mi.; **Water:** 0.0 sq. mi.

Paola   City
ZIP: 66071   **Lat:** 38-34-37 N **Long:** 94-51-58 W
Pop: 4,698 (1990); 4,557 (1980)   **Pop Density:** 1381.8
Land: 3.4 sq. mi.; **Water:** 0.3 sq. mi.   **Elev:** 900 ft.
Incorporated Dec 17, 1859.
Name origin: From a variation of the name of French linguist, Baptiste Peoria. The Indians had difficulty pronouncing *r* and the name became Paola.

*Paola   Township
ZIP: 66071   **Lat:** 38-34-41 N **Long:** 94-51-48 W
Pop: 910 (1990); 738 (1980)   **Pop Density:** 32.5
Land: 28.0 sq. mi.; **Water:** 0.2 sq. mi.

Richland   Township
                         Lat: 38-40-19 N **Long:** 94-59-34 W
Pop: 1,142 (1990); 1,036 (1980)   **Pop Density:** 17.8
Land: 64.0 sq. mi.; **Water:** 6.2 sq. mi.

Spring Hill   City
ZIP: 66083   **Lat:** 38-43-52 N **Long:** 94-49-35 W
Pop: 107 (1990); 42 (1980)   **Pop Density:** 178.3
Land: 0.6 sq. mi.; **Water:** 0.0 sq. mi.   **Elev:** 1050 ft.
Incorporated 1885. Part of the town is also in Johnson County.
Name origin: For Spring Hill, AL.

Stanton   Township
                         Lat: 38-33-57 N **Long:** 95-00-06 W
Pop: 747 (1990); 766 (1980)   **Pop Density:** 18.5
Land: 40.3 sq. mi.; **Water:** 0.2 sq. mi.

Sugar Creek   Township
                         Lat: 38-27-14 N **Long:** 94-38-57 W
Pop: 370 (1990); 322 (1980)   **Pop Density:** 9.2
Land: 40.1 sq. mi.; **Water:** 0.3 sq. mi.

Ten Mile   Township
                         Lat: 38-40-49 N **Long:** 94-45-26 W
Pop: 989 (1990); 798 (1980)   **Pop Density:** 21.1
Land: 46.8 sq. mi.; **Water:** 0.2 sq. mi.

Valley   Township
                         Lat: 38-30-53 N **Long:** 94-51-36 W
Pop: 1,401 (1990); 1,262 (1980)   **Pop Density:** 38.3
Land: 36.6 sq. mi.; **Water:** 0.1 sq. mi.

Wea   Township
                         Lat: 38-39-51 N **Long:** 94-39-41 W
Pop: 1,162 (1990); 1,087 (1980)   **Pop Density:** 25.1
Land: 46.3 sq. mi.; **Water:** 0.2 sq. mi.

Mitchell County
County Seat: Beloit (ZIP: 67420)

Pop: 7,203 (1990); 8,117 (1980)　　　　**Pop Density:** 10.3
Land: 699.9 sq. mi.; **Water:** 18.7 sq. mi.　　　　**Area Code:** 913
In north-central KS, northwest of Salina; organized Feb 26, 1867 from Kirwin Land District.
Name origin: For Capt. William D. Mitchell (?–1865), Union officer killed at Battle of Monroe's Cross Roads, NC.

Asherville　　　　Township
Lat: 39-26-31 N　**Long:** 97-59-28 W
Pop: 139 (1990); 152 (1980)　　**Pop Density:** 3.9
Land: 36.0 sq. mi.; **Water:** 0.0 sq. mi.

Beloit　　　　City
ZIP: 67420　　**Lat:** 39-27-56 N　**Long:** 98-06-28 W
Pop: 4,066 (1990); 4,367 (1980)　　**Pop Density:** 1161.7
Land: 3.5 sq. mi.; **Water:** 0.0 sq. mi.　　**Elev:** 1386 ft.
In north-central KS, 51 mi. east of Salina. Incorporated Aug 1872.
Name origin: For Beloit, WI.

*Beloit　　　　Township
ZIP: 67420　　**Lat:** 39-26-14 N　**Long:** 98-05-47 W
Pop: 269 (1990); 443 (1980)　　**Pop Density:** 8.2
Land: 32.7 sq. mi.; **Water:** 0.0 sq. mi.

Bloomfield　　　　Township
Lat: 39-21-03 N　**Long:** 98-06-01 W
Pop: 95 (1990); 117 (1980)　　**Pop Density:** 2.6
Land: 36.1 sq. mi.; **Water:** 0.1 sq. mi.

Blue Hill　　　　Township
Lat: 39-15-54 N　**Long:** 98-19-26 W
Pop: 45 (1990); 44 (1980)　　**Pop Density:** 1.3
Land: 36.0 sq. mi.; **Water:** 0.1 sq. mi.

Carr Creek　　　　Township
Lat: 39-26-23 N　**Long:** 98-25-53 W
Pop: 36 (1990); 33 (1980)　　**Pop Density:** 1.1
Land: 32.6 sq. mi.; **Water:** 3.4 sq. mi.

Cawker　　　　Township
Lat: 39-31-19 N　**Long:** 98-25-56 W
Pop: 637 (1990); 706 (1980)　　**Pop Density:** 22.0
Land: 29.0 sq. mi.; **Water:** 6.7 sq. mi.

Cawker City　　　　City
ZIP: 67430　　**Lat:** 39-30-35 N　**Long:** 98-25-55 W
Pop: 588 (1990); 640 (1980)　　**Pop Density:** 588.0
Land: 1.0 sq. mi.; **Water:** 0.0 sq. mi.　　**Elev:** 1500 ft.
Incorporated May 20, 1874.
Name origin: For E.H. Cawker, who won the right to name the town in a poker game.

Center　　　　Township
Lat: 39-20-42 N　**Long:** 98-12-44 W
Pop: 42 (1990); 62 (1980)　　**Pop Density:** 1.2
Land: 36.0 sq. mi.; **Water:** 0.0 sq. mi.

Custer　　　　Township
Lat: 39-16-05 N　**Long:** 98-26-22 W
Pop: 181 (1990); 208 (1980)　　**Pop Density:** 5.0
Land: 36.2 sq. mi.; **Water:** 0.0 sq. mi.

Eureka　　　　Township
Lat: 39-15-47 N　**Long:** 97-59-34 W
Pop: 42 (1990); 45 (1980)　　**Pop Density:** 1.2
Land: 35.8 sq. mi.; **Water:** 0.1 sq. mi.

Glen Elder　　　　City
ZIP: 67446　　**Lat:** 39-29-58 N　**Long:** 98-18-22 W
Pop: 448 (1990); 491 (1980)　　**Pop Density:** 1120.0
Land: 0.4 sq. mi.; **Water:** 0.0 sq. mi.　　**Elev:** 1424 ft.
Incorporated Nov 28, 1879. Not coextensive with the town of the same name.
Name origin: Named by pioneers from Scotland.

*Glen Elder　　　　Township
ZIP: 67446　　**Lat:** 39-31-59 N　**Long:** 98-18-57 W
Pop: 548 (1990); 599 (1980)　　**Pop Density:** 18.1
Land: 30.3 sq. mi.; **Water:** 5.8 sq. mi.

Hayes　　　　Township
Lat: 39-21-15 N　**Long:** 98-18-42 W
Pop: 29 (1990); 38 (1980)　　**Pop Density:** 0.8
Land: 36.0 sq. mi.; **Water:** 0.0 sq. mi.

Hunter　　　　City
ZIP: 67452　　**Lat:** 39-14-08 N　**Long:** 98-23-44 W
Pop: 116 (1990); 135 (1980)　　**Pop Density:** 580.0
Land: 0.2 sq. mi.; **Water:** 0.0 sq. mi.　　**Elev:** 1600 ft.
Incorporated Apr 5, 1918.
Name origin: For Al Hunter, from Marion County, IA.

Logan　　　　Township
Lat: 39-21-09 N　**Long:** 97-59-06 W
Pop: 159 (1990); 179 (1980)　　**Pop Density:** 4.4
Land: 36.0 sq. mi.; **Water:** 0.0 sq. mi.

Lulu　　　　Township
Lat: 39-31-20 N　**Long:** 97-59-02 W
Pop: 86 (1990); 121 (1980)　　**Pop Density:** 2.4
Land: 35.4 sq. mi.; **Water:** 0.0 sq. mi.

Pittsburg　　　　Township
Lat: 39-20-53 N　**Long:** 98-25-51 W
Pop: 373 (1990); 476 (1980)　　**Pop Density:** 10.3
Land: 36.1 sq. mi.; **Water:** 0.0 sq. mi.

Plum Creek　　　　Township
Lat: 39-31-09 N　**Long:** 98-05-38 W
Pop: 109 (1990); 142 (1980)　　**Pop Density:** 3.1
Land: 35.6 sq. mi.; **Water:** 0.0 sq. mi.

Round Springs　　　　Township
Lat: 39-16-04 N　**Long:** 98-13-24 W
Pop: 43 (1990); 47 (1980)　　**Pop Density:** 1.2
Land: 35.8 sq. mi.; **Water:** 0.0 sq. mi.

Salt Creek
Township
Lat: 39-15-40 N **Long:** 98-05-40 W
Pop: 35 (1990); 54 (1980) **Pop Density:** 1.0
Land: 35.8 sq. mi.; **Water:** 0.1 sq. mi.

Scottsville
City
ZIP: 67477 **Lat:** 39-32-34 N **Long:** 97-57-07 W
Pop: 26 (1990); 56 (1980) **Pop Density:** 86.7
Land: 0.3 sq. mi.; **Water:** 0.0 sq. mi.
Incorporated Jan 14, 1907.

Simpson
City
ZIP: 67478 **Lat:** 39-23-10 N **Long:** 97-56-01 W
Pop: 107 (1990); 122 (1980) **Pop Density:** 535.0
Land: 0.2 sq. mi.; **Water:** 0.0 sq. mi. **Elev:** 1337 ft.
Incorporated Apr 3, 1907. Part of the town is also in Cloud County.
Name origin: For Alfred Simpson, who donated land for the town site.

Solomon Rapids
Township
Lat: 39-31-28 N **Long:** 98-12-32 W
Pop: 86 (1990); 84 (1980) **Pop Density:** 2.4
Land: 35.3 sq. mi.; **Water:** 0.1 sq. mi.

Tipton
City
ZIP: 67485 **Lat:** 39-20-21 N **Long:** 98-28-15 W
Pop: 267 (1990); 321 (1980) **Pop Density:** 890.0
Land: 0.3 sq. mi.; **Water:** 0.0 sq. mi. **Elev:** 1604 ft.
Incorporated Jul 15, 1916.

Turkey Creek
Township
Lat: 39-26-19 N **Long:** 98-12-18 W
Pop: 135 (1990); 139 (1980) **Pop Density:** 3.8
Land: 35.7 sq. mi.; **Water:** 0.1 sq. mi.

Walnut Creek
Township
Lat: 39-26-09 N **Long:** 98-19-18 W
Pop: 48 (1990); 61 (1980) **Pop Density:** 1.4
Land: 34.0 sq. mi.; **Water:** 2.1 sq. mi.

Montgomery County
County Seat: Independence (ZIP: 67301)

Pop: 38,816 (1990); 42,281 (1980) **Pop Density:** 60.2
Land: 645.3 sq. mi.; **Water:** 6.2 sq. mi. **Area Code:** 316
On the southeastern border of KS, west of Joplin, MO; organized Feb 26, 1867 from Labette County.
Name origin: For either James M. Montgomery (1814–71), abolitionist and preacher, a nephew or more distant relative of Gen. Richard Montgomery (1738–75), officer in the American Revolution, or for Gen. Richard Montgomery himself.

Caney
City
ZIP: 67333 **Lat:** 37-00-48 N **Long:** 95-55-53 W
Pop: 2,062 (1990); 2,284 (1980) **Pop Density:** 1874.5
Land: 1.1 sq. mi.; **Water:** 0.0 sq. mi. **Elev:** 770 ft.
Incorporated Jul 5, 1887.
Name origin: For nearby Caney River.

*Caney
Township
ZIP: 67333 **Lat:** 37-03-51 N **Long:** 95-53-38 W
Pop: 1,205 (1990); 1,289 (1980) **Pop Density:** 17.7
Land: 68.0 sq. mi.; **Water:** 0.2 sq. mi.

Cherokee
Township
Lat: 37-03-50 N **Long:** 95-33-39 W
Pop: 620 (1990); 580 (1980) **Pop Density:** 16.1
Land: 38.6 sq. mi.; **Water:** 0.0 sq. mi.

Cherry
Township
Lat: 37-19-11 N **Long:** 95-33-56 W
Pop: 550 (1990); 503 (1980) **Pop Density:** 13.9
Land: 39.7 sq. mi.; **Water:** 0.0 sq. mi.

Cherryvale
City
ZIP: 67335 **Lat:** 37-16-04 N **Long:** 95-33-03 W
Pop: 2,464 (1990); 2,769 (1980) **Pop Density:** 1642.7
Land: 1.5 sq. mi.; **Water:** 0.0 sq. mi. **Elev:** 850 ft.
Incorporated 1880.
Name origin: For the wild black cherry and chokecherry that grew in the area.

Coffeyville
City
ZIP: 67337 **Lat:** 37-02-26 N **Long:** 95-37-55 W
Pop: 12,917 (1990); 15,185 (1980) **Pop Density:** 1845.3
Land: 7.0 sq. mi.; **Water:** 0.0 sq. mi. **Elev:** 736 ft.
In southeastern KS, 15 mi. south of Independence. Incorporated Mar 22, 1872.
Name origin: For Col. James Coffey, who founded a trading post here.

Dearing
City
ZIP: 67340 **Lat:** 37-03-32 N **Long:** 95-42-43 W
Pop: 428 (1990); 475 (1980) **Pop Density:** 1426.7
Land: 0.3 sq. mi.; **Water:** 0.0 sq. mi. **Elev:** 770 ft.
Incorporated Jan 25, 1909.

Drum Creek
Township
Lat: 37-13-37 N **Long:** 95-35-53 W
Pop: 488 (1990); 522 (1980) **Pop Density:** 13.8
Land: 35.4 sq. mi.; **Water:** 0.1 sq. mi.

Elk City
City
ZIP: 67344 **Lat:** 37-17-20 N **Long:** 95-54-35 W
Pop: 334 (1990); 404 (1980) **Pop Density:** 1113.3
Land: 0.3 sq. mi.; **Water:** 0.0 sq. mi. **Elev:** 835 ft.
Incorporated 1871.
Name origin: For the elk herds once common to the area.

Fawn Creek
Township
Lat: 37-04-03 N **Long:** 95-44-56 W
Pop: 2,124 (1990); 2,088 (1980) **Pop Density:** 30.8
Land: 69.0 sq. mi.; **Water:** 0.0 sq. mi.

Havana
City
ZIP: 67347 **Lat:** 37-05-32 N **Long:** 95-56-28 W
Pop: 121 (1990); 169 (1980) **Pop Density:** 1210.0
Land: 0.1 sq. mi.; **Water:** 0.0 sq. mi. **Elev:** 760 ft.
Incorporated Nov 22, 1909.
Name origin: For Havana, IL.

Independence
City
ZIP: 67301 **Lat:** 37-13-53 N **Long:** 95-42-49 W
Pop: 9,942 (1990); 10,598 (1980) **Pop Density:** 2209.3
Land: 4.5 sq. mi.; **Water:** 0.0 sq. mi. **Elev:** 826 ft.
In southeastern KS, about 15 mi. north of the OK border. Incorporated Jul 25, 1870.
Name origin: For Independence, IA.

*Independence
Township
ZIP: 67301 **Lat:** 37-10-49 N **Long:** 95-45-11 W
Pop: 2,532 (1990); 2,426 (1980) **Pop Density:** 39.9
Land: 63.5 sq. mi.; **Water:** 1.9 sq. mi.

Liberty
City
ZIP: 67351 **Lat:** 37-09-22 N **Long:** 95-35-51 W
Pop: 140 (1990); 174 (1980) **Pop Density:** 466.7
Land: 0.3 sq. mi.; **Water:** 0.0 sq. mi. **Elev:** 750 ft.
Incorporated Oct 16, 1884. Not coextensive with the town of the same name.

*Liberty
Township
ZIP: 67351 **Lat:** 37-09-32 N **Long:** 95-35-57 W
Pop: 504 (1990); 568 (1980) **Pop Density:** 11.6
Land: 43.5 sq. mi.; **Water:** 0.1 sq. mi.

Louisburg
Township
Lat: 37-19-12 N **Long:** 95-53-41 W
Pop: 669 (1990); 791 (1980) **Pop Density:** 9.4
Land: 71.5 sq. mi.; **Water:** 0.5 sq. mi.

Parker
Township
Lat: 37-03-55 N **Long:** 95-38-15 W
Pop: 1,333 (1990); 1,194 (1980) **Pop Density:** 52.1
Land: 25.6 sq. mi.; **Water:** 0.1 sq. mi.

Rutland
Township
Lat: 37-11-24 N **Long:** 95-52-58 W
Pop: 357 (1990); 282 (1980) **Pop Density:** 5.0
Land: 71.4 sq. mi.; **Water:** 0.6 sq. mi.

Sycamore
Township
Lat: 37-19-03 N **Long:** 95-44-52 W
Pop: 835 (1990); 994 (1980) **Pop Density:** 12.8
Land: 65.4 sq. mi.; **Water:** 2.6 sq. mi.

Tyro
City
ZIP: 67364 **Lat:** 37-02-12 N **Long:** 95-49-17 W
Pop: 243 (1990); 289 (1980) **Pop Density:** 486.0
Land: 0.5 sq. mi.; **Water:** 0.0 sq. mi. **Elev:** 891 ft.
Incorporated Apr 24, 1906.
Name origin: Named by settlers to reflect their inexperience; from Latin meaning 'novice'.

West Cherry
Township
Lat: 37-19-24 N **Long:** 95-38-36 W
Pop: 214 (1990); 208 (1980) **Pop Density:** 5.4
Land: 39.4 sq. mi.; **Water:** 0.0 sq. mi.

Morris County
County Seat: Council Grove (ZIP: 66846)

Pop: 6,198 (1990); 6,419 (1980) **Pop Density:** 8.9
Land: 697.4 sq. mi.; **Water:** 5.5 sq. mi. **Area Code:** 316
In east-central KS, northwest of Emporia; organized as Wise County Aug 30, 1855 (prior to statehood) from Madison County; name changed Feb 11, 1859.
Name origin: For Thomas Morris (1766–1844), opponent of slavery and U.S. senator from OH (1833–39).

Council Grove
City
ZIP: 66846 **Lat:** 38-39-38 N **Long:** 96-29-21 W
Pop: 2,228 (1990); 2,381 (1980) **Pop Density:** 1310.6
Land: 1.7 sq. mi.; **Water:** 0.0 sq. mi. **Elev:** 1233 ft.
Incorporated Mar 3, 1887.
Name origin: For the grove of trees used by the Indians for council meetings.

Dunlap
City
Lat: 38-34-32 N **Long:** 96-21-57 W
Pop: 65 (1990); 82 (1980) **Pop Density:** 325.0
Land: 0.2 sq. mi.; **Water:** 0.0 sq. mi. **Elev:** 1186 ft.
Incorporated Jan 26, 1887.
Name origin: For founder Joseph Dunlap.

Dwight
City
ZIP: 66849 **Lat:** 38-50-37 N **Long:** 96-35-30 W
Pop: 365 (1990); 320 (1980) **Pop Density:** 912.5
Land: 0.4 sq. mi.; **Water:** 0.0 sq. mi. **Elev:** 490 ft.
Incorporated Jul 7, 1905.

Herington
City
Lat: 38-40-45 N **Long:** 96-55-41 W
Pop: 0 (1990)
Land: 0.1 sq. mi.; **Water:** 0.0 sq. mi.
Incorporated Apr 11, 1887. Part of the town is also in Dickinson County.
Name origin: For pioneer rancher Monroe Herington.

Highland
Township
Lat: 38-44-24 N **Long:** 96-45-24 W
Pop: 114 (1990); 133 (1980) **Pop Density:** 3.2
Land: 36.0 sq. mi.; **Water:** 0.0 sq. mi.

Latimer
City
Lat: 38-44-20 N **Long:** 96-50-44 W
Pop: 20 (1990); 31 (1980) **Pop Density:** 200.0
Land: 0.1 sq. mi.; **Water:** 0.0 sq. mi. **Elev:** 1413 ft.
Incorporated Aug 6, 1929.

Overland
Township
Lat: 38-48-17 N **Long:** 96-51-42 W
Pop: 69 (1990); 111 (1980) **Pop Density:** 2.0
Land: 34.1 sq. mi.; **Water:** 0.0 sq. mi.

KANSAS, Morris County

Parkerville
City
Lat: 38-45-49 N Long: 96-39-44 W
Pop: 28 (1990); 42 (1980) **Pop Density:** 280.0
Land: 0.1 sq. mi.; **Water:** 0.0 sq. mi. **Elev:** 1350 ft.
Incorporated 1871.

Township No. 1
Township
Lat: 38-36-41 N Long: 96-28-07 W
Pop: 581 (1990); 589 (1980) **Pop Density:** 4.2
Land: 137.6 sq. mi.; **Water:** 0.4 sq. mi.

Township No. 2
Township
Lat: 38-44-45 N Long: 96-29-30 W
Pop: 781 (1990); 627 (1980) **Pop Density:** 7.5
Land: 104.4 sq. mi.; **Water:** 4.8 sq. mi.

Township No. 3
Township
Lat: 38-49-37 N Long: 96-34-06 W
Pop: 569 (1990); 510 (1980) **Pop Density:** 13.5
Land: 42.2 sq. mi.; **Water:** 0.0 sq. mi.

Township No. 4
Township
Lat: 38-46-03 N Long: 96-39-37 W
Pop: 232 (1990); 234 (1980) **Pop Density:** 3.9
Land: 59.8 sq. mi.; **Water:** 0.0 sq. mi.

Township No. 5
Township
Lat: 38-49-38 N Long: 96-45-24 W
Pop: 684 (1990); 707 (1980) **Pop Density:** 19.1
Land: 35.9 sq. mi.; **Water:** 0.0 sq. mi.

Township No. 6
Township
Lat: 38-44-00 N Long: 96-52-29 W
Pop: 116 (1990); 141 (1980) **Pop Density:** 3.9
Land: 30.1 sq. mi.; **Water:** 0.1 sq. mi.

Township No. 7
Township
Lat: 38-39-20 N Long: 96-49-46 W
Pop: 260 (1990); 327 (1980) **Pop Density:** 4.0
Land: 65.7 sq. mi.; **Water:** 0.1 sq. mi.

Township No. 8
Township
Lat: 38-33-40 N Long: 96-49-11 W
Pop: 230 (1990); 300 (1980) **Pop Density:** 3.2
Land: 71.9 sq. mi.; **Water:** 0.1 sq. mi.

Township No. 9
Township
Lat: 38-36-31 N Long: 96-39-23 W
Pop: 334 (1990); 359 (1980) **Pop Density:** 4.3
Land: 78.0 sq. mi.; **Water:** 0.1 sq. mi.

White City
City
ZIP: 66872 Lat: 38-47-39 N Long: 96-44-05 W
Pop: 533 (1990); 534 (1980) **Pop Density:** 444.2
Land: 1.2 sq. mi.; **Water:** 0.0 sq. mi. **Elev:** 1470 ft.
Incorporated Oct 19, 1885.
Name origin: For railroad superintendant F.C. White.

Wilsey
City
ZIP: 66873 Lat: 38-38-09 N Long: 96-40-36 W
Pop: 149 (1990); 179 (1980) **Pop Density:** 496.7
Land: 0.3 sq. mi.; **Water:** 0.0 sq. mi. **Elev:** 1510 ft.

Morton County
County Seat: Elkhart (ZIP: 67950)

Pop: 3,480 (1990); 3,454 (1980) **Pop Density:** 4.8
Land: 730.0 sq. mi.; **Water:** 0.0 sq. mi. **Area Code:** 316
In the southwestern corner of KS; organized Feb 18, 1886 from Stanton County.
Name origin: For Oliver Hazard Perry Throck Morton (1823–77), jurist, IN governor (1861–67), and U.S. senator (1867–77).

Cimarron
Township
Lat: 37-04-32 N Long: 101-46-17 W
Pop: 74 (1990); 73 (1980) **Pop Density:** 1.1
Land: 67.1 sq. mi.; **Water:** 0.0 sq. mi.

Elkhart
City
ZIP: 67950 Lat: 37-00-07 N Long: 101-53-40 W
Pop: 2,318 (1990); 2,243 (1980) **Pop Density:** 1220.0
Land: 1.9 sq. mi.; **Water:** 0.0 sq. mi. **Elev:** 3624 ft.
Incorporated Jul 1913.
Name origin: For Elkhart, IN.

Jones
Township
Lat: 37-04-17 N Long: 101-59-21 W
Pop: 11 (1990); 16 (1980) **Pop Density:** 0.2
Land: 54.2 sq. mi.; **Water:** 0.0 sq. mi.

Richfield
City
ZIP: 67953 Lat: 37-15-56 N Long: 101-46-59 W
Pop: 50 (1990); 81 (1980) **Pop Density:** 50.0
Land: 1.0 sq. mi.; **Water:** 0.0 sq. mi. **Elev:** 3400 ft.
In the southwestern corner of KS; incorporated Apr 11, 1887.
Name origin: For its descriptive connotations.

*Richfield
Township
ZIP: 67953 Lat: 37-16-57 N Long: 101-44-46 W
Pop: 269 (1990); 316 (1980) **Pop Density:** 1.1
Land: 250.4 sq. mi.; **Water:** 0.0 sq. mi.

Rolla
City
ZIP: 67954 Lat: 37-07-09 N Long: 101-37-50 W
Pop: 387 (1990); 417 (1980) **Pop Density:** 1290.0
Land: 0.3 sq. mi.; **Water:** 0.0 sq. mi. **Elev:** 3300 ft.
In the southwestern corner of KS; incorporated Aug 2, 1921.
Name origin: From a post office error. Originally called Reil.

*Rolla
Township
ZIP: 67954 Lat: 37-06-53 N Long: 101-38-11 W
Pop: 575 (1990); 561 (1980) **Pop Density:** 4.0
Land: 144.0 sq. mi.; **Water:** 0.0 sq. mi.

Taloga
Township
Lat: 37-03-41 N Long: 101-52-19 W
Pop: 2,443 (1990); 2,378 (1980) **Pop Density:** 44.4
Land: 55.0 sq. mi.; **Water:** 0.0 sq. mi.

Westola
Township
Lat: 37-15-55 N Long: 101-57-14 W
Pop: 108 (1990); 110 (1980) **Pop Density:** 0.7
Land: 159.2 sq. mi.; **Water:** 0.0 sq. mi.

Nemaha County
County Seat: Seneca (ZIP: 66538)

Pop: 10,446 (1990); 11,211 (1980) **Pop Density:** 14.5
Land: 719.1 sq. mi.; **Water:** 0.4 sq. mi. **Area Code:** 913
On northern border of KS, west of St. Joseph, MO; original county; organized Aug 25, 1855 (prior to statehood).
Name origin: For the Nemaha River, itself named from the Oto Indian *nimaha* 'muddy water.'

Adams Township
Lat: 39-47-00 N **Long:** 95-57-26 W
Pop: 205 (1990); 242 (1980) **Pop Density:** 5.7
Land: 36.0 sq. mi.; **Water:** 0.0 sq. mi.

Bern City
ZIP: 66408 **Lat:** 39-57-45 N **Long:** 95-58-20 W
Pop: 190 (1990); 220 (1980) **Pop Density:** 950.0
Land: 0.2 sq. mi.; **Water:** 0.0 sq. mi. **Elev:** 1281 ft.
Incorporated Jul 6, 1910.
Name origin: Named by Swiss settlers for Bern, Switzerland.

Berwick Township
Lat: 39-57-27 N **Long:** 95-50-41 W
Pop: 383 (1990); 346 (1980) **Pop Density:** 10.6
Land: 36.0 sq. mi.; **Water:** 0.0 sq. mi.

Capioma Township
Lat: 39-46-48 N **Long:** 95-50-19 W
Pop: 160 (1990); 202 (1980) **Pop Density:** 4.4
Land: 36.0 sq. mi.; **Water:** 0.0 sq. mi.

Center Township
Lat: 39-46-36 N **Long:** 96-11-31 W
Pop: 211 (1990); 274 (1980) **Pop Density:** 5.8
Land: 36.1 sq. mi.; **Water:** 0.0 sq. mi.

Centralia City
ZIP: 66415 **Lat:** 39-43-26 N **Long:** 96-07-50 W
Pop: 452 (1990); 486 (1980) **Pop Density:** 1130.0
Land: 0.4 sq. mi.; **Water:** 0.0 sq. mi. **Elev:** 1300 ft.
Incorporated Sep 14, 1882.

Clear Creek Township
Lat: 39-58-05 N **Long:** 96-10-57 W
Pop: 144 (1990); 170 (1980) **Pop Density:** 4.0
Land: 35.8 sq. mi.; **Water:** 0.0 sq. mi.

Corning City
ZIP: 66417 **Lat:** 39-39-23 N **Long:** 96-01-43 W
Pop: 142 (1990); 158 (1980) **Pop Density:** 473.3
Land: 0.3 sq. mi.; **Water:** 0.0 sq. mi. **Elev:** 1350 ft.
Incorporated Apr 16, 1889.
Name origin: For Corning, NY.

Gilman Township
Lat: 39-52-00 N **Long:** 95-57-13 W
Pop: 247 (1990); 318 (1980) **Pop Density:** 6.9
Land: 35.9 sq. mi.; **Water:** 0.1 sq. mi.

Goff City
ZIP: 66428 **Lat:** 39-39-48 N **Long:** 95-55-52 W
Pop: 156 (1990); 196 (1980) **Pop Density:** 780.0
Land: 0.2 sq. mi.; **Water:** 0.0 sq. mi. **Elev:** 1250 ft.
Incorporated Apr 12, 1894.
Name origin: For Central Union Pacific Railway official Edward Goff.

Granada Township
Lat: 39-41-46 N **Long:** 95-50-40 W
Pop: 106 (1990); 127 (1980) **Pop Density:** 2.9
Land: 36.1 sq. mi.; **Water:** 0.0 sq. mi.

Harrison Township
Lat: 39-41-46 N **Long:** 95-57-15 W
Pop: 379 (1990); 424 (1980) **Pop Density:** 10.5
Land: 36.1 sq. mi.; **Water:** 0.0 sq. mi.

Home Township
Lat: 39-41-39 N **Long:** 96-11-20 W
Pop: 571 (1990); 603 (1980) **Pop Density:** 15.8
Land: 36.2 sq. mi.; **Water:** 0.1 sq. mi.

Illinois Township
Lat: 39-41-21 N **Long:** 96-03-40 W
Pop: 424 (1990); 465 (1980) **Pop Density:** 11.8
Land: 35.8 sq. mi.; **Water:** 0.0 sq. mi.

Marion Township
Lat: 39-52-11 N **Long:** 96-10-58 W
Pop: 469 (1990); 475 (1980) **Pop Density:** 13.0
Land: 36.1 sq. mi.; **Water:** 0.0 sq. mi.

Mitchell Township
Lat: 39-47-22 N **Long:** 96-04-19 W
Pop: 368 (1990); 345 (1980) **Pop Density:** 10.3
Land: 35.8 sq. mi.; **Water:** 0.0 sq. mi.

Nemaha Township
Lat: 39-57-28 N **Long:** 96-04-11 W
Pop: 193 (1990); 196 (1980) **Pop Density:** 5.4
Land: 35.5 sq. mi.; **Water:** 0.0 sq. mi.

Neuchatel Township
Lat: 39-36-33 N **Long:** 96-10-54 W
Pop: 129 (1990); 165 (1980) **Pop Density:** 3.6
Land: 36.1 sq. mi.; **Water:** 0.0 sq. mi.

Oneida City
ZIP: 66522 **Lat:** 39-52-04 N **Long:** 95-56-23 W
Pop: 79 (1990); 120 (1980) **Pop Density:** 395.0
Land: 0.2 sq. mi.; **Water:** 0.0 sq. mi. **Elev:** 1213 ft.
In northeastern KS.
Name origin: For a tribe of NY State-area Iroquois Indians.

Red Vermillion Township
Lat: 39-36-38 N **Long:** 96-04-08 W
Pop: 135 (1990); 174 (1980) **Pop Density:** 3.8
Land: 35.9 sq. mi.; **Water:** 0.0 sq. mi.

Reilly Township
Lat: 39-36-41 N **Long:** 95-57-01 W
Pop: 158 (1990); 202 (1980) **Pop Density:** 4.4
Land: 36.1 sq. mi.; **Water:** 0.0 sq. mi.

Richmond
Township
Lat: 39-52-26 N **Long:** 96-03-41 W
Pop: 543 (1990); 460 (1980) **Pop Density:** 15.7
Land: 34.5 sq. mi.; **Water:** 0.0 sq. mi.

Rock Creek
Township
Lat: 39-51-48 N **Long:** 95-51-00 W
Pop: 362 (1990); 265 (1980) **Pop Density:** 10.5
Land: 34.4 sq. mi.; **Water:** 0.1 sq. mi.

Sabetha
City
ZIP: 66534 **Lat:** 39-54-11 N **Long:** 95-47-56 W
Pop: 2,335 (1990); 2,288 (1980) **Pop Density:** 1556.7
Land: 1.5 sq. mi.; **Water:** 0.0 sq. mi. **Elev:** 1318 ft.
Incorporated Jul 28, 1874. Part of the town is also in Brown County.
Name origin: Possibly for the sabbath.

Seneca
City
ZIP: 66538 **Lat:** 39-50-08 N **Long:** 96-03-56 W
Pop: 2,027 (1990); 2,389 (1980) **Pop Density:** 1689.2
Land: 1.2 sq. mi.; **Water:** 0.0 sq. mi. **Elev:** 1131 ft.
Incorporated May 17, 1870.
Name origin: For the Seneca Indians in NY.

Washington
Township
Lat: 39-57-26 N **Long:** 95-57-25 W
Pop: 457 (1990); 539 (1980) **Pop Density:** 12.7
Land: 35.9 sq. mi.; **Water:** 0.0 sq. mi.

Wetmore
City
ZIP: 66550 **Lat:** 39-38-05 N **Long:** 95-48-39 W
Pop: 284 (1990); 376 (1980) **Pop Density:** 710.0
Land: 0.4 sq. mi.; **Water:** 0.0 sq. mi. **Elev:** 1150 ft.
Incorporated Oct 4, 1882. Not coextensive with the town of the same name.
Name origin: For Central Branch Railroad vice president, W.T. Wetmore.

*Wetmore
Township
ZIP: 66550 **Lat:** 39-36-25 N **Long:** 95-50-46 W
Pop: 440 (1990); 542 (1980) **Pop Density:** 12.2
Land: 36.0 sq. mi.; **Water:** 0.0 sq. mi.

Neosho County
County Seat: Erie (ZIP: 66733)

Pop: 17,035 (1990); 18,967 (1980) **Pop Density:** 29.8
Land: 571.9 sq. mi.; **Water:** 6.2 sq. mi. **Area Code:** 316
In southeastern KS, west of Pittsburgh; organized as Dorn County Aug 25, 1855 (prior to statehood) from Labette County.
Name origin: Osage Indian 'cold, clear water' or 'main river;' unclear which river is referred to.

Big Creek
Township
Lat: 37-41-14 N **Long:** 95-18-16 W
Pop: 455 (1990); 558 (1980) **Pop Density:** 9.5
Land: 47.9 sq. mi.; **Water:** 0.2 sq. mi.

Canville
Township
Lat: 37-36-05 N **Long:** 95-27-07 W
Pop: 491 (1990); 527 (1980) **Pop Density:** 10.3
Land: 47.8 sq. mi.; **Water:** 0.2 sq. mi.

Centerville
Township
ZIP: 66740 **Lat:** 37-30-48 N **Long:** 95-18-45 W
Pop: 561 (1990); 526 (1980) **Pop Density:** 11.8
Land: 47.6 sq. mi.; **Water:** 0.4 sq. mi.

Chanute
City
ZIP: 66720 **Lat:** 37-40-15 N **Long:** 95-27-36 W
Pop: 9,488 (1990); 10,506 (1980) **Pop Density:** 1608.1
Land: 5.9 sq. mi.; **Water:** 0.1 sq. mi.
Incorporated Dec 9, 1872.
Name origin: For Octave Chanute, the chief civil engineer for the LL&G Railroad.

Chetopa
Township
Lat: 37-30-53 N **Long:** 95-27-04 W
Pop: 805 (1990); 934 (1980) **Pop Density:** 16.7
Land: 48.1 sq. mi.; **Water:** 0.1 sq. mi.

Earlton
City
ZIP: 66720 **Lat:** 37-35-14 N **Long:** 95-28-09 W
Pop: 69 (1990); 79 (1980) **Pop Density:** 690.0
Land: 0.1 sq. mi.; **Water:** 0.0 sq. mi. **Elev:** 960 ft.
Incorporated Mar 1, 1912.

Erie
City
ZIP: 66733 **Lat:** 37-34-06 N **Long:** 95-14-37 W
Pop: 1,276 (1990); 1,415 (1980) **Pop Density:** 1595.0
Land: 0.8 sq. mi.; **Water:** 0.0 sq. mi. **Elev:** 925 ft.
Incorporated Jan 1870. Not coextensive with the town of the same name.
Name origin: For Lake Erie.

*Erie
Township
ZIP: 66733 **Lat:** 37-36-04 N **Long:** 95-18-19 W
Pop: 1,615 (1990); 1,821 (1980) **Pop Density:** 34.1
Land: 47.4 sq. mi.; **Water:** 0.6 sq. mi.

Galesburg
City
ZIP: 66740 **Lat:** 37-28-20 N **Long:** 95-21-20 W
Pop: 160 (1990); 181 (1980) **Pop Density:** 800.0
Land: 0.2 sq. mi.; **Water:** 0.0 sq. mi. **Elev:** 1000 ft.
Incorporated Feb 16, 1907.
Name origin: Named by Scandinavian settlers for Galesburg, IL, their former home.

Grant
Township
Lat: 37-41-18 N Long: 95-09-46 W
Pop: 372 (1990); 471 (1980) Pop Density: 7.7
Land: 48.1 sq. mi.; Water: 0.1 sq. mi.

Ladore
Township
Lat: 37-25-39 N Long: 95-18-22 W
Pop: 384 (1990); 395 (1980) Pop Density: 8.2
Land: 46.7 sq. mi.; Water: 1.3 sq. mi.

Lincoln
Township
Lat: 37-25-33 N Long: 95-09-13 W
Pop: 393 (1990); 381 (1980) Pop Density: 8.3
Land: 47.4 sq. mi.; Water: 0.6 sq. mi.

Mission
Township
Lat: 37-30-54 N Long: 95-09-41 W
Pop: 936 (1990); 989 (1980) Pop Density: 20.3
Land: 46.0 sq. mi.; Water: 1.9 sq. mi.

St. Paul
City
Lat: 37-31-02 N Long: 95-10-29 W
Pop: 687 (1990); 746 (1980) Pop Density: 624.5
Land: 1.1 sq. mi.; Water: 0.0 sq. mi. Elev: 897 ft.
In southeastern KS; incorporated Apr 1869.
Name origin: For St. Paul of the Cross, founder of the Passionist Order, which had established a home in the Osage Mission.

Shiloh
Township
Lat: 37-25-55 N Long: 95-27-37 W
Pop: 299 (1990); 286 (1980) Pop Density: 6.2
Land: 48.2 sq. mi.; Water: 0.1 sq. mi.

Stark
City
ZIP: 66775 Lat: 37-41-22 N Long: 95-08-35 W
Pop: 79 (1990); 143 (1980) Pop Density: 395.0
Land: 0.2 sq. mi.; Water: 0.0 sq. mi. Elev: 1050 ft.
Incorporated Jan 11, 1910.
Name origin: For Revolutionary War hero John Stark (1728–1822).

Thayer
City
ZIP: 66776 Lat: 37-29-16 N Long: 95-28-26 W
Pop: 435 (1990); 517 (1980) Pop Density: 1087.5
Land: 0.4 sq. mi.; Water: 0.0 sq. mi. Elev: 1033 ft.
Incorporated Jan 3, 1871.
Name origin: For railway promoter Nathaniel Thayer.

Tioga
Township
Lat: 37-41-47 N Long: 95-27-02 W
Pop: 873 (1990); 1,194 (1980) Pop Density: 20.6
Land: 42.3 sq. mi.; Water: 0.5 sq. mi.

Walnut Grove
Township
Lat: 37-35-57 N Long: 95-09-03 W
Pop: 363 (1990); 379 (1980) Pop Density: 7.5
Land: 48.3 sq. mi.; Water: 0.1 sq. mi.

Ness County
County Seat: Ness City (ZIP: 67560)

Pop: 4,033 (1990); 4,498 (1980) Pop Density: 3.8
Land: 1074.8 sq. mi.; Water: 0.3 sq. mi. Area Code: 913
In west-central KS, north of Dodge City; established Feb 26, 1867.
Name origin: For Noah V. Ness (?–1864), a corporal in the Kansas cavalry killed in the Civil War, and the only corporal to be so honored in KS.

Bazine
City
ZIP: 67516 Lat: 38-26-45 N Long: 99-41-31 W
Pop: 373 (1990); 385 (1980) Pop Density: 746.0
Land: 0.5 sq. mi.; Water: 0.0 sq. mi. Elev: 2125 ft.
In west-central KS; incorporated Nov 3, 1924. Not coextensive with the town of the same name.
Name origin: For Achille Francois Bazaine, a French general of the Franco-Prussian War. The Post Office dropped the second *a* and the new name was allowed to stand.

*Bazine
Township
ZIP: 67516 Lat: 38-28-46 N Long: 99-41-50 W
Pop: 546 (1990); 611 (1980) Pop Density: 4.5
Land: 120.4 sq. mi.; Water: 0.0 sq. mi.

Brownell
City
ZIP: 67521 Lat: 38-38-24 N Long: 99-44-37 W
Pop: 44 (1990); 92 (1980) Pop Density: 220.0
Land: 0.2 sq. mi.; Water: 0.0 sq. mi. Elev: 2410 ft.
Incorporated Jan 1, 1927.

Center
Township
Lat: 38-29-31 N Long: 99-51-13 W
Pop: 1,775 (1990); 1,830 (1980) Pop Density: 37.2
Land: 47.7 sq. mi.; Water: 0.0 sq. mi.

Eden
Township
Lat: 38-28-57 N Long: 100-08-47 W
Pop: 91 (1990); 124 (1980) Pop Density: 0.9
Land: 102.8 sq. mi.; Water: 0.0 sq. mi.

Forrester
Township
Lat: 38-30-28 N Long: 99-59-26 W
Pop: 129 (1990); 108 (1980) Pop Density: 1.6
Land: 79.6 sq. mi.; Water: 0.0 sq. mi.

Franklin
Township
Lat: 38-21-20 N Long: 99-55-13 W
Pop: 159 (1990); 203 (1980) Pop Density: 1.1
Land: 143.5 sq. mi.; Water: 0.0 sq. mi.

Highpoint
Township
Lat: 38-20-02 N Long: 99-41-45 W
Pop: 120 (1990); 145 (1980) Pop Density: 1.0
Land: 120.6 sq. mi.; Water: 0.1 sq. mi.

Johnson
Township
Lat: 38-19-46 N Long: 100-08-06 W
Pop: 73 (1990); 96 (1980) Pop Density: 0.6
Land: 119.0 sq. mi.; Water: 0.1 sq. mi.

Ness City
ZIP: 67560   **Lat:** 38-27-12 N   **Long:** 99-54-20 W
Pop: 1,724 (1990); 1,769 (1980)   **Pop Density:** 1724.0
Land: 1.0 sq. mi.; **Water:** 0.0 sq. mi.   **Elev:** 2251 ft.
Incorporated Jul 31, 1886.
Name origin: For Corp. Noah V. Ness, who was killed in the Civil War.

Nevada
Township
Lat: 38-37-48 N   **Long:** 99-54-33 W
Pop: 581 (1990); 656 (1980)   **Pop Density:** 5.4
Land: 107.2 sq. mi.; **Water:** 0.0 sq. mi.

Ohio
Township
Lat: 38-37-21 N   **Long:** 100-08-28 W
Pop: 403 (1990); 474 (1980)   **Pop Density:** 3.5
Land: 115.0 sq. mi.; **Water:** 0.0 sq. mi.

Ransom
City
ZIP: 67572   **Lat:** 38-38-10 N   **Long:** 99-55-55 W
Pop: 386 (1990); 448 (1980)   **Pop Density:** 1286.7
Land: 0.3 sq. mi.; **Water:** 0.0 sq. mi.   **Elev:** 2511 ft.
Incorporated Mar 8, 1905.
Name origin: For Gen. Thomas E.G. Ransom.

Utica
City
ZIP: 67584   **Lat:** 38-38-34 N   **Long:** 100-10-11 W
Pop: 208 (1990); 275 (1980)   **Pop Density:** 1040.0
Land: 0.2 sq. mi.; **Water:** 0.0 sq. mi.   **Elev:** 2618 ft.
Incorporated Jul 6, 1911.
Name origin: For the ancient Roman city.

Waring
Township
Lat: 38-36-38 N   **Long:** 99-41-53 W
Pop: 156 (1990); 251 (1980)   **Pop Density:** 1.3
Land: 118.8 sq. mi.; **Water:** 0.0 sq. mi.

Norton County
County Seat: Norton (ZIP: 67654)

Pop: 5,947 (1990); 6,689 (1980)   **Pop Density:** 6.8
Land: 877.9 sq. mi.; **Water:** 3.5 sq. mi.   **Area Code:** 913

On the central northern border of KS; established as Oro County 1859 (prior to statehood) from unorganized territory; name changed to Norton Feb 26, 1867; changed to Billings Mar 6, 1873; changed back to Norton Feb 19, 1874.

Name origin: For Orloff Norton (?–1864), Kansas army officer killed during a skirmish at Cane Hill, AR. Previously for N. H. Billings, a member of the KS legislature.

Almena
City
ZIP: 67622   **Lat:** 39-53-29 N   **Long:** 99-42-35 W
Pop: 423 (1990); 517 (1980)   **Pop Density:** 705.0
Land: 0.6 sq. mi.; **Water:** 0.0 sq. mi.   **Elev:** 2155 ft.
Incorporated 1893.
Name origin: For a local pioneer settler.

Almena-District 4
Township
Lat: 39-52-16 N   **Long:** 99-41-27 W
Pop: 574 (1990); 762 (1980)   **Pop Density:** 5.3
Land: 107.4 sq. mi.; **Water:** 0.0 sq. mi.

Center-District 1
Township
Lat: 39-53-55 N   **Long:** 99-58-57 W
Pop: 1,323 (1990); 1,196 (1980)   **Pop Density:** 5.2
Land: 252.6 sq. mi.; **Water:** 0.2 sq. mi.

Clayton
City
ZIP: 67629   **Lat:** 39-44-12 N   **Long:** 100-10-29 W
Pop: 77 (1990); 93 (1980)   **Pop Density:** 192.5
Land: 0.4 sq. mi.; **Water:** 0.0 sq. mi.   **Elev:** 2450 ft.
Incorporated Feb 4, 1907. Part of the town is also in Decatur County.
Name origin: For the clay on the roads in the area.

Edmond
City
ZIP: 67636   **Lat:** 39-37-36 N   **Long:** 99-49-13 W
Pop: 37 (1990); 56 (1980)   **Pop Density:** 185.0
Land: 0.2 sq. mi.; **Water:** 0.0 sq. mi.   **Elev:** 2119 ft.
Incorporated Apr 4, 1916.

Harrison-District 6
Township
Lat: 39-57-20 N   **Long:** 99-47-55 W
Pop: 20 (1990); 33 (1980)   **Pop Density:** 0.6
Land: 35.8 sq. mi.; **Water:** 0.0 sq. mi.

Highland-District 2
Township
Lat: 39-41-23 N   **Long:** 100-01-47 W
Pop: 822 (1990); 1,016 (1980)   **Pop Density:** 2.8
Land: 288.7 sq. mi.; **Water:** 3.3 sq. mi.

Lenora
City
ZIP: 67645   **Lat:** 39-36-39 N   **Long:** 100-00-03 W
Pop: 329 (1990); 444 (1980)   **Pop Density:** 658.0
Land: 0.5 sq. mi.; **Water:** 0.0 sq. mi.   **Elev:** 2270 ft.
Incorporated 1887.
Name origin: For early pioneer, Lenora Hanson.

Norton
City
ZIP: 67654   **Lat:** 39-50-07 N   **Long:** 99-53-30 W
Pop: 3,017 (1990); 3,400 (1980)   **Pop Density:** 1587.9
Land: 1.9 sq. mi.; **Water:** 0.0 sq. mi.   **Elev:** 2300 ft.
Incorporated Sep 12, 1885.
Name origin: For the county.

Solomon-District 3
Township
Lat: 39-40-38 N   **Long:** 99-45-54 W
Pop: 191 (1990); 282 (1980)   **Pop Density:** 1.0
Land: 191.5 sq. mi.; **Water:** 0.0 sq. mi.

Osage County
County Seat: Lyndon (ZIP: 66451)

Pop: 15,248 (1990); 15,319 (1980) **Pop Density:** 21.7
Land: 703.6 sq. mi.; **Water:** 15.7 sq. mi. **Area Code:** 913
In eastern KS, south of Topeka; original county; organized as Weller County Aug 30, 1855 (prior to statehood); name changed Feb 11, 1859.

Name origin: For the Osage Indians, a tribe of Siouan linguistic stock. Name is a corruption of their name in their own language, *Wazhazhe*, meaning unknown.

Agency   Township
Lat: 38-34-32 N   Long: 95-33-17 W
Pop: 500 (1990); 565 (1980)   **Pop Density:** 15.1
Land: 33.1 sq. mi.; **Water:** 0.0 sq. mi.

Arvonia   Township
Lat: 38-28-46 N   Long: 95-52-23 W
Pop: 141 (1990); 116 (1980)   **Pop Density:** 3.3
Land: 43.2 sq. mi.; **Water:** 4.9 sq. mi.

Barclay   Township
Lat: 38-34-08 N   Long: 95-52-30 W
Pop: 181 (1990); 203 (1980)   **Pop Density:** 3.8
Land: 47.9 sq. mi.; **Water:** 0.1 sq. mi.

Burlingame   City
ZIP: 66413   Lat: 38-45-03 N   Long: 95-50-07 W
Pop: 1,074 (1990); 1,239 (1980)   **Pop Density:** 1534.3
Land: 0.7 sq. mi.; **Water:** 0.0 sq. mi.   **Elev:** 1055 ft.
Incorporated 1861. Not coextensive with the town of the same name.
Name origin: For Anson Burlingame, U.S. senator from MA and an early free-state advocate.

*Burlingame   Township
ZIP: 66413   Lat: 38-48-23 N   Long: 95-52-24 W
Pop: 1,760 (1990); 1,935 (1980)   **Pop Density:** 24.4
Land: 72.0 sq. mi.; **Water:** 0.3 sq. mi.

Carbondale   City
ZIP: 66414   Lat: 38-49-12 N   Long: 95-41-31 W
Pop: 1,526 (1990); 1,518 (1980)   **Pop Density:** 1907.5
Land: 0.8 sq. mi.; **Water:** 0.0 sq. mi.   **Elev:** 1087 ft.
Incorporated Oct 15, 1872.
Name origin: For the abundant coal resources in its area.

Dragoon   Township
Lat: 38-42-58 N   Long: 95-50-18 W
Pop: 234 (1990); 277 (1980)   **Pop Density:** 6.5
Land: 36.2 sq. mi.; **Water:** 0.0 sq. mi.

Elk   Township
Lat: 38-48-14 N   Long: 95-33-05 W
Pop: 1,630 (1990); 1,637 (1980)   **Pop Density:** 30.1
Land: 54.1 sq. mi.; **Water:** 0.2 sq. mi.

Fairfax   Township
Lat: 38-42-52 N   Long: 95-40-03 W
Pop: 435 (1990); 302 (1980)   **Pop Density:** 10.1
Land: 43.0 sq. mi.; **Water:** 1.9 sq. mi.

Grant   Township
Lat: 38-39-01 N   Long: 95-53-43 W
Pop: 311 (1990); 342 (1980)   **Pop Density:** 8.6
Land: 36.1 sq. mi.; **Water:** 0.1 sq. mi.

Junction   Township
Lat: 38-40-39 N   Long: 95-33-56 W
Pop: 849 (1990); 736 (1980)   **Pop Density:** 17.1
Land: 49.6 sq. mi.; **Water:** 0.1 sq. mi.

Lincoln   Township
Lat: 38-29-06 N   Long: 95-33-16 W
Pop: 121 (1990); 138 (1980)   **Pop Density:** 3.8
Land: 32.1 sq. mi.; **Water:** 0.0 sq. mi.

Lyndon   City
ZIP: 66451   Lat: 38-36-36 N   Long: 95-41-06 W
Pop: 964 (1990); 1,132 (1980)   **Pop Density:** 1377.1
Land: 0.7 sq. mi.; **Water:** 0.0 sq. mi.   **Elev:** 1030 ft.

Melvern   City
ZIP: 66510   Lat: 38-30-26 N   Long: 95-38-17 W
Pop: 423 (1990); 481 (1980)   **Pop Density:** 1410.0
Land: 0.3 sq. mi.; **Water:** 0.0 sq. mi.   **Elev:** 1012 ft.
Incorporated 1883. Not coextensive with the town of the same name.
Name origin: For the Malvern hills in Worcestershire, England, with a spelling variation.

*Melvern   Township
ZIP: 66510   Lat: 38-30-07 N   Long: 95-38-48 W
Pop: 735 (1990); 842 (1980)   **Pop Density:** 16.5
Land: 44.5 sq. mi.; **Water:** 0.1 sq. mi.

Olivet   City
Lat: 38-28-51 N   Long: 95-45-07 W
Pop: 59 (1990); 65 (1980)   **Pop Density:** 196.7
Land: 0.3 sq. mi.; **Water:** 0.0 sq. mi.   **Elev:** 1150 ft.
Incorporated Feb 2, 1924. Not coextensive with the town of the same name.

*Olivet   Township
Lat: 38-30-59 N   Long: 95-44-40 W
Pop: 253 (1990); 238 (1980)   **Pop Density:** 4.6
Land: 55.1 sq. mi.; **Water:** 6.6 sq. mi.

Osage City   City
ZIP: 66523   Lat: 38-37-58 N   Long: 95-49-15 W
Pop: 2,689 (1990); 2,667 (1980)   **Pop Density:** 896.3
Land: 3.0 sq. mi.; **Water:** 0.1 sq. mi.   **Elev:** 1085 ft.
Incorporated Apr 5, 1872.
Name origin: For the Osage Indians.

Overbrook   City
ZIP: 66524   Lat: 38-46-47 N   Long: 95-33-24 W
Pop: 920 (1990); 930 (1980)   **Pop Density:** 1840.0
Land: 0.5 sq. mi.; **Water:** 0.0 sq. mi.   **Elev:** 1220 ft.
Incorporated Mar 8, 1948.
Name origin: Named by early settlers for Overbrook, PA.

Quenemo
City
ZIP: 66528 **Lat:** 38-34-49 N **Long:** 95-31-34 W
Pop: 369 (1990); 413 (1980) **Pop Density:** 922.5
Land: 0.4 sq. mi.; **Water:** 0.0 sq. mi. **Elev:** 941 ft.
Incorporated 1885.

Ridgeway
Township
Lat: 38-49-05 N **Long:** 95-39-53 W
Pop: 2,502 (1990); 2,353 (1980) **Pop Density:** 60.1
Land: 41.6 sq. mi.; **Water:** 0.8 sq. mi.

Scranton
City
ZIP: 66537 **Lat:** 38-46-40 N **Long:** 95-44-26 W
Pop: 674 (1990); 664 (1980) **Pop Density:** 674.0
Land: 1.0 sq. mi.; **Water:** 0.0 sq. mi. **Elev:** 1123 ft.
Incorporated 1875. Not coextensive with the town of the same name.
Name origin: For Scranton, PA.

*Scranton
Township
ZIP: 66537 **Lat:** 38-48-11 N **Long:** 95-45-16 W
Pop: 1,158 (1990); 1,076 (1980) **Pop Density:** 32.5
Land: 35.6 sq. mi.; **Water:** 0.3 sq. mi.

Superior
Township
Lat: 38-38-58 N **Long:** 95-46-42 W
Pop: 305 (1990); 356 (1980) **Pop Density:** 8.4
Land: 36.2 sq. mi.; **Water:** 0.1 sq. mi.

Valley Brook
Township
Lat: 38-36-39 N **Long:** 95-40-16 W
Pop: 1,444 (1990); 1,536 (1980) **Pop Density:** 35.9
Land: 40.2 sq. mi.; **Water:** 0.2 sq. mi.

Osborne County
County Seat: Osborne (ZIP: 67473)

Pop: 4,867 (1990); 5,959 (1980) **Pop Density:** 5.5
Land: 892.6 sq. mi.; **Water:** 1.7 sq. mi. **Area Code:** 913
In north-central KS, northeast of Hays; organized Feb 26, 1867 from Mitchell County.
Name origin: For Vincent B. Osborne (?–1865), Kansas soldier and lawyer. The geodetic center of the U.S. is in this county.

Alton
City
ZIP: 67623 **Lat:** 39-28-05 N **Long:** 98-56-53 W
Pop: 115 (1990); 135 (1980) **Pop Density:** 383.3
Land: 0.3 sq. mi.; **Water:** 0.0 sq. mi. **Elev:** 1652 ft.
Incorporated 1880.
Name origin: For Alton, IL.

Bethany
Township
Lat: 39-31-33 N **Long:** 98-39-08 W
Pop: 221 (1990); 295 (1980) **Pop Density:** 6.1
Land: 36.0 sq. mi.; **Water:** 0.0 sq. mi.

Bloom
Township
Lat: 39-19-44 N **Long:** 98-33-06 W
Pop: 91 (1990); 148 (1980) **Pop Density:** 1.7
Land: 54.0 sq. mi.; **Water:** 0.0 sq. mi.

Corinth
Township
Lat: 39-26-15 N **Long:** 98-32-41 W
Pop: 55 (1990); 66 (1980) **Pop Density:** 1.6
Land: 35.3 sq. mi.; **Water:** 0.1 sq. mi.

Covert
Township
Lat: 39-15-16 N **Long:** 98-46-30 W
Pop: 25 (1990); 29 (1980) **Pop Density:** 0.7
Land: 35.9 sq. mi.; **Water:** 0.1 sq. mi.

Delhi
Township
Lat: 39-11-54 N **Long:** 98-32-40 W
Pop: 43 (1990); 59 (1980) **Pop Density:** 0.8
Land: 53.6 sq. mi.; **Water:** 0.2 sq. mi.

Downs
City
ZIP: 67437 **Lat:** 39-30-11 N **Long:** 98-32-48 W
Pop: 1,119 (1990); 1,324 (1980) **Pop Density:** 1243.3
Land: 0.9 sq. mi.; **Water:** 0.0 sq. mi. **Elev:** 1484 ft.
Incorporated Jul 27, 1879.
Name origin: For railroad official Maj. William F. Downs.

Grant
Township
Lat: 39-31-27 N **Long:** 98-59-14 W
Pop: 33 (1990); 54 (1980) **Pop Density:** 0.9
Land: 35.4 sq. mi.; **Water:** 0.1 sq. mi.

Hancock
Township
Lat: 39-21-09 N **Long:** 98-39-00 W
Pop: 26 (1990); 36 (1980) **Pop Density:** 0.7
Land: 36.0 sq. mi.; **Water:** 0.1 sq. mi.

Hawkeye
Township
Lat: 39-31-04 N **Long:** 98-52-27 W
Pop: 34 (1990); 35 (1980) **Pop Density:** 1.0
Land: 35.6 sq. mi.; **Water:** 0.1 sq. mi.

Independence
Township
Lat: 39-20-56 N **Long:** 98-46-02 W
Pop: 41 (1990); 63 (1980) **Pop Density:** 1.2
Land: 35.5 sq. mi.; **Water:** 0.1 sq. mi.

Jackson
Township
Lat: 39-10-45 N **Long:** 98-39-09 W
Pop: 52 (1990); 58 (1980) **Pop Density:** 1.4
Land: 35.9 sq. mi.; **Water:** 0.0 sq. mi.

Kill Creek
Township
Lat: 39-21-21 N **Long:** 98-52-51 W
Pop: 54 (1990); 48 (1980) **Pop Density:** 1.5
Land: 36.0 sq. mi.; **Water:** 0.1 sq. mi.

Lawrence
Township
Lat: 39-31-56 N Long: 98-45-54 W
Pop: 34 (1990); 56 (1980) Pop Density: 1.0
Land: 34.7 sq. mi.; Water: 0.1 sq. mi.

Liberty
Township
Lat: 39-11-05 N Long: 98-52-41 W
Pop: 27 (1990); 27 (1980) Pop Density: 0.8
Land: 35.8 sq. mi.; Water: 0.1 sq. mi.

Mount Ayr
Township
Lat: 39-21-03 N Long: 98-59-28 W
Pop: 66 (1990); 74 (1980) Pop Density: 1.8
Land: 35.7 sq. mi.; Water: 0.0 sq. mi.

Natoma
City
ZIP: 67651 Lat: 39-11-20 N Long: 99-01-28 W
Pop: 392 (1990); 515 (1980) Pop Density: 980.0
Land: 0.4 sq. mi.; Water: 0.0 sq. mi. Elev: 1834 ft.
Incorporated Jul 3, 1905. Not coextensive with the town of the same name.
Name origin: From an Indian term meaning 'newly born.'

*Natoma
Township
ZIP: 67651 Lat: 39-10-38 N Long: 98-59-22 W
Pop: 449 (1990); 570 (1980) Pop Density: 12.5
Land: 35.9 sq. mi.; Water: 0.1 sq. mi.

Osborne
City
ZIP: 67473 Lat: 39-26-21 N Long: 98-41-53 W
Pop: 1,778 (1990); 2,120 (1980) Pop Density: 1270.0
Land: 1.4 sq. mi.; Water: 0.0 sq. mi. Elev: 1554 ft.
Incorporated Jan 3, 1870.
Name origin: For Civil War veteran, Vincent B. Osborne.

Penn
Township
Lat: 39-26-00 N Long: 98-40-20 W
Pop: 139 (1990); 176 (1980) Pop Density: 3.0
Land: 46.1 sq. mi.; Water: 0.0 sq. mi.

Portis
City
ZIP: 67474 Lat: 39-33-47 N Long: 98-41-27 W
Pop: 129 (1990); 172 (1980) Pop Density: 430.0
Land: 0.3 sq. mi.; Water: 0.0 sq. mi. Elev: 1542 ft.
Incorporated Jun 1904.
Name origin: For a Missouri-Pacific Railroad vice president.

Ross
Township
Lat: 39-31-17 N Long: 98-32-38 W
Pop: 1,230 (1990); 1,456 (1980) Pop Density: 34.7
Land: 35.4 sq. mi.; Water: 0.3 sq. mi.

Round Mound
Township
Lat: 39-15-54 N Long: 98-59-33 W
Pop: 57 (1990); 78 (1980) Pop Density: 1.6
Land: 35.7 sq. mi.; Water: 0.0 sq. mi.

Sumner
Township
Lat: 39-26-50 N Long: 98-57-15 W
Pop: 231 (1990); 275 (1980) Pop Density: 4.3
Land: 53.6 sq. mi.; Water: 0.0 sq. mi.

Tilden
Township
Lat: 39-26-14 N Long: 98-48-56 W
Pop: 96 (1990); 134 (1980) Pop Density: 2.3
Land: 41.2 sq. mi.; Water: 0.1 sq. mi.

Valley
Township
Lat: 39-10-48 N Long: 98-46-05 W
Pop: 30 (1990); 29 (1980) Pop Density: 0.8
Land: 36.1 sq. mi.; Water: 0.0 sq. mi.

Victor
Township
Lat: 39-15-53 N Long: 98-52-33 W
Pop: 35 (1990); 42 (1980) Pop Density: 1.0
Land: 35.9 sq. mi.; Water: 0.0 sq. mi.

Winfield
Township
Lat: 39-15-31 N Long: 98-39-27 W
Pop: 20 (1990); 31 (1980) Pop Density: 0.6
Land: 35.9 sq. mi.; Water: 0.1 sq. mi.

Ottawa County
County Seat: Minneapolis (ZIP: 67467)

Pop: 5,634 (1990); 5,971 (1980) Pop Density: 7.8
Land: 721.2 sq. mi.; Water: 0.8 sq. mi. Area Code: 913
In north-central KS, north of Salina; established Feb 27, 1860 (prior to statehood) from Saline County.
Name origin: For the Ottawa Indians of Algonquian linguistic stock. Tribal name derived from K*adawe* 'to trade,' for their ability as intertribal traders and barterers.

Bennington
City
ZIP: 67422 Lat: 39-01-55 N Long: 97-35-38 W
Pop: 568 (1990); 579 (1980) Pop Density: 1420.0
Land: 0.4 sq. mi.; Water: 0.0 sq. mi. Elev: 1221 ft.
In northeast-central KS; incorporated May 9, 1885. Not coextensive with the town of the same name.
Name origin: For Bennington, VT.

*Bennington
Township
ZIP: 67422 Lat: 39-00-00 N Long: 97-38-35 W
Pop: 844 (1990); 781 (1980) Pop Density: 20.1
Land: 42.0 sq. mi.; Water: 0.0 sq. mi.

Blaine
Township
Lat: 39-10-24 N Long: 97-38-44 W
Pop: 120 (1990); 111 (1980) Pop Density: 3.3
Land: 36.3 sq. mi.; Water: 0.0 sq. mi.

Buckeye
Township
Lat: 39-00-12 N Long: 97-31-47 W
Pop: 84 (1990); 96 (1980) Pop Density: 2.8
Land: 30.0 sq. mi.; Water: 0.0 sq. mi.

Center
Township
Lat: 39-05-09 N Long: 97-45-33 W
Pop: 75 (1990); 84 (1980) Pop Density: 2.1
Land: 35.7 sq. mi.; Water: 0.1 sq. mi.

KANSAS, Ottawa County

Chapman Township
Lat: 39-15-51 N Long: 97-25-46 W
Pop: 72 (1990); 76 (1980) Pop Density: 2.0
Land: 35.8 sq. mi.; Water: 0.0 sq. mi.

Concord Township
Lat: 39-05-18 N Long: 97-38-53 W
Pop: 163 (1990); 177 (1980) Pop Density: 4.6
Land: 35.1 sq. mi.; Water: 0.0 sq. mi.

Culver City
ZIP: 67484 Lat: 38-58-05 N Long: 97-45-33 W
Pop: 162 (1990); 167 (1980) Pop Density: 810.0
Land: 0.2 sq. mi.; Water: 0.0 sq. mi. Elev: 1260 ft.
Incorporated 1909. Not coextensive with the town of the same name.

*Culver Township
Lat: 39-00-04 N Long: 97-45-52 W
Pop: 291 (1990); 297 (1980) Pop Density: 8.0
Land: 36.2 sq. mi.; Water: 0.0 sq. mi.

Delphos City
ZIP: 67436 Lat: 39-16-29 N Long: 97-45-57 W
Pop: 494 (1990); 570 (1980) Pop Density: 823.3
Land: 0.6 sq. mi.; Water: 0.0 sq. mi. Elev: 1300 ft.
Incorporated 1884.
Name origin: For Delphos, OH, former home of Levi Yockey, the first postmaster.

Durham Township
Lat: 39-10-32 N Long: 97-25-36 W
Pop: 36 (1990); 34 (1980) Pop Density: 1.0
Land: 35.8 sq. mi.; Water: 0.0 sq. mi.

Fountain Township
Lat: 39-10-41 N Long: 97-52-30 W
Pop: 179 (1990); 199 (1980) Pop Density: 4.9
Land: 36.2 sq. mi.; Water: 0.0 sq. mi.

Garfield Township
Lat: 39-10-37 N Long: 97-45-04 W
Pop: 95 (1990); 84 (1980) Pop Density: 2.6
Land: 36.3 sq. mi.; Water: 0.0 sq. mi.

Grant Township
Lat: 39-10-05 N Long: 97-31-58 W
Pop: 68 (1990); 94 (1980) Pop Density: 1.9
Land: 36.3 sq. mi.; Water: 0.0 sq. mi.

Henry Township
Lat: 39-05-04 N Long: 97-52-24 W
Pop: 31 (1990); 51 (1980) Pop Density: 0.9
Land: 35.7 sq. mi.; Water: 0.1 sq. mi.

Lincoln Township
Lat: 38-59-58 N Long: 97-25-39 W
Pop: 136 (1990); 161 (1980) Pop Density: 3.8
Land: 35.9 sq. mi.; Water: 0.0 sq. mi.

Logan Township
Lat: 39-15-46 N Long: 97-38-59 W
Pop: 89 (1990); 124 (1980) Pop Density: 2.5
Land: 36.1 sq. mi.; Water: 0.0 sq. mi.

Minneapolis City
ZIP: 67467 Lat: 39-07-29 N Long: 97-42-07 W
Pop: 1,983 (1990); 2,075 (1980) Pop Density: 1416.4
Land: 1.4 sq. mi.; Water: 0.0 sq. mi. Elev: 1253 ft.
Incorporated 1871.
Name origin: For Minneapolis, MN.

Morton Township
Lat: 39-00-22 N Long: 97-52-27 W
Pop: 454 (1990); 483 (1980) Pop Density: 12.6
Land: 35.9 sq. mi.; Water: 0.0 sq. mi.

Ottawa Township
Lat: 39-04-50 N Long: 97-26-09 W
Pop: 46 (1990); 46 (1980) Pop Density: 1.3
Land: 35.9 sq. mi.; Water: 0.0 sq. mi.

Richland Township
Lat: 39-04-44 N Long: 97-32-08 W
Pop: 158 (1990); 174 (1980) Pop Density: 4.4
Land: 35.6 sq. mi.; Water: 0.2 sq. mi.

Sheridan Township
Lat: 39-15-44 N Long: 97-45-47 W
Pop: 591 (1990); 699 (1980) Pop Density: 16.2
Land: 36.4 sq. mi.; Water: 0.0 sq. mi.

Sherman Township
Lat: 39-15-46 N Long: 97-32-13 W
Pop: 71 (1990); 81 (1980) Pop Density: 2.0
Land: 36.2 sq. mi.; Water: 0.0 sq. mi.

Stanton Township
Lat: 39-15-44 N Long: 97-52-26 W
Pop: 48 (1990); 44 (1980) Pop Density: 1.3
Land: 36.6 sq. mi.; Water: 0.1 sq. mi.

Tescott City
ZIP: 67484 Lat: 39-00-42 N Long: 97-52-38 W
Pop: 317 (1990); 331 (1980) Pop Density: 1056.7
Land: 0.3 sq. mi.; Water: 0.0 sq. mi. Elev: 1294 ft.
Incorporated Jul 12, 1905.
Name origin: For pioneer T.E. Scott.

American Places Dictionary   KANSAS, Pawnee County

Pawnee County
County Seat: Larned (ZIP: 67550)

Pop: 7,555 (1990); 8,065 (1980)   **Pop Density:** 10.0
Land: 754.2 sq. mi.; **Water:** 0.4 sq. mi.   **Area Code:** 316
In central KS, west of Great Bend; established Feb 26, 1867 from Rush and Stafford counties.

Name origin: For an Indian tribe of Caddoan linguistic stock. Name may mean 'horn' for the shape of their hair lock; Osages called them *Pa-in* 'long-haired'; they called themselves 'civilized people.'

Ash Valley   Township
Lat: 38-18-15 N   **Long:** 99-11-53 W
Pop: 60 (1990); 66 (1980)   **Pop Density:** 1.6
Land: 36.6 sq. mi.; **Water:** 0.0 sq. mi.

Browns Grove   Township
Lat: 38-13-16 N   **Long:** 99-30-46 W
Pop: 298 (1990); 336 (1980)   **Pop Density:** 8.3
Land: 35.8 sq. mi.; **Water:** 0.0 sq. mi.

Burdett   City
ZIP: 67523   **Lat:** 38-11-36 N   **Long:** 99-31-33 W
Pop: 248 (1990); 275 (1980)   **Pop Density:** 826.7
Land: 0.3 sq. mi.; **Water:** 0.0 sq. mi.   **Elev:** 2133 ft.
Incorporated Nov 28, 1961.

Name origin: For Robert J. Burdette, author and humorist; the final *e* was dropped.

Conkling   Township
Lat: 38-18-10 N   **Long:** 99-18-37 W
Pop: 31 (1990); 33 (1980)   **Pop Density:** 0.9
Land: 36.3 sq. mi.; **Water:** 0.0 sq. mi.

Garfield   City
ZIP: 67529   **Lat:** 38-04-39 N   **Long:** 99-14-40 W
Pop: 236 (1990); 277 (1980)   **Pop Density:** 472.0
Land: 0.5 sq. mi.; **Water:** 0.0 sq. mi.

*Garfield   Township
ZIP: 67529   **Lat:** 38-02-42 N   **Long:** 99-17-44 W
Pop: 287 (1990); 326 (1980)   **Pop Density:** 8.0
Land: 35.8 sq. mi.; **Water:** 0.0 sq. mi.

Grant   Township
Lat: 38-13-06 N   **Long:** 99-24-18 W
Pop: 238 (1990); 293 (1980)   **Pop Density:** 6.7
Land: 35.7 sq. mi.; **Water:** 0.0 sq. mi.

Keysville   Township
Lat: 38-07-44 N   **Long:** 99-24-07 W
Pop: 55 (1990); 71 (1980)   **Pop Density:** 1.5
Land: 36.1 sq. mi.; **Water:** 0.0 sq. mi.

Larned   City
ZIP: 67550   **Lat:** 38-10-59 N   **Long:** 99-06-04 W
Pop: 4,490 (1990); 4,811 (1980)   **Pop Density:** 1952.2
Land: 2.3 sq. mi.; **Water:** 0.0 sq. mi.   **Elev:** 2004 ft.
Incorporated Mar 17, 1886.

Name origin: For Col. Benjamin Larned, U.S. Army Paymaster-General in 1860.

*Larned   Township
ZIP: 67550   **Lat:** 38-13-35 N   **Long:** 99-04-30 W
Pop: 248 (1990); 333 (1980)   **Pop Density:** 7.4
Land: 33.6 sq. mi.; **Water:** 0.0 sq. mi.

Lincoln   Township
Lat: 38-18-38 N   **Long:** 99-25-34 W
Pop: 37 (1990); 54 (1980)   **Pop Density:** 1.0
Land: 36.0 sq. mi.; **Water:** 0.0 sq. mi.

Logan   Township
Lat: 38-07-34 N   **Long:** 98-57-29 W
Pop: 59 (1990); 60 (1980)   **Pop Density:** 1.6
Land: 35.8 sq. mi.; **Water:** 0.0 sq. mi.

Morton   Township
Lat: 38-13-07 N   **Long:** 99-17-41 W
Pop: 61 (1990); 89 (1980)   **Pop Density:** 1.7
Land: 35.7 sq. mi.; **Water:** 0.0 sq. mi.

Orange   Township
Lat: 38-03-02 N   **Long:** 99-10-39 W
Pop: 81 (1990); 85 (1980)   **Pop Density:** 2.3
Land: 35.7 sq. mi.; **Water:** 0.0 sq. mi.

Pawnee   Township
Lat: 38-13-05 N   **Long:** 99-11-25 W
Pop: 154 (1990); 101 (1980)   **Pop Density:** 4.3
Land: 35.7 sq. mi.; **Water:** 0.0 sq. mi.

Pleasant Grove   Township
Lat: 38-07-14 N   **Long:** 99-04-38 W
Pop: 256 (1990); 243 (1980)   **Pop Density:** 7.2
Land: 35.8 sq. mi.; **Water:** 0.1 sq. mi.

Pleasant Ridge   Township
Lat: 38-08-10 N   **Long:** 99-18-05 W
Pop: 76 (1990); 83 (1980)   **Pop Density:** 2.1
Land: 36.0 sq. mi.; **Water:** 0.0 sq. mi.

Pleasant Valley   Township
Lat: 38-02-12 N   **Long:** 99-04-56 W
Pop: 144 (1990); 134 (1980)   **Pop Density:** 4.0
Land: 36.0 sq. mi.; **Water:** 0.0 sq. mi.

River   Township
Lat: 38-13-18 N   **Long:** 98-57-42 W
Pop: 102 (1990); 111 (1980)   **Pop Density:** 2.9
Land: 35.7 sq. mi.; **Water:** 0.0 sq. mi.

Rozel   City
ZIP: 67574   **Lat:** 38-11-45 N   **Long:** 99-24-07 W
Pop: 187 (1990); 219 (1980)   **Pop Density:** 935.0
Land: 0.2 sq. mi.; **Water:** 0.0 sq. mi.   **Elev:** 2073 ft.
Incorporated Nov 4, 1929.

Name origin: For the daughter of a Pawnee County land agent.

Santa Fe   Township
Lat: 38-07-41 N   **Long:** 99-10-35 W
Pop: 632 (1990); 579 (1980)   **Pop Density:** 17.7
Land: 35.7 sq. mi.; **Water:** 0.0 sq. mi.

KANSAS, Pawnee County

Sawmill — Township
Lat: 38-07-42 N Long: 99-30-23 W
Pop: 29 (1990); 36 (1980)   Pop Density: 0.8
Land: 36.0 sq. mi.; Water: 0.0 sq. mi.

Shiley — Township
Lat: 38-18-23 N Long: 99-31-47 W
Pop: 42 (1990); 33 (1980)   Pop Density: 1.2
Land: 36.3 sq. mi.; Water: 0.1 sq. mi.

Valley Center — Township
Lat: 38-03-03 N Long: 98-57-45 W
Pop: 64 (1990); 91 (1980)   Pop Density: 1.8
Land: 35.5 sq. mi.; Water: 0.0 sq. mi.

Walnut — Township
Lat: 38-17-57 N Long: 99-05-05 W
Pop: 111 (1990); 97 (1980)   Pop Density: 3.1
Land: 36.0 sq. mi.; Water: 0.0 sq. mi.

Phillips County
County Seat: Phillipsburg (ZIP: 67661)

Pop: 6,590 (1990); 7,406 (1980)   Pop Density: 7.4
Land: 886.3 sq. mi.; Water: 8.6 sq. mi.   Area Code: 913

On the central northern border of KS; established Feb 26, 1867 from Kirwin Land District.

Name origin: Either for William A. Phillips (?–1856), a free-state man murdered at Leavenworth by a proslaver, or for a "gallant private soldier of the Union army."

Agra — City
ZIP: 67621   Lat: 39-45-39 N Long: 99-07-11 W
Pop: 322 (1990); 321 (1980)   Pop Density: 1073.3
Land: 0.3 sq. mi.; Water: 0.0 sq. mi.   Elev: 1851 ft.
Incorporated Oct 7, 1904.
Name origin: For the daughter of the president of the Chicago, Rock Island, and Pacific Railroad..

Arcade — Township
Lat: 39-46-59 N Long: 99-13-58 W
Pop: 100 (1990); 106 (1980)   Pop Density: 2.8
Land: 35.7 sq. mi.; Water: 0.0 sq. mi.

Beaver — Township
Lat: 39-47-05 N Long: 99-34-48 W
Pop: 69 (1990); 94 (1980)   Pop Density: 1.9
Land: 35.8 sq. mi.; Water: 0.0 sq. mi.

Belmont — Township
Lat: 39-41-56 N Long: 99-27-41 W
Pop: 141 (1990); 114 (1980)   Pop Density: 3.9
Land: 36.1 sq. mi.; Water: 0.0 sq. mi.

Bow Creek — Township
Lat: 39-36-46 N Long: 99-13-53 W
Pop: 40 (1990); 39 (1980)   Pop Density: 1.1
Land: 35.4 sq. mi.; Water: 0.5 sq. mi.

Crystal — Township
Lat: 39-52-08 N Long: 99-07-03 W
Pop: 53 (1990); 82 (1980)   Pop Density: 1.5
Land: 35.7 sq. mi.; Water: 0.1 sq. mi.

Dayton — Township
Lat: 39-52-20 N Long: 99-27-25 W
Pop: 52 (1990); 64 (1980)   Pop Density: 1.5
Land: 35.7 sq. mi.; Water: 0.0 sq. mi.

Deer Creek — Township
Lat: 39-41-44 N Long: 99-14-10 W
Pop: 91 (1990); 105 (1980)   Pop Density: 2.7
Land: 34.0 sq. mi.; Water: 1.7 sq. mi.

Freedom — Township
Lat: 39-52-35 N Long: 99-20-30 W
Pop: 98 (1990); 109 (1980)   Pop Density: 2.7
Land: 35.7 sq. mi.; Water: 0.0 sq. mi.

Glade — City
ZIP: 67639   Lat: 39-40-57 N Long: 99-18-38 W
Pop: 101 (1990); 131 (1980)   Pop Density: 505.0
Land: 0.2 sq. mi.; Water: 0.0 sq. mi.   Elev: 1811 ft.
Incorporated Oct 7, 1948.
Name origin: For a Pacific Railroad engineer.

Glenwood — Township
Lat: 39-57-44 N Long: 99-13-48 W
Pop: 52 (1990); 52 (1980)   Pop Density: 1.5
Land: 35.5 sq. mi.; Water: 0.1 sq. mi.

Granite — Township
Lat: 39-57-22 N Long: 99-28-11 W
Pop: 28 (1990); 68 (1980)   Pop Density: 0.8
Land: 35.6 sq. mi.; Water: 0.0 sq. mi.

Greenwood — Township
Lat: 39-52-20 N Long: 99-14-01 W
Pop: 56 (1990); 63 (1980)   Pop Density: 1.6
Land: 35.5 sq. mi.; Water: 0.0 sq. mi.

Kirwin — City
ZIP: 67644   Lat: 39-40-11 N Long: 99-07-21 W
Pop: 269 (1990); 249 (1980)   Pop Density: 298.9
Land: 0.9 sq. mi.; Water: 0.0 sq. mi.   Elev: 1696 ft.
Incorporated Mar 1, 1877. Not coextensive with the town of the same name.

*Kirwin — Township
ZIP: 67644   Lat: 39-41-27 N Long: 99-07-36 W
Pop: 348 (1990); 329 (1980)   Pop Density: 10.4
Land: 33.5 sq. mi.; Water: 2.5 sq. mi.

Logan — City
ZIP: 67646   Lat: 39-39-40 N Long: 99-33-59 W
Pop: 633 (1990); 720 (1980)   Pop Density: 422.0
Land: 1.5 sq. mi.; Water: 0.0 sq. mi.   Elev: 1970 ft.
In northern KS; incorporated Apr 19, 1880.
Name origin: For Union Gen. John Logan (1826–1886).

*Logan — Township
ZIP: 67646   Lat: 39-41-58 N Long: 99-34-34 W
Pop: 705 (1990); 802 (1980)   Pop Density: 19.6
Land: 36.0 sq. mi.; Water: 0.0 sq. mi.

Long Island
City
ZIP: 67647 **Lat:** 39-56-46 N **Long:** 99-31-58 W
Pop: 170 (1990); 187 (1980) **Pop Density:** 425.0
Land: 0.4 sq. mi.; **Water:** 0.0 sq. mi. **Elev:** 2071 ft.
Incorporated Oct 3, 1904. Not coextensive with the town of the same name.

Name origin: For its location between two creeks that run parallel to each other for several miles.

*Long Island
Township
ZIP: 67647 **Lat:** 39-57-38 N **Long:** 99-34-29 W
Pop: 271 (1990); 318 (1980) **Pop Density:** 7.7
Land: 35.2 sq. mi.; **Water:** 0.0 sq. mi.

Mound
Township
Lat: 39-47-11 N **Long:** 99-27-32 W
Pop: 178 (1990); 192 (1980) **Pop Density:** 5.0
Land: 35.9 sq. mi.; **Water:** 0.0 sq. mi.

Phillipsburg
City
ZIP: 67661 **Lat:** 39-45-05 N **Long:** 99-19-18 W
Pop: 2,828 (1990); 3,229 (1980) **Pop Density:** 1885.3
Land: 1.5 sq. mi.; **Water:** 0.0 sq. mi. **Elev:** 1951 ft.
Incorporated 1880.

Name origin: For *New York Tribune* reporter William A. Phillips.

*Phillipsburg
Township
ZIP: 67661 **Lat:** 39-47-04 N **Long:** 99-20-49 W
Pop: 407 (1990); 433 (1980) **Pop Density:** 11.8
Land: 34.5 sq. mi.; **Water:** 0.0 sq. mi.

Plainview
Township
Lat: 39-36-19 N **Long:** 99-27-36 W
Pop: 25 (1990); 21 (1980) **Pop Density:** 0.7
Land: 36.0 sq. mi.; **Water:** 0.0 sq. mi.

Plum
Township
Lat: 39-46-52 N **Long:** 99-07-32 W
Pop: 428 (1990); 462 (1980) **Pop Density:** 12.0
Land: 35.8 sq. mi.; **Water:** 0.1 sq. mi.

Prairie View
City
ZIP: 67664 **Lat:** 39-49-54 N **Long:** 99-34-22 W
Pop: 111 (1990); 145 (1980) **Pop Density:** 555.0
Land: 0.2 sq. mi.; **Water:** 0.0 sq. mi. **Elev:** 2200 ft.
Incorporated Aug 1905. Not coextensive with the town of the same name.

Name origin: For its descriptive connotations.

*Prairie View
Township
ZIP: 67664 **Lat:** 39-52-29 N **Long:** 99-34-05 W
Pop: 226 (1990); 264 (1980) **Pop Density:** 6.4
Land: 35.5 sq. mi.; **Water:** 0.0 sq. mi.

Rushville
Township
Lat: 39-36-39 N **Long:** 99-20-59 W
Pop: 16 (1990); 36 (1980) **Pop Density:** 0.4
Land: 36.0 sq. mi.; **Water:** 0.0 sq. mi.

Solomon
Township
Lat: 39-41-51 N **Long:** 99-20-49 W
Pop: 240 (1990); 258 (1980) **Pop Density:** 6.7
Land: 35.7 sq. mi.; **Water:** 0.0 sq. mi.

Speed
City
Lat: 39-40-34 N **Long:** 99-25-12 W
Pop: 64 (1990); 41 (1980) **Pop Density:** 640.0
Land: 0.1 sq. mi.; **Water:** 0.0 sq. mi. **Elev:** 1900 ft.
Incorporated Jan 3, 1928.

Name origin: For James Speed, U.S. Attorney General in Pres. Abraham Lincoln's cabinet.

Sumner
Township
Lat: 39-57-58 N **Long:** 99-07-28 W
Pop: 55 (1990); 55 (1980) **Pop Density:** 1.5
Land: 35.5 sq. mi.; **Water:** 0.1 sq. mi.

Towanda
Township
Lat: 39-36-15 N **Long:** 99-34-12 W
Pop: 30 (1990); 23 (1980) **Pop Density:** 0.8
Land: 36.0 sq. mi.; **Water:** 0.1 sq. mi.

Valley
Township
Lat: 39-36-37 N **Long:** 99-07-11 W
Pop: 38 (1990); 55 (1980) **Pop Density:** 1.2
Land: 32.9 sq. mi.; **Water:** 3.1 sq. mi.

Walnut
Township
Lat: 39-57-32 N **Long:** 99-20-45 W
Pop: 15 (1990); 33 (1980) **Pop Density:** 0.4
Land: 35.8 sq. mi.; **Water:** 0.0 sq. mi.

Pottawatomie County
County Seat: Westmoreland (ZIP: 66549)

Pop: 16,128 (1990); 14,782 (1980)   **Pop Density:** 19.1
Land: 844.3 sq. mi.; **Water:** 17.8 sq. mi.   **Area Code:** 913
In northeastern KS, east of Manhattan; organized Feb 20, 1857 (prior to statehood) from Indian lands.
Name origin: For the Potawatomie Indian tribe of Algonquian linguistic stock. Name means 'people of the place of the fire.'

Belvue — City
ZIP: 66407   Lat: 39-13-00 N   Long: 96-10-41 W
Pop: 207 (1990); 212 (1980)   Pop Density: 2070.0
Land: 0.1 sq. mi.; Water: 0.0 sq. mi.   Elev: 960 ft.
Incorporated May 1913. Not coextensive with the town of the same name.

*Belvue — Township
ZIP: 66407   Lat: 39-15-08 N   Long: 96-11-16 W
Pop: 330 (1990); 353 (1980)   Pop Density: 8.9
Land: 37.2 sq. mi.; Water: 0.4 sq. mi.

Blue — Township
Lat: 39-14-36 N   Long: 96-32-26 W
Pop: 1,620 (1990); 1,402 (1980)   Pop Density: 36.7
Land: 44.1 sq. mi.; Water: 5.3 sq. mi.

Blue Valley — Township
Lat: 39-27-29 N   Long: 96-38-30 W
Pop: 336 (1990); 293 (1980)   Pop Density: 7.6
Land: 44.5 sq. mi.; Water: 4.9 sq. mi.

Center — Township
Lat: 39-20-37 N   Long: 96-13-52 W
Pop: 102 (1990); 126 (1980)   Pop Density: 3.4
Land: 30.0 sq. mi.; Water: 0.0 sq. mi.

Clear Creek — Township
Lat: 39-30-56 N   Long: 96-24-58 W
Pop: 134 (1990); 152 (1980)   Pop Density: 3.7
Land: 36.1 sq. mi.; Water: 0.0 sq. mi.

Emmett — City
ZIP: 66422   Lat: 39-18-25 N   Long: 96-03-21 W
Pop: 165 (1990); 223 (1980)   Pop Density: 825.0
Land: 0.2 sq. mi.; Water: 0.0 sq. mi.   Elev: 1025 ft.
Incorporated Dec 6, 1920. Not coextensive with the town of the same name.

*Emmett — Township
ZIP: 66422   Lat: 39-18-26 N   Long: 96-06-32 W
Pop: 343 (1990); 377 (1980)   Pop Density: 11.5
Land: 29.8 sq. mi.; Water: 0.2 sq. mi.

Grant — Township
Lat: 39-31-26 N   Long: 96-05-02 W
Pop: 285 (1990); 365 (1980)   Pop Density: 9.6
Land: 29.8 sq. mi.; Water: 0.0 sq. mi.

Green — Township
Lat: 39-21-14 N   Long: 96-36-04 W
Pop: 160 (1990); 153 (1980)   Pop Density: 3.3
Land: 48.3 sq. mi.; Water: 5.3 sq. mi.

Havensville — City
ZIP: 66432   Lat: 39-30-41 N   Long: 96-04-33 W
Pop: 135 (1990); 183 (1980)   Pop Density: 1350.0
Land: 0.1 sq. mi.; Water: 0.0 sq. mi.   Elev: 1200 ft.
Incorporated Jul 19, 1892.
Name origin: For Paul E. Havens, an officer of the Kansas Central Railroad.

Lincoln — Township
Lat: 39-25-58 N   Long: 96-05-14 W
Pop: 124 (1990); 122 (1980)   Pop Density: 4.1
Land: 29.9 sq. mi.; Water: 0.1 sq. mi.

Lone Tree — Township
Lat: 39-31-46 N   Long: 96-17-43 W
Pop: 262 (1990); 231 (1980)   Pop Density: 7.3
Land: 36.0 sq. mi.; Water: 0.0 sq. mi.

Louisville — City
ZIP: 66450   Lat: 39-15-03 N   Long: 96-18-54 W
Pop: 215 (1990); 207 (1980)   Pop Density: 430.0
Land: 0.5 sq. mi.; Water: 0.0 sq. mi.   Elev: 1000 ft.
Incorporated 1870. Not coextensive with the town of the same name.
Name origin: For Louisville, KY.

*Louisville — Township
ZIP: 66450   Lat: 39-16-24 N   Long: 96-18-31 W
Pop: 666 (1990); 591 (1980)   Pop Density: 18.1
Land: 36.7 sq. mi.; Water: 0.0 sq. mi.

Manhattan — City
Lat: 39-11-12 N   Long: 96-33-08 W
Pop: 143 (1990); 162 (1980)   Pop Density: 158.9
Land: 0.9 sq. mi.; Water: 0.0 sq. mi.   Elev: 1020 ft.
In northeast-central KS on the Kansas River, 50 mi. west of Topeka. Settled 1854; incorporated Feb 14, 1857. Part of the town is also in Riley County.
Name origin: For Manhattan Island in NY.

Mill Creek — Township
Lat: 39-30-45 N   Long: 96-11-19 W
Pop: 1,043 (1990); 1,000 (1980)   Pop Density: 24.9
Land: 41.9 sq. mi.; Water: 0.0 sq. mi.

Olsburg — City
ZIP: 66520   Lat: 39-25-55 N   Long: 96-36-55 W
Pop: 192 (1990); 166 (1980)   Pop Density: 960.0
Land: 0.2 sq. mi.; Water: 0.0 sq. mi.
Incorporated May 15, 1926.

Onaga — City
ZIP: 66521 **Lat:** 39-29-21 N **Long:** 96-10-13 W
Pop: 761 (1990); 752 (1980) **Pop Density:** 1268.3
Land: 0.6 sq. mi.; **Water:** 0.0 sq. mi. **Elev:** 1150 ft.
Incorporated May 15, 1926.
Name origin: From a Potawatomie Indian name whose meaning is unknown.

Pottawatomie — Township
Lat: 39-19-28 N **Long:** 96-26-24 W
Pop: 356 (1990); 399 (1980) **Pop Density:** 5.9
Land: 59.9 sq. mi.; **Water:** 0.0 sq. mi.

Rock Creek — Township
Lat: 39-26-08 N **Long:** 96-24-26 W
Pop: 657 (1990); 701 (1980) **Pop Density:** 18.3
Land: 36.0 sq. mi.; **Water:** 0.1 sq. mi.

St. Clere — Township
Lat: 39-21-53 N **Long:** 96-06-08 W
Pop: 69 (1990); 82 (1980) **Pop Density:** 2.3
Land: 29.9 sq. mi.; **Water:** 0.1 sq. mi.

St. George — City
Lat: 39-11-24 N **Long:** 96-25-02 W
Pop: 397 (1990); 309 (1980) **Pop Density:** 992.5
Land: 0.4 sq. mi.; **Water:** 0.0 sq. mi.
Incorporated Dec 17, 1919. Not coextensive with the town of the same name.
Name origin: For England's St. George, the dragon killer.

*St. George — Township
Lat: 39-13-11 N **Long:** 96-24-18 W
Pop: 2,044 (1990); 1,697 (1980) **Pop Density:** 61.2
Land: 33.4 sq. mi.; **Water:** 0.6 sq. mi.

St. Marys — City
Lat: 39-11-38 N **Long:** 96-03-55 W
Pop: 1,791 (1990); 1,598 (1980) **Pop Density:** 2238.8
Land: 0.8 sq. mi.; **Water:** 0.0 sq. mi. **Elev:** 1000 ft.
Incorporated Oct 8, 1869. Not coextensive with the town of the same name. Part of the town is also in Wabaunsee County.
Name origin: For the mother of Jesus.

*St. Marys — Township
Lat: 39-13-28 N **Long:** 96-04-47 W
Pop: 2,309 (1990); 1,989 (1980) **Pop Density:** 60.3
Land: 38.3 sq. mi.; **Water:** 0.2 sq. mi.

Shannon — Township
Lat: 39-26-14 N **Long:** 96-31-22 W
Pop: 200 (1990); 196 (1980) **Pop Density:** 5.0
Land: 40.0 sq. mi.; **Water:** 0.0 sq. mi.

Sherman — Township
Lat: 39-25-50 N **Long:** 96-17-38 W
Pop: 128 (1990); 156 (1980) **Pop Density:** 3.5
Land: 36.1 sq. mi.; **Water:** 0.0 sq. mi.

Spring Creek — Township
Lat: 39-30-55 N **Long:** 96-31-07 W
Pop: 66 (1990); 72 (1980) **Pop Density:** 1.7
Land: 39.6 sq. mi.; **Water:** 0.0 sq. mi.

Union — Township
Lat: 39-20-55 N **Long:** 96-20-15 W
Pop: 179 (1990); 161 (1980) **Pop Density:** 5.0
Land: 36.1 sq. mi.; **Water:** 0.0 sq. mi.

Vienna — Township
Lat: 39-26-04 N **Long:** 96-10-41 W
Pop: 121 (1990); 120 (1980) **Pop Density:** 4.0
Land: 30.2 sq. mi.; **Water:** 0.0 sq. mi.

Wamego — City
ZIP: 66547 **Lat:** 39-12-14 N **Long:** 96-18-28 W
Pop: 3,706 (1990); 3,159 (1980) **Pop Density:** 2850.8
Land: 1.3 sq. mi.; **Water:** 0.0 sq. mi. **Elev:** 990 ft.
Incorporated 1869. Not coextensive with the town of the same name.
Name origin: For an early Potawatomie chief.

*Wamego — Township
ZIP: 66547 **Lat:** 39-12-23 N **Long:** 96-17-44 W
Pop: 4,451 (1990); 3,882 (1980) **Pop Density:** 228.3
Land: 19.5 sq. mi.; **Water:** 0.6 sq. mi.

Westmoreland — City
ZIP: 66549 **Lat:** 39-23-41 N **Long:** 96-24-49 W
Pop: 541 (1990); 598 (1980) **Pop Density:** 1082.0
Land: 0.5 sq. mi.; **Water:** 0.0 sq. mi. **Elev:** 1168 ft.
Incorporated 1884.
Name origin: For Westmoreland County in England.

Wheaton — City
ZIP: 66551 **Lat:** 39-30-09 N **Long:** 96-19-08 W
Pop: 106 (1990); 90 (1980) **Pop Density:** 1060.0
Land: 0.1 sq. mi.; **Water:** 0.0 sq. mi. **Elev:** 1500 ft.
Incorporated Jul 1926.

Pratt County
County Seat: Pratt (ZIP: 67124)

Pop: 9,702 (1990); 10,275 (1980) **Pop Density:** 13.2
Land: 735.0 sq. mi.; **Water:** 0.8 sq. mi. **Area Code:** 316

In south-central KS, west of Wichita; established Feb 26, 1867. The county was fradulently organized with no bona fide settlers at the time. Official recognition was given in 1879.

Name origin: For Lt. Caleb Pratt (?–1861), Union officer killed at battle of Wilson's Creek, MO.

Byers — City
ZIP: 67021 Lat: 37-47-16 N Long: 98-52-00 W
Pop: 46 (1990); 47 (1980) Pop Density: 230.0
Land: 0.2 sq. mi.; Water: 0.0 sq. mi. Elev: 2006 ft.
Incorporated 1915.

Coats — City
ZIP: 67028 Lat: 37-30-39 N Long: 98-49-27 W
Pop: 127 (1990); 153 (1980) Pop Density: 635.0
Land: 0.2 sq. mi.; Water: 0.0 sq. mi. Elev: 1970 ft.
Incorporated Apr 22, 1909.
Name origin: For railroad and town developer W.A. Coats.

Cullison — City
ZIP: 67124 Lat: 37-37-46 N Long: 98-54-18 W
Pop: 120 (1990); 154 (1980) Pop Density: 600.0
Land: 0.2 sq. mi.; Water: 0.0 sq. mi. Elev: 2040 ft.
Incorporated 1887.

Iuka — City
ZIP: 67066 Lat: 37-43-44 N Long: 98-43-53 W
Pop: 197 (1990); 235 (1980) Pop Density: 328.3
Land: 0.6 sq. mi.; Water: 0.0 sq. mi. Elev: 1950 ft.
Incorporated Dec 1908.
Name origin: Named by a veteran of the Civil War battle of Iuka, MS.

Pratt — City
ZIP: 67124 Lat: 37-38-47 N Long: 98-44-09 W
Pop: 6,687 (1990); 6,885 (1980) Pop Density: 2089.7
Land: 3.2 sq. mi.; Water: 0.0 sq. mi. Elev: 1890 ft.
In south-central KS, 54 mi. west-southwest of Hutchinson. Incorporated Oct 9, 1884.
Name origin: For Civil War hero Caleb Pratt.

Preston — City
ZIP: 67569 Lat: 37-45-28 N Long: 98-33-19 W
Pop: 177 (1990); 227 (1980) Pop Density: 354.0
Land: 0.5 sq. mi.; Water: 0.0 sq. mi. Elev: 1840 ft.
Incorporated Apr 15, 1909.

Sawyer — City
ZIP: 67134 Lat: 37-29-51 N Long: 98-40-57 W
Pop: 183 (1990); 213 (1980) Pop Density: 1830.0
Land: 0.1 sq. mi.; Water: 0.0 sq. mi. Elev: 1910 ft.
Incorporated Jan 7, 1914.
Name origin: For a director of the Santa Fe Railroad.

Township No. 6 — Township
Lat: 37-44-24 N Long: 98-34-56 W
Pop: 572 (1990); 720 (1980) Pop Density: 3.9
Land: 147.2 sq. mi.; Water: 0.2 sq. mi.

Township No. 7 — Township
Lat: 37-45-19 N Long: 98-43-47 W
Pop: 387 (1990); 461 (1980) Pop Density: 6.9
Land: 56.3 sq. mi.; Water: 0.1 sq. mi.

Township No. 8 — Township
Lat: 37-46-10 N Long: 98-54-45 W
Pop: 208 (1990); 246 (1980) Pop Density: 2.7
Land: 76.2 sq. mi.; Water: 0.0 sq. mi.

Township No. 9 — Township
Lat: 37-38-40 N Long: 98-54-19 W
Pop: 376 (1990); 425 (1980) Pop Density: 2.6
Land: 146.5 sq. mi.; Water: 0.1 sq. mi.

Township No. 10 — Township
Lat: 37-30-50 N Long: 98-54-24 W
Pop: 190 (1990); 222 (1980) Pop Density: 2.6
Land: 72.5 sq. mi.; Water: 0.0 sq. mi.

Township No. 11 — Township
Lat: 37-30-50 N Long: 98-37-47 W
Pop: 569 (1990); 570 (1980) Pop Density: 5.2
Land: 108.6 sq. mi.; Water: 0.1 sq. mi.

Township No. 12 — Township
Lat: 37-36-38 N Long: 98-38-33 W
Pop: 713 (1990); 746 (1980) Pop Density: 5.7
Land: 124.4 sq. mi.; Water: 0.2 sq. mi.

Rawlins County
County Seat: Atwood (ZIP: 67730)

Pop: 3,404 (1990); 4,105 (1980)   **Pop Density:** 3.2
Land: 1069.7 sq. mi.; **Water:** 0.1 sq. mi.   **Area Code:** 913
On the northwestern border of KS; organized Mar 20, 1873 from Kirwin Land District.
Name origin: For Gen. John Aaron Rawlins (1831–69), officer in the Civil War and U.S. secretary of war under Grant (1869).

Achilles   Township
Lat: 39-42-20 N   **Long:** 100-49-35 W
Pop: 88 (1990); 94 (1980)   **Pop Density:** 1.7
Land: 51.1 sq. mi.; **Water:** 0.0 sq. mi.

Atwood   City
ZIP: 67730   **Lat:** 39-48-37 N   **Long:** 101-02-27 W
Pop: 1,388 (1990); 1,665 (1980)   **Pop Density:** 1388.0
Land: 1.0 sq. mi.; **Water:** 0.1 sq. mi.   **Elev:** 2850 ft.
In northwestern KS; incorporated Oct 15, 1885. Not coextensive with the town of the same name.

*Atwood   Township
ZIP: 67730   **Lat:** 39-48-56 N   **Long:** 101-02-30 W
Pop: 1,443 (1990); 1,695 (1980)   **Pop Density:** 187.4
Land: 7.7 sq. mi.; **Water:** 0.1 sq. mi.

Center   Township
Lat: 39-43-11 N   **Long:** 101-03-54 W
Pop: 390 (1990); 461 (1980)   **Pop Density:** 1.5
Land: 265.5 sq. mi.; **Water:** 0.0 sq. mi.

Driftwood   Township
Lat: 39-57-27 N   **Long:** 101-04-35 W
Pop: 133 (1990); 143 (1980)   **Pop Density:** 1.9
Land: 71.6 sq. mi.; **Water:** 0.0 sq. mi.

Herl   Township
Lat: 39-49-52 N   **Long:** 100-50-49 W
Pop: 506 (1990); 637 (1980)   **Pop Density:** 2.7
Land: 189.6 sq. mi.; **Water:** 0.0 sq. mi.

Herndon   City
ZIP: 67739   **Lat:** 39-54-30 N   **Long:** 100-47-08 W
Pop: 170 (1990); 220 (1980)   **Pop Density:** 566.7
Land: 0.3 sq. mi.; **Water:** 0.0 sq. mi.   **Elev:** 2666 ft.
Incorporated 1906.
Name origin: For William Herndon (1818–91), Abraham Lincoln's early law partner.

Jefferson   Township
Lat: 39-36-40 N   **Long:** 100-49-16 W
Pop: 24 (1990); 64 (1980)   **Pop Density:** 0.5
Land: 47.7 sq. mi.; **Water:** 0.0 sq. mi.

Ludell   Township
ZIP: 67744   **Lat:** 39-52-23 N   **Long:** 100-56-33 W
Pop: 155 (1990); 187 (1980)   **Pop Density:** 4.4
Land: 35.4 sq. mi.; **Water:** 0.0 sq. mi.

McDonald   City
ZIP: 67745   **Lat:** 39-47-06 N   **Long:** 101-22-13 W
Pop: 184 (1990); 239 (1980)   **Pop Density:** 920.0
Land: 0.2 sq. mi.; **Water:** 0.0 sq. mi.   **Elev:** 3360 ft.
Incorporated Oct 8, 1919.

Mirage   Township
Lat: 39-39-45 N   **Long:** 101-14-51 W
Pop: 47 (1990); 70 (1980)   **Pop Density:** 0.7
Land: 71.5 sq. mi.; **Water:** 0.0 sq. mi.

Rocewood   Township
Lat: 39-49-21 N   **Long:** 101-19-07 W
Pop: 551 (1990); 680 (1980)   **Pop Density:** 1.9
Land: 286.6 sq. mi.; **Water:** 0.0 sq. mi.

Union   Township
Lat: 39-46-12 N   **Long:** 100-54-26 W
Pop: 67 (1990); 74 (1980)   **Pop Density:** 1.6
Land: 43.0 sq. mi.; **Water:** 0.0 sq. mi.

Reno County
County Seat: Hutchinson (ZIP: 67501)

Pop: 62,389 (1990); 64,983 (1980)   **Pop Density:** 49.7
Land: 1254.5 sq. mi.; **Water:** 16.8 sq. mi.   **Area Code:** 316

In south-central KS, northwest of Wichita; established Feb 26, 1867 from Sedgwick County.

Name origin: For Gen. Jesse Lee Reno (1823–62), officer in the Mexican-American War and the Civil War.

Abbyville — City
ZIP: 67510   **Lat:** 37-58-14 N   **Long:** 98-12-12 W
Pop: 140 (1990); 123 (1980)   **Pop Density:** 700.0
Land: 0.2 sq. mi.; **Water:** 0.0 sq. mi.   **Elev:** 1650 ft.
Incorporated Mar 10, 1924.
Name origin: For the first child born here, Abby McLean.

Albion — Township
Lat: 37-46-49 N   **Long:** 97-57-49 W
Pop: 823 (1990); 920 (1980)   **Pop Density:** 21.9
Land: 37.6 sq. mi.; **Water:** 0.0 sq. mi.

Arlington — City
ZIP: 67514   **Lat:** 37-53-45 N   **Long:** 98-10-39 W
Pop: 457 (1990); 631 (1980)   **Pop Density:** 380.8
Land: 1.2 sq. mi.; **Water:** 0.0 sq. mi.   **Elev:** 1610 ft.
In central KS; incorporated Oct 5, 1887. Not coextensive with the town of the same name.
Name origin: For Arlington Heights, MA.

*Arlington — Township
ZIP: 67514   **Lat:** 37-51-50 N   **Long:** 98-12-08 W
Pop: 594 (1990); 798 (1980)   **Pop Density:** 16.4
Land: 36.2 sq. mi.; **Water:** 0.0 sq. mi.

Bell — Township
Lat: 37-47-00 N   **Long:** 98-17-29 W
Pop: 89 (1990); 105 (1980)   **Pop Density:** 2.3
Land: 38.0 sq. mi.; **Water:** 0.0 sq. mi.

Buhler — City
ZIP: 67522   **Lat:** 38-08-17 N   **Long:** 97-46-16 W
Pop: 1,277 (1990); 1,188 (1980)   **Pop Density:** 2128.3
Land: 0.6 sq. mi.; **Water:** 0.0 sq. mi.   **Elev:** 1485 ft.
In central KS; incorporated Jun 6, 1913.
Name origin: For Mennonite elder Bernard Buhler.

Castleton — Township
Lat: 37-52-24 N   **Long:** 97-57-00 W
Pop: 234 (1990); 242 (1980)   **Pop Density:** 4.3
Land: 54.2 sq. mi.; **Water:** 0.0 sq. mi.

Center — Township
Lat: 37-57-38 N   **Long:** 98-05-22 W
Pop: 581 (1990); 627 (1980)   **Pop Density:** 16.0
Land: 36.2 sq. mi.; **Water:** 0.1 sq. mi.

Clay — Township
Lat: 38-03-15 N   **Long:** 97-51-29 W
Pop: 2,894 (1990); 3,238 (1980)   **Pop Density:** 84.9
Land: 34.1 sq. mi.; **Water:** 0.2 sq. mi.

Enterprise — Township
Lat: 38-02-17 N   **Long:** 98-11-21 W
Pop: 160 (1990); 146 (1980)   **Pop Density:** 4.5
Land: 35.9 sq. mi.; **Water:** 0.0 sq. mi.

Grant — Township
Lat: 38-08-21 N   **Long:** 98-01-21 W
Pop: 1,147 (1990); 1,263 (1980)   **Pop Density:** 26.1
Land: 44.0 sq. mi.; **Water:** 0.6 sq. mi.

Grove — Township
Lat: 37-51-56 N   **Long:** 98-24-53 W
Pop: 58 (1990); 93 (1980)   **Pop Density:** 1.6
Land: 36.1 sq. mi.; **Water:** 0.0 sq. mi.

Haven — City
ZIP: 67543   **Lat:** 37-54-08 N   **Long:** 97-46-50 W
Pop: 1,198 (1990); 1,125 (1980)   **Pop Density:** 2396.0
Land: 0.5 sq. mi.; **Water:** 0.0 sq. mi.   **Elev:** 1480 ft.
Incorporated Aug 1901. Not coextensive with the town of the same name.
Name origin: For the Haven Town Company.

*Haven — Township
ZIP: 67543   **Lat:** 37-53-25 N   **Long:** 97-47-01 W
Pop: 1,648 (1990); 1,539 (1980)   **Pop Density:** 29.9
Land: 55.2 sq. mi.; **Water:** 0.2 sq. mi.

Hayes — Township
Lat: 38-05-03 N   **Long:** 98-24-59 W
Pop: 85 (1990); 154 (1980)   **Pop Density:** 1.2
Land: 71.9 sq. mi.; **Water:** 0.0 sq. mi.

Huntsville — Township
Lat: 38-02-16 N   **Long:** 98-18-58 W
Pop: 139 (1990); 176 (1980)   **Pop Density:** 3.9
Land: 36.1 sq. mi.; **Water:** 0.0 sq. mi.

Hutchinson — City
ZIP: 67501   **Lat:** 38-03-55 N   **Long:** 97-54-51 W
Pop: 39,308 (1990); 40,284 (1980)   **Pop Density:** 1898.9
Land: 20.7 sq. mi.; **Water:** 0.1 sq. mi.   **Elev:** 1538 ft.
In central KS on the Arkansas River, 42 mi. west-northwest of Wichita. Incorporated Sep 25, 1872.
Name origin: For C.C. Hutchinson, an early pioneer preacher and Indian agent.

Langdon — City
ZIP: 67549   **Lat:** 37-51-12 N   **Long:** 98-19-26 W
Pop: 62 (1990); 84 (1980)   **Pop Density:** 620.0
Land: 0.1 sq. mi.; **Water:** 0.0 sq. mi.   **Elev:** 1695 ft.
Incorporated Apr 1, 1912. Not coextensive with the town of the same name.

*Langdon — Township
Lat: 37-52-14 N   **Long:** 98-18-35 W
Pop: 171 (1990); 246 (1980)   **Pop Density:** 4.7
Land: 36.4 sq. mi.; **Water:** 0.1 sq. mi.

Lincoln — Township
Lat: 37-57-46 N   **Long:** 97-58-06 W
Pop: 644 (1990); 595 (1980)   **Pop Density:** 17.9
Land: 35.9 sq. mi.; **Water:** 0.0 sq. mi.

Little River — Township
Lat: 38-07-20 N Long: 97-44-53 W
Pop: 1,854 (1990); 1,824 (1980)   Pop Density: 51.5
Land: 36.0 sq. mi.; Water: 0.2 sq. mi.

Loda — Township
Lat: 37-47-01 N Long: 98-11-23 W
Pop: 116 (1990); 128 (1980)   Pop Density: 3.1
Land: 38.0 sq. mi.; Water: 0.1 sq. mi.

Medford — Township
Lat: 38-07-20 N Long: 98-12-22 W
Pop: 162 (1990); 185 (1980)   Pop Density: 5.1
Land: 31.9 sq. mi.; Water: 0.1 sq. mi.

Medora — Township
Lat: 38-08-36 N Long: 97-51-15 W
Pop: 1,515 (1990); 1,437 (1980)   Pop Density: 50.8
Land: 29.8 sq. mi.; Water: 0.0 sq. mi.

Miami — Township
Lat: 37-46-37 N Long: 98-24-32 W
Pop: 500 (1990); 575 (1980)   Pop Density: 13.2
Land: 38.0 sq. mi.; Water: 0.1 sq. mi.

Nickerson — City
ZIP: 67561   Lat: 38-08-51 N Long: 98-05-12 W
Pop: 1,137 (1990); 1,292 (1980)   Pop Density: 812.1
Land: 1.4 sq. mi.; Water: 0.0 sq. mi.   Elev: 1593 ft.
Incorporated Jun 7, 1879.
Name origin: For a president of the Santa Fe Railroad.

Ninnescah — Township
Lat: 37-47-09 N Long: 97-51-25 W
Pop: 200 (1990); 199 (1980)   Pop Density: 6.6
Land: 30.5 sq. mi.; Water: 10.5 sq. mi.

Partridge — City
ZIP: 67566   Lat: 37-58-02 N Long: 98-05-37 W
Pop: 213 (1990); 268 (1980)   Pop Density: 426.0
Land: 0.5 sq. mi.; Water: 0.0 sq. mi.   Elev: 1610 ft.
Incorporated Dec 4, 1906.
Name origin: For the game bird.

Plevna — City
ZIP: 67568   Lat: 37-58-16 N Long: 98-18-32 W
Pop: 117 (1990); 115 (1980)   Pop Density: 585.0
Land: 0.2 sq. mi.; Water: 0.0 sq. mi.   Elev: 1684 ft.
Incorporated Jun 29, 1910. Not coextensive with the town of the same name.
Name origin: For either a province in Bulgaria or the city in IN.

*Plevna — Township
ZIP: 67568   Lat: 37-57-11 N Long: 98-18-37 W
Pop: 270 (1990); 308 (1980)   Pop Density: 7.4
Land: 36.3 sq. mi.; Water: 0.0 sq. mi.

Pretty Prairie — City
ZIP: 67570   Lat: 37-46-48 N Long: 98-01-11 W
Pop: 601 (1990); 655 (1980)   Pop Density: 2003.3
Land: 0.3 sq. mi.; Water: 0.0 sq. mi.   Elev: 1576 ft.
Incorporated Nov 1906.

Reno — Township
Lat: 38-03-00 N Long: 97-58-43 W
Pop: 4,522 (1990); 5,006 (1980)   Pop Density: 128.8
Land: 35.1 sq. mi.; Water: 0.6 sq. mi.

Roscoe — Township
Lat: 37-46-28 N Long: 98-04-21 W
Pop: 116 (1990); 128 (1980)   Pop Density: 3.1
Land: 37.9 sq. mi.; Water: 0.0 sq. mi.

Salt Creek — Township
Lat: 38-04-12 N Long: 98-05-27 W
Pop: 447 (1990); 453 (1980)   Pop Density: 8.3
Land: 53.8 sq. mi.; Water: 0.2 sq. mi.

South Hutchinson — City
ZIP: 67505   Lat: 38-01-42 N Long: 97-56-27 W
Pop: 2,444 (1990); 2,226 (1980)   Pop Density: 905.2
Land: 2.7 sq. mi.; Water: 0.0 sq. mi.   Elev: 1525 ft.
Incorporated Jan 6, 1887.

Sumner — Township
Lat: 37-47-08 N Long: 97-44-41 W
Pop: 469 (1990); 397 (1980)   Pop Density: 11.5
Land: 40.8 sq. mi.; Water: 2.7 sq. mi.

Sylvia — City
ZIP: 67581   Lat: 37-57-35 N Long: 98-24-28 W
Pop: 308 (1990); 353 (1980)   Pop Density: 1026.7
Land: 0.3 sq. mi.; Water: 0.0 sq. mi.   Elev: 1738 ft.
Incorporated Jan 27, 1887. Not coextensive with the town of the same name.
Name origin: For Sylvia Peters, the wife of the general manager of the Santa Fe Railroad.

*Sylvia — Township
ZIP: 67581   Lat: 37-57-25 N Long: 98-24-55 W
Pop: 396 (1990); 481 (1980)   Pop Density: 11.0
Land: 35.9 sq. mi.; Water: 0.1 sq. mi.

Troy — Township
Lat: 37-52-04 N Long: 98-05-12 W
Pop: 104 (1990); 140 (1980)   Pop Density: 2.9
Land: 36.1 sq. mi.; Water: 0.1 sq. mi.

Turon — City
ZIP: 67583   Lat: 37-48-26 N Long: 98-25-40 W
Pop: 393 (1990); 481 (1980)   Pop Density: 786.0
Land: 0.5 sq. mi.; Water: 0.0 sq. mi.   Elev: 1760 ft.
Incorporated Jun 15, 1905.
Name origin: For Turin, Italy, with a spelling variation.

Valley — Township
Lat: 38-00-24 N Long: 97-44-52 W
Pop: 866 (1990); 878 (1980)   Pop Density: 15.7
Land: 55.1 sq. mi.; Water: 0.5 sq. mi.

Walnut — Township
Lat: 38-07-40 N Long: 98-18-06 W
Pop: 115 (1990); 138 (1980)   Pop Density: 3.2
Land: 36.3 sq. mi.; Water: 0.0 sq. mi.

Westminster — Township
Lat: 37-57-08 N Long: 98-11-47 W
Pop: 267 (1990); 246 (1980)   Pop Density: 7.4
Land: 36.1 sq. mi.; Water: 0.0 sq. mi.

Willowbrook — City
Lat: 38-06-05 N Long: 97-59-27 W
Pop: 95 (1990); 109 (1980)   Pop Density: 316.7
Land: 0.3 sq. mi.; Water: 0.0 sq. mi.   Elev: 1538 ft.
Incorporated Jul 10, 1952.

KANSAS, Reno County   American Places Dictionary

Yoder Township
Lat: 37-57-24 N **Long:** 97-52-02 W
Pop: 758 (1990); 742 (1980)   **Pop Density:** 20.4
Land: 37.2 sq. mi.; **Water:** 0.4 sq. mi.

Republic County
County Seat: Belleville (ZIP: 66935)

Pop: 6,482 (1990); 7,569 (1980)   **Pop Density:** 9.0
Land: 716.5 sq. mi.; **Water:** 3.8 sq. mi.   **Area Code:** 316
On the central northern border of KS, north of Salina; established Feb 27, 1860 (prior to statehood) from Washington and Cloud counties.
Name origin: For the Republican River, which first enters KS in this county; named for the valley that was home of the Pawnee Republic, a division of the Pawnee Tribe. Also, possibly for the Pawnee Republic.

Agenda City
ZIP: 66930   **Lat:** 39-42-26 N **Long:** 97-25-54 W
Pop: 81 (1990); 106 (1980)   **Pop Density:** 405.0
Land: 0.2 sq. mi.; **Water:** 0.0 sq. mi.   **Elev:** 1410 ft.
Incorporated Dec 16, 1916.

Albion Township
Lat: 39-57-27 N **Long:** 97-25-28 W
Pop: 205 (1990); 256 (1980)   **Pop Density:** 5.8
Land: 35.6 sq. mi.; **Water:** 0.0 sq. mi.

Beaver Township
Lat: 39-41-59 N **Long:** 97-52-49 W
Pop: 127 (1990); 149 (1980)   **Pop Density:** 3.6
Land: 35.0 sq. mi.; **Water:** 1.1 sq. mi.

Belleville City
ZIP: 66935   **Lat:** 39-49-23 N **Long:** 97-38-00 W
Pop: 2,517 (1990); 2,805 (1980)   **Pop Density:** 1324.7
Land: 1.9 sq. mi.; **Water:** 0.0 sq. mi.   **Elev:** 1550 ft.
Incorporated 1878.
Name origin: For the local postmaster's wife.

***Belleville** Township
ZIP: 66935   **Lat:** 39-46-27 N **Long:** 97-39-22 W
Pop: 263 (1990); 254 (1980)   **Pop Density:** 7.7
Land: 34.2 sq. mi.; **Water:** 0.0 sq. mi.

Big Bend Township
Lat: 39-57-45 N **Long:** 97-52-31 W
Pop: 278 (1990); 371 (1980)   **Pop Density:** 7.8
Land: 35.5 sq. mi.; **Water:** 0.5 sq. mi.

Courtland City
ZIP: 66939   **Lat:** 39-46-58 N **Long:** 97-53-43 W
Pop: 343 (1990); 377 (1980)   **Pop Density:** 1143.3
Land: 0.3 sq. mi.; **Water:** 0.0 sq. mi.   **Elev:** 1499 ft.
Incorporated 1892. Not coextensive with the town of the same name.
Name origin: For Cortland, NY, with a spelling variation.

***Courtland** Township
ZIP: 66939   **Lat:** 39-47-00 N **Long:** 97-52-36 W
Pop: 487 (1990); 573 (1980)   **Pop Density:** 13.5
Land: 36.2 sq. mi.; **Water:** 0.0 sq. mi.

Cuba City
ZIP: 66940   **Lat:** 39-48-07 N **Long:** 97-27-24 W
Pop: 242 (1990); 286 (1980)   **Pop Density:** 806.7
Land: 0.3 sq. mi.; **Water:** 0.0 sq. mi.   **Elev:** 1590 ft.
Incorporated Jan 5, 1885.
Name origin: Named for the largest Bohemian colony in the state, probably for the Bohemian capital, Kuba, with a spelling variation.

Elk Creek Township
Lat: 39-41-46 N **Long:** 97-25-14 W
Pop: 198 (1990); 234 (1980)   **Pop Density:** 5.5
Land: 36.1 sq. mi.; **Water:** 0.1 sq. mi.

Fairview Township
Lat: 39-52-17 N **Long:** 97-32-13 W
Pop: 176 (1990); 193 (1980)   **Pop Density:** 4.8
Land: 36.4 sq. mi.; **Water:** 0.1 sq. mi.

Farmington Township
Lat: 39-52-17 N **Long:** 97-25-30 W
Pop: 108 (1990); 147 (1980)   **Pop Density:** 3.0
Land: 35.8 sq. mi.; **Water:** 0.1 sq. mi.

Freedom Township
Lat: 39-52-02 N **Long:** 97-39-15 W
Pop: 189 (1990); 250 (1980)   **Pop Density:** 5.4
Land: 34.8 sq. mi.; **Water:** 0.1 sq. mi.

Grant Township
Lat: 39-41-49 N **Long:** 97-32-16 W
Pop: 110 (1990); 127 (1980)   **Pop Density:** 3.0
Land: 36.5 sq. mi.; **Water:** 0.1 sq. mi.

Jefferson Township
Lat: 39-46-28 N **Long:** 97-32-07 W
Pop: 139 (1990); 186 (1980)   **Pop Density:** 3.8
Land: 36.6 sq. mi.; **Water:** 0.0 sq. mi.

Liberty Township
Lat: 39-57-44 N **Long:** 97-39-08 W
Pop: 84 (1990); 98 (1980)   **Pop Density:** 2.3
Land: 36.0 sq. mi.; **Water:** 0.1 sq. mi.

Lincoln Township
Lat: 39-41-49 N **Long:** 97-39-05 W
Pop: 125 (1990); 147 (1980)   **Pop Density:** 3.5
Land: 35.5 sq. mi.; **Water:** 0.0 sq. mi.

American Places Dictionary   KANSAS, Rice County

Munden   City
ZIP: 66959   **Lat:** 39-54-44 N   **Long:** 97-32-18 W
Pop: 143 (1990); 152 (1980)   **Pop Density:** 715.0
Land: 0.2 sq. mi.; **Water:** 0.0 sq. mi.   **Elev:** 1630 ft.
Incorporated Jul 8, 1903.
Name origin: For John Munden, who owned the land used for the railroad station.

Narka   City
ZIP: 66960   **Lat:** 39-57-36 N   **Long:** 97-25-37 W
Pop: 113 (1990); 120 (1980)   **Pop Density:** 565.0
Land: 0.2 sq. mi.; **Water:** 0.0 sq. mi.   **Elev:** 1585 ft.
Incorporated 1900.
Name origin: For the daughter of a Rock Island Railroad official.

Norway   Township
Lat: 39-41-51 N   **Long:** 97-46-01 W
Pop: 160 (1990); 209 (1980)   **Pop Density:** 4.5
Land: 35.5 sq. mi.; **Water:** 0.4 sq. mi.

Republic   City
ZIP: 66964   **Lat:** 39-55-25 N   **Long:** 97-49-27 W
Pop: 177 (1990); 223 (1980)   **Pop Density:** 590.0
Land: 0.3 sq. mi.; **Water:** 0.0 sq. mi.   **Elev:** 1500 ft.
Incorporated Apr 23, 1885.
Name origin: For the Pawnee Republic, a principal division of the Pawnee tribe.

Richland   Township
Lat: 39-47-20 N   **Long:** 97-25-24 W
Pop: 342 (1990); 416 (1980)   **Pop Density:** 9.6
Land: 35.6 sq. mi.; **Water:** 0.0 sq. mi.

Rose Creek   Township
Lat: 39-57-26 N   **Long:** 97-32-12 W
Pop: 179 (1990); 197 (1980)   **Pop Density:** 4.9
Land: 36.3 sq. mi.; **Water:** 0.2 sq. mi.

Scandia   City
ZIP: 66966   **Lat:** 39-47-49 N   **Long:** 97-47-00 W
Pop: 421 (1990); 480 (1980)   **Pop Density:** 842.0
Land: 0.5 sq. mi.; **Water:** 0.0 sq. mi.   **Elev:** 1450 ft.
Incorporated Apr 5, 1879. Not coextensive with the town of the same name.
Name origin: For settlers from Scandinavia. Originally called New Scandinavia; later shortened.

*Scandia   Township
ZIP: 66966   **Lat:** 39-47-05 N   **Long:** 97-45-32 W
Pop: 537 (1990); 612 (1980)   **Pop Density:** 15.1
Land: 35.5 sq. mi.; **Water:** 0.4 sq. mi.

Union   Township
Lat: 39-52-13 N   **Long:** 97-45-34 W
Pop: 84 (1990); 80 (1980)   **Pop Density:** 2.3
Land: 35.8 sq. mi.; **Water:** 0.1 sq. mi.

Washington   Township
Lat: 39-57-38 N   **Long:** 97-45-57 W
Pop: 95 (1990); 130 (1980)   **Pop Density:** 2.7
Land: 35.8 sq. mi.; **Water:** 0.1 sq. mi.

White Rock   Township
Lat: 39-52-03 N   **Long:** 97-52-41 W
Pop: 79 (1990); 135 (1980)   **Pop Density:** 2.2
Land: 35.6 sq. mi.; **Water:** 0.4 sq. mi.   **Elev:** 1522 ft.

Rice County
County Seat: Lyons (ZIP: 67554)

Pop: 10,610 (1990); 11,900 (1980)   **Pop Density:** 14.6
Land: 726.6 sq. mi.; **Water:** 1.7 sq. mi.   **Area Code:** 316
In central KS, north of Hutchinson; organized Feb 26, 1867 from Reno County.
Name origin: For Gen. Samuel Allen Rice (1828–64), attorney and Union officer in the Civil War.

Alden   City
ZIP: 67512   **Lat:** 38-14-38 N   **Long:** 98-18-40 W
Pop: 182 (1990); 214 (1980)   **Pop Density:** 910.0
Land: 0.2 sq. mi.; **Water:** 0.0 sq. mi.   **Elev:** 1680 ft.
Incorporated Jul 3, 1916.

Atlanta   Township
Lat: 38-18-19 N   **Long:** 98-12-15 W
Pop: 181 (1990); 258 (1980)   **Pop Density:** 5.2
Land: 34.9 sq. mi.; **Water:** 0.1 sq. mi.

Bell   Township
Lat: 38-12-49 N   **Long:** 98-25-23 W
Pop: 27 (1990); 43 (1980)   **Pop Density:** 0.7
Land: 36.2 sq. mi.; **Water:** 0.2 sq. mi.

Bushton   City
ZIP: 67427   **Lat:** 38-30-46 N   **Long:** 98-23-41 W
Pop: 341 (1990); 388 (1980)   **Pop Density:** 1705.0
Land: 0.2 sq. mi.; **Water:** 0.0 sq. mi.   **Elev:** 1765 ft.
Incorporated 1907.

Center   Township
Lat: 38-18-35 N   **Long:** 98-19-11 W
Pop: 126 (1990); 148 (1980)   **Pop Density:** 3.4
Land: 36.6 sq. mi.; **Water:** 0.0 sq. mi.

Chase   City
ZIP: 67524   **Lat:** 38-21-20 N   **Long:** 98-20-54 W
Pop: 577 (1990); 753 (1980)   **Pop Density:** 1923.3
Land: 0.3 sq. mi.; **Water:** 0.0 sq. mi.   **Elev:** 1718 ft.
Incorporated Jul 1902.
Name origin: For an official of the Santa Fe Railroad.

East Washington   Township
Lat: 38-12-59 N   **Long:** 97-58-34 W
Pop: 139 (1990); 107 (1980)   **Pop Density:** 3.9
Land: 36.0 sq. mi.; **Water:** 0.0 sq. mi.

Eureka   Township
Lat: 38-28-52 N   **Long:** 98-18-50 W
Pop: 81 (1990); 93 (1980)   **Pop Density:** 2.2
Land: 36.6 sq. mi.; **Water:** 0.0 sq. mi.

Farmer
Township
Lat: 38-28-50 N **Long:** 98-25-43 W
Pop: 480 (1990); 544 (1980) **Pop Density:** 13.2
Land: 36.3 sq. mi.; **Water:** 0.0 sq. mi.

Frederick
City
Lat: 38-30-47 N **Long:** 98-16-02 W
Pop: 18 (1990); 29 (1980) **Pop Density:** 90.0
Land: 0.2 sq. mi.; **Water:** 0.0 sq. mi. **Elev:** 1762 ft.
Incorporated Oct 1909.

Galt
Township
Lat: 38-28-46 N **Long:** 98-05-25 W
Pop: 73 (1990); 74 (1980) **Pop Density:** 2.0
Land: 36.2 sq. mi.; **Water:** 0.1 sq. mi.

Geneseo
City
ZIP: 67444 **Lat:** 38-31-00 N **Long:** 98-09-14 W
Pop: 382 (1990); 496 (1980) **Pop Density:** 636.7
Land: 0.6 sq. mi.; **Water:** 0.0 sq. mi. **Elev:** 1750 ft.
Incorporated Jul 15, 1887.
Name origin: For Geneseo, NY.

Harrison
Township
Lat: 38-23-32 N **Long:** 98-12-16 W
Pop: 230 (1990); 232 (1980) **Pop Density:** 6.5
Land: 35.5 sq. mi.; **Water:** 0.0 sq. mi.

Lincoln
Township
Lat: 38-23-29 N **Long:** 98-18-41 W
Pop: 669 (1990); 881 (1980) **Pop Density:** 18.3
Land: 36.6 sq. mi.; **Water:** 0.0 sq. mi.

Little River
City
ZIP: 67457 **Lat:** 38-23-51 N **Long:** 98-00-44 W
Pop: 496 (1990); 529 (1980) **Pop Density:** 1653.3
Land: 0.3 sq. mi.; **Water:** 0.0 sq. mi. **Elev:** 1590 ft.
Incorporated Nov 11, 1886.
Name origin: For its location on the Little Arkansas River.

Lyons
City
ZIP: 67554 **Lat:** 38-20-45 N **Long:** 98-12-07 W
Pop: 3,688 (1990); 4,134 (1980) **Pop Density:** 1756.2
Land: 2.1 sq. mi.; **Water:** 0.0 sq. mi. **Elev:** 1700 ft.
Incorporated Feb 28, 1880.
Name origin: For Civil War hero Gen. Nathaniel Lyon (1818–61).

Mitchell
Township
Lat: 38-23-28 N **Long:** 98-05-21 W
Pop: 127 (1990); 170 (1980) **Pop Density:** 3.5
Land: 36.4 sq. mi.; **Water:** 0.1 sq. mi.

Odessa
Township
Lat: 38-28-45 N **Long:** 97-58-41 W
Pop: 64 (1990); 76 (1980) **Pop Density:** 1.8
Land: 35.9 sq. mi.; **Water:** 0.0 sq. mi.

Pioneer
Township
Lat: 38-23-24 N **Long:** 98-25-37 W
Pop: 103 (1990); 107 (1980) **Pop Density:** 2.8
Land: 36.2 sq. mi.; **Water:** 0.0 sq. mi.

Raymond
City
ZIP: 67573 **Lat:** 38-16-42 N **Long:** 98-24-52 W
Pop: 125 (1990); 132 (1980) **Pop Density:** 416.7
Land: 0.3 sq. mi.; **Water:** 0.0 sq. mi. **Elev:** 1726 ft.
Incorporated Dec 6, 1954. Not coextensive with the town of the same name.
Name origin: For a director of the Santa Fe Railroad.

*Raymond
Township
ZIP: 67573 **Lat:** 38-18-09 N **Long:** 98-24-55 W
Pop: 227 (1990); 237 (1980) **Pop Density:** 6.4
Land: 35.7 sq. mi.; **Water:** 0.3 sq. mi.

Rockville
Township
Lat: 38-17-58 N **Long:** 97-58-44 W
Pop: 141 (1990); 144 (1980) **Pop Density:** 3.9
Land: 36.1 sq. mi.; **Water:** 0.0 sq. mi.

Sterling
City
ZIP: 67579 **Lat:** 38-12-32 N **Long:** 98-12-20 W
Pop: 2,115 (1990); 2,312 (1980) **Pop Density:** 1762.5
Land: 1.2 sq. mi.; **Water:** 0.0 sq. mi. **Elev:** 1640 ft.
Incorporated May 10, 1876.
Name origin: For Sterling Rosan, the father of two early settlers.

*Sterling
Township
ZIP: 67579 **Lat:** 38-13-04 N **Long:** 98-12-25 W
Pop: 370 (1990); 351 (1980) **Pop Density:** 8.4
Land: 44.3 sq. mi.; **Water:** 0.5 sq. mi.

Union
Township
Lat: 38-23-33 N **Long:** 97-58-37 W
Pop: 704 (1990); 774 (1980) **Pop Density:** 19.6
Land: 36.0 sq. mi.; **Water:** 0.0 sq. mi.

Valley
Township
Lat: 38-13-01 N **Long:** 98-19-00 W
Pop: 278 (1990); 311 (1980) **Pop Density:** 9.4
Land: 29.6 sq. mi.; **Water:** 0.3 sq. mi.

Victoria
Township
Lat: 38-28-38 N **Long:** 98-12-08 W
Pop: 488 (1990); 614 (1980) **Pop Density:** 13.5
Land: 36.2 sq. mi.; **Water:** 0.0 sq. mi.

West Washington
Township
Lat: 38-13-08 N **Long:** 98-04-57 W
Pop: 142 (1990); 153 (1980) **Pop Density:** 4.0
Land: 35.8 sq. mi.; **Water:** 0.0 sq. mi.

Wilson
Township
Lat: 38-18-07 N **Long:** 98-05-27 W
Pop: 157 (1990); 137 (1980) **Pop Density:** 4.3
Land: 36.3 sq. mi.; **Water:** 0.0 sq. mi.

Riley County
County Seat: Manhattan (ZIP: 66501)

Pop: 67,139 (1990); 63,505 (1980)   **Pop Density:** 110.1
Land: 609.6 sq. mi.; **Water:** 12.5 sq. mi.   **Area Code:** 913

In east-central KS, northwest of Topeka; organized Aug 25, 1855 (prior to statehood) from Wabaunsee County.

Name origin: For Fort Riley, named for Gen. Bennett Riley (1787–1853), professional soldier and territorial governor of CA (1848).

Ashland — Township
Lat: 39-06-06 N   Long: 96-35-55 W
Pop: 166 (1990); 171 (1980)   **Pop Density:** 4.8
Land: 34.5 sq. mi.; **Water:** 0.3 sq. mi.

Bala — Township
Lat: 39-21-13 N   Long: 96-53-48 W
Pop: 751 (1990); 762 (1980)   **Pop Density:** 17.9
Land: 41.9 sq. mi.; **Water:** 0.0 sq. mi.

Center — Township
Lat: 39-28-39 N   Long: 96-52-51 W
Pop: 88 (1990); 102 (1980)   **Pop Density:** 2.8
Land: 31.6 sq. mi.; **Water:** 0.0 sq. mi.

Fancy Creek — Township
Lat: 39-25-18 N   Long: 96-53-13 W
Pop: 132 (1990); 126 (1980)   **Pop Density:** 4.1
Land: 32.0 sq. mi.; **Water:** 0.0 sq. mi.

Fort Riley North — Military Facility
ZIP: 66442   Lat: 39-06-43 N   Long: 96-48-57 W
Pop: 12,165 (1990); 14,430 (1980)   **Pop Density:** 2433.0
Land: 5.0 sq. mi.; **Water:** 0.0 sq. mi.
Part of the town is also in Geary County.

Grant — Township
Lat: 39-17-56 N   Long: 96-42-10 W
Pop: 801 (1990); 675 (1980)   **Pop Density:** 22.6
Land: 35.5 sq. mi.; **Water:** 2.8 sq. mi.

Jackson — Township
Lat: 39-27-30 N   Long: 96-45-52 W
Pop: 248 (1990); 256 (1980)   **Pop Density:** 7.7
Land: 32.3 sq. mi.; **Water:** 3.7 sq. mi.

Leonardville — City
ZIP: 66449   Lat: 39-21-48 N   Long: 96-51-28 W
Pop: 374 (1990); 437 (1980)   **Pop Density:** 1246.7
Land: 0.3 sq. mi.; **Water:** 0.0 sq. mi.   **Elev:** 1385 ft.
Incorporated Aug 18, 1885.
Name origin: For Leonard T. Smith, president of the Kansas Central Railway Co.

Madison — Township
Lat: 39-12-23 N   Long: 96-49-11 W
Pop: 14,444 (1990); 16,183 (1980)   **Pop Density:** 102.1
Land: 141.4 sq. mi.; **Water:** 0.2 sq. mi.
In northeast-central KS.

Manhattan — City
ZIP: 66502   Lat: 39-11-19 N   Long: 96-35-45 W
Pop: 37,569 (1990); 32,482 (1980)   **Pop Density:** 3683.2
Land: 10.2 sq. mi.; **Water:** 0.0 sq. mi.   **Elev:** 1020 ft.
In northeast-central KS on the Kansas River, 50 mi. west of Topeka. Settled 1854; incorporated Feb 14, 1857. Part of the town is also in Pottawatomie County.
Name origin: For Manhattan Island in NY.

*Manhattan — Township
ZIP: 66502   Lat: 39-11-13 N   Long: 96-34-44 W
Pop: 9,191 (1990); 8,924 (1980)   **Pop Density:** 242.5
Land: 37.9 sq. mi.; **Water:** 1.2 sq. mi.

May Day — Township
Lat: 39-32-35 N   Long: 96-52-59 W
Pop: 95 (1990); 125 (1980)   **Pop Density:** 3.0
Land: 31.3 sq. mi.; **Water:** 0.0 sq. mi.

Ogden — City
Lat: 39-06-42 N   Long: 96-42-25 W
Pop: 1,494 (1990); 1,804 (1980)   **Pop Density:** 2988.0
Land: 0.5 sq. mi.; **Water:** 0.0 sq. mi.   **Elev:** 1048 ft.
Incorporated 1857.
Name origin: For Maj. Edmund Ogden.

*Ogden — Township
Lat: 39-07-24 N   Long: 96-40-59 W
Pop: 2,057 (1990); 2,178 (1980)   **Pop Density:** 146.9
Land: 14.0 sq. mi.; **Water:** 0.3 sq. mi.

Randolph — City
ZIP: 66554   Lat: 39-25-48 N   Long: 96-45-33 W
Pop: 129 (1990); 131 (1980)   **Pop Density:** 645.0
Land: 0.2 sq. mi.; **Water:** 0.0 sq. mi.   **Elev:** 1250 ft.
Incorporated Jul 1886.
Name origin: For the first postmaster, Gardner Randolph.

Riley — City
ZIP: 66531   Lat: 39-17-53 N   Long: 96-49-42 W
Pop: 804 (1990); 779 (1980)   **Pop Density:** 2010.0
Land: 0.4 sq. mi.; **Water:** 0.0 sq. mi.   **Elev:** 1300 ft.
Incorporated Mar 1903.
Name origin: For an Irish railwayman.

Sherman — Township
Lat: 39-21-48 N   Long: 96-45-06 W
Pop: 391 (1990); 390 (1980)   **Pop Density:** 13.3
Land: 29.5 sq. mi.; **Water:** 1.9 sq. mi.

Swede Creek — Township
Lat: 39-32-02 N   Long: 96-42-40 W
Pop: 177 (1990); 176 (1980)   **Pop Density:** 3.7
Land: 48.1 sq. mi.; **Water:** 1.5 sq. mi.

Wild Cat — Township
Lat: 39-14-04 N   Long: 96-41-52 W
Pop: 677 (1990); 647 (1980)   **Pop Density:** 22.7
Land: 29.8 sq. mi.; **Water:** 0.0 sq. mi.

Zeandale — Township
Lat: 39-06-52 N   Long: 96-27-12 W
Pop: 352 (1990); 308 (1980)   **Pop Density:** 5.9
Land: 59.6 sq. mi.; **Water:** 0.6 sq. mi.

Rooks County
County Seat: Stockton (ZIP: 67669)

Pop: 6,039 (1990); 7,006 (1980) **Pop Density:** 6.8
Land: 888.4 sq. mi.; **Water:** 7.0 sq. mi. **Area Code:** 913
In north-central KS, north of Hays; established Feb 26, 1867 from Kirwin Land District.
Name origin: For John Calvin Rooks (?–1862), soldier who died of wounds received at the Battle of Prairie Grove, AR.

Damar City
ZIP: 67632 Lat: 39-19-08 N Long: 99-35-01 W
Pop: 112 (1990); 204 (1980) **Pop Density:** 560.0
Land: 0.2 sq. mi.; **Water:** 0.0 sq. mi. **Elev:** 2106 ft.
Incorporated Feb 26, 1935.
Name origin: For D.M. Marr, owner of the original townsite.

Palco City
ZIP: 67657 Lat: 39-15-14 N Long: 99-33-50 W
Pop: 295 (1990); 329 (1980) **Pop Density:** 983.3
Land: 0.3 sq. mi.; **Water:** 0.0 sq. mi. **Elev:** 2280 ft.
Incorporated Jul 28, 1903.
Name origin: From a combination of the names of two railroad workers, Palmer and Coe.

Plainville City
ZIP: 67663 Lat: 39-14-02 N Long: 99-18-04 W
Pop: 2,173 (1990); 2,458 (1980) **Pop Density:** 1975.5
Land: 1.1 sq. mi.; **Water:** 0.0 sq. mi. **Elev:** 2143 ft.
Incorporated Apr 11, 1888.
Name origin: For its location on the Great Plains.

Stockton City
ZIP: 67669 Lat: 39-26-10 N Long: 99-16-16 W
Pop: 1,507 (1990); 1,825 (1980) **Pop Density:** 1159.2
Land: 1.3 sq. mi.; **Water:** 0.0 sq. mi. **Elev:** 1792 ft.
Incorporated Apr 21, 1880.
Name origin: For its being perfect for raising livestock.

Township No. 1 Township
Lat: 39-26-10 N Long: 99-05-52 W
Pop: 317 (1990); 371 (1980) **Pop Density:** 3.0
Land: 106.6 sq. mi.; **Water:** 0.2 sq. mi.

Township No. 2 Township
Lat: 39-26-22 N Long: 99-12-44 W
Pop: 500 (1990); 470 (1980) **Pop Density:** 4.7
Land: 107.2 sq. mi.; **Water:** 0.3 sq. mi.

Township No. 3 Township
Lat: 39-29-02 N Long: 99-19-09 W
Pop: 1,432 (1990); 1,711 (1980) **Pop Density:** 20.2
Land: 71.0 sq. mi.; **Water:** 0.1 sq. mi.

Township No. 4 Township
Lat: 39-21-02 N Long: 99-19-32 W
Pop: 46 (1990); 43 (1980) **Pop Density:** 1.3
Land: 35.8 sq. mi.; **Water:** 0.0 sq. mi.

Township No. 5 Township
Lat: 39-29-59 N Long: 99-30-29 W
Pop: 104 (1990); 138 (1980) **Pop Density:** 1.0
Land: 106.7 sq. mi.; **Water:** 0.1 sq. mi.

Township No. 6 Township
Lat: 39-23-24 N Long: 99-25-34 W
Pop: 65 (1990); 86 (1980) **Pop Density:** 1.0
Land: 66.8 sq. mi.; **Water:** 5.1 sq. mi.

Township No. 7 Township
Lat: 39-20-57 N Long: 99-32-43 W
Pop: 214 (1990); 269 (1980) **Pop Density:** 6.1
Land: 35.2 sq. mi.; **Water:** 0.3 sq. mi.

Township No. 8 Township
Lat: 39-15-44 N Long: 99-33-19 W
Pop: 384 (1990); 424 (1980) **Pop Density:** 10.6
Land: 36.1 sq. mi.; **Water:** 0.0 sq. mi.

Township No. 9 Township
Lat: 39-10-40 N Long: 99-33-17 W
Pop: 55 (1990); 76 (1980) **Pop Density:** 1.5
Land: 36.2 sq. mi.; **Water:** 0.0 sq. mi.

Township No. 10 Township
Lat: 39-13-30 N Long: 99-25-40 W
Pop: 263 (1990); 335 (1980) **Pop Density:** 3.1
Land: 84.1 sq. mi.; **Water:** 0.1 sq. mi.

Township No. 11 Township
Lat: 39-13-55 N Long: 99-16-36 W
Pop: 2,499 (1990); 2,855 (1980) **Pop Density:** 26.1
Land: 95.8 sq. mi.; **Water:** 0.5 sq. mi.

Township No. 12 Township
Lat: 39-12-07 N Long: 99-08-02 W
Pop: 160 (1990); 228 (1980) **Pop Density:** 1.5
Land: 107.0 sq. mi.; **Water:** 0.3 sq. mi.

Woodston City
ZIP: 67675 Lat: 39-27-15 N Long: 99-05-55 W
Pop: 121 (1990); 157 (1980) **Pop Density:** 605.0
Land: 0.2 sq. mi.; **Water:** 0.0 sq. mi. **Elev:** 1712 ft.
Incorporated Aug 5, 1905.
Name origin: For pioneer Charles C. Woods.

Zurich City
ZIP: 67676 Lat: 39-13-53 N Long: 99-26-04 W
Pop: 151 (1990); 185 (1980) **Pop Density:** 755.0
Land: 0.2 sq. mi.; **Water:** 0.0 sq. mi. **Elev:** 2214 ft.
Incorporated Aug 20, 1946.
Name origin: For Zurich, Switzerland.

Rush County
County Seat: La Crosse (ZIP: 67548)

Pop: 3,842 (1990); 4,516 (1980) **Pop Density:** 5.3
Land: 718.2 sq. mi.; **Water:** 0.2 sq. mi. **Area Code:** 913
In central KS, south of Hays; established Feb 26, 1867 from unorganized territory.
Name origin: For Capt. Alexander Rush (?–1864), killed in action at Jenkins Ferry, AR.

Alexander — City
ZIP: 67513 **Lat:** 38-28-09 N **Long:** 99-33-07 W
Pop: 85 (1990); 116 (1980) **Pop Density:** 425.0
Land: 0.2 sq. mi.; **Water:** 0.0 sq. mi. **Elev:** 2065 ft.
Incorporated Apr 20, 1926.
Name origin: For Alexander Harvey, whose ranch became the nucleus of the town.

Alexander-Belle Prairie — Township
Lat: 38-27-23 N **Long:** 99-31-47 W
Pop: 150 (1990); 210 (1980) **Pop Density:** 1.8
Land: 84.8 sq. mi.; **Water:** 0.0 sq. mi.

Banner — Township
Lat: 38-24-52 N **Long:** 99-11-27 W
Pop: 185 (1990); 242 (1980) **Pop Density:** 3.4
Land: 53.7 sq. mi.; **Water:** 0.0 sq. mi.

Big Timber — Township
Lat: 38-38-25 N **Long:** 99-18-38 W
Pop: 168 (1990); 234 (1980) **Pop Density:** 3.6
Land: 47.3 sq. mi.; **Water:** 0.0 sq. mi.

Bison — City
ZIP: 67520 **Lat:** 38-31-11 N **Long:** 99-11-49 W
Pop: 252 (1990); 279 (1980) **Pop Density:** 840.0
Land: 0.3 sq. mi.; **Water:** 0.0 sq. mi. **Elev:** 2011 ft.
Incorporated Mar 18, 1912.
Name origin: For the once-abundant bison in the area.

Center — Township
Lat: 38-24-42 N **Long:** 99-18-16 W
Pop: 275 (1990); 336 (1980) **Pop Density:** 5.1
Land: 53.7 sq. mi.; **Water:** 0.0 sq. mi.

Garfield — Township
Lat: 38-24-23 N **Long:** 99-05-16 W
Pop: 177 (1990); 170 (1980) **Pop Density:** 3.3
Land: 53.6 sq. mi.; **Water:** 0.0 sq. mi.

Hampton-Fairview — Township
Lat: 38-37-56 N **Long:** 99-28-44 W
Pop: 317 (1990); 424 (1980) **Pop Density:** 3.0
Land: 106.6 sq. mi.; **Water:** 0.1 sq. mi.

Illinois — Township
Lat: 38-38-47 N **Long:** 99-11-26 W
Pop: 63 (1990); 63 (1980) **Pop Density:** 1.3
Land: 48.1 sq. mi.; **Water:** 0.0 sq. mi.

La Crosse — City
ZIP: 67548 **Lat:** 38-31-54 N **Long:** 99-18-35 W
Pop: 1,427 (1990); 1,618 (1980) **Pop Density:** 1427.0
Land: 1.0 sq. mi.; **Water:** 0.0 sq. mi. **Elev:** 2060 ft.
Incorporated 1886.
Name origin: For the city in WI.

La Crosse-Brookdale — Township
Lat: 38-31-26 N **Long:** 99-21-51 W
Pop: 1,545 (1990); 1,759 (1980) **Pop Density:** 18.3
Land: 84.3 sq. mi.; **Water:** 0.0 sq. mi.

Liebenthal — City
ZIP: 67553 **Lat:** 38-39-16 N **Long:** 99-19-12 W
Pop: 112 (1990); 163 (1980) **Pop Density:** 1120.0
Land: 0.1 sq. mi.; **Water:** 0.0 sq. mi. **Elev:** 1976 ft.
Incorporated Aug 5, 1935.
Name origin: Named by German settlers, meaning 'valley of love.'

Lone Star — Township
Lat: 38-31-50 N **Long:** 99-12-06 W
Pop: 347 (1990); 370 (1980) **Pop Density:** 8.2
Land: 42.4 sq. mi.; **Water:** 0.0 sq. mi.

McCracken — City
Lat: 38-34-56 N **Long:** 99-34-08 W
Pop: 231 (1990); 292 (1980) **Pop Density:** 231.0
Land: 1.0 sq. mi.; **Water:** 0.0 sq. mi. **Elev:** 2141 ft.
Incorporated 1887.

Otis — City
ZIP: 67565 **Lat:** 38-32-05 N **Long:** 99-03-11 W
Pop: 385 (1990); 410 (1980) **Pop Density:** 1283.3
Land: 0.3 sq. mi.; **Water:** 0.0 sq. mi. **Elev:** 2035 ft.
Incorporated Dec 15, 1911.
Name origin: For Otis Modderwell.

Pioneer — Township
Lat: 38-31-47 N **Long:** 99-04-49 W
Pop: 485 (1990); 535 (1980) **Pop Density:** 11.7
Land: 41.6 sq. mi.; **Water:** 0.0 sq. mi.

Pleasantdale — Township
Lat: 38-38-19 N **Long:** 99-05-15 W
Pop: 49 (1990); 63 (1980) **Pop Density:** 1.0
Land: 47.9 sq. mi.; **Water:** 0.0 sq. mi.

Rush Center — City
ZIP: 67575 **Lat:** 38-27-53 N **Long:** 99-18-37 W
Pop: 177 (1990); 207 (1980) **Pop Density:** 442.5
Land: 0.4 sq. mi.; **Water:** 0.0 sq. mi. **Elev:** 1995 ft.
Incorporated 1959.
Name origin: For Civil War hero Capt. Alexander Rush.

Timken — City
ZIP: 67582 **Lat:** 38-28-22 N **Long:** 99-10-37 W
Pop: 87 (1990); 99 (1980) **Pop Density:** 870.0
Land: 0.1 sq. mi.; **Water:** 0.0 sq. mi. **Elev:** 1963 ft.
Incorporated Jun 16, 1930.
Name origin: For the Timken family, who came to KS from Germany.

KANSAS, Rush County

Union
Township
Lat: 38-24-58 N **Long:** 99-25-25 W
Pop: 81 (1990); 110 (1980) **Pop Density:** 1.5
Land: 54.3 sq. mi.; **Water:** 0.0 sq. mi.

Russell County
County Seat: Russell (ZIP: 67665)

Pop: 7,835 (1990); 8,868 (1980) **Pop Density:** 8.9
Land: 884.7 sq. mi.; **Water:** 14.3 sq. mi. **Area Code:** 913
In central KS, west of Salina; organized Feb 26, 1867 from Ellsworth County.
Name origin: For Capt. Avra P. Russell (?–1862), Union army officer who died of wounds received at Prairie Grove, AR.

Big Creek
Township
Lat: 38-52-07 N **Long:** 98-59-07 W
Pop: 528 (1990); 508 (1980) **Pop Density:** 7.4
Land: 71.8 sq. mi.; **Water:** 0.0 sq. mi.

Bunker Hill
City
ZIP: 67626 **Lat:** 38-52-21 N **Long:** 98-42-02 W
Pop: 111 (1990); 124 (1980) **Pop Density:** 92.5
Land: 1.2 sq. mi.; **Water:** 0.0 sq. mi. **Elev:** 1860 ft.
Incorporated Jun 1886.
Name origin: For the famous Revolutionary War battle site in MA.

Center
Township
Lat: 38-50-20 N **Long:** 98-40-41 W
Pop: 359 (1990); 350 (1980) **Pop Density:** 2.6
Land: 138.7 sq. mi.; **Water:** 3.4 sq. mi.

Dorrance
City
ZIP: 67634 **Lat:** 38-50-46 N **Long:** 98-35-24 W
Pop: 195 (1990); 220 (1980) **Pop Density:** 650.0
Land: 0.3 sq. mi.; **Water:** 0.0 sq. mi. **Elev:** 1730 ft.
Incorporated Apr 19, 1910.
Name origin: For Dorrance, IL.

Fairfield
Township
Lat: 38-44-37 N **Long:** 98-45-59 W
Pop: 63 (1990); 55 (1980) **Pop Density:** 1.6
Land: 40.2 sq. mi.; **Water:** 0.0 sq. mi.

Fairview
Township
Lat: 39-02-50 N **Long:** 98-32-35 W
Pop: 576 (1990); 660 (1980) **Pop Density:** 8.1
Land: 71.3 sq. mi.; **Water:** 0.6 sq. mi.

Gorham
City
ZIP: 67640 **Lat:** 38-52-50 N **Long:** 99-01-24 W
Pop: 284 (1990); 355 (1980) **Pop Density:** 1420.0
Land: 0.2 sq. mi.; **Water:** 0.0 sq. mi. **Elev:** 1914 ft.
Incorporated Apr 10, 1941.

Grant
Township
Lat: 38-49-35 N **Long:** 98-50-48 W
Pop: 180 (1990); 211 (1980) **Pop Density:** 3.5
Land: 52.1 sq. mi.; **Water:** 0.1 sq. mi.

Lincoln
Township
Lat: 38-44-26 N **Long:** 98-52-31 W
Pop: 136 (1990); 146 (1980) **Pop Density:** 3.8
Land: 36.1 sq. mi.; **Water:** 0.0 sq. mi.

Lucas
City
ZIP: 67648 **Lat:** 39-03-27 N **Long:** 98-32-18 W
Pop: 452 (1990); 524 (1980) **Pop Density:** 904.0
Land: 0.5 sq. mi.; **Water:** 0.0 sq. mi. **Elev:** 1500 ft.
In central KS; incorporated Jul 31, 1899.
Name origin: For Lucas Place in Saint Louis, MO.

Luray
City
ZIP: 67649 **Lat:** 39-06-54 N **Long:** 98-41-32 W
Pop: 261 (1990); 295 (1980) **Pop Density:** 870.0
Land: 0.3 sq. mi.; **Water:** 0.0 sq. mi. **Elev:** 1570 ft.
Incorporated Apr 5, 1904. Not coextensive with the town of the same name.
Name origin: Changed by postmaster John Fritts from *Lura*.

*Luray
Township
ZIP: 67649 **Lat:** 39-03-13 N **Long:** 98-39-03 W
Pop: 339 (1990); 373 (1980) **Pop Density:** 4.8
Land: 70.6 sq. mi.; **Water:** 0.7 sq. mi.

Paradise
City
ZIP: 67658 **Lat:** 39-06-52 N **Long:** 98-55-03 W
Pop: 66 (1990); 89 (1980) **Pop Density:** 220.0
Land: 0.3 sq. mi.; **Water:** 0.0 sq. mi. **Elev:** 1695 ft.
Incorporated May 19, 1924. Not coextensive with the town of the same name.
Name origin: Named by early religious settlers for its descriptive connotations.

*Paradise
Township
ZIP: 67658 **Lat:** 39-03-09 N **Long:** 98-55-29 W
Pop: 219 (1990); 271 (1980) **Pop Density:** 1.5
Land: 143.7 sq. mi.; **Water:** 0.2 sq. mi.

Plymouth
Township
Lat: 38-49-34 N **Long:** 98-32-28 W
Pop: 316 (1990); 373 (1980) **Pop Density:** 3.2
Land: 98.3 sq. mi.; **Water:** 9.1 sq. mi.

Russell
City
ZIP: 67665 **Lat:** 38-53-16 N **Long:** 98-51-12 W
Pop: 4,781 (1990); 5,427 (1980) **Pop Density:** 1111.9
Land: 4.3 sq. mi.; **Water:** 0.0 sq. mi. **Elev:** 1826 ft.
In central KS, 37 mi. north of Great Bend. Incorporated Jun 4, 1872.
Name origin: For Maj. Aura Russell, who was killed during the Civil War.

American Places Dictionary   KANSAS, Saline County

*Russell   Township
ZIP: 67665   **Lat:** 38-55-05 N **Long:** 98-50-22 W
Pop: 117 (1990); 217 (1980)   **Pop Density:** 2.3
Land: 49.8 sq. mi.; **Water:** 0.0 sq. mi.

Waldo   City
ZIP: 67673   **Lat:** 39-07-12 N **Long:** 98-47-50 W
Pop: 57 (1990); 75 (1980)   **Pop Density:** 142.5
Land: 0.4 sq. mi.; **Water:** 0.0 sq. mi.   **Elev:** 1711 ft.
Incorporated Mar 1911. Not coextensive with the town of the same name.
Name origin: For a Union Pacific Railroad official.

*Waldo   Township
ZIP: 67673   **Lat:** 39-02-18 N **Long:** 98-45-05 W
Pop: 128 (1990); 177 (1980)   **Pop Density:** 1.8
Land: 71.9 sq. mi.; **Water:** 0.1 sq. mi.

Winterset   Township
Lat: 38-44-15 N **Long:** 98-59-28 W
Pop: 93 (1990); 100 (1980)   **Pop Density:** 2.6
Land: 36.0 sq. mi.; **Water:** 0.0 sq. mi.

Saline County
County Seat: Salina (ZIP: 67401)

Pop: 49,301 (1990); 48,905 (1980)   **Pop Density:** 68.5
Land: 719.6 sq. mi.; **Water:** 1.7 sq. mi.   **Area Code:** 913
In central KS, southwest of Manhattan; original county; organized Feb 15, 1860 (prior to statehood).
Name origin: For the Saline River, which flows through the county.

Assaria   City
ZIP: 67416   **Lat:** 38-40-49 N **Long:** 97-36-13 W
Pop: 387 (1990); 414 (1980)   **Pop Density:** 1935.0
Land: 0.2 sq. mi.; **Water:** 0.0 sq. mi.   **Elev:** 1282 ft.
In central KS; incorporated Jan 14, 1886.
Name origin: Named by Swedish settlers for the name of their church, meaning 'In God is our help,' from a Hebrew term *Azariah* 'Yahweh helps.'

Brookville   City
ZIP: 67425   **Lat:** 38-46-25 N **Long:** 97-51-51 W
Pop: 226 (1990); 259 (1980)   **Pop Density:** 376.7
Land: 0.6 sq. mi.; **Water:** 0.0 sq. mi.   **Elev:** 1369 ft.
Incorporated Apr 3, 1871.

Cambria   Township
Lat: 38-54-58 N **Long:** 97-32-20 W
Pop: 390 (1990); 463 (1980)   **Pop Density:** 10.9
Land: 35.9 sq. mi.; **Water:** 0.1 sq. mi.

Dayton   Township
Lat: 38-54-43 N **Long:** 97-25-42 W
Pop: 154 (1990); 138 (1980)   **Pop Density:** 4.3
Land: 35.5 sq. mi.; **Water:** 0.0 sq. mi.

Elm Creek   Township
Lat: 38-54-51 N **Long:** 97-38-58 W
Pop: 654 (1990); 675 (1980)   **Pop Density:** 18.4
Land: 35.6 sq. mi.; **Water:** 0.1 sq. mi.

Eureka   Township
Lat: 38-44-20 N **Long:** 97-25-37 W
Pop: 587 (1990); 669 (1980)   **Pop Density:** 16.2
Land: 36.2 sq. mi.; **Water:** 0.0 sq. mi.

Falun   Township
ZIP: 67442   **Lat:** 38-39-40 N **Long:** 97-49-09 W
Pop: 226 (1990); 218 (1980)   **Pop Density:** 3.1
Land: 71.8 sq. mi.; **Water:** 0.2 sq. mi.

Glendale   Township
Lat: 38-54-44 N **Long:** 97-52-46 W
Pop: 100 (1990); 83 (1980)   **Pop Density:** 2.8
Land: 36.0 sq. mi.; **Water:** 0.1 sq. mi.

Greeley   Township
Lat: 38-49-39 N **Long:** 97-32-04 W
Pop: 848 (1990); 660 (1980)   **Pop Density:** 27.1
Land: 31.3 sq. mi.; **Water:** 0.0 sq. mi.

Gypsum   City
ZIP: 67448   **Lat:** 38-42-20 N **Long:** 97-25-35 W
Pop: 365 (1990); 423 (1980)   **Pop Density:** 912.5
Land: 0.4 sq. mi.; **Water:** 0.0 sq. mi.   **Elev:** 1229 ft.
Incorporated Apr 11, 1887.
Name origin: For nearby gypsum mineral deposits.

*Gypsum   Township
ZIP: 67448   **Lat:** 38-39-14 N **Long:** 97-25-49 W
Pop: 155 (1990); 218 (1980)   **Pop Density:** 4.3
Land: 35.9 sq. mi.; **Water:** 0.0 sq. mi.

Liberty   Township
Lat: 38-39-02 N **Long:** 97-32-05 W
Pop: 132 (1990); 147 (1980)   **Pop Density:** 3.7
Land: 35.9 sq. mi.; **Water:** 0.2 sq. mi.

New Cambria   City
ZIP: 67470   **Lat:** 38-52-46 N **Long:** 97-30-19 W
Pop: 152 (1990); 175 (1980)   **Pop Density:** 1520.0
Land: 0.1 sq. mi.; **Water:** 0.0 sq. mi.   **Elev:** 1196 ft.
Incorporated May 6, 1913.

Ohio   Township
Lat: 38-49-31 N **Long:** 97-46-03 W
Pop: 453 (1990); 402 (1980)   **Pop Density:** 12.5
Land: 36.2 sq. mi.; **Water:** 0.0 sq. mi.

Pleasant Valley   Township
Lat: 38-54-50 N **Long:** 97-45-35 W
Pop: 291 (1990); 273 (1980)   **Pop Density:** 8.1
Land: 36.1 sq. mi.; **Water:** 0.2 sq. mi.

KANSAS, Saline County

Salina — City
ZIP: 67401   **Lat:** 38-48-56 N   **Long:** 97-37-03 W
Pop: 42,303 (1990); 41,843 (1980)   **Pop Density:** 2014.4
Land: 21.0 sq. mi.; **Water:** 0.0 sq. mi.   **Elev:** 1225 ft.
In central KS on the Smoky Hill River, 58 mi. north-northeast of Hutchinson. Founded 1858; incorporated Nov 20 1870.
Name origin: For nearby salt deposits on the Saline River.

Smoky Hill — Township
Lat: 38-50-03 N   **Long:** 97-40-04 W
Pop: 408 (1990); 362 (1980)   **Pop Density:** 17.4
Land: 23.4 sq. mi.; **Water:** 0.0 sq. mi.

Smoky View — Township
Lat: 38-38-51 N   **Long:** 97-38-22 W
Pop: 761 (1990); 857 (1980)   **Pop Density:** 21.1
Land: 36.0 sq. mi.; **Water:** 0.0 sq. mi.

Smolan — City
ZIP: 67479   **Lat:** 38-44-16 N   **Long:** 97-41-01 W
Pop: 195 (1990); 169 (1980)   **Pop Density:** 1950.0
Land: 0.1 sq. mi.; **Water:** 0.0 sq. mi.   **Elev:** 1315 ft.
Incorporated Apr 30, 1962. Not coextensive with the town of the same name.
Name origin: For the province of Smoland in Sweden, with a spelling variation..

*Smolan — Township
ZIP: 67479   **Lat:** 38-44-16 N   **Long:** 97-38-44 W
Pop: 707 (1990); 717 (1980)   **Pop Density:** 21.4
Land: 33.1 sq. mi.; **Water:** 0.0 sq. mi.

Solomon — Township
Lat: 38-49-38 N   **Long:** 97-25-34 W
Pop: 259 (1990); 241 (1980)   **Pop Density:** 7.2
Land: 36.2 sq. mi.; **Water:** 0.0 sq. mi.

Spring Creek — Township
Lat: 38-46-58 N   **Long:** 97-52-20 W
Pop: 323 (1990); 359 (1980)   **Pop Density:** 4.5
Land: 71.6 sq. mi.; **Water:** 0.3 sq. mi.

Walnut — Township
Lat: 38-44-31 N   **Long:** 97-32-48 W
Pop: 455 (1990); 503 (1980)   **Pop Density:** 12.7
Land: 35.9 sq. mi.; **Water:** 0.3 sq. mi.

Washington — Township
Lat: 38-44-09 N   **Long:** 97-45-29 W
Pop: 95 (1990); 77 (1980)   **Pop Density:** 2.6
Land: 36.0 sq. mi.; **Water:** 0.0 sq. mi.

Scott County
County Seat: Scott City (ZIP: 67871)

Pop: 5,289 (1990); 5,782 (1980)   **Pop Density:** 7.4
Land: 717.6 sq. mi.; **Water:** 0.1 sq. mi.   **Area Code:** 316
In western KS, north of Garden City; organized Mar 20, 1873 from Finney County.
Name origin: For Gen. Winfield Scott (1786–1866), officer in the War of 1812 and the Mexican-American War; general in chief of the U.S. Army (1841–61) and commander of the Union armies at the beginning of the Civil War.

Beaver — Township
Lat: 38-38-03 N   **Long:** 101-00-29 W
Pop: 327 (1990); 377 (1980)   **Pop Density:** 2.7
Land: 119.2 sq. mi.; **Water:** 0.1 sq. mi.

Isbel — Township
Lat: 38-28-56 N   **Long:** 101-03-04 W
Pop: 136 (1990); 187 (1980)   **Pop Density:** 1.7
Land: 79.6 sq. mi.; **Water:** 0.0 sq. mi.

Keystone — Township
Lat: 38-29-03 N   **Long:** 100-45-01 W
Pop: 136 (1990); 143 (1980)   **Pop Density:** 1.7
Land: 79.7 sq. mi.; **Water:** 0.0 sq. mi.

Lake — Township
Lat: 38-20-06 N   **Long:** 100-48-05 W
Pop: 117 (1990); 124 (1980)   **Pop Density:** 1.0
Land: 120.2 sq. mi.; **Water:** 0.0 sq. mi.

Michigan — Township
Lat: 38-37-41 N   **Long:** 100-48-22 W
Pop: 117 (1990); 161 (1980)   **Pop Density:** 1.0
Land: 118.8 sq. mi.; **Water:** 0.0 sq. mi.

Scott — Township
Lat: 38-28-58 N   **Long:** 100-54-25 W
Pop: 4,106 (1990); 4,432 (1980)   **Pop Density:** 51.2
Land: 80.2 sq. mi.; **Water:** 0.0 sq. mi.

Scott City — City
ZIP: 67871   **Lat:** 38-28-47 N   **Long:** 100-54-30 W
Pop: 3,785 (1990); 4,154 (1980)   **Pop Density:** 2365.6
Land: 1.6 sq. mi.; **Water:** 0.0 sq. mi.   **Elev:** 2978 ft.
Incorporated Jan 10, 1887.
Name origin: For 19th-century novelist Sir Walter Scott.

Valley — Township
Lat: 38-20-33 N   **Long:** 101-00-24 W
Pop: 350 (1990); 358 (1980)   **Pop Density:** 2.9
Land: 120.0 sq. mi.; **Water:** 0.0 sq. mi.

Sedgwick County
County Seat: Wichita (ZIP: 67203)

Pop: 403,662 (1990); 367,088 (1980) **Pop Density:** 403.6
Land: 1000.2 sq. mi.; **Water:** 9.2 sq. mi. **Area Code:** 316
In south-central KS, southeast of Hutchinson; organized Feb 26, 1867 from Butler County.
Name origin: For Gen. John Sedgwick (1813–64), Indian fighter and Union officer in the Civil War.

Afton
Township
Lat: 37-36-13 N **Long:** 97-38-47 W
Pop: 846 (1990); 757 (1980) **Pop Density:** 24.0
Land: 35.3 sq. mi.; **Water:** 0.6 sq. mi.

Andale
City
ZIP: 67001 **Lat:** 37-47-33 N **Long:** 97-37-44 W
Pop: 566 (1990); 538 (1980) **Pop Density:** 1886.7
Land: 0.3 sq. mi.; **Water:** 0.0 sq. mi. **Elev:** 1437 ft.
Name origin: For a combination of the names Anderson and Dale, two prominent families.

Attica
Township
Lat: 37-41-48 N **Long:** 97-32-15 W
Pop: 4,629 (1990); 5,019 (1980) **Pop Density:** 136.1
Land: 34.0 sq. mi.; **Water:** 0.1 sq. mi.

Bel Aire
City
Lat: 37-45-52 N **Long:** 97-16-05 W
Pop: 3,695 (1990) **Pop Density:** 1679.5
Land: 2.2 sq. mi.; **Water:** 0.0 sq. mi.

Bentley
City
ZIP: 67016 **Lat:** 37-53-10 N **Long:** 97-30-56 W
Pop: 360 (1990); 311 (1980) **Pop Density:** 1800.0
Land: 0.2 sq. mi.; **Water:** 0.0 sq. mi. **Elev:** 1387 ft.
Incorporated Nov 1960.
Name origin: For lawyer and railroad developer O.H. Bentley.

Cheney
City
ZIP: 67025 **Lat:** 37-37-40 N **Long:** 97-46-48 W
Pop: 1,560 (1990); 1,404 (1980) **Pop Density:** 1200.0
Land: 1.3 sq. mi.; **Water:** 0.0 sq. mi. **Elev:** 1385 ft.
Incorporated 1884.
Name origin: For Santa Fe Railroad director B.P. Cheney.

Clearwater
City
ZIP: 67026 **Lat:** 37-30-20 N **Long:** 97-30-04 W
Pop: 1,875 (1990); 1,684 (1980) **Pop Density:** 2083.3
Land: 0.9 sq. mi.; **Water:** 0.0 sq. mi. **Elev:** 1275 ft.
Incorporated 1885.
Name origin: From the translation of an Indian term.

Colwich
City
ZIP: 67030 **Lat:** 37-46-54 N **Long:** 97-32-15 W
Pop: 1,091 (1990); 935 (1980) **Pop Density:** 2182.0
Land: 0.5 sq. mi.; **Water:** 0.0 sq. mi. **Elev:** 1380 ft.
Incorporated Jun 6, 1887.
Name origin: From the first two syllables of the Colorado and Wichita Railroad, on which the town was located.

Delano
Township
Lat: 37-43-04 N **Long:** 97-25-42 W
Pop: 378 (1990); 2,145 (1980) **Pop Density:** 64.1
Land: 5.9 sq. mi.; **Water:** 0.6 sq. mi.

Derby
City
ZIP: 67037 **Lat:** 37-32-57 N **Long:** 97-15-31 W
Pop: 14,699 (1990); 9,786 (1980) **Pop Density:** 3195.4
Land: 4.6 sq. mi.; **Water:** 0.0 sq. mi. **Elev:** 1275 ft.
In south-central KS, 15 mi. southeast of Wichita. Incorporated 1903.
Name origin: For a Santa Fe Railroad official. Originally called El Paso.

Eagle
Township
Lat: 37-52-16 N **Long:** 97-32-00 W
Pop: 895 (1990); 738 (1980) **Pop Density:** 25.1
Land: 35.6 sq. mi.; **Water:** 0.5 sq. mi.

Eastborough
City
ZIP: 67206 **Lat:** 37-41-04 N **Long:** 97-15-30 W
Pop: 896 (1990); 854 (1980) **Pop Density:** 2240.0
Land: 0.4 sq. mi.; **Water:** 0.0 sq. mi. **Elev:** 1373 ft.
Incorporated Jun 1, 1937.

Erie
Township
Lat: 37-31-04 N **Long:** 97-45-08 W
Pop: 115 (1990); 119 (1980) **Pop Density:** 3.2
Land: 36.4 sq. mi.; **Water:** 0.0 sq. mi.

Garden Plain
City
ZIP: 67050 **Lat:** 37-39-39 N **Long:** 97-40-53 W
Pop: 731 (1990); 775 (1980) **Pop Density:** 1462.0
Land: 0.5 sq. mi.; **Water:** 0.0 sq. mi. **Elev:** 1450 ft.
Incorporated Sep 2, 1902.
Name origin: For its descriptive connotations.

*Garden Plain
Township
ZIP: 67050 **Lat:** 37-41-27 N **Long:** 97-38-55 W
Pop: 1,406 (1990); 1,449 (1980) **Pop Density:** 39.5
Land: 35.6 sq. mi.; **Water:** 0.1 sq. mi.

Goddard
City
ZIP: 67052 **Lat:** 37-39-35 N **Long:** 97-34-35 W
Pop: 1,804 (1990); 1,427 (1980) **Pop Density:** 1202.7
Land: 1.5 sq. mi.; **Water:** 0.0 sq. mi. **Elev:** 1465 ft.
Incorporated 1910.
Name origin: Named in 1877 for J.E. Goddard, general manager of the Santa Fe Railroad.

Grand River
Township
Lat: 37-41-30 N **Long:** 97-45-19 W
Pop: 550 (1990); 479 (1980) **Pop Density:** 15.7
Land: 35.0 sq. mi.; **Water:** 0.8 sq. mi.

Grant
Township
Lat: 37-51-50 N **Long:** 97-19-21 W
Pop: 3,221 (1990); 2,538 (1980) **Pop Density:** 89.7
Land: 35.9 sq. mi.; **Water:** 0.1 sq. mi.

KANSAS, Sedgwick County

Greeley Township
Lat: 37-52-21 N Long: 97-39-16 W
Pop: 1,060 (1990); 1,115 (1980) Pop Density: 29.6
Land: 35.8 sq. mi.; Water: 0.5 sq. mi.

Gypsum Township
Lat: 37-36-26 N Long: 97-12-32 W
Pop: 5,581 (1990); 5,432 (1980) Pop Density: 156.8
Land: 35.6 sq. mi.; Water: 0.2 sq. mi.

Haysville City
ZIP: 67060 Lat: 37-34-01 N Long: 97-20-57 W
Pop: 8,364 (1990); 8,006 (1980) Pop Density: 2534.5
Land: 3.3 sq. mi.; Water: 0.0 sq. mi.
In south-central KS, south of Wichita. Incorporated Jul 3, 1951.
Name origin: For Will Hays, local land baron.

Illinois Township
Lat: 37-36-30 N Long: 97-31-55 W
Pop: 1,553 (1990); 1,297 (1980) Pop Density: 43.5
Land: 35.7 sq. mi.; Water: 0.0 sq. mi.

Kechi City
Lat: 37-47-43 N Long: 97-16-41 W
Pop: 517 (1990); 288 (1980) Pop Density: 646.3
Land: 0.8 sq. mi.; Water: 0.0 sq. mi. Elev: 1380 ft.
Incorporated Apr 29, 1957. Not coextensive with the town of the same name.
Name origin: For the Kechi Indians. Also called Kechi City.

*Kechi Township
Lat: 37-47-35 N Long: 97-19-03 W
Pop: 10,460 (1990); 11,584 (1980) Pop Density: 411.8
Land: 25.4 sq. mi.; Water: 0.1 sq. mi.

Lincoln Township
Lat: 37-52-25 N Long: 97-12-41 W
Pop: 427 (1990); 411 (1980) Pop Density: 11.7
Land: 36.4 sq. mi.; Water: 0.0 sq. mi.

Maize City
ZIP: 67101 Lat: 37-46-23 N Long: 97-27-50 W
Pop: 1,520 (1990); 1,294 (1980) Pop Density: 1900.0
Land: 0.8 sq. mi.; Water: 0.0 sq. mi. Elev: 1350 ft.
Incorporated May 17, 1915.
Name origin: For the abundant corn crop grown here.

Minneha Township
Lat: 37-41-34 N Long: 97-11-36 W
Pop: 6,566 (1990); 4,623 (1980) Pop Density: 279.4
Land: 23.5 sq. mi.; Water: 0.3 sq. mi.

Morton Township
Lat: 37-36-43 N Long: 97-44-44 W
Pop: 1,832 (1990); 1,668 (1980) Pop Density: 51.9
Land: 35.3 sq. mi.; Water: 0.4 sq. mi.

Mount Hope City
ZIP: 67108 Lat: 37-52-06 N Long: 97-39-51 W
Pop: 805 (1990); 791 (1980) Pop Density: 2683.3
Land: 0.3 sq. mi.; Water: 0.0 sq. mi. Elev: 1440 ft.
Incorporated 1887.
Name origin: For Mount Hope, MI.

Mulvane City
Lat: 37-29-10 N Long: 97-14-28 W
Pop: 3,466 (1990); 2,994 (1980) Pop Density: 2666.2
Land: 1.3 sq. mi.; Water: 0.0 sq. mi. Elev: 1250 ft.
Incorporated Sep 27, 1883. Part of the town is also in Sumner County. In south-central KS.
Name origin: For the Mulvane brothers, who were Topeka bankers and land developers.

Ninnescah Township
Lat: 37-30-58 N Long: 97-32-07 W
Pop: 2,453 (1990); 2,151 (1980) Pop Density: 68.1
Land: 36.0 sq. mi.; Water: 0.2 sq. mi.

Oaklawn-Sunview CDP
Lat: 37-36-24 N Long: 97-17-55 W
Pop: 3,240 (1990) Pop Density: 6480.0
Land: 0.5 sq. mi.; Water: 0.0 sq. mi.

Ohio Township
Lat: 37-31-08 N Long: 97-25-28 W
Pop: 892 (1990); 752 (1980) Pop Density: 24.7
Land: 36.1 sq. mi.; Water: 0.1 sq. mi.

Park Township
Lat: 37-46-50 N Long: 97-25-34 W
Pop: 3,954 (1990); 3,585 (1980) Pop Density: 121.3
Land: 32.6 sq. mi.; Water: 0.7 sq. mi.

Park City City
ZIP: 67219 Lat: 37-47-45 N Long: 97-19-18 W
Pop: 5,050 (1990); 3,778 (1980) Pop Density: 1741.4
Land: 2.9 sq. mi.; Water: 0.0 sq. mi. Elev: 1360 ft.

Payne Township
Lat: 37-46-59 N Long: 97-12-10 W
Pop: 724 (1990); 874 (1980) Pop Density: 23.1
Land: 31.4 sq. mi.; Water: 0.0 sq. mi.

Riverside Township
ZIP: 67203 Lat: 37-35-41 N Long: 97-18-19 W
Pop: 14,364 (1990); 11,725 (1980) Pop Density: 772.3
Land: 18.6 sq. mi.; Water: 0.4 sq. mi.
In south-central KS.

Rockford Township
Lat: 37-30-59 N Long: 97-13-00 W
Pop: 17,189 (1990); 13,919 (1980) Pop Density: 440.7
Land: 39.0 sq. mi.; Water: 0.4 sq. mi.
In south-central KS.

Salem Township
Lat: 37-30-47 N Long: 97-19-10 W
Pop: 7,827 (1990); 7,697 (1980) Pop Density: 244.6
Land: 32.0 sq. mi.; Water: 0.3 sq. mi.

Sedgwick City
Lat: 37-54-34 N Long: 97-25-27 W
Pop: 132 (1990); 128 (1980) Pop Density: 1320.0
Land: 0.1 sq. mi.; Water: 0.0 sq. mi.
Incorporated 1872. Part of the town is also in Harvey County.
Name origin: For Civil War hero Gen. John Sedgwick (1813–64).

Sherman Township
Lat: 37-47-01 N Long: 97-38-12 W
Pop: 1,251 (1990); 1,089 (1980) Pop Density: 33.8
Land: 37.0 sq. mi.; Water: 0.1 sq. mi.

American Places Dictionary — KANSAS, Seward County

Union
Township
Lat: 37-46-49 N Long: 97-32-05 W
Pop: 1,945 (1990); 1,629 (1980) Pop Density: 53.7
Land: 36.2 sq. mi.; Water: 0.1 sq. mi.

Valley Center
City
ZIP: 67147 Lat: 37-50-06 N Long: 97-22-24 W
Pop: 3,624 (1990); 3,300 (1980) Pop Density: 2265.0
Land: 1.6 sq. mi.; Water: 0.0 sq. mi. Elev: 1345 ft.
Incorporated 1885.
Name origin: For its descriptive connotations.

*Valley Center
Township
ZIP: 67147 Lat: 37-51-40 N Long: 97-26-09 W
Pop: 2,985 (1990); 2,442 (1980) Pop Density: 82.2
Land: 36.3 sq. mi.; Water: 0.1 sq. mi.

Viola
City
ZIP: 67149 Lat: 37-28-56 N Long: 97-38-40 W
Pop: 185 (1990); 199 (1980) Pop Density: 925.0
Land: 0.2 sq. mi.; Water: 0.0 sq. mi. Elev: 1335 ft.
Incorporated Apr 29, 1909. Not coextensive with the town of the same name.
Name origin: For Viola, IL.

*Viola
Township
ZIP: 67149 Lat: 37-31-10 N Long: 97-38-38 W
Pop: 484 (1990); 439 (1980) Pop Density: 13.4
Land: 36.1 sq. mi.; Water: 0.4 sq. mi.

Waco
Township
Lat: 37-36-00 N Long: 97-26-04 W
Pop: 2,369 (1990); 1,574 (1980) Pop Density: 79.0
Land: 30.0 sq. mi.; Water: 0.1 sq. mi.

Wichita
City
ZIP: 67209 Lat: 37-41-14 N Long: 97-20-33 W
Pop: 304,011 (1990); 279,838 (1980) Pop Density: 2641.3
Land: 115.1 sq. mi.; Water: 2.2 sq. mi. Elev: 1305 ft.
In south-central KS on the Arkansas River, 177 mi. southwest of Kansas City. Largest city in the state, founded 1864; incorporated Apr 5, 1871. Distribution center for farming region producing dairy products, grain, livestock; diverse manufacturing: general civilian aircraft, chemicals, and camping and recreational equipment; meat processing; petroleum center of KS.
Name origin: For one of the more important tribes of Caddoan linguistic stock. The name means either 'man,' or possibly, as taken from Choctaw *owa chito* 'big hunt.'

Seward County
County Seat: Liberal (ZIP: 67901)

Pop: 18,743 (1990); 17,071 (1980) Pop Density: 29.3
Land: 639.6 sq. mi.; Water: 1.0 sq. mi. Area Code: 316

On the southern border of KS, southwest of Dodge City; organized as Godfrey County Mar 26, 1873 from Indian lands; name changed to Seward Jun 3, 1861; changed to Howard 1867. In 1873 the name Seward was given to a new county in the present location.
Name origin: For William Henry Seward (1801–72), U.S. secretary of state (1861–69), renowned for negotiating the purchase of Alaska (1867).

Fargo
Township
Lat: 37-07-14 N Long: 100-45-01 W
Pop: 1,195 (1990); 961 (1980) Pop Density: 5.4
Land: 219.9 sq. mi.; Water: 0.6 sq. mi.

Kismet
City
ZIP: 67859 Lat: 37-12-17 N Long: 100-42-02 W
Pop: 421 (1990); 368 (1980) Pop Density: 2105.0
Land: 0.2 sq. mi.; Water: 0.0 sq. mi. Elev: 2775 ft.
Incorporated Dec 2, 1929.
Name origin: Named by railroad builders who had difficulty crossing the Cimarron River. From Turkish meaning 'destiny' or 'fate.'

Liberal
City
ZIP: 67901 Lat: 37-02-40 N Long: 100-56-07 W
Pop: 16,573 (1990); 14,911 (1980) Pop Density: 1744.5
Land: 9.5 sq. mi.; Water: 0.0 sq. mi. Elev: 2836 ft.
In southwestern KS on the OK border, 75 mi. southwest of Dodge City. Incorporated May 1, 1888.
Name origin: For generous pioneer L. E. Keefer, who "liberally" supplied well water to local travelers without charge.

*Liberal
Township
ZIP: 67901 Lat: 37-07-36 N Long: 100-58-01 W
Pop: 616 (1990); 803 (1980) Pop Density: 3.2
Land: 195.3 sq. mi.; Water: 0.2 sq. mi.

Seward
Township
Lat: 37-18-50 N Long: 100-51-09 W
Pop: 359 (1990); 396 (1980) Pop Density: 1.7
Land: 214.8 sq. mi.; Water: 0.1 sq. mi.

Shawnee County
County Seat: Topeka (ZIP: 66603)

Pop: 160,976 (1990); 154,916 (1980)   **Pop Density:** 292.8
Land: 549.9 sq. mi.; **Water:** 6.5 sq. mi.   **Area Code:** 913
In northeastern KS, west of Lawrence; original county; organized Aug 25, 1855 (prior to statehood).
Name origin: For the Indian tribe of Algonquian linguistic stock. Name means 'southerner.'

Auburn — City
ZIP: 66402   **Lat:** 38-54-20 N   **Long:** 95-49-00 W
Pop: 908 (1990); 890 (1980)   **Pop Density:** 1816.0
Land: 0.5 sq. mi.; **Water:** 0.0 sq. mi.   **Elev:** 1080 ft.
Incorporated Jun 27, 1963. Not coextensive with the town of the same name.
Name origin: For the name of the imaginary village in the famous poem "The Deserted Village" (1770) by Oliver Goldsmith (1730–74).

*Auburn — Township
ZIP: 66402   **Lat:** 38-54-26 N   **Long:** 95-51-10 W
Pop: 2,157 (1990); 1,885 (1980)   **Pop Density:** 39.1
Land: 55.2 sq. mi.; **Water:** 0.7 sq. mi.

Dover — Township
Lat: 39-00-44 N   **Long:** 95-53-26 W
Pop: 1,220 (1990); 1,124 (1980)   **Pop Density:** 21.7
Land: 56.2 sq. mi.; **Water:** 0.6 sq. mi.

Grove — Township
Lat: 39-10-15 N   **Long:** 95-51-45 W
Pop: 272 (1990); 214 (1980)   **Pop Density:** 9.1
Land: 30.0 sq. mi.; **Water:** 0.1 sq. mi.

Menoken — Township
Lat: 39-08-46 N   **Long:** 95-46-49 W
Pop: 1,203 (1990); 987 (1980)   **Pop Density:** 26.8
Land: 44.9 sq. mi.; **Water:** 0.5 sq. mi.

Mission — Township
Lat: 39-00-16 N   **Long:** 95-47-27 W
Pop: 7,370 (1990); 5,082 (1980)   **Pop Density:** 228.2
Land: 32.3 sq. mi.; **Water:** 0.8 sq. mi.

Monmouth — Township
Lat: 38-56-06 N   **Long:** 95-33-25 W
Pop: 1,912 (1990); 1,645 (1980)   **Pop Density:** 34.0
Land: 56.3 sq. mi.; **Water:** 0.0 sq. mi.

Rossville — City
ZIP: 66533   **Lat:** 39-08-09 N   **Long:** 95-56-58 W
Pop: 1,052 (1990); 1,045 (1980)   **Pop Density:** 2104.0
Land: 0.5 sq. mi.; **Water:** 0.0 sq. mi.   **Elev:** 930 ft.
Incorporated Jun 27, 1881. Not coextensive with the town of the same name.
Name origin: For prominent journalist William W. Ross, who came to KS in 1855.

*Rossville — Township
ZIP: 66533   **Lat:** 39-09-43 N   **Long:** 95-57-53 W
Pop: 1,581 (1990); 1,596 (1980)   **Pop Density:** 30.9
Land: 51.2 sq. mi.; **Water:** 0.6 sq. mi.

Silver Lake — City
ZIP: 66539   **Lat:** 39-05-55 N   **Long:** 95-51-21 W
Pop: 1,390 (1990); 1,350 (1980)   **Pop Density:** 2780.0
Land: 0.5 sq. mi.; **Water:** 0.0 sq. mi.   **Elev:** 911 ft.
Incorporated Apr 18, 1870. Not coextensive with the town of the same name.
Name origin: For the silvery appearance of the water.

*Silver Lake — Township
ZIP: 66539   **Lat:** 39-06-08 N   **Long:** 95-51-31 W
Pop: 1,882 (1990); 1,828 (1980)   **Pop Density:** 105.1
Land: 17.9 sq. mi.; **Water:** 0.5 sq. mi.

Soldier — Township
Lat: 39-09-16 N   **Long:** 95-39-38 W
Pop: 11,491 (1990); 11,017 (1980)   **Pop Density:** 182.1
Land: 63.1 sq. mi.; **Water:** 0.3 sq. mi.

Tecumseh — Township
ZIP: 66542   **Lat:** 39-01-35 N   **Long:** 95-33-43 W
Pop: 7,185 (1990); 6,314 (1980)   **Pop Density:** 204.7
Land: 35.1 sq. mi.; **Water:** 0.8 sq. mi.

Topeka — City
ZIP: 66601   **Lat:** 39-02-16 N   **Long:** 95-41-31 W
Pop: 119,883 (1990); 118,690 (1980)   **Pop Density:** 2171.8
Land: 55.2 sq. mi.; **Water:** 1.0 sq. mi.   **Elev:** 1000 ft.
In northeastern KS on the Kansas River, 55 mi. west of Kansas City. State capital since 1861; founded 1854; incorporated Feb 14, 1857. Important trade center; home of the Menninger Foundation; former headquarters of the Atchison, Topeka, and Santa Fe Railroad.
Name origin: From Siouan, 'a place to find small potatoes.' It is believed that the Indian term designated any edible root, not just the potato.

*Topeka — Township
Lat: 38-58-43 N   **Long:** 95-40-28 W
Pop: 991 (1990); 2,610 (1980)   **Pop Density:** 88.5
Land: 11.2 sq. mi.; **Water:** 0.6 sq. mi.

Willard — City
Lat: 39-05-38 N   **Long:** 95-56-35 W
Pop: 110 (1990); 123 (1980)   **Pop Density:** 1100.0
Land: 0.1 sq. mi.; **Water:** 0.0 sq. mi.   **Elev:** 930 ft.
Incorporated Oct 22, 1912. Part of the town is also in Wabaunsee County.

Williamsport — Township
Lat: 38-54-50 N   **Long:** 95-41-54 W
Pop: 3,829 (1990); 1,924 (1980)   **Pop Density:** 92.7
Land: 41.3 sq. mi.; **Water:** 0.1 sq. mi.

Sheridan County
County Seat: Hoxie (ZIP: 67740)

Pop: 3,043 (1990); 3,544 (1980) **Pop Density:** 3.4
Land: 896.4 sq. mi.; **Water:** 0.2 sq. mi. **Area Code:** 913
In northwestern KS, southwest of Norton; organized Mar 20, 1873 from unorganized territory.
Name origin: For Gen. Philip Henry Sheridan (1831–88), Union officer during the Civil War and commander in chief of the U.S. army (1883–88).

Adell
Township
Lat: 39-31-50 N **Long:** 100-14-41 W
Pop: 23 (1990); 46 (1980) **Pop Density:** 0.4
Land: 54.0 sq. mi.; **Water:** 0.0 sq. mi.

Bloomfield
Township
Lat: 39-26-07 N **Long:** 100-39-50 W
Pop: 59 (1990); 56 (1980) **Pop Density:** 1.6
Land: 36.0 sq. mi.; **Water:** 0.0 sq. mi.

Bowcreek
Township
Lat: 39-25-47 N **Long:** 100-15-51 W
Pop: 60 (1990); 71 (1980) **Pop Density:** 0.8
Land: 71.9 sq. mi.; **Water:** 0.0 sq. mi.

East Saline
Township
Lat: 39-13-10 N **Long:** 100-13-08 W
Pop: 73 (1990); 106 (1980) **Pop Density:** 1.0
Land: 71.8 sq. mi.; **Water:** 0.0 sq. mi.

Hoxie
City
ZIP: 67740 **Lat:** 39-21-19 N **Long:** 100-26-22 W
Pop: 1,342 (1990); 1,462 (1980) **Pop Density:** 1677.5
Land: 0.8 sq. mi.; **Water:** 0.0 sq. mi. **Elev:** 2700 ft.
Incorporated Aug 20, 1886.
Name origin: For railroad builder, H.M. Hoxie.

Kenneth
Township
Lat: 39-21-01 N **Long:** 100-26-32 W
Pop: 1,533 (1990); 1,640 (1980) **Pop Density:** 42.8
Land: 35.8 sq. mi.; **Water:** 0.0 sq. mi.

Logan
Township
Lat: 39-20-39 N **Long:** 100-36-55 W
Pop: 144 (1990); 213 (1980) **Pop Density:** 2.0
Land: 72.0 sq. mi.; **Water:** 0.0 sq. mi.

Parnell
Township
Lat: 39-26-22 N **Long:** 100-29-35 W
Pop: 120 (1990); 124 (1980) **Pop Density:** 1.7
Land: 71.4 sq. mi.; **Water:** 0.0 sq. mi.

Prairie Dog
Township
Lat: 39-31-27 N **Long:** 100-40-13 W
Pop: 73 (1990); 81 (1980) **Pop Density:** 2.0
Land: 35.8 sq. mi.; **Water:** 0.0 sq. mi.

Selden
City
ZIP: 67757 **Lat:** 39-32-28 N **Long:** 100-33-59 W
Pop: 248 (1990); 266 (1980) **Pop Density:** 826.7
Land: 0.3 sq. mi.; **Water:** 0.0 sq. mi. **Elev:** 2837 ft.
Incorporated 1905.

Sheridan
Township
Lat: 39-31-44 N **Long:** 100-31-35 W
Pop: 328 (1990); 386 (1980) **Pop Density:** 6.1
Land: 53.4 sq. mi.; **Water:** 0.0 sq. mi.

Solomon
Township
Lat: 39-12-52 N **Long:** 100-38-24 W
Pop: 240 (1990); 299 (1980) **Pop Density:** 2.2
Land: 107.6 sq. mi.; **Water:** 0.0 sq. mi.

Springbrook
Township
Lat: 39-13-02 N **Long:** 100-27-53 W
Pop: 106 (1990); 156 (1980) **Pop Density:** 1.0
Land: 107.6 sq. mi.; **Water:** 0.0 sq. mi.

Union
Township
Lat: 39-31-28 N **Long:** 100-22-51 W
Pop: 43 (1990); 66 (1980) **Pop Density:** 1.2
Land: 35.7 sq. mi.; **Water:** 0.0 sq. mi.

Valley
Township
Lat: 39-21-14 N **Long:** 100-16-24 W
Pop: 122 (1990); 162 (1980) **Pop Density:** 1.7
Land: 71.7 sq. mi.; **Water:** 0.1 sq. mi.

West Saline
Township
Lat: 39-13-13 N **Long:** 100-19-43 W
Pop: 119 (1990); 138 (1980) **Pop Density:** 1.7
Land: 71.7 sq. mi.; **Water:** 0.0 sq. mi.

Sherman County
County Seat: Goodland (ZIP: 67735)

Pop: 6,926 (1990); 7,759 (1980) **Pop Density:** 6.6
Land: 1055.9 sq. mi.; **Water:** 0.2 sq. mi. **Area Code:** 913
On the northwestern border of KS; organized Mar 20, 1873 from Kirwin Land District.
Name origin: For Gen. William Tecumseh Sherman (1820–91), officer in the Mexican-American War and the Civil War, leader of the "march to the sea" through the Southern states; remembered for the statement "War is hell."

Goodland — City
ZIP: 67735 **Lat:** 39-20-54 N **Long:** 101-42-33 W
Pop: 4,983 (1990); 5,708 (1980) **Pop Density:** 1158.8
Land: 4.3 sq. mi.; **Water:** 0.0 sq. mi. **Elev:** 3683 ft.
In northwestern KS, 28 mi. east of the CO border. Incorporated Sep 5, 1887.
Name origin: For Goodland, IN.

Grant — Township
Lat: 39-29-06 N **Long:** 101-56-30 W
Pop: 123 (1990); 135 (1980) **Pop Density:** 0.9
Land: 136.9 sq. mi.; **Water:** 0.0 sq. mi.

Iowa — Township
Lat: 39-12-23 N **Long:** 101-30-01 W
Pop: 46 (1990); 47 (1980) **Pop Density:** 0.4
Land: 107.6 sq. mi.; **Water:** 0.0 sq. mi.

Itasca — Township
Lat: 39-18-02 N **Long:** 101-39-38 W
Pop: 333 (1990); 327 (1980) **Pop Density:** 9.9
Land: 33.7 sq. mi.; **Water:** 0.0 sq. mi.

Kanorado — City
ZIP: 67741 **Lat:** 39-20-13 N **Long:** 102-02-12 W
Pop: 276 (1990); 217 (1980) **Pop Density:** 920.0
Land: 0.3 sq. mi.; **Water:** 0.0 sq. mi. **Elev:** 3908 ft.
Incorporated 1920.
Name origin: For its location on the border of Kansas and Colorado, a combination of the two names.

Lincoln — Township
Lat: 39-18-25 N **Long:** 101-53-04 W
Pop: 101 (1990); 169 (1980) **Pop Density:** 1.7
Land: 60.1 sq. mi.; **Water:** 0.0 sq. mi.

Llanos — Township
Lat: 39-28-30 N **Long:** 101-26-52 W
Pop: 47 (1990); 71 (1980) **Pop Density:** 0.7
Land: 71.4 sq. mi.; **Water:** 0.0 sq. mi.

Logan — Township
Lat: 39-19-31 N **Long:** 101-47-11 W
Pop: 236 (1990); 220 (1980) **Pop Density:** 4.4
Land: 53.4 sq. mi.; **Water:** 0.0 sq. mi.

McPherson — Township
Lat: 39-10-30 N **Long:** 101-56-52 W
Pop: 53 (1990); 81 (1980) **Pop Density:** 0.8
Land: 67.3 sq. mi.; **Water:** 0.0 sq. mi.

Shermanville — Township
Lat: 39-28-57 N **Long:** 101-34-00 W
Pop: 35 (1990); 41 (1980) **Pop Density:** 0.5
Land: 71.4 sq. mi.; **Water:** 0.0 sq. mi.

Smoky — Township
Lat: 39-12-03 N **Long:** 101-43-40 W
Pop: 96 (1990); 113 (1980) **Pop Density:** 0.9
Land: 108.0 sq. mi.; **Water:** 0.1 sq. mi.

Stateline — Township
Lat: 39-18-32 N **Long:** 101-59-25 W
Pop: 417 (1990); 332 (1980) **Pop Density:** 5.5
Land: 75.4 sq. mi.; **Water:** 0.0 sq. mi.

Union — Township
Lat: 39-20-02 N **Long:** 101-27-01 W
Pop: 53 (1990); 69 (1980) **Pop Density:** 1.0
Land: 53.9 sq. mi.; **Water:** 0.0 sq. mi.

Voltaire — Township
Lat: 39-28-28 N **Long:** 101-43-14 W
Pop: 290 (1990); 287 (1980) **Pop Density:** 1.8
Land: 158.7 sq. mi.; **Water:** 0.0 sq. mi.

Washington — Township
Lat: 39-20-14 N **Long:** 101-33-28 W
Pop: 113 (1990); 159 (1980) **Pop Density:** 2.1
Land: 53.7 sq. mi.; **Water:** 0.0 sq. mi.

Smith County
County Seat: Smith Center (ZIP: 66967)

Pop: 5,078 (1990); 5,947 (1980)   **Pop Density:** 5.7
Land: 895.5 sq. mi.; **Water:** 1.1 sq. mi.   **Area Code:** 913
On the central northern border of KS; established Feb 26, 1867 from unorganized territory.
Name origin: For Maj. J. Nelson Smith (?–1864), Union officer killed at the battle of Little Blue, MO.

Athol   City
ZIP: 66932   **Lat:** 39-45-56 N   **Long:** 98-55-11 W
Pop: 86 (1990); 90 (1980)   **Pop Density:** 430.0
Land: 0.2 sq. mi.; **Water:** 0.0 sq. mi.   **Elev:** 1789 ft.
Incorporated 1911.

Banner   Township
Lat: 39-41-54 N   **Long:** 98-47-16 W
Pop: 60 (1990); 52 (1980)   **Pop Density:** 1.7
Land: 36.0 sq. mi.; **Water:** 0.0 sq. mi.

Beaver   Township
Lat: 39-57-27 N   **Long:** 98-47-09 W
Pop: 83 (1990); 91 (1980)   **Pop Density:** 2.3
Land: 35.9 sq. mi.; **Water:** 0.1 sq. mi.

Blaine   Township
Lat: 39-47-09 N   **Long:** 98-40-18 W
Pop: 75 (1990); 90 (1980)   **Pop Density:** 2.1
Land: 36.0 sq. mi.; **Water:** 0.0 sq. mi.

Cedar   City
ZIP: 67628   **Lat:** 39-39-24 N   **Long:** 98-56-24 W
Pop: 25 (1990); 53 (1980)   **Pop Density:** 125.0
Land: 0.2 sq. mi.; **Water:** 0.0 sq. mi.   **Elev:** 1631 ft.
Incorporated Sep 13, 1916.

*Cedar   Township
ZIP: 67628   **Lat:** 39-46-51 N   **Long:** 99-01-01 W
Pop: 665 (1990); 774 (1980)   **Pop Density:** 18.6
Land: 35.8 sq. mi.; **Water:** 0.0 sq. mi.

Center   Township
Lat: 39-47-04 N   **Long:** 98-47-06 W
Pop: 2,233 (1990); 2,413 (1980)   **Pop Density:** 62.0
Land: 36.0 sq. mi.; **Water:** 0.0 sq. mi.

Cora   Township
Lat: 39-52-45 N   **Long:** 98-40-05 W
Pop: 63 (1990); 86 (1980)   **Pop Density:** 1.8
Land: 35.9 sq. mi.; **Water:** 0.1 sq. mi.

Crystal Plains   Township
Lat: 39-42-10 N   **Long:** 98-40-50 W
Pop: 45 (1990); 64 (1980)   **Pop Density:** 1.3
Land: 35.9 sq. mi.; **Water:** 0.0 sq. mi.

Dor   Township
Lat: 39-36-06 N   **Long:** 99-00-06 W
Pop: 62 (1990); 67 (1980)   **Pop Density:** 1.7
Land: 35.7 sq. mi.; **Water:** 0.1 sq. mi.

Garfield   Township
Lat: 39-37-04 N   **Long:** 98-40-23 W
Pop: 35 (1990); 46 (1980)   **Pop Density:** 1.0
Land: 35.9 sq. mi.; **Water:** 0.0 sq. mi.

Gaylord   City
ZIP: 67638   **Lat:** 39-38-46 N   **Long:** 98-50-48 W
Pop: 173 (1990); 203 (1980)   **Pop Density:** 576.7
Land: 0.3 sq. mi.; **Water:** 0.0 sq. mi.   **Elev:** 1592 ft.
Incorporated Jul 9, 1886.

German   Township
Lat: 39-58-07 N   **Long:** 99-00-42 W
Pop: 41 (1990); 40 (1980)   **Pop Density:** 1.2
Land: 35.4 sq. mi.; **Water:** 0.1 sq. mi.

Harlan   Township
ZIP: 67641   **Lat:** 39-36-40 N   **Long:** 98-46-53 W
Pop: 91 (1990); 145 (1980)   **Pop Density:** 2.5
Land: 35.9 sq. mi.; **Water:** 0.0 sq. mi.

Harvey   Township
Lat: 39-42-01 N   **Long:** 98-54-20 W
Pop: 119 (1990); 167 (1980)   **Pop Density:** 3.3
Land: 35.9 sq. mi.; **Water:** 0.0 sq. mi.

Houston   Township
Lat: 39-36-58 N   **Long:** 98-53-46 W
Pop: 231 (1990); 297 (1980)   **Pop Density:** 6.4
Land: 35.9 sq. mi.; **Water:** 0.1 sq. mi.

Kensington   City
ZIP: 66951   **Lat:** 39-46-02 N   **Long:** 99-01-55 W
Pop: 553 (1990); 681 (1980)   **Pop Density:** 1843.3
Land: 0.3 sq. mi.; **Water:** 0.0 sq. mi.   **Elev:** 1784 ft.
Incorporated Jun 6, 1900.
Name origin: For Kensington, England.

Lane   Township
Lat: 39-47-07 N   **Long:** 98-53-56 W
Pop: 164 (1990); 187 (1980)   **Pop Density:** 4.6
Land: 35.9 sq. mi.; **Water:** 0.0 sq. mi.

Lebanon   City
ZIP: 66952   **Lat:** 39-48-37 N   **Long:** 98-33-25 W
Pop: 364 (1990); 440 (1980)   **Pop Density:** 1213.3
Land: 0.3 sq. mi.; **Water:** 0.0 sq. mi.   **Elev:** 1821 ft.
Incorporated Jan 12, 1889.
Name origin: For Lebanon, KY, former home of an early settler.

Lincoln   Township
Lat: 39-36-11 N   **Long:** 98-33-40 W
Pop: 90 (1990); 126 (1980)   **Pop Density:** 2.5
Land: 35.8 sq. mi.; **Water:** 0.1 sq. mi.

Logan   Township
Lat: 39-57-38 N   **Long:** 98-33-25 W
Pop: 55 (1990); 89 (1980)   **Pop Density:** 1.5
Land: 35.7 sq. mi.; **Water:** 0.1 sq. mi.

KANSAS, Smith County   American Places Dictionary

Martin
Township
Lat: 39-57-29 N **Long:** 98-53-54 W
Pop: 44 (1990); 51 (1980)   **Pop Density:** 1.2
Land: 35.7 sq. mi.; **Water:** 0.1 sq. mi.

Oak
Township
Lat: 39-47-03 N **Long:** 98-33-38 W
Pop: 466 (1990); 565 (1980)   **Pop Density:** 13.0
Land: 35.9 sq. mi.; **Water:** 0.0 sq. mi.

Pawnee
Township
Lat: 39-57-35 N **Long:** 98-39-41 W
Pop: 56 (1990); 82 (1980)   **Pop Density:** 1.6
Land: 35.6 sq. mi.; **Water:** 0.2 sq. mi.

Pleasant
Township
Lat: 39-52-26 N **Long:** 98-53-45 W
Pop: 66 (1990); 83 (1980)   **Pop Density:** 1.8
Land: 35.8 sq. mi.; **Water:** 0.0 sq. mi.

Smith Center
City
ZIP: 66967   **Lat:** 39-46-46 N **Long:** 98-46-59 W
Pop: 2,016 (1990); 2,240 (1980)   **Pop Density:** 1832.7
Land: 1.1 sq. mi.; **Water:** 0.0 sq. mi.   **Elev:** 1800 ft.
Incorporated 1886.
Name origin: For Civil War hero James Nelson Smith.

Swan
Township
Lat: 39-52-20 N **Long:** 99-00-37 W
Pop: 57 (1990); 72 (1980)   **Pop Density:** 1.6
Land: 35.5 sq. mi.; **Water:** 0.1 sq. mi.

Valley
Township
Lat: 39-42-00 N **Long:** 99-00-41 W
Pop: 89 (1990); 106 (1980)   **Pop Density:** 2.5
Land: 35.8 sq. mi.; **Water:** 0.0 sq. mi.

Washington
Township
Lat: 39-52-25 N **Long:** 98-46-56 W
Pop: 75 (1990); 93 (1980)   **Pop Density:** 2.1
Land: 35.9 sq. mi.; **Water:** 0.0 sq. mi.

Webster
Township
Lat: 39-41-29 N **Long:** 98-33-51 W
Pop: 53 (1990); 79 (1980)   **Pop Density:** 1.5
Land: 35.8 sq. mi.; **Water:** 0.0 sq. mi.

White Rock
Township
Lat: 39-52-09 N **Long:** 98-33-50 W
Pop: 60 (1990); 82 (1980)   **Pop Density:** 1.7
Land: 35.9 sq. mi.; **Water:** 0.0 sq. mi.

Stafford County
County Seat: Saint John (ZIP: 67576)

Pop: 5,365 (1990); 5,694 (1980)   **Pop Density:** 6.8
Land: 792.1 sq. mi.; **Water:** 2.7 sq. mi.   **Area Code:** 316
In south-central KS, west of Hutchinson; established Feb 26, 1867 from unorganized territory.
Name origin: For Capt. Lewis Stafford (?–1863), Union army officer killed at Young's Point, LA.

Albano
Township
Lat: 37-52-17 N **Long:** 98-51-58 W
Pop: 61 (1990); 76 (1980)   **Pop Density:** 1.7
Land: 36.3 sq. mi.; **Water:** 0.0 sq. mi.

Byron
Township
Lat: 38-12-49 N **Long:** 98-38-05 W
Pop: 88 (1990); 106 (1980)   **Pop Density:** 2.4
Land: 36.4 sq. mi.; **Water:** 0.0 sq. mi.

Clear Creek
Township
Lat: 37-53-00 N **Long:** 98-57-29 W
Pop: 47 (1990); 60 (1980)   **Pop Density:** 1.3
Land: 36.1 sq. mi.; **Water:** 0.0 sq. mi.

Cleveland
Township
Lat: 38-02-27 N **Long:** 98-51-11 W
Pop: 102 (1990); 91 (1980)   **Pop Density:** 2.8
Land: 36.1 sq. mi.; **Water:** 0.0 sq. mi.   **Elev:** 2119 ft.

Douglas
Township
Lat: 38-08-15 N **Long:** 98-50-54 W
Pop: 156 (1990); 165 (1980)   **Pop Density:** 4.3
Land: 36.0 sq. mi.; **Water:** 0.0 sq. mi.

East Cooper
Township
Lat: 38-02-17 N **Long:** 98-31-55 W
Pop: 84 (1990); 77 (1980)   **Pop Density:** 2.4
Land: 35.5 sq. mi.; **Water:** 0.3 sq. mi.

Fairview
Township
Lat: 37-57-29 N **Long:** 98-31-03 W
Pop: 117 (1990); 122 (1980)   **Pop Density:** 3.3
Land: 36.0 sq. mi.; **Water:** 0.0 sq. mi.

Farmington
Township
Lat: 37-57-21 N **Long:** 98-58-00 W
Pop: 569 (1990); 614 (1980)   **Pop Density:** 15.8
Land: 36.1 sq. mi.; **Water:** 0.0 sq. mi.

Hayes
Township
Lat: 38-07-19 N **Long:** 98-37-41 W
Pop: 251 (1990); 275 (1980)   **Pop Density:** 7.0
Land: 36.0 sq. mi.; **Water:** 0.0 sq. mi.

Hudson
City
ZIP: 67545   **Lat:** 38-06-14 N **Long:** 98-39-36 W
Pop: 159 (1990); 157 (1980)   **Pop Density:** 1590.0
Land: 0.1 sq. mi.; **Water:** 0.0 sq. mi.   **Elev:** 1865 ft.
Incorporated 1905.
Name origin: For Hudson, WI.

Lincoln
Township
Lat: 38-12-37 N **Long:** 98-50-54 W
Pop: 164 (1990); 146 (1980)   **Pop Density:** 4.6
Land: 35.8 sq. mi.; **Water:** 0.0 sq. mi.

American Places Dictionary   KANSAS, Stanton County

Macksville — City
ZIP: 67557   Lat: 37-57-25 N   **Long:** 98-58-05 W
Pop: 488 (1990); 546 (1980)   Pop Density: 488.0
Land: 1.0 sq. mi.; Water: 0.0 sq. mi.   Elev: 2035 ft.
Incorporated 1886.

North Seward — Township
Lat: 38-12-46 N   **Long:** 98-44-35 W
Pop: 249 (1990); 224 (1980)   Pop Density: 6.9
Land: 36.1 sq. mi.; Water: 0.0 sq. mi.

Ohio — Township
Lat: 37-57-20 N   **Long:** 98-44-38 W
Pop: 441 (1990); 453 (1980)   Pop Density: 12.1
Land: 36.5 sq. mi.; Water: 0.0 sq. mi.

Putnam — Township
Lat: 38-10-41 N   **Long:** 98-31-47 W
Pop: 42 (1990); 39 (1980)   Pop Density: 0.6
Land: 70.4 sq. mi.; Water: 2.1 sq. mi.

Radium — City
Lat: 38-10-25 N   **Long:** 98-53-37 W
Pop: 47 (1990); 47 (1980)   Pop Density: 1175.0
Land: 0.04 sq. mi.; Water: 0.0 sq. mi.   Elev: 1951 ft.
Incorporated Jan 1934.
Name origin: For the element that is found in the area.

Richland — Township
Lat: 37-57-11 N   **Long:** 98-51-01 W
Pop: 77 (1990); 80 (1980)   Pop Density: 2.1
Land: 36.2 sq. mi.; Water: 0.0 sq. mi.

Rose Valley — Township
Lat: 37-51-41 N   **Long:** 98-44-17 W
Pop: 81 (1990); 93 (1980)   Pop Density: 2.2
Land: 36.4 sq. mi.; Water: 0.0 sq. mi.

St. John — City
ZIP: 67576   Lat: 38-00-03 N   **Long:** 98-45-38 W
Pop: 1,357 (1990); 1,501 (1980)   Pop Density: 753.9
Land: 1.8 sq. mi.; Water: 0.0 sq. mi.   Elev: 1909 ft.
Incorporated Sep 30, 1885.
Name origin: For KS governor John P. St. John.

*St. John — Township
Lat: 38-01-57 N   **Long:** 98-45-06 W
Pop: 1,093 (1990); 1,221 (1980)   Pop Density: 30.1
Land: 36.3 sq. mi.; Water: 0.0 sq. mi.

Seward — City
ZIP: 67577   Lat: 38-10-39 N   **Long:** 98-47-37 W
Pop: 71 (1990); 88 (1980)   Pop Density: 355.0
Land: 0.2 sq. mi.; Water: 0.0 sq. mi.   Elev: 1913 ft.
Incorporated Sep 5, 1927.
Name origin: For William Seward (1801–72), U.S. secretary of state during the Civil War.

South Seward — Township
Lat: 38-07-58 N   **Long:** 98-44-34 W
Pop: 87 (1990); 85 (1980)   Pop Density: 2.4
Land: 35.9 sq. mi.; Water: 0.0 sq. mi.

Stafford — City
ZIP: 67578   Lat: 37-57-45 N   **Long:** 98-35-57 W
Pop: 1,344 (1990); 1,425 (1980)   Pop Density: 1493.3
Land: 0.9 sq. mi.; Water: 0.0 sq. mi.   Elev: 1858 ft.
Incorporated Sep 10, 1885. Not coextensive with the town of the same name.
Name origin: For Civil War hero Capt. Lewis Stafford.

*Stafford — Township
ZIP: 67578   Lat: 37-57-06 N   **Long:** 98-37-48 W
Pop: 1,461 (1990); 1,574 (1980)   Pop Density: 40.5
Land: 36.1 sq. mi.; Water: 0.0 sq. mi.

Union — Township
Lat: 37-52-06 N   **Long:** 98-38-10 W
Pop: 38 (1990); 58 (1980)   Pop Density: 1.1
Land: 36.1 sq. mi.; Water: 0.0 sq. mi.

West Cooper — Township
Lat: 38-02-29 N   **Long:** 98-38-11 W
Pop: 85 (1990); 74 (1980)   Pop Density: 2.4
Land: 35.9 sq. mi.; Water: 0.1 sq. mi.

York — Township
Lat: 37-52-13 N   **Long:** 98-31-38 W
Pop: 72 (1990); 61 (1980)   Pop Density: 2.0
Land: 35.9 sq. mi.; Water: 0.1 sq. mi.

Stanton County
County Seat: Johnson (ZIP: 67855)

Pop: 2,333 (1990); 2,339 (1980)   Pop Density: 3.4
Land: 680.1 sq. mi.; Water: 0.1 sq. mi.   Area Code: 316

On the southwestern border of KS, southwest of Garden City; created Mar 6, 1873, later abolished and made part of Hamilton County; in 1887 Stanton County was reorganized from Hamilton County.

Name origin: For Edwin McMasters Stanton (1814–69), U.S. Attorney General (1860–61) and U.S. Secretary of War under Abraham Lincoln and Andrew Johnson (1862–68).

Big Bow — Township
ZIP: 67855   Lat: 37-33-18 N   **Long:** 101-36-28 W
Pop: 415 (1990); 442 (1980)   Pop Density: 1.9
Land: 215.6 sq. mi.; Water: 0.0 sq. mi.

Johnson — City
ZIP: 67855   Lat: 37-34-10 N   **Long:** 101-45-08 W
Pop: 1,348 (1990); 1,244 (1980)   Pop Density: 1225.5
Land: 1.1 sq. mi.; Water: 0.0 sq. mi.
Incorporated Jan 4, 1888.

KANSAS, Stanton County

Manter City
ZIP: 67862 Lat: 37-31-27 N Long: 101-52-57 W
Pop: 186 (1990); 205 (1980) Pop Density: 930.0
Land: 0.2 sq. mi.; Water: 0.0 sq. mi. Elev: 3490 ft.
Incorporated Jan 28, 1924.
Name origin: For local Santa Fe Railroad official.

*Manter Township
ZIP: 67862 Lat: 37-33-29 N Long: 101-56-27 W
Pop: 354 (1990); 426 (1980) Pop Density: 1.4
Land: 249.8 sq. mi.; Water: 0.0 sq. mi.

Stanton Township
Lat: 37-33-43 N Long: 101-46-22 W
Pop: 1,564 (1990); 1,471 (1980) Pop Density: 7.3
Land: 214.6 sq. mi.; Water: 0.0 sq. mi.

Stevens County
County Seat: Hugoton (ZIP: 67951)

Pop: 5,048 (1990); 4,736 (1980) Pop Density: 6.9
Land: 727.6 sq. mi.; Water: 0.2 sq. mi. Area Code: 316
On the southwestern border of KS; organized Mar 6, 1873 from Indian lands.
Name origin: For Thaddeus Stevens (1792–1868), U.S. representative from PA (1849–53; 1859–68) who strongly opposed slavery.

Banner Township
Lat: 37-03-40 N Long: 101-10-46 W
Pop: 204 (1990); 199 (1980) Pop Density: 1.9
Land: 107.0 sq. mi.; Water: 0.0 sq. mi.

Center Township
Lat: 37-10-38 N Long: 101-13-15 W
Pop: 3,735 (1990); 3,521 (1980) Pop Density: 34.6
Land: 108.0 sq. mi.; Water: 0.0 sq. mi.

Harmony Township
Lat: 37-19-21 N Long: 101-26-53 W
Pop: 146 (1990); 178 (1980) Pop Density: 1.4
Land: 108.0 sq. mi.; Water: 0.0 sq. mi.

Hugoton City
ZIP: 67951 Lat: 37-10-34 N Long: 101-20-48 W
Pop: 3,179 (1990); 3,165 (1980) Pop Density: 2270.7
Land: 1.4 sq. mi.; Water: 0.0 sq. mi. Elev: 3111 ft.
Incorporated Jan 1910.
Name origin: For 19th-century French author, Victor Hugo (1802–85).

Moscow City
ZIP: 67952 Lat: 37-19-31 N Long: 101-12-22 W
Pop: 252 (1990); 228 (1980) Pop Density: 1260.0
Land: 0.2 sq. mi.; Water: 0.0 sq. mi. Elev: 3045 ft.
Incorporated May 6, 1929.
Name origin: For the capital of Russia.

*Moscow Township
ZIP: 67952 Lat: 37-18-27 N Long: 101-12-10 W
Pop: 658 (1990); 556 (1980) Pop Density: 3.9
Land: 170.6 sq. mi.; Water: 0.2 sq. mi.

Voorhees Township
Lat: 37-03-13 N Long: 101-25-09 W
Pop: 148 (1990); 128 (1980) Pop Density: 1.1
Land: 134.9 sq. mi.; Water: 0.0 sq. mi.

West Center Township
Lat: 37-11-29 N Long: 101-27-21 W
Pop: 157 (1990); 154 (1980) Pop Density: 1.6
Land: 99.1 sq. mi.; Water: 0.0 sq. mi.

Sumner County
County Seat: Wellington (ZIP: 67152)

Pop: 25,841 (1990); 24,928 (1980) Pop Density: 21.9
Land: 1181.9 sq. mi.; Water: 3.0 sq. mi. Area Code: 316
On the central southern border of KS, south of Wichita; organized Feb 26, 1867 from Cowley County.
Name origin: For Charles Sumner (1811–74), a founder (1848) of the Free-Soil Party and U.S. senator from MA (1851–74); he was physically beaten on the floor of the Senate for his anti-slavery stand.

Argonia City
ZIP: 67004 Lat: 37-15-55 N Long: 97-45-52 W
Pop: 529 (1990); 587 (1980) Pop Density: 1322.5
Land: 0.4 sq. mi.; Water: 0.0 sq. mi. Elev: 1255 ft.
Incorporated 1885.
Name origin: For Jason's ship *Argo* in Greek mythology, with a euphonious ending.

Avon Township
Lat: 37-15-57 N Long: 97-18-54 W
Pop: 293 (1990); 278 (1980) Pop Density: 8.2
Land: 35.7 sq. mi.; Water: 0.0 sq. mi.

American Places Dictionary   KANSAS, Sumner County

Belle Plaine — City
ZIP: 67013   **Lat:** 37-23-39 N   **Long:** 97-16-43 W
Pop: 1,649 (1990); 1,706 (1980)   **Pop Density:** 2061.3
Land: 0.8 sq. mi.; **Water:** 0.0 sq. mi.   **Elev:** 1230 ft.
Incorporated May 10, 1884. Not coextensive with the town of the same name.
Name origin: From French for the 'beautiful prairie' surrounding the town.

*Belle Plaine — Township
ZIP: 67013   **Lat:** 37-25-28 N   **Long:** 97-17-30 W
Pop: 3,543 (1990); 2,926 (1980)   **Pop Density:** 87.7
Land: 40.4 sq. mi.; **Water:** 0.3 sq. mi.

Bluff — Township
Lat: 37-03-48 N   **Long:** 97-44-35 W
Pop: 106 (1990); 136 (1980)   **Pop Density:** 2.0
Land: 52.6 sq. mi.; **Water:** 0.0 sq. mi.

Caldwell — City
ZIP: 67022   **Lat:** 37-02-06 N   **Long:** 97-36-31 W
Pop: 1,351 (1990); 1,401 (1980)   **Pop Density:** 1228.2
Land: 1.1 sq. mi.; **Water:** 0.0 sq. mi.   **Elev:** 1149 ft.
Incorporated Jul 29, 1879.
Name origin: For U.S. senator from KS Alexander Caldwell.

*Caldwell — Township
Lat: 37-03-41 N   **Long:** 97-37-50 W
Pop: 195 (1990); 313 (1980)   **Pop Density:** 3.7
Land: 52.5 sq. mi.; **Water:** 0.0 sq. mi.

Chikaskia — Township
Lat: 37-10-03 N   **Long:** 97-38-02 W
Pop: 67 (1990); 112 (1980)   **Pop Density:** 1.9
Land: 36.2 sq. mi.; **Water:** 0.0 sq. mi.

Conway — Township
Lat: 37-25-59 N   **Long:** 97-38-38 W
Pop: 1,249 (1990); 1,244 (1980)   **Pop Density:** 34.5
Land: 36.2 sq. mi.; **Water:** 0.0 sq. mi.

Conway Springs — City
ZIP: 67031   **Lat:** 37-23-22 N   **Long:** 97-38-38 W
Pop: 1,384 (1990); 1,313 (1980)   **Pop Density:** 2306.7
Land: 0.6 sq. mi.; **Water:** 0.0 sq. mi.   **Elev:** 1366 ft.
Incorporated Jul 26, 1886.
Name origin: Named by J.L. Johnson for his former home in NH and for a favorite author, Moncure D. Conway.

Creek — Township
Lat: 37-20-34 N   **Long:** 97-44-51 W
Pop: 223 (1990); 177 (1980)   **Pop Density:** 6.1
Land: 36.6 sq. mi.; **Water:** 0.0 sq. mi.

Dixon — Township
Lat: 37-15-31 N   **Long:** 97-45-06 W
Pop: 726 (1990); 783 (1980)   **Pop Density:** 19.9
Land: 36.5 sq. mi.; **Water:** 0.0 sq. mi.

Downs — Township
Lat: 37-10-17 N   **Long:** 97-31-47 W
Pop: 200 (1990); 174 (1980)   **Pop Density:** 5.6
Land: 35.8 sq. mi.; **Water:** 0.0 sq. mi.

Eden — Township
Lat: 37-25-44 N   **Long:** 97-45-30 W
Pop: 353 (1990); 324 (1980)   **Pop Density:** 9.6
Land: 36.8 sq. mi.; **Water:** 0.0 sq. mi.

Falls — Township
Lat: 37-03-38 N   **Long:** 97-31-40 W
Pop: 193 (1990); 252 (1980)   **Pop Density:** 3.6
Land: 53.5 sq. mi.; **Water:** 0.0 sq. mi.

Geuda Springs — City
ZIP: 67051   **Lat:** 37-06-40 N   **Long:** 97-09-06 W
Pop: 185 (1990); 202 (1980)   **Pop Density:** 925.0
Land: 0.2 sq. mi.; **Water:** 0.0 sq. mi.   **Elev:** 1120 ft.
Incorporated Apr 1884. Part of the town is also in Cowley County.
Name origin: For nearby 'healing springs.'

Gore — Township
Lat: 37-25-30 N   **Long:** 97-11-30 W
Pop: 2,317 (1990); 2,229 (1980)   **Pop Density:** 72.6
Land: 31.9 sq. mi.; **Water:** 0.5 sq. mi.

Greene — Township
Lat: 37-10-27 N   **Long:** 97-18-58 W
Pop: 91 (1990); 92 (1980)   **Pop Density:** 2.5
Land: 35.8 sq. mi.; **Water:** 0.0 sq. mi.

Guelph — Township
Lat: 37-03-43 N   **Long:** 97-18-58 W
Pop: 158 (1990); 171 (1980)   **Pop Density:** 2.9
Land: 54.6 sq. mi.; **Water:** 0.0 sq. mi.

Harmon — Township
Lat: 37-20-15 N   **Long:** 97-19-12 W
Pop: 271 (1990); 237 (1980)   **Pop Density:** 8.9
Land: 30.6 sq. mi.; **Water:** 0.0 sq. mi.

Hunnewell — City
ZIP: 67140   **Lat:** 37-00-16 N   **Long:** 97-24-24 W
Pop: 87 (1990); 86 (1980)   **Pop Density:** 174.0
Land: 0.5 sq. mi.; **Water:** 0.0 sq. mi.   **Elev:** 1105 ft.
Incorporated 1882.

Illinois — Township
Lat: 37-26-11 N   **Long:** 97-32-27 W
Pop: 133 (1990); 130 (1980)   **Pop Density:** 3.7
Land: 36.4 sq. mi.; **Water:** 0.0 sq. mi.

Jackson — Township
Lat: 37-10-26 N   **Long:** 97-25-22 W
Pop: 173 (1990); 175 (1980)   **Pop Density:** 4.8
Land: 36.3 sq. mi.; **Water:** 0.0 sq. mi.

London — Township
Lat: 37-26-01 N   **Long:** 97-24-47 W
Pop: 617 (1990); 603 (1980)   **Pop Density:** 14.9
Land: 41.3 sq. mi.; **Water:** 0.4 sq. mi.

Mayfield — City
ZIP: 67103   **Lat:** 37-15-44 N   **Long:** 97-32-43 W
Pop: 110 (1990); 128 (1980)   **Pop Density:** 1100.0
Land: 0.1 sq. mi.; **Water:** 0.0 sq. mi.   **Elev:** 1281 ft.
Incorporated Apr 5, 1927.

Milan — City
ZIP: 67105   **Lat:** 37-15-29 N   **Long:** 97-40-22 W
Pop: 109 (1990); 135 (1980)   **Pop Density:** 1090.0
Land: 0.1 sq. mi.; **Water:** 0.0 sq. mi.   **Elev:** 1221 ft.
Incorporated 1890.
Name origin: For Milan, Italy.

Morris — Township
Lat: 37-10-11 N   **Long:** 97-44-46 W
Pop: 58 (1990); 48 (1980)   **Pop Density:** 1.6
Land: 36.5 sq. mi.; **Water:** 0.0 sq. mi.

Mulvane
City
ZIP: 67110 **Lat:** 37-28-22 N **Long:** 97-14-33 W
Pop: 1,208 (1990); 1,260 (1980) **Pop Density:** 2416.0
Land: 0.5 sq. mi.; **Water:** 0.0 sq. mi. **Elev:** 1250 ft.
Incorporated Sep 27, 1883. Part of the town is also in Sedgwick County. In south-central KS.
Name origin: For the Mulvane brothers, who were Topeka bankers and land developers.

Osborne
Township
Lat: 37-15-16 N **Long:** 97-32-02 W
Pop: 353 (1990); 278 (1980) **Pop Density:** 10.0
Land: 35.4 sq. mi.; **Water:** 0.5 sq. mi.

Oxford
City
ZIP: 67119 **Lat:** 37-16-29 N **Long:** 97-10-10 W
Pop: 1,143 (1990); 1,125 (1980) **Pop Density:** 1428.8
Land: 0.8 sq. mi.; **Water:** 0.0 sq. mi. **Elev:** 1185 ft.
Incorporated Oct 10, 1879. Not coextensive with the town of the same name.
Name origin: For Oxford University in England.

*Oxford
Township
ZIP: 67119 **Lat:** 37-15-51 N **Long:** 97-11-42 W
Pop: 1,387 (1990); 1,346 (1980) **Pop Density:** 36.4
Land: 38.1 sq. mi.; **Water:** 0.4 sq. mi.

Palestine
Township
Lat: 37-21-06 N **Long:** 97-13-03 W
Pop: 258 (1990); 271 (1980) **Pop Density:** 9.2
Land: 28.0 sq. mi.; **Water:** 0.4 sq. mi.

Ryan
Township
Lat: 37-15-24 N **Long:** 97-38-15 W
Pop: 238 (1990); 239 (1980) **Pop Density:** 6.7
Land: 35.5 sq. mi.; **Water:** 0.0 sq. mi.

Seventy-Six
Township
Lat: 37-20-39 N **Long:** 97-25-17 W
Pop: 253 (1990); 248 (1980) **Pop Density:** 7.1
Land: 35.8 sq. mi.; **Water:** 0.0 sq. mi.

South Haven
City
ZIP: 67140 **Lat:** 37-02-56 N **Long:** 97-24-01 W
Pop: 420 (1990); 439 (1980) **Pop Density:** 525.0
Land: 0.8 sq. mi.; **Water:** 0.0 sq. mi. **Elev:** 1121 ft.
Incorporated Jul 6, 1887. Not coextensive with the town of the same name.

*South Haven
Township
ZIP: 67140 **Lat:** 37-03-36 N **Long:** 97-25-18 W
Pop: 710 (1990); 733 (1980) **Pop Density:** 13.1
Land: 54.0 sq. mi.; **Water:** 0.0 sq. mi.

Springdale
Township
Lat: 37-20-38 N **Long:** 97-38-18 W
Pop: 685 (1990); 565 (1980) **Pop Density:** 19.1
Land: 35.8 sq. mi.; **Water:** 0.0 sq. mi.

Sumner
Township
Lat: 37-20-45 N **Long:** 97-31-36 W
Pop: 174 (1990); 180 (1980) **Pop Density:** 4.8
Land: 36.2 sq. mi.; **Water:** 0.0 sq. mi.

Valverde
Township
Lat: 37-10-30 N **Long:** 97-12-27 W
Pop: 128 (1990); 140 (1980) **Pop Density:** 3.6
Land: 35.8 sq. mi.; **Water:** 0.3 sq. mi.

Walton
Township
Lat: 37-03-36 N **Long:** 97-12-27 W
Pop: 503 (1990); 454 (1980) **Pop Density:** 9.4
Land: 53.6 sq. mi.; **Water:** 0.0 sq. mi.

Wellington
City
ZIP: 67152 **Lat:** 37-16-16 N **Long:** 97-23-49 W
Pop: 8,411 (1990); 8,212 (1980) **Pop Density:** 1716.5
Land: 4.9 sq. mi.; **Water:** 0.1 sq. mi. **Elev:** 1230 ft.
In southern KS, 30 mi. south of Wichita. Incorporated Nov 13, 1872.
Name origin: For the famous British general and statesman Arthur Wellesley, Duke of Wellington (1769–1852).

*Wellington
Township
ZIP: 67152 **Lat:** 37-15-22 N **Long:** 97-25-22 W
Pop: 424 (1990); 457 (1980) **Pop Density:** 13.6
Land: 31.2 sq. mi.; **Water:** 0.0 sq. mi.

Thomas County
County Seat: Colby (ZIP: 67701)

Pop: 8,258 (1990); 8,451 (1980) **Pop Density:** 7.7
Land: 1074.9 sq. mi.; **Water:** 0.1 sq. mi. **Area Code:** 913
In northwestern KS; organized Mar 6, 1873 from Kirwin Land District; reorganized Oct 8, 1895 with territory annexed from Logan County.
Name origin: For Gen. George Henry Thomas (1816–70), Union commander of the Army of the Cumberland.

Barrett
Township
Lat: 39-29-47 N **Long:** 101-16-26 W
Pop: 153 (1990); 178 (1980) **Pop Density:** 1.4
Land: 106.6 sq. mi.; **Water:** 0.0 sq. mi.

Brewster
City
ZIP: 67732 **Lat:** 39-21-46 N **Long:** 101-22-38 W
Pop: 296 (1990); 327 (1980) **Pop Density:** 986.7
Land: 0.3 sq. mi.; **Water:** 0.0 sq. mi. **Elev:** 3428 ft.
Incorporated Apr 6, 1920.
Name origin: For Rock Island Railway director L.D. Brewster.

Colby   City
ZIP: 67701   **Lat:** 39-23-15 N   **Long:** 101-02-45 W
Pop: 5,396 (1990); 5,544 (1980)   **Pop Density:** 1740.6
Land: 3.1 sq. mi.; **Water:** 0.0 sq. mi.   **Elev:** 3160 ft.
Incorporated Jul 16, 1886.

East Hale   Township
                    Lat: 39-22-52 N   **Long:** 101-13-38 W
Pop: 143 (1990); 146 (1980)   **Pop Density:** 2.7
Land: 53.9 sq. mi.; **Water:** 0.0 sq. mi.

Gem   City
ZIP: 67734   **Lat:** 39-25-32 N   **Long:** 100-53-48 W
Pop: 104 (1990); 101 (1980)   **Pop Density:** 346.7
Land: 0.3 sq. mi.; **Water:** 0.0 sq. mi.   **Elev:** 3090 ft.
Incorporated Dec 7, 1926.
Name origin: A reference to the 'precious' nature of the area.

Kingery   Township
                    Lat: 39-13-11 N   **Long:** 101-16-51 W
Pop: 100 (1990); 113 (1980)   **Pop Density:** 0.7
Land: 143.9 sq. mi.; **Water:** 0.0 sq. mi.

Lacey   Township
                    Lat: 39-25-53 N   **Long:** 100-53-09 W
Pop: 157 (1990); 158 (1980)   **Pop Density:** 4.4
Land: 35.7 sq. mi.; **Water:** 0.0 sq. mi.

Menlo   City
ZIP: 67746   **Lat:** 39-21-22 N   **Long:** 100-43-26 W
Pop: 50 (1990); 42 (1980)   **Pop Density:** 500.0
Land: 0.1 sq. mi.; **Water:** 0.0 sq. mi.   **Elev:** 2945 ft.
Incorporated Apr 25, 1926. Not coextensive with the town of the same name.

*Menlo   Township
ZIP: 67746   **Lat:** 39-20-05 N   **Long:** 100-46-51 W
Pop: 113 (1990); 125 (1980)   **Pop Density:** 2.1
Land: 54.1 sq. mi.; **Water:** 0.0 sq. mi.

Morgan   Township
                    Lat: 39-22-21 N   **Long:** 101-03-39 W
Pop: 759 (1990); 568 (1980)   **Pop Density:** 7.2
Land: 104.9 sq. mi.; **Water:** 0.0 sq. mi.

North Randall   Township
                    Lat: 39-19-43 N   **Long:** 100-52-45 W
Pop: 91 (1990); 117 (1980)   **Pop Density:** 1.7
Land: 53.3 sq. mi.; **Water:** 0.0 sq. mi.

Oakley   City
ZIP: 67748   **Lat:** 39-08-01 N   **Long:** 100-51-31 W
Pop: 58 (1990); 75 (1980)   **Pop Density:** 1933.3
Land: 0.03 sq. mi.; **Water:** 0.0 sq. mi.   **Elev:** 350 ft.
Incorporated Oct 15, 1887. Part of the town is also in Logan County.
Name origin: For Miss Eliza Oakley. Originally called Carlyle.

Rexford   City
ZIP: 67753   **Lat:** 39-28-13 N   **Long:** 100-44-36 W
Pop: 171 (1990); 204 (1980)   **Pop Density:** 570.0
Land: 0.3 sq. mi.; **Water:** 0.0 sq. mi.   **Elev:** 2955 ft.
Incorporated Apr 2, 1917.

Rovohl   Township
                    Lat: 39-30-33 N   **Long:** 101-03-13 W
Pop: 169 (1990); 171 (1980)   **Pop Density:** 1.6
Land: 107.0 sq. mi.; **Water:** 0.0 sq. mi.

Smith   Township
                    Lat: 39-26-20 N   **Long:** 100-46-53 W
Pop: 246 (1990); 280 (1980)   **Pop Density:** 6.9
Land: 35.9 sq. mi.; **Water:** 0.0 sq. mi.

South Randall   Township
                    Lat: 39-11-54 N   **Long:** 100-49-36 W
Pop: 270 (1990); 315 (1980)   **Pop Density:** 2.5
Land: 107.6 sq. mi.; **Water:** 0.0 sq. mi.

Summers   Township
                    Lat: 39-13-05 N   **Long:** 101-03-39 W
Pop: 207 (1990); 212 (1980)   **Pop Density:** 1.4
Land: 144.2 sq. mi.; **Water:** 0.0 sq. mi.

Wendell   Township
                    Lat: 39-31-03 N   **Long:** 100-49-19 W
Pop: 80 (1990); 114 (1980)   **Pop Density:** 1.1
Land: 70.8 sq. mi.; **Water:** 0.0 sq. mi.

West Hale   Township
                    Lat: 39-22-26 N   **Long:** 101-19-30 W
Pop: 374 (1990); 410 (1980)   **Pop Density:** 6.9
Land: 53.9 sq. mi.; **Water:** 0.0 sq. mi.

Trego County
County Seat: WaKeeney (ZIP: 67672)

Pop: 3,694 (1990); 4,165 (1980)   **Pop Density:** 4.2
Land: 888.4 sq. mi.; **Water:** 10.7 sq. mi.   **Area Code:** 913
In west-central KS, west of Hays; established Feb 26, 1867.
Name origin: For Capt. Edgar P. Trego (?–1863), Union army officer killed at Chickamauga, TN.

Collyer   City
ZIP: 67631   **Lat:** 39-02-16 N   **Long:** 100-07-05 W
Pop: 144 (1990); 151 (1980)   **Pop Density:** 480.0
Land: 0.3 sq. mi.; **Water:** 0.0 sq. mi.   **Elev:** 2550 ft.
Incorporated Apr 3, 1917. Not coextensive with the town of the same name.
Name origin: For pioneer settler, the Rev. Robert Collyer.

*Collyer   Township
ZIP: 67631   **Lat:** 38-59-10 N   **Long:** 100-03-32 W
Pop: 435 (1990); 523 (1980)   **Pop Density:** 2.2
Land: 199.6 sq. mi.; **Water:** 0.0 sq. mi.

KANSAS, Trego County

Franklin
Township
Lat: 38-45-36 N **Long:** 100-03-29 W
Pop: 88 (1990); 130 (1980) **Pop Density:** 0.9
Land: 99.9 sq. mi.; **Water:** 0.0 sq. mi.

Glencoe
Township
Lat: 38-54-57 N **Long:** 99-38-49 W
Pop: 82 (1990); 94 (1980) **Pop Density:** 2.3
Land: 35.9 sq. mi.; **Water:** 0.0 sq. mi.

Ogallah
Township
ZIP: 67656 **Lat:** 39-01-23 N **Long:** 99-41-45 W
Pop: 240 (1990); 288 (1980) **Pop Density:** 1.7
Land: 143.8 sq. mi.; **Water:** 0.1 sq. mi.

Riverside
Township
Lat: 38-47-10 N **Long:** 99-41-15 W
Pop: 138 (1990); 196 (1980) **Pop Density:** 1.2
Land: 114.5 sq. mi.; **Water:** 6.0 sq. mi.

WaKeeney
City
ZIP: 67672 **Lat:** 39-01-24 N **Long:** 99-52-52 W
Pop: 2,161 (1990); 2,388 (1980) **Pop Density:** 1271.2
Land: 1.7 sq. mi.; **Water:** 0.0 sq. mi. **Elev:** 2465 ft.
Incorporated Mar 29, 1880. Not coextensive with the town of the same name.
Name origin: From a combination of the names of its developers, *Wa*rren and *Keeney*.

*WaKeeney
Township
ZIP: 67672 **Lat:** 39-00-08 N **Long:** 99-52-14 W
Pop: 2,585 (1990); 2,792 (1980) **Pop Density:** 14.4
Land: 179.5 sq. mi.; **Water:** 0.1 sq. mi.

Wilcox
Township
Lat: 38-47-09 N **Long:** 99-52-22 W
Pop: 126 (1990); 142 (1980) **Pop Density:** 1.1
Land: 115.1 sq. mi.; **Water:** 4.6 sq. mi.

Wabaunsee County
County Seat: Alma (ZIP: 66401)

Pop: 6,603 (1990); 6,867 (1980) **Pop Density:** 8.3
Land: 797.5 sq. mi.; **Water:** 2.4 sq. mi. **Area Code:** 913
In east-central KS, west of Topeka; organized as Richardson County Aug 30, 1855 (prior to statehood); name changed Feb 11, 1859.
Name origin: For Wabaunsee (1760–1845), a Potawatomi chief. Meaning of the name is uncertain: possibly 'dawn of day'; others not sufficiently documented or satisfactory are 'he lives through the winter,' 'daylight,' and 'boggy day.' Citizens preferred the name of an Indian chief to that of Richardson, a proslavery advocate.

Alma
City
ZIP: 66401 **Lat:** 39-00-52 N **Long:** 96-17-18 W
Pop: 871 (1990); 925 (1980) **Pop Density:** 1742.0
Land: 0.5 sq. mi.; **Water:** 0.0 sq. mi. **Elev:** 1095 ft.
Incorporated 1868. Not coextensive with the town of the same name.
Name origin: For either a stream in the Crimea, or a city in Germany, former home of some early settlers.

*Alma
Township
ZIP: 66401 **Lat:** 39-01-09 N **Long:** 96-18-49 W
Pop: 1,160 (1990); 1,201 (1980) **Pop Density:** 29.0
Land: 40.0 sq. mi.; **Water:** 0.0 sq. mi.

Alta Vista
City
ZIP: 66834 **Lat:** 38-51-53 N **Long:** 96-29-20 W
Pop: 477 (1990); 430 (1980) **Pop Density:** 1590.0
Land: 0.3 sq. mi.; **Water:** 0.0 sq. mi. **Elev:** 1437 ft.
Incorporated Jun 1905.
Name origin: From Spanish meaning 'high view,' for its geographic location on the high divide between the Kaw (Kansas) and Neosho rivers.

Eskridge
City
ZIP: 66423 **Lat:** 38-51-34 N **Long:** 96-06-16 W
Pop: 518 (1990); 603 (1980) **Pop Density:** 1036.0
Land: 0.5 sq. mi.; **Water:** 0.0 sq. mi. **Elev:** 1400 ft.
Incorporated Jul 8, 1887.
Name origin: For journalist Charles Eskridge.

Farmer
Township
Lat: 38-55-37 N **Long:** 96-18-42 W
Pop: 108 (1990); 118 (1980) **Pop Density:** 1.6
Land: 66.3 sq. mi.; **Water:** 0.0 sq. mi.

Garfield
Township
Lat: 38-52-28 N **Long:** 96-26-31 W
Pop: 629 (1990); 619 (1980) **Pop Density:** 13.9
Land: 45.4 sq. mi.; **Water:** 0.0 sq. mi.

Harveyville
City
ZIP: 66431 **Lat:** 38-47-20 N **Long:** 95-57-43 W
Pop: 267 (1990); 280 (1980) **Pop Density:** 2670.0
Land: 0.1 sq. mi.; **Water:** 0.0 sq. mi. **Elev:** 1121 ft.
Incorporated Jan 6, 1905.
Name origin: For Quaker missionary Henry Harvey.

Kaw
Township
Lat: 39-09-40 N **Long:** 96-09-12 W
Pop: 230 (1990); 257 (1980) **Pop Density:** 5.4
Land: 42.3 sq. mi.; **Water:** 0.7 sq. mi.

McFarland
City
ZIP: 66501 **Lat:** 39-03-16 N **Long:** 96-14-16 W
Pop: 224 (1990); 242 (1980) **Pop Density:** 1120.0
Land: 0.2 sq. mi.; **Water:** 0.0 sq. mi. **Elev:** 1020 ft.
Incorporated Apr 1903.

Maple Hill — City
ZIP: 66507 Lat: 39-05-10 N Long: 96-01-36 W
Pop: 406 (1990); 381 (1980) Pop Density: 2030.0
Land: 0.2 sq. mi.; Water: 0.0 sq. mi. Elev: 960 ft.
Incorporated 1908. Not coextensive with the town of the same name.
Name origin: For its descriptive connotations.

*Maple Hill — Township
ZIP: 66507 Lat: 39-03-23 N Long: 96-01-22 W
Pop: 796 (1990); 777 (1980) Pop Density: 10.9
Land: 73.2 sq. mi.; Water: 0.4 sq. mi.

Mill Creek — Township
Lat: 38-54-34 N Long: 96-11-42 W
Pop: 263 (1990); 311 (1980) Pop Density: 3.5
Land: 74.2 sq. mi.; Water: 0.3 sq. mi.

Mission Creek — Township
Lat: 38-55-33 N Long: 96-02-00 W
Pop: 448 (1990); 453 (1980) Pop Density: 5.6
Land: 80.5 sq. mi.; Water: 0.0 sq. mi.

Newbury — Township
Lat: 39-03-42 N Long: 96-09-52 W
Pop: 934 (1990); 941 (1980) Pop Density: 11.9
Land: 78.5 sq. mi.; Water: 0.1 sq. mi.

Paxico — City
ZIP: 66526 Lat: 39-04-09 N Long: 96-10-01 W
Pop: 174 (1990); 168 (1980) Pop Density: 1740.0
Land: 0.1 sq. mi.; Water: 0.0 sq. mi. Elev: 990 ft.
Incorporated Apr 7, 1914.
Name origin: From an anglicized version of the name of Potawatomi Chief Pashqua.

Plumb — Township
Lat: 38-48-10 N Long: 95-59-49 W
Pop: 617 (1990); 654 (1980) Pop Density: 12.4
Land: 49.9 sq. mi.; Water: 0.1 sq. mi.

Rock Creek — Township
Lat: 38-46-58 N Long: 96-17-30 W
Pop: 92 (1990); 113 (1980) Pop Density: 1.4
Land: 65.9 sq. mi.; Water: 0.0 sq. mi.

St. Marys — City
Lat: 39-11-06 N Long: 96-04-31 W
Pop: 0 (1990)
Land: 0.001 sq. mi.; Water: 0.0 sq. mi.
Incorporated Oct 8, 1869. Not coextensive with the town of the same name. Part of the town is also in Pottawatomie County.
Name origin: For the mother of Jesus.

Wabaunsee — Township
Lat: 39-07-06 N Long: 96-19-21 W
Pop: 455 (1990); 455 (1980) Pop Density: 6.9
Land: 66.4 sq. mi.; Water: 0.7 sq. mi.

Washington — Township
Lat: 38-58-49 N Long: 96-26-30 W
Pop: 100 (1990); 114 (1980) Pop Density: 1.7
Land: 57.2 sq. mi.; Water: 0.0 sq. mi.

Willard — City
Lat: 39-05-37 N Long: 95-56-47 W
Pop: 0 (1990); 5 (1980)
Land: 0.005 sq. mi.; Water: 0.0 sq. mi. Elev: 930 ft.
Incorporated Oct 22, 1912. Part of the town is also in Shawnee County.

Wilmington — Township
Lat: 38-47-50 N Long: 96-06-49 W
Pop: 771 (1990); 854 (1980) Pop Density: 13.3
Land: 57.8 sq. mi.; Water: 0.0 sq. mi.

Wallace County
County Seat: Sharon Springs (ZIP: 67758)

Pop: 1,821 (1990); 2,045 (1980) Pop Density: 2.0
Land: 914.1 sq. mi.; Water: 0.1 sq. mi. Area Code: 913
On central western border of KS; organized Mar 2, 1868 from Indian lands.
Name origin: For Gen. William Harvey Lamb Wallace (?–1862), Union officer in the Civil War who died of wounds received at Shiloh, TN.

Harrison — Township
Lat: 38-45-53 N Long: 101-34-32 W
Pop: 108 (1990); 114 (1980) Pop Density: 1.3
Land: 81.2 sq. mi.; Water: 0.0 sq. mi.

Sharon Springs — City
ZIP: 67758 Lat: 38-53-39 N Long: 101-45-07 W
Pop: 872 (1990); 982 (1980) Pop Density: 968.9
Land: 0.9 sq. mi.; Water: 0.0 sq. mi. Elev: 3471 ft.
Incorporated 1890. Not coextensive with the town of the same name.
Name origin: For Sharon Springs, NY.

*Sharon Springs — Township
ZIP: 67758 Lat: 38-56-37 N Long: 101-45-19 W
Pop: 1,148 (1990); 1,264 (1980) Pop Density: 3.4
Land: 341.8 sq. mi.; Water: 0.0 sq. mi.

Wallace — City
ZIP: 67761 Lat: 38-54-49 N Long: 101-35-32 W
Pop: 75 (1990); 86 (1980) Pop Density: 187.5
Land: 0.4 sq. mi.; Water: 0.0 sq. mi. Elev: 3311 ft.
Incorporated Jul 1887. Not coextensive with the town of the same name.
Name origin: For Civil War hero Gen. William Wallace.

KANSAS, Wallace County   *American Places Dictionary*

*Wallace   Township
ZIP: 67761   Lat: 38-58-57 N Long: 101-34-27 W
Pop: 185 (1990); 218 (1980)   Pop Density: 1.0
Land: 188.5 sq. mi.; Water: 0.0 sq. mi.

Weskan   Township
ZIP: 67762   Lat: 38-53-07 N Long: 101-56-07 W
Pop: 380 (1990); 364 (1980)   Pop Density: 1.3
Land: 302.6 sq. mi.; Water: 0.0 sq. mi.

Washington County
County Seat: Washington (ZIP: 66968)

Pop: 7,073 (1990); 8,543 (1980)   **Pop Density:** 7.9
Land: 898.5 sq. mi.; **Water:** 0.4 sq. mi.   **Area Code:** 913

On the northern border of KS, northwest of Manhattan; original county; established Feb 20, 1857 (prior to statehood).

Name origin: For George Washington (1732–99), American patriot and first U.S. president.

Barnes   City
ZIP: 66933   Lat: 39-42-42 N Long: 96-52-21 W
Pop: 167 (1990); 257 (1980)   Pop Density: 835.0
Land: 0.2 sq. mi.; Water: 0.0 sq. mi.   Elev: 1331 ft.
Not coextensive with the town of the same name.
Name origin: For railroad stockholder, A. S. Barnes.

*Barnes   Township
ZIP: 66933   Lat: 39-41-59 N Long: 96-51-40 W
Pop: 283 (1990); 394 (1980)   Pop Density: 7.9
Land: 35.9 sq. mi.; Water: 0.0 sq. mi.

Brantford   Township
                        Lat: 39-41-43 N Long: 97-18-34 W
Pop: 109 (1990); 129 (1980)   Pop Density: 3.0
Land: 35.9 sq. mi.; Water: 0.0 sq. mi.

Charleston   Township
                        Lat: 39-51-49 N Long: 96-57-53 W
Pop: 115 (1990); 129 (1980)   Pop Density: 3.2
Land: 35.9 sq. mi.; Water: 0.0 sq. mi.

Clifton   City
ZIP: 66937   Lat: 39-34-11 N Long: 97-16-46 W
Pop: 334 (1990); 371 (1980)   Pop Density: 1113.3
Land: 0.3 sq. mi.; Water: 0.0 sq. mi.   Elev: 1302 ft.
Incorporated May 21, 1884. Part of the town is also in Clay County.
Name origin: For a well-liked government surveyor.

*Clifton   Township
ZIP: 66937   Lat: 39-36-39 N Long: 97-18-47 W
Pop: 463 (1990); 567 (1980)   Pop Density: 12.8
Land: 36.2 sq. mi.; Water: 0.0 sq. mi.

Coleman   Township
                        Lat: 39-46-59 N Long: 97-12-05 W
Pop: 84 (1990); 104 (1980)   Pop Density: 2.3
Land: 36.2 sq. mi.; Water: 0.0 sq. mi.

Farmington   Township
                        Lat: 39-52-09 N Long: 97-04-54 W
Pop: 181 (1990); 216 (1980)   Pop Density: 5.0
Land: 36.3 sq. mi.; Water: 0.0 sq. mi.

Franklin   Township
                        Lat: 39-58-05 N Long: 96-58-13 W
Pop: 146 (1990); 231 (1980)   Pop Density: 4.1
Land: 35.7 sq. mi.; Water: 0.1 sq. mi.

Grant   Township
                        Lat: 39-47-30 N Long: 97-18-55 W
Pop: 43 (1990); 55 (1980)   Pop Density: 1.2
Land: 35.9 sq. mi.; Water: 0.0 sq. mi.

Greenleaf   City
ZIP: 66943   Lat: 39-43-36 N Long: 96-58-47 W
Pop: 353 (1990); 462 (1980)   Pop Density: 706.0
Land: 0.5 sq. mi.; Water: 0.0 sq. mi.   Elev: 1417 ft.
Incorporated Aug 24, 1880. Not coextensive with the town of the same name.

*Greenleaf   Township
ZIP: 66943   Lat: 39-41-38 N Long: 96-58-39 W
Pop: 479 (1990); 585 (1980)   Pop Density: 13.3
Land: 35.9 sq. mi.; Water: 0.0 sq. mi.

Haddam   City
ZIP: 66944   Lat: 39-51-19 N Long: 97-18-14 W
Pop: 195 (1990); 239 (1980)   Pop Density: 650.0
Land: 0.3 sq. mi.; Water: 0.0 sq. mi.   Elev: 1400 ft.
Incorporated Jul 7, 1886. Not coextensive with the town of the same name.
Name origin: For Haddam, CT, former home of early settlers.

*Haddam   Township
ZIP: 66944   Lat: 39-52-14 N Long: 97-18-43 W
Pop: 290 (1990); 385 (1980)   Pop Density: 8.1
Land: 35.9 sq. mi.; Water: 0.0 sq. mi.

Hanover   City
ZIP: 66945   Lat: 39-53-31 N Long: 96-52-35 W
Pop: 696 (1990); 802 (1980)   Pop Density: 1392.0
Land: 0.5 sq. mi.; Water: 0.0 sq. mi.   Elev: 1231 ft.
Incorporated Jul 5, 1872. Not coextensive with the town of the same name.
Name origin: Named by German settlers for Hanover, Germany.

*Hanover   Township
ZIP: 66945   Lat: 39-52-22 N Long: 96-52-08 W
Pop: 968 (1990); 1,071 (1980)   Pop Density: 26.9
Land: 36.0 sq. mi.; Water: 0.0 sq. mi.

Highland   Township
                        Lat: 39-57-57 N Long: 97-05-46 W
Pop: 33 (1990); 80 (1980)   Pop Density: 0.9
Land: 35.6 sq. mi.; Water: 0.2 sq. mi.

Hollenberg — City
ZIP: 66946 Lat: 39-58-52 N Long: 96-59-27 W
Pop: 28 (1990); 57 (1980) Pop Density: 280.0
Land: 0.1 sq. mi.; Water: 0.0 sq. mi. Elev: 1271 ft.
Incorporated Jul 14, 1937.
Name origin: For German adventurer Henry Hollenberg, who settled here in 1858.

Independence — Township
Lat: 39-57-27 N Long: 96-51-48 W
Pop: 210 (1990); 229 (1980) Pop Density: 5.8
Land: 36.0 sq. mi.; Water: 0.0 sq. mi.

Kimeo — Township
Lat: 39-36-37 N Long: 96-58-30 W
Pop: 85 (1990); 124 (1980) Pop Density: 2.4
Land: 36.0 sq. mi.; Water: 0.0 sq. mi.

Lincoln — Township
Lat: 39-36-10 N Long: 96-51-10 W
Pop: 91 (1990); 130 (1980) Pop Density: 2.5
Land: 36.0 sq. mi.; Water: 0.0 sq. mi.

Linn — City
ZIP: 66953 Lat: 39-40-45 N Long: 97-05-11 W
Pop: 472 (1990); 483 (1980) Pop Density: 1573.3
Land: 0.3 sq. mi.; Water: 0.0 sq. mi. Elev: 1460 ft.
Incorporated Oct 1911. Not coextensive with the town of the same name.

*Linn — Township
ZIP: 66953 Lat: 39-41-23 N Long: 97-05-14 W
Pop: 666 (1990); 686 (1980) Pop Density: 18.5
Land: 36.0 sq. mi.; Water: 0.0 sq. mi.

Little Blue — Township
Lat: 39-47-03 N Long: 96-51-33 W
Pop: 100 (1990); 152 (1980) Pop Density: 2.8
Land: 35.8 sq. mi.; Water: 0.0 sq. mi.

Logan — Township
Lat: 39-47-02 N Long: 96-58-28 W
Pop: 143 (1990); 168 (1980) Pop Density: 4.0
Land: 35.7 sq. mi.; Water: 0.0 sq. mi.

Lowe — Township
Lat: 39-57-33 N Long: 97-11-57 W
Pop: 86 (1990); 120 (1980) Pop Density: 2.4
Land: 35.5 sq. mi.; Water: 0.0 sq. mi.

Mahaska — City
ZIP: 66955 Lat: 39-59-17 N Long: 97-21-09 W
Pop: 98 (1990); 119 (1980) Pop Density: 490.0
Land: 0.2 sq. mi.; Water: 0.0 sq. mi. Elev: 1600 ft.
Incorporated Jul 8, 1909.
Name origin: For Sioux Indian chief Mahaska, whose name means 'white cloud.'

Mill Creek — Township
Lat: 39-51-56 N Long: 97-11-55 W
Pop: 292 (1990); 333 (1980) Pop Density: 8.1
Land: 36.2 sq. mi.; Water: 0.0 sq. mi.

Morrowville — City
ZIP: 66958 Lat: 39-50-41 N Long: 97-10-19 W
Pop: 173 (1990); 180 (1980) Pop Density: 1730.0
Land: 0.1 sq. mi.; Water: 0.0 sq. mi. Elev: 1350 ft.
Incorporated Oct 8, 1929.
Name origin: For legislator James C. Morrow.

Palmer — City
ZIP: 66962 Lat: 39-38-01 N Long: 97-08-21 W
Pop: 121 (1990); 149 (1980) Pop Density: 403.3
Land: 0.3 sq. mi.; Water: 0.0 sq. mi. Elev: 1325 ft.
Incorporated Jan 7, 1911.

Sheridan — Township
Lat: 39-36-38 N Long: 97-11-52 W
Pop: 121 (1990); 160 (1980) Pop Density: 3.4
Land: 35.9 sq. mi.; Water: 0.0 sq. mi.

Sherman — Township
Lat: 39-36-51 N Long: 97-05-21 W
Pop: 276 (1990); 342 (1980) Pop Density: 7.6
Land: 36.1 sq. mi.; Water: 0.0 sq. mi.

Strawberry — Township
Lat: 39-41-57 N Long: 97-12-18 W
Pop: 160 (1990); 227 (1980) Pop Density: 4.4
Land: 36.2 sq. mi.; Water: 0.0 sq. mi.

Union — Township
Lat: 39-57-36 N Long: 97-18-33 W
Pop: 142 (1990); 192 (1980) Pop Density: 4.0
Land: 35.7 sq. mi.; Water: 0.0 sq. mi.

Vining — City
Lat: 39-34-05 N Long: 97-17-34 W
Pop: 20 (1990); 30 (1980) Pop Density: 200.0
Land: 0.1 sq. mi.; Water: 0.0 sq. mi. Elev: 1280 ft.
Incorporated Feb 9, 1885. Part of the town is also in Clay County.

Washington — City
ZIP: 66968 Lat: 39-49-00 N Long: 97-03-07 W
Pop: 1,304 (1990); 1,488 (1980) Pop Density: 1862.9
Land: 0.7 sq. mi.; Water: 0.0 sq. mi. Elev: 1335 ft.
Incorporated Apr 19, 1875.
Name origin: For George Washington (1732–99), first U.S. president.

*Washington — Township
ZIP: 66968 Lat: 39-47-03 N Long: 97-05-09 W
Pop: 203 (1990); 246 (1980) Pop Density: 5.8
Land: 35.3 sq. mi.; Water: 0.0 sq. mi.

KANSAS, Wichita County   *American Places Dictionary*

> ## Wichita County
> **County Seat: Leoti (ZIP: 67861)**
>
> **Pop:** 2,758 (1990); 3,041 (1980)   **Pop Density:** 3.8
> **Land:** 718.6 sq. mi.; **Water:** 0.0 sq. mi.   **Area Code:** 316
> In western KS, northwest of Garden City; organized Mar 6, 1873 from Indian lands.
> **Name origin:** For the Wichita Indians, one of the more important tribes of Caddoan linguistic stock. Name is translated 'man,' or from Choctaw *owa chito* 'big hunt.'

Leoti   City
ZIP: 67861   **Lat:** 38-28-58 N **Long:** 101-21-25 W
Pop: 1,738 (1990); 1,869 (1980)   **Pop Density:** 1336.9
Land: 1.3 sq. mi.; **Water:** 0.0 sq. mi.   **Elev:** 3305 ft.
Incorporated Feb 1887. Not coextensive with the town of the same name.

*Leoti   Township
ZIP: 67861   **Lat:** 38-28-54 N **Long:** 101-20-49 W
Pop: 2,758 (1990); 3,041 (1980)   **Pop Density:** 3.8
Land: 718.6 sq. mi.; **Water:** 0.0 sq. mi.

> ## Wilson County
> **County Seat: Fredonia (ZIP: 66736)**
>
> **Pop:** 10,289 (1990); 12,128 (1980)   **Pop Density:** 17.9
> **Land:** 573.9 sq. mi.; **Water:** 1.1 sq. mi.   **Area Code:** 316
> In southeastern KS, south of Iola; original county; organized Aug 25, 1855 (prior to statehood).
> **Name origin:** For Hiero T. Wilson (1806–?), army officer, settler, and merchant.

Altoona   City
ZIP: 66710   **Lat:** 37-31-31 N **Long:** 95-39-41 W
Pop: 456 (1990); 564 (1980)   **Pop Density:** 912.0
Land: 0.5 sq. mi.; **Water:** 0.0 sq. mi.   **Elev:** 828 ft.
Incorporated 1887.
Name origin: For Altoona, PA, also a coal-producing area.

Benedict   City
ZIP: 66714   **Lat:** 37-37-28 N **Long:** 95-44-30 W
Pop: 16 (1990); 111 (1980)   **Pop Density:** 533.3
Land: 0.03 sq. mi.; **Water:** 0.0 sq. mi.   **Elev:** 900 ft.
Incorporated 1905.
Name origin: For the Catholic order of Saint Benedict of Nursia.

Buffalo   City
ZIP: 66717   **Lat:** 37-42-30 N **Long:** 95-41-48 W
Pop: 293 (1990); 386 (1980)   **Pop Density:** 976.7
Land: 0.3 sq. mi.; **Water:** 0.0 sq. mi.   **Elev:** 945 ft.
Incorporated Oct 4, 1898.
Name origin: For the once plentiful buffalo.

Cedar   Township
                           Lat: 37-30-52 N **Long:** 95-41-20 W
Pop: 704 (1990); 862 (1980)   **Pop Density:** 19.6
Land: 36.0 sq. mi.; **Water:** 0.0 sq. mi.

Center   Township
                           Lat: 37-30-45 N **Long:** 95-48-20 W
Pop: 634 (1990); 684 (1980)   **Pop Density:** 15.9
Land: 39.8 sq. mi.; **Water:** 0.1 sq. mi.

Chetopa   Township
                           Lat: 37-30-52 N **Long:** 95-34-36 W
Pop: 201 (1990); 230 (1980)   **Pop Density:** 5.6
Land: 35.8 sq. mi.; **Water:** 0.0 sq. mi.

Clifton   Township
                           Lat: 37-41-26 N **Long:** 95-43-18 W
Pop: 455 (1990); 541 (1980)   **Pop Density:** 12.7
Land: 35.8 sq. mi.; **Water:** 0.2 sq. mi.

Colfax   Township
                           Lat: 37-41-22 N **Long:** 95-35-49 W
Pop: 442 (1990); 525 (1980)   **Pop Density:** 9.3
Land: 47.5 sq. mi.; **Water:** 0.1 sq. mi.

Coyville   City
ZIP: 66736   **Lat:** 37-41-13 N **Long:** 95-53-43 W
Pop: 78 (1990); 98 (1980)   **Pop Density:** 260.0
Land: 0.3 sq. mi.; **Water:** 0.0 sq. mi.   **Elev:** 885 ft.
Incorporated Jun 12, 1906.

Duck Creek   Township
                           Lat: 37-25-18 N **Long:** 95-54-01 W
Pop: 109 (1990); 131 (1980)   **Pop Density:** 3.0
Land: 35.9 sq. mi.; **Water:** 0.1 sq. mi.

Fall River   Township
                           Lat: 37-32-47 N **Long:** 95-54-45 W
Pop: 372 (1990); 392 (1980)   **Pop Density:** 7.4
Land: 50.5 sq. mi.; **Water:** 0.1 sq. mi.

Fredonia   City
ZIP: 66736   **Lat:** 37-31-58 N **Long:** 95-49-26 W
Pop: 2,599 (1990); 3,047 (1980)   **Pop Density:** 1130.0
Land: 2.3 sq. mi.; **Water:** 0.0 sq. mi.   **Elev:** 893 ft.
Incorporated 1871.
Name origin: For Fredonia, NY.

Guilford   Township
ZIP: 66710   **Lat:** 37-36-14 N **Long:** 95-43-27 W
Pop: 191 (1990); 236 (1980)   **Pop Density:** 5.3
Land: 35.9 sq. mi.; **Water:** 0.0 sq. mi.

Neodesha — City
ZIP: 66757 **Lat:** 37-25-24 N **Long:** 95-40-51 W
Pop: 2,837 (1990); 3,414 (1980) **Pop Density:** 2579.1
Land: 1.1 sq. mi.; **Water:** 0.0 sq. mi. **Elev:** 819 ft.
Incorporated Mar 1, 1871.
Name origin: From an Osage term meaning 'muddy water.'

*Neodesha — Township
ZIP: 66757 **Lat:** 37-25-46 N **Long:** 95-41-15 W
Pop: 599 (1990); 700 (1980) **Pop Density:** 17.2
Land: 34.8 sq. mi.; **Water:** 0.2 sq. mi.

New Albany — City
ZIP: 66759 **Lat:** 37-34-03 N **Long:** 95-56-04 W
Pop: 60 (1990); 78 (1980) **Pop Density:** 300.0
Land: 0.2 sq. mi.; **Water:** 0.0 sq. mi. **Elev:** 894 ft.

Newark — Township
Lat: 37-25-29 N **Long:** 95-34-54 W
Pop: 228 (1990); 235 (1980) **Pop Density:** 6.4
Land: 35.7 sq. mi.; **Water:** 0.1 sq. mi.

Pleasant Valley — Township
Lat: 37-36-25 N **Long:** 95-36-19 W
Pop: 182 (1990); 243 (1980) **Pop Density:** 3.8
Land: 47.5 sq. mi.; **Water:** 0.0 sq. mi.

Prairie — Township
Lat: 37-36-16 N **Long:** 95-49-25 W
Pop: 134 (1990); 113 (1980) **Pop Density:** 4.5
Land: 30.1 sq. mi.; **Water:** 0.1 sq. mi.

Talleyrand — Township
Lat: 37-25-46 N **Long:** 95-47-43 W
Pop: 216 (1990); 273 (1980) **Pop Density:** 6.1
Land: 35.5 sq. mi.; **Water:** 0.0 sq. mi.

Verdigris — Township
Lat: 37-40-35 N **Long:** 95-54-38 W
Pop: 331 (1990); 427 (1980) **Pop Density:** 8.3
Land: 39.9 sq. mi.; **Water:** 0.1 sq. mi.

Webster — Township
Lat: 37-41-23 N **Long:** 95-49-59 W
Pop: 55 (1990); 75 (1980) **Pop Density:** 1.8
Land: 29.8 sq. mi.; **Water:** 0.0 sq. mi.

Woodson County
County Seat: Yates Center (ZIP: 66783)

Pop: 4,116 (1990); 4,600 (1980) **Pop Density:** 8.2
Land: 500.7 sq. mi.; **Water:** 4.8 sq. mi. **Area Code:** 316
In southeastern KS, east of Wichita; original county; organized Aug 25, 1855 (prior to statehood).
Name origin: For Daniel Woodson, secretary of KS Territory (1854–57).

Center — Township
Lat: 37-50-13 N **Long:** 95-44-09 W
Pop: 647 (1990); 309 (1980) **Pop Density:** 4.1
Land: 158.9 sq. mi.; **Water:** 0.5 sq. mi.

Liberty — Township
Lat: 37-58-24 N **Long:** 95-43-46 W
Pop: 210 (1990); 205 (1980) **Pop Density:** 2.4
Land: 86.0 sq. mi.; **Water:** 0.2 sq. mi.

Neosho Falls — City
ZIP: 66758 **Lat:** 38-00-21 N **Long:** 95-33-18 W
Pop: 157 (1990); 157 (1980) **Pop Density:** 314.0
Land: 0.5 sq. mi.; **Water:** 0.0 sq. mi. **Elev:** 975 ft.
Incorporated 1892. Not coextensive with the town of the same name.
Name origin: From an Indian term meaning 'muddy water.'

*Neosho Falls — Township
ZIP: 66758 **Lat:** 37-56-37 N **Long:** 95-33-53 W
Pop: 549 (1990); 365 (1980) **Pop Density:** 7.2
Land: 75.8 sq. mi.; **Water:** 0.3 sq. mi.

North — Township
Lat: 37-58-50 N **Long:** 95-53-14 W
Pop: 93 (1990); 123 (1980) **Pop Density:** 1.4
Land: 64.3 sq. mi.; **Water:** 0.1 sq. mi.

Perry — Township
Lat: 37-46-50 N **Long:** 95-34-56 W
Pop: 143 (1990); 147 (1980) **Pop Density:** 2.9
Land: 48.9 sq. mi.; **Water:** 0.0 sq. mi.

Toronto — City
ZIP: 66777 **Lat:** 37-47-54 N **Long:** 95-56-57 W
Pop: 317 (1990); 466 (1980) **Pop Density:** 792.5
Land: 0.4 sq. mi.; **Water:** 0.0 sq. mi. **Elev:** 950 ft.
Incorporated Jan 13, 1885. Not coextensive with the town of the same name.
Name origin: From a Huron term menaing 'gateway.'

*Toronto — Township
ZIP: 66777 **Lat:** 37-49-20 N **Long:** 95-54-35 W
Pop: 659 (1990); 742 (1980) **Pop Density:** 10.2
Land: 64.4 sq. mi.; **Water:** 3.7 sq. mi.

Yates Center — City
ZIP: 66783 **Lat:** 37-52-20 N **Long:** 95-44-33 W
Pop: 1,815 (1990); 1,998 (1980) **Pop Density:** 789.1
Land: 2.3 sq. mi.; **Water:** 0.0 sq. mi. **Elev:** 1136 ft.
Incorporated Mar 8, 1884.

Wyandotte County
County Seat: Kansas City (ZIP: 66101)

Pop: 161,993 (1990); 172,335 (1980) **Pop Density:** 1070.0
Land: 151.4 sq. mi.; **Water:** 4.3 sq. mi. **Area Code:** 913

On northeastern border of KS, east of Topeka; original county; organized Jan 29, 1859 (prior to statehood).

Name origin: For the Wyandotte Indians, a tribe of Iroquoian linguistic stock. Name is thought to mean 'islanders' or 'those who live on a peninsula,' from their original home on islands in the St. Lawrence River and on a peninsula.

Bonner Springs City
ZIP: 66012 **Lat:** 39-04-45 N **Long:** 94-52-53 W
Pop: 6,410 (1990); 6,266 (1980) **Pop Density:** 419.0
Land: 15.3 sq. mi.; **Water:** 0.2 sq. mi. **Elev:** 850 ft.

In northeastern KS, 15 mi. west of Kansas City. Incorporated Nov 8, 1898. Part of the town is also in Johnson County.

Name origin: For Robert Bonner, editor of the *New York City Ledger*, and for the local natural springs.

Delaware Township
Lat: 39-02-23 N **Long:** 94-54-00 W
Pop: 166 (1990); 153 (1980) **Pop Density:** 40.5
Land: 4.1 sq. mi.; **Water:** 0.2 sq. mi.

Edwardsville City
Lat: 39-04-41 N **Long:** 94-49-07 W
Pop: 3,979 (1990); 3,364 (1980) **Pop Density:** 442.1
Land: 9.0 sq. mi.; **Water:** 0.2 sq. mi. **Elev:** 850 ft.

Incorporated Jun 28, 1915.

Name origin: For Union Pacific Railroad official John Edwards.

Kansas City City
ZIP: 66102 **Lat:** 39-07-06 N **Long:** 94-43-37 W
Pop: 149,767 (1990); 161,148 (1980) **Pop Density:** 1389.3
Land: 107.8 sq. mi.; **Water:** 3.5 sq. mi. **Elev:** 740 ft.

In northeastern KS on both banks of the Kansas River, on the KS-MO border just west of Kansas City, MO. Settled 1857 as Wyandotte. In 1886, the towns of Armourdale, Armstrong, and Kansas City combined with Wyandotte and were incorporated under the name of Kansas City on Mar 6; later, Argentine and Rosedale joined them. Nicknamed "Gateway to Kansas." Industrial city: food processing, automobiles, fiberglass, soap; also an agricultural center.

Name origin: For the state, which was named for the Kansa Indians.

Lake Quivira City
Lat: 39-02-47 N **Long:** 94-46-12 W
Pop: 40 (1990); 58 (1980) **Pop Density:** 133.3
Land: 0.3 sq. mi.; **Water:** 0.0 sq. mi. **Elev:** 890 ft.

Incorporated Jul 1971. Part of the town is also in Johnson County.

Name origin: For Quivira, a legendary land of treasure, which the 16th-century Spanish believed could be found in central North America.

Prairie Township
Lat: 39-10-07 N **Long:** 94-52-09 W
Pop: 1,631 (1990); 1,346 (1980) **Pop Density:** 108.7
Land: 15.0 sq. mi.; **Water:** 0.1 sq. mi.

Index to Places and Counties in Kansas

Abbyville (Reno) City 296
Abilene (Dickinson) City 235
Achilles (Rawlins) Township 295
Adams (Nemaha) Township 281
Adell (Sheridan) Township 311
Admire (Lyon) City 269
Adrian (Jackson) Township 254
Aetna (Barber) Township 215
Afton (Sedgwick) Township 307
Agency (Osage) Township 285
Agenda (Republic) City 298
Agnes City (Lyon) Township 269
Agra (Phillips) City 290
Alamota (Lane) Township 264
Albano (Stafford) Township 314
Albert (Barton) City 216
Albion (Barton) Township 216
Albion (Reno) Township 296
Albion (Republic) Township 298
Alden (Rice) City 299
Alexander (Rush) City 303
Alexander-Belle Prairie (Rush) Township 303
Alexandria (Leavenworth) Township 265
Allen (Jewell) Township 257
Allen (Kingman) Township 261
Allen (Lyon) City 269
Allen County 212
Allison (Decatur) Township 233
Allodium (Graham) Township 247
Alma (Wabaunsee) City 320
Alma (Wabaunsee) Township 320
Almena (Norton) City 284
Almena-District 4 (Norton) Township 284
Alta (Harvey) Township 252
Altamont (Labette) City 263
Alta Vista (Wabaunsee) City 320
Alton (Osborne) City 286
Altoona (Wilson) City 324
Altory (Decatur) Township 233
Americus (Lyon) City 269
Americus (Lyon) Township 269
Andale (Sedgwick) City 307
Anderson County 213
Andover (Butler) City 220
Anthony (Harper) City 251
Appanoose (Franklin) Township 244
Appleton (Clark) Township 226
Arcade (Phillips) Township 290
Arcadia (Crawford) City 232
Argonia (Sumner) City 316
Arion (Cloud) Township 228
Arkansas City (Cowley) City 231
Arlington (Reno) City 296
Arlington (Reno) Township 296
Arma (Crawford) City 232
Arvonia (Osage) Township 285
Ash Creek (Ellsworth) Township 241
Asherville (Mitchell) Township 277
Ashland (Clark) City 226
Ashland (Riley) Township 301
Ash Valley (Pawnee) Township 289
Assaria (Saline) City 305
Atchison (Atchison) City 214
Atchison County 214
Athelstane (Clay) Township 226
Athens (Jewell) Township 257
Athol (Smith) City 313
Atlanta (Cowley) City 231

Atlanta (Rice) Township 299
Attica (Harper) City 251
Attica (Sedgwick) Township 307
Atwood (Rawlins) City 295
Atwood (Rawlins) Township 295
Aubry (Johnson) Township 258
Auburn (Shawnee) City 310
Auburn (Shawnee) Township 310
Augusta (Butler) City 220
Augusta (Butler) Township 220
Augustine (Logan) Township 268
Aurora (Cloud) City 228
Aurora (Cloud) Township 228
Avilla (Comanche) Township 230
Avon (Coffey) Township 229
Avon (Sumner) Township 316
Axtell (Marshall) City 272
Bachelor (Greenwood) Township 249
Baker (Crawford) Township 232
Baker (Gove) Township 246
Bala (Riley) Township 301
Balderson (Marshall) Township 272
Baldwin City (Douglas) City 237
Banner (Dickinson) Township 235
Banner (Jackson) Township 254
Banner (Rush) Township 303
Banner (Smith) Township 313
Banner (Stevens) Township 316
Barber County 215
Barclay (Osage) Township 285
Barnard (Lincoln) City 266
Barnes (Washington) City 322
Barnes (Washington) Township 322
Barrett (Thomas) Township 318
Bartlett (Labette) City 263
Barton County 216
Basehor (Leavenworth) City 265
Bassett (Allen) City 212
Bassettville (Decatur) Township 233
Battle Creek (Lincoln) Township 266
Battle Hill (McPherson) Township 273
Baxter Springs (Cherokee) City 224
Bazaar (Chase) Township 222
Bazine (Ness) City 283
Bazine (Ness) Township 283
Bear Creek (Hamilton) Township 251
Beattie (Marshall) City 272
Beaver (Barton) Township 216
Beaver (Cowley) Township 231
Beaver (Decatur) Township 233
Beaver (Lincoln) Township 266
Beaver (Phillips) Township 290
Beaver (Republic) Township 298
Beaver (Scott) Township 306
Beaver (Smith) Township 313
Bel Aire (Sedgwick) City 307
Bell (Reno) Township 296
Bell (Rice) Township 299
Belle Plaine (Sumner) City 317
Belle Plaine (Sumner) Township 317
Belleville (Chautauqua) Township 223
Belleville (Republic) City 298
Belleville (Republic) Township 298
Belmont (Kingman) Township 261
Belmont (Phillips) Township 290
Beloit (Mitchell) City 277
Beloit (Mitchell) Township 277
Belpre (Edwards) City 238
Belpre (Edwards) Township 238
Belvue (Pottawatomie) City 292

Belvue (Pottawatomie) Township 292
Benedict (Wilson) City 324
Benkelman (Cheyenne) Township 225
Bennett (Kingman) Township 261
Bennington (Ottawa) City 287
Bennington (Ottawa) Township 287
Bentley (Sedgwick) City 307
Benton (Atchison) Township 214
Benton (Butler) City 220
Benton (Butler) Township 220
Benton (Hodgeman) Township 254
Bern (Nemaha) City 281
Berwick (Nemaha) Township 281
Bethany (Osborne) Township 286
Beverly (Lincoln) City 266
Big Bend (Republic) Township 298
Big Bow (Stanton) Township 315
Big Creek (Ellis) Township 240
Big Creek (Neosho) Township 282
Big Creek (Russell) Township 304
Bigelow (Marshall) Township 272
Big Timber (Rush) Township 303
Bird City (Cheyenne) City 225
Bird City (Cheyenne) Township 225
Bison (Rush) City 303
Black Wolf (Ellsworth) Township 241
Blaine (Clay) Township 226
Blaine (Lane) Township 264
Blaine (Marion) Township 270
Blaine (Ottawa) Township 287
Blaine (Smith) Township 313
Blakely (Geary) Township 245
Bloom (Clay) Township 226
Bloom (Ford) Township 243
Bloom (Osborne) Township 286
Bloomfield (Mitchell) Township 277
Bloomfield (Sheridan) Township 311
Bloomington (Butler) Township 220
Blue (Pottawatomie) Township 292
Blue Hill (Mitchell) Township 277
Blue Mound (Linn) City 267
Blue Mound (Linn) Township 267
Blue Rapids (Marshall) City 272
Blue Rapids (Marshall) Township 272
Blue Rapids City (Marshall) Township 272
Blue Valley (Pottawatomie) Township 292
Bluff (Sumner) Township 317
Bluff City (Harper) City 251
Bogue (Graham) City 247
Bolton (Cowley) Township 231
Bonaville (McPherson) Township 273
Bonner Springs (Johnson) City 258
Bonner Springs (Wyandotte) City 326
Bourbon County 218
Bow Creek (Phillips) Township 290
Bowcreek (Sheridan) Township 311
Brantford (Washington) Township 322
Brewster (Thomas) City 318
Bronson (Bourbon) City 218
Brookville (Saline) City 305
Brown County 219
Brownell (Ness) City 283
Browns Creek (Jewell) Township 257
Browns Grove (Pawnee) Township 289
Bruno (Butler) Township 220
Bryant (Graham) Township 247
Buckeye (Dickinson) Township 235
Buckeye (Ellis) Township 240

KANSAS
American Places Dictionary

Buckeye (Ottawa) Township...287
Bucklin (Ford) City...243
Bucklin (Ford) Township...243
Buffalo (Barton) Township...216
Buffalo (Cloud) Township...228
Buffalo (Jewell) Township...257
Buffalo (Wilson) City...324
Buhler (Reno) City...296
Bunker Hill (Russell) City...304
Burden (Cowley) City...231
Burdett (Pawnee) City...289
Burlingame (Osage) City...285
Burlingame (Osage) Township...285
Burlington (Coffey) City...229
Burlington (Coffey) Township...229
Burns (Marion) City...270
Burr Oak (Doniphan) Township...236
Burr Oak (Jewell) City...257
Burr Oak (Jewell) Township...257
Burrton (Harvey) City...252
Burrton (Harvey) Township...252
Bushong (Lyon) City...269
Bushton (Rice) City...299
Butler County...220
Byers (Pratt) City...294
Byron (Stafford) Township...314
Caldwell (Sumner) City...317
Caldwell (Sumner) Township...317
Calhoun (Cheyenne) Township...225
Calvin (Jewell) Township...257
Cambria (Saline) Township...305
Cambridge (Cowley) City...231
Camp Forsyth (Geary) Military Facility...245
Canada (Labette) Township...263
Caney (Montgomery) City...278
Caney (Montgomery) Township...278
Caneyville (Chautauqua) Township...223
Canton (Kingman) Township...261
Canton (McPherson) City...273
Canton (McPherson) Township...273
Canville (Neosho) Township...282
Capioma (Nemaha) Township...281
Carbondale (Osage) City...285
Carlton (Dickinson) City...235
Carlyle (Allen) Township...212
Carneiro (Ellsworth) Township...241
Carr Creek (Mitchell) Township...277
Cassoday (Butler) City...220
Castle (McPherson) Township...274
Castleton (Reno) Township...296
Catherine (Ellis) Township...240
Catlin (Marion) Township...270
Cawker (Mitchell) Township...277
Cawker City (Mitchell) City...277
Cedar (Chase) Township...222
Cedar (Cowley) Township...231
Cedar (Jackson) Township...254
Cedar (Smith) City...313
Cedar (Smith) Township...313
Cedar (Wilson) Township...324
Cedar Point (Chase) City...222
Cedar Vale (Chautauqua) City...223
Cedron (Lincoln) Township...266
Center (Atchison) Township...214
Center (Chautauqua) Township...223
Center (Clark) Township...226
Center (Cloud) Township...228
Center (Decatur) Township...233
Center (Dickinson) Township...235
Center (Doniphan) Township...236
Center (Hodgeman) Township...254
Center (Jewell) Township...257
Center (Lyon) Township...269
Center (Marion) Township...270
Center (Marshall) Township...272
Center (Mitchell) Township...277
Center (Nemaha) Township...281
Center (Ness) Township...283
Center (Ottawa) Township...287
Center (Pottawatomie) Township...292
Center (Rawlins) Township...295
Center (Reno) Township...296
Center (Rice) Township...299
Center (Riley) Township...301
Center (Rush) Township...303
Center (Russell) Township...304
Center (Smith) Township...313
Center (Stevens) Township...316
Center (Wilson) Township...324
Center (Woodson) Township...325
Center-District 1 (Norton) Township...284
Centerville (Linn) Township...267
Centerville (Neosho) Township...282
Centralia (Nemaha) City...281
Centropolis (Franklin) Township...244
Chanute (Neosho) City...282
Chapman (Clay) Township...226
Chapman (Dickinson) City...235
Chapman (Ottawa) Township...288
Charleston (Washington) Township...322
Chase (Rice) City...299
Chase County...222
Chautauqua (Chautauqua) City...223
Chautauqua County...223
Cheever (Dickinson) Township...235
Chelsea (Butler) Township...220
Cheney (Sedgwick) City...307
Cherokee (Cherokee) Township...224
Cherokee (Crawford) City...232
Cherokee (Montgomery) Township...278
Cherokee County...224
Cherry (Montgomery) Township...278
Cherry Creek (Cheyenne) Township...225
Cherryvale (Montgomery) City...278
Chetopa (Labette) City...263
Chetopa (Neosho) Township...282
Chetopa (Wilson) Township...324
Cheyenne (Barton) Township...216
Cheyenne (Lane) Township...264
Cheyenne County...225
Chikaskia (Kingman) Township...261
Chikaskia (Sumner) Township...317
Cimarron (Gray) City...248
Cimarron (Gray) Township...248
Cimarron (Meade) Township...275
Cimarron (Morton) Township...280
Circleville (Jackson) City...254
Claflin (Barton) City...216
Clarence (Barton) Township...216
Clark (Marion) Township...270
Clark County...226
Clay (Butler) Township...220
Clay (Reno) Township...296
Clay Center (Clay) City...227
Clay Center (Clay) Township...227
Clay County...226
Clayton (Decatur) City...234
Clayton (Norton) City...284
Clear Creek (Ellsworth) Township...241
Clear Creek (Marion) Township...270
Clear Creek (Nemaha) Township...281
Clear Creek (Pottawatomie) Township...292
Clear Creek (Stafford) Township...314
Clear Fork (Marshall) Township...272
Clearwater (Sedgwick) City...307
Cleveland (Barton) Township...216
Cleveland (Lane) Township...264
Cleveland (Marshall) Township...272
Cleveland (Stafford) Township...314
Cleveland Run (Cheyenne) Township...225
Clifford (Butler) Township...220
Clifton (Clay) City...227
Clifton (Washington) City...322
Clifton (Washington) Township...322
Clifton (Wilson) Township...324
Climax (Greenwood) City...249
Clinton (Douglas) Township...237
Cloud County...228
Clyde (Cloud) City...228
Coats (Pratt) City...294
Coffey County...229
Coffeyville (Montgomery) City...278
Colby (Thomas) City...319
Coldwater (Comanche) City...230
Coldwater (Comanche) Township...230
Coleman (Washington) Township...322
Colfax (Cloud) Township...228
Colfax (Marion) Township...270
Colfax (Wilson) Township...324
Collyer (Trego) City...319
Collyer (Trego) Township...319
Colony (Anderson) City...213
Colony (Greeley) Township...249
Colorado (Lincoln) Township...266
Columbia (Ellsworth) Township...241
Columbus (Cherokee) City...224
Colwich (Sedgwick) City...307
Comanche (Barton) Township...217
Comanche County...230
Concord (Ford) Township...243
Concord (Ottawa) Township...288
Concordia (Cloud) City...228
Conkling (Pawnee) Township...289
Conway (Sumner) Township...317
Conway Springs (Sumner) City...317
Cook (Decatur) Township...234
Coolidge (Hamilton) City...251
Coolidge (Hamilton) Township...251
Copeland (Gray) City...248
Copeland (Gray) Township...248
Cora (Smith) Township...313
Corinth (Osborne) Township...286
Corning (Nemaha) City...281
Cottage Grove (Allen) Township...212
Cottage Hill (Marshall) Township...272
Cottonwood (Chase) Township...222
Cottonwood Falls (Chase) City...222
Council Grove (Morris) City...279
Countryside (Johnson) City...258
Courtland (Republic) City...298
Courtland (Republic) Township...298
Covert (Osborne) Township...286
Cowley County...231
Coyville (Wilson) City...324
Crawford (Cherokee) Township...224
Crawford (Crawford) Township...232
Crawford County...232
Creek (Sumner) Township...317
Creswell (Cowley) Township...231
Crooked Creek (Meade) Township...275
Crystal (Phillips) Township...290
Crystal Plains (Smith) Township...313
Cuba (Republic) City...298
Cullison (Pratt) City...294
Culver (Ottawa) City...288
Culver (Ottawa) Township...288
Cunningham (Kingman) City...261
Custer (Decatur) Township...234
Custer (Mitchell) Township...277
Cutler (Franklin) Township...244
Dale (Kingman) Township...261

American Places Dictionary   KANSAS

Damar (Rooks) City ... 302
Danville (Harper) City ... 252
Darlington (Harvey) Township ... 252
Dayton (Phillips) Township ... 290
Dayton (Saline) Township ... 305
Dearing (Montgomery) City ... 278
Decatur County ... 233
Deer Creek (Allen) Township ... 212
Deer Creek (Phillips) Township ... 290
Deerfield (Kearny) City ... 260
Deerfield (Kearny) Township ... 260
Deerhead (Barber) Township ... 215
Delano (Sedgwick) Township ... 307
Delaware (Jefferson) Township ... 256
Delaware (Leavenworth) Township .. 265
Delaware (Wyandotte) Township ... 326
Delhi (Osborne) Township ... 286
Delia (Jackson) City ... 255
Delmore (McPherson) Township ... 274
Delphos (Ottawa) City ... 288
Denison (Jackson) City ... 255
Denton (Doniphan) City ... 236
Derby (Sedgwick) City ... 307
De Soto (Johnson) City ... 259
Dexter (Cowley) City ... 231
Dexter (Cowley) Township ... 231
Diamond Creek (Chase) Township ... 222
Dickinson County ... 235
Dighton (Lane) City ... 264
Dighton (Lane) Township ... 264
Dixon (Sumner) Township ... 317
Dodge (Ford) Township ... 243
Dodge City (Ford) City ... 243
Doniphan County ... 236
Dor (Smith) Township ... 313
Dorrance (Russell) City ... 304
Douglas (Jackson) Township ... 255
Douglas (Stafford) Township ... 314
Douglas County ... 237
Douglass (Butler) City ... 220
Douglass (Butler) Township ... 220
Dover (Shawnee) Township ... 310
Downs (Osborne) City ... 286
Downs (Sumner) Township ... 317
Doyle (Marion) Township ... 270
Dragoon (Osage) Township ... 285
Dresden (Decatur) City ... 234
Dresden (Decatur) Township ... 234
Dresden (Kingman) Township ... 261
Driftwood (Rawlins) Township ... 295
Drum Creek (Montgomery) Township ... 278
Drywood (Bourbon) Township ... 218
Duck Creek (Wilson) Township ... 324
Dudley (Haskell) Township ... 253
Dunlap (Morris) City ... 279
Durham (Marion) City ... 270
Durham (Ottawa) Township ... 288
Durham Park (Marion) Township 270
Dwight (Morris) City ... 279
Eagle (Barber) Township ... 215
Eagle (Kingman) Township ... 261
Eagle (Sedgwick) Township ... 307
Earlton (Neosho) City ... 282
Eastborough (Sedgwick) City ... 307
East Branch (Marion) Township ... 270
East Cooper (Stafford) Township ... 314
East Hale (Thomas) Township ... 319
East Hess (Gray) Township ... 248
East Hibbard (Kearny) Township ... 260
East Kiowa (Kiowa) Pop. Place ... 262
Easton (Leavenworth) City ... 265
Easton (Leavenworth) Township ... 265
East Saline (Sheridan) Township ... 311
East Washington (Rice) Township ... 299

Eden (Ness) Township ... 283
Eden (Sumner) Township ... 317
Edgerton (Johnson) City ... 259
Edmond (Norton) City ... 284
Edna (Labette) City ... 263
Edwards County ... 238
Edwardsville (Wyandotte) City ... 326
Effingham (Atchison) City ... 214
Elbing (Butler) City ... 221
El Dorado (Butler) City ... 221
El Dorado (Butler) Township ... 221
Elgin (Chautauqua) City ... 223
Elk (Cloud) Township ... 228
Elk (Osage) Township ... 285
Elkader (Logan) Township ... 268
Elk City (Montgomery) City ... 278
Elk County ... 239
Elk Creek (Republic) Township ... 298
Elk Falls (Elk) City ... 239
Elk Falls (Elk) Township ... 239
Elkhart (Morton) City ... 280
Elkhorn (Lincoln) Township ... 266
Ellinwood (Barton) City ... 217
Ellis (Ellis) City ... 240
Ellis (Ellis) Township ... 240
Ellis County ... 240
Ellsworth (Ellsworth) City ... 241
Ellsworth (Ellsworth) Township ... 241
Ellsworth County ... 241
Elm (Allen) Township ... 212
Elm Creek (Marshall) Township ... 272
Elm Creek (Saline) Township ... 305
Elmdale (Chase) City ... 222
Elmendaro (Lyon) Township ... 269
Elm Grove (Labette) Township ... 263
Elm Mills (Barber) Township ... 215
Elsmore (Allen) City ... 212
Elsmore (Allen) Township ... 212
Elwood (Barber) Township ... 215
Elwood (Doniphan) City ... 236
Emma (Harvey) Township ... 252
Emmett (Pottawatomie) City ... 292
Emmett (Pottawatomie) Township ... 292
Empire (Ellsworth) Township ... 241
Empire (McPherson) Township ... 274
Emporia (Lyon) City ... 269
Emporia (Lyon) Township ... 269
Englewood (Clark) City ... 226
Englewood (Clark) Township ... 226
Ensign (Gray) City ... 248
Enterprise (Dickinson) City ... 235
Enterprise (Ford) Township ... 243
Enterprise (Reno) Township ... 296
Erie (Neosho) City ... 282
Erie (Neosho) Township ... 282
Erie (Sedgwick) Township ... 307
Erving (Jewell) Township ... 257
Esbon (Jewell) City ... 257
Esbon (Jewell) Township ... 257
Eskridge (Wabaunsee) City ... 320
Eudora (Douglas) City ... 237
Eudora (Douglas) Township ... 237
Eureka (Barton) Township ... 217
Eureka (Greenwood) City ... 249
Eureka (Greenwood) Township ... 250
Eureka (Kingman) Township ... 261
Eureka (Mitchell) Township ... 277
Eureka (Rice) Township ... 299
Eureka (Saline) Township ... 305
Evan (Kingman) Township ... 261
Everest (Brown) City ... 219
Exeter (Clay) Township ... 227
Fairfax (Osage) Township ... 285
Fairfield (Russell) Township ... 304
Fairmount (Butler) Township ... 221

Fairmount (Leavenworth) Township . 265
Fairplay (Marion) Township ... 270
Fairview (Barton) Township ... 217
Fairview (Brown) City ... 219
Fairview (Butler) Township ... 221
Fairview (Cowley) Township ... 231
Fairview (Ford) Township ... 243
Fairview (Jefferson) Township ... 256
Fairview (Labette) Township ... 263
Fairview (Republic) Township ... 298
Fairview (Russell) Township ... 304
Fairview (Stafford) Township ... 314
Fairway (Johnson) City ... 259
Fall River (Greenwood) City ... 250
Fall River (Greenwood) Township 250
Fall River (Wilson) Township ... 324
Falls (Chase) Township ... 222
Falls (Sumner) Township ... 317
Falun (Saline) Township ... 305
Fancy Creek (Riley) Township ... 301
Fargo (Seward) Township ... 309
Farmer (Rice) Township ... 300
Farmer (Wabaunsee) Township ... 320
Farmington (Republic) Township ... 298
Farmington (Stafford) Township ... 314
Farmington (Washington) Township . 322
Fawn Creek (Montgomery) Township ... 278
Finley (Decatur) Township ... 234
Finney County ... 242
Five Creeks (Clay) Township ... 227
Flora (Dickinson) Township ... 235
Florence (Marion) City ... 270
Fontana (Miami) City ... 276
Foote (Gray) Township ... 248
Ford (Ford) City ... 243
Ford (Ford) Township ... 243
Ford County ... 243
Formoso (Jewell) City ... 257
Forrester (Ness) Township ... 283
Fort Riley-Camp Whiteside (Geary) Military Facility ... 245
Fort Riley North (Geary) Military Facility ... 245
Fort Riley North (Riley) Military Facility ... 301
Fort Scott (Bourbon) City ... 218
Fountain (Ottawa) Township ... 288
Fowler (Meade) City ... 275
Fowler (Meade) Township ... 275
Fragrant Hill (Dickinson) Township . 235
Frankfort (Marshall) City ... 272
Franklin (Bourbon) Township ... 218
Franklin (Edwards) Township ... 238
Franklin (Franklin) Township ... 244
Franklin (Jackson) Township ... 255
Franklin (Lincoln) Township ... 266
Franklin (Marshall) Township ... 272
Franklin (Ness) Township ... 283
Franklin (Trego) Township ... 320
Franklin (Washington) Township ... 322
Franklin County ... 244
Frederick (Rice) City ... 300
Fredonia (Wilson) City ... 324
Freedom (Bourbon) Township ... 218
Freedom (Ellis) Township ... 240
Freedom (Phillips) Township ... 290
Freedom (Republic) Township ... 298
Freeport (Harper) City ... 252
Fremont (Lyon) Township ... 269
Frontenac (Crawford) City ... 232
Fulton (Bourbon) City ... 218
Gaeland (Gove) Township ... 246
Galatia (Barton) City ... 217
Gale (Marion) Township ... 270

329

KANSAS
American Places Dictionary

Galena (Cherokee) City 224
Galesburg (Kingman) Township 261
Galesburg (Neosho) City 282
Galt (Rice) Township 300
Galva (McPherson) City 274
Garden (Cherokee) Township 224
Garden (Harvey) Township 252
Garden City (Finney) City 242
Garden City (Finney) Township 242
Garden Plain (Sedgwick) City 307
Garden Plain (Sedgwick) Township .. 307
Gardner (Johnson) City 259
Gardner (Johnson) Township 259
Garfield (Clay) Township 227
Garfield (Decatur) Township 234
Garfield (Dickinson) Township 235
Garfield (Ellsworth) Township 241
Garfield (Finney) Township 242
Garfield (Jackson) Township 255
Garfield (Ottawa) Township 288
Garfield (Pawnee) City 289
Garfield (Pawnee) Township 289
Garfield (Rush) Township 303
Garfield (Smith) Township 313
Garfield (Wabaunsee) Township 320
Garnett (Anderson) City 213
Gas (Allen) City 212
Gaylord (Smith) City 313
Geary County 245
Gem (Thomas) City 319
Geneseo (Rice) City 300
Geneva (Allen) Township 212
German (Smith) Township 313
Gettysburg (Graham) Township 247
Geuda Springs (Cowley) City 231
Geuda Springs (Sumner) City 317
Gill (Clay) Township 227
Gilman (Nemaha) Township 281
Girard (Crawford) City 233
Glade (Phillips) City 290
Glasco (Cloud) City 228
Glencoe (Butler) Township 221
Glencoe (Trego) Township 320
Glendale (Saline) Township 305
Glen Elder (Mitchell) City 277
Glen Elder (Mitchell) Township 277
Glenwood (Phillips) Township 290
Goddard (Sedgwick) City 307
Goessel (Marion) City 270
Goff (Nemaha) City 281
Golden Belt (Lincoln) Township 266
Goodland (Sherman) City 312
Gore (Sumner) Township 317
Gorham (Russell) City 304
Goshen (Clay) Township 227
Gove (Gove) Township 246
Gove City (Gove) City 246
Gove County 246
Graham (Graham) Township 247
Graham County 247
Grainfield (Gove) City 246
Grainfield (Gove) Township 246
Granada (Nemaha) Township 281
Grand River (Sedgwick) Township .. 307
Grandview (Ford) Township 243
Grandview Plaza (Geary) City 245
Granite (Phillips) Township 290
Grant (Barton) Township 217
Grant (Clay) Township 227
Grant (Cloud) Township 228
Grant (Cowley) Township 231
Grant (Crawford) Township 233
Grant (Decatur) Township 234
Grant (Dickinson) Township 235
Grant (Douglas) Township 237

Grant (Jackson) Township 255
Grant (Jewell) Township 257
Grant (Lincoln) Township 266
Grant (Marion) Township 270
Grant (Neosho) Township 283
Grant (Osage) Township 285
Grant (Osborne) Township 286
Grant (Ottawa) Township 288
Grant (Pawnee) Township 289
Grant (Pottawatomie) Township 292
Grant (Reno) Township 296
Grant (Republic) Township 298
Grant (Riley) Township 301
Grant (Russell) Township 304
Grant (Sedgwick) Township 307
Grant (Sherman) Township 312
Grant (Washington) Township 322
Grant County 248
Grasshopper (Atchison) Township 214
Gray County 248
Great Bend (Barton) City 217
Great Bend (Barton) Township 217
Greeley (Anderson) City 213
Greeley (Saline) Township 305
Greeley (Sedgwick) Township 308
Greeley County 249
Green (Clay) City 227
Green (Pottawatomie) Township 292
Greene (Sumner) Township 317
Greenfield (Elk) Township 239
Green Garden (Ellsworth) Township 241
Greenleaf (Washington) City 322
Greenleaf (Washington) Township .. 322
Greensburg (Kiowa) City 262
Greenwood (Franklin) Township 244
Greenwood (Phillips) Township 290
Greenwood County 249
Grenola (Elk) City 239
Gridley (Coffey) City 229
Grinnell (Gove) City 246
Grinnell (Gove) Township 246
Grove (Reno) Township 296
Grove (Shawnee) Township 310
Groveland (McPherson) Township ... 274
Guelph (Sumner) Township 317
Guilford (Wilson) Township 324
Guittard (Marshall) Township 272
Gypsum (Saline) City 305
Gypsum (Saline) Township 305
Gypsum (Sedgwick) Township 308
Gypsum Creek (McPherson)
   Township 274
Hackberry (Labette) Township 263
Haddam (Washington) City 322
Haddam (Washington) Township 322
Hallet (Hodgeman) Township 254
Halstead (Harvey) City 252
Halstead (Harvey) Township 252
Hamilton (Greenwood) City 250
Hamilton County 251
Hamlin (Brown) City 219
Hamlin (Brown) Township 219
Hampden (Coffey) Township 229
Hampton-Fairview (Rush) Township 303
Hancock (Osborne) Township 286
Hanover (Lincoln) Township 266
Hanover (Washington) City 322
Hanover (Washington) Township 322
Hanston (Hodgeman) City 254
Happy (Graham) Township 247
Hardtner (Barber) City 215
Harlan (Decatur) Township 234
Harlan (Smith) Township 313
Harmon (Sumner) Township 317
Harmony (Stevens) Township 316

Harper (Harper) City 252
Harper (McPherson) Township 274
Harper County 251
Harris (Anderson) City 213
Harrison (Chautauqua) Township 223
Harrison (Franklin) Township 244
Harrison (Greeley) Township 249
Harrison (Jewell) Township 257
Harrison (Nemaha) Township 281
Harrison (Rice) Township 300
Harrison (Wallace) Township 321
Harrison-District 6 (Norton)
   Township 284
Hartford (Lyon) City 269
Hartland (Kearny) Township 260
Harvey (Cowley) Township 231
Harvey (Smith) Township 313
Harvey County 252
Harveyville (Wabaunsee) City 320
Haskell (Haskell) Township 253
Haskell County 253
Havana (Montgomery) City 279
Haven (Reno) City 296
Haven (Reno) Township 296
Havensville (Pottawatomie) City 292
Haviland (Kiowa) City 262
Hawkeye (Osborne) Township 286
Hayes (Clay) Township 227
Hayes (Dickinson) Township 235
Hayes (Franklin) Township 244
Hayes (McPherson) Township 274
Hayes (Mitchell) Township 277
Hayes (Reno) Township 296
Hayes (Stafford) Township 314
Hays (Ellis) City 240
Haysville (Sedgwick) City 308
Hazelton (Barber) City 215
Hazelton (Barber) Township 215
Hendricks (Chautauqua) Township .. 223
Henry (Ottawa) Township 288
Hepler (Crawford) City 233
Herington (Dickinson) City 235
Herington (Morris) City 279
Herkimer (Marshall) Township 272
Herl (Rawlins) Township 295
Herndon (Rawlins) City 295
Herzog (Ellis) Township 240
Hesston (Harvey) City 253
Hiawatha (Brown) City 219
Hiawatha (Brown) Township 219
Hickory (Butler) Township 221
Highland (Clay) Township 227
Highland (Doniphan) City 236
Highland (Harvey) Township 253
Highland (Jewell) Township 257
Highland (Lincoln) Township 266
Highland (Morris) Township 279
Highland (Washington) Township 322
Highland-District 2 (Norton)
   Township 284
Highpoint (Ness) Township 283
High Prairie (Leavenworth)
   Township 265
Hill City (Graham) City 247
Hill City (Graham) Township 247
Hillsboro (Marion) City 271
Hodgeman County 254
Hoisington (Barton) City 217
Holcomb (Finney) City 242
Holland (Dickinson) Township 235
Hollenberg (Washington) City 323
Holmwood (Jewell) Township 257
Holton (Jackson) City 255
Holyrood (Ellsworth) City 241
Home (Nemaha) Township 281

American Places Dictionary — KANSAS

Homestead (Chase) Township............222
Homewood (Franklin) Township......244
Hoosier (Kingman) Township...........261
Hope (Dickinson) City......................235
Hope (Dickinson) Township.............235
Horace (Greeley) City......................249
Horton (Brown) City........................219
Houston (Smith) Township...............313
Howard (Elk) City............................239
Howard (Elk) Township....................239
Howard (Labette) Township..............263
Hoxie (Sheridan) City......................311
Hoyt (Jackson) City.........................255
Hudson (Stafford) City.....................314
Hugoton (Stevens) City....................316
Humboldt (Allen) City.....................212
Humboldt (Allen) Township.............212
Hunnewell (Sumner) City.................317
Hunter (Mitchell) City......................277
Huntsville (Reno) Township.............296
Huron (Atchison) City......................214
Hutchinson (Reno) City....................296
Illinois (Nemaha) Township..............281
Illinois (Rush) Township..................303
Illinois (Sedgwick) Township............308
Illinois (Sumner) Township...............317
Independence (Doniphan) Township 237
Independence (Montgomery) City....279
Independence (Montgomery)
   Township.................................279
Independence (Osborne) Township...286
Independence (Washington)
   Township.................................323
Independent (Barton) Township.......217
Indiana (Graham) Township.............247
Indiana (Lincoln) Township..............266
Indian Creek (Anderson) Township..213
Ingalls (Gray) City............................248
Ingalls (Gray) Township....................248
Inman (McPherson) City...................274
Iola (Allen) City................................212
Iola (Allen) Township........................212
Ionia (Jewell) Township.....................257
Iowa (Doniphan) Township................237
Iowa (Sherman) Township.................312
Irving (Brown) Township...................219
Isabel (Barber) City...........................215
Isbel (Scott) Township......................306
Itasca (Sherman) Township...............312
Iuka (Pratt) City................................294
Ivanhoe (Finney) Township...............242
Ivy (Lyon) Township.........................269
Jackson (Anderson) Township...........213
Jackson (Edwards) Township............238
Jackson (Geary) Township.................245
Jackson (Jewell) Township.................257
Jackson (Lyon) Township...................269
Jackson (McPherson) Township........274
Jackson (Osborne) Township.............286
Jackson (Riley) Township..................301
Jackson (Sumner) Township..............317
Jackson County............................254
Jamestown (Cloud) City....................228
Janesville (Greenwood) Township.....250
Jaqua (Cheyenne) Township..............225
Jefferson (Chautauqua) Township.....223
Jefferson (Dickinson) Township........235
Jefferson (Geary) Township...............245
Jefferson (Jackson) Township............255
Jefferson (Rawlins) Township............295
Jefferson (Republic) Township..........298
Jefferson County...........................256
Jefferson No. 10 (Jefferson)
   Township..................................256
Jennings (Decatur) City....................234

Jennings (Decatur) Township............234
Jerome (Gove) Township..................246
Jetmore (Hodgeman) City.................254
Jewell (Jewell) City...........................258
Jewell County................................257
Johnson (Ness) Township..................283
Johnson (Stanton) City......................315
Johnson County..............................258
Jones (Morton) Township..................280
Junction (Osage) Township................285
Junction City (Geary) City.................245
Kanopolis (Ellsworth) City................241
Kanorado (Sherman) City..................312
Kansas City (Wyandotte) City...........326
Kanwaka (Douglas) Township...........238
Kapioma (Atchison) Township..........214
Kaw (Jefferson) Township.................256
Kaw (Wabaunsee) Township..............320
Kearny County...............................260
Kechi (Sedgwick) City.......................308
Kechi (Sedgwick) Township..............308
Kendall (Hamilton) Township............251
Kendall (Kearny) Township...............260
Kenneth (Sheridan) Township............311
Kensington (Smith) City....................313
Kentucky (Jefferson) Township.........256
Keystone (Scott) Township................306
Keysville (Pawnee) Township............289
Key West (Coffey) Township.............229
Kickapoo (Leavenworth) Township..265
Kill Creek (Osborne) Township.........286
Kimeo (Washington) Township.........323
Kincaid (Anderson) City....................213
King City (McPherson) Township....274
Kingery (Thomas) Township.............319
Kingman (Kingman) City..................261
Kingman (Kingman) Township..........261
Kingman County............................261
Kinsley (Edwards) City......................238
Kinsley (Edwards) Township.............238
Kiowa (Barber) City...........................215
Kiowa (Barber) Township..................215
Kiowa County.................................262
Kirwin (Phillips) City.........................290
Kirwin (Phillips) Township................290
Kismet (Seward) City.........................309
Labette (Labette) City........................263
Labette (Labette) Township................263
Labette County...............................263
Lacey (Thomas) Township.................319
La Crosse (Rush) City........................303
La Crosse-Brookdale (Rush)
   Township..................................303
La Cygne (Linn) City.........................267
Ladore (Neosho) Township................283
Lafayette (Chautauqua) Township.....223
La Harpe (Allen) City........................212
Lake (Harvey) Township....................253
Lake (Scott) Township.......................306
Lake City (Barber) Township.............215
Lake Quivira (Johnson) City..............259
Lake Quivira (Wyandotte) City.........326
Lakin (Barton) Township...................217
Lakin (Harvey) Township...................253
Lakin (Kearny) City............................260
Lakin (Kearny) Township...................260
Lamont (Hamilton) Township............251
Lancaster (Atchison) City...................214
Lancaster (Atchison) Township..........214
Lane (Franklin) City..........................244
Lane (Greenwood) Township.............250
Lane (Smith) Township......................313
Lane County...................................264
Langdon (Reno) City.........................296
Langdon (Reno) Township.................296

Langley (Ellsworth) Township...........241
Lansing (Leavenworth) City..............265
Larned (Pawnee) City........................289
Larned (Pawnee) Township................289
Larrabee (Gove) Township.................246
Latham (Butler) City..........................221
Latimer (Morris) City.........................279
Lawrence (Cloud) Township..............228
Lawrence (Douglas) City...................238
Lawrence (Osborne) Township..........287
Leavenworth (Leavenworth) City.....265
Leavenworth County.....................265
Leawood (Johnson) City....................259
Lebanon (Smith) City........................313
Lebo (Coffey) City.............................229
Lecompton (Douglas) City.................238
Lecompton (Douglas) Township........238
Lees (Logan) Township.....................268
Lehigh (Marion) City.........................271
Lehigh (Marion) Township.................271
Lenexa (Johnson) City.......................259
Lenora (Norton) City.........................284
Leon (Butler) City..............................221
Leona (Doniphan) City......................237
Leonardville (Riley) City...................301
Leoti (Wichita) City............................324
Leoti (Wichita) Township...................324
Le Roy (Coffey) City..........................229
Le Roy (Coffey) Township.................229
Lewis (Edwards) City.........................238
Lewis (Gove) Township......................246
Lexington (Clark) Township...............226
Lexington (Johnson) Township..........259
Liberal (Seward) City.........................309
Liberal (Seward) Township................309
Liberty (Barton) Township.................217
Liberty (Clark) Township...................226
Liberty (Coffey) Township.................229
Liberty (Cowley) Township................231
Liberty (Decatur) Township...............234
Liberty (Dickinson) Township...........235
Liberty (Elk) Township......................239
Liberty (Geary) Township..................245
Liberty (Hamilton) Township.............251
Liberty (Jackson) Township...............255
Liberty (Kingman) Township.............261
Liberty (Labette) Township................263
Liberty (Linn) Township....................267
Liberty (Marion) Township................271
Liberty (Montgomery) City...............279
Liberty (Montgomery) Township.....279
Liberty (Osborne) Township.............287
Liberty (Republic) Township............298
Liberty (Saline) Township.................305
Liberty (Woodson) Township............325
Liebenthal (Rush) City......................303
Limestone (Jewell) Township...........258
Lincoln (Anderson) Township..........213
Lincoln (Butler) Township................221
Lincoln (Cloud) Township................228
Lincoln (Coffey) Township...............229
Lincoln (Crawford) Township...........233
Lincoln (Decatur) Township.............234
Lincoln (Dickinson) Township.........235
Lincoln (Edwards) Township............238
Lincoln (Ellsworth) Township..........241
Lincoln (Franklin) Township............244
Lincoln (Grant) Township.................248
Lincoln (Jackson) Township..............255
Lincoln (Lincoln) City.......................266
Lincoln (Linn) Township...................267
Lincoln (Marshall) Township............272
Lincoln (Neosho) Township..............283
Lincoln (Osage) Township................285
Lincoln (Ottawa) Township...............288

KANSAS

Lincoln (Pawnee) Township 289
Lincoln (Pottawatomie) Township 292
Lincoln (Reno) Township 296
Lincoln (Republic) Township 298
Lincoln (Rice) Township 300
Lincoln (Russell) Township 304
Lincoln (Sedgwick) Township 308
Lincoln (Sherman) Township 312
Lincoln (Smith) Township 313
Lincoln (Stafford) Township 314
Lincoln (Washington) Township 323
Lincoln County 266
Lincolnville (Marion) City 271
Lindsborg (McPherson) City 274
Linn (Washington) City 323
Linn (Washington) Township 323
Linn County 267
Linwood (Leavenworth) City 265
Little Blue (Washington) Township... 323
Little Caney (Chautauqua) Township 223
Little River (Reno) Township 297
Little River (Rice) City 300
Little Valley (McPherson) Township. 274
Little Walnut (Butler) Township 221
Llanos (Sherman) Township 312
Lockport (Haskell) Township 253
Loda (Reno) Township 297
Logan (Allen) Township 212
Logan (Barton) Township 217
Logan (Butler) Township 221
Logan (Decatur) Township 234
Logan (Dickinson) Township 236
Logan (Edwards) Township 238
Logan (Gray) Township 249
Logan (Lincoln) Township 266
Logan (Marion) Township 271
Logan (Marshall) Township 272
Logan (Meade) Township 275
Logan (Mitchell) Township 277
Logan (Ottawa) Township 288
Logan (Pawnee) Township 289
Logan (Phillips) City 290
Logan (Phillips) Township 290
Logan (Sheridan) Township 311
Logan (Sherman) Township 312
Logan (Smith) Township 313
Logan (Washington) Township 323
Logan County 268
Logansport (Logan) Township 268
Lola (Cherokee) Township 224
London (Sumner) Township 317
Lone Elm (Anderson) City 213
Lone Elm (Anderson) Township 213
Lone Star (Rush) Township 303
Lone Tree (McPherson) Township ... 274
Lone Tree (Pottawatomie) Township 292
Longford (Clay) City 227
Long Island (Phillips) City 291
Long Island (Phillips) Township 291
Longton (Elk) City 239
Longton (Elk) Township 239
Lookout (Ellis) Township 240
Lorraine (Ellsworth) City 241
Lost Springs (Marion) City 271
Lost Springs (Marion) Township 271
Louisburg (Miami) City 276
Louisburg (Montgomery) Township. 279
Louisville (Pottawatomie) City 292
Louisville (Pottawatomie) Township 292
Lowe (Washington) Township 323
Lowell (Cherokee) Township 224
Lucas (Russell) City 304
Ludell (Rawlins) Township 295
Lulu (Mitchell) Township 277

Luray (Russell) City 304
Luray (Russell) Township 304
Lyndon (Osage) City 285
Lyon (Cherokee) Township 224
Lyon (Cloud) Township 228
Lyon (Decatur) Township 234
Lyon (Dickinson) Township 236
Lyon (Geary) Township 245
Lyon County 269
Lyons (Rice) City 300
Macksville (Stafford) City 315
Macon (Harvey) Township 253
Madison (Greenwood) City 250
Madison (Greenwood) Township 250
Madison (Lincoln) Township 266
Madison (Riley) Township 301
Mahaska (Washington) City 323
Maize (Sedgwick) City 308
Manchester (Dickinson) City 236
Manhattan (Pottawatomie) City 292
Manhattan (Riley) City 301
Manhattan (Riley) Township 301
Mankato (Jewell) City 258
Manter (Stanton) City 316
Manter (Stanton) Township 316
Maple (Cowley) Township 231
Maple Hill (Wabaunsee) City 321
Maple Hill (Wabaunsee) Township . 321
Mapleton (Bourbon) City 218
Marena (Hodgeman) Township 254
Marion (Bourbon) Township 218
Marion (Doniphan) Township 237
Marion (Douglas) Township 238
Marion (Lincoln) Township 266
Marion (Marion) City 271
Marion (Nemaha) Township 281
Marion County 270
Marmaton (Allen) Township 212
Marmaton (Bourbon) Township 218
Marquette (McPherson) City 274
Marquette (McPherson) Township.. 274
Marshall County 272
Martin (Smith) Township 314
Marysville (Marshall) City 272
Marysville (Marshall) Township 272
Marysville (Miami) Township 276
Matfield (Chase) Township 222
Matfield Green (Chase) City 222
May Day (Riley) Township 301
Mayetta (Jackson) City 255
Mayfield (Sumner) City 317
McAdoo (Barber) Township 215
McAllaster (Logan) Township 268
McCamish (Johnson) Township 259
McCracken (Rush) City 303
McCune (Crawford) City 233
McDonald (Rawlins) City 295
McFarland (Wabaunsee) City 320
McLouth (Jefferson) City 256
McPherson (McPherson) City 274
McPherson (McPherson) Township. 274
McPherson (Sherman) Township 312
McPherson County 273
Meade (Meade) City 275
Meade Center (Meade) Township ... 275
Meade County 275
Medford (Reno) Township 297
Medicine Lodge (Barber) City 215
Medicine Lodge (Barber) Township. 216
Medora (Reno) Township 297
Medway (Hamilton) Township 251
Melvern (Osage) City 285
Melvern (Osage) Township 285
Menlo (Thomas) City 319
Menlo (Thomas) Township 319

American Places Dictionary

Menno (Marion) Township 271
Menoken (Shawnee) Township 310
Meredith (Cloud) Township 228
Meriden (Jefferson) City 256
Meridian (McPherson) Township 274
Merriam (Johnson) City 259
Mertilla (Meade) Township 275
Miami (Miami) Township 276
Miami (Reno) Township 297
Miami County 276
Michigan (Scott) Township 306
Middle Creek (Miami) Township 276
Milan (Sumner) City 317
Mildred (Allen) City 212
Milford (Geary) City 245
Milford (Geary) Township 245
Millbrook (Graham) Township 247
Mill Creek (Bourbon) Township 218
Mill Creek (Pottawatomie) Township 292
Mill Creek (Wabaunsee) Township... 321
Mill Creek (Washington) Township.. 323
Milton (Butler) Township 221
Milton (Marion) Township 271
Miltonvale (Cloud) City 228
Mineral (Cherokee) Township 224
Mingona (Barber) Township 216
Minneapolis (Ottawa) City 288
Minneha (Sedgwick) Township 308
Minneola (Clark) City 226
Mirage (Rawlins) Township 295
Mission (Brown) Township 219
Mission (Johnson) City 259
Mission (Neosho) Township 283
Mission (Shawnee) Township 310
Mission Creek (Wabaunsee) Township 321
Mission Hills (Johnson) City 259
Mission Woods (Johnson) City 259
Mitchell (Nemaha) Township 281
Mitchell (Rice) Township 300
Mitchell County 277
Moline (Elk) City 239
Monmouth (Shawnee) Township ... 310
Monroe (Anderson) Township 213
Montana (Jewell) Township 258
Montana (Labette) Township 263
Montezuma (Gray) City 249
Montezuma (Gray) Township 249
Montgomery County 278
Monticello (Johnson) Township 259
Monument (Logan) Township 268
Moore (Barber) Township 216
Moore (Marion) Township 271
Moran (Allen) City 213
Morgan (Thomas) Township 319
Morganville (Clay) City 227
Morlan (Graham) Township 247
Morland (Graham) City 247
Morrill (Brown) City 219
Morrill (Brown) Township 219
Morris (Sumner) Township 317
Morris County 279
Morrowville (Washington) City 323
Morton (Ottawa) Township 288
Morton (Pawnee) Township 289
Morton (Sedgwick) Township 308
Morton County 280
Moscow (Stevens) City 316
Moscow (Stevens) Township 316
Mound (McPherson) Township 274
Mound (Miami) Township 276
Mound (Phillips) Township 291
Mound City (Linn) City 267
Mound City (Linn) Township 267

Moundridge (McPherson) City *274*
Mound Valley (Labette) City.............*263*
Mound Valley (Labette) Township....*263*
Mount Ayr (Osborne) Township *287*
Mount Hope (Sedgwick) City...........*308*
Mount Pleasant (Atchison)
　　Township................................ *214*
Mount Pleasant (Labette) Township.*263*
Mulberry (Clay) Township *227*
Mulberry (Crawford) City *233*
Mulberry (Ellsworth) Township *241*
Mullinville (Kiowa) City *262*
Mulvane (Sedgwick) City *308*
Mulvane (Sumner) City.....................*318*
Munden (Republic) City....................*299*
Murdock (Butler) Township...............*221*
Murray (Marshall) Township *272*
Muscotah (Atchison) City *215*
Narka (Republic) City........................*299*
Nashville (Kingman) City *261*
Natoma (Osborne) City.....................*287*
Natoma (Osborne) Township............*287*
Nelson (Cloud) Township..................*228*
Nemaha (Nemaha) Township...........*281*
Nemaha County................................*281*
Neodesha (Wilson) City *325*
Neodesha (Wilson) Township............*325*
Neosho (Cherokee) Township *224*
Neosho (Coffey) Township *229*
Neosho (Labette) Township *263*
Neosho County................................*282*
Neosho Falls (Woodson) City............*325*
Neosho Falls (Woodson) Township...*325*
Neosho Rapids (Lyon) City................*269*
Ness City (Ness) City *284*
Ness County.....................................*283*
Netawaka (Jackson) City...................*255*
Netawaka (Jackson) Township..........*255*
Neuchatel (Nemaha) Township.........*281*
Nevada (Ness) Township...................*284*
New Albany (Wilson) City..................*325*
Newark (Wilson) Township................*325*
Newbern (Dickinson) Township........*236*
Newbury (Wabaunsee) Township......*321*
New Cambria (Saline) City *305*
New Gottland (McPherson)
　　Township................................ *274*
New Strawn (Coffey) City..................*230*
Newton (Harvey) City *253*
Newton (Harvey) Township...............*253*
Nickerson (Reno) City.......................*297*
Nicodemus (Graham) Township *247*
Ninnescah (Cowley) Township..........*231*
Ninnescah (Kingman) Township.......*261*
Ninnescah (Reno) Township *297*
Ninnescah (Sedgwick) Township......*308*
Niotaze (Chautauqua) City *223*
Nippawalla (Barber) Township *216*
Noble (Dickinson) Township.............*236*
Noble (Ellsworth) Township..............*241*
Noble (Marshall) Township *273*
Norcatur (Decatur) City.....................*234*
North (Labette) Township *263*
North (Woodson) Township...............*325*
North Brown (Edwards) Township ...*238*
North Homestead (Barton)
　　Township................................ *217*
North Newton (Harvey) City *253*
North Randall (Thomas) Township ...*319*
North Rich (Anderson) Township.....*213*
North Roscoe (Hodgeman)
　　Township................................ *254*
North Seward (Stafford) Township...*315*
Norton (Jefferson) Township *256*
Norton (Norton) City *284*

Norton County...................................*284*
Nortonville (Jefferson) City *256*
Norway (Republic) Township............*299*
Norwich (Kingman) City....................*261*
Oak (Smith) Township *314*
Oak Hill (Clay) City *227*
Oakland (Clay) Township...................*227*
Oakland (Cloud) Township *228*
Oaklawn-Sunview (Sedgwick) CDP ..*308*
Oakley (Logan) City *268*
Oakley (Logan) Township..................*268*
Oakley (Thomas) City *319*
Oak Valley (Elk) Township *239*
Oberlin (Decatur) City *234*
Oberlin (Decatur) Township...............*234*
Odee (Meade) Township....................*275*
Odessa (Jewell) Township *258*
Odessa (Rice) Township *300*
Offerle (Edwards) City.......................*239*
Ogallah (Trego) Township *320*
Ogden (Riley) City.............................*301*
Ogden (Riley) Township.....................*301*
Ohio (Franklin) Township..................*244*
Ohio (Ness) Township *284*
Ohio (Saline) Township *305*
Ohio (Sedgwick) Township................*308*
Ohio (Stafford) Township...................*315*
Oketo (Marshall) City.........................*273*
Oketo (Marshall) Township................*273*
Olathe (Johnson) City *259*
Olathe (Johnson) Township *259*
Olive (Decatur) Township *234*
Olivet (Osage) City............................*285*
Olivet (Osage) Township *285*
Olmitz (Barton) City *217*
Olpe (Lyon) City.................................*269*
Olsburg (Pottawatomie) City.............*292*
Omnia (Cowley) Township.................*231*
Onaga (Pottawatomie) City................*293*
Oneida (Nemaha) City *281*
Orange (Lincoln) Township...............*266*
Orange (Pawnee) Township...............*289*
Orlando (Cheyenne) Township...........*225*
Osage (Allen) Township.....................*213*
Osage (Bourbon) Township *218*
Osage (Crawford) Township...............*233*
Osage (Labette) Township *263*
Osage (Miami) Township *276*
Osage City (Osage) City....................*285*
Osage County...................................*285*
Osawatomie (Miami) City..................*276*
Osawatomie (Miami) Township..........*276*
Osborne (Osborne) City *287*
Osborne (Sumner) Township.............*318*
Osborne County................................*286*
Oskaloosa (Jefferson) City................*256*
Oskaloosa (Jefferson) Township.......*256*
Oswego (Labette) City *264*
Oswego (Labette) Township *264*
Otis (Rush) City *303*
Ottawa (Franklin) City *244*
Ottawa (Franklin) Township *244*
Ottawa (Ottawa) Township *288*
Ottawa County *287*
Otter (Cowley) Township *231*
Otter Creek (Greenwood) Township.*250*
Ottumwa (Coffey) Township *230*
Overbrook (Osage) City....................*285*
Overland (Morris) Township *279*
Overland Park (Johnson) City *259*
Oxford (Johnson) Township *260*
Oxford (Sumner) City........................*318*
Oxford (Sumner) Township................*318*
Ozark (Anderson) Township *213*
Ozawkie (Jefferson) City...................*256*

Ozawkie (Jefferson) Township *256*
Padonia (Brown) Township................*219*
Painterhood (Elk) Township..............*239*
Palacky (Ellsworth) Township...........*241*
Palco (Rooks) City............................*302*
Palestine (Sumner) Township...........*318*
Palmer (Washington) City.................*323*
Palmyra (Douglas) Township *238*
Paola (Miami) City............................*276*
Paola (Miami) Township *276*
Paradise (Russell) City *304*
Paradise (Russell) Township.............*304*
Paris (Linn) Township.......................*267*
Park (Gove) City *246*
Park (Sedgwick) Township................*308*
Park City (Sedgwick) City.................*308*
Parker (Linn) City *267*
Parker (Montgomery) Township *279*
Parkerville (Morris) City *280*
Parnell (Sheridan) Township.............*311*
Parsons (Labette) City......................*264*
Partridge (Reno) City *297*
Pawnee (Bourbon) Township *218*
Pawnee (Pawnee) Township..............*289*
Pawnee (Smith) Township *314*
Pawnee County................................*289*
Pawnee Rock (Barton) City...............*217*
Pawnee Rock (Barton) Township......*217*
Paw Paw (Elk) Township *239*
Paxico (Wabaunsee) City..................*321*
Paxton (Logan) Township..................*268*
Payne (Gove) Township *246*
Payne (Sedgwick) Township *308*
Peabody (Marion) City......................*271*
Peabody (Marion) Township..............*271*
Penalosa (Kingman) City *262*
Penn (Osborne) Township.................*287*
Peoria (Franklin) Township...............*244*
Perry (Jefferson) City *256*
Perry (Woodson) Township...............*325*
Peru (Chautauqua) City *223*
Peters (Kingman) Township...............*262*
Phillipsburg (Phillips) City.................*291*
Phillipsburg (Phillips) Township.........*291*
Phillips County *290*
Pierceville (Finney) Township...........*242*
Pike (Lyon) Township........................*269*
Pioneer (Graham) Township *247*
Pioneer (Rice) Township *300*
Pioneer (Rush) Township *303*
Pittsburg (Crawford) City..................*233*
Pittsburg (Mitchell) Township...........*277*
Plains City (Meade) City...................*275*
Plainview (Phillips) Township............*291*
Plainville (Rooks) City *302*
Pleasant (Butler) Township *221*
Pleasant (Coffey) Township...............*230*
Pleasant (Harvey) Township *253*
Pleasant (Lincoln) Township..............*266*
Pleasant (Smith) Township................*314*
Pleasantdale (Rush) Township *303*
Pleasant Grove (Greenwood)
　　Township................................ *250*
Pleasant Grove (Pawnee) Township .*289*
Pleasanton (Linn) City *267*
Pleasant Ridge (Pawnee) Township ..*289*
Pleasant Valley (Cowley) Township ..*231*
Pleasant Valley (Decatur) Township .*234*
Pleasant Valley (Finney) Township ...*242*
Pleasant Valley (Pawnee) Township..*289*
Pleasant Valley (Saline) Township *305*
Pleasant Valley (Wilson) Township...*325*
Pleasant View (Cherokee) Township.*224*
Plevna (Reno) City *297*
Plevna (Reno) Township *297*

KANSAS
American Places Dictionary

Plum (Phillips) Township...................*291*
Plumb (Wabaunsee) Township............*321*
Plum Creek (Mitchell) Township........*277*
Plum Grove (Butler) Township...........*221*
Plymouth (Russell) Township..............*304*
Pomona (Franklin) City.......................*244*
Pomona (Franklin) Township.............*244*
Portis (Osborne) City..........................*287*
Potosi (Linn) Township......................*267*
Pottawatomie (Coffey) Township........*230*
Pottawatomie (Franklin) Township *244*
Pottawatomie (Pottawatomie)
  Township..*293*
Pottawatomie County.......................*292*
Potwin (Butler) City............................*221*
Powell (Comanche) Township............*230*
Powhattan (Brown) City.....................*219*
Powhattan (Brown) Township............*219*
Prairie (Jewell) Township...................*258*
Prairie (Wilson) Township..................*325*
Prairie (Wyandotte) Township............*326*
Prairie Dog (Decatur) Township........*234*
Prairie Dog (Sheridan) Township......*311*
Prairie View (Phillips) City................*291*
Prairie View (Phillips) Township........*291*
Prairie Village (Johnson) City............*260*
Pratt (Pratt) City..................................*294*
Pratt County......................................*294*
Prescott (Linn) City.............................*267*
Preston (Pratt) City..............................*294*
Pretty Prairie (Reno) City..................*297*
Princeton (Franklin) City....................*244*
Prospect (Butler) Township.................*221*
Protection (Comanche) City................*230*
Protection (Comanche) Township.......*230*
Putnam (Anderson) Township............*213*
Putnam (Stafford) Township...............*315*
Quenemo (Osage) City........................*286*
Quincy (Greenwood) Township..........*250*
Quinter (Gove) City..............................*246*
Radium (Stafford) City.........................*315*
Ramona (Marion) City..........................*271*
Randall (Jewell) City............................*258*
Randolph (Riley) City...........................*301*
Ransom (Ness) City..............................*284*
Rantoul (Franklin) City........................*244*
Rawlins County..................................*295*
Raymond (Rice) City............................*300*
Raymond (Rice) Township..................*300*
Reading (Lyon) City.............................*270*
Reading (Lyon) Township....................*270*
Redfield (Bourbon) City.......................*218*
Red Vermillion (Nemaha) Township *281*
Reeder (Anderson) Township..............*214*
Reilly (Nemaha) Township..................*281*
Reno (Leavenworth) Township............*265*
Reno (Reno) Township.........................*297*
Reno County......................................*296*
Republic (Republic) City....................*299*
Republican (Clay) Township..............*227*
Republic County..............................*298*
Reserve (Brown) City..........................*219*
Rexford (Thomas) City........................*319*
Rice County......................................*299*
Rich (Anderson) Township.................*214*
Richfield (Morton) City.......................*280*
Richfield (Morton) Township...............*280*
Richland (Butler) Township.................*221*
Richland (Cowley) Township...............*231*
Richland (Ford) Township...................*243*
Richland (Hamilton) Township............*251*
Richland (Harvey) Township...............*253*
Richland (Jewell) Township.................*258*
Richland (Kingman) Township............*262*
Richland (Labette) Township...............*264*

Richland (Marshall) Township...........*273*
Richland (Miami) Township..............*276*
Richland (Ottawa) Township.............*288*
Richland (Republic) Township..........*299*
Richland (Stafford) Township...........*315*
Richmond (Franklin) City...................*245*
Richmond (Franklin) Township..........*245*
Richmond (Nemaha) Township.........*282*
Ridge (Barber) Township....................*216*
Ridge (Dickinson) Township..............*236*
Ridgeway (Osage) Township..............*286*
Riley (Riley) City..................................*301*
Riley County......................................*301*
Rinehart (Dickinson) Township.........*236*
Risley (Marion) Township....................*271*
River (Pawnee) Township *289*
Riverside (Sedgwick) Township..........*308*
Riverside (Trego) Township.................*320*
Robinson (Brown) City........................*219*
Robinson (Brown) Township................*219*
Rocewood (Rawlins) Township...........*295*
Rochester (Kingman) Township..........*262*
Rock (Marshall) Township..................*273*
Rock Creek (Butler) Township...........*221*
Rock Creek (Coffey) Township *230*
Rock Creek (Cowley) Township.........*232*
Rock Creek (Jefferson) Township *256*
Rock Creek (Nemaha) Township *282*
Rock Creek (Pottawatomie)
  Township..*293*
Rock Creek (Wabaunsee) Township..*321*
Rockford (Sedgwick) Township..........*308*
Rockville (Rice) Township *300*
Roeland Park (Johnson) City..............*260*
Rolla (Morton) City...............................*280*
Rolla (Morton) Township.....................*280*
Rooks County.....................................*302*
Roosevelt (Decatur) Township............*234*
Rosalia (Butler) Township....................*221*
Roscoe (Reno) Township......................*297*
Rose Creek (Republic) Township.......*299*
Rose Hill (Butler) City *221*
Roseland (Cherokee) City....................*224*
Rose Valley (Stafford) Township.........*315*
Ross (Cherokee) Township *224*
Ross (Osborne) Township.....................*287*
Rossville (Shawnee) City......................*310*
Rossville (Shawnee) Township............*310*
Round Mound (Osborne) Township...*287*
Round Springs (Mitchell) Township...*277*
Rovohl (Thomas) Township.................*319*
Royal (Ford) Township.........................*243*
Rozel (Pawnee) City..............................*289*
Rural (Jefferson) Township *256*
Rural (Kingman) Township *262*
Rush Center (Rush) City.....................*303*
Rush County.....................................*303*
Rushville (Phillips) Township.............*291*
Russell (Russell) City..........................*304*
Russell (Russell) Township.................*305*
Russell County.................................*304*
Russell Springs (Logan) City..............*268*
Russell Springs (Logan) Township....*268*
Rutland (Montgomery) Township.....*279*
Ryan (Sumner) Township....................*318*
Sabetha (Brown) City..........................*220*
Sabetha (Nemaha) City........................*282*
St. Bridget (Marshall) Township.........*273*
St. Clere (Pottawatomie) Township...*293*
St. Francis (Cheyenne) City...............*225*
St. George (Pottawatomie) City.........*293*
St. George (Pottawatomie)
  Township..*293*
St. John (Stafford) City........................*315*
St. John (Stafford) Township..............*315*

St. Marys (Pottawatomie) City..........*293*
St. Marys (Pottawatomie) Township.*293*
St. Marys (Wabaunsee) City..............*321*
St. Paul (Neosho) City..........................*283*
Salamanca (Cherokee) Township......*224*
Salem (Allen) Township.......................*213*
Salem (Cowley) Township....................*232*
Salem (Greenwood) Township............*250*
Salem (Sedgwick) Township................*308*
Salina (Saline) City...............................*306*
Saline County....................................*305*
Salt Creek (Chautauqua) Township ..*223*
Salt Creek (Lincoln) Township...........*266*
Salt Creek (Mitchell) Township..........*278*
Salt Creek (Reno) Township................*297*
Salt Springs (Greenwood) Township.*250*
Sand Creek (Meade) Township *275*
Santa Fe (Pawnee) Township..............*289*
Sappa (Decatur) Township..................*234*
Sarcoxie (Jefferson) Township............*256*
Satanta (Haskell) City...........................*253*
Savonburg (Allen) City.........................*213*
Sawlog (Hodgeman) Township............*254*
Sawmill (Pawnee) Township................*290*
Sawyer (Pratt) City................................*294*
Scammon (Cherokee) City...................*224*
Scandia (Republic) City........................*299*
Scandia (Republic) Township..............*299*
Schoenchen (Ellis) City........................*240*
Scott (Bourbon) Township....................*218*
Scott (Lincoln) Township *266*
Scott (Linn) Township..........................*267*
Scott (Scott) Township.........................*306*
Scott City (Scott) City..........................*306*
Scott County......................................*306*
Scottsville (Mitchell) City....................*278*
Scranton (Osage) City...........................*286*
Scranton (Osage) Township.................*286*
Sedan (Chautauqua) City.....................*223*
Sedan (Chautauqua) Township...........*223*
Sedgwick (Harvey) City........................*253*
Sedgwick (Harvey) Township..............*253*
Sedgwick (Sedgwick) City....................*308*
Sedgwick County..............................*307*
Selden (Sheridan) City.........................*311*
Seneca (Nemaha) City..........................*282*
Seventy-Six (Sumner) Township *318*
Severance (Doniphan) City.................*237*
Severy (Greenwood) City.....................*250*
Seward (Seward) Township..................*309*
Seward (Stafford) City..........................*315*
Seward County..................................*309*
Shannon (Atchison) Township............*215*
Shannon (Pottawatomie) Township ..*293*
Sharon (Barber) City............................*216*
Sharon (Barber) Township...................*216*
Sharon Springs (Wallace) City............*321*
Sharon Springs (Wallace) Township..*321*
Shawnee (Cherokee) Township *224*
Shawnee (Johnson) City.......................*260*
Shawnee (Johnson) Township.............*260*
Shawnee County...............................*310*
Shell Rock (Greenwood) Township...*250*
Sheridan (Cherokee) Township..........*225*
Sheridan (Cowley) Township...............*232*
Sheridan (Crawford) Township...........*233*
Sheridan (Linn) Township...................*267*
Sheridan (Ottawa) Township...............*288*
Sheridan (Sheridan) Township............*311*
Sheridan (Washington) Township......*323*
Sheridan County...............................*311*
Sherlock (Finney) Township................*242*
Sherman (Clay) Township....................*227*
Sherman (Crawford) Township...........*233*
Sherman (Decatur) Township *234*

Sherman (Dickinson) Township........236
Sherman (Ellsworth) Township........241
Sherman (Grant) Township...............248
Sherman (Leavenworth) Township...265
Sherman (Ottawa) Township.............288
Sherman (Pottawatomie) Township..293
Sherman (Riley) Township.................301
Sherman (Sedgwick) Township.........308
Sherman (Washington) Township.....323
Sherman County...................................*312*
Shermanville (Sherman) Township...*312*
Shiley (Pawnee) Township..................290
Shiloh (Neosho) Township.................283
Shirley (Cloud) Township...................229
Sibley (Cloud) Township.....................229
Silver Creek (Cowley) Township........232
Silverdale (Cowley) Township...........232
Silver Lake (Shawnee) City................310
Silver Lake (Shawnee) Township......310
Simpson (Cloud) City..........................229
Simpson (Mitchell) City.....................278
Sinclair (Jewell) Township..................258
Sitka (Clark) Township........................226
Smith (Thomas) Township..................319
Smith Center (Smith) City..................314
Smith County.......................................*313*
Smoky (Sherman) Township..............312
Smoky Hill (Geary) Township...........246
Smoky Hill (McPherson) Township..274
Smoky Hill (Saline) Township...........306
Smoky View (Saline) Township.........306
Smolan (Saline) City...........................306
Smolan (Saline) Township..................306
Sodville (Ford) Township...................243
Soldier (Jackson) City........................255
Soldier (Jackson) Township................255
Soldier (Shawnee) Township.............310
Solomon (Cloud) Township................229
Solomon (Dickinson) City..................236
Solomon (Graham) Township............247
Solomon (Phillips) Township............291
Solomon (Saline) Township................306
Solomon (Sheridan) Township...........311
Solomon-District 3 (Norton)
 Township.. 284
Solomon Rapids (Mitchell)
 Township.. 278
South Bend (Barton) Township.........217
South Brown (Edwards) Township....239
South Haven (Sumner) City...............318
South Haven (Sumner) Township.....318
South Homestead (Barton)
 Township.. 217
South Hutchinson (Reno) City..........297
South Randall (Thomas) Township..*319*
South Roscoe (Hodgeman)
 Township.. 254
South Salem (Greenwood) Township*250*
South Seward (Stafford) Township...*315*
South Sharps Creek (McPherson)
 Township.. 274
Southside (Kearny) Township............260
Spearville (Ford) City.........................243
Spearville (Ford) Township................243
Speed (Phillips) City..........................291
Spivey (Kingman) City......................262
Spring (Butler) Township...................221
Springbrook (Sheridan) Township.....311
Spring Creek (Coffey) Township........230
Spring Creek (Cowley) Township......232
Spring Creek (Greenwood)
 Township.. 250
Spring Creek (Lane) Township..........264
Spring Creek (Pottawatomie)
 Township.. 293

Spring Creek (Saline) Township........306
Springdale (Sumner) Township.........318
Spring Hill (Johnson) City.................260
Spring Hill (Johnson) Township........260
Spring Hill (Miami) City....................276
Spring Valley (Cherokee) Township..225
Spring Valley (McPherson)
 Township.. 275
Stafford (Stafford) City......................*315*
Stafford (Stafford) Township............*315*
Stafford County...................................*314*
Stanton (Linn) Township....................267
Stanton (Miami) Township.................276
Stanton (Ottawa) Township................288
Stanton (Stanton) Township...............316
Stanton County....................................*315*
Star (Coffey) Township.......................230
Stark (Neosho) City............................283
Starr (Cloud) Township......................229
Stateline (Sherman) Township..........*312*
Sterling (Hodgeman) Township.........254
Sterling (Rice) City............................300
Sterling (Rice) Township....................300
Stevens County....................................*316*
Stockton (Rooks) City........................302
Straight Creek (Jackson) Township...255
Stranger (Leavenworth) Township 265
Strawberry (Washington) Township ..323
Strong (Chase) Township....................222
Strong City (Chase) City....................223
Sublette (Haskell) City.......................253
Sugar Creek (Miami) Township........276
Sullivan (Grant) Township.................248
Summerfield (Marshall) City.............273
Summers (Thomas) Township..........*319*
Summit (Chautauqua) Township.......224
Summit (Cloud) Township..................229
Summit (Decatur) Township..............234
Summit (Marion) Township...............271
Sumner (Osborne) Township.............287
Sumner (Phillips) Township..............291
Sumner (Reno) Township...................297
Sumner (Sumner) Township...............318
Sumner County....................................*316*
Sun City (Barber) City.......................216
Sun City (Barber) Township..............216
Superior (McPherson) Township.......275
Superior (Osage) Township................286
Susank (Barton) City.........................217
Swan (Smith) Township.....................314
Swede Creek (Riley) Township.........301
Sycamore (Butler) Township..............221
Sycamore (Montgomery) Township..279
Sylvan Grove (Lincoln) City.............266
Sylvia (Reno) City..............................297
Sylvia (Reno) Township......................297
Syracuse (Hamilton) City..................251
Syracuse (Hamilton) Township..........251
Talleyrand (Wilson) Township..........325
Taloga (Morton) Township.................280
Tampa (Marion) City.........................271
Tecumseh (Shawnee) Township........310
Ten Mile (Miami) Township..............276
Terry (Finney) Township....................242
Tescott (Ottawa) City.........................288
Thayer (Neosho) City........................283
Thomas (Ellsworth) Township..........241
Thomas County...................................*318*
Tilden (Osborne) Township................287
Timberhill (Bourbon) Township........218
Timken (Rush) City............................303
Tioga (Neosho) Township..................283
Tipton (Mitchell) City........................278
Tisdale (Cowley) Township................232
Toledo (Chase) Township...................223

Tonganoxie (Leavenworth) City........265
Tonganoxie (Leavenworth)
 Township.. 265
Topeka (Shawnee) City......................310
Topeka (Shawnee) Township.............310
Toronto (Woodson) City....................325
Toronto (Woodson) Township..........325
Towanda (Butler) City.......................222
Towanda (Butler) Township..............222
Towanda (Phillips) Township............291
Township No. 1 (Harper) Township.*252*
Township No. 1 (Morris) Township..*280*
Township No. 1 (Rooks) Township ..*302*
Township No. 10 (Pratt) Township ..*294*
Township No. 10 (Rooks) Township *302*
Township No. 11 (Pratt) Township ...*294*
Township No. 11 (Rooks) Township *302*
Township No. 12 (Pratt) Township ...*294*
Township No. 12 (Rooks) Township *302*
Township No. 2 (Harper) Township.*252*
Township No. 2 (Morris) Township..*280*
Township No. 2 (Rooks) Township ..*302*
Township No. 3 (Harper) Township.*252*
Township No. 3 (Morris) Township..*280*
Township No. 3 (Rooks) Township ..*302*
Township No. 4 (Harper) Township.*252*
Township No. 4 (Morris) Township..*280*
Township No. 4 (Rooks) Township ..*302*
Township No. 5 (Harper) Township.*252*
Township No. 5 (Morris) Township..*280*
Township No. 5 (Rooks) Township ..*302*
Township No. 6 (Harper) Township.*252*
Township No. 6 (Morris) Township..*280*
Township No. 6 (Pratt) Township *294*
Township No. 6 (Rooks) Township ..*302*
Township No. 7 (Morris) Township..*280*
Township No. 7 (Pratt) Township *294*
Township No. 7 (Rooks) Township ..*302*
Township No. 8 (Morris) Township..*280*
Township No. 8 (Pratt) Township *294*
Township No. 8 (Rooks) Township ..*302*
Township No. 9 (Morris) Township..*280*
Township No. 9 (Pratt) Township *294*
Township No. 9 (Rooks) Township ..*302*
Treece (Cherokee) City......................225
Trego County.......................................*319*
Trenton (Edwards) Township............239
Tribune (Greeley) City.......................249
Tribune (Greeley) Township...............249
Trivoli (Ellsworth) Township.............241
Troy (Doniphan) City........................237
Troy (Reno) Township........................297
Turkey Creek (Barber) Township......216
Turkey Creek (McPherson)
 Township.. 275
Turkey Creek (Mitchell) Township ...278
Turon (Reno) City..............................297
Twin Grove (Greenwood) Township *250*
Tyro (Montgomery) City....................279
Udall (Cowley) City...........................232
Ulysses (Grant) City..........................248
Union (Anderson) Township..............214
Union (Barton) Township..................217
Union (Butler) Township...................222
Union (Clay) Township......................227
Union (Dickinson) Township............236
Union (Doniphan) Township.............237
Union (Jefferson) Township..............256
Union (Kingman) Township..............262
Union (McPherson) Township..........275
Union (Pottawatomie) Township......293
Union (Rawlins) Township................295
Union (Republic) Township..............299
Union (Rice) Township......................300
Union (Rush) Township.....................304

KANSAS
American Places Dictionary

Union (Sedgwick) Township *309*
Union (Sheridan) Township *311*
Union (Sherman) Township *312*
Union (Stafford) Township *315*
Union (Washington) Township *323*
Union Center (Elk) Township *239*
Uniontown (Bourbon) City *218*
Utica (Ness) City *284*
Valley (Barber) Township *216*
Valley (Ellsworth) Township *242*
Valley (Hodgeman) Township *254*
Valley (Kingman) Township *262*
Valley (Lincoln) Township *267*
Valley (Linn) Township *267*
Valley (Miami) Township *276*
Valley (Osborne) Township *287*
Valley (Phillips) Township *291*
Valley (Reno) Township *297*
Valley (Rice) Township *300*
Valley (Scott) Township *306*
Valley (Sheridan) Township *311*
Valley (Smith) Township *314*
Valley Brook (Osage) Township *286*
Valley Center (Pawnee) Township *290*
Valley Center (Sedgwick) City *309*
Valley Center (Sedgwick) Township ..*309*
Valley Falls (Jefferson) City *257*
Valverde (Sumner) Township *318*
Verdigris (Wilson) Township *325*
Vermillion (Marshall) City *273*
Vermillion (Marshall) Township *273*
Vernon (Cowley) Township *232*
Vesper (Lincoln) Township *267*
Vicksburg (Jewell) Township *258*
Victor (Osborne) Township *287*
Victoria (Ellis) City *240*
Victoria (Ellis) Township *240*
Victoria (Rice) Township *300*
Vienna (Pottawatomie) Township *293*
Vining (Clay) City *227*
Vining (Washington) City *323*
Vinita (Kingman) Township *262*
Viola (Sedgwick) City *309*
Viola (Sedgwick) Township *309*
Virgil (Greenwood) City *250*
Voltaire (Sherman) Township *312*
Voorhees (Stevens) Township *316*
Wabaunsee (Wabaunsee) Township ...*321*
Wabaunsee County *320*
Waco (Sedgwick) Township *309*
Wakarusa (Douglas) Township *238*
WaKeeney (Trego) City *320*
WaKeeney (Trego) Township *320*
Wakefield (Clay) City *227*
Waldo (Russell) City *305*
Waldo (Russell) Township *305*
Waldron (Harper) City *252*
Walker (Anderson) Township *214*
Wallace (Wallace) City *321*
Wallace (Wallace) Township *322*
Wallace County *321*
Walnut (Atchison) Township *215*
Walnut (Barton) Township *217*
Walnut (Bourbon) Township *218*
Walnut (Brown) Township *220*
Walnut (Butler) Township *222*
Walnut (Cowley) Township *232*
Walnut (Crawford) City *233*

Walnut (Crawford) Township *233*
Walnut (Jewell) Township *258*
Walnut (Marshall) Township *273*
Walnut (Pawnee) Township *290*
Walnut (Phillips) Township *291*
Walnut (Reno) Township *297*
Walnut (Saline) Township *306*
Walnut Creek (Mitchell) Township *278*
Walnut Grove (Neosho) Township *283*
Walton (Harvey) City *253*
Walton (Harvey) Township *253*
Walton (Labette) Township *264*
Walton (Sumner) Township *318*
Wamego (Pottawatomie) City *293*
Wamego (Pottawatomie) Township ...*293*
Wano (Cheyenne) Township *225*
Waring (Ness) Township *284*
Washington (Anderson) Township *214*
Washington (Brown) Township *220*
Washington (Chautauqua) Township *224*
Washington (Crawford) Township *233*
Washington (Doniphan) Township *237*
Washington (Jackson) Township *255*
Washington (Jewell) Township *258*
Washington (Nemaha) Township *282*
Washington (Republic) Township *299*
Washington (Saline) Township *306*
Washington (Sherman) Township *312*
Washington (Smith) Township *314*
Washington (Wabaunsee) Township ..*321*
Washington (Washington) City *323*
Washington (Washington) Township.*323*
Washington County *322*
Waterloo (Lyon) Township *270*
Waterville (Marshall) City *273*
Waterville (Marshall) Township *273*
Wathena (Doniphan) City *237*
Waverly (Coffey) City *230*
Wayne (Doniphan) Township *237*
Wayne (Edwards) Township *239*
Wea (Miami) Township *276*
Webber (Jewell) City *258*
Webster (Smith) Township *314*
Webster (Wilson) Township *325*
Weir (Cherokee) City *225*
Welda (Anderson) Township *214*
Wellington (Sumner) City *318*
Wellington (Sumner) Township *318*
Wells (Marshall) Township *273*
Wellsville (Franklin) City *245*
Wendell (Thomas) Township *319*
Weskan (Wallace) Township *322*
West Branch (Marion) Township *271*
West Center (Stevens) Township *316*
West Cherry (Montgomery)
  Township *279*
West Cooper (Stafford) Township *315*
Western (Logan) Township *268*
West Hale (Thomas) Township *319*
West Hibbard (Kearny) Township *261*
West Kiowa (Kiowa) Pop. Place *262*
West Mineral (Cherokee) City *225*
Westminster (Reno) Township *297*
Westmoreland (Pottawatomie) City ..*293*
Westola (Morton) Township *280*
Westphalia (Anderson) City *214*
Westphalia (Anderson) Township *214*

West Plains (Meade) Township *275*
West Saline (Sheridan) Township *311*
West Washington (Rice) Township ...*300*
Westwood (Johnson) City *260*
Westwood Hills (Johnson) City *260*
Wetmore (Nemaha) City *282*
Wetmore (Nemaha) Township *282*
Wheatland (Barton) Township *217*
Wheatland (Dickinson) Township *236*
Wheatland (Ellis) Township *240*
Wheatland (Ford) Township *243*
Wheaton (Pottawatomie) City *293*
White (Kingman) Township *262*
White City (Morris) City *280*
White Cloud (Doniphan) City *237*
White Mound (Jewell) Township *258*
White Rock (Lane) Township *264*
White Rock (Republic) Township *299*
White Rock (Smith) Township *314*
Whitewater (Butler) City *222*
Whiting (Jackson) City *255*
Whiting (Jackson) Township *255*
Wichita (Sedgwick) City *309*
Wichita County *324*
Wilburn (Ford) Township *243*
Wilcox (Trego) Township *320*
Wildcat (Elk) Township *239*
Wild Cat (Riley) Township *301*
Wildhorse (Graham) Township *247*
Willard (Shawnee) City *310*
Willard (Wabaunsee) City *321*
Williamsburg (Franklin) City *245*
Williamsburg (Franklin) Township ...*245*
Williamsport (Shawnee) Township ...*310*
Willis (Brown) City *220*
Willowbrook (Reno) City *297*
Willowdale (Dickinson) Township *236*
Willow Springs (Douglas) Township .*238*
Wilmington (Wabaunsee) Township .*321*
Wilmore (Comanche) City *230*
Wilsey (Morris) City *280*
Wilson (Ellsworth) City *242*
Wilson (Ellsworth) Township *242*
Wilson (Lane) Township *264*
Wilson (Marion) Township *271*
Wilson (Rice) Township *300*
Wilson County *324*
Winchester (Jefferson) City *257*
Windom (McPherson) City *275*
Windsor (Cowley) Township *232*
Winfield (Cowley) City *232*
Winfield (Osborne) Township *287*
Wingfield (Geary) Township *246*
Winona (Logan) City *268*
Winona (Logan) Township *268*
Winterset (Russell) Township *305*
Wolf River (Doniphan) Township *237*
Woodbine (Dickinson) City *236*
Woodson County *325*
Woodston (Rooks) City *302*
Wyandotte County *326*
Yates Center (Woodson) City *325*
Yoder (Reno) Township *298*
York (Stafford) Township *315*
Zeandale (Riley) Township *301*
Zenda (Kingman) City *262*
Zurich (Rooks) City *302*

Montana

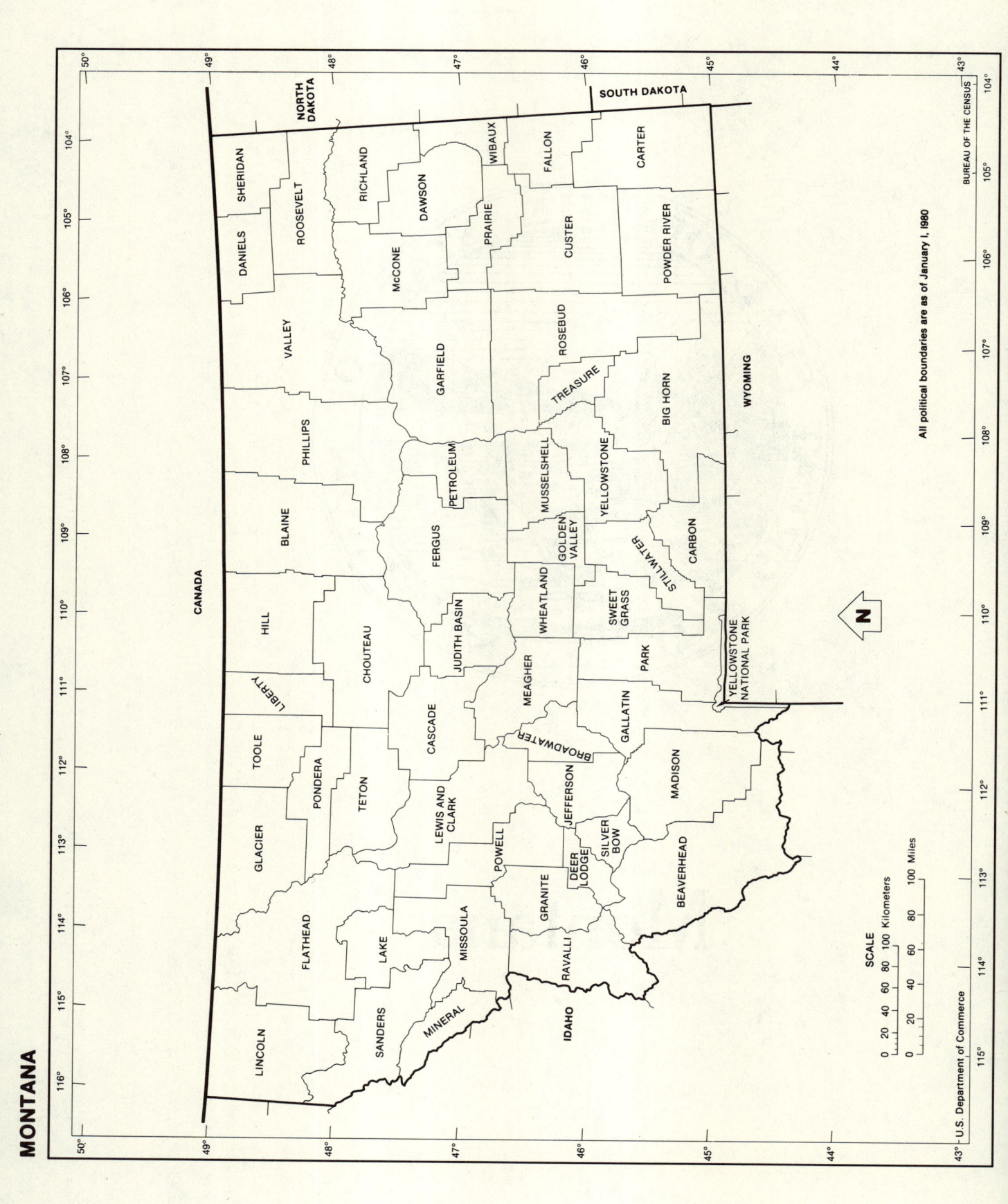

Montana

Population: 799,065 (1990); 786,690 (1980)
Population rank (1990): 44
Percent population change (1980–1990): 1.6
Population projection: 861,000 (1995); 897,000 (2000)

Area: total: 147,046 sq. mi.; 145,556 sq. mi. land, 1,490 sq. mi. water
Area rank: 4
Highest elevation: 12,799 ft., Granite Peak (Park County)
Lowest point: 1,800 ft., along the Kootenai River (Lincoln County)

State capital: Helena (Lewis and Clark County)
Largest city: Billings (81,151)
Second largest city: Great Falls (55,097)
Largest county: Yellowstone (113,419)

Total housing units: 361,155
No. of occupied housing units: 306,163
Vacant housing units (%): 15.2
Distribution of population by race and Hispanic origin (%):
White: 92.7
Black: 0.3
Hispanic (any race): 1.5
Native American: 6.0
Asian/Pacific: 0.5
Other: 0.5

Admission date: November 8, 1889 (41st state).

Location: In the northwestern United States, bordering North Dakota, South Dakota, Wyoming, Idaho, and the Canadian provinces of Saskatchewan, Alberta, and British Columbia.

Name Origin: Latin or Spanish word meaning 'mountainous.' Suggested by Rep. James M. Ashley of OH, when Montana Territory was organized.

State bird: western meadowlark *(Sturnella neglecta)*
State fish: black-spotted (cutthroat) trout *(Salmo clarki)*
State flower: bitterroot *(Lewisia rediviva)*
State gems: yogo sapphire, Montana agate
State grass: bluebunch wheatgrass *(Agropyron spicatum)*
State song: "Montana"
State tree: Ponderosa pine *(Pinus ponderosa)*

State motto: *Oro y Plata* (Spanish 'Gold and Silver')
State nicknames: Treasure State, Big Sky Country

Area code: 406
Time zone: Mountain

Abbreviations: MT (postal); Mont. (traditional)
Part of (region): Rocky Mountain

Local Government

Counties

Montana has 56 counties, most of which are governed by three elected commissioners.

Municipalities

Montana has 126 municipalities. Unified city-county governments include Anaconda-Deer Lodge and Butte-Silver Bow.

Settlement History and Early Development

Although there is some evidence of prehistoric settlement more than 4,000 years ago in the region now known as Montana, the Indian tribes living in the territory when white explorers first entered had, for the most part, been pushed westward by European settlement in the east. These tribes included the Arapaho, Assiniboine, Atsina, Blackfeet, Cheyenne, Crow, Bannock, Flathead, Kalispel, Kutenai, Shoshone, Sioux, Mandan, and Nez Perce.

French traders and trappers may have entered the Montana territory during the eighteenth century, but it was not until the Lewis and Clark expedition of 1804–06 that the exploration of the area was recorded. The land that later became Montana was part of the vast Louisiana Territory that had initially been claimed by the French but that was sold to the U.S. in 1803 as the Louisiana Purchase. The Lewis and Clark expedition crossed Montana both as they headed west and on their return trip.

Fur trappers and traders were active in Montana from 1807. In 1847 Fort Benton was built on the Missouri River by the American Fur Company. In 1859 gold was discovered near what is now Drummond, and in 1862 there was a gold strike at Grasshopper Creek. Prospectors rushed into the area and established such mining towns as Bannack, Diamond City, and Virginia City. Partly because of the wild, lawless nature of these towns, inhabitants urged Congress to create a new territory and impose order. Montana became a territory in 1864.

Montana's Indians resisted the influx of settlers, but despite the Sioux and Cheyenne victory in 1876 against Lieutenant Colonel George Custer and the 7th Cavalry at Big Horn, there was no hope that the Indians would be able to prevail. The next year the U.S. army fought a running battle against the Nez Perce tribe under Chief Joseph, who was forced to surrender about 40 miles south of the Canadian border.

In the 1860s longhorn cattle were driven up from Texas to

MONTANA

Montana and cattle ranching became common until the great cattle ranches were struck by disaster when thousands of cattle died in the bitterly cold winter of 1886–87. Ranching continued on a smaller scale after that. The arrival of the Northern Pacific Railway in 1883 had opened eastern markets and made it easier for settlers to reach the territory.

Statehood

Montana became the 41st U.S. state on November 8, 1889. Its wealth was based on minerals: first gold and silver, and then copper was discovered near Butte. A single corporation, the Anaconda Corporation, bought up copper interests and owned timberland, banks, and newspapers. The company was responsible for building a railroad and an electric power company.

Later Developments

The first woman to serve in the U.S. Congress was Jeannette Rankin, elected as a representative from Montana in 1916. She became famous for refusing to vote for war in 1941 in the wake of the attack on Pearl Harbor by the Japanese. She was the only Congressperson to vote against the declaration of war and she was unwavering in her belief that war was wrong.

The state suffered during the Great Depression of the 1930s, although the building of the Fort Peck Dam, completed in 1940, did help provide jobs as well as much-needed water for irrigation. Montana's economy rebounded during World War II as the state's agricultural products and minerals were in high demand. After the war agricultural prices dropped and farming became more mechanized. People leaving the farms for the cities found growth in the petroleum, gas, oil, and coal industries, as well as the Anaconda Aluminum Company's plant that opened in 1955. Tourism also became an important industry as visitors came to enjoy the great outdoors, dude ranches, summer resorts, and winter skiing, as well as state and national parks and historical sites.

State Boundaries

Montana was organized as a territory in 1864 from land that had been part of the Idaho Territory. The boundaries of the territory were changed very little when Montana was made a state in 1889, with the boundaries as they are currently.

Montana Counties

Beaverhead	Fallon	Lewis and	Phillips	Stillwater
Big Horn	Fergus	Clark	Pondera	Sweet Grass
Blaine	Flathead	Liberty	Powder River	Teton
Broadwater	Gallatin	Lincoln	Powell	Toole
Carbon	Garfield	McCone	Prairie	Treasure
Carter	Glacier	Madison	Ravalli	Valley
Cascade	Golden Valley	Meagher	Richland	Wheatland
Chouteau	Granite	Mineral	Roosevelt	Wibaux
Custer	Hill	Missoula	Rosebud	Yellowstone
Daniels	Jefferson	Musselshell	Sanders	Yellowstone
Dawson	Judith Basin	Park	Sheridan	National
Deer Lodge	Lake	Petroleum	Silver Bow	Park

Beaverhead County
County Seat: Dillon (ZIP: 59725)

Pop: 8,424 (1990); 8,186 (1980)   **Pop Density:** 1.5
Land: 5542.6 sq. mi.; **Water:** 29.7 sq. mi.   **Area Code:** 406

On the southwestern border of MT, south of Butte; original county; organized Feb 2, 1865 (prior to statehood); annexed part of Madison County in 1911.

Name origin: For the Beaverhead River, which contains a rock formation that the Indians thought resembled a beaver's head.

Dillon — City
ZIP: 59725   **Lat:** 45-12-58 N   **Long:** 112-38-04 W
Pop: 3,991 (1990); 3,976 (1980)   **Pop Density:** 2494.4
Land: 1.6 sq. mi.; **Water:** 0.0 sq. mi.   **Elev:** 5096 ft.
Name origin: For the president of the Union Pacific Railroad, Sidney Dillon.

Lima — Town
ZIP: 59739   **Lat:** 44-38-18 N   **Long:** 112-35-29 W
Pop: 265 (1990); 272 (1980)   **Pop Density:** 441.7
Land: 0.6 sq. mi.; **Water:** 0.0 sq. mi.   **Elev:** 6256 ft.
Name origin: Named by Henry Thompson for his hometown, Lima, WI.

Big Horn County
County Seat: Hardin (ZIP: 59034)

Pop: 11,337 (1990); 11,096 (1980)   **Pop Density:** 2.3
Land: 4994.9 sq. mi.; **Water:** 19.8 sq. mi.   **Area Code:** 406

On the central southern border of MT, south of Billings; organized Jan 13, 1913 from Rosebud and Yellowstone counties.

Name origin: For the Big Horn and Little Big Horn rivers that flow through it; the rivers named for the great droves of bighorn sheep on the hillsides.

Busby — CDP
ZIP: 59016   **Lat:** 45-31-52 N   **Long:** 106-57-20 W
Pop: 409 (1990)   **Pop Density:** 46.0
Land: 8.9 sq. mi.; **Water:** 0.0 sq. mi.

Crow Agency — CDP
ZIP: 59022   **Lat:** 45-36-01 N   **Long:** 107-27-38 W
Pop: 1,446 (1990)   **Pop Density:** 219.1
Land: 6.6 sq. mi.; **Water:** 0.0 sq. mi.

Hardin — City
ZIP: 59034   **Lat:** 45-43-54 N   **Long:** 107-36-48 W
Pop: 2,940 (1990); 3,300 (1980)   **Pop Density:** 2261.5
Land: 1.3 sq. mi.; **Water:** 0.0 sq. mi.   **Elev:** 2902 ft.
Name origin: For Samuel Hardin, friend of the president of the Lincoln Land Company.

Lodge Grass — Town
ZIP: 59050   **Lat:** 45-18-51 N   **Long:** 107-21-59 W
Pop: 517 (1990); 499 (1980)   **Pop Density:** 2585.0
Land: 0.2 sq. mi.; **Water:** 0.0 sq. mi.   **Elev:** 3363 ft.
Name origin: For the nearby creek which the Crow Indians called Greasy Grass, because it was so nourishing it made their animals greasy fat. Grease and Lodge are very similar in the Crow language, thus causing the mistaken transliteration.

Muddy — CDP
Lat: 45-35-24 N   **Long:** 106-47-41 W
Pop: 387 (1990)   **Pop Density:** 13.6
Land: 28.4 sq. mi.; **Water:** 0.0 sq. mi.

Pryor — CDP
Lat: 45-25-08 N   **Long:** 108-31-54 W
Pop: 654 (1990)   **Pop Density:** 19.0
Land: 34.4 sq. mi.; **Water:** 0.0 sq. mi.

Blaine County
County Seat: Chinook (ZIP: 59523)

Pop: 6,728 (1990); 6,999 (1980) **Pop Density:** 1.6
Land: 4226.2 sq. mi.; **Water:** 12.7 sq. mi. **Area Code:** 406

On the central northern border of MT, northeast of Great Falls; organized Feb 29, 1912 from Chouteau County.

Name origin: For James Gillespie Blaine (1830–93), U.S. representative from ME (1863–76), U.S. senator (1876–81), and U.S. secretary of state (1881; 1889–92).

Chinook — City
ZIP: 59523 **Lat:** 48-35-25 N **Long:** 109-13-52 W
Pop: 1,512 (1990); 1,660 (1980) **Pop Density:** 3024.0
Land: 0.5 sq. mi.; **Water:** 0.0 sq. mi. **Elev:** 2438 ft.
Name origin: From an Indian term for 'warm wind.' Previously called Belknap and Dawes.

Fort Belknap — CDP
Lat: 48-28-59 N **Long:** 108-45-58 W
Pop: 422 (1990) **Pop Density:** 703.3
Land: 0.6 sq. mi.; **Water:** 0.0 sq. mi.

Harlem — City
ZIP: 59526 **Lat:** 48-31-54 N **Long:** 108-47-01 W
Pop: 882 (1990); 1,023 (1980) **Pop Density:** 2205.0
Land: 0.4 sq. mi.; **Water:** 0.0 sq. mi. **Elev:** 2371 ft.
Founded 1889.

Hays — CDP
ZIP: 59527 **Lat:** 47-59-25 N **Long:** 108-38-57 W
Pop: 333 (1990) **Pop Density:** 39.2
Land: 8.5 sq. mi.; **Water:** 0.0 sq. mi.

Broadwater County
County Seat: Townsend (ZIP: 59644)

Pop: 3,318 (1990); 3,267 (1980) **Pop Density:** 2.8
Land: 1191.5 sq. mi.; **Water:** 47.5 sq. mi. **Area Code:** 406

In west-central MT, east of Helena; organized Feb 9, 1895 from Jefferson and Meagher counties.

Name origin: For Col. Charles A. Broadwater (1840–92), miner, businessman, president of the Montana Central Railroad, and local resort proprietor.

Townsend — City
ZIP: 59644 **Lat:** 46-19-08 N **Long:** 111-31-08 W
Pop: 1,635 (1990); 1,587 (1980) **Pop Density:** 1021.9
Land: 1.6 sq. mi.; **Water:** 0.0 sq. mi. **Elev:** 3848 ft.
Name origin: For an official of the Northern Pacific Railroad.

Carbon County
County Seat: Red Lodge (ZIP: 59068)

Pop: 8,080 (1990); 8,099 (1980) **Pop Density:** 3.9
Land: 2048.1 sq. mi.; **Water:** 14.2 sq. mi. **Area Code:** 406

On the central southern border of MT, southwest of Billings; organized Mar 4, 1895 from Park and Yellowstone counties.

Name origin: For the abundant coal deposits within its borders.

Bearcreek — Town
ZIP: 59007 **Lat:** 45-09-38 N **Long:** 109-09-25 W
Pop: 37 (1990); 61 (1980) **Pop Density:** 370.0
Land: 0.1 sq. mi.; **Water:** 0.0 sq. mi. **Elev:** 4578 ft.
Founded 1906.
Name origin: For the bears that came for berries along a nearby creek.

Bridger — Town
ZIP: 59014 **Lat:** 45-17-36 N **Long:** 108-54-53 W
Pop: 692 (1990); 724 (1980) **Pop Density:** 1153.3
Land: 0.6 sq. mi.; **Water:** 0.0 sq. mi.
Name origin: For explorer Jim Bridger. Originally known as Georgetown and Stringtown.

American Places Dictionary   MONTANA, Cascade County

Fromberg   Town
ZIP: 59029   **Lat:** 45-23-28 N   **Long:** 108-54-20 W
Pop: 370 (1990); 469 (1980)   **Pop Density:** 740.0
Land: 0.5 sq. mi.; **Water:** 0.0 sq. mi.   **Elev:** 3527 ft.
Post office established 1903.
Name origin: Previously called Gebo and Poverty Flats.

Joliet   Town
ZIP: 59041   **Lat:** 45-29-04 N   **Long:** 108-58-13 W
Pop: 522 (1990); 580 (1980)   **Pop Density:** 1740.0
Land: 0.3 sq. mi.; **Water:** 0.0 sq. mi.
Name origin: Named by a railroad official for his former home, Joliet, IL.

Red Lodge   City
ZIP: 59068   **Lat:** 45-11-29 N   **Long:** 109-14-49 W
Pop: 1,958 (1990); 1,896 (1980)   **Pop Density:** 932.4
Land: 2.1 sq. mi.; **Water:** 0.0 sq. mi.   **Elev:** 5553 ft.

Carter County
County Seat: Ekalaka (ZIP: 59324)

Pop: 1,503 (1990); 1,799 (1980)   **Pop Density:** 0.5
Land: 3339.7 sq. mi.; **Water:** 8.7 sq. mi.   **Area Code:** 406
In the southeastern corner of MT; organized Feb 22, 1917 from Fallon County.
Name origin: For Thomas Henry Carter (1854–1911), first U.S. senator from MT (1895–1901; 1905–11).

Ekalaka   Town
ZIP: 59324   **Lat:** 45-53-21 N   **Long:** 104-32-57 W
Pop: 439 (1990); 620 (1980)   **Pop Density:** 439.0
Land: 1.0 sq. mi.; **Water:** 0.0 sq. mi.
Name origin: Anglicization of *Ijkalaka*, the niece of Sitting Bull (c.1831–90), whose name means 'swift one.'

Cascade County
County Seat: Great Falls (ZIP: 59401)

Pop: 77,691 (1990); 80,696 (1980)   **Pop Density:** 28.8
Land: 2698.0 sq. mi.; **Water:** 13.7 sq. mi.   **Area Code:** 406
In central MT, northeast of Helena; organized Sep 12, 1887 (prior to statehood) from Chouteau and Meagher counties.
Name origin: For the falls in the Missouri River, which runs through the northern part of the county.

Belt   City
ZIP: 59412   **Lat:** 47-23-09 N   **Long:** 110-55-32 W
Pop: 571 (1990); 825 (1980)   **Pop Density:** 1903.3
Land: 0.3 sq. mi.; **Water:** 0.0 sq. mi.   **Elev:** 3571 ft.
Name origin: For nearby Belt Butte, a mountain with a belt or girdle of rocks around it. Previously called Castner.

Cascade   Town
ZIP: 59421   **Lat:** 47-16-14 N   **Long:** 111-42-08 W
Pop: 729 (1990); 773 (1980)   **Pop Density:** 1458.0
Land: 0.5 sq. mi.; **Water:** 0.0 sq. mi.   **Elev:** 3378 ft.
Name origin: For falls or cascades on the Missouri River.

Great Falls   City
ZIP: 59401   **Lat:** 47-30-17 N   **Long:** 111-17-26 W
Pop: 55,097 (1990); 56,884 (1980)   **Pop Density:** 3577.7
Land: 15.4 sq. mi.; **Water:** 0.4 sq. mi.   **Elev:** 3334 ft.
In west-central MT on the Missouri River, northeast of Helena. First post office 1884; incorporated as city 1888. Industry (flour milling, meat packing, petroleum processing, printing and publishing); important regional medical center; Malmstrom Air Force Base nearby.
Name origin: For the 'great falls' on the Missouri River, discovered by Lewis and Clark in 1805.

Malmstrom Air Force Base   Military Facility
ZIP: 59402   **Lat:** 47-30-33 N   **Long:** 111-11-26 W
Pop: 5,938 (1990); 6,675 (1980)   **Pop Density:** 2969.0
Land: 2.0 sq. mi.; **Water:** 0.0 sq. mi.

Neihart   Town
ZIP: 59465   **Lat:** 46-56-00 N   **Long:** 110-44-08 W
Pop: 53 (1990); 91 (1980)   **Pop Density:** 26.5
Land: 2.0 sq. mi.; **Water:** 0.0 sq. mi.   **Elev:** 5635 ft.
Name origin: For prospector James I. Neihart, who discovered minerals near here.

Sun Prairie   CDP
Lat: 47-32-12 N   **Long:** 111-28-49 W
Pop: 1,424 (1990)   **Pop Density:** 237.3
Land: 6.0 sq. mi.; **Water:** 0.1 sq. mi.

MONTANA, Chouteau County

Chouteau County
County Seat: Fort Benton (ZIP: 59442)

Pop: 5,452 (1990); 6,092 (1980)   **Pop Density:** 1.4
Land: 3973.4 sq. mi.; **Water:** 23.7 sq. mi.   **Area Code:** 406
In north-central MT, north of Great Falls; original county; organized Feb 2, 1865 (prior to statehood).
Name origin: For the Chouteau family, whose members included Auguste (1749–1829) and Pierre (1758–1849), fur traders.

Big Sandy   Town
ZIP: 59520   **Lat:** 48-10-44 N   **Long:** 110-06-46 W
Pop: 740 (1990); 835 (1980)   **Pop Density:** 1850.0
Land: 0.4 sq. mi.; **Water:** 0.0 sq. mi.   **Elev:** 2712 ft.
Name origin: From an Indian term *un-es-putcha-eka* meaning 'big sandy creek.'

Fort Benton   City
ZIP: 59442   **Lat:** 47-49-43 N   **Long:** 110-39-18 W
Pop: 1,660 (1990); 1,693 (1980)   **Pop Density:** 790.5
Land: 2.1 sq. mi.; **Water:** 0.0 sq. mi.   **Elev:** 2632 ft.
Name origin: For U.S. Sen. Thomas Hart Benton (1782–1858) of MO.

Geraldine   Town
ZIP: 59446   **Lat:** 47-36-12 N   **Long:** 110-15-57 W
Pop: 299 (1990); 305 (1980)   **Pop Density:** 598.0
Land: 0.5 sq. mi.; **Water:** 0.0 sq. mi.   **Elev:** 3135 ft.
Name origin: For the wife of William Rockefeller, director of the Milwaukee Railroad.

Custer County
County Seat: Miles City (ZIP: 59301)

Pop: 11,697 (1990); 13,109 (1980)   **Pop Density:** 3.1
Land: 3783.3 sq. mi.; **Water:** 10.1 sq. mi.   **Area Code:** 406
In southeastern MT; original county; organized as Big Horn County Feb 2, 1865 (prior to statehood); name changed Feb 16, 1877.
Name origin: For Gen. George Armstrong Custer (1839–76), U.S. army officer defeated at the Battle of Little Bighorn (1876).

Ismay   Town
ZIP: 59336   **Lat:** 46-30-00 N   **Long:** 104-47-35 W
Pop: 19 (1990); 31 (1980)   **Pop Density:** 47.5
Land: 0.4 sq. mi.; **Water:** 0.0 sq. mi.
Name origin: For Isabelle and Mary, daughters of George W. Peck, general consul for the railroad.

Miles City   City
ZIP: 59301   **Lat:** 46-24-26 N   **Long:** 105-50-20 W
Pop: 8,461 (1990); 9,602 (1980)   **Pop Density:** 2820.3
Land: 3.0 sq. mi.; **Water:** 0.0 sq. mi.   **Elev:** 2358 ft.
Name origin: For Gen. Nelson Miles (1873–1925). Previously called Milestown.

Daniels County
County Seat: Scobey (ZIP: 59263)

Pop: 2,266 (1990); 2,835 (1980)   **Pop Density:** 1.6
Land: 1426.1 sq. mi.; **Water:** 0.4 sq. mi.   **Area Code:** 406
On the northeastern border of MT; organized Aug 30, 1920 from Sheridan and Valley counties.
Name origin: For Mansfield A. Daniels, an early rancher and storekeeper.

Flaxville   Town
ZIP: 59222   **Lat:** 48-48-13 N   **Long:** 105-10-23 W
Pop: 88 (1990); 142 (1980)   **Pop Density:** 880.0
Land: 0.1 sq. mi.; **Water:** 0.0 sq. mi.
Name origin: For the flax that grew in the area. Originally located two and one-half miles southwest of the present site and called Boyer.

Scobey   City
ZIP: 59263   **Lat:** 48-47-26 N   **Long:** 105-25-14 W
Pop: 1,154 (1990); 1,382 (1980)   **Pop Density:** 1648.6
Land: 0.7 sq. mi.; **Water:** 0.0 sq. mi.   **Elev:** 2507 ft.
Name origin: For Maj. C.R.A. Scobey, an agent of the Fort Peck Indian Reservation.

Dawson County
County Seat: Glendive (ZIP: 59330)

Pop: 9,505 (1990); 11,805 (1980)   **Pop Density:** 4.0
Land: 2373.3 sq. mi.; **Water:** 10.0 sq. mi.   **Area Code:** 406
In central eastern MT; original county, organized Jan 15, 1869 (prior to statehood).
Name origin: For Maj. Andrew Dawson, commander of Fort Benton for the American Fur Company.

Glendive — City
ZIP: 59330   **Lat:** 47-06-30 N   **Long:** 104-42-27 W
Pop: 4,802 (1990); 5,978 (1980)   **Pop Density:** 1455.2
Land: 3.3 sq. mi.; **Water:** 0.0 sq. mi.   **Elev:** 2078 ft.
Name origin: For nearby Glendive Creek. Previously called Glendale Creek by Sir St. George Gore, a wealthy Irishman.

Richey — Town
ZIP: 59259   **Lat:** 47-38-38 N   **Long:** 105-04-06 W
Pop: 259 (1990); 417 (1980)   **Pop Density:** 863.3
Land: 0.3 sq. mi.; **Water:** 0.0 sq. mi.
Name origin: For Clyde C. Richey, the town's first postmaster.

Deer Lodge County
County Seat: Anaconda (ZIP: 59711)

Pop: 10,278 (1990); 12,518 (1980)   **Pop Density:** 13.9
Land: 736.9 sq. mi.; **Water:** 4.3 sq. mi.   **Area Code:** 406
In southwestern MT, west of Butte; original county; organized Feb 2, 1865 (prior to statehood).
Name origin: Descriptive of the area where deer came to the salt licks.

Anaconda-Deer Lodge County — City
ZIP: 59711   **Lat:** 46-03-56 N   **Long:** 113-05-00 W
Pop: 10,278 (1990); 12,518 (1980)   **Pop Density:** 13.9
Land: 736.9 sq. mi.; **Water:** 4.3 sq. mi.
City government consolidated with Deer Lodge County.
Name origin: Named by Michael Hickey, who established a copper mine here and named it from a newspaper editorial which stated that Grant's army was "encircling Lee's forces like a giant anaconda."

Fallon County
County Seat: Baker (ZIP: 59313)

Pop: 3,103 (1990); 3,763 (1980)   **Pop Density:** 1.9
Land: 1620.4 sq. mi.; **Water:** 2.7 sq. mi.   **Area Code:** 406
On southeastern border of MT; organized Dec 9, 1913 from Custer County.
Name origin: For Benjamin O'Fallon (1793–1842), army officer, Indian agent, and nephew of the explorer William Clark (1770–1838).

Baker — City
ZIP: 59313   **Lat:** 46-21-47 N   **Long:** 104-16-25 W
Pop: 1,818 (1990); 2,354 (1980)   **Pop Density:** 2020.0
Land: 0.9 sq. mi.; **Water:** 0.1 sq. mi.
Name origin: Named in 1908 for railroad man A.G. Baker. Previously called Lorraine.

Plevna — Town
ZIP: 59344   **Lat:** 46-24-58 N   **Long:** 104-31-02 W
Pop: 140 (1990); 191 (1980)   **Pop Density:** 280.0
Land: 0.5 sq. mi.; **Water:** 0.0 sq. mi.
Name origin: For the former hometown of Bulgarian settlers.

MONTANA, Fergus County · American Places Dictionary

Fergus County
County Seat: Lewistown (ZIP: 59457)

Pop: 12,083 (1990); 13,076 (1980)   **Pop Density:** 2.8
Land: 4339.3 sq. mi.; **Water:** 11.2 sq. mi.   **Area Code:** 406
In central MT, northwest of Billings; organized Mar 12, 1885 (prior to statehood) from Meagher County. Its county seat is in the exact center of MT.
Name origin: For James Fergus (1813–97), cattleman, miner, and a MT territorial legislator.

Denton   Town
ZIP: 59430   **Lat:** 47-19-23 N   **Long:** 109-56-55 W
Pop: 350 (1990); 356 (1980)   **Pop Density:** 437.5
Land: 0.8 sq. mi.; **Water:** 0.0 sq. mi.   **Elev:** 3603 ft.
Name origin: For the Dent brothers, who owned the land on which the town was built. The *on* was added because Dent was considered too short for a town.

Grass Range   Town
ZIP: 59032   **Lat:** 47-01-36 N   **Long:** 108-48-10 W
Pop: 159 (1990); 139 (1980)   **Pop Density:** 795.0
Land: 0.2 sq. mi.; **Water:** 0.0 sq. mi.

Lewistown   City
ZIP: 59457   **Lat:** 47-03-48 N   **Long:** 109-25-39 W
Pop: 6,051 (1990); 7,104 (1980)   **Pop Density:** 3361.7
Land: 1.8 sq. mi.; **Water:** 0.0 sq. mi.   **Elev:** 3963 ft.
Name origin: For Maj. William H. Lewis. Previously called Reed's Fort.

Moore   Town
ZIP: 59464   **Lat:** 46-58-29 N   **Long:** 109-41-41 W
Pop: 211 (1990); 229 (1980)   **Pop Density:** 1055.0
Land: 0.2 sq. mi.; **Water:** 0.0 sq. mi.   **Elev:** 4171 ft.
Name origin: For Mr. Moore of Philadelphia, who contributed financially to the building of the 'Jaw Bone' railroad.

Winifred   Town
ZIP: 59489   **Lat:** 47-33-41 N   **Long:** 109-22-31 W
Pop: 150 (1990); 155 (1980)   **Pop Density:** 300.0
Land: 0.5 sq. mi.; **Water:** 0.0 sq. mi.
Name origin: For either Winifred Sewall, daughter of Ed. D. Sewall, or Winifred Rockefeller.

Flathead County
County Seat: Kalispell (ZIP: 59901)

Pop: 59,218 (1990); 51,966 (1980)   **Pop Density:** 11.6
Land: 5098.6 sq. mi.; **Water:** 158.0 sq. mi.   **Area Code:** 406
On the northwestern border of MT, north of Missoula; organized Feb 6, 1893 from Missoula County; annexed part of Deer Lodge County before 1900.
Name origin: For the Salish or Flathead Indians of the Catawba group; there is no evidence that they flattened the heads of their infants, as some other tribes did. It has been suggested the name comes from their home at the 'flat' head of the Columbia River rather than in the deep canyons below.

Columbia Falls   City
Lat: 48-22-16 N   **Long:** 114-11-14 W
Pop: 2,942 (1990); 3,112 (1980)   **Pop Density:** 2451.7
Land: 1.2 sq. mi.; **Water:** 0.0 sq. mi.
Name origin: For the town's intended location near falls on the Flathead River. Previously called Monaco.

Evergreen   CDP
Lat: 48-13-32 N   **Long:** 114-16-29 W
Pop: 4,109 (1990); 3,746 (1980)   **Pop Density:** 1245.2
Land: 3.3 sq. mi.; **Water:** 0.0 sq. mi.

Kalispell   City
ZIP: 59901   **Lat:** 48-11-57 N   **Long:** 114-19-01 W
Pop: 11,917 (1990); 10,689 (1980)   **Pop Density:** 2708.4
Land: 4.4 sq. mi.; **Water:** 0.0 sq. mi.
In northwestern MT, 9 mi. northwest of Flathead Lake. Established 1881.
Name origin: For the Kalispel Indian tribe of Salishan linguistic stock, part of the Flathead tribe. Name is said to mean 'camas,' a genus of the lily family with edible roots.

Whitefish   City
ZIP: 59937   **Lat:** 48-24-56 N   **Long:** 114-20-41 W
Pop: 4,368 (1990); 3,703 (1980)   **Pop Density:** 1456.0
Land: 3.0 sq. mi.; **Water:** 0.0 sq. mi.   **Elev:** 3036 ft.
Name origin: For a nearby lake, itself named for the abundant whitefish in it.

Gallatin County
County Seat: Bozeman (ZIP: 59715)

Pop: 50,463 (1990); 42,865 (1980) **Pop Density:** 20.1
Land: 2506.9 sq. mi.; **Water:** 25.9 sq. mi. **Area Code:** 406

On the southwestern border of MT, east of Butte; original county; organized Feb 2, 1865 (prior to statehood).

Name origin: For the Gallatin River, which flows through the county; itself named by Lewis and Clark in 1805 for Abraham Alfonse Albert Gallatin (1761–1849), U.S. secretary of the treasury (1802–14) at the time.

Belgrade   Town
ZIP: 59714   **Lat:** 45-46-40 N **Long:** 111-10-38 W
Pop: 3,411 (1990); 2,336 (1980) **Pop Density:** 2623.8
Land: 1.3 sq. mi.; **Water:** 0.0 sq. mi. **Elev:** 4454 ft.

Name origin: Named in 1889 by a Serbian capitalist for his former home of Belgrade.

Bozeman   City
ZIP: 59715   **Lat:** 45-40-36 N **Long:** 111-02-32 W
Pop: 22,660 (1990); 21,645 (1980) **Pop Density:** 2312.2
Land: 9.8 sq. mi.; **Water:** 0.0 sq. mi. **Elev:** 4810 ft.

In southern MT, 81 mi. east-southeast of Butte.

Name origin: For explorer John Bozeman (1835–1867), who guided the first train of immigrants into the Gallatin Valley. Previously called Missouri.

Manhattan   Town
ZIP: 59741   **Lat:** 45-51-26 N **Long:** 111-19-48 W
Pop: 1,034 (1990); 988 (1980) **Pop Density:** 1723.3
Land: 0.6 sq. mi.; **Water:** 0.0 sq. mi. **Elev:** 4243 ft.

Name origin: Named in 1891 for the Manhattan Company of New York which had land holdings in the area. Previously called Hamilton and Moreland.

Three Forks   Town
ZIP: 59752   **Lat:** 45-53-21 N **Long:** 111-33-13 W
Pop: 1,203 (1990); 1,247 (1980) **Pop Density:** 1002.5
Land: 1.2 sq. mi.; **Water:** 0.0 sq. mi.

Name origin: For the location near the forks formed by the Madison, Gallatin and Jefferson rivers as they join to become the Missouri River.

West Yellowstone   Town
ZIP: 59758   **Lat:** 44-39-52 N **Long:** 111-06-24 W
Pop: 913 (1990); 735 (1980) **Pop Density:** 1304.3
Land: 0.7 sq. mi.; **Water:** 0.0 sq. mi. **Elev:** 6667 ft.

Name origin: Named in 1920 for the town's location at the western entrance to Yellowstone Park. Originally known as Yellowstone.

Garfield County
County Seat: Jordan (ZIP: 59337)

Pop: 1,589 (1990); 1,656 (1980) **Pop Density:** 0.3
Land: 4668.2 sq. mi.; **Water:** 179.5 sq. mi. **Area Code:** 406

In east-central MT, northeast of Billings; organized Feb 7, 1919 from Valley and McCone counties.

Name origin: For James Abram Garfield (1831–81), twentieth U.S. president.

Jordan   Town
ZIP: 59337   **Lat:** 47-19-16 N **Long:** 106-54-36 W
Pop: 494 (1990); 485 (1980) **Pop Density:** 1235.0
Land: 0.4 sq. mi.; **Water:** 0.0 sq. mi. **Elev:** 2598 ft.

Name origin: Named by founder Arthur Jordan for a friend with the same name.

MONTANA, Glacier County   American Places Dictionary

> ## Glacier County
> **County Seat: Cut Bank (ZIP: 59427)**
>
> **Pop:** 12,121 (1990); 10,628 (1980) **Pop Density:** 4.0
> **Land:** 2994.7 sq. mi.; **Water:** 42.4 sq. mi. **Area Code:** 406
>
> On the northwestern border of MT, northwest of Great Falls, bordering Alberta province, Canada and Glacier National Park; organized Feb 17, 1919 from Flathead and Teton counties.
>
> **Name origin:** For Glacier National Park on the county's western border.

Browning   Town
ZIP: 59417   **Lat:** 48-33-24 N **Long:** 113-00-49 W
Pop: 1,170 (1990); 1,226 (1980)   **Pop Density:** 3900.0
Land: 0.3 sq. mi.; **Water:** 0.0 sq. mi.

Cut Bank   City
ZIP: 59427   **Lat:** 48-38-05 N **Long:** 112-19-48 W
Pop: 3,329 (1990); 3,688 (1980)   **Pop Density:** 3329.0
Land: 1.0 sq. mi.; **Water:** 0.0 sq. mi.
Name origin: For the deep gorge made by nearby Cut Bank Creek.

East Glacier Park Village   CDP
                         Lat: 48-26-49 N **Long:** 113-13-20 W
Pop: 326 (1990)   **Pop Density:** 74.1
Land: 4.4 sq. mi.; **Water:** 0.0 sq. mi.

North Browning   CDP
                         Lat: 48-34-12 N **Long:** 113-00-30 W
Pop: 1,630 (1990)   **Pop Density:** 493.9
Land: 3.3 sq. mi.; **Water:** 0.0 sq. mi.

South Browning   CDP
                         Lat: 48-32-46 N **Long:** 113-00-48 W
Pop: 1,748 (1990)   **Pop Density:** 874.0
Land: 2.0 sq. mi.; **Water:** 0.1 sq. mi.

Starr School   CDP
                         Lat: 48-36-07 N **Long:** 113-08-57 W
Pop: 260 (1990)   **Pop Density:** 63.4
Land: 4.1 sq. mi.; **Water:** 0.0 sq. mi.

> ## Golden Valley County
> **County Seat: Ryegate (ZIP: 59074)**
>
> **Pop:** 912 (1990); 1,026 (1980) **Pop Density:** 0.8
> **Land:** 1175.3 sq. mi.; **Water:** 1.1 sq. mi. **Area Code:** 406
>
> In south-central MT, northwest of Billings; organized Oct 4, 1920 from Musselshell and Sweet Grass counties.
>
> **Name origin:** For the rich soil and plentiful streams.

Lavina   Town
ZIP: 59046   **Lat:** 46-17-46 N **Long:** 108-56-20 W
Pop: 151 (1990); 164 (1980)   **Pop Density:** 151.0
Land: 1.0 sq. mi.; **Water:** 0.0 sq. mi.
Name origin: For daughter of the housekeeper of an early settler, Mr. Vance.

Ryegate   Town
ZIP: 59074   **Lat:** 46-17-55 N **Long:** 109-15-12 W
Pop: 260 (1990); 273 (1980)   **Pop Density:** 371.4
Land: 0.7 sq. mi.; **Water:** 0.0 sq. mi.
Name origin: For rye fields in the area.

Granite County
County Seat: Philipsburg (ZIP: 59858)

Pop: 2,548 (1990); 2,700 (1980)   **Pop Density:** 1.5
Land: 1727.5 sq. mi.; **Water:** 5.6 sq. mi.   **Area Code:** 406

In west-central MT, northwest of Butte; organized Mar 2, 1893 from Deer Lodge County.

Name origin: For the Granite Mountain Silver Mine, itself named for the granite rock within the mine.

Drummond — Town
ZIP: 59832   **Lat:** 46-39-58 N   **Long:** 113-08-43 W
Pop: 264 (1990); 414 (1980)   **Pop Density:** 440.0
Land: 0.6 sq. mi.; **Water:** 0.0 sq. mi.   **Elev:** 3948 ft.

Name origin: For an early trapper named Drummond. Previously called Drummond Camp.

Philipsburg — Town
ZIP: 59858   **Lat:** 46-19-56 N   **Long:** 113-17-41 W
Pop: 925 (1990); 1,138 (1980)   **Pop Density:** 1156.3
Land: 0.8 sq. mi.; **Water:** 0.0 sq. mi.   **Elev:** 5270 ft.
Settled 1864.

Name origin: For Phillip Deidesheimer, first superintendent of the St. Louis Montana Gold and Silver Mining Company.

Hill County
County Seat: Havre (ZIP: 59501)

Pop: 17,654 (1990); 17,985 (1980)   **Pop Density:** 6.1
Land: 2896.4 sq. mi.; **Water:** 19.7 sq. mi.   **Area Code:** 406

On the central northern border of MT, northeast of Great Falls; organized Feb 28, 1912 from Chouteau County.

Name origin: For James Jerome Hill (1838–1916), president and developer of the Great Northern Railroad.

Havre — City
ZIP: 59501   **Lat:** 48-32-37 N   **Long:** 109-40-44 W
Pop: 10,201 (1990); 10,891 (1980)   **Pop Density:** 4080.4
Land: 2.5 sq. mi.; **Water:** 0.0 sq. mi.   **Elev:** 2494 ft.

In northern MT, 100 mi. northeast of Great Falls. Founded 1891.

Name origin: For Havre, France, birthplace of homesteaders Simon Pepin and Gus DesCelles. Previously called Bull Hook Bottoms and Bull Hook Siding.

Havre North — CDP
Lat: 48-33-40 N   **Long:** 109-40-07 W
Pop: 1,110 (1990); 1,230 (1980)   **Pop Density:** 317.1
Land: 3.5 sq. mi.; **Water:** 0.0 sq. mi.

Hingham — Town
ZIP: 59528   **Lat:** 48-33-20 N   **Long:** 110-25-14 W
Pop: 181 (1990); 186 (1980)   **Pop Density:** 905.0
Land: 0.2 sq. mi.; **Water:** 0.0 sq. mi.   **Elev:** 3032 ft.
Established c. 1910.

Jefferson County
County Seat: Boulder (ZIP: 59632)

Pop: 7,939 (1990); 7,029 (1980)   **Pop Density:** 4.8
Land: 1656.7 sq. mi.; **Water:** 2.2 sq. mi.   **Area Code:** 406

In west-central MT, east of Butte; original county, organized Feb 2, 1865 (prior to statehood).

Name origin: For the Jefferson River, which forms part of the county's southern border; itself named by Lewis and Clark for Thomas Jefferson (1743–1826), third U.S. president.

Boulder — Town
ZIP: 59632   **Lat:** 46-14-09 N   **Long:** 112-07-10 W
Pop: 1,316 (1990); 1,441 (1980)   **Pop Density:** 1196.4
Land: 1.1 sq. mi.; **Water:** 0.0 sq. mi.   **Elev:** 4904 ft.
Established c. 1860.

Name origin: For the massive rocks found in the valley.

Whitehall — Town
ZIP: 59759   **Lat:** 45-52-17 N   **Long:** 112-05-45 W
Pop: 1,067 (1990); 1,030 (1980)   **Pop Density:** 1524.3
Land: 0.7 sq. mi.; **Water:** 0.0 sq. mi.

Name origin: Named by E.G. Brooke for his home, which resembles a similar building in Whitehall, IL.

Judith Basin County
County Seat: Stanford (ZIP: 59479)

Pop: 2,282 (1990); 2,646 (1980) **Pop Density:** 1.2
Land: 1869.9 sq. mi.; **Water:** 0.9 sq. mi. **Area Code:** 406

In central MT, southeast of Great Falls; organized Dec 10, 1920 from Fergus and Cascade counties.

Name origin: For the basin of the Judith River, which flows through the county; named by Meriwether Lewis (1774–1809) for his cousin, Judith Hancock, who later married Lt. William Clark (1770–1838).

Hobson — Town
ZIP: 59452 Lat: 46-59-56 N Long: 109-52-23 W
Pop: 226 (1990); 261 (1980) Pop Density: 753.3
Land: 0.3 sq. mi.; Water: 0.0 sq. mi. Elev: 4078 ft.
Name origin: For local cowboy and rancher S.S. Hobson.

Stanford — Town
ZIP: 59479 Lat: 47-09-07 N Long: 110-13-06 W
Pop: 529 (1990); 595 (1980) Pop Density: 1322.5
Land: 0.4 sq. mi.; Water: 0.0 sq. mi. Elev: 4284 ft.
Name origin: For Stanfordville, NY, former home of settlers Calvin and Edward Bowers.

Lake County
County Seat: Polson (ZIP: 59860)

Pop: 21,041 (1990); 19,056 (1980) **Pop Density:** 14.1
Land: 1493.8 sq. mi.; **Water:** 159.9 sq. mi. **Area Code:** 406

In northwestern MT, north of Missoula; organized May 11, 1923 from Flathead and Missoula counties.

Name origin: For Flathead Lake, which comprises most of the northern part of the county.

Arlee — CDP
ZIP: 59821 Lat: 47-10-09 N Long: 114-05-20 W
Pop: 489 (1990) Pop Density: 75.2
Land: 6.5 sq. mi.; Water: 0.0 sq. mi.

Charlo — CDP
ZIP: 59824 Lat: 47-26-32 N Long: 114-10-14 W
Pop: 358 (1990) Pop Density: 179.0
Land: 2.0 sq. mi.; Water: 0.0 sq. mi.

Finley Point — CDP
Lat: 47-44-17 N Long: 114-03-44 W
Pop: 395 (1990) Pop Density: 94.0
Land: 4.2 sq. mi.; Water: 7.1 sq. mi.

Kicking Horse — CDP
Lat: 47-27-38 N Long: 114-04-27 W
Pop: 281 (1990) Pop Density: 112.4
Land: 2.5 sq. mi.; Water: 1.1 sq. mi.

Pablo — CDP
Lat: 47-36-15 N Long: 114-06-17 W
Pop: 1,298 (1990) Pop Density: 264.9
Land: 4.9 sq. mi.; Water: 0.0 sq. mi.

Polson — City
ZIP: 59860 Lat: 47-41-23 N Long: 114-09-28 W
Pop: 3,283 (1990); 2,798 (1980) Pop Density: 1823.9
Land: 1.8 sq. mi.; Water: 0.0 sq. mi. Elev: 2931 ft.

Ronan — City
ZIP: 59864 Lat: 47-31-42 N Long: 114-05-59 W
Pop: 1,547 (1990); 1,530 (1980) Pop Density: 1406.4
Land: 1.1 sq. mi.; Water: 0.0 sq. mi.
Name origin: For Maj. Peter Ronan, who wrote a history of the Flathead Indians.

St. Ignatius — Town
Lat: 47-19-09 N Long: 114-05-42 W
Pop: 778 (1990); 877 (1980) Pop Density: 1556.0
Land: 0.5 sq. mi.; Water: 0.0 sq. mi.
Founded 1854.
Name origin: For St. Ignatius of Loyola (1491–1556), the founder of the Society of Jesus.

Lewis and Clark County
County Seat: Helena (ZIP: 59601)

Pop: 47,495 (1990); 43,039 (1980)   **Pop Density:** 13.7
Land: 3461.0 sq. mi.; **Water:** 36.6 sq. mi.   **Area Code:** 406

In west-central MT, west of Great Falls; original county; organized as Edgerton County Feb 2, 1865 (prior to statehood); name changed Dec 20, 1867, effective Mar 1, 1868.

Name origin: For Meriwether Lewis (1774–1809) and William Clark (1770–1838), explorers and leaders of the expedition (1804–06) to explore the American northwest. Originally named for Sidney Edgerton, the first territorial governor.

East Helena — Town
ZIP: 59635   **Lat:** 46-35-18 N   **Long:** 111-55-04 W
Pop: 1,538 (1990); 1,647 (1980)   **Pop Density:** 1922.5
Land: 0.8 sq. mi.; **Water:** 0.0 sq. mi.   **Elev:** 3874 ft.
Settled c. 1900.
Name origin: For its location east of the city of Helena.

Helena — City
ZIP: 59601   **Lat:** 46-35-47 N   **Long:** 112-01-13 W
Pop: 24,569 (1990); 23,938 (1980)   **Pop Density:** 1819.9
Land: 13.5 sq. mi.; **Water:** 0.0 sq. mi.   **Elev:** 4090 ft.

In west-central MT, 45 mi. north-northeast of Butte. Incorporated as town 1870, as city 1881; state capital 1889. Trading and supply center for mining and agricultural area; lead and zinc refining.

Name origin: Named in 1864 by John Somerville, who came from Helena, MN. Originally known as Last Chance Gulch.

Helena Valley Northeast — CDP
Lat: 46-42-12 N   **Long:** 111-57-29 W
Pop: 1,585 (1990)   **Pop Density:** 35.9
Land: 44.2 sq. mi.; **Water:** 4.5 sq. mi.

Helena Valley Northwest — CDP
Lat: 46-43-38 N   **Long:** 112-03-22 W
Pop: 1,215 (1990)   **Pop Density:** 72.3
Land: 16.8 sq. mi.; **Water:** 0.0 sq. mi.

Helena Valley Southeast — CDP
Lat: 46-36-58 N   **Long:** 111-55-16 W
Pop: 4,601 (1990)   **Pop Density:** 282.3
Land: 16.3 sq. mi.; **Water:** 0.0 sq. mi.

Helena Valley West Central — CDP
Lat: 46-39-39 N   **Long:** 112-03-30 W
Pop: 6,327 (1990)   **Pop Density:** 233.5
Land: 27.1 sq. mi.; **Water:** 0.0 sq. mi.

Helena West Side — CDP
Lat: 46-35-48 N   **Long:** 112-06-25 W
Pop: 1,847 (1990)   **Pop Density:** 125.6
Land: 14.7 sq. mi.; **Water:** 0.0 sq. mi.

Liberty County
County Seat: Chester (ZIP: 59522)

Pop: 2,295 (1990); 2,329 (1980)   **Pop Density:** 1.6
Land: 1429.8 sq. mi.; **Water:** 17.4 sq. mi.   **Area Code:** 406

On the central northern border of MT, north of Great Falls; organized Feb 11, 1920 from Chouteau and Hill counties.

Name origin: For the inhabitants' 'freedom' from Hill County.

Chester — Town
ZIP: 59522   **Lat:** 48-30-40 N   **Long:** 110-57-57 W
Pop: 942 (1990); 963 (1980)   **Pop Density:** 1884.0
Land: 0.5 sq. mi.; **Water:** 0.0 sq. mi.   **Elev:** 3132 ft.
Name origin: For the first telegraph operator's hometown in PA.

Lincoln County
County Seat: Libby (ZIP: 59923)

Pop: 17,481 (1990); 17,752 (1980)   **Pop Density:** 4.8
Land: 3612.8 sq. mi.; **Water:** 62.4 sq. mi.   **Area Code:** 406
On the northwestern corner of MT; organized Mar 9, 1909 from Flathead County.
Name origin: For Abraham Lincoln (1809–65), sixteenth U.S. president.

Eureka — Town
ZIP: 59917   **Lat:** 48-52-33 N **Long:** 115-02-52 W
Pop: 1,043 (1990); 1,119 (1980)   **Pop Density:** 1043.0
Land: 1.0 sq. mi.; **Water:** 0.0 sq. mi.   **Elev:** 2566 ft.

Libby — City
ZIP: 59923   **Lat:** 48-23-20 N **Long:** 115-33-25 W
Pop: 2,532 (1990); 2,748 (1980)   **Pop Density:** 2301.8
Land: 1.1 sq. mi.; **Water:** 0.0 sq. mi.
Name origin: For the daughter of early settler George Davis.

Rexford — Town
ZIP: 59930   **Lat:** 48-54-03 N **Long:** 115-10-13 W
Pop: 132 (1990); 130 (1980)   **Pop Density:** 1320.0
Land: 0.1 sq. mi.; **Water:** 0.0 sq. mi.

Troy — Town
ZIP: 59935   **Lat:** 48-27-36 N **Long:** 115-53-23 W
Pop: 953 (1990); 1,088 (1980)   **Pop Density:** 1906.0
Land: 0.5 sq. mi.; **Water:** 0.0 sq. mi.   **Elev:** 1888 ft.
Name origin: For local resident Troy Morrow. Previously called Lake City.

Madison County
County Seat: Virginia City (ZIP: 59755)

Pop: 5,989 (1990); 5,448 (1980)   **Pop Density:** 1.7
Land: 3586.6 sq. mi.; **Water:** 16.3 sq. mi.   **Area Code:** 406
In southwestern MT, southeast of Butte; original county; organized Feb 2, 1865 (prior to statehood).
Name origin: For the Madison River, which flows through the county; itself named by Lewis and Clark for James Madison (1751–1836), then secretary of state (1801–09), later fourth U.S. president.

Ennis — Town
ZIP: 59729   **Lat:** 45-20-43 N **Long:** 111-43-46 W
Pop: 773 (1990); 660 (1980)   **Pop Density:** 1104.3
Land: 0.7 sq. mi.; **Water:** 0.0 sq. mi.   **Elev:** 4939 ft.
Name origin: For William Ennis, who settled here in 1879 and built a store.

Sheridan — Town
ZIP: 59749   **Lat:** 45-27-25 N **Long:** 112-11-29 W
Pop: 652 (1990); 646 (1980)   **Pop Density:** 592.7
Land: 1.1 sq. mi.; **Water:** 0.0 sq. mi.
Established c. 1866.
Name origin: For Civil War Gen. Philip H. Sheridan (1831–88).

Twin Bridges — Town
ZIP: 59754   **Lat:** 45-32-36 N **Long:** 112-19-57 W
Pop: 374 (1990); 437 (1980)   **Pop Density:** 374.0
Land: 1.0 sq. mi.; **Water:** 0.0 sq. mi.   **Elev:** 4627 ft.
Name origin: For two bridges which span the Jefferson River near town.

Virginia City — Town
ZIP: 59755   **Lat:** 45-17-55 N **Long:** 111-56-07 W
Pop: 142 (1990); 192 (1980)   **Pop Density:** 157.8
Land: 0.9 sq. mi.; **Water:** 0.0 sq. mi.   **Elev:** 5822 ft.
Incorporated 1864; the first incorporated town in MT.
Name origin: Named Varina for the wife of Jefferson Davis (1808–89), but this created conflict; a judge changed the name to Virginia. *City* was added later.

McCone County
County Seat: Circle (ZIP: 59215)

Pop: 2,276 (1990); 2,702 (1980) **Pop Density:** 0.9
Land: 2642.6 sq. mi.; **Water:** 40.2 sq. mi. **Area Code:** 406
In east-central MT; organized Feb 20, 1919 from Dawson and Richland counties.
Name origin: For George McCone, a MT state legislator.

Circle Town
ZIP: 59215 **Lat:** 47-25-02 N **Long:** 105-35-10 W
Pop: 805 (1990); 931 (1980) **Pop Density:** 1006.3
Land: 0.8 sq. mi.; **Water:** 0.0 sq. mi.

Name origin: For the circle brand of an early Montana cow outfit owned by Cross and Twiggly.

Meagher County
County Seat: White Sulphur Springs (ZIP: 59645)

Pop: 1,819 (1990); 2,154 (1980) **Pop Density:** 0.8
Land: 2391.8 sq. mi.; **Water:** 3.0 sq. mi. **Area Code:** 406
In central MT, east of Helena; original county; organized Nov 16, 1867 (prior to statehood) from Chouteau and Gallatin counties; annexed part of Fergus County in 1911.
Name origin: For Thomas Francis Meagher (1823–67), Irish revolutionary tried for sedition and banished to Tasmania. He escaped to New York City, where he practiced law. He became a brigadier general in the Civil War and led the "Irish Brigade." He was acting governor of MT Territory (1865–66).

White Sulphur Springs City
ZIP: 59645 **Lat:** 46-32-49 N **Long:** 110-54-13 W
Pop: 963 (1990); 1,302 (1980) **Pop Density:** 1203.8
Land: 0.8 sq. mi.; **Water:** 0.0 sq. mi.

Name origin: For white deposits around the sulphur hot springs here.

Mineral County
County Seat: Superior (ZIP: 59872)

Pop: 3,315 (1990); 3,675 (1980) **Pop Density:** 2.7
Land: 1219.9 sq. mi.; **Water:** 3.6 sq. mi. **Area Code:** 406
On the central western border of MT, west of Missoula; organized Aug 7, 1914 from Missoula County.
Name origin: For its many mines.

Alberton Town
ZIP: 59820 **Lat:** 47-00-07 N **Long:** 114-28-34 W
Pop: 354 (1990); 368 (1980) **Pop Density:** 590.0
Land: 0.6 sq. mi.; **Water:** 0.0 sq. mi.

Name origin: For the Alberts, a pioneer family who came to the area from Canada in 1870.

Superior Town
ZIP: 59872 **Lat:** 47-11-39 N **Long:** 114-53-39 W
Pop: 881 (1990); 1,054 (1980) **Pop Density:** 800.9
Land: 1.1 sq. mi.; **Water:** 0.1 sq. mi. **Elev:** 2744 ft.

Name origin: For an early settler's former home of Superior, WI.

Missoula County
County Seat: Missoula (ZIP: 59802)

Pop: 78,687 (1990); 76,016 (1980)   **Pop Density:** 30.3
Land: 2598.2 sq. mi.; **Water:** 20.2 sq. mi.   **Area Code:** 406
In west-central MT; original county; organized Feb 2, 1865 (prior to statehood).
Name origin: From a Salish (Flathead) Indian word whose meaning is in dispute: possibly 'feared water,' 'at the stream of surprise and ambush,' or 'river of awe'; believed to refer to Hell Gate Canyon where Blackfeet Indians ambushed the Salish.

Bonner-West Riverside   CDP
Lat: 46-52-40 N   **Long:** 113-53-16 W
Pop: 1,669 (1990); 1,742 (1980)   **Pop Density:** 1192.1
Land: 1.4 sq. mi.; **Water:** 0.1 sq. mi.

Lolo   CDP
ZIP: 59847   **Lat:** 46-46-03 N   **Long:** 114-06-18 W
Pop: 2,746 (1990); 2,418 (1980)   **Pop Density:** 289.1
Land: 9.5 sq. mi.; **Water:** 0.2 sq. mi.

Missoula   City
ZIP: 59801   **Lat:** 46-52-07 N   **Long:** 114-00-27 W
Pop: 42,918 (1990); 33,351 (1980)   **Pop Density:** 2585.4
Land: 16.6 sq. mi.; **Water:** 0.1 sq. mi.   **Elev:** 3200 ft.
In western MT near the Bitterroot River and Clark Fork, west of Helena. Main industry is wood products; site of University of Montana and training center for Forest Service workers who parachute into areas to fight forest fires.
Name origin: A Flathead Indian term probably meaning 'the river of awe,' 'feared water,' or with the connotation of 'dread,' believed to be in reference to Hell Gate Canyon.

Orchard Homes   CDP
ZIP: 59801   **Lat:** 46-51-35 N   **Long:** 114-03-59 W
Pop: 10,317 (1990); 10,837 (1980)   **Pop Density:** 1273.7
Land: 8.1 sq. mi.; **Water:** 0.2 sq. mi.

Musselshell County
County Seat: Roundup (ZIP: 59072)

Pop: 4,106 (1990); 4,428 (1980)   **Pop Density:** 2.2
Land: 1867.2 sq. mi.; **Water:** 3.8 sq. mi.   **Area Code:** 406
In south-central MT, north of Billings; organized Feb 11, 1911 from Fergus, Yellowstone, and Meagher counties.
Name origin: For the Musselshell River, which forms part of the county's eastern border; the river was named for the mussel shells found on its banks.

Melstone   Town
ZIP: 59054   **Lat:** 46-35-56 N   **Long:** 107-52-03 W
Pop: 166 (1990); 238 (1980)   **Pop Density:** 237.1
Land: 0.7 sq. mi.; **Water:** 0.0 sq. mi.
Name origin: For newspaper man Melvin Stone, who was on the train with railroad officials who selected the names for towns along the line.

Roundup   City
ZIP: 59072   **Lat:** 46-26-54 N   **Long:** 108-32-19 W
Pop: 1,808 (1990); 2,119 (1980)   **Pop Density:** 1390.8
Land: 1.3 sq. mi.; **Water:** 0.0 sq. mi.   **Elev:** 3226 ft.
Founded c. 1883.
Name origin: It was once the gathering point for the great herds of cattle that grazed in the valley.

Park County
County Seat: Livingston (ZIP: 59047)

Pop: 14,562 (1990); 12,869 (1980) **Pop Density:** 5.5
Land: 2656.2 sq. mi.; **Water:** 10.6 sq. mi. **Area Code:** 406

On the southern border of MT, east of Bozeman; organized Feb 23, 1887 (prior to statehood) from Gallatin County.

Name origin: For Yellowstone National Park, which is on the county's southern border.

Clyde Park — Town
ZIP: 59018 **Lat:** 45-53-01 N **Long:** 110-36-19 W
Pop: 282 (1990); 283 (1980) **Pop Density:** 705.0
Land: 0.4 sq. mi.; **Water:** 0.0 sq. mi. **Elev:** 4868 ft.

Name origin: For Clydesdale horses imported from England. Originally known as Sunnyside.

Livingston — City
ZIP: 59047 **Lat:** 45-39-46 N **Long:** 110-33-49 W
Pop: 6,701 (1990); 6,994 (1980) **Pop Density:** 2680.4
Land: 2.5 sq. mi.; **Water:** 0.0 sq. mi. **Elev:** 4503 ft.

Name origin: Named in 1882 for Crawford Livingston, director of the Northern Pacific Railroad. Previously called Clark's City.

Petroleum County
County Seat: Winnett (ZIP: 59087)

Pop: 519 (1990); 655 (1980) **Pop Density:** 0.3
Land: 1653.9 sq. mi.; **Water:** 20.1 sq. mi. **Area Code:** 406

In central MT, north of Billings; organized Feb 22, 1925 from Fergus County.

Name origin: For the petroleum production in the Cat Creek fields.

Winnett — Town
ZIP: 59087 **Lat:** 47-00-16 N **Long:** 108-20-46 W
Pop: 188 (1990); 207 (1980) **Pop Density:** 188.0
Land: 1.0 sq. mi.; **Water:** 0.0 sq. mi.

Phillips County
County Seat: Malta (ZIP: 59538)

Pop: 5,163 (1990); 5,367 (1980) **Pop Density:** 1.0
Land: 5139.9 sq. mi.; **Water:** 72.3 sq. mi. **Area Code:** 406

On central northern border of MT; organized Feb 5, 1915 from Blaine and Valley counties.

Name origin: For Benjamin D. Phillips, a local landowner and prominent citizen.

Dodson — Town
ZIP: 59524 **Lat:** 48-23-43 N **Long:** 108-14-42 W
Pop: 137 (1990); 158 (1980) **Pop Density:** 685.0
Land: 0.2 sq. mi.; **Water:** 0.0 sq. mi.

Name origin: For the owner of the trading post and saloon.

Malta — City
ZIP: 59538 **Lat:** 48-21-17 N **Long:** 107-52-11 W
Pop: 2,340 (1990); 2,367 (1980) **Pop Density:** 2127.3
Land: 1.1 sq. mi.; **Water:** 0.0 sq. mi. **Elev:** 2255 ft.

Name origin: For the island in the Mediterranean.

Saco — Town
ZIP: 59261 **Lat:** 48-27-25 N **Long:** 107-20-25 W
Pop: 261 (1990); 252 (1980) **Pop Density:** 870.0
Land: 0.3 sq. mi.; **Water:** 0.0 sq. mi. **Elev:** 2175 ft.

Name origin: For either the Sack-ow Indian tribe of ME or a contraction of *Sacajawea* (1786?–1812), a guide on the Lewis and Clark expedition (1804–06).

MONTANA, Pondera County

> ## Pondera County
> **County Seat: Conrad (ZIP: 59425)**
>
> **Pop:** 6,433 (1990); 6,731 (1980)   **Pop Density:** 4.0
> **Land:** 1624.7 sq. mi.; **Water:** 15.2 sq. mi.   **Area Code:** 406
>
> In northwest-central MT, northwest of Great Falls; organized Feb 17, 1919 from Chouteau and Teton counties.
>
> **Name origin:** From French *pend d'oreille* 'hanging ear,' first applied to a lake in ID, thought to resemble an earlobe. To avoid confusion with the lake and town, name was changed to Pondera.

Conrad
City
ZIP: 59425   **Lat:** 48-10-22 N **Long:** 111-56-46 W
Pop: 2,891 (1990); 3,074 (1980)   **Pop Density:** 2409.2
Land: 1.2 sq. mi.; **Water:** 0.0 sq. mi.
Name origin: Named c. 1884 for W.G. Conrad of the Conrad Investment Company. Previously called Rondera.

Heart Butte
CDP
Lat: 48-17-25 N **Long:** 112-49-58 W
Pop: 499 (1990)   **Pop Density:** 110.9
Land: 4.5 sq. mi.; **Water:** 0.0 sq. mi.

Valier
Town
ZIP: 59486   **Lat:** 48-18-06 N **Long:** 112-15-04 W
Pop: 519 (1990); 640 (1980)   **Pop Density:** 432.5
Land: 1.2 sq. mi.; **Water:** 0.0 sq. mi.   **Elev:** 3805 ft.
Name origin: For Peter Valier, who supervised the building of the Montana Western Railroad.

> ## Powder River County
> **County Seat: Broadus (ZIP: 59317)**
>
> **Pop:** 2,090 (1990); 2,520 (1980)   **Pop Density:** 0.6
> **Land:** 3297.3 sq. mi.; **Water:** 0.8 sq. mi.   **Area Code:** 406
>
> On the southeastern border of MT, southeast of Billings; organized Mar 7, 1919 from Custer County.
>
> **Name origin:** For the river, which runs diagonally through the county; the river's name comes either from the fine black sand resembling gunpowder that is found along its banks, or from an incident when a group of soldiers were attacked by Indians, and one yelled "hide the powder!"

Broadus
Town
ZIP: 59317   **Lat:** 45-26-34 N **Long:** 105-24-25 W
Pop: 572 (1990); 712 (1980)   **Pop Density:** 1906.7
Land: 0.3 sq. mi.; **Water:** 0.0 sq. mi.   **Elev:** 3029 ft.
Name origin: For the Broaddus family, who settled along the Powder River.

Powell County
County Seat: Deer Lodge (ZIP: 59722)

Pop: 6,620 (1990); 6,958 (1980)　　　**Pop Density:** 2.8
Land: 2326.0 sq. mi.; **Water:** 6.7 sq. mi.　　　**Area Code:** 406

In west-central MT, west of Helena; organized Jan 31, 1901 from Deer Lodge County.

Name origin: For John Wesley Powell (1834–1902), geologist and explorer of the Grand Canyon (1870), director of the U.S. Geological Survey, and first head of the U.S. Bureau of Reclamation.

Deer Lodge　　　　　　　　　　　　　　　City
ZIP: 59722　　　**Lat:** 46-23-50 N　**Long:** 112-43-55 W
Pop: 3,378 (1990); 4,023 (1980)　　**Pop Density:** 2412.9
Land: 1.4 sq. mi.; **Water:** 0.0 sq. mi.　　**Elev:** 4521 ft.
Name origin: Indians called this valley 'Lodge of the White Tailed Deer.' Previously Cottonwood and La Barge City.

Prairie County
County Seat: Terry (ZIP: 59349)

Pop: 1,383 (1990); 1,836 (1980)　　　**Pop Density:** 0.8
Land: 1736.6 sq. mi.; **Water:** 6.0 sq. mi.　　　**Area Code:** 406

In east-central MT, north of Miles City; organized Feb 5, 1915 from Custer, Dawson, and Fallon counties.

Name origin: For the topography of most of the eastern half of the state.

Terry　　　　　　　　　　　　　　　City
ZIP: 59349　　　**Lat:** 46-47-31 N　**Long:** 105-18-41 W
Pop: 659 (1990); 929 (1980)　　**Pop Density:** 941.4
Land: 0.7 sq. mi.; **Water:** 0.0 sq. mi.　　**Elev:** 2253 ft.
Founded c. 1882.
Name origin: For Gen. Alfred H. Terry (1827–90).

Ravalli County
County Seat: Hamilton (ZIP: 59840)

Pop: 25,010 (1990); 22,493 (1980)　　　**Pop Density:** 10.4
Land: 2394.3 sq. mi.; **Water:** 6.1 sq. mi.　　　**Area Code:** 406

On the central western border of MT, west of Butte; organized Feb 16, 1893 from Missoula County.

Name origin: For Father Anthony Ravalli (1812–84), Jesuit missionary to the Salish (Flathead) Indians at St. Mary's Mission, Stevensville, MT, the first white settlement in MT.

Darby　　　　　　　　　　　　　　　Town
ZIP: 59829　　　**Lat:** 46-01-19 N　**Long:** 114-10-42 W
Pop: 625 (1990); 581 (1980)　　**Pop Density:** 1250.0
Land: 0.5 sq. mi.; **Water:** 0.0 sq. mi.　　**Elev:** 3888 ft.
Name origin: For its first postmaster, James R. Darby.

Hamilton　　　　　　　　　　　　　　　City
ZIP: 59840　　　**Lat:** 46-15-04 N　**Long:** 114-09-43 W
Pop: 2,737 (1990); 2,661 (1980)　　**Pop Density:** 1520.6
Land: 1.8 sq. mi.; **Water:** 0.0 sq. mi.　　**Elev:** 3572 ft.
Name origin: For landowner J.W. Hamilton, from whom the Northern Pacific Railroad purchased a right-of-way.

Pinesdale　　　　　　　　　　　　　　　Town
ZIP: 59841　　　**Lat:** 46-20-11 N　**Long:** 114-13-09 W
Pop: 670 (1990)　　**Pop Density:** 515.4
Land: 1.3 sq. mi.; **Water:** 0.0 sq. mi.

Stevensville　　　　　　　　　　　　　　　Town
ZIP: 59870　　　**Lat:** 46-30-28 N　**Long:** 114-05-27 W
Pop: 1,221 (1990); 1,207 (1980)　　**Pop Density:** 2442.0
Land: 0.5 sq. mi.; **Water:** 0.0 sq. mi.　　**Elev:** 3370 ft.
Established c. 1868.
Name origin: For Isaac Ingle Stevens.

MONTANA, Richland County　　　　　　　　　　　　　　　　　　　　　　　　American Places Dictionary

Richland County
County Seat: Sidney (ZIP: 59270)

Pop: 10,716 (1990); 12,243 (1980)　　　　　　　　　　**Pop Density:** 5.1
Land: 2084.1 sq. mi.; **Water:** 18.9 sq. mi.　　　　　　**Area Code:** 406
On the northeastern border of MT; organized May 27, 1914 from Dawson County.
Name origin: Promotional, to attract new settlers.

Fairview　　　　　　　　　　　　　　　　City
ZIP: 59221　　　　**Lat:** 47-51-03 N **Long:** 104-03-03 W
Pop: 869 (1990); 1,366 (1980)　　　**Pop Density:** 869.0
Land: 1.0 sq. mi.; **Water:** 0.0 sq. mi.
Name origin: For the city's beautiful view of the lower Yellowstone Valley.

Sidney　　　　　　　　　　　　　　　　City
ZIP: 59270　　　　**Lat:** 47-42-44 N **Long:** 104-09-49 W
Pop: 5,217 (1990); 5,726 (1980)　　　**Pop Density:** 2371.4
Land: 2.2 sq. mi.; **Water:** 0.0 sq. mi.　　　**Elev:** 1931 ft.
Name origin: For settler Sidney Walters.

Roosevelt County
County Seat: Wolf Point (ZIP: 59201)

Pop: 10,999 (1990); 10,467 (1980)　　　　　　　　　　**Pop Density:** 4.7
Land: 2355.7 sq. mi.; **Water:** 14.0 sq. mi.　　　　　　**Area Code:** 406
On the northeastern border of MT; organized Feb 18, 1919 from Sheridan County.
Name origin: For Theodore Roosevelt (1858–1919), twenty-sixth U.S. president.

Bainville　　　　　　　　　　　　　　　　Town
ZIP: 59212　　　　**Lat:** 48-08-25 N **Long:** 104-13-06 W
Pop: 165 (1990); 245 (1980)　　　**Pop Density:** 165.0
Land: 1.0 sq. mi.; **Water:** 0.0 sq. mi.
Name origin: For early resident C.M. Bain. Previously called Kilva.

Brockton　　　　　　　　　　　　　　　　Town
ZIP: 59213　　　　**Lat:** 48-08-56 N **Long:** 104-54-48 W
Pop: 365 (1990); 374 (1980)　　　**Pop Density:** 1825.0
Land: 0.2 sq. mi.; **Water:** 0.0 sq. mi.　　　**Elev:** 1959 ft.

Culbertson　　　　　　　　　　　　　　　　Town
ZIP: 59218　　　　**Lat:** 48-08-50 N **Long:** 104-30-55 W
Pop: 796 (1990); 887 (1980)　　　**Pop Density:** 1326.7
Land: 0.6 sq. mi.; **Water:** 0.0 sq. mi.　　　**Elev:** 1933 ft.
Name origin: For fur trapper Alexander Culbertson.

Froid　　　　　　　　　　　　　　　　Town
ZIP: 59226　　　　**Lat:** 48-20-07 N **Long:** 104-29-27 W
Pop: 195 (1990); 323 (1980)　　　**Pop Density:** 650.0
Land: 0.3 sq. mi.; **Water:** 0.0 sq. mi.
Name origin: From French meaning 'cold.'

Poplar　　　　　　　　　　　　　　　　City
ZIP: 59255　　　　**Lat:** 48-06-37 N **Long:** 105-11-45 W
Pop: 881 (1990); 995 (1980)　　　**Pop Density:** 2936.7
Land: 0.3 sq. mi.; **Water:** 0.0 sq. mi.　　　**Elev:** 1993 ft.

Wolf Point　　　　　　　　　　　　　　　　City
ZIP: 59201　　　　**Lat:** 48-05-33 N **Long:** 105-38-25 W
Pop: 2,880 (1990); 3,074 (1980)　　　**Pop Density:** 3200.0
Land: 0.9 sq. mi.; **Water:** 0.0 sq. mi.　　　**Elev:** 1997 ft.

Rosebud County
County Seat: Forsyth (ZIP: 59327)

Pop: 10,505 (1990); 9,899 (1980)　　　　　　　　　　**Pop Density:** 2.1
Land: 5012.4 sq. mi.; **Water:** 14.6 sq. mi.　　　　　　**Area Code:** 406
In south-central MT, east of Billings; organized Feb 11, 1901 from Custer County.
Name origin: For Rosebud Creek, which runs through the county; named for the profusion of wild roses along its banks.

Ashland　　　　　　　　　　　　　　　　CDP
ZIP: 59003　　　　**Lat:** 45-37-24 N **Long:** 106-18-51 W
Pop: 484 (1990)　　　**Pop Density:** 63.7
Land: 7.6 sq. mi.; **Water:** 0.0 sq. mi.

Colstrip　　　　　　　　　　　　　　　　CDP
　　　　Lat: 45-53-41 N **Long:** 106-38-02 W
Pop: 3,035 (1990); 1,476 (1980)　　　**Pop Density:** 532.5
Land: 5.7 sq. mi.; **Water:** 0.3 sq. mi.

Forsyth　　　　　　　　　　　　　　　　City
ZIP: 59327　　　　**Lat:** 46-16-00 N **Long:** 106-40-37 W
Pop: 2,178 (1990); 2,553 (1980)　　　**Pop Density:** 1980.0
Land: 1.1 sq. mi.; **Water:** 0.0 sq. mi.　　　**Elev:** 2526 ft.
Name origin: For Gen. James W. Forsyth, who came up the Yellowstone River by steamer and landed here.

Lame Deer
CDP
Lat: 45-37-03 N **Long:** 106-36-35 W
Pop: 1,918 (1990) **Pop Density:** 34.5
Land: 55.6 sq. mi.; **Water:** 0.0 sq. mi.

Sanders County
County Seat: Thompson Falls (ZIP: 59873)

Pop: 8,669 (1990); 8,675 (1980) **Pop Density:** 3.1
Land: 2762.3 sq. mi.; **Water:** 27.9 sq. mi. **Area Code:** 406
On the northwestern border of MT, northwest of Missoula; organized Feb 5, 1907 from Missoula County.
Name origin: For Wilbur Fisk Sanders (1834–1905), officer in the Civil War and U.S. senator from MT (1890–93).

Hot Springs
Town
ZIP: 59845 **Lat:** 47-36-32 N **Long:** 114-40-15 W
Pop: 411 (1990); 601 (1980) **Pop Density:** 1370.0
Land: 0.3 sq. mi.; **Water:** 0.0 sq. mi. **Elev:** 2829 ft.
Name origin: For the natural hot springs located here.

Plains
Town
ZIP: 59859 **Lat:** 47-27-37 N **Long:** 114-53-00 W
Pop: 992 (1990); 1,116 (1980) **Pop Density:** 1653.3
Land: 0.6 sq. mi.; **Water:** 0.0 sq. mi. **Elev:** 2468 ft.
Name origin: Originally known as Horse Plains because the Indians spent the winters here with their horses.

Thompson Falls
Town
ZIP: 59873 **Lat:** 47-35-58 N **Long:** 115-20-01 W
Pop: 1,319 (1990); 1,478 (1980) **Pop Density:** 1099.2
Land: 1.2 sq. mi.; **Water:** 0.0 sq. mi. **Elev:** 2419 ft.
Name origin: For David Thompson, a fur trader who worked this area around 1809.

Sheridan County
County Seat: Plentywood (ZIP: 59254)

Pop: 4,732 (1990); 5,414 (1980) **Pop Density:** 2.8
Land: 1676.6 sq. mi.; **Water:** 29.7 sq. mi. **Area Code:** 406
In the northeastern corner of MT; organized Mar 4, 1913 from Valley County.
Name origin: For Gen. Philip Henry Sheridan (1831–88), Union officer during the Civil War and commander in chief of the U.S. army (1883–88).

Medicine Lake
Town
ZIP: 59247 **Lat:** 48-30-12 N **Long:** 104-30-00 W
Pop: 357 (1990); 408 (1980) **Pop Density:** 892.5
Land: 0.4 sq. mi.; **Water:** 0.0 sq. mi. **Elev:** 1951 ft.
Name origin: For nearby Medicine Lake.

Outlook
Town
ZIP: 59252 **Lat:** 48-53-19 N **Long:** 104-46-54 W
Pop: 109 (1990); 122 (1980) **Pop Density:** 83.8
Land: 1.3 sq. mi.; **Water:** 0.0 sq. mi.
Name origin: According to legend, it was named when a stranger entering the saloon here was told 'lookout!' and avoided being hit with a hurled glass. The name was reversed.

Plentywood
City
ZIP: 59254 **Lat:** 48-46-26 N **Long:** 104-33-16 W
Pop: 2,136 (1990); 2,476 (1980) **Pop Density:** 1941.8
Land: 1.1 sq. mi.; **Water:** 0.0 sq. mi.
Name origin: For firewood found here by a cattle outfit driving across the treeless prairie.

Westby
Town
ZIP: 59275 **Lat:** 48-52-13 N **Long:** 104-03-23 W
Pop: 253 (1990); 291 (1980) **Pop Density:** 506.0
Land: 0.5 sq. mi.; **Water:** 0.0 sq. mi.
Name origin: Named by Danish settlers for its location and from the Dutch term *by* for 'town.'

Silver Bow County
County Seat: Butte (ZIP: 59701)

Pop: 33,941 (1990); 38,092 (1980)   **Pop Density:** 47.3
Land: 718.3 sq. mi.; **Water:** 0.7 sq. mi.   **Area Code:** 406

In southwestern MT, southwest of Helena; organized Feb 16, 1881 (prior to statehood) from Deer Lodge County.

Name origin: For Silver Bow Creek, which runs through the county; named by prospectors who saw the sun shining "like a silver bow" on its waters.

Butte-Silver Bow
City
ZIP: 59701   **Lat:** 45-53-45 N **Long:** 112-39-27 W
Pop: 33,336 (1990); 37,205 (1980)   **Pop Density:** 46.5
Land: 716.2 sq. mi.; **Water:** 0.7 sq. mi.

In southwestern MT on a plateau of the Rocky Mountains, southwest of Helena. Founded 1864; incorporated as town 1876, as city 1879. Called *The City That is a Mile High and a Mile Deep* for the mine shafts, some of which go 5,000 ft. below the earth's surface, that produce arsenic, cadmium, gold, and silver. City government consolidated with Silver Bow County.

Name origin: For Big Butte, the peak rising 6,369 ft. above sea level.

Walkerville
City
Lat: 46-02-11 N **Long:** 112-32-25 W
Pop: 605 (1990); 887 (1980)   **Pop Density:** 288.1
Land: 2.1 sq. mi.; **Water:** 0.0 sq. mi.   **Elev:** 6468 ft.

Name origin: For the Walker brothers, who operated the Alice Mine near here.

Stillwater County
County Seat: Columbus (ZIP: 59019)

Pop: 6,536 (1990); 5,598 (1980)   **Pop Density:** 3.6
Land: 1794.7 sq. mi.; **Water:** 10.0 sq. mi.   **Area Code:** 406

In south-central MT, west of Billings; organized Mar 24, 1913 from Carbon, Sweet Grass, and Yellowstone counties.

Name origin: For the Stillwater River, which runs through the county.

Absarokee
CDP
ZIP: 59001   **Lat:** 45-31-29 N **Long:** 109-26-40 W
Pop: 1,067 (1990)   **Pop Density:** 485.0
Land: 2.2 sq. mi.; **Water:** 0.0 sq. mi.

Columbus
Town
ZIP: 59019   **Lat:** 45-38-13 N **Long:** 109-15-02 W
Pop: 1,573 (1990); 1,439 (1980)   **Pop Density:** 1310.8
Land: 1.2 sq. mi.; **Water:** 0.0 sq. mi.   **Elev:** 3600 ft.

Name origin: Renamed in 1894 for Christopher Columbus (1451–1506). Previously called Stillwater, Eagle's Nest, and Sheep Dip.

Sweet Grass County
County Seat: Big Timber (ZIP: 59011)

Pop: 3,154 (1990); 3,216 (1980)   **Pop Density:** 1.7
Land: 1855.2 sq. mi.; **Water:** 6.9 sq. mi.   **Area Code:** 406

In south-central MT, west of Billings; organized Mar 5, 1895 from Meagher, Park, and Yellowstone counties.

Name origin: For the abundant fragrant grass of the genus *Glyceria*, at the suggestion of Mrs. Paul Van Cleve, Sr.

Big Timber
City
ZIP: 59011   **Lat:** 45-50-02 N **Long:** 109-57-02 W
Pop: 1,557 (1990); 1,690 (1980)   **Pop Density:** 1946.3
Land: 0.8 sq. mi.; **Water:** 0.0 sq. mi.

Name origin: For large cottonwood trees along a nearby creek.

Teton County
County Seat: Choteau (ZIP: 59422)

Pop: 6,271 (1990); 6,491 (1980)   **Pop Density:** 2.8
Land: 2272.6 sq. mi.; **Water:** 20.0 sq. mi.   **Area Code:** 406
In west-central MT, northwest of Great Falls; organized Feb 7, 1893 from Chouteau County.
Name origin: For the Teton River and Teton Peak in the Teton Mountains or for the Teton Indian tribe.

Choteau   City
ZIP: 59422   **Lat:** 47-48-45 N **Long:** 112-10-46 W
Pop: 1,741 (1990); 1,798 (1980)   **Pop Density:** 1339.2
Land: 1.3 sq. mi.; **Water:** 0.0 sq. mi.   **Elev:** 3820 ft.
Name origin: For Pierre Chouteau, Jr., president of the American Fur Company. Previously called Old Agency.

Dutton   Town
ZIP: 59433   **Lat:** 47-50-51 N **Long:** 111-42-48 W
Pop: 392 (1990); 359 (1980)   **Pop Density:** 1306.7
Land: 0.3 sq. mi.; **Water:** 0.0 sq. mi.   **Elev:** 3716 ft.
Founded early 1900s.
Name origin: For a freight and passenger agent for the railroad.

Fairfield   Town
ZIP: 59436   **Lat:** 47-36-55 N **Long:** 111-58-48 W
Pop: 660 (1990); 650 (1980)   **Pop Density:** 2200.0
Land: 0.3 sq. mi.; **Water:** 0.0 sq. mi.   **Elev:** 3977 ft.
Name origin: For nearby hay and grain fields.

Toole County
County Seat: Shelby (ZIP: 59474)

Pop: 5,046 (1990); 5,559 (1980)   **Pop Density:** 2.6
Land: 1910.9 sq. mi.; **Water:** 34.9 sq. mi.   **Area Code:** 406
On the central northern border of MT, north of Great Falls; organized May 7, 1914 from Hill and Teton counties.
Name origin: For Joseph Kemp Toole (1851–1929), governor of MT (1889–93; 1901–08).

Kevin   Town
ZIP: 59454   **Lat:** 48-44-44 N **Long:** 111-57-55 W
Pop: 185 (1990); 208 (1980)   **Pop Density:** 616.7
Land: 0.3 sq. mi.; **Water:** 0.0 sq. mi.   **Elev:** 3329 ft.
Established c. 1910.
Name origin: For Thomas Kevin, an official of the Alberta Railway and Irrigation Company Railway.

Shelby   City
ZIP: 59474   **Lat:** 48-30-34 N **Long:** 111-51-24 W
Pop: 2,763 (1990); 3,142 (1980)   **Pop Density:** 1726.9
Land: 1.6 sq. mi.; **Water:** 0.1 sq. mi.   **Elev:** 3286 ft.
Founded 1891.
Name origin: For Peter P. Shelby, general manager of the Montana-Central Railroad.

Sunburst   Town
ZIP: 59482   **Lat:** 48-52-35 N **Long:** 111-54-22 W
Pop: 437 (1990); 476 (1980)   **Pop Density:** 273.1
Land: 1.6 sq. mi.; **Water:** 0.3 sq. mi.   **Elev:** 3348 ft.
Name origin: Named by William George Davis for the way the sun rose over the valley.

Treasure County
County Seat: Hysham (ZIP: 59038)

Pop: 874 (1990); 981 (1980) **Pop Density:** 0.9
Land: 978.9 sq. mi.; **Water:** 5.2 sq. mi. **Area Code:** 406
In south-central MT, northeast of Billings; organized Feb 7, 1919 from Rosebud County.
Name origin: For the nickname of MT, the "Treasure State."

Hysham — Town
ZIP: 59038 **Lat:** 46-17-25 N **Long:** 107-13-45 W
Pop: 361 (1990); 449 (1980) **Pop Density:** 1805.0
Land: 0.2 sq. mi.; **Water:** 0.0 sq. mi. **Elev:** 2661 ft.
Founded 1907.
Name origin: For trail herder Charles J. Hysham, who worked at a local ranch.

Valley County
County Seat: Glasgow (ZIP: 59230)

Pop: 8,239 (1990); 10,250 (1980) **Pop Density:** 1.7
Land: 4920.9 sq. mi.; **Water:** 141.1 sq. mi. **Area Code:** 406
On the northern border of MT with the province of Saskatchewan, Canada; organized Feb 6, 1893 from Dawson County.
Name origin: For the Milk and Missouri river valleys.

Fort Peck — Town
ZIP: 59223 **Lat:** 48-00-23 N **Long:** 106-27-17 W
Pop: 325 (1990) **Pop Density:** 361.1
Land: 0.9 sq. mi.; **Water:** 0.0 sq. mi.

Frazer — CDP
Lat: 48-03-08 N **Long:** 106-02-59 W
Pop: 403 (1990) **Pop Density:** 237.1
Land: 1.7 sq. mi.; **Water:** 0.0 sq. mi.

Glasgow — City
Lat: 48-11-54 N **Long:** 106-37-54 W
Pop: 3,572 (1990); 4,455 (1980) **Pop Density:** 2551.4
Land: 1.4 sq. mi.; **Water:** 0.0 sq. mi. **Elev:** 2090 ft.
Founded 1887.
Name origin: For Glasgow, Scotland.

Nashua — Town
ZIP: 59248 **Lat:** 48-08-03 N **Long:** 106-21-22 W
Pop: 375 (1990); 495 (1980) **Pop Density:** 535.7
Land: 0.7 sq. mi.; **Water:** 0.0 sq. mi. **Elev:** 2063 ft.
Located at the confluence of Porcupine Creek and the Milk River.
Name origin: From an Indian term believed to mean 'meeting of two streams.'

Opheim — Town
ZIP: 59250 **Lat:** 48-51-24 N **Long:** 106-24-27 W
Pop: 145 (1990); 210 (1980) **Pop Density:** 725.0
Land: 0.2 sq. mi.; **Water:** 0.0 sq. mi. **Elev:** 3265 ft.
Name origin: For postmaster Alfred S. Opheim.

Wheatland County
County Seat: Harlowton (ZIP: 59036)

Pop: 2,246 (1990); 2,359 (1980) **Pop Density:** 1.6
Land: 1423.2 sq. mi.; **Water:** 5.2 sq. mi. **Area Code:** 406
In south-central MT, northwest of Billings; organized Feb 22, 1917 from Meagher and Sweet Grass counties.
Name origin: For the major crop in the area.

Harlowton — City
ZIP: 59036 **Lat:** 46-26-13 N **Long:** 109-50-02 W
Pop: 1,049 (1990); 1,181 (1980) **Pop Density:** 1748.3
Land: 0.6 sq. mi.; **Water:** 0.0 sq. mi.
Name origin: Named in 1900 for railroad builder Richard Harlow. Originally known as Merino.

Judith Gap — City
ZIP: 59453 **Lat:** 46-40-44 N **Long:** 109-45-14 W
Pop: 133 (1990); 213 (1980) **Pop Density:** 332.5
Land: 0.4 sq. mi.; **Water:** 0.0 sq. mi.
Name origin: For its location in a gap in the Little Belt

Mountains, which offered the easiest way to reach Judith Basin.

Wibaux County
County Seat: Wibaux (ZIP: 59353)

Pop: 1,191 (1990); 1,476 (1980) **Pop Density:** 1.3
Land: 889.3 sq. mi.; **Water:** 0.8 sq. mi. **Area Code:** 406
On the central eastern border of MT; organized Aug 17, 1914 from Dawson, Fallon, and Richland counties.
Name origin: For Pierre Wibaux, a Huguenot immigrant who owned one of the largest herds of cattle in MT.

Wibaux — Town
ZIP: 59353 **Lat:** 46-59-13 N **Long:** 104-11-21 W
Pop: 628 (1990); 782 (1980) **Pop Density:** 570.9
Land: 1.1 sq. mi.; **Water:** 0.0 sq. mi.
Name origin: For settler Pierre Wibaux.

Yellowstone County
County Seat: Billings (ZIP: 59101)

Pop: 113,419 (1990); 108,035 (1980) **Pop Density:** 43.0
Land: 2635.2 sq. mi.; **Water:** 13.9 sq. mi. **Area Code:** 406
In south-central MT; organized Feb 26, 1883 from Custer County.
Name origin: For the Yellowstone River, which flows through the county.

Billings — City
ZIP: 59101 **Lat:** 45-47-29 N **Long:** 108-32-18 W
Pop: 81,151 (1990); 66,818 (1980) **Pop Density:** 2489.3
Land: 32.6 sq. mi.; **Water:** 0.1 sq. mi.
In south-central MT on the Yellowstone River, east of Bozeman. Founded 1882. Trade and transportation center for the "Midland Empire," a large agricultural area; also health care services and petroleum refining.
Name origin: For Frederick Billings (1823–90), lawyer, railroad promoter, and philanthropist.

Broadview — Town
ZIP: 59015 **Lat:** 46-05-51 N **Long:** 108-52-38 W
Pop: 133 (1990); 120 (1980) **Pop Density:** 665.0
Land: 0.2 sq. mi.; **Water:** 0.0 sq. mi.
Name origin: For the view from the house of local rancher Dr. Sudduth.

Laurel — City
ZIP: 59044 **Lat:** 45-40-26 N **Long:** 108-46-18 W
Pop: 5,686 (1990); 5,481 (1980) **Pop Density:** 3158.9
Land: 1.8 sq. mi.; **Water:** 0.0 sq. mi. **Elev:** 3297 ft.
Founded c. 1899.

Lockwood — CDP
Lat: 45-49-09 N **Long:** 108-24-50 W
Pop: 3,967 (1990) **Pop Density:** 536.1
Land: 7.4 sq. mi.; **Water:** 0.4 sq. mi.

Yellowstone National Park

Pop: 52 (1990); 66 (1980) **Pop Density:** 0.2
Land: 245.4 sq. mi.; **Water:** 0.7 sq. mi.
In southwest MT; that portion of the park within the state has county status.
Name origin: From the Yellowstone River, which the French called *Roche Jaune* 'yellow stone' after the Indian *mitsiadazi* 'yellow rock river.'

MONTANA

Index to Places and Counties in Montana

Absarokee (Stillwater) CDP 360
Alberton (Mineral) Town.................353
Anaconda-Deer Lodge County (Deer Lodge) City 345
Arlee (Lake) CDP 350
Ashland (Rosebud) CDP 358
Bainville (Roosevelt) Town 358
Baker (Fallon) City 345
Bearcreek (Carbon) Town..................342
Beaverhead County..........................341
Belgrade (Gallatin) Town 347
Belt (Cascade) City 343
Big Horn County..............................341
Big Sandy (Chouteau) Town 344
Big Timber (Sweet Grass) City 360
Billings (Yellowstone) City 363
Blaine County...................................342
Bonner-West Riverside (Missoula) CDP 354
Boulder (Jefferson) Town 349
Bozeman (Gallatin) City 347
Bridger (Carbon) Town......................342
Broadus (Powder River) Town..........356
Broadview (Yellowstone) Town.........363
Broadwater County..........................342
Brockton (Roosevelt) Town...............358
Browning (Glacier) Town 348
Busby (Big Horn) CDP 341
Butte-Silver Bow (Silver Bow) City ...360
Carbon County.................................342
Carter County 343
Cascade (Cascade) Town 343
Cascade County...............................343
Charlo (Lake) CDP.............................350
Chester (Liberty) Town......................351
Chinook (Blaine) City.........................342
Choteau (Teton) City..........................361
Chouteau County.............................344
Circle (McCone) Town 353
Clyde Park (Park) Town....................355
Colstrip (Rosebud) CDP 358
Columbia Falls (Flathead) City..........346
Columbus (Stillwater) Town..............360
Conrad (Pondera) City.......................356
Crow Agency (Big Horn) CDP..........341
Culbertson (Roosevelt) Town............358
Custer County 344
Cut Bank (Glacier) City 348
Daniels County.................................344
Darby (Ravalli) Town........................357
Dawson County 345
Deer Lodge (Powell) City 357
Deer Lodge County 345
Denton (Fergus) Town 346
Dillon (Beaverhead) City....................341
Dodson (Phillips) Town......................355
Drummond (Granite) Town...............349
Dutton (Teton) Town..........................361
East Glacier Park Village (Glacier) CDP 348
East Helena (Lewis and Clark) Town 351
Ekalaka (Carter) Town.......................343
Ennis (Madison) Town 352
Eureka (Lincoln) Town......................352
Evergreen (Flathead) CDP.................346
Fairfield (Teton) Town.......................361
Fairview (Richland) City....................358
Fallon County..................................345
Fergus County 346

Finley Point (Lake) CDP 350
Flathead County...............................346
Flaxville (Daniels) Town 344
Forsyth (Rosebud) City......................358
Fort Belknap (Blaine) CDP 342
Fort Benton (Chouteau) City.............344
Fort Peck (Valley) Town....................362
Frazer (Valley) CDP 362
Froid (Roosevelt) Town......................358
Fromberg (Carbon) Town..................343
Gallatin County................................347
Garfield County................................347
Geraldine (Chouteau) Town...............344
Glacier County.................................348
Glasgow (Valley) City.........................362
Glendive (Dawson) City......................345
Golden Valley County 348
Granite County 349
Grass Range (Fergus) Town...............346
Great Falls (Cascade) City.................343
Hamilton (Ravalli) City......................357
Hardin (Big Horn) City......................341
Harlem (Blaine) City..........................342
Harlowton (Wheatland) City.............362
Havre (Hill) City.................................349
Havre North (Hill) CDP 349
Hays (Blaine) CDP 342
Heart Butte (Pondera) CDP 356
Helena (Lewis and Clark) City..........351
Helena Valley Northeast (Lewis and Clark) CDP 351
Helena Valley Northwest (Lewis and Clark) CDP 351
Helena Valley Southeast (Lewis and Clark) CDP 351
Helena Valley West Central (Lewis and Clark) CDP 351
Helena West Side (Lewis and Clark) CDP 351
Hill County.......................................349
Hingham (Hill) Town 349
Hobson (Judith Basin) Town 350
Hot Springs (Sanders) Town..............359
Hysham (Treasure) Town 362
Ismay (Custer) Town 344
Jefferson County..............................349
Joliet (Carbon) Town..........................343
Jordan (Garfield) Town......................347
Judith Basin County 350
Judith Gap (Wheatland) City.............362
Kalispell (Flathead) City 346
Kevin (Toole) Town............................361
Kicking Horse (Lake) CDP 350
Lake County.....................................350
Lame Deer (Rosebud) CDP 359
Laurel (Yellowstone) City 363
Lavina (Golden Valley) Town............348
Lewis and Clark County 351
Lewistown (Fergus) City....................346
Libby (Lincoln) City...........................352
Liberty County.................................351
Lima (Beaverhead) Town...................341
Lincoln County................................352
Livingston (Park) City........................355
Lockwood (Yellowstone) CDP 363
Lodge Grass (Big Horn) Town 341
Lolo (Missoula) CDP 354
Madison County..............................352
Malmstrom Air Force Base (Cascade) Military Facility................................ 343

Malta (Phillips) City...........................355
Manhattan (Gallatin) Town...............347
McCone County 353
Meagher County..............................353
Medicine Lake (Sheridan) Town.......359
Melstone (Musselshell) Town............354
Miles City (Custer) City 344
Mineral County 353
Missoula (Missoula) City...................354
Missoula County 354
Moore (Fergus) Town 346
Muddy (Big Horn) CDP 341
Musselshell County.........................354
Nashua (Valley) Town 362
Neihart (Cascade) Town....................343
North Browning (Glacier) CDP 348
Opheim (Valley) Town.......................362
Orchard Homes (Missoula) CDP......354
Outlook (Sheridan) Town 359
Pablo (Lake) CDP...............................350
Park County 355
Petroleum County 355
Philipsburg (Granite) Town...............349
Phillips County 355
Pinesdale (Ravalli) Town 357
Plains (Sanders) Town 359
Plentywood (Sheridan) City 359
Plevna (Fallon) Town 345
Polson (Lake) City...............................350
Pondera County...............................356
Poplar (Roosevelt) City......................358
Powder River County 356
Powell County 357
Prairie County 357
Pryor (Big Horn) CDP 341
Ravalli County.................................357
Red Lodge (Carbon) City..................343
Rexford (Lincoln) Town 352
Richey (Dawson) Town 345
Richland County.............................358
Ronan (Lake) City..............................350
Roosevelt County............................358
Rosebud County..............................358
Roundup (Musselshell) City...............354
Ryegate (Golden Valley) Town..........348
Saco (Phillips) Town...........................355
St. Ignatius (Lake) Town 350
Sanders County 359
Scobey (Daniels) City.........................344
Shelby (Toole) City.............................361
Sheridan (Madison) Town 352
Sheridan County.............................359
Sidney (Richland) City 358
Silver Bow County 360
South Browning (Glacier) CDP 348
Stanford (Judith Basin) Town 350
Starr School (Glacier) CDP 348
Stevensville (Ravalli) Town................357
Stillwater County............................360
Sunburst (Toole) Town 361
Sun Prairie (Cascade) CDP 343
Superior (Mineral) Town...................353
Sweet Grass County 360
Terry (Prairie) City............................357
Teton County...................................361
Thompson Falls (Sanders) Town.......359
Three Forks (Gallatin) Town.............347
Toole County 361
Townsend (Broadwater) City.............342
Treasure County 362

Troy (Lincoln) Town............................*352*
Twin Bridges (Madison) Town...........*352*
Valier (Pondera) Town *356*
Valley County *362*
Virginia City (Madison) Town *352*
Walkerville (Silver Bow) City.............*360*
Westby (Sheridan) Town *359*
West Yellowstone (Gallatin) Town.....*347*
Wheatland County................................*362*
Whitefish (Flathead) City...................*346*
Whitehall (Jefferson) Town *349*
White Sulphur Springs (Meagher) City... *353*
Wibaux (Wibaux) Town *363*
Wibaux County......................................*363*
Winifred (Fergus) Town......................*346*
Winnett (Petroleum) Town................*355*
Wolf Point (Roosevelt) City...............*358*
Yellowstone County *363*
Yellowstone National Park.................*363*

Nebraska

NEBRASKA

All political boundaries are as of January 1, 1980

SCALE

U.S. Department of Commerce — BUREAU OF THE CENSUS

Nebraska

Population: 1,578,385 (1990); 1,569,825 (1980)
Population rank (1990): 36
Percent population change (1980–1990): 0.5
Population projection: 1,595,000 (1995); 1,583,000 (2000)

Area: total: 77,358 sq. mi.; 76,878 sq. mi. land, 481 sq. mi. water
Area rank: 16
Highest elevation: 5,426 ft., in southwestern Kimball County
Lowest point: 840 ft., in Richardson County

State capital: Lincoln (Lancaster County)
Largest city: Omaha (335,795)
Second largest city: Lincoln (191,972)
Largest county: Douglas (416,444)

Total housing units: 660,621
No. of occupied housing units: 602,363
Vacant housing units (%): 8.8
Distribution of population by race and Hispanic origin (%):
White: 93.8
Black: 3.6
Hispanic (any race): 2.3
Native American: 0.8
Asian/Pacific: 0.8
Other: 1.0

Admission date: March 1, 1867 (37th state).

Location: In the midwestern United States, bordering Kansas, Colorado, Wyoming, South Dakota, Iowa, and Missouri.

Name Origin: From the Oto Indian word *nebrathka*, meaning 'flat water'; the name was used for the Platte River, which flows through the central part of the state.

State bird: Western meadowlark *(Sturnella neglecta)*
State flower: goldenrod *(Solidago gigantea)*
State fossil: mammoth
State gem: blue agate (blue chalcedony)
State grass: little bluestem *(Schizachyrium scoparium)*, called "bunch grass" or "beard grass"
State insect: honeybee *(Apis mellifera)*
State mammal: Whitetail deer *(Odocoileus virginianus)*
State rock: prairie agate
State soil: Holdrege series
State song: "Beautiful Nebraska"
State tree: cottonwood *(Populus deltoides)*

State motto: Equality Before the Law

State nickname: Cornhusker State; Tree Planters' State

Area codes: 308 (west), 402 (east)
Time zones: Central and Mountain (western counties)
Abbreviations: NE (postal); Neb. or Nebr. (traditional)
Part of (region): Plains States; Midwest

Local Government

Counties

Nebraska has 93 counties, 29 governed by elected boards of supervisors and 64 governed by elected boards of commissioners.

Municipalities

Nebraska has 535 municipalities, most of which have the mayor-council form of government. Although the Nebraska constitution gives home rule to all cities with more than 5,000 people, only Lincoln and Omaha have chosen to adopt their own charters. There are also 471 townships and more than 1,000 special districts that provide such services as fire protection, housing, irrigation, and sewage treatment.

State Government

In 1934, Nebraska approved the adoption of a unicameral (one-house) state legislature. It is the only state in the union to have a unicameral legislature.

Settlement History and Early Development

Nebraska was inhabited by prehistoric peoples more than 10,000 years ago. European explorers arriving in the 1700s found Missouri, Omaha, Oto, Ponca, Pawnee, Sioux, Comanche, Arapaho, and Cheyenne Indians. Later, white settlement drove Winnebago Indians from Wisconsin into Nebraska.

Although the territory of Nebraska was claimed by the Spanish in 1541 and the French in 1682, it was not until the 1700s that French explorers actually entered Nebraska. The area was considered part of the Louisiana Territory and, as such, passed from France to Spain in 1762 and from Spain back to France in 1800. Under the Louisiana Purchase, France sold the territory that is now Nebraska to the United States in 1803.

French fur trappers and traders had been operating in Nebraska during the 1700s. The Lewis and Clark expedition of 1804–06 followed the Missouri River along Nebraska's eastern border. The territory was also partially explored by Zebulon Pike (1806), Stephen Long (1819–20), and John Frémont (1838–39). Various fur trading posts, including one at Fort Lisa, about 10 miles from present-day Omaha, were established by Manuel Lisa, a

Spanish-American trader. A route through Nebraska followed by fur traders heading for Oregon was taken by later settlers and became the famed Oregon Trail.

White settlement was prohibited by the Indian Intercourse Act of 1834, which reserved the Great Plains as Indian territory. No white settlement occurred until after 1854, when Congress passed the Kansas-Nebraska Act, making Nebraska a territory and opening it to settlement. A provision of the act was that the territories could decide for themselves whether to permit slavery.

Statehood

In 1862 Congress passed the Homestead Act, granting 160 acres of land to settlers, who then poured into Nebraska. With so few trees on the prairies, most settlers built their first homes of sod, which became known as "Nebraska marble." In 1865 the Union Pacific Railroad choose Omaha as the starting point of its line west.

Nebraska became the 37th state on March 1, 1867, over the veto of President Andrew Johnson, who feared that the Republican senators from the new state would tip the balance against him in impeachment proceedings.

Agriculture and Industry

Nebraska's growth as an agricultural state suffered many setbacks, including swarms of grasshoppers in the 1870s, drought, and the overuse of credit in the 1890s, and the Great Depression in the 1930s. However, irrigation and dam projects have since made agriculture less risky, so that since World War II, Nebraska has been a leading producer of beef cattle, corn, oats, potatoes, and wheat. Aside from the surface-level water sources, irrigation is also made possible by tapping a huge groundwater supply, part of the great Ogallala Aquifer.

From 1939 to 1949 oil was discovered in various sections of Nebraska. In 1948 Strategic Air Command headquarters were established near Omaha, providing a boost to the economy. In recent years the Omaha area has become a national center for telemarketing services.

State Boundaries

The original Territory of Nebraska was reduced by the formation of the Territories of Colorado, Dakota, and Idaho in the early 1860s. The boundaries laid down when the territory became a state in 1867 have altered slightly with a change in the course of the Missouri River (the state's eastern and northeastern boundary), giving Nebraska about 5 additional square miles that had formerly been part of the Dakota Territory.

Nebraska Counties

Adams	Cuming	Greeley	Loup	Saline
Antelope	Custer	Hall	McPherson	Sarpy
Arthur	Dakota	Hamilton	Madison	Saunders
Banner	Dawes	Harlan	Merrick	Scotts Bluff
Blaine	Dawson	Hayes	Morrill	Seward
Boone	Deuel	Hitchcock	Nance	Sheridan
Box Butte	Dixon	Holt	Nemaha	Sherman
Boyd	Dodge	Hooker	Nuckolls	Sioux
Brown	Douglas	Howard	Otoe	Stanton
Buffalo	Dundy	Jefferson	Pawnee	Thayer
Burt	Fillmore	Johnson	Perkins	Thomas
Butler	Franklin	Kearney	Phelps	Thurston
Cass	Frontier	Keith	Pierce	Valley
Cedar	Furnas	Keya Paha	Platte	Washington
Chase	Gage	Kimball	Polk	Wayne
Cherry	Garden	Knox	Red Willow	Webster
Cheyenne	Garfield	Lancaster	Richardson	Wheeler
Clay	Gosper	Lincoln	Rock	York
Colfax	Grant	Logan		

Multi-County Places

The following Nebraska places are in more than one county. Given here is the total population for each multi-county place, and the names of the counties it is in.

Emerson, pop. 791; Dixon (387), Dakota (312), Thurston (92)
Halsey, pop. 110; Thomas (102), Blaine (8)
Newman Grove, pop. 787; Madison (770), Platte (17)
Oxford, pop. 949; Furnas (736), Harlan (213)
Palisade, pop. 381; Hitchcock (367), Hayes (14)
Tilden, pop. 895; Madison (662), Antelope (233)
Trumbull, pop. 225; Clay (225), Adams (0)
Wakefield, pop. 1,082; Dixon (1,006), Wayne (76)

Adams County
County Seat: Hastings (ZIP: 68901)

Pop: 29,625 (1990); 30,656 (1980) **Pop Density:** 52.6
Land: 563.4 sq. mi.; **Water:** 0.8 sq. mi. **Area Code:** 402
In south-central NE, south of Grand Island; organized Feb 16, 1867 from Clay County.
Name origin: For John Adams (1735–1826), second U.S. president.

Ayr — Village
ZIP: 68925 Lat: 40-26-16 N Long: 98-26-24 W
Pop: 101 (1990); 112 (1980) Pop Density: 505.0
Land: 0.2 sq. mi.; Water: 0.0 sq. mi.
Established 1878.
Name origin: For Dr. Ayr, a director of the Burlington & Missouri River Railroad.

Blaine — Township
Lat: 40-33-51 N Long: 98-19-33 W
Pop: 586 (1990); 1,089 (1980) Pop Density: 19.7
Land: 29.8 sq. mi.; Water: 0.0 sq. mi.

Cottonwood — Township
ZIP: 68950 Lat: 40-28-51 N Long: 98-39-59 W
Pop: 320 (1990); 384 (1980) Pop Density: 8.9
Land: 35.9 sq. mi.; Water: 0.0 sq. mi.

Denver — Township
ZIP: 68950 Lat: 40-33-47 N Long: 98-26-50 W
Pop: 783 (1990); 941 (1980) Pop Density: 26.0
Land: 30.1 sq. mi.; Water: 0.1 sq. mi.

Hanover — Township
Lat: 40-28-49 N Long: 98-20-11 W
Pop: 201 (1990); 230 (1980) Pop Density: 6.1
Land: 33.2 sq. mi.; Water: 0.0 sq. mi.

Hastings — City
ZIP: 68901 Lat: 40-35-21 N Long: 98-23-24 W
Pop: 22,837 (1990); 23,045 (1980) Pop Density: 2429.5
Land: 9.4 sq. mi.; Water: 0.1 sq. mi.
Name origin: For Col. D.T. (or T.D.) Hastings of the St. Joseph & Grand Island Railroad.

Highland — Township
ZIP: 68950 Lat: 40-39-21 N Long: 98-26-13 W
Pop: 577 (1990); 512 (1980) Pop Density: 16.2
Land: 35.7 sq. mi.; Water: 0.2 sq. mi.

Holstein — Village
ZIP: 68950 Lat: 40-27-53 N Long: 98-39-03 W
Pop: 207 (1990); 241 (1980) Pop Density: 1035.0
Land: 0.2 sq. mi.; Water: 0.0 sq. mi.
Platted 1887.
Name origin: For the Schleswig-Holstein peninsula in Germany.

Juniata — Village
ZIP: 68955 Lat: 40-35-22 N Long: 98-30-19 W
Pop: 811 (1990); 703 (1980) Pop Density: 1622.0
Land: 0.5 sq. mi.; Water: 0.0 sq. mi.
Not coextensive with the township.
Name origin: For the Juniata River in PA.

*Juniata — Township
ZIP: 68955 Lat: 40-33-55 N Long: 98-33-21 W
Pop: 1,058 (1990); 978 (1980) Pop Density: 29.6
Land: 35.7 sq. mi.; Water: 0.1 sq. mi.

Kenesaw — Village
ZIP: 68956 Lat: 40-37-10 N Long: 98-39-29 W
Pop: 818 (1990); 854 (1980) Pop Density: 1022.5
Land: 0.8 sq. mi.; Water: 0.0 sq. mi.
Not coextensive with the township. Surveyed 1872.
Name origin: For the battle of Kenesaw Mountain in GA in 1864.

*Kenesaw — Township
ZIP: 68956 Lat: 40-39-50 N Long: 98-40-17 W
Pop: 922 (1990); 980 (1980) Pop Density: 25.5
Land: 36.2 sq. mi.; Water: 0.0 sq. mi.

Little Blue — Township
Lat: 40-23-22 N Long: 98-19-30 W
Pop: 244 (1990); 260 (1980) Pop Density: 7.4
Land: 33.0 sq. mi.; Water: 0.0 sq. mi.

Logan — Township
ZIP: 68950 Lat: 40-23-34 N Long: 98-39-55 W
Pop: 93 (1990); 100 (1980) Pop Density: 2.6
Land: 36.0 sq. mi.; Water: 0.0 sq. mi.

Prosser — Village
ZIP: 68868 Lat: 40-41-19 N Long: 98-34-38 W
Pop: 77 (1990); 98 (1980) Pop Density: 385.0
Land: 0.2 sq. mi.; Water: 0.0 sq. mi.
Name origin: For T. J. Prosser, superintendent of the construction crew that built the railroad through town.

Roseland — Village
ZIP: 68973 Lat: 40-28-15 N Long: 98-33-28 W
Pop: 247 (1990); 254 (1980) Pop Density: 1235.0
Land: 0.2 sq. mi.; Water: 0.0 sq. mi. Elev: 1972 ft.
Not coextensive with the township.
Name origin: Named by the town's first postmaster, B.F. Evans, for the abundant wild roses in the area.

*Roseland — Township
ZIP: 68973 Lat: 40-29-18 N Long: 98-33-06 W
Pop: 467 (1990); 517 (1980) Pop Density: 13.0
Land: 35.9 sq. mi.; Water: 0.0 sq. mi.

Silver Lake — Township
ZIP: 68973 Lat: 40-23-51 N Long: 98-33-29 W
Pop: 136 (1990); 160 (1980) Pop Density: 3.8
Land: 36.1 sq. mi.; Water: 0.0 sq. mi.

Trumbull — Village
Lat: 40-40-31 N Long: 98-16-41 W
Pop: 0 (1990); 216 (1980)
Land: 0.01 sq. mi.; Water: 0.0 sq. mi.
Part of the town is also in Clay County.

American Places Dictionary   NEBRASKA, Antelope County

Verona Township
ZIP: 68868   Lat: 40-39-17 N   Long: 98-33-15 W
Pop: 297 (1990); 330 (1980)   Pop Density: 8.3
Land: 35.7 sq. mi.; Water: 0.1 sq. mi.

Wanda Township
ZIP: 68956   Lat: 40-34-29 N   Long: 98-39-43 W
Pop: 154 (1990); 178 (1980)   Pop Density: 4.3
Land: 36.1 sq. mi.; Water: 0.0 sq. mi.

West Blue Township
Lat: 40-39-00 N   Long: 98-19-30 W
Pop: 334 (1990); 304 (1980)   Pop Density: 10.2
Land: 32.7 sq. mi.; Water: 0.0 sq. mi.

Zero Township
ZIP: 68925   Lat: 40-23-29 N   Long: 98-26-15 W
Pop: 272 (1990); 300 (1980)   Pop Density: 7.5
Land: 36.2 sq. mi.; Water: 0.0 sq. mi.

Antelope County
County Seat: Neligh (ZIP: 68756)

Pop: 7,965 (1990); 8,675 (1980)   Pop Density: 9.3
Land: 857.1 sq. mi.; Water: 1.4 sq. mi.   Area Code: 402
In east-central NE, southwest of Sioux City, IA; organized Jun 15, 1871 from Pierce County.

Name origin: The bill for establishment of the county was introduced by Leander Gerrard who once shot an antelope for food while on the trail of Indians.

Bazile Township
Lat: 42-23-56 N   Long: 97-53-29 W
Pop: 230 (1990); 189 (1980)   Pop Density: 6.4
Land: 36.1 sq. mi.; Water: 0.0 sq. mi.

Blaine Township
Lat: 42-13-16 N   Long: 98-07-50 W
Pop: 171 (1990); 198 (1980)   Pop Density: 4.8
Land: 35.9 sq. mi.; Water: 0.0 sq. mi.

Brunswick Village
ZIP: 68720   Lat: 42-20-17 N   Long: 97-58-16 W
Pop: 182 (1990); 190 (1980)   Pop Density: 303.3
Land: 0.6 sq. mi.; Water: 0.0 sq. mi.
Name origin: For Brunswick, Germany, a center for the beet industry; settler Henry Nagle suggested the name after he raised an immense sugar beet on his farm.

Burnett Township
Lat: 42-03-21 N   Long: 97-53-16 W
Pop: 279 (1990); 225 (1980)   Pop Density: 7.9
Land: 35.1 sq. mi.; Water: 0.4 sq. mi.

Cedar Township
Lat: 41-57-32 N   Long: 98-00-31 W
Pop: 153 (1990); 199 (1980)   Pop Density: 4.3
Land: 35.4 sq. mi.; Water: 0.0 sq. mi.

Clearwater Village
ZIP: 68726   Lat: 42-10-14 N   Long: 98-11-18 W
Pop: 401 (1990); 409 (1980)   Pop Density: 1002.5
Land: 0.4 sq. mi.; Water: 0.0 sq. mi.
Not coextensive with the township.
Name origin: For a nearby creek. Originally known as Antelope.

***Clearwater** Township
ZIP: 68726   Lat: 42-07-49 N   Long: 98-14-12 W
Pop: 583 (1990); 630 (1980)   Pop Density: 16.3
Land: 35.8 sq. mi.; Water: 0.0 sq. mi.

Crawford Township
Lat: 42-18-01 N   Long: 97-53-00 W
Pop: 189 (1990); 217 (1980)   Pop Density: 5.3
Land: 35.7 sq. mi.; Water: 0.0 sq. mi.

Custer Township
Lat: 42-12-44 N   Long: 98-00-18 W
Pop: 127 (1990); 154 (1980)   Pop Density: 3.6
Land: 35.7 sq. mi.; Water: 0.0 sq. mi.

Eden Township
Lat: 42-23-09 N   Long: 98-00-18 W
Pop: 163 (1990); 164 (1980)   Pop Density: 4.5
Land: 36.0 sq. mi.; Water: 0.0 sq. mi.

Elgin City
ZIP: 68636   Lat: 41-59-01 N   Long: 98-04-59 W
Pop: 731 (1990); 807 (1980)   Pop Density: 1044.3
Land: 0.7 sq. mi.; Water: 0.0 sq. mi.
Name origin: Named by post office official E. Gailey for Elgin, IL.

***Elgin** Township
ZIP: 68636   Lat: 42-03-09 N   Long: 98-06-48 W
Pop: 120 (1990); 151 (1980)   Pop Density: 3.4
Land: 35.7 sq. mi.; Water: 0.0 sq. mi.

Ellsworth Township
Lat: 42-18-49 N   Long: 98-00-18 W
Pop: 325 (1990); 348 (1980)   Pop Density: 9.1
Land: 35.6 sq. mi.; Water: 0.0 sq. mi.

Elm Township
Lat: 42-08-02 N   Long: 97-53-13 W
Pop: 114 (1990); 103 (1980)   Pop Density: 3.2
Land: 35.9 sq. mi.; Water: 0.0 sq. mi.

Frenchtown Township
Lat: 42-13-12 N   Long: 98-14-31 W
Pop: 182 (1990); 173 (1980)   Pop Density: 5.1
Land: 35.7 sq. mi.; Water: 0.2 sq. mi.

Garfield Township
Lat: 42-17-57 N   Long: 98-13-56 W
Pop: 619 (1990); 653 (1980)   Pop Density: 17.3
Land: 35.8 sq. mi.; Water: 0.0 sq. mi.

Grant Township
Lat: 41-57-33 N   Long: 97-53-32 W
Pop: 125 (1990); 141 (1980)   Pop Density: 3.5
Land: 36.0 sq. mi.; Water: 0.0 sq. mi.

NEBRASKA, Antelope County

Lincoln
Township
Lat: 41-57-46 N **Long:** 98-14-24 W
Pop: 119 (1990); 126 (1980) **Pop Density:** 3.3
Land: 35.6 sq. mi.; **Water:** 0.0 sq. mi.

Logan
Township
Lat: 41-57-37 N **Long:** 98-07-26 W
Pop: 970 (1990); 1,064 (1980) **Pop Density:** 27.2
Land: 35.6 sq. mi.; **Water:** 0.0 sq. mi.

Neligh
City
ZIP: 68756 **Lat:** 42-07-48 N **Long:** 98-01-43 W
Pop: 1,742 (1990); 1,893 (1980) **Pop Density:** 1935.6
Land: 0.9 sq. mi.; **Water:** 0.0 sq. mi.
Not coextensive with the township. Platted 1873.
Name origin: For early settler and landowner John D. Neligh.

*Neligh
Township
ZIP: 68756 **Lat:** 42-07-57 N **Long:** 98-00-31 W
Pop: 307 (1990); 369 (1980) **Pop Density:** 8.8
Land: 34.7 sq. mi.; **Water:** 0.2 sq. mi.

Oakdale
Village
ZIP: 68761 **Lat:** 42-04-11 N **Long:** 97-57-57 W
Pop: 362 (1990); 410 (1980) **Pop Density:** 603.3
Land: 0.6 sq. mi.; **Water:** 0.0 sq. mi.
Not coextensive with the township. Platted 1872.

*Oakdale
Township
ZIP: 68761 **Lat:** 42-02-44 N **Long:** 97-59-58 W
Pop: 508 (1990); 571 (1980) **Pop Density:** 14.4
Land: 35.4 sq. mi.; **Water:** 0.2 sq. mi.

Orchard
Village
ZIP: 68764 **Lat:** 42-20-09 N **Long:** 98-14-28 W
Pop: 439 (1990); 482 (1980) **Pop Density:** 1097.5
Land: 0.4 sq. mi.; **Water:** 0.0 sq. mi. **Elev:** 1946 ft.
Settled 1880.

Ord
Township
Lat: 42-07-31 N **Long:** 98-07-52 W
Pop: 106 (1990); 114 (1980) **Pop Density:** 3.0
Land: 35.6 sq. mi.; **Water:** 0.2 sq. mi.

Royal
Village
ZIP: 68773 **Lat:** 42-19-57 N **Long:** 98-07-30 W
Pop: 81 (1990); 86 (1980) **Pop Density:** 810.0
Land: 0.1 sq. mi.; **Water:** 0.0 sq. mi.
Not coextensive with the township.
Name origin: For Mr. Royal Thayer. Previously called Savage.

*Royal
Township
ZIP: 68773 **Lat:** 42-17-56 N **Long:** 98-06-57 W
Pop: 218 (1990); 253 (1980) **Pop Density:** 6.1
Land: 35.7 sq. mi.; **Water:** 0.0 sq. mi.

Sherman
Township
Lat: 42-23-26 N **Long:** 98-14-26 W
Pop: 101 (1990); 119 (1980) **Pop Density:** 2.8
Land: 35.7 sq. mi.; **Water:** 0.0 sq. mi.

Stanton
Township
Lat: 42-03-09 N **Long:** 98-13-43 W
Pop: 110 (1990); 147 (1980) **Pop Density:** 3.1
Land: 35.5 sq. mi.; **Water:** 0.0 sq. mi.

Tilden
City
ZIP: 68781 **Lat:** 42-02-34 N **Long:** 97-50-11 W
Pop: 233 (1990); 293 (1980) **Pop Density:** 776.7
Land: 0.3 sq. mi.; **Water:** 0.0 sq. mi.
Part of the town is also in Madison County.
Name origin: For Samuel J. Tilden, statesman from NY. Originally called Burnett after a railroad official.

Verdigris
Township
Lat: 42-23-53 N **Long:** 98-07-22 W
Pop: 90 (1990); 83 (1980) **Pop Density:** 2.5
Land: 35.9 sq. mi.; **Water:** 0.1 sq. mi.

Willow
Township
Lat: 42-13-07 N **Long:** 97-53-00 W
Pop: 81 (1990); 98 (1980) **Pop Density:** 2.3
Land: 35.8 sq. mi.; **Water:** 0.0 sq. mi.

Arthur County
County Seat: Arthur (ZIP: 69121)

Pop: 462 (1990); 513 (1980) **Pop Density:** 0.6
Land: 715.4 sq. mi.; **Water:** 2.9 sq. mi. **Area Code:** 308
In west-central NE, northwest of North Platte; county approved Mar 31, 1887 from unattached lands; formed Jun 7, 1913.
Name origin: For Chester A. Arthur (1830–86), twenty-first U.S. president.

Arthur
Village
ZIP: 69121 **Lat:** 41-34-20 N **Long:** 101-41-30 W
Pop: 128 (1990); 124 (1980) **Pop Density:** 426.7
Land: 0.3 sq. mi.; **Water:** 0.0 sq. mi.
Name origin: For Chester A. Arthur (1830–86), twenty-first U.S. president.

Banner County
County Seat: Harrisburg (ZIP: 69345)

Pop: 852 (1990); 918 (1980) **Pop Density:** 1.1
Land: 746.3 sq. mi.; **Water:** 0.2 sq. mi. **Area Code:** 308

On the southwestern border of NE, south of Scottsbluff; organized Nov 6, 1888 from Cheyenne County.

Name origin: Named by the citizens who wanted the county to be the "banner county" of the state.

Blaine County
County Seat: Brewster (ZIP: 68821)

Pop: 675 (1990); 867 (1980) **Pop Density:** 0.9
Land: 710.8 sq. mi.; **Water:** 3.6 sq. mi. **Area Code:** 308

In central NE, northeast of North Platte; organized Mar 5, 1885 from Custer County.

Name origin: For James Gillespie Blaine (1830–93), U.S. representative from ME (1863–76), U.S. senator (1876–81), and U.S. secretary of state (1881; 1889–92).

Brewster Village
ZIP: 68821 **Lat:** 41-56-18 N **Long:** 99-51-54 W
Pop: 22 (1990); 46 (1980) **Pop Density:** 220.0
Land: 0.1 sq. mi.; **Water:** 0.0 sq. mi. **Elev:** 2494 ft.
Name origin: For newspaperman George W. Brewster.

Dunning Village
ZIP: 68833 **Lat:** 41-49-39 N **Long:** 100-06-13 W
Pop: 131 (1990); 182 (1980) **Pop Density:** 655.0
Land: 0.2 sq. mi.; **Water:** 0.0 sq. mi.
Established in Dunning Precinct as a station on the Chicago, Burlington & Quincy Railroad.

Halsey Village
Lat: 41-54-07 N **Long:** 100-15-51 W
Pop: 8 (1990); 10 (1980)
Land: 0.03 sq. mi.; **Water:** 0.0 sq. mi.
Part of the town is also in Thomas County.
Name origin: For Halsey Yates, a surveyor for the railroad.

Purdum Pop. Place
ZIP: 69157 **Lat:** 41-57-53 N **Long:** 100-06-42 W
Pop: 204 (1990); 236 (1980) **Pop Density:** 0.7
Land: 281.0 sq. mi.; **Water:** 1.0 sq. mi.

Boone County
County Seat: Albion (ZIP: 68621)

Pop: 6,667 (1990); 7,391 (1980) **Pop Density:** 9.7
Land: 686.7 sq. mi.; **Water:** 0.6 sq. mi. **Area Code:** 402

In east-central NE, northeast of Grand Island; organized Mar 28, 1871 from Platte County.

Name origin: For Daniel Boone (1734?–1820), U.S. frontiersman and KY pioneer.

Albion City
ZIP: 68620 **Lat:** 41-41-21 N **Long:** 98-00-10 W
Pop: 1,916 (1990); 1,997 (1980) **Pop Density:** 2395.0
Land: 0.8 sq. mi.; **Water:** 0.0 sq. mi.
Name origin: For Albion, MI.

Cedar Rapids Village
ZIP: 68627 **Lat:** 41-33-31 N **Long:** 98-08-57 W
Pop: 396 (1990); 447 (1980) **Pop Density:** 990.0
Land: 0.4 sq. mi.; **Water:** 0.0 sq. mi.

Petersburg Village
ZIP: 68652 **Lat:** 41-51-16 N **Long:** 98-04-47 W
Pop: 388 (1990); 381 (1980) **Pop Density:** 970.0
Land: 0.4 sq. mi.; **Water:** 0.0 sq. mi.
Settled 1887.
Name origin: For John Peters, who owned the land on which the village was established.

Primrose Village
ZIP: 68655 **Lat:** 41-37-25 N **Long:** 98-14-13 W
Pop: 69 (1990); 102 (1980) **Pop Density:** 230.0
Land: 0.3 sq. mi.; **Water:** 0.0 sq. mi.
Name origin: For David Primrose, who owned the land on which the townsite was built.

NEBRASKA, Boone County

St. Edward
Lat: 41-34-16 N **Long:** 97-51-39 W   City
Pop: 822 (1990); 891 (1980)   **Pop Density:** 1174.3
Land: 0.7 sq. mi.; **Water:** 0.0 sq. mi.
Name origin: Named by a former resident of South Bend, IN, for Father Edward Serrels, a prominent Roman Catholic priest at Notre Dame University in IN.

Box Butte County
County Seat: Alliance (ZIP: 69301)

Pop: 13,130 (1990); 13,696 (1980)   **Pop Density:** 12.2
Land: 1075.4 sq. mi.; **Water:** 2.5 sq. mi.   **Area Code:** 308
In northwestern NE, northeast of Scottsbluff; organized Nov 2, 1886 from Dawes County.
Name origin: Descriptive of the rectangular-shaped butte near Alliance.

Alliance   City
ZIP: 69301   **Lat:** 42-06-01 N **Long:** 102-52-26 W
Pop: 9,765 (1990); 9,920 (1980)   **Pop Density:** 2077.7
Land: 4.7 sq. mi.; **Water:** 0.0 sq. mi.   **Elev:** 3960 ft.
In northwestern NE, 45 mi. northeast of Scottsbluff.
Name origin: Named by G.W. Holdrege, who is said to have selected the name because it was a single word, different from any name in the state and was near the beginning of the alphabet. Previously called Grand Lake.

Hemingford   Village
ZIP: 69348   **Lat:** 42-19-16 N **Long:** 103-04-32 W
Pop: 953 (1990); 1,023 (1980)   **Pop Density:** 1588.3
Land: 0.6 sq. mi.; **Water:** 0.0 sq. mi.
Name origin: Named by Joseph Hare for his former home of Hemmingford, Canada; one *m* was dropped through clerical error and allowed to stand.

Boyd County
County Seat: Butte (ZIP: 68722)

Pop: 2,835 (1990); 3,331 (1980)   **Pop Density:** 5.2
Land: 540.1 sq. mi.; **Water:** 4.5 sq. mi.   **Area Code:** 402
On the northern border of NE; organized Mar 20, 1891 from Holt County.
Name origin: For James E. Boyd (1834–1906), NE governor (1891; 1892–93).

Anoka   Village
Lat: 42-56-48 N **Long:** 98-49-47 W
Pop: 10 (1990); 24 (1980)   **Pop Density:** 16.7
Land: 0.6 sq. mi.; **Water:** 0.0 sq. mi.
Name origin: Probably named for Anoka, MN.

Basin   Township
Lat: 42-54-52 N **Long:** 99-09-06 W
Pop: 386 (1990); 422 (1980)   **Pop Density:** 3.0
Land: 128.7 sq. mi.; **Water:** 0.0 sq. mi.

Bristow   Village
ZIP: 68719   **Lat:** 42-50-23 N **Long:** 98-35-01 W
Pop: 107 (1990); 123 (1980)   **Pop Density:** 535.0
Land: 0.2 sq. mi.; **Water:** 0.0 sq. mi.
Not coextensive with the township.
Name origin: For Benjamin H. Bristow (1832–96), U.S. secretary of the treasury (1874–76).

*Bristow   Township
ZIP: 68719   **Lat:** 42-50-02 N **Long:** 98-35-41 W
Pop: 181 (1990); 196 (1980)   **Pop Density:** 5.5
Land: 33.0 sq. mi.; **Water:** 0.4 sq. mi.

Bush   Township
Lat: 42-50-25 N **Long:** 98-22-15 W
Pop: 88 (1990); 122 (1980)   **Pop Density:** 1.6
Land: 55.2 sq. mi.; **Water:** 2.0 sq. mi.

Butte   Village
ZIP: 68722   **Lat:** 42-54-45 N **Long:** 98-50-52 W
Pop: 452 (1990); 529 (1980)   **Pop Density:** 1130.0
Land: 0.4 sq. mi.; **Water:** 0.0 sq. mi.   **Elev:** 1811 ft.
Not coextensive with the township.
Name origin: For the rocky elevation at the south end of the village.

*Butte   Township
ZIP: 68722   **Lat:** 42-54-37 N **Long:** 98-49-49 W
Pop: 667 (1990); 798 (1980)   **Pop Density:** 10.5
Land: 63.7 sq. mi.; **Water:** 0.1 sq. mi.

Gross   Village
Lat: 42-56-48 N **Long:** 98-34-07 W
Pop: 7 (1990); 2 (1980)   **Pop Density:** 70.0
Land: 0.1 sq. mi.; **Water:** 0.0 sq. mi.
Name origin: For homesteader B.B. Gross, who also became the town's first postmaster.

Lynch   Village
ZIP: 68746   **Lat:** 42-49-51 N **Long:** 98-28-00 W
Pop: 296 (1990); 357 (1980)   **Pop Density:** 592.0
Land: 0.5 sq. mi.; **Water:** 0.0 sq. mi.
Not coextensive with the township.

*Lynch
ZIP: 68746   **Lat:** 42-49-33 N   **Long:** 98-28-50 W   Township
Pop: 371 (1990); 484 (1980)   **Pop Density:** 9.1
Land: 40.7 sq. mi.; **Water:** 0.6 sq. mi.

McCulley
Lat: 42-56-23 N   **Long:** 98-57-07 W   Township
Pop: 135 (1990); 130 (1980)   **Pop Density:** 2.5
Land: 53.0 sq. mi.; **Water:** 0.0 sq. mi.

Monowi
Lat: 42-49-48 N   **Long:** 98-19-43 W   Village
Pop: 6 (1990); 18 (1980)   **Pop Density:** 30.0
Land: 0.2 sq. mi.; **Water:** 0.0 sq. mi.
Name origin: From an Indian term meaning 'flowers.'

Morton
Lat: 42-56-27 N   **Long:** 98-36-24 W   Township
Pop: 174 (1990); 221 (1980)   **Pop Density:** 3.3
Land: 52.5 sq. mi.; **Water:** 0.0 sq. mi.

Mullen
Lat: 42-54-52 N   **Long:** 98-29-11 W   Township
Pop: 37 (1990); 66 (1980)   **Pop Density:** 0.9
Land: 39.3 sq. mi.; **Water:** 1.1 sq. mi.

Naper
ZIP: 68755   **Lat:** 42-57-51 N   **Long:** 99-05-49 W   Village
Pop: 130 (1990); 136 (1980)   **Pop Density:** 1300.0
Land: 0.1 sq. mi.; **Water:** 0.0 sq. mi.
Name origin: For homesteader Ralph Naper, who donated eighty acres for the townsite and named the village after himself.

Spencer
ZIP: 68777   **Lat:** 42-52-28 N   **Long:** 98-42-05 W   Village
Pop: 536 (1990); 596 (1980)   **Pop Density:** 1072.0
Land: 0.5 sq. mi.; **Water:** 0.0 sq. mi.
Not coextensive with the township.
Name origin: Named by the first postmaster, Mr. Sterns, for his former home in Spencer, IA.

*Spencer
ZIP: 68777   **Lat:** 42-54-18 N   **Long:** 98-43-08 W   Township
Pop: 796 (1990); 892 (1980)   **Pop Density:** 10.8
Land: 73.9 sq. mi.; **Water:** 0.2 sq. mi.

Brown County
County Seat: Ainsworth (ZIP: 69210)

Pop: 3,657 (1990); 4,377 (1980)   **Pop Density:** 3.0
Land: 1221.4 sq. mi.; **Water:** 3.8 sq. mi.   **Area Code:** 402
In north-central NE; organized Feb 19, 1883 from unorganized territory.
Name origin: Possibly for two state legislators named Brown who sponsored the bill for organization of the county.

Ainsworth
ZIP: 69210   **Lat:** 42-32-56 N   **Long:** 99-51-25 W   City
Pop: 1,870 (1990); 2,256 (1980)   **Pop Density:** 1870.0
Land: 1.0 sq. mi.; **Water:** 0.0 sq. mi.
Incorporated 1883.
Name origin: For Capt. James E. Ainsworth, a chief engineer for the railroad company.

Johnstown
ZIP: 69214   **Lat:** 42-34-20 N   **Long:** 100-03-18 W   Village
Pop: 48 (1990); 78 (1980)   **Pop Density:** 96.0
Land: 0.5 sq. mi.; **Water:** 0.0 sq. mi.
Name origin: For mail stagecoach driver John Berry.

*Long Pine
ZIP: 69217   **Lat:** 42-32-05 N   **Long:** 99-42-08 W   City
Pop: 396 (1990); 521 (1980)   **Pop Density:** 660.0
Land: 0.6 sq. mi.; **Water:** 0.0 sq. mi.
Settled 1878.

Long Pine
ZIP: 69217   **Lat:** 42-32-05 N   **Long:** 99-42-08 W   City
Pop: 396 (1990); 521 (1980)   **Pop Density:** 660.0
Land: 0.6 sq. mi.; **Water:** 0.0 sq. mi.
Settled 1878.

Buffalo County
County Seat: Kearney (ZIP: 68848)

Pop: 37,447 (1990); 34,797 (1980)　　　　**Pop Density:** 38.7
Land: 968.1 sq. mi.; **Water:** 7.2 sq. mi.　　　**Area Code:** 308
In south-central NE, west of Grand Island; original county; organized Mar 14, 1855 (prior to statehood); not officially recognized until Jan 20, 1870.
Name origin: For the former feeding grounds of the buffalo.

Amherst — Village
ZIP: 68812　　**Lat:** 40-50-19 N　**Long:** 99-16-08 W
Pop: 231 (1990); 269 (1980)　　**Pop Density:** 1155.0
Land: 0.2 sq. mi.; **Water:** 0.0 sq. mi.
Name origin: Named by railroad president John N. Hamilton for Amherst College in MA.

Armada — Township
ZIP: 68858　　**Lat:** 40-55-24 N　**Long:** 99-21-53 W
Pop: 261 (1990); 259 (1980)　　**Pop Density:** 7.4
Land: 35.4 sq. mi.; **Water:** 0.0 sq. mi.

Beaver — Township
Lat: 41-00-30 N　**Long:** 99-00-16 W
Pop: 134 (1990); 183 (1980)　　**Pop Density:** 3.8
Land: 35.6 sq. mi.; **Water:** 0.1 sq. mi.

Cedar — Township
ZIP: 68866　　**Lat:** 40-55-07 N　**Long:** 99-00-56 W
Pop: 194 (1990); 223 (1980)　　**Pop Density:** 5.4
Land: 35.8 sq. mi.; **Water:** 0.0 sq. mi.

Center — Township
Lat: 40-43-04 N　**Long:** 99-00-13 W
Pop: 610 (1990); 629 (1980)　　**Pop Density:** 11.6
Land: 52.7 sq. mi.; **Water:** 1.0 sq. mi.

Cherry Creek — Township
ZIP: 68869　　**Lat:** 40-59-51 N　**Long:** 98-46-46 W
Pop: 94 (1990); 130 (1980)　　**Pop Density:** 2.6
Land: 35.6 sq. mi.; **Water:** 0.2 sq. mi.

Collins — Township
Lat: 40-41-27 N　**Long:** 99-08-35 W
Pop: 1,280 (1990); 1,684 (1980)　　**Pop Density:** 50.4
Land: 25.4 sq. mi.; **Water:** 0.9 sq. mi.

Divide — Township
ZIP: 68870　　**Lat:** 40-49-39 N　**Long:** 99-07-29 W
Pop: 313 (1990); 345 (1980)　　**Pop Density:** 7.5
Land: 41.6 sq. mi.; **Water:** 0.0 sq. mi.

Elm Creek — Village
ZIP: 68836　　**Lat:** 40-43-11 N　**Long:** 99-22-29 W
Pop: 852 (1990); 862 (1980)　　**Pop Density:** 1217.1
Land: 0.7 sq. mi.; **Water:** 0.0 sq. mi.　　**Elev:** 2262 ft.
Not coextensive with the township.
Name origin: For a nearby creek that had elm trees growing along its banks.

*Elm Creek — Township
ZIP: 68836　　**Lat:** 40-43-25 N　**Long:** 99-22-01 W
Pop: 1,151 (1990); 1,144 (1980)　　**Pop Density:** 24.0
Land: 48.0 sq. mi.; **Water:** 1.2 sq. mi.

Gardner — Township
ZIP: 68870　　**Lat:** 40-54-42 N　**Long:** 98-46-23 W
Pop: 127 (1990); 158 (1980)　　**Pop Density:** 3.5
Land: 35.8 sq. mi.; **Water:** 0.0 sq. mi.

Garfield — Township
ZIP: 68869　　**Lat:** 41-00-16 N　**Long:** 98-53-07 W
Pop: 235 (1990); 327 (1980)　　**Pop Density:** 6.8
Land: 34.7 sq. mi.; **Water:** 0.4 sq. mi.

Gibbon — City
ZIP: 68840　　**Lat:** 40-44-47 N　**Long:** 98-50-41 W
Pop: 1,525 (1990); 1,531 (1980)　　**Pop Density:** 2178.6
Land: 0.7 sq. mi.; **Water:** 0.0 sq. mi.
Not coextensive with the township.
Name origin: For Maj. Gen. John Gibbon, who served in the Mexican and Civil wars.

*Gibbon — Township
ZIP: 68840　　**Lat:** 40-44-20 N　**Long:** 98-53-12 W
Pop: 1,901 (1990); 1,905 (1980)　　**Pop Density:** 47.8
Land: 39.8 sq. mi.; **Water:** 0.1 sq. mi.

Grant — Township
ZIP: 68812　　**Lat:** 40-49-31 N　**Long:** 99-15-11 W
Pop: 457 (1990); 457 (1980)　　**Pop Density:** 12.8
Land: 35.8 sq. mi.; **Water:** 0.0 sq. mi.

Harrison — Township
ZIP: 68858　　**Lat:** 41-00-14 N　**Long:** 99-22-06 W
Pop: 76 (1990); 80 (1980)　　**Pop Density:** 2.1
Land: 35.8 sq. mi.; **Water:** 0.1 sq. mi.

Kearney — City
ZIP: 68847　　**Lat:** 40-42-02 N　**Long:** 99-05-04 W
Pop: 24,396 (1990); 21,158 (1980)　　**Pop Density:** 2836.7
Land: 8.6 sq. mi.; **Water:** 0.0 sq. mi.　　**Elev:** 2153 ft.
In south-central NE on the Platte River, 45 mi. southwest of Grand Island.
Name origin: For Gen. Stephen Watts Kearney (1794–1848), who served in the War of 1812 and the Mexican War. Previously called Fort Childs and Kearney Junction.

Logan — Township
ZIP: 68812　　**Lat:** 40-49-47 N　**Long:** 99-22-06 W
Pop: 105 (1990); 105 (1980)　　**Pop Density:** 2.9
Land: 35.8 sq. mi.; **Water:** 0.0 sq. mi.

Loup — Township
ZIP: 68866　　**Lat:** 41-00-25 N　**Long:** 99-07-32 W
Pop: 537 (1990); 518 (1980)　　**Pop Density:** 12.8
Land: 41.9 sq. mi.; **Water:** 0.0 sq. mi.

Miller — Village
ZIP: 68858　　**Lat:** 40-55-37 N　**Long:** 99-23-25 W
Pop: 130 (1990); 147 (1980)　　**Pop Density:** 325.0
Land: 0.4 sq. mi.; **Water:** 0.0 sq. mi.
Name origin: For Dr. George L. Miller, who once owned land in the area.

Odessa — Township
Lat: 40-43-21 N　**Long:** 99-15-13 W
Pop: 379 (1990); 367 (1980)　　**Pop Density:** 7.7
Land: 49.5 sq. mi.; **Water:** 0.7 sq. mi.

Platte
Township
Lat: 40-41-04 N **Long:** 98-50-17 W
Pop: 255 (1990); 225 (1980) **Pop Density:** 11.0
Land: 23.2 sq. mi.; **Water:** 2.2 sq. mi.

Pleasanton
Village
ZIP: 68866 **Lat:** 40-58-12 N **Long:** 99-05-12 W
Pop: 372 (1990); 349 (1980) **Pop Density:** 1240.0
Land: 0.3 sq. mi.; **Water:** 0.0 sq. mi.

Ravenna
City
ZIP: 68869 **Lat:** 41-01-36 N **Long:** 98-54-46 W
Pop: 1,317 (1990); 1,296 (1980) **Pop Density:** 1646.3
Land: 0.8 sq. mi.; **Water:** 0.0 sq. mi. **Elev:** 2018 ft.
Name origin: For the ancient Italian city. Previously called Beaver Creek.

Riverdale
Village
ZIP: 68870 **Lat:** 40-47-00 N **Long:** 99-09-35 W
Pop: 208 (1990); 204 (1980) **Pop Density:** 693.3
Land: 0.3 sq. mi.; **Water:** 0.0 sq. mi.
Name origin: For its view of the Wood River in the Platte Valley.

*Riverdale
Township
ZIP: 68870 **Lat:** 40-45-22 N **Long:** 99-07-51 W
Pop: 1,328 (1990); 1,113 (1980) **Pop Density:** 47.3
Land: 28.1 sq. mi.; **Water:** 0.0 sq. mi.

Rusco
Township
ZIP: 68866 **Lat:** 40-54-59 N **Long:** 99-07-52 W
Pop: 181 (1990); 178 (1980) **Pop Density:** 4.3
Land: 42.0 sq. mi.; **Water:** 0.0 sq. mi.

Sartoria
Township
ZIP: 68866 **Lat:** 41-00-04 N **Long:** 99-15-15 W
Pop: 117 (1990); 104 (1980) **Pop Density:** 3.3
Land: 35.9 sq. mi.; **Water:** 0.0 sq. mi.

Schneider
Township
Lat: 40-54-45 N **Long:** 98-53-20 W
Pop: 154 (1990); 210 (1980) **Pop Density:** 4.3
Land: 35.8 sq. mi.; **Water:** 0.0 sq. mi.

Scott
Township
ZIP: 68858 **Lat:** 40-55-06 N **Long:** 99-15-14 W
Pop: 103 (1990); 124 (1980) **Pop Density:** 2.9
Land: 35.6 sq. mi.; **Water:** 0.0 sq. mi.

Sharon
Township
ZIP: 68876 **Lat:** 40-49-43 N **Long:** 98-46-23 W
Pop: 163 (1990); 212 (1980) **Pop Density:** 4.5
Land: 35.9 sq. mi.; **Water:** 0.0 sq. mi.

Shelton
Village
ZIP: 68876 **Lat:** 40-46-42 N **Long:** 98-43-48 W
Pop: 954 (1990); 1,046 (1980) **Pop Density:** 1362.9
Land: 0.7 sq. mi.; **Water:** 0.0 sq. mi.
Not coextensive with the township.
Name origin: For N. Shelton, an auditor for the railroad. Previously called Wood River Center.

*Shelton
Township
ZIP: 68876 **Lat:** 40-44-30 N **Long:** 98-46-59 W
Pop: 1,256 (1990); 1,337 (1980) **Pop Density:** 40.5
Land: 31.0 sq. mi.; **Water:** 0.2 sq. mi.

Thornton
Township
ZIP: 68870 **Lat:** 40-49-32 N **Long:** 99-00-40 W
Pop: 171 (1990); 190 (1980) **Pop Density:** 4.7
Land: 36.2 sq. mi.; **Water:** 0.0 sq. mi.

Valley
Township
ZIP: 68840 **Lat:** 40-49-40 N **Long:** 98-54-02 W
Pop: 152 (1990); 136 (1980) **Pop Density:** 4.2
Land: 35.9 sq. mi.; **Water:** 0.0 sq. mi.

Burt County
County Seat: Tekamah (ZIP: 68061)

Pop: 7,868 (1990); 8,813 (1980) **Pop Density:** 16.0
Land: 492.8 sq. mi.; **Water:** 4.3 sq. mi. **Area Code:** 402
On the central eastern border of NE, north of Omaha; original county; organized Feb 18, 1855 (prior to statehood).
Name origin: For Francis Burt (1807–54), SC legislator, editor, and first territorial governor of NE (1854).

Arizona
Township
Lat: 41-45-49 N **Long:** 96-09-18 W
Pop: 321 (1990); 353 (1980) **Pop Density:** 4.4
Land: 72.2 sq. mi.; **Water:** 1.2 sq. mi.

Bell Creek
Township
Lat: 41-52-11 N **Long:** 96-24-36 W
Pop: 236 (1990); 306 (1980) **Pop Density:** 6.6
Land: 35.8 sq. mi.; **Water:** 0.0 sq. mi.

Craig
Village
ZIP: 68019 **Lat:** 41-47-05 N **Long:** 96-21-41 W
Pop: 228 (1990); 237 (1980) **Pop Density:** 760.0
Land: 0.3 sq. mi.; **Water:** 0.0 sq. mi.
Not coextensive with the township.
Name origin: For William Stewart Craig, who owned the land on which the town was built.

*Craig
Township
ZIP: 68019 **Lat:** 41-45-31 N **Long:** 96-24-27 W
Pop: 574 (1990); 677 (1980) **Pop Density:** 10.2
Land: 56.4 sq. mi.; **Water:** 0.0 sq. mi.

Decatur
Village
ZIP: 68020 **Lat:** 42-00-29 N **Long:** 96-15-02 W
Pop: 641 (1990); 723 (1980) **Pop Density:** 712.2
Land: 0.9 sq. mi.; **Water:** 0.0 sq. mi.
Not coextensive with the township. Established 1855 by the Decatur Town and Ferry Company.
Name origin: For Stephen Decatur, a member of the company.

NEBRASKA, Burt County

*Decatur — Township
ZIP: 68020 Lat: 41-58-28 N Long: 96-17-05 W
Pop: 873 (1990); 998 (1980) Pop Density: 18.4
Land: 47.5 sq. mi.; Water: 1.0 sq. mi.

Everett — Township
Lat: 41-57-59 N Long: 96-31-04 W
Pop: 1,334 (1990); 1,447 (1980) Pop Density: 40.5
Land: 32.9 sq. mi.; Water: 0.0 sq. mi.

Logan — Township
Lat: 41-58-16 N Long: 96-24-30 W
Pop: 279 (1990); 339 (1980) Pop Density: 6.7
Land: 41.4 sq. mi.; Water: 0.0 sq. mi.

Lyons — City
ZIP: 68038 Lat: 41-56-10 N Long: 96-28-19 W
Pop: 1,144 (1990); 1,214 (1980) Pop Density: 1634.3
Land: 0.7 sq. mi.; Water: 0.0 sq. mi.
Name origin: For settler Waldo Lyon, who came here from AZ c. 1869.

Oakland — City
ZIP: 68045 Lat: 41-50-06 N Long: 96-27-56 W
Pop: 1,279 (1990); 1,393 (1980) Pop Density: 1598.8
Land: 0.8 sq. mi.; Water: 0.0 sq. mi. Elev: 1287 ft.
Platted 1872.

*Oakland — Township
ZIP: 68045 Lat: 41-52-35 N Long: 96-30-32 W
Pop: 162 (1990); 225 (1980) Pop Density: 5.8
Land: 27.9 sq. mi.; Water: 0.0 sq. mi.

Pershing — Township
Lat: 41-47-07 N Long: 96-30-43 W
Pop: 178 (1990); 199 (1980) Pop Density: 6.2
Land: 28.5 sq. mi.; Water: 0.0 sq. mi.

Quinnebaugh — Township
Lat: 41-57-48 N Long: 96-10-50 W
Pop: 69 (1990); 95 (1980) Pop Density: 2.9
Land: 23.4 sq. mi.; Water: 1.4 sq. mi.

Riverside — Township
Lat: 41-51-56 N Long: 96-10-47 W
Pop: 70 (1990); 152 (1980) Pop Density: 2.4
Land: 29.1 sq. mi.; Water: 0.5 sq. mi.

Silver Creek — Township
Lat: 41-52-03 N Long: 96-17-32 W
Pop: 174 (1990); 223 (1980) Pop Density: 4.8
Land: 35.9 sq. mi.; Water: 0.0 sq. mi.

Summit — Township
Lat: 41-45-25 N Long: 96-17-06 W
Pop: 467 (1990); 520 (1980) Pop Density: 7.8
Land: 59.9 sq. mi.; Water: 0.2 sq. mi.

Tekamah — City
ZIP: 68061 Lat: 41-46-38 N Long: 96-13-21 W
Pop: 1,852 (1990); 1,886 (1980) Pop Density: 1683.6
Land: 1.1 sq. mi.; Water: 0.0 sq. mi.
Founded 1854 on an old Indian camping ground.
Name origin: From an Indian term possibly meaning 'big cottonwood' or 'field of battle.' It is also possibly a variant of Tacoma.

Butler County
County Seat: David City (ZIP: 68632)

Pop: 8,601 (1990); 9,330 (1980) Pop Density: 14.7
Land: 583.6 sq. mi.; Water: 0.8 sq. mi. Area Code: 402
In east-central NE, west of Omaha; organized Jun 26, 1856 from unorganized territory.
Name origin: For David Butler (1829–91), first governor of NE (1867–71).

Abie — Village
ZIP: 68001 Lat: 41-20-01 N Long: 96-56-57 W
Pop: 106 (1990); 107 (1980) Pop Density: 1060.0
Land: 0.1 sq. mi.; Water: 0.0 sq. mi.
Name origin: Named in 1877 for Abigail Stevens, the wife of the man who filed the application for a post office.

Alexis — Township
Lat: 41-20-38 N Long: 97-18-22 W
Pop: 555 (1990); 519 (1980) Pop Density: 17.7
Land: 31.4 sq. mi.; Water: 0.1 sq. mi.

Bellwood — Village
ZIP: 68624 Lat: 41-20-31 N Long: 97-14-24 W
Pop: 395 (1990); 407 (1980) Pop Density: 1975.0
Land: 0.2 sq. mi.; Water: 0.0 sq. mi.
Name origin: For Jesse D. Bell, who founded the town and planted rows of trees here.

Bone Creek — Township
Lat: 41-21-28 N Long: 97-04-14 W
Pop: 361 (1990); 386 (1980) Pop Density: 9.5
Land: 37.9 sq. mi.; Water: 0.1 sq. mi.

Brainard — Village
ZIP: 68626 Lat: 41-10-57 N Long: 97-00-07 W
Pop: 326 (1990); 275 (1980) Pop Density: 1086.7
Land: 0.3 sq. mi.; Water: 0.0 sq. mi.
Name origin: For David Brainard, a missionary to the Indians.

Bruno — Village
ZIP: 68014 Lat: 41-16-59 N Long: 96-57-37 W
Pop: 141 (1990); 154 (1980) Pop Density: 470.0
Land: 0.3 sq. mi.; Water: 0.0 sq. mi.
Name origin: Named by Moravian settlers for the city of Brno or Brunn in Moravia; it was later corrupted to Bruno.

Center — Township
Lat: 41-10-34 N Long: 97-04-55 W
Pop: 241 (1990); 291 (1980) Pop Density: 6.7
Land: 36.0 sq. mi.; Water: 0.0 sq. mi.

NEBRASKA, Butler County

David City
City
ZIP: 68632　　Lat: 41-15-16 N　Long: 97-07-34 W
Pop: 2,522 (1990); 2,514 (1980)　　Pop Density: 1801.4
Land: 1.4 sq. mi.; Water: 0.0 sq. mi.
Name origin: For David, the maiden name of Mrs. Miles, who deeded a large tract of land for the townsite.

Dwight
Village
ZIP: 68635　　Lat: 41-04-58 N　Long: 97-01-08 W
Pop: 227 (1990); 221 (1980)　　Pop Density: 1135.0
Land: 0.2 sq. mi.; Water: 0.0 sq. mi.
Name origin: For Dwight, IL, the hometown of many of the settlers. Previously called Lone Star.

Franklin
Township
Lat: 41-15-51 N　Long: 97-05-07 W
Pop: 310 (1990); 418 (1980)　　Pop Density: 9.0
Land: 34.5 sq. mi.; Water: 0.0 sq. mi.

Garrison
Village
Lat: 41-10-31 N　Long: 97-09-46 W
Pop: 71 (1990); 68 (1980)　　Pop Density: 710.0
Land: 0.1 sq. mi.; Water: 0.0 sq. mi.
Name origin: Named by Mr. Sargent for William Lloyd Garrison (1805–79), the famous antislavery leader.

Linwood
Village
ZIP: 68036　　Lat: 41-24-42 N　Long: 96-55-56 W
Pop: 91 (1990); 119 (1980)　　Pop Density: 227.5
Land: 0.4 sq. mi.; Water: 0.0 sq. mi.
Not coextensive with the township.
Name origin: Named by settler Sara Johnson for the linn or basswood trees that grew in the area.

*Linwood
Township
ZIP: 68036　　Lat: 41-21-14 N　Long: 96-57-40 W
Pop: 282 (1990); 322 (1980)　　Pop Density: 7.9
Land: 35.9 sq. mi.; Water: 0.0 sq. mi.

Oak Creek
Township
Lat: 41-10-30 N　Long: 96-57-51 W
Pop: 570 (1990); 611 (1980)　　Pop Density: 15.9
Land: 35.8 sq. mi.; Water: 0.1 sq. mi.

Octavia
Village
ZIP: 68650　　Lat: 41-20-50 N　Long: 97-03-32 W
Pop: 132 (1990); 127 (1980)　　Pop Density: 660.0
Land: 0.2 sq. mi.; Water: 0.0 sq. mi.
Laid out 1857.
Name origin: For Octavia Speltz, wife of a prominent farmer in the area.

Olive
Township
Lat: 41-15-22 N　Long: 97-11-50 W
Pop: 241 (1990); 261 (1980)　　Pop Density: 6.7
Land: 35.9 sq. mi.; Water: 0.1 sq. mi.

Platte
Township
Lat: 41-25-06 N　Long: 96-56-55 W
Pop: 175 (1990); 193 (1980)　　Pop Density: 10.2
Land: 17.2 sq. mi.; Water: 0.1 sq. mi.

Plum Creek
Township
Lat: 41-05-35 N　Long: 97-04-39 W
Pop: 217 (1990); 282 (1980)　　Pop Density: 6.0
Land: 36.0 sq. mi.; Water: 0.1 sq. mi.

Read
Township
Lat: 41-05-26 N　Long: 97-18-34 W
Pop: 250 (1990); 317 (1980)　　Pop Density: 6.9
Land: 36.1 sq. mi.; Water: 0.0 sq. mi.

Reading
Township
Lat: 41-10-40 N　Long: 97-18-39 W
Pop: 531 (1990); 617 (1980)　　Pop Density: 14.8
Land: 36.0 sq. mi.; Water: 0.0 sq. mi.

Richardson
Township
Lat: 41-05-27 N　Long: 96-57-43 W
Pop: 462 (1990); 424 (1980)　　Pop Density: 12.9
Land: 35.9 sq. mi.; Water: 0.1 sq. mi.

Rising City
Village
ZIP: 68658　　Lat: 41-11-55 N　Long: 97-17-48 W
Pop: 341 (1990); 392 (1980)　　Pop Density: 852.5
Land: 0.4 sq. mi.; Water: 0.0 sq. mi.
Name origin: For A.W. and S.W. Rising, who owned the townsite.

Savannah
Township
Lat: 41-20-44 N　Long: 97-11-49 W
Pop: 645 (1990); 746 (1980)　　Pop Density: 21.7
Land: 29.7 sq. mi.; Water: 0.0 sq. mi.

Skull Creek
Township
Lat: 41-15-59 N　Long: 96-58-07 W
Pop: 366 (1990); 399 (1980)　　Pop Density: 10.2
Land: 35.9 sq. mi.; Water: 0.0 sq. mi.

Summit
Township
Lat: 41-16-19 N　Long: 97-18-58 W
Pop: 166 (1990); 223 (1980)　　Pop Density: 4.6
Land: 35.7 sq. mi.; Water: 0.0 sq. mi.

Surprise
Village
ZIP: 68667　　Lat: 41-06-15 N　Long: 97-18-31 W
Pop: 55 (1990); 60 (1980)　　Pop Density: 137.5
Land: 0.4 sq. mi.; Water: 0.0 sq. mi.
In southeastern NE, northwest of Lincoln.
Name origin: Named by settlers who were surprised to find much better land here than they expected. Another story has it that as newcomers came over the hills they were surprised to see George Miller's flour mill so far from civilization.

Ulysses
Village
ZIP: 68669　　Lat: 41-04-20 N　Long: 97-12-08 W
Pop: 256 (1990); 270 (1980)　　Pop Density: 1280.0
Land: 0.2 sq. mi.; Water: 0.0 sq. mi.
Not coextensive with the township.
Name origin: For Ulysses S. Grant (1822–85), eighteenth U.S. president.

*Ulysses
Township
ZIP: 68669　　Lat: 41-05-29 N　Long: 97-11-59 W
Pop: 440 (1990); 504 (1980)　　Pop Density: 12.1
Land: 36.3 sq. mi.; Water: 0.0 sq. mi.

Union
Township
Lat: 41-10-43 N　Long: 97-11-52 W
Pop: 267 (1990); 303 (1980)　　Pop Density: 7.4
Land: 36.1 sq. mi.; Water: 0.0 sq. mi.

NEBRASKA, Cass County   American Places Dictionary

> ## Cass County
> **County Seat: Plattsmouth (ZIP: 68048)**
>
> **Pop:** 21,318 (1990); 20,297 (1980)   **Pop Density:** 38.1
> **Land:** 559.3 sq. mi.; **Water:** 7.0 sq. mi.   **Area Code:** 402
> On the southeastern border of NE, northeast of Lincoln; original county; organized Mar 7, 1855 (prior to statehood).
> **Name origin:** For Gen. Lewis Cass (1782–1866), OH legislator, military and civil governor of MI Territory (1813–31), U.S. secretary of war (1831–36), and U.S. secretary of state (1857–60).

Alvo — Village
ZIP: 68304 **Lat:** 40-52-17 N **Long:** 96-23-11 W
Pop: 164 (1990); 144 (1980) **Pop Density:** 1640.0
Land: 0.1 sq. mi.; **Water:** 0.0 sq. mi.
Name origin: Named by the post office.

Avoca — Village
ZIP: 68307 **Lat:** 40-47-46 N **Long:** 96-07-04 W
Pop: 254 (1990); 242 (1980) **Pop Density:** 2540.0
Land: 0.1 sq. mi.; **Water:** 0.0 sq. mi.
Platted 1857.
Name origin: For either Avoca Precinct or for the poem "Sweet Vale of Avoca" by Thomas Moore (1779–1852).

Cedar Creek — Village
ZIP: 68016 **Lat:** 41-02-43 N **Long:** 96-05-52 W
Pop: 334 (1990); 311 (1980) **Pop Density:** 477.1
Land: 0.7 sq. mi.; **Water:** 0.4 sq. mi.
Established 1865.
Name origin: For nearby creek that had cedar trees along its banks.

Eagle — Village
ZIP: 68347 **Lat:** 40-48-57 N **Long:** 96-25-55 W
Pop: 1,047 (1990); 832 (1980) **Pop Density:** 3490.0
Land: 0.3 sq. mi.; **Water:** 0.0 sq. mi.
Name origin: Probably for the eagles that once nested in the area. Previously called Sunlight.

Elmwood — Village
ZIP: 68349 **Lat:** 40-50-31 N **Long:** 96-17-39 W
Pop: 584 (1990); 598 (1980) **Pop Density:** 1460.0
Land: 0.4 sq. mi.; **Water:** 0.0 sq. mi.
Name origin: For a grove of elm trees that grew nearby.

Greenwood — Village
ZIP: 68366 **Lat:** 40-57-41 N **Long:** 96-26-33 W
Pop: 531 (1990); 587 (1980) **Pop Density:** 1327.5
Land: 0.4 sq. mi.; **Water:** 0.0 sq. mi.
Name origin: For nearby Greenwood Creek, which was named for an early settler.

Louisville — Village
ZIP: 68037 **Lat:** 40-59-55 N **Long:** 96-09-37 W
Pop: 998 (1990); 1,022 (1980) **Pop Density:** 2495.0
Land: 0.4 sq. mi.; **Water:** 0.0 sq. mi. **Elev:** 1044 ft.
Established 1857.
Name origin: Probably named for Louisville, KY.

Manley — Village
ZIP: 68403 **Lat:** 40-55-07 N **Long:** 96-09-54 W
Pop: 170 (1990); 124 (1980) **Pop Density:** 1700.0
Land: 0.1 sq. mi.; **Water:** 0.0 sq. mi.

Murdock — Village
ZIP: 68407 **Lat:** 40-55-33 N **Long:** 96-16-49 W
Pop: 267 (1990); 242 (1980) **Pop Density:** 2670.0
Land: 0.1 sq. mi.; **Water:** 0.0 sq. mi.
Name origin: For a member of the townsite company that established this village.

Murray — Village
ZIP: 68409 **Lat:** 40-54-59 N **Long:** 95-55-40 W
Pop: 418 (1990); 465 (1980) **Pop Density:** 2090.0
Land: 0.2 sq. mi.; **Water:** 0.0 sq. mi.
Name origin: For the Rev. George L. Murray, a United Presbyterian minister and influential man in the town. Originally called Fairview.

Nehawka — Village
ZIP: 68413 **Lat:** 40-49-47 N **Long:** 95-59-21 W
Pop: 260 (1990); 270 (1980) **Pop Density:** 1300.0
Land: 0.2 sq. mi.; **Water:** 0.0 sq. mi. **Elev:** 992 ft.

Plattsmouth — City
ZIP: 68048 **Lat:** 41-00-27 N **Long:** 95-53-28 W
Pop: 6,412 (1990); 6,295 (1980) **Pop Density:** 2374.8
Land: 2.7 sq. mi.; **Water:** 0.0 sq. mi.

South Bend — Village
ZIP: 68058 **Lat:** 41-00-07 N **Long:** 96-14-46 W
Pop: 93 (1990); 107 (1980) **Pop Density:** 930.0
Land: 0.1 sq. mi.; **Water:** 0.0 sq. mi.
Laid out 1857.
Name origin: For its location on the south bend of the Platte River.

Union — Village
ZIP: 68455 **Lat:** 40-48-52 N **Long:** 95-55-14 W
Pop: 299 (1990); 307 (1980) **Pop Density:** 1495.0
Land: 0.2 sq. mi.; **Water:** 0.0 sq. mi.
Name origin: Named by townspeople for their sympathies with the North during the Civil War.

Weeping Water — City
ZIP: 68463 **Lat:** 40-52-03 N **Long:** 96-08-19 W
Pop: 1,008 (1990); 1,109 (1980) **Pop Density:** 1440.0
Land: 0.7 sq. mi.; **Water:** 0.0 sq. mi.
Name origin: For a nearby creek, which the French called *l'eau qui pleure* 'water that weeps'.

Cedar County
County Seat: Hartington (ZIP: 68739)

Pop: 10,131 (1990); 11,375 (1980)
Land: 740.3 sq. mi.; **Water:** 5.6 sq. mi.
Pop Density: 13.7
Area Code: 308

On the northeastern border of NE, west of Sioux City, IA; original county; organized Feb 12, 1855 (prior to statehood).

Name origin: For the cedar trees that are abundant locally.

Belden
Village
ZIP: 68717 **Lat:** 42-24-42 N **Long:** 97-12-27 W
Pop: 149 (1990); 151 (1980) **Pop Density:** 745.0
Land: 0.2 sq. mi.; **Water:** 0.0 sq. mi.

Name origin: For Scott Belden, who was a paymaster on the railroad from Sioux City to O'Neill.

Coleridge
Village
ZIP: 68727 **Lat:** 42-30-22 N **Long:** 97-12-08 W
Pop: 596 (1990); 673 (1980) **Pop Density:** 1192.0
Land: 0.5 sq. mi.; **Water:** 0.0 sq. mi.

Fordyce
Village
ZIP: 68736 **Lat:** 42-41-53 N **Long:** 97-21-45 W
Pop: 190 (1990); 148 (1980) **Pop Density:** 950.0
Land: 0.2 sq. mi.; **Water:** 0.0 sq. mi.

Name origin: For William B. Fordyce, a train dispatcher for the railroad.

Hartington
City
ZIP: 68739 **Lat:** 42-37-12 N **Long:** 97-15-53 W
Pop: 1,583 (1990); 1,730 (1980) **Pop Density:** 2261.4
Land: 0.7 sq. mi.; **Water:** 0.0 sq. mi.

Laurel
City
ZIP: 68745 **Lat:** 42-25-40 N **Long:** 97-05-38 W
Pop: 981 (1990); 1,031 (1980) **Pop Density:** 1090.0
Land: 0.9 sq. mi.; **Water:** 0.0 sq. mi.

Magnet
Village
ZIP: 68749 **Lat:** 42-27-26 N **Long:** 97-28-08 W
Pop: 69 (1990); 59 (1980) **Pop Density:** 690.0
Land: 0.1 sq. mi.; **Water:** 0.0 sq. mi.

Established 1893.

Name origin: Named by B.E. Smith for the magnet stone found here, saying that the place would "attract people as the magnet attracts iron."

Obert
Village
ZIP: 68762 **Lat:** 42-41-20 N **Long:** 97-01-37 W
Pop: 39 (1990); 44 (1980) **Pop Density:** 390.0
Land: 0.1 sq. mi.; **Water:** 0.0 sq. mi.

Name origin: For a railroad officer named Oberton; the name was shortened to Obert to avoid confusion with another town called Overton.

Randolph
City
ZIP: 68771 **Lat:** 42-22-38 N **Long:** 97-21-26 W
Pop: 983 (1990); 1,106 (1980) **Pop Density:** 1092.2
Land: 0.9 sq. mi.; **Water:** 0.0 sq. mi.

Name origin: Named by F. H. Peavey for Lord Randolph Churchill (1849–95) of England.

St. Helena
Village
Lat: 42-48-35 N **Long:** 97-14-55 W
Pop: 87 (1990); 111 (1980) **Pop Density:** 217.5
Land: 0.4 sq. mi.; **Water:** 0.0 sq. mi.

Wynot
Village
ZIP: 68792 **Lat:** 42-44-22 N **Long:** 97-10-10 W
Pop: 213 (1990); 222 (1980) **Pop Density:** 1065.0
Land: 0.2 sq. mi.; **Water:** 0.0 sq. mi.

Name origin: Said to be from the phrase "why not?"

Chase County
County Seat: Imperial (ZIP: 69033)

Pop: 4,381 (1990); 4,758 (1980)
Land: 894.5 sq. mi.; **Water:** 3.1 sq. mi.
Pop Density: 4.9
Area Code: 308

On the southwestern border of NE, southwest of North Platte; organized Apr 24, 1886 from Keith County.

Name origin: For Champion S. Chase (?–1898), mayor of Omaha, NE, and first attorney general of NE.

Imperial
City
ZIP: 69033 **Lat:** 40-30-58 N **Long:** 101-38-15 W
Pop: 2,007 (1990); 1,941 (1980) **Pop Density:** 802.8
Land: 2.5 sq. mi.; **Water:** 0.0 sq. mi. **Elev:** 3284 ft.

Lamar
Village
ZIP: 69035 **Lat:** 40-34-20 N **Long:** 101-58-46 W
Pop: 31 (1990); 60 (1980) **Pop Density:** 310.0
Land: 0.1 sq. mi.; **Water:** 0.0 sq. mi.

Wauneta
Village
ZIP: 69045 **Lat:** 40-24-59 N **Long:** 101-22-17 W
Pop: 675 (1990); 746 (1980) **Pop Density:** 843.8
Land: 0.8 sq. mi.; **Water:** 0.0 sq. mi.

Name origin: Named by early settlers for the popular song "Juanita"; the spelling was changed to Wauneta to avoid confusion with the town of Juniata.

Cherry County
County Seat: Valentine (ZIP: 69201)

Pop: 6,307 (1990); 6,758 (1980)
Land: 5960.7 sq. mi.; **Water:** 49.1 sq. mi.
Pop Density: 1.1
Area Code: 402

On the central northern border of NE; organized Feb 23, 1883 from unorganized territory. Claims to be the largest county in the U.S.

Name origin: For Lt. Samuel A. Cherry (?–1881), an army officer.

Cody
Village
ZIP: 69211 **Lat:** 42-56-13 N **Long:** 101-14-51 W
Pop: 177 (1990); 177 (1980) **Pop Density:** 177.0
Land: 1.0 sq. mi.; **Water:** 0.0 sq. mi.
Name origin: For Thomas Cody, a foreman of the water supply construction gang when the railroad was built here.

Crookston
Village
ZIP: 69212 **Lat:** 42-55-31 N **Long:** 100-45-10 W
Pop: 99 (1990); 86 (1980) **Pop Density:** 247.5
Land: 0.4 sq. mi.; **Water:** 0.0 sq. mi.
Platted 1894.
Name origin: For W.T. Crook, a yard master for the railroad.

Kilgore
Village
ZIP: 69216 **Lat:** 42-56-18 N **Long:** 100-57-24 W
Pop: 79 (1990); 76 (1980) **Pop Density:** 197.5
Land: 0.4 sq. mi.; **Water:** 0.0 sq. mi. **Elev:** 2919 ft.

Merriman
Village
ZIP: 69218 **Lat:** 42-55-15 N **Long:** 101-41-59 W
Pop: 151 (1990); 159 (1980) **Pop Density:** 151.0
Land: 1.0 sq. mi.; **Water:** 0.0 sq. mi.
Name origin: For John Merriman, a train master for the railroad. First spelled Merryman.

Nenzel
Village
ZIP: 69219 **Lat:** 42-55-36 N **Long:** 101-06-04 W
Pop: 8 (1990); 28 (1980) **Pop Density:** 26.7
Land: 0.3 sq. mi.; **Water:** 0.0 sq. mi.
Name origin: For George Nenzel, who owned the land on which the town was built.

Valentine
City
ZIP: 69201 **Lat:** 42-52-25 N **Long:** 100-32-59 W
Pop: 2,826 (1990); 2,829 (1980) **Pop Density:** 1570.0
Land: 1.8 sq. mi.; **Water:** 0.0 sq. mi.
Name origin: For U.S. congressman Edward Kimball Valentine of NE.

Wood Lake
Village
ZIP: 69221 **Lat:** 42-38-20 N **Long:** 100-14-12 W
Pop: 59 (1990); 89 (1980) **Pop Density:** 196.7
Land: 0.3 sq. mi.; **Water:** 0.0 sq. mi.

Cheyenne County
County Seat: Sidney (ZIP: 69162)

Pop: 9,494 (1990); 10,057 (1980)
Land: 1196.4 sq. mi.; **Water:** 0.1 sq. mi.
Pop Density: 7.9
Area Code: 402

On the southwestern border of NE, west of North Platte; organized Jun 6, 1871 from Lincoln County.

Name origin: For the Cheyenne Indians who once lived in the area.

Dalton
Village
ZIP: 69131 **Lat:** 41-24-27 N **Long:** 102-58-13 W
Pop: 282 (1990); 345 (1980) **Pop Density:** 940.0
Land: 0.3 sq. mi.; **Water:** 0.0 sq. mi. **Elev:** 4270 ft.
Name origin: For Dalton, MA.

Gurley
Village
ZIP: 69141 **Lat:** 41-19-13 N **Long:** 102-58-25 W
Pop: 198 (1990); 212 (1980) **Pop Density:** 990.0
Land: 0.2 sq. mi.; **Water:** 0.0 sq. mi.

Lodgepole
Village
ZIP: 69149 **Lat:** 41-08-54 N **Long:** 102-38-17 W
Pop: 368 (1990); 413 (1980) **Pop Density:** 736.0
Land: 0.5 sq. mi.; **Water:** 0.0 sq. mi.
Name origin: For nearby Lodgepole Creek, which got its name because Indians used to cut lodgepoles for their teepees from trees that grew near the stream.

Potter
Village
ZIP: 69156 **Lat:** 41-13-08 N **Long:** 103-18-51 W
Pop: 388 (1990); 369 (1980) **Pop Density:** 776.0
Land: 0.5 sq. mi.; **Water:** 0.0 sq. mi.

Sidney
City
ZIP: 69162 **Lat:** 41-08-01 N **Long:** 102-58-12 W
Pop: 5,959 (1990); 6,010 (1980) **Pop Density:** 1010.0
Land: 5.9 sq. mi.; **Water:** 0.0 sq. mi.
Name origin: For Sidney Dillon, an attorney for the Union Pacific Railroad Company.

Clay County
County Seat: Clay Center (ZIP: 68933)

Pop: 7,123 (1990); 8,106 (1980)   **Pop Density:** 12.4
Land: 573.1 sq. mi.; **Water:** 0.5 sq. mi.   **Area Code:** 402

In south-central NE, southeast of Grand Island; original county, organized Mar 7, 1855 (prior to statehood). According to Thorndale and Dollarhide's *Map Guide to the U.S. Federal Censuses, 1790–1920*, area originally called Clay County is now part of Lancaster and Gage counties, while present-day Clay county occupies area which was unattached in 1860.

Name origin: For Henry Clay (1777–1852), U.S. senator from KY, known as the "Great Pacificator" for his advocacy of compromise to avert national crises.

Clay Center   City
ZIP: 68933   **Lat:** 40-31-23 N **Long:** 98-03-17 W
Pop: 825 (1990); 962 (1980)   **Pop Density:** 1650.0
Land: 0.5 sq. mi.; **Water:** 0.0 sq. mi.

Name origin: Named in 1879 for its location at the center of the county.

Deweese   Village
ZIP: 68934   **Lat:** 40-21-15 N **Long:** 98-08-20 W
Pop: 74 (1990); 69 (1980)   **Pop Density:** 740.0
Land: 0.1 sq. mi.; **Water:** 0.0 sq. mi.

Name origin: For James W. Deweese, an attorney for the Burlington Railroad.

Edgar   City
ZIP: 68935   **Lat:** 40-22-06 N **Long:** 97-58-13 W
Pop: 600 (1990); 705 (1980)   **Pop Density:** 750.0
Land: 0.8 sq. mi.; **Water:** 0.0 sq. mi.

Not coextensive with the township.

Name origin: For the son of pioneer Ed Graham. Previously called Eden.

*Edgar   Township
ZIP: 68935   **Lat:** 40-23-30 N **Long:** 98-00-01 W
Pop: 687 (1990); 802 (1980)   **Pop Density:** 19.1
Land: 35.9 sq. mi.; **Water:** 0.0 sq. mi.

Eldorado   Township
    Lat: 40-39-44 N **Long:** 97-59-09 W
Pop: 159 (1990); 183 (1980)   **Pop Density:** 4.4
Land: 35.8 sq. mi.; **Water:** 0.0 sq. mi.

Fairfield   City
ZIP: 68938   **Lat:** 40-25-55 N **Long:** 98-06-11 W
Pop: 458 (1990); 543 (1980)   **Pop Density:** 654.3
Land: 0.7 sq. mi.; **Water:** 0.0 sq. mi.

Not coextensive with the township.

Name origin: Probably for either Fairfield, IL or IA. Previously called White Elm and Frankfort. Named changed to avoid confusion with another Frankfort in the state.

*Fairfield   Township
ZIP: 68938   **Lat:** 40-23-28 N **Long:** 98-06-32 W
Pop: 731 (1990); 819 (1980)   **Pop Density:** 20.2
Land: 36.1 sq. mi.; **Water:** 0.0 sq. mi.

Glenvil   Village
ZIP: 68941   **Lat:** 40-30-09 N **Long:** 98-15-17 W
Pop: 304 (1990); 363 (1980)   **Pop Density:** 1520.0
Land: 0.2 sq. mi.; **Water:** 0.0 sq. mi.

Not coextensive with the township.

Name origin: Shortened from Glenville to Glenvil to avoid confusion with other Glenvilles. Previously known as Georgetown and Dogtown, because at one time the town had more dogs than people; and Glenville.

*Glenvil   Township
ZIP: 68941   **Lat:** 40-29-07 N **Long:** 98-13-52 W
Pop: 444 (1990); 504 (1980)   **Pop Density:** 12.4
Land: 35.7 sq. mi.; **Water:** 0.0 sq. mi.

Harvard   City
ZIP: 68944   **Lat:** 40-37-09 N **Long:** 98-05-46 W
Pop: 976 (1990); 1,217 (1980)   **Pop Density:** 1394.3
Land: 0.7 sq. mi.; **Water:** 0.0 sq. mi.

Not coextensive with the township.

Name origin: Named by officials of the Chicago, Burlington & Quincy Railroad for Harvard University in MA.

*Harvard   Township
    Lat: 40-39-00 N **Long:** 98-06-12 W
Pop: 1,159 (1990); 1,410 (1980)   **Pop Density:** 32.6
Land: 35.6 sq. mi.; **Water:** 0.0 sq. mi.

Inland   Township
    Lat: 40-34-05 N **Long:** 98-13-15 W
Pop: 116 (1990); 107 (1980)   **Pop Density:** 3.2
Land: 35.7 sq. mi.; **Water:** 0.0 sq. mi.

Leicester   Township
ZIP: 68980   **Lat:** 40-39-04 N **Long:** 98-13-36 W
Pop: 381 (1990); 378 (1980)   **Pop Density:** 10.7
Land: 35.6 sq. mi.; **Water:** 0.0 sq. mi.

Lewis   Township
ZIP: 68975   **Lat:** 40-34-09 N **Long:** 98-00-01 W
Pop: 165 (1990); 200 (1980)   **Pop Density:** 4.6
Land: 35.6 sq. mi.; **Water:** 0.0 sq. mi.

Logan   Township
    Lat: 40-23-38 N **Long:** 97-52-52 W
Pop: 150 (1990); 235 (1980)   **Pop Density:** 4.1
Land: 36.2 sq. mi.; **Water:** 0.0 sq. mi.

Lone Tree   Township
ZIP: 68933   **Lat:** 40-28-35 N **Long:** 98-05-57 W
Pop: 128 (1990); 132 (1980)   **Pop Density:** 3.6
Land: 35.4 sq. mi.; **Water:** 0.3 sq. mi.

Lynn   Township
ZIP: 68933   **Lat:** 40-34-01 N **Long:** 98-06-09 W
Pop: 82 (1990); 105 (1980)   **Pop Density:** 2.3
Land: 35.7 sq. mi.; **Water:** 0.0 sq. mi.

Marshall   Township
ZIP: 68933   **Lat:** 40-28-25 N **Long:** 97-59-07 W
Pop: 54 (1990); 79 (1980)   **Pop Density:** 1.5
Land: 35.8 sq. mi.; **Water:** 0.0 sq. mi.

NEBRASKA, Clay County

Ong
Village
ZIP: 68452   Lat: 40-23-53 N Long: 97-50-20 W
Pop: 69 (1990); 104 (1980)   Pop Density: 230.0
Land: 0.3 sq. mi.; Water: 0.0 sq. mi.
Platted 1886.
Name origin: For Judge J.E. Ong, who owned the land on which the town was built. Previously called Greenberry for landowner Greenberry L. Fort.

Saronville
Village
ZIP: 68975   Lat: 40-36-10 N Long: 97-56-19 W
Pop: 38 (1990); 63 (1980)   Pop Density: 380.0
Land: 0.1 sq. mi.; Water: 0.0 sq. mi.
Name origin: For the village in Sweden. Previously called Saron.

School Creek
Township
ZIP: 68979   Lat: 40-38-57 N Long: 97-53-20 W
Pop: 215 (1990); 251 (1980)   Pop Density: 6.0
Land: 35.8 sq. mi.; Water: 0.0 sq. mi.

Sheridan
Township
Lat: 40-28-43 N Long: 97-52-56 W
Pop: 108 (1990); 128 (1980)   Pop Density: 3.0
Land: 36.0 sq. mi.; Water: 0.0 sq. mi.

Spring Ranch
Township
ZIP: 68934   Lat: 40-23-28 N Long: 98-13-11 W
Pop: 180 (1990); 174 (1980)   Pop Density: 5.1
Land: 35.6 sq. mi.; Water: 0.0 sq. mi.

Sutton
City
ZIP: 68975   Lat: 40-36-27 N Long: 97-51-30 W
Pop: 1,353 (1990); 1,416 (1980)   Pop Density: 1353.0
Land: 1.0 sq. mi.; Water: 0.0 sq. mi.   Elev: 1680 ft.
Settled c. 1870.
Name origin: For Sutton, MA.

*Sutton
Township
ZIP: 68975   Lat: 40-33-56 N Long: 97-52-39 W
Pop: 186 (1990); 221 (1980)   Pop Density: 5.3
Land: 35.1 sq. mi.; Water: 0.0 sq. mi.

Trumbull
Village
ZIP: 68980   Lat: 40-40-48 N Long: 98-16-21 W
Pop: 225 (1990); 216 (1980)   Pop Density: 562.5
Land: 0.4 sq. mi.; Water: 0.0 sq. mi.
Part of the town is also in Adams County.

Colfax County
County Seat: Schuyler (ZIP: 68661)

Pop: 9,139 (1990); 9,890 (1980)   Pop Density: 22.1
Land: 413.2 sq. mi.; Water: 5.4 sq. mi.   Area Code: 402
In east-central NE, northwest of Omaha; organized Feb 15, 1869 from Platte County.
Name origin: For Schuyler Colfax (1823–85), U.S. vice president under Ulysses S. Grant (1869–73).

Clarkson
City
ZIP: 68629   Lat: 41-43-28 N Long: 97-07-16 W
Pop: 699 (1990); 817 (1980)   Pop Density: 998.6
Land: 0.7 sq. mi.; Water: 0.0 sq. mi.
Platted 1886.
Name origin: For S. Clarkson, the first postmaster of Schuyler, NE, who helped establish an office here.

Howells
Village
ZIP: 68641   Lat: 41-43-24 N Long: 97-00-16 W
Pop: 615 (1990); 677 (1980)   Pop Density: 1025.0
Land: 0.6 sq. mi.; Water: 0.0 sq. mi.
Platted 1886.
Name origin: For prominent resident J.S. Howell.

Leigh
Village
ZIP: 68643   Lat: 41-42-14 N Long: 97-14-12 W
Pop: 447 (1990); 509 (1980)   Pop Density: 1117.5
Land: 0.4 sq. mi.; Water: 0.0 sq. mi.
Name origin: For the maiden name of A.M. Walling's wife, whose land was used for the townsite.

Richland
Village
Lat: 41-26-14 N Long: 97-12-50 W
Pop: 96 (1990); 114 (1980)   Pop Density: 480.0
Land: 0.2 sq. mi.; Water: 0.0 sq. mi.
Platted 1884.
Name origin: For its descriptive connotations. Previously called Spitley.

Rogers
Village
Lat: 41-27-52 N Long: 96-54-58 W
Pop: 89 (1990); 89 (1980)   Pop Density: 445.0
Land: 0.2 sq. mi.; Water: 0.0 sq. mi.
Platted 1866.

Schuyler
City
ZIP: 68661   Lat: 41-26-52 N Long: 97-03-35 W
Pop: 4,052 (1990); 4,151 (1980)   Pop Density: 2026.0
Land: 2.0 sq. mi.; Water: 0.0 sq. mi.
Name origin: For U.S. Vice President Schuyler Colfax.

Cuming County
County Seat: West Point (ZIP: 68788)

Pop: 10,117 (1990); 11,664 (1980)   **Pop Density:** 17.7
Land: 572.0 sq. mi.; **Water:** 2.5 sq. mi.   **Area Code:** 402
In east-central NE, northwest of Omaha; organized Mar 16, 1855 from Burt County.
Name origin: For Thomas B. Cuming (?–1858), acting governor of NE Territory (1854–55; 1857–58).

Bancroft — Village
ZIP: 68004   **Lat:** 42-00-37 N   **Long:** 96-34-22 W
Pop: 494 (1990); 552 (1980)   **Pop Density:** 1235.0
Land: 0.4 sq. mi.; **Water:** 0.0 sq. mi.
Not coextensive with the township.
Name origin: For American historian George Bancroft (1801–91).

*Bancroft — Township
ZIP: 68004   **Lat:** 42-02-37 N   **Long:** 96-36-52 W
Pop: 692 (1990); 811 (1980)   **Pop Density:** 19.3
Land: 35.8 sq. mi.; **Water:** 0.0 sq. mi.

Beemer — Village
ZIP: 68716   **Lat:** 41-55-49 N   **Long:** 96-48-34 W
Pop: 672 (1990); 853 (1980)   **Pop Density:** 1680.0
Land: 0.4 sq. mi.; **Water:** 0.0 sq. mi.
Not coextextensive with the township.
Name origin: For A.D. Beemer. Previously called Rockcreek.

*Beemer — Township
ZIP: 68716   **Lat:** 41-57-57 N   **Long:** 96-50-34 W
Pop: 948 (1990); 1,132 (1980)   **Pop Density:** 26.9
Land: 35.3 sq. mi.; **Water:** 0.4 sq. mi.

Bismarck — Township
Lat: 41-52-24 N   **Long:** 96-57-36 W
Pop: 240 (1990); 288 (1980)   **Pop Density:** 6.7
Land: 35.9 sq. mi.; **Water:** 0.0 sq. mi.

Blaine — Township
Lat: 42-02-24 N   **Long:** 96-57-58 W
Pop: 189 (1990); 213 (1980)   **Pop Density:** 5.3
Land: 35.8 sq. mi.; **Water:** 0.0 sq. mi.

Cleveland — Township
Lat: 42-03-05 N   **Long:** 96-44-16 W
Pop: 221 (1990); 298 (1980)   **Pop Density:** 6.2
Land: 35.7 sq. mi.; **Water:** 0.0 sq. mi.

Cuming — Township
Lat: 41-47-11 N   **Long:** 96-36-56 W
Pop: 282 (1990); 368 (1980)   **Pop Density:** 7.8
Land: 36.0 sq. mi.; **Water:** 0.0 sq. mi.

Elkhorn — Township
Lat: 41-52-21 N   **Long:** 96-50-44 W
Pop: 329 (1990); 418 (1980)   **Pop Density:** 9.2
Land: 35.8 sq. mi.; **Water:** 0.1 sq. mi.

Garfield — Township
Lat: 41-52-30 N   **Long:** 96-36-18 W
Pop: 320 (1990); 378 (1980)   **Pop Density:** 8.9
Land: 35.8 sq. mi.; **Water:** 0.0 sq. mi.

Grant — Township
Lat: 42-02-21 N   **Long:** 96-50-28 W
Pop: 163 (1990); 242 (1980)   **Pop Density:** 4.5
Land: 36.0 sq. mi.; **Water:** 0.0 sq. mi.

Lincoln — Township
Lat: 41-47-09 N   **Long:** 96-57-30 W
Pop: 256 (1990); 326 (1980)   **Pop Density:** 7.1
Land: 36.0 sq. mi.; **Water:** 0.0 sq. mi.

Logan — Township
Lat: 41-57-10 N   **Long:** 96-44-00 W
Pop: 274 (1990); 374 (1980)   **Pop Density:** 7.6
Land: 35.9 sq. mi.; **Water:** 0.0 sq. mi.

Monterey — Township
Lat: 41-47-12 N   **Long:** 96-50-28 W
Pop: 339 (1990); 440 (1980)   **Pop Density:** 9.4
Land: 36.1 sq. mi.; **Water:** 0.0 sq. mi.

Neligh — Township
Lat: 41-57-28 N   **Long:** 96-36-29 W
Pop: 241 (1990); 325 (1980)   **Pop Density:** 6.7
Land: 35.8 sq. mi.; **Water:** 0.0 sq. mi.

Sherman — Township
Lat: 41-50-39 N   **Long:** 96-42-57 W
Pop: 655 (1990); 532 (1980)   **Pop Density:** 16.5
Land: 39.8 sq. mi.; **Water:** 0.7 sq. mi.

St. Charles — Township
Lat: 41-48-35 N   **Long:** 96-45-28 W
Pop: 277 (1990); 324 (1980)   **Pop Density:** 9.6
Land: 29.0 sq. mi.; **Water:** 0.7 sq. mi.

West Point — City
ZIP: 68788   **Lat:** 41-50-15 N   **Long:** 96-42-26 W
Pop: 3,250 (1990); 3,609 (1980)   **Pop Density:** 1625.0
Land: 2.0 sq. mi.; **Water:** 0.0 sq. mi.
Name origin: For the fact that when it was first settled it was the most westerly populated point in the Elkhorn River valley.

Wisner — City
ZIP: 68791   **Lat:** 41-59-12 N   **Long:** 96-54-48 W
Pop: 1,253 (1990); 1,335 (1980)   **Pop Density:** 1253.0
Land: 1.0 sq. mi.; **Water:** 0.0 sq. mi.
Not coextensive with the township. Established c. 1865.
Name origin: For Samuel P. Wisner, vice president of the railroad company.

*Wisner — Township
ZIP: 68791   **Lat:** 41-57-39 N   **Long:** 96-57-43 W
Pop: 188 (1990); 251 (1980)   **Pop Density:** 5.5
Land: 34.3 sq. mi.; **Water:** 0.6 sq. mi.

NEBRASKA, Custer County

Custer County
County Seat: Broken Bow (ZIP: 68822)

Pop: 12,270 (1990); 13,877 (1980)
Land: 2575.8 sq. mi.; **Water:** 0.4 sq. mi.
Pop Density: 4.8
Area Code: 308

In south-central NE, east of North Platte; organized as Kountze County Feb 17, 1877 from unorganized territory.

Name origin: For Gen. George Armstrong Custer (1839–76), U.S. army officer and Indian fighter.

Algernon — Township
ZIP: 68855   **Lat:** 41-13-20 N   **Long:** 99-18-02 W
Pop: 320 (1990); 470 (1980)   **Pop Density:** 3.5
Land: 92.4 sq. mi.; **Water:** 0.0 sq. mi.

Anselmo — Village
ZIP: 68813   **Lat:** 41-37-06 N   **Long:** 99-51-51 W
Pop: 189 (1990); 187 (1980)   **Pop Density:** 630.0
Land: 0.3 sq. mi.; **Water:** 0.0 sq. mi.
Platted 1886.
Name origin: For Anselmo B. Smith, a civil engineer for the Lincoln Town-Site Company.

Ansley — Village
ZIP: 68814   **Lat:** 41-17-15 N   **Long:** 99-22-55 W
Pop: 555 (1990); 644 (1980)   **Pop Density:** 925.0
Land: 0.6 sq. mi.; **Water:** 0.0 sq. mi.
No coextensive with the township. Settled 1886.
Name origin: For a lady who invested in real estate when the town was founded.

*Ansley — Township
Lat: 41-17-18 N   **Long:** 99-23-43 W
Pop: 732 (1990); 823 (1980)   **Pop Density:** 14.3
Land: 51.1 sq. mi.; **Water:** 0.0 sq. mi.

Arnold — Village
ZIP: 69120   **Lat:** 41-25-25 N   **Long:** 100-11-37 W
Pop: 679 (1990); 813 (1980)   **Pop Density:** 848.8
Land: 0.8 sq. mi.; **Water:** 0.0 sq. mi.
Not coextensive with the township. Laid out 1883.
Name origin: For George Arnold, who settled in the area c. 1875.

*Arnold — Township
ZIP: 69120   **Lat:** 41-27-15 N   **Long:** 100-10-08 W
Pop: 921 (1990); 1,134 (1980)   **Pop Density:** 6.7
Land: 138.0 sq. mi.; **Water:** 0.1 sq. mi.

Berwyn — Village
ZIP: 68819   **Lat:** 41-21-04 N   **Long:** 99-30-00 W
Pop: 122 (1990); 104 (1980)   **Pop Density:** 406.7
Land: 0.3 sq. mi.; **Water:** 0.0 sq. mi.
Not coextensive with the township.
Name origin: For a railroad surveyor. Originally called Janesville.

*Berwyn — Township
Lat: 41-19-54 N   **Long:** 99-29-59 W
Pop: 318 (1990); 321 (1980)   **Pop Density:** 4.2
Land: 74.9 sq. mi.; **Water:** 0.0 sq. mi.

Broken Bow — City
ZIP: 68822   **Lat:** 41-24-19 N   **Long:** 99-38-20 W
Pop: 3,778 (1990); 3,979 (1980)   **Pop Density:** 2361.3
Land: 1.6 sq. mi.; **Water:** 0.0 sq. mi.   **Elev:** 2475 ft.
Not coextensive with the township. Platted 1882.
Name origin: For a broken bow and arrow found at an Indian campsite near here.

*Broken Bow — Township
ZIP: 68822   **Lat:** 41-25-04 N   **Long:** 99-38-16 W
Pop: 744 (1990); 802 (1980)   **Pop Density:** 6.0
Land: 124.3 sq. mi.; **Water:** 0.1 sq. mi.

Callaway — Village
ZIP: 68825   **Lat:** 41-17-28 N   **Long:** 99-55-12 W
Pop: 539 (1990); 579 (1980)   **Pop Density:** 770.0
Land: 0.7 sq. mi.; **Water:** 0.0 sq. mi.
Platted 1885.
Name origin: For S.R. Callaway, general manager of the Union Pacific Railroad.

Cliff — Township
ZIP: 69120   **Lat:** 41-29-17 N   **Long:** 99-58-17 W
Pop: 137 (1990); 153 (1980)   **Pop Density:** 1.4
Land: 99.5 sq. mi.; **Water:** 0.0 sq. mi.

Comstock — Village
ZIP: 68828   **Lat:** 41-33-28 N   **Long:** 99-14-33 W
Pop: 135 (1990); 168 (1980)   **Pop Density:** 450.0
Land: 0.3 sq. mi.; **Water:** 0.0 sq. mi.
Not coextensive with the township.
Name origin: For W.H. Comstock, who moved a store building from Wescott to this townsite.

*Comstock — Township
ZIP: 68828   **Lat:** 41-35-26 N   **Long:** 99-14-50 W
Pop: 212 (1990); 247 (1980)   **Pop Density:** 6.8
Land: 31.1 sq. mi.; **Water:** 0.0 sq. mi.

Corner — Township
ZIP: 68874   **Lat:** 41-41-52 N   **Long:** 99-15-50 W
Pop: 22 (1990); 47 (1980)   **Pop Density:** 0.6
Land: 35.6 sq. mi.; **Water:** 0.0 sq. mi.

Custer — Township
ZIP: 68825   **Lat:** 41-16-17 N   **Long:** 99-48-16 W
Pop: 68 (1990); 90 (1980)   **Pop Density:** 1.3
Land: 53.8 sq. mi.; **Water:** 0.0 sq. mi.

Delight — Township
ZIP: 68825   **Lat:** 41-15-08 N   **Long:** 99-57-33 W
Pop: 750 (1990); 798 (1980)   **Pop Density:** 9.7
Land: 77.1 sq. mi.; **Water:** 0.0 sq. mi.

Douglas Grove — Township
ZIP: 68828   **Lat:** 41-32-55 N   **Long:** 99-21-22 W
Pop: 106 (1990); 141 (1980)   **Pop Density:** 1.6
Land: 66.9 sq. mi.; **Water:** 0.0 sq. mi.

NEBRASKA, Custer County

East Custer — Township
ZIP: 68860 Lat: 41-15-37 N Long: 99-37-26 W
Pop: 49 (1990); 48 (1980) Pop Density: 0.9
Land: 53.9 sq. mi.; Water: 0.0 sq. mi.

Elim — Township
ZIP: 68825 Lat: 41-14-53 N Long: 100-08-24 W
Pop: 134 (1990); 196 (1980) Pop Density: 1.2
Land: 108.6 sq. mi.; Water: 0.0 sq. mi.

Elk Creek — Township
ZIP: 68855 Lat: 41-06-13 N Long: 99-19-24 W
Pop: 153 (1990); 187 (1980) Pop Density: 1.6
Land: 95.0 sq. mi.; Water: 0.0 sq. mi.

Garfield — Township
ZIP: 68822 Lat: 41-30-30 N Long: 99-31-40 W
Pop: 102 (1990); 122 (1980) Pop Density: 1.5
Land: 65.9 sq. mi.; Water: 0.0 sq. mi.

Grant — Township
ZIP: 68825 Lat: 41-07-00 N Long: 99-58-03 W
Pop: 53 (1990); 71 (1980) Pop Density: 0.7
Land: 79.8 sq. mi.; Water: 0.0 sq. mi.

Hayes — Township
ZIP: 68813 Lat: 41-38-35 N Long: 100-06-22 W
Pop: 41 (1990); 69 (1980) Pop Density: 0.2
Land: 181.2 sq. mi.; Water: 0.0 sq. mi.

Kilfoil — Township
ZIP: 68856 Lat: 41-29-19 N Long: 99-47-53 W
Pop: 658 (1990); 716 (1980) Pop Density: 5.7
Land: 115.3 sq. mi.; Water: 0.0 sq. mi.

Lillian — Township
Lat: 41-36-40 N Long: 99-32-21 W
Pop: 191 (1990); 220 (1980) Pop Density: 2.5
Land: 77.6 sq. mi.; Water: 0.0 sq. mi.

Loup — Township
ZIP: 68860 Lat: 41-07-56 N Long: 99-32-45 W
Pop: 165 (1990); 224 (1980) Pop Density: 1.2
Land: 143.0 sq. mi.; Water: 0.0 sq. mi.

Mason City — Village
ZIP: 68855 Lat: 41-13-20 N Long: 99-17-52 W
Pop: 160 (1990); 196 (1980) Pop Density: 320.0
Land: 0.5 sq. mi.; Water: 0.0 sq. mi.

Merna — Village
ZIP: 68856 Lat: 41-29-04 N Long: 99-45-38 W
Pop: 377 (1990); 389 (1980) Pop Density: 754.0
Land: 0.5 sq. mi.; Water: 0.0 sq. mi.
Name origin: For daughter of the first postmaster, Samuel Dunning.

Milburn — Township
Lat: 41-42-24 N Long: 99-38-28 W
Pop: 77 (1990); 93 (1980) Pop Density: 1.7
Land: 45.3 sq. mi.; Water: 0.0 sq. mi.

Myrtle — Township
Lat: 41-22-32 N Long: 99-15-44 W
Pop: 121 (1990); 149 (1980) Pop Density: 2.2
Land: 54.2 sq. mi.; Water: 0.0 sq. mi.

Oconto — Village
ZIP: 68860 Lat: 41-08-29 N Long: 99-45-39 W
Pop: 147 (1990); 176 (1980) Pop Density: 735.0
Land: 0.2 sq. mi.; Water: 0.0 sq. mi.

Ryno — Township
ZIP: 68825 Lat: 41-20-28 N Long: 99-48-31 W
Pop: 80 (1990); 107 (1980) Pop Density: 1.5
Land: 54.2 sq. mi.; Water: 0.0 sq. mi.

Sargent — City
ZIP: 68874 Lat: 41-38-27 N Long: 99-22-11 W
Pop: 710 (1990); 828 (1980) Pop Density: 788.9
Land: 0.9 sq. mi.; Water: 0.0 sq. mi.
Laid out 1883. Not coextensive with the township.
Name origin: Named by postmistress Mrs. George Sherman for friends in IL.

***Sargent** — Township
ZIP: 68874 Lat: 41-40-24 N Long: 99-22-13 W
Pop: 921 (1990); 1,060 (1980) Pop Density: 15.8
Land: 58.2 sq. mi.; Water: 0.0 sq. mi.

Spring Creek — Township
ZIP: 68881 Lat: 41-28-23 N Long: 99-16-41 W
Pop: 13 (1990); 31 (1980) Pop Density: 0.4
Land: 31.1 sq. mi.; Water: 0.0 sq. mi.

Triumph — Township
ZIP: 68825 Lat: 41-22-09 N Long: 99-59-50 W
Pop: 107 (1990); 130 (1980) Pop Density: 1.5
Land: 70.3 sq. mi.; Water: 0.0 sq. mi.

Victoria — Township
ZIP: 68813 Lat: 41-39-03 N Long: 99-48-44 W
Pop: 489 (1990); 496 (1980) Pop Density: 3.0
Land: 161.7 sq. mi.; Water: 0.1 sq. mi.

Wayne — Township
ZIP: 68860 Lat: 41-06-56 N Long: 100-08-35 W
Pop: 163 (1990); 188 (1980) Pop Density: 2.0
Land: 80.8 sq. mi.; Water: 0.0 sq. mi.

West Union — Township
ZIP: 68874 Lat: 41-41-41 N Long: 99-30-06 W
Pop: 99 (1990); 111 (1980) Pop Density: 2.4
Land: 41.7 sq. mi.; Water: 0.0 sq. mi.

Westerville — Township
ZIP: 68881 Lat: 41-24-43 N Long: 99-23-45 W
Pop: 172 (1990); 192 (1980) Pop Density: 2.5
Land: 68.9 sq. mi.; Water: 0.0 sq. mi.

Wood River — Township
ZIP: 68860 Lat: 41-07-44 N Long: 99-46-41 W
Pop: 374 (1990); 462 (1980) Pop Density: 2.6
Land: 142.9 sq. mi.; Water: 0.0 sq. mi.

NEBRASKA, Dakota County   American Places Dictionary

> ## Dakota County
> **County Seat: Dakota City (ZIP: 68731)**
>
> **Pop:** 16,742 (1990); 16,573 (1980)　　　　　　　　　　**Pop Density:** 63.4
> **Land:** 264.0 sq. mi.; **Water:** 3.4 sq. mi.　　　　　　**Area Code:** 402
> On the northeastern border of NE, south of Sioux City, IA; original county, organized Mar 7, 1855.
> **Name origin:** For the Dakota (also called the Sioux) Indian tribe.

Dakota City　　　　　　　　　　　　　City
ZIP: 68731　　　　**Lat:** 42-24-57 N **Long:** 96-25-02 W
Pop: 1,470 (1990); 1,440 (1980)　　**Pop Density:** 1336.4
Land: 1.1 sq. mi.; **Water:** 0.1 sq. mi.
Platted by the Dakota City Land Company 1855–56.
Name origin: For the Dakota Indians.

Emerson　　　　　　　　　　　　　　Village
ZIP: 68733　　　　**Lat:** 42-16-55 N **Long:** 96-43-27 W
Pop: 312 (1990); 312 (1980)　　　**Pop Density:** 3120.0
Land: 0.1 sq. mi.; **Water:** 0.0 sq. mi.
Platted 1883. Part of the town is also in Dixon and Thurston counties.
Name origin: For author Ralph Waldo Emerson (1803–82).

Homer　　　　　　　　　　　　　　Village
ZIP: 68030　　　　**Lat:** 42-19-19 N **Long:** 96-29-27 W
Pop: 553 (1990); 564 (1980)　　　**Pop Density:** 1382.5
Land: 0.4 sq. mi.; **Water:** 0.0 sq. mi.
Surveyed 1874.
Name origin: For the Greek epic poet Homer (9th–8th century B.C.).

Hubbard　　　　　　　　　　　　　Village
ZIP: 68741　　　　**Lat:** 42-23-07 N **Long:** 96-35-25 W
Pop: 199 (1990); 234 (1980)　　　**Pop Density:** 995.0
Land: 0.2 sq. mi.; **Water:** 0.0 sq. mi.　　**Elev:** 1172 ft.
Established 1880.
Name origin: For Judge Asahel W. Hubbard, president of the Covington, Columbus & Black Hills Railroad.

Jackson　　　　　　　　　　　　　　Village
ZIP: 68743　　　　**Lat:** 42-26-55 N **Long:** 96-33-57 W
Pop: 230 (1990); 287 (1980)　　　**Pop Density:** 1150.0
Land: 0.2 sq. mi.; **Water:** 0.0 sq. mi.　　**Elev:** 1120 ft.

South Sioux City　　　　　　　　　　　City
ZIP: 68776　　　　**Lat:** 42-27-57 N **Long:** 96-24-43 W
Pop: 9,677 (1990); 9,339 (1980)　　**Pop Density:** 2058.9
Land: 4.7 sq. mi.; **Water:** 0.3 sq. mi.
Name origin: For the Sioux Indians, who had a reservation near here.

> ## Dawes County
> **County Seat: Chadron (ZIP: 69337)**
>
> **Pop:** 9,021 (1990); 9,609 (1980)　　　　　　　　　　**Pop Density:** 6.5
> **Land:** 1396.3 sq. mi.; **Water:** 4.6 sq. mi.　　　　　**Area Code:** 308
> On the northwestern border of NE, northeast of Scottsbluff; organized Feb 19, 1885 from Sioux County.
> **Name origin:** For James William Dawes (1845–87), governor of NE (1883–87).

Chadron　　　　　　　　　　　　　　City
ZIP: 69337　　　　**Lat:** 42-49-37 N **Long:** 103-00-00 W
Pop: 5,588 (1990); 5,933 (1980)　　**Pop Density:** 1693.3
Land: 3.3 sq. mi.; **Water:** 0.0 sq. mi.
Platted 1885.
Name origin: For Pierre Chadron, a French-Indian trapper who lived in the area.

Crawford　　　　　　　　　　　　　City
ZIP: 69339　　　　**Lat:** 42-41-07 N **Long:** 103-24-51 W
Pop: 1,115 (1990); 1,542 (1980)　　**Pop Density:** 1238.9
Land: 0.9 sq. mi.; **Water:** 0.0 sq. mi.
Name origin: For poet, scout, and soldier Jack Crawford, who was stationed at Fort Robinson in the 1880s.

Marsland　　　　　　　　　　　　　Village
ZIP: 69354　　　　**Lat:** 42-26-40 N **Long:** 103-18-03 W
Pop: 10 (1990); 27 (1980)　　　　**Pop Density:** 20.0
Land: 0.5 sq. mi.; **Water:** 0.0 sq. mi.
Name origin: For Thomas Marsland, general freight agent of the Chicago, Burlington & Quincy Railroad.

Whitney　　　　　　　　　　　　　Village
ZIP: 69367　　　　**Lat:** 42-47-02 N **Long:** 103-15-24 W
Pop: 38 (1990); 72 (1980)　　　　**Pop Density:** 190.0
Land: 0.2 sq. mi.; **Water:** 0.0 sq. mi.
Name origin: For Peter Whitney, a townsite agent for the railroad. Previously called Dawes City and Earth Lodge.

Dawson County
County Seat: Lexington (ZIP: 68850)

Pop: 19,940 (1990); 22,304 (1980)   **Pop Density:** 19.7
Land: 1012.9 sq. mi.; **Water:** 6.4 sq. mi.   **Area Code:** 308
In south-central NE, west of Grand Island; organized Jan 11, 1860 from Buffalo County.
Name origin: For Jacob Dawson, first postmaster of Lancaster (now Lincoln).

Cozad — City
ZIP: 69130   **Lat:** 40-51-46 N **Long:** 99-59-11 W
Pop: 3,823 (1990); 4,453 (1980)   **Pop Density:** 2012.1
Land: 1.9 sq. mi.; **Water:** 0.0 sq. mi.
Settled 1873.
Name origin: For John J. Cozad, the leader of pioneers from OH.

Eddyville — Village
ZIP: 68834   **Lat:** 41-00-45 N **Long:** 99-37-23 W
Pop: 102 (1990); 121 (1980)   **Pop Density:** 340.0
Land: 0.3 sq. mi.; **Water:** 0.0 sq. mi.
Name origin: For Eddyville, IA.

Farnam — Village
ZIP: 69029   **Lat:** 40-42-22 N **Long:** 100-12-54 W
Pop: 188 (1990); 268 (1980)   **Pop Density:** 268.6
Land: 0.7 sq. mi.; **Water:** 0.0 sq. mi.
Established 1887.
Name origin: For railroad builder Henry W. Farnam.

Gothenburg — City
ZIP: 69138   **Lat:** 40-55-45 N **Long:** 100-09-40 W
Pop: 3,232 (1990); 3,479 (1980)   **Pop Density:** 1616.0
Land: 2.0 sq. mi.; **Water:** 0.0 sq. mi.   **Elev:** 2567 ft.
Name origin: Named by E.G. West for Gothenburg, Sweden.

Lexington — City
ZIP: 68850   **Lat:** 40-46-42 N **Long:** 99-44-31 W
Pop: 6,601 (1990); 7,040 (1980)   **Pop Density:** 2357.5
Land: 2.8 sq. mi.; **Water:** 0.0 sq. mi.
Name origin: For the Battle of Lexington in the Revolutionary War. Previously called Plum Creek.

Overton — Village
ZIP: 68863   **Lat:** 40-44-25 N **Long:** 99-32-13 W
Pop: 547 (1990); 633 (1980)   **Pop Density:** 1094.0
Land: 0.5 sq. mi.; **Water:** 0.0 sq. mi.
Name origin: Named in 1871 for a government official in charge of guarding workmen when they built the railroad here.

Sumner — Village
ZIP: 68878   **Lat:** 40-56-58 N **Long:** 99-30-25 W
Pop: 210 (1990); 254 (1980)   **Pop Density:** 700.0
Land: 0.3 sq. mi.; **Water:** 0.0 sq. mi.   **Elev:** 2370 ft.
Laid out 1890.
Name origin: For Sen. Charles Sumner of MA (1811–74).

Deuel County
County Seat: Chappell (ZIP: 69129)

Pop: 2,237 (1990); 2,462 (1980)   **Pop Density:** 5.1
Land: 439.9 sq. mi.; **Water:** 0.9 sq. mi.   **Area Code:** 308
On the southern border of NE, west of North Platte; organized Jan, 1889 from Cheyenne County.
Name origin: For Henry (or Harry) Porter Deuel (1836–1914), an early settler of Omaha and later a local railroad official.

Big Springs — Village
ZIP: 69122   **Lat:** 41-03-48 N **Long:** 102-04-28 W
Pop: 495 (1990); 505 (1980)   **Pop Density:** 1237.5
Land: 0.4 sq. mi.; **Water:** 0.0 sq. mi.   **Elev:** 3367 ft.

Chappell — City
ZIP: 69129   **Lat:** 41-05-38 N **Long:** 102-28-01 W
Pop: 979 (1990); 1,095 (1980)   **Pop Density:** 1958.0
Land: 0.5 sq. mi.; **Water:** 0.0 sq. mi.
Name origin: For John Chappell, president of the Union Pacific Railroad.

Dixon County
County Seat: Ponca (ZIP: 68770)

Pop: 6,143 (1990); 7,137 (1980)
Land: 476.4 sq. mi.; **Water:** 6.3 sq. mi.
Pop Density: 12.9
Area Code: 402

On the northeastern border of NE, west of Sioux City, IA; original county; organized Dec, 1858 (prior to statehood) from Dakota County.

Name origin: For an early settler.

Allen — Village
ZIP: 68710   **Lat:** 42-24-52 N **Long:** 96-50-34 W
Pop: 331 (1990); 390 (1980)   **Pop Density:** 827.5
Land: 0.4 sq. mi.; **Water:** 0.0 sq. mi.

Name origin: For pioneer Henry Allen, who homesteaded this land in 1870.

Clark — Township
Lat: 42-29-18 N **Long:** 96-56-48 W
Pop: 162 (1990); 214 (1980)   **Pop Density:** 4.5
Land: 36.1 sq. mi.; **Water:** 0.0 sq. mi.

Concord — Village
ZIP: 68728   **Lat:** 42-23-03 N **Long:** 96-59-19 W
Pop: 156 (1990); 145 (1980)   **Pop Density:** 1560.0
Land: 0.1 sq. mi.; **Water:** 0.0 sq. mi.

Not coextensive with the township.

Name origin: Named by railroad president Marvin Hughitt for the Revolutionary War battlesite in MA.

*Concord — Township
ZIP: 68728   **Lat:** 42-23-33 N **Long:** 96-57-20 W
Pop: 488 (1990); 532 (1980)   **Pop Density:** 13.6
Land: 35.9 sq. mi.; **Water:** 0.0 sq. mi.

Daily — Township
Lat: 42-33-54 N **Long:** 96-57-57 W
Pop: 117 (1990); 186 (1980)   **Pop Density:** 3.3
Land: 35.7 sq. mi.; **Water:** 0.0 sq. mi.

Dixon — Village
ZIP: 68732   **Lat:** 42-24-56 N **Long:** 96-59-40 W
Pop: 87 (1990); 127 (1980)   **Pop Density:** 435.0
Land: 0.2 sq. mi.; **Water:** 0.0 sq. mi.

Name origin: For the county.

Emerson — Village
Lat: 42-16-41 N **Long:** 96-43-42 W
Pop: 387 (1990); 460 (1980)   **Pop Density:** 1935.0
Land: 0.2 sq. mi.; **Water:** 0.0 sq. mi.

Platted 1883. Not coextensive with the town of the same name. Part of the town is also in Dakota and Thurston counties.

Name origin: For author Ralph Waldo Emerson (1803–82).

*Emerson — Township
Lat: 42-19-45 N **Long:** 96-45-19 W
Pop: 570 (1990); 689 (1980)   **Pop Density:** 21.5
Land: 26.5 sq. mi.; **Water:** 0.0 sq. mi.

Galena — Township
Lat: 42-28-53 N **Long:** 96-50-13 W
Pop: 306 (1990); 419 (1980)   **Pop Density:** 8.5
Land: 35.9 sq. mi.; **Water:** 0.1 sq. mi.

Hooker — Township
Lat: 42-41-10 N **Long:** 96-57-23 W
Pop: 218 (1990); 269 (1980)   **Pop Density:** 4.3
Land: 50.7 sq. mi.; **Water:** 2.1 sq. mi.

Logan — Township
Lat: 42-18-13 N **Long:** 96-57-44 W
Pop: 257 (1990); 314 (1980)   **Pop Density:** 7.2
Land: 35.9 sq. mi.; **Water:** 0.0 sq. mi.

Martinsburg — Village
Lat: 42-30-28 N **Long:** 96-49-53 W
Pop: 90 (1990); 100 (1980)   **Pop Density:** 900.0
Land: 0.1 sq. mi.; **Water:** 0.0 sq. mi.   **Elev:** 1252 ft.

Settled 1872.

Name origin: For early resident Jonathan Martin.

Maskell — Village
ZIP: 68751   **Lat:** 42-41-25 N **Long:** 96-58-53 W
Pop: 54 (1990); 76 (1980)   **Pop Density:** 270.0
Land: 0.2 sq. mi.; **Water:** 0.0 sq. mi.

Name origin: Named by Saint Paul Town-Site Company for A. H. Maskell, who owned land in the area.

Newcastle — Village
ZIP: 68757   **Lat:** 42-39-07 N **Long:** 96-52-29 W
Pop: 271 (1990); 348 (1980)   **Pop Density:** 903.3
Land: 0.3 sq. mi.; **Water:** 0.0 sq. mi.

Not coextensive with the township.

*Newcastle — Township
ZIP: 68757   **Lat:** 42-40-12 N **Long:** 96-51-05 W
Pop: 482 (1990); 557 (1980)   **Pop Density:** 12.7
Land: 37.9 sq. mi.; **Water:** 1.6 sq. mi.

Otter Creek — Township
Lat: 42-27-42 N **Long:** 96-45-09 W
Pop: 241 (1990); 307 (1980)   **Pop Density:** 9.0
Land: 26.8 sq. mi.; **Water:** 0.0 sq. mi.

Ponca — City
ZIP: 68770   **Lat:** 42-33-55 N **Long:** 96-42-32 W
Pop: 877 (1990); 1,057 (1980)   **Pop Density:** 1252.9
Land: 0.7 sq. mi.; **Water:** 0.0 sq. mi.

Not coextensive with the township. Surveyed 1856.

Name origin: For the Ponca Indians, who once lived in the area.

*Ponca — Township
ZIP: 68770   **Lat:** 42-35-19 N **Long:** 96-43-53 W
Pop: 439 (1990); 377 (1980)   **Pop Density:** 9.4
Land: 46.8 sq. mi.; **Water:** 2.4 sq. mi.

Silver Creek — Township
Lat: 42-34-44 N **Long:** 96-50-40 W
Pop: 164 (1990); 212 (1980)   **Pop Density:** 4.6
Land: 35.9 sq. mi.; **Water:** 0.0 sq. mi.

Spring Bank — Township
Lat: 42-23-30 N **Long:** 96-50-51 W
Pop: 539 (1990); 659 (1980)   **Pop Density:** 15.1
Land: 35.7 sq. mi.; **Water:** 0.0 sq. mi.

Wakefield — City
ZIP: 68784 Lat: 42-16-10 N Long: 96-52-01 W
Pop: 1,006 (1990); 991 (1980) Pop Density: 2515.0
Land: 0.4 sq. mi.; Water: 0.0 sq. mi.
Founded 1881. Part of the town is also in Wayne County.
Name origin: For L.W. Wakefield, an engineer for the railroad surveying party.

*Wakefield — Township
ZIP: 68784 Lat: 42-18-53 N Long: 96-51-02 W
Pop: 1,283 (1990); 1,345 (1980) Pop Density: 35.7
Land: 35.9 sq. mi.; Water: 0.0 sq. mi.

Waterbury — Village
ZIP: 68785 Lat: 42-27-25 N Long: 96-44-06 W
Pop: 95 (1990); 92 (1980) Pop Density: 950.0
Land: 0.1 sq. mi.; Water: 0.0 sq. mi.
Name origin: For a nearby spring that provided water for the railroad.

Dodge County
County Seat: Fremont (ZIP: 68025)

Pop: 34,500 (1990); 35,847 (1980) Pop Density: 64.5
Land: 534.5 sq. mi.; Water: 9.5 sq. mi. Area Code: 402
In east-central NE, northwest of Omaha; original county, organized Mar 6, 1855 (prior to statehood).
Name origin: For Augustus Caesar Dodge (1812–83), son of Henry Dodge. First U.S. senator from IA (1848–55) and an active supporter of the Kansas-Nebraska bill.

Cotterell — Township
Lat: 41-30-10 N Long: 96-43-20 W
Pop: 428 (1990); 427 (1980) Pop Density: 8.2
Land: 52.0 sq. mi.; Water: 1.6 sq. mi.

Cuming — Township
Lat: 41-41-41 N Long: 96-37-38 W
Pop: 285 (1990); 307 (1980) Pop Density: 8.1
Land: 35.4 sq. mi.; Water: 0.1 sq. mi.

Dodge — Village
ZIP: 68633 Lat: 41-43-17 N Long: 96-52-45 W
Pop: 693 (1990); 815 (1980) Pop Density: 1732.5
Land: 0.4 sq. mi.; Water: 0.0 sq. mi.
Platted 1886 by the Pioneer Town-Site Company.
Name origin: For settler George A. Dodge.

Elkhorn — Township
Lat: 41-25-35 N Long: 96-24-01 W
Pop: 425 (1990); 578 (1980) Pop Density: 13.0
Land: 32.6 sq. mi.; Water: 0.4 sq. mi.

Everett — Township
Lat: 41-36-35 N Long: 96-36-56 W
Pop: 250 (1990); 277 (1980) Pop Density: 7.0
Land: 35.6 sq. mi.; Water: 0.4 sq. mi.

Fremont — City
ZIP: 68025 Lat: 41-26-26 N Long: 96-29-31 W
Pop: 23,680 (1990); 23,979 (1980) Pop Density: 3534.3
Land: 6.7 sq. mi.; Water: 0.0 sq. mi.
In eastern NE on the Platte River, 33 mi. northwest of Omaha.
Name origin: For western explorer John C. Frémont (1813–90).

Hooper — City
ZIP: 68031 Lat: 41-36-44 N Long: 96-32-52 W
Pop: 850 (1990); 932 (1980) Pop Density: 1416.7
Land: 0.6 sq. mi.; Water: 0.0 sq. mi.
Not coextensive with the township.
Name origin: For the Hon. Samuel Hooper, a member of Congress during the Civil War.

*Hooper — Township
ZIP: 68031 Lat: 41-36-38 N Long: 96-30-08 W
Pop: 1,285 (1990); 1,425 (1980) Pop Density: 36.7
Land: 35.0 sq. mi.; Water: 0.6 sq. mi.

Inglewood — Village
ZIP: 68025 Lat: 41-25-00 N Long: 96-30-05 W
Pop: 286 (1990); 257 (1980) Pop Density: 1430.0
Land: 0.2 sq. mi.; Water: 0.0 sq. mi.

Logan — Township
Lat: 41-42-03 N Long: 96-29-49 W
Pop: 536 (1990); 601 (1980) Pop Density: 15.0
Land: 35.7 sq. mi.; Water: 0.0 sq. mi.

Maple — Township
Lat: 41-31-22 N Long: 96-36-32 W
Pop: 341 (1990); 376 (1980) Pop Density: 9.5
Land: 36.0 sq. mi.; Water: 0.0 sq. mi.

Nickerson — Village
ZIP: 68044 Lat: 41-32-06 N Long: 96-28-13 W
Pop: 291 (1990); 254 (1980) Pop Density: 727.5
Land: 0.4 sq. mi.; Water: 0.0 sq. mi.
Not coextensive with the township.
Name origin: For founder Reynolds K. Nickerson, a contractor for the railroad.

*Nickerson — Township
ZIP: 68044 Lat: 41-31-28 N Long: 96-29-53 W
Pop: 691 (1990); 634 (1980) Pop Density: 18.6
Land: 37.2 sq. mi.; Water: 0.4 sq. mi.

NEBRASKA, Dodge County

North Bend
City
Lat: 41-27-54 N Long: 96-46-59 W
Pop: 1,249 (1990); 1,368 (1980)   Pop Density: 1561.3
Land: 0.8 sq. mi.; Water: 0.0 sq. mi.
Name origin: For its location on the northernmost bend in the Platte River.

Pebble
Township
Lat: 41-42-25 N Long: 96-43-45 W
Pop: 532 (1990); 673 (1980)   Pop Density: 15.0
Land: 35.4 sq. mi.; Water: 0.5 sq. mi.

Platte
Township
Lat: 41-27-03 N Long: 96-33-56 W
Pop: 2,099 (1990); 2,172 (1980)   Pop Density: 61.0
Land: 34.4 sq. mi.; Water: 4.1 sq. mi.

Pleasant Valley
Township
Lat: 41-36-43 N Long: 96-50-36 W
Pop: 202 (1990); 286 (1980)   Pop Density: 5.6
Land: 36.0 sq. mi.; Water: 0.0 sq. mi.

Ridgeley
Township
Lat: 41-36-42 N Long: 96-43-59 W
Pop: 215 (1990); 251 (1980)   Pop Density: 6.0
Land: 36.0 sq. mi.; Water: 0.0 sq. mi.

Scribner
City
ZIP: 68057   Lat: 41-39-52 N Long: 96-39-53 W
Pop: 950 (1990); 1,011 (1980)   Pop Density: 1583.3
Land: 0.6 sq. mi.; Water: 0.0 sq. mi.
Name origin: For publisher Charles Scribner (1821–71).

Snyder
Village
ZIP: 68664   Lat: 41-42-16 N Long: 96-47-10 W
Pop: 280 (1990); 387 (1980)   Pop Density: 560.0
Land: 0.5 sq. mi.; Water: 0.0 sq. mi.
Platted 1886.
Name origin: For postmaster Conrad Schneider, who owned the townsite.

Uehling
Village
ZIP: 68063   Lat: 41-44-03 N Long: 96-30-19 W
Pop: 273 (1990); 273 (1980)   Pop Density: 1365.0
Land: 0.2 sq. mi.; Water: 0.0 sq. mi.
Platted 1906.
Name origin: For settler Theodore Uehling, who came to NE in 1860.

Union
Township
Lat: 41-30-38 N Long: 96-51-07 W
Pop: 262 (1990); 285 (1980)   Pop Density: 5.3
Land: 49.0 sq. mi.; Water: 1.3 sq. mi.

Webster
Township
Lat: 41-42-21 N Long: 96-50-55 W
Pop: 1,070 (1990); 1,197 (1980)   Pop Density: 29.6
Land: 36.2 sq. mi.; Water: 0.0 sq. mi.

Winslow
Village
ZIP: 68072   Lat: 41-36-31 N Long: 96-30-17 W
Pop: 140 (1990); 143 (1980)   Pop Density: 1400.0
Land: 0.1 sq. mi.; Water: 0.0 sq. mi.

Douglas County
County Seat: Omaha (ZIP: 68183)

Pop: 416,444 (1990); 397,038 (1980)   Pop Density: 1258.0
Land: 331.0 sq. mi.; Water: 8.6 sq. mi.   Area Code: 402
On the central eastern border of NE, west of Council Bluffs, IA; original county; organized 1854 (prior to statehood).
Name origin: For Stephen Arnold Douglas (1813–61), U.S. orator and statesman.

Bennington
Village
ZIP: 68007   Lat: 41-22-03 N Long: 96-09-24 W
Pop: 866 (1990); 631 (1980)   Pop Density: 2886.7
Land: 0.3 sq. mi.; Water: 0.0 sq. mi.
Name origin: For Bennington, VT.

Boys Town
Village
ZIP: 68010   Lat: 41-15-34 N Long: 96-07-52 W
Pop: 794 (1990); 622 (1980)   Pop Density: 397.0
Land: 2.0 sq. mi.; Water: 0.1 sq. mi.
Site of the institution for homeless boys founded by Father Flanagan (1886–1948).

Elkhorn
City
ZIP: 68022   Lat: 41-16-57 N Long: 96-14-10 W
Pop: 1,398 (1990); 1,344 (1980)   Pop Density: 1747.5
Land: 0.8 sq. mi.; Water: 0.0 sq. mi.
Incorporated 1856.
Name origin: For its location on the Elkhorn River.

Omaha
City
ZIP: 68108   Lat: 41-15-50 N Long: 96-00-42 W
Pop: 335,795 (1990); 313,939 (1980)   Pop Density: 3337.9
Land: 100.6 sq. mi.; Water: 3.0 sq. mi.
In eastern NE on the Missouri River, 15 mi. north of its confluence with the Platte River. Founded 1854. Leading cattle market and meat-packing center; manufacturing (food processing, frozen food production, meat packing); insurance; national center for telemarketing companies.
Name origin: For the Omaha or Maha tribe of Siouan linguistic stock. The name has been translated 'upstream people' or 'those going against the current or wind.' There is a French version *aux maha* 'of the Maha.' Or it is possibly a variant of Oto Indian *Nemaha* 'muddy water.'

Ralston
City
ZIP: 68127   Lat: 41-12-04 N Long: 96-02-12 W
Pop: 6,236 (1990); 5,143 (1980)   Pop Density: 3897.5
Land: 1.6 sq. mi.; Water: 0.0 sq. mi.

Skyline
CDP
Lat: 41-14-58 N Long: 96-14-57 W
Pop: 2,563 (1990)   Pop Density: 800.9
Land: 3.2 sq. mi.; Water: 0.1 sq. mi.

Valley
City
ZIP: 68064   Lat: 41-18-46 N   Long: 96-20-45 W
Pop: 1,775 (1990); 1,716 (1980)   Pop Density: 1775.0
Land: 1.0 sq. mi.; Water: 0.0 sq. mi.
Name origin: Previously called Platte Sanders for John Sanders.

Waterloo
Village
ZIP: 68069   Lat: 41-17-15 N   Long: 96-17-08 W
Pop: 479 (1990); 450 (1980)   Pop Density: 1197.5
Land: 0.4 sq. mi.; Water: 0.0 sq. mi.
Laid out 1871.
Name origin: For the battlefield in Belgium, site of Napoleon's final defeat.

Dundy County
County Seat: Benkelman (ZIP: 69021)

Pop: 2,582 (1990); 2,861 (1980)   Pop Density: 2.8
Land: 919.9 sq. mi.; Water: 0.9 sq. mi.   Area Code: 308
On the southern border of NE, west of McCook; organized Feb 27, 1873 from unorganized territory.
Name origin: For Elmer S. Dundy (1830–96), NE territorial legislator and jurist of the U.S. circuit court.

Benkelman
City
ZIP: 69021   Lat: 40-03-05 N   Long: 101-32-04 W
Pop: 1,193 (1990); 1,235 (1980)   Pop Density: 1704.3
Land: 0.7 sq. mi.; Water: 0.0 sq. mi.
Name origin: For settler J. G. Benkelman. Originally known as Collinsville for early settler Moses Collins.

Haigler
Village
ZIP: 69030   Lat: 40-00-44 N   Long: 101-56-18 W
Pop: 225 (1990); 225 (1980)   Pop Density: 1125.0
Land: 0.2 sq. mi.; Water: 0.0 sq. mi.
Name origin: For prominent landowner Jacob Haigler, who had a cattle business here.

Fillmore County
County Seat: Geneva (ZIP: 68361)

Pop: 7,103 (1990); 7,920 (1980)   Pop Density: 12.3
Land: 576.5 sq. mi.; Water: 0.2 sq. mi.   Area Code: 402
In southeastern NE, southwest of Lincoln; established Jan 26, 1856 from unorganized territory, organized 1871.
Name origin: For Millard Fillmore (1800–74), thirteenth U.S. president.

Belle Prairie
Township
ZIP: 68444   Lat: 40-23-39 N   Long: 97-32-16 W
Pop: 202 (1990); 218 (1980)   Pop Density: 5.6
Land: 36.0 sq. mi.; Water: 0.0 sq. mi.

Bennett
Township
Lat: 40-33-51 N   Long: 97-46-31 W
Pop: 94 (1990); 131 (1980)   Pop Density: 2.6
Land: 36.2 sq. mi.; Water: 0.0 sq. mi.

Bryant
Township
Lat: 40-23-39 N   Long: 97-45-55 W
Pop: 524 (1990); 617 (1980)   Pop Density: 14.5
Land: 36.1 sq. mi.; Water: 0.1 sq. mi.

Chelsea
Township
Lat: 40-28-52 N   Long: 97-32-16 W
Pop: 147 (1990); 167 (1980)   Pop Density: 4.1
Land: 35.7 sq. mi.; Water: 0.0 sq. mi.

Exeter
Village
ZIP: 68351   Lat: 40-38-40 N   Long: 97-26-57 W
Pop: 661 (1990); 807 (1980)   Pop Density: 944.3
Land: 0.7 sq. mi.; Water: 0.0 sq. mi.   Elev: 2552 ft.
Not coextensive with the township.
Name origin: For Exeter, NH, former hometown of early settlers.

*Exeter
Township
ZIP: 68351   Lat: 40-39-17 N   Long: 97-25-31 W
Pop: 796 (1990); 987 (1980)   Pop Density: 21.9
Land: 36.3 sq. mi.; Water: 0.0 sq. mi.

Fairmont
Village
ZIP: 68354   Lat: 40-38-07 N   Long: 97-35-03 W
Pop: 708 (1990); 767 (1980)   Pop Density: 1011.4
Land: 0.7 sq. mi.; Water: 0.0 sq. mi.
Not coextensive with the township.
Name origin: For its elevated location and view. Previously called Hesperia.

*Fairmont
Township
ZIP: 68354   Lat: 40-39-42 N   Long: 97-32-41 W
Pop: 829 (1990); 899 (1980)   Pop Density: 23.2
Land: 35.7 sq. mi.; Water: 0.0 sq. mi.

Franklin
Township
Lat: 40-23-41 N   Long: 97-25-33 W
Pop: 274 (1990); 323 (1980)   Pop Density: 7.6
Land: 36.0 sq. mi.; Water: 0.0 sq. mi.

NEBRASKA, Fillmore County

Geneva
City
ZIP: 68361 **Lat:** 40-31-39 N **Long:** 97-36-05 W
Pop: 2,310 (1990); 2,400 (1980) **Pop Density:** 1650.0
Land: 1.4 sq. mi.; **Water:** 0.0 sq. mi.
Name origin: Named by Emma, daughter of landowner J. A. McCaully, for Geneva, NY.

*Geneva
Township
ZIP: 68361 **Lat:** 40-34-02 N **Long:** 97-39-14 W
Pop: 1,486 (1990); 1,601 (1980) **Pop Density:** 41.3
Land: 36.0 sq. mi.; **Water:** 0.0 sq. mi.

Glengary
Township
Lat: 40-28-55 N **Long:** 97-25-29 W
Pop: 477 (1990); 517 (1980) **Pop Density:** 13.3
Land: 36.0 sq. mi.; **Water:** 0.0 sq. mi.

Grafton
Village
ZIP: 68365 **Lat:** 40-37-46 N **Long:** 97-42-54 W
Pop: 167 (1990); 185 (1980) **Pop Density:** 556.7
Land: 0.3 sq. mi.; **Water:** 0.0 sq. mi.
Not coextensive with the township.
Name origin: Probably named for Grafton, MA.

*Grafton
Township
ZIP: 68365 **Lat:** 40-39-35 N **Long:** 97-46-32 W
Pop: 302 (1990); 320 (1980) **Pop Density:** 8.3
Land: 36.3 sq. mi.; **Water:** 0.0 sq. mi.

Hamilton
Township
ZIP: 68444 **Lat:** 40-23-40 N **Long:** 97-39-31 W
Pop: 198 (1990); 208 (1980) **Pop Density:** 5.5
Land: 36.0 sq. mi.; **Water:** 0.0 sq. mi.

Liberty
Township
Lat: 40-34-07 N **Long:** 97-25-28 W
Pop: 138 (1990); 171 (1980) **Pop Density:** 3.8
Land: 36.2 sq. mi.; **Water:** 0.0 sq. mi.

Madison
Township
Lat: 40-34-04 N **Long:** 97-32-21 W
Pop: 582 (1990); 599 (1980) **Pop Density:** 16.3
Land: 35.7 sq. mi.; **Water:** 0.0 sq. mi.

Milligan
Village
ZIP: 68406 **Lat:** 40-29-59 N **Long:** 97-23-16 W
Pop: 328 (1990); 332 (1980) **Pop Density:** 1640.0
Land: 0.2 sq. mi.; **Water:** 0.0 sq. mi.
Name origin: For an official of the Kansas City & Omaha Railroad.

Momence
Township
Lat: 40-28-47 N **Long:** 97-45-57 W
Pop: 98 (1990); 136 (1980) **Pop Density:** 2.7
Land: 36.2 sq. mi.; **Water:** 0.0 sq. mi.

Ohiowa
Village
ZIP: 68416 **Lat:** 40-24-50 N **Long:** 97-27-06 W
Pop: 146 (1990); 135 (1980) **Pop Density:** 730.0
Land: 0.2 sq. mi.; **Water:** 0.0 sq. mi.
Name origin: A combination of Ohio and Iowa, the former home states of early settlers.

Shickley
Village
ZIP: 68436 **Lat:** 40-24-57 N **Long:** 97-43-24 W
Pop: 360 (1990); 413 (1980) **Pop Density:** 1200.0
Land: 0.3 sq. mi.; **Water:** 0.0 sq. mi.
Name origin: For Fillmore Schickley, owner of the townsite and an attorney for the railroad.

Stanton
Township
Lat: 40-28-47 N **Long:** 97-38-58 W
Pop: 817 (1990); 859 (1980) **Pop Density:** 22.8
Land: 35.9 sq. mi.; **Water:** 0.0 sq. mi.

Strang
Village
ZIP: 68444 **Lat:** 40-24-54 N **Long:** 97-35-13 W
Pop: 42 (1990); 59 (1980) **Pop Density:** 420.0
Land: 0.1 sq. mi.; **Water:** 0.0 sq. mi.
Name origin: For A.L. Strang, a local resident who donated a windmill for a town pump.

West Blue
Township
Lat: 40-39-25 N **Long:** 97-39-06 W
Pop: 139 (1990); 167 (1980) **Pop Density:** 3.8
Land: 36.2 sq. mi.; **Water:** 0.0 sq. mi.

Franklin County
County Seat: Franklin (ZIP: 68939)

Pop: 3,938 (1990); 4,377 (1980) **Pop Density:** 6.8
Land: 575.9 sq. mi.; **Water:** 0.2 sq. mi. **Area Code:** 308
On central southern border of NE, southwest of Grand Island; organized Mar 9, 1871 from Kearney County.
Name origin: For Benjamin Franklin (1706–90), U.S. patriot, diplomat, and statesman.

Antelope
Township
ZIP: 68981 **Lat:** 40-18-19 N **Long:** 98-53-41 W
Pop: 259 (1990); 312 (1980) **Pop Density:** 7.2
Land: 35.9 sq. mi.; **Water:** 0.0 sq. mi.

Ash Grove
Township
ZIP: 68939 **Lat:** 40-10-23 N **Long:** 99-07-33 W
Pop: 183 (1990); 214 (1980) **Pop Density:** 2.6
Land: 71.7 sq. mi.; **Water:** 0.0 sq. mi.

Bloomington
Village
ZIP: 68929 **Lat:** 40-05-36 N **Long:** 99-02-16 W
Pop: 129 (1990); 138 (1980) **Pop Density:** 161.3
Land: 0.8 sq. mi.; **Water:** 0.0 sq. mi.
Not coextensive with the township.
Name origin: Probably for Bloomington, IL.

*Bloomington
Township
ZIP: 68929 **Lat:** 40-05-22 N **Long:** 99-00-34 W
Pop: 298 (1990); 349 (1980) **Pop Density:** 4.2
Land: 71.8 sq. mi.; **Water:** 0.0 sq. mi.

Campbell — Village
ZIP: 68932 **Lat:** 40-17-48 N **Long:** 98-43-51 W
Pop: 432 (1990); 441 (1980) **Pop Density:** 1080.0
Land: 0.4 sq. mi.; **Water:** 0.0 sq. mi.
Name origin: For the town founder.

Franklin — City
ZIP: 68939 **Lat:** 40-05-47 N **Long:** 98-57-03 W
Pop: 1,112 (1990); 1,167 (1980) **Pop Density:** 1112.0
Land: 1.0 sq. mi.; **Water:** 0.0 sq. mi.
Settled 1879.
Name origin: For Benjamin Franklin (1706–90), diplomat, patriot, and statesman.

Grant — Township
ZIP: 68972 **Lat:** 40-10-31 N **Long:** 98-47-06 W
Pop: 186 (1990); 248 (1980) **Pop Density:** 2.6
Land: 72.0 sq. mi.; **Water:** 0.0 sq. mi.

Hildreth — Village
ZIP: 68947 **Lat:** 40-20-15 N **Long:** 99-02-45 W
Pop: 364 (1990); 394 (1980) **Pop Density:** 606.7
Land: 0.6 sq. mi.; **Water:** 0.0 sq. mi.
Name origin: For Carson Hildreth, who owned the land on which the village was built.

Lincoln — Township
ZIP: 68947 **Lat:** 40-17-58 N **Long:** 99-07-56 W
Pop: 167 (1990); 150 (1980) **Pop Density:** 4.7
Land: 35.9 sq. mi.; **Water:** 0.0 sq. mi.

Macon — Township
ZIP: 68939 **Lat:** 40-12-44 N **Long:** 99-00-49 W
Pop: 133 (1990); 167 (1980) **Pop Density:** 3.7
Land: 36.3 sq. mi.; **Water:** 0.0 sq. mi.

Marion — Township
ZIP: 68939 **Lat:** 40-10-59 N **Long:** 98-54-03 W
Pop: 193 (1990); 232 (1980) **Pop Density:** 2.7
Land: 71.1 sq. mi.; **Water:** 0.0 sq. mi.

Naponee — Village
ZIP: 68960 **Lat:** 40-04-26 N **Long:** 99-08-17 W
Pop: 97 (1990); 160 (1980) **Pop Density:** 485.0
Land: 0.2 sq. mi.; **Water:** 0.0 sq. mi.
Settled 1878.
Name origin: For Naponee, Canada.

North Franklin — Township
ZIP: 68932 **Lat:** 40-18-39 N **Long:** 98-47-33 W
Pop: 525 (1990); 521 (1980) **Pop Density:** 14.5
Land: 36.1 sq. mi.; **Water:** 0.0 sq. mi.

Riverton — Village
ZIP: 68972 **Lat:** 40-05-19 N **Long:** 98-45-33 W
Pop: 162 (1990); 212 (1980) **Pop Density:** 405.0
Land: 0.4 sq. mi.; **Water:** 0.0 sq. mi.
Settled 1871.
Name origin: Either for its location on the Republican River or for Riverton, IA.

Salem — Township
ZIP: 68947 **Lat:** 40-18-32 N **Long:** 99-01-06 W
Pop: 496 (1990); 536 (1980) **Pop Density:** 13.7
Land: 36.1 sq. mi.; **Water:** 0.0 sq. mi.

Turkey Creek — Township
ZIP: 68960 **Lat:** 40-02-34 N **Long:** 99-07-02 W
Pop: 178 (1990); 232 (1980) **Pop Density:** 4.9
Land: 36.0 sq. mi.; **Water:** 0.0 sq. mi.

Upland — Village
ZIP: 68981 **Lat:** 40-19-08 N **Long:** 98-54-05 W
Pop: 169 (1990); 192 (1980) **Pop Density:** 422.5
Land: 0.4 sq. mi.; **Water:** 0.0 sq. mi.

Washington — Township
ZIP: 68972 **Lat:** 40-02-50 N **Long:** 98-50-06 W
Pop: 208 (1990); 249 (1980) **Pop Density:** 2.9
Land: 72.0 sq. mi.; **Water:** 0.1 sq. mi.

Frontier County
County Seat: Stockville (ZIP: 69042)

Pop: 3,101 (1990); 3,647 (1980) **Pop Density:** 3.2
Land: 974.6 sq. mi.; **Water:** 5.5 sq. mi. **Area Code:** 308
In south-central NE, south of North Platte; organized Jan 17, 1872 from unorganized territory.
Name origin: For its location on the NE frontier at the time of naming.

Curtis — City
ZIP: 69025 **Lat:** 40-38-04 N **Long:** 100-30-51 W
Pop: 791 (1990); 1,014 (1980) **Pop Density:** 608.5
Land: 1.3 sq. mi.; **Water:** 0.0 sq. mi.
Name origin: For nearby Curtis Creek.

Eustis — Village
ZIP: 69028 **Lat:** 40-39-51 N **Long:** 100-01-43 W
Pop: 452 (1990); 460 (1980) **Pop Density:** 1130.0
Land: 0.4 sq. mi.; **Water:** 0.0 sq. mi.
Name origin: For P.S. Eustis, a passenger agent for the Burlington Railroad.

Maywood — Village
ZIP: 69038 **Lat:** 40-39-29 N **Long:** 100-37-20 W
Pop: 313 (1990); 332 (1980) **Pop Density:** 626.0
Land: 0.5 sq. mi.; **Water:** 0.0 sq. mi.
Name origin: For May Wood, daughter of Israel Wood, who owned the land on which the town was built. Originally known as Laird for James Laird.

Moorefield — Village
ZIP: 69039 **Lat:** 40-41-23 N **Long:** 100-23-59 W
Pop: 52 (1990); 36 (1980) **Pop Density:** 260.0
Land: 0.2 sq. mi.; **Water:** 0.0 sq. mi. **Elev:** 2824 ft.

NEBRASKA, Frontier County

Stockville
Village
ZIP: 69042 Lat: 40-31-59 N Long: 100-23-02 W
Pop: 32 (1990); 45 (1980) Pop Density: 106.7
Land: 0.3 sq. mi.; Water: 0.0 sq. mi.
Established 1872.

Furnas County
County Seat: Beaver City (ZIP: 68926)

Pop: 5,553 (1990); 6,486 (1980) Pop Density: 7.7
Land: 718.1 sq. mi.; Water: 2.4 sq. mi. Area Code: 308

On the central southern border of NE, east of McCook; organized Feb 27, 1873 from unorganized territory.

Name origin: For Col. Robert Wilkinson Furnas (1824–1905), an officer in the Civil War and governor of NE (1873–75).

Arapahoe
City
ZIP: 68922 Lat: 40-18-18 N Long: 99-53-53 W
Pop: 1,001 (1990); 1,107 (1980) Pop Density: 1001.0
Land: 1.0 sq. mi.; Water: 0.0 sq. mi.

Name origin: For the Arapahoe Indians; the name means 'traders.'

Beaver City
City
ZIP: 68926 Lat: 40-08-15 N Long: 99-49-38 W
Pop: 707 (1990); 775 (1980) Pop Density: 785.6
Land: 0.9 sq. mi.; Water: 0.0 sq. mi.

Cambridge
City
ZIP: 69022 Lat: 40-17-00 N Long: 100-10-13 W
Pop: 1,107 (1990); 1,206 (1980) Pop Density: 1845.0
Land: 0.6 sq. mi.; Water: 0.0 sq. mi.

Name origin: For Cambridge, MA. Previously called Medicine Creek.

Edison
Village
ZIP: 68936 Lat: 40-16-39 N Long: 99-46-32 W
Pop: 148 (1990); 210 (1980) Pop Density: 493.3
Land: 0.3 sq. mi.; Water: 0.0 sq. mi.

Hendley
Village
Lat: 40-07-51 N Long: 99-58-13 W
Pop: 42 (1990); 39 (1980) Pop Density: 210.0
Land: 0.2 sq. mi.; Water: 0.0 sq. mi.

Holbrook
Village
ZIP: 68948 Lat: 40-18-13 N Long: 100-00-37 W
Pop: 233 (1990); 297 (1980) Pop Density: 1165.0
Land: 0.2 sq. mi.; Water: 0.0 sq. mi.

Name origin: For a railroad official. Previously called Burton's Bend.

Oxford
Village
ZIP: 68967 Lat: 40-15-15 N Long: 99-38-08 W
Pop: 736 (1990); 864 (1980) Pop Density: 1226.7
Land: 0.6 sq. mi.; Water: 0.0 sq. mi.

Part of the town is also in Harlan County.

Name origin: The origin of the name is in dispute. Probably for a nearby ford in the Republican River where teams of oxen used to cross, or possibly for either Oxford, OH, or Oxford Univ. in England. Previously called Grand View.

Wilsonville
Village
ZIP: 69046 Lat: 40-06-41 N Long: 100-06-21 W
Pop: 136 (1990); 189 (1980) Pop Density: 453.3
Land: 0.3 sq. mi.; Water: 0.0 sq. mi. Elev: 2304 ft.

Name origin: For early settlers, the Wilson brothers.

Gage County
County Seat: Beatrice (ZIP: 68310)

Pop: 22,794 (1990); 24,456 (1980)　　　　**Pop Density:** 26.6
Land: 855.3 sq. mi.; **Water:** 4.7 sq. mi.　　　　**Area Code:** 402
On the southern border of NE, south of Lincoln; original county; organized Mar 16, 1855 (prior to statehood).
Name origin: For William D. Gage (1803–85), Methodist minister and a local official.

Adams　　　　Village
ZIP: 68301　　**Lat:** 40-27-22 N　**Long:** 96-30-40 W
Pop: 472 (1990); 395 (1980)　　**Pop Density:** 786.7
Land: 0.6 sq. mi.; **Water:** 0.0 sq. mi.
Not coextensive with the township.
Name origin: For settler John O. Adams, who founded the township in 1873.

*Adams　　　　Township
ZIP: 68301　　**Lat:** 40-28-28 N　**Long:** 96-30-38 W
Pop: 733 (1990); 664 (1980)　　**Pop Density:** 21.5
Land: 34.1 sq. mi.; **Water:** 0.2 sq. mi.

Barneston　　　　Village
ZIP: 68309　　**Lat:** 40-02-55 N　**Long:** 96-34-36 W
Pop: 122 (1990); 155 (1980)　　**Pop Density:** 305.0
Land: 0.4 sq. mi.; **Water:** 0.0 sq. mi.
Name origin: For Francis M. Barnes, who was a member of the townsite company that established the village.

*Barneston　　　　Township
Lat: 40-02-41 N　**Long:** 96-38-16 W
Pop: 224 (1990); 295 (1980)　　**Pop Density:** 6.2
Land: 35.9 sq. mi.; **Water:** 0.0 sq. mi.

Beatrice　　　　City
ZIP: 68310　　**Lat:** 40-16-11 N　**Long:** 96-44-44 W
Pop: 12,354 (1990); 12,891 (1980)　　**Pop Density:** 1871.8
Land: 6.6 sq. mi.; **Water:** 0.0 sq. mi.
In southeastern NE, 35 mi. south of Lincoln. Incorporated 1858.
Name origin: For Julia Beatrice Kinney, daughter of Judge J.F. Kinney of the UT Supreme Court.

Blakely　　　　Township
Lat: 40-18-18 N　**Long:** 96-51-50 W
Pop: 415 (1990); 405 (1980)　　**Pop Density:** 11.6
Land: 35.7 sq. mi.; **Water:** 0.1 sq. mi.

Blue Springs　　　　City
ZIP: 68318　　**Lat:** 40-08-13 N　**Long:** 96-39-45 W
Pop: 431 (1990); 521 (1980)　　**Pop Density:** 538.8
Land: 0.8 sq. mi.; **Water:** 0.0 sq. mi.
Not coextensive with the township. Established 1857.
Name origin: For its location on the Blue River and for the springs which feed the river.

Blue Springs-Wymore　　　　Township
Lat: 40-07-37 N　**Long:** 96-38-17 W
Pop: 2,215 (1990)　　**Pop Density:** 61.5
Land: 36.0 sq. mi.; **Water:** 0.0 sq. mi.

Clatonia　　　　Village
ZIP: 68328　　**Lat:** 40-27-53 N　**Long:** 96-51-04 W
Pop: 296 (1990); 273 (1980)　　**Pop Density:** 986.7
Land: 0.3 sq. mi.; **Water:** 0.0 sq. mi.
Not coextensive with the township. Originally part of Clay County.
Name origin: For Clatonia Creek, which traverses the northwestern corner of the county.

*Clatonia　　　　Township
ZIP: 68328　　**Lat:** 40-28-46 N　**Long:** 96-51-21 W
Pop: 502 (1990); 483 (1980)　　**Pop Density:** 14.0
Land: 35.9 sq. mi.; **Water:** 0.2 sq. mi.

Cortland　　　　Village
ZIP: 68331　　**Lat:** 40-30-22 N　**Long:** 96-42-20 W
Pop: 393 (1990); 403 (1980)　　**Pop Density:** 1965.0
Land: 0.2 sq. mi.; **Water:** 0.0 sq. mi.
Name origin: Probably for Cortland, NY.

Elm　　　　Township
Lat: 40-08-04 N　**Long:** 96-51-40 W
Pop: 196 (1990); 227 (1980)　　**Pop Density:** 5.6
Land: 35.3 sq. mi.; **Water:** 0.6 sq. mi.

Filley　　　　Village
ZIP: 68357　　**Lat:** 40-17-07 N　**Long:** 96-32-01 W
Pop: 157 (1990); 172 (1980)　　**Pop Density:** 1570.0
Land: 0.1 sq. mi.; **Water:** 0.0 sq. mi.
Not coextensive with the township. Founded 1882.
Name origin: For founder Elijah Filley.

*Filley　　　　Township
ZIP: 68357　　**Lat:** 40-18-12 N　**Long:** 96-30-37 W
Pop: 352 (1990); 366 (1980)　　**Pop Density:** 9.9
Land: 35.4 sq. mi.; **Water:** 0.4 sq. mi.

Glenwood　　　　Township
Lat: 40-02-42 N　**Long:** 96-51-26 W
Pop: 247 (1990); 321 (1980)　　**Pop Density:** 6.9
Land: 36.0 sq. mi.; **Water:** 0.3 sq. mi.

Grant　　　　Township
Lat: 40-23-36 N　**Long:** 96-51-19 W
Pop: 229 (1990); 238 (1980)　　**Pop Density:** 6.4
Land: 36.0 sq. mi.; **Water:** 0.1 sq. mi.

Hanover　　　　Township
Lat: 40-23-59 N　**Long:** 96-38-15 W
Pop: 260 (1990); 320 (1980)　　**Pop Density:** 7.3
Land: 35.7 sq. mi.; **Water:** 0.3 sq. mi.

Highland　　　　Township
ZIP: 68331　　**Lat:** 40-28-16 N　**Long:** 96-44-47 W
Pop: 691 (1990); 669 (1980)　　**Pop Density:** 19.5
Land: 35.5 sq. mi.; **Water:** 0.2 sq. mi.

Holt
Township
Lat: 40-23-31 N **Long:** 96-44-35 W
Pop: 512 (1990); 521 (1980) **Pop Density:** 14.3
Land: 35.8 sq. mi.; **Water:** 0.1 sq. mi.

Hooker
Township
Lat: 40-23-35 N **Long:** 96-31-03 W
Pop: 156 (1990); 197 (1980) **Pop Density:** 4.6
Land: 33.8 sq. mi.; **Water:** 0.3 sq. mi.

Island Grove
Township
Lat: 40-08-18 N **Long:** 96-31-43 W
Pop: 115 (1990); 166 (1980) **Pop Density:** 3.2
Land: 35.9 sq. mi.; **Water:** 0.0 sq. mi.

Liberty
Village
ZIP: 68381 **Lat:** 40-05-06 N **Long:** 96-28-58 W
Pop: 74 (1990); 105 (1980) **Pop Density:** 370.0
Land: 0.2 sq. mi.; **Water:** 0.0 sq. mi.
Not coextensive with the township.

*Liberty
Township
Lat: 40-03-07 N **Long:** 96-31-02 W
Pop: 307 (1990); 395 (1980) **Pop Density:** 8.6
Land: 35.9 sq. mi.; **Water:** 0.2 sq. mi.

Lincoln
Township
Lat: 40-13-08 N **Long:** 96-51-02 W
Pop: 180 (1990); 241 (1980) **Pop Density:** 5.0
Land: 36.0 sq. mi.; **Water:** 0.0 sq. mi.

Logan
Township
Lat: 40-18-12 N **Long:** 96-37-33 W
Pop: 295 (1990); 316 (1980) **Pop Density:** 8.3
Land: 35.5 sq. mi.; **Water:** 0.3 sq. mi.

Midland
Township
Lat: 40-18-56 N **Long:** 96-44-37 W
Pop: 894 (1990); 1,146 (1980) **Pop Density:** 28.7
Land: 31.2 sq. mi.; **Water:** 0.1 sq. mi.

Nemaha
Township
ZIP: 68331 **Lat:** 40-28-38 N **Long:** 96-37-34 W
Pop: 238 (1990); 296 (1980) **Pop Density:** 6.6
Land: 35.8 sq. mi.; **Water:** 0.2 sq. mi.

Odell
Village
ZIP: 68415 **Lat:** 40-03-01 N **Long:** 96-48-02 W
Pop: 291 (1990); 322 (1980) **Pop Density:** 970.0
Land: 0.3 sq. mi.; **Water:** 0.0 sq. mi.
Founded 1880.
Name origin: For early settler Le Grand Odell.

Paddock
Township
Lat: 40-02-41 N **Long:** 96-45-07 W
Pop: 395 (1990); 411 (1980) **Pop Density:** 11.0
Land: 35.9 sq. mi.; **Water:** 0.2 sq. mi.

Pickrell
Village
ZIP: 68422 **Lat:** 40-22-40 N **Long:** 96-43-42 W
Pop: 201 (1990); 184 (1980) **Pop Density:** 2010.0
Land: 0.1 sq. mi.; **Water:** 0.0 sq. mi.
Established 1884.
Name origin: For William Pickrell, who owned part of the original townsite.

Riverside
Township
Lat: 40-13-18 N **Long:** 96-44-35 W
Pop: 501 (1990); 452 (1980) **Pop Density:** 14.7
Land: 34.0 sq. mi.; **Water:** 0.1 sq. mi.

Rockford
Township
Lat: 40-12-44 N **Long:** 96-38-00 W
Pop: 353 (1990); 375 (1980) **Pop Density:** 9.9
Land: 35.6 sq. mi.; **Water:** 0.3 sq. mi.

Sherman
Township
Lat: 40-13-05 N **Long:** 96-30-41 W
Pop: 226 (1990); 261 (1980) **Pop Density:** 6.3
Land: 35.9 sq. mi.; **Water:** 0.1 sq. mi.

Sicily
Township
ZIP: 68466 **Lat:** 40-08-22 N **Long:** 96-44-43 W
Pop: 204 (1990); 233 (1980) **Pop Density:** 5.7
Land: 36.0 sq. mi.; **Water:** 0.2 sq. mi.

Virginia
Village
ZIP: 68458 **Lat:** 40-14-42 N **Long:** 96-29-55 W
Pop: 94 (1990); 90 (1980) **Pop Density:** 940.0
Land: 0.1 sq. mi.; **Water:** 0.0 sq. mi.
Name origin: For Virginia Lewis.

Wymore
City
ZIP: 68466 **Lat:** 40-07-21 N **Long:** 96-39-59 W
Pop: 1,611 (1990); 1,841 (1980) **Pop Density:** 1006.9
Land: 1.6 sq. mi.; **Water:** 0.0 sq. mi.
Name origin: For Samuel Wymore, who donated land to the railroad.

Garden County
County Seat: Oshkosh (ZIP: 69154)

Pop: 2,460 (1990); 2,802 (1980)   **Pop Density:** 1.4
Land: 1704.5 sq. mi.; **Water:** 26.6 sq. mi.   **Area Code:** 308
In west-central NE, southeast of Scottsbluff; organized Nov 2, 1909 from Devel County.
Name origin: Named by John T. And William R. Twiford, the developers who thought it would become the "garden spot of the West."

Lewellen   *Village*
ZIP: 69147   **Lat:** 41-19-50 N   **Long:** 102-08-35 W
Pop: 307 (1990); 368 (1980)   **Pop Density:** 767.5
Land: 0.4 sq. mi.; **Water:** 0.0 sq. mi.
Name origin: For Frank Lewellen, who ran the first store and post office here c. 1887.

Oshkosh   *City*
ZIP: 69154   **Lat:** 41-24-30 N   **Long:** 102-20-39 W
Pop: 986 (1990); 1,057 (1980)   **Pop Density:** 1408.6
Land: 0.7 sq. mi.; **Water:** 0.0 sq. mi.
Name origin: Named by Alfred W. Grumaer for his former home in WI.

Garfield County
County Seat: Burwell (ZIP: 68823)

Pop: 2,141 (1990); 2,363 (1980)   **Pop Density:** 3.8
Land: 570.1 sq. mi.; **Water:** 1.3 sq. mi.   **Area Code:** 308
In east-central NE, northwest of Grand Island; organized Nov 8, 1881 from Wheeler County.
Name origin: For James Abram Garfield (1831–81), twentieth U.S. president.

Burwell   *City*
ZIP: 68823   **Lat:** 41-46-48 N   **Long:** 99-08-01 W
Pop: 1,278 (1990); 1,383 (1980)   **Pop Density:** 1278.0
Land: 1.0 sq. mi.; **Water:** 0.0 sq. mi.
Platted 1883.
Name origin: For Miss Burwell, fiancee of platter Frank Webster's brother. Previously called Webster's Town.

Gosper County
County Seat: Elwood (ZIP: 68937)

Pop: 1,928 (1990); 2,140 (1980)   **Pop Density:** 4.2
Land: 458.2 sq. mi.; **Water:** 4.6 sq. mi.   **Area Code:** 308
In south-central NE, organized Aug 29, 1873 from unorganized territory.
Name origin: For John J. Gosper, NE secretary of state (1873–75).

Elwood   *Village*
ZIP: 68937-76   **Lat:** 40-35-22 N   **Long:** 99-51-41 W
Pop: 679 (1990); 716 (1980)   **Pop Density:** 1358.0
Land: 0.5 sq. mi.; **Water:** 0.0 sq. mi.
Name origin: For farmer Elwood Thomas.

Smithfield   *Village*
Lat: 40-34-23 N   **Long:** 99-44-27 W
Pop: 53 (1990); 68 (1980)   **Pop Density:** 265.0
Land: 0.2 sq. mi.; **Water:** 0.0 sq. mi.   **Elev:** 2545 ft.
Name origin: For E.B. Smith, who owned the field on which the town was located.

NEBRASKA, Grant County   American Places Dictionary

Grant County
County Seat: Hyannis (ZIP: 69350)

Pop: 769 (1990); 877 (1980)
Land: 776.3 sq. mi.; **Water:** 7.0 sq. mi.
Pop Density: 1.0
Area Code: 308

In west-central NE, northwest of North Platte; organized Mar 31, 1888 from unorganized territory. In 1870 a "paper" county called Grant covered parts of present-day Lincoln, Frontier, Red Willow, Furnas, Gosper, Dawson, Hayes, and Hitchcock counties, much of which was known as Shorter County in 1860.

Name origin: For Ulysses Simpson Grant (1822–85), Civil War general and eighteenth U.S. president.

Hyannis — Village
ZIP: 69350   **Lat:** 42-00-01 N **Long:** 101-45-38 W
Pop: 210 (1990); 336 (1980)   **Pop Density:** 300.0
Land: 0.7 sq. mi.; **Water:** 0.0 sq. mi.
Name origin: For Hyannis, MA.

Greeley County
County Seat: Greeley (ZIP: 68842)

Pop: 3,006 (1990); 3,462 (1980)
Land: 569.9 sq. mi.; **Water:** 0.9 sq. mi.
Pop Density: 5.3
Area Code: 308

In east-central NE, north of Grand Island; organized Mar 1, 1871 from Boone County.

Name origin: For Horace Greeley (1811–72), editor who championed westward expansion.

Greeley Center — Village
Lat: 41-32-53 N **Long:** 98-31-47 W
Pop: 562 (1990); 597 (1980)   **Pop Density:** 936.7
Land: 0.6 sq. mi.; **Water:** 0.0 sq. mi.

Spalding — Village
ZIP: 68665   **Lat:** 41-41-18 N **Long:** 98-21-43 W
Pop: 592 (1990); 645 (1980)   **Pop Density:** 1973.3
Land: 0.3 sq. mi.; **Water:** 0.0 sq. mi.
Name origin: Established by an Irish Catholic association and named for its president, Bishop Spalding.

Scotia — Village
ZIP: 68875   **Lat:** 41-28-05 N **Long:** 98-42-08 W
Pop: 318 (1990); 349 (1980)   **Pop Density:** 1060.0
Land: 0.3 sq. mi.; **Water:** 0.0 sq. mi.
Name origin: Literary name for Scotland, an early settler's former homeland.

Wolbach — Village
ZIP: 68882   **Lat:** 41-24-02 N **Long:** 98-23-30 W
Pop: 280 (1990); 301 (1980)   **Pop Density:** 400.0
Land: 0.7 sq. mi.; **Water:** 0.0 sq. mi.
Name origin: For S.N. Wolbach, who once owned a great deal of land here.

Hall County
County Seat: Grand Island (ZIP: 68801)

Pop: 48,925 (1990); 47,690 (1980)
Land: 546.4 sq. mi.; **Water:** 5.8 sq. mi.
Pop Density: 89.5
Area Code: 308

In south-central NE, west of Lincoln; original county; organized Nov 4, 1858 (prior to statehood).

Name origin: For Augustus Hall (1814–61), U.S. representative from IA (1855–57) and chief justice of NE Territory (1858–61).

Alda — Village
ZIP: 68810   **Lat:** 40-51-52 N **Long:** 98-28-07 W
Pop: 540 (1990); 601 (1980)   **Pop Density:** 1800.0
Land: 0.3 sq. mi.; **Water:** 0.0 sq. mi.   **Elev:** 1916 ft.
Name origin: For the first white child born in the town. Previously called Pawnee.

*Alda — Township
ZIP: 68810   **Lat:** 40-49-49 N **Long:** 98-26-14 W
Pop: 872 (1990); 931 (1980)   **Pop Density:** 24.6
Land: 35.4 sq. mi.; **Water:** 0.6 sq. mi.

Cairo
Village
ZIP: 68824   **Lat:** 41-00-05 N **Long:** 98-36-27 W
Pop: 733 (1990); 737 (1980)   **Pop Density:** 1832.5
Land: 0.4 sq. mi.; **Water:** 0.0 sq. mi.
Name origin: Named by the Lincoln Land Company, probably for Cairo, Egypt.

Cameron
Township
ZIP: 68883   **Lat:** 40-54-58 N **Long:** 98-39-51 W
Pop: 204 (1990); 237 (1980)   **Pop Density:** 5.7
Land: 35.9 sq. mi.; **Water:** 0.0 sq. mi.

Center
Township
Lat: 40-54-26 N **Long:** 98-26-41 W
Pop: 1,018 (1990); 5,432 (1980)   **Pop Density:** 35.6
Land: 28.6 sq. mi.; **Water:** 0.1 sq. mi.

Doniphan
Village
ZIP: 68832   **Lat:** 40-46-24 N **Long:** 98-22-16 W
Pop: 736 (1990); 696 (1980)   **Pop Density:** 1840.0
Land: 0.4 sq. mi.; **Water:** 0.0 sq. mi.   **Elev:** 1940 ft.
Name origin: For Col. John Doniphan, an attorney for the railroad, or for Col. Alexander William Doniphan.

*Doniphan
Township
ZIP: 68832   **Lat:** 40-46-41 N **Long:** 98-19-48 W
Pop: 1,063 (1990); 1,082 (1980)   **Pop Density:** 20.4
Land: 52.1 sq. mi.; **Water:** 1.5 sq. mi.

Grand Island
City
ZIP: 68802   **Lat:** 40-55-18 N **Long:** 98-21-57 W
Pop: 39,386 (1990); 33,180 (1980)   **Pop Density:** 1911.9
Land: 20.6 sq. mi.; **Water:** 0.1 sq. mi.
In southeast-central NE on the Platte River, 90 mi. west of Lincoln. Platted in 1866.
Name origin: For the large island in the Platte River.

Harrison
Township
ZIP: 68883   **Lat:** 40-55-01 N **Long:** 98-33-03 W
Pop: 224 (1990); 295 (1980)   **Pop Density:** 6.2
Land: 36.2 sq. mi.; **Water:** 0.0 sq. mi.

Jackson
Township
ZIP: 68883   **Lat:** 40-47-51 N **Long:** 98-40-26 W
Pop: 439 (1990); 564 (1980)   **Pop Density:** 7.2
Land: 61.1 sq. mi.; **Water:** 1.5 sq. mi.

Lake
Township
Lat: 41-00-21 N **Long:** 98-19-42 W
Pop: 405 (1990); 439 (1980)   **Pop Density:** 13.5
Land: 29.9 sq. mi.; **Water:** 0.0 sq. mi.

Martin
Township
ZIP: 68883   **Lat:** 40-43-58 N **Long:** 98-34-22 W
Pop: 180 (1990); 191 (1980)   **Pop Density:** 4.7
Land: 38.2 sq. mi.; **Water:** 1.2 sq. mi.

Mayfield
Township
ZIP: 68824   **Lat:** 41-00-14 N **Long:** 98-32-51 W
Pop: 544 (1990); 578 (1980)   **Pop Density:** 15.3
Land: 35.5 sq. mi.; **Water:** 0.0 sq. mi.

Prairie Creek
Township
Lat: 40-59-47 N **Long:** 98-25-33 W
Pop: 302 (1990); 287 (1980)   **Pop Density:** 8.5
Land: 35.4 sq. mi.; **Water:** 0.0 sq. mi.

South Loup
Township
ZIP: 68824   **Lat:** 41-00-21 N **Long:** 98-40-00 W
Pop: 651 (1990); 657 (1980)   **Pop Density:** 18.3
Land: 35.5 sq. mi.; **Water:** 0.0 sq. mi.

South Platte
Township
ZIP: 68832   **Lat:** 40-44-30 N **Long:** 98-26-02 W
Pop: 433 (1990); 425 (1980)   **Pop Density:** 12.1
Land: 35.9 sq. mi.; **Water:** 0.5 sq. mi.

Washington
Township
Lat: 40-54-05 N **Long:** 98-19-36 W
Pop: 1,752 (1990); 1,687 (1980)   **Pop Density:** 73.6
Land: 23.8 sq. mi.; **Water:** 0.2 sq. mi.

Wood River
City
ZIP: 68883   **Lat:** 40-49-18 N **Long:** 98-35-52 W
Pop: 1,156 (1990); 1,334 (1980)   **Pop Density:** 1651.4
Land: 0.7 sq. mi.; **Water:** 0.0 sq. mi.
Not coextensive with the township. Established c. 1871.
Name origin: For its location on the banks of the Wood River.

*Wood River
Township
ZIP: 68883   **Lat:** 40-49-20 N **Long:** 98-33-33 W
Pop: 1,452 (1990); 1,705 (1980)   **Pop Density:** 34.2
Land: 42.5 sq. mi.; **Water:** 0.0 sq. mi.

Hamilton County
County Seat: Aurora (ZIP: 68818)

Pop: 8,862 (1990); 9,301 (1980)   **Pop Density:** 16.3
Land: 543.7 sq. mi.; **Water:** 3.1 sq. mi.   **Area Code:** 402
In south-central NE, east of Grand Island; organized Feb 16, 1867 from York County.
Name origin: For Alexander Hamilton (1757–1804), first U.S. secretary of the treasury (1789–95).

Aurora
City
ZIP: 68818   **Lat:** 40-51-56 N **Long:** 98-00-11 W
Pop: 3,810 (1990); 3,717 (1980)   **Pop Density:** 2116.7
Land: 1.8 sq. mi.; **Water:** 0.0 sq. mi.
Name origin: For Aurora, IL, former home of settler David Stone's wife.

Giltner
Village
ZIP: 68841   **Lat:** 40-46-27 N **Long:** 98-09-14 W
Pop: 367 (1990); 400 (1980)   **Pop Density:** 1223.3
Land: 0.3 sq. mi.; **Water:** 0.0 sq. mi.
Platted 1886.
Name origin: For the Rev. Henry M. Giltner, a Presbyterian minister and missionary. Previously called Bromfield.

NEBRASKA, Hamilton County

Hampton
Village
ZIP: 68843   Lat: 40-52-51 N   Long: 97-53-16 W
Pop: 432 (1990); 419 (1980)   Pop Density: 1440.0
Land: 0.3 sq. mi.; Water: 0.0 sq. mi.
Platted 1879.

Hordville
Village
ZIP: 68846   Lat: 41-04-47 N   Long: 97-53-25 W
Pop: 164 (1990); 155 (1980)   Pop Density: 546.7
Land: 0.3 sq. mi.; Water: 0.0 sq. mi.
Settled 1907.
Name origin: For T.B. Hord, who once owned land in this area.

Marquette
Village
ZIP: 68854   Lat: 41-00-21 N   Long: 98-00-34 W
Pop: 211 (1990); 303 (1980)   Pop Density: 1055.0
Land: 0.2 sq. mi.; Water: 0.0 sq. mi.
Platted 1882.
Name origin: For Thomas M. Marquette, a member of the Lincoln Land Company.

Phillips
Village
ZIP: 68865   Lat: 40-53-52 N   Long: 98-12-53 W
Pop: 316 (1990); 405 (1980)   Pop Density: 1580.0
Land: 0.2 sq. mi.; Water: 0.0 sq. mi.
Name origin: For Capt. R.O. Phillips, who established townsites for the Lincoln Land Company.

Stockham
Village
ZIP: 68818   Lat: 40-43-00 N   Long: 97-56-36 W
Pop: 64 (1990); 68 (1980)   Pop Density: 320.0
Land: 0.2 sq. mi.; Water: 0.0 sq. mi.
Platted 1887.
Name origin: For Joseph Stockham, a member of the town board of trustees.

Harlan County
County Seat: Alma (ZIP: 68920)

Pop: 3,810 (1990); 4,292 (1980)   Pop Density: 6.9
Land: 552.8 sq. mi.; Water: 21.4 sq. mi.   Area Code: 308
On the central southern border of NE, southwest of Kearney; organized Jun 3, 1871 from Lincoln County.
Name origin: For either Thomas Harlan, a local official, or for his uncle, James Harlan (1820-99), U.S. senator from IA (1855-65; 1867-73) and U.S. secretary of the interior (1865-66).

Albany
Township
Lat: 40-18-35 N   Long: 99-28-01 W
Pop: 68 (1990); 87 (1980)   Pop Density: 1.9
Land: 35.6 sq. mi.; Water: 0.0 sq. mi.

Alma
City
ZIP: 68920   Lat: 40-06-06 N   Long: 99-21-44 W
Pop: 1,226 (1990); 1,369 (1980)   Pop Density: 1532.5
Land: 0.8 sq. mi.; Water: 0.0 sq. mi.
Not coextensive with the township.
Name origin: For the daughter of N.P. Cook of the Cheyenne Colony.

*Alma
Township
ZIP: 68920   Lat: 40-07-32 N   Long: 99-20-42 W
Pop: 190 (1990); 148 (1980)   Pop Density: 5.6
Land: 34.1 sq. mi.; Water: 1.0 sq. mi.

Antelope
Township
Lat: 40-18-23 N   Long: 99-14-15 W
Pop: 148 (1990); 165 (1980)   Pop Density: 4.1
Land: 35.9 sq. mi.; Water: 0.0 sq. mi.

Eldorado
Township
ZIP: 68920   Lat: 40-02-49 N   Long: 99-27-27 W
Pop: 58 (1990); 93 (1980)   Pop Density: 1.6
Land: 36.1 sq. mi.; Water: 0.0 sq. mi.

Emerson
Township
Lat: 40-13-16 N   Long: 99-34-35 W
Pop: 320 (1990); 343 (1980)   Pop Density: 9.0
Land: 35.6 sq. mi.; Water: 0.4 sq. mi.

Fairfield
Township
ZIP: 68977   Lat: 40-02-26 N   Long: 99-34-02 W
Pop: 79 (1990); 66 (1980)   Pop Density: 2.2
Land: 35.5 sq. mi.; Water: 0.0 sq. mi.

Huntley
Village
ZIP: 68951   Lat: 40-12-38 N   Long: 99-17-27 W
Pop: 58 (1990); 64 (1980)   Pop Density: 193.3
Land: 0.3 sq. mi.; Water: 0.0 sq. mi.

Mullally
Township
ZIP: 68971   Lat: 40-08-03 N   Long: 99-13-54 W
Pop: 289 (1990); 347 (1980)   Pop Density: 8.0
Land: 36.0 sq. mi.; Water: 0.0 sq. mi.

Orleans
Village
ZIP: 68966   Lat: 40-07-53 N   Long: 99-27-14 W
Pop: 490 (1990); 527 (1980)   Pop Density: 816.7
Land: 0.6 sq. mi.; Water: 0.0 sq. mi.
Not coextensive with the township.
Name origin: For either Orleans, MA, or for Orleans, France. Previously called Melrose.

*Orleans
Township
ZIP: 68966   Lat: 40-07-57 N   Long: 99-27-35 W
Pop: 570 (1990); 637 (1980)   Pop Density: 16.1
Land: 35.3 sq. mi.; Water: 0.3 sq. mi.

American Places Dictionary NEBRASKA, Hayes County

Oxford
Village
Lat: 40-15-06 N **Long:** 99-37-34 W
Pop: 213 (1990); 245 (1980)   **Pop Density:** 710.0
Land: 0.3 sq. mi.; **Water:** 0.0 sq. mi.
Part of the town is also in Furnas County.
Name origin: The origin of the name is in dispute. Probably for a nearby ford in the Republican River where teams of oxen used to cross, or possibly for either Oxford, OH, or Oxford Univ. in England. Previously called Grand View.

Prairie Dog
Township
ZIP: 68920   **Lat:** 40-02-26 N **Long:** 99-21-02 W
Pop: 27 (1990); 36 (1980)   **Pop Density:** 1.0
Land: 26.3 sq. mi.; **Water:** 9.6 sq. mi.

Ragan
Village
ZIP: 68969   **Lat:** 40-18-38 N **Long:** 99-17-24 W
Pop: 59 (1990); 71 (1980)   **Pop Density:** 196.7
Land: 0.3 sq. mi.; **Water:** 0.0 sq. mi.

Republican City
Village
ZIP: 68971   **Lat:** 40-06-00 N **Long:** 99-13-20 W
Pop: 199 (1990); 231 (1980)   **Pop Density:** 663.3
Land: 0.3 sq. mi.; **Water:** 0.0 sq. mi.
Settled 1871.
Name origin: For its location on the Republican River.

*Republican City
Township
ZIP: 68971   **Lat:** 40-02-31 N **Long:** 99-13-56 W
Pop: 111 (1990); 101 (1980)   **Pop Density:** 4.3
Land: 26.1 sq. mi.; **Water:** 9.9 sq. mi.

Reuben
Township
Lat: 40-13-11 N **Long:** 99-27-22 W
Pop: 64 (1990); 73 (1980)   **Pop Density:** 1.8
Land: 35.5 sq. mi.; **Water:** 0.0 sq. mi.

Sappa
Township
ZIP: 68977   **Lat:** 40-07-57 N **Long:** 99-34-25 W
Pop: 317 (1990); 358 (1980)   **Pop Density:** 8.8
Land: 36.0 sq. mi.; **Water:** 0.0 sq. mi.

Scandinavia
Township
Lat: 40-18-30 N **Long:** 99-20-50 W
Pop: 112 (1990); 158 (1980)   **Pop Density:** 3.1
Land: 35.9 sq. mi.; **Water:** 0.0 sq. mi.

Spring Grove
Township
Lat: 40-18-50 N **Long:** 99-34-39 W
Pop: 81 (1990); 114 (1980)   **Pop Density:** 2.2
Land: 36.1 sq. mi.; **Water:** 0.0 sq. mi.

Stamford
Village
ZIP: 68977   **Lat:** 40-07-50 N **Long:** 99-35-41 W
Pop: 188 (1990); 214 (1980)   **Pop Density:** 376.0
Land: 0.5 sq. mi.; **Water:** 0.0 sq. mi.
Name origin: For Stamford, CT. Previously called Carisbrook.

Turkey Creek
Township
Lat: 40-13-04 N **Long:** 99-13-52 W
Pop: 73 (1990); 95 (1980)   **Pop Density:** 2.0
Land: 36.0 sq. mi.; **Water:** 0.0 sq. mi.

Washington
Township
Lat: 40-13-16 N **Long:** 99-20-23 W
Pop: 77 (1990); 102 (1980)   **Pop Density:** 2.1
Land: 36.0 sq. mi.; **Water:** 0.0 sq. mi.

Hayes County
County Seat: Hayes Center (ZIP: 69032)

Pop: 1,222 (1990); 1,356 (1980)   **Pop Density:** 1.7
Land: 713.1 sq. mi.; **Water:** 0.2 sq. mi.   **Area Code:** 308
In south-central NE, southwest of North Platte; organized Feb 19, 1877 from unorganized territory.
Name origin: For Rutherford Birchard Hayes (1822–93), nineteenth U.S. president.

Hamlet
Village
ZIP: 69031   **Lat:** 40-23-03 N **Long:** 101-14-05 W
Pop: 60 (1990); 74 (1980)   **Pop Density:** 200.0
Land: 0.3 sq. mi.; **Water:** 0.0 sq. mi.

Hayes Center
Village
ZIP: 69032   **Lat:** 40-30-40 N **Long:** 101-01-11 W
Pop: 259 (1990); 231 (1980)   **Pop Density:** 863.3
Land: 0.3 sq. mi.; **Water:** 0.0 sq. mi.
Established 1885.
Name origin: For its location at the center of the county.

Palisade
Village
Lat: 40-21-07 N **Long:** 101-06-19 W
Pop: 14 (1990); 401 (1980)   **Pop Density:** 140.0
Land: 0.1 sq. mi.; **Water:** 0.0 sq. mi.
Part of the town is also in Hitchcock County.

NEBRASKA, Hitchcock County

Hitchcock County
County Seat: Trenton (ZIP: 69044)

Pop: 3,750 (1990); 4,079 (1980)
Land: 710.1 sq. mi.; **Water:** 8.5 sq. mi.
Pop Density: 5.3
Area Code: 308

On the central southern border of NE, south of North Platte; organized Feb 27, 1873 from unorganized territory.

Name origin: For Phineas Warrener Hitchcock (1831–81), U.S. senator from NE (1871–77).

Culbertson — Village
ZIP: 69024 **Lat:** 40-13-42 N **Long:** 100-50-08 W
Pop: 795 (1990); 767 (1980) **Pop Density:** 883.3
Land: 0.9 sq. mi.; **Water:** 0.0 sq. mi.
Name origin: For Mr. Culbertson, an Indian agent.

Palisade — Village
ZIP: 69040 **Lat:** 40-20-50 N **Long:** 101-06-28 W
Pop: 367 (1990); 401 (1980) **Pop Density:** 1223.3
Land: 0.3 sq. mi.; **Water:** 0.0 sq. mi.
Part of the town is also in Hayes County.

Stratton — Village
ZIP: 69043 **Lat:** 40-09-05 N **Long:** 101-13-39 W
Pop: 427 (1990); 499 (1980) **Pop Density:** 1067.5
Land: 0.4 sq. mi.; **Water:** 0.0 sq. mi.
Founded 1883.
Name origin: For Mrs. Stratton, an early settler.

Trenton — Village
ZIP: 69044 **Lat:** 40-10-27 N **Long:** 101-00-47 W
Pop: 656 (1990); 796 (1980) **Pop Density:** 1093.3
Land: 0.6 sq. mi.; **Water:** 0.0 sq. mi.
Name origin: Probably for Trenton, NJ.

Holt County
County Seat: O'Neill (ZIP: 68763)

Pop: 12,599 (1990); 13,552 (1980)
Land: 2412.8 sq. mi.; **Water:** 5.0 sq. mi.
Pop Density: 5.2
Area Code: 402

In north-central NE; organized Jan 9, 1862 from Elkhorn County.

Name origin: For Joseph Holt (1807–94), U.S. Postmaster General (1859–61); secretary of war (1861), and judge advocate general for the U.S. army (1862–75).

Antelope — Township
ZIP: 68763 **Lat:** 42-28-47 N **Long:** 98-29-10 W
Pop: 67 (1990); 89 (1980) **Pop Density:** 1.9
Land: 36.0 sq. mi.; **Water:** 0.0 sq. mi.

Atkinson — City
ZIP: 68713 **Lat:** 42-31-54 N **Long:** 98-58-35 W
Pop: 1,380 (1990); 1,521 (1980) **Pop Density:** 1150.0
Land: 1.2 sq. mi.; **Water:** 0.0 sq. mi.
Not coextensive with the township. Settled 1876.
Name origin: For Col. John Atkinson of Detroit, who had large land holdings in the area.

*Atkinson — Township
ZIP: 68713 **Lat:** 42-35-14 N **Long:** 98-58-49 W
Pop: 1,942 (1990); 2,127 (1980) **Pop Density:** 24.0
Land: 80.9 sq. mi.; **Water:** 0.1 sq. mi.

Belle — Township
Lat: 42-38-43 N **Long:** 98-50-26 W
Pop: 60 (1990); 51 (1980) **Pop Density:** 1.7
Land: 35.9 sq. mi.; **Water:** 0.0 sq. mi.

Chambers — Village
ZIP: 68725 **Lat:** 42-12-18 N **Long:** 98-44-52 W
Pop: 341 (1990); 390 (1980) **Pop Density:** 341.0
Land: 1.0 sq. mi.; **Water:** 0.0 sq. mi.
Not coextensive with the township.
Name origin: Named by W.D. Matthews for his friend B.F. Chambers, registrar of the land office in a nearby town.

*Chambers — Township
ZIP: 68725 **Lat:** 42-13-08 N **Long:** 98-46-02 W
Pop: 570 (1990); 603 (1980) **Pop Density:** 7.9
Land: 72.1 sq. mi.; **Water:** 0.0 sq. mi.

Cleveland — Township
Lat: 42-45-30 N **Long:** 99-09-45 W
Pop: 82 (1990); 99 (1980) **Pop Density:** 1.0
Land: 85.8 sq. mi.; **Water:** 0.0 sq. mi.

Coleman — Township
Lat: 42-45-41 N **Long:** 98-43-33 W
Pop: 41 (1990); 64 (1980) **Pop Density:** 0.8
Land: 52.9 sq. mi.; **Water:** 0.1 sq. mi.

Conley — Township
Lat: 42-08-12 N **Long:** 98-47-13 W
Pop: 92 (1990); 112 (1980) **Pop Density:** 1.3
Land: 72.3 sq. mi.; **Water:** 0.0 sq. mi.

Deloit — Township
Lat: 42-07-30 N **Long:** 98-23-16 W
Pop: 159 (1990); 219 (1980) **Pop Density:** 2.9
Land: 54.2 sq. mi.; **Water:** 0.1 sq. mi.

Dustin — Township
Lat: 42-50-29 N **Long:** 98-59-27 W
Pop: 48 (1990); 62 (1980) **Pop Density:** 0.8
Land: 59.8 sq. mi.; **Water:** 0.0 sq. mi.

Emmet — Village
ZIP: 68734 Lat: 42-28-34 N Long: 98-48-35 W
Pop: 70 (1990); 73 (1980) Pop Density: 233.3
Land: 0.3 sq. mi.; Water: 0.0 sq. mi.
Not coextensive with the township.
Name origin: For Irish nationalist Robert Emmet (1778–1803).

*Emmet — Township
ZIP: 68734 Lat: 42-25-45 N Long: 98-49-02 W
Pop: 190 (1990); 188 (1980) Pop Density: 2.7
Land: 71.1 sq. mi.; Water: 0.1 sq. mi.

Ewing — Village
ZIP: 68735 Lat: 42-15-30 N Long: 98-20-33 W
Pop: 449 (1990); 520 (1980) Pop Density: 1122.5
Land: 0.4 sq. mi.; Water: 0.0 sq. mi.
Established 1874.
Name origin: For first postmaster James Ewing.

*Ewing — Township
ZIP: 68735 Lat: 42-13-00 N Long: 98-22-46 W
Pop: 543 (1990); 586 (1980) Pop Density: 10.0
Land: 54.2 sq. mi.; Water: 0.1 sq. mi.

Fairview — Township
Lat: 42-18-49 N Long: 98-54-37 W
Pop: 36 (1990); 84 (1980) Pop Density: 0.7
Land: 53.7 sq. mi.; Water: 0.1 sq. mi.

Francis — Township
Lat: 42-18-48 N Long: 99-03-23 W
Pop: 47 (1990); 67 (1980) Pop Density: 0.9
Land: 53.8 sq. mi.; Water: 0.2 sq. mi.

Golden — Township
Lat: 42-18-27 N Long: 98-23-20 W
Pop: 172 (1990); 202 (1980) Pop Density: 3.2
Land: 53.6 sq. mi.; Water: 0.1 sq. mi.

Grattan — Township
ZIP: 68763 Lat: 42-26-35 N Long: 98-40-01 W
Pop: 1,046 (1990); 1,037 (1980) Pop Density: 8.9
Land: 117.8 sq. mi.; Water: 0.0 sq. mi.

Green Valley — Township
Lat: 42-26-15 N Long: 99-07-02 W
Pop: 105 (1990); 133 (1980) Pop Density: 1.5
Land: 70.5 sq. mi.; Water: 0.3 sq. mi.

Holt Creek — Township
Lat: 42-18-43 N Long: 99-10-21 W
Pop: 39 (1990); 30 (1980) Pop Density: 0.7
Land: 52.7 sq. mi.; Water: 0.8 sq. mi.

Inman — Village
ZIP: 68742 Lat: 42-22-52 N Long: 98-31-44 W
Pop: 159 (1990); 181 (1980) Pop Density: 530.0
Land: 0.3 sq. mi.; Water: 0.0 sq. mi.
Not coextensive with the township. Established c. 1881.
Name origin: For early settler and storekeeper W.H. Inman.

*Inman — Township
ZIP: 68742 Lat: 42-20-08 N Long: 98-33-23 W
Pop: 439 (1990); 489 (1980) Pop Density: 4.6
Land: 95.6 sq. mi.; Water: 0.0 sq. mi.

Iowa — Township
Lat: 42-28-32 N Long: 98-21-30 W
Pop: 92 (1990); 86 (1980) Pop Density: 2.6
Land: 36.0 sq. mi.; Water: 0.0 sq. mi.

Josie — Township
Lat: 42-07-51 N Long: 99-10-26 W
Pop: 18 (1990); 15 (1980) Pop Density: 0.5
Land: 35.9 sq. mi.; Water: 0.0 sq. mi.

Lake — Township
Lat: 42-08-02 N Long: 98-34-58 W
Pop: 110 (1990); 120 (1980) Pop Density: 2.0
Land: 53.9 sq. mi.; Water: 0.3 sq. mi.

McClure — Township
Lat: 42-13-17 N Long: 98-33-23 W
Pop: 82 (1990); 84 (1980) Pop Density: 1.5
Land: 54.1 sq. mi.; Water: 0.0 sq. mi.

O'Neill — City
ZIP: 68763 Lat: 42-27-38 N Long: 98-38-47 W
Pop: 3,852 (1990); 4,049 (1980) Pop Density: 2027.4
Land: 1.9 sq. mi.; Water: 0.0 sq. mi.
Name origin: For Gen. O'Neill, who settled here in 1874.

Paddock — Township
Lat: 42-42-16 N Long: 98-35-17 W
Pop: 113 (1990); 160 (1980) Pop Density: 1.5
Land: 74.2 sq. mi.; Water: 0.6 sq. mi.

Page — Village
ZIP: 68766 Lat: 42-23-56 N Long: 98-25-02 W
Pop: 191 (1990); 172 (1980) Pop Density: 955.0
Land: 0.2 sq. mi.; Water: 0.0 sq. mi.
Name origin: For the town's first postmistress, Mrs. Selinda Page.

Pleasant View — Township
Lat: 42-34-03 N Long: 98-50-07 W
Pop: 111 (1990); 115 (1980) Pop Density: 3.1
Land: 35.8 sq. mi.; Water: 0.1 sq. mi.

Rock Falls — Township
Lat: 42-38-02 N Long: 98-42-16 W
Pop: 33 (1990); 37 (1980) Pop Density: 0.9
Land: 36.0 sq. mi.; Water: 0.0 sq. mi.

Sand Creek — Township
Lat: 42-43-03 N Long: 98-58-50 W
Pop: 92 (1990); 131 (1980) Pop Density: 1.1
Land: 81.3 sq. mi.; Water: 0.0 sq. mi.

Saratoga — Township
Lat: 42-45-53 N Long: 98-50-25 W
Pop: 66 (1990); 61 (1980) Pop Density: 1.2
Land: 53.5 sq. mi.; Water: 0.1 sq. mi.

Scott — Township
Lat: 42-42-03 N Long: 98-29-02 W
Pop: 64 (1990); 75 (1980) Pop Density: 1.0
Land: 66.1 sq. mi.; Water: 0.4 sq. mi.

Shamrock — Township
Lat: 42-18-48 N Long: 98-43-45 W
Pop: 32 (1990); 50 (1980) Pop Density: 0.6
Land: 54.4 sq. mi.; Water: 0.0 sq. mi.

Sheridan — Township
Lat: 42-26-32 N Long: 98-57-38 W
Pop: 239 (1990); 251 (1980) Pop Density: 3.0
Land: 80.3 sq. mi.; Water: 0.0 sq. mi.

Shields — Township
ZIP: 68763 Lat: 42-33-48 N Long: 98-39-02 W
Pop: 162 (1990); 150 (1980) Pop Density: 2.3
Land: 72.0 sq. mi.; Water: 0.0 sq. mi.

NEBRASKA, Holt County

Steel Creek
Township
Lat: 42-41-26 N Long: 98-22-02 W
Pop: 63 (1990); 95 (1980) **Pop Density:** 1.0
Land: 65.4 sq. mi.; **Water:** 0.4 sq. mi.

Stuart
Village
ZIP: 68780 Lat: 42-36-00 N Long: 99-08-24 W
Pop: 650 (1990); 641 (1980) **Pop Density:** 1083.3
Land: 0.6 sq. mi.; **Water:** 0.0 sq. mi.
Not coextensive with the township. Settled c. 1879.
Name origin: For Peter Stuart, who owned the townsite.

*Stuart
Township
ZIP: 68780 Lat: 42-35-09 N Long: 99-09-25 W
Pop: 1,058 (1990); 1,102 (1980) **Pop Density:** 7.8
Land: 134.8 sq. mi.; **Water:** 0.2 sq. mi.

Swan
Township
Lat: 42-11-23 N Long: 99-05-31 W
Pop: 75 (1990); 89 (1980) **Pop Density:** 0.7
Land: 106.7 sq. mi.; **Water:** 0.7 sq. mi.

Verdigris
Township
Lat: 42-23-20 N Long: 98-23-14 W
Pop: 452 (1990); 442 (1980) **Pop Density:** 8.4
Land: 53.8 sq. mi.; **Water:** 0.0 sq. mi.

Willowdale
Township
ZIP: 68763 Lat: 42-33-57 N Long: 98-25-55 W
Pop: 104 (1990); 94 (1980) **Pop Density:** 1.4
Land: 72.0 sq. mi.; **Water:** 0.0 sq. mi.

Wyoming
Township
Lat: 42-11-27 N Long: 98-56-12 W
Pop: 103 (1990); 104 (1980) **Pop Density:** 1.4
Land: 71.7 sq. mi.; **Water:** 0.2 sq. mi.

Hooker County
County Seat: Mullen (ZIP: 69152)

Pop: 793 (1990); 990 (1980) **Pop Density:** 1.1
Land: 721.2 sq. mi.; **Water:** 0.3 sq. mi. **Area Code:** 308
In west-central NE, northwest of North Platte; organized Mar 29, 1889 from unorganized territory.
Name origin: For Joseph Hooker (1814–79), famous Union general during the Civil War.

Mullen
Village
ZIP: 69152 Lat: 42-02-31 N Long: 101-02-35 W
Pop: 554 (1990); 720 (1980) **Pop Density:** 1385.0
Land: 0.4 sq. mi.; **Water:** 0.0 sq. mi.
Name origin: Named by railroad officials for a contractor who worked in the area.

Howard County
County Seat: St. Paul (ZIP: 68873)

Pop: 6,055 (1990); 6,773 (1980)   **Pop Density:** 10.6
Land: 569.5 sq. mi.; **Water:** 6.3 sq. mi.   **Area Code:** 308

In east-central NE, north of Grand Island; organized Mar 1, 1871 from Hall County.

Name origin: For Gen. Oliver Otis Howard (1830–1909), Union officer in the Seminole War and the Civil War; president of Howard University (1869–73). Others believe it was for Howard Paul, son of an early settler, whose family founded St. Paul, the county seat.

Cotesfield   Village
ZIP: 68829   **Lat:** 41-21-27 N   **Long:** 98-37-58 W
Pop: 60 (1990); 82 (1980)   **Pop Density:** 75.0
Land: 0.8 sq. mi.; **Water:** 0.0 sq. mi.

Cushing   Village
ZIP: 68873   **Lat:** 41-17-40 N   **Long:** 98-22-08 W
Pop: 25 (1990); 48 (1980)   **Pop Density:** 83.3
Land: 0.3 sq. mi.; **Water:** 0.0 sq. mi.
Name origin: For early settler James Cushing.

Dannebrog   Village
ZIP: 68831   **Lat:** 41-07-06 N   **Long:** 98-32-42 W
Pop: 324 (1990); 356 (1980)   **Pop Density:** 810.0
Land: 0.4 sq. mi.; **Water:** 0.0 sq. mi.
Name origin: Named by Danish settlers for the flag of Denmark.

Elba   Village
ZIP: 68835   **Lat:** 41-17-03 N   **Long:** 98-34-08 W
Pop: 196 (1990); 218 (1980)   **Pop Density:** 980.0
Land: 0.2 sq. mi.; **Water:** 0.0 sq. mi.
Founded 1882.
Name origin: For the "elbow curve" in the railroad to the south of town.

Farwell   Village
ZIP: 68838   **Lat:** 41-12-57 N   **Long:** 98-37-38 W
Pop: 152 (1990); 165 (1980)   **Pop Density:** 760.0
Land: 0.2 sq. mi.; **Water:** 0.0 sq. mi.

Howard City   Village
Lat: 41-04-30 N   **Long:** 98-42-54 W
Pop: 203 (1990); 228 (1980)   **Pop Density:** 290.0
Land: 0.7 sq. mi.; **Water:** 0.0 sq. mi.
Name origin: For the county.

St. Paul   City
Lat: 41-12-49 N   **Long:** 98-27-34 W
Pop: 2,009 (1990); 2,094 (1980)   **Pop Density:** 1826.4
Land: 1.1 sq. mi.; **Water:** 0.0 sq. mi.
Name origin: Named by U.S. senator Phineas W. Hitchcock for the first settlers, J.N. and N.J. Paul.

Jefferson County
County Seat: Fairbury (ZIP: 68352)

Pop: 8,759 (1990); 9,817 (1980)   **Pop Density:** 15.3
Land: 573.1 sq. mi.; **Water:** 2.5 sq. mi.   **Area Code:** 402

On the southern border of NE, southwest of Lincoln. Organized 1864; combined with Jones County 1867; both counties dissolved 1871 and eastern part (Jones County) named Jefferson. Original Jones County probably established Jan 26, 1856. Jefferson County attached to Gage County for judicial purposes between 1857 and 1864.

Name origin: For Thomas Jefferson (1743–1826), U.S. patriot and statesman; third U.S. president.

Daykin   Village
ZIP: 68338   **Lat:** 40-19-18 N   **Long:** 97-17-50 W
Pop: 188 (1990); 207 (1980)   **Pop Density:** 940.0
Land: 0.2 sq. mi.; **Water:** 0.0 sq. mi.
Name origin: For landowner John Daykin.

Diller   Village
ZIP: 68342   **Lat:** 40-06-31 N   **Long:** 96-56-15 W
Pop: 298 (1990); 311 (1980)   **Pop Density:** 745.0
Land: 0.4 sq. mi.; **Water:** 0.0 sq. mi.
Established 1881.
Name origin: For early settler H.H. Diller.

Endicott   Village
ZIP: 68350   **Lat:** 40-04-51 N   **Long:** 97-05-43 W
Pop: 163 (1990); 198 (1980)   **Pop Density:** 326.0
Land: 0.5 sq. mi.; **Water:** 0.0 sq. mi.
Name origin: For William C. Endicott, U.S. secretary of war under Pres. Cleveland.

NEBRASKA, Jefferson County

Fairbury
City
ZIP: 68352 Lat: 40-08-27 N Long: 97-10-38 W
Pop: 4,335 (1990); 4,885 (1980) Pop Density: 2281.6
Land: 1.9 sq. mi.; Water: 0.0 sq. mi.
Platted 1869.
Name origin: For Fairbury, IL, former home of platter Woodford G. McDowell.

Harbine
Village
ZIP: 68377 Lat: 40-11-29 N Long: 96-58-24 W
Pop: 66 (1990); 50 (1980) Pop Density: 660.0
Land: 0.1 sq. mi.; Water: 0.0 sq. mi.
Established 1881.
Name origin: For Col. Thomas Harbine.

Jansen
Village
ZIP: 68377 Lat: 40-11-08 N Long: 97-04-56 W
Pop: 140 (1990); 204 (1980) Pop Density: 700.0
Land: 0.2 sq. mi.; Water: 0.0 sq. mi.
Name origin: For Mennonite immigrant Peter Jansen, who acted as proprietor of the town.

Plymouth
Village
ZIP: 68424 Lat: 40-18-12 N Long: 96-59-17 W
Pop: 455 (1990); 506 (1980) Pop Density: 1516.7
Land: 0.3 sq. mi.; Water: 0.0 sq. mi.
Name origin: For Plymouth, MA, the former home of settlers.

Reynolds
Village
ZIP: 68429 Lat: 40-03-37 N Long: 97-20-09 W
Pop: 104 (1990); 125 (1980) Pop Density: 346.7
Land: 0.3 sq. mi.; Water: 0.0 sq. mi.

Steele City
Village
ZIP: 68440 Lat: 40-02-11 N Long: 97-01-21 W
Pop: 101 (1990); 137 (1980) Pop Density: 505.0
Land: 0.2 sq. mi.; Water: 0.0 sq. mi.
Name origin: For Dudley M. Steele, president of the St. Joseph & Denver City Railroad.

Johnson County
County Seat: Tecumseh (ZIP: 68450)

Pop: 4,673 (1990); 5,285 (1980) Pop Density: 12.4
Land: 376.2 sq. mi.; Water: 0.7 sq. mi. Area Code: 402
In southeastern NE, southeast of Lincoln; original county; organized Mar 2, 1855 (prior to statehood).
Name origin: For Col. Richard Mentor Johnson (1781–1850), officer in the War of 1812, U.S. senator from KY (1819–29), and U.S. vice president under Van Buren (1837–41).

Cook
Village
ZIP: 68329 Lat: 40-30-37 N Long: 96-09-40 W
Pop: 333 (1990); 341 (1980) Pop Density: 1665.0
Land: 0.2 sq. mi.; Water: 0.0 sq. mi.

Crab Orchard
Village
ZIP: 68332 Lat: 40-20-03 N Long: 96-25-18 W
Pop: 47 (1990); 82 (1980) Pop Density: 235.0
Land: 0.2 sq. mi.; Water: 0.0 sq. mi.

Elk Creek
Village
ZIP: 68348 Lat: 40-17-14 N Long: 96-07-40 W
Pop: 116 (1990); 144 (1980) Pop Density: 1160.0
Land: 0.1 sq. mi.; Water: 0.0 sq. mi.
Name origin: For the nearby stream, which was named for the elk that lived in the area.

Sterling
Village
ZIP: 68443 Lat: 40-27-42 N Long: 96-22-41 W
Pop: 451 (1990); 526 (1980) Pop Density: 1127.5
Land: 0.4 sq. mi.; Water: 0.0 sq. mi.
Name origin: For Sterling, IL, former home of early settler John Mann.

Tecumseh
City
ZIP: 68450 Lat: 40-22-13 N Long: 96-11-19 W
Pop: 1,702 (1990); 1,926 (1980) Pop Density: 1134.7
Land: 1.5 sq. mi.; Water: 0.0 sq. mi.
Laid out 1856.
Name origin: For Shawnee Indian Chief Tecumseh (1768–1813). Previously called Frances for the wife of Gen. Johnson.

Kearney County
County Seat: Minden (ZIP: 68959)

Pop: 6,629 (1990); 7,053 (1980) **Pop Density:** 12.8
Land: 516.1 sq. mi.; **Water:** 0.1 sq. mi. **Area Code:** 308
In south-central NE, southwest of Grand Island; original county; organized Jan 10, 1860 (prior to statehood).
Name origin: For Fort Kearny, itself named for Gen. Stephen Watts Kearny (1794–1848), officer in the War of 1812 and the Mexican-American War. The *e* in the last syllable was added in 1857, reason unknown.

Axtell — Village
ZIP: 68924 **Lat:** 40-28-44 N **Long:** 99-07-41 W
Pop: 707 (1990); 602 (1980) **Pop Density:** 1767.5
Land: 0.4 sq. mi.; **Water:** 0.0 sq. mi.
Name origin: For the engineer of a Burlington passenger train.

Blaine — Township
ZIP: 68924 **Lat:** 40-35-02 N **Long:** 99-07-19 W
Pop: 528 (1990); 529 (1980) **Pop Density:** 9.7
Land: 54.5 sq. mi.; **Water:** 0.0 sq. mi.

Cosmo — Township
Lat: 40-23-37 N **Long:** 98-53-39 W
Pop: 107 (1990); 115 (1980) **Pop Density:** 3.0
Land: 36.2 sq. mi.; **Water:** 0.0 sq. mi.

Eaton — Township
ZIP: 68945 **Lat:** 40-34-06 N **Long:** 98-47-02 W
Pop: 197 (1990); 235 (1980) **Pop Density:** 5.5
Land: 35.9 sq. mi.; **Water:** 0.0 sq. mi.

Grant — Township
Lat: 40-23-12 N **Long:** 98-47-25 W
Pop: 79 (1990); 104 (1980) **Pop Density:** 2.2
Land: 36.0 sq. mi.; **Water:** 0.0 sq. mi.

Hayes — Township
Lat: 40-29-05 N **Long:** 99-00-38 W
Pop: 1,428 (1990); 1,487 (1980) **Pop Density:** 39.7
Land: 36.0 sq. mi.; **Water:** 0.0 sq. mi.

Heartwell — Village
ZIP: 68945 **Lat:** 40-34-11 N **Long:** 98-47-18 W
Pop: 69 (1990); 87 (1980) **Pop Density:** 690.0
Land: 0.1 sq. mi.; **Water:** 0.0 sq. mi.
Name origin: For J.B. Heartwell, president of the Nebraska Loan and Trust Company and former state senator.

Liberty — Township
ZIP: 68945 **Lat:** 40-34-31 N **Long:** 98-53-06 W
Pop: 186 (1990); 187 (1980) **Pop Density:** 5.2
Land: 35.9 sq. mi.; **Water:** 0.0 sq. mi.

Lincoln — Township
Lat: 40-28-56 N **Long:** 98-53-42 W
Pop: 1,715 (1990); 1,884 (1980) **Pop Density:** 47.6
Land: 36.0 sq. mi.; **Water:** 0.0 sq. mi.

Logan — Township
Lat: 40-34-08 N **Long:** 99-00-22 W
Pop: 161 (1990); 167 (1980) **Pop Density:** 4.5
Land: 36.1 sq. mi.; **Water:** 0.0 sq. mi.

Lowell — Township
Lat: 40-38-27 N **Long:** 98-48-35 W
Pop: 210 (1990); 245 (1980) **Pop Density:** 5.0
Land: 42.1 sq. mi.; **Water:** 0.0 sq. mi.

May — Township
Lat: 40-28-47 N **Long:** 98-46-59 W
Pop: 136 (1990); 166 (1980) **Pop Density:** 3.8
Land: 36.0 sq. mi.; **Water:** 0.0 sq. mi.

Minden — City
ZIP: 68959 **Lat:** 40-30-02 N **Long:** 98-57-02 W
Pop: 2,749 (1990); 2,939 (1980) **Pop Density:** 1718.1
Land: 1.6 sq. mi.; **Water:** 0.0 sq. mi. **Elev:** 2172 ft.
Name origin: Named by the city's first postmaster, Fred Bredermier, for his former home of Minden, Germany.

Mirage — Township
ZIP: 68924 **Lat:** 40-28-51 N **Long:** 99-07-15 W
Pop: 1,019 (1990); 1,038 (1980) **Pop Density:** 28.3
Land: 36.0 sq. mi.; **Water:** 0.0 sq. mi.

Newark — Township
Lat: 40-37-48 N **Long:** 98-59-38 W
Pop: 237 (1990); 218 (1980) **Pop Density:** 10.2
Land: 23.3 sq. mi.; **Water:** 0.0 sq. mi.

Norman — Village
ZIP: 68963 **Lat:** 40-28-45 N **Long:** 98-47-27 W
Pop: 48 (1990); 58 (1980) **Pop Density:** 480.0
Land: 0.1 sq. mi.; **Water:** 0.0 sq. mi.
Name origin: For John and Carl Norman, who owned eighty acres on which the town was built.

Oneida — Township
ZIP: 68982 **Lat:** 40-23-34 N **Long:** 99-06-57 W
Pop: 520 (1990); 558 (1980) **Pop Density:** 14.4
Land: 36.2 sq. mi.; **Water:** 0.0 sq. mi.

Sherman — Township
ZIP: 68982 **Lat:** 40-23-39 N **Long:** 99-00-29 W
Pop: 106 (1990); 120 (1980) **Pop Density:** 2.9
Land: 36.0 sq. mi.; **Water:** 0.0 sq. mi.

Wilcox — Village
ZIP: 68982 **Lat:** 40-21-52 N **Long:** 99-10-07 W
Pop: 349 (1990); 379 (1980) **Pop Density:** 581.7
Land: 0.6 sq. mi.; **Water:** 0.0 sq. mi.
Name origin: For founder Henry Wilcox.

Keith County
County Seat: Ogallala (ZIP: 69153)

Pop: 8,584 (1990); 9,364 (1980) **Pop Density:** 8.1
Land: 1061.3 sq. mi.; **Water:** 48.5 sq. mi. **Area Code:** 308

In west-central NE, west of North Platte; organized May 3, 1873 from Lincoln County.

Name origin: For either Morrill C. Keith, the grandfather of NE governor Keith Morrill (1917–19), or John Keith, a prominent citizen of North Platte.

Brule — Village
ZIP: 69127 **Lat:** 41-05-45 N **Long:** 101-53-18 W
Pop: 411 (1990); 438 (1980) **Pop Density:** 2055.0
Land: 0.2 sq. mi.; **Water:** 0.0 sq. mi.
Name origin: For the Brule tribe of the Teton Sioux Indians.

Ogallala — City
ZIP: 69153 **Lat:** 41-07-49 N **Long:** 101-43-13 W
Pop: 5,095 (1990); 5,638 (1980) **Pop Density:** 1543.9
Land: 3.3 sq. mi.; **Water:** 0.1 sq. mi.
Name origin: For the Oglala, tribe of the Teton Sioux Indians.

Paxton — Village
ZIP: 69155 **Lat:** 41-07-29 N **Long:** 101-21-19 W
Pop: 536 (1990); 568 (1980) **Pop Density:** 1072.0
Land: 0.5 sq. mi.; **Water:** 0.0 sq. mi.
Name origin: For resident W.A. Paxton.

Keya Paha County
County Seat: Springview (ZIP: 68778)

Pop: 1,029 (1990); 1,301 (1980) **Pop Density:** 1.3
Land: 773.3 sq. mi.; **Water:** 0.9 sq. mi. **Area Code:** 402

On the central northern border of NE; organized Nov 4, 1884 from Brown County.

Name origin: For the Keya Paha River, which flows through the northeastern part of the county. From Dakota Indian *keya* 'turtle' and *paha* 'hill,' for a turtle-shaped hill.

Burton — Village
Lat: 42-54-40 N **Long:** 99-35-26 W
Pop: 9 (1990); 12 (1980) **Pop Density:** 90.0
Land: 0.1 sq. mi.; **Water:** 0.0 sq. mi.

Springview — Village
ZIP: 68778 **Lat:** 42-49-31 N **Long:** 99-44-56 W
Pop: 304 (1990); 326 (1980) **Pop Density:** 1520.0
Land: 0.2 sq. mi.; **Water:** 0.0 sq. mi.
Name origin: For a spring that once flowed near the center of town.

Kimball County
County Seat: Kimball (ZIP: 69145)

Pop: 4,108 (1990); 4,882 (1980) **Pop Density:** 4.3
Land: 951.8 sq. mi.; **Water:** 0.6 sq. mi. **Area Code:** 308

In the southwestern corner of NE, south of Scottsbluff; organized Nov 6, 1888 from Cheyenne County.

Name origin: For Thomas Lord Kimball (1831–99), vice president of the Union Pacific Railroad.

Bushnell — Village
ZIP: 69128 **Lat:** 41-13-55 N **Long:** 103-53-25 W
Pop: 119 (1990); 187 (1980) **Pop Density:** 595.0
Land: 0.2 sq. mi.; **Water:** 0.0 sq. mi.
Name origin: For Mr. Bushnell, a civil engineer on the Union Pacific Railroad.

Dix — Village
ZIP: 69133 **Lat:** 41-14-04 N **Long:** 103-29-10 W
Pop: 229 (1990); 275 (1980) **Pop Density:** 1145.0
Land: 0.2 sq. mi.; **Water:** 0.0 sq. mi.
Name origin: For Dixon, IL, the former home of landowner Margaret Robertson.

Kimball
City
ZIP: 69145   **Lat:** 41-13-57 N   **Long:** 103-39-32 W
Pop: 2,574 (1990); 3,120 (1980)   **Pop Density:** 1716.0
Land: 1.5 sq. mi.; **Water:** 0.0 sq. mi.
Name origin: Named in 1885 for Thomas Lord Kimball, vice president and general manager of the Union Pacific Railroad. Originally named descriptively as Antelopeville.

Knox County
County Seat: Center (ZIP: 68724)

Pop: 9,534 (1990); 11,457 (1980)   **Pop Density:** 8.6
Land: 1108.2 sq. mi.; **Water:** 31.5 sq. mi.   **Area Code:** 402
On the northeastern border of NE, northwest of Sioux City, IA. Original county; organized as L'Eau Qui Court County, Feb 10, 1857 (prior to statehood); name changed to Emmett County; then to present name Feb 21, 1873.
Name origin: For Gen. Henry Knox (1750–1806), Revolutionary War officer and first U.S. secretary of war (1785–95)

Addison
Township
Lat: 42-44-27 N   **Long:** 97-40-05 W
Pop: 155 (1990); 172 (1980)   **Pop Density:** 4.3
Land: 35.8 sq. mi.; **Water:** 0.0 sq. mi.

Bazile Mills
Village
Lat: 42-30-49 N   **Long:** 97-54-36 W
Pop: 34 (1990); 54 (1980)   **Pop Density:** 68.0
Land: 0.5 sq. mi.; **Water:** 0.0 sq. mi.
Name origin: For an early mill built here on Bazile Creek, the name of which probably came from Bazeilles, France.

Bloomfield
City
ZIP: 68718   **Lat:** 42-35-55 N   **Long:** 97-38-55 W
Pop: 1,181 (1990); 1,393 (1980)   **Pop Density:** 1312.2
Land: 0.9 sq. mi.; **Water:** 0.0 sq. mi.
Name origin: For early landowner Bloomfield Dyer.

Bohemia
Township
Lat: 42-39-07 N   **Long:** 98-08-17 W
Pop: 70 (1990); 64 (1980)   **Pop Density:** 2.1
Land: 33.6 sq. mi.; **Water:** 0.0 sq. mi.

Center
Village
ZIP: 68724   **Lat:** 42-36-32 N   **Long:** 97-52-33 W
Pop: 112 (1990); 123 (1980)   **Pop Density:** 1120.0
Land: 0.1 sq. mi.; **Water:** 0.0 sq. mi.
Name origin: For its location at the center of Knox County.

Central
Township
Lat: 42-34-28 N   **Long:** 97-46-35 W
Pop: 133 (1990); 166 (1980)   **Pop Density:** 3.7
Land: 36.0 sq. mi.; **Water:** 0.0 sq. mi.

Cleveland
Township
Lat: 42-28-27 N   **Long:** 97-47-18 W
Pop: 166 (1990); 201 (1980)   **Pop Density:** 4.6
Land: 36.0 sq. mi.; **Water:** 0.0 sq. mi.

Columbia
Township
Lat: 42-28-57 N   **Long:** 97-39-39 W
Pop: 163 (1990); 231 (1980)   **Pop Density:** 4.5
Land: 36.0 sq. mi.; **Water:** 0.0 sq. mi.

Creighton
City
ZIP: 68729   **Lat:** 42-27-54 N   **Long:** 97-54-24 W
Pop: 1,223 (1990); 1,341 (1980)   **Pop Density:** 1111.8
Land: 1.1 sq. mi.; **Water:** 0.0 sq. mi.
Not coextensive with the township.
Name origin: For John A. Creighton, founder of the John A. Creighton Medical College of Creighton University.

*Creighton
Township
ZIP: 68729   **Lat:** 42-28-45 N   **Long:** 97-54-05 W
Pop: 248 (1990); 327 (1980)   **Pop Density:** 7.1
Land: 34.9 sq. mi.; **Water:** 0.0 sq. mi.

Crofton
Village
Lat: 42-43-54 N   **Long:** 97-29-51 W
Pop: 820 (1990); 948 (1980)   **Pop Density:** 1366.7
Land: 0.6 sq. mi.; **Water:** 0.0 sq. mi.
Name origin: Named by J.T.M. Pierce for his former home of Crofton Court, England, or for an Englishman named Crofton.

Dolphin
Township
Lat: 42-39-29 N   **Long:** 97-32-19 W
Pop: 251 (1990); 286 (1980)   **Pop Density:** 7.0
Land: 36.1 sq. mi.; **Water:** 0.0 sq. mi.

Dowling
Township
Lat: 42-34-18 N   **Long:** 97-32-59 W
Pop: 166 (1990); 240 (1980)   **Pop Density:** 4.6
Land: 36.1 sq. mi.; **Water:** 0.0 sq. mi.

Eastern
Township
Lat: 42-44-31 N   **Long:** 97-32-45 W
Pop: 261 (1990); 1,310 (1980)   **Pop Density:** 7.4
Land: 35.5 sq. mi.; **Water:** 0.0 sq. mi.

Frankfort
Township
Lat: 42-48-38 N   **Long:** 97-32-21 W
Pop: 83 (1990); 229 (1980)   **Pop Density:** 4.6
Land: 18.1 sq. mi.; **Water:** 0.0 sq. mi.

Harrison
Township
Lat: 42-39-21 N   **Long:** 97-46-28 W
Pop: 73 (1990); 120 (1980)   **Pop Density:** 2.0
Land: 35.8 sq. mi.; **Water:** 0.0 sq. mi.

NEBRASKA, Knox County

Herrick
Township
Lat: 42-49-39 N **Long:** 97-39-40 W
Pop: 60 (1990); 54 (1980) **Pop Density:** 3.2
Land: 19.0 sq. mi.; **Water:** 6.2 sq. mi.

Hill
Township
Lat: 42-44-27 N **Long:** 97-46-22 W
Pop: 159 (1990); 198 (1980) **Pop Density:** 4.4
Land: 36.2 sq. mi.; **Water:** 0.0 sq. mi.

Jefferson
Township
Lat: 42-34-02 N **Long:** 98-07-53 W
Pop: 107 (1990); 136 (1980) **Pop Density:** 3.0
Land: 35.6 sq. mi.; **Water:** 0.2 sq. mi.

Lincoln
Township
Lat: 42-28-52 N **Long:** 97-32-29 W
Pop: 795 (1990); 930 (1980) **Pop Density:** 22.0
Land: 36.1 sq. mi.; **Water:** 0.0 sq. mi.

Logan
Township
Lat: 42-28-56 N **Long:** 98-08-01 W
Pop: 94 (1990); 159 (1980) **Pop Density:** 2.6
Land: 35.7 sq. mi.; **Water:** 0.2 sq. mi.

Miller
Township
Lat: 42-28-26 N **Long:** 98-00-13 W
Pop: 227 (1990); 276 (1980) **Pop Density:** 6.3
Land: 36.0 sq. mi.; **Water:** 0.0 sq. mi.

Morton
Township
Lat: 42-34-09 N **Long:** 97-39-17 W
Pop: 231 (1990); 278 (1980) **Pop Density:** 6.6
Land: 35.0 sq. mi.; **Water:** 0.0 sq. mi.

Niobrara
Village
ZIP: 68760 **Lat:** 42-45-01 N **Long:** 98-01-48 W
Pop: 376 (1990); 419 (1980) **Pop Density:** 537.1
Land: 0.7 sq. mi.; **Water:** 0.0 sq. mi.
Not coextensive with the town of the same name.
Name origin: For the Niobrara River, which was called *nibthatha* meaning 'spreading water' by the Omaha and Ponca Indians.

*Niobrara
Township
ZIP: 68760 **Lat:** 42-43-21 N **Long:** 97-59-56 W
Pop: 420 (1990); 477 (1980) **Pop Density:** 18.8
Land: 22.4 sq. mi.; **Water:** 0.9 sq. mi.

North Frankfort
Township
Lat: 42-50-47 N **Long:** 97-32-42 W
Pop: 67 (1990) **Pop Density:** 20.3
Land: 3.3 sq. mi.; **Water:** 5.6 sq. mi.

Peoria
Township
Lat: 42-39-15 N **Long:** 97-39-48 W
Pop: 209 (1990); 241 (1980) **Pop Density:** 5.9
Land: 35.7 sq. mi.; **Water:** 0.0 sq. mi.

Raymond
Township
Lat: 42-47-03 N **Long:** 98-11-00 W
Pop: 246 (1990); 355 (1980) **Pop Density:** 2.5
Land: 100.3 sq. mi.; **Water:** 6.0 sq. mi.

Santee
Village
Lat: 42-50-18 N **Long:** 97-50-57 W
Pop: 365 (1990); 388 (1980) **Pop Density:** 608.3
Land: 0.6 sq. mi.; **Water:** 0.0 sq. mi.
Not coextensive with the township.
Name origin: For the Santee Sioux Indians.

*Santee
Township
Lat: 42-49-40 N **Long:** 97-48-37 W
Pop: 385 (1990); 438 (1980) **Pop Density:** 12.5
Land: 30.7 sq. mi.; **Water:** 11.3 sq. mi.

Spade
Township
ZIP: 68724 **Lat:** 42-39-12 N **Long:** 97-53-29 W
Pop: 54 (1990); 71 (1980) **Pop Density:** 1.5
Land: 35.5 sq. mi.; **Water:** 0.0 sq. mi.

Sparta
Township
Lat: 42-38-55 N **Long:** 98-00-40 W
Pop: 94 (1990); 121 (1980) **Pop Density:** 2.7
Land: 34.8 sq. mi.; **Water:** 0.3 sq. mi.

Union
Township
Lat: 42-44-14 N **Long:** 97-53-39 W
Pop: 87 (1990); 87 (1980) **Pop Density:** 2.5
Land: 34.7 sq. mi.; **Water:** 0.3 sq. mi.

Valley
Township
Lat: 42-34-07 N **Long:** 97-53-38 W
Pop: 219 (1990); 262 (1980) **Pop Density:** 6.1
Land: 35.8 sq. mi.; **Water:** 0.0 sq. mi.

Verdel
Village
ZIP: 68782 **Lat:** 42-48-41 N **Long:** 98-11-34 W
Pop: 59 (1990); 72 (1980) **Pop Density:** 295.0
Land: 0.2 sq. mi.; **Water:** 0.0 sq. mi.

Verdigre
Village
ZIP: 68783 **Lat:** 42-35-51 N **Long:** 98-02-06 W
Pop: 607 (1990); 617 (1980) **Pop Density:** 1011.7
Land: 0.6 sq. mi.; **Water:** 0.0 sq. mi.
Not coextensive with the township.
Name origin: A corruption of the spelling of nearby Verdigris Creek, which took its name from the green copper ore in the area. Previously called Verdigris.

*Verdigre
Township
ZIP: 68783 **Lat:** 42-34-11 N **Long:** 98-00-42 W
Pop: 759 (1990); 830 (1980) **Pop Density:** 21.4
Land: 35.5 sq. mi.; **Water:** 0.2 sq. mi.

Walnut Grove
Township
Lat: 42-30-07 N **Long:** 98-14-30 W
Pop: 142 (1990); 219 (1980) **Pop Density:** 2.7
Land: 53.3 sq. mi.; **Water:** 0.0 sq. mi.

Washington
Township
Lat: 42-37-25 N **Long:** 98-14-47 W
Pop: 111 (1990); 153 (1980) **Pop Density:** 2.3
Land: 47.8 sq. mi.; **Water:** 0.0 sq. mi.

Wausa
Village
ZIP: 68786 **Lat:** 42-29-52 N **Long:** 97-32-17 W
Pop: 598 (1990); 647 (1980) **Pop Density:** 1196.0
Land: 0.5 sq. mi.; **Water:** 0.0 sq. mi.
Name origin: For the first Protestant king of Sweden, Gustavus Vasa (1523–60); the spelling was altered to reflect pronunciation.

Western
Township
Lat: 42-42-36 N **Long:** 98-14-59 W
Pop: 75 (1990); 92 (1980) **Pop Density:** 2.7
Land: 28.0 sq. mi.; **Water:** 0.1 sq. mi.

American Places Dictionary   NEBRASKA, Lancaster County

Winnetoon   Village
ZIP: 68789   **Lat:** 42-30-51 N   **Long:** 97-57-41 W
Pop: 59 (1990); 82 (1980)   **Pop Density:** 196.7
Land: 0.3 sq. mi.; **Water:** 0.0 sq. mi.
Name origin: Named by railroad official W.F. Fitch for a farm in WI.

Lancaster County
County Seat: Lincoln (ZIP: 68508)

Pop: 213,641 (1990); 192,884 (1980)   **Pop Density:** 254.7
Land: 838.9 sq. mi.; **Water:** 7.8 sq. mi.   **Area Code:** 402
In southeastern NE, southwest of Omaha; original county, organized Mar 6, 1855 (prior to statehood).
Name origin: For Lancaster County, PA, former home of many settlers.

Bennet   Village
ZIP: 68317   **Lat:** 40-40-52 N   **Long:** 96-30-21 W
Pop: 544 (1990); 523 (1980)   **Pop Density:** 1813.3
Land: 0.3 sq. mi.; **Water:** 0.0 sq. mi.
Platted 1871.
Name origin: For John Bennett, a railroad official and local resident.

Davey   Village
ZIP: 68336   **Lat:** 40-58-57 N   **Long:** 96-40-06 W
Pop: 160 (1990); 190 (1980)   **Pop Density:** 800.0
Land: 0.2 sq. mi.; **Water:** 0.0 sq. mi.
Platted 1886.
Name origin: For Michael Davey, who owned the land on which the townsite was located.

Denton   Village
ZIP: 68339   **Lat:** 40-44-22 N   **Long:** 96-50-40 W
Pop: 161 (1990); 164 (1980)   **Pop Density:** 1610.0
Land: 0.1 sq. mi.; **Water:** 0.0 sq. mi.
Established 1871.
Name origin: For homesteader Daniel M. Denton.

Firth   Village
ZIP: 68358   **Lat:** 40-32-03 N   **Long:** 96-36-14 W
Pop: 471 (1990); 384 (1980)   **Pop Density:** 1570.0
Land: 0.3 sq. mi.; **Water:** 0.0 sq. mi.
Established 1873.
Name origin: For Superintendent Firth of the Atchison & Nebraska Railroad.

Hallam   Village
ZIP: 68368   **Lat:** 40-32-12 N   **Long:** 96-47-09 W
Pop: 309 (1990); 290 (1980)   **Pop Density:** 1545.0
Land: 0.2 sq. mi.; **Water:** 0.0 sq. mi.
Established 1892 by the Kansas Town and Land Company.

Hickman   Village
ZIP: 68372   **Lat:** 40-37-17 N   **Long:** 96-37-53 W
Pop: 1,081 (1990); 687 (1980)   **Pop Density:** 2702.5
Land: 0.4 sq. mi.; **Water:** 0.0 sq. mi.
Established 1872.
Name origin: For C.H. Hickman.

Lincoln   City
ZIP: 68501   **Lat:** 40-48-59 N   **Long:** 96-41-17 W
Pop: 191,972 (1990); 171,932 (1980)   **Pop Density:** 3032.7
Land: 63.3 sq. mi.; **Water:** 0.8 sq. mi.
In southeastern NE, 52 mi. southwest of Omaha. State capital since 1867. Business and industrial center (defense and aerospace equipment, drugs, laboratory equipment, commercial printing), and agricultural (dairy and grain products, meat).
Name origin: For Abraham Lincoln (1809–65), sixteenth U.S. president. Previously called Lancaster.

Malcolm   Village
ZIP: 68402   **Lat:** 40-54-30 N   **Long:** 96-51-57 W
Pop: 181 (1990); 355 (1980)   **Pop Density:** 1810.0
Land: 0.1 sq. mi.; **Water:** 0.0 sq. mi.
Established 1877.
Name origin: For landowner Malcolm A. Showers.

Panama   Village
ZIP: 68419   **Lat:** 40-35-58 N   **Long:** 96-30-40 W
Pop: 207 (1990); 160 (1980)   **Pop Density:** 690.0
Land: 0.3 sq. mi.; **Water:** 0.0 sq. mi.
Name origin: Probably for the Isthmus of Panama and the Panama Canal, which were in the news about the time the town was established.

Raymond   Village
ZIP: 68428   **Lat:** 40-57-23 N   **Long:** 96-46-53 W
Pop: 167 (1990); 179 (1980)   **Pop Density:** 1670.0
Land: 0.1 sq. mi.; **Water:** 0.0 sq. mi.
Platted 1860.
Name origin: For grocer I.M. Raymond.

Roca   Village
ZIP: 68430   **Lat:** 40-39-29 N   **Long:** 96-39-41 W
Pop: 84 (1990); 130 (1980)   **Pop Density:** 840.0
Land: 0.1 sq. mi.; **Water:** 0.0 sq. mi.
Laid out 1876.

Sprague   Village
ZIP: 68438   **Lat:** 40-37-35 N   **Long:** 96-44-42 W
Pop: 157 (1990); 168 (1980)   **Pop Density:** 1570.0
Land: 0.1 sq. mi.; **Water:** 0.0 sq. mi.
Surveyed 1888.

NEBRASKA, Lancaster County

Waverly
City
ZIP: 68462 **Lat:** 40-54-53 N **Long:** 96-31-47 W
Pop: 1,869 (1990); 1,726 (1980) **Pop Density:** 2336.3
Land: 0.8 sq. mi.; **Water:** 0.0 sq. mi.
Established 1868.
Name origin: For *Waverley*, the historical novel by Sir Walter Scott (1771–1832).

Lincoln County
County Seat: North Platte (ZIP: 69101)

Pop: 32,508 (1990); 36,455 (1980) **Pop Density:** 12.7
Land: 2564.2 sq. mi.; **Water:** 11.1 sq. mi. **Area Code:** 308
In south-central NE, north of McCook; organized as Shorter County Jan 7, 1860 (prior to statehood) from unorganized territory (contained the "paper" counties of Grant and Jackson in 1870); name changed 1866.
Name origin: For Abraham Lincoln (1809–65), sixteenth U.S. president.

Brady
Village
ZIP: 69123 **Lat:** 41-01-22 N **Long:** 100-22-02 W
Pop: 331 (1990); 377 (1980) **Pop Density:** 1103.3
Land: 0.3 sq. mi.; **Water:** 0.0 sq. mi.

Dickens
Village
ZIP: 69132 **Lat:** 40-49-32 N **Long:** 100-59-36 W
Pop: 16 (1990); 24 (1980) **Pop Density:** 160.0
Land: 0.1 sq. mi.; **Water:** 0.0 sq. mi.
Name origin: For English author Charles Dickens (1812–70).

Hershey
Village
ZIP: 69143 **Lat:** 41-09-29 N **Long:** 101-00-04 W
Pop: 579 (1990); 633 (1980) **Pop Density:** 1158.0
Land: 0.5 sq. mi.; **Water:** 0.0 sq. mi.
Name origin: Named c. 1890 for J.H. Hershey, a rancher and prominent landowner.

Maxwell
Village
ZIP: 69151 **Lat:** 41-04-42 N **Long:** 100-31-32 W
Pop: 285 (1990); 410 (1980) **Pop Density:** 950.0
Land: 0.3 sq. mi.; **Water:** 0.0 sq. mi. **Elev:** 2711 ft.

North Platte
City
ZIP: 69101 **Lat:** 41-07-58 N **Long:** 100-46-18 W
Pop: 22,605 (1990); 24,509 (1980) **Pop Density:** 2430.6
Land: 9.3 sq. mi.; **Water:** 0.1 sq. mi.
In southwest-central NE at the confluence of the North Platte and South Platte rivers. Laid out 1866.
Name origin: For its location on the river.

Sutherland
Village
ZIP: 69165 **Lat:** 41-09-27 N **Long:** 101-07-35 W
Pop: 1,032 (1990); 1,238 (1980) **Pop Density:** 1290.0
Land: 0.8 sq. mi.; **Water:** 0.0 sq. mi.
Laid out 1869.
Name origin: For Mr. Sutherland, an official of the Union Pacific Railroad.

Wallace
Village
ZIP: 69169 **Lat:** 40-50-13 N **Long:** 101-09-48 W
Pop: 308 (1990); 349 (1980) **Pop Density:** 440.0
Land: 0.7 sq. mi.; **Water:** 0.0 sq. mi.
Name origin: For the son-in-law of the head of the Lincoln Town-Site Company.

Wellfleet
Village
ZIP: 69170 **Lat:** 40-45-09 N **Long:** 100-43-49 W
Pop: 63 (1990); 83 (1980) **Pop Density:** 210.0
Land: 0.3 sq. mi.; **Water:** 0.0 sq. mi.
Name origin: For Wellfleet, MA.

Logan County
County Seat: Stapleton (ZIP: 69163)

Pop: 878 (1990); 983 (1980) **Pop Density:** 1.5
Land: 570.7 sq. mi.; **Water:** 0.5 sq. mi. **Area Code:** 308
In central NE, north of North Platte; organized Feb 24, 1885 from Custer County.
Name origin: For Gen. John Alexander Logan (1826–86), officer in the Mexican-American War and Civil War; U.S. senator from IL (1871–77; 1879–86).

Gandy
Village
ZIP: 69163 **Lat:** 41-28-12 N **Long:** 100-27-26 W
Pop: 51 (1990); 53 (1980) **Pop Density:** 255.0
Land: 0.2 sq. mi.; **Water:** 0.0 sq. mi.

Stapleton
Village
ZIP: 69163 **Lat:** 41-28-47 N **Long:** 100-30-44 W
Pop: 299 (1990); 340 (1980) **Pop Density:** 1495.0
Land: 0.2 sq. mi.; **Water:** 0.0 sq. mi.
Name origin: Named by Harry O'Neill for a friend who helped promote the townsite.

Loup County
County Seat: Taylor (ZIP: 68879)

Pop: 683 (1990); 859 (1980) **Pop Density:** 1.2
Land: 569.7 sq. mi.; **Water:** 1.3 sq. mi. **Area Code:** 308
In central NE, northeast of North Platte; organized as Taylor County Mar 6, 1855 from unorganized territory (prior to statehood); name changed Jul 23, 1883.
Name origin: For the Loup River, which flows through the county; itself named for the Pawnee Loup Indians. Name is French translation of Pawnee *skidi* 'wolf.'

Taylor
Village
ZIP: 68879 **Lat:** 41-46-10 N **Long:** 99-22-52 W
Pop: 186 (1990); 278 (1980) **Pop Density:** 620.0
Land: 0.3 sq. mi.; **Water:** 0.0 sq. mi.
Established c. 1881.
Name origin: For pioneer Ed Taylor.

Madison County
County Seat: Madison (ZIP: 68748)

Pop: 32,655 (1990); 31,382 (1980) **Pop Density:** 57.0
Land: 572.6 sq. mi.; **Water:** 2.5 sq. mi. **Area Code:** 402
In east-central NE, northwest of Omaha; organized Dec, 1867 from Platte County.
Name origin: For either James Madison (1751–1836), fourth U.S. president, or for Madison County, WI, former home of early German settlers.

Battle Creek
Village
ZIP: 68715 **Lat:** 41-59-56 N **Long:** 97-35-55 W
Pop: 997 (1990); 948 (1980) **Pop Density:** 1661.7
Land: 0.6 sq. mi.; **Water:** 0.0 sq. mi.
Name origin: For a nearby creek, which was said to be the site of a battle between NE volunteer militiamen and Pawnee Indians.

Madison
City
ZIP: 68748 **Lat:** 41-49-42 N **Long:** 97-27-23 W
Pop: 2,135 (1990); 1,950 (1980) **Pop Density:** 1940.9
Land: 1.1 sq. mi.; **Water:** 0.0 sq. mi.
Settled 1868.
Name origin: Probably named for the county.

Meadow Grove
Village
ZIP: 68752 **Lat:** 42-01-44 N **Long:** 97-44-10 W
Pop: 332 (1990); 400 (1980) **Pop Density:** 1106.7
Land: 0.3 sq. mi.; **Water:** 0.0 sq. mi.

Newman Grove
City
ZIP: 68758 **Lat:** 41-44-50 N **Long:** 97-46-37 W
Pop: 770 (1990); 909 (1980) **Pop Density:** 1540.0
Land: 0.5 sq. mi.; **Water:** 0.0 sq. mi.
Part of the town is also in Platte County.
Name origin: For a grove of cottonwood trees that grew nearby on land belonging to Newman Warren.

NEBRASKA, Madison County

Norfolk — City
ZIP: 68701   **Lat:** 42-02-03 N   **Long:** 97-25-06 W
Pop: 21,476 (1990); 19,449 (1980)   **Pop Density:** 2413.0
Land: 8.9 sq. mi.; **Water:** 0.1 sq. mi.   **Elev:** 1520 ft.

Tilden — City
Lat: 42-02-38 N   **Long:** 97-49-50 W
Pop: 662 (1990); 719 (1980)   **Pop Density:** 1324.0
Land: 0.5 sq. mi.; **Water:** 0.0 sq. mi.
Part of the town is also in Antelope County.
Name origin: For Samuel J. Tilden, statesman from NY. Originally called Burnett after a railroad official.

McPherson County
County Seat: Tryon (ZIP: 69167)

Pop: 546 (1990); 593 (1980)   **Pop Density:** 0.6
Land: 859.0 sq. mi.; **Water:** 1.0 sq. mi.   **Area Code:** 308
In central NE, north of North Platte; boundaries set Mar 31, 1887 from Lincoln and Keith counties.
Name origin: For Gen. James Birdseye McPherson (1828–64), commander of the Union army in Tennessee during the Civil War.

Merrick County
County Seat: Central City (ZIP: 68826)

Pop: 8,042 (1990); 8,945 (1980)   **Pop Density:** 16.6
Land: 484.6 sq. mi.; **Water:** 9.7 sq. mi.   **Area Code:** 308
In east-central NE, northeast of Grand Island; original county; organized Nov 4, 1858 (prior to statehood).
Name origin: For Elvira Merrick De Puy, wife of Rep. Henry W. De Puy, who introduced the bill for the county's establishment.

Central — Township
Lat: 41-10-05 N   **Long:** 97-54-35 W
Pop: 89 (1990); 109 (1980)   **Pop Density:** 5.7
Land: 15.5 sq. mi.; **Water:** 0.9 sq. mi.

Central City — City
ZIP: 68826   **Lat:** 41-06-51 N   **Long:** 98-00-09 W
Pop: 2,868 (1990); 3,083 (1980)   **Pop Density:** 1593.3
Land: 1.8 sq. mi.; **Water:** 0.0 sq. mi.   **Elev:** 1703 ft.

Chapman — Village
ZIP: 68827   **Lat:** 41-01-22 N   **Long:** 98-09-34 W
Pop: 292 (1990); 349 (1980)   **Pop Density:** 730.0
Land: 0.4 sq. mi.; **Water:** 0.0 sq. mi.
Not coextensive with the township.
Name origin: For the roadmaster of the Pacific Railroad.

*Chapman — Township
ZIP: 68827   **Lat:** 41-01-47 N   **Long:** 98-09-15 W
Pop: 553 (1990); 632 (1980)   **Pop Density:** 17.8
Land: 31.0 sq. mi.; **Water:** 0.7 sq. mi.

Clarks — Village
ZIP: 68628   **Lat:** 41-12-58 N   **Long:** 97-50-21 W
Pop: 379 (1990); 445 (1980)   **Pop Density:** 1263.3
Land: 0.3 sq. mi.; **Water:** 0.0 sq. mi.
Name origin: For Silas Henry H. Clark, one-time acting head of the Union Pacific Railroad.

Clarksville — Township
Lat: 41-15-16 N   **Long:** 97-51-15 W
Pop: 749 (1990); 901 (1980)   **Pop Density:** 10.7
Land: 69.8 sq. mi.; **Water:** 0.7 sq. mi.

Lone Tree — Township
ZIP: 68826   **Lat:** 41-07-16 N   **Long:** 98-01-34 W
Pop: 606 (1990); 628 (1980)   **Pop Density:** 9.3
Land: 65.3 sq. mi.; **Water:** 2.1 sq. mi.

Loup — Township
ZIP: 68864   **Lat:** 41-13-38 N   **Long:** 98-13-07 W
Pop: 753 (1990); 845 (1980)   **Pop Density:** 13.4
Land: 56.0 sq. mi.; **Water:** 0.1 sq. mi.

Mead — Township
Lat: 41-14-13 N   **Long:** 98-01-07 W
Pop: 177 (1990); 241 (1980)   **Pop Density:** 3.3
Land: 53.1 sq. mi.; **Water:** 0.0 sq. mi.

Midland — Township
ZIP: 68816   **Lat:** 41-10-45 N   **Long:** 98-06-20 W
Pop: 237 (1990); 265 (1980)   **Pop Density:** 6.6
Land: 36.1 sq. mi.; **Water:** 0.0 sq. mi.

Palmer — Village
ZIP: 68864   **Lat:** 41-13-38 N   **Long:** 98-13-07 W
Pop: 753 (1990); 487 (1980)   **Pop Density:** 13.4
Land: 56.0 sq. mi.; **Water:** 0.1 sq. mi.

Prairie Creek — Township
Lat: 41-06-26 N   **Long:** 98-12-41 W
Pop: 396 (1990); 435 (1980)   **Pop Density:** 7.0
Land: 56.5 sq. mi.; **Water:** 0.0 sq. mi.

Prairie Island — Township
Lat: 41-08-24 N   **Long:** 97-52-55 W
Pop: 39 (1990); 53 (1980)   **Pop Density:** 3.0
Land: 13.1 sq. mi.; **Water:** 2.0 sq. mi.

Silver Creek — Village
ZIP: 68663   **Lat:** 41-19-57 N   **Long:** 97-39-56 W
Pop: 625 (1990); 496 (1980)   **Pop Density:** 14.9
Land: 42.0 sq. mi.; **Water:** 2.1 sq. mi.
Not coextensive with the township.
Name origin: For the nearby stream.

*Silver Creek — Township
ZIP: 68663   **Lat:** 41-19-57 N   **Long:** 97-39-56 W
Pop: 625 (1990); 709 (1980)   **Pop Density:** 14.9
Land: 42.0 sq. mi.; **Water:** 2.1 sq. mi.

Vieregg — Township
ZIP: 68827   **Lat:** 40-58-51 N   **Long:** 98-14-07 W
Pop: 950 (1990); 1,044 (1980)   **Pop Density:** 21.4
Land: 44.4 sq. mi.; **Water:** 1.2 sq. mi.

Morrill County
County Seat: Bridgeport (ZIP: 69336)

Pop: 5,423 (1990); 6,085 (1980)   **Pop Density:** 3.8
Land: 1423.9 sq. mi.; **Water:** 6.1 sq. mi.   **Area Code:** 308
In western NE, east of Scottsbluff; organized Nov 3, 1908 from Cheyenne County.
Name origin: For Charles Henry Morrill, regent of the University of Nebraska (1890–1903).

Bayard — City
ZIP: 69334   **Lat:** 41-45-25 N   **Long:** 103-19-22 W
Pop: 1,196 (1990); 1,435 (1980)   **Pop Density:** 1708.6
Land: 0.7 sq. mi.; **Water:** 0.0 sq. mi.
Name origin: Named in 1887 for the former IL hometown of Millard and Jap Senteny.

Bridgeport — City
ZIP: 69336   **Lat:** 41-39-59 N   **Long:** 103-05-53 W
Pop: 1,581 (1990); 1,668 (1980)   **Pop Density:** 1581.0
Land: 1.0 sq. mi.; **Water:** 0.0 sq. mi.
Name origin: For a local bridge over the North Platte River.

Broadwater — Village
ZIP: 69125   **Lat:** 41-35-51 N   **Long:** 102-51-05 W
Pop: 160 (1990); 161 (1980)   **Pop Density:** 800.0
Land: 0.2 sq. mi.; **Water:** 0.0 sq. mi.
Name origin: Named by the president of the Union Pacific Railroad, Mr. Moeller, for his personal friend, Gen. Broadwater.

Nance County
County Seat: Fullerton (ZIP: 68638)

Pop: 4,275 (1990); 4,740 (1980)   **Pop Density:** 9.7
Land: 441.3 sq. mi.; **Water:** 6.7 sq. mi.   **Area Code:** 308
In east-central NE, northeast of Grand Island; organized Feb 4, 1879 from Merrick County, encompassing the entire former Pawnee Reservation.
Name origin: For Albinus Nance (1848–1911), governor of NE (1879–83).

Beaver — Township
Lat: 41-29-54 N   **Long:** 97-49-36 W
Pop: 150 (1990); 196 (1980)   **Pop Density:** 3.6
Land: 41.5 sq. mi.; **Water:** 0.0 sq. mi.

Belgrade — Village
ZIP: 68623   **Lat:** 41-28-16 N   **Long:** 98-04-01 W
Pop: 157 (1990); 195 (1980)   **Pop Density:** 785.0
Land: 0.2 sq. mi.; **Water:** 0.0 sq. mi.
Name origin: Named by James Main for Belgrade, Serbia, because he thought the landscape resembled that of the city on the Danube.

Cedar — Township
Lat: 41-27-15 N   **Long:** 98-00-03 W
Pop: 127 (1990); 167 (1980)   **Pop Density:** 3.1
Land: 41.0 sq. mi.; **Water:** 0.2 sq. mi.

Cottonwood — Township
Lat: 41-20-06 N   **Long:** 98-13-29 W
Pop: 86 (1990); 122 (1980)   **Pop Density:** 1.9
Land: 45.6 sq. mi.; **Water:** 0.9 sq. mi.

Council Creek — Township
Lat: 41-24-45 N   **Long:** 97-53-24 W
Pop: 121 (1990); 136 (1980)   **Pop Density:** 3.5
Land: 34.7 sq. mi.; **Water:** 0.7 sq. mi.

East Newman — Township
Lat: 41-20-37 N   **Long:** 97-52-40 W
Pop: 137 (1990); 186 (1980)   **Pop Density:** 4.3
Land: 31.9 sq. mi.; **Water:** 0.7 sq. mi.

NEBRASKA, Nance County

Fullerton — City
ZIP: 68638 **Lat:** 41-21-50 N **Long:** 97-58-21 W
Pop: 1,452 (1990); 1,506 (1980) **Pop Density:** 1210.0
Land: 1.2 sq. mi.; **Water:** 0.0 sq. mi.
Not coextensive with the township. Platted 1878.
Name origin: For early settler Randall Fuller.

*Fullerton — Township
ZIP: 68638 **Lat:** 41-22-04 N **Long:** 98-00-34 W
Pop: 161 (1990); 163 (1980) **Pop Density:** 5.8
Land: 27.9 sq. mi.; **Water:** 1.0 sq. mi.

Genoa — City
ZIP: 68640 **Lat:** 41-26-45 N **Long:** 97-43-58 W
Pop: 1,082 (1990); 1,090 (1980) **Pop Density:** 1202.2
Land: 0.9 sq. mi.; **Water:** 0.0 sq. mi.
Not coextensive with the township.
Name origin: Named by Mormons in 1857 for Genoa, Italy.

*Genoa — Township
ZIP: 68640 **Lat:** 41-26-25 N **Long:** 97-46-51 W
Pop: 220 (1990); 222 (1980) **Pop Density:** 6.9
Land: 32.1 sq. mi.; **Water:** 0.7 sq. mi.

Loup Ferry — Township
Lat: 41-20-43 N **Long:** 98-06-48 W
Pop: 107 (1990); 105 (1980) **Pop Density:** 2.7
Land: 40.3 sq. mi.; **Water:** 0.4 sq. mi.

Prairie Creek — Township
Lat: 41-21-30 N **Long:** 97-45-43 W
Pop: 217 (1990); 266 (1980) **Pop Density:** 4.9
Land: 44.1 sq. mi.; **Water:** 0.2 sq. mi.

South Branch — Township
Lat: 41-26-06 N **Long:** 98-13-20 W
Pop: 71 (1990); 89 (1980) **Pop Density:** 2.0
Land: 35.7 sq. mi.; **Water:** 0.0 sq. mi.

Timber Creek — Township
Lat: 41-26-46 N **Long:** 98-06-37 W
Pop: 268 (1990); 345 (1980) **Pop Density:** 7.1
Land: 37.5 sq. mi.; **Water:** 0.2 sq. mi.

West Newman — Township
Lat: 41-18-04 N **Long:** 98-02-43 W
Pop: 76 (1990); 122 (1980) **Pop Density:** 2.8
Land: 26.8 sq. mi.; **Water:** 1.7 sq. mi.

Nemaha County
County Seat: Auburn (ZIP: 68305)

Pop: 7,980 (1990); 8,367 (1980) **Pop Density:** 19.5
Land: 409.3 sq. mi.; **Water:** 2.6 sq. mi. **Area Code:** 402
On the southeastern border of NE, southeast of Lincoln; original county, organized Mar 7, 1855 (prior to statehood).
Name origin: For the Nemaha River, which flows through the county; itself named from the Otoe Indian word *nimaha* 'murky water.'

Auburn — City
ZIP: 68305 **Lat:** 40-23-17 N **Long:** 95-50-31 W
Pop: 3,443 (1990); 3,482 (1980) **Pop Density:** 2295.3
Land: 1.5 sq. mi.; **Water:** 0.0 sq. mi.
Name origin: For Auburn, NY. Originally comprised of two towns named Sheridan and Calvert.

Brock — Village
ZIP: 68320 **Lat:** 40-28-52 N **Long:** 95-57-34 W
Pop: 143 (1990); 189 (1980) **Pop Density:** 476.7
Land: 0.3 sq. mi.; **Water:** 0.0 sq. mi.
Name origin: For a railroad superintendent and local resident.

Brownville — Village
ZIP: 68321 **Lat:** 40-23-49 N **Long:** 95-39-41 W
Pop: 148 (1990); 203 (1980) **Pop Density:** 246.7
Land: 0.6 sq. mi.; **Water:** 0.0 sq. mi.
Founded 1856.
Name origin: For Richard Brown, who owned the site.

Johnson — Village
ZIP: 68378 **Lat:** 40-24-40 N **Long:** 95-59-54 W
Pop: 323 (1990); 341 (1980) **Pop Density:** 1615.0
Land: 0.2 sq. mi.; **Water:** 0.0 sq. mi.
Established 1869.
Name origin: For Julius A. Johnson, who owned the land on which the village was built.

Julian — Village
ZIP: 68379 **Lat:** 40-31-13 N **Long:** 95-52-01 W
Pop: 71 (1990); 87 (1980) **Pop Density:** 710.0
Land: 0.1 sq. mi.; **Water:** 0.0 sq. mi.
Name origin: For Frenchman Julian Bahaud, who owned several farms in the area.

Nemaha — Village
ZIP: 68414 **Lat:** 40-20-16 N **Long:** 95-40-33 W
Pop: 188 (1990); 209 (1980) **Pop Density:** 626.7
Land: 0.3 sq. mi.; **Water:** 0.0 sq. mi.
Incorporated 1856.
Name origin: For the Nemaha River, itself named from the Otoe Indian term meaning 'murky water.'

Peru — City
ZIP: 68421 **Lat:** 40-28-43 N **Long:** 95-43-51 W
Pop: 1,110 (1990); 998 (1980) **Pop Density:** 2220.0
Land: 0.5 sq. mi.; **Water:** 0.0 sq. mi.
Name origin: For Peru, IN, former hometown of settlers.

Nuckolls County
County Seat: Nelson (ZIP: 68961)

Pop: 5,786 (1990); 6,726 (1980) **Pop Density:** 10.1
Land: 575.3 sq. mi.; **Water:** 0.7 sq. mi. **Area Code:** 402

On the southern border of NE, southeast of Grand Island; organized Jun 27, 1871 from unorganized territory; a county originally named Nuckolls is now Thayer County.

Name origin: For Stephen Friel Nuckolls (1825–79), pioneer, NE territorial legislator (1859), and U.S. representative from WY (1869–71).

Hardy   Village
ZIP: 68943   **Lat:** 40-00-41 N **Long:** 97-55-23 W
Pop: 206 (1990); 232 (1980)   **Pop Density:** 343.3
Land: 0.6 sq. mi.; **Water:** 0.0 sq. mi.

Lawrence   Village
ZIP: 68957   **Lat:** 40-17-24 N **Long:** 98-15-32 W
Pop: 323 (1990); 350 (1980)   **Pop Density:** 807.5
Land: 0.4 sq. mi.; **Water:** 0.0 sq. mi.

Nelson   City
ZIP: 68961   **Lat:** 40-12-03 N **Long:** 98-04-08 W
Pop: 627 (1990); 733 (1980)   **Pop Density:** 783.8
Land: 0.8 sq. mi.; **Water:** 0.0 sq. mi.
Surveyed 1873.
Name origin: For C. Nelson, who owned the land on which the city was established.

Nora   Village
                        Lat: 40-09-49 N **Long:** 97-58-25 W
Pop: 24 (1990); 24 (1980)   **Pop Density:** 60.0
Land: 0.4 sq. mi.; **Water:** 0.0 sq. mi.

Oak   Village
ZIP: 68964   **Lat:** 40-14-14 N **Long:** 97-54-14 W
Pop: 68 (1990); 79 (1980)   **Pop Density:** 340.0
Land: 0.2 sq. mi.; **Water:** 0.0 sq. mi.
Name origin: For a grove of oak trees that grew along the Little Blue River.

Ruskin   Village
ZIP: 68974   **Lat:** 40-08-39 N **Long:** 97-51-59 W
Pop: 187 (1990); 224 (1980)   **Pop Density:** 467.5
Land: 0.4 sq. mi.; **Water:** 0.0 sq. mi.
Name origin: For English author and art critic John Ruskin (1819–1900).

Superior   City
ZIP: 68978   **Lat:** 40-01-20 N **Long:** 98-04-03 W
Pop: 2,397 (1990); 2,502 (1980)   **Pop Density:** 1712.1
Land: 1.4 sq. mi.; **Water:** 0.0 sq. mi.
Name origin: For the superior land along the railroad here.

Otoe County
County Seat: Nebraska City (ZIP: 68410)

Pop: 14,252 (1990); 15,183 (1980)   **Pop Density:** 23.1
Land: 615.9 sq. mi.; **Water:** 3.3 sq. mi. **Area Code:** 402

On the southeastern border of NE, southeast of Lincoln; original county; organized Mar 2, 1855 (prior to statehood).

Name origin: For the Indian tribe of Siouan linguistic stock; meaning uncertain, but said to be 'lechers,' either as 'lovers' or in the pejorative sense. The name seems to be a shortened version of a Siouan or possibly French name.

Burr   Village
ZIP: 68324   **Lat:** 40-32-09 N **Long:** 96-17-55 W
Pop: 75 (1990); 101 (1980)   **Pop Density:** 750.0
Land: 0.1 sq. mi.; **Water:** 0.0 sq. mi.
Name origin: For a grove of burr trees near here. Previously called Burr Oak, the name was shortened to avoid confusion with Burr Oak, KS.

Douglas   Village
ZIP: 68344   **Lat:** 40-35-32 N **Long:** 96-23-18 W
Pop: 199 (1990); 207 (1980)   **Pop Density:** 995.0
Land: 0.2 sq. mi.; **Water:** 0.0 sq. mi.
Name origin: For a girl from the Douglas family that owned land here. Previously called Hendricks.

Dunbar   Village
ZIP: 68346   **Lat:** 40-40-07 N **Long:** 96-01-49 W
Pop: 171 (1990); 216 (1980)   **Pop Density:** 855.0
Land: 0.2 sq. mi.; **Water:** 0.0 sq. mi.
Name origin: For early resident Thomas Dunbar or landowner John Dunbar. Previously called Wilson and Dennison.

Lorton Village   Village
                        Lat: 40-35-51 N **Long:** 96-01-24 W
Pop: 61 (1990); 47 (1980)   **Pop Density:** 1525.0
Land: 0.04 sq. mi.; **Water:** 0.0 sq. mi.
Platted 1881.
Name origin: For Robert Lorton, who owned a wholesale grocery business. Originally known as Delta and Cio.

Nebraska City — City
ZIP: 68410　　Lat: 40-40-34 N　Long: 95-51-38 W
Pop: 6,547 (1990); 7,127 (1980)　　Pop Density: 1769.5
Land: 3.7 sq. mi.; Water: 0.0 sq. mi.
Incorporated 1855.
Name origin: For the state.

Otoe — Village
ZIP: 68417　　Lat: 40-43-28 N　Long: 96-07-12 W
Pop: 196 (1990); 197 (1980)　　Pop Density: 980.0
Land: 0.2 sq. mi.; Water: 0.0 sq. mi.
Name origin: For the county. Originally known as Berlin.

Palmyra — Village
ZIP: 68418　　Lat: 40-42-20 N　Long: 96-23-29 W
Pop: 545 (1990); 512 (1980)　　Pop Density: 1816.7
Land: 0.3 sq. mi.; Water: 0.0 sq. mi.
Founded 1870.
Name origin: For the ancient city in Asia Minor.

Syracuse — City
ZIP: 68446　　Lat: 40-39-42 N　Long: 96-10-58 W
Pop: 1,646 (1990); 1,638 (1980)　　Pop Density: 1828.9
Land: 0.9 sq. mi.; Water: 0.0 sq. mi.
Name origin: Named by George Warner for his former hometown in NY.

Talmage — Village
ZIP: 68448　　Lat: 40-31-54 N　Long: 96-01-24 W
Pop: 246 (1990); 246 (1980)　　Pop Density: 1230.0
Land: 0.2 sq. mi.; Water: 0.0 sq. mi.
Platted 1881.
Name origin: For Thomas DeWitt Talmage, superintendent of a division of the Missouri Railroad.

Unadilla — Village
ZIP: 68454　　Lat: 40-40-58 N　Long: 96-16-12 W
Pop: 294 (1990); 291 (1980)　　Pop Density: 980.0
Land: 0.3 sq. mi.; Water: 0.0 sq. mi.
Name origin: Named by I.N. White for his former hometown in NY.

Pawnee County
County Seat: Pawnee City (ZIP: 68420)

Pop: 3,317 (1990); 3,937 (1980)　　Pop Density: 7.7
Land: 431.7 sq. mi.; Water: 1.3 sq. mi.　　Area Code: 402
In southeastern NE, southeast of Lincoln; original county; organized Mar 6, 1855 (prior to statehood).
Name origin: For the Indian tribe of Caddoan linguistic stock. The name may mean 'horn,' for the shape of their forelock; they called themselves 'civilized people.'

Burchard — Village
ZIP: 68323　　Lat: 40-08-59 N　Long: 96-20-52 W
Pop: 105 (1990); 122 (1980)　　Pop Density: 525.0
Land: 0.2 sq. mi.; Water: 0.0 sq. mi.

Du Bois — Village
ZIP: 68345　　Lat: 40-02-02 N　Long: 96-02-45 W
Pop: 119 (1990); 178 (1980)　　Pop Density: 238.0
Land: 0.5 sq. mi.; Water: 0.0 sq. mi.　　Elev: 1065 ft.

Lewiston — Village
ZIP: 68380　　Lat: 40-14-36 N　Long: 96-24-26 W
Pop: 64 (1990); 102 (1980)　　Pop Density: 640.0
Land: 0.1 sq. mi.; Water: 0.0 sq. mi.

Pawnee City — City
ZIP: 68420　　Lat: 40-06-38 N　Long: 96-09-07 W
Pop: 1,008 (1990); 1,156 (1980)　　Pop Density: 840.0
Land: 1.2 sq. mi.; Water: 0.0 sq. mi.
Name origin: For the Pawnee Indians.

Steinauer — Village
ZIP: 68441　　Lat: 40-12-25 N　Long: 96-14-00 W
Pop: 92 (1990); 108 (1980)　　Pop Density: 920.0
Land: 0.1 sq. mi.; Water: 0.0 sq. mi.
Settled 1856.
Name origin: For Joseph A. Steinauer, the town's first postmaster.

Table Rock — Village
ZIP: 68447　　Lat: 40-10-43 N　Long: 96-05-21 W
Pop: 308 (1990); 393 (1980)　　Pop Density: 513.3
Land: 0.6 sq. mi.; Water: 0.0 sq. mi.
Incorporated 1860.
Name origin: For a large, flat-topped rock east of town.

Perkins County
County Seat: Grant (ZIP: 69140)

Pop: 3,367 (1990); 3,637 (1980) **Pop Density:** 3.8
Land: 883.2 sq. mi.; **Water:** 1.2 sq. mi. **Area Code:** 308
In west-central NE, west of North Platte; organized Nov 8, 1887 from Keith County.
Name origin: For Charles Elliott Perkins (1807–1907), president of the Chicago, Burlington, and Quincy Railroad. Locally it is also said to be for Joseph Perkins, an early resident.

Elsie Village
ZIP: 69134 **Lat:** 40-50-48 N **Long:** 101-23-20 W
Pop: 153 (1990); 133 (1980) **Pop Density:** 765.0
Land: 0.2 sq. mi.; **Water:** 0.0 sq. mi.
Name origin: For the daughter of county namesake, Charles E. Perkins.

Grainton Village
Lat: 40-49-20 N **Long:** 101-17-11 W
Pop: 16 (1990); 20 (1980) **Pop Density:** 160.0
Land: 0.1 sq. mi.; **Water:** 0.0 sq. mi.

Grant City
ZIP: 69140 **Lat:** 40-50-39 N **Long:** 101-43-32 W
Pop: 1,239 (1990); 1,270 (1980) **Pop Density:** 1770.0
Land: 0.7 sq. mi.; **Water:** 0.0 sq. mi. **Elev:** 3418 ft.
Name origin: For Ulysses S. Grant (1822–85), eighteenth U.S. president.

Madrid Village
ZIP: 69150 **Lat:** 40-50-58 N **Long:** 101-32-33 W
Pop: 288 (1990); 284 (1980) **Pop Density:** 720.0
Land: 0.4 sq. mi.; **Water:** 0.0 sq. mi. **Elev:** 3300 ft.
Name origin: For Madrid, Spain. Originally known as Trail City.

Venango Village
ZIP: 69168 **Lat:** 40-45-42 N **Long:** 102-02-26 W
Pop: 192 (1990); 230 (1980) **Pop Density:** 960.0
Land: 0.2 sq. mi.; **Water:** 0.0 sq. mi. **Elev:** 359 ft.
Name origin: Probably for Venango, PA.

Phelps County
County Seat: Holdrege (ZIP: 68949)

Pop: 9,715 (1990); 9,769 (1980) **Pop Density:** 18.0
Land: 540.0 sq. mi.; **Water:** 0.6 sq. mi. **Area Code:** 308
In south-central NE, southwest of Grand Island; organized Feb 11, 1873 from unorganized territory.
Name origin: For Capt. William Phelps (1808–?), an early settler and former Missouri River steamboat captain.

Anderson Township
ZIP: 68940 **Lat:** 40-34-16 N **Long:** 99-14-06 W
Pop: 173 (1990); 177 (1980) **Pop Density:** 4.4
Land: 39.4 sq. mi.; **Water:** 0.0 sq. mi.

Atlanta Village
ZIP: 68923 **Lat:** 40-22-05 N **Long:** 99-28-20 W
Pop: 114 (1990); 102 (1980) **Pop Density:** 570.0
Land: 0.2 sq. mi.; **Water:** 0.0 sq. mi. **Elev:** 2339 ft.
Name origin: For either Atlanta, GA, or Atlanta, IL.

Bertrand Village
ZIP: 68927 **Lat:** 40-31-36 N **Long:** 99-37-57 W
Pop: 708 (1990); 775 (1980) **Pop Density:** 1180.0
Land: 0.6 sq. mi.; **Water:** 0.0 sq. mi.
Organized 1885.
Name origin: For an official of the Chicago, Burlington & Quincy Railroad.

Center Township
Lat: 40-34-16 N **Long:** 99-21-32 W
Pop: 196 (1990); 217 (1980) **Pop Density:** 5.4
Land: 36.2 sq. mi.; **Water:** 0.0 sq. mi.

Cottonwood Township
Lat: 40-38-57 N **Long:** 99-17-20 W
Pop: 95 (1990); 106 (1980) **Pop Density:** 2.5
Land: 37.5 sq. mi.; **Water:** 0.0 sq. mi.

Divide Township
ZIP: 68940 **Lat:** 40-28-57 N **Long:** 99-14-16 W
Pop: 385 (1990); 383 (1980) **Pop Density:** 9.8
Land: 39.4 sq. mi.; **Water:** 0.0 sq. mi.

Funk Village
ZIP: 68940 **Lat:** 40-27-46 N **Long:** 99-14-58 W
Pop: 198 (1990); 189 (1980) **Pop Density:** 660.0
Land: 0.3 sq. mi.; **Water:** 0.0 sq. mi.
Settled 1887.
Name origin: For early resident P.C. Funk.

Garfield Township
ZIP: 68927 **Lat:** 40-33-59 N **Long:** 99-35-17 W
Pop: 560 (1990); 563 (1980) **Pop Density:** 15.6
Land: 35.9 sq. mi.; **Water:** 0.0 sq. mi.

Holdrege
City
ZIP: 68949　　　Lat: 40-26-26 N　Long: 99-22-31 W
Pop: 5,671 (1990); 5,624 (1980)　　Pop Density: 1620.3
Land: 3.5 sq. mi.; Water: 0.0 sq. mi.
Established 1883.
Name origin: For George W. Holdredge, superintendent of the Chicago, Burlington & Quincy Railroad.

Industry-Rock Falls
Township
Lat: 40-23-49 N　Long: 99-32-08 W
Pop: 261 (1990); 250 (1980)　　Pop Density: 3.7
Land: 71.2 sq. mi.; Water: 0.0 sq. mi.

Laird
Township
ZIP: 68958　　　Lat: 40-28-55 N　Long: 99-28-27 W
Pop: 586 (1990); 616 (1980)　　Pop Density: 16.4
Land: 35.7 sq. mi.; Water: 0.1 sq. mi.

Lake
Township
Lat: 40-23-37 N　Long: 99-14-20 W
Pop: 165 (1990); 174 (1980)　　Pop Density: 4.2
Land: 39.4 sq. mi.; Water: 0.0 sq. mi.

Loomis
Village
ZIP: 68958　　　Lat: 40-28-41 N　Long: 99-30-26 W
Pop: 376 (1990); 447 (1980)　　Pop Density: 1253.3
Land: 0.3 sq. mi.; Water: 0.0 sq. mi.
Established c. 1885.
Name origin: For railroad man N.H. Loomis.

Prairie
Township
Lat: 40-23-32 N　Long: 99-21-36 W
Pop: 372 (1990); 338 (1980)　　Pop Density: 10.7
Land: 34.8 sq. mi.; Water: 0.0 sq. mi.

Sheridan
Township
Lat: 40-29-22 N　Long: 99-21-15 W
Pop: 245 (1990); 209 (1980)　　Pop Density: 7.2
Land: 33.9 sq. mi.; Water: 0.0 sq. mi.

Union
Township
Lat: 40-28-53 N　Long: 99-35-10 W
Pop: 472 (1990); 536 (1980)　　Pop Density: 13.2
Land: 35.8 sq. mi.; Water: 0.0 sq. mi.

Westmark
Township
ZIP: 68927　　　Lat: 40-34-08 N　Long: 99-28-24 W
Pop: 205 (1990); 234 (1980)　　Pop Density: 5.7
Land: 36.0 sq. mi.; Water: 0.0 sq. mi.

Westside
Township
ZIP: 68927　　　Lat: 40-38-32 N　Long: 99-35-17 W
Pop: 162 (1990); 166 (1980)　　Pop Density: 5.8
Land: 28.0 sq. mi.; Water: 0.4 sq. mi.

Williamsburg
Township
ZIP: 68927　　　Lat: 40-38-37 N　Long: 99-27-28 W
Pop: 167 (1990); 176 (1980)　　Pop Density: 5.0
Land: 33.2 sq. mi.; Water: 0.1 sq. mi.

Pierce County
County Seat: Pierce (ZIP: 68767)

Pop: 7,827 (1990); 8,481 (1980)　　Pop Density: 13.6
Land: 574.0 sq. mi.; Water: 1.3 sq. mi.　　Area Code: 402
In northeast NE, southwest of Sioux City, IA; organized Jan 26, 1856 from Madison County.
Name origin: For Franklin Pierce (1804–69), fourteenth U.S. president.

Foster
Village
ZIP: 68737　　　Lat: 42-16-25 N　Long: 97-39-54 W
Pop: 57 (1990); 81 (1980)　　Pop Density: 285.0
Land: 0.2 sq. mi.; Water: 0.0 sq. mi.
Name origin: For railroad station agent George Foster, who owned land near here.

Hadar
Village
ZIP: 68738　　　Lat: 42-06-20 N　Long: 97-27-05 W
Pop: 291 (1990); 286 (1980)　　Pop Density: 727.5
Land: 0.4 sq. mi.; Water: 0.0 sq. mi.

McLean
Village
ZIP: 68747　　　Lat: 42-23-10 N　Long: 97-28-03 W
Pop: 49 (1990); 46 (1980)　　Pop Density: 490.0
Land: 0.1 sq. mi.; Water: 0.0 sq. mi.

Osmond
City
ZIP: 68765　　　Lat: 42-21-29 N　Long: 97-35-56 W
Pop: 774 (1990); 871 (1980)　　Pop Density: 1105.7
Land: 0.7 sq. mi.; Water: 0.0 sq. mi.

Pierce
City
ZIP: 68767　　　Lat: 42-11-58 N　Long: 97-31-39 W
Pop: 1,615 (1990); 1,535 (1980)　　Pop Density: 1794.4
Land: 0.9 sq. mi.; Water: 0.0 sq. mi.　　Elev: 1579 ft.
Settled 1870.
Name origin: For Franklin Pierce (1804–69), fourteenth U.S. president.

Plainview
City
Lat: 42-21-14 N　Long: 97-47-12 W
Pop: 1,333 (1990); 1,483 (1980)　　Pop Density: 1211.8
Land: 1.1 sq. mi.; Water: 0.0 sq. mi.
Name origin: For its location on high ground and for the town of Plainview, MN. Previously called Roseville for postmaster Charles Rose.

Platte County
County Seat: Columbus (ZIP: 68601)

Pop: 29,820 (1990); 28,852 (1980) **Pop Density:** 44.0
Land: 678.1 sq. mi.; **Water:** 11.1 sq. mi. Area Code: 402

In east-central NE, northwest of Omaha; original county; organized as Loup County Jan 26, 1856 (prior to statehood); name changed 1859.

Name origin: For the Platte River, which forms part of its southern border; from French for 'flat' or 'still.'

Bismark — Township
Lat: 41-31-15 N **Long:** 97-18-27 W
Pop: 483 (1990); 471 (1980) **Pop Density:** 13.8
Land: 35.1 sq. mi.; **Water:** 0.9 sq. mi.

Burrows — Township
Lat: 41-37-00 N **Long:** 97-31-58 W
Pop: 334 (1990); 369 (1980) **Pop Density:** 9.3
Land: 35.9 sq. mi.; **Water:** 0.0 sq. mi.

Butler — Township
Lat: 41-23-19 N **Long:** 97-30-02 W
Pop: 688 (1990); 696 (1980) **Pop Density:** 22.8
Land: 30.2 sq. mi.; **Water:** 3.4 sq. mi.

Columbus — City
ZIP: 68601 **Lat:** 41-26-04 N **Long:** 97-21-20 W
Pop: 19,480 (1990); 17,328 (1980) **Pop Density:** 2239.1
Land: 8.7 sq. mi.; **Water:** 0.2 sq. mi.

At the confluence of the Loup and Platte rivers. Not coextensive with the township. Laid out 1856.
Name origin: For Columbus, OH.

*Columbus — Township
Lat: 41-26-19 N **Long:** 97-20-40 W
Pop: 2,557 (1990); 3,050 (1980) **Pop Density:** 46.5
Land: 55.0 sq. mi.; **Water:** 4.3 sq. mi.

Cornlea — Village
ZIP: 68630 **Lat:** 41-40-50 N **Long:** 97-34-01 W
Pop: 39 (1990); 40 (1980) **Pop Density:** 390.0
Land: 0.1 sq. mi.; **Water:** 0.0 sq. mi.

Creston — Village
ZIP: 68631 **Lat:** 41-42-25 N **Long:** 97-21-41 W
Pop: 220 (1990); 210 (1980) **Pop Density:** 1100.0
Land: 0.2 sq. mi.; **Water:** 0.0 sq. mi.

Not coextensive with the township.
Name origin: For its location on the crest of a hill overlooking the Elkhorn and Platte rivers.

*Creston — Township
ZIP: 68631 **Lat:** 41-41-54 N **Long:** 97-18-44 W
Pop: 481 (1990); 511 (1980) **Pop Density:** 13.4
Land: 35.9 sq. mi.; **Water:** 0.0 sq. mi.

Duncan — Village
ZIP: 68634 **Lat:** 41-23-23 N **Long:** 97-29-36 W
Pop: 387 (1990); 410 (1980) **Pop Density:** 967.5
Land: 0.4 sq. mi.; **Water:** 0.0 sq. mi.

Laid out 1871.
Name origin: Originally known as Jackson.

Grand Prairie — Township
Lat: 41-36-49 N **Long:** 97-25-38 W
Pop: 436 (1990); 455 (1980) **Pop Density:** 12.0
Land: 36.2 sq. mi.; **Water:** 0.0 sq. mi.

Granville — Township
Lat: 41-41-57 N **Long:** 97-32-18 W
Pop: 1,030 (1990); 1,200 (1980) **Pop Density:** 28.9
Land: 35.7 sq. mi.; **Water:** 0.0 sq. mi.

Humphrey — City
ZIP: 68642 **Lat:** 41-41-17 N **Long:** 97-29-14 W
Pop: 741 (1990); 799 (1980) **Pop Density:** 1852.5
Land: 0.4 sq. mi.; **Water:** 0.0 sq. mi.

Platted 1880.
Name origin: For Humphrey, NY, the former home of Mrs. Leach, the town's postmistress.

*Humphrey — Township
ZIP: 68642 **Lat:** 41-42-08 N **Long:** 97-25-20 W
Pop: 380 (1990); 428 (1980) **Pop Density:** 10.6
Land: 35.9 sq. mi.; **Water:** 0.0 sq. mi.

Joliet — Township
Lat: 41-36-40 N **Long:** 97-39-35 W
Pop: 185 (1990); 226 (1980) **Pop Density:** 5.1
Land: 36.0 sq. mi.; **Water:** 0.0 sq. mi.

Lindsay — Village
ZIP: 68644 **Lat:** 41-42-02 N **Long:** 97-41-39 W
Pop: 321 (1990); 383 (1980) **Pop Density:** 1070.0
Land: 0.3 sq. mi.; **Water:** 0.0 sq. mi.

Name origin: Named by early settler, John Walker, for Lindsay, Ontario, Canada.

Lost Creek — Township
Lat: 41-31-25 N **Long:** 97-32-42 W
Pop: 638 (1990); 636 (1980) **Pop Density:** 17.7
Land: 36.0 sq. mi.; **Water:** 0.0 sq. mi.

Loup — Township
Lat: 41-24-47 N **Long:** 97-35-21 W
Pop: 132 (1990); 172 (1980) **Pop Density:** 3.1
Land: 42.1 sq. mi.; **Water:** 1.0 sq. mi.

Monroe — Village
ZIP: 68647 **Lat:** 41-28-25 N **Long:** 97-36-00 W
Pop: 309 (1990); 294 (1980) **Pop Density:** 1545.0
Land: 0.2 sq. mi.; **Water:** 0.0 sq. mi.

Founded 1889 by Leander Gerrard and his brother.
Name origin: For James Monroe (1758–1831), fifth U.S. president.

*Monroe — Township
ZIP: 68647 **Lat:** 41-31-46 N **Long:** 97-39-35 W
Pop: 210 (1990); 212 (1980) **Pop Density:** 6.2
Land: 34.0 sq. mi.; **Water:** 0.0 sq. mi.

NEBRASKA, Platte County

Newman Grove
City
ZIP: 68758 Lat: 41-44-30 N Long: 97-46-33 W
Pop: 17 (1990); 21 (1980) Pop Density: 850.0
Land: 0.02 sq. mi.; Water: 0.0 sq. mi.
Part of the town is also in Madison County.
Name origin: For a grove of cottonwood trees that grew nearby on land belonging to Newman Warren.

Oconee
Township
Lat: 41-27-55 N Long: 97-35-36 W
Pop: 457 (1990); 521 (1980) Pop Density: 18.2
Land: 25.1 sq. mi.; Water: 0.9 sq. mi.

Platte Center
Village
ZIP: 68653 Lat: 41-32-16 N Long: 97-29-13 W
Pop: 387 (1990); 367 (1980) Pop Density: 1290.0
Land: 0.3 sq. mi.; Water: 0.0 sq. mi.

Shell Creek
Township
Lat: 41-31-02 N Long: 97-25-55 W
Pop: 761 (1990); 769 (1980) Pop Density: 21.3
Land: 35.7 sq. mi.; Water: 0.4 sq. mi.

Sherman
Township
Lat: 41-36-57 N Long: 97-18-03 W
Pop: 347 (1990); 372 (1980) Pop Density: 9.6
Land: 36.0 sq. mi.; Water: 0.0 sq. mi.

St. Bernard
Township
Lat: 41-42-00 N Long: 97-39-27 W
Pop: 674 (1990); 786 (1980) Pop Density: 18.9
Land: 35.6 sq. mi.; Water: 0.0 sq. mi.

Tarnov
Village
Lat: 41-36-53 N Long: 97-30-10 W
Pop: 61 (1990); 63 (1980) Pop Density: 2033.3
Land: 0.03 sq. mi.; Water: 0.0 sq. mi.
Name origin: Probably for Tarnow, Galicia. Previously called Burrows.

Walker
Township
Lat: 41-40-59 N Long: 97-46-25 W
Pop: 341 (1990); 378 (1980) Pop Density: 6.4
Land: 53.6 sq. mi.; Water: 0.0 sq. mi.

Woodville
Township
Lat: 41-33-40 N Long: 97-46-20 W
Pop: 189 (1990); 251 (1980) Pop Density: 5.3
Land: 35.4 sq. mi.; Water: 0.0 sq. mi.

Polk County
County Seat: Osceola (ZIP: 68651)

Pop: 5,675 (1990); 6,320 (1980) Pop Density: 12.9
Land: 439.1 sq. mi.; Water: 2.0 sq. mi. Area Code: 402
In east-central NE, west of Omaha; boundaries established Jan 26, 1856 (prior to statehood) from Butler County.
Name origin: For James Knox Polk (1795–1849), eleventh U.S. president.

Osceola
City
ZIP: 68651 Lat: 41-10-40 N Long: 97-32-54 W
Pop: 879 (1990); 975 (1980) Pop Density: 976.7
Land: 0.9 sq. mi.; Water: 0.0 sq. mi.
Platted 1872.
Name origin: For the Seminole chief (c. 1804–38).

Polk
Village
ZIP: 68654 Lat: 41-04-30 N Long: 97-46-57 W
Pop: 345 (1990); 440 (1980) Pop Density: 690.0
Land: 0.5 sq. mi.; Water: 0.0 sq. mi.
Name origin: For James K. Polk (1795–1849), eleventh U.S. president.

Shelby
Village
ZIP: 68662 Lat: 41-11-39 N Long: 97-25-35 W
Pop: 690 (1990); 724 (1980) Pop Density: 1380.0
Land: 0.5 sq. mi.; Water: 0.0 sq. mi.
Laid out 1879.
Name origin: For a Union Pacific Railroad official. Previously called Arcade.

Stromsburg
City
ZIP: 68666 Lat: 41-06-58 N Long: 97-35-25 W
Pop: 1,241 (1990); 1,290 (1980) Pop Density: 1241.0
Land: 1.0 sq. mi.; Water: 0.0 sq. mi.
Surveyed 1872.
Name origin: Named by Swedish settlers for a suburb of Stockholm, Sweden.

Red Willow County
County Seat: McCook (ZIP: 69001)

Pop: 11,705 (1990); 12,615 (1980)　　**Pop Density:** 16.3
Land: 716.7 sq. mi.; **Water:** 1.4 sq. mi.　　**Area Code:** 308
On the central southern border of NE, south of North Platte; organized Feb 27, 1873 from unorganized territory.
Name origin: For Red Willow Creek, which runs through the county; a mistranslation of the Dakota term for 'Red Dogwood Creek,' for the trees that grow there.

Bartley — Village
ZIP: 69020　　Lat: 40-15-09 N　Long: 100-18-33 W
Pop: 339 (1990); 342 (1980)　　Pop Density: 484.3
Land: 0.7 sq. mi.; Water: 0.0 sq. mi.
Platted 1886.
Name origin: For the Rev. Allen Bartley, a homesteader and Methodist Episcopal minister.

Danbury — Village
ZIP: 69026　　Lat: 40-02-15 N　Long: 100-24-15 W
Pop: 109 (1990); 143 (1980)　　Pop Density: 363.3
Land: 0.3 sq. mi.; Water: 0.0 sq. mi.
Name origin: Named by first postmaster, George Gilbert, for his former home of Danbury, CT.

Indianola — City
ZIP: 69034　　Lat: 40-14-05 N　Long: 100-25-08 W
Pop: 672 (1990); 856 (1980)　　Pop Density: 560.0
Land: 1.2 sq. mi.; Water: 0.0 sq. mi.
Name origin: Named by I. Starbuck for his former home of Indianola, IA.

Lebanon — Village
ZIP: 69036　　Lat: 40-02-57 N　Long: 100-16-33 W
Pop: 75 (1990); 102 (1980)　　Pop Density: 375.0
Land: 0.2 sq. mi.; Water: 0.0 sq. mi.
Name origin: Named by the first postmaster, Mr. Bradbury, for the biblical cedars of Lebanon.

McCook — City
ZIP: 69001　　Lat: 40-12-14 N　Long: 100-37-13 W
Pop: 8,112 (1990); 8,404 (1980)　　Pop Density: 1530.6
Land: 5.3 sq. mi.; Water: 0.0 sq. mi.
Established 1882.
Name origin: For Civil War hero Maj. Gen. Alexander McDowell McCook (1831–1903). Previously called Fairview.

Richardson County
County Seat: Falls City (ZIP: 68355)

Pop: 9,937 (1990); 11,315 (1980)　　**Pop Density:** 18.0
Land: 553.5 sq. mi.; **Water:** 2.5 sq. mi.　　**Area Code:** 402
In the southeastern corner of NE, southeast of Lincoln; original county; organized Mar 7, 1855 (prior to statehood).
Name origin: For Maj. William A. Richardson (1811–75), officer in the Mexican-American War, U.S. senator from IL (1863–65), and governor of NE Territory (1858).

Barada — Village
ZIP: 68355　　Lat: 40-13-05 N　Long: 95-34-43 W
Pop: 24 (1990); 36 (1980)　　Pop Density: 240.0
Land: 0.1 sq. mi.; Water: 0.0 sq. mi.
Name origin: For its location in Barada Precinct, which was named for an early settler, Antoine Barada.

Dawson — Village
ZIP: 68337　　Lat: 40-07-51 N　Long: 95-49-47 W
Pop: 157 (1990); 215 (1980)　　Pop Density: 785.0
Land: 0.2 sq. mi.; Water: 0.0 sq. mi.
Established 1871.
Name origin: For settler Joshua Dawson, who built a flour and feed mill here. Also called Doraville.

Falls City — City
ZIP: 68355　　Lat: 40-03-55 N　Long: 95-35-58 W
Pop: 4,769 (1990); 5,374 (1980)　　Pop Density: 1834.2
Land: 2.6 sq. mi.; Water: 0.0 sq. mi.
Incorporated 1860.
Name origin: For its location near the falls on the Great Nemaha River.

Humboldt — City
ZIP: 68376　　Lat: 40-09-58 N　Long: 95-56-39 W
Pop: 1,003 (1990); 1,176 (1980)　　Pop Density: 771.5
Land: 1.3 sq. mi.; Water: 0.0 sq. mi.
Name origin: Named by founder O.J. Tinker for the German scientist and explorer Alexander von Humboldt (1769–1859).

NEBRASKA, Richardson County

Preston
Village
ZIP: 68355 Lat: 40-02-02 N Long: 95-31-02 W
Pop: 40 (1990); 45 (1980) Pop Density: 400.0
Land: 0.1 sq. mi.; Water: 0.0 sq. mi.
Name origin: Named by storekeeper James S. Eatough for his hometown of Preston, England. Previously called Bluffton.

Rulo
City
ZIP: 68431 Lat: 40-03-07 N Long: 95-25-47 W
Pop: 191 (1990); 261 (1980) Pop Density: 318.3
Land: 0.6 sq. mi.; Water: 0.0 sq. mi.
Laid out 1857.
Name origin: For Mrs. Rouleau, who owned the townsite. The spelling altered to reflect pronunciation.

Salem
Village
ZIP: 68433 Lat: 40-04-37 N Long: 95-43-36 W
Pop: 160 (1990); 221 (1980) Pop Density: 266.7
Land: 0.6 sq. mi.; Water: 0.0 sq. mi.
Laid out 1855.
Name origin: For the biblical name.

Shubert
Village
ZIP: 68437 Lat: 40-14-08 N Long: 95-40-59 W
Pop: 237 (1990); 267 (1980) Pop Density: 1185.0
Land: 0.2 sq. mi.; Water: 0.0 sq. mi. Elev: 1123 ft.
Name origin: For early settler Henry W. Shubert.

Stella
Village
ZIP: 68442 Lat: 40-13-53 N Long: 95-46-21 W
Pop: 248 (1990); 289 (1980) Pop Density: 1240.0
Land: 0.2 sq. mi.; Water: 0.0 sq. mi.
Laid out 1881.
Name origin: For Stella Clark, daughter of J.W. Clark, owner of the townsite.

Verdon
Village
ZIP: 68457 Lat: 40-08-55 N Long: 95-42-38 W
Pop: 242 (1990); 278 (1980) Pop Density: 1210.0
Land: 0.2 sq. mi.; Water: 0.0 sq. mi.
Laid out 1882.

Rock County
County Seat: Bassett (ZIP: 68714)

Pop: 2,019 (1990); 2,383 (1980) Pop Density: 2.0
Land: 1008.5 sq. mi.; Water: 3.4 sq. mi. Area Code: 402
In north-central NE; organized Nov 6, 1888 from Brown County.
Name origin: For the rocky soil.

Bassett
City
ZIP: 68714 Lat: 42-34-57 N Long: 99-32-08 W
Pop: 739 (1990); 1,009 (1980) Pop Density: 1847.5
Land: 0.4 sq. mi.; Water: 0.0 sq. mi.
Name origin: For rancher J.W. Bassett, who brought the first herd of cattle into the state in 1871.

Newport
Village
Lat: 42-36-02 N Long: 99-19-39 W
Pop: 136 (1990); 141 (1980) Pop Density: 453.3
Land: 0.3 sq. mi.; Water: 0.0 sq. mi.
Name origin: For the Newport Bridge, which spans the Niobrara River about 10 mi. north of town.

Saline County
County Seat: Wilber (ZIP: 68465)

Pop: 12,715 (1990); 13,131 (1980) Pop Density: 22.1
Land: 575.4 sq. mi.; Water: 0.7 sq. mi. Area Code: 402
In southeastern NE, southwest of Lincoln; organized Feb 18, 1867 from Gage and Lancaster counties.
Name origin: In the unfounded belief that extensive salt springs or deposits could be found within its boundaries.

Crete
City
ZIP: 68333 Lat: 40-37-32 N Long: 96-57-29 W
Pop: 4,841 (1990); 4,872 (1980) Pop Density: 2305.2
Land: 2.1 sq. mi.; Water: 0.0 sq. mi.
Platted 1870.
Name origin: For Crete, IL. Originally known as Blue River City.

De Witt
Village
ZIP: 68341 Lat: 40-23-41 N Long: 96-55-18 W
Pop: 598 (1990); 642 (1980) Pop Density: 1495.0
Land: 0.4 sq. mi.; Water: 0.0 sq. mi.
Incorporated 1857.

Dorchester
Village
ZIP: 68343 Lat: 40-38-51 N Long: 97-06-53 W
Pop: 614 (1990); 611 (1980) Pop Density: 1228.0
Land: 0.5 sq. mi.; Water: 0.0 sq. mi.
Name origin: For Dorchester, MA, or for Dorchester, England. Originally called DeWitt.

Friend
City
ZIP: 68359   **Lat:** 40-39-03 N **Long:** 97-17-02 W
Pop: 1,111 (1990); 1,079 (1980)   **Pop Density:** 1388.8
Land: 0.8 sq. mi.; **Water:** 0.0 sq. mi.
Surveyed 1873.
Name origin: For farm owner Charles E. Friend, the town's first postmaster and storekeeper.

Swanton
Village
ZIP: 68445   **Lat:** 40-22-45 N **Long:** 97-04-46 W
Pop: 145 (1990); 131 (1980)   **Pop Density:** 725.0
Land: 0.2 sq. mi.; **Water:** 0.0 sq. mi.
Name origin: For nearby Swan Creek. Previously called Morris.

Tobias
Village
ZIP: 68453   **Lat:** 40-25-06 N **Long:** 97-20-10 W
Pop: 127 (1990); 138 (1980)   **Pop Density:** 423.3
Land: 0.3 sq. mi.; **Water:** 0.0 sq. mi.
Name origin: For prominent citizen Tobias Castor. Previously called Castor.

Western
Village
ZIP: 68464   **Lat:** 40-23-35 N **Long:** 97-11-57 W
Pop: 264 (1990); 336 (1980)   **Pop Density:** 660.0
Land: 0.4 sq. mi.; **Water:** 0.0 sq. mi.
Established 1872.

Wilber
City
ZIP: 68465   **Lat:** 40-28-51 N **Long:** 96-57-47 W
Pop: 1,527 (1990); 1,624 (1980)   **Pop Density:** 1908.8
Land: 0.8 sq. mi.; **Water:** 0.0 sq. mi.
Laid out c. 1872.
Name origin: For Professor C.D. Wilber.

Sarpy County
County Seat: Papillion (ZIP: 68046)

Pop: 102,583 (1990); 86,015 (1980)   **Pop Density:** 426.2
Land: 240.7 sq. mi.; **Water:** 6.6 sq. mi.   **Area Code:** 402
On the central eastern border of NE, south of Omaha; organized Feb 7, 1857 from Douglas County.
Name origin: For Col. Peter A. Sarpy (1805–65), an early settler, trader, and quartermaster for NE volunteer regiment (1855).

Bellevue
City
ZIP: 68005   **Lat:** 41-09-23 N **Long:** 95-55-21 W
Pop: 30,982 (1990); 21,813 (1980)   **Pop Density:** 3872.8
Land: 8.0 sq. mi.; **Water:** 0.0 sq. mi.
In eastern NE on the Missouri River, 8 mi. south of Omaha. Oldest city in NE.
Name origin: Named 1805 by fur trader Manuel Lisa; from French 'beautiful view.'

Chalco
CDP
Lat: 41-11-00 N **Long:** 96-08-02 W
Pop: 7,337 (1990)   **Pop Density:** 2620.4
Land: 2.8 sq. mi.; **Water:** 0.0 sq. mi.

Gretna
City
ZIP: 68028   **Lat:** 41-08-26 N **Long:** 96-14-37 W
Pop: 2,249 (1990); 1,609 (1980)   **Pop Density:** 2811.3
Land: 0.8 sq. mi.; **Water:** 0.0 sq. mi.
Name origin: Probably for Gretna Green, in Dumfriesshire, Scotland.

La Vista
City
ZIP: 68128   **Lat:** 41-11-03 N **Long:** 96-02-20 W
Pop: 9,840 (1990); 9,588 (1980)   **Pop Density:** 5788.2
Land: 1.7 sq. mi.; **Water:** 0.0 sq. mi.   **Elev:** 1050 ft.
Name origin: From Spanish meaning 'the view'.

Offutt AFB West
Military Facility
ZIP: 68113   **Lat:** 41-06-41 N **Long:** 95-55-07 W
Pop: 10,883 (1990); 8,787 (1980)   **Pop Density:** 2473.4
Land: 4.4 sq. mi.; **Water:** 0.0 sq. mi.

Papillion
City
ZIP: 68046   **Lat:** 41-09-26 N **Long:** 96-02-25 W
Pop: 10,372 (1990); 6,399 (1980)   **Pop Density:** 4509.6
Land: 2.3 sq. mi.; **Water:** 0.0 sq. mi.   **Elev:** 1029 ft.
Name origin: For nearby Papillion Creek.

Springfield
City
ZIP: 68059   **Lat:** 41-04-59 N **Long:** 96-07-55 W
Pop: 1,426 (1990); 782 (1980)   **Pop Density:** 2852.0
Land: 0.5 sq. mi.; **Water:** 0.0 sq. mi.
Platted 1881.

NEBRASKA, Saunders County

Saunders County
County Seat: Wahoo (ZIP: 68066)

Pop: 18,285 (1990); 18,716 (1980)
Land: 754.1 sq. mi.; **Water:** 4.8 sq. mi.
Pop Density: 24.2
Area Code: 402

In east-central NE, west of Omaha; organized as Calhoun County Jan 26, 1856 (prior to statehood); name changed Jan 8, 1862.

Name origin: For Alvin Saunders (1817–99), NE Territory governor (1861–67) and U.S. senator from NE (1877–83).

Ashland — City
ZIP: 68003 **Lat:** 41-02-25 N **Long:** 96-22-15 W
Pop: 2,136 (1990); 2,274 (1980) **Pop Density:** 2136.0
Land: 1.0 sq. mi.; **Water:** 0.0 sq. mi.
Organized 1870.
Name origin: For the KY home of statesman Henry Clay (1777–1852).

*Ashland — Township
ZIP: 68003 **Lat:** 41-02-00 N **Long:** 96-23-59 W
Pop: 2,229 (1990); 2,400 (1980) **Pop Density:** 153.7
Land: 14.5 sq. mi.; **Water:** 0.1 sq. mi.

Bohemia — Township
Lat: 41-24-32 N **Long:** 96-51-27 W
Pop: 169 (1990); 194 (1980) **Pop Density:** 6.1
Land: 27.8 sq. mi.; **Water:** 0.1 sq. mi.

Cedar Bluffs — Village
ZIP: 68015 **Lat:** 41-23-52 N **Long:** 96-36-33 W
Pop: 591 (1990); 632 (1980) **Pop Density:** 1477.5
Land: 0.4 sq. mi.; **Water:** 0.0 sq. mi.
Name origin: For its descriptive connotations.

Center — Township
Lat: 41-15-56 N **Long:** 96-37-07 W
Pop: 466 (1990); 541 (1980) **Pop Density:** 13.1
Land: 35.6 sq. mi.; **Water:** 0.0 sq. mi.

Ceresco — Village
ZIP: 68017 **Lat:** 41-03-27 N **Long:** 96-38-43 W
Pop: 825 (1990); 836 (1980) **Pop Density:** 2062.5
Land: 0.4 sq. mi.; **Water:** 0.0 sq. mi.
Name origin: For the former MI hometown of Richard Nelson and Hod Andrus.

Chapman — Township
Lat: 41-10-42 N **Long:** 96-44-02 W
Pop: 599 (1990); 623 (1980) **Pop Density:** 16.5
Land: 36.2 sq. mi.; **Water:** 0.0 sq. mi.

Chester — Township
Lat: 41-20-27 N **Long:** 96-50-58 W
Pop: 496 (1990); 510 (1980) **Pop Density:** 16.7
Land: 29.7 sq. mi.; **Water:** 0.1 sq. mi.

Clear Creek — Township
Lat: 41-05-36 N **Long:** 96-23-47 W
Pop: 796 (1990); 748 (1980) **Pop Density:** 20.0
Land: 39.8 sq. mi.; **Water:** 0.8 sq. mi.

Colon — Village
ZIP: 68018 **Lat:** 41-17-51 N **Long:** 96-36-23 W
Pop: 128 (1990); 148 (1980) **Pop Density:** 1280.0
Land: 0.1 sq. mi.; **Water:** 0.0 sq. mi.
Name origin: For the first postmaster's former MI hometown.

Douglas — Township
Lat: 41-21-06 N **Long:** 96-44-12 W
Pop: 219 (1990); 245 (1980) **Pop Density:** 6.8
Land: 32.0 sq. mi.; **Water:** 0.0 sq. mi.

Elk — Township
Lat: 41-15-50 N **Long:** 96-51-07 W
Pop: 323 (1990); 380 (1980) **Pop Density:** 9.0
Land: 35.8 sq. mi.; **Water:** 0.1 sq. mi.

Green — Township
Lat: 41-05-21 N **Long:** 96-31-01 W
Pop: 270 (1990); 276 (1980) **Pop Density:** 8.6
Land: 31.3 sq. mi.; **Water:** 0.0 sq. mi.

Ithaca — Village
ZIP: 68033 **Lat:** 41-09-37 N **Long:** 96-32-22 W
Pop: 133 (1990); 156 (1980) **Pop Density:** 665.0
Land: 0.2 sq. mi.; **Water:** 0.0 sq. mi.
Name origin: Named by the county surveyor for Ithaca, NY.

Leshara — Village
Lat: 41-19-48 N **Long:** 96-25-43 W
Pop: 118 (1990); 133 (1980) **Pop Density:** 1180.0
Land: 0.1 sq. mi.; **Water:** 0.0 sq. mi.
Not coextensive with the township.
Name origin: For Petalesharo, a Pawnee chief; spelling changed by the post office.

*Leshara — Township
Lat: 41-20-02 N **Long:** 96-26-50 W
Pop: 492 (1990); 556 (1980) **Pop Density:** 21.8
Land: 22.6 sq. mi.; **Water:** 1.1 sq. mi.

Malmo — Village
ZIP: 68040 **Lat:** 41-15-58 N **Long:** 96-43-15 W
Pop: 114 (1990); 100 (1980) **Pop Density:** 1140.0
Land: 0.1 sq. mi.; **Water:** 0.0 sq. mi.
Name origin: Named by Swedes for Malmo, Sweden.

Marble — Township
Lat: 41-10-15 N **Long:** 96-23-47 W
Pop: 293 (1990); 321 (1980) **Pop Density:** 7.1
Land: 41.3 sq. mi.; **Water:** 0.8 sq. mi.

Marietta — Township
Lat: 41-15-52 N **Long:** 96-31-11 W
Pop: 786 (1990); 846 (1980) **Pop Density:** 25.9
Land: 30.3 sq. mi.; **Water:** 0.0 sq. mi.

Mariposa — Township
Lat: 41-15-48 N **Long:** 96-44-09 W
Pop: 349 (1990); 381 (1980) **Pop Density:** 9.7
Land: 35.9 sq. mi.; **Water:** 0.0 sq. mi.

American Places Dictionary   NEBRASKA, Saunders County

Mead
Village
ZIP: 68041   **Lat:** 41-13-44 N   **Long:** 96-29-21 W
Pop: 513 (1990); 506 (1980)   **Pop Density:** 1710.0
Land: 0.3 sq. mi.; **Water:** 0.0 sq. mi.
Name origin: For Mr. Mead, a railroad official. Previously called Alvin and Saunders.

Memphis
Village
ZIP: 68042   **Lat:** 41-05-40 N   **Long:** 96-25-57 W
Pop: 117 (1990); 89 (1980)   **Pop Density:** 1170.0
Land: 0.1 sq. mi.; **Water:** 0.0 sq. mi.
Name origin: Named by settlers from TN for their former home.

Morse Bluff
Village
ZIP: 68648   **Lat:** 41-25-52 N   **Long:** 96-45-56 W
Pop: 128 (1990); 132 (1980)   **Pop Density:** 640.0
Land: 0.2 sq. mi.; **Water:** 0.0 sq. mi.
Not coextensive with the township.
Name origin: For Charles W. Morse, who once owned the land on which the town was located. "Bluff" was added to the name to avoid confusion with another place along the railroad line with the same name.

*Morse Bluff
Township
ZIP: 68648   **Lat:** 41-24-31 N   **Long:** 96-44-32 W
Pop: 333 (1990); 342 (1980)   **Pop Density:** 15.4
Land: 21.6 sq. mi.; **Water:** 0.3 sq. mi.

Newman
Township
Lat: 41-10-24 N   **Long:** 96-51-13 W
Pop: 235 (1990); 250 (1980)   **Pop Density:** 6.5
Land: 36.2 sq. mi.; **Water:** 0.0 sq. mi.

North Cedar
Township
Lat: 41-24-15 N   **Long:** 96-36-47 W
Pop: 808 (1990); 869 (1980)   **Pop Density:** 37.1
Land: 21.8 sq. mi.; **Water:** 0.3 sq. mi.

Oak Creek
Township
Lat: 41-05-30 N   **Long:** 96-50-56 W
Pop: 807 (1990); 834 (1980)   **Pop Density:** 22.4
Land: 36.1 sq. mi.; **Water:** 0.0 sq. mi.

Pohocco
Township
Lat: 41-21-35 N   **Long:** 96-31-17 W
Pop: 863 (1990); 740 (1980)   **Pop Density:** 29.6
Land: 29.2 sq. mi.; **Water:** 0.1 sq. mi.

Prague
Village
ZIP: 68050   **Lat:** 41-18-34 N   **Long:** 96-48-30 W
Pop: 282 (1990); 285 (1980)   **Pop Density:** 940.0
Land: 0.3 sq. mi.; **Water:** 0.0 sq. mi.
Name origin: For the capital of Czechoslovakia, former home of early settlers.

Richland
Township
Lat: 41-05-28 N   **Long:** 96-37-18 W
Pop: 1,237 (1990); 1,283 (1980)   **Pop Density:** 34.2
Land: 36.2 sq. mi.; **Water:** 0.0 sq. mi.

Rock Creek
Township
Lat: 41-05-21 N   **Long:** 96-44-08 W
Pop: 288 (1990); 342 (1980)   **Pop Density:** 8.0
Land: 36.1 sq. mi.; **Water:** 0.0 sq. mi.

South Cedar
Township
Lat: 41-20-38 N   **Long:** 96-36-57 W
Pop: 240 (1990); 264 (1980)   **Pop Density:** 8.0
Land: 29.9 sq. mi.; **Water:** 0.0 sq. mi.

Stocking
Township
Lat: 41-10-28 N   **Long:** 96-37-01 W
Pop: 401 (1990); 391 (1980)   **Pop Density:** 11.6
Land: 34.6 sq. mi.; **Water:** 0.0 sq. mi.

Union
Township
Lat: 41-15-20 N   **Long:** 96-24-55 W
Pop: 1,545 (1990); 1,448 (1980)   **Pop Density:** 58.3
Land: 26.5 sq. mi.; **Water:** 0.8 sq. mi.

Valparaiso
Village
ZIP: 68065   **Lat:** 41-04-45 N   **Long:** 96-49-55 W
Pop: 481 (1990); 484 (1980)   **Pop Density:** 962.0
Land: 0.5 sq. mi.; **Water:** 0.0 sq. mi.
Name origin: For its being considered the "valley of paradise." Previously called Raccoon Forks for three creeks that joined here.

Wahoo
City
ZIP: 68066   **Lat:** 41-12-54 N   **Long:** 96-37-11 W
Pop: 3,681 (1990); 3,555 (1980)   **Pop Density:** 2045.0
Land: 1.8 sq. mi.; **Water:** 0.0 sq. mi.
Name origin: From the 'wahoo' or burning bush that grows in the area, or from an Indian term for 'elm.'

*Wahoo
Township
ZIP: 68066   **Lat:** 41-10-17 N   **Long:** 96-30-21 W
Pop: 360 (1990); 377 (1980)   **Pop Density:** 11.5
Land: 31.2 sq. mi.; **Water:** 0.0 sq. mi.

Weston
Village
ZIP: 68070   **Lat:** 41-11-31 N   **Long:** 96-44-28 W
Pop: 299 (1990); 286 (1980)   **Pop Density:** 996.7
Land: 0.3 sq. mi.; **Water:** 0.0 sq. mi.

Yutan
Village
ZIP: 68073   **Lat:** 41-14-35 N   **Long:** 96-23-50 W
Pop: 626 (1990); 631 (1980)   **Pop Density:** 2086.7
Land: 0.3 sq. mi.; **Water:** 0.0 sq. mi.
Name origin: For Otoe chief Ietan.

Scotts Bluff County
County Seat: Gering (ZIP: 69341)

Pop: 36,025 (1990); 38,344 (1980) **Pop Density:** 48.7
Land: 739.3 sq. mi.; **Water:** 6.2 sq. mi. **Area Code:** 308
On western border of NE; organized Nov 6, 1888 from Cheyenne County.
Name origin: For the prominent bluff on the North Platte River, named for Hiram Scott, a member of the Bonneville expedition of 1832, who died there.

Gering City
ZIP: 69341 **Lat:** 41-49-42 N **Long:** 103-39-54 W
Pop: 7,946 (1990); 7,760 (1980) **Pop Density:** 2483.1
Land: 3.2 sq. mi.; **Water:** 0.0 sq. mi.
Name origin: For Martin Gering, a member of the original townsite company and a Civil War veteran.

Henry Village
ZIP: 69349 **Lat:** 41-59-53 N **Long:** 104-02-46 W
Pop: 145 (1990); 155 (1980) **Pop Density:** 483.3
Land: 0.3 sq. mi.; **Water:** 0.0 sq. mi.
Name origin: For Henry Nichols, a boy who drowned in the Platte River a year before the town was established.

Lyman Village
ZIP: 69352 **Lat:** 41-55-05 N **Long:** 104-02-11 W
Pop: 452 (1990); 551 (1980) **Pop Density:** 1130.0
Land: 0.4 sq. mi.; **Water:** 0.0 sq. mi.

McGrew Village
ZIP: 69353 **Lat:** 41-44-50 N **Long:** 103-25-01 W
Pop: 99 (1990); 110 (1980) **Pop Density:** 247.5
Land: 0.4 sq. mi.; **Water:** 0.0 sq. mi.

Melbeta Village
ZIP: 69355 **Lat:** 41-46-55 N **Long:** 103-31-00 W
Pop: 116 (1990); 151 (1980) **Pop Density:** 1160.0
Land: 0.1 sq. mi.; **Water:** 0.0 sq. mi.
Originally a railroad shipping place for beets.
Name origin: From German meaning 'sugar beet.'

Minatare City
ZIP: 69356 **Lat:** 41-48-39 N **Long:** 103-30-08 W
Pop: 807 (1990); 969 (1980) **Pop Density:** 2017.5
Land: 0.4 sq. mi.; **Water:** 0.0 sq. mi.
Name origin: For the Minnetare tribe of the Sioux Indians.

Mitchell City
ZIP: 69357 **Lat:** 41-56-31 N **Long:** 103-48-32 W
Pop: 1,743 (1990); 1,956 (1980) **Pop Density:** 2490.0
Land: 0.7 sq. mi.; **Water:** 0.0 sq. mi.

Morrill Village
ZIP: 69358 **Lat:** 41-57-50 N **Long:** 103-55-25 W
Pop: 974 (1990); 1,097 (1980) **Pop Density:** 1623.3
Land: 0.6 sq. mi.; **Water:** 0.0 sq. mi.
Name origin: For Charles H. Morrill, who owned property here and was president of the Lincoln Land Company.

Scottsbluff City
ZIP: 69361 **Lat:** 41-52-02 N **Long:** 103-39-41 W
Pop: 13,711 (1990); 14,156 (1980) **Pop Density:** 2323.9
Land: 5.9 sq. mi.; **Water:** 0.0 sq. mi.
In western NE on the North Platte River, 20 mi. east of the WY border.
Name origin: For a high ridge in the Platte Valley where the body of mountaineer Hiram Scott was found.

Terrytown Village
ZIP: 69341 **Lat:** 41-51-00 N **Long:** 103-40-06 W
Pop: 656 (1990); 727 (1980) **Pop Density:** 1640.0
Land: 0.4 sq. mi.; **Water:** 0.0 sq. mi.

Seward County
County Seat: Seward (ZIP: 68434)

Pop: 15,450 (1990); 15,789 (1980) **Pop Density:** 26.9
Land: 574.8 sq. mi.; **Water:** 1.0 sq. mi. **Area Code:** 402

In east-central NE, west of Lincoln; organized as Greene County Jan 26, 1856 (prior to statehood) from Lancaster County; name changed Jan 3, 1862 when Gen. Greene of Missouri joined the Confederacy.

Name origin: For William Henry Seward (1801–72), U.S. secretary of state (1861–69) who negotiated the purchase of Alaska (1867).

Beaver Crossing — Village
ZIP: 68313   **Lat:** 40-46-39 N **Long:** 97-16-54 W
Pop: 448 (1990); 458 (1980)   **Pop Density:** 640.0
Land: 0.7 sq. mi.; **Water:** 0.0 sq. mi.
Platted 1887.
Name origin: For its location near where the overland trail from Leavenworth crossed Beaver Creek.

Bee — Village
ZIP: 68314   **Lat:** 41-00-24 N **Long:** 97-03-27 W
Pop: 209 (1990); 192 (1980)   **Pop Density:** 1045.0
Land: 0.2 sq. mi.; **Water:** 0.0 sq. mi.
Name origin: For its location in Precinct B, one of sixteen precincts in Seward County labeled A through P.

Cordova — Village
ZIP: 68330   **Lat:** 40-42-59 N **Long:** 97-21-03 W
Pop: 147 (1990); 129 (1980)   **Pop Density:** 490.0
Land: 0.3 sq. mi.; **Water:** 0.0 sq. mi.
Established 1887.
Name origin: For Cordoba, Spain. Previously called Hunkins for the first postmaster. Spelling altered to reflect pronunciation.

Garland — Village
ZIP: 68360   **Lat:** 40-56-39 N **Long:** 96-59-06 W
Pop: 247 (1990); 257 (1980)   **Pop Density:** 1235.0
Land: 0.2 sq. mi.; **Water:** 0.0 sq. mi.
Name origin: For local soldier Ray Garland, who died in France during the World War. Previously called Germantown.

Goehner — Village
ZIP: 68364   **Lat:** 40-49-57 N **Long:** 97-13-11 W
Pop: 192 (1990); 165 (1980)   **Pop Density:** 960.0
Land: 0.2 sq. mi.; **Water:** 0.0 sq. mi.
Platted 1887.

Milford — City
ZIP: 68405   **Lat:** 40-46-21 N **Long:** 97-03-07 W
Pop: 1,886 (1990); 2,108 (1980)   **Pop Density:** 3143.3
Land: 0.6 sq. mi.; **Water:** 0.0 sq. mi.
Settled 1864.
Name origin: Named by J.L. Davison, who built a mill at Weeping Water Falls just above a ford on the Blue River.

Pleasant Dale — Village
ZIP: 68423   **Lat:** 40-47-30 N **Long:** 96-55-57 W
Pop: 253 (1990); 259 (1980)   **Pop Density:** 2530.0
Land: 0.1 sq. mi.; **Water:** 0.0 sq. mi.

Seward — City
ZIP: 68434   **Lat:** 40-54-43 N **Long:** 97-05-47 W
Pop: 5,634 (1990); 5,713 (1980)   **Pop Density:** 3130.0
Land: 1.8 sq. mi.; **Water:** 0.0 sq. mi.
Name origin: For the county.

Staplehurst — Village
ZIP: 68439   **Lat:** 40-58-29 N **Long:** 97-10-19 W
Pop: 281 (1990); 306 (1980)   **Pop Density:** 2810.0
Land: 0.1 sq. mi.; **Water:** 0.0 sq. mi.
Name origin: Named in 1873 by settler Ebenezar Jull for his former home town in England.

Tamora — Village
ZIP: 68434   **Lat:** 40-53-44 N **Long:** 97-13-26 W
Pop: 51 (1990); 50 (1980)   **Pop Density:** 255.0
Land: 0.2 sq. mi.; **Water:** 0.0 sq. mi.
Surveyed 1879.
Name origin: Coined from the word "tomorrow" because after each discussion about which townsite donor's name would be given to the town, it was decided to put off the final decision "until tomorrow."

Utica — Village
ZIP: 68456   **Lat:** 40-53-44 N **Long:** 97-20-42 W
Pop: 718 (1990); 689 (1980)   **Pop Density:** 1795.0
Land: 0.4 sq. mi.; **Water:** 0.0 sq. mi.
Name origin: For Utica, NY.

Sheridan County
County Seat: Rushville (ZIP: 69360)

Pop: 6,750 (1990); 7,544 (1980)   **Pop Density:** 2.8
Land: 2441.2 sq. mi.; **Water:** 28.9 sq. mi.   **Area Code:** 308

On the northern border of NE, northeast of Scottsbluff; organized Feb 25, 1885 from Sioux County.

Name origin: For Gen. Philip Henry Sheridan (1831–88), Union officer during the Civil War and commander in chief of the U.S. army (1883–88).

Clinton — Village
ZIP: 69343   Lat: 42-45-33 N   Long: 102-20-53 W
Pop: 33 (1990); 80 (1980)   **Pop Density:** 330.0
Land: 0.1 sq. mi.; **Water:** 0.0 sq. mi.

Gordon — City
ZIP: 69343   Lat: 42-48-22 N   Long: 102-12-13 W
Pop: 1,803 (1990); 2,167 (1980)   **Pop Density:** 2003.3
Land: 0.9 sq. mi.; **Water:** 0.0 sq. mi.

Hay Springs — Village
ZIP: 69347   Lat: 42-40-59 N   Long: 102-41-20 W
Pop: 693 (1990); 794 (1980)   **Pop Density:** 1732.5
Land: 0.4 sq. mi.; **Water:** 0.0 sq. mi.

Rushville — City
ZIP: 69360   Lat: 42-42-46 N   Long: 102-27-56 W
Pop: 1,127 (1990); 1,217 (1980)   **Pop Density:** 1024.5
Land: 1.1 sq. mi.; **Water:** 0.0 sq. mi.

Name origin: For nearby Rush Creek, which got its name from the rushes growing in the area.

Sherman County
County Seat: Loup City (ZIP: 68853)

Pop: 3,718 (1990); 4,226 (1980)   **Pop Density:** 6.6
Land: 565.9 sq. mi.; **Water:** 5.8 sq. mi.   **Area Code:** 308

In central NE, northwest of Grand Island; organized Mar 1, 1871 from Buffalo County.

Name origin: For Gen. William Tecumseh Sherman (1820–91), officer in the Mexican-American War and the Civil War, remembered for his "march to the sea" through the South.

Ashton — Village
ZIP: 68817   Lat: 41-14-51 N   Long: 98-47-40 W
Pop: 251 (1990); 273 (1980)   **Pop Density:** 418.3
Land: 0.6 sq. mi.; **Water:** 0.0 sq. mi.

Name origin: For settler John P. Taylor's former home in Ashton, IL.

Hazard — Village
ZIP: 68844   Lat: 41-05-28 N   Long: 99-04-41 W
Pop: 78 (1990); 75 (1980)   **Pop Density:** 260.0
Land: 0.3 sq. mi.; **Water:** 0.0 sq. mi.

Not coextensive with the township.

Name origin: Supposedly named when a conference was held to decide the village name, and one man said he would "hazard some name."

Litchfield — Village
ZIP: 68852   Lat: 41-09-21 N   Long: 99-09-06 W
Pop: 314 (1990); 256 (1980)   **Pop Density:** 1046.7
Land: 0.3 sq. mi.; **Water:** 0.0 sq. mi.

Established 1886.

Name origin: Probably named for Litchfield, CT.

Loup City — City
ZIP: 68853   Lat: 41-16-34 N   Long: 98-58-03 W
Pop: 1,104 (1990); 1,368 (1980)   **Pop Density:** 1226.7
Land: 0.9 sq. mi.; **Water:** 0.0 sq. mi.

Not coextensive with the township.

Name origin: From French meaning 'wolf,' for its location in the Loup Valley.

Rockville — Village
ZIP: 68871   Lat: 41-07-09 N   Long: 98-49-51 W
Pop: 87 (1990); 116 (1980)   **Pop Density:** 290.0
Land: 0.3 sq. mi.; **Water:** 0.0 sq. mi.

Name origin: For nearby Rock Creek, itself named for the lime rocks in its bed.

Sioux County
County Seat: Harrison (ZIP: 69346)

Pop: 1,549 (1990); 1,845 (1980)   **Pop Density:** 0.7
Land: 2066.7 sq. mi.; **Water:** 0.7 sq. mi.   **Area Code:** 308

On the northwestern border of NE, north of Scottsbluff; organized Feb 19, 1877 from unorganized territory.
Name origin: For the Sioux Indian tribe, also known as the Dakotas.

Harrison   Village
ZIP: 69346   **Lat:** 42-41-16 N   **Long:** 103-52-53 W
Pop: 291 (1990); 361 (1980)   **Pop Density:** 970.0
Land: 0.3 sq. mi.; **Water:** 0.0 sq. mi.
Name origin: For Benjamin Harrison (1833–1901), twenty-third U.S. president. Previously called Bowen.

Stanton County
County Seat: Stanton (ZIP: 68779)

Pop: 6,244 (1990); 6,549 (1980)   **Pop Density:** 14.5
Land: 429.9 sq. mi.; **Water:** 1.2 sq. mi.   **Area Code:** 402

In east-central NE, west of Norfolk; organized Jan 10, 1862 from Dodge County; previously called Izard County.
Name origin: For Edwin McMasters Stanton (1814–69), U.S. secretary of war under Abraham Lincoln and Andrew Johnson (1862–68).

Pilger   Village
ZIP: 68768   **Lat:** 42-00-27 N   **Long:** 97-03-14 W
Pop: 361 (1990); 400 (1980)   **Pop Density:** 1203.3
Land: 0.3 sq. mi.; **Water:** 0.0 sq. mi.
Name origin: For Peter Pilger, who owned the land on which the village was located.

Stanton   City
ZIP: 68779   **Lat:** 41-56-55 N   **Long:** 97-13-26 W
Pop: 1,549 (1990); 1,603 (1980)   **Pop Density:** 1549.0
Land: 1.0 sq. mi.; **Water:** 0.0 sq. mi.
Platted 1871.
Name origin: For the maiden name of S.L. Halman's wife.

Union Creek   Pop. Place
Lat: 41-52-21 N   **Long:** 97-18-15 W
Pop: 152 (1990)   **Pop Density:** 4.2
Land: 35.9 sq. mi.; **Water:** 0.0 sq. mi.

Thayer County
County Seat: Hebron (ZIP: 68370)

Pop: 6,635 (1990); 7,582 (1980)   **Pop Density:** 11.5
Land: 574.6 sq. mi.; **Water:** 0.8 sq. mi.   **Area Code:** 402

On the southern border of NE, southwest of Lincoln; organized as Jefferson County 1867; name changed 1871.
Name origin: For Gen. John Milton Thayer (1820–1906), an officer in the Civil War, U.S. senator from NE (1867–71), and governor (1887–92).

Alexandria   Village
ZIP: 68303   **Lat:** 40-14-50 N   **Long:** 97-23-12 W
Pop: 224 (1990); 255 (1980)   **Pop Density:** 560.0
Land: 0.4 sq. mi.; **Water:** 0.0 sq. mi.
Established 1871.
Name origin: For NE secretary of state, S.J. Alexander.

Belvidere   Village
ZIP: 68315   **Lat:** 40-15-15 N   **Long:** 97-33-24 W
Pop: 117 (1990); 158 (1980)   **Pop Density:** 234.0
Land: 0.5 sq. mi.; **Water:** 0.0 sq. mi.
Name origin: Possibly for Belvidere, IL or NJ.

Bruning
Village
ZIP: 68322 **Lat:** 40-20-08 N **Long:** 97-33-52 W
Pop: 332 (1990); 330 (1980) **Pop Density:** 1106.7
Land: 0.3 sq. mi.; **Water:** 0.0 sq. mi.
Name origin: For early settlers Frank Bruning and his brother.

Byron
Village
ZIP: 68325 **Lat:** 40-00-18 N **Long:** 97-46-05 W
Pop: 140 (1990); 154 (1980) **Pop Density:** 700.0
Land: 0.2 sq. mi.; **Water:** 0.0 sq. mi.
Name origin: For English poet George Gordon Lord Byron (1788–1824).

Carleton
Village
ZIP: 68326 **Lat:** 40-18-06 N **Long:** 97-40-24 W
Pop: 144 (1990); 160 (1980) **Pop Density:** 288.0
Land: 0.5 sq. mi.; **Water:** 0.0 sq. mi.
Name origin: For the son of the townsite owner. Originally known as Coldrain or Coleraine.

Chester
Village
ZIP: 68327 **Lat:** 40-00-34 N **Long:** 97-37-03 W
Pop: 351 (1990); 435 (1980) **Pop Density:** 702.0
Land: 0.5 sq. mi.; **Water:** 0.0 sq. mi.

Davenport
Village
ZIP: 68335 **Lat:** 40-18-41 N **Long:** 97-48-36 W
Pop: 383 (1990); 445 (1980) **Pop Density:** 547.1
Land: 0.7 sq. mi.; **Water:** 0.0 sq. mi.
Established 1872.
Name origin: For Davenport, IA.

Deshler
City
ZIP: 68340 **Lat:** 40-08-20 N **Long:** 97-43-23 W
Pop: 892 (1990); 997 (1980) **Pop Density:** 1784.0
Land: 0.5 sq. mi.; **Water:** 0.0 sq. mi.
Name origin: For John Deshler, who was the original owner of the townsite.

Gilead
Village
ZIP: 68362 **Lat:** 40-08-47 N **Long:** 97-24-53 W
Pop: 37 (1990); 69 (1980) **Pop Density:** 370.0
Land: 0.1 sq. mi.; **Water:** 0.0 sq. mi.
Name origin: For Mount Gilead in Palestine.

Hebron
City
ZIP: 68370 **Lat:** 40-10-06 N **Long:** 97-35-15 W
Pop: 1,765 (1990); 1,906 (1980) **Pop Density:** 1260.7
Land: 1.4 sq. mi.; **Water:** 0.0 sq. mi.
Name origin: Settlers associated with the Disciples of Christ named this city for the biblical Hebron in Palestine.

Hubbell
Village
ZIP: 68375 **Lat:** 40-00-27 N **Long:** 97-29-48 W
Pop: 55 (1990); 71 (1980) **Pop Density:** 183.3
Land: 0.3 sq. mi.; **Water:** 0.0 sq. mi.
Established 1880 by the Lincoln Land and Loan Company.
Name origin: For Hubbell H. Johnson, who owned the land on which the site was located.

Thomas County
County Seat: Thedford (ZIP: 69166)

Pop: 851 (1990); 973 (1980) **Pop Density:** 1.2
Land: 712.9 sq. mi.; **Water:** 0.8 sq. mi. **Area Code:** 308
In central NE, north of North Platte; organized Mar 31, 1887 from Blaine County.
Name origin: For Gen. George Henry Thomas (1816–70), Union commander of the Army of the Cumberland.

Halsey
Village
ZIP: 69142 **Lat:** 41-54-12 N **Long:** 100-16-13 W
Pop: 102 (1990); 134 (1980) **Pop Density:** 510.0
Land: 0.2 sq. mi.; **Water:** 0.0 sq. mi.
Part of the town is also in Blaine County.
Name origin: For Halsey Yates, a surveyor for the railroad.

Seneca
Village
ZIP: 69161 **Lat:** 42-02-33 N **Long:** 100-49-52 W
Pop: 78 (1990); 90 (1980) **Pop Density:** 780.0
Land: 0.1 sq. mi.; **Water:** 0.0 sq. mi.
Name origin: For the Seneca Indians.

Thedford
Village
ZIP: 69166 **Lat:** 41-58-43 N **Long:** 100-34-28 W
Pop: 243 (1990); 313 (1980) **Pop Density:** 1215.0
Land: 0.2 sq. mi.; **Water:** 0.0 sq. mi.
Name origin: Probably for the town of Thedford, Ontario, Canada.

Thurston County
County Seat: Pender (ZIP: 68047)

Pop: 6,936 (1990); 7,186 (1980)   **Pop Density:** 17.6
Land: 393.8 sq. mi.; **Water:** 2.4 sq. mi.   **Area Code:** 402
On the northeastern border of NE, south of Sioux City, IA; organized as Blackbird County Mar 7, 1865 from Burt County; name changed in 1889.
Name origin: For John Mellen Thurston (1847–1916), U.S. senator from NE (1895–1901), active in establishing the county. Originally named for either Chief Blackbird of the Omaha Indians, or Black Bird, for their mythological Thunder Bird.

Anderson   Township
Lat: 42-04-03 N   **Long:** 96-19-50 W
Pop: 202 (1990); 144 (1980)   **Pop Density:** 6.6
Land: 30.6 sq. mi.; **Water:** 0.3 sq. mi.

Blackbird   Township
Lat: 42-08-43 N   **Long:** 96-21-10 W
Pop: 1,292 (1990); 1,149 (1980)   **Pop Density:** 49.3
Land: 26.2 sq. mi.; **Water:** 0.8 sq. mi.

Bryan   Township
Lat: 42-07-35 N   **Long:** 96-34-47 W
Pop: 118 (1990); 157 (1980)   **Pop Density:** 5.8
Land: 20.4 sq. mi.; **Water:** 0.0 sq. mi.

Dawes   Township
Lat: 42-04-00 N   **Long:** 96-28-20 W
Pop: 424 (1990); 554 (1980)   **Pop Density:** 8.0
Land: 52.8 sq. mi.; **Water:** 0.0 sq. mi.

Emerson   Village
Lat: 42-16-28 N   **Long:** 96-43-27 W
Pop: 92 (1990); 102 (1980)   **Pop Density:** 920.0
Land: 0.1 sq. mi.; **Water:** 0.0 sq. mi.
Platted 1883. Part of the town is also in Dakota and Dixon counties.
Name origin: For author Ralph Waldo Emerson (1803–82).

Flournoy   Township
Lat: 42-12-05 N   **Long:** 96-42-48 W
Pop: 306 (1990); 364 (1980)   **Pop Density:** 8.5
Land: 35.9 sq. mi.; **Water:** 0.0 sq. mi.

Macy   CDP
ZIP: 68039   **Lat:** 42-06-45 N   **Long:** 96-21-46 W
Pop: 836 (1990)   **Pop Density:** 696.7
Land: 1.2 sq. mi.; **Water:** 0.0 sq. mi.

Merry   Township
Lat: 42-13-26 N   **Long:** 96-35-49 W
Pop: 106 (1990); 163 (1980)   **Pop Density:** 3.4
Land: 31.4 sq. mi.; **Water:** 0.0 sq. mi.

Omaha   Township
Lat: 42-08-53 N   **Long:** 96-28-56 W
Pop: 1,212 (1990); 1,146 (1980)   **Pop Density:** 27.1
Land: 44.8 sq. mi.; **Water:** 0.0 sq. mi.

Pender   Village
ZIP: 68047   **Lat:** 42-06-36 N   **Long:** 96-42-38 W
Pop: 1,208 (1990); 1,318 (1980)   **Pop Density:** 2013.3
Land: 0.6 sq. mi.; **Water:** 0.0 sq. mi.
Not coextensive with the township.
Name origin: For John Pender, director of the Chicago, St. Paul, Minneapolis & Omaha Railroad. Originally known as Athens.

*Pender   Township
ZIP: 68047   **Lat:** 42-07-59 N   **Long:** 96-41-09 W
Pop: 1,393 (1990); 1,552 (1980)   **Pop Density:** 46.3
Land: 30.1 sq. mi.; **Water:** 0.0 sq. mi.

Perry   Township
Lat: 42-14-23 N   **Long:** 96-42-57 W
Pop: 329 (1990); 319 (1980)   **Pop Density:** 9.5
Land: 34.6 sq. mi.; **Water:** 0.0 sq. mi.

Rosalie   Village
ZIP: 68055   **Lat:** 42-03-24 N   **Long:** 96-30-45 W
Pop: 178 (1990); 224 (1980)   **Pop Density:** 890.0
Land: 0.2 sq. mi.; **Water:** 0.0 sq. mi.
Name origin: For daughter of Omaha chief Joseph LaFlesche.

Thayer   Township
Lat: 42-07-58 N   **Long:** 96-46-55 W
Pop: 155 (1990); 194 (1980)   **Pop Density:** 6.5
Land: 24.0 sq. mi.; **Water:** 0.0 sq. mi.

Thurston   Village
ZIP: 68062   **Lat:** 42-10-35 N   **Long:** 96-41-59 W
Pop: 98 (1990); 139 (1980)   **Pop Density:** 980.0
Land: 0.1 sq. mi.; **Water:** 0.0 sq. mi.
Name origin: For U.S. senator John M. Thurston of NE. Originally known as Flournoy.

Walthill   Village
ZIP: 68067   **Lat:** 42-08-55 N   **Long:** 96-29-34 W
Pop: 747 (1990); 847 (1980)   **Pop Density:** 1867.5
Land: 0.4 sq. mi.; **Water:** 0.0 sq. mi.
Settled c. 1906.
Name origin: For Walter Hill, who helped organize the town.

Winnebago   Village
ZIP: 68071   **Lat:** 42-14-13 N   **Long:** 96-28-22 W
Pop: 705 (1990); 902 (1980)   **Pop Density:** 2350.0
Land: 0.3 sq. mi.; **Water:** 0.0 sq. mi.
Not coextensive with the township.
Name origin: For the Winnebago Indian tribe.

*Winnebago   Township
ZIP: 68071   **Lat:** 42-14-03 N   **Long:** 96-26-38 W
Pop: 1,399 (1990); 1,444 (1980)   **Pop Density:** 22.2
Land: 62.9 sq. mi.; **Water:** 1.3 sq. mi.

NEBRASKA, Valley County — American Places Dictionary

Valley County
County Seat: Ord (ZIP: 68862)

Pop: 5,169 (1990); 5,633 (1980) **Pop Density:** 9.1
Land: 568.1 sq. mi.; **Water:** 2.4 sq. mi. **Area Code:** 308
In central NE, northwest of Grand Island; organized Mar 1, 1871 from unorganized territory.
Name origin: For the North Loup River valley, which comprises the county.

Arcadia Village
ZIP: 68815 Lat: 41-25-28 N Long: 99-07-32 W
Pop: 385 (1990); 412 (1980) Pop Density: 641.7
Land: 0.6 sq. mi.; Water: 0.0 sq. mi.
Not coextensive with the township.

*Arcadia Township
ZIP: 68815 Lat: 41-26-16 N Long: 99-09-15 W
Pop: 530 (1990); 556 (1980) Pop Density: 14.8
Land: 35.9 sq. mi.; Water: 0.0 sq. mi.

Davis Creek Township
ZIP: 68815 Lat: 41-26-18 N Long: 98-55-09 W
Pop: 98 (1990); 109 (1980) Pop Density: 2.7
Land: 36.0 sq. mi.; Water: 0.0 sq. mi.

Elyria Village
ZIP: 68837 Lat: 41-40-46 N Long: 99-00-18 W
Pop: 61 (1990); 62 (1980) Pop Density: 203.3
Land: 0.3 sq. mi.; Water: 0.0 sq. mi.
Not coextensive with the township.

*Elyria Township
Lat: 41-42-00 N Long: 99-00-55 W
Pop: 229 (1990); 226 (1980) Pop Density: 4.4
Land: 52.3 sq. mi.; Water: 0.8 sq. mi.

Enterprise Township
ZIP: 68859 Lat: 41-31-20 N Long: 98-55-08 W
Pop: 122 (1990); 160 (1980) Pop Density: 3.4
Land: 35.8 sq. mi.; Water: 0.0 sq. mi.

Eureka Township
ZIP: 68859 Lat: 41-40-56 N Long: 99-09-13 W
Pop: 76 (1990); 114 (1980) Pop Density: 2.1
Land: 35.5 sq. mi.; Water: 0.0 sq. mi.

Geranium Township
Lat: 41-36-35 N Long: 99-09-24 W
Pop: 113 (1990); 139 (1980) Pop Density: 3.2
Land: 35.8 sq. mi.; Water: 0.0 sq. mi.

Independent Township
ZIP: 68859 Lat: 41-26-02 N Long: 98-49-03 W
Pop: 87 (1990); 90 (1980) Pop Density: 2.4
Land: 35.8 sq. mi.; Water: 0.0 sq. mi.

Liberty Township
ZIP: 68815 Lat: 41-32-22 N Long: 99-09-34 W
Pop: 60 (1990); 80 (1980) Pop Density: 1.7
Land: 35.8 sq. mi.; Water: 0.0 sq. mi.

Michigan Township
ZIP: 68862 Lat: 41-37-06 N Long: 99-02-10 W
Pop: 83 (1990); 103 (1980) Pop Density: 2.3
Land: 35.7 sq. mi.; Water: 0.0 sq. mi.

Noble Township
ZIP: 68862 Lat: 41-41-37 N Long: 98-50-14 W
Pop: 120 (1990); 130 (1980) Pop Density: 2.3
Land: 52.7 sq. mi.; Water: 0.0 sq. mi.

North Loup Village
ZIP: 68859 Lat: 41-29-41 N Long: 98-46-18 W
Pop: 361 (1990); 405 (1980) Pop Density: 902.5
Land: 0.4 sq. mi.; Water: 0.0 sq. mi.
Not coextensive with the township.
Name origin: For its location in the valley of the North Loup River.

*North Loup Township
ZIP: 68859 Lat: 41-32-06 N Long: 98-49-12 W
Pop: 539 (1990); 615 (1980) Pop Density: 13.5
Land: 40.0 sq. mi.; Water: 0.8 sq. mi.

Ord City
ZIP: 68862 Lat: 41-36-09 N Long: 98-55-46 W
Pop: 2,481 (1990); 2,658 (1980) Pop Density: 1550.6
Land: 1.6 sq. mi.; Water: 0.0 sq. mi.
Not coextensive with the township. Surveyed 1874.
Name origin: For Gen. E.O.C. Ord, who commanded the military department of the Platte.

*Ord Township
ZIP: 68862 Lat: 41-36-43 N Long: 98-55-28 W
Pop: 2,878 (1990); 2,978 (1980) Pop Density: 81.8
Land: 35.2 sq. mi.; Water: 0.4 sq. mi.

Springdale Township
ZIP: 68862 Lat: 41-37-06 N Long: 98-48-34 W
Pop: 66 (1990); 97 (1980) Pop Density: 2.2
Land: 30.3 sq. mi.; Water: 0.3 sq. mi.

Vinton Township
ZIP: 68815 Lat: 41-32-19 N Long: 99-02-13 W
Pop: 89 (1990); 127 (1980) Pop Density: 2.5
Land: 35.6 sq. mi.; Water: 0.0 sq. mi.

Yale Township
ZIP: 68815 Lat: 41-26-41 N Long: 99-02-27 W
Pop: 79 (1990); 109 (1980) Pop Density: 2.2
Land: 35.8 sq. mi.; Water: 0.0 sq. mi.

Washington County
County Seat: Blair (ZIP: 68008)

Pop: 16,607 (1990); 15,508 (1980)   **Pop Density:** 42.5
Land: 390.5 sq. mi.; **Water:** 3.3 sq. mi.   **Area Code:** 402
On the central eastern border of NE, north of Omaha; original county; organized Feb 22, 1855 (prior to statehood).
Name origin: For George Washington (1732–99), American patriot and first U.S. president.

Arlington   Village
ZIP: 68002   **Lat:** 41-27-15 N   **Long:** 96-21-19 W
Pop: 1,178 (1990); 1,117 (1980)   **Pop Density:** 1963.3
Land: 0.6 sq. mi.; **Water:** 0.0 sq. mi.
Name origin: Named in 1882 for Arlington, VA. Originally called Bell Creek for the Bell family, who settled at a nearby creek.

Blair   City
ZIP: 68008   **Lat:** 41-32-39 N   **Long:** 96-08-12 W
Pop: 6,860 (1990); 6,418 (1980)   **Pop Density:** 1673.2
Land: 4.1 sq. mi.; **Water:** 0.0 sq. mi.
Platted 1869.
Name origin: For railroad financier John I. Blair, who owned land here.

Fort Calhoun   City
ZIP: 68023   **Lat:** 41-27-18 N   **Long:** 96-01-32 W
Pop: 648 (1990); 641 (1980)   **Pop Density:** 1296.0
Land: 0.5 sq. mi.; **Water:** 0.0 sq. mi.
Not coextensive with the township.
Name origin: For John C. Calhoun (1782–1850), U.S. secretary of war. Originally known as Fort Atkinson.

Herman   Village
ZIP: 68029   **Lat:** 41-40-23 N   **Long:** 96-12-59 W
Pop: 186 (1990); 340 (1980)   **Pop Density:** 930.0
Land: 0.2 sq. mi.; **Water:** 0.0 sq. mi.
Platted 1871.
Name origin: For Samuel Herman, a conductor on the Omaha & Northwestern Railroad.

Kennard   Village
ZIP: 68034   **Lat:** 41-28-27 N   **Long:** 96-12-12 W
Pop: 371 (1990); 372 (1980)   **Pop Density:** 1236.7
Land: 0.3 sq. mi.; **Water:** 0.0 sq. mi.
Incorporated 1895.
Name origin: For the Hon. Thomas P. Kennard, NE's first secretary of state.

Washington   Village
ZIP: 68068   **Lat:** 41-23-53 N   **Long:** 96-12-31 W
Pop: 125 (1990); 113 (1980)   **Pop Density:** 625.0
Land: 0.2 sq. mi.; **Water:** 0.0 sq. mi.
Platted 1887.
Name origin: For the county.

Wayne County
County Seat: Wayne (ZIP: 68787)

Pop: 9,364 (1990); 9,858 (1980)   **Pop Density:** 21.1
Land: 443.5 sq. mi.; **Water:** 0.0 sq. mi.   **Area Code:** 402
In northeastern NE, southwest of Sioux City, IA; organized 1870 from Thurston County.
Name origin: For Gen. Anthony Wayne (1745–96), PA soldier and statesman, nicknamed "Mad Anthony" for his daring during the Revolutionary War.

Carroll   Village
ZIP: 68723   **Lat:** 42-16-34 N   **Long:** 97-11-27 W
Pop: 237 (1990); 246 (1980)   **Pop Density:** 2370.0
Land: 0.1 sq. mi.; **Water:** 0.0 sq. mi.
Name origin: For Charles Carroll (1737–1832), one of the signers of the Declaration of Independence.

Hoskins   Village
ZIP: 68740   **Lat:** 42-06-49 N   **Long:** 97-18-16 W
Pop: 307 (1990); 306 (1980)   **Pop Density:** 767.5
Land: 0.4 sq. mi.; **Water:** 0.0 sq. mi.
Name origin: For a member of the land company that established the town.

Sholes   Village
Lat: 42-20-06 N   **Long:** 97-17-38 W
Pop: 22 (1990); 27 (1980)   **Pop Density:** 220.0
Land: 0.1 sq. mi.; **Water:** 0.0 sq. mi.
Established 1902.
Name origin: For railroad official Lyman Sholes.

Wakefield   City
Lat: 42-15-49 N   **Long:** 96-52-06 W
Pop: 76 (1990); 134 (1980)   **Pop Density:** 380.0
Land: 0.2 sq. mi.; **Water:** 0.0 sq. mi.
Founded 1881. Part of the town is also in Dixon County.
Name origin: For L.W. Wakefield, an engineer for the railroad surveying party.

NEBRASKA, Wayne County

Wayne
City
ZIP: 68787 **Lat:** 42-14-13 N **Long:** 97-01-00 W
Pop: 5,142 (1990); 5,240 (1980) **Pop Density:** 2706.3
Land: 1.9 sq. mi.; **Water:** 0.0 sq. mi.
Name origin: For the county.

Winside
Village
ZIP: 68790 **Lat:** 42-10-40 N **Long:** 97-10-26 W
Pop: 434 (1990); 439 (1980) **Pop Density:** 1446.7
Land: 0.3 sq. mi.; **Water:** 0.0 sq. mi.
Name origin: For what was considered to be a "winning location at the side of the railroad tracks."

Webster County
County Seat: Red Cloud (ZIP: 68970)

Pop: 4,279 (1990); 4,858 (1980) **Pop Density:** 7.4
Land: 574.9 sq. mi.; **Water:** 0.1 sq. mi. **Area Code:** 402

On the central southern border of NE, south of Grand Island; organized Feb 16, 1867 (prior to statehood) from unorganized territory.

Name origin: For Daniel Webster (1782–1852), U.S. statesman and orator from MA.

Bladen
Village
ZIP: 68928 **Lat:** 40-19-24 N **Long:** 98-35-42 W
Pop: 280 (1990); 298 (1980) **Pop Density:** 700.0
Land: 0.4 sq. mi.; **Water:** 0.0 sq. mi.
Platted 1886 by the Lincoln Land Company.

Blue Hill
City
ZIP: 68930 **Lat:** 40-19-58 N **Long:** 98-26-51 W
Pop: 810 (1990); 883 (1980) **Pop Density:** 1157.1
Land: 0.7 sq. mi.; **Water:** 0.0 sq. mi.
Name origin: For its location in the hills near the Blue River. Previously called Belmont.

Cowles
Village
ZIP: 68930 **Lat:** 40-10-15 N **Long:** 98-26-52 W
Pop: 42 (1990); 48 (1980) **Pop Density:** 84.0
Land: 0.5 sq. mi.; **Water:** 0.0 sq. mi.
Platted 1878.
Name origin: For W.D. Cowles, a freight agent for the Burlington & Missouri River Railroad.

Guide Rock
Village
ZIP: 68942 **Lat:** 40-04-22 N **Long:** 98-19-45 W
Pop: 290 (1990); 344 (1980) **Pop Density:** 580.0
Land: 0.5 sq. mi.; **Water:** 0.0 sq. mi.
Name origin: For a nearby rocky bluff that rises above the old bed of the Republican River and was a prominent landmark for early pioneers.

Red Cloud
City
ZIP: 68970 **Lat:** 40-05-09 N **Long:** 98-31-20 W
Pop: 1,204 (1990); 1,300 (1980) **Pop Density:** 1204.0
Land: 1.0 sq. mi.; **Water:** 0.0 sq. mi.
Name origin: For Chief Red Cloud (Mahpiua Luta, 1822–1909) of the Oglala-Sioux Indians.

Wheeler County
County Seat: Bartlett (ZIP: 68622)

Pop: 948 (1990); 1,060 (1980) **Pop Density:** 1.6
Land: 575.2 sq. mi.; **Water:** 0.4 sq. mi. **Area Code:** 308

In north-central NE, north of Grand Island; organized Feb 17, 1877 from Boone County.

Name origin: For Daniel H. Wheeler (1834–?), a state official.

Bartlett
Village
ZIP: 68622 **Lat:** 41-53-02 N **Long:** 98-33-04 W
Pop: 131 (1990); 144 (1980) **Pop Density:** 1310.0
Land: 0.1 sq. mi.; **Water:** 0.0 sq. mi.
Founded c. 1885.
Name origin: For founder Ezra Bartlett Hitchell.

Ericson
Village
ZIP: 68637 **Lat:** 41-46-49 N **Long:** 98-40-39 W
Pop: 111 (1990); 132 (1980) **Pop Density:** 370.0
Land: 0.3 sq. mi.; **Water:** 0.0 sq. mi.
Name origin: For Christensen Erickson and his two sons, Eric and Peter.

American Places Dictionary   NEBRASKA, York County

York County
County Seat: York (ZIP: 68467)

Pop: 14,428 (1990); 14,798 (1980)   **Pop Density:** 25.1
Land: 575.7 sq. mi.; **Water:** 0.4 sq. mi.   **Area Code:** 402
In south-central NE, west of Lincoln; original county; boundaries defined Mar 13, 1855 (prior to statehood).
Name origin: Either for York, England, named by Alfred D. Jones. Or for York County, PA, former home of early settlers.

Benedict — Village
ZIP: 68316   **Lat:** 41-00-23 N **Long:** 97-36-24 W
Pop: 230 (1990); 228 (1980)   **Pop Density:** 1150.0
Land: 0.2 sq. mi.; **Water:** 0.0 sq. mi.
Incorporated 1898.
Name origin: For E.C. Benedict, president of the Kansas City & Omaha Railroad.

Bradshaw — Village
ZIP: 68319   **Lat:** 40-53-01 N **Long:** 97-44-46 W
Pop: 330 (1990); 373 (1980)   **Pop Density:** 1100.0
Land: 0.3 sq. mi.; **Water:** 0.0 sq. mi.
Established 1890.
Name origin: For the maiden name of J.M. Richard's wife.

Gresham — Village
ZIP: 68367   **Lat:** 41-01-39 N **Long:** 97-24-04 W
Pop: 253 (1990); 320 (1980)   **Pop Density:** 843.3
Land: 0.3 sq. mi.; **Water:** 0.0 sq. mi.
Platted 1887 by the Pioneer Town-Site Company.
Name origin: For Walter Quinton Gresham (1832–95), U.S. secretary of state under Pres. Cleveland.

Henderson — City
ZIP: 68371   **Lat:** 40-46-44 N **Long:** 97-48-41 W
Pop: 999 (1990); 1,072 (1980)   **Pop Density:** 1998.0
Land: 0.5 sq. mi.; **Water:** 0.0 sq. mi.
Settled c. 1866.
Name origin: For pioneers David Henderson and his son, John.

Lushton — Village
ZIP: 68371   **Lat:** 40-43-25 N **Long:** 97-43-26 W
Pop: 28 (1990); 33 (1980)   **Pop Density:** 280.0
Land: 0.1 sq. mi.; **Water:** 0.0 sq. mi.
Surveyed 1887.

McCool Junction — Village
ZIP: 68401   **Lat:** 40-44-39 N **Long:** 97-35-42 W
Pop: 372 (1990); 404 (1980)   **Pop Density:** 1240.0
Land: 0.3 sq. mi.; **Water:** 0.0 sq. mi.

Thayer — Village
ZIP: 68460   **Lat:** 40-58-10 N **Long:** 97-29-40 W
Pop: 64 (1990); 70 (1980)   **Pop Density:** 213.3
Land: 0.3 sq. mi.; **Water:** 0.0 sq. mi.

Waco — Village
ZIP: 68460   **Lat:** 40-53-47 N **Long:** 97-27-40 W
Pop: 211 (1990); 225 (1980)   **Pop Density:** 1055.0
Land: 0.2 sq. mi.; **Water:** 0.0 sq. mi.
Name origin: Named by Miss Chapin, who donated land for the townsite, for her former home in TX.

York — City
ZIP: 68467   **Lat:** 40-52-16 N **Long:** 97-35-44 W
Pop: 7,884 (1990); 7,723 (1980)   **Pop Density:** 1407.9
Land: 5.6 sq. mi.; **Water:** 0.0 sq. mi.
Platted 1896.

Index to Places and Counties in Nebraska

Abie (Butler) Village....................*380*
Adams (Gage) Township *399*
Adams (Gage) Village *399*
Adams County.................................*372*
Addison (Knox) Township *413*
Ainsworth (Brown) City *377*
Albany (Harlan) Township *404*
Albion (Boone) City *375*
Alda (Hall) Township *402*
Alda (Hall) Village *402*
Alexandria (Thayer) Village *435*
Alexis (Butler) Township *380*
Algernon (Custer) Township..............*388*
Allen (Dixon) Village *392*
Alliance (Box Butte) City *376*
Alma (Harlan) City............................*404*
Alma (Harlan) Township *404*
Alvo (Cass) Village *382*
Amherst (Buffalo) Village..................*378*
Anderson (Phelps) Township.............*423*
Anderson (Thurston) Township *437*
Anoka (Boyd) Village *376*
Anselmo (Custer) Village...................*388*
Ansley (Custer) Township *388*
Ansley (Custer) Village......................*388*
Antelope (Franklin) Township *396*
Antelope (Harlan) Township *404*
Antelope (Holt) Township *406*
Antelope County.............................*373*
Arapahoe (Furnas) City *398*
Arcadia (Valley) Township *438*
Arcadia (Valley) Village.....................*438*
Arizona (Burt) Township...................*379*
Arlington (Washington) Village.........*439*
Armada (Buffalo) Township..............*378*
Arnold (Custer) Township *388*
Arnold (Custer) Village......................*388*
Arthur (Arthur) Village......................*374*
Arthur County................................*374*
Ash Grove (Franklin) Township *396*
Ashland (Saunders) City....................*430*
Ashland (Saunders) Township...........*430*
Ashton (Sherman) Village *434*
Atkinson (Holt) City..........................*406*
Atkinson (Holt) Township.................*406*
Atlanta (Phelps) Village.....................*423*
Auburn (Nemaha) City......................*420*
Aurora (Hamilton) City.....................*403*
Avoca (Cass) Village *382*
Axtell (Kearney) Village....................*411*
Ayr (Adams) Village *372*
Bancroft (Cuming) Township............*387*
Bancroft (Cuming) Village.................*387*
Banner County...............................*375*
Barada (Richardson) Village.............*427*
Barneston (Gage) Township *399*
Barneston (Gage) Village...................*399*
Bartlett (Wheeler) Village..................*440*
Bartley (Red Willow) Village *427*
Basin (Boyd) Township *376*
Bassett (Rock) City............................*428*
Battle Creek (Madison) Village..........*417*
Bayard (Morrill) City.........................*419*
Bazile (Antelope) Township *373*
Bazile Mills (Knox) Village *413*
Beatrice (Gage) City *399*
Beaver (Buffalo) Township................*378*
Beaver (Nance) Township..................*419*
Beaver City (Furnas) City *398*
Beaver Crossing (Seward) Village *433*

Bee (Seward) Village..........................*433*
Beemer (Cuming) Township..............*387*
Beemer (Cuming) Village *387*
Belden (Cedar) Village.......................*383*
Belgrade (Nance) Village *419*
Bell Creek (Burt) Township...............*379*
Belle (Holt) Township........................*406*
Belle Prairie (Fillmore) Township.....*395*
Bellevue (Sarpy) City.........................*429*
Bellwood (Butler) Village *380*
Belvidere (Thayer) Village.................*435*
Benedict (York) Village *441*
Benkelman (Dundy) City *395*
Bennet (Lancaster) Village................*415*
Bennett (Fillmore) Township *395*
Bennington (Douglas) Village............*394*
Bertrand (Phelps) Village *423*
Berwyn (Custer) Township *388*
Berwyn (Custer) Village.....................*388*
Big Springs (Deuel) Village *391*
Bismarck (Cuming) Township...........*387*
Bismark (Platte) Township................*425*
Blackbird (Thurston) Township *437*
Bladen (Webster) Village *440*
Blaine (Adams) Township *372*
Blaine (Antelope) Township *373*
Blaine (Cuming) Township *387*
Blaine (Kearney) Township *411*
Blaine County.................................*375*
Blair (Washington) City....................*439*
Blakely (Gage) Township *399*
Bloomfield (Knox) City.....................*413*
Bloomington (Franklin) Township....*396*
Bloomington (Franklin) Village........*396*
Blue Hill (Webster) City....................*440*
Blue Springs (Gage) City *399*
Blue Springs-Wymore (Gage)
  Township...*399*
Bohemia (Knox) Township................*413*
Bohemia (Saunders) Township..........*430*
Bone Creek (Butler) Township..........*380*
Boone County *375*
Box Butte County *376*
Boyd County...................................*376*
Boys Town (Douglas) Village *394*
Bradshaw (York) Village....................*441*
Brady (Lincoln) Village *416*
Brainard (Butler) Village *380*
Brewster (Blaine) Village *375*
Bridgeport (Morrill) City...................*419*
Bristow (Boyd) Township..................*376*
Bristow (Boyd) Village.......................*376*
Broadwater (Morrill) Village *419*
Brock (Nemaha) Village *420*
Broken Bow (Custer) City *388*
Broken Bow (Custer) Township *388*
Brown County *377*
Brownville (Nemaha) Village *420*
Brule (Keith) Village..........................*412*
Bruning (Thayer) Village *436*
Bruno (Butler) Village *380*
Brunswick (Antelope) Village............*373*
Bryan (Thurston) Township..............*437*
Bryant (Fillmore) Township *395*
Buffalo County *378*
Burchard (Pawnee) Village *422*
Burnett (Antelope) Township *373*
Burr (Otoe) Village............................*421*
Burrows (Platte) Township................*425*
Burt County....................................*379*

Burton (Keya Paha) Village *412*
Burwell (Garfield) City......................*401*
Bush (Boyd) Township *376*
Bushnell (Kimball) Village *412*
Butler (Platte) Township *425*
Butler County.................................*380*
Butte (Boyd) Township......................*376*
Butte (Boyd) Village *376*
Byron (Thayer) Village *436*
Cairo (Hall) Village *403*
Callaway (Custer) Village..................*388*
Cambridge (Furnas) City...................*398*
Cameron (Hall) Township *403*
Campbell (Franklin) Village..............*397*
Carleton (Thayer) Village *436*
Carroll (Wayne) Village *439*
Cass County....................................*382*
Cedar (Antelope) Township *373*
Cedar (Buffalo) Township *378*
Cedar (Nance) Township...................*419*
Cedar Bluffs (Saunders) Village........*430*
Cedar County.................................*383*
Cedar Creek (Cass) Village................*382*
Cedar Rapids (Boone) Village...........*375*
Center (Buffalo) Township *378*
Center (Butler) Township *380*
Center (Hall) Township *403*
Center (Knox) Village *413*
Center (Phelps) Township *423*
Center (Saunders) Township *430*
Central (Knox) Township *413*
Central (Merrick) Township *418*
Central City (Merrick) City...............*418*
Ceresco (Saunders) Village *430*
Chadron (Dawes) City.......................*390*
Chalco (Sarpy) CDP..........................*429*
Chambers (Holt) Township *406*
Chambers (Holt) Village....................*406*
Chapman (Merrick) Township *418*
Chapman (Merrick) Village...............*418*
Chapman (Saunders) Township *430*
Chappell (Deuel) City........................*391*
Chase County *383*
Chelsea (Fillmore) Township.............*395*
Cherry County *384*
Cherry Creek (Buffalo) Township *378*
Chester (Saunders) Township............*430*
Chester (Thayer) Village....................*436*
Cheyenne County *384*
Clark (Dixon) Township....................*392*
Clarks (Merrick) Village....................*418*
Clarkson (Colfax) City......................*386*
Clarksville (Merrick) Township.........*418*
Clatonia (Gage) Township *399*
Clatonia (Gage) Village *399*
Clay Center (Clay) City.....................*385*
Clay County....................................*385*
Clear Creek (Saunders) Township....*430*
Clearwater (Antelope) Township.......*373*
Clearwater (Antelope) Village *373*
Cleveland (Cuming) Township..........*387*
Cleveland (Holt) Township *406*
Cleveland (Knox) Township *413*
Cliff (Custer) Township.....................*388*
Clinton (Sheridan) Village.................*434*
Cody (Cherry) Village.......................*384*
Coleman (Holt) Township *406*
Coleridge (Cedar) Village *383*
Colfax County *386*
Collins (Buffalo) Township................*378*

Colon (Saunders) Village....................430	Dixon County..392	Fairview (Holt) Township....................407
Columbia (Knox) Township...............413	Dodge (Dodge) Village........................393	Falls City (Richardson) City...............427
Columbus (Platte) City........................425	**Dodge County**....................................393	Farnam (Dawson) Village....................391
Columbus (Platte) Township..............425	Dolphin (Knox) Township..................413	Farwell (Howard) Village....................409
Comstock (Custer) Township.............388	Doniphan (Hall) Township.................403	Filley (Gage) Township.......................399
Comstock (Custer) Village..................388	Doniphan (Hall) Village......................403	Filley (Gage) Village...........................399
Concord (Dixon) Township................392	Dorchester (Saline) Village.................428	**Fillmore County**...............................395
Concord (Dixon) Village.....................392	Douglas (Otoe) Village........................421	Firth (Lancaster) Village......................415
Conley (Holt) Township......................406	Douglas (Saunders) Township............430	Flournoy (Thurston) Township............437
Cook (Johnson) Village.......................410	**Douglas County**................................394	Fordyce (Cedar) Village.......................383
Cordova (Seward) Village...................433	Douglas Grove (Custer) Township.....388	Fort Calhoun (Washington) City........439
Corner (Custer) Township...................388	Dowling (Knox) Township.................413	Foster (Pierce) Village.........................424
Cornlea (Platte) Village.......................425	Du Bois (Pawnee) Village...................422	Francis (Holt) Township......................407
Cortland (Gage) Village......................399	Dunbar (Otoe) Village.........................421	Frankfort (Knox) Township................413
Cosmo (Kearney) Township................411	Duncan (Platte) Village.......................425	Franklin (Butler) Township.................381
Cotesfield (Howard) Village...............409	**Dundy County**..................................395	Franklin (Fillmore) Township.............395
Cotterell (Dodge) Township................393	Dunning (Blaine) Village....................375	Franklin (Franklin) City.......................397
Cottonwood (Adams) Township.........372	Dustin (Holt) Township.......................406	**Franklin County**...............................396
Cottonwood (Nance) Township..........419	Dwight (Butler) Village.......................381	Fremont (Dodge) City..........................393
Cottonwood (Phelps) Township..........423	Eagle (Cass) Village.............................382	Frenchtown (Antelope) Township.......373
Council Creek (Nance) Township.......419	East Custer (Custer) Township............389	Friend (Saline) City..............................429
Cowles (Webster) Village....................440	Eastern (Knox) Township....................413	**Frontier County**................................397
Cozad (Dawson) City...........................391	East Newman (Nance) Township........419	Fullerton (Nance) City..........................420
Crab Orchard (Johnson) Village..........410	Eaton (Kearney) Township..................411	Fullerton (Nance) Township................420
Craig (Burt) Township.........................379	Eddyville (Dawson) Village................391	Funk (Phelps) Village...........................423
Craig (Burt) Village.............................379	Eden (Antelope) Township.................373	**Furnas County**..................................398
Crawford (Antelope) Township..........373	Edgar (Clay) City.................................385	**Gage County**.....................................399
Crawford (Dawes) City........................390	Edgar (Clay) Township........................385	Galena (Dixon) Township....................392
Creighton (Knox) City.........................413	Edison (Furnas) Village.......................398	Gandy (Logan) Village.........................417
Creighton (Knox) Township................413	Elba (Howard) Village.........................409	**Garden County**.................................401
Creston (Platte) Township...................425	Eldorado (Clay) Township..................385	Gardner (Buffalo) Township................378
Creston (Platte) Village........................425	Eldorado (Harlan) Township...............404	Garfield (Antelope) Township.............373
Crete (Saline) City...............................428	Elgin (Antelope) City...........................373	Garfield (Buffalo) Township................378
Crofton (Knox) Village........................413	Elgin (Antelope) Township.................373	Garfield (Cuming) Township...............387
Crookston (Cherry) Village.................384	Elim (Custer) Township.......................389	Garfield (Custer) Township.................389
Culbertson (Hitchcock) Village...........406	Elk (Saunders) Township....................430	Garfield (Phelps) Township.................423
Cuming (Cuming) Township...............387	Elk Creek (Custer) Township..............389	**Garfield County**................................401
Cuming (Dodge) Township.................393	Elk Creek (Johnson) Village................410	Garland (Seward) Village....................433
Cuming County................................387	Elkhorn (Cuming) Township..............387	Garrison (Butler) Village.....................381
Curtis (Frontier) City...........................397	Elkhorn (Dodge) Township.................393	Geneva (Fillmore) City........................396
Cushing (Howard) Village..................409	Elkhorn (Douglas) City........................394	Geneva (Fillmore) Township...............396
Custer (Antelope) Township................373	Ellsworth (Antelope) Township..........373	Genoa (Nance) City..............................420
Custer (Custer) Township....................388	Elm (Antelope) Township...................373	Genoa (Nance) Township.....................420
Custer County...................................388	Elm (Gage) Township..........................399	Geranium (Valley) Township...............438
Daily (Dixon) Township......................392	Elm Creek (Buffalo) Township...........378	Gering (Scotts Bluff) City....................432
Dakota City (Dakota) City...................390	Elm Creek (Buffalo) Village................378	Gibbon (Buffalo) City..........................378
Dakota County..................................390	Elmwood (Cass) Village......................382	Gibbon (Buffalo) Township.................378
Dalton (Cheyenne) Village..................384	Elsie (Perkins) Village.........................423	Gilead (Thayer) Village.......................436
Danbury (Red Willow) Village............427	Elwood (Gosper) Village.....................401	Giltner (Hamilton) Village...................403
Dannebrog (Howard) Village..............409	Elyria (Valley) Township.....................438	Glengary (Fillmore) Township............396
Davenport (Thayer) Village.................436	Elyria (Valley) Village.........................438	Glenvil (Clay) Township.....................385
Davey (Lancaster) Village...................415	Emerson (Dakota) Village...................390	Glenvil (Clay) Village..........................385
David City (Butler) City......................381	Emerson (Dixon) Township................392	Glenwood (Gage) Township................399
Davis Creek (Valley) Township..........438	Emerson (Dixon) Village.....................392	Goehner (Seward) Village...................433
Dawes (Thurston) Township...............437	Emerson (Harlan) Township................404	Golden (Holt) Township......................407
Dawes County...................................390	Emerson (Thurston) Village................437	Gordon (Sheridan) City........................434
Dawson (Richardson) Village.............427	Emmet (Holt) Township......................407	**Gosper County**..................................401
Dawson County................................391	Emmet (Holt) Village...........................407	Gothenburg (Dawson) City..................391
Daykin (Jefferson) Village..................409	Endicott (Jefferson) Village................409	Grafton (Fillmore) Township...............396
Decatur (Burt) Township.....................380	Enterprise (Valley) Township.............438	Grafton (Fillmore) Village...................396
Decatur (Burt) Village..........................379	Ericson (Wheeler) Village...................440	Grainton (Perkins) Village...................423
Delight (Custer) Township..................388	Eureka (Valley) Township...................438	Grand Island (Hall) City......................403
Deloit (Holt) Township........................406	Eustis (Frontier) Village......................397	Grand Prairie (Platte) Township..........425
Denton (Lancaster) Village..................415	Everett (Burt) Township......................380	Grant (Antelope) Township.................373
Denver (Adams) Township..................372	Everett (Dodge) Township...................393	Grant (Buffalo) Township....................378
Deshler (Thayer) City..........................436	Ewing (Holt) Township.......................407	Grant (Cuming) Township...................387
Deuel County....................................391	Ewing (Holt) Village............................407	Grant (Custer) Township......................389
Deweese (Clay) Village.......................385	Exeter (Fillmore) Township................395	Grant (Franklin) Township..................397
De Witt (Saline) Village......................428	Exeter (Fillmore) Village....................395	Grant (Gage) Township.......................399
Dickens (Lincoln) Village...................416	Fairbury (Jefferson) City.....................410	Grant (Kearney) Township..................411
Diller (Jefferson) Village.....................409	Fairfield (Clay) City............................385	Grant (Perkins) City.............................423
Divide (Buffalo) Township..................378	Fairfield (Clay) Township...................385	**Grant County**....................................402
Divide (Phelps) Township...................423	Fairfield (Harlan) Township................404	Granville (Platte) Township................425
Dix (Kimball) Village..........................412	Fairmont (Fillmore) Township............395	Grattan (Holt) Township......................407
Dixon (Dixon) Village.........................392	Fairmont (Fillmore) Village................395	Greeley Center (Greeley) Village........402

NEBRASKA

Greeley County..................402
Green (Saunders) Township..........430
Green Valley (Holt) Township........407
Greenwood (Cass) Village............382
Gresham (York) Village..............441
Gretna (Sarpy) City.................429
Gross (Boyd) Village................376
Guide Rock (Webster) Village........440
Gurley (Cheyenne) Village...........384
Hadar (Pierce) Village..............424
Haigler (Dundy) Village.............395
Hallam (Lancaster) Village..........415
Hall County.....................402
Halsey (Blaine) Village.............375
Halsey (Thomas) Village.............436
Hamilton (Fillmore) Township........396
Hamilton County.................403
Hamlet (Hayes) Village..............405
Hampton (Hamilton) Village..........404
Hanover (Adams) Township............372
Hanover (Gage) Township.............399
Harbine (Jefferson) Village.........410
Hardy (Nuckolls) Village............421
Harlan County...................404
Harrison (Buffalo) Township.........378
Harrison (Hall) Township............403
Harrison (Knox) Township............413
Harrison (Sioux) Village............435
Hartington (Cedar) City.............383
Harvard (Clay) City.................385
Harvard (Clay) Township.............385
Hastings (Adams) City...............372
Hayes (Custer) Township.............389
Hayes (Kearney) Township............411
Hayes Center (Hayes) Village........405
Hayes County....................405
Hay Springs (Sheridan) Village......434
Hazard (Sherman) Village............434
Heartwell (Kearney) Village.........411
Hebron (Thayer) City................436
Hemingford (Box Butte) Village......376
Henderson (York) City...............441
Hendley (Furnas) Village............398
Henry (Scotts Bluff) Village........432
Herman (Washington) Village.........439
Herrick (Knox) Township.............414
Hershey (Lincoln) Village...........416
Hickman (Lancaster) Village.........415
Highland (Adams) Township...........372
Highland (Gage) Township............399
Hildreth (Franklin) Village.........397
Hill (Knox) Township................414
Hitchcock County................406
Holbrook (Furnas) Village...........398
Holdrege (Phelps) City..............424
Holstein (Adams) Village............372
Holt (Gage) Township................400
Holt County.....................406
Holt Creek (Holt) Township..........407
Homer (Dakota) Village..............390
Hooker (Dixon) Township.............392
Hooker (Gage) Township..............400
Hooker County...................408
Hooper (Dodge) City.................393
Hooper (Dodge) Township.............393
Hordville (Hamilton) Village........404
Hoskins (Wayne) Village.............439
Howard County...................409
Howard City (Howard) Village........409
Howells (Colfax) Village............386
Hubbard (Dakota) Village............390
Hubbell (Thayer) Village............436
Humboldt (Richardson) City..........427
Humphrey (Platte) City..............425
Humphrey (Platte) Township..........425

Huntley (Harlan) Village............404
Hyannis (Grant) Village.............402
Imperial (Chase) City...............383
Independent (Valley) Township.......438
Indianola (Red Willow) City.........427
Industry-Rock Falls (Phelps)
 Township..........................424
Inglewood (Dodge) Village...........393
Inland (Clay) Township..............385
Inman (Holt) Township...............407
Inman (Holt) Village................407
Iowa (Holt) Township................407
Island Grove (Gage) Township........400
Ithaca (Saunders) Village...........430
Jackson (Dakota) Village............390
Jackson (Hall) Township.............403
Jansen (Jefferson) Village..........410
Jefferson (Knox) Township...........414
Jefferson County................409
Johnson (Nemaha) Village............420
Johnson County..................410
Johnstown (Brown) Village...........377
Joliet (Platte) Township............425
Josie (Holt) Township...............407
Julian (Nemaha) Village.............420
Juniata (Adams) Township............372
Juniata (Adams) Village.............372
Kearney (Buffalo) City..............378
Kearney County..................411
Keith County....................412
Kenesaw (Adams) Township............372
Kenesaw (Adams) Village.............372
Kennard (Washington) Village........439
Keya Paha County................412
Kilfoil (Custer) Township...........389
Kilgore (Cherry) Village............384
Kimball (Kimball) City..............413
Kimball County..................412
Knox County.....................413
Laird (Phelps) Township.............424
Lake (Hall) Township................403
Lake (Holt) Township................407
Lake (Phelps) Township..............424
Lamar (Chase) Village...............383
Lancaster County................415
Laurel (Cedar) City.................383
La Vista (Sarpy) City...............429
Lawrence (Nuckolls) Village.........421
Lebanon (Red Willow) Village........427
Leicester (Clay) Township...........385
Leigh (Colfax) Village..............386
Leshara (Saunders) Township.........430
Leshara (Saunders) Village..........430
Lewellen (Garden) Village...........401
Lewis (Clay) Township...............385
Lewiston (Pawnee) Village...........422
Lexington (Dawson) City.............391
Liberty (Fillmore) Township.........396
Liberty (Gage) Township.............400
Liberty (Gage) Village..............400
Liberty (Kearney) Township..........411
Liberty (Valley) Township...........438
Lillian (Custer) Township...........389
Lincoln (Antelope) Township.........374
Lincoln (Cuming) Township...........387
Lincoln (Franklin) Township.........397
Lincoln (Gage) Township.............400
Lincoln (Kearney) Township..........411
Lincoln (Knox) Township.............414
Lincoln (Lancaster) City............415
Lincoln County..................416
Lindsay (Platte) Village............425
Linwood (Butler) Township...........381
Linwood (Butler) Village............381
Litchfield (Sherman) Village........434

Little Blue (Adams) Township........372
Lodgepole (Cheyenne) Village........384
Logan (Adams) Township..............372
Logan (Antelope) Township...........374
Logan (Buffalo) Township............378
Logan (Burt) Township...............380
Logan (Clay) Township...............385
Logan (Cuming) Township.............387
Logan (Dixon) Township..............392
Logan (Dodge) Township..............393
Logan (Gage) Township...............400
Logan (Kearney) Township............411
Logan (Knox) Township...............414
Logan County....................417
Lone Tree (Clay) Township...........385
Lone Tree (Merrick) Township........418
Long Pine (Brown) City..............377
Long Pine (Brown) City..............377
Loomis (Phelps) Village.............424
Lorton Village (Otoe) Village.......421
Lost Creek (Platte) Township........425
Louisville (Cass) Village...........382
Loup (Buffalo) Township.............378
Loup (Custer) Township..............389
Loup (Merrick) Township.............418
Loup (Platte) Township..............425
Loup City (Sherman) City............434
Loup County.....................417
Loup Ferry (Nance) Township.........420
Lowell (Kearney) Township...........411
Lushton (York) Village..............441
Lyman (Scotts Bluff) Village........432
Lynch (Boyd) Township...............377
Lynch (Boyd) Village................376
Lynn (Clay) Township................385
Lyons (Burt) City...................380
Macon (Franklin) Township...........397
Macy (Thurston) CDP.................437
Madison (Fillmore) Township.........396
Madison (Madison) City..............417
Madison County..................417
Madrid (Perkins) Village............423
Magnet (Cedar) Village..............383
Malcolm (Lancaster) Village.........415
Malmo (Saunders) Village............430
Manley (Cass) Village...............382
Maple (Dodge) Township..............393
Marble (Saunders) Township..........430
Marietta (Saunders) Township........430
Marion (Franklin) Township..........397
Mariposa (Saunders) Township........430
Marquette (Hamilton) Village........404
Marshall (Clay) Township............385
Marsland (Dawes) Village............390
Martin (Hall) Township..............403
Martinsburg (Dixon) Village.........392
Maskell (Dixon) Village.............392
Mason City (Custer) Village.........389
Maxwell (Lincoln) Village...........416
May (Kearney) Township..............411
Mayfield (Hall) Township............403
Maywood (Frontier) Village..........397
McClure (Holt) Township.............407
McCook (Red Willow) City............427
McCool Junction (York) Village......441
McCulley (Boyd) Township............377
McGrew (Scotts Bluff) Village.......432
McLean (Pierce) Village.............424
McPherson County................418
Mead (Merrick) Township.............418
Mead (Saunders) Village.............431
Meadow Grove (Madison) Village......417
Melbeta (Scotts Bluff) Village......432
Memphis (Saunders) Village..........431
Merna (Custer) Village..............389

American Places Dictionary NEBRASKA

Name	Page
Merrick County	418
Merriman (Cherry) Village	384
Merry (Thurston) Township	437
Michigan (Valley) Township	438
Midland (Gage) Township	400
Midland (Merrick) Township	418
Milburn (Custer) Township	389
Milford (Seward) City	433
Miller (Buffalo) Village	378
Miller (Knox) Township	414
Milligan (Fillmore) Village	396
Minatare (Scotts Bluff) City	432
Minden (Kearney) City	411
Mirage (Kearney) Township	411
Mitchell (Scotts Bluff) City	432
Momence (Fillmore) Township	396
Monowi (Boyd) Village	377
Monroe (Platte) Township	425
Monroe (Platte) Village	425
Monterey (Cuming) Township	387
Moorefield (Frontier) Village	397
Morrill (Scotts Bluff) Village	432
Morrill County	419
Morse Bluff (Saunders) Township	431
Morse Bluff (Saunders) Village	431
Morton (Boyd) Township	377
Morton (Knox) Township	414
Mullally (Harlan) Township	404
Mullen (Boyd) Township	377
Mullen (Hooker) Village	408
Murdock (Cass) Village	382
Murray (Cass) Village	382
Myrtle (Custer) Township	389
Nance County	419
Naper (Boyd) Village	377
Naponee (Franklin) Village	397
Nebraska City (Otoe) City	422
Nehawka (Cass) Village	382
Neligh (Antelope) City	374
Neligh (Antelope) Township	374
Neligh (Cuming) Township	387
Nelson (Nuckolls) City	421
Nemaha (Gage) Township	400
Nemaha (Nemaha) Village	420
Nemaha County	420
Nenzel (Cherry) Village	384
Newark (Kearney) Township	411
Newcastle (Dixon) Township	392
Newcastle (Dixon) Village	392
Newman (Saunders) Township	431
Newman Grove (Madison) City	417
Newman Grove (Platte) City	426
Newport (Rock) Village	428
Nickerson (Dodge) Township	393
Nickerson (Dodge) Village	393
Niobrara (Knox) Township	414
Niobrara (Knox) Village	414
Noble (Valley) Township	438
Nora (Nuckolls) Village	421
Norfolk (Madison) City	418
Norman (Kearney) Village	411
North Bend (Dodge) City	394
North Cedar (Saunders) Township	431
North Frankfort (Knox) Township	414
North Franklin (Franklin) Township	397
North Loup (Valley) Township	438
North Loup (Valley) Village	438
North Platte (Lincoln) City	416
Nuckolls County	421
Oak (Nuckolls) Village	421
Oak Creek (Butler) Township	381
Oak Creek (Saunders) Township	431
Oakdale (Antelope) Township	374
Oakdale (Antelope) Village	374
Oakland (Burt) City	380
Oakland (Burt) Township	380
Obert (Cedar) Village	383
Oconee (Platte) Township	426
Oconto (Custer) Village	389
Octavia (Butler) Village	381
Odell (Gage) Village	400
Odessa (Buffalo) Township	378
Offutt AFB West (Sarpy) Military Facility	429
Ogallala (Keith) City	412
Ohiowa (Fillmore) Village	396
Olive (Butler) Township	381
Omaha (Douglas) City	394
Omaha (Thurston) Township	437
Oneida (Kearney) Township	411
O'Neill (Holt) City	407
Ong (Clay) Village	386
Orchard (Antelope) Village	374
Ord (Antelope) Township	374
Ord (Valley) City	438
Ord (Valley) Township	438
Orleans (Harlan) Township	404
Orleans (Harlan) Village	404
Osceola (Polk) City	426
Oshkosh (Garden) City	401
Osmond (Pierce) City	424
Otoe (Otoe) Village	422
Otoe County	421
Otter Creek (Dixon) Township	392
Overton (Dawson) Village	391
Oxford (Furnas) Village	398
Oxford (Harlan) Village	405
Paddock (Gage) Township	400
Paddock (Holt) Township	407
Page (Holt) Village	407
Palisade (Hayes) Village	405
Palisade (Hitchcock) Village	406
Palmer (Merrick) Village	418
Palmyra (Otoe) Village	422
Panama (Lancaster) Village	415
Papillion (Sarpy) City	429
Pawnee City (Pawnee) City	422
Pawnee County	422
Paxton (Keith) Village	412
Pebble (Dodge) Township	394
Pender (Thurston) Township	437
Pender (Thurston) Village	437
Peoria (Knox) Township	414
Perkins County	423
Perry (Thurston) Township	437
Pershing (Burt) Township	380
Peru (Nemaha) City	420
Petersburg (Boone) Village	375
Phelps County	423
Phillips (Hamilton) Village	404
Pickrell (Gage) Village	400
Pierce (Pierce) City	424
Pierce County	424
Pilger (Stanton) Village	435
Plainview (Pierce) City	424
Platte (Buffalo) Township	379
Platte (Butler) Township	381
Platte (Dodge) Township	394
Platte Center (Platte) Village	426
Platte County	425
Plattsmouth (Cass) City	382
Pleasant Dale (Seward) Village	433
Pleasanton (Buffalo) Village	379
Pleasant Valley (Dodge) Township	394
Pleasant View (Holt) Township	407
Plum Creek (Butler) Township	381
Plymouth (Jefferson) Village	410
Pohocco (Saunders) Township	431
Polk (Polk) Village	426
Polk County	426
Ponca (Dixon) City	392
Ponca (Dixon) Township	392
Potter (Cheyenne) Village	384
Prague (Saunders) Village	431
Prairie (Phelps) Township	424
Prairie Creek (Hall) Township	403
Prairie Creek (Merrick) Township	418
Prairie Creek (Nance) Township	420
Prairie Dog (Harlan) Township	405
Prairie Island (Merrick) Township	418
Preston (Richardson) Village	428
Primrose (Boone) Village	375
Prosser (Adams) Village	372
Purdum (Blaine) Pop. Place	375
Quinnebaugh (Burt) Township	380
Ragan (Harlan) Village	405
Ralston (Douglas) City	394
Randolph (Cedar) City	383
Ravenna (Buffalo) City	379
Raymond (Knox) Township	414
Raymond (Lancaster) Village	415
Read (Butler) Township	381
Reading (Butler) Township	381
Red Cloud (Webster) City	440
Red Willow County	427
Republican City (Harlan) Township	405
Republican City (Harlan) Village	405
Reuben (Harlan) Township	405
Reynolds (Jefferson) Village	410
Richardson (Butler) Township	381
Richardson County	427
Richland (Colfax) Village	386
Richland (Saunders) Township	431
Ridgeley (Dodge) Township	394
Rising City (Butler) Village	381
Riverdale (Buffalo) Township	379
Riverdale (Buffalo) Village	379
Riverside (Burt) Township	380
Riverside (Gage) Township	400
Riverton (Franklin) Village	397
Roca (Lancaster) Village	415
Rock County	428
Rock Creek (Saunders) Township	431
Rock Falls (Holt) Township	407
Rockford (Gage) Township	400
Rockville (Sherman) Village	434
Rogers (Colfax) Village	386
Rosalie (Thurston) Village	437
Roseland (Adams) Township	372
Roseland (Adams) Village	372
Royal (Antelope) Township	374
Royal (Antelope) Village	374
Rulo (Richardson) City	428
Rusco (Buffalo) Township	379
Rushville (Sheridan) City	434
Ruskin (Nuckolls) Village	421
Ryno (Custer) Township	389
St. Bernard (Platte) Township	426
St. Charles (Cuming) Township	387
St. Edward (Boone) City	376
St. Helena (Cedar) Village	383
St. Paul (Howard) City	409
Salem (Franklin) Township	397
Salem (Richardson) Village	428
Saline County	428
Sand Creek (Holt) Township	407
Santee (Knox) Township	414
Santee (Knox) Village	414
Sappa (Harlan) Township	405
Saratoga (Holt) Township	407
Sargent (Custer) City	389
Sargent (Custer) Township	389
Saronville (Clay) Village	386
Sarpy County	429
Sartoria (Buffalo) Township	379

NEBRASKA

Saunders County *430*
Savannah (Butler) Township *381*
Scandinavia (Harlan) Township *405*
Schneider (Buffalo) Township *379*
School Creek (Clay) Township *386*
Schuyler (Colfax) City *386*
Scotia (Greeley) Village *402*
Scott (Buffalo) Township *379*
Scott (Holt) Township *407*
Scottsbluff (Scotts Bluff) City *432*
Scotts Bluff County *432*
Scribner (Dodge) City *394*
Seneca (Thomas) Village *436*
Seward (Seward) City *433*
Seward County *433*
Shamrock (Holt) Township *407*
Sharon (Buffalo) Township *379*
Shelby (Polk) Village *426*
Shell Creek (Platte) Township *426*
Shelton (Buffalo) Township *379*
Shelton (Buffalo) Village *379*
Sheridan (Clay) Township *386*
Sheridan (Holt) Township *407*
Sheridan (Phelps) Township *424*
Sheridan County *434*
Sherman (Antelope) Township *374*
Sherman (Cuming) Township *387*
Sherman (Gage) Township *400*
Sherman (Kearney) Township *411*
Sherman (Platte) Township *426*
Sherman County *434*
Shickley (Fillmore) Village *396*
Shields (Holt) Township *407*
Sholes (Wayne) Village *439*
Shubert (Richardson) Village *428*
Sicily (Gage) Township *400*
Sidney (Cheyenne) City *384*
Silver Creek (Burt) Township *380*
Silver Creek (Dixon) Township *392*
Silver Creek (Merrick) Township *419*
Silver Creek (Merrick) Village *419*
Silver Lake (Adams) Township *372*
Sioux County *435*
Skull Creek (Butler) Township *381*
Skyline (Douglas) CDP *394*
Smithfield (Gosper) Village *401*
Snyder (Dodge) Village *394*
South Bend (Cass) Village *382*
South Branch (Nance) Township *420*
South Cedar (Saunders) Township *431*
South Loup (Hall) Township *403*
South Platte (Hall) Township *403*
South Sioux City (Dakota) City *390*
Spade (Knox) Township *414*
Spalding (Greeley) Village *402*
Sparta (Knox) Township *414*
Spencer (Boyd) Township *377*
Spencer (Boyd) Village *377*
Sprague (Lancaster) Village *415*
Spring Bank (Dixon) Township *392*
Spring Creek (Custer) Township *389*
Springdale (Valley) Township *438*
Springfield (Sarpy) City *429*
Spring Grove (Harlan) Township *405*
Spring Ranch (Clay) Township *386*
Springview (Keya Paha) Village *412*
Stamford (Harlan) Village *405*
Stanton (Antelope) Township *374*
Stanton (Fillmore) Township *396*
Stanton (Stanton) City *435*
Stanton County *435*
Staplehurst (Seward) Village *433*
Stapleton (Logan) Village *417*
Steel Creek (Holt) Township *408*
Steele City (Jefferson) Village *410*

Steinauer (Pawnee) Village *422*
Stella (Richardson) Village *428*
Sterling (Johnson) Village *410*
Stockham (Hamilton) Village *404*
Stocking (Saunders) Township *431*
Stockville (Frontier) Village *398*
Strang (Fillmore) Village *396*
Stratton (Hitchcock) Village *406*
Stromsburg (Polk) City *426*
Stuart (Holt) Township *408*
Stuart (Holt) Village *408*
Summit (Burt) Township *380*
Summit (Butler) Township *381*
Sumner (Dawson) Village *391*
Superior (Nuckolls) City *421*
Surprise (Butler) Village *381*
Sutherland (Lincoln) Village *416*
Sutton (Clay) City *386*
Sutton (Clay) Township *386*
Swan (Holt) Township *408*
Swanton (Saline) Village *429*
Syracuse (Otoe) City *422*
Table Rock (Pawnee) Village *422*
Talmage (Otoe) Village *422*
Tamora (Seward) Village *433*
Tarnov (Platte) Village *426*
Taylor (Loup) Village *417*
Tecumseh (Johnson) City *410*
Tekamah (Burt) City *380*
Terrytown (Scotts Bluff) Village *432*
Thayer (Thurston) Township *437*
Thayer (York) Village *441*
Thayer County *435*
Thedford (Thomas) Village *436*
Thomas County *436*
Thornton (Buffalo) Township *379*
Thurston (Thurston) Village *437*
Thurston County *437*
Tilden (Antelope) City *374*
Tilden (Madison) City *418*
Timber Creek (Nance) Township *420*
Tobias (Saline) Village *429*
Trenton (Hitchcock) Village *406*
Triumph (Custer) Township *389*
Trumbull (Adams) Village *372*
Trumbull (Clay) Village *386*
Turkey Creek (Franklin) Township ... *397*
Turkey Creek (Harlan) Township *405*
Uehling (Dodge) Village *394*
Ulysses (Butler) Township *381*
Ulysses (Butler) Village *381*
Unadilla (Otoe) Village *422*
Union (Butler) Township *381*
Union (Cass) Village *382*
Union (Dodge) Township *394*
Union (Knox) Township *414*
Union (Phelps) Township *424*
Union (Saunders) Township *431*
Union Creek (Stanton) Pop. Place *435*
Upland (Franklin) Village *397*
Utica (Seward) Village *433*
Valentine (Cherry) City *384*
Valley (Buffalo) Township *379*
Valley (Douglas) City *395*
Valley (Knox) Township *414*
Valley County *438*
Valparaiso (Saunders) Village *431*
Venango (Perkins) Village *423*
Verdel (Knox) Village *414*
Verdigre (Knox) Township *414*
Verdigre (Knox) Village *414*
Verdigris (Antelope) Township *374*
Verdigris (Holt) Township *408*
Verdon (Richardson) Village *428*

American Places Dictionary

Verona (Adams) Township *373*
Victoria (Custer) Township *389*
Vieregg (Merrick) Township *419*
Vinton (Valley) Township *438*
Virginia (Gage) Village *400*
Waco (York) Village *441*
Wahoo (Saunders) City *431*
Wahoo (Saunders) Township *431*
Wakefield (Dixon) City *393*
Wakefield (Dixon) Township *393*
Wakefield (Wayne) City *439*
Walker (Platte) Township *426*
Wallace (Lincoln) Village *416*
Walnut Grove (Knox) Township *414*
Walthill (Thurston) Village *437*
Wanda (Adams) Township *373*
Washington (Franklin) Township *397*
Washington (Hall) Township *403*
Washington (Harlan) Township *405*
Washington (Knox) Township *414*
Washington (Washington) Village *439*
Washington County *439*
Waterbury (Dixon) Village *393*
Waterloo (Douglas) Village *395*
Wauneta (Chase) Village *383*
Wausa (Knox) Village *414*
Waverly (Lancaster) City *416*
Wayne (Custer) Township *389*
Wayne (Wayne) City *440*
Wayne County *439*
Webster (Dodge) Township *394*
Webster County *440*
Weeping Water (Cass) City *382*
Wellfleet (Lincoln) Village *416*
West Blue (Adams) Township *373*
West Blue (Fillmore) Township *396*
Western (Knox) Township *414*
Western (Saline) Village *429*
Westerville (Custer) Township *389*
Westmark (Phelps) Township *424*
West Newman (Nance) Township *420*
Weston (Saunders) Village *431*
West Point (Cuming) City *387*
Westside (Phelps) Township *424*
West Union (Custer) Township *389*
Wheeler County *440*
Whitney (Dawes) Village *390*
Wilber (Saline) City *429*
Wilcox (Kearney) Village *411*
Williamsburg (Phelps) Township *424*
Willow (Antelope) Township *374*
Willowdale (Holt) Township *408*
Wilsonville (Furnas) Village *398*
Winnebago (Thurston) Township *437*
Winnebago (Thurston) Village *437*
Winnetoon (Knox) Village *415*
Winside (Wayne) Village *440*
Winslow (Dodge) Village *394*
Wisner (Cuming) City *387*
Wisner (Cuming) Township *387*
Wolbach (Greeley) Village *402*
Wood Lake (Cherry) Village *384*
Wood River (Custer) Township *389*
Wood River (Hall) City *403*
Wood River (Hall) Township *403*
Woodville (Platte) Township *426*
Wymore (Gage) City *400*
Wynot (Cedar) Village *383*
Wyoming (Holt) Township *408*
Yale (Valley) Township *438*
York (York) City *441*
York County *441*
Yutan (Saunders) Village *431*
Zero (Adams) Township *373*

Nevada

NEVADA

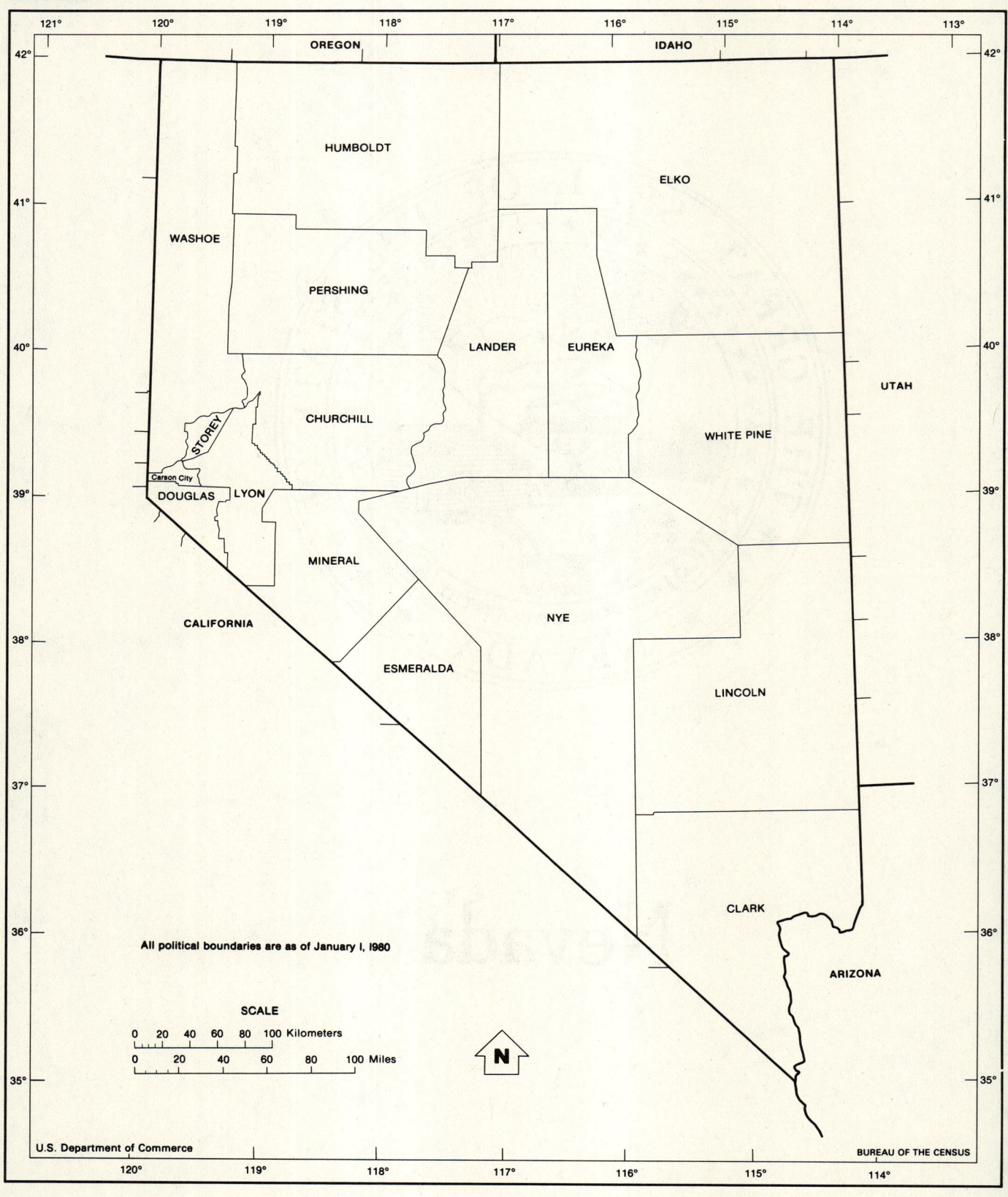

Nevada

Population: 1,201,833 (1990); 800,493 (1980)
Population rank (1990): 39
Percent population change (1980–1990): 50.1
Population projection: 1,279,000 (1995); 1,414,000 (2000)

Area: total: 110,567 sq. mi.; 109,806 sq. mi. land, 761 sq. mi. water
Area rank: 7
Highest elevation: 13,140 ft., Boundary Peak (Esmeralda County)
Lowest point: 470 ft., along the Colorado River (Clark County)

State capital: Carson City (independent city)
Largest city: Las Vegas (258,295)
Second largest city: Reno (133,850)
Largest county: Clark (741,459)

Total housing units: 518,858
No. of occupied housing units: 466,297
Vacant housing units (%): 10.1
Distribution of population by race and Hispanic origin (%):
  White: 84.3
  Black: 6.6
  Hispanic (any race): 10.4
  Native American: 1.6
  Asian/Pacific: 3.2
  Other: 4.4

Admission date: October 31, 1864 (36th state).

Location: In the western United States, bordering California, Oregon, Idaho, Utah, and Arizona.

Name Origin: Shortened from Sierra Nevada, the mountain range in western Nevada along the CA border. From Spanish *nevada* 'snow-covered.'

State animal: desert bighorn sheep *(Ovis canadensis)*
State bird: mountain bluebird *(Sialia currucoides)*
State fish: Lahontan cutthroat trout *(Salmo clarki henshawi)*
State flower: sagebrush *(Artemisia tridentata)*
State fossil: ichthyosaur *(Stenopterygius quadriscissus)*
State grass: Indian ricegrass *(Oryzopsis hymenoides)*
State metal: silver
State precious gemstone: Virgin Valley Black Fire opal
State reptile: desert tortoise *(Gopherus agassizii)*
State rock: sandstone
State semi-precious gemstone: turquoise
State song: "Home Means Nevada"
State tree: single-leaf piñon *(Pinus monophylla)*; bristlecone pine *(Pinus aristata)*

State motto: All for Our Country
State nicknames: Silver State, Sagebrush State

Area code: 702
Time zone: Pacific
Abbreviations: NV (postal); Nev. (traditional)
Part of (region): Rocky Mountain States

Local Government

Counties

Nevada has 16 counties, most of which are governed by three-member boards of county commissioners. Carson City, the exception, operates as an independent city, having consolidated with the former Ormsby County.

Municipalities

Nevada has a total of 19 incorporated cities, including Carson City.

Settlement History and Early Development

Earliest human presence in what is now Nevada may date as far back as 20,000 years ago, according to the evidence of artifacts and cave paintings. Early white explorers found Mohave, Paiute, Shoshone, and Washoe Indians in the area. The first white visitor was probably Francisco Garcés, a Spanish priest who passed through the southern portion of present-day Nevada in 1776 on his way to California. The territory was under Spanish control as part of Alta California, then becoming a division of the Republic of Mexico with Mexican independence in 1821. Fur trappers and traders explored the area in the 1820s and 1830s, and American John Frémont explored Nevada between 1843 and 1845.

In 1848 the U.S. acquired Nevada as part of the huge Mexican Cession at the end of the Mexican War. The same year gold was discovered in California and eager prospectors traveled through Nevada, buying provisions there on the way.

In 1849 the area was included as part of the area called Deseret by the Mormon leader Brigham Young. He was named governor of the territory of Utah, established in 1850, which then included most of what is now Nevada. But the early Mormon settlers left Nevada for Salt Lake City in large numbers in 1857, responding to a call from Brigham Young to defend against federal government attack.

Mining and Statehood

In 1859 the Comstock Lode was discovered at the site of present-day Virginia City. The rush of prospectors and miners swelled the population, and in 1861 the Nevada

Territory was created. Because of the valuable mineral resources needed by the North during the Civil War and the state's antislavery stance, it was quickly granted statehood on October 31, 1864.

Later Development

During the last three decades of the nineteenth century mining declined drastically in Nevada. New discoveries of silver, copper, and gold in the first few years of the twentieth century quickly revived the economy, however. During World War I, discoveries of tungsten and zinc added to Nevada's mineral wealth.

In 1936 the Hoover Dam project was completed, providing both hydroelectric power and irrigation to Nevada, Arizona, and California. Nevada had already begun to attract tourists with the legalization of gambling in 1931. The growth of casinos after World War II, especially around Las Vegas, was made possible by the availability of water from Lake Mead, formed on the Colorado River by the Hoover Dam.

Mining experienced a resurgence during World War II; after the war, Nevada became the site of nuclear testing and research into nuclear power. However, tourism and gambling remain the state's leading industries, with visitors (and new residents) flocking to Las Vegas and the Reno-Lake Tahoe area year-round. Nevada has experienced phenomenal growth in recent years, recording the highest percentage of population increase of any state between 1980–90, more than 50 percent. Most of this increase has been in the Las Vegas area, with the continuing expansion of casinos, new residential communities, recreational facilities, and service industries.

State Boundaries

Although Nevada became a state in 1864, the present boundaries were established after the addition of territory taken from Utah and Arizona in 1866. The boundary between Nevada and Arizona, the Colorado River, was more precisely defined by compact in 1961.

Nevada Counties

Carson	Eureka	Nye
Churchill	Humboldt	Pershing
Clark	Lander	Storey
Douglas	Lincoln	Washoe
Elko	Lyon	White Pine
Esmeralda	Mineral	

Carson City (Independent City)
County Seat: Carson City (ZIP: 89701)

Pop: 40,443 (1990); 32,022 (1980)   **Pop Density:** 281.8
Land: 143.5 sq. mi.; **Water:** 12.3 sq. mi.   **Area Code:** 702

In western NV near the Carson River and Lake Tahoe, 28 mi. south of Reno. Laid out 1858 by Maj. William M. Omsby; county seat since 1861; independent city 1969; state capital. City government consolidated with county.

Name origin: For frontiersman Christopher "Kit" Carson (1809–68). Previously called Eagle Station.

Carson City   City
ZIP: 89701   **Lat:** 39-08-53 N   **Long:** 119-44-35 W
Pop: 40,443 (1990); 32,022 (1980)   **Pop Density:** 281.8
Land: 143.5 sq. mi.; **Water:** 12.3 sq. mi.   **Elev:** 4665 ft.
In western NV near the Carson River and Lake Tahoe, 28 mi. south of Reno. Laid out 1858 by Maj. William M. Omsby; county seat since 1861; independent city 1969; state capital. City government consolidated with county.

Name origin: For frontiersman Christopher "Kit" Carson (1809–68). Previously called Eagle Station.

Churchill County
County Seat: Fallon (ZIP: 89406)

Pop: 17,938 (1990); 13,917 (1980)   **Pop Density:** 3.6
Land: 4929.3 sq. mi.; **Water:** 94.3 sq. mi.   **Area Code:** 702

In west-central NV, east of Reno; original county, organized Nov 25, 1861 (prior to statehood).

Name origin: For Fort Churchill, which was named for either Charles C. Churchill, an officer of the Third U.S. Artillery Regiment, or possibly Gen. Sylvester Churchill (1783–1862), an officer in the War of 1812 and the Mexican-American War.

Fallon   City
ZIP: 89406   **Lat:** 39-28-32 N   **Long:** 118-46-40 W
Pop: 6,438 (1990); 4,262 (1980)   **Pop Density:** 2476.2
Land: 2.6 sq. mi.; **Water:** 0.0 sq. mi.   **Elev:** 3963 ft.
Established 1896.
Name origin: For settler Michael Fallon.

Fallon Station   Military Facility
Lat: 39-25-06 N   **Long:** 118-43-12 W
Pop: 1,092 (1990); 1,256 (1980)   **Pop Density:** 436.8
Land: 2.5 sq. mi.; **Water:** 0.0 sq. mi.

Clark County
County Seat: Las Vegas (ZIP: 89101)

Pop: 741,459 (1990); 463,087 (1980)   **Pop Density:** 93.7
Land: 7910.7 sq. mi.; **Water:** 180.3 sq. mi.   **Area Code:** 702

In the southeastern corner of NV; organized Feb 5, 1908 from Lincoln County.

Name origin: For William Andrews Clark (1839–1925), U.S. senator from MT (1899-1900; 1901–07).

Boulder City   City
ZIP: 89005   **Lat:** 35-57-57 N   **Long:** 114-50-17 W
Pop: 12,567 (1990); 9,590 (1980)   **Pop Density:** 374.0
Land: 33.6 sq. mi.; **Water:** 0.0 sq. mi.
Name origin: For huge rock formations in Boulder Canyon. Previously called Boulder Dam.

East Las Vegas   CDP
ZIP: 89112   **Lat:** 36-05-47 N   **Long:** 115-02-36 W
Pop: 11,087 (1990); 6,449 (1980)   **Pop Density:** 3576.5
Land: 3.1 sq. mi.; **Water:** 0.0 sq. mi.

Enterprise   CDP
Lat: 36-01-31 N   **Long:** 115-14-28 W
Pop: 6,412 (1990)   **Pop Density:** 92.8
Land: 69.1 sq. mi.; **Water:** 0.0 sq. mi.

Henderson   City
ZIP: 89015   **Lat:** 36-02-01 N   **Long:** 115-00-08 W
Pop: 64,942 (1990); 24,363 (1980)   **Pop Density:** 908.3
Land: 71.5 sq. mi.; **Water:** 0.0 sq. mi.
In southeastern NV, south of Las Vegas. Established c. 1944.
Name origin: For Sen. Charles Belknap Henderson (1873–1954).

NEVADA, Clark County

Indian Springs CDP
Lat: 36-34-14 N **Long:** 115-39-59 W
Pop: 1,164 (1990) **Pop Density:** 776.0
Land: 1.5 sq. mi.; **Water:** 0.0 sq. mi.

Las Vegas City
ZIP: 89125 **Lat:** 36-12-20 N **Long:** 115-13-22 W
Pop: 258,295 (1990); 164,674 (1980) **Pop Density:** 3100.8
Land: 83.3 sq. mi.; **Water:** 0.1 sq. mi.
In southeastern NV, 23 mi. northwest of Boulder Dam. County seat 1909; created as City of Las Vegas 1911. A major tourist center of the U.S., famous for gambling casinos and nightclubs.
Name origin: Named by traders on the Old Spanish Trail from Spanish 'fertile or marshy plains.'

Laughlin CDP
ZIP: 89029 **Lat:** 35-09-02 N **Long:** 114-37-37 W
Pop: 4,791 (1990) **Pop Density:** 173.0
Land: 27.7 sq. mi.; **Water:** 1.0 sq. mi.

Mesquite Township
ZIP: 89024 **Lat:** 36-48-08 N **Long:** 114-06-25 W
Pop: 1,871 (1990) **Pop Density:** 128.2
Land: 14.6 sq. mi.; **Water:** 0.3 sq. mi. **Elev:** 1608 ft.
Name origin: For the abundant mesquite shrubs and trees in the area.

Moapa Valley CDP
Lat: 36-34-49 N **Long:** 114-28-10 W
Pop: 3,444 (1990) **Pop Density:** 395.9
Land: 8.7 sq. mi.; **Water:** 0.0 sq. mi.

Nellis Air Force Base Military Facility
ZIP: 89191 **Lat:** 36-14-39 N **Long:** 115-03-13 W
Pop: 8,377 (1990); 7,476 (1980) **Pop Density:** 2702.3
Land: 3.1 sq. mi.; **Water:** 0.0 sq. mi.

North Las Vegas City
ZIP: 89030 **Lat:** 36-16-04 N **Long:** 115-08-39 W
Pop: 47,707 (1990); 42,739 (1980) **Pop Density:** 782.1
Land: 61.0 sq. mi.; **Water:** 0.0 sq. mi.
Name origin: For its location north of the city of Las Vegas.

Paradise CDP
ZIP: 89109 **Lat:** 36-04-50 N **Long:** 115-08-00 W
Pop: 124,682 (1990) **Pop Density:** 2613.9
Land: 47.7 sq. mi.; **Water:** 0.0 sq. mi.

Spring Valley CDP
ZIP: 89125 **Lat:** 36-06-28 N **Long:** 115-14-39 W
Pop: 51,726 (1990) **Pop Density:** 2599.3
Land: 19.9 sq. mi.; **Water:** 0.0 sq. mi.

Sunrise Manor CDP
ZIP: 89110 **Lat:** 36-11-14 N **Long:** 115-02-59 W
Pop: 95,362 (1990) **Pop Density:** 2732.4
Land: 34.9 sq. mi.; **Water:** 0.0 sq. mi.

Winchester CDP
ZIP: 89101 **Lat:** 36-08-11 N **Long:** 115-07-47 W
Pop: 23,365 (1990); 19,728 (1980) **Pop Density:** 5310.2
Land: 4.4 sq. mi.; **Water:** 0.0 sq. mi.

Douglas County
County Seat: Minden (ZIP: 89423)

Pop: 27,637 (1990); 19,421 (1980) **Pop Density:** 38.9
Land: 709.9 sq. mi.; **Water:** 27.8 sq. mi. **Area Code:** 702
On the southwestern border of NV, south of Reno; original county; organized Nov 25, 1861 (prior to statehood).
Name origin: For Stephen Arnold Douglas (1813–61), U.S. orator and statesman.

Gardnerville CDP
ZIP: 89410 **Lat:** 38-56-21 N **Long:** 119-44-09 W
Pop: 2,177 (1990); 2,638 (1980) **Pop Density:** 473.3
Land: 4.6 sq. mi.; **Water:** 0.0 sq. mi.

Gardnerville Ranchos CDP
ZIP: 89410 **Lat:** 38-53-17 N **Long:** 119-44-24 W
Pop: 7,455 (1990); 3,542 (1980) **Pop Density:** 507.1
Land: 14.7 sq. mi.; **Water:** 0.0 sq. mi.

Indian Hills CDP
Lat: 39-05-09 N **Long:** 119-46-58 W
Pop: 2,544 (1990) **Pop Density:** 265.0
Land: 9.6 sq. mi.; **Water:** 0.0 sq. mi.

Johnson Lane CDP
Lat: 39-02-52 N **Long:** 119-43-16 W
Pop: 2,551 (1990) **Pop Density:** 119.8
Land: 21.3 sq. mi.; **Water:** 0.0 sq. mi.

Kingsbury CDP
Lat: 38-58-33 N **Long:** 119-52-55 W
Pop: 2,238 (1990); 2,695 (1980) **Pop Density:** 89.5
Land: 25.0 sq. mi.; **Water:** 0.0 sq. mi.

Minden CDP
ZIP: 89423 **Lat:** 38-57-37 N **Long:** 119-46-19 W
Pop: 1,441 (1990) **Pop Density:** 327.5
Land: 4.4 sq. mi.; **Water:** 0.0 sq. mi.

Stateline CDP
Lat: 38-58-07 N **Long:** 119-56-35 W
Pop: 1,379 (1990) **Pop Density:** 1970.0
Land: 0.7 sq. mi.; **Water:** 0.1 sq. mi.

Zephyr Cove-Round Hill Village CDP
Lat: 38-59-40 N **Long:** 119-54-58 W
Pop: 1,434 (1990); 1,316 (1980) **Pop Density:** 181.5
Land: 7.9 sq. mi.; **Water:** 0.3 sq. mi.

Elko County
County Seat: Elko (ZIP: 89801)

Pop: 33,530 (1990); 17,269 (1980)　　**Pop Density:** 2.0
Land: 17181.5 sq. mi.; **Water:** 22.5 sq. mi.　　**Area Code:** 702
On the northeastern border of NV; organized Mar 5, 1869 from Lander County.

Name origin: For the town; meaning of name is undetermined, possibly *elk* plus *-o*, a typical railroad name. It has been suggested that the town was named for elk (the animal) or that the word is an Indian term meaning 'first white woman.'

Carlin　　City
ZIP: 89822　　**Lat:** 40-43-01 N **Long:** 116-06-45 W
Pop: 2,220 (1990); 1,232 (1980)　　**Pop Density:** 244.0
Land: 9.1 sq. mi.; **Water:** 0.0 sq. mi.
Settled 1860s.
Name origin: For Union army officer, William Passmore Carlin.

Elko　　City
ZIP: 89801　　**Lat:** 40-50-19 N **Long:** 115-45-38 W
Pop: 14,736 (1990); 8,758 (1980)　　**Pop Density:** 1503.7
Land: 9.8 sq. mi.; **Water:** 0.0 sq. mi.　　**Elev:** 5067 ft.
In northeastern NV on the Humboldt River, 30 mi. northwest of Franklin Lake. Laid out c. 1869.
Name origin: Named by railway official Charles Crocker. Meaning is undetermined.

Owyhee　　CDP
ZIP: 89832　　**Lat:** 41-54-51 N **Long:** 116-11-16 W
Pop: 908 (1990)　　**Pop Density:** 4.0
Land: 224.3 sq. mi.; **Water:** 1.1 sq. mi.

Spring Creek　　CDP
ZIP: 89801　　**Lat:** 40-44-18 N **Long:** 115-35-45 W
Pop: 5,866 (1990)　　**Pop Density:** 102.2
Land: 57.4 sq. mi.; **Water:** 0.0 sq. mi.

Wells　　City
ZIP: 89833　　**Lat:** 41-06-51 N **Long:** 114-56-53 W
Pop: 1,256 (1990); 1,218 (1980)　　**Pop Density:** 190.3
Land: 6.6 sq. mi.; **Water:** 0.0 sq. mi.
Name origin: For nearby springs, locally called wells. Previously called Humboldt Wells.

West Wendover　　CDP
　　Lat: 40-46-03 N **Long:** 114-06-55 W
Pop: 2,007 (1990)　　**Pop Density:** 39.7
Land: 50.6 sq. mi.; **Water:** 0.0 sq. mi.

Esmeralda County
County Seat: Goldfield (ZIP: 89013)

Pop: 1,344 (1990); 777 (1980)　　**Pop Density:** 0.4
Land: 3588.7 sq. mi.; **Water:** 0.5 sq. mi.　　**Area Code:** 702
On the central southern border of NV with CA; original county; organized Nov 25, 1861 (prior to statehood).
Name origin: For the Esmeralda Mining District, from Spanish 'emerald,' for the stones found there.

Eureka County
County Seat: Eureka (ZIP: 89316)

Pop: 1,547 (1990); 1,198 (1980)　　**Pop Density:** 0.4
Land: 4176.0 sq. mi.; **Water:** 4.3 sq. mi.　　**Area Code:** 702
In east-central NV; organized Mar 1, 1873 from Lander County.
Name origin: For the Eureka Mining District, from Greek 'I have found it.'

Humboldt County
County Seat: Winnemucca (ZIP: 89445)

Pop: 12,844 (1990); 9,449 (1980)   **Pop Density:** 1.3
Land: 9648.4 sq. mi.; **Water:** 10.0 sq. mi.   **Area Code:** 702
On the northern border of NV; original county; organized Nov 25, 1861 (prior to statehood).
Name origin: For the Little Humboldt River, which runs through the county; named for Alexander von Humboldt (1769–1859), German explorer and naturalist.

McDermitt   CDP
Lat: 41-58-22 N   **Long:** 117-36-16 W
Pop: 373 (1990)   **Pop Density:** 28.3
Land: 13.2 sq. mi.; **Water:** 0.0 sq. mi.

Winnemucca   City
ZIP: 89445   **Lat:** 40-58-05 N   **Long:** 117-43-32 W
Pop: 6,134 (1990); 4,140 (1980)   **Pop Density:** 807.1
Land: 7.6 sq. mi.; **Water:** 0.0 sq. mi.   **Elev:** 4299 ft.
Name origin: Named in 1868 by C.B.O. Bannon for the famous Indian chief. Previously called French Ford, French Bridge, and Centerville.

Lander County
County Seat: Battle Mountain (ZIP: 89820)

Pop: 6,266 (1990); 4,076 (1980)   **Pop Density:** 1.1
Land: 5493.8 sq. mi.; **Water:** 25.8 sq. mi.   **Area Code:** 702
In central NV; organized Dec 19, 1862 (prior to statehood). Originally encompassed a third of the state and was called "Great East" and later "mother of counties."
Name origin: For Gen. Frederick William Lander (1822–62), Union army officer, surveyor, and Indian agent.

Battle Mountain   CDP
ZIP: 89820   **Lat:** 40-38-29 N   **Long:** 116-56-15 W
Pop: 3,542 (1990); 2,749 (1980)   **Pop Density:** 1967.8
Land: 1.8 sq. mi.; **Water:** 0.0 sq. mi.

Lincoln County
County Seat: Pioche (ZIP: 89043)

Pop: 3,775 (1990); 3,732 (1980)   **Pop Density:** 0.4
Land: 10634.7 sq. mi.; **Water:** 2.8 sq. mi.   **Area Code:** 702
On the southeast border of NV, north of Las Vegas; organized Feb 25, 1866.
Name origin: For Abraham Lincoln (1809–65), sixteenth U.S. president.

Caliente   City
ZIP: 89008   **Lat:** 37-36-56 N   **Long:** 114-30-52 W
Pop: 1,111 (1990); 982 (1980)   **Pop Density:** 740.7
Land: 1.5 sq. mi.; **Water:** 0.0 sq. mi.   **Elev:** 4395 ft.
Name origin: Named in 1901 from Spanish 'hot,' a reference to nearby hot springs. Originally known as Dutch Flat, Culverwell Ranch, and Clover or Cloverdale Station.

Pioche   Pop. Place
ZIP: 89043
Pop: 830 (1990); 130 (1980)

Elev: 6064 ft.

Lyon County
County Seat: Yerington (ZIP: 89447)

Pop: 20,001 (1990); 13,594 (1980)   **Pop Density:** 10.0
Land: 1993.8 sq. mi.; **Water:** 22.7 sq. mi.   **Area Code:** 702

In southwestern NV, southeast of Reno; original county; organized Nov 25, 1861 (prior to statehood).

Name origin: For either Gen. Nathaniel Lyon (1818–61), an officer in the Seminole War, Mexican-American War, and Civil War, or for Capt. Robert Lyon, a hero of the Indian Wars.

Dayton   CDP
ZIP: 89403   **Lat:** 39-15-22 N   **Long:** 119-34-10 W
Pop: 2,217 (1990)   **Pop Density:** 70.2
Land: 31.6 sq. mi.; **Water:** 0.0 sq. mi.

Fernley   CDP
ZIP: 89408   **Lat:** 39-35-01 N   **Long:** 119-12-03 W
Pop: 5,164 (1990)   **Pop Density:** 148.8
Land: 34.7 sq. mi.; **Water:** 0.0 sq. mi.

Silver Springs   CDP
ZIP: 89429   **Lat:** 39-22-50 N   **Long:** 119-12-50 W
Pop: 2,253 (1990)   **Pop Density:** 32.9
Land: 68.5 sq. mi.; **Water:** 6.2 sq. mi.

Smith Valley   CDP
Lat: 38-47-10 N   **Long:** 119-20-26 W
Pop: 1,033 (1990)   **Pop Density:** 8.6
Land: 119.9 sq. mi.; **Water:** 2.0 sq. mi.

Yerington   City
ZIP: 89447   **Lat:** 38-59-17 N   **Long:** 119-09-47 W
Pop: 2,367 (1990); 2,021 (1980)   **Pop Density:** 1479.4
Land: 1.6 sq. mi.; **Water:** 0.0 sq. mi.   **Elev:** 4384 ft.
Name origin: For Henry Marvin Yerington, superintendent of the Virginia and Truckee Railroad. Originally known as Poison, Pizen, Switch, and Greenfield.

Mineral County
County Seat: Hawthorne (ZIP: 89415)

Pop: 6,475 (1990); 6,217 (1980)   **Pop Density:** 1.7
Land: 3756.6 sq. mi.; **Water:** 56.6 sq. mi.   **Area Code:** 702

On the southwestern border of NV with CA, southeast of Reno; organized Feb 10, 1911 from Esmeralda County.

Name origin: For the profusion of various minerals in the area.

Hawthorne   CDP
ZIP: 89415   **Lat:** 38-31-30 N   **Long:** 118-37-37 W
Pop: 4,162 (1990); 3,741 (1980)   **Pop Density:** 2774.7
Land: 1.5 sq. mi.; **Water:** 0.0 sq. mi.

Schurz   CDP
Lat: 38-59-34 N   **Long:** 118-49-58 W
Pop: 617 (1990)   **Pop Density:** 17.5
Land: 35.3 sq. mi.; **Water:** 0.0 sq. mi.

Nye County
County Seat: Tonopah (ZIP: 89049)

Pop: 17,781 (1990); 9,048 (1980)   **Pop Density:** 1.0
Land: 18147.2 sq. mi.; **Water:** 12.5 sq. mi.   **Area Code:** 702

In south-central NV; organized Feb 16, 1864 from Esmeralda County; largest county in NV.

Name origin: For James Warren Nye (1814–76), NY statesman, governor of NV Territory (1861–64), and U.S. senator from NV (1864–73).

Beatty   CDP
Lat: 36-56-24 N   **Long:** 116-42-25 W
Pop: 1,623 (1990)   **Pop Density:** 9.2
Land: 175.7 sq. mi.; **Water:** 0.0 sq. mi.

Gabbs   City
ZIP: 89409   **Lat:** 38-52-03 N   **Long:** 117-55-17 W
Pop: 667 (1990); 811 (1980)   **Pop Density:** 222.3
Land: 3.0 sq. mi.; **Water:** 0.0 sq. mi.
Name origin: Named in 1943 for paleontologist William M. Gabbs. Previously called Toiyabe.

NEVADA, Nye County   American Places Dictionary

Pahrump   CDP
ZIP: 89041   Lat: 36-15-10 N Long: 116-01-05 W
Pop: 7,424 (1990)   Pop Density: 26.8
Land: 277.1 sq. mi.; Water: 0.0 sq. mi.

Tonopah   CDP
ZIP: 89049   Lat: 38-05-51 N Long: 117-14-51 W
Pop: 3,616 (1990)   Pop Density: 223.2
Land: 16.2 sq. mi.; Water: 0.0 sq. mi.

Pershing County
County Seat: Lovelock (ZIP: 89419)

Pop: 4,336 (1990); 3,408 (1980)   **Pop Density:** 0.7
Land: 6009.1 sq. mi.; **Water:** 58.8 sq. mi.   **Area Code:** 702

In west-central NV, northeast of Reno; organized Mar 18, 1919 from Humboldt County.

Name origin: For Gen. John Joseph "Black Jack" Pershing (1860–1948), an officer who served in Cuba, the Philippines, and Manchuria; commander in chief of the American Expeditionary Force (1917–18) during WW I, and U.S. army chief of staff (1921–24).

Lovelock   City
ZIP: 89419   Lat: 40-10-47 N Long: 118-28-36 W
Pop: 2,069 (1990); 1,680 (1980)   Pop Density: 2955.7
Land: 0.7 sq. mi.; Water: 0.0 sq. mi.

Name origin: For settler George Lovelock. Previously called Big Meadows.

Storey County
County Seat: Virginia City (ZIP: 89440-0139)

Pop: 2,526 (1990); 1,503 (1980)   **Pop Density:** 9.6
Land: 263.5 sq. mi.; **Water:** 0.3 sq. mi.   **Area Code:** 702

In southwestern NV, east of Reno; original county; organized Nov 25, 1861 (prior to statehood).

Name origin: For Capt. Edward Faris Storey (?–1860), army officer killed by Paiute Indians at Pyramid Lake.

Washoe County
County Seat: Reno (ZIP: 89520)

Pop: 254,667 (1990); 193,623 (1980)   **Pop Density:** 40.2
Land: 6342.5 sq. mi.; **Water:** 209.0 sq. mi.   **Area Code:** 702

On the western border of NV; original county; organized Nov 25, 1861 (prior to statehood); in 1883 annexed Roop County (called Lake County until 1862), which was also an original county.

Name origin: For the Washo or Washiu Indian tribe in northwestern NV and adjacent areas of CA. Their name has been translated as 'person,' 'tall bunch grass,' and 'rye grass.' The first seems most probable.

Incline Village-Crystal Bay   CDP
ZIP: 89450   Lat: 39-16-01 N Long: 119-57-50 W
Pop: 7,119 (1990)   Pop Density: 512.2
Land: 13.9 sq. mi.; Water: 1.7 sq. mi.

New Washoe City   CDP
                    Lat: 39-18-04 N Long: 119-46-18 W
Pop: 2,875 (1990); 2,543 (1980)   Pop Density: 338.2
Land: 8.5 sq. mi.; Water: 0.9 sq. mi.

Reno   City
ZIP: 89501   Lat: 39-32-19 N Long: 119-49-20 W
Pop: 133,850 (1990); 100,756 (1980)   Pop Density: 2327.8
Land: 57.5 sq. mi.; Water: 0.2 sq. mi.   Elev: 4498 ft.

In northwestern NV on the Truckee River, 18 mi. north of Lake Tahoe. Settled 1859; incorporated as city 1879.

Name origin: For army officer Jesse Lee Reno (1823–62), Union general and surveyor of Utah Territory. Originally known as Fuller's Crossing and Lakes Crossing.

Sparks
City
ZIP: 89431 **Lat:** 39-32-39 N **Long:** 119-44-12 W
Pop: 53,367 (1990); 40,780 (1980) **Pop Density:** 3758.2
Land: 14.2 sq. mi.; **Water:** 0.0 sq. mi.

In northwestern NV on the Truckee River, 4 mi. east of Reno. Founded c. 1903. Major tourist center with gambling casinos and nightclubs. Also known for its short residency requirement for divorces.
Name origin: For John Sparks, governor of NV. Previously called Harriman.

Sun Valley
CDP
ZIP: 89433 **Lat:** 39-35-53 N **Long:** 119-46-42 W
Pop: 11,391 (1990) **Pop Density:** 1294.4
Land: 8.8 sq. mi.; **Water:** 0.0 sq. mi.

Wadsworth
CDP
Lat: 39-37-57 N **Long:** 119-17-24 W
Pop: 640 (1990) **Pop Density:** 173.0
Land: 3.7 sq. mi.; **Water:** 0.0 sq. mi.

White Pine County
County Seat: Ely (ZIP: 89301)

Pop: 9,264 (1990); 8,167 (1980) **Pop Density:** 1.0
Land: 8876.6 sq. mi.; **Water:** 20.6 sq. mi. **Area Code:** 702

On the central eastern border of NV; organized Mar 2, 1869 from Lander county.
Name origin: For the White Pine Mining District, itself named for the area's many pine trees.

Ely
City
ZIP: 89301 **Lat:** 39-14-56 N **Long:** 114-52-40 W
Pop: 4,756 (1990); 4,882 (1980) **Pop Density:** 1358.9
Land: 3.5 sq. mi.; **Water:** 0.0 sq. mi. **Elev:** 6427 ft.
Located 1869 or 1870.
Name origin: For Smith Ely, who built a copper furnace in the town. Previously called Murry Creek Station.

McGill
CDP
Lat: 39-23-58 N **Long:** 114-46-44 W
Pop: 1,258 (1990) **Pop Density:** 1572.5
Land: 0.8 sq. mi.; **Water:** 0.0 sq. mi.

Index to Places and Counties in Nevada

Battle Mountain (Lander) CDP *454*
Beatty (Nye) CDP *455*
Boulder City (Clark) City *451*
Caliente (Lincoln) City *454*
Carlin (Elko) City *453*
Carson City (Carson City (Independent City)) City *451*
Carson City (Independent City) *451*
Churchill County *451*
Clark County *451*
Dayton (Lyon) CDP *455*
Douglas County *452*
East Las Vegas (Clark) CDP *451*
Elko (Elko) City *453*
Elko County *453*
Ely (White Pine) City *457*
Enterprise (Clark) CDP *451*
Esmeralda County *453*
Eureka County *453*
Fallon (Churchill) City *451*
Fallon Station (Churchill) Military Facility *451*
Fernley (Lyon) CDP *455*
Gabbs (Nye) City *455*
Gardnerville (Douglas) CDP *452*
Gardnerville Ranchos (Douglas) CDP *452*
Hawthorne (Mineral) CDP *455*
Henderson (Clark) City *451*
Humboldt County *454*
Incline Village-Crystal Bay (Washoe) CDP *456*
Indian Hills (Douglas) CDP *452*
Indian Springs (Clark) CDP *452*
Johnson Lane (Douglas) CDP *452*
Kingsbury (Douglas) CDP *452*
Lander County *454*
Las Vegas (Clark) City *452*
Laughlin (Clark) CDP *452*
Lincoln County *454*
Lovelock (Pershing) City *456*
Lyon County *455*
McDermitt (Humboldt) CDP *454*
McGill (White Pine) CDP *457*
Mesquite (Clark) Township *452*
Minden (Douglas) CDP *452*
Mineral County *455*
Moapa Valley (Clark) CDP *452*
Nellis Air Force Base (Clark) Military Facility *452*
New Washoe City (Washoe) CDP *456*
North Las Vegas (Clark) City *452*
Nye County *455*
Owyhee (Elko) CDP *453*
Pahrump (Nye) CDP *456*
Paradise (Clark) CDP *452*
Pershing County *456*
Pioche (Lincoln) Pop. Place *454*
Reno (Washoe) City *456*
Schurz (Mineral) CDP *455*
Silver Springs (Lyon) CDP *455*
Smith Valley (Lyon) CDP *455*
Sparks (Washoe) City *457*
Spring Creek (Elko) CDP *453*
Spring Valley (Clark) CDP *452*
Stateline (Douglas) CDP *452*
Storey County *456*
Sunrise Manor (Clark) CDP *452*
Sun Valley (Washoe) CDP *457*
Tonopah (Nye) CDP *456*
Wadsworth (Washoe) CDP *457*
Washoe County *456*
Wells (Elko) City *453*
West Wendover (Elko) CDP *453*
White Pine County *457*
Winchester (Clark) CDP *452*
Winnemucca (Humboldt) City *454*
Yerington (Lyon) City *455*
Zephyr Cove-Round Hill Village (Douglas) CDP *452*

New Mexico

NEW MEXICO

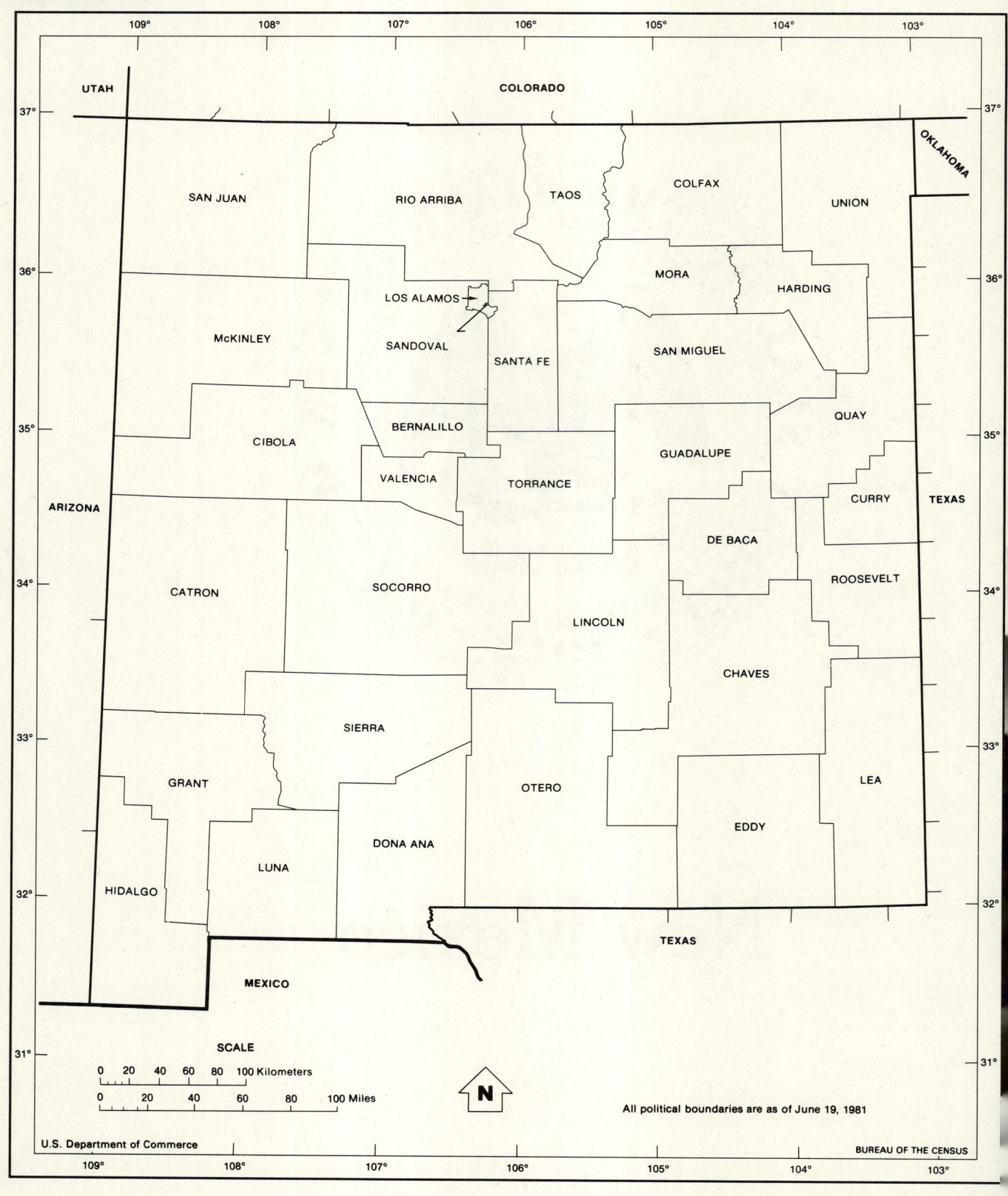

New Mexico

Population: 1,515,069 (1990); 1,302,894 (1980)
Population rank (1990): 37
Percent population change (1980–1990): 16.3
Population projection: 1,642,000 (1995); 1,727,000 (2000)

Area: total: 121,598 sq. mi.; 121,365 sq. mi. land, 234 sq. mi. water
Area rank: 5
Highest elevation: 13,161 ft., Wheeler Peak (Taos County)
Lowest point: 2,817 ft., at Red Bluff Reservoir (Eddy County)

State capital: Santa Fe (Santa Fe County)
Largest city: Albuquerque (384,736)
Second largest city: Las Cruces (62,126)
Largest county: Bernalillo (480,577)

Total housing units: 632,058
No. of occupied housing units: 542,709
Vacant housing units (%): 14.1
Distribution of population by race and Hispanic origin (%):
White: 75.6
Black: 2.0
Hispanic (any race): 38.2
Native American: 8.9
Asian/Pacific: 0.9
Other: 12.6

Admission date: January 6, 1912 (47th state).

Location: In the southwestern United States, bordering Texas, Mexico, Arizona, Utah, Colorado, and Oklahoma.

Name Origin: Named by Spanish explorer Francisco de Ibarra in 1562 for the country of Mexico, of which it was a territory until the end of the Mexican War (1846–48). The name was originally applied to all territory north of New Spain, the Spanish colony that became Mexico.

State animal: black bear *(Ursus americanus)*
State bird: Chaparral bird or roadrunner *(Geococcyx californianus)*
State cookie: biscochito
State fish: cutthroat trout *(Salmo clarki)*
State flower: yucca
State fossil: *Coelophysis* dinosaur
State gem: turquoise
State grass: Blue grama *(Bouteloua gracilis)*
State insect: tarantula hawk wasp *(Pepsis formosa)*
State song: "O, Fair New Mexico"

State tree: piñon *(Pinus edulis)*
State vegetables: chile *(Capsicum annum)* and frijol or pinto bean *(Phaseolus vulgaris)*

State motto: *Crescit Eundo* (Latin 'It Grows as It Goes')
State nickname: Land of Enchantment

Area code: 505
Time zone: Mountain
Abbreviations: NM (postal); N.M. or N. Mex. (traditional)
Part of (region): Southwest

Local Government

Counties

New Mexico has 33 counties, each governed by elected county commissioners with the exception of Los Alamos County, which is administered by a city-county council.

New Mexico's large American Indian population has its own government bodies on four reservations and nineteen pueblos. The Pueblo elect governors to form the All-Indian Pueblo Council. The Apache and Navajo each elect council members to their respective governing councils. The Ute Mountain group has its tribal government at Towaoc, CO.

Municipalities

New Mexico's municipalities may adopt their own charters and choose from the mayor-council, commission, city manager-commission, or other forms of government.

Settlement History and Early Development

Indian settlement in the area that is now New Mexico began as much as 12,000 years ago. Among the ancient Indian groups were the Mogollon and the Anasazi, who were the predecessors of the Pueblo Indians. The Anasazi built multi-roomed dwellings that resemble apartment buildings; some Anasazi were cliff dwellers. Later immigrants to the area included the Navajo, Apache, Ute, and Comanche Indians.

From 1536 Spanish explorers had heard tales of the "Seven Cities of Cibola," legendary centers of great wealth, for which they searched for most of the rest of the century. In 1598, Juan de Oñate established a colony at the Pueblo of San Juan de Los Caballeros; he became governor of the province of New Mexico. His successor moved the capital to Sante Fe in 1609 or 1610, making it the oldest seat of government in the United States.

The Spanish spent the rest of the seventeenth century in conflict with the Indians, whom they were simultaneously trying to convert to Christianity and use as forced labor.

NEW MEXICO

The Spanish eventually prevailed and hostilities were much less common during the eighteenth century.

Mexican Rule

When Mexico won its freedom from Spain in 1821, it retained New Mexico as a province. The same year the Sante Fe Trail was opened to bring goods from Missouri to New Mexico. New Mexico was occupied by the forces of U.S. General Stephen Kearny during the Mexican-American War (1846–1848), and the territory became part of the U.S. by the Treaty of Guadalupe Hidalgo (1848). It was organized as a territory as part of the Compromise of 1850, then enlarged to its south by the Gadsden Purchase in 1853.

The Civil War and Statehood

New Mexico was held by both Confederate and Union forces during the Civil War. The decades following the war were a time of both economic growth and turbulence in New Mexico. The Atchison, Topeka, and Santa Fe Railroad came to New Mexico in 1879 and, with its affiliates, linked all regions of the territory, leading to growth for the livestock, farming, mining, and timber industries. This was also the time of the "Wild West," with much of the territory at the periphery of effective law enforcement. Kit Carson battled the Indians, cattlemen and landowners vied for their own interests, Sheriff Pat Garrett killed Billy the Kid in 1881, and Geronimo terrorized the area before surrendering in 1886.

New Mexico became the 47th state on January 6, 1912. In 1916, the state was raided by Mexican revolutionary Pancho Villa, whom the U.S. Army was unsuccessful in apprehending.

Business and Commerce

Economic woes beset the state's farming and ranching industries in the 1920s and 1930s. These troubles were only partly mitigated by the discovery of oil, potash, and the caverns near Carlsbad that became a national park and major tourist attraction. New Mexico was the site of Los Alamos, a secretly built town where the world's first atomic bombs were developed during World War II. The first test of a nuclear device was successfully conducted near Alamogordo in July 1945. After the war nuclear research continued in the state, and the discovery of uranium in 1950 benefited the industry. Nuclear research, the defense industry, and tourism continue to be important industries in New Mexico, although the state faces economic losses because of expected military cutbacks in the 1990s.

State Boundaries

The present boundaries of New Mexico were determined in 1863, when the territories of Colorado and Arizona were organized. In 1920 New Mexico and Texas agreed to fix their boundary at the midchannel of the Rio Grande as it flowed in 1850, but it ultimately took a Supreme Court case (1931) to determine where that line actually was.

New Mexico Counties

Bernalillo	Doña Ana	Lincoln	Rio Arriba	Sierra
Catron	Eddy	Los Alamos	Roosevelt	Socorro
Chaves	Grant	Luna	Sandoval	Taos
Cibola	Guadalupe	McKinley	San Juan	Torrance
Colfax	Harding	Mora	San Miguel	Union
Curry	Hidalgo	Otero	Santa Fe	Valencia
DeBaca	Lea	Quay		

Multi-County Places

The following New Mexico places are in more than one county. Given here is the total population for each multi-county place, and the names of the counties it is in.

Chimayo, pop. 2,789; Rio Arriba (2,150), Santa Fe (639)
Corrales, pop. 5,453; Sandoval (4,918), Bernalillo (535)
Edgewood, pop. 3,324; Santa Fe (2,880), Torrance (444)
Espanola, pop. 8,389; Rio Arriba (6,210), Santa Fe (2,179)
Isleta Pueblo, pop. 1,703; Bernalillo (1,355), Valencia (348)
Mosquero, pop. 164; Harding (164), San Miguel (0)

Bernalillo County
County Seat: Albuquerque (ZIP: 87102)

Pop: 480,577 (1990); 420,261 (1980) **Pop Density:** 412.1
Land: 1166.2 sq. mi.; **Water:** 2.6 sq. mi. **Area Code:** 505

In west-central NM, southwest of Santa Fe; original county; organized Jan 8, 1852 (prior to statehood); annexed Santa Ana County 1876.

Name origin: Spanish for 'little Bernal,' possibly for a young member of the Gonzales-Bernal family who lived in the area as early as 1680. It may also have been named for Fray Juan Bernal, a friend of one of the community leaders.

Albuquerque   City
ZIP: 87101   **Lat:** 35-07-01 N **Long:** 106-37-28 W
Pop: 384,736 (1990); 332,920 (1980)   **Pop Density:** 2910.3
Land: 132.2 sq. mi.; **Water:** 0.6 sq. mi.

In central NM on the Rio Grande, 55 mi. southwest of Santa Fe. Established Apr 23, 1706. Incorporated as town 1885; as city 1891. Industrial, trade, and transportation center of the Southwest. Also, leading center for energy research programs and U.S. government defense research.

Name origin: For Alburquerque, Spain. Derivation is uncertain, but possibly *albus quercus* 'white oak'; an oak tree appears on the seal of the Spanish city. And in honor of Don Francisco Enriquez, the Duque de Alburquerque and the 34th viceroy of New Spain. The *r* in the second syllable was dropped in the early 1800s by English-speakers.

Corrales   Village
ZIP: 87048   **Lat:** 35-12-44 N **Long:** 106-37-59 W
Pop: 535 (1990); 123 (1980)   **Pop Density:** 334.4
Land: 1.6 sq. mi.; **Water:** 0.1 sq. mi.

Incorporated 1971. Part of the town is also in Sandoval County.

Name origin: From Spanish meaning 'enclosures.'

Isleta Pueblo   CDP
                    Lat: 34-54-33 N **Long:** 106-41-50 W
Pop: 1,355 (1990); 1,246 (1980)   **Pop Density:** 967.9
Land: 1.4 sq. mi.; **Water:** 0.0 sq. mi.

Part of the town is also in Valencia County.

Los Ranchos de Albuquerque   Village
                    Lat: 35-09-54 N **Long:** 106-38-56 W
Pop: 3,955 (1990); 2,741 (1980)   **Pop Density:** 1068.9
Land: 3.7 sq. mi.; **Water:** 0.0 sq. mi.

Incorporated 1958.

Name origin: For Los Ranchos de Albuquerque Grant, a large land grant north of Albuquerque made in 1694 by Spain to Diego Montoya.

North Valley   CDP
ZIP: 87107   **Lat:** 35-10-23 N **Long:** 106-37-21 W
Pop: 12,507 (1990); 5,096 (1980)   **Pop Density:** 1583.2
Land: 7.9 sq. mi.; **Water:** 0.0 sq. mi.

Paradise Hills   CDP
ZIP: 87114   **Lat:** 35-11-47 N **Long:** 106-41-39 W
Pop: 5,513 (1990)   **Pop Density:** 3675.3
Land: 1.5 sq. mi.; **Water:** 0.0 sq. mi.

Sandia   CDP
ZIP: 87047   **Lat:** 35-03-12 N **Long:** 106-33-54 W
Pop: 6,742 (1990); 5,288 (1980)   **Pop Density:** 1605.2
Land: 4.2 sq. mi.; **Water:** 0.0 sq. mi.

Sandia Heights   CDP
                    Lat: 35-10-36 N **Long:** 106-29-26 W
Pop: 3,519 (1990)   **Pop Density:** 1005.4
Land: 3.5 sq. mi.; **Water:** 0.0 sq. mi.

South Valley   CDP
ZIP: 87102   **Lat:** 35-00-36 N **Long:** 106-40-39 W
Pop: 35,701 (1990); 38,916 (1980)   **Pop Density:** 1170.5
Land: 30.5 sq. mi.; **Water:** 0.7 sq. mi.

Tijeras   Village
ZIP: 87059   **Lat:** 35-05-18 N **Long:** 106-22-29 W
Pop: 340 (1990); 311 (1980)   **Pop Density:** 425.0
Land: 0.8 sq. mi.; **Water:** 0.0 sq. mi.

Incorporated 1973.

Name origin: For a pioneer whose surname translates as 'scissors.'

Catron County
County Seat: Reserve (ZIP: 87830)

Pop: 2,563 (1990); 2,720 (1980) **Pop Density:** 0.4
Land: 6928.3 sq. mi.; **Water:** 1.2 sq. mi. **Area Code:** 505

On the central western border of NM, southwest of Albuquerque; organized Feb 25, 1921 from Socorro County.

Name origin: For Thomas Benton Catron (1840–1921), Confederate officer during the Civil War and U.S. senator from NM (1912–17).

Reserve   Village
ZIP: 87830   **Lat:** 33-42-30 N **Long:** 108-45-40 W
Pop: 319 (1990); 439 (1980)   **Pop Density:** 531.7
Land: 0.6 sq. mi.; **Water:** 0.0 sq. mi.

Incorporated 1974.

Name origin: For the adjacent U.S. forest reserves.

Chaves County
County Seat: Roswell (ZIP: 88201)

Pop: 57,849 (1990); 51,103 (1980) **Pop Density:** 9.5
Land: 6071.4 sq. mi.; **Water:** 4.2 sq. mi. **Area Code:** 505

In southeastern NM, northeast of Las Cruces; organized Feb 25, 1889 from Lincoln County (prior to statehood).

Name origin: For Lt. Col. José Francisco Cháves (1833–1904), an officer during the Civil War and U.S. representative from NM (1865–67; 1869–71).

Dexter   Town
ZIP: 88230   **Lat:** 33-11-40 N **Long:** 104-22-06 W
Pop: 898 (1990); 882 (1980)   **Pop Density:** 1282.9
Land: 0.7 sq. mi.; **Water:** 0.1 sq. mi.   **Elev:** 3462 ft.

Founded 1903; incorporated 1903.

Name origin: For Dexter, IA.

Hagerman   Town
ZIP: 88232   **Lat:** 33-06-48 N **Long:** 104-19-41 W
Pop: 961 (1990); 936 (1980)   **Pop Density:** 739.2
Land: 1.3 sq. mi.; **Water:** 0.0 sq. mi.   **Elev:** 3425 ft.

Incorporated 1905.

Name origin: For J. J. Hagerman, president of a local railroad.

Lake Arthur   Town
ZIP: 88253   **Lat:** 32-59-59 N **Long:** 104-21-48 W
Pop: 336 (1990); 327 (1980)   **Pop Density:** 560.0
Land: 0.6 sq. mi.; **Water:** 0.0 sq. mi.   **Elev:** 3378 ft.

Incorporated 1906.

Name origin: For pioneer Arthur Russell, who settled here in 1893.

Roswell   City
ZIP: 88201   **Lat:** 33-22-15 N **Long:** 104-31-45 W
Pop: 44,654 (1990); 39,676 (1980)   **Pop Density:** 1534.5
Land: 29.1 sq. mi.; **Water:** 0.0 sq. mi.   **Elev:** 3573 ft.

In southeastern NM, northeast of Alamogordo. Settled 1869; incorporated 1903.

Name origin: For Roswell·Smith, a gambler who helped found the town.

Cibola County
County Seat: Grants (ZIP: 87020)

Pop: 23,794 (1990); 30,346 (1980)   **Pop Density:** 5.2
Land: 4539.6 sq. mi.; **Water:** 2.5 sq. mi.   **Area Code:** 505

On the central western border of NM, west of Albuquerque; organized Jun 19, 1981 from Valencia County.

Name origin: For the Cibola National Forest, part of which is within the county. Origin and meaning of name unknown: possibly a transliteration of Zuni Indian *shiwina*, the name for their tribal range; or possibly from Isleta Indian *sibulada* 'buffalo.'

Acomita Lake   CDP
Lat: 35-04-12 N   **Long:** 107-36-46 W
Pop: 273 (1990)   **Pop Density:** 80.3
Land: 3.4 sq. mi.; **Water:** 0.1 sq. mi.

Grants   City
ZIP: 87020   **Lat:** 35-09-12 N   **Long:** 107-50-17 W
Pop: 8,626 (1990); 11,439 (1980)   **Pop Density:** 629.6
Land: 13.7 sq. mi.; **Water:** 0.0 sq. mi.
Incorporated 1933.
Name origin: For the Grant brothers, local railroad contractors.

Laguna   CDP
ZIP: 87026   **Lat:** 35-02-19 N   **Long:** 107-23-33 W
Pop: 434 (1990)   **Pop Density:** 188.7
Land: 2.3 sq. mi.; **Water:** 0.0 sq. mi.

Mesita   CDP
ZIP: 87026   **Lat:** 35-00-47 N   **Long:** 107-19-50 W
Pop: 627 (1990)   **Pop Density:** 64.6
Land: 9.7 sq. mi.; **Water:** 0.0 sq. mi.

Milan   Village
ZIP: 87021   **Lat:** 35-11-20 N   **Long:** 107-53-31 W
Pop: 1,911 (1990); 3,747 (1980)   **Pop Density:** 707.8
Land: 2.7 sq. mi.; **Water:** 0.0 sq. mi.
Incorporated 1957.
Name origin: For the original landowner.

North Acomita Village   CDP
Lat: 35-03-47 N   **Long:** 107-33-55 W
Pop: 314 (1990)   **Pop Density:** 116.3
Land: 2.7 sq. mi.; **Water:** 0.0 sq. mi.

Paguate   CDP
ZIP: 87040   **Lat:** 35-08-04 N   **Long:** 107-21-49 W
Pop: 492 (1990)   **Pop Density:** 66.5
Land: 7.4 sq. mi.; **Water:** 0.0 sq. mi.

Paraje   CDP
ZIP: 87007   **Lat:** 35-02-45 N   **Long:** 107-28-02 W
Pop: 622 (1990)   **Pop Density:** 132.3
Land: 4.7 sq. mi.; **Water:** 0.0 sq. mi.

Seama   CDP
ZIP: 87014   **Lat:** 35-02-50 N   **Long:** 107-31-38 W
Pop: 403 (1990)   **Pop Density:** 74.6
Land: 5.4 sq. mi.; **Water:** 0.0 sq. mi.

Skyline-Ganipa   CDP
Lat: 35-02-04 N   **Long:** 107-36-54 W
Pop: 946 (1990)   **Pop Density:** 155.1
Land: 6.1 sq. mi.; **Water:** 0.0 sq. mi.

Colfax County
County Seat: Raton (ZIP: 87740)

Pop: 12,925 (1990); 13,667 (1980)   **Pop Density:** 3.4
Land: 3756.9 sq. mi.; **Water:** 11.4 sq. mi.   **Area Code:** 505

On the northern border of NM, northeast of Santa Fe; organized Jan 25, 1869 from Mora County (prior to statehood).

Name origin: For Schuyler Colfax (1823-85), U.S. vice president under Ulysses S. Grant (1869-73).

Angel Fire   Village
Lat: 36-23-26 N   **Long:** 105-16-43 W
Pop: 93 (1990)   **Pop Density:** 310.0
Land: 0.3 sq. mi.; **Water:** 0.0 sq. mi.

Cimarron   Village
ZIP: 87714   **Lat:** 36-30-35 N   **Long:** 104-54-45 W
Pop: 774 (1990); 888 (1980)   **Pop Density:** 407.4
Land: 1.9 sq. mi.; **Water:** 0.0 sq. mi.   **Elev:** 6428 ft.
Incorporated 1910.
Name origin: From Spanish meaning 'wild' or 'unruly.'

NEW MEXICO, Colfax County

Eagle Nest
Village
ZIP: 87718 Lat: 36-33-10 N Long: 105-15-38 W
Pop: 189 (1990); 202 (1980) Pop Density: 315.0
Land: 0.6 sq. mi.; Water: 0.0 sq. mi. Elev: 8203 ft.
Incorporated 1976.
Name origin: For the golden eagles nesting in nearby mountains.

Maxwell
Village
ZIP: 87728 Lat: 36-32-25 N Long: 104-32-31 W
Pop: 247 (1990); 316 (1980) Pop Density: 494.0
Land: 0.5 sq. mi.; Water: 0.0 sq. mi. Elev: 5931 ft.
Incorporated 1912.
Name origin: For pioneer Lucien Maxwell, who received a land grant here.

Raton
City
ZIP: 87740 Lat: 36-53-08 N Long: 104-26-29 W
Pop: 7,372 (1990); 8,225 (1980) Pop Density: 1038.3
Land: 7.1 sq. mi.; Water: 0.0 sq. mi.
Incorporated 1891.
Name origin: From Spanish meaning 'mouse' but in NM also applied to rock squirrel and kangaroo rats.

Springer
Town
ZIP: 87747 Lat: 36-21-58 N Long: 104-35-35 W
Pop: 1,262 (1990); 1,657 (1980) Pop Density: 841.3
Land: 1.5 sq. mi.; Water: 0.0 sq. mi. Elev: 5832 ft.
Settled 1879; incorporated 1910.
Name origin: For the Springer brothers.

Curry County
County Seat: Clovis (ZIP: 88101)

Pop: 42,207 (1990); 42,019 (1980) Pop Density: 30.0
Land: 1406.1 sq. mi.; Water: 1.7 sq. mi. Area Code: 505

On the central eastern border of NM, southeast of Albuquerque; organized Feb 25, 1909 from Quay and Roosevelt counties (prior to statehood).

Name origin: For Capt. George Curry (1863–1947), an officer in the Spanish-American War, NM territorial governor (1907–11), and U.S. representative (1912–13).

Cannon Air Force Base
Military Facility
Lat: 34-22-49 N Long: 103-18-50 W
Pop: 3,312 (1990); 3,798 (1980) Pop Density: 624.9
Land: 5.3 sq. mi.; Water: 0.0 sq. mi.

Clovis
City
ZIP: 88101 Lat: 34-24-36 N Long: 103-12-09 W
Pop: 30,954 (1990); 31,194 (1980) Pop Density: 2243.0
Land: 13.8 sq. mi.; Water: 0.1 sq. mi.
Settled 1906; incorporated 1909.
Name origin: For an early Frankish king.

Grady
Village
ZIP: 88112 Lat: 34-49-19 N Long: 103-18-55 W
Pop: 110 (1990); 122 (1980) Pop Density: 366.7
Land: 0.3 sq. mi.; Water: 0.0 sq. mi.
Incorporated 1936.
Name origin: For Pearl Grady, an early postmaster.

Melrose
Village
ZIP: 88124 Lat: 34-25-45 N Long: 103-37-43 W
Pop: 662 (1990); 649 (1980) Pop Density: 389.4
Land: 1.7 sq. mi.; Water: 0.0 sq. mi.
Incorporated 1916.
Name origin: For Melrose, OH, so named by railway officials in 1906.

Texico
City
ZIP: 88135 Lat: 34-23-21 N Long: 103-03-06 W
Pop: 966 (1990); 958 (1980) Pop Density: 1207.5
Land: 0.8 sq. mi.; Water: 0.0 sq. mi.
Incorporated 1908.
Name origin: From a combination of Texas and New Mexico, for its location on that border.

DeBaca County
County Seat: Fort Sumner (ZIP: 88119)

Pop: 2,252 (1990); 2,454 (1980)　　**Pop Density:** 1.0
Land: 2325.1 sq. mi.; **Water:** 9.0 sq. mi.　　**Area Code:** 505

In east-central NM, west of Clovis; organized Feb 28, 1917 from Chaves, Guadalupe, and Roosevelt counties.

Name origin: For Ezequiel Cabeza de Baca (1864–1917), lt. governor (1911–16) and governor (1917) who died after six weeks in office.

Fort Sumner　　　　　　　　　　Village
ZIP: 88119　　**Lat:** 34-28-41 N　**Long:** 104-14-13 W
Pop: 1,269 (1990); 1,421 (1980)　　**Pop Density:** 384.5
Land: 3.3 sq. mi.; **Water:** 0.0 sq. mi.　　**Elev:** 4049 ft.
Incorporated 1916.
Name origin: For Gen. Edmond Sumner, a Civil War commander.

Doña Ana County
County Seat: Las Cruces (ZIP: 88005)

Pop: 135,510 (1990); 96,340 (1980)　　**Pop Density:** 35.6
Land: 3807.4 sq. mi.; **Water:** 7.4 sq. mi.　　**Area Code:** 505

On the central southern border of NM, south of Albuquerque; original county; organized Jan 9, 1852 (prior to statehood); annexed Arizona County 1861.

Name origin: For either Doña Ana Robledo, a woman famous for charity in the 1600s, or for Doña Ana Maria Niña de Cordova, a girl captured during an Apache raid and never seen again.

Anthony　　　　　　　　　　CDP
ZIP: 88021　　**Lat:** 32-00-19 N　**Long:** 106-35-44 W
Pop: 5,160 (1990)　　**Pop Density:** 5160.0
Land: 1.0 sq. mi.; **Water:** 0.0 sq. mi.

Chaparral　　　　　　　　　　CDP
　　Lat: 32-01-33 N　**Long:** 106-23-58 W
Pop: 2,962 (1990)　　**Pop Density:** 548.5
Land: 5.4 sq. mi.; **Water:** 0.0 sq. mi.

Doña Ana　　　　　　　　　　CDP
ZIP: 88032　　**Lat:** 32-23-28 N　**Long:** 106-48-55 W
Pop: 1,202 (1990)　　**Pop Density:** 4006.7
Land: 0.3 sq. mi.; **Water:** 0.0 sq. mi.

Hatch　　　　　　　　　　Village
ZIP: 87937　　**Lat:** 32-40-03 N　**Long:** 107-09-20 W
Pop: 1,136 (1990); 1,028 (1980)　　**Pop Density:** 1420.0
Land: 0.8 sq. mi.; **Water:** 0.0 sq. mi.　　**Elev:** 4057 ft.
Incorporated 1927.
Name origin: For Gen. Edward Hatch, who commanded the local military district in the 1880s.

Las Cruces　　　　　　　　　　City
ZIP: 88001　　**Lat:** 32-20-09 N　**Long:** 106-45-20 W
Pop: 62,126 (1990); 45,086 (1980)　　**Pop Density:** 1656.7
Land: 37.5 sq. mi.; **Water:** 0.1 sq. mi.
In south-central NM, northwest of El Paso, TX. Incorporated 1907.
Name origin: Spanish 'the crosses'; there is an old burial ground with crosses there.

Mesilla　　　　　　　　　　Town
ZIP: 88046　　**Lat:** 32-16-12 N　**Long:** 106-48-24 W
Pop: 1,975 (1990); 2,029 (1980)　　**Pop Density:** 365.7
Land: 5.4 sq. mi.; **Water:** 0.0 sq. mi.
Incorporated 1959.
Name origin: From Spanish meaning 'little table,' for its location on a small tableland that rises above the Rio Grande.

Sunland Park　　　　　　　　　　City
ZIP: 88063　　**Lat:** 31-47-56 N　**Long:** 106-34-37 W
Pop: 8,179 (1990)　　**Pop Density:** 870.1
Land: 9.4 sq. mi.; **Water:** 0.2 sq. mi.
Incorporated 1983.

University Park　　　　　　　　　　CDP
　　Lat: 32-16-41 N　**Long:** 106-44-50 W
Pop: 4,520 (1990); 4,353 (1980)　　**Pop Density:** 2825.0
Land: 1.6 sq. mi.; **Water:** 0.0 sq. mi.

White Sands　　　　　　　Military Facility
　　Lat: 32-22-57 N　**Long:** 106-29-32 W
Pop: 2,616 (1990); 3,120 (1980)　　**Pop Density:** 1046.4
Land: 2.5 sq. mi.; **Water:** 0.0 sq. mi.

NEW MEXICO, Eddy County   American Places Dictionary

Eddy County
County Seat: Carlsbad (ZIP: 88221)

Pop: 48,605 (1990); 47,855 (1980) **Pop Density:** 11.6
Land: 4182.2 sq. mi.; **Water:** 15.6 sq. mi. **Area Code:** 505
On the southern border of NM, east of Las Cruces; organized Feb 25, 1889 from Lincoln County (prior to statehood).
Name origin: For Charles B. Eddy, rancher, promoter of the Carlsbad Irrigation Project, and railroad builder.

Artesia City
ZIP: 88210 **Lat:** 32-50-50 N **Long:** 104-25-46 W
Pop: 10,610 (1990); 10,385 (1980) **Pop Density:** 1293.9
Land: 8.2 sq. mi.; **Water:** 0.0 sq. mi. **Elev:** 3379 ft.
In southeastern NM, 38 mi. south of Roswell. Founded 1903; incorporated 1905.
Name origin: For the artesian water wells nearby.

Carlsbad City
ZIP: 88220 **Lat:** 32-24-14 N **Long:** 104-14-11 W
Pop: 24,952 (1990); 25,496 (1980) **Pop Density:** 917.4
Land: 27.2 sq. mi.; **Water:** 0.0 sq. mi. **Elev:** 3111 ft.
In southeastern NM on the Pecos River, 70 mi. south of Roswell. Established 1888; incorporated 1918.
Name origin: For the famous Carlsbad Springs in Bohemia, after a local mineral spring was discovered.

Carlsbad North CDP
Lat: 32-26-46 N **Long:** 104-13-21 W
Pop: 1,167 (1990); 1,271 (1980) **Pop Density:** 729.4
Land: 1.6 sq. mi.; **Water:** 0.0 sq. mi.

Hope Village
ZIP: 88250 **Lat:** 32-49-02 N **Long:** 104-44-12 W
Pop: 101 (1990); 111 (1980) **Pop Density:** 84.2
Land: 1.2 sq. mi.; **Water:** 0.0 sq. mi. **Elev:** 4086 ft.
Settled 1884; incorporated 1910.
Name origin: For a bet between two homesteaders, one of whom hoped the other would lose the toss to name the town.

Loving Village
ZIP: 88256 **Lat:** 32-17-11 N **Long:** 104-05-45 W
Pop: 1,243 (1990); 1,355 (1980) **Pop Density:** 1130.0
Land: 1.1 sq. mi.; **Water:** 0.0 sq. mi.
Incorporated 1945.
Name origin: For early rancher John Loving.

Grant County
County Seat: Silver City (ZIP: 88062)

Pop: 27,676 (1990); 26,204 (1980) **Pop Density:** 7.0
Land: 3966.2 sq. mi.; **Water:** 1.6 sq. mi. **Area Code:** 505
On the western border of NM, northwest of Las Cruces; organized Jan 30, 1868 from Socorro County (prior to statehood).
Name origin: For Ulysses Simpson Grant (1822–85), Civil War general and eighteenth U.S. president.

Bayard Village
ZIP: 88023 **Lat:** 32-45-34 N **Long:** 108-08-00 W
Pop: 2,598 (1990); 3,036 (1980) **Pop Density:** 3247.5
Land: 0.8 sq. mi.; **Water:** 0.0 sq. mi.
Incorporated 1938.
Name origin: For Fort Bayard, an early military post.

Central Village
ZIP: 88026 **Lat:** 32-46-31 N **Long:** 108-09-15 W
Pop: 1,835 (1990); 1,968 (1980) **Pop Density:** 1835.0
Land: 1.0 sq. mi.; **Water:** 0.0 sq. mi.
Incorporated 1947.
Name origin: For its central location in the county, so named 1887.

Hurley Town
ZIP: 88043 **Lat:** 32-41-51 N **Long:** 108-07-52 W
Pop: 1,534 (1990); 1,616 (1980) **Pop Density:** 1534.0
Land: 1.0 sq. mi.; **Water:** 0.0 sq. mi.
Incorporated 1956.
Name origin: For J. E. Hurley, the Chino mine's manager.

Silver City Town
ZIP: 88061 **Lat:** 32-46-58 N **Long:** 108-16-00 W
Pop: 10,683 (1990); 9,887 (1980) **Pop Density:** 1214.0
Land: 8.8 sq. mi.; **Water:** 0.0 sq. mi. **Elev:** 5938 ft.
In southwestern NM, 45 mi. northwest of Deming. Settled 1878; incorporated 1870.
Name origin: For the local silver deposits.

Guadalupe County
County Seat: Santa Rosa (ZIP: 88435)

Pop: 4,156 (1990); 4,496 (1980) **Pop Density:** 1.4
Land: 3030.6 sq. mi.; **Water:** 1.2 sq. mi. **Area Code:** 505

In east-central NM, east of Albuquerque; organized Feb 26, 1891 from Lincoln and San Miguel counties (prior to statehood).
Name origin: For Our Lady of Guadalupe, patron saint of Mexico.

Santa Rosa — City
ZIP: 88435 **Lat:** 34-56-36 N **Long:** 104-40-36 W
Pop: 2,263 (1990); 2,469 (1980) **Pop Density:** 808.2
Land: 2.8 sq. mi.; **Water:** 0.0 sq. mi. **Elev:** 4599 ft.
Settled 1865; incorporated 1914.
Name origin: For Saint Rose of Lima (1586–1617).

Vaughn — Town
ZIP: 88353 **Lat:** 34-36-23 N **Long:** 105-12-44 W
Pop: 633 (1990); 737 (1980) **Pop Density:** 113.0
Land: 5.6 sq. mi.; **Water:** 0.0 sq. mi.
Founded c. 1900; incorporated 1919.
Name origin: For Maj. G. W. Vaughn, a civil engineer for the AT & SF Railroad.

Harding County
County Seat: Mosquero (ZIP: 87733)

Pop: 987 (1990); 1,090 (1980) **Pop Density:** 0.5
Land: 2125.5 sq. mi.; **Water:** 0.6 sq. mi. **Area Code:** 505

In northeastern NM, northeast of Santa Fe; organized Mar 4, 1921 from Mora and Union counties.
Name origin: For Warren Gamaliel Harding (1865–1923), twenty-ninth U.S. president.

Mosquero — Village
ZIP: 87733 **Lat:** 35-46-35 N **Long:** 103-57-09 W
Pop: 164 (1990); 197 (1980) **Pop Density:** 234.3
Land: 0.7 sq. mi.; **Water:** 0.0 sq. mi. **Elev:** 5688 ft.
Incorporated 1922. Part of the town is also in San Miguel County.
Name origin: From Spanish meaning 'swarm of flies, fleas, or mosquitoes.' Literally 'flytrap' but not so used in NM.

Roy — Village
ZIP: 87743 **Lat:** 35-56-43 N **Long:** 104-11-46 W
Pop: 362 (1990); 381 (1980) **Pop Density:** 181.0
Land: 2.0 sq. mi.; **Water:** 0.0 sq. mi. **Elev:** 5888 ft.
Incorporated 1916.
Name origin: For the Roy brothers, who settled here in 1901.

Hidalgo County
County Seat: Lordsburg (ZIP: 88045)

Pop: 5,958 (1990); 6,049 (1980) **Pop Density:** 1.7
Land: 3445.9 sq. mi.; **Water:** 0.3 sq. mi. **Area Code:** 505

In the southwestern corner of NM, southwest of Las Cruces; organized Feb 25, 1919 from Grant County.
Name origin: Probably for the Treaty of Guadalupe Hidalgo, which ended the Mexican War; others claim for Miguel Hidalgo y Costilla (1753–1811), leader of the Mexican war for independence from Spain.

Lordsburg — City
ZIP: 88045 **Lat:** 32-20-35 N **Long:** 108-42-07 W
Pop: 2,951 (1990); 3,195 (1980) **Pop Density:** 355.5
Land: 8.3 sq. mi.; **Water:** 0.0 sq. mi. **Elev:** 4258 ft.
Settled 1880; incorporated 1916.
Name origin: For a local railroad construction engineer.

Virden — Village
Lat: 32-41-18 N **Long:** 109-00-07 W
Pop: 108 (1990); 246 (1980) **Pop Density:** 540.0
Land: 0.2 sq. mi.; **Water:** 0.0 sq. mi.
Incorporated 1932.
Name origin: For the original landowner.

NEW MEXICO, Lea County   American Places Dictionary

> ## Lea County
> **County Seat: Lovington (ZIP: 88260)**
>
> **Pop:** 55,765 (1990); 55,993 (1980) **Pop Density:** 12.7
> **Land:** 4393.3 sq. mi.; **Water:** 1.1 sq. mi. **Area Code:** 505
> In the southeastern corner of NM, east of Roswell; organized Mar 7, 1917 from Chaves and Eddy counties.
> **Name origin:** For Gen. Joseph C. Lea (?–1904), Confederate officer in the Civil War, "father of [the town of] Roswell," and founder of the New Mexico Military Institute there.

Eunice   City
ZIP: 88231   Lat: 32-26-33 N Long: 103-11-35 W
Pop: 2,676 (1990); 2,970 (1980)   Pop Density: 922.8
Land: 2.9 sq. mi.; Water: 0.0 sq. mi.
Incorporated 1936.
Name origin: For Eunice Carlson, daughter of the original homesteader.

Hobbs   City
ZIP: 88240   Lat: 32-44-03 N Long: 103-09-45 W
Pop: 29,115 (1990); 29,153 (1980)   Pop Density: 1540.5
Land: 18.9 sq. mi.; Water: 0.0 sq. mi.
Incorporated 1937.
Name origin: For the first homesteaders, the Hobbs family.

Jal   City
ZIP: 88252   Lat: 32-06-48 N Long: 103-11-21 W
Pop: 2,156 (1990); 2,675 (1980)   Pop Density: 449.2
Land: 4.8 sq. mi.; Water: 0.0 sq. mi.
Incorporated 1950.
Name origin: For nearby JAL Ranch, founded by pioneer rancher John A. Lynch.

Lovington   City
ZIP: 88260   Lat: 32-56-43 N Long: 103-21-01 W
Pop: 9,322 (1990); 9,727 (1980)   Pop Density: 1942.1
Land: 4.8 sq. mi.; Water: 0.0 sq. mi.
Founded c. 1900; incorporated 1917.
Name origin: For settler R. F. Love.

Tatum   Town
ZIP: 88267   Lat: 33-15-19 N Long: 103-18-55 W
Pop: 768 (1990); 896 (1980)   Pop Density: 640.0
Land: 1.2 sq. mi.; Water: 0.0 sq. mi.
Incorporated 1948.
Name origin: For James Tatum, who founded the first store here in 1909.

> ## Lincoln County
> **County Seat: Carrizozo (ZIP: 88301)**
>
> **Pop:** 12,219 (1990); 10,997 (1980) **Pop Density:** 2.5
> **Land:** 4831.4 sq. mi.; **Water:** 0.2 sq. mi. **Area Code:** 505
> In south-central NM, west of Roswell; organized Jan 16, 1869 (prior to statehood).
> **Name origin:** For Abraham Lincoln (1809–65), sixteenth U.S. president.

Capitan   Village
ZIP: 88316   Lat: 33-32-25 N Long: 105-35-38 W
Pop: 842 (1990); 762 (1980)   Pop Density: 263.1
Land: 3.2 sq. mi.; Water: 0.0 sq. mi.   Elev: 6351 ft.
Incorporated 1937.
Name origin: For the nearby Capitan Mountains.

Carrizozo   Town
ZIP: 88301   Lat: 33-38-37 N Long: 105-52-59 W
Pop: 1,075 (1990); 1,222 (1980)   Pop Density: 398.1
Land: 2.7 sq. mi.; Water: 0.0 sq. mi.
Founded 1900; incorporated 1917.
Name origin: For the Carrizo Springs; the extra *zo* indicates abundance.

Corona   Village
ZIP: 88318   Lat: 34-14-58 N Long: 105-35-48 W
Pop: 215 (1990); 236 (1980)   Pop Density: 215.0
Land: 1.0 sq. mi.; Water: 0.0 sq. mi.
Settled 1902; incorporated 1947.
Name origin: For a local, crown-shaped hill.

Ruidoso   Village
ZIP: 88345   Lat: 33-21-57 N Long: 105-38-32 W
Pop: 4,600 (1990); 4,260 (1980)   Pop Density: 323.9
Land: 14.2 sq. mi.; Water: 0.0 sq. mi.
Incorporated 1945.
Name origin: For the Ruidoso River that runs through the town. From Spanish meaning 'noisy.'

Ruidoso Downs Village
ZIP: 88346 **Lat:** 33-19-53 N **Long:** 105-36-13 W
Pop: 920 (1990); 949 (1980) **Pop Density:** 438.1
Land: 2.1 sq. mi.; **Water:** 0.0 sq. mi.
Incorporated 1947.

Los Alamos County
County Seat: Los Alamos (ZIP: 87544)

Pop: 18,115 (1990); 17,599 (1980) **Pop Density:** 165.7
Land: 109.4 sq. mi.; **Water:** 0.0 sq. mi. **Area Code:** 505
In north-central NM, northwest of Santa Fe; organized Mar 16, 1949 from Sandoval and Santa Fe counties. Site of the Manhattan Project that produced the first atomic bomb.
Name origin: For its county seat, itself named for the Los Alamos School for Boys, established 1925 by Ashley Pond; from Spanish 'poplars' or 'cottonwoods.'

Los Alamos CDP
ZIP: 87544 **Lat:** 35-53-37 N **Long:** 106-17-01 W
Pop: 11,455 (1990); 11,039 (1980) **Pop Density:** 1050.9
Land: 10.9 sq. mi.; **Water:** 0.0 sq. mi.

White Rock CDP
ZIP: 87544 **Lat:** 35-48-13 N **Long:** 106-12-37 W
Pop: 6,192 (1990); 6,560 (1980) **Pop Density:** 860.0
Land: 7.2 sq. mi.; **Water:** 0.0 sq. mi.

Luna County
County Seat: Deming (ZIP: 88031)

Pop: 18,110 (1990); 15,585 (1980) **Pop Density:** 6.1
Land: 2965.3 sq. mi.; **Water:** 0.2 sq. mi. **Area Code:** 505
On the southern border of NM, west of Las Cruces; organized Mar 16, 1901 from Doña Ana and Grant counties (prior to statehood).
Name origin: For Don Salomon Luna, a sheep rancher and a leader of the Republican party in the state.

Columbus Village
ZIP: 88029 **Lat:** 31-49-43 N **Long:** 107-38-26 W
Pop: 641 (1990); 414 (1980) **Pop Density:** 305.2
Land: 2.1 sq. mi.; **Water:** 0.0 sq. mi. **Elev:** 4064 ft.
Founded 1891; incorporated 1913.
Name origin: For Christopher Columbus (1451–1506).

Deming City
ZIP: 88030 **Lat:** 32-15-42 N **Long:** 107-45-01 W
Pop: 10,970 (1990); 9,964 (1980) **Pop Density:** 1891.4
Land: 5.8 sq. mi.; **Water:** 0.0 sq. mi.
In southwestern NM, west of Las Cruces. Incorporated 1902.
Name origin: For an early pioneer, Mary Ann Deming.

McKinley County
County Seat: Gallup (ZIP: 87305)

Pop: 60,686 (1990); 56,536 (1980) **Pop Density:** 11.1
Land: 5449.1 sq. mi.; **Water:** 6.5 sq. mi. **Area Code:** 505
On the northwestern border of NM, west of Santa Fe; organized Feb 23, 1899 from Bernalillo, Valencia, and San Juan counties.
Name origin: For William McKinley (1843–1901), twenty-fifth U.S. president.

Black Rock CDP
ZIP: 87327 **Lat:** 35-05-09 N **Long:** 108-47-24 W
Pop: 858 (1990) **Pop Density:** 1072.5
Land: 0.8 sq. mi.; **Water:** 0.0 sq. mi.

Crownpoint CDP
ZIP: 87313 **Lat:** 35-41-17 N **Long:** 108-08-45 W
Pop: 2,108 (1990); 1,134 (1980) **Pop Density:** 314.6
Land: 6.7 sq. mi.; **Water:** 0.0 sq. mi.

NEW MEXICO, McKinley County   American Places Dictionary

Gallup   City
ZIP: 87301   **Lat:** 35-31-13 N **Long:** 108-44-07 W
Pop: 19,154 (1990); 18,167 (1980)   **Pop Density:** 1741.3
Land: 11.0 sq. mi.; **Water:** 0.0 sq. mi.
Established 1881; incorporated 1891.
Name origin: For AT & SF Railroad official David Gallup.

Mexican Springs   CDP
                        Lat: 35-47-15 N **Long:** 108-48-26 W
Pop: 242 (1990)   **Pop Density:** 49.4
Land: 4.9 sq. mi.; **Water:** 0.0 sq. mi.

Navajo   CDP
                        Lat: 35-53-46 N **Long:** 109-01-53 W
Pop: 1,985 (1990)   **Pop Density:** 863.0
Land: 2.3 sq. mi.; **Water:** 0.0 sq. mi.

Tohatchi   CDP
ZIP: 87325   **Lat:** 35-51-00 N **Long:** 108-45-00 W
Pop: 661 (1990); 1,011 (1980)   **Pop Density:** 194.4
Land: 3.4 sq. mi.; **Water:** 0.1 sq. mi.

Zuni Pueblo   CDP
ZIP: 87327   **Lat:** 35-04-20 N **Long:** 108-50-59 W
Pop: 5,857 (1990); 5,551 (1980)   **Pop Density:** 802.3
Land: 7.3 sq. mi.; **Water:** 0.0 sq. mi.

Mora County
County Seat: Mora (ZIP: 87732)

Pop: 4,264 (1990); 4,205 (1980)   **Pop Density:** 2.2
Land: 1931.2 sq. mi.; **Water:** 2.4 sq. mi.   **Area Code:** 505
In east-central NM, northeast of Santa Fe; organized Feb 1, 1860 from San Miguel County (prior to statehood).
Name origin: Either from personal and family names of early settlers, such as Mora Pineda and García de la Mora, or possibly from the Spanish word meaning 'blackberry' or 'mulberry,' referring to the abundance of fruit locally.

Mora   Pop. Place
ZIP: 87732
Pop: 1,200 (1990)   **Elev:** 7179 ft.

Wagon Mound   Village
ZIP: 87752   **Lat:** 36-00-10 N **Long:** 104-42-51 W
Pop: 319 (1990); 416 (1980)   **Pop Density:** 177.2
Land: 1.8 sq. mi.; **Water:** 0.0 sq. mi.   **Elev:** 6195 ft.
Incorporated 1918.
Name origin: For a local rocky formation that resembles a covered wagon.

Otero County
County Seat: Alamogordo (ZIP: 88310)

Pop: 51,928 (1990); 44,665 (1980)   **Pop Density:** 7.8
Land: 6626.9 sq. mi.; **Water:** 0.9 sq. mi.   **Area Code:** 505
On the central southern border of NM, east of Las Cruces; organized Jan 30, 1899 from Doña Ana and Lincoln counties.
Name origin: For Miguel Antonio Otero (1859–1944), territorial governor of New Mexico (1896–1906).

Alamogordo   City
ZIP: 88310   **Lat:** 32-53-04 N **Long:** 105-57-27 W
Pop: 27,596 (1990); 24,024 (1980)   **Pop Density:** 1613.8
Land: 17.1 sq. mi.; **Water:** 0.0 sq. mi.   **Elev:** 4334 ft.
In southern NM, 60 mi. northeast of Las Cruces, west of the Sacramento Mountains. Settled 1898; incorporated 1912.
Name origin: From Spanish 'large cottonwood [tree].'

Boles Acres   CDP
                        Lat: 32-48-31 N **Long:** 105-59-12 W
Pop: 1,409 (1990)   **Pop Density:** 128.1
Land: 11.0 sq. mi.; **Water:** 0.0 sq. mi.

Cloudcroft   Village
ZIP: 88317   **Lat:** 32-57-10 N **Long:** 105-44-21 W
Pop: 636 (1990); 521 (1980)   **Pop Density:** 578.2
Land: 1.1 sq. mi.; **Water:** 0.0 sq. mi.   **Elev:** 8663 ft.
Incorporated 1948.
Name origin: For its position "in the clouds."

Holloman Air Force Base   Military Facility
ZIP: 88330   **Lat:** 32-51-04 N **Long:** 106-06-22 W
Pop: 5,891 (1990); 7,245 (1980)   **Pop Density:** 471.3
Land: 12.5 sq. mi.; **Water:** 0.1 sq. mi.

La Luz
CDP
ZIP: 88337 **Lat:** 32-58-13 N **Long:** 105-56-14 W
Pop: 1,625 (1990); 1,194 (1980) **Pop Density:** 151.9
Land: 10.7 sq. mi.; **Water:** 0.0 sq. mi.

Mescalero
CDP
ZIP: 88340 **Lat:** 33-09-02 N **Long:** 105-47-45 W
Pop: 1,159 (1990); 1,259 (1980) **Pop Density:** 75.8
Land: 15.3 sq. mi.; **Water:** 0.0 sq. mi.

Tularosa
Village
ZIP: 88352 **Lat:** 33-04-33 N **Long:** 106-01-11 W
Pop: 2,615 (1990); 2,536 (1980) **Pop Density:** 1307.5
Land: 2.0 sq. mi.; **Water:** 0.0 sq. mi.
Incorporated 1916.
Name origin: From Spanish meaning 'reddish reeds or willows.'

Quay County
County Seat: Tucumcari (ZIP: 88401)

Pop: 10,823 (1990); 10,577 (1980) **Pop Density:** 3.8
Land: 2875.1 sq. mi.; **Water:** 6.9 sq. mi. **Area Code:** 505
On the central eastern border of NM; organized Jan 28, 1903 (prior to statehood).
Name origin: For Lt. Col. Matthew S. Quay (1833–1904), U.S. senator from PA (1887–99; 1901–04) who was active in establishing the area.

House
Village
ZIP: 88121 **Lat:** 34-38-52 N **Long:** 103-54-11 W
Pop: 85 (1990); 117 (1980) **Pop Density:** 94.4
Land: 0.9 sq. mi.; **Water:** 0.0 sq. mi.
Incorporated 1959.
Name origin: For Lucie House, who settled here in 1902.

Logan
Village
ZIP: 88426 **Lat:** 35-21-39 N **Long:** 103-26-36 W
Pop: 870 (1990); 735 (1980) **Pop Density:** 108.8
Land: 8.0 sq. mi.; **Water:** 0.5 sq. mi. **Elev:** 3819 ft.
Incorporated 1959.
Name origin: For a Texas Ranger commander.

San Jon
Village
ZIP: 88411 **Lat:** 35-06-46 N **Long:** 103-19-38 W
Pop: 277 (1990); 341 (1980) **Pop Density:** 230.8
Land: 1.2 sq. mi.; **Water:** 0.0 sq. mi. **Elev:** 4022 ft.
Incorporated 1946.
Name origin: Probably from a corruption of Spanish *zanjon* 'deep gully.'

Tucumcari
City
ZIP: 88401 **Lat:** 35-10-02 N **Long:** 103-43-38 W
Pop: 6,831 (1990); 6,765 (1980) **Pop Density:** 923.1
Land: 7.4 sq. mi.; **Water:** 0.0 sq. mi. **Elev:** 4086 ft.
Incorporated 1908.
Name origin: For the nearby Tucumcari Mountains.

Rio Arriba County
County Seat: Tierra Amarilla (ZIP: 87575)

Pop: 34,365 (1990); 29,282 (1980) **Pop Density:** 5.9
Land: 5858.1 sq. mi.; **Water:** 38.5 sq. mi. **Area Code:** 505
On the central northern border of NM, northwest of Santa Fe; original county; organized Jan 9, 1852 (prior to statehood).
Name origin: Spanish 'upper river,' the Spanish designation for the upper Rio Grande in NM.

Alcalde
CDP
ZIP: 87511 **Lat:** 36-05-05 N **Long:** 106-03-30 W
Pop: 308 (1990) **Pop Density:** 616.0
Land: 0.5 sq. mi.; **Water:** 0.0 sq. mi.

Chama
Village
ZIP: 87520 **Lat:** 36-53-36 N **Long:** 106-34-57 W
Pop: 1,048 (1990); 1,090 (1980) **Pop Density:** 403.1
Land: 2.6 sq. mi.; **Water:** 0.0 sq. mi.
Incorporated 1961.
Name origin: For the Chama River, which traverses the southeastern part of the county.

Chimayo
CDP
ZIP: 87522 **Lat:** 36-00-30 N **Long:** 105-56-40 W
Pop: 2,150 (1990); 1,424 (1980) **Pop Density:** 796.3
Land: 2.7 sq. mi.; **Water:** 0.0 sq. mi.
Part of the town is also in Santa Fe County.

Dulce
CDP
ZIP: 87528 **Lat:** 36-56-00 N **Long:** 106-59-45 W
Pop: 2,438 (1990); 1,648 (1980) **Pop Density:** 217.7
Land: 11.2 sq. mi.; **Water:** 0.0 sq. mi.

Espanola
City
ZIP: 87532 **Lat:** 36-00-25 N **Long:** 106-04-39 W
Pop: 6,210 (1990); 5,665 (1980) **Pop Density:** 985.7
Land: 6.3 sq. mi.; **Water:** 0.1 sq. mi. **Elev:** 5589 ft.
Incorporated 1925. Part of the town is also in Santa Fe County.
Name origin: Meaning of the name is not clear. It is a variation of *Hispaniola* 'New Spain' and also means 'Spanish lady.'

San Juan
CDP
Lat: 36-03-06 N **Long:** 106-04-06 W
Pop: 465 (1990) **Pop Density:** 930.0
Land: 0.5 sq. mi.; **Water:** 0.0 sq. mi.

Santa Clara Pueblo
CDP
Lat: 35-58-18 N **Long:** 106-05-33 W
Pop: 1,156 (1990) **Pop Density:** 550.5
Land: 2.1 sq. mi.; **Water:** 0.0 sq. mi.

Tierra Amarilla
Pop. Place
ZIP: 87575
Pop: 900 (1990)
Elev: 7524 ft.

Roosevelt County
County Seat: Portales (ZIP: 88130)

Pop: 16,702 (1990); 15,695 (1980) **Pop Density:** 6.8
Land: 2448.7 sq. mi.; **Water:** 6.4 sq. mi. **Area Code:** 505
On the central eastern border of NM, south of Clovis; organized Feb 28, 1903 from Chaves and Guadalupe counties (prior to statehood).
Name origin: For Theodore Roosevelt (1858–1919), twenty-sixth U.S. president.

Causey
Village
ZIP: 88113 **Lat:** 33-51-54 N **Long:** 103-07-00 W
Pop: 57 (1990); 81 (1980) **Pop Density:** 18.4
Land: 3.1 sq. mi.; **Water:** 0.0 sq. mi.
Incorporated 1959.
Name origin: For a pioneer buffalo hunter.

Dora
Village
ZIP: 88115 **Lat:** 33-55-59 N **Long:** 103-20-07 W
Pop: 167 (1990); 168 (1980) **Pop Density:** 59.6
Land: 2.8 sq. mi.; **Water:** 0.0 sq. mi. **Elev:** 4288 ft.
Incorporated 1959.
Name origin: For Dora Humphrey, the first postmaster's daughter.

Elida
Town
ZIP: 88116 **Lat:** 33-56-39 N **Long:** 103-39-16 W
Pop: 201 (1990); 202 (1980) **Pop Density:** 251.3
Land: 0.8 sq. mi.; **Water:** 0.0 sq. mi.
Settled 1902; incorporated 1907.
Name origin: For Elida, OH.

Floyd
Village
ZIP: 88118 **Lat:** 34-12-52 N **Long:** 103-32-56 W
Pop: 117 (1990); 146 (1980) **Pop Density:** 37.7
Land: 3.1 sq. mi.; **Water:** 0.0 sq. mi. **Elev:** 4153 ft.
Incorporated 1959.
Name origin: For a friend of the first postmaster, Simon Lane.

Portales
City
ZIP: 88123 **Lat:** 34-10-51 N **Long:** 103-20-43 W
Pop: 10,690 (1990); 9,940 (1980) **Pop Density:** 2138.0
Land: 5.0 sq. mi.; **Water:** 0.0 sq. mi. **Elev:** 4009 ft.
In eastern NM, 18 mi. southwest of Clovis. Founded 1898; incorporated 1909.
Name origin: For the nearby caves, or 'portales.'

Sandoval County
County Seat: Bernalillo (ZIP: 87004)

Pop: 63,319 (1990); 34,400 (1980) **Pop Density:** 17.1
Land: 3709.7 sq. mi.; **Water:** 5.0 sq. mi. **Area Code:** 505
In north-central NM, west of Santa Fe; organized Mar 10, 1903 from Rio Arriba County (prior to statehood).
Name origin: For the Sandoval family, descendants of Juan de Diós Sandoval Martínez, who came to the area in 1692.

Bernalillo Town
ZIP: 87004 **Lat:** 35-18-57 N **Long:** 106-33-20 W
Pop: 5,960 (1990); 2,988 (1980) **Pop Density:** 1083.6
Land: 5.5 sq. mi.; **Water:** 0.1 sq. mi. **Elev:** 5052 ft.
Incorporated 1948.
Name origin: Spanish 'little Bernal,' possibly for Fray Juan Bernal, a Catholic missionary, martyred 1680.

Cochiti CDP
Lat: 35-36-31 N **Long:** 106-20-58 W
Pop: 434 (1990) **Pop Density:** 868.0
Land: 0.5 sq. mi.; **Water:** 0.0 sq. mi.

Corrales Village
ZIP: 87048 **Lat:** 35-14-23 N **Long:** 106-37-16 W
Pop: 4,918 (1990); 2,668 (1980) **Pop Density:** 540.4
Land: 9.1 sq. mi.; **Water:** 0.4 sq. mi.
Incorporated 1971. Part of the town is also in Bernalillo County.
Name origin: From Spanish meaning 'enclosures.'

Cuba Village
ZIP: 87013 **Lat:** 36-01-20 N **Long:** 106-57-15 W
Pop: 760 (1990); 609 (1980) **Pop Density:** 584.6
Land: 1.3 sq. mi.; **Water:** 0.0 sq. mi. **Elev:** 6908 ft.
Settled 1879; incorporated 1964.
Name origin: Spanish 'trough, tank.' Previously called Nacimiento.

Jemez Pueblo CDP
ZIP: 87024 **Lat:** 35-36-58 N **Long:** 106-43-34 W
Pop: 1,301 (1990); 1,503 (1980) **Pop Density:** 2602.0
Land: 0.5 sq. mi.; **Water:** 0.0 sq. mi.

Jemez Springs Village
ZIP: 87025 **Lat:** 35-46-25 N **Long:** 106-41-18 W
Pop: 413 (1990); 316 (1980) **Pop Density:** 86.0
Land: 4.8 sq. mi.; **Water:** 0.0 sq. mi.
Incorporated 1955.
Name origin: From a Spanish translation of the Indian term *hay mish* 'people.'

Pena Blanca CDP
Lat: 35-34-17 N **Long:** 106-20-10 W
Pop: 300 (1990) **Pop Density:** 125.0
Land: 2.4 sq. mi.; **Water:** 0.0 sq. mi.

Placitas CDP
ZIP: 87043 **Lat:** 35-19-12 N **Long:** 106-27-57 W
Pop: 1,611 (1990) **Pop Density:** 108.1
Land: 14.9 sq. mi.; **Water:** 0.0 sq. mi.

Rio Rancho City
ZIP: 87124 **Lat:** 35-16-24 N **Long:** 106-39-37 W
Pop: 32,505 (1990); 9,985 (1980) **Pop Density:** 711.3
Land: 45.7 sq. mi.; **Water:** 0.1 sq. mi.

San Felipe Pueblo CDP
ZIP: 87001 **Lat:** 35-26-03 N **Long:** 106-25-42 W
Pop: 1,557 (1990); 1,465 (1980) **Pop Density:** 130.8
Land: 11.9 sq. mi.; **Water:** 0.3 sq. mi.

Santa Ana Pueblo CDP
ZIP: 87004 **Lat:** 35-21-09 N **Long:** 106-31-06 W
Pop: 476 (1990) **Pop Density:** 68.0
Land: 7.0 sq. mi.; **Water:** 0.5 sq. mi.

Santo Domingo Pueblo CDP
ZIP: 87052 **Lat:** 35-30-57 N **Long:** 106-21-56 W
Pop: 2,866 (1990); 2,082 (1980) **Pop Density:** 1433.0
Land: 2.0 sq. mi.; **Water:** 0.0 sq. mi.

San Ysidro Village
ZIP: 87053 **Lat:** 35-33-23 N **Long:** 106-46-18 W
Pop: 233 (1990); 199 (1980) **Pop Density:** 101.3
Land: 2.3 sq. mi.; **Water:** 0.0 sq. mi.
Incorporated 1967.
Name origin: For Saint Isidore, an 11th-century Spanish saint.

Zia Pueblo CDP
ZIP: 87053 **Lat:** 35-30-50 N **Long:** 106-43-31 W
Pop: 637 (1990) **Pop Density:** 28.6
Land: 22.3 sq. mi.; **Water:** 0.0 sq. mi.

NEW MEXICO, San Juan County

San Juan County
County Seat: Aztec (ZIP: 87410)

Pop: 91,605 (1990); 81,433 (1980) **Pop Density:** 16.6
Land: 5514.4 sq. mi.; **Water:** 24.3 sq. mi. **Area Code:** 505
On the northwestern border of NM; organized Jan 24, 1887 from Rio Arriba County (prior to statehood).
Name origin: For the San Juan River, which flows through the county; Spanish for St. John (the Baptist).

Aztec City
ZIP: 87410 Lat: 36-49-42 N Long: 108-00-16 W
Pop: 5,479 (1990); 5,512 (1980) Pop Density: 1369.8
Land: 4.0 sq. mi.; Water: 0.1 sq. mi.
Founded in 1890; incorporated 1905.
Name origin: For the Aztec Indians of Mexico.

Bloomfield City
ZIP: 87413 Lat: 36-42-42 N Long: 107-58-38 W
Pop: 5,214 (1990); 4,881 (1980) Pop Density: 1158.7
Land: 4.5 sq. mi.; Water: 0.1 sq. mi.
Settled 1878; incorporated 1958.

Farmington City
ZIP: 87401 Lat: 36-45-16 N Long: 108-11-08 W
Pop: 33,997 (1990); 31,222 (1980) Pop Density: 1446.7
Land: 23.5 sq. mi.; Water: 0.4 sq. mi.
In northwestern NM on the San Juan River. Incorporated 1901.
Name origin: For the area's function as a farming town, so named by early ranchers.

Flora Vista CDP
ZIP: 87415 Lat: 36-48-07 N Long: 108-04-55 W
Pop: 1,021 (1990) Pop Density: 638.1
Land: 1.6 sq. mi.; Water: 0.0 sq. mi.

Kirtland CDP
ZIP: 87417 Lat: 36-44-22 N Long: 108-20-35 W
Pop: 3,552 (1990) Pop Density: 582.3
Land: 6.1 sq. mi.; Water: 0.2 sq. mi.

Naschitti CDP
Lat: 36-03-43 N Long: 108-40-51 W
Pop: 323 (1990) Pop Density: 146.8
Land: 2.2 sq. mi.; Water: 0.0 sq. mi.

Newcomb CDP
Lat: 36-16-59 N Long: 108-42-24 W
Pop: 388 (1990) Pop Density: 70.5
Land: 5.5 sq. mi.; Water: 0.0 sq. mi.

Ojo Amarillo CDP
Lat: 36-41-35 N Long: 108-22-06 W
Pop: 955 (1990) Pop Density: 502.6
Land: 1.9 sq. mi.; Water: 0.0 sq. mi.

Sanostee CDP
ZIP: 87420 Lat: 36-26-05 N Long: 108-52-21 W
Pop: 626 (1990) Pop Density: 115.9
Land: 5.4 sq. mi.; Water: 0.0 sq. mi.

Shiprock CDP
ZIP: 87420 Lat: 36-47-31 N Long: 108-41-45 W
Pop: 7,687 (1990) Pop Density: 483.5
Land: 15.9 sq. mi.; Water: 0.3 sq. mi.

San Miguel County
County Seat: Las Vegas (ZIP: 87701)

Pop: 25,743 (1990); 22,751 (1980) **Pop Density:** 5.5
Land: 4717.4 sq. mi.; **Water:** 18.6 sq. mi. **Area Code:** 505
In east-central NM, east of Santa Fe; original county; organized Jan 9, 1852 (prior to statehood).
Name origin: For the town of San Miguel del Bado, Spanish 'Saint Michael of the ford,' a river crossing on the Pecos River on the Old Santa Fe Trail.

Las Vegas City
ZIP: 87701 Lat: 35-35-57 N Long: 105-13-10 W
Pop: 14,753 (1990); 14,322 (1980) Pop Density: 1993.6
Land: 7.4 sq. mi.; Water: 0.0 sq. mi.
In northeast-central NM, 40 mi. southeast of Santa Fe. Incorporated 1888.
Name origin: From Spanish 'the meadows.'

Mosquero Village
ZIP: 87733 Lat: 35-46-20 N Long: 103-57-39 W
Pop: 0 (1990)
Land: 0.3 sq. mi.; Water: 0.0 sq. mi. Elev: 5688 ft.
Incorporated 1922. Part of the town is also in Harding County.
Name origin: From Spanish meaning 'swarm of flies, fleas, or mosquitoes.' Literally 'flytrap' but not so used in NM.

Pecos
Village
ZIP: 87552   **Lat:** 35-34-30 N   **Long:** 105-40-43 W
Pop: 1,012 (1990); 885 (1980)   **Pop Density:** 632.5
Land: 1.6 sq. mi.; **Water:** 0.0 sq. mi.   **Elev:** 6923 ft.
Incorporated 1953.

Name origin: From a Spanish translation of an Indian term meaning 'place of water.'

Santa Fe County
County Seat: Santa Fe (ZIP: 87504)

Pop: 98,928 (1990); 75,519 (1980)   **Pop Density:** 51.8
Land: 1909.4 sq. mi.; **Water:** 1.6 sq. mi.   **Area Code:** 505
In north-central NM, northeast of Albuquerque; original county; organized Jan 9, 1852 (prior to statehood).
Name origin: For the capital of NM and the county seat; Spanish 'Holy Faith.'

Agua Fria
CDP
Lat: 35-38-51 N   **Long:** 106-01-17 W
Pop: 3,717 (1990)   **Pop Density:** 1616.1
Land: 2.3 sq. mi.; **Water:** 0.0 sq. mi.

Chimayo
CDP
Lat: 35-59-22 N   **Long:** 105-54-54 W
Pop: 639 (1990); 569 (1980)   **Pop Density:** 159.8
Land: 4.0 sq. mi.; **Water:** 0.1 sq. mi.
Part of the town is also in Rio Arriba County.

Cuyamungue
CDP
Lat: 35-52-11 N   **Long:** 106-00-30 W
Pop: 329 (1990)   **Pop Density:** 822.5
Land: 0.4 sq. mi.; **Water:** 0.0 sq. mi.

Edgewood
CDP
ZIP: 87015   **Lat:** 35-05-02 N   **Long:** 106-10-29 W
Pop: 2,880 (1990)   **Pop Density:** 55.5
Land: 51.9 sq. mi.; **Water:** 0.0 sq. mi.
Part of the town is also in Torrance county.

Eldorado at Santa Fe
CDP
Lat: 35-31-34 N   **Long:** 105-56-03 W
Pop: 2,260 (1990)   **Pop Density:** 105.6
Land: 21.4 sq. mi.; **Water:** 0.0 sq. mi.

Espanola
City
ZIP: 87532   **Lat:** 35-59-50 N   **Long:** 106-03-07 W
Pop: 2,179 (1990); 1,138 (1980)   **Pop Density:** 1676.2
Land: 1.3 sq. mi.; **Water:** 0.0 sq. mi.   **Elev:** 5589 ft.
Incorporated 1925. Part of the town is also in Rio Arriba County.
Name origin: Meaning of the name is not clear. It is a variation of *Hispaniola* 'New Spain' and also means 'Spanish lady.'

Jaconita
CDP
Lat: 35-53-33 N   **Long:** 106-02-05 W
Pop: 375 (1990)   **Pop Density:** 535.7
Land: 0.7 sq. mi.; **Water:** 0.0 sq. mi.

La Cienega
CDP
Lat: 35-34-35 N   **Long:** 106-06-37 W
Pop: 1,066 (1990)   **Pop Density:** 98.7
Land: 10.8 sq. mi.; **Water:** 0.0 sq. mi.

Nambe
CDP
Lat: 35-54-00 N   **Long:** 105-58-18 W
Pop: 1,246 (1990); 1,017 (1980)   **Pop Density:** 270.9
Land: 4.6 sq. mi.; **Water:** 0.0 sq. mi.

Pojoaque
CDP
Lat: 35-53-36 N   **Long:** 106-00-35 W
Pop: 1,037 (1990)   **Pop Density:** 450.9
Land: 2.3 sq. mi.; **Water:** 0.0 sq. mi.

San Ildefonso Pueblo
CDP
Lat: 35-53-52 N   **Long:** 106-07-39 W
Pop: 447 (1990)   **Pop Density:** 144.2
Land: 3.1 sq. mi.; **Water:** 0.2 sq. mi.

Santa Cruz
CDP
ZIP: 87567   **Lat:** 35-59-07 N   **Long:** 106-00-57 W
Pop: 2,504 (1990)   **Pop Density:** 368.2
Land: 6.8 sq. mi.; **Water:** 0.0 sq. mi.

Santa Fe
City
ZIP: 87501   **Lat:** 35-40-42 N   **Long:** 105-57-14 W
Pop: 55,859 (1990); 49,160 (1980)   **Pop Density:** 1526.2
Land: 36.6 sq. mi.; **Water:** 0.1 sq. mi.   **Elev:** 6989 ft.
In north-central NM, northeast of Albuquerque. State capital; founded in 1610 by Spaniards as part of New Spain; incorporated 1891. When statehood was granted in 1910, it remained the capital and is the oldest capital city in the U.S. Major tourist center of the Southwest. Largest employers, in addition to tourism, are federal, state, and city government agencies.
Name origin: Spanish 'holy faith.' Full name is *La Villa Real de la Santa Fe de San Francisco de Assisi* 'the royal town of the Holy Faith of St. Francis of Assisi.'

Tesuque
CDP
ZIP: 87574   **Lat:** 35-45-59 N   **Long:** 105-55-23 W
Pop: 1,490 (1990); 1,014 (1980)   **Pop Density:** 141.9
Land: 10.5 sq. mi.; **Water:** 0.0 sq. mi.

NEW MEXICO, Sierra County / American Places Dictionary

Sierra County
County Seat: Truth or Consequences (ZIP: 87901)

Pop: 9,912 (1990); 8,454 (1980) **Pop Density:** 2.4
Land: 4180.5 sq. mi.; **Water:** 56.1 sq. mi. **Area Code:** 505

In west-central NM, northwest of Las Cruces; organized Apr 3, 1884 from Socorro County (prior to statehood).

Name origin: For the Sierra de los Caballos Range, Spanish 'saw' for the shape of the mountains, thus 'saw-toothed mountain of the horses.' The county may have been named for the Sierra family, whose members included Nicholas de la Sierra.

Truth or Consequences — City
ZIP: 87901 **Lat:** 33-08-08 N **Long:** 107-14-53 W
Pop: 6,221 (1990); 5,219 (1980) **Pop Density:** 489.8
Land: 12.7 sq. mi.; **Water:** 0.1 sq. mi. **Elev:** 4242 ft.

In southwestern NM, northwest of Alamogordo. Incorporated 1916.

Name origin: For the popular radio (later television) show, so-named in 1950 when Ralph Edwards, the master of ceremonies, promised to hold an annual program here if they would rename their town. Originally called Hot Springs.

Williamsburg — Village
ZIP: 87942 **Lat:** 33-06-57 N **Long:** 107-17-38 W
Pop: 456 (1990); 433 (1980) **Pop Density:** 1140.0
Land: 0.4 sq. mi.; **Water:** 0.0 sq. mi.

Incorporated 1949.

Socorro County
County Seat: Socorro (ZIP: 87801)

Pop: 14,764 (1990); 12,566 (1980) **Pop Density:** 2.2
Land: 6647.1 sq. mi.; **Water:** 2.0 sq. mi. **Area Code:** 505

In west-central NM, south of Albuquerque; original county; organized Jul 1850 (prior to statehood).

Name origin: Name given to the Piro Indian pueblo of Teypana in 1598 by Juan de Oñate (1550?–1630) because "they gave us much corn." Spanish 'aid, help, succor, assistance.'

Magdalena — Village
ZIP: 87825 **Lat:** 34-06-37 N **Long:** 107-14-04 W
Pop: 861 (1990); 1,022 (1980) **Pop Density:** 138.9
Land: 6.2 sq. mi.; **Water:** 0.0 sq. mi. **Elev:** 6573 ft.

Settled 1884; incorporated 1918.

Name origin: For Mary Magdalene of the New Testament.

Socorro — City
ZIP: 87801 **Lat:** 34-03-18 N **Long:** 106-54-15 W
Pop: 8,159 (1990); 7,173 (1980) **Pop Density:** 566.6
Land: 14.4 sq. mi.; **Water:** 0.0 sq. mi.

Incorporated 1894.

Name origin: Name given by Juan de Oñate (1550?–1630) to the Piro Indian pueblo of Teypana; from Spanish meaning 'help, aid' because the Piro Indians "gave us much corn."

Taos County
County Seat: Taos (ZIP: 87571)

Pop: 23,118 (1990); 19,456 (1980) **Pop Density:** 10.5
Land: 2203.3 sq. mi.; **Water:** 1.5 sq. mi. **Area Code:** 505

On the central northern border of NM, north of Santa Fe; original county; organized Jan 9, 1852 (prior to statehood).

Name origin: A Spanish transliteration for a town of the Tewa Pueblos, located in what is now Taos County. From either *tuota* 'red willow place,' or *tuatah* 'at the village.'

Chamisal — CDP
ZIP: 87521 **Lat:** 36-10-35 N **Long:** 105-44-56 W
Pop: 272 (1990) **Pop Density:** 170.0
Land: 1.6 sq. mi.; **Water:** 0.0 sq. mi.

Penasco — CDP
Lat: 36-10-16 N **Long:** 105-41-30 W
Pop: 648 (1990) **Pop Density:** 540.0
Land: 1.2 sq. mi.; **Water:** 0.0 sq. mi.

Questa
Village
ZIP: 87556 **Lat:** 36-42-39 N **Long:** 105-35-33 W
Pop: 1,707 (1990); 1,202 (1980) **Pop Density:** 334.7
Land: 5.1 sq. mi.; **Water:** 0.0 sq. mi. **Elev:** 7392 ft.
Incorporated 1964.
Name origin: A corruption of Spanish *cuesta* meaning 'slope.'

Ranchos De Taos
CDP
ZIP: 87557 **Lat:** 36-21-46 N **Long:** 105-36-11 W
Pop: 1,779 (1990); 1,411 (1980) **Pop Density:** 555.9
Land: 3.2 sq. mi.; **Water:** 0.0 sq. mi.

Red River
Town
ZIP: 87558 **Lat:** 36-42-27 N **Long:** 105-24-23 W
Pop: 387 (1990); 332 (1980) **Pop Density:** 552.9
Land: 0.7 sq. mi.; **Water:** 0.0 sq. mi. **Elev:** 8650 ft.
Incorporated 1971.
Name origin: For the Red River, on which it is located.

Taos
Town
ZIP: 87571 **Lat:** 36-23-10 N **Long:** 105-34-37 W
Pop: 4,065 (1990); 3,369 (1980) **Pop Density:** 829.6
Land: 4.9 sq. mi.; **Water:** 0.0 sq. mi. **Elev:** 6952 ft.
In north-central NM, northeast of Santa Fe. Incorporated 1934.
Name origin: Spanish translation of either *tuota* 'red willow place,' or *tuatah* 'at the village,' in reference to a town of the Tewa Pueblo Indians.

Taos Pueblo
CDP
ZIP: 87571 **Lat:** 36-28-09 N **Long:** 105-33-34 W
Pop: 1,187 (1990) **Pop Density:** 76.1
Land: 15.6 sq. mi.; **Water:** 0.0 sq. mi.

Vadito
CDP
ZIP: 87579 **Lat:** 36-11-27 N **Long:** 105-40-37 W
Pop: 283 (1990) **Pop Density:** 314.4
Land: 0.9 sq. mi.; **Water:** 0.0 sq. mi.

Torrance County
County Seat: Estancia (ZIP: 87016)

Pop: 10,285 (1990); 7,491 (1980) **Pop Density:** 3.1
Land: 3345.1 sq. mi.; **Water:** 1.0 sq. mi. **Area Code:** 505
In central NM, southeast of Albuquerque; organized Mar 16, 1903 (prior to statehood).
Name origin: For the town of Torrance, itself named for Francis J. Torrance, a New Mexico Central Railroad promoter.

Edgewood
CDP
Lat: 35-02-00 N **Long:** 106-10-54 W
Pop: 444 (1990) **Pop Density:** 193.0
Land: 2.3 sq. mi.; **Water:** 0.0 sq. mi.
Part of the town is also in Santa Fe county.

Encino
Village
ZIP: 88321 **Lat:** 34-39-03 N **Long:** 105-27-28 W
Pop: 131 (1990); 155 (1980) **Pop Density:** 65.5
Land: 2.0 sq. mi.; **Water:** 0.0 sq. mi.
Incorporated 1938.
Name origin: From Spanish meaning 'oak grove.'

Estancia
Town
ZIP: 87016 **Lat:** 34-45-37 N **Long:** 106-03-36 W
Pop: 792 (1990); 830 (1980) **Pop Density:** 1131.4
Land: 0.7 sq. mi.; **Water:** 0.0 sq. mi. **Elev:** 6107 ft.
Incorporated 1909.
Name origin: From Spanish meaning 'large estate.'

Moriarty
City
Lat: 35-00-04 N **Long:** 106-02-37 W
Pop: 1,399 (1990); 1,276 (1980) **Pop Density:** 466.3
Land: 3.0 sq. mi.; **Water:** 0.0 sq. mi. **Elev:** 6217 ft.
Incorporated 1953.
Name origin: For Michael Moriarty, who came to the area in the 1880s for a health cure and settled permanently.

Mountainair
Town
ZIP: 87036 **Lat:** 34-31-14 N **Long:** 106-14-34 W
Pop: 926 (1990); 1,170 (1980) **Pop Density:** 1028.9
Land: 0.9 sq. mi.; **Water:** 0.0 sq. mi. **Elev:** 6499 ft.
Incorporated 1921.
Name origin: For its location at the top of Abo Pass.

Willard
Village
ZIP: 87063 **Lat:** 34-35-39 N **Long:** 106-02-01 W
Pop: 183 (1990); 166 (1980) **Pop Density:** 228.8
Land: 0.8 sq. mi.; **Water:** 0.0 sq. mi. **Elev:** 6107 ft.
Incorporated 1910.
Name origin: For Willard Hopewell, son of railroad promoter W. S. Hopewell.

NEW MEXICO, Union County

Union County
County Seat: Clayton (ZIP: 88415)

Pop: 4,124 (1990); 4,725 (1980)
Land: 3830.2 sq. mi.; **Water:** 0.8 sq. mi.
Pop Density: 1.1
Area Code: 505

In the northeastern corner of NM; organized Feb 13, 1893 from Colfax, Mora, and San Miguel counties (prior to statehood).

Name origin: For the union of the three counties.

Clayton — Town
ZIP: 88415 **Lat:** 36-27-02 N **Long:** 103-10-30 W
Pop: 2,484 (1990); 2,968 (1980) **Pop Density:** 564.5
Land: 4.4 sq. mi.; **Water:** 0.0 sq. mi. **Elev:** 5053 ft.
Founded 1887; incorporated 1912.
Name origin: For Clayton Dorsey, son of an AR senator.

Des Moines — Village
ZIP: 88418 **Lat:** 36-45-40 N **Long:** 103-49-59 W
Pop: 168 (1990); 178 (1980) **Pop Density:** 140.0
Land: 1.2 sq. mi.; **Water:** 0.0 sq. mi.
Incorporated 1915.
Name origin: For Des Moines, IA.

Folsom — Village
ZIP: 88419 **Lat:** 36-50-53 N **Long:** 103-55-03 W
Pop: 71 (1990); 73 (1980) **Pop Density:** 142.0
Land: 0.5 sq. mi.; **Water:** 0.0 sq. mi.
Incorporated 1908.
Name origin: For Frances Folsom, the wife of Pres. Grover Cleveland (1837–1908).

Grenville — Village
ZIP: 88424 **Lat:** 36-35-34 N **Long:** 103-36-45 W
Pop: 24 (1990); 39 (1980) **Pop Density:** 40.0
Land: 0.6 sq. mi.; **Water:** 0.0 sq. mi.
Founded 1880s; incorporated 1920.

Valencia County
County Seat: Los Lunas (ZIP: 87031)

Pop: 45,235 (1990); 30,769 (1980)
Land: 1067.6 sq. mi.; **Water:** 0.6 sq. mi.
Pop Density: 42.4
Area Code: 505

In west-central NM, south of Albuquerque; original county; organized Jan 9, 1852 (prior to statehood).

Name origin: Either for the town, itself named for Juan de Valencia, a seventeenth-century Spanish settler, or for the seventeenth-century home of Francisco de Valencia, a Spanish official.

Belen — City
ZIP: 87002 **Lat:** 34-39-31 N **Long:** 106-46-44 W
Pop: 6,547 (1990); 5,617 (1980) **Pop Density:** 1558.8
Land: 4.2 sq. mi.; **Water:** 0.0 sq. mi.
Founded in 1740; incorporated 1914.
Name origin: From Spanish 'Bethlehem.'

Bosque Farms — Village
ZIP: 87068 **Lat:** 34-51-17 N **Long:** 106-42-03 W
Pop: 3,791 (1990); 3,353 (1980) **Pop Density:** 972.1
Land: 3.9 sq. mi.; **Water:** 0.0 sq. mi.
Incorporated 1974.
Name origin: From Spanish meaning 'woods.'

Isleta Pueblo — CDP
Lat: 34-52-19 N **Long:** 106-40-43 W
Pop: 348 (1990) **Pop Density:** 99.4
Land: 3.5 sq. mi.; **Water:** 0.0 sq. mi.
Part of the town is also in Bernadillo County.

Los Chaves — CDP
Lat: 34-43-47 N **Long:** 106-45-39 W
Pop: 3,872 (1990) **Pop Density:** 330.9
Land: 11.7 sq. mi.; **Water:** 0.0 sq. mi.

Los Lunas — Village
ZIP: 87031 **Lat:** 34-48-47 N **Long:** 106-44-17 W
Pop: 6,013 (1990); 3,525 (1980) **Pop Density:** 985.7
Land: 6.1 sq. mi.; **Water:** 0.0 sq. mi. **Elev:** 4852 ft.
Incorporated 1928.
Name origin: From Spanish 'the Luna family,' for the descendants of Diego de Luna.

Los Trujillos-Gabaldon — CDP
Lat: 34-39-40 N **Long:** 106-45-18 W
Pop: 1,841 (1990) **Pop Density:** 306.8
Land: 6.0 sq. mi.; **Water:** 0.0 sq. mi.

Meadow Lake — CDP
Lat: 34-48-07 N **Long:** 106-35-26 W
Pop: 1,590 (1990) **Pop Density:** 130.3
Land: 12.2 sq. mi.; **Water:** 0.0 sq. mi.

Peralta — CDP
ZIP: 87042 **Lat:** 34-49-46 N **Long:** 106-41-14 W
Pop: 3,182 (1990) **Pop Density:** 691.7
Land: 4.6 sq. mi.; **Water:** 0.0 sq. mi.

Rio Communities — CDP
Lat: 34-38-38 N **Long:** 106-43-04 W
Pop: 3,233 (1990); 2,089 (1980) **Pop Density:** 538.8
Land: 6.0 sq. mi.; **Water:** 0.0 sq. mi.

Tome-Adelino CDP
Lat: 34-43-53 N Long: 106-43-14 W
Pop: 1,695 (1990) **Pop Density:** 269.0
Land: 6.3 sq. mi.; **Water:** 0.0 sq. mi.

Valencia CDP
Lat: 34-47-45 N Long: 106-41-27 W
Pop: 3,917 (1990) **Pop Density:** 712.2
Land: 5.5 sq. mi.; **Water:** 0.0 sq. mi.

NEW MEXICO

Index to Places and Counties in New Mexico

Acomita Lake (Cibola) CDP 465
Agua Fria (Santa Fe) CDP 477
Alamogordo (Otero) City 472
Albuquerque (Bernalillo) City 463
Alcalde (Rio Arriba) CDP 473
Angel Fire (Colfax) Village 465
Anthony (Doña Ana) CDP 467
Artesia (Eddy) City 468
Aztec (San Juan) City 476
Bayard (Grant) Village 468
Belen (Valencia) City 480
Bernalillo (Sandoval) Town 475
Bernalillo County 463
Black Rock (McKinley) CDP 471
Bloomfield (San Juan) City 476
Boles Acres (Otero) CDP 472
Bosque Farms (Valencia) Village 480
Cannon Air Force Base (Curry) Military Facility 466
Capitan (Lincoln) Village 470
Carlsbad (Eddy) City 468
Carlsbad North (Eddy) CDP 468
Carrizozo (Lincoln) Town 470
Catron County 464
Causey (Roosevelt) Village 474
Central (Grant) Village 468
Chama (Rio Arriba) Village 473
Chamisal (Taos) CDP 478
Chaparral (Doña Ana) CDP 467
Chaves County 464
Chimayo (Rio Arriba) CDP 473
Chimayo (Santa Fe) CDP 477
Cibola County 465
Cimarron (Colfax) Village 465
Clayton (Union) Town 480
Cloudcroft (Otero) Village 472
Clovis (Curry) City 466
Cochiti (Sandoval) CDP 475
Colfax County 465
Columbus (Luna) Village 471
Corona (Lincoln) Village 470
Corrales (Bernalillo) Village 463
Corrales (Sandoval) Village 475
Crownpoint (McKinley) CDP 471
Cuba (Sandoval) Village 475
Curry County 466
Cuyamungue (Santa Fe) CDP 477
DeBaca County 467
Deming (Luna) City 471
Des Moines (Union) Village 480
Dexter (Chaves) Town 464
Dora (Roosevelt) Village 474
Doña Ana (Doña Ana) CDP 467
Doña Ana County 467
Dulce (Rio Arriba) CDP 473
Eagle Nest (Colfax) Village 466
Eddy County 468
Edgewood (Santa Fe) CDP 477
Edgewood (Torrance) CDP 479
Eldorado at Santa Fe (Santa Fe) CDP 477
Elida (Roosevelt) Town 474
Encino (Torrance) Village 479
Espanola (Rio Arriba) City 474
Espanola (Santa Fe) City 477
Estancia (Torrance) Town 479
Eunice (Lea) City 470
Farmington (San Juan) City 476
Flora Vista (San Juan) CDP 476
Floyd (Roosevelt) Village 474

Folsom (Union) Village 480
Fort Sumner (DeBaca) Village 467
Gallup (McKinley) City 472
Grady (Curry) Village 466
Grant County 468
Grants (Cibola) City 465
Grenville (Union) Village 480
Guadalupe County 469
Hagerman (Chaves) Town 464
Harding County 469
Hatch (Doña Ana) Village 467
Hidalgo County 469
Hobbs (Lea) City 470
Holloman Air Force Base (Otero) Military Facility 472
Hope (Eddy) Village 468
House (Quay) Village 473
Hurley (Grant) Town 468
Isleta Pueblo (Bernalillo) CDP 463
Isleta Pueblo (Valencia) CDP 480
Jaconita (Santa Fe) CDP 477
Jal (Lea) City 470
Jemez Pueblo (Sandoval) CDP 475
Jemez Springs (Sandoval) Village 475
Kirtland (San Juan) CDP 476
La Cienega (Santa Fe) CDP 477
Laguna (Cibola) CDP 465
Lake Arthur (Chaves) Town 464
La Luz (Otero) CDP 473
Las Cruces (Doña Ana) City 467
Las Vegas (San Miguel) City 476
Lea County 470
Lincoln County 470
Logan (Quay) Village 473
Lordsburg (Hidalgo) City 469
Los Alamos (Los Alamos) CDP 471
Los Alamos County 471
Los Chaves (Valencia) CDP 480
Los Lunas (Valencia) Village 480
Los Ranchos de Albuquerque (Bernalillo) Village 463
Los Trujillos-Gabaldon (Valencia) CDP 480
Loving (Eddy) Village 468
Lovington (Lea) City 470
Luna County 471
Magdalena (Socorro) Village 478
Maxwell (Colfax) Village 466
McKinley County 471
Meadow Lake (Valencia) CDP 480
Melrose (Curry) Village 466
Mescalero (Otero) CDP 473
Mesilla (Doña Ana) Town 467
Mesita (Cibola) CDP 465
Mexican Springs (McKinley) CDP 472
Milan (Cibola) Village 465
Mora (Mora) Pop. Place 472
Mora County 472
Moriarty (Torrance) City 479
Mosquero (Harding) Village 469
Mosquero (San Miguel) Village 476
Mountainair (Torrance) Town 479
Nambe (Santa Fe) CDP 477
Naschitti (San Juan) CDP 476
Navajo (McKinley) Village 472
Newcomb (San Juan) CDP 476
North Acomita Village (Cibola) CDP 465
North Valley (Bernalillo) CDP 463
Ojo Amarillo (San Juan) CDP 476

Otero County 472
Paguate (Cibola) CDP 465
Paradise Hills (Bernalillo) CDP 463
Paraje (Cibola) CDP 465
Pecos (San Miguel) Village 477
Pena Blanca (Sandoval) CDP 475
Penasco (Taos) CDP 478
Peralta (Valencia) CDP 480
Placitas (Sandoval) CDP 475
Pojoaque (Santa Fe) CDP 477
Portales (Roosevelt) City 474
Quay County 473
Questa (Taos) Village 479
Ranchos De Taos (Taos) CDP 479
Raton (Colfax) City 466
Red River (Taos) Town 479
Reserve (Catron) Village 464
Rio Arriba County 473
Rio Communities (Valencia) CDP 480
Rio Rancho (Sandoval) City 475
Roosevelt County 474
Roswell (Chaves) City 464
Roy (Harding) Village 469
Ruidoso (Lincoln) Village 470
Ruidoso Downs (Lincoln) Village 471
Sandia (Bernalillo) CDP 463
Sandia Heights (Bernalillo) CDP 463
Sandoval County 475
San Felipe Pueblo (Sandoval) CDP .. 475
San Ildefonso Pueblo (Santa Fe) CDP 477
San Jon (Quay) Village 473
San Juan (Rio Arriba) CDP 474
San Juan County 476
San Miguel County 476
Sanostee (San Juan) CDP 476
Santa Ana Pueblo (Sandoval) CDP .. 475
Santa Clara Pueblo (Rio Arriba) CDP 474
Santa Cruz (Santa Fe) CDP 477
Santa Fe (Santa Fe) City 477
Santa Fe County 477
Santa Rosa (Guadalupe) City 469
Santo Domingo Pueblo (Sandoval) CDP 475
San Ysidro (Sandoval) Village 475
Seama (Cibola) CDP 465
Shiprock (San Juan) CDP 476
Sierra County 478
Silver City (Grant) Town 468
Skyline-Ganipa (Cibola) CDP 465
Socorro (Socorro) City 478
Socorro County 478
South Valley (Bernalillo) CDP 463
Springer (Colfax) Town 466
Sunland Park (Doña Ana) City 467
Taos (Taos) Town 479
Taos County 478
Taos Pueblo (Taos) CDP 479
Tatum (Lea) Town 470
Tesuque (Santa Fe) CDP 477
Texico (Curry) City 466
Tierra Amarilla (Rio Arriba) Pop. Place 474
Tijeras (Bernalillo) Village 463
Tohatchi (McKinley) CDP 472
Tome-Adelino (Valencia) CDP 481
Torrance County 479
Truth or Consequences (Sierra) City 478
Tucumcari (Quay) City 473

Tularosa (Otero) Village 473
Union County 480
University Park (Doña Ana) CDP 467
Vadito (Taos) CDP 479
Valencia (Valencia) CDP 481
Valencia County 480
Vaughn (Guadalupe) Town 469
Virden (Hidalgo) Village 469
Wagon Mound (Mora) Village 472
White Rock (Los Alamos) CDP 471
White Sands (Doña Ana) Military Facility 467
Willard (Torrance) Village 479
Williamsburg (Sierra) Village 478
Zia Pueblo (Sandoval) CDP 475
Zuni Pueblo (McKinley) CDP 472

North Dakota

NORTH DAKOTA

All political boundaries are as of January 1, 1980

U.S. Department of Commerce — BUREAU OF THE CENSUS

North Dakota

Population: 638,800 (1990); 652,717 (1980)
Population rank (1990): 47
Percent population change (1980–1990): -2.1
Population projection: 635,000 (1995); 615,000 (2000)

Area: total: 70,704 sq. mi.; 68,994 sq. mi. land, 1,710 sq. mi. water
Area rank: 19
Highest elevation: 3,506 ft., White Butte (Slope County)
Lowest point: 750 ft. (Pembina County)

State capital: Bismarck (Burleigh County)
Largest city: Fargo (74,111)
Second largest city: Grand Forks (49,425)
Largest county: Cass (102,874)

Total housing units: 276,340
No. of occupied housing units: 240,878
Vacant housing units (%): 12.8
Distribution of population by race and Hispanic origin (%):
White: 94.6
Black: 0.6
Hispanic (any race): 0.7
Native American: 4.1
Asian/Pacific: 0.5
Other: 0.3

Admission date: November 2, 1889 (39th state).

Location: In the north central United States bordering South Dakota, Montana, the Canadian provinces of Manitoba and Saskatchewan, and Minnesota.

Name Origin: For the Dakota (Sioux) Indian confederation, in whose language the word means 'allies,' referring to the friendly compact that joined seven smaller tribes. The name was originally applied to the entire Dakota Territory, which was divided into North and South in 1889.

State beverage: milk
State bird: Western meadowlark *(Sturnella neglecta)*
State fish: northern pike *(Esox lucius)*
State flower: wild prairie rose *(Rosa blanda* or *arkansana)*
State fossil: Teredo petrified wood
State grass: western wheatgrass *(Agropyron smithii)*
State march: "Spirit of the Land"
State song: "North Dakota Hymn"
State stone: Teredo petrified wood
State tree: American elm *(Ulmus americana)*

State motto: Liberty and Union, Now and Forever, One and Inseparable
State nicknames: Flickertail State, Sioux State, Land of the Dakotas, Peace Garden State

Area code: 701
Time zones: Central and Mountain
Abbreviations: ND (postal); N.D. or N. Dak. (traditional)
Part of (region): Plains States; Midwest

Local Government

Counties

North Dakota has 53 counties, each governed by a board of commissioners.

Municipalities

North Dakota's 366 cities have limited home rule and are governed by either a mayor and council or a commission. There are also more than 1300 townships, either organized or unorganized. The organized townships have elected officials for government. The unorganized townships are under the jurisdiction of the county board of commissioners.

Settlement History and Early Development

Although there was some prehistoric settlement in North Dakota as long as 13,000 years ago, those settlers were forced by drought to seek new lands elsewhere, and it was not until relatively recently—about 2,000 years ago—that Indians began returning to the Dakotas. Among the tribes that settled in the Dakotas were the Mandan, Hidatsa, Arikara, Yanktonai Sioux, Teton Sioux, Cheyenne, Assiniboine, Chippewa, and Ojibwa Indians.

French explorers, led by Robert Cavelier, Sieur de La Salle, claimed all of the land drained by the Mississippi River system for France in 1682. Because the Missouri River in the Dakotas flows into the Mississippi, this area was included. The northeastern section of present-day North Dakota was given by France to Great Britain in 1713. The southern part of the state was included in the vast Louisiana territory that was owned by France, then Spain (1762), then France again (1800). Under Napoleon Bonaparte France sold the territory to the U.S. in 1803 in the Louisiana Purchase.

The first white visitor to the region was a fur trader, Pierre Gaultier de Varennes, Sieur de la Vérendrye, in 1738. The fur trade grew throughout the area, with trading posts established by the North West Company, the Hudson's Bay Company, and, after the Lewis and Clark Expedition of 1804–06, the American Fur Company. The most important commodity was buffalo hides. Lewis and Clark built Fort Mandan on the east bank of the Missouri

NORTH DAKOTA

River and stayed there in the winter of 1804–05 during their famous expedition.

A farming settlement was established in 1812 at Pembina by settlers from Canada. In 1818, a treaty between Great Britain and the U.S. made the northeastern part of North Dakota part of the U.S. and established the U.S.-Canadian border at the 49th parallel. Most of the Pembina settlers moved north to make sure they were in Canadian territory.

Dakota Territory

In 1861 the Dakota Territory was organized, comprising the Dakotas, Montana, and Wyoming. During and after the Civil War army action against the Sioux led to American settlement in the region, which was opened to homesteading in 1863. Settlement grew as treaties forced the Indians onto reservations and the Northern Pacific Railroad arrived in Fargo in 1872. Peace with the Indians was assured after Sioux leader Sitting Bull surrendered to U.S. troops in 1881. There was a land boom during which many settlers arrived from Canada, and profitable farming of wheat led to these farms being known as "bonanza" farms. Cattle grazing also became common. However, drought and falling farm prices in the 1880s drove many of these settlers from the area.

Statehood

Because centers of population had developed in opposite corners of the Dakota territory, inhabitants asked Congress to divide the area into two parts. The boundary between North Dakota and South Dakota was established in February 1889, and North Dakota became the 39th U.S. state on November 2, 1889. During the next two decades the American and Canadian farmers who had left the state were replaced by an influx of Europeans, especially Norwegian and German immigrants.

Business and Industry

During the 1920s and 1930s bank failures, low farm prices, drought, and the Great Depression all had an adverse effect on the state's economy and led to another exodus by many of the inhabitants. The economy rebounded modestly during World War II, as the state supplied food for the armed forces. After the war, increased mechanization led to fewer jobs on the farms. The state's economy has been aided by the construction of the Garrison Dam (1946–60) and by state and local development commissions formed to attract new industry to the state. U.S. Air Force Strategic Air Command bases were built during the 1960s. Since the 1970s there has been increased drilling for oil, mining of lignite for electrical generation, and coal and natural gas production.

State Boundaries

The Dakota Territory was organized in 1861; its area was changed by the formation of the Idaho Territory (1863), the Montana Territory (1864), and the Wyoming Territory (1868). The North Dakota-Canadian border was established at the 49th parallel by treaty between the U.S. and Great Britain in 1818. The North Dakota—South Dakota border was established in February 1889 before the two areas became states in November 1889.

North Dakota Counties

Adams	Divide	LaMoure	Pembina	Slope
Barnes	Dunn	Logan	Pierce	Stark
Benson	Eddy	McHenry	Ramsey	Steele
Billings	Emmons	McIntosh	Ransom	Stutsman
Bottineau	Foster	McKenzie	Renville	Towner
Bowman	Golden Valley	McLean	Richland	Traill
Burke	Grand Forks	Mercer	Rolette	Walsh
Burleigh	Grant	Morton	Sargent	Ward
Cass	Griggs	Mountrail	Sheridan	Wells
Cavalier	Hettinger	Nelson	Sioux	Williams
Dickey	Kidder	Oliver		

Multi-County Places

The following North Dakota places are in more than one county. Given here is the total population for each multi-county place, and the names of the counties it is in.

Enderlin, pop. 997; Ransom (980), Cass (17)
Grandin, pop. 213; Cass (213), Traill (0)
Lehr, pop. 191; McIntosh (147), Logan (44)
Reynolds, pop. 299; Traill (192), Grand Forks (107)
Sarles, pop. 86; Cavalier (83), Towner (3)
Tower City, pop. 233; Cass (233), Barnes (0)
Wilton, pop. 728; McLean (552), Burleigh (176)

NORTH DAKOTA, Adams County

Adams County
County Seat: Hettinger (ZIP: 58639)

Pop: 3,174 (1990); 3,584 (1980)   **Pop Density:** 3.2
Land: 988.0 sq. mi.; **Water:** 0.9 sq. mi.   **Area Code:** 701
On the southwestern border of ND, south of Dickinson; organized Apr 24, 1907 from Hettinger County.

Name origin: For John Quincy Adams (1848–1919), land and townsite agent for the Chicago, Milwaukee and St. Paul Railway whose main line to the Pacific coast was built through the area (1906–07). Adams was distantly related to the president of the same name.

Beisigl   Township
Lat: 46-09-23 N   Long: 102-03-34 W
Pop: 25 (1990); 37 (1980)   **Pop Density:** 0.7
Land: 36.1 sq. mi.; **Water:** 0.0 sq. mi.

Bucyrus   City
ZIP: 58639   Lat: 46-03-48 N   Long: 102-47-17 W
Pop: 22 (1990); 32 (1980)   **Pop Density:** 73.3
Land: 0.3 sq. mi.; **Water:** 0.0 sq. mi.   **Elev:** 2780 ft.
Not coextensive with township.

*Bucyrus   Township
Lat: 46-04-37 N   Long: 102-48-25 W
Pop: 36 (1990); 49 (1980)   **Pop Density:** 1.0
Land: 35.6 sq. mi.; **Water:** 0.0 sq. mi.

Cedar   Township
Lat: 46-14-57 N   Long: 102-41-03 W
Pop: 21 (1990); 30 (1980)   **Pop Density:** 0.7
Land: 31.6 sq. mi.; **Water:** 0.0 sq. mi.

Central Adams   Pop. Place
Lat: 46-07-09 N   Long: 102-41-04 W
Pop: 95 (1990); 91 (1980)   **Pop Density:** 1.3
Land: 71.9 sq. mi.; **Water:** 0.0 sq. mi.

Chandler   Township
Lat: 46-09-46 N   Long: 102-26-10 W
Pop: 29 (1990); 23 (1980)   **Pop Density:** 0.8
Land: 36.0 sq. mi.; **Water:** 0.0 sq. mi.

Clermont   Township
Lat: 45-59-14 N   Long: 102-25-58 W
Pop: 32 (1990); 38 (1980)   **Pop Density:** 0.9
Land: 35.9 sq. mi.; **Water:** 0.0 sq. mi.

Darling Springs   Township
Lat: 46-15-04 N   Long: 102-48-28 W
Pop: 31 (1990); 42 (1980)   **Pop Density:** 1.0
Land: 31.1 sq. mi.; **Water:** 0.0 sq. mi.

Duck Creek   Township
Lat: 46-04-23 N   Long: 102-33-23 W
Pop: 41 (1990); 32 (1980)   **Pop Density:** 1.1
Land: 36.0 sq. mi.; **Water:** 0.0 sq. mi.

East Adams   Pop. Place
Lat: 46-05-49 N   Long: 102-16-38 W
Pop: 146 (1990); 186 (1980)   **Pop Density:** 0.8
Land: 179.6 sq. mi.; **Water:** 0.0 sq. mi.

Gilstrap   Township
Lat: 45-59-18 N   Long: 102-18-38 W
Pop: 36 (1990); 28 (1980)   **Pop Density:** 1.0
Land: 36.0 sq. mi.; **Water:** 0.0 sq. mi.

Haynes   City
ZIP: 58637   Lat: 45-58-25 N   Long: 102-28-17 W
Pop: 37 (1990); 58 (1980)   **Pop Density:** 370.0
Land: 0.1 sq. mi.; **Water:** 0.0 sq. mi.   **Elev:** 2548 ft.

Hettinger   City
ZIP: 58639   Lat: 46-00-13 N   Long: 102-38-03 W
Pop: 1,574 (1990); 1,739 (1980)   **Pop Density:** 1967.5
Land: 0.8 sq. mi.; **Water:** 0.0 sq. mi.   **Elev:** 2700 ft.
Not coextensive with township.

Name origin: For Mathias Hettinger, the father-in-law of surveyor E.A. Williams.

*Hettinger   Township
ZIP: 58639   Lat: 45-59-18 N   Long: 102-40-30 W
Pop: 218 (1990); 192 (1980)   **Pop Density:** 6.2
Land: 34.9 sq. mi.; **Water:** 0.2 sq. mi.

Holden   Township
Lat: 45-59-03 N   Long: 102-48-33 W
Pop: 44 (1990); 43 (1980)   **Pop Density:** 1.2
Land: 36.0 sq. mi.; **Water:** 0.0 sq. mi.

Lemmon   Pop. Place
Lat: 46-10-09 N   Long: 102-56-10 W
Pop: 30 (1990); 47 (1980)   **Pop Density:** 0.8
Land: 35.7 sq. mi.; **Water:** 0.0 sq. mi.

Lightning Creek   Township
Lat: 45-59-12 N   Long: 102-55-20 W
Pop: 22 (1990); 27 (1980)   **Pop Density:** 0.6
Land: 36.1 sq. mi.; **Water:** 0.0 sq. mi.

Maine   Township
Lat: 46-14-11 N   Long: 102-33-55 W
Pop: 32 (1990); 34 (1980)   **Pop Density:** 1.0
Land: 31.7 sq. mi.; **Water:** 0.0 sq. mi.

North Lemmon   Township
Lat: 45-59-09 N   Long: 102-11-34 W
Pop: 81 (1990); 109 (1980)   **Pop Density:** 2.2
Land: 36.1 sq. mi.; **Water:** 0.1 sq. mi.

Orange   Township
Lat: 45-58-48 N   Long: 102-03-45 W
Pop: 40 (1990); 48 (1980)   **Pop Density:** 1.1
Land: 35.9 sq. mi.; **Water:** 0.1 sq. mi.

Reeder   City
ZIP: 58649   Lat: 46-06-25 N   Long: 102-56-31 W
Pop: 252 (1990); 355 (1980)   **Pop Density:** 630.0
Land: 0.4 sq. mi.; **Water:** 0.0 sq. mi.   **Elev:** 2830 ft.
Not coextensive with township.

Name origin: For Milwaukee Railroad engineer E. A. Reeder.

*Reeder — Township
ZIP: 58649 Lat: 46-04-33 N Long: 102-55-40 W
Pop: 51 (1990); 63 (1980) Pop Density: 1.4
Land: 35.3 sq. mi.; Water: 0.2 sq. mi.

Scott — Township
Lat: 45-59-07 N Long: 102-33-42 W
Pop: 150 (1990); 139 (1980) Pop Density: 4.2
Land: 35.9 sq. mi.; Water: 0.1 sq. mi.

South Fork — Township
Lat: 46-04-56 N Long: 102-03-55 W
Pop: 17 (1990); 14 (1980) Pop Density: 0.5
Land: 36.0 sq. mi.; Water: 0.0 sq. mi.

Taylor Butte — Township
Lat: 46-09-18 N Long: 102-33-23 W
Pop: 34 (1990); 41 (1980) Pop Density: 0.9
Land: 35.9 sq. mi.; Water: 0.0 sq. mi.

Whetstone — Township
Lat: 46-14-34 N Long: 102-55-58 W
Pop: 26 (1990); 41 (1980) Pop Density: 0.8
Land: 31.1 sq. mi.; Water: 0.0 sq. mi.

Wolf Butte — Township
Lat: 46-10-11 N Long: 102-49-08 W
Pop: 52 (1990); 46 (1980) Pop Density: 1.4
Land: 35.9 sq. mi.; Water: 0.1 sq. mi.

Barnes County
County Seat: Valley City (ZIP: 58072)

Pop: 12,545 (1990); 13,960 (1980) Pop Density: 8.4
Land: 1491.8 sq. mi.; Water: 21.6 sq. mi. Area Code: 701
In southeastern ND, west of Fargo; organized as Burbank County by the 1872–1873 territorial legislature (prior to statehood) from Cass County; renamed Jan 14, 1875.
Name origin: For Alanson H. Barnes (1818–90), judge of the federal district court (1872–81). Originally for John A. Burbank (1827–1905), governor of Dakota Territory (1869–73).

Alta — Township
Lat: 46-56-07 N Long: 97-52-20 W
Pop: 107 (1990); 116 (1980) Pop Density: 3.0
Land: 36.1 sq. mi.; Water: 0.0 sq. mi.

Anderson — Township
Lat: 47-00-57 N Long: 98-15-58 W
Pop: 64 (1990); 70 (1980) Pop Density: 1.8
Land: 35.8 sq. mi.; Water: 0.3 sq. mi.

Ashtabula — Township
Lat: 47-06-24 N Long: 98-01-03 W
Pop: 119 (1990); 100 (1980) Pop Density: 3.6
Land: 32.7 sq. mi.; Water: 3.4 sq. mi.

Baldwin — Township
Lat: 47-12-14 N Long: 97-53-30 W
Pop: 39 (1990); 56 (1980) Pop Density: 1.1
Land: 35.6 sq. mi.; Water: 0.7 sq. mi.

Binghampton — Township
Lat: 46-45-53 N Long: 97-44-02 W
Pop: 113 (1990); 118 (1980) Pop Density: 3.2
Land: 35.6 sq. mi.; Water: 0.1 sq. mi.

Brimer — Township
Lat: 47-01-40 N Long: 98-24-06 W
Pop: 70 (1990); 82 (1980) Pop Density: 2.0
Land: 35.5 sq. mi.; Water: 0.5 sq. mi.

Cuba — Township
Lat: 46-50-54 N Long: 97-51-59 W
Pop: 85 (1990); 93 (1980) Pop Density: 2.4
Land: 35.8 sq. mi.; Water: 0.0 sq. mi.

Dazey — City
ZIP: 58429 Lat: 47-11-17 N Long: 98-12-01 W
Pop: 129 (1990); 143 (1980) Pop Density: 322.5
Land: 0.4 sq. mi.; Water: 0.0 sq. mi. Elev: 1433 ft.
Not coextensive with township.

*Dazey — Township
ZIP: 58429 Lat: 47-11-24 N Long: 98-08-30 W
Pop: 72 (1990); 76 (1980) Pop Density: 2.1
Land: 35.0 sq. mi.; Water: 0.4 sq. mi.

Eckelson — Township
Lat: 46-56-24 N Long: 98-22-35 W
Pop: 100 (1990); 146 (1980) Pop Density: 2.9
Land: 35.0 sq. mi.; Water: 1.4 sq. mi.

Edna — Township
Lat: 47-06-13 N Long: 98-16-34 W
Pop: 95 (1990); 100 (1980) Pop Density: 2.8
Land: 34.5 sq. mi.; Water: 1.3 sq. mi.

Ellsbury — Township
Lat: 47-11-47 N Long: 97-46-03 W
Pop: 59 (1990); 77 (1980) Pop Density: 1.6
Land: 36.0 sq. mi.; Water: 0.0 sq. mi.

Fingal — City
ZIP: 58031 Lat: 46-45-43 N Long: 97-47-32 W
Pop: 138 (1990); 151 (1980) Pop Density: 345.0
Land: 0.4 sq. mi.; Water: 0.0 sq. mi. Elev: 1280 ft.

Getchell — Township
Lat: 47-01-47 N Long: 98-00-53 W
Pop: 81 (1990); 75 (1980) Pop Density: 2.3
Land: 34.8 sq. mi.; Water: 1.0 sq. mi.

Grand Prairie — Township
Lat: 47-06-35 N Long: 97-54-01 W
Pop: 43 (1990); 53 (1980) Pop Density: 1.2
Land: 36.2 sq. mi.; Water: 0.0 sq. mi.

Green — Township
Lat: 46-50-58 N Long: 98-07-30 W
Pop: 88 (1990); 113 (1980) Pop Density: 2.5
Land: 35.4 sq. mi.; Water: 0.5 sq. mi.

NORTH DAKOTA, Barnes County

Greenland Township
Lat: 46-40-16 N Long: 98-22-21 W
Pop: 75 (1990); 92 (1980) Pop Density: 2.1
Land: 36.1 sq. mi.; Water: 0.0 sq. mi.

Hemen Township
Lat: 46-50-55 N Long: 98-14-54 W
Pop: 50 (1990); 64 (1980) Pop Density: 1.4
Land: 35.2 sq. mi.; Water: 0.9 sq. mi.

Hobart Township
Lat: 46-56-10 N Long: 98-06-57 W
Pop: 137 (1990); 197 (1980) Pop Density: 4.0
Land: 34.4 sq. mi.; Water: 1.7 sq. mi.

Kathryn City
ZIP: 58049 Lat: 46-40-47 N Long: 97-58-03 W
Pop: 72 (1990); 95 (1980) Pop Density: 120.0
Land: 0.6 sq. mi.; Water: 0.0 sq. mi. Elev: 1200 ft.

Lake Town Township
Lat: 47-12-00 N Long: 98-17-20 W
Pop: 56 (1990); 78 (1980) Pop Density: 1.6
Land: 34.5 sq. mi.; Water: 1.0 sq. mi.

Leal City
Lat: 47-06-18 N Long: 98-18-50 W
Pop: 35 (1990); 45 (1980) Pop Density: 350.0
Land: 0.1 sq. mi.; Water: 0.0 sq. mi. Elev: 1465 ft.

Litchville City
ZIP: 58461 Lat: 46-39-26 N Long: 98-11-28 W
Pop: 205 (1990); 251 (1980) Pop Density: 136.7
Land: 1.5 sq. mi.; Water: 0.0 sq. mi. Elev: 1467 ft.

Mansfield Township
Lat: 46-50-39 N Long: 98-21-52 W
Pop: 38 (1990); 43 (1980) Pop Density: 1.1
Land: 35.7 sq. mi.; Water: 0.5 sq. mi.

Marsh Township
Lat: 46-50-46 N Long: 98-00-01 W
Pop: 246 (1990); 209 (1980) Pop Density: 6.9
Land: 35.9 sq. mi.; Water: 0.1 sq. mi.

Meadow Lake Township
Lat: 46-45-20 N Long: 98-22-35 W
Pop: 95 (1990); 97 (1980) Pop Density: 2.6
Land: 36.3 sq. mi.; Water: 0.0 sq. mi.

Minnie Lake Township
Lat: 47-06-24 N Long: 97-46-15 W
Pop: 75 (1990); 84 (1980) Pop Density: 2.1
Land: 36.1 sq. mi.; Water: 0.0 sq. mi.

Nelson Township
Lat: 46-45-42 N Long: 97-59-11 W
Pop: 79 (1990); 87 (1980) Pop Density: 2.2
Land: 36.0 sq. mi.; Water: 0.0 sq. mi.

Noltimier Township
Lat: 47-01-46 N Long: 97-53-07 W
Pop: 91 (1990); 117 (1980) Pop Density: 2.5
Land: 35.9 sq. mi.; Water: 0.1 sq. mi.

Nome City
ZIP: 58062 Lat: 46-40-32 N Long: 97-48-56 W
Pop: 67 (1990); 67 (1980) Pop Density: 167.5
Land: 0.4 sq. mi.; Water: 0.0 sq. mi. Elev: 1330 ft.

Norma Township
Lat: 46-45-52 N Long: 97-52-25 W
Pop: 58 (1990); 79 (1980) Pop Density: 1.6
Land: 35.7 sq. mi.; Water: 0.3 sq. mi.

Oakhill Township
Lat: 46-39-48 N Long: 97-59-44 W
Pop: 95 (1990); 119 (1980) Pop Density: 2.7
Land: 35.4 sq. mi.; Water: 0.1 sq. mi.

Oriska City
ZIP: 58063 Lat: 46-55-52 N Long: 97-47-19 W
Pop: 103 (1990); 125 (1980) Pop Density: 343.3
Land: 0.3 sq. mi.; Water: 0.0 sq. mi. Elev: 1265 ft.
Not coextensive with township.

*Oriska Township
ZIP: 58063 Lat: 46-55-55 N Long: 97-44-27 W
Pop: 128 (1990); 128 (1980) Pop Density: 3.6
Land: 35.1 sq. mi.; Water: 0.1 sq. mi.

Pierce Township
Lat: 47-11-23 N Long: 98-23-36 W
Pop: 79 (1990); 97 (1980) Pop Density: 2.2
Land: 35.2 sq. mi.; Water: 0.2 sq. mi.

Pillsbury City
ZIP: 58065 Lat: 47-12-24 N Long: 97-47-45 W
Pop: 31 (1990); 46 (1980) Pop Density: 155.0
Land: 0.2 sq. mi.; Water: 0.0 sq. mi. Elev: 1280 ft.

Potter Township
Lat: 46-56-29 N Long: 98-14-25 W
Pop: 90 (1990); 97 (1980) Pop Density: 2.7
Land: 32.8 sq. mi.; Water: 2.8 sq. mi.

Raritan Township
Lat: 46-40-25 N Long: 97-44-43 W
Pop: 139 (1990); 138 (1980) Pop Density: 3.9
Land: 36.0 sq. mi.; Water: 0.0 sq. mi.

Rogers City
ZIP: 58479 Lat: 47-04-23 N Long: 98-12-07 W
Pop: 69 (1990); 68 (1980) Pop Density: 69.0
Land: 1.0 sq. mi.; Water: 0.0 sq. mi. Elev: 1425 ft.
Not coextensive with township.

*Rogers Township
ZIP: 58479 Lat: 47-07-02 N Long: 98-08-25 W
Pop: 44 (1990); 70 (1980) Pop Density: 1.3
Land: 34.8 sq. mi.; Water: 0.2 sq. mi.

Rosebud Township
Lat: 46-40-35 N Long: 98-15-15 W
Pop: 65 (1990); 86 (1980) Pop Density: 1.9
Land: 35.0 sq. mi.; Water: 0.1 sq. mi.

Sanborn City
ZIP: 58480 Lat: 46-56-33 N Long: 98-13-23 W
Pop: 164 (1990); 237 (1980) Pop Density: 328.0
Land: 0.5 sq. mi.; Water: 0.0 sq. mi. Elev: 1450 ft.

Sibley City
ZIP: 58429 Lat: 47-13-02 N Long: 97-57-54 W
Pop: 41 (1990); 21 (1980) Pop Density: 1025.0
Land: 0.04 sq. mi.; Water: 0.0 sq. mi. Elev: 1270 ft.

Sibley Trail Township
Lat: 47-12-15 N Long: 98-00-54 W
Pop: 78 (1990); 118 (1980) Pop Density: 2.3
Land: 33.9 sq. mi.; Water: 2.2 sq. mi.

Skandia
Township
Lat: 46-45-32 N **Long:** 98-07-04 W
Pop: 67 (1990); 76 (1980)   **Pop Density:** 1.9
Land: 35.2 sq. mi.; **Water:** 0.7 sq. mi.

Spring Creek
Township
Lat: 46-40-41 N **Long:** 98-07-28 W
Pop: 84 (1990); 87 (1980)   **Pop Density:** 2.4
Land: 35.5 sq. mi.; **Water:** 0.0 sq. mi.

Springvale
Township
Lat: 46-50-49 N **Long:** 97-44-47 W
Pop: 82 (1990); 112 (1980)   **Pop Density:** 2.3
Land: 35.9 sq. mi.; **Water:** 0.0 sq. mi.

Stewart
Township
Lat: 47-01-45 N **Long:** 98-08-21 W
Pop: 88 (1990); 117 (1980)   **Pop Density:** 2.4
Land: 36.1 sq. mi.; **Water:** 0.0 sq. mi.

Svea
Township
Lat: 46-46-00 N **Long:** 98-14-45 W
Pop: 67 (1990); 78 (1980)   **Pop Density:** 1.9
Land: 35.9 sq. mi.; **Water:** 0.0 sq. mi.

Thordenskjold
Township
Lat: 46-40-08 N **Long:** 97-52-14 W
Pop: 95 (1990); 107 (1980)   **Pop Density:** 2.7
Land: 35.6 sq. mi.; **Water:** 0.0 sq. mi.

Tower City
City
Lat: 46-55-23 N **Long:** 97-41-02 W
Pop: 0 (1990); 293 (1980)
Land: 0.6 sq. mi.; **Water:** 0.0 sq. mi.   **Elev:** 1172 ft.
Part of the town is also in Cass County.

Uxbridge
Township
Lat: 47-06-16 N **Long:** 98-24-41 W
Pop: 106 (1990); 113 (1980)   **Pop Density:** 3.0
Land: 35.1 sq. mi.; **Water:** 0.8 sq. mi.

Valley
Township
Lat: 46-56-10 N **Long:** 97-59-43 W
Pop: 539 (1990); 565 (1980)   **Pop Density:** 16.4
Land: 32.9 sq. mi.; **Water:** 0.0 sq. mi.

Valley City
City
ZIP: 58072   **Lat:** 46-55-23 N **Long:** 98-00-20 W
Pop: 7,163 (1990); 7,774 (1980)   **Pop Density:** 2170.6
Land: 3.3 sq. mi.; **Water:** 0.0 sq. mi.   **Elev:** 1222 ft.
Founded 1881.
Name origin: For its descriptive connotations.

Weimer
Township
Lat: 47-01-35 N **Long:** 97-45-41 W
Pop: 72 (1990); 77 (1980)   **Pop Density:** 2.0
Land: 36.0 sq. mi.; **Water:** 0.0 sq. mi.

Wimbledon
City
ZIP: 58492   **Lat:** 47-10-14 N **Long:** 98-27-34 W
Pop: 275 (1990); 330 (1980)   **Pop Density:** 550.0
Land: 0.5 sq. mi.; **Water:** 0.0 sq. mi.   **Elev:** 1485 ft.

Benson County
County Seat: Minnewaukan (ZIP: 58351)

Pop: 7,198 (1990); 7,944 (1980)   **Pop Density:** 5.2
Land: 1388.6 sq. mi.; **Water:** 50.8 sq. mi.   **Area Code:** 701
In east-central ND, east of Minot; organized Mar 9, 1883 (prior to statehood) from Ramsey County.
Name origin: For Bertil W. Benson, a Dakota Territory legislator at the time the county was organized.

Albert
Township
Lat: 48-04-18 N **Long:** 99-32-03 W
Pop: 81 (1990); 83 (1980)   **Pop Density:** 2.3
Land: 35.6 sq. mi.; **Water:** 0.3 sq. mi.

Arne
Township
Lat: 47-53-30 N **Long:** 99-37-32 W
Pop: 57 (1990); 85 (1980)   **Pop Density:** 1.6
Land: 35.3 sq. mi.; **Water:** 0.5 sq. mi.

Aurora
Township
Lat: 47-58-37 N **Long:** 99-21-49 W
Pop: 35 (1990); 51 (1980)   **Pop Density:** 1.0
Land: 35.7 sq. mi.; **Water:** 0.2 sq. mi.

Beaver
Township
Lat: 48-14-51 N **Long:** 99-31-23 W
Pop: 35 (1990); 46 (1980)   **Pop Density:** 1.1
Land: 33.0 sq. mi.; **Water:** 2.9 sq. mi.

Brinsmade
City
ZIP: 58320   **Lat:** 48-10-59 N **Long:** 99-19-27 W
Pop: 21 (1990); 54 (1980)   **Pop Density:** 210.0
Land: 0.1 sq. mi.; **Water:** 0.0 sq. mi.   **Elev:** 1563 ft.
Incorporated 1967.

Broe
Township
Lat: 48-08-36 N **Long:** 99-39-36 W
Pop: 55 (1990); 89 (1980)   **Pop Density:** 1.5
Land: 35.5 sq. mi.; **Water:** 0.5 sq. mi.

Butte Valley
Township
Lat: 48-09-35 N **Long:** 99-31-16 W
Pop: 113 (1990); 143 (1980)   **Pop Density:** 3.2
Land: 35.4 sq. mi.; **Water:** 0.6 sq. mi.

East Fork
Township
Lat: 47-53-52 N **Long:** 99-45-29 W
Pop: 49 (1990); 51 (1980)   **Pop Density:** 1.4
Land: 35.7 sq. mi.; **Water:** 0.0 sq. mi.

NORTH DAKOTA, Benson County

Eldon Township
Lat: 48-03-54 N Long: 99-24-12 W
Pop: 70 (1990); 74 (1980) Pop Density: 1.9
Land: 36.0 sq. mi.; Water: 0.1 sq. mi.

Esmond City
ZIP: 58332 Lat: 48-01-58 N Long: 99-45-53 W
Pop: 196 (1990); 337 (1980) Pop Density: 392.0
Land: 0.5 sq. mi.; Water: 0.0 sq. mi. Elev: 1623 ft.
Not coextensive with township. Founded 1901.
Name origin: Named by railroad construction engineer E. Smith for the novel *Henry Esmond* (1852) by William Makepeace Thackeray (1811–63).

Esmond Township
ZIP: 58332 Lat: 48-04-19 N Long: 99-46-32 W
Pop: 73 (1990); 114 (1980) Pop Density: 2.1
Land: 34.7 sq. mi.; Water: 0.9 sq. mi.

Fort Totten Pop. Place
Lat: 47-58-57 N Long: 98-59-10 W
Pop: 1,359 (1990); 1,141 (1980) Pop Density: 41.9
Land: 32.4 sq. mi.; Water: 2.7 sq. mi.

Hesper Township
ZIP: 58348 Lat: 47-58-41 N Long: 99-36-48 W
Pop: 86 (1990); 110 (1980) Pop Density: 2.4
Land: 35.4 sq. mi.; Water: 0.7 sq. mi.

Impark Township
Lat: 48-09-14 N Long: 99-47-21 W
Pop: 65 (1990); 71 (1980) Pop Density: 2.1
Land: 31.7 sq. mi.; Water: 4.3 sq. mi.

Iowa Township
Lat: 48-14-09 N Long: 99-46-59 W
Pop: 30 (1990); 35 (1980) Pop Density: 0.9
Land: 33.6 sq. mi.; Water: 2.3 sq. mi.

Irvine Township
Lat: 48-19-40 N Long: 99-16-15 W
Pop: 43 (1990); 63 (1980) Pop Density: 1.2
Land: 35.9 sq. mi.; Water: 0.7 sq. mi.

Isabel Township
Lat: 48-03-51 N Long: 99-39-14 W
Pop: 93 (1990); 114 (1980) Pop Density: 2.6
Land: 35.5 sq. mi.; Water: 0.6 sq. mi.

Knox City
ZIP: 58343 Lat: 48-20-33 N Long: 99-41-21 W
Pop: 45 (1990); 69 (1980) Pop Density: 90.0
Land: 0.5 sq. mi.; Water: 0.0 sq. mi. Elev: 1604 ft.
Not coextensive with township.

Knox Township
ZIP: 58343 Lat: 48-19-41 N Long: 99-38-33 W
Pop: 55 (1990); 52 (1980) Pop Density: 1.5
Land: 35.8 sq. mi.; Water: 0.6 sq. mi.

Lake Ibsen Township
Lat: 48-14-18 N Long: 99-23-38 W
Pop: 35 (1990); 41 (1980) Pop Density: 1.0
Land: 33.6 sq. mi.; Water: 2.3 sq. mi.

Lallie Township
Lat: 47-58-40 N Long: 99-07-31 W
Pop: 295 (1990); 290 (1980) Pop Density: 6.0
Land: 48.9 sq. mi.; Water: 5.4 sq. mi.

Lallie North Pop. Place
Lat: 48-03-36 N Long: 99-07-56 W
Pop: 16 (1990); 21 (1980) Pop Density: 0.7
Land: 24.6 sq. mi.; Water: 3.9 sq. mi.

Leeds City
ZIP: 58346 Lat: 48-17-21 N Long: 99-26-18 W
Pop: 542 (1990); 678 (1980) Pop Density: 1084.0
Land: 0.5 sq. mi.; Water: 0.0 sq. mi. Elev: 1514 ft.
Not coextensive with township.
Name origin: Named by Great Northern & Northern Pacific Railroad officials for Leeds, England.

Leeds Township
ZIP: 58346 Lat: 48-19-29 N Long: 99-23-06 W
Pop: 86 (1990); 101 (1980) Pop Density: 2.4
Land: 35.7 sq. mi.; Water: 0.7 sq. mi.

Lohnes Township
Lat: 47-58-06 N Long: 98-42-46 W
Pop: 26 (1990); 13 (1980) Pop Density: 1.3
Land: 19.8 sq. mi.; Water: 0.9 sq. mi.

McClellan Township
Lat: 48-09-00 N Long: 99-23-55 W
Pop: 69 (1990); 64 (1980) Pop Density: 1.9
Land: 35.8 sq. mi.; Water: 0.2 sq. mi.

Maddock City
ZIP: 58348 Lat: 47-57-43 N Long: 99-31-44 W
Pop: 559 (1990); 677 (1980) Pop Density: 621.1
Land: 0.9 sq. mi.; Water: 0.0 sq. mi. Elev: 588 ft.
Name origin: Originally called Ellwood.

Minco Township
Lat: 47-52-09 N Long: 98-35-50 W
Pop: 44 (1990); 51 (1980) Pop Density: 1.5
Land: 28.6 sq. mi.; Water: 0.4 sq. mi.

Minnewaukan City
ZIP: 58351 Lat: 48-04-11 N Long: 99-15-00 W
Pop: 401 (1990); 461 (1980) Pop Density: 1336.7
Land: 0.3 sq. mi.; Water: 0.0 sq. mi. Elev: 1461 ft.

Mission Township
Lat: 47-59-05 N Long: 98-50-05 W
Pop: 1,044 (1990); 857 (1980) Pop Density: 26.4
Land: 39.6 sq. mi.; Water: 5.2 sq. mi.

Normania Township
Lat: 48-14-19 N Long: 99-16-31 W
Pop: 63 (1990); 74 (1980) Pop Density: 1.8
Land: 34.4 sq. mi.; Water: 1.5 sq. mi.

North Viking Township
Lat: 47-58-20 N Long: 99-29-01 W
Pop: 82 (1990); 95 (1980) Pop Density: 2.3
Land: 35.0 sq. mi.; Water: 0.2 sq. mi.

Oberon City
ZIP: 58357 Lat: 47-55-25 N Long: 99-12-18 W
Pop: 103 (1990); 150 (1980) Pop Density: 343.3
Land: 0.3 sq. mi.; Water: 0.0 sq. mi. Elev: 1562 ft.
Not coextensive with township.

Oberon Township
ZIP: 58357 Lat: 47-55-33 N Long: 99-14-37 W
Pop: 87 (1990); 137 (1980) Pop Density: 1.5
Land: 57.5 sq. mi.; Water: 0.5 sq. mi.

American Places Dictionary   NORTH DAKOTA, Billings County

Pleasant Lake
Township
Lat: 48-19-32 N **Long:** 99-47-11 W
Pop: 73 (1990); 104 (1980)   **Pop Density:** 2.1
Land: 34.0 sq. mi.; **Water:** 2.5 sq. mi.

Rich Valley
Township
Lat: 47-59-05 N **Long:** 99-45-30 W
Pop: 59 (1990); 93 (1980)   **Pop Density:** 1.6
Land: 36.0 sq. mi.; **Water:** 0.1 sq. mi.

Riggin
Township
Lat: 48-08-51 N **Long:** 99-13-55 W
Pop: 78 (1990); 92 (1980)   **Pop Density:** 1.7
Land: 46.6 sq. mi.; **Water:** 1.5 sq. mi.

Rock
Township
Lat: 47-53-01 N **Long:** 99-05-33 W
Pop: 55 (1990); 58 (1980)   **Pop Density:** 1.5
Land: 36.1 sq. mi.; **Water:** 0.3 sq. mi.

South Viking
Township
Lat: 47-52-55 N **Long:** 99-29-03 W
Pop: 74 (1990); 80 (1980)   **Pop Density:** 2.1
Land: 35.6 sq. mi.; **Water:** 0.2 sq. mi.

Twin Lake
Township
Lat: 48-14-35 N **Long:** 99-39-10 W
Pop: 63 (1990); 77 (1980)   **Pop Density:** 1.9
Land: 33.9 sq. mi.; **Water:** 2.1 sq. mi.

Twin Tree
Township
Lat: 47-53-40 N **Long:** 98-58-07 W
Pop: 66 (1990); 53 (1980)   **Pop Density:** 1.8
Land: 36.4 sq. mi.; **Water:** 0.2 sq. mi.

Warwick
City
ZIP: 58381   **Lat:** 47-51-20 N **Long:** 98-42-25 W
Pop: 80 (1990); 108 (1980)   **Pop Density:** 114.3
Land: 0.7 sq. mi.; **Water:** 0.4 sq. mi.   **Elev:** 1471 ft.
Not coextensive with township.

*Warwick
Township
ZIP: 58381   **Lat:** 47-53-43 N **Long:** 98-43-44 W
Pop: 45 (1990); 54 (1980)   **Pop Density:** 1.3
Land: 33.7 sq. mi.; **Water:** 2.3 sq. mi.

West Antelope
Township
Lat: 47-53-32 N **Long:** 99-22-15 W
Pop: 44 (1990); 60 (1980)   **Pop Density:** 1.2
Land: 35.9 sq. mi.; **Water:** 0.1 sq. mi.

West Bay
Township
Lat: 48-03-49 N **Long:** 99-16-12 W
Pop: 83 (1990); 114 (1980)   **Pop Density:** 2.4
Land: 35.0 sq. mi.; **Water:** 0.5 sq. mi.

Wood Lake
Township
Lat: 47-53-46 N **Long:** 98-50-39 W
Pop: 391 (1990); 440 (1980)   **Pop Density:** 11.2
Land: 34.8 sq. mi.; **Water:** 1.3 sq. mi.

York
City
ZIP: 58386   **Lat:** 48-18-48 N **Long:** 99-34-24 W
Pop: 35 (1990); 69 (1980)   **Pop Density:** 175.0
Land: 0.2 sq. mi.; **Water:** 0.0 sq. mi.   **Elev:** 1607 ft.
Not coextensive with township.

*York
Township
ZIP: 58386   **Lat:** 48-19-30 N **Long:** 99-32-06 W
Pop: 39 (1990); 50 (1980)   **Pop Density:** 1.1
Land: 36.1 sq. mi.; **Water:** 0.3 sq. mi.

Billings County
County Seat: Medora (ZIP: 58645)

Pop: 1,108 (1990); 1,138 (1980)   **Pop Density:** 1.0
Land: 1151.5 sq. mi.; **Water:** 2.0 sq. mi.   **Area Code:** 701
In southwestern ND, west of Dickinson; organized Feb 10, 1879 (prior to statehood) from unorganized territory.
Name origin: For Frederick K. Billings (1823–90), president of the Northern Pacific railroad (1879–81).

Medora
City
ZIP: 58645   **Lat:** 46-54-49 N **Long:** 103-31-27 W
Pop: 101 (1990); 94 (1980)   **Pop Density:** 252.5
Land: 0.4 sq. mi.; **Water:** 0.0 sq. mi.   **Elev:** 2271 ft.

North Billings
Pop. Place
Lat: 47-07-27 N **Long:** 103-20-45 W
Pop: 729 (1990); 717 (1980)   **Pop Density:** 0.9
Land: 806.9 sq. mi.; **Water:** 1.9 sq. mi.

South Billings
Pop. Place
Lat: 46-45-21 N **Long:** 103-25-01 W
Pop: 278 (1990); 327 (1980)   **Pop Density:** 0.8
Land: 344.2 sq. mi.; **Water:** 0.1 sq. mi.

NORTH DAKOTA, Bottineau County *American Places Dictionary*

> ## Bottineau County
> **County Seat: Bottineau (ZIP: 58318)**
>
> **Pop:** 8,011 (1990); 9,239 (1980) **Pop Density:** 4.8
> **Land:** 1668.7 sq. mi.; **Water:** 29.2 sq. mi. **Area Code:** 701
>
> On the central northern border of ND, northeast of Minot; organized Jan 4, 1873 (prior to statehood) from unorganized territory.
>
> **Name origin:** For Pierre Bottineau (c. 1814–95), a French-Canadian frontiersman, guide, and land speculator.

Amity — Township
Lat: 48-45-41 N Long: 100-22-30 W
Pop: 47 (1990); 69 (1980) Pop Density: 1.3
Land: 36.0 sq. mi.; Water: 0.1 sq. mi.

Antler — City
ZIP: 58711 Lat: 48-58-16 N Long: 101-16-58 W
Pop: 74 (1990); 101 (1980) Pop Density: 370.0
Land: 0.2 sq. mi.; Water: 0.0 sq. mi. Elev: 1535 ft.
Not coextensive with township. Incorporated 1906.
Name origin: For two streams whose flow pattern through the area resembles a deer's horns.

***Antler** — Township
ZIP: 58711 Lat: 48-56-39 N Long: 101-17-19 W
Pop: 83 (1990); 102 (1980) Pop Density: 1.9
Land: 43.6 sq. mi.; Water: 0.0 sq. mi.

Bentinck — Township
Lat: 48-50-40 N Long: 101-09-50 W
Pop: 52 (1990); 85 (1980) Pop Density: 1.5
Land: 35.8 sq. mi.; Water: 0.2 sq. mi.

Blaine — Township
Lat: 48-41-00 N Long: 101-22-30 W
Pop: 37 (1990); 37 (1980) Pop Density: 1.0
Land: 36.0 sq. mi.; Water: 0.0 sq. mi.

Bottineau — City
ZIP: 58318 Lat: 48-49-31 N Long: 100-26-35 W
Pop: 2,598 (1990); 2,829 (1980) Pop Density: 2598.0
Land: 1.0 sq. mi.; Water: 0.0 sq. mi. Elev: 1635 ft.
Incorporated 1904.
Name origin: For early explorer Pierre Bottineau (c. 1814–95).

Brander — Township
Lat: 48-46-12 N Long: 101-01-35 W
Pop: 53 (1990); 65 (1980) Pop Density: 1.5
Land: 35.7 sq. mi.; Water: 0.3 sq. mi.

Cecil — Township
Lat: 48-40-31 N Long: 100-13-09 W
Pop: 36 (1990); 42 (1980) Pop Density: 1.0
Land: 35.2 sq. mi.; Water: 0.2 sq. mi.

Chatfield — Township
Lat: 48-35-18 N Long: 101-07-11 W
Pop: 61 (1990); 74 (1980) Pop Density: 1.7
Land: 35.9 sq. mi.; Water: 0.1 sq. mi.

Cordelia — Township
Lat: 48-51-10 N Long: 100-15-34 W
Pop: 110 (1990); 119 (1980) Pop Density: 3.2
Land: 34.6 sq. mi.; Water: 1.1 sq. mi.

Cut Bank — Township
Lat: 48-46-13 N Long: 101-25-12 W
Pop: 81 (1990); 102 (1980) Pop Density: 2.3
Land: 35.9 sq. mi.; Water: 0.0 sq. mi.

Dalen — Township
Lat: 48-57-06 N Long: 100-30-06 W
Pop: 131 (1990); 137 (1980) Pop Density: 3.1
Land: 42.7 sq. mi.; Water: 1.1 sq. mi.

Eidsvold — Township
Lat: 48-51-26 N Long: 100-48-27 W
Pop: 63 (1990); 93 (1980) Pop Density: 1.1
Land: 58.7 sq. mi.; Water: 0.9 sq. mi.

Elms — Township
Lat: 48-35-16 N Long: 101-15-22 W
Pop: 58 (1990); 74 (1980) Pop Density: 1.6
Land: 36.1 sq. mi.; Water: 0.0 sq. mi.

Elysian — Township
Lat: 48-40-07 N Long: 100-35-28 W
Pop: 62 (1990); 89 (1980) Pop Density: 1.7
Land: 35.7 sq. mi.; Water: 0.1 sq. mi.

Gardena — City
ZIP: 58739 Lat: 48-42-03 N Long: 100-29-53 W
Pop: 41 (1990); 66 (1980) Pop Density: 136.7
Land: 0.3 sq. mi.; Water: 0.0 sq. mi. Elev: 1470 ft.

Haram — Township
Lat: 48-57-07 N Long: 100-38-45 W
Pop: 92 (1990); 98 (1980) Pop Density: 2.1
Land: 43.6 sq. mi.; Water: 0.1 sq. mi.

Hastings — Township
Lat: 48-46-12 N Long: 101-09-27 W
Pop: 74 (1990); 121 (1980) Pop Density: 2.1
Land: 35.8 sq. mi.; Water: 0.1 sq. mi.

Hoffman — Township
Lat: 48-50-51 N Long: 101-25-10 W
Pop: 14 (1990); 15 (1980) Pop Density: 0.4
Land: 35.7 sq. mi.; Water: 0.1 sq. mi.

Homen — Township
Lat: 48-56-37 N Long: 100-15-05 W
Pop: 129 (1990); 124 (1980) Pop Density: 3.3
Land: 38.7 sq. mi.; Water: 5.8 sq. mi.

Kane — Township
Lat: 48-45-20 N Long: 100-55-01 W
Pop: 92 (1990); 115 (1980) Pop Density: 2.9
Land: 31.5 sq. mi.; Water: 1.3 sq. mi.

Kramer — City
ZIP: 58748 Lat: 48-41-28 N Long: 100-42-25 W
Pop: 51 (1990); 84 (1980) Pop Density: 255.0
Land: 0.2 sq. mi.; Water: 0.0 sq. mi. Elev: 1455 ft.

American Places Dictionary NORTH DAKOTA, Bottineau County

Landa City
ZIP: 58749   Lat: 48-53-43 N   Long: 100-54-39 W
Pop: 38 (1990); 62 (1980)   Pop Density: 380.0
Land: 0.1 sq. mi.; Water: 0.0 sq. mi.   Elev: 1480 ft.

Lansford City
ZIP: 58750   Lat: 48-37-35 N   Long: 101-22-34 W
Pop: 249 (1990); 294 (1980)   Pop Density: 830.0
Land: 0.3 sq. mi.; Water: 0.0 sq. mi.   Elev: 1610 ft.
Not coextensive with township.

*Lansford Township
ZIP: 58750   Lat: 48-34-56 N   Long: 101-23-49 W
Pop: 65 (1990); 92 (1980)   Pop Density: 1.8
Land: 35.6 sq. mi.; Water: 0.0 sq. mi.

Lewis Township
Lat: 48-40-58 N   Long: 101-08-07 W
Pop: 45 (1990); 50 (1980)   Pop Density: 1.3
Land: 35.9 sq. mi.; Water: 0.0 sq. mi.

Lordsburg Township
Lat: 48-45-42 N   Long: 100-15-20 W
Pop: 32 (1990); 53 (1980)   Pop Density: 0.9
Land: 35.3 sq. mi.; Water: 0.8 sq. mi.

Maxbass City
ZIP: 58760   Lat: 48-43-20 N   Long: 101-08-30 W
Pop: 123 (1990); 141 (1980)   Pop Density: 615.0
Land: 0.2 sq. mi.; Water: 0.0 sq. mi.   Elev: 1505 ft.

Mount Rose Township
Lat: 48-40-06 N   Long: 101-14-39 W
Pop: 65 (1990); 63 (1980)   Pop Density: 1.8
Land: 36.0 sq. mi.; Water: 0.0 sq. mi.

Newborg Township
Lat: 48-40-58 N   Long: 100-59-44 W
Pop: 54 (1990); 74 (1980)   Pop Density: 1.5
Land: 35.6 sq. mi.; Water: 0.4 sq. mi.

Newburg City
ZIP: 58762   Lat: 48-42-52 N   Long: 100-54-44 W
Pop: 104 (1990); 151 (1980)   Pop Density: 1040.0
Land: 0.1 sq. mi.; Water: 0.0 sq. mi.   Elev: 1465 ft.

Oak Creek Township
Lat: 48-39-53 N   Long: 100-28-09 W
Pop: 41 (1990); 49 (1980)   Pop Density: 1.2
Land: 35.4 sq. mi.; Water: 0.0 sq. mi.

Oak Valley Township
Lat: 48-45-20 N   Long: 100-30-01 W
Pop: 62 (1990); 83 (1980)   Pop Density: 1.7
Land: 36.0 sq. mi.; Water: 0.1 sq. mi.

Ostby Township
ZIP: 58384   Lat: 48-34-51 N   Long: 100-21-08 W
Pop: 73 (1990); 102 (1980)   Pop Density: 2.1
Land: 35.5 sq. mi.; Water: 0.0 sq. mi.

Overly City
ZIP: 58360   Lat: 48-40-52 N   Long: 100-09-02 W
Pop: 25 (1990); 25 (1980)   Pop Density: 62.5
Land: 0.4 sq. mi.; Water: 0.0 sq. mi.   Elev: 1538 ft.

Peabody Township
Lat: 48-50-33 N   Long: 100-38-00 W
Pop: 12 (1990); 33 (1980)   Pop Density: 0.3
Land: 35.6 sq. mi.; Water: 0.4 sq. mi.

Pickering Township
Lat: 48-51-25 N   Long: 100-30-41 W
Pop: 218 (1990); 200 (1980)   Pop Density: 6.1
Land: 35.6 sq. mi.; Water: 0.0 sq. mi.

Renville Township
Lat: 48-46-13 N   Long: 101-17-19 W
Pop: 36 (1990); 50 (1980)   Pop Density: 1.0
Land: 35.9 sq. mi.; Water: 0.1 sq. mi.

Richburg Township
Lat: 48-56-40 N   Long: 101-01-56 W
Pop: 98 (1990); 99 (1980)   Pop Density: 2.3
Land: 43.3 sq. mi.; Water: 2.1 sq. mi.

Roland Township
Lat: 48-56-52 N   Long: 100-22-57 W
Pop: 426 (1990); 433 (1980)   Pop Density: 11.2
Land: 38.1 sq. mi.; Water: 5.9 sq. mi.

Russell City
ZIP: 58762   Lat: 48-40-24 N   Long: 100-54-07 W
Pop: 14 (1990); 18 (1980)   Pop Density: 46.7
Land: 0.3 sq. mi.; Water: 0.0 sq. mi.   Elev: 1465 ft.

Scandia Township
Lat: 48-56-40 N   Long: 100-45-48 W
Pop: 88 (1990); 108 (1980)   Pop Density: 2.0
Land: 43.9 sq. mi.; Water: 0.0 sq. mi.

Scotia Township
Lat: 48-56-40 N   Long: 100-53-43 W
Pop: 89 (1990); 84 (1980)   Pop Density: 2.2
Land: 40.2 sq. mi.; Water: 1.1 sq. mi.

Sergius Township
Lat: 48-50-34 N   Long: 101-00-17 W
Pop: 91 (1990); 116 (1980)   Pop Density: 1.9
Land: 47.7 sq. mi.; Water: 1.1 sq. mi.

Sherman Township
Lat: 48-50-33 N   Long: 101-17-18 W
Pop: 76 (1990); 73 (1980)   Pop Density: 2.1
Land: 35.9 sq. mi.; Water: 0.0 sq. mi.

Souris City
ZIP: 58783   Lat: 48-54-37 N   Long: 100-40-49 W
Pop: 97 (1990); 122 (1980)   Pop Density: 970.0
Land: 0.1 sq. mi.; Water: 0.0 sq. mi.   Elev: 1510 ft.

Starbuck Township
Lat: 48-46-12 N   Long: 100-47-07 W
Pop: 29 (1990); 40 (1980)   Pop Density: 0.8
Land: 38.5 sq. mi.; Water: 1.1 sq. mi.

Stone Creek Township
Lat: 48-41-20 N   Long: 100-43-21 W
Pop: 32 (1990); 55 (1980)   Pop Density: 1.1
Land: 28.6 sq. mi.; Water: 0.6 sq. mi.

Tacoma Township
Lat: 48-40-08 N   Long: 100-51-09 W
Pop: 93 (1990); 94 (1980)   Pop Density: 2.4
Land: 39.2 sq. mi.; Water: 2.7 sq. mi.

Wayne Township
Lat: 48-56-14 N   Long: 101-09-47 W
Pop: 36 (1990); 44 (1980)   Pop Density: 0.8
Land: 43.6 sq. mi.; Water: 0.3 sq. mi.

NORTH DAKOTA, Bottineau County   American Places Dictionary

Wellington Township
Lat: 48-35-32 N Long: 100-11-59 W
Pop: 53 (1990); 68 (1980)   Pop Density: 1.5
Land: 35.9 sq. mi.; Water: 0.1 sq. mi.

Westhope City
ZIP: 58793 Lat: 48-54-42 N Long: 101-00-59 W
Pop: 578 (1990); 741 (1980)   Pop Density: 1926.7
Land: 0.3 sq. mi.; Water: 0.0 sq. mi.   Elev: 1496 ft.

Wheaton Township
Lat: 48-56-10 N Long: 101-26-06 W
Pop: 65 (1990); 73 (1980)   Pop Density: 1.5
Land: 43.4 sq. mi.; Water: 0.3 sq. mi.

Whitby Township
Lat: 48-45-33 N Long: 100-38-22 W
Pop: 27 (1990); 35 (1980)   Pop Density: 0.7
Land: 36.3 sq. mi.; Water: 0.0 sq. mi.

Whitteron Township
Lat: 48-50-32 N Long: 100-22-48 W
Pop: 511 (1990); 462 (1980)   Pop Density: 14.7
Land: 34.8 sq. mi.; Water: 0.5 sq. mi.

Willow City City
ZIP: 58384 Lat: 48-36-16 N Long: 100-17-33 W
Pop: 281 (1990); 329 (1980)   Pop Density: 562.0
Land: 0.5 sq. mi.; Water: 0.0 sq. mi.   Elev: 1471 ft.

Willow Vale Township
Lat: 48-40-24 N Long: 100-19-58 W
Pop: 46 (1990); 72 (1980)   Pop Density: 1.3
Land: 35.9 sq. mi.; Water: 0.2 sq. mi.

Bowman County
County Seat: Bowman (ZIP: 58623)

Pop: 3,596 (1990); 4,229 (1980)   **Pop Density:** 3.1
Land: 1162.1 sq. mi.; **Water:** 4.9 sq. mi.   **Area Code:** 701

In the southwestern corner of ND; organized Mar 8, 1883 (prior to statehood) from Billings County. Eliminated in 1903 for lack of settlement; reestablished Jun 10, 1907.

Name origin: Possibly for Edward M. Bowman, a Dakota Territory representative. Another source says that William Bowman was the territorial legislator, and Edward M. Bowman was an official of the Milwaukee Road Railroad that ran through the county.

Adelaide Township
Lat: 46-09-45 N Long: 103-41-00 W
Pop: 37 (1990); 48 (1980)   Pop Density: 1.0
Land: 35.7 sq. mi.; Water: 0.0 sq. mi.

Amor Township
Lat: 46-04-35 N Long: 103-33-16 W
Pop: 28 (1990); 35 (1980)   Pop Density: 0.8
Land: 35.9 sq. mi.; Water: 0.0 sq. mi.

Bowman City
ZIP: 58623 Lat: 46-11-01 N Long: 103-23-59 W
Pop: 1,741 (1990); 2,071 (1980)   Pop Density: 1339.2
Land: 1.3 sq. mi.; Water: 0.0 sq. mi.   Elev: 2960 ft.
Not coextensive with township. Incorporated 1956.
Name origin: For either Edward or William Bowman. Originally called Lowden.

*Bowman Township
ZIP: 58623 Lat: 46-10-04 N Long: 103-25-53 W
Pop: 278 (1990); 259 (1980)   Pop Density: 8.1
Land: 34.5 sq. mi.; Water: 0.1 sq. mi.

Boyesen Township
Lat: 46-04-10 N Long: 103-18-36 W
Pop: 42 (1990); 54 (1980)   Pop Density: 1.2
Land: 35.8 sq. mi.; Water: 0.1 sq. mi.

Buena Vista Township
Lat: 46-15-02 N Long: 103-03-20 W
Pop: 39 (1990); 42 (1980)   Pop Density: 1.3
Land: 30.6 sq. mi.; Water: 0.0 sq. mi.

Fischbein Township
Lat: 46-09-37 N Long: 103-03-44 W
Pop: 27 (1990); 43 (1980)   Pop Density: 0.8
Land: 35.1 sq. mi.; Water: 0.3 sq. mi.

Gascoyne City
ZIP: 58653 Lat: 46-07-02 N Long: 103-04-45 W
Pop: 22 (1990); 23 (1980)   Pop Density: 22.0
Land: 1.0 sq. mi.; Water: 0.0 sq. mi.   Elev: 2755 ft.

*Gascoyne Township
Lat: 46-04-36 N Long: 103-04-04 W
Pop: 25 (1990); 30 (1980)   Pop Density: 0.7
Land: 35.5 sq. mi.; Water: 0.1 sq. mi.

Gem Township
Lat: 46-04-30 N Long: 103-25-58 W
Pop: 27 (1990); 24 (1980)   Pop Density: 0.8
Land: 35.9 sq. mi.; Water: 0.1 sq. mi.

Goldfield Township
Lat: 45-59-19 N Long: 103-10-55 W
Pop: 42 (1990); 56 (1980)   Pop Density: 1.2
Land: 36.0 sq. mi.; Water: 0.0 sq. mi.

Grainbelt Township
Lat: 46-14-20 N Long: 103-18-09 W
Pop: 42 (1990); 61 (1980)   Pop Density: 1.4
Land: 30.5 sq. mi.; Water: 0.0 sq. mi.

Grand River Township
Lat: 45-59-48 N Long: 103-33-21 W
Pop: 36 (1990); 32 (1980)   Pop Density: 1.0
Land: 36.0 sq. mi.; Water: 0.0 sq. mi.

Haley Township
ZIP: 58653 Lat: 45-59-23 N Long: 103-03-10 W
Pop: 28 (1990); 46 (1980) Pop Density: 0.8
Land: 36.0 sq. mi.; Water: 0.0 sq. mi.

Hart Pop. Place
Lat: 46-09-44 N Long: 103-32-43 W
Pop: 18 (1990); 42 (1980) Pop Density: 0.5
Land: 35.8 sq. mi.; Water: 0.0 sq. mi.

Ladd Township
ZIP: 58623 Lat: 45-59-45 N Long: 103-26-29 W
Pop: 34 (1990); 25 (1980) Pop Density: 0.9
Land: 36.0 sq. mi.; Water: 0.0 sq. mi.

Langberg Township
Lat: 45-59-44 N Long: 103-41-03 W
Pop: 42 (1990); 26 (1980) Pop Density: 1.2
Land: 35.9 sq. mi.; Water: 0.1 sq. mi.

Marion Township
Lat: 46-14-49 N Long: 103-33-39 W
Pop: 15 (1990); 24 (1980) Pop Density: 0.5
Land: 30.7 sq. mi.; Water: 0.0 sq. mi.

Minnehaha Township
Lat: 45-59-21 N Long: 103-19-01 W
Pop: 30 (1990); 35 (1980) Pop Density: 0.9
Land: 32.9 sq. mi.; Water: 3.1 sq. mi.

Nebo Township
Lat: 46-04-53 N Long: 103-40-42 W
Pop: 44 (1990); 44 (1980) Pop Density: 1.2
Land: 35.8 sq. mi.; Water: 0.0 sq. mi.

Rhame City
ZIP: 58651 Lat: 46-14-02 N Long: 103-39-15 W
Pop: 186 (1990); 222 (1980) Pop Density: 124.0
Land: 1.5 sq. mi.; Water: 0.0 sq. mi. Elev: 3200 ft.
Not coextensive with township. Settled 1907.
Name origin: For railroad district engineer Mitchell Rhame.

***Rhame** Township
ZIP: 58651 Lat: 46-14-40 N Long: 103-40-37 W
Pop: 43 (1990); 46 (1980) Pop Density: 1.5
Land: 29.1 sq. mi.; Water: 0.1 sq. mi.

Scranton City
ZIP: 58653 Lat: 46-08-52 N Long: 103-08-32 W
Pop: 294 (1990); 415 (1980) Pop Density: 326.7
Land: 0.9 sq. mi.; Water: 0.0 sq. mi. Elev: 2800 ft.
Not coextensive with township. Established 1907.
Name origin: For Scranton, PA, another coal-mining town.

***Scranton** Township
ZIP: 58653 Lat: 46-09-24 N Long: 103-11-33 W
Pop: 130 (1990); 99 (1980) Pop Density: 3.7
Land: 34.9 sq. mi.; Water: 0.1 sq. mi.

Star Township
Lat: 46-14-56 N Long: 103-25-58 W
Pop: 43 (1990); 50 (1980) Pop Density: 1.4
Land: 30.6 sq. mi.; Water: 0.0 sq. mi.

Stillwater Township
Lat: 46-14-15 N Long: 103-11-04 W
Pop: 38 (1990); 49 (1980) Pop Density: 1.2
Land: 30.6 sq. mi.; Water: 0.0 sq. mi.

Sunny Slope Township
Lat: 46-09-38 N Long: 103-57-19 W
Pop: 8 (1990); 13 (1980) Pop Density: 0.2
Land: 51.1 sq. mi.; Water: 0.1 sq. mi.

Talbot Township
Lat: 46-09-40 N Long: 103-18-11 W
Pop: 98 (1990); 108 (1980) Pop Density: 2.7
Land: 35.8 sq. mi.; Water: 0.0 sq. mi.

West Bowman Pop. Place
Lat: 46-06-07 N Long: 103-52-33 W
Pop: 107 (1990); 151 (1980) Pop Density: 0.4
Land: 285.0 sq. mi.; Water: 0.5 sq. mi.

Whiting Township
Lat: 46-04-38 N Long: 103-10-33 W
Pop: 52 (1990); 56 (1980) Pop Density: 1.4
Land: 35.9 sq. mi.; Water: 0.1 sq. mi.

Burke County
County Seat: Bowbells (ZIP: 58721)

Pop: 3,002 (1990); 3,822 (1980) Pop Density: 2.7
Land: 1103.6 sq. mi.; Water: 25.7 sq. mi. Area Code: 701
On the northwestern border of ND, northwest of Minot; organized Jul 12, 1910 from Ward County.
Name origin: For John Burke (1859–1937), ND governor (1907–13), treasurer of the U.S. (1913–21), and justice of ND Supreme Court (1925–37).

Battleview Township
ZIP: 58714 Lat: 48-35-10 N Long: 102-49-09 W
Pop: 138 (1990); 167 (1980) Pop Density: 3.9
Land: 35.6 sq. mi.; Water: 0.3 sq. mi.

Bowbells City
ZIP: 58721 Lat: 48-48-10 N Long: 102-14-48 W
Pop: 498 (1990); 587 (1980) Pop Density: 622.5
Land: 0.8 sq. mi.; Water: 0.0 sq. mi. Elev: 1959 ft.
Incorporated 1906.
Name origin: Named by English stockholders of the Soo Railroad for the famous bow bells at the Church of St. Mary-le-Bow in London, England.

NORTH DAKOTA, Burke County

*Bowbells
Township
Lat: 48-45-48 N Long: 102-13-07 W
Pop: 57 (1990); 53 (1980) Pop Density: 1.6
Land: 35.2 sq. mi.; Water: 0.4 sq. mi.

Carter
Township
Lat: 48-50-59 N Long: 102-20-52 W
Pop: 20 (1990); 31 (1980) Pop Density: 0.6
Land: 35.1 sq. mi.; Water: 0.8 sq. mi.

Clayton
Township
Lat: 48-45-47 N Long: 102-28-44 W
Pop: 34 (1990); 49 (1980) Pop Density: 1.0
Land: 35.4 sq. mi.; Water: 0.6 sq. mi.

Cleary
Township
Lat: 48-41-20 N Long: 102-40-53 W
Pop: 47 (1990); 53 (1980) Pop Density: 1.3
Land: 35.3 sq. mi.; Water: 0.7 sq. mi.

Columbus
City
ZIP: 58727 Lat: 48-54-16 N Long: 102-46-51 W
Pop: 223 (1990); 325 (1980) Pop Density: 743.3
Land: 0.3 sq. mi.; Water: 0.0 sq. mi. Elev: 1930 ft.
Name origin: For its second postmaster, Columbus Larson.

Colville
Township
Lat: 48-35-22 N Long: 102-41-24 W
Pop: 59 (1990); 68 (1980) Pop Density: 1.8
Land: 33.2 sq. mi.; Water: 1.4 sq. mi.

Dale
Township
Lat: 48-51-05 N Long: 102-28-30 W
Pop: 37 (1990); 59 (1980) Pop Density: 1.0
Land: 35.4 sq. mi.; Water: 0.6 sq. mi.

Dimond
Township
Lat: 48-40-31 N Long: 102-25-29 W
Pop: 29 (1990); 40 (1980) Pop Density: 0.9
Land: 32.7 sq. mi.; Water: 2.9 sq. mi.

Fay
Township
Lat: 48-50-39 N Long: 102-44-50 W
Pop: 43 (1990); 57 (1980) Pop Density: 1.2
Land: 35.9 sq. mi.; Water: 0.0 sq. mi.

Flaxton
City
ZIP: 58737 Lat: 48-53-50 N Long: 102-23-33 W
Pop: 121 (1990); 182 (1980) Pop Density: 403.3
Land: 0.3 sq. mi.; Water: 0.0 sq. mi. Elev: 1935 ft.

Foothills
Township
Lat: 48-45-40 N Long: 102-37-03 W
Pop: 58 (1990); 58 (1980) Pop Density: 1.6
Land: 35.2 sq. mi.; Water: 0.8 sq. mi.

Forthun
Township
Lat: 48-56-59 N Long: 102-52-05 W
Pop: 21 (1990); 27 (1980) Pop Density: 0.5
Land: 43.3 sq. mi.; Water: 0.1 sq. mi.

Garness
Township
Lat: 48-34-54 N Long: 102-34-14 W
Pop: 75 (1990); 93 (1980) Pop Density: 2.1
Land: 35.8 sq. mi.; Water: 0.2 sq. mi.

Harmonious
Township
Lat: 48-45-47 N Long: 102-52-18 W
Pop: 39 (1990); 45 (1980) Pop Density: 1.1
Land: 35.5 sq. mi.; Water: 0.6 sq. mi.

Kandiyohi
Township
Lat: 48-35-49 N Long: 102-17-45 W
Pop: 30 (1990); 43 (1980) Pop Density: 0.9
Land: 33.3 sq. mi.; Water: 2.7 sq. mi.

Keller
Township
Lat: 48-50-58 N Long: 102-52-19 W
Pop: 33 (1990); 27 (1980) Pop Density: 0.9
Land: 35.3 sq. mi.; Water: 0.3 sq. mi.

Lakeview
Township
Lat: 48-55-57 N Long: 102-04-33 W
Pop: 15 (1990); 30 (1980) Pop Density: 0.3
Land: 49.7 sq. mi.; Water: 1.9 sq. mi.

Larson
City
ZIP: 58727 Lat: 48-53-28 N Long: 102-51-56 W
Pop: 26 (1990); 21 (1980) Pop Density: 65.0
Land: 0.4 sq. mi.; Water: 0.0 sq. mi. Elev: 1925 ft.

Leaf Mountain
Township
Lat: 48-45-48 N Long: 102-44-17 W
Pop: 34 (1990); 61 (1980) Pop Density: 1.0
Land: 34.7 sq. mi.; Water: 1.2 sq. mi.

Lignite
City
ZIP: 58752 Lat: 48-52-36 N Long: 102-33-49 W
Pop: 242 (1990); 332 (1980) Pop Density: 2420.0
Land: 0.1 sq. mi.; Water: 0.0 sq. mi. Elev: 1975 ft.

Lucy
Township
Lat: 48-40-54 N Long: 102-33-22 W
Pop: 36 (1990); 54 (1980) Pop Density: 1.0
Land: 34.4 sq. mi.; Water: 1.7 sq. mi.

Minnesota
Township
Lat: 48-51-28 N Long: 102-11-04 W
Pop: 35 (1990); 43 (1980) Pop Density: 0.7
Land: 52.5 sq. mi.; Water: 1.0 sq. mi.

North Burke
Pop. Place
Lat: 48-54-56 N Long: 102-07-11 W
Pop: 4 (1990); 8 (1980) Pop Density: 0.3
Land: 11.6 sq. mi.; Water: 0.8 sq. mi.

North Star
Township
Lat: 48-56-40 N Long: 102-13-35 W
Pop: 62 (1990); 83 (1980) Pop Density: 1.6
Land: 39.8 sq. mi.; Water: 0.7 sq. mi.

Portal
City
ZIP: 58772 Lat: 48-59-44 N Long: 102-32-52 W
Pop: 192 (1990); 238 (1980) Pop Density: 320.0
Land: 0.6 sq. mi.; Water: 0.0 sq. mi. Elev: 1953 ft.
Founded 1890s.
Name origin: Name coined by Soo Railroad officials to indicate that it was a major port of entry into Canada.

*Portal
Township
ZIP: 58772 Lat: 48-56-41 N Long: 102-37-20 W
Pop: 47 (1990); 69 (1980) Pop Density: 1.1
Land: 42.5 sq. mi.; Water: 0.3 sq. mi.

Powers Lake
City
ZIP: 58773 Lat: 48-33-49 N Long: 102-38-36 W
Pop: 408 (1990); 466 (1980) Pop Density: 408.0
Land: 1.0 sq. mi.; Water: 0.2 sq. mi. Elev: 2206 ft.

Richland
Township
Lat: 48-56-41 N Long: 102-20-16 W
Pop: 36 (1990); 58 (1980) Pop Density: 0.8
Land: 42.6 sq. mi.; Water: 0.2 sq. mi.

Roseland
Township
Lat: 48-41-02 N **Long:** 102-17-46 W
Pop: 32 (1990); 31 (1980) **Pop Density:** 0.9
Land: 35.7 sq. mi.; **Water:** 0.2 sq. mi.

Short Creek
Township
Lat: 48-57-11 N **Long:** 102-44-20 W
Pop: 65 (1990); 74 (1980) **Pop Density:** 1.5
Land: 42.7 sq. mi.; **Water:** 0.3 sq. mi.

Soo
Township
Lat: 48-56-25 N **Long:** 102-28-10 W
Pop: 47 (1990); 50 (1980) **Pop Density:** 1.1
Land: 42.8 sq. mi.; **Water:** 0.3 sq. mi.

Thorson
Township
Lat: 48-40-09 N **Long:** 102-49-34 W
Pop: 32 (1990); 51 (1980) **Pop Density:** 0.9
Land: 35.6 sq. mi.; **Water:** 0.4 sq. mi.

Vale
Township
Lat: 48-50-56 N **Long:** 102-36-51 W
Pop: 28 (1990); 37 (1980) **Pop Density:** 0.8
Land: 34.8 sq. mi.; **Water:** 1.0 sq. mi.

Vanville
Township
Lat: 48-35-32 N **Long:** 102-25-39 W
Pop: 34 (1990); 55 (1980) **Pop Density:** 1.0
Land: 33.4 sq. mi.; **Water:** 2.4 sq. mi.

Ward
Township
Lat: 48-45-57 N **Long:** 102-20-32 W
Pop: 65 (1990); 97 (1980) **Pop Density:** 1.9
Land: 35.0 sq. mi.; **Water:** 1.0 sq. mi.

Burleigh County
County Seat: Bismarck (ZIP: 58502)

Pop: 60,131 (1990); 54,811 (1980) **Pop Density:** 36.8
Land: 1633.2 sq. mi.; **Water:** 34.9 sq. mi. **Area Code:** 701
In south-central ND; organized Jan 4, 1873 (prior to statehood) from Buffalo County, which was discontinued.
Name origin: For Walter Atwood Burleigh (1820–96), attorney, physician, Dakota Territory delegate to Congress (1865–69), and legislator.

Apple Creek
Township
Lat: 46-46-00 N **Long:** 100-38-35 W
Pop: 1,039 (1990); 843 (1980) **Pop Density:** 29.6
Land: 35.1 sq. mi.; **Water:** 0.0 sq. mi.

Bismarck
City
ZIP: 58501 **Lat:** 46-48-19 N **Long:** 100-46-02 W
Pop: 49,256 (1990); 44,485 (1980) **Pop Density:** 2027.0
Land: 24.3 sq. mi.; **Water:** 0.5 sq. mi. **Elev:** 1700 ft.
In south-central ND on the Missouri River. State capital. Incorporated 1875. Important shipping center for the farm and ranch region; major products cattle, flour, butter, poultry, coal, and petroleum.
Name origin: Named by Northern Pacific Railroad officials for Germany's chancellor Otto von Bismark (1815–98), in recognition of financial aid given by the Germans to the railroad.

*Bismarck
Pop. Place
Lat: 46-43-47 N **Long:** 100-45-35 W
Pop: 2,259 (1990); 2,233 (1980) **Pop Density:** 82.4
Land: 27.4 sq. mi.; **Water:** 2.3 sq. mi.

Boyd
Township
Lat: 46-45-56 N **Long:** 100-30-56 W
Pop: 96 (1990); 94 (1980) **Pop Density:** 2.7
Land: 36.0 sq. mi.; **Water:** 0.0 sq. mi.

Canfield
Township
Lat: 47-12-26 N **Long:** 100-26-32 W
Pop: 24 (1990); 31 (1980) **Pop Density:** 0.7
Land: 35.5 sq. mi.; **Water:** 0.4 sq. mi.

Christiania
Township
Lat: 46-56-42 N **Long:** 100-16-32 W
Pop: 47 (1990); 53 (1980) **Pop Density:** 1.3
Land: 36.0 sq. mi.; **Water:** 0.0 sq. mi.

Clear Lake
Township
Lat: 46-56-41 N **Long:** 100-07-41 W
Pop: 31 (1990); 48 (1980) **Pop Density:** 0.9
Land: 35.9 sq. mi.; **Water:** 0.2 sq. mi.

Crofte
Township
Lat: 47-01-36 N **Long:** 100-41-00 W
Pop: 152 (1990); 123 (1980) **Pop Density:** 4.2
Land: 36.2 sq. mi.; **Water:** 0.0 sq. mi.

Cromwell
Township
Lat: 47-01-48 N **Long:** 100-33-19 W
Pop: 35 (1990); 43 (1980) **Pop Density:** 1.0
Land: 36.2 sq. mi.; **Water:** 0.0 sq. mi.

Driscoll
Township
ZIP: 58532 **Lat:** 46-50-51 N **Long:** 100-08-30 W
Pop: 177 (1990); 223 (1980) **Pop Density:** 4.9
Land: 36.0 sq. mi.; **Water:** 0.1 sq. mi.

East Burleigh
Pop. Place
Lat: 47-11-59 N **Long:** 100-10-12 W
Pop: 20 (1990); 90 (1980) **Pop Density:** 0.6
Land: 34.8 sq. mi.; **Water:** 1.1 sq. mi.

Ecklund
Township
Lat: 47-06-47 N **Long:** 100-43-21 W
Pop: 124 (1990); 124 (1980) **Pop Density:** 2.3
Land: 53.9 sq. mi.; **Water:** 0.0 sq. mi.

Estherville
Township
Lat: 47-12-27 N **Long:** 100-33-03 W
Pop: 33 (1990); 63 (1980) **Pop Density:** 0.9
Land: 35.5 sq. mi.; **Water:** 0.0 sq. mi.

NORTH DAKOTA, Burleigh County

Florence Lake
Township
Lat: 47-17-42 N Long: 100-18-49 W
Pop: 25 (1990); 41 (1980) Pop Density: 0.8
Land: 32.1 sq. mi.; Water: 2.8 sq. mi.

Francis
Township
Lat: 46-57-06 N Long: 100-31-05 W
Pop: 39 (1990); 37 (1980) Pop Density: 1.1
Land: 35.8 sq. mi.; Water: 0.0 sq. mi.

Ghylin
Township
Lat: 47-06-41 N Long: 100-33-22 W
Pop: 39 (1990); 54 (1980) Pop Density: 1.1
Land: 35.6 sq. mi.; Water: 0.0 sq. mi.

Gibbs
Township
Lat: 46-51-34 N Long: 100-38-44 W
Pop: 739 (1990); 770 (1980) Pop Density: 21.1
Land: 35.1 sq. mi.; Water: 0.0 sq. mi.

Glenview
Township
Lat: 47-01-42 N Long: 100-49-22 W
Pop: 160 (1990); 160 (1980) Pop Density: 4.1
Land: 38.8 sq. mi.; Water: 0.6 sq. mi.

Grass Lake
Township
Lat: 47-12-27 N Long: 100-41-24 W
Pop: 67 (1990); 65 (1980) Pop Density: 1.9
Land: 35.5 sq. mi.; Water: 0.6 sq. mi.

Harriet
Township
Lat: 47-07-12 N Long: 100-11-06 W
Pop: 70 (1990); 88 (1980) Pop Density: 2.1
Land: 32.9 sq. mi.; Water: 3.0 sq. mi.

Hay Creek
Township
Lat: 46-52-13 N Long: 100-47-53 W
Pop: 1,924 (1990); 1,658 (1980) Pop Density: 59.0
Land: 32.6 sq. mi.; Water: 0.8 sq. mi.

Hazel Grove
Township
Lat: 47-17-16 N Long: 100-10-23 W
Pop: 23 (1990); 34 (1980) Pop Density: 0.7
Land: 34.2 sq. mi.; Water: 0.8 sq. mi.

Lein
Township
Lat: 47-01-56 N Long: 100-10-41 W
Pop: 27 (1990); 32 (1980) Pop Density: 0.8
Land: 36.0 sq. mi.; Water: 0.0 sq. mi.

Lincoln
City
Lat: 46-45-54 N Long: 100-42-03 W
Pop: 1,132 (1990); 656 (1980) Pop Density: 1257.8
Land: 0.9 sq. mi.; Water: 0.0 sq. mi. Elev: 1680 ft.

Logan
Township
Lat: 46-45-44 N Long: 100-24-18 W
Pop: 47 (1990); 50 (1980) Pop Density: 1.3
Land: 35.8 sq. mi.; Water: 0.2 sq. mi.

Long Lake
Township
Lat: 46-40-57 N Long: 100-16-21 W
Pop: 100 (1990); 144 (1980) Pop Density: 3.1
Land: 32.2 sq. mi.; Water: 3.8 sq. mi.

Lyman
Pop. Place
Lat: 47-01-30 N Long: 100-17-40 W
Pop: 11 (1990); 21 (1980) Pop Density: 0.3
Land: 36.0 sq. mi.; Water: 0.2 sq. mi.

McKenzie
Township
Lat: 46-50-55 N Long: 100-23-51 W
Pop: 85 (1990); 108 (1980) Pop Density: 2.4
Land: 35.9 sq. mi.; Water: 0.1 sq. mi.

Menoken
Township
ZIP: 58558 Lat: 46-50-55 N Long: 100-30-55 W
Pop: 137 (1990); 148 (1980) Pop Density: 3.8
Land: 35.9 sq. mi.; Water: 0.1 sq. mi.

Missouri
Township
Lat: 46-41-15 N Long: 100-39-03 W
Pop: 86 (1990); 83 (1980) Pop Density: 3.6
Land: 24.2 sq. mi.; Water: 5.2 sq. mi.

Morton
Township
Lat: 46-40-31 N Long: 100-24-21 W
Pop: 45 (1990); 54 (1980) Pop Density: 1.3
Land: 35.9 sq. mi.; Water: 0.0 sq. mi.

Naughton
Township
Lat: 46-56-22 N Long: 100-38-36 W
Pop: 144 (1990); 110 (1980) Pop Density: 4.0
Land: 36.0 sq. mi.; Water: 0.0 sq. mi.

Painted Woods
Township
Lat: 47-07-10 N Long: 100-52-20 W
Pop: 110 (1990); 115 (1980) Pop Density: 3.0
Land: 36.7 sq. mi.; Water: 1.0 sq. mi.

Regan
City
ZIP: 58477 Lat: 47-09-26 N Long: 100-31-39 W
Pop: 51 (1990); 71 (1980) Pop Density: 51.0
Land: 1.0 sq. mi.; Water: 0.0 sq. mi. Elev: 2032 ft.

Richmond
Township
Lat: 47-11-40 N Long: 100-18-02 W
Pop: 45 (1990) Pop Density: 1.3
Land: 34.9 sq. mi.; Water: 1.1 sq. mi.

Rock Hill
Township
Lat: 47-07-27 N Long: 100-25-32 W
Pop: 44 (1990); 61 (1980) Pop Density: 1.2
Land: 36.0 sq. mi.; Water: 0.0 sq. mi.

Schrunk
Township
Lat: 47-17-53 N Long: 100-25-54 W
Pop: 29 (1990); 34 (1980) Pop Density: 0.9
Land: 32.7 sq. mi.; Water: 1.7 sq. mi.

Sibley Butte
Township
Lat: 46-56-14 N Long: 100-23-39 W
Pop: 31 (1990); 52 (1980) Pop Density: 0.9
Land: 36.0 sq. mi.; Water: 0.0 sq. mi.

Steiber
Township
Lat: 47-17-14 N Long: 100-33-32 W
Pop: 29 (1990); 35 (1980) Pop Density: 0.8
Land: 34.2 sq. mi.; Water: 0.1 sq. mi.

Sterling
Township
ZIP: 58572 Lat: 46-50-37 N Long: 100-16-03 W
Pop: 183 (1990); 177 (1980) Pop Density: 5.1
Land: 36.0 sq. mi.; Water: 0.0 sq. mi.

Taft
Township
Lat: 46-46-17 N Long: 100-16-43 W
Pop: 33 (1990); 48 (1980) Pop Density: 0.9
Land: 35.8 sq. mi.; Water: 0.2 sq. mi.

Telfer
Township
Lat: 46-40-35 N Long: 100-31-41 W
Pop: 61 (1990); 94 (1980)   Pop Density: 1.7
Land: 36.0 sq. mi.; Water: 0.1 sq. mi.

Thelma
Township
Lat: 46-47-03 N Long: 100-07-50 W
Pop: 27 (1990); 33 (1980)   Pop Density: 0.8
Land: 34.1 sq. mi.; Water: 1.9 sq. mi.

Trygg
Township
Lat: 47-01-59 N Long: 100-26-31 W
Pop: 44 (1990); 57 (1980)   Pop Density: 1.2
Land: 36.1 sq. mi.; Water: 0.0 sq. mi.

West Burleigh
Pop. Place
Lat: 46-56-33 N Long: 100-48-42 W
Pop: 754 (1990); 628 (1980)   Pop Density: 13.0
Land: 58.0 sq. mi.; Water: 0.9 sq. mi.

Wild Rose
Township
Lat: 46-41-03 N Long: 100-08-34 W
Pop: 31 (1990); 54 (1980)   Pop Density: 1.0
Land: 31.7 sq. mi.; Water: 4.3 sq. mi.

Wilson
Township
Lat: 47-16-29 N Long: 100-41-11 W
Pop: 49 (1990); 62 (1980)   Pop Density: 1.5
Land: 33.7 sq. mi.; Water: 0.8 sq. mi.

Wilton
City
Lat: 47-09-20 N Long: 100-46-48 W
Pop: 176 (1990); 262 (1980)   Pop Density: 880.0
Land: 0.2 sq. mi.; Water: 0.0 sq. mi.   Elev: 2183 ft.
Founded 1898. Part of the town is also in McLean County.
Name origin: Named by Minneapolis flour magnate, W. D. Washburn, for Wilton, ME, his former home.

Wing
City
ZIP: 58494   Lat: 47-08-33 N Long: 100-16-55 W
Pop: 208 (1990); 220 (1980)   Pop Density: 346.7
Land: 0.6 sq. mi.; Water: 0.0 sq. mi.   Elev: 1888 ft.
Not coextensive with township.

*Wing
Township
ZIP: 58494   Lat: 47-06-32 N Long: 100-17-39 W
Pop: 33 (1990); 42 (1980)   Pop Density: 0.9
Land: 35.5 sq. mi.; Water: 0.0 sq. mi.

Cass County
County Seat: Fargo (ZIP: 58103)

Pop: 102,874 (1990); 88,247 (1980)   Pop Density: 58.3
Land: 1765.7 sq. mi.; Water: 2.2 sq. mi.   Area Code: 701
On the southeastern border of ND, south of Grand Forks; original county; organized Jan 4, 1873 (prior to statehood).
Name origin: For George W. Cass (1810–88), president of the Northern Pacific railroad (1856).

Addison
Township
Lat: 46-45-40 N Long: 97-06-47 W
Pop: 95 (1990); 103 (1980)   Pop Density: 2.6
Land: 36.1 sq. mi.; Water: 0.0 sq. mi.

Alice
City
ZIP: 58003   Lat: 46-45-37 N Long: 97-33-22 W
Pop: 62 (1990); 62 (1980)   Pop Density: 62.0
Land: 1.0 sq. mi.; Water: 0.0 sq. mi.   Elev: 1125 ft.
Incorporated 1967.

Amenia
City
ZIP: 58004   Lat: 47-00-29 N Long: 97-13-26 W
Pop: 82 (1990); 93 (1980)   Pop Density: 58.6
Land: 1.4 sq. mi.; Water: 0.0 sq. mi.   Elev: 952 ft.
Not coextensive with township. Incorporated 1967.

*Amenia
Township
Lat: 47-00-57 N Long: 97-16-15 W
Pop: 132 (1990); 135 (1980)   Pop Density: 3.8
Land: 34.5 sq. mi.; Water: 0.0 sq. mi.

Argusville
City
ZIP: 58005   Lat: 47-03-02 N Long: 96-56-27 W
Pop: 161 (1990); 147 (1980)   Pop Density: 40.3
Land: 4.0 sq. mi.; Water: 0.0 sq. mi.   Elev: 886 ft.
Incorporated 1967.
Name origin: Coined from *Fargo Argus*, the first daily newspaper in ND.

Arthur
City
ZIP: 58006   Lat: 47-06-12 N Long: 97-13-05 W
Pop: 400 (1990); 445 (1980)   Pop Density: 266.7
Land: 1.5 sq. mi.; Water: 0.0 sq. mi.   Elev: 990 ft.
Not coextensive with township. Incorporated 1967.
Name origin: For Chester A. Arthur (1829–86), twenty-first U.S. president.

*Arthur
Township
ZIP: 58006   Lat: 47-06-54 N Long: 97-16-16 W
Pop: 71 (1990); 103 (1980)   Pop Density: 2.1
Land: 34.5 sq. mi.; Water: 0.0 sq. mi.

Ayr
City
ZIP: 58007   Lat: 47-02-26 N Long: 97-29-28 W
Pop: 19 (1990); 42 (1980)   Pop Density: 190.0
Land: 0.1 sq. mi.; Water: 0.0 sq. mi.   Elev: 1205 ft.
Not coextensive with township. Incorporated 1967.

*Ayr
Township
ZIP: 58007   Lat: 47-01-43 N Long: 97-31-32 W
Pop: 78 (1990); 96 (1980)   Pop Density: 2.2
Land: 36.0 sq. mi.; Water: 0.0 sq. mi.

Barnes
Township
Lat: 46-49-50 N Long: 96-52-37 W
Pop: 291 (1990); 490 (1980)   Pop Density: 19.0
Land: 15.3 sq. mi.; Water: 0.0 sq. mi.

NORTH DAKOTA, Cass County

Bell
Township
Lat: 47-11-17 N **Long:** 97-07-23 W
Pop: 52 (1990); 56 (1980) **Pop Density:** 1.4
Land: 35.9 sq. mi.; **Water:** 0.0 sq. mi.

Berlin
Township
Lat: 47-01-27 N **Long:** 97-01-00 W
Pop: 133 (1990); 147 (1980) **Pop Density:** 3.9
Land: 34.0 sq. mi.; **Water:** 0.0 sq. mi.

Briarwood
City
Lat: 46-47-10 N **Long:** 96-47-37 W
Pop: 88 (1990); 47 (1980) **Pop Density:** 440.0
Land: 0.2 sq. mi.; **Water:** 0.0 sq. mi.
Incorporated 1978.

Buffalo
City
ZIP: 58011 **Lat:** 46-55-17 N **Long:** 97-33-01 W
Pop: 204 (1990); 226 (1980) **Pop Density:** 1020.0
Land: 0.2 sq. mi.; **Water:** 0.0 sq. mi. **Elev:** 1197 ft.
Not coextensive with township.
Name origin: For Buffalo, NY.

*Buffalo
Township
ZIP: 58011 **Lat:** 46-56-00 N **Long:** 97-29-30 W
Pop: 77 (1990); 99 (1980) **Pop Density:** 2.1
Land: 35.9 sq. mi.; **Water:** 0.0 sq. mi.

Casselton
City
ZIP: 58012 **Lat:** 46-54-02 N **Long:** 97-12-42 W
Pop: 1,601 (1990); 1,661 (1980) **Pop Density:** 1455.5
Land: 1.1 sq. mi.; **Water:** 0.0 sq. mi. **Elev:** 936 ft.
Not coextensive with township.
Name origin: For Northern Pacific Railway president George Cass.

*Casselton
Township
Lat: 46-56-29 N **Long:** 97-15-07 W
Pop: 111 (1990); 111 (1980) **Pop Density:** 3.2
Land: 34.3 sq. mi.; **Water:** 0.0 sq. mi.

Clifton
Township
Lat: 46-45-33 N **Long:** 97-36-48 W
Pop: 78 (1990); 113 (1980) **Pop Density:** 2.2
Land: 35.2 sq. mi.; **Water:** 0.2 sq. mi.

Cornell
Township
Lat: 47-01-32 N **Long:** 97-38-15 W
Pop: 90 (1990); 84 (1980) **Pop Density:** 2.5
Land: 36.0 sq. mi.; **Water:** 0.0 sq. mi.

Davenport
City
ZIP: 58021 **Lat:** 46-42-49 N **Long:** 97-04-07 W
Pop: 218 (1990); 195 (1980) **Pop Density:** 2180.0
Land: 0.1 sq. mi.; **Water:** 0.0 sq. mi. **Elev:** 920 ft.
Not coextensive with township. Founded 1872.
Name origin: Named by G.E. Channing for a friend, Alice Davenport, who became the second wife of William Claflin, governor of MA (1869–72).

*Davenport
Township
ZIP: 58021 **Lat:** 46-39-55 N **Long:** 97-06-53 W
Pop: 131 (1990); 165 (1980) **Pop Density:** 3.6
Land: 36.0 sq. mi.; **Water:** 0.0 sq. mi.

Dows
Township
Lat: 47-11-17 N **Long:** 97-23-50 W
Pop: 76 (1990); 93 (1980) **Pop Density:** 2.1
Land: 36.0 sq. mi.; **Water:** 0.0 sq. mi.

Durbin
Township
Lat: 46-50-23 N **Long:** 97-07-06 W
Pop: 106 (1990); 124 (1980) **Pop Density:** 3.0
Land: 35.2 sq. mi.; **Water:** 0.0 sq. mi.

Eldred
Township
Lat: 46-45-48 N **Long:** 97-29-49 W
Pop: 115 (1990); 124 (1980) **Pop Density:** 3.3
Land: 35.3 sq. mi.; **Water:** 0.1 sq. mi.

Empire
Township
Lat: 47-01-38 N **Long:** 97-23-54 W
Pop: 124 (1990); 150 (1980) **Pop Density:** 3.5
Land: 35.8 sq. mi.; **Water:** 0.0 sq. mi.

Enderlin
City
Lat: 46-37-48 N **Long:** 97-36-11 W
Pop: 17 (1990); 11 (1980) **Pop Density:** 566.7
Land: 0.03 sq. mi.; **Water:** 0.0 sq. mi. **Elev:** 1090 ft.
Part of the town is also in Ransom County.
Name origin: From a humorous corruption of "end of the line."

Erie
Township
ZIP: 58029 **Lat:** 47-06-27 N **Long:** 97-23-17 W
Pop: 135 (1990); 136 (1980) **Pop Density:** 3.8
Land: 35.8 sq. mi.; **Water:** 0.2 sq. mi.

Everest
Township
Lat: 46-50-36 N **Long:** 97-13-53 W
Pop: 126 (1990); 122 (1980) **Pop Density:** 3.6
Land: 35.4 sq. mi.; **Water:** 0.0 sq. mi.

Fargo
City
ZIP: 58102 **Lat:** 46-52-35 N **Long:** 96-49-01 W
Pop: 74,111 (1990); 61,383 (1980) **Pop Density:** 2486.9
Land: 29.8 sq. mi.; **Water:** 0.0 sq. mi. **Elev:** 900 ft.
In eastern ND on the Red River near the MN border. Founded 1871; incorporated 1875. Stockyards; manufacturing (tractors, sugar beet harvesters and cultivators, computer software, dairy and other food products); wholesale distribution center. Nicknamed "Transportation Hub of the Northwest."
Name origin: Named by Northern Pacific Railroad officials for William Fargo (1818–81), the founder of Wells-Fargo Express Co. Previously called The Crossing, Tent City, and Centralia.

*Fargo
Township
Lat: 46-56-20 N **Long:** 96-47-39 W
Pop: 0 (1990); 10 (1980)
Land: 0.2 sq. mi.; **Water:** 0.0 sq. mi.

Frontier
City
Lat: 46-48-01 N **Long:** 96-49-58 W
Pop: 218 (1990); 160 (1980) **Pop Density:** 1090.0
Land: 0.2 sq. mi.; **Water:** 0.0 sq. mi.

Gardner
City
ZIP: 58036 **Lat:** 47-08-36 N **Long:** 96-58-07 W
Pop: 85 (1990); 94 (1980) **Pop Density:** 170.0
Land: 0.5 sq. mi.; **Water:** 0.0 sq. mi. **Elev:** 887 ft.
Not coextensive with township.

*Gardner
Township
ZIP: 58036 **Lat:** 47-06-04 N **Long:** 97-00-59 W
Pop: 115 (1990); 114 (1980) **Pop Density:** 3.2
Land: 35.6 sq. mi.; **Water:** 0.0 sq. mi.

American Places Dictionary   NORTH DAKOTA, Cass County

Gill
Township
Lat: 46-50-55 N   **Long:** 97-21-38 W
Pop: 115 (1990); 114 (1980)   **Pop Density:** 3.2
Land: 36.1 sq. mi.; **Water:** 0.0 sq. mi.

Grandin
City
ZIP: 58038   **Lat:** 47-14-09 N   **Long:** 97-00-08 W
Pop: 213 (1990); 210 (1980)   **Pop Density:** 2130.0
Land: 0.1 sq. mi.; **Water:** 0.0 sq. mi.   **Elev:** 892 ft.
Part of the town is also in Traill County.

Gunkel
Township
Lat: 47-06-56 N   **Long:** 97-07-33 W
Pop: 72 (1990); 93 (1980)   **Pop Density:** 2.0
Land: 36.2 sq. mi.; **Water:** 0.0 sq. mi.

Harmony
Township
Lat: 46-55-56 N   **Long:** 97-07-25 W
Pop: 93 (1990); 110 (1980)   **Pop Density:** 2.7
Land: 34.5 sq. mi.; **Water:** 0.0 sq. mi.

Harwood
City
ZIP: 58042   **Lat:** 46-58-48 N   **Long:** 96-52-47 W
Pop: 590 (1990); 326 (1980)   **Pop Density:** 655.6
Land: 0.9 sq. mi.; **Water:** 0.0 sq. mi.   **Elev:** 889 ft.
Not coextensive with township.
Name origin: For Fargo real estate agent, A.J. Harwood, who invested heavily in the region.

*Harwood
Township
ZIP: 58042   **Lat:** 47-01-12 N   **Long:** 96-52-49 W
Pop: 322 (1990); 530 (1980)   **Pop Density:** 10.4
Land: 31.0 sq. mi.; **Water:** 0.0 sq. mi.

Highland
Township
Lat: 46-40-32 N   **Long:** 97-29-19 W
Pop: 144 (1990); 130 (1980)   **Pop Density:** 4.0
Land: 35.7 sq. mi.; **Water:** 0.2 sq. mi.

Hill
Township
Lat: 46-50-47 N   **Long:** 97-36-50 W
Pop: 64 (1990); 76 (1980)   **Pop Density:** 1.8
Land: 35.9 sq. mi.; **Water:** 0.0 sq. mi.

Horace
City
ZIP: 58047   **Lat:** 46-45-26 N   **Long:** 96-54-14 W
Pop: 662 (1990); 494 (1980)   **Pop Density:** 2206.7
Land: 0.3 sq. mi.; **Water:** 0.0 sq. mi.   **Elev:** 915 ft.

Howes
Township
Lat: 46-50-58 N   **Long:** 97-29-51 W
Pop: 99 (1990); 98 (1980)   **Pop Density:** 2.8
Land: 35.7 sq. mi.; **Water:** 0.1 sq. mi.

Hunter
City
ZIP: 58048   **Lat:** 47-11-31 N   **Long:** 97-12-58 W
Pop: 341 (1990); 369 (1980)   **Pop Density:** 189.4
Land: 1.8 sq. mi.; **Water:** 0.0 sq. mi.   **Elev:** 978 ft.
Not coextensive with township.
Name origin: For landowner John C. Hunter.

*Hunter
Township
ZIP: 58048   **Lat:** 47-11-40 N   **Long:** 97-15-50 W
Pop: 95 (1990); 117 (1980)   **Pop Density:** 2.8
Land: 34.1 sq. mi.; **Water:** 0.1 sq. mi.

Kindred
City
ZIP: 58051   **Lat:** 46-39-03 N   **Long:** 97-01-15 W
Pop: 569 (1990); 568 (1980)   **Pop Density:** 569.0
Land: 1.0 sq. mi.; **Water:** 0.0 sq. mi.   **Elev:** 942 ft.

Kinyon
Township
Lat: 47-11-43 N   **Long:** 97-00-20 W
Pop: 100 (1990); 119 (1980)   **Pop Density:** 2.8
Land: 35.9 sq. mi.; **Water:** 0.0 sq. mi.

Lake
Township
Lat: 47-06-40 N   **Long:** 97-38-42 W
Pop: 59 (1990); 62 (1980)   **Pop Density:** 1.6
Land: 36.0 sq. mi.; **Water:** 0.1 sq. mi.

Leonard
City
ZIP: 58052   **Lat:** 46-39-04 N   **Long:** 97-14-43 W
Pop: 310 (1990); 289 (1980)   **Pop Density:** 620.0
Land: 0.5 sq. mi.; **Water:** 0.0 sq. mi.   **Elev:** 1050 ft.
Not coextensive with township.
Name origin: For pioneer settler Leonard Stroble.

*Leonard
Township
ZIP: 58052   **Lat:** 46-40-29 N   **Long:** 97-14-34 W
Pop: 121 (1990); 142 (1980)   **Pop Density:** 3.4
Land: 35.5 sq. mi.; **Water:** 0.0 sq. mi.

Maple River
Township
Lat: 46-45-38 N   **Long:** 97-14-21 W
Pop: 125 (1990); 155 (1980)   **Pop Density:** 3.5
Land: 35.8 sq. mi.; **Water:** 0.0 sq. mi.

Mapleton
City
ZIP: 58059   **Lat:** 46-53-26 N   **Long:** 97-03-12 W
Pop: 682 (1990); 306 (1980)   **Pop Density:** 170.5
Land: 4.0 sq. mi.; **Water:** 0.0 sq. mi.   **Elev:** 908 ft.
Founded 1876.
Name origin: For its location on the Maple River, which traverses the southern portion of the county.

*Mapleton
Township
ZIP: 58059   **Lat:** 46-51-10 N   **Long:** 96-59-46 W
Pop: 269 (1990); 244 (1980)   **Pop Density:** 7.8
Land: 34.7 sq. mi.; **Water:** 0.0 sq. mi.

Noble
Township
Lat: 47-11-40 N   **Long:** 96-53-02 W
Pop: 99 (1990); 107 (1980)   **Pop Density:** 3.2
Land: 31.4 sq. mi.; **Water:** 0.0 sq. mi.

Normanna
Township
Lat: 46-40-51 N   **Long:** 96-58-43 W
Pop: 340 (1990); 331 (1980)   **Pop Density:** 9.7
Land: 35.0 sq. mi.; **Water:** 0.0 sq. mi.

North River
City
Lat: 46-56-57 N   **Long:** 96-48-07 W
Pop: 68 (1990); 65 (1980)   **Pop Density:** 680.0
Land: 0.1 sq. mi.; **Water:** 0.0 sq. mi.

Oxbow
City
Lat: 46-40-14 N   **Long:** 96-48-05 W
Pop: 100 (1990)   **Pop Density:** 250.0
Land: 0.4 sq. mi.; **Water:** 0.0 sq. mi.

Page
City
ZIP: 58064   **Lat:** 47-09-28 N   **Long:** 97-34-14 W
Pop: 266 (1990); 329 (1980)   **Pop Density:** 1330.0
Land: 0.2 sq. mi.; **Water:** 0.0 sq. mi.   **Elev:** 1175 ft.
Not coextensive with township.
Name origin: For E.E. Page, brother-in-law of major landowner Col. M.B. Morton.

NORTH DAKOTA, Cass County

*Page
Township
ZIP: 58064 **Lat:** 47-11-53 N **Long:** 97-31-29 W
Pop: 59 (1990); 78 (1980) **Pop Density:** 1.6
Land: 35.8 sq. mi.; **Water:** 0.0 sq. mi.

Pleasant
Township
Lat: 46-40-51 N **Long:** 96-51-51 W
Pop: 354 (1990); 398 (1980) **Pop Density:** 9.3
Land: 37.9 sq. mi.; **Water:** 0.0 sq. mi.

Pontiac
Township
Lat: 46-39-49 N **Long:** 97-37-32 W
Pop: 108 (1990); 140 (1980) **Pop Density:** 3.1
Land: 35.2 sq. mi.; **Water:** 0.8 sq. mi.

Prairie Rose
City
Lat: 46-49-02 N **Long:** 96-50-03 W
Pop: 49 (1990); 76 (1980) **Pop Density:** 490.0
Land: 0.1 sq. mi.; **Water:** 0.0 sq. mi.

Raymond
Township
Lat: 46-56-07 N **Long:** 96-59-17 W
Pop: 284 (1990); 255 (1980) **Pop Density:** 8.3
Land: 34.4 sq. mi.; **Water:** 0.1 sq. mi.

Reed
Township
Lat: 46-56-30 N **Long:** 96-52-18 W
Pop: 1,046 (1990); 848 (1980) **Pop Density:** 37.9
Land: 27.6 sq. mi.; **Water:** 0.1 sq. mi.

Reile's Acres
City
Lat: 46-55-21 N **Long:** 96-51-44 W
Pop: 210 (1990); 191 (1980) **Pop Density:** 1050.0
Land: 0.2 sq. mi.; **Water:** 0.0 sq. mi.

Rich
Township
Lat: 47-06-28 N **Long:** 97-31-17 W
Pop: 81 (1990); 108 (1980) **Pop Density:** 2.2
Land: 36.1 sq. mi.; **Water:** 0.0 sq. mi.

Rochester
Township
Lat: 47-11-19 N **Long:** 97-38-05 W
Pop: 46 (1990); 76 (1980) **Pop Density:** 1.3
Land: 36.1 sq. mi.; **Water:** 0.0 sq. mi.

Rush River
Township
Lat: 47-01-25 N **Long:** 97-07-20 W
Pop: 107 (1990); 141 (1980) **Pop Density:** 2.9
Land: 36.4 sq. mi.; **Water:** 0.0 sq. mi.

Stanley
Township
Lat: 46-45-11 N **Long:** 96-51-03 W
Pop: 1,933 (1990); 1,706 (1980) **Pop Density:** 50.1
Land: 38.6 sq. mi.; **Water:** 0.0 sq. mi.

Tower
Township
Lat: 46-55-42 N **Long:** 97-36-46 W
Pop: 66 (1990); 69 (1980) **Pop Density:** 1.9
Land: 34.5 sq. mi.; **Water:** 0.0 sq. mi.

Tower City
City
ZIP: 58071 **Lat:** 46-55-37 N **Long:** 97-40-22 W
Pop: 233 (1990); 293 (1980) **Pop Density:** 155.3
Land: 1.5 sq. mi.; **Water:** 0.0 sq. mi. **Elev:** 1172 ft.
Part of the town is also in Barnes County.

Walburg
Township
Lat: 46-45-53 N **Long:** 97-22-13 W
Pop: 189 (1990); 206 (1980) **Pop Density:** 5.2
Land: 36.1 sq. mi.; **Water:** 0.0 sq. mi.

Warren
Township
ZIP: 58021 **Lat:** 46-45-13 N **Long:** 96-58-43 W
Pop: 133 (1990); 158 (1980) **Pop Density:** 3.7
Land: 36.1 sq. mi.; **Water:** 0.0 sq. mi.

Watson
Township
Lat: 46-40-23 N **Long:** 97-21-58 W
Pop: 123 (1990); 138 (1980) **Pop Density:** 3.4
Land: 36.0 sq. mi.; **Water:** 0.0 sq. mi.

West Fargo
City
ZIP: 58078 **Lat:** 46-52-22 N **Long:** 96-53-49 W
Pop: 12,287 (1990); 10,099 (1980) **Pop Density:** 1730.6
Land: 7.1 sq. mi.; **Water:** 0.0 sq. mi. **Elev:** 900 ft.
Incorporated 1947.
Name origin: For its location in relation to Fargo. Originally called Haggart.

Wheatland
Township
ZIP: 58079 **Lat:** 46-56-00 N **Long:** 97-21-32 W
Pop: 153 (1990); 183 (1980) **Pop Density:** 4.2
Land: 36.2 sq. mi.; **Water:** 0.0 sq. mi.

Wiser
Township
Lat: 47-06-26 N **Long:** 96-53-21 W
Pop: 93 (1990); 94 (1980) **Pop Density:** 2.8
Land: 33.8 sq. mi.; **Water:** 0.0 sq. mi.

Cavalier County
County Seat: Langdon (ZIP: 58249)

Pop: 6,064 (1990); 7,636 (1980) **Pop Density:** 4.1
Land: 1489.1 sq. mi.; **Water:** 21.1 sq. mi. **Area Code:** 701
On the northeastern border of ND, northwest of Grand Forks; organized Jan 4, 1873 (prior to statehood) from Pembina County.
Name origin: For either Charles T. Cavileer (1818–1902), an early white settler and public official (with the spelling changed to seem French); or Rene Robert Cavalier, Sieur de la Salle (1643–87), the explorer.

Alma
Township
Lat: 48-40-27 N **Long:** 98-07-26 W
Pop: 62 (1990); 70 (1980) **Pop Density:** 1.7
Land: 35.7 sq. mi.; **Water:** 0.1 sq. mi.

Alsen
City
ZIP: 58311 **Lat:** 48-37-46 N **Long:** 98-42-19 W
Pop: 113 (1990); 169 (1980) **Pop Density:** 3.9
Land: 29.3 sq. mi.; **Water:** 0.5 sq. mi. **Elev:** 1580 ft.
Incorporated 1967.

American Places Dictionary NORTH DAKOTA, Cavalier County

Banner
Township
Lat: 48-34-40 N Long: 98-46-52 W
Pop: 58 (1990); 70 (1980) Pop Density: 2.0
Land: 29.0 sq. mi.; Water: 0.8 sq. mi.

Billings
Township
Lat: 48-34-47 N Long: 98-31-02 W
Pop: 37 (1990); 122 (1980) Pop Density: 1.3
Land: 28.3 sq. mi.; Water: 0.3 sq. mi.

Bruce
Township
Lat: 48-46-04 N Long: 98-55-37 W
Pop: 56 (1990); 60 (1980) Pop Density: 1.6
Land: 35.3 sq. mi.; Water: 0.8 sq. mi.

Byron
Township
Lat: 48-56-07 N Long: 98-48-48 W
Pop: 46 (1990); 74 (1980) Pop Density: 1.0
Land: 44.4 sq. mi.; Water: 0.5 sq. mi.

Calio
City
ZIP: 58322 Lat: 48-37-24 N Long: 98-56-16 W
Pop: 43 (1990); 60 (1980) Pop Density: 5.2
Land: 8.2 sq. mi.; Water: 0.7 sq. mi. Elev: 1540 ft.

Calvin
City
ZIP: 58323 Lat: 48-51-04 N Long: 98-56-13 W
Pop: 27 (1990); 61 (1980) Pop Density: 135.0
Land: 0.2 sq. mi.; Water: 0.0 sq. mi. Elev: 1617 ft.

Cypress
Township
Lat: 48-56-22 N Long: 98-56-17 W
Pop: 89 (1990); 96 (1980) Pop Density: 2.0
Land: 44.4 sq. mi.; Water: 0.0 sq. mi.

Dresden
Township
Lat: 48-56-14 N Long: 98-32-19 W
Pop: 74 (1990); 93 (1980) Pop Density: 1.7
Land: 44.0 sq. mi.; Water: 0.7 sq. mi.

Easby
Township
Lat: 48-40-30 N Long: 98-15-06 W
Pop: 48 (1990); 96 (1980) Pop Density: 1.3
Land: 35.7 sq. mi.; Water: 0.2 sq. mi.

East Alma
Township
Lat: 48-40-25 N Long: 97-59-36 W
Pop: 35 (1990); 70 (1980) Pop Density: 1.0
Land: 35.9 sq. mi.; Water: 0.0 sq. mi.

Elgin
Township
Lat: 48-45-46 N Long: 98-24-18 W
Pop: 310 (1990); 413 (1980) Pop Density: 9.1
Land: 34.2 sq. mi.; Water: 0.3 sq. mi.

Fremont
Township
Lat: 48-57-06 N Long: 98-02-16 W
Pop: 110 (1990); 119 (1980) Pop Density: 2.0
Land: 55.4 sq. mi.; Water: 0.1 sq. mi.

Glenila
Township
Lat: 48-50-53 N Long: 98-55-58 W
Pop: 34 (1990); 61 (1980) Pop Density: 0.9
Land: 35.9 sq. mi.; Water: 0.1 sq. mi.

Gordon
Township
Lat: 48-40-40 N Long: 98-38-13 W
Pop: 31 (1990); 67 (1980) Pop Density: 1.2
Land: 26.7 sq. mi.; Water: 0.4 sq. mi.

Grey
Township
Lat: 48-51-10 N Long: 98-48-03 W
Pop: 46 (1990); 82 (1980) Pop Density: 1.3
Land: 35.5 sq. mi.; Water: 0.6 sq. mi.

Hannah
City
ZIP: 58239 Lat: 48-58-23 N Long: 98-41-24 W
Pop: 49 (1990); 90 (1980) Pop Density: 245.0
Land: 0.2 sq. mi.; Water: 0.0 sq. mi. Elev: 1650 ft.

Harvey
Township
Lat: 48-50-53 N Long: 98-16-39 W
Pop: 79 (1990); 85 (1980) Pop Density: 2.2
Land: 35.8 sq. mi.; Water: 0.1 sq. mi.

Hay
Township
Lat: 48-45-38 N Long: 98-08-43 W
Pop: 67 (1990); 89 (1980) Pop Density: 1.9
Land: 35.9 sq. mi.; Water: 0.1 sq. mi.

Henderson
Township
Lat: 48-41-01 N Long: 98-46-49 W
Pop: 63 (1990); 109 (1980) Pop Density: 2.2
Land: 28.1 sq. mi.; Water: 1.2 sq. mi.

Hope
Township
Lat: 48-55-44 N Long: 98-09-51 W
Pop: 63 (1990); 92 (1980) Pop Density: 2.1
Land: 29.6 sq. mi.; Water: 0.1 sq. mi.

Huron
Township
Lat: 48-45-48 N Long: 98-47-30 W
Pop: 48 (1990); 79 (1980) Pop Density: 1.3
Land: 35.7 sq. mi.; Water: 0.4 sq. mi.

Langdon
City
ZIP: 58249 Lat: 48-45-45 N Long: 98-22-22 W
Pop: 2,241 (1990); 2,335 (1980) Pop Density: 1318.2
Land: 1.7 sq. mi.; Water: 0.0 sq. mi. Elev: 1617 ft.

*Langdon
Township
ZIP: 58249 Lat: 48-50-53 N Long: 98-24-33 W
Pop: 54 (1990); 62 (1980) Pop Density: 1.5
Land: 35.9 sq. mi.; Water: 0.2 sq. mi.

Linden
Township
Lat: 48-57-03 N Long: 98-40-07 W
Pop: 46 (1990); 65 (1980) Pop Density: 1.1
Land: 42.6 sq. mi.; Water: 1.8 sq. mi.

Loam
Township
Lat: 48-51-04 N Long: 98-09-24 W
Pop: 58 (1990); 97 (1980) Pop Density: 1.7
Land: 33.4 sq. mi.; Water: 0.1 sq. mi.

Loma
City
ZIP: 58311 Lat: 48-38-16 N Long: 98-31-30 W
Pop: 27 (1990); 39 (1980) Pop Density: 1.0
Land: 26.4 sq. mi.; Water: 0.4 sq. mi. Elev: 1568 ft.

Manilla
Township
Lat: 48-45-13 N Long: 98-16-37 W
Pop: 172 (1990); 183 (1980) Pop Density: 4.8
Land: 35.7 sq. mi.; Water: 0.3 sq. mi.

Milton
City
ZIP: 58260 Lat: 48-37-37 N Long: 98-02-37 W
Pop: 133 (1990); 195 (1980) Pop Density: 332.5
Land: 0.4 sq. mi.; Water: 0.0 sq. mi. Elev: 1586 ft.

NORTH DAKOTA, Cavalier County

Minto
Township
Lat: 48-50-48 N Long: 98-40-56 W
Pop: 45 (1990); 68 (1980) Pop Density: 1.3
Land: 35.0 sq. mi.; Water: 0.8 sq. mi.

Montrose
Township
Lat: 48-35-37 N Long: 97-59-13 W
Pop: 75 (1990); 121 (1980) Pop Density: 2.1
Land: 35.4 sq. mi.; Water: 0.1 sq. mi.

Moscow
Township
ZIP: 58311 Lat: 48-45-32 N Long: 98-40-22 W
Pop: 46 (1990); 84 (1980) Pop Density: 1.3
Land: 35.0 sq. mi.; Water: 1.0 sq. mi.

Mount Carmel
Township
Lat: 48-56-32 N Long: 98-23-51 W
Pop: 104 (1990); 164 (1980) Pop Density: 2.3
Land: 44.3 sq. mi.; Water: 0.7 sq. mi.

Munich
City
ZIP: 58352 Lat: 48-40-08 N Long: 98-49-56 W
Pop: 310 (1990); 300 (1980) Pop Density: 516.7
Land: 0.6 sq. mi.; Water: 0.0 sq. mi. Elev: 1595 ft.
Name origin: Named by founder William Budge for Munich, Germany.

Nekoma
City
ZIP: 58355 Lat: 48-34-33 N Long: 98-22-34 W
Pop: 63 (1990); 102 (1980) Pop Density: 157.5
Land: 0.4 sq. mi.; Water: 0.0 sq. mi. Elev: 1630 ft.
Not coextensive with township.

*Nekoma
Township
Lat: 48-35-34 N Long: 98-22-46 W
Pop: 53 (1990); 90 (1980) Pop Density: 1.5
Land: 35.1 sq. mi.; Water: 0.5 sq. mi.

North Loma
Township
Lat: 48-41-44 N Long: 98-30-13 W
Pop: 34 (1990); 33 (1980) Pop Density: 1.9
Land: 18.1 sq. mi.; Water: 0.1 sq. mi.

North Olga
Township
Lat: 48-51-23 N Long: 98-01-40 W
Pop: 75 (1990); 100 (1980) Pop Density: 1.8
Land: 42.1 sq. mi.; Water: 0.0 sq. mi.

Osford
Township
Lat: 48-35-08 N Long: 98-07-01 W
Pop: 55 (1990); 89 (1980) Pop Density: 1.5
Land: 35.8 sq. mi.; Water: 0.0 sq. mi.

Osnabrock
City
ZIP: 58269 Lat: 48-40-12 N Long: 98-08-56 W
Pop: 214 (1990); 222 (1980) Pop Density: 713.3
Land: 0.3 sq. mi.; Water: 0.0 sq. mi. Elev: 1615 ft.
Not coextensive with township.

*Osnabrock
Township
ZIP: 58269 Lat: 48-35-39 N Long: 98-15-00 W
Pop: 53 (1990); 87 (1980) Pop Density: 1.5
Land: 35.5 sq. mi.; Water: 0.4 sq. mi.

Perry
Township
Lat: 48-40-44 N Long: 98-22-37 W
Pop: 72 (1990); 105 (1980) Pop Density: 2.0
Land: 35.8 sq. mi.; Water: 0.2 sq. mi.

Sarles
City
ZIP: 58372 Lat: 48-56-42 N Long: 98-59-42 W
Pop: 83 (1990); 102 (1980) Pop Density: 415.0
Land: 0.2 sq. mi.; Water: 0.0 sq. mi. Elev: 1588 ft.
Part of the town is also in Towner County.

Seivert
Township
Lat: 48-34-59 N Long: 98-54-05 W
Pop: 31 (1990); 53 (1980) Pop Density: 1.1
Land: 28.0 sq. mi.; Water: 1.9 sq. mi.

South Dresden
Township
Lat: 48-50-46 N Long: 98-31-58 W
Pop: 67 (1990); 107 (1980) Pop Density: 1.9
Land: 35.4 sq. mi.; Water: 0.5 sq. mi.

South Olga
Township
Lat: 48-45-36 N Long: 98-01-05 W
Pop: 77 (1990); 99 (1980) Pop Density: 2.1
Land: 36.4 sq. mi.; Water: 0.1 sq. mi.

Storlie
Township
Lat: 48-34-42 N Long: 98-38-04 W
Pop: 30 (1990); 39 (1980) Pop Density: 1.2
Land: 25.1 sq. mi.; Water: 0.3 sq. mi.

Trier
Township
Lat: 48-40-31 N Long: 98-54-05 W
Pop: 67 (1990); 119 (1980) Pop Density: 2.2
Land: 31.1 sq. mi.; Water: 1.9 sq. mi.

Wales
City
ZIP: 58281 Lat: 48-53-38 N Long: 98-36-04 W
Pop: 48 (1990); 74 (1980) Pop Density: 240.0
Land: 0.2 sq. mi.; Water: 0.0 sq. mi. Elev: 1565 ft.

Waterloo
Township
Lat: 48-46-06 N Long: 98-32-44 W
Pop: 65 (1990); 65 (1980) Pop Density: 1.8
Land: 35.4 sq. mi.; Water: 0.6 sq. mi.

West Hope
Township
Lat: 48-56-32 N Long: 98-16-38 W
Pop: 78 (1990); 107 (1980) Pop Density: 1.8
Land: 44.4 sq. mi.; Water: 0.6 sq. mi.

American Places Dictionary   NORTH DAKOTA, Dickey County

Dickey County
County Seat: Ellendale (ZIP: 58436)

Pop: 6,107 (1990); 7,207 (1980)   **Pop Density:** 5.4
Land: 1131.1 sq. mi.; **Water:** 10.7 sq. mi.   **Area Code:** 701
On the southern border of ND, southwest of Fargo; organized Mar 5, 1881 (prior to statehood) from La Moure County.
Name origin: For either Alfred M. Dickey (1846–1901), a homesteader in the county and lt. governor of ND (1889–90), or for George H. Dickey (1858–1923), an attorney and ND legislator.

Ada   Township
Lat: 45-59-13 N   Long: 98-19-44 W
Pop: 54 (1990); 101 (1980)   **Pop Density:** 1.5
Land: 35.9 sq. mi.; **Water:** 0.0 sq. mi.

Albertha   Township
Lat: 45-58-48 N   Long: 98-56-24 W
Pop: 33 (1990); 42 (1980)   **Pop Density:** 1.0
Land: 33.5 sq. mi.; **Water:** 2.3 sq. mi.

Albion   Township
Lat: 46-04-21 N   Long: 98-41-50 W
Pop: 59 (1990); 61 (1980)   **Pop Density:** 1.6
Land: 36.1 sq. mi.; **Water:** 0.1 sq. mi.

Bear Creek   Township
Lat: 46-09-17 N   Long: 98-03-18 W
Pop: 181 (1990); 208 (1980)   **Pop Density:** 6.0
Land: 30.0 sq. mi.; **Water:** 0.1 sq. mi.

Clement   Township
Lat: 46-09-37 N   Long: 98-10-59 W
Pop: 126 (1990); 172 (1980)   **Pop Density:** 2.8
Land: 45.1 sq. mi.; **Water:** 0.4 sq. mi.

Divide   Township
Lat: 46-13-49 N   Long: 98-03-41 W
Pop: 81 (1990); 108 (1980)   **Pop Density:** 2.3
Land: 35.2 sq. mi.; **Water:** 0.2 sq. mi.

Elden   Township
Lat: 46-04-04 N   Long: 98-34-09 W
Pop: 79 (1990); 108 (1980)   **Pop Density:** 2.2
Land: 36.1 sq. mi.; **Water:** 0.0 sq. mi.

Ellendale   City
ZIP: 58436   Lat: 46-00-14 N   Long: 98-31-29 W
Pop: 1,798 (1990); 1,967 (1980)   **Pop Density:** 1383.1
Land: 1.3 sq. mi.; **Water:** 0.0 sq. mi.   **Elev:** 1456 ft.
Not coextensive with township.
Name origin: For Mary Ellen Dale Merrill, the wife of the local railroad superintendent.

*Ellendale   Township
ZIP: 58436   Lat: 45-58-54 N   Long: 98-33-55 W
Pop: 136 (1990); 163 (1980)   **Pop Density:** 3.9
Land: 34.6 sq. mi.; **Water:** 0.1 sq. mi.

Elm   Township
Lat: 45-58-56 N   Long: 98-42-12 W
Pop: 76 (1990); 88 (1980)   **Pop Density:** 2.1
Land: 35.9 sq. mi.; **Water:** 0.3 sq. mi.

Forbes   City
ZIP: 58439   Lat: 45-56-31 N   Long: 98-46-57 W
Pop: 56 (1990); 84 (1980)   **Pop Density:** 280.0
Land: 0.2 sq. mi.; **Water:** 0.0 sq. mi.   **Elev:** 1560 ft.

Fullerton   City
ZIP: 58441   Lat: 46-09-49 N   Long: 98-25-32 W
Pop: 94 (1990); 107 (1980)   **Pop Density:** 235.0
Land: 0.4 sq. mi.; **Water:** 0.0 sq. mi.   **Elev:** 1455 ft.
Name origin: Named by Edwin F. Sweet for Philo Case Fuller, his wife's grandfather and a former Congressman.

German   Township
Lat: 46-09-04 N   Long: 98-56-20 W
Pop: 46 (1990); 46 (1980)   **Pop Density:** 1.4
Land: 34.0 sq. mi.; **Water:** 1.5 sq. mi.

Grand Valley   Township
Lat: 46-04-08 N   Long: 98-49-06 W
Pop: 38 (1990); 55 (1980)   **Pop Density:** 1.1
Land: 36.1 sq. mi.; **Water:** 0.2 sq. mi.

Hamburg   Township
Lat: 46-09-40 N   Long: 98-41-36 W
Pop: 27 (1990); 59 (1980)   **Pop Density:** 0.7
Land: 36.2 sq. mi.; **Water:** 0.1 sq. mi.

Hudson   Township
Lat: 46-04-24 N   Long: 98-11-37 W
Pop: 97 (1990); 108 (1980)   **Pop Density:** 2.9
Land: 33.9 sq. mi.; **Water:** 0.3 sq. mi.

James River Valley   Township
Lat: 46-14-51 N   Long: 98-10-58 W
Pop: 50 (1990); 90 (1980)   **Pop Density:** 1.7
Land: 28.8 sq. mi.; **Water:** 0.0 sq. mi.

Kent   Township
Lat: 46-04-24 N   Long: 98-19-21 W
Pop: 34 (1990); 46 (1980)   **Pop Density:** 0.9
Land: 35.9 sq. mi.; **Water:** 0.0 sq. mi.

Kentner   Township
Lat: 46-03-35 N   Long: 98-26-33 W
Pop: 150 (1990); 156 (1980)   **Pop Density:** 4.1
Land: 36.2 sq. mi.; **Water:** 0.0 sq. mi.

Keystone   Township
Lat: 46-08-52 N   Long: 98-33-50 W
Pop: 51 (1990); 69 (1980)   **Pop Density:** 1.4
Land: 35.9 sq. mi.; **Water:** 0.0 sq. mi.

Lorraine   Township
Lat: 45-58-54 N   Long: 98-49-18 W
Pop: 70 (1990); 76 (1980)   **Pop Density:** 2.0
Land: 35.5 sq. mi.; **Water:** 0.0 sq. mi.

Lovell   Township
Lat: 45-58-46 N   Long: 98-04-49 W
Pop: 69 (1990); 66 (1980)   **Pop Density:** 1.6
Land: 43.4 sq. mi.; **Water:** 0.5 sq. mi.

NORTH DAKOTA, Dickey County

Ludden City
Lat: 46-00-28 N Long: 98-07-29 W
Pop: 41 (1990); 47 (1980) Pop Density: 51.3
Land: 0.8 sq. mi.; Water: 0.0 sq. mi. Elev: 1301 ft.

Maple Township
ZIP: 58441 Lat: 46-09-25 N Long: 98-25-57 W
Pop: 75 (1990); 90 (1980) Pop Density: 2.1
Land: 35.9 sq. mi.; Water: 0.0 sq. mi.

Merricourt City
ZIP: 58469 Lat: 46-12-28 N Long: 98-45-40 W
Pop: 9 (1990); 17 (1980) Pop Density: 90.0
Land: 0.1 sq. mi.; Water: 0.0 sq. mi. Elev: 1644 ft.

Monango City
ZIP: 58471 Lat: 46-10-21 N Long: 98-35-42 W
Pop: 53 (1990); 59 (1980) Pop Density: 132.5
Land: 0.4 sq. mi.; Water: 0.0 sq. mi. Elev: 1509 ft.

Northwest Township
Lat: 46-14-33 N Long: 98-56-16 W
Pop: 37 (1990); 52 (1980) Pop Density: 1.1
Land: 32.6 sq. mi.; Water: 0.5 sq. mi.

Oakes City
ZIP: 58474 Lat: 46-08-21 N Long: 98-05-10 W
Pop: 1,775 (1990); 2,112 (1980) Pop Density: 1109.4
Land: 1.6 sq. mi.; Water: 0.0 sq. mi. Elev: 1313 ft.
Name origin: For Northern Pacific Railway manager Thomas Oakes.

Port Emma Township
Lat: 45-58-47 N Long: 98-12-49 W
Pop: 62 (1990); 96 (1980) Pop Density: 2.3
Land: 26.5 sq. mi.; Water: 0.5 sq. mi.

Porter Township
Lat: 46-14-27 N Long: 98-25-45 W
Pop: 66 (1990); 78 (1980) Pop Density: 1.9
Land: 35.2 sq. mi.; Water: 0.3 sq. mi.

Potsdam Township
Lat: 46-14-46 N Long: 98-42-00 W
Pop: 59 (1990); 55 (1980) Pop Density: 1.7
Land: 34.5 sq. mi.; Water: 0.0 sq. mi.

Riverdale Township
Lat: 46-03-32 N Long: 98-04-48 W
Pop: 87 (1990); 116 (1980) Pop Density: 2.3
Land: 37.1 sq. mi.; Water: 0.3 sq. mi.

Spring Valley Township
Lat: 46-04-46 N Long: 98-56-18 W
Pop: 31 (1990); 49 (1980) Pop Density: 0.9
Land: 33.2 sq. mi.; Water: 2.3 sq. mi.

Valley Township
Lat: 46-14-25 N Long: 98-33-58 W
Pop: 68 (1990); 72 (1980) Pop Density: 1.9
Land: 35.3 sq. mi.; Water: 0.0 sq. mi.

Van Meter Township
Lat: 45-58-31 N Long: 98-26-22 W
Pop: 119 (1990); 121 (1980) Pop Density: 3.3
Land: 36.0 sq. mi.; Water: 0.0 sq. mi.

Whitestone Township
Lat: 46-09-31 N Long: 98-48-57 W
Pop: 40 (1990); 46 (1980) Pop Density: 1.1
Land: 36.1 sq. mi.; Water: 0.4 sq. mi.

Wright Township
Lat: 46-13-59 N Long: 98-18-17 W
Pop: 92 (1990); 102 (1980) Pop Density: 2.6
Land: 35.3 sq. mi.; Water: 0.2 sq. mi.

Yorktown Township
Lat: 46-09-12 N Long: 98-19-05 W
Pop: 48 (1990); 69 (1980) Pop Density: 1.3
Land: 35.8 sq. mi.; Water: 0.0 sq. mi.

Young Township
Lat: 46-14-44 N Long: 98-49-42 W
Pop: 40 (1990); 46 (1980) Pop Density: 1.2
Land: 34.2 sq. mi.; Water: 0.1 sq. mi.

Divide County
County Seat: Crosby (ZIP: 58730)

Pop: 2,899 (1990); 3,494 (1980) Pop Density: 2.3
Land: 1259.4 sq. mi.; Water: 34.8 sq. mi. Area Code: 701
In the northwestern corner of ND; organized Dec 9, 1910 from Williams County.
Name origin: For the division of Williams County to form it, or possibly for the mountains that divide the county.

Alexandria Township
Lat: 48-45-15 N Long: 103-39-22 W
Pop: 27 (1990); 35 (1980) Pop Density: 0.8
Land: 35.8 sq. mi.; Water: 0.4 sq. mi.

Ambrose City
ZIP: 58833 Lat: 48-57-18 N Long: 103-28-50 W
Pop: 48 (1990); 60 (1980) Pop Density: 43.6
Land: 1.1 sq. mi.; Water: 0.0 sq. mi. Elev: 2059 ft.
Incorporated 1911.

*Ambrose Township
ZIP: 58833 Lat: 48-57-10 N Long: 103-31-32 W
Pop: 43 (1990); 57 (1980) Pop Density: 1.0
Land: 41.6 sq. mi.; Water: 0.8 sq. mi.

Blooming Prairie Township
Lat: 48-57-02 N Long: 103-24-02 W
Pop: 62 (1990); 77 (1980) Pop Density: 1.5
Land: 42.2 sq. mi.; Water: 1.2 sq. mi.

Blooming Valley
Township
Lat: 48-51-04 N **Long:** 103-08-06 W
Pop: 57 (1990); 55 (1980) **Pop Density:** 1.6
Land: 35.5 sq. mi.; **Water:** 0.5 sq. mi.

Border
Township
Lat: 48-45-23 N **Long:** 102-59-38 W
Pop: 44 (1990); 55 (1980) **Pop Density:** 1.3
Land: 35.2 sq. mi.; **Water:** 0.8 sq. mi.

Burg
Township
Lat: 48-46-00 N **Long:** 103-31-08 W
Pop: 31 (1990); 57 (1980) **Pop Density:** 0.9
Land: 35.7 sq. mi.; **Water:** 0.5 sq. mi.

Clinton
Township
Lat: 48-50-40 N **Long:** 103-47-37 W
Pop: 19 (1990); 26 (1980) **Pop Density:** 0.5
Land: 35.4 sq. mi.; **Water:** 0.6 sq. mi.

Coalfield
Township
Lat: 48-51-04 N **Long:** 103-00-21 W
Pop: 64 (1990); 65 (1980) **Pop Density:** 1.8
Land: 35.4 sq. mi.; **Water:** 0.2 sq. mi.

Crosby
City
ZIP: 58730 **Lat:** 48-54-41 N **Long:** 103-17-41 W
Pop: 1,312 (1990); 1,469 (1980) **Pop Density:** 1640.0
Land: 0.8 sq. mi.; **Water:** 0.0 sq. mi. **Elev:** 1964 ft.
Founded 1903.
Name origin: For lawyer S.A. Crosby, who platted the area and founded the town.

Daneville
Township
Lat: 48-45-36 N **Long:** 103-57-15 W
Pop: 52 (1990); 76 (1980) **Pop Density:** 1.0
Land: 50.5 sq. mi.; **Water:** 1.3 sq. mi.

De Witt
Township
Lat: 48-56-26 N **Long:** 103-47-58 W
Pop: 32 (1990); 48 (1980) **Pop Density:** 0.8
Land: 41.1 sq. mi.; **Water:** 1.2 sq. mi.

Elkhorn
Township
Lat: 48-56-43 N **Long:** 103-56-48 W
Pop: 38 (1990); 57 (1980) **Pop Density:** 0.6
Land: 59.5 sq. mi.; **Water:** 3.0 sq. mi.

Fertile Valley
Township
Lat: 48-40-51 N **Long:** 103-55-21 W
Pop: 23 (1990); 43 (1980) **Pop Density:** 0.4
Land: 64.7 sq. mi.; **Water:** 4.2 sq. mi.

Fillmore
Township
Lat: 48-56-59 N **Long:** 103-16-12 W
Pop: 46 (1990); 58 (1980) **Pop Density:** 1.1
Land: 41.2 sq. mi.; **Water:** 1.4 sq. mi.

Fortuna
City
ZIP: 58844 **Lat:** 48-54-39 N **Long:** 103-46-36 W
Pop: 53 (1990); 98 (1980) **Pop Density:** 53.0
Land: 1.0 sq. mi.; **Water:** 0.0 sq. mi. **Elev:** 2200 ft.

Frazier
Township
Lat: 48-45-50 N **Long:** 103-16-07 W
Pop: 32 (1990); 28 (1980) **Pop Density:** 0.9
Land: 35.1 sq. mi.; **Water:** 1.0 sq. mi.

Frederick
Township
Lat: 48-40-10 N **Long:** 103-21-04 W
Pop: 43 (1990); 40 (1980) **Pop Density:** 1.2
Land: 35.8 sq. mi.; **Water:** 0.1 sq. mi.

Garnet
Township
Lat: 48-41-01 N **Long:** 103-27-38 W
Pop: 28 (1990); 42 (1980) **Pop Density:** 0.8
Land: 35.5 sq. mi.; **Water:** 0.3 sq. mi.

Gooseneck
Township
Lat: 48-56-56 N **Long:** 103-39-04 W
Pop: 54 (1990); 65 (1980) **Pop Density:** 1.3
Land: 42.5 sq. mi.; **Water:** 0.8 sq. mi.

Hawkeye
Township
Lat: 48-51-14 N **Long:** 103-15-53 W
Pop: 48 (1990); 43 (1980) **Pop Density:** 1.4
Land: 35.1 sq. mi.; **Water:** 0.9 sq. mi.

Hayland
Township
Lat: 48-41-02 N **Long:** 103-04-50 W
Pop: 40 (1990); 48 (1980) **Pop Density:** 1.1
Land: 35.1 sq. mi.; **Water:** 0.9 sq. mi.

Lincoln Valley
Township
Lat: 48-51-15 N **Long:** 103-39-27 W
Pop: 39 (1990); 31 (1980) **Pop Density:** 1.1
Land: 35.3 sq. mi.; **Water:** 0.7 sq. mi.

Long Creek
Township
Lat: 48-56-57 N **Long:** 103-08-25 W
Pop: 49 (1990); 72 (1980) **Pop Density:** 1.2
Land: 42.4 sq. mi.; **Water:** 1.1 sq. mi.

Mentor
Township
Lat: 48-56-41 N **Long:** 102-59-42 W
Pop: 31 (1990); 43 (1980) **Pop Density:** 0.7
Land: 42.7 sq. mi.; **Water:** 0.6 sq. mi.

Noonan
City
ZIP: 58765 **Lat:** 48-53-25 N **Long:** 103-00-35 W
Pop: 231 (1990); 283 (1980) **Pop Density:** 770.0
Land: 0.3 sq. mi.; **Water:** 0.0 sq. mi. **Elev:** 1975 ft.

Palmer
Township
Lat: 48-40-49 N **Long:** 103-12-58 W
Pop: 17 (1990); 32 (1980) **Pop Density:** 0.5
Land: 35.2 sq. mi.; **Water:** 0.6 sq. mi.

Plumer
Township
Lat: 48-46-10 N **Long:** 103-24-00 W
Pop: 8 (1990); 15 (1980) **Pop Density:** 0.2
Land: 34.8 sq. mi.; **Water:** 1.3 sq. mi.

Sioux Trail
Township
Lat: 48-41-08 N **Long:** 103-43-54 W
Pop: 43 (1990); 60 (1980) **Pop Density:** 1.2
Land: 35.7 sq. mi.; **Water:** 0.2 sq. mi.

Smoky Butte
Township
Lat: 48-40-44 N **Long:** 103-35-54 W
Pop: 34 (1990); 44 (1980) **Pop Density:** 1.0
Land: 35.2 sq. mi.; **Water:** 0.8 sq. mi.

Stoneview
Township
Lat: 48-40-37 N **Long:** 102-57-00 W
Pop: 24 (1990); 38 (1980) **Pop Density:** 0.7
Land: 35.2 sq. mi.; **Water:** 0.5 sq. mi.

Troy
Township
Lat: 48-51-00 N **Long:** 103-23-56 W
Pop: 68 (1990); 81 (1980) **Pop Density:** 2.0
Land: 34.2 sq. mi.; **Water:** 1.7 sq. mi.

NORTH DAKOTA, Divide County   American Places Dictionary

Twin Butte Township
Lat: 48-51-22 N Long: 103-31-35 W
Pop: 33 (1990); 38 (1980)   Pop Density: 1.0
Land: 34.5 sq. mi.; Water: 1.5 sq. mi.

Westby Township
Lat: 48-51-27 N Long: 103-57-23 W
Pop: 74 (1990); 88 (1980)   Pop Density: 1.5
Land: 48.1 sq. mi.; Water: 3.7 sq. mi.

Upland Township
Lat: 48-45-51 N Long: 103-08-22 W
Pop: 31 (1990); 39 (1980)   Pop Density: 0.9
Land: 35.1 sq. mi.; Water: 1.0 sq. mi.

Writing Rock Township
Lat: 48-46-12 N Long: 103-47-36 W
Pop: 21 (1990); 28 (1980)   Pop Density: 0.6
Land: 35.2 sq. mi.; Water: 1.0 sq. mi.

Dunn County
County Seat: Manning (ZIP: 58642)

Pop: 4,005 (1990); 4,627 (1980)   Pop Density: 2.0
Land: 2010.0 sq. mi.; Water: 72.4 sq. mi.   Area Code: 701

In west-central ND, north of Dickinson; organized Mar 9, 1883 (prior to statehood) from Howard County, which was discontinued.

Name origin: For John P. Dunn (1839–1917), early settler and mayor of Bismarck, ND.

Dodge City
ZIP: 58625   Lat: 47-18-19 N Long: 102-12-07 W
Pop: 135 (1990); 199 (1980)   Pop Density: 270.0
Land: 0.5 sq. mi.; Water: 0.0 sq. mi.   Elev: 1988 ft.

Killdeer Pop. Place
Lat: 47-27-49 N Long: 102-47-23 W
Pop: 1,055 (1990); 1,206 (1980)   Pop Density: 1.1
Land: 927.3 sq. mi.; Water: 50.3 sq. mi.

Dunn Center City
ZIP: 58626   Lat: 47-21-11 N Long: 102-37-25 W
Pop: 128 (1990); 170 (1980)   Pop Density: 320.0
Land: 0.4 sq. mi.; Water: 0.0 sq. mi.   Elev: 2182 ft.

***Killdeer** City
ZIP: 58640   Lat: 47-21-55 N Long: 102-45-09 W
Pop: 722 (1990); 790 (1980)   Pop Density: 656.4
Land: 1.1 sq. mi.; Water: 0.0 sq. mi.   Elev: 2242 ft.
Name origin: For the nearby 10-mile-long Killdeer hills.

Halliday Pop. Place
Lat: 47-23-37 N Long: 102-25-45 W
Pop: 847 (1990); 1,010 (1980)   Pop Density: 1.4
Land: 585.4 sq. mi.; Water: 22.0 sq. mi.

Manning City
ZIP: 58642
Pop: 50 (1990)
                                         Elev: 2219 ft.

***Halliday** City
ZIP: 58636   Lat: 47-21-09 N Long: 102-20-14 W
Pop: 288 (1990); 355 (1980)   Pop Density: 576.0
Land: 0.5 sq. mi.; Water: 0.0 sq. mi.   Elev: 2044 ft.
Name origin: For its first postmaster, Nathan Haliday.

South Dunn Pop. Place
Lat: 47-04-57 N Long: 102-33-26 W
Pop: 830 (1990); 897 (1980)   Pop Density: 1.7
Land: 494.9 sq. mi.; Water: 0.1 sq. mi.

Eddy County
County Seat: New Rockford (ZIP: 58356)

Pop: 2,951 (1990); 3,554 (1980)   Pop Density: 4.7
Land: 632.1 sq. mi.; Water: 12.2 sq. mi.   Area Code: 701

In east-central ND, west of Grand Forks; organized Mar 9, 1885 (prior to statehood) from Foster County.

Name origin: For Ezra B. Eddy (1830–85), founder of the First National Bank of Fargo.

Bush Township
Lat: 47-47-45 N Long: 98-57-52 W
Pop: 58 (1990); 80 (1980)   Pop Density: 1.6
Land: 35.5 sq. mi.; Water: 0.7 sq. mi.

Columbia Township
Lat: 47-37-25 N Long: 98-49-31 W
Pop: 61 (1990); 70 (1980)   Pop Density: 1.7
Land: 34.9 sq. mi.; Water: 0.1 sq. mi.

Cherry Lake Township
Lat: 47-37-38 N Long: 98-42-35 W
Pop: 49 (1990); 56 (1980)   Pop Density: 1.5
Land: 33.6 sq. mi.; Water: 1.4 sq. mi.

Colvin Township
Lat: 47-42-58 N Long: 98-35-23 W
Pop: 64 (1990); 96 (1980)   Pop Density: 1.8
Land: 35.5 sq. mi.; Water: 0.5 sq. mi.

Eddy
Township
Lat: 47-48-00 N **Long:** 98-43-13 W
Pop: 46 (1990); 61 (1980) **Pop Density:** 1.3
Land: 35.9 sq. mi.; **Water:** 0.6 sq. mi.

Freeborn
Township
Lat: 47-47-32 N **Long:** 98-35-10 W
Pop: 91 (1990); 142 (1980) **Pop Density:** 2.5
Land: 36.1 sq. mi.; **Water:** 0.3 sq. mi.

Gates
Township
Lat: 47-48-46 N **Long:** 99-06-38 W
Pop: 75 (1990); 103 (1980) **Pop Density:** 2.1
Land: 35.6 sq. mi.; **Water:** 0.4 sq. mi.

Grandfield
Township
Lat: 47-48-11 N **Long:** 99-13-47 W
Pop: 56 (1990); 62 (1980) **Pop Density:** 1.6
Land: 35.8 sq. mi.; **Water:** 0.1 sq. mi.

Hillsdale
Township
Lat: 47-48-47 N **Long:** 98-50-18 W
Pop: 44 (1990); 63 (1980) **Pop Density:** 1.3
Land: 34.8 sq. mi.; **Water:** 1.6 sq. mi.

Lake Washington
Township
Lat: 47-42-43 N **Long:** 98-43-18 W
Pop: 32 (1990); 54 (1980) **Pop Density:** 1.0
Land: 32.4 sq. mi.; **Water:** 3.5 sq. mi.

Munster
Township
ZIP: 58356 **Lat:** 47-42-30 N **Long:** 99-14-12 W
Pop: 87 (1990); 88 (1980) **Pop Density:** 2.4
Land: 36.0 sq. mi.; **Water:** 0.1 sq. mi.

New Rockford
City
ZIP: 58356 **Lat:** 47-40-50 N **Long:** 99-08-08 W
Pop: 1,604 (1990); 1,791 (1980) **Pop Density:** 1233.8
Land: 1.3 sq. mi.; **Water:** 0.0 sq. mi. **Elev:** 1536 ft.
Not coextensive with township.
Name origin: Named by pioneer Charles Gregory for his former home, Rockford, IL.

*New Rockford
Township
ZIP: 58356 **Lat:** 47-43-44 N **Long:** 99-06-06 W
Pop: 88 (1990); 141 (1980) **Pop Density:** 2.5
Land: 34.6 sq. mi.; **Water:** 0.2 sq. mi.

Paradise
Township
Lat: 47-37-24 N **Long:** 98-33-50 W
Pop: 31 (1990); 71 (1980) **Pop Density:** 0.9
Land: 34.1 sq. mi.; **Water:** 1.3 sq. mi.

Pleasant Prairie
Township
Lat: 47-37-45 N **Long:** 98-56-53 W
Pop: 57 (1990); 66 (1980) **Pop Density:** 1.6
Land: 34.6 sq. mi.; **Water:** 0.3 sq. mi.

Rosefield
Township
Lat: 47-38-18 N **Long:** 99-11-28 W
Pop: 61 (1990); 58 (1980) **Pop Density:** 1.7
Land: 34.9 sq. mi.; **Water:** 0.2 sq. mi.

Sheldon
Township
Lat: 47-44-06 N **Long:** 98-58-32 W
Pop: 45 (1990); 54 (1980) **Pop Density:** 1.3
Land: 35.7 sq. mi.; **Water:** 0.3 sq. mi.

Sheyenne
City
ZIP: 58374 **Lat:** 47-49-36 N **Long:** 99-06-59 W
Pop: 272 (1990); 307 (1980) **Pop Density:** 1360.0
Land: 0.2 sq. mi.; **Water:** 0.0 sq. mi. **Elev:** 1475 ft.
Name origin: For the Sheyenne River, which traverses the northeastern portion of the state, itself named for the Cheyenne Indians. The misspelling of the river has been perpetuated in other place names within the state.

Superior
Township
Lat: 47-38-03 N **Long:** 99-04-27 W
Pop: 86 (1990); 119 (1980) **Pop Density:** 2.5
Land: 34.9 sq. mi.; **Water:** 0.3 sq. mi.

Tiffany
Township
Lat: 47-42-57 N **Long:** 98-50-43 W
Pop: 44 (1990); 72 (1980) **Pop Density:** 1.2
Land: 36.0 sq. mi.; **Water:** 0.1 sq. mi.

Emmons County
County Seat: Linton (ZIP: 58552)

Pop: 4,830 (1990); 5,877 (1980) **Pop Density:** 3.2
Land: 1510.0 sq. mi.; **Water:** 44.8 sq. mi. **Area Code:** 701
On the central southern border of ND, southeast of Bismarck; organized Feb 10, 1879 (prior to statehood) from unorganized territory.
Name origin: For James A. Emmons (1845–1919), steamboat captain, early settler, and merchant.

Braddock
City
ZIP: 58524 **Lat:** 46-33-48 N **Long:** 100-05-20 W
Pop: 56 (1990); 86 (1980) **Pop Density:** 280.0
Land: 0.2 sq. mi.; **Water:** 0.0 sq. mi. **Elev:** 1859 ft.
Incorporated 1967.

Buchanan Valley
Township
Lat: 46-35-27 N **Long:** 100-21-14 W
Pop: 44 (1990); 78 (1980) **Pop Density:** 1.2
Land: 36.2 sq. mi.; **Water:** 0.0 sq. mi.

Campbell
Township
Lat: 46-35-15 N **Long:** 99-58-44 W
Pop: 83 (1990); 119 (1980) **Pop Density:** 2.4
Land: 34.9 sq. mi.; **Water:** 1.9 sq. mi.

Danbury
Township
Lat: 46-24-58 N **Long:** 100-13-55 W
Pop: 68 (1990); 80 (1980) **Pop Density:** 1.9
Land: 36.3 sq. mi.; **Water:** 0.0 sq. mi.

NORTH DAKOTA, Emmons County   American Places Dictionary

Hague
City
ZIP: 58542   Lat: 46-01-45 N   Long: 99-59-53 W
Pop: 109 (1990); 127 (1980)   Pop Density: 363.3
Land: 0.3 sq. mi.; Water: 0.0 sq. mi.   Elev: 1900 ft.

Harding
Township
Lat: 46-04-08 N   Long: 100-03-36 W
Pop: 64 (1990); 80 (1980)   Pop Density: 1.8
Land: 34.6 sq. mi.; Water: 1.3 sq. mi.

Hazelton
City
ZIP: 58544   Lat: 46-29-03 N   Long: 100-16-42 W
Pop: 240 (1990); 266 (1980)   Pop Density: 1200.0
Land: 0.2 sq. mi.; Water: 0.0 sq. mi.   Elev: 1978 ft.
Not coextensive with township.

*Hazelton
Township
ZIP: 58544   Lat: 46-29-46 N   Long: 100-13-14 W
Pop: 83 (1990); 126 (1980)   Pop Density: 2.3
Land: 35.8 sq. mi.; Water: 0.0 sq. mi.

Lincoln
Township
Lat: 46-29-57 N   Long: 100-05-55 W
Pop: 41 (1990)   Pop Density: 1.1
Land: 36.0 sq. mi.; Water: 0.1 sq. mi.

Linton
City
ZIP: 58552   Lat: 46-16-06 N   Long: 100-13-59 W
Pop: 1,410 (1990); 1,561 (1980)   Pop Density: 2014.3
Land: 0.7 sq. mi.; Water: 0.0 sq. mi.   Elev: 1708 ft.
Established 1899.
Name origin: For George Lynn, a prominent pioneer attorney.

McCulley
Township
Lat: 46-19-49 N   Long: 100-13-45 W
Pop: 79 (1990); 96 (1980)   Pop Density: 2.2
Land: 36.4 sq. mi.; Water: 0.0 sq. mi.

North Emmons
Pop. Place
Lat: 46-35-16 N   Long: 100-09-59 W
Pop: 79 (1990)   Pop Density: 1.1
Land: 72.2 sq. mi.; Water: 0.0 sq. mi.

Northeast Emmons
Pop. Place
Lat: 46-16-59 N   Long: 100-04-54 W
Pop: 550 (1990); 845 (1980)   Pop Density: 2.2
Land: 244.9 sq. mi.; Water: 0.6 sq. mi.

Prairie View
Township
Lat: 46-24-50 N   Long: 100-21-16 W
Pop: 44 (1990); 44 (1980)   Pop Density: 1.2
Land: 36.3 sq. mi.; Water: 0.1 sq. mi.

South Emmons
Pop. Place
Lat: 46-03-56 N   Long: 100-09-36 W
Pop: 775 (1990); 989 (1980)   Pop Density: 2.0
Land: 386.1 sq. mi.; Water: 2.1 sq. mi.

Strasburg
City
ZIP: 58573   Lat: 46-07-59 N   Long: 100-09-37 W
Pop: 553 (1990); 623 (1980)   Pop Density: 1843.3
Land: 0.3 sq. mi.; Water: 0.0 sq. mi.   Elev: 1804 ft.
Founded 1902.
Name origin: For Strasburg in Europe's Rhineland, former home of early settlers.

Tell
Township
Lat: 46-30-08 N   Long: 99-59-10 W
Pop: 52 (1990); 72 (1980)   Pop Density: 1.5
Land: 35.5 sq. mi.; Water: 0.5 sq. mi.

West Emmons
Pop. Place
Lat: 46-18-15 N   Long: 100-27-45 W
Pop: 441 (1990); 616 (1980)   Pop Density: 1.0
Land: 446.4 sq. mi.; Water: 38.1 sq. mi.

Wood
Township
Lat: 46-25-26 N   Long: 99-58-49 W
Pop: 59 (1990); 69 (1980)   Pop Density: 1.6
Land: 36.4 sq. mi.; Water: 0.0 sq. mi.

Foster County
County Seat: Carrington (ZIP: 58421)

Pop: 3,983 (1990); 4,611 (1980)   Pop Density: 6.3
Land: 635.3 sq. mi.; Water: 11.5 sq. mi.   Area Code: 701
In east-central ND, southwest of Grand Forks; organized Jan 4, 1873 (prior to statehood) from Pembina County.
Name origin: For either James S. Foster, commissioner of immigration, or possibly his brother, George I. Foster. Both were prominent in Dakota territorial affairs.

Birtsell
Township
Lat: 47-32-13 N   Long: 99-11-29 W
Pop: 121 (1990); 131 (1980)   Pop Density: 3.4
Land: 35.8 sq. mi.; Water: 0.1 sq. mi.

Bordulac
Township
Lat: 47-22-10 N   Long: 98-57-02 W
Pop: 104 (1990); 120 (1980)   Pop Density: 3.1
Land: 33.9 sq. mi.; Water: 1.9 sq. mi.

Bucephalia
Township
Lat: 47-21-38 N   Long: 98-48-48 W
Pop: 63 (1990); 74 (1980)   Pop Density: 1.8
Land: 35.4 sq. mi.; Water: 0.7 sq. mi.

Carrington
City
ZIP: 58421   Lat: 47-27-00 N   Long: 99-07-24 W
Pop: 2,267 (1990); 2,641 (1980)   Pop Density: 1511.3
Land: 1.5 sq. mi.; Water: 0.0 sq. mi.   Elev: 1587 ft.
Not coextensive with township.
Name origin: For M. D. Carrington, general manager of a land company with large holdings in the area.

American Places Dictionary   NORTH DAKOTA, Golden Valley County

*Carrington   Township
ZIP: 58421   **Lat:** 47-27-25 N **Long:** 99-04-29 W
Pop: 183 (1990); 186 (1980)   **Pop Density:** 5.4
Land: 34.2 sq. mi.; **Water:** 0.3 sq. mi.

Eastman   Township
Lat: 47-22-07 N **Long:** 98-34-00 W
Pop: 39 (1990); 54 (1980)   **Pop Density:** 1.1
Land: 35.6 sq. mi.; **Water:** 0.5 sq. mi.

Estabrook   Township
Lat: 47-32-42 N **Long:** 99-04-10 W
Pop: 72 (1990); 89 (1980)   **Pop Density:** 2.0
Land: 35.9 sq. mi.; **Water:** 0.1 sq. mi.

Florance   Township
Lat: 47-32-36 N **Long:** 98-41-16 W
Pop: 89 (1990); 82 (1980)   **Pop Density:** 2.6
Land: 34.7 sq. mi.; **Water:** 1.2 sq. mi.

Glenfield   City
ZIP: 58443   **Lat:** 47-27-17 N **Long:** 98-33-58 W
Pop: 118 (1990); 164 (1980)   **Pop Density:** 1180.0
Land: 0.1 sq. mi.; **Water:** 0.0 sq. mi.   **Elev:** 1502 ft.
Not coextensive with township.

*Glenfield   Township
ZIP: 58443   **Lat:** 47-27-24 N **Long:** 98-34-08 W
Pop: 85 (1990); 114 (1980)   **Pop Density:** 2.4
Land: 35.7 sq. mi.; **Water:** 0.2 sq. mi.

Grace City   City
ZIP: 58445   **Lat:** 47-33-01 N **Long:** 98-48-14 W
Pop: 108 (1990)   **Pop Density:** 216.0
Land: 0.5 sq. mi.; **Water:** 0.0 sq. mi.   **Elev:** 1510 ft.

Haven   Township
ZIP: 58421   **Lat:** 47-26-59 N **Long:** 98-48-41 W
Pop: 50 (1990); 64 (1980)   **Pop Density:** 1.4
Land: 35.3 sq. mi.; **Water:** 0.6 sq. mi.

Larrabee   Township
Lat: 47-32-30 N **Long:** 98-49-29 W
Pop: 60 (1990); 166 (1980)   **Pop Density:** 1.7
Land: 34.7 sq. mi.; **Water:** 0.7 sq. mi.

Longview   Township
Lat: 47-21-35 N **Long:** 99-12-21 W
Pop: 56 (1990); 63 (1980)   **Pop Density:** 1.6
Land: 35.4 sq. mi.; **Water:** 0.7 sq. mi.

McHenry   City
ZIP: 58464   **Lat:** 47-34-33 N **Long:** 98-35-26 W
Pop: 85 (1990); 113 (1980)   **Pop Density:** 283.3
Land: 0.3 sq. mi.; **Water:** 0.0 sq. mi.   **Elev:** 1507 ft.
Not coextensive with township.

*McHenry   Township
ZIP: 58464   **Lat:** 47-32-11 N **Long:** 98-34-28 W
Pop: 87 (1990); 85 (1980)   **Pop Density:** 2.5
Land: 35.0 sq. mi.; **Water:** 0.7 sq. mi.

McKinnon   Township
Lat: 47-21-48 N **Long:** 98-40-51 W
Pop: 43 (1990); 70 (1980)   **Pop Density:** 1.2
Land: 35.7 sq. mi.; **Water:** 0.4 sq. mi.

Melville   Township
Lat: 47-22-28 N **Long:** 99-04-39 W
Pop: 55 (1990); 61 (1980)   **Pop Density:** 1.6
Land: 34.3 sq. mi.; **Water:** 1.8 sq. mi.

Nordmore   Township
Lat: 47-33-04 N **Long:** 98-56-50 W
Pop: 90 (1990); 91 (1980)   **Pop Density:** 2.5
Land: 35.5 sq. mi.; **Water:** 0.1 sq. mi.

Rolling Prairie   Township
Lat: 47-27-06 N **Long:** 98-41-49 W
Pop: 52 (1990); 53 (1980)   **Pop Density:** 1.5
Land: 35.7 sq. mi.; **Water:** 0.3 sq. mi.

Rose Hill   Township
ZIP: 58421   **Lat:** 47-27-28 N **Long:** 98-56-37 W
Pop: 94 (1990); 118 (1980)   **Pop Density:** 2.7
Land: 35.1 sq. mi.; **Water:** 0.6 sq. mi.

Wyard   Township
Lat: 47-26-56 N **Long:** 99-12-01 W
Pop: 62 (1990); 72 (1980)   **Pop Density:** 1.8
Land: 35.0 sq. mi.; **Water:** 0.8 sq. mi.

Golden Valley County
County Seat: Beach (ZIP: 58621)

Pop: 2,108 (1990); 2,391 (1980)   **Pop Density:** 2.1
Land: 1002.0 sq. mi.; **Water:** 0.4 sq. mi.   **Area Code:** 701
On the southwestern border of ND, west of Dickinson; organized Nov 11, 1912 from Billings County.
Name origin: Descriptive, or for the Golden Valley Land and Cattle Company.

Beach   City
ZIP: 58621   **Lat:** 46-54-50 N **Long:** 104-00-27 W
Pop: 1,205 (1990); 1,381 (1980)   **Pop Density:** 669.4
Land: 1.8 sq. mi.; **Water:** 0.0 sq. mi.   **Elev:** 2793 ft.
Not coextensive with township. Incorporated 1909.
Name origin: For a local settler.

*Beach   Township
ZIP: 58621   **Lat:** 46-53-32 N **Long:** 103-57-14 W
Pop: 201 (1990); 218 (1980)   **Pop Density:** 1.9
Land: 105.1 sq. mi.; **Water:** 0.0 sq. mi.

Bullion   Township
Lat: 46-41-01 N **Long:** 103-48-06 W
Pop: 50 (1990); 63 (1980)   **Pop Density:** 1.2
Land: 41.8 sq. mi.; **Water:** 0.0 sq. mi.

Delhi   Township
Lat: 47-01-26 N **Long:** 103-51-11 W
Pop: 46 (1990); 33 (1980)   **Pop Density:** 1.3
Land: 35.9 sq. mi.; **Water:** 0.0 sq. mi.

NORTH DAKOTA, Golden Valley County

East Golden Valley — Pop. Place
Lat: 46-43-31 N Long: 103-40-38 W
Pop: 13 (1990); 13 (1980) Pop Density: 0.2
Land: 71.4 sq. mi.; Water: 0.0 sq. mi.

Elk Creek — Township
Lat: 47-06-13 N Long: 103-51-08 W
Pop: 10 (1990); 5 (1980) Pop Density: 0.3
Land: 35.7 sq. mi.; Water: 0.0 sq. mi.

Elmwood — Township
Lat: 47-06-27 N Long: 103-59-08 W
Pop: 13 (1990); 16 (1980) Pop Density: 0.4
Land: 35.6 sq. mi.; Water: 0.0 sq. mi.

Garner — Township
Lat: 46-45-57 N Long: 103-47-30 W
Pop: 25 (1990); 27 (1980) Pop Density: 0.8
Land: 29.9 sq. mi.; Water: 0.0 sq. mi.

Golva — City
ZIP: 58632 Lat: 46-44-04 N Long: 103-58-57 W
Pop: 101 (1990); 101 (1980) Pop Density: 336.7
Land: 0.3 sq. mi.; Water: 0.0 sq. mi. Elev: 2832 ft.

Henry — Township
Lat: 47-14-51 N Long: 103-58-50 W
Pop: 27 (1990); 38 (1980) Pop Density: 0.4
Land: 72.5 sq. mi.; Water: 0.0 sq. mi.

Lone Tree — Township
Lat: 46-42-49 N Long: 103-56-58 W
Pop: 166 (1990); 209 (1980) Pop Density: 1.6
Land: 105.1 sq. mi.; Water: 0.0 sq. mi.

North Golden Valley — Pop. Place
Lat: 47-08-12 N Long: 103-43-47 W
Pop: 35 (1990); 55 (1980) Pop Density: 0.2
Land: 143.3 sq. mi.; Water: 0.0 sq. mi.

Pearl — Township
Lat: 47-14-01 N Long: 103-50-41 W
Pop: 12 (1990); 5 (1980) Pop Density: 0.2
Land: 72.3 sq. mi.; Water: 0.0 sq. mi.

Saddle Butte — Township
Lat: 47-01-00 N Long: 103-59-01 W
Pop: 40 (1990); 61 (1980) Pop Density: 1.1
Land: 35.3 sq. mi.; Water: 0.2 sq. mi.

Sentinel — Township
ZIP: 58654 Lat: 46-53-56 N Long: 103-44-07 W
Pop: 62 (1990); 62 (1980) Pop Density: 0.4
Land: 143.4 sq. mi.; Water: 0.1 sq. mi.

Sentinel Butte — City
ZIP: 58654 Lat: 46-55-09 N Long: 103-50-23 W
Pop: 79 (1990); 86 (1980) Pop Density: 71.8
Land: 1.1 sq. mi.; Water: 0.0 sq. mi. Elev: 3410 ft.

South Golden Valley — Pop. Place
Lat: 46-35-08 N Long: 103-55-26 W
Pop: 23 (1990); 18 (1980) Pop Density: 0.3
Land: 71.4 sq. mi.; Water: 0.0 sq. mi.

Grand Forks County
County Seat: Grand Forks (ZIP: 58206)

Pop: 70,683 (1990); 66,100 (1980) Pop Density: 49.2
Land: 1437.9 sq. mi.; Water: 2.0 sq. mi. Area Code: 701

On the central eastern border of ND; organized Jan 4, 1873 (prior to statehood) from Pembina County.

Name origin: For the village of Grand Forks, itself named for the forks of the Red River of the North and Red Lake River.

Agnes — Township
Lat: 48-03-49 N Long: 97-42-32 W
Pop: 94 (1990); 121 (1980) Pop Density: 2.6
Land: 36.1 sq. mi.; Water: 0.0 sq. mi.

Allendale — Township
Lat: 47-48-07 N Long: 97-10-21 W
Pop: 284 (1990); 261 (1980) Pop Density: 7.9
Land: 35.9 sq. mi.; Water: 0.0 sq. mi.

Americus — Township
Lat: 47-43-22 N Long: 97-02-42 W
Pop: 161 (1990); 214 (1980) Pop Density: 4.5
Land: 36.0 sq. mi.; Water: 0.0 sq. mi.

Arvilla — Township
ZIP: 58214 Lat: 47-53-22 N Long: 97-33-23 W
Pop: 322 (1990); 350 (1980) Pop Density: 9.0
Land: 35.9 sq. mi.; Water: 0.0 sq. mi.

Avon — Township
Lat: 47-48-34 N Long: 97-32-55 W
Pop: 141 (1990); 128 (1980) Pop Density: 3.9
Land: 35.9 sq. mi.; Water: 0.0 sq. mi.

Bentru — Township
Lat: 47-42-30 N Long: 96-56-54 W
Pop: 53 (1990); 65 (1980) Pop Density: 3.0
Land: 17.7 sq. mi.; Water: 0.0 sq. mi.

Blooming — Township
Lat: 47-58-28 N Long: 97-17-37 W
Pop: 1,456 (1990); 786 (1980) Pop Density: 42.2
Land: 34.5 sq. mi.; Water: 0.3 sq. mi.

Brenna — Township
Lat: 47-53-19 N Long: 97-10-35 W
Pop: 523 (1990); 530 (1980) Pop Density: 14.5
Land: 36.1 sq. mi.; Water: 0.0 sq. mi.

American Places Dictionary NORTH DAKOTA, Grand Forks County

Chester Township
Lat: 47-53-15 N Long: 97-26-18 W
Pop: 150 (1990); 191 (1980) **Pop Density:** 4.1
Land: 36.2 sq. mi.; **Water:** 0.0 sq. mi.

Elkmount Township
Lat: 48-09-05 N Long: 97-50-20 W
Pop: 53 (1990); 67 (1980) **Pop Density:** 1.5
Land: 35.9 sq. mi.; **Water:** 0.1 sq. mi.

Elm Grove Township
Lat: 47-58-53 N Long: 97-40-58 W
Pop: 134 (1990); 168 (1980) **Pop Density:** 3.7
Land: 36.5 sq. mi.; **Water:** 0.0 sq. mi.

Emerado City
ZIP: 58228 Lat: 47-55-17 N Long: 97-21-50 W
Pop: 483 (1990); 596 (1980) **Pop Density:** 1610.0
Land: 0.3 sq. mi.; **Water:** 0.0 sq. mi. **Elev:** 902 ft.
Name origin: For Emery Farm, part of the original townsite.

Fairfield Township
Lat: 47-48-11 N Long: 97-18-01 W
Pop: 106 (1990); 97 (1980) **Pop Density:** 3.0
Land: 35.5 sq. mi.; **Water:** 0.0 sq. mi.

Falconer Township
Lat: 47-58-44 N Long: 97-05-21 W
Pop: 314 (1990); 283 (1980) **Pop Density:** 23.8
Land: 13.2 sq. mi.; **Water:** 0.1 sq. mi.

Ferry Township
Lat: 48-03-49 N Long: 97-10-01 W
Pop: 373 (1990); 366 (1980) **Pop Density:** 8.1
Land: 46.0 sq. mi.; **Water:** 0.2 sq. mi.

Gilby City
ZIP: 58235 Lat: 48-05-01 N Long: 97-28-05 W
Pop: 262 (1990); 283 (1980) **Pop Density:** 2620.0
Land: 0.1 sq. mi.; **Water:** 0.0 sq. mi. **Elev:** 875 ft.
Not coextensive with township.
Name origin: For the Gibley brothers, early settlers.

***Gilby** Township
ZIP: 58235 Lat: 48-03-37 N Long: 97-27-03 W
Pop: 133 (1990); 127 (1980) **Pop Density:** 3.7
Land: 36.1 sq. mi.; **Water:** 0.0 sq. mi.

Grace Township
Lat: 47-48-07 N Long: 97-41-17 W
Pop: 90 (1990); 127 (1980) **Pop Density:** 2.5
Land: 36.4 sq. mi.; **Water:** 0.0 sq. mi.

Grand Forks City
ZIP: 58201 Lat: 47-55-00 N Long: 97-04-19 W
Pop: 49,425 (1990); 43,765 (1980) **Pop Density:** 3432.3
Land: 14.4 sq. mi.; **Water:** 0.0 sq. mi. **Elev:** 834 ft.
In eastern ND on the Red River, 73 mi. north of Fargo. Incorporated 1881.
Name origin: A translation from French *La Grand Fourche* for the forks of the Red River of the North and Red Lake River.

***Grand Forks** Township
Lat: 47-51-37 N Long: 97-03-58 W
Pop: 465 (1990); 789 (1980) **Pop Density:** 30.8
Land: 15.1 sq. mi.; **Water:** 0.0 sq. mi.

Grand Forks Air Force Base Military Facility
ZIP: 58205 Lat: 47-57-43 N Long: 97-23-02 W
Pop: 9,343 (1990); 527 (1980) **Pop Density:** 1099.2
Land: 8.5 sq. mi.; **Water:** 0.0 sq. mi.

Hegton Township
Lat: 47-59-00 N Long: 97-33-31 W
Pop: 195 (1990); 182 (1980) **Pop Density:** 5.4
Land: 36.3 sq. mi.; **Water:** 0.1 sq. mi.

Inkster City
ZIP: 58244 Lat: 48-09-07 N Long: 97-38-39 W
Pop: 95 (1990); 135 (1980) **Pop Density:** 95.0
Land: 1.0 sq. mi.; **Water:** 0.0 sq. mi. **Elev:** 1029 ft.
Name origin: For the first settler, George Inkster.

***Inkster** Township
ZIP: 58244 Lat: 48-08-38 N Long: 97-43-09 W
Pop: 127 (1990); 127 (1980) **Pop Density:** 3.6
Land: 35.4 sq. mi.; **Water:** 0.2 sq. mi.

Johnstown Township
Lat: 48-08-56 N Long: 97-26-15 W
Pop: 109 (1990); 113 (1980) **Pop Density:** 3.0
Land: 36.3 sq. mi.; **Water:** 0.0 sq. mi.

Lakeville Township
Lat: 48-03-22 N Long: 97-19-11 W
Pop: 91 (1990); 87 (1980) **Pop Density:** 2.6
Land: 35.5 sq. mi.; **Water:** 0.5 sq. mi.

Larimore City
ZIP: 58251 Lat: 47-54-30 N Long: 97-37-38 W
Pop: 1,464 (1990); 1,524 (1980) **Pop Density:** 2440.0
Land: 0.6 sq. mi.; **Water:** 0.0 sq. mi. **Elev:** 1136 ft.
Name origin: For farmer N.G. Larimore, who held 15,000 acres in the area.

***Larimore** Township
ZIP: 58251 Lat: 47-53-30 N Long: 97-41-15 W
Pop: 151 (1990); 202 (1980) **Pop Density:** 4.2
Land: 35.9 sq. mi.; **Water:** 0.0 sq. mi.

Levant Township
Lat: 48-09-26 N Long: 97-19-07 W
Pop: 59 (1990); 83 (1980) **Pop Density:** 1.6
Land: 36.0 sq. mi.; **Water:** 0.0 sq. mi.

Lind Township
Lat: 47-42-56 N Long: 97-41-19 W
Pop: 86 (1990); 119 (1980) **Pop Density:** 2.4
Land: 36.2 sq. mi.; **Water:** 0.0 sq. mi.

Logan Center Township
Lat: 47-48-04 N Long: 97-48-27 W
Pop: 63 (1990); 77 (1980) **Pop Density:** 1.8
Land: 36.0 sq. mi.; **Water:** 0.0 sq. mi.

Loretta Township
Lat: 47-42-37 N Long: 97-48-21 W
Pop: 69 (1990); 66 (1980) **Pop Density:** 1.9
Land: 36.2 sq. mi.; **Water:** 0.0 sq. mi.

Manvel City
ZIP: 58256 Lat: 48-04-23 N Long: 97-10-32 W
Pop: 333 (1990); 308 (1980) **Pop Density:** 1110.0
Land: 0.3 sq. mi.; **Water:** 0.0 sq. mi. **Elev:** 815 ft.

Mekinock Township
ZIP: 58258 Lat: 47-58-17 N Long: 97-25-18 W
Pop: 8,316 (1990); 9,011 (1980) **Pop Density:** 227.8
Land: 36.5 sq. mi.; **Water:** 0.0 sq. mi.

NORTH DAKOTA, Grand Forks County

Michigan Township
Lat: 47-42-30 N Long: 97-11-05 W
Pop: 162 (1990); 198 (1980) **Pop Density:** 4.5
Land: 36.1 sq. mi.; **Water:** 0.0 sq. mi.

Moraine Township
Lat: 47-53-13 N Long: 97-48-53 W
Pop: 121 (1990); 126 (1980) **Pop Density:** 3.4
Land: 35.9 sq. mi.; **Water:** 0.0 sq. mi.

Niagara City
ZIP: 58266 Lat: 47-59-50 N Long: 97-52-13 W
Pop: 73 (1990); 76 (1980) **Pop Density:** 81.1
Land: 0.9 sq. mi.; **Water:** 0.0 sq. mi. **Elev:** 1440 ft.
Not coextensive with township.

*Niagara Township
ZIP: 58266 Lat: 47-58-41 N Long: 97-48-58 W
Pop: 91 (1990); 107 (1980) **Pop Density:** 2.6
Land: 35.1 sq. mi.; **Water:** 0.1 sq. mi.

Northwood City
ZIP: 58267 Lat: 47-44-08 N Long: 97-34-07 W
Pop: 1,166 (1990); 1,240 (1980) **Pop Density:** 1295.6
Land: 0.9 sq. mi.; **Water:** 0.0 sq. mi. **Elev:** 1113 ft.
Not coextensive with township.
Name origin: Named by early settlers for Northwood, IA.

*Northwood Township
ZIP: 58267 Lat: 47-43-00 N Long: 97-33-24 W
Pop: 160 (1990); 204 (1980) **Pop Density:** 4.6
Land: 35.0 sq. mi.; **Water:** 0.0 sq. mi.

Oakville Township
Lat: 47-53-49 N Long: 97-17-52 W
Pop: 176 (1990); 182 (1980) **Pop Density:** 5.0
Land: 35.0 sq. mi.; **Water:** 0.0 sq. mi.

Pleasant View Township
Lat: 47-47-42 N Long: 97-25-49 W
Pop: 163 (1990); 154 (1980) **Pop Density:** 4.5
Land: 36.1 sq. mi.; **Water:** 0.0 sq. mi.

Plymouth Township
Lat: 48-03-54 N Long: 97-50-27 W
Pop: 107 (1990); 121 (1980) **Pop Density:** 3.0
Land: 36.1 sq. mi.; **Water:** 0.1 sq. mi.

Reynolds City
ZIP: 58275 Lat: 47-40-29 N Long: 97-06-32 W
Pop: 107 (1990); 115 (1980) **Pop Density:** 535.0
Land: 0.2 sq. mi.; **Water:** 0.0 sq. mi. **Elev:** 911 ft.
Part of the town is also in Traill County.

Rye Township
Lat: 47-58-21 N Long: 97-09-48 W
Pop: 213 (1990); 271 (1980) **Pop Density:** 6.3
Land: 34.0 sq. mi.; **Water:** 0.0 sq. mi.

Strabane Township
Lat: 48-09-30 N Long: 97-34-43 W
Pop: 154 (1990); 153 (1980) **Pop Density:** 4.3
Land: 35.5 sq. mi.; **Water:** 0.0 sq. mi.

Thompson City
ZIP: 58278 Lat: 47-46-30 N Long: 97-06-20 W
Pop: 930 (1990); 785 (1980) **Pop Density:** 1860.0
Land: 0.5 sq. mi.; **Water:** 0.0 sq. mi. **Elev:** 867 ft.
Name origin: For the first postmaster, Albert Thompson. Originally called Norton.

Turtle River Township
Lat: 48-08-34 N Long: 97-12-05 W
Pop: 177 (1990); 226 (1980) **Pop Density:** 5.3
Land: 33.4 sq. mi.; **Water:** 0.2 sq. mi.

Union Township
Lat: 47-42-47 N Long: 97-18-16 W
Pop: 201 (1990); 206 (1980) **Pop Density:** 5.6
Land: 36.0 sq. mi.; **Water:** 0.0 sq. mi.

Walle Township
Lat: 47-48-04 N Long: 97-02-31 W
Pop: 277 (1990); 323 (1980) **Pop Density:** 7.1
Land: 39.0 sq. mi.; **Water:** 0.0 sq. mi.

Washington Township
Lat: 47-42-29 N Long: 97-25-52 W
Pop: 125 (1990); 171 (1980) **Pop Density:** 3.5
Land: 36.1 sq. mi.; **Water:** 0.0 sq. mi.

Wheatfield Township
Lat: 48-03-51 N Long: 97-35-23 W
Pop: 100 (1990); 94 (1980) **Pop Density:** 2.8
Land: 36.1 sq. mi.; **Water:** 0.0 sq. mi.

Grant County
County Seat: Carson (ZIP: 58529)

Pop: 3,549 (1990); 4,274 (1980) **Pop Density:** 2.1
Land: 1659.6 sq. mi.; **Water:** 6.5 sq. mi. **Area Code:** 701
In south-central ND, southwest of Bismarck; organized Nov 25, 1916 from Morton County.
Name origin: For Ulysses Simpson Grant (1822–85), Civil War general and eighteenth U.S. president.

Carson City
ZIP: 58529 Lat: 46-25-18 N Long: 101-34-11 W
Pop: 383 (1990); 469 (1980) **Pop Density:** 95.8
Land: 4.0 sq. mi.; **Water:** 0.0 sq. mi. **Elev:** 2305 ft.
Name origin: For pioneer businessmen Frank Carter and the Pederson brothers, coined by combining parts of both names.

Central Grant Pop. Place
Lat: 46-07-05 N Long: 101-41-06 W
Pop: 78 (1990); 75 (1980) **Pop Density:** 1.0
Land: 74.6 sq. mi.; **Water:** 0.1 sq. mi.

East Grant Pop. Place
Lat: 46-21-05 N Long: 101-26-34 W
Pop: 714 (1990); 888 (1980) **Pop Density:** 1.2
Land: 604.1 sq. mi.; **Water:** 0.2 sq. mi.

Elgin City
ZIP: 58533 Lat: 46-24-05 N Long: 101-50-47 W
Pop: 765 (1990); 930 (1980) Pop Density: 956.3
Land: 0.8 sq. mi.; Water: 0.0 sq. mi. Elev: 2351 ft.
Name origin: For a local citizen's Elgin watch after many hours of disagreement over a name. Originally called Staley.

Elm Township
Lat: 46-25-03 N Long: 101-43-59 W
Pop: 70 (1990); 86 (1980) Pop Density: 2.0
Land: 34.7 sq. mi.; Water: 0.0 sq. mi.

Fisher Township
Lat: 46-15-07 N Long: 101-40-59 W
Pop: 36 (1990); 30 (1980) Pop Density: 1.1
Land: 33.0 sq. mi.; Water: 0.1 sq. mi.

Freda Township
Lat: 46-19-39 N Long: 101-06-40 W
Pop: 21 (1990); 23 (1980) Pop Density: 0.6
Land: 36.0 sq. mi.; Water: 0.0 sq. mi.

Howe Township
Lat: 46-04-30 N Long: 101-48-48 W
Pop: 16 (1990); 29 (1980) Pop Density: 0.5
Land: 31.6 sq. mi.; Water: 0.0 sq. mi.

Lark Township
Lat: 46-23-56 N Long: 101-21-16 W
Pop: 68 (1990); 64 (1980) Pop Density: 1.9
Land: 36.0 sq. mi.; Water: 0.0 sq. mi.

Leipzig Township
Lat: 46-30-03 N Long: 101-51-38 W
Pop: 83 (1990); 82 (1980) Pop Density: 2.3
Land: 35.9 sq. mi.; Water: 0.0 sq. mi.

Leith City
ZIP: 58551 Lat: 46-21-35 N Long: 101-38-14 W
Pop: 43 (1990); 59 (1980) Pop Density: 35.8
Land: 1.2 sq. mi.; Water: 0.0 sq. mi. Elev: 2350 ft.

Minnie Township
Lat: 46-24-47 N Long: 101-51-48 W
Pop: 102 (1990); 104 (1980) Pop Density: 2.9
Land: 35.0 sq. mi.; Water: 0.0 sq. mi.

New Leipzig City
ZIP: 58562 Lat: 46-22-34 N Long: 101-56-58 W
Pop: 326 (1990); 352 (1980) Pop Density: 362.2
Land: 0.9 sq. mi.; Water: 0.0 sq. mi. Elev: 2326 ft.

Otter Creek Township
Lat: 46-30-10 N Long: 101-21-22 W
Pop: 52 (1990); 60 (1980) Pop Density: 1.5
Land: 35.7 sq. mi.; Water: 0.0 sq. mi.

Pretty Rock Township
Lat: 46-09-59 N Long: 101-49-19 W
Pop: 31 (1990); 41 (1980) Pop Density: 0.9
Land: 35.8 sq. mi.; Water: 0.0 sq. mi.

Raleigh Township
Lat: 46-19-43 N Long: 101-21-51 W
Pop: 86 (1990); 113 (1980) Pop Density: 2.4
Land: 36.0 sq. mi.; Water: 0.0 sq. mi.

Rock Township
Lat: 46-19-41 N Long: 101-44-14 W
Pop: 32 (1990); 43 (1980) Pop Density: 0.9
Land: 35.6 sq. mi.; Water: 0.0 sq. mi.

Schultz Township
Lat: 46-09-06 N Long: 101-33-26 W
Pop: 45 (1990); 62 (1980) Pop Density: 1.3
Land: 35.8 sq. mi.; Water: 0.0 sq. mi.

West Grant Pop. Place
Lat: 46-27-01 N Long: 101-55-55 W
Pop: 559 (1990); 688 (1980) Pop Density: 1.1
Land: 512.5 sq. mi.; Water: 5.9 sq. mi.

Winona Township
Lat: 46-03-05 N Long: 101-33-40 W
Pop: 39 (1990); 33 (1980) Pop Density: 1.0
Land: 40.3 sq. mi.; Water: 0.1 sq. mi.

Griggs County
County Seat: Cooperstown (ZIP: 58425)

Pop: 3,303 (1990); 3,714 (1980) Pop Density: 4.7
Land: 708.5 sq. mi.; Water: 7.7 sq. mi. Area Code: 701

In east-central ND, southwest of Grand Forks; organized Feb 18, 1881 (prior to statehood) from Foster County.

Name origin: For Alexander Griggs (1838–1903), a Red River pilot known as "Captain," closely identified with the earliest navigation on the Red River.

Addie Township
Lat: 47-32-27 N Long: 98-18-23 W
Pop: 70 (1990); 85 (1980) Pop Density: 2.1
Land: 33.2 sq. mi.; Water: 2.3 sq. mi.

Ball Hill Township
Lat: 47-22-03 N Long: 98-10-07 W
Pop: 109 (1990); 119 (1980) Pop Density: 3.0
Land: 36.6 sq. mi.; Water: 0.0 sq. mi.

Bartley Township
Lat: 47-17-05 N Long: 98-16-58 W
Pop: 46 (1990); 48 (1980) Pop Density: 1.3
Land: 34.3 sq. mi.; Water: 0.6 sq. mi.

NORTH DAKOTA, Griggs County

Binford — City
ZIP: 58416 **Lat:** 47-33-35 N **Long:** 98-20-43 W
Pop: 233 (1990); 293 (1980) **Pop Density:** 776.7
Land: 0.3 sq. mi.; **Water:** 0.0 sq. mi. **Elev:** 1520 ft.
Incorporated 1967.
Name origin: For the attorney who represented the original landowners. Originally called Blooming Prairie.

Broadview — Township
Lat: 47-16-37 N **Long:** 98-02-05 W
Pop: 53 (1990); 68 (1980) **Pop Density:** 1.6
Land: 33.9 sq. mi.; **Water:** 1.5 sq. mi.

Bryan — Township
Lat: 47-32-11 N **Long:** 98-25-30 W
Pop: 70 (1990); 63 (1980) **Pop Density:** 1.9
Land: 35.9 sq. mi.; **Water:** 0.0 sq. mi.

Clearfield — Township
Lat: 47-27-24 N **Long:** 98-19-05 W
Pop: 65 (1990); 94 (1980) **Pop Density:** 1.8
Land: 35.4 sq. mi.; **Water:** 0.6 sq. mi.

Cooperstown — City
ZIP: 58425 **Lat:** 47-26-38 N **Long:** 98-07-26 W
Pop: 1,247 (1990); 1,308 (1980) **Pop Density:** 1558.8
Land: 0.8 sq. mi.; **Water:** 0.0 sq. mi. **Elev:** 1437 ft.
Not coextensive with township.
Name origin: For Rollin C. and Thomas Cooper, well-to-do brothers, who settled the area in 1880.

***Cooperstown** — Township
ZIP: 58425 **Lat:** 47-27-51 N **Long:** 98-10-36 W
Pop: 86 (1990); 104 (1980) **Pop Density:** 2.4
Land: 35.6 sq. mi.; **Water:** 0.3 sq. mi.

Dover — Township
Lat: 47-16-36 N **Long:** 98-23-36 W
Pop: 57 (1990); 75 (1980) **Pop Density:** 1.6
Land: 35.2 sq. mi.; **Water:** 0.2 sq. mi.

Greenfield — Township
Lat: 47-17-43 N **Long:** 98-08-52 W
Pop: 117 (1990); 137 (1980) **Pop Density:** 3.4
Land: 34.9 sq. mi.; **Water:** 0.0 sq. mi.

Hannaford — City
ZIP: 58448 **Lat:** 47-18-49 N **Long:** 98-11-16 W
Pop: 204 (1990); 201 (1980) **Pop Density:** 1020.0
Land: 0.2 sq. mi.; **Water:** 0.0 sq. mi. **Elev:** 1414 ft.

Helena — Township
Lat: 47-21-58 N **Long:** 98-18-53 W
Pop: 64 (1990); 71 (1980) **Pop Density:** 1.8
Land: 36.0 sq. mi.; **Water:** 0.1 sq. mi.

Kingsley — Township
ZIP: 58416 **Lat:** 47-27-18 N **Long:** 98-26-00 W
Pop: 74 (1990); 100 (1980) **Pop Density:** 2.1
Land: 36.0 sq. mi.; **Water:** 0.0 sq. mi.

Lenora — Township
Lat: 47-38-04 N **Long:** 98-02-50 W
Pop: 97 (1990); 101 (1980) **Pop Density:** 2.8
Land: 34.7 sq. mi.; **Water:** 0.5 sq. mi.

Mabel — Township
Lat: 47-22-37 N **Long:** 98-25-28 W
Pop: 110 (1990); 126 (1980) **Pop Density:** 3.1
Land: 36.0 sq. mi.; **Water:** 0.1 sq. mi.

Pilot Mound — Township
Lat: 47-37-58 N **Long:** 98-09-59 W
Pop: 81 (1990); 88 (1980) **Pop Density:** 2.3
Land: 36.0 sq. mi.; **Water:** 0.1 sq. mi.

Romness — Township
Lat: 47-32-34 N **Long:** 98-02-24 W
Pop: 50 (1990); 73 (1980) **Pop Density:** 1.4
Land: 35.6 sq. mi.; **Water:** 0.1 sq. mi.

Rosendal — Township
Lat: 47-38-16 N **Long:** 98-25-30 W
Pop: 54 (1990); 68 (1980) **Pop Density:** 1.6
Land: 34.8 sq. mi.; **Water:** 0.5 sq. mi.

Sverdrup — Township
Lat: 47-22-06 N **Long:** 98-02-39 W
Pop: 109 (1990); 112 (1980) **Pop Density:** 3.0
Land: 36.0 sq. mi.; **Water:** 0.0 sq. mi.

Tyrol — Township
Lat: 47-33-07 N **Long:** 98-11-14 W
Pop: 161 (1990); 179 (1980) **Pop Density:** 4.4
Land: 36.6 sq. mi.; **Water:** 0.2 sq. mi.

Washburn — Township
Lat: 47-27-49 N **Long:** 98-02-27 W
Pop: 67 (1990); 90 (1980) **Pop Density:** 1.9
Land: 35.8 sq. mi.; **Water:** 0.1 sq. mi.

Willow — Township
Lat: 47-38-07 N **Long:** 98-18-28 W
Pop: 79 (1990); 111 (1980) **Pop Density:** 2.3
Land: 34.5 sq. mi.; **Water:** 0.6 sq. mi.

Hettinger County
County Seat: Mott (ZIP: 58646)

Pop: 3,445 (1990); 4,275 (1980) **Pop Density:** 3.0
Land: 1132.3 sq. mi.; **Water:** 1.5 sq. mi. **Area Code:** 701
In southwestern ND, south of Dickinson; organized Mar 9, 1883 (prior to statehood) from Stark County.
Name origin: For Mathias K. Hettinger of IL; named by his son-in-law, Erastus A. Williams, a ND territorial legislator and county founder.

Acme   Township
Lat: 46-30-13 N Long: 102-21-09 W
Pop: 34 (1990); 59 (1980) **Pop Density:** 0.9
Land: 36.0 sq. mi.; **Water:** 0.0 sq. mi.

Alden   Township
Lat: 46-19-18 N Long: 102-36-32 W
Pop: 30 (1990); 38 (1980) **Pop Density:** 0.8
Land: 36.2 sq. mi.; **Water:** 0.0 sq. mi.

Ashby   Township
Lat: 46-14-59 N Long: 102-26-21 W
Pop: 10 (1990); 21 (1980) **Pop Density:** 0.3
Land: 32.2 sq. mi.; **Water:** 0.0 sq. mi.

Baer   Township
Lat: 46-14-30 N Long: 102-02-58 W
Pop: 41 (1990); 38 (1980) **Pop Density:** 1.3
Land: 32.2 sq. mi.; **Water:** 0.1 sq. mi.

Berry   Township
Lat: 46-24-39 N Long: 102-14-16 W
Pop: 29 (1990); 37 (1980) **Pop Density:** 0.8
Land: 35.3 sq. mi.; **Water:** 0.2 sq. mi.

Black Butte   Township
Lat: 46-30-25 N Long: 102-36-10 W
Pop: 47 (1990); 71 (1980) **Pop Density:** 1.3
Land: 35.8 sq. mi.; **Water:** 0.0 sq. mi.

Brittian   Township
Lat: 46-19-50 N Long: 102-14-18 W
Pop: 25 (1990); 35 (1980) **Pop Density:** 0.7
Land: 35.7 sq. mi.; **Water:** 0.1 sq. mi.

Campbell   Township
Lat: 46-35-15 N Long: 102-21-38 W
Pop: 62 (1990); 63 (1980) **Pop Density:** 1.8
Land: 35.1 sq. mi.; **Water:** 0.0 sq. mi.

Cannon Ball   Township
Lat: 46-19-43 N Long: 102-06-40 W
Pop: 104 (1990); 95 (1980) **Pop Density:** 2.9
Land: 35.9 sq. mi.; **Water:** 0.0 sq. mi.

Castle Rock   Township
Lat: 46-19-20 N Long: 102-21-13 W
Pop: 96 (1990); 117 (1980) **Pop Density:** 2.7
Land: 35.9 sq. mi.; **Water:** 0.0 sq. mi.

Chilton   Township
Lat: 46-19-36 N Long: 102-29-02 W
Pop: 36 (1990); 44 (1980) **Pop Density:** 1.0
Land: 36.2 sq. mi.; **Water:** 0.0 sq. mi.

Clark   Township
Lat: 46-35-05 N Long: 102-44-29 W
Pop: 32 (1990); 50 (1980) **Pop Density:** 0.9
Land: 35.5 sq. mi.; **Water:** 0.0 sq. mi.

Farina   Township
Lat: 46-25-21 N Long: 102-29-25 W
Pop: 52 (1990); 60 (1980) **Pop Density:** 1.4
Land: 36.3 sq. mi.; **Water:** 0.2 sq. mi.

Havelock   Township
ZIP: 58647 Lat: 46-29-54 N Long: 102-43-53 W
Pop: 34 (1990); 47 (1980) **Pop Density:** 1.0
Land: 35.6 sq. mi.; **Water:** 0.0 sq. mi.

Highland   Township
Lat: 46-35-19 N Long: 102-14-08 W
Pop: 34 (1990); 51 (1980) **Pop Density:** 1.0
Land: 34.3 sq. mi.; **Water:** 0.0 sq. mi.

Indian Creek   Township
Lat: 46-24-46 N Long: 102-36-22 W
Pop: 34 (1990); 38 (1980) **Pop Density:** 1.0
Land: 35.4 sq. mi.; **Water:** 0.0 sq. mi.

Kennedy   Township
Lat: 46-19-47 N Long: 102-51-17 W
Pop: 63 (1990); 84 (1980) **Pop Density:** 1.7
Land: 36.1 sq. mi.; **Water:** 0.1 sq. mi.

Kern   Township
Lat: 46-14-39 N Long: 102-19-12 W
Pop: 22 (1990); 30 (1980) **Pop Density:** 0.7
Land: 32.3 sq. mi.; **Water:** 0.0 sq. mi.

Kunze   Township
Lat: 46-35-14 N Long: 102-51-35 W
Pop: 66 (1990); 93 (1980) **Pop Density:** 1.8
Land: 36.4 sq. mi.; **Water:** 0.0 sq. mi.

Madison   Township
Lat: 46-35-35 N Long: 102-29-12 W
Pop: 55 (1990); 54 (1980) **Pop Density:** 1.5
Land: 36.3 sq. mi.; **Water:** 0.0 sq. mi.

Merrill   Township
Lat: 46-14-30 N Long: 102-10-29 W
Pop: 11 (1990); 25 (1980) **Pop Density:** 0.3
Land: 32.1 sq. mi.; **Water:** 0.3 sq. mi.

Mott   City
ZIP: 58646 Lat: 46-22-29 N Long: 102-19-05 W
Pop: 1,019 (1990); 1,315 (1980) **Pop Density:** 1019.0
Land: 1.0 sq. mi.; **Water:** 0.0 sq. mi. **Elev:** 2377 ft.
Not coextensive with township.
Name origin: For C.W. Mott, a general agent for the Northern Pacific Railroad.

*Mott   Township
ZIP: 58646 Lat: 46-24-43 N Long: 102-22-16 W
Pop: 69 (1990); 101 (1980) **Pop Density:** 2.0
Land: 35.1 sq. mi.; **Water:** 0.1 sq. mi.

NORTH DAKOTA, Hettinger County

New England City
ZIP: 58647 **Lat:** 46-32-27 N **Long:** 102-52-00 W
Pop: 663 (1990); 825 (1980) **Pop Density:** 1326.0
Land: 0.5 sq. mi.; **Water:** 0.0 sq. mi. **Elev:** 2592 ft.
Founded 1887.
Name origin: Originally named Mayflower, then New England City; shortened to present form in 1894 by H.W. Smith, who noted that most early settlers were from VT and MA.

*New England Township
ZIP: 58647 **Lat:** 46-29-59 N **Long:** 102-52-18 W
Pop: 124 (1990); 111 (1980) **Pop Density:** 3.5
Land: 35.5 sq. mi.; **Water:** 0.0 sq. mi.

Odessa Township
Lat: 46-34-58 N **Long:** 102-06-09 W
Pop: 25 (1990); 40 (1980) **Pop Density:** 0.7
Land: 35.8 sq. mi.; **Water:** 0.0 sq. mi.

Regent City
ZIP: 58650 **Lat:** 46-25-21 N **Long:** 102-33-27 W
Pop: 268 (1990); 297 (1980) **Pop Density:** 536.0
Land: 0.5 sq. mi.; **Water:** 0.0 sq. mi. **Elev:** 2460 ft.

Rifle Township
Lat: 46-35-05 N **Long:** 102-37-04 W
Pop: 55 (1990); 68 (1980) **Pop Density:** 1.5
Land: 35.5 sq. mi.; **Water:** 0.0 sq. mi.

St. Croix Township
Lat: 46-29-39 N **Long:** 102-29-45 W
Pop: 48 (1990); 56 (1980) **Pop Density:** 1.3
Land: 36.7 sq. mi.; **Water:** 0.0 sq. mi.

Solon Township
Lat: 46-24-35 N **Long:** 102-07-07 W
Pop: 42 (1990); 44 (1980) **Pop Density:** 1.2
Land: 35.9 sq. mi.; **Water:** 0.1 sq. mi.

Steiner Township
Lat: 46-30-04 N **Long:** 102-14-15 W
Pop: 33 (1990); 70 (1980) **Pop Density:** 0.9
Land: 35.1 sq. mi.; **Water:** 0.0 sq. mi.

Strehlow Township
Lat: 46-24-52 N **Long:** 102-52-06 W
Pop: 46 (1990); 49 (1980) **Pop Density:** 1.3
Land: 35.9 sq. mi.; **Water:** 0.1 sq. mi.

Tepee Butte Township
Lat: 46-24-36 N **Long:** 102-44-12 W
Pop: 54 (1990); 53 (1980) **Pop Density:** 1.5
Land: 35.8 sq. mi.; **Water:** 0.0 sq. mi.

Wagendorf Township
Lat: 46-19-29 N **Long:** 102-44-30 W
Pop: 46 (1990); 50 (1980) **Pop Density:** 1.3
Land: 36.0 sq. mi.; **Water:** 0.0 sq. mi.

Walker Township
Lat: 46-30-06 N **Long:** 102-06-58 W
Pop: 36 (1990); 46 (1980) **Pop Density:** 1.0
Land: 36.1 sq. mi.; **Water:** 0.0 sq. mi.

Kidder County
County Seat: Steele (ZIP: 58482)

Pop: 3,332 (1990); 3,833 (1980) **Pop Density:** 2.5
Land: 1351.6 sq. mi.; **Water:** 81.7 sq. mi. **Area Code:** 701
In central ND, east of Bismarck; organized Jan 4, 1873 (prior to statehood) from Buffalo County, which was discontinued.
Name origin: For Jefferson Parrish Kidder (1815–83), VT legislator and lieutenant governor, MN legislator (1863–64), and associate justice of the Dakota territorial supreme court (1865–76; 1879–83).

Allen Township
Lat: 46-55-54 N **Long:** 99-52-54 W
Pop: 66 (1990); 78 (1980) **Pop Density:** 1.9
Land: 34.1 sq. mi.; **Water:** 1.1 sq. mi.

Atwood Township
Lat: 47-11-48 N **Long:** 99-55-32 W
Pop: 47 (1990); 46 (1980) **Pop Density:** 1.4
Land: 33.3 sq. mi.; **Water:** 2.2 sq. mi.

Baker Township
Lat: 46-41-18 N **Long:** 100-00-56 W
Pop: 60 (1990); 87 (1980) **Pop Density:** 1.5
Land: 39.3 sq. mi.; **Water:** 0.6 sq. mi.

Buckeye Township
Lat: 47-01-00 N **Long:** 99-39-38 W
Pop: 34 (1990); 40 (1980) **Pop Density:** 1.0
Land: 32.5 sq. mi.; **Water:** 3.3 sq. mi.

Bunker Township
Lat: 46-40-33 N **Long:** 99-45-45 W
Pop: 48 (1990); 61 (1980) **Pop Density:** 1.3
Land: 36.1 sq. mi.; **Water:** 0.0 sq. mi.

Chestina Township
Lat: 47-02-16 N **Long:** 100-02-36 W
Pop: 40 (1990); 47 (1980) **Pop Density:** 1.1
Land: 35.8 sq. mi.; **Water:** 0.3 sq. mi.

Clear Lake Township
Lat: 47-06-51 N **Long:** 99-56-01 W
Pop: 65 (1990); 74 (1980) **Pop Density:** 1.9
Land: 34.6 sq. mi.; **Water:** 1.0 sq. mi.

Crown Hill Township
Lat: 46-46-16 N **Long:** 100-00-16 W
Pop: 25 (1990); 33 (1980) **Pop Density:** 0.8
Land: 30.8 sq. mi.; **Water:** 1.5 sq. mi.

Crystal Springs
Township
Lat: 46-50-27 N Long: 99-30-15 W
Pop: 64 (1990); 48 (1980) Pop Density: 1.8
Land: 35.4 sq. mi.; Water: 0.6 sq. mi.

Dawson
City
ZIP: 58428 Lat: 46-52-05 N Long: 99-45-07 W
Pop: 78 (1990); 144 (1980) Pop Density: 195.0
Land: 0.4 sq. mi.; Water: 0.0 sq. mi. Elev: 1750 ft.
Founded 1873.
Name origin: For farmer and banker J. Dawson Thompson.

Excelsior
Township
Lat: 46-56-16 N Long: 100-01-21 W
Pop: 46 (1990); 44 (1980) Pop Density: 1.3
Land: 35.4 sq. mi.; Water: 0.6 sq. mi.

Frettim
Township
Lat: 47-12-01 N Long: 99-40-35 W
Pop: 39 (1990); 61 (1980) Pop Density: 1.2
Land: 33.2 sq. mi.; Water: 2.6 sq. mi.

Graf
Township
Lat: 46-40-20 N Long: 99-30-38 W
Pop: 39 (1990); 48 (1980) Pop Density: 1.2
Land: 31.4 sq. mi.; Water: 4.6 sq. mi.

Haynes
Township
Lat: 47-01-24 N Long: 99-55-33 W
Pop: 27 (1990); 39 (1980) Pop Density: 0.8
Land: 34.3 sq. mi.; Water: 1.5 sq. mi.

Kickapoo
Township
Lat: 47-13-12 N Long: 100-03-42 W
Pop: 29 (1990); 39 (1980) Pop Density: 0.9
Land: 33.2 sq. mi.; Water: 2.3 sq. mi.

Lake Williams
Township
Lat: 47-06-47 N Long: 99-40-10 W
Pop: 39 (1990); 73 (1980) Pop Density: 1.2
Land: 31.6 sq. mi.; Water: 4.3 sq. mi.

Manning
Township
Lat: 46-43-55 N Long: 99-53-17 W
Pop: 103 (1990); 98 (1980) Pop Density: 1.5
Land: 69.2 sq. mi.; Water: 2.3 sq. mi.

Merkel
Township
Lat: 47-14-01 N Long: 99-47-50 W
Pop: 65 (1990); 84 (1980) Pop Density: 1.0
Land: 65.7 sq. mi.; Water: 6.0 sq. mi.

Northwest
Township
Lat: 47-16-17 N Long: 100-02-28 W
Pop: 34 (1990); 35 (1980) Pop Density: 1.0
Land: 32.8 sq. mi.; Water: 1.7 sq. mi.

Peace
Township
Lat: 46-40-08 N Long: 99-38-36 W
Pop: 49 (1990); 63 (1980) Pop Density: 1.4
Land: 34.0 sq. mi.; Water: 2.1 sq. mi.

Petersville
Township
Lat: 47-11-04 N Long: 99-32-33 W
Pop: 43 (1990); 79 (1980) Pop Density: 1.3
Land: 34.0 sq. mi.; Water: 1.9 sq. mi.

Pettibone
City
ZIP: 58475 Lat: 47-07-04 N Long: 99-31-12 W
Pop: 93 (1990); 127 (1980) Pop Density: 465.0
Land: 0.2 sq. mi.; Water: 0.0 sq. mi. Elev: 1838 ft.
Not coextensive with township.

*Pettibone
Township
ZIP: 58475 Lat: 47-06-47 N Long: 99-32-40 W
Pop: 70 (1990); 88 (1980) Pop Density: 2.2
Land: 32.1 sq. mi.; Water: 3.7 sq. mi.

Pleasant Hill
Township
Lat: 46-51-27 N Long: 100-00-50 W
Pop: 59 (1990); 76 (1980) Pop Density: 1.7
Land: 35.4 sq. mi.; Water: 0.5 sq. mi.

Quinby
Township
Lat: 47-01-01 N Long: 99-47-30 W
Pop: 23 (1990); 29 (1980) Pop Density: 0.8
Land: 29.2 sq. mi.; Water: 6.7 sq. mi.

Rexine
Township
Lat: 47-16-57 N Long: 99-32-41 W
Pop: 28 (1990); 15 (1980) Pop Density: 0.8
Land: 34.0 sq. mi.; Water: 1.6 sq. mi.

Robinson
City
ZIP: 58478 Lat: 47-08-35 N Long: 99-46-48 W
Pop: 87 (1990); 129 (1980) Pop Density: 435.0
Land: 0.2 sq. mi.; Water: 0.0 sq. mi. Elev: 1776 ft.
Not coextensive with township.

*Robinson
Township
ZIP: 58478 Lat: 47-06-46 N Long: 99-48-00 W
Pop: 61 (1990); 59 (1980) Pop Density: 1.8
Land: 34.4 sq. mi.; Water: 1.6 sq. mi.

Sibley
Township
Lat: 46-50-54 N Long: 99-45-30 W
Pop: 91 (1990); 48 (1980) Pop Density: 2.9
Land: 31.6 sq. mi.; Water: 4.1 sq. mi.

South Kidder
Pop. Place
Lat: 46-45-30 N Long: 99-46-30 W
Pop: 36 (1990); 46 (1980) Pop Density: 1.1
Land: 33.2 sq. mi.; Water: 2.9 sq. mi.

Steele
City
ZIP: 58482 Lat: 46-51-21 N Long: 99-54-58 W
Pop: 762 (1990); 796 (1980) Pop Density: 1270.0
Land: 0.6 sq. mi.; Water: 0.0 sq. mi. Elev: 1865 ft.
Platted 1881.
Name origin: For Col. Wilbur Steele, on whose homesite the town was platted.

Stewart
Township
Lat: 47-16-27 N Long: 99-55-53 W
Pop: 34 (1990); 37 (1980) Pop Density: 1.0
Land: 33.3 sq. mi.; Water: 1.4 sq. mi.

Tanner
Township
Lat: 46-46-17 N Long: 99-30-39 W
Pop: 41 (1990); 55 (1980) Pop Density: 1.2
Land: 34.1 sq. mi.; Water: 2.2 sq. mi.

Tappen
City
ZIP: 58487 Lat: 46-52-22 N Long: 99-37-24 W
Pop: 239 (1990); 271 (1980) Pop Density: 183.8
Land: 1.3 sq. mi.; Water: 0.0 sq. mi. Elev: 1775 ft.
Not coextensive with township.
Name origin: For farmer S. Tappen, who ran a 10,000-acre farm here in the 1880s.

*Tappen
Township
ZIP: 58487 Lat: 46-51-01 N Long: 99-38-20 W
Pop: 95 (1990); 83 (1980) Pop Density: 2.8
Land: 34.5 sq. mi.; Water: 0.2 sq. mi.

NORTH DAKOTA, Kidder County   American Places Dictionary

Tuttle   City
ZIP: 58488   Lat: 47-08-38 N Long: 99-59-36 W
Pop: 160 (1990); 202 (1980)   Pop Density: 800.0
Land: 0.2 sq. mi.; Water: 0.0 sq. mi.   Elev: 1859 ft.
Not coextensive with township.

*Tuttle   Township
ZIP: 58488   Lat: 47-06-28 N Long: 100-02-30 W
Pop: 89 (1990); 104 (1980)   Pop Density: 2.6
Land: 34.5 sq. mi.; Water: 1.0 sq. mi.

Valley   Township
                      Lat: 46-45-28 N Long: 99-38-41 W
Pop: 42 (1990); 53 (1980)   Pop Density: 1.2
Land: 34.7 sq. mi.; Water: 1.3 sq. mi.

Vernon   Township
                      Lat: 46-55-37 N Long: 99-46-12 W
Pop: 45 (1990); 62 (1980)   Pop Density: 1.5
Land: 30.0 sq. mi.; Water: 6.1 sq. mi.

Wallace   Township
                      Lat: 47-16-30 N Long: 99-39-56 W
Pop: 33 (1990); 38 (1980)   Pop Density: 1.0
Land: 34.2 sq. mi.; Water: 1.4 sq. mi.

Weiser   Township
                      Lat: 47-01-24 N Long: 99-32-41 W
Pop: 53 (1990); 48 (1980)   Pop Density: 1.5
Land: 34.8 sq. mi.; Water: 1.1 sq. mi.

Westford   Township
                      Lat: 46-56-31 N Long: 99-38-05 W
Pop: 40 (1990); 45 (1980)   Pop Density: 1.2
Land: 33.4 sq. mi.; Water: 2.7 sq. mi.

Williams   Township
                      Lat: 46-55-53 N Long: 99-31-00 W
Pop: 22 (1990); 30 (1980)   Pop Density: 0.7
Land: 33.8 sq. mi.; Water: 2.4 sq. mi.

Woodlawn   Township
                      Lat: 46-51-12 N Long: 99-52-45 W
Pop: 89 (1990); 71 (1980)   Pop Density: 2.6
Land: 34.8 sq. mi.; Water: 0.1 sq. mi.

LaMoure County
County Seat: La Moure (ZIP: 58458)

Pop: 5,383 (1990); 6,473 (1980)   **Pop Density:** 4.7
Land: 1147.2 sq. mi.; **Water:** 3.6 sq. mi.   **Area Code:** 701

In southeastern ND, southwest of Fargo; organized Jan 4, 1873 (prior to statehood) from Pembina County.

Name origin: For Judson LaMoure (1839–1918), pioneer, legislator, and commissioner of Dakota Territory (1890).

Adrian   Township
                      Lat: 46-35-15 N Long: 98-36-00 W
Pop: 132 (1990); 160 (1980)   Pop Density: 3.7
Land: 36.1 sq. mi.; Water: 0.0 sq. mi.

Badger   Township
                      Lat: 46-19-51 N Long: 98-28-18 W
Pop: 64 (1990); 86 (1980)   Pop Density: 1.8
Land: 35.8 sq. mi.; Water: 0.3 sq. mi.

Berlin   City
ZIP: 58415   Lat: 46-22-42 N Long: 98-29-14 W
Pop: 32 (1990); 57 (1980)   Pop Density: 320.0
Land: 0.1 sq. mi.; Water: 0.0 sq. mi.   Elev: 1471 ft.
Incorporated 1967.

Black Loam   Township
                      Lat: 46-30-27 N Long: 98-05-46 W
Pop: 79 (1990); 81 (1980)   Pop Density: 2.2
Land: 35.9 sq. mi.; Water: 0.1 sq. mi.

Bluebird   Township
                      Lat: 46-29-58 N Long: 98-50-52 W
Pop: 68 (1990); 115 (1980)   Pop Density: 1.9
Land: 35.5 sq. mi.; Water: 0.1 sq. mi.

Dean   Township
                      Lat: 46-19-41 N Long: 98-21-26 W
Pop: 215 (1990); 248 (1980)   Pop Density: 6.2
Land: 34.4 sq. mi.; Water: 0.4 sq. mi.

Dickey   City
ZIP: 58431   Lat: 46-32-11 N Long: 98-28-02 W
Pop: 53 (1990); 74 (1980)   Pop Density: 265.0
Land: 0.2 sq. mi.; Water: 0.0 sq. mi.   Elev: 1360 ft.

Edgeley   City
ZIP: 58433   Lat: 46-21-45 N Long: 98-42-42 W
Pop: 680 (1990); 843 (1980)   Pop Density: 971.4
Land: 0.7 sq. mi.; Water: 0.0 sq. mi.   Elev: 1559 ft.

Gladstone   Township
                      Lat: 46-29-49 N Long: 98-13-02 W
Pop: 90 (1990); 110 (1980)   Pop Density: 2.5
Land: 35.9 sq. mi.; Water: 0.0 sq. mi.

Glen   Township
                      Lat: 46-35-20 N Long: 98-58-19 W
Pop: 58 (1990); 100 (1980)   Pop Density: 1.6
Land: 35.3 sq. mi.; Water: 0.1 sq. mi.

Glenmore   Township
                      Lat: 46-29-34 N Long: 98-43-05 W
Pop: 74 (1990); 106 (1980)   Pop Density: 2.1
Land: 35.8 sq. mi.; Water: 0.0 sq. mi.

Golden Glen   Township
                      Lat: 46-19-25 N Long: 98-44-03 W
Pop: 136 (1990); 162 (1980)   Pop Density: 3.9
Land: 35.3 sq. mi.; Water: 0.1 sq. mi.

American Places Dictionary   NORTH DAKOTA, LaMoure County

Grand Rapids
Township
Lat: 46-24-52 N Long: 98-20-43 W
Pop: 120 (1990); 117 (1980)   Pop Density: 3.3
Land: 36.1 sq. mi.; Water: 0.0 sq. mi.

Grandview
Township
Lat: 46-30-02 N Long: 98-20-23 W
Pop: 85 (1990); 92 (1980)   Pop Density: 2.4
Land: 35.7 sq. mi.; Water: 0.1 sq. mi.

Greenville
Township
Lat: 46-24-52 N Long: 98-06-02 W
Pop: 94 (1990); 112 (1980)   Pop Density: 2.6
Land: 35.9 sq. mi.; Water: 0.1 sq. mi.

Henrietta
Township
Lat: 46-24-51 N Long: 98-28-59 W
Pop: 91 (1990); 100 (1980)   Pop Density: 2.5
Land: 36.0 sq. mi.; Water: 0.0 sq. mi.

Jud
City
ZIP: 58454   Lat: 46-31-30 N Long: 98-53-52 W
Pop: 84 (1990); 118 (1980)   Pop Density: 420.0
Land: 0.2 sq. mi.; Water: 0.0 sq. mi.   Elev: 1738 ft.

Kennison
Township
Lat: 46-34-48 N Long: 98-42-52 W
Pop: 120 (1990); 187 (1980)   Pop Density: 3.3
Land: 35.9 sq. mi.; Water: 0.0 sq. mi.

Kulm
City
ZIP: 58456   Lat: 46-18-06 N Long: 98-56-51 W
Pop: 514 (1990); 570 (1980)   Pop Density: 1713.3
Land: 0.3 sq. mi.; Water: 0.0 sq. mi.   Elev: 1970 ft.
Name origin: Named by German settlers from Kulm, Russia.

La Moure
City
ZIP: 58458   Lat: 46-21-27 N Long: 98-17-47 W
Pop: 970 (1990); 1,077 (1980)   Pop Density: 808.3
Land: 1.2 sq. mi.; Water: 0.0 sq. mi.   Elev: 462126N-0981739W ft.
Founded 1882.
Name origin: For pioneer and territorial politician, Judson La Moure.

Litchville
Township
Lat: 46-35-46 N Long: 98-06-03 W
Pop: 90 (1990); 90 (1980)   Pop Density: 2.5
Land: 36.0 sq. mi.; Water: 0.1 sq. mi.

Marion
City
ZIP: 58466   Lat: 46-36-34 N Long: 98-20-05 W
Pop: 169 (1990); 214 (1980)   Pop Density: 211.3
Land: 0.8 sq. mi.; Water: 0.2 sq. mi.   Elev: 1460 ft.

Mikkelson
Township
Lat: 46-35-14 N Long: 98-51-19 W
Pop: 63 (1990); 69 (1980)   Pop Density: 1.8
Land: 35.6 sq. mi.; Water: 0.1 sq. mi.

Nora
Township
Lat: 46-24-35 N Long: 98-44-03 W
Pop: 87 (1990); 107 (1980)   Pop Density: 2.4
Land: 36.0 sq. mi.; Water: 0.1 sq. mi.

Norden
Township
Lat: 46-20-06 N Long: 98-58-44 W
Pop: 77 (1990); 87 (1980)   Pop Density: 2.2
Land: 35.6 sq. mi.; Water: 0.1 sq. mi.

Ovid
Township
Lat: 46-19-46 N Long: 98-05-33 W
Pop: 81 (1990); 112 (1980)   Pop Density: 2.3
Land: 35.3 sq. mi.; Water: 0.5 sq. mi.

Pearl Lake
Township
Lat: 46-24-56 N Long: 98-13-23 W
Pop: 81 (1990); 87 (1980)   Pop Density: 2.3
Land: 35.3 sq. mi.; Water: 0.8 sq. mi.

Pomona View
Township
Lat: 46-19-14 N Long: 98-50-57 W
Pop: 43 (1990); 53 (1980)   Pop Density: 1.2
Land: 35.8 sq. mi.; Water: 0.1 sq. mi.

Prairie
Township
Lat: 46-35-33 N Long: 98-13-28 W
Pop: 84 (1990); 114 (1980)   Pop Density: 2.3
Land: 36.1 sq. mi.; Water: 0.0 sq. mi.

Raney
Township
Lat: 46-29-46 N Long: 98-58-20 W
Pop: 33 (1990); 60 (1980)   Pop Density: 0.9
Land: 35.4 sq. mi.; Water: 0.0 sq. mi.

Ray
Township
Lat: 46-24-56 N Long: 98-50-37 W
Pop: 64 (1990); 77 (1980)   Pop Density: 1.8
Land: 36.0 sq. mi.; Water: 0.0 sq. mi.

Roscoe
Township
Lat: 46-30-13 N Long: 98-29-02 W
Pop: 96 (1990); 118 (1980)   Pop Density: 2.7
Land: 35.9 sq. mi.; Water: 0.0 sq. mi.

Russell
Township
Lat: 46-30-27 N Long: 98-35-20 W
Pop: 71 (1990); 100 (1980)   Pop Density: 2.0
Land: 35.8 sq. mi.; Water: 0.0 sq. mi.

Ryan
Township
Lat: 46-20-00 N Long: 98-13-00 W
Pop: 107 (1990); 114 (1980)   Pop Density: 3.0
Land: 35.8 sq. mi.; Water: 0.3 sq. mi.

Saratoga
Township
Lat: 46-35-20 N Long: 98-28-31 W
Pop: 62 (1990); 81 (1980)   Pop Density: 1.7
Land: 36.2 sq. mi.; Water: 0.0 sq. mi.

Sheridan
Township
Lat: 46-35-32 N Long: 98-21-07 W
Pop: 51 (1990); 60 (1980)   Pop Density: 1.5
Land: 34.9 sq. mi.; Water: 0.1 sq. mi.

Swede
Township
Lat: 46-24-59 N Long: 98-58-21 W
Pop: 61 (1990); 98 (1980)   Pop Density: 1.7
Land: 35.8 sq. mi.; Water: 0.1 sq. mi.

Verona
City
ZIP: 58490   Lat: 46-21-54 N Long: 98-04-15 W
Pop: 103 (1990); 126 (1980)   Pop Density: 343.3
Land: 0.3 sq. mi.; Water: 0.0 sq. mi.   Elev: 1385 ft.

Wano
Township
ZIP: 58433   Lat: 46-24-49 N Long: 98-35-57 W
Pop: 62 (1990); 65 (1980)   Pop Density: 1.7
Land: 36.1 sq. mi.; Water: 0.0 sq. mi.

NORTH DAKOTA, LaMoure County

Willowbank
Township
Lat: 46-19-43 N **Long:** 98-35-20 W
Pop: 139 (1990); 126 (1980) **Pop Density:** 3.8
Land: 36.2 sq. mi.; **Water:** 0.0 sq. mi.

Logan County
County Seat: Napoleon (ZIP: 58561)

Pop: 2,847 (1990); 3,493 (1980) **Pop Density:** 2.9
Land: 992.7 sq. mi.; **Water:** 18.4 sq. mi. **Area Code:** 701
In south-central ND, southeast of Bismarck; organized Jan 4, 1873 (prior to statehood) from Buffalo County, which was discontinued.
Name origin: For Gen. John Alexander Logan (1826–86), officer in the Mexican-American War and Civil War; U.S. senator from IL (1871–77; 1879–86).

Bryant
Township
Lat: 46-30-22 N **Long:** 99-43-10 W
Pop: 93 (1990); 90 (1980) **Pop Density:** 2.7
Land: 34.4 sq. mi.; **Water:** 0.0 sq. mi.

Dixon
Township
Lat: 46-30-01 N **Long:** 99-36-06 W
Pop: 30 (1990); 37 (1980) **Pop Density:** 0.8
Land: 35.8 sq. mi.; **Water:** 0.1 sq. mi.

East Logan
Pop. Place
Lat: 46-27-54 N **Long:** 99-22-28 W
Pop: 594 (1990); 719 (1980) **Pop Density:** 1.3
Land: 462.3 sq. mi.; **Water:** 12.0 sq. mi.

Finn
Township
Lat: 46-35-23 N **Long:** 99-06-10 W
Pop: 29 (1990); 53 (1980) **Pop Density:** 0.9
Land: 33.8 sq. mi.; **Water:** 0.8 sq. mi.

Fredonia
City
ZIP: 58440 **Lat:** 46-19-42 N **Long:** 99-05-41 W
Pop: 66 (1990); 82 (1980) **Pop Density:** 330.0
Land: 0.2 sq. mi.; **Water:** 0.0 sq. mi. **Elev:** 2054 ft.

Gackle
City
ZIP: 58442 **Lat:** 46-37-34 N **Long:** 99-08-29 W
Pop: 450 (1990); 456 (1980) **Pop Density:** 900.0
Land: 0.5 sq. mi.; **Water:** 0.0 sq. mi. **Elev:** 1930 ft.
Founded 1903.
Name origin: For merchant George Gackle.

Glendale
Township
Lat: 46-35-39 N **Long:** 99-43-27 W
Pop: 67 (1990); 84 (1980) **Pop Density:** 1.8
Land: 36.7 sq. mi.; **Water:** 0.1 sq. mi.

Gutschmidt
Township
Lat: 46-30-24 N **Long:** 99-05-58 W
Pop: 48 (1990); 59 (1980) **Pop Density:** 1.3
Land: 36.0 sq. mi.; **Water:** 0.5 sq. mi.

Haag
Township
Lat: 46-19-22 N **Long:** 99-06-09 W
Pop: 47 (1990); 55 (1980) **Pop Density:** 1.3
Land: 36.0 sq. mi.; **Water:** 0.0 sq. mi.

Janke
Township
Lat: 46-25-05 N **Long:** 99-05-46 W
Pop: 41 (1990); 64 (1980) **Pop Density:** 1.1
Land: 36.0 sq. mi.; **Water:** 0.2 sq. mi.

Lehr
City
Lat: 46-17-08 N **Long:** 99-21-11 W
Pop: 44 (1990); 57 (1980) **Pop Density:** 440.0
Land: 0.1 sq. mi.; **Water:** 0.0 sq. mi. **Elev:** 2050 ft.
Part of the town is also in McIntosh County.

Napoleon
City
ZIP: 58561 **Lat:** 46-30-12 N **Long:** 99-46-04 W
Pop: 930 (1990); 1,103 (1980) **Pop Density:** 664.3
Land: 1.4 sq. mi.; **Water:** 0.0 sq. mi. **Elev:** 1955 ft.
Founded 1886.
Name origin: For Napoleon Goodsill, the president of the local land company.

Red Lake
Township
Lat: 46-24-29 N **Long:** 99-35-42 W
Pop: 59 (1990); 88 (1980) **Pop Density:** 1.8
Land: 33.6 sq. mi.; **Water:** 2.1 sq. mi.

Sealy
Township
Lat: 46-34-51 N **Long:** 99-51-23 W
Pop: 40 (1990); 66 (1980) **Pop Density:** 1.1
Land: 36.4 sq. mi.; **Water:** 0.2 sq. mi.

Starkey
Township
Lat: 46-24-52 N **Long:** 99-44-16 W
Pop: 43 (1990); 69 (1980) **Pop Density:** 1.2
Land: 36.1 sq. mi.; **Water:** 0.0 sq. mi.

West Logan
Pop. Place
Lat: 46-22-22 N **Long:** 99-47-42 W
Pop: 266 (1990); 354 (1980) **Pop Density:** 1.5
Land: 173.4 sq. mi.; **Water:** 2.5 sq. mi.

McHenry County
County Seat: Towner (ZIP: 58788)

Pop: 6,528 (1990); 7,858 (1980)　　　　**Pop Density:** 3.5
Land: 1874.2 sq. mi.; **Water:** 37.6 sq. mi.　　**Area Code:** 701

In north-central ND, east of Minot; organized Jan 4, 1873 (prior to statehood) from Buffalo County, which was discontinued.
Name origin: For James McHenry, an early settler of Vermillion, SD.

Anamoose — City
ZIP: 58710　**Lat:** 47-52-59 N　**Long:** 100-14-29 W
Pop: 277 (1990); 355 (1980)　**Pop Density:** 461.7
Land: 0.6 sq. mi.; **Water:** 0.0 sq. mi.　**Elev:** 1610 ft.
Not coextensive with township. Incorporated 1922.
Name origin: From the Chippewa Indian term *uhnemoosh* meaning 'female dog.'

*Anamoose — Township
ZIP: 58710　**Lat:** 47-53-36 N　**Long:** 100-15-46 W
Pop: 89 (1990); 109 (1980)　**Pop Density:** 2.5
Land: 35.1 sq. mi.; **Water:** 0.4 sq. mi.

Balfour — City
ZIP: 58712　**Lat:** 47-57-08 N　**Long:** 100-32-04 W
Pop: 33 (1990); 51 (1980)　**Pop Density:** 66.0
Land: 0.5 sq. mi.; **Water:** 0.0 sq. mi.　**Elev:** 1615 ft.
Not coextensive with township. Incorporated 1921.

*Balfour — Township
ZIP: 58712　**Lat:** 47-58-53 N　**Long:** 100-31-18 W
Pop: 49 (1990); 99 (1980)　**Pop Density:** 1.4
Land: 35.0 sq. mi.; **Water:** 0.7 sq. mi.

Bantry — City
ZIP: 58713　**Lat:** 48-29-52 N　**Long:** 100-36-33 W
Pop: 16 (1990); 28 (1980)　**Pop Density:** 80.0
Land: 0.2 sq. mi.; **Water:** 0.0 sq. mi.　**Elev:** 1455 ft.
Not coextensive with township. Incorporated 1967.

*Bantry — Township
ZIP: 58713　**Lat:** 48-29-54 N　**Long:** 100-36-22 W
Pop: 66 (1990); 64 (1980)　**Pop Density:** 1.8
Land: 35.7 sq. mi.; **Water:** 0.1 sq. mi.

Bergen — City
ZIP: 58792　**Lat:** 48-00-16 N　**Long:** 100-43-05 W
Pop: 12 (1990); 24 (1980)　**Pop Density:** 17.1
Land: 0.7 sq. mi.; **Water:** 0.0 sq. mi.　**Elev:** 1587 ft.
Incorporated 1967.

Berwick — Township
Lat: 48-20-01 N　**Long:** 100-17-27 W
Pop: 93 (1990); 100 (1980)　**Pop Density:** 2.6
Land: 36.1 sq. mi.; **Water:** 0.2 sq. mi.

Bjornson — Township
Lat: 47-53-43 N　**Long:** 100-54-31 W
Pop: 56 (1990); 52 (1980)　**Pop Density:** 1.6
Land: 35.4 sq. mi.; **Water:** 0.3 sq. mi.

Brown — Township
Lat: 47-58-38 N　**Long:** 100-54-34 W
Pop: 81 (1990); 84 (1980)　**Pop Density:** 2.3
Land: 35.2 sq. mi.; **Water:** 0.2 sq. mi.

Cottonwood Lake — Township
Lat: 47-54-02 N　**Long:** 100-38-57 W
Pop: 36 (1990); 35 (1980)　**Pop Density:** 1.0
Land: 34.3 sq. mi.; **Water:** 1.8 sq. mi.

Deep River — Township
Lat: 48-35-15 N　**Long:** 100-51-08 W
Pop: 59 (1990); 79 (1980)　**Pop Density:** 1.6
Land: 36.1 sq. mi.; **Water:** 0.1 sq. mi.

Deering — City
ZIP: 58731　**Lat:** 48-23-42 N　**Long:** 101-02-57 W
Pop: 99 (1990); 85 (1980)　**Pop Density:** 990.0
Land: 0.1 sq. mi.; **Water:** 0.0 sq. mi.　**Elev:** 1542 ft.
Not coextensive with township.

*Deering — Township
ZIP: 58731　**Lat:** 48-24-40 N　**Long:** 100-59-00 W
Pop: 101 (1990); 135 (1980)　**Pop Density:** 2.8
Land: 36.0 sq. mi.; **Water:** 0.1 sq. mi.

Denbigh — Township
Lat: 48-19-12 N　**Long:** 100-33-01 W
Pop: 71 (1990); 77 (1980)　**Pop Density:** 2.0
Land: 36.2 sq. mi.; **Water:** 0.3 sq. mi.

Drake — City
ZIP: 58736　**Lat:** 47-55-18 N　**Long:** 100-22-33 W
Pop: 361 (1990); 479 (1980)　**Pop Density:** 180.5
Land: 2.0 sq. mi.; **Water:** 0.0 sq. mi.　**Elev:** 1682 ft.
Name origin: Named by Soo Railroad Company officials for Herman Drake, who homesteaded the town in 1899.

East McHenry — Pop. Place
Lat: 48-11-33 N　**Long:** 100-24-22 W
Pop: 122 (1990); 179 (1980)　**Pop Density:** 0.7
Land: 175.7 sq. mi.; **Water:** 4.2 sq. mi.

Egg Creek — Township
Lat: 48-19-54 N　**Long:** 100-49-56 W
Pop: 55 (1990); 75 (1980)　**Pop Density:** 1.6
Land: 34.3 sq. mi.; **Water:** 2.1 sq. mi.

Falsen — Township
Lat: 48-09-40 N　**Long:** 100-41-32 W
Pop: 43 (1990); 79 (1980)　**Pop Density:** 1.2
Land: 35.9 sq. mi.; **Water:** 0.1 sq. mi.

Gilmore — Township
Lat: 48-25-10 N　**Long:** 100-44-37 W
Pop: 20 (1990); 15 (1980)　**Pop Density:** 0.6
Land: 35.6 sq. mi.; **Water:** 0.7 sq. mi.

Granville — City
ZIP: 58741　**Lat:** 48-16-02 N　**Long:** 100-50-34 W
Pop: 236 (1990); 281 (1980)　**Pop Density:** 1180.0
Land: 0.2 sq. mi.; **Water:** 0.0 sq. mi.　**Elev:** 1515 ft.
Not coextensive with townshp.

NORTH DAKOTA, McHenry County

*Granville — Township
ZIP: 58741   Lat: 48-14-24 N   Long: 100-49-19 W
Pop: 114 (1990); 114 (1980)   Pop Density: 3.2
Land: 35.2 sq. mi.; Water: 0.8 sq. mi.

Grilley — Township
Lat: 48-30-00 N   Long: 100-59-15 W
Pop: 78 (1990); 84 (1980)   Pop Density: 2.2
Land: 35.9 sq. mi.; Water: 0.1 sq. mi.

Hendrickson — Township
Lat: 48-09-18 N   Long: 100-48-36 W
Pop: 71 (1990); 81 (1980)   Pop Density: 2.0
Land: 36.1 sq. mi.; Water: 0.0 sq. mi.

Karlsruhe — City
ZIP: 58744   Lat: 48-05-26 N   Long: 100-37-01 W
Pop: 143 (1990); 164 (1980)   Pop Density: 178.8
Land: 0.8 sq. mi.; Water: 0.0 sq. mi.   Elev: 1540 ft.
Not coextensive with township.

*Karlsruhe — Township
ZIP: 58744   Lat: 48-03-43 N   Long: 100-33-49 W
Pop: 63 (1990); 71 (1980)   Pop Density: 1.8
Land: 34.3 sq. mi.; Water: 1.1 sq. mi.

Kief — City
ZIP: 58747   Lat: 47-51-37 N   Long: 100-30-45 W
Pop: 24 (1990); 36 (1980)   Pop Density: 20.0
Land: 1.2 sq. mi.; Water: 0.0 sq. mi.   Elev: 1668 ft.

Kottke Valley — Township
Lat: 48-19-38 N   Long: 100-57-10 W
Pop: 43 (1990); 61 (1980)   Pop Density: 1.2
Land: 35.7 sq. mi.; Water: 0.0 sq. mi.

Lake George — Township
Lat: 48-03-29 N   Long: 100-25-53 W
Pop: 77 (1990); 95 (1980)   Pop Density: 2.2
Land: 34.8 sq. mi.; Water: 1.2 sq. mi.

Lake Hester — Township
Lat: 48-03-58 N   Long: 100-41-22 W
Pop: 74 (1990); 119 (1980)   Pop Density: 2.1
Land: 35.6 sq. mi.; Water: 0.3 sq. mi.

Land — Township
Lat: 47-53-40 N   Long: 100-30-37 W
Pop: 64 (1990); 51 (1980)   Pop Density: 1.9
Land: 34.3 sq. mi.; Water: 0.4 sq. mi.

Layton — Township
Lat: 48-30-09 N   Long: 100-43-49 W
Pop: 39 (1990); 55 (1980)   Pop Density: 1.1
Land: 35.9 sq. mi.; Water: 0.1 sq. mi.

Lebanon — Township
Lat: 48-04-23 N   Long: 100-49-51 W
Pop: 111 (1990); 110 (1980)   Pop Density: 3.1
Land: 35.5 sq. mi.; Water: 0.6 sq. mi.

Little Deep — Township
Lat: 48-29-41 N   Long: 100-52-23 W
Pop: 54 (1990); 60 (1980)   Pop Density: 1.5
Land: 36.2 sq. mi.; Water: 0.1 sq. mi.

Meadow — Township
Lat: 48-35-19 N   Long: 100-44-05 W
Pop: 80 (1990); 76 (1980)   Pop Density: 2.6
Land: 31.2 sq. mi.; Water: 4.5 sq. mi.

Mouse River — Township
Lat: 48-35-00 N   Long: 100-36-37 W
Pop: 36 (1990); 35 (1980)   Pop Density: 1.2
Land: 31.3 sq. mi.; Water: 4.7 sq. mi.

Newport — Township
Lat: 48-19-51 N   Long: 100-25-32 W
Pop: 140 (1990); 149 (1980)   Pop Density: 3.9
Land: 35.8 sq. mi.; Water: 0.0 sq. mi.

Normal — Township
Lat: 48-29-56 N   Long: 100-20-39 W
Pop: 80 (1990); 101 (1980)   Pop Density: 2.2
Land: 35.6 sq. mi.; Water: 0.1 sq. mi.

Northeast McHenry — Pop. Place
Lat: 48-26-40 N   Long: 100-25-20 W
Pop: 136 (1990); 135 (1980)   Pop Density: 1.3
Land: 107.6 sq. mi.; Water: 0.5 sq. mi.

North Prairie — Township
Lat: 48-08-53 N   Long: 100-56-21 W
Pop: 110 (1990); 112 (1980)   Pop Density: 3.1
Land: 35.8 sq. mi.; Water: 0.0 sq. mi.

Norwich — Township
ZIP: 58768   Lat: 48-14-46 N   Long: 100-56-23 W
Pop: 167 (1990); 183 (1980)   Pop Density: 4.7
Land: 35.6 sq. mi.; Water: 0.1 sq. mi.

Odin — Township
Lat: 47-59-04 N   Long: 100-38-36 W
Pop: 59 (1990); 78 (1980)   Pop Density: 1.7
Land: 34.4 sq. mi.; Water: 1.7 sq. mi.

Olivia — Township
Lat: 47-53-24 N   Long: 100-46-37 W
Pop: 66 (1990); 83 (1980)   Pop Density: 1.8
Land: 35.9 sq. mi.; Water: 0.0 sq. mi.

Pratt — Township
Lat: 48-35-46 N   Long: 100-58-59 W
Pop: 51 (1990); 76 (1980)   Pop Density: 1.4
Land: 36.0 sq. mi.; Water: 0.0 sq. mi.

Riga — Township
Lat: 48-19-11 N   Long: 100-40-48 W
Pop: 91 (1990); 71 (1980)   Pop Density: 2.6
Land: 34.9 sq. mi.; Water: 1.5 sq. mi.

Rose Hill — Township
Lat: 48-13-57 N   Long: 100-40-45 W
Pop: 26 (1990); 59 (1980)   Pop Density: 0.7
Land: 35.8 sq. mi.; Water: 0.1 sq. mi.

Round Lake — Township
Lat: 48-04-10 N   Long: 100-18-05 W
Pop: 49 (1990); 70 (1980)   Pop Density: 1.5
Land: 32.6 sq. mi.; Water: 3.5 sq. mi.

Saline — Township
Lat: 48-24-27 N   Long: 100-52-28 W
Pop: 31 (1990); 35 (1980)   Pop Density: 0.9
Land: 36.1 sq. mi.; Water: 0.1 sq. mi.

Schiller — Township
Lat: 47-58-13 N   Long: 100-15-37 W
Pop: 95 (1990); 104 (1980)   Pop Density: 2.7
Land: 35.4 sq. mi.; Water: 1.0 sq. mi.

Spring Grove
Township
Lat: 47-53-42 N **Long:** 100-23-53 W
Pop: 48 (1990); 68 (1980) **Pop Density:** 1.5
Land: 32.2 sq. mi.; **Water:** 1.8 sq. mi.

Strege
Township
Lat: 47-58-40 N **Long:** 100-23-04 W
Pop: 67 (1990); 87 (1980) **Pop Density:** 1.9
Land: 35.3 sq. mi.; **Water:** 0.9 sq. mi.

Towner
City
ZIP: 58788 **Lat:** 48-20-51 N **Long:** 100-24-25 W
Pop: 669 (1990); 867 (1980) **Pop Density:** 836.3
Land: 0.8 sq. mi.; **Water:** 0.0 sq. mi. **Elev:** 1486 ft.
Settled 1886.
Name origin: For Col. O. M. Towner, a Civil War veteran and an early rancher.

Upham
City
ZIP: 58789 **Lat:** 48-34-49 N **Long:** 100-43-41 W
Pop: 205 (1990); 227 (1980) **Pop Density:** 1025.0
Land: 0.2 sq. mi.; **Water:** 0.0 sq. mi. **Elev:** 1445 ft.
Founded 1905.
Name origin: For explorer and geologist Dr. Warren Upham.

Velva
City
ZIP: 58790 **Lat:** 48-03-29 N **Long:** 100-55-52 W
Pop: 968 (1990); 1,101 (1980) **Pop Density:** 1210.0
Land: 0.8 sq. mi.; **Water:** 0.0 sq. mi. **Elev:** 1505 ft.
Not coextensive with township.
Name origin: Named by Soo Railroad officials for the velvet-like appearance of the Mouse River Valley.

*Velva
Township
ZIP: 58790 **Lat:** 48-03-45 N **Long:** 100-56-55 W
Pop: 163 (1990); 194 (1980) **Pop Density:** 4.6
Land: 35.1 sq. mi.; **Water:** 0.1 sq. mi.

Villard
Township
Lat: 48-08-42 N **Long:** 100-33-42 W
Pop: 43 (1990); 65 (1980) **Pop Density:** 1.2
Land: 35.9 sq. mi.; **Water:** 0.3 sq. mi.

Voltaire
City
ZIP: 58792 **Lat:** 48-01-09 N **Long:** 100-50-38 W
Pop: 63 (1990); 65 (1980) **Pop Density:** 157.5
Land: 0.4 sq. mi.; **Water:** 0.0 sq. mi. **Elev:** 1588 ft.

*Voltaire
Township
ZIP: 58792 **Lat:** 47-58-14 N **Long:** 100-47-12 W
Pop: 39 (1990); 53 (1980) **Pop Density:** 1.1
Land: 35.1 sq. mi.; **Water:** 0.4 sq. mi.

Wagar
Township
Lat: 48-24-27 N **Long:** 100-36-47 W
Pop: 54 (1990); 77 (1980) **Pop Density:** 1.5
Land: 36.0 sq. mi.; **Water:** 0.1 sq. mi.

Willow Creek
Township
Lat: 48-34-50 N **Long:** 100-28-38 W
Pop: 62 (1990); 79 (1980) **Pop Density:** 1.7
Land: 36.3 sq. mi.; **Water:** 0.1 sq. mi.

McIntosh County
County Seat: Ashley (ZIP: 58413)

Pop: 4,021 (1990); 4,800 (1980) **Pop Density:** 4.1
Land: 975.3 sq. mi.; **Water:** 19.8 sq. mi. **Area Code:** 701
On the central southern border of ND, southeast of Bismarck; organized Mar 9, 1883 (prior to statehood) from Logan County.
Name origin: For either John J. McIntosh, a state legislator, or for Edward H. McIntosh (1922–1901), a Dakota territorial legislator.

Ashley
City
ZIP: 58413 **Lat:** 46-02-05 N **Long:** 99-22-24 W
Pop: 1,052 (1990); 1,192 (1980) **Pop Density:** 1753.3
Land: 0.6 sq. mi.; **Water:** 0.0 sq. mi. **Elev:** 2005 ft.
Incorporated 1920.
Name origin: For Ashley Morrow, who was part of the construction company that built the railroad here in 1887.

East McIntosh
Pop. Place
Lat: 46-04-19 N **Long:** 99-11-35 W
Pop: 454 (1990); 573 (1980) **Pop Density:** 1.3
Land: 347.8 sq. mi.; **Water:** 12.3 sq. mi.

Lehr
City
ZIP: 58460 **Lat:** 46-16-53 N **Long:** 99-21-06 W
Pop: 147 (1990); 197 (1980) **Pop Density:** 1470.0
Land: 0.1 sq. mi.; **Water:** 0.0 sq. mi. **Elev:** 2050 ft.
Part of the town is also in Logan County.

Northwest McIntosh
Pop. Place
Lat: 46-12-01 N **Long:** 99-35-20 W
Pop: 498 (1990); 654 (1980) **Pop Density:** 1.5
Land: 321.5 sq. mi.; **Water:** 4.8 sq. mi.

Roloff
Township
Lat: 46-14-35 N **Long:** 99-03-46 W
Pop: 38 (1990); 36 (1980) **Pop Density:** 1.1
Land: 33.9 sq. mi.; **Water:** 0.2 sq. mi.

Southwest McIntosh
Pop. Place
Lat: 46-02-06 N **Long:** 99-38-19 W
Pop: 434 (1990); 510 (1980) **Pop Density:** 1.6
Land: 269.5 sq. mi.; **Water:** 2.6 sq. mi.

Venturia
City
ZIP: 58489 **Lat:** 45-59-50 N **Long:** 99-32-57 W
Pop: 30 (1990); 40 (1980) **Pop Density:** 300.0
Land: 0.1 sq. mi.; **Water:** 0.0 sq. mi. **Elev:** 2078 ft.

NORTH DAKOTA, McIntosh County

Wishek City
ZIP: 58495 **Lat:** 46-15-20 N **Long:** 99-33-18 W
Pop: 1,171 (1990); 1,345 (1980) **Pop Density:** 780.7
Land: 1.5 sq. mi.; **Water:** 0.0 sq. mi. **Elev:** 2038 ft.
Surveyed 1898.
Name origin: For original landowner John Wishek.

Zeeland City
ZIP: 58581 **Lat:** 45-58-23 N **Long:** 99-49-56 W
Pop: 197 (1990); 253 (1980) **Pop Density:** 656.7
Land: 0.3 sq. mi.; **Water:** 0.0 sq. mi. **Elev:** 2005 ft.

McKenzie County
County Seat: Watford City (ZIP: 58854)

Pop: 6,383 (1990); 7,132 (1980) **Pop Density:** 2.3
Land: 2742.2 sq. mi.; **Water:** 118.9 sq. mi. **Area Code:** 701

On the central western border of ND, southwest of Minot; organized Mar 9, 1883 (prior to statehood) from Howard County, which was discontinued. McKenzie County eliminated in 1891 for lack of settlement; present county formed 1905.

Name origin: For Alexander McKenzie (1851–1922), sheriff of Burleigh County and a powerful political leader.

Alex Township
Lat: 47-47-41 N **Long:** 103-36-18 W
Pop: 56 (1990); 51 (1980) **Pop Density:** 1.6
Land: 34.8 sq. mi.; **Water:** 0.0 sq. mi.

Alexander City
ZIP: 58831 **Lat:** 47-50-27 N **Long:** 103-38-33 W
Pop: 216 (1990); 358 (1980) **Pop Density:** 216.0
Land: 1.0 sq. mi.; **Water:** 0.0 sq. mi. **Elev:** 2180 ft.
Founded 1906. Incorporated 1967.
Name origin: For political leader Alexander McKenzie (1851–1922).

Antelope Creek Township
Lat: 47-42-38 N **Long:** 103-35-36 W
Pop: 18 (1990); 21 (1980) **Pop Density:** 0.5
Land: 36.0 sq. mi.; **Water:** 0.0 sq. mi.

Arnegard City
ZIP: 58835 **Lat:** 47-48-29 N **Long:** 103-26-17 W
Pop: 122 (1990); 193 (1980) **Pop Density:** 406.7
Land: 0.3 sq. mi.; **Water:** 0.0 sq. mi. **Elev:** 2244 ft.
Not coextensive with townshp. Incorporated 1967.

*Arnegard Township
ZIP: 58835 **Lat:** 47-48-29 N **Long:** 103-28-32 W
Pop: 68 (1990); 89 (1980) **Pop Density:** 1.9
Land: 35.4 sq. mi.; **Water:** 0.1 sq. mi.

Blue Butte Township
Lat: 47-52-57 N **Long:** 102-57-43 W
Pop: 81 (1990); 98 (1980) **Pop Density:** 2.3
Land: 34.5 sq. mi.; **Water:** 1.2 sq. mi.

Central McKenzie Pop. Place
Lat: 47-41-58 N **Long:** 103-12-21 W
Pop: 862 (1990); 239 (1980) **Pop Density:** 2.2
Land: 399.9 sq. mi.; **Water:** 1.8 sq. mi.

Charbon Township
Lat: 47-53-17 N **Long:** 103-44-23 W
Pop: 59 (1990); 60 (1980) **Pop Density:** 1.6
Land: 35.8 sq. mi.; **Water:** 0.0 sq. mi.

East McKenzie Pop. Place
Lat: 47-51-49 N **Long:** 102-42-06 W
Pop: 919 (1990); 927 (1980) **Pop Density:** 5.0
Land: 183.1 sq. mi.; **Water:** 14.6 sq. mi.

Elk Township
Lat: 47-58-41 N **Long:** 103-44-24 W
Pop: 21 (1990); 26 (1980) **Pop Density:** 0.6
Land: 36.2 sq. mi.; **Water:** 0.3 sq. mi.

Elm Tree Township
Lat: 48-05-10 N **Long:** 102-53-55 W
Pop: 60 (1990); 71 (1980) **Pop Density:** 1.5
Land: 39.1 sq. mi.; **Water:** 4.9 sq. mi.

Four Bears Village CDP
Lat: 47-59-21 N **Long:** 102-35-49 W
Pop: 309 (1990) **Pop Density:** 280.9
Land: 1.1 sq. mi.; **Water:** 0.0 sq. mi.

Grail Township
Lat: 47-48-20 N **Long:** 102-49-53 W
Pop: 62 (1990); 64 (1980) **Pop Density:** 2.0
Land: 31.6 sq. mi.; **Water:** 0.0 sq. mi.

Hawkeye Township
Lat: 47-58-53 N **Long:** 102-50-06 W
Pop: 73 (1990); 67 (1980) **Pop Density:** 2.2
Land: 33.5 sq. mi.; **Water:** 0.0 sq. mi.

Keene Township
ZIP: 58847 **Lat:** 47-58-39 N **Long:** 102-57-44 W
Pop: 44 (1990); 42 (1980) **Pop Density:** 1.2
Land: 36.9 sq. mi.; **Water:** 0.0 sq. mi.

Mandaree CDP
ZIP: 58757 **Lat:** 47-44-18 N **Long:** 102-40-36 W
Pop: 367 (1990) **Pop Density:** 32.8
Land: 11.2 sq. mi.; **Water:** 0.0 sq. mi.

North McKenzie Pop. Place
Lat: 47-55-17 N **Long:** 103-15-58 W
Pop: 503 (1990); 225 (1980) **Pop Density:** 1.3
Land: 379.7 sq. mi.; **Water:** 20.1 sq. mi.

Poe Township
Lat: 47-59-17 N **Long:** 103-35-41 W
Pop: 23 (1990); 29 (1980) **Pop Density:** 0.6
Land: 35.5 sq. mi.; **Water:** 1.1 sq. mi.

Randolph Township
Lat: 47-48-42 N **Long:** 103-43-38 W
Pop: 15 (1990); 23 (1980) **Pop Density:** 0.4
Land: 35.8 sq. mi.; **Water:** 0.0 sq. mi.

Rawson
City
ZIP: 58831 Lat: 47-49-11 N Long: 103-32-26 W
Pop: 9 (1990); 12 (1980) Pop Density: 45.0
Land: 0.2 sq. mi.; Water: 0.0 sq. mi. Elev: 2256 ft.

Red Wing
Township
Lat: 47-38-43 N Long: 103-32-46 W
Pop: 49 (1990); 51 (1980) Pop Density: 1.4
Land: 35.5 sq. mi.; Water: 0.0 sq. mi.

Riverview
Township
Lat: 48-02-17 N Long: 102-43-40 W
Pop: 5 (1990); 20 (1980) Pop Density: 0.1
Land: 42.4 sq. mi.; Water: 14.3 sq. mi.

Sioux
Township
Lat: 47-55-30 N Long: 103-52-23 W
Pop: 146 (1990); 174 (1980) Pop Density: 2.3
Land: 64.3 sq. mi.; Water: 7.9 sq. mi.

Southeast McKenzie
Pop. Place
Lat: 47-27-19 N Long: 103-21-09 W
Pop: 282 (1990) Pop Density: 0.7
Land: 400.2 sq. mi.; Water: 2.6 sq. mi.

Southwest McKenzie
Pop. Place
Lat: 47-33-59 N Long: 103-50-01 W
Pop: 284 (1990); 566 (1980) Pop Density: 0.4
Land: 665.3 sq. mi.; Water: 2.8 sq. mi.

Twin Valley
Township
Lat: 48-02-18 N Long: 103-11-39 W
Pop: 81 (1990); 105 (1980) Pop Density: 1.0
Land: 79.1 sq. mi.; Water: 19.6 sq. mi.

Watford City
City
ZIP: 58854 Lat: 47-48-08 N Long: 103-16-17 W
Pop: 1,784 (1990); 2,119 (1980) Pop Density: 1115.0
Land: 1.6 sq. mi.; Water: 0.0 sq. mi. Elev: 2100 ft.
Name origin: For the city in Ontario, Canada, the former home of local physician V. G. Morris.

Wilbur
Township
Lat: 48-04-35 N Long: 103-40-31 W
Pop: 27 (1990); 31 (1980) Pop Density: 1.0
Land: 27.1 sq. mi.; Water: 24.6 sq. mi.

Yellowstone
Township
Lat: 47-53-16 N Long: 104-00-22 W
Pop: 514 (1990); 687 (1980) Pop Density: 13.8
Land: 37.3 sq. mi.; Water: 3.0 sq. mi.

McLean County
County Seat: Washburn (ZIP: 58577)

Pop: 10,457 (1990); 12,383 (1980) Pop Density: 5.0
Land: 2110.4 sq. mi.; Water: 217.8 sq. mi. Area Code: 701
In west-central ND, northwest of Bismarck; organized Mar 8, 1883 (prior to statehood) from Stevens County.
Name origin: For John A. McLean (1849–1916), first mayor of Bismarck, ND.

Amundsville
Township
Lat: 47-47-49 N Long: 101-56-05 W
Pop: 80 (1990); 91 (1980) Pop Density: 2.2
Land: 36.0 sq. mi.; Water: 0.1 sq. mi.

Andrews
Township
Lat: 47-47-49 N Long: 101-02-07 W
Pop: 47 (1990); 76 (1980) Pop Density: 1.3
Land: 35.8 sq. mi.; Water: 0.0 sq. mi.

Aurena
Township
Lat: 47-43-03 N Long: 100-46-02 W
Pop: 36 (1990); 57 (1980) Pop Density: 1.0
Land: 35.6 sq. mi.; Water: 0.4 sq. mi.

Benedict
City
ZIP: 58716 Lat: 47-49-49 N Long: 101-05-01 W
Pop: 52 (1990); 68 (1980) Pop Density: 173.3
Land: 0.3 sq. mi.; Water: 0.0 sq. mi. Elev: 2090 ft.
Incorporated 1967.

Blackwater
Township
Lat: 47-37-43 N Long: 101-45-03 W
Pop: 59 (1990); 89 (1980) Pop Density: 1.7
Land: 35.1 sq. mi.; Water: 0.1 sq. mi.

Blue Hill
Township
Lat: 47-48-11 N Long: 101-40-47 W
Pop: 29 (1990); 49 (1980) Pop Density: 0.8
Land: 35.9 sq. mi.; Water: 0.1 sq. mi.

Butte
City
ZIP: 58723 Lat: 47-50-14 N Long: 100-39-57 W
Pop: 129 (1990); 157 (1980) Pop Density: 430.0
Land: 0.3 sq. mi.; Water: 0.0 sq. mi. Elev: 1740 ft.

*Butte
Township
ZIP: 58723 Lat: 47-48-19 N Long: 100-46-41 W
Pop: 29 (1990); 23 (1980) Pop Density: 0.8
Land: 35.7 sq. mi.; Water: 0.4 sq. mi.

Byersville
Township
Lat: 47-42-40 N Long: 100-39-32 W
Pop: 39 (1990); 41 (1980) Pop Density: 1.1
Land: 34.9 sq. mi.; Water: 1.3 sq. mi.

Coleharbor
City
ZIP: 58531 Lat: 47-32-32 N Long: 101-13-16 W
Pop: 88 (1990); 150 (1980) Pop Density: 440.0
Land: 0.2 sq. mi.; Water: 0.0 sq. mi. Elev: 1897 ft.
Name origin: Named by Soo Railroad officials for one of their employees, W. A. Cole.

NORTH DAKOTA, McLean County

Cremerville — Township
Lat: 47-48-13 N Long: 102-03-54 W
Pop: 63 (1990); 59 (1980) Pop Density: 1.8
Land: 35.7 sq. mi.; Water: 0.1 sq. mi.

Deepwater — Township
Lat: 47-43-28 N Long: 101-56-47 W
Pop: 32 (1990); 61 (1980) Pop Density: 0.9
Land: 36.1 sq. mi.; Water: 0.0 sq. mi.

Dogden — Township
Lat: 47-48-13 N Long: 100-38-36 W
Pop: 73 (1990); 81 (1980) Pop Density: 2.1
Land: 35.3 sq. mi.; Water: 0.4 sq. mi.

Douglas — Township
Lat: 47-48-11 N Long: 101-32-42 W
Pop: 53 (1990); 58 (1980) Pop Density: 1.5
Land: 35.7 sq. mi.; Water: 0.3 sq. mi.

East McLean — Pop. Place
Lat: 47-37-35 N Long: 100-55-31 W
Pop: 111 (1990); 152 (1980) Pop Density: 1.6
Land: 67.9 sq. mi.; Water: 2.7 sq. mi.

Economy — Township
Lat: 47-47-54 N Long: 101-17-29 W
Pop: 52 (1990); 104 (1980) Pop Density: 1.5
Land: 34.9 sq. mi.; Water: 0.3 sq. mi.

Garrison — City
ZIP: 58540 Lat: 47-39-13 N Long: 101-25-24 W
Pop: 1,530 (1990); 1,830 (1980) Pop Density: 1176.9
Land: 1.3 sq. mi.; Water: 0.0 sq. mi. Elev: 1920 ft.
Name origin: For Garrison Stream, which was named in 1864 by troops garrisoned at nearby Fort Stevenson.

Gate — Township
Lat: 47-48-13 N Long: 101-48-18 W
Pop: 33 (1990); 59 (1980) Pop Density: 0.9
Land: 35.7 sq. mi.; Water: 0.2 sq. mi.

Greatstone — Township
Lat: 47-42-46 N Long: 101-01-35 W
Pop: 50 (1990); 62 (1980) Pop Density: 1.4
Land: 36.0 sq. mi.; Water: 0.0 sq. mi.

Horseshoe Valley — Township
Lat: 47-43-07 N Long: 100-54-28 W
Pop: 55 (1990); 60 (1980) Pop Density: 1.6
Land: 35.3 sq. mi.; Water: 0.8 sq. mi.

Lake Williams — Township
Lat: 47-32-37 N Long: 100-51-47 W
Pop: 82 (1990); 112 (1980) Pop Density: 2.5
Land: 32.4 sq. mi.; Water: 3.2 sq. mi.

Longfellow — Township
Lat: 47-27-48 N Long: 101-15-30 W
Pop: 55 (1990); 66 (1980) Pop Density: 1.5
Land: 36.1 sq. mi.; Water: 0.1 sq. mi.

Loquemont — Township
Lat: 47-43-07 N Long: 102-04-00 W
Pop: 80 (1990); 76 (1980) Pop Density: 2.2
Land: 35.9 sq. mi.; Water: 0.0 sq. mi.

McGinnis — Township
Lat: 47-42-37 N Long: 101-24-38 W
Pop: 89 (1990); 93 (1980) Pop Density: 2.5
Land: 35.6 sq. mi.; Water: 0.5 sq. mi.

Malcolm — Township
Lat: 47-38-22 N Long: 101-07-14 W
Pop: 86 (1990); 98 (1980) Pop Density: 3.2
Land: 26.8 sq. mi.; Water: 8.5 sq. mi.

Max — City
ZIP: 58759 Lat: 47-49-11 N Long: 101-17-27 W
Pop: 301 (1990); 330 (1980) Pop Density: 376.3
Land: 0.8 sq. mi.; Water: 0.0 sq. mi. Elev: 2100 ft.

Medicine Hill — Township
Lat: 47-37-30 N Long: 100-43-33 W
Pop: 68 (1990); 105 (1980) Pop Density: 2.0
Land: 34.3 sq. mi.; Water: 0.8 sq. mi.

Mercer — City
ZIP: 58559 Lat: 47-29-27 N Long: 100-42-36 W
Pop: 104 (1990); 134 (1980) Pop Density: 520.0
Land: 0.2 sq. mi.; Water: 0.0 sq. mi. Elev: 1926 ft.
Not coextensive with township.

*Mercer — Township
ZIP: 58559 Lat: 47-27-34 N Long: 100-43-56 W
Pop: 38 (1990); 50 (1980) Pop Density: 1.1
Land: 35.1 sq. mi.; Water: 0.7 sq. mi.

North Central McLean — Pop. Place
Lat: 47-39-18 N Long: 101-21-59 W
Pop: 393 (1990); 369 (1980) Pop Density: 6.1
Land: 64.6 sq. mi.; Water: 25.6 sq. mi.

Otis — Township
Lat: 47-48-10 N Long: 100-54-46 W
Pop: 65 (1990); 101 (1980) Pop Density: 1.9
Land: 35.1 sq. mi.; Water: 0.7 sq. mi.

Poplar — Pop. Place
Lat: 47-45-31 N Long: 101-09-26 W
Pop: 120 (1990); 92 (1980) Pop Density: 1.7
Land: 71.4 sq. mi.; Water: 0.7 sq. mi.

Riverdale — City
Lat: 47-29-47 N Long: 101-21-55 W
Pop: 283 (1990) Pop Density: 202.1
Land: 1.4 sq. mi.; Water: 0.0 sq. mi.

Roseglen — Township
ZIP: 58775 Lat: 47-43-28 N Long: 101-48-51 W
Pop: 86 (1990); 77 (1980) Pop Density: 2.4
Land: 35.6 sq. mi.; Water: 0.3 sq. mi.

Rosemont — Township
Lat: 47-48-45 N Long: 101-25-40 W
Pop: 50 (1990); 51 (1980) Pop Density: 1.4
Land: 35.8 sq. mi.; Water: 0.2 sq. mi.

Ruso — City
ZIP: 58778 Lat: 47-50-11 N Long: 100-56-00 W
Pop: 8 (1990); 12 (1980) Pop Density: 26.7
Land: 0.3 sq. mi.; Water: 0.0 sq. mi. Elev: 2080 ft.

St. Mary — Township
Lat: 47-38-24 N Long: 101-30-19 W
Pop: 100 (1990); 116 (1980) Pop Density: 3.0
Land: 33.1 sq. mi.; Water: 1.8 sq. mi.

Snow — Township
Lat: 47-37-31 N Long: 101-15-07 W
Pop: 77 (1990); 78 (1980) Pop Density: 3.6
Land: 21.3 sq. mi.; Water: 14.1 sq. mi.

NORTH DAKOTA, Mercer County

South McLean
Pop. Place
Lat: 47-20-06 N **Long:** 100-56-21 W
Pop: 765 (1990); 805 (1980) **Pop Density:** 2.1
Land: 370.5 sq. mi.; **Water:** 6.5 sq. mi.

Turtle Lake
City
ZIP: 58575 **Lat:** 47-31-17 N **Long:** 100-53-25 W
Pop: 681 (1990); 802 (1980) **Pop Density:** 1362.0
Land: 0.5 sq. mi.; **Water:** 0.0 sq. mi. **Elev:** 1875 ft.
Name origin: For the nearby turtle-shaped lake.

*Turtle Lake
Township
ZIP: 58575 **Lat:** 47-33-05 N **Long:** 100-59-22 W
Pop: 69 (1990); 75 (1980) **Pop Density:** 2.0
Land: 34.0 sq. mi.; **Water:** 2.0 sq. mi.

Underwood
City
ZIP: 58576 **Lat:** 47-27-15 N **Long:** 101-08-28 W
Pop: 976 (1990); 1,329 (1980) **Pop Density:** 1084.4
Land: 0.9 sq. mi.; **Water:** 0.0 sq. mi. **Elev:** 2026 ft.
Founded 1903.
Name origin: For a local railroad vice president, Fred Underwood.

*Underwood
Pop. Place
Lat: 47-27-25 N **Long:** 101-10-51 W
Pop: 370 (1990); 722 (1980) **Pop Density:** 2.0
Land: 181.2 sq. mi.; **Water:** 20.7 sq. mi.

Victoria
Township
Lat: 47-32-49 N **Long:** 101-15-07 W
Pop: 41 (1990); 33 (1980) **Pop Density:** 1.3
Land: 31.0 sq. mi.; **Water:** 4.9 sq. mi.

Washburn
City
ZIP: 58577 **Lat:** 47-17-28 N **Long:** 101-01-38 W
Pop: 1,506 (1990); 1,767 (1980) **Pop Density:** 836.7
Land: 1.8 sq. mi.; **Water:** 0.1 sq. mi. **Elev:** 1731 ft.
Founded 1882.
Name origin: Named by its founders for C. C. Washburn, the governor of WI in 1872.

West McLean
Pop. Place
Lat: 47-39-04 N **Long:** 101-55-16 W
Pop: 724 (1990); 752 (1980) **Pop Density:** 2.3
Land: 317.4 sq. mi.; **Water:** 117.0 sq. mi.

White Shield
CDP
Lat: 47-39-40 N **Long:** 101-50-41 W
Pop: 274 (1990) **Pop Density:** 74.1
Land: 3.7 sq. mi.; **Water:** 0.0 sq. mi.

Wilton
City
ZIP: 58579 **Lat:** 47-09-36 N **Long:** 100-47-11 W
Pop: 552 (1990); 688 (1980) **Pop Density:** 1840.0
Land: 0.3 sq. mi.; **Water:** 0.0 sq. mi. **Elev:** 2183 ft.
Founded 1898. Part of the town is also in Burleigh County.
Name origin: Named by Minneapolis flour magnate, W. D. Washburn, for Wilton, ME, his former home.

Wise
Township
Lat: 47-32-52 N **Long:** 100-44-28 W
Pop: 48 (1990); 65 (1980) **Pop Density:** 1.4
Land: 33.4 sq. mi.; **Water:** 2.5 sq. mi.

Mercer County
County Seat: Stanton (ZIP: 58571)

Pop: 9,808 (1990); 9,404 (1980) **Pop Density:** 9.4
Land: 1045.4 sq. mi.; **Water:** 67.1 sq. mi. **Area Code:** 701
In west-central ND, northwest of Bismarck; organized Jan 14, 1875 (prior to statehood) from original territory.
Name origin: For William Henry Harrison Mercer (1884–1901), an early rancher.

Beulah
City
ZIP: 58523 **Lat:** 47-16-00 N **Long:** 101-46-24 W
Pop: 3,363 (1990); 2,908 (1980) **Pop Density:** 1401.3
Land: 2.4 sq. mi.; **Water:** 0.0 sq. mi. **Elev:** 1780 ft.
Incorporated 1967.
Name origin: For a niece of the land company agent. Originally called Troy.

East Mercer
Pop. Place
Lat: 47-23-35 N **Long:** 101-33-25 W
Pop: 1,254 (1990); 1,220 (1980) **Pop Density:** 3.6
Land: 345.4 sq. mi.; **Water:** 34.2 sq. mi.

Golden Valley
City
ZIP: 58541 **Lat:** 47-17-25 N **Long:** 102-03-52 W
Pop: 239 (1990); 287 (1980) **Pop Density:** 341.4
Land: 0.7 sq. mi.; **Water:** 0.0 sq. mi.

Hazen
City
ZIP: 58545 **Lat:** 47-17-58 N **Long:** 101-37-29 W
Pop: 2,818 (1990); 2,365 (1980) **Pop Density:** 2167.7
Land: 1.3 sq. mi.; **Water:** 0.0 sq. mi. **Elev:** 1743 ft.
Founded 1885.
Name origin: For assistant postmaster, A.D. Hazen.

Pick City
City
ZIP: 58545 **Lat:** 47-30-42 N **Long:** 101-27-21 W
Pop: 203 (1990); 182 (1980) **Pop Density:** 1015.0
Land: 0.2 sq. mi.; **Water:** 0.0 sq. mi. **Elev:** 1952 ft.

Stanton
City
ZIP: 58571 **Lat:** 47-19-06 N **Long:** 101-22-55 W
Pop: 517 (1990); 623 (1980) **Pop Density:** 1292.5
Land: 0.4 sq. mi.; **Water:** 0.0 sq. mi. **Elev:** 1701 ft.
Name origin: The McGrath brothers, who settled here 1882, gave it their mother's maiden name.

West Mercer
Pop. Place
Lat: 47-16-13 N **Long:** 101-58-35 W
Pop: 1,127 (1990); 1,308 (1980) **Pop Density:** 1.6
Land: 694.1 sq. mi.; **Water:** 32.8 sq. mi.

Zap — City
ZIP: 58580 Lat: 47-17-05 N Long: 101-55-18 W
Pop: 287 (1990); 511 (1980) Pop Density: 287.0
Land: 1.0 sq. mi.; Water: 0.0 sq. mi. Elev: 1845 ft.

Morton County
County Seat: Mandan (ZIP: 58554)

Pop: 23,700 (1990); 25,177 (1980) Pop Density: 12.3
Land: 1926.4 sq. mi.; Water: 19.0 sq. mi. Area Code: 701
In south-central ND, west of Bismarck; organized Jan 8, 1873 (prior to statehood) from original territory.
Name origin: For Oliver Hazard Perry Throck Morton (1823–77), jurist, IN governor (1861–67), and U.S. senator (1867–77).

Almont — City
ZIP: 58520 Lat: 46-43-40 N Long: 101-30-09 W
Pop: 117 (1990); 146 (1980) Pop Density: 45.0
Land: 2.6 sq. mi.; Water: 0.0 sq. mi. Elev: 1910 ft.
Founded 1906. Incorporated 1967.
Name origin: A contraction of the nearby Altamount Buttes, a glacial moraine.

Captain's Landing — Township
Lat: 46-48-45 N Long: 100-49-42 W
Pop: 138 (1990) Pop Density: 460.0
Land: 0.3 sq. mi.; Water: 0.1 sq. mi.

East Morton — Pop. Place
Lat: 46-37-29 N Long: 100-59-41 W
Pop: 2,609 (1990); 2,838 (1980) Pop Density: 2.5
Land: 1027.8 sq. mi.; Water: 15.1 sq. mi.

Engelter — Township
Lat: 46-51-15 N Long: 101-24-04 W
Pop: 108 (1990); 114 (1980) Pop Density: 3.1
Land: 34.5 sq. mi.; Water: 0.0 sq. mi.

Flasher — City
Lat: 46-27-07 N Long: 101-13-55 W
Pop: 317 (1990); 410 (1980) Pop Density: 452.9
Land: 0.7 sq. mi.; Water: 0.0 sq. mi. Elev: 1920 ft.
Founded 1902.
Name origin: For homesteader Mabel Flasher.

Glen Ullin — City
ZIP: 58631 Lat: 46-48-44 N Long: 101-49-55 W
Pop: 927 (1990); 1,125 (1980) Pop Density: 927.0
Land: 1.0 sq. mi.; Water: 0.0 sq. mi. Elev: 2072 ft.
Founded 1883.
Name origin: Coined by land agent Alvin E. Bovay from *glen* Gaelic for 'valley' and *Ullin* from an English ballad, "Lord Ullin's Daughter."

Hebron — City
ZIP: 58638 Lat: 46-54-10 N Long: 102-02-38 W
Pop: 888 (1990); 1,078 (1980) Pop Density: 592.0
Land: 1.5 sq. mi.; Water: 0.0 sq. mi. Elev: 2167 ft.
Name origin: Named in 1904 for the biblical valley. Originally called Knife River.

Mandan — City
ZIP: 58554 Lat: 46-49-45 N Long: 100-53-16 W
Pop: 15,177 (1990); 15,513 (1980) Pop Density: 1517.7
Land: 10.0 sq. mi.; Water: 0.1 sq. mi. Elev: 1651 ft.
In southwest-central ND, across the Missouri River from Bismarck. Incorporated 1883.
Name origin: For the Mandan Indians.

*Mandan — Pop. Place
Lat: 46-51-24 N Long: 100-56-01 W
Pop: 1,265 (1990); 1,408 (1980) Pop Density: 20.0
Land: 63.2 sq. mi.; Water: 1.9 sq. mi.

New Salem — City
ZIP: 58563 Lat: 46-50-34 N Long: 101-25-02 W
Pop: 909 (1990); 1,081 (1980) Pop Density: 757.5
Land: 1.2 sq. mi.; Water: 0.0 sq. mi. Elev: 2161 ft.

West Morton — Pop. Place
Lat: 46-48-52 N Long: 101-40-30 W
Pop: 1,245 (1990); 1,368 (1980) Pop Density: 1.6
Land: 783.5 sq. mi.; Water: 1.8 sq. mi.

Mountrail County
County Seat: Stanley (ZIP: 58784)

Pop: 7,021 (1990); 7,679 (1980) **Pop Density:** 3.8
Land: 1824.0 sq. mi.; **Water:** 117.2 sq. mi. **Area Code:** 701

In north-central ND, west of Minot; organized as Mountraille County Jan 4, 1873 (prior to statehood) from Ward County. Eliminated in 1891; reestablished with present spelling Jan 25, 1909.

Name origin: For "Savage" Joseph Mountraille, prominent voyageur who carried the mail.

Alger Township
Lat: 48-13-53 N **Long:** 102-30-22 W
Pop: 43 (1990); 63 (1980) **Pop Density:** 1.2
Land: 35.3 sq. mi.; **Water:** 0.5 sq. mi.

Austin Township
Lat: 48-08-58 N **Long:** 102-14-05 W
Pop: 35 (1990); 44 (1980) **Pop Density:** 1.0
Land: 35.7 sq. mi.; **Water:** 0.2 sq. mi.

Banner Township
Lat: 47-53-44 N **Long:** 102-04-05 W
Pop: 49 (1990); 41 (1980) **Pop Density:** 1.4
Land: 36.0 sq. mi.; **Water:** 0.0 sq. mi.

Bicker Township
Lat: 48-30-39 N **Long:** 102-49-25 W
Pop: 58 (1990); 64 (1980) **Pop Density:** 1.6
Land: 35.8 sq. mi.; **Water:** 0.1 sq. mi.

Big Bend Township
Lat: 47-53-05 N **Long:** 102-34-56 W
Pop: 56 (1990); 42 (1980) **Pop Density:** 1.8
Land: 31.4 sq. mi.; **Water:** 5.1 sq. mi.

Brookbank Township
Lat: 48-09-14 N **Long:** 102-30-13 W
Pop: 41 (1990); 40 (1980) **Pop Density:** 1.1
Land: 35.9 sq. mi.; **Water:** 0.0 sq. mi.

Burke Township
Lat: 48-13-59 N **Long:** 102-14-44 W
Pop: 43 (1990); 51 (1980) **Pop Density:** 1.2
Land: 35.5 sq. mi.; **Water:** 0.2 sq. mi.

Clearwater Township
Lat: 48-25-30 N **Long:** 102-17-55 W
Pop: 31 (1990); 53 (1980) **Pop Density:** 0.9
Land: 35.1 sq. mi.; **Water:** 0.9 sq. mi.

Cottonwood Township
Lat: 48-25-09 N **Long:** 102-33-41 W
Pop: 51 (1990); 54 (1980) **Pop Density:** 1.5
Land: 33.6 sq. mi.; **Water:** 2.3 sq. mi.

Crane Creek Township
Lat: 48-03-37 N **Long:** 102-22-23 W
Pop: 39 (1990); 62 (1980) **Pop Density:** 1.1
Land: 35.7 sq. mi.; **Water:** 0.3 sq. mi.

Crowfoot Township
Lat: 48-30-18 N **Long:** 102-09-51 W
Pop: 27 (1990); 38 (1980) **Pop Density:** 0.8
Land: 34.4 sq. mi.; **Water:** 1.4 sq. mi.

Debing Township
Lat: 48-14-04 N **Long:** 102-37-37 W
Pop: 56 (1990); 67 (1980) **Pop Density:** 1.6
Land: 35.6 sq. mi.; **Water:** 0.3 sq. mi.

Egan Township
Lat: 48-19-42 N **Long:** 101-59-31 W
Pop: 66 (1990); 69 (1980) **Pop Density:** 1.9
Land: 34.0 sq. mi.; **Water:** 2.6 sq. mi.

Fertile Township
Lat: 47-53-35 N **Long:** 102-12-13 W
Pop: 75 (1990); 71 (1980) **Pop Density:** 2.1
Land: 35.7 sq. mi.; **Water:** 0.0 sq. mi.

Howie Township
Lat: 47-53-28 N **Long:** 102-26-35 W
Pop: 41 (1990); 38 (1980) **Pop Density:** 1.5
Land: 26.9 sq. mi.; **Water:** 8.9 sq. mi.

Idaho Township
Lat: 48-19-28 N **Long:** 102-22-06 W
Pop: 171 (1990); 150 (1980) **Pop Density:** 5.1
Land: 33.7 sq. mi.; **Water:** 1.2 sq. mi.

James Hill Township
Lat: 48-25-14 N **Long:** 102-25-45 W
Pop: 50 (1990); 37 (1980) **Pop Density:** 1.6
Land: 31.8 sq. mi.; **Water:** 4.3 sq. mi.

Kickapoo Township
Lat: 48-14-41 N **Long:** 101-59-20 W
Pop: 17 (1990); 44 (1980) **Pop Density:** 0.5
Land: 33.2 sq. mi.; **Water:** 2.6 sq. mi.

Knife River Township
Lat: 48-04-25 N **Long:** 102-29-58 W
Pop: 23 (1990); 33 (1980) **Pop Density:** 0.6
Land: 35.7 sq. mi.; **Water:** 0.3 sq. mi.

Liberty Township
Lat: 47-54-03 N **Long:** 102-17-56 W
Pop: 19 (1990); 11 (1980) **Pop Density:** 1.4
Land: 13.4 sq. mi.; **Water:** 22.2 sq. mi.

Lostwood Township
Lat: 48-30-11 N **Long:** 102-25-06 W
Pop: 47 (1990); 64 (1980) **Pop Density:** 1.4
Land: 34.3 sq. mi.; **Water:** 1.6 sq. mi.

Lowland Township
Lat: 48-30-10 N **Long:** 102-02-20 W
Pop: 71 (1990); 75 (1980) **Pop Density:** 2.1
Land: 34.4 sq. mi.; **Water:** 1.6 sq. mi.

Manitou Township
ZIP: 58776 **Lat:** 48-20-04 N **Long:** 102-38-25 W
Pop: 60 (1990); 70 (1980) **Pop Density:** 1.7
Land: 36.2 sq. mi.; **Water:** 0.5 sq. mi.

McAlmond Township
Lat: 48-14-13 N **Long:** 102-06-19 W
Pop: 36 (1990); 56 (1980) **Pop Density:** 1.0
Land: 35.0 sq. mi.; **Water:** 0.8 sq. mi.

McGahan
Township
Lat: 48-20-13 N **Long:** 102-06-49 W
Pop: 68 (1990); 67 (1980) **Pop Density:** 2.0
Land: 34.6 sq. mi.; **Water:** 1.9 sq. mi.

Model
Township
Lat: 47-58-41 N **Long:** 102-03-55 W
Pop: 78 (1990); 81 (1980) **Pop Density:** 2.1
Land: 36.5 sq. mi.; **Water:** 0.1 sq. mi.

Mountrail
Township
Lat: 47-53-31 N **Long:** 101-55-24 W
Pop: 43 (1990); 64 (1980) **Pop Density:** 1.2
Land: 35.8 sq. mi.; **Water:** 0.0 sq. mi.

Myrtle
Township
Lat: 48-19-42 N **Long:** 102-45-59 W
Pop: 44 (1990); 35 (1980) **Pop Density:** 1.2
Land: 36.4 sq. mi.; **Water:** 0.1 sq. mi.

New Town
City
ZIP: 58763 **Lat:** 47-58-50 N **Long:** 102-29-22 W
Pop: 1,388 (1990); 1,335 (1980) **Pop Density:** 2313.3
Land: 0.6 sq. mi.; **Water:** 0.0 sq. mi. **Elev:** 1900 ft.
Founded 1950.
Name origin: For its role as a replacement for several towns flooded by the Garrison Dam Reservoir.

Oakland
Township
Lat: 48-09-18 N **Long:** 102-06-52 W
Pop: 33 (1990); 53 (1980) **Pop Density:** 0.9
Land: 35.2 sq. mi.; **Water:** 0.8 sq. mi.

Osborn
Township
Lat: 47-58-35 N **Long:** 102-27-09 W
Pop: 375 (1990); 281 (1980) **Pop Density:** 12.1
Land: 30.9 sq. mi.; **Water:** 5.0 sq. mi.

Osloe
Township
Lat: 48-09-16 N **Long:** 101-58-42 W
Pop: 54 (1990); 62 (1980) **Pop Density:** 1.5
Land: 35.1 sq. mi.; **Water:** 1.0 sq. mi.

Palermo
City
ZIP: 58769 **Lat:** 48-20-17 N **Long:** 102-13-42 W
Pop: 95 (1990); 97 (1980) **Pop Density:** 43.2
Land: 2.2 sq. mi.; **Water:** 0.0 sq. mi. **Elev:** 2200 ft.
Not coextensive with township.

*Palermo
Township
ZIP: 58769 **Lat:** 48-19-39 N **Long:** 102-15-16 W
Pop: 38 (1990); 30 (1980) **Pop Density:** 1.2
Land: 33.0 sq. mi.; **Water:** 1.2 sq. mi.

Parshall
City
ZIP: 58770 **Lat:** 47-57-17 N **Long:** 102-08-01 W
Pop: 943 (1990); 1,059 (1980) **Pop Density:** 1886.0
Land: 0.5 sq. mi.; **Water:** 0.0 sq. mi. **Elev:** 1940 ft.
No coextensive with township. Founded 1913.
Name origin: For George Parshall, a pioneer stage coach driver.

*Parshall
Township
ZIP: 58770 **Lat:** 47-58-40 N **Long:** 102-11-37 W
Pop: 70 (1990); 73 (1980) **Pop Density:** 1.9
Land: 36.0 sq. mi.; **Water:** 0.0 sq. mi.

Plaza
City
ZIP: 58771 **Lat:** 48-01-32 N **Long:** 101-57-33 W
Pop: 193 (1990); 222 (1980) **Pop Density:** 175.5
Land: 1.1 sq. mi.; **Water:** 0.0 sq. mi. **Elev:** 2096 ft.
Founded 1906.
Name origin: For the central plaza in the town's business district.

*Plaza
Township
ZIP: 58771 **Lat:** 47-58-44 N **Long:** 101-56-04 W
Pop: 44 (1990); 66 (1980) **Pop Density:** 1.2
Land: 36.1 sq. mi.; **Water:** 0.0 sq. mi.

Powers
Township
Lat: 48-30-40 N **Long:** 102-33-38 W
Pop: 15 (1990); 46 (1980) **Pop Density:** 0.4
Land: 34.4 sq. mi.; **Water:** 1.6 sq. mi.

Powers Lake
Township
Lat: 48-30-36 N **Long:** 102-41-23 W
Pop: 68 (1990); 87 (1980) **Pop Density:** 1.9
Land: 35.6 sq. mi.; **Water:** 0.3 sq. mi.

Purcell
Township
Lat: 48-14-53 N **Long:** 102-22-50 W
Pop: 60 (1990); 45 (1980) **Pop Density:** 1.7
Land: 35.5 sq. mi.; **Water:** 0.4 sq. mi.

Rat Lake
Township
Lat: 48-08-45 N **Long:** 102-37-49 W
Pop: 27 (1990); 39 (1980) **Pop Density:** 0.8
Land: 35.7 sq. mi.; **Water:** 0.1 sq. mi.

Redmond
Township
Lat: 48-25-06 N **Long:** 102-10-04 W
Pop: 19 (1990); 25 (1980) **Pop Density:** 0.6
Land: 33.6 sq. mi.; **Water:** 2.4 sq. mi.

Ross
City
ZIP: 58776 **Lat:** 48-18-47 N **Long:** 102-32-34 W
Pop: 61 (1990); 104 (1980) **Pop Density:** 203.3
Land: 0.3 sq. mi.; **Water:** 0.0 sq. mi. **Elev:** 2287 ft.
Not coextensive with township.

*Ross
Township
ZIP: 58776 **Lat:** 48-20-04 N **Long:** 102-29-36 W
Pop: 43 (1990); 39 (1980) **Pop Density:** 1.2
Land: 35.6 sq. mi.; **Water:** 0.7 sq. mi.

Shell
Township
Lat: 48-03-45 N **Long:** 102-07-13 W
Pop: 38 (1990); 46 (1980) **Pop Density:** 1.1
Land: 36.0 sq. mi.; **Water:** 0.0 sq. mi.

Sidonia
Township
Lat: 48-30-33 N **Long:** 102-18-21 W
Pop: 31 (1990); 47 (1980) **Pop Density:** 0.9
Land: 34.5 sq. mi.; **Water:** 1.4 sq. mi.

Sikes
Township
Lat: 48-08-37 N **Long:** 102-22-16 W
Pop: 55 (1990); 60 (1980) **Pop Density:** 1.5
Land: 35.5 sq. mi.; **Water:** 0.5 sq. mi.

Sorkness
Township
Lat: 48-24-33 N **Long:** 102-41-48 W
Pop: 38 (1990); 36 (1980) **Pop Density:** 1.1
Land: 35.7 sq. mi.; **Water:** 0.5 sq. mi.

Southwest Mountrail
Pop. Place
Lat: 47-48-03 N **Long:** 102-29-01 W
Pop: 41 (1990); 56 (1980) **Pop Density:** 0.9
Land: 45.0 sq. mi.; **Water:** 13.3 sq. mi.

Spring Coulee
Township
Lat: 48-04-13 N **Long:** 101-58-53 W
Pop: 72 (1990); 86 (1980) **Pop Density:** 2.1
Land: 35.1 sq. mi.; **Water:** 0.1 sq. mi.

Stanley
City
ZIP: 58784 **Lat:** 48-19-00 N **Long:** 102-23-11 W
Pop: 1,371 (1990); 1,631 (1980) **Pop Density:** 806.5
Land: 1.7 sq. mi.; **Water:** 0.0 sq. mi. **Elev:** 2250 ft.
Settled 1895.
Name origin: For early homesteader King Stanley.

Stave
Township
Lat: 48-25-15 N **Long:** 102-02-16 W
Pop: 48 (1990); 54 (1980) **Pop Density:** 1.4
Land: 33.3 sq. mi.; **Water:** 2.8 sq. mi.

Van Hook
Township
Lat: 47-59-01 N **Long:** 102-19-07 W
Pop: 72 (1990); 57 (1980) **Pop Density:** 2.2
Land: 32.9 sq. mi.; **Water:** 3.6 sq. mi.

Wayzetta
Township
Lat: 48-03-59 N **Long:** 102-14-53 W
Pop: 38 (1990); 42 (1980) **Pop Density:** 1.1
Land: 35.9 sq. mi.; **Water:** 0.1 sq. mi.

West Mountrail
Pop. Place
Lat: 48-07-56 N **Long:** 102-42-40 W
Pop: 139 (1990); 174 (1980) **Pop Density:** 1.5
Land: 93.6 sq. mi.; **Water:** 21.2 sq. mi.

White Earth
City
ZIP: 58794 **Lat:** 48-22-48 N **Long:** 102-46-18 W
Pop: 73 (1990); 98 (1980) **Pop Density:** 48.7
Land: 1.5 sq. mi.; **Water:** 0.0 sq. mi. **Elev:** 2090 ft.
Not coextensive with township.

*White Earth
Township
ZIP: 58794 **Lat:** 48-24-11 N **Long:** 102-49-29 W
Pop: 41 (1990); 45 (1980) **Pop Density:** 1.2
Land: 34.3 sq. mi.; **Water:** 0.1 sq. mi.

Nelson County
County Seat: Lakota (ZIP: 58344)

Pop: 4,410 (1990); 5,233 (1980) **Pop Density:** 4.5
Land: 981.7 sq. mi.; **Water:** 27.1 sq. mi. **Area Code:** 701
In east-central ND, west of Grand Forks; organized Mar 9, 1883 (prior to statehood) from Foster and Grand Forks counties.
Name origin: For Nelson E. Nelson (1830–1913), a ND legislator at the time.

Adler
Township
Lat: 47-53-16 N **Long:** 97-56-39 W
Pop: 56 (1990); 78 (1980) **Pop Density:** 1.6
Land: 35.8 sq. mi.; **Water:** 0.1 sq. mi.

Aneta
City
ZIP: 58212 **Lat:** 47-40-44 N **Long:** 97-59-19 W
Pop: 314 (1990); 341 (1980) **Pop Density:** 314.0
Land: 1.0 sq. mi.; **Water:** 0.0 sq. mi. **Elev:** 1503 ft.
Incorporated 1903.
Name origin: For *An*na Ros*eta* Mitchell, wife of the postmaster.

Bergen
Township
Lat: 47-43-22 N **Long:** 98-19-18 W
Pop: 89 (1990); 94 (1980) **Pop Density:** 2.5
Land: 35.4 sq. mi.; **Water:** 0.6 sq. mi.

Central
Township
Lat: 47-53-03 N **Long:** 98-12-10 W
Pop: 63 (1990); 83 (1980) **Pop Density:** 1.8
Land: 34.9 sq. mi.; **Water:** 1.2 sq. mi.

Clara
Township
Lat: 48-09-17 N **Long:** 98-21-24 W
Pop: 41 (1990); 75 (1980) **Pop Density:** 1.2
Land: 34.6 sq. mi.; **Water:** 1.4 sq. mi.

Dahlen
Township
Lat: 48-09-36 N **Long:** 97-58-06 W
Pop: 103 (1990); 131 (1980) **Pop Density:** 2.9
Land: 35.7 sq. mi.; **Water:** 0.2 sq. mi.

Dayton
Township
Lat: 47-48-35 N **Long:** 98-27-01 W
Pop: 81 (1990); 124 (1980) **Pop Density:** 2.3
Land: 34.5 sq. mi.; **Water:** 0.4 sq. mi.

Dodds
Township
Lat: 47-59-01 N **Long:** 98-20-37 W
Pop: 59 (1990); 83 (1980) **Pop Density:** 1.6
Land: 35.9 sq. mi.; **Water:** 0.4 sq. mi.

Enterprise
Township
Lat: 48-09-07 N **Long:** 98-13-34 W
Pop: 58 (1990); 65 (1980) **Pop Density:** 1.6
Land: 35.2 sq. mi.; **Water:** 0.9 sq. mi.

Field
Township
Lat: 47-47-43 N **Long:** 98-03-51 W
Pop: 58 (1990); 69 (1980) **Pop Density:** 1.6
Land: 35.8 sq. mi.; **Water:** 0.1 sq. mi.

Forde
Township
Lat: 47-42-29 N **Long:** 98-27-18 W
Pop: 61 (1990); 80 (1980) **Pop Density:** 1.7
Land: 35.3 sq. mi.; **Water:** 0.6 sq. mi.

NORTH DAKOTA, Nelson County

Hamlin
Township
Lat: 47-48-35 N Long: 98-12-52 W
Pop: 70 (1990); 97 (1980) Pop Density: 2.0
Land: 34.7 sq. mi.; Water: 0.1 sq. mi.

Illinois
Township
Lat: 47-58-37 N Long: 98-28-10 W
Pop: 34 (1990); 63 (1980) Pop Density: 1.0
Land: 35.0 sq. mi.; Water: 1.2 sq. mi.

Lakota
City
ZIP: 58344 Lat: 48-02-34 N Long: 98-20-49 W
Pop: 898 (1990); 963 (1980) Pop Density: 898.0
Land: 1.0 sq. mi.; Water: 0.0 sq. mi. Elev: 1518 ft.
Not coextensive with township.

*Lakota
Township
ZIP: 58344 Lat: 48-03-30 N Long: 98-21-17 W
Pop: 79 (1990); 65 (1980) Pop Density: 2.3
Land: 34.2 sq. mi.; Water: 0.9 sq. mi.

Lee
Township
Lat: 47-42-55 N Long: 98-04-27 W
Pop: 88 (1990); 120 (1980) Pop Density: 2.5
Land: 35.8 sq. mi.; Water: 0.2 sq. mi.

Leval
Township
Lat: 47-53-02 N Long: 98-27-01 W
Pop: 48 (1990); 65 (1980) Pop Density: 1.5
Land: 31.8 sq. mi.; Water: 4.1 sq. mi.

McVille
City
ZIP: 58254 Lat: 47-45-54 N Long: 98-10-34 W
Pop: 559 (1990); 626 (1980) Pop Density: 399.3
Land: 1.4 sq. mi.; Water: 0.1 sq. mi. Elev: 1470 ft.

Melvin
Township
Lat: 47-53-48 N Long: 98-04-30 W
Pop: 38 (1990); 60 (1980) Pop Density: 1.1
Land: 34.7 sq. mi.; Water: 1.2 sq. mi.

Michigan
Township
ZIP: 58259 Lat: 48-01-43 N Long: 98-05-31 W
Pop: 82 (1990); 110 (1980) Pop Density: 1.4
Land: 57.3 sq. mi.; Water: 2.3 sq. mi.

Michigan City
City
Lat: 48-01-28 N Long: 98-07-13 W
Pop: 413 (1990); 502 (1980) Pop Density: 826.0
Land: 0.5 sq. mi.; Water: 0.0 sq. mi.
Name origin: Named in 1880s for either the state, or the city in IN.

Nash
Township
Lat: 48-04-17 N Long: 97-57-26 W
Pop: 75 (1990); 75 (1980) Pop Density: 2.1
Land: 35.7 sq. mi.; Water: 0.3 sq. mi.

Nesheim
Township
Lat: 47-43-18 N Long: 98-11-49 W
Pop: 49 (1990); 80 (1980) Pop Density: 1.4
Land: 35.8 sq. mi.; Water: 0.1 sq. mi.

Ora
Township
Lat: 47-43-12 N Long: 97-56-48 W
Pop: 61 (1990); 79 (1980) Pop Density: 1.8
Land: 34.4 sq. mi.; Water: 0.7 sq. mi.

Osago
Township
Lat: 47-47-38 N Long: 98-20-12 W
Pop: 39 (1990); 59 (1980) Pop Density: 1.1
Land: 35.4 sq. mi.; Water: 0.2 sq. mi.

Pekin
City
ZIP: 58361 Lat: 47-47-27 N Long: 98-19-35 W
Pop: 101 (1990); 101 (1980) Pop Density: 336.7
Land: 0.3 sq. mi.; Water: 0.0 sq. mi. Elev: 1468 ft.

Petersburg
City
ZIP: 58272 Lat: 48-00-42 N Long: 97-59-58 W
Pop: 219 (1990); 230 (1980) Pop Density: 219.0
Land: 1.0 sq. mi.; Water: 0.0 sq. mi. Elev: 1530 ft.
Not coextensive with township.

*Petersburg
Township
ZIP: 58272 Lat: 47-58-14 N Long: 97-58-30 W
Pop: 54 (1990); 68 (1980) Pop Density: 1.2
Land: 46.2 sq. mi.; Water: 1.1 sq. mi.

Rubin
Township
Lat: 48-03-51 N Long: 98-12-59 W
Pop: 62 (1990); 89 (1980) Pop Density: 1.8
Land: 34.1 sq. mi.; Water: 2.1 sq. mi.

Rugh
Township
Lat: 47-48-33 N Long: 97-56-44 W
Pop: 51 (1990); 51 (1980) Pop Density: 1.4
Land: 35.8 sq. mi.; Water: 0.1 sq. mi.

Sarnia
Township
Lat: 48-09-02 N Long: 98-06-00 W
Pop: 83 (1990); 151 (1980) Pop Density: 2.4
Land: 34.8 sq. mi.; Water: 1.2 sq. mi.

Tolna
City
ZIP: 58380 Lat: 47-49-30 N Long: 98-26-14 W
Pop: 230 (1990); 241 (1980) Pop Density: 287.5
Land: 0.8 sq. mi.; Water: 0.0 sq. mi. Elev: 1458 ft.

Wamduska
Township
Lat: 47-53-24 N Long: 98-19-51 W
Pop: 48 (1990); 45 (1980) Pop Density: 1.5
Land: 31.1 sq. mi.; Water: 4.8 sq. mi.

Williams
Township
Lat: 47-58-17 N Long: 98-11-35 W
Pop: 46 (1990); 70 (1980) Pop Density: 1.3
Land: 35.7 sq. mi.; Water: 0.7 sq. mi.

> ## Oliver County
> **County Seat: Center (ZIP: 58530)**
>
> **Pop:** 2,381 (1990); 2,495 (1980)   **Pop Density:** 3.3
> **Land:** 723.6 sq. mi.; **Water:** 7.7 sq. mi.   **Area Code:** 701
> In south-central ND, northwest of Bismarck; organized Mar 12, 1885 (prior to statehood) from Mercer County.
> **Name origin:** For Harry S. Oliver (1855–1909), a Dakota Territory legislator.

Center   City
ZIP: 58530   **Lat:** 47-06-53 N **Long:** 101-17-48 W
Pop: 826 (1990); 900 (1980)   **Pop Density:** 2753.3
Land: 0.3 sq. mi.; **Water:** 0.0 sq. mi.   **Elev:** 1980 ft.
Name origin: For its central location in the county.

East Oliver   Pop. Place
Lat: 47-07-08 N **Long:** 101-10-29 W
Pop: 980 (1990); 964 (1980)   **Pop Density:** 2.2
Land: 437.1 sq. mi.; **Water:** 7.1 sq. mi.

West Oliver   Pop. Place
Lat: 47-06-43 N **Long:** 101-36-05 W
Pop: 575 (1990); 631 (1980)   **Pop Density:** 2.0
Land: 286.1 sq. mi.; **Water:** 0.6 sq. mi.

> ## Pembina County
> **County Seat: Cavalier (ZIP: 58220)**
>
> **Pop:** 9,238 (1990); 10,399 (1980)   **Pop Density:** 8.3
> **Land:** 1118.8 sq. mi.; **Water:** 3.0 sq. mi.   **Area Code:** 701
> In the northeast corner of ND; organized Jan 9, 1867 (prior to statehood) from Indian lands.
> **Name origin:** From Ojibway Indian *anepeminan* 'high bush cranberries,' which grew abundantly in the area.

Advance   Township
Lat: 48-50-58 N **Long:** 97-44-48 W
Pop: 205 (1990); 222 (1980)   **Pop Density:** 5.7
Land: 35.8 sq. mi.; **Water:** 0.0 sq. mi.

Akra   Township
Lat: 48-46-11 N **Long:** 97-45-12 W
Pop: 260 (1990); 243 (1980)   **Pop Density:** 7.3
Land: 35.6 sq. mi.; **Water:** 0.4 sq. mi.

Bathgate   City
ZIP: 58216   **Lat:** 48-52-49 N **Long:** 97-28-22 W
Pop: 75 (1990); 67 (1980)   **Pop Density:** 250.0
Land: 0.3 sq. mi.; **Water:** 0.0 sq. mi.   **Elev:** 820 ft.
Not coextensive with township. Incorporated 1907.

*Bathgate   Township
ZIP: 58216   **Lat:** 48-51-19 N **Long:** 97-30-02 W
Pop: 94 (1990); 118 (1980)   **Pop Density:** 3.5
Land: 26.5 sq. mi.; **Water:** 0.0 sq. mi.

Beaulieu   Township
Lat: 48-45-43 N **Long:** 97-53-03 W
Pop: 205 (1990); 180 (1980)   **Pop Density:** 5.7
Land: 35.8 sq. mi.; **Water:** 0.2 sq. mi.

Canton City   City
Lat: 48-41-15 N **Long:** 97-40-00 W
Pop: 64 (1990); 68 (1980)   **Pop Density:** 640.0
Land: 0.1 sq. mi.; **Water:** 0.0 sq. mi.

Carlisle   Township
Lat: 48-48-12 N **Long:** 97-21-43 W
Pop: 163 (1990); 180 (1980)   **Pop Density:** 2.3
Land: 71.6 sq. mi.; **Water:** 0.0 sq. mi.

Cavalier   City
ZIP: 58220   **Lat:** 48-47-43 N **Long:** 97-37-27 W
Pop: 1,508 (1990); 1,505 (1980)   **Pop Density:** 2154.3
Land: 0.7 sq. mi.; **Water:** 0.0 sq. mi.   **Elev:** 891 ft.
Not coextensive with township.
Name origin: For the first settler, Charles Cavalier.

*Cavalier   Township
ZIP: 58220   **Lat:** 48-48-13 N **Long:** 97-37-03 W
Pop: 672 (1990); 731 (1980)   **Pop Density:** 9.5
Land: 70.9 sq. mi.; **Water:** 0.0 sq. mi.

Crystal   City
ZIP: 58222   **Lat:** 48-35-54 N **Long:** 97-40-06 W
Pop: 199 (1990); 256 (1980)   **Pop Density:** 284.3
Land: 0.7 sq. mi.; **Water:** 0.0 sq. mi.   **Elev:** 905 ft.

*Crystal   Township
ZIP: 58222   **Lat:** 48-35-14 N **Long:** 97-43-42 W
Pop: 103 (1990); 101 (1980)   **Pop Density:** 2.9
Land: 35.5 sq. mi.; **Water:** 0.0 sq. mi.

NORTH DAKOTA, Pembina County

Drayton City
ZIP: 58225 Lat: 48-33-52 N Long: 97-10-46 W
Pop: 961 (1990); 1,082 (1980) Pop Density: 1922.0
Land: 0.5 sq. mi.; Water: 0.0 sq. mi. Elev: 801 ft.
Not coextensive with township.
Name origin: Named by Canadian settlers for Drayton, Ontario, Canada.

*Drayton Township
ZIP: 58225 Lat: 48-34-41 N Long: 97-12-55 W
Pop: 47 (1990); 62 (1980) Pop Density: 1.4
Land: 34.7 sq. mi.; Water: 0.8 sq. mi.

Elora Township
Lat: 48-35-51 N Long: 97-35-42 W
Pop: 82 (1990); 79 (1980) Pop Density: 2.3
Land: 35.8 sq. mi.; Water: 0.0 sq. mi.

Felson Township
Lat: 48-56-30 N Long: 97-36-42 W
Pop: 113 (1990); 118 (1980) Pop Density: 2.5
Land: 44.8 sq. mi.; Water: 0.0 sq. mi.

Gardar Township
Lat: 48-35-18 N Long: 97-51-35 W
Pop: 112 (1990); 158 (1980) Pop Density: 3.1
Land: 35.9 sq. mi.; Water: 0.0 sq. mi.

Hamilton City
ZIP: 58238 Lat: 48-48-29 N Long: 97-27-05 W
Pop: 74 (1990); 109 (1980) Pop Density: 246.7
Land: 0.3 sq. mi.; Water: 0.0 sq. mi. Elev: 825 ft.
Not coextensive with township.

*Hamilton Township
ZIP: 58238 Lat: 48-46-02 N Long: 97-29-34 W
Pop: 61 (1990); 100 (1980) Pop Density: 1.4
Land: 44.5 sq. mi.; Water: 0.0 sq. mi.

Joliette Township
Lat: 48-47-47 N Long: 97-13-40 W
Pop: 118 (1990); 145 (1980) Pop Density: 1.7
Land: 70.1 sq. mi.; Water: 0.7 sq. mi.

La Moure Township
Lat: 48-50-26 N Long: 97-53-39 W
Pop: 134 (1990); 156 (1980) Pop Density: 3.7
Land: 35.9 sq. mi.; Water: 0.1 sq. mi.

Lincoln Township
Lat: 48-40-27 N Long: 97-11-19 W
Pop: 92 (1990); 148 (1980) Pop Density: 2.0
Land: 46.6 sq. mi.; Water: 0.3 sq. mi.

Lodema Township
Lat: 48-40-41 N Long: 97-35-23 W
Pop: 121 (1990); 136 (1980) Pop Density: 3.3
Land: 36.2 sq. mi.; Water: 0.0 sq. mi.

Midland Township
Lat: 48-38-13 N Long: 97-19-53 W
Pop: 133 (1990); 162 (1980) Pop Density: 1.9
Land: 69.8 sq. mi.; Water: 0.0 sq. mi.

Mountain City
ZIP: 58262 Lat: 48-41-00 N Long: 97-51-48 W
Pop: 134 (1990); 156 (1980) Pop Density: 1340.0
Land: 0.1 sq. mi.; Water: 0.0 sq. mi. Elev: 1034 ft.

Neche City
ZIP: 58265 Lat: 48-58-55 N Long: 97-33-03 W
Pop: 434 (1990); 471 (1980) Pop Density: 1085.0
Land: 0.4 sq. mi.; Water: 0.0 sq. mi. Elev: 830 ft.
Not coextensive with township.

*Neche Township
ZIP: 58265 Lat: 48-56-37 N Long: 97-29-10 W
Pop: 66 (1990); 87 (1980) Pop Density: 1.3
Land: 49.0 sq. mi.; Water: 0.0 sq. mi.

Park Township
Lat: 48-40-31 N Long: 97-43-29 W
Pop: 83 (1990); 86 (1980) Pop Density: 2.3
Land: 35.9 sq. mi.; Water: 0.1 sq. mi.

Pembina City
ZIP: 58271 Lat: 48-58-04 N Long: 97-14-44 W
Pop: 642 (1990); 673 (1980) Pop Density: 1070.0
Land: 0.6 sq. mi.; Water: 0.0 sq. mi. Elev: 780 ft.
Not coextensive with township.
Name origin: From Ojibway Indian *anepeminan* 'high bush cranberries,' which grew abundantly in the area.

*Pembina Township
ZIP: 58271 Lat: 48-56-48 N Long: 97-18-45 W
Pop: 102 (1990); 145 (1980) Pop Density: 1.6
Land: 64.6 sq. mi.; Water: 0.3 sq. mi.

St. Joseph Township
Lat: 48-57-11 N Long: 97-44-51 W
Pop: 164 (1990); 139 (1980) Pop Density: 3.7
Land: 44.9 sq. mi.; Water: 0.0 sq. mi.

St. Thomas City
Lat: 48-37-12 N Long: 97-26-48 W
Pop: 444 (1990); 528 (1980) Pop Density: 403.6
Land: 1.1 sq. mi.; Water: 0.0 sq. mi.
Not coextensive with township.

*St. Thomas Township
Lat: 48-37-49 N Long: 97-28-00 W
Pop: 163 (1990); 203 (1980) Pop Density: 2.3
Land: 72.0 sq. mi.; Water: 0.0 sq. mi.

Thingvalla Township
Lat: 48-40-30 N Long: 97-51-03 W
Pop: 154 (1990); 195 (1980) Pop Density: 4.3
Land: 36.0 sq. mi.; Water: 0.0 sq. mi.

Walhalla City
ZIP: 58282 Lat: 48-55-16 N Long: 97-55-00 W
Pop: 1,131 (1990); 1,429 (1980) Pop Density: 1028.2
Land: 1.1 sq. mi.; Water: 0.0 sq. mi. Elev: 980 ft.
Not coextensive with township.
Name origin: From German *Valhalla* 'home of the gods'; spelling altered to reflect pronunciation.

*Walhalla Township
ZIP: 58282 Lat: 48-56-55 N Long: 97-52-59 W
Pop: 125 (1990); 161 (1980) Pop Density: 2.8
Land: 44.1 sq. mi.; Water: 0.0 sq. mi.

Pierce County
County Seat: Rugby (ZIP: 58368)

Pop: 5,052 (1990); 6,166 (1980) **Pop Density:** 5.0
Land: 1017.9 sq. mi.; **Water:** 64.3 sq. mi. **Area Code:** 701
In north-central ND, east of Minot; organized Mar 11, 1887 (prior to statehood) from parts of Rolette, Bottineau, and McHenry counties and all of De Smet County; annexed part of Church County in 1891.
Name origin: For Lt. Col. Gilbert Ashville Pierce (1839–1901), officer in the Civil War, governor of Dakota Territory (1884–87), and U.S. senator from ND (1889–91).

Alexander
Township
Lat: 47-58-14 N **Long:** 99-51-56 W
Pop: 53 (1990); 84 (1980) **Pop Density:** 1.5
Land: 35.2 sq. mi.; **Water:** 0.7 sq. mi.

Antelope Lake
Township
Lat: 47-59-12 N **Long:** 100-07-42 W
Pop: 31 (1990); 58 (1980) **Pop Density:** 1.0
Land: 31.7 sq. mi.; **Water:** 4.4 sq. mi.

Balta
City
ZIP: 58313 **Lat:** 48-09-58 N **Long:** 100-02-13 W
Pop: 79 (1990); 139 (1980) **Pop Density:** 395.0
Land: 0.2 sq. mi.; **Water:** 0.0 sq. mi. **Elev:** 1542 ft.
Not coextensive with township. Incorporated 1967.
Name origin: Named by early Russian immigrants for Balta in the Russian Ukraine.

*Balta
Township
Lat: 48-08-58 N **Long:** 100-02-32 W
Pop: 53 (1990); 89 (1980) **Pop Density:** 1.6
Land: 33.9 sq. mi.; **Water:** 1.7 sq. mi.

Barton
City
Lat: 48-30-21 N **Long:** 100-10-41 W
Pop: 24 (1990); 38 (1980) **Pop Density:** 48.0
Land: 0.5 sq. mi.; **Water:** 0.0 sq. mi. **Elev:** 1505 ft.
Incorporated 1967.

Central Pierce
Pop. Place
Lat: 48-09-31 N **Long:** 100-10-42 W
Pop: 29 (1990); 43 (1980) **Pop Density:** 0.9
Land: 33.3 sq. mi.; **Water:** 2.9 sq. mi.

Elling
Township
Lat: 48-04-00 N **Long:** 100-10-23 W
Pop: 76 (1990); 102 (1980) **Pop Density:** 2.2
Land: 34.2 sq. mi.; **Water:** 2.0 sq. mi.

Elverum
Township
Lat: 48-09-21 N **Long:** 99-54-36 W
Pop: 72 (1990); 100 (1980) **Pop Density:** 2.2
Land: 32.2 sq. mi.; **Water:** 3.8 sq. mi.

Hagel
Township
Lat: 47-53-53 N **Long:** 99-51-56 W
Pop: 97 (1990); 156 (1980) **Pop Density:** 2.7
Land: 35.7 sq. mi.; **Water:** 0.1 sq. mi.

Jefferson
Township
Lat: 48-14-22 N **Long:** 100-09-38 W
Pop: 65 (1990); 85 (1980) **Pop Density:** 1.9
Land: 35.0 sq. mi.; **Water:** 1.1 sq. mi.

Meyer
Township
Lat: 48-19-16 N **Long:** 99-54-45 W
Pop: 97 (1990); 101 (1980) **Pop Density:** 2.8
Land: 34.1 sq. mi.; **Water:** 2.8 sq. mi.

Ness
Township
Lat: 48-19-35 N **Long:** 100-10-55 W
Pop: 103 (1990); 105 (1980) **Pop Density:** 2.8
Land: 36.6 sq. mi.; **Water:** 0.2 sq. mi.

North Pierce
Pop. Place
Lat: 48-28-03 N **Long:** 99-55-02 W
Pop: 781 (1990); 896 (1980) **Pop Density:** 2.1
Land: 369.0 sq. mi.; **Water:** 25.7 sq. mi.

Reno Valley
Township
Lat: 48-13-51 N **Long:** 99-54-52 W
Pop: 47 (1990); 74 (1980) **Pop Density:** 1.4
Land: 34.6 sq. mi.; **Water:** 1.4 sq. mi.

Rugby
City
ZIP: 58368 **Lat:** 48-22-01 N **Long:** 99-59-27 W
Pop: 2,909 (1990); 3,335 (1980) **Pop Density:** 1531.1
Land: 1.9 sq. mi.; **Water:** 0.0 sq. mi. **Elev:** 1550 ft.
Founded 1885.
Name origin: Named by English railroad stockholders for Rugby, England.

Rush Lake
Township
Lat: 48-24-57 N **Long:** 99-40-53 W
Pop: 47 (1990); 63 (1980) **Pop Density:** 1.4
Land: 34.8 sq. mi.; **Water:** 1.3 sq. mi.

South Pierce
Pop. Place
Lat: 48-02-11 N **Long:** 99-59-16 W
Pop: 129 (1990); 189 (1980) **Pop Density:** 1.3
Land: 97.1 sq. mi.; **Water:** 10.8 sq. mi.

Torgerson
Township
Lat: 48-24-45 N **Long:** 99-56-56 W
Pop: 87 (1990); 100 (1980) **Pop Density:** 2.6
Land: 33.1 sq. mi.; **Water:** 2.3 sq. mi.

Truman
Township
Lat: 47-53-13 N **Long:** 100-00-55 W
Pop: 65 (1990); 111 (1980) **Pop Density:** 1.8
Land: 35.3 sq. mi.; **Water:** 0.5 sq. mi.

Tuscarora
Township
Lat: 48-14-08 N **Long:** 100-02-51 W
Pop: 91 (1990); 113 (1980) **Pop Density:** 2.6
Land: 34.6 sq. mi.; **Water:** 1.2 sq. mi.

White
Township
Lat: 47-53-42 N **Long:** 100-07-23 W
Pop: 61 (1990); 109 (1980) **Pop Density:** 1.8
Land: 34.6 sq. mi.; **Water:** 1.3 sq. mi.

NORTH DAKOTA, Pierce County   *American Places Dictionary*

Wolford   City
ZIP: 58385   **Lat:** 48-29-52 N **Long:** 99-42-16 W
Pop: 56 (1990); 76 (1980)   **Pop Density:** 280.0
Land: 0.2 sq. mi.; **Water:** 0.0 sq. mi.   **Elev:** 1630 ft.

Ramsey County
County Seat: Devils Lake (ZIP: 58301)

Pop: 12,681 (1990); 13,048 (1980)   **Pop Density:** 10.7
Land: 1186.2 sq. mi.; **Water:** 114.7 sq. mi.   **Area Code:** 701
In east-central ND, northwest of Grand Forks; organized Jan 4, 1873 (prior to statehood) from Pembina County.
Name origin: For Alexander Ramsey (1815–1903), first governor of MN Territory, U.S. senator from MN (1863–75), and U.S. secretary of war (1879–81).

Bartlett   Township
                            Lat: 48-03-50 N **Long:** 98-29-12 W
Pop: 92 (1990); 138 (1980)   **Pop Density:** 2.7
Land: 34.7 sq. mi.; **Water:** 1.3 sq. mi.

Brocket   City
ZIP: 58321   **Lat:** 48-12-40 N **Long:** 98-21-22 W
Pop: 81 (1990); 74 (1980)   **Pop Density:** 101.3
Land: 0.8 sq. mi.; **Water:** 0.0 sq. mi.   **Elev:** 1513 ft.
Incorporated 1967.

Cato   Township
                            Lat: 48-19-25 N **Long:** 98-37-05 W
Pop: 42 (1990); 51 (1980)   **Pop Density:** 1.2
Land: 35.7 sq. mi.; **Water:** 0.5 sq. mi.

Chain Lakes   Township
                            Lat: 48-20-03 N **Long:** 99-07-55 W
Pop: 24 (1990); 37 (1980)   **Pop Density:** 0.9
Land: 25.6 sq. mi.; **Water:** 11.2 sq. mi.

Churchs Ferry   City
ZIP: 58325   **Lat:** 48-16-06 N **Long:** 99-11-39 W
Pop: 118 (1990); 139 (1980)   **Pop Density:** 295.0
Land: 0.4 sq. mi.; **Water:** 0.0 sq. mi.

Coulee   Township
                            Lat: 48-14-19 N **Long:** 99-07-57 W
Pop: 135 (1990); 141 (1980)   **Pop Density:** 3.8
Land: 35.3 sq. mi.; **Water:** 0.2 sq. mi.

Crary   City
ZIP: 58327   **Lat:** 48-04-17 N **Long:** 98-38-24 W
Pop: 145 (1990); 139 (1980)   **Pop Density:** 161.1
Land: 0.9 sq. mi.; **Water:** 0.0 sq. mi.   **Elev:** 1487 ft.

Creel   Township
                            Lat: 48-06-46 N **Long:** 98-53-11 W
Pop: 1,572 (1990); 1,622 (1980)   **Pop Density:** 33.9
Land: 46.4 sq. mi.; **Water:** 16.8 sq. mi.

De Groat   Township
                            Lat: 48-19-30 N **Long:** 99-00-02 W
Pop: 40 (1990); 50 (1980)   **Pop Density:** 1.3
Land: 31.8 sq. mi.; **Water:** 4.7 sq. mi.

Devils Lake   City
ZIP: 58301   **Lat:** 48-06-45 N **Long:** 98-52-26 W
Pop: 7,782 (1990); 7,442 (1980)   **Pop Density:** 1525.9
Land: 5.1 sq. mi.; **Water:** 0.0 sq. mi.   **Elev:** 1475 ft.
Name origin: For a nearby lake. Originally called Creelsburg.

Dry Lake   Township
                            Lat: 48-14-47 N **Long:** 99-00-53 W
Pop: 54 (1990); 62 (1980)   **Pop Density:** 1.8
Land: 29.6 sq. mi.; **Water:** 6.4 sq. mi.

Edmore   City
ZIP: 58330   **Lat:** 48-24-45 N **Long:** 98-27-11 W
Pop: 329 (1990); 416 (1980)   **Pop Density:** 1096.7
Land: 0.3 sq. mi.; **Water:** 0.0 sq. mi.   **Elev:** 1513 ft.

Fancher   Township
                            Lat: 48-24-39 N **Long:** 98-30-45 W
Pop: 67 (1990); 68 (1980)   **Pop Density:** 1.9
Land: 35.2 sq. mi.; **Water:** 0.5 sq. mi.

Freshwater   Township
                            Lat: 48-14-30 N **Long:** 98-52-52 W
Pop: 77 (1990); 85 (1980)   **Pop Density:** 2.8
Land: 27.8 sq. mi.; **Water:** 8.3 sq. mi.

Grand Harbor   Township
                            Lat: 48-06-32 N **Long:** 98-59-58 W
Pop: 331 (1990); 274 (1980)   **Pop Density:** 6.5
Land: 50.6 sq. mi.; **Water:** 20.5 sq. mi.

Hammer   Township
                            Lat: 48-24-30 N **Long:** 98-54-22 W
Pop: 76 (1990); 74 (1980)   **Pop Density:** 2.2
Land: 35.1 sq. mi.; **Water:** 0.8 sq. mi.

Hampden   City
ZIP: 58338   **Lat:** 48-32-22 N **Long:** 98-39-16 W
Pop: 89 (1990); 126 (1980)   **Pop Density:** 445.0
Land: 0.2 sq. mi.; **Water:** 0.0 sq. mi.   **Elev:** 1565 ft.

Harding   Township
                            Lat: 48-19-29 N **Long:** 98-44-36 W
Pop: 51 (1990); 71 (1980)   **Pop Density:** 1.4
Land: 36.5 sq. mi.; **Water:** 0.1 sq. mi.

Highland Center   Township
                            Lat: 48-30-29 N **Long:** 98-22-23 W
Pop: 66 (1990); 89 (1980)   **Pop Density:** 1.8
Land: 35.9 sq. mi.; **Water:** 0.2 sq. mi.

Klingstrup   Township
                            Lat: 48-30-23 N **Long:** 98-54-24 W
Pop: 72 (1990); 96 (1980)   **Pop Density:** 2.1
Land: 35.0 sq. mi.; **Water:** 0.9 sq. mi.

Lawton City
ZIP: 58345 Lat: 48-18-10 N Long: 98-22-02 W
Pop: 63 (1990); 101 (1980) Pop Density: 70.0
Land: 0.9 sq. mi.; Water: 0.1 sq. mi. Elev: 1517 ft.
Not coextensive with township.

*Lawton Township
ZIP: 58345 Lat: 48-19-50 N Long: 98-21-16 W
Pop: 44 (1990); 75 (1980) Pop Density: 1.3
Land: 34.4 sq. mi.; Water: 0.9 sq. mi.

Lillehoff Township
Lat: 48-14-35 N Long: 98-21-24 W
Pop: 50 (1990); 81 (1980) Pop Density: 1.5
Land: 33.7 sq. mi.; Water: 1.4 sq. mi.

Minnewaukan Township
Lat: 48-09-16 N Long: 98-45-02 W
Pop: 133 (1990); 141 (1980) Pop Density: 3.8
Land: 34.6 sq. mi.; Water: 1.5 sq. mi.

Morris Township
Lat: 48-14-04 N Long: 98-44-51 W
Pop: 66 (1990); 55 (1980) Pop Density: 2.0
Land: 33.0 sq. mi.; Water: 3.1 sq. mi.

Newbre Township
Lat: 48-14-34 N Long: 98-29-07 W
Pop: 24 (1990); 44 (1980) Pop Density: 0.7
Land: 34.0 sq. mi.; Water: 2.1 sq. mi.

Newland Township
Lat: 48-24-48 N Long: 98-23-09 W
Pop: 64 (1990); 56 (1980) Pop Density: 1.8
Land: 35.6 sq. mi.; Water: 0.5 sq. mi.

Nixon Township
Lat: 48-09-06 N Long: 98-29-26 W
Pop: 29 (1990); 28 (1980) Pop Density: 0.8
Land: 34.3 sq. mi.; Water: 1.8 sq. mi.

Noonan Township
Lat: 48-14-19 N Long: 98-37-13 W
Pop: 57 (1990); 59 (1980) Pop Density: 1.7
Land: 33.8 sq. mi.; Water: 2.1 sq. mi.

Northfield Township
Lat: 48-29-57 N Long: 98-38-27 W
Pop: 59 (1990); 93 (1980) Pop Density: 1.7
Land: 34.8 sq. mi.; Water: 0.9 sq. mi.

Odessa Township
Lat: 47-58-17 N Long: 98-36-03 W
Pop: 56 (1990); 76 (1980) Pop Density: 1.5
Land: 38.1 sq. mi.; Water: 8.0 sq. mi.

Ontario Township
Lat: 48-08-55 N Long: 98-37-18 W
Pop: 78 (1990); 74 (1980) Pop Density: 2.3
Land: 34.0 sq. mi.; Water: 2.0 sq. mi.

Overland Township
Lat: 48-25-01 N Long: 98-38-42 W
Pop: 28 (1990); 39 (1980) Pop Density: 0.8
Land: 35.6 sq. mi.; Water: 0.4 sq. mi.

Pelican Township
Lat: 48-09-38 N Long: 99-07-49 W
Pop: 63 (1990); 74 (1980) Pop Density: 2.4
Land: 25.8 sq. mi.; Water: 1.0 sq. mi.

Prospect Township
Lat: 48-30-29 N Long: 98-30-41 W
Pop: 46 (1990); 72 (1980) Pop Density: 1.3
Land: 35.8 sq. mi.; Water: 0.2 sq. mi.

Royal Township
Lat: 48-30-19 N Long: 98-46-12 W
Pop: 35 (1990); 61 (1980) Pop Density: 1.0
Land: 34.8 sq. mi.; Water: 1.2 sq. mi.

South Minnewaukan Township
Lat: 48-02-53 N Long: 98-44-05 W
Pop: 72 (1990); 142 (1980) Pop Density: 2.5
Land: 29.1 sq. mi.; Water: 12.4 sq. mi.

Starkweather City
ZIP: 58377 Lat: 48-27-08 N Long: 98-52-39 W
Pop: 197 (1990); 210 (1980) Pop Density: 1970.0
Land: 0.1 sq. mi.; Water: 0.0 sq. mi. Elev: 1495 ft.

Stevens Township
Lat: 48-04-02 N Long: 98-36-40 W
Pop: 71 (1990); 94 (1980) Pop Density: 2.1
Land: 33.7 sq. mi.; Water: 1.3 sq. mi.

Sullivan Township
Lat: 48-24-46 N Long: 98-46-41 W
Pop: 48 (1990); 64 (1980) Pop Density: 1.4
Land: 35.5 sq. mi.; Water: 0.5 sq. mi.

Triumph Township
Lat: 48-19-47 N Long: 98-29-30 W
Pop: 47 (1990); 59 (1980) Pop Density: 1.3
Land: 36.1 sq. mi.; Water: 0.5 sq. mi.

Webster Township
ZIP: 58382 Lat: 48-19-37 N Long: 98-52-32 W
Pop: 108 (1990); 156 (1980) Pop Density: 3.0
Land: 36.0 sq. mi.; Water: 0.4 sq. mi.

Ransom County
County Seat: Lisbon (ZIP: 58054)

Pop: 5,921 (1990); 6,698 (1980)   **Pop Density:** 6.9
Land: 862.8 sq. mi.; **Water:** 1.4 sq. mi.   **Area Code:** 701
In southeastern ND, southwest of Fargo; organized Jan 4, 1873 (prior to statehood) from Pembina County.
Name origin: For Fort Ransom, built in 1867 and named for Gen. Thomas E. G. Ransom (1834–64), a Union officer from IL.

Aliceton   Township
Lat: 46-19-49 N   **Long:** 97-35-11 W
Pop: 132 (1990); 162 (1980)   **Pop Density:** 3.6
Land: 36.3 sq. mi.; **Water:** 0.1 sq. mi.

Alleghany   Township
Lat: 46-19-08 N   **Long:** 97-50-09 W
Pop: 62 (1990); 87 (1980)   **Pop Density:** 1.7
Land: 36.1 sq. mi.; **Water:** 0.0 sq. mi.

Bale   Township
Lat: 46-20-00 N   **Long:** 97-43-14 W
Pop: 95 (1990); 130 (1980)   **Pop Density:** 2.6
Land: 36.2 sq. mi.; **Water:** 0.0 sq. mi.

Big Bend   Township
Lat: 46-24-11 N   **Long:** 97-35-54 W
Pop: 149 (1990); 156 (1980)   **Pop Density:** 4.1
Land: 36.4 sq. mi.; **Water:** 0.1 sq. mi.

Casey   Township
Lat: 46-29-57 N   **Long:** 97-35-31 W
Pop: 87 (1990); 85 (1980)   **Pop Density:** 2.4
Land: 36.3 sq. mi.; **Water:** 0.0 sq. mi.

Coburn   Township
Lat: 46-34-46 N   **Long:** 97-21-09 W
Pop: 76 (1990); 94 (1980)   **Pop Density:** 2.1
Land: 35.8 sq. mi.; **Water:** 0.0 sq. mi.

Elliott   City
Lat: 46-24-08 N   **Long:** 97-48-49 W
Pop: 32 (1990); 44 (1980)   **Pop Density:** 320.0
Land: 0.1 sq. mi.; **Water:** 0.0 sq. mi.   **Elev:** 1330 ft.
Not coextensive with township.

*Elliott   Township
Lat: 46-24-57 N   **Long:** 97-50-39 W
Pop: 78 (1990); 119 (1980)   **Pop Density:** 2.2
Land: 35.8 sq. mi.; **Water:** 0.0 sq. mi.

Enderlin   City
ZIP: 58027   **Lat:** 46-37-18 N   **Long:** 97-35-55 W
Pop: 980 (1990); 1,140 (1980)   **Pop Density:** 816.7
Land: 1.2 sq. mi.; **Water:** 0.0 sq. mi.   **Elev:** 1090 ft.
Part of the town is also in Cass County.
Name origin: From a humorous corruption of "end of the line."

Fort Ransom   City
ZIP: 58033   **Lat:** 46-31-28 N   **Long:** 97-55-49 W
Pop: 111 (1990); 99 (1980)   **Pop Density:** 370.0
Land: 0.3 sq. mi.; **Water:** 0.0 sq. mi.   **Elev:** 1135 ft.
Not coextensive with township.

*Fort Ransom   Township
ZIP: 58033   **Lat:** 46-29-59 N   **Long:** 97-57-49 W
Pop: 85 (1990); 103 (1980)   **Pop Density:** 2.4
Land: 35.5 sq. mi.; **Water:** 0.0 sq. mi.

Greene   Township
Lat: 46-35-19 N   **Long:** 97-28-07 W
Pop: 146 (1990); 192 (1980)   **Pop Density:** 4.2
Land: 34.8 sq. mi.; **Water:** 0.5 sq. mi.

Hanson   Township
Lat: 46-24-06 N   **Long:** 97-58-12 W
Pop: 96 (1990); 123 (1980)   **Pop Density:** 2.7
Land: 35.9 sq. mi.; **Water:** 0.0 sq. mi.

Island Park   Township
Lat: 46-24-27 N   **Long:** 97-43-50 W
Pop: 300 (1990); 400 (1980)   **Pop Density:** 8.9
Land: 33.8 sq. mi.; **Water:** 0.1 sq. mi.

Isley   Township
Lat: 46-19-51 N   **Long:** 97-58-56 W
Pop: 44 (1990); 69 (1980)   **Pop Density:** 1.2
Land: 35.9 sq. mi.; **Water:** 0.2 sq. mi.

Liberty   Township
Lat: 46-34-48 N   **Long:** 97-35-48 W
Pop: 132 (1990); 133 (1980)   **Pop Density:** 3.8
Land: 34.6 sq. mi.; **Water:** 0.0 sq. mi.

Lisbon   City
ZIP: 58054   **Lat:** 46-26-17 N   **Long:** 97-40-59 W
Pop: 2,177 (1990); 2,283 (1980)   **Pop Density:** 989.5
Land: 2.2 sq. mi.; **Water:** 0.0 sq. mi.   **Elev:** 1091 ft.
Name origin: For the cities in IL and NY, former homes of early settlers.

Moore   Township
Lat: 46-35-27 N   **Long:** 97-42-53 W
Pop: 116 (1990); 133 (1980)   **Pop Density:** 3.2
Land: 35.7 sq. mi.; **Water:** 0.0 sq. mi.

Northland   Township
Lat: 46-35-01 N   **Long:** 97-57-49 W
Pop: 80 (1990); 96 (1980)   **Pop Density:** 2.2
Land: 35.7 sq. mi.; **Water:** 0.0 sq. mi.

Owego   Township
Lat: 46-29-25 N   **Long:** 97-20-34 W
Pop: 32 (1990); 30 (1980)   **Pop Density:** 0.9
Land: 36.1 sq. mi.; **Water:** 0.0 sq. mi.

Preston   Township
Lat: 46-35-11 N   **Long:** 97-51-04 W
Pop: 94 (1990); 120 (1980)   **Pop Density:** 2.6
Land: 35.7 sq. mi.; **Water:** 0.0 sq. mi.

Rosemeade
Township
Lat: 46-19-06 N **Long:** 97-21-12 W
Pop: 55 (1990); 65 (1980) **Pop Density:** 1.5
Land: 36.3 sq. mi.; **Water:** 0.0 sq. mi.

Sandoun
Township
Lat: 46-23-37 N **Long:** 97-19-51 W
Pop: 70 (1990); 94 (1980) **Pop Density:** 1.9
Land: 36.1 sq. mi.; **Water:** 0.0 sq. mi.

Scoville
Township
Lat: 46-23-28 N **Long:** 97-28-42 W
Pop: 37 (1990); 33 (1980) **Pop Density:** 2.1
Land: 18.0 sq. mi.; **Water:** 0.0 sq. mi.

Sheldon
City
ZIP: 58068 **Lat:** 46-35-13 N **Long:** 97-29-31 W
Pop: 149 (1990); 173 (1980) **Pop Density:** 745.0
Land: 0.2 sq. mi.; **Water:** 0.0 sq. mi. **Elev:** 1075 ft.

Shenford
Township
Lat: 46-28-44 N **Long:** 97-28-41 W
Pop: 143 (1990); 183 (1980) **Pop Density:** 2.7
Land: 53.5 sq. mi.; **Water:** 0.1 sq. mi.

Springer
Township
Lat: 46-29-57 N **Long:** 97-50-47 W
Pop: 82 (1990); 93 (1980) **Pop Density:** 2.3
Land: 35.9 sq. mi.; **Water:** 0.1 sq. mi.

Sydna
Township
Lat: 46-19-48 N **Long:** 97-28-15 W
Pop: 133 (1990); 88 (1980) **Pop Density:** 3.7
Land: 36.3 sq. mi.; **Water:** 0.0 sq. mi.

Tuller
Township
Lat: 46-30-25 N **Long:** 97-43-11 W
Pop: 148 (1990); 171 (1980) **Pop Density:** 4.1
Land: 36.0 sq. mi.; **Water:** 0.0 sq. mi.

Renville County
County Seat: Mohall (ZIP: 58761)

Pop: 3,160 (1990); 3,608 (1980) **Pop Density:** 3.6
Land: 874.8 sq. mi.; **Water:** 17.3 sq. mi. **Area Code:** 701
On the central northern border of ND, northwest of Minot; organized Jan 4, 1873 (prior to statehood) from Pembina County. Dissolved in 1891 for lack of settlement; present county created Jul 23, 1910.
Name origin: For Gabriel Renville, an early settler and trader.

Brandon
Township
Lat: 48-46-14 N **Long:** 101-34-22 W
Pop: 80 (1990); 97 (1980) **Pop Density:** 2.3
Land: 35.0 sq. mi.; **Water:** 0.1 sq. mi.

Callahan
Township
Lat: 48-35-10 N **Long:** 101-39-28 W
Pop: 56 (1990); 52 (1980) **Pop Density:** 1.8
Land: 31.5 sq. mi.; **Water:** 4.2 sq. mi.

Clay
Township
Lat: 48-40-39 N **Long:** 101-30-47 W
Pop: 42 (1990); 54 (1980) **Pop Density:** 1.2
Land: 35.7 sq. mi.; **Water:** 0.1 sq. mi.

Colquhoun
Township
Lat: 48-56-39 N **Long:** 101-42-14 W
Pop: 97 (1990); 94 (1980) **Pop Density:** 2.2
Land: 43.2 sq. mi.; **Water:** 0.0 sq. mi.

Eden Valley
Township
Lat: 48-56-57 N **Long:** 101-33-49 W
Pop: 59 (1990); 70 (1980) **Pop Density:** 1.4
Land: 43.5 sq. mi.; **Water:** 0.2 sq. mi.

Ensign
Township
Lat: 48-30-07 N **Long:** 101-15-22 W
Pop: 75 (1990); 74 (1980) **Pop Density:** 2.1
Land: 35.7 sq. mi.; **Water:** 0.0 sq. mi.

Fairbanks
Township
Lat: 48-46-15 N **Long:** 101-57-58 W
Pop: 77 (1990); 77 (1980) **Pop Density:** 2.2
Land: 35.6 sq. mi.; **Water:** 0.4 sq. mi.

Glenburn
City
ZIP: 58740 **Lat:** 48-30-47 N **Long:** 101-13-13 W
Pop: 439 (1990); 454 (1980) **Pop Density:** 1463.3
Land: 0.3 sq. mi.; **Water:** 0.0 sq. mi. **Elev:** 1565 ft.

Grano
City
Lat: 48-37-01 N **Long:** 101-35-11 W
Pop: 9 (1990); 6 (1980) **Pop Density:** 30.0
Land: 0.3 sq. mi.; **Water:** 0.0 sq. mi. **Elev:** 1731 ft.

Grassland
Township
Lat: 48-40-10 N **Long:** 101-39-28 W
Pop: 47 (1990); 62 (1980) **Pop Density:** 1.4
Land: 33.2 sq. mi.; **Water:** 2.5 sq. mi.

Grover
Township
Lat: 48-50-43 N **Long:** 101-49-04 W
Pop: 46 (1990); 51 (1980) **Pop Density:** 1.3
Land: 35.7 sq. mi.; **Water:** 0.0 sq. mi.

Hamerly
Township
Lat: 48-50-57 N **Long:** 101-41-43 W
Pop: 44 (1990); 56 (1980) **Pop Density:** 1.2
Land: 35.9 sq. mi.; **Water:** 0.0 sq. mi.

Hamlet
Township
Lat: 48-45-22 N **Long:** 101-42-14 W
Pop: 77 (1990); 78 (1980) **Pop Density:** 2.2
Land: 35.7 sq. mi.; **Water:** 0.2 sq. mi.

Hurley
Township
Lat: 48-50-58 N **Long:** 101-33-53 W
Pop: 65 (1990); 61 (1980) **Pop Density:** 1.8
Land: 35.6 sq. mi.; **Water:** 0.0 sq. mi.

NORTH DAKOTA, Renville County

Ivanhoe
Township
Lat: 48-35-49 N Long: 101-45-59 W
Pop: 54 (1990); 76 (1980) Pop Density: 1.5
Land: 36.0 sq. mi.; Water: 0.0 sq. mi.

Lockwood
Township
Lat: 48-34-56 N Long: 101-30-20 W
Pop: 23 (1990); 39 (1980) Pop Density: 0.7
Land: 35.3 sq. mi.; Water: 0.5 sq. mi.

Loraine
City
Lat: 48-52-01 N Long: 101-34-02 W
Pop: 15 (1990); 21 (1980) Pop Density: 75.0
Land: 0.2 sq. mi.; Water: 0.0 sq. mi. Elev: 1625 ft.

McKinney
Township
Lat: 48-46-15 N Long: 101-50-06 W
Pop: 64 (1990); 85 (1980) Pop Density: 1.8
Land: 35.0 sq. mi.; Water: 0.8 sq. mi.

Mohall
City
ZIP: 58761 Lat: 48-45-57 N Long: 101-30-38 W
Pop: 931 (1990); 1,049 (1980) Pop Density: 1163.8
Land: 0.8 sq. mi.; Water: 0.0 sq. mi. Elev: 1639 ft.
Name origin: For Martin O. Hall, who settled in the area in 1901.

Muskego
Township
Lat: 48-29-43 N Long: 101-30-19 W
Pop: 80 (1990); 92 (1980) Pop Density: 2.6
Land: 31.2 sq. mi.; Water: 4.8 sq. mi.

Plain
Township
Lat: 48-29-58 N Long: 101-38-53 W
Pop: 46 (1990); 74 (1980) Pop Density: 1.3
Land: 35.7 sq. mi.; Water: 0.4 sq. mi.

Prescott
Township
Lat: 48-29-53 N Long: 101-07-52 W
Pop: 37 (1990); 39 (1980) Pop Density: 1.0
Land: 35.7 sq. mi.; Water: 0.1 sq. mi.

Prosperity
Township
Lat: 48-56-40 N Long: 101-48-48 W
Pop: 48 (1990); 72 (1980) Pop Density: 1.1
Land: 43.3 sq. mi.; Water: 0.0 sq. mi.

Rockford
Township
Lat: 48-51-27 N Long: 101-57-58 W
Pop: 81 (1990); 108 (1980) Pop Density: 2.3
Land: 35.7 sq. mi.; Water: 0.2 sq. mi.

Roosevelt
Township
Lat: 48-40-24 N Long: 101-46-10 W
Pop: 41 (1990); 62 (1980) Pop Density: 1.2
Land: 33.2 sq. mi.; Water: 2.6 sq. mi.

Sherwood
City
ZIP: 58782 Lat: 48-57-41 N Long: 101-37-59 W
Pop: 286 (1990); 294 (1980) Pop Density: 953.3
Land: 0.3 sq. mi.; Water: 0.0 sq. mi. Elev: 1640 ft.
Name origin: For original landowner Sherwood Sleeper.

Stafford
Township
Lat: 48-57-18 N Long: 101-57-36 W
Pop: 56 (1990); 72 (1980) Pop Density: 1.3
Land: 43.4 sq. mi.; Water: 0.1 sq. mi.

Tolley
City
ZIP: 58787 Lat: 48-43-49 N Long: 101-49-35 W
Pop: 79 (1990); 103 (1980) Pop Density: 790.0
Land: 0.1 sq. mi.; Water: 0.0 sq. mi. Elev: 1850 ft.

Van Buren
Township
Lat: 48-30-11 N Long: 101-23-02 W
Pop: 59 (1990); 72 (1980) Pop Density: 1.6
Land: 36.1 sq. mi.; Water: 0.0 sq. mi.

White Ash
Township
Lat: 48-29-58 N Long: 101-47-18 W
Pop: 47 (1990); 64 (1980) Pop Density: 1.3
Land: 35.9 sq. mi.; Water: 0.0 sq. mi.

Richland County
County Seat: Wahpeton (ZIP: 58075)

Pop: 18,148 (1990); 19,207 (1980) Pop Density: 12.6
Land: 1436.9 sq. mi.; Water: 8.9 sq. mi. Area Code: 701
In the southeastern corner of ND, south of Fargo; original county; organized Jan 4, 1873 (prior to statehood).
Name origin: For Morgan T. Rich (1832–98), settler and founder of the city of Wahpeton.

Abercrombie
City
ZIP: 58001 Lat: 46-26-50 N Long: 96-43-34 W
Pop: 252 (1990); 260 (1980) Pop Density: 420.0
Land: 0.6 sq. mi.; Water: 0.0 sq. mi. Elev: 936 ft.
Incorporated 1967.
Name origin: For Fort Abercrombie, a military post in intermittent use in the 1860s.

*Abercrombie
Township
Lat: 46-24-44 N Long: 96-47-21 W
Pop: 286 (1990); 306 (1980) Pop Density: 4.7
Land: 60.7 sq. mi.; Water: 0.0 sq. mi.

Antelope
Township
Lat: 46-19-39 N Long: 96-57-28 W
Pop: 127 (1990); 148 (1980) Pop Density: 3.5
Land: 36.0 sq. mi.; Water: 0.0 sq. mi.

Barney
City
ZIP: 58008 Lat: 46-15-59 N Long: 96-59-57 W
Pop: 79 (1990); 70 (1980) Pop Density: 395.0
Land: 0.2 sq. mi.; Water: 0.0 sq. mi. Elev: 1035 ft.
Incorporated 1967.

*Barney
Township
Lat: 46-14-19 N Long: 96-57-18 W
Pop: 143 (1990); 147 (1980) Pop Density: 4.1
Land: 35.2 sq. mi.; Water: 0.0 sq. mi.

American Places Dictionary — NORTH DAKOTA, Richland County

Barrie
Township
Lat: 46-35-06 N **Long:** 97-05-48 W
Pop: 150 (1990); 133 (1980) **Pop Density:** 4.3
Land: 35.2 sq. mi.; **Water:** 0.0 sq. mi.

Belford
Township
Lat: 46-09-08 N **Long:** 96-57-09 W
Pop: 162 (1990); 172 (1980) **Pop Density:** 4.5
Land: 35.7 sq. mi.; **Water:** 0.0 sq. mi.

Brandenburg
Township
Lat: 46-08-53 N **Long:** 96-49-45 W
Pop: 127 (1990); 160 (1980) **Pop Density:** 3.6
Land: 35.3 sq. mi.; **Water:** 0.0 sq. mi.

Brightwood
Township
Lat: 46-03-30 N **Long:** 96-56-42 W
Pop: 184 (1990); 178 (1980) **Pop Density:** 5.6
Land: 32.9 sq. mi.; **Water:** 1.8 sq. mi.

Center
Township
Lat: 46-13-55 N **Long:** 96-40-42 W
Pop: 423 (1990); 337 (1980) **Pop Density:** 9.5
Land: 44.5 sq. mi.; **Water:** 0.0 sq. mi.

Christine
City
ZIP: 58015 **Lat:** 46-34-31 N **Long:** 96-48-24 W
Pop: 140 (1990); 147 (1980) **Pop Density:** 700.0
Land: 0.2 sq. mi.; **Water:** 0.0 sq. mi. **Elev:** 929 ft.

Colfax
City
ZIP: 58018 **Lat:** 46-28-12 N **Long:** 96-52-26 W
Pop: 80 (1990); 101 (1980) **Pop Density:** 88.9
Land: 0.9 sq. mi.; **Water:** 0.0 sq. mi. **Elev:** 960 ft.
Not coextensive with township.

*Colfax
Township
ZIP: 58018 **Lat:** 46-30-25 N **Long:** 96-55-34 W
Pop: 201 (1990); 219 (1980) **Pop Density:** 3.4
Land: 59.2 sq. mi.; **Water:** 0.0 sq. mi.

Danton
Township
Lat: 46-14-13 N **Long:** 97-04-49 W
Pop: 159 (1990); 161 (1980) **Pop Density:** 4.5
Land: 35.1 sq. mi.; **Water:** 0.0 sq. mi.

Devillo
Township
Lat: 46-03-40 N **Long:** 96-41-59 W
Pop: 121 (1990); 142 (1980) **Pop Density:** 3.4
Land: 36.0 sq. mi.; **Water:** 0.0 sq. mi.

Dexter
Township
Lat: 46-08-47 N **Long:** 97-11-49 W
Pop: 106 (1990); 132 (1980) **Pop Density:** 3.0
Land: 35.0 sq. mi.; **Water:** 0.8 sq. mi.

Duerr
Township
Lat: 45-59-07 N **Long:** 97-07-31 W
Pop: 173 (1990); 210 (1980) **Pop Density:** 2.7
Land: 63.0 sq. mi.; **Water:** 1.2 sq. mi.

Dwight
City
Lat: 46-18-10 N **Long:** 96-44-19 W
Pop: 83 (1990); 72 (1980) **Pop Density:** 415.0
Land: 0.2 sq. mi.; **Water:** 0.0 sq. mi. **Elev:** 956 ft.
Not coextensive with township.

*Dwight
Township
Lat: 46-19-41 N **Long:** 96-41-56 W
Pop: 260 (1990); 240 (1980) **Pop Density:** 5.7
Land: 45.4 sq. mi.; **Water:** 0.1 sq. mi.

Eagle
Township
Lat: 46-31-59 N **Long:** 96-46-38 W
Pop: 237 (1990); 234 (1980) **Pop Density:** 5.6
Land: 42.4 sq. mi.; **Water:** 0.0 sq. mi.

Elma
Township
Lat: 45-58-25 N **Long:** 96-57-12 W
Pop: 102 (1990); 125 (1980) **Pop Density:** 2.9
Land: 35.5 sq. mi.; **Water:** 0.9 sq. mi.

Fairmount
City
ZIP: 58030 **Lat:** 46-03-16 N **Long:** 96-36-09 W
Pop: 427 (1990); 480 (1980) **Pop Density:** 1423.3
Land: 0.3 sq. mi.; **Water:** 0.0 sq. mi. **Elev:** 984 ft.
Not coextensive with township. Founded 1881.
Name origin: Named by original settlers for Fairmount Park in Philadelphia.

*Fairmount
Township
ZIP: 58030 **Lat:** 46-01-18 N **Long:** 96-36-05 W
Pop: 130 (1990); 177 (1980) **Pop Density:** 3.2
Land: 40.9 sq. mi.; **Water:** 0.0 sq. mi.

Freeman
Township
Lat: 46-24-20 N **Long:** 97-13-41 W
Pop: 58 (1990); 65 (1980) **Pop Density:** 1.6
Land: 35.9 sq. mi.; **Water:** 0.0 sq. mi.

Garborg
Township
Lat: 46-24-21 N **Long:** 97-06-07 W
Pop: 105 (1990); 123 (1980) **Pop Density:** 2.9
Land: 36.1 sq. mi.; **Water:** 0.0 sq. mi.

Grant
Township
Lat: 46-04-05 N **Long:** 97-12-27 W
Pop: 190 (1990); 202 (1980) **Pop Density:** 5.7
Land: 33.6 sq. mi.; **Water:** 1.7 sq. mi.

Great Bend
City
ZIP: 58039 **Lat:** 46-09-16 N **Long:** 96-48-03 W
Pop: 108 (1990); 113 (1980) **Pop Density:** 180.0
Land: 0.6 sq. mi.; **Water:** 0.0 sq. mi. **Elev:** 975 ft.

Greendale
Township
Lat: 45-58-19 N **Long:** 96-49-49 W
Pop: 121 (1990); 142 (1980) **Pop Density:** 3.3
Land: 36.3 sq. mi.; **Water:** 0.1 sq. mi.

Hankinson
City
ZIP: 58041 **Lat:** 46-04-17 N **Long:** 96-53-37 W
Pop: 1,038 (1990); 1,158 (1980) **Pop Density:** 741.4
Land: 1.4 sq. mi.; **Water:** 0.0 sq. mi. **Elev:** 1067 ft.
Name origin: For homesteader and Civil War soldier Richard Hankinson.

Helendale
Township
Lat: 46-34-46 N **Long:** 97-12-29 W
Pop: 108 (1990); 86 (1980) **Pop Density:** 3.1
Land: 35.0 sq. mi.; **Water:** 0.0 sq. mi.

Homestead
Township
Lat: 46-19-07 N **Long:** 97-06-08 W
Pop: 118 (1990); 118 (1980) **Pop Density:** 3.3
Land: 36.1 sq. mi.; **Water:** 0.0 sq. mi.

Ibsen
Township
Lat: 46-19-07 N **Long:** 96-50-09 W
Pop: 144 (1990); 167 (1980) **Pop Density:** 4.0
Land: 36.4 sq. mi.; **Water:** 0.0 sq. mi.

NORTH DAKOTA, Richland County

La Mars
Township
Lat: 45-58-19 N **Long:** 96-41-44 W
Pop: 102 (1990); 118 (1980) **Pop Density:** 2.8
Land: 35.9 sq. mi.; **Water:** 0.0 sq. mi.

Liberty Grove
Township
Lat: 46-09-16 N **Long:** 97-04-21 W
Pop: 117 (1990); 146 (1980) **Pop Density:** 3.3
Land: 35.8 sq. mi.; **Water:** 0.0 sq. mi.

Lidgerwood
City
ZIP: 58053 **Lat:** 46-04-29 N **Long:** 97-08-46 W
Pop: 799 (1990); 971 (1980) **Pop Density:** 1331.7
Land: 0.6 sq. mi.; **Water:** 0.0 sq. mi. **Elev:** 1114 ft.

Mantador
City
ZIP: 58058 **Lat:** 46-09-57 N **Long:** 96-58-39 W
Pop: 77 (1990); 76 (1980) **Pop Density:** 770.0
Land: 0.1 sq. mi.; **Water:** 0.0 sq. mi. **Elev:** 1027 ft.

Mooreton
City
ZIP: 58061 **Lat:** 46-16-08 N **Long:** 96-52-34 W
Pop: 193 (1990); 216 (1980) **Pop Density:** 643.3
Land: 0.3 sq. mi.; **Water:** 0.0 sq. mi. **Elev:** 970 ft.
Not coextensive with township.

*Mooreton
Township
ZIP: 58061 **Lat:** 46-14-21 N **Long:** 96-49-18 W
Pop: 120 (1990); 146 (1980) **Pop Density:** 3.4
Land: 35.2 sq. mi.; **Water:** 0.1 sq. mi.

Moran
Township
Lat: 46-03-58 N **Long:** 97-04-22 W
Pop: 89 (1990); 117 (1980) **Pop Density:** 2.7
Land: 33.5 sq. mi.; **Water:** 2.1 sq. mi.

Nansen
Township
Lat: 46-24-18 N **Long:** 96-57-59 W
Pop: 112 (1990); 118 (1980) **Pop Density:** 3.1
Land: 35.9 sq. mi.; **Water:** 0.0 sq. mi.

Sheyenne
Township
Lat: 46-29-32 N **Long:** 97-12-26 W
Pop: 62 (1990); 62 (1980) **Pop Density:** 1.7
Land: 35.8 sq. mi.; **Water:** 0.0 sq. mi.

Summit
Township
Lat: 46-08-42 N **Long:** 96-40-04 W
Pop: 245 (1990); 268 (1980) **Pop Density:** 4.6
Land: 53.4 sq. mi.; **Water:** 0.0 sq. mi.

Viking
Township
Lat: 46-29-58 N **Long:** 97-06-10 W
Pop: 71 (1990); 88 (1980) **Pop Density:** 2.0
Land: 36.0 sq. mi.; **Water:** 0.0 sq. mi.

Wahpeton
City
ZIP: 58075 **Lat:** 46-16-15 N **Long:** 96-36-36 W
Pop: 8,751 (1990); 9,064 (1980) **Pop Density:** 1750.2
Land: 5.0 sq. mi.; **Water:** 0.0 sq. mi. **Elev:** 963 ft.
Name origin: For local Wahpeton Indians.

Walcott
City
ZIP: 58077 **Lat:** 46-33-01 N **Long:** 96-56-13 W
Pop: 178 (1990); 186 (1980) **Pop Density:** 178.0
Land: 1.0 sq. mi.; **Water:** 0.0 sq. mi. **Elev:** 960 ft.
Not coextensive with township.

*Walcott
Township
ZIP: 58077 **Lat:** 46-34-46 N **Long:** 96-55-00 W
Pop: 302 (1990); 279 (1980) **Pop Density:** 5.2
Land: 58.6 sq. mi.; **Water:** 0.0 sq. mi.

Waldo
Township
Lat: 46-03-43 N **Long:** 96-49-49 W
Pop: 101 (1990); 112 (1980) **Pop Density:** 2.8
Land: 35.6 sq. mi.; **Water:** 0.0 sq. mi.

West End
Township
Lat: 46-19-23 N **Long:** 97-12-43 W
Pop: 52 (1990); 54 (1980) **Pop Density:** 1.4
Land: 36.2 sq. mi.; **Water:** 0.0 sq. mi.

Wyndmere
City
ZIP: 58081 **Lat:** 46-15-51 N **Long:** 97-07-51 W
Pop: 501 (1990); 550 (1980) **Pop Density:** 556.7
Land: 0.9 sq. mi.; **Water:** 0.0 sq. mi. **Elev:** 1059 ft.
Settled 1880s.
Name origin: For Windermere Lake, Westmorelandshire, England, with spelling deviation. From *wynd* 'narrow lane' and *mere* 'pool, lake.'

*Wyndmere
Township
ZIP: 58081 **Lat:** 46-14-46 N **Long:** 97-12-27 W
Pop: 134 (1990); 111 (1980) **Pop Density:** 3.8
Land: 35.5 sq. mi.; **Water:** 0.0 sq. mi.

Rolette County
County Seat: Rolla (ZIP: 58367)

Pop: 12,772 (1990); 12,177 (1980) **Pop Density:** 14.2
Land: 902.5 sq. mi.; **Water:** 36.9 sq. mi. **Area Code:** 701
On the central northern border of ND, northeast of Minot; organized Jan 4, 1873 (prior to statehood) from Buffalo County, which was discontinued.
Name origin: For Joseph Rolette (1820–71), pioneer and fur trader who opened a post for the American Fur Co.

Belcourt
CDP
ZIP: 58316 **Lat:** 48-50-29 N **Long:** 99-44-46 W
Pop: 2,458 (1990); 1,803 (1980) **Pop Density:** 416.6
Land: 5.9 sq. mi.; **Water:** 0.2 sq. mi.

Currie
Township
Lat: 48-45-44 N **Long:** 100-07-40 W
Pop: 90 (1990); 124 (1980) **Pop Density:** 2.5
Land: 35.9 sq. mi.; **Water:** 0.3 sq. mi.

Dunseith
City
ZIP: 58329 **Lat:** 48-48-45 N **Long:** 100-03-40 W
Pop: 723 (1990); 625 (1980) **Pop Density:** 723.0
Land: 1.0 sq. mi.; **Water:** 0.0 sq. mi. **Elev:** 1700 ft.

East Dunseith
CDP
Lat: 48-51-55 N **Long:** 100-00-58 W
Pop: 260 (1990) **Pop Density:** 162.5
Land: 1.6 sq. mi.; **Water:** 0.1 sq. mi.

East Rolette
Pop. Place
Lat: 48-41-23 N **Long:** 99-36-45 W
Pop: 585 (1990); 586 (1980) **Pop Density:** 2.8
Land: 207.9 sq. mi.; **Water:** 5.8 sq. mi.

Fairview
Township
Lat: 48-56-42 N **Long:** 99-35-06 W
Pop: 46 (1990); 57 (1980) **Pop Density:** 1.0
Land: 44.0 sq. mi.; **Water:** 0.3 sq. mi.

Kohlmeier
Township
Lat: 48-40-29 N **Long:** 100-05-06 W
Pop: 49 (1990); 67 (1980) **Pop Density:** 1.4
Land: 35.2 sq. mi.; **Water:** 0.4 sq. mi.

Leonard
Township
Lat: 48-40-29 N **Long:** 99-49-45 W
Pop: 203 (1990); 213 (1980) **Pop Density:** 6.0
Land: 33.6 sq. mi.; **Water:** 1.1 sq. mi.

Maryville
Township
Lat: 48-46-09 N **Long:** 99-42-42 W
Pop: 49 (1990); 62 (1980) **Pop Density:** 1.4
Land: 35.7 sq. mi.; **Water:** 0.3 sq. mi.

Mylo
City
ZIP: 58353 **Lat:** 48-38-09 N **Long:** 99-37-04 W
Pop: 20 (1990); 31 (1980) **Pop Density:** 22.2
Land: 0.9 sq. mi.; **Water:** 0.0 sq. mi. **Elev:** 1646 ft.

North Rolette
Pop. Place
Lat: 48-54-57 N **Long:** 99-57-07 W
Pop: 3,045 (1990); 2,871 (1980) **Pop Density:** 13.3
Land: 228.1 sq. mi.; **Water:** 19.0 sq. mi.

Rolette
City
ZIP: 58366 **Lat:** 48-39-40 N **Long:** 99-50-25 W
Pop: 623 (1990); 667 (1980) **Pop Density:** 623.0
Land: 1.0 sq. mi.; **Water:** 0.0 sq. mi. **Elev:** 1623 ft.
Name origin: For pioneer fur trader and legislator Joseph Rolette.

Rolla
City
ZIP: 58367 **Lat:** 48-51-31 N **Long:** 99-37-04 W
Pop: 1,286 (1990); 1,538 (1980) **Pop Density:** 1607.5
Land: 0.8 sq. mi.; **Water:** 0.0 sq. mi. **Elev:** 1805 ft.
Name origin: For either a contraction of Rollette County or for Rolla, MO.

Russell
Township
Lat: 48-45-49 N **Long:** 99-58-43 W
Pop: 69 (1990); 77 (1980) **Pop Density:** 1.9
Land: 35.7 sq. mi.; **Water:** 0.3 sq. mi.

St. John
City
Lat: 48-56-37 N **Long:** 99-42-38 W
Pop: 368 (1990); 401 (1980) **Pop Density:** 1840.0
Land: 0.2 sq. mi.; **Water:** 0.0 sq. mi. **Elev:** 1950 ft.
Name origin: For St. John, Canada, former home of an early settler.

Shell Valley
CDP
Lat: 48-47-52 N **Long:** 99-51-51 W
Pop: 343 (1990) **Pop Density:** 343.0
Land: 1.0 sq. mi.; **Water:** 0.0 sq. mi.

*Shell Valley
Township
Lat: 48-45-43 N **Long:** 99-51-17 W
Pop: 426 (1990); 269 (1980) **Pop Density:** 12.0
Land: 35.5 sq. mi.; **Water:** 0.5 sq. mi.

South Rolette
Pop. Place
Lat: 48-37-36 N **Long:** 99-54-08 W
Pop: 210 (1990); 235 (1980) **Pop Density:** 2.0
Land: 103.8 sq. mi.; **Water:** 4.0 sq. mi.

South Valley
Township
Lat: 48-35-21 N **Long:** 100-04-42 W
Pop: 40 (1990); 43 (1980) **Pop Density:** 1.1
Land: 35.5 sq. mi.; **Water:** 0.5 sq. mi.

Turtle Mountains
Pop. Place
Lat: 48-50-48 N **Long:** 99-47-11 W
Pop: 4,940 (1990); 4,311 (1980) **Pop Density:** 73.1
Land: 67.6 sq. mi.; **Water:** 4.3 sq. mi.

Sargent County
County Seat: Forman (ZIP: 58032)

Pop: 4,549 (1990); 5,512 (1980) **Pop Density:** 5.3
Land: 858.8 sq. mi.; **Water:** 8.3 sq. mi. **Area Code:** 701

On the southeastern border of ND, southwest of Fargo; organized Mar 3, 1883 (prior to statehood) from Ransom County.

Name origin: For Gen. Homer E. Sargent, superintendent of the Northern Pacific Railroad Company and developer of the Red River Valley.

Bowen
Township
Lat: 46-09-37 N **Long:** 97-41-24 W
Pop: 110 (1990); 146 (1980) **Pop Density:** 3.1
Land: 35.6 sq. mi.; **Water:** 0.0 sq. mi.

Brampton
Township
Lat: 45-58-44 N **Long:** 97-48-35 W
Pop: 93 (1990); 132 (1980) **Pop Density:** 2.6
Land: 36.3 sq. mi.; **Water:** 0.1 sq. mi.

Cayuga
City
ZIP: 58013 Lat: 46-04-33 N Long: 97-23-00 W
Pop: 60 (1990); 75 (1980) Pop Density: 60.0
Land: 1.0 sq. mi.; Water: 0.0 sq. mi. Elev: 1141 ft.

Cogswell
City
ZIP: 58017 Lat: 46-06-25 N Long: 97-47-02 W
Pop: 184 (1990); 227 (1980) Pop Density: 613.3
Land: 0.3 sq. mi.; Water: 0.0 sq. mi. Elev: 1300 ft.
Founded 1889.
Name origin: For a Soo Railroad official.

Denver
Township
Lat: 46-13-57 N Long: 97-56-02 W
Pop: 92 (1990); 111 (1980) Pop Density: 2.6
Land: 34.8 sq. mi.; Water: 0.6 sq. mi.

Dunbar
Township
Lat: 46-09-45 N Long: 97-34-23 W
Pop: 112 (1990); 142 (1980) Pop Density: 3.1
Land: 36.0 sq. mi.; Water: 0.0 sq. mi.

Forman
City
ZIP: 58032 Lat: 46-06-18 N Long: 97-38-12 W
Pop: 586 (1990); 629 (1980) Pop Density: 732.5
Land: 0.8 sq. mi.; Water: 0.0 sq. mi. Elev: 1250 ft.
Founded 1883.
Name origin: For Col. Cornelius Forman, who settled in the area and donated land for the town.

*Forman
Township
ZIP: 58032 Lat: 46-03-58 N Long: 97-41-43 W
Pop: 72 (1990); 86 (1980) Pop Density: 2.0
Land: 35.3 sq. mi.; Water: 0.0 sq. mi.

Gwinner
City
ZIP: 58040 Lat: 46-13-27 N Long: 97-39-30 W
Pop: 585 (1990); 725 (1980) Pop Density: 531.8
Land: 1.1 sq. mi.; Water: 0.0 sq. mi. Elev: 1263 ft.
Name origin: Named by Northern Pacific Railway officials for Arthur Gwinner, a major stockholder and European banker.

Hall
Township
Lat: 46-14-06 N Long: 97-18-58 W
Pop: 165 (1990); 193 (1980) Pop Density: 4.6
Land: 36.0 sq. mi.; Water: 0.0 sq. mi.

Harlem
Township
Lat: 46-09-46 N Long: 97-48-50 W
Pop: 32 (1990); 61 (1980) Pop Density: 0.9
Land: 36.1 sq. mi.; Water: 0.1 sq. mi. Elev: 1315 ft.

Havana
City
ZIP: 58043 Lat: 45-57-02 N Long: 97-37-03 W
Pop: 124 (1990); 148 (1980) Pop Density: 310.0
Land: 0.4 sq. mi.; Water: 0.0 sq. mi. Elev: 1294 ft.

Herman
Township
Lat: 46-09-33 N Long: 97-19-38 W
Pop: 122 (1990); 153 (1980) Pop Density: 3.4
Land: 36.0 sq. mi.; Water: 0.0 sq. mi.

Jackson
Township
Lat: 46-03-32 N Long: 97-56-07 W
Pop: 42 (1990); 65 (1980) Pop Density: 1.2
Land: 35.7 sq. mi.; Water: 0.0 sq. mi.

Kingston
Township
Lat: 46-03-43 N Long: 97-19-09 W
Pop: 136 (1990); 194 (1980) Pop Density: 3.2
Land: 42.0 sq. mi.; Water: 0.4 sq. mi.

Marboe
Township
Lat: 45-58-21 N Long: 97-18-04 W
Pop: 72 (1990); 81 (1980) Pop Density: 2.7
Land: 26.6 sq. mi.; Water: 0.9 sq. mi.

Milnor
City
ZIP: 58060 Lat: 46-15-38 N Long: 97-27-23 W
Pop: 651 (1990); 716 (1980) Pop Density: 723.3
Land: 0.9 sq. mi.; Water: 0.1 sq. mi. Elev: 1090 ft.
Not coextensive with township.
Name origin: Named by Northern Pacific Railroad officials for two of their employees.

*Milnor
Township
ZIP: 58060 Lat: 46-14-37 N Long: 97-27-00 W
Pop: 111 (1990); 113 (1980) Pop Density: 3.4
Land: 32.7 sq. mi.; Water: 1.5 sq. mi.

Ransom
Township
Lat: 46-03-59 N Long: 97-26-34 W
Pop: 107 (1990); 106 (1980) Pop Density: 3.0
Land: 35.1 sq. mi.; Water: 0.1 sq. mi.

Rutland
City
ZIP: 58067 Lat: 46-03-13 N Long: 97-30-28 W
Pop: 212 (1990); 250 (1980) Pop Density: 424.0
Land: 0.5 sq. mi.; Water: 0.0 sq. mi. Elev: 1224 ft.

*Rutland
Township
ZIP: 58067 Lat: 46-04-23 N Long: 97-34-16 W
Pop: 65 (1990); 99 (1980) Pop Density: 1.8
Land: 35.3 sq. mi.; Water: 0.3 sq. mi.

Sargent
Township
Lat: 46-03-58 N Long: 97-49-58 W
Pop: 75 (1990); 71 (1980) Pop Density: 2.1
Land: 36.0 sq. mi.; Water: 0.0 sq. mi.

Shuman
Township
Lat: 46-09-04 N Long: 97-26-39 W
Pop: 80 (1990); 113 (1980) Pop Density: 2.3
Land: 34.9 sq. mi.; Water: 0.7 sq. mi.

Southwest
Township
Lat: 45-59-12 N Long: 97-55-55 W
Pop: 37 (1990); 36 (1980) Pop Density: 1.0
Land: 36.0 sq. mi.; Water: 0.1 sq. mi.

Taylor
Township
Lat: 45-58-44 N Long: 97-41-44 W
Pop: 44 (1990); 63 (1980) Pop Density: 1.2
Land: 36.1 sq. mi.; Water: 0.2 sq. mi.

Tewaukon
Township
Lat: 45-58-33 N Long: 97-25-36 W
Pop: 76 (1990); 91 (1980) Pop Density: 2.0
Land: 37.7 sq. mi.; Water: 1.5 sq. mi.

Verner
Township
Lat: 46-09-37 N Long: 97-56-04 W
Pop: 58 (1990); 87 (1980) Pop Density: 1.6
Land: 35.3 sq. mi.; Water: 0.4 sq. mi.

Vivian
Township
Lat: 46-13-58 N Long: 97-49-46 W
Pop: 151 (1990); 198 (1980) Pop Density: 4.3
Land: 35.1 sq. mi.; Water: 0.5 sq. mi.

NORTH DAKOTA, Sheridan County

Weber — Township
Lat: 45-58-35 N Long: 97-33-49 W
Pop: 104 (1990); 137 (1980) Pop Density: 2.6
Land: 39.7 sq. mi.; Water: 0.5 sq. mi.

Whitestone Hill — Township
Lat: 46-14-24 N Long: 97-42-18 W
Pop: 97 (1990); 153 (1980) Pop Density: 2.8
Land: 34.1 sq. mi.; Water: 0.1 sq. mi.

Willey — Township
Lat: 46-14-48 N Long: 97-34-02 W
Pop: 94 (1990); 111 (1980) Pop Density: 2.6
Land: 35.5 sq. mi.; Water: 0.1 sq. mi.

Sheridan County
County Seat: McClusky (ZIP: 58463)

Pop: 2,148 (1990); 2,819 (1980) Pop Density: 2.2
Land: 971.8 sq. mi.; Water: 34.0 sq. mi. Area Code: 701
In central ND, northeast of Bismarck; organized Nov 1908 (prior to statehood) from McLean County.
Name origin: For Gen. Philip Henry Sheridan (1831–88), Union officer during the Civil War and commander in chief of the U.S. army (1883–88).

Berlin — Township
Lat: 47-43-01 N Long: 100-08-39 W
Pop: 60 (1990); 84 (1980) Pop Density: 1.7
Land: 34.5 sq. mi.; Water: 1.6 sq. mi.

Boone — Township
Lat: 47-33-05 N Long: 100-06-09 W
Pop: 35 (1990); 57 (1980) Pop Density: 1.0
Land: 35.3 sq. mi.; Water: 0.6 sq. mi.

Central Sheridan — Pop. Place
Lat: 47-34-44 N Long: 100-23-48 W
Pop: 350 (1990); 357 (1980) Pop Density: 1.4
Land: 252.4 sq. mi.; Water: 4.2 sq. mi.

Denhoff — Township
ZIP: 58430 Lat: 47-27-28 N Long: 100-13-09 W
Pop: 56 (1990); 89 (1980) Pop Density: 1.6
Land: 34.2 sq. mi.; Water: 1.9 sq. mi.

Edgemont — Township
Lat: 47-21-54 N Long: 100-36-47 W
Pop: 18 (1990); 38 (1980) Pop Density: 0.5
Land: 35.4 sq. mi.; Water: 0.8 sq. mi.

Fairview — Township
Lat: 47-37-58 N Long: 100-05-55 W
Pop: 33 (1990); 34 (1980) Pop Density: 0.9
Land: 35.0 sq. mi.; Water: 0.2 sq. mi.

Goodrich — City
ZIP: 58444 Lat: 47-28-34 N Long: 100-07-28 W
Pop: 192 (1990); 288 (1980) Pop Density: 640.0
Land: 0.3 sq. mi.; Water: 0.0 sq. mi. Elev: 1977 ft.
Not coextensive with township.

*Goodrich — Township
ZIP: 58444 Lat: 47-27-28 N Long: 100-05-51 W
Pop: 81 (1990); 91 (1980) Pop Density: 2.4
Land: 33.5 sq. mi.; Water: 2.2 sq. mi.

Highland — Township
Lat: 47-42-47 N Long: 100-31-27 W
Pop: 55 (1990); 59 (1980) Pop Density: 1.6
Land: 35.3 sq. mi.; Water: 0.8 sq. mi.

Holmes — Township
Lat: 47-38-02 N Long: 100-37-33 W
Pop: 18 (1990); 52 (1980) Pop Density: 0.5
Land: 34.5 sq. mi.; Water: 0.9 sq. mi.

Lincoln Dale — Township
Lat: 47-38-13 N Long: 100-21-37 W
Pop: 38 (1990); 54 (1980) Pop Density: 1.1
Land: 35.0 sq. mi.; Water: 0.3 sq. mi.

Martin — City
ZIP: 58758 Lat: 47-49-36 N Long: 100-06-51 W
Pop: 117 (1990); 114 (1980) Pop Density: 1170.0
Land: 0.1 sq. mi.; Water: 0.0 sq. mi. Elev: 1629 ft.
Not coextensive with township.

*Martin — Township
ZIP: 58758 Lat: 47-48-14 N Long: 100-07-22 W
Pop: 69 (1990); 94 (1980) Pop Density: 2.0
Land: 34.7 sq. mi.; Water: 1.2 sq. mi.

Mauch — Township
Lat: 47-22-15 N Long: 100-05-36 W
Pop: 31 (1990); 45 (1980) Pop Density: 0.9
Land: 32.8 sq. mi.; Water: 3.4 sq. mi.

McClusky — City
ZIP: 58463 Lat: 47-29-03 N Long: 100-26-30 W
Pop: 492 (1990); 658 (1980) Pop Density: 1230.0
Land: 0.4 sq. mi.; Water: 0.0 sq. mi. Elev: 1925 ft.
Not coextensive with township.
Name origin: For William McClusky, who settled in the area in 1902.

*McClusky — Township
ZIP: 58463 Lat: 47-27-54 N Long: 100-29-28 W
Pop: 85 (1990); 101 (1980) Pop Density: 2.4
Land: 35.3 sq. mi.; Water: 0.6 sq. mi.

New Germantown — Township
Lat: 47-43-03 N Long: 100-15-42 W
Pop: 60 (1990); 87 (1980) Pop Density: 1.7
Land: 34.3 sq. mi.; Water: 1.8 sq. mi.

NORTH DAKOTA, Sheridan County   American Places Dictionary

North Sheridan   Pop. Place
                    Lat: 47-48-14 N Long: 100-16-23 W
Pop: 74 (1990); 215 (1980)   Pop Density: 2.2
Land: 33.8 sq. mi.; Water: 2.3 sq. mi.

Pickard   Township
                    Lat: 47-27-39 N Long: 100-36-35 W
Pop: 49 (1990); 56 (1980)   Pop Density: 1.4
Land: 34.9 sq. mi.; Water: 1.2 sq. mi.

Rosenfield   Township
                    Lat: 47-48-16 N Long: 100-23-10 W
Pop: 58 (1990)   Pop Density: 1.7
Land: 33.8 sq. mi.; Water: 2.1 sq. mi.

South Sheridan   Pop. Place
                    Lat: 47-22-57 N Long: 100-20-36 W
Pop: 116 (1990); 165 (1980)   Pop Density: 0.9
Land: 134.1 sq. mi.; Water: 4.5 sq. mi.

Strassburg   Township
                    Lat: 47-48-37 N Long: 100-31-25 W
Pop: 61 (1990); 81 (1980)   Pop Density: 1.9
Land: 32.4 sq. mi.; Water: 3.6 sq. mi.

Sioux County
County Seat: Fort Yates (ZIP: 58538)

Pop: 3,761 (1990); 3,620 (1980)   Pop Density: 3.4
Land: 1094.2 sq. mi.; Water: 34.2 sq. mi.   Area Code: 701
On the central southern border of ND, south of Bismarck; organized Sep 3, 1914 from the Standing Rock Indian Reservation.
Name origin: For the Sioux Indians, sometimes known as the Dakotas.

Cannon Ball   CDP
                    Lat: 46-18-44 N Long: 100-37-55 W
Pop: 702 (1990)   Pop Density: 8.1
Land: 86.8 sq. mi.; Water: 8.4 sq. mi.

Fort Yates   City
ZIP: 58538   Lat: 46-05-13 N Long: 100-37-47 W
Pop: 183 (1990); 771 (1980)   Pop Density: 1830.0
Land: 0.1 sq. mi.; Water: 0.0 sq. mi.   Elev: 1642 ft.
Name origin: For Capt. George Yates, who was killed at Custer's last stand in 1876.

*Fort Yates   Pop. Place
                    Lat: 46-02-06 N Long: 100-42-02 W
Pop: 1,913 (1990); 943 (1980)   Pop Density: 11.4
Land: 167.6 sq. mi.; Water: 20.6 sq. mi.

Menz   Township
                    Lat: 45-59-55 N Long: 101-55-39 W
Pop: 39 (1990); 70 (1980)   Pop Density: 0.8
Land: 46.8 sq. mi.; Water: 0.0 sq. mi.

North Sioux   Pop. Place
                    Lat: 46-16-57 N Long: 100-47-04 W
Pop: 926 (1990); 971 (1980)   Pop Density: 3.0
Land: 310.0 sq. mi.; Water: 13.1 sq. mi.

Selfridge   City
ZIP: 58568   Lat: 46-02-31 N Long: 100-55-27 W
Pop: 242 (1990); 273 (1980)   Pop Density: 806.7
Land: 0.3 sq. mi.; Water: 0.0 sq. mi.   Elev: 2184 ft.
Name origin: For either a Soo Railroad official or an early army aviator hero.

Solen   City
ZIP: 58570   Lat: 46-23-19 N Long: 100-47-43 W
Pop: 92 (1990); 138 (1980)   Pop Density: 306.7
Land: 0.3 sq. mi.; Water: 0.0 sq. mi.   Elev: 1680 ft.

Southwest Sioux   Pop. Place
                    Lat: 46-02-43 N Long: 101-13-20 W
Pop: 366 (1990); 454 (1980)   Pop Density: 0.6
Land: 569.1 sq. mi.; Water: 0.5 sq. mi.

Slope County
County Seat: Amidon (ZIP: 58620)

Pop: 907 (1990); 1,157 (1980)   Pop Density: 0.7
Land: 1218.0 sq. mi.; Water: 1.3 sq. mi.   Area Code: 701
On the southwestern border of ND, southwest of Dickinson; organized Jan 14, 1915 from Billings County.
Name origin: For the Missouri Slope, a popular name for western ND, especially the area west of the Missouri River.

Amidon   City
ZIP: 58620   Lat: 46-28-55 N Long: 103-19-07 W
Pop: 24 (1990); 43 (1980)   Pop Density: 40.0
Land: 0.6 sq. mi.; Water: 0.0 sq. mi.   Elev: 2908 ft.
Incorporated 1967.

Bucklin   Township
                    Lat: 46-19-21 N Long: 103-59-49 W
Pop: 8 (1990); 11 (1980)   Pop Density: 0.2
Land: 32.2 sq. mi.; Water: 0.0 sq. mi.

NORTH DAKOTA, Slope County

Carroll
Township
Lat: 46-24-37 N **Long:** 102-59-12 W
Pop: 20 (1990); 34 (1980) **Pop Density:** 0.6
Land: 36.0 sq. mi.; **Water:** 0.0 sq. mi.

Cash
Township
Lat: 46-19-38 N **Long:** 103-28-53 W
Pop: 24 (1990); 34 (1980) **Pop Density:** 0.7
Land: 35.8 sq. mi.; **Water:** 0.2 sq. mi.

Cedar Creek
Township
Lat: 46-19-19 N **Long:** 102-58-47 W
Pop: 36 (1990); 38 (1980) **Pop Density:** 1.0
Land: 35.8 sq. mi.; **Water:** 0.3 sq. mi.

Chalky Butte
Pop. Place
Lat: 46-24-33 N **Long:** 103-21-27 W
Pop: 22 (1990); 15 (1980) **Pop Density:** 0.6
Land: 35.9 sq. mi.; **Water:** 0.0 sq. mi.

Connor
Township
Lat: 46-24-41 N **Long:** 103-13-49 W
Pop: 30 (1990); 61 (1980) **Pop Density:** 0.8
Land: 35.9 sq. mi.; **Water:** 0.1 sq. mi.

Crawford
Township
Lat: 46-19-37 N **Long:** 103-44-47 W
Pop: 31 (1990); 28 (1980) **Pop Density:** 0.9
Land: 35.9 sq. mi.; **Water:** 0.0 sq. mi.

Deep Creek
Pop. Place
Lat: 46-19-29 N **Long:** 103-36-32 W
Pop: 27 (1990); 50 (1980) **Pop Density:** 0.8
Land: 35.9 sq. mi.; **Water:** 0.0 sq. mi.

Dovre
Township
Lat: 46-35-46 N **Long:** 103-06-35 W
Pop: 21 (1990); 18 (1980) **Pop Density:** 0.6
Land: 36.1 sq. mi.; **Water:** 0.0 sq. mi.

E-Six
Pop. Place
Lat: 46-35-23 N **Long:** 102-59-38 W
Pop: 79 (1990); 120 (1980) **Pop Density:** 2.2
Land: 36.5 sq. mi.; **Water:** 0.1 sq. mi.

Harper
Township
Lat: 46-24-44 N **Long:** 103-37-22 W
Pop: 7 (1990); 5 (1980) **Pop Density:** 0.2
Land: 35.7 sq. mi.; **Water:** 0.0 sq. mi.

Hughes
Township
Lat: 46-18-23 N **Long:** 103-51-48 W
Pop: 11 (1990); 17 (1980) **Pop Density:** 0.3
Land: 35.3 sq. mi.; **Water:** 0.0 sq. mi.

Hume
Township
Lat: 46-24-14 N **Long:** 103-06-11 W
Pop: 25 (1990); 44 (1980) **Pop Density:** 0.7
Land: 35.5 sq. mi.; **Water:** 0.0 sq. mi.

Marmarth
City
ZIP: 58643 **Lat:** 46-17-45 N **Long:** 103-56-02 W
Pop: 144 (1990); 190 (1980) **Pop Density:** 57.6
Land: 2.5 sq. mi.; **Water:** 0.0 sq. mi. **Elev:** 2706 ft.

Mineral Springs
Township
Lat: 46-19-15 N **Long:** 103-14-41 W
Pop: 37 (1990); 36 (1980) **Pop Density:** 1.0
Land: 35.9 sq. mi.; **Water:** 0.0 sq. mi.

Moord
Township
Lat: 46-29-53 N **Long:** 103-06-39 W
Pop: 17 (1990); 27 (1980) **Pop Density:** 0.5
Land: 35.2 sq. mi.; **Water:** 0.0 sq. mi.

Mound
Township
Lat: 46-24-56 N **Long:** 103-44-29 W
Pop: 13 (1990); 25 (1980) **Pop Density:** 0.4
Land: 35.9 sq. mi.; **Water:** 0.0 sq. mi. **Elev:** 3030 ft.

Northwest Slope
Pop. Place
Lat: 46-35-11 N **Long:** 103-32-59 W
Pop: 74 (1990); 58 (1980) **Pop Density:** 0.5
Land: 146.9 sq. mi.; **Water:** 0.1 sq. mi.

Peaceful Valley
Township
Lat: 46-35-21 N **Long:** 103-13-55 W
Pop: 30 (1990); 36 (1980) **Pop Density:** 0.8
Land: 36.9 sq. mi.; **Water:** 0.0 sq. mi.

Rainy Butte
Township
Lat: 46-29-50 N **Long:** 102-58-57 W
Pop: 29 (1990); 63 (1980) **Pop Density:** 0.8
Land: 35.8 sq. mi.; **Water:** 0.0 sq. mi.

Richland Center
Township
Lat: 46-30-12 N **Long:** 103-36-18 W
Pop: 7 (1990); 11 (1980) **Pop Density:** 0.2
Land: 35.7 sq. mi.; **Water:** 0.0 sq. mi.

Sand Creek
Township
Lat: 46-29-35 N **Long:** 103-25-20 W
Pop: 49 (1990); 47 (1980) **Pop Density:** 0.7
Land: 70.9 sq. mi.; **Water:** 0.1 sq. mi.

Sheets
Township
Lat: 46-18-57 N **Long:** 103-22-03 W
Pop: 46 (1990); 32 (1980) **Pop Density:** 1.3
Land: 35.9 sq. mi.; **Water:** 0.1 sq. mi.

Slope Center
Township
Lat: 46-24-55 N **Long:** 103-28-57 W
Pop: 12 (1990); 11 (1980) **Pop Density:** 0.3
Land: 35.8 sq. mi.; **Water:** 0.0 sq. mi.

Sunshine
Township
Lat: 46-29-14 N **Long:** 103-44-32 W
Pop: 2 (1990); 4 (1980) **Pop Density:** 0.1
Land: 35.9 sq. mi.; **Water:** 0.0 sq. mi.

West Slope
Pop. Place
Lat: 46-27-54 N **Long:** 103-55-42 W
Pop: 25 (1990); 31 (1980) **Pop Density:** 0.2
Land: 139.9 sq. mi.; **Water:** 0.0 sq. mi.

White Lake
Township
Lat: 46-29-56 N **Long:** 103-14-09 W
Pop: 27 (1990); 36 (1980) **Pop Density:** 0.8
Land: 35.6 sq. mi.; **Water:** 0.3 sq. mi.

Woodberry
Township
Lat: 46-19-23 N **Long:** 103-06-51 W
Pop: 30 (1990); 32 (1980) **Pop Density:** 0.8
Land: 35.9 sq. mi.; **Water:** 0.0 sq. mi.

Stark County
County Seat: Dickinson (ZIP: 58602)

Pop: 22,832 (1990); 23,697 (1980)   **Pop Density:** 17.1
Land: 1338.3 sq. mi.; **Water:** 2.3 sq. mi.   **Area Code:** 701
In southwestern ND, west of Bismarck; organized Feb 10, 1879 (prior to statehood) from unorganized territory.
Name origin: For George Stark, vice president of the Northern Pacific Railroad Co. (1875–79).

Belfield — City
ZIP: 58622   Lat: 46-53-13 N   Long: 103-11-43 W
Pop: 887 (1990); 1,274 (1980)   Pop Density: 985.6
Land: 0.9 sq. mi.; Water: 0.0 sq. mi.   Elev: 2592 ft.
Incorporated 1915.

Dickinson — City
ZIP: 58601   Lat: 46-53-10 N   Long: 102-46-57 W
Pop: 16,097 (1990); 15,924 (1980)   Pop Density: 1609.7
Land: 10.0 sq. mi.; Water: 0.0 sq. mi.   Elev: 2417 ft.
In southwestern ND, 100 mi. west of Bismarck. Incorporated 1900.
Name origin: For original landowner, Wells S. Dickinson.

Dickinson North — Pop. Place
Lat: 46-53-27 N   Long: 102-44-36 W
Pop: 2,315 (1990); 2,432 (1980)   Pop Density: 8.6
Land: 269.1 sq. mi.; Water: 1.3 sq. mi.

Dickinson South — Pop. Place
Lat: 46-43-17 N   Long: 102-45-44 W
Pop: 601 (1990); 669 (1980)   Pop Density: 2.9
Land: 205.2 sq. mi.; Water: 0.0 sq. mi.

East Stark — Pop. Place
Lat: 46-48-46 N   Long: 102-19-16 W
Pop: 904 (1990); 1,106 (1980)   Pop Density: 1.7
Land: 547.7 sq. mi.; Water: 0.8 sq. mi.

Gladstone — City
ZIP: 58630   Lat: 46-51-35 N   Long: 102-34-02 W
Pop: 224 (1990); 317 (1980)   Pop Density: 560.0
Land: 0.4 sq. mi.; Water: 0.0 sq. mi.   Elev: 2354 ft.
Name origin: Named by early settlers for English statesman William Gladstone (1809–1898).

Richardton — City
ZIP: 58652   Lat: 46-53-04 N   Long: 102-18-53 W
Pop: 625 (1990); 699 (1980)   Pop Density: 1562.5
Land: 0.4 sq. mi.; Water: 0.0 sq. mi.   Elev: 2470 ft.

South Heart — City
ZIP: 58655   Lat: 46-51-49 N   Long: 102-59-30 W
Pop: 322 (1990); 294 (1980)   Pop Density: 1073.3
Land: 0.3 sq. mi.; Water: 0.0 sq. mi.   Elev: 2482 ft.

Taylor — City
ZIP: 58656   Lat: 46-54-07 N   Long: 102-25-20 W
Pop: 163 (1990); 239 (1980)   Pop Density: 326.0
Land: 0.5 sq. mi.; Water: 0.0 sq. mi.   Elev: 2492 ft.

West Stark — Pop. Place
Lat: 46-47-28 N   Long: 103-05-48 W
Pop: 694 (1990); 743 (1980)   Pop Density: 2.3
Land: 304.0 sq. mi.; Water: 0.1 sq. mi.

Steele County
County Seat: Finley (ZIP: 58230)

Pop: 2,420 (1990); 3,106 (1980)   **Pop Density:** 3.4
Land: 712.4 sq. mi.; **Water:** 3.1 sq. mi.   **Area Code:** 701
In east-central ND, southwest of Grand Forks; organized Mar 8, 1883 (prior to statehood) from Traill County.
Name origin: For Edward H. Steele (1846–99), an officer of the Red River Land Co., which figured prominently in the establishment of the county.

Beaver Creek — Township
Lat: 47-37-57 N   Long: 97-40-08 W
Pop: 114 (1990); 112 (1980)   Pop Density: 3.3
Land: 34.8 sq. mi.; Water: 0.9 sq. mi.

Broadlawn — Township
Lat: 47-16-44 N   Long: 97-30-28 W
Pop: 59 (1990); 73 (1980)   Pop Density: 1.7
Land: 35.2 sq. mi.; Water: 0.1 sq. mi.

Carpenter — Township
Lat: 47-16-44 N   Long: 97-45-40 W
Pop: 53 (1990); 72 (1980)   Pop Density: 1.5
Land: 35.0 sq. mi.; Water: 0.0 sq. mi.

Colgate — Township
Lat: 47-16-58 N   Long: 97-38-31 W
Pop: 98 (1990); 112 (1980)   Pop Density: 2.8
Land: 35.3 sq. mi.; Water: 0.0 sq. mi.

Easton — Township
Lat: 47-27-45 N   Long: 97-46-56 W
Pop: 78 (1990); 118 (1980)   Pop Density: 2.2
Land: 36.0 sq. mi.; Water: 0.0 sq. mi.

Edendale — Township
Lat: 47-22-32 N   Long: 97-31-37 W
Pop: 72 (1990); 94 (1980)   Pop Density: 2.0
Land: 36.0 sq. mi.; Water: 0.0 sq. mi.

Enger
Township
Lat: 47-32-28 N **Long:** 97-32-18 W
Pop: 98 (1990); 105 (1980) **Pop Density:** 2.7
Land: 35.8 sq. mi.; **Water:** 0.0 sq. mi.

Finley
City
ZIP: 58230 **Lat:** 47-30-41 N **Long:** 97-50-13 W
Pop: 543 (1990); 718 (1980) **Pop Density:** 155.1
Land: 3.5 sq. mi.; **Water:** 0.0 sq. mi. **Elev:** 1457 ft.
Not coextensive with township.
Name origin: Named in 1896 for Great Northern Railway vice president W.W. Finley. Originally called Gilbert.

*Finley
Township
ZIP: 58230 **Lat:** 47-32-24 N **Long:** 97-46-56 W
Pop: 65 (1990); 81 (1980) **Pop Density:** 2.0
Land: 32.4 sq. mi.; **Water:** 0.1 sq. mi.

Franklin
Township
Lat: 47-32-47 N **Long:** 97-54-45 W
Pop: 49 (1990); 79 (1980) **Pop Density:** 1.4
Land: 35.8 sq. mi.; **Water:** 0.1 sq. mi.

Golden Lake
Township
Lat: 47-32-31 N **Long:** 97-39-58 W
Pop: 68 (1990); 87 (1980) **Pop Density:** 2.0
Land: 34.8 sq. mi.; **Water:** 1.2 sq. mi.

Greenview
Township
Lat: 47-27-37 N **Long:** 97-55-03 W
Pop: 64 (1990); 76 (1980) **Pop Density:** 1.8
Land: 36.0 sq. mi.; **Water:** 0.0 sq. mi.

Hope
City
Lat: 47-19-29 N **Long:** 97-43-10 W
Pop: 281 (1990); 406 (1980) **Pop Density:** 468.3
Land: 0.6 sq. mi.; **Water:** 0.0 sq. mi. **Elev:** 1240 ft.
Founded 1882.
Name origin: For Hope Steele, wife of the land company treasurer, who bought 50,000 acres of wheat land from the railroad for $1 per acre.

Hugo
Township
Lat: 47-22-01 N **Long:** 97-40-35 W
Pop: 61 (1990); 71 (1980) **Pop Density:** 1.7
Land: 35.9 sq. mi.; **Water:** 0.0 sq. mi.

Luverne
City
ZIP: 58056 **Lat:** 47-15-01 N **Long:** 97-56-04 W
Pop: 41 (1990); 65 (1980) **Pop Density:** 136.7
Land: 0.3 sq. mi.; **Water:** 0.0 sq. mi. **Elev:** 1430 ft.

Melrose
Township
Lat: 47-22-06 N **Long:** 97-47-42 W
Pop: 73 (1990); 91 (1980) **Pop Density:** 2.0
Land: 36.0 sq. mi.; **Water:** 0.0 sq. mi.

Newburgh
Township
Lat: 47-37-55 N **Long:** 97-32-00 W
Pop: 102 (1990); 103 (1980) **Pop Density:** 2.8
Land: 35.8 sq. mi.; **Water:** 0.0 sq. mi.

Primrose
Township
Lat: 47-27-54 N **Long:** 97-32-14 W
Pop: 90 (1990); 114 (1980) **Pop Density:** 2.5
Land: 36.0 sq. mi.; **Water:** 0.0 sq. mi.

Riverside
Township
Lat: 47-21-59 N **Long:** 97-55-25 W
Pop: 55 (1990); 65 (1980) **Pop Density:** 1.5
Land: 36.1 sq. mi.; **Water:** 0.1 sq. mi.

Sharon
City
ZIP: 58277 **Lat:** 47-35-49 N **Long:** 97-53-54 W
Pop: 119 (1990); 166 (1980) **Pop Density:** 79.3
Land: 1.5 sq. mi.; **Water:** 0.0 sq. mi. **Elev:** 1510 ft.
Not coextensive with township.

*Sharon
Township
ZIP: 58277 **Lat:** 47-37-46 N **Long:** 97-55-19 W
Pop: 44 (1990); 62 (1980) **Pop Density:** 1.3
Land: 33.8 sq. mi.; **Water:** 0.0 sq. mi.

Sherbrooke
Township
Lat: 47-27-28 N **Long:** 97-39-17 W
Pop: 59 (1990); 85 (1980) **Pop Density:** 1.6
Land: 36.0 sq. mi.; **Water:** 0.0 sq. mi.

Westfield
Township
Lat: 47-37-44 N **Long:** 97-47-28 W
Pop: 73 (1990); 76 (1980) **Pop Density:** 2.1
Land: 35.4 sq. mi.; **Water:** 0.0 sq. mi.

Willow Lake
Township
Lat: 47-17-21 N **Long:** 97-53-25 W
Pop: 61 (1990); 75 (1980) **Pop Density:** 1.8
Land: 34.5 sq. mi.; **Water:** 0.4 sq. mi.

Stutsman County
County Seat: Jamestown (ZIP: 58401)

Pop: 22,241 (1990); 24,154 (1980)
Land: 2221.5 sq. mi.; **Water:** 76.9 sq. mi.
Pop Density: 10.0
Area Code: 701

In south-central ND, west of Fargo; organized Jan 4, 1873 (prior to statehood) from Pembina County.

Name origin: For Enos Stutsman (1926–74), member of the Dakota Council and a special agent of the U.S. Treasury Dept.

Alexander
Township
Lat: 46-40-07 N Long: 99-00-08 W
Pop: 49 (1990); 48 (1980) Pop Density: 1.4
Land: 35.7 sq. mi.; Water: 0.3 sq. mi.

Ashland
Township
Lat: 47-06-52 N Long: 98-39-27 W
Pop: 86 (1990); 89 (1980) Pop Density: 2.5
Land: 34.0 sq. mi.; Water: 1.4 sq. mi.

Bloom
Township
Lat: 46-55-49 N Long: 98-37-37 W
Pop: 511 (1990); 347 (1980) Pop Density: 14.9
Land: 34.2 sq. mi.; Water: 0.6 sq. mi.

Bloomenfield
Township
Lat: 46-45-15 N Long: 99-15-39 W
Pop: 51 (1990); 53 (1980) Pop Density: 1.5
Land: 34.3 sq. mi.; Water: 1.7 sq. mi.

Buchanan
City
ZIP: 58420 Lat: 47-03-46 N Long: 98-49-45 W
Pop: 40 (1990) Pop Density: 400.0
Land: 0.1 sq. mi.; Water: 0.0 sq. mi. Elev: 1551 ft.
Not coextensive with township. Incorporated 1983.

*Buchanan
Township
ZIP: 58420 Lat: 47-01-43 N Long: 98-47-23 W
Pop: 123 (1990); 187 (1980) Pop Density: 3.6
Land: 33.9 sq. mi.; Water: 2.0 sq. mi.

Chase Lake
Pop. Place
Lat: 47-02-14 N Long: 99-25-12 W
Pop: 6 (1990); 5 (1980) Pop Density: 0.2
Land: 30.9 sq. mi.; Water: 4.9 sq. mi.

Chicago
Township
Lat: 46-51-10 N Long: 99-16-05 W
Pop: 55 (1990); 74 (1980) Pop Density: 1.6
Land: 33.7 sq. mi.; Water: 1.9 sq. mi.

Cleveland
City
ZIP: 58424 Lat: 46-53-27 N Long: 99-07-11 W
Pop: 121 (1990); 130 (1980) Pop Density: 605.0
Land: 0.2 sq. mi.; Water: 0.0 sq. mi. Elev: 1850 ft.

Conklin
Township
Lat: 47-16-58 N Long: 99-17-28 W
Pop: 16 (1990); 27 (1980) Pop Density: 0.5
Land: 34.3 sq. mi.; Water: 1.6 sq. mi.

Corinne
Township
Lat: 47-16-35 N Long: 98-31-12 W
Pop: 38 (1990); 67 (1980) Pop Density: 1.1
Land: 35.5 sq. mi.; Water: 0.1 sq. mi.

Corwin
Township
Lat: 46-45-31 N Long: 98-37-19 W
Pop: 95 (1990); 182 (1980) Pop Density: 2.6
Land: 36.0 sq. mi.; Water: 0.0 sq. mi.

Courtenay
City
ZIP: 58426 Lat: 47-13-28 N Long: 98-34-07 W
Pop: 70 (1990); 110 (1980) Pop Density: 175.0
Land: 0.4 sq. mi.; Water: 0.0 sq. mi. Elev: 1525 ft.
Not coextensive with township.

*Courtenay
Township
ZIP: 58426 Lat: 47-11-57 N Long: 98-31-35 W
Pop: 58 (1990); 63 (1980) Pop Density: 1.6
Land: 35.2 sq. mi.; Water: 0.3 sq. mi.

Cusator
Township
Lat: 46-45-30 N Long: 99-00-26 W
Pop: 58 (1990); 55 (1980) Pop Density: 1.7
Land: 34.9 sq. mi.; Water: 0.7 sq. mi.

Deer Lake
Township
Lat: 47-01-20 N Long: 99-02-04 W
Pop: 30 (1990); 49 (1980) Pop Density: 0.9
Land: 34.4 sq. mi.; Water: 1.4 sq. mi.

Durham
Township
Lat: 47-12-24 N Long: 98-39-28 W
Pop: 77 (1990); 89 (1980) Pop Density: 2.2
Land: 35.5 sq. mi.; Water: 0.5 sq. mi.

Edmunds
Township
Lat: 47-16-44 N Long: 98-54-40 W
Pop: 74 (1990); 67 (1980) Pop Density: 2.1
Land: 34.8 sq. mi.; Water: 0.6 sq. mi.

Eldridge
Township
Lat: 46-55-59 N Long: 98-52-44 W
Pop: 162 (1990); 204 (1980) Pop Density: 4.7
Land: 34.7 sq. mi.; Water: 1.2 sq. mi.

Flint
Township
Lat: 46-56-25 N Long: 99-15-18 W
Pop: 53 (1990); 76 (1980) Pop Density: 1.6
Land: 32.9 sq. mi.; Water: 2.6 sq. mi.

Fried
Township
Lat: 47-01-21 N Long: 98-39-34 W
Pop: 177 (1990); 152 (1980) Pop Density: 5.0
Land: 35.4 sq. mi.; Water: 0.7 sq. mi. Elev: 1521 ft.

Gerber
Township
Lat: 47-11-28 N Long: 99-25-17 W
Pop: 19 (1990); 28 (1980) Pop Density: 0.6
Land: 33.6 sq. mi.; Water: 2.1 sq. mi.

NORTH DAKOTA, Stutsman County

Germania
Township
Lat: 46-40-14 N Long: 99-15-38 W
Pop: 45 (1990); 53 (1980) Pop Density: 1.3
Land: 35.6 sq. mi.; Water: 0.3 sq. mi.

Glacier
Township
Lat: 47-16-47 N Long: 99-09-43 W
Pop: 46 (1990); 44 (1980) Pop Density: 1.3
Land: 34.7 sq. mi.; Water: 0.9 sq. mi.

Gray
Township
Lat: 47-06-05 N Long: 98-31-59 W
Pop: 55 (1990); 50 (1980) Pop Density: 1.6
Land: 33.8 sq. mi.; Water: 0.9 sq. mi.

Griffin
Township
Lat: 46-40-46 N Long: 99-08-22 W
Pop: 68 (1990); 80 (1980) Pop Density: 1.9
Land: 35.9 sq. mi.; Water: 0.1 sq. mi.

Hidden
Township
Lat: 47-01-20 N Long: 98-54-00 W
Pop: 58 (1990); 75 (1980) Pop Density: 1.6
Land: 35.3 sq. mi.; Water: 0.7 sq. mi.

Homer
Township
Lat: 46-50-27 N Long: 98-37-04 W
Pop: 312 (1990); 309 (1980) Pop Density: 8.9
Land: 35.1 sq. mi.; Water: 0.0 sq. mi.

Iosco
Township
Lat: 47-01-16 N Long: 99-17-22 W
Pop: 15 (1990); 27 (1980) Pop Density: 0.4
Land: 33.6 sq. mi.; Water: 2.3 sq. mi.

Jamestown
City
ZIP: 58401 Lat: 46-54-36 N Long: 98-41-53 W
Pop: 15,571 (1990); 16,280 (1980) Pop Density: 1402.8
Land: 11.1 sq. mi.; Water: 0.1 sq. mi. Elev: 1413 ft.
In southeast-central ND on the James River, 95 mi. west of Fargo. Incorporated 1883.
Name origin: Named by Virginian construction engineer, T.L. Rosser, for Jamestown, VA.

Jim River Valley
Township
Lat: 47-06-49 N Long: 98-47-18 W
Pop: 61 (1990); 75 (1980) Pop Density: 1.8
Land: 34.2 sq. mi.; Water: 1.7 sq. mi.

Kensal
City
ZIP: 58455 Lat: 47-18-01 N Long: 98-43-57 W
Pop: 191 (1990); 210 (1980) Pop Density: 318.3
Land: 0.6 sq. mi.; Water: 0.0 sq. mi. Elev: 1540 ft.
Not coextensive with township.

*Kensal
Township
ZIP: 58455 Lat: 47-17-04 N Long: 98-47-02 W
Pop: 48 (1990); 63 (1980) Pop Density: 1.5
Land: 32.2 sq. mi.; Water: 2.7 sq. mi.

Lenton
Township
Lat: 46-45-43 N Long: 98-53-01 W
Pop: 72 (1990); 79 (1980) Pop Density: 2.0
Land: 36.2 sq. mi.; Water: 0.0 sq. mi.

Lippert
Township
Lat: 46-50-59 N Long: 98-53-11 W
Pop: 110 (1990); 112 (1980) Pop Density: 3.1
Land: 35.8 sq. mi.; Water: 0.4 sq. mi.

Lowery
Township
Lat: 47-16-44 N Long: 99-25-06 W
Pop: 48 (1990); 46 (1980) Pop Density: 1.4
Land: 34.3 sq. mi.; Water: 1.1 sq. mi.

Lyon
Township
Lat: 47-11-44 N Long: 98-46-43 W
Pop: 25 (1990); 45 (1980) Pop Density: 0.8
Land: 33.0 sq. mi.; Water: 2.8 sq. mi.

Manns
Township
Lat: 46-40-54 N Long: 98-30-00 W
Pop: 74 (1990); 98 (1980) Pop Density: 2.0
Land: 36.1 sq. mi.; Water: 0.0 sq. mi.

Marston Moor
Township
Lat: 47-07-01 N Long: 99-24-26 W
Pop: 39 (1990); 55 (1980) Pop Density: 1.1
Land: 34.5 sq. mi.; Water: 1.4 sq. mi.

Medina
City
ZIP: 58467 Lat: 46-53-42 N Long: 99-17-59 W
Pop: 387 (1990); 521 (1980) Pop Density: 387.0
Land: 1.0 sq. mi.; Water: 0.0 sq. mi. Elev: 1810 ft.
Founded 1873.
Name origin: Originally called Midway.

Midway
Township
Lat: 46-55-56 N Long: 98-46-38 W
Pop: 599 (1990); 806 (1980) Pop Density: 22.6
Land: 26.5 sq. mi.; Water: 2.2 sq. mi.

Montpelier
City
ZIP: 58472 Lat: 46-41-55 N Long: 98-35-13 W
Pop: 82 (1990); 96 (1980) Pop Density: 273.3
Land: 0.3 sq. mi.; Water: 0.0 sq. mi. Elev: 1362 ft.
Not coextensive with township.

*Montpelier
Township
ZIP: 58472 Lat: 46-40-20 N Long: 98-37-58 W
Pop: 76 (1990); 85 (1980) Pop Density: 2.1
Land: 35.7 sq. mi.; Water: 0.0 sq. mi.

Moon Lake
Township
Lat: 46-50-55 N Long: 98-59-53 W
Pop: 78 (1990); 93 (1980) Pop Density: 2.3
Land: 34.3 sq. mi.; Water: 0.7 sq. mi.

Newbury
Township
Lat: 46-45-45 N Long: 99-23-08 W
Pop: 56 (1990); 69 (1980) Pop Density: 1.6
Land: 34.6 sq. mi.; Water: 1.5 sq. mi.

Nogosek
Township
Lat: 47-17-19 N Long: 98-38-49 W
Pop: 43 (1990); 49 (1980) Pop Density: 1.2
Land: 35.0 sq. mi.; Water: 0.5 sq. mi.

Northwest Stutsman
Pop. Place
Lat: 47-12-00 N Long: 99-09-50 W
Pop: 24 (1990); 22 (1980) Pop Density: 0.7
Land: 34.4 sq. mi.; Water: 1.4 sq. mi.

Paris
Township
Lat: 47-06-24 N Long: 99-10-01 W
Pop: 42 (1990); 76 (1980) Pop Density: 1.3
Land: 32.8 sq. mi.; Water: 3.2 sq. mi.

Peterson
Township
Lat: 46-55-59 N Long: 99-22-45 W
Pop: 56 (1990); 63 (1980) Pop Density: 1.6
Land: 34.5 sq. mi.; Water: 1.7 sq. mi.

NORTH DAKOTA, Stutsman County — American Places Dictionary

Pingree — City
ZIP: 58476 Lat: 47-09-47 N Long: 98-54-32 W
Pop: 61 (1990); 88 (1980) Pop Density: 305.0
Land: 0.2 sq. mi.; Water: 0.0 sq. mi. Elev: 1551 ft.
Not coextensive with township.

*Pingree — Township
ZIP: 58476 Lat: 47-11-40 N Long: 98-55-09 W
Pop: 42 (1990); 86 (1980) Pop Density: 1.2
Land: 35.0 sq. mi.; Water: 0.7 sq. mi.

Pipestem Valley — Township
Lat: 47-11-42 N Long: 99-02-51 W
Pop: 50 (1990); 75 (1980) Pop Density: 1.4
Land: 35.6 sq. mi.; Water: 0.3 sq. mi.

Plainview — Township
Lat: 47-07-01 N Long: 98-54-02 W
Pop: 63 (1990); 75 (1980) Pop Density: 1.8
Land: 35.9 sq. mi.; Water: 0.0 sq. mi.

Rose — Township
Lat: 47-01-19 N Long: 98-31-42 W
Pop: 76 (1990); 92 (1980) Pop Density: 2.2
Land: 35.1 sq. mi.; Water: 0.9 sq. mi.

Round Top — Township
Lat: 47-07-05 N Long: 99-02-28 W
Pop: 32 (1990); 30 (1980) Pop Density: 1.0
Land: 33.6 sq. mi.; Water: 2.2 sq. mi.

St. Paul — Township
Lat: 46-50-37 N Long: 99-22-38 W
Pop: 71 (1990); 83 (1980) Pop Density: 2.2
Land: 32.2 sq. mi.; Water: 3.8 sq. mi.

Severn — Township
Lat: 46-40-26 N Long: 98-45-16 W
Pop: 55 (1990); 82 (1980) Pop Density: 1.5
Land: 36.0 sq. mi.; Water: 0.1 sq. mi.

Sharlow — Township
Lat: 46-40-25 N Long: 98-52-59 W
Pop: 70 (1990); 61 (1980) Pop Density: 1.9
Land: 36.2 sq. mi.; Water: 0.0 sq. mi.

Sinclair — Township
Lat: 46-45-48 N Long: 99-07-37 W
Pop: 39 (1990); 49 (1980) Pop Density: 1.1
Land: 34.2 sq. mi.; Water: 1.7 sq. mi.

Spiritwood — Township
ZIP: 58481 Lat: 46-56-07 N Long: 98-29-55 W
Pop: 99 (1990); 124 (1980) Pop Density: 2.8
Land: 35.9 sq. mi.; Water: 0.3 sq. mi.

Spiritwood Lake — City
ZIP: 58401 Lat: 47-04-28 N Long: 98-35-13 W
Pop: 61 (1990); 50 (1980) Pop Density: 55.5
Land: 1.1 sq. mi.; Water: 0.7 sq. mi.

Stirton — Township
Lat: 46-50-49 N Long: 99-08-02 W
Pop: 82 (1990); 72 (1980) Pop Density: 2.5
Land: 32.9 sq. mi.; Water: 3.0 sq. mi.

Streeter — City
ZIP: 58483 Lat: 46-39-24 N Long: 99-21-25 W
Pop: 161 (1990); 264 (1980) Pop Density: 536.7
Land: 0.3 sq. mi.; Water: 0.0 sq. mi. Elev: 1030 ft.
Not coextensive with township.

*Streeter — Township
ZIP: 58483 Lat: 46-40-50 N Long: 99-22-30 W
Pop: 62 (1990); 87 (1980) Pop Density: 1.8
Land: 34.7 sq. mi.; Water: 1.0 sq. mi.

Strong — Township
Lat: 47-06-29 N Long: 99-17-20 W
Pop: 60 (1990); 68 (1980) Pop Density: 1.8
Land: 33.8 sq. mi.; Water: 1.9 sq. mi.

Sydney — Township
Lat: 46-45-15 N Long: 98-45-00 W
Pop: 92 (1990); 112 (1980) Pop Density: 2.5
Land: 36.2 sq. mi.; Water: 0.1 sq. mi.

Valley Spring — Township
Lat: 47-01-14 N Long: 99-09-41 W
Pop: 33 (1990); 54 (1980) Pop Density: 1.0
Land: 33.8 sq. mi.; Water: 2.2 sq. mi.

Wadsworth — Township
Lat: 47-11-32 N Long: 99-17-07 W
Pop: 35 (1990); 43 (1980) Pop Density: 1.1
Land: 32.6 sq. mi.; Water: 3.0 sq. mi.

Walters — Township
Lat: 47-16-57 N Long: 99-02-35 W
Pop: 69 (1990); 66 (1980) Pop Density: 1.9
Land: 35.4 sq. mi.; Water: 0.1 sq. mi.

Weld — Township
Lat: 46-55-32 N Long: 99-07-12 W
Pop: 39 (1990); 65 (1980) Pop Density: 1.2
Land: 33.9 sq. mi.; Water: 2.4 sq. mi.

Windsor — Township
Lat: 46-56-07 N Long: 99-00-06 W
Pop: 58 (1990); 80 (1980) Pop Density: 1.7
Land: 34.2 sq. mi.; Water: 0.7 sq. mi.

Winfield — Township
Lat: 46-50-35 N Long: 98-29-55 W
Pop: 81 (1990); 74 (1980) Pop Density: 2.3
Land: 36.0 sq. mi.; Water: 0.1 sq. mi.

Woodbury — Township
Lat: 46-50-50 N Long: 98-45-47 W
Pop: 244 (1990); 264 (1980) Pop Density: 7.0
Land: 34.9 sq. mi.; Water: 0.2 sq. mi.

Woodworth — City
ZIP: 58496 Lat: 47-08-32 N Long: 99-18-13 W
Pop: 102 (1990); 137 (1980) Pop Density: 510.0
Land: 0.2 sq. mi.; Water: 0.0 sq. mi. Elev: 2052 ft.

Ypsilanti — Township
ZIP: 58497 Lat: 46-45-32 N Long: 98-30-11 W
Pop: 154 (1990); 190 (1980) Pop Density: 4.3
Land: 36.1 sq. mi.; Water: 0.0 sq. mi.

Towner County
County Seat: Cando (ZIP: 58324)

Pop: 3,627 (1990); 4,052 (1980)   **Pop Density:** 3.5
Land: 1025.4 sq. mi.; **Water:** 16.2 sq. mi.   **Area Code:** 701
On the central northern border of ND; organized Mar 8, 1883 (prior to statehood) from Rolette County.
Name origin: For Oscar M. Towner (1842–97), Dakota Territory legislator.

Armourdale — Township
ZIP: 58365   Lat: 48-50-46 N   Long: 99-19-29 W
Pop: 66 (1990); 77 (1980)   Pop Density: 1.8
Land: 35.8 sq. mi.; Water: 0.3 sq. mi.

Atkins — Township
Lat: 48-25-17 N   Long: 99-17-29 W
Pop: 52 (1990); 50 (1980)   Pop Density: 1.5
Land: 35.1 sq. mi.; Water: 1.0 sq. mi.

Bethel — Township
Lat: 48-30-29 N   Long: 99-02-27 W
Pop: 24 (1990); 36 (1980)   Pop Density: 0.7
Land: 35.6 sq. mi.; Water: 0.3 sq. mi.

Bisbee — City
ZIP: 58317   Lat: 48-37-35 N   Long: 99-22-41 W
Pop: 227 (1990); 257 (1980)   Pop Density: 756.7
Land: 0.3 sq. mi.; Water: 0.0 sq. mi.   Elev: 1600 ft.
Incorporated 1950.
Name origin: For Civil War veteran Col. Bisbee, who lived nearby.

Cando — City
ZIP: 58324   Lat: 48-29-15 N   Long: 99-12-09 W
Pop: 1,564 (1990); 1,496 (1980)   Pop Density: 2606.7
Land: 0.6 sq. mi.; Water: 0.0 sq. mi.   Elev: 1486 ft.
Not coextensive with township. Established 1884.
Name origin: For the words "can do" by county commissioners, who overruled a challenge to their authority.

*Cando — Township
ZIP: 58324   Lat: 48-29-37 N   Long: 99-09-17 W
Pop: 119 (1990); 129 (1980)   Pop Density: 3.4
Land: 35.1 sq. mi.; Water: 0.5 sq. mi.

Coolin — Township
Lat: 48-24-33 N   Long: 99-02-35 W
Pop: 45 (1990); 59 (1980)   Pop Density: 1.3
Land: 35.9 sq. mi.; Water: 0.2 sq. mi.

Crocus — Township
ZIP: 58365   Lat: 48-40-37 N   Long: 99-09-34 W
Pop: 69 (1990); 79 (1980)   Pop Density: 2.0
Land: 35.0 sq. mi.; Water: 0.9 sq. mi.

Dash — Township
Lat: 48-56-54 N   Long: 99-03-52 W
Pop: 56 (1990); 82 (1980)   Pop Density: 1.3
Land: 44.3 sq. mi.; Water: 0.8 sq. mi.

Egeland — City
ZIP: 58331   Lat: 48-37-40 N   Long: 99-05-51 W
Pop: 103 (1990); 112 (1980)   Pop Density: 257.5
Land: 0.4 sq. mi.; Water: 0.0 sq. mi.   Elev: 1519 ft.

Gerrard — Township
Lat: 48-35-30 N   Long: 99-18-02 W
Pop: 39 (1990); 53 (1980)   Pop Density: 1.1
Land: 35.5 sq. mi.; Water: 0.4 sq. mi.

Grainfield — Township
Lat: 48-40-47 N   Long: 99-26-16 W
Pop: 57 (1990); 76 (1980)   Pop Density: 1.6
Land: 35.6 sq. mi.; Water: 0.1 sq. mi.

Hansboro — City
ZIP: 58339   Lat: 48-57-08 N   Long: 99-22-50 W
Pop: 20 (1990); 43 (1980)   Pop Density: 100.0
Land: 0.2 sq. mi.; Water: 0.0 sq. mi.   Elev: 1606 ft.

Howell — Township
Lat: 48-45-47 N   Long: 99-19-22 W
Pop: 73 (1990); 82 (1980)   Pop Density: 2.1
Land: 35.6 sq. mi.; Water: 0.3 sq. mi.

Lansing — Township
Lat: 48-50-35 N   Long: 99-03-19 W
Pop: 13 (1990); 34 (1980)   Pop Density: 0.4
Land: 36.1 sq. mi.; Water: 0.1 sq. mi.

Maza — City
ZIP: 58324   Lat: 48-23-41 N   Long: 99-11-58 W
Pop: 12 (1990); 21 (1980)   Pop Density: 1.3
Land: 9.0 sq. mi.; Water: 0.1 sq. mi.
Not coextensive with township.

*Maza — Township
Lat: 48-25-16 N   Long: 99-09-18 W
Pop: 36 (1990); 57 (1980)   Pop Density: 1.3
Land: 26.9 sq. mi.; Water: 0.3 sq. mi.

Monroe — Township
Lat: 48-45-34 N   Long: 99-27-43 W
Pop: 30 (1990); 47 (1980)   Pop Density: 0.8
Land: 36.0 sq. mi.; Water: 0.0 sq. mi.

Mount View — Township
Lat: 48-50-43 N   Long: 99-27-51 W
Pop: 64 (1990); 69 (1980)   Pop Density: 1.8
Land: 35.3 sq. mi.; Water: 0.5 sq. mi.

New City — Township
Lat: 48-35-34 N   Long: 99-25-23 W
Pop: 34 (1990); 34 (1980)   Pop Density: 1.0
Land: 35.7 sq. mi.; Water: 0.0 sq. mi.

Olson — Township
Lat: 48-30-12 N   Long: 99-17-46 W
Pop: 58 (1990); 65 (1980)   Pop Density: 1.7
Land: 35.0 sq. mi.; Water: 1.0 sq. mi.

Paulson — Township
Lat: 48-35-23 N   Long: 99-10-11 W
Pop: 58 (1990); 72 (1980)   Pop Density: 1.7
Land: 34.9 sq. mi.; Water: 1.2 sq. mi.

NORTH DAKOTA, Towner County   American Places Dictionary

Perth — City
ZIP: 58363   Lat: 48-42-52 N   Long: 99-27-25 W
Pop: 22 (1990); 20 (1980)   Pop Density: 220.0
Land: 0.1 sq. mi.; Water: 0.0 sq. mi.   Elev: 1720 ft.

Picton — Township
Lat: 48-56-55 N   Long: 99-27-51 W
Pop: 50 (1990); 53 (1980)   Pop Density: 1.1
Land: 44.1 sq. mi.; Water: 0.2 sq. mi.

Rocklake — City
ZIP: 58365   Lat: 48-47-26 N   Long: 99-14-41 W
Pop: 221 (1990); 287 (1980)   Pop Density: 1105.0
Land: 0.2 sq. mi.; Water: 0.0 sq. mi.   Elev: 1543 ft.

Rock Lake — Township
ZIP: 58365   Lat: 48-51-20 N   Long: 99-11-52 W
Pop: 36 (1990); 50 (1980)   Pop Density: 1.1
Land: 33.4 sq. mi.; Water: 2.2 sq. mi.

Sarles — City
ZIP: 58372   Lat: 48-56-36 N   Long: 99-00-09 W
Pop: 3 (1990); 9 (1980)   Pop Density: 30.0
Land: 0.1 sq. mi.; Water: 0.0 sq. mi.   Elev: 1588 ft.
Part of the town is also in Cavalier County.

Sidney — Township
Lat: 48-56-23 N   Long: 99-19-57 W
Pop: 87 (1990); 97 (1980)   Pop Density: 2.0
Land: 44.0 sq. mi.; Water: 0.4 sq. mi.

Smith — Township
Lat: 48-56-46 N   Long: 99-11-24 W
Pop: 46 (1990); 56 (1980)   Pop Density: 1.1
Land: 43.3 sq. mi.; Water: 0.7 sq. mi.

Sorenson — Township
Lat: 48-40-40 N   Long: 99-17-45 W
Pop: 46 (1990); 59 (1980)   Pop Density: 1.3
Land: 35.1 sq. mi.; Water: 0.7 sq. mi.

Springfield — Township
Lat: 48-24-25 N   Long: 99-25-41 W
Pop: 47 (1990); 63 (1980)   Pop Density: 1.4
Land: 34.6 sq. mi.; Water: 1.4 sq. mi.

Teddy — Township
Lat: 48-46-07 N   Long: 99-04-37 W
Pop: 82 (1990); 92 (1980)   Pop Density: 2.3
Land: 35.9 sq. mi.; Water: 0.2 sq. mi.

Twin Hill — Township
Lat: 48-40-28 N   Long: 99-02-07 W
Pop: 44 (1990); 51 (1980)   Pop Density: 1.3
Land: 34.9 sq. mi.; Water: 0.9 sq. mi.

Victor — Township
Lat: 48-34-40 N   Long: 99-02-11 W
Pop: 23 (1990); 52 (1980)   Pop Density: 0.7
Land: 34.9 sq. mi.; Water: 0.8 sq. mi.

Virginia — Township
Lat: 48-45-37 N   Long: 99-12-03 W
Pop: 51 (1990); 65 (1980)   Pop Density: 1.5
Land: 35.0 sq. mi.; Water: 0.7 sq. mi.

Zion — Township
Lat: 48-30-12 N   Long: 99-25-03 W
Pop: 50 (1990); 68 (1980)   Pop Density: 1.4
Land: 35.9 sq. mi.; Water: 0.1 sq. mi.

Traill County
County Seat: Hillsboro (ZIP: 58045)

Pop: 8,752 (1990); 9,624 (1980)   Pop Density: 10.2
Land: 861.9 sq. mi.; Water: 0.6 sq. mi.   Area Code: 701

On the central eastern border of ND, south of Grand Forks; organized Jan 12, 1875 (prior to statehood) from Grand Forks County.

Name origin: For Walter J. S. Traill (1847–1933) of the Hudson Bay Company; he was a founder of the county.

Belmont — Township
Lat: 47-37-16 N   Long: 96-54-56 W
Pop: 77 (1990); 94 (1980)   Pop Density: 3.1
Land: 25.0 sq. mi.; Water: 0.0 sq. mi.

Bingham — Township
Lat: 47-32-28 N   Long: 96-54-45 W
Pop: 108 (1990); 119 (1980)   Pop Density: 3.6
Land: 30.1 sq. mi.; Water: 0.0 sq. mi.

Blanchard — Township
Lat: 47-21-48 N   Long: 97-16-57 W
Pop: 117 (1990); 140 (1980)   Pop Density: 3.3
Land: 36.0 sq. mi.; Water: 0.0 sq. mi.

Bloomfield — Township
Lat: 47-21-58 N   Long: 97-09-17 W
Pop: 153 (1990); 153 (1980)   Pop Density: 4.2
Land: 36.1 sq. mi.; Water: 0.0 sq. mi.

Bohnsack — Township
Lat: 47-17-24 N   Long: 97-07-51 W
Pop: 64 (1990); 90 (1980)   Pop Density: 1.8
Land: 35.1 sq. mi.; Water: 0.0 sq. mi.

Buxton — City
ZIP: 58218   Lat: 47-36-07 N   Long: 97-05-57 W
Pop: 343 (1990); 336 (1980)   Pop Density: 1715.0
Land: 0.2 sq. mi.; Water: 0.0 sq. mi.   Elev: 935 ft.
Not coextensive with township.

*Buxton — Township
Lat: 47-38-00 N   Long: 97-08-40 W
Pop: 81 (1990); 140 (1980)   Pop Density: 2.3
Land: 35.2 sq. mi.; Water: 0.0 sq. mi.

Caledonia — Township
Lat: 47-27-30 N   Long: 96-54-26 W
Pop: 154 (1990); 220 (1980)   Pop Density: 5.2
Land: 29.6 sq. mi.; Water: 0.0 sq. mi.

Clifford
City
ZIP: 58016 Lat: 47-20-53 N Long: 97-24-33 W
Pop: 51 (1990); 51 (1980) Pop Density: 510.0
Land: 0.1 sq. mi.; Water: 0.0 sq. mi. Elev: 1050 ft.

Eldorado
Township
Lat: 47-27-41 N Long: 97-02-16 W
Pop: 175 (1990); 229 (1980) Pop Density: 4.9
Land: 35.6 sq. mi.; Water: 0.5 sq. mi.

Elm River
Township
Lat: 47-17-02 N Long: 96-53-24 W
Pop: 47 (1990); 73 (1980) Pop Density: 1.6
Land: 29.0 sq. mi.; Water: 0.0 sq. mi.

Ervin
Township
Lat: 47-33-01 N Long: 97-01-11 W
Pop: 178 (1990); 217 (1980) Pop Density: 4.9
Land: 36.3 sq. mi.; Water: 0.0 sq. mi.

Galesburg
City
ZIP: 58035 Lat: 47-16-14 N Long: 97-24-30 W
Pop: 161 (1990); 165 (1980) Pop Density: 805.0
Land: 0.2 sq. mi.; Water: 0.0 sq. mi. Elev: 1075 ft.
Not coextensive with township.
Name origin: For original landowner, J.H. Gale, who settled in the area in 1883.

*Galesburg
Township
ZIP: 58035 Lat: 47-17-17 N Long: 97-23-32 W
Pop: 127 (1990); 143 (1980) Pop Density: 3.6
Land: 34.9 sq. mi.; Water: 0.1 sq. mi.

Garfield
Township
Lat: 47-38-08 N Long: 97-24-10 W
Pop: 170 (1990); 185 (1980) Pop Density: 4.9
Land: 35.0 sq. mi.; Water: 0.0 sq. mi.

Grandin
City
ZIP: 58038 Lat: 47-14-22 N Long: 97-00-22 W
Pop: 0 (1990)
Land: 0.01 sq. mi.; Water: 0.0 sq. mi. Elev: 892 ft.
Part of the town is also in Cass County.

Greenfield
Township
Lat: 47-16-29 N Long: 97-15-00 W
Pop: 56 (1990); 74 (1980) Pop Density: 1.6
Land: 35.4 sq. mi.; Water: 0.0 sq. mi.

Hatton
City
ZIP: 58240 Lat: 47-38-09 N Long: 97-27-27 W
Pop: 800 (1990); 787 (1980) Pop Density: 1333.3
Land: 0.6 sq. mi.; Water: 0.0 sq. mi. Elev: 1081 ft.
Name origin: For assistant postmaster Frank Hatton.

Herberg
Township
Lat: 47-22-03 N Long: 96-54-36 W
Pop: 124 (1990); 136 (1980) Pop Density: 3.7
Land: 33.8 sq. mi.; Water: 0.0 sq. mi.

Hillsboro
City
ZIP: 58045 Lat: 47-24-10 N Long: 97-03-40 W
Pop: 1,488 (1990); 1,600 (1980) Pop Density: 1488.0
Land: 1.0 sq. mi.; Water: 0.0 sq. mi. Elev: 908 ft.
Not coextensive with township. Founded 1880.
Name origin: For railroad magnate James J. Hill.

*Hillsboro
Township
ZIP: 58045 Lat: 47-22-01 N Long: 97-01-00 W
Pop: 106 (1990); 151 (1980) Pop Density: 3.0
Land: 34.8 sq. mi.; Water: 0.0 sq. mi.

Kelso
Township
Lat: 47-16-55 N Long: 97-00-45 W
Pop: 96 (1990); 92 (1980) Pop Density: 2.7
Land: 35.0 sq. mi.; Water: 0.0 sq. mi.

Lindaas
Township
Lat: 47-32-01 N Long: 97-16-29 W
Pop: 127 (1990); 153 (1980) Pop Density: 3.6
Land: 34.8 sq. mi.; Water: 0.0 sq. mi.

Mayville
City
ZIP: 58257 Lat: 47-30-00 N Long: 97-19-41 W
Pop: 2,092 (1990); 2,255 (1980) Pop Density: 1307.5
Land: 1.6 sq. mi.; Water: 0.0 sq. mi. Elev: 976 ft.
Name origin: For May, the second daughter of early settler Alvin Arnold.

*Mayville
Township
ZIP: 58257 Lat: 47-27-17 N Long: 97-16-33 W
Pop: 159 (1990); 168 (1980) Pop Density: 4.5
Land: 35.3 sq. mi.; Water: 0.0 sq. mi.

Morgan
Township
Lat: 47-38-07 N Long: 97-16-18 W
Pop: 111 (1990); 126 (1980) Pop Density: 3.1
Land: 36.0 sq. mi.; Water: 0.0 sq. mi.

Norman
Township
Lat: 47-22-01 N Long: 97-24-55 W
Pop: 77 (1990); 102 (1980) Pop Density: 2.2
Land: 35.8 sq. mi.; Water: 0.0 sq. mi.

Norway
Township
Lat: 47-27-25 N Long: 97-08-45 W
Pop: 172 (1990); 177 (1980) Pop Density: 4.8
Land: 35.7 sq. mi.; Water: 0.0 sq. mi.

Portland
City
ZIP: 58274 Lat: 47-29-56 N Long: 97-22-07 W
Pop: 602 (1990); 627 (1980) Pop Density: 668.9
Land: 0.9 sq. mi.; Water: 0.0 sq. mi. Elev: 984 ft.

Reynolds
City
Lat: 47-40-06 N Long: 97-06-28 W
Pop: 192 (1990); 194 (1980) Pop Density: 480.0
Land: 0.4 sq. mi.; Water: 0.0 sq. mi. Elev: 911 ft.
Part of the town is also in Grand Forks County.

Roseville
Township
Lat: 47-26-51 N Long: 97-24-25 W
Pop: 115 (1990); 112 (1980) Pop Density: 3.2
Land: 35.6 sq. mi.; Water: 0.0 sq. mi.

Stavanger
Township
Lat: 47-38-08 N Long: 97-02-06 W
Pop: 115 (1990); 135 (1980) Pop Density: 3.2
Land: 36.1 sq. mi.; Water: 0.0 sq. mi.

Viking
Township
Lat: 47-32-33 N Long: 97-24-16 W
Pop: 170 (1990); 213 (1980) Pop Density: 4.9
Land: 34.8 sq. mi.; Water: 0.0 sq. mi.

Wold
Township
Lat: 47-32-19 N Long: 97-08-42 W
Pop: 144 (1990); 167 (1980) Pop Density: 4.0
Land: 35.8 sq. mi.; Water: 0.0 sq. mi.

Walsh County
County Seat: Grafton (ZIP: 58237)

Pop: 13,840 (1990); 15,371 (1980)　　**Pop Density:** 10.8
Land: 1282.0 sq. mi.; **Water:** 12.2 sq. mi.　　**Area Code:** 701
On the northeastern border of ND, north of Grand Forks; organized Feb 18, 1881 (prior to statehood) from Grand Forks and Pembina counties.
Name origin: For George H. Walsh (1868–1913), newspaper publisher and member of the ND legislative council (1881, 1883, 1885, 1889).

Acton　　Township
Lat: 48-24-18 N　Long: 97-12-03 W
Pop: 154 (1990); 161 (1980)　　**Pop Density:** 4.1
Land: 37.7 sq. mi.; **Water:** 0.4 sq. mi.

Adams　　City
ZIP: 58210　　Lat: 48-25-10 N　Long: 98-04-25 W
Pop: 248 (1990); 303 (1980)　　**Pop Density:** 248.0
Land: 1.0 sq. mi.; **Water:** 0.0 sq. mi.　　**Elev:** 1565 ft.
Incorporated 1967.
Name origin: For Adams County, WI.

*Adams　　Township
ZIP: 58210　　Lat: 48-24-37 N　Long: 98-07-14 W
Pop: 64 (1990); 85 (1980)　　**Pop Density:** 1.9
Land: 34.3 sq. mi.; **Water:** 0.7 sq. mi.

Ardoch　　City
ZIP: 58213　　Lat: 48-12-21 N　Long: 97-20-27 W
Pop: 49 (1990); 78 (1980)　　**Pop Density:** 163.3
Land: 0.3 sq. mi.; **Water:** 0.0 sq. mi.　　**Elev:** 825 ft.
Not coextensive with township. Incorporated 1967.

*Ardoch　　Township
Lat: 48-14-27 N　Long: 97-18-37 W
Pop: 115 (1990); 124 (1980)　　**Pop Density:** 3.4
Land: 34.1 sq. mi.; **Water:** 1.4 sq. mi.

Cleveland　　Township
Lat: 48-14-00 N　Long: 97-57-52 W
Pop: 123 (1990); 123 (1980)　　**Pop Density:** 3.4
Land: 35.7 sq. mi.; **Water:** 0.2 sq. mi.

Conway　　City
ZIP: 58233　　Lat: 48-14-02 N　Long: 97-40-27 W
Pop: 24 (1990); 33 (1980)　　**Pop Density:** 120.0
Land: 0.2 sq. mi.; **Water:** 0.0 sq. mi.　　**Elev:** 982 ft.

Dewey　　Township
Lat: 48-25-21 N　Long: 98-14-52 W
Pop: 48 (1990); 79 (1980)　　**Pop Density:** 1.3
Land: 35.6 sq. mi.; **Water:** 0.5 sq. mi.

Dundee　　Township
Lat: 48-30-29 N　Long: 97-44-07 W
Pop: 123 (1990); 165 (1980)　　**Pop Density:** 3.4
Land: 36.0 sq. mi.; **Water:** 0.0 sq. mi.

Eden　　Township
Lat: 48-13-51 N　Long: 97-43-08 W
Pop: 72 (1990); 64 (1980)　　**Pop Density:** 2.0
Land: 35.8 sq. mi.; **Water:** 0.0 sq. mi.

Edinburg　　City
ZIP: 58227　　Lat: 48-29-44 N　Long: 97-51-43 W
Pop: 284 (1990); 300 (1980)　　**Pop Density:** 946.7
Land: 0.3 sq. mi.; **Water:** 0.0 sq. mi.　　**Elev:** 1187 ft.

Fairdale　　City
ZIP: 58229　　Lat: 48-29-22 N　Long: 98-13-53 W
Pop: 76 (1990); 97 (1980)　　**Pop Density:** 253.3
Land: 0.3 sq. mi.; **Water:** 0.0 sq. mi.　　**Elev:** 1623 ft.

Farmington　　Township
Lat: 48-30-24 N　Long: 97-28-48 W
Pop: 204 (1990); 246 (1980)　　**Pop Density:** 5.6
Land: 36.2 sq. mi.; **Water:** 0.0 sq. mi.

Fertile　　Township
Lat: 48-24-45 N　Long: 97-35-57 W
Pop: 285 (1990); 277 (1980)　　**Pop Density:** 7.9
Land: 36.1 sq. mi.; **Water:** 0.0 sq. mi.

Fordville　　City
ZIP: 58231　　Lat: 48-13-00 N　Long: 97-47-40 W
Pop: 299 (1990); 326 (1980)　　**Pop Density:** 299.0
Land: 1.0 sq. mi.; **Water:** 0.0 sq. mi.　　**Elev:** 1144 ft.
Name origin: From a combination of Medford and Belleville. Originally called Medford. Name changed in 1910 when the two post offices merged.

Forest River　　City
ZIP: 58233　　Lat: 48-13-01 N　Long: 97-28-12 W
Pop: 148 (1990); 152 (1980)　　**Pop Density:** 296.0
Land: 0.5 sq. mi.; **Water:** 0.0 sq. mi.　　**Elev:** 865 ft.

*Forest River　　Township
ZIP: 58233　　Lat: 48-14-01 N　Long: 97-26-57 W
Pop: 136 (1990); 111 (1980)　　**Pop Density:** 3.8
Land: 35.6 sq. mi.; **Water:** 0.0 sq. mi.

Glenwood　　Township
Lat: 48-30-03 N　Long: 97-35-33 W
Pop: 245 (1990); 300 (1980)　　**Pop Density:** 6.9
Land: 35.7 sq. mi.; **Water:** 0.0 sq. mi.

Golden　　Township
Lat: 48-24-48 N　Long: 97-51-55 W
Pop: 131 (1990); 113 (1980)　　**Pop Density:** 3.7
Land: 35.8 sq. mi.; **Water:** 0.2 sq. mi.

Grafton　　City
ZIP: 58237　　Lat: 48-24-54 N　Long: 97-24-11 W
Pop: 4,840 (1990); 5,293 (1980)　　**Pop Density:** 1613.3
Land: 3.0 sq. mi.; **Water:** 0.0 sq. mi.　　**Elev:** 826 ft.
Name origin: Named by Thomas Cooper for his wife's former home in Grafton County, NH.

*Grafton　　Township
ZIP: 58237　　Lat: 48-24-19 N　Long: 97-28-51 W
Pop: 369 (1990); 327 (1980)　　**Pop Density:** 10.6
Land: 34.7 sq. mi.; **Water:** 0.0 sq. mi.

Harriston　　Township
Lat: 48-19-55 N　Long: 97-18-37 W
Pop: 172 (1990); 167 (1980)　　**Pop Density:** 5.0
Land: 34.3 sq. mi.; **Water:** 0.0 sq. mi.

Hoople
City
ZIP: 58243   **Lat:** 48-32-07 N **Long:** 97-38-14 W
Pop: 310 (1990); 350 (1980)   **Pop Density:** 775.0
Land: 0.4 sq. mi.; **Water:** 0.0 sq. mi.   **Elev:** 890 ft.

Kensington
Township
Lat: 48-24-46 N **Long:** 97-43-57 W
Pop: 291 (1990); 258 (1980)   **Pop Density:** 8.6
Land: 33.9 sq. mi.; **Water:** 0.1 sq. mi.

Kinloss
Township
Lat: 48-30-01 N **Long:** 98-15-04 W
Pop: 75 (1990); 85 (1980)   **Pop Density:** 2.1
Land: 35.4 sq. mi.; **Water:** 0.4 sq. mi.

Lampton
Township
Lat: 48-30-04 N **Long:** 97-52-06 W
Pop: 169 (1990); 209 (1980)   **Pop Density:** 4.7
Land: 35.6 sq. mi.; **Water:** 0.0 sq. mi.

Lankin
City
ZIP: 58250   **Lat:** 48-18-53 N **Long:** 97-55-14 W
Pop: 152 (1990); 175 (1980)   **Pop Density:** 506.7
Land: 0.3 sq. mi.; **Water:** 0.0 sq. mi.   **Elev:** 1349 ft.

Latona
Township
Lat: 48-19-48 N **Long:** 98-05-55 W
Pop: 82 (1990); 114 (1980)   **Pop Density:** 2.3
Land: 35.0 sq. mi.; **Water:** 1.1 sq. mi.

Martin
Township
Lat: 48-30-22 N **Long:** 97-20-21 W
Pop: 114 (1990); 135 (1980)   **Pop Density:** 3.3
Land: 34.1 sq. mi.; **Water:** 0.8 sq. mi.

Medford
Township
Lat: 48-14-10 N **Long:** 97-50-52 W
Pop: 78 (1990); 102 (1980)   **Pop Density:** 2.2
Land: 34.9 sq. mi.; **Water:** 0.0 sq. mi.

Minto
City
ZIP: 58261   **Lat:** 48-17-32 N **Long:** 97-22-19 W
Pop: 560 (1990); 592 (1980)   **Pop Density:** 400.0
Land: 1.4 sq. mi.; **Water:** 0.0 sq. mi.   **Elev:** 820 ft.
Name origin: Named by settlers for their former home in Canada.

Norton
Township
Lat: 48-19-24 N **Long:** 97-58-33 W
Pop: 115 (1990); 130 (1980)   **Pop Density:** 3.2
Land: 35.7 sq. mi.; **Water:** 0.1 sq. mi.

Oakwood
Township
Lat: 48-24-19 N **Long:** 97-19-54 W
Pop: 348 (1990); 477 (1980)   **Pop Density:** 10.4
Land: 33.5 sq. mi.; **Water:** 0.0 sq. mi.

Ops
Township
ZIP: 58233   **Lat:** 48-14-03 N **Long:** 97-34-04 W
Pop: 74 (1990); 86 (1980)   **Pop Density:** 2.1
Land: 36.0 sq. mi.; **Water:** 0.0 sq. mi.

Park River
City
ZIP: 58270   **Lat:** 48-23-36 N **Long:** 97-44-41 W
Pop: 1,725 (1990); 1,844 (1980)   **Pop Density:** 821.4
Land: 2.1 sq. mi.; **Water:** 0.0 sq. mi.   **Elev:** 1006 ft.
Name origin: For the Park River, which flows through the town.

Perth
Township
Lat: 48-13-59 N **Long:** 98-06-02 W
Pop: 84 (1990); 116 (1980)   **Pop Density:** 2.4
Land: 34.7 sq. mi.; **Water:** 1.2 sq. mi.

Pisek
City
ZIP: 58273   **Lat:** 48-18-39 N **Long:** 97-42-37 W
Pop: 130 (1990); 156 (1980)   **Pop Density:** 1300.0
Land: 0.1 sq. mi.; **Water:** 0.0 sq. mi.   **Elev:** 985 ft.

Prairie Center
Township
Lat: 48-19-18 N **Long:** 97-34-04 W
Pop: 131 (1990); 196 (1980)   **Pop Density:** 3.6
Land: 36.1 sq. mi.; **Water:** 0.0 sq. mi.

Pulaski
Township
Lat: 48-19-18 N **Long:** 97-11-59 W
Pop: 119 (1990); 150 (1980)   **Pop Density:** 3.5
Land: 34.2 sq. mi.; **Water:** 0.3 sq. mi.

Rushford
Township
Lat: 48-19-17 N **Long:** 97-42-48 W
Pop: 124 (1990); 172 (1980)   **Pop Density:** 3.4
Land: 36.0 sq. mi.; **Water:** 0.0 sq. mi.

St. Andrews
Township
Lat: 48-29-32 N **Long:** 97-12-05 W
Pop: 68 (1990); 79 (1980)   **Pop Density:** 1.9
Land: 36.3 sq. mi.; **Water:** 0.5 sq. mi.

Sauter
Township
Lat: 48-14-16 N **Long:** 98-13-34 W
Pop: 61 (1990); 82 (1980)   **Pop Density:** 1.7
Land: 34.9 sq. mi.; **Water:** 1.2 sq. mi.

Shepherd
Township
Lat: 48-19-39 N **Long:** 98-13-33 W
Pop: 55 (1990); 75 (1980)   **Pop Density:** 1.6
Land: 34.6 sq. mi.; **Water:** 1.5 sq. mi.

Silvesta
Township
Lat: 48-29-54 N **Long:** 98-07-04 W
Pop: 75 (1990); 108 (1980)   **Pop Density:** 2.1
Land: 35.2 sq. mi.; **Water:** 0.7 sq. mi.

Tiber
Township
Lat: 48-29-43 N **Long:** 97-59-23 W
Pop: 124 (1990); 124 (1980)   **Pop Density:** 3.5
Land: 35.8 sq. mi.; **Water:** 0.1 sq. mi.

Vernon
Township
Lat: 48-19-30 N **Long:** 97-49-59 W
Pop: 124 (1990); 139 (1980)   **Pop Density:** 3.4
Land: 36.1 sq. mi.; **Water:** 0.0 sq. mi.

Vesta
Township
Lat: 48-24-55 N **Long:** 97-59-31 W
Pop: 44 (1990); 60 (1980)   **Pop Density:** 1.2
Land: 35.9 sq. mi.; **Water:** 0.2 sq. mi.

Walsh Centre
Township
Lat: 48-19-30 N **Long:** 97-26-48 W
Pop: 208 (1990); 186 (1980)   **Pop Density:** 5.7
Land: 36.3 sq. mi.; **Water:** 0.0 sq. mi.

Walshville
Township
Lat: 48-14-15 N **Long:** 97-11-22 W
Pop: 191 (1990); 247 (1980)   **Pop Density:** 5.8
Land: 33.2 sq. mi.; **Water:** 0.4 sq. mi.

Ward County
County Seat: Minot (ZIP: 58701)

Pop: 57,921 (1990); 58,392 (1980) **Pop Density:** 28.8
Land: 2013.0 sq. mi.; **Water:** 43.4 sq. mi. **Area Code:** 701

In north-central ND; organized Apr 14, 1885 (prior to statehood) from Renville County.

Name origin: For either J. P. Ward or Mark Ward (1844–1902), or both, members of the Dakota Territory legislature in 1885 when the county was formed.

Afton Township
Lat: 48-08-53 N Long: 101-20-01 W
Pop: 506 (1990); 575 (1980) **Pop Density:** 14.2
Land: 35.7 sq. mi.; **Water:** 0.2 sq. mi.

Anna Township
Lat: 47-59-07 N Long: 101-40-03 W
Pop: 37 (1990); 47 (1980) **Pop Density:** 1.1
Land: 35.1 sq. mi.; **Water:** 1.3 sq. mi.

Baden Township
Lat: 48-35-30 N Long: 102-02-51 W
Pop: 48 (1990); 58 (1980) **Pop Density:** 1.4
Land: 34.9 sq. mi.; **Water:** 0.9 sq. mi.

Berthold City
ZIP: 58718 Lat: 48-18-54 N Long: 101-44-07 W
Pop: 409 (1990); 485 (1980) **Pop Density:** 1363.3
Land: 0.3 sq. mi.; **Water:** 0.0 sq. mi. **Elev:** 2080 ft.
Not coextensive with township. Incorporated 1967.
Name origin: For Bartholmew Berthold, who established a trading post here in 1845, which later became a fort.

*Berthold Township
Lat: 48-19-42 N Long: 101-43-58 W
Pop: 83 (1990); 98 (1980) **Pop Density:** 2.3
Land: 35.9 sq. mi.; **Water:** 0.3 sq. mi.

Brillian Township
Lat: 47-58-46 N Long: 101-02-13 W
Pop: 43 (1990); 56 (1980) **Pop Density:** 1.2
Land: 36.3 sq. mi.; **Water:** 0.0 sq. mi.

Burlington City
ZIP: 58722 Lat: 48-16-31 N Long: 101-25-32 W
Pop: 995 (1990); 762 (1980) **Pop Density:** 2487.5
Land: 0.4 sq. mi.; **Water:** 0.0 sq. mi. **Elev:** 1580 ft.
Not coextensive with township.
Name origin: For Burlington, IA. Originally called Colton.

*Burlington Township
ZIP: 58722 Lat: 48-14-15 N Long: 101-27-52 W
Pop: 288 (1990); 341 (1980) **Pop Density:** 8.1
Land: 35.5 sq. mi.; **Water:** 0.1 sq. mi.

Burt Township
Lat: 48-09-08 N Long: 101-27-30 W
Pop: 90 (1990); 102 (1980) **Pop Density:** 2.5
Land: 35.7 sq. mi.; **Water:** 0.4 sq. mi.

Cameron Township
Lat: 47-52-55 N Long: 101-32-53 W
Pop: 42 (1990); 64 (1980) **Pop Density:** 1.2
Land: 34.6 sq. mi.; **Water:** 0.9 sq. mi.

Carbondale Township
Lat: 48-29-34 N Long: 101-54-56 W
Pop: 64 (1990); 98 (1980) **Pop Density:** 1.8
Land: 35.5 sq. mi.; **Water:** 0.0 sq. mi.

Carpio City
ZIP: 58725 Lat: 48-26-32 N Long: 101-42-55 W
Pop: 178 (1990); 244 (1980) **Pop Density:** 296.7
Land: 0.6 sq. mi.; **Water:** 0.0 sq. mi. **Elev:** 1697 ft.

*Carpio Township
ZIP: 58725 Lat: 48-24-40 N Long: 101-47-00 W
Pop: 63 (1990); 89 (1980) **Pop Density:** 1.8
Land: 35.7 sq. mi.; **Water:** 0.0 sq. mi.

Denmark Township
Lat: 48-45-49 N Long: 102-05-09 W
Pop: 65 (1990); 80 (1980) **Pop Density:** 1.9
Land: 33.7 sq. mi.; **Water:** 2.2 sq. mi.

Des Lacs City
ZIP: 58733 Lat: 48-15-24 N Long: 101-33-47 W
Pop: 216 (1990); 212 (1980) **Pop Density:** 432.0
Land: 0.5 sq. mi.; **Water:** 0.0 sq. mi. **Elev:** 1931 ft.
Not coextensive with township.
Name origin: For the river, which traverses the county.

*Des Lacs Township
ZIP: 58733 Lat: 48-14-31 N Long: 101-36-06 W
Pop: 90 (1990); 94 (1980) **Pop Density:** 2.6
Land: 35.0 sq. mi.; **Water:** 0.3 sq. mi.

Donnybrook City
ZIP: 58734 Lat: 48-30-28 N Long: 101-53-08 W
Pop: 106 (1990); 139 (1980) **Pop Density:** 151.4
Land: 0.7 sq. mi.; **Water:** 0.0 sq. mi. **Elev:** 1760 ft.

Douglas City
ZIP: 58735 Lat: 47-51-30 N Long: 101-30-02 W
Pop: 93 (1990); 112 (1980) **Pop Density:** 310.0
Land: 0.3 sq. mi.; **Water:** 0.0 sq. mi. **Elev:** 2055 ft.

Elmdale Township
Lat: 48-40-05 N Long: 102-10-30 W
Pop: 64 (1990); 91 (1980) **Pop Density:** 1.8
Land: 35.5 sq. mi.; **Water:** 0.5 sq. mi.

Eureka Township
Lat: 48-19-38 N Long: 101-20-12 W
Pop: 305 (1990); 253 (1980) **Pop Density:** 8.5
Land: 36.0 sq. mi.; **Water:** 0.5 sq. mi.

Evergreen Township
Lat: 48-14-45 N Long: 101-51-01 W
Pop: 8 (1990); 9 (1980) **Pop Density:** 0.2
Land: 33.5 sq. mi.; **Water:** 2.3 sq. mi.

NORTH DAKOTA, Ward County

Foxholm
Township
Lat: 48-19-43 N **Long:** 101-36-09 W
Pop: 88 (1990); 175 (1980) **Pop Density:** 2.4
Land: 36.4 sq. mi.; **Water:** 0.0 sq. mi.

Freedom
Township
Lat: 48-04-05 N **Long:** 101-20-31 W
Pop: 143 (1990); 168 (1980) **Pop Density:** 4.0
Land: 35.5 sq. mi.; **Water:** 0.6 sq. mi.

Gasman
Township
Lat: 47-58-41 N **Long:** 101-17-30 W
Pop: 100 (1990); 73 (1980) **Pop Density:** 2.9
Land: 35.0 sq. mi.; **Water:** 1.2 sq. mi.

Greely
Township
Lat: 47-53-37 N **Long:** 101-02-31 W
Pop: 37 (1990); 50 (1980) **Pop Density:** 1.1
Land: 34.8 sq. mi.; **Water:** 1.0 sq. mi.

Greenbush
Township
Lat: 48-35-49 N **Long:** 101-53-48 W
Pop: 44 (1990); 52 (1980) **Pop Density:** 1.2
Land: 35.8 sq. mi.; **Water:** 0.0 sq. mi.

Harrison
Township
Lat: 48-14-25 N **Long:** 101-21-20 W
Pop: 1,268 (1990); 1,906 (1980) **Pop Density:** 51.8
Land: 24.5 sq. mi.; **Water:** 0.0 sq. mi.

Hiddenwood
Township
Lat: 47-53-01 N **Long:** 101-48-51 W
Pop: 60 (1990); 53 (1980) **Pop Density:** 1.7
Land: 35.3 sq. mi.; **Water:** 0.6 sq. mi.

Hilton
Township
Lat: 47-58-21 N **Long:** 101-25-28 W
Pop: 49 (1990); 50 (1980) **Pop Density:** 1.4
Land: 35.8 sq. mi.; **Water:** 0.3 sq. mi.

Iota Flat
Township
Lat: 47-53-17 N **Long:** 101-10-05 W
Pop: 85 (1990); 99 (1980) **Pop Density:** 2.4
Land: 35.3 sq. mi.; **Water:** 0.7 sq. mi.

Kenmare
City
ZIP: 58746 **Lat:** 48-40-26 N **Long:** 102-04-47 W
Pop: 1,214 (1990); 1,456 (1980) **Pop Density:** 1517.5
Land: 0.8 sq. mi.; **Water:** 0.0 sq. mi. **Elev:** 1900 ft.
Not coextensive with township. Settled 1890s.
Name origin: For Kenmare, Ireland.

*Kenmare
Township
ZIP: 58746 **Lat:** 48-41-01 N **Long:** 102-01-39 W
Pop: 106 (1990); 110 (1980) **Pop Density:** 3.1
Land: 33.7 sq. mi.; **Water:** 1.2 sq. mi.

Kirkelie
Township
Lat: 48-19-31 N **Long:** 101-28-18 W
Pop: 372 (1990); 288 (1980) **Pop Density:** 10.2
Land: 36.6 sq. mi.; **Water:** 0.1 sq. mi.

Linton
Township
Lat: 48-04-28 N **Long:** 101-42-55 W
Pop: 35 (1990); 49 (1980) **Pop Density:** 1.0
Land: 34.5 sq. mi.; **Water:** 1.6 sq. mi.

Lund
Township
Lat: 48-03-36 N **Long:** 101-51-10 W
Pop: 49 (1990); 49 (1980) **Pop Density:** 1.4
Land: 34.9 sq. mi.; **Water:** 1.2 sq. mi.

McKinley
Township
Lat: 48-19-47 N **Long:** 101-12-13 W
Pop: 152 (1990); 157 (1980) **Pop Density:** 4.2
Land: 36.5 sq. mi.; **Water:** 0.0 sq. mi.

Makoti
City
ZIP: 58756 **Lat:** 47-57-37 N **Long:** 101-48-16 W
Pop: 145 (1990); 199 (1980) **Pop Density:** 725.0
Land: 0.2 sq. mi.; **Water:** 0.0 sq. mi. **Elev:** 2080 ft.

Mandan
Township
Lat: 48-14-26 N **Long:** 101-43-14 W
Pop: 65 (1990); 67 (1980) **Pop Density:** 1.9
Land: 34.1 sq. mi.; **Water:** 1.7 sq. mi.

Margaret
Township
Lat: 48-25-13 N **Long:** 101-06-50 W
Pop: 67 (1990); 72 (1980) **Pop Density:** 1.9
Land: 36.1 sq. mi.; **Water:** 0.1 sq. mi.

Maryland
Township
Lat: 48-19-16 N **Long:** 101-04-23 W
Pop: 85 (1990); 76 (1980) **Pop Density:** 2.3
Land: 36.2 sq. mi.; **Water:** 0.1 sq. mi.

Mayland
Township
Lat: 48-24-54 N **Long:** 101-38-58 W
Pop: 57 (1990); 78 (1980) **Pop Density:** 1.6
Land: 35.8 sq. mi.; **Water:** 0.1 sq. mi.

Minot
City
ZIP: 58701 **Lat:** 48-14-01 N **Long:** 101-17-45 W
Pop: 34,544 (1990); 32,843 (1980) **Pop Density:** 2597.3
Land: 13.3 sq. mi.; **Water:** 0.0 sq. mi. **Elev:** 1555 ft.
In northwest-central ND on the Souris River, 100 mi. north of Bismarck. Founded 1886. Incorporated 1887.
Name origin: For Henry Davis Minot (1859–90), a director of the Great Northern Railroad.

Minot Air Force Base
Military Facility
ZIP: 58701 **Lat:** 48-25-11 N **Long:** 101-20-10 W
Pop: 9,095 (1990); 5,153 (1980) **Pop Density:** 1263.2
Land: 7.2 sq. mi.; **Water:** 0.4 sq. mi.

Nedrose
Township
Lat: 48-14-16 N **Long:** 101-12-20 W
Pop: 2,077 (1990); 1,661 (1980) **Pop Density:** 62.0
Land: 33.5 sq. mi.; **Water:** 0.7 sq. mi.

Newman
Township
Lat: 47-58-50 N **Long:** 101-09-35 W
Pop: 85 (1990); 106 (1980) **Pop Density:** 2.4
Land: 35.9 sq. mi.; **Water:** 0.2 sq. mi.

New Prairie
Township
Lat: 48-08-45 N **Long:** 101-04-06 W
Pop: 221 (1990); 234 (1980) **Pop Density:** 6.1
Land: 36.0 sq. mi.; **Water:** 0.1 sq. mi.

Orlien
Township
Lat: 47-58-38 N **Long:** 101-48-23 W
Pop: 53 (1990); 82 (1980) **Pop Density:** 1.5
Land: 35.7 sq. mi.; **Water:** 0.7 sq. mi.

Passport
Township
Lat: 48-19-39 N **Long:** 101-51-23 W
Pop: 51 (1990); 59 (1980) **Pop Density:** 1.5
Land: 33.5 sq. mi.; **Water:** 3.1 sq. mi.

NORTH DAKOTA, Ward County

Ree Township
Lat: 48-25-06 N Long: 101-54-43 W
Pop: 38 (1990); 57 (1980) Pop Density: 1.1
Land: 34.2 sq. mi.; Water: 1.9 sq. mi.

Rice Lake Township
Lat: 47-58-26 N Long: 101-32-36 W
Pop: 54 (1990); 56 (1980) Pop Density: 1.6
Land: 34.4 sq. mi.; Water: 1.8 sq. mi.

Rolling Green Township
Lat: 48-08-43 N Long: 101-35-34 W
Pop: 96 (1990); 97 (1980) Pop Density: 2.8
Land: 34.1 sq. mi.; Water: 1.8 sq. mi.

Rushville Township
Lat: 47-53-55 N Long: 101-17-40 W
Pop: 81 (1990); 104 (1980) Pop Density: 2.3
Land: 35.3 sq. mi.; Water: 0.7 sq. mi.

Ryder City
ZIP: 58779 Lat: 47-55-02 N Long: 101-40-23 W
Pop: 121 (1990); 158 (1980) Pop Density: 403.3
Land: 0.3 sq. mi.; Water: 0.0 sq. mi. Elev: 2106 ft.
Not coextensive with township.

*Ryder Township
ZIP: 58779 Lat: 47-53-26 N Long: 101-40-54 W
Pop: 53 (1990); 61 (1980) Pop Density: 1.5
Land: 34.8 sq. mi.; Water: 0.7 sq. mi.

St. Marys Township
Lat: 48-24-37 N Long: 101-31-20 W
Pop: 51 (1990); 60 (1980) Pop Density: 1.5
Land: 34.9 sq. mi.; Water: 1.2 sq. mi.

Sauk Prairie Township
Lat: 48-40-10 N Long: 101-53-47 W
Pop: 38 (1990); 42 (1980) Pop Density: 1.1
Land: 35.4 sq. mi.; Water: 0.5 sq. mi.

Sawyer City
ZIP: 58781 Lat: 48-05-21 N Long: 101-03-14 W
Pop: 319 (1990); 417 (1980) Pop Density: 797.5
Land: 0.4 sq. mi.; Water: 0.0 sq. mi. Elev: 1542 ft.
Not coextensive with township. Founded 1882.
Name origin: Named by Soo Railroad officials for an employee.

*Sawyer Township
ZIP: 58781 Lat: 48-04-14 N Long: 101-05-10 W
Pop: 174 (1990); 218 (1980) Pop Density: 4.9
Land: 35.5 sq. mi.; Water: 0.0 sq. mi.

Shealey Township
Lat: 48-08-27 N Long: 101-51-20 W
Pop: 48 (1990); 51 (1980) Pop Density: 1.4
Land: 35.1 sq. mi.; Water: 0.8 sq. mi.

Spencer Township
ZIP: 58746 Lat: 48-35-39 N Long: 102-10-17 W
Pop: 100 (1990); 100 (1980) Pop Density: 2.9
Land: 35.0 sq. mi.; Water: 1.0 sq. mi.

Spring Lake Township
Lat: 47-53-22 N Long: 101-24-49 W
Pop: 36 (1990); 53 (1980) Pop Density: 1.0
Land: 34.7 sq. mi.; Water: 1.2 sq. mi.

Sundre Township
Lat: 48-09-05 N Long: 101-12-22 W
Pop: 900 (1990); 901 (1980) Pop Density: 25.2
Land: 35.7 sq. mi.; Water: 0.2 sq. mi.

Surrey City
ZIP: 58785 Lat: 48-14-09 N Long: 101-07-57 W
Pop: 856 (1990); 999 (1980) Pop Density: 856.0
Land: 1.0 sq. mi.; Water: 0.0 sq. mi. Elev: 1625 ft.
Not coextensive with township. Founded 1900.
Name origin: Named by railroad officials for Surrey, England.

*Surrey Township
ZIP: 58785 Lat: 48-14-30 N Long: 101-04-39 W
Pop: 253 (1990); 272 (1980) Pop Density: 7.2
Land: 35.0 sq. mi.; Water: 0.0 sq. mi.

Tatman Township
Lat: 48-24-58 N Long: 101-14-50 W
Pop: 6,126 (1990); 5,439 (1980) Pop Density: 170.6
Land: 35.9 sq. mi.; Water: 0.2 sq. mi.

Tolgen Township
Lat: 48-08-41 N Long: 101-43-53 W
Pop: 29 (1990); 28 (1980) Pop Density: 0.9
Land: 33.7 sq. mi.; Water: 2.2 sq. mi.

Torning Township
Lat: 48-03-55 N Long: 101-27-56 W
Pop: 54 (1990); 68 (1980) Pop Density: 1.6
Land: 34.4 sq. mi.; Water: 1.8 sq. mi.

Vang Township
Lat: 48-03-33 N Long: 101-35-54 W
Pop: 57 (1990); 72 (1980) Pop Density: 1.7
Land: 34.3 sq. mi.; Water: 1.7 sq. mi.

Waterford Township
Lat: 48-24-50 N Long: 101-22-45 W
Pop: 3,277 (1990); 4,801 (1980) Pop Density: 91.5
Land: 35.8 sq. mi.; Water: 0.4 sq. mi.

Willis Township
Lat: 48-04-05 N Long: 101-12-33 W
Pop: 115 (1990); 117 (1980) Pop Density: 3.2
Land: 36.0 sq. mi.; Water: 0.0 sq. mi.

Wells County
County Seat: Fessenden (ZIP: 58438)

Pop: 5,864 (1990); 6,979 (1980)   **Pop Density:** 4.6
Land: 1271.4 sq. mi.; **Water:** 19.3 sq. mi.   **Area Code:** 701
In central ND, northeast of Bismarck; organized as Gingras County Jan 4, 1873 (prior to statehood) from Sheridan County; name changed Feb 26, 1881.
Name origin: For Edward Payson Wells (1847–1936), ND territorial legislator (1881), banker, and developer of the James River valley.

Berlin — Township
Lat: 47-22-10 N   Long: 99-35-07 W
Pop: 54 (1990); 67 (1980)   Pop Density: 1.5
Land: 34.9 sq. mi.; Water: 1.3 sq. mi.

Bilodeau — Township
Lat: 47-27-35 N   Long: 99-19-08 W
Pop: 61 (1990); 80 (1980)   Pop Density: 1.7
Land: 35.6 sq. mi.; Water: 0.2 sq. mi.

Bowdon — City
ZIP: 58418   Lat: 47-28-08 N   Long: 99-42-29 W
Pop: 196 (1990); 220 (1980)   Pop Density: 653.3
Land: 0.3 sq. mi.; Water: 0.0 sq. mi.   Elev: 1811 ft.
Incorporated 1952.

Bremen — Township
Lat: 47-43-10 N   Long: 99-21-04 W
Pop: 108 (1990); 154 (1980)   Pop Density: 3.0
Land: 35.8 sq. mi.; Water: 0.2 sq. mi.

Bull Moose — Township
Lat: 47-27-44 N   Long: 99-57-53 W
Pop: 67 (1990); 77 (1980)   Pop Density: 2.0
Land: 33.6 sq. mi.; Water: 2.1 sq. mi.

Cathay — City
ZIP: 58422   Lat: 47-33-14 N   Long: 99-24-39 W
Pop: 54 (1990); 66 (1980)   Pop Density: 270.0
Land: 0.2 sq. mi.; Water: 0.0 sq. mi.   Elev: 1580 ft.
Not coextensive with township.

*Cathay — Township
ZIP: 58422   Lat: 47-33-05 N   Long: 99-27-41 W
Pop: 61 (1990); 81 (1980)   Pop Density: 1.7
Land: 35.6 sq. mi.; Water: 0.1 sq. mi.

Chaseley — Township
ZIP: 58423   Lat: 47-27-42 N   Long: 99-50-55 W
Pop: 68 (1990); 106 (1980)   Pop Density: 1.9
Land: 35.3 sq. mi.; Water: 0.8 sq. mi.

Crystal Lake — Township
Lat: 47-31-59 N   Long: 99-58-01 W
Pop: 45 (1990); 53 (1980)   Pop Density: 1.3
Land: 35.5 sq. mi.; Water: 0.4 sq. mi.

Delger — Township
Lat: 47-32-35 N   Long: 99-50-21 W
Pop: 52 (1990); 71 (1980)   Pop Density: 1.5
Land: 35.8 sq. mi.; Water: 0.2 sq. mi.

Fairville — Township
Lat: 47-37-25 N   Long: 99-19-09 W
Pop: 53 (1990); 87 (1980)   Pop Density: 1.5
Land: 35.2 sq. mi.; Water: 0.0 sq. mi.

Fessenden — City
ZIP: 58438   Lat: 47-38-58 N   Long: 99-37-32 W
Pop: 655 (1990); 761 (1980)   Pop Density: 1637.5
Land: 0.4 sq. mi.; Water: 0.0 sq. mi.   Elev: 1608 ft.
Name origin: For Gen. Cortez Fessenden, who surveyed the area in the early 1880s.

Forward — Township
Lat: 47-43-27 N   Long: 99-53-12 W
Pop: 105 (1990); 109 (1980)   Pop Density: 2.9
Land: 35.8 sq. mi.; Water: 0.4 sq. mi.

Fram — Township
Lat: 47-48-27 N   Long: 99-45-27 W
Pop: 95 (1990); 110 (1980)   Pop Density: 2.6
Land: 36.0 sq. mi.; Water: 0.0 sq. mi.

Germantown — Township
Lat: 47-37-25 N   Long: 99-26-50 W
Pop: 51 (1990); 50 (1980)   Pop Density: 1.5
Land: 35.1 sq. mi.; Water: 0.2 sq. mi.

Haaland — Township
Lat: 47-27-40 N   Long: 99-42-38 W
Pop: 59 (1990); 79 (1980)   Pop Density: 1.7
Land: 35.4 sq. mi.; Water: 0.2 sq. mi.

Hamberg — City
ZIP: 58337   Lat: 47-45-45 N   Long: 99-30-53 W
Pop: 19 (1990); 41 (1980)   Pop Density: 47.5
Land: 0.4 sq. mi.; Water: 0.0 sq. mi.   Elev: 1547 ft.

Hamburg — Township
ZIP: 58337   Lat: 47-43-26 N   Long: 99-28-44 W
Pop: 61 (1990); 93 (1980)   Pop Density: 1.7
Land: 35.3 sq. mi.; Water: 0.8 sq. mi.

Harvey — City
ZIP: 58341   Lat: 47-46-12 N   Long: 99-55-50 W
Pop: 2,263 (1990); 2,527 (1980)   Pop Density: 2057.3
Land: 1.1 sq. mi.; Water: 0.0 sq. mi.   Elev: 1600 ft.
Name origin: For Col. James Harvey, a director and stockholder of the Soo Railroad.

Hawksnest — Township
Lat: 47-22-31 N   Long: 99-19-08 W
Pop: 45 (1990); 62 (1980)   Pop Density: 1.3
Land: 35.9 sq. mi.; Water: 0.2 sq. mi.

Heimdal — Township
ZIP: 58342   Lat: 47-48-07 N   Long: 99-37-15 W
Pop: 85 (1990); 104 (1980)   Pop Density: 2.4
Land: 35.7 sq. mi.; Water: 0.3 sq. mi.

Hillsdale — Township
Lat: 47-48-09 N   Long: 100-00-52 W
Pop: 149 (1990); 145 (1980)   Pop Density: 4.2
Land: 35.6 sq. mi.; Water: 0.2 sq. mi.

NORTH DAKOTA, Wells County

Hurdsfield — City
ZIP: 58451 Lat: 47-26-52 N Long: 99-55-48 W
Pop: 92 (1990); 113 (1980) Pop Density: 306.7
Land: 0.3 sq. mi.; Water: 0.0 sq. mi. Elev: 1906 ft.

Johnson — Township
Lat: 47-22-32 N Long: 99-26-48 W
Pop: 57 (1990); 78 (1980) Pop Density: 1.6
Land: 35.2 sq. mi.; Water: 0.9 sq. mi.

Lynn — Township
Lat: 47-22-05 N Long: 99-58-01 W
Pop: 35 (1990); 49 (1980) Pop Density: 1.0
Land: 34.7 sq. mi.; Water: 1.5 sq. mi.

Manfred — Township
ZIP: 58465 Lat: 47-43-26 N Long: 99-45-29 W
Pop: 73 (1990); 106 (1980) Pop Density: 2.0
Land: 35.9 sq. mi.; Water: 0.2 sq. mi.

Norway Lake — Township
Lat: 47-47-55 N Long: 99-29-18 W
Pop: 88 (1990); 98 (1980) Pop Density: 2.5
Land: 34.7 sq. mi.; Water: 0.9 sq. mi.

Oshkosh — Township
Lat: 47-37-54 N Long: 99-35-01 W
Pop: 55 (1990); 71 (1980) Pop Density: 1.6
Land: 34.7 sq. mi.; Water: 0.1 sq. mi.

Pony Gulch — Township
Lat: 47-37-28 N Long: 99-57-51 W
Pop: 58 (1990); 96 (1980) Pop Density: 1.7
Land: 35.1 sq. mi.; Water: 0.0 sq. mi.

Progress — Township
Lat: 47-21-57 N Long: 99-43-04 W
Pop: 45 (1990); 46 (1980) Pop Density: 1.3
Land: 34.9 sq. mi.; Water: 1.0 sq. mi.

Rusland — Township
Lat: 47-37-37 N Long: 99-50-12 W
Pop: 54 (1990); 79 (1980) Pop Density: 1.6
Land: 34.7 sq. mi.; Water: 0.5 sq. mi.

St. Anna — Township
Lat: 47-37-45 N Long: 99-43-14 W
Pop: 34 (1990); 54 (1980) Pop Density: 1.0
Land: 33.2 sq. mi.; Water: 1.8 sq. mi.

Silver Lake — Township
Lat: 47-22-19 N Long: 99-50-29 W
Pop: 33 (1990); 54 (1980) Pop Density: 0.9
Land: 34.8 sq. mi.; Water: 1.2 sq. mi.

South Cottonwood — Township
Lat: 47-32-48 N Long: 99-34-44 W
Pop: 78 (1990); 84 (1980) Pop Density: 2.2
Land: 35.4 sq. mi.; Water: 0.5 sq. mi.

Speedwell — Township
Lat: 47-27-25 N Long: 99-35-04 W
Pop: 76 (1990); 99 (1980) Pop Density: 2.1
Land: 35.6 sq. mi.; Water: 0.3 sq. mi.

Sykeston — City
ZIP: 58486 Lat: 47-27-56 N Long: 99-23-54 W
Pop: 167 (1990); 193 (1980) Pop Density: 417.5
Land: 0.4 sq. mi.; Water: 0.0 sq. mi. Elev: 1638 ft.
Not coextensive with township.

*Sykeston — Township
ZIP: 58486 Lat: 47-27-46 N Long: 99-26-49 W
Pop: 54 (1990); 75 (1980) Pop Density: 1.5
Land: 35.0 sq. mi.; Water: 0.5 sq. mi.

Valhalla — Township
Lat: 47-48-13 N Long: 99-21-37 W
Pop: 45 (1990); 77 (1980) Pop Density: 1.3
Land: 35.5 sq. mi.; Water: 0.5 sq. mi.

Wells — Township
Lat: 47-47-59 N Long: 99-51-55 W
Pop: 137 (1990); 160 (1980) Pop Density: 4.0
Land: 34.5 sq. mi.; Water: 0.6 sq. mi.

Western — Township
Lat: 47-42-35 N Long: 99-59-38 W
Pop: 115 (1990); 127 (1980) Pop Density: 3.2
Land: 35.6 sq. mi.; Water: 0.4 sq. mi.

West Norway — Township
Lat: 47-42-34 N Long: 99-36-28 W
Pop: 73 (1990); 58 (1980) Pop Density: 2.0
Land: 35.8 sq. mi.; Water: 0.2 sq. mi.

West Ontario — Township
Lat: 47-32-03 N Long: 99-42-48 W
Pop: 44 (1990); 57 (1980) Pop Density: 1.2
Land: 35.4 sq. mi.; Water: 0.3 sq. mi.

Woodward — Township
Lat: 47-32-23 N Long: 99-20-26 W
Pop: 45 (1990); 62 (1980) Pop Density: 1.3
Land: 35.7 sq. mi.; Water: 0.3 sq. mi.

Williams County
County Seat: Williston (ZIP: 58802)

Pop: 21,129 (1990); 22,237 (1980) **Pop Density:** 10.2
Land: 2070.6 sq. mi.; **Water:** 77.5 sq. mi. **Area Code:** 701

On the northwestern border of ND, west of Minot; established Jan 8, 1873 by absorbing both Buford and Flannery counties. Originally located south of the Missouri River, near present-day Dunn and Mercer counties; established in present location in 1892.

Name origin: For Erastus A. Williams (1850–1930), Dakota Territory legislator, ND surveyor general, and a founder of Hettinger County.

Alamo City
ZIP: 58830 **Lat:** 48-34-55 N **Long:** 103-28-01 W
Pop: 69 (1990); 122 (1980) **Pop Density:** 138.0
Land: 0.5 sq. mi.; **Water:** 0.0 sq. mi. **Elev:** 2115 ft.
Incorporated 1967.
Name origin: From the Spanish 'cottonwood', for the nearby cottonwood stands and also for the Alamo mission in TX.

Athens Township
Lat: 48-25-16 N **Long:** 103-36-43 W
Pop: 28 (1990); 20 (1980) **Pop Density:** 0.8
Land: 35.9 sq. mi.; **Water:** 0.1 sq. mi.

Barr Butte Township
Lat: 48-34-58 N **Long:** 103-51-07 W
Pop: 19 (1990); 26 (1980) **Pop Density:** 0.5
Land: 35.1 sq. mi.; **Water:** 0.1 sq. mi.

Big Meadow Township
Lat: 48-35-50 N **Long:** 103-04-52 W
Pop: 31 (1990); 40 (1980) **Pop Density:** 0.9
Land: 34.9 sq. mi.; **Water:** 1.0 sq. mi.

Big Stone Township
Lat: 48-35-23 N **Long:** 103-20-27 W
Pop: 39 (1990); 50 (1980) **Pop Density:** 1.1
Land: 35.7 sq. mi.; **Water:** 0.2 sq. mi.

Blacktail Township
Lat: 48-25-44 N **Long:** 103-43-54 W
Pop: 44 (1990); 41 (1980) **Pop Density:** 1.2
Land: 35.9 sq. mi.; **Water:** 0.2 sq. mi.

Blue Ridge Township
Lat: 48-35-36 N **Long:** 103-36-11 W
Pop: 40 (1990); 69 (1980) **Pop Density:** 1.2
Land: 34.0 sq. mi.; **Water:** 2.1 sq. mi.

Bonetraill Township
Lat: 48-24-33 N **Long:** 103-52-04 W
Pop: 24 (1990); 35 (1980) **Pop Density:** 0.7
Land: 36.0 sq. mi.; **Water:** 0.0 sq. mi.

Brooklyn Township
Lat: 48-14-32 N **Long:** 103-16-37 W
Pop: 35 (1990); 38 (1980) **Pop Density:** 1.0
Land: 35.6 sq. mi.; **Water:** 0.0 sq. mi.

Buford Township
Lat: 48-00-07 N **Long:** 103-55-43 W
Pop: 193 (1990); 188 (1980) **Pop Density:** 5.7
Land: 33.8 sq. mi.; **Water:** 1.7 sq. mi.

Bull Butte Township
Lat: 48-19-44 N **Long:** 103-57-37 W
Pop: 23 (1990); 39 (1980) **Pop Density:** 0.4
Land: 51.4 sq. mi.; **Water:** 0.1 sq. mi.

Champion Township
Lat: 48-24-36 N **Long:** 103-12-00 W
Pop: 20 (1990); 37 (1980) **Pop Density:** 0.6
Land: 35.9 sq. mi.; **Water:** 0.1 sq. mi.

Climax Township
Lat: 48-30-14 N **Long:** 103-59-31 W
Pop: 19 (1990); 30 (1980) **Pop Density:** 0.6
Land: 32.8 sq. mi.; **Water:** 0.0 sq. mi.

Cow Creek Township
Lat: 48-19-24 N **Long:** 103-48-12 W
Pop: 21 (1990); 16 (1980) **Pop Density:** 0.6
Land: 36.4 sq. mi.; **Water:** 0.0 sq. mi.

Dry Fork Township
Lat: 48-14-26 N **Long:** 102-53-44 W
Pop: 36 (1990); 56 (1980) **Pop Density:** 1.0
Land: 35.8 sq. mi.; **Water:** 0.0 sq. mi.

Dublin Township
Lat: 48-24-49 N **Long:** 103-28-03 W
Pop: 15 (1990); 14 (1980) **Pop Density:** 0.4
Land: 35.8 sq. mi.; **Water:** 0.2 sq. mi.

East Fork Township
Lat: 48-19-33 N **Long:** 103-32-24 W
Pop: 24 (1990); 35 (1980) **Pop Density:** 0.7
Land: 36.3 sq. mi.; **Water:** 0.0 sq. mi.

Ellisville Township
Lat: 48-30-18 N **Long:** 103-28-04 W
Pop: 29 (1990); 30 (1980) **Pop Density:** 0.8
Land: 35.8 sq. mi.; **Water:** 0.1 sq. mi.

Epping City
ZIP: 58843 **Lat:** 48-16-50 N **Long:** 103-21-27 W
Pop: 64 (1990); 104 (1980) **Pop Density:** 160.0
Land: 0.4 sq. mi.; **Water:** 0.0 sq. mi. **Elev:** 2218 ft.

Equality Township
Lat: 48-19-34 N **Long:** 103-08-56 W
Pop: 48 (1990); 70 (1980) **Pop Density:** 1.4
Land: 34.9 sq. mi.; **Water:** 0.3 sq. mi.

Farmvale Township
Lat: 48-14-22 N **Long:** 103-00-59 W
Pop: 39 (1990); 44 (1980) **Pop Density:** 1.1
Land: 35.9 sq. mi.; **Water:** 0.0 sq. mi.

Golden Valley Township
Lat: 48-24-31 N **Long:** 103-04-50 W
Pop: 32 (1990); 42 (1980) **Pop Density:** 0.9
Land: 35.9 sq. mi.; **Water:** 0.1 sq. mi.

NORTH DAKOTA, Williams County

Good Luck Township
Lat: 48-30-38 N Long: 103-51-26 W
Pop: 32 (1990); 45 (1980) Pop Density: 0.9
Land: 35.8 sq. mi.; Water: 0.0 sq. mi.

Grenora City
ZIP: 58845 Lat: 48-37-09 N Long: 103-56-09 W
Pop: 261 (1990); 362 (1980) Pop Density: 435.0
Land: 0.6 sq. mi.; Water: 0.0 sq. mi. Elev: 2105 ft.
Not coextensive with township.

*Grenora Township
ZIP: 58845 Lat: 48-35-31 N Long: 103-58-48 W
Pop: 22 (1990); 15 (1980) Pop Density: 0.7
Land: 31.5 sq. mi.; Water: 0.9 sq. mi.

Hanks City
ZIP: 58856 Lat: 48-36-09 N Long: 103-48-07 W
Pop: 11 (1990); 10 (1980) Pop Density: 13.8
Land: 0.8 sq. mi.; Water: 0.0 sq. mi. Elev: 2114 ft.

Hardscrabble Township
Lat: 48-04-15 N Long: 103-57-15 W
Pop: 88 (1990); 75 (1980) Pop Density: 1.8
Land: 50.2 sq. mi.; Water: 0.0 sq. mi.

Hazel Township
Lat: 48-35-23 N Long: 103-12-39 W
Pop: 45 (1990); 54 (1980) Pop Density: 1.3
Land: 35.2 sq. mi.; Water: 0.4 sq. mi.

Hebron Township
Lat: 48-14-54 N Long: 103-57-37 W
Pop: 34 (1990); 50 (1980) Pop Density: 0.7
Land: 50.4 sq. mi.; Water: 0.0 sq. mi.

Hofflund Township
Lat: 48-09-53 N Long: 103-01-57 W
Pop: 24 (1990); 32 (1980) Pop Density: 1.5
Land: 16.5 sq. mi.; Water: 9.7 sq. mi.

Judson Township
Lat: 48-09-11 N Long: 103-47-39 W
Pop: 164 (1990); 113 (1980) Pop Density: 4.6
Land: 35.9 sq. mi.; Water: 0.0 sq. mi.

Lindahl Township
Lat: 48-30-36 N Long: 102-57-01 W
Pop: 37 (1990); 42 (1980) Pop Density: 1.0
Land: 35.7 sq. mi.; Water: 0.2 sq. mi.

Marshall Township
Lat: 48-19-39 N Long: 103-24-35 W
Pop: 43 (1990); 48 (1980) Pop Density: 1.2
Land: 36.3 sq. mi.; Water: 0.0 sq. mi.

Missouri Ridge Township
Lat: 48-14-28 N Long: 103-40-03 W
Pop: 446 (1990); 550 (1980) Pop Density: 12.4
Land: 35.9 sq. mi.; Water: 0.1 sq. mi.

Mont Township
Lat: 48-15-03 N Long: 103-48-12 W
Pop: 45 (1990); 66 (1980) Pop Density: 1.3
Land: 35.9 sq. mi.; Water: 0.0 sq. mi.

Nesson Valley Pop. Place
Lat: 48-10-17 N Long: 103-09-00 W
Pop: 19 (1990); 11 (1980) Pop Density: 1.0
Land: 19.7 sq. mi.; Water: 4.9 sq. mi.

New Home Township
Lat: 48-30-11 N Long: 103-12-44 W
Pop: 30 (1990); 39 (1980) Pop Density: 0.8
Land: 36.0 sq. mi.; Water: 0.0 sq. mi.

Oliver Township
Lat: 48-24-41 N Long: 103-20-48 W
Pop: 17 (1990); 24 (1980) Pop Density: 0.5
Land: 36.0 sq. mi.; Water: 0.0 sq. mi.

Orthell Township
Lat: 48-30-15 N Long: 103-43-51 W
Pop: 19 (1990); 21 (1980) Pop Density: 0.5
Land: 35.9 sq. mi.; Water: 0.0 sq. mi.

Pherrin Township
Lat: 48-14-10 N Long: 103-32-05 W
Pop: 225 (1990); 192 (1980) Pop Density: 6.4
Land: 35.1 sq. mi.; Water: 0.8 sq. mi.

Pleasant Valley Township
Lat: 48-19-34 N Long: 102-53-16 W
Pop: 173 (1990); 157 (1980) Pop Density: 4.8
Land: 36.3 sq. mi.; Water: 0.0 sq. mi.

Rainbow Township
Lat: 48-30-38 N Long: 103-20-01 W
Pop: 17 (1990); 13 (1980) Pop Density: 0.5
Land: 35.7 sq. mi.; Water: 0.2 sq. mi.

Ray City
ZIP: 58849 Lat: 48-20-28 N Long: 103-09-45 W
Pop: 603 (1990); 766 (1980) Pop Density: 603.0
Land: 1.0 sq. mi.; Water: 0.0 sq. mi. Elev: 2280 ft.
Founded 1901.
Name origin: For early pioneer Ray Payton.

Rock Island Township
Lat: 48-35-47 N Long: 103-27-58 W
Pop: 8 (1990); 8 (1980) Pop Density: 0.2
Land: 34.4 sq. mi.; Water: 0.8 sq. mi.

Round Prairie Township
Lat: 48-09-25 N Long: 103-57-08 W
Pop: 133 (1990); 97 (1980) Pop Density: 2.6
Land: 50.6 sq. mi.; Water: 0.0 sq. mi.

Sauk Valley Township
Lat: 48-35-14 N Long: 102-56-31 W
Pop: 94 (1990); 134 (1980) Pop Density: 2.6
Land: 35.5 sq. mi.; Water: 0.2 sq. mi.

Scorio Township
Lat: 48-35-33 N Long: 103-43-57 W
Pop: 54 (1990); 70 (1980) Pop Density: 1.5
Land: 34.9 sq. mi.; Water: 0.7 sq. mi.

Southeast Williams Pop. Place
Lat: 48-10-32 N Long: 102-54-14 W
Pop: 10 (1990); 15 (1980) Pop Density: 0.5
Land: 18.5 sq. mi.; Water: 9.4 sq. mi.

South Meadow Township
Lat: 48-30-36 N Long: 103-04-50 W
Pop: 35 (1990); 34 (1980) Pop Density: 1.0
Land: 35.7 sq. mi.; Water: 0.2 sq. mi.

Spring Brook City
Lat: 48-15-06 N Long: 103-27-43 W
Pop: 29 (1990); 52 (1980) Pop Density: 72.5
Land: 0.4 sq. mi.; Water: 0.0 sq. mi. Elev: 2066 ft.
Not coextensive with township.

*Springbrook — Township
Lat: 48-14-19 N **Long:** 103-23-58 W
Pop: 67 (1990); 35 (1980) **Pop Density:** 1.9
Land: 34.8 sq. mi.; **Water:** 0.3 sq. mi.

Stony Creek — Township
Lat: 48-07-12 N **Long:** 103-32-04 W
Pop: 474 (1990); 394 (1980) **Pop Density:** 9.6
Land: 49.4 sq. mi.; **Water:** 14.0 sq. mi.

Strandahl — Township
Lat: 48-25-25 N **Long:** 103-58-56 W
Pop: 32 (1990); 29 (1980) **Pop Density:** 1.0
Land: 32.5 sq. mi.; **Water:** 0.2 sq. mi.

Tioga — City
ZIP: 58852 **Lat:** 48-23-36 N **Long:** 102-56-18 W
Pop: 1,278 (1990); 1,597 (1980) **Pop Density:** 1161.8
Land: 1.1 sq. mi.; **Water:** 0.0 sq. mi. **Elev:** 2238 ft.
Not coextensive with township.
Name origin: Named in 1902 by settlers for Tioga, NY, from an Iroquois Indian term meaning 'peaceful valley.'

*Tioga — Township
ZIP: 58852 **Lat:** 48-25-02 N **Long:** 102-56-48 W
Pop: 137 (1990); 153 (1980) **Pop Density:** 3.9
Land: 34.7 sq. mi.; **Water:** 0.2 sq. mi.

Trenton — Township
Lat: 48-04-15 N **Long:** 103-47-51 W
Pop: 525 (1990); 401 (1980) **Pop Density:** 20.4
Land: 25.7 sq. mi.; **Water:** 6.8 sq. mi.

Truax — Township
Lat: 48-07-01 N **Long:** 103-17-20 W
Pop: 97 (1990); 72 (1980) **Pop Density:** 2.0
Land: 49.3 sq. mi.; **Water:** 7.8 sq. mi.

Twelve Mile — Township
Lat: 48-07-22 N **Long:** 103-24-30 W
Pop: 111 (1990); 104 (1980) **Pop Density:** 1.8
Land: 62.2 sq. mi.; **Water:** 7.7 sq. mi.

Tyrone — Township
Lat: 48-19-33 N **Long:** 103-39-19 W
Pop: 49 (1990); 59 (1980) **Pop Density:** 1.3
Land: 36.3 sq. mi.; **Water:** 0.0 sq. mi.

View — Township
Lat: 48-14-21 N **Long:** 103-08-35 W
Pop: 41 (1990); 37 (1980) **Pop Density:** 1.1
Land: 35.8 sq. mi.; **Water:** 0.1 sq. mi.

West Bank — Township
Lat: 48-19-56 N **Long:** 103-01-57 W
Pop: 68 (1990); 64 (1980) **Pop Density:** 1.9
Land: 36.6 sq. mi.; **Water:** 0.0 sq. mi.

Wheelock — City
ZIP: 58849 **Lat:** 48-17-41 N **Long:** 103-15-08 W
Pop: 23 (1990); 34 (1980) **Pop Density:** 28.8
Land: 0.8 sq. mi.; **Water:** 0.0 sq. mi. **Elev:** 2393 ft.
No coextensive with township.

*Wheelock — Township
Lat: 48-19-14 N **Long:** 103-16-51 W
Pop: 39 (1990); 27 (1980) **Pop Density:** 1.1
Land: 35.2 sq. mi.; **Water:** 0.0 sq. mi.

Wildrose — City
ZIP: 58795 **Lat:** 48-37-45 N **Long:** 103-10-59 W
Pop: 193 (1990); 214 (1980) **Pop Density:** 643.3
Land: 0.3 sq. mi.; **Water:** 0.0 sq. mi. **Elev:** 2254 ft.

Williston — City
ZIP: 58801 **Lat:** 48-09-44 N **Long:** 103-37-51 W
Pop: 13,131 (1990); 13,336 (1980) **Pop Density:** 1903.0
Land: 6.9 sq. mi.; **Water:** 0.1 sq. mi. **Elev:** 1882 ft.
In northwestern ND on the Missouri River, 20 mi. east of the MT border. Not coextensive with township. Incorporated 1904.
Name origin: Named by Great Northern Railroad director James Hill for his friend, D. Willis James of NY.

*Williston — Township
Lat: 48-09-32 N **Long:** 103-40-46 W
Pop: 1,209 (1990); 1,384 (1980) **Pop Density:** 55.0
Land: 22.0 sq. mi.; **Water:** 4.8 sq. mi.

Winner — Township
Lat: 48-29-54 N **Long:** 103-36-20 W
Pop: 45 (1990); 56 (1980) **Pop Density:** 1.3
Land: 35.8 sq. mi.; **Water:** 0.2 sq. mi.

Index to Places and Counties in North Dakota

Abercrombie (Richland) City 546
Abercrombie (Richland) Township ... 546
Acme (Hettinger) Township 521
Acton (Walsh) Township 562
Ada (Dickey) Township 509
Adams (Walsh) City 562
Adams (Walsh) Township 562
Adams County 490
Addie (Griggs) Township 519
Addison (Cass) Township 503
Adelaide (Bowman) Township 498
Adler (Nelson) Township 537
Adrian (LaMoure) Township 524
Advance (Pembina) Township 539
Afton (Ward) Township 564
Agnes (Grand Forks) Township 516
Akra (Pembina) Township 539
Alamo (Williams) City 569
Albert (Benson) Township 493
Albertha (Dickey) Township 509
Albion (Dickey) Township 509
Alden (Hettinger) Township 521
Alex (McKenzie) Township 530
Alexander (McKenzie) City 530
Alexander (Pierce) Township 541
Alexander (Stutsman) Township 556
Alexandria (Divide) Township 510
Alger (Mountrail) Township 535
Alice (Cass) City 503
Aliceton (Ransom) Township 544
Alleghany (Ransom) Township 544
Allen (Kidder) Township 522
Allendale (Grand Forks) Township ... 516
Alma (Cavalier) Township 506
Almont (Morton) City 534
Alsen (Cavalier) City 506
Alta (Barnes) Township 491
Ambrose (Divide) City 510
Ambrose (Divide) Township 510
Amenia (Cass) City 503
Amenia (Cass) Township 503
Americus (Grand Forks) Township ... 516
Amidon (Slope) City 552
Amity (Bottineau) Township 496
Amor (Bowman) Township 498
Amundsville (McLean) Township 531
Anamoose (McHenry) City 527
Anamoose (McHenry) Township 527
Anderson (Barnes) Township 491
Andrews (McLean) Township 531
Aneta (Nelson) City 537
Anna (Ward) Township 564
Antelope (Richland) Township 546
Antelope Creek (McKenzie)
 Township 530
Antelope Lake (Pierce) Township ... 541
Antler (Bottineau) City 496
Antler (Bottineau) Township 496
Apple Creek (Burleigh) Township ... 501
Ardoch (Walsh) City 562
Ardoch (Walsh) Township 562
Argusville (Cass) City 503
Armourdale (Towner) Township 559
Arne (Benson) Township 493
Arnegard (McKenzie) City 530
Arnegard (McKenzie) Township 530
Arthur (Cass) City 503
Arthur (Cass) Township 503
Arvilla (Grand Forks) Township 516
Ashby (Hettinger) Township 521

Ashland (Stutsman) Township 556
Ashley (McIntosh) City 529
Ashtabula (Barnes) Township 491
Athens (Williams) Township 569
Atkins (Towner) Township 559
Atwood (Kidder) Township 522
Aurena (McLean) Township 531
Aurora (Benson) Township 493
Austin (Mountrail) Township 535
Avon (Grand Forks) Township 516
Ayr (Cass) City 503
Ayr (Cass) Township 503
Baden (Ward) Township 564
Badger (LaMoure) Township 524
Baer (Hettinger) Township 521
Baker (Kidder) Township 522
Baldwin (Barnes) Township 491
Bale (Ransom) Township 544
Balfour (McHenry) City 527
Balfour (McHenry) Township 527
Ball Hill (Griggs) Township 519
Balta (Pierce) City 541
Balta (Pierce) Township 541
Banner (Cavalier) Township 507
Banner (Mountrail) Township 535
Bantry (McHenry) City 527
Bantry (McHenry) Township 527
Barnes (Cass) Township 503
Barnes County 491
Barney (Richland) City 546
Barney (Richland) Township 546
Barr Butte (Williams) Township 569
Barrie (Richland) Township 547
Bartlett (Ramsey) Township 542
Bartley (Griggs) Township 519
Barton (Pierce) City 541
Bathgate (Pembina) City 539
Bathgate (Pembina) Township 539
Battleview (Burke) Township 499
Beach (Golden Valley) City 515
Beach (Golden Valley) Township ... 515
Bear Creek (Dickey) Township 509
Beaulieu (Pembina) Township 539
Beaver (Benson) Township 493
Beaver Creek (Steele) Township 554
Beisigl (Adams) Township 490
Belcourt (Rolette) CDP 548
Belfield (Stark) City 554
Belford (Richland) Township 547
Bell (Cass) Township 504
Belmont (Traill) Township 560
Benedict (McLean) City 531
Benson County 493
Bentinck (Bottineau) Township 496
Bentru (Grand Forks) Township 516
Bergen (McHenry) City 527
Bergen (Nelson) Township 537
Berlin (Cass) Township 504
Berlin (LaMoure) City 524
Berlin (Sheridan) Township 551
Berlin (Wells) Township 567
Berry (Hettinger) Township 521
Berthold (Ward) City 564
Berthold (Ward) Township 564
Berwick (McHenry) Township 527
Bethel (Towner) Township 559
Beulah (Mercer) City 533
Bicker (Mountrail) Township 535
Big Bend (Mountrail) Township 535
Big Bend (Ransom) Township 544

Big Meadow (Williams) Township ... 569
Big Stone (Williams) Township 569
Billings (Cavalier) Township 507
Billings County 495
Bilodeau (Wells) Township 567
Binford (Griggs) City 520
Bingham (Traill) Township 560
Binghampton (Barnes) Township ... 491
Birtsell (Foster) Township 514
Bisbee (Towner) City 559
Bismarck (Burleigh) City 501
Bismarck (Burleigh) Pop. Place 501
Bjornson (McHenry) Township 527
Black Butte (Hettinger) Township ... 521
Black Loam (LaMoure) Township ... 524
Blacktail (Williams) Township 569
Blackwater (McLean) Township 531
Blaine (Bottineau) Township 496
Blanchard (Traill) Township 560
Bloom (Stutsman) Township 556
Bloomenfield (Stutsman) Township ... 556
Bloomfield (Traill) Township 560
Blooming (Grand Forks) Township ... 516
Blooming Prairie (Divide) Township ... 510
Blooming Valley (Divide) Township ... 511
Bluebird (LaMoure) Township 524
Blue Butte (McKenzie) Township ... 530
Blue Hill (McLean) Township 531
Blue Ridge (Williams) Township ... 569
Bohnsack (Traill) Township 560
Bonetraill (Williams) Township 569
Boone (Sheridan) Township 551
Border (Divide) Township 511
Bordulac (Foster) Township 514
Bottineau (Bottineau) City 496
Bottineau County 496
Bowbells (Burke) City 499
Bowbells (Burke) Township 500
Bowdon (Wells) City 567
Bowen (Sargent) Township 549
Bowman (Bowman) City 498
Bowman (Bowman) Township 498
Bowman County 498
Boyd (Burleigh) Township 501
Boyesen (Bowman) Township 498
Braddock (Emmons) City 513
Brampton (Sargent) Township 549
Brandenburg (Richland) Township ... 547
Brander (Bottineau) Township 496
Brandon (Renville) Township 545
Bremen (Wells) Township 567
Brenna (Grand Forks) Township 516
Briarwood (Cass) City 504
Brightwood (Richland) Township ... 547
Brillian (Ward) Township 564
Brimer (Barnes) Township 491
Brinsmade (Benson) City 493
Brittian (Hettinger) Township 521
Broadlawn (Steele) Township 554
Broadview (Griggs) Township 520
Brocket (Ramsey) City 542
Broe (Benson) Township 493
Brookbank (Mountrail) Township ... 535
Brooklyn (Williams) Township 569
Brown (McHenry) Township 527
Bruce (Cavalier) Township 507
Bryan (Griggs) Township 520
Bryant (Logan) Township 526
Bucephalia (Foster) Township 514
Buchanan (Stutsman) City 556

Buchanan (Stutsman) Township........556
Buchanan Valley (Emmons)
   Township...........................513
Buckeye (Kidder) Township..............522
Bucklin (Slope) Township...............552
Bucyrus (Adams) City...................490
Bucyrus (Adams) Township...............490
Buena Vista (Bowman) Township.........498
Buffalo (Cass) City....................504
Buffalo (Cass) Township................504
Buford (Williams) Township.............569
Bull Butte (Williams) Township.........569
Bullion (Golden Valley) Township.....515
Bull Moose (Wells) Township............567
Bunker (Kidder) Township...............522
Burg (Divide) Township.................511
Burke (Mountrail) Township.............535
Burke County...........................499
Burleigh County........................501
Burlington (Ward) City.................564
Burlington (Ward) Township.............564
Burt (Ward) Township...................564
Bush (Eddy) Township...................512
Butte (McLean) City....................531
Butte (McLean) Township................531
Butte Valley (Benson) Township.......493
Buxton (Traill) City...................560
Buxton (Traill) Township...............560
Byersville (McLean) Township...........531
Byron (Cavalier) Township..............507
Caledonia (Traill) Township............560
Calio (Cavalier) City..................507
Callahan (Renville) Township...........545
Calvin (Cavalier) City.................507
Cameron (Ward) Township................564
Campbell (Emmons) Township.............513
Campbell (Hettinger) Township..........521
Cando (Towner) City....................559
Cando (Towner) Township................559
Canfield (Burleigh) Township...........501
Cannon Ball (Hettinger) Township.....521
Cannon Ball (Sioux) CDP................552
Canton City (Pembina) City.............539
Captain's Landing (Morton)
   Township...........................534
Carbondale (Ward) Township.............564
Carlisle (Pembina) Township............539
Carpenter (Steele) Township............554
Carpio (Ward) City.....................564
Carpio (Ward) Township.................564
Carrington (Foster) City...............514
Carrington (Foster) Township...........515
Carroll (Slope) Township...............553
Carson (Grant) City....................518
Carter (Burke) Township................500
Casey (Ransom) Township................544
Cash (Slope) Township..................553
Cass County............................503
Casselton (Cass) City..................504
Casselton (Cass) Township..............504
Castle Rock (Hettinger) Township.....521
Cathay (Wells) City....................567
Cathay (Wells) Township................567
Cato (Ramsey) Township.................542
Cavalier (Pembina) City................539
Cavalier (Pembina) Township............539
Cavalier County........................506
Cayuga (Sargent) City..................550
Cecil (Bottineau) Township.............496
Cedar (Adams) Township.................490
Cedar Creek (Slope) Township...........553
Center (Oliver) City...................539
Center (Richland) Township.............547
Central (Nelson) Township..............537
Central Adams (Adams) Pop. Place..490

Central Grant (Grant) Pop. Place.....518
Central McKenzie (McKenzie) Pop.
   Place..............................530
Central Pierce (Pierce) Pop. Place....541
Central Sheridan (Sheridan) Pop.
   Place..............................551
Chain Lakes (Ramsey) Township.......542
Chalky Butte (Slope) Pop. Place.....553
Champion (Williams) Township........569
Chandler (Adams) Township.............490
Charbon (McKenzie) Township.........530
Chase Lake (Stutsman) Pop. Place...556
Chaseley (Wells) Township.............567
Chatfield (Bottineau) Township........496
Cherry Lake (Eddy) Township...........512
Chester (Grand Forks) Township......517
Chestina (Kidder) Township............522
Chicago (Stutsman) Township...........556
Chilton (Hettinger) Township..........521
Christiania (Burleigh) Township.......501
Christine (Richland) City.............547
Churchs Ferry (Ramsey) City...........542
Clara (Nelson) Township...............537
Clark (Hettinger) Township............521
Clay (Renville) Township..............545
Clayton (Burke) Township..............500
Clearfield (Griggs) Township..........520
Clear Lake (Burleigh) Township........501
Clear Lake (Kidder) Township..........522
Clearwater (Mountrail) Township.....535
Cleary (Burke) Township...............500
Clement (Dickey) Township.............509
Clermont (Adams) Township.............490
Cleveland (Stutsman) City.............556
Cleveland (Walsh) Township............562
Clifford (Traill) City................561
Clifton (Cass) Township...............504
Climax (Williams) Township............569
Clinton (Divide) Township.............511
Coalfield (Divide) Township...........511
Coburn (Ransom) Township..............544
Cogswell (Sargent) City...............550
Colehabor (McLean) City...............531
Colfax (Richland) City................547
Colfax (Richland) Township............547
Colgate (Steele) Township.............554
Colquhoun (Renville) Township.......545
Columbia (Eddy) Township..............512
Columbus (Burke) City.................500
Colville (Burke) Township.............500
Colvin (Eddy) Township................512
Conklin (Stutsman) Township...........556
Connor (Slope) Township...............553
Conway (Walsh) City...................562
Coolin (Towner) Township..............559
Cooperstown (Griggs) City.............520
Cooperstown (Griggs) Township.......520
Cordelia (Bottineau) Township........496
Corinne (Stutsman) Township...........556
Cornell (Cass) Township...............504
Corwin (Stutsman) Township............556
Cottonwood (Mountrail) Township ..535
Cottonwood Lake (McHenry)
   Township...........................527
Coulee (Ramsey) Township..............542
Courtenay (Stutsman) City.............556
Courtenay (Stutsman) Township........556
Cow Creek (Williams) Township......569
Crane Creek (Mountrail) Township..535
Crary (Ramsey) City...................542
Crawford (Slope) Township.............553
Creel (Ramsey) Township...............542
Cremerville (McLean) Township........532
Crocus (Towner) Township..............559
Crofte (Burleigh) Township............501

Cromwell (Burleigh) Township 501
Crosby (Divide) City..................511
Crowfoot (Mountrail) Township......535
Crown Hill (Kidder) Township..........522
Crystal (Pembina) City................539
Crystal (Pembina) Township............539
Crystal Lake (Wells) Township.........567
Crystal Springs (Kidder) Township...523
Cuba (Barnes) Township................491
Currie (Rolette) Township.............548
Cusator (Stutsman) Township...........556
Cut Bank (Bottineau) Township........496
Cypress (Cavalier) Township...........507
Dahlen (Nelson) Township..............537
Dale (Burke) Township.................500
Dalen (Bottineau) Township............496
Danbury (Emmons) Township.............513
Daneville (Divide) Township...........511
Danton (Richland) Township............547
Darling Springs (Adams) Township..490
Dash (Towner) Township................559
Davenport (Cass) City.................504
Davenport (Cass) Township.............504
Dawson (Kidder) City..................523
Dayton (Nelson) Township..............537
Dazey (Barnes) City...................491
Dazey (Barnes) Township...............491
Dean (LaMoure) Township...............524
Debing (Mountrail) Township...........535
Deep Creek (Slope) Pop. Place.........553
Deep River (McHenry) Township......527
Deepwater (McLean) Township..........532
Deering (McHenry) City................527
Deering (McHenry) Township............527
Deer Lake (Stutsman) Township........556
De Groat (Ramsey) Township 542
Delger (Wells) Township...............567
Delhi (Golden Valley) Township.......515
Denbigh (McHenry) Township............527
Denhoff (Sheridan) Township...........551
Denmark (Ward) Township...............564
Denver (Sargent) Township.............550
Des Lacs (Ward) City..................564
Des Lacs (Ward) Township..............564
Devillo (Richland) Township...........547
Devils Lake (Ramsey) City.............542
Dewey (Walsh) Township................562
De Witt (Divide) Township.............511
Dexter (Richland) Township............547
Dickey (LaMoure) City.................524
Dickey County..........................509
Dickinson (Stark) City................554
Dickinson North (Stark) Pop. Place..554
Dickinson South (Stark) Pop. Place..554
Dimond (Burke) Township...............500
Divide (Dickey) Township..............509
Divide County..........................510
Dixon (Logan) Township................526
Dodds (Nelson) Township...............537
Dodge (Dunn) City.....................512
Dogden (McLean) Township..............532
Donnybrook (Ward) City................564
Douglas (McLean) Township.............532
Douglas (Ward) City...................564
Dover (Griggs) Township...............520
Dovre (Slope) Township................553
Dows (Cass) Township..................504
Drake (McHenry) City..................527
Drayton (Pembina) City................540
Drayton (Pembina) Township............540
Dresden (Cavalier) Township...........507
Driscoll (Burleigh) Township..........501
Dry Fork (Williams) Township..........569
Dry Lake (Ramsey) Township............542
Dublin (Williams) Township............569

NORTH DAKOTA

Duck Creek (Adams) Township *490*
Duerr (Richland) Township *547*
Dunbar (Sargent) Township *550*
Dundee (Walsh) Township *562*
Dunn Center (Dunn) City *512*
Dunn County *512*
Dunseith (Rolette) City *549*
Durbin (Cass) Township *504*
Durham (Stutsman) Township *556*
Dwight (Richland) City *547*
Dwight (Richland) Township *547*
Eagle (Richland) Township *547*
Easby (Cavalier) Township *507*
East Adams (Adams) Pop. Place *490*
East Alma (Cavalier) Township *507*
East Burleigh (Burleigh) Pop. Place .. *501*
East Dunseith (Rolette) CDP *549*
East Fork (Benson) Township *493*
East Fork (Williams) Township *569*
East Golden Valley (Golden Valley) Pop. Place *516*
East Grant (Grant) Pop. Place *518*
East Logan (Logan) Pop. Place *526*
Eastman (Foster) Township *515*
East McHenry (McHenry) Pop. Place *527*
East McIntosh (McIntosh) Pop. Place *529*
East McKenzie (McKenzie) Pop. Place *530*
East McLean (McLean) Pop. Place ... *532*
East Mercer (Mercer) Pop. Place *533*
East Morton (Morton) Pop. Place *534*
East Oliver (Oliver) Pop. Place *539*
Easton (Steele) Township *554*
East Rolette (Rolette) Pop. Place *549*
East Stark (Stark) Pop. Place *554*
Eckelson (Barnes) Township *491*
Ecklund (Burleigh) Township *501*
Economy (McLean) Township *532*
Eddy (Eddy) Township *513*
Eddy County *512*
Eden (Walsh) Township *562*
Edendale (Steele) Township *554*
Eden Valley (Renville) Township *545*
Edgeley (LaMoure) City *524*
Edgemont (Sheridan) Township *551*
Edinburg (Walsh) City *562*
Edmore (Ramsey) City *542*
Edmunds (Stutsman) Township *556*
Edna (Barnes) Township *491*
Egan (Mountrail) Township *535*
Egeland (Towner) City *559*
Egg Creek (McHenry) Township *527*
Eidsvold (Bottineau) Township *496*
Elden (Dickey) Township *509*
Eldon (Benson) Township *494*
Eldorado (Traill) Township *561*
Eldred (Cass) Township *504*
Eldridge (Stutsman) Township *556*
Elgin (Cavalier) Township *507*
Elgin (Grant) City *519*
Elk (McKenzie) Township *530*
Elk Creek (Golden Valley) Township *516*
Elkhorn (Divide) Township *511*
Elkmount (Grand Forks) Township .. *517*
Ellendale (Dickey) City *509*
Ellendale (Dickey) Township *509*
Elling (Pierce) Township *541*
Elliott (Ransom) City *544*
Elliott (Ransom) Township *544*
Ellisville (Williams) Township *569*
Ellsbury (Barnes) Township *491*
Elm (Dickey) Township *509*
Elm (Grant) Township *519*

Elma (Richland) Township *547*
Elmdale (Ward) Township *564*
Elm Grove (Grand Forks) Township *517*
Elm River (Traill) Township *561*
Elms (Bottineau) Township *496*
Elm Tree (McKenzie) Township *530*
Elmwood (Golden Valley) Township *516*
Elora (Pembina) Township *540*
Elverum (Pierce) Township *541*
Elysian (Bottineau) Township *496*
Emerado (Grand Forks) City *517*
Emmons County *513*
Empire (Cass) Township *504*
Enderlin (Cass) City *504*
Enderlin (Ransom) City *544*
Engelter (Morton) Township *534*
Enger (Steele) Township *555*
Ensign (Renville) Township *545*
Enterprise (Nelson) Township *537*
Epping (Williams) City *569*
Equality (Williams) Township *569*
Erie (Cass) Township *504*
Ervin (Traill) Township *561*
E-Six (Slope) Pop. Place *553*
Esmond (Benson) City *494*
Esmond (Benson) Township *494*
Estabrook (Foster) Township *515*
Estherville (Burleigh) Township *501*
Eureka (Ward) Township *564*
Everest (Cass) Township *504*
Evergreen (Ward) Township *564*
Excelsior (Kidder) Township *523*
Fairbanks (Renville) Township *545*
Fairdale (Walsh) City *562*
Fairfield (Grand Forks) Township *517*
Fairmount (Richland) City *547*
Fairmount (Richland) Township *547*
Fairview (Rolette) Township *549*
Fairview (Sheridan) Township *551*
Fairville (Wells) Township *567*
Falconer (Grand Forks) Township ... *517*
Falsen (McHenry) Township *527*
Fancher (Ramsey) Township *542*
Fargo (Cass) City *504*
Fargo (Cass) Township *504*
Farina (Hettinger) Township *521*
Farmington (Walsh) Township *562*
Farmvale (Williams) Township *569*
Fay (Burke) Township *500*
Felson (Pembina) Township *540*
Ferry (Grand Forks) Township *517*
Fertile (Mountrail) Township *535*
Fertile (Walsh) Township *562*
Fertile Valley (Divide) Township *511*
Fessenden (Wells) City *567*
Field (Nelson) Township *537*
Fillmore (Divide) Township *511*
Fingal (Barnes) City *491*
Finley (Steele) City *555*
Finley (Steele) Township *555*
Finn (Logan) Township *526*
Fischbein (Bowman) Township *498*
Fisher (Grant) Township *519*
Flasher (Morton) City *534*
Flaxton (Burke) City *500*
Flint (Stutsman) Township *556*
Florance (Foster) Township *515*
Florence Lake (Burleigh) Township .. *502*
Foothills (Burke) Township *500*
Forbes (Dickey) City *509*
Forde (Nelson) Township *537*
Fordville (Walsh) City *562*
Forest River (Walsh) City *562*
Forest River (Walsh) Township *562*
Forman (Sargent) City *550*

Forman (Sargent) Township *550*
Forthun (Burke) Township *500*
Fort Ransom (Ransom) City *544*
Fort Ransom (Ransom) Township ... *544*
Fort Totten (Benson) Pop. Place *494*
Fortuna (Divide) City *511*
Fort Yates (Sioux) City *552*
Fort Yates (Sioux) Pop. Place *552*
Forward (Wells) Township *567*
Foster County *514*
Four Bears Village (McKenzie) CDP *530*
Foxholm (Ward) Township *565*
Fram (Wells) Township *567*
Francis (Burleigh) Township *502*
Franklin (Steele) Township *555*
Frazier (Divide) Township *511*
Freda (Grant) Township *519*
Frederick (Divide) Township *511*
Fredonia (Logan) City *526*
Freeborn (Eddy) Township *513*
Freedom (Ward) Township *565*
Freeman (Richland) Township *547*
Fremont (Cavalier) Township *507*
Freshwater (Ramsey) Township *542*
Frettim (Kidder) Township *523*
Fried (Stutsman) Township *556*
Frontier (Cass) City *504*
Fullerton (Dickey) City *509*
Gackle (Logan) City *526*
Galesburg (Traill) City *561*
Galesburg (Traill) Township *561*
Garborg (Richland) Township *547*
Gardar (Pembina) Township *540*
Gardena (Bottineau) City *496*
Gardner (Cass) City *504*
Gardner (Cass) Township *504*
Garfield (Traill) Township *561*
Garner (Golden Valley) Township ... *516*
Garness (Burke) Township *500*
Garnet (Divide) Township *511*
Garrison (McLean) City *532*
Gascoyne (Bowman) City *498*
Gascoyne (Bowman) Township *498*
Gasman (Ward) Township *565*
Gate (McLean) Township *532*
Gates (Eddy) Township *513*
Gem (Bowman) Township *498*
Gerber (Stutsman) Township *556*
German (Dickey) Township *509*
Germania (Stutsman) Township *557*
Germantown (Wells) Township *567*
Gerrard (Towner) Township *559*
Getchell (Barnes) Township *491*
Ghylin (Burleigh) Township *502*
Gibbs (Burleigh) Township *502*
Gilby (Grand Forks) City *517*
Gilby (Grand Forks) Township *517*
Gill (Cass) Township *505*
Gilmore (McHenry) Township *527*
Gilstrap (Adams) Township *490*
Glacier (Stutsman) Township *557*
Gladstone (LaMoure) Township *524*
Gladstone (Stark) City *554*
Glen (LaMoure) Township *524*
Glenburn (Renville) City *545*
Glendale (Logan) Township *526*
Glenfield (Foster) City *515*
Glenfield (Foster) Township *515*
Glenila (Cavalier) Township *507*
Glenmore (LaMoure) Township *524*
Glen Ullin (Morton) City *534*
Glenview (Burleigh) Township *502*
Glenwood (Walsh) Township *562*
Golden (Walsh) Township *562*
Golden Glen (LaMoure) Township .. *524*

American Places Dictionary — NORTH DAKOTA

Golden Lake (Steele) Township 555
Golden Valley (Mercer) City 533
Golden Valley (Williams) Township .569
Golden Valley County 515
Goldfield (Bowman) Township 498
Golva (Golden Valley) City 516
Good Luck (Williams) Township 570
Goodrich (Sheridan) City 551
Goodrich (Sheridan) Township 551
Gooseneck (Divide) Township 511
Gordon (Cavalier) Township 507
Grace (Grand Forks) Township 517
Grace City (Foster) City 515
Graf (Kidder) Township 523
Grafton (Walsh) City 562
Grafton (Walsh) Township 562
Grail (McKenzie) Township 530
Grainbelt (Bowman) Township 498
Grainfield (Towner) Township 559
Grandfield (Eddy) Township 513
Grand Forks (Grand Forks) City 517
Grand Forks (Grand Forks) Township 517
Grand Forks Air Force Base (Grand Forks) Military Facility 517
Grand Forks County 516
Grand Harbor (Ramsey) Township ...542
Grandin (Cass) City 505
Grandin (Traill) City 561
Grand Prairie (Barnes) Township 491
Grand Rapids (LaMoure) Township .525
Grand River (Bowman) Township 498
Grand Valley (Dickey) Township 509
Grandview (LaMoure) Township 525
Grano (Renville) City 545
Grant (Richland) Township 547
Grant County 518
Granville (McHenry) City 527
Granville (McHenry) Township 528
Grass Lake (Burleigh) Township 502
Grassland (Renville) Township 545
Gray (Stutsman) Township 557
Great Bend (Richland) City 547
Greatstone (McLean) Township 532
Greely (Ward) Township 565
Green (Barnes) Township 491
Greenbush (Ward) Township 565
Greendale (Richland) Township 547
Greene (Ransom) Township 544
Greenfield (Griggs) Township 520
Greenfield (Traill) Township 561
Greenland (Barnes) Township 492
Greenview (Steele) Township 555
Greenville (LaMoure) Township 525
Grenora (Williams) City 570
Grenora (Williams) Township 570
Grey (Cavalier) Township 507
Griffin (Stutsman) Township 557
Griggs County 519
Grilley (McHenry) Township 528
Grover (Renville) Township 545
Gunkel (Cass) Township 505
Gutschmidt (Logan) Township 526
Gwinner (Sargent) City 550
Haag (Logan) Township 526
Haaland (Wells) Township 567
Hagel (Pierce) Township 541
Hague (Emmons) City 514
Haley (Bowman) Township 499
Hall (Sargent) Township 550
Halliday (Dunn) City 512
Halliday (Dunn) Pop. Place 512
Hamberg (Wells) City 567
Hamburg (Dickey) Township 509
Hamburg (Wells) Township 567

Hamerly (Renville) Township 545
Hamilton (Pembina) City 540
Hamilton (Pembina) Township 540
Hamlet (Renville) Township 545
Hamlin (Nelson) Township 538
Hammer (Ramsey) Township 542
Hampden (Ramsey) City 542
Hankinson (Richland) City 547
Hanks (Williams) City 570
Hannaford (Griggs) City 520
Hannah (Cavalier) City 507
Hansboro (Towner) City 559
Hanson (Ransom) Township 544
Haram (Bottineau) Township 496
Harding (Emmons) Township 514
Harding (Ramsey) Township 542
Hardscrabble (Williams) Township ...570
Harlem (Sargent) Township 550
Harmonious (Burke) Township 500
Harmony (Cass) Township 505
Harper (Slope) Township 553
Harriet (Burleigh) Township 502
Harrison (Ward) Township 565
Harriston (Walsh) Township 562
Hart (Bowman) Pop. Place 499
Harvey (Cavalier) Township 507
Harvey (Wells) City 567
Harwood (Cass) City 505
Harwood (Cass) Township 505
Hastings (Bottineau) Township 496
Hatton (Traill) City 561
Havana (Sargent) City 550
Havelock (Hettinger) Township 521
Haven (Foster) Township 515
Hawkeye (Divide) Township 511
Hawkeye (McKenzie) Township 530
Hawksnest (Wells) Township 567
Hay (Cavalier) Township 507
Hay Creek (Burleigh) Township 502
Hayland (Divide) Township 511
Haynes (Adams) City 490
Haynes (Kidder) Township 523
Hazel (Williams) Township 570
Hazel Grove (Burleigh) Township 502
Hazelton (Emmons) City 514
Hazelton (Emmons) Township 514
Hazen (Mercer) City 533
Hebron (Morton) City 534
Hebron (Williams) Township 570
Hegton (Grand Forks) Township 517
Heimdal (Wells) Township 567
Helena (Griggs) Township 520
Helendale (Richland) Township 547
Hemen (Barnes) Township 492
Henderson (Cavalier) Township 507
Hendrickson (McHenry) Township 528
Henrietta (LaMoure) Township 525
Henry (Golden Valley) Township 516
Herberg (Traill) Township 561
Herman (Sargent) Township 550
Hesper (Benson) Township 494
Hettinger (Adams) City 490
Hettinger (Adams) Township 490
Hettinger County 521
Hidden (Stutsman) Township 557
Hiddenwood (Ward) Township 565
Highland (Cass) Township 505
Highland (Hettinger) Township 521
Highland (Sheridan) Township 551
Highland Center (Ramsey) Township........ 542
Hill (Cass) Township 505
Hillsboro (Traill) City 561
Hillsboro (Traill) Township 561
Hillsdale (Eddy) Township 513

Hillsdale (Wells) Township 567
Hilton (Ward) Township 565
Hobart (Barnes) Township 492
Hofflund (Williams) Township 570
Hoffman (Bottineau) Township 496
Holden (Adams) Township 490
Holmes (Sheridan) Township 551
Homen (Bottineau) Township 496
Homer (Stutsman) Township 557
Homestead (Richland) Township 547
Hoople (Walsh) City 563
Hope (Cavalier) Township 507
Hope (Steele) City 555
Horace (Cass) City 505
Horseshoe Valley (McLean) Township........ 532
Howe (Grant) Township 519
Howell (Towner) Township 559
Howes (Cass) Township 505
Howie (Mountrail) Township 535
Hudson (Dickey) Township 509
Hughes (Slope) Township 553
Hugo (Steele) Township 555
Hume (Slope) Township 553
Hunter (Cass) City 505
Hunter (Cass) Township 505
Hurdsfield (Wells) City 568
Hurley (Renville) Township 545
Huron (Cavalier) Township 507
Ibsen (Richland) Township 547
Idaho (Mountrail) Township 535
Illinois (Nelson) Township 538
Impark (Benson) Township 494
Indian Creek (Hettinger) Township ..521
Inkster (Grand Forks) City 517
Inkster (Grand Forks) Township 517
Iosco (Stutsman) Township 557
Iota Flat (Ward) Township 565
Iowa (Benson) Township 494
Irvine (Benson) Township 494
Isabel (Benson) Township 494
Island Park (Ransom) Township 544
Isley (Ransom) Township 544
Ivanhoe (Renville) Township 546
Jackson (Sargent) Township 550
James Hill (Mountrail) Township 535
James River Valley (Dickey) Township........ 509
Jamestown (Stutsman) City 557
Janke (Logan) Township 526
Jefferson (Pierce) Township 541
Jim River Valley (Stutsman) Township........ 557
Johnson (Wells) Township 568
Johnstown (Grand Forks) Township..517
Joliette (Pembina) Township 540
Jud (LaMoure) City 525
Judson (Williams) Township 570
Kandiyohi (Burke) Township 500
Kane (Bottineau) Township 496
Karlsruhe (McHenry) City 528
Karlsruhe (McHenry) Township 528
Kathryn (Barnes) City 492
Keene (McKenzie) Township 530
Keller (Burke) Township 500
Kelso (Traill) Township 561
Kenmare (Ward) City 565
Kenmare (Ward) Township 565
Kennedy (Hettinger) Township 521
Kennison (LaMoure) Township 525
Kensal (Stutsman) City 557
Kensal (Stutsman) Township 557
Kensington (Walsh) Township 563
Kent (Dickey) Township 509
Kentner (Dickey) Township 509

575

NORTH DAKOTA

Kern (Hettinger) Township *521*
Keystone (Dickey) Township *509*
Kickapoo (Kidder) Township............. *523*
Kickapoo (Mountrail) Township *535*
Kidder County *522*
Kief (McHenry) City *528*
Killdeer (Dunn) City *512*
Killdeer (Dunn) Pop. Place *512*
Kindred (Cass) City *505*
Kingsley (Griggs) Township *520*
Kingston (Sargent) Township *550*
Kinloss (Walsh) Township *563*
Kinyon (Cass) Township *505*
Kirkelie (Ward) Township *565*
Klingstrup (Ramsey) Township........... *542*
Knife River (Mountrail) Township ... *535*
Knox (Benson) City *494*
Knox (Benson) Township *494*
Kohlmeier (Rolette) Township............ *549*
Kottke Valley (McHenry) Township .*528*
Kramer (Bottineau) City *496*
Kulm (LaMoure) City.......................... *525*
Kunze (Hettinger) Township *521*
Ladd (Bowman) Township *499*
Lake (Cass) Township.......................... *505*
Lake George (McHenry) Township ...*528*
Lake Hester (McHenry) Township....*528*
Lake Ibsen (Benson) Township *494*
Lake Town (Barnes) Township........... *492*
Lakeview (Burke) Township *500*
Lakeville (Grand Forks) Township *517*
Lake Washington (Eddy) Township ..*513*
Lake Williams (Kidder) Township....*523*
Lake Williams (McLean) Township ..*532*
Lakota (Nelson) City *538*
Lakota (Nelson) Township *538*
Lallie (Benson) Township *494*
Lallie North (Benson) Pop. Place *494*
La Mars (Richland) Township *548*
La Moure (LaMoure) City................... *525*
La Moure (Pembina) Township *540*
LaMoure County............................... *524*
Lampton (Walsh) Township *563*
Land (McHenry) Township *528*
Landa (Bottineau) City....................... *497*
Langberg (Bowman) Township........... *499*
Langdon (Cavalier) City...................... *507*
Langdon (Cavalier) Township............. *507*
Lankin (Walsh) City *563*
Lansford (Bottineau) City *497*
Lansford (Bottineau) Township.......... *497*
Lansing (Towner) Township *559*
Larimore (Grand Forks) City............. *517*
Larimore (Grand Forks) Township ...*517*
Lark (Grant) Township....................... *519*
Larrabee (Foster) Township................ *515*
Larson (Burke) City............................. *500*
Latona (Walsh) Township *563*
Lawton (Ramsey) City......................... *543*
Lawton (Ramsey) Township................ *543*
Layton (McHenry) Township *528*
Leaf Mountain (Burke) Township..... *500*
Leal (Barnes) City................................ *492*
Lebanon (McHenry) Township *528*
Lee (Nelson) Township........................ *538*
Leeds (Benson) City............................. *494*
Leeds (Benson) Township.................... *494*
Lehr (Logan) City *526*
Lehr (McIntosh) City........................... *529*
Lein (Burleigh) Township *502*
Leipzig (Grant) Township *519*
Leith (Grant) City................................ *519*
Lemmon (Adams) Pop. Place *490*
Lenora (Griggs) Township *520*
Lenton (Stutsman) Township *557*

Leonard (Cass) City............................. *505*
Leonard (Cass) Township.................... *505*
Leonard (Rolette) Township............... *549*
Leval (Nelson) Township..................... *538*
Levant (Grand Forks) Township........ *517*
Lewis (Bottineau) Township *497*
Liberty (Mountrail) Township *535*
Liberty (Ransom) Township................ *544*
Liberty Grove (Richland) Township .*548*
Lidgerwood (Richland) City............... *548*
Lightning Creek (Adams) Township .*490*
Lignite (Burke) City............................. *500*
Lillehoff (Ramsey) Township.............. *543*
Lincoln (Burleigh) City....................... *502*
Lincoln (Emmons) Township.............. *514*
Lincoln (Pembina) Township.............. *540*
Lincoln Dale (Sheridan) Township ...*551*
Lincoln Valley (Divide) Township *511*
Lind (Grand Forks) Township *517*
Lindaas (Traill) Township................... *561*
Lindahl (Williams) Township............. *570*
Linden (Cavalier) Township................ *507*
Linton (Emmons) City *514*
Linton (Ward) Township..................... *565*
Lippert (Stutsman) Township *557*
Lisbon (Ransom) City.......................... *544*
Litchville (Barnes) City *492*
Litchville (LaMoure) Township *525*
Little Deep (McHenry) Township *528*
Loam (Cavalier) Township.................. *507*
Lockwood (Renville) Township.......... *546*
Lodema (Pembina) Township............. *540*
Logan (Burleigh) Township *502*
Logan Center (Grand Forks) Township... *517*
Logan County *526*
Lohnes (Benson) Township................. *494*
Loma (Cavalier) City........................... *507*
Lone Tree (Golden Valley) Township... *516*
Long Creek (Divide) Township.......... *511*
Longfellow (McLean) Township......... *532*
Long Lake (Burleigh) Township......... *502*
Longview (Foster) Township............... *515*
Loquemont (McLean) Township........ *532*
Loraine (Renville) Township............... *546*
Lordsburg (Bottineau) Township........ *497*
Loretta (Grand Forks) Township *517*
Lorraine (Dickey) Township *509*
Lostwood (Mountrail) Township........ *535*
Lovell (Dickey) Township *509*
Lowery (Stutsman) Township............. *557*
Lowland (Mountrail) Township......... *535*
Lucy (Burke) Township *500*
Ludden (Dickey) City.......................... *510*
Lund (Ward) Township *565*
Luverne (Steele) City *555*
Lyman (Burleigh) Pop. Place *502*
Lynn (Wells) Township....................... *568*
Lyon (Stutsman) Township................. *557*
Mabel (Griggs) Township *520*
Maddock (Benson) City...................... *494*
Madison (Hettinger) Township *521*
Maine (Adams) Township *490*
Makoti (Ward) City *565*
Malcolm (McLean) Township............ *532*
Mandan (Morton) City........................ *534*
Mandan (Morton) Pop. Place *534*
Mandan (Ward) Township *565*
Mandaree (McKenzie) CDP................ *530*
Manfred (Wells) Township *568*
Manilla (Cavalier) Township.............. *507*
Manitou (Mountrail) Township *535*
Manning (Dunn) City.......................... *512*
Manning (Kidder) Township.............. *523*

American Places Dictionary

Manns (Stutsman) Township............... *557*
Mansfield (Barnes) Township.............. *492*
Mantador (Richland) City................... *548*
Manvel (Grand Forks) City................. *517*
Maple (Dickey) Township *510*
Maple River (Cass) Township............. *505*
Mapleton (Cass) City........................... *505*
Mapleton (Cass) Township.................. *505*
Marboe (Sargent) Township................ *550*
Margaret (Ward) Township *565*
Marion (Bowman) Township............... *499*
Marion (LaMoure) City....................... *525*
Marmarth (Slope) City *553*
Marsh (Barnes) Township................... *492*
Marshall (Williams) Township *570*
Marston Moor (Stutsman) Township*557*
Martin (Sheridan) City *551*
Martin (Sheridan) Township *551*
Martin (Walsh) Township................... *563*
Maryland (Ward) Township................ *565*
Maryville (Rolette) Township............. *549*
Mauch (Sheridan) Township *551*
Max (McLean) City *532*
Maxbass (Bottineau) City.................... *497*
Mayland (Ward) Township.................. *565*
Mayville (Traill) City........................... *561*
Mayville (Traill) Township.................. *561*
Maza (Towner) City............................. *559*
Maza (Towner) Township.................... *559*
McAlmond (Mountrail) Township *535*
McClellan (Benson) Township *494*
McClusky (Sheridan) City................... *551*
McClusky (Sheridan) Township *551*
McCulley (Emmons) Township........... *514*
McGahan (Mountrail) Township *536*
McGinnis (McLean) Township *532*
McHenry (Foster) City *515*
McHenry (Foster) Township............... *515*
McHenry County................................ *527*
McIntosh County *529*
McKenzie (Burleigh) Township.......... *502*
McKenzie County *530*
McKinley (Ward) Township................ *565*
McKinney (Renville) Township *546*
McKinnon (Foster) Township *515*
McLean County *531*
McVille (Nelson) City.......................... *538*
Meadow (McHenry) Township............ *528*
Meadow Lake (Barnes) Township.....*492*
Medford (Walsh) Township *563*
Medicine Hill (McLean) Township ...*532*
Medina (Stutsman) City *557*
Medora (Billings) City......................... *495*
Mekinock (Grand Forks) Township ..*517*
Melrose (Steele) Township *555*
Melville (Foster) Township.................. *515*
Melvin (Nelson) Township.................. *538*
Menoken (Burleigh) Township *502*
Mentor (Divide) Township.................. *511*
Menz (Sioux) Township....................... *552*
Mercer (McLean) City *532*
Mercer (McLean) Township *532*
Mercer County *533*
Merkel (Kidder) Township................. *523*
Merricourt (Dickey) City.................... *510*
Merrill (Hettinger) Township *521*
Meyer (Pierce) Township.................... *541*
Michigan (Grand Forks) Township ...*518*
Michigan (Nelson) Township.............. *538*
Michigan City (Nelson) City.............. *538*
Midland (Pembina) Township............ *540*
Midway (Stutsman) Township *557*
Mikkelson (LaMoure) Township *525*
Milnor (Sargent) City *550*
Milnor (Sargent) Township................. *550*

Milton (Cavalier) City 507
Minco (Benson) Township.................494
Mineral Springs (Slope) Township 553
Minnehaha (Bowman) Township 499
Minnesota (Burke) Township 500
Minnewaukan (Benson) City.............494
Minnewaukan (Ramsey) Township...543
Minnie (Grant) Township 519
Minnie Lake (Barnes) Township 492
Minot (Ward) City 565
Minot Air Force Base (Ward) Military
  Facility 565
Minto (Cavalier) Township 508
Minto (Walsh) City 563
Mission (Benson) Township 494
Missouri (Burleigh) Township 502
Missouri Ridge (Williams)
  Township... 570
Model (Mountrail) Township............536
Mohall (Renville) City........................546
Monango (Dickey) City 510
Monroe (Towner) Township...............559
Mont (Williams) Township 570
Montpelier (Stutsman) City 557
Montpelier (Stutsman) Township......557
Montrose (Cavalier) Township..........508
Moon Lake (Stutsman) Township 557
Moord (Slope) Township....................553
Moore (Ransom) Township 544
Mooreton (Richland) City 548
Mooreton (Richland) Township 548
Moraine (Grand Forks) Township 518
Moran (Richland) Township 548
Morgan (Traill) Township 561
Morris (Ramsey) Township 543
Morton (Burleigh) Township 502
Morton County.....................................534
Moscow (Cavalier) Township............508
Mott (Hettinger) City 521
Mott (Hettinger) Township................521
Mound (Slope) Township...................553
Mountain (Pembina) City 540
Mount Carmel (Cavalier) Township .508
Mountrail (Mountrail) Township.......536
Mountrail County................................535
Mount Rose (Bottineau) Township ...497
Mount View (Towner) Township 559
Mouse River (McHenry) Township ..528
Munich (Cavalier) City......................508
Munster (Eddy) Township..................513
Muskego (Renville) Township...........546
Mylo (Rolette) City.............................549
Myrtle (Mountrail) Township............536
Nansen (Richland) Township 548
Napoleon (Logan) City 526
Nash (Nelson) Township 538
Naughton (Burleigh) Township 502
Nebo (Bowman) Township................499
Neche (Pembina) City 540
Neche (Pembina) Township...............540
Nedrose (Ward) Township 565
Nekoma (Cavalier) City 508
Nekoma (Cavalier) Township............508
Nelson (Barnes) Township 492
Nelson County.....................................537
Nesheim (Nelson) Township 538
Ness (Pierce) Township 541
Nesson Valley (Williams) Pop. Place 570
Newborg (Bottineau) Township 497
Newbre (Ramsey) Township 543
Newburg (Bottineau) City 497
Newburgh (Steele) Township 555
Newbury (Stutsman) Township.........557
New City (Towner) Township 559
New England (Hettinger) City...........522

New England (Hettinger) Township..522
New Germantown (Sheridan)
  Township... 551
New Home (Williams) Township......570
Newland (Ramsey) Township............543
New Leipzig (Grant) City..................519
Newman (Ward) Township................565
Newport (McHenry) Township 528
New Prairie (Ward) Township 565
New Rockford (Eddy) City 513
New Rockford (Eddy) Township.......513
New Salem (Morton) City 534
New Town (Mountrail) City..............536
Niagara (Grand Forks) City 518
Niagara (Grand Forks) Township 518
Nixon (Ramsey) Township 543
Noble (Cass) Township......................505
Nogosek (Stutsman) Township..........557
Noltimier (Barnes) Township............492
Nome (Barnes) City...........................492
Noonan (Divide) City.........................511
Noonan (Ramsey) Township 543
Nora (LaMoure) Township 525
Norden (LaMoure) Township............525
Nordmore (Foster) Township 515
Norma (Barnes) Township 492
Normal (McHenry) Township 528
Norman (Traill) Township.................561
Normania (Benson) Township 494
Normanna (Cass) Township 505
North Billings (Billings) Pop. Place ..495
North Burke (Burke) Pop. Place 500
North Central McLean (McLean) Pop.
  Place.. 532
Northeast Emmons (Emmons) Pop.
  Place.. 514
Northeast McHenry (McHenry) Pop.
  Place.. 528
North Emmons (Emmons) Pop.
  Place.. 514
Northfield (Ramsey) Township 543
North Golden Valley (Golden Valley)
  Pop. Place 516
Northland (Ransom) Township.........544
North Lemmon (Adams) Township ..490
North Loma (Cavalier) Township.....508
North McKenzie (McKenzie) Pop.
  Place.. 530
North Olga (Cavalier) Township.......508
North Pierce (Pierce) Pop. Place 541
North Prairie (McHenry) Township .528
North River (Cass) City 505
North Rolette (Rolette) Pop. Place ...549
North Sheridan (Sheridan) Pop.
  Place.. 552
North Sioux (Sioux) Pop. Place 552
North Star (Burke) Township............500
North Viking (Benson) Township 494
Northwest (Dickey) Township...........510
Northwest (Kidder) Township...........523
Northwest McIntosh (McIntosh) Pop.
  Place.. 529
Northwest Slope (Slope) Pop. Place..553
Northwest Stutsman (Stutsman) Pop.
  Place.. 557
Northwood (Grand Forks) City.........518
Northwood (Grand Forks) Township518
Norton (Walsh) Township 563
Norway (Traill) Township 561
Norway Lake (Wells) Township 568
Norwich (McHenry) Township.........528
Oak Creek (Bottineau) Township......497
Oakes (Dickey) City..........................510
Oakhill (Barnes) Township 492
Oakland (Mountrail) Township.........536

Oak Valley (Bottineau) Township 497
Oakville (Grand Forks) Township.....518
Oakwood (Walsh) Township..............563
Oberon (Benson) City........................494
Oberon (Benson) Township...............494
Odessa (Hettinger) Township............522
Odessa (Ramsey) Township...............543
Odin (McHenry) Township 528
Oliver (Williams) Township 570
Oliver County 539
Olivia (McHenry) Township 528
Olson (Towner) Township 559
Ontario (Ramsey) Township 543
Ops (Walsh) Township.......................563
Ora (Nelson) Township 538
Orange (Adams) Township................490
Oriska (Barnes) City..........................492
Oriska (Barnes) Township 492
Orlien (Ward) Township....................565
Orthell (Williams) Township.............570
Osago (Nelson) Township..................538
Osborn (Mountrail) Township...........536
Osford (Cavalier) Township 508
Oshkosh (Wells) Township 568
Osloe (Mountrail) Township.............536
Osnabrock (Cavalier) City.................508
Osnabrock (Cavalier) Township........508
Ostby (Bottineau) Township..............497
Otis (McLean) Township...................532
Otter Creek (Grant) Township...........519
Overland (Ramsey) Township 543
Overly (Bottineau) City 497
Ovid (LaMoure) Township 525
Owego (Ransom) Township 544
Oxbow (Cass) City.............................505
Page (Cass) City.................................505
Page (Cass) Township........................506
Painted Woods (Burleigh) Township.502
Palermo (Mountrail) City..................536
Palermo (Mountrail) Township.........536
Palmer (Divide) Township.................511
Paradise (Eddy) Township.................513
Paris (Stutsman) Township 557
Park (Pembina) Township..................540
Park River (Walsh) City 563
Parshall (Mountrail) City 536
Parshall (Mountrail) Township..........536
Passport (Ward) Township.................565
Paulson (Towner) Township 559
Peabody (Bottineau) Township 497
Peace (Kidder) Township 523
Peaceful Valley (Slope) Township 553
Pearl (Golden Valley) Township 516
Pearl Lake (LaMoure) Township 525
Pekin (Nelson) City 538
Pelican (Ramsey) Township 543
Pembina (Pembina) City 540
Pembina (Pembina) Township 540
Pembina County 539
Perry (Cavalier) Township 508
Perth (Towner) City...........................560
Perth (Walsh) Township 563
Petersburg (Nelson) City 538
Petersburg (Nelson) Township..........538
Peterson (Stutsman) Township..........557
Petersville (Kidder) Township...........523
Pettibone (Kidder) City.....................523
Pettibone (Kidder) Township 523
Pherrin (Williams) Township............570
Pickard (Sheridan) Township............552
Pick City (Mercer) City 533
Pickering (Bottineau) Township........497
Picton (Towner) Township 560
Pierce (Barnes) Township..................492
Pierce County 541

NORTH DAKOTA

Pillsbury (Barnes) City 492
Pilot Mound (Griggs) Township 520
Pingree (Stutsman) City 558
Pingree (Stutsman) Township 558
Pipestem Valley (Stutsman)
    Township.......................................558
Pisek (Walsh) City 563
Plain (Renville) Township..................546
Plainview (Stutsman) Township........558
Plaza (Mountrail) City.......................536
Plaza (Mountrail) Township..............536
Pleasant (Cass) Township 506
Pleasant Hill (Kidder) Township 523
Pleasant Lake (Benson) Township 495
Pleasant Prairie (Eddy) Township.....513
Pleasant Valley (Williams) Township 570
Pleasant View (Grand Forks)
    Township.......................................518
Plumer (Divide) Township................511
Plymouth (Grand Forks) Township ..518
Poe (McKenzie) Township 530
Pomona View (LaMoure) Township .525
Pontiac (Cass) Township 506
Pony Gulch (Wells) Township...........568
Poplar (McLean) Pop. Place 532
Portal (Burke) City............................500
Portal (Burke) Township 500
Port Emma (Dickey) Township.........510
Porter (Dickey) Township 510
Portland (Traill) City 561
Potsdam (Dickey) Township 510
Potter (Barnes) Township..................492
Powers (Mountrail) Township...........536
Powers Lake (Burke) City 500
Powers Lake (Mountrail) Township..536
Prairie (LaMoure) Township.............525
Prairie Center (Walsh) Township 563
Prairie Rose (Cass) City 506
Prairie View (Emmons) Township....514
Pratt (McHenry) Township 528
Prescott (Renville) Township.............546
Preston (Ransom) Township..............544
Pretty Rock (Grant) Township..........519
Primrose (Steele) Township...............555
Progress (Wells) Township.................568
Prospect (Ramsey) Township 543
Prosperity (Renville) Township.........546
Pulaski (Walsh) Township 563
Purcell (Mountrail) Township 536
Quinby (Kidder) Township 523
Rainbow (Williams) Township..........570
Rainy Butte (Slope) Township...........553
Raleigh (Grant) Township.................519
Ramsey County...................................542
Randolph (McKenzie) Township 530
Raney (LaMoure) Township..............525
Ransom (Sargent) Township.............550
Ransom County...................................544
Raritan (Barnes) Township................492
Rat Lake (Mountrail) Township 536
Rawson (McKenzie) City 531
Ray (LaMoure) Township 525
Ray (Williams) City...........................570
Raymond (Cass) Township................506
Red Lake (Logan) Township 526
Redmond (Mountrail) Township.......536
Red Wing (McKenzie) Township......531
Ree (Ward) Township........................566
Reed (Cass) Township........................506
Reeder (Adams) City..........................490
Reeder (Adams) Township.................491
Regan (Burleigh) City........................502
Regent (Hettinger) City 522
Reile's Acres (Cass) City....................506
Reno Valley (Pierce) Township 541

Renville (Bottineau) Township..........497
Renville County 545
Rexine (Kidder) Township 523
Reynolds (Grand Forks) City 518
Reynolds (Traill) City........................561
Rhame (Bowman) City......................499
Rhame (Bowman) Township.............499
Rice Lake (Ward) Township..............566
Rich (Cass) Township........................506
Richardton (Stark) City.....................554
Richburg (Bottineau) Township........497
Richland (Burke) Township...............500
Richland Center (Slope) Township ...553
Richland County..................................546
Richmond (Burleigh) Township........502
Rich Valley (Benson) Township 495
Rifle (Hettinger) Township................522
Riga (McHenry) Township 528
Riggin (Benson) Township 495
Riverdale (Dickey) Township............510
Riverdale (McLean) City...................532
Riverside (Steele) Township..............555
Riverview (McKenzie) Township......531
Robinson (Kidder) City......................523
Robinson (Kidder) Township.............523
Rochester (Cass) Township 506
Rock (Benson) Township...................495
Rock (Grant) Township.....................519
Rockford (Renville) Township 546
Rock Hill (Burleigh) Township 502
Rock Island (Williams) Township.....570
Rocklake (Towner) City.....................560
Rock Lake (Towner) Township 560
Rogers (Barnes) City..........................492
Rogers (Barnes) Township.................492
Roland (Bottineau) Township 497
Rolette (Rolette) City 549
Rolette County....................................548
Rolla (Rolette) City 549
Rolling Green (Ward) Township.......566
Rolling Prairie (Foster) Township.....515
Roloff (McIntosh) Township 529
Romness (Griggs) Township..............520
Roosevelt (Renville) Township..........546
Roscoe (LaMoure) Township 525
Rose (Stutsman) Township................558
Rosebud (Barnes) Township..............492
Rosefield (Eddy) Township 513
Roseglen (McLean) Township 532
Rose Hill (Foster) Township..............515
Rose Hill (McHenry) Township........528
Roseland (Burke) Township...............501
Rosemeade (Ransom) Township.......545
Rosemont (McLean) Township 532
Rosendal (Griggs) Township..............520
Rosenfield (Sheridan) Township........552
Roseville (Traill) Township................561
Ross (Mountrail) City........................536
Ross (Mountrail) Township...............536
Round Lake (McHenry) Township ...528
Round Prairie (Williams) Township .570
Round Top (Stutsman) Township 558
Royal (Ramsey) Township.................543
Rubin (Nelson) Township..................538
Rugby (Pierce) City 541
Rugh (Nelson) Township...................538
Rushford (Walsh) Township..............563
Rush Lake (Pierce) Township............541
Rush River (Cass) Township.............506
Rushville (Ward) Township...............566
Rusland (Wells) Township.................568
Ruso (McLean) City..........................532
Russell (Bottineau) City 497
Russell (LaMoure) Township.............525
Russell (Rolette) Township 549

Rutland (Sargent) City.......................550
Rutland (Sargent) Township..............550
Ryan (LaMoure) Township 525
Ryder (Ward) City 566
Ryder (Ward) Township....................566
Rye (Grand Forks) Township............518
Saddle Butte (Golden Valley)
    Township.......................................516
St. Andrews (Walsh) Township 563
St. Anna (Wells) Township................568
St. Croix (Hettinger) Township.........522
St. John (Rolette) City.......................549
St. Joseph (Pembina) Township 540
St. Mary (McLean) Township 532
St. Marys (Ward) Township 566
St. Paul (Stutsman) Township...........558
St. Thomas (Pembina) City...............540
St. Thomas (Pembina) Township......540
Saline (McHenry) Township..............528
Sanborn (Barnes) City 492
Sand Creek (Slope) Township 553
Sandoun (Ransom) Township 545
Saratoga (LaMoure) Township..........525
Sargent (Sargent) Township...............550
Sargent County....................................549
Sarles (Cavalier) City.........................508
Sarles (Towner) City 560
Sarnia (Nelson) Township..................538
Sauk Prairie (Ward) Township..........566
Sauk Valley (Williams) Township 570
Sauter (Walsh) Township...................563
Sawyer (Ward) City 566
Sawyer (Ward) Township..................566
Scandia (Bottineau) Township 497
Schiller (McHenry) Township 528
Schrunk (Burleigh) Township............502
Schultz (Grant) Township 519
Scorio (Williams) Township..............570
Scotia (Bottineau) Township.............497
Scott (Adams) Township 491
Scoville (Ransom) Township.............545
Scranton (Bowman) City...................499
Scranton (Bowman) Township 499
Sealy (Logan) Township 526
Seivert (Cavalier) Township...............508
Selfridge (Sioux) City.........................552
Sentinel (Golden Valley) Township...516
Sentinel Butte (Golden Valley) City ..516
Sergius (Bottineau) Township 497
Severn (Stutsman) Township.............558
Sharlow (Stutsman) Township...........558
Sharon (Steele) City...........................555
Sharon (Steele) Township..................555
Shealey (Ward) Township..................566
Sheets (Slope) Township....................553
Sheldon (Eddy) Township 513
Sheldon (Ransom) City......................545
Shell (Mountrail) Township...............536
Shell Valley (Rolette) CDP................549
Shell Valley (Rolette) Township........549
Shenford (Ransom) Township...........545
Shepherd (Walsh) Township..............563
Sherbrooke (Steele) Township...........555
Sheridan (LaMoure) Township..........525
Sheridan County.................................551
Sherman (Bottineau) Township.........497
Sherwood (Renville) City 546
Sheyenne (Eddy) City........................513
Sheyenne (Richland) Township.........548
Short Creek (Burke) Township 501
Shuman (Sargent) Township 550
Sibley (Barnes) City...........................492
Sibley (Kidder) Township..................523
Sibley Butte (Burleigh) Township 502
Sibley Trail (Barnes) Township 492

Sidney (Towner) Township *560*	Stark County *554*	Tower City (Cass) City *506*
Sidonia (Mountrail) Township *536*	Starkey (Logan) Township *526*	Towner (McHenry) City *529*
Sikes (Mountrail) Township *536*	Starkweather (Ramsey) City *543*	**Towner County** *559*
Silver Lake (Wells) Township *568*	Stavanger (Traill) Township *561*	**Traill County** *560*
Silvesta (Walsh) Township *563*	Stave (Mountrail) Township *537*	Trenton (Williams) Township *571*
Sinclair (Stutsman) Township *558*	Steele (Kidder) City *523*	Trier (Cavalier) Township *508*
Sioux (McKenzie) Township *531*	**Steele County** *554*	Triumph (Ramsey) Township *543*
Sioux County *552*	Steiber (Burleigh) Township *502*	Troy (Divide) Township *511*
Sioux Trail (Divide) Township *511*	Steiner (Hettinger) Township *522*	Truax (Williams) Township *571*
Skandia (Barnes) Township *493*	Sterling (Burleigh) Township *502*	Truman (Pierce) Township *541*
Slope Center (Slope) Township *553*	Stevens (Ramsey) Township *543*	Trygg (Burleigh) Township *503*
Slope County *552*	Stewart (Barnes) Township *493*	Tuller (Ransom) Township *545*
Smith (Towner) Township *560*	Stewart (Kidder) Township *523*	Turtle Lake (McLean) City *533*
Smoky Butte (Divide) Township *511*	Stillwater (Bowman) Township *499*	Turtle Lake (McLean) Township *533*
Snow (McLean) Township *532*	Stirton (Stutsman) Township *558*	Turtle Mountains (Rolette) Pop.
Solen (Sioux) City *552*	Stone Creek (Bottineau) Township ... *497*	Place *549*
Solon (Hettinger) Township *522*	Stoneview (Divide) Township *511*	Turtle River (Grand Forks)
Soo (Burke) Township *501*	Stony Creek (Williams) Township *571*	Township *518*
Sorenson (Towner) Township *560*	Storlie (Cavalier) Township *508*	Tuscarora (Pierce) Township *541*
Sorkness (Mountrail) Township *536*	Strabane (Grand Forks) Township *518*	Tuttle (Kidder) City *524*
Souris (Bottineau) City *497*	Strandahl (Williams) Township *571*	Tuttle (Kidder) Township *524*
South Billings (Billings) Pop. Place .. *495*	Strasburg (Emmons) City *514*	Twelve Mile (Williams) Township *571*
South Cottonwood (Wells) Township *568*	Strassburg (Sheridan) Township *552*	Twin Butte (Divide) Township *512*
South Dresden (Cavalier) Township . *508*	Streeter (Stutsman) City *558*	Twin Hill (Towner) Township *560*
South Dunn (Dunn) Pop. Place *512*	Streeter (Stutsman) Township *558*	Twin Lake (Benson) Township *495*
Southeast McKenzie (McKenzie) Pop.	Strege (McHenry) Township *529*	Twin Tree (Benson) Township *495*
Place *531*	Strehlow (Hettinger) Township *522*	Twin Valley (McKenzie) Township ... *531*
Southeast Williams (Williams) Pop.	Strong (Stutsman) Township *558*	Tyrol (Griggs) Township *520*
Place *570*	**Stutsman County** *556*	Tyrone (Williams) Township *571*
South Emmons (Emmons) Pop.	Sullivan (Ramsey) Township *543*	Underwood (McLean) City *533*
Place *514*	Summit (Richland) Township *548*	Underwood (McLean) Pop. Place *533*
South Fork (Adams) Township *491*	Sundre (Ward) Township *566*	Union (Grand Forks) Township *518*
South Golden Valley (Golden Valley)	Sunny Slope (Bowman) Township *499*	Upham (McHenry) City *529*
Pop. Place *516*	Sunshine (Slope) Township *553*	Upland (Divide) Township *512*
South Heart (Stark) City *554*	Superior (Eddy) Township *513*	Uxbridge (Barnes) Township *493*
South Kidder (Kidder) Pop. Place *523*	Surrey (Ward) City *566*	Vale (Burke) Township *501*
South McLean (McLean) Pop. Place *533*	Surrey (Ward) Township *566*	Valhalla (Wells) Township *568*
South Meadow (Williams) Township *570*	Svea (Barnes) Township *493*	Valley (Barnes) Township *493*
South Minnewaukan (Ramsey)	Sverdrup (Griggs) Township *520*	Valley (Dickey) Township *510*
Township *543*	Swede (LaMoure) Township *525*	Valley (Kidder) Township *524*
South Olga (Cavalier) Township *508*	Sydna (Ransom) Township *545*	Valley City (Barnes) City *493*
South Pierce (Pierce) Pop. Place *541*	Sydney (Stutsman) Township *558*	Valley Spring (Stutsman) Township .. *558*
South Rolette (Rolette) Pop. Place ... *549*	Sykeston (Wells) City *568*	Van Buren (Renville) Township *546*
South Sheridan (Sheridan) Pop.	Sykeston (Wells) Township *568*	Vang (Ward) Township *566*
Place *552*	Tacoma (Bottineau) Township *497*	Van Hook (Mountrail) Township *537*
South Valley (Rolette) Township *549*	Taft (Burleigh) Township *502*	Van Meter (Dickey) Township *510*
South Viking (Benson) Township *495*	Talbot (Bowman) Township *499*	Vanville (Burke) Township *501*
Southwest (Sargent) Township *550*	Tanner (Kidder) Township *523*	Velva (McHenry) City *529*
Southwest McIntosh (McIntosh) Pop.	Tappen (Kidder) City *523*	Velva (McHenry) Township *529*
Place *529*	Tappen (Kidder) Township *523*	Venturia (McIntosh) City *529*
Southwest McKenzie (McKenzie) Pop.	Tatman (Ward) Township *566*	Verner (Sargent) Township *550*
Place *531*	Taylor (Sargent) Township *550*	Vernon (Kidder) Township *524*
Southwest Mountrail (Mountrail) Pop.	Taylor (Stark) City *554*	Vernon (Walsh) Township *563*
Place *537*	Taylor Butte (Adams) Township *491*	Verona (LaMoure) City *525*
Southwest Sioux (Sioux) Pop. Place . *552*	Teddy (Towner) Township *560*	Vesta (Walsh) Township *563*
Speedwell (Wells) Township *568*	Telfer (Burleigh) Township *503*	Victor (Towner) Township *560*
Spencer (Ward) Township *566*	Tell (Emmons) Township *514*	Victoria (McLean) Township *533*
Spiritwood (Stutsman) Township *558*	Tepee Butte (Hettinger) Township *522*	View (Williams) Township *571*
Spiritwood Lake (Stutsman) City *558*	Tewaukon (Sargent) Township *550*	Viking (Richland) Township *548*
Spring Brook (Williams) City *570*	Thelma (Burleigh) Township *503*	Viking (Traill) Township *561*
Springbrook (Williams) Township *571*	Thingvalla (Pembina) Township *540*	Villard (McHenry) Township *529*
Spring Coulee (Mountrail) Township *537*	Thompson (Grand Forks) City *518*	Virginia (Towner) Township *560*
Spring Creek (Barnes) Township *493*	Thordenskjold (Barnes) Township *493*	Vivian (Sargent) Township *550*
Springer (Ransom) Township *545*	Thorson (Burke) Township *501*	Voltaire (McHenry) City *529*
Springfield (Towner) Township *560*	Tiber (Walsh) Township *563*	Voltaire (McHenry) Township *529*
Spring Grove (McHenry) Township .. *529*	Tiffany (Eddy) Township *513*	Wadsworth (Stutsman) Township *558*
Spring Lake (Ward) Township *566*	Tioga (Williams) City *571*	Wagar (McHenry) Township *529*
Springvale (Barnes) Township *493*	Tioga (Williams) Township *571*	Wagendorf (Hettinger) Township *522*
Spring Valley (Dickey) Township *510*	Tolgen (Ward) Township *566*	Wahpeton (Richland) City *548*
Stafford (Renville) Township *546*	Tolley (Renville) City *546*	Walburg (Cass) Township *506*
Stanley (Cass) Township *506*	Tolna (Nelson) City *538*	Walcott (Richland) City *548*
Stanley (Mountrail) City *537*	Torgerson (Pierce) Township *541*	Walcott (Richland) Township *548*
Stanton (Mercer) City *533*	Torning (Ward) Township *566*	Waldo (Richland) Township *548*
Star (Bowman) Township *499*	Tower (Cass) Township *506*	Wales (Cavalier) City *508*
Starbuck (Bottineau) Township *497*	Tower City (Barnes) City *493*	Walhalla (Pembina) City *540*

NORTH DAKOTA

Walhalla (Pembina) Township 540
Walker (Hettinger) Township 522
Wallace (Kidder) Township 524
Walle (Grand Forks) Township 518
Walsh Centre (Walsh) Township 563
Walsh County 562
Walshville (Walsh) Township 563
Walters (Stutsman) Township.............558
Wamduska (Nelson) Township..........538
Wano (LaMoure) Township................525
Ward (Burke) Township 501
Ward County 564
Warren (Cass) Township.....................506
Warwick (Benson) City......................495
Warwick (Benson) Township.............495
Washburn (Griggs) Township.............520
Washburn (McLean) City 533
Washington (Grand Forks)
  Township.. 518
Waterford (Ward) Township...............566
Waterloo (Cavalier) Township...........508
Watford City (McKenzie) City..........531
Watson (Cass) Township 506
Wayne (Bottineau) Township 497
Wayzetta (Mountrail) Township........537
Weber (Sargent) Township..................551
Webster (Ramsey) Township 543
Weimer (Barnes) Township 493
Weiser (Kidder) Township..................524
Weld (Stutsman) Township.................558
Wellington (Bottineau) Township......498
Wells (Wells) Township......................568
Wells County 567
West Antelope (Benson) Township ...495
West Bank (Williams) Township.......571
West Bay (Benson) Township............495
West Bowman (Bowman) Pop. Place499
West Burleigh (Burleigh) Pop. Place.503
Westby (Divide) Township 512
West Emmons (Emmons) Pop. Place514
West End (Richland) Township 548
Western (Wells) Township 568
West Fargo (Cass) City 506

Westfield (Steele) Township 555
Westford (Kidder) Township..............524
West Grant (Grant) Pop. Place 519
Westhope (Bottineau) City 498
West Hope (Cavalier) Township 508
West Logan (Logan) Pop. Place 526
West McLean (McLean) Pop. Place..533
West Mercer (Mercer) Pop. Place 533
West Morton (Morton) Pop. Place....534
West Mountrail (Mountrail) Pop.
  Place.. 537
West Norway (Wells) Township 568
West Oliver (Oliver) Pop. Place........539
West Ontario (Wells) Township........568
West Slope (Slope) Pop. Place...........553
West Stark (Stark) Pop. Place 554
Wheatfield (Grand Forks) Township 518
Wheatland (Cass) Township...............506
Wheaton (Bottineau) Township 498
Wheelock (Williams) City 571
Wheelock (Williams) Township 571
Whetstone (Adams) Township 491
Whitby (Bottineau) Township............498
White (Pierce) Township 541
White Ash (Renville) Township.........546
White Earth (Mountrail) City 537
White Earth (Mountrail) Township ..537
White Lake (Slope) Township 553
White Shield (McLean) CDP 533
Whitestone (Dickey) Township 510
Whitestone Hill (Sargent) Township.551
Whiting (Bowman) Township 499
Whitteron (Bottineau) Township 498
Wilbur (McKenzie) Township...........531
Wild Rose (Burleigh) Township 503
Wildrose (Williams) City...................571
Willey (Sargent) Township 551
Williams (Kidder) Township..............524
Williams (Nelson) Township..............538
Williams County 569
Willis (Ward) Township.....................566
Williston (Williams) City...................571
Williston (Williams) Township 571

Willow (Griggs) Township.................520
Willowbank (LaMoure) Township 526
Willow City (Bottineau) City 498
Willow Creek (McHenry) Township .529
Willow Lake (Steele) Township.........555
Willow Vale (Bottineau) Township ...498
Wilson (Burleigh) Township...............503
Wilton (Burleigh) City......................503
Wilton (McLean) City 533
Wimbledon (Barnes) City..................493
Windsor (Stutsman) Township..........558
Winfield (Stutsman) Township..........558
Wing (Burleigh) City 503
Wing (Burleigh) Township.................503
Winner (Williams) Township 571
Winona (Grant) Township 519
Wise (McLean) Township...................533
Wiser (Cass) Township.......................506
Wishek (McIntosh) City 530
Wold (Traill) Township......................561
Wolf Butte (Adams) Township..........491
Wolford (Pierce) City........................542
Wood (Emmons) Township 514
Woodberry (Slope) Township 553
Woodbury (Stutsman) Township.......558
Wood Lake (Benson) Township 495
Woodlawn (Kidder) Township 524
Woodward (Wells) Township.............568
Woodworth (Stutsman) City..............558
Wright (Dickey) Township 510
Writing Rock (Divide) Township......512
Wyard (Foster) Township 515
Wyndmere (Richland) City 548
Wyndmere (Richland) Township 548
Yellowstone (McKenzie) Township...531
York (Benson) City 495
York (Benson) Township 495
Yorktown (Dickey) Township............510
Young (Dickey) Township 510
Ypsilanti (Stutsman) Township.........558
Zap (Mercer) City 534
Zeeland (McIntosh) City 530
Zion (Towner) Township...................560

Oregon

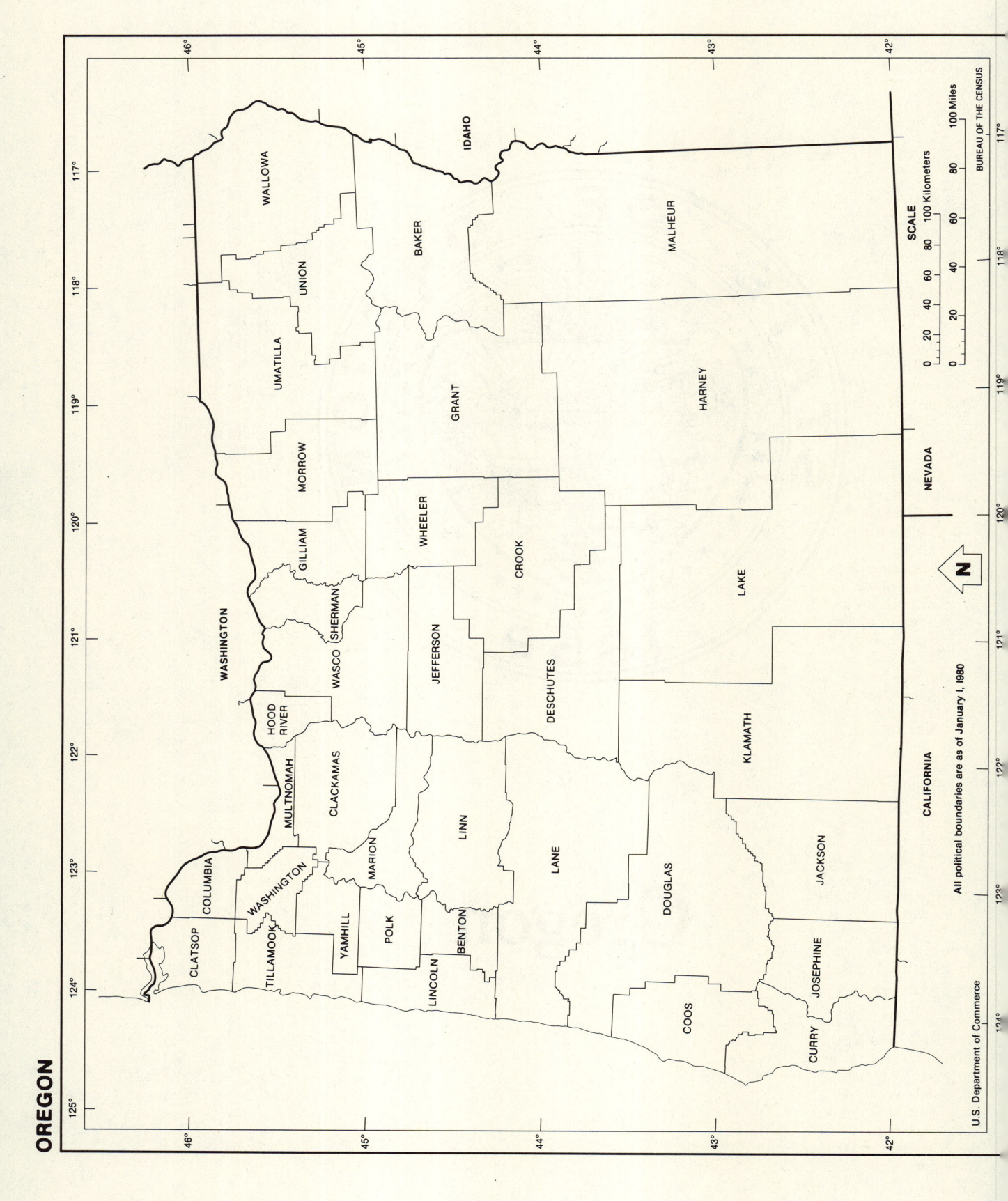

Oregon

Population: 2,842,321 (1990); 2,633,105 (1980)
Population rank (1990): 29
Percent population change (1980–1990): 7.9
Population projection: 2,960,000 (1995); 3,086,000 (2000)

Area: total: 98,386 sq. mi.; 96,003 sq. mi. land, 2,383 sq. mi. water
Area rank: 9
Highest elevation: 11,239 ft., Mount Hood (Clackamas County)
Lowest point: sea level along the Pacific coast

State capital: Salem (Marion and Polk Counties)
Largest city: Portland (437,319)
Second largest city: Eugene (112,669)
Largest county: Multnomah (583,887)

Total housing units: 1,193,567
No. of occupied housing units: 1,103,313
Vacant housing units (%): 7.6
Distribution of population by race and Hispanic origin (%):
  White: 92.8
  Black: 1.6
  Hispanic (any race): 4.0
  Native American: 1.4
  Asian/Pacific: 2.4
  Other: 1.8

Admission date: February 14, 1859 (33rd state).

Location: In the northwestern United States on the Pacific Ocean, bordering California, Washington, Idaho, and Nevada.

Name Origin: From a former name of the Columbia River; its first use with the present spelling recorded by Jonathan Carver in *Travels through the Interior Parts of North America* (1778). The exact origin of the name is in dispute.

State animal: beaver *(Castor canadensis)*
State bird: western meadowlark *(Sturnella neglecta)*
State colors: navy blue and gold
State dance: square dance
State fish: chinook salmon *(Oncorhynchus tshawytscha)*
State flower: Oregon grape *(Berberis aquifolium)*
State gemstone: Oregon sunstone
State insect: swallowtail butterfly *(Papilio oregonius)*
State nut: hazelnut *(Corylus avellana)*
State rock: thunderegg (geode)
State song: "Oregon, My Oregon"
State tree: Douglas fir *(Pseudotsuga menziesii)*

State motto: The Union
State nicknames: Beaver State, Pacific Wonderland

Area code: 503
Time zone: Pacific
Abbreviations: OR (postal); Ore. or Oreg. (traditional)
Part of (region): Pacific Coast

Local Government

Counties

Oregon has 36 counties, of which only 7 have taken advantage of the home rule granted by a 1958 amendment to the state's constitution. Most of the counties are governed by a board of commissioners.

Municipalities

Oregon has 241 incorporated cities and towns.

Settlement History and Early Development

The earliest inhabitants of the area that became Oregon were immigrants from Asia who crossed the land bridge into North America more than 10,000 years ago. Later Indian tribes were the descendants of these people and included the Chinook, Clackama, Kalapuya, Multnomah, Tillamook, Bannock, Cayuse, Paiute, Umatilla, Klamath, and Nez Perce. Both English and Spanish explorers sailed into the waters of the Pacific Northwest during the 1500s, including Sir Francis Drake, who is believed to have sighted the coast of Oregon in 1578.

Despite occasional sightings of the coast over the next two centuries, serious exploration did not occur until 1778, when James Cook sailed into the area, as did George Vancouver and Peter Puget in 1792–94, leading England to claim the territory. Spanish explorers encountered Vancouver's expedition; Vancouver in turn encountered an expedition led by an American, Robert Gray, who reached the mouth of the Columbia River in 1792. In 1805, Lewis and Clark reached the Columbia River by land and followed it to the Pacific. The explorations of Gray and of Lewis and Clark (1804–06) became the basis of American claims to the area.

During the early 1800s both British-Canadian and American fur traders established posts in the area, including Astoria, founded by John Jacob Astor. Great Britain and the U.S. signed a treaty in 1818 that permitted both to trade in the area. Missionaries soon followed the fur traders into the region. In 1834 Jason Lee, a Methodist missionary, established a mission in the Willamette Valley near present-day Salem.

Wagon trains started to arrive by way of the Oregon Trail during the 1840s. This route, used by thousands moving

West from the 1840s to the 1870s, began in Missouri and proceeded to the Columbia River country; the Columbia was then called the Oregon. Settlers agreed in 1843 (just before the arrival of nearly 1,000 settlers in the Willamette Valley) to form a provisional government, which remained in power until Oregon became a territory in 1848. As more and more Americans settled in the area, the northern boundary question continued to be disputed between Great Britain and the U.S. until the U.S.-Canadian boundary was set by treaty at the 49th parallel in 1846.

Indian Wars

During the late 1840s and the 1850s, settlers fought the Indians in a series of wars that included the Cayuse War of 1847–48, the Rogue River Indian War (which ended in 1856), the Modoc War (1872–73), and the Nez Perce War (1877). A band of Nez Perce Indians led by Chief Joseph attempted to flee to Canada but were forced to surrender to U.S. troops about 40 miles south of the Canadian border. Most of the Indians were placed on reservations.

Statehood

Oregon became a territory in 1848 and received its present boundaries in 1853 when Washington Territory was formed. Throughout the 1850s the Donation Land Law (1850) provided land to settlers who would stay and farm it. Oregon became the 33rd state on February 14, 1859, with Salem as the state capital. After the Civil War, despite continued problems with Indian attacks, settlement in Oregon increased rapidly, especially after the arrival of the railroads in the 1880s. The discovery of gold in the 1860s also brought more people to the state.

During the Great Depression of the 1930s federal funds built the Bonneville Dam on the Columbia River and provided electric power and improved navigation. The state's economy improved during World War II as the state became a center of shipbuilding and shipping of supplies to the Pacific forces.

After the war the construction of the McNary and The Dalles dams on the Columbia River, as well as the supply of natural gas through pipelines, contributed to Oregon's supply of cheap power and brought such industries as electrical and electronic manufacturing to the state. The timber industry expanded but also faced the need to replant the trees that had been cut over the years. Other important industries in Oregon include aluminum and nursery products, fruit, wine, and tourism.

State Boundaries

The territory of Oregon organized by Congress in 1848 included present-day Oregon, Washington, Idaho, and parts of Montana and Wyoming. The territory north of the Columbia River was organized as Washington in 1853. When Oregon was admitted as a state in 1859 its boundaries were as they are at present.

Oregon Counties

Baker	Deschutes	Jefferson	Malheur	Umatilla
Benton	Douglas	Josephine	Marion	Union
Clackamas	Gilliam	Klamath	Morrow	Wallowa
Clatsop	Grant	Lake	Multnomah	Wasco
Columbia	Harney	Lane	Polk	Washington
Coos	Hood River	Lincoln	Sherman	Wheeler
Crook	Jackson	Linn	Tillamook	Yamhill
Curry				

Multi-County Places

The following Oregon places are in more than one county. Given here is the total population for each multi-county place, and the names of the counties it is in.

Albany, pop. 29,462; Linn (29,441), Benton (21)
Gates, pop. 499; Marion (458), Linn (41)
Greenhorn, pop. 0; Baker (0), Grant (0)
Idanha, pop. 289; Marion (177), Linn (112)
Lake Oswego, pop. 30,576; Clackamas (28,317), Multnomah (2,253), Washington (6)
Mill City, pop. 1,555; Linn (1,247), Marion (308)
Milwaukie, pop. 18,692; Clackamas (18,692), Multnomah (0)
Portland, pop. 437,319; Multnomah (435,415), Washington (1,197), Clackamas (707)
Rivergrove, pop. 294; Clackamas (267), Washington (27)
Salem, pop. 107,786; Marion (94,983), Polk (12,803)
Tualatin, pop. 15,013; Washington (13,257), Clackamas (1,756)
Willamina, pop. 1,717; Yamhill (1,194), Polk (523)
Wilsonville, pop. 7,106; Clackamas (7,096), Washington (10)

Baker County
County Seat: Baker (ZIP: 97814)

Pop: 15,317 (1990); 16,134 (1980)
Land: 3068.3 sq. mi.; **Water:** 20.3 sq. mi.
Pop Density: 5.0
Area Code: 503
On the northeastern border of OR; organized Sep 22, 1862 from Wasco County.
Name origin: For Col. Edward Dickinson Baker (1811–61), officer in the Civil War, U.S. representative from IL (1845–47; 1849–51), and U.S. senator from OR (1860–61).

Baker — City
ZIP: 97814 **Lat:** 44-46-27 N **Long:** 117-49-53 W
Pop: 9,140 (1990); 9,471 (1980) **Pop Density:** 1344.1
Land: 6.8 sq. mi.; **Water:** 0.0 sq. mi. **Elev:** 3443 ft.
Incorporated 1874.
Name origin: For Edward Dickinson Baker, U.S. senator from OR and Civil War hero.

Greenhorn — City
Lat: 44-42-31 N **Long:** 118-29-44 W
Pop: 0 (1990)
Land: 0.1 sq. mi.; **Water:** 0.0 sq. mi.
Incorporated 1912. Inactive incorporated place. Part of the town is also in Grant County.
Name origin: For the many amateur miners who came to the area in the 1860s gold rush.

Haines — City
ZIP: 97833 **Lat:** 44-54-42 N **Long:** 117-56-20 W
Pop: 405 (1990); 341 (1980) **Pop Density:** 506.3
Land: 0.8 sq. mi.; **Water:** 0.0 sq. mi. **Elev:** 3333 ft.
Founded 1884; incorporated 1909.
Name origin: For its original landowner, "Judge" I.D. Haines.

Halfway — Town
ZIP: 97834 **Lat:** 44-52-36 N **Long:** 117-06-32 W
Pop: 311 (1990); 380 (1980) **Pop Density:** 1036.7
Land: 0.3 sq. mi.; **Water:** 0.0 sq. mi. **Elev:** 2663 ft.
Founded 1887; incorporated 1909.
Name origin: For its location between Pine and Cornucopia.

Huntington — City
ZIP: 97907 **Lat:** 44-21-01 N **Long:** 117-15-57 W
Pop: 522 (1990); 539 (1980) **Pop Density:** 745.7
Land: 0.7 sq. mi.; **Water:** 0.0 sq. mi. **Elev:** 2108 ft.
Incorporated 1891.
Name origin: For the Huntington brothers, who settled here in 1882.

Richland — Town
ZIP: 97870 **Lat:** 44-46-03 N **Long:** 117-10-03 W
Pop: 161 (1990); 181 (1980) **Pop Density:** 1610.0
Land: 0.1 sq. mi.; **Water:** 0.0 sq. mi.
Incorporated 1917.
Name origin: For its descriptive connotations.

Sumpter — City
ZIP: 97877 **Lat:** 44-44-37 N **Long:** 118-11-45 W
Pop: 119 (1990); 133 (1980) **Pop Density:** 54.1
Land: 2.2 sq. mi.; **Water:** 0.0 sq. mi.
Incorporated 1901.

Unity — City
ZIP: 97884 **Lat:** 44-26-12 N **Long:** 118-11-14 W
Pop: 87 (1990); 115 (1980) **Pop Density:** 870.0
Land: 0.1 sq. mi.; **Water:** 0.0 sq. mi.
Incorporated 1972.
Name origin: For the "unity" meeting held to determine its post office's new location.

Benton County
County Seat: Corvallis (ZIP: 97330)

Pop: 70,811 (1990); 68,211 (1980)
Land: 676.5 sq. mi.; **Water:** 2.5 sq. mi.
Pop Density: 104.7
Area Code: 503
In west-central OR, north of Eugene; original county; organized Dec 23, 1847 (prior to statehood).
Name origin: For Thomas Hart Benton (1782–1858), U.S. journalist and statesman; nicknamed "Old Bullion" for championing the use of gold and silver currency rather than paper money.

Adair Village — City
Lat: 44-40-27 N **Long:** 123-13-03 W
Pop: 554 (1990); 589 (1980) **Pop Density:** 2770.0
Land: 0.2 sq. mi.; **Water:** 0.0 sq. mi. **Elev:** 320 ft.
Incorporated 1976.
Name origin: For former U.S. Army base Camp Adair, so named for World War I hero Henry Adair.

Albany — City
ZIP: 97321 **Lat:** 44-38-36 N **Long:** 123-06-31 W
Pop: 21 (1990); 6 (1980) **Pop Density:** 105.0
Land: 0.2 sq. mi.; **Water:** 0.0 sq. mi. **Elev:** 212 ft.
In western OR on the Willamette River, 40 mi. north of Eugene. Founded 1848; incorporated 1864. Part of the town is also in Linn County.
Name origin: For Albany, NY.

Corvallis City
ZIP: 97333　　　**Lat:** 44-34-15 N **Long:** 123-16-33 W
Pop: 44,757 (1990); 40,960 (1980)　　**Pop Density:** 3469.5
Land: 12.9 sq. mi.; **Water:** 0.1 sq. mi.　　**Elev:** 225 ft.
In western OR on the Willamette River, 30 mi. southwest of Salem. Incorporated 1857.
Name origin: Coined by Joseph C. Avery, pioneer and landowner, from Latin *cor* and *vallis*, which he intended to mean 'heart of the valley.'

Monroe City
ZIP: 97456　　　**Lat:** 44-19-00 N **Long:** 123-17-54 W
Pop: 448 (1990); 412 (1980)　　**Pop Density:** 896.0
Land: 0.5 sq. mi.; **Water:** 0.0 sq. mi.　　**Elev:** 288 ft.
Founded 1853; incorporated 1914.
Name origin: For James Monroe (1758–1831), fifth U.S. president.

North Albany CDP
　　　Lat: 44-39-42 N **Long:** 123-06-48 W
Pop: 4,325 (1990); 4,499 (1980)　　**Pop Density:** 540.6
Land: 8.0 sq. mi.; **Water:** 0.2 sq. mi.

Philomath City
ZIP: 97370　　　**Lat:** 44-32-25 N **Long:** 123-21-25 W
Pop: 2,983 (1990); 2,673 (1980)　　**Pop Density:** 2983.0
Land: 1.0 sq. mi.; **Water:** 0.0 sq. mi.　　**Elev:** 280 ft.
Incorporated 1882.

Clackamas County
County Seat: Oregon City (ZIP: 97045)

Pop: 278,850 (1990); 241,911 (1980)　　**Pop Density:** 149.3
Land: 1868.3 sq. mi.; **Water:** 10.8 sq. mi.　　**Area Code:** 503
In northern OR, south of Portland; original county; organized Jul 5, 1843 (prior to statehood).
Name origin: For the Clackamas tribe of Chinook Indians; meaning of name is unknown.

Barlow City
ZIP: 97013　　　**Lat:** 45-15-08 N **Long:** 122-43-12 W
Pop: 118 (1990); 105 (1980)　　**Pop Density:** 1180.0
Land: 0.1 sq. mi.; **Water:** 0.0 sq. mi.　　**Elev:** 101 ft.
Incorporated 1903.
Name origin: For pioneer settler William Barlow.

Canby City
ZIP: 97013　　　**Lat:** 45-15-59 N **Long:** 122-41-30 W
Pop: 8,983 (1990); 7,659 (1980)　　**Pop Density:** 3097.6
Land: 2.9 sq. mi.; **Water:** 0.0 sq. mi.　　**Elev:** 153 ft.
Incorporated 1893.
Name origin: For Gen. Edward Canby, killed by Modoc Indians on Apr. 11, 1873.

Clackamas CDP
ZIP: 97015　　　**Lat:** 45-24-30 N **Long:** 122-33-09 W
Pop: 2,578 (1990)　　**Pop Density:** 1227.6
Land: 2.1 sq. mi.; **Water:** 0.0 sq. mi.

Estacada City
ZIP: 97023　　　**Lat:** 45-17-31 N **Long:** 122-19-59 W
Pop: 2,016 (1990); 1,419 (1980)　　**Pop Density:** 1832.7
Land: 1.1 sq. mi.; **Water:** 0.0 sq. mi.
Incorporated 1905.
Name origin: From Spanish meaning 'staked out' or 'marked off.' The name was chosen because it had a pleasing sound.

Gladstone City
ZIP: 97027　　　**Lat:** 45-23-08 N **Long:** 122-35-29 W
Pop: 10,152 (1990); 9,500 (1980)　　**Pop Density:** 4230.0
Land: 2.4 sq. mi.; **Water:** 0.0 sq. mi.
In northwestern OR on Clackamus River, 9 mi. south of Portland. Established 1890; incorporated 1911.
Name origin: For British statesman William E. Gladstone (1809–98).

Happy Valley City
　　　Lat: 45-26-37 N **Long:** 122-32-08 W
Pop: 1,519 (1990); 1,499 (1980)　　**Pop Density:** 660.4
Land: 2.3 sq. mi.; **Water:** 0.0 sq. mi.
Incorporated 1965.
Name origin: For its hospitable and happy residents, so named by an early settler.

Jennings Lodge CDP
ZIP: 97222　　　**Lat:** 45-23-34 N **Long:** 122-36-50 W
Pop: 6,530 (1990)　　**Pop Density:** 4081.3
Land: 1.6 sq. mi.; **Water:** 0.1 sq. mi.

Johnson City City
　　　Lat: 45-24-16 N **Long:** 122-34-40 W
Pop: 586 (1990); 378 (1980)　　**Pop Density:** 5860.0
Land: 0.1 sq. mi.; **Water:** 0.0 sq. mi.
Incorporated 1970.
Name origin: For its developer, Delbert Johnson.

Lake Oswego City
ZIP: 97034　　　**Lat:** 45-24-40 N **Long:** 122-41-49 W
Pop: 28,317 (1990); 21,313 (1980)　　**Pop Density:** 3146.3
Land: 9.0 sq. mi.; **Water:** 0.6 sq. mi.
In northwestern OR, 8 mi. south of Portland. Incorporated 1910. Part of the town is also in Multnomah and Washington counties.
Name origin: For its position on Lake Oswego, which is named for Oswego, NY.

Milwaukie — City
ZIP: 97222 **Lat:** 45-26-39 N **Long:** 122-37-11 W
Pop: 18,692 (1990); 17,931 (1980) **Pop Density:** 3894.2
Land: 4.8 sq. mi.; **Water:** 0.0 sq. mi.
Settled 1847; incorporated 1903. Part of the town is also in Multnomah County.
Name origin: For Milwaukee, WI, with a spelling variation.

Molalla — City
ZIP: 97038 **Lat:** 45-08-59 N **Long:** 122-34-40 W
Pop: 3,651 (1990); 2,992 (1980) **Pop Density:** 2281.9
Land: 1.6 sq. mi.; **Water:** 0.0 sq. mi. **Elev:** 373 ft.
Incorporated 1913.

Mount Hood Village — CDP
Lat: 45-21-19 N **Long:** 121-58-46 W
Pop: 2,234 (1990) **Pop Density:** 328.5
Land: 6.8 sq. mi.; **Water:** 0.0 sq. mi.

Oak Grove — CDP
ZIP: 97267 **Lat:** 45-24-48 N **Long:** 122-38-15 W
Pop: 12,576 (1990); 11,640 (1980) **Pop Density:** 4336.6
Land: 2.9 sq. mi.; **Water:** 0.2 sq. mi.

Oatfield — CDP
Lat: 45-24-49 N **Long:** 122-35-46 W
Pop: 15,348 (1990) **Pop Density:** 3488.2
Land: 4.4 sq. mi.; **Water:** 0.0 sq. mi.

Oregon City — City
ZIP: 97045 **Lat:** 45-20-41 N **Long:** 122-35-48 W
Pop: 14,698 (1990); 14,673 (1980) **Pop Density:** 3127.2
Land: 4.7 sq. mi.; **Water:** 0.2 sq. mi.
In northwestern OR on the Willamette River, 11 mi. south of Portland. Founded 1842; incorporated 1844.
Name origin: For the state.

Portland — City
ZIP: 97201-99 **Lat:** 45-27-40 N **Long:** 122-32-47 W
Pop: 707 (1990); 695 (1980) **Pop Density:** 1414.0
Land: 0.5 sq. mi.; **Water:** 0.0 sq. mi.
In northwestern OR on the Willamette River, 10 mi. east of its confluence with the Columbia River. OR's largest city and principal port. Founded 1845; incorporated 1851. Diverse manufacturing city: metal processing, electric equipment, lumber and wood products. Part of the town is also in Multnomah and Washington counties.
Name origin: For Portland, ME, arrived at by flipping a coin to choose between it and Boston, homes of the founders, Asa L. Lovejoy of Boston and Francis W. Pettygrove.

Rivergrove — City
Lat: 45-23-07 N **Long:** 122-43-57 W
Pop: 267 (1990); 287 (1980) **Pop Density:** 1335.0
Land: 0.2 sq. mi.; **Water:** 0.0 sq. mi.
Incorporated 1971. Part of the town is also in Washington County.
Name origin: From a combination of the nearby Tualatin River and Lake Grove.

Sandy — City
ZIP: 97055 **Lat:** 45-23-58 N **Long:** 122-15-59 W
Pop: 4,152 (1990); 2,905 (1980) **Pop Density:** 2442.4
Land: 1.7 sq. mi.; **Water:** 0.0 sq. mi.
In northwestern OR on the Sandy River, 22 mi. southeast of Portland. Incorporated 1913.
Name origin: For its river, which traverses the county.

Sunnyside — CDP
Lat: 45-25-55 N **Long:** 122-33-20 W
Pop: 4,423 (1990) **Pop Density:** 1701.2
Land: 2.6 sq. mi.; **Water:** 0.0 sq. mi.

Tualatin — City
ZIP: 97062 **Lat:** 45-22-54 N **Long:** 122-44-08 W
Pop: 1,756 (1990); 41 (1980) **Pop Density:** 2195.0
Land: 0.8 sq. mi.; **Water:** 0.0 sq. mi. **Elev:** 123 ft.
Incorporated 1913. Part of the town is also in Washington County.
Name origin: From an Indian term meaning 'sluggish' and referring to the Tualatin River.

West Linn — City
ZIP: 97068 **Lat:** 45-22-06 N **Long:** 122-38-17 W
Pop: 16,367 (1990); 11,358 (1980) **Pop Density:** 2479.8
Land: 6.6 sq. mi.; **Water:** 0.5 sq. mi. **Elev:** 128 ft.
In northwestern OR on the Willamette River, 10 mi. south of Portland. Settled 1840s; incorporated 1913.
Name origin: For U.S. Sen. Lewis Linn of MO, who urged the American settlement of OR.

Wilsonville — City
ZIP: 97070 **Lat:** 45-18-28 N **Long:** 122-45-59 W
Pop: 7,096 (1990); 2,900 (1980) **Pop Density:** 1202.7
Land: 5.9 sq. mi.; **Water:** 0.2 sq. mi.
Settled 1870s; incorporated 1969. Part of the town is also in Washington County.
Name origin: For pioneer Charles Wilson.

Clatsop County
County Seat: Astoria (ZIP: 97103)

Pop: 33,301 (1990); 32,489 (1980)   **Pop Density:** 40.3
Land: 827.3 sq. mi.; **Water:** 257.5 sq. mi.   **Area Code:** 503
In the northwestern corner of OR; original county; organized Jun 22, 1844 (prior to statehood) from the Tuality district.
Name origin: For the Clatsop Indian tribe of Chinook Indians, whose name means 'dried salmon.'

Astoria   City
ZIP: 97103   **Lat:** 46-11-16 N   **Long:** 123-49-13 W
Pop: 10,069 (1990); 9,998 (1980)   **Pop Density:** 1766.5
Land: 5.7 sq. mi.; **Water:** 3.9 sq. mi.   **Elev:** 18 ft.
Founded 1813; incorporated 1856.
Name origin: For fur-trading magnate Jacob Astor.

Cannon Beach   City
Lat: 45-53-19 N   **Long:** 123-57-35 W
Pop: 1,221 (1990); 1,187 (1980)   **Pop Density:** 872.1
Land: 1.4 sq. mi.; **Water:** 0.0 sq. mi.
In the northwestern corner of OR on the Pacific coast, 22 mi. southwest of Astoria. Incorporated 1956.
Name origin: For its beach, so named for an iron cannon from the U.S. Navy schooner *Shark*, wrecked near the Columbia River shore.

Gearhart   City
ZIP: 97138   **Lat:** 46-01-29 N   **Long:** 123-55-02 W
Pop: 1,027 (1990); 967 (1980)   **Pop Density:** 933.6
Land: 1.1 sq. mi.; **Water:** 0.0 sq. mi.   **Elev:** 16 ft.
Incorporated 1918.
Name origin: For pioneer Philip Gearhart.

Hammond   Town
ZIP: 97121   **Lat:** 46-11-53 N   **Long:** 123-56-48 W
Pop: 589 (1990); 516 (1980)   **Pop Density:** 490.8
Land: 1.2 sq. mi.; **Water:** 0.3 sq. mi.   **Elev:** 9 ft.
Incorporated 1899.
Name origin: For Pacific coast businessman Andrew H. Hammond.

Seaside   City
ZIP: 97138   **Lat:** 45-59-24 N   **Long:** 123-55-12 W
Pop: 5,359 (1990); 5,193 (1980)   **Pop Density:** 1448.4
Land: 3.7 sq. mi.; **Water:** 0.2 sq. mi.
Incorporated 1899.
Name origin: For the Seaside House, a well-known hotel and resort about a mile south of the present business section.

Warrenton   City
ZIP: 97146   **Lat:** 46-10-12 N   **Long:** 123-55-15 W
Pop: 2,681 (1990); 2,493 (1980)   **Pop Density:** 248.2
Land: 10.8 sq. mi.; **Water:** 4.0 sq. mi.
Incorporated 1899.
Name origin: For D.K. Warrenton, an early settler.

Columbia County
County Seat: St. Helens (ZIP: 97051)

Pop: 37,557 (1990); 35,646 (1980)   **Pop Density:** 57.2
Land: 656.8 sq. mi.; **Water:** 31.6 sq. mi.   **Area Code:** 503
On the northwestern border of OR, northwest of Portland; organized Jan 16, 1854 (prior to statehood) from Washington County.
Name origin: For the Columbia River, which forms its northern and eastern borders.

Clatskanie   City
ZIP: 97016   **Lat:** 46-06-13 N   **Long:** 123-12-18 W
Pop: 1,629 (1990); 1,648 (1980)   **Pop Density:** 1357.5
Land: 1.2 sq. mi.; **Water:** 0.0 sq. mi.   **Elev:** 33 ft.
Incorporated 1893.
Name origin: From an Indian place name for a spot in the Nehalem Valley.

Columbia City   City
ZIP: 97018   **Lat:** 45-53-50 N   **Long:** 122-48-38 W
Pop: 1,003 (1990); 678 (1980)   **Pop Density:** 1432.9
Land: 0.7 sq. mi.; **Water:** 0.3 sq. mi.   **Elev:** 24 ft.
Founded 1867; incorporated 1926.
Name origin: For the Columbia River.

Prescott   City
Lat: 46-02-50 N   **Long:** 122-53-08 W
Pop: 63 (1990); 73 (1980)   **Pop Density:** 630.0
Land: 0.1 sq. mi.; **Water:** 0.0 sq. mi.   **Elev:** 25 ft.
Incorporated 1948.
Name origin: For the local sawmill owners.

Rainier   City
ZIP: 97048   **Lat:** 46-05-32 N   **Long:** 122-56-47 W
Pop: 1,674 (1990); 1,655 (1980)   **Pop Density:** 1116.0
Land: 1.5 sq. mi.; **Water:** 1.0 sq. mi.   **Elev:** 24 ft.
Inthe northwest corner of OR on the Columbia River across from Kelso, WA. Settled 1851; incorporated 1885.
Name origin: For WA's Mount Rainier.

OREGON, Columbia County

St. Helens City
ZIP: 97051 **Lat:** 45-51-38 N **Long:** 122-48-39 W
Pop: 7,535 (1990); 7,064 (1980) **Pop Density:** 2093.1
Land: 3.6 sq. mi.; **Water:** 0.9 sq. mi. **Elev:** 73 ft.
In the northwestern corner of OR on the Columbia River. Incorporated 1889.
Name origin: For its location near Mount St. Helens, which is 38 mi. to its northeast in WA.

Scappoose City
ZIP: 97056 **Lat:** 45-45-05 N **Long:** 122-52-49 W
Pop: 3,529 (1990); 3,213 (1980) **Pop Density:** 1764.5
Land: 2.0 sq. mi.; **Water:** 0.0 sq. mi. **Elev:** 61 ft.
Incorporated 1921.
Name origin: From an Indian term meaning 'gravel plain.'

Vernonia City
ZIP: 97064 **Lat:** 45-51-37 N **Long:** 123-11-06 W
Pop: 1,808 (1990); 1,785 (1980) **Pop Density:** 1291.4
Land: 1.4 sq. mi.; **Water:** 0.0 sq. mi. **Elev:** 621 ft.
Incorporated 1891.
Name origin: For founder Ozias Cherrington's daughter.

Coos County
County Seat: Coquille (ZIP: 97423)

Pop: 60,273 (1990); 64,047 (1980) **Pop Density:** 37.7
Land: 1600.5 sq. mi.; **Water:** 205.9 sq. mi. **Area Code:** 503
On the southwestern coast of OR, southwest of Eugene; organized Dec 22, 1853 (prior to statehood) from Umpqua and Jackson counties.
Name origin: For the Coos Bay Indian tribe, the name being interpreted as either 'lake' or 'place of pines.'

Bandon City
ZIP: 97411 **Lat:** 43-06-57 N **Long:** 124-24-52 W
Pop: 2,215 (1990); 2,311 (1980) **Pop Density:** 851.9
Land: 2.6 sq. mi.; **Water:** 0.3 sq. mi. **Elev:** 67 ft.
Settled 1870s; incorporated 1891.
Name origin: For Bandon, Ireland, so named by an Irish settler.

Barview CDP
ZIP: 97420 **Lat:** 43-20-51 N **Long:** 124-18-28 W
Pop: 1,402 (1990); 1,462 (1980) **Pop Density:** 1001.4
Land: 1.4 sq. mi.; **Water:** 0.4 sq. mi.

Bunker Hill CDP
ZIP: 97420 **Lat:** 43-21-00 N **Long:** 124-12-32 W
Pop: 1,242 (1990); 1,555 (1980) **Pop Density:** 887.1
Land: 1.4 sq. mi.; **Water:** 0.1 sq. mi.

Coos Bay City
ZIP: 97420 **Lat:** 43-22-42 N **Long:** 124-13-51 W
Pop: 15,076 (1990); 14,424 (1980) **Pop Density:** 1422.3
Land: 10.6 sq. mi.; **Water:** 5.3 sq. mi. **Elev:** 11 ft.
In western OR on the Pacific coast, 65 mi. southwest of Eugene. Incorporated 1874.
Name origin: For its bay, named for the Coos Indians. Previously called Marshfield.

Coquille City
ZIP: 97423 **Lat:** 43-10-52 N **Long:** 124-10-54 W
Pop: 4,121 (1990); 4,481 (1980) **Pop Density:** 1421.0
Land: 2.9 sq. mi.; **Water:** 0.0 sq. mi. **Elev:** 50 ft.
Incorporated 1891.
Name origin: From French trappers' translation of *Ku-kwil-tunne*, the name of Indians who once lived here.

Lakeside City
ZIP: 97449 **Lat:** 43-34-44 N **Long:** 124-10-23 W
Pop: 1,437 (1990); 1,453 (1980) **Pop Density:** 718.5
Land: 2.0 sq. mi.; **Water:** 0.3 sq. mi. **Elev:** 29 ft.
In western OR on the Pacific coast on Tenmile Lake, 62 mi. southwest of Eugene. Incorporated 1974.
Name origin: For its descriptive connotations.

Myrtle Point City
ZIP: 97458 **Lat:** 43-03-43 N **Long:** 124-07-54 W
Pop: 2,712 (1990); 2,859 (1980) **Pop Density:** 1695.0
Land: 1.6 sq. mi.; **Water:** 0.0 sq. mi. **Elev:** 90 ft.
Incorporated 1887.
Name origin: For the abundance of Oregon myrtle.

North Bend City
ZIP: 97459 **Lat:** 43-24-21 N **Long:** 124-14-10 W
Pop: 9,614 (1990); 9,779 (1980) **Pop Density:** 2465.1
Land: 3.9 sq. mi.; **Water:** 1.2 sq. mi. **Elev:** 23 ft.
In southeast OR on Coos Bay. Incorporated 1903.
Name origin: For it location, so named by Capt. A. M. Simpson in 1856.

Powers City
ZIP: 97466 **Lat:** 42-53-07 N **Long:** 124-04-19 W
Pop: 682 (1990); 819 (1980) **Pop Density:** 852.5
Land: 0.8 sq. mi.; **Water:** 0.0 sq. mi. **Elev:** 286 ft.
Incorporated 1947.
Name origin: For lumber businessman A. H. Powers, in 1914.

Crook County
County Seat: Prineville (ZIP: 97754)

Pop: 14,111 (1990); 13,091 (1980)   **Pop Density:** 4.7
Land: 2979.5 sq. mi.; **Water:** 8.0 sq. mi.   **Area Code:** 503
In central OR; organized Oct 24, 1882 from Wasco and Grant counties.
Name origin: For Gen. George Crook (1829–90), army officer in the OR Territory (1852–60).

Prineville   City
ZIP: 97754   **Lat:** 44-18-19 N   **Long:** 120-50-29 W
Pop: 5,355 (1990); 5,276 (1980)   **Pop Density:** 2231.3
Land: 2.4 sq. mi.; **Water:** 0.0 sq. mi.
Incorporated 1880.
Name origin: For Barney Prine, the town's first merchant.

Curry County
County Seat: Gold Beach (ZIP: 97444)

Pop: 19,327 (1990); 16,992 (1980)   **Pop Density:** 11.9
Land: 1627.4 sq. mi.; **Water:** 361.2 sq. mi.   **Area Code:** 503
On the southwestern coast of OR; organized Dec 18, 1855 (prior to statehood) from Coos County.
Name origin: For George Law Curry (1820–78), governor of OR Territory (1853–59).

Brookings   City
ZIP: 97415   **Lat:** 42-03-35 N   **Long:** 124-17-26 W
Pop: 4,400 (1990); 3,384 (1980)   **Pop Density:** 1571.4
Land: 2.8 sq. mi.; **Water:** 0.0 sq. mi.
Settled early 1900s; incorporated 1951.
Name origin: For lumberman Robert S. Brookings.

Gold Beach   City
ZIP: 97444   **Lat:** 42-24-46 N   **Long:** 124-25-06 W
Pop: 1,546 (1990); 1,515 (1980)   **Pop Density:** 1405.5
Land: 1.1 sq. mi.; **Water:** 0.2 sq. mi.   **Elev:** 51 ft.
Incorporated 1948.
Name origin: For the placer gold operations here in the 1850s.

Harbor   CDP
Lat: 42-02-20 N   **Long:** 124-15-16 W
Pop: 2,143 (1990); 2,856 (1980)   **Pop Density:** 1530.7
Land: 1.4 sq. mi.; **Water:** 0.4 sq. mi.

Port Orford   City
ZIP: 97465   **Lat:** 42-44-59 N   **Long:** 124-29-43 W
Pop: 1,025 (1990); 1,061 (1980)   **Pop Density:** 640.6
Land: 1.6 sq. mi.; **Water:** 0.0 sq. mi.
Incorporated 1935.

Deschutes County
County Seat: Bend (ZIP: 97701)

Pop: 74,958 (1990); 62,142 (1980)   **Pop Density:** 24.8
Land: 3018.3 sq. mi.; **Water:** 36.6 sq. mi.   **Area Code:** 503
In central OR, east of Eugene; organized Dec 13, 1916 from Crook County.
Name origin: For the Deschutes River, which traverses the county; from French '[river] of the falls.'

Bend   City
ZIP: 97701   **Lat:** 44-03-57 N   **Long:** 121-18-39 W
Pop: 20,469 (1990); 17,263 (1980)   **Pop Density:** 1527.5
Land: 13.4 sq. mi.; **Water:** 0.2 sq. mi.   **Elev:** 3629 ft.
In central OR on the Deschutes River, 95 mi. east of Eugene. Incorporated 1905.
Name origin: For its location on a bend of the river.

Deschutes River Woods   CDP
Lat: 43-59-30 N   **Long:** 121-21-25 W
Pop: 2,373 (1990)   **Pop Density:** 474.6
Land: 5.0 sq. mi.; **Water:** 0.0 sq. mi.

OREGON, Deschutes County

Redmond — City
ZIP: 97756   **Lat:** 44-15-34 N   **Long:** 121-10-16 W
Pop: 7,163 (1990); 6,452 (1980)   **Pop Density:** 852.7
Land: 8.4 sq. mi.; **Water:** 0.0 sq. mi.   **Elev:** 2997 ft.
Incorporated 1910.
Name origin: For pioneer Frank Redmond, who settled here 1905.

Sisters — City
ZIP: 97759   **Lat:** 44-17-27 N   **Long:** 121-32-53 W
Pop: 679 (1990); 696 (1980)   **Pop Density:** 848.8
Land: 0.8 sq. mi.; **Water:** 0.0 sq. mi.   **Elev:** 3186 ft.
In west-central OR, just east of Cascade Range. Incorporated 1946.
Name origin: For the nearby Cascade peaks known as the Three Sisters.

Terrebonne — CDP
ZIP: 97760   **Lat:** 44-20-31 N   **Long:** 121-10-38 W
Pop: 1,143 (1990)   **Pop Density:** 357.2
Land: 3.2 sq. mi.; **Water:** 0.0 sq. mi.

Three Rivers — CDP
Lat: 43-49-12 N   **Long:** 121-28-04 W
Pop: 1,268 (1990)   **Pop Density:** 154.6
Land: 8.2 sq. mi.; **Water:** 0.0 sq. mi.

Douglas County
County Seat: Roseburg (ZIP: 97470)

Pop: 94,649 (1990); 93,748 (1980)   **Pop Density:** 18.8
Land: 5036.8 sq. mi.; **Water:** 97.2 sq. mi.   **Area Code:** 503
In southwestern OR, south of Eugene; organized Jan 7, 1852 (prior to statehood) from Umpqua County, which was organized in 1851 and whose remnant, after Coos County was broken off in 1855, was annexed to Douglas County in 1862
Name origin: For Stephen Arnold Douglas (1813–61), U.S. orator and statesman.

Canyonville — City
ZIP: 97417   **Lat:** 42-55-43 N   **Long:** 123-16-42 W
Pop: 1,219 (1990); 1,288 (1980)   **Pop Density:** 1741.4
Land: 0.7 sq. mi.; **Water:** 0.0 sq. mi.   **Elev:** 785 ft.
Incorporated 1901.
Name origin: For its location at the end of Canyon Creek Canyon.

Drain — City
ZIP: 97435   **Lat:** 43-39-43 N   **Long:** 123-18-50 W
Pop: 1,011 (1990); 1,148 (1980)   **Pop Density:** 2022.0
Land: 0.5 sq. mi.; **Water:** 0.0 sq. mi.   **Elev:** 292 ft.
Incorporated 1887.
Name origin: For pioneer-settler Charles Drain.

Elkton — City
ZIP: 97436   **Lat:** 43-38-14 N   **Long:** 123-33-57 W
Pop: 172 (1990); 155 (1980)   **Pop Density:** 860.0
Land: 0.2 sq. mi.; **Water:** 0.0 sq. mi.   **Elev:** 149 ft.
Settled 1850; incorporated 1948.
Name origin: For its location on Elk Creek.

Glendale — City
ZIP: 97442   **Lat:** 42-44-15 N   **Long:** 123-25-42 W
Pop: 707 (1990); 712 (1980)   **Pop Density:** 1767.5
Land: 0.4 sq. mi.; **Water:** 0.0 sq. mi.   **Elev:** 1423 ft.
Settled 1890s; incorporated 1901.
Name origin: For either Glendale, MA, or Glendale, Scotland.

Green — CDP
ZIP: 97470   **Lat:** 43-08-57 N   **Long:** 123-22-55 W
Pop: 5,076 (1990); 3,897 (1980)   **Pop Density:** 906.4
Land: 5.6 sq. mi.; **Water:** 0.2 sq. mi.

Myrtle Creek — City
ZIP: 97457   **Lat:** 43-01-32 N   **Long:** 123-16-57 W
Pop: 3,063 (1990); 3,365 (1980)   **Pop Density:** 2042.0
Land: 1.5 sq. mi.; **Water:** 0.0 sq. mi.   **Elev:** 640 ft.
Incorporated 1903.
Name origin: For the groves of Oregon myrtle in the area.

Oakland — City
ZIP: 97462   **Lat:** 43-25-22 N   **Long:** 123-17-44 W
Pop: 844 (1990); 886 (1980)   **Pop Density:** 1205.7
Land: 0.7 sq. mi.; **Water:** 0.0 sq. mi.   **Elev:** 430 ft.
Incorporated 1878.
Name origin: For the oak trees around the original townsite.

Reedsport — City
ZIP: 97467   **Lat:** 43-41-56 N   **Long:** 124-06-39 W
Pop: 4,796 (1990); 4,984 (1980)   **Pop Density:** 2283.8
Land: 2.1 sq. mi.; **Water:** 0.2 sq. mi.   **Elev:** 10 ft.
Incorporated 1919.
Name origin: For Alfred Reed, an early pioneer in the area.

Riddle — City
ZIP: 97469   **Lat:** 42-57-13 N   **Long:** 123-21-58 W
Pop: 1,143 (1990); 1,265 (1980)   **Pop Density:** 1632.9
Land: 0.7 sq. mi.; **Water:** 0.0 sq. mi.   **Elev:** 705 ft.
Incorporated 1893.
Name origin: For pioneer William Riddle, who settled here 1851.

Roseburg — City
ZIP: 97470   **Lat:** 43-13-10 N   **Long:** 123-21-27 W
Pop: 17,032 (1990); 16,644 (1980)   **Pop Density:** 2301.6
Land: 7.4 sq. mi.; **Water:** 0.2 sq. mi.   **Elev:** 459 ft.
In southwestern OR, 52 mi. southwest of Eugene. Incorporated 1872.
Name origin: For Aaron Rose, who settled here 1851.

Roseburg North — CDP
Lat: 43-15-13 N **Long:** 123-19-15 W
Pop: 6,831 (1990) **Pop Density:** 281.1
Land: 24.3 sq. mi.; **Water:** 0.3 sq. mi.

Sutherlin — City
ZIP: 97479 **Lat:** 43-23-18 N **Long:** 123-18-53 W
Pop: 5,020 (1990); 4,560 (1980) **Pop Density:** 1004.0
Land: 5.0 sq. mi.; **Water:** 0.1 sq. mi. **Elev:** 540 ft.
Incorporated 1952.
Name origin: For pioneer horticulturalist Fendel Sutherlin.

Tri-City — CDP
ZIP: 97457 **Lat:** 42-59-04 N **Long:** 123-18-37 W
Pop: 3,585 (1990); 3,439 (1980) **Pop Density:** 407.4
Land: 8.8 sq. mi.; **Water:** 0.0 sq. mi.

Winston — City
ZIP: 97496 **Lat:** 43-07-13 N **Long:** 123-24-40 W
Pop: 3,773 (1990); 3,359 (1980) **Pop Density:** 2902.3
Land: 1.3 sq. mi.; **Water:** 0.0 sq. mi. **Elev:** 534 ft.
Founded 1893; incorporated 1955.
Name origin: For its first postmaster, Elijah Winston.

Yoncalla — City
ZIP: 97499 **Lat:** 43-36-00 N **Long:** 123-17-07 W
Pop: 919 (1990); 805 (1980) **Pop Density:** 1531.7
Land: 0.6 sq. mi.; **Water:** 0.0 sq. mi.
Incorporated 1901.
Name origin: From an Indian term meaning 'eagle.'

Gilliam County
County Seat: Condon (ZIP: 97823)

Pop: 1,717 (1990); 2,057 (1980) **Pop Density:** 1.4
Land: 1204.1 sq. mi.; **Water:** 18.8 sq. mi. **Area Code:** 503
On the central northern border of OR; organized Feb 25, 1885 from Wasco County.
Name origin: For Col. Cornelius Gilliam (1798–1848), veteran of Indian wars and former county official in MT.

Arlington — City
ZIP: 97812 **Lat:** 45-43-04 N **Long:** 120-11-33 W
Pop: 425 (1990); 521 (1980) **Pop Density:** 236.1
Land: 1.8 sq. mi.; **Water:** 0.3 sq. mi. **Elev:** 2851 ft.
Established 1881; incorporated 1885.
Name origin: For Gen. Robert E. Lee's VA estate.

Condon — City
ZIP: 97823 **Lat:** 45-14-12 N **Long:** 120-11-02 W
Pop: 635 (1990); 783 (1980) **Pop Density:** 705.6
Land: 0.9 sq. mi.; **Water:** 0.0 sq. mi. **Elev:** 2844 ft.
Established 1884; incorporated 1893.
Name origin: For lawyer Harvey C. Condon.

Lonerock — City
Lat: 45-05-21 N **Long:** 119-52-59 W
Pop: 11 (1990); 26 (1980) **Pop Density:** 11.0
Land: 1.0 sq. mi.; **Water:** 0.0 sq. mi. **Elev:** 2840 ft.
Incorporated 1901.
Name origin: For a 100-ft.-high rock landmark near its center.

Grant County
County Seat: Canyon City (ZIP: 97820)

Pop: 7,853 (1990); 8,210 (1980) **Pop Density:** 1.7
Land: 4528.8 sq. mi.; **Water:** 0.7 sq. mi. **Area Code:** 503
In northeastern OR; organized Oct 14, 1864.
Name origin: For Ulysses Simpson Grant (1822–85), Civil War general and eighteenth U.S. president.

Canyon City — Town
ZIP: 97820 **Lat:** 44-23-31 N **Long:** 118-56-54 W
Pop: 648 (1990); 639 (1980) **Pop Density:** 462.9
Land: 1.4 sq. mi.; **Water:** 0.0 sq. mi. **Elev:** 3198 ft.
Incorporated 1864.
Name origin: For its descriptive connotations.

Dayville — Town
ZIP: 97825 **Lat:** 44-28-00 N **Long:** 119-31-56 W
Pop: 144 (1990); 199 (1980) **Pop Density:** 288.0
Land: 0.5 sq. mi.; **Water:** 0.0 sq. mi.
Incorporated 1914.
Name origin: For John Day River, which traverses the center of the county, itself named for John Day, an explorer with the 1811 Astor expedition.

Granite
City
Lat: 44-48-38 N **Long:** 118-25-09 W
Pop: 8 (1990); 17 (1980) **Pop Density:** 20.0
Land: 0.4 sq. mi.; **Water:** 0.0 sq. mi. **Elev:** 4689 ft.
Incorporated 1901.
Name origin: For the region's abundant granite.

Greenhorn
City
Lat: 44-42-43 N **Long:** 118-29-49 W
Pop: 0 (1990)
Land: 0.01 sq. mi.; **Water:** 0.0 sq. mi.
Incorporated 1912. Inactive incorporated place. Part of the town is also in Baker County.
Name origin: For the many amateur miners who came to the area in the 1860s gold rush.

John Day
City
ZIP: 97845 **Lat:** 44-25-06 N **Long:** 118-56-57 W
Pop: 1,836 (1990); 2,012 (1980) **Pop Density:** 1080.0
Land: 1.7 sq. mi.; **Water:** 0.0 sq. mi. **Elev:** 3084 ft.
Incorporated 1901.
Name origin: For the John Day River, which flows across the center of the county, itself named for John Day, an explorer and trapper with the 1811 Astor expedition.

Long Creek
Town
ZIP: 97856 **Lat:** 44-42-49 N **Long:** 119-06-06 W
Pop: 249 (1990); 252 (1980) **Pop Density:** 249.0
Land: 1.0 sq. mi.; **Water:** 0.0 sq. mi. **Elev:** 3772 ft.
Incorporated 1891.
Name origin: For the nearby creek.

Monument
City
ZIP: 97864 **Lat:** 44-49-11 N **Long:** 119-25-07 W
Pop: 162 (1990); 192 (1980) **Pop Density:** 324.0
Land: 0.5 sq. mi.; **Water:** 0.0 sq. mi. **Elev:** 2008 ft.
Settled 1870s; incorporated 1947.
Name origin: For a nearby mountain.

Mount Vernon
City
ZIP: 97865 **Lat:** 44-25-04 N **Long:** 119-06-43 W
Pop: 538 (1990); 569 (1980) **Pop Density:** 768.6
Land: 0.7 sq. mi.; **Water:** 0.0 sq. mi. **Elev:** 2871 ft.
Incorporated 1948.
Name origin: For a well-known prized black stallion of the 1870s.

Prairie City
City
ZIP: 97817 **Lat:** 44-27-41 N **Long:** 118-42-34 W
Pop: 1,117 (1990); 1,106 (1980) **Pop Density:** 1241.1
Land: 0.9 sq. mi.; **Water:** 0.0 sq. mi.
Incorporated 1891.
Name origin: For its descriptive connotations.

Seneca
City
ZIP: 97873 **Lat:** 44-08-04 N **Long:** 118-58-32 W
Pop: 191 (1990); 285 (1980) **Pop Density:** 238.8
Land: 0.8 sq. mi.; **Water:** 0.0 sq. mi. **Elev:** 4666 ft.
Incorporated 1970.
Name origin: For Judge Seneca Smith of Portland.

Harney County
County Seat: Burns (ZIP: 97720)

Pop: 7,060 (1990); 8,314 (1980) **Pop Density:** 0.7
Land: 10134.9 sq. mi.; **Water:** 92.2 sq. mi. **Area Code:** 503
In southeastern OR; organized Feb 25, 1889 from Grant County.
Name origin: For Gen. William Selby Harney (1800–89), officer in the Black Hawk War, Seminole War, and Mexican-American War; commander of department of OR who was instrumental in opening eastern OR for settlement.

Burns
City
ZIP: 97720 **Lat:** 43-35-15 N **Long:** 119-03-40 W
Pop: 2,913 (1990); 3,579 (1980) **Pop Density:** 809.2
Land: 3.6 sq. mi.; **Water:** 0.0 sq. mi. **Elev:** 4148 ft.
Incorporated 1891.
Name origin: For Scottish poet Robert Burns (1759–96), so named by pioneer George McGowan.

Hines
City
ZIP: 97738 **Lat:** 43-34-02 N **Long:** 119-04-43 W
Pop: 1,452 (1990); 1,632 (1980) **Pop Density:** 1452.0
Land: 1.0 sq. mi.; **Water:** 0.0 sq. mi. **Elev:** 4157 ft.
Incorporated 1930.
Name origin: For the Edward Hines Lumber Company.

Hood River County
County Seat: Hood River (ZIP: 97031)

Pop: 16,903 (1990); 15,835 (1980) **Pop Density:** 32.4
Land: 522.4 sq. mi.; **Water:** 11.2 sq. mi. **Area Code:** 503
On northwestern border of OR, east of Portland; organized Jun 23, 1908 from Wasco County.
Name origin: For the river and the town; the river was named for either Samuel Hood (1724–1816), or for Arthur William Acland Hood (1824–1901), admirals in the British Navy.

Cascade Locks   City
ZIP: 97014   **Lat:** 45-40-40 N **Long:** 121-52-21 W
Pop: 930 (1990); 838 (1980)   **Pop Density:** 422.7
Land: 2.2 sq. mi.; **Water:** 0.8 sq. mi.
Incorporated 1935.
Name origin: For the cascade locks constructed in 1888.

Hood River   City
ZIP: 97031   **Lat:** 45-42-35 N **Long:** 121-31-18 W
Pop: 4,632 (1990); 4,329 (1980)   **Pop Density:** 2437.9
Land: 1.9 sq. mi.; **Water:** 0.6 sq. mi.
Incorporated 1895.
Name origin: For the nearby river, which traverses the county.

Jackson County
County Seat: Medford (ZIP: 97501)

Pop: 146,389 (1990); 132,456 (1980) **Pop Density:** 52.6
Land: 2785.4 sq. mi.; **Water:** 16.6 sq. mi. **Area Code:** 503
On the southwestern border of OR; organized Jan 12, 1852 (prior to statehood) from the original Yamhill and Champoeg districts
Name origin: For Andrew Jackson (1767–1845), seventh U.S. president.

Ashland   City
ZIP: 97520   **Lat:** 42-11-24 N **Long:** 122-41-58 W
Pop: 16,234 (1990); 14,943 (1980)   **Pop Density:** 2536.6
Land: 6.4 sq. mi.; **Water:** 0.0 sq. mi.   **Elev:** 1951 ft.
In southwestern OR, 58 mi. southeast of Eugene. Incorporated 1874.
Name origin: For Ashland, KY.

Butte Falls   Town
ZIP: 97522   **Lat:** 42-32-31 N **Long:** 122-34-04 W
Pop: 252 (1990); 428 (1980)   **Pop Density:** 840.0
Land: 0.3 sq. mi.; **Water:** 0.0 sq. mi.   **Elev:** 2536 ft.
Incorporated 1911.
Name origin: For its location on the falls of Big Butte Creek.

Central Point   City
ZIP: 97502   **Lat:** 42-22-25 N **Long:** 122-54-39 W
Pop: 7,509 (1990); 6,357 (1980)   **Pop Density:** 3128.7
Land: 2.4 sq. mi.; **Water:** 0.0 sq. mi.   **Elev:** 1278 ft.
Incorporated 1889.
Name origin: For the crossing of two pioneer wagon trails of the Rogue River valley.

Eagle Point   City
ZIP: 97524   **Lat:** 42-27-57 N **Long:** 122-47-58 W
Pop: 3,008 (1990); 2,764 (1980)   **Pop Density:** 1769.4
Land: 1.7 sq. mi.; **Water:** 0.0 sq. mi.   **Elev:** 1305 ft.
Settled 1872; incorporated 1911.
Name origin: For nearby rocky cliffs, nesting place of many eagles.

Gold Hill   City
ZIP: 97525   **Lat:** 42-26-04 N **Long:** 123-03-01 W
Pop: 964 (1990); 904 (1980)   **Pop Density:** 1606.7
Land: 0.6 sq. mi.; **Water:** 0.0 sq. mi.
Incorporated 1895.
Name origin: For the discovery of gold here.

Jacksonville   City
ZIP: 97530   **Lat:** 42-18-47 N **Long:** 122-58-03 W
Pop: 1,896 (1990); 2,030 (1980)   **Pop Density:** 1053.3
Land: 1.8 sq. mi.; **Water:** 0.0 sq. mi.   **Elev:** 1569 ft.
Incorporated 1860.
Name origin: For its location on Jackson Creek.

Medford   City
ZIP: 97501   **Lat:** 42-20-23 N **Long:** 122-51-11 W
Pop: 46,951 (1990); 39,746 (1980)   **Pop Density:** 2565.6
Land: 18.3 sq. mi.; **Water:** 0.0 sq. mi.   **Elev:** 383 ft.
In southwestern OR, 120 mi. south-southeast of Eugene. Incorporated 1885.
Name origin: For the town's location on the middle ford of Bear Creek, so named by railroad engineer David Loring.

Phoenix   City
ZIP: 97535   **Lat:** 42-16-28 N **Long:** 122-48-57 W
Pop: 3,239 (1990); 2,309 (1980)   **Pop Density:** 3598.9
Land: 0.9 sq. mi.; **Water:** 0.0 sq. mi.   **Elev:** 1543 ft.
Incorporated 1911.

Rogue River — City
ZIP: 97537 **Lat:** 42-26-08 N **Long:** 123-10-01 W
Pop: 1,759 (1990); 1,308 (1980) **Pop Density:** 1759.0
Land: 1.0 sq. mi.; **Water:** 0.0 sq. mi. **Elev:** 1001 ft.
Incorporated 1911.
Name origin: For its location on the river at the mouth of Evans Creek.

Shady Cove — City
ZIP: 97539 **Lat:** 42-36-42 N **Long:** 122-49-07 W
Pop: 1,351 (1990); 1,097 (1980) **Pop Density:** 711.1
Land: 1.9 sq. mi.; **Water:** 0.0 sq. mi. **Elev:** 1399 ft.
In southwest OR on the Rogue River, 30 mi. northeast of Grants Pass. Incorporated 1972.
Name origin: For a nook on the river bank.

Talent — City
ZIP: 97540 **Lat:** 42-14-24 N **Long:** 122-46-51 W
Pop: 3,274 (1990); 2,577 (1980) **Pop Density:** 2976.4
Land: 1.1 sq. mi.; **Water:** 0.0 sq. mi. **Elev:** 1635 ft.
In southeastern OR, 15 mi. north of CA border. Founded 1880s; incorporated 1911.
Name origin: For its founder, A. P. Talent.

White City — CDP
ZIP: 97503 **Lat:** 42-25-55 N **Long:** 122-49-48 W
Pop: 5,891 (1990); 5,445 (1980) **Pop Density:** 3272.8
Land: 1.8 sq. mi.; **Water:** 0.0 sq. mi.

Jefferson County
County Seat: Madras (ZIP: 97741)

Pop: 13,676 (1990); 11,599 (1980) **Pop Density:** 7.7
Land: 1780.9 sq. mi.; **Water:** 10.4 sq. mi. **Area Code:** 503
In north-central OR; organized Dec 12, 1914 from Crook County.
Name origin: For Mount Jefferson on the county's western border, itself named for Thomas Jefferson (1743–1826), third U.S. president.

Culver — City
ZIP: 97734 **Lat:** 44-31-29 N **Long:** 121-12-33 W
Pop: 570 (1990); 514 (1980) **Pop Density:** 1140.0
Land: 0.5 sq. mi.; **Water:** 0.0 sq. mi. **Elev:** 2636 ft.
Incorporated 1946.
Name origin: From the ancestral name of its first postmaster, O. G. Collver.

Madras — City
ZIP: 97741 **Lat:** 44-37-47 N **Long:** 121-07-44 W
Pop: 3,443 (1990); 2,235 (1980) **Pop Density:** 1639.5
Land: 2.1 sq. mi.; **Water:** 0.0 sq. mi.
Name origin: For cotton cloth from Madras, India, so named by an early merchant.

Metolius — City
ZIP: 97741 **Lat:** 44-35-15 N **Long:** 121-10-35 W
Pop: 450 (1990); 451 (1980) **Pop Density:** 1500.0
Land: 0.3 sq. mi.; **Water:** 0.0 sq. mi. **Elev:** 2530 ft.
Incorporated 1913.
Name origin: For a Deschutes River tributary, from an Indian term meaning 'salmon-water.'

Warm Springs — CDP
Lat: 44-46-09 N **Long:** 121-17-08 W
Pop: 2,287 (1990) **Pop Density:** 57.0
Land: 40.1 sq. mi.; **Water:** 0.2 sq. mi.

Josephine County
County Seat: Grants Pass (ZIP: 97526)

Pop: 62,649 (1990); 58,855 (1980) **Pop Density:** 38.2
Land: 1639.6 sq. mi.; **Water:** 2.0 sq. mi. **Area Code:** 503
On the southwestern border of OR, west of Jackson; organized Jan 22, 1856 from Jackson County.
Name origin: For either Josephine Rollins (1835–c.1911), daughter of the leader of a wagon train bound for California and first white woman to settle in the county, or for Josephine Creek, which was also named in her honor.

Cave Junction — City
ZIP: 97523 **Lat:** 42-10-02 N **Long:** 123-38-40 W
Pop: 1,126 (1990); 1,023 (1980) **Pop Density:** 750.7
Land: 1.5 sq. mi.; **Water:** 0.0 sq. mi. **Elev:** 1295 ft.
Incorporated 1948.
Name origin: For its location on the highway that branches to the OR caves.

Grants Pass — City
ZIP: 97527 **Lat:** 42-26-28 N **Long:** 123-19-27 W
Pop: 17,488 (1990); 15,032 (1980) **Pop Density:** 2690.5
Land: 6.5 sq. mi.; **Water:** 0.1 sq. mi. **Elev:** 948 ft.
In southwestern OR on the Rogue River, 112 mi. south of Eugene. Founded 1860s; incorporated 1887.
Name origin: For Ulysses S. Grant (1822–85), eighteenth U.S. president.

Harbeck-Fruitdale CDP
Lat: 42-24-57 N **Long:** 123-19-13 W
Pop: 3,982 (1990); 4,733 (1980) **Pop Density:** 2095.8
Land: 1.9 sq. mi.; **Water:** 0.0 sq. mi.

Redwood CDP
Lat: 42-25-19 N **Long:** 123-23-10 W
Pop: 3,702 (1990); 3,171 (1980) **Pop Density:** 755.5
Land: 4.9 sq. mi.; **Water:** 0.1 sq. mi.

Klamath County
County Seat: Klamath Falls (ZIP: 97601)

Pop: 57,702 (1990); 59,117 (1980) **Pop Density:** 9.7
Land: 5944.6 sq. mi.; **Water:** 191.6 sq. mi. **Area Code:** 503
On central southern border of OR; organized Oct 17, 1882 from Lake County.
Name origin: For the Klamath Indians; the name is probably from Chinook *tlamatl*, their name for the sister tribe of the Modocs; the meaning is unknown. Also spelled *Claminitt* and *Clammitte*.

Altamont CDP
ZIP: 97601 **Lat:** 42-11-53 N **Long:** 121-43-10 W
Pop: 18,591 (1990); 19,805 (1980) **Pop Density:** 1840.7
Land: 10.1 sq. mi.; **Water:** 0.0 sq. mi.

Bonanza Town
ZIP: 97623 **Lat:** 42-11-58 N **Long:** 121-24-21 W
Pop: 323 (1990); 270 (1980) **Pop Density:** 403.8
Land: 0.8 sq. mi.; **Water:** 0.0 sq. mi. **Elev:** 4116 ft.
Incorporated 1901.
Name origin: From the Spanish term for 'prosperity.'

Chiloquin City
ZIP: 97624 **Lat:** 42-34-35 N **Long:** 121-52-00 W
Pop: 673 (1990); 778 (1980) **Pop Density:** 841.3
Land: 0.8 sq. mi.; **Water:** 0.0 sq. mi. **Elev:** 4179 ft.
Incorporated 1926.
Name origin: For the Klamath chief Chaloquin.

Klamath Falls City
ZIP: 97601 **Lat:** 42-13-15 N **Long:** 121-46-20 W
Pop: 17,737 (1990); 16,661 (1980) **Pop Density:** 1081.5
Land: 16.4 sq. mi.; **Water:** 0.8 sq. mi.
In southern OR on the falls of the Link River at the south end of Upper Klamath Lake and on the east slope of Cascade Range, 15 mi. north of the CA border. Incorporated 1905.
Name origin: For the falls in the Klamath River, probably from Chinook *tlamatl*, their name for the sister tribe of the Modocs.

Malin City
ZIP: 97632 **Lat:** 42-00-50 N **Long:** 121-24-27 W
Pop: 725 (1990); 539 (1980) **Pop Density:** 2416.7
Land: 0.3 sq. mi.; **Water:** 0.0 sq. mi.
In south-central OR on the CA border. Founded 1909; incorporated 1922.
Name origin: For Malin, in the former Czechoslovakia.

Merrill City
ZIP: 97633 **Lat:** 42-01-35 N **Long:** 121-35-58 W
Pop: 837 (1990); 809 (1980) **Pop Density:** 2092.5
Land: 0.4 sq. mi.; **Water:** 0.0 sq. mi. **Elev:** 4067 ft.
Incorporated 1903.
Name origin: For early pioneer Nathan S. Merrill.

Lake County
County Seat: Lakeview (ZIP: 97630)

Pop: 7,186 (1990); 7,532 (1980) **Pop Density:** 0.9
Land: 8136.3 sq. mi.; **Water:** 222.7 sq. mi. **Area Code:** 503
On central southern border of OR; organized Oct 24, 1874 from Jackson County.
Name origin: For the many lakes in the area.

Lakeview Town
ZIP: 97630 **Lat:** 42-11-21 N **Long:** 120-20-43 W
Pop: 2,526 (1990); 2,770 (1980) **Pop Density:** 1804.3
Land: 1.4 sq. mi.; **Water:** 0.0 sq. mi. **Elev:** 4798 ft.
In south-central OR near the CA border. Incorporated 1889.
Name origin: For its view of Goose Lake.

Paisley City
ZIP: 97636 **Lat:** 42-41-34 N **Long:** 120-32-39 W
Pop: 350 (1990); 343 (1980) **Pop Density:** 875.0
Land: 0.4 sq. mi.; **Water:** 0.0 sq. mi. **Elev:** 4369 ft.
Incorporated 1911.
Name origin: Named by early Scottish settlers for Paisley, Scotland.

Lane County
County Seat: Eugene (ZIP: 97401)

Pop: 282,912 (1990); 275,226 (1980) **Pop Density:** 62.1
Land: 4554.1 sq. mi.; **Water:** 167.8 sq. mi. **Area Code:** 503
On central-western coast of OR; organized Jan 28, 1851 (prior to statehood) from Linn and Benton counties.
Name origin: For Gen. Joseph Lane (1801–81), OR territorial governor (1849–50; 1853) and first U.S. senator from OR (1859–61).

Coburg City
ZIP: 97401 **Lat:** 44-08-17 N **Long:** 123-03-35 W
Pop: 763 (1990); 699 (1980) **Pop Density:** 1090.0
Land: 0.7 sq. mi.; **Water:** 0.0 sq. mi. **Elev:** 400 ft.
Incorporated 1893.
Name origin: For a well-known local stallion, so named by blacksmith Thomas Kane.

Cottage Grove City
ZIP: 97424 **Lat:** 43-47-51 N **Long:** 123-03-20 W
Pop: 7,402 (1990); 7,148 (1980) **Pop Density:** 2741.5
Land: 2.7 sq. mi.; **Water:** 0.0 sq. mi. **Elev:** 641 ft.
Incorporated 1887.
Name origin: For the location of the house of the first postmaster, G. C. Pearce, in a nearby oak grove.

Creswell City
ZIP: 97426 **Lat:** 43-55-05 N **Long:** 123-01-09 W
Pop: 2,431 (1990); 1,770 (1980) **Pop Density:** 2701.1
Land: 0.9 sq. mi.; **Water:** 0.0 sq. mi. **Elev:** 547 ft.
Incorporated 1909.
Name origin: For John A. Creswell, U.S. postmaster general (1869–74).

Dunes City City
ZIP: 97439 **Lat:** 43-54-29 N **Long:** 124-05-42 W
Pop: 1,081 (1990); 1,124 (1980) **Pop Density:** 415.8
Land: 2.6 sq. mi.; **Water:** 0.8 sq. mi. **Elev:** 80 ft.
Incorporated 1963.

Eugene City
ZIP: 97401 **Lat:** 44-03-10 N **Long:** 123-06-43 W
Pop: 112,669 (1990); 105,664 (1980) **Pop Density:** 2965.0
Land: 38.0 sq. mi.; **Water:** 0.0 sq. mi. **Elev:** 419 ft.
In western OR on the Willamette River, 62 mi. south of Salem. Incorporated 1862. Major industries are lumbering and manufacture of wood products.
Name origin: For Eugene Skinner (1809–1911), who claimed this land in 1847.

Florence City
ZIP: 97439 **Lat:** 43-59-10 N **Long:** 124-06-11 W
Pop: 5,162 (1990); 4,411 (1980) **Pop Density:** 1474.9
Land: 3.5 sq. mi.; **Water:** 0.4 sq. mi. **Elev:** 23 ft.
Incorporated 1893.
Name origin: For early OR state senator A.B. Florence.

Junction City City
ZIP: 97448 **Lat:** 44-13-04 N **Long:** 123-12-13 W
Pop: 3,670 (1990); 3,320 (1980) **Pop Density:** 2823.1
Land: 1.3 sq. mi.; **Water:** 0.0 sq. mi. **Elev:** 327 ft.
Incorporated 1872.
Name origin: For being the site of an important railroad intersection.

Lowell City
ZIP: 97452 **Lat:** 43-55-14 N **Long:** 122-46-46 W
Pop: 785 (1990); 661 (1980) **Pop Density:** 872.2
Land: 0.9 sq. mi.; **Water:** 0.3 sq. mi. **Elev:** 741 ft.
Settled 1850s; incorporated 1954.
Name origin: For Lowell, MA.

North Springfield CDP
ZIP: 97477 **Lat:** 44-04-30 N **Long:** 123-00-06 W
Pop: 5,451 (1990); 6,140 (1980) **Pop Density:** 1946.8
Land: 2.8 sq. mi.; **Water:** 0.0 sq. mi.

Oakridge City
ZIP: 97463 **Lat:** 43-44-50 N **Long:** 122-28-19 W
Pop: 3,063 (1990); 3,729 (1980) **Pop Density:** 2187.9
Land: 1.4 sq. mi.; **Water:** 0.0 sq. mi. **Elev:** 1209 ft.
Established 1912; incorporated 1935.
Name origin: For the oak-covered ridge forming part of town.

River Road CDP
ZIP: 97404 **Lat:** 44-05-03 N **Long:** 123-07-57 W
Pop: 9,443 (1990); 10,370 (1980) **Pop Density:** 3497.4
Land: 2.7 sq. mi.; **Water:** 0.0 sq. mi.

Santa Clara CDP
ZIP: 97404 **Lat:** 44-06-52 N **Long:** 123-07-54 W
Pop: 12,834 (1990); 14,288 (1980) **Pop Density:** 2212.8
Land: 5.8 sq. mi.; **Water:** 0.1 sq. mi.

Springfield City
ZIP: 97477 **Lat:** 44-03-10 N **Long:** 122-58-37 W
Pop: 44,683 (1990); 41,621 (1980) **Pop Density:** 3334.6
Land: 13.4 sq. mi.; **Water:** 0.0 sq. mi. **Elev:** 456 ft.
In western OR, 5 mi. east of Eugene. Settled 1849; incorporated 1885.
Name origin: For a natural spring on the site.

Veneta City
ZIP: 97487 **Lat:** 44-02-54 N **Long:** 123-21-08 W
Pop: 2,519 (1990); 2,449 (1980) **Pop Density:** 1007.6
Land: 2.5 sq. mi.; **Water:** 0.0 sq. mi.
Founded 1913; incorporated 1962.
Name origin: For Veneta Hunter, daughter of its founder, E.E. Hunter.

Westfir City
ZIP: 97492 **Lat:** 43-45-29 N **Long:** 122-30-23 W
Pop: 278 (1990); 312 (1980) **Pop Density:** 926.7
Land: 0.3 sq. mi.; **Water:** 0.0 sq. mi.
Incorporated 1979.

Lincoln County
County Seat: Newport (ZIP: 97365)

Pop: 38,889 (1990); 35,264 (1980) **Pop Density:** 39.7
Land: 979.6 sq. mi.; **Water:** 214.2 sq. mi. **Area Code:** 503
On central western coast of OR; organized Feb 20, 1893 from Benton and Polk counties.
Name origin: For Abraham Lincoln (1809–65), sixteenth U.S. president.

Depoe Bay   City
ZIP: 97341   Lat: 44-48-36 N Long: 124-03-29 W
Pop: 870 (1990); 723 (1980)   Pop Density: 483.3
Land: 1.8 sq. mi.; Water: 0.0 sq. mi.   Elev: 58 ft.
Incorporated 1973.
Name origin: For an Indian nicknamed "Depot" for his association with an early army supply depot; spelling apparently altered to reflect pronunciation.

Lincoln Beach   CDP
ZIP: 97341   Lat: 44-52-26 N Long: 124-01-42 W
Pop: 1,507 (1990)   Pop Density: 456.7
Land: 3.3 sq. mi.; Water: 0.8 sq. mi.

Lincoln City   City
ZIP: 97367   Lat: 44-58-21 N Long: 124-00-25 W
Pop: 5,892 (1990); 5,469 (1980) Pop Density: 1111.7
Land: 5.3 sq. mi.; Water: 0.0 sq. mi.
Incorporated 1965.
Name origin: For its county.

Newport   City
ZIP: 97365   Lat: 44-37-00 N Long: 124-03-14 W
Pop: 8,437 (1990); 7,519 (1980) Pop Density: 1068.0
Land: 7.9 sq. mi.; Water: 0.4 sq. mi.   Elev: 177 ft.
Incorporated 1882.
Name origin: For Newport, RI, so named in 1868.

Rose Lodge   CDP
                Lat: 45-01-19 N Long: 123-52-47 W
Pop: 1,257 (1990)   Pop Density: 273.3
Land: 4.6 sq. mi.; Water: 0.0 sq. mi.

Siletz   City
ZIP: 97357   Lat: 44-43-19 N Long: 123-54-59 W
Pop: 926 (1990); 1,001 (1980)   Pop Density: 1543.3
Land: 0.6 sq. mi.; Water: 0.0 sq. mi.   Elev: 131 ft.
In eastern OR on Siletz River, 12 mi. northeast of Newport. Incorporated 1946.
Name origin: For the river, itself named for Siletz Lake; from an Indian term *silis* meaning 'black bear.'

Toledo   City
ZIP: 97391   Lat: 44-37-15 N Long: 123-55-57 W
Pop: 3,174 (1990); 3,151 (1980) Pop Density: 1670.5
Land: 1.9 sq. mi.; Water: 0.2 sq. mi.   Elev: 59 ft.
Settled 1868; incorporated 1905.
Name origin: For Toledo, OH, the former home of a pioneer.

Waldport   City
ZIP: 97376   Lat: 44-25-17 N Long: 124-03-50 W
Pop: 1,595 (1990); 1,274 (1980) Pop Density: 759.5
Land: 2.1 sq. mi.; Water: 0.5 sq. mi.   Elev: 11 ft.
Incorporated 1911.
Name origin: From German *wald* 'forest' plus *port*.

Yachats   City
ZIP: 97498   Lat: 44-18-45 N Long: 124-06-01 W
Pop: 533 (1990); 482 (1980)   Pop Density: 592.2
Land: 0.9 sq. mi.; Water: 0.0 sq. mi.
Incorporated 1966.

Linn County
County Seat: Albany (ZIP: 97321)

Pop: 91,227 (1990); 89,495 (1980) **Pop Density:** 39.8
Land: 2291.4 sq. mi.; **Water:** 17.9 sq. mi. **Area Code:** 503
In northwest OR, northeast of Eugene; original county; organized 1847 (prior to statehood).
Name origin: For Lewis Fields Linn (1795–1843), physician and U.S. senator from MO (1833–43); author of the Donation Land Law, which gave free land in the west to settlers.

Albany   City
ZIP: 97321   Lat: 44-37-01 N Long: 123-05-28 W
Pop: 29,441 (1990); 26,505 (1980) Pop Density: 2605.4
Land: 11.3 sq. mi.; Water: 0.1 sq. mi.   Elev: 212 ft.
In western OR on the Willamette River, 40 mi. north of Eugene. Founded 1848; incorporated 1864. Part of the town is also in Benton County.
Name origin: For Albany, NY.

Brownsville   City
ZIP: 97327   Lat: 44-23-34 N Long: 122-58-54 W
Pop: 1,281 (1990); 1,261 (1980) Pop Density: 985.4
Land: 1.3 sq. mi.; Water: 0.0 sq. mi.   Elev: 356 ft.
Established 1853; incorporated 1876.
Name origin: For storeowner Hugh Brown.

OREGON, Linn County

Gates — City
ZIP: 97346 **Lat:** 44-45-15 N **Long:** 122-24-27 W
Pop: 41 (1990); 38 (1980) **Pop Density:** 820.0
Land: 0.05 sq. mi.; **Water:** 0.0 sq. mi. **Elev:** 942 ft.
Settled 1882; incorporated 1950. Part of the town is also in Marion County.
Name origin: For Mrs. Gates, one of the oldest pioneer settlers.

Halsey — City
ZIP: 97348 **Lat:** 44-22-59 N **Long:** 123-06-29 W
Pop: 667 (1990); 693 (1980) **Pop Density:** 1334.0
Land: 0.5 sq. mi.; **Water:** 0.0 sq. mi. **Elev:** 280 ft.
Incorporated 1876.

Harrisburg — City
ZIP: 97446 **Lat:** 44-16-06 N **Long:** 123-09-53 W
Pop: 1,939 (1990); 1,881 (1980) **Pop Density:** 1615.8
Land: 1.2 sq. mi.; **Water:** 0.0 sq. mi. **Elev:** 309 ft.
Incorporated 1866.
Name origin: For Harrisburg, PA.

Idanha — City
ZIP: 97350 **Lat:** 44-41-51 N **Long:** 122-04-15 W
Pop: 112 (1990); 117 (1980) **Pop Density:** 560.0
Land: 0.2 sq. mi.; **Water:** 0.0 sq. mi. **Elev:** 1718 ft.
In northwestern OR on the North Santiam River near Detroit Lake. Incorporated 1895. Part of the town is also in Marion County.

Lebanon — City
ZIP: 97355 **Lat:** 44-32-05 N **Long:** 122-54-15 W
Pop: 10,950 (1990); 10,413 (1980) **Pop Density:** 2281.3
Land: 4.8 sq. mi.; **Water:** 0.2 sq. mi.
In western OR, 32 mi. southeast of Salem. Incorporated 1878.
Name origin: For Lebanon, TN, so named by early settlers.

Lyons — City
ZIP: 97358 **Lat:** 44-46-38 N **Long:** 122-36-24 W
Pop: 938 (1990); 877 (1980) **Pop Density:** 1042.2
Land: 0.9 sq. mi.; **Water:** 0.0 sq. mi.
Incorporated 1958.
Name origin: For the pioneer family that established the town.

Mill City — City
ZIP: 97360 **Lat:** 44-44-59 N **Long:** 122-28-37 W
Pop: 1,247 (1990); 1,257 (1980) **Pop Density:** 2078.3
Land: 0.6 sq. mi.; **Water:** 0.0 sq. mi. **Elev:** 827 ft.
In northwestern OR on the North Santiam River, 30 mi. southeast of Salem. Incorporated 1947. Part of the town is also in Marion County.
Name origin: For an early sawmill.

Millersburg — City
ZIP: 97321 **Lat:** 44-40-50 N **Long:** 123-04-14 W
Pop: 715 (1990); 562 (1980) **Pop Density:** 162.5
Land: 4.4 sq. mi.; **Water:** 0.2 sq. mi. **Elev:** 242 ft.
Incorporated 1974.
Name origin: For the Miller family, who have lived here for more than a century.

Scio — City
ZIP: 97374 **Lat:** 44-42-19 N **Long:** 122-50-54 W
Pop: 623 (1990); 579 (1980) **Pop Density:** 2076.7
Land: 0.3 sq. mi.; **Water:** 0.0 sq. mi. **Elev:** 317 ft.
Incorporated 1866.
Name origin: For Scio, OH.

Sodaville — Town
ZIP: 97355 **Lat:** 44-29-02 N **Long:** 122-52-02 W
Pop: 192 (1990); 145 (1980) **Pop Density:** 640.0
Land: 0.3 sq. mi.; **Water:** 0.0 sq. mi.
Incorporated 1880.
Name origin: For a nearby mineral springs.

South Lebanon — CDP
Lat: 44-30-23 N **Long:** 122-54-07 W
Pop: 1,203 (1990); 1,309 (1980) **Pop Density:** 802.0
Land: 1.5 sq. mi.; **Water:** 0.0 sq. mi.

Sweet Home — City
ZIP: 97386 **Lat:** 44-24-06 N **Long:** 122-42-07 W
Pop: 6,850 (1990); 6,921 (1980) **Pop Density:** 1292.5
Land: 5.3 sq. mi.; **Water:** 0.4 sq. mi. **Elev:** 525 ft.
Incorporated 1893.
Name origin: From an early pioneer's description of it: "sweet home valley."

Tangent — City
ZIP: 97389 **Lat:** 44-33-04 N **Long:** 123-06-28 W
Pop: 556 (1990); 478 (1980) **Pop Density:** 146.3
Land: 3.8 sq. mi.; **Water:** 0.0 sq. mi. **Elev:** 246 ft.
Incorporated 1893.
Name origin: For its location on a straight 20-mi. segment of the Southern Pacific Railroad Line.

Waterloo — Town
ZIP: 97355 **Lat:** 44-29-42 N **Long:** 122-49-17 W
Pop: 191 (1990); 221 (1980) **Pop Density:** 955.0
Land: 0.2 sq. mi.; **Water:** 0.0 sq. mi.
Incorporated 1893.
Name origin: For the site of the famous defeat of Napoleon (1769–1821) by British and Prussian forces.

Malheur County
County Seat: Vale (ZIP: 97918)

Pop: 26,038 (1990); 26,896 (1980) **Pop Density:** 2.6
Land: 9887.7 sq. mi.; **Water:** 42.8 sq. mi. **Area Code:** 503
On eastern border of OR; organized Feb 17, 1887 from Baker county.
Name origin: For the Malheur River, which flows through it; from French 'misfortune', given to the river by trappers who were attacked by Indians and lost all their furs.

Adrian   City
ZIP: 97901 **Lat:** 43-44-27 N **Long:** 117-04-12 W
Pop: 131 (1990); 162 (1980) **Pop Density:** 655.0
Land: 0.2 sq. mi.; **Water:** 0.0 sq. mi.
Founded early 1900s; incorporated 1972.
Name origin: For sheepman James Adrian.

Jordan Valley   Town
ZIP: 97910 **Lat:** 42-58-35 N **Long:** 117-03-15 W
Pop: 364 (1990); 473 (1980) **Pop Density:** 173.3
Land: 2.1 sq. mi.; **Water:** 0.0 sq. mi. **Elev:** 4389 ft.
Established 1870s; incorporated 1911.
Name origin: For the biblical location.

Nyssa   Town
ZIP: 97913 **Lat:** 43-52-42 N **Long:** 116-59-50 W
Pop: 2,629 (1990); 2,862 (1980) **Pop Density:** 2629.0
Land: 1.0 sq. mi.; **Water:** 0.0 sq. mi. **Elev:** 2177 ft.
Incorporated 1903.
Name origin: Named by Greek residents for the mythological Nysaean nymphs, who reared the infant Bacchus.

Ontario   City
ZIP: 97914 **Lat:** 44-01-28 N **Long:** 116-58-27 W
Pop: 9,392 (1990); 8,814 (1980) **Pop Density:** 2290.7
Land: 4.1 sq. mi.; **Water:** 0.0 sq. mi. **Elev:** 2154 ft.
Incorporated 1899.
Name origin: For Ontario, Canada, the birthplace of pioneer James Virtue.

Vale   City
ZIP: 97918 **Lat:** 43-58-59 N **Long:** 117-14-25 W
Pop: 1,491 (1990); 1,558 (1980) **Pop Density:** 1491.0
Land: 1.0 sq. mi.; **Water:** 0.0 sq. mi.
Incorporated 1889.

Marion County
County Seat: Salem (ZIP: 97301)

Pop: 228,483 (1990); 204,692 (1980) **Pop Density:** 192.8
Land: 1185.0 sq. mi.; **Water:** 10.2 sq. mi. **Area Code:** 503
In northwest OR, south of Portland; original county; organized as Champoick County Jul 5, 1843 (prior to statehood); name changed 1849.
Name origin: For Gen. Francis Marion (c. 1732–95), SC soldier and legislator, known as "The Swamp Fox" for his tactics during the Revolutionary War.

Aumsville   City
ZIP: 97325 **Lat:** 44-50-44 N **Long:** 122-52-05 W
Pop: 1,650 (1990); 1,432 (1980) **Pop Density:** 2062.5
Land: 0.8 sq. mi.; **Water:** 0.0 sq. mi. **Elev:** 363 ft.
Incorporated 1911.
Name origin: For early settler Amos "Aumus" M. Davis.

Aurora   City
ZIP: 97002 **Lat:** 45-13-41 N **Long:** 122-45-20 W
Pop: 567 (1990); 523 (1980) **Pop Density:** 1417.5
Land: 0.4 sq. mi.; **Water:** 0.0 sq. mi. **Elev:** 133 ft.
Settled 1857; incorporated 1893.
Name origin: For the Roman goddess of dawn.

Detroit   City
ZIP: 97342 **Lat:** 44-44-01 N **Long:** 122-09-03 W
Pop: 331 (1990); 367 (1980) **Pop Density:** 662.0
Land: 0.5 sq. mi.; **Water:** 0.3 sq. mi.
Established 1891; incorporated 1952.
Name origin: For Detroit, MI.

Donald   City
Lat: 45-13-22 N **Long:** 122-50-15 W
Pop: 316 (1990); 267 (1980) **Pop Density:** 1580.0
Land: 0.2 sq. mi.; **Water:** 0.0 sq. mi. **Elev:** 195 ft.
Incorporated 1912.
Name origin: For R.L. Donald, a railroad construction official.

OREGON, Marion County

Four Corners CDP
ZIP: 97301 Lat: 44-55-44 N Long: 122-58-11 W
Pop: 12,156 (1990); 11,331 (1980) Pop Density: 4052.0
Land: 3.0 sq. mi.; Water: 0.0 sq. mi.

Gates City
ZIP: 97346 Lat: 44-45-22 N Long: 122-25-12 W
Pop: 458 (1990); 417 (1980) Pop Density: 763.3
Land: 0.6 sq. mi.; Water: 0.0 sq. mi. Elev: 942 ft.
Settled 1882; incorporated 1950. Part of the town is also in Linn County.
Name origin: For Mrs. Gates, one of the oldest pioneer settlers.

Gervais City
ZIP: 97026 Lat: 45-06-30 N Long: 122-53-41 W
Pop: 992 (1990); 799 (1980) Pop Density: 2480.0
Land: 0.4 sq. mi.; Water: 0.0 sq. mi. Elev: 184 ft.
Incorporated 1878.
Name origin: For French trapper Joseph Gervais, who came to OR in 1811.

Hayesville CDP
ZIP: 97303 Lat: 44-59-04 N Long: 122-58-13 W
Pop: 14,318 (1990); 9,213 (1980) Pop Density: 3254.1
Land: 4.4 sq. mi.; Water: 0.0 sq. mi.

Hubbard City
ZIP: 97032 Lat: 45-10-52 N Long: 122-48-21 W
Pop: 1,881 (1990); 1,640 (1980) Pop Density: 3135.0
Land: 0.6 sq. mi.; Water: 0.0 sq. mi. Elev: 182 ft.
Incorporated 1891.
Name origin: For pioneer settler Charles Hubbard, who came to OR in 1847.

Idanha City
ZIP: 97350 Lat: 44-42-17 N Long: 122-05-14 W
Pop: 177 (1990); 202 (1980) Pop Density: 177.0
Land: 1.0 sq. mi.; Water: 0.0 sq. mi. Elev: 1718 ft.
In northwestern OR on the North Santiam River near Detroit Lake. Incorporated 1895. Part of the town is also in Linn County.

Jefferson City
ZIP: 97352 Lat: 44-43-04 N Long: 123-00-18 W
Pop: 1,805 (1990); 1,702 (1980) Pop Density: 2578.6
Land: 0.7 sq. mi.; Water: 0.0 sq. mi. Elev: 230 ft.
Incorporated 1870.
Name origin: For Thomas Jefferson (1743–1826), third U.S. president.

Keizer City
ZIP: 97303 Lat: 45-00-14 N Long: 123-01-16 W
Pop: 21,884 (1990); 18,592 (1980) Pop Density: 3039.4
Land: 7.2 sq. mi.; Water: 0.1 sq. mi. Elev: 134 ft.
In northwestern OR, 4 mi. north of Salem. Incorporated 1982.

Mill City City
ZIP: 97346 Lat: 44-45-20 N Long: 122-28-35 W
Pop: 308 (1990); 308 (1980) Pop Density: 1540.0
Land: 0.2 sq. mi.; Water: 0.0 sq. mi. Elev: 827 ft.
In northwestern OR on the North Santiam River, 30 mi. southeast of Salem. Incorporated 1947. Part of the town is also in Linn County.
Name origin: For an early sawmill.

Mount Angel City
ZIP: 97362 Lat: 45-04-09 N Long: 122-47-39 W
Pop: 2,778 (1990); 2,876 (1980) Pop Density: 3086.7
Land: 0.9 sq. mi.; Water: 0.0 sq. mi.
Incorporated 1893.
Name origin: For Engelberg, Switzerland (anglicized to 'Mount Angel').

St. Paul City
Lat: 45-12-46 N Long: 122-58-31 W
Pop: 322 (1990); 312 (1980) Pop Density: 1073.3
Land: 0.3 sq. mi.; Water: 0.0 sq. mi. Elev: 170 ft.
Incorporated 1901.
Name origin: For the Saint Paul Mission.

Salem City
ZIP: 97301 Lat: 44-55-08 N Long: 123-00-54 W
Pop: 94,983 (1990); 78,552 (1980) Pop Density: 2574.1
Land: 36.9 sq. mi.; Water: 0.4 sq. mi. Elev: 154 ft.
In northwestern OR on the Willamette River, 44 mi. south-southwest of Portland. State capital; settled 1840; incorporated 1857. Commercial center for the surrounding agricultural area. Part of the town is also in Polk County.
Name origin: Anglicization of the Hebrew word *Shalom*; its popularity is partly due to the fact that it serves as a shortened form of Jeru*salem* 'the City of Peace.' Originally called Chemetka, an Indian term for 'place of peace.'

Scotts Mills City
ZIP: 97375 Lat: 45-02-27 N Long: 122-40-05 W
Pop: 283 (1990); 249 (1980) Pop Density: 943.3
Land: 0.3 sq. mi.; Water: 0.0 sq. mi.
Incorporated 1916.
Name origin: For pioneers Robert and Thomas Scott's 1860s sawmill.

Silverton City
ZIP: 97381 Lat: 45-00-27 N Long: 122-46-50 W
Pop: 5,635 (1990); 5,168 (1980) Pop Density: 2965.8
Land: 1.9 sq. mi.; Water: 0.0 sq. mi. Elev: 249 ft.
In northwestern OR on Silver Creek, 12 mi. northeast of Salem. Settled 1840s; incorporated 1885.
Name origin: For the creek.

Stayton City
ZIP: 97383 Lat: 44-48-06 N Long: 122-47-46 W
Pop: 5,011 (1990); 4,396 (1980) Pop Density: 2004.4
Land: 2.5 sq. mi.; Water: 0.0 sq. mi. Elev: 457 ft.
Established 1872; incorporated 1901.
Name origin: For its founder, Drury S. Stayton.

Sublimity City
ZIP: 97385 Lat: 44-49-45 N Long: 122-47-30 W
Pop: 1,491 (1990); 1,077 (1980) Pop Density: 1491.0
Land: 1.0 sq. mi.; Water: 0.0 sq. mi. Elev: 548 ft.
Founded 1852; incorporated 1903.
Name origin: For its "sublime scenery."

Turner City
ZIP: 97392 Lat: 44-50-45 N Long: 122-57-05 W
Pop: 1,281 (1990); 1,116 (1980) Pop Density: 1067.5
Land: 1.2 sq. mi.; Water: 0.0 sq. mi.
Incorporated 1905.
Name origin: For pioneer Henry L. Turner.

Woodburn — City
ZIP: 97071 **Lat:** 45-08-54 N **Long:** 122-51-20 W
Pop: 13,404 (1990); 11,196 (1980) **Pop Density:** 3191.4
Land: 4.2 sq. mi.; **Water:** 0.0 sq. mi. **Elev:** 183 ft.
In northwestern OR, 16 mi. north-northeast of Salem. Incorporated 1889.
Name origin: For the main energy source of its settlers.

Morrow County
County Seat: Heppner (ZIP: 97836)

Pop: 7,625 (1990); 7,519 (1980) **Pop Density:** 3.8
Land: 2032.8 sq. mi.; **Water:** 15.8 sq. mi. **Area Code:** 503
On central northern border of OR; organized Feb 16, 1885 from Umatilla County.
Name origin: For Jackson L. Morrow (1827–99), member of the first state legislature.

Boardman — City
ZIP: 97818 **Lat:** 45-50-15 N **Long:** 119-42-08 W
Pop: 1,387 (1990); 1,261 (1980) **Pop Density:** 513.7
Land: 2.7 sq. mi.; **Water:** 0.4 sq. mi.
Settled 1916; incorporated 1927.
Name origin: For its founder, Sam Boardman.

Heppner — City
ZIP: 97836 **Lat:** 45-21-14 N **Long:** 119-33-10 W
Pop: 1,412 (1990); 1,498 (1980) **Pop Density:** 1176.7
Land: 1.2 sq. mi.; **Water:** 0.0 sq. mi. **Elev:** 1955 ft.
Incorporated 1887.
Name origin: For Henry Heppner, who opened its first store in 1873.

Ione — City
ZIP: 97843 **Lat:** 45-30-03 N **Long:** 119-49-20 W
Pop: 255 (1990); 345 (1980) **Pop Density:** 510.0
Land: 0.5 sq. mi.; **Water:** 0.0 sq. mi. **Elev:** 1085 ft.
Incorporated 1903.
Name origin: For Ione Arthur, so named by pioneer E. G. Sperry.

Irrigon — City
ZIP: 97844 **Lat:** 45-53-48 N **Long:** 119-29-16 W
Pop: 737 (1990); 700 (1980) **Pop Density:** 737.0
Land: 1.0 sq. mi.; **Water:** 0.2 sq. mi. **Elev:** 297 ft.
On the central-northern border of WA, northwest of Pendleton. Incorporated 1957.
Name origin: From a combination of *irri*gation and Ore*gon*, for the large irrigation project being constructed in 1905, when the name was changed from Stokes.

Lexington — Town
ZIP: 97839 **Lat:** 45-26-44 N **Long:** 119-41-11 W
Pop: 286 (1990); 307 (1980) **Pop Density:** 715.0
Land: 0.4 sq. mi.; **Water:** 0.0 sq. mi.
Incorporated 1903.
Name origin: For Lexington, KY, the former home of pioneer William Penland.

Multnomah County
County Seat: Portland (ZIP: 97204)

Pop: 583,887 (1990); 562,647 (1980) **Pop Density:** 1341.5
Land: 435.3 sq. mi.; **Water:** 30.4 sq. mi. **Area Code:** 503
On central northern border of OR; organized Dec 22, 1854 (prior to statehood) from Clackamas and Washington counties. The smallest county in OR by size and largest by population.
Name origin: For the Multnomah Indian village on Sauvie Island; Lewis and Clark applied the name to all local Indians. From *nemathlonamaq* probably meaning 'downriver.'

Fairview — City
ZIP: 97024 **Lat:** 45-32-46 N **Long:** 122-26-05 W
Pop: 2,391 (1990); 1,749 (1980) **Pop Density:** 747.2
Land: 3.2 sq. mi.; **Water:** 0.2 sq. mi.
Settled 1850s; incorporated 1908.
Name origin: From the name of a Methodist Church.

Gresham — City
ZIP: 97030 **Lat:** 45-30-13 N **Long:** 122-26-17 W
Pop: 68,235 (1990); 33,005 (1980) **Pop Density:** 3087.6
Land: 22.1 sq. mi.; **Water:** 0.1 sq. mi. **Elev:** 323 ft.
In northwestern OR, 14 mi. east of Portland. Incorporated 1905.
Name origin: For politician and general Walter Q. Gresham.

OREGON, Multnomah County

Hazelwood
CDP
ZIP: 97230 **Lat:** 45-30-59 N **Long:** 122-31-21 W
Pop: 11,480 (1990); 25,541 (1980) **Pop Density:** 5466.7
Land: 2.1 sq. mi.; **Water:** 0.0 sq. mi.

Lake Oswego
City
ZIP: 97034-35 **Lat:** 45-26-04 N **Long:** 122-42-46 W
Pop: 2,253 (1990); 1,209 (1980) **Pop Density:** 4506.0
Land: 0.5 sq. mi.; **Water:** 0.0 sq. mi.
In northwestern OR, 8 mi. south of Portland. Incorporated 1910. Part of the town is also in Clackamas and Washington counties.
Name origin: For its position on Lake Oswego, which is named for Oswego, NY.

Maywood Park
City
ZIP: 97220 **Lat:** 45-33-09 N **Long:** 122-33-39 W
Pop: 781 (1990); 845 (1980) **Pop Density:** 3905.0
Land: 0.2 sq. mi.; **Water:** 0.0 sq. mi.
Incorporated 1967.
Name origin: Descriptively named by its developers.

Milwaukie
City
ZIP: 97222 **Lat:** 45-27-41 N **Long:** 122-36-38 W
Pop: 0 (1990); 17,931 (1980)
Land: 0.005 sq. mi.; **Water:** 0.0 sq. mi.
Settled 1847; incorporated 1903. Part of the town is also in Clackamas County.
Name origin: For Milwaukee, WI, with a spelling variation.

Portland
City
ZIP: 97208 **Lat:** 45-32-20 N **Long:** 122-39-30 W
Pop: 435,415 (1990); 366,792 (1980) **Pop Density:** 3511.4
Land: 124.0 sq. mi.; **Water:** 9.7 sq. mi.
In northwestern OR on the Willamette River, 10 mi. east of its confluence with the Columbia River. OR's largest city and principal port. Founded 1845; incorporated 1851. Diverse manufacturing city: metal processing, electric equipment, lumber and wood products. Part of the town is also in Clackamas and Washington counties, but Multnomah is the county in which the city of Portland has its greatest population.
Name origin: For Portland, ME, arrived at by flipping a coin to choose between it and Boston, homes of the founders, Asa L. Lovejoy of Boston and Francis W. Pettygrove.

Powellhurst-Centennial
CDP
Lat: 45-29-46 N **Long:** 122-30-54 W
Pop: 28,756 (1990); 20,132 (1980) **Pop Density:** 5325.2
Land: 5.4 sq. mi.; **Water:** 0.0 sq. mi.

Troutdale
City
ZIP: 97060 **Lat:** 45-32-12 N **Long:** 122-23-26 W
Pop: 7,852 (1990); 5,908 (1980) **Pop Density:** 1570.4
Land: 5.0 sq. mi.; **Water:** 0.0 sq. mi. **Elev:** 73 ft.
Incorporated 1907.
Name origin: For a nearby pond stocked with trout. Originally called Sandy.

Wood Village
City
ZIP: 97060 **Lat:** 45-32-00 N **Long:** 122-25-13 W
Pop: 2,814 (1990); 2,253 (1980) **Pop Density:** 3517.5
Land: 0.8 sq. mi.; **Water:** 0.0 sq. mi.
Incorporated 1951.
Name origin: For Portland real estate agent Lester J. Wood.

Polk County
County Seat: Dallas (ZIP: 97338)

Pop: 49,541 (1990); 45,203 (1980) **Pop Density:** 66.8
Land: 741.1 sq. mi.; **Water:** 3.1 sq. mi. **Area Code:** 503
In northwest OR, west of Salem; original county; organized Dec 22, 1845 (prior to statehood) from the Yamhill district.
Name origin: For James Knox Polk (1795–1849), eleventh U.S. president.

Dallas
City
ZIP: 97338 **Lat:** 44-55-16 N **Long:** 123-18-44 W
Pop: 9,422 (1990); 8,530 (1980) **Pop Density:** 2191.2
Land: 4.3 sq. mi.; **Water:** 0.0 sq. mi. **Elev:** 326 ft.
Incorporated 1874.
Name origin: For George M. Dallas, Pres. James K. Polk's vice president (1845–49).

Falls City
City
ZIP: 97344 **Lat:** 44-51-56 N **Long:** 123-26-12 W
Pop: 818 (1990); 804 (1980) **Pop Density:** 681.7
Land: 1.2 sq. mi.; **Water:** 0.0 sq. mi. **Elev:** 370 ft.
Incorporated 1893.
Name origin: For the nearby falls on the Little Luckiamute River.

Independence
City
ZIP: 97351 **Lat:** 44-51-19 N **Long:** 123-11-32 W
Pop: 4,425 (1990); 4,024 (1980) **Pop Density:** 2107.1
Land: 2.1 sq. mi.; **Water:** 0.1 sq. mi. **Elev:** 168 ft.
Incorporated 1874.
Name origin: For Indpendence, MO, so named by settler E. A. Thorp, who came to OR in 1845.

Monmouth
City
ZIP: 97361 **Lat:** 44-51-01 N **Long:** 123-13-43 W
Pop: 6,288 (1990); 5,594 (1980) **Pop Density:** 3930.0
Land: 1.6 sq. mi.; **Water:** 0.0 sq. mi. **Elev:** 201 ft.
Settled 1853; incorporated 1880.
Name origin: For Monmouth, IL.

Salem City
ZIP: 97301 **Lat:** 44-57-08 N **Long:** 123-04-01 W
Pop: 12,803 (1990); 10,539 (1980) **Pop Density:** 2724.0
Land: 4.7 sq. mi.; **Water:** 0.2 sq. mi. **Elev:** 154 ft.
In northwestern OR on the Willamette River, 44 mi. south-southwest of Portland. State capital; settled 1840; incorporated 1857. Commercial center for the surrounding agricultural area. Part of the town is also in Marion County.
Name origin: Anglicization of the Hebrew word *Shalom*; its popularity is partly due to the fact that it serves as a shortened form of Jeru*salem* 'the City of Peace.' Originally called Chemetka, an Indian term for 'place of peace.'

Willamina City
ZIP: 97396 **Lat:** 45-04-26 N **Long:** 123-29-07 W
Pop: 523 (1990); 563 (1980) **Pop Density:** 2615.0
Land: 0.2 sq. mi.; **Water:** 0.0 sq. mi. **Elev:** 225 ft.
In northwestern OR on Willamina Creek, 25 mi. northwest of Salem. Incorporated 1903. Part of the town is also in Yamhill County.
Name origin: For its creek, itself named for Mrs. Willamina Williams, the area's first European woman.

Sherman County
County Seat: Moro (ZIP: 97039)

Pop: 1,918 (1990); 2,172 (1980) **Pop Density:** 2.3
Land: 823.3 sq. mi.; **Water:** 8.0 sq. mi. **Area Code:** 503
On central northern border of OR; organized Feb 25, 1889 from Wasco County.
Name origin: For Gen. William Tecumseh Sherman (1820–91), officer in the Mexican-American War and the Civil War, remembered for his "march to the sea" through the South.

Grass Valley City
ZIP: 97029 **Lat:** 45-21-35 N **Long:** 120-46-59 W
Pop: 160 (1990); 164 (1980) **Pop Density:** 320.0
Land: 0.5 sq. mi.; **Water:** 0.0 sq. mi. **Elev:** 2252 ft.
Incorporated 1901.

Moro City
ZIP: 97039 **Lat:** 45-29-08 N **Long:** 120-43-54 W
Pop: 292 (1990); 336 (1980) **Pop Density:** 584.0
Land: 0.5 sq. mi.; **Water:** 0.0 sq. mi. **Elev:** 1808 ft.
Founded late 1860s; incorporated 1899.
Name origin: For Moro, IL.

Rufus City
ZIP: 97050 **Lat:** 45-41-37 N **Long:** 120-44-22 W
Pop: 295 (1990); 352 (1980) **Pop Density:** 245.8
Land: 1.2 sq. mi.; **Water:** 0.0 sq. mi. **Elev:** 206 ft.
Incorporated 1965.
Name origin: For its original settler, Rufus C. Wallis.

Wasco City
ZIP: 97065 **Lat:** 45-35-29 N **Long:** 120-41-44 W
Pop: 374 (1990); 415 (1980) **Pop Density:** 374.0
Land: 1.0 sq. mi.; **Water:** 0.0 sq. mi. **Elev:** 1270 ft.
Incorporated 1898.
Name origin: For the Wasco Indians, who once lived on the Columbia River.

Tillamook County
County Seat: Tillamook (ZIP: 97141)

Pop: 21,570 (1990); 21,164 (1980) **Pop Density:** 19.6
Land: 1102.2 sq. mi.; **Water:** 230.6 sq. mi. **Area Code:** 503
On the northwestern coast of OR, west of Portland; organized Dec 15, 1853 (prior to statehood) from Clatsop and Yamhill counties.
Name origin: For the Tillamook Indians, from Chinook 'people of Nekelim,' because the tribe lived on the Nehalem and Salmon rivers.

Bay City City
ZIP: 97107 **Lat:** 45-31-16 N **Long:** 123-53-06 W
Pop: 1,027 (1990); 986 (1980) **Pop Density:** 790.0
Land: 1.3 sq. mi.; **Water:** 0.4 sq. mi. **Elev:** 18 ft.
Established 1888; incorporated 1910.
Name origin: For Bay City, MI.

Garibaldi City
ZIP: 97118 **Lat:** 45-33-37 N **Long:** 123-54-36 W
Pop: 877 (1990); 999 (1980) **Pop Density:** 877.0
Land: 1.0 sq. mi.; **Water:** 0.4 sq. mi.
Incorporated 1946.
Name origin: Named in the 1860s by pioneer settler Daniel Bayley for the Italian patriot Giuseppe Garibaldi (1807–82).

OREGON, Tillamook County

Manzanita — City
ZIP: 97130 Lat: 45-43-02 N Long: 123-56-00 W
Pop: 513 (1990); 443 (1980) Pop Density: 732.9
Land: 0.7 sq. mi.; Water: 0.0 sq. mi. Elev: 111 ft.
Incorporated 1946.

Nehalem — Town
ZIP: 97131 Lat: 45-43-15 N Long: 123-53-29 W
Pop: 232 (1990); 258 (1980) Pop Density: 773.3
Land: 0.3 sq. mi.; Water: 0.0 sq. mi.
Incorporated 1899.
Name origin: For the Nehalem Indians, who lived here.

Rockaway Beach — City
ZIP: 97136 Lat: 45-36-53 N Long: 123-56-17 W
Pop: 970 (1990); 906 (1980) Pop Density: 692.9
Land: 1.4 sq. mi.; Water: 0.1 sq. mi. Elev: 16 ft.
Incorporated 1942.
Name origin: For Rockaway Beach, Long Island, NY.

Tillamook — City
ZIP: 97141 Lat: 45-27-24 N Long: 123-50-15 W
Pop: 4,001 (1990); 3,981 (1980) Pop Density: 2667.3
Land: 1.5 sq. mi.; Water: 0.0 sq. mi. Elev: 16 ft.
On the northwestern coast of OR, southwest of Portland. Incorporated 1891.
Name origin: From Chinook 'people of Nekelim,' referring to the indigenous Tillamook tribe.

Wheeler — City
ZIP: 97147 Lat: 45-41-13 N Long: 123-53-02 W
Pop: 335 (1990); 319 (1980) Pop Density: 558.3
Land: 0.6 sq. mi.; Water: 0.0 sq. mi. Elev: 18 ft.
Incorporated 1914.
Name origin: For Portland lumberman C.H. Wheeler.

Umatilla County
County Seat: Pendleton (ZIP: 97801)

Pop: 59,249 (1990); 58,861 (1980) Pop Density: 18.4
Land: 3215.3 sq. mi.; Water: 16.0 sq. mi. Area Code: 503
On northeastern border of OR; organized Sep 27, 1862 from Wasco County.
Name origin: For the Umatilla River, which runs through the county; the river is itself named for the Umatilla Indian tribe. The meaning of the name is disputed: possibly 'water rippling over sand.'

Adams — City
ZIP: 97810 Lat: 45-46-02 N Long: 118-33-45 W
Pop: 223 (1990); 240 (1980) Pop Density: 743.3
Land: 0.3 sq. mi.; Water: 0.0 sq. mi. Elev: 1513 ft.
Incorporated 1893.
Name origin: For original settler John F. Adams.

Athena — City
ZIP: 97813 Lat: 45-48-46 N Long: 118-29-29 W
Pop: 997 (1990); 965 (1980) Pop Density: 1994.0
Land: 0.5 sq. mi.; Water: 0.0 sq. mi. Elev: 1710 ft.
Incorporated 1905.
Name origin: For the Greek goddess of wisdom, war, and industry. Originally called Centerville.

Echo — City
ZIP: 97826 Lat: 45-44-38 N Long: 119-11-31 W
Pop: 499 (1990); 624 (1980) Pop Density: 831.7
Land: 0.6 sq. mi.; Water: 0.0 sq. mi. Elev: 638 ft.
Incorporated 1904.
Name origin: For Echo Koontz, daughter of a pioneer family.

Helix — City
ZIP: 97835 Lat: 45-51-00 N Long: 118-39-26 W
Pop: 150 (1990); 155 (1980) Pop Density: 1500.0
Land: 0.1 sq. mi.; Water: 0.0 sq. mi. Elev: 1754 ft.
Incorporated 1919.
Name origin: From the fact that a resident's helix (external ear rim) was infected at the time of the town's naming.

Hermiston — City
ZIP: 97838 Lat: 45-49-58 N Long: 119-17-00 W
Pop: 10,040 (1990); 9,408 (1980) Pop Density: 1792.9
Land: 5.6 sq. mi.; Water: 0.0 sq. mi. Elev: 457 ft.
Incorporated 1907.
Name origin: For *Wier of Hermiston*, an unfinished novel by Robert Louis Stevenson (1850–94); so named by pioneer Col. F. McNaught.

Milton-Freewater — City
ZIP: 97862 Lat: 45-56-05 N Long: 118-23-25 W
Pop: 5,533 (1990); 5,086 (1980) Pop Density: 3254.7
Land: 1.7 sq. mi.; Water: 0.0 sq. mi. Elev: 1033 ft.
Incorporated 1950.
Name origin: From a merger in 1951 of Milton and Freewater.

Mission — CDP
Lat: 45-40-01 N Long: 118-40-18 W
Pop: 664 (1990) Pop Density: 288.7
Land: 2.3 sq. mi.; Water: 0.0 sq. mi.

Pendleton — City
ZIP: 97801 Lat: 45-40-25 N Long: 118-49-02 W
Pop: 15,126 (1990); 14,521 (1980) Pop Density: 1527.9
Land: 9.9 sq. mi.; Water: 0.0 sq. mi. Elev: 1068 ft.
In northeastern OR on the Umatilla River, 192 mi. east of Portland. Incorporated 1880.
Name origin: For George Hunt Pendleton (1825–89), an OH senator and vice presidential candidate.

Pilot Rock — City
ZIP: 97868   **Lat:** 45-28-53 N   **Long:** 118-49-55 W
Pop: 1,478 (1990); 1,630 (1980)   **Pop Density:** 2956.0
Land: 0.5 sq. mi.; **Water:** 0.0 sq. mi.   **Elev:** 1636 ft.
Incorporated 1912.

Stanfield — City
ZIP: 97875   **Lat:** 45-47-10 N   **Long:** 119-13-10 W
Pop: 1,568 (1990); 1,568 (1980)   **Pop Density:** 1120.0
Land: 1.4 sq. mi.; **Water:** 0.0 sq. mi.
In north-central OR on Birch Creek near the WA border, 22 mi. northwest of Pendleton. Founded 1880s; incorporated 1910.
Name origin: For U.S. senator Robert N. Stanfield.

Ukiah — City
ZIP: 97880   **Lat:** 45-08-01 N   **Long:** 118-55-54 W
Pop: 250 (1990); 249 (1980)   **Pop Density:** 1250.0
Land: 0.2 sq. mi.; **Water:** 0.0 sq. mi.   **Elev:** 3353 ft.
Settled 1898; incorporated 1969.
Name origin: For Ukiah, CA.

Umatilla — City
ZIP: 97882   **Lat:** 45-54-47 N   **Long:** 119-19-40 W
Pop: 3,046 (1990); 3,199 (1980)   **Pop Density:** 1128.1
Land: 2.7 sq. mi.; **Water:** 0.2 sq. mi.   **Elev:** 296 ft.
Incorporated 1864.
Name origin: For the Umatilla, among the area's original Indians.

Weston — City
ZIP: 97886   **Lat:** 45-48-56 N   **Long:** 118-25-29 W
Pop: 606 (1990); 719 (1980)   **Pop Density:** 1212.0
Land: 0.5 sq. mi.; **Water:** 0.0 sq. mi.   **Elev:** 1838 ft.
Established 1860s; incorporated 1878.
Name origin: For Weston, MO.

Union County
County Seat: La Grande (ZIP: 97850)

Pop: 23,598 (1990); 23,921 (1980)   **Pop Density:** 11.6
Land: 2036.7 sq. mi.; **Water:** 1.7 sq. mi.   **Area Code:** 503
In northeastern OR; organized Oct 14, 1864 from Baker County.
Name origin: For the town of Union, named in 1862 in support of the Union forces in the Civil War.

Cove — City
ZIP: 97824   **Lat:** 45-17-48 N   **Long:** 117-48-34 W
Pop: 507 (1990); 451 (1980)   **Pop Density:** 633.8
Land: 0.8 sq. mi.; **Water:** 0.0 sq. mi.
Incorporated 1904.
Name origin: For its location where Mill Creek flows from the Wallowa Mountains.

Elgin — City
ZIP: 97827   **Lat:** 45-33-52 N   **Long:** 117-55-12 W
Pop: 1,586 (1990); 1,701 (1980)   **Pop Density:** 1586.0
Land: 1.0 sq. mi.; **Water:** 0.0 sq. mi.   **Elev:** 2716 ft.
Incorporated 1891.
Name origin: From the song "Wreck of the Lady Elgin," so named by its postmaster. Formerly called Fishtrap.

Imbler — City
ZIP: 97841   **Lat:** 45-27-44 N   **Long:** 117-57-44 W
Pop: 299 (1990); 292 (1980)   **Pop Density:** 1495.0
Land: 0.2 sq. mi.; **Water:** 0.0 sq. mi.   **Elev:** 2731 ft.
Settled 19th century; incorporated 1922.
Name origin: For the Imblers, a pioneer family.

Island City — Town
Lat: 45-20-19 N   **Long:** 118-02-45 W
Pop: 696 (1990); 477 (1980)   **Pop Density:** 1740.0
Land: 0.4 sq. mi.; **Water:** 0.0 sq. mi.
Incorporated 1904.
Name origin: For its location on an island formed by a slough of the Grande Ronde River.

La Grande — City
ZIP: 97850   **Lat:** 45-19-31 N   **Long:** 118-05-14 W
Pop: 11,766 (1990); 11,354 (1980)   **Pop Density:** 2941.5
Land: 4.0 sq. mi.; **Water:** 0.0 sq. mi.   **Elev:** 2771 ft.
In northeastern OR on the Grande Ronde River, which traverses the county. Settled 1860s; incorporated 1865.
Name origin: For the impressive views of the surrounding Grande Ronde Valley.

North Powder — City
ZIP: 97867   **Lat:** 45-01-50 N   **Long:** 117-55-07 W
Pop: 448 (1990); 430 (1980)   **Pop Density:** 746.7
Land: 0.6 sq. mi.; **Water:** 0.0 sq. mi.   **Elev:** 3256 ft.
In northeast OR on the Powder River, 20 mi. southeast of La Grande. Incorporated 1903.
Name origin: For its location on the river's northernmost bend.

Summerville — Town
ZIP: 97876   **Lat:** 45-29-23 N   **Long:** 118-00-09 W
Pop: 111 (1990); 143 (1980)   **Pop Density:** 370.0
Land: 0.3 sq. mi.; **Water:** 0.0 sq. mi.
Settled 1865; incorporated 1885.
Name origin: For pioneer Alexander Sommerville; spelling altered to reflect pronunciation.

Union
ZIP: 97883   **Lat:** 45-12-32 N   **Long:** 117-52-01 W
Pop: 1,847 (1990); 2,062 (1980)   **Pop Density:** 738.8
Land: 2.5 sq. mi.; **Water:** 0.0 sq. mi.   **Elev:** 2788 ft.
Founded 1862; incorporated 1878.
Name origin: For the embattled "Union," so named during the Civil War by patriotic citizens.

Wallowa County
County Seat: Enterprise (ZIP: 97828)

Pop: 6,911 (1990); 7,273 (1980)   **Pop Density:** 2.2
Land: 3145.4 sq. mi.; **Water:** 6.4 sq. mi.   **Area Code:** 503
On northeastern border of OR; organized Feb 11, 1887 from Union County.
Name origin: A Nez Perce word for the 'tripod' used to support netting to catch fish.

Enterprise City
ZIP: 97828   **Lat:** 45-25-30 N   **Long:** 117-16-33 W
Pop: 1,905 (1990); 2,003 (1980)   **Pop Density:** 1465.4
Land: 1.3 sq. mi.; **Water:** 0.0 sq. mi.   **Elev:** 3756 ft.
Incorporated 1889.
Name origin: For the pioneer virtue, so named in 1887.

Joseph City
ZIP: 97846   **Lat:** 45-21-07 N   **Long:** 117-13-40 W
Pop: 1,073 (1990); 999 (1980)   **Pop Density:** 1532.9
Land: 0.7 sq. mi.; **Water:** 0.0 sq. mi.   **Elev:** 4190 ft.
Incorporated 1887.
Name origin: For Nez Perce chief Hinmaton-Yalaktit (known as "Chief Joseph," c.1840–1904), captured by the U.S. Army in 1877.

Lostine City
ZIP: 97857   **Lat:** 45-29-13 N   **Long:** 117-25-44 W
Pop: 231 (1990); 250 (1980)   **Pop Density:** 770.0
Land: 0.3 sq. mi.; **Water:** 0.0 sq. mi.   **Elev:** 3363 ft.
Incorporated 1903.
Name origin: For Lostine, KS, the former home of a pioneer.

Wallowa City
ZIP: 97885   **Lat:** 45-34-14 N   **Long:** 117-31-39 W
Pop: 748 (1990); 847 (1980)   **Pop Density:** 1246.7
Land: 0.6 sq. mi.; **Water:** 0.0 sq. mi.   **Elev:** 2948 ft.
Incorporated 1899.
Name origin: From a Nez Perce term that describes a structure of stakes for catching fish.

Wasco County
County Seat: The Dalles (ZIP: 97058)

Pop: 21,683 (1990); 21,732 (1980)   **Pop Density:** 9.1
Land: 2381.2 sq. mi.; **Water:** 14.3 sq. mi.   **Area Code:** 503
On the central northern border of OR; organized Jan 11, 1854 (prior to statehood), from the original Champoeg district; it covered all of Oregon east of the Cascade Range, most of Idaho, and parts of MT and WY.
Name origin: For the Wasco or Wascopam Indian tribe of Chinookan linguistic stock; the name means 'cup' or 'bowl.'

Antelope City
ZIP: 97001   **Lat:** 44-54-39 N   **Long:** 120-43-21 W
Pop: 34 (1990); 39 (1980)   **Pop Density:** 68.0
Land: 0.5 sq. mi.; **Water:** 0.0 sq. mi.   **Elev:** 2632 ft.
Incorporated 1896.
Name origin: For the area's once-abundant antelope.

Chenoweth CDP
Lat: 45-37-38 N   **Long:** 121-13-48 W
Pop: 3,246 (1990); 2,820 (1980)   **Pop Density:** 541.0
Land: 6.0 sq. mi.; **Water:** 0.1 sq. mi.

The Dalles City
ZIP: 97058   **Lat:** 45-35-56 N   **Long:** 121-10-29 W
Pop: 11,060 (1990); 10,820 (1980)   **Pop Density:** 2257.1
Land: 4.9 sq. mi.; **Water:** 0.3 sq. mi.
In northern OR on the Columbia River, 72 mi. east of Portland. Incorporated 1857.
Name origin: For its location on the river's Dalles Narrows, so named from the French for 'flagstone.'

Dufur Town
ZIP: 97021   **Lat:** 45-27-12 N   **Long:** 121-07-37 W
Pop: 527 (1990); 560 (1980)   **Pop Density:** 878.3
Land: 0.6 sq. mi.; **Water:** 0.0 sq. mi.   **Elev:** 1320 ft.
Founded 1878; incorporated 1893.
Name origin: For local farmers Andrew and Burnham Dufur.

Maupin   City
ZIP: 97037   **Lat:** 45-10-30 N   **Long:** 121-04-58 W
Pop: 456 (1990); 495 (1980)   **Pop Density:** 414.5
Land: 1.1 sq. mi.; **Water:** 0.1 sq. mi.   **Elev:** 1041 ft.
In north-central OR on the Deschutes River, 28 mi. south of The Dalles. Incorporated 1922.
Name origin: For central OR pioneer Howard Maupin.

Mosier   City
ZIP: 97040   **Lat:** 45-41-01 N   **Long:** 121-23-41 W
Pop: 244 (1990); 340 (1980)   **Pop Density:** 488.0
Land: 0.5 sq. mi.; **Water:** 0.2 sq. mi.   **Elev:** 121 ft.
Begun 1853; incorporated 1914.
Name origin: For its founder, J. H. Mosier.

Shaniko   City
ZIP: 97057   **Lat:** 45-00-15 N   **Long:** 120-45-01 W
Pop: 26 (1990); 30 (1980)   **Pop Density:** 52.0
Land: 0.5 sq. mi.; **Water:** 0.0 sq. mi.   **Elev:** 3341 ft.
Incorporated 1901.
Name origin: For pioneer rancher August Scherneckau, who settled in OR after the Civil War; the spelling reflects the Indian pronunciation.

Washington County
County Seat: Hillsboro (**ZIP:** 97124)

Pop: 311,554 (1990); 245,860 (1980)   **Pop Density:** 430.4
Land: 723.8 sq. mi.; **Water:** 2.6 sq. mi.   **Area Code:** 503
In northwest OR, west of Portland; original county; organized as Tuality County Jul 5, 1843 (prior to statehood); name changed Sep 3, 1849.
Name origin: For George Washington (1732–99), American patriot and first U.S. president.

Aloha   CDP
ZIP: 97006   **Lat:** 45-29-31 N   **Long:** 122-52-18 W
Pop: 34,284 (1990); 28,353 (1980)   **Pop Density:** 4633.0
Land: 7.4 sq. mi.; **Water:** 0.0 sq. mi.

Banks   City
ZIP: 97106   **Lat:** 45-36-55 N   **Long:** 123-06-36 W
Pop: 563 (1990); 489 (1980)   **Pop Density:** 1876.7
Land: 0.3 sq. mi.; **Water:** 0.0 sq. mi.
Incorporated 1921.
Name origin: For pioneer resident Robert Banks.

Beaverton   City
ZIP: 97005   **Lat:** 45-28-31 N   **Long:** 122-48-59 W
Pop: 53,310 (1990); 31,962 (1980)   **Pop Density:** 3863.0
Land: 13.8 sq. mi.; **Water:** 0.0 sq. mi.   **Elev:** 189 ft.
In western OR, 10 mi. west of Portland. Settled 1869; incorporated 1893.
Name origin: For the many beaver once in the area.

Cedar Hills   CDP
ZIP: 97005   **Lat:** 45-30-13 N   **Long:** 122-48-20 W
Pop: 9,294 (1990); 9,619 (1980)   **Pop Density:** 3872.5
Land: 2.4 sq. mi.; **Water:** 0.0 sq. mi.

Cedar Mill   CDP
ZIP: 97229   **Lat:** 45-32-11 N   **Long:** 122-47-58 W
Pop: 9,697 (1990)   **Pop Density:** 2424.3
Land: 4.0 sq. mi.; **Water:** 0.0 sq. mi.

Cornelius   City
ZIP: 97113   **Lat:** 45-31-07 N   **Long:** 123-03-14 W
Pop: 6,148 (1990); 4,462 (1980)   **Pop Density:** 3415.6
Land: 1.8 sq. mi.; **Water:** 0.0 sq. mi.   **Elev:** 179 ft.
Incorporated 1893.
Name origin: For pioneer Col. T. R. Cornelius, who came to OR in 1845.

Durham   City
ZIP: 97224   **Lat:** 45-23-40 N   **Long:** 122-45-26 W
Pop: 748 (1990); 707 (1980)   **Pop Density:** 1870.0
Land: 0.4 sq. mi.; **Water:** 0.0 sq. mi.   **Elev:** 142 ft.
Incorporated 1966.
Name origin: For pioneer lumberman Albert A. Durham.

Forest Grove   City
ZIP: 97116   **Lat:** 45-31-20 N   **Long:** 123-06-15 W
Pop: 13,559 (1990); 11,499 (1980)   **Pop Density:** 3307.1
Land: 4.1 sq. mi.; **Water:** 0.1 sq. mi.
In northwestern OR, 22 mi. west of Portland. Incorporated 1872.
Name origin: For the homestead of pioneer settler J.Q. Thornton, so named in 1851.

Garden Home-Whitford   CDP
ZIP: 97223   **Lat:** 45-27-54 N   **Long:** 122-45-24 W
Pop: 6,652 (1990); 6,926 (1980)   **Pop Density:** 3167.6
Land: 2.1 sq. mi.; **Water:** 0.0 sq. mi.

Gaston   City
ZIP: 97119   **Lat:** 45-26-08 N   **Long:** 123-08-26 W
Pop: 563 (1990); 471 (1980)   **Pop Density:** 2815.0
Land: 0.2 sq. mi.; **Water:** 0.0 sq. mi.
Incorporated 1914.
Name origin: For Joseph Gaston, pioneer railroad promoter.

Hillsboro   City
ZIP: 97123   **Lat:** 45-31-39 N   **Long:** 122-56-20 W
Pop: 37,520 (1990); 27,664 (1980)   **Pop Density:** 1944.0
Land: 19.3 sq. mi.; **Water:** 0.0 sq. mi.
In northwestern OR, 15 mi. west of Portland. Incorporated 1876.
Name origin: For early settler and legislator David Hill.

OREGON, Washington County

King City
City
ZIP: 97224 **Lat:** 45-24-19 N **Long:** 122-48-05 W
Pop: 2,060 (1990); 1,853 (1980) **Pop Density:** 5150.0
Land: 0.4 sq. mi.; **Water:** 0.0 sq. mi. **Elev:** 160 ft.
Incorporated 1966.

Lake Oswego
City
ZIP: 97034-35 **Lat:** 45-23-27 N **Long:** 122-44-38 W
Pop: 6 (1990); 5 (1980) **Pop Density:** 300.0
Land: 0.02 sq. mi.; **Water:** 0.0 sq. mi.
In northwestern OR, 8 mi. south of Portland. Incorporated 1910. Part of the town is also in Clackamas and Multnomah counties.
Name origin: For its position on Lake Oswego, which is named for Oswego, NY.

Metzger
CDP
Lat: 45-26-59 N **Long:** 122-45-41 W
Pop: 3,149 (1990); 5,544 (1980) **Pop Density:** 3936.3
Land: 0.8 sq. mi.; **Water:** 0.0 sq. mi.

North Plains
City
ZIP: 97133 **Lat:** 45-35-48 N **Long:** 122-59-55 W
Pop: 972 (1990); 715 (1980) **Pop Density:** 1388.6
Land: 0.7 sq. mi.; **Water:** 0.0 sq. mi.
Incorporated 1963.

Oak Hills
CDP
Lat: 45-32-28 N **Long:** 122-50-23 W
Pop: 6,450 (1990) **Pop Density:** 4031.3
Land: 1.6 sq. mi.; **Water:** 0.0 sq. mi.

Portland
City
ZIP: 97201-99 **Lat:** 45-28-02 N **Long:** 122-44-42 W
Pop: 1,197 (1990); 661 (1980) **Pop Density:** 5985.0
Land: 0.2 sq. mi.; **Water:** 0.0 sq. mi.
In northwestern OR on the Willamette River, 10 mi. east of its confluence with the Columbia River. OR's largest city and principal port. Founded 1845; incorporated 1851. Diverse manufacturing city: metal processing, electric equipment, lumber and wood products. Part of the town is also in Clackamas and Multnomah counties.
Name origin: For Portland, ME, arrived at by flipping a coin to choose between it and Boston, homes of the founders, Asa L. Lovejoy of Boston and Francis W. Pettygrove.

Raleigh Hills
CDP
ZIP: 97225 **Lat:** 45-29-05 N **Long:** 122-45-15 W
Pop: 6,066 (1990); 6,517 (1980) **Pop Density:** 3568.2
Land: 1.7 sq. mi.; **Water:** 0.0 sq. mi.

Rivergrove
City
Lat: 45-23-14 N **Long:** 122-44-49 W
Pop: 27 (1990); 27 (1980) **Pop Density:** 1350.0
Land: 0.02 sq. mi.; **Water:** 0.0 sq. mi.
Incorporated 1971. Part of the town is also in Clackamas County.
Name origin: From a combination of the nearby Tualatin River and Lake Grove.

Rockcreek
CDP
Lat: 45-33-01 N **Long:** 122-52-33 W
Pop: 8,282 (1990) **Pop Density:** 4141.0
Land: 2.0 sq. mi.; **Water:** 0.0 sq. mi.

Sherwood
City
ZIP: 97140 **Lat:** 45-21-35 N **Long:** 122-50-30 W
Pop: 3,093 (1990); 2,386 (1980) **Pop Density:** 966.6
Land: 3.2 sq. mi.; **Water:** 0.0 sq. mi. **Elev:** 205 ft.
Incorporated 1893.
Name origin: For either Sherwood, MI, or England's Sherwood Forest. Originally called Smockville.

Tigard
City
ZIP: 97223 **Lat:** 45-25-30 N **Long:** 122-46-26 W
Pop: 29,344 (1990); 14,799 (1980) **Pop Density:** 2876.9
Land: 10.2 sq. mi.; **Water:** 0.0 sq. mi. **Elev:** 166 ft.
In northwestern OR, 7 mi. south-southwest of Portland. Incorporated 1961.
Name origin: For Wilson M. Tigard, who came to OR in 1852.

Tualatin
City
ZIP: 97062 **Lat:** 45-22-39 N **Long:** 122-46-35 W
Pop: 13,257 (1990); 7,442 (1980) **Pop Density:** 2104.3
Land: 6.3 sq. mi.; **Water:** 0.0 sq. mi. **Elev:** 123 ft.
Incorporated 1913. Part of the town is also in Clackamas County.
Name origin: From an Indian term meaning 'sluggish' and referring to the Tualatin River.

West Haven-Sylvan
CDP
Lat: 45-31-04 N **Long:** 122-46-03 W
Pop: 6,009 (1990) **Pop Density:** 2225.6
Land: 2.7 sq. mi.; **Water:** 0.0 sq. mi.

West Slope
CDP
ZIP: 97225 **Lat:** 45-29-49 N **Long:** 122-46-09 W
Pop: 7,959 (1990); 5,364 (1980) **Pop Density:** 3460.4
Land: 2.3 sq. mi.; **Water:** 0.0 sq. mi.

Wilsonville
City
ZIP: 97070 **Lat:** 45-20-08 N **Long:** 122-46-03 W
Pop: 10 (1990); 20 (1980) **Pop Density:** 20.0
Land: 0.5 sq. mi.; **Water:** 0.0 sq. mi.
Settled 1870s; incorporated 1969. Part of the town is also in Clackamas County.
Name origin: For pioneer Charles Wilson.

Wheeler County
County Seat: Fossil (ZIP: 97830)

Pop: 1,396 (1990); 1,513 (1980)   **Pop Density:** 0.8
Land: 1715.0 sq. mi.; **Water:** 0.5 sq. mi.   **Area Code:** 503
In north-central OR; organized Feb 17, 1899 from Crook, Gilliam, and Grant counties.
Name origin: For Henry H. Wheeler (1826–1915), who operated the first stage line through the county and later became a prominent rancher in the area.

Fossil — Town
ZIP: 97830   **Lat:** 44-59-54 N   **Long:** 120-12-47 W
Pop: 399 (1990); 535 (1980)   **Pop Density:** 498.8
Land: 0.8 sq. mi.; **Water:** 0.0 sq. mi.   **Elev:** 2654 ft.
Founded 1870s; incorporated 1891.
Name origin: For the numerous fossils in the area.

Mitchell — Town
ZIP: 97750   **Lat:** 44-34-02 N   **Long:** 120-09-08 W
Pop: 163 (1990); 183 (1980)   **Pop Density:** 135.8
Land: 1.2 sq. mi.; **Water:** 0.0 sq. mi.   **Elev:** 2767 ft.
Incorporated 1891.
Name origin: For J. H. Mitchell, U.S. senator from OR (1873–79).

Spray — Town
ZIP: 97874   **Lat:** 44-49-55 N   **Long:** 119-47-35 W
Pop: 149 (1990); 155 (1980)   **Pop Density:** 745.0
Land: 0.2 sq. mi.; **Water:** 0.0 sq. mi.   **Elev:** 1798 ft.
In north-central OR on the John Day River. Founded 1900; incorporated 1958.
Name origin: For its founder, John Spray, who came to OR 1864.

Yamhill County
County Seat: McMinnville (ZIP: 97128)

Pop: 65,551 (1990); 55,332 (1980)   **Pop Density:** 91.6
Land: 715.6 sq. mi.; **Water:** 2.8 sq. mi.   **Area Code:** 503
In northwest OR, southwest of Portland; original county; organized 1843 (prior to statehood).
Name origin: For the Yamhela or Yamhill Indian tribe; meaning of name is unknown.

Amity — City
ZIP: 97101   **Lat:** 45-06-56 N   **Long:** 123-12-11 W
Pop: 1,175 (1990); 1,092 (1980)   **Pop Density:** 1958.3
Land: 0.6 sq. mi.; **Water:** 0.0 sq. mi.
Settled mid-1800s; incorporated 1880.
Name origin: For an amicable settlement of a local school dispute.

Carlton — City
ZIP: 97111   **Lat:** 45-17-41 N   **Long:** 123-10-29 W
Pop: 1,289 (1990); 1,302 (1980)   **Pop Density:** 1432.2
Land: 0.9 sq. mi.; **Water:** 0.0 sq. mi.   **Elev:** 199 ft.
Established 1874; incorporated 1899.
Name origin: For early settler John Carl.

Dayton — City
ZIP: 97114   **Lat:** 45-13-13 N   **Long:** 123-04-35 W
Pop: 1,526 (1990); 1,409 (1980)   **Pop Density:** 2543.3
Land: 0.6 sq. mi.; **Water:** 0.0 sq. mi.
Settled 1848; incorporated 1880.
Name origin: For Dayton, OH.

Dundee — City
ZIP: 97115   **Lat:** 45-16-35 N   **Long:** 123-00-21 W
Pop: 1,663 (1990); 1,223 (1980)   **Pop Density:** 1187.9
Land: 1.4 sq. mi.; **Water:** 0.0 sq. mi.   **Elev:** 190 ft.
Incorporated 1895.
Name origin: For Dundee, Scotland, so named by pioneer William Reid.

Lafayette — City
ZIP: 97127   **Lat:** 45-14-46 N   **Long:** 123-06-37 W
Pop: 1,292 (1990); 1,215 (1980)   **Pop Density:** 1435.6
Land: 0.9 sq. mi.; **Water:** 0.0 sq. mi.
Founded 1846; incorporated 1878.
Name origin: For Lafayette, IN.

McMinnville — City
ZIP: 97128   **Lat:** 45-12-40 N   **Long:** 123-11-24 W
Pop: 17,894 (1990); 14,080 (1980)   **Pop Density:** 2105.2
Land: 8.5 sq. mi.; **Water:** 0.0 sq. mi.   **Elev:** 160 ft.
In northwestern OR, 21 mi. north-northwest of Salem. Incorporated 1882.
Name origin: For McMinnville, TN, the birthplace of pioneer William Newby.

Newberg City
ZIP: 97132 **Lat:** 45-18-24 N **Long:** 122-57-35 W
Pop: 13,086 (1990); 10,394 (1980) **Pop Density:** 3115.7
Land: 4.2 sq. mi.; **Water:** 0.0 sq. mi. **Elev:** 176 ft.
In northwestern OR, 21 mi. southwest of Portland. Incorporated 1889.
Name origin: For Neuberg, Germany, named by the first postmaster, Sebastian Brutscher.

Sheridan City
ZIP: 97378 **Lat:** 45-05-43 N **Long:** 123-23-42 W
Pop: 3,979 (1990); 2,249 (1980) **Pop Density:** 2340.6
Land: 1.7 sq. mi.; **Water:** 0.0 sq. mi.
Incorporated 1880.
Name origin: For Union general Philip H. Sheridan (1831–88), Civil War hero.

Willamina City
ZIP: 97396 **Lat:** 45-04-51 N **Long:** 123-28-55 W
Pop: 1,194 (1990); 1,186 (1980) **Pop Density:** 1990.0
Land: 0.6 sq. mi.; **Water:** 0.0 sq. mi. **Elev:** 225 ft.
In northwestern OR on Willamina Creek, 25 mi. northwest of Salem. Incorporated 1903. Part of the town is also in Polk County.
Name origin: For its creek, itself named for Mrs. Willamina Williams, the area's first European woman.

Yamhill City
ZIP: 97148 **Lat:** 45-20-28 N **Long:** 123-11-03 W
Pop: 867 (1990); 690 (1980) **Pop Density:** 2167.5
Land: 0.4 sq. mi.; **Water:** 0.0 sq. mi. **Elev:** 183 ft.

Index to Places and Counties in Oregon

Adair Village (Benton) City 586
Adams (Umatilla) City 606
Adrian (Malheur) City....................601
Albany (Benton) City........................586
Albany (Linn) City...........................599
Aloha (Washington) CDP.................609
Altamont (Klamath) CDP 597
Amity (Yamhill) City........................611
Antelope (Wasco) City....................608
Arlington (Gilliam) City..................593
Ashland (Jackson) City....................595
Astoria (Clatsop) City......................589
Athena (Umatilla) City....................606
Aumsville (Marion) City..................601
Aurora (Marion) City......................601
Baker (Baker) City...........................586
Baker County 586
Bandon (Coos) City 590
Banks (Washington) City..................609
Barlow (Clackamas) City..................587
Barview (Coos) CDP 590
Bay City (Tillamook) City.................605
Beaverton (Washington) City 609
Bend (Deschutes) City.....................591
Benton County............................586
Boardman (Morrow) City..................603
Bonanza (Klamath) Town 597
Brookings (Curry) City....................591
Brownsville (Linn) City...................599
Bunker Hill (Coos) CDP 590
Burns (Harney) City.........................594
Butte Falls (Jackson) Town 595
Canby (Clackamas) City..................587
Cannon Beach (Clatsop) City............589
Canyon City (Grant) Town 593
Canyonville (Douglas) City..............592
Carlton (Yamhill) City.....................611
Cascade Locks (Hood River) City 595
Cave Junction (Josephine) City 596
Cedar Hills (Washington) CDP.........609
Cedar Mill (Washington) CDP..........609
Central Point (Jackson) City............595
Chenoweth (Wasco) CDP 608
Chiloquin (Klamath) City................597
Clackamas (Clackamas) CDP...........587
Clackamas County......................587
Clatskanie (Columbia) City.............589
Clatsop County..........................589
Coburg (Lane) City..........................598
Columbia City (Columbia) City........589
Columbia County........................589
Condon (Gilliam) City 593
Coos Bay (Coos) City 590
Coos County...............................590
Coquille (Coos) City........................590
Cornelius (Washington) City...........609
Corvallis (Benton) City....................587
Cottage Grove (Lane) City 598
Cove (Union) City...........................607
Creswell (Lane) City........................598
Crook County..............................591
Culver (Jefferson) City....................596
Curry County..............................591
Dallas (Polk) City............................604
The Dalles (Wasco) City...................608
Dayton (Yamhill) City......................611
Dayville (Grant) Town.....................593
Depoe Bay (Lincoln) City 599
Deschutes County......................591

Deschutes River Woods (Deschutes) CDP 591
Detroit (Marion) City......................601
Donald (Marion) City......................601
Douglas County..........................592
Drain (Douglas) City.......................592
Dufur (Wasco) Town 608
Dundee (Yamhill) City.....................611
Dunes City (Lane) City....................598
Durham (Washington) City..............609
Eagle Point (Jackson) City 595
Echo (Umatilla) City.......................606
Elgin (Union) City...........................607
Elkton (Douglas) City......................592
Enterprise (Wallowa) City 608
Estacada (Clackamas) City..............587
Eugene (Lane) City..........................598
Fairview (Multnomah) City..............603
Falls City (Polk) City.......................604
Florence (Lane) City........................598
Forest Grove (Washington) City 609
Fossil (Wheeler) Town.....................611
Four Corners (Marion) CDP............602
Garden Home-Whitford (Washington) CDP 609
Garibaldi (Tillamook) City..............605
Gaston (Washington) City...............609
Gates (Linn) City.............................600
Gates (Marion) City.........................602
Gearhart (Clatsop) City...................589
Gervais (Marion) City......................602
Gilliam County...........................593
Gladstone (Clackamas) City............587
Glendale (Douglas) City..................592
Gold Beach (Curry) City..................591
Gold Hill (Jackson) City..................595
Granite (Grant) City........................594
Grant County..............................593
Grants Pass (Josephine) City 596
Grass Valley (Sherman) City............605
Green (Douglas) CDP 592
Greenhorn (Baker) City...................586
Greenhorn (Grant) City...................594
Gresham (Multnomah) City.............603
Haines (Baker) City.........................586
Halfway (Baker) Town.....................586
Halsey (Linn) City............................600
Hammond (Clatsop) City.................589
Happy Valley (Clackamas) City 587
Harbeck-Fruitdale (Josephine) CDP.597
Harbor (Curry) CDP 591
Harney County............................594
Harrisburg (Linn) City.....................600
Hayesville (Marion) CDP.................602
Hazelwood (Multnomah) CDP 604
Helix (Umatilla) City.......................606
Heppner (Morrow) City....................603
Hermiston (Umatilla) City...............606
Hillsboro (Washington) City............609
Hines (Harney) City.........................594
Hood River (Hood River) City.........595
Hood River County....................595
Hubbard (Marion) City....................602
Huntington (Baker) City..................586
Idanha (Linn) City..........................600
Idanha (Marion) City......................602
Imbler (Union) City.........................607
Independence (Polk) City................604
Ione (Morrow) City.........................603
Irrigon (Morrow) City 603

Island City (Union) Town 607
Jackson County..........................595
Jacksonville (Jackson) City..............595
Jefferson (Marion) City...................602
Jefferson County........................596
Jennings Lodge (Clackamas) CDP....587
John Day (Grant) City.....................594
Johnson City (Clackamas) City........587
Jordan Valley (Malheur) Town.........601
Joseph (Wallowa) City 608
Josephine County 596
Junction City (Lane) City.................598
Keizer (Marion) City........................602
King City (Washington) City............610
Klamath County.........................597
Klamath Falls (Klamath) City..........597
Lafayette (Yamhill) City..................611
La Grande (Union) City...................607
Lake County 597
Lake Oswego (Clackamas) City........587
Lake Oswego (Multnomah) City 604
Lake Oswego (Washington) City 610
Lakeside (Coos) City 590
Lakeview (Lake) Town 597
Lane County...............................598
Lebanon (Linn) City........................600
Lexington (Morrow) Town 603
Lincoln Beach (Lincoln) CDP..........599
Lincoln City (Lincoln) City..............599
Lincoln County..........................599
Linn County...............................599
Lonerock (Gilliam) City...................593
Long Creek (Grant) Town 594
Lostine (Wallowa) City....................608
Lowell (Lane) City...........................598
Lyons (Linn) City.............................600
Madras (Jefferson) City...................596
Malheur County.........................601
Malin (Klamath) City.......................597
Manzanita (Tillamook) City.............606
Marion County...........................601
Maupin (Wasco) City.......................609
Maywood Park (Multnomah) City....604
McMinnville (Yamhill) City..............611
Medford (Jackson) City...................595
Merrill (Klamath) City.....................597
Metolius (Jefferson) City.................596
Metzger (Washington) CDP 610
Mill City (Linn) City........................600
Mill City (Marion) City....................602
Millersburg (Linn) City....................600
Milton-Freewater (Umatilla) City.....606
Milwaukie (Clackamas) City............588
Milwaukie (Multnomah) City 604
Mission (Umatilla) CDP 606
Mitchell (Wheeler) Town..................611
Molalla (Clackamas) City................588
Monmouth (Polk) City.....................604
Monroe (Benton) City......................587
Monument (Grant) City...................594
Moro (Sherman) City.......................605
Morrow County...........................603
Mosier (Wasco) City........................609
Mount Angel (Marion) City 602
Mount Hood Village (Clackamas) CDP 588
Mount Vernon (Grant) City..............594
Multnomah County 603
Myrtle Creek (Douglas) City............592
Myrtle Point (Coos) City..................590

OREGON

Nehalem (Tillamook) Town 606
Newberg (Yamhill) City 612
Newport (Lincoln) City 599
North Albany (Benton) CDP 587
North Bend (Coos) City 590
North Plains (Washington) City 610
North Powder (Union) City 607
North Springfield (Lane) CDP 598
Nyssa (Malheur) Town 601
Oak Grove (Clackamas) CDP 588
Oak Hills (Washington) CDP 610
Oakland (Douglas) City 592
Oakridge (Lane) City 598
Oatfield (Clackamas) CDP 588
Ontario (Malheur) City 601
Oregon City (Clackamas) City 588
Paisley (Lake) City 597
Pendleton (Umatilla) City 606
Philomath (Benton) City 587
Phoenix (Jackson) City 595
Pilot Rock (Umatilla) City 607
Polk County 604
Portland (Clackamas) City 588
Portland (Multnomah) City 604
Portland (Washington) City 610
Port Orford (Curry) City 591
Powellhurst-Centennial (Multnomah)
   CDP 604
Powers (Coos) City 590
Prairie City (Grant) City 594
Prescott (Columbia) City 589
Prineville (Crook) City 591
Rainier (Columbia) City 589
Raleigh Hills (Washington) CDP 610
Redmond (Deschutes) City 592
Redwood (Josephine) CDP 597
Reedsport (Douglas) City 592
Richland (Baker) Town 586
Riddle (Douglas) City 592
Rivergrove (Clackamas) City 588
Rivergrove (Washington) City 610
River Road (Lane) CDP 598
Rockaway Beach (Tillamook) City ... 606
Rockcreek (Washington) CDP 610

Rogue River (Jackson) City 596
Roseburg (Douglas) City 592
Roseburg North (Douglas) CDP 593
Rose Lodge (Lincoln) CDP 599
Rufus (Sherman) City 605
St. Helens (Columbia) City 590
St. Paul (Marion) City 602
Salem (Marion) City 602
Salem (Polk) City 605
Sandy (Clackamas) City 588
Santa Clara (Lane) CDP 598
Scappoose (Columbia) City 590
Scio (Linn) City 600
Scotts Mills (Marion) City 602
Seaside (Clatsop) City 589
Seneca (Grant) City 594
Shady Cove (Jackson) City 596
Shaniko (Wasco) City 609
Sheridan (Yamhill) City 612
Sherman County 605
Sherwood (Washington) City............. 610
Siletz (Lincoln) City 599
Silverton (Marion) City 602
Sisters (Deschutes) City 592
Sodaville (Linn) Town 600
South Lebanon (Linn) CDP 600
Spray (Wheeler) Town 611
Springfield (Lane) City 598
Stanfield (Umatilla) City 607
Stayton (Marion) City 602
Sublimity (Marion) City 602
Summerville (Union) Town 607
Sumpter (Baker) City 586
Sunnyside (Clackamas) CDP 588
Sutherlin (Douglas) City 593
Sweet Home (Linn) City 600
Talent (Jackson) City 596
Tangent (Linn) City 600
Terrebonne (Deschutes) CDP............. 592
Three Rivers (Deschutes) CDP 592
Tigard (Washington) City 610
Tillamook (Tillamook) City 606
Tillamook County 605
Toledo (Lincoln) City 599

Tri-City (Douglas) CDP..................... 593
Troutdale (Multnomah) City 604
Tualatin (Clackamas) City 588
Tualatin (Washington) City 610
Turner (Marion) City 602
Ukiah (Umatilla) City 607
Umatilla (Umatilla) City 607
Umatilla County 606
Union (Union) City 608
Union County 607
Unity (Baker) City 586
Vale (Malheur) City 601
Veneta (Lane) City 598
Vernonia (Columbia) City 590
Waldport (Lincoln) City 599
Wallowa (Wallowa) City 608
Wallowa County 608
Warm Springs (Jefferson) CDP 596
Warrenton (Clatsop) City 589
Wasco (Sherman) City 605
Wasco County 608
Washington County 609
Waterloo (Linn) Town 600
Westfir (Lane) City 598
West Haven-Sylvan (Washington)
   CDP 610
West Linn (Clackamas) City.............. 588
Weston (Umatilla) City 607
West Slope (Washington) CDP 610
Wheeler (Tillamook) City 606
Wheeler County 611
White City (Jackson) CDP 596
Willamina (Polk) City 605
Willamina (Yamhill) City 612
Wilsonville (Clackamas) City 588
Wilsonville (Washington) City 610
Winston (Douglas) City 593
Woodburn (Marion) City................... 603
Wood Village (Multnomah) City....... 604
Yachats (Lincoln) City....................... 599
Yamhill (Yamhill) City 612
Yamhill County 611
Yoncalla (Douglas) City..................... 593

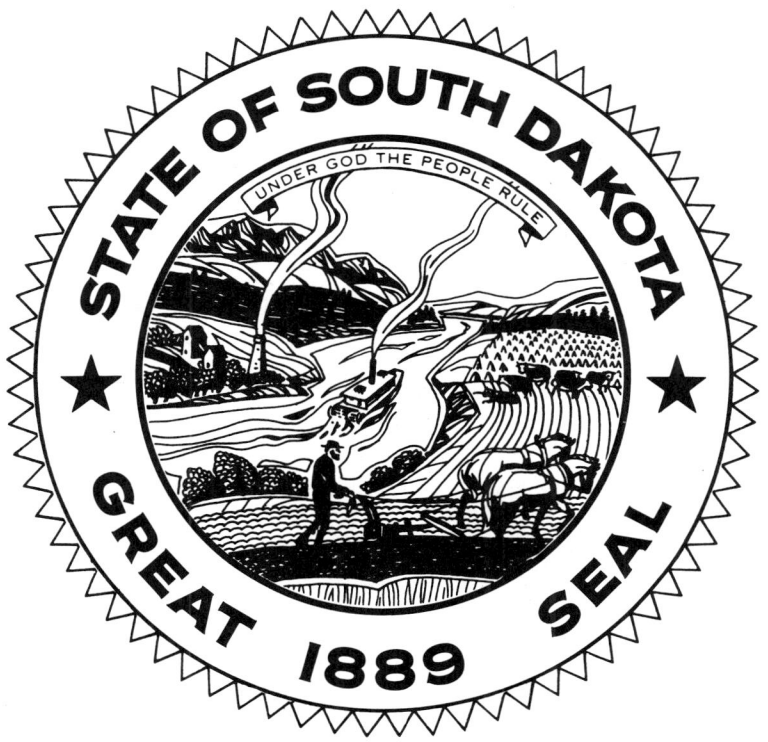

South Dakota

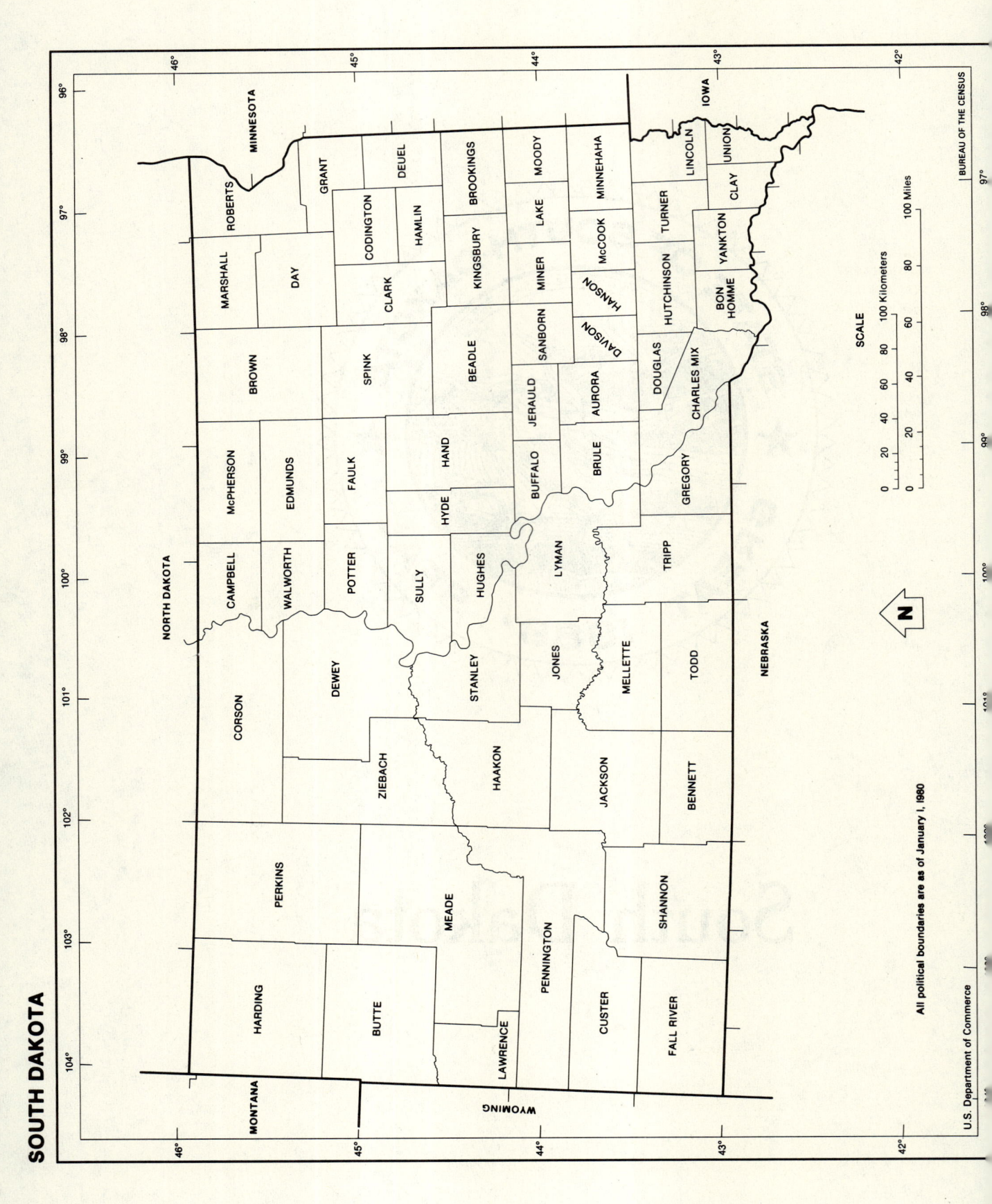

South Dakota

Population: 696,004 (1990); 690,768 (1980)
Population rank (1990): 45
Percent population change (1980–1990): 0.8
Population projection: 720,000 (1995); 723,000 (2000)

Area: total: 77,121 sq. mi.; 75,898 sq. mi. land, 1,224 sq. mi. water
Area rank: 17
Highest elevation: 7,242 ft., Harney Peak (Pennington County)
Lowest point: 962 ft., Big Stone Lake (Roberts County)

State capital: Pierre (Hughes County)
Largest city: Sioux Falls (100,814)
Second largest city: Rapid City (54,523)
Largest county: Minnehaha (123,809)

Total housing units: 292,436
No. of occupied housing units: 259,034
Vacant housing units (%): 11.4
Distribution of population by race and Hispanic origin (%):
White: 91.6
Black: 0.5
Hispanic (any race): 0.8
Native American: 7.3
Asian/Pacific: 0.4
Other: 0.2

Admission date: November 2, 1889 (40th state).

Location: In the north central United States bordering Nebraska, Wyoming, Montana, North Dakota, Minnesota, and Iowa.

Name Origin: For the Dakota (Sioux) Indian confederation, in whose language the word means 'allies,' referring to the friendly compact that joined seven smaller tribes. The name was originally applied to the entire Dakota Territory, which was divided into North and South in 1889.

State animal: coyote *(Canis latrans)*
State bird: ring-necked pheasant *(Phasianus colchicus)*
State drink: milk
State fish: walleye *(Stizostedion vitreum)*
State flower: American pasque *(Pulsatilla hisutissima)*
State gem: Fairburn agate
State grass: western wheatgrass *(Agropyron smithii)*
State insect: honey bee *(Apis mellifera)*
State mineral: rose quartz
State song: "Hail, South Dakota"
State tree: Black Hills spruce *(Picea glauca densata)*
State motto: Under God the People Rule

State nicknames: Coyote State, Sunshine State

Area code: 605
Time zones: Central and Mountain (western counties)
Abbreviations: SD (postal); S.D. or S. Dak. (traditional)
Part of (region): Plains States; Midwest

Local Government

Counties
South Dakota has 66 counties, each governed by county commissioners.

Municipalities
South Dakota has 310 cities separated into three classes by population. The cities have the power of home rule under the state's constitution. There are also 996 townships.

Settlement History and Early Development

The area that became South Dakota has been inhabited for at least 20,000 years, first by nomadic hunters and then by the ancestors of the Mandan, Hidatsa, Cheyenne, and Arikara Indians. These tribes were in the area at the time of the first European penetration but were driven out by the Dakota (Sioux) Indians, who moved westward from the Minnesota area in the 1820s and 1830s.

Present-day South Dakota was included in the vast Louisiana territory claimed by the French in 1682. It was first visited by French-Canadian explorers François and Louis-Joseph La Vérendrye in 1743. The two brothers buried a lead plate near what is now Fort Pierre as proof that they had been there; it was found in 1913.

The Louisiana territory passed from the French to the Spanish in 1762 and then back to the French in 1800. In 1803 the U.S. acquired the territory from France under the terms of the Louisiana Purchase. The Lewis and Clark expedition (1804–06) followed the Missouri River through the area of South Dakota, establishing friendly relations with the Indians there. French fur traders were already active in the area; in 1817 Joseph La Framboise established a trading post on the site of what is now Fort Pierre.

During the 1830s steamboats traveled the Missouri, opening broader markets for the fur trade in South Dakota. After 1850 the fur trade declined but agricultural settlement began in eastern South Dakota. Land companies acquired land and planned towns, including Sioux Falls, Medary, and Flandreau. When the Yankton Sioux signed a treaty relinquishing their claim to land in southeastern South Dakota, the farming communities of Yankton, Vermillion, and Bon Homme were founded.

SOUTH DAKOTA

Dakota Territory

In 1861 Congress created the Dakota Territory, which included present-day North Dakota and South Dakota, as well as parts of present-day Montana and Wyoming. There were problems with the Indians throughout much of the 1860s. The Sioux Indians fought Red Cloud's War to protect hunting grounds until the Laramie Treaty of 1868, by which the U.S. government created the Great Sioux Reservation.

In 1874 a military expedition led by Lieutenant Colonel George A. Custer discovered gold in the Black Hills. Prospectors flooded into the territory. Further gold discoveries brought more prospectors and led to the establishment of the town of Deadwood, legendary among wild frontier towns. Wild Bill Hickok and Calamity Jane were among Deadwood's most famous inhabitants.

Indians

Indians led by Crazy Horse and Sitting Bull resisted the white settlement of the Black Hills. After signing a treaty in 1876, most of the Indians were settled on reservations west of the Missouri River, but Sitting Bull, who fled to Canada, returned in 1881 and eventually settled on Standing Rock Reservation. In 1890 a religious movement called the Ghost Dance, started by a Paiute Indian named Wovoka, spread among the Sioux. The army feared the movement would lead to an uprising, so officials sent Indian police to arrest Sitting Bull. He resisted and was killed. Some of his followers joined Chief Big Foot and the Sioux on the Cheyenne River. This group was taken by federal troops to Wounded Knee Creek, where some 200 Indians were shot to death.

Statehood

From 1878 the influx of settlers into South Dakota was steady, with people coming from areas to the east and from Europe to farm the land. The railroads were well established by the 1880s and cattle ranchers joined miners and farmers in the rush to South Dakota.

Because the larger towns had grown up in opposite parts of the Dakota Territory, settlers asked Congress to divide the territory into two parts. In February 1889 Congress set the boundary between North Dakota and South Dakota. On November 2, 1889, South Dakota became the 40th U.S. state, and on the same day North Dakota became the 39th state. Pierre was chosen as the state capital.

Business and Commerce

Settlement slowed in South Dakota, partly because of a drought that lasted most of the 1890s. But after 1900 the weather improved and settlers continued to seek land in South Dakota, sometimes by means of state land lotteries. However, in 1911 drought hit the state again and population dropped. South Dakota's farm products brought prosperity during World War I and the early 1920s, but during the late 1920s South Dakota suffered from falling farm prices. During the 1930s the state was plagued by drought, grasshoppers, and huge dust storms called "black blizzards." During these years of the Great Depression federal programs such as the Civilian Conservations Corps and the Works Progress Administration provided jobs in South Dakota.

World War II brought increased demand for South Dakota's food products, but while mechanization improved productivity, it caused many farm workers to lose their jobs. Many young people left the state, prompting South Dakota to try to diversify its economy after the war. The Missouri River Basin Project (now the Pick-Sloan Missouri Basin Project), authorized by Congress in 1944, provided for the construction of four dams that not only produced hydroelectric power and irrigation but also formed Francis Case, Lewis and Clark, Oahe, and Sharpe lakes. Known as the "Great Lakes of South Dakota," these lakes helped spur the state's tourist industry.

During the 1960s the U.S. government built several defense projects, including missile sites, in South Dakota. In 1980 the U.S. Supreme Court ordered the payment of more than $120 million to the Sioux in payment for the land in the Black Hills that was taken from them. The Sioux have refused the money and seek the return of their land.

State Boundaries

The Dakota Territory was organized in 1861; its area was changed by the formation of the Idaho Territory (1863), the Montana Territory (1864), and the Wyoming Territory (1868). The North Dakota-South Dakota border was established in February 1889, months before the two areas became states in November 1889.

South Dakota Counties

Aurora	Corson	Hamlin	Lincoln	Roberts
Beadle	Custer	Hand	Lyman	Sanborn
Bennett	Davison	Hanson	Marshall	Shannon
Bon Homme	Day	Harding	McCook	Spink
Brookings	Deuel	Hughes	McPherson	Stanley
Brown	Dewey	Hutchinson	Meade	Sully
Brule	Douglas	Hyde	Mellette	Todd
Buffalo	Edmunds	Jackson	Miner	Tripp
Butte	Fall River	Jerauld	Minnehaha	Turner
Campbell	Faulk	Jones	Moody	Union
Charles Mix	Grant	Kingsbury	Pennington	Walworth
Clark	Gregory	Lake	Perkins	Yankton
Clay	Haakon	Lawrence	Potter	Ziebach
Codington				

Multi-County Places

The following South Dakota places are in more than one county. Given here is the total population for each multi-county place, and the names of the counties it is in.

Arlington, pop. 908; Kingsbury (902), Brookings (6)
Beresford, pop. 1,849; Union (1,500), Lincoln (349)
Eagle Butte, pop. 489; Dewey (475), Ziebach (14)
Ellsworth AFB, pop. 7,017; Meade (4,330), Pennington (2,687)
Irene, pop. 464; Turner (253), Clay (209), Yankton (2)
Iroquois, pop. 328; Kingsbury (271), Beadle (57)
Sioux Falls, pop. 100,814; Minnehaha (99,405), Lincoln (1,409)
Wessington, pop. 265; Beadle (241), Hand (24)

Aurora County
County Seat: Plankinton (ZIP: 57368)

Pop: 3,135 (1990); 3,628 (1980) **Pop Density:** 4.4
Land: 708.2 sq. mi.; **Water:** 4.4 sq. mi. **Area Code:** 605
In south-central SD, west of Sioux Falls; created Feb 22, 1879 and organized 1882 (prior to statehood) from land that had been parts of Hanson County (what was later Davison, Jerauld and Cragin counties).
Name origin: For the Roman goddess of dawn.

Aurora Township
Lat: 43-32-13 N Long: 98-22-18 W
Pop: 130 (1990); 138 (1980) Pop Density: 3.7
Land: 35.4 sq. mi.; Water: 0.0 sq. mi.

Belford Township
Lat: 43-53-29 N Long: 98-23-42 W
Pop: 190 (1990); 205 (1980) Pop Density: 5.3
Land: 35.9 sq. mi.; Water: 0.0 sq. mi.

Bristol Township
Lat: 43-53-53 N Long: 98-31-14 W
Pop: 62 (1990); 81 (1980) Pop Density: 1.7
Land: 35.7 sq. mi.; Water: 0.1 sq. mi.

Center Township
Lat: 43-32-51 N Long: 98-37-31 W
Pop: 116 (1990); 177 (1980) Pop Density: 3.3
Land: 35.5 sq. mi.; Water: 0.0 sq. mi.

Cooper Township
ZIP: 57383 Lat: 43-48-07 N Long: 98-37-14 W
Pop: 20 (1990); 27 (1980) Pop Density: 0.6
Land: 33.9 sq. mi.; Water: 0.0 sq. mi.

Crystal Lake Township
Lat: 43-37-14 N Long: 98-36-15 W
Pop: 57 (1990); 73 (1980) Pop Density: 1.6
Land: 35.8 sq. mi.; Water: 0.3 sq. mi.

Dudley Township
Lat: 43-37-33 N Long: 98-22-46 W
Pop: 111 (1990); 106 (1980) Pop Density: 3.2
Land: 34.8 sq. mi.; Water: 0.0 sq. mi.

Eureka Township
Lat: 43-42-32 N Long: 98-36-58 W
Pop: 38 (1990); 77 (1980) Pop Density: 1.1
Land: 34.3 sq. mi.; Water: 0.1 sq. mi.

Firesteel Township
Lat: 43-48-29 N Long: 98-30-49 W
Pop: 70 (1990); 89 (1980) Pop Density: 1.9
Land: 36.8 sq. mi.; Water: 0.1 sq. mi.

Gales Township
ZIP: 57383 Lat: 43-37-42 N Long: 98-44-35 W
Pop: 89 (1990); 93 (1980) Pop Density: 2.5
Land: 36.3 sq. mi.; Water: 0.0 sq. mi.

Hopper Township
ZIP: 57368 Lat: 43-43-06 N Long: 98-23-17 W
Pop: 83 (1990); 103 (1980) Pop Density: 2.3
Land: 36.1 sq. mi.; Water: 0.0 sq. mi.

Lake Township
Lat: 43-48-03 N Long: 98-44-14 W
Pop: 57 (1990); 85 (1980) Pop Density: 1.7
Land: 34.2 sq. mi.; Water: 3.2 sq. mi.

Palatine Township
ZIP: 57368 Lat: 43-48-24 N Long: 98-23-26 W
Pop: 71 (1990); 85 (1980) Pop Density: 1.9
Land: 36.9 sq. mi.; Water: 0.2 sq. mi.

Patten Township
ZIP: 57383 Lat: 43-53-34 N Long: 98-44-36 W
Pop: 53 (1990); 61 (1980) Pop Density: 1.5
Land: 35.6 sq. mi.; Water: 0.1 sq. mi.

Plankinton City
ZIP: 57368 Lat: 43-42-56 N Long: 98-29-02 W
Pop: 604 (1990); 644 (1980) Pop Density: 862.9
Land: 0.7 sq. mi.; Water: 0.0 sq. mi. Elev: 1525 ft.
Organized 1881.
Name origin: For John H. Plankinton, a Milwaukee Railroad director.

*Plankinton Township
ZIP: 57368 Lat: 43-42-52 N Long: 98-29-57 W
Pop: 239 (1990); 218 (1980) Pop Density: 7.0
Land: 34.2 sq. mi.; Water: 0.0 sq. mi.

Pleasant Lake Township
ZIP: 57368 Lat: 43-37-17 N Long: 98-29-20 W
Pop: 97 (1990); 113 (1980) Pop Density: 2.9
Land: 33.8 sq. mi.; Water: 0.0 sq. mi.

Pleasant Valley Township
Lat: 43-53-23 N Long: 98-37-37 W
Pop: 44 (1990); 58 (1980) Pop Density: 1.2
Land: 35.3 sq. mi.; Water: 0.2 sq. mi.

Stickney Town
ZIP: 57375 Lat: 43-35-22 N Long: 98-26-15 W
Pop: 323 (1990); 409 (1980) Pop Density: 1076.7
Land: 0.3 sq. mi.; Water: 0.0 sq. mi. Elev: 1630 ft.
Platted 1905.
Name origin: For J. B. Stickney, a Milwaukee Railroad official.

Truro Township
ZIP: 57375 Lat: 43-32-06 N Long: 98-29-20 W
Pop: 100 (1990); 165 (1980) Pop Density: 2.9
Land: 34.9 sq. mi.; Water: 0.0 sq. mi.

Washington Township
Lat: 43-32-31 N Long: 98-44-05 W
Pop: 76 (1990); 109 (1980) Pop Density: 2.1
Land: 35.5 sq. mi.; Water: 0.0 sq. mi.

White Lake City
ZIP: 57383 Lat: 43-43-42 N Long: 98-42-46 W
Pop: 419 (1990); 414 (1980) Pop Density: 1047.5
Land: 0.4 sq. mi.; Water: 0.0 sq. mi. Elev: 1650 ft.
Name origin: For nearby White Lake. Originally called Siding 36.

White Lake Township
ZIP: 57383 **Lat:** 43-43-06 N **Long:** 98-44-17 W
Pop: 86 (1990); 98 (1980) **Pop Density:** 2.4
Land: 36.0 sq. mi.; **Water:** 0.0 sq. mi.

Beadle County
County Seat: Huron (ZIP: 57350)

Pop: 18,253 (1990); 19,195 (1980) **Pop Density:** 14.5
Land: 1259.4 sq. mi.; **Water:** 5.5 sq. mi. **Area Code:** 605
In east-central SD, northwest of Sioux Falls; created Feb 22, 1879 (prior to statehood) from Spink and Clark counties.
Name origin: For Gen. William Henry Harrison Beadle (1838–1915), officer in the Civil War, surveyor general of the Dakota Territory (1869–73), and educator.

Allen Township
Lat: 44-29-57 N **Long:** 98-31-05 W
Pop: 95 (1990); 114 (1980) **Pop Density:** 2.6
Land: 36.6 sq. mi.; **Water:** 0.0 sq. mi.

Altoona Township
ZIP: 57348 **Lat:** 44-35-39 N **Long:** 98-23-47 W
Pop: 135 (1990); 98 (1980) **Pop Density:** 3.8
Land: 35.7 sq. mi.; **Water:** 0.0 sq. mi.

Banner Township
Lat: 44-24-17 N **Long:** 97-54-20 W
Pop: 49 (1990); 59 (1980) **Pop Density:** 1.4
Land: 35.2 sq. mi.; **Water:** 0.0 sq. mi.

Barrett Township
Lat: 44-35-37 N **Long:** 97-55-10 W
Pop: 33 (1990); 61 (1980) **Pop Density:** 0.9
Land: 35.9 sq. mi.; **Water:** 0.1 sq. mi.

Belle Prairie Township
Lat: 44-14-41 N **Long:** 97-54-21 W
Pop: 50 (1990); 74 (1980) **Pop Density:** 1.4
Land: 35.8 sq. mi.; **Water:** 0.0 sq. mi.

Bonilla Township
ZIP: 57348 **Lat:** 44-35-10 N **Long:** 98-30-47 W
Pop: 80 (1990); 117 (1980) **Pop Density:** 2.2
Land: 36.0 sq. mi.; **Water:** 0.0 sq. mi.

Broadland Town
ZIP: 57350 **Lat:** 44-29-36 N **Long:** 98-20-53 W
Pop: 40 (1990); 49 (1980) **Pop Density:** 40.0
Land: 1.0 sq. mi.; **Water:** 0.0 sq. mi. **Elev:** 1303 ft.
Name origin: For its location on the broad rolling prairie.

*Broadland Township
ZIP: 57350 **Lat:** 44-29-57 N **Long:** 98-23-56 W
Pop: 86 (1990); 88 (1980) **Pop Density:** 2.4
Land: 35.7 sq. mi.; **Water:** 0.0 sq. mi.

Burr Oak Township
Lat: 44-14-32 N **Long:** 98-38-14 W
Pop: 43 (1990); 50 (1980) **Pop Density:** 1.2
Land: 36.3 sq. mi.; **Water:** 0.1 sq. mi.

Carlyle Township
Lat: 44-14-19 N **Long:** 98-23-53 W
Pop: 94 (1990); 94 (1980) **Pop Density:** 2.6
Land: 36.4 sq. mi.; **Water:** 0.1 sq. mi.

Cavour Town
ZIP: 57324 **Lat:** 44-22-22 N **Long:** 98-02-27 W
Pop: 166 (1990); 117 (1980) **Pop Density:** 415.0
Land: 0.4 sq. mi.; **Water:** 0.0 sq. mi. **Elev:** 1310 ft.
Name origin: Named 1880 for Camillo Benso, Count di Cavour (1810–61), Italian statesman and patriot.

*Cavour Township
ZIP: 57324 **Lat:** 44-24-52 N **Long:** 98-02-12 W
Pop: 124 (1990); 136 (1980) **Pop Density:** 3.5
Land: 35.4 sq. mi.; **Water:** 0.0 sq. mi.

Clifton Township
Lat: 44-14-48 N **Long:** 98-09-49 W
Pop: 131 (1990); 147 (1980) **Pop Density:** 3.7
Land: 35.8 sq. mi.; **Water:** 0.0 sq. mi.

Clyde Township
Lat: 44-19-41 N **Long:** 98-16-47 W
Pop: 627 (1990); 617 (1980) **Pop Density:** 18.7
Land: 33.6 sq. mi.; **Water:** 0.0 sq. mi.

Custer Township
Lat: 44-19-10 N **Long:** 98-08-37 W
Pop: 397 (1990); 427 (1980) **Pop Density:** 11.8
Land: 33.6 sq. mi.; **Water:** 0.6 sq. mi.

Dearborn Township
Lat: 44-19-45 N **Long:** 98-23-39 W
Pop: 134 (1990); 155 (1980) **Pop Density:** 3.8
Land: 35.2 sq. mi.; **Water:** 0.1 sq. mi.

Fairfield Township
Lat: 44-30-00 N **Long:** 98-15-59 W
Pop: 104 (1990); 133 (1980) **Pop Density:** 2.8
Land: 36.6 sq. mi.; **Water:** 0.0 sq. mi.

Foster Township
Lat: 44-30-13 N **Long:** 97-54-26 W
Pop: 75 (1990); 78 (1980) **Pop Density:** 2.1
Land: 35.9 sq. mi.; **Water:** 0.1 sq. mi.

Grant Township
Lat: 44-14-41 N **Long:** 98-16-27 W
Pop: 149 (1990); 164 (1980) **Pop Density:** 4.1
Land: 36.3 sq. mi.; **Water:** 0.0 sq. mi.

Hartland Township
Lat: 44-24-42 N **Long:** 98-23-49 W
Pop: 106 (1990); 137 (1980) **Pop Density:** 2.9
Land: 36.3 sq. mi.; **Water:** 0.0 sq. mi.

SOUTH DAKOTA, Beadle County

Hitchcock Town
ZIP: 57348 Lat: 44-37-45 N Long: 98-24-28 W
Pop: 95 (1990); 132 (1980) Pop Density: 316.7
Land: 0.3 sq. mi.; Water: 0.0 sq. mi. Elev: 1340 ft.

Huron City
ZIP: 57350 Lat: 44-21-50 N Long: 98-13-04 W
Pop: 12,448 (1990); 13,000 (1980) Pop Density: 2109.8
Land: 5.9 sq. mi.; Water: 0.1 sq. mi. Elev: 1270 ft.
In east-central SD, 47 mi. north of Mitchell. Settled 1880.
Name origin: For the Huron Indians.

Iowa Township
Lat: 44-30-01 N Long: 98-08-36 W
Pop: 206 (1990); 197 (1980) Pop Density: 5.7
Land: 35.9 sq. mi.; Water: 0.4 sq. mi.

Iroquois City
Lat: 44-21-59 N Long: 97-51-19 W
Pop: 57 (1990); 49 (1980) Pop Density: 570.0
Land: 0.1 sq. mi.; Water: 0.0 sq. mi. Elev: 1398 ft.
Founded 1880s. Part of the town is also in Kingsbury County.
Name origin: For the Iroquois Indians.

Kellogg Township
Lat: 44-14-18 N Long: 98-30-57 W
Pop: 80 (1990); 84 (1980) Pop Density: 2.2
Land: 36.3 sq. mi.; Water: 0.0 sq. mi.

Lake Byron Township
ZIP: 57350 Lat: 44-35-10 N Long: 98-09-43 W
Pop: 237 (1990); 182 (1980) Pop Density: 7.2
Land: 32.9 sq. mi.; Water: 3.1 sq. mi.

Liberty Township
Lat: 44-30-25 N Long: 98-02-31 W
Pop: 81 (1990); 126 (1980) Pop Density: 2.2
Land: 36.4 sq. mi.; Water: 0.0 sq. mi.

Logan Township
Lat: 44-19-39 N Long: 97-54-52 W
Pop: 127 (1990); 154 (1980) Pop Density: 3.5
Land: 35.8 sq. mi.; Water: 0.0 sq. mi.

Milford Township
ZIP: 57386 Lat: 44-35-06 N Long: 98-02-22 W
Pop: 92 (1990); 107 (1980) Pop Density: 2.6
Land: 35.7 sq. mi.; Water: 0.1 sq. mi.

Nance Township
ZIP: 57381 Lat: 44-35-17 N Long: 98-39-07 W
Pop: 40 (1990); 55 (1980) Pop Density: 1.1
Land: 35.9 sq. mi.; Water: 0.0 sq. mi.

Pearl Creek Township
Lat: 44-14-51 N Long: 98-02-10 W
Pop: 110 (1990); 106 (1980) Pop Density: 3.1
Land: 35.9 sq. mi.; Water: 0.0 sq. mi.

Pleasant View Township
Lat: 44-35-24 N Long: 98-16-36 W
Pop: 56 (1990); 72 (1980) Pop Density: 1.6
Land: 35.8 sq. mi.; Water: 0.2 sq. mi.

Richland Township
Lat: 44-19-07 N Long: 98-02-35 W
Pop: 158 (1990); 167 (1980) Pop Density: 4.4
Land: 35.6 sq. mi.; Water: 0.0 sq. mi.

Sand Creek Township
ZIP: 57381 Lat: 44-19-47 N Long: 98-37-45 W
Pop: 57 (1990); 63 (1980) Pop Density: 1.6
Land: 36.3 sq. mi.; Water: 0.0 sq. mi.

Theresa Township
Lat: 44-24-43 N Long: 98-16-40 W
Pop: 266 (1990); 264 (1980) Pop Density: 7.6
Land: 34.9 sq. mi.; Water: 0.0 sq. mi.

Valley Township
Lat: 44-24-24 N Long: 98-08-35 W
Pop: 257 (1990); 233 (1980) Pop Density: 7.3
Land: 35.3 sq. mi.; Water: 0.5 sq. mi.

Vernon Township
Lat: 44-19-58 N Long: 98-30-29 W
Pop: 106 (1990); 105 (1980) Pop Density: 2.9
Land: 36.0 sq. mi.; Water: 0.0 sq. mi.

Virgil Town
ZIP: 57379 Lat: 44-17-24 N Long: 98-25-36 W
Pop: 33 (1990); 37 (1980) Pop Density: 33.0
Land: 1.0 sq. mi.; Water: 0.0 sq. mi. Elev: 1310 ft.
Founded 1880s.
Name origin: For Virgil (70–19 B.C.), the Latin poet.

Wessington City
ZIP: 57381 Lat: 44-27-17 N Long: 98-41-46 W
Pop: 241 (1990); 304 (1980) Pop Density: 803.3
Land: 0.3 sq. mi.; Water: 0.0 sq. mi. Elev: 1415 ft.
Settled 1880. Part of the town is also in Hand County.
Name origin: For the nearby Wessington Hills.

***Wessington** Township
ZIP: 57381 Lat: 44-24-26 N Long: 98-38-23 W
Pop: 61 (1990); 73 (1980) Pop Density: 1.7
Land: 36.0 sq. mi.; Water: 0.0 sq. mi.

Whiteside Township
ZIP: 57381 Lat: 44-29-52 N Long: 98-38-44 W
Pop: 60 (1990); 77 (1980) Pop Density: 1.6
Land: 36.8 sq. mi.; Water: 0.0 sq. mi.

Wolsey Town
ZIP: 57384 Lat: 44-24-39 N Long: 98-28-25 W
Pop: 442 (1990); 437 (1980) Pop Density: 192.2
Land: 2.3 sq. mi.; Water: 0.0 sq. mi. Elev: 1350 ft.
Settled 1882.
Name origin: For Cardinal Thomas Wolsey, a 16th-century British prelate.

***Wolsey** Township
ZIP: 57384 Lat: 44-25-03 N Long: 98-31-31 W
Pop: 97 (1990); 120 (1980) Pop Density: 2.9
Land: 33.7 sq. mi.; Water: 0.0 sq. mi.

Yale Town
ZIP: 57386 Lat: 44-26-00 N Long: 97-59-20 W
Pop: 128 (1990); 136 (1980) Pop Density: 640.0
Land: 0.2 sq. mi.; Water: 0.0 sq. mi. Elev: 1235 ft.

Bennett County
County Seat: Martin (ZIP: 57551)

Pop: 3,206 (1990); 3,044 (1980) **Pop Density:** 2.7
Land: 1185.4 sq. mi.; **Water:** 5.3 sq. mi. **Area Code:** 605
On the central southern border of SD, southeast of Rapid City; created Mar 9, 1909 from Indian lands.
Name origin: For either John E. Bennett, SD supreme court judge, or jointly for John E. Bennett and Granville G. Bennett, IL legislator and federally appointed judge in Dakota Territory.

East Bennett — Pop. Place
Lat: 43-11-37 N **Long:** 101-28-22 W
Pop: 926 (1990); 1,001 (1980) **Pop Density:** 1.4
Land: 658.1 sq. mi.; **Water:** 4.5 sq. mi.

West Bennett — Pop. Place
Lat: 43-11-22 N **Long:** 101-54-22 W
Pop: 1,129 (1990); 1,025 (1980) **Pop Density:** 2.1
Land: 526.4 sq. mi.; **Water:** 0.8 sq. mi.

Martin — City
ZIP: 57551 **Lat:** 43-10-29 N **Long:** 101-43-25 W
Pop: 1,151 (1990); 1,018 (1980) **Pop Density:** 1278.9
Land: 0.9 sq. mi.; **Water:** 0.0 sq. mi. **Elev:** 3314 ft.
Name origin: For U.S. Congressman Eben Martin, who represented SD (1908–12).

Bon Homme County
County Seat: Tyndall (ZIP: 57066)

Pop: 7,089 (1990); 8,059 (1980) **Pop Density:** 12.6
Land: 563.4 sq. mi.; **Water:** 17.9 sq. mi. **Area Code:** 605
On the southeastern border of SD, west of Sioux Falls; original county; organized Apr 5, 1862 (prior to statehood) from unorganized territory.
Name origin: For a village, which was named for a nearby large island in the Missouri River; mentioned in Lewis and Clark's journals. French 'good man,' name used by fourteenth-century French aristocracy for peasants.

Avon — City
ZIP: 57315 **Lat:** 43-00-18 N **Long:** 98-03-32 W
Pop: 576 (1990); 576 (1980) **Pop Density:** 960.0
Land: 0.6 sq. mi.; **Water:** 0.0 sq. mi. **Elev:** 1608 ft.
Founded 1879.
Name origin: For the Avon River in England, near William Shakespeare's home, so named by the first postmaster.

Northeast Bon Homme — Pop. Place
Lat: 43-04-48 N **Long:** 97-45-27 W
Pop: 695 (1990); 836 (1980) **Pop Density:** 4.9
Land: 140.9 sq. mi.; **Water:** 0.3 sq. mi.

Northwest Bon Homme — Pop. Place
Lat: 43-05-00 N **Long:** 97-59-27 W
Pop: 592 (1990); 772 (1980) **Pop Density:** 4.3
Land: 138.2 sq. mi.; **Water:** 0.2 sq. mi.

Scotland — City
ZIP: 57059 **Lat:** 43-08-53 N **Long:** 97-43-10 W
Pop: 968 (1990); 1,022 (1980) **Pop Density:** 1210.0
Land: 0.8 sq. mi.; **Water:** 0.0 sq. mi. **Elev:** 1348 ft.
Platted 1879.
Name origin: Named by Scottish settlers for their former home.

Southeast Bon Homme — Pop. Place
Lat: 42-55-38 N **Long:** 97-44-30 W
Pop: 547 (1990); 644 (1980) **Pop Density:** 5.7
Land: 96.7 sq. mi.; **Water:** 10.8 sq. mi.

Southwest Bon Homme — Pop. Place
Lat: 42-53-09 N **Long:** 97-58-58 W
Pop: 1,273 (1990); 1,119 (1980) **Pop Density:** 6.9
Land: 183.6 sq. mi.; **Water:** 6.7 sq. mi.

Springfield — City
ZIP: 57062 **Lat:** 42-51-17 N **Long:** 97-53-34 W
Pop: 834 (1990); 1,377 (1980) **Pop Density:** 1390.0
Land: 0.6 sq. mi.; **Water:** 0.0 sq. mi.
Incorporated 1879.

Tabor — Town
ZIP: 57063 **Lat:** 42-56-51 N **Long:** 97-39-34 W
Pop: 403 (1990); 460 (1980) **Pop Density:** 1343.3
Land: 0.3 sq. mi.; **Water:** 0.0 sq. mi. **Elev:** 1364 ft.
Settled 1872.
Name origin: Named by Czech emigrants for a city in Bohemia.

SOUTH DAKOTA, Bon Homme County

Tyndall   City
ZIP: 57066   **Lat:** 42-59-23 N **Long:** 97-51-52 W
Pop: 1,201 (1990); 1,253 (1980)   **Pop Density:** 750.6
Land: 1.6 sq. mi.; **Water:** 0.0 sq. mi.   **Elev:** 1422 ft.
Incorporated 1887.
Name origin: For John Tyndall (1820–93), an Irish scientist.

Brookings County
County Seat: Brookings (ZIP: 57006)

Pop: 25,207 (1990); 24,332 (1980)   **Pop Density:** 31.7
Land: 794.5 sq. mi.; **Water:** 10.3 sq. mi.   **Area Code:** 605
On the central eastern border of SD, north of Sioux Falls; created Apr 5, 1862 (prior to statehood) from unorganized territory.
Name origin: For Wilmot W. Brookings (1833–85), prominent legislator and associate justice on the Dakota Territory supreme court (1869–73). He promoted the Southern Dakota Railway, and "Judge Brookings" was the name of the first locomotive to enter what is now SD.

Afton   Township
Lat: 44-24-37 N **Long:** 96-41-57 W
Pop: 185 (1990); 224 (1980)   **Pop Density:** 5.2
Land: 35.6 sq. mi.; **Water:** 0.0 sq. mi.

Alton   Township
Lat: 44-19-06 N **Long:** 96-35-02 W
Pop: 284 (1990); 286 (1980)   **Pop Density:** 8.1
Land: 35.1 sq. mi.; **Water:** 0.0 sq. mi.

Argo   Township
ZIP: 57276   **Lat:** 44-29-56 N **Long:** 96-42-01 W
Pop: 153 (1990); 165 (1980)   **Pop Density:** 4.2
Land: 36.1 sq. mi.; **Water:** 0.0 sq. mi.

Arlington   City
Lat: 44-21-36 N **Long:** 97-07-31 W
Pop: 6 (1990); 3 (1980)   **Pop Density:** 12.0
Land: 0.5 sq. mi.; **Water:** 0.0 sq. mi.   **Elev:** 1842 ft.
Part of the town is also in Kingsbury County.
Name origin: For Arlington, VA.

Aurora   Town
ZIP: 57002   **Lat:** 44-16-57 N **Long:** 96-41-11 W
Pop: 619 (1990); 507 (1980)   **Pop Density:** 1238.0
Land: 0.5 sq. mi.; **Water:** 0.0 sq. mi.   **Elev:** 1625 ft.
Founded 1880.
Name origin: For the Roman goddess of dawn.

*Aurora   Township
ZIP: 57002   **Lat:** 44-19-35 N **Long:** 96-42-31 W
Pop: 300 (1990); 330 (1980)   **Pop Density:** 8.9
Land: 33.6 sq. mi.; **Water:** 0.0 sq. mi.

Bangor   Township
Lat: 44-19-41 N **Long:** 97-03-50 W
Pop: 176 (1990); 185 (1980)   **Pop Density:** 5.0
Land: 35.1 sq. mi.; **Water:** 0.6 sq. mi.

Brookings   City
ZIP: 57006   **Lat:** 44-18-22 N **Long:** 96-47-10 W
Pop: 16,270 (1990); 14,951 (1980)   **Pop Density:** 1564.4
Land: 10.4 sq. mi.; **Water:** 0.1 sq. mi.   **Elev:** 1623 ft.
In eastern SD, 53 mi. north of Sioux Falls. Platted 1879.
Name origin: For prominent early pioneer, Judge Wilmot Brookings. Originally called Ada.

*Brookings   Township
Lat: 44-20-00 N **Long:** 96-50-17 W
Pop: 430 (1990); 425 (1980)   **Pop Density:** 15.4
Land: 27.9 sq. mi.; **Water:** 0.0 sq. mi.

Bruce   City
ZIP: 57220   **Lat:** 44-26-17 N **Long:** 96-53-21 W
Pop: 235 (1990); 254 (1980)   **Pop Density:** 587.5
Land: 0.4 sq. mi.; **Water:** 0.0 sq. mi.   **Elev:** 1620 ft.
Founded 1881.
Name origin: For either the son of one of the early North Western railroad officials, or for B.K. Bruce, a well-known African-American statesman. Originally called Lee.

Bushnell   Town
ZIP: 57276   **Lat:** 44-19-42 N **Long:** 96-38-35 W
Pop: 81 (1990); 76 (1980)   **Pop Density:** 115.7
Land: 0.7 sq. mi.; **Water:** 0.0 sq. mi.   **Elev:** 1693 ft.
Name origin: For Frank Bushnell, who owned the land upon which the town was founded.

Elkton   City
ZIP: 57026   **Lat:** 44-14-04 N **Long:** 96-28-47 W
Pop: 602 (1990); 632 (1980)   **Pop Density:** 376.3
Land: 1.6 sq. mi.; **Water:** 0.0 sq. mi.   **Elev:** 1751 ft.
Platted 1880s.
Name origin: For Elkton, MD.

*Elkton   Township
Lat: 44-14-24 N **Long:** 96-29-19 W
Pop: 104 (1990); 135 (1980)   **Pop Density:** 5.1
Land: 20.3 sq. mi.; **Water:** 0.0 sq. mi.

Eureka   Township
Lat: 44-30-26 N **Long:** 96-49-36 W
Pop: 154 (1990); 208 (1980)   **Pop Density:** 4.3
Land: 36.1 sq. mi.; **Water:** 0.0 sq. mi.

Lake Hendricks   Township
ZIP: 57276   **Lat:** 44-28-26 N **Long:** 96-29-19 W
Pop: 141 (1990); 161 (1980)   **Pop Density:** 4.6
Land: 30.9 sq. mi.; **Water:** 1.8 sq. mi.

Lake Sinai
Township
Lat: 44-14-26 N **Long:** 97-03-48 W
Pop: 176 (1990); 211 (1980) **Pop Density:** 5.1
Land: 34.5 sq. mi.; **Water:** 1.0 sq. mi.

Laketon
Township
Lat: 44-30-18 N **Long:** 97-04-09 W
Pop: 120 (1990); 151 (1980) **Pop Density:** 3.5
Land: 34.6 sq. mi.; **Water:** 1.3 sq. mi.

Medary
Township
Lat: 44-14-15 N **Long:** 96-50-01 W
Pop: 950 (1990); 939 (1980) **Pop Density:** 27.5
Land: 34.5 sq. mi.; **Water:** 1.2 sq. mi.

Oak Lake
Township
Lat: 44-30-00 N **Long:** 96-34-52 W
Pop: 108 (1990); 164 (1980) **Pop Density:** 3.0
Land: 35.8 sq. mi.; **Water:** 0.4 sq. mi.

Oakwood
Township
Lat: 44-24-40 N **Long:** 96-56-29 W
Pop: 190 (1990); 215 (1980) **Pop Density:** 5.8
Land: 32.5 sq. mi.; **Water:** 2.6 sq. mi.

Oslo
Township
Lat: 44-14-36 N **Long:** 96-57-06 W
Pop: 229 (1990); 212 (1980) **Pop Density:** 6.5
Land: 35.5 sq. mi.; **Water:** 0.1 sq. mi.

Parnell
Township
Lat: 44-14-21 N **Long:** 96-35-12 W
Pop: 147 (1990); 171 (1980) **Pop Density:** 4.1
Land: 35.8 sq. mi.; **Water:** 0.0 sq. mi.

Preston
Township
ZIP: 57220 **Lat:** 44-30-24 N **Long:** 96-56-17 W
Pop: 189 (1990); 226 (1980) **Pop Density:** 5.3
Land: 35.4 sq. mi.; **Water:** 0.2 sq. mi.

Richland
Township
Lat: 44-21-01 N **Long:** 96-29-46 W
Pop: 160 (1990); 219 (1980) **Pop Density:** 4.8
Land: 33.1 sq. mi.; **Water:** 0.0 sq. mi.

Sherman
Township
Lat: 44-25-05 N **Long:** 96-35-34 W
Pop: 145 (1990); 194 (1980) **Pop Density:** 4.1
Land: 35.4 sq. mi.; **Water:** 0.0 sq. mi.

Sinai
Town
Lat: 44-14-42 N **Long:** 97-02-34 W
Pop: 120 (1990); 129 (1980) **Pop Density:** 300.0
Land: 0.4 sq. mi.; **Water:** 0.0 sq. mi. **Elev:** 1770 ft.
Name origin: Named in 1907 for nearby Lake Sinai.

Sterling
Township
Lat: 44-24-45 N **Long:** 96-49-47 W
Pop: 326 (1990); 341 (1980) **Pop Density:** 9.2
Land: 35.4 sq. mi.; **Water:** 0.0 sq. mi.

Trenton
Township
Lat: 44-14-46 N **Long:** 96-42-03 W
Pop: 333 (1990); 381 (1980) **Pop Density:** 9.3
Land: 35.7 sq. mi.; **Water:** 0.0 sq. mi.

Volga
City
ZIP: 57071 **Lat:** 44-19-23 N **Long:** 96-55-21 W
Pop: 1,263 (1990); 1,221 (1980) **Pop Density:** 1578.8
Land: 0.8 sq. mi.; **Water:** 0.0 sq. mi. **Elev:** 1634 ft.
Settled 1880s.
Name origin: For the Volga River in Russia.

*Volga
Township
ZIP: 57071 **Lat:** 44-19-33 N **Long:** 96-57-02 W
Pop: 299 (1990); 328 (1980) **Pop Density:** 8.8
Land: 34.1 sq. mi.; **Water:** 0.5 sq. mi.

White
City
ZIP: 57276 **Lat:** 44-26-00 N **Long:** 96-38-43 W
Pop: 536 (1990); 474 (1980) **Pop Density:** 765.7
Land: 0.7 sq. mi.; **Water:** 0.0 sq. mi. **Elev:** 1777 ft.
Platted 1884.
Name origin: For the original settler, W.H. White.

Winsor
Township
Lat: 44-24-11 N **Long:** 97-04-14 W
Pop: 176 (1990); 214 (1980) **Pop Density:** 4.9
Land: 35.6 sq. mi.; **Water:** 0.4 sq. mi.

Brown County
County Seat: Aberdeen (ZIP: 57401)

Pop: 35,580 (1990); 36,962 (1980) **Pop Density:** 20.8
Land: 1712.8 sq. mi.; **Water:** 18.5 sq. mi. **Area Code:** 605
On the northeastern border of SD; created Feb 22, 1879 (prior to statehood) from Beadle County.
Name origin: For Alfred Brown (1836–?), member of the Dakota Territory legislature instrumental in consolidating the then existing counties, which earned him the nickname "Consolidation Brown."

Aberdeen
City
ZIP: 57401 **Lat:** 45-28-03 N **Long:** 98-28-56 W
Pop: 24,927 (1990); 25,851 (1980) **Pop Density:** 2967.5
Land: 8.4 sq. mi.; **Water:** 0.0 sq. mi. **Elev:** 1304 ft.
In northeastern SD, 90 mi. west of Big Stone Lake. Founded 1881.
Name origin: For Aberdeen, Scotland, so named by railroad officials.

*Aberdeen
Township
Lat: 45-27-45 N **Long:** 98-30-37 W
Pop: 1,669 (1990); 1,473 (1980) **Pop Density:** 36.6
Land: 45.6 sq. mi.; **Water:** 0.2 sq. mi.

Allison
Township
Lat: 45-48-37 N **Long:** 98-40-17 W
Pop: 26 (1990); 28 (1980) **Pop Density:** 0.7
Land: 35.9 sq. mi.; **Water:** 0.0 sq. mi.

SOUTH DAKOTA, Brown County

Bates Township
Lat: 45-17-04 N Long: 98-02-11 W
Pop: 44 (1990); 67 (1980)   Pop Density: 1.2
Land: 35.8 sq. mi.; Water: 0.0 sq. mi.

Bath Township
ZIP: 57427   Lat: 45-27-34 N Long: 98-20-13 W
Pop: 593 (1990); 630 (1980)   Pop Density: 14.1
Land: 42.2 sq. mi.; Water: 0.0 sq. mi.

Brainard Township
Lat: 45-43-37 N Long: 98-22-59 W
Pop: 119 (1990); 149 (1980)   Pop Density: 2.3
Land: 52.6 sq. mi.; Water: 3.7 sq. mi.

Cambria Township
ZIP: 57433   Lat: 45-32-17 N Long: 98-16-57 W
Pop: 124 (1990); 170 (1980)   Pop Density: 3.4
Land: 36.3 sq. mi.; Water: 0.0 sq. mi.

Carlisle Township
ZIP: 57481   Lat: 45-38-30 N Long: 98-39-38 W
Pop: 58 (1990); 66 (1980)   Pop Density: 1.6
Land: 36.1 sq. mi.; Water: 0.2 sq. mi.

Claremont Town
ZIP: 57432   Lat: 45-40-19 N Long: 98-00-52 W
Pop: 135 (1990); 180 (1980)   Pop Density: 450.0
Land: 0.3 sq. mi.; Water: 0.0 sq. mi.   Elev: 1300 ft.
Founded 1886 by the Great Northern Railway.
Name origin: For Claremont, NH.

*Claremont Township
ZIP: 57432   Lat: 45-37-50 N Long: 98-04-38 W
Pop: 165 (1990); 159 (1980)   Pop Density: 3.1
Land: 53.9 sq. mi.; Water: 0.0 sq. mi.

Columbia City
ZIP: 57433   Lat: 45-36-53 N Long: 98-18-41 W
Pop: 133 (1990); 161 (1980)   Pop Density: 83.1
Land: 1.6 sq. mi.; Water: 0.0 sq. mi.   Elev: 1304 ft.
Name origin: Changed due to a postal conflict. Originally called Richmond.

*Columbia Township
ZIP: 57433   Lat: 45-38-22 N Long: 98-14-18 W
Pop: 127 (1990); 171 (1980)   Pop Density: 2.7
Land: 47.6 sq. mi.; Water: 0.6 sq. mi.

East Hanson Township
Lat: 45-22-26 N Long: 98-01-56 W
Pop: 139 (1990); 141 (1980)   Pop Density: 3.9
Land: 36.0 sq. mi.; Water: 0.1 sq. mi.

East Rondell Township
Lat: 45-17-13 N Long: 98-16-43 W
Pop: 91 (1990); 105 (1980)   Pop Density: 2.5
Land: 36.0 sq. mi.; Water: 0.0 sq. mi.

Franklyn Township
Lat: 45-43-43 N Long: 98-39-09 W
Pop: 45 (1990); 58 (1980)   Pop Density: 1.3
Land: 35.9 sq. mi.; Water: 0.2 sq. mi.

Frederick Town
ZIP: 57441   Lat: 45-49-58 N Long: 98-30-23 W
Pop: 241 (1990); 307 (1980)   Pop Density: 602.5
Land: 0.4 sq. mi.; Water: 0.0 sq. mi.   Elev: 1375 ft.
Established 1882.
Name origin: For the son of a Milwaukee Railroad official.

*Frederick Township
Lat: 45-48-28 N Long: 98-32-54 W
Pop: 86 (1990); 74 (1980)   Pop Density: 2.4
Land: 35.8 sq. mi.; Water: 0.0 sq. mi.

Garden Prairie Township
Lat: 45-16-38 N Long: 98-10-31 W
Pop: 155 (1990); 102 (1980)   Pop Density: 4.3
Land: 36.0 sq. mi.; Water: 0.0 sq. mi.

Garland Township
ZIP: 57433   Lat: 45-38-35 N Long: 98-23-00 W
Pop: 69 (1990); 90 (1980)   Pop Density: 2.3
Land: 29.7 sq. mi.; Water: 0.0 sq. mi.

Gem Township
ZIP: 57479   Lat: 45-22-49 N Long: 98-20-23 W
Pop: 225 (1990); 235 (1980)   Pop Density: 3.4
Land: 66.2 sq. mi.; Water: 0.0 sq. mi.

Greenfield Township
Lat: 45-48-15 N Long: 98-17-47 W
Pop: 72 (1990); 88 (1980)   Pop Density: 2.2
Land: 32.6 sq. mi.; Water: 3.4 sq. mi.

Groton City
ZIP: 57445   Lat: 45-27-07 N Long: 98-06-00 W
Pop: 1,196 (1990); 1,230 (1980)   Pop Density: 854.3
Land: 1.4 sq. mi.; Water: 0.0 sq. mi.   Elev: 1308 ft.
Name origin: For Groton, MA.

*Groton Township
ZIP: 57445   Lat: 45-27-26 N Long: 98-03-34 W
Pop: 111 (1990); 128 (1980)   Pop Density: 2.4
Land: 46.6 sq. mi.; Water: 0.0 sq. mi.

Hecla City
ZIP: 57446   Lat: 45-52-55 N Long: 98-09-05 W
Pop: 398 (1990); 435 (1980)   Pop Density: 1326.7
Land: 0.3 sq. mi.; Water: 0.0 sq. mi.   Elev: 1299 ft.
Settled 1886.
Name origin: For a volcano in Iceland.

*Hecla Township
ZIP: 57446   Lat: 45-53-18 N Long: 98-08-53 W
Pop: 49 (1990); 71 (1980)   Pop Density: 2.0
Land: 24.0 sq. mi.; Water: 0.3 sq. mi.

Henry Township
Lat: 45-27-31 N Long: 98-12-15 W
Pop: 123 (1990); 136 (1980)   Pop Density: 3.4
Land: 35.9 sq. mi.; Water: 0.0 sq. mi.

Highland Township
Lat: 45-22-08 N Long: 98-39-26 W
Pop: 92 (1990); 95 (1980)   Pop Density: 2.5
Land: 36.2 sq. mi.; Water: 0.1 sq. mi.

Lansing Township
Lat: 45-47-57 N Long: 98-10-33 W
Pop: 63 (1990); 84 (1980)   Pop Density: 1.8
Land: 34.2 sq. mi.; Water: 1.8 sq. mi.

Liberty Township
Lat: 45-53-54 N Long: 98-16-32 W
Pop: 91 (1990); 123 (1980)   Pop Density: 1.9
Land: 46.8 sq. mi.; Water: 0.2 sq. mi.

Lincoln Township
Lat: 45-34-06 N Long: 98-32-45 W
Pop: 1,042 (1990); 1,029 (1980)   Pop Density: 21.7
Land: 48.0 sq. mi.; Water: 0.1 sq. mi.

Mercier Township
Lat: 45-28-04 N Long: 98-38-59 W
Pop: 140 (1990); 150 (1980) Pop Density: 3.9
Land: 36.0 sq. mi.; Water: 0.1 sq. mi.

New Hope Township
Lat: 45-17-38 N Long: 98-38-59 W
Pop: 126 (1990); 132 (1980) Pop Density: 3.5
Land: 36.2 sq. mi.; Water: 0.2 sq. mi.

North Detroit Township
Lat: 45-47-55 N Long: 98-02-45 W
Pop: 84 (1990); 87 (1980) Pop Density: 2.4
Land: 35.6 sq. mi.; Water: 0.6 sq. mi.

Oneota Township
Lat: 45-43-41 N Long: 98-32-53 W
Pop: 127 (1990); 132 (1980) Pop Density: 3.5
Land: 35.9 sq. mi.; Water: 0.2 sq. mi.

Ordway Township
Lat: 45-33-02 N Long: 98-24-39 W
Pop: 233 (1990); 387 (1980) Pop Density: 5.6
Land: 41.4 sq. mi.; Water: 0.0 sq. mi.

Osceola Township
Lat: 45-53-58 N Long: 98-31-54 W
Pop: 68 (1990); 64 (1980) Pop Density: 1.9
Land: 35.7 sq. mi.; Water: 0.0 sq. mi.

Palmyra Township
Lat: 45-53-52 N Long: 98-39-46 W
Pop: 35 (1990); 56 (1980) Pop Density: 1.0
Land: 34.1 sq. mi.; Water: 1.6 sq. mi.

Portage Township
ZIP: 57446 Lat: 45-53-09 N Long: 98-03-03 W
Pop: 82 (1990); 79 (1980) Pop Density: 2.3
Land: 35.7 sq. mi.; Water: 0.1 sq. mi.

Prairiewood Township
Lat: 45-30-42 N Long: 98-25-12 W
Pop: 186 (1990) Pop Density: 310.0
Land: 0.6 sq. mi.; Water: 0.0 sq. mi.

Putney Township
ZIP: 57445 Lat: 45-33-08 N Long: 98-10-10 W
Pop: 102 (1990); 107 (1980) Pop Density: 2.8
Land: 36.2 sq. mi.; Water: 0.0 sq. mi.

Ravinia Township
Lat: 45-32-40 N Long: 98-39-09 W
Pop: 247 (1990); 168 (1980) Pop Density: 7.0
Land: 35.1 sq. mi.; Water: 1.0 sq. mi.

Richland Township
Lat: 45-48-51 N Long: 98-24-13 W
Pop: 62 (1990); 86 (1980) Pop Density: 1.7
Land: 35.9 sq. mi.; Water: 0.0 sq. mi.

Riverside Township
Lat: 45-33-07 N Long: 98-01-52 W
Pop: 70 (1990); 88 (1980) Pop Density: 1.9
Land: 36.0 sq. mi.; Water: 0.0 sq. mi.

Savo Township
Lat: 45-53-11 N Long: 98-24-13 W
Pop: 68 (1990); 96 (1980) Pop Density: 1.9
Land: 35.6 sq. mi.; Water: 0.0 sq. mi.

Shelby Township
Lat: 45-42-43 N Long: 98-11-47 W
Pop: 137 (1990); 155 (1980) Pop Density: 2.8
Land: 48.5 sq. mi.; Water: 3.6 sq. mi.

South Detroit Township
Lat: 45-43-08 N Long: 98-03-05 W
Pop: 100 (1990); 121 (1980) Pop Density: 2.8
Land: 36.3 sq. mi.; Water: 0.0 sq. mi.

Stratford Town
ZIP: 57474 Lat: 45-19-01 N Long: 98-18-13 W
Pop: 85 (1990); 82 (1980) Pop Density: 425.0
Land: 0.2 sq. mi.; Water: 0.0 sq. mi. Elev: 1290 ft.

Verdon Town
Lat: 45-14-40 N Long: 98-05-53 W
Pop: 7 (1990); 7 (1980) Pop Density: 35.0
Land: 0.2 sq. mi.; Water: 0.0 sq. mi. Elev: 1305 ft.
Name origin: Named 1886 for Verdun, France; a slight misspelling was allowed to stand.

Warner Town
ZIP: 57479 Lat: 45-19-27 N Long: 98-29-42 W
Pop: 336 (1990); 322 (1980) Pop Density: 1120.0
Land: 0.3 sq. mi.; Water: 0.0 sq. mi. Elev: 1298 ft.
Name origin: For early settler Warren Tarbox.

*Warner Township
ZIP: 57479 Lat: 45-19-55 N Long: 98-31-48 W
Pop: 499 (1990); 550 (1980) Pop Density: 6.3
Land: 79.8 sq. mi.; Water: 0.2 sq. mi.

West Hanson Township
Lat: 45-22-22 N Long: 98-09-52 W
Pop: 73 (1990); 92 (1980) Pop Density: 2.0
Land: 35.9 sq. mi.; Water: 0.0 sq. mi.

Westport Town
ZIP: 57481 Lat: 45-38-52 N Long: 98-29-50 W
Pop: 112 (1990); 122 (1980) Pop Density: 373.3
Land: 0.3 sq. mi.; Water: 0.0 sq. mi.

*Westport Township
ZIP: 57481 Lat: 45-38-27 N Long: 98-31-40 W
Pop: 106 (1990); 135 (1980) Pop Density: 3.7
Land: 28.9 sq. mi.; Water: 0.0 sq. mi.

West Rondell Township
Lat: 45-16-40 N Long: 98-24-07 W
Pop: 87 (1990); 108 (1980) Pop Density: 2.6
Land: 34.1 sq. mi.; Water: 0.0 sq. mi.

SOUTH DAKOTA, Brule County

Brule County
County Seat: Chamberlain (ZIP: 57325)

Pop: 5,485 (1990); 5,245 (1980)   **Pop Density:** 6.7
Land: 819.0 sq. mi.; **Water:** 27.5 sq. mi.   **Area Code:** 605

In south-central SD, west of Sioux Falls; created Jan 14, 1875 (prior to statehood) from Buffalo County.

Name origin: For the Brule tribe of Sioux Indians. French 'burned,' partial transliteration of *sicangu* 'burned thighs,' a name derisively given to a group of Sioux who tried to raid the Pawnees, who set the plains on fire. Many of the unsuccessful raiders were badly burned but escaped.

America   Township
Lat: 43-32-32 N   **Long:** 99-13-08 W
Pop: 62 (1990); 76 (1980)   **Pop Density:** 1.5
Land: 42.3 sq. mi.; **Water:** 3.8 sq. mi.

Brule   Township
Lat: 43-42-33 N   **Long:** 99-21-41 W
Pop: 100 (1990); 81 (1980)   **Pop Density:** 2.4
Land: 41.9 sq. mi.; **Water:** 3.5 sq. mi.

Chamberlain   City
ZIP: 57325   **Lat:** 43-48-27 N   **Long:** 99-19-12 W
Pop: 2,347 (1990); 2,258 (1980)   **Pop Density:** 733.4
Land: 3.2 sq. mi.; **Water:** 0.0 sq. mi.   **Elev:** 1465 ft.
Founded 1881.
Name origin: For Milwaukee Railroad director Selah Chamberlain.

*Chamberlain   Township
Lat: 43-47-17 N   **Long:** 99-19-08 W
Pop: 392 (1990); 186 (1980)   **Pop Density:** 18.4
Land: 21.3 sq. mi.; **Water:** 2.7 sq. mi.

Cleveland   Township
Lat: 43-48-26 N   **Long:** 99-05-34 W
Pop: 104 (1990); 106 (1980)   **Pop Density:** 2.8
Land: 36.9 sq. mi.; **Water:** 0.0 sq. mi.

Eagle   Township
Lat: 43-32-38 N   **Long:** 99-05-11 W
Pop: 82 (1990); 103 (1980)   **Pop Density:** 2.3
Land: 35.5 sq. mi.; **Water:** 0.1 sq. mi.

Grandview   Pop. Place
Lat: 43-37-44 N   **Long:** 99-18-36 W
Pop: 31 (1990); 41 (1980)   **Pop Density:** 1.4
Land: 22.8 sq. mi.; **Water:** 7.7 sq. mi.

Highland   Township
Lat: 43-38-11 N   **Long:** 98-57-47 W
Pop: 59 (1990); 60 (1980)   **Pop Density:** 1.6
Land: 35.8 sq. mi.; **Water:** 0.0 sq. mi.

Kimball   City
ZIP: 57355   **Lat:** 43-44-46 N   **Long:** 98-57-25 W
Pop: 743 (1990); 752 (1980)   **Pop Density:** 239.7
Land: 3.1 sq. mi.; **Water:** 0.0 sq. mi.   **Elev:** 1788 ft.
Incorporated 1883.
Name origin: For surveyor J.W. Kimball.

*Kimball   Township
ZIP: 57355   **Lat:** 43-42-10 N   **Long:** 98-58-14 W
Pop: 49 (1990); 88 (1980)   **Pop Density:** 1.5
Land: 32.5 sq. mi.; **Water:** 0.0 sq. mi.

Lyon   Township
ZIP: 57355   **Lat:** 43-53-42 N   **Long:** 98-58-35 W
Pop: 58 (1990); 73 (1980)   **Pop Density:** 1.6
Land: 35.8 sq. mi.; **Water:** 0.0 sq. mi.

Ola   Township
Lat: 43-37-20 N   **Long:** 99-13-16 W
Pop: 132 (1990); 114 (1980)   **Pop Density:** 3.7
Land: 35.9 sq. mi.; **Water:** 0.0 sq. mi.

Plainfield   Township
ZIP: 57355   **Lat:** 43-42-50 N   **Long:** 98-51-20 W
Pop: 45 (1990); 56 (1980)   **Pop Density:** 1.3
Land: 35.5 sq. mi.; **Water:** 0.0 sq. mi.

Pleasant Grove   Township
ZIP: 57355   **Lat:** 43-32-07 N   **Long:** 98-57-45 W
Pop: 41 (1990); 53 (1980)   **Pop Density:** 1.2
Land: 35.5 sq. mi.; **Water:** 0.0 sq. mi.

Plummer   Township
ZIP: 57355   **Lat:** 43-53-06 N   **Long:** 98-51-45 W
Pop: 39 (1990); 45 (1980)   **Pop Density:** 1.1
Land: 35.7 sq. mi.; **Water:** 0.1 sq. mi.

Pukwana   Town
ZIP: 57370   **Lat:** 43-46-44 N   **Long:** 99-10-56 W
Pop: 263 (1990); 234 (1980)   **Pop Density:** 328.8
Land: 0.8 sq. mi.; **Water:** 0.0 sq. mi.   **Elev:** 1549 ft.
Founded 1881.
Name origin: For an Indian name in the poem *The Song of Hiawatha* by Henry Wadsworth Longfellow (1807–82).

*Pukwana   Township
ZIP: 57370   **Lat:** 43-48-22 N   **Long:** 99-12-48 W
Pop: 128 (1990); 136 (1980)   **Pop Density:** 3.6
Land: 35.4 sq. mi.; **Water:** 0.1 sq. mi.

Red Lake   Township
ZIP: 57370   **Lat:** 43-42-20 N   **Long:** 99-12-41 W
Pop: 82 (1990); 78 (1980)   **Pop Density:** 2.7
Land: 30.2 sq. mi.; **Water:** 5.6 sq. mi.

Richland   Township
Lat: 43-37-18 N   **Long:** 99-04-54 W
Pop: 69 (1990); 108 (1980)   **Pop Density:** 1.9
Land: 35.7 sq. mi.; **Water:** 0.0 sq. mi.

Smith   Township
ZIP: 57355   **Lat:** 43-43-49 N   **Long:** 99-05-31 W
Pop: 61 (1990); 66 (1980)   **Pop Density:** 1.7
Land: 35.9 sq. mi.; **Water:** 0.0 sq. mi.

Torrey Lake   Township
ZIP: 57355   **Lat:** 43-32-24 N   **Long:** 98-51-21 W
Pop: 191 (1990); 159 (1980)   **Pop Density:** 5.4
Land: 35.6 sq. mi.; **Water:** 0.0 sq. mi.

Union Township
Lat: 43-53-23 N Long: 99-06-13 W
Pop: 61 (1990); 78 (1980) **Pop Density:** 1.7
Land: 35.6 sq. mi.; **Water:** 0.0 sq. mi.

Waldro Township
ZIP: 57355 Lat: 43-48-20 N Long: 98-58-04 W
Pop: 74 (1990); 85 (1980) **Pop Density:** 2.0
Land: 36.9 sq. mi.; **Water:** 0.0 sq. mi.

West Point Township
Lat: 43-53-51 N Long: 99-15-22 W
Pop: 86 (1990); 105 (1980) **Pop Density:** 1.8
Land: 47.4 sq. mi.; **Water:** 3.6 sq. mi.

Wilbur Township
ZIP: 57355 Lat: 43-37-54 N Long: 98-51-01 W
Pop: 132 (1990); 45 (1980) **Pop Density:** 3.7
Land: 35.8 sq. mi.; **Water:** 0.0 sq. mi.

Willow Lake Township
Lat: 43-47-51 N Long: 98-51-28 W
Pop: 54 (1990); 59 (1980) **Pop Density:** 1.5
Land: 36.0 sq. mi.; **Water:** 0.0 sq. mi.

Buffalo County
County Seat: Gannvalley (ZIP: 57341)

Pop: 1,759 (1990); 1,795 (1980) **Pop Density:** 3.7
Land: 470.6 sq. mi.; **Water:** 16.8 sq. mi. **Area Code:** 605
In south-central SD, southeast of Pierre; organized 1871 (prior to statehood) from territorial country.
Name origin: For the once-plentiful herds of buffalo.

Crow Creek Pop. Place
ZIP: 57339 Lat: 44-04-21 N Long: 99-19-51 W
Pop: 1,495 (1990); 1,439 (1980) **Pop Density:** 6.2
Land: 239.4 sq. mi.; **Water:** 16.3 sq. mi.

Elvira Township
ZIP: 57341 Lat: 44-03-44 N Long: 99-00-08 W
Pop: 63 (1990); 96 (1980) **Pop Density:** 1.3
Land: 47.6 sq. mi.; **Water:** 0.1 sq. mi.

Fort Thompson CDP
ZIP: 57339 Lat: 44-02-59 N Long: 99-24-43 W
Pop: 1,088 (1990) **Pop Density:** 105.6
Land: 10.3 sq. mi.; **Water:** 2.3 sq. mi.

Gannvalley Pop. Place
ZIP: 57341
Pop: 130 (1990)

North Buffalo Pop. Place
Lat: 44-08-44 N Long: 99-07-10 W
Pop: 123 (1990); 176 (1980) **Pop Density:** 0.9
Land: 130.4 sq. mi.; **Water:** 0.3 sq. mi.

Southeast Buffalo Pop. Place
Lat: 43-59-53 N Long: 99-00-51 W
Pop: 78 (1990); 84 (1980) **Pop Density:** 1.5
Land: 53.3 sq. mi.; **Water:** 0.1 sq. mi.

Butte County
County Seat: Belle Fourche (ZIP: 57717)

Pop: 7,914 (1990); 8,372 (1980) **Pop Density:** 3.5
Land: 2248.6 sq. mi.; **Water:** 17.9 sq. mi. **Area Code:** 605
On the central western border of SD; organized Mar 2, 1883 (prior to statehood) from Harding County.
Name origin: For nearby buttes (flat-topped mounds or mountains).

Belle Fourche City
ZIP: 57717 Lat: 44-39-51 N Long: 103-51-07 W
Pop: 4,335 (1990); 4,692 (1980) **Pop Density:** 1667.3
Land: 2.6 sq. mi.; **Water:** 0.0 sq. mi. **Elev:** 3023 ft.
Name origin: For its location on the Belle Fourche River.

East Butte Pop. Place
Lat: 44-53-13 N Long: 103-12-42 W
Pop: 729 (1990); 631 (1980) **Pop Density:** 0.9
Land: 836.8 sq. mi.; **Water:** 3.5 sq. mi.

Fruitdale Town
ZIP: 57742 Lat: 44-40-05 N Long: 103-41-43 W
Pop: 43 (1990); 88 (1980) **Pop Density:** 143.3
Land: 0.3 sq. mi.; **Water:** 0.0 sq. mi. **Elev:** 2950 ft.
Founded 1910.
Name origin: Named by original landowner Henry Stearns for the many varieties of fruit growing in the area.

SOUTH DAKOTA, Butte County

Newell
City
ZIP: 57760 **Lat:** 44-42-54 N **Long:** 103-25-03 W
Pop: 675 (1990); 638 (1980) **Pop Density:** 675.0
Land: 1.0 sq. mi.; **Water:** 0.0 sq. mi. **Elev:** 2853 ft.
Founded 1910.
Name origin: For F.H. Newell, a reclamation engineer.

Nisland
Town
ZIP: 57762 **Lat:** 44-40-24 N **Long:** 103-33-08 W
Pop: 174 (1990); 216 (1980) **Pop Density:** 580.0
Land: 0.3 sq. mi.; **Water:** 0.0 sq. mi. **Elev:** 2857 ft.
Founded 1909.
Name origin: For pioneer Nils Sorenson, on whose land the town was built.

Union
Township
Lat: 44-57-13 N **Long:** 103-00-39 W
Pop: 24 (1990); 52 (1980) **Pop Density:** 0.2
Land: 140.8 sq. mi.; **Water:** 0.8 sq. mi.

Vale
Township
ZIP: 57788 **Lat:** 44-37-11 N **Long:** 103-23-59 W
Pop: 98 (1990); 315 (1980) **Pop Density:** 245.0
Land: 0.4 sq. mi.; **Water:** 0.0 sq. mi.

West Butte
Pop. Place
Lat: 44-55-03 N **Long:** 103-45-14 W
Pop: 1,836 (1990); 1,733 (1980) **Pop Density:** 1.4
Land: 1266.5 sq. mi.; **Water:** 13.6 sq. mi.

Campbell County
County Seat: Mound City (ZIP: 57646)

Pop: 1,965 (1990); 2,243 (1980) **Pop Density:** 2.7
Land: 735.8 sq. mi.; **Water:** 35.5 sq. mi. **Area Code:** 605
On the central northern border of SD, northwest of Aberdeen; created Jan 8, 1873 (prior to statehood) from Buffalo County.
Name origin: For Norman B. Campbell, Dakota Territory legislator (1872–73).

Artas
Town
Lat: 45-53-15 N **Long:** 99-48-21 W
Pop: 28 (1990); 43 (1980) **Pop Density:** 280.0
Land: 0.1 sq. mi.; **Water:** 0.0 sq. mi. **Elev:** 1813 ft.
Name origin: From *artos*, a Greek term meaning 'bread', so named because of the region's importance as a wheat-growing area; with a spelling variation.

Herreid
City
ZIP: 57632 **Lat:** 45-50-12 N **Long:** 100-04-30 W
Pop: 488 (1990); 570 (1980) **Pop Density:** 488.0
Land: 1.0 sq. mi.; **Water:** 0.0 sq. mi. **Elev:** 1682 ft.
Name origin: For Charles Herreid, governor of SD in 1907.

Mound City
Town
ZIP: 57646 **Lat:** 45-43-36 N **Long:** 100-04-03 W
Pop: 89 (1990); 111 (1980) **Pop Density:** 890.0
Land: 0.1 sq. mi.; **Water:** 0.0 sq. mi. **Elev:** 1722 ft.
Name origin: For nearby Indian mounds.

North Campbell
Pop. Place
Lat: 45-51-51 N **Long:** 100-03-30 W
Pop: 522 (1990); 599 (1980) **Pop Density:** 1.4
Land: 380.6 sq. mi.; **Water:** 22.6 sq. mi.

Pollock
Town
ZIP: 57648 **Lat:** 45-54-05 N **Long:** 100-17-24 W
Pop: 379 (1990); 355 (1980) **Pop Density:** 1895.0
Land: 0.2 sq. mi.; **Water:** 0.0 sq. mi. **Elev:** 1665 ft.
Name origin: For pioneer settler James Pollock. Originally called Harba.

South Campbell
Pop. Place
Lat: 45-40-50 N **Long:** 100-01-37 W
Pop: 459 (1990); 565 (1980) **Pop Density:** 1.3
Land: 353.8 sq. mi.; **Water:** 12.9 sq. mi.

Charles Mix County
County Seat: Lake Andes (ZIP: 57356)

Pop: 9,131 (1990); 9,680 (1980) **Pop Density:** 8.3
Land: 1098.3 sq. mi.; **Water:** 52.0 sq. mi. **Area Code:** 605
On the southeastern border of SD, southwest of Sioux Falls; original county; created May 8, 1862 (prior to statehood).
Name origin: For either Charles E. Mix, a commissioner of Indian affairs, or Charles H. Mix, a scout during the Civil War.

Bryan
Township
ZIP: 57380 **Lat:** 43-07-28 N **Long:** 98-17-11 W
Pop: 352 (1990); 257 (1980) **Pop Density:** 9.8
Land: 36.1 sq. mi.; **Water:** 0.0 sq. mi.

Carroll
Township
ZIP: 57369 **Lat:** 43-28-01 N **Long:** 98-45-55 W
Pop: 56 (1990); 73 (1980) **Pop Density:** 1.9
Land: 29.3 sq. mi.; **Water:** 0.1 sq. mi.

Castalia
Pop. Place
Lat: 43-23-20 N **Long:** 98-59-33 W
Pop: 85 (1990) **Pop Density:** 2.4
Land: 35.5 sq. mi.; **Water:** 0.0 sq. mi.

Choteau Creek
Township
ZIP: 57380 **Lat:** 43-09-06 N **Long:** 98-09-27 W
Pop: 221 (1990); 280 (1980) **Pop Density:** 3.6
Land: 62.1 sq. mi.; **Water:** 0.0 sq. mi.

Dante
Town
Lat: 43-02-23 N **Long:** 98-11-11 W
Pop: 98 (1990); 83 (1980) **Pop Density:** 245.0
Land: 0.4 sq. mi.; **Water:** 0.0 sq. mi. **Elev:** 1400 ft.
Founded 1908.
Name origin: For Italian author and poet Dante Alighieri (1265–1321).

Darlington
Township
Lat: 43-23-08 N **Long:** 98-45-47 W
Pop: 139 (1990); 167 (1980) **Pop Density:** 3.6
Land: 38.6 sq. mi.; **Water:** 0.0 sq. mi.

Forbes
Township
ZIP: 57369 **Lat:** 43-27-28 N **Long:** 98-52-52 W
Pop: 88 (1990); 119 (1980) **Pop Density:** 3.0
Land: 29.5 sq. mi.; **Water:** 0.0 sq. mi.

Geddes
City
ZIP: 57342 **Lat:** 43-15-14 N **Long:** 98-41-50 W
Pop: 280 (1990); 303 (1980) **Pop Density:** 466.7
Land: 0.6 sq. mi.; **Water:** 0.0 sq. mi. **Elev:** 1620 ft.
Founded 1900.
Name origin: For D.C. Geddes, a Milwaukee railroad official.

Goose Lake
Township
Lat: 43-12-56 N **Long:** 98-34-43 W
Pop: 204 (1990); 268 (1980) **Pop Density:** 3.2
Land: 64.1 sq. mi.; **Water:** 0.4 sq. mi.

Hamilton
Township
Lat: 43-17-49 N **Long:** 98-59-19 W
Pop: 51 (1990); 53 (1980) **Pop Density:** 2.3
Land: 22.5 sq. mi.; **Water:** 4.4 sq. mi.

Highland
Township
Lat: 43-02-04 N **Long:** 98-24-30 W
Pop: 461 (1990); 387 (1980) **Pop Density:** 12.7
Land: 36.4 sq. mi.; **Water:** 0.0 sq. mi.

Howard
Township
Lat: 43-14-08 N **Long:** 98-24-41 W
Pop: 236 (1990); 147 (1980) **Pop Density:** 5.3
Land: 44.8 sq. mi.; **Water:** 4.5 sq. mi.

Jackson
Township
Lat: 43-10-48 N **Long:** 98-44-43 W
Pop: 166 (1990); 201 (1980) **Pop Density:** 2.8
Land: 60.1 sq. mi.; **Water:** 8.4 sq. mi.

Kennedy
Township
ZIP: 57380 **Lat:** 43-12-19 N **Long:** 98-17-49 W
Pop: 85 (1990); 138 (1980) **Pop Density:** 2.5
Land: 34.4 sq. mi.; **Water:** 0.0 sq. mi.

Lake Andes
City
ZIP: 57356 **Lat:** 43-09-20 N **Long:** 98-32-06 W
Pop: 846 (1990); 1,029 (1980) **Pop Density:** 846.0
Land: 1.0 sq. mi.; **Water:** 0.0 sq. mi. **Elev:** 1466 ft.
Founded 1904.
Name origin: For the nearby lake.

Lake George
Township
Lat: 43-27-47 N **Long:** 99-00-43 W
Pop: 48 (1990); 54 (1980) **Pop Density:** 1.6
Land: 29.9 sq. mi.; **Water:** 0.0 sq. mi.

La Roche
Township
Lat: 43-27-00 N **Long:** 99-09-06 W
Pop: 161 (1990); 239 (1980) **Pop Density:** 2.7
Land: 60.3 sq. mi.; **Water:** 12.8 sq. mi.

Lawrence
Township
Lat: 43-01-50 N **Long:** 98-17-53 W
Pop: 386 (1990); 425 (1980) **Pop Density:** 11.3
Land: 34.3 sq. mi.; **Water:** 0.2 sq. mi.

Lone Tree
Township
Lat: 43-02-03 N **Long:** 98-10-26 W
Pop: 206 (1990); 190 (1980) **Pop Density:** 5.5
Land: 37.2 sq. mi.; **Water:** 0.2 sq. mi.

Marty
CDP
Lat: 42-59-34 N **Long:** 98-25-45 W
Pop: 436 (1990) **Pop Density:** 136.3
Land: 3.2 sq. mi.; **Water:** 0.0 sq. mi.

Moore
Township
Lat: 43-18-28 N **Long:** 98-35-39 W
Pop: 144 (1990); 238 (1980) **Pop Density:** 2.3
Land: 62.1 sq. mi.; **Water:** 0.0 sq. mi.

Pickstown
Town
Lat: 43-04-00 N **Long:** 98-31-49 W
Pop: 95 (1990) **Pop Density:** 158.3
Land: 0.6 sq. mi.; **Water:** 0.0 sq. mi.

Plain Center
Township
Lat: 43-07-05 N **Long:** 98-24-02 W
Pop: 192 (1990); 207 (1980) **Pop Density:** 5.5
Land: 35.2 sq. mi.; **Water:** 0.9 sq. mi.

Platte
City
ZIP: 57369 **Lat:** 43-23-14 N **Long:** 98-50-37 W
Pop: 1,311 (1990); 1,334 (1980) **Pop Density:** 1456.7
Land: 0.9 sq. mi.; **Water:** 0.0 sq. mi. **Elev:** 1612 ft.
Name origin: Named in 1882 by Dutch settlers for nearby Platte Creek.

*Platte
Township
ZIP: 57369 **Lat:** 43-23-00 N **Long:** 98-53-12 W
Pop: 282 (1990); 264 (1980) **Pop Density:** 8.1
Land: 34.7 sq. mi.; **Water:** 0.2 sq. mi.

Ravinia
Town
Lat: 43-08-09 N **Long:** 98-25-37 W
Pop: 79 (1990); 88 (1980) **Pop Density:** 395.0
Land: 0.2 sq. mi.; **Water:** 0.0 sq. mi. **Elev:** 1495 ft.
Name origin: Named in 1909 either for its location in a ravine or for an Indian woman whose property comprised part of the town site.

Ree
Township
ZIP: 57380 **Lat:** 42-56-34 N **Long:** 98-16-43 W
Pop: 159 (1990); 183 (1980) **Pop Density:** 3.4
Land: 46.8 sq. mi.; **Water:** 0.6 sq. mi.

Rhoda
Township
ZIP: 57342 **Lat:** 43-18-12 N **Long:** 98-45-15 W
Pop: 135 (1990); 158 (1980) **Pop Density:** 3.1
Land: 42.9 sq. mi.; **Water:** 0.0 sq. mi.

SOUTH DAKOTA, Charles Mix County

Rouse
Township
Lat: 42-54-58 N **Long:** 98-10-10 W
Pop: 215 (1990); 211 (1980) **Pop Density:** 3.5
Land: 61.0 sq. mi.; **Water:** 0.4 sq. mi.

Signal
Township
ZIP: 57342 **Lat:** 43-16-16 N **Long:** 98-52-07 W
Pop: 60 (1990); 75 (1980) **Pop Density:** 1.3
Land: 47.6 sq. mi.; **Water:** 7.4 sq. mi.

Wagner
City
ZIP: 57380 **Lat:** 43-04-41 N **Long:** 98-18-05 W
Pop: 1,462 (1990); 1,453 (1980) **Pop Density:** 913.8
Land: 1.6 sq. mi.; **Water:** 0.0 sq. mi. **Elev:** 1448 ft.
Platted 1900.
Name origin: For postmaster Walt Wagner.

Wahehe
Township
Lat: 42-57-28 N **Long:** 98-23-40 W
Pop: 306 (1990); 441 (1980) **Pop Density:** 10.9
Land: 28.1 sq. mi.; **Water:** 0.9 sq. mi.

White Swan
Township
Lat: 43-05-56 N **Long:** 98-33-39 W
Pop: 522 (1990); 516 (1980) **Pop Density:** 6.6
Land: 79.1 sq. mi.; **Water:** 10.7 sq. mi.

Clark County
County Seat: Clark (ZIP: 57225)

Pop: 4,403 (1990); 4,894 (1980) **Pop Density:** 4.6
Land: 958.0 sq. mi.; **Water:** 9.9 sq. mi. **Area Code:** 605
In east-central SD, southeast of Aberdeen; created Jan 8, 1873 (prior to statehood) from Hanson County.
Name origin: For Newton Clark, pioneer schoolteacher and Dakota territorial legislator.

Ash
Township
Lat: 45-01-23 N **Long:** 97-55-05 W
Pop: 47 (1990); 60 (1980) **Pop Density:** 1.3
Land: 35.5 sq. mi.; **Water:** 0.0 sq. mi.

Blaine
Township
Lat: 45-06-31 N **Long:** 97-33-54 W
Pop: 58 (1990); 76 (1980) **Pop Density:** 1.7
Land: 33.6 sq. mi.; **Water:** 2.2 sq. mi.

Bradley
Town
ZIP: 57217 **Lat:** 45-05-24 N **Long:** 97-38-29 W
Pop: 117 (1990); 135 (1980) **Pop Density:** 585.0
Land: 0.2 sq. mi.; **Water:** 0.0 sq. mi. **Elev:** 1795 ft.
Name origin: Named by railroad officials for E.R. Bradley, who broke up a fight between a railroad official and a group of laborers.

Clark
City
ZIP: 57225 **Lat:** 44-52-50 N **Long:** 97-44-01 W
Pop: 1,292 (1990); 1,351 (1980) **Pop Density:** 993.8
Land: 1.3 sq. mi.; **Water:** 0.0 sq. mi. **Elev:** 1845 ft.
Founded 1882.
Name origin: For territorial legislator Newton Clark.

Collins
Township
ZIP: 57278 **Lat:** 44-35-23 N **Long:** 97-41-01 W
Pop: 100 (1990); 105 (1980) **Pop Density:** 2.8
Land: 35.5 sq. mi.; **Water:** 0.0 sq. mi.

Cottonwood
Township
Lat: 45-06-40 N **Long:** 97-40-30 W
Pop: 109 (1990); 140 (1980) **Pop Density:** 3.1
Land: 34.9 sq. mi.; **Water:** 0.7 sq. mi.

Darlington
Township
Lat: 44-46-11 N **Long:** 97-47-38 W
Pop: 91 (1990); 92 (1980) **Pop Density:** 2.5
Land: 35.8 sq. mi.; **Water:** 0.0 sq. mi.

Day
Township
ZIP: 57225 **Lat:** 44-50-33 N **Long:** 97-40-32 W
Pop: 87 (1990); 131 (1980) **Pop Density:** 2.5
Land: 34.5 sq. mi.; **Water:** 0.6 sq. mi.

Eden
Township
Lat: 44-56-05 N **Long:** 97-33-16 W
Pop: 82 (1990); 100 (1980) **Pop Density:** 2.3
Land: 35.1 sq. mi.; **Water:** 0.4 sq. mi.

Elrod
Township
ZIP: 57225 **Lat:** 44-50-53 N **Long:** 97-33-05 W
Pop: 96 (1990); 131 (1980) **Pop Density:** 2.6
Land: 36.3 sq. mi.; **Water:** 0.0 sq. mi.

Fordham
Township
ZIP: 57258 **Lat:** 44-45-52 N **Long:** 97-55-11 W
Pop: 151 (1990); 121 (1980) **Pop Density:** 4.2
Land: 35.6 sq. mi.; **Water:** 0.1 sq. mi.

Foxton
Township
Lat: 44-45-14 N **Long:** 97-32-49 W
Pop: 70 (1990); 77 (1980) **Pop Density:** 1.9
Land: 36.0 sq. mi.; **Water:** 0.0 sq. mi.

Garden City
Town
ZIP: 57236 **Lat:** 44-57-28 N **Long:** 97-34-50 W
Pop: 93 (1990); 104 (1980) **Pop Density:** 232.5
Land: 0.4 sq. mi.; **Water:** 0.0 sq. mi. **Elev:** 1840 ft.
Settled 1889.

Garfield
Township
Lat: 44-56-09 N **Long:** 97-48-09 W
Pop: 91 (1990); 110 (1980) **Pop Density:** 2.5
Land: 36.0 sq. mi.; **Water:** 0.0 sq. mi.

Hague
Township
ZIP: 57278 **Lat:** 44-40-28 N **Long:** 97-47-52 W
Pop: 51 (1990); 78 (1980) **Pop Density:** 1.4
Land: 35.8 sq. mi.; **Water:** 0.0 sq. mi.

American Places Dictionary   SOUTH DAKOTA, Clay County

Lake   Township
Lat: 44-40-58 N   **Long:** 97-40-28 W
Pop: 110 (1990); 131 (1980)   **Pop Density:** 3.2
Land: 34.5 sq. mi.; **Water:** 1.2 sq. mi.

Lincoln   Township
Lat: 44-50-55 N   **Long:** 97-47-59 W
Pop: 95 (1990); 106 (1980)   **Pop Density:** 2.7
Land: 35.1 sq. mi.; **Water:** 0.1 sq. mi.

Logan   Township
Lat: 44-51-03 N   **Long:** 97-54-24 W
Pop: 50 (1990); 66 (1980)   **Pop Density:** 1.4
Land: 35.6 sq. mi.; **Water:** 0.1 sq. mi.

Maydell   Township
ZIP: 57217   **Lat:** 45-01-17 N   **Long:** 97-33-17 W
Pop: 49 (1990); 50 (1980)   **Pop Density:** 1.4
Land: 34.7 sq. mi.; **Water:** 1.1 sq. mi.

Merton   Township
ZIP: 57225   **Lat:** 44-45-31 N   **Long:** 97-40-04 W
Pop: 73 (1990); 83 (1980)   **Pop Density:** 2.1
Land: 35.6 sq. mi.; **Water:** 0.0 sq. mi.

Mount Pleasant   Township
ZIP: 57225   **Lat:** 44-56-18 N   **Long:** 97-40-09 W
Pop: 177 (1990); 164 (1980)   **Pop Density:** 4.9
Land: 35.9 sq. mi.; **Water:** 0.0 sq. mi.

Naples   Town
ZIP: 57271   **Lat:** 44-46-16 N   **Long:** 97-30-45 W
Pop: 35 (1990); 45 (1980)   **Pop Density:** 350.0
Land: 0.1 sq. mi.; **Water:** 0.0 sq. mi.   **Elev:** 1789 ft.
Name origin: Named by Italian workers on the Milwaukee Railroad for Naples, Italy.

Pleasant   Township
Lat: 44-40-18 N   **Long:** 97-33-15 W
Pop: 167 (1990); 104 (1980)   **Pop Density:** 4.7
Land: 35.3 sq. mi.; **Water:** 0.0 sq. mi.

Raymond   Town
ZIP: 57258   **Lat:** 44-54-40 N   **Long:** 97-56-11 W
Pop: 96 (1990); 106 (1980)   **Pop Density:** 320.0
Land: 0.3 sq. mi.; **Water:** 0.0 sq. mi.   **Elev:** 1456 ft.

*****Raymond**   Township
ZIP: 57258   **Lat:** 44-56-15 N   **Long:** 97-55-04 W
Pop: 71 (1990); 91 (1980)   **Pop Density:** 2.0
Land: 35.7 sq. mi.; **Water:** 0.0 sq. mi.

Richland   Township
Lat: 44-40-25 N   **Long:** 97-55-02 W
Pop: 101 (1990); 105 (1980)   **Pop Density:** 2.8
Land: 35.9 sq. mi.; **Water:** 0.0 sq. mi.

Rosedale   Township
Lat: 44-35-05 N   **Long:** 97-47-40 W
Pop: 83 (1990); 109 (1980)   **Pop Density:** 2.3
Land: 35.8 sq. mi.; **Water:** 0.0 sq. mi.

Spring Valley   Township
Lat: 45-06-14 N   **Long:** 97-47-52 W
Pop: 73 (1990); 77 (1980)   **Pop Density:** 2.1
Land: 35.1 sq. mi.; **Water:** 0.9 sq. mi.

Thorp   Township
ZIP: 57217   **Lat:** 45-01-15 N   **Long:** 97-40-50 W
Pop: 66 (1990); 79 (1980)   **Pop Density:** 1.9
Land: 35.1 sq. mi.; **Water:** 0.7 sq. mi.

Vienna   Town
ZIP: 57271   **Lat:** 44-42-11 N   **Long:** 97-29-56 W
Pop: 93 (1990); 90 (1980)   **Pop Density:** 116.3
Land: 0.8 sq. mi.; **Water:** 0.0 sq. mi.   **Elev:** 1830 ft.
Name origin: Named in 1888 for Vienna, Austria. Originally named Stusted.

Warren   Township
Lat: 45-06-22 N   **Long:** 97-55-10 W
Pop: 63 (1990); 77 (1980)   **Pop Density:** 1.8
Land: 35.0 sq. mi.; **Water:** 0.3 sq. mi.

Washington   Township
Lat: 44-35-05 N   **Long:** 97-32-58 W
Pop: 89 (1990); 126 (1980)   **Pop Density:** 2.5
Land: 35.6 sq. mi.; **Water:** 0.4 sq. mi.

Willow Lake   City
ZIP: 57278   **Lat:** 44-37-40 N   **Long:** 97-38-16 W
Pop: 317 (1990); 375 (1980)   **Pop Density:** 792.5
Land: 0.4 sq. mi.; **Water:** 0.0 sq. mi.   **Elev:** 1780 ft.
Settled 1882.

Woodland   Township
ZIP: 57278   **Lat:** 45-01-15 N   **Long:** 97-47-46 W
Pop: 60 (1990); 99 (1980)   **Pop Density:** 1.7
Land: 35.0 sq. mi.; **Water:** 0.9 sq. mi.

Clay County
County Seat: Vermillion (ZIP: 57069)

Pop: 13,186 (1990); 13,689 (1980)   **Pop Density:** 32.0
Land: 411.6 sq. mi.; **Water:** 5.1 sq. mi.   **Area Code:** 605
In southeastern SD, south of Sioux Falls; original county; organized Apr 5, 1862 (prior to statehood) from unorganized territory.
Name origin: For Henry Clay (1777–1852), U.S. senator from KY, known as the "Great Pacificator" for his advocacy of compromise to avert national crises.

Bethel   Township
ZIP: 57073   **Lat:** 42-57-07 N   **Long:** 97-06-13 W
Pop: 213 (1990); 239 (1980)   **Pop Density:** 5.9
Land: 35.8 sq. mi.; **Water:** 0.0 sq. mi.

Fairview   Township
Lat: 42-46-19 N   **Long:** 96-51-28 W
Pop: 393 (1990); 395 (1980)   **Pop Density:** 11.3
Land: 34.9 sq. mi.; **Water:** 1.5 sq. mi.

SOUTH DAKOTA, Clay County

Garfield Township
ZIP: 57069 Lat: 42-57-16 N Long: 96-52-13 W
Pop: 255 (1990); 273 (1980) Pop Density: 7.1
Land: 36.0 sq. mi.; Water: 0.0 sq. mi.

Glenwood Township
Lat: 43-02-28 N Long: 96-52-03 W
Pop: 187 (1990); 255 (1980) Pop Density: 5.2
Land: 35.9 sq. mi.; Water: 0.0 sq. mi.

Irene Town
ZIP: 57037 Lat: 43-04-53 N Long: 97-09-29 W
Pop: 209 (1990); 250 (1980) Pop Density: 2090.0
Land: 0.1 sq. mi.; Water: 0.0 sq. mi. Elev: 1364 ft.
Part of the town is also in Turner and Yankton counties.
Name origin: For Irene Fry, the daughter of the original landowner.

Meckling Township
ZIP: 57044 Lat: 42-51-56 N Long: 97-06-37 W
Pop: 228 (1990); 268 (1980) Pop Density: 6.3
Land: 36.1 sq. mi.; Water: 0.0 sq. mi.

Norway Township
Lat: 42-47-50 N Long: 97-04-35 W
Pop: 168 (1990); 176 (1980) Pop Density: 6.5
Land: 26.0 sq. mi.; Water: 1.9 sq. mi.

Pleasant Valley Township
Lat: 42-57-25 N Long: 96-58-42 W
Pop: 182 (1990); 221 (1980) Pop Density: 5.1
Land: 35.9 sq. mi.; Water: 0.0 sq. mi.

Prairie Center Township
Lat: 42-51-58 N Long: 96-51-50 W
Pop: 210 (1990); 220 (1980) Pop Density: 5.8
Land: 36.1 sq. mi.; Water: 0.1 sq. mi.

Riverside Township
Lat: 43-02-25 N Long: 96-58-20 W
Pop: 162 (1990); 199 (1980) Pop Density: 4.5
Land: 35.9 sq. mi.; Water: 0.0 sq. mi. Elev: 1230 ft.

Spirit Mound Township
ZIP: 57069 Lat: 42-51-50 N Long: 96-59-21 W
Pop: 192 (1990); 234 (1980) Pop Density: 5.3
Land: 36.1 sq. mi.; Water: 0.0 sq. mi.

Star Township
ZIP: 57073 Lat: 43-02-24 N Long: 97-06-43 W
Pop: 188 (1990); 193 (1980) Pop Density: 5.3
Land: 35.4 sq. mi.; Water: 0.0 sq. mi.

Vermillion City
ZIP: 57069 Lat: 42-46-55 N Long: 96-55-35 W
Pop: 10,034 (1990); 10,136 (1980) Pop Density: 3236.8
Land: 3.1 sq. mi.; Water: 0.0 sq. mi. Elev: 1221 ft.
Founded 1859. Site of the University of South Dakota.
Name origin: For the adjacent Vermillion River.

*Vermillion Township
ZIP: 57069 Lat: 42-47-03 N Long: 96-57-32 W
Pop: 236 (1990); 247 (1980) Pop Density: 9.8
Land: 24.1 sq. mi.; Water: 1.6 sq. mi.

Wakonda Town
ZIP: 57073 Lat: 43-00-29 N Long: 97-06-19 W
Pop: 329 (1990); 383 (1980) Pop Density: 822.5
Land: 0.4 sq. mi.; Water: 0.0 sq. mi. Elev: 1377 ft.
Platted 1888.
Name origin: From a Sioux Indian term meaning 'holy.'

Codington County
County Seat: Watertown (ZIP: 57201)

Pop: 22,698 (1990); 20,885 (1980) Pop Density: 33.0
Land: 687.8 sq. mi.; Water: 29.4 sq. mi. Area Code: 605
In east-central SD, southeast of Aberdeen; organized Aug 7, 1878 (prior to statehood) from Indian lands.
Name origin: For the Rev. G. S. S. Codington, clergyman and Dakota Territory legislator.

Dexter Township
ZIP: 57235 Lat: 45-06-31 N Long: 97-16-13 W
Pop: 188 (1990); 200 (1980) Pop Density: 3.1
Land: 59.7 sq. mi.; Water: 1.0 sq. mi.

Eden Township
Lat: 45-06-34 N Long: 97-26-09 W
Pop: 116 (1990); 131 (1980) Pop Density: 3.5
Land: 33.4 sq. mi.; Water: 2.4 sq. mi.

Elmira Township
Lat: 44-56-09 N Long: 97-03-40 W
Pop: 311 (1990); 326 (1980) Pop Density: 9.7
Land: 32.0 sq. mi.; Water: 0.0 sq. mi.

Florence Town
ZIP: 57235 Lat: 45-03-20 N Long: 97-19-33 W
Pop: 192 (1990); 190 (1980) Pop Density: 320.0
Land: 0.6 sq. mi.; Water: 0.0 sq. mi. Elev: 1770 ft.

Fuller Township
ZIP: 57235 Lat: 45-01-23 N Long: 97-16-26 W
Pop: 284 (1990); 278 (1980) Pop Density: 5.3
Land: 54.0 sq. mi.; Water: 3.1 sq. mi.

Germantown Township
Lat: 45-06-34 N Long: 97-04-39 W
Pop: 164 (1990); 204 (1980) Pop Density: 3.5
Land: 47.0 sq. mi.; Water: 0.0 sq. mi.

Graceland Township
ZIP: 57243 Lat: 44-56-03 N Long: 97-26-04 W
Pop: 108 (1990); 149 (1980) Pop Density: 3.3
Land: 33.2 sq. mi.; Water: 3.0 sq. mi.

Henry
Town
ZIP: 57243 **Lat:** 44-52-51 N **Long:** 97-27-45 W
Pop: 215 (1990); 217 (1980) **Pop Density:** 134.4
Land: 1.6 sq. mi.; **Water:** 0.0 sq. mi. **Elev:** 1790 ft.
Name origin: For its first settler, J E. Henry.

*Henry
Township
ZIP: 57243 **Lat:** 44-50-59 N **Long:** 97-26-07 W
Pop: 112 (1990); 125 (1980) **Pop Density:** 3.3
Land: 34.2 sq. mi.; **Water:** 0.0 sq. mi.

Kampeska
Township
Lat: 44-50-52 N **Long:** 97-18-34 W
Pop: 226 (1990); 273 (1980) **Pop Density:** 6.4
Land: 35.1 sq. mi.; **Water:** 0.8 sq. mi.

Kranzburg
Town
ZIP: 57245 **Lat:** 44-53-11 N **Long:** 96-54-35 W
Pop: 132 (1990); 136 (1980) **Pop Density:** 188.6
Land: 0.7 sq. mi.; **Water:** 0.0 sq. mi. **Elev:** 1960 ft.
Platted 1879.
Name origin: For the four Kranz brothers, pioneer settlers.

*Kranzburg
Township
Lat: 44-53-00 N **Long:** 96-56-05 W
Pop: 340 (1990); 363 (1980) **Pop Density:** 5.6
Land: 60.5 sq. mi.; **Water:** 0.0 sq. mi.

Lake
Township
Lat: 44-56-56 N **Long:** 97-10-57 W
Pop: 690 (1990); 551 (1980) **Pop Density:** 32.4
Land: 21.3 sq. mi.; **Water:** 0.6 sq. mi.

Leola
Township
Lat: 45-06-25 N **Long:** 96-56-36 W
Pop: 63 (1990); 103 (1980) **Pop Density:** 1.9
Land: 33.2 sq. mi.; **Water:** 1.0 sq. mi.

Pelican
Township
Lat: 44-50-23 N **Long:** 97-11-50 W
Pop: 547 (1990); 460 (1980) **Pop Density:** 17.9
Land: 30.5 sq. mi.; **Water:** 4.4 sq. mi.

Phipps
Township
ZIP: 57235 **Lat:** 45-00-57 N **Long:** 97-25-50 W
Pop: 77 (1990); 105 (1980) **Pop Density:** 2.3
Land: 33.3 sq. mi.; **Water:** 2.8 sq. mi.

Rauville
Township
Lat: 45-01-20 N **Long:** 97-05-32 W
Pop: 272 (1990); 325 (1980) **Pop Density:** 5.4
Land: 50.2 sq. mi.; **Water:** 0.0 sq. mi.

Richland
Township
Lat: 44-56-00 N **Long:** 97-18-17 W
Pop: 156 (1990); 169 (1980) **Pop Density:** 4.6
Land: 33.6 sq. mi.; **Water:** 2.3 sq. mi.

Sheridan
Township
Lat: 44-50-42 N **Long:** 97-03-27 W
Pop: 407 (1990); 368 (1980) **Pop Density:** 12.1
Land: 33.5 sq. mi.; **Water:** 0.0 sq. mi.

South Shore
Town
ZIP: 57263 **Lat:** 45-06-06 N **Long:** 96-55-48 W
Pop: 260 (1990); 241 (1980) **Pop Density:** 185.7
Land: 1.4 sq. mi.; **Water:** 0.0 sq. mi. **Elev:** 1862 ft.
Name origin: For its location on the south shore of Punished Woman Lake.

Wallace
Town
ZIP: 57272 **Lat:** 45-05-06 N **Long:** 97-28-38 W
Pop: 83 (1990); 90 (1980) **Pop Density:** 830.0
Land: 0.1 sq. mi.; **Water:** 0.0 sq. mi. **Elev:** 1770 ft.

Watertown
City
ZIP: 57201 **Lat:** 44-54-45 N **Long:** 97-09-59 W
Pop: 17,592 (1990); 15,649 (1980) **Pop Density:** 1332.7
Land: 13.2 sq. mi.; **Water:** 7.9 sq. mi. **Elev:** 1739 ft.
In northeastern SD, 70 mi. northeast of Huron. Founded 1875.
Name origin: For Watertown, NY.

Waverly
Township
Lat: 45-00-23 N **Long:** 96-56-42 W
Pop: 163 (1990); 232 (1980) **Pop Density:** 3.6
Land: 45.3 sq. mi.; **Water:** 0.0 sq. mi.

Corson County
County Seat: McIntosh (ZIP: 57641)

Pop: 4,195 (1990); 5,196 (1980) **Pop Density:** 1.7
Land: 2473.1 sq. mi.; **Water:** 56.5 sq. mi. **Area Code:** 605
On the central northern border of SD; organized Mar 2, 1909 from Dewey County.
Name origin: For Dighton Corson (1827–1915), WI legislator, a framer of the SD constitution, and SD Supreme Court Justice (1889–1913).

Bullhead
CDP
Lat: 45-46-04 N **Long:** 101-04-48 W
Pop: 179 (1990) **Pop Density:** 74.6
Land: 2.4 sq. mi.; **Water:** 0.1 sq. mi.

Cadillac
Township
Lat: 45-52-48 N **Long:** 101-00-45 W
Pop: 39 (1990); 43 (1980) **Pop Density:** 0.8
Land: 51.5 sq. mi.; **Water:** 0.2 sq. mi.

Central Corson
Pop. Place
Lat: 45-39-06 N **Long:** 101-00-27 W
Pop: 1,632 (1990); 1,399 (1980) **Pop Density:** 2.0
Land: 828.1 sq. mi.; **Water:** 8.8 sq. mi.

Custer
Township
Lat: 45-53-12 N **Long:** 101-45-48 W
Pop: 55 (1990); 65 (1980) **Pop Density:** 1.1
Land: 51.3 sq. mi.; **Water:** 0.2 sq. mi.

SOUTH DAKOTA, Corson County

Delaney
Township
Lat: 45-36-03 N **Long:** 101-54-59 W
Pop: 16 (1990); 22 (1980) **Pop Density:** 0.3
Land: 46.5 sq. mi.; **Water:** 0.1 sq. mi.

Grand Valley
Township
Lat: 45-41-14 N **Long:** 101-55-33 W
Pop: 28 (1990); 38 (1980) **Pop Density:** 0.6
Land: 45.8 sq. mi.; **Water:** 0.0 sq. mi.

Lake
Township
Lat: 45-55-29 N **Long:** 101-19-27 W
Pop: 32 (1990); 40 (1980) **Pop Density:** 1.1
Land: 30.4 sq. mi.; **Water:** 0.3 sq. mi.

Lemon, No. 2
Pop. Place
Lat: 45-52-10 N **Long:** 101-54-37 W
Pop: 72 (1990) **Pop Density:** 1.0
Land: 73.7 sq. mi.; **Water:** 0.1 sq. mi.

Lincoln
Township
Lat: 45-53-27 N **Long:** 100-49-52 W
Pop: 90 (1990); 87 (1980) **Pop Density:** 0.9
Land: 103.7 sq. mi.; **Water:** 0.1 sq. mi.

Little Eagle
CDP
Lat: 45-40-53 N **Long:** 100-47-46 W
Pop: 294 (1990) **Pop Density:** 210.0
Land: 1.4 sq. mi.; **Water:** 0.0 sq. mi.

McIntosh
City
ZIP: 57641 **Lat:** 45-55-14 N **Long:** 101-20-58 W
Pop: 302 (1990); 418 (1980) **Pop Density:** 335.6
Land: 0.9 sq. mi.; **Water:** 0.0 sq. mi. **Elev:** 2301 ft.
Name origin: For the McIntosh Construction Co., which worked here on the Milwaukee Railroad in 1909.

McLaughlin
City
ZIP: 57642 **Lat:** 45-48-46 N **Long:** 100-48-39 W
Pop: 780 (1990); 754 (1980) **Pop Density:** 1950.0
Land: 0.4 sq. mi.; **Water:** 0.0 sq. mi. **Elev:** 2001 ft.

Mahto
Township
Lat: 45-46-46 N **Long:** 100-39-18 W
Pop: 31 (1990); 36 (1980) **Pop Density:** 0.9
Land: 36.0 sq. mi.; **Water:** 0.1 sq. mi.

Mission
Township
Lat: 45-38-59 N **Long:** 100-27-34 W
Pop: 148 (1990); 268 (1980) **Pop Density:** 1.7
Land: 88.3 sq. mi.; **Water:** 22.4 sq. mi.

Morristown
Town
ZIP: 57645 **Lat:** 45-56-20 N **Long:** 101-43-05 W
Pop: 64 (1990); 127 (1980) **Pop Density:** 213.3
Land: 0.3 sq. mi.; **Water:** 0.0 sq. mi. **Elev:** 2250 ft.
Name origin: For Nels P. Morris, head of the packing company that shipped 30,000 head of cattle on the new Milwaukee railroad to the local C-7 Ranch he also owned.

Northeast Corson
Pop. Place
Lat: 45-50-48 N **Long:** 100-32-00 W
Pop: 190 (1990); 272 (1980) **Pop Density:** 1.1
Land: 171.4 sq. mi.; **Water:** 16.0 sq. mi.

Pioneer
Township
Lat: 45-52-34 N **Long:** 101-37-44 W
Pop: 71 (1990); 76 (1980) **Pop Density:** 1.4
Land: 51.7 sq. mi.; **Water:** 0.2 sq. mi.

Pleasant Ridge
Township
Lat: 45-30-41 N **Long:** 101-24-26 W
Pop: 30 (1990); 42 (1980) **Pop Density:** 0.8
Land: 35.8 sq. mi.; **Water:** 0.2 sq. mi.

Prairie View
Township
ZIP: 57660 **Lat:** 45-51-38 N **Long:** 101-30-56 W
Pop: 23 (1990); 35 (1980) **Pop Density:** 0.6
Land: 35.8 sq. mi.; **Water:** 0.1 sq. mi.

Ridgeland
Township
Lat: 45-30-52 N **Long:** 100-34-29 W
Pop: 68 (1990); 82 (1980) **Pop Density:** 0.8
Land: 82.1 sq. mi.; **Water:** 6.4 sq. mi.

Riverside
Township
Lat: 45-42-09 N **Long:** 101-46-46 W
Pop: 13 (1990); 22 (1980) **Pop Density:** 0.4
Land: 34.8 sq. mi.; **Water:** 0.1 sq. mi.

Rolling Green
Township
Lat: 45-46-22 N **Long:** 101-55-05 W
Pop: 51 (1990); 39 (1980) **Pop Density:** 1.0
Land: 50.9 sq. mi.; **Water:** 0.2 sq. mi.

Sherman
Township
Lat: 45-47-23 N **Long:** 101-45-42 W
Pop: 34 (1990); 45 (1980) **Pop Density:** 0.9
Land: 35.9 sq. mi.; **Water:** 0.1 sq. mi.

Twin Butte
Township
Lat: 45-31-26 N **Long:** 101-54-43 W
Pop: 22 (1990); 36 (1980) **Pop Density:** 0.5
Land: 46.6 sq. mi.; **Water:** 0.0 sq. mi.

Wakpala
Township
ZIP: 57658 **Lat:** 45-41-48 N **Long:** 100-34-03 W
Pop: 176 (1990); 282 (1980) **Pop Density:** 9.4
Land: 18.7 sq. mi.; **Water:** 0.0 sq. mi.

Walker
Township
Lat: 45-53-39 N **Long:** 101-08-13 W
Pop: 36 (1990); 38 (1980) **Pop Density:** 0.7
Land: 51.8 sq. mi.; **Water:** 0.1 sq. mi.

Watauga
Township
ZIP: 57660 **Lat:** 45-55-09 N **Long:** 101-30-53 W
Pop: 56 (1990); 62 (1980) **Pop Density:** 3.5
Land: 15.9 sq. mi.; **Water:** 0.0 sq. mi.

West Corson
Pop. Place
Lat: 45-39-58 N **Long:** 101-34-20 W
Pop: 136 (1990); 184 (1980) **Pop Density:** 0.3
Land: 484.7 sq. mi.; **Water:** 0.8 sq. mi.

Custer County
County Seat: Custer (ZIP: 57730)

Pop: 6,179 (1990); 6,000 (1980)   **Pop Density:** 4.0
Land: 1557.8 sq. mi.; **Water:** 1.5 sq. mi.   **Area Code:** 605
On the southwestern border of SD, south of Rapid City; created Jan 11, 1875 (prior to statehood) from Indian lands.
Name origin: For Gen. George Armstrong Custer (1839–76), U.S. soldier and Indian fighter.

Buffalo Gap — Town
ZIP: 57722   **Lat:** 43-29-33 N   **Long:** 103-18-49 W
Pop: 173 (1990); 186 (1980)   **Pop Density:** 865.0
Land: 0.2 sq. mi.; **Water:** 0.0 sq. mi.   **Elev:** 3260 ft.
Name origin: For the large buffalo herds once found in the area.

Custer — City
ZIP: 57730   **Lat:** 43-45-59 N   **Long:** 103-36-02 W
Pop: 1,741 (1990); 1,830 (1980)   **Pop Density:** 1243.6
Land: 1.4 sq. mi.; **Water:** 0.0 sq. mi.   **Elev:** 5318 ft.
Established 1875.
Name origin: For Gen. George Armstrong Custer (1839–76), who led the expedition that discovered gold there in 1874. Originally called Stonewall.

East Custer — Pop. Place
Lat: 43-42-34 N   **Long:** 103-09-38 W
Pop: 921 (1990); 816 (1980)   **Pop Density:** 1.1
Land: 808.2 sq. mi.; **Water:** 1.1 sq. mi.

Fairburn — Town
ZIP: 57738   **Lat:** 43-41-12 N   **Long:** 103-12-29 W
Pop: 62 (1990); 41 (1980)   **Pop Density:** 155.0
Land: 0.4 sq. mi.; **Water:** 0.0 sq. mi.   **Elev:** 3289 ft.
Name origin: For its location on a scenic creek, *burn* being the Scottish term meaning 'stream.'

Hermosa — Town
ZIP: 57744   **Lat:** 43-50-24 N   **Long:** 103-11-29 W
Pop: 242 (1990); 251 (1980)   **Pop Density:** 605.0
Land: 0.4 sq. mi.; **Water:** 0.0 sq. mi.   **Elev:** 3303 ft.
Founded 1886.
Name origin: From Spanish meaning 'beautiful.'

Pringle — Town
ZIP: 57773   **Lat:** 43-36-32 N   **Long:** 103-35-37 W
Pop: 96 (1990); 105 (1980)   **Pop Density:** 480.0
Land: 0.2 sq. mi.; **Water:** 0.0 sq. mi.   **Elev:** 4880 ft.
Name origin: For rancher W.H. Pringle, who owned the local water rights.

West Custer — Pop. Place
Lat: 43-39-53 N   **Long:** 103-46-21 W
Pop: 2,944 (1990); 2,771 (1980)   **Pop Density:** 3.9
Land: 747.0 sq. mi.; **Water:** 0.4 sq. mi.

Davison County
County Seat: Mitchell (ZIP: 57301)

Pop: 17,503 (1990); 17,820 (1980)   **Pop Density:** 40.2
Land: 435.5 sq. mi.; **Water:** 1.4 sq. mi.   **Area Code:** 605
In southeastern SD, west of Sioux Falls; created Jan 8, 1873 (prior to statehood) from Hanson County.
Name origin: For Henry C. Davison, prominent merchant and homesteader.

Badger — Township
Lat: 43-48-25 N   **Long:** 98-08-11 W
Pop: 170 (1990); 166 (1980)   **Pop Density:** 4.5
Land: 37.4 sq. mi.; **Water:** 0.0 sq. mi.

Baker — Township
Lat: 43-32-31 N   **Long:** 98-15-44 W
Pop: 171 (1990); 182 (1980)   **Pop Density:** 4.7
Land: 36.1 sq. mi.; **Water:** 0.0 sq. mi.

Beulah — Township
Lat: 43-43-00 N   **Long:** 98-08-47 W
Pop: 369 (1990); 393 (1980)   **Pop Density:** 10.3
Land: 35.9 sq. mi.; **Water:** 0.0 sq. mi.

Blendon — Township
ZIP: 57301   **Lat:** 43-48-42 N   **Long:** 98-15-21 W
Pop: 111 (1990); 123 (1980)   **Pop Density:** 3.0
Land: 37.4 sq. mi.; **Water:** 0.0 sq. mi.

Ethan — Town
ZIP: 57334   **Lat:** 43-32-45 N   **Long:** 97-58-58 W
Pop: 312 (1990); 351 (1980)   **Pop Density:** 1560.0
Land: 0.2 sq. mi.; **Water:** 0.0 sq. mi.   **Elev:** 1344 ft.
Platted 1883.
Name origin: For Revolutionary War patriot Ethan Allen (1738–89).

SOUTH DAKOTA, Davison County

Lisbon
Township
ZIP: 57301 Lat: 43-37-44 N Long: 98-08-38 W
Pop: 124 (1990); 164 (1980) Pop Density: 3.4
Land: 36.2 sq. mi.; Water: 0.0 sq. mi.

Mitchell
City
ZIP: 57301 Lat: 43-43-57 N Long: 98-02-01 W
Pop: 13,798 (1990); 13,916 (1980) Pop Density: 1467.9
Land: 9.4 sq. mi.; Water: 1.0 sq. mi. Elev: 1300 ft.
In southeastern SD, 72 mi. west of Sioux Falls.
Name origin: For Alexander Mitchell, president of the Milwaukee Railroad in 1879.

*Mitchell
Township
ZIP: 57301 Lat: 43-43-34 N Long: 98-02-22 W
Pop: 759 (1990); 697 (1980) Pop Density: 27.0
Land: 28.1 sq. mi.; Water: 0.0 sq. mi.

Mount Vernon
City
ZIP: 57363 Lat: 43-42-43 N Long: 98-15-39 W
Pop: 368 (1990); 402 (1980) Pop Density: 1226.7
Land: 0.3 sq. mi.; Water: 0.0 sq. mi. Elev: 1411 ft.
Founded 1880s.
Name origin: For the VA estate of George Washington (1732–99).

*Mount Vernon
Township
ZIP: 57363 Lat: 43-43-00 N Long: 98-15-54 W
Pop: 179 (1990); 186 (1980) Pop Density: 5.0
Land: 36.1 sq. mi.; Water: 0.0 sq. mi.

Perry
Township
Lat: 43-48-40 N Long: 98-01-53 W
Pop: 174 (1990); 198 (1980) Pop Density: 5.1
Land: 34.3 sq. mi.; Water: 0.1 sq. mi.

Prosper
Township
ZIP: 57301 Lat: 43-38-13 N Long: 98-01-50 W
Pop: 500 (1990); 493 (1980) Pop Density: 14.0
Land: 35.8 sq. mi.; Water: 0.1 sq. mi.

Rome
Township
Lat: 43-32-50 N Long: 98-02-02 W
Pop: 238 (1990); 275 (1980) Pop Density: 6.6
Land: 35.8 sq. mi.; Water: 0.0 sq. mi.

Tobin
Township
ZIP: 57301 Lat: 43-32-31 N Long: 98-08-31 W
Pop: 157 (1990); 173 (1980) Pop Density: 4.3
Land: 36.2 sq. mi.; Water: 0.0 sq. mi.

Union
Township
Lat: 43-38-04 N Long: 98-16-30 W
Pop: 73 (1990); 101 (1980) Pop Density: 2.0
Land: 36.2 sq. mi.; Water: 0.0 sq. mi.

Day County
County Seat: Webster (ZIP: 57274)

Pop: 6,978 (1990); 8,133 (1980) Pop Density: 6.8
Land: 1028.6 sq. mi.; Water: 62.7 sq. mi. Area Code: 605
In northeastern SD, east of Aberdeen; created Feb 22, 1879 (prior to statehood) from Clark County.
Name origin: For Merritt H. Day (1844–1900), Dakota Territory legislator.

Andover
Town
ZIP: 57422 Lat: 45-24-38 N Long: 97-54-11 W
Pop: 106 (1990); 139 (1980) Pop Density: 353.3
Land: 0.3 sq. mi.; Water: 0.0 sq. mi. Elev: 1482 ft.
Name origin: For Andover, MA.

*Andover
Township
ZIP: 57422 Lat: 45-24-50 N Long: 97-55-07 W
Pop: 127 (1990); 162 (1980) Pop Density: 1.8
Land: 71.1 sq. mi.; Water: 0.4 sq. mi.

Bristol
City
ZIP: 57219 Lat: 45-20-47 N Long: 97-44-56 W
Pop: 419 (1990); 445 (1980) Pop Density: 838.0
Land: 0.5 sq. mi.; Water: 0.0 sq. mi. Elev: 1790 ft.
Founded 1881.
Name origin: For Bristol, England.

*Bristol
Township
ZIP: 57219 Lat: 45-22-11 N Long: 97-47-46 W
Pop: 65 (1990); 111 (1980) Pop Density: 1.9
Land: 34.4 sq. mi.; Water: 1.0 sq. mi.

Butler
Town
Lat: 45-15-29 N Long: 97-42-40 W
Pop: 17 (1990); 22 (1980) Pop Density: 24.3
Land: 0.7 sq. mi.; Water: 0.0 sq. mi. Elev: 1822 ft.
Established 1887.
Name origin: For Harrison Butler, who deeded the land to the town.

*Butler
Township
Lat: 45-16-58 N Long: 97-40-18 W
Pop: 83 (1990); 91 (1980) Pop Density: 2.4
Land: 34.4 sq. mi.; Water: 0.7 sq. mi.

Central Point
Township
ZIP: 57273 Lat: 45-16-45 N Long: 97-17-52 W
Pop: 104 (1990); 132 (1980) Pop Density: 3.0
Land: 34.3 sq. mi.; Water: 6.6 sq. mi.

Egeland
Township
ZIP: 57274 Lat: 45-11-15 N Long: 97-17-47 W
Pop: 109 (1990); 128 (1980) Pop Density: 2.6
Land: 41.5 sq. mi.; Water: 1.5 sq. mi.

Farmington
Township
Lat: 45-32-47 N **Long:** 97-55-17 W
Pop: 76 (1990); 88 (1980) **Pop Density:** 2.1
Land: 35.5 sq. mi.; **Water:** 0.6 sq. mi.

Grenville
Town
ZIP: 57239 **Lat:** 45-27-59 N **Long:** 97-23-22 W
Pop: 81 (1990); 119 (1980) **Pop Density:** 405.0
Land: 0.2 sq. mi.; **Water:** 0.0 sq. mi. **Elev:** 1850 ft.
Incorporated 1918.

*Grenville
Township
ZIP: 57239 **Lat:** 45-27-38 N **Long:** 97-25-35 W
Pop: 152 (1990); 148 (1980) **Pop Density:** 4.5
Land: 33.6 sq. mi.; **Water:** 6.0 sq. mi.

Highland
Township
Lat: 45-11-47 N **Long:** 97-33-21 W
Pop: 111 (1990); 164 (1980) **Pop Density:** 3.1
Land: 35.4 sq. mi.; **Water:** 1.0 sq. mi.

Homer
Township
ZIP: 57468 **Lat:** 45-32-43 N **Long:** 97-47-55 W
Pop: 68 (1990); 91 (1980) **Pop Density:** 1.9
Land: 36.0 sq. mi.; **Water:** 0.1 sq. mi.

Independence
Township
Lat: 45-33-06 N **Long:** 97-40-35 W
Pop: 83 (1990); 118 (1980) **Pop Density:** 2.4
Land: 34.0 sq. mi.; **Water:** 2.1 sq. mi.

Kidder
Township
Lat: 45-22-01 N **Long:** 97-40-31 W
Pop: 94 (1990); 100 (1980) **Pop Density:** 2.7
Land: 34.9 sq. mi.; **Water:** 1.0 sq. mi.

Kosciusko
Township
ZIP: 57239 **Lat:** 45-30-19 N **Long:** 97-17-08 W
Pop: 195 (1990); 243 (1980) **Pop Density:** 4.9
Land: 39.7 sq. mi.; **Water:** 2.1 sq. mi.

Liberty
Township
Lat: 45-32-29 N **Long:** 97-33-18 W
Pop: 89 (1990); 108 (1980) **Pop Density:** 2.9
Land: 30.2 sq. mi.; **Water:** 5.3 sq. mi.

Lily
Town
Lat: 45-10-52 N **Long:** 97-40-52 W
Pop: 26 (1990); 38 (1980) **Pop Density:** 65.0
Land: 0.4 sq. mi.; **Water:** 0.0 sq. mi. **Elev:** 1845 ft.
Settled 1887.
Name origin: For the first postmaster's sister.

Lynn
Township
Lat: 45-27-14 N **Long:** 97-40-14 W
Pop: 72 (1990); 85 (1980) **Pop Density:** 2.0
Land: 35.4 sq. mi.; **Water:** 0.6 sq. mi.

Morton
Township
ZIP: 57274 **Lat:** 45-17-10 N **Long:** 97-24-57 W
Pop: 105 (1990); 126 (1980) **Pop Density:** 3.0
Land: 35.5 sq. mi.; **Water:** 0.5 sq. mi.

Nutley
Township
ZIP: 57239 **Lat:** 45-32-16 N **Long:** 97-25-47 W
Pop: 101 (1990); 126 (1980) **Pop Density:** 3.0
Land: 33.7 sq. mi.; **Water:** 4.1 sq. mi.

Oak Gulch
Township
Lat: 45-11-22 N **Long:** 97-54-57 W
Pop: 35 (1990); 54 (1980) **Pop Density:** 1.0
Land: 34.6 sq. mi.; **Water:** 0.5 sq. mi.

Pierpont
Town
ZIP: 57468 **Lat:** 45-29-48 N **Long:** 97-49-52 W
Pop: 173 (1990); 184 (1980) **Pop Density:** 576.7
Land: 0.3 sq. mi.; **Water:** 0.0 sq. mi. **Elev:** 1500 ft.
Settled 1883.

Racine
Township
ZIP: 57274 **Lat:** 45-22-08 N **Long:** 97-25-26 W
Pop: 98 (1990); 122 (1980) **Pop Density:** 3.5
Land: 28.0 sq. mi.; **Water:** 8.0 sq. mi.

Raritan
Township
ZIP: 57261 **Lat:** 45-27-28 N **Long:** 97-33-06 W
Pop: 110 (1990); 121 (1980) **Pop Density:** 3.2
Land: 34.7 sq. mi.; **Water:** 0.9 sq. mi.

Roslyn
Town
ZIP: 57261 **Lat:** 45-29-47 N **Long:** 97-29-36 W
Pop: 251 (1990); 261 (1980) **Pop Density:** 1255.0
Land: 0.2 sq. mi.; **Water:** 0.0 sq. mi. **Elev:** 1865 ft.
Name origin: A coined word made by combining the names of nearby Lakes Rosholt and Linn, with a spelling variation.

Rusk
Township
ZIP: 57274 **Lat:** 45-16-55 N **Long:** 97-33-07 W
Pop: 153 (1990); 208 (1980) **Pop Density:** 4.3
Land: 35.3 sq. mi.; **Water:** 0.7 sq. mi.

Scotland
Township
Lat: 45-16-34 N **Long:** 97-54-11 W
Pop: 39 (1990); 60 (1980) **Pop Density:** 1.1
Land: 35.9 sq. mi.; **Water:** 0.0 sq. mi.

Troy
Township
Lat: 45-11-57 N **Long:** 97-48-00 W
Pop: 65 (1990); 69 (1980) **Pop Density:** 1.9
Land: 34.2 sq. mi.; **Water:** 2.2 sq. mi.

Union
Township
Lat: 45-27-24 N **Long:** 97-47-50 W
Pop: 87 (1990); 120 (1980) **Pop Density:** 2.5
Land: 35.4 sq. mi.; **Water:** 0.1 sq. mi.

Valley
Township
Lat: 45-16-57 N **Long:** 97-47-40 W
Pop: 51 (1990); 103 (1980) **Pop Density:** 1.4
Land: 35.7 sq. mi.; **Water:** 0.2 sq. mi.

Waubay
City
ZIP: 57273 **Lat:** 45-19-59 N **Long:** 97-18-23 W
Pop: 647 (1990); 675 (1980) **Pop Density:** 462.1
Land: 1.4 sq. mi.; **Water:** 0.0 sq. mi. **Elev:** 1814 ft.
Name origin: Named in 1885 for nearby Waubay Lake.

*Waubay
Township
ZIP: 57273 **Lat:** 45-23-29 N **Long:** 97-18-01 W
Pop: 491 (1990); 516 (1980) **Pop Density:** 10.7
Land: 46.0 sq. mi.; **Water:** 13.7 sq. mi.

Webster
City
ZIP: 57274 **Lat:** 45-20-08 N **Long:** 97-31-18 W
Pop: 2,017 (1990); 2,417 (1980) **Pop Density:** 1344.7
Land: 1.5 sq. mi.; **Water:** 0.0 sq. mi. **Elev:** 1847 ft.
Platted 1881.
Name origin: For the first settler, J.B. Webster.

Wheatland
Township
ZIP: 57274 **Lat:** 45-11-40 N **Long:** 97-25-55 W
Pop: 111 (1990); 122 (1980) **Pop Density:** 3.1
Land: 36.2 sq. mi.; **Water:** 0.2 sq. mi.

SOUTH DAKOTA, Day County

York
Lat: 45-11-38 N **Long:** 97-40-27 W
Pop: 43 (1990); 68 (1980)   **Pop Density:** 1.3
Land: 34.2 sq. mi.; **Water:** 1.5 sq. mi.
Township

Deuel County
County Seat: Clear Lake (ZIP: 57226)

Pop: 4,522 (1990); 5,289 (1980)   **Pop Density:** 7.3
Land: 623.6 sq. mi.; **Water:** 13.2 sq. mi.   **Area Code:** 605
On central eastern border of SD, north of Sioux Falls; created Apr 5, 1862 (prior to statehood) from Brookings County.
Name origin: For Jacob S. Deuel (1830–?), sawmill owner and a member of the first Territorial legislature (1862–63).

Altamont
Town
Lat: 44-50-25 N **Long:** 96-41-24 W
Pop: 48 (1990); 58 (1980)   **Pop Density:** 34.3
Land: 1.4 sq. mi.; **Water:** 0.0 sq. mi.   **Elev:** 1850 ft.
Founded 1880s.
Name origin: For the highest point in the county.

*Altamont
Township
Lat: 44-50-50 N **Long:** 96-40-27 W
Pop: 109 (1990); 143 (1980)   **Pop Density:** 3.0
Land: 36.5 sq. mi.; **Water:** 3.2 sq. mi.

Antelope Valley
Township
Lat: 44-56-07 N **Long:** 96-29-15 W
Pop: 45 (1990); 82 (1980)   **Pop Density:** 2.3
Land: 19.2 sq. mi.; **Water:** 0.0 sq. mi.

Astoria
Town
ZIP: 57213   **Lat:** 44-33-27 N **Long:** 96-32-45 W
Pop: 155 (1990); 154 (1980)   **Pop Density:** 775.0
Land: 0.2 sq. mi.; **Water:** 0.0 sq. mi.   **Elev:** 1820 ft.
Established 1900.
Name origin: For Astoria, OR.

Blom
Township
ZIP: 57268   **Lat:** 44-35-12 N **Long:** 96-42-09 W
Pop: 140 (1990); 150 (1980)   **Pop Density:** 3.9
Land: 35.8 sq. mi.; **Water:** 0.0 sq. mi.

Brandt
Town
ZIP: 57218   **Lat:** 44-39-55 N **Long:** 96-37-30 W
Pop: 123 (1990); 129 (1980)   **Pop Density:** 94.6
Land: 1.3 sq. mi.; **Water:** 0.0 sq. mi.   **Elev:** 1851 ft.
Founded 1884.
Name origin: For the Rev. P.O. Brandt.

*Brandt
Township
ZIP: 57218   **Lat:** 44-40-25 N **Long:** 96-42-20 W
Pop: 159 (1990); 162 (1980)   **Pop Density:** 4.4
Land: 35.8 sq. mi.; **Water:** 0.0 sq. mi.

Clear Lake
City
ZIP: 57226   **Lat:** 44-45-57 N **Long:** 96-40-52 W
Pop: 1,247 (1990); 1,310 (1980)   **Pop Density:** 415.7
Land: 3.0 sq. mi.; **Water:** 0.2 sq. mi.   **Elev:** 1800 ft.
Settled 1884.
Name origin: For a nearby lake whose bottom can be seen through the clear water.

*Clear Lake
Township
ZIP: 57226   **Lat:** 44-46-15 N **Long:** 96-40-03 W
Pop: 188 (1990); 248 (1980)   **Pop Density:** 5.0
Land: 37.4 sq. mi.; **Water:** 1.3 sq. mi.

Gary
City
ZIP: 57237   **Lat:** 44-47-42 N **Long:** 96-27-28 W
Pop: 274 (1990); 354 (1980)   **Pop Density:** 391.4
Land: 0.7 sq. mi.; **Water:** 0.0 sq. mi.   **Elev:** 1483 ft.
Established 1877.
Name origin: For H.B. Gary, an early mail agent.

Glenwood
Township
Lat: 44-50-52 N **Long:** 96-31-50 W
Pop: 102 (1990); 155 (1980)   **Pop Density:** 2.4
Land: 42.9 sq. mi.; **Water:** 0.7 sq. mi.

Goodwin
Town
ZIP: 57238   **Lat:** 44-52-37 N **Long:** 96-50-54 W
Pop: 126 (1990); 139 (1980)   **Pop Density:** 252.0
Land: 0.5 sq. mi.; **Water:** 0.0 sq. mi.   **Elev:** 2000 ft.
Name origin: For George Goodwin, a local railroad official. Originally called Prairie Siding.

*Goodwin
Township
ZIP: 57238   **Lat:** 44-51-06 N **Long:** 96-48-49 W
Pop: 188 (1990); 219 (1980)   **Pop Density:** 4.7
Land: 40.4 sq. mi.; **Water:** 0.0 sq. mi.

Grange
Township
ZIP: 57268   **Lat:** 44-35-17 N **Long:** 96-49-06 W
Pop: 128 (1990); 167 (1980)   **Pop Density:** 3.6
Land: 36.0 sq. mi.; **Water:** 0.0 sq. mi.

Havana
Township
ZIP: 57226   **Lat:** 44-45-37 N **Long:** 96-48-27 W
Pop: 194 (1990); 247 (1980)   **Pop Density:** 4.7
Land: 41.5 sq. mi.; **Water:** 0.0 sq. mi.

Herrick
Township
Lat: 44-45-32 N **Long:** 96-31-54 W
Pop: 171 (1990); 162 (1980)   **Pop Density:** 4.0
Land: 43.1 sq. mi.; **Water:** 0.7 sq. mi.

Hidewood
Township
ZIP: 57218   **Lat:** 44-40-41 N **Long:** 96-49-39 W
Pop: 110 (1990); 148 (1980)   **Pop Density:** 3.1
Land: 35.8 sq. mi.; **Water:** 0.0 sq. mi.

Lowe — Township
Lat: 44-55-33 N Long: 96-34-37 W
Pop: 141 (1990); 198 (1980) Pop Density: 3.9
Land: 35.8 sq. mi.; Water: 0.0 sq. mi.

Norden — Township
Lat: 44-40-53 N Long: 96-33-04 W
Pop: 263 (1990); 312 (1980) Pop Density: 4.9
Land: 54.0 sq. mi.; Water: 1.4 sq. mi.

Portland — Township
Lat: 44-55-49 N Long: 96-41-50 W
Pop: 93 (1990); 112 (1980) Pop Density: 2.6
Land: 35.3 sq. mi.; Water: 0.3 sq. mi.

Rome — Township
Lat: 44-56-31 N Long: 96-49-10 W
Pop: 102 (1990); 143 (1980) Pop Density: 3.2
Land: 32.2 sq. mi.; Water: 3.7 sq. mi.

Scandinavia — Township
ZIP: 57213 Lat: 44-35-32 N Long: 96-32-45 W
Pop: 215 (1990); 261 (1980) Pop Density: 3.9
Land: 54.7 sq. mi.; Water: 1.5 sq. mi.

Toronto — Town
ZIP: 57268 Lat: 44-34-20 N Long: 96-38-29 W
Pop: 201 (1990); 236 (1980) Pop Density: 670.0
Land: 0.3 sq. mi.; Water: 0.0 sq. mi. Elev: 1997 ft.
Established 1884, by a settler from Canada.
Name origin: For the capital of the province of Ontario, Canada.

Dewey County
County Seat: Timber Lake (ZIP: 57656)

Pop: 5,523 (1990); 5,366 (1980) Pop Density: 2.4
Land: 2302.8 sq. mi.; Water: 143.0 sq. mi. Area Code: 605

In north-central SD, north of Pierre; created as Rusk County in 1883 (prior to statehood); organized 1909 from Indian lands.

Name origin: For William Pitt Dewey (?–1900), surveyor general of the Dakota Territory (1873–77).

Eagle Butte — Town
ZIP: 57625 Lat: 44-59-51 N Long: 101-14-00 W
Pop: 475 (1990); 435 (1980) Pop Density: 2375.0
Land: 0.2 sq. mi.; Water: 0.0 sq. mi. Elev: 2390 ft.
Founded 1910. Part of the town is also in Ziebach County.
Name origin: For the nearby butte.

Isabel — City
ZIP: 57633 Lat: 45-23-44 N Long: 101-25-42 W
Pop: 319 (1990); 332 (1980) Pop Density: 531.7
Land: 0.6 sq. mi.; Water: 0.0 sq. mi. Elev: 2400 ft.

North Dewey — Pop. Place
Lat: 45-17-28 N Long: 101-08-55 W
Pop: 3,393 (1990); 2,982 (1980) Pop Density: 3.7
Land: 905.4 sq. mi.; Water: 2.1 sq. mi.

North Eagle Butte — CDP
Lat: 45-00-04 N Long: 101-13-37 W
Pop: 1,423 (1990); 1,354 (1980) Pop Density: 2032.9
Land: 0.7 sq. mi.; Water: 0.0 sq. mi.

South Dewey — Pop. Place
Lat: 45-04-51 N Long: 100-42-16 W
Pop: 819 (1990); 957 (1980) Pop Density: 0.6
Land: 1396.2 sq. mi.; Water: 141.0 sq. mi.

Timber Lake — City
ZIP: 57656 Lat: 45-25-39 N Long: 101-04-27 W
Pop: 517 (1990); 660 (1980) Pop Density: 1292.5
Land: 0.4 sq. mi.; Water: 0.0 sq. mi. Elev: 2159 ft.
Name origin: For the nearby lake.

Douglas County
County Seat: Armour (ZIP: 57313)

Pop: 3,746 (1990); 4,181 (1980)
Land: 433.6 sq. mi.; **Water:** 0.5 sq. mi.
Pop Density: 8.6
Area Code: 605

In south-central SD, southwest of Sioux Falls; created Jan 8, 1873 (prior to statehood) from Charles Mix County.

Name origin: For Stephen Arnold Douglas (1813–61), U.S. orator and statesman.

Armour — City
ZIP: 57313 **Lat:** 43-19-09 N **Long:** 98-20-37 W
Pop: 854 (1990); 819 (1980) **Pop Density:** 854.0
Land: 1.0 sq. mi.; **Water:** 0.0 sq. mi. **Elev:** 1523 ft.
Founded 1886.
Name origin: For Phillip D. Armour, industrialist and railroad director.

Belmont — Township
Lat: 43-17-38 N **Long:** 98-10-43 W
Pop: 82 (1990); 117 (1980) **Pop Density:** 2.4
Land: 34.3 sq. mi.; **Water:** 0.0 sq. mi.

Chester — Township
Lat: 43-18-52 N **Long:** 98-25-13 W
Pop: 89 (1990); 164 (1980) **Pop Density:** 3.1
Land: 28.3 sq. mi.; **Water:** 0.0 sq. mi.

Clark — Township
Lat: 43-23-29 N **Long:** 98-38-26 W
Pop: 177 (1990); 206 (1980) **Pop Density:** 6.3
Land: 28.0 sq. mi.; **Water:** 0.0 sq. mi.

Corsica — City
ZIP: 57328 **Lat:** 43-25-27 N **Long:** 98-24-20 W
Pop: 619 (1990); 644 (1980) **Pop Density:** 884.3
Land: 0.7 sq. mi.; **Water:** 0.0 sq. mi. **Elev:** 1540 ft.
Name origin: Named in 1905 for the many Corsicans who helped build the railroad in the area.

Delmont — City
ZIP: 57330 **Lat:** 43-15-57 N **Long:** 98-09-35 W
Pop: 235 (1990); 290 (1980) **Pop Density:** 293.8
Land: 0.8 sq. mi.; **Water:** 0.0 sq. mi. **Elev:** 1470 ft.
Founded 1886.
Name origin: For an official of the Milwaukee Railroad Co.

East Choteau — Township
ZIP: 57330 **Lat:** 43-13-48 N **Long:** 98-09-31 W
Pop: 151 (1990); 153 (1980) **Pop Density:** 9.6
Land: 15.8 sq. mi.; **Water:** 0.0 sq. mi.

Garfield — Township
Lat: 43-27-49 N **Long:** 98-17-11 W
Pop: 97 (1990); 104 (1980) **Pop Density:** 3.3
Land: 29.5 sq. mi.; **Water:** 0.0 sq. mi.

Grandview — Township
Lat: 43-23-16 N **Long:** 98-24-35 W
Pop: 116 (1990); 169 (1980) **Pop Density:** 3.3
Land: 34.9 sq. mi.; **Water:** 0.2 sq. mi. **Elev:** 1593 ft.

Holland — Township
Lat: 43-27-36 N **Long:** 98-32-07 W
Pop: 233 (1990); 209 (1980) **Pop Density:** 7.9
Land: 29.4 sq. mi.; **Water:** 0.0 sq. mi.

Independence — Township
Lat: 43-17-32 N **Long:** 98-16-44 W
Pop: 175 (1990); 204 (1980) **Pop Density:** 4.9
Land: 36.0 sq. mi.; **Water:** 0.0 sq. mi.

Iowa — Township
Lat: 43-23-02 N **Long:** 98-31-43 W
Pop: 144 (1990); 167 (1980) **Pop Density:** 4.0
Land: 35.9 sq. mi.; **Water:** 0.0 sq. mi.

Joubert — Township
Lat: 43-27-24 N **Long:** 98-39-05 W
Pop: 181 (1990); 193 (1980) **Pop Density:** 6.2
Land: 29.1 sq. mi.; **Water:** 0.1 sq. mi.

Lincoln — Township
Lat: 43-23-02 N **Long:** 98-10-13 W
Pop: 144 (1990); 189 (1980) **Pop Density:** 4.1
Land: 35.5 sq. mi.; **Water:** 0.0 sq. mi.

Valley — Township
Lat: 43-23-20 N **Long:** 98-17-15 W
Pop: 148 (1990); 180 (1980) **Pop Density:** 4.1
Land: 36.2 sq. mi.; **Water:** 0.2 sq. mi.

Walnut Grove — Township
Lat: 43-27-49 N **Long:** 98-25-11 W
Pop: 152 (1990); 201 (1980) **Pop Density:** 5.2
Land: 29.1 sq. mi.; **Water:** 0.0 sq. mi.

Washington — Township
Lat: 43-27-47 N **Long:** 98-10-55 W
Pop: 149 (1990); 172 (1980) **Pop Density:** 5.1
Land: 29.2 sq. mi.; **Water:** 0.0 sq. mi.

Edmunds County
County Seat: Ipswich (ZIP: 57451)

Pop: 4,356 (1990); 5,159 (1980)　　　　**Pop Density:** 3.8
Land: 1145.7 sq. mi.; **Water:** 5.6 sq. mi.　　**Area Code:** 605
In north-central SD, west of Aberdeen; created Jan 8, 1873 (prior to statehood) from Buffalo County.
Name origin: For Newton Edmunds (1819–1908), governor of Dakota Territory (1863–66).

Adrian　　　　　　　　　　　　　　　Township
　　　　　　　Lat: 45-32-55 N　Long: 99-09-20 W
Pop: 20 (1990); 24 (1980)　　**Pop Density:** 0.6
Land: 35.6 sq. mi.; **Water:** 0.0 sq. mi.

Belle　　　　　　　　　　　　　　　Township
　　　　　　　Lat: 45-33-22 N　Long: 98-54-50 W
Pop: 105 (1990); 146 (1980)　　**Pop Density:** 2.9
Land: 36.1 sq. mi.; **Water:** 0.0 sq. mi.

Bowdle　　　　　　　　　　　　　　　City
ZIP: 57428　　Lat: 45-27-05 N　Long: 99-39-21 W
Pop: 589 (1990); 644 (1980)　**Pop Density:** 981.7
Land: 0.6 sq. mi.; **Water:** 0.0 sq. mi.　**Elev:** 2004 ft.
Laid out 1886.
Name origin: For C. C. Bowdle, pioneer banker.

*Bowdle　　　　　　　　　　　　　　Township
ZIP: 57428　　Lat: 45-28-01 N　Long: 99-38-51 W
Pop: 76 (1990); 89 (1980)　　**Pop Density:** 2.2
Land: 35.2 sq. mi.; **Water:** 0.0 sq. mi.

Bryant　　　　　　　　　　　　　　　Township
　　　　　　　Lat: 45-27-52 N　Long: 99-16-38 W
Pop: 36 (1990); 65 (1980)　　**Pop Density:** 1.0
Land: 35.4 sq. mi.; **Water:** 0.1 sq. mi.

Clear Lake　　　　　　　　　　　　　Township
　　　　　　　Lat: 45-17-42 N　Long: 98-47-38 W
Pop: 52 (1990); 66 (1980)　　**Pop Density:** 1.5
Land: 34.7 sq. mi.; **Water:** 1.5 sq. mi.

Cleveland　　　　　　　　　　　　　　Township
　　　　　　　Lat: 45-22-21 N　Long: 99-09-02 W
Pop: 31 (1990); 65 (1980)　　**Pop Density:** 0.9
Land: 36.1 sq. mi.; **Water:** 0.1 sq. mi.

Cloyd Valley　　　　　　　　　　　　Township
ZIP: 57428　　Lat: 45-22-59 N　Long: 99-31-05 W
Pop: 33 (1990); 42 (1980)　　**Pop Density:** 0.9
Land: 36.0 sq. mi.; **Water:** 0.2 sq. mi.

Cortlandt　　　　　　　　　　　　　　Township
　　　　　　　Lat: 45-27-15 N　Long: 98-46-24 W
Pop: 424 (1990); 372 (1980)　**Pop Density:** 12.3
Land: 34.4 sq. mi.; **Water:** 1.0 sq. mi.

Cottonwood Lake　　　　　　　　　　Township
ZIP: 57428　　Lat: 45-27-24 N　Long: 99-32-00 W
Pop: 72 (1990); 77 (1980)　　**Pop Density:** 2.0
Land: 36.0 sq. mi.; **Water:** 0.0 sq. mi.

Fountain　　　　　　　　　　　　　　Township
　　　　　　　Lat: 45-27-55 N　Long: 98-54-16 W
Pop: 80 (1990); 90 (1980)　　**Pop Density:** 2.2
Land: 36.1 sq. mi.; **Water:** 0.0 sq. mi.

Glen　　　　　　　　　　　　　　　Township
ZIP: 57471　　Lat: 45-28-13 N　Long: 99-24-21 W
Pop: 35 (1990); 70 (1980)　　**Pop Density:** 1.0
Land: 35.7 sq. mi.; **Water:** 0.0 sq. mi.

Glover　　　　　　　　　　　　　　Township
ZIP: 57471　　Lat: 45-22-39 N　Long: 99-24-06 W
Pop: 53 (1990); 60 (1980)　　**Pop Density:** 1.5
Land: 36.1 sq. mi.; **Water:** 0.0 sq. mi.

Harmony　　　　　　　　　　　　　Township
　　　　　　　Lat: 45-22-53 N　Long: 99-01-09 W
Pop: 169 (1990)　　　　　　**Pop Density:** 4.7
Land: 36.3 sq. mi.; **Water:** 0.1 sq. mi.

Hillside　　　　　　　　　　　　　　Township
　　　　　　　Lat: 45-17-02 N　Long: 99-24-18 W
Pop: 41 (1990); 65 (1980)　　**Pop Density:** 1.1
Land: 36.0 sq. mi.; **Water:** 0.1 sq. mi.

Hosmer　　　　　　　　　　　　　　City
ZIP: 57448　　Lat: 45-34-43 N　Long: 99-28-25 W
Pop: 310 (1990); 385 (1980)　**Pop Density:** 310.0
Land: 1.0 sq. mi.; **Water:** 0.0 sq. mi.　**Elev:** 1906 ft.

*Hosmer　　　　　　　　　　　　　　Township
ZIP: 57448　　Lat: 45-33-23 N　Long: 99-31-46 W
Pop: 32 (1990); 76 (1980)　　**Pop Density:** 0.9
Land: 35.0 sq. mi.; **Water:** 0.1 sq. mi.

Hudson　　　　　　　　　　　　　　Township
　　　　　　　Lat: 45-17-05 N　Long: 99-39-04 W
Pop: 53 (1990); 67 (1980)　　**Pop Density:** 1.5
Land: 34.8 sq. mi.; **Water:** 1.2 sq. mi.

Huntley　　　　　　　　　　　　　　Township
　　　　　　　Lat: 45-27-36 N　Long: 99-09-23 W
Pop: 48 (1990); 71 (1980)　　**Pop Density:** 1.3
Land: 35.9 sq. mi.; **Water:** 0.0 sq. mi.

Ipswich　　　　　　　　　　　　　　City
ZIP: 57451　　Lat: 45-26-38 N　Long: 99-01-47 W
Pop: 965 (1990); 1,153 (1980)　**Pop Density:** 742.3
Land: 1.3 sq. mi.; **Water:** 0.0 sq. mi.　**Elev:** 1540 ft.
Settled 1883.
Name origin: For Ipswich, England.

*Ipswich　　　　　　　　　　　　　　Township
　　　　　　　Lat: 45-27-46 N　Long: 99-01-33 W
Pop: 71 (1990); 77 (1980)　　**Pop Density:** 2.0
Land: 35.0 sq. mi.; **Water:** 0.0 sq. mi.

Kent　　　　　　　　　　　　　　　Township
　　　　　　　Lat: 45-17-40 N　Long: 98-53-57 W
Pop: 33 (1990); 39 (1980)　　**Pop Density:** 0.9
Land: 35.9 sq. mi.; **Water:** 0.0 sq. mi.

SOUTH DAKOTA, Edmunds County

Liberty   Township
Lat: 45-17-18 N   Long: 99-09-17 W
Pop: 32 (1990); 44 (1980)   **Pop Density:** 0.9
Land: 36.0 sq. mi.; **Water:** 0.2 sq. mi.

Madison   Township
Lat: 45-17-05 N   Long: 99-31-18 W
Pop: 23 (1990); 52 (1980)   **Pop Density:** 0.6
Land: 36.0 sq. mi.; **Water:** 0.2 sq. mi.

Modena   Township
Lat: 45-32-50 N   Long: 99-38-43 W
Pop: 48 (1990); 54 (1980)   **Pop Density:** 1.4
Land: 35.4 sq. mi.; **Water:** 0.3 sq. mi.

Montpelier   Township
ZIP: 57471   Lat: 45-22-26 N   Long: 99-16-49 W
Pop: 50 (1990); 77 (1980)   **Pop Density:** 1.4
Land: 36.2 sq. mi.; **Water:** 0.0 sq. mi.

North Bryant   Township
ZIP: 57471   Lat: 45-33-20 N   Long: 99-16-27 W
Pop: 48 (1990); 71 (1980)   **Pop Density:** 1.4
Land: 35.4 sq. mi.; **Water:** 0.3 sq. mi.

Odessa   Township
ZIP: 57428   Lat: 45-22-43 N   Long: 99-38-32 W
Pop: 36 (1990); 54 (1980)   **Pop Density:** 1.0
Land: 36.0 sq. mi.; **Water:** 0.0 sq. mi.

Pembrook   Township
Lat: 45-32-50 N   Long: 98-47-12 W
Pop: 61 (1990); 67 (1980)   **Pop Density:** 1.7
Land: 34.9 sq. mi.; **Water:** 0.0 sq. mi.

Powell   Township
Lat: 45-17-20 N   Long: 99-01-28 W
Pop: 37 (1990); 55 (1980)   **Pop Density:** 1.0
Land: 36.2 sq. mi.; **Water:** 0.0 sq. mi.

Richland   Township
Lat: 45-22-32 N   Long: 98-46-53 W
Pop: 39 (1990); 46 (1980)   **Pop Density:** 1.1
Land: 35.7 sq. mi.; **Water:** 0.0 sq. mi.

Roscoe   City
ZIP: 57471   Lat: 45-27-01 N   Long: 99-20-05 W
Pop: 362 (1990); 370 (1980)   **Pop Density:** 724.0
Land: 0.5 sq. mi.; **Water:** 0.0 sq. mi.   **Elev:** 1830 ft.
Founded 1877.
Name origin: For U.S. Sen. Roscoe Conkling (1829–88) of NY.

Rosette   Township
Lat: 45-33-00 N   Long: 99-01-29 W
Pop: 140 (1990); 144 (1980)   **Pop Density:** 3.9
Land: 36.3 sq. mi.; **Water:** 0.1 sq. mi.

Sangamon   Township
ZIP: 57448   Lat: 45-33-09 N   Long: 99-24-21 W
Pop: 64 (1990); 90 (1980)   **Pop Density:** 1.8
Land: 35.6 sq. mi.; **Water:** 0.0 sq. mi.

Union   Township
Lat: 45-23-04 N   Long: 98-54-14 W
Pop: 40 (1990); 67 (1980)   **Pop Density:** 1.1
Land: 36.1 sq. mi.; **Water:** 0.0 sq. mi.

Vermont   Township
ZIP: 57471   Lat: 45-17-16 N   Long: 99-16-42 W
Pop: 48 (1990); 52 (1980)   **Pop Density:** 1.3
Land: 36.2 sq. mi.; **Water:** 0.0 sq. mi.

Fall River County
County Seat: Hot Springs (ZIP: 57747)

Pop: 7,353 (1990); 8,439 (1980)   **Pop Density:** 4.2
Land: 1739.9 sq. mi.; **Water:** 9.3 sq. mi.   **Area Code:** 605
On the southwestern border of SD, south of Rapid City; organized Mar 6, 1883 (prior to statehood) from Custer County. Seat of government for Shannon County.
Name origin: For the Fall River, which flows through the county. Literal translation of the Indian name.

Antelope   Township
ZIP: 57763   Lat: 43-05-24 N   Long: 103-09-28 W
Pop: 58 (1990); 55 (1980)   **Pop Density:** 0.6
Land: 104.9 sq. mi.; **Water:** 0.2 sq. mi.

Argentine   Township
ZIP: 57735   Lat: 43-26-11 N   Long: 103-59-47 W
Pop: 22 (1990); 25 (1980)   **Pop Density:** 0.6
Land: 35.8 sq. mi.; **Water:** 0.0 sq. mi.

Cottonwood   Township
Lat: 43-15-37 N   Long: 103-52-38 W
Pop: 31 (1990); 51 (1980)   **Pop Density:** 0.9
Land: 34.9 sq. mi.; **Water:** 0.0 sq. mi.

Edgemont   City
ZIP: 57735   Lat: 43-17-54 N   Long: 103-49-37 W
Pop: 906 (1990); 1,468 (1980)   **Pop Density:** 906.0
Land: 1.0 sq. mi.; **Water:** 0.0 sq. mi.   **Elev:** 3459 ft.

Harmony   Township
ZIP: 57763   Lat: 43-04-17 N   Long: 103-17-33 W
Pop: 29 (1990); 44 (1980)   **Pop Density:** 0.5
Land: 53.2 sq. mi.; **Water:** 0.1 sq. mi.

Hot Springs   City
ZIP: 57747   Lat: 43-25-58 N   Long: 103-28-49 W
Pop: 4,325 (1990); 4,742 (1980)   **Pop Density:** 1491.4
Land: 2.9 sq. mi.; **Water:** 0.0 sq. mi.   **Elev:** 3464 ft.
County seat for Fall River and Shannon counties.
Name origin: For its location on the site of an Indian camping ground called *Minne-kahta* 'warm waters.'

Northeast Fall River Pop. Place
Lat: 43-19-58 N Long: 103-19-19 W
Pop: 1,492 (1990); 1,265 (1980) Pop Density: 2.3
Land: 659.0 sq. mi.; Water: 8.2 sq. mi.

Oelrichs Town
ZIP: 57763 Lat: 43-10-53 N Long: 103-13-59 W
Pop: 138 (1990); 124 (1980) Pop Density: 345.0
Land: 0.4 sq. mi.; Water: 0.0 sq. mi. Elev: 3365 ft.
Established 1885.
Name origin: For Harry Oelrichs, a prominent rancher.

Provo Township
ZIP: 57774 Lat: 43-10-18 N Long: 103-52-38 W
Pop: 32 (1990); 139 (1980) Pop Density: 0.9
Land: 35.5 sq. mi.; Water: 0.1 sq. mi.

Robins Township
ZIP: 57763 Lat: 43-14-51 N Long: 103-10-37 W
Pop: 15 (1990); 28 (1980) Pop Density: 0.4
Land: 35.9 sq. mi.; Water: 0.0 sq. mi.

Southwest Fall River Pop. Place
Lat: 43-11-21 N Long: 103-44-15 W
Pop: 305 (1990); 418 (1980) Pop Density: 0.4
Land: 776.6 sq. mi.; Water: 0.7 sq. mi.

Faulk County
County Seat: Faulkton (ZIP: 57438)

Pop: 2,744 (1990); 3,327 (1980) **Pop Density:** 2.7
Land: 1000.2 sq. mi.; **Water:** 5.5 sq. mi. **Area Code:** 605
In north-central SD, southwest of Aberdeen; created Jan 8, 1873 (prior to statehood) from Buffalo County and unorganized territory.
Name origin: For Andrew Jackson Faulk (1814–98), a governor of Dakota Territory.

Arcade Township
ZIP: 57438 Lat: 44-56-34 N Long: 99-01-36 W
Pop: 32 (1990); 72 (1980) Pop Density: 0.9
Land: 35.9 sq. mi.; Water: 0.1 sq. mi.

Bryant Township
Lat: 45-01-52 N Long: 99-16-28 W
Pop: 52 (1990); 67 (1980) Pop Density: 1.5
Land: 35.6 sq. mi.; Water: 0.3 sq. mi.

Centerville Township
Lat: 45-01-45 N Long: 98-54-00 W
Pop: 39 (1990); 62 (1980) Pop Density: 1.1
Land: 35.8 sq. mi.; Water: 0.2 sq. mi.

Chelsea Town
Lat: 45-10-01 N Long: 98-44-31 W
Pop: 33 (1990); 41 (1980) Pop Density: 110.0
Land: 0.3 sq. mi.; Water: 0.0 sq. mi. Elev: 1344 ft.
Name origin: Named in 1907 for Chelsea, England.

Clark Township
Lat: 45-11-52 N Long: 99-23-01 W
Pop: 44 (1990); 78 (1980) Pop Density: 1.2
Land: 35.5 sq. mi.; Water: 0.4 sq. mi.

Cresbard Town
ZIP: 57435 Lat: 45-10-10 N Long: 98-56-51 W
Pop: 185 (1990); 221 (1980) Pop Density: 462.5
Land: 0.4 sq. mi.; Water: 0.0 sq. mi. Elev: 1450 ft.
Founded 1906.
Name origin: A coined name made by combining the names of two early settlers, John Cressey and Fred Baird.

Devoe Township
ZIP: 57435 Lat: 45-06-59 N Long: 98-53-43 W
Pop: 47 (1990); 59 (1980) Pop Density: 1.3
Land: 36.1 sq. mi.; Water: 0.0 sq. mi.

Ellisville Township
ZIP: 57473 Lat: 44-56-28 N Long: 99-30-46 W
Pop: 45 (1990); 68 (1980) Pop Density: 1.3
Land: 35.9 sq. mi.; Water: 0.1 sq. mi.

Emerson Township
ZIP: 57435 Lat: 45-11-46 N Long: 99-00-39 W
Pop: 36 (1990); 50 (1980) Pop Density: 1.0
Land: 35.8 sq. mi.; Water: 0.1 sq. mi.

Enterprise Township
Lat: 45-11-37 N Long: 99-15-56 W
Pop: 104 (1990); 159 (1980) Pop Density: 3.0
Land: 35.2 sq. mi.; Water: 0.3 sq. mi.

Fairview Township
Lat: 45-12-22 N Long: 98-54-16 W
Pop: 44 (1990); 50 (1980) Pop Density: 1.2
Land: 35.7 sq. mi.; Water: 0.0 sq. mi.

Faulkton City
ZIP: 57438 Lat: 45-02-03 N Long: 99-07-39 W
Pop: 809 (1990); 981 (1980) Pop Density: 809.0
Land: 1.0 sq. mi.; Water: 0.0 sq. mi. Elev: 1589 ft.
Platted 1886.
Name origin: For Andrew Faulk, third governor of the Dakota territory.

Freedom Township
Lat: 45-12-09 N Long: 99-08-38 W
Pop: 159 (1990); 162 (1980) Pop Density: 4.4
Land: 35.9 sq. mi.; Water: 0.2 sq. mi.

Hillsdale Township
ZIP: 57438 Lat: 44-57-11 N Long: 98-53-57 W
Pop: 59 (1990); 59 (1980) Pop Density: 1.6
Land: 35.9 sq. mi.; Water: 0.2 sq. mi.

SOUTH DAKOTA, Faulk County

Irving
Township
Lat: 44-56-32 N **Long:** 99-15-48 W
Pop: 18 (1990) **Pop Density:** 0.5
Land: 35.8 sq. mi.; **Water:** 0.3 sq. mi.

Lafoon
Township
ZIP: 57438 **Lat:** 45-02-03 N **Long:** 99-01-22 W
Pop: 63 (1990); 75 (1980) **Pop Density:** 1.8
Land: 35.8 sq. mi.; **Water:** 0.1 sq. mi.

Myron
Township
ZIP: 57438 **Lat:** 45-06-48 N **Long:** 99-01-43 W
Pop: 71 (1990); 58 (1980) **Pop Density:** 2.0
Land: 36.1 sq. mi.; **Water:** 0.0 sq. mi.

Onaka
Town
ZIP: 57466 **Lat:** 45-11-28 N **Long:** 99-27-52 W
Pop: 52 (1990); 70 (1980) **Pop Density:** 173.3
Land: 0.3 sq. mi.; **Water:** 0.0 sq. mi. **Elev:** 1850 ft.

O'Neil
Township
Lat: 45-06-32 N **Long:** 99-23-03 W
Pop: 15 (1990); 15 (1980) **Pop Density:** 0.4
Land: 36.1 sq. mi.; **Water:** 0.2 sq. mi.

Orient
Town
ZIP: 57467 **Lat:** 44-54-10 N **Long:** 99-05-17 W
Pop: 59 (1990); 87 (1980) **Pop Density:** 196.7
Land: 0.3 sq. mi.; **Water:** 0.0 sq. mi. **Elev:** 1590 ft.
Founded 1887.
Name origin: Named by Milwaukee railroad officials for the Far East.

*Orient
Township
ZIP: 57467 **Lat:** 44-55-56 N **Long:** 99-09-16 W
Pop: 48 (1990); 68 (1980) **Pop Density:** 1.3
Land: 35.6 sq. mi.; **Water:** 0.1 sq. mi.

Pioneer
Township
ZIP: 57470 **Lat:** 45-01-45 N **Long:** 98-46-52 W
Pop: 37 (1990); 58 (1980) **Pop Density:** 1.0
Land: 35.7 sq. mi.; **Water:** 0.0 sq. mi.

Pulaski
Pop. Place
Lat: 45-06-58 N **Long:** 99-08-51 W
Pop: 19 (1990) **Pop Density:** 0.5
Land: 36.2 sq. mi.; **Water:** 0.1 sq. mi.

Rockham
Town
ZIP: 57470 **Lat:** 44-54-18 N **Long:** 98-49-22 W
Pop: 48 (1990); 52 (1980) **Pop Density:** 96.0
Land: 0.5 sq. mi.; **Water:** 0.0 sq. mi. **Elev:** 1396 ft.
Name origin: Named in 1886 for Rockham, Australia.

Saratoga
Township
ZIP: 57438 **Lat:** 45-07-25 N **Long:** 99-15-41 W
Pop: 94 (1990); 24 (1980) **Pop Density:** 2.6
Land: 35.5 sq. mi.; **Water:** 0.2 sq. mi.

Seneca
Town
ZIP: 57473 **Lat:** 45-03-39 N **Long:** 99-30-29 W
Pop: 81 (1990); 103 (1980) **Pop Density:** 202.5
Land: 0.4 sq. mi.; **Water:** 0.0 sq. mi. **Elev:** 1907 ft.
Name origin: Named by its founders for Seneca, NY.

Sherman
Township
Lat: 45-12-09 N **Long:** 99-30-57 W
Pop: 47 (1990); 53 (1980) **Pop Density:** 1.3
Land: 35.7 sq. mi.; **Water:** 0.1 sq. mi.

Southwest Faulk
Pop. Place
Lat: 45-01-16 N **Long:** 99-26-24 W
Pop: 87 (1990); 141 (1980) **Pop Density:** 0.6
Land: 142.9 sq. mi.; **Water:** 0.8 sq. mi.

Tamworth
Township
ZIP: 57438 **Lat:** 45-01-43 N **Long:** 99-09-05 W
Pop: 92 (1990); 110 (1980) **Pop Density:** 2.7
Land: 34.7 sq. mi.; **Water:** 0.2 sq. mi.

Union
Township
Lat: 45-12-04 N **Long:** 98-46-49 W
Pop: 75 (1990); 80 (1980) **Pop Density:** 2.3
Land: 33.0 sq. mi.; **Water:** 1.3 sq. mi.

Wesley
Township
Lat: 45-06-38 N **Long:** 98-46-28 W
Pop: 46 (1990); 69 (1980) **Pop Density:** 1.3
Land: 35.3 sq. mi.; **Water:** 0.0 sq. mi.

Zell
Township
ZIP: 57483 **Lat:** 44-56-05 N **Long:** 98-46-57 W
Pop: 104 (1990); 107 (1980) **Pop Density:** 3.0
Land: 35.2 sq. mi.; **Water:** 0.1 sq. mi.

Grant County
County Seat: Milbank (ZIP: 57252)

Pop: 8,372 (1990); 9,013 (1980) **Pop Density:** 12.3
Land: 682.5 sq. mi.; **Water:** 5.4 sq. mi. **Area Code:** 605
On the northeastern border of SD, northeast of Watertown; organized Jun 12, 1878 (prior to statehood) from Codington and Deuel counties.
Name origin: For Ulysses Simpson Grant (1822–85), Civil War general and eighteenth U.S. president.

Adams
Township
ZIP: 57259 **Lat:** 45-01-17 N **Long:** 96-32-47 W
Pop: 190 (1990); 242 (1980) **Pop Density:** 3.5
Land: 54.5 sq. mi.; **Water:** 0.0 sq. mi.

Alban
Township
Lat: 45-11-21 N **Long:** 96-32-51 W
Pop: 622 (1990); 624 (1980) **Pop Density:** 11.4
Land: 54.5 sq. mi.; **Water:** 0.4 sq. mi.

Albee
Town
Lat: 45-03-04 N **Long:** 96-33-15 W
Pop: 15 (1990); 23 (1980) **Pop Density:** 150.0
Land: 0.1 sq. mi.; **Water:** 0.0 sq. mi. **Elev:** 1177 ft.
Name origin: For an early train dispatcher, W. C. Albee.

SOUTH DAKOTA, Grant County

Big Stone — Township
ZIP: 57216   **Lat:** 45-16-34 N   **Long:** 96-31-02 W
Pop: 318 (1990); 285 (1980)   **Pop Density:** 10.0
Land: 31.7 sq. mi.; **Water:** 2.0 sq. mi.

Big Stone City — City
ZIP: 57216   **Lat:** 45-17-42 N   **Long:** 96-27-51 W
Pop: 669 (1990); 672 (1980)   **Pop Density:** 477.9
Land: 1.4 sq. mi.; **Water:** 0.0 sq. mi.   **Elev:** 977 ft.
Name origin: For its location on Big Stone Lake.

Blooming Valley — Township
ZIP: 57251   **Lat:** 45-15-13 N   **Long:** 97-09-52 W
Pop: 118 (1990); 130 (1980)   **Pop Density:** 3.3
Land: 36.2 sq. mi.; **Water:** 0.1 sq. mi.

Farmington — Township
Lat: 45-15-37 N   **Long:** 97-04-11 W
Pop: 53 (1990); 65 (1980)   **Pop Density:** 2.4
Land: 21.9 sq. mi.; **Water:** 0.1 sq. mi.

Georgia — Township
Lat: 45-00-46 N   **Long:** 96-41-22 W
Pop: 97 (1990); 140 (1980)   **Pop Density:** 2.7
Land: 35.3 sq. mi.; **Water:** 0.2 sq. mi.

Grant Center — Township
Lat: 45-11-45 N   **Long:** 96-42-30 W
Pop: 298 (1990); 316 (1980)   **Pop Density:** 8.3
Land: 36.0 sq. mi.; **Water:** 0.0 sq. mi.

Kilborn — Township
ZIP: 57269   **Lat:** 45-17-02 N   **Long:** 96-48-18 W
Pop: 172 (1990); 197 (1980)   **Pop Density:** 4.8
Land: 35.8 sq. mi.; **Water:** 0.0 sq. mi.

La Bolt — Town
Lat: 45-03-00 N   **Long:** 96-40-27 W
Pop: 91 (1990); 94 (1980)   **Pop Density:** 455.0
Land: 0.2 sq. mi.; **Water:** 0.0 sq. mi.
Name origin: For Alfred La Bolt, an early landowner.

Lura — Township
ZIP: 57251   **Lat:** 45-11-07 N   **Long:** 97-08-20 W
Pop: 89 (1990); 121 (1980)   **Pop Density:** 2.8
Land: 31.8 sq. mi.; **Water:** 0.2 sq. mi.

Madison — Township
Lat: 45-06-21 N   **Long:** 96-41-48 W
Pop: 147 (1990); 179 (1980)   **Pop Density:** 4.1
Land: 35.8 sq. mi.; **Water:** 0.0 sq. mi.

Marvin — Town
ZIP: 57251   **Lat:** 45-15-39 N   **Long:** 96-54-45 W
Pop: 38 (1990); 52 (1980)   **Pop Density:** 38.0
Land: 1.0 sq. mi.; **Water:** 0.0 sq. mi.   **Elev:** 1650 ft.
Name origin: For a Marvin Safe Co. vault in the town. Originally called Grant's Siding.

Mazeppa — Township
Lat: 45-11-36 N   **Long:** 96-58-27 W
Pop: 96 (1990); 136 (1980)   **Pop Density:** 1.9
Land: 51.8 sq. mi.; **Water:** 0.4 sq. mi.

Melrose — Township
Lat: 45-16-45 N   **Long:** 96-40-03 W
Pop: 409 (1990); 412 (1980)   **Pop Density:** 8.6
Land: 47.8 sq. mi.; **Water:** 0.1 sq. mi.

Milbank — City
ZIP: 57252   **Lat:** 45-13-10 N   **Long:** 96-38-05 W
Pop: 3,879 (1990); 4,120 (1980)   **Pop Density:** 1616.2
Land: 2.4 sq. mi.; **Water:** 0.1 sq. mi.   **Elev:** 1150 ft.
Name origin: For railroad director Jeremiah Milbank, who donated a $15,000 church to the town.

Osceola — Township
Lat: 45-16-34 N   **Long:** 96-56-03 W
Pop: 108 (1990); 156 (1980)   **Pop Density:** 2.6
Land: 42.3 sq. mi.; **Water:** 0.8 sq. mi.

Revillo — Town
ZIP: 57259   **Lat:** 45-00-52 N   **Long:** 96-34-13 W
Pop: 152 (1990); 158 (1980)   **Pop Density:** 760.0
Land: 0.2 sq. mi.; **Water:** 0.0 sq. mi.   **Elev:** 1200 ft.
Name origin: For a popular railroad man, J. S. Oliver; his name was spelled backward with an extra *l* added.

Stockholm — Town
ZIP: 57264   **Lat:** 45-06-08 N   **Long:** 96-47-54 W
Pop: 89 (1990); 95 (1980)   **Pop Density:** 222.5
Land: 0.4 sq. mi.; **Water:** 0.0 sq. mi.   **Elev:** 1650 ft.
Founded 1896.
Name origin: For the capital of Sweden.

*Stockholm — Township
ZIP: 57264   **Lat:** 45-06-31 N   **Long:** 96-49-17 W
Pop: 124 (1990); 109 (1980)   **Pop Density:** 3.6
Land: 34.9 sq. mi.; **Water:** 0.2 sq. mi.

Strandburg — Town
ZIP: 57265   **Lat:** 45-02-36 N   **Long:** 96-45-39 W
Pop: 74 (1990); 79 (1980)   **Pop Density:** 740.0
Land: 0.1 sq. mi.; **Water:** 0.0 sq. mi.   **Elev:** 1690 ft.
Name origin: For John Strandburg, the first postmaster.

Troy — Township
ZIP: 57265   **Lat:** 45-00-43 N   **Long:** 96-49-11 W
Pop: 59 (1990); 92 (1980)   **Pop Density:** 1.7
Land: 34.8 sq. mi.; **Water:** 0.8 sq. mi.

Twin Brooks — Town
ZIP: 57269   **Lat:** 45-12-27 N   **Long:** 96-47-12 W
Pop: 54 (1990); 87 (1980)   **Pop Density:** 135.0
Land: 0.4 sq. mi.; **Water:** 0.0 sq. mi.   **Elev:** 1260 ft.

*Twin Brooks — Township
ZIP: 57269   **Lat:** 45-11-21 N   **Long:** 96-49-02 W
Pop: 122 (1990); 118 (1980)   **Pop Density:** 3.4
Land: 36.4 sq. mi.; **Water:** 0.0 sq. mi.

Vernon — Township
Lat: 45-06-29 N   **Long:** 96-32-29 W
Pop: 289 (1990); 311 (1980)   **Pop Density:** 5.3
Land: 54.7 sq. mi.; **Water:** 0.1 sq. mi.

Gregory County
County Seat: Burke (ZIP: 57523)

Pop: 5,359 (1990); 6,015 (1980)
Land: 1016.0 sq. mi.; **Water:** 37.5 sq. mi.
Pop Density: 5.3
Area Code: 605

On the central southern border of SD, east of Winner; created May 8, 1862 (prior to statehood) from Yankton County.

Name origin: For John Shaw Gregory (1831–?), Indian agent and Dakota territorial legislator (1862–64).

Bonesteel — City
ZIP: 57317 **Lat:** 43-04-41 N **Long:** 98-56-48 W
Pop: 297 (1990); 358 (1980) **Pop Density:** 990.0
Land: 0.3 sq. mi.; **Water:** 0.0 sq. mi. **Elev:** 1963 ft.
Name origin: For pioneer H.E. Bonesteel, who settled in the territory 1872 and later started a freight company.

Burke — City
ZIP: 57523 **Lat:** 43-10-58 N **Long:** 99-17-33 W
Pop: 756 (1990); 859 (1980) **Pop Density:** 1260.0
Land: 0.6 sq. mi.; **Water:** 0.0 sq. mi. **Elev:** 2213 ft.
Founded 1904.
Name origin: For state legislator Charles Burke.

*Burke — Township
ZIP: 57523 **Lat:** 43-12-51 N **Long:** 99-14-12 W
Pop: 99 (1990); 105 (1980) **Pop Density:** 2.8
Land: 35.2 sq. mi.; **Water:** 0.1 sq. mi.

Carlock — Township
ZIP: 57533 **Lat:** 43-02-04 N **Long:** 99-28-53 W
Pop: 87 (1990); 106 (1980) **Pop Density:** 2.5
Land: 34.8 sq. mi.; **Water:** 0.0 sq. mi.

Dallas — Town
ZIP: 57529 **Lat:** 43-14-16 N **Long:** 99-31-03 W
Pop: 142 (1990); 199 (1980) **Pop Density:** 284.0
Land: 0.5 sq. mi.; **Water:** 0.0 sq. mi. **Elev:** 2194 ft.
Name origin: For Dallas, TX.

Dickens — Township
Lat: 43-07-45 N **Long:** 99-28-38 W
Pop: 92 (1990); 112 (1980) **Pop Density:** 2.6
Land: 35.9 sq. mi.; **Water:** 0.1 sq. mi.

Dixon — Township
Lat: 43-24-50 N **Long:** 99-28-39 W
Pop: 159 (1990); 132 (1980) **Pop Density:** 2.5
Land: 64.6 sq. mi.; **Water:** 0.2 sq. mi.

East Gregory — Pop. Place
Lat: 43-07-53 N **Long:** 98-53-08 W
Pop: 22 (1990); 26 (1980) **Pop Density:** 1.0
Land: 21.6 sq. mi.; **Water:** 2.1 sq. mi.

Edens — Township
ZIP: 57529 **Lat:** 43-17-32 N **Long:** 99-28-47 W
Pop: 64 (1990); 86 (1980) **Pop Density:** 1.8
Land: 35.7 sq. mi.; **Water:** 0.0 sq. mi.

Ellston — Township
Lat: 43-02-23 N **Long:** 99-07-07 W
Pop: 98 (1990); 115 (1980) **Pop Density:** 2.8
Land: 34.4 sq. mi.; **Water:** 0.1 sq. mi.

Fairfax — Town
ZIP: 57335 **Lat:** 43-01-41 N **Long:** 98-53-20 W
Pop: 144 (1990); 225 (1980) **Pop Density:** 480.0
Land: 0.3 sq. mi.; **Water:** 0.0 sq. mi. **Elev:** 1932 ft.
Established 1890.
Name origin: For Fairfax County, VA.

*Fairfax — Township
ZIP: 57335 **Lat:** 43-02-34 N **Long:** 98-52-47 W
Pop: 118 (1990); 145 (1980) **Pop Density:** 3.6
Land: 32.5 sq. mi.; **Water:** 0.0 sq. mi.

Gregory — City
ZIP: 57533 **Lat:** 43-13-54 N **Long:** 99-25-30 W
Pop: 1,384 (1990); 1,503 (1980) **Pop Density:** 988.6
Land: 1.4 sq. mi.; **Water:** 0.0 sq. mi. **Elev:** 2166 ft.
Settled 1904.
Name origin: For the county.

Herrick — Town
ZIP: 57538 **Lat:** 43-06-55 N **Long:** 99-11-13 W
Pop: 139 (1990); 115 (1980) **Pop Density:** 278.0
Land: 0.5 sq. mi.; **Water:** 0.0 sq. mi. **Elev:** 2155 ft.
Name origin: For town founder Samuel Herrick.

Jones — Township
Lat: 43-07-30 N **Long:** 99-21-23 W
Pop: 69 (1990); 96 (1980) **Pop Density:** 1.9
Land: 36.0 sq. mi.; **Water:** 0.0 sq. mi.

Landing Creek — Township
Lat: 43-25-05 N **Long:** 99-21-41 W
Pop: 24 (1990); 50 (1980) **Pop Density:** 0.4
Land: 61.8 sq. mi.; **Water:** 1.5 sq. mi.

Lone Star — Township
Lat: 43-02-19 N **Long:** 99-21-19 W
Pop: 93 (1990); 94 (1980) **Pop Density:** 2.7
Land: 34.9 sq. mi.; **Water:** 0.0 sq. mi.

North Gregory — Pop. Place
Lat: 43-17-03 N **Long:** 99-15-58 W
Pop: 829 (1990) **Pop Density:** 3.2
Land: 259.2 sq. mi.; **Water:** 9.1 sq. mi.

Pleasant Valley — Township
Lat: 43-02-46 N **Long:** 99-00-25 W
Pop: 235 (1990); 224 (1980) **Pop Density:** 6.5
Land: 36.3 sq. mi.; **Water:** 0.0 sq. mi.

St. Charles — Township
Lat: 43-07-29 N **Long:** 99-05-36 W
Pop: 85 (1990); 118 (1980) **Pop Density:** 1.6
Land: 53.5 sq. mi.; **Water:** 0.0 sq. mi.

Schriever
ZIP: 57317   **Lat:** 43-07-07 N   **Long:** 98-56-50 W   Township
Pop: 58 (1990); 75 (1980)   **Pop Density:** 2.4
Land: 23.8 sq. mi.; **Water:** 0.0 sq. mi.

Southeast Gregory
Pop. Place
Lat: 43-01-39 N   **Long:** 98-36-57 W
Pop: 55 (1990); 69 (1980)   **Pop Density:** 1.4
Land: 39.4 sq. mi.; **Water:** 6.4 sq. mi.

Spring Valley
Pop. Place
Lat: 43-02-39 N   **Long:** 99-14-11 W
Pop: 85 (1990)   **Pop Density:** 2.4
Land: 34.8 sq. mi.; **Water:** 0.0 sq. mi.

Star Valley
Township
Lat: 43-04-22 N   **Long:** 98-46-31 W
Pop: 84 (1990); 101 (1980)   **Pop Density:** 1.7
Land: 48.3 sq. mi.; **Water:** 6.8 sq. mi.

Union
Township
Lat: 43-07-36 N   **Long:** 99-13-59 W
Pop: 113 (1990); 172 (1980)   **Pop Density:** 3.2
Land: 35.4 sq. mi.; **Water:** 0.0 sq. mi.

Whetstone
Township
ZIP: 57317   **Lat:** 43-12-35 N   **Long:** 98-59-32 W
Pop: 28 (1990); 36 (1980)   **Pop Density:** 0.5
Land: 54.4 sq. mi.; **Water:** 11.0 sq. mi.

Haakon County
County Seat: Philip (ZIP: 57567)

Pop: 2,624 (1990); 2,794 (1980)   **Pop Density:** 1.4
Land: 1813.1 sq. mi.; **Water:** 14.3 sq. mi.   **Area Code:** 605

In west-central SD, west of Pierre; created Nov, 1914 from Stanley County.

Name origin: For Haakon VII (1872–1957), king of Norway; the name was suggested by Hugh J. McMahon, an Irish immigrant who wished to gain the votes of the Norwegian immigrants in favor of the division of Stanley County into two new counties.

East Haakon
Pop. Place
Lat: 44-19-06 N   **Long:** 101-21-57 W
Pop: 556 (1990); 616 (1980)   **Pop Density:** 0.5
Land: 1099.0 sq. mi.; **Water:** 9.1 sq. mi.

Midland
Town
ZIP: 57552   **Lat:** 44-04-15 N   **Long:** 101-09-16 W
Pop: 233 (1990); 277 (1980)   **Pop Density:** 776.7
Land: 0.3 sq. mi.; **Water:** 0.0 sq. mi.   **Elev:** 1879 ft.
Established 1890.
Name origin: For its location halfway between the Missouri and Cheyenne rivers.

Philip
City
ZIP: 57567   **Lat:** 44-02-25 N   **Long:** 101-39-49 W
Pop: 1,077 (1990); 1,088 (1980)   **Pop Density:** 1795.0
Land: 0.6 sq. mi.; **Water:** 0.0 sq. mi.   **Elev:** 2162 ft.
Name origin: Named in 1907 for cattleman James Philip.

West Haakon
Pop. Place
Lat: 44-15-46 N   **Long:** 101-47-45 W
Pop: 758 (1990); 763 (1980)   **Pop Density:** 1.1
Land: 713.2 sq. mi.; **Water:** 5.2 sq. mi.

Hamlin County
County Seat: Hayti (ZIP: 57241)

Pop: 4,974 (1990); 5,261 (1980)   **Pop Density:** 9.7
Land: 511.2 sq. mi.; **Water:** 26.8 sq. mi.   **Area Code:** 605

In east-central SD, northwest of Sioux Falls; created Jan 8, 1873 (prior to statehood) from Deuel County.

Name origin: For Hannibal Hamlin (1809–91), governor of ME (1857), U.S. senator from ME (1848–67; 1857–61; 1869–81), and vice president (1861–65) under Lincoln.

Brantford
Township
ZIP: 57242   **Lat:** 44-45-13 N   **Long:** 97-23-59 W
Pop: 158 (1990); 185 (1980)   **Pop Density:** 3.0
Land: 53.4 sq. mi.; **Water:** 0.1 sq. mi.

Bryant
City
ZIP: 57221   **Lat:** 44-35-23 N   **Long:** 97-28-02 W
Pop: 374 (1990); 388 (1980)   **Pop Density:** 748.0
Land: 0.5 sq. mi.; **Water:** 0.0 sq. mi.   **Elev:** 1840 ft.
Platted in 1887.
Name origin: Named for an official of the Milwaukee land company.

SOUTH DAKOTA, Hamlin County — American Places Dictionary

Castlewood City
ZIP: 57223 Lat: 44-43-27 N Long: 97-01-50 W
Pop: 549 (1990); 557 (1980) Pop Density: 499.1
Land: 1.1 sq. mi.; Water: 0.0 sq. mi. Elev: 1690 ft.
Name origin: For "Castlewood," the home of hero Henry Esmond in the novel *The History of Henry Esmond* by William Makepeace Thackeray (1811–63).

*Castlewood Township
ZIP: 57223 Lat: 44-46-04 N Long: 97-04-19 W
Pop: 171 (1990); 158 (1980) Pop Density: 4.9
Land: 34.6 sq. mi.; Water: 0.1 sq. mi.

Cleveland Township
Lat: 44-35-11 N Long: 97-18-29 W
Pop: 159 (1990); 195 (1980) Pop Density: 4.5
Land: 35.6 sq. mi.; Water: 0.3 sq. mi.

Dempster Township
Lat: 44-40-23 N Long: 96-56-38 W
Pop: 245 (1990); 289 (1980) Pop Density: 6.8
Land: 35.9 sq. mi.; Water: 0.0 sq. mi.

Dixon Township
Lat: 44-40-32 N Long: 97-25-47 W
Pop: 89 (1990); 96 (1980) Pop Density: 2.5
Land: 35.9 sq. mi.; Water: 0.0 sq. mi.

Estelline City
ZIP: 57234 Lat: 44-34-34 N Long: 96-54-00 W
Pop: 658 (1990); 719 (1980) Pop Density: 658.0
Land: 1.0 sq. mi.; Water: 0.0 sq. mi. Elev: 1640 ft.
Name origin: For the daughter of the D.J. Spalding, original landowner.

*Estelline Township
ZIP: 57234 Lat: 44-34-55 N Long: 96-57-58 W
Pop: 245 (1990); 292 (1980) Pop Density: 5.2
Land: 47.3 sq. mi.; Water: 5.6 sq. mi.

Florence Township
Lat: 44-40-41 N Long: 97-04-37 W
Pop: 124 (1990); 136 (1980) Pop Density: 3.6
Land: 34.4 sq. mi.; Water: 1.4 sq. mi.

Garfield Township
Lat: 44-35-22 N Long: 97-25-28 W
Pop: 164 (1990); 187 (1980) Pop Density: 4.6
Land: 35.3 sq. mi.; Water: 0.0 sq. mi.

Hamlin Township
ZIP: 57223 Lat: 44-46-06 N Long: 96-56-59 W
Pop: 239 (1990); 204 (1980) Pop Density: 6.7
Land: 35.9 sq. mi.; Water: 0.0 sq. mi.

Hayti Town
ZIP: 57241 Lat: 44-39-23 N Long: 97-12-14 W
Pop: 372 (1990); 371 (1980) Pop Density: 1240.0
Land: 0.3 sq. mi.; Water: 0.0 sq. mi. Elev: 1680 ft.
Name origin: For the hay tied together to make fuel that inspired early settlers who were meeting to discuss possibilities for the town's name. Another claim is that it is named for a pioneer hay dealer named Tie.

*Hayti Township
ZIP: 57241 Lat: 44-40-50 N Long: 97-11-42 W
Pop: 146 (1990); 184 (1980) Pop Density: 4.5
Land: 32.7 sq. mi.; Water: 2.9 sq. mi.

Hazel Town
ZIP: 57242 Lat: 44-45-28 N Long: 97-22-48 W
Pop: 103 (1990); 94 (1980) Pop Density: 515.0
Land: 0.2 sq. mi.; Water: 0.0 sq. mi. Elev: 1766 ft.
Founded 1888.
Name origin: For the daughter of landowner C.A. Bowley.

Lake Norden City
ZIP: 57248 Lat: 44-34-44 N Long: 97-12-28 W
Pop: 427 (1990); 417 (1980) Pop Density: 610.0
Land: 0.7 sq. mi.; Water: 0.0 sq. mi. Elev: 1680 ft.
Platted 1908.
Name origin: For the nearby lake.

Norden Township
Lat: 44-34-45 N Long: 97-09-29 W
Pop: 314 (1990); 310 (1980) Pop Density: 7.8
Land: 40.5 sq. mi.; Water: 12.6 sq. mi.

Opdahl Township
ZIP: 57241 Lat: 44-40-27 N Long: 97-18-22 W
Pop: 202 (1990); 217 (1980) Pop Density: 5.9
Land: 34.0 sq. mi.; Water: 1.9 sq. mi.

Oxford Township
ZIP: 57241 Lat: 44-45-30 N Long: 97-12-57 W
Pop: 235 (1990); 262 (1980) Pop Density: 4.5
Land: 52.0 sq. mi.; Water: 1.7 sq. mi.

Hand County
County Seat: Miller (ZIP: 57362)

Pop: 4,272 (1990); 4,948 (1980) Pop Density: 3.0
Land: 1436.7 sq. mi.; Water: 3.6 sq. mi. Area Code: 605
In east-central SD, southwest of Aberdeen; created 1873 (prior to statehood) from Buffalo County.
Name origin: For George H. Hand (1837–91), secretary of Dakota Territory (1874–83).

Alden Township
ZIP: 57371 Lat: 44-40-39 N Long: 99-07-13 W
Pop: 42 (1990); 52 (1980) Pop Density: 1.2
Land: 36.4 sq. mi.; Water: 0.0 sq. mi.

Alpha Township
ZIP: 57362 Lat: 44-35-28 N Long: 99-00-29 W
Pop: 41 (1990); 59 (1980) Pop Density: 1.1
Land: 35.9 sq. mi.; Water: 0.0 sq. mi.

SOUTH DAKOTA, Hand County

Bates — Township
ZIP: 57362　　Lat: 44-14-24 N　Long: 98-45-39 W
Pop: 59 (1990); 82 (1980)　　Pop Density: 1.6
Land: 36.2 sq. mi.; Water: 0.2 sq. mi.

Burdette — Township
ZIP: 57362　　Lat: 44-41-06 N　Long: 98-45-22 W
Pop: 57 (1990); 71 (1980)　　Pop Density: 1.6
Land: 35.6 sq. mi.; Water: 0.0 sq. mi.

Campbell — Township
ZIP: 57371　　Lat: 44-39-23 N　Long: 99-15-39 W
Pop: 28 (1990); 33 (1980)　　Pop Density: 0.8
Land: 35.8 sq. mi.; Water: 0.0 sq. mi.

Carlton — Township
ZIP: 57362　　Lat: 44-46-04 N　Long: 98-52-47 W
Pop: 43 (1990); 55 (1980)　　Pop Density: 1.2
Land: 36.0 sq. mi.; Water: 0.0 sq. mi.

Cedar — Township
ZIP: 57362　　Lat: 44-19-15 N　Long: 99-13-55 W
Pop: 46 (1990); 51 (1980)　　Pop Density: 1.3
Land: 34.1 sq. mi.; Water: 0.0 sq. mi.

Como — Township
ZIP: 57362　　Lat: 44-14-26 N　Long: 99-15-02 W
Pop: 40 (1990); 60 (1980)　　Pop Density: 1.2
Land: 34.2 sq. mi.; Water: 0.0 sq. mi.

Florence — Township
Lat: 44-41-01 N　Long: 99-00-44 W
Pop: 32 (1990); 65 (1980)　　Pop Density: 0.9
Land: 35.9 sq. mi.; Water: 0.0 sq. mi.

Gilbert — Township
ZIP: 57373　　Lat: 44-35-13 N　Long: 98-45-38 W
Pop: 65 (1990); 78 (1980)　　Pop Density: 1.8
Land: 35.8 sq. mi.; Water: 0.0 sq. mi.

Glendale — Township
ZIP: 57362　　Lat: 44-20-29 N　Long: 99-07-28 W
Pop: 29 (1990); 35 (1980)　　Pop Density: 0.8
Land: 36.1 sq. mi.; Water: 0.1 sq. mi.

Grand — Township
ZIP: 57373　　Lat: 44-29-59 N　Long: 98-45-06 W
Pop: 74 (1990); 94 (1980)　　Pop Density: 2.0
Land: 37.2 sq. mi.; Water: 0.0 sq. mi.

Greenleaf — Township
ZIP: 57362　　Lat: 44-35-24 N　Long: 99-07-58 W
Pop: 36 (1990); 35 (1980)　　Pop Density: 1.0
Land: 35.8 sq. mi.; Water: 0.4 sq. mi.

Hiland — Township
ZIP: 57373　　Lat: 44-19-37 N　Long: 98-53-02 W
Pop: 33 (1990); 47 (1980)　　Pop Density: 0.9
Land: 35.7 sq. mi.; Water: 0.0 sq. mi.

Holden — Township
ZIP: 57362　　Lat: 44-40-40 N　Long: 98-53-17 W
Pop: 60 (1990); 76 (1980)　　Pop Density: 1.7
Land: 36.2 sq. mi.; Water: 0.0 sq. mi.

Hulbert — Township
Lat: 44-25-06 N　Long: 98-45-05 W
Pop: 72 (1990); 79 (1980)　　Pop Density: 2.0
Land: 36.3 sq. mi.; Water: 0.0 sq. mi.

Linn — Township
Lat: 44-50-34 N　Long: 98-53-29 W
Pop: 65 (1990); 65 (1980)　　Pop Density: 1.8
Land: 36.3 sq. mi.; Water: 0.0 sq. mi.

Logan — Township
Lat: 44-24-39 N　Long: 99-00-46 W
Pop: 39 (1990); 38 (1980)　　Pop Density: 1.1
Land: 35.9 sq. mi.; Water: 0.0 sq. mi.

Midland — Township
Lat: 44-29-58 N　Long: 99-07-14 W
Pop: 46 (1990); 37 (1980)　　Pop Density: 1.2
Land: 37.0 sq. mi.; Water: 0.1 sq. mi.

Miller — City
ZIP: 57362　　Lat: 44-31-11 N　Long: 98-59-15 W
Pop: 1,678 (1990); 1,931 (1980)　　Pop Density: 1864.4
Land: 0.9 sq. mi.; Water: 0.0 sq. mi.　　Elev: 1578 ft.

*Miller — Township
ZIP: 57362　　Lat: 44-30-04 N　Long: 99-00-16 W
Pop: 147 (1990); 164 (1980)　　Pop Density: 4.2
Land: 35.3 sq. mi.; Water: 0.2 sq. mi.

Mondamin — Township
ZIP: 57362　　Lat: 44-14-29 N　Long: 99-07-37 W
Pop: 27 (1990); 39 (1980)　　Pop Density: 0.8
Land: 35.9 sq. mi.; Water: 0.1 sq. mi.

Northwest Hand — Pop. Place
Lat: 44-48-18 N　Long: 99-08-21 W
Pop: 285 (1990)　　Pop Density: 2.0
Land: 144.6 sq. mi.; Water: 0.4 sq. mi.

Ohio — Township
ZIP: 57362　　Lat: 44-19-37 N　Long: 99-00-13 W
Pop: 134 (1990); 100 (1980)　　Pop Density: 3.7
Land: 36.0 sq. mi.; Water: 0.0 sq. mi.

Ontario — Township
ZIP: 57371　　Lat: 44-45-45 N　Long: 99-15-20 W
Pop: 46 (1990); 73 (1980)　　Pop Density: 1.3
Land: 35.8 sq. mi.; Water: 0.0 sq. mi.

Park — Township
Lat: 44-51-02 N　Long: 99-00-49 W
Pop: 49 (1990); 74 (1980)　　Pop Density: 1.4
Land: 36.0 sq. mi.; Water: 0.1 sq. mi.

Pearl — Township
Lat: 44-25-14 N　Long: 98-52-44 W
Pop: 30 (1990); 46 (1980)　　Pop Density: 0.8
Land: 35.4 sq. mi.; Water: 0.1 sq. mi.

Plato — Township
Lat: 44-50-41 N　Long: 98-45-22 W
Pop: 66 (1990); 65 (1980)　　Pop Density: 1.8
Land: 36.1 sq. mi.; Water: 0.0 sq. mi.

Pleasant Valley — Township
Lat: 44-14-50 N　Long: 99-00-48 W
Pop: 49 (1990); 48 (1980)　　Pop Density: 1.4
Land: 35.5 sq. mi.; Water: 0.5 sq. mi.

Ree Heights — Town
ZIP: 57371　　Lat: 44-30-57 N　Long: 99-12-01 W
Pop: 91 (1990); 88 (1980)　　Pop Density: 303.3
Land: 0.3 sq. mi.; Water: 0.0 sq. mi.　　Elev: 1729 ft.
Name origin: For its location near the Ree Hills.

*Ree Heights
Township
ZIP: 57371   Lat: 44-30-35 N   Long: 99-14-22 W
Pop: 42 (1990); 41 (1980)   Pop Density: 1.2
Land: 35.1 sq. mi.; Water: 0.0 sq. mi.

Riverside
Township
Lat: 44-35-21 N   Long: 99-15-07 W
Pop: 31 (1990); 48 (1980)   Pop Density: 0.9
Land: 35.9 sq. mi.; Water: 0.0 sq. mi.

Rockdale
Township
ZIP: 57362   Lat: 44-25-21 N   Long: 99-07-11 W
Pop: 147 (1990); 107 (1980)   Pop Density: 4.1
Land: 36.1 sq. mi.; Water: 0.1 sq. mi.

Rose Hill
Township
Lat: 44-20-03 N   Long: 98-46-17 W
Pop: 60 (1990); 93 (1980)   Pop Density: 1.6
Land: 36.4 sq. mi.; Water: 0.0 sq. mi.

St. Lawrence
Town
Lat: 44-31-01 N   Long: 98-56-23 W
Pop: 223 (1990); 223 (1980)   Pop Density: 148.7
Land: 1.5 sq. mi.; Water: 0.0 sq. mi.   Elev: 1560 ft.
Settled 1881.
Name origin: For a county and river in NY.

*St. Lawrence
Township
Lat: 44-30-00 N   Long: 98-53-12 W
Pop: 63 (1990); 90 (1980)   Pop Density: 1.8
Land: 35.9 sq. mi.; Water: 0.0 sq. mi.

Spring Hill
Township
ZIP: 57371   Lat: 44-24-39 N   Long: 99-14-22 W
Pop: 50 (1990); 54 (1980)   Pop Density: 1.5
Land: 34.3 sq. mi.; Water: 0.2 sq. mi.

Spring Lake
Township
Lat: 44-14-26 N   Long: 98-53-07 W
Pop: 37 (1990); 46 (1980)   Pop Density: 1.1
Land: 35.0 sq. mi.; Water: 0.9 sq. mi.

Wessington
City
Lat: 44-27-04 N   Long: 98-42-09 W
Pop: 24 (1990); 23 (1980)   Pop Density: 600.0
Land: 0.04 sq. mi.; Water: 0.0 sq. mi.   Elev: 1415 ft.
Settled 1880. Part of the town is also in Beadle County.
Name origin: For the nearby Wessington Hills.

Wheaton
Township
ZIP: 57362   Lat: 44-46-20 N   Long: 98-45-21 W
Pop: 47 (1990); 62 (1980)   Pop Density: 1.3
Land: 35.6 sq. mi.; Water: 0.0 sq. mi.

York
Township
Lat: 44-35-19 N   Long: 98-52-37 W
Pop: 39 (1990); 54 (1980)   Pop Density: 1.1
Land: 36.3 sq. mi.; Water: 0.0 sq. mi.

Hanson County
County Seat: Alexandria (ZIP: 57311)

Pop: 2,994 (1990); 3,415 (1980)   Pop Density: 6.9
Land: 434.7 sq. mi.; Water: 1.0 sq. mi.   Area Code: 605
In southeastern SD, west of Sioux Falls; organized Jan 13, 1871 (prior to statehood) from Buffalo and Deuel counties.
Name origin: For Maj. Joseph R. Hanson (1837–1917), Dakota Territory legislator and Indian affairs official.

Alexandria
City
ZIP: 57311   Lat: 43-39-14 N   Long: 97-46-44 W
Pop: 518 (1990); 588 (1980)   Pop Density: 863.3
Land: 0.6 sq. mi.; Water: 0.0 sq. mi.   Elev: 1350 ft.
Name origin: For Alexander Mitchell, one-time president of the Milwaukee Railroad.

Beulah
Township
Lat: 43-32-43 N   Long: 97-47-05 W
Pop: 224 (1990); 262 (1980)   Pop Density: 6.2
Land: 36.2 sq. mi.; Water: 0.0 sq. mi.

Edgerton
Township
Lat: 43-43-13 N   Long: 97-40-34 W
Pop: 129 (1990); 169 (1980)   Pop Density: 3.6
Land: 35.8 sq. mi.; Water: 0.2 sq. mi.

Emery
City
ZIP: 57332   Lat: 43-36-09 N   Long: 97-37-12 W
Pop: 417 (1990); 399 (1980)   Pop Density: 1042.5
Land: 0.4 sq. mi.; Water: 0.0 sq. mi.   Elev: 1382 ft.
Settled 1881.
Name origin: For original landowner S. M. Emery.

Fairview
Township
Lat: 43-48-20 N   Long: 97-47-36 W
Pop: 132 (1990); 152 (1980)   Pop Density: 3.6
Land: 37.0 sq. mi.; Water: 0.1 sq. mi.

Farmer
Town
ZIP: 57336   Lat: 43-43-29 N   Long: 97-41-17 W
Pop: 23 (1990); 27 (1980)   Pop Density: 46.0
Land: 0.5 sq. mi.; Water: 0.0 sq. mi.   Elev: 1394 ft.
Name origin: For the fertile landscape that inspired early settler Joseph Altenhofer to describe the area as a "farmer's paradise."

Fulton
Town
ZIP: 57340   Lat: 43-43-41 N   Long: 97-49-20 W
Pop: 70 (1990); 108 (1980)   Pop Density: 77.8
Land: 0.9 sq. mi.; Water: 0.0 sq. mi.   Elev: 1328 ft.
Name origin: For inventor Robert Fulton (1765–1815).

Hanson
Township
Lat: 43-43-15 N   Long: 97-53-52 W
Pop: 193 (1990); 216 (1980)   Pop Density: 5.4
Land: 36.0 sq. mi.; Water: 0.1 sq. mi.

Jasper Township
Lat: 43-43-04 N **Long:** 97-47-36 W
Pop: 147 (1990); 157 (1980) **Pop Density:** 4.2
Land: 35.4 sq. mi.; **Water:** 0.0 sq. mi.

Plano Township
ZIP: 57340 **Lat:** 43-48-40 N **Long:** 97-54-21 W
Pop: 130 (1990); 140 (1980) **Pop Density:** 3.5
Land: 36.9 sq. mi.; **Water:** 0.0 sq. mi.

Pleasant Township
Lat: 43-37-50 N **Long:** 97-39-37 W
Pop: 153 (1990); 172 (1980) **Pop Density:** 4.3
Land: 35.6 sq. mi.; **Water:** 0.1 sq. mi.

Rosedale Township
Lat: 43-37-59 N **Long:** 97-54-20 W
Pop: 293 (1990); 281 (1980) **Pop Density:** 8.1
Land: 36.0 sq. mi.; **Water:** 0.1 sq. mi.

Spring Lake Township
Lat: 43-47-48 N **Long:** 97-40-15 W
Pop: 130 (1990); 162 (1980) **Pop Density:** 3.6
Land: 36.6 sq. mi.; **Water:** 0.2 sq. mi.

Taylor Township
Lat: 43-33-02 N **Long:** 97-40-32 W
Pop: 146 (1990); 181 (1980) **Pop Density:** 4.1
Land: 36.0 sq. mi.; **Water:** 0.0 sq. mi.

Wayne Township
Lat: 43-37-25 N **Long:** 97-47-35 W
Pop: 192 (1990); 254 (1980) **Pop Density:** 5.5
Land: 35.2 sq. mi.; **Water:** 0.2 sq. mi.

Worthen Township
Lat: 43-33-01 N **Long:** 97-53-45 W
Pop: 97 (1990); 147 (1980) **Pop Density:** 2.7
Land: 35.8 sq. mi.; **Water:** 0.1 sq. mi.

Harding County
County Seat: Buffalo (ZIP: 57720)

Pop: 1,669 (1990); 1,700 (1980) **Pop Density:** 0.6
Land: 2670.6 sq. mi.; **Water:** 7.1 sq. mi. **Area Code:** 605
On the northwest border of SD; organized Feb 26, 1909 from Butte County.
Name origin: For J. A. Harding, a Dakota Territory legislator.

Buffalo Town
ZIP: 57720 **Lat:** 45-35-09 N **Long:** 103-32-34 W
Pop: 488 (1990); 453 (1980) **Pop Density:** 976.0
Land: 0.5 sq. mi.; **Water:** 0.0 sq. mi. **Elev:** 2877 ft.
Name origin: For the once-numerous buffalo herds.

Camp Crook Town
ZIP: 57724 **Lat:** 45-32-59 N **Long:** 103-58-29 W
Pop: 146 (1990); 100 (1980) **Pop Density:** 1460.0
Land: 0.1 sq. mi.; **Water:** 0.0 sq. mi. **Elev:** 3110 ft.
Founded 1884.
Name origin: For Gen. George Crook (1829–90), a well-known Indian fighter in the 1870s.

North Harding Pop. Place
Lat: 45-44-49 N **Long:** 103-29-37 W
Pop: 697 (1990); 742 (1980) **Pop Density:** 0.5
Land: 1503.9 sq. mi.; **Water:** 3.8 sq. mi.

South Harding Pop. Place
Lat: 45-22-23 N **Long:** 103-29-16 W
Pop: 338 (1990); 405 (1980) **Pop Density:** 0.3
Land: 1165.9 sq. mi.; **Water:** 3.3 sq. mi.

Hughes County
County Seat: Pierre (ZIP: 57501)

Pop: 14,817 (1990); 14,220 (1980) **Pop Density:** 20.0
Land: 741.0 sq. mi.; **Water:** 59.4 sq. mi. **Area Code:** 605
In central SD, east of Pierre; organized Nov 26, 1880 (prior to statehood) from Buffalo County.
Name origin: For Alexander Hughes, Dakota Territory legislator.

Blunt City
ZIP: 57522 **Lat:** 44-30-55 N **Long:** 99-59-16 W
Pop: 342 (1990); 424 (1980) **Pop Density:** 684.0
Land: 0.5 sq. mi.; **Water:** 0.0 sq. mi. **Elev:** 1619 ft.
Settled 1882.
Name origin: For John Blunt, chief engineer of the North Western Railroad.

Butte Township
ZIP: 57536 **Lat:** 44-19-19 N **Long:** 99-43-51 W
Pop: 28 (1990); 34 (1980) **Pop Density:** 0.8
Land: 36.1 sq. mi.; **Water:** 0.1 sq. mi.

Crow Creek Pop. Place
Lat: 44-11-28 N **Long:** 99-46-26 W
Pop: 171 (1990); 205 (1980) **Pop Density:** 1.7
Land: 99.7 sq. mi.; **Water:** 20.8 sq. mi.

SOUTH DAKOTA, Hughes County

Harrold
Town
ZIP: 57536 Lat: 44-31-23 N Long: 99-44-18 W
Pop: 167 (1990); 196 (1980) Pop Density: 556.7
Land: 0.3 sq. mi.; Water: 0.0 sq. mi. Elev: 1796 ft.
Settled 1881.
Name origin: For railroad official Harrold McCullough.

Logan
Township
ZIP: 57522 Lat: 44-30-15 N Long: 100-04-39 W
Pop: 19 (1990); 30 (1980) Pop Density: 0.5
Land: 37.5 sq. mi.; Water: 0.0 sq. mi.

North Hughes
Pop. Place
Lat: 44-27-43 N Long: 99-48-57 W
Pop: 170 (1990); 184 (1980) Pop Density: 0.9
Land: 187.4 sq. mi.; Water: 0.4 sq. mi.

Pierre
City
ZIP: 57501 Lat: 44-22-22 N Long: 100-19-20 W
Pop: 12,906 (1990); 11,973 (1980) Pop Density: 992.8
Land: 13.0 sq. mi.; Water: 0.0 sq. mi. Elev: 1484 ft.
In central SD on the Missouri River; state capital. Settled 1878.
Name origin: For Fort Pierre, a former fort and town across the Missouri River, which was named for Pierre Choteau, Jr., French fur trader.

Raber
Township
Lat: 44-18-21 N Long: 99-51-20 W
Pop: 41 (1990); 59 (1980) Pop Density: 0.8
Land: 51.7 sq. mi.; Water: 1.4 sq. mi.

Valley
Township
ZIP: 57522 Lat: 44-24-21 N Long: 99-57-48 W
Pop: 10 (1990); 35 (1980) Pop Density: 0.3
Land: 36.0 sq. mi.; Water: 0.0 sq. mi.

West Hughes
Pop. Place
Lat: 44-25-37 N Long: 100-13-04 W
Pop: 963 (1990); 963 (1980) Pop Density: 3.5
Land: 278.8 sq. mi.; Water: 36.5 sq. mi.

Hutchinson County
County Seat: Olivet (ZIP: 57052)

Pop: 8,262 (1990); 9,350 (1980) Pop Density: 10.2
Land: 813.0 sq. mi.; Water: 1.4 sq. mi. Area Code: 605
In southeastern SD, southwest of Sioux Falls; created May 8, 1862 (prior to statehood) from unorganized territory.
Name origin: For John S. Hutchinson (1821–?), secretary of the Dakota Territory (1861–65), during which time he was frequently acting governor; member of the Hutchinson family singing and bell-ringing group, famous during the mid-1850s.

Capital
Township
ZIP: 57052 Lat: 43-13-20 N Long: 97-41-14 W
Pop: 103 (1990); 141 (1980) Pop Density: 2.9
Land: 35.8 sq. mi.; Water: 0.0 sq. mi.

Clayton
Township
Lat: 43-26-13 N Long: 97-41-51 W
Pop: 172 (1990); 232 (1980) Pop Density: 3.6
Land: 48.1 sq. mi.; Water: 0.0 sq. mi.

Cross Plains
Township
ZIP: 57331 Lat: 43-27-35 N Long: 97-56-23 W
Pop: 118 (1990); 150 (1980) Pop Density: 4.0
Land: 29.5 sq. mi.; Water: 0.1 sq. mi.

Dimock
Town
ZIP: 57331 Lat: 43-28-33 N Long: 97-59-15 W
Pop: 157 (1990); 140 (1980) Pop Density: 785.0
Land: 0.2 sq. mi.; Water: 0.0 sq. mi. Elev: 1370 ft.
Name origin: Named in 1910 for a surveyor who charted the railroad link in 1885.

Fair
Township
ZIP: 57376 Lat: 43-12-38 N Long: 97-56-01 W
Pop: 146 (1990); 166 (1980) Pop Density: 4.2
Land: 34.8 sq. mi.; Water: 0.0 sq. mi.

Foster
Township
Lat: 43-27-25 N Long: 97-49-18 W
Pop: 144 (1990); 196 (1980) Pop Density: 4.9
Land: 29.2 sq. mi.; Water: 0.3 sq. mi.

Freeman
City
ZIP: 57029 Lat: 43-21-03 N Long: 97-25-56 W
Pop: 1,293 (1990); 1,462 (1980) Pop Density: 1847.1
Land: 0.7 sq. mi.; Water: 0.0 sq. mi. Elev: 1514 ft.

German
Township
ZIP: 57366 Lat: 43-17-49 N Long: 97-55-43 W
Pop: 142 (1990); 156 (1980) Pop Density: 4.0
Land: 35.1 sq. mi.; Water: 0.1 sq. mi.

Grandview
Township
Lat: 43-23-08 N Long: 97-27-53 W
Pop: 253 (1990); 234 (1980) Pop Density: 7.1
Land: 35.4 sq. mi.; Water: 0.0 sq. mi.

Kassel
Township
ZIP: 57029 Lat: 43-17-35 N Long: 97-34-46 W
Pop: 131 (1990); 152 (1980) Pop Density: 3.6
Land: 35.9 sq. mi.; Water: 0.1 sq. mi.

Kaylor
Township
Lat: 43-12-41 N Long: 97-49-13 W
Pop: 223 (1990); 269 (1980) Pop Density: 6.3
Land: 35.6 sq. mi.; Water: 0.0 sq. mi.

Kulm
ZIP: 57366   **Lat:** 43-17-53 N   **Long:** 98-03-17 W   Township
Pop: 108 (1990); 137 (1980)   **Pop Density:** 3.1
Land: 35.3 sq. mi.; **Water:** 0.0 sq. mi.

Liberty
Township
Lat: 43-22-38 N   **Long:** 97-55-36 W
Pop: 162 (1990); 190 (1980)   **Pop Density:** 4.7
Land: 34.7 sq. mi.; **Water:** 0.0 sq. mi.

Menno
City
ZIP: 57045   **Lat:** 43-14-16 N   **Long:** 97-34-37 W
Pop: 768 (1990); 793 (1980)   **Pop Density:** 1536.0
Land: 0.5 sq. mi.; **Water:** 0.0 sq. mi.   **Elev:** 1326 ft.
Founded 1879.
Name origin: For a large colony of Mennonites in the area.

Milltown
Township
ZIP: 57366   **Lat:** 43-23-03 N   **Long:** 97-49-11 W
Pop: 146 (1990); 186 (1980)   **Pop Density:** 4.1
Land: 35.7 sq. mi.; **Water:** 0.0 sq. mi.

Molan
Township
ZIP: 57045   **Lat:** 43-12-32 N   **Long:** 97-27-32 W
Pop: 180 (1990); 213 (1980)   **Pop Density:** 5.0
Land: 36.0 sq. mi.; **Water:** 0.0 sq. mi.

Oak Hollow
Township
ZIP: 57376   **Lat:** 43-13-05 N   **Long:** 98-02-24 W
Pop: 68 (1990); 135 (1980)   **Pop Density:** 2.1
Land: 32.3 sq. mi.; **Water:** 0.0 sq. mi.

Olivet
Town
ZIP: 57052   **Lat:** 43-14-30 N   **Long:** 97-40-24 W
Pop: 74 (1990); 96 (1980)   **Pop Density:** 370.0
Land: 0.2 sq. mi.; **Water:** 0.0 sq. mi.   **Elev:** 1220 ft.
Name origin: For Olivet, MI, former home of two early settlers.

Parkston
City
ZIP: 57366   **Lat:** 43-23-35 N   **Long:** 97-59-07 W
Pop: 1,572 (1990); 1,545 (1980)   **Pop Density:** 1746.7
Land: 0.9 sq. mi.; **Water:** 0.0 sq. mi.   **Elev:** 1396 ft.
Name origin: For R.S. Parke, the original landowner.

Pleasant
Township
Lat: 43-27-55 N   **Long:** 97-34-14 W
Pop: 62 (1990); 80 (1980)   **Pop Density:** 2.1
Land: 29.0 sq. mi.; **Water:** 0.0 sq. mi.

Sharon
Township
ZIP: 57376   **Lat:** 43-18-07 N   **Long:** 97-49-07 W
Pop: 111 (1990); 143 (1980)   **Pop Density:** 3.1
Land: 35.5 sq. mi.; **Water:** 0.0 sq. mi.

Silver Lake
Township
Lat: 43-28-22 N   **Long:** 97-27-46 W
Pop: 114 (1990); 146 (1980)   **Pop Density:** 4.0
Land: 28.3 sq. mi.; **Water:** 0.6 sq. mi.

Starr
Township
ZIP: 57331   **Lat:** 43-27-48 N   **Long:** 98-02-48 W
Pop: 151 (1990); 188 (1980)   **Pop Density:** 5.3
Land: 28.5 sq. mi.; **Water:** 0.0 sq. mi.

Susquehanna
Township
ZIP: 57366   **Lat:** 43-23-08 N   **Long:** 98-02-38 W
Pop: 207 (1990); 262 (1980)   **Pop Density:** 5.9
Land: 34.9 sq. mi.; **Water:** 0.0 sq. mi.

Sweet
Township
ZIP: 57045   **Lat:** 43-13-13 N   **Long:** 97-34-20 W
Pop: 258 (1990); 340 (1980)   **Pop Density:** 7.2
Land: 35.9 sq. mi.; **Water:** 0.0 sq. mi.

Tripp
City
ZIP: 57376   **Lat:** 43-13-29 N   **Long:** 97-57-59 W
Pop: 664 (1990); 804 (1980)   **Pop Density:** 1106.7
Land: 0.6 sq. mi.; **Water:** 0.0 sq. mi.   **Elev:** 1531 ft.
Name origin: For Barlett Tripp, who served as territorial Chief Justice in 1886 when the town was founded.

Valley
Township
Lat: 43-17-32 N   **Long:** 97-28-09 W
Pop: 220 (1990); 249 (1980)   **Pop Density:** 6.1
Land: 36.1 sq. mi.; **Water:** 0.0 sq. mi.

Wittenberg
Township
ZIP: 57052   **Lat:** 43-19-16 N   **Long:** 97-42-28 W
Pop: 267 (1990); 300 (1980)   **Pop Density:** 5.0
Land: 53.2 sq. mi.; **Water:** 0.0 sq. mi.

Wolf Creek
Township
ZIP: 57052   **Lat:** 43-23-08 N   **Long:** 97-34-55 W
Pop: 248 (1990); 245 (1980)   **Pop Density:** 7.0
Land: 35.5 sq. mi.; **Water:** 0.1 sq. mi.

Hyde County
County Seat: Highmore (ZIP: 57345)

Pop: 1,696 (1990); 2,069 (1980)   **Pop Density:** 2.0
Land: 861.1 sq. mi.; **Water:** 5.6 sq. mi.   **Area Code:** 605
In central SD, east of Pierre; created Jan 8, 1873 (prior to statehood) from Buffalo County.
Name origin: For James Hyde (1842–1902), Civil War prisoner of war at Andersonville and Dakota territorial legislator.

Central Hyde
Pop. Place
Lat: 44-28-31 N   **Long:** 99-29-04 W
Pop: 459 (1990); 481 (1980)   **Pop Density:** 1.1
Land: 423.3 sq. mi.; **Water:** 1.1 sq. mi.

Crow Creek
Pop. Place
Lat: 44-12-59 N   **Long:** 99-29-37 W
Pop: 90 (1990); 143 (1980)   **Pop Density:** 1.1
Land: 82.7 sq. mi.; **Water:** 2.3 sq. mi.

SOUTH DAKOTA, Hyde County

Dewey
Township
Lat: 44-19-40 N Long: 99-28-41 W
Pop: 14 (1990); 24 (1980)   Pop Density: 0.4
Land: 36.1 sq. mi.; Water: 0.3 sq. mi.

Highmore
City
ZIP: 57345   Lat: 44-31-14 N Long: 99-26-20 W
Pop: 835 (1990); 1,055 (1980)   Pop Density: 463.9
Land: 1.8 sq. mi.; Water: 0.0 sq. mi.   Elev: 1888 ft.

North Hyde
Pop. Place
Lat: 44-47-39 N Long: 99-28-49 W
Pop: 249 (1990); 291 (1980)   Pop Density: 1.0
Land: 245.5 sq. mi.; Water: 1.6 sq. mi.

Valley
Township
Lat: 44-39-58 N Long: 99-37-16 W
Pop: 39 (1990); 24 (1980)   Pop Density: 1.1
Land: 36.0 sq. mi.; Water: 0.2 sq. mi.

William Hamilton
Township
Lat: 44-35-29 N Long: 99-22-26 W
Pop: 10 (1990); 11 (1980)   Pop Density: 0.3
Land: 35.7 sq. mi.; Water: 0.1 sq. mi.

Jackson County
County Seat: Kadoka (ZIP: 57543)

Pop: 2,811 (1990); 3,437 (1980)   Pop Density: 1.5
Land: 1869.3 sq. mi.; Water: 2.1 sq. mi.   Area Code: 605

In south-central SD, southwest of Pierre; created Nov, 1914 from Stanley County. In 1976 annexed Washabaugh County, which was organized 1883 from Indian lands and continued as an Indian reservation. An original Jackson County, formed in 1883, gradually disappeared as parts of its territory joined other counties.

Name origin: For John R. Jackson, Dakota Territory legislator when the original Jackson county was formed in 1883. A claim has been made for Andrew Jackson, but seems to be unjustified.

Belvidere
Town
ZIP: 57521   Lat: 43-49-52 N Long: 101-16-13 W
Pop: 63 (1990); 80 (1980)   Pop Density: 78.8
Land: 0.8 sq. mi.; Water: 0.1 sq. mi.   Elev: 2320 ft.
Name origin: For Belvidere, IL, the former home of settlers.

Cottonwood
Town
Lat: 43-57-55 N Long: 101-54-06 W
Pop: 12 (1990); 4 (1980)   Pop Density: 13.3
Land: 0.9 sq. mi.; Water: 0.0 sq. mi.   Elev: 2415 ft.
Name origin: For nearby Cottonwood Creek. Originally called Ingham.

East Jackson
Pop. Place
Lat: 43-53-34 N Long: 101-22-01 W
Pop: 236 (1990); 244 (1980)   Pop Density: 0.7
Land: 358.9 sq. mi.; Water: 0.8 sq. mi.

Grandview
Township
Lat: 43-57-35 N Long: 101-43-54 W
Pop: 17 (1990); 20 (1980)   Pop Density: 0.5
Land: 35.5 sq. mi.; Water: 0.0 sq. mi.

Interior
Town
ZIP: 57750   Lat: 43-43-38 N Long: 101-59-00 W
Pop: 67 (1990); 62 (1980)   Pop Density: 51.5
Land: 1.3 sq. mi.; Water: 0.0 sq. mi.   Elev: 2378 ft.
Name origin: For its position inside the Badlands' Wall.

*Interior
Township
ZIP: 57750   Lat: 43-46-18 N Long: 101-53-18 W
Pop: 60 (1990); 110 (1980)   Pop Density: 0.6
Land: 101.3 sq. mi.; Water: 0.1 sq. mi.

Jewett
Township
ZIP: 57543   Lat: 43-57-19 N Long: 101-28-56 W
Pop: 21 (1990); 24 (1980)   Pop Density: 0.6
Land: 35.7 sq. mi.; Water: 0.0 sq. mi.

Kadoka
City
ZIP: 57543   Lat: 43-49-55 N Long: 101-30-31 W
Pop: 736 (1990); 832 (1980)   Pop Density: 320.0
Land: 2.3 sq. mi.; Water: 0.0 sq. mi.   Elev: 2458 ft.
Founded 1906.
Name origin: From a Sioux Indian term meaning 'opening,' a reference to its location along the Badlands' Wall.

Little Buffalo
Township
ZIP: 57543   Lat: 43-51-50 N Long: 101-42-54 W
Pop: 20 (1990); 18 (1980)   Pop Density: 0.6
Land: 35.8 sq. mi.; Water: 0.1 sq. mi.

Northwest Jackson
Pop. Place
Lat: 43-54-32 N Long: 101-53-49 W
Pop: 64 (1990); 92 (1980)   Pop Density: 0.5
Land: 141.9 sq. mi.; Water: 0.1 sq. mi.

Southeast Jackson
Pop. Place
Lat: 43-34-53 N Long: 101-21-30 W
Pop: 214 (1990); 233 (1980)   Pop Density: 0.6
Land: 380.9 sq. mi.; Water: 0.3 sq. mi.

Southwest Jackson
Pop. Place
Lat: 43-33-04 N Long: 101-48-21 W
Pop: 1,269 (1990); 1,673 (1980)   Pop Density: 1.9
Land: 684.3 sq. mi.; Water: 0.2 sq. mi.

Wall
Township
Lat: 43-46-56 N Long: 101-36-24 W
Pop: 19 (1990); 27 (1980)   Pop Density: 0.5
Land: 39.4 sq. mi.; Water: 0.3 sq. mi.

Wanblee
CDP
ZIP: 57577   Lat: 43-34-27 N Long: 101-39-42 W
Pop: 654 (1990)   Pop Density: 297.3
Land: 2.2 sq. mi.; Water: 0.0 sq. mi.

Weta Township
ZIP: 57543 **Lat:** 43-45-48 N **Long:** 101-43-04 W
Pop: 13 (1990); 18 (1980) **Pop Density:** 0.3
Land: 50.2 sq. mi.; **Water:** 0.1 sq. mi.

Jerauld County
County Seat: Wessington Springs (ZIP: 57382)

Pop: 2,425 (1990); 2,929 (1980) **Pop Density:** 4.6
Land: 530.3 sq. mi.; **Water:** 2.4 sq. mi. **Area Code:** 605
In south-central SD, northwest of Sioux Falls; organized Mar 9, 1883 (prior to statehood) from Aurora County.
Name origin: For H. A. Jerauld, Dakota Territory legislator when the county was formed.

Alpena Town
ZIP: 57312 **Lat:** 44-11-00 N **Long:** 98-22-04 W
Pop: 251 (1990); 288 (1980) **Pop Density:** 156.9
Land: 1.6 sq. mi.; **Water:** 0.0 sq. mi. **Elev:** 1310 ft.
Plotted 1883.
Name origin: For Alpena, MI, so named by local railroad officials.

*****Alpena** Township
ZIP: 57312 **Lat:** 44-09-08 N **Long:** 98-24-08 W
Pop: 108 (1990); 136 (1980) **Pop Density:** 3.2
Land: 33.5 sq. mi.; **Water:** 0.0 sq. mi.

Anina Township
ZIP: 57382 **Lat:** 43-58-29 N **Long:** 98-37-38 W
Pop: 55 (1990); 76 (1980) **Pop Density:** 1.6
Land: 35.1 sq. mi.; **Water:** 0.0 sq. mi.

Blaine Township
Lat: 43-59-08 N **Long:** 98-23-30 W
Pop: 86 (1990); 110 (1980) **Pop Density:** 2.4
Land: 35.7 sq. mi.; **Water:** 0.2 sq. mi.

Chery Township
ZIP: 57382 **Lat:** 44-09-15 N **Long:** 98-37-20 W
Pop: 67 (1990); 91 (1980) **Pop Density:** 1.9
Land: 35.1 sq. mi.; **Water:** 0.0 sq. mi.

Crow Township
ZIP: 57382 **Lat:** 44-03-30 N **Long:** 98-52-04 W
Pop: 119 (1990); 162 (1980) **Pop Density:** 3.4
Land: 35.4 sq. mi.; **Water:** 0.0 sq. mi.

Crow Lake Township
ZIP: 57382 **Lat:** 43-58-24 N **Long:** 98-44-31 W
Pop: 61 (1990); 73 (1980) **Pop Density:** 1.8
Land: 34.6 sq. mi.; **Water:** 0.8 sq. mi.

Dale Township
ZIP: 57312 **Lat:** 44-09-14 N **Long:** 98-30-46 W
Pop: 50 (1990); 87 (1980) **Pop Density:** 1.4
Land: 34.9 sq. mi.; **Water:** 0.1 sq. mi.

Franklin Township
Lat: 44-04-06 N **Long:** 98-23-20 W
Pop: 81 (1990); 114 (1980) **Pop Density:** 2.3
Land: 35.5 sq. mi.; **Water:** 0.0 sq. mi.

Harmony Township
Lat: 44-09-06 N **Long:** 98-45-06 W
Pop: 50 (1990); 63 (1980) **Pop Density:** 1.4
Land: 34.9 sq. mi.; **Water:** 0.8 sq. mi.

Lane Town
ZIP: 57358 **Lat:** 44-04-08 N **Long:** 98-25-26 W
Pop: 71 (1990); 83 (1980) **Pop Density:** 142.0
Land: 0.5 sq. mi.; **Water:** 0.0 sq. mi. **Elev:** 1376 ft.
Name origin: For T.W. Lane, the original landowner.

Logan Township
Lat: 43-58-36 N **Long:** 98-52-35 W
Pop: 21 (1990); 38 (1980) **Pop Density:** 0.6
Land: 35.6 sq. mi.; **Water:** 0.0 sq. mi.

Marlar Township
ZIP: 57382 **Lat:** 44-09-26 N **Long:** 98-51-39 W
Pop: 46 (1990); 49 (1980) **Pop Density:** 1.3
Land: 36.0 sq. mi.; **Water:** 0.1 sq. mi.

Media Township
ZIP: 57382 **Lat:** 44-03-43 N **Long:** 98-37-20 W
Pop: 63 (1990); 77 (1980) **Pop Density:** 1.8
Land: 34.2 sq. mi.; **Water:** 0.2 sq. mi.

Pleasant Township
Lat: 44-03-50 N **Long:** 98-45-02 W
Pop: 78 (1990); 100 (1980) **Pop Density:** 2.2
Land: 35.4 sq. mi.; **Water:** 0.0 sq. mi.

Viola Township
ZIP: 57382 **Lat:** 43-58-47 N **Long:** 98-30-05 W
Pop: 52 (1990); 67 (1980) **Pop Density:** 1.5
Land: 35.6 sq. mi.; **Water:** 0.0 sq. mi.

Wessington Springs City
ZIP: 57382 **Lat:** 44-04-50 N **Long:** 98-34-16 W
Pop: 1,083 (1990); 1,203 (1980) **Pop Density:** 601.7
Land: 1.8 sq. mi.; **Water:** 0.0 sq. mi. **Elev:** 1687 ft.
Name origin: For the fact that the town's springs arise from the Wessington Hills.

*****Wessington Springs** Township
ZIP: 57382 **Lat:** 44-03-59 N **Long:** 98-30-55 W
Pop: 83 (1990); 112 (1980) **Pop Density:** 2.4
Land: 34.9 sq. mi.; **Water:** 0.0 sq. mi.

Jones County
County Seat: Murdo (ZIP: 57559)

Pop: 1,324 (1990); 1,463 (1980)
Land: 970.6 sq. mi.; **Water:** 1.1 sq. mi.
Pop Density: 1.4
Area Code: 605
In south-central SD, south of Pierre; organized Jan 16, 1917 from Lyman County.
Name origin: For Jones County, IA, former home of some settlers.

Buffalo
Township
Lat: 43-51-55 N Long: 100-39-07 W
Pop: 42 (1990); 42 (1980) Pop Density: 1.2
Land: 35.8 sq. mi.; Water: 0.0 sq. mi.

Central Jones
Pop. Place
Lat: 43-55-26 N Long: 100-43-22 W
Pop: 111 (1990) Pop Density: 1.0
Land: 106.4 sq. mi.; Water: 0.2 sq. mi.

Draper
Town
ZIP: 57531 Lat: 43-55-33 N Long: 100-32-15 W
Pop: 123 (1990); 138 (1980) Pop Density: 205.0
Land: 0.6 sq. mi.; Water: 0.0 sq. mi. Elev: 2257 ft.
Established 1906.
Name origin: For C.A. Draper, a Milwaukee Railroad conductor.

*Draper
Township
ZIP: 57531 Lat: 43-56-58 N Long: 100-31-54 W
Pop: 42 (1990); 44 (1980) Pop Density: 1.2
Land: 35.1 sq. mi.; Water: 0.0 sq. mi.

Dunkel
Township
ZIP: 57531 Lat: 43-51-35 N Long: 100-31-26 W
Pop: 16 (1990); 24 (1980) Pop Density: 0.4
Land: 36.0 sq. mi.; Water: 0.0 sq. mi.

Grandview
Township
ZIP: 57562 Lat: 43-51-31 N Long: 100-59-45 W
Pop: 13 (1990); 19 (1980) Pop Density: 0.5
Land: 28.3 sq. mi.; Water: 0.1 sq. mi.

Kolls
Township
ZIP: 57531 Lat: 44-02-36 N Long: 100-37-31 W
Pop: 19 (1990); 30 (1980) Pop Density: 0.5
Land: 35.5 sq. mi.; Water: 0.1 sq. mi.

Morgan
Township
ZIP: 57562 Lat: 43-56-44 N Long: 101-00-12 W
Pop: 29 (1990); 45 (1980) Pop Density: 0.8
Land: 35.6 sq. mi.; Water: 0.1 sq. mi.

Mullen
Township
ZIP: 57559 Lat: 43-46-44 N Long: 100-45-43 W
Pop: 6 (1990); 11 (1980) Pop Density: 0.2
Land: 36.1 sq. mi.; Water: 0.0 sq. mi.

Murdo
City
ZIP: 57559 Lat: 43-53-21 N Long: 100-42-48 W
Pop: 679 (1990); 723 (1980) Pop Density: 1131.7
Land: 0.6 sq. mi.; Water: 0.0 sq. mi. Elev: 2326 ft.
Name origin: For Murdo McKenzie, an early cattleman.

Mussman
Township
ZIP: 57531 Lat: 43-57-33 N Long: 100-25-29 W
Pop: 19 (1990); 15 (1980) Pop Density: 0.6
Land: 30.0 sq. mi.; Water: 0.0 sq. mi.

North Jones
Pop. Place
Lat: 44-06-09 N Long: 100-45-47 W
Pop: 40 (1990) Pop Density: 0.2
Land: 214.5 sq. mi.; Water: 0.2 sq. mi.

Okaton
Township
ZIP: 57562 Lat: 43-50-31 N Long: 100-52-00 W
Pop: 64 (1990); 67 (1980) Pop Density: 1.4
Land: 46.0 sq. mi.; Water: 0.0 sq. mi.

Richland
Township
Lat: 44-07-37 N Long: 100-24-04 W
Pop: 5 (1990); 8 (1980) Pop Density: 0.2
Land: 23.5 sq. mi.; Water: 0.1 sq. mi.

Rich Valley
Pop. Place
ZIP: 57531 Lat: 44-01-38 N Long: 100-24-34 W
Pop: 4 (1990); 7 (1980) Pop Density: 0.2
Land: 23.6 sq. mi.; Water: 0.1 sq. mi.

Scovil
Township
ZIP: 57559 Lat: 43-56-42 N Long: 100-53-25 W
Pop: 21 (1990); 25 (1980) Pop Density: 0.6
Land: 35.7 sq. mi.; Water: 0.0 sq. mi.

South Creek
Township
Lat: 44-02-30 N Long: 100-59-40 W
Pop: 22 (1990); 26 (1980) Pop Density: 0.6
Land: 35.7 sq. mi.; Water: 0.0 sq. mi.

Union
Township
Lat: 44-02-29 N Long: 100-44-48 W
Pop: 0 (1990); 13 (1980)
Land: 35.6 sq. mi.; Water: 0.0 sq. mi.

Virgil
Township
Lat: 44-02-30 N Long: 100-29-44 W
Pop: 16 (1990); 9 (1980) Pop Density: 0.4
Land: 35.7 sq. mi.; Water: 0.1 sq. mi.

Westover
Township
Lat: 43-47-48 N Long: 100-39-28 W
Pop: 3 (1990); 17 (1980) Pop Density: 0.1
Land: 33.7 sq. mi.; Water: 0.0 sq. mi.

Williams Creek
Township
ZIP: 57531 Lat: 43-49-07 N Long: 100-24-24 W
Pop: 38 (1990); 51 (1980) Pop Density: 0.5
Land: 73.9 sq. mi.; Water: 0.1 sq. mi.

Zickrick
Township
ZIP: 57531 Lat: 43-46-58 N Long: 100-31-37 W
Pop: 12 (1990); 18 (1980) Pop Density: 0.4
Land: 32.7 sq. mi.; Water: 0.0 sq. mi.

Kingsbury County
County Seat: De Smet (ZIP: 57231)

Pop: 5,925 (1990); 6,679 (1980)　　**Pop Density:** 7.1
Land: 838.4 sq. mi.; **Water:** 25.3 sq. mi.　　**Area Code:** 605
In east-central SD, northwest of Sioux Falls; created Jan 8, 1873 (prior to statehood) from Hanson County.
Name origin: For George Washington Kingsbury (1837–1925) and T.A. Kingsbury, brothers prominent in territorial affairs and members of several Territorial legislatures. George was a newspaper publisher and author of *History of Dakota Territory*.

Arlington　　City
ZIP: 57212　　**Lat:** 44-21-47 N　**Long:** 97-08-19 W
Pop: 902 (1990); 988 (1980)　　**Pop Density:** 820.0
Land: 1.1 sq. mi.; **Water:** 0.0 sq. mi.　　**Elev:** 1842 ft.
Part of the town is also in Brookings County.
Name origin: For Arlington, VA.

Badger　　Town
ZIP: 57214　　**Lat:** 44-29-08 N　**Long:** 97-12-33 W
Pop: 114 (1990); 99 (1980)　　**Pop Density:** 114.0
Land: 1.0 sq. mi.; **Water:** 0.0 sq. mi.　　**Elev:** 1710 ft.
Founded 1906.
Name origin: For the nearby lake.

*Badger　　Township
Lat: 44-29-32 N　**Long:** 97-13-11 W
Pop: 240 (1990); 272 (1980)　　**Pop Density:** 4.5
Land: 53.5 sq. mi.; **Water:** 5.4 sq. mi.

Baker　　Township
Lat: 44-22-06 N　**Long:** 97-23-09 W
Pop: 280 (1990); 276 (1980)　　**Pop Density:** 3.9
Land: 71.4 sq. mi.; **Water:** 3.3 sq. mi.

Bancroft　　Town
ZIP: 57316　　**Lat:** 44-29-19 N　**Long:** 97-45-01 W
Pop: 30 (1990); 41 (1980)　　**Pop Density:** 150.0
Land: 0.2 sq. mi.; **Water:** 0.0 sq. mi.　　**Elev:** 1517 ft.
Name origin: For L.L. Bancroft, who started a newspaper in the town in 1884.

Denver　　Township
ZIP: 57212　　**Lat:** 44-23-01 N　**Long:** 97-12-10 W
Pop: 245 (1990); 285 (1980)　　**Pop Density:** 3.7
Land: 65.4 sq. mi.; **Water:** 1.0 sq. mi.

De Smet　　City
ZIP: 57231　　**Lat:** 44-23-11 N　**Long:** 97-32-51 W
Pop: 1,172 (1990); 1,237 (1980)　　**Pop Density:** 1065.5
Land: 1.1 sq. mi.; **Water:** 0.0 sq. mi.　　**Elev:** 1724 ft.
Incorporated 1883.
Name origin: For Father Pierre–Jean De Smet (1801–73), who spent his life ministering to the Indians in the 19th century.

*De Smet　　Township
ZIP: 57231　　**Lat:** 44-22-44 N　**Long:** 97-31-38 W
Pop: 328 (1990); 435 (1980)　　**Pop Density:** 5.1
Land: 64.7 sq. mi.; **Water:** 3.8 sq. mi.

Erwin　　Town
ZIP: 57233　　**Lat:** 44-29-17 N　**Long:** 97-26-27 W
Pop: 42 (1990); 66 (1980)　　**Pop Density:** 84.0
Land: 0.5 sq. mi.; **Water:** 0.0 sq. mi.　　**Elev:** 1830 ft.
Name origin: For first postmaster James Erwin Hollister.

Esmond　　Township
ZIP: 57353　　**Lat:** 44-15-54 N　**Long:** 97-45-40 W
Pop: 57 (1990); 84 (1980)　　**Pop Density:** 0.7
Land: 78.6 sq. mi.; **Water:** 0.0 sq. mi.

Hartland　　Township
Lat: 44-29-33 N　**Long:** 97-23-51 W
Pop: 183 (1990); 202 (1980)　　**Pop Density:** 2.9
Land: 62.9 sq. mi.; **Water:** 0.0 sq. mi.

Hetland　　Town
ZIP: 57244　　**Lat:** 44-22-35 N　**Long:** 97-14-04 W
Pop: 53 (1990); 66 (1980)　　**Pop Density:** 530.0
Land: 0.1 sq. mi.; **Water:** 0.0 sq. mi.　　**Elev:** 1733 ft.
Established 1880.
Name origin: For pioneer homesteader John Hetland.

Iroquois　　City
ZIP: 57353　　**Lat:** 44-21-59 N　**Long:** 97-50-52 W
Pop: 271 (1990); 299 (1980)　　**Pop Density:** 542.0
Land: 0.5 sq. mi.; **Water:** 0.0 sq. mi.　　**Elev:** 1398 ft.
Founded 1880s. Part of the town is also in Beadle County.
Name origin: For the Iroquois Indians.

*Iroquois　　Township
ZIP: 57353　　**Lat:** 44-22-33 N　**Long:** 97-48-09 W
Pop: 64 (1990); 73 (1980)　　**Pop Density:** 1.5
Land: 41.3 sq. mi.; **Water:** 0.0 sq. mi.

Lake Preston　　City
ZIP: 57249　　**Lat:** 44-21-42 N　**Long:** 97-22-34 W
Pop: 663 (1990); 789 (1980)　　**Pop Density:** 947.1
Land: 0.7 sq. mi.; **Water:** 0.0 sq. mi.　　**Elev:** 1719 ft.
Name origin: Named in 1881 for the nearby lake.

Le Sueur　　Township
ZIP: 57316　　**Lat:** 44-29-30 N　**Long:** 97-45-47 W
Pop: 170 (1990); 145 (1980)　　**Pop Density:** 2.7
Land: 63.2 sq. mi.; **Water:** 0.1 sq. mi.

Manchester　　Township
ZIP: 57353　　**Lat:** 44-22-54 N　**Long:** 97-41-03 W
Pop: 136 (1990); 131 (1980)　　**Pop Density:** 2.4
Land: 55.7 sq. mi.; **Water:** 0.0 sq. mi.

Mathews　　Township
ZIP: 57353　　**Lat:** 44-15-12 N　**Long:** 97-34-38 W
Pop: 153 (1990); 212 (1980)　　**Pop Density:** 1.8
Land: 85.7 sq. mi.; **Water:** 4.2 sq. mi.

Oldham　　City
ZIP: 57051　　**Lat:** 44-13-41 N　**Long:** 97-18-31 W
Pop: 189 (1990); 222 (1980)　　**Pop Density:** 945.0
Land: 0.2 sq. mi.; **Water:** 0.0 sq. mi.　　**Elev:** 1710 ft.
Name origin: Named by Milwaukee Railroad officials for Oldham Carrot, a farmer who granted the right-of-way to the railroad. Originally called Huffman.

SOUTH DAKOTA, Kingsbury County

Spirit Lake — Township
ZIP: 57233 Lat: 44-30-11 N Long: 97-34-36 W
Pop: 167 (1990); 188 (1980) Pop Density: 2.7
Land: 61.0 sq. mi.; Water: 2.9 sq. mi.

Spring Lake — Township
Lat: 44-16-05 N Long: 97-13-11 W
Pop: 327 (1990); 382 (1980) Pop Density: 4.1
Land: 79.8 sq. mi.; Water: 1.6 sq. mi.

Whitewood — Township
Lat: 44-15-01 N Long: 97-22-50 W
Pop: 139 (1990); 187 (1980) Pop Density: 2.8
Land: 49.9 sq. mi.; Water: 3.1 sq. mi.

Lake County
County Seat: Madison (ZIP: 57042)

Pop: 10,550 (1990); 10,724 (1980) Pop Density: 18.7
Land: 563.3 sq. mi.; Water: 11.8 sq. mi. Area Code: 605
In east-central SD, northwest of Sioux Falls; organized Jan 8, 1873 (prior to statehood) from Brookings and Hanson counties.
Name origin: For the area's numerous lakes.

Badus — Township
ZIP: 57054 Lat: 44-09-01 N Long: 97-11-43 W
Pop: 146 (1990); 171 (1980) Pop Density: 4.2
Land: 35.1 sq. mi.; Water: 0.4 sq. mi.

Chester — Township
ZIP: 57016 Lat: 43-53-19 N Long: 96-56-33 W
Pop: 571 (1990); 522 (1980) Pop Density: 17.0
Land: 33.5 sq. mi.; Water: 2.4 sq. mi.

Clarno — Township
ZIP: 57076 Lat: 43-53-37 N Long: 97-18-21 W
Pop: 190 (1990); 202 (1980) Pop Density: 5.3
Land: 36.1 sq. mi.; Water: 0.0 sq. mi.

Concord — Township
ZIP: 57076 Lat: 44-04-05 N Long: 97-19-05 W
Pop: 125 (1990); 153 (1980) Pop Density: 3.4
Land: 36.3 sq. mi.; Water: 0.0 sq. mi.

Farmington — Township
Lat: 44-04-00 N Long: 97-11-18 W
Pop: 188 (1990); 236 (1980) Pop Density: 5.2
Land: 35.9 sq. mi.; Water: 0.0 sq. mi.

Franklin — Township
ZIP: 57016 Lat: 43-53-23 N Long: 97-04-13 W
Pop: 228 (1990); 244 (1980) Pop Density: 6.3
Land: 36.0 sq. mi.; Water: 0.1 sq. mi.

Herman — Township
ZIP: 57042 Lat: 43-58-38 N Long: 97-11-11 W
Pop: 556 (1990); 551 (1980) Pop Density: 16.9
Land: 32.9 sq. mi.; Water: 2.9 sq. mi.

Lake View — Township
Lat: 43-58-38 N Long: 97-03-59 W
Pop: 468 (1990); 399 (1980) Pop Density: 16.1
Land: 29.1 sq. mi.; Water: 3.0 sq. mi.

Le Roy — Township
ZIP: 57042 Lat: 44-04-04 N Long: 97-04-04 W
Pop: 239 (1990); 216 (1980) Pop Density: 6.6
Land: 36.0 sq. mi.; Water: 0.0 sq. mi.

Madison — City
ZIP: 57042 Lat: 44-00-30 N Long: 97-06-26 W
Pop: 6,257 (1990); 6,210 (1980) Pop Density: 1604.4
Land: 3.9 sq. mi.; Water: 0.0 sq. mi. Elev: 1670 ft.

Nunda — Town
ZIP: 57050 Lat: 44-09-39 N Long: 97-01-04 W
Pop: 45 (1990); 60 (1980) Pop Density: 45.0
Land: 1.0 sq. mi.; Water: 0.0 sq. mi. Elev: 1740 ft.
Name origin: For Nunda, VT, former home of pioneer settler John Fleming.

*Nunda — Township
ZIP: 57050 Lat: 44-08-58 N Long: 97-03-34 W
Pop: 103 (1990); 129 (1980) Pop Density: 3.0
Land: 34.6 sq. mi.; Water: 0.3 sq. mi.

Orland — Township
ZIP: 57042 Lat: 43-53-03 N Long: 97-10-42 W
Pop: 135 (1990); 163 (1980) Pop Density: 3.8
Land: 35.7 sq. mi.; Water: 0.2 sq. mi.

Ramona — Town
ZIP: 57054 Lat: 44-07-12 N Long: 97-12-54 W
Pop: 194 (1990); 241 (1980) Pop Density: 646.7
Land: 0.3 sq. mi.; Water: 0.0 sq. mi. Elev: 1800 ft.
Platted 1886.

Rutland — Township
Lat: 44-03-31 N Long: 96-56-19 W
Pop: 213 (1990); 226 (1980) Pop Density: 5.9
Land: 35.8 sq. mi.; Water: 0.1 sq. mi.

Summit — Township
Lat: 44-09-20 N Long: 96-56-19 W
Pop: 186 (1990); 214 (1980) Pop Density: 5.3
Land: 34.9 sq. mi.; Water: 0.7 sq. mi.

Wayne — Township
ZIP: 57054 Lat: 44-08-45 N Long: 97-19-11 W
Pop: 124 (1990); 140 (1980) Pop Density: 3.5
Land: 35.5 sq. mi.; Water: 0.0 sq. mi.

Wentworth — Village
ZIP: 57075 Lat: 43-59-48 N Long: 96-57-51 W
Pop: 181 (1990); 193 (1980) Pop Density: 603.3
Land: 0.3 sq. mi.; Water: 0.0 sq. mi. Elev: 1680 ft.
Founded 1879.
Name origin: For the first settler, George Wentworth.

*Wentworth — Township
ZIP: 57075   **Lat:** 43-58-18 N   **Long:** 96-57-15 W
Pop: 213 (1990); 226 (1980)   **Pop Density:** 6.3
Land: 34.0 sq. mi.; **Water:** 1.6 sq. mi.

Winfred — Town
ZIP: 57076   **Lat:** 43-59-51 N   **Long:** 97-21-45 W
Pop: 54 (1990); 81 (1980)   **Pop Density:** 77.1
Land: 0.7 sq. mi.; **Water:** 0.0 sq. mi.   **Elev:** 1710 ft.
Founded 1882.

*Winfred — Township
ZIP: 57076   **Lat:** 43-59-10 N   **Long:** 97-18-38 W
Pop: 134 (1990); 147 (1980)   **Pop Density:** 3.8
Land: 35.7 sq. mi.; **Water:** 0.0 sq. mi.

Lawrence County
County Seat: Deadwood (ZIP: 57732)

Pop: 20,655 (1990); 18,339 (1980)   **Pop Density:** 25.8
Land: 800.1 sq. mi.; **Water:** 0.3 sq. mi.   **Area Code:** 605
On the central western border of SD, northwest of Rapid City; created Jan 11, 1875 (prior to statehood) from unorganized territory.
Name origin: For John Lawrence, Dakota Territory legislator and first treasurer of the county.

Central City — City
ZIP: 57754   **Lat:** 44-22-09 N   **Long:** 103-46-09 W
Pop: 185 (1990); 177 (1980)   **Pop Density:** 1850.0
Land: 0.1 sq. mi.; **Water:** 0.0 sq. mi.   **Elev:** 4920 ft.
Founded 1877.
Name origin: For its location between Lead and Deadwood.

Deadwood — City
ZIP: 57732   **Lat:** 44-22-55 N   **Long:** 103-43-23 W
Pop: 1,830 (1990); 2,035 (1980)   **Pop Density:** 494.6
Land: 3.7 sq. mi.; **Water:** 0.0 sq. mi.   **Elev:** 4537 ft.
Name origin: Named in 1876 for its location in Deadwood Gulch.

Lead — City
ZIP: 57754   **Lat:** 44-21-07 N   **Long:** 103-46-00 W
Pop: 3,632 (1990); 4,330 (1980)   **Pop Density:** 1911.6
Land: 1.9 sq. mi.; **Water:** 0.0 sq. mi.   **Elev:** 4960 ft.
Founded 1876.
Name origin: For a *lead* or 'gold-bearing vein'. Originally called Washington.

North Lawrence — Pop. Place
Lat: 44-28-28 N   **Long:** 103-49-23 W
Pop: 4,741 (1990); 3,582 (1980)   **Pop Density:** 14.3
Land: 332.0 sq. mi.; **Water:** 0.2 sq. mi.

North Spearfish — CDP
Lat: 44-30-24 N   **Long:** 103-53-30 W
Pop: 2,274 (1990)   **Pop Density:** 541.4
Land: 4.2 sq. mi.; **Water:** 0.0 sq. mi.

St. Onge — Township
Lat: 44-33-33 N   **Long:** 103-44-51 W
Pop: 317 (1990); 257 (1980)   **Pop Density:** 8.9
Land: 35.7 sq. mi.; **Water:** 0.1 sq. mi.

South Lawrence — Pop. Place
Lat: 44-14-56 N   **Long:** 103-46-09 W
Pop: 2,093 (1990); 1,886 (1980)   **Pop Density:** 5.0
Land: 422.4 sq. mi.; **Water:** 0.1 sq. mi.

Spearfish — City
ZIP: 57783   **Lat:** 44-29-19 N   **Long:** 103-50-49 W
Pop: 6,966 (1990); 5,251 (1980)   **Pop Density:** 1833.2
Land: 3.8 sq. mi.; **Water:** 0.0 sq. mi.   **Elev:** 3643 ft.
Founded 1876.
Name origin: For nearby Spearfish Creek.

Whitewood — City
ZIP: 57793   **Lat:** 44-27-41 N   **Long:** 103-38-24 W
Pop: 891 (1990); 821 (1980)   **Pop Density:** 1782.0
Land: 0.5 sq. mi.; **Water:** 0.0 sq. mi.   **Elev:** 3648 ft.
Platted 1888.
Name origin: For the numerous white-barked birch and aspen trees in the area.

SOUTH DAKOTA, Lincoln County

Lincoln County
County Seat: Canton (ZIP: 57013)

Pop: 15,427 (1990); 13,942 (1980)
Land: 578.1 sq. mi.; **Water:** 0.5 sq. mi.
Pop Density: 26.7
Area Code: 605

On the southeastern border of SD, south of Sioux Falls; created Dec 30, 1867 (prior to statehood) from Minnehaha County.

Name origin: For Abraham Lincoln (1809–65), sixteenth U.S. president.

Beresford — City
Lat: 43-05-04 N **Long:** 96-46-51 W
Pop: 349 (1990); 361 (1980) **Pop Density:** 698.0
Land: 0.5 sq. mi.; **Water:** 0.0 sq. mi. **Elev:** 1498 ft.
Part of the town is also in Union County.
Name origin: For Adm. Lord Charles Beresford (1846–1919), who had a financial interest in the local railroad. Originally called Paris.

Brooklyn — Township
Lat: 43-07-38 N **Long:** 96-51-45 W
Pop: 234 (1990); 259 (1980) **Pop Density:** 6.5
Land: 36.0 sq. mi.; **Water:** 0.0 sq. mi.

Canton — City
ZIP: 57013 **Lat:** 43-18-11 N **Long:** 96-34-51 W
Pop: 2,787 (1990); 2,886 (1980) **Pop Density:** 961.0
Land: 2.9 sq. mi.; **Water:** 0.0 sq. mi. **Elev:** 1300 ft.
Name origin: For Canton, China, because early settlers thought their town was located opposite that great Chinese city.

*Canton — Township
ZIP: 57013 **Lat:** 43-18-05 N **Long:** 96-37-21 W
Pop: 423 (1990); 441 (1980) **Pop Density:** 11.1
Land: 38.2 sq. mi.; **Water:** 0.0 sq. mi.

Dayton — Township
Lat: 43-22-50 N **Long:** 96-37-05 W
Pop: 460 (1990); 484 (1980) **Pop Density:** 10.3
Land: 44.7 sq. mi.; **Water:** 0.0 sq. mi.

Delapre — Township
Lat: 43-28-06 N **Long:** 96-50-09 W
Pop: 1,419 (1990); 995 (1980) **Pop Density:** 34.4
Land: 41.2 sq. mi.; **Water:** 0.0 sq. mi.

Delaware — Township
ZIP: 57039 **Lat:** 43-12-43 N **Long:** 96-51-31 W
Pop: 194 (1990); 223 (1980) **Pop Density:** 5.4
Land: 36.0 sq. mi.; **Water:** 0.0 sq. mi.

Eden — Township
Lat: 43-07-11 N **Long:** 96-31-07 W
Pop: 165 (1990); 220 (1980) **Pop Density:** 4.7
Land: 34.9 sq. mi.; **Water:** 0.0 sq. mi.

Fairview — Town
ZIP: 57027 **Lat:** 43-13-19 N **Long:** 96-29-20 W
Pop: 73 (1990); 90 (1980) **Pop Density:** 730.0
Land: 0.1 sq. mi.; **Water:** 0.0 sq. mi. **Elev:** 1213 ft.

*Fairview — Township
ZIP: 57027 **Lat:** 43-11-32 N **Long:** 96-31-10 W
Pop: 145 (1990); 155 (1980) **Pop Density:** 8.1
Land: 17.8 sq. mi.; **Water:** 0.2 sq. mi.

Grant — Township
Lat: 43-18-14 N **Long:** 96-51-37 W
Pop: 337 (1990); 391 (1980) **Pop Density:** 9.4
Land: 35.8 sq. mi.; **Water:** 0.0 sq. mi.

Harrisburg — Town
ZIP: 57032 **Lat:** 43-25-49 N **Long:** 96-41-44 W
Pop: 727 (1990); 558 (1980) **Pop Density:** 1817.5
Land: 0.4 sq. mi.; **Water:** 0.0 sq. mi. **Elev:** 1428 ft.

Highland — Township
Lat: 43-13-16 N **Long:** 96-37-06 W
Pop: 254 (1990); 289 (1980) **Pop Density:** 6.9
Land: 36.6 sq. mi.; **Water:** 0.0 sq. mi.

Hudson — Town
ZIP: 57034 **Lat:** 43-07-47 N **Long:** 96-27-19 W
Pop: 332 (1990); 388 (1980) **Pop Density:** 1106.7
Land: 0.3 sq. mi.; **Water:** 0.0 sq. mi. **Elev:** 1221 ft.
Settled 1868.
Name origin: For Hudson, IA, former home of early settlers.

La Valley — Township
ZIP: 57032 **Lat:** 43-23-29 N **Long:** 96-44-20 W
Pop: 410 (1990); 443 (1980) **Pop Density:** 11.5
Land: 35.7 sq. mi.; **Water:** 0.0 sq. mi.

Lennox — City
ZIP: 57039 **Lat:** 43-21-10 N **Long:** 96-53-47 W
Pop: 1,767 (1990); 1,827 (1980) **Pop Density:** 1472.5
Land: 1.2 sq. mi.; **Water:** 0.0 sq. mi. **Elev:** 1338 ft.
Settled 1879.
Name origin: For Ben Lennox, a Milwaukee railroad official.

Lincoln — Township
Lat: 43-12-50 N **Long:** 96-44-58 W
Pop: 221 (1990); 230 (1980) **Pop Density:** 6.1
Land: 36.1 sq. mi.; **Water:** 0.0 sq. mi.

Lynn — Township
Lat: 43-17-38 N **Long:** 96-44-12 W
Pop: 290 (1990); 289 (1980) **Pop Density:** 8.1
Land: 35.7 sq. mi.; **Water:** 0.0 sq. mi.

Norway — Township
Lat: 43-07-34 N **Long:** 96-37-38 W
Pop: 277 (1990); 305 (1980) **Pop Density:** 7.7
Land: 36.0 sq. mi.; **Water:** 0.0 sq. mi.

Perry — Township
ZIP: 57039 **Lat:** 43-23-19 N **Long:** 96-51-57 W
Pop: 554 (1990); 504 (1980) **Pop Density:** 16.0
Land: 34.7 sq. mi.; **Water:** 0.0 sq. mi.

Pleasant — Township
Lat: 43-07-28 N **Long:** 96-44-10 W
Pop: 382 (1990); 407 (1980) **Pop Density:** 10.8
Land: 35.5 sq. mi.; **Water:** 0.0 sq. mi.

Sioux Falls — City
ZIP: 57055 **Lat:** 43-29-55 N **Long:** 96-44-41 W
Pop: 1,409 (1990); 161 (1980) **Pop Density:** 828.8
Land: 1.7 sq. mi.; **Water:** 0.0 sq. mi. **Elev:** 1442 ft.
In southeastern SD on the Big Sioux River, 75 mi. north of Sioux City, IA. Largest city; settled 1857. Products include packaged meats, processed dairy foods, fabricated steel, electromagnetic equipment. Part of the town is also in Minnehaha County.
Name origin: For its location on the falls of the Big Sioux River.

Springdale — Township
Lat: 43-27-56 N **Long:** 96-39-48 W
Pop: 1,061 (1990); 919 (1980) **Pop Density:** 29.8
Land: 35.6 sq. mi.; **Water:** 0.2 sq. mi.

Tea — Town
Lat: 43-26-53 N **Long:** 96-50-14 W
Pop: 786 (1990); 729 (1980) **Pop Density:** 2620.0
Land: 0.3 sq. mi.; **Water:** 0.0 sq. mi. **Elev:** 1486 ft.
Name origin: For the fact that a postal conflict required a town meeting that went on until "tea time." Originally called Byron.

Worthing — Town
ZIP: 57077 **Lat:** 43-19-43 N **Long:** 96-45-53 W
Pop: 371 (1990); 388 (1980) **Pop Density:** 1236.7
Land: 0.3 sq. mi.; **Water:** 0.0 sq. mi. **Elev:** 1362 ft.

Lyman County
County Seat: Kennebec (ZIP: 57544)

Pop: 3,638 (1990); 3,864 (1980) **Pop Density:** 2.2
Land: 1640.1 sq. mi.; **Water:** 67.1 sq. mi. **Area Code:** 605
In south-central SD, southeast of Pierre; created Jan 8, 1873 (prior to statehood) from unorganized territory.
Name origin: For W. P. Lyman, member of the Dakota territorial legislature and first settler in Yankton County.

Applegate — Township
ZIP: 57568 **Lat:** 44-09-24 N **Long:** 100-04-31 W
Pop: 3 (1990); 4 (1980) **Pop Density:** 0.1
Land: 35.8 sq. mi.; **Water:** 0.0 sq. mi.

Bailey — Township
ZIP: 57569 **Lat:** 43-48-33 N **Long:** 99-40-51 W
Pop: 38 (1990); 53 (1980) **Pop Density:** 0.9
Land: 43.4 sq. mi.; **Water:** 0.1 sq. mi.

Black Dog — Pop. Place
Lat: 43-41-15 N **Long:** 99-34-24 W
Pop: 12 (1990) **Pop Density:** 0.3
Land: 34.9 sq. mi.; **Water:** 0.0 sq. mi.

Butte — Township
Lat: 43-47-51 N **Long:** 99-33-25 W
Pop: 49 (1990); 63 (1980) **Pop Density:** 1.2
Land: 40.8 sq. mi.; **Water:** 0.1 sq. mi.

Dorman — Township
ZIP: 57544 **Lat:** 43-58-30 N **Long:** 99-49-57 W
Pop: 17 (1990); 34 (1980) **Pop Density:** 0.5
Land: 32.7 sq. mi.; **Water:** 0.1 sq. mi.

Earling — Township
ZIP: 57544 **Lat:** 43-53-14 N **Long:** 99-56-48 W
Pop: 33 (1990); 50 (1980) **Pop Density:** 0.9
Land: 35.8 sq. mi.; **Water:** 0.1 sq. mi.

Fairland — Township
ZIP: 57569 **Lat:** 43-53-08 N **Long:** 99-28-27 W
Pop: 28 (1990); 23 (1980) **Pop Density:** 0.8
Land: 35.7 sq. mi.; **Water:** 0.1 sq. mi.

Hilmoe — Township
ZIP: 57568 **Lat:** 43-48-12 N **Long:** 100-09-44 W
Pop: 16 (1990); 37 (1980) **Pop Density:** 0.4
Land: 35.9 sq. mi.; **Water:** 0.0 sq. mi.

Hope — Township
ZIP: 57576 **Lat:** 43-58-54 N **Long:** 100-18-47 W
Pop: 17 (1990); 28 (1980) **Pop Density:** 0.5
Land: 36.1 sq. mi.; **Water:** 0.0 sq. mi.

Iona — Township
ZIP: 57542 **Lat:** 43-35-58 N **Long:** 99-26-24 W
Pop: 107 (1990); 120 (1980) **Pop Density:** 0.9
Land: 125.7 sq. mi.; **Water:** 12.1 sq. mi.

Kennebec — Town
ZIP: 57544 **Lat:** 43-54-15 N **Long:** 99-51-44 W
Pop: 284 (1990); 334 (1980) **Pop Density:** 355.0
Land: 0.8 sq. mi.; **Water:** 0.0 sq. mi. **Elev:** 1690 ft.
Established 1905.

*Kennebec — Township
ZIP: 57544 **Lat:** 43-53-25 N **Long:** 99-49-34 W
Pop: 36 (1990); 26 (1980) **Pop Density:** 1.0
Land: 34.9 sq. mi.; **Water:** 0.2 sq. mi.

Liberty — Township
ZIP: 57568 **Lat:** 43-48-23 N **Long:** 100-02-43 W
Pop: 21 (1990); 30 (1980) **Pop Density:** 0.6
Land: 35.8 sq. mi.; **Water:** 0.0 sq. mi.

Lower Brule — CDP
ZIP: 57548 **Lat:** 44-04-26 N **Long:** 99-34-56 W
Pop: 655 (1990) **Pop Density:** 1637.5
Land: 0.4 sq. mi.; **Water:** 0.0 sq. mi.

McClure — Pop. Place
ZIP: 57576 **Lat:** 44-08-52 N **Long:** 100-11-20 W
Pop: 9 (1990) **Pop Density:** 0.3
Land: 35.9 sq. mi.; **Water:** 0.1 sq. mi.

SOUTH DAKOTA, Lyman County

Moore Township
ZIP: 57568 Lat: 43-53-23 N Long: 100-11-15 W
Pop: 28 (1990); 30 (1980) Pop Density: 0.8
Land: 35.9 sq. mi.; Water: 0.0 sq. mi.

Morningside Township
Lat: 43-33-37 N Long: 99-34-24 W
Pop: 27 (1990); 26 (1980) Pop Density: 0.7
Land: 40.2 sq. mi.; Water: 0.0 sq. mi.

Northeast Lyman Pop. Place
Lat: 44-02-35 N Long: 99-47-59 W
Pop: 1,188 (1990); 1,037 (1980) Pop Density: 2.8
Land: 424.5 sq. mi.; Water: 40.6 sq. mi.

Oacoma Town
ZIP: 57365 Lat: 43-47-57 N Long: 99-23-03 W
Pop: 367 (1990); 289 (1980) Pop Density: 244.7
Land: 1.5 sq. mi.; Water: 1.7 sq. mi. Elev: 1390 ft.
Founded 1890.
Name origin: From a Sioux term meaning 'place between', referring to its location between the Missouri River and its bluffs.

*Oacoma Township
Lat: 43-48-45 N Long: 99-25-07 W
Pop: 59 (1990); 56 (1980) Pop Density: 1.0
Land: 59.8 sq. mi.; Water: 9.7 sq. mi.

Pleasant Township
ZIP: 57544 Lat: 43-57-23 N Long: 99-42-42 W
Pop: 10 (1990); 17 (1980) Pop Density: 0.3
Land: 33.0 sq. mi.; Water: 0.0 sq. mi.

Pratt Township
ZIP: 57568 Lat: 43-43-51 N Long: 100-09-38 W
Pop: 14 (1990); 15 (1980) Pop Density: 0.6
Land: 25.4 sq. mi.; Water: 0.3 sq. mi.

Presho City
ZIP: 57568 Lat: 43-54-25 N Long: 100-03-27 W
Pop: 654 (1990); 760 (1980) Pop Density: 934.3
Land: 0.7 sq. mi.; Water: 0.0 sq. mi. Elev: 1800 ft.
Settled 1905.
Name origin: For J.S. Presho, an early trader.

*Presho Township
ZIP: 57568 Lat: 43-53-28 N Long: 100-03-52 W
Pop: 39 (1990); 76 (1980) Pop Density: 1.1
Land: 35.4 sq. mi.; Water: 0.0 sq. mi.

Reliance Town
ZIP: 57569 Lat: 43-52-49 N Long: 99-36-08 W
Pop: 169 (1990); 190 (1980) Pop Density: 153.6
Land: 1.1 sq. mi.; Water: 0.1 sq. mi. Elev: 1796 ft.
Settled 1905.

*Reliance Township
ZIP: 57569 Lat: 43-53-18 N Long: 99-35-23 W
Pop: 80 (1990); 80 (1980) Pop Density: 2.3
Land: 34.7 sq. mi.; Water: 0.1 sq. mi.

Rex Township
ZIP: 57544 Lat: 43-53-35 N Long: 99-41-48 W
Pop: 42 (1990); 45 (1980) Pop Density: 1.2
Land: 35.8 sq. mi.; Water: 0.1 sq. mi.

Rose Township
ZIP: 57544 Lat: 43-48-10 N Long: 99-55-37 W
Pop: 29 (1990); 48 (1980) Pop Density: 0.8
Land: 35.8 sq. mi.; Water: 0.0 sq. mi.

Rowe Township
Lat: 44-08-42 N Long: 100-17-53 W
Pop: 12 (1990); 3 (1980) Pop Density: 0.3
Land: 35.5 sq. mi.; Water: 0.1 sq. mi.

Sioux Township
Lat: 43-46-29 N Long: 100-15-10 W
Pop: 20 (1990); 30 (1980) Pop Density: 0.4
Land: 56.3 sq. mi.; Water: 0.3 sq. mi.

South Lyman Pop. Place
Lat: 43-44-48 N Long: 99-50-29 W
Pop: 48 (1990); 7 (1980) Pop Density: 0.6
Land: 86.0 sq. mi.; Water: 0.7 sq. mi.

Stony Butte Township
ZIP: 57576 Lat: 44-03-34 N Long: 100-18-21 W
Pop: 20 (1990); 18 (1980) Pop Density: 0.6
Land: 35.6 sq. mi.; Water: 0.0 sq. mi.

Sylvia Township
ZIP: 57568 Lat: 43-43-35 N Long: 100-02-15 W
Pop: 15 (1990); 10 (1980) Pop Density: 0.6
Land: 26.3 sq. mi.; Water: 0.3 sq. mi.

Tracy Township
ZIP: 57568 Lat: 44-04-45 N Long: 100-11-11 W
Pop: 4 (1990); 10 (1980) Pop Density: 0.1
Land: 36.4 sq. mi.; Water: 0.1 sq. mi.

Vivian Township
ZIP: 57576 Lat: 43-53-29 N Long: 100-18-15 W
Pop: 143 (1990); 135 (1980) Pop Density: 4.0
Land: 36.1 sq. mi.; Water: 0.0 sq. mi.

Marshall County
County Seat: Britton (ZIP: 57430)

Pop: 4,844 (1990); 5,404 (1980) **Pop Density:** 5.8
Land: 838.9 sq. mi.; **Water:** 46.8 sq. mi. **Area Code:** 605

On the northeastern border of SD, northeast of Aberdeen; organized Mar 10, 1885 (prior to statehood) from Day County.

Name origin: For Marshall Vincent of NY, an early homesteader and one of the first Marshall County commissioners.

Britton — City
ZIP: 57430 Lat: 45-47-22 N Long: 97-44-58 W
Pop: 1,394 (1990); 1,590 (1980) Pop Density: 995.7
Land: 1.4 sq. mi.; Water: 0.0 sq. mi. Elev: 1358 ft.
Platted 1881.
Name origin: For Col. Issac Britton, the general manager of the Dakota and Great Southern Railroad.

Buffalo — Township
Lat: 45-35-53 N Long: 97-17-25 W
Pop: 111 (1990); 107 (1980) Pop Density: 3.9
Land: 28.6 sq. mi.; Water: 7.7 sq. mi.

Dayton — Township
Lat: 45-53-32 N Long: 97-54-39 W
Pop: 36 (1990); 48 (1980) Pop Density: 1.0
Land: 35.4 sq. mi.; Water: 0.4 sq. mi.

Dumarce — Township
ZIP: 57270 Lat: 45-47-01 N Long: 97-24-20 W
Pop: 71 (1990); 71 (1980) Pop Density: 2.6
Land: 27.4 sq. mi.; Water: 3.0 sq. mi.

Eden — Town
ZIP: 57232 Lat: 45-36-58 N Long: 97-25-12 W
Pop: 97 (1990); 142 (1980) Pop Density: 485.0
Land: 0.2 sq. mi.; Water: 0.0 sq. mi. Elev: 1836 ft.

*Eden — Township
ZIP: 57232 Lat: 45-37-31 N Long: 97-25-07 W
Pop: 110 (1990); 129 (1980) Pop Density: 3.4
Land: 32.3 sq. mi.; Water: 3.6 sq. mi.

Fort — Township
ZIP: 57232 Lat: 45-37-52 N Long: 97-32-59 W
Pop: 56 (1990); 73 (1980) Pop Density: 1.9
Land: 29.8 sq. mi.; Water: 6.0 sq. mi.

Hamilton — Township
Lat: 45-42-48 N Long: 97-32-57 W
Pop: 43 (1990); 65 (1980) Pop Density: 1.4
Land: 31.2 sq. mi.; Water: 4.2 sq. mi.

Hickman — Township
ZIP: 57454 Lat: 45-37-18 N Long: 97-47-42 W
Pop: 83 (1990); 96 (1980) Pop Density: 2.3
Land: 35.8 sq. mi.; Water: 0.1 sq. mi.

La Belle — Township
ZIP: 57270 Lat: 45-52-47 N Long: 97-24-32 W
Pop: 80 (1990); 110 (1980) Pop Density: 1.9
Land: 41.7 sq. mi.; Water: 0.6 sq. mi.

Lake — Township
Lat: 45-42-07 N Long: 97-25-07 W
Pop: 129 (1990); 127 (1980) Pop Density: 4.7
Land: 27.4 sq. mi.; Water: 8.6 sq. mi.

Lake City — Town
ZIP: 57247 Lat: 45-43-25 N Long: 97-24-48 W
Pop: 43 (1990); 46 (1980) Pop Density: 215.0
Land: 0.2 sq. mi.; Water: 0.0 sq. mi. Elev: 1864 ft.
Established 1914.
Name origin: For its location in the lake region of northeastern SD.

Langford — Town
ZIP: 57454 Lat: 45-36-08 N Long: 97-49-46 W
Pop: 298 (1990); 307 (1980) Pop Density: 993.3
Land: 0.3 sq. mi.; Water: 0.0 sq. mi. Elev: 1373 ft.
Name origin: For the original landowner, Sam Langford.

Lowell — Township
Lat: 45-42-49 N Long: 97-47-12 W
Pop: 81 (1990); 74 (1980) Pop Density: 2.2
Land: 36.2 sq. mi.; Water: 0.1 sq. mi.

McKinley — Township
ZIP: 57270 Lat: 45-46-19 N Long: 97-17-14 W
Pop: 57 (1990); 75 (1980) Pop Density: 1.7
Land: 34.4 sq. mi.; Water: 1.6 sq. mi.

Miller — Township
Lat: 45-48-29 N Long: 97-47-15 W
Pop: 209 (1990); 229 (1980) Pop Density: 6.1
Land: 34.3 sq. mi.; Water: 0.5 sq. mi.

Newark — Township
ZIP: 57430 Lat: 45-53-07 N Long: 97-47-01 W
Pop: 85 (1990); 91 (1980) Pop Density: 2.4
Land: 35.7 sq. mi.; Water: 0.1 sq. mi.

Newport — Township
ZIP: 57454 Lat: 45-37-56 N Long: 97-55-07 W
Pop: 96 (1990); 106 (1980) Pop Density: 2.8
Land: 34.5 sq. mi.; Water: 1.5 sq. mi.

Nordland — Township
ZIP: 57430 Lat: 45-49-56 N Long: 97-31-26 W
Pop: 31 (1990); 48 (1980) Pop Density: 1.3
Land: 23.4 sq. mi.; Water: 0.8 sq. mi.

Pleasant Valley — Township
Lat: 45-48-22 N Long: 97-40-11 W
Pop: 143 (1990); 174 (1980) Pop Density: 4.0
Land: 35.8 sq. mi.; Water: 0.2 sq. mi.

Red Iron Lake — Township
ZIP: 57247 Lat: 45-41-02 N Long: 97-17-14 W
Pop: 229 (1990); 188 (1980) Pop Density: 7.4
Land: 31.1 sq. mi.; Water: 4.8 sq. mi.

Sisseton — Township
Lat: 45-38-01 N Long: 97-39-59 W
Pop: 93 (1990); 100 (1980) Pop Density: 2.7
Land: 34.9 sq. mi.; Water: 1.0 sq. mi.

SOUTH DAKOTA, Marshall County

Stena Township
ZIP: 57430 Lat: 45-47-54 N Long: 97-54-21 W
Pop: 142 (1990); 169 (1980) Pop Density: 4.0
Land: 35.9 sq. mi.; Water: 0.2 sq. mi.

Veblen City
ZIP: 57270 Lat: 45-51-42 N Long: 97-17-12 W
Pop: 321 (1990); 368 (1980) Pop Density: 1070.0
Land: 0.3 sq. mi.; Water: 0.0 sq. mi. Elev: 1270 ft.
Founded 1900.
Name origin: For the first homesteader, J.E. Veblen.

*Veblen Township
ZIP: 57270 Lat: 45-52-16 N Long: 97-17-34 W
Pop: 236 (1990); 243 (1980) Pop Density: 5.0
Land: 47.5 sq. mi.; Water: 0.2 sq. mi.

Victor Township
Lat: 45-53-33 N Long: 97-32-22 W
Pop: 49 (1990); 91 (1980) Pop Density: 1.3
Land: 38.5 sq. mi.; Water: 0.3 sq. mi.

Waverly Township
Lat: 45-43-06 N Long: 97-40-01 W
Pop: 86 (1990); 94 (1980) Pop Density: 2.4
Land: 36.0 sq. mi.; Water: 0.1 sq. mi.

Weston Township
ZIP: 57421 Lat: 45-43-25 N Long: 97-55-37 W
Pop: 227 (1990); 191 (1980) Pop Density: 6.3
Land: 35.9 sq. mi.; Water: 0.2 sq. mi.

White Township
Lat: 45-53-05 N Long: 97-40-37 W
Pop: 182 (1990); 206 (1980) Pop Density: 5.1
Land: 35.6 sq. mi.; Water: 0.3 sq. mi.

Wismer Township
ZIP: 57430 Lat: 45-46-22 N Long: 97-32-55 W
Pop: 26 (1990); 46 (1980) Pop Density: 1.5
Land: 17.1 sq. mi.; Water: 0.7 sq. mi.

McCook County
County Seat: Salem (ZIP: 57058)

Pop: 5,688 (1990); 6,444 (1980) **Pop Density:** 9.9
Land: 574.6 sq. mi.; **Water:** 2.6 sq. mi. **Area Code:** 605
In southeastern SD, west of Sioux Falls; created Jan 8, 1873 (prior to statehood) from Hanson County.
Name origin: For Edwin S. McCook (1837–73), secretary of the Dakota Territory, killed in a political dispute.

Benton Township
Lat: 43-43-02 N Long: 97-32-52 W
Pop: 111 (1990); 133 (1980) Pop Density: 3.2
Land: 35.1 sq. mi.; Water: 0.2 sq. mi.

Bridgewater City
ZIP: 57319 Lat: 43-33-00 N Long: 97-29-54 W
Pop: 533 (1990); 653 (1980) Pop Density: 484.5
Land: 1.1 sq. mi.; Water: 0.0 sq. mi. Elev: 1410 ft.
Name origin: Named by the railroad workers, who had to carry their drinking water across a bridge. Originally called Nation.

*Bridgewater Township
ZIP: 57319 Lat: 43-32-33 N Long: 97-33-14 W
Pop: 173 (1990); 173 (1980) Pop Density: 5.0
Land: 34.6 sq. mi.; Water: 0.1 sq. mi.

Brookfield Township
ZIP: 57058 Lat: 43-48-50 N Long: 97-18-41 W
Pop: 141 (1990); 192 (1980) Pop Density: 3.9
Land: 36.4 sq. mi.; Water: 0.0 sq. mi.

Canistota City
ZIP: 57012 Lat: 43-35-51 N Long: 97-17-29 W
Pop: 608 (1990); 626 (1980) Pop Density: 1013.3
Land: 0.6 sq. mi.; Water: 0.0 sq. mi. Elev: 1549 ft.
Founded 1883.
Name origin: For Canastota, NY, from an Indian term meaning 'board on the water'. A spelling error was allowed to remain.

*Canistota Township
ZIP: 57012 Lat: 43-37-51 N Long: 97-18-27 W
Pop: 132 (1990); 194 (1980) Pop Density: 3.7
Land: 35.7 sq. mi.; Water: 0.0 sq. mi.

Emery Township
Lat: 43-37-45 N Long: 97-25-35 W
Pop: 108 (1990); 157 (1980) Pop Density: 3.0
Land: 35.8 sq. mi.; Water: 0.2 sq. mi.

Grant Township
Lat: 43-32-27 N Long: 97-18-23 W
Pop: 175 (1990); 201 (1980) Pop Density: 4.8
Land: 36.1 sq. mi.; Water: 0.0 sq. mi.

Greenland Township
Lat: 43-37-55 N Long: 97-11-30 W
Pop: 183 (1990); 182 (1980) Pop Density: 5.3
Land: 34.8 sq. mi.; Water: 1.0 sq. mi.

Jefferson Township
Lat: 43-37-38 N Long: 97-32-44 W
Pop: 132 (1990); 130 (1980) Pop Density: 3.7
Land: 35.4 sq. mi.; Water: 0.3 sq. mi.

Montrose City
ZIP: 57048 Lat: 43-42-05 N Long: 97-10-58 W
Pop: 420 (1990); 396 (1980) Pop Density: 1050.0
Land: 0.4 sq. mi.; Water: 0.0 sq. mi. Elev: 1480 ft.
Settled 1880.
Name origin: For *The Legend of Montrose* (1819), a novel by Sir Walter Scott (1771–1832).

American Places Dictionary — SOUTH DAKOTA, McPherson County

*Montrose Township
ZIP: 57048 **Lat:** 43-42-46 N **Long:** 97-11-19 W
Pop: 219 (1990); 201 (1980) **Pop Density:** 6.2
Land: 35.5 sq. mi.; **Water:** 0.0 sq. mi.

Pearl Township
Lat: 43-48-26 N **Long:** 97-33-17 W
Pop: 100 (1990); 164 (1980) **Pop Density:** 2.8
Land: 36.3 sq. mi.; **Water:** 0.0 sq. mi.

Ramsey Township
ZIP: 57048 **Lat:** 43-48-07 N **Long:** 97-11-13 W
Pop: 136 (1990); 148 (1980) **Pop Density:** 3.8
Land: 36.1 sq. mi.; **Water:** 0.3 sq. mi.

Richland Township
Lat: 43-42-57 N **Long:** 97-18-06 W
Pop: 199 (1990); 219 (1980) **Pop Density:** 5.5
Land: 35.9 sq. mi.; **Water:** 0.0 sq. mi.

Salem City
ZIP: 57058 **Lat:** 43-43-27 N **Long:** 97-23-19 W
Pop: 1,289 (1990); 1,486 (1980) **Pop Density:** 1289.0
Land: 1.0 sq. mi.; **Water:** 0.0 sq. mi. **Elev:** 1527 ft.
Name origin: For Salem, MA, former home of the first postmaster, O.S. Pender.

*Salem Township
ZIP: 57058 **Lat:** 43-43-05 N **Long:** 97-25-34 W
Pop: 182 (1990); 207 (1980) **Pop Density:** 5.2
Land: 34.9 sq. mi.; **Water:** 0.4 sq. mi.

Spencer City
ZIP: 57374 **Lat:** 43-43-40 N **Long:** 97-35-30 W
Pop: 317 (1990); 380 (1980) **Pop Density:** 792.5
Land: 0.4 sq. mi.; **Water:** 0.0 sq. mi. **Elev:** 1381 ft.
Settled 1880s.
Name origin: For Omaha Railroad official Hugh Spencer.

Spring Valley Township
Lat: 43-32-18 N **Long:** 97-11-44 W
Pop: 232 (1990); 260 (1980) **Pop Density:** 6.5
Land: 35.8 sq. mi.; **Water:** 0.0 sq. mi.

Sun Prairie Township
ZIP: 57058 **Lat:** 43-48-07 N **Long:** 97-26-07 W
Pop: 152 (1990); 159 (1980) **Pop Density:** 4.2
Land: 36.5 sq. mi.; **Water:** 0.0 sq. mi.

Union Township
Lat: 43-32-28 N **Long:** 97-26-15 W
Pop: 146 (1990); 183 (1980) **Pop Density:** 4.0
Land: 36.2 sq. mi.; **Water:** 0.0 sq. mi.

McPherson County
County Seat: Leola (ZIP: 57456)

Pop: 3,228 (1990); 4,027 (1980) **Pop Density:** 2.8
Land: 1137.0 sq. mi.; **Water:** 14.9 sq. mi. **Area Code:** 605
On the central northern border of SD, northwest of Aberdeen; created Jan 8, 1873 (prior to statehood) from Buffalo County.
Name origin: For Gen. James Birdseye McPherson (1828–64), commander of the Union Army of the Tennessee during the Civil War.

Carl Township
Lat: 45-48-45 N **Long:** 98-47-34 W
Pop: 43 (1990); 63 (1980) **Pop Density:** 1.2
Land: 35.2 sq. mi.; **Water:** 0.0 sq. mi.

Central McPherson Pop. Place
Lat: 45-44-36 N **Long:** 99-06-41 W
Pop: 753 (1990); 922 (1980) **Pop Density:** 1.3
Land: 599.2 sq. mi.; **Water:** 9.5 sq. mi.

Eureka City
ZIP: 57437 **Lat:** 45-46-07 N **Long:** 99-37-22 W
Pop: 1,197 (1990); 1,360 (1980) **Pop Density:** 1710.0
Land: 0.7 sq. mi.; **Water:** 0.1 sq. mi. **Elev:** 1891 ft.
Settled 1887.
Name origin: From the Greek term meaning 'I have found it.'

Hillsview Town
ZIP: 57437 **Lat:** 45-39-54 N **Long:** 99-33-34 W
Pop: 4 (1990); 9 (1980) **Pop Density:** 6.7
Land: 0.6 sq. mi.; **Water:** 0.0 sq. mi. **Elev:** 1851 ft.

Hoffman Township
ZIP: 57456 **Lat:** 45-48-06 N **Long:** 99-02-09 W
Pop: 23 (1990); 45 (1980) **Pop Density:** 0.7
Land: 35.2 sq. mi.; **Water:** 0.5 sq. mi.

Leola City
ZIP: 57456 **Lat:** 45-43-16 N **Long:** 98-56-17 W
Pop: 521 (1990); 645 (1980) **Pop Density:** 744.3
Land: 0.7 sq. mi.; **Water:** 0.0 sq. mi. **Elev:** 1596 ft.
Name origin: For Leola Hayes, daughter of a pioneer family.

Long Lake Town
Lat: 45-51-22 N **Long:** 99-12-22 W
Pop: 64 (1990); 117 (1980) **Pop Density:** 213.3
Land: 0.3 sq. mi.; **Water:** 0.0 sq. mi. **Elev:** 1950 ft.

Wachter Township
Lat: 45-54-14 N **Long:** 98-47-11 W
Pop: 39 (1990); 68 (1980) **Pop Density:** 1.1
Land: 34.5 sq. mi.; **Water:** 0.3 sq. mi.

Wacker Township
ZIP: 57457 **Lat:** 45-53-50 N **Long:** 99-02-10 W
Pop: 22 (1990); 29 (1980) **Pop Density:** 0.6
Land: 34.7 sq. mi.; **Water:** 1.1 sq. mi.

Weber Township
Lat: 45-53-26 N **Long:** 98-54-11 W
Pop: 93 (1990); 113 (1980) **Pop Density:** 2.5
Land: 36.6 sq. mi.; **Water:** 0.1 sq. mi.

West McPherson Pop. Place
Lat: 45-45-35 N **Long:** 99-33-44 W
Pop: 457 (1990); 634 (1980) **Pop Density:** 1.3
Land: 359.0 sq. mi.; **Water:** 3.2 sq. mi.

Wetonka
Town
Lat: 45-37-28 N **Long:** 98-46-11 W
Pop: 12 (1990); 22 (1980) **Pop Density:** 60.0
Land: 0.2 sq. mi.; **Water:** 0.0 sq. mi. **Elev:** 1471 ft.
Name origin: From an Indian term meaning 'to grow big.'

Meade County
County Seat: Sturgis (ZIP: 57785)

Pop: 21,878 (1990); 20,717 (1980) **Pop Density:** 6.3
Land: 3470.8 sq. mi.; **Water:** 11.8 sq. mi. **Area Code:** 605
In west-central SD, north of Rapid City; created Feb 7, 1889 from Lawrence County.
Name origin: For Fort Meade, named for Gen. George Gordon Meade (1815–72), officer in the Mexican-American War and the Civil War, Union commander who defeated Gen. Lee at Gettysburg.

Belle Fourche-Cheyenne Valleys
Pop. Place
Lat: 44-27-33 N **Long:** 102-43-21 W
Pop: 5,804 (1990); 6,451 (1980) **Pop Density:** 3.4
Land: 1723.6 sq. mi.; **Water:** 6.6 sq. mi.

Blackhawk
CDP
ZIP: 57718 **Lat:** 44-09-06 N **Long:** 103-18-54 W
Pop: 1,995 (1990); 1,608 (1980) **Pop Density:** 906.8
Land: 2.2 sq. mi.; **Water:** 0.0 sq. mi.

Eagle
Township
Lat: 44-59-28 N **Long:** 102-46-14 W
Pop: 12 (1990); 16 (1980) **Pop Density:** 0.3
Land: 36.2 sq. mi.; **Water:** 0.2 sq. mi.

Ellsworth Air Force Base
Military Facility
Lat: 44-08-53 N **Long:** 103-04-38 W
Pop: 4,330 (1990); 4,766 (1980) **Pop Density:** 3330.8
Land: 1.3 sq. mi.; **Water:** 0.0 sq. mi.
Part of the facility is also in Pennington County.

Faith
City
ZIP: 57626 **Lat:** 45-01-33 N **Long:** 102-02-11 W
Pop: 548 (1990); 576 (1980) **Pop Density:** 421.5
Land: 1.3 sq. mi.; **Water:** 0.0 sq. mi. **Elev:** 2575 ft.
Name origin: Believed to be for Faith Rockefeller, wife of an important Milwaukee Railroad stockholder.

Howard
Township
Lat: 44-38-13 N **Long:** 102-03-37 W
Pop: 13 (1990); 13 (1980) **Pop Density:** 0.4
Land: 34.9 sq. mi.; **Water:** 0.2 sq. mi.

Lakeside
Township
Lat: 44-12-07 N **Long:** 102-34-43 W
Pop: 50 (1990); 55 (1980) **Pop Density:** 0.8
Land: 63.4 sq. mi.; **Water:** 0.0 sq. mi.

North Meade
Pop. Place
Lat: 44-51-49 N **Long:** 102-26-49 W
Pop: 447 (1990); 493 (1980) **Pop Density:** 0.5
Land: 990.1 sq. mi.; **Water:** 3.6 sq. mi.

Smithville
Township
Lat: 44-13-12 N **Long:** 102-25-44 W
Pop: 3 (1990) **Pop Density:** 0.1
Land: 52.6 sq. mi.; **Water:** 0.0 sq. mi.

Southwest Meade
Pop. Place
Lat: 44-20-49 N **Long:** 103-22-31 W
Pop: 9,640 (1990); 7,861 (1980) **Pop Density:** 19.5
Land: 495.2 sq. mi.; **Water:** 1.0 sq. mi.

Sturgis
City
ZIP: 57785 **Lat:** 44-24-41 N **Long:** 103-30-52 W
Pop: 5,330 (1990); 5,184 (1980) **Pop Density:** 2050.0
Land: 2.6 sq. mi.; **Water:** 0.0 sq. mi. **Elev:** 3440 ft.
Name origin: For Lt. J.G. Sturgis, killed in 1876 in the battle of Little Bighorn.

Union
Township
Lat: 44-38-49 N **Long:** 102-10-19 W
Pop: 15 (1990); 28 (1980) **Pop Density:** 0.4
Land: 35.1 sq. mi.; **Water:** 0.2 sq. mi.

Upper Red Owl
Township
ZIP: 57777 **Lat:** 44-43-56 N **Long:** 102-39-22 W
Pop: 16 (1990); 40 (1980) **Pop Density:** 0.4
Land: 35.9 sq. mi.; **Water:** 0.0 sq. mi.

Mellette County
County Seat: White River (ZIP: 57579)

Pop: 2,137 (1990); 2,249 (1980)　　　　　　　　　　**Pop Density:** 1.6
Land: 1306.6 sq. mi.; **Water:** 3.3 sq. mi.　　　　　**Area Code:** 605
In south-central SD, south of Pierre; organized May 25, 1911 from Tripp County.
Name origin: For Arthur C. Mellette (1842–96), first governor of SD (1889–93).

Bad Nation　　　　　　　　　　　Township
ZIP: 57585　　　　**Lat:** 43-36-11 N **Long:** 100-20-56 W
Pop: 44 (1990); 35 (1980)　　　　**Pop Density:** 0.6
Land: 72.3 sq. mi.; **Water:** 0.0 sq. mi.

Blackpipe　　　　　　　　　　　Township
ZIP: 57560　　　　**Lat:** 43-25-41 N **Long:** 101-05-57 W
Pop: 52 (1990); 62 (1980)　　　　**Pop Density:** 1.4
Land: 36.0 sq. mi.; **Water:** 0.1 sq. mi.

Butte　　　　　　　　　　　　　Township
　　　　　　　　　　　Lat: 43-26-22 N **Long:** 100-23-22 W
Pop: 2 (1990); 8 (1980)　　　　　**Pop Density:** 0.1
Land: 36.6 sq. mi.; **Water:** 0.1 sq. mi.

Cedarbutte　　　　　　　　　　Pop. Place
　　　　　　　　　　　Lat: 43-36-27 N **Long:** 101-08-17 W
Pop: 118 (1990); 120 (1980)　　　**Pop Density:** 2.3
Land: 50.5 sq. mi.; **Water:** 0.1 sq. mi.　　**Elev:** 2359 ft.

Central Mellette　　　　　　　　Pop. Place
　　　　　　　　　　　Lat: 43-34-54 N **Long:** 100-44-47 W
Pop: 694 (1990); 618 (1980)　　　**Pop Density:** 1.6
Land: 444.4 sq. mi.; **Water:** 0.8 sq. mi.

Cody　　　　　　　　　　　　　Township
ZIP: 57579　　　　**Lat:** 43-39-03 N **Long:** 100-31-33 W
Pop: 43 (1990); 51 (1980)　　　　**Pop Density:** 0.6
Land: 73.3 sq. mi.; **Water:** 0.0 sq. mi.

Corn Creek　　　　　　　　　　Township
ZIP: 57560　　　　**Lat:** 43-31-30 N **Long:** 101-08-16 W
Pop: 69 (1990); 83 (1980)　　　　**Pop Density:** 1.4
Land: 50.5 sq. mi.; **Water:** 0.0 sq. mi.

Fairview　　　　　　　　　　　Township
　　　　　　　　　　　Lat: 43-26-28 N **Long:** 100-31-06 W
Pop: 27 (1990); 47 (1980)　　　　**Pop Density:** 0.7
Land: 37.1 sq. mi.; **Water:** 0.2 sq. mi.

Mosher　　　　　　　　　　　　Township
　　　　　　　　　　　Lat: 43-25-54 N **Long:** 100-16-32 W
Pop: 27 (1990); 42 (1980)　　　　**Pop Density:** 0.8
Land: 35.9 sq. mi.; **Water:** 0.2 sq. mi.

New Surprise Valley　　　　　　　Township
　　　　　　　　　　　Lat: 43-31-02 N **Long:** 101-00-17 W
Pop: 3 (1990)　　　　　　　　　**Pop Density:** 0.1
Land: 35.6 sq. mi.; **Water:** 0.1 sq. mi.

Norris　　　　　　　　　　　　Township
ZIP: 57560　　　　**Lat:** 43-26-07 N **Long:** 101-11-26 W
Pop: 171 (1990); 213 (1980)　　　**Pop Density:** 8.1
Land: 21.2 sq. mi.; **Water:** 0.1 sq. mi.

Prospect　　　　　　　　　　　Township
　　　　　　　　　　　Lat: 43-41-12 N **Long:** 101-04-58 W
Pop: 14 (1990); 22 (1980)　　　　**Pop Density:** 0.2
Land: 85.7 sq. mi.; **Water:** 0.4 sq. mi.

Red Fish　　　　　　　　　　　Township
　　　　　　　　　　　Lat: 43-47-15 N **Long:** 101-00-08 W
Pop: 32 (1990); 35 (1980)　　　　**Pop Density:** 0.7
Land: 43.3 sq. mi.; **Water:** 0.1 sq. mi.

Ring Thunder　　　　　　　　　Township
ZIP: 57579　　　　**Lat:** 43-25-45 N **Long:** 100-52-14 W
Pop: 24 (1990); 17 (1980)　　　　**Pop Density:** 0.7
Land: 36.1 sq. mi.; **Water:** 0.2 sq. mi.

Riverside　　　　　　　　　　　Township
ZIP: 57585　　　　**Lat:** 43-41-03 N **Long:** 100-21-54 W
Pop: 24 (1990); 27 (1980)　　　　**Pop Density:** 0.4
Land: 55.5 sq. mi.; **Water:** 0.3 sq. mi.

Rocky Ford　　　　　　　　　　Township
　　　　　　　　　　　Lat: 43-46-24 N **Long:** 101-08-18 W
Pop: 16 (1990); 10 (1980)　　　　**Pop Density:** 0.3
Land: 50.3 sq. mi.; **Water:** 0.1 sq. mi.

Rosebud　　　　　　　　　　　Township
　　　　　　　　　　　Lat: 43-31-35 N **Long:** 100-21-15 W
Pop: 48 (1990); 48 (1980)　　　　**Pop Density:** 0.7
Land: 71.6 sq. mi.; **Water:** 0.2 sq. mi.

Running Bird　　　　　　　　　Township
　　　　　　　　　　　Lat: 43-36-20 N **Long:** 100-59-39 W
Pop: 28 (1990); 40 (1980)　　　　**Pop Density:** 0.8
Land: 36.1 sq. mi.; **Water:** 0.0 sq. mi.

Surprise Valley　　　　　　　　Township
　　　　　　　　　　　Lat: 43-25-49 N **Long:** 100-58-53 W
Pop: 33 (1990); 47 (1980)　　　　**Pop Density:** 1.0
Land: 33.7 sq. mi.; **Water:** 0.2 sq. mi.

White River　　　　　　　　　　City
ZIP: 57579　　　　**Lat:** 43-34-02 N **Long:** 100-44-39 W
Pop: 595 (1990); 561 (1980)　　　**Pop Density:** 1190.0
Land: 0.5 sq. mi.; **Water:** 0.0 sq. mi.　　**Elev:** 2135 ft.
Founded 1911.
Name origin: For the adjacent White River.

Wood　　　　　　　　　　　　　Town
ZIP: 57585　　　　**Lat:** 43-29-48 N **Long:** 100-28-47 W
Pop: 73 (1990); 134 (1980)　　　　**Pop Density:** 365.0
Land: 0.2 sq. mi.; **Water:** 0.0 sq. mi.
Founded 1910.
Name origin: For founder A.K. Wood.

SOUTH DAKOTA, Miner County   American Places Dictionary

> ## Miner County
> **County Seat: Howard (ZIP: 57349)**
>
> **Pop:** 3,272 (1990); 3,739 (1980) **Pop Density:** 5.7
> **Land:** 570.4 sq. mi.; **Water:** 1.7 sq. mi. **Area Code:** 605
> In east-central SD, northwest of Sioux Falls; created Jan 8, 1873 (prior to statehood) from Hanson County.
> **Name origin:** For Capt. Nelson Miner (1827–79) and Ephraim Miner (1833–?), members of the Dakota Territory legislature when the county was formed.

Adams   Township
Lat: 44-04-24 N **Long:** 97-32-25 W
Pop: 143 (1990); 176 (1980) **Pop Density:** 4.0
Land: 36.0 sq. mi.; **Water:** 0.0 sq. mi.

Beaver   Township
ZIP: 57337 **Lat:** 43-54-11 N **Long:** 97-47-20 W
Pop: 78 (1990); 108 (1980) **Pop Density:** 2.2
Land: 35.4 sq. mi.; **Water:** 0.7 sq. mi.

Belleview   Township
ZIP: 57349 **Lat:** 44-08-43 N **Long:** 97-26-14 W
Pop: 100 (1990); 129 (1980) **Pop Density:** 2.8
Land: 35.2 sq. mi.; **Water:** 0.0 sq. mi.

Canova   Town
ZIP: 57321 **Lat:** 43-52-50 N **Long:** 97-30-10 W
Pop: 172 (1990); 194 (1980) **Pop Density:** 573.3
Land: 0.3 sq. mi.; **Water:** 0.0 sq. mi. **Elev:** 1523 ft.
Settled 1883.
Name origin: For Antonio Canova (1757–1822), a famous Italian sculptor.

*Canova   Township
ZIP: 57321 **Lat:** 43-53-36 N **Long:** 97-33-08 W
Pop: 102 (1990); 106 (1980) **Pop Density:** 2.8
Land: 35.8 sq. mi.; **Water:** 0.0 sq. mi.

Carthage   City
ZIP: 57323 **Lat:** 44-10-07 N **Long:** 97-42-50 W
Pop: 221 (1990); 274 (1980) **Pop Density:** 147.3
Land: 1.5 sq. mi.; **Water:** 0.0 sq. mi. **Elev:** 1430 ft.
Established early 1880s.
Name origin: For Carthage, NY.

*Carthage   Township
ZIP: 57323 **Lat:** 44-09-01 N **Long:** 97-40-04 W
Pop: 52 (1990); 61 (1980) **Pop Density:** 1.6
Land: 33.1 sq. mi.; **Water:** 0.3 sq. mi.

Clearwater   Township
ZIP: 57349 **Lat:** 43-58-11 N **Long:** 97-25-50 W
Pop: 186 (1990); 220 (1980) **Pop Density:** 5.2
Land: 36.0 sq. mi.; **Water:** 0.0 sq. mi.

Clinton   Township
ZIP: 57337 **Lat:** 43-59-03 N **Long:** 97-47-01 W
Pop: 132 (1990); 181 (1980) **Pop Density:** 3.7
Land: 35.9 sq. mi.; **Water:** 0.1 sq. mi.

Grafton   Township
ZIP: 57323 **Lat:** 44-08-46 N **Long:** 97-33-11 W
Pop: 114 (1990); 133 (1980) **Pop Density:** 3.3
Land: 34.9 sq. mi.; **Water:** 0.0 sq. mi.

Green Valley   Township
Lat: 44-03-33 N **Long:** 97-39-54 W
Pop: 62 (1990); 93 (1980) **Pop Density:** 1.7
Land: 35.9 sq. mi.; **Water:** 0.0 sq. mi.

Henden   Township
ZIP: 57349 **Lat:** 44-03-40 N **Long:** 97-25-41 W
Pop: 159 (1990); 158 (1980) **Pop Density:** 4.4
Land: 36.0 sq. mi.; **Water:** 0.0 sq. mi.

Howard   City
ZIP: 57349 **Lat:** 44-00-42 N **Long:** 97-31-23 W
Pop: 1,156 (1990); 1,169 (1980) **Pop Density:** 1284.4
Land: 0.9 sq. mi.; **Water:** 0.0 sq. mi. **Elev:** 1572 ft.
Name origin: For the son of Judge J.D. Farmer, the original townsite owner, who died while a young man.

*Howard   Township
ZIP: 57349 **Lat:** 43-58-48 N **Long:** 97-33-11 W
Pop: 129 (1990); 126 (1980) **Pop Density:** 3.9
Land: 32.8 sq. mi.; **Water:** 0.0 sq. mi.

Miner   Township
ZIP: 57337 **Lat:** 44-03-56 N **Long:** 97-47-15 W
Pop: 78 (1990); 97 (1980) **Pop Density:** 2.2
Land: 36.0 sq. mi.; **Water:** 0.1 sq. mi.

Redstone   Township
ZIP: 57323 **Lat:** 44-08-49 N **Long:** 97-46-48 W
Pop: 45 (1990); 50 (1980) **Pop Density:** 1.3
Land: 34.8 sq. mi.; **Water:** 0.0 sq. mi.

Rock Creek   Township
ZIP: 57321 **Lat:** 43-53-38 N **Long:** 97-40-17 W
Pop: 127 (1990); 172 (1980) **Pop Density:** 3.5
Land: 35.9 sq. mi.; **Water:** 0.2 sq. mi.

Roswell   Town
Lat: 43-59-56 N **Long:** 97-42-03 W
Pop: 19 (1990); 19 (1980) **Pop Density:** 13.6
Land: 1.4 sq. mi.; **Water:** 0.0 sq. mi. **Elev:** 1405 ft.
Name origin: Named in 1883 for Roswell Miller, Milwaukee Railroad president.

*Roswell   Township
Lat: 43-58-53 N **Long:** 97-39-50 W
Pop: 64 (1990); 88 (1980) **Pop Density:** 1.9
Land: 34.3 sq. mi.; **Water:** 0.3 sq. mi.

Vermillion   Township
Lat: 43-53-22 N **Long:** 97-25-57 W
Pop: 105 (1990); 157 (1980) **Pop Density:** 2.9
Land: 36.0 sq. mi.; **Water:** 0.0 sq. mi.

Vilas
Town
ZIP: 57349 **Lat:** 44-00-30 N **Long:** 97-35-44 W
Pop: 28 (1990); 28 (1980) **Pop Density:** 12.2
Land: 2.3 sq. mi.; **Water:** 0.0 sq. mi. **Elev:** 1478 ft.
Established 1883.
Name origin: For W.F. Vilas, a U.S. Postmaster General.

Minnehaha County
County Seat: Sioux Falls (ZIP: 57102)

Pop: 123,809 (1990); 109,435 (1980) **Pop Density:** 153.0
Land: 809.2 sq. mi.; **Water:** 4.6 sq. mi. **Area Code:** 605
On the southeastern border of SD; original county; organized Apr 5, 1862 (prior to statehood) from Big Sioux, a territorial county.
Name origin: Siouan, literally 'waterfall,' popularly 'laughing water.'

Baltic
Town
ZIP: 57003 **Lat:** 43-45-34 N **Long:** 96-44-18 W
Pop: 666 (1990); 679 (1980) **Pop Density:** 1332.0
Land: 0.5 sq. mi.; **Water:** 0.0 sq. mi. **Elev:** 1510 ft.
Founded 1881.
Name origin: For the Baltic Sea.

Benton
Township
Lat: 43-37-55 N **Long:** 96-49-40 W
Pop: 630 (1990); 544 (1980) **Pop Density:** 17.8
Land: 35.4 sq. mi.; **Water:** 0.0 sq. mi.

Brandon
City
Lat: 43-35-28 N **Long:** 96-34-40 W
Pop: 3,543 (1990); 2,589 (1980) **Pop Density:** 1221.7
Land: 2.9 sq. mi.; **Water:** 0.0 sq. mi.

*Brandon
Township
Lat: 43-38-01 N **Long:** 96-35-36 W
Pop: 612 (1990); 624 (1980) **Pop Density:** 18.0
Land: 34.0 sq. mi.; **Water:** 0.1 sq. mi.

Buffalo
Township
Lat: 43-47-52 N **Long:** 97-04-25 W
Pop: 238 (1990); 260 (1980) **Pop Density:** 6.9
Land: 34.7 sq. mi.; **Water:** 1.1 sq. mi.

Burk
Township
Lat: 43-48-19 N **Long:** 96-49-44 W
Pop: 306 (1990); 339 (1980) **Pop Density:** 8.5
Land: 36.0 sq. mi.; **Water:** 0.0 sq. mi.

Clear Lake
Township
Lat: 43-43-27 N **Long:** 97-03-42 W
Pop: 175 (1990); 195 (1980) **Pop Density:** 4.9
Land: 35.5 sq. mi.; **Water:** 0.6 sq. mi.

Colton
City
ZIP: 57018 **Lat:** 43-47-10 N **Long:** 96-55-37 W
Pop: 657 (1990); 757 (1980) **Pop Density:** 938.6
Land: 0.7 sq. mi.; **Water:** 0.0 sq. mi. **Elev:** 1605 ft.
Name origin: For railroad builder J. E. Colton in 1898 after he donated a park to the community.

Crooks
Town
ZIP: 57020 **Lat:** 43-39-36 N **Long:** 96-48-26 W
Pop: 671 (1990); 594 (1980) **Pop Density:** 1118.3
Land: 0.6 sq. mi.; **Water:** 0.0 sq. mi. **Elev:** 1592 ft.
Name origin: For W.A. Crooks, the town's first postmaster.

Dell Rapids
City
ZIP: 57022 **Lat:** 43-49-29 N **Long:** 96-42-44 W
Pop: 2,484 (1990); 2,389 (1980) **Pop Density:** 1461.2
Land: 1.7 sq. mi.; **Water:** 0.0 sq. mi. **Elev:** 1498 ft.
Incorporated 1871.

*Dell Rapids
Township
ZIP: 57022 **Lat:** 43-48-16 N **Long:** 96-42-29 W
Pop: 338 (1990); 463 (1980) **Pop Density:** 9.9
Land: 34.2 sq. mi.; **Water:** 0.0 sq. mi.

Edison
Township
ZIP: 57030 **Lat:** 43-43-03 N **Long:** 96-35-26 W
Pop: 346 (1990); 389 (1980) **Pop Density:** 9.6
Land: 36.1 sq. mi.; **Water:** 0.0 sq. mi.

Garretson
City
ZIP: 57030 **Lat:** 43-43-00 N **Long:** 96-30-01 W
Pop: 924 (1990); 963 (1980) **Pop Density:** 924.0
Land: 1.0 sq. mi.; **Water:** 0.0 sq. mi. **Elev:** 1481 ft.
Incorporated 1891.
Name origin: For A.S. Garretson, Sioux City banker.

Grand Meadow
Township
ZIP: 57033 **Lat:** 43-43-08 N **Long:** 96-56-41 W
Pop: 268 (1990); 313 (1980) **Pop Density:** 7.5
Land: 35.6 sq. mi.; **Water:** 0.1 sq. mi.

Hartford
City
ZIP: 57033 **Lat:** 43-37-24 N **Long:** 96-56-41 W
Pop: 1,262 (1990); 1,207 (1980) **Pop Density:** 1262.0
Land: 1.0 sq. mi.; **Water:** 0.0 sq. mi. **Elev:** 1568 ft.
Name origin: Named in 1881 for Hartford, CT, the former home of early settlers.

*Hartford
Township
ZIP: 57033 **Lat:** 43-38-16 N **Long:** 96-56-42 W
Pop: 542 (1990); 421 (1980) **Pop Density:** 15.6
Land: 34.7 sq. mi.; **Water:** 0.2 sq. mi.

Highland
Township
Lat: 43-48-03 N **Long:** 96-29-23 W
Pop: 164 (1990); 235 (1980) **Pop Density:** 6.9
Land: 23.7 sq. mi.; **Water:** 0.0 sq. mi.

SOUTH DAKOTA, Minnehaha County

Humboldt
Town
ZIP: 57035   Lat: 43-38-41 N   Long: 97-04-26 W
Pop: 468 (1990); 487 (1980)   Pop Density: 780.0
Land: 0.6 sq. mi.; Water: 0.0 sq. mi.   Elev: 1710 ft.
Founded 1880s.
Name origin: For Baron Alexander von Humboldt (1769–1859), the famous German naturalist and explorer.

*Humboldt
Township
ZIP: 57035   Lat: 43-38-16 N   Long: 97-04-11 W
Pop: 318 (1990); 309 (1980)   Pop Density: 9.1
Land: 34.9 sq. mi.; Water: 0.7 sq. mi.

Logan
Township
Lat: 43-48-15 N   Long: 96-35-28 W
Pop: 277 (1990); 287 (1980)   Pop Density: 7.8
Land: 35.6 sq. mi.; Water: 0.0 sq. mi.

Lyons
Township
Lat: 43-43-04 N   Long: 96-49-44 W
Pop: 559 (1990); 569 (1980)   Pop Density: 15.6
Land: 35.8 sq. mi.; Water: 0.0 sq. mi.

Mapleton
Township
Lat: 43-37-59 N   Long: 96-43-03 W
Pop: 1,686 (1990); 1,712 (1980)   Pop Density: 52.2
Land: 32.3 sq. mi.; Water: 0.0 sq. mi.

Palisade
Township
ZIP: 57030   Lat: 43-43-02 N   Long: 96-29-25 W
Pop: 276 (1990); 264 (1980)   Pop Density: 12.4
Land: 22.2 sq. mi.; Water: 0.0 sq. mi.

Red Rock
Township
ZIP: 57068   Lat: 43-37-50 N   Long: 96-29-35 W
Pop: 342 (1990); 323 (1980)   Pop Density: 14.6
Land: 23.5 sq. mi.; Water: 0.0 sq. mi.

Sherman
Town
ZIP: 57060   Lat: 43-45-27 N   Long: 96-28-31 W
Pop: 66 (1990); 100 (1980)   Pop Density: 220.0
Land: 0.3 sq. mi.; Water: 0.0 sq. mi.   Elev: 1495 ft.
Name origin: Named in 1888 for territorial banker E. A. Sherman.

Sioux Falls
City
ZIP: 57101   Lat: 43-32-48 N   Long: 96-43-48 W
Pop: 99,405 (1990); 81,182 (1980)   Pop Density: 2295.7
Land: 43.3 sq. mi.; Water: 0.0 sq. mi.   Elev: 1442 ft.
In southeastern SD on the Big Sioux River, 75 mi. north of Sioux City, IA. Largest city; settled 1857. Products include packaged meats, processed dairy foods, fabricated steel, electromagnetic equipment. Part of the town is also in Lincoln County.
Name origin: For its location on the falls of the Big Sioux River.

Split Rock
Township
Lat: 43-32-21 N   Long: 96-35-58 W
Pop: 2,137 (1990); 1,802 (1980)   Pop Density: 54.8
Land: 39.0 sq. mi.; Water: 0.0 sq. mi.

Sverdrup
Township
Lat: 43-42-53 N   Long: 96-42-56 W
Pop: 614 (1990); 577 (1980)   Pop Density: 17.2
Land: 35.8 sq. mi.; Water: 0.1 sq. mi.

Taopi
Township
ZIP: 57018   Lat: 43-48-23 N   Long: 96-56-45 W
Pop: 347 (1990); 357 (1980)   Pop Density: 10.0
Land: 34.7 sq. mi.; Water: 0.1 sq. mi.

Valley Springs
City
ZIP: 57068   Lat: 43-34-59 N   Long: 96-27-52 W
Pop: 739 (1990); 801 (1980)   Pop Density: 923.8
Land: 0.8 sq. mi.; Water: 0.0 sq. mi.   Elev: 1392 ft.
Settled 1872.

*Valley Springs
Township
ZIP: 57068   Lat: 43-32-31 N   Long: 96-29-46 W
Pop: 275 (1990); 313 (1980)   Pop Density: 11.9
Land: 23.1 sq. mi.; Water: 0.0 sq. mi.

Wall Lake
Township
ZIP: 57033   Lat: 43-32-35 N   Long: 96-56-59 W
Pop: 863 (1990); 844 (1980)   Pop Density: 24.4
Land: 35.4 sq. mi.; Water: 0.6 sq. mi.

Wayne
Township
Lat: 43-32-49 N   Long: 96-50-23 W
Pop: 1,307 (1990); 3,953 (1980)   Pop Density: 46.3
Land: 28.2 sq. mi.; Water: 0.0 sq. mi.

Wellington
Township
ZIP: 57035   Lat: 43-32-29 N   Long: 97-04-18 W
Pop: 304 (1990); 311 (1980)   Pop Density: 8.5
Land: 35.6 sq. mi.; Water: 0.7 sq. mi.

Moody County
County Seat: Flandreau (ZIP: 57028)

Pop: 6,507 (1990); 6,692 (1980)   Pop Density: 12.5
Land: 519.7 sq. mi.; Water: 1.4 sq. mi.   Area Code: 605
On the central eastern border of SD, north of Sioux Falls; organized Jan 8, 1873 (prior to statehood) from Brookings and Minnehaha counties.
Name origin: For Col. Gideon Curtis Moody (1832–1906), officer in the Civil War, Dakota Territory legislator, and one of the first two U.S. senators from SD (1889–91).

Alliance
Township
ZIP: 57065   Lat: 43-53-29 N   Long: 96-29-11 W
Pop: 114 (1990); 141 (1980)   Pop Density: 5.2
Land: 21.8 sq. mi.; Water: 0.0 sq. mi.

Blinsmon
Township
ZIP: 57065   Lat: 43-53-38 N   Long: 96-34-50 W
Pop: 258 (1990); 276 (1980)   Pop Density: 7.1
Land: 36.5 sq. mi.; Water: 0.0 sq. mi.

American Places Dictionary — SOUTH DAKOTA, Pennington County

Clare — Township
ZIP: 57028 Lat: 44-03-45 N Long: 96-42-32 W
Pop: 179 (1990); 229 (1980) Pop Density: 5.0
Land: 35.8 sq. mi.; Water: 0.0 sq. mi.

Colman — City
ZIP: 57017 Lat: 43-59-04 N Long: 96-48-57 W
Pop: 482 (1990); 501 (1980) Pop Density: 283.5
Land: 1.7 sq. mi.; Water: 0.0 sq. mi. Elev: 1680 ft.
Name origin: For the Colman Lumber Co. Originally called Sankey.

*Colman — Township
ZIP: 57017 Lat: 43-59-01 N Long: 96-49-45 W
Pop: 235 (1990); 267 (1980) Pop Density: 7.0
Land: 33.8 sq. mi.; Water: 0.4 sq. mi.

Egan — City
ZIP: 57024 Lat: 43-59-58 N Long: 96-39-01 W
Pop: 208 (1990); 248 (1980) Pop Density: 693.3
Land: 0.3 sq. mi.; Water: 0.0 sq. mi. Elev: 1520 ft.
Settled 1880.

*Egan — Township
ZIP: 57024 Lat: 43-58-47 N Long: 96-42-06 W
Pop: 211 (1990); 211 (1980) Pop Density: 5.9
Land: 35.7 sq. mi.; Water: 0.0 sq. mi.

Enterprise — Township
Lat: 43-53-30 N Long: 96-43-04 W
Pop: 282 (1990); 316 (1980) Pop Density: 8.0
Land: 35.1 sq. mi.; Water: 0.0 sq. mi.

Flandreau — City
ZIP: 57028 Lat: 44-02-48 N Long: 96-35-51 W
Pop: 2,311 (1990); 2,114 (1980) Pop Density: 1283.9
Land: 1.8 sq. mi.; Water: 0.1 sq. mi. Elev: 1570 ft.
Settled 1857.
Name origin: For Judge Charles Flandreau of St. Paul, MN.

*Flandreau — Township
ZIP: 57028 Lat: 44-04-09 N Long: 96-35-04 W
Pop: 367 (1990); 334 (1980) Pop Density: 10.6
Land: 34.7 sq. mi.; Water: 0.3 sq. mi.

Fremont — Township
Lat: 44-08-57 N Long: 96-50-11 W
Pop: 243 (1990); 296 (1980) Pop Density: 6.9
Land: 35.2 sq. mi.; Water: 0.5 sq. mi.

Grovena — Township
ZIP: 57024 Lat: 43-58-40 N Long: 96-35-02 W
Pop: 239 (1990); 223 (1980) Pop Density: 6.5
Land: 36.6 sq. mi.; Water: 0.0 sq. mi.

Jefferson — Township
Lat: 44-03-56 N Long: 96-49-08 W
Pop: 153 (1990); 181 (1980) Pop Density: 4.3
Land: 35.8 sq. mi.; Water: 0.0 sq. mi.

Lone Rock — Township
ZIP: 57028 Lat: 43-58-48 N Long: 96-29-18 W
Pop: 99 (1990); 125 (1980) Pop Density: 4.5
Land: 21.9 sq. mi.; Water: 0.0 sq. mi.

Lynn — Township
Lat: 43-53-13 N Long: 96-49-32 W
Pop: 296 (1990); 320 (1980) Pop Density: 8.2
Land: 36.0 sq. mi.; Water: 0.2 sq. mi.

Riverview — Township
Lat: 44-09-10 N Long: 96-42-21 W
Pop: 190 (1990); 193 (1980) Pop Density: 5.3
Land: 35.8 sq. mi.; Water: 0.0 sq. mi.

Spring Creek — Township
Lat: 44-09-09 N Long: 96-35-25 W
Pop: 146 (1990); 179 (1980) Pop Density: 4.1
Land: 35.5 sq. mi.; Water: 0.0 sq. mi.

Trent — Town
ZIP: 57065 Lat: 43-54-24 N Long: 96-39-26 W
Pop: 211 (1990); 197 (1980) Pop Density: 211.0
Land: 1.0 sq. mi.; Water: 0.0 sq. mi. Elev: 1510 ft.

Union — Township
Lat: 44-03-58 N Long: 96-29-23 W
Pop: 163 (1990); 197 (1980) Pop Density: 7.3
Land: 22.4 sq. mi.; Water: 0.0 sq. mi.

Ward — Town
ZIP: 57074 Lat: 44-09-19 N Long: 96-27-38 W
Pop: 35 (1990); 43 (1980) Pop Density: 116.7
Land: 0.3 sq. mi.; Water: 0.0 sq. mi. Elev: 1740 ft.
Settled 1880s.
Name origin: For Dakota railroad promoter James A. Ward.

*Ward — Township
Lat: 44-09-20 N Long: 96-29-10 W
Pop: 85 (1990); 101 (1980) Pop Density: 3.9
Land: 21.9 sq. mi.; Water: 0.0 sq. mi.

Pennington County
County Seat: Rapid City (ZIP: 57709)

Pop: 81,343 (1990); 70,361 (1980) Pop Density: 29.3
Land: 2776.4 sq. mi.; Water: 8.1 sq. mi. Area Code: 605
On the southwestern border of SD; created Jan 11, 1875 (prior to statehood) from unorganized territory.
Name origin: For John L. Pennington, Dakota Territory governor (1874–78).

Ash No. 16 — Township
Lat: 44-12-36 N Long: 102-11-17 W
Pop: 22 (1990); 34 (1980) Pop Density: 0.6
Land: 35.6 sq. mi.; Water: 0.1 sq. mi.

Box Elder — City
ZIP: 57719 Lat: 44-07-10 N Long: 103-04-19 W
Pop: 2,680 (1990); 3,186 (1980) Pop Density: 788.2
Land: 3.4 sq. mi.; Water: 0.0 sq. mi. Elev: 3030 ft.
Name origin: For Box Elder Creek.

SOUTH DAKOTA, Pennington County

Castle Butte No. 18
Township
Lat: 43-45-20 N Long: 102-04-09 W
Pop: 39 (1990); 25 (1980) Pop Density: 0.8
Land: 51.1 sq. mi.; Water: 0.1 sq. mi.

Cedar Butte No. 4
Township
Lat: 44-07-46 N Long: 102-17-51 W
Pop: 50 (1990); 61 (1980) Pop Density: 1.4
Land: 35.4 sq. mi.; Water: 0.1 sq. mi.

Central Pennington
Pop. Place
Lat: 44-03-27 N Long: 103-14-10 W
Pop: 14,435 (1990); 12,021 (1980) Pop Density: 161.8
Land: 89.2 sq. mi.; Water: 0.0 sq. mi.

Cheyenne No. 21
Township
Lat: 44-22-39 N Long: 102-11-53 W
Pop: 8 (1990); 16 (1980) Pop Density: 0.1
Land: 53.5 sq. mi.; Water: 0.4 sq. mi.

Colonial Pine Hills
CDP
Lat: 44-00-27 N Long: 103-18-53 W
Pop: 1,553 (1990) Pop Density: 88.7
Land: 17.5 sq. mi.; Water: 0.0 sq. mi.

Conata No. 20
Township
Lat: 43-48-28 N Long: 102-12-11 W
Pop: 6 (1990); 13 (1980) Pop Density: 0.1
Land: 89.3 sq. mi.; Water: 0.3 sq. mi.

Crooked Creek No. 25
Township
Lat: 43-57-19 N Long: 102-23-11 W
Pop: 33 (1990); 23 (1980) Pop Density: 0.5
Land: 71.1 sq. mi.; Water: 0.3 sq. mi.

Dalzell Canyon
Pop. Place
Lat: 44-17-46 N Long: 102-16-48 W
Pop: 4 (1990); 6 (1980) Pop Density: 0.1
Land: 41.0 sq. mi.; Water: 0.1 sq. mi.

East Central Pennington
Pop. Place
Lat: 43-56-26 N Long: 102-40-46 W
Pop: 266 (1990); 308 (1980) Pop Density: 0.7
Land: 387.4 sq. mi.; Water: 0.7 sq. mi.

Ellsworth Air Force Base
Military Facility
Lat: 44-07-57 N Long: 103-04-06 W
Pop: 2,687 (1990) Pop Density: 4478.3
Land: 0.6 sq. mi.; Water: 0.0 sq. mi.
Part of the facility is also in Meade County.

Fairview No. 22
Township
Lat: 43-56-50 N Long: 102-12-01 W
Pop: 22 (1990); 75 (1980) Pop Density: 0.6
Land: 34.6 sq. mi.; Water: 0.2 sq. mi.

Flat Butte No. 12
Township
Lat: 43-50-49 N Long: 102-04-24 W
Pop: 12 (1990); 11 (1980) Pop Density: 0.3
Land: 35.5 sq. mi.; Water: 0.3 sq. mi.

Hill City
Town
ZIP: 57745 Lat: 43-55-55 N Long: 103-34-17 W
Pop: 650 (1990); 535 (1980) Pop Density: 812.5
Land: 0.8 sq. mi.; Water: 0.0 sq. mi. Elev: 4979 ft.
Settled 1876 during the gold rush.
Name origin: For its location in the Black Hills.

Huron No. 10
Township
Lat: 44-07-19 N Long: 102-11-08 W
Pop: 52 (1990); 37 (1980) Pop Density: 1.5
Land: 35.6 sq. mi.; Water: 0.2 sq. mi.

Imlay No. 24
Township
Lat: 43-43-31 N Long: 102-21-06 W
Pop: 14 (1990); 6 (1980) Pop Density: 0.2
Land: 74.4 sq. mi.; Water: 0.1 sq. mi.

Keystone
Town
ZIP: 57751 Lat: 43-53-39 N Long: 103-25-43 W
Pop: 232 (1990); 295 (1980) Pop Density: 80.0
Land: 2.9 sq. mi.; Water: 0.0 sq. mi. Elev: 4323 ft.
Founded 1891.
Name origin: For a nearby mine.

Lake Creek
Pop. Place
Lat: 44-02-00 N Long: 102-04-34 W
Pop: 52 (1990); 64 (1980) Pop Density: 1.4
Land: 35.9 sq. mi.; Water: 0.0 sq. mi.

Lake Flat No. 8
Township
Lat: 44-02-21 N Long: 102-18-31 W
Pop: 30 (1990); 40 (1980) Pop Density: 0.9
Land: 35.1 sq. mi.; Water: 0.4 sq. mi.

Lake Hill No. 5
Township
Lat: 44-02-50 N Long: 102-11-24 W
Pop: 17 (1990); 24 (1980) Pop Density: 0.5
Land: 35.1 sq. mi.; Water: 0.3 sq. mi.

Mount Rushmore
Pop. Place
Lat: 43-57-44 N Long: 103-22-43 W
Pop: 4,197 (1990); 3,369 (1980) Pop Density: 18.4
Land: 228.2 sq. mi.; Water: 0.6 sq. mi.
Site of the famous Mount Rushmore National Memorial.

New Underwood
Town
ZIP: 57761 Lat: 44-05-37 N Long: 102-50-00 W
Pop: 553 (1990); 517 (1980) Pop Density: 1106.0
Land: 0.5 sq. mi.; Water: 0.0 sq. mi. Elev: 2839 ft.
Established 1906.
Name origin: For Johnny Underwood, partner of the original landowner.

Northeast Pennington
Pop. Place
Lat: 44-20-30 N Long: 102-03-19 W
Pop: 38 (1990); 57 (1980) Pop Density: 0.3
Land: 127.2 sq. mi.; Water: 0.5 sq. mi.

Owanka No. 13
Township
Lat: 44-02-43 N Long: 102-33-51 W
Pop: 50 (1990); 42 (1980) Pop Density: 1.4
Land: 36.0 sq. mi.; Water: 0.0 sq. mi.

Peno No. 9
Township
Lat: 44-07-54 N Long: 102-04-17 W
Pop: 37 (1990); 38 (1980) Pop Density: 1.0
Land: 35.7 sq. mi.; Water: 0.2 sq. mi.

Quinn
Town
ZIP: 57775 Lat: 43-59-18 N Long: 102-07-40 W
Pop: 72 (1990); 80 (1980) Pop Density: 72.0
Land: 1.0 sq. mi.; Water: 0.0 sq. mi. Elev: 2606 ft.
Established 1907.
Name origin: For pioneer rancher Michael Quinn.

Quinn No. 1
Township
Lat: 43-57-23 N Long: 102-04-53 W
Pop: 11 (1990); 9 (1980) Pop Density: 0.3
Land: 34.4 sq. mi.; Water: 0.3 sq. mi.

Rainy Creek No. 19 — Township
Lat: 44-17-53 N **Long:** 102-11-13 W
Pop: 33 (1990); 56 (1980) **Pop Density:** 0.9
Land: 36.3 sq. mi.; **Water:** 0.1 sq. mi.

Rapid City — City
ZIP: 57701 **Lat:** 44-04-30 N **Long:** 103-13-58 W
Pop: 54,523 (1990); 46,492 (1980) **Pop Density:** 1544.6
Land: 35.3 sq. mi.; **Water:** 0.1 sq. mi. **Elev:** 3247 ft.
In southwestern SD in the eastern part of the Black Hills, 45 mi. east of the WY border. Settled 1876. Diverse manufacturing city: cement, computer parts, jewelry, meat products. Site of SD School of Mines and Technology; Ellsworth Air Force Base.
Name origin: For Rapid Creek, which flows through the town.

Rapid Valley — CDP
ZIP: 57701 **Lat:** 44-04-21 N **Long:** 103-07-46 W
Pop: 5,968 (1990); 3,265 (1980) **Pop Density:** 568.4
Land: 10.5 sq. mi.; **Water:** 0.0 sq. mi.

Scenic No. 7 — Township
Lat: 43-49-25 N **Long:** 102-29-58 W
Pop: 71 (1990); 108 (1980) **Pop Density:** 0.5
Land: 142.7 sq. mi.; **Water:** 0.2 sq. mi.

Shyne No. 27 — Township
Lat: 44-07-15 N **Long:** 102-25-49 W
Pop: 20 (1990); 11 (1980) **Pop Density:** 0.7
Land: 26.9 sq. mi.; **Water:** 0.1 sq. mi.

Sunnyside No. 26 — Township
Lat: 44-12-39 N **Long:** 102-19-21 W
Pop: 22 (1990); 14 (1980) **Pop Density:** 0.6
Land: 38.9 sq. mi.; **Water:** 0.1 sq. mi.

Wall — Town
ZIP: 57790 **Lat:** 43-59-29 N **Long:** 102-14-20 W
Pop: 834 (1990); 770 (1980) **Pop Density:** 490.6
Land: 1.7 sq. mi.; **Water:** 0.0 sq. mi. **Elev:** 2818 ft.
Founded 1907.
Name origin: For its location near the Badlands National Monument wall.

Wasta — Town
ZIP: 57791 **Lat:** 44-04-09 N **Long:** 102-26-45 W
Pop: 82 (1990); 99 (1980) **Pop Density:** 410.0
Land: 0.2 sq. mi.; **Water:** 0.0 sq. mi. **Elev:** 2313 ft.
Name origin: From a Sioux Indian term meaning 'good.'

Wasta No. 2 — Township
Lat: 44-01-15 N **Long:** 102-25-14 W
Pop: 13 (1990); 27 (1980) **Pop Density:** 0.4
Land: 35.8 sq. mi.; **Water:** 0.0 sq. mi.

West Pennington — Pop. Place
Lat: 44-00-18 N **Long:** 103-46-57 W
Pop: 1,276 (1990); 1,092 (1980) **Pop Density:** 2.4
Land: 535.4 sq. mi.; **Water:** 1.8 sq. mi.

Perkins County
County Seat: Bison (ZIP: 57620)

Pop: 3,932 (1990); 4,700 (1980) **Pop Density:** 1.4
Land: 2873.5 sq. mi.; **Water:** 17.3 sq. mi. **Area Code:** 605
On the northwestern border of SD; organized Feb 26, 1909 from Harding and Butte counties.
Name origin: For Henry E. Perkins, state senator who helped pass the act that established the county.

Ada — Township
Lat: 45-20-27 N **Long:** 102-24-24 W
Pop: 27 (1990); 34 (1980) **Pop Density:** 0.8
Land: 35.4 sq. mi.; **Water:** 0.2 sq. mi.

Anderson — Township
ZIP: 57644 **Lat:** 45-41-25 N **Long:** 102-15-12 W
Pop: 30 (1990); 27 (1980) **Pop Density:** 0.9
Land: 32.3 sq. mi.; **Water:** 3.2 sq. mi.

Antelope — Township
Lat: 45-21-06 N **Long:** 102-45-49 W
Pop: 28 (1990); 34 (1980) **Pop Density:** 0.8
Land: 35.6 sq. mi.; **Water:** 0.1 sq. mi.

Barrett — Township
Lat: 45-46-22 N **Long:** 102-29-47 W
Pop: 16 (1990); 21 (1980) **Pop Density:** 0.4
Land: 35.8 sq. mi.; **Water:** 0.2 sq. mi.

Beck — Township
Lat: 45-10-03 N **Long:** 102-38-49 W
Pop: 9 (1990); 16 (1980) **Pop Density:** 0.3
Land: 35.9 sq. mi.; **Water:** 0.1 sq. mi.

Bison — Town
ZIP: 57620 **Lat:** 45-31-18 N **Long:** 102-28-00 W
Pop: 451 (1990); 457 (1980) **Pop Density:** 451.0
Land: 1.0 sq. mi.; **Water:** 0.0 sq. mi. **Elev:** 2695 ft.
Founded 1907.
Name origin: For the American bison, commonly called the buffalo.

*Bison — Township
Lat: 45-31-11 N **Long:** 102-30-39 W
Pop: 35 (1990); 37 (1980) **Pop Density:** 1.0
Land: 34.8 sq. mi.; **Water:** 0.2 sq. mi.

Brushy — Township
Lat: 45-14-46 N **Long:** 102-31-34 W
Pop: 9 (1990); 24 (1980) **Pop Density:** 0.3
Land: 35.7 sq. mi.; **Water:** 0.2 sq. mi.

Burdick — Township
Lat: 45-46-18 N **Long:** 102-22-48 W
Pop: 38 (1990); 58 (1980) **Pop Density:** 1.1
Land: 36.0 sq. mi.; **Water:** 0.1 sq. mi.

SOUTH DAKOTA, Perkins County

Cash
Township
Lat: 45-36-08 N **Long:** 102-38-44 W
Pop: 27 (1990); 34 (1980) **Pop Density:** 0.8
Land: 35.6 sq. mi.; **Water:** 0.1 sq. mi.

Castle Butte
Township
Lat: 45-53-18 N **Long:** 102-31-03 W
Pop: 24 (1990); 23 (1980) **Pop Density:** 0.5
Land: 51.8 sq. mi.; **Water:** 0.1 sq. mi.

Chance
Township
Lat: 45-23-18 N **Long:** 102-16-19 W
Pop: 41 (1990); 46 (1980) **Pop Density:** 0.6
Land: 71.3 sq. mi.; **Water:** 0.4 sq. mi.

Chaudoin
Township
Lat: 45-15-02 N **Long:** 102-24-19 W
Pop: 12 (1990); 14 (1980) **Pop Density:** 0.3
Land: 36.1 sq. mi.; **Water:** 0.1 sq. mi.

Clark
Township
Lat: 45-35-24 N **Long:** 102-09-32 W
Pop: 27 (1990); 38 (1980) **Pop Density:** 0.8
Land: 35.8 sq. mi.; **Water:** 0.2 sq. mi.

De Witt
Township
Lat: 45-46-47 N **Long:** 102-05-54 W
Pop: 54 (1990); 81 (1980) **Pop Density:** 1.0
Land: 56.3 sq. mi.; **Water:** 0.6 sq. mi.

Duck Creek
Pop. Place
Lat: 45-46-26 N **Long:** 102-46-12 W
Pop: 29 (1990); 42 (1980) **Pop Density:** 0.8
Land: 36.0 sq. mi.; **Water:** 0.1 sq. mi.

Duell
Township
Lat: 45-20-28 N **Long:** 102-39-42 W
Pop: 19 (1990); 18 (1980) **Pop Density:** 0.5
Land: 35.4 sq. mi.; **Water:** 0.1 sq. mi.

East Perkins
Pop. Place
Lat: 45-33-32 N **Long:** 102-06-38 W
Pop: 152 (1990); 111 (1980) **Pop Density:** 0.6
Land: 237.3 sq. mi.; **Water:** 6.3 sq. mi.

Englewood
Township
Lat: 45-16-28 N **Long:** 102-07-29 W
Pop: 8 (1990); 17 (1980) **Pop Density:** 0.1
Land: 64.8 sq. mi.; **Water:** 0.1 sq. mi.

Flat Creek
Township
Lat: 45-51-23 N **Long:** 102-16-14 W
Pop: 12 (1990); 172 (1980) **Pop Density:** 0.3
Land: 35.8 sq. mi.; **Water:** 0.1 sq. mi.

Foster
Township
Lat: 45-20-34 N **Long:** 102-06-46 W
Pop: 22 (1990); 27 (1980) **Pop Density:** 0.3
Land: 64.2 sq. mi.; **Water:** 0.1 sq. mi.

Fredlund
Township
Lat: 45-42-04 N **Long:** 102-38-37 W
Pop: 48 (1990); 42 (1980) **Pop Density:** 1.4
Land: 35.4 sq. mi.; **Water:** 0.1 sq. mi.

Glendo
Township
ZIP: 57649 **Lat:** 45-41-03 N **Long:** 102-53-29 W
Pop: 16 (1990); 26 (1980) **Pop Density:** 0.5
Land: 35.3 sq. mi.; **Water:** 0.0 sq. mi.

Grand River
Township
ZIP: 57640 **Lat:** 45-53-12 N **Long:** 102-37-44 W
Pop: 35 (1990); 34 (1980) **Pop Density:** 0.7
Land: 51.8 sq. mi.; **Water:** 0.2 sq. mi.

Hall
Township
Lat: 45-19-53 N **Long:** 102-32-00 W
Pop: 19 (1990); 22 (1980) **Pop Density:** 0.5
Land: 35.5 sq. mi.; **Water:** 0.1 sq. mi.

Highland
Township
Lat: 45-14-48 N **Long:** 102-39-33 W
Pop: 9 (1990); 17 (1980) **Pop Density:** 0.3
Land: 36.0 sq. mi.; **Water:** 0.1 sq. mi.

Horse Creek
Township
Lat: 45-51-53 N **Long:** 102-52-29 W
Pop: 48 (1990); 77 (1980) **Pop Density:** 0.9
Land: 51.9 sq. mi.; **Water:** 0.1 sq. mi.

Independence
Pop. Place
Lat: 45-36-32 N **Long:** 102-16-44 W
Pop: 30 (1990) **Pop Density:** 0.8
Land: 35.7 sq. mi.; **Water:** 0.2 sq. mi.

Lemmon
City
ZIP: 57638 **Lat:** 45-56-18 N **Long:** 102-09-29 W
Pop: 1,614 (1990); 1,871 (1980) **Pop Density:** 1614.0
Land: 1.0 sq. mi.; **Water:** 0.0 sq. mi. **Elev:** 2577 ft.
Name origin: For G.E. Lemmon, a well-known early cowboy.

Liberty
Township
Lat: 45-51-46 N **Long:** 102-23-16 W
Pop: 23 (1990); 30 (1980) **Pop Density:** 0.6
Land: 35.8 sq. mi.; **Water:** 0.1 sq. mi.

Lincoln
Township
Lat: 45-53-05 N **Long:** 102-06-13 W
Pop: 166 (1990); 156 (1980) **Pop Density:** 2.0
Land: 81.2 sq. mi.; **Water:** 0.1 sq. mi.

Lodgepole
Township
ZIP: 57640 **Lat:** 45-46-47 N **Long:** 102-37-04 W
Pop: 51 (1990); 51 (1980) **Pop Density:** 1.4
Land: 36.0 sq. mi.; **Water:** 0.0 sq. mi.

Lone Tree
Township
Lat: 45-25-55 N **Long:** 102-23-36 W
Pop: 44 (1990); 51 (1980) **Pop Density:** 1.2
Land: 35.7 sq. mi.; **Water:** 0.4 sq. mi.

Maltby
Township
Lat: 45-25-32 N **Long:** 102-46-09 W
Pop: 9 (1990); 25 (1980) **Pop Density:** 0.3
Land: 35.9 sq. mi.; **Water:** 0.1 sq. mi.

Marshfield
Township
Lat: 45-36-18 N **Long:** 102-27-32 W
Pop: 29 (1990); 30 (1980) **Pop Density:** 0.4
Land: 71.5 sq. mi.; **Water:** 0.3 sq. mi.

Martin
Township
Lat: 45-09-56 N **Long:** 102-24-00 W
Pop: 9 (1990); 9 (1980) **Pop Density:** 0.2
Land: 36.1 sq. mi.; **Water:** 0.0 sq. mi.

Meadow
Township
ZIP: 57644 **Lat:** 45-30-57 N **Long:** 102-16-07 W
Pop: 45 (1990); 60 (1980) **Pop Density:** 1.3
Land: 35.6 sq. mi.; **Water:** 0.3 sq. mi.

SOUTH DAKOTA, Perkins County

Moreau Township
Lat: 45-12-07 N Long: 102-16-47 W
Pop: 16 (1990); 7 (1980) Pop Density: 0.2
Land: 72.0 sq. mi.; Water: 0.0 sq. mi.

Plateau Township
ZIP: 57649 Lat: 45-31-35 N Long: 102-53-10 W
Pop: 21 (1990); 24 (1980) Pop Density: 0.6
Land: 35.7 sq. mi.; Water: 0.4 sq. mi.

Pleasant Valley Township
Lat: 45-41-50 N Long: 102-31-03 W
Pop: 6 (1990); 20 (1980) Pop Density: 0.2
Land: 35.4 sq. mi.; Water: 0.1 sq. mi.

Rainbow Township
Lat: 45-30-32 N Long: 102-23-24 W
Pop: 34 (1990); 34 (1980) Pop Density: 1.0
Land: 35.4 sq. mi.; Water: 0.6 sq. mi.

Rockford Township
Lat: 45-41-49 N Long: 102-23-31 W
Pop: 28 (1990); 24 (1980) Pop Density: 0.8
Land: 35.4 sq. mi.; Water: 0.1 sq. mi.

Scotch Cap Township
Lat: 45-30-41 N Long: 102-38-12 W
Pop: 41 (1990); 29 (1980) Pop Density: 1.2
Land: 35.4 sq. mi.; Water: 0.5 sq. mi.

Sidney Township
ZIP: 57640 Lat: 45-41-06 N Long: 102-46-46 W
Pop: 32 (1990); 40 (1980) Pop Density: 0.9
Land: 35.5 sq. mi.; Water: 0.0 sq. mi.

South Perkins Pop. Place
Lat: 45-06-42 N Long: 102-19-59 W
Pop: 124 (1990); 165 (1980) Pop Density: 0.4
Land: 309.9 sq. mi.; Water: 0.4 sq. mi.

Southwest Perkins Pop. Place
Lat: 45-08-27 N Long: 102-51-43 W
Pop: 25 (1990); 35 (1980) Pop Density: 0.2
Land: 107.5 sq. mi.; Water: 0.0 sq. mi.

Strool Township
ZIP: 57649 Lat: 45-30-41 N Long: 102-45-43 W
Pop: 81 (1990); 99 (1980) Pop Density: 2.3
Land: 35.8 sq. mi.; Water: 0.2 sq. mi.

Trail Township
Lat: 45-55-39 N Long: 102-14-55 W
Pop: 40 (1990); 39 (1980) Pop Density: 2.5
Land: 16.0 sq. mi.; Water: 0.0 sq. mi.

Vail Township
Lat: 45-36-11 N Long: 102-46-11 W
Pop: 14 (1990); 18 (1980) Pop Density: 0.4
Land: 35.8 sq. mi.; Water: 0.1 sq. mi.

Vickers Township
Lat: 45-25-46 N Long: 102-30-34 W
Pop: 21 (1990); 21 (1980) Pop Density: 0.6
Land: 36.0 sq. mi.; Water: 0.0 sq. mi.

Viking Township
ZIP: 57640 Lat: 45-53-20 N Long: 102-45-32 W
Pop: 13 (1990); 26 (1980) Pop Density: 0.3
Land: 51.7 sq. mi.; Water: 0.1 sq. mi.

Vrooman Township
Lat: 45-04-34 N Long: 102-47-30 W
Pop: 9 (1990); 11 (1980) Pop Density: 0.3
Land: 35.6 sq. mi.; Water: 0.0 sq. mi.

Wells Township
Lat: 45-20-52 N Long: 102-54-17 W
Pop: 17 (1990); 13 (1980) Pop Density: 0.5
Land: 35.3 sq. mi.; Water: 0.0 sq. mi.

West Central Perkins Pop. Place
Lat: 45-25-46 N Long: 102-38-20 W
Pop: 28 (1990); 27 (1980) Pop Density: 0.8
Land: 36.0 sq. mi.; Water: 0.0 sq. mi.

West Perkins Pop. Place
Lat: 45-26-01 N Long: 102-53-49 W
Pop: 23 (1990); 21 (1980) Pop Density: 0.6
Land: 35.9 sq. mi.; Water: 0.0 sq. mi.

White Butte Township
Lat: 45-55-31 N Long: 102-22-52 W
Pop: 38 (1990); 30 (1980) Pop Density: 2.4
Land: 16.0 sq. mi.; Water: 0.0 sq. mi.

White Hill Township
Lat: 45-36-12 N Long: 102-53-53 W
Pop: 8 (1990); 22 (1980) Pop Density: 0.2
Land: 35.9 sq. mi.; Water: 0.1 sq. mi.

Wilson Township
Lat: 45-46-34 N Long: 102-52-12 W
Pop: 40 (1990); 42 (1980) Pop Density: 1.1
Land: 36.0 sq. mi.; Water: 0.0 sq. mi.

Wyandotte Township
ZIP: 57795 Lat: 45-16-34 N Long: 102-49-29 W
Pop: 8 (1990); 19 (1980) Pop Density: 0.1
Land: 71.9 sq. mi.; Water: 0.0 sq. mi.

SOUTH DAKOTA, Potter County   American Places Dictionary

> ## Potter County
> **County Seat: Gettysburg (ZIP: 57442)**
>
> **Pop:** 3,190 (1990); 3,674 (1980)   **Pop Density:** 3.7
> **Land:** 866.5 sq. mi.; **Water:** 31.9 sq. mi.   **Area Code:** 605
> In north-central SD, northeast of Pierre; created as Ashmore County Jan 14, 1875 (prior to statehood) from Buffalo County; name changed 1877.
> **Name origin:** For Dr. Joel A. Potter, legislator and steward of the State Hospital for the Insane, Yankton. Originally named for Samuel Ashmore, legislator (1872–73).

Central Potter   Pop. Place
                    Lat: 45-04-27 N **Long:** 99-56-55 W
Pop: 319 (1990); 460 (1980)   **Pop Density:** 1.2
Land: 263.1 sq. mi.; **Water:** 0.2 sq. mi.

East Potter   Pop. Place
                    Lat: 45-03-53 N **Long:** 99-42-06 W
Pop: 419 (1990); 488 (1980)   **Pop Density:** 1.4
Land: 307.6 sq. mi.; **Water:** 0.7 sq. mi.

Gettysburg   City
ZIP: 57442   **Lat:** 45-00-23 N **Long:** 99-57-12 W
Pop: 1,510 (1990); 1,623 (1980)   **Pop Density:** 794.7
Land: 1.9 sq. mi.; **Water:** 0.0 sq. mi.   **Elev:** 2061 ft.
Settled 1880s by Civil War veterans.
Name origin: For the great Civil War battle.

Hoven   Town
ZIP: 57450   **Lat:** 45-14-30 N **Long:** 99-46-34 W
Pop: 522 (1990); 615 (1980)   **Pop Density:** 1740.0
Land: 0.3 sq. mi.; **Water:** 0.0 sq. mi.   **Elev:** 1902 ft.
Founded 1883.
Name origin: For townsite landowners Peter and Matt Hoven.

Lebanon   Town
ZIP: 57455   **Lat:** 45-04-08 N **Long:** 99-45-57 W
Pop: 115 (1990); 129 (1980)   **Pop Density:** 230.0
Land: 0.5 sq. mi.; **Water:** 0.0 sq. mi.   **Elev:** 1953 ft.
Platted 1887.
Name origin: For the country in the Middle East.

Tolstoy   Town
ZIP: 57475   **Lat:** 45-12-24 N **Long:** 99-36-53 W
Pop: 69 (1990); 97 (1980)   **Pop Density:** 345.0
Land: 0.2 sq. mi.; **Water:** 0.0 sq. mi.   **Elev:** 1940 ft.
Founded 1907.
Name origin: For the Russian writer Leo Tolstoy (1828–1910).

West Potter   Pop. Place
                    Lat: 45-02-39 N **Long:** 100-11-55 W
Pop: 236 (1990); 262 (1980)   **Pop Density:** 0.8
Land: 293.0 sq. mi.; **Water:** 31.0 sq. mi.

> ## Roberts County
> **County Seat: Sisseton (ZIP: 57262)**
>
> **Pop:** 9,914 (1990); 10,911 (1980)   **Pop Density:** 9.0
> **Land:** 1101.3 sq. mi.; **Water:** 34.1 sq. mi.   **Area Code:** 605
> On the northeastern border of SD, east of Aberdeen; organized Mar 8, 1883 (prior to statehood) from Grant County.
> **Name origin:** Most likely for S. G. Roberts, a publisher and a member of the Dakota territorial legislature when the county was established.

Agency   Township
                    Lat: 45-30-40 N **Long:** 97-02-33 W
Pop: 315 (1990); 242 (1980)   **Pop Density:** 8.8
Land: 35.9 sq. mi.; **Water:** 0.1 sq. mi.

Alto   Township
                    Lat: 45-25-19 N **Long:** 97-10-17 W
Pop: 83 (1990); 88 (1980)   **Pop Density:** 2.4
Land: 35.0 sq. mi.; **Water:** 1.1 sq. mi.

Becker   Township
ZIP: 57257   **Lat:** 45-32-02 N **Long:** 96-50-31 W
Pop: 141 (1990); 154 (1980)   **Pop Density:** 4.9
Land: 28.6 sq. mi.; **Water:** 1.3 sq. mi.

Bossko   Township
ZIP: 57224   **Lat:** 45-46-17 N **Long:** 97-10-01 W
Pop: 82 (1990); 99 (1980)   **Pop Density:** 2.3
Land: 36.0 sq. mi.; **Water:** 0.0 sq. mi.

Bryant   Township
                    Lat: 45-42-20 N **Long:** 96-47-40 W
Pop: 197 (1990); 217 (1980)   **Pop Density:** 9.2
Land: 21.5 sq. mi.; **Water:** 6.1 sq. mi.

Claire City   Town
ZIP: 57224   **Lat:** 45-51-23 N **Long:** 97-06-08 W
Pop: 85 (1990); 87 (1980)   **Pop Density:** 425.0
Land: 0.2 sq. mi.; **Water:** 0.0 sq. mi.   **Elev:** 1200 ft.
Established 1913.
Name origin: For the wife of town founder A. Feeney.

SOUTH DAKOTA, Roberts County

Corona Town
ZIP: 57227 Lat: 45-20-05 N Long: 96-45-54 W
Pop: 118 (1990); 126 (1980) Pop Density: 590.0
Land: 0.2 sq. mi.; Water: 0.0 sq. mi. Elev: 1165 ft.
Name origin: For Corona, NY.

Dry Wood Lake Township
ZIP: 57262 Lat: 45-36-34 N Long: 97-10-01 W
Pop: 124 (1990); 97 (1980) Pop Density: 3.9
Land: 31.6 sq. mi.; Water: 4.5 sq. mi.

Easter Township
ZIP: 57257 Lat: 45-36-06 N Long: 96-55-25 W
Pop: 184 (1990); 198 (1980) Pop Density: 5.5
Land: 33.4 sq. mi.; Water: 0.6 sq. mi.

Enterprise Township
Lat: 45-46-31 N Long: 97-02-30 W
Pop: 120 (1990); 152 (1980) Pop Density: 3.4
Land: 35.8 sq. mi.; Water: 0.2 sq. mi.

Garfield Township
Lat: 45-22-04 N Long: 96-48-28 W
Pop: 187 (1990); 185 (1980) Pop Density: 5.3
Land: 35.0 sq. mi.; Water: 0.2 sq. mi.

Geneseo Township
ZIP: 57227 Lat: 45-22-29 N Long: 96-41-17 W
Pop: 216 (1990); 266 (1980) Pop Density: 6.4
Land: 33.7 sq. mi.; Water: 1.4 sq. mi.

Goodwill Township
ZIP: 57262 Lat: 45-36-09 N Long: 97-02-26 W
Pop: 713 (1990); 664 (1980) Pop Density: 19.7
Land: 36.2 sq. mi.; Water: 0.0 sq. mi.

Grant Township
Lat: 45-41-06 N Long: 96-55-09 W
Pop: 176 (1990); 190 (1980) Pop Density: 4.9
Land: 35.8 sq. mi.; Water: 0.4 sq. mi.

Harmon Township
ZIP: 57260 Lat: 45-46-31 N Long: 96-44-41 W
Pop: 230 (1990); 295 (1980) Pop Density: 3.7
Land: 61.6 sq. mi.; Water: 3.9 sq. mi.

Hart Township
ZIP: 57255 Lat: 45-46-26 N Long: 96-54-44 W
Pop: 111 (1990); 126 (1980) Pop Density: 3.1
Land: 36.0 sq. mi.; Water: 0.4 sq. mi.

Lake Township
Lat: 45-26-57 N Long: 96-47-26 W
Pop: 170 (1990); 180 (1980) Pop Density: 4.6
Land: 36.8 sq. mi.; Water: 2.9 sq. mi.

Lawrence Township
Lat: 45-31-01 N Long: 96-56-38 W
Pop: 170 (1990); 191 (1980) Pop Density: 7.7
Land: 22.2 sq. mi.; Water: 0.0 sq. mi.

Lee Township
ZIP: 57279 Lat: 45-26-58 N Long: 96-54-47 W
Pop: 136 (1990); 141 (1980) Pop Density: 4.8
Land: 28.1 sq. mi.; Water: 0.1 sq. mi.

Lien Township
ZIP: 57255 Lat: 45-52-33 N Long: 96-55-16 W
Pop: 172 (1990); 179 (1980) Pop Density: 3.6
Land: 47.3 sq. mi.; Water: 0.5 sq. mi.

Lockwood Township
Lat: 45-21-05 N Long: 96-33-56 W
Pop: 185 (1990); 186 (1980) Pop Density: 8.5
Land: 21.7 sq. mi.; Water: 3.9 sq. mi.

Long Hollow Township
ZIP: 57262 Lat: 45-41-19 N Long: 97-09-44 W
Pop: 273 (1990); 245 (1980) Pop Density: 7.6
Land: 35.7 sq. mi.; Water: 0.5 sq. mi.

Minnesota Township
ZIP: 57224 Lat: 45-52-11 N Long: 97-02-18 W
Pop: 149 (1990); 203 (1980) Pop Density: 3.2
Land: 47.2 sq. mi.; Water: 0.9 sq. mi.

New Effington Town
ZIP: 57255 Lat: 45-51-18 N Long: 96-55-04 W
Pop: 219 (1990); 261 (1980) Pop Density: 730.0
Land: 0.3 sq. mi.; Water: 0.0 sq. mi. Elev: 1108 ft.
Name origin: For Effie, the first girl born in the town. Originally called Effington, until 1913 when it was moved to a new site.

Norway Township
Lat: 45-52-38 N Long: 97-09-40 W
Pop: 160 (1990); 178 (1980) Pop Density: 3.3
Land: 48.1 sq. mi.; Water: 0.1 sq. mi.

One Road Township
ZIP: 57262 Lat: 45-30-31 N Long: 97-09-52 W
Pop: 88 (1990); 103 (1980) Pop Density: 2.6
Land: 34.4 sq. mi.; Water: 1.6 sq. mi.

Ortley Town
ZIP: 57256 Lat: 45-20-06 N Long: 97-12-14 W
Pop: 63 (1990); 80 (1980) Pop Density: 28.6
Land: 2.2 sq. mi.; Water: 0.0 sq. mi. Elev: 1840 ft.
Name origin: For an Indian who lived in the area. Originally called Anderson.

*Ortley Township
Lat: 45-20-30 N Long: 97-09-33 W
Pop: 88 (1990); 105 (1980) Pop Density: 2.6
Land: 33.6 sq. mi.; Water: 0.2 sq. mi.

Peever Town
ZIP: 57257 Lat: 45-32-32 N Long: 96-57-20 W
Pop: 195 (1990); 232 (1980) Pop Density: 1950.0
Land: 0.1 sq. mi.; Water: 0.0 sq. mi. Elev: 1200 ft.
Name origin: For landowner T.H. Peever, who named the town after himself.

Rosholt Town
ZIP: 57260 Lat: 45-51-58 N Long: 96-43-54 W
Pop: 408 (1990); 446 (1980) Pop Density: 1360.0
Land: 0.3 sq. mi.; Water: 0.0 sq. mi. Elev: 1047 ft.
Established 1913.
Name origin: For Julius Rosholt, a railroad construction man.

Sisseton City
ZIP: 57262 Lat: 45-39-44 N Long: 97-02-45 W
Pop: 2,181 (1990); 2,789 (1980) Pop Density: 1454.0
Land: 1.5 sq. mi.; Water: 0.0 sq. mi. Elev: 1204 ft.
Settled late 1860s.
Name origin: For Fort Sisseton.

SOUTH DAKOTA, Roberts County

*Sisseton   Township
ZIP: 57262   **Lat:** 45-41-21 N **Long:** 97-01-48 W
Pop: 577 (1990); 324 (1980)   **Pop Density:** 16.8
Land: 34.4 sq. mi.; **Water:** 0.0 sq. mi.

Springdale   Township
    Lat: 45-22-16 N **Long:** 96-55-37 W
Pop: 130 (1990); 173 (1980)   **Pop Density:** 3.7
Land: 34.8 sq. mi.; **Water:** 0.0 sq. mi.

Spring Grove   Township
    Lat: 45-25-39 N **Long:** 97-02-34 W
Pop: 150 (1990); 248 (1980)   **Pop Density:** 4.2
Land: 36.0 sq. mi.; **Water:** 0.3 sq. mi.

Summit   Town
ZIP: 57266   **Lat:** 45-18-13 N **Long:** 97-02-12 W
Pop: 267 (1990); 290 (1980)   **Pop Density:** 667.5
Land: 0.4 sq. mi.; **Water:** 0.0 sq. mi.   **Elev:** 1999 ft.
Name origin: For the town's nearly 2000-ft. altitude.

*Summit   Township
ZIP: 57266   **Lat:** 45-20-40 N **Long:** 97-02-47 W
Pop: 52 (1990); 78 (1980)   **Pop Density:** 1.6
Land: 32.5 sq. mi.; **Water:** 0.6 sq. mi.

Victor   Township
ZIP: 57260   **Lat:** 45-52-38 N **Long:** 96-47-11 W
Pop: 169 (1990); 268 (1980)   **Pop Density:** 3.6
Land: 46.9 sq. mi.; **Water:** 0.9 sq. mi.

White Rock   Town
ZIP: 57260   **Lat:** 45-55-30 N **Long:** 96-34-21 W
Pop: 7 (1990); 10 (1980)   **Pop Density:** 4.4
Land: 1.6 sq. mi.; **Water:** 0.0 sq. mi.   **Elev:** 976 ft.
Name origin: For a former large grey rock landmark near the town.

*White Rock   Township
ZIP: 57260   **Lat:** 45-52-15 N **Long:** 96-39-24 W
Pop: 257 (1990); 308 (1980)   **Pop Density:** 4.4
Land: 58.2 sq. mi.; **Water:** 1.2 sq. mi.

Wilmot   City
ZIP: 57279   **Lat:** 45-24-33 N **Long:** 96-51-24 W
Pop: 566 (1990); 507 (1980)   **Pop Density:** 1132.0
Land: 0.5 sq. mi.; **Water:** 0.0 sq. mi.   **Elev:** 1190 ft.
Name origin: For distinguished Judge Wilmot Brookings, a well-known early pioneer.

Sanborn County
County Seat: Woonsocket (ZIP: 57385)

Pop: 2,833 (1990); 3,213 (1980)   **Pop Density:** 5.0
Land: 569.0 sq. mi.; **Water:** 1.2 sq. mi.   **Area Code:** 605
In south-central SD, northwest of Sioux Falls; organized Mar 9, 1883 (prior to statehood) from Miner County.
Name origin: For George W. Sanborn, a Milwaukee Railroad official.

Afton   Township
    Lat: 44-09-14 N **Long:** 97-54-15 W
Pop: 55 (1990); 83 (1980)   **Pop Density:** 1.6
Land: 34.5 sq. mi.; **Water:** 0.0 sq. mi.

Artesian   Town
ZIP: 57314   **Lat:** 44-00-30 N **Long:** 97-55-22 W
Pop: 217 (1990); 227 (1980)   **Pop Density:** 361.7
Land: 0.6 sq. mi.; **Water:** 0.0 sq. mi.   **Elev:** 1317 ft.
Name origin: For its location in a great artesian basin. Originally called Dianna.

Benedict   Township
ZIP: 57314   **Lat:** 44-04-10 N **Long:** 97-54-53 W
Pop: 49 (1990); 51 (1980)   **Pop Density:** 1.4
Land: 35.9 sq. mi.; **Water:** 0.0 sq. mi.

Butler   Township
    Lat: 43-53-53 N **Long:** 98-02-26 W
Pop: 252 (1990); 228 (1980)   **Pop Density:** 7.0
Land: 36.1 sq. mi.; **Water:** 0.0 sq. mi.

Diana   Township
ZIP: 57314   **Lat:** 43-58-26 N **Long:** 97-55-15 W
Pop: 49 (1990); 81 (1980)   **Pop Density:** 1.4
Land: 35.3 sq. mi.; **Water:** 0.0 sq. mi.

Elliott   Township
ZIP: 57359   **Lat:** 43-53-43 N **Long:** 98-16-41 W
Pop: 121 (1990); 151 (1980)   **Pop Density:** 3.4
Land: 35.9 sq. mi.; **Water:** 0.0 sq. mi.

Floyd   Township
ZIP: 57385   **Lat:** 44-09-30 N **Long:** 98-02-22 W
Pop: 95 (1990); 121 (1980)   **Pop Density:** 2.8
Land: 34.3 sq. mi.; **Water:** 0.0 sq. mi.

Jackson   Township
    Lat: 44-08-47 N **Long:** 98-08-27 W
Pop: 101 (1990); 118 (1980)   **Pop Density:** 2.9
Land: 34.5 sq. mi.; **Water:** 0.0 sq. mi.

Letcher   Town
ZIP: 57359   **Lat:** 43-53-51 N **Long:** 98-08-36 W
Pop: 164 (1990); 221 (1980)   **Pop Density:** 273.3
Land: 0.6 sq. mi.; **Water:** 0.0 sq. mi.   **Elev:** 1308 ft.
Name origin: For O.T. Letcher, an original landowner.

*Letcher   Township
ZIP: 57359   **Lat:** 43-53-45 N **Long:** 98-09-08 W
Pop: 185 (1990); 139 (1980)   **Pop Density:** 5.2
Land: 35.5 sq. mi.; **Water:** 0.0 sq. mi.

Logan   Township
    Lat: 43-59-22 N **Long:** 98-09-04 W
Pop: 134 (1990); 195 (1980)   **Pop Density:** 3.7
Land: 35.9 sq. mi.; **Water:** 0.0 sq. mi.

Oneida   Township
    Lat: 44-03-56 N **Long:** 98-01-45 W
Pop: 49 (1990); 57 (1980)   **Pop Density:** 1.4
Land: 35.7 sq. mi.; **Water:** 0.2 sq. mi.

American Places Dictionary   SOUTH DAKOTA, Shannon County

Ravenna   Township
ZIP: 57314   **Lat:** 43-53-38 N   **Long:** 97-54-37 W
Pop: 61 (1990); 79 (1980)   **Pop Density:** 1.7
Land: 35.5 sq. mi.; **Water:** 0.3 sq. mi.

Silver Creek   Township
ZIP: 57385   **Lat:** 44-03-57 N   **Long:** 98-09-12 W
Pop: 108 (1990); 135 (1980)   **Pop Density:** 3.0
Land: 36.0 sq. mi.; **Water:** 0.0 sq. mi.

Twin Lake   Township
ZIP: 57385   **Lat:** 43-58-28 N   **Long:** 98-15-39 W
Pop: 117 (1990); 141 (1980)   **Pop Density:** 3.3
Land: 35.7 sq. mi.; **Water:** 0.3 sq. mi.

Union   Township
     Lat: 43-58-42 N   **Long:** 98-01-37 W
Pop: 65 (1990); 96 (1980)   **Pop Density:** 1.8
Land: 35.8 sq. mi.; **Water:** 0.0 sq. mi.

Warren   Township
     Lat: 44-09-16 N   **Long:** 98-16-01 W
Pop: 75 (1990); 80 (1980)   **Pop Density:** 2.1
Land: 35.2 sq. mi.; **Water:** 0.0 sq. mi.

Woonsocket   City
ZIP: 57385   **Lat:** 44-03-16 N   **Long:** 98-16-25 W
Pop: 766 (1990); 799 (1980)   **Pop Density:** 1094.3
Land: 0.7 sq. mi.; **Water:** 0.0 sq. mi.   **Elev:** 1307 ft.
Settled 1883.
Name origin: For Woonsocket, RI.

*Woonsocket   Township
ZIP: 57385   **Lat:** 44-03-57 N   **Long:** 98-16-32 W
Pop: 170 (1990); 211 (1980)   **Pop Density:** 4.8
Land: 35.5 sq. mi.; **Water:** 0.1 sq. mi.

Shannon County
County Seat: Hot Springs (ZIP: 57747)

Pop: 9,902 (1990); 11,323 (1980)   **Pop Density:** 4.7
Land: 2094.0 sq. mi.; **Water:** 2.8 sq. mi.   **Area Code:** 605
On the southwestern border of SD, southeast of Rapid City; created Jan 11, 1875 (prior to statehood) from territorial county. Unorganized; attached to Fall River County for government purposes. County seat is in Fall River County.
Name origin: For Peter C. Shannon (1821–?), chief justice of the Dakota Territory Supreme Court (1873–82).

Batesland   Town
ZIP: 57716   **Lat:** 43-07-39 N   **Long:** 102-06-04 W
Pop: 124 (1990); 163 (1980)   **Pop Density:** 1240.0
Land: 0.1 sq. mi.; **Water:** 0.0 sq. mi.
Name origin: For C.A. Bates, the government surveyor who plotted the area.

East Shannon   Pop. Place
     Lat: 43-20-55 N   **Long:** 102-18-13 W
Pop: 4,083 (1990); 4,652 (1980)   **Pop Density:** 4.6
Land: 881.9 sq. mi.; **Water:** 1.0 sq. mi.

Hot Springs. *See* **Hot Springs, Fall River County**

Kyle   CDP
ZIP: 57752   **Lat:** 43-25-38 N   **Long:** 102-09-52 W
Pop: 914 (1990)   **Pop Density:** 481.1
Land: 1.9 sq. mi.; **Water:** 0.0 sq. mi.

Manderson-White Horse Creek   CDP
     Lat: 43-13-46 N   **Long:** 102-28-14 W
Pop: 243 (1990)   **Pop Density:** 220.9
Land: 1.1 sq. mi.; **Water:** 0.0 sq. mi.

Oglala   CDP
     Lat: 43-10-58 N   **Long:** 102-43-46 W
Pop: 422 (1990)   **Pop Density:** 31.5
Land: 13.4 sq. mi.; **Water:** 0.9 sq. mi.

Pine Ridge   CDP
ZIP: 57770   **Lat:** 43-01-39 N   **Long:** 102-33-30 W
Pop: 2,596 (1990); 3,059 (1980)   **Pop Density:** 1298.0
Land: 2.0 sq. mi.; **Water:** 0.0 sq. mi.

Porcupine   CDP
ZIP: 57772   **Lat:** 43-16-19 N   **Long:** 102-19-58 W
Pop: 783 (1990)   **Pop Density:** 82.4
Land: 9.5 sq. mi.; **Water:** 0.0 sq. mi.

West Shannon   Pop. Place
     Lat: 43-19-29 N   **Long:** 102-43-35 W
Pop: 5,695 (1990); 6,508 (1980)   **Pop Density:** 4.7
Land: 1212.0 sq. mi.; **Water:** 1.7 sq. mi.

Wounded Knee   CDP
ZIP: 57794   **Lat:** 43-08-32 N   **Long:** 102-21-52 W
Pop: 18 (1990)   **Pop Density:** 25.7
Land: 0.7 sq. mi.; **Water:** 0.0 sq. mi.

SOUTH DAKOTA, Spink County

> ## Spink County
> **County Seat: Redfield (ZIP: 57469)**
>
> **Pop:** 7,981 (1990); 9,201 (1980) **Pop Density:** 5.3
> **Land:** 1504.0 sq. mi.; **Water:** 6.2 sq. mi. **Area Code:** 605
> In east-central SD, south of Aberdeen; created Jan 8, 1873 (prior to statehood) from Hanson and Walworth counties.
> **Name origin:** For Solomon Lewis Spink (1831–81), Dakota Territory secretary and territorial delegate to Congress (1869–71).

Antelope — Township
Lat: 44-39-55 N **Long:** 98-09-11 W
Pop: 96 (1990); 93 (1980) **Pop Density:** 2.7
Land: 35.9 sq. mi.; **Water:** 0.0 sq. mi.

Ashton — City
ZIP: 57424 **Lat:** 44-59-36 N **Long:** 98-29-53 W
Pop: 148 (1990); 154 (1980) **Pop Density:** 370.0
Land: 0.4 sq. mi.; **Water:** 0.0 sq. mi. **Elev:** 1291 ft.
Founded 1879.
Name origin: For its groves of ash trees.

Athol — Township
Lat: 45-02-01 N **Long:** 98-38-12 W
Pop: 110 (1990); 137 (1980) **Pop Density:** 2.3
Land: 47.8 sq. mi.; **Water:** 0.0 sq. mi.

Belle Plaine — Township
ZIP: 57436 **Lat:** 44-51-24 N **Long:** 98-10-10 W
Pop: 118 (1990); 96 (1980) **Pop Density:** 3.3
Land: 36.2 sq. mi.; **Water:** 0.0 sq. mi.

Belmont — Township
Lat: 44-41-00 N **Long:** 98-24-42 W
Pop: 68 (1990); 98 (1980) **Pop Density:** 1.9
Land: 35.9 sq. mi.; **Water:** 0.0 sq. mi.

Benton — Township
Lat: 45-06-58 N **Long:** 98-09-45 W
Pop: 35 (1990); 66 (1980) **Pop Density:** 1.0
Land: 36.1 sq. mi.; **Water:** 0.0 sq. mi.

Beotia — Township
ZIP: 57434 **Lat:** 45-11-59 N **Long:** 98-09-37 W
Pop: 53 (1990); 66 (1980) **Pop Density:** 1.5
Land: 35.5 sq. mi.; **Water:** 0.0 sq. mi.

Brentford — Town
ZIP: 57429 **Lat:** 45-09-33 N **Long:** 98-19-17 W
Pop: 69 (1990); 91 (1980) **Pop Density:** 345.0
Land: 0.2 sq. mi.; **Water:** 0.0 sq. mi. **Elev:** 1297 ft.
Established 1905.
Name origin: For Brentford, England.

Buffalo — Township
Lat: 44-40-47 N **Long:** 98-39-07 W
Pop: 77 (1990); 89 (1980) **Pop Density:** 2.2
Land: 35.8 sq. mi.; **Water:** 0.0 sq. mi.

Capitola — Township
ZIP: 57436 **Lat:** 44-45-47 N **Long:** 98-02-08 W
Pop: 227 (1990); 254 (1980) **Pop Density:** 6.3
Land: 35.9 sq. mi.; **Water:** 0.1 sq. mi.

Clifton — Township
Lat: 45-01-31 N **Long:** 98-18-33 W
Pop: 78 (1990); 89 (1980) **Pop Density:** 1.6
Land: 48.2 sq. mi.; **Water:** 0.0 sq. mi.

Conde — City
ZIP: 57434 **Lat:** 45-09-28 N **Long:** 98-05-48 W
Pop: 203 (1990); 259 (1980) **Pop Density:** 338.3
Land: 0.6 sq. mi.; **Water:** 0.0 sq. mi. **Elev:** 1314 ft.
Name origin: Named in 1886 by French settlers for the famous French Conde family.

*Conde — Township
ZIP: 57434 **Lat:** 45-12-15 N **Long:** 98-02-08 W
Pop: 32 (1990); 32 (1980) **Pop Density:** 0.9
Land: 35.4 sq. mi.; **Water:** 0.0 sq. mi.

Cornwall — Township
Lat: 44-40-32 N **Long:** 98-17-16 W
Pop: 61 (1990); 79 (1980) **Pop Density:** 1.7
Land: 35.5 sq. mi.; **Water:** 0.2 sq. mi.

Crandon — Township
ZIP: 57476 **Lat:** 44-45-47 N **Long:** 98-24-05 W
Pop: 103 (1990); 104 (1980) **Pop Density:** 2.9
Land: 35.8 sq. mi.; **Water:** 0.0 sq. mi.

Doland — City
ZIP: 57436 **Lat:** 44-53-39 N **Long:** 98-05-56 W
Pop: 306 (1990); 381 (1980) **Pop Density:** 510.0
Land: 0.6 sq. mi.; **Water:** 0.0 sq. mi. **Elev:** 1358 ft.
Settled 1882.
Name origin: For F.H. Doland, who was a director of the North Western Railroad and a local landowner.

Exline — Township
ZIP: 57469 **Lat:** 44-51-38 N **Long:** 98-38-35 W
Pop: 77 (1990); 84 (1980) **Pop Density:** 2.1
Land: 36.7 sq. mi.; **Water:** 0.1 sq. mi.

Frankfort — City
ZIP: 57440 **Lat:** 44-52-38 N **Long:** 98-18-30 W
Pop: 192 (1990); 209 (1980) **Pop Density:** 240.0
Land: 0.8 sq. mi.; **Water:** 0.0 sq. mi. **Elev:** 1296 ft.
Settled 1882.
Name origin: For Frankfurt, Germany.

*Frankfort — Township
ZIP: 57440 **Lat:** 44-51-25 N **Long:** 98-16-17 W
Pop: 64 (1990); 81 (1980) **Pop Density:** 1.8
Land: 35.2 sq. mi.; **Water:** 0.2 sq. mi.

Garfield — Township
Lat: 44-40-10 N **Long:** 98-30-52 W
Pop: 59 (1990); 65 (1980) **Pop Density:** 1.6
Land: 35.9 sq. mi.; **Water:** 0.0 sq. mi.

Great Bend — Township
ZIP: 57469 **Lat:** 44-56-14 N **Long:** 98-25-07 W
Pop: 56 (1990); 71 (1980) **Pop Density:** 1.6
Land: 36.0 sq. mi.; **Water:** 0.0 sq. mi.

SOUTH DAKOTA, Spink County

Groveland Township
ZIP: 57469 Lat: 44-56-18 N Long: 98-39-11 W
Pop: 84 (1990); 97 (1980) Pop Density: 2.3
Land: 36.1 sq. mi.; Water: 0.0 sq. mi.

Harmony Township
Lat: 44-56-42 N Long: 98-16-41 W
Pop: 70 (1990); 72 (1980) Pop Density: 1.9
Land: 36.1 sq. mi.; Water: 0.0 sq. mi.

Harrison Township
Lat: 44-46-04 N Long: 98-08-58 W
Pop: 59 (1990); 61 (1980) Pop Density: 1.6
Land: 35.8 sq. mi.; Water: 0.1 sq. mi.

Jefferson Township
Lat: 45-02-12 N Long: 98-28-10 W
Pop: 80 (1990); 89 (1980) Pop Density: 1.7
Land: 47.7 sq. mi.; Water: 0.0 sq. mi.

Lake Township
Lat: 44-46-04 N Long: 98-39-10 W
Pop: 91 (1990); 103 (1980) Pop Density: 2.7
Land: 33.3 sq. mi.; Water: 2.4 sq. mi.

La Prairie Township
Lat: 45-11-33 N Long: 98-19-06 W
Pop: 71 (1990); 93 (1980) Pop Density: 1.4
Land: 49.9 sq. mi.; Water: 0.0 sq. mi.

Lincoln Township
Lat: 44-46-15 N Long: 98-16-30 W
Pop: 216 (1990); 242 (1980) Pop Density: 6.1
Land: 35.4 sq. mi.; Water: 0.3 sq. mi.

Lodi Township
ZIP: 57469 Lat: 44-50-49 N Long: 98-24-28 W
Pop: 84 (1990); 102 (1980) Pop Density: 2.3
Land: 36.7 sq. mi.; Water: 0.0 sq. mi.

Mellette City
ZIP: 57461 Lat: 45-09-14 N Long: 98-29-52 W
Pop: 184 (1990); 192 (1980) Pop Density: 613.3
Land: 0.3 sq. mi.; Water: 0.0 sq. mi. Elev: 1296 ft.
Settled 1878.
Name origin: For Arthur Melette, the first governor of SD.

*Mellette** Township
ZIP: 57461 Lat: 45-09-28 N Long: 98-28-38 W
Pop: 178 (1990); 224 (1980) Pop Density: 2.4
Land: 75.0 sq. mi.; Water: 0.0 sq. mi.

Northville Town
ZIP: 57465 Lat: 45-09-17 N Long: 98-34-42 W
Pop: 105 (1990); 138 (1980) Pop Density: 262.5
Land: 0.4 sq. mi.; Water: 0.0 sq. mi. Elev: 1279 ft.
Platted 1881.
Name origin: For its location as the northern point of the North Western Railroad.

*Northville** Township
ZIP: 57465 Lat: 45-09-35 N Long: 98-37-58 W
Pop: 209 (1990); 279 (1980) Pop Density: 2.1
Land: 99.7 sq. mi.; Water: 0.3 sq. mi.

Olean Township
ZIP: 57477 Lat: 45-06-16 N Long: 98-02-56 W
Pop: 66 (1990); 66 (1980) Pop Density: 1.8
Land: 36.1 sq. mi.; Water: 0.0 sq. mi.

Prairie Center Township
Lat: 44-55-48 N Long: 98-09-57 W
Pop: 47 (1990); 54 (1980) Pop Density: 1.3
Land: 36.0 sq. mi.; Water: 0.0 sq. mi.

Redfield City
ZIP: 57469 Lat: 44-52-22 N Long: 98-31-13 W
Pop: 2,770 (1990); 3,027 (1980) Pop Density: 1538.9
Land: 1.8 sq. mi.; Water: 0.0 sq. mi. Elev: 1303 ft.
Name origin: For J.B. Redfield, a North Western Railroad official.

*Redfield** Township
ZIP: 57469 Lat: 44-51-10 N Long: 98-32-00 W
Pop: 654 (1990); 864 (1980) Pop Density: 18.6
Land: 35.2 sq. mi.; Water: 0.5 sq. mi.

Richfield Township
ZIP: 57436 Lat: 44-51-15 N Long: 98-01-44 W
Pop: 35 (1990); 55 (1980) Pop Density: 1.0
Land: 35.6 sq. mi.; Water: 0.0 sq. mi.

Spring Township
Lat: 44-56-16 N Long: 98-02-26 W
Pop: 31 (1990); 70 (1980) Pop Density: 0.9
Land: 35.7 sq. mi.; Water: 0.0 sq. mi.

Sumner Township
ZIP: 57477 Lat: 45-01-33 N Long: 98-09-43 W
Pop: 37 (1990); 46 (1980) Pop Density: 1.0
Land: 36.0 sq. mi.; Water: 0.0 sq. mi.

Tetonka Township
Lat: 45-06-19 N Long: 98-19-30 W
Pop: 117 (1990); 104 (1980) Pop Density: 2.0
Land: 58.8 sq. mi.; Water: 0.0 sq. mi.

Three Rivers Township
ZIP: 57469 Lat: 44-56-27 N Long: 98-31-22 W
Pop: 67 (1990); 90 (1980) Pop Density: 1.9
Land: 36.1 sq. mi.; Water: 0.0 sq. mi.

Tulare Town
ZIP: 57476 Lat: 44-44-19 N Long: 98-30-31 W
Pop: 244 (1990); 238 (1980) Pop Density: 813.3
Land: 0.3 sq. mi.; Water: 0.0 sq. mi. Elev: 1322 ft.
Name origin: For its location in a marshy region with abundant rushes or tules.

*Tulare** Township
ZIP: 57476 Lat: 44-45-23 N Long: 98-30-50 W
Pop: 55 (1990); 71 (1980) Pop Density: 1.6
Land: 33.9 sq. mi.; Water: 1.8 sq. mi.

Turton Town
ZIP: 57477 Lat: 45-02-56 N Long: 98-05-47 W
Pop: 76 (1990); 101 (1980) Pop Density: 190.0
Land: 0.4 sq. mi.; Water: 0.0 sq. mi. Elev: 1320 ft.

*Turton** Township
ZIP: 57477 Lat: 45-01-18 N Long: 98-02-21 W
Pop: 41 (1990); 51 (1980) Pop Density: 1.1
Land: 35.7 sq. mi.; Water: 0.0 sq. mi.

Union Township
Lat: 44-40-23 N Long: 98-01-48 W
Pop: 78 (1990); 74 (1980) Pop Density: 2.2
Land: 35.9 sq. mi.; Water: 0.0 sq. mi.

Stanley County
County Seat: Fort Pierre (ZIP: 57532)

Pop: 2,453 (1990); 2,533 (1980)   **Pop Density:** 1.7
Land: 1443.4 sq. mi.; **Water:** 73.7 sq. mi.   **Area Code:** 605
In central SD; created Jan 8, 1873 (prior to statehood) from unorganized territory.
Name origin: For Gen. David Sloane Stanley (1829–1902), army officer; after retirement, he served as director of the U.S. Soldiers' Home in Washington, D.C. (1893–98).

Fort Pierre — City
ZIP: 57532   **Lat:** 44-21-45 N   **Long:** 100-22-45 W
Pop: 1,854 (1990); 1,789 (1980)   **Pop Density:** 713.1
Land: 2.6 sq. mi.; **Water:** 0.0 sq. mi.   **Elev:** 1460 ft.
One of the oldest white settlements in SD.
Name origin: For the pioneer fort.

North Stanley — Pop. Place
Lat: 44-31-58 N   **Long:** 100-50-15 W
Pop: 268 (1990); 350 (1980)   **Pop Density:** 0.4
Land: 706.7 sq. mi.; **Water:** 63.3 sq. mi.

South Stanley — Pop. Place
Lat: 44-16-07 N   **Long:** 100-37-10 W
Pop: 331 (1990); 394 (1980)   **Pop Density:** 0.5
Land: 734.1 sq. mi.; **Water:** 10.3 sq. mi.

Sully County
County Seat: Onida (ZIP: 57564)

Pop: 1,589 (1990); 1,990 (1980)   **Pop Density:** 1.6
Land: 1007.0 sq. mi.; **Water:** 63.5 sq. mi.   **Area Code:** 605
In central SD, north of Pierre; created Jan 8, 1873 (prior to statehood) from Potter County.
Name origin: For Fort Sully, which was named for Gen. Alfred Sully (1821–79), its builder and commander; famous as an Indian fighter and cited several times for bravery during the Civil War.

Agar — Town
ZIP: 57520   **Lat:** 44-50-19 N   **Long:** 100-04-20 W
Pop: 82 (1990); 139 (1980)   **Pop Density:** 410.0
Land: 0.2 sq. mi.; **Water:** 0.0 sq. mi.   **Elev:** 1851 ft.
Founded 1910.
Name origin: For county commissioner Charles Agar.

Onida — City
ZIP: 57564   **Lat:** 44-42-16 N   **Long:** 100-03-59 W
Pop: 761 (1990); 851 (1980)   **Pop Density:** 1268.3
Land: 0.6 sq. mi.; **Water:** 0.0 sq. mi.   **Elev:** 1870 ft.
Founded 1883.
Name origin: For Oneida, NY, former home of its settlers. Spelling altered to reflect pronunciation.

East Sully — Pop. Place
Lat: 44-43-42 N   **Long:** 99-53-13 W
Pop: 340 (1990); 478 (1980)   **Pop Density:** 0.7
Land: 477.5 sq. mi.; **Water:** 3.4 sq. mi.

West Sully — Pop. Place
Lat: 44-42-52 N   **Long:** 100-20-03 W
Pop: 406 (1990); 522 (1980)   **Pop Density:** 0.8
Land: 528.7 sq. mi.; **Water:** 60.0 sq. mi.

Todd County
County Seat: Winner (ZIP: 57580)

Pop: 8,352 (1990); 7,328 (1980)   **Pop Density:** 6.0
Land: 1388.2 sq. mi.; **Water:** 2.8 sq. mi.   **Area Code:** 605

On the central southern border of SD, south of Pierre; created Mar 9, 1909 from Indian lands. Unorganized; attached to Tripp County for governmental purposes. County seat is in Tripp County.

Name origin: For Gen. John Blair Smith Todd (1814–72), officer in the Seminole War and the Mexican-American War, U.S. congressional delegate from the Dakota Territory (1862–65), and territorial legislator (1866–67).

Antelope   CDP
Lat: 43-18-20 N **Long:** 100-37-41 W
Pop: 744 (1990)   **Pop Density:** 323.5
Land: 2.3 sq. mi.; **Water:** 0.0 sq. mi.

East Todd   Pop. Place
Lat: 43-11-51 N **Long:** 100-27-59 W
Pop: 2,439 (1990); 2,255 (1980)   **Pop Density:** 3.4
Land: 723.6 sq. mi.; **Water:** 1.9 sq. mi.

Mission   City
ZIP: 57555   **Lat:** 43-18-23 N **Long:** 100-39-37 W
Pop: 730 (1990); 748 (1980)   **Pop Density:** 1216.7
Land: 0.6 sq. mi.; **Water:** 0.0 sq. mi.   **Elev:** 2581 ft.
Founded 1915.
Name origin: Named by founder S.J. Kimmel for the many churches in the area.

Parmelee   CDP
ZIP: 57566   **Lat:** 43-19-27 N **Long:** 101-02-11 W
Pop: 618 (1990)   **Pop Density:** 134.3
Land: 4.6 sq. mi.; **Water:** 0.1 sq. mi.

Rosebud   CDP
Lat: 43-14-07 N **Long:** 100-50-19 W
Pop: 1,538 (1990)   **Pop Density:** 147.9
Land: 10.4 sq. mi.; **Water:** 0.0 sq. mi.

St. Francis   Town
Lat: 43-08-32 N **Long:** 100-54-07 W
Pop: 815 (1990); 766 (1980)   **Pop Density:** 2037.5
Land: 0.4 sq. mi.; **Water:** 0.0 sq. mi.   **Elev:** 2980 ft.
Name origin: For the nearby St. Francis Indian School.

Spring Creek   CDP
ZIP: 57572   **Lat:** 43-07-13 N **Long:** 101-01-38 W
Pop: 231 (1990)   **Pop Density:** 27.5
Land: 8.4 sq. mi.; **Water:** 0.0 sq. mi.

Two Strike   CDP
Lat: 43-12-46 N **Long:** 100-52-30 W
Pop: 112 (1990)   **Pop Density:** 43.1
Land: 2.6 sq. mi.; **Water:** 0.0 sq. mi.

West Todd   Pop. Place
Lat: 43-11-29 N **Long:** 100-59-24 W
Pop: 4,368 (1990); 3,559 (1980)   **Pop Density:** 6.6
Land: 663.7 sq. mi.; **Water:** 0.9 sq. mi.

White Horse   CDP
Lat: 43-18-29 N **Long:** 100-35-45 W
Pop: 152 (1990)   **Pop Density:** 47.5
Land: 3.2 sq. mi.; **Water:** 0.0 sq. mi.

Winner. *See* **Winner, Tripp County**

Tripp County
County Seat: Winner (ZIP: 57580)

Pop: 6,924 (1990); 7,268 (1980)   **Pop Density:** 4.3
Land: 1613.6 sq. mi.; **Water:** 3.9 sq. mi.   **Area Code:** 605

On the central southern border of SD, southeast of Pierre; created Jan 8, 1873 (prior to statehood) from unorganized territory. Seat of government for Todd County.

Name origin: For Bartlett Tripp (1842–1911), promoter of SD's statehood, U.S. minister to Austria-Hungary (1893), chief justice of the Dakota Territory (1886–89), and trustee of Yankton College.

Banner   Township
Lat: 43-27-57 N **Long:** 99-56-56 W
Pop: 18 (1990); 19 (1980)   **Pop Density:** 0.6
Land: 28.5 sq. mi.; **Water:** 0.0 sq. mi.

Beaver Creek   Township
ZIP: 57545   **Lat:** 43-02-28 N **Long:** 100-10-11 W
Pop: 24 (1990); 22 (1980)   **Pop Density:** 1.1
Land: 21.0 sq. mi.; **Water:** 0.0 sq. mi.

Black   Township
ZIP: 57580   **Lat:** 43-23-45 N **Long:** 99-57-01 W
Pop: 150 (1990); 136 (1980)   **Pop Density:** 4.2
Land: 35.7 sq. mi.; **Water:** 0.0 sq. mi.

Brunson   Township
Lat: 43-28-10 N **Long:** 99-50-07 W
Pop: 53 (1990); 65 (1980)   **Pop Density:** 1.8
Land: 28.8 sq. mi.; **Water:** 0.0 sq. mi.

SOUTH DAKOTA, Tripp County

Bull Creek Township
ZIP: 57534   Lat: 43-28-40 N **Long:** 99-35-11 W
Pop: 43 (1990); 43 (1980)   **Pop Density:** 1.5
Land: 29.1 sq. mi.; **Water:** 0.0 sq. mi.

Carter Town
ZIP: 57526   **Lat:** 43-22-57 N **Long:** 100-10-14 W
Pop: 52 (1990); 65 (1980)   **Pop Density:** 2.0
Land: 26.3 sq. mi.; **Water:** 0.1 sq. mi.
Platted 1909.
Name origin: For Jervis Carter, a local U.S. land office registrar.

Colome City
ZIP: 57528   **Lat:** 43-15-35 N **Long:** 99-42-56 W
Pop: 309 (1990); 361 (1980)   **Pop Density:** 1030.0
Land: 0.3 sq. mi.; **Water:** 0.0 sq. mi.   **Elev:** 2268 ft.
Founded 1905.
Name origin: For the Colome brothers, who established the town.

***Colome** Township
ZIP: 57528   **Lat:** 43-17-57 N **Long:** 99-42-06 W
Pop: 108 (1990); 104 (1980)   **Pop Density:** 3.0
Land: 35.5 sq. mi.; **Water:** 0.0 sq. mi.

Condon Township
ZIP: 57534   **Lat:** 43-32-53 N **Long:** 99-41-16 W
Pop: 47 (1990); 58 (1980)   **Pop Density:** 1.3
Land: 36.0 sq. mi.; **Water:** 0.1 sq. mi.

Curlew Township
Lat: 43-32-05 N **Long:** 100-09-59 W
Pop: 38 (1990); 41 (1980)   **Pop Density:** 1.0
Land: 39.4 sq. mi.; **Water:** 0.0 sq. mi.

Dog Ear Township
Lat: 43-13-11 N **Long:** 99-56-56 W
Pop: 62 (1990); 77 (1980)   **Pop Density:** 1.7
Land: 35.7 sq. mi.; **Water:** 0.1 sq. mi.

Elliston Township
Lat: 43-12-53 N **Long:** 99-35-14 W
Pop: 47 (1990); 62 (1980)   **Pop Density:** 1.3
Land: 35.7 sq. mi.; **Water:** 0.1 sq. mi.

Greenwood Township
Lat: 43-38-02 N **Long:** 100-02-06 W
Pop: 21 (1990); 29 (1980)   **Pop Density:** 0.5
Land: 44.7 sq. mi.; **Water:** 0.3 sq. mi.

Holsclaw Township
ZIP: 57545   **Lat:** 43-07-51 N **Long:** 100-10-26 W
Pop: 24 (1990); 34 (1980)   **Pop Density:** 1.0
Land: 23.8 sq. mi.; **Water:** 0.0 sq. mi.

Huggins Township
ZIP: 57545   **Lat:** 43-02-20 N **Long:** 100-04-10 W
Pop: 29 (1990); 43 (1980)   **Pop Density:** 0.8
Land: 34.9 sq. mi.; **Water:** 0.0 sq. mi.

Ideal Township
ZIP: 57541   **Lat:** 43-32-31 N **Long:** 99-55-20 W
Pop: 208 (1990); 223 (1980)   **Pop Density:** 5.8
Land: 36.0 sq. mi.; **Water:** 0.0 sq. mi.

Irwin Township
ZIP: 57528   **Lat:** 43-17-56 N **Long:** 99-35-34 W
Pop: 39 (1990); 60 (1980)   **Pop Density:** 1.1
Land: 35.7 sq. mi.; **Water:** 0.1 sq. mi.

Jordan Township
ZIP: 57580   **Lat:** 43-23-38 N **Long:** 100-04-18 W
Pop: 44 (1990); 50 (1980)   **Pop Density:** 1.2
Land: 35.7 sq. mi.; **Water:** 0.1 sq. mi.

Keyapaha Township
ZIP: 57545   **Lat:** 43-02-07 N **Long:** 99-42-32 W
Pop: 36 (1990); 43 (1980)   **Pop Density:** 1.0
Land: 34.9 sq. mi.; **Water:** 0.0 sq. mi.

King Township
ZIP: 57534   **Lat:** 43-32-30 N **Long:** 99-48-15 W
Pop: 41 (1990); 56 (1980)   **Pop Density:** 1.1
Land: 35.9 sq. mi.; **Water:** 0.0 sq. mi.

Lake Township
Lat: 43-07-49 N **Long:** 99-50-16 W
Pop: 86 (1990); 89 (1980)   **Pop Density:** 2.4
Land: 36.0 sq. mi.; **Water:** 0.0 sq. mi.

Lamro Township
ZIP: 57580   **Lat:** 43-23-24 N **Long:** 99-49-30 W
Pop: 589 (1990); 368 (1980)   **Pop Density:** 17.1
Land: 34.5 sq. mi.; **Water:** 0.0 sq. mi.

Lincoln Township
Lat: 43-07-05 N **Long:** 99-36-10 W
Pop: 55 (1990); 61 (1980)   **Pop Density:** 1.5
Land: 35.8 sq. mi.; **Water:** 0.1 sq. mi.

Lone Star Township
ZIP: 57534   **Lat:** 43-37-23 N **Long:** 99-47-32 W
Pop: 23 (1990); 24 (1980)   **Pop Density:** 0.6
Land: 35.8 sq. mi.; **Water:** 0.1 sq. mi.

Lone Tree Township
ZIP: 57580   **Lat:** 43-32-46 N **Long:** 100-03-02 W
Pop: 44 (1990); 56 (1980)   **Pop Density:** 1.2
Land: 35.8 sq. mi.; **Water:** 0.0 sq. mi.

McNeely Township
ZIP: 57580   **Lat:** 43-13-11 N **Long:** 99-50-24 W
Pop: 75 (1990); 117 (1980)   **Pop Density:** 2.1
Land: 35.9 sq. mi.; **Water:** 0.0 sq. mi.

Millboro Township
Lat: 43-02-19 N **Long:** 99-56-19 W
Pop: 56 (1990); 58 (1980)   **Pop Density:** 1.6
Land: 34.9 sq. mi.; **Water:** 0.0 sq. mi.

New Witten Town
Lat: 43-26-25 N **Long:** 100-04-58 W
Pop: 87 (1990); 134 (1980)   **Pop Density:** 290.0
Land: 0.3 sq. mi.; **Water:** 0.0 sq. mi.
Settled 1910.

North Tripp Pop. Place
Lat: 43-42-00 N **Long:** 99-42-47 W
Pop: 27 (1990); 34 (1980)   **Pop Density:** 0.7
Land: 41.4 sq. mi.; **Water:** 0.4 sq. mi.

Pahapesto Township
Lat: 43-38-15 N **Long:** 100-09-46 W
Pop: 25 (1990); 27 (1980)   **Pop Density:** 0.5
Land: 50.3 sq. mi.; **Water:** 0.3 sq. mi.

Plainview Township
Lat: 43-22-43 N **Long:** 99-42-07 W
Pop: 112 (1990); 83 (1980)   **Pop Density:** 3.1
Land: 35.6 sq. mi.; **Water:** 0.1 sq. mi.

American Places Dictionary   SOUTH DAKOTA, Turner County

Pleasant Valley   Township
ZIP: 57580   **Lat:** 43-27-56 N   **Long:** 99-42-43 W
Pop: 23 (1990); 31 (1980)   **Pop Density:** 0.8
Land: 28.8 sq. mi.; **Water:** 0.0 sq. mi.

Pleasant View   Township
ZIP: 57528   **Lat:** 43-12-44 N   **Long:** 99-42-51 W
Pop: 129 (1990); 148 (1980)   **Pop Density:** 3.6
Land: 35.9 sq. mi.; **Water:** 0.0 sq. mi.

Progressive   Township
ZIP: 57584   **Lat:** 43-28-16 N   **Long:** 100-10-31 W
Pop: 30 (1990); 36 (1980)   **Pop Density:** 1.3
Land: 22.6 sq. mi.; **Water:** 0.1 sq. mi.

Rames   Township
Lat: 43-02-05 N   **Long:** 99-50-02 W
Pop: 39 (1990); 57 (1980)   **Pop Density:** 1.1
Land: 34.9 sq. mi.; **Water:** 0.0 sq. mi.

Rosedale   Township
ZIP: 57580   **Lat:** 43-18-32 N   **Long:** 100-03-51 W
Pop: 52 (1990); 76 (1980)   **Pop Density:** 1.5
Land: 35.8 sq. mi.; **Water:** 0.1 sq. mi.

Roseland   Township
ZIP: 57534   **Lat:** 43-38-57 N   **Long:** 99-41-17 W
Pop: 51 (1990); 58 (1980)   **Pop Density:** 1.4
Land: 35.9 sq. mi.; **Water:** 0.1 sq. mi.

Star Prairie   Township
Lat: 43-12-44 N   **Long:** 100-04-15 W
Pop: 51 (1990); 71 (1980)   **Pop Density:** 1.4
Land: 35.9 sq. mi.; **Water:** 0.0 sq. mi.

Star Valley   Township
ZIP: 57541   **Lat:** 43-37-47 N   **Long:** 99-54-59 W
Pop: 26 (1990); 37 (1980)   **Pop Density:** 0.6
Land: 42.1 sq. mi.; **Water:** 0.4 sq. mi.

Stewart   Township
ZIP: 57528   **Lat:** 43-07-29 N   **Long:** 99-42-51 W
Pop: 115 (1990); 127 (1980)   **Pop Density:** 3.2
Land: 36.0 sq. mi.; **Water:** 0.0 sq. mi.

Sully   Township
ZIP: 57580   **Lat:** 43-22-58 N   **Long:** 99-35-16 W
Pop: 54 (1990); 50 (1980)   **Pop Density:** 1.5
Land: 35.7 sq. mi.; **Water:** 0.1 sq. mi.

Taylor   Township
Lat: 43-18-25 N   **Long:** 100-10-33 W
Pop: 21 (1990); 21 (1980)   **Pop Density:** 0.8
Land: 26.3 sq. mi.; **Water:** 0.1 sq. mi.

Valley   Township
Lat: 43-02-13 N   **Long:** 99-35-53 W
Pop: 46 (1990); 61 (1980)   **Pop Density:** 1.3
Land: 34.8 sq. mi.; **Water:** 0.0 sq. mi.

Weaver   Township
ZIP: 57580   **Lat:** 43-18-04 N   **Long:** 99-57-12 W
Pop: 70 (1990); 76 (1980)   **Pop Density:** 2.0
Land: 35.7 sq. mi.; **Water:** 0.0 sq. mi.

Willow Creek   Township
ZIP: 57580   **Lat:** 43-07-58 N   **Long:** 99-57-30 W
Pop: 71 (1990); 62 (1980)   **Pop Density:** 2.0
Land: 35.8 sq. mi.; **Water:** 0.2 sq. mi.

Wilson   Township
ZIP: 57580   **Lat:** 43-18-17 N   **Long:** 99-49-38 W
Pop: 135 (1990); 110 (1980)   **Pop Density:** 3.8
Land: 35.8 sq. mi.; **Water:** 0.0 sq. mi.

Winner   City
ZIP: 57580   **Lat:** 43-22-25 N   **Long:** 99-51-31 W
Pop: 3,354 (1990); 3,472 (1980)   **Pop Density:** 2395.7
Land: 1.4 sq. mi.; **Water:** 0.0 sq. mi.   **Elev:** 1950 ft.
County seat for Todd and Tripp counties.
Name origin: For being the winner in establishing a town along the railroad right-of-way.

Witten   Township
ZIP: 57584   **Lat:** 43-28-03 N   **Long:** 100-03-45 W
Pop: 31 (1990); 34 (1980)   **Pop Density:** 1.1
Land: 28.2 sq. mi.; **Water:** 0.2 sq. mi.

Wortman   Township
ZIP: 57545   **Lat:** 43-07-25 N   **Long:** 100-03-44 W
Pop: 39 (1990); 64 (1980)   **Pop Density:** 1.1
Land: 35.9 sq. mi.; **Water:** 0.1 sq. mi.

Wright   Township
ZIP: 57545   **Lat:** 43-12-55 N   **Long:** 100-10-33 W
Pop: 15 (1990); 28 (1980)   **Pop Density:** 0.6
Land: 26.3 sq. mi.; **Water:** 0.0 sq. mi.

Turner County
County Seat: Parker (ZIP: 57053)

Pop: 8,576 (1990); 9,255 (1980)   **Pop Density:** 13.9
Land: 616.9 sq. mi.; **Water:** 0.6 sq. mi.   **Area Code:** 605
In southeastern SD, southwest of Sioux Falls; organized Jan 13, 1871 (prior to statehood) from Lincoln County and part of the now-defunct Jayne County.
Name origin: For John W. Turner (1800–83), member of the Dakota Territory legislature (1865–66; 1872) and a superintendent of public instruction.

Brothersfield   Township
Lat: 43-27-37 N   **Long:** 97-06-02 W
Pop: 148 (1990); 168 (1980)   **Pop Density:** 5.2
Land: 28.4 sq. mi.; **Water:** 0.0 sq. mi.

Centerville   City
ZIP: 57014   **Lat:** 43-07-03 N   **Long:** 96-57-31 W
Pop: 887 (1990); 892 (1980)   **Pop Density:** 1108.8
Land: 0.8 sq. mi.; **Water:** 0.0 sq. mi.   **Elev:** 1226 ft.
Name origin: Named in 1872 for its location between Swan Lake and Vermillion.

SOUTH DAKOTA, Turner County

*Centerville — Township
ZIP: 57014   Lat: 43-07-36 N   Long: 96-58-50 W
Pop: 211 (1990); 212 (1980)   Pop Density: 6.0
Land: 35.1 sq. mi.; Water: 0.0 sq. mi.

Chancellor — Town
ZIP: 57015   Lat: 43-22-20 N   Long: 96-59-14 W
Pop: 276 (1990); 257 (1980)   Pop Density: 1380.0
Land: 0.2 sq. mi.; Water: 0.0 sq. mi.   Elev: 1367 ft.
Name origin: Named by early German settlers for Otto Bismarck (1815–98), Germany's "Iron Chancellor."

Childstown — Township
ZIP: 57036   Lat: 43-18-03 N   Long: 97-20-09 W
Pop: 283 (1990); 322 (1980)   Pop Density: 7.8
Land: 36.5 sq. mi.; Water: 0.0 sq. mi.

Daneville — Township
Lat: 43-07-23 N   Long: 97-06-01 W
Pop: 213 (1990); 230 (1980)   Pop Density: 6.0
Land: 35.7 sq. mi.; Water: 0.0 sq. mi.

Davis — Town
ZIP: 57021   Lat: 43-15-29 N   Long: 96-59-44 W
Pop: 87 (1990); 100 (1980)   Pop Density: 217.5
Land: 0.4 sq. mi.; Water: 0.0 sq. mi.   Elev: 1250 ft.
Founded 1893.
Name origin: For Jackson Davis, the original landowner.

Dolton — Town
ZIP: 57023   Lat: 43-29-29 N   Long: 97-23-05 W
Pop: 43 (1990); 47 (1980)   Pop Density: 143.3
Land: 0.3 sq. mi.; Water: 0.0 sq. mi.   Elev: 1440 ft.
Incorporated 1907.

*Dolton — Township
Lat: 43-28-13 N   Long: 97-20-36 W
Pop: 169 (1990); 199 (1980)   Pop Density: 5.8
Land: 29.1 sq. mi.; Water: 0.0 sq. mi.

Germantown — Township
ZIP: 57015   Lat: 43-23-35 N   Long: 96-59-10 W
Pop: 326 (1990); 357 (1980)   Pop Density: 9.2
Land: 35.5 sq. mi.; Water: 0.0 sq. mi.

Home — Township
ZIP: 57053   Lat: 43-27-47 N   Long: 96-59-32 W
Pop: 279 (1990); 254 (1980)   Pop Density: 10.0
Land: 27.9 sq. mi.; Water: 0.0 sq. mi.

Hurley — City
ZIP: 57036   Lat: 43-16-47 N   Long: 97-05-24 W
Pop: 372 (1990); 419 (1980)   Pop Density: 744.0
Land: 0.5 sq. mi.; Water: 0.0 sq. mi.   Elev: 1293 ft.
Platted 1883.
Name origin: For R.E. Hurley, chief engineer of the North Western Railroad.

*Hurley — Township
ZIP: 57036   Lat: 43-18-02 N   Long: 97-06-05 W
Pop: 152 (1990); 181 (1980)   Pop Density: 4.3
Land: 35.1 sq. mi.; Water: 0.3 sq. mi.

Irene — Town
Lat: 43-05-04 N   Long: 97-09-12 W
Pop: 253 (1990); 268 (1980)   Pop Density: 2530.0
Land: 0.1 sq. mi.; Water: 0.0 sq. mi.   Elev: 1364 ft.
Part of the town is also in Clay and Yankton counties.
Name origin: For Irene Fry, the daughter of the original landowner.

Marion — City
Lat: 43-25-26 N   Long: 97-15-38 W
Pop: 831 (1990); 830 (1980)   Pop Density: 923.3
Land: 0.9 sq. mi.; Water: 0.0 sq. mi.   Elev: 1440 ft.
Established 1879.
Name origin: For the daughter of a Milwaukee Railroad official.

*Marion — Township
Lat: 43-23-01 N   Long: 97-12-46 W
Pop: 237 (1990); 242 (1980)   Pop Density: 6.8
Land: 35.0 sq. mi.; Water: 0.0 sq. mi.

Middleton — Township
ZIP: 57021   Lat: 43-18-01 N   Long: 96-58-48 W
Pop: 248 (1990); 287 (1980)   Pop Density: 7.0
Land: 35.4 sq. mi.; Water: 0.0 sq. mi.

Monroe — Town
ZIP: 57047   Lat: 43-29-13 N   Long: 97-12-57 W
Pop: 151 (1990); 170 (1980)   Pop Density: 377.5
Land: 0.4 sq. mi.; Water: 0.0 sq. mi.   Elev: 1480 ft.
Name origin: For James Monroe (1758–1831), fifth U.S. president.

*Monroe — Township
Lat: 43-27-51 N   Long: 97-12-53 W
Pop: 157 (1990); 184 (1980)   Pop Density: 5.6
Land: 28.1 sq. mi.; Water: 0.0 sq. mi.

Norway — Township
Lat: 43-18-00 N   Long: 97-13-13 W
Pop: 208 (1990); 212 (1980)   Pop Density: 5.8
Land: 35.8 sq. mi.; Water: 0.0 sq. mi.

Parker — City
ZIP: 57053   Lat: 43-23-46 N   Long: 97-08-18 W
Pop: 984 (1990); 999 (1980)   Pop Density: 1093.3
Land: 0.9 sq. mi.; Water: 0.0 sq. mi.   Elev: 1372 ft.
Settled 1879.
Name origin: For Kimball Parker, a railroad official.

*Parker — Township
ZIP: 57053   Lat: 43-23-15 N   Long: 97-06-01 W
Pop: 249 (1990); 326 (1980)   Pop Density: 7.1
Land: 35.0 sq. mi.; Water: 0.0 sq. mi.

Rosefield — Township
Lat: 43-22-51 N   Long: 97-20-32 W
Pop: 218 (1990); 266 (1980)   Pop Density: 6.0
Land: 36.4 sq. mi.; Water: 0.0 sq. mi.

Salem — Township
Lat: 43-13-06 N   Long: 97-20-26 W
Pop: 213 (1990); 264 (1980)   Pop Density: 5.9
Land: 36.4 sq. mi.; Water: 0.0 sq. mi.

Spring Valley — Township
Lat: 43-13-05 N   Long: 97-13-14 W
Pop: 205 (1990); 255 (1980)   Pop Density: 5.7
Land: 35.7 sq. mi.; Water: 0.0 sq. mi.

Swan Lake — Township
ZIP: 57070   Lat: 43-13-01 N   Long: 97-06-13 W
Pop: 208 (1990); 260 (1980)   Pop Density: 5.9
Land: 35.5 sq. mi.; Water: 0.3 sq. mi.

Turner — Township
ZIP: 57021   Lat: 43-13-06 N   Long: 96-58-54 W
Pop: 205 (1990); 242 (1980)   Pop Density: 5.8
Land: 35.5 sq. mi.; Water: 0.1 sq. mi.

Viborg
City
ZIP: 57070 **Lat:** 43-10-16 N **Long:** 97-04-49 W
Pop: 763 (1990); 812 (1980) **Pop Density:** 1907.5
Land: 0.4 sq. mi.; **Water:** 0.0 sq. mi. **Elev:** 1304 ft.
Settled 1886.
Name origin: Named by Danish setters for Viborg, Denmark.

Union County
County Seat: Elk Point (ZIP: 57025)

Pop: 10,189 (1990); 10,938 (1980) **Pop Density:** 22.1
Land: 460.4 sq. mi.; **Water:** 6.7 sq. mi. **Area Code:** 605
In southeastern SD, south of Sioux Falls; organized as Cole County Apr 10, 1862 (prior to statehood) from unorganized territory; name changed 1864.
Name origin: For support of the Union in the Civil War. Originally for Austin Cole, member of the first Territorial legislature.

Alcester
City
ZIP: 57001 **Lat:** 43-01-23 N **Long:** 96-37-43 W
Pop: 843 (1990); 885 (1980) **Pop Density:** 2810.0
Land: 0.3 sq. mi.; **Water:** 0.0 sq. mi. **Elev:** 1370 ft.
Founded 1879.
Name origin: For a colonel in the British Army.

Alcester
Township
ZIP: 57001 **Lat:** 43-02-48 N **Long:** 96-37-58 W
Pop: 339 (1990); 352 (1980) **Pop Density:** 9.5
Land: 35.5 sq. mi.; **Water:** 0.1 sq. mi.

Beresford
City
ZIP: 57004 **Lat:** 43-04-35 N **Long:** 96-46-42 W
Pop: 1,500 (1990); 1,504 (1980) **Pop Density:** 1153.8
Land: 1.3 sq. mi.; **Water:** 0.0 sq. mi. **Elev:** 1498 ft.
Part of the town is also in Lincoln County.
Name origin: For Adm. Lord Charles Beresford (1846–1919), who had a financial interest in the local railroad. Originally called Paris.

Big Sioux
Township
ZIP: 57049 **Lat:** 42-31-26 N **Long:** 96-30-33 W
Pop: 382 (1990); 403 (1980) **Pop Density:** 26.5
Land: 14.4 sq. mi.; **Water:** 1.9 sq. mi.

Big Springs
Township
Lat: 42-57-26 N **Long:** 96-37-46 W
Pop: 302 (1990); 331 (1980) **Pop Density:** 8.3
Land: 36.6 sq. mi.; **Water:** 0.0 sq. mi.

Brule
Township
Lat: 42-47-01 N **Long:** 96-45-19 W
Pop: 243 (1990); 271 (1980) **Pop Density:** 6.7
Land: 36.3 sq. mi.; **Water:** 0.0 sq. mi.

Civil Bend
Township
ZIP: 57025 **Lat:** 42-35-54 N **Long:** 96-39-17 W
Pop: 302 (1990); 358 (1980) **Pop Density:** 10.1
Land: 29.8 sq. mi.; **Water:** 3.0 sq. mi.

Elk Point
City
ZIP: 57025 **Lat:** 42-40-57 N **Long:** 96-40-50 W
Pop: 1,423 (1990); 1,661 (1980) **Pop Density:** 1094.6
Land: 1.3 sq. mi.; **Water:** 0.0 sq. mi. **Elev:** 1127 ft.
Name origin: For nearby Elk Point on the Missouri River.

*Elk Point
Township
ZIP: 57025 **Lat:** 42-41-32 N **Long:** 96-41-47 W
Pop: 280 (1990); 338 (1980) **Pop Density:** 5.0
Land: 55.5 sq. mi.; **Water:** 0.9 sq. mi.

Emmet
Township
ZIP: 57004 **Lat:** 42-57-08 N **Long:** 96-44-34 W
Pop: 278 (1990); 347 (1980) **Pop Density:** 7.7
Land: 36.0 sq. mi.; **Water:** 0.0 sq. mi.

Jefferson
Town
ZIP: 57038 **Lat:** 42-36-12 N **Long:** 96-33-41 W
Pop: 527 (1990); 592 (1980) **Pop Density:** 2635.0
Land: 0.2 sq. mi.; **Water:** 0.0 sq. mi. **Elev:** 1119 ft.
Name origin: For Thomas Jefferson (1743–1826), third U.S. president.

*Jefferson
Township
ZIP: 57038 **Lat:** 42-35-29 N **Long:** 96-33-44 W
Pop: 523 (1990); 531 (1980) **Pop Density:** 14.3
Land: 36.7 sq. mi.; **Water:** 0.7 sq. mi.

North Sioux City
City
ZIP: 57049 **Lat:** 42-32-11 N **Long:** 96-30-07 W
Pop: 2,019 (1990); 1,992 (1980) **Pop Density:** 961.4
Land: 2.1 sq. mi.; **Water:** 0.0 sq. mi. **Elev:** 1100 ft.
Name origin: For the Sioux Indians.

Prairie
Township
Lat: 43-02-21 N **Long:** 96-45-01 W
Pop: 218 (1990); 246 (1980) **Pop Density:** 6.3
Land: 34.5 sq. mi.; **Water:** 0.0 sq. mi.

Richland
Pop. Place
ZIP: 57025 **Lat:** 42-47-38 N **Long:** 96-38-48 W
Pop: 199 (1990); 227 (1980) **Pop Density:** 8.9
Land: 22.3 sq. mi.; **Water:** 0.1 sq. mi.

Sioux Valley
Township
Lat: 42-52-05 N **Long:** 96-37-10 W
Pop: 275 (1990); 274 (1980) **Pop Density:** 6.5
Land: 42.1 sq. mi.; **Water:** 0.0 sq. mi.

Spink
Township
ZIP: 57025 **Lat:** 42-51-53 N **Long:** 96-44-31 W
Pop: 278 (1990); 328 (1980) **Pop Density:** 7.7
Land: 36.3 sq. mi.; **Water:** 0.0 sq. mi.

SOUTH DAKOTA, Union County   American Places Dictionary

Virginia
Township
Lat: 43-00-15 N **Long:** 96-32-01 W
Pop: 258 (1990); 298 (1980) **Pop Density:** 6.6
Land: 39.1 sq. mi.; **Water:** 0.0 sq. mi.

Walworth County
County Seat: Selby (ZIP: 57472)

Pop: 6,087 (1990); 7,011 (1980) **Pop Density:** 8.6
Land: 707.8 sq. mi.; **Water:** 36.4 sq. mi. **Area Code:** 605
In north-central SD, west of Aberdeen; created Jan 8, 1873 (prior to statehood) from territorial county.
Name origin: For Walworth County, WI, former home of early settlers.

Akaska
Town
ZIP: 57420 **Lat:** 45-19-54 N **Long:** 100-07-14 W
Pop: 52 (1990); 49 (1980) **Pop Density:** 74.3
Land: 0.7 sq. mi.; **Water:** 0.0 sq. mi. **Elev:** 1768 ft.
Name origin: From a Sioux Indian term meaning 'a woman who lives with several men' or 'to eat up.'

East Walworth
Pop. Place
Lat: 45-24-47 N **Long:** 99-53-01 W
Pop: 584 (1990); 705 (1980) **Pop Density:** 1.5
Land: 392.3 sq. mi.; **Water:** 5.4 sq. mi.

Glenham
Town
ZIP: 57631 **Lat:** 45-31-59 N **Long:** 100-16-13 W
Pop: 134 (1990); 169 (1980) **Pop Density:** 446.7
Land: 0.3 sq. mi.; **Water:** 0.0 sq. mi. **Elev:** 1709 ft.
Established 1900.

Java
City
ZIP: 57452 **Lat:** 45-30-12 N **Long:** 99-53-03 W
Pop: 161 (1990); 261 (1980) **Pop Density:** 322.0
Land: 0.5 sq. mi.; **Water:** 0.0 sq. mi. **Elev:** 2079 ft.
Name origin: Named by Milwaukee Railroad officials for the slang name for coffee.

Lowry
Town
ZIP: 57472 **Lat:** 45-18-55 N **Long:** 99-58-55 W
Pop: 15 (1990); 22 (1980) **Pop Density:** 75.0
Land: 0.2 sq. mi.; **Water:** 0.0 sq. mi. **Elev:** 1866 ft.
Settled 1907.
Name origin: For a Minneapolis and St. Louis Railroad official.

Mobridge
City
Lat: 45-32-26 N **Long:** 100-26-08 W
Pop: 3,768 (1990); 4,174 (1980) **Pop Density:** 2093.3
Land: 1.8 sq. mi.; **Water:** 0.0 sq. mi. **Elev:** 1676 ft.
Established 1906.
Name origin: For a railroad bridge across the Missouri River.

Selby
City
ZIP: 57472 **Lat:** 45-30-17 N **Long:** 100-01-56 W
Pop: 707 (1990); 884 (1980) **Pop Density:** 883.8
Land: 0.8 sq. mi.; **Water:** 0.0 sq. mi. **Elev:** 1912 ft.
Founded 1899.

West Walworth
Pop. Place
Lat: 45-26-32 N **Long:** 100-12-57 W
Pop: 666 (1990); 747 (1980) **Pop Density:** 2.1
Land: 311.2 sq. mi.; **Water:** 31.0 sq. mi.

Yankton County
County Seat: Yankton (ZIP: 57078)

Pop: 19,252 (1990); 18,952 (1980) **Pop Density:** 36.9
Land: 521.6 sq. mi.; **Water:** 11.0 sq. mi. **Area Code:** 605
On the southeastern border of SD, southwest of Sioux Falls; original county; organized Apr 5, 1862 (prior to statehood) from territorial county.
Name origin: For the city of Yankton.

Gayville
Town
ZIP: 57031 **Lat:** 42-53-17 N **Long:** 97-10-21 W
Pop: 401 (1990); 407 (1980) **Pop Density:** 2005.0
Land: 0.2 sq. mi.; **Water:** 0.0 sq. mi. **Elev:** 1165 ft.
Established 1872.
Name origin: For Elkanah Gay, the town's first postmaster.

*Gayville
Township
ZIP: 57031 **Lat:** 42-52-07 N **Long:** 97-12-29 W
Pop: 171 (1990); 207 (1980) **Pop Density:** 5.5
Land: 31.2 sq. mi.; **Water:** 1.6 sq. mi.

Irene
Town
Lat: 43-05-03 N **Long:** 97-09-37 W
Pop: 2 (1990); 5 (1980) **Pop Density:** 20.0
Land: 0.1 sq. mi.; **Water:** 0.0 sq. mi. **Elev:** 1364 ft.
Part of the town is also in Clay and Turner counties.
Name origin: For Irene Fry, the daughter of the original landowner.

Jamesville
Township
ZIP: 57067 **Lat:** 43-07-25 N **Long:** 97-27-38 W
Pop: 275 (1990); 258 (1980) **Pop Density:** 7.6
Land: 36.2 sq. mi.; **Water:** 0.0 sq. mi.

Lesterville
Town
ZIP: 57040 **Lat:** 43-02-19 N **Long:** 97-35-25 W
Pop: 168 (1990); 156 (1980) **Pop Density:** 840.0
Land: 0.2 sq. mi.; **Water:** 0.0 sq. mi. **Elev:** 1380 ft.
Name origin: For the first grandson of the town's first postmaster, A.S. Duning. Originally called Moscow.

Marindahl
Township
Lat: 43-02-48 N **Long:** 97-12-51 W
Pop: 187 (1990); 220 (1980) **Pop Density:** 5.2
Land: 35.7 sq. mi.; **Water:** 0.2 sq. mi.

Mayfield
Township
Lat: 43-07-35 N **Long:** 97-20-14 W
Pop: 229 (1990); 266 (1980) **Pop Density:** 6.3
Land: 36.6 sq. mi.; **Water:** 0.0 sq. mi.

Mission Hill
Town
ZIP: 57046 **Lat:** 42-55-16 N **Long:** 97-16-44 W
Pop: 180 (1990); 197 (1980) **Pop Density:** 600.0
Land: 0.3 sq. mi.; **Water:** 0.0 sq. mi. **Elev:** 1200 ft.
Name origin: Named in 1894 by the Rev. C.B. Nichols for a nearby hill.

*Mission Hill
Township
ZIP: 57046 **Lat:** 42-56-37 N **Long:** 97-19-56 W
Pop: 332 (1990); 341 (1980) **Pop Density:** 9.4
Land: 35.2 sq. mi.; **Water:** 0.0 sq. mi.

Southeast Yankton
Pop. Place
Lat: 42-53-00 N **Long:** 97-19-48 W
Pop: 694 (1990); 644 (1980) **Pop Density:** 45.7
Land: 15.2 sq. mi.; **Water:** 1.4 sq. mi.

Turkey Valley
Township
Lat: 43-07-33 N **Long:** 97-13-11 W
Pop: 218 (1990); 265 (1980) **Pop Density:** 6.1
Land: 35.8 sq. mi.; **Water:** 0.0 sq. mi.

Utica
Town
ZIP: 57067 **Lat:** 42-58-52 N **Long:** 97-29-46 W
Pop: 115 (1990); 100 (1980) **Pop Density:** 383.3
Land: 0.3 sq. mi.; **Water:** 0.0 sq. mi. **Elev:** 1370 ft.
Name origin: For Utica, NY.

*Utica
Township
ZIP: 57067 **Lat:** 42-57-10 N **Long:** 97-27-15 W
Pop: 846 (1990); 867 (1980) **Pop Density:** 23.6
Land: 35.9 sq. mi.; **Water:** 0.1 sq. mi.

Volin
Town
ZIP: 57072 **Lat:** 42-57-32 N **Long:** 97-10-50 W
Pop: 175 (1990); 156 (1980) **Pop Density:** 875.0
Land: 0.2 sq. mi.; **Water:** 0.0 sq. mi. **Elev:** 1185 ft.
Name origin: For pioneer settler Henry Volin.

*Volin
Township
ZIP: 57072 **Lat:** 42-56-57 N **Long:** 97-13-44 W
Pop: 240 (1990); 290 (1980) **Pop Density:** 6.7
Land: 35.6 sq. mi.; **Water:** 0.0 sq. mi.

Walshtown
Township
ZIP: 57067 **Lat:** 43-02-19 N **Long:** 97-20-43 W
Pop: 214 (1990); 235 (1980) **Pop Density:** 5.9
Land: 36.2 sq. mi.; **Water:** 0.0 sq. mi.

West Yankton
Pop. Place
Lat: 43-00-00 N **Long:** 97-32-19 W
Pop: 2,102 (1990); 2,327 (1980) **Pop Density:** 11.7
Land: 179.5 sq. mi.; **Water:** 7.4 sq. mi.

Yankton
City
ZIP: 57078 **Lat:** 42-53-23 N **Long:** 97-23-31 W
Pop: 12,703 (1990); 12,011 (1980) **Pop Density:** 1716.6
Land: 7.4 sq. mi.; **Water:** 0.2 sq. mi. **Elev:** 1205 ft.
In southeastern SD on Missouri River, 60 mi. southwest of Sioux Falls.
Name origin: From the Sioux Indian term *ihanktonwane* meaning 'end village.'

Ziebach County
County Seat: Dupree (ZIP: 57623)

Pop: 2,220 (1990); 2,308 (1980) **Pop Density:** 1.1
Land: 1962.5 sq. mi.; **Water:** 8.7 sq. mi. **Area Code:** 605
In west-central SD, northwest of Pierre; organized Feb 1, 1911 from Pennington County.
Name origin: For Frank M. Ziebach (1830–1929), publisher of the *Weekly Dakotian*.

Dupree   City
ZIP: 57623   **Lat:** 45-02-56 N **Long:** 101-36-02 W
Pop: 484 (1990); 562 (1980)   **Pop Density:** 1210.0
Land: 0.4 sq. mi.; **Water:** 0.0 sq. mi.   **Elev:** 727 ft.
Settled 1910.
Name origin: For Fred Dupree, an early rancher and trader.

*Dupree   Pop. Place
                              Lat: 45-02-57 N **Long:** 101-34-41 W
Pop: 154 (1990); 150 (1980)   **Pop Density:** 1.8
Land: 84.4 sq. mi.; **Water:** 0.2 sq. mi.

Eagle Butte   City
                              Lat: 44-59-10 N **Long:** 101-13-23 W
Pop: 14 (1990)   **Pop Density:** 20.0
Land: 0.7 sq. mi.; **Water:** 0.0 sq. mi.
Founded 1910. Part of the town is also in Dewey County.
Name origin: For the nearby butte.

North Ziebach   Pop. Place
                              Lat: 45-15-46 N **Long:** 101-44-19 W
Pop: 346 (1990); 442 (1980)   **Pop Density:** 0.5
Land: 700.2 sq. mi.; **Water:** 5.0 sq. mi.

South Ziebach   Pop. Place
                              Lat: 44-48-34 N **Long:** 101-36-34 W
Pop: 1,222 (1990); 1,154 (1980)   **Pop Density:** 1.0
Land: 1176.8 sq. mi.; **Water:** 3.6 sq. mi.

Index to Places and Counties in South Dakota

Aberdeen (Brown) City......625
Aberdeen (Brown) Township......625
Ada (Perkins) Township......675
Adams (Grant) Township......646
Adams (Miner) Township......670
Adrian (Edmunds) Township......643
Afton (Brookings) Township......624
Afton (Sanborn) Township......680
Agar (Sully) Town......684
Agency (Roberts) Township......678
Akaska (Walworth) Town......690
Alban (Grant) Township......646
Albee (Grant) Town......646
Alcester (Union) City......689
Alcester (Union) Township......689
Alden (Hand) Township......650
Alexandria (Hanson) City......652
Allen (Beadle) Township......621
Alliance (Moody) Township......672
Allison (Brown) Township......625
Alpena (Jerauld) Town......657
Alpena (Jerauld) Township......657
Alpha (Hand) Township......650
Altamont (Deuel) Town......640
Altamont (Deuel) Township......640
Alto (Roberts) Township......678
Alton (Brookings) Township......624
Altoona (Beadle) Township......621
America (Brule) Township......628
Anderson (Perkins) Township......675
Andover (Day) Town......638
Andover (Day) Township......638
Anina (Jerauld) Township......657
Antelope (Fall River) Township......644
Antelope (Perkins) Township......675
Antelope (Spink) Township......682
Antelope (Todd) CDP......685
Antelope Valley (Deuel) Township......640
Applegate (Lyman) Township......663
Arcade (Faulk) Township......645
Argentine (Fall River) Township......644
Argo (Brookings) Township......624
Arlington (Brookings) City......624
Arlington (Kingsbury) City......659
Armour (Douglas) City......642
Artas (Campbell) Town......630
Artesian (Sanborn) Town......680
Ash (Clark) Township......632
Ash No. 16 (Pennington) Township..673
Ashton (Spink) City......682
Astoria (Deuel) Town......640
Athol (Spink) Township......682
Aurora (Aurora) Township......620
Aurora (Brookings) Town......624
Aurora (Brookings) Township......624
Aurora County......620
Avon (Bon Homme) City......623
Badger (Davison) Township......637
Badger (Kingsbury) Town......659
Badger (Kingsbury) Township......659
Bad Nation (Mellette) Township......669
Badus (Lake) Township......660
Bailey (Lyman) Township......663
Baker (Davison) Township......637
Baker (Kingsbury) Township......659
Baltic (Minnehaha) Town......671
Bancroft (Kingsbury) Town......659
Bangor (Brookings) Township......624
Banner (Beadle) Township......621
Banner (Tripp) Township......685

Barrett (Beadle) Township......621
Barrett (Perkins) Township......675
Bates (Brown) Township......626
Bates (Hand) Township......651
Batesland (Shannon) Town......681
Bath (Brown) Township......626
Beadle County......621
Beaver (Miner) Township......670
Beaver Creek (Tripp) Township......685
Beck (Perkins) Township......675
Becker (Roberts) Township......678
Belford (Aurora) Township......620
Belle (Edmunds) Township......643
Belle Fourche (Butte) City......629
Belle Fourche-Cheyenne Valleys (Meade) Pop. Place......668
Belle Plaine (Spink) Township......682
Belle Prairie (Beadle) Township......621
Belleview (Miner) Township......670
Belmont (Douglas) Township......642
Belmont (Spink) Township......682
Belvidere (Jackson) Town......656
Benedict (Sanborn) Township......680
Bennett County......623
Benton (McCook) Township......666
Benton (Minnehaha) Township......671
Benton (Spink) Township......682
Beotia (Spink) Township......682
Beresford (Lincoln) City......662
Beresford (Union) City......689
Bethel (Clay) Township......633
Beulah (Davison) Township......637
Beulah (Hanson) Township......652
Big Sioux (Union) Township......689
Big Springs (Union) Township......689
Big Stone (Grant) Township......647
Big Stone City (Grant) City......647
Bison (Perkins) Town......675
Bison (Perkins) Township......675
Black (Tripp) Township......685
Black Dog (Lyman) Pop. Place......663
Blackhawk (Meade) CDP......668
Blackpipe (Mellette) Township......669
Blaine (Clark) Township......632
Blaine (Jerauld) Township......657
Blendon (Davison) Township......637
Blinsmon (Moody) Township......672
Blom (Deuel) Township......640
Blooming Valley (Grant) Township..647
Blunt (Hughes) City......653
Bonesteel (Gregory) City......648
Bon Homme County......623
Bonilla (Beadle) Township......621
Bossko (Roberts) Township......678
Bowdle (Edmunds) City......643
Bowdle (Edmunds) Township......643
Box Elder (Pennington) City......673
Bradley (Clark) Town......632
Brainard (Brown) Township......626
Brandon (Minnehaha) City......671
Brandon (Minnehaha) Township......671
Brandt (Deuel) Town......640
Brandt (Deuel) Township......640
Brantford (Hamlin) Township......649
Brentford (Spink) Town......682
Bridgewater (McCook) City......666
Bridgewater (McCook) Township......666
Bristol (Aurora) Township......620
Bristol (Day) City......638
Bristol (Day) Township......638

Britton (Marshall) City......665
Broadland (Beadle) Town......621
Broadland (Beadle) Township......621
Brookfield (McCook) Township......666
Brookings (Brookings) City......624
Brookings (Brookings) Township......624
Brookings County......624
Brooklyn (Lincoln) Township......662
Brothersfield (Turner) Township......687
Brown County......625
Bruce (Brookings) City......624
Brule (Brule) Township......628
Brule (Union) Township......689
Brule County......628
Brunson (Tripp) Township......685
Brushy (Perkins) Township......675
Bryan (Charles Mix) Township......630
Bryant (Edmunds) Township......643
Bryant (Faulk) Township......645
Bryant (Hamlin) City......649
Bryant (Roberts) Township......678
Buffalo (Harding) Town......653
Buffalo (Jones) Township......658
Buffalo (Marshall) Township......665
Buffalo (Minnehaha) Township......671
Buffalo (Spink) Township......682
Buffalo County......629
Buffalo Gap (Custer) Town......637
Bull Creek (Tripp) Township......686
Bullhead (Corson) CDP......635
Burdette (Hand) Township......651
Burdick (Perkins) Township......675
Burk (Minnehaha) Township......671
Burke (Gregory) City......648
Burke (Gregory) Township......648
Burr Oak (Beadle) Township......621
Bushnell (Brookings) Town......624
Butler (Day) Town......638
Butler (Day) Township......638
Butler (Sanborn) Township......680
Butte (Hughes) Township......653
Butte (Lyman) Township......663
Butte (Mellette) Township......669
Butte County......629
Cadillac (Corson) Township......635
Cambria (Brown) Township......626
Campbell (Hand) Township......651
Campbell County......630
Camp Crook (Harding) Town......653
Canistota (McCook) City......666
Canistota (McCook) Township......666
Canova (Miner) Town......670
Canova (Miner) Township......670
Canton (Lincoln) City......662
Canton (Lincoln) Township......662
Capital (Hutchinson) Township......654
Capitola (Spink) Township......682
Carl (McPherson) Township......667
Carlisle (Brown) Township......626
Carlock (Gregory) Township......648
Carlton (Hand) Township......651
Carlyle (Beadle) Township......621
Carroll (Charles Mix) Township......630
Carter (Tripp) Town......686
Carthage (Miner) City......670
Carthage (Miner) Township......670
Cash (Perkins) Township......676
Castalia (Charles Mix) Pop. Place......631
Castle Butte (Perkins) Township......676

SOUTH DAKOTA

Castle Butte No. 18 (Pennington) Township ... 674
Castlewood (Hamlin) City ... 650
Castlewood (Hamlin) Township ... 650
Cavour (Beadle) Town ... 621
Cavour (Beadle) Township ... 621
Cedar (Hand) Township ... 651
Cedarbutte (Mellette) Pop. Place ... 669
Cedar Butte No. 4 (Pennington) Township ... 674
Center (Aurora) Township ... 620
Centerville (Faulk) Township ... 645
Centerville (Turner) City ... 687
Centerville (Turner) Township ... 688
Central City (Lawrence) City ... 661
Central Corson (Corson) Pop. Place ... 635
Central Hyde (Hyde) Pop. Place ... 655
Central Jones (Jones) Pop. Place ... 658
Central McPherson (McPherson) Pop. Place ... 667
Central Mellette (Mellette) Pop. Place ... 669
Central Pennington (Pennington) Pop. Place ... 674
Central Point (Day) Township ... 638
Central Potter (Potter) Pop. Place ... 678
Chamberlain (Brule) City ... 628
Chamberlain (Brule) Township ... 628
Chance (Perkins) Township ... 676
Chancellor (Turner) Town ... 688
Charles Mix County ... 630
Chaudoin (Perkins) Township ... 676
Chelsea (Faulk) Town ... 645
Chery (Jerauld) Township ... 657
Chester (Douglas) Township ... 642
Chester (Lake) Township ... 660
Cheyenne No. 21 (Pennington) Township ... 674
Childstown (Turner) Township ... 688
Choteau Creek (Charles Mix) Township ... 631
Civil Bend (Union) Township ... 689
Hot Springs. *See* **Hot Springs, Fall River County (Shannon)** ... 681
Winner. *See* **Winner, Tripp County (Todd)** ... 685
Claire City (Roberts) Town ... 678
Clare (Moody) Township ... 673
Claremont (Brown) Town ... 626
Claremont (Brown) Township ... 626
Clark (Clark) City ... 632
Clark (Douglas) Township ... 642
Clark (Faulk) Township ... 645
Clark (Perkins) Township ... 676
Clark County ... 632
Clarno (Lake) Township ... 660
Clay County ... 633
Clayton (Hutchinson) Township ... 654
Clear Lake (Deuel) City ... 640
Clear Lake (Deuel) Township ... 640
Clear Lake (Edmunds) Township ... 643
Clear Lake (Minnehaha) Township ... 671
Clearwater (Miner) Township ... 670
Cleveland (Brule) Township ... 628
Cleveland (Edmunds) Township ... 643
Cleveland (Hamlin) Township ... 650
Clifton (Beadle) Township ... 621
Clifton (Spink) Township ... 682
Clinton (Miner) Township ... 670
Cloyd Valley (Edmunds) Township ... 643
Clyde (Beadle) Township ... 621
Codington County ... 634
Cody (Mellette) Township ... 669
Collins (Clark) Township ... 632

Colman (Moody) City ... 673
Colman (Moody) Township ... 673
Colome (Tripp) City ... 686
Colome (Tripp) Township ... 686
Colonial Pine Hills (Pennington) CDP ... 674
Colton (Minnehaha) City ... 671
Columbia (Brown) City ... 626
Columbia (Brown) Township ... 626
Como (Hand) Township ... 651
Conata No. 20 (Pennington) Township ... 674
Concord (Lake) Township ... 660
Conde (Spink) City ... 682
Conde (Spink) Township ... 682
Condon (Tripp) Township ... 686
Cooper (Aurora) Township ... 620
Corn Creek (Mellette) Township ... 669
Cornwall (Spink) Township ... 682
Corona (Roberts) Town ... 679
Corsica (Douglas) City ... 642
Corson County ... 635
Cortlandt (Edmunds) Township ... 643
Cottonwood (Clark) Township ... 632
Cottonwood (Fall River) Township ... 644
Cottonwood (Jackson) Town ... 656
Cottonwood Lake (Edmunds) Township ... 643
Crandon (Spink) Township ... 682
Cresbard (Faulk) Town ... 645
Crooked Creek No. 25 (Pennington) Township ... 674
Crooks (Minnehaha) Town ... 671
Cross Plains (Hutchinson) Township ... 654
Crow (Jerauld) Township ... 657
Crow Creek (Buffalo) Pop. Place ... 629
Crow Creek (Hughes) Pop. Place ... 653
Crow Creek (Hyde) Pop. Place ... 655
Crow Lake (Jerauld) Township ... 657
Crystal Lake (Aurora) Township ... 620
Curlew (Tripp) Township ... 686
Custer (Beadle) Township ... 621
Custer (Corson) Township ... 635
Custer (Custer) City ... 637
Custer County ... 637
Dale (Jerauld) Township ... 657
Dallas (Gregory) Town ... 648
Dalzell Canyon (Pennington) Pop. Place ... 674
Daneville (Turner) Township ... 688
Dante (Charles Mix) Town ... 631
Darlington (Charles Mix) Township ... 631
Darlington (Clark) Township ... 632
Davis (Turner) Town ... 688
Davison County ... 637
Day (Clark) Township ... 632
Day County ... 638
Dayton (Lincoln) Township ... 662
Dayton (Marshall) Township ... 665
Deadwood (Lawrence) City ... 661
Dearborn (Beadle) Township ... 621
Delaney (Corson) Township ... 636
Delapre (Lincoln) Township ... 662
Delaware (Lincoln) Township ... 662
Dell Rapids (Minnehaha) City ... 671
Dell Rapids (Minnehaha) Township ... 671
Delmont (Douglas) City ... 642
Dempster (Hamlin) Township ... 650
Denver (Kingsbury) Township ... 659
De Smet (Kingsbury) City ... 659
De Smet (Kingsbury) Township ... 659
Deuel County ... 640
Devoe (Faulk) Township ... 645
Dewey (Hyde) Township ... 656
Dewey County ... 641

De Witt (Perkins) Township ... 676
Dexter (Codington) Township ... 634
Diana (Sanborn) Township ... 680
Dickens (Gregory) Township ... 648
Dimock (Hutchinson) Town ... 654
Dixon (Gregory) Township ... 648
Dixon (Hamlin) Township ... 650
Dog Ear (Tripp) Township ... 686
Doland (Spink) City ... 682
Dolton (Turner) Town ... 688
Dolton (Turner) Township ... 688
Dorman (Lyman) Township ... 663
Douglas County ... 642
Draper (Jones) Town ... 658
Draper (Jones) Township ... 658
Dry Wood Lake (Roberts) Township ... 679
Duck Creek (Perkins) Pop. Place ... 676
Dudley (Aurora) Township ... 620
Duell (Perkins) Township ... 676
Dumarce (Marshall) Township ... 665
Dunkel (Jones) Township ... 658
Dupree (Ziebach) City ... 692
Dupree (Ziebach) Pop. Place ... 692
Eagle (Brule) Township ... 628
Eagle (Meade) Township ... 668
Eagle Butte (Dewey) Town ... 641
Eagle Butte (Ziebach) City ... 692
Earling (Lyman) Township ... 663
East Bennett (Bennett) Pop. Place ... 623
East Butte (Butte) Pop. Place ... 629
East Central Pennington (Pennington) Pop. Place ... 674
East Choteau (Douglas) Township ... 642
East Custer (Custer) Pop. Place ... 637
Easter (Roberts) Township ... 679
East Gregory (Gregory) Pop. Place ... 648
East Haakon (Haakon) Pop. Place ... 649
East Hanson (Brown) Township ... 626
East Jackson (Jackson) Pop. Place ... 656
East Perkins (Perkins) Pop. Place ... 676
East Potter (Potter) Pop. Place ... 678
East Rondell (Brown) Township ... 626
East Shannon (Shannon) Pop. Place ... 681
East Sully (Sully) Pop. Place ... 684
East Todd (Todd) Pop. Place ... 685
East Walworth (Walworth) Pop. Place ... 690
Eden (Clark) Township ... 632
Eden (Codington) Township ... 634
Eden (Lincoln) Township ... 662
Eden (Marshall) Town ... 665
Eden (Marshall) Township ... 665
Edens (Gregory) Township ... 648
Edgemont (Fall River) City ... 644
Edgerton (Hanson) Township ... 652
Edison (Minnehaha) Township ... 671
Edmunds County ... 643
Egan (Moody) City ... 673
Egan (Moody) Township ... 673
Egeland (Day) Township ... 638
Elk Point (Union) City ... 689
Elk Point (Union) Township ... 689
Elkton (Brookings) City ... 624
Elkton (Brookings) Township ... 624
Elliott (Sanborn) Township ... 680
Elliston (Tripp) Township ... 686
Ellisville (Faulk) Township ... 645
Ellston (Gregory) Township ... 648
Ellsworth Air Force Base (Meade) Military Facility ... 668
Ellsworth Air Force Base (Pennington) Military Facility ... 674
Elmira (Codington) Township ... 634
Elrod (Clark) Township ... 632
Elvira (Buffalo) Township ... 629

Emerson (Faulk) Township............645
Emery (Hanson) City.....................652
Emery (McCook) Township 666
Emmet (Union) Township................689
Englewood (Perkins) Township.......676
Enterprise (Faulk) Township...........645
Enterprise (Moody) Township..........673
Enterprise (Roberts) Township........679
Erwin (Kingsbury) Town 659
Esmond (Kingsbury) Township........659
Estelline (Hamlin) City...................650
Estelline (Hamlin) Township...........650
Ethan (Davison) Town 637
Eureka (Aurora) Township 620
Eureka (Brookings) Township.........624
Eureka (McPherson) City...............667
Exline (Spink) Township 682
Fair (Hutchinson) Township............654
Fairburn (Custer) Town 637
Fairfax (Gregory) Town 648
Fairfax (Gregory) Township 648
Fairfield (Beadle) Township............621
Fairland (Lyman) Township 663
Fairview (Clay) Township 633
Fairview (Faulk) Township 645
Fairview (Hanson) Township...........652
Fairview (Lincoln) Town 662
Fairview (Lincoln) Township...........662
Fairview (Mellette) Township..........669
Fairview No. 22 (Pennington)
  Township........................... 674
Faith (Meade) City 668
Fall River County.........................644
Farmer (Hanson) Town 652
Farmington (Day) Township............639
Farmington (Grant) Township.........647
Farmington (Lake) Township 660
Faulk County...............................645
Faulkton (Faulk) City 645
Firesteel (Aurora) Township...........620
Flandreau (Moody) City..................673
Flandreau (Moody) Township..........673
Flat Butte No. 12 (Pennington)
  Township........................... 674
Flat Creek (Perkins) Township........676
Florence (Codington) Town............634
Florence (Hamlin) Township...........650
Florence (Hand) Township..............651
Floyd (Sanborn) Township..............680
Forbes (Charles Mix) Township.......631
Fordham (Clark) Township............632
Fort (Marshall) Township...............665
Fort Pierre (Stanley) City...............684
Fort Thompson (Buffalo) CDP........629
Foster (Beadle) Township 621
Foster (Hutchinson) Township........654
Foster (Perkins) Township..............676
Fountain (Edmunds) Township........643
Foxton (Clark) Township................632
Frankfort (Spink) City...................682
Frankfort (Spink) Township...........682
Franklin (Jerauld) Township...........657
Franklin (Lake) Township 660
Franklyn (Brown) Township 626
Frederick (Brown) Town 626
Frederick (Brown) Township...........626
Fredlund (Perkins) Township..........676
Freedom (Faulk) Township.............645
Freeman (Hutchinson) City............654
Fremont (Moody) Township............673
Fruitdale (Butte) Town 629
Fuller (Codington) Township..........634
Fulton (Hanson) Town 652
Gales (Aurora) Township 620
Gannvalley (Buffalo) Pop. Place.....629

Garden City (Clark) Town 632
Garden Prairie (Brown) Township....626
Garfield (Clark) Township 632
Garfield (Clay) Township................634
Garfield (Douglas) Township 642
Garfield (Hamlin) Township............650
Garfield (Roberts) Township..........679
Garfield (Spink) Township 682
Garland (Brown) Township.............626
Garretson (Minnehaha) City 671
Gary (Deuel) City...........................640
Gayville (Yankton) Town 690
Gayville (Yankton) Township...........690
Geddes (Charles Mix) City..............631
Gem (Brown) Township 626
Geneseo (Roberts) Township 679
Georgia (Grant) Township 647
German (Hutchinson) Township......654
Germantown (Codington) Township 634
Germantown (Turner) Township......688
Gettysburg (Potter) City 678
Gilbert (Hand) Township 651
Glen (Edmunds) Township.............643
Glendale (Hand) Township.............651
Glendo (Perkins) Township.............676
Glenham (Walworth) Town 690
Glenwood (Clay) Township 634
Glenwood (Deuel) Township..........640
Glover (Edmunds) Township 643
Goodwill (Roberts) Township 679
Goodwin (Deuel) Town 640
Goodwin (Deuel) Township............640
Goose Lake (Charles Mix) Township 631
Graceland (Codington) Township....634
Grafton (Miner) Township..............670
Grand (Hand) Township 651
Grand Meadow (Minnehaha)
  Township........................... 671
Grand River (Perkins) Township......676
Grand Valley (Corson) Township.....636
Grandview (Brule) Pop. Place........628
Grandview (Douglas) Township.......642
Grandview (Hutchinson) Township..654
Grandview (Jackson) Township......656
Grandview (Jones) Township 658
Grange (Deuel) Township 640
Grant (Beadle) Township 621
Grant (Lincoln) Township................662
Grant (McCook) Township 666
Grant (Roberts) Township 679
Grant Center (Grant) Township 647
Grant County...............................646
Great Bend (Spink) Township.........682
Greenfield (Brown) Township..........626
Greenland (McCook) Township.......666
Greenleaf (Hand) Township...........651
Green Valley (Miner) Township.......670
Greenwood (Tripp) Township.........686
Gregory (Gregory) City 648
Gregory County.............................648
Grenville (Day) Town.....................639
Grenville (Day) Township................639
Groton (Brown) City 626
Groton (Brown) Township..............626
Groveland (Spink) Township 683
Grovena (Moody) Township 673
Haakon County.............................649
Hague (Clark) Township.................632
Hall (Perkins) Township..................676
Hamilton (Charles Mix) Township ...631
Hamilton (Marshall) Township 665
Hamlin (Hamlin) Township 650
Hamlin County.............................649
Hand County 650
Hanson (Hanson) Township............652

Hanson County.............................652
Harding County.............................653
Harmon (Roberts) Township............679
Harmony (Edmunds) Township........643
Harmony (Fall River) Township 644
Harmony (Jerauld) Township...........657
Harmony (Spink) Township 683
Harrisburg (Lincoln) Town..............662
Harrison (Spink) Township 683
Harrold (Hughes) Town...................654
Hart (Roberts) Township................679
Hartford (Minnehaha) City 671
Hartford (Minnehaha) Township 671
Hartland (Beadle) Township 621
Hartland (Kingsbury) Township........659
Havana (Deuel) Township..............640
Hayti (Hamlin) Town 650
Hayti (Hamlin) Township 650
Hazel (Hamlin) Town 650
Hecla (Brown) City........................626
Hecla (Brown) Township................626
Henden (Miner) Township 670
Henry (Brown) Township 626
Henry (Codington) Town 635
Henry (Codington) Township 635
Herman (Lake) Township...............660
Hermosa (Custer) Town 637
Herreid (Campbell) City.................630
Herrick (Deuel) Township..............640
Herrick (Gregory) Town 648
Hetland (Kingsbury) Town 659
Hickman (Marshall) Township.........665
Hidewood (Deuel) Township..........640
Highland (Brown) Township...........626
Highland (Brule) Township.............628
Highland (Charles Mix) Township....631
Highland (Day) Township 639
Highland (Lincoln) Township 662
Highland (Minnehaha) Township 671
Highland (Perkins) Township..........676
Highmore (Hyde) City....................656
Hiland (Hand) Township.................651
Hill City (Pennington) Town............674
Hillsdale (Faulk) Township 645
Hillside (Edmunds) Township 643
Hillsview (McPherson) Town 667
Hilmoe (Lyman) Township..............663
Hitchcock (Beadle) Town 622
Hoffman (McPherson) Township......667
Holden (Hand) Township 651
Holland (Douglas) Township 642
Holsclaw (Tripp) Township.............686
Home (Turner) Township 688
Homer (Day) Township...................639
Hope (Lyman) Township.................663
Hopper (Aurora) Township.............620
Horse Creek (Perkins) Township....676
Hosmer (Edmunds) City 643
Hosmer (Edmunds) Township.........643
Hot Springs (Fall River) City 644
Hoven (Potter) Town.....................678
Howard (Charles Mix) Township......631
Howard (Meade) Township 668
Howard (Miner) City......................670
Howard (Miner) Township..............670
Hudson (Edmunds) Township 643
Hudson (Lincoln) Town 662
Huggins (Tripp) Township..............686
Hughes County............................653
Hulbert (Hand) Township 651
Humboldt (Minnehaha) Town 672
Humboldt (Minnehaha) Township....672
Huntley (Edmunds) Township 643
Hurley (Turner) City.......................688
Hurley (Turner) Township...............688

SOUTH DAKOTA

Huron (Beadle) City *622*
Huron No. 10 (Pennington)
 Township *674*
Hutchinson County *654*
Hyde County *655*
Ideal (Tripp) Township *686*
Imlay No. 24 (Pennington)
 Township *674*
Independence (Day) Township *639*
Independence (Douglas) Township ... *642*
Independence (Perkins) Pop. Place ... *676*
Interior (Jackson) Town *656*
Interior (Jackson) Township *656*
Iona (Lyman) Township *663*
Iowa (Beadle) Township *622*
Iowa (Douglas) Township *642*
Ipswich (Edmunds) City *643*
Ipswich (Edmunds) Township *643*
Irene (Clay) Town *634*
Irene (Turner) Town *688*
Irene (Yankton) Town *690*
Iroquois (Beadle) City *622*
Iroquois (Kingsbury) City *659*
Iroquois (Kingsbury) Township *659*
Irving (Faulk) Township *646*
Irwin (Tripp) Township *686*
Isabel (Dewey) City *641*
Jackson (Charles Mix) Township *631*
Jackson (Sanborn) Township *680*
Jackson County *656*
Jamesville (Yankton) Township *691*
Jasper (Hanson) Township *653*
Java (Walworth) City *690*
Jefferson (McCook) Township *666*
Jefferson (Moody) Township *673*
Jefferson (Spink) Township *683*
Jefferson (Union) Town *689*
Jefferson (Union) Township *689*
Jerauld County *657*
Jewett (Jackson) Township *656*
Jones (Gregory) Township *648*
Jones County *658*
Jordan (Tripp) Township *686*
Joubert (Douglas) Township *642*
Kadoka (Jackson) City *656*
Kampeska (Codington) Township *635*
Kassel (Hutchinson) Township *654*
Kaylor (Hutchinson) Township *654*
Kellogg (Beadle) Township *622*
Kennebec (Lyman) Town *663*
Kennebec (Lyman) Township *663*
Kennedy (Charles Mix) Township *631*
Kent (Edmunds) Township *643*
Keyapaha (Tripp) Township *686*
Keystone (Pennington) Town *674*
Kidder (Day) Township *639*
Kilborn (Grant) Township *647*
Kimball (Brule) City *628*
Kimball (Brule) Township *628*
King (Tripp) Township *686*
Kingsbury County *659*
Kolls (Jones) Township *658*
Kosciusko (Day) Township *639*
Kranzburg (Codington) Town *635*
Kranzburg (Codington) Township *635*
Kulm (Hutchinson) Township *655*
Kyle (Shannon) CDP *681*
La Belle (Marshall) Township *665*
La Bolt (Grant) Town *647*
Lafoon (Faulk) Township *646*
Lake (Aurora) Township *620*
Lake (Clark) Township *633*
Lake (Codington) Township *635*
Lake (Corson) Township *636*
Lake (Marshall) Township *665*

Lake (Roberts) Township *679*
Lake (Spink) Township *683*
Lake (Tripp) Township *686*
Lake Andes (Charles Mix) City *631*
Lake Byron (Beadle) Township *622*
Lake City (Marshall) Town *665*
Lake County *660*
Lake Creek (Pennington) Pop. Place *674*
Lake Flat No. 8 (Pennington)
 Township *674*
Lake George (Charles Mix)
 Township *631*
Lake Hendricks (Brookings)
 Township *624*
Lake Hill No. 5 (Pennington)
 Township *674*
Lake Norden (Hamlin) City *650*
Lake Preston (Kingsbury) City *659*
Lakeside (Meade) Township *668*
Lake Sinai (Brookings) Township *625*
Laketon (Brookings) Township *625*
Lake View (Lake) Township *660*
Lamro (Tripp) Township *686*
Landing Creek (Gregory) Township .. *648*
Lane (Jerauld) Town *657*
Langford (Marshall) Town *665*
Lansing (Brown) Township *626*
La Prairie (Spink) Township *683*
La Roche (Charles Mix) Township ... *631*
La Valley (Lincoln) Township *662*
Lawrence (Charles Mix) Township ... *631*
Lawrence (Roberts) Township *679*
Lawrence County *661*
Lead (Lawrence) City *661*
Lebanon (Potter) Town *678*
Lee (Roberts) Township *679*
Lemmon (Perkins) City *676*
Lemon, No. 2 (Corson) Pop. Place *636*
Lennox (Lincoln) City *662*
Leola (Codington) Township *635*
Leola (McPherson) City *667*
Le Roy (Lake) Township *660*
Lesterville (Yankton) Town *691*
Le Sueur (Kingsbury) Township *659*
Letcher (Sanborn) Town *680*
Letcher (Sanborn) Township *680*
Liberty (Beadle) Township *622*
Liberty (Brown) Township *626*
Liberty (Day) Township *639*
Liberty (Edmunds) Township *644*
Liberty (Hutchinson) Township *655*
Liberty (Lyman) Township *663*
Liberty (Perkins) Township *676*
Lien (Roberts) Township *679*
Lily (Day) Town *639*
Lincoln (Brown) Township *626*
Lincoln (Clark) Township *633*
Lincoln (Corson) Township *636*
Lincoln (Douglas) Township *642*
Lincoln (Lincoln) Township *662*
Lincoln (Perkins) Township *676*
Lincoln (Spink) Township *683*
Lincoln (Tripp) Township *686*
Lincoln County *662*
Linn (Hand) Township *651*
Lisbon (Davison) Township *638*
Little Buffalo (Jackson) Township *656*
Little Eagle (Corson) CDP *636*
Lockwood (Roberts) Township *679*
Lodgepole (Perkins) Township *676*
Lodi (Spink) Township *683*
Logan (Beadle) Township *622*
Logan (Clark) Township *633*
Logan (Hand) Township *651*
Logan (Hughes) Township *654*

American Places Dictionary

Logan (Jerauld) Township *657*
Logan (Minnehaha) Township *672*
Logan (Sanborn) Township *680*
Lone Rock (Moody) Township *673*
Lone Star (Gregory) Township *648*
Lone Star (Tripp) Township *686*
Lone Tree (Charles Mix) Township .. *631*
Lone Tree (Perkins) Township *676*
Lone Tree (Tripp) Township *686*
Long Hollow (Roberts) Township *679*
Long Lake (McPherson) Town *667*
Lowe (Deuel) Township *641*
Lowell (Marshall) Township *665*
Lower Brule (Lyman) CDP *663*
Lowry (Walworth) Town *690*
Lura (Grant) Township *647*
Lyman County *663*
Lynn (Day) Township *639*
Lynn (Lincoln) Township *662*
Lynn (Moody) Township *673*
Lyon (Brule) Township *628*
Lyons (Minnehaha) Township *672*
Madison (Edmunds) Township *644*
Madison (Grant) Township *647*
Madison (Lake) City *660*
Mahto (Corson) Township *636*
Maltby (Perkins) Township *676*
Manchester (Kingsbury) Township *659*
Manderson-White Horse Creek (Shan-
 non) CDP *681*
Mapleton (Minnehaha) Township *672*
Marindahl (Yankton) Township *691*
Marion (Turner) City *688*
Marion (Turner) Township *688*
Marlar (Jerauld) Township *657*
Marshall County *665*
Marshfield (Perkins) Township *676*
Martin (Bennett) City *623*
Martin (Perkins) Township *676*
Marty (Charles Mix) CDP *631*
Marvin (Grant) Town *647*
Mathews (Kingsbury) Township *659*
Maydell (Clark) Township *633*
Mayfield (Yankton) Township *691*
Mazeppa (Grant) Township *647*
McClure (Lyman) Pop. Place *663*
McCook County *666*
McIntosh (Corson) City *636*
McKinley (Marshall) Township *665*
McLaughlin (Corson) City *636*
McNeely (Tripp) Township *686*
McPherson County *667*
Meade County *668*
Meadow (Perkins) Township *676*
Meckling (Clay) Township *634*
Medary (Brookings) Township *625*
Media (Jerauld) Township *657*
Mellette (Spink) City *683*
Mellette (Spink) Township *683*
Mellette County *669*
Melrose (Grant) Township *647*
Menno (Hutchinson) City *655*
Mercier (Brown) Township *627*
Merton (Clark) Township *633*
Middleton (Turner) Township *688*
Midland (Haakon) Town *649*
Midland (Hand) Township *651*
Milbank (Grant) City *647*
Milford (Beadle) Township *622*
Millboro (Tripp) Township *686*
Miller (Hand) City *651*
Miller (Hand) Township *651*
Miller (Marshall) Township *665*
Milltown (Hutchinson) Township *655*
Miner (Miner) Township *670*

South Dakota

- Miner County 670
- **Minnehaha County** 671
- Minnesota (Roberts) Township 679
- Mission (Corson) Township 636
- Mission (Todd) City 685
- Mission Hill (Yankton) Town 691
- Mission Hill (Yankton) Township 691
- Mitchell (Davison) City 638
- Mitchell (Davison) Township 638
- Mobridge (Walworth) City 690
- Modena (Edmunds) Township 644
- Molan (Hutchinson) Township 655
- Mondamin (Hand) Township 651
- Monroe (Turner) Town 688
- Monroe (Turner) Township 688
- Montpelier (Edmunds) Township 644
- Montrose (McCook) City 666
- Montrose (McCook) Township 667
- **Moody County** 672
- Moore (Charles Mix) Township 631
- Moore (Lyman) Township 664
- Moreau (Perkins) Township 677
- Morgan (Jones) Township 658
- Morningside (Lyman) Township 664
- Morristown (Corson) Town 636
- Morton (Day) Township 639
- Mosher (Mellette) Township 669
- Mound City (Campbell) Town 630
- Mount Pleasant (Clark) Township 633
- Mount Rushmore (Pennington) Pop. Place 674
- Mount Vernon (Davison) City 638
- Mount Vernon (Davison) Township .638
- Mullen (Jones) Township 658
- Murdo (Jones) City 658
- Mussman (Jones) Township 658
- Myron (Faulk) Township 646
- Nance (Beadle) Township 622
- Naples (Clark) Town 633
- Newark (Marshall) Township 665
- New Effington (Roberts) Town 679
- Newell (Butte) City 630
- New Hope (Brown) Township 627
- Newport (Marshall) Township 665
- New Surprise Valley (Mellette) Township 669
- New Underwood (Pennington) Town 674
- New Witten (Tripp) Town 686
- Nisland (Butte) Town 630
- Norden (Deuel) Township 641
- Norden (Hamlin) Township 650
- Nordland (Marshall) Township 665
- Norris (Mellette) Township 669
- North Bryant (Edmunds) Township .644
- North Buffalo (Buffalo) Pop. Place ...629
- North Campbell (Campbell) Pop. Place 630
- North Detroit (Brown) Township 627
- North Dewey (Dewey) Pop. Place 641
- North Eagle Butte (Dewey) CDP 641
- Northeast Bon Homme (Bon Homme) Pop. Place 623
- Northeast Corson (Corson) Pop. Place 636
- Northeast Fall River (Fall River) Pop. Place 645
- Northeast Lyman (Lyman) Pop. Place 664
- Northeast Pennington (Pennington) Pop. Place 674
- North Gregory (Gregory) Pop. Place 648
- North Harding (Harding) Pop. Place653
- North Hughes (Hughes) Pop. Place ..654
- North Hyde (Hyde) Pop. Place 656
- North Jones (Jones) Pop. Place 658
- North Lawrence (Lawrence) Pop. Place 661
- North Meade (Meade) Pop. Place 668
- North Sioux City (Union) City 689
- North Spearfish (Lawrence) CDP 661
- North Stanley (Stanley) Pop. Place ..684
- North Tripp (Tripp) Pop. Place 686
- Northville (Spink) Town 683
- Northville (Spink) Township 683
- Northwest Bon Homme (Bon Homme) Pop. Place 623
- Northwest Hand (Hand) Pop. Place .651
- Northwest Jackson (Jackson) Pop. Place 656
- North Ziebach (Ziebach) Pop. Place.692
- Norway (Clay) Township 634
- Norway (Lincoln) Township 662
- Norway (Roberts) Township 679
- Norway (Turner) Township 688
- Nunda (Lake) Town 660
- Nunda (Lake) Township 660
- Nutley (Day) Township 639
- Oacoma (Lyman) Town 664
- Oacoma (Lyman) Township 664
- Oak Gulch (Day) Township 639
- Oak Hollow (Hutchinson) Township 655
- Oak Lake (Brookings) Township 625
- Oakwood (Brookings) Township 625
- Odessa (Edmunds) Township 644
- Oelrichs (Fall River) Town 645
- Oglala (Shannon) CDP 681
- Ohio (Hand) Township 651
- Okaton (Jones) Township 658
- Ola (Brule) Township 628
- Oldham (Kingsbury) City 659
- Olean (Spink) Township 683
- Olivet (Hutchinson) Town 655
- Onaka (Faulk) Town 646
- Oneida (Sanborn) Township 680
- O'Neil (Faulk) Township 646
- Oneota (Brown) Township 627
- One Road (Roberts) Township........... 679
- Onida (Sully) City 684
- Ontario (Hand) Township 651
- Opdahl (Hamlin) Township 650
- Ordway (Brown) Township 627
- Orient (Faulk) Town 646
- Orient (Faulk) Township 646
- Orland (Lake) Township 660
- Ortley (Roberts) Town 679
- Ortley (Roberts) Township 679
- Osceola (Brown) Township 627
- Osceola (Grant) Township 647
- Oslo (Brookings) Township 625
- Owanka No. 13 (Pennington) Township 674
- Oxford (Hamlin) Township 650
- Pahapesto (Tripp) Township 686
- Palatine (Aurora) Township 620
- Palisade (Minnehaha) Township 672
- Palmyra (Brown) Township 627
- Park (Hand) Township 651
- Parker (Turner) City 688
- Parker (Turner) Township 688
- Parkston (Hutchinson) City 655
- Parmelee (Todd) CDP 685
- Parnell (Brookings) Township 625
- Patten (Aurora) Township 620
- Pearl (Hand) Township 651
- Pearl (McCook) Township 667
- Pearl Creek (Beadle) Township 622
- Peever (Roberts) Town 679
- Pelican (Codington) Township 635
- Pembrook (Edmunds) Township........ 644
- **Pennington County** 673
- Peno No. 9 (Pennington) Township..674
- **Perkins County** 675
- Perry (Davison) Township 638
- Perry (Lincoln) Township 662
- Philip (Haakon) City 649
- Phipps (Codington) Township 635
- Pickstown (Charles Mix) Town 631
- Pierpont (Day) Town 639
- Pierre (Hughes) City 654
- Pine Ridge (Shannon) CDP 681
- Pioneer (Corson) Township 636
- Pioneer (Faulk) Township 646
- Plain Center (Charles Mix) Township 631
- Plainfield (Brule) Township 628
- Plainview (Tripp) Township 686
- Plankinton (Aurora) City 620
- Plankinton (Aurora) Township 620
- Plano (Hanson) Township 653
- Plateau (Perkins) Township............... 677
- Plato (Hand) Township 651
- Platte (Charles Mix) City 631
- Platte (Charles Mix) Township 631
- Pleasant (Clark) Township 633
- Pleasant (Hanson) Township 653
- Pleasant (Hutchinson) Township 655
- Pleasant (Jerauld) Township 657
- Pleasant (Lincoln) Township 662
- Pleasant (Lyman) Township 664
- Pleasant Grove (Brule) Township 628
- Pleasant Lake (Aurora) Township..... 620
- Pleasant Ridge (Corson) Township...636
- Pleasant Valley (Aurora) Township...620
- Pleasant Valley (Clay) Township 634
- Pleasant Valley (Gregory) Township.648
- Pleasant Valley (Hand) Township 651
- Pleasant Valley (Marshall) Township665
- Pleasant Valley (Perkins) Township..677
- Pleasant Valley (Tripp) Township 687
- Pleasant View (Beadle) Township.....622
- Pleasant View (Tripp) Township 687
- Plummer (Brule) Township 628
- Pollock (Campbell) Town 630
- Porcupine (Shannon) CDP 681
- Portage (Brown) Township 627
- Portland (Deuel) Township 641
- **Potter County** 678
- Powell (Edmunds) Township............. 644
- Prairie (Union) Township 689
- Prairie Center (Clay) Township 634
- Prairie Center (Spink) Township 683
- Prairie View (Corson) Township........ 636
- Prairiewood (Brown) Township 627
- Pratt (Lyman) Township 664
- Presho (Lyman) City 664
- Presho (Lyman) Township 664
- Preston (Brookings) Township 625
- Pringle (Custer) Town 637
- Progressive (Tripp) Township 687
- Prospect (Mellette) Township............ 669
- Prosper (Davison) Township 638
- Provo (Fall River) Township 645
- Pukwana (Brule) Town 628
- Pukwana (Brule) Township 628
- Pulaski (Faulk) Pop. Place 646
- Putney (Brown) Township 627
- Quinn (Pennington) Town 674
- Quinn No. 1 (Pennington) Township 674
- Raber (Hughes) Township 654
- Racine (Day) Township 639
- Rainbow (Perkins) Township 677
- Rainy Creek No. 19 (Pennington) Township 675

SOUTH DAKOTA

Rames (Tripp) Township................687
Ramona (Lake) Town.....................660
Ramsey (McCook) Township............667
Rapid City (Pennington) City..........675
Rapid Valley (Pennington) CDP........675
Raritan (Day) Township..................639
Rauville (Codington) Township........635
Ravenna (Sanborn) Township...........681
Ravinia (Brown) Township...............627
Ravinia (Charles Mix) Town.............631
Raymond (Clark) Town....................633
Raymond (Clark) Township..............633
Redfield (Spink) City.......................683
Redfield (Spink) Township................683
Red Fish (Mellette) Township...........669
Red Iron Lake (Marshall) Township..665
Red Lake (Brule) Township..............628
Red Rock (Minnehaha) Township....672
Redstone (Miner) Township.............670
Ree (Charles Mix) Township............631
Ree Heights (Hand) Town................651
Ree Heights (Hand) Township..........652
Reliance (Lyman) Town...................664
Reliance (Lyman) Township..............664
Revillo (Grant) Town......................647
Rex (Lyman) Township....................664
Rhoda (Charles Mix) Township........631
Richfield (Spink) Township..............683
Richland (Beadle) Township.............622
Richland (Brookings) Township........625
Richland (Brown) Township..............627
Richland (Brule) Township................628
Richland (Clark) Township...............633
Richland (Codington) Township.......635
Richland (Edmunds) Township.........644
Richland (Jones) Township...............658
Richland (McCook) Township..........667
Richland (Union) Pop. Place............689
Rich Valley (Jones) Pop. Place.........658
Ridgeland (Corson) Township..........636
Ring Thunder (Mellette) Township...669
Riverside (Brown) Township.............627
Riverside (Clay) Township................634
Riverside (Corson) Township...........636
Riverside (Hand) Township..............652
Riverside (Mellette) Township..........669
Riverview (Moody) Township...........673
Roberts County..........................678
Robins (Fall River) Township............645
Rock Creek (Miner) Township..........670
Rockdale (Hand) Township..............652
Rockford (Perkins) Township...........677
Rockham (Faulk) Town...................646
Rocky Ford (Mellette) Township......669
Rolling Green (Corson) Township....636
Rome (Davison) Township...............638
Rome (Deuel) Township...................641
Roscoe (Edmunds) City..................644
Rose (Lyman) Township..................664
Rosebud (Mellette) Township..........669
Rosebud (Todd) CDP.....................685
Rosedale (Clark) Township..............633
Rosedale (Hanson) Township...........653
Rosedale (Tripp) Township..............687
Rosefield (Turner) Township.............688
Rose Hill (Hand) Township..............652
Roseland (Tripp) Township..............687
Rosette (Edmunds) Township...........644
Rosholt (Roberts) Town...................679
Roslyn (Day) Town........................639
Roswell (Miner) Town....................670
Roswell (Miner) Township...............670
Rouse (Charles Mix) Township........632
Rowe (Lyman) Township.................664
Running Bird (Mellette) Township...669

Rusk (Day) Township......................639
Rutland (Lake) Township.................660
St. Charles (Gregory) Township.......648
St. Francis (Todd) Town..................685
St. Lawrence (Hand) Town..............652
St. Lawrence (Hand) Township........652
St. Onge (Lawrence) Township.........661
Salem (McCook) City.....................667
Salem (McCook) Township..............667
Salem (Turner) Township.................688
Sanborn County..........................680
Sand Creek (Beadle) Township........622
Sangamon (Edmunds) Township......644
Saratoga (Faulk) Township..............646
Savo (Brown) Township..................627
Scandinavia (Deuel) Township.........641
Scenic No. 7 (Pennington)
  Township...................................675
Schriever (Gregory) Township..........649
Scotch Cap (Perkins) Township.......677
Scotland (Bon Homme) City...........623
Scotland (Day) Township................639
Scovil (Jones) Township..................658
Selby (Walworth) City...................690
Seneca (Faulk) Town......................646
Shannon County........................681
Sharon (Hutchinson) Township........655
Shelby (Brown) Township................627
Sheridan (Codington) Township.......635
Sherman (Brookings) Township........625
Sherman (Corson) Township............636
Sherman (Faulk) Township..............646
Sherman (Minnehaha) Town............672
Shyne No. 27 (Pennington)
  Township...................................675
Sidney (Perkins) Township..............677
Signal (Charles Mix) Township........632
Silver Creek (Sanborn) Township....681
Silver Lake (Hutchinson) Township..655
Sinai (Brookings) Town..................625
Sioux (Lyman) Township.................664
Sioux Falls (Lincoln) City...............663
Sioux Falls (Minnehaha) City..........672
Sioux Valley (Union) Township.......689
Sisseton (Marshall) Township..........665
Sisseton (Roberts) City..................679
Sisseton (Roberts) Township...........680
Smith (Brule) Township..................628
Smithville (Meade) Township..........668
South Campbell (Campbell) Pop.
  Place..630
South Creek (Jones) Township........658
South Detroit (Brown) Township.....627
South Dewey (Dewey) Pop. Place...641
Southeast Bon Homme (Bon Homme)
  Pop. Place................................623
Southeast Buffalo (Buffalo) Pop.
  Place..629
Southeast Gregory (Gregory) Pop.
  Place..649
Southeast Jackson (Jackson) Pop.
  Place..656
Southeast Yankton (Yankton) Pop.
  Place..691
South Harding (Harding) Pop. Place.653
South Lawrence (Lawrence) Pop.
  Place..661
South Lyman (Lyman) Pop. Place...664
South Perkins (Perkins) Pop. Place..677
South Shore (Codington) Town.......635
South Stanley (Stanley) Pop. Place..684
Southwest Bon Homme (Bon Homme)
  Pop. Place................................623
Southwest Fall River (Fall River) Pop.
  Place..645

Southwest Faulk (Faulk) Pop. Place..646
Southwest Jackson (Jackson) Pop.
  Place..656
Southwest Meade (Meade) Pop.
  Place..668
Southwest Perkins (Perkins) Pop.
  Place..677
South Ziebach (Ziebach) Pop. Place.692
Spearfish (Lawrence) City...............661
Spencer (McCook) City..................667
Spink (Union) Township..................689
Spink County..............................682
Spirit Lake (Kingsbury) Township....660
Spirit Mound (Clay) Township........634
Split Rock (Minnehaha) Township...672
Spring (Spink) Township.................683
Spring Creek (Moody) Township.....673
Spring Creek (Todd) CDP..............685
Springdale (Lincoln) Township........663
Springdale (Roberts) Township........680
Springfield (Bon Homme) City........623
Spring Grove (Roberts) Township...680
Spring Hill (Hand) Township..........652
Spring Lake (Hand) Township.........652
Spring Lake (Hanson) Township.....653
Spring Lake (Kingsbury) Township..660
Spring Valley (Clark) Township.......633
Spring Valley (Gregory) Pop. Place..649
Spring Valley (McCook) Township...667
Spring Valley (Turner) Township......688
Stanley County..........................684
Star (Clay) Township.....................634
Star Prairie (Tripp) Township..........687
Starr (Hutchinson) Township..........655
Star Valley (Gregory) Township.......649
Star Valley (Tripp) Township..........687
Stena (Marshall) Township..............666
Sterling (Brookings) Township........625
Stewart (Tripp) Township...............687
Stickney (Aurora) Town..................620
Stockholm (Grant) Town................647
Stockholm (Grant) Township..........647
Stony Butte (Lyman) Township......664
Strandburg (Grant) Town...............647
Stratford (Brown) Town..................627
Strool (Perkins) Township...............677
Sturgis (Meade) City.....................668
Sully (Tripp) Township..................687
Sully County..............................684
Summit (Lake) Township.................660
Summit (Roberts) Town..................680
Summit (Roberts) Township............680
Sumner (Spink) Township...............683
Sunnyside No. 26 (Pennington)
  Township..................................675
Sun Prairie (McCook) Township......667
Surprise Valley (Mellette) Township.669
Susquehanna (Hutchinson)
  Township..................................655
Sverdrup (Minnehaha) Township....672
Swan Lake (Turner) Township........688
Sweet (Hutchinson) Township........655
Sylvia (Lyman) Township...............664
Tabor (Bon Homme) Town............623
Tamworth (Faulk) Township..........646
Taopi (Minnehaha) Township.........672
Taylor (Hanson) Township.............653
Taylor (Tripp) Township................687
Tea (Lincoln) Town......................663
Tetonka (Spink) Township.............683
Theresa (Beadle) Township............622
Thorp (Clark) Township.................633
Three Rivers (Spink) Township.......683
Timber Lake (Dewey) City............641
Tobin (Davison) Township.............638

Todd County 685	Virgil (Beadle) Town............................622	West Pennington (Pennington) Pop. Place..675
Tolstoy (Potter) Town..........................678	Virgil (Jones) Township........................658	West Perkins (Perkins) Pop. Place....677
Toronto (Deuel) Town 641	Virginia (Union) Township...................690	West Point (Brule) Township...............629
Torrey Lake (Brule) Township 628	Vivian (Lyman) Township....................664	Westport (Brown) Town 627
Tracy (Lyman) Township....................664	Volga (Brookings) City 625	Westport (Brown) Township................627
Trail (Perkins) Township.....................677	Volga (Brookings) Township................625	West Potter (Potter) Pop. Place 678
Trent (Moody) Town 673	Volin (Yankton) Town 691	West Rondell (Brown) Township 627
Trenton (Brookings) Township..........625	Volin (Yankton) Township....................691	West Shannon (Shannon) Pop. Place681
Tripp (Hutchinson) City......................655	Vrooman (Perkins) Township 677	West Sully (Sully) Pop. Place 684
Tripp County 685	Wachter (McPherson) Township 667	West Todd (Todd) Pop. Place 685
Troy (Day) Township............................639	Wacker (McPherson) Township 667	West Walworth (Walworth) Pop. Place..690
Troy (Grant) Township........................647	Wagner (Charles Mix) City.................632	West Yankton (Yankton) Pop. Place.691
Truro (Aurora) Township 620	Wahehe (Charles Mix) Township.....632	Weta (Jackson) Township....................657
Tulare (Spink) Town 683	Wakonda (Clay) Town 634	Wetonka (McPherson) Town 668
Tulare (Spink) Township.....................683	Wakpala (Corson) Township...............636	Wheatland (Day) Township.................639
Turkey Valley (Yankton) Township...691	Waldro (Brule) Township 629	Wheaton (Hand) Township 652
Turner (Turner) Township..................688	Walker (Corson) Township..................636	Whetstone (Gregory) Township 649
Turner County 687	Wall (Jackson) Township....................656	White (Brookings) City.........................625
Turton (Spink) Town 683	Wall (Pennington) Town......................675	White (Marshall) Township..................666
Turton (Spink) Township.....................683	Wallace (Codington) Town 635	White Butte (Perkins) Township........677
Twin Brooks (Grant) Town 647	Wall Lake (Minnehaha) Township....672	White Hill (Perkins) Township 677
Twin Brooks (Grant) Township 647	Walnut Grove (Douglas) Township...642	White Horse (Todd) CDP 685
Twin Butte (Corson) Township 636	Walshtown (Yankton) Township 691	White Lake (Aurora) City 620
Twin Lake (Sanborn) Township 681	**Walworth County** 690	White Lake (Aurora) Township 621
Two Strike (Todd) CDP 685	Wanblee (Jackson) CDP 656	White River (Mellette) City 669
Tyndall (Bon Homme) City..................624	Ward (Moody) Town 673	White Rock (Roberts) Town 680
Union (Brule) Township........................629	Ward (Moody) Township......................673	White Rock (Roberts) Township........680
Union (Butte) Township........................630	Warner (Brown) Town 627	Whiteside (Beadle) Township............622
Union (Davison) Township...................638	Warner (Brown) Township...................627	White Swan (Charles Mix) Township...632
Union (Day) Township..........................639	Warren (Clark) Township 633	Whitewood (Kingsbury) Township ...660
Union (Edmunds) Township 644	Warren (Sanborn) Township 681	Whitewood (Lawrence) City...............661
Union (Faulk) Township 646	Washington (Aurora) Township 620	Wilbur (Brule) Township 629
Union (Gregory) Township..................649	Washington (Clark) Township............633	William Hamilton (Hyde) Township 656
Union (Jones) Township 658	Washington (Douglas) Township........642	Williams Creek (Jones) Township....658
Union (McCook) Township...................667	Wasta (Pennington) Town...................675	Willow Creek (Tripp) Township........687
Union (Meade) Township.....................668	Wasta No. 2 (Pennington) Township 675	Willow Lake (Brule) Township 629
Union (Moody) Township.....................673	Watauga (Corson) Township 636	Willow Lake (Clark) City 633
Union (Sanborn) Township 681	Watertown (Codington) City 635	Wilmot (Roberts) Town.......................680
Union (Spink) Township.......................683	Waubay (Day) City 639	Wilson (Perkins) Township 677
Union County 689	Waubay (Day) Township......................639	Wilson (Tripp) Township......................687
Upper Red Owl (Meade) Township..668	Waverly (Codington) Township..........635	Winfred (Lake) Town 661
Utica (Yankton) Town..........................691	Waverly (Marshall) Township 666	Winfred (Lake) Township....................661
Utica (Yankton) Township...................691	Wayne (Hanson) Township 653	Winner (Tripp) City...............................687
Vail (Perkins) Township 677	Wayne (Lake) Township 660	Winsor (Brookings) Township.............625
Vale (Butte) Township 630	Wayne (Minnehaha) Township...........672	Wismer (Marshall) Township..............666
Valley (Beadle) Township 622	Weaver (Tripp) Township....................687	Witten (Tripp) Township......................687
Valley (Day) Township.........................639	Weber (McPherson) Township 667	Wittenberg (Hutchinson) Township..655
Valley (Douglas) Township..................642	Webster (Day) City................................639	Wolf Creek (Hutchinson) Township..655
Valley (Hughes) Township....................654	Wellington (Minnehaha) Township ...672	Wolsey (Beadle) Town 622
Valley (Hutchinson) Township 655	Wells (Perkins) Township 677	Wolsey (Beadle) Township..................622
Valley (Hyde) Township 656	Wentworth (Lake) Township 661	Wood (Mellette) Town..........................669
Valley (Tripp) Township......................687	Wentworth (Lake) Village...................660	Woodland (Clark) Township 633
Valley Springs (Minnehaha) City 672	Wesley (Faulk) Township....................646	Woonsocket (Sanborn) City................681
Valley Springs (Minnehaha) Township...672	Wessington (Beadle) City....................622	Woonsocket (Sanborn) Township......681
Veblen (Marshall) City 666	Wessington (Beadle) Township..........622	Worthen (Hanson) Township 653
Veblen (Marshall) Township...............666	Wessington (Hand) City 652	Worthing (Lincoln) Town 663
Verdon (Brown) Town 627	Wessington Springs (Jerauld) City 657	Wortman (Tripp) Township..................687
Vermillion (Clay) City...........................634	Wessington Springs (Jerauld) Township...657	Wounded Knee (Shannon) CDP 681
Vermillion (Clay) Township.................634	West Bennett (Bennett) Pop. Place ...623	Wright (Tripp) Township......................687
Vermillion (Miner) Township..............670	West Butte (Butte) Pop. Place...........630	Wyandotte (Perkins) Township..........677
Vermont (Edmunds) Township 644	West Central Perkins (Perkins) Pop. Place..677	Yale (Beadle) Town...............................622
Vernon (Beadle) Township 622	West Corson (Corson) Pop. Place....636	Yankton (Yankton) City 691
Vernon (Grant) Township....................647	West Custer (Custer) Pop. Place.....637	**Yankton County**.................................690
Viborg (Turner) City.............................689	West Haakon (Haakon) Pop. Place...649	York (Day) Township 640
Vickers (Perkins) Township................677	West Hanson (Brown) Township.......627	York (Hand) Township 652
Victor (Marshall) Township.................666	West Hughes (Hughes) Pop. Place 654	Zell (Faulk) Township..........................646
Victor (Roberts) Township..................680	West McPherson (McPherson) Pop. Place..667	Zickrick (Jones) Township 658
Vienna (Clark) Town 633	Weston (Marshall) Township..............666	**Ziebach County** 692
Viking (Perkins) Township..................677	Westover (Jones) Township................658	
Vilas (Miner) Town 671		
Viola (Jerauld) Township 657		

Utah

UTAH

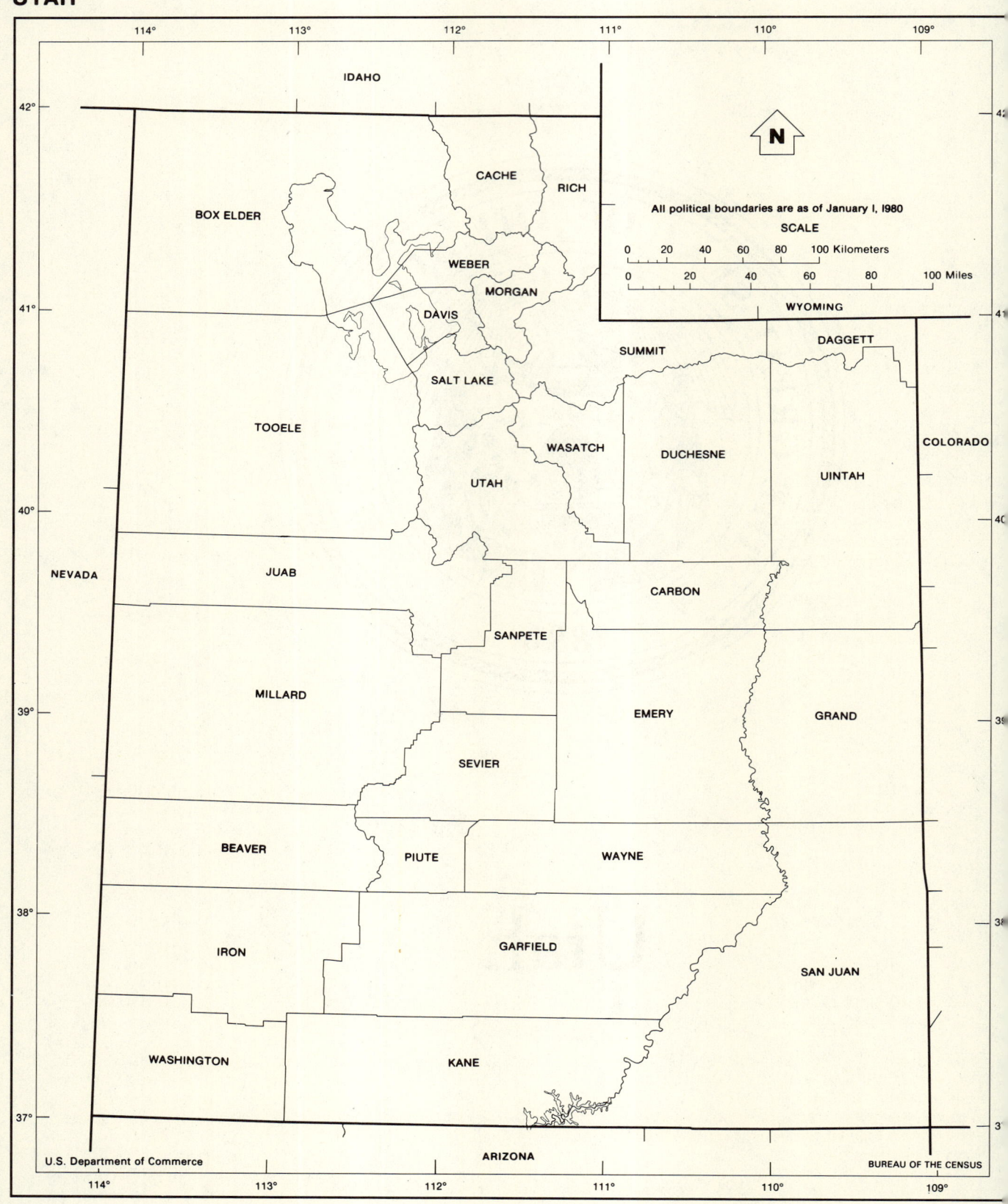

Utah

Population: 1,722,850 (1990); 1,461,037 (1980)
Population rank (1990): 35
Percent population change (1980–1990): 17.9
Population projection: 1,841,000 (1995); 1,929,000 (2000)

Area: total: 84,904 sq. mi.; 82,168 sq. mi. land, 2,736 sq. mi. water
Area rank: 13
Highest elevation: 13,528 ft., Kings Peak (Duchesne County)
Lowest point: 2,000 ft., Beaverdam Creek (Washington County)

State capital: Salt Lake City (Salt Lake County)
Largest city: Salt Lake City (159,936)
Second largest city: West Valley (86,976)
Largest county: Salt Lake (725,956)

Total housing units: 598,388
No. of occupied housing units: 537,273
Vacant housing units (%): 10.2
Distribution of population by race and Hispanic origin (%):
  White: 93.8
  Black: 0.7
  Hispanic (any race): 4.9
  Native American: 1.4
  Asian/Pacific: 1.9
  Other: 2.2

Admission date: January 4, 1896 (45th state).

Location: In the western United States, bordering Arizona, Nevada, Idaho, Wyoming, Colorado, and New Mexico.

Name Origin: For the Ute Indians, who lived in the area. *Ute* or *Eutaw* is variously defined as 'in the tops of the mountains,' 'high up,' 'the hill dwellers,' 'the land of the sun,' or 'the land of plenty.'

State animal: elk *(Cervus canadensis)*
State bird: California gull *(Larus californius)*
State emblem: beehive
State fish: rainbow trout *(Salmo gairdnerii)*
State flower: sego lily *(Calochortus nuttallii)*
State fossil: allosaurus
State gem: topaz
State grass: Indian ricegrass *(Oryzopsis hymenoides)*
State insect: honey bee *(Apis mellifera)*
State rock: coal
State song: "Utah, We Love Thee"
State tree: blue spruce *(Picea pungens)*

State motto: Industry
State nickname: Beehive State

Area code: 801
Time zone: Mountain
Abbreviations: UT (postal); Ut. (traditional)
Part of (region): Rocky Mountain

Local Government

Counties

Utah has 29 counties, each governed by a board of commissioners.

Municipalities

Utah has 229 cities and towns. Utah's state constitution gives municipalities the right of home rule, but few have chosen to adopt their own charters.

Settlement History and Early Development

Utah's earliest inhabitants were Indians who lived in pueblos and cliff dwellings. In the late 1770s white explorers of the area that is now Utah found Gosiute, Paiute, Shoshone, and Ute Indians; the Navajo arrived in Utah in the 1860s.

The first white men to see what is now Utah were probably two Spanish Franciscan friars, Silvestre Vélez de Escalante and Francisco Atanasio Domínguez, who reached Utah Lake in 1775. An American fur-trading expedition may have crossed northern Utah in 1811–12, and Jim Bridger, an American scout, saw the Great Salt Lake in 1824–25. Fur trappers and traders came to the area, and by 1830 travelers from Santa Fe, New Mexico, were crossing central Utah to reach California.

The area that became Utah had been claimed by Spain; it passed to Mexico when Mexico became independent of Spain in 1821. After the Mexican-American War (1846–48) Utah was part of the land ceded by Mexico to the U.S. under the Treaty of Guadalupe-Hidalgo.

The first permanent white settlers in Utah were the Mormons, or members of the Church of Jesus Christ of Latter-Day Saints, a religious group that had been persecuted elsewhere. Joseph Smith had established the church in New York State in 1830; after Smith's death in 1844 the new leader, Brigham Young, led the group west. Young and some of his followers settled in the Great Salt Lake area in 1847. The Mormons irrigated the land and began to farm. In 1849 the Mormons established a Perpetual Emigrating Fund to pay the traveling expenses of other Mormons who wished to come to the Utah settlement.

After initially peaceful relations, Mormons encountered difficulties with the Indians during the Walker War (1853–54) and the Black Hawk War (1865–67). Occasional raids on the settlers continued until the early 1870s. Most of the Ute Indians were eventually settled on reservations.

Territory of Utah and Statehood

In 1849 the Mormons established a state called Deseret, with Brigham Young as its leader. The settlers asked to be admitted to the Union, but a debate in Congress over slavery resulted in the Compromise of 1850, which established the Territory of Utah with Brigham Young as governor. Although the settlers continued to request admission to the Union, Congress refused because of the Mormon practice of polygamy. In an attempt to take control of Utah from the Mormons, President James Buchanan sent federal troops to enforce his appointment of a new governor in place of Brigham Young in 1857. The Utah War or Mormon War, 1857–60, included the Mountain Meadows Massacre, during which Mormons attacked and killed most of a group of 140 travelers. Federal troops left Utah when the Civil War began in 1861.

In 1863 gold and silver were discovered in Bingham Canyon, but initial profits were small and it was some years before Utah had a sizable mining industry. Utah attracted more settlers after the Central Pacific Railroad and the Union Pacific Railroad met at Promontory, Utah, in 1869, completing the first transcontinental railroad.

In 1862 Congress had passed a law forbidding polygamy. During the 1880s federal courts began enforcing the law against polygamy, fining and imprisoning about 1,000 Mormons. In 1890 the church president advised Mormons to give up polygamy, which the church prohibited after 1904.

In 1895 Utah submitted a constitution to Congress that prohibited polygamy and prevented church control of the state. Utah was admitted as the 45th state on January 4, 1896.

Business and Industry

Utah prospered in the early 1900s with expansion of the railroads, increased farming and livestock production, and copper mining. Utah provided both food and metals during World War I, but both farming and mining suffered during the Great Depression of the 1930s, when Utah had one of the country's highest unemployment rates. During World War II the state's economy rebounded, and after the war the federal government constructed military installations in Utah. The state became a center of missile production.

Utah changed from an agricultural to an industrial state during the 1950s and 1960s. Steel manufacturing, uranium mining, and the development of oil and gas fields became important industries. In 1967 construction began on the Central Utah Project, a long-running plan to increase Utah's water supplies. Tourists began to visit Utah in increasing numbers as outdoor recreation areas, including ski areas, were developed.

State Boundaries

Utah's boundaries were changed several times during the 1860s as parts of the territory were given to Nevada, Colorado, and Wyoming. The present boundaries were established in 1868.

Utah Counties

Beaver	Garfield	Piute	Tooele
Box Elder	Grand	Rich	Uintah
Cache	Iron	Salt Lake	Utah
Carbon	Juab	San Juan	Wasatch
Daggett	Kane	Sanpete	Washington
Davis	Millard	Sevier	Wayne
Duchesne	Morgan	Summit	Weber
Emery			

Multi-County Places

The following Utah places are in more than one county. Given here is the total population for each multi-county place, and the names of the counties it is in.

Draper, pop. 7,257; Salt Lake (7,257), Utah (0)
Green River, pop. 866; Emery (744), Grand (122)
Hiawatha, pop. 43; Carbon (43), Emery (0)
Park City, pop. 4,468; Summit (4,468), Wasatch (0)

Beaver County
County Seat: Beaver (ZIP: 84713)

Pop: 4,765 (1990); 4,378 (1980)   **Pop Density:** 1.8
Land: 2590.1 sq. mi.; **Water:** 2.3 sq. mi.   **Area Code:** 801
On the southwestern border of UT; organized Jan 5, 1856 (prior to statehood) from Iron County.
Name origin: For the beaver once plentiful in the area.

Beaver   City
ZIP: 84713   **Lat:** 38-16-44 N **Long:** 112-38-23 W
Pop: 1,998 (1990); 1,792 (1980)   **Pop Density:** 1332.0
Land: 1.5 sq. mi.; **Water:** 0.0 sq. mi.   **Elev:** 5898 ft.
Incorporated Jan 10, 1867.

Milford   City
ZIP: 84751   **Lat:** 38-23-40 N **Long:** 113-00-39 W
Pop: 1,107 (1990); 1,293 (1980)   **Pop Density:** 1230.0
Land: 0.9 sq. mi.; **Water:** 0.0 sq. mi.   **Elev:** 4957 ft.
Incorporated 1903.

Minersville   Town
ZIP: 84752   **Lat:** 38-12-47 N **Long:** 112-55-26 W
Pop: 608 (1990); 552 (1980)   **Pop Density:** 1013.3
Land: 0.6 sq. mi.; **Water:** 0.0 sq. mi.   **Elev:** 5625 ft.
Incorporated Apr 4, 1899.

Box Elder County
County Seat: Brigham City (ZIP: 84302)

Pop: 36,485 (1990); 33,222 (1980)   **Pop Density:** 6.4
Land: 5723.7 sq. mi.; **Water:** 1005.8 sq. mi.   **Area Code:** 801
On the northwestern border of UT, west of Ogden; organized Jan 5, 1856 (prior to statehood) from Weber County.
Name origin: For the abundant box elder trees in the area. It is more commonly known as the North American maple tree *Acer negundo*.

Bear River City   Town
ZIP: 84301   **Lat:** 41-36-51 N **Long:** 112-07-23 W
Pop: 700 (1990); 540 (1980)   **Pop Density:** 437.5
Land: 1.6 sq. mi.; **Water:** 0.0 sq. mi.   **Elev:** 4253 ft.

Brigham City   City
ZIP: 84302   **Lat:** 41-30-32 N **Long:** 112-00-34 W
Pop: 15,644 (1990); 15,596 (1980)   **Pop Density:** 1251.5
Land: 12.5 sq. mi.; **Water:** 0.0 sq. mi.   **Elev:** 4439 ft.
In northwestern UT, 20 mi. north of Ogden. Incorporated 1867.
Name origin: For Mormon elder Brigham Young (1801–77). A former name was Box Elder.

Corinne   City
ZIP: 84307   **Lat:** 41-32-51 N **Long:** 112-06-59 W
Pop: 639 (1990); 512 (1980)   **Pop Density:** 177.5
Land: 3.6 sq. mi.; **Water:** 0.1 sq. mi.   **Elev:** 4230 ft.
Incorporated Feb. 18, 1870.

Deweyville   Town
Lat: 41-41-23 N **Long:** 112-05-23 W
Pop: 318 (1990); 311 (1980)   **Pop Density:** 48.9
Land: 6.5 sq. mi.; **Water:** 0.0 sq. mi.   **Elev:** 4323 ft.
Incorporated Mar 7, 1939.

Elwood   Town
ZIP: 84337   **Lat:** 41-40-43 N **Long:** 112-08-21 W
Pop: 575 (1990); 481 (1980)   **Pop Density:** 74.7
Land: 7.7 sq. mi.; **Water:** 0.0 sq. mi.   **Elev:** 4285 ft.
Incorporated 1929.

Fielding   Town
ZIP: 84311   **Lat:** 41-48-43 N **Long:** 112-06-58 W
Pop: 422 (1990); 325 (1980)   **Pop Density:** 1055.0
Land: 0.4 sq. mi.; **Water:** 0.0 sq. mi.   **Elev:** 4367 ft.
Incorporated 1911.

Garland   City
ZIP: 84312   **Lat:** 41-44-12 N **Long:** 112-09-40 W
Pop: 1,637 (1990); 1,405 (1980)   **Pop Density:** 1091.3
Land: 1.5 sq. mi.; **Water:** 0.0 sq. mi.   **Elev:** 4344 ft.
Incorporated Jan 1, 1915.

Honeyville   City
ZIP: 84314   **Lat:** 41-38-05 N **Long:** 112-04-58 W
Pop: 1,112 (1990); 915 (1980)   **Pop Density:** 94.2
Land: 11.8 sq. mi.; **Water:** 0.0 sq. mi.   **Elev:** 4269 ft.
Incorporated Jul 8, 1911.

Howell   Town
ZIP: 84316   **Lat:** 41-46-16 N **Long:** 112-26-41 W
Pop: 237 (1990); 176 (1980)   **Pop Density:** 6.7
Land: 35.4 sq. mi.; **Water:** 0.2 sq. mi.   **Elev:** 4556 ft.
Incorporated Jun 16, 1941.

Mantua   Town
ZIP: 84302   **Lat:** 41-30-09 N **Long:** 111-55-56 W
Pop: 665 (1990); 484 (1980)   **Pop Density:** 266.0
Land: 2.5 sq. mi.; **Water:** 0.7 sq. mi.   **Elev:** 5175 ft.
Incorporated Mar 6, 1911

Perry — City
Lat: 41-27-53 N Long: 112-02-03 W
Pop: 1,211 (1990); 1,084 (1980) **Pop Density:** 173.0
Land: 7.0 sq. mi.; **Water:** 0.0 sq. mi.
Incorporated Oct 1971.

Plymouth — Town
ZIP: 84330 **Lat:** 41-52-34 N **Long:** 112-08-41 W
Pop: 267 (1990); 238 (1980) **Pop Density:** 534.0
Land: 0.5 sq. mi.; **Water:** 0.0 sq. mi. **Elev:** 4400 ft.

Portage — Town
ZIP: 84331 **Lat:** 41-58-35 N **Long:** 112-14-16 W
Pop: 218 (1990); 196 (1980) **Pop Density:** 94.8
Land: 2.3 sq. mi.; **Water:** 0.0 sq. mi.
Incorporated 1922.

Snowville — Town
ZIP: 84336 **Lat:** 41-58-11 N **Long:** 112-42-53 W
Pop: 251 (1990); 237 (1980) **Pop Density:** 167.3
Land: 1.5 sq. mi.; **Water:** 0.0 sq. mi. **Elev:** 4551 ft.
Incorporated 1933.

Tremonton — City
ZIP: 84337 **Lat:** 41-42-54 N **Long:** 112-10-39 W
Pop: 4,264 (1990); 3,464 (1980) **Pop Density:** 888.3
Land: 4.8 sq. mi.; **Water:** 0.0 sq. mi. **Elev:** 4290 ft.
Incorporated Jul 8, 1918.

Willard — City
ZIP: 84340 **Lat:** 41-24-42 N **Long:** 112-02-38 W
Pop: 1,298 (1990); 1,241 (1980) **Pop Density:** 231.8
Land: 5.6 sq. mi.; **Water:** 1.5 sq. mi. **Elev:** 4266 ft.
Incorporated Mar 3, 1851.

Cache County
County Seat: Logan (ZIP: 84321)

Pop: 70,183 (1990); 57,176 (1980) **Pop Density:** 60.3
Land: 1164.6 sq. mi.; **Water:** 8.5 sq. mi. **Area Code:** 801
On the central northern border of UT, northeast of Ogden; organized Jan 5, 1856 (prior to statehood) from unorganized territory.
Name origin: For Cache Valley, from the French for 'hiding place,' because early trappers or hunters stored furs and supplies in the valley.

Amalga — Town
ZIP: 84335 **Lat:** 41-51-27 N **Long:** 111-53-48 W
Pop: 366 (1990); 323 (1980) **Pop Density:** 107.6
Land: 3.4 sq. mi.; **Water:** 0.2 sq. mi. **Elev:** 4425 ft.
Incorporated Jul 15, 1938.

Clarkston — Town
ZIP: 84305 **Lat:** 41-55-15 N **Long:** 112-02-54 W
Pop: 645 (1990); 562 (1980) **Pop Density:** 645.0
Land: 1.0 sq. mi.; **Water:** 0.0 sq. mi. **Elev:** 4884 ft.
Incorporated 1901.

Cornish — Town
ZIP: 84308 **Lat:** 41-58-23 N **Long:** 111-57-03 W
Pop: 205 (1990); 181 (1980) **Pop Density:** 42.7
Land: 4.8 sq. mi.; **Water:** 0.0 sq. mi. **Elev:** 4480 ft.

Hyde Park — City
ZIP: 84318 **Lat:** 41-47-52 N **Long:** 111-48-52 W
Pop: 2,190 (1990); 1,495 (1980) **Pop Density:** 684.4
Land: 3.2 sq. mi.; **Water:** 0.0 sq. mi. **Elev:** 4448 ft.
Incorporated Jan 16, 1892.

Hyrum — City
ZIP: 84319 **Lat:** 41-37-58 N **Long:** 111-50-40 W
Pop: 4,829 (1990); 3,952 (1980) **Pop Density:** 1305.1
Land: 3.7 sq. mi.; **Water:** 0.0 sq. mi. **Elev:** 4706 ft.
Incorporated Feb 10, 1870.

Lewiston — City
ZIP: 84320 **Lat:** 41-57-39 N **Long:** 111-52-29 W
Pop: 1,532 (1990); 1,438 (1980) **Pop Density:** 59.8
Land: 25.6 sq. mi.; **Water:** 0.1 sq. mi. **Elev:** 4506 ft.
Incorporated Sep 12, 1921.

Logan — City
ZIP: 84321 **Lat:** 41-44-24 N **Long:** 111-50-06 W
Pop: 32,762 (1990); 26,844 (1980) **Pop Density:** 2323.5
Land: 14.1 sq. mi.; **Water:** 0.5 sq. mi. **Elev:** 4535 ft.
In northern UT, 36 mi. north of Ogden at the mouth of Logan Canyon. Incorporated 1867.
Name origin: The source of the name is in dispute. Probably for the Logan River, but others claim that it was for a friendly Indian chief named Logan.

Mendon — City
ZIP: 84325 **Lat:** 41-42-39 N **Long:** 111-58-46 W
Pop: 684 (1990); 663 (1980) **Pop Density:** 684.0
Land: 1.0 sq. mi.; **Water:** 0.0 sq. mi. **Elev:** 4520 ft.
Incorporated 1870.

Millville — City
ZIP: 84326 **Lat:** 41-40-50 N **Long:** 111-49-07 W
Pop: 1,202 (1990); 848 (1980) **Pop Density:** 924.6
Land: 1.3 sq. mi.; **Water:** 0.0 sq. mi. **Elev:** 4542 ft.
Incorporated Mar 2, 1867.

Newton — Town
ZIP: 84327 **Lat:** 41-51-40 N **Long:** 111-59-20 W
Pop: 659 (1990); 623 (1980) **Pop Density:** 823.8
Land: 0.8 sq. mi.; **Water:** 0.0 sq. mi. **Elev:** 4525 ft.
Incorporated Mar 12, 1900.

Nibley — City
ZIP: 84332 **Lat:** 41-40-21 N **Long:** 111-50-30 W
Pop: 1,167 (1990); 1,036 (1980) **Pop Density:** 402.4
Land: 2.9 sq. mi.; **Water:** 0.0 sq. mi. **Elev:** 4553 ft.
Incorporated 1936.

North Logan — City
ZIP: 84321 **Lat:** 41-46-17 N **Long:** 111-48-50 W
Pop: 3,768 (1990); 2,258 (1980) **Pop Density:** 801.7
Land: 4.7 sq. mi.; **Water:** 0.0 sq. mi. **Elev:** 4640 ft.
Incorporated 1934.

Paradise — Town
ZIP: 84328 **Lat:** 41-34-03 N **Long:** 111-49-59 W
Pop: 561 (1990); 542 (1980) **Pop Density:** 510.0
Land: 1.1 sq. mi.; **Water:** 0.0 sq. mi. **Elev:** 4860 ft.
Incorporated Apr 1, 1901.

Providence — City
ZIP: 84332 **Lat:** 41-42-18 N **Long:** 111-48-48 W
Pop: 3,344 (1990); 2,675 (1980) **Pop Density:** 1238.5
Land: 2.7 sq. mi.; **Water:** 0.0 sq. mi. **Elev:** 4600 ft.
Incorporated Jul 1929.

Richmond — City
ZIP: 84333 **Lat:** 41-55-09 N **Long:** 111-48-33 W
Pop: 1,955 (1990); 1,705 (1980) **Pop Density:** 674.1
Land: 2.9 sq. mi.; **Water:** 0.0 sq. mi. **Elev:** 4607 ft.
Incorporated 1865.

River Heights — City
ZIP: 84321 **Lat:** 41-43-21 N **Long:** 111-49-13 W
Pop: 1,274 (1990); 1,211 (1980) **Pop Density:** 2123.3
Land: 0.6 sq. mi.; **Water:** 0.0 sq. mi. **Elev:** 4560 ft.
Incorporated Oct 31, 1934.

Smithfield — City
ZIP: 84335 **Lat:** 41-50-07 N **Long:** 111-49-46 W
Pop: 5,566 (1990); 4,993 (1980) **Pop Density:** 1391.5
Land: 4.0 sq. mi.; **Water:** 0.0 sq. mi. **Elev:** 4595 ft.
Incorporated Apr 1, 1868.

Trenton — Town
ZIP: 84338 **Lat:** 41-54-50 N **Long:** 111-56-06 W
Pop: 464 (1990); 447 (1980) **Pop Density:** 64.4
Land: 7.2 sq. mi.; **Water:** 0.1 sq. mi. **Elev:** 4461 ft.

Wellsville — City
ZIP: 84339 **Lat:** 41-37-56 N **Long:** 111-55-54 W
Pop: 2,206 (1990); 1,952 (1980) **Pop Density:** 787.9
Land: 2.8 sq. mi.; **Water:** 0.0 sq. mi. **Elev:** 4495 ft.
Incorporated Mar 1866.

Carbon County
County Seat: Price (ZIP: 84501)

Pop: 20,228 (1990); 22,179 (1980) **Pop Density:** 13.7
Land: 1478.6 sq. mi.; **Water:** 6.1 sq. mi. **Area Code:** 801
In east-central UT, southeast of Provo; organized 1894 (prior to statehood) from Emery County.
Name origin: For the abundant coal deposits within its borders.

East Carbon — City
ZIP: 84520 **Lat:** 39-32-08 N **Long:** 110-24-23 W
Pop: 1,270 (1990); 1,942 (1980) **Pop Density:** 244.2
Land: 5.2 sq. mi.; **Water:** 0.0 sq. mi. **Elev:** 6300 ft.
Incorporated Jul 19, 1973.

Helper — City
Lat: 39-41-22 N **Long:** 110-51-32 W
Pop: 2,148 (1990); 2,724 (1980) **Pop Density:** 1193.3
Land: 1.8 sq. mi.; **Water:** 0.0 sq. mi. **Elev:** 5830 ft.
Incorporated Oct 9, 1915.

Hiawatha — Town
ZIP: 84527 **Lat:** 39-29-46 N **Long:** 111-01-44 W
Pop: 43 (1990); 249 (1980) **Pop Density:** 5.5
Land: 7.8 sq. mi.; **Water:** 0.0 sq. mi. **Elev:** 7050 ft.
Incorporated Sep 26, 1911. Part of the town is also in Emery County.

Price — City
ZIP: 84501 **Lat:** 39-36-05 N **Long:** 110-48-04 W
Pop: 8,712 (1990); 9,086 (1980) **Pop Density:** 2124.9
Land: 4.1 sq. mi.; **Water:** 0.0 sq. mi. **Elev:** 5566 ft.
Incorporated 1911.

Scofield — Town
Lat: 39-43-30 N **Long:** 111-09-40 W
Pop: 43 (1990); 105 (1980) **Pop Density:** 86.0
Land: 0.5 sq. mi.; **Water:** 0.0 sq. mi. **Elev:** 7702 ft.
Incorporated Mar 7, 1892.

Sunnyside — City
ZIP: 84539 **Lat:** 39-33-07 N **Long:** 110-24-00 W
Pop: 339 (1990); 611 (1980) **Pop Density:** 109.4
Land: 3.1 sq. mi.; **Water:** 0.0 sq. mi. **Elev:** 6710 ft.
Incorporated May 11, 1916.

Wellington — City
ZIP: 84542 **Lat:** 39-32-16 N **Long:** 110-44-14 W
Pop: 1,632 (1990); 1,406 (1980) **Pop Density:** 466.3
Land: 3.5 sq. mi.; **Water:** 0.0 sq. mi. **Elev:** 5413 ft.
Incorporated Mar 21, 1907.

Daggett County
County Seat: Manila (ZIP: 84046)

Pop: 690 (1990); 769 (1980)   **Pop Density:** 1.0
Land: 698.4 sq. mi.; **Water:** 24.7 sq. mi.   **Area Code:** 801
On the northeastern border of UT; organized Jan 7, 1918 from Uintah County.
Name origin: For Ellsworth Daggett (1845–1923), mining engineer and first surveyor-general of UT.

Manila   Town
ZIP: 84046   **Lat:** 40-59-33 N   **Long:** 109-43-13 W
Pop: 207 (1990); 272 (1980)   **Pop Density:** 258.8
Land: 0.8 sq. mi.; **Water:** 0.0 sq. mi.   **Elev:** 6375 ft.
Incorporated 1958.

Davis County
County Seat: Farmington (ZIP: 84025)

Pop: 187,941 (1990); 146,540 (1980)   **Pop Density:** 617.2
Land: 304.5 sq. mi.; **Water:** 329.1 sq. mi.   **Area Code:** 801
In north-central UT, north of Salt Lake City; original county; organized Oct 5, 1850 (prior to statehood).
Name origin: For Daniel C. Davis (1804–50), commander of "The Mormon Volunteers."

Bountiful   City
ZIP: 84010   **Lat:** 40-52-33 N   **Long:** 111-51-54 W
Pop: 36,659 (1990); 32,877 (1980)   **Pop Density:** 3426.1
Land: 10.7 sq. mi.; **Water:** 0.0 sq. mi.   **Elev:** 4408 ft.
In northern UT, 8 mi. north of Salt Lake City. Incorporated Dec 14, 1892.
Name origin: Named by early settlers for the fertility of the soil.

Centerville   City
ZIP: 84014   **Lat:** 40-55-35 N   **Long:** 111-53-09 W
Pop: 11,500 (1990); 8,069 (1980)   **Pop Density:** 1854.8
Land: 6.2 sq. mi.; **Water:** 0.0 sq. mi.   **Elev:** 4246 ft.
In northern UT, 12 mi. north of Salt Lake City. Incorporated May 4, 1915.
Name origin: Reason for name is unknown. Formerly called Deuel Creek and Cherry Settlement.

Clearfield   City
ZIP: 84015   **Lat:** 41-06-16 N   **Long:** 112-01-21 W
Pop: 21,435 (1990); 17,982 (1980)   **Pop Density:** 2858.0
Land: 7.5 sq. mi.; **Water:** 0.0 sq. mi.   **Elev:** 4487 ft.
In northern UT, south of Ogden. Incorporated 1942.
Name origin: For its descriptive connotations.

Clinton   City
ZIP: 84015   **Lat:** 41-08-27 N   **Long:** 112-03-45 W
Pop: 7,945 (1990); 5,777 (1980)   **Pop Density:** 1444.5
Land: 5.5 sq. mi.; **Water:** 0.0 sq. mi.   **Elev:** 5410 ft.
Incorporated Aug 17, 1936.

Farmington   City
ZIP: 84025   **Lat:** 40-59-19 N   **Long:** 111-53-41 W
Pop: 9,028 (1990); 4,691 (1980)   **Pop Density:** 1703.4
Land: 5.3 sq. mi.; **Water:** 0.0 sq. mi.   **Elev:** 4302 ft.
Incorporated Nov 16, 1892.

Fruit Heights   City
ZIP: 84037   **Lat:** 41-01-41 N   **Long:** 111-54-20 W
Pop: 3,900 (1990); 2,728 (1980)   **Pop Density:** 1772.7
Land: 2.2 sq. mi.; **Water:** 0.0 sq. mi.   **Elev:** 4680 ft.
Incorporated Aug 23, 1939.

Kaysville   City
ZIP: 84037   **Lat:** 41-01-50 N   **Long:** 111-56-39 W
Pop: 13,961 (1990); 9,811 (1980)   **Pop Density:** 1469.6
Land: 9.5 sq. mi.; **Water:** 0.0 sq. mi.   **Elev:** 4349 ft.
In northern UT, 18 mi. south of Ogden. Incorporated Mar 15, 1868.
Name origin: For William Kay, first Mormon bishop of the district.

Layton   City
ZIP: 84041   **Lat:** 41-04-40 N   **Long:** 111-57-16 W
Pop: 41,784 (1990); 22,862 (1980)   **Pop Density:** 2283.3
Land: 18.3 sq. mi.; **Water:** 0.1 sq. mi.   **Elev:** 4356 ft.
In northern UT, north of Salt Lake City. Incorporated Jul 1920.
Name origin: For Christopher Layton, member of the Mormon Battalion and an early bishop, who brought the first alfalfa seed into the community. Previously called Little Fort, Kaysville Second Ward, and Laytona.

North Salt Lake   City
ZIP: 84054   **Lat:** 40-50-39 N   **Long:** 111-55-22 W
Pop: 6,474 (1990); 5,548 (1980)   **Pop Density:** 886.8
Land: 7.3 sq. mi.; **Water:** 0.0 sq. mi.   **Elev:** 4305 ft.
Incorporated Oct 1946.

South Weber   City
Lat: 41-08-02 N   **Long:** 111-56-05 W
Pop: 2,863 (1990); 1,575 (1980)   **Pop Density:** 622.4
Land: 4.6 sq. mi.; **Water:** 0.0 sq. mi.   **Elev:** 4510 ft.
Incorporated Aug 1936.

Sunset — City
ZIP: 84015 **Lat:** 41-08-19 N **Long:** 112-01-37 W
Pop: 5,128 (1990); 5,733 (1980) **Pop Density:** 3418.7
Land: 1.5 sq. mi.; **Water:** 0.0 sq. mi. **Elev:** 4567 ft.
Incorporated Sep 3, 1935.

Syracuse — City
ZIP: 84075 **Lat:** 41-05-46 N **Long:** 112-03-26 W
Pop: 4,658 (1990); 3,702 (1980) **Pop Density:** 763.6
Land: 6.1 sq. mi.; **Water:** 0.0 sq. mi. **Elev:** 4280 ft.
Incorporated Oct 14, 1935.

Val Verda — CDP
Lat: 40-51-13 N **Long:** 111-53-19 W
Pop: 3,712 (1990); 6,422 (1980) **Pop Density:** 4640.0
Land: 0.8 sq. mi.; **Water:** 0.0 sq. mi.

West Bountiful — City
ZIP: 84087 **Lat:** 40-54-00 N **Long:** 111-54-07 W
Pop: 4,477 (1990); 3,556 (1980) **Pop Density:** 2035.0
Land: 2.2 sq. mi.; **Water:** 0.0 sq. mi. **Elev:** 4260 ft.
Incorporated 1948.

West Point — City
ZIP: 84015 **Lat:** 41-07-17 N **Long:** 112-05-49 W
Pop: 4,258 (1990); 2,170 (1980) **Pop Density:** 591.4
Land: 7.2 sq. mi.; **Water:** 0.0 sq. mi. **Elev:** 4315 ft.
Incorporated Sep 3, 1935.

Woods Cross — City
ZIP: 84087 **Lat:** 40-52-24 N **Long:** 111-54-42 W
Pop: 5,384 (1990); 4,263 (1980) **Pop Density:** 1583.5
Land: 3.4 sq. mi.; **Water:** 0.0 sq. mi. **Elev:** 4292 ft.
Incorporated Oct 23, 1961.

Duchesne County
County Seat: Duchesne (ZIP: 84021)

Pop: 12,645 (1990); 12,565 (1980) **Pop Density:** 3.9
Land: 3238.4 sq. mi.; **Water:** 17.9 sq. mi. **Area Code:** 801
In north-central UT, east of Provo; organized Aug 13, 1914 from Wasatch County.
Name origin: For the Duchesne River, which flows through the county. Origin of name unknown. Possibly for Rose Du Chesne (1769–1852), founder of the Society of the Sacred Heart in America; for a fur trapper of that name; or for Fort Duquesne, PA.

Altamont — Town
ZIP: 84001 **Lat:** 40-21-30 N **Long:** 110-17-10 W
Pop: 167 (1990); 247 (1980) **Pop Density:** 835.0
Land: 0.2 sq. mi.; **Water:** 0.0 sq. mi. **Elev:** 6375 ft.
Incorporated 1954.

Duchesne — City
ZIP: 84021 **Lat:** 40-10-31 N **Long:** 110-23-32 W
Pop: 1,308 (1990); 1,677 (1980) **Pop Density:** 568.7
Land: 2.3 sq. mi.; **Water:** 0.0 sq. mi. **Elev:** 5517 ft.
Incorporated May 16, 1917.

Myton — City
ZIP: 84052 **Lat:** 40-11-36 N **Long:** 110-03-42 W
Pop: 468 (1990); 500 (1980) **Pop Density:** 468.0
Land: 1.0 sq. mi.; **Water:** 0.0 sq. mi. **Elev:** 5084 ft.
Incorporated 1905.

Neola — CDP
ZIP: 84053 **Lat:** 40-26-24 N **Long:** 110-02-12 W
Pop: 511 (1990) **Pop Density:** 72.0
Land: 7.1 sq. mi.; **Water:** 0.0 sq. mi.

Roosevelt — City
ZIP: 84066 **Lat:** 40-17-43 N **Long:** 110-00-00 W
Pop: 3,915 (1990); 3,842 (1980) **Pop Density:** 752.9
Land: 5.2 sq. mi.; **Water:** 0.0 sq. mi. **Elev:** 5100 ft.

Tabiona — Town
ZIP: 84072 **Lat:** 40-21-14 N **Long:** 110-42-30 W
Pop: 120 (1990); 152 (1980) **Pop Density:** 1200.0
Land: 0.1 sq. mi.; **Water:** 0.0 sq. mi. **Elev:** 6517 ft.
Incorporated 1938.

> ## Emery County
> **County Seat: Castle Dale (ZIP: 84513)**
>
> **Pop:** 10,332 (1990); 11,451 (1980) **Pop Density:** 2.3
> **Land:** 4452.1 sq. mi.; **Water:** 9.7 sq. mi. **Area Code:** 801
> In east-central UT; organized Feb 12, 1880 (prior to statehood) from Sanpete and Sevier counties.
> **Name origin:** For George W. Emery, a territorial governor (1875–80).

Castle Dale   City
ZIP: 84513   **Lat:** 39-13-16 N **Long:** 111-01-11 W
Pop: 1,704 (1990); 1,910 (1980)   **Pop Density:** 896.8
Land: 1.9 sq. mi.; **Water:** 0.0 sq. mi.   **Elev:** 5771 ft.
Incorporated Jul 1920.

Clawson   Town
ZIP: 84516   **Lat:** 39-07-58 N **Long:** 111-05-49 W
Pop: 151 (1990)   **Pop Density:** 302.0
Land: 0.5 sq. mi.; **Water:** 0.0 sq. mi.   **Elev:** 5944 ft.
Incorporated Jan 1, 1982.

Cleveland   Town
ZIP: 84518   **Lat:** 39-20-56 N **Long:** 110-51-23 W
Pop: 498 (1990); 522 (1980)   **Pop Density:** 553.3
Land: 0.9 sq. mi.; **Water:** 0.0 sq. mi.   **Elev:** 5735 ft.
Incorporated 1916.

Elmo   Town
ZIP: 84521   **Lat:** 39-23-19 N **Long:** 110-48-55 W
Pop: 267 (1990); 300 (1980)   **Pop Density:** 534.0
Land: 0.5 sq. mi.; **Water:** 0.0 sq. mi.   **Elev:** 5694 ft.
Incorporated 1935.

Emery   Town
ZIP: 84522   **Lat:** 38-55-30 N **Long:** 111-15-02 W
Pop: 300 (1990); 372 (1980)   **Pop Density:** 250.0
Land: 1.2 sq. mi.; **Water:** 0.0 sq. mi.   **Elev:** 6262 ft.
Incorporated 1901.

Ferron   City
ZIP: 84523   **Lat:** 39-05-26 N **Long:** 111-07-56 W
Pop: 1,606 (1990); 1,718 (1980)   **Pop Density:** 803.0
Land: 2.0 sq. mi.; **Water:** 0.0 sq. mi.   **Elev:** 5949 ft.
Incorporated Mar 7, 1900.

Green River   City
ZIP: 84525   **Lat:** 38-59-41 N **Long:** 110-09-50 W
Pop: 744 (1990); 956 (1980)   **Pop Density:** 310.0
Land: 2.4 sq. mi.; **Water:** 0.0 sq. mi.   **Elev:** 4079 ft.
Incorporated May 1, 1911. Part of the town is also in Grand County.

Hiawatha   Town
ZIP: 84527   **Lat:** 39-29-14 N **Long:** 111-04-30 W
Pop: 0 (1990)
Land: 0.1 sq. mi.; **Water:** 0.0 sq. mi.   **Elev:** 7050 ft.
Incorporated Sep 26, 1911. Part of the town is also in Carbon County.

Huntington   City
ZIP: 84528   **Lat:** 39-19-51 N **Long:** 110-57-46 W
Pop: 1,875 (1990); 2,316 (1980)   **Pop Density:** 937.5
Land: 2.0 sq. mi.; **Water:** 0.0 sq. mi.   **Elev:** 5791 ft.
Incorporated Jan 3, 1920.

Orangeville   City
ZIP: 84537   **Lat:** 39-13-52 N **Long:** 111-03-32 W
Pop: 1,459 (1990); 1,309 (1980)   **Pop Density:** 1122.3
Land: 1.3 sq. mi.; **Water:** 0.0 sq. mi.   **Elev:** 5772 ft.
Incorporated 1921.

> ## Garfield County
> **County Seat: Panguitch (ZIP: 84759)**
>
> **Pop:** 3,980 (1990); 3,673 (1980) **Pop Density:** 0.8
> **Land:** 5174.5 sq. mi.; **Water:** 34.0 sq. mi. **Area Code:** 801
> In south-central UT; organized Mar 9, 1882 (prior to statehood) from Iron County.
> **Name origin:** For James Abram Garfield (1831–81), twentieth U.S. president.

Antimony   Town
ZIP: 84712   **Lat:** 38-06-03 N **Long:** 111-59-00 W
Pop: 83 (1990); 94 (1980)   **Pop Density:** 8.2
Land: 10.1 sq. mi.; **Water:** 0.0 sq. mi.   **Elev:** 6500 ft.
Incorporated 1934.

Boulder   Town
ZIP: 84716   **Lat:** 37-55-44 N **Long:** 111-25-39 W
Pop: 126 (1990); 113 (1980)   **Pop Density:** 6.0
Land: 20.9 sq. mi.; **Water:** 0.0 sq. mi.
Incorporated Dec 3, 1956.

Cannonville   Town
ZIP: 84718   **Lat:** 37-33-57 N **Long:** 112-03-14 W
Pop: 131 (1990); 134 (1980)   **Pop Density:** 1310.0
Land: 0.1 sq. mi.; **Water:** 0.0 sq. mi.   **Elev:** 6000 ft.
Incorporated 1935.

Escalante   Town
Lat: 37-45-53 N **Long:** 111-36-02 W
Pop: 818 (1990); 652 (1980)   **Pop Density:** 282.1
Land: 2.9 sq. mi.; **Water:** 0.0 sq. mi.   **Elev:** 5812 ft.

Hatch
Town
ZIP: 84735 **Lat:** 37-39-08 N **Long:** 112-25-57 W
Pop: 103 (1990); 121 (1980) **Pop Density:** 343.3
Land: 0.3 sq. mi.; **Water:** 0.0 sq. mi. **Elev:** 6917 ft.
Incorporated Jan 3, 1934.

Henrieville
Town
ZIP: 84736 **Lat:** 37-33-52 N **Long:** 111-59-40 W
Pop: 163 (1990); 167 (1980) **Pop Density:** 815.0
Land: 0.2 sq. mi.; **Water:** 0.0 sq. mi. **Elev:** 6000 ft.
Incorporated Jan 3, 1934.

Panguitch
City
ZIP: 84759 **Lat:** 37-49-25 N **Long:** 112-26-15 W
Pop: 1,444 (1990); 1,343 (1980) **Pop Density:** 1031.4
Land: 1.4 sq. mi.; **Water:** 0.0 sq. mi. **Elev:** 6624 ft.
Incorporated Jun 2, 1899.

Tropic
Town
ZIP: 84776 **Lat:** 37-37-28 N **Long:** 112-05-15 W
Pop: 374 (1990); 338 (1980) **Pop Density:** 748.0
Land: 0.5 sq. mi.; **Water:** 0.0 sq. mi. **Elev:** 6295 ft.
Incorporated Nov 3, 1905.

Grand County
County Seat: Moab (ZIP: 84532)

Pop: 6,620 (1990); 8,241 (1980) **Pop Density:** 1.8
Land: 3681.8 sq. mi.; **Water:** 12.5 sq. mi. **Area Code:** 801
On the central eastern border of UT; organized Mar 13, 1890 (prior to statehood).
Name origin: For the Grand River, which flows through the county; the river was renamed the Colorado in 1921.

Castle Valley
Town
Lat: 38-37-57 N **Long:** 109-23-57 W
Pop: 211 (1990) **Pop Density:** 26.4
Land: 8.0 sq. mi.; **Water:** 0.0 sq. mi. **Elev:** 4800 ft.
Incorporated Nov 27, 1985.

Green River
City
ZIP: 84525 **Lat:** 38-57-55 N **Long:** 110-03-40 W
Pop: 122 (1990); 92 (1980) **Pop Density:** 12.0
Land: 10.2 sq. mi.; **Water:** 0.1 sq. mi. **Elev:** 4079 ft.
Incorporated May 1, 1911. Part of the town is also in Emery County.

Moab
City
ZIP: 84532 **Lat:** 38-34-21 N **Long:** 109-32-49 W
Pop: 3,971 (1990); 5,333 (1980) **Pop Density:** 1323.7
Land: 3.0 sq. mi.; **Water:** 0.0 sq. mi. **Elev:** 4025 ft.
Incorporated Dec 30, 1902.

Iron County
County Seat: Parowan (ZIP: 84761)

Pop: 20,789 (1990); 17,349 (1980) **Pop Density:** 6.3
Land: 3298.5 sq. mi.; **Water:** 3.6 sq. mi. **Area Code:** 801
On the southwestern border of UT; organized as Little Salt Lake County in 1850 (prior to statehood) from unorganized territory; name changed later that year.
Name origin: For the county's iron ore deposits and mines.

Brian Head
Town
ZIP: 84719 **Lat:** 37-41-54 N **Long:** 112-50-30 W
Pop: 109 (1990); 77 (1980) **Pop Density:** 35.2
Land: 3.1 sq. mi.; **Water:** 0.0 sq. mi. **Elev:** 9800 ft.
Incorporated Mar 1975.

Cedar City
City
ZIP: 84720 **Lat:** 37-41-23 N **Long:** 113-04-24 W
Pop: 13,443 (1990); 10,972 (1980) **Pop Density:** 1200.3
Land: 11.2 sq. mi.; **Water:** 0.0 sq. mi. **Elev:** 5834 ft.
In southwestern UT. Founded 1851; incorporated Feb 18, 1868.
Name origin: For the abundant scrub cedar trees in the area.

Enoch
City
ZIP: 84720 **Lat:** 37-45-43 N **Long:** 113-02-31 W
Pop: 1,947 (1990); 678 (1980) **Pop Density:** 608.4
Land: 3.2 sq. mi.; **Water:** 0.0 sq. mi. **Elev:** 5500 ft.
Incorporated c. 1965.

Kanarraville
Town
ZIP: 84742 **Lat:** 37-32-14 N **Long:** 113-10-46 W
Pop: 228 (1990); 255 (1980) **Pop Density:** 570.0
Land: 0.4 sq. mi.; **Water:** 0.0 sq. mi. **Elev:** 5541 ft.

Paragonah
Town
ZIP: 84760 **Lat:** 37-53-12 N **Long:** 112-46-17 W
Pop: 307 (1990); 310 (1980) **Pop Density:** 614.0
Land: 0.5 sq. mi.; **Water:** 0.0 sq. mi. **Elev:** 5897 ft.
Incorporated Apr 3, 1916.

Parowan City
ZIP: 84761 **Lat:** 37-49-56 N **Long:** 112-49-12 W
Pop: 1,873 (1990); 1,836 (1980) **Pop Density:** 346.9
Land: 5.4 sq. mi.; **Water:** 0.0 sq. mi. **Elev:** 5990 ft.
Incorporated Sep 25, 1874.

Juab County
County Seat: Nephi (ZIP: 84648)

Pop: 5,817 (1990); 5,530 (1980) **Pop Density:** 1.7
Land: 3391.9 sq. mi.; **Water:** 14.6 sq. mi. **Area Code:** 801
On the central western border of UT, southwest of Provo; original county; organized Mar 3, 1852 (prior to statehood).
Name origin: From the Juab Valley, named by the local Indians, the Uabs, Yuabs, or Yoabs of the Piute tribe. Meaning is either 'flat, level plain,' or possibly 'thirsty plain.'

Eureka City
 Lat: 39-57-18 N **Long:** 112-06-56 W
Pop: 562 (1990); 670 (1980) **Pop Density:** 624.4
Land: 0.9 sq. mi.; **Water:** 0.0 sq. mi. **Elev:** 6442 ft.
Incorporated Dec 1, 1892.

Mona Town
ZIP: 84645 **Lat:** 39-48-55 N **Long:** 111-51-27 W
Pop: 584 (1990); 536 (1980) **Pop Density:** 449.2
Land: 1.3 sq. mi.; **Water:** 0.0 sq. mi. **Elev:** 4916 ft.
Incorporated 1924.

Levan Town
ZIP: 84639 **Lat:** 39-33-24 N **Long:** 111-51-36 W
Pop: 416 (1990); 453 (1980) **Pop Density:** 594.3
Land: 0.7 sq. mi.; **Water:** 0.0 sq. mi. **Elev:** 5314 ft.
Incorporated Oct 8, 1906.

Nephi City
ZIP: 84648 **Lat:** 39-42-38 N **Long:** 111-49-43 W
Pop: 3,515 (1990); 3,285 (1980) **Pop Density:** 925.0
Land: 3.8 sq. mi.; **Water:** 0.0 sq. mi. **Elev:** 5133 ft.
Incorporated 1889.

Kane County
County Seat: Kanab (ZIP: 84741)

Pop: 5,169 (1990); 4,024 (1980) **Pop Density:** 1.3
Land: 3992.2 sq. mi.; **Water:** 116.4 sq. mi. **Area Code:** 801
On the central southern border of UT; organized Jan 16, 1864 (prior to statehood) from Washington County.
Name origin: For Gen. Thomas Leiper Kane (1822–83), Union army officer and friend to the Mormons who acted as an intermediary in the so-called Mormon War of 1858.

Alton Town
ZIP: 84710 **Lat:** 37-26-19 N **Long:** 112-28-59 W
Pop: 93 (1990); 75 (1980) **Pop Density:** 232.5
Land: 0.4 sq. mi.; **Water:** 0.0 sq. mi. **Elev:** 6875 ft.
Incorporated 1936.

Kanab City
ZIP: 84741 **Lat:** 37-01-12 N **Long:** 112-31-01 W
Pop: 3,289 (1990); 2,148 (1980) **Pop Density:** 238.3
Land: 13.8 sq. mi.; **Water:** 0.0 sq. mi. **Elev:** 4909 ft.
Incorporated Sep 7, 1885.

Big Water Town
ZIP: 84741 **Lat:** 37-04-06 N **Long:** 111-39-41 W
Pop: 326 (1990) **Pop Density:** 53.4
Land: 6.1 sq. mi.; **Water:** 0.0 sq. mi.
Incorporated Dec 29, 1983.

Orderville Town
 Lat: 37-16-34 N **Long:** 112-37-57 W
Pop: 422 (1990); 423 (1980) **Pop Density:** 263.8
Land: 1.6 sq. mi.; **Water:** 0.0 sq. mi. **Elev:** 5250 ft.
Incorporated 1936.

Glendale Town
ZIP: 84729 **Lat:** 37-19-55 N **Long:** 112-36-02 W
Pop: 282 (1990); 237 (1980) **Pop Density:** 36.2
Land: 7.8 sq. mi.; **Water:** 0.0 sq. mi. **Elev:** 5824 ft.
Incorporated 1935.

Millard County
County Seat: Fillmore (ZIP: 84631)

Pop: 11,333 (1990); 8,970 (1980)   **Pop Density:** 1.7
Land: 6589.6 sq. mi.; **Water:** 238.9 sq. mi.   **Area Code:** 801
On the central western border of UT, southwest of Provo; organized Oct 4, 1851 (prior to statehood) from Juab County.
Name origin: For Millard Fillmore (1800-74), 13th U.S. president, who signed the act creating the Territory of Utah and appointed Brigham Young (1801–77) the first governor.

Delta — City
Lat: 39-21-11 N **Long:** 112-33-56 W
Pop: 2,998 (1990); 1,930 (1980)   **Pop Density:** 1033.8
Land: 2.9 sq. mi.; **Water:** 0.0 sq. mi.   **Elev:** 4649 ft.
Incorporated Jan 19, 1955.

Fillmore — City
ZIP: 84631   **Lat:** 38-58-03 N **Long:** 112-20-12 W
Pop: 1,956 (1990); 2,083 (1980)   **Pop Density:** 416.2
Land: 4.7 sq. mi.; **Water:** 0.0 sq. mi.   **Elev:** 5135 ft.
Incorporated Jan 12, 1867.

Hinckley — Town
ZIP: 84635   **Lat:** 39-19-56 N **Long:** 112-40-21 W
Pop: 658 (1990); 464 (1980)   **Pop Density:** 131.6
Land: 5.0 sq. mi.; **Water:** 0.0 sq. mi.   **Elev:** 4600 ft.

Holden — Town
ZIP: 84636   **Lat:** 39-05-59 N **Long:** 112-16-08 W
Pop: 402 (1990); 364 (1980)   **Pop Density:** 804.0
Land: 0.5 sq. mi.; **Water:** 0.0 sq. mi.   **Elev:** 5115 ft.
Incorporated 1922.

Kanosh — Town
ZIP: 84637   **Lat:** 38-48-16 N **Long:** 112-26-17 W
Pop: 386 (1990); 435 (1980)   **Pop Density:** 386.0
Land: 1.0 sq. mi.; **Water:** 0.0 sq. mi.   **Elev:** 5015 ft.
Incorporated Mar 13, 1903.

Leamington — Town
ZIP: 84638   **Lat:** 39-31-51 N **Long:** 112-17-21 W
Pop: 253 (1990); 113 (1980)   **Pop Density:** 158.1
Land: 1.6 sq. mi.; **Water:** 0.0 sq. mi.   **Elev:** 4738 ft.
Incorporated Feb 20, 1936.

Lynndyl — Town
ZIP: 84640   **Lat:** 39-30-29 N **Long:** 112-23-20 W
Pop: 120 (1990); 90 (1980)   **Pop Density:** 34.3
Land: 3.5 sq. mi.; **Water:** 0.0 sq. mi.   **Elev:** 4784 ft.
Incorporated 1945.

Meadow — Town
ZIP: 84644   **Lat:** 38-53-12 N **Long:** 112-24-21 W
Pop: 250 (1990); 265 (1980)   **Pop Density:** 416.7
Land: 0.6 sq. mi.; **Water:** 0.0 sq. mi.   **Elev:** 5000 ft.
Incorporated 1926.

Oak City — Town
ZIP: 84649   **Lat:** 39-22-33 N **Long:** 112-20-09 W
Pop: 587 (1990); 389 (1980)   **Pop Density:** 978.3
Land: 0.6 sq. mi.; **Water:** 0.0 sq. mi.   **Elev:** 5105 ft.
Incorporated 1921.

Scipio — Town
Lat: 39-14-51 N **Long:** 112-06-07 W
Pop: 291 (1990); 257 (1980)   **Pop Density:** 323.3
Land: 0.9 sq. mi.; **Water:** 0.0 sq. mi.   **Elev:** 5305 ft.
Incorporated Jan 1900.

Morgan County
County Seat: Morgan (ZIP: 84050)

Pop: 5,528 (1990); 4,917 (1980)   **Pop Density:** 9.1
Land: 609.1 sq. mi.; **Water:** 1.7 sq. mi.   **Area Code:** 801
In north-central UT, east of Bountiful; organized Jan 17, 1862 (prior to statehood) from Davis and Summit counties.
Name origin: For Jedediah Morgan Grant (1816–56), prominent Mormon churchman.

Morgan — City
ZIP: 84050   **Lat:** 41-02-33 N **Long:** 111-40-57 W
Pop: 2,023 (1990); 1,896 (1980)   **Pop Density:** 697.6
Land: 2.9 sq. mi.; **Water:** 0.0 sq. mi.

Piute County
County Seat: Junction (ZIP: 84740)

Pop: 1,277 (1990); 1,329 (1980)
Land: 757.9 sq. mi.; **Water:** 8.0 sq. mi.
Pop Density: 1.7
Area Code: 801
In south-central UT; organized Jan 16, 1865 (prior to statehood) from Beaver County.
Name origin: For the sub-tribe of the Ute Indians. The name means 'water Ute.'

Circleville — Town
ZIP: 84723 **Lat:** 38-09-48 N **Long:** 112-15-42 W
Pop: 417 (1990); 445 (1980) **Pop Density:** 45.8
Land: 9.1 sq. mi.; **Water:** 0.0 sq. mi. **Elev:** 6063 ft.
Incorporated Aug 24, 1921.

Junction — Town
ZIP: 84740 **Lat:** 38-14-18 N **Long:** 112-13-26 W
Pop: 132 (1990); 151 (1980) **Pop Density:** 9.2
Land: 14.4 sq. mi.; **Water:** 0.6 sq. mi. **Elev:** 6002 ft.
Incorporated Apr 7, 1913.

Kingston — Town
ZIP: 84743 **Lat:** 38-12-17 N **Long:** 112-10-45 W
Pop: 134 (1990); 146 (1980) **Pop Density:** 25.3
Land: 5.3 sq. mi.; **Water:** 0.0 sq. mi. **Elev:** 6000 ft.

Marysvale — Town
Lat: 38-26-15 N **Long:** 112-15-29 W
Pop: 364 (1990); 359 (1980) **Pop Density:** 24.1
Land: 15.1 sq. mi.; **Water:** 0.0 sq. mi. **Elev:** 5866 ft.

Rich County
County Seat: Randolph (ZIP: 84064)

Pop: 1,725 (1990); 2,100 (1980)
Land: 1028.6 sq. mi.; **Water:** 57.8 sq. mi.
Pop Density: 1.7
Area Code: 801
On the northern border of UT, northeast of Ogden; original county. Created as Richland in 1863; organized and name changed Jan 16, 1864 (prior to statehood).
Name origin: For Charles Coulson Rich, a Mormon apostle.

Garden City — Town
ZIP: 84028 **Lat:** 41-56-02 N **Long:** 111-24-34 W
Pop: 193 (1990); 259 (1980) **Pop Density:** 46.0
Land: 4.2 sq. mi.; **Water:** 0.0 sq. mi. **Elev:** 5950 ft.
Incorporated 1934.

Laketown — Town
ZIP: 84038 **Lat:** 41-49-20 N **Long:** 111-19-03 W
Pop: 261 (1990); 271 (1980) **Pop Density:** 435.0
Land: 0.6 sq. mi.; **Water:** 0.0 sq. mi. **Elev:** 5988 ft.

Randolph — City
ZIP: 84064 **Lat:** 41-39-52 N **Long:** 111-10-57 W
Pop: 488 (1990); 659 (1980) **Pop Density:** 542.2
Land: 0.9 sq. mi.; **Water:** 0.0 sq. mi. **Elev:** 6289 ft.

Woodruff — Town
ZIP: 84086 **Lat:** 41-31-22 N **Long:** 111-09-48 W
Pop: 135 (1990); 222 (1980) **Pop Density:** 270.0
Land: 0.5 sq. mi.; **Water:** 0.0 sq. mi. **Elev:** 6340 ft.
Incorporated Dec 4, 1933.

Salt Lake County
County Seat: Salt Lake City (ZIP: 84111)

Pop: 725,956 (1990); 619,066 (1980)
Land: 737.4 sq. mi.; **Water:** 70.4 sq. mi.
Pop Density: 984.5
Area Code: 801
In north-central UT, on the eastern shore of Great Salt Lake; original county. Organized as Great Salt Lake County in 1849 (prior to statehood); name changed Jan 29, 1868.
Name origin: For the Great Salt Lake.

Alta — Town
Lat: 40-34-44 N **Long:** 111-37-08 W
Pop: 397 (1990); 381 (1980) **Pop Density:** 96.8
Land: 4.1 sq. mi.; **Water:** 0.0 sq. mi. **Elev:** 8583 ft.
Incorporated Aug 4, 1970.

Bluffdale — City
ZIP: 84065 **Lat:** 40-28-33 N **Long:** 111-57-19 W
Pop: 2,152 (1990); 1,300 (1980) **Pop Density:** 131.2
Land: 16.4 sq. mi.; **Water:** 0.0 sq. mi. **Elev:** 4435 ft.

UTAH, Salt Lake County

Canyon Rim
CDP
Lat: 40-42-23 N **Long:** 111-49-16 W
Pop: 10,527 (1990) **Pop Density:** 5012.9
Land: 2.1 sq. mi.; **Water:** 0.0 sq. mi.

Cottonwood Heights
CDP
ZIP: 84121 **Lat:** 40-36-36 N **Long:** 111-48-34 W
Pop: 28,766 (1990); 22,665 (1980) **Pop Density:** 4230.3
Land: 6.8 sq. mi.; **Water:** 0.0 sq. mi.

Cottonwood West
CDP
Lat: 40-38-47 N **Long:** 111-51-01 W
Pop: 17,476 (1990) **Pop Density:** 4598.9
Land: 3.8 sq. mi.; **Water:** 0.0 sq. mi.

Draper
City
ZIP: 84020 **Lat:** 40-30-18 N **Long:** 111-52-11 W
Pop: 7,257 (1990); 5,521 (1980) **Pop Density:** 322.5
Land: 22.5 sq. mi.; **Water:** 0.0 sq. mi. **Elev:** 4525 ft.
Incorporated Feb 22, 1978. Part of the town is also in Utah County.

East Millcreek
CDP
Lat: 40-41-19 N **Long:** 111-49-13 W
Pop: 21,184 (1990); 24,150 (1980) **Pop Density:** 4707.6
Land: 4.5 sq. mi.; **Water:** 0.0 sq. mi.

Granite
CDP
Lat: 40-34-02 N **Long:** 111-48-20 W
Pop: 3,300 (1990) **Pop Density:** 846.2
Land: 3.9 sq. mi.; **Water:** 0.0 sq. mi.

Holladay-Cottonwood
CDP
Lat: 40-38-54 N **Long:** 111-48-33 W
Pop: 14,095 (1990); 22,189 (1980) **Pop Density:** 2013.6
Land: 7.0 sq. mi.; **Water:** 0.0 sq. mi.

Kearns
CDP
ZIP: 84118 **Lat:** 40-39-08 N **Long:** 112-00-29 W
Pop: 28,374 (1990); 21,353 (1980) **Pop Density:** 5790.6
Land: 4.9 sq. mi.; **Water:** 0.0 sq. mi.

Little Cottonwood Creek Valley
CDP
Lat: 40-36-15 N **Long:** 111-49-43 W
Pop: 5,042 (1990) **Pop Density:** 2521.0
Land: 2.0 sq. mi.; **Water:** 0.0 sq. mi.

Magna
CDP
ZIP: 84044 **Lat:** 40-42-14 N **Long:** 112-05-10 W
Pop: 17,829 (1990); 13,138 (1980) **Pop Density:** 2377.2
Land: 7.5 sq. mi.; **Water:** 0.0 sq. mi.

Midvale
City
ZIP: 84047 **Lat:** 40-36-42 N **Long:** 111-54-08 W
Pop: 11,886 (1990); 10,146 (1980) **Pop Density:** 3495.9
Land: 3.4 sq. mi.; **Water:** 0.0 sq. mi. **Elev:** 4354 ft.
In northern UT, 11 mi. south of Salt Lake City. Incorporated Jul 1, 1909.
Name origin: For its location in the surrounding valley.

Millcreek
CDP
ZIP: 84109 **Lat:** 40-41-12 N **Long:** 111-52-28 W
Pop: 32,230 (1990) **Pop Density:** 4415.1
Land: 7.3 sq. mi.; **Water:** 0.0 sq. mi.

Mount Olympus
CDP
ZIP: 84117 **Lat:** 40-41-07 N **Long:** 111-47-16 W
Pop: 7,413 (1990); 6,068 (1980) **Pop Density:** 2180.3
Land: 3.4 sq. mi.; **Water:** 0.0 sq. mi.

Murray
City
ZIP: 84107 **Lat:** 40-39-08 N **Long:** 111-53-32 W
Pop: 31,282 (1990); 25,750 (1980) **Pop Density:** 3292.8
Land: 9.5 sq. mi.; **Water:** 0.0 sq. mi. **Elev:** 4350 ft.
In northern UT on the Jordan River, 8 mi. south of Salt Lake City. Incorporated 1902.
Name origin: For UT Territorial Gov. Eli Murray.

Oquirrh
CDP
Lat: 40-37-50 N **Long:** 112-01-59 W
Pop: 7,593 (1990) **Pop Density:** 2920.4
Land: 2.6 sq. mi.; **Water:** 0.0 sq. mi.

Riverton
City
ZIP: 84065 **Lat:** 40-31-11 N **Long:** 111-56-42 W
Pop: 11,261 (1990); 7,032 (1980) **Pop Density:** 1390.2
Land: 8.1 sq. mi.; **Water:** 0.0 sq. mi. **Elev:** 4435 ft.
In north-central UT, 15 mi. south of Salt Lake City. Incorporated 1948.
Name origin: For its location near the Jordan River.

Salt Lake City
City
ZIP: 84101 **Lat:** 40-46-38 N **Long:** 111-55-47 W
Pop: 159,936 (1990); 163,034 (1980) **Pop Density:** 1467.3
Land: 109.0 sq. mi.; **Water:** 1.3 sq. mi. **Elev:** 4266 ft.
In north-central UT on the Jordan River, 13 mi. east of Great Salt Lake. State capital and largest city. Founded by Mormons under Brigham Young on Jul 24, 1847; incorporated Jan 6, 1851. World headquarters of the Church of Latter Day Saints (Mormons). Tourism, diverse manufacturing (chemicals, electronics, food products, petroleum, steel), and banking center. Site of University of Utah.

Sandy
City
ZIP: 84070 **Lat:** 40-34-10 N **Long:** 111-51-15 W
Pop: 75,058 (1990); 52,210 (1980) **Pop Density:** 3752.9
Land: 20.0 sq. mi.; **Water:** 0.0 sq. mi.

South Jordan
City
ZIP: 84065 **Lat:** 40-33-31 N **Long:** 111-58-23 W
Pop: 12,220 (1990); 7,492 (1980) **Pop Density:** 608.0
Land: 20.1 sq. mi.; **Water:** 0.2 sq. mi. **Elev:** 4300 ft.
In northern UT, 14 mi. south of Salt Lake City. Incorporated Nov 1935.

South Salt Lake
City
ZIP: 84115 **Lat:** 40-42-36 N **Long:** 111-53-48 W
Pop: 10,129 (1990); 10,413 (1980) **Pop Density:** 2250.9
Land: 4.5 sq. mi.; **Water:** 0.0 sq. mi. **Elev:** 4263 ft.
Incorporated Aug 1, 1950.

Taylorsville-Bennion
CDP
Lat: 40-39-20 N **Long:** 111-56-41 W
Pop: 52,351 (1990); 17,448 (1980) **Pop Density:** 4716.3
Land: 11.1 sq. mi.; **Water:** 0.0 sq. mi.

Union
CDP
ZIP: 84047 **Lat:** 40-37-08 N **Long:** 111-52-21 W
Pop: 13,684 (1990); 9,665 (1980) **Pop Density:** 4887.1
Land: 2.8 sq. mi.; **Water:** 0.0 sq. mi.

West Jordan
City
ZIP: 84084 **Lat:** 40-35-59 N **Long:** 111-59-40 W
Pop: 42,892 (1990); 27,325 (1980) **Pop Density:** 1600.4
Land: 26.8 sq. mi.; **Water:** 0.0 sq. mi. **Elev:** 4370 ft.
Settled 1848; incorporated 1941.
Name origin: At the time of settlement it included the area west of the Jordan River and south to Herriman.

UTAH, Salt Lake County   *American Places Dictionary*

West Valley City   City
ZIP: 84120   Lat: 40-41-27 N   Long: 112-00-30 W
Pop: 86,976 (1990); 72,378 (1980)   Pop Density: 2558.1
Land: 34.0 sq. mi.; Water: 0.1 sq. mi.

White City   CDP
ZIP: 84070   Lat: 40-34-02 N   Long: 111-51-39 W
Pop: 6,506 (1990)   Pop Density: 6506.0
Land: 1.0 sq. mi.; Water: 0.0 sq. mi.

San Juan County
County Seat: Monticello (ZIP: 84535)

Pop: 12,621 (1990); 12,253 (1980)   Pop Density: 1.6
Land: 7820.7 sq. mi.; Water: 112.9 sq. mi.   Area Code: 801

On the southeastern border of UT; organized Feb 17, 1880 (prior to statehood) from Kane, Iron, Sevier, and Piute counties.

Name origin: For the San Juan River, which runs through the county; Spanish 'Saint John.' The origin of the river's name is in dispute.

Blanding   City
ZIP: 84511   Lat: 37-37-28 N   Long: 109-28-48 W
Pop: 3,162 (1990); 3,118 (1980)   Pop Density: 1664.2
Land: 1.9 sq. mi.; Water: 0.0 sq. mi.   Elev: 6105 ft.

Mexican Hat   CDP
Lat: 37-07-42 N   Long: 109-54-55 W
Pop: 259 (1990)   Pop Density: 17.5
Land: 14.8 sq. mi.; Water: 0.0 sq. mi.

Montezuma Creek   CDP
Lat: 37-15-36 N   Long: 109-18-47 W
Pop: 345 (1990)   Pop Density: 69.0
Land: 5.0 sq. mi.; Water: 0.2 sq. mi.

Monticello   City
ZIP: 84535   Lat: 37-52-17 N   Long: 109-20-07 W
Pop: 1,806 (1990); 1,929 (1980)   Pop Density: 668.9
Land: 2.7 sq. mi.; Water: 0.0 sq. mi.   Elev: 7066 ft.
Incorporated Oct 10, 1950.

Sanpete County
County Seat: Manti (ZIP: 84642)

Pop: 16,259 (1990); 14,620 (1980)   Pop Density: 10.2
Land: 1588.2 sq. mi.; Water: 14.6 sq. mi.   Area Code: 801

In central UT, south of Provo; original county; organized 1850 (prior to statehood).

Name origin: Corruption of *San Pitch*, name of the Ute Indian chieftain whose people lived in the region.

Centerfield   Town
ZIP: 84622   Lat: 39-07-39 N   Long: 111-49-01 W
Pop: 766 (1990); 653 (1980)   Pop Density: 425.6
Land: 1.8 sq. mi.; Water: 0.0 sq. mi.   Elev: 5125 ft.
Incorporated Jun 2, 1909.

Ephraim   City
ZIP: 84627   Lat: 39-21-34 N   Long: 111-35-03 W
Pop: 3,363 (1990); 2,810 (1980)   Pop Density: 1293.5
Land: 2.6 sq. mi.; Water: 0.0 sq. mi.   Elev: 5543 ft.
Incorporated Feb 14, 1868.

Fairview   City
ZIP: 84629   Lat: 39-37-49 N   Long: 111-26-07 W
Pop: 960 (1990); 916 (1980)   Pop Density: 600.0
Land: 1.6 sq. mi.; Water: 0.0 sq. mi.   Elev: 6033 ft.
Incorporated Feb 16, 1872.

Fayette   Town
ZIP: 84630   Lat: 39-13-33 N   Long: 111-51-10 W
Pop: 183 (1990); 165 (1980)   Pop Density: 366.0
Land: 0.5 sq. mi.; Water: 0.0 sq. mi.   Elev: 5050 ft.
Incorporated Mar 18, 1948.

Fountain Green   City
ZIP: 84632   Lat: 39-37-39 N   Long: 111-38-18 W
Pop: 578 (1990); 578 (1980)   Pop Density: 412.9
Land: 1.4 sq. mi.; Water: 0.0 sq. mi.   Elev: 6025 ft.
Incorporated Jan 3, 1910.

Gunnison   City
Lat: 39-09-29 N   Long: 111-48-45 W
Pop: 1,298 (1990); 1,255 (1980)   Pop Density: 249.6
Land: 5.2 sq. mi.; Water: 0.0 sq. mi.   Elev: 5125 ft.
Incorporated Sep 13, 1909.

Manti   City
ZIP: 84642   Lat: 39-16-00 N   Long: 111-38-10 W
Pop: 2,268 (1990); 2,080 (1980)   Pop Density: 1193.7
Land: 1.9 sq. mi.; Water: 0.0 sq. mi.   Elev: 5530 ft.
Incorporated 1851.

Mayfield   Town
ZIP: 84643   Lat: 39-06-58 N   Long: 111-42-26 W
Pop: 438 (1990); 397 (1980)   Pop Density: 625.7
Land: 0.7 sq. mi.; Water: 0.0 sq. mi.   Elev: 5500 ft.
Incorporated 1909.

Moroni　　　　　　　　　　　　　　　　City
ZIP: 84646　　　**Lat:** 39-31-41 N　**Long:** 111-34-56 W
Pop: 1,115 (1990); 1,086 (1980)　**Pop Density:** 1115.0
Land: 1.0 sq. mi.; **Water:** 0.0 sq. mi.　**Elev:** 5520 ft.
Incorporated 1857.

Mount Pleasant　　　　　　　　　　　City
ZIP: 84647　　　**Lat:** 39-32-30 N　**Long:** 111-27-20 W
Pop: 2,092 (1990); 2,049 (1980)　**Pop Density:** 774.8
Land: 2.7 sq. mi.; **Water:** 0.0 sq. mi.　**Elev:** 5924 ft.
Incorporated 1868.

Spring City　　　　　　　　　　　　　City
　　　　　　　　Lat: 39-28-48 N　**Long:** 111-29-25 W
Pop: 715 (1990); 671 (1980)　**Pop Density:** 550.0
Land: 1.3 sq. mi.; **Water:** 0.0 sq. mi.　**Elev:** 5826 ft.

Sterling　　　　　　　　　　　　　　Town
ZIP: 84665　　　**Lat:** 39-11-39 N　**Long:** 111-41-27 W
Pop: 191 (1990); 199 (1980)　**Pop Density:** 955.0
Land: 0.2 sq. mi.; **Water:** 0.0 sq. mi.　**Elev:** 5414 ft.
Incorporated 1934.

Wales　　　　　　　　　　　　　　　Town
ZIP: 84667　　　**Lat:** 39-29-10 N　**Long:** 111-38-07 W
Pop: 189 (1990); 153 (1980)　**Pop Density:** 630.0
Land: 0.3 sq. mi.; **Water:** 0.0 sq. mi.　**Elev:** 5500 ft.
Incorporated Oct 18, 1909.

Sevier County
County Seat: Richfield (ZIP: 84701)

Pop: 15,431 (1990); 14,727 (1980)　　**Pop Density:** 8.1
Land: 1910.4 sq. mi.; **Water:** 8.0 sq. mi.　　**Area Code:** 801
In south-central UT; organized Jan 16, 1865 (prior to statehood) from Sanpete County.
Name origin: For the Sevier River, which runs through the county. Anglicization of Spanish *Río Severo* 'violent river.'

Annabella　　　　　　　　　　　　　Town
　　　　　　　　Lat: 38-42-22 N　**Long:** 112-03-27 W
Pop: 487 (1990); 463 (1980)　**Pop Density:** 1217.5
Land: 0.4 sq. mi.; **Water:** 0.0 sq. mi.　**Elev:** 5301 ft.
Incorporated Feb 1, 1910.

Aurora　　　　　　　　　　　　　　City
ZIP: 84620　　　**Lat:** 38-55-13 N　**Long:** 111-55-56 W
Pop: 911 (1990); 874 (1980)　**Pop Density:** 911.0
Land: 1.0 sq. mi.; **Water:** 0.0 sq. mi.　**Elev:** 5187 ft.
Incorporated 1914.

Elsinore　　　　　　　　　　　　　　Town
ZIP: 84724　　　**Lat:** 38-41-01 N　**Long:** 112-08-55 W
Pop: 608 (1990); 612 (1980)　**Pop Density:** 467.7
Land: 1.3 sq. mi.; **Water:** 0.0 sq. mi.　**Elev:** 5335 ft.
Incorporated 1891.

Glenwood　　　　　　　　　　　　　Town
ZIP: 84730　　　**Lat:** 38-45-44 N　**Long:** 111-59-18 W
Pop: 437 (1990); 447 (1980)　**Pop Density:** 874.0
Land: 0.5 sq. mi.; **Water:** 0.0 sq. mi.　**Elev:** 5300 ft.
Incorporated Apr 15, 1897.

Joseph　　　　　　　　　　　　　　Town
ZIP: 84739　　　**Lat:** 38-37-30 N　**Long:** 112-13-07 W
Pop: 198 (1990); 217 (1980)　**Pop Density:** 220.0
Land: 0.9 sq. mi.; **Water:** 0.0 sq. mi.　**Elev:** 5435 ft.

Koosharem　　　　　　　　　　　　Town
ZIP: 84744　　　**Lat:** 38-30-41 N　**Long:** 111-52-49 W
Pop: 266 (1990); 183 (1980)　**Pop Density:** 532.0
Land: 0.5 sq. mi.; **Water:** 0.0 sq. mi.　**Elev:** 6914 ft.
Incorporated 1914.

Monroe　　　　　　　　　　　　　　City
ZIP: 84754　　　**Lat:** 38-37-27 N　**Long:** 112-07-10 W
Pop: 1,472 (1990); 1,476 (1980)　**Pop Density:** 420.6
Land: 3.5 sq. mi.; **Water:** 0.0 sq. mi.　**Elev:** 4375 ft.
Incorporated 1918.

Redmond　　　　　　　　　　　　　Town
ZIP: 84652　　　**Lat:** 39-00-19 N　**Long:** 111-51-52 W
Pop: 648 (1990); 619 (1980)　**Pop Density:** 810.0
Land: 0.8 sq. mi.; **Water:** 0.0 sq. mi.　**Elev:** 5135 ft.
Incorporated 1897.

Richfield　　　　　　　　　　　　　City
ZIP: 84701　　　**Lat:** 38-45-57 N　**Long:** 112-05-25 W
Pop: 5,593 (1990); 5,482 (1980)　**Pop Density:** 1598.0
Land: 3.5 sq. mi.; **Water:** 0.0 sq. mi.　**Elev:** 5308 ft.
Incorporated Feb 22, 1878.

Salina　　　　　　　　　　　　　　City
ZIP: 84654　　　**Lat:** 38-56-56 N　**Long:** 111-51-33 W
Pop: 1,943 (1990); 1,992 (1980)　**Pop Density:** 844.8
Land: 2.3 sq. mi.; **Water:** 0.0 sq. mi.　**Elev:** 5160 ft.
Incorporated Apr 14, 1913.

Sigurd　　　　　　　　　　　　　　Town
ZIP: 84657　　　**Lat:** 38-51-01 N　**Long:** 111-57-55 W
Pop: 385 (1990); 386 (1980)　**Pop Density:** 385.0
Land: 1.0 sq. mi.; **Water:** 0.0 sq. mi.　**Elev:** 5270 ft.
Incorporated Aug 24, 1935.

UTAH, Summit County   *American Places Dictionary*

> ## Summit County
> **County Seat: Coalville (ZIP: 84017)**
>
> **Pop:** 15,518 (1990); 10,198 (1980)   **Pop Density:** 8.3
> **Land:** 1871.1 sq. mi.; **Water:** 11.0 sq. mi.   **Area Code:** 801
>
> On the central northern border of UT, east of Salt Lake City; organized Jan 13, 1854 (prior to statehood) from Green River County.
>
> **Name origin:** For its location on the divide between the Colorado River Valley and the Salt Lake Valley.

Coalville   City
ZIP: 84017   **Lat:** 40-55-03 N   **Long:** 111-23-39 W
Pop: 1,065 (1990); 1,031 (1980)   **Pop Density:** 367.2
Land: 2.9 sq. mi.; **Water:** 0.4 sq. mi.   **Elev:** 5586 ft.
Incorporated Sep 1, 1899.

Francis   Town
ZIP: 84036   **Lat:** 40-36-43 N   **Long:** 111-16-31 W
Pop: 381 (1990); 371 (1980)   **Pop Density:** 272.1
Land: 1.4 sq. mi.; **Water:** 0.0 sq. mi.   **Elev:** 6560 ft.
Incorporated Dec 19, 1939.

Henefer   Town
ZIP: 84033   **Lat:** 41-01-08 N   **Long:** 111-29-33 W
Pop: 554 (1990); 547 (1980)   **Pop Density:** 615.6
Land: 0.9 sq. mi.; **Water:** 0.0 sq. mi.   **Elev:** 5337 ft.
Incorporated Feb 18, 1938.

Kamas   City
    Lat: 40-38-35 N   **Long:** 111-16-25 W
Pop: 1,061 (1990); 1,064 (1980)   **Pop Density:** 707.3
Land: 1.5 sq. mi.; **Water:** 0.0 sq. mi.   **Elev:** 6473 ft.
Incorporated Jul 5, 1911.

Oakley   Town
ZIP: 84055   **Lat:** 40-43-19 N   **Long:** 111-17-15 W
Pop: 522 (1990); 470 (1980)   **Pop Density:** 193.3
Land: 2.7 sq. mi.; **Water:** 0.0 sq. mi.   **Elev:** 6517 ft.
Incorporated Dec 20, 1933.

Park City   City
ZIP: 84060   **Lat:** 40-39-23 N   **Long:** 111-29-34 W
Pop: 4,468 (1990); 2,823 (1980)   **Pop Density:** 531.9
Land: 8.4 sq. mi.; **Water:** 0.0 sq. mi.   **Elev:** 6980 ft.
Incorporated Mar 15, 1884. Part of the town is also in Wasatch County.

> ## Tooele County
> **County Seat: Tooele (ZIP: 84074)**
>
> **Pop:** 26,601 (1990); 26,033 (1980)   **Pop Density:** 3.8
> **Land:** 6945.9 sq. mi.; **Water:** 341.8 sq. mi.   **Area Code:** 801
>
> On the northwestern border of UT, west of Salt Lake City; original county. Organized as Tuilla County Jan 31, 1850 (prior to statehood); includes Shambip County, which was abolished in 1862. Spelling was changed Mar 1852.
>
> **Name origin:** Possibly for Tuilla, a Goshute Indian chief, or for the bulrushes (tules) in the swamps, or for Mat Tooele, an Austrian village.

Dugway   Military Facility
ZIP: 84022   **Lat:** 40-13-52 N   **Long:** 112-45-01 W
Pop: 1,761 (1990); 1,646 (1980)   **Pop Density:** 338.7
Land: 5.2 sq. mi.; **Water:** 0.0 sq. mi.

Erda   CDP
ZIP: 84074   **Lat:** 40-35-26 N   **Long:** 112-19-18 W
Pop: 1,113 (1990)   **Pop Density:** 42.6
Land: 26.1 sq. mi.; **Water:** 0.0 sq. mi.

Grantsville   City
ZIP: 84029   **Lat:** 40-35-49 N   **Long:** 112-28-02 W
Pop: 4,500 (1990); 4,419 (1980)   **Pop Density:** 260.1
Land: 17.3 sq. mi.; **Water:** 0.0 sq. mi.   **Elev:** 4304 ft.
Incorporated Jan 12, 1867.

Ophir   Town
ZIP: 84071   **Lat:** 40-22-10 N   **Long:** 112-15-15 W
Pop: 25 (1990); 42 (1980)   **Pop Density:** 125.0
Land: 0.2 sq. mi.; **Water:** 0.0 sq. mi.   **Elev:** 6498 ft.

Rush Valley   Town
ZIP: 84069   **Lat:** 40-21-46 N   **Long:** 112-26-58 W
Pop: 339 (1990); 356 (1980)   **Pop Density:** 18.5
Land: 18.3 sq. mi.; **Water:** 0.0 sq. mi.
Incorporated 1935.

Stansbury Park   CDP
ZIP: 84074   **Lat:** 40-38-16 N   **Long:** 112-18-12 W
Pop: 1,049 (1990)   **Pop Density:** 806.9
Land: 1.3 sq. mi.; **Water:** 0.2 sq. mi.

Stockton
Town
ZIP: 84071 **Lat:** 40-27-09 N **Long:** 112-21-43 W
Pop: 426 (1990); 437 (1980) **Pop Density:** 473.3
Land: 0.9 sq. mi.; **Water:** 0.0 sq. mi. **Elev:** 5068 ft.
Incorporated Aug 5, 1901.

Tooele
City
ZIP: 84074 **Lat:** 40-32-11 N **Long:** 112-18-04 W
Pop: 13,887 (1990); 14,335 (1980) **Pop Density:** 1119.9
Land: 12.4 sq. mi.; **Water:** 0.0 sq. mi. **Elev:** 4923 ft.
In northwestern UT, 25 mi. southwest of Salt Lake City. Incorporated Jun 19, 1853.
Name origin: For either the Goshute Indian Chief, Tuilla, or a reference to the rushes and reeds common in the tules, the swampy areas in the valley.

Vernon
Town
ZIP: 84080 **Lat:** 40-05-28 N **Long:** 112-26-59 W
Pop: 181 (1990); 181 (1980) **Pop Density:** 24.1
Land: 7.5 sq. mi.; **Water:** 0.0 sq. mi. **Elev:** 5511 ft.
Incorporated Feb 22, 1972.

Wendover
City
ZIP: 84083 **Lat:** 40-44-08 N **Long:** 114-02-09 W
Pop: 1,127 (1990); 1,099 (1980) **Pop Density:** 5635.0
Land: 0.2 sq. mi.; **Water:** 0.0 sq. mi. **Elev:** 4246 ft.
Incorporated Aug 7, 1950.

Uintah County
County Seat: Vernal (ZIP: 84078)

Pop: 22,211 (1990); 20,506 (1980) **Pop Density:** 5.0
Land: 4477.3 sq. mi.; **Water:** 21.9 sq. mi. **Area Code:** 801
On the northeastern border of UT; original county; organized Jan 31, 1850 (prior to statehood).
Name origin: For a subtribe of the Utes; name said to mean 'pineland.'

Ballard
Town
Lat: 40-17-03 N **Long:** 109-56-49 W
Pop: 644 (1990); 558 (1980) **Pop Density:** 31.7
Land: 20.3 sq. mi.; **Water:** 0.0 sq. mi. **Elev:** 5054 ft.
Incorporated Aug 2, 1976.

Fort Duchesne
CDP
Lat: 40-16-41 N **Long:** 109-52-15 W
Pop: 655 (1990) **Pop Density:** 109.2
Land: 6.0 sq. mi.; **Water:** 0.6 sq. mi.

Maeser
CDP
Lat: 40-28-24 N **Long:** 109-34-51 W
Pop: 2,598 (1990); 2,216 (1980) **Pop Density:** 399.7
Land: 6.5 sq. mi.; **Water:** 0.0 sq. mi.

Naples
City
ZIP: 84078 **Lat:** 40-25-47 N **Long:** 109-29-27 W
Pop: 1,334 (1990) **Pop Density:** 196.2
Land: 6.8 sq. mi.; **Water:** 0.0 sq. mi. **Elev:** 5260 ft.
Incorporated May 13, 1982.

Randlett
CDP
Lat: 40-13-50 N **Long:** 109-49-39 W
Pop: 283 (1990) **Pop Density:** 54.4
Land: 5.2 sq. mi.; **Water:** 0.0 sq. mi.

Vernal
City
ZIP: 84078 **Lat:** 40-27-07 N **Long:** 109-32-07 W
Pop: 6,644 (1990); 6,600 (1980) **Pop Density:** 1444.3
Land: 4.6 sq. mi.; **Water:** 0.0 sq. mi. **Elev:** 5322 ft.
Incorporated 1898.

Whiterocks
CDP
ZIP: 84085 **Lat:** 40-28-22 N **Long:** 109-56-34 W
Pop: 312 (1990) **Pop Density:** 135.7
Land: 2.3 sq. mi.; **Water:** 0.0 sq. mi.

Utah County
County Seat: Provo (ZIP: 84601)

Pop: 263,590 (1990); 218,106 (1980)   **Pop Density:** 131.9
Land: 1998.4 sq. mi.; **Water:** 142.6 sq. mi.   **Area Code:** 801

In north-central UT, south of Salt Lake City; original county; organized Jan 31, 1850 (prior to statehood); includes Cedar County, which was abolished in 1862.

Name origin: For the Ute Indians. *Ute* or *Eutaw* is variously defined as 'in the tops of the mountains,' 'high up,' 'the hill dwellers,' 'the land of the sun,' or 'the land of plenty.'

Alpine   City
Lat: 40-27-36 N   **Long:** 111-46-28 W
Pop: 3,492 (1990); 2,649 (1980)   **Pop Density:** 506.1
Land: 6.9 sq. mi.; **Water:** 0.0 sq. mi.   **Elev:** 4957 ft.
Incorporated Jan 19, 1855.

American Fork   City
ZIP: 84003   **Lat:** 40-23-03 N   **Long:** 111-47-37 W
Pop: 15,696 (1990); 12,564 (1980)   **Pop Density:** 2573.1
Land: 6.1 sq. mi.; **Water:** 0.0 sq. mi.   **Elev:** 4566 ft.
In north-central UT near the Fork River on Utah Lake, 14 mi. northwest of Provo. Settled 1850; incorporated Jun 4, 1853.
Name origin: For contrast with nearby Spanish Fork.

Cedar Fort   Town
Lat: 40-19-51 N   **Long:** 112-05-46 W
Pop: 284 (1990); 269 (1980)   **Pop Density:** 202.9
Land: 1.4 sq. mi.; **Water:** 0.0 sq. mi.   **Elev:** 5125 ft.

Cedar Hills   Town
ZIP: 84062   **Lat:** 40-24-16 N   **Long:** 111-45-02 W
Pop: 769 (1990); 571 (1980)   **Pop Density:** 480.6
Land: 1.6 sq. mi.; **Water:** 0.0 sq. mi.
Incorporated Nov 10, 1977.

Draper   City
Lat: 40-27-52 N   **Long:** 111-50-08 W
Pop: 0 (1990)
Land: 7.8 sq. mi.; **Water:** 0.0 sq. mi.
Part of the town is also in Salt Lake County.

Elk Ridge   Town
ZIP: 84651   **Lat:** 40-00-23 N   **Long:** 111-40-43 W
Pop: 771 (1990); 381 (1980)   **Pop Density:** 285.6
Land: 2.7 sq. mi.; **Water:** 0.0 sq. mi.
Incorporated 1976.

Genola   Town
ZIP: 84655   **Lat:** 40-01-02 N   **Long:** 111-51-10 W
Pop: 803 (1990); 630 (1980)   **Pop Density:** 63.2
Land: 12.7 sq. mi.; **Water:** 0.2 sq. mi.   **Elev:** 4598 ft.

Goshen   Town
ZIP: 84633   **Lat:** 39-57-06 N   **Long:** 111-54-03 W
Pop: 578 (1990); 582 (1980)   **Pop Density:** 825.7
Land: 0.7 sq. mi.; **Water:** 0.0 sq. mi.   **Elev:** 4530 ft.

Highland   City
ZIP: 84003   **Lat:** 40-25-17 N   **Long:** 111-47-19 W
Pop: 5,002 (1990); 2,435 (1980)   **Pop Density:** 757.9
Land: 6.6 sq. mi.; **Water:** 0.0 sq. mi.   **Elev:** 5000 ft.
Incorporated Jul 13, 1977.

Lehi   City
ZIP: 84043   **Lat:** 40-24-08 N   **Long:** 111-51-15 W
Pop: 8,475 (1990); 6,848 (1980)   **Pop Density:** 1486.8
Land: 5.7 sq. mi.; **Water:** 0.0 sq. mi.   **Elev:** 4562 ft.
Incorporated Feb 5, 1852.

Lindon   City
Lat: 40-20-28 N   **Long:** 111-42-59 W
Pop: 3,818 (1990); 2,796 (1980)   **Pop Density:** 454.5
Land: 8.4 sq. mi.; **Water:** 0.2 sq. mi.   **Elev:** 4640 ft.
Incorporated 1924.

Mapleton   City
Lat: 40-07-18 N   **Long:** 111-34-22 W
Pop: 3,572 (1990); 2,726 (1980)   **Pop Density:** 388.3
Land: 9.2 sq. mi.; **Water:** 0.0 sq. mi.   **Elev:** 4724 ft.
Incorporated Sep 3, 1901.

Orem   City
ZIP: 84057   **Lat:** 40-17-53 N   **Long:** 111-41-53 W
Pop: 67,561 (1990); 52,399 (1980)   **Pop Density:** 3774.4
Land: 17.9 sq. mi.; **Water:** 0.0 sq. mi.   **Elev:** 4756 ft.
In north-central UT, 7 mi. northwest of Provo. Incorporated May 5, 1919.
Name origin: For Walter C. Orem, president of the Salt Lake and Utah Electric Interurban RR.

Payson   City
ZIP: 84651   **Lat:** 40-02-02 N   **Long:** 111-43-41 W
Pop: 9,510 (1990); 8,246 (1980)   **Pop Density:** 1668.4
Land: 5.7 sq. mi.; **Water:** 0.0 sq. mi.   **Elev:** 4700 ft.
Incorporated Apr 1853.

Pleasant Grove   City
ZIP: 84042   **Lat:** 40-22-13 N   **Long:** 111-43-59 W
Pop: 13,476 (1990); 10,833 (1980)   **Pop Density:** 1953.0
Land: 6.9 sq. mi.; **Water:** 0.0 sq. mi.   **Elev:** 4621 ft.
In north-central UT, 10 mi. northwest of Provo. Incorporated May 1855.
Name origin: Named euphoniously. Previously called Battle Creek.

Provo   City
ZIP: 84601   **Lat:** 40-14-49 N   **Long:** 111-38-33 W
Pop: 86,835 (1990); 74,111 (1980)   **Pop Density:** 2249.6
Land: 38.6 sq. mi.; **Water:** 2.1 sq. mi.   **Elev:** 4549 ft.
In north-central UT on the Provo River, 3 mi. from Utah Lake and 45 mi. southeast of Salt Lake City. Founded 1850 as Fort Utah; incorporated Feb 6, 1851.
Name origin: For French Canadian explorer and mountain man Etienne Provot (also spelled Proveau, Provost, Provaux). After an incident between whites and Indians, it became known as Proveau's Hole. Later shortened; spelling altered to reflect pronunciation.

American Places Dictionary UTAH, Wasatch County

Salem City
ZIP: 84653 **Lat:** 40-03-08 N **Long:** 111-40-17 W
Pop: 2,284 (1990); 2,233 (1980) **Pop Density:** 2284.0
Land: 1.0 sq. mi.; **Water:** 0.0 sq. mi. **Elev:** 4600 ft.
Incorporated Jun 1920.

Santaquin City
ZIP: 84655 **Lat:** 39-58-29 N **Long:** 111-47-00 W
Pop: 2,386 (1990); 2,175 (1980) **Pop Density:** 1988.3
Land: 1.2 sq. mi.; **Water:** 0.0 sq. mi. **Elev:** 4887 ft.

Spanish Fork City
ZIP: 84660 **Lat:** 40-06-51 N **Long:** 111-38-21 W
Pop: 11,272 (1990); 9,825 (1980) **Pop Density:** 1483.2
Land: 7.6 sq. mi.; **Water:** 0.0 sq. mi. **Elev:** 4549 ft.
In north-central UT, 10 mi. south of Provo. Incorporated Jan 17, 1855.
Name origin: For the nearby Spanish Fork River.

Springville City
ZIP: 84663 **Lat:** 40-09-53 N **Long:** 111-36-52 W
Pop: 13,950 (1990); 12,101 (1980) **Pop Density:** 1438.1
Land: 9.7 sq. mi.; **Water:** 0.0 sq. mi. **Elev:** 4515 ft.
In north-central UT, 5 mi. south of Provo. Incorporated Apr 4, 1853.
Name origin: For a nearby large freshwater spring at the base of the Wasatch Mountains.

Vineyard Town
Lat: 40-18-26 N **Long:** 111-45-07 W
Pop: 151 (1990) **Pop Density:** 36.0
Land: 4.2 sq. mi.; **Water:** 0.5 sq. mi.

Woodland Hills Town
ZIP: 84653 **Lat:** 40-00-53 N **Long:** 111-38-59 W
Pop: 301 (1990); 60 (1980) **Pop Density:** 130.9
Land: 2.3 sq. mi.; **Water:** 0.0 sq. mi. **Elev:** 5320 ft.
Incorporated Dec 1979.

Wasatch County
County Seat: Heber City (ZIP: 84032)

Pop: 10,089 (1990); 8,523 (1980) **Pop Density:** 8.5
Land: 1180.9 sq. mi.; **Water:** 28.3 sq. mi. **Area Code:** 801
In east-central UT, east of Provo; organized Jan 17, 1862 (prior to statehood) from Summit County.
Name origin: For the Wasatch Mountains, a Ute word meaning 'mountain pass' or 'low place in a high mountain,' referring to the place where the Weber River cuts through.

Charleston Town
ZIP: 84032 **Lat:** 40-27-55 N **Long:** 111-28-04 W
Pop: 336 (1990); 320 (1980) **Pop Density:** 197.6
Land: 1.7 sq. mi.; **Water:** 0.2 sq. mi. **Elev:** 5433 ft.
Incorporated Jan 3, 1890.

Heber City
ZIP: 84032 **Lat:** 40-30-24 N **Long:** 111-24-41 W
Pop: 4,782 (1990); 4,362 (1980) **Pop Density:** 2277.1
Land: 2.1 sq. mi.; **Water:** 0.0 sq. mi. **Elev:** 5595 ft.
Incorporated Mar 4, 1889.

Midway City
ZIP: 84049 **Lat:** 40-30-52 N **Long:** 111-28-28 W
Pop: 1,554 (1990); 1,194 (1980) **Pop Density:** 535.9
Land: 2.9 sq. mi.; **Water:** 0.0 sq. mi. **Elev:** 5567 ft.
Incorporated Jun 1891.

Park City City
ZIP: 84060 **Lat:** 40-37-15 N **Long:** 111-28-58 W
Pop: 0 (1990)
Land: 0.1 sq. mi.; **Water:** 0.0 sq. mi. **Elev:** 6980 ft.
Incorporated Mar 15, 1884. Part of the town is also in Summit County.

Wallsburg Town
ZIP: 84082 **Lat:** 40-23-12 N **Long:** 111-25-15 W
Pop: 252 (1990); 239 (1980) **Pop Density:** 504.0
Land: 0.5 sq. mi.; **Water:** 0.0 sq. mi. **Elev:** 5301 ft.
Incorporated Apr 2, 1917.

Washington County
County Seat: St. George (ZIP: 84770)

Pop: 48,560 (1990); 26,065 (1980)
Land: 2427.2 sq. mi.; **Water:** 2.9 sq. mi.
Pop Density: 20.0
Area Code: 801
On the southwestern border of UT; organized Mar 2, 1852 (prior to statehood) from unorganized territory.
Name origin: For George Washington (1732–1799), American patriot and first U.S. president.

Enterprise City
Lat: 37-34-13 N **Long:** 113-42-52 W
Pop: 936 (1990); 905 (1980) **Pop Density:** 585.0
Land: 1.6 sq. mi.; **Water:** 0.0 sq. mi. **Elev:** 5500 ft.
Incorporated Mar 17, 1913.

Hildale Town
Lat: 37-00-29 N **Long:** 112-58-05 W
Pop: 1,325 (1990); 1,009 (1980) **Pop Density:** 1325.0
Land: 1.0 sq. mi.; **Water:** 0.0 sq. mi. **Elev:** 5042 ft.
Incorporated Dec 9, 1963.

Hurricane City
Lat: 37-09-35 N **Long:** 113-20-21 W
Pop: 3,915 (1990); 2,361 (1980) **Pop Density:** 177.1
Land: 22.1 sq. mi.; **Water:** 0.0 sq. mi. **Elev:** 3266 ft.
Incorporated 1912.

Ivins Town
ZIP: 84738 **Lat:** 37-10-29 N **Long:** 113-41-04 W
Pop: 1,630 (1990); 600 (1980) **Pop Density:** 206.3
Land: 7.9 sq. mi.; **Water:** 0.1 sq. mi. **Elev:** 3074 ft.
Incorporated 1926.

La Verkin City
ZIP: 84745 **Lat:** 37-12-23 N **Long:** 113-16-20 W
Pop: 1,771 (1990); 1,174 (1980) **Pop Density:** 520.9
Land: 3.4 sq. mi.; **Water:** 0.0 sq. mi. **Elev:** 3313 ft.
Incorporated 1927.

Leeds Town
ZIP: 84746 **Lat:** 37-14-13 N **Long:** 113-21-28 W
Pop: 254 (1990); 218 (1980) **Pop Density:** 141.1
Land: 1.8 sq. mi.; **Water:** 0.0 sq. mi. **Elev:** 2750 ft.

New Harmony Town
ZIP: 84757 **Lat:** 37-28-42 N **Long:** 113-18-29 W
Pop: 101 (1990); 117 (1980) **Pop Density:** 505.0
Land: 0.2 sq. mi.; **Water:** 0.0 sq. mi. **Elev:** 5306 ft.

Rockville Town
Lat: 37-09-12 N **Long:** 113-03-33 W
Pop: 182 (1990) **Pop Density:** 24.9
Land: 7.3 sq. mi.; **Water:** 0.0 sq. mi.

St. George City
ZIP: 84770 **Lat:** 37-04-42 N **Long:** 113-34-42 W
Pop: 28,502 (1990); 11,350 (1980) **Pop Density:** 495.7
Land: 57.5 sq. mi.; **Water:** 0.3 sq. mi. **Elev:** 2761 ft.
In southwestern UT, 50 mi. southwest of Cedar City. Incorporated Jan 17, 1862.
Name origin: For George Albert Smith, presiding Mormon elder and "Father of the South."

Santa Clara City
ZIP: 84765 **Lat:** 37-08-02 N **Long:** 113-39-04 W
Pop: 2,322 (1990); 1,091 (1980) **Pop Density:** 725.6
Land: 3.2 sq. mi.; **Water:** 0.0 sq. mi. **Elev:** 2759 ft.
Incorporated Jan 4, 1915.

Springdale Town
ZIP: 84767 **Lat:** 37-11-02 N **Long:** 112-59-56 W
Pop: 275 (1990); 258 (1980) **Pop Density:** 59.8
Land: 4.6 sq. mi.; **Water:** 0.0 sq. mi. **Elev:** 3913 ft.
Incorporated 1959.

Toquerville Town
ZIP: 84774 **Lat:** 37-14-11 N **Long:** 113-17-07 W
Pop: 488 (1990); 277 (1980) **Pop Density:** 57.4
Land: 8.5 sq. mi.; **Water:** 0.0 sq. mi. **Elev:** 3200 ft.
Incorporated 1916.

Virgin Town
ZIP: 84779 **Lat:** 37-12-02 N **Long:** 113-11-54 W
Pop: 229 (1990); 169 (1980) **Pop Density:** 190.8
Land: 1.2 sq. mi.; **Water:** 0.0 sq. mi. **Elev:** 3550 ft.
Incorporated Apr 16, 1929.

Washington City
ZIP: 84780 **Lat:** 37-08-04 N **Long:** 113-29-36 W
Pop: 4,198 (1990); 3,092 (1980) **Pop Density:** 166.6
Land: 25.2 sq. mi.; **Water:** 0.0 sq. mi. **Elev:** 2800 ft.
Incorporated 1858.

American Places Dictionary UTAH, Weber County

Wayne County
County Seat: Loa (ZIP: 84747)

Pop: 2,177 (1990); 1,911 (1980)   **Pop Density:** 0.9
Land: 2460.5 sq. mi.; **Water:** 6.1 sq. mi.   **Area Code:** 801

In south-central UT; organized Mar 10, 1892 (prior to statehood) from Piute County.

Name origin: Named by Willis Robinson, a delegate to the state constitutional convention, for his deceased son, Wayne.

Bicknell — Town
ZIP: 84715   **Lat:** 38-20-29 N   **Long:** 111-32-41 W
Pop: 327 (1990); 296 (1980)   **Pop Density:** 654.0
Land: 0.5 sq. mi.; **Water:** 0.0 sq. mi.   **Elev:** 7125 ft.
Incorporated Feb 1939.

Loa — Town
ZIP: 84747   **Lat:** 38-24-10 N   **Long:** 111-38-35 W
Pop: 444 (1990); 364 (1980)   **Pop Density:** 493.3
Land: 0.9 sq. mi.; **Water:** 0.0 sq. mi.   **Elev:** 7000 ft.

Lyman — Town
ZIP: 84749   **Lat:** 38-23-46 N   **Long:** 111-35-17 W
Pop: 198 (1990)   **Pop Density:** 104.2
Land: 1.9 sq. mi.; **Water:** 0.0 sq. mi.   **Elev:** 7177 ft.
Incorporated Jan 1, 1983.

Torrey — Town
ZIP: 84775   **Lat:** 38-18-05 N   **Long:** 111-25-09 W
Pop: 122 (1990); 140 (1980)   **Pop Density:** 305.0
Land: 0.4 sq. mi.; **Water:** 0.0 sq. mi.   **Elev:** 7000 ft.
Incorporated Feb 5, 1939.

Weber County
County Seat: Ogden (ZIP: 84401)

Pop: 158,330 (1990); 144,616 (1980)   **Pop Density:** 275.1
Land: 575.6 sq. mi.; **Water:** 83.9 sq. mi.   **Area Code:** 801

In north-central UT, north of Salt Lake City; original county; organized Jan 31, 1850 (prior to statehood).

Name origin: For the Weber River, which runs through the county. The river is itself named for John H. Weber (?–1859), a Dutch sea captain and trapper who traveled west with Gen. Ashby and was killed near the river, or for another trapper named Weber.

Farr West — City
ZIP: 84404   **Lat:** 41-17-52 N   **Long:** 112-01-48 W
Pop: 2,178 (1990)   **Pop Density:** 410.9
Land: 5.3 sq. mi.; **Water:** 0.0 sq. mi.   **Elev:** 4260 ft.
Incorporated Nov 19, 1980.

Harrisville — City
ZIP: 84404   **Lat:** 41-16-51 N   **Long:** 111-59-03 W
Pop: 3,004 (1990); 1,371 (1980)   **Pop Density:** 1072.9
Land: 2.8 sq. mi.; **Water:** 0.0 sq. mi.   **Elev:** 4290 ft.
Incorporated Apr 1962.

Hooper — CDP
ZIP: 84315   **Lat:** 41-10-22 N   **Long:** 112-07-28 W
Pop: 3,468 (1990)   **Pop Density:** 309.6
Land: 11.2 sq. mi.; **Water:** 0.1 sq. mi.

Huntsville — Town
ZIP: 84317   **Lat:** 41-15-35 N   **Long:** 111-46-21 W
Pop: 561 (1990); 577 (1980)   **Pop Density:** 935.0
Land: 0.6 sq. mi.; **Water:** 0.1 sq. mi.   **Elev:** 4929 ft.
Incorporated 1924.

North Ogden — City
ZIP: 84404   **Lat:** 41-18-41 N   **Long:** 111-57-32 W
Pop: 11,668 (1990); 9,309 (1980)   **Pop Density:** 1881.9
Land: 6.2 sq. mi.; **Water:** 0.0 sq. mi.   **Elev:** 4275 ft.
In northern UT, 14 mi. north of Ogden. Incorporated 1934.

Ogden — City
ZIP: 84401   **Lat:** 41-13-40 N   **Long:** 111-57-56 W
Pop: 63,909 (1990); 64,407 (1980)   **Pop Density:** 2448.6
Land: 26.1 sq. mi.; **Water:** 0.0 sq. mi.   **Elev:** 4299 ft.
In northern UT, 33 mi. north of Salt Lake City. Incorporated Feb 6, 1851.

Name origin: For Peter Skene Ogden, an early Hudson Bay co-agent. Before 1850, known as Brownsville.

Plain City — City
ZIP: 84404   **Lat:** 41-17-55 N   **Long:** 112-04-30 W
Pop: 2,722 (1990); 2,379 (1980)   **Pop Density:** 850.6
Land: 3.2 sq. mi.; **Water:** 0.0 sq. mi.   **Elev:** 4237 ft.
Incorporated Jan 13, 1944.

Pleasant View — City
ZIP: 84404   **Lat:** 41-19-25 N   **Long:** 111-59-55 W
Pop: 3,603 (1990); 3,983 (1980)   **Pop Density:** 537.8
Land: 6.7 sq. mi.; **Water:** 0.0 sq. mi.   **Elev:** 4398 ft.
Incorporated Aug 27, 1945.

Riverdale — City
ZIP: 84405   **Lat:** 41-10-16 N   **Long:** 112-00-08 W
Pop: 6,419 (1990); 6,031 (1980)   **Pop Density:** 1458.9
Land: 4.4 sq. mi.; **Water:** 0.0 sq. mi.   **Elev:** 4355 ft.
Incorporated Mar 4, 1946.

UTAH, Weber County

Roy — City
ZIP: 84067 **Lat:** 41-10-21 N **Long:** 112-02-41 W
Pop: 24,603 (1990); 19,694 (1980) **Pop Density:** 3618.1
Land: 6.8 sq. mi.; **Water:** 0.0 sq. mi. **Elev:** 4436 ft.
In northeastern UT, southwest of Ogden. Incorporated 1937.
Name origin: For the recently deceased young son of David P. Peebles.

South Ogden — City
ZIP: 84403 **Lat:** 41-10-27 N **Long:** 111-57-28 W
Pop: 12,105 (1990); 11,366 (1980) **Pop Density:** 3904.8
Land: 3.1 sq. mi.; **Water:** 0.0 sq. mi. **Elev:** 4300 ft.
Incorporated Jul 6, 1936.

Uintah — Town
ZIP: 84403 **Lat:** 41-08-34 N **Long:** 111-56-01 W
Pop: 760 (1990); 439 (1980) **Pop Density:** 844.4
Land: 0.9 sq. mi.; **Water:** 0.0 sq. mi. **Elev:** 4497 ft.
Incorporated Feb 10, 1937.

Washington Terrace — City
ZIP: 84403 **Lat:** 41-10-12 N **Long:** 111-58-46 W
Pop: 8,189 (1990); 8,212 (1980) **Pop Density:** 4817.1
Land: 1.7 sq. mi.; **Water:** 0.0 sq. mi. **Elev:** 4600 ft.
Incorporated Dec 12, 1958.

Index to Places and Counties in Utah

Alpine (Utah) City.............................720
Alta (Salt Lake) Town.....................714
Altamont (Duchesne) Town............709
Alton (Kane) Town.........................712
Amalga (Cache) Town.....................706
American Fork (Utah) City.............720
Annabella (Sevier) Town.................717
Antimony (Garfield) Town...............710
Aurora (Sevier) City........................717
Ballard (Uintah) Town.....................719
Bear River City (Box Elder) Town...705
Beaver (Beaver) City 705
Beaver County.................................705
Bicknell (Wayne) Town....................723
Big Water (Kane) Town...................712
Blanding (San Juan) City.................716
Bluffdale (Salt Lake) City.................714
Boulder (Garfield) Town 710
Bountiful (Davis) City.....................708
Box Elder County...........................705
Brian Head (Iron) Town...................711
Brigham City (Box Elder) City..........705
Cache County 706
Cannonville (Garfield) Town 710
Canyon Rim (Salt Lake) CDP 715
Carbon County 707
Castle Dale (Emery) City.................710
Castle Valley (Grand) Town.............711
Cedar City (Iron) City.....................711
Cedar Fort (Utah) Town..................720
Cedar Hills (Utah) Town..................720
Centerfield (Sanpete) Town..............716
Centerville (Davis) City...................708
Charleston (Wasatch) Town.............721
Circleville (Piute) Town....................714
Clarkston (Cache) Town..................706
Clawson (Emery) Town 710
Clearfield (Davis) City.....................708
Cleveland (Emery) Town 710
Clinton (Davis) City........................708
Coalville (Summit) City...................718
Corinne (Box Elder) City.................705
Cornish (Cache) Town.....................706
Cottonwood Heights (Salt Lake) CDP 715
Cottonwood West (Salt Lake) CDP ..715
Daggett County 708
Davis County...................................708
Delta (Millard) City.........................713
Deweyville (Box Elder) Town 705
Draper (Salt Lake) City...................715
Draper (Utah) City 720
Duchesne (Duchesne) City 709
Duchesne County............................709
Dugway (Tooele) Military Facility....718
East Carbon (Carbon) City..............707
East Millcreek (Salt Lake) CDP 715
Elk Ridge (Utah) Town 720
Elmo (Emery) Town 710
Elsinore (Sevier) Town....................717
Elwood (Box Elder) Town...............705
Emery (Emery) Town 710
Emery County.................................710
Enoch (Iron) City............................711
Enterprise (Washington) City...........722
Ephraim (Sanpete) City 716
Erda (Tooele) CDP 718
Escalante (Garfield) Town 710
Eureka (Juab) City..........................712
Fairview (Sanpete) City 716

Farmington (Davis) City 708
Farr West (Weber) City...................723
Fayette (Sanpete) Town 716
Ferron (Emery) City........................710
Fielding (Box Elder) Town 705
Fillmore (Millard) City....................713
Fort Duchesne (Uintah) CDP 719
Fountain Green (Sanpete) City 716
Francis (Summit) Town...................718
Fruit Heights (Davis) City 708
Garden City (Rich) Town................714
Garfield County..............................710
Garland (Box Elder) City 705
Genola (Utah) Town.......................720
Glendale (Kane) Town 712
Glenwood (Sevier) Town.................717
Goshen (Utah) Town.......................720
Grand County.................................711
Granite (Salt Lake) CDP 715
Grantsville (Tooele) City..................718
Green River (Emery) City................710
Green River (Grand) City................711
Gunnison (Sanpete) City..................716
Harrisville (Weber) City 723
Hatch (Garfield) Town 711
Heber (Wasatch) City......................721
Helper (Carbon) City.......................707
Henefer (Summit) Town..................718
Henrieville (Garfield) Town..............711
Hiawatha (Carbon) Town................707
Hiawatha (Emery) Town..................710
Highland (Utah) City......................720
Hildale (Washington) Town.............722
Hinckley (Millard) Town..................713
Holden (Millard) Town 713
Holladay-Cottonwood (Salt Lake) CDP 715
Honeyville (Box Elder) City.............705
Hooper (Weber) CDP 723
Howell (Box Elder) Town................705
Huntington (Emery) City 710
Huntsville (Weber) Town 723
Hurricane (Washington) City 722
Hyde Park (Cache) City 706
Hyrum (Cache) City 706
Iron County 711
Ivins (Washington) Town 722
Joseph (Sevier) Town......................717
Juab County 712
Junction (Piute) Town.....................714
Kamas (Summit) City......................718
Kanab (Kane) City 712
Kanarraville (Iron) Town 711
Kane County 712
Kanosh (Millard) Town 713
Kaysville (Davis) City......................708
Kearns (Salt Lake) CDP 715
Kingston (Piute) Town 714
Koosharem (Sevier) Town................717
Laketown (Rich) Town 714
La Verkin (Washington) City...........722
Layton (Davis) City.........................708
Leamington (Millard) Town.............713
Leeds (Washington) Town 722
Lehi (Utah) City 720
Levan (Juab) Town 712
Lewiston (Cache) City.....................706
Lindon (Utah) City.........................720
Little Cottonwood Creek Valley (Salt Lake) CDP 715

Loa (Wayne) Town..........................723
Logan (Cache) City.........................706
Lyman (Wayne) Town.....................723
Lynndyl (Millard) Town..................713
Maeser (Uintah) CDP 719
Magna (Salt Lake) CDP 715
Manila (Daggett) Town....................708
Manti (Sanpete) City.......................716
Mantua (Box Elder) Town...............705
Mapleton (Utah) City......................720
Marysvale (Piute) Town 714
Mayfield (Sanpete) Town 716
Meadow (Millard) Town..................713
Mendon (Cache) City......................706
Mexican Hat (San Juan) CDP 716
Midvale (Salt Lake) City..................715
Midway (Wasatch) City...................721
Milford (Beaver) City 705
Millard County...............................713
Millcreek (Salt Lake) CDP 715
Millville (Cache) City......................706
Minersville (Beaver) Town...............705
Moab (Grand) City 711
Mona (Juab) Town..........................712
Monroe (Sevier) City.......................717
Montezuma Creek (San Juan) CDP..716
Monticello (San Juan) City 716
Morgan (Morgan) City....................713
Morgan County 713
Moroni (Sanpete) City.....................717
Mount Olympus (Salt Lake) CDP.....715
Mount Pleasant (Sanpete) City 717
Murray (Salt Lake) City...................715
Myton (Duchesne) City 709
Naples (Uintah) City 719
Neola (Duchesne) CDP 709
Nephi (Juab) City............................712
New Harmony (Washington) Town ..722
Newton (Cache) Town.....................706
Nibley (Cache) City.........................706
North Logan (Cache) City...............707
North Ogden (Weber) City..............723
North Salt Lake (Davis) City 708
Oak City (Millard) Town.................713
Oakley (Summit) Town 718
Ogden (Weber) City........................723
Ophir (Tooele) Town 718
Oquirrh (Salt Lake) CDP 715
Orangeville (Emery) City.................710
Orderville (Kane) Town...................712
Orem (Utah) City 720
Panguitch (Garfield) City.................711
Paradise (Cache) Town....................707
Paragonah (Iron) Town....................711
Park City (Summit) City..................718
Park City (Wasatch) City.................721
Parowan (Iron) City........................712
Payson (Utah) City 720
Perry (Box Elder) City.....................706
Piute County...................................714
Plain City (Weber) City...................723
Pleasant Grove (Utah) City..............720
Pleasant View (Weber) City 723
Plymouth (Box Elder) Town............706
Portage (Box Elder) Town...............706
Price (Carbon) City 707
Providence (Cache) City..................707
Provo (Utah) City...........................720
Randlett (Uintah) CDP 719
Randolph (Rich) City......................714

UTAH

Redmond (Sevier) Town.....................717
Rich County..*714*
Richfield (Sevier) City.........................717
Richmond (Cache) City......................707
Riverdale (Weber) City.......................723
River Heights (Cache) City................707
Riverton (Salt Lake) City...................715
Rockville (Washington) Town............722
Roosevelt (Duchesne) City.................709
Roy (Weber) City................................724
Rush Valley (Tooele) Town 718
St. George (Washington) City............722
Salem (Utah) City................................721
Salina (Sevier) City..............................717
Salt Lake City (Salt Lake) City 715
Salt Lake County *714*
Sandy (Salt Lake) City........................715
San Juan County..................................*716*
Sanpete County *716*
Santa Clara (Washington) City..........722
Santaquin (Utah) City.........................721
Scipio (Millard) Town 713
Scofield (Carbon) Town.....................707
Sevier County *717*
Sigurd (Sevier) Town..........................717
Smithfield (Cache) City......................707
Snowville (Box Elder) Town..............706
South Jordan (Salt Lake) City............715
South Ogden (Weber) City 724
South Salt Lake (Salt Lake) City........715
South Weber (Davis) City 708
Spanish Fork (Utah) City 721
Spring City (Sanpete) City 717
Springdale (Washington) Town 722
Springville (Utah) City 721
Stansbury Park (Tooele) CDP............718
Sterling (Sanpete) Town 717
Stockton (Tooele) Town.....................719
Summit County....................................*718*
Sunnyside (Carbon) City 707
Sunset (Davis) City.............................709
Syracuse (Davis) City 709
Tabiona (Duchesne) Town.................709
Taylorsville-Bennion (Salt Lake)
 CDP *715*
Tooele (Tooele) City 719
Tooele County......................................*718*
Toquerville (Washington) Town 722
Torrey (Wayne) Town 723
Tremonton (Box Elder) City 706
Trenton (Cache) Town.......................707
Tropic (Garfield) Town 711
Uintah (Weber) Town........................724
Uintah County......................................*719*
Union (Salt Lake) CDP......................715

American Places Dictionary

Utah County...*720*
Val Verda (Davis) CDP......................709
Vernal (Uintah) City............................719
Vernon (Tooele) Town 719
Vineyard (Utah) Town 721
Virgin (Washington) Town 722
Wales (Sanpete) Town 717
Wallsburg (Wasatch) Town 721
Wasatch County *721*
Washington (Washington) City..........722
Washington County *722*
Washington Terrace (Weber) City 724
Wayne County *723*
Weber County *723*
Wellington (Carbon) City 707
Wellsville (Cache) City 707
Wendover (Tooele) City.....................719
West Bountiful (Davis) City..............709
West Jordan (Salt Lake) City............715
West Point (Davis) City 709
West Valley City (Salt Lake) City 716
White City (Salt Lake) CDP 716
Whiterocks (Uintah) CDP..................719
Willard (Box Elder) City 706
Woodland Hills (Utah) Town............721
Woodruff (Rich) Town 714
Woods Cross (Davis) City 709

Washington

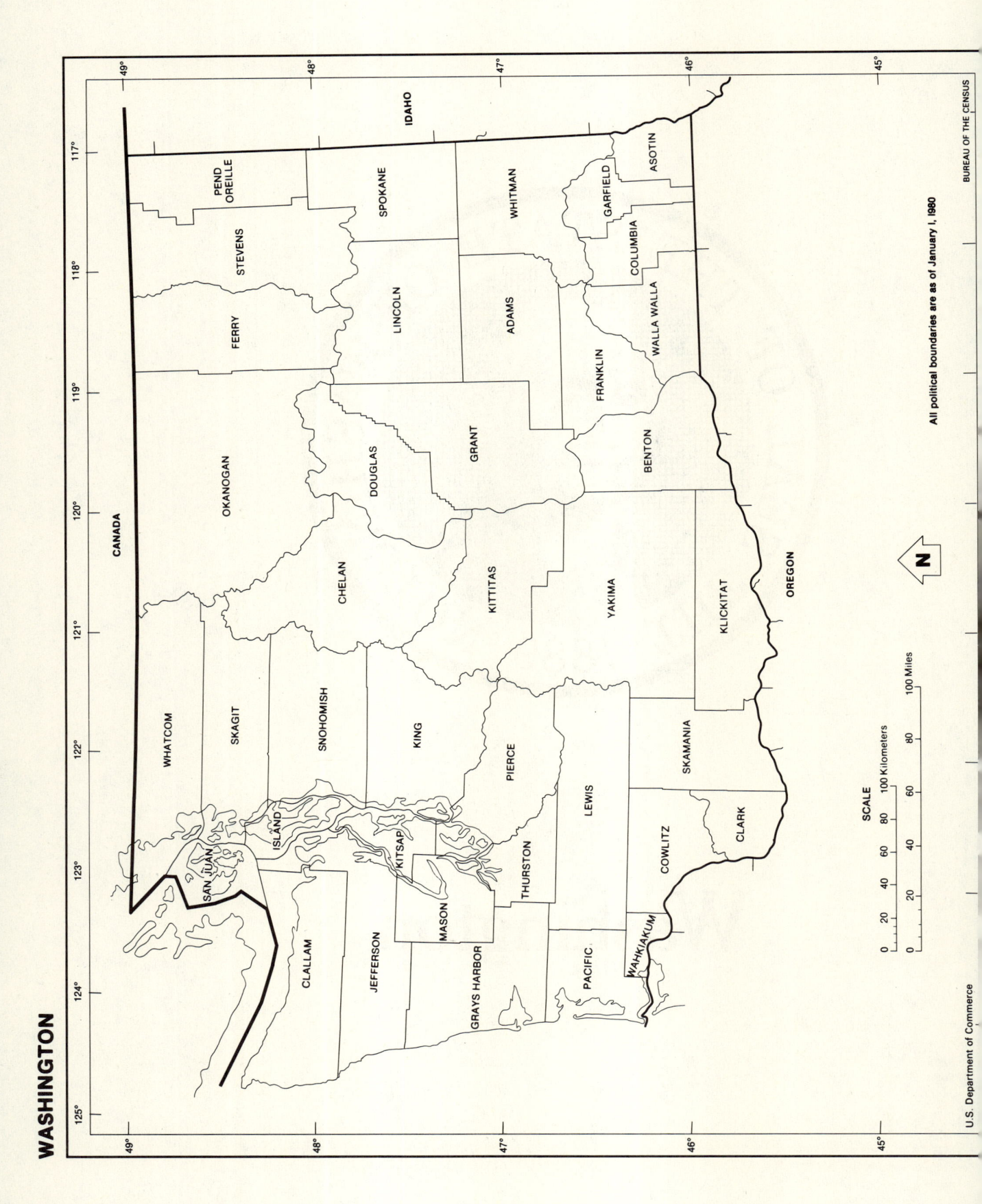

Washington

Population: 4,866,692 (1990); 4,132,156 (1980)
Population rank (1990): 18
Percent population change (1980–1990): 17.8
Population projection: 5,157,000 (1995); 5,477,000 (2000)

Area: total: 71,303 sq. mi.; 66,582 sq. mi. land, 4,721 sq. mi. water
Area rank: 18
Highest elevation: 14,410 ft., Mount Rainier (Pierce County)
Lowest point: sea level along the Pacific coast

State capital: Olympia (Thurston County)
Largest city: Seattle (516,259)
Second largest city: Spokane (177,196)
Largest county: King (1,507,319)

Total housing units: 2,032,378
No. of occupied housing units: 1,872,431
Vacant housing units (%): 7.9
Distribution of population by race and Hispanic origin (%):
  White: 88.5
  Black: 3.1
  Hispanic (any race): 4.4
  Native American: 1.7
  Asian/Pacific: 4.3
  Other: 2.4

Admission date: November 11, 1889 (42nd state).

Location: In the northwestern U.S. on the Pacific Ocean, bordering Oregon, Idaho, and the Canadian province of British Columbia.

Name Origin: For George Washington (1732–99), first U.S. president. The name *Columbia* was originally suggested for the territory, but the present name was chosen because the District of Columbia already existed but no territory name honored the national hero.

State bird: willow goldfinch *(Spinus tristis salicamans)*
State colors: green and gold
State dance: square dance
State fish: steelhead trout *(Salmo gairdnerii)*
State flower: coast rhododendron *(Rhododendron macrophyllum)*
State folk song: "Roll on, Columbia, Roll on"
State fruit: apple
State gem: petrified wood
State grass: bluebunch wheatgrass *(Agropyron spicatum)*
State ship: container ship "President Washington"
State song: "Washington, My Home"
State tree: western hemlock *(Tsuga heterophylla)*

State motto: Alki (Indian for 'By and By')
State nickname: Evergreen State

Area codes: 206 (west); 509 (east)
Time zone: Pacific
Abbreviations: WA (postal); Wash. (traditional)
Part of (region): Pacific Coast

Local Government

Counties

Washington has 39 counties, most of which are governed by a three-member board of commissioners.

Municipalities

Washington has 268 incorporated cities and towns, governed variously by the council-manager, commission, or mayor-council form of government. Ten of the larger cities have their own charters under the state constitution's home rule provision.

Settlement History and Early Development

The first settlers in Washington were the prehistoric peoples who made their way from Asia across the land bridge to North America and slowly spread southward at least 10,000 years ago. At the time white explorers first arrived in the area, Cayuse, Colville, Nez Perce, Okanogan, Spokane, and Yakima Indians lived east of the Cascade Mountains; west of the mountains lived the Chinook, Clallam, Clatsop, Makah, Lummi, Nisqually, Nooksack, and Puyallup Indians. Although both English and Spanish explorers sailed into the waters of the Pacific Northwest during the 1500s, no attempt was made to settle the area until the 1700s, when fear that the Russians would expand south from their settlements in Alaska led to Spanish expeditions into the region. In 1775 Bruno Heceta and Juan Francisco de la Bodega y Quadra claimed the area for Spain when they landed near what is now Point Grenville. Explorations by Manuel Quimper in 1790 and Francisco de Eliza in 1791 led to a Spanish settlement at Neah Bay in 1792.

James Cook (in 1778) and George Vancouver and Peter Puget (in 1792–94) sailed into the area and claimed the territory for England. Spanish explorers encountered Vancouver's expedition; Vancouver in turn encountered an expedition led by an American, Robert Gray, who reached the mouth of the Columbia River in 1792. In 1805 Lewis and Clark reached the Columbia River by land and followed it to the Pacific. The explorations of Gray and of Lewis and Clark became the basis of American claims to the area.

During the early 1800s both British-Canadian and American fur traders established posts in the area, including

Spokane House, near present-day Spokane, and Astoria (Oregon), founded by John Jacob Astor. After the War of 1812 Great Britain and the U.S. signed a treaty that permitted both to trade in the area. Missionaries soon followed the fur traders into the region.

In 1838–42 U.S. naval officer Charles Wilkes led an expedition to survey the inland waters and surrounding land. As more and more Americans settled in the area, the boundary question continued to be disputed between Great Britain and the U.S. until the U.S.-Canadian boundary was set at the 49th parallel in 1846.

Territory and Statehood

Washington was a part of the Oregon Territory created in 1848 by Congress. Washington Territory was created in 1853, with a capital at Olympia. After less than a decade of conflict with the Indians, settlement in Washington was spurred by the discovery of gold in nearby areas. However, no major gold strikes were made in Washington, and settlers remained to become loggers, ranchers, and farmers. After the Northern Pacific Railroad was completed in 1883, settlement increased rapidly. The territory became the 42nd state on November 11, 1889, with Olympia continuing as the capital.

Business and Industry

The next decade saw the growth of farming, lumbering, fishing, and shipping businesses. The port of Seattle became a supply center for prospectors headed for the Yukon and Alaska.

Washington's economy profited by World War I but suffered after the war and throughout the 1930s. During World War II Washington produced not only food products but also aircraft and ships. Along with military bases, the aerospace contractor Boeing has been an important economic force in the Seattle region for decades, despite periodic slumps in the industry. Recent years have seen growth and prosperity from the computer industry, led by software manufacturer Microsoft in Redmond, near Seattle.

State Boundaries

The boundary dispute between the U.S. and Great Britain over what was then called the Oregon Country became an issue in the 1844 presidential campaign, when James Polk used the slogan "Fifty-Four Forty or Fight!" to champion the U.S. claim to all territory south of 54 degrees, 40 minutes north latitude. As president, Polk signed a treaty with Great Britain in 1846 that set the northern boundary of Washington with Canada at its present location of the 49th parallel, with the exception of the part of Vancouver Island that lies south of the parallel. The exact boundary between the mainland and Vancouver Island was defined by the Treaty of Washington in 1871. Washington's other boundaries were established in 1853 when the Washington Territory became separate from the Oregon Territory (the Columbia River marked the boundary), and in 1863, when the Idaho Territory was formed.

Washington Counties

Adams	Douglas	King	Pacific	Stevens
Asotin	Ferry	Kitsap	Pend Oreille	Thurston
Benton	Franklin	Kittitas	Pierce	Wahkiakum
Chelan	Garfield	Klickitat	San Juan	Walla Walla
Clallam	Grant	Lewis	Skagit	Whatcom
Clark	Grays Harbor	Lincoln	Skamania	Whitman
Columbia	Island	Mason	Snohomish	Yakima
Cowlitz	Jefferson	Okanogan	Spokane	

Multi-County Places

The following Washington places are in more than one county. Given here is the total population for each multi-county place, and the names of the counties it is in.

Bothell, pop. 12,345; King (11,986), Snohomish (359)
Coulee Dam, pop. 1,087; Okanogan (879), Douglas (207), Grant (1)
Milton, pop. 4,995; Pierce (4,298), King (697)
Pacific, pop. 4,622; King (4,622), Pierce (0)
Woodland, pop. 2,500; Cowlitz (2,406), Clark (94)

Adams County
County Seat: Ritzville (ZIP: 99169)

Pop: 13,603 (1990); 13,267 (1980) **Pop Density:** 7.1
Land: 1925.0 sq. mi.; **Water:** 4.7 sq. mi. **Area Code:** 509

In southeast WA, southwest of Spokane; organized Nov 28, 1883 (prior to statehood) from Whitman County.
Name origin: For John Adams (1735–1826), second U.S. president.

Hatton — Town
ZIP: 99332 **Lat:** 46-46-31 N **Long:** 118-49-40 W
Pop: 71 (1990); 81 (1980) **Pop Density:** 177.5
Land: 0.4 sq. mi.; **Water:** 0.0 sq. mi.
Name origin: A combination of the names of postmaster J.D. Hackett and local settler Mr. Sutton.

Lind — Town
ZIP: 99341 **Lat:** 46-58-17 N **Long:** 118-36-48 W
Pop: 472 (1990); 567 (1980) **Pop Density:** 472.0
Land: 1.0 sq. mi.; **Water:** 0.0 sq. mi.
Established c. 1900.

Othello — City
ZIP: 99344 **Lat:** 46-49-13 N **Long:** 119-10-01 W
Pop: 4,638 (1990); 4,454 (1980) **Pop Density:** 2016.5
Land: 2.3 sq. mi.; **Water:** 0.0 sq. mi. **Elev:** 1038 ft.
Name origin: For William Shakespeare's tragic hero.

Ritzville — City
ZIP: 99169 **Lat:** 47-07-35 N **Long:** 118-22-33 W
Pop: 1,725 (1990); 1,800 (1980) **Pop Density:** 1437.5
Land: 1.2 sq. mi.; **Water:** 0.0 sq. mi.
Name origin: For early pioneer Phillip Ritz, who settled here in 1878.

Washtucna — Town
ZIP: 99371 **Lat:** 46-45-12 N **Long:** 118-18-41 W
Pop: 231 (1990); 266 (1980) **Pop Density:** 462.0
Land: 0.5 sq. mi.; **Water:** 0.0 sq. mi. **Elev:** 1024 ft.
Name origin: From the name of a Palouse Indian chief.

Asotin County
County Seat: Asotin (ZIP: 99402)

Pop: 17,605 (1990); 16,823 (1980) **Pop Density:** 27.7
Land: 635.9 sq. mi.; **Water:** 4.8 sq. mi. **Area Code:** 509

On the southeastern border of WA; organized Oct 27, 1883 (prior to statehood) from Garfield County.
Name origin: For Asotin Creek, which runs through the county; Nez Perce word meaning 'eel creek.'

Asotin — City
ZIP: 99402 **Lat:** 46-20-19 N **Long:** 117-02-38 W
Pop: 981 (1990); 943 (1980) **Pop Density:** 1401.4
Land: 0.7 sq. mi.; **Water:** 0.2 sq. mi. **Elev:** 770 ft.
Name origin: From a Nez Perce term meaning 'eel creek.'

Clarkston — City
ZIP: 99403 **Lat:** 46-24-55 N **Long:** 117-02-56 W
Pop: 6,753 (1990); 6,903 (1980) **Pop Density:** 3554.2
Land: 1.9 sq. mi.; **Water:** 0.1 sq. mi.
Name origin: For Capt. William Clark (1770–1838) of Lewis and Clark expedition fame.

Clarkston Heights-Vineland — CDP
Lat: 46-23-10 N **Long:** 117-04-35 W
Pop: 2,832 (1990) **Pop Density:** 1048.9
Land: 2.7 sq. mi.; **Water:** 0.0 sq. mi.

West Clarkston-Highland — CDP
Lat: 46-23-54 N **Long:** 117-03-26 W
Pop: 3,913 (1990); 3,683 (1980) **Pop Density:** 1778.6
Land: 2.2 sq. mi.; **Water:** 0.2 sq. mi.

Benton County
County Seat: Prosser (ZIP: 99350)

Pop: 112,560 (1990); 109,444 (1980) **Pop Density:** 66.1
Land: 1703.1 sq. mi.; **Water:** 57.1 sq. mi. **Area Code:** 509

On the south-central border of WA; organized Mar 8, 1905 from Yakima and Klickitat counties.

Name origin: For Thomas Hart Benton (1782–1858), U.S. journalist and statesman; nicknamed "Old Bullion" for championing the use of gold and silver currency rather than paper money.

Benton City — City
ZIP: 99320 **Lat:** 46-16-04 N **Long:** 119-29-13 W
Pop: 1,806 (1990); 1,980 (1980) **Pop Density:** 1062.4
Land: 1.7 sq. mi.; **Water:** 0.0 sq. mi. **Elev:** 494 ft.

Finley — CDP
Lat: 46-10-08 N **Long:** 119-02-31 W
Pop: 4,897 (1990) **Pop Density:** 425.8
Land: 11.5 sq. mi.; **Water:** 3.0 sq. mi.

Highland — CDP
Lat: 46-07-53 N **Long:** 119-06-46 W
Pop: 3,656 (1990) **Pop Density:** 137.4
Land: 26.6 sq. mi.; **Water:** 0.0 sq. mi.

Kennewick — City
ZIP: 99336 **Lat:** 46-12-10 N **Long:** 119-10-13 W
Pop: 42,155 (1990); 34,397 (1980) **Pop Density:** 2097.3
Land: 20.1 sq. mi.; **Water:** 1.4 sq. mi.

In south-central WA on Columbia River, 10 mi. southeast of Richland. Incorporated 1904.

Name origin: From an Indian term meaning 'grassy place.'

Prosser — City
ZIP: 99350 **Lat:** 46-12-22 N **Long:** 119-45-58 W
Pop: 4,476 (1990); 3,896 (1980) **Pop Density:** 1091.7
Land: 4.1 sq. mi.; **Water:** 0.1 sq. mi.

Richland — City
ZIP: 99352 **Lat:** 46-17-38 N **Long:** 119-17-26 W
Pop: 32,315 (1990); 33,578 (1980) **Pop Density:** 1009.8
Land: 32.0 sq. mi.; **Water:** 2.9 sq. mi.

In south-central WA on the Columbia River, 50 mi. northwest of Walla Walla. Site of Hanford Nuclear Reservation. Incorporated 1958.

Name origin: For landowner Nelson Rich.

West Richland — City
ZIP: 99352 **Lat:** 46-19-28 N **Long:** 119-23-50 W
Pop: 3,962 (1990); 2,938 (1980) **Pop Density:** 188.7
Land: 21.0 sq. mi.; **Water:** 0.0 sq. mi.

Chelan County
County Seat: Wenatchee (ZIP: 98801)

Pop: 52,250 (1990); 45,061 (1980) **Pop Density:** 17.9
Land: 2921.6 sq. mi.; **Water:** 72.2 sq. mi. **Area Code:** 509

In north-central WA, east of Seattle; organized Mar 13, 1899 from Kittitas and Okanogan counties.

Name origin: For Chelan Lake; from a Salish Indian tribal name, *tsill-anne*, said to mean 'deep water.'

Cashmere — City
ZIP: 98815 **Lat:** 47-31-06 N **Long:** 120-28-03 W
Pop: 2,544 (1990); 2,240 (1980) **Pop Density:** 3180.0
Land: 0.8 sq. mi.; **Water:** 0.0 sq. mi. **Elev:** 795 ft.

Name origin: For the Vale of Kashmir in India; with a spelling variation. Formerly called Mission.

Chelan — City
ZIP: 98816 **Lat:** 47-50-46 N **Long:** 120-01-39 W
Pop: 2,969 (1990); 2,802 (1980) **Pop Density:** 957.7
Land: 3.1 sq. mi.; **Water:** 0.1 sq. mi.

Name origin: For the lake on which the town is located; from an Indian term meaning 'deep water' or 'bubbling water.'

Entiat — Town
ZIP: 98822 **Lat:** 47-40-31 N **Long:** 120-12-41 W
Pop: 449 (1990); 445 (1980) **Pop Density:** 561.3
Land: 0.8 sq. mi.; **Water:** 0.5 sq. mi.

Leavenworth — City
ZIP: 98826 **Lat:** 47-35-28 N **Long:** 120-39-51 W
Pop: 1,692 (1990); 1,522 (1980) **Pop Density:** 1692.0
Land: 1.0 sq. mi.; **Water:** 0.0 sq. mi.

Name origin: For the U.S. Army post in KS, so named by early settlers.

South Wenatchee — CDP
Lat: 47-23-28 N **Long:** 120-17-33 W
Pop: 1,207 (1990); 1,376 (1980) **Pop Density:** 635.3
Land: 1.9 sq. mi.; **Water:** 0.4 sq. mi.

Sunnyslope — CDP
Lat: 47-29-30 N **Long:** 120-20-28 W
Pop: 1,907 (1990); 1,485 (1980) **Pop Density:** 198.6
Land: 9.6 sq. mi.; **Water:** 0.4 sq. mi.

Wenatchee City
ZIP: 98801　　　　Lat: 47-25-32 N　Long: 120-19-29 W
Pop: 21,756 (1990); 17,257 (1980)　　Pop Density: 3566.6
Land: 6.1 sq. mi.; Water: 0.4 sq. mi.
In central WA on the Columbia River, 60 mi. north of Yakima. Incorporated 1893.
Name origin: From a Yakima term meaning 'river flowing from canyon.'

West Wenatchee CDP
　　　　　　　　Lat: 47-26-38 N　Long: 120-21-08 W
Pop: 2,220 (1990); 2,187 (1980)　　Pop Density: 472.3
Land: 4.7 sq. mi.; Water: 0.2 sq. mi.

Clallam County
County Seat: Port Angeles (ZIP: 98362)

Pop: 56,464 (1990); 51,648 (1980)　　　　Pop Density: 32.4
Land: 1745.2 sq. mi.; Water: 931.0 sq. mi.　　Area Code: 206

On the northwest coast of WA, bordered on the north by the Strait of Juan de Fuca; organized as Clalm County Apr 26, 1854 (prior to statehood) from Jefferson County; spelling changed soon after.
Name origin: For the Indian tribe; name means 'strong people.'

Forks Town
ZIP: 98331　　　　Lat: 47-56-49 N　Long: 124-23-23 W
Pop: 2,862 (1990); 3,060 (1980)　　Pop Density: 1908.0
Land: 1.5 sq. mi.; Water: 0.0 sq. mi.

Neah Bay CDP
　　　　　　　　Lat: 48-21-52 N　Long: 124-36-39 W
Pop: 916 (1990)　　Pop Density: 398.3
Land: 2.3 sq. mi.; Water: 0.0 sq. mi.

Port Angeles City
ZIP: 98362　　　　Lat: 48-11-27 N　Long: 123-27-34 W
Pop: 17,710 (1990); 17,311 (1980)　　Pop Density: 1807.1
Land: 9.8 sq. mi.; Water: 52.9 sq. mi.　　Elev: 32 ft.
In northwestern WA on the Strait of Juan de Fuca, 60 mi. northwest of Seattle, across the strait from Vancouver Island, British Columbia, Canada. Incorporated 1890.
Name origin: For the bay, itself originally named *Puerto de Nuestra Señora de los Angeles* 'Port of our Lady of the Angels' in 1791 by Juan Francisco de Eliza. Capt. George Vancouver (1757–98) shortened it to its present form in 1792.

Port Angeles East CDP
　　　　　　　　Lat: 48-06-21 N　Long: 123-22-33 W
Pop: 2,672 (1990); 2,786 (1980)　　Pop Density: 861.9
Land: 3.1 sq. mi.; Water: 0.5 sq. mi.

Sequim City
ZIP: 98382　　　　Lat: 48-04-38 N　Long: 123-06-18 W
Pop: 3,616 (1990); 3,013 (1980)　　Pop Density: 1506.7
Land: 2.4 sq. mi.; Water: 0.0 sq. mi.　　Elev: 183 ft.
Name origin: From a Clallum Indian term meaning 'quiet water.'

Clark County
County Seat: Vancouver (ZIP: 98660)

Pop: 238,053 (1990); 192,227 (1980)　　Pop Density: 379.1
Land: 627.9 sq. mi.; Water: 28.4 sq. mi.　　Area Code: 206

On the southwestern border of WA, north of Portland, OR; original county. Organized as Vancouver County Dec 21, 1845 (prior to statehood); name changed Sep 3, 1849.
Name origin: For William Clark (1770–1838), explorer and co-leader of the Lewis and Clark expedition (1804–06).

Battle Ground City
ZIP: 98604　　　　Lat: 45-46-55 N　Long: 122-32-27 W
Pop: 3,758 (1990); 2,774 (1980)　　Pop Density: 1503.2
Land: 2.5 sq. mi.; Water: 0.0 sq. mi.
Name origin: For a battle between the U.S. Army and local Indians during pioneer days.

Brush Prairie CDP
ZIP: 98606　　　　Lat: 45-43-53 N　Long: 122-33-04 W
Pop: 2,650 (1990)　　Pop Density: 339.7
Land: 7.8 sq. mi.; Water: 0.0 sq. mi.

Camas City
ZIP: 98607　　　　Lat: 45-35-16 N　Long: 122-25-24 W
Pop: 6,442 (1990); 5,681 (1980)　　Pop Density: 847.6
Land: 7.6 sq. mi.; Water: 1.7 sq. mi.
Name origin: For *Camassia esculenta*, an edible root of the lily family.

Cascade Park East CDP
　　　　　　　　Lat: 45-36-19 N　Long: 122-30-48 W
Pop: 6,996 (1990)　　Pop Density: 4372.5
Land: 1.6 sq. mi.; Water: 0.0 sq. mi.

Cascade Park West   CDP
Lat: 45-36-41 N Long: 122-32-16 W
Pop: 6,656 (1990)   Pop Density: 3915.3
Land: 1.7 sq. mi.; Water: 0.0 sq. mi.

Ellsworth North   CDP
Lat: 45-37-58 N Long: 122-34-16 W
Pop: 5,796 (1990)   Pop Density: 3864.0
Land: 1.5 sq. mi.; Water: 0.0 sq. mi.

Ellsworth South   CDP
Lat: 45-36-35 N Long: 122-34-01 W
Pop: 4,423 (1990)   Pop Density: 2106.2
Land: 2.1 sq. mi.; Water: 0.2 sq. mi.

Evergreen   CDP
ZIP: 98662   Lat: 45-37-38 N Long: 122-31-38 W
Pop: 11,249 (1990)   Pop Density: 2499.8
Land: 4.5 sq. mi.; Water: 0.0 sq. mi.

Felida   CDP
Lat: 45-43-00 N Long: 122-42-29 W
Pop: 3,109 (1990)   Pop Density: 1110.4
Land: 2.8 sq. mi.; Water: 0.1 sq. mi.

Five Corners   CDP
Lat: 45-41-05 N Long: 122-34-26 W
Pop: 6,776 (1990)   Pop Density: 1882.2
Land: 3.6 sq. mi.; Water: 0.0 sq. mi.

Hazel Dell North   CDP
Lat: 45-41-13 N Long: 122-38-52 W
Pop: 6,924 (1990); 15,386 (1980) Pop Density: 2564.4
Land: 2.7 sq. mi.; Water: 0.0 sq. mi.

Hazel Dell South   CDP
Lat: 45-40-12 N Long: 122-39-34 W
Pop: 5,796 (1990)   Pop Density: 2520.0
Land: 2.3 sq. mi.; Water: 0.0 sq. mi.

La Center   Town
ZIP: 98629   Lat: 45-51-50 N Long: 122-39-59 W
Pop: 451 (1990); 439 (1980)   Pop Density: 1127.5
Land: 0.4 sq. mi.; Water: 0.0 sq. mi.

Lake Shore   CDP
ZIP: 98665   Lat: 45-41-26 N Long: 122-41-23 W
Pop: 6,268 (1990)   Pop Density: 3687.1
Land: 1.7 sq. mi.; Water: 0.0 sq. mi.

Meadow Glade   CDP
Lat: 45-45-16 N Long: 122-33-14 W
Pop: 1,584 (1990)   Pop Density: 337.0
Land: 4.7 sq. mi.; Water: 0.0 sq. mi.

Minnehaha   CDP
Lat: 45-39-25 N Long: 122-37-34 W
Pop: 9,661 (1990)   Pop Density: 2611.1
Land: 3.7 sq. mi.; Water: 0.0 sq. mi.

Orchards North   CDP
Lat: 45-41-00 N Long: 122-31-32 W
Pop: 6,479 (1990); 8,828 (1980) Pop Density: 1751.1
Land: 3.7 sq. mi.; Water: 0.0 sq. mi.

Orchards South   CDP
Lat: 45-39-21 N Long: 122-32-17 W
Pop: 12,956 (1990)   Pop Density: 2195.9
Land: 5.9 sq. mi.; Water: 0.0 sq. mi.

Ridgefield   Town
ZIP: 98642   Lat: 45-49-02 N Long: 122-44-24 W
Pop: 1,297 (1990); 1,062 (1980) Pop Density: 1621.3
Land: 0.8 sq. mi.; Water: 0.0 sq. mi.

Salmon Creek   CDP
Lat: 45-42-48 N Long: 122-39-39 W
Pop: 11,989 (1990)   Pop Density: 1903.0
Land: 6.3 sq. mi.; Water: 0.0 sq. mi.

Vancouver   City
ZIP: 98661   Lat: 45-38-03 N Long: 122-38-35 W
Pop: 46,380 (1990); 42,834 (1980) Pop Density: 3289.4
Land: 14.1 sq. mi.; Water: 1.3 sq. mi.

In southwestern WA on the Columbia River, 35 mi. southeast of Longview on the WA-OR border. Founded 1824; incorporated 1857.

Name origin: For British explorer George Vancouver (1757–98).

Vancouver Mall   CDP
ZIP: 98662   Lat: 45-39-11 N Long: 122-35-01 W
Pop: 6,938 (1990)   Pop Density: 2312.7
Land: 3.0 sq. mi.; Water: 0.0 sq. mi.

Walnut Grove   CDP
Lat: 45-40-36 N Long: 122-36-27 W
Pop: 3,906 (1990)   Pop Density: 1220.6
Land: 3.2 sq. mi.; Water: 0.0 sq. mi.

Washougal   City
ZIP: 98671   Lat: 45-34-44 N Long: 122-20-38 W
Pop: 4,764 (1990); 3,834 (1980) Pop Density: 1832.3
Land: 2.6 sq. mi.; Water: 0.0 sq. mi.

Name origin: From an Indian term meaning 'rushing water.'

Woodland   City
ZIP: 98674   Lat: 45-53-58 N Long: 122-44-30 W
Pop: 94 (1990); 85 (1980)   Pop Density: 3133.3
Land: 0.03 sq. mi.; Water: 0.0 sq. mi.

Part of the town is also in Cowlitz County.

Yacolt   Town
ZIP: 98675   Lat: 45-51-56 N Long: 122-24-21 W
Pop: 600 (1990); 544 (1980)   Pop Density: 1200.0
Land: 0.5 sq. mi.; Water: 0.0 sq. mi.

Name origin: From an Indian term meaning 'haunted place.'

Columbia County
County Seat: Dayton (ZIP: 99328)

Pop: 4,024 (1990); 4,057 (1980)
Land: 868.8 sq. mi.; **Water:** 4.7 sq. mi.
Pop Density: 4.6
Area Code: 509

On the southeastern border of WA; organized Nov 11, 1875 (prior to statehood) from Walla Walla County.

Name origin: For the Columbia River.

Dayton — City
ZIP: 99328 **Lat:** 46-19-03 N **Long:** 117-58-36 W
Pop: 2,468 (1990); 2,565 (1980) **Pop Density:** 1645.3
Land: 1.5 sq. mi.; **Water:** 0.0 sq. mi. **Elev:** 1613 ft.
Founded 1870s.
Name origin: For founders Jesse and Elizabeth Day.

Starbuck — Town
ZIP: 99359 **Lat:** 46-31-08 N **Long:** 118-07-29 W
Pop: 170 (1990); 198 (1980) **Pop Density:** 850.0
Land: 0.2 sq. mi.; **Water:** 0.0 sq. mi. **Elev:** 645 ft.
Name origin: For NY businessman Gen. Starbuck, who gave the town church its first bell.

Cowlitz County
County Seat: Kelso (ZIP: 98626)

Pop: 82,119 (1990); 79,548 (1980)
Land: 1138.7 sq. mi.; **Water:** 27.7 sq. mi.
Pop Density: 72.1
Area Code: 206

In southwestern WA, north of Portland, OR; organized Apr 21, 1854 (prior to statehood) from Lewis County.

Name origin: For the Cowlitz River, which flows through the county; from an Indian tribal name; meaning uncertain but possibly 'river of shifting sand.'

Castle Rock — City
ZIP: 98611 **Lat:** 46-16-22 N **Long:** 122-54-05 W
Pop: 2,067 (1990); 2,162 (1980) **Pop Density:** 1722.5
Land: 1.2 sq. mi.; **Water:** 0.0 sq. mi.
Name origin: For its 150-ft.-high rock that resembles a castle.

Kalama — City
ZIP: 98625 **Lat:** 46-00-37 N **Long:** 122-50-27 W
Pop: 1,210 (1990); 1,216 (1980) **Pop Density:** 1008.3
Land: 1.2 sq. mi.; **Water:** 0.0 sq. mi.

Kelso — City
ZIP: 98626 **Lat:** 46-07-35 N **Long:** 122-53-28 W
Pop: 11,820 (1990); 11,129 (1980) **Pop Density:** 1535.1
Land: 7.7 sq. mi.; **Water:** 0.3 sq. mi.
In southwestern WA on the Cowlitz River, 60 mi. south of Olympia, near the OR border. Incorporated 1890.
Name origin: For surveyor Peter Crawford's former hometown in Scotland.

Longview — City
ZIP: 98632 **Lat:** 46-08-47 N **Long:** 122-57-17 W
Pop: 31,499 (1990); 31,052 (1980) **Pop Density:** 2624.9
Land: 12.0 sq. mi.; **Water:** 0.1 sq. mi. **Elev:** 21 ft.
In southwest WA at the confluence of the Columbia and Cowlitz rivers, 60 mi. south of Olympia, on the OR border. Incorporated 1924.
Name origin: For its long view of the Columbia River.

Longview Heights — CDP
Lat: 46-10-49 N **Long:** 122-57-21 W
Pop: 3,310 (1990) **Pop Density:** 788.1
Land: 4.2 sq. mi.; **Water:** 0.0 sq. mi.

West Longview — CDP
Lat: 46-10-04 N **Long:** 122-59-51 W
Pop: 3,163 (1990) **Pop Density:** 1317.9
Land: 2.4 sq. mi.; **Water:** 0.0 sq. mi.

West Side Highway — CDP
Lat: 46-11-05 N **Long:** 122-54-39 W
Pop: 3,641 (1990) **Pop Density:** 1456.4
Land: 2.5 sq. mi.; **Water:** 0.1 sq. mi.

Woodland — City
ZIP: 98674 **Lat:** 45-54-54 N **Long:** 122-44-34 W
Pop: 2,406 (1990); 2,256 (1980) **Pop Density:** 1266.3
Land: 1.9 sq. mi.; **Water:** 0.1 sq. mi.
Part of the town is also in Clark County.

Douglas County
County Seat: Waterville (ZIP: 98858)

Pop: 26,205 (1990); 22,144 (1980) **Pop Density:** 14.4
Land: 1820.6 sq. mi.; **Water:** 28.2 sq. mi. **Area Code:** 509
In east-central WA, west of Spokane; organized Nov 28, 1883 (prior to statehood) from Lincoln County, just four days after Lincoln Co. was formed.
Name origin: For Stephen Arnold Douglas (1813–61), U.S. orator and statesman.

Bridgeport — Town
ZIP: 98813 **Lat:** 48-00-20 N **Long:** 119-40-16 W
Pop: 1,498 (1990); 1,174 (1980) **Pop Density:** 1498.0
Land: 1.0 sq. mi.; **Water:** 0.0 sq. mi. **Elev:** 829 ft.

Coulee Dam — Town
ZIP: 99116 **Lat:** 47-57-53 N **Long:** 118-59-08 W
Pop: 207 (1990); 234 (1980) **Pop Density:** 2070.0
Land: 0.1 sq. mi.; **Water:** 0.0 sq. mi. **Elev:** 1145 ft.
Part of the town is also in Grant and Okanogan counties.

East Wenatchee — City
Lat: 47-25-01 N **Long:** 120-17-17 W
Pop: 2,701 (1990); 1,640 (1980) **Pop Density:** 2701.0
Land: 1.0 sq. mi.; **Water:** 0.0 sq. mi.

East Wenatchee Bench — CDP
ZIP: 98801 **Lat:** 47-25-33 N **Long:** 120-16-48 W
Pop: 12,539 (1990); 11,410 (1980) **Pop Density:** 1548.0
Land: 8.1 sq. mi.; **Water:** 0.7 sq. mi.

Mansfield — Town
ZIP: 98830 **Lat:** 47-48-41 N **Long:** 119-38-13 W
Pop: 311 (1990); 315 (1980) **Pop Density:** 1036.7
Land: 0.3 sq. mi.; **Water:** 0.0 sq. mi. **Elev:** 2262 ft.
Name origin: For Mansfield, OH, settler R.E. Darling's former home.

Rock Island — Town
ZIP: 98850 **Lat:** 47-22-18 N **Long:** 120-08-13 W
Pop: 524 (1990); 491 (1980) **Pop Density:** 873.3
Land: 0.6 sq. mi.; **Water:** 0.0 sq. mi.

Waterville — Town
ZIP: 98858 **Lat:** 47-38-52 N **Long:** 120-04-10 W
Pop: 995 (1990); 908 (1980) **Pop Density:** 1243.8
Land: 0.8 sq. mi.; **Water:** 0.0 sq. mi. **Elev:** 2622 ft.
Name origin: For a 30-ft. well that produced water. Originally called Jumper's Flat.

Ferry County
County Seat: Republic (ZIP: 99166)

Pop: 6,295 (1990); 5,811 (1980) **Pop Density:** 2.9
Land: 2204.0 sq. mi.; **Water:** 53.5 sq. mi. **Area Code:** 509
On northeastern border of WA, northwest of Spokane; organized as Eureka County Jan 12, 1899 from Stevens County; name changed Feb 16, 1899. Northern half is part of Colville National Forest; southern half comprises the Colville Indian Reservation.
Name origin: For Elisha Peyre Ferry (1825–95), first governor of WA (1889–93).

Inchelium — CDP
ZIP: 99138 **Lat:** 48-20-28 N **Long:** 118-14-50 W
Pop: 393 (1990) **Pop Density:** 14.8
Land: 26.5 sq. mi.; **Water:** 0.0 sq. mi.

Republic — Town
ZIP: 99166 **Lat:** 48-38-56 N **Long:** 118-43-54 W
Pop: 940 (1990); 1,018 (1980) **Pop Density:** 587.5
Land: 1.6 sq. mi.; **Water:** 0.0 sq. mi.

Franklin County
County Seat: Pasco (ZIP: 99301)

Pop: 37,473 (1990); 35,025 (1980)   **Pop Density:** 30.2
Land: 1242.2 sq. mi.; **Water:** 23.2 sq. mi.   **Area Code:** 509

In southeastern WA; organized Nov 28, 1883 (prior to statehood) from Whitman County.
Name origin: For Benjamin Franklin (1706–90), U.S. patriot, diplomat, and statesman.

Connell   Town
ZIP: 99326   **Lat:** 46-39-35 N   **Long:** 118-51-39 W
Pop: 2,005 (1990); 1,981 (1980)   **Pop Density:** 1542.3
Land: 1.3 sq. mi.; **Water:** 0.0 sq. mi.   **Elev:** 840 ft.

Kahlotus   Town
ZIP: 99335   **Lat:** 46-38-37 N   **Long:** 118-33-08 W
Pop: 167 (1990); 203 (1980)   **Pop Density:** 417.5
Land: 0.4 sq. mi.; **Water:** 0.0 sq. mi.   **Elev:** 901 ft.

Mesa   Town
ZIP: 99343   **Lat:** 46-34-23 N   **Long:** 118-59-58 W
Pop: 252 (1990); 278 (1980)   **Pop Density:** 157.5
Land: 1.6 sq. mi.; **Water:** 0.0 sq. mi.

Pasco   City
ZIP: 99301   **Lat:** 46-15-07 N   **Long:** 119-07-39 W
Pop: 20,337 (1990); 18,428 (1980)   **Pop Density:** 892.0
Land: 22.8 sq. mi.; **Water:** 0.5 sq. mi.

In south-central WA on the Columbia River, 35 mi. northwest of Walla Walla. Incorporated 1884.
Name origin: For Pasco, Mexico, so named by surveyor Virgil Bogue.

West Pasco   CDP
ZIP: 99301   **Lat:** 46-14-44 N   **Long:** 119-10-54 W
Pop: 7,312 (1990); 6,210 (1980)   **Pop Density:** 1044.6
Land: 7.0 sq. mi.; **Water:** 1.5 sq. mi.

Garfield County
County Seat: Pomeroy (ZIP: 99347)

Pop: 2,248 (1990); 2,468 (1980)   **Pop Density:** 3.2
Land: 710.5 sq. mi.; **Water:** 7.6 sq. mi.   **Area Code:** 509

In southeastern WA; organized Nov 29, 1881 (prior to statehood) from Columbia County.
Name origin: For James Abram Garfield (1831–81), twentieth U.S. president.

Pomeroy   City
ZIP: 99347   **Lat:** 46-28-26 N   **Long:** 117-35-43 W
Pop: 1,393 (1990); 1,716 (1980)   **Pop Density:** 773.9
Land: 1.8 sq. mi.; **Water:** 0.0 sq. mi.
Founded 1878.
Name origin: For its founder, Joseph Pomeroy.

Grant County
County Seat: Ephrata (ZIP: 98823)

Pop: 54,758 (1990); 48,522 (1980)   **Pop Density:** 20.5
Land: 2676.4 sq. mi.; **Water:** 115.0 sq. mi.   **Area Code:** 509

In east-central WA; organized Feb 24, 1909 from Douglas County.
Name origin: For Ulysses Simpson Grant (1822–85), Civil War general and eighteenth U.S. president.

Cascade Valley   CDP
Lat: 47-08-05 N   **Long:** 119-19-37 W
Pop: 1,288 (1990)   **Pop Density:** 536.7
Land: 2.4 sq. mi.; **Water:** 1.0 sq. mi.

Coulee City   Town
ZIP: 99115   **Lat:** 47-36-42 N   **Long:** 119-17-23 W
Pop: 568 (1990); 510 (1980)   **Pop Density:** 1136.0
Land: 0.5 sq. mi.; **Water:** 0.0 sq. mi.

In central WA at Grand Coulee Dam on the Columbia River, 78 mi. northwest of Spokane.

WASHINGTON, Grant County

Coulee Dam — Town
ZIP: 99116   **Lat:** 47-57-42 N   **Long:** 118-59-08 W
Pop: 1 (1990); 4 (1980)   **Pop Density:** 100.0
Land: 0.01 sq. mi.; **Water:** 0.0 sq. mi.   **Elev:** 1145 ft.
Part of the town is also in Douglas and Okanogan counties.

Electric City — Town
ZIP: 99123   **Lat:** 47-55-48 N   **Long:** 119-02-10 W
Pop: 910 (1990); 927 (1980)   **Pop Density:** 1820.0
Land: 0.5 sq. mi.; **Water:** 0.0 sq. mi.   **Elev:** 1655 ft.
Name origin: For its being a center of hydroelectric power.

Ephrata — City
ZIP: 98823   **Lat:** 47-18-44 N   **Long:** 119-32-12 W
Pop: 5,349 (1990); 5,359 (1980)   **Pop Density:** 810.5
Land: 6.6 sq. mi.; **Water:** 0.0 sq. mi.
Name origin: For the ancient name for Bethlehem, so named by Great Northern Railway surveyors.

George — Town
ZIP: 98824   **Lat:** 47-04-42 N   **Long:** 119-51-21 W
Pop: 253 (1990); 261 (1980)   **Pop Density:** 421.7
Land: 0.6 sq. mi.; **Water:** 0.0 sq. mi.   **Elev:** 222 ft.
Name origin: For Indian George, an early trapper and fur trader.

Grand Coulee — City
ZIP: 99133   **Lat:** 47-56-22 N   **Long:** 119-00-14 W
Pop: 984 (1990); 1,180 (1980)   **Pop Density:** 984.0
Land: 1.0 sq. mi.; **Water:** 0.0 sq. mi.
Name origin: For its location near the gigantic coulee that was the ancient bed of the Columbia River.

Hartline — Town
ZIP: 99135   **Lat:** 47-41-21 N   **Long:** 119-06-21 W
Pop: 176 (1990); 165 (1980)   **Pop Density:** 586.7
Land: 0.3 sq. mi.; **Water:** 0.0 sq. mi.
Name origin: For early settler John Hartline.

Krupp — Town
Lat: 47-24-35 N   **Long:** 118-59-16 W
Pop: 53 (1990); 83 (1980)   **Pop Density:** 88.3
Land: 0.6 sq. mi.; **Water:** 0.0 sq. mi.

Mattawa — Town
Lat: 46-44-11 N   **Long:** 119-54-02 W
Pop: 941 (1990); 299 (1980)   **Pop Density:** 2352.5
Land: 0.4 sq. mi.; **Water:** 0.0 sq. mi.   **Elev:** 778 ft.

Moses Lake — City
ZIP: 98837   **Lat:** 47-06-56 N   **Long:** 119-17-10 W
Pop: 11,235 (1990); 10,629 (1980)   **Pop Density:** 1234.6
Land: 9.1 sq. mi.; **Water:** 1.6 sq. mi.
In central WA on Moses Lake, 60 mi. north of Richland. Incorporated 1938.
Name origin: For the lake, itself named for Chief Moses, whose tribe lived near the shores of the lake.

Moses Lake North — CDP
ZIP: 98837   **Lat:** 47-11-42 N   **Long:** 119-19-21 W
Pop: 3,677 (1990); 3,348 (1980)   **Pop Density:** 602.8
Land: 6.1 sq. mi.; **Water:** 0.0 sq. mi.

Quincy — Town
ZIP: 98848   **Lat:** 47-14-01 N   **Long:** 119-51-04 W
Pop: 3,738 (1990); 3,525 (1980)   **Pop Density:** 2076.7
Land: 1.8 sq. mi.; **Water:** 0.0 sq. mi.

Royal City — Town
ZIP: 99357   **Lat:** 46-53-56 N   **Long:** 119-36-50 W
Pop: 1,104 (1990); 676 (1980)   **Pop Density:** 849.2
Land: 1.3 sq. mi.; **Water:** 0.0 sq. mi.

Soap Lake — City
ZIP: 98851   **Lat:** 47-23-17 N   **Long:** 119-29-22 W
Pop: 1,149 (1990); 1,196 (1980)   **Pop Density:** 1149.0
Land: 1.0 sq. mi.; **Water:** 0.0 sq. mi.

Warden — Town
ZIP: 98857   **Lat:** 46-58-04 N   **Long:** 119-02-49 W
Pop: 1,639 (1990); 1,479 (1980)   **Pop Density:** 1092.7
Land: 1.5 sq. mi.; **Water:** 0.0 sq. mi.
Name origin: For an eastern investor named Warden, so named by railroad official H. R. Williams.

Wilson Creek — Town
Lat: 47-25-21 N   **Long:** 119-06-56 W
Pop: 148 (1990); 222 (1980)   **Pop Density:** 148.0
Land: 1.0 sq. mi.; **Water:** 0.0 sq. mi.

Grays Harbor County
County Seat: Montesano (ZIP: 98563)

Pop: 64,175 (1990); 66,314 (1980)   **Pop Density:** 33.5
Land: 1917.3 sq. mi.; **Water:** 307.3 sq. mi.   **Area Code:** 206
On the west-central coast of WA, E of Olympia; organized as Chehalis County Apr 14, 1854 (prior to statehood); name changed Mar 15, 1915.
Name origin: For Robert Gray (1755–1806), an American who discovered Grays Harbor and named it *Bulfinch* for an owner of his ship. Formerly called *Puerto Grek* by Spanish explorer Martinez y Zayas and *Whidbey* or *Whitbey Harbor* by British explorer David Douglas.

Aberdeen — City
ZIP: 98520   **Lat:** 46-58-37 N   **Long:** 123-48-30 W
Pop: 16,565 (1990); 18,739 (1980)   **Pop Density:** 1562.7
Land: 10.6 sq. mi.; **Water:** 1.6 sq. mi.
In southwestern WA on Grays Harbor, 45 mi. west of Olympia. Incorporated 1890.
Name origin: For the town in Scotland.

Central Park — CDP
ZIP: 98520   **Lat:** 46-58-14 N   **Long:** 123-42-05 W
Pop: 2,669 (1990); 2,709 (1980)   **Pop Density:** 762.6
Land: 3.5 sq. mi.; **Water:** 0.0 sq. mi.

Chehalis Village
CDP
Lat: 46-48-13 N Long: 123-10-04 W
Pop: 282 (1990) **Pop Density:** 282.0
Land: 1.0 sq. mi.; **Water:** 0.0 sq. mi.

Cosmopolis
City
ZIP: 98537 **Lat:** 46-57-19 N **Long:** 123-46-11 W
Pop: 1,372 (1990); 1,575 (1980) **Pop Density:** 1143.3
Land: 1.2 sq. mi.; **Water:** 0.1 sq. mi. **Elev:** 12 ft.

Elma
City
ZIP: 98541 **Lat:** 47-00-18 N **Long:** 123-24-03 W
Pop: 3,011 (1990); 2,720 (1980) **Pop Density:** 2007.3
Land: 1.5 sq. mi.; **Water:** 0.0 sq. mi.
Name origin: For early Puget Sound pioneer Elma Austin.

Hoquiam
City
ZIP: 98550 **Lat:** 46-58-31 N **Long:** 123-53-11 W
Pop: 8,972 (1990); 9,719 (1980) **Pop Density:** 1401.9
Land: 6.4 sq. mi.; **Water:** 4.1 sq. mi.
Name origin: For the Hoquiam River, at the mouth of which the town is located. From the name of an Indian band meaning 'hungry for wood,' a reference to their custom of using driftwood from the river for fuel.

McCleary
Town
ZIP: 98557 **Lat:** 47-03-18 N **Long:** 123-16-03 W
Pop: 1,235 (1990); 1,419 (1980) **Pop Density:** 1235.0
Land: 1.0 sq. mi.; **Water:** 0.0 sq. mi. **Elev:** 257 ft.
Name origin: For a local timber company president, Henry McCleary.

Montesano
City
ZIP: 98563 **Lat:** 47-00-52 N **Long:** 123-35-02 W
Pop: 3,064 (1990); 3,247 (1980) **Pop Density:** 306.4
Land: 10.0 sq. mi.; **Water:** 0.1 sq. mi. **Elev:** 66 ft.
In western WA on the Chehalis River, 11 mi. east of Aberdeen.
Name origin: From Spanish *monte* 'mountain' and *sano* 'healthy.'

Oakville
City
ZIP: 98568 **Lat:** 46-50-25 N **Long:** 123-14-00 W
Pop: 493 (1990); 537 (1980) **Pop Density:** 1232.5
Land: 0.4 sq. mi.; **Water:** 0.0 sq. mi. **Elev:** 90 ft.

Ocean Shores
City
ZIP: 98569 **Lat:** 46-58-15 N **Long:** 124-09-08 W
Pop: 2,301 (1990); 1,692 (1980) **Pop Density:** 267.6
Land: 8.6 sq. mi.; **Water:** 3.4 sq. mi.
In western WA on the Pacific coast at North Bay, 12 mi. west of Hoquiam.

Taholah
CDP
Lat: 47-20-24 N Long: 124-16-48 W
Pop: 788 (1990) **Pop Density:** 463.5
Land: 1.7 sq. mi.; **Water:** 0.3 sq. mi.

Westport
City
ZIP: 98595 **Lat:** 46-53-31 N **Long:** 124-06-39 W
Pop: 1,892 (1990); 1,954 (1980) **Pop Density:** 525.6
Land: 3.6 sq. mi.; **Water:** 0.6 sq. mi. **Elev:** 12 ft.
Name origin: For its location on the west side of Chehalis Point Spit. Formerly called Peterson's Point.

Island County
County Seat: Coupeville (ZIP: 98239)

Pop: 60,195 (1990); 44,048 (1980) **Pop Density:** 288.6
Land: 208.6 sq. mi.; **Water:** 308.8 sq. mi. **Area Code:** 206
In northwestern WA, bounded on the north by Deception Pass, on the east by Skagit Bay, on the south by Admiralty Inlet, and on the west by the Strait of Juan de Fuca. Organized Jan 6, 1853 (prior to statehood) from either King County or Thurston County.
Name origin: So named because the county is wholly composed of islands.

Ault Field
Military Facility
Lat: 48-20-13 N Long: 122-40-34 W
Pop: 3,795 (1990); 2,553 (1980) **Pop Density:** 550.0
Land: 6.9 sq. mi.; **Water:** 3.5 sq. mi.

Clinton
CDP
ZIP: 98236 **Lat:** 47-58-44 N **Long:** 122-21-29 W
Pop: 1,564 (1990) **Pop Density:** 332.8
Land: 4.7 sq. mi.; **Water:** 4.3 sq. mi.

Coupeville
Town
ZIP: 98239 **Lat:** 48-13-02 N **Long:** 122-40-32 W
Pop: 1,377 (1990); 1,006 (1980) **Pop Density:** 1059.2
Land: 1.3 sq. mi.; **Water:** 0.0 sq. mi.
Name origin: For founder Capt. Thomas Coupe.

Freeland
CDP
ZIP: 98249 **Lat:** 48-00-46 N **Long:** 122-32-15 W
Pop: 1,278 (1990) **Pop Density:** 277.8
Land: 4.6 sq. mi.; **Water:** 0.9 sq. mi.

Langley
City
ZIP: 98260 **Lat:** 48-02-13 N **Long:** 122-24-26 W
Pop: 845 (1990); 650 (1980) **Pop Density:** 1056.3
Land: 0.8 sq. mi.; **Water:** 0.0 sq. mi.
Name origin: For Judge J.W. Langley of Seattle, an original landowner.

Oak Harbor
City
ZIP: 98277 **Lat:** 48-17-34 N **Long:** 122-37-21 W
Pop: 17,176 (1990); 12,271 (1980) **Pop Density:** 2260.0
Land: 7.6 sq. mi.; **Water:** 0.0 sq. mi.
In northwestern WA, 50 mi. northwest of Seattle. Incorporated 1915.

WASHINGTON, Jefferson County　　　　　　　　　　　　　　　　　　　　　　　　　　　　　　*American Places Dictionary*

Jefferson County
County Seat: Port Townsend (ZIP: 98368)

Pop: 20,146 (1990); 15,965 (1980)　　　　**Pop Density:** 11.1
Land: 1808.8 sq. mi.; **Water:** 369.2 sq. mi.　　**Area Code:** 206

On the northwestern coast of WA, E of Seattle; original county; organized Dec 23, 1852 (prior to statehood).

Name origin: For Thomas Jefferson (1743–1826), U.S. patriot and statesman; third U.S. president.

Hadlock-Irondale　　　　　　　　　　CDP
Lat: 48-02-56 N **Long:** 122-46-17 W
Pop: 2,742 (1990); 1,752 (1980)　　**Pop Density:** 609.3
Land: 4.5 sq. mi.; **Water:** 2.2 sq. mi.

Port Townsend　　　　　　　　　　City
ZIP: 98368　　**Lat:** 48-07-19 N **Long:** 122-46-45 W
Pop: 7,001 (1990); 6,067 (1980)　　**Pop Density:** 1000.1
Land: 7.0 sq. mi.; **Water:** 2.5 sq. mi.

In western WA at the entrance to Puget Sound, 30 mi. northwest of Everett. Settled 1851; chartered as city 1860.

Name origin: For Marquis Townsend, so named by British explorer George Vancouver (1757–98).

King County
County Seat: Seattle (ZIP: 98104)

Pop: 1,507,320 (1990); 1,269,900 (1980)　　**Pop Density:** 709.0
Land: 2126.1 sq. mi.; **Water:** 180.7 sq. mi.　　**Area Code:** 206

In west-central WA, bounded on west by Puget Sound; organized Dec 22, 1852 (prior to statehood) from Thurston County.

Name origin: For William Rufus King (1786–1853), U.S. senator from AL (1819–44; 1848–52) and vice president for six weeks before his death. In 1986 it was decided the name would honor Martin Luther King, Jr. (1929–68), slain civil rights leader.

Algona　　　　　　　　　　　　　　City
Lat: 47-17-01 N **Long:** 122-15-00 W
Pop: 1,694 (1990); 1,467 (1980)　　**Pop Density:** 1303.1
Land: 1.3 sq. mi.; **Water:** 0.0 sq. mi.

Name origin: From an Indian term meaning 'valley of flowers.'

Auburn　　　　　　　　　　　　　　City
ZIP: 98002　　**Lat:** 47-17-56 N **Long:** 122-12-42 W
Pop: 33,102 (1990); 26,417 (1980)　　**Pop Density:** 1680.3
Land: 19.7 sq. mi.; **Water:** 0.0 sq. mi.

In west-central WA on Puget Sound, 20 mi. south of Seattle. Incorporated 1891.

Name origin: For Auburn, Yorkshire, England. Originally called Slaughter.

Beaux Arts Village　　　　　　　　Town
Lat: 47-35-09 N **Long:** 122-12-11 W
Pop: 303 (1990); 328 (1980)　　**Pop Density:** 3030.0
Land: 0.1 sq. mi.; **Water:** 0.1 sq. mi.

Bellevue　　　　　　　　　　　　　City
ZIP: 98009　　**Lat:** 47-36-12 N **Long:** 122-09-18 W
Pop: 86,874 (1990); 73,903 (1980)　　**Pop Density:** 3290.7
Land: 26.4 sq. mi.; **Water:** 3.1 sq. mi.

In west-central WA directly east of Seattle. Incorporated 1953.

Name origin: For an old English name or from French 'beautiful view.'

Black Diamond　　　　　　　　　　City
ZIP: 98010　　**Lat:** 47-18-42 N **Long:** 122-00-35 W
Pop: 1,422 (1990); 1,170 (1980)　　**Pop Density:** 444.4
Land: 3.2 sq. mi.; **Water:** 0.1 sq. mi.

Name origin: For the Black River, which runs through the county.

Bothell　　　　　　　　　　　　　　City
ZIP: 98011　　**Lat:** 47-45-36 N **Long:** 122-11-48 W
Pop: 11,986 (1990); 7,943 (1980)　　**Pop Density:** 2305.0
Land: 5.2 sq. mi.; **Water:** 0.0 sq. mi.

In west-central WA, 12 mi. north of Seattle. Incorporated 1909. Part of the town is also in Snohomish County.

Name origin: For the Bothell family, who were local businessmen and politicians.

Bryn Mawr-Skyway　　　　　　　　CDP
ZIP: 98178　　**Lat:** 47-29-42 N **Long:** 122-14-17 W
Pop: 12,514 (1990)　　**Pop Density:** 3910.6
Land: 3.2 sq. mi.; **Water:** 0.2 sq. mi.

Burien　　　　　　　　　　　　　　CDP
ZIP: 98166　　**Lat:** 47-27-53 N **Long:** 122-20-47 W
Pop: 25,089 (1990); 23,189 (1980)　　**Pop Density:** 3920.2
Land: 6.4 sq. mi.; **Water:** 1.3 sq. mi.

Carnation
City
ZIP: 98014   Lat: 47-38-46 N   Long: 121-54-33 W
Pop: 1,243 (1990); 913 (1980)   Pop Density: 1553.8
Land: 0.8 sq. mi.; Water: 0.0 sq. mi.
Name origin: For the state flower, so named by the state legislature in 1917.

Cascade-Fairwood
CDP
ZIP: 98055   Lat: 47-26-57 N   Long: 122-09-45 W
Pop: 30,107 (1990)   Pop Density: 3272.5
Land: 9.2 sq. mi.; Water: 0.0 sq. mi.

Clyde Hill
Town
Lat: 47-37-45 N   Long: 122-13-03 W
Pop: 2,972 (1990); 3,229 (1980)   Pop Density: 2972.0
Land: 1.0 sq. mi.; Water: 0.0 sq. mi.
Name origin: For an early pioneer.

Covington-Sawyer-Wilderness
CDP
Lat: 47-21-10 N   Long: 122-04-23 W
Pop: 24,321 (1990)   Pop Density: 1198.1
Land: 20.3 sq. mi.; Water: 0.7 sq. mi.

Des Moines
City
ZIP: 98188   Lat: 47-23-43 N   Long: 122-18-34 W
Pop: 17,283 (1990); 7,378 (1980)   Pop Density: 5083.2
Land: 3.4 sq. mi.; Water: 0.0 sq. mi.
In west-central WA on Puget Sound, 15 mi. south of Seattle. Incorporated 1959.
Name origin: For Des Moines, IA.

Duvall
City
ZIP: 98019   Lat: 47-44-01 N   Long: 121-58-09 W
Pop: 2,770 (1990); 729 (1980)   Pop Density: 1978.6
Land: 1.4 sq. mi.; Water: 0.0 sq. mi.
Name origin: For its first landowner, pioneer James Duval.

Eastgate
CDP
Lat: 47-34-20 N   Long: 122-08-05 W
Pop: 4,434 (1990); 8,341 (1980)   Pop Density: 3695.0
Land: 1.2 sq. mi.; Water: 0.0 sq. mi.

East Hill-Meridian
CDP
Lat: 47-23-23 N   Long: 122-10-19 W
Pop: 42,696 (1990)   Pop Density: 2439.8
Land: 17.5 sq. mi.; Water: 0.3 sq. mi.

East Renton Highlands
CDP
ZIP: 98024   Lat: 47-29-06 N   Long: 122-06-40 W
Pop: 13,218 (1990); 12,033 (1980)   Pop Density: 1283.3
Land: 10.3 sq. mi.; Water: 0.1 sq. mi.

Enumclaw
City
ZIP: 98022   Lat: 47-12-03 N   Long: 121-59-20 W
Pop: 7,227 (1990); 5,427 (1980)   Pop Density: 1901.8
Land: 3.8 sq. mi.; Water: 0.0 sq. mi.
Name origin: From an Indian term meaning 'home of the evil spirit.'

Fall City
CDP
ZIP: 98024   Lat: 47-33-58 N   Long: 121-54-07 W
Pop: 1,582 (1990); 1,528 (1980)   Pop Density: 1216.9
Land: 1.3 sq. mi.; Water: 0.0 sq. mi.

Federal Way
CDP
ZIP: 98003   Lat: 47-18-42 N   Long: 122-20-26 W
Pop: 67,554 (1990)   Pop Density: 3429.1
Land: 19.7 sq. mi.; Water: 1.1 sq. mi.

Hunts Point
Town
Lat: 47-38-19 N   Long: 122-13-38 W
Pop: 513 (1990); 480 (1980)   Pop Density: 1710.0
Land: 0.3 sq. mi.; Water: 0.0 sq. mi.

Inglewood-Finn Hill
CDP
ZIP: 98011   Lat: 47-43-33 N   Long: 122-14-05 W
Pop: 29,132 (1990); 12,467 (1980)   Pop Density: 3236.9
Land: 9.0 sq. mi.; Water: 2.2 sq. mi.

Issaquah
City
ZIP: 98027   Lat: 47-31-56 N   Long: 122-02-18 W
Pop: 7,786 (1990); 5,536 (1980)   Pop Density: 1526.7
Land: 5.1 sq. mi.; Water: 0.0 sq. mi.

Kenmore
CDP
ZIP: 98028   Lat: 47-45-52 N   Long: 122-14-33 W
Pop: 8,917 (1990); 7,281 (1980)   Pop Density: 2622.6
Land: 3.4 sq. mi.; Water: 0.1 sq. mi.

Kent
City
ZIP: 98031   Lat: 47-23-39 N   Long: 122-14-18 W
Pop: 37,960 (1990); 22,961 (1980)   Pop Density: 2008.5
Land: 18.9 sq. mi.; Water: 0.0 sq. mi.
In west-central WA, 15 mi. south of Seattle. Incorporated 1890.
Name origin: For the county of Kent, England.

Kingsgate
CDP
ZIP: 98011   Lat: 47-43-50 N   Long: 122-10-01 W
Pop: 14,259 (1990); 12,652 (1980)   Pop Density: 4193.8
Land: 3.4 sq. mi.; Water: 0.0 sq. mi.

Kirkland
City
ZIP: 98033   Lat: 47-41-04 N   Long: 122-11-38 W
Pop: 40,052 (1990); 18,785 (1980)   Pop Density: 3743.2
Land: 10.7 sq. mi.; Water: 1.8 sq. mi.
In west-central WA, 10 mi. northeast of Seattle. Incorporated 1905.
Name origin: For millionaire ironmaker Peter Kirk, who lived and died nearby.

Lake Forest North
CDP
ZIP: 98155   Lat: 47-46-03 N   Long: 122-17-07 W
Pop: 8,002 (1990); 7,995 (1980)   Pop Density: 4211.6
Land: 1.9 sq. mi.; Water: 0.2 sq. mi.

Lake Forest Park
City
ZIP: 98155   Lat: 47-45-45 N   Long: 122-17-10 W
Pop: 4,031 (1990); 2,485 (1980)   Pop Density: 3664.5
Land: 1.1 sq. mi.; Water: 0.0 sq. mi.

Lakeland North
CDP
ZIP: 98002   Lat: 47-19-45 N   Long: 122-16-40 W
Pop: 14,402 (1990); 5,236 (1980)   Pop Density: 2149.6
Land: 6.7 sq. mi.; Water: 0.1 sq. mi.

Lakeland South
CDP
ZIP: 98002   Lat: 47-16-38 N   Long: 122-16-57 W
Pop: 9,027 (1990); 5,225 (1980)   Pop Density: 1556.4
Land: 5.8 sq. mi.; Water: 0.1 sq. mi.

Lea Hill
CDP
Lat: 47-19-34 N   Long: 122-10-49 W
Pop: 6,876 (1990)   Pop Density: 1206.3
Land: 5.7 sq. mi.; Water: 0.0 sq. mi.

Maple Valley
CDP
ZIP: 98038   Lat: 47-24-04 N   Long: 122-01-32 W
Pop: 1,211 (1990)   Pop Density: 637.4
Land: 1.9 sq. mi.; Water: 0.0 sq. mi.

WASHINGTON, King County

Medina — City
ZIP: 98039 **Lat:** 47-36-58 N **Long:** 122-14-11 W
Pop: 2,981 (1990); 3,220 (1980) **Pop Density:** 2129.3
Land: 1.4 sq. mi.; **Water:** 2.5 sq. mi.
Name origin: For Medina, Turkey.

Mercer Island — City
ZIP: 98040 **Lat:** 47-34-09 N **Long:** 122-13-51 W
Pop: 20,816 (1990); 21,522 (1980) **Pop Density:** 3252.5
Land: 6.4 sq. mi.; **Water:** 6.7 sq. mi.
In west-central WA on Lake Washington, 5 mi. east of Seattle. Incorporated 1960.
Name origin: For early settler, Asa Mercer.

Milton — Town
ZIP: 98354 **Lat:** 47-15-41 N **Long:** 122-18-47 W
Pop: 697 (1990); 218 (1980) **Pop Density:** 1742.5
Land: 0.4 sq. mi.; **Water:** 0.0 sq. mi.
Part of the town is also in Pierce County.

Mirrormont — CDP
Lat: 47-27-45 N **Long:** 121-59-39 W
Pop: 2,360 (1990) **Pop Density:** 786.7
Land: 3.0 sq. mi.; **Water:** 0.0 sq. mi.

Newport Hills — CDP
ZIP: 98002 **Lat:** 47-32-51 N **Long:** 122-10-26 W
Pop: 14,736 (1990); 12,245 (1980) **Pop Density:** 2497.6
Land: 5.9 sq. mi.; **Water:** 0.1 sq. mi.

Normandy Park — City
ZIP: 98166 **Lat:** 47-26-41 N **Long:** 122-21-20 W
Pop: 6,709 (1990); 4,268 (1980) **Pop Density:** 2795.4
Land: 2.4 sq. mi.; **Water:** 4.2 sq. mi.
Name origin: For Normandy, France.

North Bend — City
ZIP: 98045 **Lat:** 47-29-44 N **Long:** 121-47-19 W
Pop: 2,578 (1990); 1,701 (1980) **Pop Density:** 889.0
Land: 2.9 sq. mi.; **Water:** 0.0 sq. mi. **Elev:** 442 ft.
Name origin: From its location at the north bend of the South Fork of the Snoqualmie River.

North City-Ridgecrest — CDP
ZIP: 98155 **Lat:** 47-45-03 N **Long:** 122-18-47 W
Pop: 13,832 (1990) **Pop Density:** 4940.0
Land: 2.8 sq. mi.; **Water:** 0.0 sq. mi.

North Hill — CDP
ZIP: 98166 **Lat:** 47-25-09 N **Long:** 122-19-20 W
Pop: 5,706 (1990); 10,170 (1980) **Pop Density:** 3804.0
Land: 1.5 sq. mi.; **Water:** 0.0 sq. mi.

Pacific — City
ZIP: 98047 **Lat:** 47-15-56 N **Long:** 122-14-48 W
Pop: 4,622 (1990); 2,261 (1980) **Pop Density:** 2311.0
Land: 2.0 sq. mi.; **Water:** 0.0 sq. mi.
Part of the town is also in Pierce County.
Name origin: For the Pacific Ocean.

Pine Lake — CDP
ZIP: 98027 **Lat:** 47-34-44 N **Long:** 122-02-41 W
Pop: 13,940 (1990) **Pop Density:** 1315.1
Land: 10.6 sq. mi.; **Water:** 2.1 sq. mi.

Redmond — City
ZIP: 98052 **Lat:** 47-40-27 N **Long:** 122-06-53 W
Pop: 35,800 (1990); 23,318 (1980) **Pop Density:** 2486.1
Land: 14.4 sq. mi.; **Water:** 0.7 sq. mi.
In west-central WA, 10 mi. northeast of Seattle. Incorporated 1912.
Name origin: For founder and first postmaster, Luke McRedmond, who arrived in 1852.

Renton — City
ZIP: 98058 **Lat:** 47-28-54 N **Long:** 122-11-47 W
Pop: 41,688 (1990); 31,031 (1980) **Pop Density:** 2573.3
Land: 16.2 sq. mi.; **Water:** 0.3 sq. mi.
In west-central WA, 10 mi. southeast of Seattle. Incorporated 1901.
Name origin: For Capt. William Renton of the Port Blakely Mill Company.

Richmond Beach-Innis Arden — CDP
ZIP: 98160 **Lat:** 47-45-18 N **Long:** 122-22-24 W
Pop: 7,242 (1990); 6,700 (1980) **Pop Density:** 2336.1
Land: 3.1 sq. mi.; **Water:** 1.0 sq. mi.

Richmond Highlands — CDP
ZIP: 98133 **Lat:** 47-45-32 N **Long:** 122-20-34 W
Pop: 26,037 (1990); 24,463 (1980) **Pop Density:** 5105.3
Land: 5.1 sq. mi.; **Water:** 0.0 sq. mi.

Riverton-Boulevard Park — CDP
ZIP: 98188 **Lat:** 47-29-51 N **Long:** 122-18-33 W
Pop: 15,337 (1990); 14,182 (1980) **Pop Density:** 3651.7
Land: 4.2 sq. mi.; **Water:** 0.1 sq. mi.

Sahalee — CDP
Lat: 47-38-05 N **Long:** 122-03-14 W
Pop: 13,951 (1990) **Pop Density:** 1743.9
Land: 8.0 sq. mi.; **Water:** 1.1 sq. mi.

Sea-Tac — CDP
ZIP: 98188 **Lat:** 47-26-36 N **Long:** 122-17-51 W
Pop: 22,694 (1990) **Pop Density:** 2315.7
Land: 9.8 sq. mi.; **Water:** 0.2 sq. mi.

Seattle — City
ZIP: 98101 **Lat:** 47-37-18 N **Long:** 122-21-01 W
Pop: 516,259 (1990); 493,846 (1980) **Pop Density:** 6153.3
Land: 83.9 sq. mi.; **Water:** 58.7 sq. mi.
In west-central WA on Puget Sound. Settled 1851; incorporated 1865. Largest city and a major port. Major industries: airplane production; lumbering; commercial fishing. Site of the University of Washington.
Name origin: For Chief Seattle (or Sealth, 1786?–1866) of the Suquamish tribe, who was very friendly to white settlers. From an Indian term meaning 'little place where one crosses over,' a reference to an Indian trail terminating at Lake Washington.

Sheridan Beach — CDP
ZIP: 98155 **Lat:** 47-44-41 N **Long:** 122-17-12 W
Pop: 6,518 (1990); 6,873 (1980) **Pop Density:** 4345.3
Land: 1.5 sq. mi.; **Water:** 0.6 sq. mi.

Skykomish — Town
ZIP: 98288 **Lat:** 47-42-40 N **Long:** 121-21-26 W
Pop: 273 (1990); 209 (1980) **Pop Density:** 910.0
Land: 0.3 sq. mi.; **Water:** 0.0 sq. mi. **Elev:** 931 ft.

American Places Dictionary   WASHINGTON, Kitsap County

Snoqualmie   City
ZIP: 98065   **Lat:** 47-31-27 N   **Long:** 121-49-03 W
Pop: 1,546 (1990); 1,370 (1980)   **Pop Density:** 498.7
Land: 3.1 sq. mi.; **Water:** 0.0 sq. mi.

Tukwila   City
ZIP: 98188   **Lat:** 47-28-39 N   **Long:** 122-16-05 W
Pop: 11,874 (1990); 3,578 (1980)   **Pop Density:** 1448.0
Land: 8.2 sq. mi.; **Water:** 0.1 sq. mi.   **Elev:** 134 ft.
Incorporated 1908.
Name origin: From an Indian term meaning 'land of the hazelnuts.'

West Lake Sammamish   CDP
Lat: 47-34-40 N   **Long:** 122-05-59 W
Pop: 6,087 (1990)   **Pop Density:** 4347.9
Land: 1.4 sq. mi.; **Water:** 2.0 sq. mi.

White Center-Shorewood   CDP
ZIP: 98106   **Lat:** 47-30-07 N   **Long:** 122-20-59 W
Pop: 20,531 (1990); 19,362 (1980)   **Pop Density:** 5264.4
Land: 3.9 sq. mi.; **Water:** 0.2 sq. mi.

Woodinville   CDP
ZIP: 98072   **Lat:** 47-44-46 N   **Long:** 122-06-42 W
Pop: 23,654 (1990)   **Pop Density:** 1314.1
Land: 18.0 sq. mi.; **Water:** 0.1 sq. mi.

Woodmont Beach   CDP
Lat: 47-21-42 N   **Long:** 122-18-58 W
Pop: 7,493 (1990)   **Pop Density:** 3122.1
Land: 2.4 sq. mi.; **Water:** 1.1 sq. mi.

Yarrow Point   Town
Lat: 47-38-44 N   **Long:** 122-12-55 W
Pop: 962 (1990); 1,064 (1980)   **Pop Density:** 2405.0
Land: 0.4 sq. mi.; **Water:** 0.0 sq. mi.

Kitsap County
County Seat: Port Orchard (ZIP: 98366)

Pop: 189,731 (1990); 147,152 (1980)   **Pop Density:** 479.1
Land: 396.0 sq. mi.; **Water:** 170.0 sq. mi.   **Area Code:** 206

A peninsula in western WA, bounded on east by Puget Sound, west of Seattle. Organized as Slaughter County Jan 16, 1857 (prior to statehood) from Jefferson and King counties; name changed Jul 13, 1857.

Name origin: For an Indian chief, whose name means 'brave,' said to have saved area settlers by warning them of a planned massacre. Originally named for Lt. W. A. Slaughter (?–1855).

Bangor Trident Base   Military Facility
Lat: 47-41-31 N   **Long:** 122-42-57 W
Pop: 3,702 (1990)   **Pop Density:** 1276.6
Land: 2.9 sq. mi.; **Water:** 0.0 sq. mi.

Bremerton   City
ZIP: 98310   **Lat:** 47-32-56 N   **Long:** 122-42-07 W
Pop: 38,142 (1990); 36,208 (1980)   **Pop Density:** 1916.7
Land: 19.9 sq. mi.; **Water:** 3.4 sq. mi.
In western WA on Puget Sound, 15 mi. west of Seattle. Incorporated 1901.
Name origin: For early pioneer William Bremer, who founded the town.

East Port Orchard   CDP
ZIP: 98366   **Lat:** 47-31-16 N   **Long:** 122-37-25 W
Pop: 5,409 (1990); 4,631 (1980)   **Pop Density:** 1931.8
Land: 2.8 sq. mi.; **Water:** 0.0 sq. mi.

Erlands Point-Kitsap Lake   CDP
Lat: 47-35-46 N   **Long:** 122-42-10 W
Pop: 2,764 (1990); 1,254 (1980)   **Pop Density:** 1454.7
Land: 1.9 sq. mi.; **Water:** 0.6 sq. mi.

Indianola   CDP
Lat: 47-45-16 N   **Long:** 122-30-47 W
Pop: 1,729 (1990)   **Pop Density:** 352.9
Land: 4.9 sq. mi.; **Water:** 0.5 sq. mi.

Kingston   CDP
ZIP: 98346   **Lat:** 47-47-52 N   **Long:** 122-29-47 W
Pop: 1,270 (1990)   **Pop Density:** 846.7
Land: 1.5 sq. mi.; **Water:** 0.8 sq. mi.

Manchester   CDP
Lat: 47-33-07 N   **Long:** 122-32-30 W
Pop: 4,031 (1990)   **Pop Density:** 1390.0
Land: 2.9 sq. mi.; **Water:** 3.1 sq. mi.

Navy Yard City   CDP
Lat: 47-33-05 N   **Long:** 122-40-01 W
Pop: 2,905 (1990); 2,382 (1980)   **Pop Density:** 3227.8
Land: 0.9 sq. mi.; **Water:** 0.4 sq. mi.

Parkwood   CDP
ZIP: 98366   **Lat:** 47-31-33 N   **Long:** 122-35-48 W
Pop: 6,853 (1990); 4,599 (1980)   **Pop Density:** 2538.1
Land: 2.7 sq. mi.; **Water:** 0.0 sq. mi.

Port Orchard   City
ZIP: 98366   **Lat:** 47-31-44 N   **Long:** 122-38-28 W
Pop: 4,984 (1990); 4,787 (1980)   **Pop Density:** 1607.7
Land: 3.1 sq. mi.; **Water:** 0.7 sq. mi.
Name origin: For H.M. Orchard, clerk of the ship *Discovery*, so named by Capt. George Vancouver (1757–98) in 1792.

Poulsbo   City
ZIP: 98370   **Lat:** 47-44-13 N   **Long:** 122-38-24 W
Pop: 4,848 (1990); 3,453 (1980)   **Pop Density:** 1939.2
Land: 2.5 sq. mi.; **Water:** 0.6 sq. mi.   **Elev:** 15 ft.
Name origin: For the former home of Norwegian settlers.

Silverdale   CDP
Lat: 47-39-07 N   **Long:** 122-40-59 W
Pop: 7,660 (1990)   **Pop Density:** 1418.5
Land: 5.4 sq. mi.; **Water:** 0.9 sq. mi.

Suquamish
CDP
ZIP: 98392 Lat: 47-43-44 N Long: 122-35-03 W
Pop: 3,105 (1990); 1,498 (1980) Pop Density: 456.6
Land: 6.8 sq. mi.; Water: 0.6 sq. mi.

Tracyton
CDP
Lat: 47-36-34 N Long: 122-39-16 W
Pop: 2,621 (1990); 2,304 (1980) Pop Density: 1747.3
Land: 1.5 sq. mi.; Water: 0.9 sq. mi.

Winslow
City
ZIP: Lat: 47-37-46 N Long: 122-31-04 W
Pop: 3,081 (1990); 2,196 (1980) Pop Density: 1925.6
Land: 1.6 sq. mi.; Water: 0.3 sq. mi.

Name origin: For Winslow Hall, a founder of Hall Brothers Shipbuilding Company.

Kittitas County
County Seat: Ellensburg (ZIP: 98926)

Pop: 26,725 (1990); 24,877 (1980) Pop Density: 11.6
Land: 2297.3 sq. mi.; Water: 35.9 sq. mi. Area Code: 509

In central WA, southeast of Tacoma; organized Nov 2, 1883 (prior to statehood) from Yakima County.

Name origin: Probably from a subtribal name of the Yakima Indians. Meaning uncertain, with 'shoal people' most appropriate, but 'land of bread' has also been suggested, as has 'gray gravel bank,' said to refer to a gravel bank on a river shoal.

Cle Elum
City
ZIP: 98922 Lat: 47-11-38 N Long: 120-55-59 W
Pop: 1,778 (1990); 1,773 (1980) Pop Density: 1270.0
Land: 1.4 sq. mi.; Water: 0.0 sq. mi. Elev: 1905 ft.
Name origin: From an Indian term meaning 'swift waters.'

Ellensburg
City
ZIP: 98926 Lat: 46-59-49 N Long: 120-32-52 W
Pop: 12,361 (1990); 11,752 (1980) Pop Density: 2522.7
Land: 4.9 sq. mi.; Water: 0.0 sq. mi.
In central WA on the Yakima River, 25 mi. north of Yakima. Incorporated 1883.
Name origin: For Mary Ellen, wife of pioneer founder John Shoudy.

Kittitas
City
ZIP: 98934 Lat: 46-59-06 N Long: 120-25-01 W
Pop: 843 (1990); 782 (1980) Pop Density: 1405.0
Land: 0.6 sq. mi.; Water: 0.0 sq. mi. Elev: 1647 ft.

Name origin: Probably from a subtribal name of the Yakima Indians. Meaning uncertain, with 'shoal people' most appropriate, but 'land of bread' has also been suggested, as has 'gray gravel bank,' said to refer to a gravel bank on a river shoal.

Roslyn
City
ZIP: 98941 Lat: 47-14-41 N Long: 121-06-09 W
Pop: 869 (1990); 938 (1980) Pop Density: 184.9
Land: 4.7 sq. mi.; Water: 0.0 sq. mi.
Name origin: For Roslyn, NY, the home of the sweetheart of a manager of the Northern Pacific Railroad Company.

South Cle Elum
Town
ZIP: 98943 Lat: 47-11-12 N Long: 120-57-06 W
Pop: 457 (1990); 449 (1980) Pop Density: 1142.5
Land: 0.4 sq. mi.; Water: 0.0 sq. mi.

Klickitat County
County Seat: Goldendale (ZIP: 98620)

Pop: 16,616 (1990); 15,822 (1980) Pop Density: 8.9
Land: 1872.5 sq. mi.; Water: 31.8 sq. mi. Area Code: 509

On central southern border of WA; original county; organized Dec 20, 1859 (prior to statehood).

Name origin: For an Indian nation that lived in the area; name possibly means 'beyond' or 'those who live beyond the mountains,' or even 'thief.'

Bingen
City
ZIP: 98605 Lat: 45-42-51 N Long: 121-28-05 W
Pop: 645 (1990); 644 (1980) Pop Density: 921.4
Land: 0.7 sq. mi.; Water: 0.1 sq. mi. Elev: 1131 ft.
Founded 1892.
Name origin: For Bingen, Germany.

Goldendale
City
ZIP: 98620 Lat: 45-49-19 N Long: 120-49-05 W
Pop: 3,319 (1990); 3,575 (1980) Pop Density: 1659.5
Land: 2.0 sq. mi.; Water: 0.0 sq. mi. Elev: 1633 ft.
Name origin: For homesteader John J. Golden, who settled here in 1863.

White Salmon City
ZIP: 98672 **Lat:** 45-43-39 N **Long:** 121-29-01 W
Pop: 1,861 (1990); 1,853 (1980) **Pop Density:** 1691.8
Land: 1.1 sq. mi.; **Water:** 0.0 sq. mi.
Name origin: For the White Salmon River, itself named for the color of spawning salmon during their fall runs.

Lewis County
County Seat: Chehalis (ZIP: 98532)

Pop: 59,358 (1990); 56,025 (1980) **Pop Density:** 24.7
Land: 2407.8 sq. mi.; **Water:** 28.6 sq. mi. **Area Code:** 206

In southwestern WA, south of Tacoma; original county; organized Dec 21, 1845 (prior to statehood).

Name origin: For Meriwether Lewis (1774–1809), co-leader of the Lewis and Clark expedition (1804–06).

Centralia City
ZIP: 98531 **Lat:** 46-43-16 N **Long:** 122-57-43 W
Pop: 12,101 (1990); 11,555 (1980) **Pop Density:** 2051.0
Land: 5.9 sq. mi.; **Water:** 0.0 sq. mi. **Elev:** 189 ft.
In southwestern WA on the Chehalis River, 23 mi. south of Olympia. Incorporated 1886.
Name origin: For Centralia, IL. Originally called Centerville.

Chehalis City
ZIP: 98532 **Lat:** 46-39-53 N **Long:** 122-57-54 W
Pop: 6,527 (1990); 6,100 (1980) **Pop Density:** 1165.5
Land: 5.6 sq. mi.; **Water:** 0.0 sq. mi. **Elev:** 226 ft.
Name origin: An Indian term meaning 'sand,' which early settlers incorrectly applied to local Indians.

Fords Prairie CDP
ZIP: 98531 **Lat:** 46-44-24 N **Long:** 123-00-05 W
Pop: 2,480 (1990); 2,582 (1980) **Pop Density:** 496.0
Land: 5.0 sq. mi.; **Water:** 0.1 sq. mi.

Morton City
ZIP: 98356 **Lat:** 46-33-28 N **Long:** 122-16-48 W
Pop: 1,130 (1990); 1,264 (1980) **Pop Density:** 1412.5
Land: 0.8 sq. mi.; **Water:** 0.0 sq. mi.
Name origin: For Benjamin Harrison's vice-president, Levi Morton (1824–1920).

Mossyrock City
ZIP: 98564 **Lat:** 46-31-48 N **Long:** 122-28-52 W
Pop: 452 (1990); 463 (1980) **Pop Density:** 1130.0
Land: 0.4 sq. mi.; **Water:** 0.0 sq. mi. **Elev:** 698 ft.
Name origin: For a nearby moss-covered rock about 200 ft. high.

Napavine City
ZIP: 98565 **Lat:** 46-34-37 N **Long:** 122-54-30 W
Pop: 745 (1990); 611 (1980) **Pop Density:** 1064.3
Land: 0.7 sq. mi.; **Water:** 0.0 sq. mi. **Elev:** 444 ft.

Pe Ell Town
ZIP: 98572 **Lat:** 46-34-17 N **Long:** 123-17-48 W
Pop: 547 (1990); 617 (1980) **Pop Density:** 911.7
Land: 0.6 sq. mi.; **Water:** 0.0 sq. mi. **Elev:** 412 ft.

Toledo City
ZIP: 98591 **Lat:** 46-26-25 N **Long:** 122-50-51 W
Pop: 586 (1990); 637 (1980) **Pop Density:** 1953.3
Land: 0.3 sq. mi.; **Water:** 0.0 sq. mi.
Name origin: For the riverboat *Toledo*, which worked in the area in 1879.

Vader City
ZIP: 98593 **Lat:** 46-24-10 N **Long:** 122-57-20 W
Pop: 414 (1990); 406 (1980) **Pop Density:** 460.0
Land: 0.9 sq. mi.; **Water:** 0.0 sq. mi.

Winlock City
ZIP: 98596 **Lat:** 46-29-29 N **Long:** 122-56-09 W
Pop: 1,027 (1990); 1,052 (1980) **Pop Density:** 1027.0
Land: 1.0 sq. mi.; **Water:** 0.0 sq. mi. **Elev:** 309 ft.
Name origin: For its original landowner, Gen. Winlock E. Miller.

Lincoln County
County Seat: Davenport (ZIP: 99122)

Pop: 8,864 (1990); 9,604 (1980)   **Pop Density:** 3.8
Land: 2311.2 sq. mi.; **Water:** 28.5 sq. mi.   **Area Code:** 509
In eastern WA, W of Spokane; organized Nov 24, 1883 (prior to statehood) from Spokane County.
Name origin: For Abraham Lincoln (1809–65), sixteenth U.S. president.

Almira   Town
ZIP: 99103   **Lat:** 47-42-38 N **Long:** 118-56-21 W
Pop: 310 (1990); 330 (1980)   **Pop Density:** 775.0
Land: 0.4 sq. mi.; **Water:** 0.0 sq. mi.   **Elev:** 1915 ft.
Name origin: For Almira Davis, wife of its first merchant.

Creston   Town
ZIP: 99117   **Lat:** 47-45-35 N **Long:** 118-31-09 W
Pop: 230 (1990); 309 (1980)   **Pop Density:** 575.0
Land: 0.4 sq. mi.; **Water:** 0.0 sq. mi.   **Elev:** 2436 ft.
Name origin: For a local butte, the highest point in the country, so named by Northern Pacific Railway engineers.

Davenport   City
ZIP: 99122   **Lat:** 47-39-04 N **Long:** 118-09-11 W
Pop: 1,502 (1990); 1,559 (1980)   **Pop Density:** 1155.4
Land: 1.3 sq. mi.; **Water:** 0.0 sq. mi.   **Elev:** 2369 ft.

Harrington   Town
ZIP: 99134   **Lat:** 47-28-49 N **Long:** 118-15-15 W
Pop: 449 (1990); 507 (1980)   **Pop Density:** 1122.5
Land: 0.4 sq. mi.; **Water:** 0.0 sq. mi.   **Elev:** 2140 ft.
Name origin: For W.P. Harrington, a CA banker who invested in the town in 1882.

Odessa   Town
ZIP: 99159   **Lat:** 47-19-59 N **Long:** 118-41-13 W
Pop: 935 (1990); 1,009 (1980)   **Pop Density:** 1168.8
Land: 0.8 sq. mi.; **Water:** 0.0 sq. mi.   **Elev:** 1544 ft.
Name origin: For Odessa, Russia, in honor of the Russian settlers living in the area, so named in 1892 by Great Northern Railway officials.

Reardan   Town
ZIP: 99029   **Lat:** 47-40-09 N **Long:** 117-52-38 W
Pop: 482 (1990); 498 (1980)   **Pop Density:** 1205.0
Land: 0.4 sq. mi.; **Water:** 0.0 sq. mi.   **Elev:** 2496 ft.
Name origin: For a civil engineer who worked for the Washington Central Railroad Company.

Sprague   City
ZIP: 99032   **Lat:** 47-18-00 N **Long:** 117-58-26 W
Pop: 410 (1990); 473 (1980)   **Pop Density:** 683.3
Land: 0.6 sq. mi.; **Water:** 0.0 sq. mi.   **Elev:** 1899 ft.
Name origin: For Gen. John W. Sprague, a director of the Northern Pacific Railroad.

Wilbur   Town
ZIP: 99185   **Lat:** 47-45-29 N **Long:** 118-42-16 W
Pop: 863 (1990); 1,122 (1980)   **Pop Density:** 863.0
Land: 1.0 sq. mi.; **Water:** 0.0 sq. mi.   **Elev:** 2163 ft.
Founded 1887.
Name origin: For its founder, Samuel Wilbur Condit.

Mason County
County Seat: Shelton (ZIP: 98584)

Pop: 38,341 (1990); 31,184 (1980)   **Pop Density:** 39.9
Land: 961.1 sq. mi.; **Water:** 90.0 sq. mi.   **Area Code:** 206
In western WA, bordered on east by Puget Sound, west of Tacoma; organized as Sawamish County Mar 13, 1854 from Thurston County; name changed Jan 8, 1864.
Name origin: For Charles H. Mason (?–1859), secretary and sometimes acting governor of WA Territory.

Allyn-Grapeview   CDP
     Lat: 47-20-39 N **Long:** 122-49-52 W
Pop: 1,526 (1990)   **Pop Density:** 263.1
Land: 5.8 sq. mi.; **Water:** 5.2 sq. mi.

Shelton   City
ZIP: 98584   **Lat:** 47-12-53 N **Long:** 123-06-18 W
Pop: 7,241 (1990); 7,629 (1980)   **Pop Density:** 1766.1
Land: 4.1 sq. mi.; **Water:** 0.3 sq. mi.   **Elev:** 6 ft.
Name origin: For pioneer David Shelton, who became its mayor.

Skokomish   CDP
     Lat: 47-20-00 N **Long:** 123-09-22 W
Pop: 532 (1990)   **Pop Density:** 80.6
Land: 6.6 sq. mi.; **Water:** 0.2 sq. mi.

Okanogan County
County Seat: Okanogan (ZIP: 98840)

Pop: 33,350 (1990); 30,663 (1980) **Pop Density:** 6.3
Land: 5268.3 sq. mi.; **Water:** 47.1 sq. mi. **Area Code:** 509

On the central northern border of WA; organized Feb 2, 1888 (prior to statehood) from Stevens County.

Name origin: For the Okanogan River, which traverses the county. From a Salish Indian name possibly meaning 'meeting place [of water]' for the confluence of the Okanogan and Columbia rivers, or 'rendezvous' because they met here for their potlaches.

Brewster   City
ZIP: 98812 **Lat:** 48-06-10 N **Long:** 119-46-46 W
Pop: 1,633 (1990); 1,337 (1980) **Pop Density:** 1484.5
Land: 1.1 sq. mi.; **Water:** 0.0 sq. mi.

Conconully   Town
ZIP: 98819 **Lat:** 48-33-31 N **Long:** 119-45-03 W
Pop: 153 (1990); 157 (1980) **Pop Density:** 765.0
Land: 0.2 sq. mi.; **Water:** 0.0 sq. mi.
Name origin: From an Indian term meaning 'cloudy.'

Coulee Dam   Town
ZIP: 99116 **Lat:** 47-58-10 N **Long:** 118-58-18 W
Pop: 879 (1990); 1,174 (1980) **Pop Density:** 1465.0
Land: 0.6 sq. mi.; **Water:** 0.0 sq. mi. **Elev:** 1145 ft.
Part of the town is also in Douglas and Grant counties.

Elmer City   Town
ZIP: 99124 **Lat:** 47-59-56 N **Long:** 118-57-08 W
Pop: 290 (1990); 312 (1980) **Pop Density:** 1450.0
Land: 0.2 sq. mi.; **Water:** 0.0 sq. mi.

Nespelem   Town
ZIP: 99155 **Lat:** 48-10-03 N **Long:** 118-58-17 W
Pop: 187 (1990); 284 (1980) **Pop Density:** 935.0
Land: 0.2 sq. mi.; **Water:** 0.0 sq. mi.

Nespelem Community   CDP
Lat: 48-10-01 N **Long:** 119-01-08 W
Pop: 291 (1990) **Pop Density:** 12.6
Land: 23.1 sq. mi.; **Water:** 0.0 sq. mi.

North Omak   CDP
Lat: 48-26-43 N **Long:** 119-26-36 W
Pop: 515 (1990) **Pop Density:** 46.0
Land: 11.2 sq. mi.; **Water:** 0.0 sq. mi.

Okanogan   City
ZIP: 98840 **Lat:** 48-22-07 N **Long:** 119-34-34 W
Pop: 2,370 (1990); 2,326 (1980) **Pop Density:** 1481.3
Land: 1.6 sq. mi.; **Water:** 0.1 sq. mi. **Elev:** 860 ft.
Name origin: For the Okanogan River, which traverses the county. From a Salish Indian name possibly meaning 'meeting place [of water]' for the confluence of the Okanogan and Columbia rivers, or 'rendezvous' because they met here for their potlaches.

Omak   City
ZIP: 98841 **Lat:** 48-24-34 N **Long:** 119-31-31 W
Pop: 4,117 (1990); 4,007 (1980) **Pop Density:** 2573.1
Land: 1.6 sq. mi.; **Water:** 0.1 sq. mi. **Elev:** 837 ft.
Name origin: From an Indian term meaning 'great medicine' and referring to a nearby lake with supposed curative powers.

Oroville   Town
ZIP: 98844 **Lat:** 48-56-32 N **Long:** 119-25-53 W
Pop: 1,505 (1990); 1,483 (1980) **Pop Density:** 1254.2
Land: 1.2 sq. mi.; **Water:** 0.0 sq. mi.
Name origin: From Spanish *oro* meaning 'gold.'

Pateros   Town
ZIP: 98846 **Lat:** 48-03-17 N **Long:** 119-53-59 W
Pop: 570 (1990); 555 (1980) **Pop Density:** 1140.0
Land: 0.5 sq. mi.; **Water:** 0.0 sq. mi. **Elev:** 776 ft.

Riverside   Town
ZIP: 98849 **Lat:** 48-30-09 N **Long:** 119-30-27 W
Pop: 223 (1990); 243 (1980) **Pop Density:** 318.6
Land: 0.7 sq. mi.; **Water:** 0.1 sq. mi.

Tonasket   Town
ZIP: 98855 **Lat:** 48-42-17 N **Long:** 119-26-16 W
Pop: 847 (1990); 985 (1980) **Pop Density:** 1694.0
Land: 0.5 sq. mi.; **Water:** 0.0 sq. mi.
Name origin: For Chief Tonasket of the Colville Indians.

Twisp   Town
ZIP: 98856 **Lat:** 48-21-47 N **Long:** 120-07-10 W
Pop: 872 (1990); 911 (1980) **Pop Density:** 872.0
Land: 1.0 sq. mi.; **Water:** 0.0 sq. mi. **Elev:** 1614 ft.
Name origin: For the nearby Twisp River.

Winthrop   Town
ZIP: 98862 **Lat:** 48-28-22 N **Long:** 120-10-41 W
Pop: 302 (1990); 413 (1980) **Pop Density:** 377.5
Land: 0.8 sq. mi.; **Water:** 0.0 sq. mi. **Elev:** 1760 ft.
Name origin: For New England author Theodore Winthrop (1828–61), whose novel *Canoe and the Saddle* (1863) was located in the Washington region.

Pacific County
County Seat: South Bend (ZIP: 98586)

Pop: 18,882 (1990); 17,237 (1980)   **Pop Density:** 19.4
Land: 974.6 sq. mi.; **Water:** 249.0 sq. mi.   **Area Code:** 206
On the southwestern coast of WA; original county; organized Feb 4, 1851 (prior to statehood).
Name origin: For the Pacific Ocean, which forms the county's western border.

Ilwaco   Town
ZIP: 98624   **Lat:** 46-18-39 N   **Long:** 124-01-58 W
Pop: 815 (1990); 604 (1980)   **Pop Density:** 626.9
Land: 1.3 sq. mi.; **Water:** 0.3 sq. mi.   **Elev:** 11 ft.

Long Beach   Town
ZIP: 98631   **Lat:** 46-21-19 N   **Long:** 124-03-11 W
Pop: 1,236 (1990); 1,199 (1980)   **Pop Density:** 1030.0
Land: 1.2 sq. mi.; **Water:** 0.0 sq. mi.
Name origin: For the area's 20-mi.-long beach.

Ocean Park   CDP
ZIP: 98640   **Lat:** 46-29-44 N   **Long:** 124-02-35 W
Pop: 1,409 (1990)   **Pop Density:** 402.6
Land: 3.5 sq. mi.; **Water:** 0.4 sq. mi.

Raymond   City
ZIP: 98577   **Lat:** 46-41-00 N   **Long:** 123-44-12 W
Pop: 2,901 (1990); 2,991 (1980)   **Pop Density:** 743.8
Land: 3.9 sq. mi.; **Water:** 0.5 sq. mi.   **Elev:** 14 ft.
Name origin: For L.U. Raymond, its original landowner.

South Bend   City
ZIP: 98586   **Lat:** 46-40-14 N   **Long:** 123-48-10 W
Pop: 1,551 (1990); 1,686 (1980)   **Pop Density:** 1193.1
Land: 1.3 sq. mi.; **Water:** 0.4 sq. mi.   **Elev:** 80 ft.

Pend Oreille County
County Seat: Newport (ZIP: 99156)

Pop: 8,915 (1990); 8,580 (1980)   **Pop Density:** 6.4
Land: 1400.5 sq. mi.; **Water:** 24.9 sq. mi.   **Area Code:** 509
On northeastern border of WA; organized Mar 1, 1911 from Stevens County.
Name origin: For the Pend Oreille River, which runs through the county, or for the name given to the Kalispel Indians by French-Canadian traders; from the French meaning 'pendant ears' because the Indians wore ear ornaments that probably lengthened their lobes.

Cusick   Town
ZIP: 99119   **Lat:** 48-20-04 N   **Long:** 117-17-38 W
Pop: 195 (1990); 246 (1980)   **Pop Density:** 650.0
Land: 0.3 sq. mi.; **Water:** 0.0 sq. mi.

Ione   Town
ZIP: 99139   **Lat:** 48-44-26 N   **Long:** 117-25-15 W
Pop: 507 (1990); 594 (1980)   **Pop Density:** 1014.0
Land: 0.5 sq. mi.; **Water:** 0.1 sq. mi.

Metaline   Town
ZIP: 99152   **Lat:** 48-51-16 N   **Long:** 117-23-17 W
Pop: 198 (1990); 190 (1980)   **Pop Density:** 660.0
Land: 0.3 sq. mi.; **Water:** 0.0 sq. mi.

Metaline Falls   Town
ZIP: 99153   **Lat:** 48-51-44 N   **Long:** 117-22-09 W
Pop: 210 (1990); 296 (1980)   **Pop Density:** 1050.0
Land: 0.2 sq. mi.; **Water:** 0.0 sq. mi.
In northeastern WA at the falls on the Pend Oreille River.

Newport   City
ZIP: 99156   **Lat:** 48-10-50 N   **Long:** 117-03-02 W
Pop: 1,691 (1990); 1,665 (1980)   **Pop Density:** 1691.0
Land: 1.0 sq. mi.; **Water:** 0.0 sq. mi.

Pierce County
County Seat: Tacoma (ZIP: 98402)

Pop: 586,203 (1990); 485,667 (1980) **Pop Density:** 349.9
Land: 1675.5 sq. mi.; **Water:** 131.1 sq. mi. **Area Code:** 206
In west-central WA at the southeastern end of Puget Sound; original county; organized Dec 22, 1852 (prior to statehood).
Name origin: For Franklin Pierce (1804–69), fourteenth U.S. president.

Artondale CDP
ZIP: 98335 **Lat:** 47-18-49 N **Long:** 122-38-04 W
Pop: 7,141 (1990) **Pop Density:** 673.7
Land: 10.6 sq. mi.; **Water:** 0.3 sq. mi.

Bonney Lake City
ZIP: 98390 **Lat:** 47-11-14 N **Long:** 122-10-07 W
Pop: 7,494 (1990); 5,328 (1980) **Pop Density:** 1972.1
Land: 3.8 sq. mi.; **Water:** 0.5 sq. mi.
Name origin: For the nearby lake.

Buckley City
ZIP: 98321 **Lat:** 47-09-45 N **Long:** 122-01-07 W
Pop: 3,516 (1990); 3,143 (1980) **Pop Density:** 901.5
Land: 3.9 sq. mi.; **Water:** 0.0 sq. mi. **Elev:** 726 ft.

Carbonado Town
ZIP: 98323 **Lat:** 47-04-51 N **Long:** 122-03-12 W
Pop: 495 (1990); 456 (1980) **Pop Density:** 1650.0
Land: 0.3 sq. mi.; **Water:** 0.0 sq. mi.
Name origin: For the adjacent Carbon River, so called for the coal deposits on its banks.

DuPont City
ZIP: 98327 **Lat:** 47-06-24 N **Long:** 122-39-11 W
Pop: 592 (1990); 559 (1980) **Pop Density:** 103.9
Land: 5.7 sq. mi.; **Water:** 0.0 sq. mi.
Name origin: For the nearby Du Pont explosives factory.

Eatonville Town
ZIP: 98328 **Lat:** 46-52-06 N **Long:** 122-16-07 W
Pop: 1,374 (1990); 998 (1980) **Pop Density:** 1526.7
Land: 0.9 sq. mi.; **Water:** 0.0 sq. mi.

Edgewood-North Hill CDP
Lat: 47-13-55 N **Long:** 122-16-49 W
Pop: 9,120 (1990) **Pop Density:** 1048.3
Land: 8.7 sq. mi.; **Water:** 0.0 sq. mi.

Elk Plain CDP
ZIP: 98387 **Lat:** 47-03-12 N **Long:** 122-22-40 W
Pop: 12,197 (1990) **Pop Density:** 1069.9
Land: 11.4 sq. mi.; **Water:** 0.0 sq. mi.

Fife City
ZIP: 98424 **Lat:** 47-14-23 N **Long:** 122-21-40 W
Pop: 3,864 (1990); 1,823 (1980) **Pop Density:** 1332.4
Land: 2.9 sq. mi.; **Water:** 0.0 sq. mi.

Fircrest Town
ZIP: 98466 **Lat:** 47-13-52 N **Long:** 122-30-46 W
Pop: 5,258 (1990); 5,477 (1980) **Pop Density:** 4780.0
Land: 1.1 sq. mi.; **Water:** 0.0 sq. mi.

Fort Lewis Military Facility
ZIP: 98433 **Lat:** 47-06-22 N **Long:** 122-34-54 W
Pop: 22,224 (1990) **Pop Density:** 1554.1
Land: 14.3 sq. mi.; **Water:** 0.6 sq. mi.

Fox Island CDP
ZIP: 98333 **Lat:** 47-15-06 N **Long:** 122-37-40 W
Pop: 2,017 (1990); 23,761 (1980) **Pop Density:** 387.9
Land: 5.2 sq. mi.; **Water:** 1.2 sq. mi.

Frederickson CDP
Lat: 47-05-11 N **Long:** 122-21-42 W
Pop: 3,502 (1990) **Pop Density:** 454.8
Land: 7.7 sq. mi.; **Water:** 0.0 sq. mi.

Gig Harbor Town
ZIP: 98335 **Lat:** 47-19-43 N **Long:** 122-35-16 W
Pop: 3,236 (1990); 2,429 (1980) **Pop Density:** 2022.5
Land: 1.6 sq. mi.; **Water:** 0.0 sq. mi.
Name origin: Named by members of the 1841 Wilkes expedition for its harbor that has sufficient depth for small gigs, light, oared boats.

Lakewood CDP
Lat: 47-09-42 N **Long:** 122-31-48 W
Pop: 58,412 (1990) **Pop Density:** 3300.1
Land: 17.7 sq. mi.; **Water:** 1.7 sq. mi.

McChord Air Force Base Military Facility
Lat: 47-08-01 N **Long:** 122-29-47 W
Pop: 4,538 (1990); 5,746 (1980) **Pop Density:** 782.4
Land: 5.8 sq. mi.; **Water:** 0.0 sq. mi.

Midland CDP
ZIP: 98444 **Lat:** 47-10-20 N **Long:** 122-24-32 W
Pop: 5,587 (1990) **Pop Density:** 1802.3
Land: 3.1 sq. mi.; **Water:** 0.0 sq. mi.

Milton Town
ZIP: 98354 **Lat:** 47-14-54 N **Long:** 122-18-45 W
Pop: 4,298 (1990); 2,944 (1980) **Pop Density:** 2387.8
Land: 1.8 sq. mi.; **Water:** 0.0 sq. mi.
Part of the town is also in King County.

North Puyallup CDP
Lat: 47-12-42 N **Long:** 122-18-41 W
Pop: 2,886 (1990) **Pop Density:** 1068.9
Land: 2.7 sq. mi.; **Water:** 0.1 sq. mi.

Orting Town
ZIP: 98360 **Lat:** 47-05-19 N **Long:** 122-12-19 W
Pop: 2,106 (1990); 1,787 (1980) **Pop Density:** 1316.3
Land: 1.6 sq. mi.; **Water:** 0.0 sq. mi.

Pacific City
Lat: 47-15-28 N **Long:** 122-15-09 W
Pop: 0 (1990)
Land: 0.01 sq. mi.; **Water:** 0.0 sq. mi.
Part of the town is also in King County.
Name origin: For the Pacific Ocean.

WASHINGTON, Pierce County

Parkland — CDP
ZIP: 98444 **Lat:** 47-08-16 N **Long:** 122-25-45 W
Pop: 20,882 (1990); 23,355 (1980) **Pop Density:** 3026.4
Land: 6.9 sq. mi.; **Water:** 0.0 sq. mi.

Prairie Ridge — CDP
ZIP: 98390 **Lat:** 47-08-16 N **Long:** 122-08-50 W
Pop: 8,278 (1990) **Pop Density:** 973.9
Land: 8.5 sq. mi.; **Water:** 0.0 sq. mi.

Puyallup — City
ZIP: 98371 **Lat:** 47-10-55 N **Long:** 122-17-02 W
Pop: 23,875 (1990); 18,251 (1980) **Pop Density:** 2318.0
Land: 10.3 sq. mi.; **Water:** 0.1 sq. mi.

In west-central WA on the Puyallup River, 25 mi. south of Seattle. Incorporated 1890.

Name origin: For the river, itself named from the Indian term meaning 'generous people,' referring to the Indians who lived along its banks.

Roy — City
ZIP: 98580 **Lat:** 47-00-04 N **Long:** 122-32-39 W
Pop: 258 (1990); 417 (1980) **Pop Density:** 1290.0
Land: 0.2 sq. mi.; **Water:** 0.0 sq. mi.

Ruston — Town
ZIP: 98407 **Lat:** 47-17-52 N **Long:** 122-30-33 W
Pop: 693 (1990); 612 (1980) **Pop Density:** 2310.0
Land: 0.3 sq. mi.; **Water:** 0.0 sq. mi.

Name origin: For W.R. Rust, one-time president of the Tacoma Smelting Company.

South Hill — CDP
Lat: 47-08-28 N **Long:** 122-16-08 W
Pop: 12,963 (1990) **Pop Density:** 1851.9
Land: 7.0 sq. mi.; **Water:** 0.1 sq. mi.

South Prairie — Town
ZIP: 98385 **Lat:** 47-08-18 N **Long:** 122-05-30 W
Pop: 180 (1990); 202 (1980) **Pop Density:** 600.0
Land: 0.3 sq. mi.; **Water:** 0.0 sq. mi.

Name origin: For its location on South Prairie Creek.

Spanaway — CDP
ZIP: 98387 **Lat:** 47-06-22 N **Long:** 122-25-35 W
Pop: 15,001 (1990); 8,868 (1980) **Pop Density:** 2941.4
Land: 5.1 sq. mi.; **Water:** 0.4 sq. mi.

Steilacoom — Town
ZIP: 98388 **Lat:** 47-10-10 N **Long:** 122-35-32 W
Pop: 5,728 (1990); 4,886 (1980) **Pop Density:** 2727.6
Land: 2.1 sq. mi.; **Water:** 0.0 sq. mi. **Elev:** 51 ft.
Founded 1851.

Name origin: For an Indian term *tchil-ac-cum* meaning 'pink flower.'

Summit — CDP
Lat: 47-10-19 N **Long:** 122-21-28 W
Pop: 6,312 (1990) **Pop Density:** 1315.0
Land: 4.8 sq. mi.; **Water:** 0.0 sq. mi.

Sumner — City
ZIP: 98390 **Lat:** 47-12-37 N **Long:** 122-14-09 W
Pop: 6,281 (1990); 4,936 (1980) **Pop Density:** 1652.9
Land: 3.8 sq. mi.; **Water:** 0.0 sq. mi.

Name origin: For U.S. senator and antislavery proponent Charles Sumner (1811–74), so named by founder John Kincaid.

Tacoma — City
ZIP: 98402 **Lat:** 47-15-07 N **Long:** 122-27-35 W
Pop: 176,664 (1990); 158,501 (1980) **Pop Density:** 3680.5
Land: 48.0 sq. mi.; **Water:** 12.5 sq. mi.

In west-central WA on Commencement Bay at the mouth of the Puyallup River, 25 mi. south of Seattle. Incorporated 1884.

Name origin: From the Indian term for Mt. Rainier; meaning uncertain.

University Place — CDP
ZIP: 98465 **Lat:** 47-13-08 N **Long:** 122-32-32 W
Pop: 27,701 (1990); 20,381 (1980) **Pop Density:** 3506.5
Land: 7.9 sq. mi.; **Water:** 1.4 sq. mi.

Waller — CDP
Lat: 47-12-03 N **Long:** 122-22-05 W
Pop: 6,415 (1990) **Pop Density:** 1018.3
Land: 6.3 sq. mi.; **Water:** 0.0 sq. mi.

Wilkeson — Town
ZIP: 98396 **Lat:** 47-06-25 N **Long:** 122-02-49 W
Pop: 366 (1990); 316 (1980) **Pop Density:** 732.0
Land: 0.5 sq. mi.; **Water:** 0.0 sq. mi.

Name origin: For Samuel Wilkeson, an official of the Northern Pacific Railroad, which began a coal mine here 1879.

San Juan County
County Seat: Friday Harbor (ZIP: 98250)

Pop: 10,035 (1990); 7,838 (1980)   **Pop Density:** 57.4
Land: 174.9 sq. mi.; **Water:** 446.1 sq. mi.   **Area Code:** 206

Islands in northwestern WA, bounded on west and northwest by Haro Strait, on north and northeast by Georgia Strait, and on south by Juan de Fuca Strait. Organized Oct 31, 1873 (prior to statehood) from Whatcom County.

Name origin: For St. John the Baptist, cousin and baptizer of Jesus. Some sources suggest the county may have been named for San Juan Island, for Juan Francisco de Eliza, governor of the Spanish settlement at Nootka Sound in the late 18th century, or for Juan de Fuca, supposedly a Greek navigator in Spanish service.

Friday Harbor   Town
ZIP: 98250   **Lat:** 48-32-12 N **Long:** 123-01-52 W
Pop: 1,492 (1990); 1,200 (1980)   **Pop Density:** 1147.7
Land: 1.3 sq. mi.; **Water:** 0.4 sq. mi.   **Elev:** 91 ft.

Name origin: For a Hawaiian sheepherder for Hudson's Bay Company named John Friday. Previously called Bellvue, Bellvue Farm, Friday's Place, and Kanaka's Place.

Skagit County
County Seat: Mount Vernon (ZIP: 98273)

Pop: 79,555 (1990); 64,138 (1980)   **Pop Density:** 45.8
Land: 1735.3 sq. mi.; **Water:** 185.2 sq. mi.   **Area Code:** 206

In northwestern WA, bordered on west by upper Puget Sound, north of Seattle. Organized Nov 28, 1883 (prior to statehood) from Whatcom County.

Name origin: For the Indian tribe; meaning of name is unknown.

Anacortes   City
ZIP: 98221   **Lat:** 48-29-32 N **Long:** 122-37-45 W
Pop: 11,451 (1990); 9,013 (1980)   **Pop Density:** 1050.6
Land: 10.9 sq. mi.; **Water:** 1.7 sq. mi.

In northwestern WA on Puget Sound, 65 mi. northwest of Seattle. Incorporated 1889.

Name origin: For the wife of civil engineer Amos Bowman, who plotted the townsite and gave it his wife's maiden name: Anna Curtis. The spelling was later changed to give it a Spanish sound.

Burlington   City
ZIP: 98233   **Lat:** 48-28-08 N **Long:** 122-19-54 W
Pop: 4,349 (1990); 3,894 (1980)   **Pop Density:** 1449.7
Land: 3.0 sq. mi.; **Water:** 0.0 sq. mi.

Founded 1891.

Concrete   Town
ZIP: 98237   **Lat:** 48-32-13 N **Long:** 121-44-55 W
Pop: 735 (1990); 592 (1980)   **Pop Density:** 612.5
Land: 1.2 sq. mi.; **Water:** 0.0 sq. mi.

Settled 1888.

Name origin: For the local cement industry. Originally called Cement City.

Hamilton   Town
ZIP: 98255   **Lat:** 48-31-23 N **Long:** 121-59-17 W
Pop: 228 (1990); 268 (1980)   **Pop Density:** 380.0
Land: 0.6 sq. mi.; **Water:** 0.0 sq. mi.

La Conner   Town
ZIP: 98257   **Lat:** 48-23-33 N **Long:** 122-29-35 W
Pop: 656 (1990); 633 (1980)   **Pop Density:** 1640.0
Land: 0.4 sq. mi.; **Water:** 0.1 sq. mi.

Name origin: For Louisa Ann Connor, the wife of early merchant J.J. Connor.

Lyman   Town
ZIP: 98263   **Lat:** 48-31-24 N **Long:** 122-03-49 W
Pop: 275 (1990); 285 (1980)   **Pop Density:** 458.3
Land: 0.6 sq. mi.; **Water:** 0.1 sq. mi.

Name origin: For its first postmaster, B.L. Lyman.

Mount Vernon   City
ZIP: 98273   **Lat:** 48-25-18 N **Long:** 122-18-52 W
Pop: 17,647 (1990); 13,009 (1980)   **Pop Density:** 2100.8
Land: 8.4 sq. mi.; **Water:** 0.2 sq. mi.

In northwestern WA on the Skagit River, 55 mi. north of Seattle. Incorporated 1890.

Name origin: For the VA estate of George Washington (1732–99).

Sedro-Woolley   City
ZIP: 98284   **Lat:** 48-30-29 N **Long:** 122-14-06 W
Pop: 6,031 (1990); 6,110 (1980)   **Pop Density:** 1827.6
Land: 3.3 sq. mi.; **Water:** 0.0 sq. mi.

Shelter Bay   CDP
Lat: 48-22-57 N **Long:** 122-30-50 W
Pop: 1,069 (1990)   **Pop Density:** 1069.0
Land: 1.0 sq. mi.; **Water:** 0.1 sq. mi.

WASHINGTON, Skagit County

Snee Oosh CDP
Lat: 48-25-21 N Long: 122-33-11 W
Pop: 302 (1990) **Pop Density:** 377.5
Land: 0.8 sq. mi.; **Water:** 0.0 sq. mi.

Swinomish Village CDP
Lat: 48-24-30 N Long: 122-30-35 W
Pop: 563 (1990) **Pop Density:** 296.3
Land: 1.9 sq. mi.; **Water:** 0.0 sq. mi.

Skamania County
County Seat: Stevenson (ZIP: 98648)

Pop: 8,289 (1990); 7,919 (1980) **Pop Density:** 5.0
Land: 1656.5 sq. mi.; **Water:** 27.4 sq. mi. **Area Code:** 509

On the southern border of WA, northeast of Portland, OR; organized Mar 9, 1854 (prior to statehood) from Clark County.

Name origin: From the Indian name for parts of the Columbia River, which forms the county's southern border. The usual interpretation is 'swift water.'

Carson River Valley CDP
Lat: 45-43-54 N Long: 121-49-00 W
Pop: 1,678 (1990) **Pop Density:** 357.0
Land: 4.7 sq. mi.; **Water:** 0.0 sq. mi.

North Bonneville City
ZIP: 98639 Lat: 45-38-34 N Long: 121-58-10 W
Pop: 411 (1990); 394 (1980) **Pop Density:** 178.7
Land: 2.3 sq. mi.; **Water:** 0.2 sq. mi.

Stevenson City
ZIP: 98648 Lat: 45-41-37 N Long: 121-53-35 W
Pop: 1,147 (1990); 1,172 (1980) **Pop Density:** 955.8
Land: 1.2 sq. mi.; **Water:** 0.1 sq. mi. **Elev:** 103 ft.
Founded 1894.
Name origin: For its founder, George Stevenson.

Snohomish County
County Seat: Everett (ZIP: 98201)

Pop: 465,642 (1990); 337,720 (1980) **Pop Density:** 222.8
Land: 2090.2 sq. mi.; **Water:** 106.3 sq. mi. **Area Code:** 206

In northwestern WA, bordered on west by Puget Sound, northeast of Seattle. Organized Jan 14, 1861 (prior to statehood) from Island County.

Name origin: For the Snohomish Indians; name is believed to mean 'tidewater people' or 'union.'

Alderwood Manor-Bothell North CDP
Lat: 47-47-58 N Long: 122-14-31 W
Pop: 22,945 (1990); 16,524 (1980) **Pop Density:** 2868.1
Land: 8.0 sq. mi.; **Water:** 0.0 sq. mi.

Arlington City
ZIP: 98223 Lat: 48-10-32 N Long: 122-08-17 W
Pop: 4,037 (1990); 3,282 (1980) **Pop Density:** 734.0
Land: 5.5 sq. mi.; **Water:** 0.0 sq. mi.
Name origin: For Arlington National Cemetery, which was named for Lord Henry Bennet, Earl of Arlington (1618–85), a member of the cabinet of King Charles II of England. Name suggested by two railroad contractors who purchased the townsite in 1890.

Bothell City
Lat: 47-46-43 N Long: 122-11-54 W
Pop: 359 (1990); 7,943 (1980) **Pop Density:** 3590.0
Land: 0.1 sq. mi.; **Water:** 0.0 sq. mi.
In west-central WA, 12 mi. north of Seattle. Incorporated 1909. Part of the town is also in King County.
Name origin: For the Bothell family, who were local businessmen and politicians.

Brier City
ZIP: 98036 Lat: 47-47-33 N Long: 122-16-18 W
Pop: 5,633 (1990); 2,915 (1980) **Pop Density:** 2682.4
Land: 2.1 sq. mi.; **Water:** 0.0 sq. mi.

Cathan CDP
Lat: 48-06-51 N Long: 122-16-34 W
Pop: 428 (1990) **Pop Density:** 237.8
Land: 1.8 sq. mi.; **Water:** 0.0 sq. mi.

Darrington Town
ZIP: 98241 Lat: 48-15-08 N Long: 121-36-14 W
Pop: 1,042 (1990); 1,064 (1980) **Pop Density:** 1302.5
Land: 0.8 sq. mi.; **Water:** 0.0 sq. mi. **Elev:** 549 ft.
Name origin: For a man named Barrington, but the first letter was changed by clerical error in the application.

Edmonds City
ZIP: 98020 Lat: 47-49-33 N Long: 122-22-04 W
Pop: 30,744 (1990); 27,679 (1980) **Pop Density:** 4211.5
Land: 7.3 sq. mi.; **Water:** 9.5 sq. mi.
In west-central WA on Puget Sound, 13 mi. north of Seattle. Incorporated 1890.
Name origin: The town site was called Point Edmund by the Wilkes Expedition in 1841. Name altered to its present form when the post office was established in the 1880s.

American Places Dictionary   WASHINGTON, Snohomish County

Esperance   CDP
ZIP: 98043   **Lat:** 47-47-20 N   **Long:** 122-21-15 W
Pop: 11,236 (1990); 11,120 (1980)   **Pop Density:** 5107.3
Land: 2.2 sq. mi.; **Water:** 0.0 sq. mi.

Everett   City
ZIP: 98271   **Lat:** 47-57-47 N   **Long:** 122-11-54 W
Pop: 69,961 (1990); 54,413 (1980)   **Pop Density:** 2339.8
Land: 29.9 sq. mi.; **Water:** 15.3 sq. mi.
In west-central WA on Puget Sound, 25 mi. north of Seattle. Incorporated 1893.
Name origin: For Everett Colby, son of prominent landowner Charles Colby.

Gold Bar   Town
ZIP: 98251   **Lat:** 47-51-27 N   **Long:** 121-41-44 W
Pop: 1,078 (1990); 794 (1980)   **Pop Density:** 1796.7
Land: 0.6 sq. mi.; **Water:** 0.0 sq. mi.

Granite Falls   Town
ZIP: 98252   **Lat:** 48-04-58 N   **Long:** 121-58-01 W
Pop: 1,060 (1990); 911 (1980)   **Pop Density:** 1514.3
Land: 0.7 sq. mi.; **Water:** 0.0 sq. mi.   **Elev:** 391 ft.
Name origin: For the falls in the granite canyon of the Stillaguamish River.

Harbour Pointe   CDP
Lat: 47-53-09 N   **Long:** 122-18-14 W
Pop: 9,107 (1990)   **Pop Density:** 1570.2
Land: 5.8 sq. mi.; **Water:** 0.3 sq. mi.

Index   Town
ZIP: 98256   **Lat:** 47-49-14 N   **Long:** 121-33-08 W
Pop: 139 (1990); 147 (1980)   **Pop Density:** 463.3
Land: 0.3 sq. mi.; **Water:** 0.0 sq. mi.   **Elev:** 532 ft.
Name origin: For nearby Index Mountain, which resembles an index finger pointing to the sky.

John Sam Lake   CDP
Lat: 48-06-33 N   **Long:** 122-14-40 W
Pop: 432 (1990)   **Pop Density:** 86.4
Land: 5.0 sq. mi.; **Water:** 0.1 sq. mi.

Lake Goodwin   CDP
Lat: 48-08-20 N   **Long:** 122-16-42 W
Pop: 2,437 (1990)   **Pop Density:** 609.3
Land: 4.0 sq. mi.; **Water:** 1.3 sq. mi.

Lake Serene-North Lynnwood   CDP
Lat: 47-51-18 N   **Long:** 122-17-02 W
Pop: 14,290 (1990)   **Pop Density:** 2463.8
Land: 5.8 sq. mi.; **Water:** 0.1 sq. mi.

Lake Stevens   City
ZIP: 98258   **Lat:** 48-01-01 N   **Long:** 122-03-55 W
Pop: 3,380 (1990); 1,660 (1980)   **Pop Density:** 1988.2
Land: 1.7 sq. mi.; **Water:** 0.0 sq. mi.   **Elev:** 210 ft.

Lynnwood   City
ZIP: 98036   **Lat:** 47-49-38 N   **Long:** 122-18-15 W
Pop: 28,695 (1990); 22,641 (1980)   **Pop Density:** 4099.3
Land: 7.0 sq. mi.; **Water:** 0.0 sq. mi.
Incorporated 1959.

Martha Lake   CDP
ZIP: 98012   **Lat:** 47-51-03 N   **Long:** 122-14-16 W
Pop: 10,155 (1990); 3,054 (1980)   **Pop Density:** 2072.4
Land: 4.9 sq. mi.; **Water:** 0.1 sq. mi.

Marysville   City
ZIP: 98270   **Lat:** 48-03-34 N   **Long:** 122-09-16 W
Pop: 10,328 (1990); 5,080 (1980)   **Pop Density:** 2197.4
Land: 4.7 sq. mi.; **Water:** 0.0 sq. mi.
Founded 1870s. Incorporated 1891.
Name origin: For Marysville, CA, so named by early settlers.

Mill Creek   City
ZIP: 98012   **Lat:** 47-51-27 N   **Long:** 122-12-21 W
Pop: 7,172 (1990)   **Pop Density:** 2561.4
Land: 2.8 sq. mi.; **Water:** 0.0 sq. mi.

Monroe   City
ZIP: 98272   **Lat:** 47-51-29 N   **Long:** 121-58-54 W
Pop: 4,278 (1990); 2,869 (1980)   **Pop Density:** 1125.8
Land: 3.8 sq. mi.; **Water:** 0.0 sq. mi.
Name origin: For James Monroe (1758–1831), fifth U.S. president.

Mountlake Terrace   City
ZIP: 98043   **Lat:** 47-47-28 N   **Long:** 122-18-23 W
Pop: 19,320 (1990); 16,534 (1980)   **Pop Density:** 4953.8
Land: 3.9 sq. mi.; **Water:** 0.1 sq. mi.
In west-central WA north of Seattle. Incorporated 1954.

Mukilteo   City
ZIP: 98275   **Lat:** 47-55-36 N   **Long:** 122-18-31 W
Pop: 7,007 (1990); 1,426 (1980)   **Pop Density:** 2595.2
Land: 2.7 sq. mi.; **Water:** 3.1 sq. mi.
Name origin: From an Indian term meaning 'good camping ground.'

North Creek-Canyon Park   CDP
Lat: 47-48-38 N   **Long:** 122-11-10 W
Pop: 23,236 (1990)   **Pop Density:** 1408.2
Land: 16.5 sq. mi.; **Water:** 0.0 sq. mi.

North Marysville   CDP
ZIP: 98201   **Lat:** 48-05-57 N   **Long:** 122-08-51 W
Pop: 18,711 (1990)   **Pop Density:** 1281.6
Land: 14.6 sq. mi.; **Water:** 0.0 sq. mi.

Paine Field-Lake Stickney   CDP
Lat: 47-53-13 N   **Long:** 122-15-44 W
Pop: 18,670 (1990)   **Pop Density:** 2424.7
Land: 7.7 sq. mi.; **Water:** 0.0 sq. mi.

Priest Point   CDP
Lat: 48-02-12 N   **Long:** 122-14-59 W
Pop: 703 (1990)   **Pop Density:** 703.0
Land: 1.0 sq. mi.; **Water:** 2.8 sq. mi.

Shaker Church   CDP
Lat: 48-03-10 N   **Long:** 122-13-37 W
Pop: 670 (1990)   **Pop Density:** 134.0
Land: 5.0 sq. mi.; **Water:** 0.0 sq. mi.

Silver Lake-Fircrest   CDP
ZIP: 98201   **Lat:** 47-52-25 N   **Long:** 122-10-11 W
Pop: 24,474 (1990); 10,299 (1980)   **Pop Density:** 1699.6
Land: 14.4 sq. mi.; **Water:** 0.0 sq. mi.

Smokey Point   CDP
ZIP: 98223   **Lat:** 48-09-01 N   **Long:** 122-11-36 W
Pop: 2,620 (1990)   **Pop Density:** 770.6
Land: 3.4 sq. mi.; **Water:** 0.0 sq. mi.

WASHINGTON, Snohomish County

Snohomish — City
ZIP: 98290 **Lat:** 47-55-10 N **Long:** 122-05-36 W
Pop: 6,499 (1990); 5,294 (1980) **Pop Density:** 3094.8
Land: 2.1 sq. mi.; **Water:** 0.1 sq. mi.
Name origin: For the area's dominant Indian tribe.

Stanwood — City
Lat: 48-14-35 N **Long:** 122-20-53 W
Pop: 1,961 (1990); 1,646 (1980) **Pop Density:** 1307.3
Land: 1.5 sq. mi.; **Water:** 0.0 sq. mi.
Settled 1866.
Name origin: For the maiden name of the wife of postmaster D.O. Pearson.

Stimson Crossing — CDP
Lat: 48-06-28 N **Long:** 122-12-25 W
Pop: 591 (1990) **Pop Density:** 164.2
Land: 3.6 sq. mi.; **Water:** 0.0 sq. mi.

Sultan — Town
ZIP: 98294 **Lat:** 47-51-52 N **Long:** 121-48-15 W
Pop: 2,236 (1990); 1,578 (1980) **Pop Density:** 931.7
Land: 2.4 sq. mi.; **Water:** 0.0 sq. mi. **Elev:** 114 ft.
Name origin: For the Sultan River, so named by Chief Tseultud.

Tulalip Bay — CDP
Lat: 48-02-14 N **Long:** 122-18-32 W
Pop: 1,395 (1990) **Pop Density:** 871.9
Land: 1.6 sq. mi.; **Water:** 8.2 sq. mi.

Weallup Lake — CDP
Lat: 48-06-37 N **Long:** 122-18-17 W
Pop: 681 (1990) **Pop Density:** 131.0
Land: 5.2 sq. mi.; **Water:** 0.0 sq. mi.

West Lake Stevens — CDP
Lat: 47-59-36 N **Long:** 122-06-02 W
Pop: 12,453 (1990) **Pop Density:** 1082.9
Land: 11.5 sq. mi.; **Water:** 1.6 sq. mi.

Woodway — Town
ZIP: 98020 **Lat:** 47-47-40 N **Long:** 122-24-55 W
Pop: 914 (1990); 832 (1980) **Pop Density:** 830.9
Land: 1.1 sq. mi.; **Water:** 2.8 sq. mi.
Name origin: For its tree-lined streets.

Spokane County
County Seat: Spokane (ZIP: 99201)

Pop: 361,364 (1990); 341,835 (1980) **Pop Density:** 204.9
Land: 1763.8 sq. mi.; **Water:** 17.0 sq. mi. **Area Code:** 509

On central eastern border of WA; organized Jan 29, 1864 (prior to statehood) from Stevens County (an earlier Spokane County was merged with Stevens County in 1863). It is the only WA county with township governments in each township.

Name origin: For the Spokane Indians, or for the city or river also named for the tribe. The meaning of the name is uncertain: possibly 'sun people' or 'children of the sun,' or the name may be from Chief Illum Spokane, whose village was at the base of what became known as Spokane Falls.

Airway Heights — City
ZIP: 99001 **Lat:** 47-38-39 N **Long:** 117-34-58 W
Pop: 1,971 (1990); 1,730 (1980) **Pop Density:** 419.4
Land: 4.7 sq. mi.; **Water:** 0.0 sq. mi.

Cheney — City
ZIP: 99004 **Lat:** 47-29-26 N **Long:** 117-34-46 W
Pop: 7,723 (1990); 7,630 (1980) **Pop Density:** 2970.4
Land: 2.6 sq. mi.; **Water:** 0.0 sq. mi.
Name origin: For Benjamin P. Cheney, a founder of the Northern Pacific Railroad.

Country Homes — CDP
ZIP: 99218 **Lat:** 47-44-56 N **Long:** 117-25-22 W
Pop: 5,126 (1990) **Pop Density:** 2697.9
Land: 1.9 sq. mi.; **Water:** 0.0 sq. mi.

Deer Park — City
ZIP: 99006 **Lat:** 47-57-48 N **Long:** 117-26-02 W
Pop: 2,278 (1990); 2,140 (1980) **Pop Density:** 361.6
Land: 6.3 sq. mi.; **Water:** 0.0 sq. mi.

Dishman — CDP
ZIP: 99213 **Lat:** 47-39-32 N **Long:** 117-16-31 W
Pop: 9,671 (1990); 10,169 (1980) **Pop Density:** 2844.4
Land: 3.4 sq. mi.; **Water:** 0.0 sq. mi.

Fairchild Air Force Base — Military Facility
ZIP: 99011 **Lat:** 47-36-47 N **Long:** 117-38-37 W
Pop: 4,854 (1990); 5,353 (1980) **Pop Density:** 746.8
Land: 6.5 sq. mi.; **Water:** 0.0 sq. mi.

Fairfield — Town
ZIP: 99012 **Lat:** 47-23-06 N **Long:** 117-10-26 W
Pop: 446 (1990); 582 (1980) **Pop Density:** 743.3
Land: 0.6 sq. mi.; **Water:** 0.0 sq. mi. **Elev:** 2559 ft.

Fairwood — CDP
ZIP: 99218 **Lat:** 47-46-01 N **Long:** 117-24-58 W
Pop: 5,807 (1990); 5,337 (1980) **Pop Density:** 1528.2
Land: 3.8 sq. mi.; **Water:** 0.0 sq. mi.

Green Acres — CDP
Lat: 47-39-48 N **Long:** 117-09-39 W
Pop: 4,626 (1990) **Pop Density:** 1401.8
Land: 3.3 sq. mi.; **Water:** 0.1 sq. mi.

Latah — Town
ZIP: 99018 **Lat:** 47-16-54 N **Long:** 117-09-15 W
Pop: 175 (1990); 155 (1980) **Pop Density:** 583.3
Land: 0.3 sq. mi.; **Water:** 0.0 sq. mi.
Name origin: From an Indian term meaning 'place where fish are caught.'

Liberty Lake
CDP
ZIP: 99019 **Lat:** 47-39-15 N **Long:** 117-04-56 W
Pop: 2,015 (1990); 1,599 (1980) **Pop Density:** 959.5
Land: 2.1 sq. mi.; **Water:** 1.1 sq. mi.

Medical Lake
Town
ZIP: 99022 **Lat:** 47-34-12 N **Long:** 117-41-31 W
Pop: 3,664 (1990); 3,600 (1980) **Pop Density:** 1221.3
Land: 3.0 sq. mi.; **Water:** 0.2 sq. mi.
Name origin: For the nearby lake thought by Indians to cure rheumatism.

Millwood
Town
ZIP: 99212 **Lat:** 47-41-08 N **Long:** 117-16-45 W
Pop: 1,559 (1990); 1,717 (1980) **Pop Density:** 2598.3
Land: 0.6 sq. mi.; **Water:** 0.0 sq. mi.

Opportunity
CDP
ZIP: 99206 **Lat:** 47-38-58 N **Long:** 117-14-25 W
Pop: 22,326 (1990); 21,241 (1980) **Pop Density:** 3332.2
Land: 6.7 sq. mi.; **Water:** 0.0 sq. mi.

Otis Orchards-East Farms
CDP
ZIP: 99025 **Lat:** 47-42-00 N **Long:** 117-05-24 W
Pop: 5,811 (1990); 4,597 (1980) **Pop Density:** 830.1
Land: 7.0 sq. mi.; **Water:** 0.1 sq. mi.

Rockford
Town
ZIP: 99030 **Lat:** 47-27-03 N **Long:** 117-07-45 W
Pop: 481 (1990); 442 (1980) **Pop Density:** 687.1
Land: 0.7 sq. mi.; **Water:** 0.0 sq. mi. **Elev:** 2361 ft.
Name origin: For the many fords crossing Rock Creek, which runs through the town.

Spangle
City
ZIP: 99031 **Lat:** 47-25-49 N **Long:** 117-22-43 W
Pop: 229 (1990); 276 (1980) **Pop Density:** 763.3
Land: 0.3 sq. mi.; **Water:** 0.0 sq. mi.
Platted 1886.
Name origin: For homesteader William Spangle.

Spokane
City
ZIP: 99210 **Lat:** 47-40-20 N **Long:** 117-24-50 W
Pop: 177,196 (1990); 171,300 (1980) **Pop Density:** 3169.9
Land: 55.9 sq. mi.; **Water:** 0.7 sq. mi.
In east-central WA on the Spokane River, 125 mi. northeast of Richland. Settled 1872; incorporated 1881.
Name origin: For the Spokane Indians, or for the city or river also named for the tribe. The meaning of the name is uncertain: possibly 'sun people' or 'children of the sun,' or the name may be from Chief Illum Spokane, whose village was at the base of what became known as Spokane Falls.

Town and Country
CDP
Lat: 47-43-38 N **Long:** 117-25-13 W
Pop: 4,921 (1990); 5,578 (1980) **Pop Density:** 3515.0
Land: 1.4 sq. mi.; **Water:** 0.0 sq. mi.

Trentwood
CDP
Lat: 47-41-52 N **Long:** 117-12-48 W
Pop: 4,060 (1990) **Pop Density:** 2255.6
Land: 1.8 sq. mi.; **Water:** 0.0 sq. mi.

Veradale
CDP
ZIP: 99037 **Lat:** 47-38-58 N **Long:** 117-12-27 W
Pop: 7,836 (1990); 7,256 (1980) **Pop Density:** 2527.7
Land: 3.1 sq. mi.; **Water:** 0.0 sq. mi.

Waverly
Town
ZIP: 99039 **Lat:** 47-20-22 N **Long:** 117-13-43 W
Pop: 37 (1990); 99 (1980) **Pop Density:** 92.5
Land: 0.4 sq. mi.; **Water:** 0.0 sq. mi.
Name origin: For Waverly, IA, the former home of early settlers.

Stevens County
County Seat: Colville (ZIP: 99114)

Pop: 30,948 (1990); 28,979 (1980) **Pop Density:** 12.5
Land: 2478.3 sq. mi.; **Water:** 62.3 sq. mi. **Area Code:** 509
On the northeastern border of WA, northwest of Spokane; original county. Organized 1854 (prior to statehood).
Name origin: For Gen. Isaac Ingalls Stevens (1818–62), an officer in the Mexican-American War and the Civil War; first governor of WA Territory (1853–57).

Chewelah
City
ZIP: 99109 **Lat:** 48-17-09 N **Long:** 117-43-46 W
Pop: 1,945 (1990); 1,888 (1980) **Pop Density:** 810.4
Land: 2.4 sq. mi.; **Water:** 0.0 sq. mi. **Elev:** 1671 ft.
Name origin: From an Indian term meaning 'snake,' possibly descriptive of meandering streams.

Colville
City
ZIP: 99114 **Lat:** 48-32-35 N **Long:** 117-53-42 W
Pop: 4,360 (1990); 4,510 (1980) **Pop Density:** 2076.2
Land: 2.1 sq. mi.; **Water:** 0.0 sq. mi.
Name origin: For Andrew Colville, governor of Hudson Bay Company in the early 1800s.

Kettle Falls
City
Lat: 48-36-21 N **Long:** 118-03-32 W
Pop: 1,272 (1990); 1,087 (1980) **Pop Density:** 1413.3
Land: 0.9 sq. mi.; **Water:** 0.0 sq. mi. **Elev:** 1625 ft.

Marcus
Town
ZIP: 99151 **Lat:** 48-39-47 N **Long:** 118-03-28 W
Pop: 135 (1990); 174 (1980) **Pop Density:** 675.0
Land: 0.2 sq. mi.; **Water:** 0.0 sq. mi.
Name origin: For Marcus Oppenheimer, one of its two original settlers.

Northport Town
ZIP: 99157 **Lat:** 48-55-00 N **Long:** 117-46-41 W
Pop: 308 (1990); 368 (1980) **Pop Density:** 513.3
Land: 0.6 sq. mi.; **Water:** 0.0 sq. mi.

Springdale Town
ZIP: 99173 **Lat:** 48-03-24 N **Long:** 117-44-46 W
Pop: 260 (1990); 281 (1980) **Pop Density:** 260.0
Land: 1.0 sq. mi.; **Water:** 0.0 sq. mi. **Elev:** 2070 ft.

Name origin: For nearby Spring Creek. Originally called Squire.

Thurston County
County Seat: Olympia (ZIP: 98502)

Pop: 161,238 (1990); 124,264 (1980) **Pop Density:** 221.8
Land: 727.1 sq. mi.; **Water:** 46.6 sq. mi. **Area Code:** 206

In west-central WA at the southern end of Puget Sound, southwest of Tacoma; organized Jan 12, 1852 (prior to statehood) from Lewis County.

Name origin: For Samuel Royal Thurston (1816–51), first delegate to Congress from the Oregon territory (1849–51).

Bucoda Town
ZIP: 98530 **Lat:** 46-47-53 N **Long:** 122-52-04 W
Pop: 536 (1990); 519 (1980) **Pop Density:** 1340.0
Land: 0.4 sq. mi.; **Water:** 0.0 sq. mi.

Grand Mound CDP
Lat: 46-48-35 N **Long:** 123-00-45 W
Pop: 1,394 (1990) **Pop Density:** 449.7
Land: 3.1 sq. mi.; **Water:** 0.0 sq. mi.

Lacey City
ZIP: 98503 **Lat:** 47-01-58 N **Long:** 122-48-20 W
Pop: 19,279 (1990); 13,940 (1980) **Pop Density:** 1908.8
Land: 10.1 sq. mi.; **Water:** 0.4 sq. mi.

In western WA directly east of Olympia.

Name origin: For O.C. Lacey, a local businessman who owned much local property. Formerly called Woodland but changed to present name because there was another town of the same name in the state.

Nisqually Indian Community CDP
Lat: 47-00-21 N **Long:** 122-40-11 W
Pop: 558 (1990) **Pop Density:** 214.6
Land: 2.6 sq. mi.; **Water:** 0.0 sq. mi.

North Yelm CDP
Lat: 46-57-47 N **Long:** 122-36-06 W
Pop: 2,075 (1990) **Pop Density:** 532.1
Land: 3.9 sq. mi.; **Water:** 0.0 sq. mi.

Olympia City
ZIP: 98501 **Lat:** 47-02-30 N **Long:** 122-53-37 W
Pop: 33,840 (1990); 27,447 (1980) **Pop Density:** 2101.9
Land: 16.1 sq. mi.; **Water:** 1.8 sq. mi.

In southwestern WA on Puget Sound, 25 mi. southwest of Tacoma. State capital. Settled 1845; incorporated 1859.

Name origin: Suggested by Col. Isaac N. Ebey from the book *Life of Olympia*.

Rainier Town
ZIP: 98576 **Lat:** 46-53-25 N **Long:** 122-41-04 W
Pop: 991 (1990); 891 (1980) **Pop Density:** 660.7
Land: 1.5 sq. mi.; **Water:** 0.0 sq. mi. **Elev:** 428 ft.

Name origin: For nearby Mt. Rainier.

Rochester CDP
ZIP: 98579 **Lat:** 46-49-44 N **Long:** 123-04-14 W
Pop: 1,250 (1990) **Pop Density:** 543.5
Land: 2.3 sq. mi.; **Water:** 0.0 sq. mi.

Tanglewilde-Thompson Place CDP
ZIP: 98506 **Lat:** 47-03-08 N **Long:** 122-46-41 W
Pop: 6,061 (1990); 5,910 (1980) **Pop Density:** 3565.3
Land: 1.7 sq. mi.; **Water:** 0.0 sq. mi.

Tenino Town
ZIP: 98589 **Lat:** 46-51-26 N **Long:** 122-50-50 W
Pop: 1,292 (1990); 1,280 (1980) **Pop Density:** 1615.0
Land: 0.8 sq. mi.; **Water:** 0.0 sq. mi.

Name origin: From a Chinook term meaning 'fork' or 'junction.'

Tumwater City
ZIP: 98502 **Lat:** 46-59-53 N **Long:** 122-55-04 W
Pop: 9,976 (1990); 6,705 (1980) **Pop Density:** 1039.2
Land: 9.6 sq. mi.; **Water:** 0.1 sq. mi.

For its location at the falls of the Deschutes River.

Name origin: From 'tun-wat-er,' Chinook jargon descriptive of falls.

Yelm Town
ZIP: 98597 **Lat:** 46-56-44 N **Long:** 122-36-12 W
Pop: 1,337 (1990); 1,294 (1980) **Pop Density:** 1028.5
Land: 1.3 sq. mi.; **Water:** 0.0 sq. mi.

Wahkiakum County
County Seat: Cathlamet (ZIP: 98612)

Pop: 3,327 (1990); 3,832 (1980)   **Pop Density:** 12.6
Land: 264.3 sq. mi.; **Water:** 22.4 sq. mi.   **Area Code:** 206

On the southwestern border of WA at the mouth of the Columbia River; organized Apr 25, 1854 (prior to statehood) from Lewis County.

Name origin: For a Chinook tribe and chief, *Wakiacum*, a name believed to mean 'tall trees' or 'big timber.' The spelling was probably changed to reflect the Indian pronunciation.

Cathlamet   Town
ZIP: 98612   **Lat:** 46-12-00 N **Long:** 123-22-46 W
Pop: 508 (1990); 635 (1980)   **Pop Density:** 1270.0
Land: 0.4 sq. mi.; **Water:** 0.0 sq. mi.   **Elev:** 53 ft.

Name origin: From an Indian term meaning 'stone,' a reference to the bed of the adjacent Columbia River.

Walla Walla County
County Seat: Walla Walla (ZIP: 99362)

Pop: 48,439 (1990); 47,435 (1980)   **Pop Density:** 38.1
Land: 1270.5 sq. mi.; **Water:** 28.7 sq. mi.   **Area Code:** 509

On the southeastern border of WA; original county; organized Apr 25, 1854 (prior to statehood).

Name origin: Apparently for a small tribe, closely related to the Nez Perce, which took its name from the Walla Walla River, 'place of many waters,' referring to the many tributaries, springs, and streams in the area. Lewis and Clark recorded the name as *Wollah Wollah*.

Burbank   CDP
Lat: 46-11-29 N **Long:** 118-58-53 W
Pop: 1,745 (1990)   **Pop Density:** 484.7
Land: 3.6 sq. mi.; **Water:** 0.0 sq. mi.

College Place   City
ZIP: 99324   **Lat:** 46-02-38 N **Long:** 118-23-01 W
Pop: 6,308 (1990); 5,771 (1980)   **Pop Density:** 3710.6
Land: 1.7 sq. mi.; **Water:** 0.0 sq. mi.

Name origin: From a local Seventh Day Adventist college.

Garrett   CDP
Lat: 46-03-40 N **Long:** 118-22-59 W
Pop: 1,004 (1990); 1,134 (1980)   **Pop Density:** 478.1
Land: 2.1 sq. mi.; **Water:** 0.0 sq. mi.

Prescott   Town
ZIP: 99348   **Lat:** 46-17-56 N **Long:** 118-18-41 W
Pop: 267 (1990); 341 (1980)   **Pop Density:** 890.0
Land: 0.3 sq. mi.; **Water:** 0.0 sq. mi.   **Elev:** 1055 ft.

Name origin: For C.H. Prescott, general superintendent of the Oregon Railway and Navigation Company.

Waitsburg   City
ZIP: 99361   **Lat:** 46-16-08 N **Long:** 118-09-01 W
Pop: 990 (1990); 1,035 (1980)   **Pop Density:** 1100.0
Land: 0.9 sq. mi.; **Water:** 0.0 sq. mi.

Name origin: For Sylvester M. Wait, who built a flour mill in the area 1864.

Walla Walla   City
ZIP: 99362   **Lat:** 46-04-00 N **Long:** 118-20-28 W
Pop: 26,478 (1990); 25,618 (1980)   **Pop Density:** 2570.7
Land: 10.3 sq. mi.; **Water:** 0.0 sq. mi.

In southeastern WA, 50 mi. southeast of Richland, near the WA-OR border. Incorporated 1862.

Name origin: Apparently for a small tribe, closely related to the Nez Perce, which took its name from the Walla Walla River, 'place of many waters,' referring to the many tributaries, springs, and streams in the area. Lewis and Clark recorded the name as *Wollah Wollah*.

Walla Walla East   CDP
Lat: 46-03-16 N **Long:** 118-18-09 W
Pop: 2,959 (1990); 3,285 (1980)   **Pop Density:** 1557.4
Land: 1.9 sq. mi.; **Water:** 0.0 sq. mi.

Whatcom County
County Seat: Bellingham (ZIP: 98225)

Pop: 127,780 (1990); 106,701 (1980) **Pop Density:** 60.3
Land: 2120.1 sq. mi.; **Water:** 383.6 sq. mi. **Area Code:** 206

On the northwestern border of WA, bordered on west by Georgia Strait; organized Mar 9, 1854 (prior to statehood) from Island County.

Name origin: From the Lummi Indian word *what-coom* or *whuks-qua-koos-ta-qua*, said to mean 'noisy, rumbling water,' referring to Whatcom Falls on Bellingham Bay.

Bellingham City
ZIP: 98225 **Lat:** 48-44-38 N **Long:** 122-28-00 W
Pop: 52,179 (1990); 45,794 (1980) **Pop Density:** 2371.8
Land: 22.0 sq. mi.; **Water:** 2.5 sq. mi.

In northwestern WA on Bellingham Bay, 80 mi. north of Seattle, near the U.S.-Canadian border. Incorporated 1903.

Name origin: For Bellingham Bay, which was named for Sir William Bellingham by the expedition led by George Vancouver (1757–98).

Birch Bay CDP
ZIP: 98230 **Lat:** 48-55-24 N **Long:** 122-45-11 W
Pop: 2,656 (1990) **Pop Density:** 166.0
Land: 16.0 sq. mi.; **Water:** 5.4 sq. mi.

Blaine City
ZIP: 98230 **Lat:** 48-59-20 N **Long:** 122-45-29 W
Pop: 2,489 (1990); 2,363 (1980) **Pop Density:** 732.1
Land: 3.4 sq. mi.; **Water:** 2.9 sq. mi.

Name origin: For James G. Blaine, the Republican presidential nominee in 1884.

Everson City
ZIP: 98247 **Lat:** 48-54-53 N **Long:** 122-21-03 W
Pop: 1,490 (1990); 898 (1980) **Pop Density:** 1354.5
Land: 1.1 sq. mi.; **Water:** 0.0 sq. mi. **Elev:** 90 ft.

Name origin: For Ever Everson, the first European settler north of the Nooksack River.

Ferndale City
ZIP: 98248 **Lat:** 48-51-03 N **Long:** 122-35-13 W
Pop: 5,398 (1990); 3,855 (1980) **Pop Density:** 1199.6
Land: 4.5 sq. mi.; **Water:** 0.0 sq. mi.

Name origin: For the first school location, a fern patch.

Lynden City
ZIP: 98264 **Lat:** 48-56-54 N **Long:** 122-27-21 W
Pop: 5,709 (1990); 4,022 (1980) **Pop Density:** 2038.9
Land: 2.8 sq. mi.; **Water:** 0.0 sq. mi. **Elev:** 103 ft.

Name origin: Spelled *Linden* in a poem, but Phoebe Judson changed it to its present form because she thought it more poetic.

Marietta-Alderwood CDP
Lat: 48-47-20 N **Long:** 122-33-17 W
Pop: 2,766 (1990); 2,324 (1980) **Pop Density:** 461.0
Land: 6.0 sq. mi.; **Water:** 1.4 sq. mi.

Nooksack City
ZIP: 98276 **Lat:** 48-55-42 N **Long:** 122-19-16 W
Pop: 584 (1990); 429 (1980) **Pop Density:** 973.3
Land: 0.6 sq. mi.; **Water:** 0.0 sq. mi. **Elev:** 84 ft.

Sudden Valley CDP
Lat: 48-43-15 N **Long:** 122-20-41 W
Pop: 2,615 (1990) **Pop Density:** 415.1
Land: 6.3 sq. mi.; **Water:** 1.9 sq. mi.

Sumas City
ZIP: 98295 **Lat:** 48-59-46 N **Long:** 122-15-53 W
Pop: 744 (1990); 712 (1980) **Pop Density:** 826.7
Land: 0.9 sq. mi.; **Water:** 0.0 sq. mi.

Name origin: From an Indian term meaning 'big level opening.'

Whitman County
County Seat: Colfax (ZIP: 99111)

Pop: 38,775 (1990); 40,103 (1980)   **Pop Density:** 18.0
Land: 2159.4 sq. mi.; **Water:** 18.2 sq. mi.   **Area Code:** 509
On the southeastern border of WA, S of Spokane; organized Nov 29, 1871 (prior to statehood) from Stevens County.
Name origin: For Dr. Marcus Whitman (1802–47), massacred leader of a missionary colony.

Albion   Town
ZIP: 99102   **Lat:** 46-47-33 N   **Long:** 117-14-58 W
Pop: 632 (1990); 631 (1980)   **Pop Density:** 1580.0
Land: 0.4 sq. mi.; **Water:** 0.0 sq. mi.
Name origin: From the literary name for England, in honor of early English exploration of the region.

Colfax   City
ZIP: 99111   **Lat:** 46-53-02 N   **Long:** 117-21-45 W
Pop: 2,713 (1990); 2,780 (1980)   **Pop Density:** 1808.7
Land: 1.5 sq. mi.; **Water:** 0.0 sq. mi.   **Elev:** 1962 ft.
Founded 1872.
Name origin: For Ulysses S. Grant's first-term vice president, Schuyler Colfax (1823–85).

Colton   Town
ZIP: 99113   **Lat:** 46-34-06 N   **Long:** 117-07-37 W
Pop: 325 (1990); 307 (1980)   **Pop Density:** 541.7
Land: 0.6 sq. mi.; **Water:** 0.0 sq. mi.   **Elev:** 2562 ft.

Endicott   Town
ZIP: 99125   **Lat:** 46-55-43 N   **Long:** 117-41-05 W
Pop: 320 (1990); 290 (1980)   **Pop Density:** 1066.7
Land: 0.3 sq. mi.; **Water:** 0.0 sq. mi.   **Elev:** 1706 ft.

Farmington   Town
ZIP: 99128   **Lat:** 47-05-20 N   **Long:** 117-02-42 W
Pop: 126 (1990); 176 (1980)   **Pop Density:** 315.0
Land: 0.4 sq. mi.; **Water:** 0.0 sq. mi.   **Elev:** 2626 ft.
Name origin: For Farmington, MN, so named by settler G.W. Truax.

Garfield   Town
ZIP: 99130   **Lat:** 47-00-30 N   **Long:** 117-08-26 W
Pop: 544 (1990); 599 (1980)   **Pop Density:** 906.7
Land: 0.6 sq. mi.; **Water:** 0.0 sq. mi.   **Elev:** 2467 ft.
Name origin: For James Garfield (1831–81), twentieth U.S. president.

La Crosse   Town
ZIP: 99143   **Lat:** 46-48-51 N   **Long:** 117-52-44 W
Pop: 336 (1990); 373 (1980)   **Pop Density:** 1120.0
Land: 0.3 sq. mi.; **Water:** 0.0 sq. mi.

Lamont   Town
ZIP: 99017   **Lat:** 47-12-02 N   **Long:** 117-54-12 W
Pop: 91 (1990); 101 (1980)   **Pop Density:** 303.3
Land: 0.3 sq. mi.; **Water:** 0.0 sq. mi.   **Elev:** 1949 ft.
Name origin: For Daniel Lamont, vice president of the Northern Pacific Railway Company.

Malden   The Whitman County
ZIP: 99149   **Lat:** 47-13-52 N   **Long:** 117-28-18 W
Pop: 189 (1990); 200 (1980)   **Pop Density:** 315.0
Land: 0.6 sq. mi.; **Water:** 0.0 sq. mi.
Name origin: For Malden, MA, so named by a railroad company official.

Oakesdale   Town
ZIP: 99158   **Lat:** 47-07-51 N   **Long:** 117-14-43 W
Pop: 346 (1990); 444 (1980)   **Pop Density:** 346.0
Land: 1.0 sq. mi.; **Water:** 0.0 sq. mi.   **Elev:** 2461 ft.

Palouse   City
ZIP: 99161   **Lat:** 46-54-39 N   **Long:** 117-04-25 W
Pop: 915 (1990); 1,005 (1980)   **Pop Density:** 915.0
Land: 1.0 sq. mi.; **Water:** 0.0 sq. mi.   **Elev:** 2426 ft.
Name origin: From *palouse* 'grasslands,' used by early French-Canadian fur trappers to describe the grass-covered hills north of the Snake River.

Pullman   City
ZIP: 99163   **Lat:** 46-43-59 N   **Long:** 117-09-43 W
Pop: 23,478 (1990); 23,579 (1980)   **Pop Density:** 3504.2
Land: 6.7 sq. mi.; **Water:** 0.0 sq. mi.
In southeastern WA, 65 mi. southeast of Spokane. Incorporated 1888.
Name origin: For sleeping-car manufacturer George Pullman (1831–97).

Rosalia   Town
ZIP: 99170   **Lat:** 47-14-13 N   **Long:** 117-22-04 W
Pop: 552 (1990); 572 (1980)   **Pop Density:** 1104.0
Land: 0.5 sq. mi.; **Water:** 0.0 sq. mi.   **Elev:** 2232 ft.

St. John   Town
Lat: 47-05-19 N   **Long:** 117-34-51 W
Pop: 499 (1990); 529 (1980)   **Pop Density:** 1247.5
Land: 0.4 sq. mi.; **Water:** 0.0 sq. mi.
Name origin: For E.T. St. John, an early settler in the area.

Tekoa   City
ZIP: 99033   **Lat:** 47-13-32 N   **Long:** 117-04-23 W
Pop: 750 (1990); 854 (1980)   **Pop Density:** 681.8
Land: 1.1 sq. mi.; **Water:** 0.0 sq. mi.   **Elev:** 2494 ft.
Name origin: For the biblical town in Judah.

Uniontown   Town
ZIP: 99179   **Lat:** 46-32-14 N   **Long:** 117-05-04 W
Pop: 277 (1990); 286 (1980)   **Pop Density:** 307.8
Land: 0.9 sq. mi.; **Water:** 0.0 sq. mi.   **Elev:** 2572 ft.
Settled 1879.

WASHINGTON, Yakima County

Yakima County
County Seat: Yakima (ZIP: 98901)

Pop: 188,823 (1990); 172,508 (1980)
Land: 4296.1 sq. mi.; **Water:** 15.7 sq. mi.
Pop Density: 44.0
Area Code: 509

In south-central WA; organized Jan 1, 1865 (prior to statehood) from Indian Territory.

Name origin: For a tribe of Shahaptian Indians; name is believed to mean either 'runaway,' for a chief's errant daughter, or possibly 'black bear.'

Fairview-Sumach CDP
Lat: 46-35-15 N Long: 120-28-28 W
Pop: 2,749 (1990); 2,788 (1980) **Pop Density:** 1963.6
Land: 1.4 sq. mi.; **Water:** 0.1 sq. mi.

Fruitvale CDP
Lat: 46-37-01 N Long: 120-32-30 W
Pop: 4,125 (1990); 3,967 (1980) **Pop Density:** 1793.5
Land: 2.3 sq. mi.; **Water:** 0.1 sq. mi.

Grandview City
ZIP: 98930 Lat: 46-14-39 N Long: 119-54-39 W
Pop: 7,169 (1990); 5,615 (1980) **Pop Density:** 1525.3
Land: 4.7 sq. mi.; **Water:** 0.1 sq. mi.
Founded 1906.
Name origin: For its view of Mt. Adams and Mt. Rainier.

Granger Town
ZIP: 98932 Lat: 46-20-34 N Long: 120-11-22 W
Pop: 2,053 (1990); 1,812 (1980) **Pop Density:** 1866.4
Land: 1.1 sq. mi.; **Water:** 0.0 sq. mi. **Elev:** 731 ft.
Founded 1902.
Name origin: For irrigation canal company president, Walter N. Granger.

Harrah Town
ZIP: 98933 Lat: 46-24-15 N Long: 120-32-28 W
Pop: 341 (1990); 343 (1980) **Pop Density:** 1136.7
Land: 0.3 sq. mi.; **Water:** 0.0 sq. mi.
Name origin: For prominent rancher J.T. Harrah. Originally called Saluskin for a Yakima chief.

Mabton Town
ZIP: 98935 Lat: 46-12-46 N Long: 119-59-44 W
Pop: 1,482 (1990); 1,248 (1980) **Pop Density:** 3705.0
Land: 0.4 sq. mi.; **Water:** 0.0 sq. mi.
Name origin: Coined from the first name of Mabel Anderson, daughter of pioneer railroad builder Dorset Boker.

Moxee Town
ZIP: 98936 Lat: 46-33-48 N Long: 120-23-55 W
Pop: 814 (1990); 687 (1980) **Pop Density:** 814.0
Land: 1.0 sq. mi.; **Water:** 0.0 sq. mi.

Naches Town
ZIP: 98929 Lat: 46-43-46 N Long: 120-41-50 W
Pop: 596 (1990); 644 (1980) **Pop Density:** 1490.0
Land: 0.4 sq. mi.; **Water:** 0.0 sq. mi.

Satus CDP
Lat: 46-13-55 N Long: 120-07-06 W
Pop: 1,343 (1990) **Pop Density:** 19.6
Land: 68.5 sq. mi.; **Water:** 0.8 sq. mi.

Selah City
ZIP: 98942 Lat: 46-39-22 N Long: 120-32-02 W
Pop: 5,113 (1990); 4,500 (1980) **Pop Density:** 1893.7
Land: 2.7 sq. mi.; **Water:** 0.0 sq. mi.
Name origin: From an Indian term meaning 'still water,' referring to a quiet section of the Yakima River.

South Broadway CDP
Lat: 46-33-59 N Long: 120-30-56 W
Pop: 2,735 (1990); 3,500 (1980) **Pop Density:** 2735.0
Land: 1.0 sq. mi.; **Water:** 0.0 sq. mi.

Sunnyside City
ZIP: 98944 Lat: 46-19-15 N Long: 120-00-45 W
Pop: 11,238 (1990); 9,225 (1980) **Pop Density:** 3121.7
Land: 3.6 sq. mi.; **Water:** 0.0 sq. mi.
Founded 1893. Incorporated 1902.
Name origin: For its founder, Walter Granger, president of Sunnyside Canal Company.

Terrace Heights CDP
Lat: 46-36-21 N Long: 120-26-15 W
Pop: 4,223 (1990); 3,199 (1980) **Pop Density:** 1141.4
Land: 3.7 sq. mi.; **Water:** 0.0 sq. mi.

Tieton Town
ZIP: 98947 Lat: 46-42-06 N Long: 120-45-10 W
Pop: 693 (1990); 528 (1980) **Pop Density:** 1386.0
Land: 0.5 sq. mi.; **Water:** 0.0 sq. mi.
Name origin: For the Tieton River, itself named from an Indian term meaning 'roaring water.'

Toppenish City
ZIP: 98948 Lat: 46-22-52 N Long: 120-18-41 W
Pop: 7,419 (1990); 6,517 (1980) **Pop Density:** 4121.7
Land: 1.8 sq. mi.; **Water:** 0.0 sq. mi.
Name origin: From a Yakima Indian term meaning 'people from the foot of the hills.'

Union Gap City
ZIP: 98903 Lat: 46-33-18 N Long: 120-29-14 W
Pop: 3,120 (1990); 3,184 (1980) **Pop Density:** 800.0
Land: 3.9 sq. mi.; **Water:** 0.0 sq. mi.

Wapato City
ZIP: 98951 Lat: 46-26-44 N Long: 120-25-14 W
Pop: 3,795 (1990); 3,307 (1980) **Pop Density:** 4216.7
Land: 0.9 sq. mi.; **Water:** 0.0 sq. mi.
Name origin: From the Chinook term meaning 'potato,' so named 1902.

West Valley CDP
Lat: 46-35-32 N Long: 120-36-14 W
Pop: 6,594 (1990) **Pop Density:** 1998.2
Land: 3.3 sq. mi.; **Water:** 0.0 sq. mi.

White Swan
CDP
ZIP: 98952 **Lat:** 46-23-17 N **Long:** 120-43-14 W
Pop: 2,669 (1990) **Pop Density:** 25.8
Land: 103.6 sq. mi.; **Water:** 0.0 sq. mi.

Yakima
City
ZIP: 98903 **Lat:** 46-35-33 N **Long:** 120-31-44 W
Pop: 54,827 (1990); 49,826 (1980) **Pop Density:** 3655.1
Land: 15.0 sq. mi.; **Water:** 0.2 sq. mi. **Elev:** 1066 ft.
In south-central WA on the Yakima River, 60 mi. northwest of Richland. Incorporated 1886.
Name origin: For the Indian tribe of the Shahaptian branch of Shapwailutan linguistic stock that lived along the river. The name is believed to mean 'runaway,' but the connotation is unclear.

Zillah
City
ZIP: 98953 **Lat:** 46-24-13 N **Long:** 120-15-34 W
Pop: 1,911 (1990); 1,599 (1980) **Pop Density:** 1737.3
Land: 1.1 sq. mi.; **Water:** 0.0 sq. mi.

WASHINGTON

Index to Places and Counties in Washington

Aberdeen (Grays Harbor) City..........*738*
Adams County..............................*731*
Airway Heights (Spokane) City.........*754*
Albion (Whitman) Town *759*
Alderwood Manor-Bothell North (Snohomish) CDP *752*
Algona (King) City............................*740*
Allyn-Grapeview (Mason) CDP *746*
Almira (Lincoln) Town.....................*746*
Anacortes (Skagit) City....................*751*
Arlington (Snohomish) City *752*
Artondale (Pierce) CDP *749*
Asotin (Asotin) City *731*
Asotin County...............................*731*
Auburn (King) City...........................*740*
Ault Field (Island) Military Facility..*739*
Bangor Trident Base (Kitsap) Military Facility *743*
Battle Ground (Clark) City *733*
Beaux Arts Village (King) Town *740*
Bellevue (King) City..........................*740*
Bellingham (Whatcom) City............*758*
Benton City (Benton) City *732*
Benton County..............................*732*
Bingen (Klickitat) City *744*
Birch Bay (Whatcom) CDP *758*
Black Diamond (King) City *740*
Blaine (Whatcom) City.....................*758*
Bonney Lake (Pierce) City...............*749*
Bothell (King) City............................*740*
Bothell (Snohomish) City *752*
Bremerton (Kitsap) City...................*743*
Brewster (Okanogan) City *747*
Bridgeport (Douglas) Town *736*
Brier (Snohomish) City *752*
Brush Prairie (Clark) CDP *733*
Bryn Mawr-Skyway (King) CDP.......*740*
Buckley (Pierce) City........................*749*
Bucoda (Thurston) Town..................*756*
Burbank (Walla Walla) CDP *757*
Burien (King) CDP.............................*740*
Burlington (Skagit) City....................*751*
Camas (Clark) City...........................*733*
Carbonado (Pierce) Town.................*749*
Carnation (King) City.......................*741*
Carson River Valley (Skamania) CDP *752*
Cascade-Fairwood (King) CDP *741*
Cascade Park East (Clark) CDP.......*733*
Cascade Park West (Clark) CDP.....*734*
Cascade Valley (Grant) CDP............*737*
Cashmere (Chelan) City *732*
Castle Rock (Cowlitz) City...............*735*
Cathan (Snohomish) CDP *752*
Cathlamet (Wahkiakum) Town *757*
Centralia (Lewis) City *745*
Central Park (Grays Harbor) CDP ...*738*
Chehalis (Lewis) City *745*
Chehalis Village (Grays Harbor) CDP *739*
Chelan (Chelan) City *732*
Chelan County..............................*732*
Cheney (Spokane) City *754*
Chewelah (Stevens) City..................*755*
Clallam County *733*
Clark County.................................*733*
Clarkston (Asotin) City *731*
Clarkston Heights-Vineland (Asotin) CDP *731*
Cle Elum (Kittitas) City *744*

Clinton (Island) CDP *739*
Clyde Hill (King) Town *741*
Colfax (Whitman) City.....................*759*
College Place (Walla Walla) City......*757*
Colton (Whitman) Town *759*
Columbia County..........................*735*
Colville (Stevens) City.....................*755*
Conconully (Okanogan) Town...........*747*
Concrete (Skagit) Town *751*
Connell (Franklin) Town *737*
Cosmopolis (Grays Harbor) City *739*
Coulee City (Grant) Town................*737*
Coulee Dam (Douglas) Town *736*
Coulee Dam (Grant) Town *738*
Coulee Dam (Okanogan) Town........*747*
Country Homes (Spokane) CDP *754*
Coupeville (Island) Town *739*
Covington-Sawyer-Wilderness (King) CDP *741*
Cowlitz County *735*
Creston (Lincoln) Town....................*746*
Cusick (Pend Oreille) Town *748*
Darrington (Snohomish) Town *752*
Davenport (Lincoln) City..................*746*
Dayton (Columbia) City....................*735*
Deer Park (Spokane) City *754*
Des Moines (King) City *741*
Dishman (Spokane) CDP *754*
Douglas County.............................*736*
DuPont (Pierce) City.........................*749*
Duvall (King) City.............................*741*
Eastgate (King) CDP *741*
East Hill-Meridian (King) CDP *741*
East Port Orchard (Kitsap) CDP *743*
East Renton Highlands (King) CDP.*741*
East Wenatchee (Douglas) City *736*
East Wenatchee Bench (Douglas) CDP *736*
Eatonville (Pierce) Town *749*
Edgewood-North Hill (Pierce) CDP .*749*
Edmonds (Snohomish) City *752*
Electric City (Grant) Town................*738*
Elk Plain (Pierce) CDP......................*749*
Ellensburg (Kittitas) City..................*744*
Ellsworth North (Clark) CDP *734*
Ellsworth South (Clark) CDP...........*734*
Elma (Grays Harbor) City.................*739*
Elmer City (Okanogan) Town *747*
Endicott (Whitman) Town *759*
Entiat (Chelan) Town *732*
Enumclaw (King) City *741*
Ephrata (Grant) City *738*
Erlands Point-Kitsap Lake (Kitsap) CDP *743*
Esperance (Snohomish) CDP...........*753*
Everett (Snohomish) City.................*753*
Evergreen (Clark) CDP......................*734*
Everson (Whatcom) City..................*758*
Fairchild Air Force Base (Spokane) Military Facility..................................... *754*
Fairfield (Spokane) Town *754*
Fairview-Sumach (Yakima) CDP *760*
Fairwood (Spokane) CDP..................*754*
Fall City (King) CDP..........................*741*
Farmington (Whitman) Town *759*
Federal Way (King) CDP *741*
Felida (Clark) CDP............................*734*
Ferndale (Whatcom) City.................*758*
Ferry County..................................*736*
Fife (Pierce) City *749*

Finley (Benton) CDP.........................*732*
Fircrest (Pierce) Town *749*
Five Corners (Clark) CDP.................*734*
Fords Prairie (Lewis) CDP................*745*
Forks (Clallam) City *733*
Fort Lewis (Pierce) Military Facility.*749*
Fox Island (Pierce) CDP *749*
Franklin County *737*
Frederickson (Pierce) CDP...............*749*
Freeland (Island) CDP *739*
Friday Harbor (San Juan) Town *751*
Fruitvale (Yakima) CDP *760*
Garfield (Whitman) Town................*759*
Garfield County............................*737*
Garrett (Walla Walla) CDP...............*757*
George (Grant) Town *738*
Gig Harbor (Pierce) Town.................*749*
Gold Bar (Snohomish) Town *753*
Goldendale (Klickitat) City...............*744*
Grand Coulee (Grant) City *738*
Grand Mound (Thurston) CDP *756*
Grandview (Yakima) City *760*
Granger (Yakima) Town....................*760*
Granite Falls (Snohomish) Town *753*
Grant County.................................*737*
Grays Harbor County....................*738*
Green Acres (Spokane) CDP............*754*
Hadlock-Irondale (Jefferson) CDP...*740*
Hamilton (Skagit) Town *751*
Harbour Pointe (Snohomish) CDP...*753*
Harrah (Yakima) Town......................*760*
Harrington (Lincoln) Town *746*
Hartline (Grant) Town......................*738*
Hatton (Adams) Town......................*731*
Hazel Dell North (Clark) CDP..........*734*
Hazel Dell South (Clark) CDP..........*734*
Highland (Benton) CDP....................*732*
Hoquiam (Grays Harbor) City..........*739*
Hunts Point (King) Town..................*741*
Ilwaco (Pacific) Town *748*
Inchelium (Ferry) CDP......................*736*
Index (Snohomish) Town *753*
Indianola (Kitsap) CDP.....................*743*
Inglewood-Finn Hill (King) CDP......*741*
Ione (Pend Oreille) Town *748*
Island County.................................*739*
Issaquah (King) City..........................*741*
Jefferson County *740*
John Sam Lake (Snohomish) CDP ...*753*
Kahlotus (Franklin) Town.................*737*
Kalama (Cowlitz) City......................*735*
Kelso (Cowlitz) City..........................*735*
Kenmore (King) CDP........................*741*
Kennewick (Benton) City *732*
Kent (King) City.................................*741*
Kettle Falls (Stevens) City...............*755*
King County...................................*740*
Kingsgate (King) CDP.......................*741*
Kingston (Kitsap) CDP......................*743*
Kirkland (King) City *741*
Kitsap County................................*743*
Kittitas (Kittitas) City *744*
Kittitas County..............................*744*
Klickitat County *744*
Krupp (Grant) Town.........................*738*
La Center (Clark) Town....................*734*
Lacey (Thurston) City.......................*756*
La Conner (Skagit) Town..................*751*
La Crosse (Whitman) Town *759*
Lake Forest North (King) CDP.........*741*

American Places Dictionary WASHINGTON

Lake Forest Park (King) City 741
Lake Goodwin (Snohomish) CDP 753
Lakeland North (King) CDP 741
Lakeland South (King) CDP 741
Lake Serene-North Lynnwood (Snohomish) CDP 753
Lake Shore (Clark) CDP 734
Lake Stevens (Snohomish) City 753
Lakewood (Pierce) CDP 749
Lamont (Whitman) Town 759
Langley (Island) City 739
Latah (Spokane) Town 754
Lea Hill (King) CDP 741
Leavenworth (Chelan) City 732
Lewis County 745
Liberty Lake (Spokane) CDP 755
Lincoln County 746
Lind (Adams) Town 731
Long Beach (Pacific) Town 748
Longview (Cowlitz) City 735
Longview Heights (Cowlitz) CDP 735
Lyman (Skagit) Town 751
Lynden (Whatcom) City 758
Lynnwood (Snohomish) City 753
Mabton (Yakima) Town 760
Malden (Whitman) The Whitman County 759
Manchester (Kitsap) CDP 743
Mansfield (Douglas) Town 736
Maple Valley (King) CDP 741
Marcus (Stevens) Town 755
Marietta-Alderwood (Whatcom) CDP 758
Martha Lake (Snohomish) CDP 753
Marysville (Snohomish) City 753
Mason County 746
Mattawa (Grant) Town 738
McChord Air Force Base (Pierce) Military Facility 749
McCleary (Grays Harbor) Town 739
Meadow Glade (Clark) CDP 734
Medical Lake (Spokane) Town 755
Medina (King) City 742
Mercer Island (King) City 742
Mesa (Franklin) Town 737
Metaline (Pend Oreille) Town 748
Metaline Falls (Pend Oreille) Town .. 748
Midland (Pierce) CDP 749
Mill Creek (Snohomish) City 753
Millwood (Spokane) Town 755
Milton (King) Town 742
Milton (Pierce) Town 749
Minnehaha (Clark) CDP 734
Mirrormont (King) CDP 742
Monroe (Snohomish) City 753
Montesano (Grays Harbor) City 739
Morton (Lewis) City 745
Moses Lake (Grant) City 738
Moses Lake North (Grant) CDP 738
Mossyrock (Lewis) City 745
Mountlake Terrace (Snohomish) City 753
Mount Vernon (Skagit) City 751
Moxee (Yakima) Town 760
Mukilteo (Snohomish) City 753
Naches (Yakima) Town 760
Napavine (Lewis) City 745
Navy Yard City (Kitsap) CDP 743
Neah Bay (Clallam) CDP 733
Nespelem (Okanogan) Town 747
Nespelem Community (Okanogan) CDP 747
Newport (Pend Oreille) City 748
Newport Hills (King) CDP 742

Nisqually Indian Community (Thurston) CDP 756
Nooksack (Whatcom) City 758
Normandy Park (King) City 742
North Bend (King) City 742
North Bonneville (Skamania) City 752
North City-Ridgecrest (King) CDP ... 742
North Creek-Canyon Park (Snohomish) CDP 753
North Hill (King) CDP 742
North Marysville (Snohomish) CDP 753
North Omak (Okanogan) CDP 747
Northport (Stevens) Town 756
North Puyallup (Pierce) CDP 749
North Yelm (Thurston) CDP 756
Oakesdale (Whitman) Town 759
Oak Harbor (Island) City 739
Oakville (Grays Harbor) City 739
Ocean Park (Pacific) CDP 748
Ocean Shores (Grays Harbor) City ... 739
Odessa (Lincoln) Town 746
Okanogan (Okanogan) City 747
Okanogan County 747
Olympia (Thurston) City 756
Omak (Okanogan) City 747
Opportunity (Spokane) CDP 755
Orchards North (Clark) CDP 734
Orchards South (Clark) CDP 734
Oroville (Okanogan) Town 747
Orting (Pierce) Town 749
Othello (Adams) City 731
Otis Orchards-East Farms (Spokane) CDP 755
Pacific (King) City 742
Pacific (Pierce) City 749
Pacific County 748
Paine Field-Lake Stickney (Snohomish) CDP 753
Palouse (Whitman) City 759
Parkland (Pierce) CDP 750
Parkwood (Kitsap) CDP 743
Pasco (Franklin) City 737
Pateros (Okanogan) Town 747
Pe Ell (Lewis) Town 745
Pend Oreille County 748
Pierce County 749
Pine Lake (King) CDP 742
Pomeroy (Garfield) City 737
Port Angeles (Clallam) City 733
Port Angeles East (Clallam) CDP 733
Port Orchard (Kitsap) City 743
Port Townsend (Jefferson) City 740
Poulsbo (Kitsap) City 743
Prairie Ridge (Pierce) CDP 750
Prescott (Walla Walla) Town 757
Priest Point (Snohomish) CDP 753
Prosser (Benton) City 732
Pullman (Whitman) City 759
Puyallup (Pierce) City 750
Quincy (Grant) Town 738
Rainier (Thurston) Town 756
Raymond (Pacific) City 748
Reardan (Lincoln) Town 746
Redmond (King) City 742
Renton (King) City 742
Republic (Ferry) Town 736
Richland (Benton) City 732
Richmond Beach-Innis Arden (King) CDP 742
Richmond Highlands (King) CDP ... 742
Ridgefield (Clark) Town 734
Ritzville (Adams) City 731
Riverside (Okanogan) Town 747
Riverton-Boulevard Park (King) CDP 742

Rochester (Thurston) CDP 756
Rockford (Spokane) Town 755
Rock Island (Douglas) Town 736
Rosalia (Whitman) Town 759
Roslyn (Kittitas) City 744
Roy (Pierce) City 750
Royal City (Grant) Town 738
Ruston (Pierce) Town 750
Sahalee (King) CDP 742
St. John (Whitman) Town 759
Salmon Creek (Clark) CDP 734
San Juan County 751
Satus (Yakima) CDP 760
Sea-Tac (King) CDP 742
Seattle (King) City 742
Sedro-Woolley (Skagit) City 751
Selah (Yakima) City 760
Sequim (Clallam) City 733
Shaker Church (Snohomish) CDP 753
Shelter Bay (Skagit) CDP 751
Shelton (Mason) City 746
Sheridan Beach (King) CDP 742
Silverdale (Kitsap) CDP 743
Silver Lake-Fircrest (Snohomish) CDP 753
Skagit County 751
Skamania County 752
Skokomish (Mason) CDP 746
Skykomish (King) Town 742
Smokey Point (Snohomish) CDP 753
Snee Oosh (Skagit) CDP 752
Snohomish (Snohomish) City 754
Snohomish County 752
Snoqualmie (King) City 743
Soap Lake (Grant) City 738
South Bend (Pacific) City 748
South Broadway (Yakima) CDP 760
South Cle Elum (Kittitas) Town 744
South Hill (Pierce) CDP 750
South Prairie (Pierce) Town 750
South Wenatchee (Chelan) CDP 732
Spanaway (Pierce) CDP 750
Spangle (Spokane) City 755
Spokane (Spokane) City 755
Spokane County 754
Sprague (Lincoln) City 746
Springdale (Stevens) Town 756
Stanwood (Snohomish) City 754
Starbuck (Columbia) Town 735
Steilacoom (Pierce) Town 750
Stevens County 755
Stevenson (Skamania) City 752
Stimson Crossing (Snohomish) CDP 754
Sudden Valley (Whatcom) CDP 758
Sultan (Snohomish) Town 754
Sumas (Whatcom) City 758
Summit (Pierce) CDP 750
Sumner (Pierce) City 750
Sunnyside (Yakima) City 760
Sunnyslope (Chelan) CDP 732
Suquamish (Kitsap) CDP 744
Swinomish Village (Skagit) CDP 752
Tacoma (Pierce) City 750
Taholah (Grays Harbor) CDP 739
Tanglewilde-Thompson Place (Thurston) CDP 756
Tekoa (Whitman) City 759
Tenino (Thurston) Town 756
Terrace Heights (Yakima) CDP 760
Thurston County 756
Tieton (Yakima) Town 760
Toledo (Lewis) City 745
Tonasket (Okanogan) Town 747
Toppenish (Yakima) City 760
Town and Country (Spokane) CDP .. 755

WASHINGTON

Tracyton (Kitsap) CDP 744
Trentwood (Spokane) CDP 755
Tukwila (King) City 743
Tulalip Bay (Snohomish) CDP 754
Tumwater (Thurston) City 756
Twisp (Okanogan) Town 747
Union Gap (Yakima) City 760
Uniontown (Whitman) Town 759
University Place (Pierce) CDP 750
Vader (Lewis) City 745
Vancouver (Clark) City 734
Vancouver Mall (Clark) CDP 734
Veradale (Spokane) CDP 755
Wahkiakum County 757
Waitsburg (Walla Walla) City 757
Walla Walla (Walla Walla) City 757
Walla Walla County 757
Walla Walla East (Walla Walla) CDP 757
Waller (Pierce) CDP 750
Walnut Grove (Clark) CDP 734
Wapato (Yakima) City 760
Warden (Grant) Town 738
Washougal (Clark) City 734
Washtucna (Adams) Town 731
Waterville (Douglas) Town 736
Waverly (Spokane) Town 755
Weallup Lake (Snohomish) CDP 754
Wenatchee (Chelan) City 733
West Clarkston-Highland (Asotin)
  CDP 731
West Lake Sammamish (King) CDP . 743
West Lake Stevens (Snohomish)
  CDP 754
West Longview (Cowlitz) CDP 735
West Pasco (Franklin) CDP 737
Westport (Grays Harbor) City 739
West Richland (Benton) City 732
West Side Highway (Cowlitz) CDP ... 735
West Valley (Yakima) CDP 760
West Wenatchee (Chelan) CDP 733
Whatcom County 758
White Center-Shorewood (King)
  CDP 743
White Salmon (Klickitat) City 745
White Swan (Yakima) CDP 761
Whitman County 759
Wilbur (Lincoln) Town 746
Wilkeson (Pierce) Town 750
Wilson Creek (Grant) Town 738
Winlock (Lewis) City 745
Winslow (Kitsap) City 744
Winthrop (Okanogan) Town 747
Woodinville (King) CDP 743
Woodland (Clark) City 734
Woodland (Cowlitz) City 735
Woodmont Beach (King) CDP 743
Woodway (Snohomish) Town 754
Yacolt (Clark) Town 734
Yakima (Yakima) City 761
Yakima County 760
Yarrow Point (King) Town 743
Yelm (Thurston) Town 756
Zillah (Yakima) City 761

Wyoming

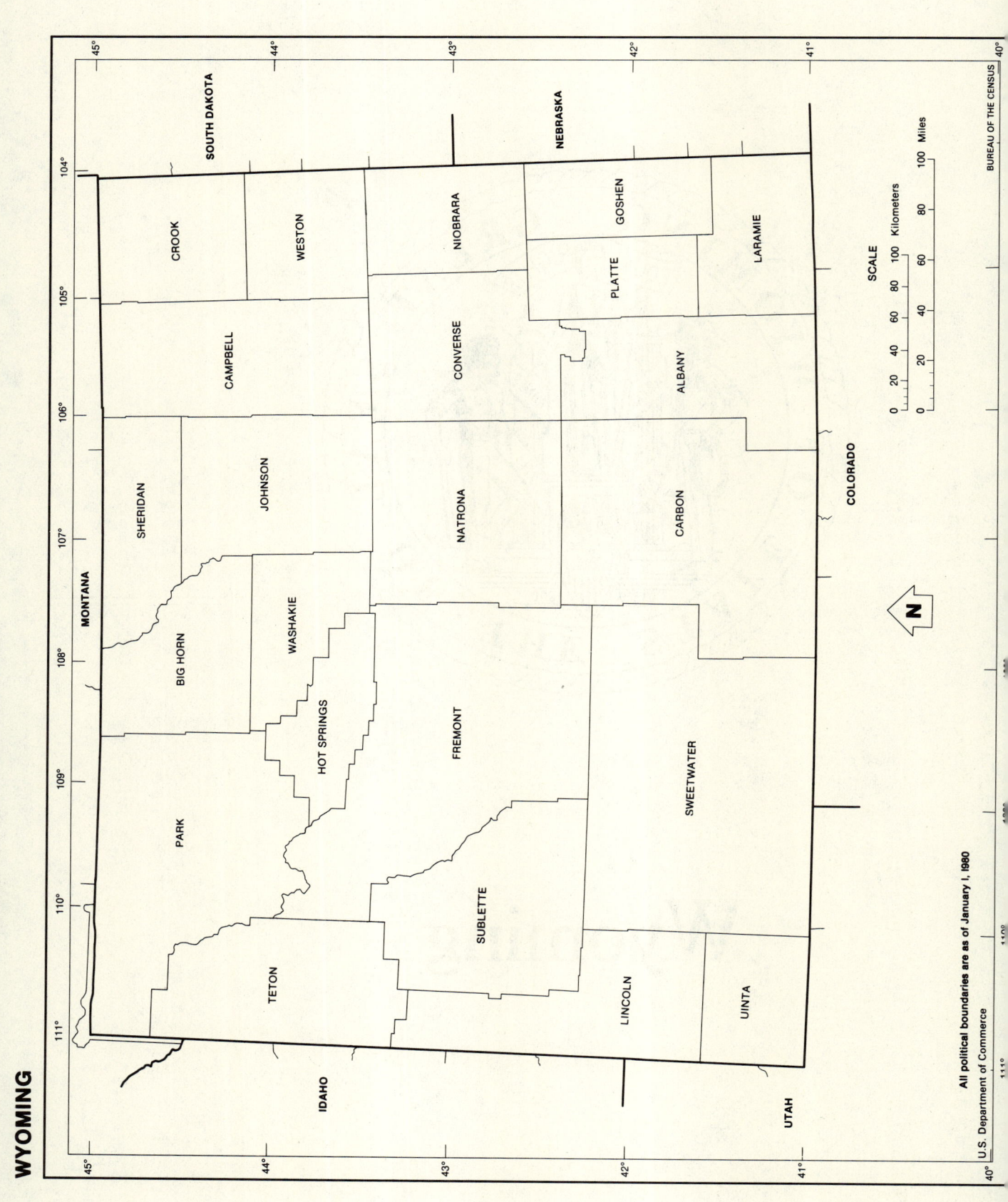

Wyoming

Population: 453,588 (1990); 469,557 (1980)
Population rank (1990): 50
Percent population change (1980–1990): -3.4
Population projection: 446,000 (1995); 430,000 (2000)

Area: total: 97,818 sq. mi.; 97,105 sq. mi. land, 714 sq. mi. water
Area rank: 10
Highest elevation: 13,804 ft., Gannett Peak (Fremont County)
Lowest point: 3,100 ft., Belle Fourche River (Crook County)

State capital: Cheyenne (Laramie County)
Largest city: Cheyenne (50,008)
Second largest city: Casper (46,742)
Largest county: Laramie (73,142)

Total housing units: 203,411
No. of occupied housing units: 168,839
Vacant housing units (%): 17.0
Distribution of population by race and Hispanic origin (%):
  White: 94.2
  Black: 0.8
  Hispanic (any race): 5.7
  Native American: 2.1
  Asian/Pacific: 0.6
  Other: 2.3

Admission date: July 10, 1890 (44th state).

Location: In the west-central United States, bordering Colorado, Utah, Idaho, Montana, South Dakota, and Nebraska.

Name Origin: For the Wyoming Valley in northeastern PA; this name for the Wyoming Territory was suggested to Congress by U.S. Representative J. M. Ashbey of Ohio. The name was made popular by the poem "Gertrude of Wyoming" (1809), by British poet Thomas Campbell, and is used in many localities. From the Delaware Indian words *maugh-wau-wa-ma,* meaning 'large plains' or 'upon the great plain.'

State bird: meadowlark *(Sturnella neglecta)*
State flower: Indian paintbrush *(Castilleja linariaefolia)*
State fossil: Knightia
State gemstone: jade (nephrite)
State mammal: bison *(Bison bison)*
State song: "Wyoming"
State tree: plains cottonwood *(Populus sargentii)*
State motto: Equal Rights
State nickname: Equality State, Cowboy State

Area code: 307
Time zone: Mountain
Abbreviations: WY (postal); Wyo. (traditional)
Part of (region): Rocky Mountains

Local Government

Counties

Wyoming has 23 counties, each governed by a board of commissioners.

Municipalities

Wyoming has 97 municipalities. Most of the cities and towns have the mayor-council form of government, except for Casper and Laramie, both of which employ city managers.

Settlement History and Early Development

The first settlers were probably prehistoric immigrants from Asia, who crossed the land bridge to North America and slowly made their way southward and eastward more than 10,000 years ago. They were the ancestors of Wyoming's Arapaho, Sioux, Bannock, Blackfeet, Cheyenne, Crow, Shoshone, and Ute Indians. The first white explorers were two French Canadian brothers, François and Louis-Joseph de la Vérendrye, in 1743. An American fur trader, John Colter, who had been a member of the Lewis and Clark expedition (1804–06), explored the northern part of the state in 1806–07. In 1812 a group led by Robert Stuart, traveling east from Oregon, discovered South Pass, a relatively easy route through the Rockies.

The part of Wyoming east of the Rockies was included in the territory called Louisiana, which was owned successively by the French, the Spanish, and the French again, who then, under Napoleon Bonaparte, sold it to the U.S. in 1803 as part of the Louisiana Purchase. Wyoming west of the Rockies consisted of three sections: one that passed from Spain to Mexico, who ceded it to the U.S. in 1848 after the Mexican-American War; a second small section that was part of Texas from its 1836 independence from Mexico until 1850; and the third, northwestern section that was part of the Oregon Country. Wyoming's land was classified at different times as part of the Louisiana, Missouri, Nebraska, Dakota, Utah, Oregon, and Washington territories.

The first permanent settlement was in 1834 at Fort William, later called Fort Laramie. In 1842 and 1843 John Frémont, guided by Kit Carson, explored the area. From about 1840, settlers crossed Wyoming on the Oregon Trail, the Mormon Trail, and the California Trail. All three trails used South Pass to cross the Rockies. After the discovery of gold in California in 1848, thousands used these routes on their way west.

Real settlement in Wyoming itself, however, occurred after the Union Pacific Railroad came through in 1867–68. In 1868 Wyoming was organized as a territory and became the first territory to pass a women's suffrage act; this, plus having the first women on juries, first woman justice of the peace, and first woman governor (Nellie Tayloe Ross, in 1924), earned for Wyoming the later nickname "Equality State."

Cattle Wars

Hostilities between Indians and whites were mostly settled by the late 1870s. Cattle ranching began in earnest, and problems between cattlemen and small ranchers culminated in the Johnson County War (1891–92). Cattlemen suspected the small ranchers of cattle rustling; two men who were suspected were killed by hired guns, but federal troops arrived before the trouble escalated. Cattlemen also faced difficulties in the early 1900s as the increase in sheep farming led to competition for grazing lands.

Statehood and Commerce

Wyoming became the 44th state on July 10, 1890. The twentieth century has seen economic growth as oil, trona (a mineral from which sodium carbonate is derived), coal, uranium, and natural gas have been discovered in Wyoming. Livestock production has continued to play a large part in the state's economy.

Almost half of Wyoming's land is owned by the federal government, which controls the rights to graze, log, mine, and produce oil. Tourists visit the state for its many natural attractions, including Yellowstone National Park, the Grand Tetons, and Devils Tower. In 1985, when Alaska's population surpassed Wyoming's, Wyoming became the least populous U.S. state.

State Boundaries

In 1863 the present area of Wyoming, except for a small section in the southwest, was included in the Idaho Territory; in 1864 all of the present area except for a small section was transferred to the Dakota Territory. The present boundaries were determined in 1868, when Wyoming was organized as a territory.

Wyoming Counties

Albany	Hot Springs	Sheridan
Big Horn	Johnson	Sublette
Campbell	Laramie	Sweetwater
Carbon	Lincoln	Teton
Converse	Natrona	Uinta
Crook	Niobrara	Washakie
Fremont	Park	Weston
Goshen	Platte	

Multi-County Places

The following Wyoming place is in more than one county. Given here is the total population and the names of the counties it is in.

Frannie, pop. 148; Big Horn (142), Park (6)

Albany County
County Seat: Laramie (ZIP: 82070)

Pop: 30,797 (1990); 29,062 (1980) **Pop Density:** 7.2
Land: 4273.8 sq. mi.; **Water:** 35.2 sq. mi. **Area Code:** 307
On the southeastern border of WY, west of Cheyenne; organized Dec 16, 1868 (prior to statehood) from Laramie County.
Name origin: For Albany, NY, former home of Charles D. Bradley, a member of the legislature.

Laramie — City
ZIP: 82070 **Lat:** 41-18-39 N **Long:** 105-34-58 W
Pop: 26,687 (1990); 24,410 (1980) **Pop Density:** 2404.2
Land: 11.1 sq. mi.; **Water:** 0.0 sq. mi. **Elev:** 7163 ft.
In southeastern WY, 45 mi. west-northwest of Cheyenne. Incorporated Jan 13, 1874. Site of the University of Wyoming.
Name origin: For its location on the Laramie River, which traverses the county.

Rock River — Town
ZIP: 82083 **Lat:** 41-43-52 N **Long:** 105-58-21 W
Pop: 190 (1990); 415 (1980) **Pop Density:** 82.6
Land: 2.3 sq. mi.; **Water:** 0.0 sq. mi. **Elev:** 6891 ft.
Incorporated May 12, 1909.

Big Horn County
County Seat: Basin (ZIP: 82410)

Pop: 10,525 (1990); 11,896 (1980) **Pop Density:** 3.4
Land: 3137.1 sq. mi.; **Water:** 22.0 sq. mi. **Area Code:** 307
On the central northern border of WY; organized 1896 from Fremont and Johnson counties.
Name origin: For the Big Horn River, which traverses the county, and the Big Horn Mountains, which form its eastern border; both are named for the bighorn sheep in the area.

Basin — Town
ZIP: 82410 **Lat:** 44-22-46 N **Long:** 108-02-32 W
Pop: 1,180 (1990); 1,349 (1980) **Pop Density:** 842.9
Land: 1.4 sq. mi.; **Water:** 0.0 sq. mi. **Elev:** 3873 ft.
Settled 1897; incorporated May 1, 1903.
Name origin: For nearby Bighorn Basin.

Burlington — Town
ZIP: 82411 **Lat:** 44-26-50 N **Long:** 108-25-54 W
Pop: 184 (1990) **Pop Density:** 184.0
Land: 1.0 sq. mi.; **Water:** 0.0 sq. mi.

Byron — Town
ZIP: 82412 **Lat:** 44-47-43 N **Long:** 108-30-27 W
Pop: 470 (1990); 633 (1980) **Pop Density:** 587.5
Land: 0.8 sq. mi.; **Water:** 0.1 sq. mi.
Incorporated Feb 1912.
Name origin: For early Mormon settler Byron Sessions, who influenced the region's development.

Cowley — Town
ZIP: 82420 **Lat:** 44-53-09 N **Long:** 108-28-11 W
Pop: 477 (1990); 455 (1980) **Pop Density:** 681.4
Land: 0.7 sq. mi.; **Water:** 0.0 sq. mi.
Settled 1901; incorporated May 1907.
Name origin: For Mormon apostle Mathias F. Cowley.

Deaver — Town
ZIP: 82421 **Lat:** 44-53-21 N **Long:** 108-35-41 W
Pop: 199 (1990); 178 (1980) **Pop Density:** 199.0
Land: 1.0 sq. mi.; **Water:** 0.0 sq. mi.
Incorporated 1919.
Name origin: For Burlington railroad agent D.C. Deaver.

Frannie — Town
Lat: 44-58-11 N **Long:** 108-37-03 W
Pop: 142 (1990); 121 (1980) **Pop Density:** 710.0
Land: 0.2 sq. mi.; **Water:** 0.0 sq. mi.
Incorporated Jun 29, 1954. Part of the town is also in Park County.
Name origin: Named by railroad officials for pioneer Frannie Morris.

Greybull — Town
ZIP: 82426 **Lat:** 44-29-27 N **Long:** 108-03-26 W
Pop: 1,789 (1990); 2,277 (1980) **Pop Density:** 1052.4
Land: 1.7 sq. mi.; **Water:** 0.0 sq. mi. **Elev:** 3787 ft.
Incorporated May 1909.

Lovell — Town
ZIP: 82431 **Lat:** 44-50-12 N **Long:** 108-23-29 W
Pop: 2,131 (1990); 2,447 (1980) **Pop Density:** 2131.0
Land: 1.0 sq. mi.; **Water:** 0.0 sq. mi. **Elev:** 3837 ft.
Founded 1900; incorporated 1906–09.
Name origin: For area rancher Henry T. Lovell.

Manderson
Town
ZIP: 82432 **Lat:** 44-16-11 N **Long:** 107-57-48 W
Pop: 83 (1990); 174 (1980) **Pop Density:** 103.8
Land: 0.8 sq. mi.; **Water:** 0.1 sq. mi.
Incorporated 1921.
Name origin: Named in 1889 for a lawyer with the Burlington Railroad. Previously called the Alamo.

Campbell County
County Seat: Gillette (ZIP: 82716)

Pop: 29,370 (1990); 24,367 (1980) **Pop Density:** 6.1
Land: 4796.9 sq. mi.; **Water:** 4.8 sq. mi. **Area Code:** 307
On northeastern border of WY; organized Feb 13, 1911 from Crook and Weston counties.
Name origin: Probably for Gen. John Allen Campbell (1835–80), Civil War officer and first territorial governor of WY (1869–75); or possibly for Robert Campell, member of an expedition into the Missouri River area in 1822.

Antelope Valley-Crestview
CDP
Lat: 44-13-31 N **Long:** 105-27-34 W
Pop: 1,099 (1990) **Pop Density:** 1373.8
Land: 0.8 sq. mi.; **Water:** 0.0 sq. mi.

Gillette
City
ZIP: 82716 **Lat:** 44-16-54 N **Long:** 105-31-04 W
Pop: 17,635 (1990); 12,134 (1980) **Pop Density:** 1367.1
Land: 12.9 sq. mi.; **Water:** 0.0 sq. mi. **Elev:** 4550 ft.
In northeastern WY, 80 mi. southeast of Sheridan. Incorporated Jan 6 & 7, 1892.
Name origin: For surveyor and civil engineer Weston Gillette, who directed the railroad's construction through the area.

Sleepy Hollow
CDP
Lat: 44-14-27 N **Long:** 105-25-17 W
Pop: 1,194 (1990) **Pop Density:** 259.6
Land: 4.6 sq. mi.; **Water:** 0.0 sq. mi.

Wright
Town
ZIP: 82732 **Lat:** 43-45-02 N **Long:** 105-29-53 W
Pop: 1,236 (1990); 1,117 (1980) **Pop Density:** 457.8
Land: 2.7 sq. mi.; **Water:** 0.0 sq. mi.
Incorporated Nov 27, 1984.

Carbon County
County Seat: Rawlins (ZIP: 82301)

Pop: 16,659 (1990); 21,896 (1980) **Pop Density:** 2.1
Land: 7896.6 sq. mi.; **Water:** 67.9 sq. mi. **Area Code:** 307
On the central southern border of WY; organized Dec 16, 1868 (prior to statehood) from Laramie County.
Name origin: For the vast coal deposits within its boundaries.

Baggs
Town
ZIP: 82321 **Lat:** 41-02-08 N **Long:** 107-39-21 W
Pop: 272 (1990); 433 (1980) **Pop Density:** 906.7
Land: 0.3 sq. mi.; **Water:** 0.0 sq. mi. **Elev:** 6247 ft.
Established 1876; incorporated 1910.
Name origin: For a nearby prominent ranch family. Previously called Dixon.

Dixon
Town
ZIP: 82323 **Lat:** 41-02-02 N **Long:** 107-32-03 W
Pop: 70 (1990); 82 (1980) **Pop Density:** 700.0
Land: 0.1 sq. mi.; **Water:** 0.0 sq. mi. **Elev:** 6359 ft.
Incorporated 1917.
Name origin: For trapper Robert Dixon.

Elk Mountain
Town
ZIP: 82324 **Lat:** 41-41-16 N **Long:** 106-24-46 W
Pop: 174 (1990); 338 (1980) **Pop Density:** 580.0
Land: 0.3 sq. mi.; **Water:** 0.0 sq. mi.
Incorporated Oct 1909.
Name origin: For the nearby mountain.

Grand Encampment
Town
Lat: 41-12-31 N **Long:** 106-47-40 W
Pop: 490 (1990); 611 (1980) **Pop Density:** 306.3
Land: 1.6 sq. mi.; **Water:** 0.0 sq. mi.

Hanna
Town
ZIP: 82327 **Lat:** 41-52-11 N **Long:** 106-33-31 W
Pop: 1,076 (1990); 2,288 (1980) **Pop Density:** 538.0
Land: 2.0 sq. mi.; **Water:** 0.0 sq. mi.
Incorporated Sep 9, 1935.
Name origin: Named in 1886 for financier Mark Hanna.

Medicine Bow
Town
ZIP: 82329 **Lat:** 41-53-59 N **Long:** 106-12-03 W
Pop: 389 (1990); 953 (1980) **Pop Density:** 111.1
Land: 3.5 sq. mi.; **Water:** 0.0 sq. mi. **Elev:** 6563 ft.
Incorporated Jun 6, 1909.
Name origin: For the Medicine Bow Mountains, a source of ash wood for bows and the site for Indian ceremonial or "medicinal" rituals and dances.

Rawlins
City
ZIP: 82301 **Lat:** 41-47-04 N **Long:** 107-13-40 W
Pop: 9,380 (1990); 11,547 (1980) **Pop Density:** 1321.1
Land: 7.1 sq. mi.; **Water:** 0.0 sq. mi. **Elev:** 6769 ft.
In southern WY, 28 mi. southwest of the confluence of the Medicine Bow and North Platte rivers. Incorporated Mar 12, 1886.
Name origin: For Gen. John A. Rawlins, who helped build the Transcontinental Railroad in 1868.

Riverside
Town
ZIP: 82325 **Lat:** 41-12-51 N **Long:** 106-46-50 W
Pop: 85 (1990); 55 (1980) **Pop Density:** 283.3
Land: 0.3 sq. mi.; **Water:** 0.0 sq. mi. **Elev:** 7136 ft.
Incorporated Nov 1902.

Saratoga
Town
ZIP: 82331 **Lat:** 41-27-05 N **Long:** 106-48-44 W
Pop: 1,969 (1990); 2,410 (1980) **Pop Density:** 656.3
Land: 3.0 sq. mi.; **Water:** 0.1 sq. mi.
Founded 1878; incorporated Jul 1, 1900.
Name origin: For Saratoga Hot Springs in NY.

Sinclair
Town
ZIP: 82334 **Lat:** 41-46-38 N **Long:** 107-07-00 W
Pop: 500 (1990); 586 (1980) **Pop Density:** 208.3
Land: 2.4 sq. mi.; **Water:** 0.0 sq. mi. **Elev:** 6593 ft.
Incorporated Apr 1, 1925.
Name origin: Named in 1934 for Sinclair Oil Company.

Converse County
County Seat: Douglas (ZIP: 82633)

Pop: 11,128 (1990); 14,069 (1980) **Pop Density:** 2.6
Land: 4254.9 sq. mi.; **Water:** 10.4 sq. mi. **Area Code:** 307
In east-central WY, east of Casper; organized Mar 9, 1888 (prior to statehood) from Albany County.
Name origin: For Amasa Converse (1842–85), WY Territory official and Cheyenne businessman who established the Converse Cattle Company.

Douglas
Town
ZIP: 82633 **Lat:** 42-45-20 N **Long:** 105-23-33 W
Pop: 5,076 (1990); 6,030 (1980) **Pop Density:** 995.3
Land: 5.1 sq. mi.; **Water:** 0.1 sq. mi.
Incorporated Jun 8, 1887.
Name origin: For Stephen A. Douglas (1813–61), orator and U.S. senator from IL.

Glenrock
Town
ZIP: 82637 **Lat:** 42-51-25 N **Long:** 105-51-25 W
Pop: 2,153 (1990); 2,736 (1980) **Pop Density:** 1133.2
Land: 1.9 sq. mi.; **Water:** 0.0 sq. mi.
Incorporated 1907.

Lost Springs
Town
ZIP: 82224 **Lat:** 42-45-55 N **Long:** 104-55-25 W
Pop: 4 (1990); 9 (1980) **Pop Density:** 40.0
Land: 0.1 sq. mi.; **Water:** 0.0 sq. mi.
Incorporated Aug 1911.

Rolling Hills
Town
Lat: 42-54-08 N **Long:** 105-50-45 W
Pop: 330 (1990) **Pop Density:** 471.4
Land: 0.7 sq. mi.; **Water:** 0.0 sq. mi.

Crook County
County Seat: Sundance (ZIP: 82729)

Pop: 5,294 (1990); 5,308 (1980)
Land: 2858.7 sq. mi.; **Water:** 11.9 sq. mi.
Pop Density: 1.9
Area Code: 307
On the northeastern border of WY, northeast of Gillette; created Dec 8, 1875 (prior to statehood).
Name origin: For Gen. George H. Crook (1829–90), officer in the Oregon Territory and Indian fighter; called "Gray Fox" by the Shoshones.

Hulett — Town
ZIP: 82720 **Lat:** 44-41-09 N **Long:** 104-35-59 W
Pop: 429 (1990); 291 (1980) **Pop Density:** 2145.0
Land: 0.2 sq. mi.; **Water:** 0.0 sq. mi.
Incorporated May 1, 1951.
Name origin: For first postmaster

Moorcroft — Town
ZIP: 82721 **Lat:** 44-15-53 N **Long:** 104-57-05 W
Pop: 768 (1990); 1,014 (1980) **Pop Density:** 698.2
Land: 1.1 sq. mi.; **Water:** 0.0 sq. mi.
Incorporated Oct 2, 1906.
Name origin: For first white settler, Alexander Moorcroft.

Pine Haven — Town
Lat: 44-20-55 N **Long:** 104-48-36 W
Pop: 141 (1990) **Pop Density:** 88.1
Land: 1.6 sq. mi.; **Water:** 0.0 sq. mi.

Sundance — Town
ZIP: 82710 **Lat:** 44-24-16 N **Long:** 104-22-27 W
Pop: 1,139 (1990); 1,087 (1980) **Pop Density:** 813.6
Land: 1.4 sq. mi.; **Water:** 0.0 sq. mi.
Elev: 4765 ft.
Founded 1879; incorporated Oct 5, 1887.
Name origin: For the nearby Sundance Mountains.

Fremont County
County Seat: Lander (ZIP: 82520)

Pop: 33,662 (1990); 38,992 (1980)
Land: 9182.7 sq. mi.; **Water:** 83.5 sq. mi.
Pop Density: 3.7
Area Code: 307
In west-central WY, west of Casper; organized Mar 5, 1884 (prior to statehood) from Sweetwater County.
Name origin: For John Charles Frémont (1813–90), soldier and explorer who led five expeditions to the West, U.S. senator from CA (1850–51), and governor of the AZ Territory (1878–81).

Arapahoe — CDP
Lat: 42-58-13 N **Long:** 108-28-30 W
Pop: 393 (1990) **Pop Density:** 53.1
Land: 7.4 sq. mi.; **Water:** 0.0 sq. mi.

Dubois — Town
ZIP: 82513 **Lat:** 43-32-10 N **Long:** 109-38-31 W
Pop: 895 (1990); 1,067 (1980) **Pop Density:** 344.2
Land: 2.6 sq. mi.; **Water:** 0.0 sq. mi.
Founded 1880s; incorporated May 14, 1914.

Ethete — CDP
Lat: 43-01-18 N **Long:** 108-45-25 W
Pop: 1,059 (1990) **Pop Density:** 67.9
Land: 15.6 sq. mi.; **Water:** 0.0 sq. mi.

Fort Washakie — CDP
ZIP: 82514 **Lat:** 43-00-28 N **Long:** 108-55-33 W
Pop: 1,334 (1990) **Pop Density:** 64.1
Land: 20.8 sq. mi.; **Water:** 0.0 sq. mi.

Hudson — Town
ZIP: 82515 **Lat:** 42-54-07 N **Long:** 108-34-53 W
Pop: 392 (1990); 514 (1980) **Pop Density:** 980.0
Land: 0.4 sq. mi.; **Water:** 0.0 sq. mi.
Incorporated Feb 4, 1909.
Name origin: For rancher John G. Hudson, who was the original landowner.

Lander — City
ZIP: 82520 **Lat:** 42-49-48 N **Long:** 108-43-42 W
Pop: 7,023 (1990); 7,867 (1980) **Pop Density:** 1633.3
Land: 4.3 sq. mi.; **Water:** 0.0 sq. mi.
Incorporated Jul 17, 1890.
Name origin: Named in 1857 for surveyor Gen. F. W. Lander. Previously called Push Root.

Pavillion — Town
ZIP: 82523 **Lat:** 43-14-38 N **Long:** 108-41-26 W
Pop: 126 (1990); 287 (1980) **Pop Density:** 1260.0
Land: 0.1 sq. mi.; **Water:** 0.0 sq. mi.
Incorporated 1939.

Riverton
City
ZIP: 82501 **Lat:** 43-02-08 N **Long:** 108-24-53 W
Pop: 9,202 (1990); 9,562 (1980) **Pop Density:** 1011.2
Land: 9.1 sq. mi.; **Water:** 0.0 sq. mi.
Incorporated Oct 2, 1900.

Shoshoni
Town
ZIP: 82649 **Lat:** 43-14-16 N **Long:** 108-06-10 W
Pop: 497 (1990); 879 (1980) **Pop Density:** 160.3
Land: 3.1 sq. mi.; **Water:** 0.0 sq. mi.
Incorporated Jun 1906.
Name origin: For the Shoshone Indians, with a spelling variation.

Goshen County
County Seat: Torrington (ZIP: 82240)

Pop: 12,373 (1990); 12,040 (1980) **Pop Density:** 5.6
Land: 2225.5 sq. mi.; **Water:** 6.8 sq. mi. **Area Code:** 307
On the southeastern border of WY, northeast of Cheyenne; created Feb 9, 1911 from Platte and Laramie counties.
Name origin: For Goshen Hole Valley, which was probably named for the Biblical Egyptian home of the Israelites before the Exodus; generally interpreted as 'land of abundance or plenty.'

Fort Laramie
Town
ZIP: 82212 **Lat:** 42-12-44 N **Long:** 104-30-59 W
Pop: 243 (1990); 356 (1980) **Pop Density:** 810.0
Land: 0.3 sq. mi.; **Water:** 0.0 sq. mi.
Incorporated 1925.
Name origin: For the Laramie River, which was named for French-Canadian trapper Jacques LaRamie, who was killed by the Indians in 1818.

La Grange
Town
Lat: 41-38-21 N **Long:** 104-09-49 W
Pop: 224 (1990); 232 (1980) **Pop Density:** 560.0
Land: 0.4 sq. mi.; **Water:** 0.0 sq. mi.
Incorporated Apr 18, 1938.
Name origin: For rancher Kale La Grange.

Lingle
Town
ZIP: 82223 **Lat:** 42-08-19 N **Long:** 104-20-45 W
Pop: 473 (1990); 475 (1980) **Pop Density:** 1576.7
Land: 0.3 sq. mi.; **Water:** 0.0 sq. mi. **Elev:** 4171 ft.
Incorporated Nov 1918.
Name origin: For Hiram Lingle, who was a major promoter of the valley's agriculture.

Torrington
Town
ZIP: 82240 **Lat:** 42-04-03 N **Long:** 104-10-55 W
Pop: 5,651 (1990); 5,441 (1980) **Pop Density:** 2691.0
Land: 2.1 sq. mi.; **Water:** 0.0 sq. mi.
Incorporated Jan 4, 1908.
Name origin: Named by William Albert Curtis for Torrington, CT.

Yoder
Town
ZIP: 82244 **Lat:** 41-55-03 N **Long:** 104-17-40 W
Pop: 136 (1990); 110 (1980) **Pop Density:** 680.0
Land: 0.2 sq. mi.; **Water:** 0.0 sq. mi.
Incorporated Dec 13, 1921.
Name origin: For pioneers Jess and Frank Yoder.

Hot Springs County
County Seat: Thermopolis (ZIP: 82443)

Pop: 4,809 (1990); 5,710 (1980) **Pop Density:** 2.4
Land: 2004.0 sq. mi.; **Water:** 2.3 sq. mi. **Area Code:** 307
In west-central WY; created Feb 9, 1911 from Fremont, Johnson, and Big Horn counties.
Name origin: For the hot springs located in the county seat.

East Thermopolis
Town
Lat: 43-38-43 N **Long:** 108-11-55 W
Pop: 221 (1990); 359 (1980) **Pop Density:** 2210.0
Land: 0.1 sq. mi.; **Water:** 0.0 sq. mi.
Incorporated 1948.

Kirby
Town
ZIP: 82430 **Lat:** 43-48-14 N **Long:** 108-10-48 W
Pop: 59 (1990); 129 (1980) **Pop Density:** 590.0
Land: 0.1 sq. mi.; **Water:** 0.0 sq. mi.
Incorporated 1918.
Name origin: For cowboy Kris Kirby, who settled here in 1878.

Thermopolis Town
ZIP: 82443 **Lat:** 43-38-52 N **Long:** 108-12-49 W
Pop: 3,247 (1990); 3,852 (1980) **Pop Density:** 1352.9
Land: 2.4 sq. mi.; **Water:** 0.1 sq. mi.
Incorporated Feb 14, 1899.
Name origin: From Latin *therma* 'hot baths' and Greek *polis* 'city.'

Johnson County
County Seat: Buffalo (ZIP: 82834)

Pop: 6,145 (1990); 6,700 (1980) **Pop Density:** 1.5
Land: 4166.4 sq. mi.; **Water:** 8.4 sq. mi. **Area Code:** 307
In north-central WY, north of Casper; created as Pease County Dec 8, 1875 (prior to statehood) from Pease County; name changed Dec 13, 1879.
Name origin: For E. P. Johnson, a Cheyenne lawyer. Originally named for Dr. E. L. Pease.

Buffalo City
ZIP: 82834 **Lat:** 44-20-32 N **Long:** 106-43-02 W
Pop: 3,302 (1990); 3,799 (1980) **Pop Density:** 1031.9
Land: 3.2 sq. mi.; **Water:** 0.0 sq. mi.
Settled 1879; incorporated Apr 4, 1884.
Name origin: For the old buffalo trail that became main street.

Kaycee Town
ZIP: 82639 **Lat:** 43-42-35 N **Long:** 106-38-15 W
Pop: 256 (1990); 271 (1980) **Pop Density:** 853.3
Land: 0.3 sq. mi.; **Water:** 0.0 sq. mi.
Incorporated c. Jul 1, 1913.
Name origin: For the K. C. Ranch, which flourished here in the 1880s.

Laramie County
County Seat: Cheyenne (ZIP: 82001)

Pop: 73,142 (1990); 68,649 (1980) **Pop Density:** 27.2
Land: 2686.2 sq. mi.; **Water:** 1.6 sq. mi. **Area Code:** 307
On the southeastern border of WY; first county in WY; created Jan 9, 1867 (prior to statehood).
Name origin: For Jacques LaRamie (?–c.1818), a respected French-Canadian trapper killed by Indians near the river, which was later named for him. Also spelled *LaRamie* or *LaRamee*.

Albin Town
ZIP: 82050 **Lat:** 41-25-01 N **Long:** 104-05-58 W
Pop: 120 (1990); 128 (1980) **Pop Density:** 1200.0
Land: 0.1 sq. mi.; **Water:** 0.0 sq. mi. **Elev:** 5340 ft.
Founded 1905; incorporated Sep 13, 1930.
Name origin: For the first postmaster John Albin Anderson.

Burns Town
ZIP: 82053 **Lat:** 41-11-24 N **Long:** 104-21-31 W
Pop: 254 (1990); 268 (1980) **Pop Density:** 81.9
Land: 3.1 sq. mi.; **Water:** 0.0 sq. mi.
Founded 1907; incorporated May 1917.

Cheyenne City
ZIP: 82001 **Lat:** 41-08-43 N **Long:** 104-47-32 W
Pop: 50,008 (1990); 47,283 (1980) **Pop Density:** 2660.0
Land: 18.8 sq. mi.; **Water:** 0.1 sq. mi.
In southeastern WY, 10 mi. north of the CO border; state capital and largest city. Founded 1867; incorporated Dec 10, 1869. First town in the world to have incandescent street lights; first county library in U.S. established here in 1886. Trade center for surrounding agricultural area; major U.S. defense center (Warren Air Force Base nearby is headquarters of an intercontinental ballistic missile network).
Name origin: From the Dakota Indian name meaning 'red talkers.'

Fox Farm-College CDP
 Lat: 41-06-36 N **Long:** 104-47-14 W
Pop: 2,965 (1990); 2,850 (1980) **Pop Density:** 872.1
Land: 3.4 sq. mi.; **Water:** 0.0 sq. mi.

Pine Bluffs Town
ZIP: 82082 **Lat:** 41-10-49 N **Long:** 104-04-05 W
Pop: 1,054 (1990); 1,077 (1980) **Pop Density:** 329.4
Land: 3.2 sq. mi.; **Water:** 0.0 sq. mi. **Elev:** 5040 ft.
Incorporated May 14, 1909.

Ranchettes CDP
 Lat: 41-13-06 N **Long:** 104-47-22 W
Pop: 4,038 (1990) **Pop Density:** 98.0
Land: 41.2 sq. mi.; **Water:** 0.0 sq. mi.

South Greeley CDP
Lat: 41-05-49 N **Long:** 104-48-20 W
Pop: 3,723 (1990) **Pop Density:** 1959.5
Land: 1.9 sq. mi.; **Water:** 0.0 sq. mi.

Warren Air Force Base Military Facility
Lat: 41-09-11 N **Long:** 104-51-38 W
Pop: 3,832 (1990); 3,627 (1980) **Pop Density:** 580.6
Land: 6.6 sq. mi.; **Water:** 0.0 sq. mi.

Lincoln County
County Seat: Kemmerer (ZIP: 83101)

Pop: 12,625 (1990); 12,177 (1980) **Pop Density:** 3.1
Land: 4069.3 sq. mi.; **Water:** 19.9 sq. mi. **Area Code:** 307
On the southwestern border of WY; created Feb 20, 1911 from Uinta County.
Name origin: For Abraham Lincoln (1809–65), sixteenth U.S. president.

Afton Town
ZIP: 83110 **Lat:** 42-43-34 N **Long:** 110-55-42 W
Pop: 1,394 (1990); 1,481 (1980) **Pop Density:** 1394.0
Land: 1.0 sq. mi.; **Water:** 0.0 sq. mi.
Founded 1879; incorporated Apr 24, 1902.
Name origin: Named by a Scots settler for a line by poet Robert Burns (1759–96): "Flow gently, sweet Afton," referring to a river in Scotland.

Alpine Town
Lat: 43-09-39 N **Long:** 111-00-49 W
Pop: 200 (1990) **Pop Density:** 500.0
Land: 0.4 sq. mi.; **Water:** 0.0 sq. mi.

Cokeville Town
ZIP: 83114 **Lat:** 42-04-59 N **Long:** 110-57-18 W
Pop: 493 (1990); 515 (1980) **Pop Density:** 704.3
Land: 0.7 sq. mi.; **Water:** 0.0 sq. mi.
Settled 1874; incorporated May 31, 1910.

Diamondville Town
ZIP: 83116 **Lat:** 41-46-39 N **Long:** 110-32-11 W
Pop: 864 (1990); 1,000 (1980) **Pop Density:** 664.6
Land: 1.3 sq. mi.; **Water:** 0.0 sq. mi.
Settled 1890s; incorporated Mar 2, 1901.

Kemmerer Town
ZIP: 83101 **Lat:** 41-46-55 N **Long:** 110-33-05 W
Pop: 3,020 (1990); 3,273 (1980) **Pop Density:** 413.7
Land: 7.3 sq. mi.; **Water:** 0.0 sq. mi.
Founded 1897; incorporated Jan 23, 1899.
Name origin: For Kemmerer Coal Company.

La Barge Town
ZIP: 83123 **Lat:** 42-15-40 N **Long:** 110-11-46 W
Pop: 493 (1990); 302 (1980) **Pop Density:** 616.3
Land: 0.8 sq. mi.; **Water:** 0.0 sq. mi.
Incorporated Feb 13, 1973.
Name origin: For nearby La Barge Creek, named for Missouri River pilot Capt. Joseph La Barge.

Opal Town
ZIP: 83124 **Lat:** 41-46-11 N **Long:** 110-19-14 W
Pop: 95 (1990) **Pop Density:** 237.5
Land: 0.4 sq. mi.; **Water:** 0.0 sq. mi.
Incorporated Aug 3, 1914.

Thayne Town
ZIP: 83127 **Lat:** 42-55-11 N **Long:** 111-00-03 W
Pop: 267 (1990); 256 (1980) **Pop Density:** 381.4
Land: 0.7 sq. mi.; **Water:** 0.0 sq. mi.
Incorporated Jun 1917.
Name origin: For first postmaster Henry Thayne.

Natrona County
County Seat: Casper (ZIP: 82601)

Pop: 61,226 (1990); 71,856 (1980) **Pop Density:** 11.5
Land: 5340.0 sq. mi.; **Water:** 35.9 sq. mi. **Area Code:** 307
In east-central WY; created Mar 9, 1888 (prior to statehood) from Carbon County.
Name origin: For the mineral natron, or trona, a sodium carbonate, found in the area.

Bar Nunn Town
Lat: 42-55-34 N **Long:** 106-20-46 W
Pop: 835 (1990) **Pop Density:** 417.5
Land: 2.0 sq. mi.; **Water:** 0.0 sq. mi.

Casper City
ZIP: 82601 **Lat:** 42-49-57 N **Long:** 106-19-45 W
Pop: 46,742 (1990); 51,016 (1980) **Pop Density:** 2269.0
Land: 20.6 sq. mi.; **Water:** 0.3 sq. mi.
In east-central WY on the North Platte River. Incorporated Jul 8, 1889. Summer/winter resort; administrative and production center for coal, gas, oil, and uranium developing companies.
Name origin: For Fort Caspar, which was named for Lt. Caspar Collins, who was killed by Indians near here; railroad misspelling allowed to stand. Previously a military post called Platte Bridge Station.

Edgerton
Town
ZIP: 82635 **Lat:** 43-24-52 N **Long:** 106-14-50 W
Pop: 247 (1990); 510 (1980) **Pop Density:** 823.3
Land: 0.3 sq. mi.; **Water:** 0.0 sq. mi.
Incorporated Nov 3, 1925.

Evansville
Town
ZIP: 82636 **Lat:** 42-52-20 N **Long:** 106-15-31 W
Pop: 1,403 (1990); 2,335 (1980) **Pop Density:** 561.2
Land: 2.5 sq. mi.; **Water:** 0.0 sq. mi.
Incorporated Jul 1923.
Name origin: For homesteader and blacksmith W. T. Evans.

Midwest
Town
ZIP: 82643 **Lat:** 43-24-40 N **Long:** 106-16-39 W
Pop: 495 (1990); 638 (1980) **Pop Density:** 1237.5
Land: 0.4 sq. mi.; **Water:** 0.0 sq. mi.
Incorporated Apr 26, 1973.
Name origin: For Midwest Oil Company. Originally known as Shannon Camp.

Mills
Town
ZIP: 82644 **Lat:** 42-50-44 N **Long:** 106-22-33 W
Pop: 1,574 (1990); 2,139 (1980) **Pop Density:** 1311.7
Land: 1.2 sq. mi.; **Water:** 0.0 sq. mi.
Founded 1919; incorporated 1921.
Name origin: For the Mills brothers, who helped found the town.

Mountain View
CDP
Lat: 42-53-02 N **Long:** 106-26-41 W
Pop: 1,345 (1990) **Pop Density:** 94.7
Land: 14.2 sq. mi.; **Water:** 0.0 sq. mi.

Niobrara County
County Seat: Lusk (ZIP: 82225)

Pop: 2,499 (1990); 2,924 (1980) **Pop Density:** 1.0
Land: 2625.9 sq. mi.; **Water:** 2.1 sq. mi. **Area Code:** 307
On the central eastern border of WY, east of Casper; created Feb 14, 1911 from Converse County.
Name origin: For the Niobrara River, which flows through the county, or for the Niobrara Indian tribe; from an Omaha-Poca Indian word *ni obthantha ko* 'spreading water river.'

Lusk
Town
ZIP: 82225 **Lat:** 42-45-38 N **Long:** 104-27-12 W
Pop: 1,504 (1990); 1,650 (1980) **Pop Density:** 1156.9
Land: 1.3 sq. mi.; **Water:** 0.0 sq. mi.
Incorporated Jun 17, 1898.
Name origin: For rancher Frank Lusk.

Manville
Town
ZIP: 82227 **Lat:** 42-46-46 N **Long:** 104-37-00 W
Pop: 97 (1990); 94 (1980) **Pop Density:** 323.3
Land: 0.3 sq. mi.; **Water:** 0.0 sq. mi.
Incorporated 1913.
Name origin: For H. S. Manville, who organized the Converse Cattle Co. in 1880.

Van Tassell
Town
ZIP: 82242 **Lat:** 42-39-49 N **Long:** 104-05-26 W
Pop: 8 (1990); 10 (1980) **Pop Density:** 4.4
Land: 1.8 sq. mi.; **Water:** 0.0 sq. mi.
Incorporated Mar 8, 1916.

Park County
County Seat: Cody (ZIP: 82414)

Pop: 23,178 (1990); 21,639 (1980)　　**Pop Density:** 3.3
Land: 6942.7 sq. mi.; **Water:** 26.1 sq. mi.　　**Area Code:** 307
On the northwestern border of WY; organized Feb 15, 1909 from Sweetwater, Fremont, and Big Horn counties.
Name origin: For Yellowstone National Park, which forms the northwestern part of the county.

Cody — City
ZIP: 82414　　**Lat:** 44-31-10 N **Long:** 109-03-14 W
Pop: 7,897 (1990); 6,599 (1980)　　**Pop Density:** 877.4
Land: 9.0 sq. mi.; **Water:** 0.2 sq. mi.
Incorporated Oct 1, 1901.
Name origin: For William Frederick "Buffalo Bill" Cody (1846–1917), Army scout, Indian fighter, and showman.

Frannie — Town
Lat: 44-58-15 N **Long:** 108-37-27 W
Pop: 6 (1990); 17 (1980)　　**Pop Density:** 30.0
Land: 0.2 sq. mi.; **Water:** 0.0 sq. mi.
Incorporated Jun 29, 1954. Part of the town is also in Big Horn County.
Name origin: Named by railroad officials for pioneer Frannie Morris.

Meeteetse — Town
ZIP: 82433　　**Lat:** 44-09-19 N **Long:** 108-52-16 W
Pop: 368 (1990); 512 (1980)　　**Pop Density:** 1840.0
Land: 0.2 sq. mi.; **Water:** 0.0 sq. mi.　　**Elev:** 6795 ft.
Incorporated Aug 7, 1901.
Name origin: For nearby Meeteetse Creek, a Shoshone name meaning 'meeting place' or 'place of rest.'

Powell — City
ZIP: 82435　　**Lat:** 44-47-30 N **Long:** 108-44-09 W
Pop: 5,292 (1990); 5,310 (1980)　　**Pop Density:** 1512.0
Land: 3.5 sq. mi.; **Water:** 0.0 sq. mi.
Incorporated May 10, 1910.
Name origin: For engineer and explorer Maj. John Wesley Powell (1834–1902).

Platte County
County Seat: Wheatland (ZIP: 82201)

Pop: 8,145 (1990); 11,975 (1980)　　**Pop Density:** 3.9
Land: 2085.0 sq. mi.; **Water:** 26.0 sq. mi.　　**Area Code:** 307
In southeastern WY, north of Cheyenne; created Feb 9, 1911 from Laramie County.
Name origin: For the North Platte River, which flows through the county; French 'flat' or 'still.'

Chugwater — Town
ZIP: 82210　　**Lat:** 41-45-20 N **Long:** 104-49-16 W
Pop: 192 (1990); 282 (1980)　　**Pop Density:** 61.9
Land: 3.1 sq. mi.; **Water:** 0.0 sq. mi.
Incorporated 1913.
Name origin: For nearby Chugwater Creek.

Glendo — Town
ZIP: 82213　　**Lat:** 42-30-14 N **Long:** 105-01-29 W
Pop: 195 (1990); 367 (1980)　　**Pop Density:** 390.0
Land: 0.5 sq. mi.; **Water:** 0.0 sq. mi.　　**Elev:** 4714 ft.
Incorporated May 1, 1922.

Guernsey — Town
ZIP: 82214　　**Lat:** 42-15-58 N **Long:** 104-44-39 W
Pop: 1,155 (1990); 1,512 (1980)　　**Pop Density:** 1155.0
Land: 1.0 sq. mi.; **Water:** 0.0 sq. mi.
Incorporated Apr 4, 1902.
Name origin: For rancher and author Charles A. Guernsey.

Hartville — Town
ZIP: 82215　　**Lat:** 42-19-38 N **Long:** 104-43-27 W
Pop: 78 (1990); 149 (1980)　　**Pop Density:** 260.0
Land: 0.3 sq. mi.; **Water:** 0.0 sq. mi.
Incorporated Feb 17, 1900.
Name origin: For copper mine owner Maj. V.K. Hart.

Wheatland — Town
ZIP: 82201　　**Lat:** 42-03-04 N **Long:** 104-57-32 W
Pop: 3,271 (1990); 5,816 (1980)　　**Pop Density:** 817.8
Land: 4.0 sq. mi.; **Water:** 0.0 sq. mi.　　**Elev:** 4748 ft.
Incorporated Nov 18, 1905.
Name origin: For its descriptive connotation. Previously called Gilchrist.

Sheridan County
County Seat: Sheridan (ZIP: 82801)

Pop: 23,562 (1990); 25,048 (1980)
Land: 2523.4 sq. mi.; **Water:** 3.7 sq. mi.
Pop Density: 9.3
Area Code: 307

On the central northern border of WY; created Mar 9, 1888 from Johnson County.

Name origin: For the county's major town and county seat, itself named for Gen. Philip Henry Sheridan (1831–88), Union officer during the Civil War and commander in chief of the U.S. army (1883–88).

Clearmont — Town
ZIP: 82835 **Lat:** 44-38-25 N **Long:** 106-22-49 W
Pop: 119 (1990); 191 (1980) **Pop Density:** 595.0
Land: 0.2 sq. mi.; **Water:** 0.0 sq. mi.
Incorporated 1920.

Dayton — Town
ZIP: 82836 **Lat:** 44-52-22 N **Long:** 107-15-48 W
Pop: 565 (1990); 701 (1980) **Pop Density:** 1412.5
Land: 0.4 sq. mi.; **Water:** 0.0 sq. mi.
Founded 1882; incorporated 1906.
Name origin: For banker Joseph Dayton Thorn.

Ranchester — Town
ZIP: 82839 **Lat:** 44-54-26 N **Long:** 107-09-50 W
Pop: 676 (1990); 655 (1980) **Pop Density:** 1126.7
Land: 0.6 sq. mi.; **Water:** 0.0 sq. mi.
Founded 1894; incorporated Sep 28, 1919.
Name origin: Named by Englishman S.H. Hardin for *ranch* combined with Chester, the name of an English city.

Sheridan — City
ZIP: 82801 **Lat:** 44-47-31 N **Long:** 106-57-25 W
Pop: 13,900 (1990); 15,146 (1980) **Pop Density:** 1828.9
Land: 7.6 sq. mi.; **Water:** 0.0 sq. mi.
In north-central WY, about 15 mi. south of the MT border. Settled 1878; incorporated Jul 8, 1907.
Name origin: Named by Jim Loucks for his Civil War commander, Gen. Phillip Henry Sheridan.

Sublette County
County Seat: Pinedale (ZIP: 82941)

Pop: 4,843 (1990); 4,548 (1980)
Land: 4881.6 sq. mi.; **Water:** 54.4 sq. mi.
Pop Density: 1.0
Area Code: 307

In west-central WY; organized Feb 15, 1921 from Fremont County.

Name origin: For William Lewis Sublette (1799–1845), fur trader and explorer of the Rocky Mountain region.

Big Piney — Town
ZIP: 83113 **Lat:** 42-32-27 N **Long:** 110-07-01 W
Pop: 454 (1990); 530 (1980) **Pop Density:** 756.7
Land: 0.6 sq. mi.; **Water:** 0.0 sq. mi.
Incorporated Apr 1, 1913.
Name origin: For nearby Big Piney Creek.

Marbleton — Town
ZIP: 83113 **Lat:** 42-33-26 N **Long:** 110-05-57 W
Pop: 634 (1990); 537 (1980) **Pop Density:** 905.7
Land: 0.7 sq. mi.; **Water:** 0.0 sq. mi.
Founded 1912; incorporated Aug 4, 1914.
Name origin: For A.H. Marble.

Pinedale — Town
ZIP: 82941 **Lat:** 42-51-59 N **Long:** 109-51-52 W
Pop: 1,181 (1990); 1,066 (1980) **Pop Density:** 984.2
Land: 1.2 sq. mi.; **Water:** 0.0 sq. mi.
Incorporated Mar 15, 1912.
Name origin: Named by postmaster Charles Peterson for its location on Pine Creek.

Sweetwater County
County Seat: Green River (ZIP: 82935)

Pop: 38,823 (1990); 41,723 (1980) **Pop Density:** 3.7
Land: 10425.9 sq. mi.; **Water:** 65.9 sq. mi. **Area Code:** 307

On the southern border of WY; largest county in WY. Created as Carter County Dec 27, 1867 (prior to statehood) from Laramie County; name changed Dec 13, 1869.

Name origin: For the Sweetwater River, which flows through Fremont County, at that time still part of Sweetwater County. Originally named for Judge W. A. Carter.

Bairoil — Town
ZIP: 82322 **Lat:** 42-14-16 N **Long:** 107-33-32 W
Pop: 228 (1990) **Pop Density:** 1140.0
Land: 0.2 sq. mi.; **Water:** 0.0 sq. mi.
Incorporated Jun 1980.

Granger — Town
ZIP: 82934 **Lat:** 41-35-38 N **Long:** 109-57-57 W
Pop: 126 (1990); 177 (1980) **Pop Density:** 50.4
Land: 2.5 sq. mi.; **Water:** 0.0 sq. mi. **Elev:** 6268 ft.
Incorporated 1914.

Green River — City
ZIP: 82935 **Lat:** 41-30-57 N **Long:** 109-28-04 W
Pop: 12,711 (1990); 12,807 (1980) **Pop Density:** 1134.9
Land: 11.2 sq. mi.; **Water:** 0.3 sq. mi. **Elev:** 6109 ft.

In southwestern WY on the Green River, 15 mi. west of Rock Springs. Incorporated Jun 10, 1891.

Name origin: For the town's location on the Green River; so called for its deep green color.

North Rock Springs — CDP
Lat: 41-38-32 N **Long:** 109-15-08 W
Pop: 2,471 (1990) **Pop Density:** 69.4
Land: 35.6 sq. mi.; **Water:** 0.0 sq. mi.

Rock Springs — City
ZIP: 82901 **Lat:** 41-35-53 N **Long:** 109-13-17 W
Pop: 19,050 (1990); 19,458 (1980) **Pop Density:** 1035.3
Land: 18.4 sq. mi.; **Water:** 0.0 sq. mi.

In southwestern WY, 40 mi. north of UT border. Incorporated 1888.

Name origin: Named by a pony express rider, who discovered springs of good water here in 1861.

Superior — Town
ZIP: 82945 **Lat:** 41-45-38 N **Long:** 108-57-48 W
Pop: 273 (1990); 586 (1980) **Pop Density:** 248.2
Land: 1.1 sq. mi.; **Water:** 0.0 sq. mi.
Incorporated Feb 1911.

Wamsutter — Town
ZIP: 82336 **Lat:** 41-40-07 N **Long:** 107-58-33 W
Pop: 240 (1990); 681 (1980) **Pop Density:** 184.6
Land: 1.3 sq. mi.; **Water:** 0.0 sq. mi.
Incorporated Apr 21, 1914.

Name origin: For a bridge-builder on the Union Pacific Railroad. Originally known as Washakie.

Teton County
County Seat: Jackson (ZIP: 83001)

Pop: 11,172 (1990); 9,355 (1980) **Pop Density:** 2.8
Land: 4007.9 sq. mi.; **Water:** 214.0 sq. mi. **Area Code:** 307

On the northwestern border of WY; created Feb 15, 1921 from Lincoln County.

Name origin: For the Teton Mountains.

Jackson — Town
ZIP: 83001 **Lat:** 43-28-26 N **Long:** 110-45-49 W
Pop: 4,472 (1990); 4,511 (1980) **Pop Density:** 2236.0
Land: 2.0 sq. mi.; **Water:** 0.0 sq. mi.
Incorporated Aug 7, 1914.

Name origin: For Jackson's Hole, a nearby protected mountain valley.

Rafter J Ranch — CDP
Lat: 43-25-34 N **Long:** 110-47-54 W
Pop: 1,092 (1990) **Pop Density:** 321.2
Land: 3.4 sq. mi.; **Water:** 0.0 sq. mi.

WYOMING, Uinta County   American Places Dictionary

Uinta County
County Seat: Evanston (ZIP: 82930)

Pop: 18,705 (1990); 13,021 (1980)   **Pop Density:** 9.0
Land: 2081.8 sq. mi.; **Water:** 5.9 sq. mi.   **Area Code:** 307

On the southwestern border of WY; original county, organized Dec 1, 1869 (prior to statehood); smallest county in WY.

Name origin: For the Uintah Mountains or the Uinta Indian tribe.

Evanston   City
ZIP: 82930   **Lat:** 41-15-31 N **Long:** 110-57-48 W
Pop: 10,903 (1990); 6,265 (1980)   **Pop Density:** 1135.7
Land: 9.6 sq. mi.; **Water:** 0.1 sq. mi.   **Elev:** 6749 ft.

In southwestern WY on the Bear River, 5 mi. east of the UT border. Founded 1869 by Union Pacific Railroad officials; incorporated Jun 1, 1888.

Name origin: For surveyor James A. Evans.

Lyman   Town
ZIP: 82937   **Lat:** 41-19-39 N **Long:** 110-18-01 W
Pop: 1,896 (1990); 2,284 (1980)   **Pop Density:** 1580.0
Land: 1.2 sq. mi.; **Water:** 0.0 sq. mi.

Established 1898; incorporated 1915.

Name origin: For Mormon apostle Francis Lyman.

Mountain View   Town
ZIP: 82939   **Lat:** 41-16-17 N **Long:** 110-20-08 W
Pop: 1,189 (1990); 628 (1980)   **Pop Density:** 1486.3
Land: 0.8 sq. mi.; **Water:** 0.0 sq. mi.

Founded 1891; incorporated Apr 1971.

Washakie County
County Seat: Worland (ZIP: 82401)

Pop: 8,388 (1990); 9,496 (1980)   **Pop Density:** 3.7
Land: 2240.2 sq. mi.; **Water:** 2.7 sq. mi.   **Area Code:** 307

In north-central WY; created Feb 9, 1911 from Big Horn and Johnson counties.

Name origin: For Washakie (1804–1900), the Shoshone Indian chief and ally of the whites; meaning of name is uncertain but possibly 'rattler,' for the one he made and used to lead his men to battle.

Ten Sleep   Town
ZIP: 82442   **Lat:** 44-02-05 N **Long:** 107-26-50 W
Pop: 311 (1990); 407 (1980)   **Pop Density:** 1555.0
Land: 0.2 sq. mi.; **Water:** 0.0 sq. mi.

Incorporated Jan 11, 1932.

Name origin: From the Indian method of telling time: the town was ten days travel or "sleeps" from Yellowstone Park and also from Fort Laramie.

Worland   City
ZIP: 82401   **Lat:** 44-00-19 N **Long:** 107-57-28 W
Pop: 5,742 (1990); 6,391 (1980)   **Pop Density:** 1400.5
Land: 4.1 sq. mi.; **Water:** 0.1 sq. mi.

Incorporated Apr 4, 1906.

Name origin: For early settler C.R. "Dad" Worland, who built an early camp in the area.

Weston County
County Seat: Newcastle (ZIP: 82701)

Pop: 6,518 (1990); 7,106 (1980)   **Pop Density:** 2.7
Land: 2397.9 sq. mi.; **Water:** 2.2 sq. mi.   **Area Code:** 307

On the northeastern border of WY; organized Mar 12, 1890 from Crook County.

Name origin: For John B. Weston, geologist and surveyor who located large anthracite deposits that eventually brought the railroad to WY.

Newcastle   City
ZIP: 82701   **Lat:** 43-50-56 N **Long:** 104-12-36 W
Pop: 3,003 (1990); 3,596 (1980)   **Pop Density:** 1580.5
Land: 1.9 sq. mi.; **Water:** 0.0 sq. mi.   **Elev:** 4317 ft.

Settled 1889; incorporated Oct 25, 1889.

Name origin: For the English city, Newcastle-upon-Tyne.

Upton   Town
ZIP: 82730   **Lat:** 44-06-05 N **Long:** 104-37-24 W
Pop: 980 (1990); 1,193 (1980)   **Pop Density:** 753.8
Land: 1.3 sq. mi.; **Water:** 0.0 sq. mi.

Incorporated Oct 18, 1909.

Name origin: For surveyor George S. Upton.

Index to Places and Counties in Wyoming

Afton (Lincoln) Town 775
Albany County 769
Albin (Laramie) Town 774
Alpine (Lincoln) Town 775
Antelope Valley-Crestview (Campbell) CDP 770
Arapahoe (Fremont) CDP 772
Baggs (Carbon) Town 770
Bairoil (Sweetwater) Town 779
Bar Nunn (Natrona) Town 775
Basin (Big Horn) Town 769
Big Horn County 769
Big Piney (Sublette) Town 778
Buffalo (Johnson) City 774
Burlington (Big Horn) Town 769
Burns (Laramie) Town 774
Byron (Big Horn) Town 769
Campbell County 770
Carbon County 770
Casper (Natrona) City 775
Cheyenne (Laramie) City 774
Chugwater (Platte) Town 777
Clearmont (Sheridan) Town 778
Cody (Park) City 777
Cokeville (Lincoln) Town 775
Converse County 771
Cowley (Big Horn) Town 769
Crook County 772
Dayton (Sheridan) Town 778
Deaver (Big Horn) Town 769
Diamondville (Lincoln) Town 775
Dixon (Carbon) Town 770
Douglas (Converse) Town 771
Dubois (Fremont) Town 772
East Thermopolis (Hot Springs) Town 773
Edgerton (Natrona) Town 776
Elk Mountain (Carbon) Town 770
Ethete (Fremont) CDP 772
Evanston (Uinta) City 780
Evansville (Natrona) Town 776
Fort Laramie (Goshen) Town 773
Fort Washakie (Fremont) CDP 772
Fox Farm-College (Laramie) CDP ... 774
Frannie (Big Horn) Town 769
Frannie (Park) Town 777

Fremont County 772
Gillette (Campbell) City 770
Glendo (Platte) Town 777
Glenrock (Converse) Town 771
Goshen County 773
Grand Encampment (Carbon) Town 770
Granger (Sweetwater) Town 779
Green River (Sweetwater) City 779
Greybull (Big Horn) Town 769
Guernsey (Platte) Town 777
Hanna (Carbon) Town 771
Hartville (Platte) Town 777
Hot Springs County 773
Hudson (Fremont) Town 772
Hulett (Crook) Town 772
Jackson (Teton) Town 779
Johnson County 774
Kaycee (Johnson) Town 774
Kemmerer (Lincoln) Town 775
Kirby (Hot Springs) Town 773
La Barge (Lincoln) Town 775
La Grange (Goshen) Town 773
Lander (Fremont) City 772
Laramie (Albany) City 769
Laramie County 774
Lincoln County 775
Lingle (Goshen) Town 773
Lost Springs (Converse) Town 771
Lovell (Big Horn) Town 769
Lusk (Niobrara) Town 776
Lyman (Uinta) Town 780
Manderson (Big Horn) Town 770
Manville (Niobrara) Town 776
Marbleton (Sublette) Town 778
Medicine Bow (Carbon) Town 771
Meeteetse (Park) Town 777
Midwest (Natrona) Town 776
Mills (Natrona) Town 776
Moorcroft (Crook) Town 772
Mountain View (Natrona) CDP 776
Mountain View (Uinta) Town 780
Natrona County 775
Newcastle (Weston) City 780
Niobrara County 776
North Rock Springs (Sweetwater) CDP 779

Opal (Lincoln) Town 775
Park County 777
Pavillion (Fremont) Town 772
Pine Bluffs (Laramie) Town 774
Pinedale (Sublette) Town 778
Pine Haven (Crook) Town 772
Platte County 777
Powell (Park) City 777
Rafter J Ranch (Teton) CDP 779
Ranchester (Sheridan) Town 778
Ranchettes (Laramie) CDP 774
Rawlins (Carbon) City 771
Riverside (Carbon) Town 771
Riverton (Fremont) City 773
Rock River (Albany) Town 769
Rock Springs (Sweetwater) City 779
Rolling Hills (Converse) Town 771
Saratoga (Carbon) Town 771
Sheridan (Sheridan) City 778
Sheridan County 778
Shoshoni (Fremont) Town 773
Sinclair (Carbon) Town 771
Sleepy Hollow (Campbell) CDP 770
South Greeley (Laramie) CDP 775
Sublette County 778
Sundance (Crook) Town 772
Superior (Sweetwater) Town 779
Sweetwater County 779
Ten Sleep (Washakie) Town 780
Teton County 779
Thayne (Lincoln) Town 775
Thermopolis (Hot Springs) Town 774
Torrington (Goshen) Town 773
Uinta County 780
Upton (Weston) Town 780
Van Tassell (Niobrara) Town 776
Wamsutter (Sweetwater) Town 779
Warren Air Force Base (Laramie) Military Facility 775
Washakie County 780
Weston County 780
Wheatland (Platte) Town 777
Worland (Washakie) City 780
Wright (Campbell) Town 770
Yoder (Goshen) Town 773

Appendixes

American Indian Reservations

This section includes entries for 341 federal- and state-recognized American Indian reservations and trust lands. In addition to these, Oklahoma also has Tribal Jurisdiction Statistical Areas (TJSAs), which are those areas delineated by federally-recognized tribes without a reservation, for Census Bureau use. They usually contain American Indians over which one or more tribal governments have jurisdiction. A rancheria is a village or settlement, especially one on a reservation. A Tribal Designated Statistical Area (TDSA) is an area outside of Oklahoma delineated by federally- and state-recognized tribes without land, for use by the Census Bureau. They represent areas that contain an American Indian population governed by federally-recognized tribes and also those governed by state tribes.

Absentee Shawnee-Citizen Band Potawatomi
HQ: Shawnee, OK
Status: Federal
Area Code: 405
County: Cleveland, Oklahoma, Pottawatomi
Pop: 6,457: AmInd; 91,166: total

Federal trust areas in central OK, near Shawnee. Total area 1115 sq. mi.

Acoma Pueblo & Trust Lands
Tribe: Keresan Tribe
HQ: Acoma Pueblo, NM
Status: Federal
Area Code: 505
County: Valencia
Pop: 2,551: AmInd; 2,590: total

In central AZ, 50 mi. west of Albuquerque. Total area 417 sq. mi.; pueblo located on top of a 357-ft.-high mesa. Original Spanish land grant made Sep 20, 1689; Congress of U.S. confirmed the grant on Dec 22, 1858, and approved by Pres. Lincoln (1809–65) with the gift of a silver-headed cane. The canes are still passed on as a badge of office when the governors of each pueblo are elected.

Name origin: From Kero Indian *ako* 'white rock' and *ma* 'people.'

Agua Caliente Reservation
Tribe: Agua Caliente Band
HQ: Palm Springs, CA
Status: Federal
Area Code: 619
County: Riverside
Pop: 117: AmInd; 20,206: total

In southern CA, 3 mi. from Palm Springs. Total area 50 sq. mi. Established on May 14, 1896.

Name origin: Spanish 'hot water,' for the nearby hot springs.

Alabama and Coushatta Reservation
Tribe: Alabama and Coushatta
HQ: Livingston, TX
Status: Federal
Area Code: 409
County: Polk
Pop: 477: AmInd; 478: total
Lat: 30-42-41 N **Long:** 09-44-20 W

In southeastern TX, northeast of Houston. Total area 7 sq. mi. In 1854, through efforts of Gen. Sam Houston (1793–1863), 1,280 acres were bought for Alabama and Coushattas; in 1928, state and federal governments enlarged it to present size.

Name origin: *Alabama* from Choctaw *alba* 'thicket, plants,' and *amo* 'cleaners, reapers.' *Coushatta* from Choctaw *Koasati* 'white reed brake' because they lived near the brake.

Alamo Navajo Reservation
Tribe: Navajo Tribe
HQ: NM
Status: Federal
Area Code: 602
County: Socorro
Pop: 1,228: AmInd; 1,271: total
Lat: 34-24-00 N **Long:** 10-72-70 W

In west-central AZ, 30 mi. north of Socorro. Total area 99 sq. mi. Established c.1868 by those Navajo not wanting to continue the march to the Navajo Reservation.

Name origin: *Navajo*, Indian tribe of Athapascan linguistic stock; meaning of name unknown. Called by other tribes 'those with reed knives,' 'bastards,' 'wild coyotes,' and 'those who live on the border of the Utes.'

Allegany Reservation
Tribe: Seneca Tribe
HQ: Saylor Building, Irving, NY
Status: State
Area Code: 315
County: Cattaraugus
Pop: 1,062: AmInd; 7,315: total
Lat: 42-09-30 N **Long:** 07-84-50 W

In northwestern NY, east of Jamestown. Total area 41 sq. mi. Established as part of the Seneca Nation, whose boundaries were set by the 1794 Pickering Treaty.

Name origin: Probably for the Allegheny River, named from Delaware Indian, but origin and meaning are uncertain. It has been derived from *welhik-hanna* or *oolik-hanna* 'fine river' or 'beautiful river.' Its stem *-aha[n]* 'lapping' or 'alternate motion,' may also refer to the river.

Alturas Rancheria
Tribe: Pit River Tribe
HQ: Alturas, CA
Status: Federal
Area Code: 916
County: Modoc
Pop: 5: AmInd; 5: total
Lat: 41-28-40 N **Long:** 12-03-12 W

In northern CA, 1 mi. east of Alturas. Total area less than 0.1 sq. mi. Established Jun 21, 1906; rancheria purchased on Sep 8, 1924.

Name origin: Spanish 'heights.'

Apache Choctaw TDSA
Tribe: Apache Choctaw
HQ: LA
Status: State
Area Code: 318
County: Sabine
Pop: 639: AmInd; 22,646: total

In west-central LA, south of Shreveport; total area 865 sq. mi.

Augustine Reservation
Tribe: Augustine Band of Mission Indians **Status:** Federal
HQ: Thermal, CA **Area Code:** 619
County: Riverside
Pop: 0: AmInd; 0: total
Lat: 33-38-55 N **Long:** 11-61-12 W

In southern CA, 15 mi. from Indio. Total area 1 sq. mi. Established in Feb 1893.

Bad River Reservation
Tribe: Chippewa Tribe **Status:** Federal
HQ: Odanah, WI **Area Code:** 715
County: Ashland, Iron
Pop: 868: AmInd; 1,070: total
Lat: 46-32-00 N **Long:** 09-04-00 W

On Lake Superior coast of WI, southeast of Washburn. Total area 192 sq. mi. Established 1854.

Name origin: For the river, from Chippewa *maski* 'swamp,' which was mistaken for *matchi* 'bad.'

Barona Rancheria
Tribe: Barona Group of Capitan Band of Mission Indians **Status:** Federal
HQ: Lakeside, CA **Area Code:** 619
County: San Diego
Pop: 373: AmInd; 537: total
Lat: 32-57-06 N **Long:** 11-65-03 W

In southwestern CA, 31 mi. east of San Diego. Total area 9 sq. mi. Established Dec 27, 1875; May 3, 1877, portions were restored to public domain; Jun 19, 1883, certain lands were set apart for the reservation. Barona Tract purchased for the Barona group.

Bay Mills Reservation
Tribe: Chippewa Tribe **Status:** Federal
HQ: Brimley, MI **Area Code:** 906
County: Chippewa
Pop: 403: AmInd; 461: total
Lat: 46-27-00 N **Long:** 08-43-60 W

On northeastern coast of Upper Peninsula of MI, 21 mi. from Sault Ste. Marie. Total area 4 sq. mi.

Name origin: *Chippewa*, more properly Ojibway, large tribe of Algonquian linguistic stock; 'puckered,' with reference to the puckered seam in their moccasins.

Benton Paiute Reservation
Tribe: Paiute **Status:** Federal
HQ: CA **Area Code:** 916
County: Mono
Pop: 52: AmInd; 63: total

On central-eastern border of CA, southeast of Mono Lake; total area 0.2 sq. mi.

Name origin: The Pah-Utes (Paiutes) are a sub-tribe of the Ute Indians of Shoshonean linguistic stock; name means 'water Ute.'

Berry Creek Rancheria
Tribe: Maidu Tribe **Status:** Federal
HQ: Berry Creek, CA **Area Code:** 916
County: Butte
Pop: 2: AmInd; 2: total

In north-central CA, near Oroville. Total area 0.1 sq. mi. Purchased in Mar 1916.

Name origin: For the creek, possibly named for Henry Berry of PA.

Big Bend Rancheria
Tribe: Pitts Tribe **Status:** Federal
HQ: Big Bend, CA **Area Code:** 707
County: Shasta
Pop: 3: AmInd; 3: total
Lat: 41-01-31 N **Long:** 12-15-44 W

In northern CA, near Redding. Total area 0.1 sq. mi. Established Jul 28, 1916.

Big Cypress Reservation
Tribe: Seminole Indian Tribe **Status:** Federal
HQ: Hollywood, FL **Area Code:** 305
County: Hendry
Pop: 447: AmInd; 484: total

In south-central Florida, south of Lake Okeechobee. Total area 82 sq. mi. The State of Florida has set aside an additional 104,000 acres adjoining the reservation called the Florida State Indian Reservation; the Seminole and Miccosukee tribes have hunting and fishing rights on this land.

Name origin: A Muskhogean tribe; name is from Creek 'the separate ones'; also recorded as 'runaway,' but with a connotation of separateness.

Big Lagoon Rancheria
Tribe: Yurok and Tolowa **Status:** Federal
HQ: CA **Area Code:** 707
County: Humboldt
Pop: 19: AmInd; 22: total
Lat: 41-09-48 N **Long:** 12-40-70 W

On the northern Pacific coast of CA, north of Eureka; total area less than 0.1 sq. mi.

Big Pine Rancheria
Tribe: Paiute-Shoshone Tribes **Status:** Federal
HQ: Big Pine, CA **Area Code:** 619
County: Inyo
Pop: 331: AmInd; 452: total
Lat: 37-09-34 N **Long:** 11-81-70 W

On central-eastern border of CA. Total area 0.4 sq. mi. The Act of Apr 20, 1937, authorized the U.S. government to exchange Indian lands and water rights for land owned by the City of Los Angeles in Inyo and Mono Counties; in 1939 exchanged 3,000 acres of property for 1,500 acres of level valley land.

Big Sandy Rancheria
Tribe: Mono **Status:** Federal
HQ: CA **Area Code:** 209
County: Fresno
Pop: 38: AmInd; 51: total

In central CA, northeast of Fresno; total area 0.4 sq. mi.

Big Valley Rancheria
Status: Federal
HQ: CA **Area Code:** 707
County: Lake
Pop: 90: AmInd; 108: total
Lat: 39-01-17 N **Long:** 12-25-31 W

In northwestern CA, south of Clear Lake; total area 0.2 sq. mi.

Bishop Rancheria
Tribe: Paiute-Shoshone Tribes **Status:** Federal
HQ: Bishop, CA **Area Code:** 714
County: Inyo
Pop: 935: AmInd; 1,408: total

In eastern CA near Bishop. Total area 1 sq. mi. Established Mar 11, 1912 (see Big Pine Rancheria).
Name origin: For the town, named for Samuel A. Bishop, army officer and local cattleman.

Blackfeet Reservation
Tribe: Blackfeet Tribe **Status:** Federal
HQ: Browning, MT **Area Code:** 406
County: Glacier, Pondera
Pop: 7,025: AmInd; 8,549: total
Lat: 48-40-00 N **Long:** 11-25-50 W

In north-central MT, 125 mi. northwest of Great Falls. Total area 2371 sq. mi. Established in late 19th century.

Blue Lake Rancheria
Tribe: Various **Status:** Federal
HQ: CA **Area Code:** 707
County: Humboldt
Pop: 30: AmInd; 58: total

In northwestern CA, northeast of Eureka; total area less than 0.1 sq. mi.

Bois Forte (Nett Lake)
Tribe: Chippewa Tribe **Status:** Federal
HQ: Nett Lake, MN **Area Code:** 218
County: Koochiching, Saint Louis
Pop: 346: AmInd; 358: total

In north-central MN, 80 mi. south of International Falls. Total area 163 sq. mi.
Name origin: Named by the French 'hard wood' for their location in thick fir woods.

Bridgeport Colony
Tribe: Paiute **Status:** Federal
HQ: CA **Area Code:** 209
County: Mono
Pop: 37: AmInd; 49: total

In central-eastern CA, north of Mono Lake; total area 0.1 sq. mi.

Brighton Reservation
Tribe: Seminole Indian Tribe **Status:** Federal
HQ: Hollywood, FL **Area Code:** 305
County: Glades
Pop: 402: AmInd; 524: total
Lat: 27-06-08 N **Long:** 08-10-42 W

In south-central Florida, northwest of Lake Okeechobee. Total area 57 sq. mi. See also Big Cypress Reservation.

Burns Paiute Reservation and Trust Lands
Tribe: Paiute **Status:** Federal
HQ: OR **Area Code:** 503
County: Harney
Pop: 151: AmInd; 163: total
Lat: 43-36-04 N **Long:** 11-90-41 W

In southeastern OR, north of Malheur and Harney lakes. Total area 19 sq. mi. Established 1863.

Cabazon Reservation
Tribe: Cabazon Band of Mission Indians **Status:** Federal
HQ: Indio, CA **Area Code:** 617
County: Riverside
Pop: 20: AmInd; 819: total

In south-central CA, near Indio. Total area 3 sq. mi. Established May 15, 1876; May 3, 1877, one section restored to public domain; 1895 area increased to present size.
Name origin: Misspelling of Spanish *cabezón* 'big head,' name given to head chief and supreme authority of the Coahuilla Indians.

Caddo-Wichita-Delaware TJSA
Status: Federal
HQ: Binger, OK **Area Code:** 405
County: Caddo, Canadian, Grady
Pop: 545: AmInd; 8,195: total

Federal trust areas in west-central OK. Total area 647 sq. mi. Established 1891.
Name origin: *Caddo* from *Kadohadacho* 'real chiefs' Confederacy; name applied to a group of tribes of Caddoan linguistic stock. *Wichita* 'man,' or if from Choctaw *owa chita* 'big hunt.' *Delaware* for the bay; also called Leni-Lenape.

Cahuilla Reservation
Tribe: Cahuilla Band of Mission Indians **Status:** Federal
HQ: Hemet, CA **Area Code:** 617
County: Riverside
Pop: 82: AmInd; 104: total
Lat: 33-31-01 N **Long:** 11-64-31 W

In south-central CA, 38 mi. from Hemet. Total area 29 sq. mi. Established Dec 17, 1875; area decreased in 1877, but increased by subsequent orders.
Name origin: A Shoshonean Indian tribal name meaning 'leader.' Indians prefer the spelling *Ka-we-a*, both pronounced the same.

Campo Reservation
Tribe: Mission Band of Indians of Campo Community **Status:** Federal
HQ: Campo, CA **Area Code:** 619
County: San Diego
Pop: 143: AmInd; 281: total
Lat: 32-40-40 N **Long:** 11-62-15 W

In southwestern CA, 37 mi. east of El Cajon. Total area 26 sq. mi. Established Feb 10, 1893; enlarged Feb 2, 1907, and again Dec 14, 1911.
Name origin: Spanish 'field,' but in California 'camp.'

Camp Verde
Tribe: Yavapai and Apache **Status:** Federal
HQ: AZ **Area Code:** 602
County: Yavapai
Pop: 569: AmInd; 618: total
Lat: 34-37-01 N **Long:** 11-15-34 W

In west-central AZ, north of Phoenix; area 1 sq. mi.

Canoncito Reservation
Tribe: Navajo Tribe **Status:** Federal
HQ: Canoncito, NM **Area Code:** 505
County: Bernalillo, Valencia
Pop: 1,177: AmInd; 1,189: total

In north-central NM. Total area 122 sq. mi. Navajo Reservation established 1868; this reservation founded by Navajo who settled there rather than continue the march to the Navajo Reservation.
Name origin: Spanish 'little canyon.'

Capitan Grande Reservation
Tribe: Mission Tribes **Status:** Federal
HQ: Alpine, CA **Area Code:** 619
County: San Diego
Pop: 0: AmInd; 0: total
Lat: 32-54-27 N **Long:** 11-64-34 W

In southwestern CA, 38 mi. east of San Diego; total area 21 sq. mi. Established Dec 27, 1875; May 3, 1877, portions returned to public domain; Jun 19, 1883, separated certain lands for the reservation; May 10, 1894, a patent issued to the Capitan Grande Band for lands chosen by the Indian Mission Commission.

Name origin: Spanish 'Big Captain,' former name for the canyon in which the reservation lies; possibly named for J.F. Ortega, an early grantee.

Carson Colony
Tribe: Washoe Tribe **Status:** Federal
HQ: Carson City, NV **Area Code:** 702
County: Washoe
Pop: 235: AmInd; 248: total
Lat: 39-08-23 N **Long:** 11-94-62 W

Three communities near Reno, on western border of NV. Total area 0.2 sq. mi. Land purchased in 1917.

Catawba Reservation
Tribe: Catawba Tribe **Status:** State
HQ: Rock Hill, SC **Area Code:** 803
County: York
Pop: 124: AmInd; 174: total

On north-central border of SC, east of Spartanburg. Total area 1 sq. mi. Their 15 sq. mi. reservation was confirmed in 1793 then leased almost entirely to whites in 1826; in 1841 all but 640 acres were sold to SC. Tribe terminated relations with U.S. government in 1962.

Name origin: *Catawba*, meaning of name unknown; member of the Siouan linguistic stock.

Cattaraugus Reservation
Tribe: Seneca Tribe **Status:** State
HQ: Irving, NY **Area Code:** 716
County: Cattaraugus, Erie, Chautauqua
Pop: 2,051: AmInd; 2,178: total
Lat: 42-33-03 N **Long:** 07-90-22 W

In northwestern NY near Lake Erie. Total area 34 sq. mi. Established in Pickering Treaty of 1794.

Name origin: Probably from Seneca 'bad smelling shore.'

Cedarville Rancheria
Tribe: Paiute Tribe **Status:** Federal
HQ: Cedarville, CA **Area Code:** 916
County: Modoc
Pop: 6: AmInd; 8: total
Lat: 41-31-32 N **Long:** 12-01-10 W

In northern CA, 164 mi. from Redding. Total area less than 0.1 sq. mi. Land purchased in 1915.

Chehalis Reservation
Tribe: Chehalis **Status:** Federal
HQ: Oakville, WA **Area Code:** 206
County: Grays Harbor, Thurston
Pop: 308: AmInd; 491: total
Lat: 46-49-12 N **Long:** 12-31-21 W

In western WA, 35 mi. from Olympia. Total area 7 sq. mi. Established 1864.

Name origin: *Chehalis* 'shining sands.'

Chemehuevi Reservation
Tribe: Chemehuevi Tribe **Status:** Federal
HQ: CA **Area Code:** 602
County: San Bernardino
Pop: 95: AmInd; 358: total

On southeastern CA border, east of Lake Havasu; total area 50 sq. mi.

Name origin: Name of a Shoshonean tribe, meaning unknown; apparently an offshoot of the Paiute. Also spelled *Chemehuevis* or *Chemehuevitz*.

Cherokee TJSA
Tribe: Cherokee **Status:** Federal
HQ: Tahlequah, OK **Area Code:** 918
County: parts of 14 counties
Pop: 66,356: AmInd; 399,385: total

Federal trust areas in northeast OK, in Adair, Cherokee, Craig, Delaware, Mayes, McIntosh, Muskogee, Nowata, Ottawa, Rogers, Sequoyah, Tulsa, Wagoner, and Washington counties. Total area 6700 sq. mi. Under treaties of 1828 and 1833 they established the Cherokee Nation with its capital at Tahlequah; nation was disbanded in 1906.

Name origin: *Cherokee* possibly from Creek *tciloki* 'people of a different speech'; a tribe of Iroquoian linguistic stock.

Cheyenne-Arapaho TJSA
Tribe: Cheyenne and Arapahoe **Status:** Federal
HQ: Concho, OK **Area Code:** 405
County: parts of 10 counties
Pop: 6,719: AmInd; 150,826: total

Federal trust areas in central OK, in Beckham, Blaine, Caddo, Canadian, Custer, Dewey, Ellis, Kingfisher, Roger Mills, and Washita counties. Total area 8123 sq. mi. Established 1869.

Name origin: *Cheyenne* from Dakota Indian 'red talkers'; tribe of Algonquian linguistic stock. *Arapaho* 'blue-sky men' or 'cloud men.'

Cheyenne River Reservation
Tribe: Sioux Tribe **Status:** Federal
HQ: Eagle Butte, SD **Area Code:** 605
County: Perkins, Dewey, Ziebach
Pop: 5,100: AmInd; 7,743: total

In northern SD, 60 mi. northwest of Pierre. Total area 4265 sq. mi. Established 1889.

Chickahominy TDSA
Tribe: Chickahominy **Status:** State
HQ: VA **Area Code:** 804
County: Chesterfield
Pop: 466: AmInd; 2,791: total

In southeastern VA, south of Richmond; total area 50 sq. mi.

Name origin: Probably from Algonquian 'land of grain,' but this is speculation. The latter part certainly refers to grain, the boiled Indian maize *rokahamen*.

Chickasaw TJSA
Tribe: Chickasaw **Status:** Federal
HQ: Ada, OK **Area Code:** 405
County: parts of 13 counties
Pop: 21,248: AmInd; 257,858: total

Federal trust area in central through south-central OK, in Bryan, Carter, Cleveland, Garvin, Grady, Jefferson, Johnston, Love, Marshall, McClain, Murray, Pontotoc, and Stephens counties. Total area 7304 sq. mi. In 1855 their lands in Indian Territory were separated from those of the Choctaw.

Name origin: Indian tribe closely connected with the Choctaw, and of Muskhogean linguistic stock; meaning of name unknown.

Chicken Ranch Rancheria
Status: Federal
HQ: CA **Area Code:** 916
County: San Joaquin
Pop: 10: AmInd; 73: total

In central CA, southeast of Stockton; total area 0.1 sq. mi.

Chitimacha Reservation
Tribe: Chitimacha Indian Tribe **Status:** Federal
HQ: Charenton, LA **Area Code:** 601
County: Saint Mary Parish
Pop: 212: AmInd; 286: total

In southern LA, 40 mi. north of Patterson. Total area 0.4 sq. mi. Land put into trust, at request of tribe, in 1935.

Choctaw TJSA
Tribe: Choctaw **Status:** Federal
HQ: Durant, OK **Area Code:** 405
County: parts of 11 counties
Pop: 28,411: AmInd; 209,339: total

Federal trust area in southern and southeastern OK, in Atoka, Bryan, Choctaw, Coal, Haskell, Hughes, Latimer, Le Flore, McCurtain, Pittsburg, and Pushmataha counties. Total area 10,612 sq. mi. Established 1898.

Name origin: An Indian tribe of Muskhogean linguistic stock; meaning of name is unknown.

Clifton Choctaw TDSA
Tribe: Choctaw **Status:** State
HQ: LA **Area Code:** 0
Pop: 153: AmInd; 411: total

In west-central LA, west of Alexandria; total area 40 sq. mi.

Cochiti Pueblo
Tribe: Keresan Tribe **Status:** Federal
HQ: Cochiti Pueblo, NM **Area Code:** 505
County: Sandoval
Pop: 666: AmInd; 1,342: total

In north-central AZ, 30 mi. southwest of Santa Fe. Total area 80 sq. mi.

Name origin: Probably a Spanish pronunciation of Keresan *k-ot yayte*, the meaning of which is obscure.

Cocopah Reservation
Tribe: Yuma Tribe **Status:** Federal
HQ: Somerton, AZ **Area Code:** 602
County: Yuma
Pop: 436: AmInd; 515: total
Lat: 32-37-15 N **Long:** 11-44-54 W

In southwestern AZ on the Colorado River, about 10 mi. south of Yuma. Total area 10 sq. mi. Established in 1917. On Mar 21, 1956, 62 acres were set aside from public domain for the temporary use of the Cocopah Indians.

Name origin: *Cocopah*, a Papago Indian name probably meaning 'those who live on the river.'

Coeur d'Alene Reservation & Trust Lands
Tribe: Coeur d'Alene Tribe **Status:** Federal
HQ: Plummer, ID **Area Code:** 208
County: Benewah, Kootenai
Pop: 749: AmInd; 5,802: total
Lat: 47-17-00 N **Long:** 11-65-00 W

On northwest border of ID, 30 mi. southeast of Spokane, WA. Total area 598 sq. mi. Established in 1859.

Name origin: Name *Coeur d'Alene* 'awl; pointed; needle-hearted,' given to Indians by French in reference to their trading ability.

Coharie TDSA
Tribe: Coharie **Status:** State
HQ: NC **Area Code:** 919
County: Sampson
Pop: 1,306: AmInd; 116,053: total

In southeastern NC, southwest of Goldsboro; total area 639 sq. mi.

Name origin: For the Coharie River.

Cold Springs Rancheria
Tribe: Mono Tribe **Status:** Federal
HQ: Tollhouse, CA **Area Code:** 209
County: Fresno
Pop: 159: AmInd; 192: total

In central CA, 42 mi. from Fresno. Total area 0.2 sq. mi.

Colorado River Reservation
Tribe: Mojave and Chemehuevi Tribes **Status:** Federal
HQ: Parker, AZ **Area Code:** 602
County: La Paz, AZ, San Bernardino, CA, Riverside, CA
Pop: 2,345: AmInd; 7,865: total
Lat: 33-47-30 N **Long:** 11-42-50 W

In southwestern AZ, about 50 mi. north of Yuma. Total area 433 sq. mi., of which 73 sq. mi. are in CA. Under the Treaty of Guadalupe Hidalgo in 1848, the U.S. agreed to preserve recognition of the Indians' right to their land, inhabited by them since recorded history.

Name origin: Mojave (Mohave) Indians are a tribe of Yuman linguistic stock. Name means 'three mountains,' in reference to the Needles. The Chemehuevi are a Shoshone tribe of the Paiute; meaning of name unknown.

Colusa (Cachil Dehe) Rancheria
Tribe: Cachil Dehe Band of Wintun Indians **Status:** Federal
HQ: Colusa, CA **Area Code:** 916
County: Colusa
Pop: 19: AmInd; 22: total

In north-central CA, 60 mi. northwest of Sacramento; Sacramento River runs through rancheria. Total area 0.3 sq. mi. Established Jun 21, 1907; additional lands acquired 1938.

Name origin: From the name of an Indian village; meaning unknown.

Colville Reservation
Tribe: Confederated Tribes **Status:** Federal
HQ: Nespelem, WA **Area Code:** 509
County: Ferry, Okanogan
Pop: 3,788: AmInd; 6,957: total
Lat: 48-12-00 N **Long:** 11-85-20 W

In northeastern WA, 97 mi. northwest of Spokane. Total area 2117 sq. mi. Established Jul 2, 1872.

Coos, Lower Umpqua, and Siuslaw Res.
Tribe: Coos, Lower Umpqua, Siuslaw Tribes **Status:** Federal
HQ: OR **Area Code:** 503
County: Coos
Pop: 1: AmInd; 4: total

On southern Pacific coast of OR, near Coos Bay; total area less than 0.1 sq. mi.

Name origin: *Coos* 'lake' or 'place of pines'; a tribe of Kusan linguistic stock; recorded as *cook-koo-oose* in Lewis and Clark journals. *Umpqua*, of Athapascan linguistic stock; meaning unknown. *Siuslaw* tribal name, meaning unknown.

Coquille Indian TDSA
Tribe: Upper and Lower Coquilles **Status:** Federal
HQ: OR **Area Code:** 503
County: Douglas
Pop: 5,483: AmInd; 404,117: total

In southwestern OR, southwest of Eugene; total area 3806 sq. mi.

Name origin: French 'shell,' but the name almost certainly has an Indian origin not satisfactorily explained. The Miluk and Mishikhwutmetunne tribes were both called Coquilles by the French, from their location in the Coquille River area, but they were from different tribal stocks.

Cortina Rancheria
Tribe: Wintun Tribe **Status:** Federal
HQ: Williams, CA **Area Code:** 916
County: Colusa
Pop: 22: AmInd; 30: total
Lat: 39-00-58 N **Long:** 12-21-71 W

In north-central CA, 50 mi. west of Yuba City. Total area 1 sq. mi. Established Jun 25, 1907.

Name origin: Probably for Kotina, a captain or head man of a Southern Wintun village.

Coushatta Tribe
Tribe: Coushatta **Status:** Federal
HQ: LA **Area Code:** 601
County: Allen
Pop: 33: AmInd; 36: total

In southwestern LA, northeast of Lake Charles. Total area 0.4 sq. mi.

Name origin: A small tribe; name from Choctaw 'white reed brake' because they lived near one. Also spelled *Koasati*.

Cow Creek Reservation
Tribe: Umpqua **Status:** Federal
HQ: OR **Area Code:** 503
County: Douglas
Pop: 11: AmInd; 58: total

In southwestern OR, northwest of Medford; total area 0.1 sq. mi.

Coyote Valley Reservation
Status: Federal
HQ: CA **Area Code:** 916
County: Mendocino
Pop: 122: AmInd; 135: total

In northwestern CA, northeast of Mendocino; total area 1 sq. mi.

Creek-Seminole Joint Area TJSA
Tribe: Creek and Seminole **Status:** Federal
HQ: OK **Area Code:** 405
County: Seminole
Pop: 518: AmInd; 2,448: total

In south-central OK. Total area 65 sq. mi.

Name origin: See Creek and Seminole.

Creek TJSA
Tribe: Creek **Status:** Federal
HQ: OK **Area Code:** 918
County: Okmulgee
Pop: 44,964: AmInd; 635,250: total

In east-central OK, south of Tulsa; total area 4648 sq. mi.

Name origin: A loose confederation of southeastern tribes of Muskhogean linguistic stock. Name given to them by settlers in TN. They were probably the Yuchi Indians who lived on Ocheese Creek.

Crow Creek Reservation
Tribe: Sioux Tribe **Status:** Federal
HQ: Fort Thompson, SD **Area Code:** 605
County: Buffalo, Hyde, Hughes
Pop: 1,531: AmInd; 1,756: total
Lat: 44-05-05 N **Long:** 09-92-05 W

In central SD, 60 mi. southeast of Pierre; total area 422 sq. mi. Established in 1870s.

Crow Reservation & Trust Lands
Tribe: Crow Tribe **Status:** Federal
HQ: Crow Agency, MT **Area Code:** 406
County: Big Horn, Yellowstone
Pop: 4,724: AmInd; 6,370: total
Lat: 45-23-00 N **Long:** 10-75-00 W

On south-central border of MT, 75 mi. southeast of Billings. Total area 3574 sq. mi. Treaty of 1851 gave the Crows 38.5 million acres in MT; by 1888 they were confined to the present reservation, also the site of the Custer battlefield.

Cuyapaipe Reservation
Tribe: Cuyapaipe Band of Mission Indians **Status:** Federal
HQ: Mount Laguna, CA **Area Code:** 619
County: San Diego
Pop: 0: AmInd; 0: total
Lat: 32-50-44 N **Long:** 11-62-31 W

In southwestern CA, 75 mi. east of San Diego. Total area 8 sq. mi. Established Feb 10, 1893.

Name origin: Possibly from Diegueo Indian *ewi-apaip* or *awi-apaip* 'rock lie on.' Also spelled *Guyapipe, Cuiapaipa*.

Deer Creek Reservation
Status: Federal
HQ: MN **Area Code:** 218
County: Itasca
Pop: 6: AmInd; 186: total

In north-central MN, north of Grand Rapids; total area 35 sq. mi.

Delaware-Muncie TDSA
Status: State
HQ: KS **Area Code:** 913
County: Franklin
Pop: 10: AmInd; 265: total

In east-central KS, southeast of Topeka; total area 13 sq. mi.

Devils Lake Sioux Reservation
Tribe: Devils Lake Sioux **Status:** Federal
HQ: Fort Totten, ND **Area Code:** 701
County: Benson, Nelson, Eddy
Pop: 2,676: AmInd; 3,588: total

In east-central ND, south of Devils Lake. Total area 392 sq. mi; originally 360 sq. mi. Fort built in 1867.

Name origin: From Siouan *miniwaukan* 'lake hole one,' which was misunderstood by white settlers as 'devil's lake.'

Dresslerville Colony
Tribe: Washoe Tribe **Status:** Federal
HQ: Dresslerville, NV **Area Code:** 702
County: Douglas
Pop: 144: AmInd; 152: total

In southwestern corner of NV, 60 mi. south of Reno. Total area 0.1 sq. mi. Land given "in trust" with the U.S. government on Mar 16, 1917, by William F. Dressler.

Dry Creek Rancheria
Tribe: Pomo **Status:** Federal
HQ: CA **Area Code:** 707
County: Sonoma
Pop: 38: AmInd; 75: total
Lat: 38-42-09 N **Long:** 12-25-12 W

In northwestern CA, northeast of Santa Rosa; total area less than 0.1 sq. mi.

Duck Valley Reservation
Tribe: Shoshone and Paiute Tribes **Status:** Federal
HQ: Owyhee, NV **Area Code:** 702
County: Elko, NV, Owyhee, ID
Pop: 1,022: AmInd; 1,101: total
Lat: 42-00-00 N **Long:** 11-61-10 W

In north-central NV and south-central ID, 100 mi. north of Elko. Total area 506 sq. mi., of which 281 is in ID and 225 in NV. Established 1877 for the Western Shoshone. In 1886, a group of Paiute settled on the north side; both groups combined into one tribe in 1938. The present reservation, by executive orders, is larger than the original.

Name origin: For the wild duck. Also called Western Shoshone Indian Reservation, Geyser Valley, and Lake Valley.

Duckwater Reservation
Tribe: Shoshone Tribe **Status:** Federal
HQ: Duckwater, NV **Area Code:** 702
County: Nye
Pop: 115: AmInd; 135: total
Lat: 38-56-23 N **Long:** 11-54-24 W

In east-central NV, 160 mi. south of Elko. Total area 6 sq. mi. Lands purchased from 1940 through 1944 declared an Indian reservation on Nov 13, 1940.

Name origin: Probably for Duckwater Valley, whose marshy areas are good feeding ground for wintering wild ducks.

Eastern Cherokee Reservation
Tribe: Eastern Band of Cherokee **Status:** Federal
HQ: Cherokee, NC **Area Code:** 704
County: parts of 5 counties
Pop: 5,388: AmInd; 6,527: total

In southwestern corner of NC, 56 mi. southwest of Asheville, in Cherokee, Graham, Jackson, Macon, and Swain counties. Total area 81 sq. mi. Established in 1925 at petition of the tribe.

Eastern Chickahominy TDSA
Tribe: Eastern Chickahominy **Status:** State
HQ: VA **Area Code:** 804
County: Henrico
Pop: 30: AmInd; 99: total

In east-central VA, east of Richmond; total area 2 sq. mi.

Elk Valley Rancheria
Status: Federal
HQ: CA **Area Code:** 707
County: Del Norte
Pop: 32: AmInd; 77: total

On northern Pacific coast of CA, south of the OR border; total area less than 0.1 sq. mi.

Ely Colony
Tribe: Shoshone Tribe **Status:** Federal
HQ: Ely, NV **Area Code:** 702
County: White Pine
Pop: 52: AmInd; 59: total
Lat: 39-14-26 N **Long:** 11-45-34 W

In eastern NV, 1 mi. from Ely. Total area 0.2 sq. mi. Established 1931.

Name origin: Probably for the town, which was named for Smith Ely who financed the construction of a small copper furnace in the 1870s.

Enterprise Rancheria
Tribe: Maidu Tribe **Status:** Federal
HQ: Oroville, CA **Area Code:** 916
County: Butte
Pop: 5: AmInd; 5: total
Lat: 39-33-45 N **Long:** 12-12-11 W

In north-central CA, 20 mi. northeast of Oroville. Total area less than 0.1 sq. mi. Land purchased in 1915.

Name origin: For the town, which was probably named for the Enterprise Co., which built flumes there in 1852.

Fallon Colony
Tribe: Paiute-Shoshone Tribe **Status:** Federal
HQ: Fallon, NV **Area Code:** 702
County: Churchill
Pop: 150: AmInd; 165: total
Lat: 39-30-50 N **Long:** 11-83-70 W

In west-central NV, 71 mi. east of Reno. Total area 0.1 sq. mi. Established 1906.

Name origin: For the town, named for Michael Fallon, who began its first post office.

Fallon Reservation
Tribe: Paiute and Shoshone **Status:** Federal
HQ: NV **Area Code:** 702
County: Churchill
Pop: 356: AmInd; 381: total
Lat: 39-30-50 N **Long:** 11-83-70 W

In west-central NV, east of Reno; total area 13 sq. mi.

Name origin: See Fallon Colony.

Flandreau Reservation
Tribe: Flandreau Santee Sioux Tribe **Status:** Federal
HQ: Flandreau, SD **Area Code:** 605
County: Moody
Pop: 249: AmInd; 279: total

On east coast of SD, north of Sioux Falls. Total area 4 sq. mi. Reservation established 1935; prior to that they had no reservation but had taken homesteads at Flandreau as authorized by the Sioux Treaty of 1868.
Name origin: For the town, named for Charles E. Flandrau, a jurist. The Frenchified *e* was added later.

Flathead Reservation
Tribe: Salish and Kootenai Tribes **Status:** Federal
HQ: Dixon, MT **Area Code:** 406
County: in parts of 4 counties
Pop: 5,130: AmInd; 21,259: total
Lat: 47-30-01 N **Long:** 11-42-00 W

In northwestern MT, 28 mi. north of Missoula, in Flathead, Lake, Missoula, and Sanders counties. Total area 1938 sq. mi. Established Jul 16, 1855, by Hellgate Treaty which ceded most of MT to the U.S. for 1,234,969 acres for a reservation for the Kootenai and Salish. Land allotment and non-Indian homesteading reduced area by about half.
Name origin: *Kootenai* 'water people.' Also spelled Kutenai.

Florida Tribe of Eastern Creek TDSA
Tribe: Eastern Creek **Status:** State
HQ: FL **Area Code:** 904
County: Walton
Pop: 0: AmInd; 195: total

In northwestern FL, east of Pensacola; total area 2 sq. mi.

Fond Du Lac Reservation
Tribe: Mississippi Band of Chippewa **Status:** Federal
HQ: Cloquet, MN **Area Code:** 218
County: Carlton, Saint Louis
Pop: 1,106: AmInd; 3,229: total
Lat: 46-45-01 N **Long:** 09-23-60 W

In northeastern MN, 20 mi. west of Duluth, immediately adjacent to Cloquet. Total area 165 sq. mi.
Name origin: French 'end of the lake,' translated from Wanikamiu, an Indian village with the similar meaning 'farthest point of the lake.'

Fort Apache Reservation
Tribe: White Mountain Apache (Coyoteros) Tribe **Status:** Federal
HQ: Whiteriver, AZ **Area Code:** 602
County: Apache, Gila, Navajo
Pop: 9,825: AmInd; 10,394: total
Lat: 33-55-00 N **Long:** 11-01-00 W

In east-central AZ, northeast of Phoenix. Total area 2627 sq. mi. Established in 1871 as part of the White Mountain Indian Reservation; divided into the San Carlos (south) and Fort Apache (north) reservations in 1897. Also used by Tonto Apaches; Warm Spring and Chiricahua Apaches used it before being removed to FL.
Name origin: Apache Indians are a tribe of Athapascan linguistic stock; name derives from Zuni term for 'enemy.' Reservation also called "White Mountain Apache" and "Apache Indian Reservation."

Fort Belknap Reservation & Trust Lands
Tribe: Gros Ventre and Assiniboine Tribes **Status:** Federal
HQ: Harlem, MT **Area Code:** 406
County: Blaine, Phillips
Pop: 2,338: AmInd; 2,508: total
Lat: 48-12-00 N **Long:** 10-83-20 W

In north-central MT, 47 mi. east of Havre. Total area 1014 sq. mi. Established in 1888; reduced to present size in 1895.
Name origin: *Assiniboine* from Ojibway *usini* 'stone,' and *upwana* 'he cooks by roasting,' thus 'one who cooks by the use of stones.'

Fort Berthold Reservation
Tribe: Mandan, Hidatsa, and Arikara Tribes **Status:** Federal
HQ: New Town, ND **Area Code:** 701
County: parts of 5 counties
Pop: 2,999: AmInd; 5,395: total

In west-central ND, around Lake Sakakawea, in Dunn, McLean, McKenzie, Mountrail, and Mercer counties. Total area 1318 sq. mi. Established 1871.
Name origin: *Arikara* 'horns' or 'elk' with reference to their hair style; tribe of Caddoan linguistic stock.

Fort Bidwell Reservation
Tribe: Paiute Tribe **Status:** Federal
HQ: Fort Bidwell, CA **Area Code:** 619
County: Modoc
Pop: 107: AmInd; 118: total
Lat: 41-51-51 N **Long:** 12-01-14 W

In northeastern CA, 59 mi. south of Alturas. Total area 5 sq. mi. Established Jan 30, 1897, by using former lands of the Fort Bidwell Military Reserve for an Indian training school. Enlarged in 1913 and 1917.
Name origin: Named in 1865 for John Bidwell (1819–1900), U.S. congressman and general of CA militia.

Fort Hall Reservation & Trust Lands
Tribe: Shoshone and Bannock Tribes **Status:** Federal
HQ: Fort Hall, ID **Area Code:** 208
County: parts of 4 counties
Pop: 3,035: AmInd; 5,114: total
Lat: 43-00-01 N **Long:** 11-22-50 W

In southeastern ID, 5 mi. from Pocatello, in Bannock, Bingham, Caribou, and Power counties. Total area 815 sq. mi. Established in late 1700s.
Name origin: For the town, named for a fort and trading post on the Oregon Trail, built in 1834.

Fort Independence Reservation
Tribe: Paiute Tribe **Status:** Federal
HQ: Independence, CA **Area Code:** 619
County: Inyo
Pop: 38: AmInd; 69: total
Lat: 36-50-09 N **Long:** 11-81-31 W

In eastern CA, 3 mi. from Independence. Total area 0.6 sq. mi. Established in 1915 and 1916; Camp Independence, established during the Indian Way on Jul 4, 1862, was later abandoned.
Name origin: For Camp Independence, established on Jul 4, 1862, by Lt. Col. George S. Evans of the Second Cavalry.

Fort McDermitt Reservation
Tribe: Paiute and Shoshone Tribes **Status:** Federal
HQ: McDermitt, NV **Area Code:** 702
County: Humboldt, NV, Malheur, OR
Pop: 387: AmInd; 396: total
Lat: 41-56-27 N **Long:** 11-74-24 W

In north-central NV and south-central OR, 75 mi. north of Winnemucca. Total area 55 sq. mi., of which 26 are in NV and 29 in OR. Military post established in 1867 and later abandoned; became public domain in 1889. Under the Homestead Law of Aug 1, 1890, it became disposable and was allotted to the Indians in 1892.
Name origin: For Lt. Col. Charles McDermit, commander of the military district of NV, killed by Indians on Aug 7, 1865.

Fort McDowell Reservation
Tribe: Mojave, Apache, and Yavapai Tribes **Status:** Federal
HQ: Scottsdale, AZ **Area Code:** 602
County: Maricopa
Pop: 560: AmInd; 640: total
Lat: 33-40-00 N **Long:** 11-14-00 W

In south-central AZ on the Verde River, 28 mi. northeast of Phoenix. Total area 39 sq. mi. set aside in 1891, of which about two-thirds will be inundated by the Orme Dam. Negotiations are in progress to transfer an equal amount of adjoining federal lands.
Name origin: For the town.

Fort Mojave Reservation & Trust Lands
Tribe: Mojave Tribe **Status:** Federal
HQ: Needles, CA **Area Code:** 619
County: Clark County, NV, San Bernardino County, CA, Mohave, AZ
Pop: 592: AmInd; 758: total
Lat: 34-57-43 N **Long:** 11-43-82 W

On CA-AZ-NV border, north of Needles. Total area 51 sq. mi., of which 36 sq. mi. are in AZ, 9 sq. mi. are in CA, and 6 sq. mi. are in NV. The U.S. government, in the 1848 Treaty of Guadalupe Hidalgo, agreed to preserve the Indians' right to their land, inhabited by them since prehistoric times.
Name origin: For the tribe of Yuman linguistic stock. The name means 'three mountains' and refers to the Needles. Also spelled *Mohave*.

Fort Peck Reservation
Tribe: Assiniboine and Sioux Tribes **Status:** Federal
HQ: Poplar, MT **Area Code:** 406
County: parts of 4 counties
Pop: 5,782: AmInd; 10,595: total

In northeastern MT, in Valley, Roosevelt, Daniels, and Sheridan counties. Total area 3289 sq. mi.

Fort Yuma (Quechan) Reservation
Tribe: Quechan Tribe **Status:** Federal
HQ: Fort Yuma, AZ **Area Code:** 619
County: Imperial County, CA, Yuma, AZ
Pop: 1,160: AmInd; 2,084: total
Lat: 32-37-00 N **Long:** 11-43-23 W

In southeastern CA and northwestern AZ, on both sides of the Colorado River, near Yuma. Total area 68 sq. mi., of which 3 sq. mi. are in AZ and the rest in CA. Established in 1884. Since then, the tribe has lost most of the AZ lands.
Name origin: For the town.

Gila River Reservation
Tribe: Pima-Maricopa Tribes **Status:** Federal
HQ: Sacaton, AZ **Area Code:** 602
County: Maricopa, Pinal
Pop: 9,116: AmInd; 9,540: total
Lat: 32-10-00 N **Long:** 11-15-20 W

In south-central AZ, 25 mi. southeast of Phoenix. Total area 584 sq. mi. Reservation of 64,000 acres established in 1859; subsequently increased to its present size.
Name origin: Pima Indians are a tribe of Piman linguistic stock. *Pima*, misapplied by missionaries, means 'I don't know, I don't understand.' The Maricopas are of Yuman linguistic stock; meaning of name uncertain. Possibly variant of Spanish *mariposa* 'butterfly'; tribe said 'people.'

Golden Hill Indian Reservation
Tribe: Pequot **Status:** State
HQ: CT **Area Code:** 203
County: Fairfield
Pop: 2: AmInd; 10: total

In southwestern CT; area 0.2 sq. mi.

Goshute Reservation
Tribe: Goshute Tribe **Status:** Federal
HQ: NV **Area Code:** 702
County: White Pine, NV, Juab, UT, Tooele, UT
Pop: 98: AmInd; 99: total
Lat: 39-46-00 N **Long:** 11-40-60 W

In eastern NV and western UT, 100 mi. northeast of Ely, NV. Total area 177 sq. mi., of which 110 are in NV and 67 in UT.
Name origin: For the *Goshute*, a sub-tribe of the Utes. Name means 'dust people.'

Grand Portage Reservation
Tribe: Chippewa Tribe **Status:** Federal
HQ: Grand Portage, MN **Area Code:** 218
County: Cook
Pop: 207: AmInd; 306: total
Lat: 47-58-00 N **Long:** 08-94-60 W

On northeasternmost tip of MN on Lake Superior. Total area 73 sq. mi. Established in 1854.
Name origin: For the town at the head of the Grand Portage Bay and at the southeast end of the 9 mi.-long grand portage to the Pigeon River.

Grand Ronde Reservation
Tribe: Grand Ronde **Status:** Federal
HQ: OR **Area Code:** 503
County: Yamhill
Pop: 1: AmInd; 57: total

In northwestern OR, southwest of Portland; total area 15 sq. mi.

Grand Traverse & Trust Lands
Tribe: Chippewa **Status:** Federal
HQ: MI **Area Code:** 906
County: Leelanau
Pop: 208: AmInd; 228: total

On northwestern coast of Lower Peninsula of MI, on West Arm of Grand Traverse Bay. Total area 54 sq. mi.
Name origin: For the bay.

Greenville Rancheria
HQ: CA
County: Plumas
Pop: 7: AmInd; 24: total
Status: Federal
Area Code: 916

In northeastern CA, northeast of Chico. Total area less than 0.1 sq. mi.

Name origin: For the town, named for the Greens: the wife served meals to miners and their house became known as Green's Hotel.

Grindstone Rancheria
Tribe: Nomalaki-Wailaki Tribe
HQ: Elk Creek, CA
County: Glenn
Pop: 102: AmInd; 103: total
Lat: 39-40-20 N **Long:** 12-23-10 W
Status: Federal
Area Code: 916

In north-central CA, 29 mi. from Willows. Total area less than 0.1 sq. mi. Established Jan 7, 1909.

Name origin: Possibly a site where such stones could be found.

Haliwa-Saponi TDSA
HQ: NC
County: Halifax
Pop: 2,244: AmInd; 6,436: total
Status: State
Area Code: 919

In northeastern NC, north of Rocky Mount; total area 162 sq. mi.

Hannahville Community & Trust Lands
Tribe: Potawatomi Indian Tribe
HQ: Wilson, MI
County: Menominee
Pop: 173: AmInd; 181: total
Lat: 45-43-00 N **Long:** 08-72-50 W
Status: Federal
Area Code: 906

In southwestern Upper Peninsula of MI, 17 mi. west of Escanaba. Total area 46 sq. mi. Established Jun 30, 1913; 39 acres added in 1942.

Name origin: *Potawatomie* 'people of the place of the fire'; an Indian tribe of Algonquian linguistic stock. Variant spelling of Pottawatomi.

Havasupai Reservation
Tribe: Havasupai Tribe
HQ: Supai, AZ
County: Coconino
Pop: 400: AmInd; 423: total
Lat: 36-14-15 N **Long:** 11-24-15 W
Status: Federal
Area Code: 602

In northwestern AZ, 3,000 ft. below the rim of the Grand Canyon; total area 274 sq. mi. Reservation established in 1880; reduced to 519 acres in 1882; to offset the loss, the Havasupai were given grazing rights on 245,760 acres of federal land. They have inhabited this area for centuries.

Name origin: *Havasupai* 'blue or green water people,' from color of water in the springs coming from the canyon's side.

Hoh Reservation
Tribe: Hoh
HQ: Forks, WA
County: Jefferson
Pop: 74: AmInd; 96: total
Lat: 47-44-26 N **Long:** 12-41-50 W
Status: Federal
Area Code: 206

On northwestern coast of WA, 85 mi. southwest of Port Angeles. Total area 1 sq. mi. Established Sep 11, 1893.

Name origin: Branch of the Quillayute tribe. Name is a simplified form of *Oh-la-qu-hoh* or *Hooh-oh-ah-lat* 'can speak Quinault at that place.'

Hollywood Reservation
Tribe: Seminole Indian Tribe
HQ: Hollywood, FL
County: Broward
Pop: 481: AmInd; 1,394: total
Lat: 26-02-22 N **Long:** 08-01-23 W
Status: Federal
Area Code: 305

In southeastern FL, southwest of Ft. Lauderdale. Total area 0.7 sq. mi. See also Big Cypress Reservation.

Name origin: For the town.

Hoopa Valley Reservation
Tribe: Hoopa Tribe
HQ: Hoopa, CA
County: Humboldt, Del Norte
Pop: 1,733: AmInd; 2,143: total
Lat: 41-10-00 N **Long:** 12-34-20 W
Status: Federal
Area Code: 707

In northwestern CA, northeast of Eureka. Total area 137 sq. mi. Established Jun 23, 1876.

Name origin: Name given by the Weits-pek and Klamath Indians to the lower part of the Trinity River and its inhabitants. Also spelled *Hupa*.

Hopi Reservation & Trust Lands
Tribe: Hopi Tribe
HQ: Oraibi, AZ
County: Coconino, Navajo
Pop: 7,061: AmInd; 7,360: total
Lat: 34-57-00 N **Long:** 11-03-01 W
Status: Federal
Area Code: 602

In northeastern AZ, northeast of Flagstaff. Total area 2436 sq. mi. Established with 2,600,000 acres in 1882, entirely surrounded by Navajo Reservation. Hopi are presently living on only 650,000 acres, the Navajo having occupied the rest. The ownership and boundary disputes are now in court.

Name origin: A tribe of Shoshonean linguistic stock, *Hopi* is contraction of *Hopitu* 'peaceful people.' *Mogi* 'monkey,' Navajo word of contempt for Hopis, possibly source of *Moki, Moqui* used from 1540 till 1895 when Smithsonian Institution adopted *Hopi*.

Hopland Rancheria
Tribe: Hopland Band of Pomo Indians
HQ: CA
County: Mendocino
Pop: 142: AmInd; 189: total
Lat: 39-00-05 N **Long:** 12-30-21 W
Status: Federal
Area Code: 916

In northwestern CA, west of Clear Lake. Total area less than 0.1 sq. mi.

Name origin: For the town, named for a successful hop-growing experiment.

Hualapai Reservation & Trust Lands
Tribe: Hualapai Tribe **Status:** Federal
HQ: Peach Springs, AZ **Area Code:** 602
County: Mohave, Coconino, Yavapai
Pop: 802: AmInd; 822: total
Lat: 35-40-00 N **Long:** 11-32-40 W

In northwest AZ, 50 mi. northeast of Kingman. Total area 1601 sq. mi. Established 500,000 acres in Jan 1883; additional acreage added subsequently by Executive Order and the Santa Fe Railroad.

Name origin: *Hualapai* 'pine tree folk,' Indian sub-tribe of Yuman linguistic stock.

Inaja-Cosmit Reservation
Tribe: Inaja-Cosmit Tribe **Status:** Federal
HQ: Julian, CA **Area Code:** 619
County: San Diego
Pop: 0: AmInd; 0: total
Lat: 33-00-36 N **Long:** 11-63-83 W

In southwestern CA, 75 mi. east of San Diego. Total area 1 sq. mi. Established Dec 27, 1875; Inaja Reservation enlarged Feb 10, 1893.

Name origin: *Inaja* from Digueo Indian *any-aha* 'my water.' Meaning of Cosmit unknown.

Indian Township Reservation
Tribe: Passamaquoddy **Status:** Federal
HQ: Peter Dana Point, ME **Area Code:** 207
County: Washington
Pop: 541: AmInd; 617: total

In southeastern ME, near Princeton. Total area 38 sq. mi.

Iowa Reservation
Tribe: Iowa Tribe **Status:** Federal
HQ: Horton, KS **Area Code:** 913
County: Richardson, NE, Brown, Doniphan, KS
Pop: 83: AmInd; 172: total
Lat: 39-59-15 N **Long:** 09-52-10 W

In northeastern KS and southeastern NE, northeast of Topeka, KS. Total area 20 sq. mi., of which 14 is in KS and 6 in NE. Established 1836, reduced May 17, 1854, and Mar 6, 1861.

Name origin: Iowa tribe of Siouan linguistic stock; name is a French version of the Dakota name for the tribe; believed to mean 'sleepy ones.' Other tribes called them 'snakes,' 'dusty heads,' 'dusty noses,' 'snowheads.' Variously spelled *Ayuhwa, Ouaouia, Aiouez, Ioways*.

Iowa-Sac and Fox Joint Area TJSA
Tribe: Iowa-Sac and Fox **Status:** Federal
HQ: OK **Area Code:** 405
County: Lincoln, Payne
Pop: 39: AmInd; 908: total

In north-central OK; total area 48 sq. mi.

Iowa Tribe TJSA
Tribe: Various **Status:** Federal
HQ: Perkins, OK **Area Code:** 405
County: parts of 4 counties
Pop: 239: AmInd; 3,979: total

Federal trust area in central OK, near Oklahoma City, in Lincoln, Logan, Oklahoma, and Payne counties. Total area 311 sq. mi. Established 1883.

Name origin: *Iowa* is a French version of the Dakota name *Ayuhway, Ouaouia, Aiouez, Ioways* believed to mean 'the sleepy ones.' Other tribes called them 'snakes,' 'dusty heads,' 'dusty noses,' and 'snowheads.'

Isabella Reservation & Trust Lands
Tribe: Saginaw Chippewa Tribe **Status:** Federal
HQ: Mount Pleasant, MI **Area Code:** 517
County: Isabella
Pop: 795: AmInd; 22,944: total
Lat: 43-36-15 N **Long:** 08-44-14 W

In central Lower Peninsula of MI, 3 mi. east of Mt. Pleasant. Total area 49 sq. mi. Established by treaties signed in 1864 and 1885.

Name origin: *Saginaw* from Ojibway 'the place of the Sacs.' *Chippewa* from Ojibway 'puckered,' with reference to the seams in their moccasins.

Isleta Pueblo
Tribe: Isleta Tribe **Status:** Federal
HQ: Isleta, NM **Area Code:** 505
County: Bernalillo, Valencia
Pop: 2,699: AmInd; 2,915: total

In west-central AZ, 15 mi. south of Albuquerque. Total area 328 sq. mi. Spanish land grant confirmed by U.S. Congress in 1858.

Name origin: *Isleta* Spanish 'little island,' because the pueblo was almost surrounded by the Rio Grande when the Spanish first saw it.

Jackson Rancheria
Tribe: Me-Wuk (Miwok) Tribe **Status:** Federal
HQ: Jackson, CA **Area Code:** 916
County: Amador
Pop: 13: AmInd; 21: total
Lat: 38-23-04 N **Long:** 12-04-32 W

In central CA near Jackson. Total area 0.5 sq. mi. Established Jan 7, 1895; is in process of termination by authority of the Rancheria Act.

Name origin: For the town, which was named for "Col." Alden M. Jackson, liked for settling quarrels out of court.

Jamestown Klallam Res. & Trust Lands
Tribe: Jamestown S'Klallam **Status:** Federal
HQ: WA **Area Code:** 206
County: Clallam
Pop: 4: AmInd; 22: total

On northwestern coast of WA, southeast of Port Angeles; total area less than 0.1 sq. mi.

Name origin: Jamestown for the beach settlement, named in 1875 for "Lord" James Balch, head chief of the Clallam tribe, or possibly "Chief" Billie James, an Amerindian Shaker preacher. *Clallam* or *Klallam* 'big brave nation'; a tribe of Salishan linguistic stock.

Jamul Village
Tribe: Diegueno **Status:** Federal
HQ: CA **Area Code:** 619
County: San Diego
Pop: 0: AmInd; 0: total

In southwestern CA, southeast of San Diego; no land.

Name origin: Digueo Indian *ha-mul* 'foam, lather' (from *aha* 'water'). Called *Jamol* in 1776.

Jemez Pueblo
Tribe: Jemez Tribe
HQ: Jemez Pueblo, NM
County: Sandoval
Pop: 1,738: AmInd; 1,750: total
Status: Federal
Area Code: 505

In north-central AZ, 45 mi. north of Albuquerque. Total area 140 sq. mi. Original Spanish land grant confirmed by U.S. Congress on Dec 22, 1858.

Name origin: Spanish *Jemez* from Tanoan *hay mish* 'people.'

Jena Band of Choctaw TDSA
Tribe: Jena Band of Choctaw
HQ: LA
County: Grant
Pop: 265: AmInd; 60,334: total
Status: State
Area Code: 318

In west-central LA, north of Alexandria; total area 704 sq. mi.

Jicarilla Apache Reservation
Tribe: Jicarilla Apache Tribe
HQ: Dulce, NM
County: Rio Arriba, Sandoval
Pop: 2,375: AmInd; 2,617: total
Status: Federal
Area Code: 505

In north-central AZ, 86 mi. east of Farmington. Total area 1286 sq. mi. Established 1887; amendments in 1907 and 1908 adjusted the western border adjoining Carson National Forest.

Name origin: Spanish *Jicarilla* 'little basketcup'; reason for name unknown.

Kaibab Reservation
Tribe: Paiute Tribe
HQ: Fredonia, AZ
County: Mohave, Coconino
Pop: 102: AmInd; 165: total
Lat: 36-55-00 N **Long:** 11-24-20 W
Status: Federal
Area Code: 801

In northern AZ, 1 mi. west of Fredonia. Total area 189 sq. mi. Established 1907.

Name origin: For the Paiute word 'mountain lying down' or 'on the mountain.'

Kalispel Reservation
Tribe: Kalispel
HQ: Usk, WA
County: Pend Oreille
Pop: 91: AmInd; 100: total
Lat: 48-23-00 N **Long:** 11-71-70 W
Status: Federal
Area Code: 509

In northeastern WA, 50 mi. north of Spokane. Total area 7 sq. mi. Established 1855.

Name origin: *Kalispell* 'camas,' a genus of lily with edible roots; a tribe of Salishan linguistic stock.

Karok Reservation and Trust Lands
HQ: CA
County: Siskiyou
Pop: 33: AmInd; 421: total
Status: Federal
Area Code: 916

In north-central CA, south of the OR border. Total area 0.7 sq. mi.

Kaw TJSA
Tribe: Kaw
HQ: Kaw City, OK
County: Kay
Pop: 673: AmInd; 13,110: total
Status: Federal
Area Code: 918

Federal trust area in north-central OK, north of Ponca City. Total area 306 sq. mi. Established 1872.

Kickapoo Reservation
Tribe: Kickapoo Tribe
HQ: Horton, KS
County: Brown
Pop: 370: AmInd; 478: total
Lat: 39-42-30 N **Long:** 09-54-00 W
Status: State
Area Code: 913

In northeastern KS, due north of Topeka. Total area 30 sq. mi. In 1832 the Kickapoo ceded their lands in Missouri for 768,000 acres in KS. In 1854, they ceded 618,000 acres to the U.S. for $300,000.

Name origin: An Indian tribe of Algonquian stock; name means 'he moves about.'

Kiowa-Comanche-Apache-Fort Sill Apache
HQ: Carnegie, OK
County: parts of 11 counties
Pop: 13,108: AmInd; 205,400: total
Status: Federal
Area Code: 918

Federal trust area in western OK, in Caddo, Comanche, Cotton, Grady, Greer, Harmon, Jackson, Jefferson, Kiowa, Stephens, and Tillman counties. Total area 6542 sq. mi. Established 1868.

Name origin: *Kiowa* 'principal people'; tribe of Tanoan linguistic stock. *Comanche*, meaning of name unknown; tribe of Shoshonean linguistic stock. *Apache* from Zuni for 'enemy'; tribe of Athapascan linguistic stock.

Klamath Tribe TDSA
Tribe: Klamath Tribe
HQ: OR
County: Klamath
Pop: 1,839: AmInd; 41,035: total
Status: Federal
Area Code: 503

In south-central OR, east of Medford; total area 109 sq. mi.

Name origin: Probably from Chinook *tlamatl*, their name for the sister tribe of the Modocs, who called themselves *maklaks* 'people, community.' Other names bestowed by rival tribes 'people of the chipmunks,' 'those above the lakes.' Meaning unknown. Also spelled Claminitt and Clammitte.

Kootenai Reservation
Tribe: Kootenai Tribe
HQ: Bonners Ferry, ID
County: Boundary
Pop: 61: AmInd; 65: total
Status: Federal
Area Code: 208

In northwestern ID, 115 mi. northeast of Spokane, WA. Total area less than 0.1 sq. mi. Established c. 1855.

Name origin: Kootenai or *Kutenai* 'water people.'

Lac Courte Oreilles Res. & Trust Lands
Tribe: Chippewa Tribe
HQ: Reserve, WI
County: Sawyer
Pop: 1,771: AmInd; 2,408: total
Lat: 45-52-00 N **Long:** 09-12-00 W
Status: Federal
Area Code: 715

In northwest WI, 70 mi. southeast of Duluth. Total area 107 sq. mi. Established 1854; in 1860 U.S. Land Office retook the land; in 1873 U.S. government reallotted 69,136 acres to the tribe.

Name origin: French name for a band of Indians who lived at Ottawa Lake; the name means 'lake short ears': the French thought they had cut the rims off their ears.

Lac Du Flambeau Reservation
Tribe: Lac du Flambeau Band of Chippewa
Indians **Status:** Federal
HQ: Lac du Flambeau, WI **Area Code:** 715
County: Iron, Vilas, Oneida
Pop: 1,432: AmInd; 2,434: total
Lat: 45-58-00 N **Long:** 08-95-30 W

In north-central WI, 35 mi. northwest of Rhinelander. Total area 108 sq. mi. Established 1854; later enlarged.

Name origin: For the lake, 'lake of the flaming torches,' named by the French when they saw Chippewa Indians fishing at night from their canoes with torches.

Lac Vieux Desert Reservation
Tribe: Chippewa **Status:** Federal
HQ: MI **Area Code:** 906
County: Gogebic
Pop: 119: AmInd; 124: total

On western border of Upper Peninsula of MI with WI; no land.

Name origin: French 'lake of the sand plains.'

Laguna Pueblo & Trust Lands
Tribe: Keresan Tribe **Status:** Federal
HQ: Laguna, NM **Area Code:** 505
County: Valencia, Bernalillo, Sandoval
Pop: 3,634: AmInd; 3,731: total

In west-central AZ, 40 mi. west of Albuquerque. Total area 761 sq. mi., in three locations. Original Spanish land grant.

Name origin: Spanish 'lake' from the name of a Keresan group's locality *pokwindiwe onwi* 'pueblo by the lake.'

La Jolla Reservation
Tribe: La Jolla Band of Mission Indians **Status:** Federal
HQ: Escondido, CA **Area Code:** 619
County: San Diego
Pop: 121: AmInd; 152: total
Lat: 33-16-12 N **Long:** 11-65-15 W

In southwestern CA, 25 mi. east of Escondido. Total area 14 sq. mi. Established 1892.

Name origin: Mexican spelling of Castilian *hoya* 'the hole' (in the rocks) which Yosemite Indian women used for milling; appears on a land grant dated Nov 7, 1845.

Lake Traverse (Sisseton) Reservation
Tribe: Sisseton and Wahpeton Sioux **Status:** Federal
HQ: Sisseton, SD **Area Code:** 605
County: parts of 5 counties, SD, parts of 2 counties, ND
Pop: 2,821: AmInd; 10,733: total

In northeastern SD in Day, Coddington, Grant, Marshall, and Roberts counties; and southeastern ND in Richland and Sargent counties. Total area 1450 sq. mi. Created in 1867.

Name origin: French *lac travers*, a translation of Siouan *mdehdakinyan* 'lake lying crosswise.'

L'Anse Reservation & Trust Lands
Tribe: Lake Superior Band, Chippewa Tribe **Status:** Federal
HQ: L'Anse, MI **Area Code:** 906
County: Baraga
Pop: 724: AmInd; 3,293: total
Lat: 46-46-00 N **Long:** 08-83-60 W

On northern coast of Upper Peninsula of MI, 33 mi. south of Houghton. Total area 56 sq. mi. Established Sep 30, 1854.

Name origin: French 'the bay.'

La Posta Reservation
Tribe: La Posta Band of Mission Indians **Status:** Federal
HQ: CA **Area Code:** 619
County: San Diego
Pop: 3: AmInd; 10: total
Lat: 32-44-07 N **Long:** 11-62-32 W

In southwestern CA, east of San Diego. Total area 6 sq. mi.

Las Vegas Colony
Tribe: Paiute Tribe **Status:** Federal
HQ: Las Vegas, NV **Area Code:** 702
County: Clark
Pop: 72: AmInd; 80: total

In southeastern NV, around Las Vegas. Total area 6 sq. mi. Land purchased 1911.

Name origin: For the city; name is Spanish for 'the meadows.'

Laytonville Rancheria
Tribe: Cahto Tribe **Status:** Federal
HQ: Laytonville, CA **Area Code:** 707
County: Mendocino
Pop: 129: AmInd; 142: total
Lat: 39-40-09 N **Long:** 12-32-94 W

In northwestern CA, 2 mi. from Laytonville. Total area 0.3 sq. mi.

Name origin: For the town, named for Frank B. Layton from Nova Scotia, who settled here in 1875.

Leech Lake Reservation
Tribe: Chippewa Tribe **Status:** Federal
HQ: Ball Club, MN **Area Code:** 218
County: parts of 4 counties
Pop: 3,390: AmInd; 8,669: total
Lat: 47-20-00 N **Long:** 09-41-30 W

In north-central MN, east of Bemidji, in Beltrami, Cass, Huibbard, and Itasca counties. Total area 972 sq. mi. Ceded to Chippewas in 1854; original million acres reduced to present size by Congress and Presidential Acts.

Likely Rancheria
Tribe: Pit River Tribe **Status:** Federal
HQ: Likely, CA **Area Code:** 916
County: Modoc
Pop: 0: AmInd; 0: total

In northeastern CA; no land. Reservation purchased on Jun 28, 1922.

Name origin: For the town, because it "wasn't likely" that another town would have a P.O. with the same name.

Lone Pine Rancheria
Tribe: Paiute-Shoshone Tribe **Status:** Federal
HQ: Lone Pine, CA **Area Code:** 619
County: Inyo
Pop: 168: AmInd; 244: total

In eastern CA near Bishop. Total area 0.4 sq. mi. Reservation acquired through a land exchange in 1939 between the federal government and the city of Los Angeles: 3,000 acres of trust property were exchanged for 1,500 acres of level valley land.

Name origin: For the town, named for a landmark tall pine.

Lookout Rancheria
Tribe: Pit River Tribe **Status:** Federal
HQ: Lookout, CA **Area Code:** 916
County: Modoc
Pop: 12: AmInd; 17: total
Lat: 41-12-32 N **Long:** 12-11-23 W

In northeastern CA. Total area 0.1 sq. mi. Reservation purchased Oct 11, 1913.

Name origin: For the town, named, according to legend, for the hill above town on which Pit River Indians kept a lookout when Modoc Indians were on wife-stealing expeditions.

Los Coyotes Reservation
Tribe: Los Coyotes Band of Mission Indians **Status:** Federal
HQ: Warner Springs, CA **Area Code:** 619
County: San Diego
Pop: 42: AmInd; 58: total
Lat: 33-17-56 N **Long:** 11-63-31 W

In southwestern CA, northeast of Escondido. Total area 39 sq. mi. Established Jun 19, 1900; Apr 13, 1914, lands from the Cleveland National Forest were transferred to the reservation.

Name origin: For the animal, believed by many Indians to be a god.

Lovelock Colony
Tribe: Paiute Tribe **Status:** Federal
HQ: Lovelock, NV **Area Code:** 702
County: Pershing
Pop: 80: AmInd; 94: total

In west-central NV, northeast of Reno. Total area less than 0.1 sq. mi. Established 1907.

Name origin: For George Lovelock, who donated land for the townsite.

Lower Brule Reservation
Tribe: Sioux Tribe **Status:** Federal
HQ: Lower Brule, SD **Area Code:** 605
County: Lyman, Stanley
Pop: 994: AmInd; 1,123: total
Lat: 44-04-25 N **Long:** 09-94-55 W

In south-central SD, southeast of Pierre; total area 339 sq. mi. Established 1890.

Name origin: French partial translation of the Indian tribal name 'burned thighs.'

Lower Elwah Reservation & Trust Lands
Tribe: Clallam **Status:** Federal
HQ: Port Angeles, WA **Area Code:** 206
County: Clallam
Pop: 130: AmInd; 137: total
Lat: 48-08-30 N **Long:** 12-33-30 W

In northwestern WA, 10 mi. from Port Angeles. Total area 1 sq. mi. Established 1934.

Name origin: For the Elwah River, from the Quillayute name *E-ilth-quatl* 'elk.'

Lower Sioux Community
Tribe: Eastern or Mississippi Sioux Tribe **Status:** Federal
HQ: Morton, MN **Area Code:** 612
County: Redwood
Pop: 225: AmInd; 259: total
Lat: 44-32-00 N **Long:** 09-45-90 W

In southwestern MN, southwest of Minneapolis. Total area 3 sq. mi. Established between 1887 and 1893.

Name origin: Sioux, sometimes known as Dakotas; name from Ojibway *nadouessioux* 'snakes' or 'enemies'; transliterated through French.

Lumbee TDSA
Tribe: Lumbee **Status:** State
HQ: NC **Area Code:** 919
County: Robeson
Pop: 28,863: AmInd; 50,039: total

In southeastern NC, south of Fayetteville; total area 390 sq. mi.

Lummi Reservation
Tribe: Lummi and Nooksack **Status:** Federal
HQ: Bellingham, WA **Area Code:** 206
County: Whatcom
Pop: 1,594: AmInd; 3,147: total
Lat: 48-46-00 N **Long:** 12-23-80 W

In northwestern coast of WA, on peninsula 5 mi. west of Bellingham. Total area 21 sq. mi. Established 1859.

Name origin: Lummi tribe; meaning of name unknown. *Nooksack* from *noot* 'people,' and *saak* 'bracken fern'; part of the Squawmish tribe. Variously spelled *Nootsack, Nooksak, Nooksahk.*

Makah Reservation
Tribe: Makah Tribe **Status:** Federal
HQ: Neah Bay, WA **Area Code:** 206
County: Clallam
Pop: 940: AmInd; 1,214: total
Lat: 48-20-00 N **Long:** 12-43-70 W

On nothwestern tip of WA, 66 mi. west of Port Angeles. Total area 43 sq. mi.; includes Cape Flattery and Neah Bay. Established 1855.

Name origin: *Makah* 'people who live on point projecting into the sea.'

Manchester (Point Arena) Rancheria
 Status: Federal
HQ: CA **Area Code:** 916
County: Mendocino
Pop: 178: AmInd; 200: total
Lat: 38-56-17 N **Long:** 12-34-04 W

On northwestern Pacific coast of CA, near Point Arena. Total area 0.6 sq. mi.

Name origin: For the town, which was probably named after one of the Manchesters already existing in the U.S.

Manzanita Reservation
Tribe: Manzanita Band of Mission Indians **Status:** Federal
HQ: Boulevard, CA **Area Code:** 619
County: San Diego
Pop: 47: AmInd; 84: total
Lat: 32-45-24 N **Long:** 11-62-02 W

In southwestern CA, 57 mi. from San Diego. Total area 6 sq. mi. Established Feb 10, 1893.

Name origin: Spanish 'little apple,' with reference to the shrub *Arctostaphylos*, whose little berries resemble apples and are valued by Indians.

American Places Dictionary   American Indian Reservations

Maricopa (Ak-Chin) Reservation
Tribe: Papago and Pima   **Status:** Federal
HQ: AZ   **Area Code:** 602
County: Pinal
Pop: 405: AmInd; 446: total

In south-central AZ, south of Phoenix; area 33 sq. mi.

Name origin: Tribal name of Yuman linguistic stock. Meaning is uncertain: may be variant of Spanish *mariposa* 'butterfly'; tribe said it meant 'people.'

Mashantucket Pequot Tribe
Tribe: Pequot   **Status:** Federal
HQ: CT   **Area Code:** 203
County: New London
Pop: 55: AmInd; 83: total

In east-central CT; area 2 sq. mi.

Mattapony Reservation
Tribe: Mattapony Indians (Powhatan)   **Status:** State
HQ: VA   **Area Code:** 804
County: King William
Pop: 65: AmInd; 70: total

In east-central VA, east of Richmond. Total area 1 sq. mi. Deed to reservation granted to Mattapony Indians in 1658 by the Virginia House of Burgesses.

Name origin: *Mattaponi*, meaning uncertain, possibly 'bad breath.'

Meherrin TDSA
Tribe: Meherrin   **Status:** State
HQ: NC   **Area Code:** 0
Pop: 296: AmInd; 55,306: total

In northeastern NC, northeast of Rocky Mount; total area 1415 sq. mi.

Name origin: For the Indian tribe of Iroquoian linguistic stock; meaning of name unknown.

Menominee Reservation
Tribe: Menominee   **Status:** Federal
HQ: WI   **Area Code:** 612
County: Menominee
Pop: 3,182: AmInd; 3,397: total

In northeastern WI, east of Wausau; reservation co-extensive with county; total area 356 sq. mi.

Name origin: *Menominee* 'wild rice people'; an Indian tribe of Algonquian linguistic stock, living where wild rice grows.

Mesa Grande Reservation
Tribe: Mesa Grande Band of Mission Indians   **Status:** Federal
HQ: Pala, CA   **Area Code:** 619
County: San Diego
Pop: 72: AmInd; 96: total

In southeastern CA, 40 mi. from Escondido. Total area 12 sq. mi. Reservation established 1882; additional lands set apart Aug 25, 1925.

Name origin: Spanish 'big tableland,' with reference to a nearby slope-sided, flat-topped hill.

Mescalero Apache Reservation
Tribe: Apache Tribe   **Status:** Federal
HQ: Mescalero, NM   **Area Code:** 505
County: Otero
Pop: 2,516: AmInd; 2,695: total

In south-central AZ, 30 mi. northeast of Alamogordo. Total area 719 sq. mi. Established 1880.

Name origin: From Spanish *mezcal*, the agave plant used for intoxicating drinks and narcotics; the Mescaleros 'ate mescal.'

Miccosukee Reservation
Tribe: Miccosukee (Seminole)   **Status:** Federal
HQ: Homestead, FL   **Area Code:** 305
County: Dade, Broward
Pop: 94: AmInd; 94: total

In southeast FL. Total area 128 sq. mi., includes a strip of land 5.5 mi. by 500 ft., called the Tamiami Trail; additional tracts 600 ft. by 65 ft. dedicated by state for the tribe; State Reservation of 76,000 acres dedicated to the tribe also available to them.

Name origin: Possibly from *nikasuki* 'hog eaters,' name for an Indian tribe that lived near Tallahassee.

Middletown Rancheria
Tribe: Pomo-Patwin Tribe   **Status:** Federal
HQ: Middletown, CA   **Area Code:** 707
County: Lake
Pop: 18: AmInd; 79: total
Lat: 38-43-48 N   **Long:** 12-23-73 W

In west-central CA, 90 mi. east of Ukiah. Total area 0.2 sq. mi. Established Jul 30, 1910.

Name origin: For the town, which was a stage stop midway between Lower Lake and Calistoga in the 1860s.

Mille Lacs Reservation
Tribe: Chippewa Tribe   **Status:** Federal
HQ: Onamia, MN   **Area Code:** 218
County: Mille Lacs, Aitkin, Pine
Pop: 428: AmInd; 470: total

In east-central MN, southeast of Brainerd. Total area 5 sq. mi. Established 1855.

Name origin: For the large lake, Mille Lacs, French 'thousand lakes.' The name was first applied to the region, then specifically to this lake.

Minnesota Chippewa Trust Lands
Status: Federal
HQ: MN   **Area Code:** 612
County: Pine, Mille Lacs, Aitkin
Pop: 28: AmInd; 43: total

In east-central MN; total area 1 sq. mi.

Mississippi Choctaw Res. & Trust Lands
Tribe: Choctaw Tribe   **Status:** Federal
HQ: Pearl River, Neshoba County, MS   **Area Code:** 601
County: parts of 7 counties
Pop: 3,932: AmInd; 4,073: total

In central MS, in Neshoba, Newton, Leake, Scott, Jones, Attala, Kemper, and Winston counties. Total area 33 sq. mi. In 1830, 104,320 acres was awarded to those Choctaw not moving to Oklahoma. By 1918 only 640 acres remained, so the U.S. government acquired an additional 16,805 acres for them.

Name origin: *Choctaw*, an Indian tribe of Muskohgean linguistic stock; meaning of name unknown.

Moapa River Reservation
Tribe: Paiute Tribe **Status:** Federal
HQ: Moapa, NV **Area Code:** 801
County: Clark
Pop: 190: AmInd; 375: total
Lat: 36-40-30 N **Long:** 11-44-00 W

In southeastern NV, 55 mi. northeast of Las Vegas. Total area 112 sq. mi. Established 1875.

Name origin: For a Southern Paiute band named *Moapariats* 'mosquito creek people,' referring to the Muddy River.

Mohegan TDSA
Tribe: Mohegan **Status:** State
HQ: CT **Area Code:** 203
County: New London
Pop: 219: AmInd; 24,636: total

In southeastern CT, north of New London; total area 15 sq. mi.

Name origin: Algonquian tribal name; meaning unknown.

Montgomery Creek Rancheria
Tribe: Pit River Tribe **Status:** Federal
HQ: Montgomery Creek, CA **Area Code:** 916
County: Shasta
Pop: 9: AmInd; 11: total
Lat: 40-50-06 N **Long:** 12-15-45 W

In northern CA, 34 mi. from Redding. Total area 0.1 sq. mi. Established Oct 13, 1915.

Name origin: For the town, named for the creek from which Zack Montgomery once hauled a lot of fish.

Morongo Reservation
Tribe: Morongo Band of Mission Indians **Status:** Federal
HQ: Banning, CA **Area Code:** 619
County: Riverside
Pop: 527: AmInd; 1,072: total

In southwestern CA, northwest of Palm Springs. Total area 49 sq. mi. Patented to the Morongo Band on Dec 14, 1908.

Name origin: From *Maronga* 'the largest village,' the name of a Serrano Shoshonean village.

Muckleshoot Reservation & Trust Lands
Tribe: Muckleshoot Tribe **Status:** Federal
HQ: Auburn, WA **Area Code:** 206
County: King
Pop: 864: AmInd; 3,841: total
Lat: 47-16-00 N **Long:** 12-20-90 W

In west-central WA, 35 mi. east of Tacoma. Total area 6 sq. mi. Established 1857.

Name origin: A branch of the Duwamish tribe; meaning of name unknown, possibly 'green prairie.'

Nambe Pueblo & Trust Lands
Tribe: Tano-Tewa Tribe **Status:** Federal
HQ: Nambe Pueblo, NM **Area Code:** 505
County: Santa Fe
Pop: 329: AmInd; 1,402: total

In north-central AZ, 17 mi. north of Santa Fe. Total area 32 sq. mi. Spanish land grant confirmed by U.S. 1858; patented in 1864.

Name origin: Tewa Indian *nambay-ongwee* 'people of the roundish earth.'

Narragansett Tribe
Tribe: Narragansett **Status:** Federal
HQ: RI **Area Code:** 401
County: Washington
Pop: 17: AmInd; 31: total

In southwestern RI, north of Westerly; area 3 sq. mi.

Name origin: *Narragansett* from *nanhiggonsick* 'back and forth' or 'people of the point'; the predominant Algonquian tribe.

Navajo Reservation and Trust Lands
Tribe: Navajo **Status:** Federal
HQ: AZ **Area Code:** 602
County: parts of 3 counties in AZ, parts of 2 counties in NM, San Juan, UT
Pop: 143,405: AmInd; 148,451: total
Lat: 36-30-01 N **Long:** 10-90-00 W

In northeastern AZ, in Apache, Coconino, and Navajo counties; in northwestern NM, in McKinley and San Juan counties; and in San Juan County, UT. Total area 24,426 sq. mi., of which 15,972 sq. mi. are in AZ; 6451 sq. mi. in NM; and 2003 sq. mi. in UT. Home of the most populous Indian people in the U.S.

Name origin: An Indian tribe, meaning of name unknown; possibilities: Spanish *navaja* 'knife, razor,' for their sharp trading; a corruption of Wichita Indians' name for themselves; Tewa word 'place of large plantings,' with reference to Navajo cornfields. Navajos call themselves *Dine* 'people.'

Nez Perce Reservation
Tribe: Nez Perce Tribe **Status:** Federal
HQ: Lapwai, ID **Area Code:** 208
County: parts of 4 counties
Pop: 1,863: AmInd; 16,160: total
Lat: 46-18-00 N **Long:** 11-62-50 W

In north-central Idaho, 11 mi. east of Lewiston, in Clearwater, Idaho, Lewis, and Nez Perce counties. Total area 1195 sq. mi. Established under the 1855 treaty in which the tribe ceded much of its land in Idaho and Oregon; in 1863 Indian commissioners tried to persuade them to adjust the boundaries of the reservation, being overrun by gold prospectors. This led to the Nez Perce War of 1877; they lost and settled on the present reservation.

Name origin: *Nez Perce* French name for Indian tribe that called itself *Chopunnish*; literally 'pierced nose,' but also translated as 'mashed, flattened nose.'

Nisqually Reservation
Tribe: Nisqually Tribe **Status:** Federal
HQ: Yelm, WA **Area Code:** 206
County: Thurston, Pierce
Pop: 365: AmInd; 578: total
Lat: 47-01-15 N **Long:** 12-04-04 W

In western WA, 10 mi. southeast of Olympia. Total area 8 sq. mi. Established 1857.

Name origin: Indian tribal name, meaning unknown. Variously spelled *Nasqually, Nezqually, Niskwalli, N'skwali, Sigwal-it-chie*.

Nooksack Reservation & Trust Lands
Tribe: Nooksack **Status:** Federal
HQ: WA **Area Code:** 206
County: Whatcom
Pop: 412: AmInd; 556: total

In northwestern WA, east of Bellingham; total area 4 sq. mi.
Name origin: Name of the tribe, originally part of the Squawmish tribe; possibly 'mountain men' or 'fern-eating people.'

Northern Cheyenne Res. & Trust Lands
Tribe: Northern Cheyenne Tribe **Status:** Federal
HQ: Lame Deer, MT **Area Code:** 406
County: Big Horn, MT, Rosebud, MT, Meade, SD
Pop: 3,542: AmInd; 3,923: total

On south-central border of MT, southeast of Billings. Total area 700 sq. mi. Established in 1884.
Name origin: *Cheyenne* from Dakota Indian 'red talkers'; tribe of Algonquian linguistic stock.

North Fork Rancheria
 Status: Federal
HQ: CA **Area Code:** 916
County: Madera
Pop: 0: AmInd; 4: total

In north-central CA, northeast of Fresno. Total area 0.1 sq. mi.

Northwestern Shoshone
Tribe: Shoshone **Status:** Federal
HQ: UT **Area Code:** 208
County: Box Elder
Pop: 0: AmInd; 0: total

In north-central UT, west of Logan; total area 0.3 sq. mi.

Omaha Reservation
Tribe: Omaha Tribe **Status:** Federal
HQ: Macy, NE **Area Code:** 402
County: parts of 3 counties in NE, Monona, IA
Pop: 1,908: AmInd; 5,227: total
Lat: 42-06-00 N **Long:** 09-63-00 W

On northeastern border of NE, in Burt, Cuming, and Thurston counties; and in Monona County, south of Sioux Falls, IA. Total area 312 sq. mi., of which 303 are in NE and 9 in IA.
Name origin: *Omaha* (or *Maha* 'those going against the wind or current' or 'those who live upstream beyond others'; anglicization of ancient tribal name, but there is a French version, *aux maha* 'of the Maha.'

Oneida (East) Reservation
 Status: Federal
HQ: NY **Area Code:** 315
County: Cattaraugus
Pop: 37: AmInd; 37: total

In north-central NY, southwest of Rome. Total area 0.1 sq. mi.
Name origin: *Oneida* probably 'stone people,' perhaps for their bravery; a tribe of Iroquoian linguistic stock, one of the Five Nations of the Iroquois.

Oneida (West) Reservation
Tribe: Oneida Tribe **Status:** Federal
HQ: Oneida, WI **Area Code:** 715
County: Brown, Outagamie
Pop: 2,447: AmInd; 18,033: total
Lat: 44-35-00 N **Long:** 08-81-10 W

In eastern WI, west of Green Bay. Total area 102 sq. mi. Established 1838. Eastern Oneidas are in NY.
Name origin: For the Indian tribe of Iroquoian linguistic stock, one of the Five Nations of the Iroquois. Name probably means 'stone people,' perhaps for their bravery.

Onondaga Reservation
Tribe: Onondaga and Oneida Tribes **Status:** State
HQ: Nedrow, NY **Area Code:** 315
County: Onondaga
Pop: 2: AmInd; 771: total
Lat: 42-56-27 N **Long:** 07-60-93 W

In northern NY, 6 mi. south of Syracuse. Total area 9 sq. mi. The Onondaga have lived on this land since before the Revolutionary War.
Name origin: *Onondaga* 'hill people'; one of the Five Nations of the Iroquois.

Ontonagon Reservation
 Status: Federal
HQ: MI **Area Code:** 906
County: Ontonagon
Pop: 0: AmInd; 0: total

On northwestern border of Upper Peninsula of MI. Total area 4 sq. mi.
Name origin: For the town on the Ontonagon River; from a Chippewa word *nan-ton-a-gon* 'bowl,' referring to the shape of the river's mouth.

Osage Reservation
Tribe: Osage **Status:** Federal
HQ: Pawhuska, OK **Area Code:** 918
County: Osage
Pop: 6,088: AmInd; 41,299: total
Lat: 36-35-00 N **Long:** 09-62-00 W

Reservation in north-central OK, coterminous with Osage County. Total area 2243 sq. mi. Established 1870.
Name origin: *Osage* is a corruption of *Wazhazhe*, their name in their own language; meaning uncertain; tribe of Siouan linguistic stock.

Otoe-Missouria TJSA
Tribe: Otoe-Missouria **Status:** Federal
HQ: Red Rock, OK **Area Code:** 918
County: Noble, Pawnee
Pop: 478: AmInd; 2,775: total

Federal trust area in north-central OK, east of Enid. Total area 278 sq. mi.
Name origin: *Otoe* 'lechers,' either as "lovers" or in the pejorative sense; tribe of Siouan linguistic stock. *Missouri* because the tribe lived near the mouth of the river.

Ozette Reservation
Tribe: Makah Tribe
HQ: Clallam County, WA
County: Clallam
Pop: 0: AmInd; 12: total
Lat: 48-10-15 N **Long:** 12-44-24 W
Status: Federal
Area Code: 206

In northwestern WA near the Olympic National Park; total area 1 sq. mi. It has no Native-American population; the Makah Tribe is trying to have Congress allow it to become part of the Makah Reservation. The Secretary of the Interior wants it to become part of the Olympic National Park.

Name origin: *Ozette* from *O-se-ilth* or *O-se-elth* 'middle tribe,' Makah Indian name for the lake and those who lived on its shores.

Paiute of Utah
Tribe: Paiute
HQ: UT
County: Washington
Pop: 323: AmInd; 645: total
Lat: 37-10-00 N **Long:** 11-34-61 W
Status: Federal
Area Code: 801

In southwestern UT; total area 51 sq. mi.

Pala Reservation
Tribe: Pala Band of Mission Indians
HQ: Pala, CA
County: San Diego
Pop: 563: AmInd; 1,071: total
Lat: 33-20-57 N **Long:** 11-70-40 W
Status: Federal
Area Code: 619

In southwestern CA, 25 mi. northeast of Oceanside. Total area 25 sq. mi. Established Dec 27, 1875; in 1877 and 1882 portions were restored to public domain. On May 27, 1962, $100,000 was appropriated to purchase land for the Mission Indians, part of which was used for moving the Indians to the new land.

Name origin: Luiseo Indian 'water.' Name appears in mission records of Sep 28, 1781.

Pamunkey Reservation
Tribe: Pamunkey Indians (Powhatan)
HQ: Pamunkey, VA
County: King William
Pop: 35: AmInd; 49: total
Lat: 37-34-23 N **Long:** 07-70-01 W
Status: State
Area Code: 804

In southeastern VA, 20 mi. east of Richmond. Total area 2 sq. mi. Established 1677 by the VA House of Burgesses.

Name origin: *Pamunkey*, from Algonquian *pam* 'sloping,' and *anki* 'uplands'; a subtribe of the Powhatans.

Papago Reservation
Tribe: Papago Tribe
HQ: Ak Chin Community, AZ
County: Pinal, Pima, Maricopa
Pop: 8,480: AmInd; 8,730: total
Lat: 32-08-00 N **Long:** 11-20-50 W
Status: Federal
Area Code: 602

In south-central AZ, west and north of Tucson; total area 4342 sq. mi. Small reservation created Jul 1, 1874, at San Xavier Mission, Tucson. On Jun 16, 1911, a very large reservation was created in Pima County, west of Tucson.

Name origin: Papago from *papah* 'beans,' and *ootam* 'people': 'beanspeople.' Spanish called them *frijoleros* 'bean eaters'; Pimas call them *Too-no-oo-tain* 'desert people.'

Pascua Yaqui Reservation
Tribe: Pascua Yaqui
HQ: AZ
County: Pima
Pop: 2,284: AmInd; 2,412: total
Lat: 32-14-54 N **Long:** 11-05-90 W
Status: Federal
Area Code: 602

Part of Tucson, in southeastern AZ; total area 1 sq. mi.

Name origin: The Yaqui (meaning of name unknown) hold a large *Pascua* 'Easter' celebration.

Passamaquody Trust Lands
HQ: ME
County: Washington
Pop: 1: AmInd; 3: total
Status: Federal
Area Code: 207

In southeastern ME, southeast of Calais. Total area 147 sq. mi.

Name origin: For Passamaquoddy Bay, a Malecite Indian name 'location of plenty of pollack,' referring to the fish.

Paucatuck Eastern Pequot Reservation
HQ: CT
County: New London
Pop: 15: AmInd; 18: total
Status: State
Area Code: 203

In southeastern CT; area 0.3 sq. mi.

Pauma Reservation
Tribe: Pauma Band of Mission Indians
HQ: Pauma Valley, CA
County: San Diego
Pop: 137: AmInd; 148: total
Lat: 33-19-58 N **Long:** 11-65-90 W
Status: Federal
Area Code: 619

In southwestern CA, 25 mi. east of Oceanside. Total area 9 sq. mi. Established Aug 18, 1892.

Name origin: Possibly from Luiseo Indian *pame* 'little water.'

Pawnee TJSA
Tribe: Pawnee
HQ: Pawnee, OK
County: Pawnee
Pop: 1,624: AmInd; 15,443: total
Status: Federal
Area Code: 918

Federal trust area in north-central OK, near Stillwater. Total area 509 sq. mi. Land deeded in trust to the tribe Oct 2, 1868.

Name origin: *Pawnee* may mean 'horn' for the shape in which they wore their hair lock; Osages called them *Pa-in* 'long-haired'; they called themselves 'civilized people.'

Payson (Yavapai-Apache) Reservation
Tribe: Yavapai Apache
HQ: Payson, AZ
County: Gila
Pop: 97: AmInd; 102: total
Lat: 13-13-17 N **Long:** 11-11-94 W
Status: Federal
Area Code: 602

In central AZ, near town of Payson; total area 0.1 sq. mi.

Name origin: For the town of Payson, named for Sen. Payson of IL c. 1882.

Pechanga Reservation
Tribe: Pechanga Band of Mission Indians **Status:** Federal
HQ: Temecula, CA **Area Code:** 619
County: Riverside
Pop: 289: AmInd; 398: total
Lat: 33-26-45 N **Long:** 11-70-32 W

In southern CA, 60 mi. north of San Diego. Total area 7 sq. mi. Established by Executive Order of Jun 27, 1882, which set aside land in Riverside County for Indian use. Present reservation established Aug 29, 1893.

Penobscot & Trust Lands
Status: Federal
HQ: ME **Area Code:** 207
County: Penobscot
Pop: 417: AmInd; 485: total

In south-central ME, northeast of Bangor. Total area 101 sq. mi.

Name origin: *Penobscob* from Algonquian *penobskeag* 'rocky place' or 'river of rocks.'

Picayune Rancheria
Tribe: Chuckchansi **Status:** Federal
HQ: CA **Area Code:** 916
County: Madera
Pop: 15: AmInd; 32: total

In north-central CA, northeast of Fresno. Total area 0.1 sq. mi.

Name origin: For the 'small' valley in which the rancheria is located.

Picuris Pueblo
Tribe: Tewa Tribe **Status:** Federal
HQ: Picuris Pueblo, NM **Area Code:** 505
County: Taos
Pop: 147: AmInd; 1,882: total

In north-central AZ, southwest of Taos. Total area 27 sq. mi. Spanish land grant of 1689 confirmed by U.S. Congress in 1858 and patented in 1864.

Name origin: Meaning unclear. May be Spanish corruption of Jemez *pay kwee lay ta* 'at mountain gap'; possibly Jemez name for Picuris people *pay kwee layish*; or Keresan *pee-koo-ree-a* 'those who paint.'

Pine Creek Reservation
Status: State
HQ: MI **Area Code:** 507
County: Calhoun
Pop: 20: AmInd; 24: total

In southwestern MI; total area 0.2 sq. mi.

Pine Ridge Reservation & Trust Lands
Tribe: Oglala Sioux Tribe **Status:** Federal
HQ: Pine Ridge, SD **Area Code:** 605
County: Shannon, parts of 3 counties, SD
Pop: 11,182: AmInd; 12,215: total

In southwest SD, in Bennett, Shannon, and Jackson counties, with a small part in northwest NE; 25 mi. north of Rushville, NE. Total area 3468 sq. mi. Established 1890.

Name origin: *Oglala* 'to scatter one's own'; a Teton tribe of Siouan linguistic stock.

Pinoleville Rancheria
Status: Federal
HQ: CA **Area Code:** 916
County: Mendocino
Pop: 77: AmInd; 130: total
Lat: 39-10-48 N **Long:** 12-31-30 W

In northwest CA, southeast of Fort Bragg. Total area 0.2 sq. mi.

Name origin: From Aztec *pinolli* 'parched or toasted grain or seeds; meal,' an Indian staple.

Pit River Trust Lands
Tribe: Pit River **Status:** Federal
HQ: CA **Area Code:** 916
County: Shasta
Pop: 1: AmInd; 7: total

In north-central WA, northeast of Redding. Total area 0.4 sq. mi.

Name origin: For the river, named for the pits dug by the Indians in which to trap game or enemies.

Pleasant Point Reservation
Tribe: Passamaquoddy **Status:** State
HQ: Peter Dana Point, ME **Area Code:** 207
County: Washington
Pop: 523: AmInd; 572: total
Lat: 44-57-24 N **Long:** 06-70-24 W

In southeastern ME near Princeton. Total area 0.8 sq. mi.

Poarch Creek Reservation & Trust Lands
Tribe: Poarch Creek **Status:** Federal
HQ: AL **Area Code:** 205
County: Baldwin, Escambia
Pop: 149: AmInd; 212: total

In southwestern AL; total area 0.4 sq. mi.

Pojoaque Pueblo
Tribe: Tano-Tewa Tribe **Status:** Federal
HQ: Pojoaque Pueblo, NM **Area Code:** 505
County: Santa Fe
Pop: 177: AmInd; 2,556: total

In north-central AZ, 16 mi. northwest of Santa Fe. Total area 21 sq. mi. Reservation grant confirmed in 1858 and patented in 1865.

Name origin: Possibly a Spanish approximation of Tewa *posoong wa ghay* 'drink water place'; or a corruption of a Santa Clara word *povi age* 'place where the flowers grow along the stream.'

Ponca TDSA
Tribe: Ponca **Status:** State
HQ: NE **Area Code:** 0
Pop: 0: AmInd; 8: total

On northeastern border of NE with SD; total area 6 sq. mi.

Name origin: For the Indian tribe of Siouan linguistic stock; meaning of name has been lost.

Poospatuck Reservation
Tribe: Poospatuck Tribe **Status:** State
HQ: NY **Area Code:** 516
County: Suffolk
Pop: 95: AmInd; 136: total

On eastern end of Long Island, NY. Total area 0.1 sq. mi. Reservation granted by the colonial government in the name of the King.

Port Gamble Reservation
Tribe: Clallam Tribe **Status:** Federal
HQ: Kingston, WA **Area Code:** 206
County: Kitsap
Pop: 377: AmInd; 552: total
Lat: 47-51-21 N **Long:** 12-23-33 W

In northwestern WA, 30 mi. north of Seattle. Total area 2 sq. mi. Federal government bought the site on Mar 12, 1936, under authority of a congressional act dated Jun 18, 1894. The reservation provided an official home for the descendants of Amerindians who were evicted from Teekalet village in 1853.

Name origin: For the town, which was named for Lt. Robert Gamble, U.S. Navy, a hero of the War of 1812.

Port Madison Reservation
Tribe: Suquamish Tribe **Status:** Federal
HQ: Bremerton, WA **Area Code:** 206
County: Kitsap
Pop: 388: AmInd; 4,834: total
Lat: 47-43-29 N **Long:** 12-23-54 W

In northwestern WA, 25 mi. north of Seattle. Total area 12 sq. mi. Established 1855, enlarged 1864.

Name origin: Named for the city, which was named in 1841 by the Wilkes Expedition for James Madison (1751–1836), fourth U.S. president.

Potawatomi (WI) Res. & Trust Lands
Tribe: Potawatomi Tribe **Status:** Federal
HQ: Potawatomi, WI **Area Code:** 715
County: Forest, Oconto
Pop: 266: AmInd; 279: total
Lat: 45-17-00 N **Long:** 08-83-50 W

In northeastern WI, 35 mi. northeast of Antigo. Total area 19 sq. mi. Established 1913.

Name origin: For the Indian tribe of Algonquian linguistic stock. Name means 'people of the place of the fire.' Also spelled *Pottawatomie*.

Pottawatomi (Kansas) Reservation
Tribe: Prairie Band of Potawatomi Tribe **Status:** Federal
HQ: Horton, KS **Area Code:** 913
County: Jackson
Pop: 502: AmInd; 1,082: total
Lat: 39-20-00 N **Long:** 09-55-00 W

In northeastern KS, north of Topeka. Total area 120 sq. mi. Original reservation covered 77,440 acres; sales, fee patents, and inheritance by non-Indians have reduced it to present size. Established c.1840.

Name origin: Indian tribe of Algonquian linguistic stock; name means 'people of the place of the fire.' Spelling is variant of *Pottawatomie*.

Prairie Island Community
Tribe: Eastern or Mississippi Sioux **Status:** Federal
HQ: Welch, MN **Area Code:** 612
County: Goodhue
Pop: 56: AmInd; 60: total
Lat: 44-38-30 N **Long:** 09-23-90 W

In southeastern MN, north of Rochester. Total area 1 sq. mi. Established between 1887 and 1893.

Puyallup Reservation & Trust Lands
Tribe: Puyallup Tribe **Status:** Federal
HQ: Puyallup, WA **Area Code:** 206
County: Pierce
Pop: 937: AmInd; 32,406: total

In west-central WA, southeast of Tacoma. Total area 29 sq. mi. Established 1855.

Name origin: *Puyallup* 'generous people,' from *pough* 'to add more and *allup* 'people'; the Amerindians living along Puyallup River were noted for their generosity in dealing with travelers.

Pyramid Lake Reservation
Tribe: Paiute Tribe **Status:** Federal
HQ: Nixon, NV **Area Code:** 702
County: Washoe, Lyon, Storey
Pop: 959: AmInd; 1,388: total
Lat: 40-05-00 N **Long:** 11-93-50 W

In western NV, 40 mi. northeast of Reno, surrounding and including Pyramid Lake. Total area 554 sq. mi. Established 1874.

Name origin: For the lake, from which rises a 600-ft. rock, thought by John C. Frémont (1813–90), who discovered it on Jan 10, 1844, to resemble the Great Pyramid of Cheops.

Quartz Valley Rancheria
Status: Federal
HQ: CA **Area Code:** 916
County: Siskiyou
Pop: 19: AmInd; 124: total
Lat: 41-36-47 N **Long:** 12-25-81 W

In north-central CA, west of Yreka. Total area 1 sq. mi.

Quileute Reservation
Tribe: Quileute Tribe **Status:** Federal
HQ: La Push, WA **Area Code:** 206
County: Clallam
Pop: 303: AmInd; 381: total
Lat: 47-54-08 N **Long:** 12-43-65 W

In northwestern WA, on the Pacific Ocean at the mouth of the Quillayute River. Total area 2 sq. mi. Designated in the Quinault River Treaty of Jul 1, 1855, and established by an executive order dated Feb 19, 1889.

Name origin: *Quileute* possibly 'joining together of rivers' (the Bogachiel and Soleduck rivers), or 'river with no head,' because the Quillayute River flows only six miles from its beginning to the Pacific Ocean. Variously spelled *Quillyhuyte*, *Kwilleute*, *Quallayute*.

Quinault Reservation
Tribe: Quinault Tribe **Status:** Federal
HQ: Taholah, WA **Area Code:** 206
County: Grays Harbor, Jefferson
Pop: 943: AmInd; 1,216: total

On western coast of WA, 40 mi. north of Aberdeen. Total area 325 sq. mi. Established Jul 1, 1855, by the Quinault River Treaty; enlarged by an executive order dated Nov 4, 1873.

Name origin: *Quinault* French form for *Kwle-ni-lth* or *Wi-ni-nlth*, the name of the tribe.

Ramah Navajo Community
Tribe: Navajo Tribe **Status:** Federal
HQ: Ramah, NM **Area Code:** 505
County: McKinley, Valencia
Pop: 191: AmInd; 194: total

In west-central AZ, 31 mi. southeast of Gallup. Total area 28 sq. mi. Established c. 1868 by those Navajos not wanting to continue the march to the Navajo Reservation.
Name origin: For the town, named by Mormons for a figure in the Book of Mormon.

Ramapough TDSA
Tribe: Ramapough **Status:** State
HQ: NJ **Area Code:** 0
Pop: 273: AmInd; 809: total

In northeastern NJ, north of Newark; total area 8 sq. mi.

Ramona Reservation
Tribe: Cahuilla Band of Mission Indians **Status:** Federal
HQ: CA **Area Code:** 619
County: Riverside
Pop: 0: AmInd; 0: total
Lat: 33-36-18 N **Long:** 11-64-13 W

In southwestern CA, 21 mi. from Hemet. Total area 0.9 sq. mi. Established Feb 10, 1893.
Name origin: For the nearby Ramona Hot Springs.

Red Cliff Reservation & Trust Lands
Tribe: Red Cliff Band of Chippewa Indians **Status:** Federal
HQ: Red Cliff, WI **Area Code:** 715
County: Bayfield
Pop: 727: AmInd; 857: total
Lat: 46-55-00 N **Long:** 09-04-80 W

At tip of peninsula into Lake Superior, southwest of the Apostle Islands. Total area 23 sq. mi. Established 1854.
Name origin: The Indian village here was originally called *Passa-bikang* 'steep cliff.' Reason for change is unknown.

Redding Rancheria
Status: Federal
HQ: CA **Area Code:** 916
County: Shasta
Pop: 79: AmInd; 101: total

In north-central CA, near town of Redding. Total area less than 0.1 sq. mi.
Name origin: For the town, named *Reading* for Pierson B. Reading, an early settler; later changed to present spelling for B.B. Redding, CA bureaucrat and land agent of the Central Pacific Railroad. Originally named *Latona*.

Red Lake Reservation
Tribe: Chippewa Tribe **Status:** Federal
HQ: Redlake, MN **Area Code:** 218
County: Beltrami, Clearwater
Pop: 3,602: AmInd; 3,699: total

In north-central MN, 32 mi. east of Red Lake. Total area 880 sq. mi. Tribe also owns additional scattered holdings of 156,690 acres up to the Canadian border. Their reservations are part of their traditional homelands.

Redwood Valley Rancheria
Status: Federal
HQ: CA **Area Code:** 916
County: Mendocino
Pop: 14: AmInd; 142: total
Lat: 39-17-04 N **Long:** 12-31-24 W

In northwestern CA, southeast of Fort Bragg. Total area 0.1 sq. mi.
Name origin: For the popular name of the *Sequoia sempervirens* tree.

Reno-Sparks Colony
Tribe: Washoe-Paiute Tribe **Status:** Federal
HQ: Reno-Sparks, NV **Area Code:** 702
County: Washoe
Pop: 262: AmInd; 264: total

In southwestern NV, 1 mi. from Reno. Total area 3 sq. mi. Established 1917.
Name origin: For the two cities: Reno, named for Jesse Lee Reno (1823–62), Union general and Western surveyor; and Sparks, named for John Sparks (1843–1908), governor of NV at the time.

Resighini Rancheria
Status: Federal
HQ: CA **Area Code:** 916
County: Del Norte
Pop: 26: AmInd; 28: total

On northwestern Pacific coast of CA, near Klamath. Total area 0.4 sq. mi.

Rincon Reservation
Tribe: San Luiseno Band of Mission Indians **Status:** State
HQ: Valley Center, CA **Area Code:** 619
County: San Diego
Pop: 379: AmInd; 1,352: total
Lat: 33-15-48 N **Long:** 11-65-73 W

In southwestern CA, 45 mi. from San Diego. Total area 6 sq. mi. Established Dec 27, 1875; enlarged Mar 2, 1881. Present reservation established Sep 13, 1892.
Name origin: Spanish 'small portion of land,' but in CA used interchangeably with *rinconada* 'inside corner' of anything projecting into something else: into another's property, into a bay, etc.

Roaring Creek Rancheria
Tribe: Pit River Tribe **Status:** Federal
HQ: Montgomery Creek, CA **Area Code:** 916
County: Shasta
Pop: 18: AmInd; 18: total
Lat: 40-53-37 N **Long:** 12-15-71 W

In northern CA near Redding. Total area 0.1 sq. mi. Land purchased Aug 31, 1915, for any landless CA Indians.

Robinson Rancheria
Tribe: Pomo **Status:** Federal
HQ: CA **Area Code:** 916
County: Lake
Pop: 113: AmInd; 139: total
Lat: 39-08-22 N **Long:** 12-25-43 W

In northwestern CA, north of Santa Rosa. Total area 0.4 sq. mi.

Rocky Boy's Reservation & Trust Lands
Tribe: Chippewa-Cree Tribe **Status:** Federal
HQ: Rocky Boy's, MT **Area Code:** 406
County: Chouteau, Hill
Pop: 1,882: AmInd; 1,954: total
Lat: 48-15-01 N **Long:** 10-94-80 W

In north-central MT, 20 mi. south of Havre. Total area 168 sq. mi. Established Apr 1916; additional lands added later.
Name origin: *Cree* Indians of Algonquian linguistic stock; meaning of name unknown.

Rohnerville Rancheria
Status: Federal
HQ: CA **Area Code:** 916
County: Humboldt
Pop: 1: AmInd; 14: total
Lat: 40-34-50 N **Long:** 12-40-71 W

In northwestern CA, southeast of Eureka. Total area less than 0.1 sq. mi.
Name origin: For the town, named for Henry Rohner, of Switzerland, who started a store here in 1859.

Rosebud Reservation & Trust Lands
Tribe: Sioux Tribe **Status:** Federal
HQ: Rosebud, SD **Area Code:** 605
County: Mellette, Todd, Tripp
Pop: 8,043: AmInd; 9,696: total

In south-central SD, south of Pierre; total area 1975 sq. mi. Established 1890.

Round Valley Reservation & Trust Lands
Tribe: various **Status:** Federal
HQ: Covelo, CA **Area Code:** 707
County: Mendocino
Pop: 577: AmInd; 1,183: total
Lat: 39-54-30 N **Long:** 12-31-91 W

On central Pacific coast, 45 mi. north of Willits. Total area 95 sq. mi. Establishment of four Indian reservations in CA authorized Apr 8, 1864, for the Yuki, Pit River, Little Lake, Konkow, Wylacki, Pomo, Nomalaki, and Wintun tribes. Round Valley Reservation enlarged Mar 30, 1870; Camp Wright Military Reserve added to reservation in 1876.

Rumsey Rancheria
Tribe: Wintun Tribe **Status:** Federal
HQ: Brooks, CA **Area Code:** 916
County: Yolo
Pop: 4: AmInd; 8: total
Lat: 38-53-18 N **Long:** 12-21-45 W

In north-central CA, northwest of Sacramento. Total area 0.1 sq. mi. Original land purchased in 1907 and 1908.
Name origin: For the town, named for Capt. D.C. Rumsey who owned the land.

Sac and Fox Reservation
Tribe: Sac and Fox (Mesquakie) Tribes **Status:** Federal
HQ: BIA Indian School, Tama, IA **Area Code:** 515
County: Tama
Pop: 564: AmInd; 577: total
Lat: 41-59-13 N **Long:** 09-23-91 W

In central IA, 48 mi. west of Cedar Rapids. Total area 6 sq. mi. Established by tribal leaders in 1856 by purchase of 80 acres, placed in trust with the governor of IA. Additional purchases increased it to present size.
Name origin: *Sac* 'outlet' is an Indian tribal name; also spelled *Sauk*. Fox is an Indian tribe of Algonquian linguistic stock.

Sac and Fox Reservation & Trust Lands
Tribe: Sac and Fox Tribes **Status:** Federal
HQ: Horton, KS **Area Code:** 913
County: Brown, KS, Richardson, NE
Pop: 49: AmInd; 210: total
Lat: 39-59-15 N **Long:** 09-52-73 W

In northeastern KS and southeastern NE, north of Topeka. Total area 24 sq. mi., of which 8 are in KS and 16 in NE; original reservation was 7,924 acres. Established 1861.
Name origin: *Sac* 'outlet.' Also spelled *Sauk*. Fox is a tribe of Algonquian linguistic stock.

Sac and Fox TJSA
Tribe: Sac and Fox **Status:** Federal
HQ: Stroud, OK **Area Code:** 405
County: Lincoln, Payne, Pottawatomi
Pop: 4,704: AmInd; 51,042: total

Federal trust area in central OK. Total area 770 sq. mi. Established 1869.
Name origin: *Sac* 'outlet.' Also spelled *Sauk*. Fox is a tribe of Algonquian linguistic stock.

Saint Croix Reservation
Tribe: St. Croix Band of Chippewa **Status:** Federal
HQ: Danbury, WI **Area Code:** 715
County: Burnett, Barron, Polk
Pop: 462: AmInd; 505: total

In northwestern WI, 55 mi. south of Duluth. Total area 3 sq. mi. Established 1938.
Name origin: For the St. Croix River, probably named for a French explorer who drowned in it.

St. Regis Mohawk Reservation
Tribe: St. Regis Mohawk **Status:** State
HQ: Hogansburg, NY **Area Code:** 315
County: Franklin
Pop: 1,923: AmInd; 1,978: total
Lat: 44-59-17 N **Long:** 07-43-92 W

In northeastern NY on St. Lawrence River, 5 mi. east of Massena. Total area 19 sq. mi. The Canadian portion of the reservation is the Caughnawaga Reserve.
Name origin: For the St. Regis river, named for a Jesuit missionary. *Mohawk* 'cannibals,' from Iroquois tribal name given to them by their enemies, the Algonquins, with reference to the custom of eating the bodies of captured enemies.

Salt River Reservation
Tribe: Pima-Maricopa Tribes **Status:** Federal
HQ: Scottsdale, AZ **Area Code:** 602
County: Maricopa
Pop: 3,533: AmInd; 4,852: total
Lat: 33-31-00 N **Long:** 11-14-60 W

In central AZ, 10 mi. northeast of Phoenix. Total area 80 sq. mi. Established in 1879.

San Carlos Reservation
Tribe: Apache Tribe **Status:** Federal
HQ: San Carlos, AZ **Area Code:** 602
County: Gila, Graham, Pinal
Pop: 7,110: AmInd; 7,294: total
Lat: 33-23-00 N **Long:** 11-00-60 W

In southeastern AZ, 100 mi. southeast of Phoenix. Total area 2911 sq. mi. Established in 1873.
Name origin: Name of an Apache tribe, possibly for the San Carlos River.

Sandia Pueblo
Tribe: Tano-Tigua Tribe **Status:** Federal
HQ: Sandia Pueblo, NM **Area Code:** 505
County: Sandoval
Pop: 358: AmInd; 3,971: total

In north-central AZ, 15 mi. north of Albuquerque. Total area 39 sq. mi. Original Spanish grant confirmed by U.S. Congress in 1858 and patented in 1864.

Name origin: Spanish 'watermelon,' meaning unclear. Watermelons are not native to the area; could refer to pumpkin or squash; or to the striped appearance of the rocks or their pinkish reflection at sunset.

Sandy Lake Reservation
Status: Federal
HQ: MN **Area Code:** 715
County: Aitkin
Pop: 36: AmInd; 37: total

In east-central MN, northeast of Mille Lacs Lake; total area 0.4 sq. mi.

San Felipe Pueblo
Tribe: Keresan Tribe **Status:** Federal
HQ: San Felipe Pueblo, NM **Area Code:** 505
County: Sandoval
Pop: 1,859: AmInd; 2,434: total

In north-central AZ, 25 mi. north of Albuquerque. Total area 79 sq. mi. Original Spanish grant confirmed by U.S. Congress and patented in 1864; additional grants increased reservation to present size.

Name origin: For St. Philip the Apostle.

San Ildefonso Pueblo
Tribe: Tewa Tribe **Status:** Federal
HQ: San Ildefonso Pueblo, NM **Area Code:** 505
County: Santa Fe, Sandoval
Pop: 347: AmInd; 1,499: total
Lat: 35-53-00 N **Long:** 10-61-05 W

In central AZ, 18 mi. north of Santa Fe. Total area 44 sq. mi. Original grant confirmed by U.S. Congress in 1858 and patented in 1864.

Name origin: For St. Ildephonse, Archbishop of Toledo in the 7th century.

San Juan Pueblo
Tribe: Tano-Tewa Tribe **Status:** Federal
HQ: San Juan, NM **Area Code:** 505
County: Rio Arriba
Pop: 1,276: AmInd; 5,209: total

In north-central AZ, 24 mi. north of Santa Fe. Total area 27 sq. mi. Original land grant confirmed by U.S. Congress in 1858 and patented in 1864.

Name origin: For St. John the Baptist.

San Manuel Reservation
Tribe: San Manuel Band **Status:** Federal
HQ: Highland, CA **Area Code:** 213
County: San Bernardino
Pop: 56: AmInd; 80: total
Lat: 34-09-25 N **Long:** 11-71-25 W

In southwestern CA, east of Los Angeles. Total area 1 sq. mi. Established Aug 31, 1893.

San Pasqual Reservation
Tribe: San Pasqual Band of Mission Indians **Status:** Federal
HQ: Valley Center, CA **Area Code:** 619
County: San Diego
Pop: 212: AmInd; 512: total

In southwestern CA, 10 mi. from Escondido. Total area 2 sq. mi. Established July 1910.

Name origin: Probably for St. Paschal, a 16th-century Franciscan. Also spelled *Pascal*.

Santa Ana Pueblo
Tribe: Keresan Tribe **Status:** Federal
HQ: Santa Ana Pueblo, NM **Area Code:** 505
County: Sandoval
Pop: 481: AmInd; 593: total

In north-central AZ, 23 mi. north of Albuquerque. Total area 101 sq. mi. Original grant confirmed by U.S. Congress in 1869 and patented in 1883; additional grants brought reservation to present size.

Name origin: For St. Anne, the traditional name for the mother of the Virgin Mary.

Santa Clara Pueblo
Tribe: Tano-Tewa Tribe **Status:** Federal
HQ: Santa Clara Pueblo, NM **Area Code:** 505
County: Rio Arriba, Sandoval
Pop: 1,246: AmInd; 10,193: total

In north-central AZ, 22 mi. west of Santa Fe. Total area 77 sq. mi. Original grant confirmed by U.S. Congress in 1858 and patented in 1909; subsequent grant brought reservation to present size.

Name origin: For St. Clare (1194–1253) of Assisi.

Santa Rosa Rancheria
Tribe: Tache Tribe **Status:** Federal
HQ: Lemoore, CA **Area Code:** 209
County: Kings
Pop: 284: AmInd; 323: total

In central CA, 30 mi. west of Visalia. Total area 0.3 sq. mi. Established Feb 1921; additional lands added Jul 1939.

Name origin: Probably for St. Rose (1586–1617) of Lima, the only female saint of the Americans until recently.

Santa Rosa Reservation
Tribe: Santa Rosa Band of Mission Indians
Status: Federal
HQ: Hemet, CA **Area Code:** 619
County: Riverside
Pop: 37: AmInd; 50: total

In southern CA, 50 mi. southwest of Palm Springs. Total area 17 sq. mi. Established Feb 2, 1907; 640 acres added in Apr 1937.

Name origin: See Santa Rosa Rancheria.

Santa Ynez Reservation
Tribe: Santa Ynez Band of Mission Indians **Status:** Federal
HQ: Sun Valley, CA **Area Code:** 805
County: Santa Barbara
Pop: 213: AmInd; 179: total
Lat: 34-36-08 N **Long:** 12-00-52 W

On Pacific coast of CA, 32 mi. north of Santa Barbara. Total area 0.2 sq. mi. Established Dec 27, 1901.

Name origin: Spanish form for St. Agnes (?–c. 350).

Santa Ysabel Reservation
Tribe: Santa Ysabel Band of Mission
Indians
HQ: Santa Ysabel, CA
County: San Diego
Pop: 150: AmInd; 169: total
Status: Federal
Area Code: 619

In southwestern CA, east of Escondido. Total area 14 sq. mi. Reservation set aside by executive order of President Ulysses S. Grant (1822–85), December 27, 1875.

Name origin: Spanish form for St. Elizabeth, probably of Portugal, daughter of the King of Aragon.

Santee Reservation
Tribe: Santee Sioux Tribe
HQ: Niobrara, NE
County: Knox
Pop: 425: AmInd; 758: total
Status: Federal
Area Code: 402

On northern border of Nebraska, a bit west of Yankton, South Dakota. Total area 173 sq. mi. Established Feb 27, 1866, though several adjustments lost them the lands west of the Niobrara River. In 1887 tribal members were given allotments and the rest of the reservation was opened to settlement by non-Indians.

Name origin: A Siouan tribe; meaning of name not known, for no words from the language have survived.

Santo Domingo Pueblo
Tribe: Keresan Tribe
HQ: Santo Domingo Pueblo, NM
County: Sandoval
Pop: 2,947: AmInd; 2,992: total
Status: Federal
Area Code: 505

In north-central AZ, 25 mi. northeast of Bernalillo. Total area 107 sq. mi. Original grant confirmed by U.S. Congress in 1858 and patented Nov 1, 1864. In 1924 the Pueblo Land Boards found that this grant was in conflict with another, prior claim: 150 acres are in conflict with Cochiti Grant.

Name origin: For St. Dominic, 13th-century founder of the Dominican religious order.

San Xavier Reservation
Tribe: Papago
HQ: AZ
County: Pima
Pop: 1,073: AmInd; 1,172: total
Lat: 32-03-00 N **Long:** 11-10-50 W
Status: Federal
Area Code: 602

In south-central AZ, south of Tucson; area 111 sq. mi.

Name origin: For the mission founded by Jesuits for the Papago Indians.

Sauk-Suiattle Reservation
Tribe: Sauk-Suiattle
HQ: WA
County: Skagit
Pop: 69: AmInd; 124: total
Status: Federal
Area Code: 206

In northwestern WA, southeast of Mt. Vernon; total area 0.1 sq. mi.

Name origin: *Sauk* is from *Sah-kee-me-hue*, an Indian band that lived along the Sauk River; meaning of the name is unknown. *Suiattle*, Indian origin but meaning unknown.

Sault Ste. Marie Res. & Trust Lands
HQ: MI
County: Chippewa
Pop: 554: AmInd; 768: total
Status: Federal
Area Code: 906

On northeastern coast of Upper Peninsula of MI, near border of Ontario province, Canada; total area 1 sq. mi.

Name origin: French 'the rapids of Saint Mary,' referring to the St. Mary River.

Schaghticoke Reservation
Tribe: Schaghticoke
HQ: CT
County: Litchfield
Pop: 7: AmInd; 10: total
Lat: 41-41-34 N **Long:** 07-33-03 W
Status: State
Area Code: 203

In northwestern CT, southwest of Hartford; area 0.4 sq. mi.

Seminole TJSA
Tribe: Seminole
HQ: Wewoka, OK
County: Seminole
Pop: 3,786: AmInd; 22,964: total
Status: Federal
Area Code: 405

Federal trust area in east-central OK, southeast of Oklahoma City. Total area 567 sq. mi. Tribe relocated from Florida in 1842–43.

Name origin: *Seminola* from Creek 'the separate ones'; also recorded as 'runaway,' but with connotation of separateness; a Muskhogean tribe.

Seminole Trust Lands
Tribe: Miccosukee and Seminole Indian Tribes
HQ: FL
County: Broward
Pop: 93: AmInd; 114: total
Lat: 26-11-47 N **Long:** 08-05-23 W
Status: State
Area Code: 305

In south-central FL; area 0.1 sq. mi.

Name origin: A Muskhogean tribe. Name is from Creek 'the separate ones.'

Shakopee Sioux Community
Tribe: Shakopee Mdewakanton Sioux
HQ: Prior Lake, MN
County: Carver
Pop: 153: AmInd; 203: total
Lat: 44-45-13 N **Long:** 09-32-71 W
Status: Federal
Area Code: 612

In south-central MN. Total area 0.5 sq. mi. Reservation lands acquired Mar 2, and Jun 29, 1888, and Aug 19, 1890. Until Nov 28, 1969, Prior Lake Reservation had been part of the Lower Sioux Reservation.

Name origin: From Siouan 'Six,' the hereditary name of successive chiefs.

Sheep Ranch Rancheria
Tribe: Me-Wuk (Miwok) Tribe
HQ: Sheepranch, CA
County: Calaveras
Pop: 0: AmInd; 0: total
Status: Federal
Area Code: 916

In central CA, southeast of Sacramento. No land. Established in 1916 for homeless CA Indians without designation of tribe.

Sherwood Valley Rancheria
Tribe: Pomo **Status:** Federal
HQ: CA **Area Code:** 916
County: Mendocino
Pop: 9: AmInd; 15: total

In northwestern CA, northeast of Fort Bragg. Total area 0.5 sq. mi.

Name origin: For the valley named for settler, Alfred Sherwood (?–1900).

Shingle Springs Rancheria
Tribe: Me-Wuk (Miwok) **Status:** Federal
HQ: CA **Area Code:** 916
County: El Dorado
Pop: 7: AmInd; 18: total
Lat: 38-41-42 N **Long:** 12-05-41 W

In north-central CA, northeast of Sacramento. Total area 0.3 sq. mi.

Name origin: For the town, named for a shingle machine located at a cluster of springs.

Shinnecock Reservation
Tribe: Shinnecock Tribe **Status:** State
HQ: Southhampton, Long Island, NY **Area Code:** 516
County: Suffolk
Pop: 339: AmInd; 375: total
Lat: 40-52-28 N **Long:** 07-22-55 W

At eastern end of Long Island, NY. Total area 1 sq. mi. Land given to Indians by the colonial government in the name of the King.

Shoalwater Reservation
Tribe: Quinault, Chinook, and Chehalis Tribes **Status:** Federal
HQ: Tokeland, WA **Area Code:** 206
County: Pacific
Pop: 66: AmInd; 131: total
Lat: 46-43-42 N **Long:** 12-40-12 W

On western coast of WA, 25 mi. southwest of Aberdeen. Total area 1 sq. mi. Established by executive order on Sep 22, 1866.

Name origin: *Chinook*, anglicization of *Tsinuk*; tribe also known as *Flatheads* for their custom of deforming the head. Their trade with inland and coastal tribes, then with French and English arrivals affected their language which became the Chinook jargon.

Siletz Reservation
Tribe: Siletz **Status:** Federal
HQ: OR **Area Code:** 503
County: Lincoln
Pop: 0: AmInd; 5: total
Lat: 44-47-00 N **Long:** 12-34-80 W

In northwestern OR, west of Salem; total area 6 sq. mi.

Skokomish Reservation
Tribe: Skokomish Tribe **Status:** Federal
HQ: Shelton, WA **Area Code:** 206
County: Mason
Pop: 431: AmInd; 614: total
Lat: 47-20-19 N **Long:** 12-30-92 W

In western WA, 25 mi. northwest of Olympia. Total area 8 sq. mi. Established 1855.

Name origin: *Skokomish* from *s'kaw* 'fresh water' and *mish* 'people.'

Skull Valley Reservation
Tribe: Goshute Tribe **Status:** Federal
HQ: Grantsville, UT **Area Code:** 801
County: Tooele
Pop: 32: AmInd; 32: total
Lat: 40-23-23 N **Long:** 11-24-20 W

In western UT, southwest of Salt Lake City. Total area 28 sq. mi.

Name origin: Possibly for the prehistoric buffalo skulls found there in 1853–54; or for Amerindian skulls supposedly found in area springs.

Smith River Rancheria
Status: Federal
HQ: CA **Area Code:** 916
County: Del Norte
Pop: 72: AmInd; 104: total

On northwestern Pacific coast of CA, south of the OR border. Total area 0.2 sq. mi.

Name origin: For the town, name given to the lower Klamath River by Jedediah Smith.

Soboba Reservation
Tribe: Soboba Band of Mission Indians **Status:** Federal
HQ: San Jacinto, CA **Area Code:** 619
County: Riverside
Pop: 308: AmInd; 369: total
Lat: 33-46-34 N **Long:** 11-65-35 W

In southwestern CA, 7 mi. east of Hemet. Total area 9 sq. mi. Established Jun 10, 1913.

Name origin: Name of a Luiseo Indian village; meaning unknown. Variously spelled, including *Sovova*.

Sokaogon Chippewa Community & Trust Land
Tribe: Sokoagon Chippewa Band **Status:** Federal
HQ: Mole Lake, WI **Area Code:** 715
County: Forest
Pop: 311: AmInd; 357: total
Lat: 45-29-30 N **Long:** 08-85-90 W

In northeastern WI, 36 mi. east of Rhinelander. Total area 3 sq. mi. Established 1826.

Southern Ute Reservation
Tribe: Mouache and Capote Ute Tribes **Status:** Federal
HQ: Ignacio, CO **Area Code:** 303
County: La Plata, Archuleta, Montezuma
Pop: 1,044: AmInd; 7,804: total
Lat: 37-05-00 N **Long:** 10-85-70 W

In southwestern CO along NM border, 25 mi. southwest of Durango. Total area 1059 sq. mi. Established 1873.

Spokane Reservation
Tribe: Spokane Tribe **Status:** Federal
HQ: Wellpinit, WA **Area Code:** 509
County: Stevens, Lincoln
Pop: 1,229: AmInd; 1,502: total
Lat: 47-54-00 N **Long:** 11-75-80 W

In northeastern WA, 40 mi. northwest of Spokane. Total area 238 sq. mi. Established Jan 18, 1881, by executive order.

Name origin: From *Spehkunne*, name of an Indian tribe of Salishan linguistic stock. Name seems to have as part of its meaning 'sun,' which has given rise to poetic renderings such as 'child of the sun' and 'chief of the sun'; may mean 'toward the sun.' All is doubtful.

Squaxin Island Reservation & Trust Lands
Tribe: Squaxin Island Tribe **Status:** Federal
HQ: Shelton, WA **Area Code:** 206
County: Mason
Pop: 127: AmInd; 157: total
Lat: 47-22-41 N **Long:** 12-25-43 W

In western WA, 15 mi. north of Olympia. Total area 3 sq. mi. Established 1854.

Name origin: *Squaxin* from *Skwaks-namish* 'alone people.'

Standing Rock Reservation
Tribe: Sioux Tribe **Status:** Federal
HQ: Fort Yates, ND **Area Code:** 701
County: Sioux, ND, Corson, SD
Pop: 4,870: AmInd; 7,956: total

In north-central SD and south-central ND, 40 mi. from Bismarck, ND. Total area 3567 sq. mi., of which 1092 are in ND, and 2473 in SD. Established 1890.

Stewarts Point Rancheria
Tribe: Kashia Pomo **Status:** Federal
HQ: CA **Area Code:** 916
County: Sonoma
Pop: 86: AmInd; 91: total
Lat: 38-39-24 N **Long:** 12-32-01 W

On northwestern Pacific coast of CA, northwest of Santa Rosa. Total area 0.1 sq. mi.

Name origin: Possibly for Lt. Col. C.S. Stewart of the Corps of Engineers, who did a coastal survey in 1875.

Stillaguamish Reservation
Tribe: Stillaguamish **Status:** Federal
HQ: WA **Area Code:** 206
County: Skagit
Pop: 96: AmInd; 113: total

In northwestern WA, south of Mount Vernon; total area less than 0.1 sq. mi.

Name origin: *Stillaguamish* from *Sta-luk-qua-mish* 'river people,' a tribal name.

Stockbridge Reservation
Tribe: Stockbridge (Mohican) and Munsee Tribes **Status:** Federal
HQ: Bowler, WI **Area Code:** 715
County: Shawano
Pop: 447: AmInd; 581: total
Lat: 44-54-00 N **Long:** 08-85-20 W

In northeastern WI, 40 mi. east of Wausau. Total area 35 sq. mi. Established 1856.

Name origin: For the town in western MA, named for Stockbridge, England, on land granted by the General Court in 1734 for the establishment of an Indian mission. The original Indians were the Mukhekanews, a branch of the Algonquins. In 1785 they migrated westward and became known as Stockbridge Indians.

Sulphur Bank (El-Em) Rancheria
Tribe: Pomo Tribe **Status:** Federal
HQ: Clearlake Oaks, CA **Area Code:** 916
County: Lake
Pop: 90: AmInd; 93: total
Lat: 39-00-30 N **Long:** 12-24-01 W

In northwestern CA, 45 mi. east of Ukiah. Total area 0.1 sq. mi. Established Jan 10, 1949.

Summit Lake Reservation
Tribe: Paiute Tribe **Status:** Federal
HQ: NV **Area Code:** 702
County: Humboldt
Pop: 6: AmInd; 7: total
Lat: 41-31-30 N **Long:** 11-90-30 W

In northwestern NV, 100 mi. east of Alturas, CA. Total area 17 sq. mi. Established 1913.

Susanville Rancheria
Tribe: Paiute, Maidu, Pit River, and Washoe Tribes **Status:** Federal
HQ: Susanville, CA **Area Code:** 916
County: Lassen
Pop: 154: AmInd; 454: total
Lat: 40-25-43 N **Long:** 12-03-92 W

In northeastern CA, 85 mi. northwest of Reno, NV. Total area 0.2 sq. mi. Land purchased Aug 15, 1923, for homeless California Indians without designation of tribe.

Name origin: For the town, named by Isaac Roop for his daughter.

Swinomish Reservation
Tribe: Swinomish Tribe **Status:** Federal
HQ: La Conner, WA **Area Code:** 206
County: Skagit
Pop: 585: AmInd; 2,282: total
Lat: 48-26-00 N **Long:** 12-23-20 W

On Haro Strait coast of WA, 35 mi. northwest of Everett. Total area 11 sq. mi. Established Jan 22, 1855, by the Point Elliott Treaty; enlarged by executive order on Sep 9, 1873.

Name origin: Name for a branch of the Skagit tribe; meaning unknown.

Sycuan Reservation
Tribe: Sycuan Band of Mission Indians **Status:** Federal
HQ: El Cajon, CA **Area Code:** 619
County: San Diego
Pop: 0: AmInd; 4: total

In southwestern CA, 14 mi. east of San Diego. Total area 0.1 sq. mi.

Table Bluff Rancheria
Tribe: Wiyot **Status:** Federal
HQ: CA **Area Code:** 916
County: Humboldt
Pop: 43: AmInd; 48: total
Lat: 40-41-03 N **Long:** 12-41-44 W

On northwestern Pacific coast of CA, southwest of Eureka. Total area less than 0.1 sq. mi.

Table Mountain Rancheria
Status: Federal
HQ: CA **Area Code:** 916
County: Fresno
Pop: 48: AmInd; 51: total

In north-central CA, northeast of Fresno. Total area 0.2 sq. mi.

Taos Pueblo & Trust Lands
Tribe: Tano-Tigua Tribe **Status:** Federal
HQ: Taos Pueblo, NM **Area Code:** 505
County: Taos
Pop: 1,212: AmInd; 4,745: total

In north-central AZ, 60 mi. northeast of Santa Fe. Total area 156 sq. mi. Present land grant confirmed Dec 22, 1858.

Name origin: Spanish approximation of Tewa *tu-o-ta* 'red willow place,' or *tua-tah* 'down at the village.'

Te-Moak Reservation & Trust Lands
HQ: NV
County: Elko
Pop: 831: AmInd; 949: total
Lat: 40-34-46 N **Long:** 11-53-61 W
Status: Federal
Area Code: 702

In north-central NV, east of Battle Mountain; total area 28 sq. mi.

Name origin: For *Tim-oak*, a Shoshone chief. Name is said to mean 'rope,' and given to him because he braided rope.

Tesuque Pueblo & Trust Lands
Tribe: Tano-Tewa Tribe
HQ: Tesuque Pueblo, NM
County: Santa Fe
Pop: 232: AmInd; 697: total
Status: Federal
Area Code: 505

In north-central AZ, 10 mi. north of Santa Fe. Total area 27 sq. mi. Grant was confirmed in 1858 and patented in 1864.

Name origin: Spanish approximation of Tewa *tat' unge' onwi* 'spotted dry place': the river disappears in the sand and comes through only in spots.

Tonawanda Reservation
Tribe: Tonawanda Band of Seneca Tribe
HQ: Tonawanda Indian Community, NY
County: Niagara, Erie, Genesee
Pop: 453: AmInd; 501: total
Lat: 43-04-20 N **Long:** 07-82-65 W
Status: State
Area Code: 315

In northwestern NY along Lake Erie, and Ontario (Canada) border. Total area 12 sq. mi. Established 1863.

Name origin: From Iroquoian 'swift water,' for the rapids on the Niagara River into which Tonawanda Creek flows.

Tonkawa TJSA
Tribe: Tonkawa
HQ: Tonkawa, OK
County: Kay
Pop: 920: AmInd; 12,289: total
Status: Federal
Area Code: 918

Federal trust area in north-central OK near Ponca City. Total area 255 sq. mi. Established 1884.

Name origin: *Tonkawa* probably from Waco *tonkaweya* 'they all stay together.' Tribe is also called *kadiko* or *kuikogo* 'man-eating men, cannibals.'

Torres-Martinez Reservation
Tribe: Torres-Martinez Band of Mission Indians
HQ: Mecca, CA
County: Riverside
Pop: 143: AmInd; 1,462: total
Status: Federal
Area Code: 619

In south-central CA, 9 mi. south of Indio. Total area 35 sq. mi., a part of which are submerged under the rising Salton Sea. Established May 15, 1876; 640 acres added Feb 11, 1903, in exchange for lands to be set apart for the Torres Band under the Act of 1891.

Trinidad Rancheria
Tribe: Me-Wuk (Miwok)
HQ: CA
County: Humboldt
Pop: 59: AmInd; 78: total
Status: Federal
Area Code: 707

On northwestern Pacific coast of CA, north of Eureka. Total area 0.1 sq. mi.

Name origin: Spanish form for 'Trinity' [Sunday], the day the Bruno de Hezeta expedition took possession of the town, on June 10, 1775.

Tulalip Reservation
Tribe: Snohomish Tribe
HQ: Marysville, WA
County: Snohomish
Pop: 1,204: AmInd; 7,103: total
Lat: 48-04-30 N **Long:** 12-21-50 W
Status: Federal
Area Code: 206

On Puget Sound coast of WA, 10 mi. northwest of Everett. Total area 35 sq. mi. and is part of their ancestral lands.

Name origin: From Indian *duh-hlay-lup* 'small mouth bay,' referring to the inlet north of the Snohomish River estuary.

Tule River Reservation
Tribe: Tule River Tribe
HQ: Porterville, CA
County: Tulare
Pop: 745: AmInd; 798: total
Lat: 36-02-30 N **Long:** 11-81-90 W
Status: Federal
Area Code: 916

In west-central CA, 45 mi. southeast of Tulare. Total area 84 sq. mi. Established Jan 9, 1873; boundaries changed May 17, 1928.

Name origin: For the river, named for the cattails and other reeds growing along its banks.

Tunica-Biloxi Tribe
Tribe: Tunica-Biloxi
HQ: LA
County: Concordia
Pop: 16: AmInd; 29: total
Status: Federal
Area Code: 601

On central eastern LA border with southwestern MS, northwest of Baton Rouge. Total area 0.2 sq. mi.

Name origin: *Tunica* 'the people' or 'those who are the people'; *Biloxi* 'broken pot.'

Tuolumne Rancheria
Tribe: Tuolumne Band of Me-Wuk (Miwok) Indians
HQ: Tuolumne, CA
County: Tuolumne
Pop: 107: AmInd; 135: total
Lat: 37-59-01 N **Long:** 12-01-41 W
Status: Federal
Area Code: 916

In east-central CA, east of Stockton. Total area 0.5 sq. mi. Land purchased in Oct 1910; land added Apr 1912.

Name origin: For a subtribe of the Miwok Indians of Penutian linguistic stock. The meaning is not clear: *-umne* means 'people,' a common designation among Indians.

Turtle Mountain Res. & Trust Lands
Tribe: Chippewa Tribe
HQ: Belcourt, ND
County: Rolette
Pop: 6,772: AmInd; 7,106: total
Status: Federal
Area Code: 701

In north-central ND. Total area 139 sq. mi., of which 138 are in ND, and 1 sq. mi. in SD. Established by treaty of Oct 2, 1892.

Tuscarora Reservation
Tribe: Tuscarora
HQ: Tuscarora Rural Community, NY
County: Niagara
Pop: 310: AmInd; 772: total
Lat: 43-09-30 N **Long:** 07-85-63 W
Status: State
Area Code: 315

In northwestern NY, 12 mi. northeast of Niagara Falls. Total area 9 sq. mi.

Name origin: From the Iroquoian tribal name meaning 'hemp gatherers.'

Twenty Nine Palms Reservation
Tribe: Twenty-Nine Palms Band of Indians **Status:** Federal
HQ: North Palm Springs, CA **Area Code:** 619
County: San Bernardino
Pop: 0: AmInd; 0: total
Lat: 34-07-04 N **Long:** 11-60-25 W

In south-central CA, northeast of Palm Springs. Total area 0.2 sq. mi. Established Nov 11, 1895.

Uintah & Ouray Reservation
Tribe: Ute **Status:** Federal
HQ: Fort Duchesne, UT **Area Code:** 801
County: parts of 6 counties
Pop: 2,650: AmInd; 17,224: total
Lat: 40-20-00 N **Long:** 11-01-00 W

In eastern UT, east of Provo, in Duchesne, Carbon, Grand, Uintah, Utah, and Wasatch counties; total area 6768 sq. mi. plus subsurface rights on 192,000 acres. Established 1863.

Name origin: *Uinta* name of a subtribe of the Utes, of Shoshonean linguistic stock; name said to mean 'pineland.' *Ouray*, probably 'the arrow,' for the Ute Indian chief (1820–80).

Umatilla Reservation
Tribe: Cayuse, Walla Walla, and Umatilla **Status:** Federal
HQ: Pendleton, OR **Area Code:** 503
County: Umatilla
Pop: 1,029: AmInd; 2,502: total
Lat: 45-40-00 N **Long:** 11-83-30 W

In northern OR, 5 mi. from Pendleton. Total area 271 sq. mi. Established c.1854.

Name origin: *Umatilla*, meaning unknown, possibly 'water rippling over sand'; tribe of Shapwailutan linguistic stock.

United Houma Nation TDSA
Tribe: Houma **Status:** State
HQ: LA **Area Code:** 318
County: Lafourche
Pop: 10,079: AmInd; 817,386: total

In southeastern LA, southwest of New Orleans; total area 4612 sq. mi.

Name origin: From Choctaw *humma* 'red,' but significance is disputed: for body paint; for color of moccasins; or for red crawfish, a tribal war symbol.

Upper Lake Rancheria
Status: Federal
HQ: CA **Area Code:** 707
County: Lake
Pop: 28: AmInd; 76: total
Lat: 39-11-07 N **Long:** 12-25-45 W

In northwestern CA, north of Clear Lake. Total area 0.7 sq. mi.

Upper Sioux Reservation
Tribe: Eastern or Mississippi Sioux **Status:** Federal
HQ: Granite Falls, MN **Area Code:** 612
County: Yellow Medicine
Pop: 43: AmInd; 49: total
Lat: 44-45-40 N **Long:** 09-53-10 W

On southwestern coast of MN, 3 mi. south of Granite Falls. Total area 1 sq. mi. In 1938 the Secretary of the Interior proclaimed certain lands bought for the Upper Sioux Indian community in MN to be a reservation.

Upper Skagit Reservation
Tribe: Upper Skagit **Status:** Federal
HQ: WA **Area Code:** 206
County: Skagit
Pop: 162: AmInd; 180: total

On northwestern coast of WA, south of Bellingham; total area 0.2 sq. mi.

Name origin: Indian tribe of Salishan linguistic stock; meaning of name unknown.

Ute Mountain Reservation & Trust Lands
Tribe: Wiminuche Ute Tribe **Status:** Federal
HQ: Towaoc, CO **Area Code:** 303
County: Montezuma, La Plata, CO; San Juan, NM; San Juan, UT
Pop: 1,264: AmInd; 1,320: total
Lat: 37-11-15 N **Long:** 10-84-11 W

In southwestern CO, northeastern NM, and southeastern UT. Total area 901 sq. mi., of which 716 are in CO, 161 in NM, and 23 in UT.

Vermillion Lake Reservation
Status: Federal
HQ: MN **Area Code:** 313
County: St. Louis
Pop: 87: AmInd; 91: total

On northern border in eastern MI, northeast of Hibbings; total area 2 sq. mi.

Name origin: Possibly for the red color of the water at sunset.

Viejas Reservation
Tribe: Viejas Grp, Capitan Grande Band of Mission Indians **Status:** Federal
HQ: Alpine, CA **Area Code:** 619
County: San Diego
Pop: 227: AmInd; 411: total
Lat: 32-50-58 N **Long:** 11-64-12 W

In southwestern CA, 33 mi. northeast of San Diego. Total area 3 sq. mi. Established Dec 27, 1875; a portion restored to public domain May 3, 1877.

Name origin: Spanish 'old women.' According to legend the name was given by the Spanish to the Indian village because the braves fled at their approach, leaving only the old women.

Waccamaw Siouan TDSA
Tribe: Waccamaw Sioux **Status:** State
HQ: NC **Area Code:** 919
County: Columbus
Pop: 1,226: AmInd; 2,667: total

In southeastern NC, west of Wilmington; total area 63 sq. mi.

Walker River Reservation
Tribe: Paiute Tribe **Status:** Federal
HQ: Schurz, NV **Area Code:** 702
County: Churchill, Lyon, Mineral
Pop: 620: AmInd; 802: total
Lat: 38-58-00 N **Long:** 11-84-20 W

In southwestern NV, 100 mi. southeast of Reno. Total area 534 sq. mi. Established Mar 19, 1874.

Name origin: Named by John C. Frémont (1813–90) for Joseph Reddeford Walker (1798–1876), a celebrated leader and guide.

Wampanoag-Gay Head TDSA
HQ: MA **Status:** Federal
County: Dukes **Area Code:** 508
Pop: 253: AmInd; 11,639: total

On Martha's Vineyard, off southeastern coast of MA; total area 104 sq. mi.

Warm Springs Reservation & Trust Lands
Tribe: various **Status:** Federal
HQ: Warm Springs, OR **Area Code:** 503
County: parts of 4 counties
Pop: 2,820: AmInd; 3,076: total
Lat: 44-51-00 N **Long:** 12-12-40 W

In northwest OR, 60 mi. north of Bend, in Jefferson, Wasco, Marion, and Clackamas counties. Total area 1019 sq. mi. Established c.1854 for the Warm Springs, Northern Paiute, and Wasco Confederated tribes.

Washoe Reservation
Tribe: Washoe, Paiute, and Shoshone **Status:** Federal
HQ: NV **Area Code:** 702
County: Douglas
Pop: 65: AmInd; 157: total
Lat: 38-54-00 N **Long:** 11-94-23 W

On central western border with CA, south of Minden. Total area 5 sq. mi.

Name origin: For the *Washo* or *Washiu* tribe. Their name has been translated as 'person,' 'tall bunch grass,' and 'rye grass.' The first seems most probable.

White Earth Reservation
Tribe: Chippewa Tribe **Status:** Federal
HQ: MN **Area Code:** 218
County: Mahnomen, Becker, Clearwater
Pop: 2,759: AmInd; 8,727: total

In west-central MN, west of Bemidji. Total area 1088 sq. mi. The reservation, established on March 19, 1867, is part of their traditional lands; the county is wholly within it.

Name origin: For the lake, for the white clay that crops up along the shore.

Wind River Reservation
Tribe: Shoshone and Arapahoe Tribes **Status:** Federal
HQ: Riverton, WY **Area Code:** 307
County: Fremont, Hot Springs
Pop: 5,676: AmInd; 21,851: total
Lat: 43-17-00 N **Long:** 10-85-00 W

In west-central WY, southeast of Yellowstone National Park. Total area 3471 sq. mi. Established 1863.

Name origin: *Arapaho* probably from a Pawnee word *tirapihu* 'trader'; 'blue-sky men' and 'cloud men' have also been suggested but are undocumented.

Winnebago Reservation
Tribe: Winnebago Tribe **Status:** Federal
HQ: Winnebago, NE **Area Code:** 402
County: Thurston, Dixon
Pop: 1,156: AmInd; 2,341: total
Lat: 42-14-00 N **Long:** 09-63-40 W

On northeastern border of NE, south of Sioux City, IA. Total area 173 sq. mi. Established Mar 6, 1865.

Name origin: *Winnebago* thought to mean 'fish eaters'; an Indian tribe of Siouan linguistic stock.

Winnemuca Colony
Tribe: Paiute Tribe **Status:** Federal
HQ: Winnemucca, NV **Area Code:** 702
County: Humboldt
Pop: 61: AmInd; 67: total
Lat: 40-57-20 N **Long:** 11-74-32 W

In northern NV, 1 mi. from Winnemucca. Total area 1 sq. mi. Established 1917 for homeless Shoshone Indians. Act of May 21, 1928, authorized purchase of land near Winnemucca for an Indian colony, but did not specify a tribe.

Name origin: For a hereditary name of Paiute chiefs; meaning is in dispute: possibly 'one moccasin,' 'the charitable man,' 'the bread giver,' 'place by the river.'

Wisconsin Winnebago Res. & Trust Lands
Tribe: Winnebago **Status:** Federal
HQ: Wisconsin Dells, WI **Area Code:** 715
County: parts of 10 counties
Pop: 570: AmInd; 700: total

In central and western WI, in Shawano, Marathon, Clark, Wood, Adams, Juneau, Monroe, Jackson, LaCrosse, and Crawford counties. Total area 4116.62 acres. The most concentrated period of land transfer to tribe members was between 1825 and 1837.

Name origin: For the Indian tribe of Siouan linguistic stock. Name is thought to mean 'fish eaters.'

Woodfords Community
Tribe: Washoe **Status:** Federal
HQ: CA **Area Code:** 702
County: Alpine
Pop: 0: AmInd; 14: total

In eastern CA, northeast of Sacramento. Total area 0.6 sq. mi.

Name origin: For Daniel Woodford, owner of a sawmill. Previously called *Carey's Mill* for the original owner.

XL Ranch Reservation
Tribe: Pit River-Paiute Tribe **Status:** Federal
HQ: Alturas, CA **Area Code:** 916
County: Modoc
Pop: 27: AmInd; 35: total
Lat: 41-47-51 N **Long:** 12-01-84 W

In northeastern CA near Goose Lake. Total area 14 sq. mi. Established Oct 13, 1938.

Yakima Reservation and Trust Lands
Tribe: Fourteen Confederated Tribes of the Yakima Nation **Status:** Federal
HQ: Toppenish, WA **Area Code:** 509
County: Klickitat, Yakima
Pop: 6,307: AmInd; 27,668: total
Lat: 46-09-00 N **Long:** 12-00-20 W

In south-central WA, 4 mi. south of Yakima. Total area 2138 sq. mi. Established Apr 18, 1859, for 14 tribes and named for the largest tribe there at the time.

Name origin: Indian tribe belonging to the Shahaptian branch of the Shapwailutan linguistic stock. Name believed to mean 'runaway,' but connotation is unclear.

Yankton Reservation
Tribe: Yankton Sioux
HQ: Wagner, SD
County: Charles Mix
Pop: 1,994: AmInd; 6,269: total
Status: Federal
Area Code: 605

In southern SD, 45 mi. northwest of Yankton. Total area 666 sq. mi. Established 1853.
Name origin: An Indian tribe of Siouan linguistic stock. The name is from Siouan *ihanktonwan* 'end village,' probably a site designation.

Yavapai Prescott Reservation
Tribe: Yavapai Tribe
HQ: Prescott, AZ
County: Yavapai
Pop: 134: AmInd; 176: total
Lat: 34-33-30 N **Long:** 11-22-64 W
Status: Federal
Area Code: 602

In west-central AZ one mile from Prescott. Total area 2 sq. mi. Established 75 acres in 1935; in May 1965, 1,298 acres added.
Name origin: Yavapai tribe of Yuman linguistic stock. Name variously defined 'sun people' *enyaeva* 'sun' and *pai* 'people'; 'hill country' *yava* 'hill' and Spanish *país* 'country'; also 'crooked-mouth (surly) people.' First meaning seems most probable.

Yerington Reservation & Trust Lands
Tribe: Paiute Tribe
HQ: Campbell Ranch, NV
County: Lyon
Pop: 324: AmInd; 428: total
Lat: 39-04-45 N **Long:** 11-91-23 W
Status: Federal
Area Code: 702

In southwestern NV, 82 mi. southeast of Reno. Total area 3 sq. mi. Land purchased for the reservation in 1936 and 1941. Land within the city limits of Yerington was purchased for non-reservation Indians in 1917.
Name origin: For the town named for Henry Marvin Yerington, a railroad official.

Yomba Reservation
Tribe: Shoshone Tribe
HQ: Austin, NV
County: Nye
Pop: 88: AmInd; 95: total
Lat: 39-05-46 N **Long:** 11-72-32 W
Status: Federal
Area Code: 702

In central NV, 180 mi. east of Reno. Total area 7 sq. mi. Land purchased 1937.

Ysleta del Sur Pueblo
Tribe: Southern Pueblos
HQ: TX
County: El Paso
Pop: 211: AmInd; 292: total
Status: Federal
Area Code: 505

On western border of TX with Mexico, near El Paso; total area 0.2 sq. mi.
Name origin: Spanish 'little southern island'; reason for name unknown.

Yurok (formerly Hoopa Valley Extension)
Tribe: Yurok Tribe
HQ: Hoopa, CA
County: Humboldt, Del Norte
Pop: 463: AmInd; 1,357: total
Status: Federal
Area Code: 707

In northwestern CA. Total area 85 sq. mi. Established Oct 16, 1891, adding the Klamath strip, a one-mile-wide tract of land on each side of the Klamath River, from the Hoopa Valley Reservation to the Pacific Ocean.

Zia Pueblo & Trust Lands
Tribe: Keresan Tribe
HQ: Zia Pueblo, NM
County: Sandoval
Pop: 637: AmInd; 637: total
Status: Federal
Area Code: 505

In north-central AZ, 40 mi. north of Albuquerque. Total area 190 sq. mi. Spanish grant confirmed by U.S. Congress in 1858; enlarged to present size by purchase and grant.
Name origin: From *Tsia*, Keresan name for the pueblo.

Zuni Pueblo
Tribe: Zuni Tribe
HQ: Zuni, NM
County: parts of 3 counties in NM, Apache, AZ
Pop: 7,073: AmInd; 7,412: total
Status: Federal
Area Code: 505

On western border of AZ, 40 mi. south of Gallup, in Catron, Cibola, and McKinley counties, and in Apache County, AZ. Total area 654 sq. mi., of which 637 are in NM and 18 in AZ.
Name origin: Spanish approximation of Keresan *sunyi'tsi* or *su'nyitsa*, meaning unknown.

Military Bases

Listed below are more than 150 of the major military bases in the U.S., excluding those whose closure was announced in 1993.

Aberdeen Proving Ground
Branch: Army
Aberdeen, MD, 21005 **County:** Harford
Size: 72518 acres
Agency: 6,680 (Active); 3,847 (Dependents); 8,260 (Civilians)
Name origin: In north-central MD, 25 miles northeast of Baltimore; U.S. Army Test and Evaluation Command; U.S. Army Ordnance Center & School.

Adak Naval Air Station
Branch: Navy
Box 2, Navsta, Adak, AK, 98791 **County:** Aleutian Islands
Size: 52,180 acres
Agency: 1,470 (Active); 1,500 (Dependents); 193 (Civilians)
Name origin: On Adak Island in the Andreanof Islands of the Aleutian Chain. About 1200 mi. from Anchorage; 2000 mi. from Tokyo and Seattle. Provides base for ships and patrol aircraft operating in North Pacific; fleet communications and oceanographic research.

Alameda Coast Guard Island
Branch: Coast Guard
Alameda, CA, 94501-5100 **County:** Alameda
Size: 43 acres **Lat:** 37-46-56 N **Long:** 12-21-45 W
Agency: 600 (Active); 300 (Civilians)
Name origin: In middle of the Oakland Estuary between Alameda and Oakland, CA. Coast Guard Pacific Area Headquarters.

Andrews Air Force Base
Branch: Air Force
Camp Springs, MD, 20331 **County:** Prince George's
Size: 7507 acres **Lat:** 38-48-22 N **Long:** 07-65-25 W
Agency: 7,480 (Active); 3,240 (Civilians)
Name origin: For Lt. Gen. Frank M. Andrews (1884–1943), European commander of operations for Army Air Forces, WWII. About 12 mi. east of Washington, DC; 89th Military Airlift Wing; home of Continental Air Command, SAC, and MATS and AF Systems Command; main port of entry for foreign military and government officials; established in July 1961 as the home of the official presidential aircraft, *Air Force One*.

Bangor Naval Submarine Base
Branch: Navy
Bremerton, WA, 98315-5000 **County:** Kitsap
Size: 6691 acres
Agency: 5,320 (Active); 2,157 (Dependents); 1,750 (Civilians)
Name origin: On the Hood Canal, near Seattle/Tacoma; submarine base; Trident Training and Refit Facilities; homeport for OHIO-class submarine.

Barksdale Air Force Base
Branch: Air Force
Bossier City, LA, 71110 **County:** Bossier
Size: 22,382 acres **Lat:** 32-30-11 N **Long:** 09-34-04 W
Agency: 6,090 (Active); 7,873 (Dependents); 1,160 (Civilians)
Name origin: For Lt. Eugene H. Barksdale, killed in test flight, 1926. In northwestern LA, 4 mi. east of Shreveport; 2nd Bombardment Wing; headquarters, 8th Air Force; Strategic Air Command NCO Academy.

Beale Air Force Base
Branch: Air Force
9th SRW, Marysville, CA, 95903-5000 **County:** Nevada, Yuba
Size: 23,000 acres **Lat:** 39-05-58 N **Long:** 12-12-40 W
Agency: 4,010 (Active); 5,531 (Dependents); 470 (Civilians)
Name origin: For founder of U.S. Camel Corps, Edward Fitzgerald Beale, minister to Austria. About 40 mi. north of Sacramento; 9th Strategic Reconaissance Wing.

Bolling Air Force Base
Branch: Air Force
Washington, DC, 20332 **County:** District of Columbia
Size: 611 acres **Lat:** 38-50-28 N **Long:** 07-70-05 W
Agency: 3,330 (Active); 1,170 (Civilians)
Name origin: For Col. Raynal C. Bollings, first high-ranking Air Service officer killed in WWI. In southwestern D.C., on the east side of the Potomac River; administrative and technological center of Air Force in Washington, D.C.

Buckley Air National Guard Base
Branch: Air National Guard
18500 E. 6th Ave, Aurora, CO, 80011-9599 **County:** Arapahoe
Size: 7113 acres **Lat:** 39-43-03 N **Long:** 10-44-61 W
Agency: 630 (Active); 650 (Civilians)
Name origin: For 1st Lt. John H. Buckley, WWI pilot killed in Meuse-Argonne offensive. seven mi. east of Denver; 140th Tactical Fighter Wing (Air National Guard).

Camp Grayling Army & Air National Guard Training Center
Branch: Air National Guard; Army National Guard
Camp Grayling, Grayling, MI, 49739-0001 **County:** Crawford
Size: 147,000 acres **Lat:** 44-43-52 N **Long:** 08-43-34 W
Agency: 36 (Active); 140 (Civilians)
Name origin: In north-central MI, 200 miles northwest of Detroit; largest National Guard training center in U.S.

Camp H. M. Smith
Branch: Marines
Headquarters, Fleet Marine Force, Pacific (FMFPac), Honolulu, HI, 96861-5001 **County:** Honolulu
Size: 420 acres
Agency: 1,900 (Active); 4,865 (Dependents); 20 (Civilians)
Name origin: For Lt. Gen. Holland M. "Hollin' Mad" Smith (1882–1967), pioneer of amphibious warfare techniques and first commander of the camp. Northwest of Honolulu; nerve center of all U.S. military forces in region.

Camp Lejeune Marine Corps Base
Branch: Marines
Jacksonville, NC, 28542 **County:** Onslow
Size: 88,432 acres
Agency: 37,620 (Active); 12,000 (Dependents); 2,080 (Civilians)
Name origin: For Lt. Gen. John A. Lejeune (1867–1942), 13th Commandant of Marine Corps. In southeastern NC, southeast of Jacksonville; amphibious training base; operating seaport.

Camp Pendleton Marine Corps Base
Branch: Marines
Oceanside, CA, 92055-5001 **County:** San Diego
Size: 186,140 acres
Agency: 46,220 (Active); 12,700 (Dependents); 1,550 (Civilians)
Name origin: For Gen. Joseph H. Pendleton, Corps veteran. Thirty-five mi. north of San Diego; world's second largest Marine installation (see Twentynine Palms MCB).

Cannon Air Force Base
Branch: Air Force
Clovis, NM, 88101 **County:** Curry
Size: 26,638 acres **Lat:** 34-23-31 N **Long:** 10-31-91 W
Agency: 4,260 (Active); 450 (Civilians)
Name origin: For Gen. John K. Cannon, former commander of TAC. Previously named Clovis Army Air Base. On central eastern border of NM, southwest of Clovis; 27th Tactical Fighter Wing.

Carlisle Barracks
Branch: Army
Carlisle, PA, 17013 **County:** Cumberland
Size: 403 acres **Lat:** 40-12-42 N **Long:** 07-71-01 W
Agency: 600 (Active); 880 (Civilians)
Name origin: In south-central PA, southwest of Harrisburg; U.S. Army War College.

Carswell Air Force Base
Branch: Air Force
Fort Worth, TX, 76127 **County:** Tarrant
Size: 3426 acres **Lat:** 32-46-17 N **Long:** 09-72-51 W
Agency: 4,740 (Active); 1,131 (Dependents); 810 (Civilians)
Name origin: For Maj. Horace S. Carswell, Jr., WWII hero from Ft. Worth. In north-central TX; 7th Bombardment Wing (SAC). Only AFB to have namesake interred on base.

Castle Air Force Base
Branch: Air Force
93rd Bombardment Wing, Merced, CA, 95342 **County:** Merced
Size: 3257 acres **Lat:** 37-21-54 N **Long:** 12-03-40 W
Agency: 4,940 (Active); 2,412 (Dependents); 410 (Civilians)
Name origin: For Brig. Gen. Frederick W. Castle, killed in action, 1944. In central CA, 7 mi. northwest of Merced; 93rd Bomb Wing.

Chanute Air Force Base
Branch: Air Force
Rantoul, IL, 61868-5000 **County:** Champaign
Size: 2174 acres
Agency: 2,360 (Active); 6,448 (Dependents); 1,030 (Civilians)
Name origin: Probably for Octave Chanute (1832–1910), pioneer exponent of heavier-than-air flight, nicknamed the "Father of Aviation." At Rantoul, IL, about 20 miles north of Champaign-Urbana, IL. Third oldest AFB in U.S. and oldest technical training center, May 1917.

Charleston Air Force Base
Branch: Air Force
Charleston, SC, 29404 **County:** Charleston
Size: 6232 acres **Lat:** 32-54-03 N **Long:** 08-00-32 W
Agency: 4,320 (Active); 5,289 (Dependents); 1,230 (Civilians)
Name origin: In southeastern SC, 10 mi. northwest of Charleston; 437th Military Airlift Wing.

Charleston Naval Base
Branch: Navy
Charleston, SC, 29408 **County:** Charleston
Size: 20,500 acres
Agency: 26,140 (Active); 30,000 (Dependents); 15,000 (Civilians)
Name origin: In southeastern SC, on the Cooper River, 6 mi. north of Charleston; Naval Base Headquarters; Charleston Naval Shipyard; Naval Weapons Station. Closure of shipyard and naval station announced in 1993.

Cheyenne Mountain Complex
Branch: Joint Service Installation; Dual-Nation (US-Can)
Cheyenne Mtn Support Group Stop #4, Colorado Springs, CO, 80914 **County:** El Paso
Size: 520 acres
Agency: 1,540 (Active); 350 (Civilians)
Name origin: About 6 mi. from Colorado Springs; communications command and control.

Coast Guard Communication Area Master Station
Branch: Coast Guard
P.O. Box 5601700 Sir Francis Drake Blvd, Point Reyes Station, CA, 94956-0560 **County:** Marin
Size: 266 acres **Lat:** 37-54-22 N **Long:** 12-24-05 W
Agency: 90 (Active)

Columbus Air Force Base
Branch: Air Force
Columbus, MS, 39701 **County:** Lowndes
Size: 5467 acres **Lat:** 33-38-34 N **Long:** 08-82-70 W
Agency: 1,420 (Active); 390 (Civilians)
Name origin: In east-central MS, 10 mi. north of Columbus; 14th Flying Training Wing.

Davis-Monthan Air Force Base
Branch: Air Force
Tucson, AZ, 85707 **County:** Pima
Size: 11,651 acres **Lat:** 32-09-58 N **Long:** 11-05-25 W
Agency: 4,320 (Active); 3,055 (Dependents); 1,370 (Civilians)
Name origin: For two Air Corps officers, Lt. Samuel H. Davis, who died in an air crash at Carlstrom Field, FL, 1921; and Lt. Oscar Monthan, who died in a crash near Honolulu, HI, 1924. In Tucson; 836th Air Division; Aerospace Maintenance and Regeneration Center; storage yard for U.S. military aircraft.

Detroit Arsenal
Branch: Army
Warren, MI, 48397 **County:** Macomb
Size: 261 acres
Agency: 310 (Active); 5,730 (Civilians)
Name origin: In southeastern MI, north of Detroit; research and development; tank production.

Dobbins Air Force Base
Branch: Air Force; Air National Guard
HQ 94 Tactical Airlift Wing, Marietta, GA, 30060 **County:** Cobb
Size: 1900 acres **Lat:** 33-54-58 N **Long:** 08-43-03 W
Agency: 100 (Active); 620 (Civilians)
Name origin: For Capt. Charles Dobbins, flyer from Marietta, GA, killed 1943. Formerly Rickenbacker Field, named for the WWI flying ace. Sixteen miles northwest of Atlanta; 94 Tactical Airlift Wing and busiest Air Reserve training base in world.

Dover Air Force Base
Branch: Air Force
HQ 436th Military Airlift Wing, Dover, DE, 19901 **County:** Kent
Size: 3735 acres **Lat:** 39-07-36 N **Long:** 07-52-75 W
Agency: 4,780 (Active); 1,390 (Civilians)
Name origin: A few miles south of Dover; 436th Military Airlift Wing; site for development of air-launched rockets; strategic airlift base.

Dyess Air Force Base
Branch: Air Force
Abilene, TX, 79607-5000 **County:** Taylor
Size: 6434 acres **Lat:** 32-25-20 N **Long:** 09-95-02 W
Agency: 5,223 (Active); 7,606 (Dependents); 440 (Civilians)
Name origin: For LTC William Edwin Dyess. In north-central TX, on the west side of Abilene; 96th Bombardment Wing (SAC).

Edwards Air Force Base
Branch: Air Force
Rosamond, CA, 93523 **County:** Kern, San Bernardino
Size: 307,970 acres **Lat:** 34-55-18 N **Long:** 11-75-30 W
Agency: 4,650 (Active); 6,100 (Dependents); 2,540 (Civilians)
Name origin: For Capt. Glen W. Edwards, of Lincoln, CA, killed during performance test of YB-49, the Flying Wing. In southwest CA on the western edge of the Mojave Desert about 100 mi. northeast of Los Angeles. Air Force Flight Test Center. Prime landing site for all space shuttle flights.

Eglin Air Force Base
Branch: Air Force
Valparaiso, FL, 32542 **County:** Okalossa, Walton, Santa Rosa
Size: 455,817 acres **Lat:** 30-28-59 N **Long:** 08-63-01 W
Agency: 8,700 (Active); 13,600 (Dependents); 3,920 (Civilians)
Name origin: For LTC Frederick I. Eglin, US Air Corps. On the southern coast of the FL panhandle, east of Pensacola; pioneer in missile and armament development and testing; one of four Vietnamese Refugee Processing Centers; Processing Center for Cuban refugees.

El Centro Naval Air Facility
Branch: Navy
El Centro, CA, 92243-5001 **County:** Imperial
Size: 63,137 acres
Agency: 270 (Active); 80 (Civilians)
Name origin: 120 mi. east of San Diego; Fleet Air Training Support. Much of film 'Top Gun' shot here in 1986. Winter home of the Blue Angels Air Demonstration Team.

Ellsworth Air Force Base
Branch: Air Force
Box Elder, SD, 57706-5000 **County:** Meade, Pennington
Size: 25,494 acres **Lat:** 44-08-50 N **Long:** 10-30-54 W
Agency: 6,840 (Active); 5,000 (Dependents); 610 (Civilians)
Name origin: Renamed in 1953 by President Dwight D. Eisenhower (1890–1969) in honor of Brig. Gen. Richard E. Ellsworth, killed in RB-36 crash. Formerly called Rapid City Army Air Force Base; Weaver Air Force Base. In southeast SD, 12 mi. east of Rapid City; 44th Strategic Missile Wing; 28th Bombardment Wing.

Elmendorf Air Force Base
Branch: Air Force
Anchorage, AK, 99506-5000 **County:** Anchorage
Size: 13,166 acres **Lat:** 61-15-05 N **Long:** 14-94-74 W
Agency: 6,460 (Active); 5,500 (Dependents); 1,030 (Civilians)
Name origin: For Capt. Hugh M. Elmendorf, test pilot killed when flying new pursuit plane at Wright Field, OH, 1933. On the north edge of Anchorage; headquarters, Alaskan Air Command; 21st Tactical Air Command Fighter Wing.

El Toro Marine Corps Air Station
Branch: Marines
Irvine, CA, 92709 **County:** Orange
Size: 5220 acres **Lat:** 33-40-19 N **Long:** 11-74-33 W
Agency: 6,450 (Active); 2,989 (Dependents); 860 (Civilians)
Name origin: Between Irvine and El Toro; hdq. 3rd Marine Air Wing; jet training. First point of arrival for 50,000 Vietnamese refugees in 1975.

Fallon Naval Air Station
Branch: Navy
Fallon, NV, 89406 **County:** Churchill
Size: 141,059 acres
Agency: 870 (Active); 260 (Civilians)
Name origin: In west-central NV, 65 mi. east of Reno; Naval Strike Warfare Center; attack aircraft training.

Fleet Combat Training Center
Branch: Navy
Virginia Beach, VA, 23461-5200 **County:** Virginia Beach (city)
Size: 1038 acres
Agency: 5,660 (Active); 630 (Civilians)
Name origin: On the southeastern coast of VA, about 5 miles south of Virginia Beach; Fleet Combat Training Center, Atlantic; Naval Guided Missiles School.

Fort Belvoir
Branch: Army
Alexandria, VA, 22060 **County:** Alexandria (city)
Size: 8656 acres
Agency: 4,950 (Active); 6,490 (Civilians)
Name origin: In northeastern VA, bordering Alexandria; U.S. Army Engineer Center and School.

Fort Benjamin Harrison
Branch: Army
Indianapolis, IN, 46216 **County:** Marion
Size: 2501 acres **Lat:** 39-51-37 N **Long:** 08-60-03 W
Agency: 4,290 (Active); 4,570 (Civilians)
Name origin: For the twenty-third U.S. president (1833–1901). In central IN, northeast of Indianapolis; Army personnel center; Defense Information School.

Fort Benning
Branch: Army
HQ, US Army Infantry Center, Columbus, GA,
31905 **County:** Chattahoochee, Muscogee
Size: 169,285 acres
Agency: 25,280 (Active); 11,339 (Dependents); 4,710 (Civilians)
Name origin: For Confederazte Maj. Gen. Henry Lewis Benning. Less than 1 mi. south of Columbus, GA; 'Home of the Infantry'; HQ, US Army Infantry Center and School.

Fort Bliss
Branch: Army
El Paso, TX, 79916 **County:** El Paso
Size: 118,218 acres
Agency: 17,480 (Active); 9,143 (Dependents); 4,640 (Civilians)
Name origin: For Lt. Col. William Bliss, a son-in-law of President Zachary Taylor (1784–1850). In northwestern TX; U.S. Army Air Defense Center and School.

Fort Bragg
Branch: Army
Fayetteville, NC, 28307 **County:** Moore, Hoke
Size: 130,696 acres **Lat:** 35-08-58 N **Long:** 07-85-90 W
Agency: 42,880 (Active); 11,318 (Dependents); 4,430 (Civilians)
Name origin: For Confederate Gen. Braxton Bragg (1817–76), artillery officer from NC. In south-central NC, about 10 mi. west of Fayetteville; 82nd Airborne Division; John F. Kennedy Special Warfare Center and School; U.S. Army Parachute Team (Golden Knights); headquarters for special forces; Fort Bragg and neighboring Pope AFB form one of world's largest military complexes.

Fort Campbell (KY)
Branch: Army
Clarksville, TN, 42223-5000 **County:** Christian, Trigg
Size: 105,397 acres **Lat:** 36-38-19 N **Long:** 08-72-65 W
Agency: 22,760 (Active); 27,800 (Dependents); 2,560 (Civilians)
Name origin: For William Campbell, army veteran of Seminole, FL and Mexican Wars, and governor of TN. On the KY-TN border, about 60 miles northwest of Nashville, TN. 101st Airborne Division, the 'Screaming Eagles.'

Fort Carson
Branch: Army
Colorado Springs, CO, 80913-5000
Size: 137,391 acres **Lat:** 38-43-54 N **Long:** 10-44-74 W
Agency: 15,940 (Active); 6,396 (Dependents); 2,150 (Civilians)
Name origin: For Brig. Gen. Christopher ("Kit") Carson (1809–68), American frontiersman. Bordering the south side of Colorado Springs; 4th Infantry Division (Mechanized).

Fort Detrick
Branch: Army
Frederick, MD, 21701-5000 **County:** Frederick
Size: 1151 acres **Lat:** 39-26-07 N **Long:** 07-72-54 W
Agency: 850 (Active); 381 (Dependents); 3,000 (Civilians)
Name origin: For Maj. Frederick L. Detrick, Army medical officer. In north-central MD; research and development; Army Medical Department's leading microbiological containment research campus.

Fort Devens
Branch: Army
P.O. Box 3, Ayer, MA, 01433-5030 **County:** Worcester, Middlesex
Size: 9380 acres
Agency: 5,980 (Active); 6,404 (Dependents); 1,910 (Civilians)
Name origin: For Maj. Gen. Charles Devens, Union Army general and attorney general under Pres. Rutherford B. Hayes (1822–93). In northeastern MA, 35 mi. northwest of Boston; U.S. Army Intelligence School; 10th Special Forces.

Fort Dix
Branch: Army
US Army Training Center & Fort Dix, Trenton, NJ,
08640-5000 **County:** Burlington, Ocean
Size: 31,110 acres **Lat:** 39-59-36 N **Long:** 07-43-80 W
Agency: 11,950 (Active); 6,800 (Dependents); 2,140 (Civilians)
Name origin: For Maj. Gen. John Adams Dix, 19th-century soldier-statesman. In west-central NJ, 25 mi. southeast of Trenton; U.S. Army Training Center; largest military installation in northeast.

Fort Drum
Branch: Army
Watertown, NY, 13602-5000 **County:** Jefferson
Size: 107,265 acres
Agency: 10,940 (Active); 1,850 (Civilians)
Name origin: For Lt. Gen. Hugh A. Drum, Commander of First U.S. Army during early years of WWII. In northwestern NY, about 75 mi. north of Syracuse; Reserve Corps and Active Army Training.

Fort Eustis
Branch: Army
Newport News, VA, 23604　　**County:** Newport News (city)
Size: 8323 acres　　**Lat:** 37-09-39 N　**Long:** 07-63-45 W
Agency: 8,590 (Active); 3,180 (Civilians)

Name origin: For Brevet Brig. Gen. Abraham Eustis, artillery officer. In southeastern VA, on the west side of Newport News on Mulberry Island. U.S. Army Transportation Center and School; U.S. Army Aviation Logistics School; NCO Academy; Joint Strategic Deployment Training Center; National Oceanic and Atmospheric Administration Officer Training Center.

Fort George G. Meade
Branch: Air Force; Army; Marines; Navy
Baltimore, MD, 20755-5000　　**County:** Anne Arundel
Size: 13,457 acres　　**Lat:** 39-06-30 N　**Long:** 07-64-33 W
Agency: 7,680 (Active); 26,460 (Civilians)

Name origin: For Maj. Gen. George Gordon Meade (1815-72), Civil War general. In west-central MD, midway between Baltimore and Washington, DC. Headquarters Command Battalion; headquarters, First U.S. Army; command and supervision of all Reserve units and Army NG in First U.S. Army area.

Fort Gordon
Branch: Army
US Army Signal Center, Fort Gordon, Augusta, GA,
30905-5000　　**County:** Jefferson, Columbia, R
Size: 55,588 acres
Agency: 12,430 (Active); 27,464 (Dependents); 3,130 (Civilians)

Name origin: For Confederate Lt. Gen. John Brown Gordon (1832-1904). Fifteen mi. southwest of Augusta, GA; signal center and school; world's largest communications electronics facility.

Fort Hood
Branch: Army
Killeen, TX, 76544　　**County:** Coryell, Bell
Size: 216,946 acres　　**Lat:** 31-08-18 N　**Long:** 09-74-61 W
Agency: 40,160 (Active); 14,642 (Dependents); 4,000 (Civilians)

Name origin: For Confederate Gen. John Bell Hood (1831-79), Civil War commander of Hood's Texas Brigade. In central TX, about 60 mi. north of Austin; 1st Cavalry Div.; 2nd Armored Div.; largest U.S. military base.

Fort Huachuca
Branch: Army
Commander, ATTN: AS-PI, Sierra Vista, AZ, 85613-5000　　**County:** Cochise
Size: 73,517 acres　　**Lat:** 31-33-11 N　**Long:** 11-02-05 W
Agency: 6,610 (Active); 4,826 (Dependents); 3,940 (Civilians)

Name origin: For a Pima Indian village; meaning unknown. Seventy mi. southeast of Tucson. Communications Command and Intelligence School; in 1886 was General Nelson A. Miles' (1839-1925) headquarters and forward supply base for campaign against Geronimo (1829-1909) and the Apaches.

Fort Irwin, National Training Center
Branch: Army
Ft. Irwin, CA, 92310　　**County:** San Bernardino
Size: 640,000 acres
Agency: 4,387 (Active); 5,326 (Dependents); 2,414 (Civilians)

Name origin: For Maj. Gen. George Leroy Irwin, commander of 57th Field Artillery Brigade in WWI. In south-central CA, in the Mojave Desert, 38 mi. northeast of Barstow; training center for all Army line units.

Fort Jackson
Branch: Army
Columbia, SC, 29207　　**County:** Richland
Size: 52,537 acres
Agency: 15,110 (Active); 3,050 (Dependents); 2,250 (Civilians)

Name origin: For Andrew Jackson (1767-1845), seventh U.S. president. In central SC, west of Columbia; U.S. Army Training Center. In 1917, first all-black regiment of WWI, 1st provisional Infantry Regiment (Colored) organized. Birthplace of Army unit patch, beginning with 81st 'Wildcat' Division. WWII 'Old Hickory' Division trained. 1974, first all female brigade, 5th Basic Training Brigade established.

Fort Knox
Branch: Army
Louisville, KY, 40121-5000　**County:** Hardin, Bullitt, Meade
Size: 109,220 acres
Agency: 19,500 (Active); 5,000 (Dependents); 4,300 (Civilians)

Name origin: For Gen. Henry Knox (1750-1806), Chief of Artillery during the American Revolution, and first secretary of war. In north-central KY, southeast of Louisville; Army training center; U.S. Bullion Depository; home of Armor and Cavalry. During WWII stored the Constitution, Bill of Rights, Declaration of Independence, British crown jewels, Magna Carta, and the gold reserves of several occupied European nations.

Fort Leavenworth
Branch: Army
Leavenworth, KS, 66027　　**County:** Leavenworth
Size: 6995 acres
Agency: 4,500 (Active); 7,000 (Dependents); 2,290 (Civilians)

Name origin: For Henry Leavenworth (1783-1834), Army general who fought in the War of 1812 and later against the Indians. In northeastern KS, northwest of Kansas City; Command and General Staff College. Tom Custer, brother of George A. Custer (1839-76), and the first man to earn two Medals of Honor, is buried in the National Cemetery here.

Fort Leonard Wood
Branch: Army
Jefferson City, MO, 65473-5000　　**County:** Pulaski
Size: 62,910 acres　　**Lat:** 37-44-02 N　**Long:** 09-20-83 W
Agency: 16,640 (Active); 7,158 (Dependents); 4,570 (Civilians)

Name origin: For Maj. Gen. Leonard Wood (1860-1927), Army surgeon, Rough Rider, Medal of Honor recipient, and Military Governor of Cuba and the Philippines. In central eastern MO, 125 mi. southwest of St. Louis; U.S. Army Training Center, Engineer.

Fort Lesley J. McNair
Branch: Army
Hdq, US Mil. Dist., Wash., D.C., Washington, DC, 20319-5050 **County:** District of Columbia
Size: 89 acres **Lat:** 38-51-59 N **Long:** 07-70-10 W
Agency: 920 (Active); 63 (Dependents); 1,360 (Civilians)

Name origin: For the commander (1883–1944) of Army Ground Forces during WWII, killed at Normandy 1944. Located at the confluence of the Anacostia and Potomac rivers in the southwest part of DC. National Defense University, including National War College and Inter-American College. In continuous use as military reservation since 1794; site for first federal penitentiary in 1826; forerunner of Walter Reed Army Hospital, 1898–1909.

Fort Lewis
Branch: Army
HQ I Corps and Fort Lewis, Tacoma, WA, 98433-5000 **County:** Pierce
Size: 86,451 acres **Lat:** 47-05-25 N **Long:** 12-23-61 W
Agency: 22,090 (Active); 9,800 (Dependents); 4,140 (Civilians)

Name origin: For Meriweather Lewis (1774–1809) of the Lewis and Clark expedition. In west-central WA, 10 mi. south of Tacoma; 9th Infantry Division; Headquarters I Corps. New home (by 1994) of the 7th Infantry Division when Fort Ord (CA) is closed down.

Fort McClellan
Branch: Army
Fort McClellan, Anniston, AL, 36205-5000 **County:** Calhoun
Size: 41,640 acres
Agency: 7,980 (Active); 1,976 (Dependents); 1,450 (Civilians)

Name origin: At the north edge of Anniston; US Army Military Police School and Training Center; served as POW camp for Germans and Italians in WWII.

Fort Monmouth
Branch: Army
Red Bank, NJ, 07703 **County:** Monmouth
Size: 637 acres
Agency: 2,920 (Active); 8,360 (Civilians)

Name origin: In honor of soldiers of American Revolution who fought in nearby fields. Former names Signal Corps Camp, Little Silver; Camp Alfred Vail. In northeastern NJ, south of Perth Amboy; Research and Development Headquarters.

Fort Monroe
Branch: Army
Hampton, VA, 23651-6000 **County:** Hampton
Size: 1068 acres **Lat:** 37-00-11 N **Long:** 07-61-82 W
Agency: 2,000 (Active); 982 (Dependents); 2,710 (Civilians)

Name origin: For James Monroe (1758–1831), fifth U.S. president. On the southeastern coast of VA, northeast of Newport News. Training and Doctrine Command Headquarters; largest stone fort in U.S. Nicknamed 'Gibraltar of the Chesapeake,' one of few federal military installations in South not to fall to Confederate forces at outbreak of Civil War.

Fort Myer
Branch: Army
Post Headquarters, Bldg 59, Arlington, VA, 22211 **County:** Arlington
Size: 256 acres
Agency: 2,830 (Active); 200 (Civilians)

Name origin: For Brig. Gen. Albert J. Myer (1829–80), Army's first Chief Signal Officer and Commander during 1860s. In northeastern VA, adjacent to Arlington National Cemetery. U.S. Army Band (Pershing's Own); 3rd U.S. Infantry Regiment (The Old Guard); First military test flight of an aircraft made from parade grounds Sept. 1908 by Orville Wright (1871–1948). Since early 1900s, known as 'Home of the Generals.' Quarters Number One, official residence of Chief of Staff of Army since 1899.

Fort Ord
Branch: Army
7th Infantry Division (Light), Fort Ord, CA, 93941-5000 **County:** Monterey
Size: 28,057 acres
Agency: 20,264 (Active); 26,434 (Dependents); 3,000 (Civilians)

Name origin: For Maj. Gen. Edward Ord, commanded Union troops in Civil War. On the central CA coast, 105 mi. south of San Francisco. Designated home of 7th Infantry Division 1972. Base to be shut down by 1994 as part of military budget cut-back; 7th Division to be transferred to Fort Lewis, WA.

Fort Polk
Branch: Army
5th Infantry Division and Fort Polk, Leesville, LA, 71459-5000 **County:** Vernon
Size: 198,325 acres **Lat:** 31-02-47 N **Long:** 09-31-21 W
Agency: 15,740 (Active); 9,975 (Dependents); 2,760 (Civilians)

Name origin: For Leonidas Polk (1806–64), graduate of the U.S. Military Academy, first Episcopal bishop of LA, then Confederate general. In west-central LA, southwest of Alexandria; 5th Infantry Division (Red Devils). During Vietnam War years (1957–75), trained soldiers in basic and advanced infantry skills; has varying terrain, from jungle-type vegetation to broad, rolling plains.

Fort Riley
Branch: Army
Junction City, KS, 66442 **County:** Geary, Riley
Size: 100,980 acres
Agency: 15,710 (Active); 31,700 (Dependents); 2,270 (Civilians)

Name origin: For Gen. Bennett Riley (1787–1853), professional soldier and territorial governor of CA (1848). In east-central KS, west of Topeka; 1st Infantry Division (Mechanized), nicknamed 'Big Red One'; first division to go to Vietnam.

Fort Sam Houston
Branch: Army
San Antonio, TX, 78234-5000 **County:** Bexar
Size: 3159 acres **Lat:** 29-26-56 N **Long:** 09-82-72 W
Agency: 10,980 (Active); 3,207 (Dependents); 9,380 (Civilians)

Name origin: For the Texas patriot and statesman (1793–1863). In central TX, adjacent to downtown San Antonio; Medical Training Headquarters; HQ Fifth U.S. Army.

Fort Sill
Branch: Army
Lawton, OK, 73503-5000   **County:** Comanche
Size: 94,220 acres   **Lat:** 34-39-33 N   **Long:** 09-82-51 W
Agency: 18,790 (Active); 3,803 (Dependents); 2,950 (Civilians)
Name origin: In southwestern OK, northwest of Lawton; U.S. Army Field Artillery Training Center and School. Established in 1869 by General Phillip Sheridan (1831–88) as a frontier post for pacifying Comanche and Kiowa Indian tribes of Southern Great Plains.

Fort Stewart
Branch: Army
Fort Stewart, Hinesville, GA, 31314-5000   **County:** Liberty, Tattnall, Evans
Size: 284,369 acres
Agency: 14,560 (Active); 14,000 (Dependents); 3,760 (Civilians)
Name origin: Probably for Gen. Daniel Stewart (1759–1829), a general in the American Revolution. Forty-one mi. southwest of Savannah. 24th Infantry Division (Mechanized), and Victory Brigade, the "First to Fight"; largest Army installation east of Mississippi River.

Fort Wainwright
Branch: Army
Fairbanks, AK, 99703   **County:** Fairbanks North Star
Size: 656,250 acres
Agency: 4,860 (Active); 4,100 (Dependents); 1,008 (Civilians)
Name origin: Originally Ladd Army Airfield; renamed 1947 for Gen. Jonathan M. Wainwright (1883–1953), defender of Bataan Peninsula in WWII. About 0.25 mi. from downtown Fairbanks; 172nd Infantry Brigade. Was used as resupply base for Distant Early Warning radar sites and experimental ice stations in Arctic Ocean.

Francis E. Warren Air Force Base
Branch: Air Force
Cheyenne, WY, 82001   **County:** Laramie
Size: 33,466 acres   **Lat:** 41-08-32 N   **Long:** 10-45-15 W
Agency: 3,700 (Active); 770 (Civilians)
Name origin: For Francis E. Warren (1944–1929), first governor of WY and Congressional Medal of Honor recipient in the Civil War. Former name Fort D. A. Russell. In southeastern WY, west of Cheyenne; 90th Strategic Missile Wing.

George Air Force Base
Branch: Air Force
George AFB, CA, 92394-5000   **County:** San Bernardino
Size: 6000 acres; plus 7583 acres in Cuddeback Range   **Lat:** 34-35-13 N   **Long:** 11-72-22 W
Agency: 5,200 (Active); 6,300 (Dependents); 520 (Civilians)
Name origin: For Brig. Gen. Harold S. George, WWI fighter ace, killed in airplane crash 1942. Four and one-half mi. northeast of Victorville; began as Victorville Army Flying School.

Grand Forks Air Force Base
Branch: Air Force
Emerado, ND, 58201   **County:** Grand Forks
Size: 23,100 acres   **Lat:** 47-56-52 N   **Long:** 09-72-31 W
Agency: 5,150 (Active); 520 (Civilians)
Name origin: On the central eastern border of ND, north of Grand Forks; 321st Strategic Missile Wing; 319th Bombardment Wing.

Great Lakes Naval Training Center
Branch: Navy
Commander, NTC, Bldg. 1, Great Lakes, IL, 60088-5000   **County:** Lake
Size: 1010 acres   **Lat:** 42-18-09 N   **Long:** 08-75-20 W
Agency: 21,810 (Active); 5,500 (Dependents); 1,270 (Civilians)
Name origin: On Lake Michigan about 35 mi. north of Chicago. Navy's largest recruit and skill training facility. During WWI, Seabees originated with 12th Regiment, 'Fighting Tradesmen.'

Griffiss Air Force Base
Branch: Air Force
Rome, NY, 13440   **County:** Oneida
Size: 5444 acres
Agency: 3,940 (Active); 2,710 (Civilians)
Name origin: For Lt. Col. Townsend E. Griffiss, Army Air Force pilot, Buffalo native, and first American flyer killed in European operations of WWII. In west-central NY; 416th Bombardment Wing.

Hickam Air Force Base
Branch: Air Force
15th Air Base Wing, Honolulu, HI, 96853-5000   **County:** Honolulu
Size: 7818 acres   **Lat:** 21-20-00 N   **Long:** 15-75-70 W
Agency: 4,980 (Active); 6,813 (Dependents); 2,180 (Civilians)
Name origin: For LTC Horace Meek Hickam, killed in aircraft accident 1934. Nine mi. from downtown Honolulu; headquarters of the Pacific Air Force.

Hill Air Force Base
Branch: Air Force
Clearfield, UT, 84406   **County:** Davis
Size: 374,574 acres   **Lat:** 41-07-32 N   **Long:** 11-15-95 W
Agency: 5,000 (Active); 13,820 (Civilians)
Name origin: For Maj. Ployer P. Hill, killed while flying the original model of the B-17. In north-central UT, south of Ogden; Air Logistics Center.

Holloman Air Force Base
Branch: Air Force
Hwy 70, Alamogordo, NM, 88330-5000   **County:** Otero
Size: 50,273 acres   **Lat:** 32-50-26 N   **Long:** 10-60-43 W
Agency: 5,340 (Active); 1,107 (Civilians)
Name origin: For Col. George V. Holloman, pioneer in guided missile research. In south-central NM; 49th Tactical Fighter Wing. In 1945 first atomic bomb detonated in northwest corner of airfield's bombing range, known as Trinity Site. Since 1981, provides contingency support for Space Shuttle at White Sands Space Harbor.

Homestead Air Force Base
Branch: Air Force
Homestead AFB, Homestead, FL, 33030   **County:** Dade
Size: 3382 acres   **Lat:** 25-29-45 N   **Long:** 08-02-34 W
Agency: 4,100 (Active); 2,791 (Dependents); 1,060 (Civilians)
Name origin: About 35 mi. south of Miami; 31st Tactical Fighter Wing.

Military Bases | American Places Dictionary

Jacksonville Naval Air Station
Branch: Navy
Jacksonville, FL, 32212-5000   **County:** Duval
Size: 12,376 acres
Agency: 7,140 (Active); 5,380 (Civilians)
Name origin: About 13 mi. south of Jacksonville; patrol and anti-submarine aircraft. During WWII base had POW camp for German soldiers; in 1946 was first home of the Blue Angels, the Navy's Flight Demonstration Team.

Kaneohe Bay Marine Corps Air Station
Branch: Marines
Kailua, HI, 96863-5001
Size: 39,392 acres   **Lat:** 21-27-11 N   **Long:** 15-74-51 W
Agency: 9,780 (Active); 4,844 (Dependents); 400 (Civilians)
Name origin: 11 mi. from Honolulu on the north shore of Oahu on Mokapu Peninsula; 1st Marine Air Base; jet and helicopter training operations.

Keesler Air Force Base
Branch: Air Force
Biloxi, MS, 39534   **County:** Harrison
Size: 3600 acres   **Lat:** 30-24-27 N   **Long:** 08-85-50 W
Agency: 5,740 (Active); 2,270 (Civilians)
Name origin: For 2nd Lt. Samuel Reeves Keesler, of Greenwood, MS, killed in action in France, WWI. On the southern coast of MS; Keesler Technical Training Center. During WWII, Air-Sea Rescue School, Chemical Warfare School, first Rotary Wing School; in 1943 began training women and foreign nationals.

Kelly Air Force Base
Branch: Air Force
San Antonio, TX, 78241   **County:** Bexar
Size: 4706 acres   **Lat:** 29-23-08 N   **Long:** 09-83-42 W
Agency: 1,940 (Active); 17,340 (Civilians)
Name origin: For Lt. George E.M. Kelly, who died in WWI, the first American military pilot to be killed in a military plane crash. In south-central TX, 5 mi. southwest of downtown San Antonio; Air Logistics Center. Site of the 1926 filming of silent movie 'Wings.'; provides refueling facilities for space shuttle's 'piggy-back' mother ship.

Kirtland Air Force Base
Branch: Air Force; Army; Navy; Department of Energy
Albuquerque, NM, 87117-5000   **County:** Bernalillo
Size: 43,881 acres   **Lat:** 35-02-51 N   **Long:** 10-63-61 W
Agency: 4,910 (Active); 7,000 (Dependents); 4,880 (Civilians)
Name origin: For Col. Roy C. Kirtland, military aviation pioneer. In central NM. 1550th Combat Crew Training Wing; Sandia National Laboratories; Naval Weapons Evaluation Facility; Air Force Weapons Laboratory; Field Command, Defense Nuclear Agency; Air Force Test and Evaluation Center; Air Force Space Technology Center.

Lackland Air Force Base
Branch: Air Force
San Antonio, TX, 78236-5000   **County:** Bexar
Size: 6766 acres   **Lat:** 29-23-06 N   **Long:** 09-83-70 W
Agency: 6,430 (Active); 1,960 (Dependents); 2,660 (Civilians)
Name origin: For Brig. Gen. Frank D. Lackland, pioneer of military flying. In south-central TX, 6 mi. southwest of San Antonio, adjacent to Kelly AFB. U.S.A.F. Basic Military Training School; Defense Language Institute English Language Center; Officer Training School.

Langley Air Force Base
Branch: Air Force
Hampton, VA, 23665   **County:** Hampton (city)
Size: 3440 acres   **Lat:** 37-05-07 N   **Long:** 07-62-12 W
Agency: 9,390 (Active); 4,423 (Dependents); 1,840 (Civilians)
Name origin: For Samuel Pierpont Langley (1834–1906), pioneer in American aviation. In southeastern VA, 3 mi. north of Hampton on Virginia Peninsula. 1st Tactical Fighter Wing; Tactical Air Command Headquarters; Headquarters First Air Force; Commander-in-Chief, Atlantic Airborne Command Post.

Lemoore Naval Air Station
Branch: Navy
Lemoore, CA, 93246   **County:** Fresno, Kings
Size: 18,000 acres; 12,000 leased back to farmers
Agency: 5,717 (Active); 9,100 (Dependents); 1,200 (Civilians)
Name origin: 40 mi. south of Fresno. Primary mission to support fleet carrier squadrons and serve as master training center for carrier base light attack squadrons of U.S. Pacific Fleet.

Little Rock Air Force Base
Branch: Air Force
Jacksonville, AR, 72076   **County:** Pulaski
Size: 11548 acres   **Lat:** 34-54-29 N   **Long:** 09-20-83 W
Agency: 5,300 (Active); 3,575 (Dependents); 960 (Civilians)
Name origin: 17 mi. northeast of Little Rock; 314th Tactical Airlift Wing; Army's Joint Readiness Training Center.

Long Beach Naval Station
Branch: Navy
Long Beach, CA, 90822-5000   **County:** Los Angeles
Size: 614 acres
Agency: 17,000 (Active); 14,200 (Dependents); 2,000 (Civilians)
Name origin: 22 mi. from downtown LA. Home port for units of the Pacific Fleet.

Loring Air Force Base
Branch: Air Force
Limestone, ME, 04751   **County:** Aroostook
Size: 11,116 acres   **Lat:** 46-56-44 N   **Long:** 06-75-32 W
Agency: 3,230 (Active); 510 (Civilians)
Name origin: For Maj. Charles J. Loring, Jr., Portland native killed during Korean War. Original name Limestone AFB. On the northeastern border of VT; 42nd Bombardment Wing.

Lowry Air Force Base
Branch: Air Force
Lowry Technical Train. Center, Denver, CO, 80230-5000
Size: 5530 acres   **Lat:** 39-43-16 N   **Long:** 10-45-33 W
Agency: 3,430 (Active); 6,000 (Dependents); 4,110 (Civilians)
Name origin: For Lt. Francis Brown Lowry, Denver aviator killed in action in WWI. Five mi. east of downtown Denver; Technical Training Center. Served as President Dwight D. Eisenhower's (1890–1969) 'Summer White House 1953–55'; home to USAF Academy (1955–58).

Luke Air Force Base
Branch: Air Force
Litchfield Park, AZ, 85321 **County:** Maricopa
Size: 5396 acres **Lat:** 33-32-30 N **Long:** 11-22-23 W
Agency: 5,590 (Active); 15,000 (Dependents); 1,290 (Civilians)

Name origin: For Lt. Frank Luke, Jr., Phoenix native and WWI pilot; first aviator to receive the Medal of Honor. Twenty mi. west of Phoenix; 832nd Air Division; advanced training facility for pilots of fighter aircraft.

MacDill Air Force Base
Branch: Air Force
56th Tactical Training Wing, Tampa, FL, 33608-5000 **County:** Hillsborough
Size: 5770 acres **Lat:** 27-51-09 N **Long:** 08-22-91 W
Agency: 6,330 (Active); 12,489 (Dependents); 910 (Civilians)

Name origin: For Col. Leslie MacDill, aviation pioneer. Five mi. south of Tampa; 56th Tactical Training Wing.

Malmstrom Air Force Base
Branch: Air Force
Great Falls, MT, 59402-5000 **County:** Cascade
Size: 29,118 acres **Lat:** 47-30-45 N **Long:** 11-11-12 W
Agency: 4,300 (Active); 5,338 (Dependents); 520 (Civilians)

Name origin: For Col. Einar Axel Malmstrom, vice wing commander who died in aircrash. In west-central MT, east of Great Falls; 341st Strategic Missile Wing, nicknamed by President John F. Kennedy (1917–63) during Cuban Missile Crisis as America's "Ace in the Hole."

Marine Barracks, Washington, D.C.
Branch: Marines
8th & I Sts., SE, Washington, DC, 20390 **County:** District of Columbia
Size: 5 acres
Agency: 1,070 (Active); 40 (Civilians)

Name origin: Oldest post of Marine Corps and residence of the Commandant since 1805; home of U.S. Marine Band, 'The President's Own.'

Marine Corps Recruit Depot
Branch: Marines
Parris Island, SC, 29905-5001 **County:** Beaufort
Size: 8081 acres **Lat:** 32-20-06 N **Long:** 08-04-13 W
Agency: 7,443 (Active); 5,500 (Dependents); 281 (Civilians)

Name origin: For Alexander Parris, public treasurer of SC, who bought the island in 1715. Off the southeastern coast of SC, 5 mi. south of Beaufort. Recruit Training Regiment; 1915, male recruit training started here and continuous since. Separate battalion (now 4th Recruit Training Battalion), activated 1949 for sole purpose of training women Marine recruits. Parris Island also has Drill Instructor School.

Mather Air Force Base
Branch: Air Force
Mather AFB, CA, 95655-5000 **County:** Sacramento
Size: 5845 acres **Lat:** 38-33-25 N **Long:** 12-11-75 W
Agency: 6,183 (Active); 3,578 (Dependents); 2,094 (Civilians)

Name origin: For Lt. Carl Mather of Paw Paw, MI, killed in aircraft accident, Ellington Field, TX. Near Rancho Cordova, CA; originally called Mills Field. 323rd Flying Training Wing single supplier of DOD basic navigation training and AF advanced navigator training.

Maxwell Air Force Base
Branch: Air Force
3800th ABW, Montgomery, AL, 36112-5000 **County:** Montgomery
Size: 3541 acres **Lat:** 32-23-00 N **Long:** 08-62-13 W
Agency: 2,450 (Active); 7,400 (Dependents); 1,663 (Civilians)

Name origin: For Atmore, AL native 2nd Lt. William C. Maxwell, aircraft accident victim. In central AL, about 3 mi. north-northwest of downtown Montgomery; Headquarters AF Reserve Officer Training Corps; Air University.

Mayport Naval Station
Branch: Navy
Mayport, FL, 32228-5000 **County:** Duval
Size: 818 acres **Lat:** 30-22-39 N **Long:** 08-12-53 W
Agency: 15,970 (Active); 19,000 (Dependents); 660 (Civilians)

Name origin: At the mouth of the St. Johns River, 18 mi. east of downtown Jacksonville; operating base; served as advance staging area in Cuban Missile Crisis.

McChord Air Force Base
Branch: Air Force
Tacoma, WA, 98438 **County:** Pierce
Size: 5786 acres **Lat:** 47-08-00 N **Long:** 12-22-90 W
Agency: 4,190 (Active); 1,380 (Civilians)

Name origin: For Col. William C. McChord, killed in a bomber crash in VA in 1937. In central western WA, 3 mi. south of Tacoma; 62nd Military Airlift Wing.

McClellan Air Force Base
Branch: Air Force
Sacramento, CA, 95652-5990 **County:** Sacramento
Size: 3850 acres **Lat:** 38-39-36 N **Long:** 12-12-35 W
Agency: 3,460 (Active); 12,920 (Civilians)

Name origin: For Maj. Hezekiah McClellan, pioneer in charting Alaskan air routes. In northeastern Sacramento; one of five Air Logistics Centers.

McConnell Air Force Base
Branch: Air Force
384th BMW, Wichita, KS, 67221 **County:** Sedgwick
Size: 41,555 acres **Lat:** 37-37-35 N **Long:** 09-71-60 W
Agency: 3,160 (Active); 7,136 (Dependents); 1,270 (Civilians)

Name origin: In south-central KS, southeast of Wichita; 384th Air Refueling Wing (Heavy); host B-1B bomber.

McGuire Air Force Base
Branch: Air Force
438th Military Airlift Wing, Wrightstown, NJ, 08641-5154
Size: 6758 acres **Lat:** 40-00-56 N **Long:** 07-43-53 W
County: Burlington
Agency: 4,910 (Active); 1,980 (Civilians)

Name origin: For Maj. Thomas B. McGuire, of Ridgewood, NJ, second leading WWII flying ace. In southwestern NJ, 45 mi. northeast of Philadelphia; 438th Military Airlift Wing; largest military Airlift Command port of embarkation/debarkation on East Coast.

Memphis Naval Air Station
Branch: Navy
Millington, TN, 38054-5000 **County:** Shelby
Size: 3499 acres
Agency: 8,790 (Active); 2,800 (Dependents); 890 (Civilians)

Name origin: In southwestern TN, about 11 mi. north of Memphis; naval technical training; world's largest inland naval complex.

Meridian Naval Air Station
Branch: Navy
Meridian, MS, 39309 **County:** Lauderdale
Size: 13,507 acres **Lat:** 32-33-00 N **Long:** 08-83-40 W
Agency: 2,570 (Active); 340 (Civilians)

Name origin: In central eastern MS, northeast of Meridian; flight training.

Miami Coast Guard Air Station
Branch: Coast Guard
Opa-Locka Airport, Opa-Locka, FL, 33054
Size: 20 acres
Agency: 339 (Active); 2 (Civilians)

Name origin: World's busiest air/sea rescue unit.

Minot Air Force Base
Branch: Air Force
Minot, ND, 58701 **County:** Ward
Size: 22,731 acres
Agency: 5,370 (Active); 7,549 (Dependents); 610 (Civilians)

Name origin: In north-central ND, 13 mi. north of Minot; 91st Strategic Missile Wing (SMW); 5th Bombardment Wing.

Miramar Naval Air Station
Branch: Navy
San Diego, CA, 92145 **County:** San Diego
Size: 24,000 acres **Lat:** 32-52-08 N **Long:** 11-70-62 W
Agency: 8,930 (Active); 1,120 (Civilians)

Name origin: Ten mi. north of San Diego; home base for all Pacific Fleet fighter and airborne early warning squadrons.

Moffett Field Naval Air Station
Branch: Navy
Naval Air Station, Moffett Field, CA, 94035 **County:** Santa Clara
Size: 3920 acres
Agency: 5,120 (Active); 8,500 (Dependents); 760 (Civilians)

Name origin: For Rear Adm. William A. Moffett, killed in crash of the dirigible *Akron*. Thirty-four mi. south of San Francisco; hub of anti-submarine warfare patrol operations in Pacific and largest P-3 Orion base.

Mountain Home Air Force Base
Branch: Air Force
Mountain Home, ID, 83648 **County:** Elmore
Size: 118,579 acres **Lat:** 43-03-12 N **Long:** 11-55-14 W
Agency: 3,830 (Active); 590 (Civilians)

Name origin: In southwestern ID, about 40 mi. southeast of Boise; 366th Tactical Fighter Wing.

National Naval Medical Center
Branch: Navy
8901 Wisconsin Ave., Bethesda, MD, 20814-5000
County: Montgomery
Size: 250 acres **Lat:** 39-00-06 N **Long:** 07-70-53 W
Agency: 3,680 (Active); 2,609 (Civilians)

Name origin: Northwest of Washington, D.C. Naval Medical Command National Capital Region; Naval Hospital; Naval Health Sciences Education and Training Command; Naval Dental Clinic; Naval Medical Research Institute.

Naval Air Engineering Center
Branch: Navy
Lakehurst, NJ, 08733-5000 **County:** Ocean
Size: 7400 acres
Agency: 800 (Active); 2,610 (Civilians)

Name origin: In east-central NJ, southeast of Trenton; aircraft launch and recovery system; one of Navy's largest research, engineering, development, testing, and evaluation complexes.

Naval Air Station
Branch: Navy
Corpus Christi, TX, 78419 **County:** Nueces
Size: 4400 acres
Agency: 1,880 (Active); 4,920 (Civilians)

Name origin: In southeastern TX; flight training.

Naval Air Test Center, Patuxent River
Branch: Navy
Patuxent River, MD, 20670-5409 **County:** St. Mary's
Size: 7127 acres
Agency: 3,410 (Active); 2,222 (Dependents); 3,350 (Civilians)

Name origin: On Chesapeake Bay, 60 mi. southeast of Washington, D.C. Naval Test Pilot School; principal site for testing and evaluating aircraft systems.

Naval Construction Battalion Center, Pt. Hueneme
Branch: Navy
Port Hueneme, CA, 93043-5000 **County:** Ventura
Size: 2410 acres
Agency: 4,050 (Active); 1,500 (Dependents); 4,540 (Civilians)

Name origin: Sixty mi. northwest of Los Angeles; construction force (Seabees) support.

Naval Education and Training Center
Branch: Navy
Newport, RI, 02841-5000 **County:** Newport
Size: 1199 acres
Agency: 5,560 (Active); 1,040 (Civilians)

Name origin: In south-central RI; Naval War College; officer indoctrination and skill training.

Naval Postgraduate School
Branch: Navy
Monterey, CA, 93943 **County:** Monterey
Size: 620 acres
Agency: 1,430 (Active); 2,141 (Dependents); 1,270 (Civilians)
Name origin: In Monterey. Professional development training; more than 1700 students enrolled in over 30 academic programs, representing all services, NOAA, DOD civilians, and 20 allied countries.

Naval Research Laboratory
Branch: Navy
4555 Overlook Ave., SW, Washington, DC, 20375-5000 **County:** District of Columbia
Size: 1160 acres
Agency: 200 (Active); 3,930 (Civilians)
Name origin: Physical sciences research, including Deep Ocean Search System, space satellites, experiments, and investigation, and NAVSTAR Global Positioning System program.

Naval Station, Guam
Branch: Navy
Agana, Guam, 96630 **County:** Guam
Size: 4779 acres
Agency: 3,880 (Active); 480 (Civilians)
Name origin: In the North Pacific Ocean, in the Marianas east of the Philippines, on the central western coast of Guam; fleet support.

Naval Surface Weapons Center
Branch: Navy
Code C12, Dahlgren, VA, 22448-5000 **County:** Virginia Beach (city)
Size: 4320 acres
Agency: 510 (Active); 384 (Dependents); 3,390 (Civilians)
Name origin: In northeastern VA, east of Fredericksburg. Research, development, testing, and experimental-ordinance technology; Naval Space Command; Naval Space Surveillance Center; AEGIS Training Center.

Nellis Air Force Base
Branch: Air Force
Las Vegas, NV, 89110
Size: 3,124,302 acres **Lat:** 36-14-09 N **Long:** 11-50-15 W
Agency: 11,400 (Active); 34,000 (Dependents); 1,130 (Civilians)
Name origin: For Lt. William Harrell Nellis, of Nevada, killed in action over Luxembourg during WWII. In southeastern NV, north of Las Vegas; U.S.A.F. Tactical Fighter Weapons Center. During Korean War, virtually every fighter pilot trained here. Today, provides training for composite strike forces of air and ground units of Army, Navy, Marines, and NATO and allied air units.

New London Naval Submarine Base
Branch: Navy
Box 00, Groton, CT, 06349-5000 **County:** New London
Size: 1394 acres
Agency: 10,490 (Active); 25,000 (Dependents); 1,200 (Civilians)
Name origin: On the east bank of the Thames River about 6 mi. upstream from the estuary and within the townships of Ledyard and Groton; submarine forces support; birthplace of U.S. submarine force.

Norfolk Naval Air Station
Branch: Navy
Norfolk, VA, 23511 **County:** Norfolk (city)
Size: 1386 acres
Agency: 10,900 (Active); 5,930 (Civilians)
Name origin: On the southeastern coast of VA, bounded on the north and west by the James and Elizabeth rivers and on the east by Chesapeake Bay (part of Norfolk Naval Station). Commander, Naval Air Force, U.S. Atlantic Fleet; early warning and anti-submarine warfare aircraft.

Norfolk Naval Shipyard
Branch: Navy
Portsmouth, VA, 23709 **County:** Portsmouth (city)
Size: 1340 acres
Agency: 730 (Active); 14,390 (Civilians)
Name origin: In southeastern VA, on the Elizabeth River southeast of Norfolk; ship alterations and repair. First dry dock in Western Hemisphere opened 1833; converted USS *Merrimack* into first ironclad, CSS *Virginia*, 1862; built first battleship commissioned by Navy (USS *Texas*); built first platform for first plane flight from ship; and converted a collier into first aircraft carrier (USS *Langley*), 1922.

Norfolk Naval Station
Branch: Navy
Norfolk, VA, 23511 **County:** Norfolk (city)
Size: 181 acres
Agency: 62,500 (Active); 2,840 (Civilians)
Name origin: In southeastern VA, bounded on the north and west by the James and Elizabeth rivers, and on the east by Chesapeake Bay; operating base.

North Island Naval Air Station
Branch: Navy
San Diego, CA, 92135 **County:** San Diego
Size: 47864 acres
Agency: 18,760 (Active); 7,044 (Dependents); 6,510 (Civilians)
Name origin: On Coronado Island, west of San Diego; important training, staging, and deployment center.

Norton Air Force Base
Branch: Air Force
San Bernardino, CA, 92409-5154 **County:** San Bernardino
Size: 2410 acres **Lat:** 34-05-52 N **Long:** 11-71-40 W
Agency: 5,395 (Active); 2,770 (Civilians)
Name origin: For Capt. Leland F. Norton, WWII pilot and San Bernardino native. In San Bernardino, 60 mi. east of Los Angeles; 63rd Military Airlift Wing.

Oakland Naval Supply Center
Branch: Navy
Oakland, CA, 94625-5000 **County:** Alameda
Size: 1130 acres **Lat:** 37-48-10 N **Long:** 12-21-85 W
Agency: 1,712 (Active); 3,630 (Civilians)
Name origin: Home of Navy's prototype computerized warehouse. When fully operational, NISTARS (Naval Integrated Storage Trucking and Retrieval System) will be largest single fully computer-controlled distribution facility.

Oceana Naval Air Station
Branch: Navy
Virginia Beach, VA, 23460 **County:** Suffolk (city)
Size: 15,180 acres **Lat:** 36-49-06 N **Long:** 07-60-14 W
Agency: 9,670 (Active); 770 (Civilians)
Name origin: On the southeastern coast of VA, east of Norfolk; Commander Tactical Wings, Atlantic.

Offutt Air Force
Branch: Air Force
Bellevue, NE, 68113-5000 **County:** Sarpy
Size: 3884 acres **Lat:** 41-07-41 N **Long:** 09-55-45 W
Agency: 5,200 (Active); 1,960 (Civilians)
Name origin: For Lt. Jarvis J. Offutt, Omaha's first air casualty in WWI. In east-central NE, 10 mi. south of Omaha; 55th Strategic Reconaissance Wing; Strategic Air Command (SAC) Headquarters.

Pacific Missile Test Center
Branch: Navy
Point Mugu, CA, 93042 **County:** Ventura
Size: 27,100 acres
Agency: 2,550 (Active); 3,031 (Dependents); 4,320 (Civilians)
Name origin: About 50 mi. northwest of Los Angeles. Since 1946 more missiles launched and tested from here than from any other major test range.

Patrick Air Force Base
Branch: Air Force
Cocoa Beach, FL, 32925 **County:** Brevard
Size: 8722 acres **Lat:** 28-14-18 N **Long:** 08-03-62 W
Agency: 3,560 (Active); 4,826 (Dependents); 1,280 (Civilians)
Name origin: For Maj. Gen. Mason M. Patrick, Chief of Army Air Service, 1921–27. Three mi. south of Cocoa Beach; Eastern Space and Missile Center; Air Force eastern test range.

Pearl Harbor Naval Station
Branch: Navy
Pearl Harbor, HI, 96860 **County:** Honolulu
Size: 5846 acres
Agency: 9,740 (Active); 1,380 (Civilians)
Name origin: Two mi. west of Honolulu; operating base. Site of Japanese attack on Dec. 7, 1941, starting WWII; Navy's most important base in Pacific.

Pensacola Naval Air Station
Branch: Navy
Pensacola, FL, 32508-5000 **County:** Escambia
Size: 7512 acres (16,500 acres entire complex)
Lat: 30-21-25 N **Long:** 08-71-82 W
Agency: 6,040 (Active); 10,500 (Dependents); 6,450 (Civilians)
Name origin: On the southern coast of the FL panhandle, near the AL border. Established 1914, oldest Naval air station; nicknamed 'Annapolis of the Air' and 'Cradle of Naval Aviation.' Activities and facilities include Naval Air Basic Training Command, Pre-Flight School, Naval School of Aviation Medicine, and Naval Aviation Museum.

Pentagon, The
Branch: Joint Service Installation
Arlington, VA, 22211 **County:** Arlington
Size: 583 acres **Lat:** 38-52-15 N **Long:** 07-70-32 W
Agency: 11,500 (Active); 11,500 (Civilians)
Name origin: For the five-sided shape of the building. Adjacent to Arlington National Cemetery and Fort Myer. Houses the Department of Defense.

Petaluma Coast Guard Training Center
Branch: Coast Guard
Petaluma, CA, 94952-5000
Size: 800 acres
Agency: 237 (Active); 400 (Dependents); 50 (Civilians)
Name origin: Fifty-eight mi. north of San Francisco in an area known as Two Rock. Facilities available for conferences and workshops. Addition of Electronics Technician and Telephone Technician schools 1989. Center now operates ten schools offering 40 courses for 5000 students a year.

Peterson Air Force Base
Branch: Air Force
3rd Space Support Wing, Colorado Springs, CO, 80914-5000 **County:** El Paso
Size: 1156 acres
Agency: 3,290 (Active); 8,188 (Dependents); 1,710 (Civilians)
Name origin: For 1st Lt. Edward J. Peterson, of Englewood, CO, photo reconnaissance pilot killed 1942. Eight mi. northeast of Colorado Springs; 1st Space Wing; headquarters North American Aerospace Defense Command (NORAD).

Pope Air Force Base
Branch: Air Force
Fayetteville, NC, 28308-5000 **County:** Cumberland
Size: 1858 acres **Lat:** 35-10-17 N **Long:** 07-90-03 W
Agency: 4,200 (Active); 6,000 (Dependents); 400 (Civilians)
Name origin: For 1st Lt. Harley Halbert Pope, killed in air crash near Fayetteville. In south-central NC, adjacent to Fort Bragg, 12 mi. northwest of Fayetteville. 317th Tactical Airlift Wing; USAF Airlift Center; pioneered development of Adverse Weather Aerial Delivery System (AWADS).

Presidio of Monterey
Branch: Air Force; Army; Marines; Navy; Coast Guard
Monterey, CA, 93940 **County:** Monterey
Size: 390 acres **Lat:** 36-36-22 N **Long:** 12-15-43 W
Agency: 3,600 (Active); 250 (Dependents); 1,200 (Civilians)
Name origin: Spanish 'garrisoned fortress.' Defense Language Institute; Foreign Language Center.

Presidio of San Francisco
Branch: Army
Bldg 37, San Francisco, CA, 94129-6520 **County:** San Francisco
Size: 180 acres
Agency: 2,190 (Active); 6,200 (Dependents); 2,940 (Civilians)
Name origin: Spanish 'garrisoned fortress.' In the northwest corner of San Francisco, adjacent to the south end of the Golden Gate Bridge. Headquarters, Sixth U.S. Army.

Quantico Marine Corps Combat Development Command
Branch: Marines
Quantico, VA, 22134 **County:** Prince William, Stafford
Size: 60,647 acres
Agency: 8,870 (Active); 4,200 (Dependents); 1,380 (Civilians)
Name origin: In northeastern VA, about 30 mi. south of Washington, DC. Marine Corps Base Quantico; Marine Air-Ground Task Force Warfighting Center; Marine Corps Wargaming and Assessment Center; The Intelligence Center.

Randolph Air Force Base
Branch: Air Force
Universal City, TX, 78148   **County:** Bexar
Size: 3953 acres   **Lat:** 29-31-56 N **Long:** 09-81-64 W
Agency: 5,140 (Active); 16,000 (Dependents); 2,820 (Civilians)
Name origin: For Texan Capt. William Millican Randolph, former adjutant of Advanced Flying School, Kelly Field. In south-central TX, 17 mi. northeast of San Antonio. 12th Flying Training Wing; nicknamed 'West Point of the Air' and 'Showplace of the Air Force.'

Redstone
Branch: Army
Huntsville, AL, 35898   **County:** Madison
Size: 38,410 acres   **Lat:** 34-39-40 N **Long:** 08-64-02 W
Agency: 3,660 (Active); 18,340 (Civilians)
Name origin: Adjacent to Huntsville; Army Rocket and Guided Missile and Munitions Center and School.

Robins Air Force Base
Branch: Air Force
2853 ABG/CC, Robins AFB, GA, 31098   **County:** Houston
Size: 8700 acres
Agency: 4,000 (Active); 5,967 (Dependents); 16,000 (Civilians)
Name origin: For Brig. Gen. Augustine Warner Robins, chief of Materiel Division of Army Air Corps. Original name Wellston Air Depot for the town. In central GA, adjacent to Warner Robins, 15 mi. southeast of Macon. Hdq. of Air Force Reserve; Museum of Aviation.

Rock Island Arsenal
Branch: Army
Rock Island, IL, 61299-5000   **County:** Rock Island
Size: 907 acres   **Lat:** 41-31-04 N **Long:** 09-03-23 W
Agency: 360 (Active); 8,280 (Civilians)
Name origin: In the metropolitan area of Moline and Rock Island, IL, and Davenport and Bettendorf, IA. Research and development, and production of tank components. Authorized in 1862; Civil War site for Confederate prison.

San Diego Marine Corps Recruit Depot
Branch: Marines
San Diego, CA, 92140-5000   **County:** San Diego
Size: 500 acres
Agency: 7,430 (Active); 2,100 (Dependents); 260 (Civilians)
Name origin: Drill Instructor School.

San Diego Naval Station
Branch: Navy
San Diego, CA, 92136   **County:** San Diego
Size: 1510 acres   **Lat:** 32-40-47 N **Long:** 11-70-71 W
Agency: 33,170 (Active); 2,730 (Civilians)
Name origin: Operating base, homeport to 74 surface warships.

San Diego Naval Submarine Base
Branch: Navy
140 Sylvester Rd., San Diego, CA, 92106-3521 **County:** San Diego
Size: 310 acres
Agency: 5,960 (Active); 25 (Dependents); 480 (Civilians)
Name origin: At tip of Ballast Point (harbor entrance) on Point Loma peninsula; submarine force support.

Schofield Barracks
Branch: Army
Honolulu, HI, 96857   **County:** Honolulu
Size: 13777 acres   **Lat:** 21-29-42 N **Long:** 15-80-35 W
Agency: 13,300 (Active); 10,000 (Dependents); 990 (Civilians)
Name origin: Probably for John M. Schofield (1831–1906), Union general during Civil War. In the center of Oahu; 25th Infantry Division.

Scott Air Force Base
Branch: Air Force
Belleville, IL, 62225-0000   **County:** St. Clair
Size: 3170 acres   **Lat:** 38-32-24 N **Long:** 08-95-14 W
Agency: 7,140 (Active); 5,000 (Dependents); 3,380 (Civilians)
Name origin: For Army Cpl. Frank S. Scott, killed in Wright biplane crash 1912. About 20 mi. east of St. Louis, MO. Headquarters Military Airlift Command; C-9 medical aircraft, C-12 and C-21 support aircraft, C-140 flight checking aircraft, and H-60 Army (Reserve) helicopters.

Seymour Johnson Air Force Base
Branch: Air Force
Goldsboro, NC, 27531   **County:** Wayne
Size: 50,730 acres   **Lat:** 35-21-16 N **Long:** 07-75-75 W
Agency: 4,780 (Active); 680 (Civilians)
Name origin: For Navy Lt. Seymour Andrew Johnson, Goldsboro native, killed in an aircraft crash. In east-central NC, south of Goldsboro; 4th Tactical Fighter Wing.

Shaw Air Force Base
Branch: Air Force
Sumter, SC, 29152   **County:** Sumter
Size: 11,450 acres   **Lat:** 33-58-09 N **Long:** 08-02-90 W
Agency: 5,650 (Active); 10,023 (Dependents); 590 (Civilians)
Name origin: For 1st Lt. Ervin D. Shaw of Sumter County, SC, shot down in WWI. In central SC, 10 mi. west of Sumter; 363rd Tactical Fighter Wing.

Sheppard Air Force Base
Branch: Air Force
Wichita Falls, TX, 76311-5000   **County:** Wichita
Size: 5397 acres   **Lat:** 33-58-20 N **Long:** 09-83-02 W
Agency: 3,460 (Active); 5,632 (Dependents); 1,230 (Civilians)
Name origin: For Morris Sheppard, chairman of Senate Military Affairs Committee 1941. In north-central TX, 4 mi. north of Wichita Falls; Technical Training Center.

Tinker Air Force Base
Branch: Air Force
Midwest City, OK, 73145   **County:** Oklahoma
Size: 4766 acres   **Lat:** 35-25-42 N **Long:** 09-72-32 W
Agency: 7,180 (Active); 17,470 (Civilians)
Name origin: For Maj. Gen. Clarence L. Tinker, Oklahoman killed on Wake Island, 1942. In central OK, 9 mi. southeast of Oklahoma City; Air Logistics Center.

Travis Air Force Base
Branch: Air Force
Fairfield, CA, 94535 **County:** Solano
Size: 7620 acres **Lat:** 38-16-04 N **Long:** 12-15-55 W
Agency: 8,000 (Active); 12,500 (Dependents); 2,230 (Civilians)
Name origin: For Brig. Gen. Robert F. Travis, killed in B-29 crash. Fifty mi. northeast of San Francisco; 60th Military Airlift Wing.

Tripler Army Medical Center
Branch: Army
Honolulu, HI, 96859-5000 **County:** Honolulu
Size: 367 acres
Agency: 1,350 (Active); 1,000 (Civilians)
Name origin: For Brevet Brig. Gen. Charles Stuart Tripler, for contributions to Army medicine during Civil War. On the island of Oahu, at the top of Moanalua Ridge. Largest military medical treatment facility in Pacific; only Army medical center not located on U.S. mainland; major graduate teaching center.

Twentynine Palms Marine Corps Air Ground Combat Center
Branch: Marines
Palm Springs, CA, 92278-5000 **County:** San Bernardino
Size: 595,590 acres **Lat:** 35-14-12 N **Long:** 11-60-31 W
Agency: 12,420 (Active); 4,028 (Dependents); 560 (Civilians)
Name origin: At the southern tip of the Mojave Desert, 60 mi. northeast of Palm Springs. Largest marine installation in the world; combined arms training.

U.S. Air Force Academy
Branch: Air Force
Colorado Springs, CO, 80840 **County:** El Paso
Size: 19,270 acres **Lat:** 38-59-25 N **Long:** 10-45-12 W
Agency: 2,450 (Active); 2,527 (Dependents); 1,940 (Civilians)
Name origin: Just north of Colorado Springs; officer acquisition training.

U.S. Army Corps of Engineers, Little Rock District
Branch: Army
PO Box 867, 700 W. Capitol St., Little Rock, AR, 72203-0867
Agency: 6 (Active); 875 (Civilians)
Name origin: Manages Arkansas River watershed between Fort Smith and Pine Bluff, White River watershed above Peach Orchard Bluff, near Georgetown, AR, and Little River Basin in Southwest AR; both civil works and military construction missions.

U.S. Coast Guard Academy
Branch: Coast Guard
Mohegan Drive, New London, CT, 06320-4195 **County:** New London
Size: 100 acres **Lat:** 41-22-20 N **Long:** 07-20-60 W
Agency: 600/9 (Active); 200 (Civilians)
Name origin: On the west bank of the Thames River, about 8 mi. upstream of the estuary; officer acquisition training.

U.S. Coast Guard Yard
Branch: Coast Guard
Curtis Bay, MD, 21226-1797 **County:** Anne Arundel
Size: 112 acres
Agency: 250 (Active); 830 (Civilians)
Name origin: On Curtis Creek 2 mi. east of Baltimore. Founded in 1899, only ship-building and repair facility of USCG. Until 1910, Yard first permanent home of Coast Guard Academy; Coast Guard's largest, most modern industrial plant, responsible for contruction, repairs, and renovation of vessel and various aids to navigation, and manufacturing of miscellaneous Coast Guard peculiar equipment.

U.S. Military Academy
Branch: Army
West Point, NY, 10996-5000 **County:** Orange
Size: 15,975 acres
Agency: 7,010 (Active); 3,500 (Dependents); 2,650 (Civilians)
Name origin: In southeastern NY, about 50 mi. north of New York City. Oldest U.S. service academy located on the oldest military post in continuous operation.

U.S. Naval Academy
Branch: Navy
Annapolis, MD, 21402 **County:** Anne Arundel
Size: 1747 acres
Agency: 5,550 (Active); 2,700 (Dependents); 2,940 (Civilians)
Name origin: On the south bank of the Severn River; 30 mi. south of Baltimore. Officer acquisition training.

U.S. Naval Observatory
Branch: Navy
34th & Massachusetts Ave. NW, Washington, DC, 20392-5100 **County:** District of Columbia
Size: 364 acres **Lat:** 38-55-17 N **Long:** 07-70-40 W
Agency: 40 (Active); 3 (Dependents); 520 (Civilians)
Name origin: In northwestern Washington, D.C. Official residence of the Vice President of US; Office of the Oceanographer of the Navy. Founded in 1830 as Depot of Charts and Instruments, one of oldest scientific agencies in U.S.

Vandenberg Air Force Base
Branch: Air Force
2392nd Aerospace Support Wing, Lompoc, CA, 93437-5000 **County:** Santa Barbara
Size: 98,950 acres
Agency: 3,550 (Active); 5,330 (Dependents); 1,410 (Civilians)
Name origin: For Gen. Hoyt S. Vandenberg, second Air Force Chief of Staff and early advocate of aerospace preparedness. Fifty-five mi. north of Santa Barbara on the central coast of CA. Space and missile test center; in 1944 POW camp established for German and Italian prisoners and 16 branch POW camps.

Walter Reed Army Medical Center
Branch: Army
7100 Georgia Ave NW, Washington, DC, 20012 **County:** District of Columbia
Size: 113 acres **Lat:** 38-58-31 N **Long:** 07-70-14 W
Agency: 3,160 (Active); 4,100 (Civilians)
Name origin: For Walter Reed (1851–1902), U.S. Army medical officer who learned to control yellow fever and typhoid fever. The main section is located between Rock Creek Park and Georgia Ave. near the MD-DC boundary. Established to integrate patient care, teaching, and research.

Westover Air Force Base
Branch: Air Force Reserve
Chicopee, MA, 01022-5000 **County:** Hampden
Size: 2850 acres
Agency: 8 (Active); 1,000 (Civilians)
Name origin: In 1940 for Maj. Gen. Oscar Westover, then top-ranking U.S. military pilot and first Chief of Air Corps. In south-central MA, 8 mi. south of Springfield. Air Force Reserve base with 439th MAW, used especially during 1990 Desert Storm (war against Iraq's invasion of Kuwait).

Whidbey Island Naval Air Station
Branch: Navy
Oak Harbor, WA, 98278-5000 **County:** Island
Size: 70,998 acres **Lat:** 48-20-45 N **Long:** 12-23-91 W
Agency: 8,420 (Active); 13,600 (Dependents); 800 (Civilians)
Name origin: In northwestern WA, in the middle of Puget Sound, 80 mi. northwest of Seattle. Attack and electronic warfare aircraft; home of all Navy electronic warfare squadrons flying EA-6B 'Prowler,' carrier-based tactical jamming aircraft; west coast training and operations center for A-6 'Intruder' attack bomber squadrons.

Whiteman Air Force Base
Branch: Air Force
351 SMW, Knob Noster, MO, 65301 **County:** Johnson
Size: 24,928 acres **Lat:** 38-43-46 N **Long:** 09-33-24 W
Agency: 3,540 (Active); 1,200 (Dependents); 500 (Civilians)
Name origin: For 2nd Lt. George A. Whiteman, of Sedalia, MO, who died in Japanese attack on Pearl Harbor 1941. In northwestern MO, 60 mi. southeast of Kansas City; 351st Strategic Missile Wing.

White Sands Missile Range
Branch: Army
USA White Sands Missile Range, White Sands, NM, 88002 **County:** Sierra, Lincoln, Otero
Size: 1,746,720 acres
Agency: 1,170 (Active); 1,424 (Dependents); 3,700 (Civilians)
Name origin: In south-central NM, in the Tularosa Basin between the Sacramento Mountains on the east and the San Andres and Organ mountains on the west. Research and Development Weapons Test Center; largest land test facility in U.S. Test bed of Army, Navy, Air Force, other government agencies, some foreign governments, and private companies. White Sands Space Harbor and alternate landing site for space shuttle and training site for NASA shuttle pilots.

Wright-Patterson Air Force Base
Branch: Air Force
Fairborn, OH, 45433 **County:** Montgomery, Greene
Size: 8312 acres **Lat:** 39-49-20 N **Long:** 08-40-21 W
Agency: 4,530 (Active); 8,010 (Civilians)
Name origin: Established 1917 as McCook Field. Renamed Wilbur Wright Field 1924, then Patterson Field in 1931 for Lt. Frank Patterson killed in airplane crash. Present name designated 1948. In southwestern OH, 10 mi. northeast of Dayton. Headquarters Air Force Logistics Command; Harry G. Armstrong Aerospace Medical Research Laboratory.

Wurtsmith Air Force Base
Branch: Air Force
379th Bombardment Wing, Oscoda, MI, 48753-5000 **County:** Iosco
Size: 5221 acres **Lat:** 44-27-14 N **Long:** 08-32-25 W
Agency: 3,220 (Active); 4,319 (Dependents); 360 (Civilians)
Name origin: For Maj. Gen. Paul Bernard Wurtsmith, WWII hero from Detroit, killed in training flight in NC. On the northeastern coast of MI, northeast of Bay City. 379th Bombardment Wing; in 1943 home of 100th Pursuit Squadron, famous all-black fighter unit 'Black Panthers'.

Yuma Proving Ground
Branch: Army
Yuma, AZ, 85365 **County:** La Paz, Yuma
Size: 1,000,000 acres
Agency: 310 (Active); 570 (Dependents); 880 (Civilians)
Name origin: About 26 mi. northeast of Yuma; research and development test center.

Major Geographical Features

Listed below are more than 500 of the major geographical features of the United States, including:

bays	deserts	oceans	rivers
beaches	gaps	passes	seas
canals	glaciers	peninsulas	sounds
canyons	gorges	plains	trails
capes	gulfs	plateaus	valleys
caves	islands	regions	volcanoes
currents	lakes	reservoirs	waterfalls
dams	mountain ranges and peaks		

Absaroka Range   Feature: range
Part of the Middle Rocky Mountains. Range from S MT across Northeast Yellowstone Park to NW WY. About 175 mi. long. Highest points: Franks Peak (13,140 ft.), Mt. Crosby (12,435 ft.), and Dead Indian Peak (12,216 ft.).
Name origin: An Indian word of disputed origin and meaning, applied to the Crow Indian tribe and the lands they inhabited.

Adirondack Mountains   Feature: range
County: St. Lawrence **State:** NY
Lat: 44-00-01 N **Long:** 07-43-00 W
In NE NY. Highest peak is Mt. Marcy, 5,344 ft. Includes many lakes, among them Saranac, Placid, and Raquette. Source of Hudson and Ausable rivers. Noted especially for winter sports; site of 1980 Winter Olympic Games (Lake Placid). In center of mountain region is Adirondack Forest Preserve, with more than 5 million acres set aside by the state for public recreation, and forest and water conservation; largest wilderness area E of Mississippi River.
Name origin: For an Algonquian tribe, called 'tree-eaters' by their enemies, as first recorded by Roger Williams, who confused the tribe with the Mohawks. Meaning of name is unknown; present spelling is a semblance of the sound form.

Agate Fossil Beds   Feature: locale
County: Sioux **State:** NE
In northwestern NE, north of Scottsbluff. Fossils of 20-million-year-old animals, including a two-horned rhinocerous about the size of a Shetland pony, and a 'terrible pig,' ten feet long and seven feet tall, with huge tusks. Part of the Agate Fossil Beds National Monument.

Akaka Falls   Feature: falls
County: Hawaii **State:** HI
Lat: 19-51-23 N **Long:** 15-50-93 W
On island of Hawaii, near Hilo. Long, thin waterfall on Kolekole stream. Height 442 ft.

Alabama River   Feature: stream
County: Baldwin **State:** AL
Lat: 31-08-09 N **Long:** 08-75-63 W
In center of state; 315 mi. long. Formed by confluence of Tallapoosa and Coosa rivers north of Montgomery. Unites with the Tombigbee River 45 mi. north of Mobile to form Mobile River.
Name origin: Possibly for an Indian tribe whose name derived from Choctaw *alba* 'thicket' or 'plants,' and *amo* 'cleaners' or 'reapers.' Territory and state named for the river.

Alaska, Gulf of   Feature: bay
County: Valdez-Cordova **State:** AK
Lat: 59-04-16 N **Long:** 14-45-75 W
Inlet of the North Pacific Ocean on southern coast of AK, bounded on east by Alexander Archipelago, and on west by Alaska Peninsula and Aleutian Islands.

Alaska Peninsula   Feature: cape
County: Dillingham **State:** AK
Lat: 57-10-00 N **Long:** 15-73-00 W
In southwest AK. Begins at Iliamna Lake and extends southwest about 475 mi. to the beginning of the Aleutian Islands.
Name origin: For the state.

Alaska Range   Feature: range
County: Yukon-Kayukuk **State:** AK
Lat: 62-35-00 N **Long:** 15-30-50 W
Forms the backbone of the Alaskan Peninsula and Aleutian Islands; extends 1,600 mi. from southeastern AK to the Attu, westernmost Aleutian Is. Includes Mt. McKinley (20,320 ft.), highest peak in North America, and Mt. Foraker (17,400 ft.).
Name origin: For the state.

Alava, Cape   Feature: cape
County: Clallam **State:** WA
Lat: 48-09-58 N **Long:** 12-44-35 W
Point farthest W of the lower 48 states, on NW coast of WA, S of Cape Flattery.
Name origin: For José Manuel de Alava, a Spanish commissioner.

Alcatraz Island   Feature: island
County: San Francisco **State:** CA
Lat: 37-49-36 N **Long:** 12-22-52 W
In San Francisco Bay about 1 mi. from mainland. Area 12 acres. Site of former federal prison 1934-63.
Name origin: Spanish 'pelican.' Also called The Rock.

Aleutian Islands
Feature: islands
County: Aleutian West **State:** AK
Lat: 52-05-49 N **Long:** 17-33-00 W

A chain of volcanic islands extending 900 mi. W from the end of the Alaska Peninsula; they separate the Bering Sea from the Atlantic Ocean. Area 6,777 sq. mi. Include 14 large islands and about 55 smaller ones, divided into five main groups from E to W: Fox Islands, Islands of Four Mountains, Andreanof Islands, Rat Islands, and Near Islands. Mountains on the islands are part of the Alaska Range. Unimak is largest island; Unalaska is second largest and trading center of the Aleutians; both in Fox Islands.

Name origin: Adjective form of *Aleut*, the natives of the islands; first used by Adm. Adam Johann von Krusenstern (1770–1846) in 1827; meaning uncertain. Other names were Billy Mitchell Islands and Katerina Archipelago.

Alexander Archipelago
Feature: cape
County: Wrangell-Petersburg **State:** AK
Lat: 56-40-00 N **Long:** 13-40-50 W

Extends southward along the coast of British Columbia in the Gulf of Alaska. Includes the islands of Prince of Wales (the largest), Revillagido, Baranof, Admiralty, Chichagof, and Kupreanof.

Name origin: Named in 1867 by U.S. Coast and Geolodetic Survey in honor of Alexander (1777–1825), Czar of Russia.

Allegheny (Alleghany) Mountains *or* Alleghenies
Feature: range

Part of the Appalachian Mountains, in PA, extreme MD and VA, and WV. Southern portion is west of and parallel to Blue Ridge Mountains. Height from 2,000 to over 4,800 ft. Tallest peak is Spruce Knod, (4,862 ft.) in WV. East slope sometimes called Allegheny Front.

Name origin: For the river.

Allegheny River
Feature: stream

In northwest PA and southwest NY. 325 mi. long; navigable about 200 mi. Joins Monongahela River at Pittsburgh to form Ohio River.

Name origin: Probaby from Delaware Indian; origin and meaning are uncertain. Derived from *welhik-hanna* or *oolik-hanne* 'fine river' or 'beautiful river.'

Alverstone, Mount
Feature: summit
County: Skagway-Yakutat-Angoon **State:** AK
Lat: 60-21-01 N **Long:** 13-90-43 W

Height 14,565 ft.; in the St. Elias Mountains on the border of SE AK with the Yukon Territory, Canada.

Name origin: For Everard Webster Alverstone (1842–1915), a mediator for several Alaska-Canada disputes.

Andreanof Islands
Feature: islands
County: Aleutians West **State:** AK
Lat: 51-55-22 N **Long:** 17-61-14 W

Part of the Aleutian Islands. Main islands are Seguam, Amlia, Atka, Adak, Kanaga, Tanaga, and Great Sitkin.

Name origin: For Andrean Tolstykh, Russian explorer of the islands in the 1760s.

Apalachee Bay
Feature: bay
County: Jefferson **State:** FL
Lat: 30-04-20 N **Long:** 08-40-15 W

An arm of the Gulf of Mexico on the S coast of the FL panhandle; Tallahassee is to the N.

Name origin: For the Indian tribe, of Muskhogean linguistic stock. Name may be Hitchiti for 'on the other side' or derive from Choctaw *apelachi* 'helper.'

Apostle Islands
Feature: islands
County: Ashland **State:** WI
Lat: 45-56-18 N **Long:** 09-03-91 W

Group of about 20 islands in southwest Lake Superior off northwest coast of WI.

Name origin: Also called the Twelve Apostles.

Appalachian Mountains
Feature: range

Second largest mountain system in North America. Extends about 1,500 mi. from Newfoundland, Quebec, and New Brunswick in northeast Canada south to central Alabama. Includes White Mts. of NH; Green Mts. of VT; the Catskills of NY; the Alleghenies of PA; the Blue Ridge Mts. in VA and NC; and the Cumberland Mts. in TN. Highest peak Mount Mitchell (6,684 ft.) in NC.

Name origin: First recorded in 1528 as *Apalachen* by Spanish explorer Álvar Núñez Cabeza de Vaca (c. 1490–c. 1560), said to be the Indian name of a province. Derived from the name of the Apalachee Indian tribe of Muskhogean linguistic stock who lived in northern Florida. Applied to the general mountainous interior, first in the south, then generalized in the late 19th century to the entire range.

Appalachian Trail
Feature: trail

Extends more than 2,000 mi. from Mt. Katahdin in ME to Springer Mountain in north GA. Traverses the Appalachian range; passes through 14 states, two national parks, and eight national forests. Highest peak Clingmans Dome. Part of the national park system since 1968.

Name origin: Full name: Appalachian National Scenic Trail

Arctic Ocean
Feature: sea

Borders the northern coasts of Alaska, Greenland, Europe, and Asia. Smallest ocean in the world. Greatest width 2,630 mi.; average depth 4,362 ft. Area 3,662,000 sq. mi.; most of it covered by ice much of the year. North Pole near center. Discovered in late 300s B.C. by Greek explorer, Pytheas. Coastal waters divided into seven seas: Greenland, Barents, Kara, Laptev, East Siberian, Chukchi, and Beaufort.

Name origin: Derived from the name of the northern constellation *Arktos*, the Greek name for what is now called Ursa Major or the Great Bear.

Arkansas River
Feature: stream

Flows southeast from central CO near Leadville, through KS and OK and empties into the Mississippi River in southeastern AR. 1,450 mi. long; navigable 650 mi.

Name origin: For the name of the Indian tribe.

Ascension Island
Feature: island

See Pohnpei Island

American Places Dictionary   Major Geographical Features

Atlantic Intracoastal Waterway   Feature: channel
A continuous series of connecting bodies of water, natural and manmade, between Boston, MA, and the southern tip of FL. About 1,200 mi. long; 12 ft.-deep channel. By using it boats need to go into the ocean for only about 50 mi. from Boston to Fishers Is. Sound at CT-RI border, and for 37 mi. along NJ coast to Delaware Bay. The Gulf Intracoastal connects FL and Brownsville, TX.

Atlantic Ocean   Feature: sea
Eastern coast of U.S. Area 31,530,000 sq. mi. not including its gulfs and bays; covers more than a fifth of the earth's surface. Bounded by Europe and Africa on east, and North and South America on west. Runs into Arctic Ocean on north, and Antarctic Ocean on south. Length is 9,000 to 10,000 mi., depending on boundaries. Greatest width 4,150 mi.; average depth approx. 13,000 ft.
Name origin: Named by the ancient Greeks 'the sea beyond Mount Atlas,' (in present-day Morocco), considered the western end of the known world.

Backbone Mountain   Feature: summit
Highest point in MD; height 3,360 ft. Extends from western tip of MD into northern WV.

Badlands   Feature: area
County: Pennington   **State:** SD & NE
Lat: 43-50-52 N   **Long:** 102-18-24 W
Barren, eroded region in southwest SD, east of the Black Hills, and in northwest NE. Includes Badland National Park.
Name origin: Translation of French name *Mauvaises Terres* 'bad lands (in which to travel).'

Baffin Bay   Feature: bay
County: Kennedy   **State:** TX
Lat: 27-15-20 N   **Long:** 09-73-05 W
An inlet of Laguna Madre, on SE coast of TX, S of Corpus Christi.
Name origin: For the bay off the coast of Greenland named for William Baffin (1584–1622), English explorer and navigator.

Baker, Mt   Feature: summit
State: WA
Peak in the Cascade Range, in northwest WA; height 10,778 ft.
Name origin: For Joseph Baker, an officer in an expedition with English explorer Captain George Vancouver (1757–98), who gave it this name.

Baranof Island   Feature: island
County: Sitka   **State:** AK
Lat: 56-57-05 N   **Long:** 13-45-65 W
Part of the Alexander Archipelago off southeastern AK. About 100 mi. long, 1,597 sq. mi. Town of Sitka is on its west coast.
Name origin: Named in 1805 for Alexander Andreievich Baranof (1746–1819), first governor of the Russian American colonies.

Barnegat Bay   Feature: bay
County: Ocean   **State:** NJ
Lat: 39-48-17 N   **Long:** 07-40-84 W
Inlet of the Atlantic Ocean along the central coast of NJ; about 30 mi. long.
Name origin: Dutch *barende gat* 'breaker's inlet', referring to a nearby break in the barrier islands along the NJ coast.

Beaufort Sea   Feature: sea
County: North Slope   **State:** AK
Part of the Arctic Ocean bordering northeast AK, northwest Canada, and the west of Banks Island in the Arctic Archipelago. Maximum depth about 15,000 ft.
Name origin: For Sir Francis Beaufort (1774–1857), hydrographer to the British Admiralty.

Becharof Lake   Feature: lake
County: Lake and Peninsula   **State:** AK
Lat: 57-57-08 N   **Long:** 15-62-23 W
Located in the northern Alaska Peninsula, southwest of Katmai National Monument. About 30 mi. long; area 458 sq. mi.
Name origin: For Bocharov, a navigator of the imperial Russian Navy.

Bedloes Island
See Liberty Island

Belau Islands
See Palau Islands

Belle Fourche River   Feature: stream
Rises in northeast Wyoming and flows into Cheyenne River in western SD. About 350 mi. long. Linked by canal to Belle Fourche Reservoir.
Name origin: French 'beautiful fork,' probably a translation of an earlier Indian name.

Bering Sea   Feature: sea
Northern part of the Pacific Ocean between Siberia and Alaska. About 1,200 mi. wide, 950 mi. long; greatest depth 13,422 ft.
Name origin: For Iran Ivanovitch Bering (1681–1741), also known as Vitus Bering; Danish navigator.

Bering Strait   Feature: channel
County: Nome   **Lat:** 65-43-33 N   **Long:** 16-82-51 W
Water passage separating Asia (U.S.S.R.) and North America (Alaska), and connecting the Bering Sea and the Arctic Ocean. Narrowest part 53 mi. wide.
Name origin: For the Bering Sea.

Berkshire Hills (The Berkshires)   Feature: range
County: Berkshire   **State:** MA
Lat: 42-10-00 N   **Long:** 07-30-90 W   **Elevation:** 3,487
In western MA, running north-south from the Green Mountains of VT to the Litchfield Hills of CT. Highest peak Mt. Greylock, 3491 ft.
Name origin: For Berkshire county in England.

Big Cypress Swamp   Feature: swamp
State: FL
Area in the western Everglades. A national preserve since 1974. Area about 2,400 sq. mi.

Bighorn Mountains   Feature: range
State: WY
Range in north-central WY, extending north to MT border. Forms the eastern front of Rocky Mtns. Highest point Cloud Peak 13,175 ft.
Name origin: For the sheep (the river was named first).

Big Sur
Feature: area
State: CA
Coastal resort region of great natural beauty. Extends from Carmel about 80 mi. southeast along the Pacific, west of the Santa Lucia Range, to the Hearst Castle at San Simeon.
Name origin: Spanish 'south' (of Carmel).

Big Thicket
Feature: forest
State: TX
In eastern TX, north of Beaumont, near the LA border. Contains a large variety of plants, birds, and mammals; now an 80,000-acre national preserve.

Billy Mitchell Islands
See Aleutian Islands

Biscayne Bay
Feature: bay
County: Dade **State:** FL
Lat: 25-33-56 N **Long:** 08-01-30 W
Inlet of the Atlantic Ocean in SE FL. Miami is on NW shore and Biscayne Key on northeast.
Name origin: Named by early Spanish explorers for a man from the province of Viscaya known as El Biscaino.

Bitterroot Range *or* Mountains
Feature: range
A range of the Rocky Mountains on the ID-MT border. 300 mi. long; highest point Scott Peak 11,393 ft.
Name origin: For the bitterroot, the state flower of MT.

Black Belt
Feature: area
Rolling prairie land across central AL and MS; its black clay soil is good for growing cotton.

Black Hills, the
Feature: range
Mountain region in northeast WY and western SD, extending over an area of 6,000 sq. mi. Highest mountain Harney Peak (SD); at 7,242 ft., the greatest elevation between the Rocky Mountains and the Alps.
Name origin: Translation of the Lakota term *paha sapa*, referring to the darkness of their pine-covered slopes seen at a distance.

Black Mesa
Feature: summit
County: Cimarron **State:** OK
Lat: 36-59-50 N **Long:** 10-30-80 W
In northwest corner of OK; highest point in the state (4,973 ft.)
Name origin: For the color of volcanic ash found there.

Black Mountains
Feature: range
State: NC
Part of the Blue Ridge Mountains, in western NC; highest peak Mount Mitchell, 6,684 ft.

Black Rock Desert
Feature: basin
County: Pershing **State:** NV
Lat: 40-54-39 N **Long:** 11-90-31 W
Alkaline sink in northwest NV. About 70 mi. long, 20 mi. wide. Area 1,000 sq. mi. Black Rock Range is along its western border.

Blanco, Cape
Feature: cape
County: Curry **State:** OR
Lat: 42-50-16 N **Long:** 12-43-34 W
Westernmost point of OR, on southwest Pacific coast.
Name origin: Spanish 'white'; reason unknown.

Block Island
Feature: island
County: Washington **State:** RI
Lat: 41-11-30 N **Long:** 07-13-43 W
In Atlantic Ocean at eastern end of Long Island Sound, about 9 mi. southwest of Point Judith, RI. Seven mi. long, 3.5 mi. wide; area about 11 sq. mi. Coextensive with town of New Shoreham. Settled 1661; admitted to colony 1664.
Name origin: Discovered and named in 1614 by Adrian Block, Dutch navigator.

Bluegrass Region
Feature: area
State: KY
Region in central KY where Kentucky bluegrass (*poa pratensis*) is plentiful; area noted for thoroughbred horse breeding.
Name origin: From the bluish-green color of the native grass.

Blue Ridge Mountains
Feature: range
Eastern range of the Appalachian Mountains; extend southwest from near Harpers Ferry, WV, across VA, NC, SC, and northern GA; some include the northern extension into MD and PA. Includes Black Mountains and Great Smokies. Highest peak Mt. Mitchell, 6,684 ft; elevation generally 2,000 to 4,000 ft.
Name origin: Descriptive of the color the pine-covered, linear slopes have when seen from a distance.

Bona, Mt.
Feature: summit
County: Valdez-Cordova **State:** AK
Lat: 61-23-08 N **Long:** 14-14-45 W
Southeastern AK, at eastern end of Wrangell Mountains, near Yukon border; height 16,500 ft.
Name origin: Named in 1897 by the mountaineer Prince Luigi Amedeo di Savoia (1873–1933), Duke of the Abruzzi, for his racing yacht *Bona*.

Bonneville Dam
Feature: dam
A power and waterway project in WA and OR, 40 mi. east of Portland, OR. Controls the flow of the Columbia River. 197 ft. high, 1,690 ft. long. Single lock 76 ft. wide, 500 ft. long permits large ships to travel upriver 188 mi. Dedicated in 1937, ten new generators added in 1982.
Name origin: For Benjamin L.E. Bonneville (1796–1878), a U.S. Army captain and explorer.

Bonneville Salt Flats
Feature: flats
County: Tooele **State:** UT
Lat: 40-47-59 N **Long:** 11-34-75 W
Barren salt flatland in northwestern UT, western part of Great Salt Lake Desert. Area 100 sq. mi. of ancient bed of Lake Bonneville, Pleistocene Era. Its International Speedway long used for land speed record attempts. In recent years decreasing in size with rising level of Great Salt Lake.
Name origin: For Benjamin L.E. Bonneville (1796–1878), a U.S. Army captain and explorer.

Bon Secour Bay
Feature: bay
County: Baldwin **State:** AL
Lat: 30-18-33 N **Long:** 08-75-21 W
An arm of Mobile Bay on Gulf coast of AL.
Name origin: Translation of French 'good help'.

Borah Peak
Feature: summit
County: Custer **State:** ID
Lat: 44-08-14 N **Long:** 11-34-64 W
Mountain in Lost River range, central ID. Highest point in the state, 12,662 ft.
Name origin: For William Edgar Borah (1865–1940), U.S. senator from Idaho (1907–40).

Boston Mountains
Feature: range
County: Johnson **State:** AR
Lat: 35-42-44 N **Long:** 09-32-03 W
Ridge in the Ozark Plateau in northwest AR. Highest peak more than 2,800 ft.
Name origin: For the city in Massachusetts.

Boulder Dam
See Hoover Dam

Boundary Peak
Feature: summit
County: Esmeralda **State:** NV
Lat: 37-50-46 N **Long:** 11-82-10 W
Mountain in southwest NV on border with CA. Highest point in NV, 13,140 ft.
Name origin: Descriptive of border location. Also called East Peak.

Brasstown Bald
Feature: summit
County: Towns **State:** GA
Lat: 34-52-20 N **Long:** 08-34-83 W
Mountain in north GA. Highest point in the state, 4,784 ft.
Name origin: Folk-etymologized translation of a Cherokee name meaning 'green valley place.' Also called Mount Etonah.

Brazos River
Feature: stream
County: Brazoria **State:** TX
Lat: 28-52-32 N **Long:** 09-52-24 W
In north-central TX, formed by confluence of Salt Fork and Double Mountain Fork rivers. Flows 1,210 mi. to the Gulf of Mexico. Chief tributaries are Paluxy, Little, and Navasota. Drainage basin extends over 44,000 sq. mi. Waco is largest city on the river. Along it are the Possum Kingdom Dam (1940), and the Whitney Dam (1953).
Name origin: Shortened from Spanish *Brazos de Dios* 'Arms of God.'

Breton Sound
Feature: bay
County: Saint Bernard **State:** LA
Lat: 29-30-00 N **Long:** 08-91-50 W
In southeast LA; inlet of the Gulf of Mexico east of the Mississippi delta.
Name origin: For the nearby island, possibly named for a former inhabitant of Brittany, western France.

Bridalveil Fall
Feature: falls
County: Mariposa **State:** CA
Lat: 37-43-00 N **Long:** 11-93-85 W
Located on the western slope of the Sierra Nevada in Yosemite National Park, east-central CA, 150 mi. east of San Francisco. Fed mainly by melting snow, the water falls 620 ft. to the Merced River.
Name origin: Named in 1850 for the diaphanous appearance of the fall's mist.

Bristol Bay
Feature: bay
County: Dillingham **State:** AK
Arm of the southeast Bering Sea between southwestern AK and the northern end of the Alaskan Peninsula.
Name origin: Named by Capt. James Cook (1728–79) in 1778 for the Earl of Bristol.

Brooklyn Bridge
Feature: bridge
County: New York **State:** NY
Lat: 40-42-19 N **Long:** 07-35-94 W **Elevation:** G
Suspension bridge over the East River, New York City, connecting boroughs of Brooklyn and Manhattan. Span 1,595 ft.; was largest suspension bridge in world when completed in 1883. Designated a national historic landmark in 1964.
Name origin: For the borough.

Brooks Range
Feature: range
County: North Slope **State:** AK
Mountains across northern AK from Kotzebue Sound to Canadian border, northwest end of the Rockies; watershed between Yukon basin on south and Arctic coast on north. Highest peak Mt. Michelson, 9,239 ft. Includes De Long, Baird, and Endicott mountains.
Name origin: Named by U.S. Geological Survey for Alfred Hulse Brooks (1871–1924), chief Alaskan geologist of the survey.

Buzzards Bay
Feature: bay
County: Barnstable **State:** MA
Lat: 41-43-00 N **Long:** 07-04-00 W
Inlet of the Atlantic Ocean between southwest Cape Cod and southeast MA mainland. 30 mi. long, 5 to 10 mi. wide. West end of Cape Cod Canal is at northeast tip of bay.

Campbell Hill
Feature: summit
County: Logan **State:** OH
Lat: 40-22-11 N **Long:** 08-34-31 W
In western OH near Bellefontaine. Highest point in the state, 1,550 ft.
Name origin: For Edward Campbell, who owned the land.

Camp David
Feature: summit
State: MD
Official U.S. presidential retreat in Catoctin Mountains, foothills of the Appalachian, about 70 mi. northwest of Washington, D.C. Site established as a presidential summer home by Franklin D. Roosevelt (1882–1945) in 1942. Operated by the U.S. Navy.
Name origin: Named *Shangri-La* by Pres. Franklin D. Roosevelt for the perfect kingdom in the novel, *Lost Horizon*, by James Hilton (1900–54). Present name given by Pres. Dwight D. Eisenhower (1890–1969) for his grandson, David Eisenhower.

Canaveral, Cape
Feature: cape
County: Brevard **State:** FL
Lat: 28-27-30 N **Long:** 08-03-20 W

Located off the east-central coast of FL, 10 mi. north of Cocoa Beach. Site of John F. Kennedy Space Center, the first tracking station in the 9,000 mi. Atlantic Missile Range, and the National Aeronautics and Space Administration (NASA) Launch Operations Center. U.S. space exploration began here, continues with the space shuttle program.

Name origin: Spanish for 'canebrake'; one of the oldest place names in the U.S. Name changed to Cape Kennedy in 1963 after the assassination of John F. Kennedy (1917–63), 35th president of the U.S. Original name restored to the cape itself in 1973 at the request of Floridians.

Cape Cod Bay
Feature: bay
County: Barnstable **State:** MA
Lat: 42-02-00 N **Long:** 07-02-50 W

Southern arm of Massachusetts Bay off east coast of MA; enclosed by hook of Cape Cod.

Name origin: For Cape Cod.

Cape Cod Canal
Feature: canal
County: Barnstable **State:** MA
Lat: 41-46-05 N **Long:** 07-03-40 W

Cuts through the strip of land joining Cape Cod to mainland MA, connecting Cape Cod Bay with Buzzards Bay. 17.5 mi. long, 450 to 700 ft. wide, 32 ft. deep at low water; permits two-way traffic. Owned and operated toll-free by U.S. government.

Name origin: For Cape Cod.

Capulin Mountain
Feature: summit
State: NM

An extinct volcano in northeastern NM, near CO border. Almost perfectly symmetrical with high sloping sides. Last eruption about 2,000 years ago. Crater is 1,450 ft. wide, 415 ft. deep; rises 8,215 ft. above sea level and 1,500 ft. above the surrounding plain. Established as a national monument in 1916.

Caribbean Sea
Feature: sea

Arm of the Atlantic Ocean south of Puerto Rico and the U.S. Virgin Islands. Bordered by West Indies on north and east, northern South America on the south, and Central America on the west. Yucatan Channel on northwest connects it with the Gulf of Mexico. Area about 1,049,500 sq. mi; maximum depth 24,720 ft.

Name origin: For the Carib Indians.

Carlsbad Caverns
Feature: caves
County: Eddy **State:** NM
Lat: 32-10-31 N **Long:** 10-42-63 W

Huge network of subterranean limestone caves in southeastern NM. Largest chamber, the Big Room over 1/2 mi. long, 650 ft. wide, 285 ft. high.

Name origin: For Karlsbad, Bohemia, a spa with medicinal springs.

Cascade Range
Feature: range

Northern continuation of the Sierra Nevada Mountains, extending north from Lassen Peak in northeastern California, across OR and WA. Highest peak Mt. Rainier (14,410 ft.) in WA; includes Mt. Shasta, Mt. Hood, Mt. St. Helens. Continuation into Canada called Coast Mountains.

Name origin: For the narrows of the Columbia River, known as the Cascades, which cut through the area.

Catskill Mountains
Feature: range
State: NY

Part of the Appalachian system in southeastern NY, along west bank of Hudson River. Southern end about 100 mi. north of New York City. About 50 mi. long, 30 mi. wide. Highest peaks Slide Mountain 4,204 ft. and Hunter Mountain 4,025 ft.

Name origin: From a Dutch name, *Kats Kill,* 'cat's stream,' probably from a personal name respelled into English and folk-etymologized to appear to be named because of a wildcat seen in the region.

Central Valley
Feature: valley
County: Santa Barbara **State:** CA
Lat: 34-01-07 N **Long:** 11-94-05 W

Extensive valley running obliquely through central CA between the Sierra Nevada and Coast Ranges. About 500 mi. long, up to 50 mi. wide. To the north is the Sacramento Valley and Sacramento River; the San Joaquin Valley and San Joaquin River are south. Irrigation provided by the Central Valley Project, completed in 1951 (later expanded), makes this the most important farming region west of the Rockies.

Chaco Canyon
Feature: valley
State: NM

In northwestern NM, site of ruins representing the height of Pre-Colombian civilization of the Anastazi Indians, also known as Basket Makers or Flat Heads, for their custom of flattening the back of the skulls of their babies. One of the largest homes is *Pueblo Bonito,* a 500-room adobe apartment house. Now part of the Chaco Culture National Historic Park.

Name origin: From Spanish 'desert,' but possibly influenced by an Indian word.

Champlain, Lake
Feature: lake

Running north and south on NY-VT border, the northern tip extends into Quebec, Canada. 107 mi. long, 1/2 to 14 mi. wide; area 435 sq. mi.; greatest depth 400 ft. Fed by Lake George and streams from the Adirondack and Green Mountains, drains into St. Lawrence via Richelien River. Popular area for summer homes and resorts, both along the shore and on islands in the lake. Main link between the Hudson and St. Lawrence rivers via Champlain Barge Canal (Hudson) and Richelien River (St. Lawrence).

Name origin: For Samuel de Champlain (1567–1635), French explorer who founded Quebec, and first European to reach the lake (1609).

Chappaquiddick Island
Feature: island
County: Dukes **State:** MA
Lat: 41-22-30 N **Long:** 07-02-83 W

In Nantucket Sound, MA, off eastern end of Martha's Vineyard. About 4 mi. at widest point. Site of incident on July 18, 1969, in which Mary Jo Kopechne died in a car driven by Sen. Edward M. Kennedy of MA.

Name origin: From Wampanoag 'place of the separated island.'

Charles Mound
Feature: summit
County: Jo Daviess **State:** IL
Lat: 42-30-15 N **Long:** 09-01-42 W

In northwest part of IL; highest point in state, 1,235 ft.

Name origin: For Elijah Charles, who settled in a log house at the base of the mound.

Chattahoochee River
Feature: stream
Rises in northeastern GA, flows 436 mi. southwest to AL border at Lanett, then south to form part of AL-GA border, and part of GA-FL border. Navigable. Dammed to form Lake Seminole in southwest corner of GA. Below the lake, known as Apalachicola River.
Name origin: From an Indian word, probably 'marked rocks,' for painted stones found in the river.

Cheaha Mountain
Feature: summit
County: Cleburne **State:** AL
Lat: 33-29-08 N **Long:** 08-54-83 W
Mountain in eastern AL; highest point in state, 2,407 ft.
Name origin: Probably from Choctaw *chaha*, 'high.' May also be from the name of an Indian tribe.

Cherokees, Lake o' the
Feature: reservoir
County: Delaware **State:** OK
Lat: 36-33-15 N **Long:** 09-44-45 W
Near Pensacola in northeastern OK. Created in 1940 by the Pensacola Dam (formerly called Grand River Dam) on the Neosho (Grand) River. 66 mi. long, 1,300 mi. of shoreline, area 64 sq. mi.
Name origin: Also called Grand Lake, Pensacola Reservoir.

Chesapeake and Delaware Canal
Feature: canal
East-west cut through northern DE and MD, from Delaware City, DE, to Chesapeake City, MD. Connects Chesapeake and Delaware Bays. About 14 mi. long, 90 ft. wide, 12 ft. deep at medium low water.
Name origin: For the bays it connects.

Chesapeake and Ohio Canal
Feature: canal
Former waterway from Washington, D.C. to Cumberland, MD, with a small section in WV; extends 185 mi. along the north bank of the Potomac River. Planned by George Washington (1732–99); begun in 1828; reached Cumberland 1850; planned extension to Pittsburgh, PA, proved unfeasible, its function made obsolete by railroads. In use until damaged by floods in 1924. Now part of the Chesapeake and Ohio Canal National Park.
Name origin: For Chesapeake Bay and the Ohio River, which the canal would have connected had it been extended to Pittsburgh, PA.

Chesapeake Bay
Feature: bay
Inlet of the Atlantic Ocean, primarily in MD but extending down into VA, the western side of the Delmarva Peninsula. From 3 to 25 mi. wide, 193 mi. long; area about 3,230 sq. mi. The Susquehanna, Patuxent, Potomac, Chester, Choptank, Nanticoke, Rappahannock, York, and James rivers empty into it. Connected to Delaware Bay by Chesapeake and Delaware Canal.
Name origin: From Algonquian; meaning is disputed, but possibly 'on the big bay,' from an Indian village name first recorded in 1585 as *Chesepiooc*, 1608 as Chesapeak.

Chesapeake Bay Bridge-Tunnel
Feature: bridge/tunnel
A series of trestles, bridges, and tunnels across mouth of Chesapeake Bay; 17.6 mi. long. Provides a 2-lane vehicular crossing between Norfolk, VA, and Cape Charles, VA. Completed in 1964.
Name origin: For the bay.

Chicago Sanitary and Ship Canal
Feature: canal
County: Du Page **State:** IL
Lat: 41-42-18 N **Long:** 08-75-60 W
Connects Lake Michigan with the Des Plaines River by way of the Chicago River. Carries treated sewage into the Des Plaines River. Before its completion in 1900, Chicago sewage was dumped into Lake Michigan, polluting the city water system. The river's natural eastward flow into Lake Michigan was changed to flow westward through the Drainage Canal, making the Chicago River the first in the world to flow away from its natural mouth. Thirty mi. long, 202 ft. wide, and 24 ft. deep. In 1967 the Supreme Court ruled that no more than 3,200 cu. ft. of water per second could be removed from Lake Michigan.
Name origin: Also called the Chicago Drainage Canal.

Chichagof Island
Feature: island
County: Sitka **State:** AK
Lat: 57-52-25 N **Long:** 13-54-63 W
In southeastern AK, in northwestern part of Alexander Archipelago, north of Baranof Island.
Name origin: Named in 1805 for Adm. Vasili Yakov Chichagov, of the Imperial Russian Navy, who explored the area (1765–66).

Chisholm Trail
Feature: trail
Famous early cattle trail from San Antonio, TX, north to Abilene, KS. Begun immediately after the Civil War to drive large herds of cattle to KS railroad terminals for shipment to market.
Name origin: For Jesse Chisholm (1806?–68?), a guide and trader, said to be part Cherokee, who first drove a wagon to mark the route in 1866.

Chukchi Sea
Feature: sea
That part of the Arctic Ocean north of the Bering Strait; divides Asia (U.S.S.R.) and North America (Alaska).
Name origin: From the name of the people inhabiting the western shore of the sea, in eastern Siberia.

Churchill, Mt.
Feature: summit
County: Valdez-Cordova **State:** AK
Lat: 61-25-10 N **Long:** 14-14-25 W
In southeast AK, peak 15,638 ft., in the Wrangell Mountains.
Name origin: Named in 1965 for Winston Churchill (1874–1965), British prime minister during World War II.

Clingmans Dome
Feature: summit
County: Sevier **State:** TN
Lat: 35-33-46 N **Long:** 08-32-95 W
Highest point (6,643 ft.) in TN, located 35 mi. southeast of Knoxville in the Great Smoky Mountains National Park on the TN-NC border.
Name origin: For Thomas Lanier Clingman (1812–97), U.S. senator from NC, who helped develop the region.

Major Geographical Features — American Places Dictionary

Coast Ranges
State: CA
Feature: range

Bolt of mountain ranges (not continuous) extending along the Pacific coast from southern CA (where they meet the Sierra Nevada Mountains), through OR, WA, British Columbia province of Canada, and into AK. Includes the Los Angeles Ranges, California Coast Range, Klamath Mountains, Oregon Coast Range, Olympic Mountains, Vancouver Range, Queen Charlotte Islands, Kodiak, Kenai, St. Elias, and Chugach Ranges, and the islands of the Alexander Archipelago. The Coast Mountains of British Columbia are separate, part of the Cascade Range.
Name origin: Also called Coast Mountains.

Cod, Cape
County: Barnstable **State:** MA
Lat: 42-03-50 N **Long:** 07-01-44 W
Feature: cape

Hook-shaped peninsula on the southeast coast of MA, enclosing Cape Cod Bay. About 65 mi. long, 1 to 20 mi. wide. Buzzards Bay is to the west, Nantucket Sound to south, the Atlantic Ocean to the east, and Massachusetts Bay to the north. Popular tourist and summer resort area. Comprising Barnstable county. Cape Cod National Seashore is along its eastern coast.
Name origin: For the species of fish once abundant in local waters; named in 1602 by Bartholomew Gosnold, an Englishman credited as being the first European to sight the cape. Also referred to as 'the Cape.'

Coeur d'Alene Lake
County: Kootenai **State:** ID
Lat: 47-42-15 N **Long:** 11-54-24 W
Feature: lake

In northern ID. About 30 mi. long; area about 60 sq. mi.
Name origin: French 'heart of awl,' origin uncertain. It is the French name for the Skitswich tribe.

Colorado Desert
State: CA
Feature: plain

In southeastern CA, east of the Santa Rosa and Coast ranges and west of the Colorado River; extends into northwestern Mexico. Includes Salton Sea, Coachella Valley, and Imperial Valley. Area about 2,000 sq. mi. Parts are 245 ft. below sea level.

Colorado Plateau
State: AZ
Feature: plain

Vast arid upland western U.S. covering parts of southeastern UT, southwestern CO, northwestern NM, and much of northern AZ. Area about 50,000 sq. mi. Includes elevations of 2,000 to 12,000 ft., and deep canyons including the Grand Canyon. Bounded on east by Rocky Mountains and on the west by the Great Basin region.
Name origin: For the river.

Colorado River
Feature: stream

Rises in Rocky Mountains in northern CO, flows southwest across western CO, southeast corner of UT, and northwest corner of AZ; then south to become the lower western NV-AZ border and entire CA-AZ border. Dammed by Hoover Dam at AZ-NV border near Las Vegas to form Lake Mead. Empties into Gulf of California in Mexico. Passes through Grand Canyon and Black Canyon. About 1,450 mi. long; total fall of more than 10,000 ft. from source to mouth. Its basin drains an area of 246,000 sq. mi., about 7% of continental U.S. (excluding AK); system includes more than 50 tributaries.
Name origin: From Spanish *colorado* 'reddish-brown,' for the color of the water in that part of the river (in CA and AZ) first encountered by Spanish explorers in 1602. Name gradually extended upriver, applied officially to its entire course in 1921. Portion in CO called Grand River until 1921. Originally named *Rio de Tison* 'firebrand river,' Bernal Diaz del Castillo (c. 1491–1581), Spanish explorer.

Columbia Plateau
Feature: plain

Vast region of varied topography, more than 200,000 sq. mi. in area, in eastern WA and OR and southern ID. Bordered on west by Cascade Range, on south by the Great Basin region, and on north and east by Rocky Mountains. Comprises high lava plains, basins, plateaus, hills, and mountains with elevations above 10,000 ft. Includes Snake River Plain.
Name origin: Because it is drained by Columbia River and its tributaries.

Columbia River
Feature: stream

Rises in British Columbia, Canada; flows into WA, forms large curve to west called Big Bend below its junction with its principal tributary, the Snake River; becomes the western part of WA-OR border; empties into Pacific Ocean. 1,214 mi. long; drainage area about 259,000 sq. mi. of which 219,000 sq. mi. are in U.S. Volume of flow second to that of Mississippi among U.S. rivers. Dammed at many points along its course, largest being Grand Coulee Dam in western WA. Navigable 95 mi. to Portland, OR, for seagoing ships. Discovered 1792 by Capt. Robert Gray (1755–1806) of Boston.
Name origin: Named in 1792 by Robert Gray who explored the river in his ship *Columbia*.

Coney Island Beach
County: Kings **State:** NY
Lat: 40-34-19 N **Long:** 07-35-85 W
Feature: beach

Beach resort and amusement park on a peninsula between Gravesend and Lower bays in south Brooklyn, south of Manhattan. Six-mi. long beach used by up to one million people; two-mi. long boardwalk. Famous Steeplechase Amusement Park is now a fairgrounds.
Name origin: Believed to be anglicization of Dutch for 'rabbit.'

Congaree Swamp
State: SC
Feature: swamp

In central SC, southeast of Columbia. Possibly the largest remaining preserve of southern bottomland hardwood forest. Believed to contain the largest examples of several native trees: swamp tupelo, loblolly pine, and American holly. Since 1976 part of Congaree Swamp National Monument.
Name origin: Siouan Indian, meaning unknown.

Connecticut River
Feature: stream

Rises in Connecticut Lakes, northern NH; flows south forming entire NH-VT border; crosses west-central MA and central CT; empties into Long Island Sound at Old Saybrook. 407 mi. long. Lower 60 mi. is tidal; navigable as far as Hartford, CT for 15-ft. drafts.
Name origin: Mohican *Quonehtacut* or *Quinnehtukguet* or *Connittecock* 'the long (tidal) river.' Colony and state were named for the river. Second *c* in present spelling is silent, and irrelevant to original Indian forms; probably inserted by analogy to connect.

Continental Divide
Feature: ridge

The high ridge of the Rocky Mountains and watershed of North American continent; the line of highest points of land separating rivers that flow generally east and south into the Mississippi River and the Gulf of Mexico from those that flow generally west into the Pacific. Extends from northwest Canada south through western U.S., including MT, WY, CO, NM, then into Mexico and Central America, and South America where it joins the Andes Mountains.

Name origin: Also called the Great Divide; 'Backbone of the Nation.'

Coos Bay
Feature: bay
County: Coos **State:** OR
Lat: 43-25-46 N **Long:** 12-41-34 W

Inlet on the southwest coast of OR, at mouth of the Coos River.

Name origin: For an Indian tribe of Kusan linguistic stock. First mentioned as *cook-koo-oose* in Lewis and Clark Expedition (1803–06) journals. Interpreted as either 'lake' or 'place of pines.'

Coteau des Prairies
Feature: plain

Plateau in the Drift Prairie region of northeastern SD and western MN. Elevation 2000 ft. Its northeastern corner drops in a 600-ft. escarpment to the Minnesota River Valley. Its western edge is marked by a 300-ft. escarpment to the border of the James River Basin.

Name origin: French 'hill of the prairies.'

Crater Lake
Feature: lake
County: Klamath **State:** OR
Lat: 42-56-38 N **Long:** 12-20-62 W **Elevation:** 6,176

Fills a deep bowl formed by the prehistoric eruption of a volcano, now called Mt. Mazama in the Cascade Range in southern part of state. About 6 mi. long; 5 mi. wide; 1,932 ft. deep. Site established as a national park in 1902. Noted for deep blue color of the water.

Name origin: For the volcanic crater that forms it.

Craters of the Moon
Feature: locale
State: ID

In south-central ID, west of Idaho Falls. An area of volcanoes and lava floes create a landscape similar to that of the moon as seen through a telescope. Since 1924 part of Craters of the Moon National Monument.

Cross-Florida Waterway
See Okeechobee Waterway

Crystal Ice Cave
Feature: cave
County: Power **State:** ID
Lat: 42-57-05 N **Long:** 11-31-25 W

Underground cave with ice formations near American Falls in southeast ID; 160 ft. below lava beds of the Columbia Plateau region. Has frozen waterfall and river; some formations are hundreds of years old. Year round temperature 32°F.

Cumberland Gap
Feature: gap

Narrow, natural pass through the Cumberland Mountains at junction of VA, KY, and TN. 1,600 ft. above sea level. Discovered 1750; became "Gateway to the West" as part of pioneer Daniel Boone's (c. 1734–1820) "Wilderness Road," used by 200,000 westward-bound travelers from 1775–1800. Route of Union armies invading TN during Civil War. Part of Cumberland Gap National Historical Park.

Name origin: For the mountains.

Cumberland Mountains
Feature: range

Tableland running from southern WV to northeastern AL north of Birmingham; along KY-VA border. Average height about 2,000 ft; average width about 50 mi. Part of the Appalachian Mountains and the Allegheny highlands.

Name origin: For the river. Also called Cumberland Plateau.

Cumberland Plateau
See Cumberland Mtns.

Cumberland River
Feature: stream

Flows through southern KY and northern TN. 687 mi. long; navigable. Cumberland Falls are part of it in KY.

Name origin: For the county of Cumberland, England. Name made popular by Prince William Augustus (1721–65), Duke of Cumberland, victor over Highlander Scots at Culloden in 1746.

Cumberland Road
See National Road

Curwood, Mt.
Feature: summit
County: Buraga **State:** MI
Lat: 46-42-12 N **Long:** 08-81-42 W

In northwestern Upper Peninsula; highest peak in the state, 1,980 ft.

Name origin: Probably for MI native James O. Curwood (1878–1927), noted author and outdoorsman.

Cuyahoga River
Feature: stream
County: Cuyahoga **State:** OH
Lat: 41-30-13 N **Long:** 08-14-24 W

Rises in northeastern part of the state, flows north, emptying into Lake Erie at Cleveland. About 100 mi. long.

Name origin: From an Indian word, but exact origin is uncertain. Attributed to *Cayahaga* 'crooked'; to *Cuyahoganuk* 'lake river'; or to Iroquoian word for 'river,' usually applied to an important one.

Dauphin Island
Feature: island
County: Mobile **State:** AL
Lat: 30-14-58 N **Long:** 08-81-10 W

Barrier island, 15 mi. long, 5 mi. average width, at entrance to Mobile Bay, off southwest coast of AL, part of Mobile County. Discovered by Pierre (1661–1706), Sieur d'Iberville 1699.

Name origin: Honoring the dauphin, heir to the French throne.

Davis, Mt.
Feature: summit
County: Somerset **State:** PA
Lat: 39-47-09 N **Long:** 07-91-03 W

In Allegheny Mtns., southern PA; highest point in state, 3,213 ft.

Name origin: For a local settler.

Davis Mountains
Feature: range
County: Jeff Davis **State:** TX
Lat: 30-45-00 N **Long:** 10-40-50 W

Small range in west TX. Includes Mt. Livermore 8,382 ft.

Name origin: For Jefferson Davis (1808–1889), president of the Confederate States (1862–65).

Daytona Beach
Feature: beach
County: Volusia **State:** FL
Lat: 29-12-38 N **Long:** 08-10-12 W

Year-round resort on northeastern Atlantic coast of FL. The hard, white sand beach is 25 mi. long and 500 ft. wide at low tide. From 1903, site of auto races and speed trials. Popular destination for college students on spring vacations.

Name origin: For Mathias Day, founder in 1870 of the city of Daytona Beach. His name extended with the suffixes *-ton* and *-a* (used for town names).

Death Valley
Feature: basin
County: Inyo **State:** CA
Lat: 36-14-45 N **Long:** 11-65-03 W

Arid desert basin in east-central CA, along border with NV; about 130 mi. long; 6 to 14 mi. wide. Lies between Panamint Mountains to west and Amargosa Range to east. Lowest elevation in Western Hemisphere near Badwater, 282 ft. below sea level.

Name origin: Named in 1849 by a party of gold seekers, for its forbidding appearance and desolation, and also possibly for some members of the group who died while trying to cross it.

Delaware Bay
Feature: bay

Arm of the Atlantic Ocean between east coast of DE and southwest coast of NJ. About 50 mi. long, 35 mi. wide. Channel running entire length is 30 to 60 ft. deep, allowing oceangoing vessels to reach Philadelphia via Delaware River, which empties into bay. Connected to Chesapeake Bay by the Chesapeake and Delaware Canal, northern DE. Cape Henlopen is at bay entrance. Discovered by Henry Hudson (d. 1611) in 1609.

Name origin: For Thomas West, Lord de la Warr (1577–1618), first British governor of the colony of VA. The river, Indian tribe (also called Leni or Leni-Lenape), and state are named for the bay.

Delaware River
Feature: stream

Rises in southern NY, flows southeast to form entire eastern boundary of PA with NY and NJ, and part of boundary of NJ and DE. About 280 mi. long; empties into Delaware Bay below Wilmington, DE. Navigable to Trenton, NJ. Discovered by Henry Hudson (d. 1611) in 1609.

Name origin: For the bay.

Delaware Water Gap
Feature: gap
County: Monroe **State:** PA
Lat: 40-58-03 N **Long:** 07-50-72 W

Deep, narrow gorge through Kittatinny Mountains east of Stroudsburg, PA; carved by Delaware River. About 3 mi. long; steep walls rise as high as 1,400 ft. on each side. Mt. Tammany is on New Jersey side, Mt. Minsi on Pennsylvania.

Name origin: For the river.

Delmarva Peninsula
Feature: cape

Lies between DE and the Atlantic Ocean to the east, Chesapeake Bay to the west.

Name origin: Formed from the names of the three states forming it: Delaware, Maryland, and Virginia.

Detroit Dam
Feature: dam
County: Marion **State:** OR
Lat: 44-43-16 N **Long:** 12-21-45 W

Gravity dam on North Santiam River about 45 mi. southeast of Salem, OR. Height 454 ft., 1,528 ft. long; completed 1953. Reservoir holds 455,000 acre-feet of water.

Detroit River
Feature: stream
County: Wayne **State:** MI
Lat: 42-02-28 N **Long:** 08-30-85 W

In southeastern MI. Flows south from Lake St. Clair into Lake Erie; forms part of U.S.-Canada border. About 30 mi. long, 1/2 to 3 mi. wide. Railroad tunnel (2,668 ft. long) and vehicular tunnel (2,200 ft. long) connect Detroit, MI, with Windsor, Canada. Ambassador Bridge spans river at Detroit. Carries more shipping than almost any other river in North America.

Name origin: For the city. Also referred to as the *Dardanelles of America*.

Devils Tower
Feature: summit
County: Crook **State:** WY
Lat: 44-35-26 N **Long:** 10-44-25 W

Massive tower of volcanic rock in northeastern WY, along Belle Fourche River; 865 ft. high from base, 5,112 ft. elevation. First national monument in U.S., 1906.

Name origin: Claimed by the Indians to have been inhabited by 'bad spirits.'

Diamond Head
Feature: summit
County: Honolulu **State:** HI
Lat: 21-15-47 N **Long:** 15-74-85 W **Elevation:** 760

Famous Honolulu landmark, an extinct volcano rising 760 ft., about 5 mi. southeast of the city on southeastern coast of Oahu. At north end is Fort Ruger, a former site for coastal artillery emplacements.

Name origin: For the calcite crystals in the rocks that reflect like diamonds when the sun strikes them. Formerly called *Lae-'ahi* 'brow of the ahi fish' and Diamond Hill.

Disappointment, Cape
Feature: cape
County: Pacific **State:** WA
Lat: 46-17-24 N **Long:** 12-40-33 W

Located on southwestern peninsula of WA, at mouth of the Columbia River.

Name origin: Named by English explorer John Meares in 1788 because he could not find a river there that the maps of earlier Spanish explorers had mistakenly shown.

Donner Pass
Feature: gap
County: Nevada **State:** CA
Lat: 39-19-09 N **Long:** 12-01-93 W

A cut through the Sierra Nevada Mountains, 7,088 ft. above sea level, about 35 mi. southwest of Reno, Nevada. First transcontinental railroad system, completed in 1869, went through the pass.

Name origin: For George and Jacob Donner, leaders of a party of 82 pioneers that met with disaster in 1846–47. Only 47 survived the severe winter in the snowbound pass, having resorted to cannibalism.

Door Peninsula
Feature: cape
County: Door **State:** WI
Lat: 44-55-00 N **Long:** 08-72-20 W

In eastern WI, jutting north into Lake Michigan and separating it from Green Bay. Includes Door County and parts of Kewaunee and Brown counties.

Name origin: From the English translation of the first word in the French *Porte des Morts* ('Door of Deaths'), the name of the strait at the tip of the peninsula that separates it from Washington Island. The French name apparently alludes to an incident that involved loss of life.

American Places Dictionary Major Geographical Features

Driskill Mountain
Feature: summit
County: Bienville **State:** LA
Lat: 32-25-28 N **Long:** 09-25-35 W
In northwest LA; highest peak in state, 535 ft.
Name origin: For a local settler.

Dry Tortugas
Feature: islands
County: Monroe **State:** FL
Lat: 24-39-53 N **Long:** 08-25-12 W
Group of coral islands, or keys, in southwest FL; about 60 mi. west of Key West, at entrance to Gulf of Mexico. Discovered by Spanish explorer Juan Ponce de León (1460–1521) in 1513. Fort Jefferson built on Garden Key in 1846. Federal bird reservation since 1908.
Name origin: Originally called Tortugas, Spanish for 'turtles,' by Ponce de León for the many turtles found in local waters.

Dust Bowl
Feature: area
Region of about 50 million acres in the southern Great Plains; parts of CO, KS, NM, OK, and TX.
Name origin: For the great dust storms that blew away the topsoil between 1935 and 1938, devastating the entire agricultural economy of the region. Caused by a seven-year drought, overgrazing, and farming techniques that did not protect the soil against erosion.

Eagle Mountain
Feature: summit
County: Cook **State:** MN
Lat: 47-53-51 N **Long:** 09-03-33 W
In northeastern MN; highest peak in state, 2,301 ft.

East Peak
See Boundary Peak

East River
Feature: channel
County: Queens **State:** NY
Lat: 40-47-13 N **Long:** 07-35-50 W
In southeastern NY; 16-mi. strait connecting Long Island Sound and Upper New York Bay. Separates boroughs of Queens and Brooklyn from Manhattan, and Queens from the Bronx. Harlem River and Spuyten Duyvil Creek connect it with the Hudson River.
Name origin: For its location along the eastern side of Manhattan.

Elbert, Mt.
Feature: summit
County: Lake **State:** CO
Lat: 39-07-04 N **Long:** 10-62-64 W
In central CO. Highest peak in the state and in the Rockies, 14,433 ft.
Name origin: For Samuel H. Elbert (1833–1907), CO territorial governor (1873–74).

Ellis Island
Feature: island
State: NY
27-acre island in New York Harbor, about 1 mi. southwest of Manhattan, 1/2 mi. north of Liberty Island, 1300 ft. from the NJ shore. Sold by NY to federal government 1808 for $10,000; used as a fort and powder magazine. Used from 1892–1924 as the chief reception center for European immigrants: functions transferred to NY City in 1943, detention center for enemy aliens until closed in 1954. Made part of Statue of Liberty National Monument. Restored main building opened as Ellis Island Immigration Museum, September 1990. Dispute over jurisdiction between NY and NJ decided in favor of NY in Feb 1992.
Name origin: For Samuel Ellis, merchant and farmer, who owned the island during the Revolutionary War. Formerly called Oyster Island, Bucking Island, and Gibbet Island.

Erie, Lake
Feature: lake
Borders western NY, corner of northwestern PA, northern OH, southeastern MI, and southern Ontario, Canada. About 240 mi. long, up to 57 mi. wide. Area 9,910 sq. mi., 4th largest of the Great Lakes. Deepest point 210 ft., shallowest of Great Lakes.
Name origin: For an Indian tribe of Iroquoian linguistic stock sometimes referred to as the Cat Nation, who lived along the southern shore of the lake. They were called *Erieehronons* 'People of the Panther' by the Iroquois (whence the name *Lac du Chat* 'Lake of the Cat' used by French explorers).

Etonah, Mount
See Brasstown Bald

Everglades, the
Feature: swamp
State: FL
Low-lying region, 1,500,000 acres (2,746 sq. mi) of swampland and flooded sawgrass plains in southern Florida. Extend from Lake Okeechobee south about 40 mi. wide, 100 mi. long, merging into saltwater marshes and mangrove swamps near Bay of Florida and Gulf of Mexico. Bounded on the west by Big Cypress Swamp, on the east by a limestone ridge. Haven of plentiful wildlife. Southwestern part forms Everglades National Park.
Name origin: Recorded as early as 1822, perhaps a corruption of 'river glades,' term applied to the area by a British surveyor. *Glade* is used in southeastern U.S. to refer to marshland.

Fairweather, Mt.
Feature: summit
County: Skagway-Yakutat-Angson **State:** AK
Lat: 58-54-26 N **Long:** 13-73-13 W
On Alaska-British Columbia (Canada) border, north of Alexander Archipelago, on Glacier Bay. Height 15,300 ft.
Name origin: Named in 1778 by British explorer Capt. James Cook, presumably because of the good weather at the time.

Fairy Falls
Feature: falls
County: Pierce **State:** WA
Lat: 46-47-41 N **Long:** 12-14-15 W
Water fall on Stevens Creek in Mount Rainier National Park, western WA. Situated 5,500 ft. above sea level, at head of Stevens Canyon. One of the highest falls in the U.S., 700 ft.

Fall Line
Geologic feature of the eastern U.S., from southern NY to AL, along which series of waterfalls and rapids form as hard rock meets softer rock. Nearly every stream along the Fall Line has rapids or waterfalls. Generally marks the farthest inland point for navigation. Dividing line between the Atlantic Coastal Plain and the Piedmont regions.

Fear, Cape
Feature: cape
County: Brunswick   State: NC
Lat: 33-50-25 N   Long: 07-75-73 W

Located on Smith Island at mouth of Cape Fear River, on southeastern Atlantic coast.

Name origin: So named because a shipwreck nearly occurred off the point of the cape during an English expedition in 1585.

Feather Falls
Feature: falls
County: Butte   State: CA
Lat: 39-38-35 N   Long: 12-11-62 W

In middle fork of Feather River, north-central CA. Height 640 ft.

Name origin: For the river also known by the Spanish version of the name, *Rio de las Plumas*. Name refers to many feathers used by the local Indians for decoration.

Finger Lakes
Feature: lakes
County: Seneca   State: NY
Lat: 42-50-00 N   Long: 07-70-00 W

Chain of long, thin lakes in north-central NY, west of Syracuse. Comprise at least 11 lakes, including notably Seneca, Cayuga, Keuka, Canandaigua, Owasco, and Skaneateles. Frontenac Island in Cayuga Lake is one of the few islands in the lakes. Seneca is the largest: 37 mi. long, 4 mi. wide; lies 444 ft. above sea level; 600 ft. deep. Cayuga and Seneca are connected at their northern ends by Cayuga and Seneca Canal, part of the NY State Barge Canal System. Lakes area is center of NY wine industry. Taughannock Falls (215 ft.) near head of Cayuga Lake is one of highest east of Rockies.

Name origin: Descriptive of their shape, and the general appearance of the largest lakes on a map, which resemble the fingers of an open hand.

Fire Island
Feature: island
County: Suffolk   State: NY
Lat: 40-40-04 N   Long: 07-30-31 W

Long narrow sandy spit off south-central Long Island, NY, separating Great South Bay from the Atlantic Ocean. Beach resort area. About 30 mi. long, 1/4 to 1/2 mi. wide. Accessible by two bridges and several passenger ferries. Has a lighthouse and signal station for transatlantic ships approaching NY harbor. Fire Island National Seashore created in 1964 to preserve natural features.

Name origin: Believed to have come from the practice in the 1700s of lighting fires to lure or warn shipping.

Flathead Lake
Feature: lake
State: MT

In northwest MT. About 30 mi. long, 12 to 14 mi. wide; area 197 sq. mi. Flathead River enters the lake at its northern end and drains it at the southern end. Largest naturally occurring freshwater lake west of the Mississippi.

Name origin: From the Flathead Indians, who formerly lived in the area.

Flattery, Cape
Feature: cape
County: Clallam   State: WA
Lat: 48-23-00 N   Long: 12-44-24 W

Located on northwest tip of WA; extends into the Pacific; Strait of Juan de Fuca to the north separates it from Vancouver Island (Canada).

Name origin: Named March 22, 1778, by British Capt. James Cook (1728–79) because a small opening near it falsely "flattered us . . . with hopes of finding a harbour there."

Florida Bay
Feature: bay
County: Monroe   State: FL
Lat: 25-00-00 N   Long: 08-04-50 W

Arm of the Gulf of Mexico between southern tip of FL and the Florida Keys, filled with many small islands.

Name origin: For the state.

Florida Keys
Feature: islands
State: FL

Chain of coral islands or reefs; extend southwest from Biscayne Bay about 150 mi. into Gulf of Mexico. Straits of Florida to the south separate them from Cuba. Key West is farthest from mainland, has most important harbor; Key Largo, nearest the mainland, is the largest. Popular tourist area. Linked and joined to mainland by Overseas Highway.

Name origin: Spanish *cayo* 'small island.'

Florida Panhandle
Feature: area
State: FL

That part of the state extending west from about Tallahassee to the AL border; bordered on the south by the Gulf of Mexico and on the north by GA and AL.

Florida, Straits of
Feature: channel
State: FL

Channel at southern tip of FL, connecting the Atlantic Ocean and the Gulf of Mexico. Separates southeast Florida and the Florida Keys from the Bahamas to the east and from Cuba to the south. 300 mi. long, 50 to 150 mi. wide. Main channel has depths of 6,000 ft. Eastern half includes Great Bahama Bank.

Name origin: For the state. Also called Florida Strait, or Gulf of Florida. Formerly called New Bahama Channel.

Floyd Collins Crystal Cave
Feature: cave
State: KY

In central KY, about 100 mi. south of Louisville, within Mammoth Cave National Park. Part of the Flint Ridge cave system now combined into the Mammoth-Flint Ridge cave system.

Name origin: For the cave explorer who discovered it in 1917.

Flume
Feature: valley
County: Grafton   State: NH
Lat: 44-06-00 N   Long: 07-14-03 W

In center of state. A canyon on west side of Flume Mountain, in the Franconia Mountains. 12 ft. wide at narrowest, about 70 ft. deep.

Foraker, Mt.
Feature: summit
County: Yukon-Koyukuk   State: AK
Lat: 62-57-39 N   Long: 15-12-35 W

In south-central AK in the Alaska Range, southwest of Mt. McKinley; 17,400 ft.

Name origin: For Joseph Benson Foraker (1846–1917), jurist and U.S. senator from Ohio (1897–1909).

American Places Dictionary Major Geographical Features

Fort Peck Dam
Feature: dam
County: McCone **State:** MT
Lat: 48-00-10 N **Long:** 10-62-45 W
On Missouri River about 15 mi. upstream from Frazer. Largest earthen structure in the world: 250 ft. high, 4 mi. long. Completed 1940.
Name origin: For the fort, a trading post, named for Campbell K. Peck, a trader.

Fort Peck Lake
Feature: reservoir
County: McCone **State:** MT
Lat: 48-00-10 N **Long:** 10-62-45 W
About 15 mi. upstream from Frazer. Formed by Fort Peck Dam on Missouri River. About 135 mi. long, 16 mi. at widest, storage capacity of 19.4 million acre-ft.
Name origin: For Fort Peck dam.

Fort Randall Dam
Feature: dam
County: Gregory **State:** SD
Lat: 43-03-35 N **Long:** 09-83-34 W
About 80 mi. upstream from Yankton on Missouri River. Earth-filled, 165 ft. high, about 2 mi. long. Seventh largest dam in U.S. Completed 1956.
Name origin: Built near abandoned Fort Randall, named for Col. Daniel Randall, an army paymaster.

Four Mountains, Islands of
Feature: islands
County: Aleutians West **State:** AK
Lat: 52-40-25 N **Long:** 17-03-81 W
Five islands in the east-central Aleutian Islands, west of Umnak Island. Islands are Chuginadak, Kagamil, Uliaga, Carlisle, and Herbert.
Name origin: From Russian *O(strova) Chetyre Soposhnye,* 'Islands of Four Volcanoes.' Four of the five have volcanic peaks.

Fox Islands
Feature: islands
County: Aleutians East **State:** AK
Lat: 53-47-00 N **Long:** 16-63-50 W
Easternmost group of the Aleutians at southwestern tip of the Alaskan Peninsula; consists of Akutan, Unimak, Unalaska, and Umnak Islands; chief settlements Dutch Harbor and Unalaska.
Name origin: For the number of foxes found there by Russian explorers.

Francis Case, Lake
Feature: reservoir
County: Charles Mix **State:** SD
Lat: 43-03-35 N **Long:** 09-83-34 W **Elevation:** 1,354
Formed in 1986 by Fort Randall Dam about 80 mi. upstream from Yankton on Missouri River. About 107 mi. long, capacity of 6.1 million acre-ft.

Franklin D. Roosevelt Lake
Feature: reservoir
County: Grant **State:** WA
Lat: 47-57-22 N **Long:** 11-85-84 W
Long, narrow artificial lake in north-central part of the state; 151 mi. long. Formed in Columbia River by Grand Coulee Dam. Source of irrigation water.
Name origin: For the president (1882–1945), during whose term the Grand Coulee Dam that formed it was constructed. Also infrequently called Grand Coulee Reservoir.

Freedom Trail
Feature: trail
State: MA
A 1.5-mi. historic route through downtown Boston and into city's North End. It passes by fifteen historic landmarks from colonial to Revolutionary War times, including Faneuil Hall, the site of the Boston Massacre, the Old North Church, and the State House.
Name origin: All the sites pertain to the American Revolution.

Frissell, Mt.
Feature: summit
State: CT
A ridge in northwest CT on the south shoulder of Mt. Frissell (whose peak is in southeastern MA.) Highest point in state 2,380 ft.

Front Range
Feature: range
County: Routt **State:** CO
Lat: 40-47-30 N **Long:** 10-64-02 W
Highest part of the Southern Rocky Mountains in north-central CO and east-central WY, stretching 300 mi. north and south; borders the Great Plains. Includes the Laramie Mountains and Medicine Bow Mountains; part of Rocky Mountain National Park. Highest peak is Gray's, 14,274 ft., but Pike's Peak, near its southern extent, is the more famous.

Fur Seal Islands
See Pribilof Islands

Gallatin River
Feature: stream
Rises in Gallatin Range, northwestern WY in Yellowstone National Park, flows north into MT. Unites with Jefferson and Madison rivers to form the Missouri near Three Forks, MT; 125 mi. long. Flows in a deep canyon for 60 mi. between Madison and Gallatin ranges in Gallatin County, WY, near one of the entrances to Yellowstone National Park.

Galveston Bay
Feature: bay
County: Chambers **State:** TX
Lat: 29-34-10 N **Long:** 09-45-61 W
Inlet of the Gulf of Mexico on the coast of TX, SE of Houston. Separated from the Gulf by Bolivar Peninsula and Galveston Island.
Name origin: For Bernardo de Galvez (1746–86), Spanish colonial statesman active especially in southern U.S. and along the Gulf of Mexico.

Gannett Peak
Feature: summit
County: Fremont **State:** WY
Lat: 43-11-04 N **Long:** 10-93-91 W
In central WY; highest peak in state 13,804 ft; part of Wind River Range.
Name origin: For Henry Gannett (1846–1914) of the U.S. Geological Survey.

Garden of the Gods
Feature: park
County: El Paso **State:** CO
Lat: 38-52-04 N **Long:** 10-45-32 W
A region of about 500 acres NW of Colorado Springs in central CO. Noted for unusual formations of red and white sandstone.

Gardiner's Island
Feature: island
County: Suffolk **State:** NY
Lat: 41-05-52 N **Long:** 07-20-61 W

In Gardiner's Bay, west of Montauk Point, on eastern end of Long Island. About 7 mi. long, 3 mi. wide; area 3,300 acres. Settled in 1639; became part of East Hampton township in 1683. Capt. William Kidd's (c. 1645–1701) pirate loot was recovered here in 1699.
Name origin: For Lion Gardiner, English military engineer. After receiving a royal charter in 1639, he bought the island from the Montaukett Indians; established the first English settlement in what would become NY state. Family has kept intact the lordship and manor for 330 years, and has preserved its 17th-century character.

Gateway Arch
Feature: other
State: MO

A 630-ft. high stainless steel arch, designed by Finnish-American architect Eero Saarinen (1910–61), on the Mississippi River waterfront of St. Louis. Tallest monument in the U.S. Part of the Jefferson National Expansion Memorial, commemorating U.S. Pres. Thomas Jefferson (1743–1826), the Louisiana Purchase, and the city's role in the settlement of the West.
Name origin: Commemorative of St. Louis as the gateway to the West.

George, Lake
Feature: lake
State: NY
Lat: 43-50-13 N **Long:** 07-32-55 W **Elevation:** 319

Long, narrow lake in northeastern NY in foothills of Adirondack Mountains, near VT border. Popular resort area. About 35 mi. long, 1 to 3 miles wide. Empties into Lake Champlain to the north.
Name origin: Named by Gen. William Johnson (1715–74) in 1755 for British king, George II (1683–1760). Early settlers called it Lake Horicon.

George Washington Bridge
Feature: bridge

Major commuter route spanning the Hudson River to connect New York City at 178th St. with Fort Lee, NJ. 3,500 ft. long, 119 ft. wide, 212 ft. above river; 8 lanes; completed 1931. A second deck with 6 lanes was completed in 1962, making it the world's first 14-lane suspension bridge.
Name origin: For the first U.S. president (1732–99).

Georgia, Strait of
Feature: channel
County: Whatcom **State:** WA
Lat: 48-49-54 N **Long:** 12-25-63 W

Channel between Vancouver Is. (Canada) on west and northwestern Washington on east. 150 mi. long, 30 mi. wide, mid-channel depth of 900 to 1,200 ft.; enters Haro Strait on south. Part of inland water route from U.S. mainland to Alaska.
Name origin: Named by Capt. George Vancouver (1757–98) in 1792 for George III (1738–1820), king of England. Locally called the Gulf.

Gila River
Feature: stream

Flows west 630 mi. from southwest NM across southern AZ to the Colorado River.
Name origin: For the gila monster, a poisonous lizard whose habitat includes the Gila River valley.

Gila Wilderness Area
Feature: area
State: NM

In southwest corner of state; first area in the country set aside as a national wilderness. Includes Gila Cliff Dwellings National Monument.
Name origin: For the gila monster.

Golden Gate Bridge
Feature: bridge
County: San Francisco **State:** CA
Lat: 37-49-11 N **Long:** 12-22-84 W

One of the world's longest spans at the entrance to San Francisco Bay, connecting Marin County to San Francisco. Total length 8,981 ft., 90 ft. wide; section between its two towers is 4,200 ft., one of the world's longest spans; deck is 220 ft. above the water. Completed 1937.
Name origin: Originally named for the Golden Gate, as the strait between San Francisco Bay and the Pacific, was named by John C. Frémont (1813–90) in 1846, in expectation of the flow of riches from the Orient. Frémont actually wanted to use the Greek name *Chrysophylae*. Fancifully associated with the painted color of the bridge in the sun.

Governors Island
Feature: island
County: New York **State:** NY
Lat: 40-41-20 N **Long:** 07-40-11 W

Fortified island in Upper New York Bay at entrance to East River, east of Liberty Island. Area 173 acres. State ceded it to U.S. govt. in 1800; used entirely for military purposes since then. Site of Fort Jay (early 1800s) and Castle Williams military prison.
Name origin: For Wouter van Twiller, a Dutch governor of NY (1632–37), who bought the island from the Indians.

Grand Canyon
Feature: valley
County: Mohave **State:** AZ
Lat: 36-06-46 N **Long:** 11-35-94 W

Enormous gorge of the Colorado River in NW AZ. Usual boundaries are from mouth of Little Colorado River to Grand Wash Cliffs near AZ-NV border; when boundaries include Marble Canyon it is about 280 mi. long, 4 to 18 mi. wide, and more than a mile deep in places. Multi-colored rock strata exposed by erosion caused by the Colorado River over millions of years reveal geologic eras spanning two billion years. Surrounding plateau is 5000-9000 ft. above sea level. Area N of canyon in northeast Mohave Co. is Grand Canyon National Park, established 1919, expanded 1974.
Name origin: Named by American geologist John Wesley Powell (1834–1902), who led the first river expedition through the canyon in 1869.

Grand Canyon of the Snake
See Hells Canyon

Grand Coulee Dam
Feature: dam
County: Grant **State:** WA
Lat: 47-57-23 N **Long:** 11-85-85 W

About 90 mi. northwest of Spokane, across the Columbia River. Largest concrete dam and greatest single source of water power in U.S.; 5,223 ft. long, 500 ft. thick at base, 550 ft. high. Has three power plants. Originally completed 1942; further construction since. Forms Franklin D. Roosevelt Lake.
Name origin: For its location near the head of the Grand Coulee, a steep-walled dry canyon where the Columbia River flowed in prehistoric times; now site of a reservoir.

Grand Lake
See Cherokee, Lake o' the

American Places Dictionary Major Geographical Features

Grand River Dam
See Pensacola Dam

Grand Strand
See Myrtle Beach

Grand Teton Feature: summit
County: Teton   State: WY
Lat: 43-44-28 N   Long: 11-04-80 W

Highest peak of the Teton Mts., 13,770 ft. in northwest WY. Surrounded by Grand Teton National Park.

Name origin: See Teton Mountains.

Grand Traverse Bay Feature: bay
County: Grand Traverse   State: MI
Lat: 45-05-00 N   Long: 08-52-80 W

Inlet of NE Lake Michigan on NW coast of MI.

Name origin: French 'the long crossing,' for the trail across the foot of the bay.

Granite Peak Feature: summit
County: Park   State: MT
Lat: 45-09-48 N   Long: 10-94-82 W

In Beartooth Range, southern MT; highest point in state, 12,799 ft.

Name origin: For the massive granite formations in the area.

Great American Desert Feature: plain
Term for the vast, semiarid region west of the Rockies and east of the Sierra Nevada, including the Great Basin and the Colorado Plateau. Also used to refer collectively to the deserts in southwest AZ and southeast CA.

Name origin: Applied in the 19th century to the vast uninhabited areas of the country from the Great Plains west. Has specialized and localized to refer to more arid regions farther west.

Great Basin Feature: area
Elevated region between Wasatch and Sierra Nevada Mountains, once covered by the Pacific Ocean; includes most of NV and parts of UT, CA, ID, WY, and OR. Area 189,000 sq. mi. Includes Great Salt Lake Desert, Carson Sink, Mojave Desert, and Death Valley. Chief drainage center Great Salt Lake; none to the ocean. Main rivers are Humboldt in northern NV and Sevier in southwest-central UT.

Name origin: Also called Basin and Range region. Arid portions were once referred to as the Great American Desert.

Great Dismal Swamp Feature: swamp
In southeast Virginia and northeast North Carolina. One of largest swamps in U.S.; about 30 mi. long, 10 mi. wide, area about 750 sq. mi. Traversed by Dismal Swamp Canal (frequently too shallow to use), connecting Chesapeake Bay with Albemarle Sound.

Great Divide
See Continental Divide

Great Lakes Feature: lakes
Group of five lakes on the U.S.-Canada border, including Huron, Ontario, Michigan, Erie, Superior. Largest freshwater source in the world. Important inland exploration and freight transportation route, with access to the Atlantic via the St. Lawrence Seaway since 1959.

Name origin: Clear evidence of the use of this term dates to the mid-1700s. Applied also to the region, especially the states of MI, OH, IN, IL, WI, and MN, also known as Lake States.

Great National Pike
See National Road

Great Plains Feature: plains
Dry grassland highlands extending from northern Canada to southern Texas, and 400 mi. east from the Rocky Mountains. Along western boundary, elevation varies from 4,500 to 6,500 ft.; along eastern boundary from 1,500 to 2,000 ft. Includes eastern Montana, Wyoming, Colorado, and New Mexico; and western North and South Dakota, Nebraska, Kansas, Oklahoma, and Texas.

Name origin: Term in use in the early 1800s. Extended to apply to the states in the region, also called the Plains States.

Great Salt Lake Feature: lake
County: Davis   State: UT
Lat: 41-10-00 N   Long: 11-23-00 W

Inland salt sea in northwest UT with no outlet. Area of lake is affected greatly by amount of rainfall and rate of evaporation; expanded to an average 2,300 sq. miles in mid-1980s, but receding since. 4,210 ft. above sea level, up to 43 ft. deep, about 70 mi. long, as much as 30 mi. wide. Southern Pacific railroad crosses it via a 13-mi. long rock-fill causeway on the Lucin Cutoff, completed in 1959. This caused an imbalance between north and south parts in lake depth, salt content, and algae growth; in 1984 a 300-ft.-wide breach was made in causeway to restore balance.

Great Salt Lake Desert Feature: plain
County: Tooele   State: UT
Lat: 40-39-11 N   Long: 11-33-13 W

In northwest UT, west of Salt Lake City. A low, flat, arid region extending south about 110 mi. from the Grouse Creek Mountains, bordering NV to the west. Area about 4,000 sq. mi. Includes Bonneville Salt Flats near NV border.

Great Sand Dunes Feature: summit
State: CO

Dunes rising up to 700 ft. in south-central CO, northeast of Alamosa, at eastern edge of the San Luis Valley. Formed by southwesterly winds, they parallel the base of the forested, snow-capped Sangre de Cristo Mountains for 10 mi. Since 1932 part of Great Sand Dunes National Monument.

Great Smoky Mountains Feature: range
Form the boundary between Tennessee and North Carolina. Among the highest and most rugged peaks of the Appalachian mountain system. Highest peak is Clingmans Dome, 6,643 ft. within Great Smoky Mountains National Park (established 1930); there are 15 other parks over 6,000 ft.

Name origin: For the mist or haze usually covering them, caused by the humidity from the thick forestation.

Great Stone Face, The
See Old Man of the Mountains

Green Bay Feature: bay
State: WI

Inlet of Lake Michigan along northeast coast of WI and the S coast of the Upper Peninsula of MI, enclosed by the Door Peninsula. About 120 mi. long, 10 to 20 mi. wide, average depth about 100 ft. Connected to Lake Michigan by canal across Door Peninsula at Sturgeon Bay. Head of important portage route between the Great Lakes and the Mississippi River via the Fox and Wisconsin rivers.

Name origin: A translation of the name given by French explorers, referring to an effect given by the color of the water.

Green Mountains
Feature: range
County: Addison **State:** VT
Lat: 42-34-20 N **Long:** 07-23-61 W

Generally low mountains and hills that extend north and south through central Vermont; part of the Appalachian system. Part of the mountain chain that continues south through MA and CT, where they are called the Berkshire Hills and the Hoosac Mountains. Popular winter resort area. Large areas are within Green Mountain National Forest. Highest peak Mt. Mansfield, 4,393 ft.

Name origin: Named by early settlers for the dense evergreen forests that covered them.

Guadalupe Peak
Feature: summit
County: Culberson **State:** TX
Lat: 31-53-28 N **Long:** 10-45-13 W

In west TX, part of the Guadalupe Mountains. Highest point in Texas, 8,751 ft. Within Guadalupe Mountains National Park.

Name origin: For Our Lady of Guadalupe, patron saint of Mexico.

Gulf Intracoastal Waterway
Feature: channel

Protected inland water route along the Gulf of Mexico from Carrabelle on S coast of Florida Panhandle to Brownsville, Texas, at Mexican border. 12 ft. deep, 125 ft. wide at bottom, 1065 mi. long. Completed 1949. Extension of the Atlantic Intracoastal Waterway.

Gulf Stream

Ocean current at the NW edge of a system of clockwise currents in the N Atlantic Ocean. Forms in the W Caribbean and flows through the Gulf of Mexico and the Straits of Florida where it reaches a surface speed of 5 knots; runs N along the E coast of the U.S.; turns NE at Cape Hatteras, NC. Splits S of Newfoundland, part reversing course as a counter current, part continuing toward Great Britain and Norway to form the North Atlantic Current. Important for its effects on water circulation on East coast of U.S., as a route for ships sailing north along U.S. Atlantic coast, and for its warming influence on prevailing westerlies that reach the British Isles and Norway, making winters milder.

Name origin: Named by Benjamin Franklin (1706–90), who thought it started in the Gulf of Mexico.

Haleakala
Feature: summit
County: Maui **State:** HI
Lat: 20-42-17 N **Long:** 15-61-03 W

On island of Maui; largest dormant volcano in world. Summit 10,023 ft.; crater about 21 mi. in circumference. Crater floor similar to moon; used for astronaut training.

Name origin: Hawaiian 'house of the sun'.

Half Dome
Feature: summit
County: Mariposa **State:** CA
Lat: 37-44-45 N **Long:** 11-93-15 W

In Yosemite National Park in NE CA. A rock mass 8,842 ft. high at head of Yosemite Valley.

Name origin: Named in 1851 by the Mariposa Battalion because of its flat, half-circular shape. Indians called it *Tissaack*.

Harney Peak
Feature: summit
County: Pennington **State:** SD
Lat: 43-51-58 N **Long:** 10-33-15 W

In Black Hills in southwest SD. Highest point in state 7,242 ft., and highest point in U.S. east of Rocky Mountains.

Name origin: For Gen. William S. Harney (1800–89), who campaigned in the 1850s against the Sioux in the Platte valley.

Harvard, Mt.
Feature: summit
County: Chaffee **State:** CO
Lat: 38-55-28 N **Long:** 10-61-91 W

In the Collegiate Range of the Sawatch Mountains, central CO. Third highest peak (14,414 ft.) in the Rocky Mountains of the U.S.

Name origin: Named in 1869 by explorer Josiah D. Whitney (1819–96) to honor Harvard College, where he taught.

Hatteras, Cape
Feature: cape
State: NC

A curved sandbar forming a promontory on the southern tip of Hatteras Island. Located 30 mi. E of the central NC coast, it extends 70 mi. along the Outer Banks, with Pamlico Sound to the W and the Atlantic Ocean on the E. The nearby Diamond Shoals are dangerous for ships. The warm current of the Gulf Stream meeting with the colder waters from the N create extremely dangerous storms, hence the nickname, "Graveyard of the Atlantic."

Name origin: For an Indian tribe of Algonquian linguistic stock; meaning is unknown but was first recorded by English explorers in the 16th century.

Hawaii
Feature: island
County: Hawaii **State:** HI

Largest, southernmost, and geologically the youngest of the seven populated islands of the state of Hawaii, 4,037 sq. mi.; separated from Maui to northwest by the Alenuihaha Channel coextensive with Hawaii county. Comprise three volcanic mountains: Mauna Kea, 13,796 ft, highest point in the state; Mauna Loa, 13,675 ft; and Hualalai, 8,275 ft.

Name origin: Also called the Big Island.

Hells Canyon
Feature: valley

Formed by the Snake River on ID-OR border. Runs N-S between Wallowa Mountains, OR, and Seven Devils Mountains, ID. North America's deepest gorge: 40 mi. long, max. height 8,032 ft.

Name origin: Descriptive of the forbidding terrain. Also called Grand Canyon of the Snake.

High Desert
Feature: plain
State: OR
Lat: 43-40-00 N **Long:** 12-02-00 W

In central part of state S of Blue Mountains and N of the Basin and Range Region. Part of Columbia Plateau, ranging in elevation from 4,000 to 5,000 ft. Much of area covered by volcanic ash.

Name origin: Descriptive of its elevation and relative lack of habitation.

High Plains
Feature: plains

A part of the Great Plains, especially southward from NE. Name also used in reference to the western portion of the Texas Panhandle.

High Point
Feature: summit
State: NJ
In northern New Jersey; highest point in state, 1,803 ft.

Hilton Head Island
Feature: island
County: Beaufort **State:** SC
Lat: 32-11-37 N **Long:** 08-04-41 W
Off SC coast south of Port Royal Sound and the mouth of the Broad River. Area 42 sq. mi. Site of Sea Pines Plantation resort.
Name origin: For William Hilton, English sea captain and adventurer who explored the island in 1663.

Hood, Mt.
Feature: summit
County: Clackamas **State:** OR
Lat: 45-22-25 N **Long:** 12-14-13 W
In northwest OR, 50 mi. E of Portland. Inactive volcanic peak in Cascade Range; highest mountain in state, 11,239 ft.
Name origin: Named by Capt. George Vancouver (1757–98) in 1792 for Lord Samuel Hood (1724–1816), admiral in British Navy.

Hoover Dam
Feature: dam
On AZ-NV border, about 25 mi. southeast of Las Vegas, NV. One of highest concrete dams in world; in Black Canyon of the Colorado River. 726 ft. high, 1,244 ft. long, base is 660 ft. thick. Built 1931–36. Caused the formation of Lake Mead.
Name origin: For Pres. Herbert Hoover (1874–1964) under whose administration construction began. For a time called Boulder Dam or Boulder Canyon Dam, officially given present name by Congress in 1947.

Hot Springs
Feature: spring
State: AR
A spa containing 47 hot springs in central AR, southwest of Little Rock. The hot mineral waters (avg. temp. 143°) are believed to relieve pain and joint disease. Bathhouses are regulated by U.S. Dept of Interior; eight of them form Bathhouse Row. Native Indians were first to use the springs. Part of Hot Springs National Park; first national health and recreation center in U.S.

Housatonic River
Feature: stream
Rises in western Massachusetts, flows south 148 mi. across western Connecticut into Long Island Sound at Stratford.
Name origin: Mohican 'at the place beyond the mountain.'

Houston Ship Canal (*or* Channel)
Feature: channel
County: Chambers **State:** TX
Lat: 29-39-57 N **Long:** 09-45-83 W
Connects Houston with the Gulf of Mexico through Buffalo Bayou and Galveston Bay. 57.3 mi. long, 200 ft. wide, 34 ft. deep.

Howe Caverns
Feature: caves
County: Schoharie **State:** NY
Lat: 42-41-45 N **Long:** 07-42-40 W
In east-central NY, 38 mi. west of Albany. Limestone caves 160 to 300 ft. deep; gondola boat rides on 1/4 mi. long underground Lake of Venus. Secret Caverns are nearby; waterfalls and fossilized marine life.
Name origin: For Lester Howe, credited with their discovery in 1842.

Hubbard, Mt.
Feature: summit
County: Akagway-Yakutat-Angson **State:** AK
Lat: 60-19-07 N **Long:** 13-90-41 W
On Alaska-Yukon (Canada) border in Coast Mountains; height 14,950 ft.
Name origin: Named in 1890 by explorer I.C. Russell for Gardiner G. Hubbard (1822–97), founder and first president of National Geographic Society, which had sponsored Russell's expedition.

Hudson River
Feature: stream
County: New York **State:** NY
Lat: 40-42-10 N **Long:** 07-40-13 W
Most important commercial waterway throughout the history of the Northeast. Rises in northern NY in Lake Tear-of-the-Clouds in Adirondack Mountains, 4,322 ft. above sea level. Flows south 306 mi. near eastern NY border; forms border with NJ for 17 mi.; empties into Atlantic Ocean at New York City. Tidal and navigable by large ships for 144 mi. from New York City to Albany; small craft can continue 6 mi. farther to Troy. Connections to the Great Lakes via the Erie Canal and to Lake Champlain and the St. Lawrence via the Champlain Canal. The Palisades line the west bank along the NJ border. In 1524, Giovanni da Verrazano (1485?–1528?), Italian sailor, became the first European to reach the river.
Name origin: For Henry Hudson (?–1611), English explorer and sea captain; in 1609 became the first white person to explore the river. Indian name *Shatemuc*; Hudson named it "Great River of the Mountains"; Dutch official name "River of Prince Mauritius"; sometimes descriptively called the "Rhine of America."

Humboldt River
Feature: stream
County: Churchill **State:** NV
Lat: 39-59-17 N **Long:** 11-83-60 W
Rises in northeastern NV and flows southwest for 290 mi.; empties into Humboldt Sink. Largest waterway in the state.
Name origin: For Alexander von Humboldt (1769–1859), German naturalist and traveler.

Humphreys Peak
Feature: summit
County: Coconino **State:** AZ
Lat: 35-20-47 N **Long:** 11-14-04 W
In western AZ; highest point in the state, 12,633 ft.
Name origin: For Gen. Andrew A. Humphreys (1812?–1883), an officer in the Ives expedition to Arizona in 1851. Also called San Francisco Mountain.

Huron, Lake
Feature: lake
Second largest of the Great Lakes. Bounded on N and E by Ontario province, Canada, and on S and W by state of MI. About 206 mi. long, about 183 mi. at its widest. Area, including North Channel and Georgian Bay, 23,050 sq. mi.; 2nd largest of the Great Lakes. Deepest point 750 ft. Connects with Lake Michigan at Straits of Mackinac and with Lake Superior via St. Mary's River. To the south, connects with Lake Erie via St. Clair River, Lake St. Clair and Detroit River.
Name origin: For a tribe of Iroquoian linguistic stock, later known as the Wyandot; from a French word for 'rough,' with a derogatory suffix, *-on*, probably indicating the Huron were formidable opponents. Originally named *Mer Douce* (French 'sea fresh'), then *Lac des Hurons*.

Idaho Panhandle
Feature: area
State: ID

The narrow, northern portion of the state between the WA border to the west and the northwestern border of MT to the east.

Iliamna Lake
Feature: lake
County: Lake and Peninsula **State:** AK
Lat: 59-32-12 N **Long:** 15-50-12 W

In southwest Alaska, west of Cook Inlet; the beginning of the Alaskan Peninsula. Area 1,033 sq. mi.
Name origin: From the Inuit name for a mythical great blackfish that inhabited the lake.

Illilouette Fall
Feature: falls
County: Mariposa **State:** CA
Lat: 37-42-50 N **Long:** 11-93-33 W

Waterfall in Yosemite National Park, east-central CA; 370 ft. high.
Name origin: Possibly from a Miwok Indian word.

Illinois River
Feature: stream
County: Calhoun **State:** IL
Lat: 38-57-52 N **Long:** 09-02-54 W

Rises in northeast IL; navigable; formed by confluence of Des Plaines and Kankakee rivers; flows 273 mi. southwest, empties into Mississippi River in western IL.
Name origin: For the Inini Indian tribe whom the French called Illini and Illinois. Their name reportedly means '(perfect and accomplished) men.'

Imperial Valley
Feature: valley
County: Imperial **State:** CA
Lat: 33-03-30 N **Long:** 11-53-33 W

Part of the Colorado Desert in south-central CA. Lies in the southern basin of the Salton Sea, near the Mexican border. Below sea level; once part of the Gulf of California (Mexico). Now irrigated from the Colorado River via the All-American Canal, one of the most productive farming areas in the U.S., with year-round farming.

Isle Royale
Feature: island
State: MI

In Lake Superior, north of the northernmost tip of the Upper Peninsula. Part of MI, though actually nearer Ontario and MN. About 45 mi. long, 9 mi. wide. Copper pits mined by Indians are still in evidence. Part of Isle Royale National Park, established 1931, which includes many other nearby small islands.

James River
Feature: stream
County: Isle of Wight **State:** VA
Lat: 36-56-29 N **Long:** 07-62-63 W

Begins in the Allegheny Mountains in central VA by confluence of the Jackson and Cowpasture rivers; flows 340 mi. east into Chesapeake Bay through the Hampton Roads channel. Jamestown, first permanent English colony in America, established on its banks in 1607. Largest waterway in the state; navigable to Richmond.
Name origin: For English King James I (1566-1625), who chartered the Virginia colony.

Jefferson, Mt.
Feature: summit
County: Linn **State:** OR
Lat: 44-40-28 N **Long:** 12-14-75 W

Peak in Cascade Range, north-central Oregon, 10,495 ft.
Name origin: For Thomas Jefferson (1743-1826), third U.S. president.

Jerimoth Hill
Feature: summit
County: Providence **State:** RI
Lat: 41-50-58 N **Long:** 07-14-64 W

In western RI, on Connecticut border. Highest point in state, 812 ft.
Name origin: Biblical name, from Hebrew meaning 'elevation.'

John Day Fossil Beds
Feature: locale
County: Wheeler **State:** OR

Three areas in north-central OR containing plant and animal fossils from five consecutive epochs: Eocene, Oligocene, Miocene, Pliocene, and Pleistocene; from 55 million to 10 million years old. Since 1974 part of John Day Fossil Beds National Monument.
Name origin: For John Day (1771-1819), a frontiersman in the Astor-Hunt overland party in the 1810s.

John Day River
Feature: stream
County: Gilliam **State:** OR
Lat: 45-43-58 N **Long:** 12-03-85 W

Rises in east-central OR, flows 281 mi. west and north into the Columbia River on southern border of WA near Rufus, OR, past John Day Fossil Beds National Monument (three sites), established 1974.
Name origin: For John Day (1771-1819), a frontiersman in the Astor-Hunt overland party in the 1810s.

Jones Beach State Park
Feature: beach
County: Nassau **State:** NY
Lat: 40-35-40 N **Long:** 07-33-01 W

Six-mi. wide, 1/4-mi. deep white sand beaches on Atlantic Ocean and Great South Bay. 5 mi. south of Wantagh on a barrier island off the southwestern coast of Long Island. 2,413-acre Jones Beach State Park created by Robert Moses opened in 1929; marine theatre; boardwalk; and many recreational facilities. The landmark water tower, above a freshwater well 1,000 ft. deep, was modeled after the campanile of St. Mark's Church in Venice. Visited by up to 9 million people each year; half of these during summer.
Name origin: For Thomas Jones, privateer, who bought the land in 1692. Name in use since 1713.

Juan de Fuca, Strait of
Feature: channel
County: Clallam **State:** WA
Lat: 48-12-01 N **Long:** 12-33-41 W

Body of water separating Vancouver Island, Canada, from WA. About 100 mi. long, 11 to 17 mi. wide. With Puget Sound and the Strait of Georgia, it forms an important waterway to the Pacific Ocean from Seattle, WA, and Vancouver, British Columbia.
Name origin: For a (perhaps legendary) Greek navigator in Spanish service, Juan de Fuca, who claimed to have found a passage between the Pacific and Atlantic oceans in 1592. His real name is said to have been Apostolos Valerianos. Name given by English explorer John Meares in 1788.

Katahdin, Mt.
Feature: summit
County: Piscataquis **State:** ME
Lat: 45-54-16 N **Long:** 06-85-52 W

Peak in north-central ME; highest point in the state, 5,268 ft. Northern terminus of Appalachian Trail.
Name origin: Abnaki Indian for 'main mountain.'

Katerina Archipelago
See Aleutian Islands

Katmai, Mt.
Feature: summit
County: Lake and Peninsula **State:** AK
Lat: 58-16-46 N **Long:** 15-45-70 W

Volcano in southern Alaska, at north end of Alaska Peninsula on Shelikof Strait; height 6,715 ft. Main crater is one of largest in world. In 1912 it produced one of the largest eruptions ever recorded; created the ash-filled Valley of the Ten Thousand Smokes. Part of Katmai National Monument, established 1918.

Name origin: For a former Eskimo village, whose name was recorded as *Katmay* in 1827 by Russian explorer Adam Johann von Krusenstern (1770–1846). Village was abandoned after 1912 eruption. Meaning unknown.

Kauai
Feature: island
State: HI

Fourth largest, oldest, and northernmost of the seven populated islands of the state of Hawaii, roughly circular, 32 mi. in diameter. Separated from Oahu to southeast by Kanai Channel.

Name origin: Descriptively called the Garden Island.

Kennebec River
Feature: stream
County: Sagadahoc **State:** ME
Lat: 43-44-06 N **Long:** 06-94-62 W

Rises in Moosehead Lake in west-central ME; flows about 165 mi. west through southern half of state, empties into Atlantic Ocean near Bath. River drops more than 1,000 ft. along its course; a series of waterfalls along the river furnish hydroelectric power. Mouth of the river was site of Fort St. George, first attempt at permanent English settlement in Maine, 1607.

Name origin: Algonquian 'long lake.' Recorded as Kinibeki by French explorers, 1609.

Kentucky Lake *or* Reservoir
Feature: reservoir

In western KY and TN, about 15 mi. southeast of Paducah. Formed by Kentucky Dam (completed 1944) across Tennessee River. About 185 mi. long, 2.5 mi. wide, area 247 sq. mi. Holds more than 6 million acre-ft.

Kilauea (Mount)
Feature: summit
County: Hawaii **State:** HI
Lat: 19-24-59 N **Long:** 15-51-63 W

Active volcano on south-central Hawaii Island on eastern slope of Mauna Loa. In Hawaii Volcanoes National Park. Crater is 2 mi. wide, elevation 4,090 ft. Largest active crater in world. Halemaumau is the fire pit; about 470 ft. deep; when active, contains from 48 to 190 acres of red-hot lava.

Name origin: Hawaiian 'spewing.'

Kings Peak
Feature: summit
County: Duchesne **State:** UT
Lat: 40-46-43 N **Long:** 11-02-22 W

In northeastern UT in the Uinta Mountains. Highest point in state, 13,528 ft.

Name origin: For Clarence King (1842–1901), U.S. geologist and explorer; first head of U.S. Geological Survey.

Klamath Mountains
Feature: range

Range of the Coast Ranges in northwestern CA; extends north into OR. In northern part, includes the Siskiyou Mountains.

Name origin: For the Indian tribe of southwestern OR.

Klamath River
Feature: stream

Rises in Upper Klamath Lake in southern OR; flows about 250 mi.; joins the Trinity River in CA; empties into Pacific at Requa, CA.

Name origin: For the Indian tribe of southwestern OR.

Kodiak Island
Feature: island
County: Kodiak Island **State:** AK
Lat: 57-23-46 N **Long:** 15-32-90 W

Largest island in AK, home of Kodiak bear, in Gulf of Alaska southeast of Alaska Peninsula; Shelikof Strait between its west coast and Alaskan mainland. Area 5,363 sq. mi. Site of first Russian colony in America, founded 1784; headquarters of Russian Trading Co. until 1805.

Name origin: At time of discovery (1763), island was called *Kadyak* by inhabitants. Island referred to as *kikhtak* 'island' by Inuit (Eskimo) natives. *Kodiak* first recorded 1778 by English explorer Capt. James Cook (1728–79). Spellings have varied since, but present form, influenced by local usage, became official in 1901.

La Brea Pits
Feature: mine
County: Los Angeles **State:** CA
Lat: 34-03-47 N **Long:** 11-82-11 W

Oil and tar-filled bog in Hancock Park in Los Angeles, CA; one of the world's best known sources of Ice Age fossils. Since 1906 skeletons of thousands of prehistoric animals have been dug up: saber-toothed tigers, giant wolves, llamas, camels, horses, giant ground sloths, etc. George C. Page Museum, on the site, displays many of the skeletons.

Name origin: Spanish 'tar,' or 'pitch.'

Laguna Beach
Feature: beach
County: Orange **State:** CA
Lat: 33-32-32 N **Long:** 11-74-65 W

Resort on the Pacific coast of CA, about 27 mi southeast of Long Beach.

Name origin: For Laguna Canyon, so-named for the two 'lagoons' at its head.

Lake Okeechobee-Cross Florida Waterway
See Okeechobee Waterway

Lake Pontchartrain
See Pontchartrain, Lake

Lake Washington Ship Canal
Feature: canal
County: King **State:** WA
Lat: 47-39-21 N **Long:** 12-22-20 W

Together with the Hiram M. Chittenden Locks and Lake Union, connects Puget Sound on the W of Seattle with Lake Washington on its E.

Name origin: For the first U.S. president, George Washington (1732–99).

Lanai
Feature: island
State: HI

One of the seven populated islands of the state of Hawaii. 18 mi. long, 10 mi. wide, area 140 sq. mi. About 7 mi. west of Maui, separated by Auau Channel.

Name origin: From Hawaiian 'day (of) conquest.' Variant form *Nanai*. Also called the Pineapple Island because all its cultivated land (98% of island) is part of a single pineapple plantation.

Laramie Mountains
Feature: range
County: Albany **State:** WY
Lat: 41-31-36 N **Long:** 10-52-95 W **Elevation:** 10,272
Part of the Southern Rockies. They are used for geologically dating the mountain-building era of the Rocky Mountain chain.
Name origin: For Jacques Laramie (?–1818), French-Canadian trapper. Also called Snowy Mountains.

Lassen Peak *or* Mount
Feature: summit
County: Shasta **State:** CA
Lat: 40-29-16 N **Long:** 12-13-01 W
Volcano in northeastern CA, 10,547 ft. high, near southern end of Cascade Mountains. Prominent landmark for westward pioneers of mid-1800s. In Lassen Volcanic National Park. Long inactive until 1914; last erupted February 1921.
Name origin: For Peter Lassen (1793–1895), Danish immigrant and important pioneer of the 1840s, who blazed a trail near it and established Lassen's Route on the California Trail. Peak was first of many area features to be named for him.

Lewes River
See Yukon River

Lewis Range
Feature: range
County: Glacier **State:** MT
Lat: 48-53-00 N **Long:** 11-35-10 W
Part of the Northern Rocky Mountains, extending from western MT north along east side of Waterton-Glacier International Peace Park into Alberta, Canada. Called "the backbone of the world" by Blackfoot Indians because the mountains rise suddenly from the plains without foothills.
Name origin: For Meriwether Lewis (1774-1809), the explorer.

Liberty Island
Feature: island
State: NY
In Upper New York Bay, southwest of Manhattan Island, site of the Statue of Liberty. Owned by U.S. government. Fort Wood, built in the shape of an 11-point star and completed in 1841, is the base on which the statue stands. Part of Statue of Liberty National Monument.
Name origin: Officially renamed in 1956; previously known as Bedloe's Island.

Little River
Feature: stream
State: AL
Along the ridge known as Lookout Mountain in northeastern AL near Chattanooga, TN. Forms the Little River Canyon, known as 'Grand Canyon of the South'; deepest gorge east of Mississippi River.

Llano Estacado
See Texas Panhandle

Long Island
Feature: island
State: NY
Long, narrow island stretching east from New York City, protecting most of the CT coastline. On west separated from Manhattan by the East River, from NJ by Upper New York Bay, and from Staten Island by the Narrows. Atlantic Ocean is to east and south; separated from CT to the north by Long Island Sound. 120 mi. long, from 12 to 23 mi. wide, area 1,701 sq. mi. Consists of Kings (Borough of Brooklyn) and Queens Counties, both part of New York City, and Nassau and Suffolk Counties; population 6,861,474. Eastern tip divides into North and South Forks; Montauk Lighthouse at tip of North Fork.
Name origin: Name in use since early 17th century.

Long Island Sound
Feature: bay
County: Suffolk **Lat:** 41-05-00 N **Long:** 07-30-00 W
Waterway separating Long Island from Connecticut. Connected by East River with New York Bay at west end; joins Atlantic Ocean at eastern end. Nearly 110 mi. long, from 3–20 mi. wide.
Name origin: For the island.

Lookout, Cape
Feature: cape
County: Carteret **State:** NC
Lat: 34-35-53 N **Long:** 07-63-21 W
In eastern NC on southern tip of Core Bank, E of Morehead City.

Lookout Mountain
Feature: summit
State: TN
Ridge in southeast TN with magnificent view of seven states; extends into GA and AL. Highest point 2,126 ft., near Chattanooga. Site of Civil War battle.

Los Angeles Ranges
Feature: ranges
State: CA
Group of small mountain ranges between Santa Barbara and San Diego along the southern coast of CA, including the Santa Ynez, Santa Monica, San Gabriel, and San Bernardino mountains; include the San Jacinto and Santa Ana mountains.
Name origin: Also called Transverse Ranges because they extend in a general east-west direction.

Lower Red Lake
See Red Lake

Lower Yosemite Falls
See Yosemite Falls

Luray Caverns
Feature: caves
County: Page **State:** VA
Lat: 38-39-51 N **Long:** 07-82-90 W
In the Shenandoah Valley of VA, west of the Blue Ridge Mountains. A series of limestone caves, some of the rooms are more than 140 ft. high; some of the stalactites 50 ft. long. Discovered by Andrew J. Campbell and friends, Aug 1878.
Name origin: Near Luray, VA.

American Places Dictionary   Major Geographical Features

Mackinac Island
Feature: island
County: Mackinac   **State:** MI
Lat: 45-51-52 N   **Long:** 08-43-73 W

Resort island off southeastern tip of the Upper Peninsula of MI in the Straits of Mackinac, 5 mi. east of St. Ignace; area 4 sq. mi.

Name origin: From Ojibway *Michilimackinak* 'island of the large turtle.' Also spelled Mackinaw, reflecting pronunciation.

Mackinac Straits Bridge
Feature: bridge
County: Mackinac   **State:** MI
Lat: 45-48-54 N   **Long:** 08-44-34 W

Spans the Straits of Mackinac to connect Mackinaw City in the Lower Peninsula of MI with St. Ignace in the Upper Peninsula. Third longest suspension bridge in the world: center span 3,800 ft.; completed 1957.

Mackinac, Straits of
Feature: channel
County: Mackinac   **State:** MI
Lat: 45-49-00 N   **Long:** 08-44-50 W

Between the Upper Peninsula and lower MI; connects lakes Michigan and Huron. About 40 mi. long, 5 mi. wide at narrowest point. Spanned by the Mackinac Straits Bridge.

Name origin: For the island.

Madre, Laguna
Feature: lake
County: Brooks   **State:** TX
Lat: 27-09-59 N   **Long:** 09-80-74 W

Long inlet of the Gulf of Mexico off southeastern coast of Texas, sheltered from Gulf by barrier islands, notably Padre Island. Extends south for 120 mi. from Corpus Christi.

Name origin: Spanish 'mother lake.'

Magazine Mountain
Feature: summit
County: Logan   **State:** AR
Lat: 35-10-02 N   **Long:** 09-33-84 W

In west-central Arkansas in the Ouachita Mountains. Highest peak in state, 2,753 ft.

Name origin: Probably from French 'storehouse.'

Malaspina Glacier
Feature: glacier
County: Skagway-Yakutat-Angson   **State:** AK
Lat: 59-58-53 N   **Long:** 14-04-30 W

On southeastern coast of AK in Saint Elias Mountains extending south from Mt. St. Elias to Yakutat Bay. Larger than Rhode Island: about 90 mi. long; area 1,500 sq. mi.; fronts the Pacific for about 60 mi.; more than 1,000 ft. thick.

Name origin: For Capt. Alessandro Malaspina, Italian explorer for the Spanish government who explored the Alaskan coast in 1791.

Malibu Beach
Feature: beach
County: Los Angeles   **State:** CA
Lat: 34-01-58 N   **Long:** 11-84-11 W

Secluded sandspit west of Los Angeles, extending into Santa Monica Bay on the southwestern Pacific coast of CA. Noted for the oceanview homes of celebrities.

Name origin: For the beach community, named for the Indian settlement (rancheria) *Umaliba*, probably Chumash, meaning unknown. Present spelling first appeared 1805. Variants include *Maligo, Malago, Malaga, Malico*.

Mammoth Cave
Feature: cave
County: Edmonson   **State:** KY
Lat: 37-11-15 N   **Long:** 08-60-61 W

In central KY about 100 mi. south of Louisville; part of the Mammoth-Flint Ridge cave system. Has 12 mi. of corridors on five levels; lowest level is 360 ft. below the earth's surface. Contains lakes, rivers, and waterfalls; Echo River is the largest: 20 to 60 ft. wide, 5 to 25 ft. deep. Artifacts show it was known to prehistoric Indians; discovered by white settlers in 1799. Opened to the public 1816. Part of Mammoth Cave National Park.

Mammoth-Flint Ridge Cave System
Feature: cave
State: KY

In central KY, about 100 mi. south of Louisville, part of Mammoth Cave National Park. In 1972 explorers discovered a connection between Mammoth Cave and the Flint Ridge cave system, which contains Floyd Collins Crystal Cave. It is the largest known cave system in the world with about 200 mi. of explored passages.

Manhattan
Feature: borough
County: New York   **State:** NY
Lat: 40-47-00 N   **Long:** 07-35-80 W   **Elevation:** 107

Forms the borough of Manhattan (popularly referred to as New York City), which is co-extensive with New York County. In southeastern NY at mouth of the Hudson River. Area 34 sq. mi., including 12 sq. mi. of inland water. Bordered on E by the East River, on the S with Upper New York Bay, on the W by the Hudson River, and on the N by the Harlem River and Spuyten Duyvil Creek. Connected to other boroughs and NJ by bridges and tunnels, including George Washington Bridge, Brooklyn Bridge, and Verrazzano-Narrows Bridges; and the Lincoln, Holland, and Queens-Mid tunnels. Bought from the Manhattan Indians in 1626 by Peter Minuit of the Dutch West Indies Co.

Name origin: For the tribe of Indians living in the area at the time of the arrival of the Dutch. As a Dutch settlement called New Amsterdam.

Mansfield, Mt.
Feature: summit
County: Lomsille   **State:** VT
Lat: 44-31-35 N   **Long:** 07-24-85 W

Peak in winter sports area of northern VT. Highest point in the state and the Green Mountains, 4,393 ft. Smugglers Notch, a deep gorge, is at base of mountain.

Marcy, Mt.
Feature: summit
County: Essex   **State:** NY
Lat: 44-06-45 N   **Long:** 07-35-52 W

Peak in northeast NY. Highest peak in the state and in the Adirondacks, 5,344 ft.

Name origin: For William Learned Marcy (1786–1857), statesman and governor of NY (1833–39) who instituted a geological survey of the Adirondack Mountains in 1837.

Marion, Lake
Feature: reservoir
County: Clarendon   **State:** SC
Lat: 33-27-13 N   **Long:** 08-00-95 W   **Elevation:** 77

In east-central SC. Formed in 1942 by the Santee Dam across the Santee River. Lake is broad and 40 mi. long. Connected to Charleston by a navigable waterway, Lake Moultrie, and by the Cooper River.

Name origin: For Francis Marion (c. 1732–95), SC soldier and legislator, known as the 'Swamp Fox' for his tactics during the American Revolution. Also called Santee Reservoir.

Martha's Vineyard
Feature: island
County: Dukes **State:** MA
Lat: 41-25-00 N **Long:** 07-03-70 W

Island summer resort south of southwestern Cape Cod. Coextensive with Dukes County. Population 11,639, but swells to 65,000 in summer season. To the north and west is Vineyard Sound, to north and east is Nantucket Sound, to the south the Atlantic Ocean. Muskeget Channel separates it from Nantucket Island to the southeast. Area about 100 sq. mi. Settled by English from MA in 1642.
Name origin: Named by Gabriel Archer in 1602 for a woman, reason unknown, plus *Vineyard* for the vines growing on the island.

Massive, Mt.
Feature: summit
County: Lake **State:** CO
Lat: 39-11-14 N **Long:** 10-62-82 W

In Sawatch Range, central CO. Second highest mountain in the state, 14,421 ft.

Matagorda Bay
Feature: bay
State: TX

Inlet of the Gulf of Mexico on southeast Texas coast between Galveston and Corpus Christi; about 50 mi. long, 3-12 mi. wide. The Colorado River of Texas empties into it on the northeast; the Gulf Intracoastal Waterway crosses it.
Name origin: Spanish 'thicket' or 'rough area.'

Matanuska Valley
Feature: valley
County: Matanuska-Susitna **State:** AK
Lat: 61-36-27 N **Long:** 14-90-44 W

In south-central AK northeast of Anchorage. Mountains to the north and warm ocean currents from Cook Inlet to the south provide temperate climate. Site of a large-scale farming experiment by the federal government during the Great Depression. Alaska's chief center of agriculture until reliable air freight service from outside became available during the 1960s.
Name origin: For the river, name derived from the Russian term for the 'copper river people,' variously spelled *Matanooski*, *Mednotski*, *Miduuski*, etc., applied to Ahtena Indians on Copper River, and possibly used in 1800s to imply a route from Cook Inlet to the Copper River.

Maui
Feature: island
County: Maui **State:** HI

Second largest of the seven populated islands of the state of Hawaii, 728 sq. mi.; northwest of the island of Hawaii. Hallakala volcano highest point on island, 10,023 ft.
Name origin: For the demigod, Maui. Called the Valley Island because of the many canyons cut into the mountains that form the island.

Mauna Kea
Feature: summit
State: HI

Dormant volcano on island of Hawaii. The world's highest island peak 13,796 ft. Measured from its underwater base it is 33,476 ft., 4,448 ft. higher than Mount Everest. At the peak is the 150-in. United Kingdom Infrared Telescope, largest in the world, and the 142-in. Canada-France-Hawaii reflector.
Name origin: Hawaiian 'white mountain,' because it is frequently snow-capped.

Mauna Loa
Feature: summit
State: HI

Volcanic mountain in south-central part of the island of Hawaii, in Hawaii Volcanoes National Park. 13,680 ft. above sea level; world's largest volcano. At top is Mokuaweoweo crater; on southeastern slop is Kilauea volcano. Most lava comes from the sides, not the peak crater.
Name origin: Hawaiian 'long mountain.'

McKinley, Mt.
Feature: summit
County: Yukon-Koyukuk **State:** AK
Lat: 63-04-10 N **Long:** 15-10-01 W

In central AK; highest peak in North America; part of the Alaska Range in Denali National Park. South Peak is 20,320 ft., North Peak 19,470 ft. Prior to 1956, South Peak was believed to be 20,269 ft. but later surveys established the present height.
Name origin: For William McKinley (1843–1901), 25th U.S. president. Also known by its Indian name *Denali* 'The Great One' or 'The High One.' Nicknamed Top of the Continent.

Mead, Lake
Feature: reservoir

Largest artificial lake in the U.S. and one of largest in the world; formed by Hoover (Boulder) Dam on the Colorado River; completed 1935; about 15 mi. E of Las Vegas on NV-AZ border. About 115 mi. long; stores about 29,755,000 acre-feet of water; area 250 sq. mi.
Name origin: For Dr. Elwood Mead, a reclamation commissioner.

Medicine Bow Mountains
Feature: range

Range of the Rocky Mountains; extending north and south in CO and WY. Highest points are Medicine Bow Peak, 12,013 ft. and Elk Mountain, 11,156 ft.
Name origin: Indians came to the mountains to obtain wood for their bows and to hold ceremonial, "medicinal" rituals and dances.

Mendenhall Glacier
Feature: glacier
County: Juneau **State:** AK
Lat: 58-29-45 N **Long:** 13-43-15 W

Flows from southern part of Juneau Icefield in the Boundary Ranges in southeast AK northwest of Juneau. About 14 mi. long, 4 mi. wide at face. Only glacier in the region accessible by highway year round. Mendenhall Lake began to form about 1900; now 1.5 mi. long, 1 mi. wide, 115 ft. deep near the face of the glacier.
Name origin: Originally named *Auke* for the Indians. Renamed in 1892 for Thomas Corwin Mendenhall (1841–1924) of the U.S. Coast and Geodetic Survey.

Meramec Caverns
Feature: caves
County: Franklin **State:** MO
Lat: 38-14-28 N **Long:** 09-10-53 W

In east-central MO, near Sullivan. The first room has space for 300 automobiles. Legendary hideout of Jesse James (1847–82).
Name origin: From an Indian tribal name meaning 'cat fish.'

Merrimack River
Feature: stream

Flows south from south-central NH about 110 mi. into northeastern MA, then northeast to the Atlantic Ocean at Newburyport, MA. Formed by confluence of Winnepesaukee and Pemigewasset rivers at Franklin, NH. Total drop of 270 ft. along its 110 mi. length, with many rapids and falls. As an abundant source of water power was important to the industrial development of the region in the 19th century as woolen and cotton mills were built along its banks. River towns include Franklin, Concord, Manchester, and Nashua, NH; and Lawrence, Lowell, and Haverhill, MA.

Name origin: Algonquian for 'swift water'.

Mesabi Range
Feature: range
County: St. Louis **State:** MN
Lat: 47-28-00 N **Long:** 09-24-50 W

Chain of low hills in northeastern MN, 60 to 75 mi. northwest of Lake Superior. One of the world's greatest iron-ore mining regions from 1892 until the 1950s.

Name origin: From Ojibway 'hidden giant,' for a legendary creature who supposedly lived in the hills.

Mesa Verde
Feature: locale
State: CO

Stone cliff-dwellings in southwestern CO, southwest of Durango. Probably built in the 1200s, they were constructed in alcoves along the high walls of the canyon. *Cliff Palace*, the largest, had 200 rooms, and was up to four stories high; also has many underground rooms, *kivas*, for religious ceremonies. Nearby are examples of pit houses, built before 400, and pueblos, built about 700. Part of Mesa Verde National Park.

Name origin: Spanish 'green table' for the pion and juniper forests.

Mexico, Gulf of
Feature: sea

Arm of the Atlantic Ocean bordered on east and north by the southern coast of the U.S. from FL to TX, on west by eastern coast of Mexico; to the south in Cuba. The Gulf is connected to the Atlantic Ocean by the Straits of Florida and south of Cuba to the Caribbean Sea by the Yucatán Channel. About 800 mi. long (north to south), 1,100 mi. wide; area 700,000 sq. mi. Greatest depth 12,700 ft. near coast of Mexico. The Mississippi, Rio Grande, Mobile, and Apalachicola are some of the major rivers that empty into it.

Michigan, Lake
Feature: lake

Borders NW IN, northeast IL, eastern WI, W MI, and the S coast of MI's Upper Peninsula, and western Lower MI. Largest body of fresh water in the U.S.; 3rd largest of the Great Lakes and the only one entirely within the U.S. 307 mi. long, 118 mi. at its widest, 923 ft. at deepest. Area 22,300 sq. mi. Green Bay is at NW corner. Empties into Lake Huron via the Straits of Mackinac; connected to the Atlantic Ocean through lakes Huron, Erie, and Ontario and by the St. Lawrence Seaway, and to the Mississippi River by the Chicago Ship Canal and the Chicago and Illinois rivers.

Name origin: Possibly from Indian *Michi-guma* 'big water.' The territory that became the state was named for the lake in 1805.

Milk River
Feature: stream
County: Valley **State:** MT
Lat: 48-03-26 N **Long:** 10-61-90 W

Two branches rise and join in western MT near the Continental Divide. Flows about 625 mi. into Alberta (Canada); then empties into Missouri River near Fort Peck Dam in northeastern MT. A major tributary of the Missouri.

Name origin: Named in 1805 by Meriwether Lewis (1774–1809) for the cloudy appearance of its waters.

Mille Lacs Lake
Feature: lake
County: Mille Lacs **State:** MN
Lat: 46-14-00 N **Long:** 09-33-90 W **Elevation:** 1,251

In east-central MN on boundary between Aitkin and Mille Lacs counties north of Minneapolis. Popular tourist and outdoor sports attraction. About 16 mi. in diameter; area 207 sq. mi.

Name origin: Probably for the county; French 'thousand lakes.'

Minnehaha Falls
Feature: falls
County: Hennepin **State:** MN
Lat: 44-54-53 N **Long:** 09-31-23 W

Near Minneapolis in southeastern MN. About 53 ft. high; occasionally necessary to pump water over the top to keep the falls going. Made famous by Henry Wadsworth Longfellow's (1807–82) poem *The Song of Hiawatha*. Bronze statue of Hiawatha and his bride stand at the top.

Name origin: Siouan 'waterfall' or 'laughing water.'

Minnesota River
Feature: stream

A major arm of the Mississippi River, it rises in the Coteau des Prairies hills in northeastern SD. Flows 332 mi., empties into Mississippi River south of St. Paul, MN. Important trade route.

Name origin: From Dakota Indian term first applied to the river. *Minne* means 'water,' but there is disagreement about *sota*. It may refer to reflection of sky upon water, so *Minnesota* would connote 'water reflecting cloudy skies.' Formerly called the St. Peter or St. Pierre.

Mississippi Alluvial Plain
Feature: plain

Area of 35,000 sq. mi. of fertile lowlands along the Mississippi River primarily in AR, MS, LA. Silt from the floodwaters of the Mississippi and its tributaries makes the soil unusually rich. Area produces large cotton and soybean crops.

Mississippi Delta
Feature: area
State: LA

Low-lying bayou region along the Mississippi River from the mouth of the Red River south to the Gulf of Mexico. Actual outlet of the Mississippi into the sea is in several distinct channels in the Delta.

Mississippi River — Feature: stream

Chief river of North America and, with its tributaries, the third largest river system in the world in volume; longest and chief inland waterway in U.S. Rises in Lake Itasca in northwestern MN, 2,348 mi., empties into the Gulf of Mexico. It and its tributaries drain almost all plains between Appalachian and Rocky mountains, including all or part of 31 states, 40% of continental U.S. Land area of the drainage basin 1,247,000 sq. mi. Navigable about 1,800 mi. from Minneapolis to Gulf. From 9 to 100 feet deep; widest at Cairo, IL, 4,500 ft. Dams, levees, and floodways are used to help control flooding. Main tributaries: Illinois and Missouri; the latter gives the Mississippi its muddy color; also Ohio, Arkansas, and Atchafalaya rivers. Its western shore forms part of the boundaries between MN, IA, MO, AR, and part of LA, and its eastern shore those of WI, IL, KY, TN, and MS.

Name origin: From words common to several Indian languages: *Meeche* or *mescha* 'great' and *cebe* 'river, water.' Territory and state named for river. Also called "Old Man River."

Mississippi Sound — Feature: bay

Inlet of Gulf of Mexico off southeast coast of MS and southwest coast of AL. The Pascagoula River empties into it.

Name origin: For the Mississippi River.

Missouri River — Feature: stream

Second longest river in U.S., after the Mississippi, and with the Ohio, one of the two main tributaries of the Mississippi. Formed in southern MT by confluence of Jefferson, Madison, and Gallatin rivers; 2,315 mi. through MT, ND, SD, forms part of the boundary between NE and IA, NE and MO, and KS and MO, joining the Mississippi River about 20 mi. north of St. Louis, MO. Navigable to Sioux City, IA. Its muddy waters color the Mississippi River. Flooding controlled by six dams, including Fort Peck, Oake, and Fort Randall. Its full course explored in 1804–1806 by Lewis and Clark Expedition.

Name origin: For an Indian tribe who inhabited an area near the mouth of the river. Original name for river was *Pekitanoul* or *Pokitanou* 'muddy water.' Territory and state named for the river. Nicknamed "Big Muddy."

Mitchell, Mt. — Feature: summit
County: Henderson **State:** NC
Lat: 35-27-10 N **Long:** 08-21-95 W

In the Black Mountain range of the Appalachians in western NC northeast of Asheville. Highest peak east of the Mississippi River, 6,684 ft.

Name origin: For Elisha Mitchell (1793–1857), professor at University of North Carolina, who fell to his death while trying to measure the height of the peak.

Mobile Bay — Feature: bay
County: Mobile **State:** AL
Lat: 30-26-33 N **Long:** 08-80-03 W

Inlet of the Gulf of Mexico on SW coast of AL. 30 mi. long, 10 to 12 mi. wide, city of Mobile on northwestern shore. The Mobile River empties into it.

Name origin: Named from the river, whose name derives from the French form of an Indian word of unknown origin, applied to a tribe related to the Choctaws who lived in the area. A possible origin is *moeil* 'to paddle.' Tribe called themselves *Moila*, and their town *Mabila, Mavilla, Mavila, Mauvila*.

Mohawk River — Feature: stream
County: Saratoga **State:** NY
Lat: 42-45-39 N **Long:** 07-34-11 W

Flows west-to-east across NY state; largest tributary of the Hudson River which it enters at Cohoes, above Albany. 148 mi. long. The Mohawk River Valley was vital in colonial and early U.S. development as a principal route from the east coast to the Great Lakes. The Erie Canal was built in the valley, paralleling the river as far as Rome, NY, and the fertile soil attracted settlement. New York Central Railroad was built along the route, and the important industrial cities of Rome, Utica, and Schenectady flourished.

Name origin: For the Iroquois tribal name given to them by their enemies, meaning *cannibals* with reference to their eating their enemies.

Mojave Desert — Feature: plain
County: San Bernardino **State:** CA
Lat: 34-45-00 N **Long:** 11-70-00 W

Area about 25,000 sq. mi. in southeastern CA, between the Sierra Nevada Mountains and the Colorado River, part of the Great Basin; bordered on southeast by the Colorado Desert. Dry lake beds in it are world's chief source of boron, a mineral used for jet-engine and rocket fuels and for nuclear reactor controls. Site of Death Valley and Joshua Tree National Monuments.

Name origin: For a tribe of Yuman linguistic stock living along the Colorado River. The name means 'three mountains,' referring to the Needles, a rock formation in the Sierra Nevadas with several sharply pointed peaks. Variant spelling *Mohave* more common in AZ, while Spanish-influenced *Mojave* is used in CA and is the standard spelling for the desert.

Molokai — Feature: island
County: Maui **State:** HI

One of the seven populated islands of the state of Hawaii, 676 sq. mi.; separated from Oahu to the northwest by the Kaiwi Channel and from Maui, to southeast by the Pailolo Channel. Site of the noted leper colony where Fr. Joseph Damien de Veuster (1840–1889) worked is on north coast on Kalaupapa peninsula.

Name origin: Nicknamed the Friendly Island.

Monongahela River — Feature: stream

Formed in northern WV by confluence of the Tygart and West Fork rivers; flows 128 mi. north into Pennsylvania and unites with the Allegheny River at Pittsburgh to form the Ohio River. Almost completely navigable by means of locks.

Name origin: From Indian *menaungehilla* 'river with the sliding banks,' or 'high banks that break off and fall down.'

Monterey Bay — Feature: bay
County: Monterey **State:** CA
Lat: 36-48-00 N **Long:** 12-15-40 W

Inlet of the Pacific Ocean on the central coast of CA, south of San Francisco; Santa Cruz is at the northern end and Monterey at the southern.

Name origin: Named by Spanish explorer Sebastián Vizcaino (1550?–1616) in 1603 for Gaspar de Acevedo y Zúñiga, Count of Monterey (c. 1560–1606), viceroy of Mexico.

Monument Valley
Feature: plain

Sandy plain in northeastern AZ and southeastern UT with red sandstone monument-like buttes 1,000 ft. high; one formation, called the Totem Pole, casts a shadow up to 35 mi. long in the evening. To the west is Rainbow Bridge National Monument, to the north Natural Bridges National Monument.

Moosehead Lake
Feature: lake
County: Piscataquis **State:** ME
Lat: 45-38-38 N **Long:** 06-94-00 W

Resort lake in central ME. About 35 mi. long, 10 mi. wide; area 117 sq. mi., largest lake in ME; maximum depth 246 ft.; elevation 1,029 ft.

Name origin: Translated from Abnaki *mozodup nebes* meaning 'moosehead lake.'

Mount Desert Island
Feature: island
County: Hancock **State:** ME
Lat: 44-22-41 N **Long:** 06-81-85 W

Resort island off the central-eastern coast of ME. Area 144 sq. mi. In 1604 French explorer Samuel de Champlain (c. 1567–1635) was first European to reach it. Highest peak is Cadillac Mountain, 1,530 ft. above sea level. Acadia National Park, first national park east of the Mississippi River established on the island in 1919.

Name origin: Named by Champlain *Ile de Monts Deserts* 'island of bald (treeless) mountains.' Pronounced like English "dessert" by locals, possibly reflecting French pronunciation.

Mud Mountain Dam
Feature: dam
County: King **State:** WA
Lat: 47-08-29 N **Long:** 12-15-55 W

Rock-fill dam on the White River in western WA, about 30 mi. east of Tacoma. 425 ft. high, 700 ft. long at top; volume is 2,360,000 cu. yds. Reservoir holds 106,000 acre-feet of water.

Name origin: Formerly called Stevens Dam.

Muir Woods
Feature: woods
County: Marin **State:** CA

At foot of Mt. Tamalpais about 15 mi. north of San Francisco on Pacific coast. A 424-acre stand of virgin coast redwoods (*Sequoia sempervirens*). The tallest here is 246 ft., 17 ft. in diameter, and about 2,000 years old. Part of Muir Woods National Monument.

Name origin: For John Muir (1838–1914), geologist, explorer, naturalist, and author.

Multnomah Falls
Feature: falls
State: OR

In northwest OR, east of Portland. On Multnomah Creek near the summit of Larch Mountain in the Cascades. Upper falls are 542 ft. high; upper and lower falls together are 620 ft. high.

Name origin: For a tribe of the Clackamas division of the Chinook Indians. Name said to be a corruption of words meaning 'down river,' or may be derived from the name of an Indian maid who, according to tribal legend, leaped off a cliff into the Columbia River to save her people from a plague. The falls appeared while the Indians prayed, and they believe them to be her soul.

Myrtle Beach
Feature: beach
County: Horry **State:** SC
Lat: 33-39-21 N **Long:** 07-85-55 W

Year-round family resort on northeastern Atlantic coast of SC. Its famous 60-mi.-long beach extends from the NC border south to Pawleys Island; entire area referred to as the Grand Strand. In the summer season population of the city rises from 30,000 to over 80,000.

Name origin: For the abundant wax myrtle bushes in the area.

Nantucket Island
Feature: island
County: Nantucket **State:** MA
Lat: 41-17-00 N **Long:** 07-00-50 W

A summer resort and artist's colony in the Atlantic Ocean 18 mi. south of Cape Cod. Coextensive with Nantucket County, MA, population 6,012 year-round; summertime approx. 40,000 (peak season July-August). Separated from Cape Cod by Nantucket Sound, and from the island of Martha's Vineyard to the west by the Muskeget Channel. Area 57 sq. mi. One of the world's greatest whaling centers from late 1700s to 1850s.

Name origin: From an Indian word of uncertain meaning. An early map names the island as *Natocko*, which may mean 'far away.' Possibly from *Nantuck* supposedly meaning 'the sandy, sterile soil tempted no one.' Or from Algonquian meaning 'narrow tidal river' with reference to the channel separating Nantucket and Tuckernuck Island to the west.

Narragansett Bay
Feature: bay
County: Bristol **State:** RI
Lat: 41-36-04 N **Long:** 07-11-92 W

Inlet of the Atlantic Ocean, in eastern RI, between Point Judith to the west and Sakonnet Point to the east. 30 mi. long, 3-12 mi. wide. Largest islands are Rhode Island, Conanicut, and Prudence.

Name origin: For the predominant Algonquian tribe; from *nanhiggonsick* meaning either 'back and forth' or 'people of the point'.

Natchez Trace
Feature: trail

Road or trail about 500 mi. long between Nashville, TN, and Natchez, MS. First a series of Indian trails, then a post road in the early 1800s, later improved. Important commercial and military route from the 1780s to 1830s. Used by traders returning to Nashville after shipping their goods down the Mississippi River, and by settlers. Explorer Meriwether Lewis (1774–1809) was killed on it near Hohenwald, TN. Natchez Trace Parkway follows its route.

Name origin: For the city, which was named probably from a Caddoan name or word believed to mean 'woods, timber.'

National Road *or* National Old Trail Road
Feature: trail

First federal road in U.S. (authorized by Congrss 1806; begun 1815) and for many years the major route west. When finished in 1852 the road stretched more than 500 mi. from Cumberland, MD, across southwestern PA, to Wheeling, WV, through OH and IN to Vandalia, IL. The state of IL later completed the road to St. Louis, MO. Old road is largely the route of modern highways U.S. 40 and Interstate 70. At some points along the route statues of the *Madonna of the Trail* honor women pioneers.

Name origin: Originally called the *Great National Pike*, later the *National Road* or *Cumberland Road* (for its beginning at Cumberland, MD). Also referred to as the *National Old Trail Road*.

Major Geographical Features

Near Islands
Feature: islands
County: Aleutian, West **State:** AK
Lat: 54-56-37 N **Long:** 16-00-24 W **Elevation:** 1,289
Westernmost group of the Aleutians about 1500 mi. west of the end of the Alaska Peninsula. Includes Attu (largest island), Agattu, and Semichi Islands.
Name origin: Translation of the name given them by Russian explorers for their proximity to Russia.

New Madrid Fault Zone
Feature: fault
County: New Madrid **State:** MO
Geologic fault on the southeastern border of MO on the Mississippi River. In 1811 and 1812, Reelfoot Lake was formed by severe earthquakes in the area that caused the Mississippi River to flow backward.
Name origin: For the nearby town.

New York State Barge Canal System
Feature: canal
State: NY
Canal system, 524 mi. long, linking the Great Lakes to Lake Champlain and the Hudson River. Comprises four canals: the 338-mi. Erie Canal, 60-mi. Champlain Canal, 24-mi. Oswego Canal, and 92-mi. Cayuga and Seneca canals. System opened in 1918; has 57 locks, channel depth is 14 ft. from Waterford to Oswego, and 12 ft. on other canals. Now used primarily by pleasure craft.

Niagara Falls
Feature: falls
County: Niagara **State:** NY
Lat: 43-05-00 N **Long:** 07-90-41 W
Spectacular water falls and major tourist attraction in northwestern NY on the Niagara River, between Lake Erie and Lake Ontario. River forms part of the U.S.-Canadian border. Divided by Goat Island into Horseshoe, (Canadian) Falls: 158 ft. high, 2,600 ft. wide; and American Falls: 176 ft. high, 1,000 ft. wide; about 85% of the water goes over Horseshoe Falls. At base of American Falls is Cave of the Winds, 100 ft. by 75 ft., formed by erosion. River below the falls runs through a 200 ft.-deep, 7-mi. long gorge; Whirlpool Rapids are about 3 mi. from the Falls.
Name origin: For the Iroquoian settlement of *Ongniaahra* near the mouth of the Niagara River. French explorers called it *Ongiara* and *Niagara*. Originally, meant 'bisected bottom lands', 'at the neck,' or 'across the neck.'

Niihau Island
Feature: island
County: Kauai **State:** HI
Lat: 21-54-24 N **Long:** 16-00-85 W
Westernmost of the seven populated islands of Hawaii; separated from Kauai Island to the northeast by Kaulakahi Channel. Area 72 sq. mi.: Tableland 1,300 ft. high. Privately owned; used as a cattle ranch.
Name origin: From Hawaiian, possibly 'bound with hau bark.' Nicknamed the Forbidden Island because no one can visit without the owner's permission.

North Platte River
Feature: stream
Rises in northern CO, flows a total of 680 mi., first north then east and southeast through WY and NE; unites with the South Platte River in southwest NE near the city of North Platte to form the Platte River.
Name origin: French 'shallow.'

Nunivak Island
Feature: island
County: Dillingham **State:** AK
Lat: 60-05-42 N **Long:** 16-61-24 W
Off southwest coast of Alaska; separated from the mainland by Etolin Strait. Second largest island in Bering Sea; area 1,625 sq. mi. Site of Nunivak National Wildlife Refuge.
Name origin: From Eskimo, meaning unknown, possibly descriptive for a large island. Originally named after the ship *Otkritie* 'Discovery' by Capt. Lt. M.N. Vasiliev of the Imperial Russian Navy, who explored it in July 1821.

Oahe Dam
Feature: dam
County: Stanley **State:** SD
Lat: 44-27-04 N **Long:** 10-02-40 W
In central SD, near Pierre. One of the ten largest earth-fill dams in world. On Missouri River; 9,300 ft. long, 245 ft. high, volume of 92 million cu. yds. The reservoir, Lake Oahe, stores 23,600,000 acre-ft. of water. Completed 1960.
Name origin: Sioux 'place of the big building,' for a council hall that once stood nearby.

Oahu
Feature: island
County: Honolulu **State:** HI
Third largest and most populous of the seven populated islands of the state of Hawaii; 593 sq. mi. Separated from Kauai to northwest by Kauai Channel and from Molokai to southeast by Kaiwi Channel. Site of Diamond Head, Pearl Harbor, Honolulu, the state capital, and Waikiki Beach.
Name origin: Nicknamed the Gathering Place because it is home to about 80 per cent of the state's population.

Ocracoke Island
Feature: island
County: Hyde **State:** NC
Lat: 35-07-55 N **Long:** 07-55-42 W
Fishing and summer resort off central NC coast, separating Pamlico Sound from the Atlantic Ocean. Part of a chain of narrow, barrier islands. Area 9 sq. mi. Hatteras Inlet to northeast and Ocracoke Inlet to southwest connect the Sound with the Atlantic.
Name origin: From Algonquian, meaning uncertain. First recorded in 1585 as *Wocokon*. Has been translated as 'bend' or 'curve,' for shape of the island; and as 'enclosed place' or 'fort,' perhaps for a village.

Ohio River
Feature: stream
Major eastern tributary of the Mississippi River and one of the most important commercial waterways in U.S. Flows through PA, forms the southern borders of OH, IN, and IL. Formed by the confluence of the Allegheny and Monongahela rivers at Pittsburgh, PA; 975 mi. long. Forms OH-WV, OH-KY, IN-KY, and IL-KY borders. Empties into Mississippi River at Cairo, IL.
Name origin: Named by French explorers after similar words in several Indian languages meaning 'beautiful.' French called it *La Belle Riviere* 'the beautiful river' and applied it to the Allegheny, as well as the Ohio. Territory and state named for the river.

American Places Dictionary Major Geographical Features

Okeechobee, Lake
Feature: lake
County: Palm Beach **State:** FL
Lat: 26-56-15 N **Long:** 08-04-84 W **Elevation:** 16
Largest freshwater lake in southern U.S., third largest wholly within the U.S. In southeastern FL, about 35 mi. west of the Atlantic coast, on northern border of the Everglades. Area about 700 sq. mi., average depth 7 ft. Connected to the Atlantic Ocean and the Gulf of Mexico by the Okeechobee Waterway.
Name origin: Muskogean (Hitchiti) Indian *oki* 'water' and *chobi* 'big.'

Okeechobee Waterway
Feature: channel
County: Glades **State:** FL
Lat: 26-48-21 N **Long:** 08-10-64 W
A 155-mi. long, 6-ft. deep series of canals, rivers, and lakes across the southern FL peninsula from near Stuart on the Atlantic Coast to the Gulf of Mexico at mouth of the Caloosahatchee River at Fort Myers. Comprises St. Lucie and Caloosahatchee canals, and Lakes Okeechobee and Hicpochee. Used by small commercial and pleasure craft.
Name origin: For the lake. Also called Cross-Florida Waterway or Lake Okeechobee-Cross Florida Waterway.

Okefenokee Swamp
Feature: swamp
Marshy, subtropical swamp, 45 mi. long, 30 mi. wide. Mostly in southeastern GA; small part extends into northeastern FL. About 460 sq. mi. in GA is set aside as the Okeefenokee National Wildlife Refuge.
Name origin: From Muskogean (Hitchiti) *oke* 'water,' and *finoki* 'trembling,' for quaking nature of the growth floating on the lakes. Area known locally as Land of Trembling Earth.

Oklahoma Panhandle
Feature: area
State: OK
Narrow northwest extension of the state lying between KS and CO on the north, NM on the west, and TX to the south.

Old Faithful
Feature: geyser
State: WY
Most famous geyser in Yellowstone National Park, northwestern WY, northwest of Shoshone Lake. Erupts on an average of every 73 minutes, shooting a stream of boiling water over 100 ft. into the air.
Name origin: For the regularity of its eruptions, which have been observed since its discovery in 1870.

Old Man of the Mountains
Feature: summit
County: Grafton **State:** NH
Lat: 44-09-23 N **Long:** 07-14-15 W
Natural granite formation 48 feet high resembling a man's profile, on south peak of Profile Peak Mountain. In the White Mountains of NH, visible from Franconia Notch. Immortalized in the story "The Great Stone Face," by Nathaniel Hawthorne (1804–64).
Name origin: Also called Great Stone Face or Profile.

Old Orchard Beach
Feature: beach
County: York **State:** ME
Resort area southwest of Portland on the southeastern Atlantic coast of ME. Seven miles of hard-packed sand; in 1929 many trans-Atlantic flights took off from the beach. Summer population increases from 10,000 to 85-100,000 in the nearby town.

Old Spanish Trail
Feature: trail
Continuation of the Santa Fe Trail, from Santa Fe, NM to Los Angeles via Durango, CO, the Green and Virgin rivers in UT, the Colorado River, and across the Mojave Desert in CA. Used for travel before railroads; especially heavy use in 1850s and 1860s by pioneers.

Olympic Mountains
Feature: range
County: Clallam **State:** WA
Lat: 48-02-04 N **Long:** 12-34-11 W
Highest part of the Pacific Coast Ranges, in northwest WA, south of Juan de Fuca Strait, on the Olympic Peninsula. Chief peaks Mount Olympus, 7,965 ft., and Mount Constance, 7,777 ft.; area about 3,500 sq. mi., largely in Olympic National Park.
Name origin: For Mount Olympus in Greece, home of the gods in Greek myth.

Oneida Lake
Feature: lake
County: Oswego **State:** NY
Lat: 43-12-25 N **Long:** 07-55-55 W **Elevation:** 369
In central NY, 12 mi. northeast of Syracuse. Connected to NY State Barge Canal system. About 22 mi. long, 6 mi. wide at its widest, area 80 sq. mi.
Name origin: For the Indian tribe of Iroquoian linguistic stock, one of the Five Nations of the Iroquois. The name means 'stone people,' perhaps for their bravery.

Ontario, Lake
Feature: lake
Smallest and easternmost of the Great Lakes. Borders state of NY on east and south, and province of Ontario, Canada, on west and north. About 193 mi. long, 53 mi. wide, 500 to 802 ft. deep. Area 7,550 sq. mi., with about 480 mi. of shoreline. A link in St. Lawrence Seaway system, connects at its northeastern end with the Atlantic Ocean via the St. Lawrence River and, at the southwestern end with Lake Erie via the Niagara River and the Welland Canal. The NY State Barge Canal System connects it to the Hudson River and thus New York City.
Name origin: Of Iroquoian origin, but meaning disputed: either from *ontare* 'lake' plus *io* 'beautiful,' or from *Entouhonorons*, name French explorer Samuel de Champlain (c. 1567–1635) used to designate Lake of the Seneca or Iroquois.

Oregon Trail
Feature: trail
Longest of the westward pioneers' routes; 200 mi. long, from Independence, MO, to Oregon Territory. First tracked by hunters and explorers in early 1800s. Followed the Platte and North Platte rivers across NE; crossed WY; traversed the Rocky Mountains through South Pass in the Wind River Range; followed the Snake River across ID to the Columbia River, thence to terminus at Fort Vancouver, OR, and the Willamette Valley. Wagon travel became very heavy 1842–60.

Oroville Dam
Feature: dam
County: Butte **State:** CA
Lat: 39-32-20 N **Long:** 12-12-90 W
In north-central CA, north of Sacramento. Highest dam in U.S.; 771 ft. high, more than a mile across the Feather River; earth-fill dam; completed 1968. Its reservoir, Lake Oroville, contains about 3.5 million acre-ft. of water.
Name origin: For the nearby town, a former gold-mining camp; from Spanish *oro* 'gold.'

Major Geographical Features — American Places Dictionary

Osage River
Feature: stream
County: Osage **State:** MO
Lat: 38-35-49 N **Long:** 09-15-64 W

Rises in west-central MO at junction of the Marais des Cygnes and Little Osage rivers. About 500 mi. long; largest tributary of the Missouri River, into which it empties east of Jefferson City. Its Bagnell Dam created (1931) The Lake of the Ozarks.

Name origin: For the Indian tribe of Siouan linguistic stock. The name is a corruption of their name in their language, *Wazhazhe*; meaning unknown.

Ouachita Mountains
Feature: range

Range in west-central AR and eastern OK; southern continuation of Ozark Plateau. Highest peak Blue Mountain, 2,660 ft. Known for its hot springs.

Name origin: For an Indian tribe, of Ceddoan linguistic stock, of the Natchitoches Confederacy. Meaning is unclear; possible translations are 'big Aunt,' 'country of large buffaloes,' 'sparkling water,' or 'large hunting grounds.' Similarity of *Ouachita* and *Wichita* may only be coincidental.

Ouachita River
Feature: stream

Rises in western AR, flows east and south for 605 mi. and joins Black River in central LA. Navigable 350 mi. up to Camden, AR.

Name origin: For the Ouachita Mountains, where it originates. Also spelled *Washita*.

Outer Banks
Feature: island
State: NC

A chain of low, narrow barrier islands cut by many inlets, along the NC coast from the NC-VA border in Currituck County south to Cape Hatteras and Cape Lookout, then west to Bogue Inlet. They separate the Atlantic Ocean and several sounds along the inner NC coast, including Pamlico, Albemarle, and Currituck. Roanoke Island was site of the first English colony in North America (1585), which finally failed. Kill Devil Hill off Albemarle Sound was the site of Wright brothers' first flight.

Name origin: Bankers first applied to islands' residents in 1849 in J.F. Cooper's Sea Lions.

Overseas Highway
Feature: bridge
State: FL

Connects the Florida Keys to mainland FL. Longest overwater road in the world; 42 bridges, one span is 7-mi. long. Built over the old route of the Florida East Coast Railroad. Crosses Card Sound to Key Largo then extends to Key West. 128 mi. long; completed 1938.

Owyhee Dam
Feature: dam
County: Malheur **State:** OR
Lat: 43-38-31 N **Long:** 11-71-42 W

On Owyhee River in east-central OR about 11 mi. southwest of Adrian, near the ID border; on Owyhee River. One of the largest concrete arch gravity dams in world: 417 ft. high, 830 ft. long; stores 1,120,000 acre-ft. of water. Reservoir 52 mi. long.

Name origin: Named for the river, which was named in 1826 by Peter Skene Ogden, explorer for Hudson's Bay Co., because 2 Hawaiians in his party were killed there by Indians.

Ozark, the
Feature: range
State: MO

Range of hills, actually an eroded tableland or dissected plateau in south-central U.S., extending from southern IL, across MO, AR and into eastern OK. Referred to locally as mountains; sometimes also referred to as Ozark Plateaus. Height 1,500 to 2,300 ft.; area about 40,000 sq. mi. Highest peaks are in Boston Mountains of AR; also includes St. Francois Mountains and Salem Plateau in MO, and Springfield Plateau in MO, AR, OK.

Name origin: Anglicized phonetic spelling of French *aux arcs* 'in the country of the Arkansas Indians.' Also called Ozark Plateau.

Ozark Plateaus
See Ozark Mountains

Ozarks, Lake of the
Feature: reservoir
State: MO

Reservoir formed in 1931 by the Bagnell Dam on the Osage River; about 130 mi. long in Ozarks of central MO.

Pacific Crest Trail
Feature: trail

Longest continuous footpath in the U.S.; about 600 mi. longer than the Appalachian Trail. Runs from the Canadian-Washington border near Lake Ross south along mountain crests for more than 2,600 mi. to the California-Mexican border.

Pacific Ocean
Feature: sea

World's largest and deepest body of water, covers about one-third of earth's surface. Bounded on east by North and South America; on south by Antarctica; on west by New Zealand, Australia, and Asia; Bering Strait connects it to the Arctic Ocean on north. Widest near equator; about 11,000 mi.; area about 70,000,000 sq. mi.; maximum depth in Mariana Trench, 36,198 ft.

Name origin: Named by Ferdinand Magellan (c. 1480–1521) for its calmness during his voyage to the Philippines (1520–21).

Padre Island
Feature: island
County: Kenedy **State:** TX
Lat: 26-50-39 N **Long:** 09-72-20 W

Off the southeast TX coast; separated from mainland by Laguna Madre. Connected to Corpus Christi and Brownsville by causeways. About 100 mi. long. A national seashore since 1962.

Name origin: For Padre Nicolas Baille, Spanish priest who was given a grant to the island by the king of Spain.

Painted Desert
Feature: plain
County: Coconino **State:** AZ
Lat: 35-30-01 N **Long:** 11-00-50 W

Wasteland in north-central AZ with brilliantly colored natural features. Extends about 200 mi. east of and along the Colorado and Little Colorado rivers east of the Grand Canyon; area about 7,500 sq. mi. Erosion has formed buttes, mesas, and valleys with exposed multi-colored rock surfaces. Also in its area is Petrified Forest National Park.

Name origin: Translation of Spanish *el Desierto Pintado*.

Palisades, the
Feature: cliff

High, scenic cliffs rising almost from the water's edge, about 15 mi. along the west bank of Hudson River in southeast NY and northeast NJ. Extend from Ft. Lee, near George Washington Bridge, to Piermont, NY. Height 350 to 540 ft. Part of Palisades State Park.

Pamlico Sound
Feature: bay
County: Hyde **State:** NC
Lat: 35-18-45 N **Long:** 07-55-61 W

Off east central coast of North Carolina. Enclosed and separated from the Atlantic Ocean by the barrier islands, the Outer Banks. Largest inland body of water along east coast, 80 mi. long, 8 to 30 mi. wide. Openings to the Atlantic are Oregon Inlet, Hatteras Inlet, and Ocracoke Inlet. Pamlico River empties into it on the west, and Neuse River on the southwest.

Name origin: For an Indian tribe of Algonquian linguistic stock, destroyed by the Tuscarora Indians in the early 1700s.

Parker Dam
Feature: dam

On the Colorado River about 145 mi. south of Hoover Dam, near the southern CA-western AZ border. Concrete-arch type dam, 320 ft. high and 856 ft. long. Dam bed was excavated 235 ft., making it the deepest underwater dam in world. Lake Havasu, its reservoir, can hold 717,000 acre-ft. of water. Completed in 1938.

Name origin: For Gen. Eli Parker, a commissioner of Indian affairs.

Park Range
Feature: range

Part of the southern Rocky Mountains in CO; runs parallel on the western side with the Front Range.

Name origin: Possibly for the large mountain valley called the 'South Park.' In the region *park* is a generic term for an open valley amoung mountains.

Passamaquoddy Bay
Feature: bay
County: Washington **State:** ME
Lat: 45-01-24 N **Long:** 06-70-40 W

Inlet of the Bay of Fundy between SW province of New Brunswick, Canada, and SE ME, at mouth of the St. Croix River. About 15 mi. long and 10 mi. wide. Tidal range is as much as 27 ft. Deer and Campobello islands are in it.

Name origin: From Algonquian name meaning 'location of plenty of pollack,' in reference to its abundance of the fish.

Pearl Harbor
Feature: bay
County: Honolulu **State:** HI
Lat: 21-21-18 N **Long:** 15-75-82 W

Landlocked inlet of Mamala Bay on the southern coast of Oahu, 6 mi. west of Honolulu. One of the world's largest sheltered harbors with 10 sq. mi. of navigable water. Made accessible after completion in 1911 of the dredging of a deep channel through the sand and coral bar blocking its entrance. Used since 1916 as operating base for U.S. Navy; still headquarters for U.S. Pacific fleet. Wairio Peninsula separates West and Middle Lochs; East Loch is north of Ford Island in eastern part of harbor. Site of U.S. naval base attacked by Japan on December 7, 1941, precipitating U.S. entry in WWII. The *USS Arizona* was the only ship permanently lost by the attack; the USS Arizona Memorial was erected above the sunken hull in commemoration.

Name origin: Anglicization of Hawaiian name *Pu'u-loa* 'long hill,' perhaps influenced by the fact that pearl oysters thrive in its waters.

Pecos River
Feature: stream

Largest branch of the Rio Grande; rises in eastern NM, near Santa Fe; flows 800 mi. across TX and empties into the Rio Grande 36 mi. north of Del Rio in the southwest. Drains over 33,000 sq. mi.

Name origin: Origin and meaning uncertain. Believed to be the name of an Indian tribe now lost or unidentified, or a Spanish translation of a Keresan word 'watering place.' Spanish form *Rio Pecos*.

Peninsular Ranges
See San Diego Ranges

Penobscot River
Feature: stream
County: Hancock **State:** ME
Lat: 44-26-27 N **Long:** 06-84-94 W

Longest river in Maine; rises near Canadian border and flows 350 mi. east and south, emptying into Penobscot Bay on the Atlantic. Forms Chesuncook and Pemadumcook lakes. Navigable for ocean vessels to Bangor, 10 mi. inland.

Name origin: Algonquian *penobskeag* 'rocky river, rocky place' usually applied to a 10-mi. stretch of the river above Bangor.

Pensacola Dam
Feature: dam
County: Mayes **State:** OK
Lat: 36-28-18 N **Long:** 09-50-15 W

Near Pensacola, in northeast OK. On the Neosho (Grand) River; multiple-arch, hollow-buttress dam; height 145 ft.; 6,500 ft. long at top. Completed 1940. Forms 64 sq. mi. lake called variously Lake of the Cherokees, Grand Lake, and Pensacola Reservoir.

Name origin: Formerly Grand River Dam.

Pensacola Reservoir
See Cherokee, Lake o' the

Petrified Forest
Feature: locale
County: Apache **State:** AZ
Lat: 35-54-32 N **Long:** 10-93-44 W

Largest known concentration of petrified wood in the world; in the Painted Desert near Adamana in northern AZ. Part of the Petrified Forest National Park, area about 40 sq. mi. Contains six 'forests' of petrified trunks of Norfolk Island pine trees, which were submerged in sediment-laden waters about 150 million years ago. The minerals seeped into the wood, solidifying it into chalcedony and agate which show every detail of the original wood structure. Prehistoric petroglyphs can be seen on some of the rocks.

Piedmont Region *or* Plateau
Feature: plain

Gently rolling, fertile land between the Blue Ridge and Appalachian mountains and the Atlantic Coastal Plain of eastern U.S. Extends from mouth of the Hudson River in NY to central AL. Area 80,000 sq. mi; about 50 mi. wide in north, 125 mi. wide in south. Division between Piedmont Region and the Atlantic Coastal Plain is marked by the Fall Line.

Name origin: For the Piedmont region of Italy 'foot of the mountain,' applied to the region in the mid-1700s as a learned term.

Pikes Peak
Feature: summit
County: El Paso **State:** CO
Lat: 38-50-26 N **Long:** 10-50-23 W

Peak in Front Range of the Rocky Mountains, 12 mi. west of Colorado Springs. First peak seen by travelers from the east. Height 14,110 ft.; site of auto race known as Pike's Peak Hill Climb.

Name origin: For Lt. Zebulon Montgomery Pike (1779-1813), American soldier and explorer who discovered it in 1806.

Placid, Lake
Feature: lake
County: Essex **State:** NY
Lat: 44-18-16 N **Long:** 07-35-94 W **Elevation:** 1,857

Glacial lake in northeastern NY, southwest of Lake Champlain, in the Adirondack Mountains. About 4 mi. long, 1/2 mi. wide. Summer and winter resort area, site of winter Olympics in 1932 and 1980.

Platte River
Feature: stream
County: Saunders **State:** NE
Lat: 41-03-14 N **Long:** 09-55-25 W

The North and South Platte rivers join in west-central NE to form the Platte River; the most important river in NE; one of largest branches of Missouri River. Flows 310 mi. eastward, empties into the Missouri at Plattsmouth, south of Omaha.

Name origin: Translation of an Omaha Indian word, also recorded as *Nebraska* referring to a stream widely spread out, not running between high banks.

Point Reyes
See Reyes, Point

Pontchartrain, Lake
Feature: lake
County: Orleans **State:** LA
Lat: 30-11-19 N **Long:** 09-00-60 W

Tidal, brackish lake, north of New Orleans. About 40 mi. long and 25 mi. wide; area 625 sq. mi. Major recreational and resort area. Connected to Mississippi River via Inner Harbor navigation canal and to Gulf of Mexico via a strait (the Rigolets) and Lake Borgne to the East. Spanned by Lake Pontchartrain Causeway, world's longest bridge and longest over-water highway, 29.2 mi. long, with 23.9 miles over water.

Name origin: For Louis, Comte de Pontchartrain (1643-1727), French political figure and explorer; name given by French colonists.

Potomac River
Feature: stream

Formed by confluence of North Branch and South Branch in northeast WV in the Allegheny Mountains. Flows 287 mi. past Harpers Ferry, WV, northwest of Washington, DC, and Mount Vernon, George Washington's (1732-99) VA home, south of Washington to its mouth in Chesapeake Bay, forming MD-WV boundary and separating VA from MD and from Washington, D.C. Navigable by ships for 115 mi. inland to Washington, D.C.; 2 to 7 mi. wide for last 100 mi. About 15 mi. above Washington are Great Falls of the Potomac, where river descends about 90 ft. in a series of falls (highest 35 ft.) and rapids within a 200-ft. gorge.

Name origin: From an Indian word meaning 'where goods are brought in.' This became the name of the river where Indians were known to do trading. Possibly a mixture of Iroquoian, Delaware, and Powhatan forms. First recorded by English colonist John Smith (c. 1580-1631) in 1608 as *Patawomeck*.

Powell, Lake
Feature: reservoir
County: San Juan **State:** UT
Lat: 36-56-10 N **Long:** 11-12-90 W **Elevation:** 3,700

Resort area and one of the largest artificially created lakes in the world, on the UT-AZ border, mostly in UT. Created by Glen Canyon Dam across Glen Canyon on the Colorado River. 186 mi. long, covers about 262-mi. area, about 500 ft. deep.

Name origin: For American geologist and explorer John Wesley Powell (1834-1902), who explored and named Glen Canyon on an expedition in 1870.

Presidential Range
Feature: range
County: Coos **State:** NH
Lat: 44-14-31 N **Long:** 07-12-04 W

Range of peaks, most named for U.S. presidents, in the White Mountains, chiefly in northern NH, between Pinkham Notch to the east and Crawford Notch to the west. Highest peak Mount Washington, 6,288 ft.

Pribilof Islands
Feature: island
County: Aleutian, West **State:** AK
Lat: 57-24-00 N **Long:** 17-01-44 W

Group of 4 Alaskan islands in southeast Bering Sea, west of the Aleutian Islands. Comprise the large islands of Saint Paul and Saint George, and the smaller Otter and Walrus. Area 76 sq. mi. World's largest fur seal grounds.

Name origin: For Gavril Pribilof, Russian explorer, who discovered them in 1786. Also called Fur Seal Islands.

Prince of Wales Island
Feature: island
County: Prince of Wales-Outer Ketchikan **State:** AK
Lat: 55-37-55 N **Long:** 13-25-42 W

Largest island in Alaska's Alexander Archipelago, off the west coast of British Columbia. About 135 mi. long; 40 mi. wide; area 2,587 sq. mi. Chief towns Hydaburg and Craig.

Name origin: Honoring Britain's Prince of Wales; earliest known use in 1825 in treaty between Great Britain and Russia.

Prince William Sound
Feature: bay
County: Valdez-Cordova **State:** AK
Lat: 60-36-54 N **Long:** 14-71-00 W

Inlet of the Gulf of Alaska in southern AK, bounded on the east by the Kenai Peninsula, on the north by Chugach Mountains. About 90 to 100 mi. across. Montague and Hinchinbrook Islands lie across its mouth. Site of major oil spill from tanker *Exxon Valdez* in 1989.

Name origin: Named by Capt. James Cook (1728-79) about May 20, 1778, for the third son of King George III (1738-1820).

Puerto Rico
Feature: island

Island and commonwealth in the West Indies easternmost of the Greater Antilles group, bounded on west by the Dominican Republic, on the south by the Caribbean Sea, on the north by the Atlantic Ocean and on the east by the Virgin Islands. About 111 mi. east to west, 39 mi. north to south; area, including Culebra, Mona, and Vieques islands, 3,515 sq. mi.; 56 sq. mi. of inland water. Capital San Juan. Highest point Cerro de Punta, 4,389 ft. A self-governing commonwealth with sovereignty similar to that of a state, its people are U.S. citizens, but cannot vote in national elections, and do not pay federal income tax while living on the island.

Name origin: Spanish 'rich port,' originally used for San Juan, the capital, but used eventually for the whole island. Originally named by Christopher Columbus (1451–1506) in 1493 San Juan Bautista (St. John the Baptist). Also called *Borinquen*, from Arawak Indian name.

Puget Sound
Feature: bay
County: Kitsap **State:** WA
Lat: 47-50-00 N **Long:** 12-22-60 W

Inlet from the Pacific in northwestern corner of WA; Seattle, Tacoma, Bremerton, Olympia, and Everett are along its shores. About 80 mi. long, 180 to 925 ft. deep; area about 2,000 sq. mi. Connected to Pacific Ocean by Strait of Juan de Fuca. From the strait, Puget Sound extends south about 35 mi. south, then divides into Admiralty Inlet and Hood Canal. Lake Washington Ship Canal connects the Sound to Lake Washington at Seattle. Many islands, area industries include fisheries, lumber, and shipping.

Name origin: For Peter Puget, lieutenant from 1791–1795 in the expeditionary group, led by British Capt. George Vancouver (1757–98), that explored the north Pacific coast of North America.

Pyramid Lake
Feature: lake
State: NV

Lake in mountainous area of western NV, about 30 mi. northeast of Reno, within the Pyramid Lake Indian Reservation. With Walker Lake 90 mi. south, one of the remnants on ancient Lake Lahontan, which once covered 10% of present-day NV. About 30 mi. long, 4 to 13 mi. wide; area, 188 sq. mi.

Name origin: Named by John C. Frémont (1813–90) in 1844 for the island rock formation that extended out of the lake and seemed to him to resemble "the great pyramid of Cheops."

Quabbin Reservoir
Feature: reservoir
County: Franklin **State:** MA
Lat: 42-17-12 N **Long:** 07-22-01 W **Elevation:** 524

Near Ware in central MA. Formed in valley of the Swift River by Winsor Dam and Quabbin Dike. Creation of the reservoir in 1937 inundated several towns, whose residents were relocated to accomodate the purpose. One of largest reservoirs of drinking water in U.S.; area, 39 sq. mi. Supplies Boston area with water via Quabbin Aqueduct to Wachusett Reservoir.

Name origin: From Nipmuc, meaning uncertain, possibly 'it twists and turns about,' 'crooked streams,' or from the name of an Indian chieftain.

Queens
Feature: borough
County: Queens **State:** NY

One of the five boroughs of New York City, co-extensive with the county. Largest in area, 126 sq. mi.; population 1,951,598. On northwest corner of Long Island; abuts Brooklyn to the south. The East River separates it from Manhattan to the west and from the Bronx to the north; connected to both by various bridges and the Queens Midtown Tunnel.

Name origin: For Queen Catherine of Braganza (1638–1705), wife of Charles II (1630–85) of England.

Rainbow Bridge
Feature: arch
State: UT

Natural sandstone bridge in southeastern UT, just north of AZ border, spanning Bridge Canyon. Span is 175 ft., 290 ft. high. Since 1910 part of Rainbow Bridge National Monument.

Name origin: Named by the Navajo and Paiute Indians because the arch, curved above as well as below, reminded them of a rainbow.

Rainier, Mt.
Feature: summit
County: Pierce **State:** WA
Lat: 46-51-10 N **Long:** 12-14-53 W

Dormant volcanic peak in west-central WA, in Mount Rainier National Park, 40 mi. southeast of Tacoma. Highest point in the Cascade Range and the state: 14,410 ft. Scenic tourist area.

Name origin: Named in 1792 by British explorer Capt. George Vancouver (1757–98) for Peter Rainier, an admiral in the British navy. Sometimes called by its Indian name, Tacoma.

Rainy Lake
Feature: lake
County: St. Louis **State:** MN
Lat: 48-37-30 N **Long:** 09-30-00 W **Elevation:** 1,325

Along international boundary between MN and province of Ontario, Canada, east of International Falls. Outlet of Rainy River; area 360 sq. mi. Irregular shape with many islands, peninsulas, and bays.

Name origin: Adaptation of an Indian word meaning 'it rains all the time,' in reference to the mist surrounding the waterfall where the lake empties into the river. French called it *La Pluie*, 'the Rain.'

Rappahannock River
Feature: stream
County: Lancaster **State:** VA
Lat: 37-35-15 N **Long:** 07-61-72 W

Rises in Blue Ridge Mountains in northeast VA. About 212 mi. long. Navigable to Fredericksburg; from there becomes a tidal stream for nearly 100 mi.; empties into Chesapeake Bay about 20 mi. south of the mouth of the Potomac River. Main tributary is Rapidan River.

Name origin: From an Indian word meaning 'stream that ebbs and rises' or 'river of quick-rising water.'

Rat Islands
Feature: island
County: Aleutian West **State:** AK
Lat: 51-47-17 N **Long:** 17-81-81 W

Group of Alaskan islands in western Aleutians between the Near Islands and the Andreanof Islands. Largest are Semispochnoi, Kiska, and Amchitka.

Name origin: For the hordes of rodents Russian explorers found there. Listed as Krissey Island, from Russian *Krysi* 'rat', by Commodore Billings of the Imperial Russian Navy in 1802. Aleut name is *Ayugadak* 'rat.'

Red Lake
Feature: lake
County: Beltrami **State:** MN
Lat: 47-52-35 N **Long:** 09-50-10 W **Elevation:** 1,216

In north central MN, largely within Red Lake Indian Reservation. Lower Red Lake to the south is connected with Upper Red Lake through a strait; each is about 20 mi. wide; total area 451 sq. mi. Once part of prehistoric Lake Agassiz.

Name origin: Ojibway 'red', perhaps for the effects of sunset on its waters. Eponymous for Red Lake River and County, MN.

Red River
Feature: stream

Rises in high plains of eastern NM in south-central U.S. Flows generally south-eastward; forms southern border of OK with TX, and part of TX-AR border; then through AR and LA; empties into Mississippi River southeast of Alexandria. Southernmost major tributary of the Mississippi; about 1,018 mi. long. Denison Dam forms Lake Texoma, one of the largest reservoirs in the U.S., at TX-OK border.

Name origin: For red clay soil in the lands of its upper basin.

Red River of the North
Feature: stream

In north-central U.S. and south-central Canada. Flows north for 530 mi., past Fargo, ND, Grand Forks, ND, and Winnipeg, Manitoba. Formed by confluence in southeastern ND of the Otter Tail and Bois de Sioux rivers; forms MN-ND border; continues north to Lake Winnipeg in province of Manitoba, Canada. Chief tributaries are Sheyenne and Red Lake rivers in U.S., and Assiniboine in Canada.

Name origin: For cranberries that grew along its banks in ND.

Red River Valley
Feature: valley
State: ND

Level plain along the Red River on ND-MN border. Part of the bed of the ancient, glacial Lake Agassiz. One of most fertile farming areas in world.

Rehoboth Beach
Feature: beach
County: Sussex **State:** DE
Lat: 38-43-00 N **Long:** 07-50-43 W

A family-type summer resort in southeastern DE, 5 mi. south of the Lewes on Atlantic Ocean. Popular with vacationers from Washington, D.C.; locally called the "Nation's Summer Capital." Beach is one mi. long, with town extending one mi. inland, surrounded by trees and flowers. Summer population rises from 2,000 to over 80,000.

Name origin: Hebrew biblical name 'enlargement,' used by settlers about 1645 because they found more room there.

Revillagigedo Island
Feature: island
County: Ketchikan Gateway **State:** AK
Lat: 55-39-32 N **Long:** 13-13-02 W

Island in southeastern Alexander Archipelago off southeastern AK, on British Columbia border. Prince of Wales Island is to the west. About 50 mi. long, 25 mi. wide; area 1,145 sq. mi. Ketchikan is on southwest coast.

Name origin: Named by British explorer Capt. George Vancouver (1757-98) on Aug. 13, 1793, for Don Juan Vicente de Güemes Pacheco de Pedilla (1740-99), Count of Revilla Gigedo and Viceroy of Mexico (1789-94). Jacinto Caamao had given this name in 1792 to the nearby channel.

Reyes, Point
Feature: cape
State: CA

Promontory on Pacific coast, Marin County, CA, at the tip of a peninsula enclosing Drakes Bay, about 30 mi. northwest of Golden Gate. Said to be windiest and foggiest place on west coast of U.S. south of the Bering Sea; averages 137 days of fog per year. At southern end of Point Reyes National Seashore.

Name origin: From Spanish 'kings,' for the Feast of the Three Kings, Jan. 6, the date in 1603 when Spanish explorer Sebastián Vizcaíno's (1550?-1616) expedition passed and named it.

Rhode Island Sound
Feature: bay
County: Washington **State:** RI
Lat: 41-12-20 N **Long:** 07-13-12 W

That part of the Atlantic Ocean south of Narragansett Bay and eastern RI; Block Island Sound is to the west, Buzzards Bay to the east.

Ribbon Falls
Feature: falls
County: Mariposa **State:** CA
Lat: 37-44-09 N **Long:** 11-93-85 W

In the Yosemite Valley, Yosemite National Park, east-central CA. Height 1,612 ft., second highest in North America, after Yosemite Falls. Fed by a mountain creek, falls enters Merced River.

Name origin: For its long, narrow appearance.

Rio Grande
Feature: stream

Major river in southwest U.S., one of the longest rivers in North America: 1,885 mi. long; forms two-thirds of the US-Mexico border from El Paso, TX/Juarez, Mexico to Brownsville, TX/Matamoros, Mexico (1,240 mi.). Rises in southwest CO on Continental Divide in the Rocky Mountains, flows south through NM, forms entire southern border of TX, empties into Gulf of Mexico. For the most part too shallow for navigation; parts even dry up completely during late summer from lack of rain and its use for irrigation. Dams and reservoirs used to control floodwaters.

Name origin: Spanish 'big river.' In Mexico called Río Bravo (del Norte) 'bold river' (of the north).

River of No Return
See Salmon River

Roanoke Island
Feature: island
State: NC
Lat: 35-52-57 N **Long:** 07-53-92 W

In Croatan Sound along the northeastern coast of NC, within the Outer Banks. Site of the first attempt at English settlement in North America (1585), dispatched by Walter Raleigh (1554-1618), and where Virginia Dare, the first English child in the New World, was born in August 1587. After the colony's first failure in 1585, a new settlement was established in 1587, but by the time a supply ship arrived from England in 1590, the whole colony had disappeared, leaving only part of the word "Croatan" carved on a tree. The fate of the colony has remained a mystery.

Name origin: From an Indian word spelled *Roanoak* by the first English settlers. The Indians applied it to an island, meaning 'place where white shells are found' or perhaps 'shells which are used for money.'

Rocky Mountains *or* the Rockies Feature: range
Largest mountain system in North America: extends more than 3,000 mi. from Mexican border to AK; about 350 mi. east-west at its widest. Forms the Continental Divide. Four major divisions: Arctic Rockies, in Canada and AK; Northern Rockies in Canada, and ID and MT, including the Lewis Range; Middle Rockies in MT, WY, and UT, including the Grand Tetons; and Southern Rockies from WY to NM, including Front Range, Sawatch Range, San Juan Mountains, Laramie Mountains, and Sangre de Cristo Mountains.

Rogers, Mt. Feature: summit
County: Grayson **State:** VA
Lat: 36-39-35 N **Long:** 08-13-24 W
Peak in southwest VA in the southern portion of the Blue Ridge Mountains, near the NC border. Highest point in state, 5,927 ft.
Name origin: For William Barton Rogers (1804–82), geologist.

Roosevelt Dam Feature: dam
County: Gila **State:** AZ
Lat: 33-40-18 N **Long:** 11-10-93 W **Elevation:** 2,141
In central AZ, about 50 mi. east of Phoenix, part of the Salt River irrigation project. Rubble-masonry arch-gravity dam, 280 ft. high, crest length 723 ft.; reservoir 23 mi. long, can store 1,398,430 acre-ft. of water. Completed 1911.
Name origin: Official name Theodore Roosevelt Dam, for the twenty-sixth U.S. president (1858–1919), under whose administration construction began.

Ross Dam Feature: dam
County: Whatcom **State:** WA
Lat: 48-43-55 N **Long:** 12-10-35 W
In a narrow gorge of the Skagit River, north of Seattle. One of the world's highest arch-type dams, 540 ft. high, 1,300 ft. long.; forms Ruby Reservoir, 24 mi. long, extending to the Canadian border; can store 1,405,000 acre-ft. of water; part of Ross Lake National Recreation Area.

Royal Gorge Feature: valley
County: Fremont **State:** CO
Lat: 38-25-52 N **Long:** 10-51-60 W
In the Grand Canyon of the Arkansas River, west of Canon City, south-central CO. More than 1,000 ft. deep, only 30 ft. wide in places. A railroad provides a water-level route through the Rockies. Spanned at the top by world's highest suspension bridge, 1,053 ft. above the river.

Rushmore, Mt. Feature: summit
County: Pennington **State:** SD
Lat: 43-52-49 N **Long:** 10-32-73 W **Elevation:** 5,728
Granite cliff in the Black Hills of SD, 25 mi. from Rapid City. Huge carving on it shows the faces of four U.S. presidents: George Washington (1732–99), Thomas Jefferson (1743–1826), Theodore Roosevelt (1858–1919), and Abraham Lincoln (1809–65). Head of Washington about 60 ft. high. Designed and supervised by Gutzon Borglum (1867–1941); begun 1927; he died in 1941; his son, Lincoln, completed the work that year. Rises 5,725 ft. above sea level, more than 500 ft. above the valley; thus taller than the Great Pyramid of Egypt. Part of Mount Rushmore National Memorial.
Name origin: For Carlos E. Rushmore, an attorney from New York who was representing investors in the Etta Mine.

Russell Cave Feature: cave
County: Jackson **State:** AL
Lat: 34-58-37 N **Long:** 08-54-83 W
Near Bridgeport in northeast AL. Contains evidence of human use from about 7000 B.C. to about 1000 A.D., then sporadic use to about 1650; includes vestiges of a 9,000-year-old campfire.
Name origin: For an early white settler and landowner.

Sabine River Feature: stream
Rises in northeast TX, flows southeast to form southern portion of TX-LA border. Empties into Gulf of Mexico through Sabine Lake and Sabine Pass, southeast of Port Arthur. Length 580 mi.
Name origin: The French form of Spanish *sabinas* 'red cedars,' for the trees along the river banks.

Sacramento River Feature: stream
County: Contra Costa **State:** CA
Lat: 38-04-00 N **Long:** 12-15-10 W
Longest river in CA. Rises near Mt. Shasta in northwest CA. Flows about 380 mi. into Suisun Bay, the eastern extension of San Francisco Bay. Navigable for 180 mi.
Name origin: Spanish '(holy) sacrament,' referring to the Christian Eucharist. City and county are named for the river.

Sacramento Valley
See Central Valley

Saginaw Bay Feature: bay
County: Bay **State:** MI
Lat: 43-45-00 N **Long:** 08-34-00 W **Elevation:** 580
Inlet of Lake Huron on east-central coast of the lower peninsula of MI; Bay City is at the head; city of Saginaw farther inland.
Name origin: Ojibway 'place of the Sacs (Indians).'

St. Clair, Lake Feature: lake
County: St. Clair **State:** MI
Lat: 42-25-00 N **Long:** 08-24-00 W **Elevation:** 575
Part of the boundary between province of Ontario, Canada, and MI. Forms a waterway, together with the St. Clair River on the north and the Detroit River to the south, connecting Lake Huron and Lake Erie. Roughly circular, 25 mi. across at center; area 460 sq. mi. Its western shore is along the eastern suburbs of Detroit.
Name origin: Named, originally to honor St. Clare, by French explorer Robert Cavelier, Sieur de LaSalle (1643–87). Spelling changed to honor Arthur St. Clair (1736–1818), American Revolutionary general and first governor of the Northwest Territory.

St. Elias Mountains *or* Range Feature: range
County: Skagway-Yakutat-Angoon **State:** AK
Extend along Pacific coast of eastern AK and into Yukon Territory. A part of the Coast Ranges, the world's highest coastal mountains. Nearly 300 mi. long; maximum width 100 mi. Many glaciers, including Malaspina. Mount St. Elias, 18,008 ft., is fourth highest peak in North America.
Name origin: Named in 1741, by Danish explorer Vitus Bering (1681–1741) to honor the Old Testament prophet Elias.

St. Helens, Mt.
Feature: summit
County: Skamania **State:** WA
Lat: 46-11-52 N **Long:** 12-21-12 W

Active volcano in the Cascade Mountains, 95 mi. south of Seattle, WA. The noted 1980 eruption was the first in the lower U.S. since 1921. More than 1,000 ft. were blown away from the peak producing a huge crater; latest elevation, 8,364 ft. Smaller eruptions have occurred since.

Name origin: Named by Capt. George Vancouver (1757–98) for Alleyne Fitzherbert, Baron St. Helens (1753–1839), British ambassador to Spain (1790–94).

St. Lawrence and Great Lakes Waterway
See St. Lawrence Seaway

St. Lawrence Island
Feature: island
County: Nome **State:** AK
Lat: 63-30-10 N **Long:** 17-02-64 W

In the Bering Sea 118 mi. west of Nome on the west coast of AK, 150 mi. south of the Bering Strait. About 95 mi. long, 10 to 35 mi. wide; area 1,712 sq. mi. Highest point, 2,204 ft. Chief settlements Gambell and Savoonga; inhabited by Eskimos. Univ. of Alaska archaeological excavations can trace development of Eskimo culture for 2000 years.

Name origin: For Saint Lawrence; discovered in 1728 by Danish explorer Vitus Bering (1681-1741) on the saint's day, Aug 10.

St. Lawrence, Lake
Feature: reservoir
County: Saint Lawrence **State:** NY
Lat: 45-00-21 N **Long:** 09-44-74 W

Name for the wide part of the St. Lawrence River in northern NY near Massena. 28 mi. long, 1 to 4 mi. wide, 84 ft. deep. Created in 1958 after dam construction, part of the St. Lawrence Seaway project, to drown the rapids of the St. Lawrence River and permit navigation.

Name origin: For the river.

St. Lawrence River
Feature: stream

River primarily in Canada, but after leaving its source Lake Ontario it flows 744 mi. through the Thousand Islands, and for about 120 mi. forms boundary between NY state and the province of Ontario, Canada. Main route for shipping on the Great Lakes, though closed by ice from December to April. Historically vital route for early European explorers, traders, and colonists. Part of the St. Lawrence Seaway.

Name origin: Named in 1535 by French explorer Jacques Cartier (1491–1557) on the saint's day, Aug 10. Name originally applied to the Gulf of St. Lawrence, but later was used of the river.

St. Lawrence Seaway
Feature: channel
County: Saint Lawrence **State:** NY
Lat: 44-57-40 N **Long:** 07-45-74 W

A international commercial waterway for oceangoing ships, connecting the Atlantic Ocean and the Great Lakes via Lake Ontario and Lake Erie. Built by Canada and the U.S., completed in 1959; each nation built and operates its own section. Composed of the St. Lawrence River, several lakes, and a system of canals and locks, including the Welland Canal. About 450 mi. long from E end of Lake Erie to Montreal; goes from 570 ft. to 20 ft. above sea level. Together with channels between the Great Lakes, forms the St. Lawrence and Great Lakes Waterway.

Name origin: For the river.

Saint Mary's Falls Canal and Locks
See Sault Sainte Marie Canals

St. Marys River
Feature: stream
County: Chippewa **State:** MI
Lat: 45-57-35 N **Long:** 08-35-34 W

In eastern Upper Peninsula of MI between Lake Superior and Lake Huron. Flows about 63 mi. from Whitefish Bay on Lake Superior and empties into the northern end of Lake Huron. Forms boundary between U.S. and province of Ontario, Canada. The rapids fall 20 ft. within a mile to create St. Marys Falls at Sault Sainte Marie canals.

Name origin: For Mary, mother of Jesus Christ.

Sakakawea, Lake
Feature: reservoir
County: McLean **State:** ND
Lat: 47-29-40 N **Long:** 10-12-40 W

On Missouri River in west-central ND. About 200 mi. long; formed 1956 after the completion of the Garrison Dam, about 50 mi. northwest of Bismarck.

Name origin: Alternate spelling of *Sacajawea*, the Shoshone (1787?–1812?) interpreter and guide for the Lewis and Clark expedition. Formerly called Garrison Reservoir.

Salmon River
Feature: stream
County: Nez Perce **State:** ID
Lat: 45-51-24 N **Long:** 11-64-73 W

Rises in the Salmon River Mountains and Sawtooth Mountins of central ID; 420 mi. long; empties into the Snake River at ID-OR border in Hells Canyon National Recreational Area. Filled with rapids that are navigable downstream, but impassable upstream; thus its alternate name, River of No Return. The Salmon River Canyon, with a 1-mile gorge, is along its lower course.

Name origin: For a salmon run on the river.

Salton Sea
Feature: lake
State: CA
Lat: 33-20-00 N **Long:** 11-55-00 W

Shallow saline lake, the largest lake in CA; about 80 mi. northeast of San Diego, in southern CA. About 30 mi. long, 10 mi. wide, 240 ft. below sea level. Situated in the Salton Trough, which includes the Coachella Valley and the Imperial Valley. The valley area had become a salt-covered depression, called the Salton Sink, but between 1905–07 the swollen Colorado River flooded the depression, creating a 450 sq. mi. salt lake. Evaporation has reduced it to its present size.

Name origin: Coined from 'salt,' referring to its high salt content.

San Andreas Fault *or* San Andreas Rift Zone
Feature: valley
State: CA

An extensive zone of fracture in the earth's crust, part of the boundary between the Pacific Plate to the west and the North American Plate to the east, the recording geological theory of plate tectonics. Movement of the plates along the fault causes frequent earthquakes. Fault extends for 750 mi. along the coast of northern CA, through the San Francisco peninsula, then southeast toward the heart of the Gulf of California (Mexico).

Name origin: For the San Andreas Valley, which is along the fault line in San Mateo County. The San Andreas Lake, a reservoir, was formed in the valley in 1875, and is about 10 mi. south of San Francisco. The valley was named *Caada de San Andres* 'Valley of St. Andrew,' by Spanish missionary Padre Francisco Palou. He named it on the saint's feast day, Nov 30, 1774. The present spelling is modified from the Spanish form.

Sand Hills
Feature: summit
State: NE

In west-central NE, north of the Platte River. 20,000 sq. mi. of sand, formed into hills and ridges, covered by grasses; largest area of sand dunes in North America. Used for cattle grazing. Absorbs most of the area's limited rainfall into underground reservoirs.

Sandstone Hills
Feature: range
State: OK

Region extending south from KS border to near the Red River in southern OK; height 250 to 400 ft. Site of early oil development.

Sandy Hook
Feature: cape
County: Monmouth **State:** NJ
Lat: 40-26-35 N **Long:** 07-35-92 W

Sandy spit at tip of northeastern coast of NJ, extending into New York Bay; 18 mi. south of Manhattan Island. Bordered on west by Sandy Hook Bay, on east by the Atlantic Ocean. About 6 mi. long, 1 mi. at widest. A 103-ft. lighthouse about 1.5 mi. inland from the tip, completed in 1764, is the oldest lighthouse still in use.

San Francisco Bay
Feature: bay
County: San Mateo **State:** CA
Lat: 37-42-29 N **Long:** 12-21-64 W **Elevation:** 1943

Inlet of the Pacific Ocean on west-central coast of CA. About 60 mi. long north to south (including San Pablo Bay to the north) and 3 to 12 mi. wide. Connects with the Pacific through Golden Gate a strait at which the Golden Gate Bridge was built. Oakland is on E shore, San Francisco on NW shore; Palo Alto at southern end.
Name origin: For St. Francis of Assisi (c. 1181–1226); name applied to a bay or port in the region as early as 1595 by Spanish explorer Rodríguez Cermeo. The christening was performed November 6, 1595, by a member of the Franciscan order of priests, and the name honors the patron of the order. The name was firmly fixed to this bay by the Gaspar de Portolá (c. 1723–c. 1784) expedition in 1769. The city and county are named for the bay.

Sangre de Cristo Mountains
Feature: range

Southernmost range of the southern Rocky Mountains, an extension of the Front Range. Extend from central CO to north-central NM. Highest is Blanca Peak, 14,317 ft. Sangre de Cristo Pass, in southern CO, 9,459 ft.; was used before 1800.
Name origin: Spanish 'blood of Christ,' possibly for the reddish tint on the snow at sundown, with a devotional aspect. Believed to have been first used in early 1800s.

Sanibel Island
Feature: island
County: Lee **State:** FL
Lat: 26-26-24 N **Long:** 08-20-65 W

Resort area in Gulf of Mexico, off west coast of FL, southwest of Fort Myers. Area 16 sq. mi. Noted for quantity and variety of seashells found on its beaches.
Name origin: Believed to combine (Spanish?) roots for 'health' and 'beauty.'

San Joaquin River
Feature: stream
County: Contra Costa **State:** CA
Lat: 38-04-00 N **Long:** 12-15-10 W

In central California; chief body of water in southern Central Valley. Rises on western slope of Sierra Nevada Mountains; flows 350 mi.; crosses Joaquin Valley; joins Sacramento River and forms delta near San Francisco Bay. Navigable by ocean-going vessels for about 88 mi. to Stockton. Friant Dam on river.
Name origin: Spanish form of Saint Joachim, traditionally the father of the Virgin Mary. Named 1805 by Spanish explorer Gabriel Moraga. County and valley named for the river.

San Joaquin Valley
Feature: valley
County: San Joaquin **State:** CA
Lat: 38-00-01 N **Long:** 12-13-00 W

Rich agricultural area, in the southern portion of the Central Valley. Irrigation is provided by construction of the Central Valley Project, channeling water from northern CA down the Sacramento River to the San Joaquin River, and from Millerton Lake, behind Friant Dam on the San Joaquin.
Name origin: For the river.

San Juan Islands
Feature: islands
County: San Juan **State:** WA

Archipelago of 172 islands lying at the juncture of the Strait of Georgia and the Strait of San Juan de Fuca, north of Puget Sound in northwestern WA. Haro Strait and Victoria, British Columbia are west and Rosario Strait and Bellingham, WA, to the east. Include Orcas Island, 59 sq. mi.; San Juan Island, 56 sq. mi.; and Lopez Island, 26 sq. mi.
Name origin: Named in 1791 by Spanish explorer Francisco Eliza, th honor St. John the Baptist, but with a nod to his patron, Juan Vicente de Guemes, viceroy of Mexico.

San Juan Mountains
Feature: range

Range of the southern Rocky Mountains in southwestern CO, extending into NM. Highest peaks Uncompahgre Peak, 14,309 ft.; Mt. Wilson, 14,246 ft.; and Mt. Sneffels, 14,150 ft.
Name origin: Spanish form, for St. John (the Baptist).

San Juan River
Feature: stream

Rises in San Juan Mountains in southwestern CO. Flows west 360 mi. across CO and NM, and empties into Colorado River in southeastern UT. Important in development projects of the upper Colorado River.
Name origin: Spanish form, for St. John (the Baptist).

Santa Catalina, Gulf of
Feature: bay
County: San Diego **State:** CA
Lat: 33-15-01 N **Long:** 11-74-50 W

Inlet of Pacific Ocean, off southwest coast of CA. Open to the Pacific Ocean on the south and west via the Outer Santa Barbara Channel, and on the north via the San Pedro Channel. Santa Catalina and San Clemente islands are to the west.
Name origin: For Santa Catalina island.

Santa Catalina Island
Feature: island
County: Los Angeles **State:** CA
Lat: 33-23-00 N **Long:** 11-82-50 W

One of the Santa Barbara Islands, in Pacific Ocean south of Los Angeles, of which it is part. To its south is the Gulf of Santa Catalina. Tourist resort served by passenger ferry; 22 mi. long, area 70 sq. mi.

Name origin: Named by Spanish explorer Sebastián Vizcaíno (1550?–1616) on Nov. 25, 1602, the feast day of Saint Catherine (Spanish *Catalina*) of Alexandria. Also called Catalina Island.

Santa Fe Trail
Feature: trail

Important overland trade route from 1821–80, 780 mi. long from Independence, MO, to Santa Fe, NM. The trail divided into two branches at Council Grove, KS; one went up the Arkansas River to Bent's Fort, CO, then southwest across Raton Pass to upper Canadian River in NM. The second branch went through the valley of the Cimarron River; a shorter route but more dangerous because of Indian attacks. Opened by William Becknell (1796–1865), trader, known as "father of the Santa Fe trade." See also Old Spanish Trail. Replaced by the Atchison, Topeka, and Santa Fe railroad.

Name origin: For its western terminus at Santa Fe.

Santee Reservoir
See Marion, Lake

Santee River
Feature: stream
County: Georgetown **State:** SC
Lat: 33-14-06 N **Long:** 07-92-73 W

In eastern SC, formed by the confluence of Wateree and Congaree rivers; flows 143 mi. southeast, emptying into Atlantic Ocean south of Georgetown, SC. Navigable to Camden, SC. Part of the Santee-Wateree-Catawba river system (438 mi. long), most important in SC. Santee Dam forms Lake Marion.

Name origin: For the Santee Indians.

Sardis Dam
Feature: dam
County: Panola **State:** MS
Lat: 34-24-32 N **Long:** 08-94-74 W

In northwestern MS, one of largest earth-filled flood control dams in U.S. 118 ft. high, almost 1/4 mi. wide at base, 15,300 ft. long at top on Little Tallahatchie River. Completed 1940, forming the Sardis Reservoir, more than 30 mi. long.

Name origin: For the ancient city in Asia Minor, the capital of Lydia; near present-day Izmir, Turkey. City is mentioned in Revelation (1:11; 3:1,4).

Sassafras Mountain
Feature: summit
County: Pickens **State:** SC
Lat: 35-03-53 N **Long:** 08-24-63 W

Peak in Blue Ridge Mountains in northwest SC. Highest point in state, 3,560 ft.

Name origin: For the tree *Sassafras albidum*.

Sault Sainte Marie Canals
Feature: canal
County: Chippewa **State:** MI
Lat: 46-30-10 N **Long:** 08-42-14 W

At U.S.-Canadian border on eastern tip of the Upper Peninsula of MI. Two U.S. canals and one Canadian permit ships to travel between Lakes Superior and Huron, by-passing St. Mary's Falls on St. Mary's River. The North canal completed 1919; 1.61 mi. long, 80 ft. wide, 24.5 ft. deep. South canal completed 1896; 1.56 mi. long, 100 ft. wide, 18 ft. deep; both administered by U.S. government. Canadian canal, completed 1895; 1.38 mi. long, 150 ft. wide, 22 ft. deep. Five locks, one on Canadian canal.

Name origin: Also Soo Canals, anglicized spelling reflects pronunciation of *Sault* (French 'falls, rapids') Sainte Marie. American canals also called Saint Marys Falls Canal and Locks.

Savannah River
Feature: stream
County: Chatham **State:** GA
Lat: 32-02-15 N **Long:** 08-05-10 W

Formed in northwestern SC by confluence of the Tugaloo and Seneca rivers. Flows southeast 314 mi., forming GA-SC border; empties into Atlantic Ocean at Tybee Roads, north of Savannah. Channel 18 mi. long, 30 mi. wide, connects Savannah to the Atlantic; used by large ships; smaller ships can navigate 230 mi. to Augusta, GA. Clark Hill Dam is on river above Augusta.

Name origin: Spanish form of Carib Indian *zabana*, possibly 'level grassy plain, often marshy.' Also said to be a Spanish rendering of the Shawnee name for the river, near which that tribe lived. The city in GA is named for the river.

Sawatch Range
Feature: range
State: CO

Part of the Southern Rocky Mountains, in west-central CO. Includes the highest point in CO and the American Rockies, Mt. Elbert, 14,331 ft. Middle portion usually called Collegiate Range, so-named for Mts. Yale, Harvard, and Princeton. Mount of the Holy Cross, 13,986 ft., has snow-filled crevices near its peak, shaped like a cross 1,000 ft. long with 375-ft. arms.

Name origin: A shortening of Ute *sa-gua-gua-chi-pa* 'blue-earth-spring,' from the blue clay found there.

Schuylkill River
Feature: stream
County: Philadelphia **State:** PA
Lat: 39-52-52 N **Long:** 07-51-15 W

Rises in central PA; flows 131 mi. southeast, empties into Delaware River at Philadelphia. Used by coal barges, furnishes hydroelectric power, and part of Philadelphia's water supply.

Name origin: Dutch *schuy* 'hidden' and *kill* 'stream.'

Sea Islands
Feature: island

Chain of low-lying, sandy islands in the Atlantic Ocean off coasts of SC, GA, and FL between the mouths of Santee and St. Johns rivers, and along the Intracoastal Waterway. Some are deserted, others are resorts or wildlife sanctuaries. Noted for production of long-stapled sea-island cotton. After the Civil War, the land was given to freed slaves who remain predominantly on the islands off SC; gullah is their dialect. St. Helena and Port Royal are the most important islands. Jekyll, St. Simons, and Sea Island are important resorts.

Sebago Lake
Feature: lake
County: Cumberland **State:** ME
Lat: 53-42-18 N **Long:** 07-03-40 W **Elevation:** 267
Resort lake in southern ME 15 mi. northwest of Portland; 13 mi. long, 10 mi. wide, second largest lake in ME.
Name origin: Abnaki 'big lake.'

Sevier Lake
Feature: lake
County: Millard **State:** UT
Lat: 38-56-20 N **Long:** 11-30-94 W
Salt-water lake, dry in some years, in western UT; lake bed is about 28 mi. long, 10 mi. wide. Has been shrinking owing to diversion of the Sevier River, which flows into it from north for irrigation.
Name origin: From the Sevier River; its name is adapted from 19th-century Spanish name *Rio Severo*, probably for San Severo, a 4th-century Spanish-born bishop. Spelling shifted to *Sevier* under English-speaking pioneers, perhaps influenced by the fame of American pioneer John Sevier.

Shasta Dam
Feature: dam
County: Shasta **State:** CA
Lat: 40-43-07 N **Long:** 12-22-50 W
On the Sacramento River in northern CA, about 12 mi. north of Redding, CA. One of the highest concrete dams in the U.S.: 602 ft. high, 3,460 ft. long, with 8,430,000 cu. yds. concrete. Highest overflow dam in the world: spillway drops 480 ft. Completed in 1945, part of the Central Valley project. Forms Shasta Lake from waters of the McCloud, Pit, and Sacramento rivers, used for irrigation.
Name origin: For Mount Shasta; name officially bestowed Sept. 12, 1937.

Shasta, Mt.
Feature: summit
County: Siskiyou **State:** CA
Lat: 41-24-34 N **Long:** 12-21-13 W
Dramatic, solitary peak in the Cascade Range, in northern CA. An extinct volcano, it was formed by lava flows in prehistoric times; steam vents are still evident. Smaller peak to the west, Shastina, has a nearly perfect volcanic cone. Height, 14,162 ft; discovered 1827; first climbed 1854.
Name origin: For an Indian tribe that inhabited the area; name recorded as *Shatasla*, *Sastise*, and *Sasty*, *Shaste*, and *Chasty*. Present spelling apparently close to the native pronunciation, established by the 1850s, and used for the mountain, county, river, town, and later the dam.

Shelter Island
Feature: island
County: Suffolk **State:** NY
Lat: 41-03-52 N **Long:** 07-22-00 W
Island and township between the north and south forks of eastern Long Island; between Little Peconic and Gardiners bays. About 7 mi. long, 6 mi. wide; resort and yachting center.

Shenandoah River
Feature: stream
Formed by confluence of two forks at Riverton in northern VA. This main body, the river proper, is 55 mi. long; together with North Fork, 172 mi.; main body with South Fork is 206 mi. Flows through the Shenandoah Valley, between the Blue Ridge Mountains and the Allegheny Mountains, primarily in VA, but also across northeastern WV joining the main stream of the Potomac River at Harper's Ferry. Largest tributary of the Potomac River, but not navigable.
Name origin: Algonquian, probably *schind-han-dowi* 'spruce stream.' Also been translated as 'great plains,' and even 'beautiful daughter of the stars.'

Shenandoah Valley
Feature: valley
State: VA
Scenic, rural valley, extends southwest from Harper's Ferry, WV; about 110 mi. long; 25 mi. wide. Fertile area drained by the Shenandoah River; also much of the area drained by the James River west of the Blue Ridge Mountains; lies between the Alleghenies to the west and the Blue Ridge Mountains to the east. During Civil War, was the avenue for Confederate incursions into the North. Portion is within Shenandoah National Park.
Name origin: For the Shenandoah River.

Ship Rock
Feature: summit
County: San Juan **State:** NM
Lat: 36-41-15 N **Long:** 10-85-00 W **Elevation:** 7178
Volcanic neck in the Colorado Plateaus of northwestern NM. It stands 1678 ft. above the surrounding tableland, and was the basis for many Navajo legends.
Name origin: For its supposed resemblance to a ship in full sail.

Shishaldin, Mt.
Feature: summit
County: Aleutians East **State:** AK
Largest volcano in the Aleutian Islands, 9,387 ft. On Unimak Island in the Fox Island group.
Name origin: Named in 1790 by Lt. G.A. Sarichev, who published the first Alaskan atlas in 1826. Transliteration from Russian *sopka shishaldinskaya*. Sarichev said Aleut name was 'Agajedan.'

Shoshone Falls
Feature: falls
County: Twin Falls **State:** ID
Lat: 42-35-43 N **Long:** 11-42-40 W
In southern ID in the Snake River near Twin Falls; height 210 ft., width 900 ft. Now reduced by upstream irrigation projects.
Name origin: For the Shoshone Indians.

Silicon Valley
Feature: valley
State: CA
Area from San Jose northwest to Palo Alto near San Francisco.
Name origin: For the many computer-related industries located there, which use many components that rely on silicon-based semiconductors. Usage began in the 1970s.

Snake River
Feature: stream
Rises near the Continental Divide in Yellowstone National Park, WY; flows 1038 mi. south and west through ID, then north to form part of ID-OR and ID-WA borders; empties into the Columbia River near Pasco, WA. Chief branch of the Columbia; important source of irrigation and hydroelectric power. On ID-OR border river flows through Hell's Canyon, more than 125 mi. long and more than 7,000 ft. deep. Many notable springs; number of cascades in southern ID north of Twin Falls, especially Twin Falls and Shoshone Falls.
Name origin: For the Snake tribe of the Shoshone Indians.

Snoqualmie Falls
Feature: falls
County: King **State:** WA
Lat: 47-32-31 N **Long:** 12-15-01 W
In west-central Washington. Waterfall on Snoqualmie River 270 ft. high. A hydroelectric power plant is also at the site.
Name origin: From the tribal name *sdoh-kwaheb-bluh*, based on *sdoh-kwaheb* 'moon,' believed to be the life source of their tribe.

Major Geographical Features — American Places Dictionary

Soo Canals
See Sault Sainte Marie Canals

Spruce Knob   Feature: summit
County: Pocahontas **State:** WV
Lat: 38-19-35 N **Long:** 08-00-91 W
In eastern WV. Highest point in state, 4,862 ft.

Staked Plains
See Texas Panhandle

Staten Island   Feature: island, borough
County: Richmond **State:** NY
Lat: 40-35-00 N **Long:** 07-40-90 W
One of the five boroughs of New York City, coextensive with Richmond county in New York Bay, about 5 mi. southwest of Manhattan Island. About 14 mi. long, 7.5 mi. at widest; area 65 sq. mi. Commuter service to Manhattan via Staten Island ferry. Verrazano-Narrows Bridge connects it to Brooklyn; three bridges connect it to New Jersey.
Name origin: For the Staten Generaal, governing body of the Netherlands; name established in the period Dutch rule. Borough formerly named Richmond; officially renamed Staten Island in 1975.

Stevens Dam
See Mud Mountain Dam

Stone Mountain   Feature: summit
County: De Kalb **State:** GA
Lat: 33-48-22 N **Long:** 08-40-84 W **Elevation:** 1683
Largest stone mountain in North America, 16 mi. east of Atlanta in northwestern GA, bearing the world's largest bas-relief sculpture. Mountain is light grey granite, elev. 1,683 ft., rising 700 ft. over surrounding terrain; stone mass is about 2 mi. long, 1 mi. wide. Sculpture is a memorial to the Confederacy, depicting Confederate heroes Jefferson Davis (1808–89), Gen. Robert E. Lee (1807–70) and Gen. Stonewall Jackson (1824–63). Work was begun 1923 but discontinued in 1928 for lack of funds; Gutzon Borglum (1867–1941) was first sculptor (see Mount Rushmore); work resumed in 1964 and completed in 1969 under direction of Walker Kirtland Hancock. Part of 3,200-acre Stone Mountain Memorial State Park.

Sunflower, Mt.   Feature: summit
County: Sheman **State:** KS
Lat: 39-01-19 N **Long:** 10-20-21 W
On west-central border of KS. Highest point in state, 4,039 ft.
Name origin: For the sunflower, *Helianthus annuus*, state flower of KS.

Superior, Lake   Feature: lake
Largest body of fresh water in the world. To the northwest, north, and east is province of Ontario, Canada; on the south are the Upper Peninsula of MI and WI; with MN to the west. Of the Great Lakes, it is the deepest, and farthest north and west. Area, 31,700 sq. mi.; greatest length east-west, 350 mi.; greatest width, 160 mi.; 1,333 ft. deep. Drains into Lake Huron through St. Mary's River.
Name origin: Name *Lac Superieur* 'Upper Lake' given by French explorers and traders in the 17th century, referring to its geographical position relative to Lake Huron.

Susquehanna River   Feature: stream
Rises in Otsego Lake in central NY; flows southward 444 mi. across NY, PA, and MD; empties into northern Chesapeake Bay at Havre de Grace. Generally too shallow for navigation.
Name origin: For an Indian tribe of Iroquoian linguistic stock who lived along the river. Name recorded by English colonist John Smith (c. 1580–1631) in 1608 as *Sasquesahanough*; other spellings include *Sasquesahonock* and *Susquehannock*. Origin is uncertain.

Suwanee River   Feature: stream
Rises in southeast GA below Waycross; flows about 250 mi. across FL; empties into Gulf of Mexico at Suwannee Sound. Navigable only by very small boats. Made famous by Stephen Foster (1826–64), who called it *Swanee* in his song, "Old Folks at Home."
Name origin: A seminole name of uncertain origin and meaning; possibly *Sawni* 'echo.' Or may be an English rendering of *San Juan*.

Tacoma, Mount
See Rainier, Mount

Taconic Mountains   Feature: range
Range of the Appalachian Mountains extending about 150 mi. along NY-CT border, the entire NY-MA border, and into VT. Highest peak Mt. Equinox 3,816 ft., in VT. The Berkshire Hills are part of the range.
Name origin: Algonquian origin, meaning disputed. May mean 'steep ascent' or 'small field,' or may be from the root *tugk*, 'tree,' 'wood,' or 'forest.'

Tahoe, Lake   Feature: lake
Oval-shaped glacial resort lake on CA-NV border, 10 mi. west of Carron City, in a valley of the Sierra Nevada. 23 mi. long, 12 mi. wide, 1,640 ft. deep; 6,228 ft. above sea level; its depth keeps it from freezing. Empties through Truckee River into Pyramid Lake to the north. John C. Frémont (1813–90) discovered it in 1844.
Name origin: Named in 1862 from Washo Indian name meaning 'big water.' Previously called *Lake Bigler*.

Tampa Bay   Feature: bay
County: Hillsborough **State:** FL
Lat: 27-41-18 N **Long:** 08-23-42 W
Inlet of the Gulf of Mexico on west-central coast of FL; 25 mi. long, up to 12 mi. wide. Tampa is at northeast end and St. Petersburg at the mouth on western shore.
Name origin: Possibly from Cree 'near it'; referring to proximity of an Indian village to the bay; also possibly for a 16th-century Indian settlement found by the Spanish. Hernando de Escalante Fontaneda, shipwrecked off the coast and rescued by the Indians in 1545, records the use of the name.

Tanana River   Feature: stream
County: Yukon-Koyukuk **State:** AK
Lat: 65-09-38 N **Long:** 15-15-73 W
Rises in glaciers in northeastern Wrangell Mountains in east and central AK. Chief southern tributary of the Yukon River. Flows northwest about 475 mi. to join the Yukon at Tanana in central AK. Navigable by large ships for about 225 mi; smaller vessels can go nearly to source. Alaska Highway follows almost its entire course.
Name origin: For the Tanana Indian tribe, of Athapascan linguistic stock. Name means 'mountain river.'

Taum Sauk Mountain
Feature: summit
County: Iron **State:** MO
Lat: 37-34-13 N **Long:** 09-04-34 W
Peak in southeastern MO; highest point in state, 1,772 ft.
Name origin: Uncertain, although *Sauk* is the name of an Indian tribe.

Tennessee River
Feature: stream
Largest tributary of the Ohio River. Begins in Knoxville, TN, at the confluence of the Holston and French Broad rivers; flows southwest 652 mi. through TN, AL, and KY; river valley extends into VA, NC, GA, and MS; empties into the Ohio River at Paducah, KY. A series of dams, begun in 1933 by the Tennessee Valley Authority, converted the river into a chain of narrow lakes that control flooding and ensure uniform depth during wet and dry seasons. The full length of the river is now navigable. Tennessee-Tombigbee Waterway, completed in 1985, connects the Tennessee with the Tombigbee River of MS and AL.
Name origin: For a Cherokee town, recorded by the Spanish (1597) as *Tanasqui*, by the English (1709) *Tinnase*. Long established name, but meaning unknown. Name used for a small stream; carried westward where the stream fed into the river. Original name *Cherokee River*.

Tennessee-Tombigbee Waterway
Feature: canal
In TN and AL; connects the Tennessee and Tombigbee rivers. Includes a canal from the east fork of the Tombigbee source north to the Tennessee River; deepening and widening the Tombigbee from its source south to Demopolis, AL. Ten locks and dams along both rivers, about 234 mi. long; completed in 1985. Ranked among the world's largest navigational projects.
Name origin: Also called Tenn-Tom Waterway.

Ten Thousand Smokes, Valley of
Feature: valley
County: Lake and Peninsula **State:** AK
Lat: 58-23-38 N **Long:** 15-52-30 W
Volcanic region at northern end of Alaska Peninsula, in southwestern AK, created by eruption of Mt. Katmai in June 1912. The valley of the River Lethe, it is 17 mi. long, 4 mi. wide, covered by flow of volcanic ash. When discovered by expedition of National Geographic Society in 1916, valley floor had thousands of various-sized steam vents, largest 150 ft. in diameter; some with temperatures as high as 1200°F. Steam vents are now largely dissipated.
Name origin: Named July 31, 1916, by R.F. Griggs and L.G. Folsum of the Katmai Expedition of the National Geographic Society.

Teton Mountains
Feature: range
In western Wyoming, south of Yellowstone National Park, part of the Middle Rockies. Group of ten Rocky Mountain peaks; highest Grand Teton: 13,770 ft. Range forms part of Grand Teton National Park. Peaks are a prime example of fault blocks.
Name origin: From French 'breast.' So named by early French fur trappers who thought the peaks resembled women's breasts. Also possibly for the Teton tribe of the Sioux Nation, whose name means 'at or on land without trees,' referring to any Indians living on the prairie, according to a letter from Maj. J.W. Powell to the Smithsonian Institution.

Texas Panhandle
Feature: plain
State: TX
The northwestern part of the state that extends between OK and NM, a treeless plateau with rich farming land.
Name origin: Western portion also called *Llano Estacado* 'Staked Plains', or the High Plains.

Texoma, Lake
Feature: reservoir
One of the largest artificial lakes in the U.S., about 80 mi. south of Oklahoma City. Formed in 1944 by Denison Dam on the Red River. Area 140 sq. mi.
Name origin: From location on Texas-Oklahoma border.

Thousand Islands
Feature: island
County: Jefferson **State:** NY
Lat: 42-20-00 N **Long:** 07-60-00 W
Group of more than 1,700 islands that lie in a 40-mi. stretch of the St. Lawrence River where it runs up to 7 mi. wide as it leaves Lake Ontario; on the border of NY and the province of Ontario, Canada. Popular resort area. Some islands are as long as 5 mi.; many just a rock above water. Thousand Islands International Bridge spans some of the islands. Seventeen islands are within St. Lawrence Island National Park.

Timms Hill
Feature: summit
County: Price **State:** WI
Lat: 45-27-04 N **Long:** 09-01-14 W
In central WI; highest point in state, 1,952 ft.
Name origin: For a local settler.

Toledo Bend Reservoir
Feature: reservoir
Largest reservoir in TX, formed by the Toledo Bend Dam on Sabine River. Extends 70 mi. along western border of TX-LA. Sabine National Forest along western shore.

Tombigbee River
Feature: stream
Rises in northeastern MS, flows south about 400 mi. into AL. In southwestern AL it joins the Alabama River and forms the Mobile River, which flows into Mobile Bay and the Gulf of Mexico. Black Warrior River is chief tributary. Tennessee-Tombigbee Waterway connects it to the Tennessee River, and links the Tennessee Valley to the Gulf of Mexico.
Name origin: From Choctaw *itombi* 'coffin,' plus *ikbi* 'makers'; for a class of tribesmen who cleaned the bones of the dead and boxed them.

Transverse Ranges
See Los Angeles Ranges

Uinta Mountains
Feature: range
County: Daggett **Lat:** 40-52-58 N **Long:** 10-90-74 W
Range in northeastern UT, east of Salt Lake City, with a small part in the southwestern corner of WY. Tallest peak is Kings Peak; 13,528 ft., highest point in UT.
Name origin: A Ute Indian tribal name.

Upper Red Lake
See Red Lake

Upper Yosemite Falls
See Yosemite Falls

Vernal Fall
Feature: falls
County: Mariposa **State:** CA
Lat: 37-43-38 N **Long:** 11-93-23 W
In east-central CA in Yosemite National Park, height 317 ft.
Name origin: Named in 1851 by Lafayette Bunnell for the cool spray created by the waterfall, which makes the area vernal or spring-like. Previous Indian name was *Yan-o-pah* 'little cloud.'

Verrazano-Narrows Bridge
Feature: bridge
County: Staten Island **State:** NY
Lat: 40-36-23 N **Long:** 07-40-24 W
Connects the New York City boroughs of Brooklyn and Staten Island. The longest suspension bridge in the U.S.; spans The Narrows connecting Upper and Lower New York bays. Main span 4,260 ft.; completed 1964.
Name origin: For Giovanni da Verrazano (1485?–1528?), Italian navigator and explorer; believed to have entered New York harbor, reached the Hudson River, and explored the New England coast.

Wabash River
Feature: stream
Main waterway of Indiana. Rises in western OH; flows southwesterly 475 mi. across IN then south to form IN-IL border from near Terre Haute, IN, to the IN-IL-KY border where it empties into the Ohio River.
Name origin: From Miami *wahba* 'white,' and *shik-ki* 'color-bright,' usually translated as 'white water.'

Waialeale, Mt.
Feature: summit
County: Kauai **State:** HI
Lat: 22-04-26 N **Long:** 15-92-95 W
Highest mountain in Kauai Island, HI, 5,148 ft. Rainiest place on earth with 486 in. annually.
Name origin: Hawaiian 'rippling or overflowing water.'

Waikiki Beach
Feature: beach
County: Honolulu **State:** HI
Lat: 21-16-46 N **Long:** 15-74-95 W
Resort on Mamala Bay, on southeastern coast of Oahu, about 4 mi. east of downtown Honolulu. Tourist center of HI; about 2.5 mi. long, backed by the Ala Wai Canal about 0.5 mi. inland; includes Kapiolani Park. Worldwide surfing competitions are held in the waves formed by the ocean crashing on a submerged coral reef about a half mile offshore.
Name origin: Hawaiian 'spouting water,' believed to refer to swamps drained to form Ala Wai Canal; also the name of a female chief.

Walden Pond
Feature: lake
County: Middlesex **State:** MA
Lat: 42-26-20 N **Long:** 07-12-02 W **Elevation:** 158
A 64-acre pond in northeast MA, south of Concord. Made famous by Henry Thoreau's (1817–62) *Walden*, an account of the two years he spent on its shore in his experiment at living closely to nature 1845–47.
Name origin: Possibly a local family name.

Wasatch Range
Feature: range
Extends about 250 mi. from southern ID into northern UT. Its western face forms the western front of the Rocky Mountains and eastern rim of the Great Basin. Salt Lake City is at foot of the range. Mount Timpanogos is highest peak; 12,008 ft.; site of Timpanogos Cave National Monument.
Name origin: Ute 'mountain pass,' but meaning uncertain.

Washington, Mt.
Feature: summit
County: Coos **State:** NH
Lat: 44-16-14 N **Long:** 07-11-81 W
In the Presidential Range of the White Mountains of NH. The highest peak in the range, the state, and northeastern U.S.: 6,288 ft. Mt. Washington Observatory keeps daily records of temperature, wind, and radioactive fallout in the mountains, also tests for cloud seeding to produce rain. Highest wind speed ever recorded on Earth, 231 m.p.h., registered here in 1934.
Name origin: For George Washington (1732–99), the first U.S. president.

Welland Ship Canal
Feature: canal
A 27-mi long canal with eight locks in the province of Ontario, Canada, connecting Lakes Ontario and Erie; an important part of the St. Lawrence Seaway. Officially opened Aug 6, 1932, present canal is an enlargement and improvement of original canal completed in 1829; further improved in 1973 by straightening it and constructing several tunnels and bridges. Extends from Port Weller on Lake Ontario to Port Colborne on Lake Erie. The natural connection between the two lakes is the Niagara River, which is too full of falls and rapids to be commercially navigable.
Name origin: For the Welland River in Lincolnshire, England.

West Quoddy Head
Feature: cape
County: Washington **State:** ME
Lat: 44-48-47 N **Long:** 06-65-74 W
The easternmost point of the continental U.S. (see also Cape Wrangell). Cape in southeast ME, south of Eastport at entrance to Passamaquoddy Bay.

Wheeler Peak
Feature: summit
County: Taos **State:** NM
Lat: 36-33-24 N **Long:** 10-52-45 W
In northern NM; highest point in state, 13,161 ft.
Name origin: For Capt. G.M. Wheeler. who led a surveying expedition in the area in 1869–70.

White Butte
Feature: summit
County: Slope **State:** ND
Lat: 46-23-12 N **Long:** 10-31-80 W
Peak in southwestern ND; highest peak in the state, 3,506 ft.

Whitefish Bay
Feature: bay
County: Alpena **State:** MI
Lat: 46-28-44 N **Long:** 08-44-85 W
Inlet of Lake Superior on northeast coast of Upper Peninsula of MI; Sault Ste. Marie is at E end. Traversed by international boundary with province of Ontario, Canada.

White Mountains
Feature: range
Mountains primarily in NH; partly in ME. Part of the Appalachian Mountain system; include a number of ranges, the Presidential Range in NH the most notable. Area about 1,000 sq. mi. Best-known of the deep canyons (called *notches*) are Franconia and Crawford. Franconia Notch features the Old Man of the Mountain. Mt. Washington is highest peak in NH: 6,288 ft.
Name origin: For the granite peaks, appearing white when sunshine hits them.

American Places Dictionary — Major Geographical Features

White Sands
Feature: area
State: NM

In south-central NM, southwest of Alamogordo. A 144,458-acre alkali flat, with dunes of white gypsum up to 60 ft. high, constantly reshaped by the wind. Plants and animals have adapted to survive the harsh environment. Established as White Sands National Monument in 1933.

Whitney, Mt.
Feature: summit
County: Tulare **State:** CA
Lat: 36-34-45 N **Long:** 11-81-73 W

In south-central CA in Sequoia National Park. Snow-capped, granite peak in Sierra Nevada Range, highest in CA, 14,495 ft.
Name origin: For Josiah Dwight Whitney (1819–96), CA state geologist.

Willamette River
Feature: stream
County: Multnomah **State:** OR
Lat: 45-39-21 N **Long:** 12-24-54 W

Formed by junction of forks in the Cascade and Coast Mountains in northern OR. Flows northward about 300 mi., empties into the Columbia River near Portland. Navigable for most of its length.
Name origin: Probably of Indian derivation, with French influence in the recording, though stress is on the second syllable. Meaning unknown.

Wind Cave
Feature: cave
County: Custer **State:** SD
Lat: 43-33-29 N **Long:** 10-32-84 W

Limestone cavern featuring unusual crystal formations in the Black Hills of southwestern SD about 10 mi. north of Hot Springs. Discovered by Tom Bingham, a Black Hills pioneer, in 1881. Part of Wind Cave National Park.
Name origin: For the strong wind currents that alternately blow in and out of the cave.

Wind River Range
Feature: range
County: Sublette **State:** WY
Lat: 43-00-00 N **Long:** 10-93-00 W

Range of the Rocky Mountains, part of the Continental Divide, in west-central WY; highest point, Gannett Peak 13,785 ft. (highest point in WY).
Name origin: For the river that flows on the eastern side of the range.

Winnebago, Lake
Feature: lake
County: Winnebago **State:** WI
Lat: 44-01-20 N **Long:** 08-82-52 W **Elevation:** 747

Largest lake in WI, in east-central part of state, below Green Bay. Fond du Lac is at southern end. Area 215 sq. mi; 30 mi. long, up to 10 mi. wide.
Name origin: For the name of an Indian tribe of Siouan linguistic stock. Name thought to mean 'fish eaters.' Other tribes called them 'stinkers' or 'people who live in filthy water.'

Winnipesaukee, Lake
Feature: lake
County: Belknap **State:** NH
Lat: 43-35-56 N **Long:** 07-11-92 W

Largest lake in NH; in east central part of state. About 22 mi. long, 1 to 10 mi. wide; area: 71 sq. mi. Has 365 islands in it.
Name origin: Meaning uncertain. The most favored translation is 'good outlet.' Formerly spelled *Winnepesaukee*.

Wisconsin Dells
Feature: valley
State: WI

Deep gorge along the Wisconsin River in south-central WI, about 50 miles north of Madison. 7 mi. long, 100 ft. deep, cut by the river through soft sandstone. Varied and strange formations are found in the rock.

Wisconsin River
Feature: stream
County: Crawford **State:** WI
Lat: 42-59-22 N **Long:** 09-10-91 W

Rises in the lake region of northern WI near the border with MI. Flows south and west 430 mi.; entire course within the state. Empties into Mississippi River below Prairie du Chien. At Portage, a short canal connects it with the Fox River and so with Lake Michigan.
Name origin: Probably from Ojibway *Wees-kon-san* 'the gathering of the waters'; name first applied to the river.

Wolf Creek Dam
Feature: dam
County: Russell **State:** KY
Lat: 36-52-05 N **Long:** 08-50-85 W

Major flood control and hydroelectric power project, on the Cumberland River near Jamestown, KY. Combination concrete and earth dam, 258 ft. high, 5,736 ft. long; completed 1951. Forms Wolf Creek Reservoir, 101 mi. long, area 63,530 acres.

Woodall Mountain
Feature: summit
County: Tishomingo **State:** MS
Lat: 34-47-16 N **Long:** 08-81-43 W

In northeastern MS; highest point in state, 806 ft.

Woods, Lake of the
Feature: lake
County: Lake of the Woods **State:** MN
Lat: 49-15-00 N **Long:** 09-44-50 W

Lake along the U.S. border with Canada 65 mi. long, 10 to 50 mi. wide, covers about 1,485 sq. mi., most of it in province of Ontario, with 2 small bays in province of Manitoba, the rest in north central MN. The northwest shore is the northernmost part of the U.S., excluding Alaska.

Worth, Lake
Feature: lake
County: Palm Beach **State:** FL
Lat: 26-40-52 N **Long:** 08-00-24 W

Lagoon in southeast FL; 22 mi. long. Between mainland and the coastal island containing the resort town of Palm Beach. Part of the Intracoastal Waterway.
Name origin: For American army officer Gen. William Jenkins Worth (1794–1849), who defeated the Seminole Indians in 1842.

Wrangell, Cape
Feature: cape
County: Aleutians West **State:** AK

Westernmost point in U.S. As it lies technically in the eastern hemisphere (172° 28' east latitude), it is also sometimes considered the easternmost point in the U.S. (see also West Quoddy Head). Located at the tip of Attu in the Near Islands of AK.
Name origin: Named about 1836 for Russian explorer Adm. Baron Ferdinand Petrovich von Wrangell (1794–1870).

Wrangell, Mt.   Feature: summit
County: Valdez-Cordova   **State:** AK
Lat: 62-00-25 N   **Long:** 14-40-05 W

Active volcano in central part of Wrangell Mountains in southern AK; height, 14,163 ft. In Wrangell-St. Elias National Park.

Name origin: Named by Russian explorers for Baron von Wrangell (1794–1870). Called Mt. Tillman by U.S. explorer H.T. Allen in his 1885 expedition; for Samuel Escue Tillman, a professor at West Point.

Wyandotte Cave   Feature: cave
County: Crawford   **State:** IN
Lat: 38-13-41 N   **Long:** 08-61-74 W

In south-central IN, 25 mi. west of New Albany. Limestone cavern, one of the largest in U.S., 25 mi. of walkways on 5 levels. Discovered 1798; source of saltpeter until 1850, when opened to public. Some chambers 350 ft. long, 180 ft. high. Includes the Pillar of the Constitution, a combined stalagmite/stalactite, 75 ft. in circumference.

Name origin: For the Indian tribe, probably meaning 'people of one speech.'

Wyoming Valley   Feature: valley
County: Luzerne   **State:** PA
Lat: 41-15-04 N   **Long:** 07-55-42 W

In northeastern PA, along Susquehanna River. About 20 mi. long, 4 mi. wide; rich deposits of anthracite coal. Historic gateway to central PA from New England and NY; center of boundary controversy between CT and PA in 1770s; site of Indian-Tory massacre of colonists in 1778.

Name origin: From Delaware Indian *maughwauwama* 'large meadows,' originally applied to the valley. Immortalized in narrative poem "Gertrude of Wyoming" (1809) by Thomas Campbell (1777–1844); popularity of the poem led to the use of *Wyoming* as a name for various localities and later as the state name.

Yellowstone Falls   Feature: falls
State: WY

In Yellowstone National Park, northeastern WY. North of Yellowstone Lake, upper falls of the Yellowstone River plunge 109 ft., lower falls 308 ft. into Yellowstone Canyon.

Name origin: For Yellowstone River.

Yellowstone Lake   Feature: lake
County: Teton   **State:** WY
Lat: 44-26-47 N   **Long:** 11-02-15 W

In Yellowstone National Park, northwestern WY. Largest high-elevation body of water in North America: 7,731 ft. 20 mi. long; area 137 sq. mi. Yellowstone River flows into it at the south and north out of it.

Name origin: For Yellowstone River.

Yellowstone River   Feature: stream

Rises near the Continental Divide in northwestern WY; about 671 mi. long; navigable for 300 mi. during high water. Flows north through Yellowstone National Park, along it are Yellowstone Lake, Yellowstone Falls, and the Grand Canyon of the Yellowstone. Continues across Great Plains of MT; empties into Missouri River on MT-ND border.

Name origin: From French *Roche Jaune* 'yellow stone,' French translation of Indian *mitsiadazi* 'yellow rock river,' for a yellow rock near the river's mouth.

Yosemite Falls   Feature: falls
State: CA

In east-central CA, in Yosemite National Park. Formed by Yosemite Creek 2,425 ft. above valley floor. Divided into Upper Falls (1,430 ft.), and Lower Falls (320 ft.), separated by cascades tumbling another 675 ft.

Name origin: For the Yosemite Indians, name meaning '*grizzly bear*.' First applied in 1851 to the Yosemite Valley.

Yukon River   Feature: stream
County: Wade Hampton   **State:** AK
Lat: 62-35-55 N   **Long:** 16-44-80 W

Third longest (1,875 mi.) navigable river in North America. Flows from SW Yukon Territory, Canada, through AK into Norton Sound on the Bering Sea. Major transportation route during Klondike gold rush (1897–98). Chief tributaries are White, Klondike, and Chandalar. River freezes from Oct to Jun.

Name origin: From an Athapascan Indian word recorded in 1846, meaning 'big river' or 'the river.' Named by John Bell of the Hudson Bay's Co. Main channel was known as Lewes River until 1945.

Yuma Desert   Feature: plain
County: Yuma   **State:** AZ
Lat: 32-31-40 N   **Long:** 11-43-41 W

In central and southwestern AZ, and in Sonora (Mexico). Arid part of Sonoran Desert east and south of Colorado River. Papago and Pima Indians have many reservations here.

Name origin: For the Yuma Indians; meaning of name uncertain; possibly 'sons of the river.'

General Index

General Index

This index includes all entries appearing in the text of *American Places Dictionary:* populated places (cities, towns, townships, etc.), all counties and their equivalents, and the entries from the appendices in Volume Four that cover American Indian reservations, military installations, and U.S. geographic features.

Populated places are indexed alphabetically by their name, then state, county, and political description. Other entries are indexed by name and state. County entries appear in **boldface** type. To the right after each entry are the section (state abbreviation or appendix) and the number of the volume in which the entry appears.

Aastad (Township)—Otter Tail..... *MN-3*
Abbeville (City)—Henry *AL-2*
Abbeville (City)—Dodge *GA-2*
Abbeville (City)—Wilcox *GA-2*
Abbeville (City)—Vermilion
  Parish *LA-2*
Abbeville (Town)—Lafayette *MS-2*
Abbeville (City)—Abbeville *SC-2*
Abbeville County.........................*SC-2*
Abbot (Town)—Piscataquis...........*ME-1*
Abbotsford (City)—Clark *WI-3*
Abbotsford (City)—Marathon *WI-3*
Abbott (Township)—Potter *PA-1*
Abbott (City)—Hill........................ *TX-2*
Abbottstown (Borough)—Adams....*PA-1*
Abbyville (City)—Reno...................*KS-4*
Abercrombie (City)—Richland *ND-4*
Abercrombie (Township)—
  Richland *ND-4*
Aberdeen (CDP)—Palm Beach.......*FL-2*
Aberdeen (City)—Bingham *ID-4*
Aberdeen (Town)—Harford *MD-1*
Aberdeen (City)—Monroe..............*MS-2*
Aberdeen (Township)—
  Monmouth *NJ-1*
Aberdeen (Town)—Moore..............*NC-2*
Aberdeen (Village)—Brown............*OH-3*
Aberdeen (City)—Brown................*SD-4*
Aberdeen (Township)—Brown........*SD-4*
Aberdeen (City)—Grays Harbor....*WA-4*
Aberdeen Proving Ground (MD)...*Mil-4*
Aberdeen Proving Ground (Mil.
  facil.)—Harford *MD-1*
Abernathy (City)—Hale *TX-2*
Abernathy (City)—Lubbock *TX-2*
Abie (Village)—Butler *NE-4*
Abilene (City)—Dickinson..............*KS-4*
Abilene (City)—Jones.....................*TX-2*
Abilene (City)—Taylor *TX-2*
Abingdon (City)—Knox *IL-3*
Abingdon (Town)—Washington....... *VA-2*
Abington (Township)—Mercer........ *IL-3*
Abington (Township)—Wayne *IN-3*
Abington (Town)—Plymouth........ *MA-1*
Abington (Township)—
  Lackawanna *PA-1*
Abington (Township)—
  Montgomery..............................*PA-1*
Abita Springs (City)—St. Tammany
  Parish *LA-2*
Aboite (Township)—Allen............... *IN-3*
Abram-Perezville (CDP)—
  Hidalgo *TX-2*
Abrams (Town)—Oconto *WI-3*
Absaroka Range () *Geog-4*
Absarokee (CDP)—Stillwater........ *MT-4*
Absecon (City)—Atlantic *NJ-1*
Absentee Shawnee-Citizen Band
  Potawatomi (OK) *IndRes-4*
Acadia Parish................................*LA-2*
Accident (Town)—Garrett............. *MD-1*

Accokeek (CDP)—Prince
  George's *MD-1*
Accomac (Town)—Accomack *VA-2*
Accomack County......................... *VA-2*
Acequia (City)—Minidoka *ID-4*
Achille (Town)—Bryan *OK-2*
Achilles (Township)—Rawlins *KS-4*
Ackerly (City)—Dawson................. *TX-2*
Ackerly (City)—Martin *TX-2*
Ackerman (Town)—Choctaw *MS-2*
Ackley (City)—Franklin *IA-3*
Ackley (City)—Hardin *IA-3*
Ackley (Town)—Langlade *WI-3*
Ackworth (City)—Warren *IA-3*
Acme (Township)—Grand
  Traverse.................................. *MI-3*
Acme (Township)—Hettinger *ND-4*
Acoma (Township)—McLeod *MN-3*
Acoma Pueblo & Trust Lands
  (NM) *IndRes-4*
Acomita Lake (CDP)—Cibola *NM-4*
Acton (CDP)—Los Angeles............ *CA-4*
Acton (Town)—York *ME-1*
Acton (Town)—Middlesex *MA-1*
Acton (Township)—Meeker *MN-3*
Acton (Township)—Walsh...............*ND-4*
Acushnet (Town)—Bristol *MA-1*
Acworth (City)—Cobb....................*GA-2*
Acworth (Town)—Sullivan *NH-1*
Ada (Township)—Kent................... *MI-3*
Ada (City)—Norman *MN-3*
Ada (Township)—Dickey *ND-4*
Ada (Village)—Hardin *OH-3*
Ada (City)—Pontotoc *OK-2*
Ada (Township)—Perkins *SD-4*
Ada County....................................*ID-4*
Adair (City)—Adair........................*IA-3*
Adair (City)—Guthrie *IA-3*
Adair (Township)—Camden *MO-3*
Adair (Town)—Mayes *OK-2*
Adair County.................................. *IA-3*
Adair County *KY-2*
Adair County *MO-3*
Adair County *OK-2*
Adairsville (City)—Bartow..............*GA-2*
Adair Village (City)—Benton *OR-4*
Adairville (City)—Logan.................*KY-2*
Adak Naval Air Station (AK) *Mil-4*
Adak Station (Military Facility)—
  Aleutians West Census Area *AK-4*
Adams (Township)—La Salle......... *IL-3*
Adams (Township)—Allen *IN-3*
Adams (Township)—Carroll *IN-3*
Adams (Township)—Cass *IN-3*
Adams (Township)—Decatur......... *IN-3*
Adams (Township)—Hamilton *IN-3*
Adams (Township)—Madison......... *IN-3*
Adams (Township)—Morgan.......... *IN-3*
Adams (Township)—Parke............. *IN-3*
Adams (Township)—Ripley *IN-3*
Adams (Township)—Warren *IN-3*

Adams (Township)—Nemaha *KS-4*
Adams (Town)—Berkshire *MA-1*
Adams (Township)—Arenac *MI-3*
Adams (Township)—Hillsdale *MI-3*
Adams (Township)—Houghton...... *MI-3*
Adams (City)—Mower *MN-3*
Adams (Township)—Mower *MN-3*
Adams (Township)—DeKalb *MO-3*
Adams (Township)—Harrison *MO-3*
Adams (Township)—Gage............. *NE-4*
Adams (Village)—Gage *NE-4*
Adams (Town)—Jefferson *NY-1*
Adams (Village)—Jefferson........... *NY-1*
Adams (City)—Walsh *ND-4*
Adams (Township)—Walsh *ND-4*
Adams (Township)—Champaign ...*OH-3*
Adams (Township)—Clinton..........*OH-3*
Adams (Township)—Coshocton *OH-3*
Adams (Township)—Darke *OH-3*
Adams (Township)—Defiance *OH-3*
Adams (Township)—Guernsey *OH-3*
Adams (Township)—Monroe.........*OH-3*
Adams (Township)—Muskingum...*OH-3*
Adams (Township)—Seneca *OH-3*
Adams (Township)—Washington...*OH-3*
Adams (City)—Umatilla *OR-4*
Adams (Township)—Butler *PA-1*
Adams (Township)—Cambria........*PA-1*
Adams (Township)—Snyder *PA-1*
Adams (Township)—Grant *SD-4*
Adams (Township)—Miner *SD-4*
Adams (Town)—Robertson *TN-2*
Adams (City)—Adams *WI-3*
Adams (Town)—Adams *WI-3*
Adams (Town)—Green.................. *WI-3*
Adams (Town)—Jackson................ *WI-3*
Adamsburg (Borough)—
  Westmoreland *PA-1*
Adams County *CO-4*
Adams County *ID-4*
Adams County *IL-3*
Adams County *IN-3*
Adams County *IA-3*
Adams County *MS-2*
Adams County *NE-4*
Adams County *ND-4*
Adams County *OH-3*
Adams County *PA-1*
Adams County *WA-4*
Adams County *WI-3*
Adamstown (Borough)—Berks........*PA-1*
Adamstown (Borough)—
  Lancaster...................................*PA-1*
Adamsville (City)—Jefferson *AL-2*
Adamsville (Village)—
  Muskingum *OH-3*
Adamsville (Town)—McNairy *TN-2*
Addie (Township)—Griggs *ND-4*
Addieville (Village)—Washington... *IL-3*
Addington (Town)—Jefferson *OK-2*

General Index

American Places Dictionary

Addis (Town)—West Baton Rouge Parish *LA-2*
Addison (Town)—Winston *AL-2*
Addison (Township)—DuPage *IL-3*
Addison (Village)—DuPage *IL-3*
Addison (Township)—Shelby *IN-3*
Addison (Town)—Washington *ME-1*
Addison (Village)—Lenawee *MI-3*
Addison (Township)—Oakland *MI-3*
Addison (Township)—Knox *NE-4*
Addison (Town)—Steuben *NY-1*
Addison (Village)—Steuben *NY-1*
Addison (Township)—Cass *ND-4*
Addison (Township)—Gallia *OH-3*
Addison (Borough)—Somerset *PA-1*
Addison (Township)—Somerset ... *PA-1*
Addison (City)—Dallas *TX-2*
Addison (Town)—Addison *VT-1*
Addison (Town)—Washington *WI-3*
Addison County *VT-1*
Addyston (Village)—Hamilton *OH-3*
Adel (City)—Cook *GA-2*
Adel (City)—Dallas *IA-3*
Adelaide (Township)—Bowman ... *ND-4*
Adelanto (City)—San Bernardino .. *CA-4*
Adeline (Village)—Ogle *IL-3*
Adell (Township)—Sheridan *KS-4*
Adell (Village)—Sheboygan *WI-3*
Adelphi (CDP)—Montgomery *MD-1*
Adelphi (CDP)—Prince George's *MD-1*
Adelphi (Village)—Ross *OH-3*
Adena (Village)—Harrison *OH-3*
Adena (Village)—Jefferson *OH-3*
Adirondack Mountains (NY) *Geog-4*
Adler (Township)—Nelson *ND-4*
Admire (City)—Lyon *KS-4*
Adona (Town)—Perry *AR-2*
Adrian (City)—Emanuel *GA-2*
Adrian (City)—Johnson *GA-2*
Adrian (Township)—Jackson *KS-4*
Adrian (City)—Lenawee *MI-3*
Adrian (Township)—Lenawee *MI-3*
Adrian (City)—Nobles *MN-3*
Adrian (Township)—Watonwan ... *MN-3*
Adrian (City)—Bates *MO-3*
Adrian (Township)—LaMoure *ND-4*
Adrian (City)—Malheur *OR-4*
Adrian (Township)—Edmunds *SD-4*
Adrian (City)—Oldham *TX-2*
Adrian (Town)—Monroe *WI-3*
Advance (Town)—Boone *IN-3*
Advance (City)—Stoddard *MO-3*
Advance (Township)—Pembina ... *ND-4*
Adwolf (CDP)—Smyth *VA-2*
Aetna (Township)—Logan *IL-3*
Aetna (Township)—Barber *KS-4*
Aetna (Township)—Mecosta *MI-3*
Aetna (Township)—Missaukee *MI-3*
Aetna (Township)—Pipestone *MN-3*
Affton (CDP)—St. Louis *MO-3*
Afton (Township)—DeKalb *IL-3*
Afton (City)—Union *IA-3*
Afton (Township)—Sedgwick *KS-4*
Afton (City)—Washington *MN-3*
Afton (Town)—Chenango *NY-1*
Afton (Village)—Chenango *NY-1*
Afton (Township)—Ward *ND-4*
Afton (Town)—Ottawa *OK-2*
Afton (Township)—Brookings *SD-4*
Afton (Township)—Sanborn *SD-4*
Afton (Town)—Lincoln *WY-4*
Agar (Town)—Sully *SD-4*
Agassiz (Township)—Lac qui Parle *MN-3*

Agate Fossil Beds (NE) *Geog-4*
Agawam (Town)—Hampden *MA-1*
Agder (Township)—Marshall *MN-3*
Agency (City)—Wapello *IA-3*
Agency (Township)—Osage *KS-4*
Agency (Town)—Buchanan *MO-3*
Agency (Township)—Buchanan ... *MO-3*
Agency (Township)—Roberts *SD-4*
Agenda (City)—Republic *KS-4*
Agenda (Town)—Ashland *WI-3*
Agnes (Township)—Grand Forks .. *ND-4*
Agnes City (Township)—Lyon *KS-4*
Agoura Hills (City)—Los Angeles .. *CA-4*
Agra (City)—Phillips *KS-4*
Agra (Town)—Lincoln *OK-2*
Agram (Township)—Morrison *MN-3*
Agua Caliente Reservation (CA) *IndRes-4*
Agua Dulce (City)—Nueces *TX-2*
Agua Fria (CDP)—Santa Fe *NM-4*
Aguilar (Town)—Las Animas *CO-4*
Ahmeek (Village)—Keweenaw *MI-3*
Ahnapee (Town)—Kewaunee *WI-3*
Ahoskie (Town)—Hertford *NC-2*
Ahuimanu (CDP)—Honolulu *HI-4*
Aid (Township)—Lawrence *OH-3*
Aiea (CDP)—Honolulu *HI-4*
Aiken (City)—Aiken *SC-2*
Aiken County *SC-2*
Ailey (Town)—Montgomery *GA-2*
Ainsworth (City)—Washington ... *IA-3*
Ainsworth (City)—Brown *NE-4*
Ainsworth (Town)—Langlade *WI-3*
Air Force Academy (Military Facility)— El Paso *CO-4*
Airmont (CDP)—Rockland *NY-1*
Airport (Township)—St. Louis ... *MO-3*
Airport Drive (Village)—Jasper .. *MO-3*
Airway Heights (City)—Spokane .. *WA-4*
Aitkin (City)—Aitkin *MN-3*
Aitkin (Township)—Aitkin *MN-3*
Aitkin County *MN-3*
Ajo (CDP)—Pima *AZ-4*
Akaka Falls (HI) *Geog-4*
Akan (Town)—Richland *WI-3*
Akaska (Town)—Walworth *SD-4*
Ak-Chin Village (CDP)—Pinal ... *AZ-4*
Akeley (City)—Hubbard *MN-3*
Akeley (Township)—Hubbard *MN-3*
Akhiok (City)—Kodiak Island Borough *AK-4*
Akiachak (City)—Bethel Census Area *AK-4*
Akiak (City)—Bethel Census Area *AK-4*
Akra (Township)—Pembina *ND-4*
Akron (Town)—Hale *AL-2*
Akron (Township)—Washington .. *CO-4*
Akron (Township)—Peoria *IL-3*
Akron (Town)—Fulton *IN-3*
Akron (City)—Plymouth *IA-3*
Akron (Township)—Tuscola *MI-3*
Akron (Village)—Tuscola *MI-3*
Akron (Township)—Big Stone *MN-3*
Akron (Township)—Wilkin *MN-3*
Akron (Village)—Erie *NY-1*
Akron (City)—Summit *OH-3*
Akron (Borough)—Lancaster *PA-1*
Akutan (City)—Aleutians East Borough *AK-4*
Alabama (Town)—Genesee *NY-1*
Alabama and Coushatta Reservation (TX) *IndRes-4*
Alabama River (AL) *Geog-4*
Alabaster (City)—Shelby *AL-2*

Alabaster (Township)—Iosco *MI-3*
Alachua (City)—Alachua *FL-2*
Alachua County *FL-2*
Alaiedon (Township)—Ingham ... *MI-3*
Alakanuk (City)—Wade Hampton Census Area *AK-4*
Alamance (Village)—Alamance ... *NC-2*
Alamance County *NC-2*
Alameda (City)—Alameda *CA-4*
Alameda Coast Guard Island (CA) *Mil-4*
Alameda County *CA-4*
Alamo (CDP)—Contra Costa *CA-4*
Alamo (Town)—Wheeler *GA-2*
Alamo (Town)—Montgomery *IN-3*
Alamo (Township)—Kalamazoo ... *MI-3*
Alamo (City)—Williams *ND-4*
Alamo (Town)—Crockett *TN-2*
Alamo (City)—Hidalgo *TX-2*
Alamogordo (City)—Otero *NM-4*
Alamo Heights (City)—Bexar *TX-2*
Alamo Navajo Reservation (NM) *IndRes-4*
Alamosa (City)—Alamosa *CO-4*
Alamosa County *CO-4*
Alamosa East (CDP)—Alamosa ... *CO-4*
Alamota (Township)—Lane *KS-4*
Alango (Township)—St. Louis ... *MN-3*
Alanson (Village)—Emmet *MI-3*
Alapaha (Town)—Berrien *GA-2*
Alaska (Township)—Beltrami *MN-3*
Alaska, Gulf of (AK) *Geog-4*
Alaska Peninsula (AK) *Geog-4*
Alaska Range (AK) *Geog-4*
Alava, Cape (WA) *Geog-4*
Alba (Township)—Henry *IL-3*
Alba (Township)—Jackson *MN-3*
Alba (City)—Jasper *MO-3*
Alba (Borough)—Bradford *PA-1*
Alba (Town)—Rains *TX-2*
Alba (Town)—Wood *TX-2*
Alban (Township)—Grant *SD-4*
Alban (Town)—Portage *WI-3*
Albano (Township)—Stafford *KS-4*
Albany (City)—Alameda *CA-4*
Albany (City)—Dougherty *GA-2*
Albany (Township)—Whiteside .. *IL-3*
Albany (Village)—Whiteside *IL-3*
Albany (Town)—Delaware *IN-3*
Albany (Town)—Randolph *IN-3*
Albany (City)—Clinton *KY-3*
Albany (Village)—Livingston Parish *LA-2*
Albany (City)—Stearns *MN-3*
Albany (Township)—Stearns *MN-3*
Albany (City)—Gentry *MO-3*
Albany (Township)—Harlan *NE-4*
Albany (Town)—Carroll *NH-1*
Albany (City)—Albany *NY-1*
Albany (Village)—Athens *OH-3*
Albany (City)—Benton *OR-4*
Albany (City)—Linn *OR-4*
Albany (Township)—Berks *PA-1*
Albany (Township)—Bradford ... *PA-1*
Albany (City)—Shackelford *TX-2*
Albany (Town)—Orleans *VT-1*
Albany (Village)—Orleans *VT-1*
Albany (Town)—Green *WI-3*
Albany (Village)—Green *WI-3*
Albany (Town)—Pepin *WI-3*
Albany County *NY-1*
Albany County *WY-4*
Albee (Township)—Saginaw *MI-3*
Albee (Town)—Grant *SD-4*
Albemarle (City)—Stanly *NC-2*

American Places Dictionary — General Index

Albemarle County *VA-2*
Albers (Village)—Clinton *IL-3*
Albert (City)—Barton *KS-4*
Albert (Township)—
  Montmorency *MI-3*
Albert (Township)—Benson *ND-4*
Alberta (Township)—Benton *MN-3*
Alberta (City)—Stevens *MN-3*
Alberta (Town)—Brunswick *VA-2*
Albert City (City)—Buena Vista *IA-3*
Albertha (Township)—Dickey *ND-4*
Albert Lea (City)—Freeborn *MN-3*
Albert Lea (Township)—
  Freeborn *MN-3*
Alberton (Town)—Mineral *MT-4*
Albertson (CDP)—Nassau *NY-1*
Albertville (City)—Marshall *AL-2*
Albertville (City)—Wright *MN-3*
Albia (City)—Monroe *IA-3*
Albin (Township)—Brown *MN-3*
Albin (Town)—Laramie *WY-4*
Albion (City)—Cassia *ID-4*
Albion (City)—Edwards *IL-3*
Albion (Town)—Noble *IN-3*
Albion (Township)—Noble *IN-3*
Albion (City)—Marshall *IA-3*
Albion (Township)—Barton *KS-4*
Albion (Township)—Reno *KS-4*
Albion (Township)—Republic *KS-4*
Albion (Town)—Kennebec *ME-1*
Albion (City)—Calhoun *MI-3*
Albion (Township)—Calhoun *MI-3*
Albion (Township)—Wright *MN-3*
Albion (City)—Boone *NE-4*
Albion (Town)—Orleans *NY-1*
Albion (Village)—Orleans *NY-1*
Albion (Town)—Oswego *NY-1*
Albion (Township)—Dickey *ND-4*
Albion (Town)—Pushmataha *OK-2*
Albion (Borough)—Erie *PA-1*
Albion (Town)—Whitman *WA-4*
Albion (Town)—Dane *WI-3*
Albion (Town)—Jackson *WI-3*
Albion (Town)—Trempealeau *WI-3*
Alborn (Township)—St. Louis *MN-3*
Albright (Town)—Preston *WV-2*
Albuquerque (City)—Bernalillo ... *NM-4*
Alburg (Town)—Grand Isle *VT-1*
Alburg (Village)—Grand Isle *VT-1*
Alburnett (City)—Linn *IA-3*
Alburtis (Borough)—Lehigh *PA-1*
Alcalde (CDP)—Rio Arriba *NM-4*
Alcan (CDP)—Southeast Fairbanks
  Census Area *AK-4*
Alcatraz Island (CA) *Geog-4*
Alcester (City)—Union *SD-4*
Alcester (Township)—Union *SD-4*
Alcoa (City)—Blount *TN-2*
Alcona (Township)—Alcona *MI-3*
Alcona County *MI-3*
Alcorn County *MS-2*
Alda (Township)—Hall *NE-4*
Alda (Village)—Hall *NE-4*
Aldan (Borough)—Delaware *PA-1*
Alden (Township)—McHenry *IL-3*
Alden (City)—Hardin *IA-3*
Alden (City)—Rice *KS-4*
Alden (City)—Freeborn *MN-3*
Alden (Township)—Freeborn *MN-3*
Alden (Township)—St. Louis *MN-3*
Alden (Town)—Erie *NY-1*
Alden (Village)—Erie *NY-1*
Alden (Township)—Hettinger *ND-4*
Alden (Township)—Hand *SD-4*
Alden (Town)—Polk *WI-3*

Alderson (Town)—Pittsburg *OK-2*
Alderson (Town)—Greenbrier *WV-2*
Alderson (Town)—Monroe *WV-2*
Alderwood Manor-Bothell North
  (CDP)—Snohomish *WA-4*
Aldine (CDP)—Harris *TX-2*
Aldora (Town)—Lamar *GA-2*
Aldrich (City)—Wadena *MN-3*
Aldrich (Township)—Wadena *MN-3*
Aldrich (Village)—Polk *MO-3*
Aledo (City)—Mercer *IL-3*
Aledo (City)—Parker *TX-2*
Aleknagik (City)—Dillingham Census
  Area *AK-4*
Aleppo (Township)—Allegheny *PA-1*
Aleppo (Township)—Greene *PA-1*
Aleutian Islands (AK) *Geog-4*
Aleutians East Borough *AK-4*
Aleutians West Census Area ... *AK-4*
Alex (Township)—McKenzie *ND-4*
Alex (Town)—Grady *OK-2*
Alexander (Town)—Pulaski *AR-2*
Alexander (City)—Franklin *IA-3*
Alexander (City)—Rush *KS-4*
Alexander (Town)—Washington ... *ME-1*
Alexander (Township)—Benton .. *MO-3*
Alexander (Town)—Genesee *NY-1*
Alexander (Village)—Genesee *NY-1*
Alexander (City)—McKenzie *ND-4*
Alexander (Township)—Pierce ... *ND-4*
Alexander (Township)—
  Stutsman *ND-4*
Alexander (Township)—Athens ... *OH-3*
Alexander Archipelago (AK) *Geog-4*
Alexander-Belle Prairie (Township)—
  Rush *KS-4*
Alexander City (City)—
  Tallapoosa *AL-2*
Alexander County *IL-3*
Alexander County *NC-2*
Alexander Mills (Town)—
  Rutherford *NC-2*
Alexandria (City)—Madison *IN-3*
Alexandria (Township)—
  Leavenworth *KS-4*
Alexandria (City)—Campbell *KY-2*
Alexandria (City)—Rapides
  Parish *LA-2*
Alexandria (City)—Douglas *MN-3*
Alexandria (Township)—
  Douglas *MN-3*
Alexandria (City)—Clark *MO-3*
Alexandria (Village)—Thayer *NE-4*
Alexandria (Town)—Grafton *NH-1*
Alexandria (Township)—
  Hunterdon *NJ-1*
Alexandria (Town)—Jefferson *NY-1*
Alexandria (Township)—Divide .. *ND-4*
Alexandria (Village)—Licking *OH-3*
Alexandria (Borough)—
  Huntingdon *PA-1*
Alexandria (City)—Hanson *SD-4*
Alexandria (Town)—DeKalb *TN-2*
Alexandria Bay (Village)—
  Jefferson *NY-1*
Alexandria (Independent City) ... *VA-2*
Alexis (Village)—Mercer *IL-3*
Alexis (Village)—Warren *IL-3*
Alexis (Township)—Butler *NE-4*
Alfalfa County *OK-2*
Alford (Town)—Jackson *FL-2*
Alford (Town)—Berkshire *MA-1*
Alfordsville (Town)—Daviess *IN-3*
Alfred (Town)—York *ME-1*
Alfred (Town)—Allegany *NY-1*

Alfred (Village)—Allegany *NY-1*
Alfsborg (Township)—Sibley *MN-3*
Algansee (Township)—Branch ... *MI-3*
Alger (Township)—Mountrail *ND-4*
Alger (Village)—Hardin *OH-3*
Alger County *MI-3*
Algernon (Township)—Custer *NE-4*
Algoma (Township)—Kent *MI-3*
Algoma (Town)—Pontotoc *MS-2*
Algoma (City)—Kewaunee *WI-3*
Algoma (Town)—Winnebago *WI-3*
Algona (City)—Kossuth *IA-3*
Algona (City)—King *WA-4*
Algonac (City)—St. Clair *MI-3*
Algonquin (Village)—Kane *IL-3*
Algonquin (Township)—McHenry.. *IL-3*
Algonquin (Village)—McHenry ... *IL-3*
Algood (Town)—Putnam *TN-2*
Alhambra (City)—Los Angeles *CA-4*
Alhambra (Township)—Madison .. *IL-3*
Alhambra (Village)—Madison *IL-3*
Aliamanu (Military Facility)—
  Honolulu *HI-4*
Alice (City)—Cass *ND-4*
Alice (City)—Jim Wells *TX-2*
Aliceton (Township)—Ransom ... *ND-4*
Aliceville (Municipality)—
  Pickens *AL-2*
Alicia (Town)—Lawrence *AR-2*
Aline (Town)—Alfalfa *OK-2*
Aliquippa (Borough)—Beaver *PA-1*
Aliso Viejo (CDP)—Orange *CA-4*
Allagash (Town)—Aroostook *ME-1*
Allakaket (City)—Yukon-Koyukuk
  Census Area *AK-4*
Allamakee County *IA-3*
Allamuchy (Township)—Warren .. *NJ-1*
Allardt (City)—Fentress *TN-2*
Allegan (City)—Allegan *MI-3*
Allegan (Township)—Allegan *MI-3*
Allegan County *MI-3*
Allegany (Town)—Cattaraugus ... *NY-1*
Allegany (Village)—Cattaraugus ... *NY-1*
Allegany (Township)—Potter *PA-1*
Allegany County *MD-1*
Allegany County *NY-1*
Allegany Reservation (NY) *IndRes-4*
Allegany Reservation (Pop. Place)—
  Cattaraugus *NY-1*
Alleghany (Township)—Ransom ... *ND-4*
Alleghany County *NC-2*
Alleghany County *VA-2*
Allegheny (Township)—Blair *PA-1*
Allegheny (Township)—Butler ... *PA-1*
Allegheny (Township)—Cambria ... *PA-1*
Allegheny (Township)—Somerset ... *PA-1*
Allegheny (Township)—Venango ... *PA-1*
Allegheny (Township)—
  Westmoreland *PA-1*
Allegheny (Alleghany) Mountains *or*
  Alleghenies (AK) *Geog-4*
Allegheny County *PA-1*
Allegheny River (AK) *Geog-4*
Alleman (City)—Polk *IA-3*
Allen (Township)—La Salle *IL-3*
Allen (Township)—Miami *IN-3*
Allen (Township)—Noble *IN-3*
Allen (Township)—Jewell *KS-4*
Allen (Township)—Kingman *KS-4*
Allen (City)—Lyon *KS-4*
Allen (City)—Floyd *KY-2*
Allen (Township)—Hillsdale *MI-3*
Allen (Village)—Hillsdale *MI-3*
Allen (Township)—Worth *MO-3*
Allen (Village)—Dixon *NE-4*

903

General Index — American Places Dictionary

Allen (Town)—Allegany NY-1
Allen (Township)—Kidder ND-4
Allen (Township)—Darke OH-3
Allen (Township)—Hancock OH-3
Allen (Township)—Ottawa OH-3
Allen (Township)—Union OH-3
Allen (Town)—Hughes OK-2
Allen (Town)—Pontotoc OK-2
Allen (Township)—Northampton ... PA-1
Allen (Township)—Beadle SD-4
Allen (City)—Collin TX-2
Allen County IN-3
Allen County KS-4
Allen County KY-2
Allen County OH-3
Allendale (Village)—Wabash IL-3
Allendale (Township)—Ottawa MI-3
Allendale (Town)—Worth MO-3
Allendale (Borough)—Bergen NJ-1
Allendale (Township)—Grand
    Forks ND-4
Allendale (Town)—Allendale SC-2
Allendale County SC-2
Allen Grove (Township)—Mason ... IL-3
Allenhurst (Town)—Liberty GA-2
Allenhurst (Borough)—
    Monmouth NJ-1
Allen Parish LA-2
Allen Park (City)—Wayne MI-3
Allenport (Borough)—Washington .. PA-1
Allenstown (Town)—Merrimack NH-1
Allensville (City)—Todd KY-2
Allentown (Town)—Bleckley GA-2
Allentown (Town)—Laurens GA-2
Allentown (Town)—Twiggs GA-2
Allentown (Town)—Wilkinson GA-2
Allentown (Borough)—
    Monmouth NJ-1
Allentown (City)—Lehigh PA-1
Allenville (Village)—Moultrie IL-3
Allenville (Village)—Cape
    Girardeau MO-3
Allerton (Village)—Champaign IL-3
Allerton (Village)—Vermilion IL-3
Allerton (City)—Wayne IA-3
Allgood (Town)—Blount AL-2
Alliance (Township)—Clay MN-3
Alliance (City)—Box Butte NE-4
Alliance (Town)—Pamlico NC-2
Alliance (City)—Mahoning OH-3
Alliance (City)—Stark OH-3
Alliance (Township)—Moody SD-4
Alligator (Town)—Bolivar MS-2
Allin (Township)—McLean IL-3
Allis (Township)—Presque Isle MI-3
Allison (Township)—Lawrence IL-3
Allison (City)—Butler IA-3
Allison (Township)—Decatur KS-4
Allison (Township)—Clinton PA-1
Allison (Township)—Brown SD-4
Allodium (Township)—Graham KS-4
Alloue (Township)—Keweenaw MI-3
Allouez (Village)—Brown WI-3
Alloway (Township)—Salem NJ-1
Allport (Town)—Lonoke AR-2
Allyn-Grapeview (CDP)—Mason .. WA-4
Alma (City)—Crawford AR-2
Alma (Town)—Park CO-4
Alma (City)—Bacon GA-2
Alma (Township)—Marion IL-3
Alma (Village)—Marion IL-3
Alma (City)—Wabaunsee KS-4
Alma (Township)—Wabaunsee KS-4
Alma (City)—Gratiot MI-3
Alma (Township)—Marshall MN-3

Alma (City)—Lafayette MO-3
Alma (City)—Harlan NE-4
Alma (Township)—Harlan NE-4
Alma (Town)—Allegany NY-1
Alma (Township)—Cavalier ND-4
Alma (Town)—Ellis TX-2
Alma (City)—Buffalo WI-3
Alma (Town)—Buffalo WI-3
Alma (Town)—Jackson WI-3
Alma Center (Village)—Jackson WI-3
Almedia (CDP)—Columbia PA-1
Almena (City)—Norton KS-4
Almena (Township)—Van Buren ... MI-3
Almena (Township)—Barron WI-3
Almena (Village)—Barron WI-3
Almena-District 4 (Township)—
    Norton KS-4
Almer (Township)—Tuscola MI-3
Almira (Township)—Benzie MI-3
Almira (Town)—Lincoln WA-4
Almon (Town)—Shawano WI-3
Almond (Township)—Big Stone ... MN-3
Almond (Town)—Allegany NY-1
Almond (Village)—Allegany NY-1
Almond (Village)—Steuben NY-1
Almond (Town)—Portage WI-3
Almond (Village)—Portage WI-3
Almont (Township)—Lapeer MI-3
Almont (Village)—Lapeer MI-3
Almont (City)—Morton ND-4
Almyra (Town)—Arkansas AR-2
Alna (Town)—Lincoln ME-1
Aloha (Township)—Cheboygan MI-3
Aloha (CDP)—Washington OR-4
Alondra Park (CDP)—Los
    Angeles CA-4
Alorton (Village)—St. Clair IL-3
Alpena (Town)—Boone AR-2
Alpena (City)—Alpena MI-3
Alpena (Township)—Alpena MI-3
Alpena (Town)—Jerauld SD-4
Alpena (Township)—Jerauld SD-4
Alpena County MI-3
Alpha (Village)—Henry IL-3
Alpha (Village)—Iron MI-3
Alpha (City)—Jackson MN-3
Alpha (Borough)—Warren NJ-1
Alpha (Township)—Hand SD-4
Alpharetta (City)—Fulton GA-2
Alpine (CDP)—San Diego CA-4
Alpine (Township)—Kent MI-3
Alpine (Township)—Stone MO-3
Alpine (Borough)—Bergen NJ-1
Alpine (City)—Brewster TX-2
Alpine (City)—Utah UT-4
Alpine (Town)—Lincoln WY-4
Alpine County CA-4
Alsace (Township)—Berks PA-1
Alsen (Township)—Cavalier ND-4
Alsey (Village)—Scott IL-3
Alsip (Suburban village)—Cook IL-3
Alstead (Town)—Cheshire NH-1
Alston (Town)—Montgomery GA-2
Alta (City)—Buena Vista IA-3
Alta (Township)—Harvey KS-4
Alta (Township)—Barnes ND-4
Alta (Town)—Salt Lake UT-4
Altadena (CDP)—Los Angeles CA-4
Altamahaw-Ossipee (CDP)—
    Alamance NC-2
Altamont (City)—Effingham IL-3
Altamont (City)—Labette KS-4
Altamont (Town)—Daviess MO-3
Altamont (Village)—Albany NY-1
Altamont (Town)—Franklin NY-1

Altamont (CDP)—Klamath OR-4
Altamont (Town)—Deuel SD-4
Altamont (Township)—Deuel SD-4
Altamont (Town)—Grundy TN-2
Altamont (Town)—Duchesne UT-4
Altamonte Springs (City)—
    Seminole FL-2
Alta Sierra (CDP)—Nevada CA-4
Alta Vista (City)—Chickasaw IA-3
Alta Vista (City)—Wabaunsee KS-4
Alta Vista (Township)—Lincoln ... MN-3
Altavista (Town)—Campbell VA-2
Altenburg (City)—Perry MO-3
Altha (Town)—Calhoun FL-2
Altheimer (City)—Jefferson AR-2
Altmar (Village)—Oswego NY-1
Alto (Town)—Banks GA-2
Alto (Town)—Habersham GA-2
Alto (Township)—Lee IL-3
Alto (Township)—Roberts SD-4
Alto (Town)—Cherokee TX-2
Alto (Town)—Fond du Lac WI-3
Alton (City)—Madison IL-3
Alton (Township)—Madison IL-3
Alton (Town)—Crawford IN-3
Alton (City)—Sioux IA-3
Alton (City)—Osborne KS-4
Alton (Town)—Penobscot ME-1
Alton (Township)—Waseca MN-3
Alton (City)—Oregon MO-3
Alton (Town)—Belknap NH-1
Alton (Township)—Brookings SD-4
Alton (City)—Hidalgo TX-2
Alton (Town)—Kane UT-4
Altona (Village)—Knox IL-3
Altona (Town)—Dekalb IN-3
Altona (Township)—Pipestone MN-3
Altona (Town)—Clinton NY-1
Altoona (Municipality)—Blount AL-2
Altoona (Municipality)—Etowah ... AL-2
Altoona (City)—Polk IA-3
Altoona (City)—Wilson KS-4
Altoona (City)—Blair PA-1
Altoona (Township)—Beadle SD-4
Altoona (City)—Eau Claire WI-3
Alto Pass (Village)—Union IL-3
Altory (Township)—Decatur KS-4
Altura (City)—Winona MN-3
Alturas (City)—Modoc CA-4
Alturas Rancheria (CA) IndRes-4
Altus (City)—Franklin AR-2
Altus (City)—Jackson OK-2
Alum Creek (CDP)—Lincoln WV-2
Alva (CDP)—Lee FL-2
Alva (City)—Woods OK-2
Alvarado (City)—Marshall MN-3
Alvarado (City)—Johnson TX-2
Alverstone, Mount (AK) Geog-4
Alvin (Village)—Vermilion IL-3
Alvin (City)—Brazoria TX-2
Alvin (Town)—Forest WI-3
Alvo (Village)—Cass NE-4
Alvord (City)—Lyon IA-3
Alvord (Town)—Wise TX-2
Alvordton (Village)—Williams OH-3
Alvwood (Township)—Itasca MN-3
Amador (Township)—Chisago MN-3
Amador City (City)—Amador CA-4
Amador County CA-4
Amagon (Town)—Jackson AR-2
Amalga (Town)—Cache UT-4
Amanda (Township)—Allen OH-3
Amanda (Township)—Fairfield OH-3
Amanda (Village)—Fairfield OH-3
Amanda (Township)—Hancock OH-3

Amarillo (City)—Potter.................. *TX-2*
Amarillo (City)—Randall................ *TX-2*
Amazonia (Town)—Andrew.......... *MO-3*
Amber (Township)—Mason *MI-3*
Amber (Town)—Grady................... *OK-2*
Amberg (Town)—Marinette *WI-3*
Amberley (Village)—Hamilton *OH-3*
Ambia (Town)—Benton *IN-3*
Ambler (City)—Northwest Arctic
 Borough... *AK-4*
Ambler (Borough)—Montgomery ... *PA-1*
Amboy (City)—Lee *IL-3*
Amboy (Township)—Lee *IL-3*
Amboy (Town)—Miami *IN-3*
Amboy (Township)—Hillsdale *MI-3*
Amboy (City)—Blue Earth *MN-3*
Amboy (Township)—
 Cottonwood..................................... *MN-3*
Amboy (Town)—Oswego *NY-1*
Amboy (Township)—Fulton........... *OH-3*
Ambridge (Borough)—Beaver *PA-1*
Ambrose (City)—Coffee *GA-2*
Ambrose (City)—Divide *ND-4*
Ambrose (Township)—Divide *ND-4*
Amchitka (CDP)—Aleutians West
 Census Area................................... *AK-4*
Amelia (CDP)—St. Mary Parish..... *LA-2*
Amelia (Village)—Clermont........... *OH-3*
Amelia County *VA-2*
Amenia (Town)—Dutchess *NY-1*
Amenia (City)—Cass *ND-4*
Amenia (Township)—Cass *ND-4*
America (Township)—Brule........... *SD-4*
American (Township)—Allen......... *OH-3*
American Canyon (CDP)—Napa... *CA-4*
American Falls (City)—Power *ID-4*
American Fork (City)—Utah *UT-4*
Americus (City)—Sumter *GA-2*
Americus (City)—Lyon................... *KS-4*
Americus (Township)—Lyon........... *KS-4*
Americus (Township)—Grand
 Forks *ND-4*
Amery (City)—Polk *WI-3*
Ames (City)—Story *IA-3*
Ames (Village)—Montgomery........ *NY-1*
Ames (Township)—Athens............. *OH-3*
Ames (Town)—Major *OK-2*
Ames (City)—Liberty *TX-2*
Amesbury (Town)—Essex............... *MA-1*
Amesville (Village)—Athens *OH-3*
Amherst (Town)—Hancock *ME-1*
Amherst (Town)—Hampshire *MA-1*
Amherst (Township)—Fillmore *MN-3*
Amherst (Village)—Buffalo *NE-4*
Amherst (Town)—Hillsborough *NH-1*
Amherst (Town)—Erie *NY-1*
Amherst (City)—Lorain *OH-3*
Amherst (Township)—Lorain......... *OH-3*
Amherst (City)—Lamb *TX-2*
Amherst (Town)—Amherst *VA-2*
Amherst (Town)—Portage.............. *WI-3*
Amherst (Village)—Portage............ *WI-3*
Amherst County *VA-2*
Amherstdale-Robinette (CDP)—
 Logan *WV-2*
Amherst Junction (Village)—
 Portage.. *WI-3*
Amidon (City)—Slope *ND-4*
Amiret (Township)—Lyon.............. *MN-3*
Amite City (Town)—Tangipahoa
 Parish.. *LA-2*
Amite County *MS-2*
Amity (City)—Clark *AR-2*
Amity (Township)—Livingston....... *IL-3*
Amity (Town)—Aroostook *ME-1*

Amity (Town)—DeKalb *MO-3*
Amity (Town)—Allegany *NY-1*
Amity (Township)—Bottineau *ND-4*
Amity (City)—Yamhill *OR-4*
Amity (Township)—Berks *PA-1*
Amity (Township)—Erie *PA-1*
Amity Gardens (CDP)—Berks *PA-1*
Amityville (Village)—Suffolk *NY-1*
Ammon (City)—Bonneville *ID-4*
Amnicon (Town)—Douglas............. *WI-3*
Amo (Town)—Hendricks *IN-3*
Amo (Township)—Cottonwood *MN-3*
Amor (Township)—Otter Tail...... *MN-3*
Amor (Township)—Bowman.......... *ND-4*
Amoret (City)—Bates *MO-3*
Amorita (Town)—Alfalfa *OK-2*
Amory (City)—Monroe *MS-2*
Amsterdam (City)—Bates *MO-3*
Amsterdam (City)—Montgomery .. *NY-1*
Amsterdam (Town)—
 Montgomery................................... *NY-1*
Amsterdam (Village)—Jefferson *OH-3*
Amundsville (Township)—
 McLean *ND-4*
Amwell (Township)—Washington... *PA-1*
Anacoco (Village)—Vernon
 Parish.. *LA-2*
Anaconda-Deer Lodge County (City)—
 Deer Lodge *MT-4*
Anacortes (City)—Skagit................. *WA-4*
Anadarko (City)—Caddo *OK-2*
Anaheim (City)—Orange................ *CA-4*
Anahola (CDP)—Kauai.................. *HI-4*
Anahuac (City)—Chambers *TX-2*
Anaktuvuk Pass (City)—North Slope
 Borough.. *AK-4*
Anamoose (City)—McHenry.......... *ND-4*
Anamoose (Township)—
 McHenry *ND-4*
Anamosa (City)—Jones *IA-3*
Anawalt (Town)—McDowell......... *WV-2*
Anchor (Township)—McLean *IL-3*
Anchor (Village)—McLean *IL-3*
Anchorage (City)—Jefferson *KY-2*
Anchorage Borough and City *AK-4*
Anchor Point (CDP)—Kenai Peninsula
 Borough.. *AK-4*
Anchorville (CDP)—St. Clair *MI-3*
Ancient Oaks (CDP)—Lehigh........ *PA-1*
Ancram (Town)—Columbia *NY-1*
Andale (City)—Sedgwick................ *KS-4*
Andalusia (City)—Covington......... *AL-2*
Andalusia (Township)—Rock
 Island.. *IL-3*
Andalusia (Village)—Rock Island... *IL-3*
Anderson (Town)—Lauderdale *AL-2*
Anderson (Town)—Yukon-Koyukuk
 Census Area................................... *AK-4*
Anderson (City)—Shasta *CA-4*
Anderson (Township)—Clark......... *IL-3*
Anderson (City)—Madison *IN-3*
Anderson (Township)—Madison *IN-3*
Anderson (Township)—Perry......... *IN-3*
Anderson (Township)—Rush *IN-3*
Anderson (Township)—Warrick...... *IN-3*
Anderson (City)—McDonald *MO-3*
Anderson (Township)—New
 Madrid *MO-3*
Anderson (Township)—Phelps....... *NE-4*
Anderson (Township)—Thurston.... *NE-4*
Anderson (Township)—Barnes...... *ND-4*
Anderson (Township)—
 Hamilton *OH-3*
Anderson (City)—Anderson............*SC-2*
Anderson (Township)—Perkins *SD-4*

Anderson (Pop. Place)—Grimes.... *TX-2*
Anderson (Town)—Burnett *WI-3*
Anderson (Town)—Iron *WI-3*
Anderson County..............................*KS-4*
Anderson County *KY-2*
Anderson County *SC-2*
Anderson County *TN-2*
Anderson County *TX-2*
Anderson East (Township)—
 McDonald *MO-3*
Anderson Mill (CDP)—Travis *TX-2*
Anderson Mill (CDP)—
 Williamson..................................... *TX-2*
Andersonville (Village)—Sumter ... *GA-2*
Anderson West (Township)—
 McDonald *MO-3*
Andes (Town)—Delaware................ *NY-1*
Andes (Village)—Delaware *NY-1*
Andover (Town)—Tolland *CT-1*
Andover (CDP)—Dade *FL-2*
Andover (Township)—Henry *IL-3*
Andover (Village)—Henry............... *IL-3*
Andover (City)—Clinton................ *IA-3*
Andover (City)—Butler *KS-4*
Andover (Town)—Oxford *ME-1*
Andover (Town)—Essex *MA-1*
Andover (City)—Anoka *MN-3*
Andover (Township)—Polk *MN-3*
Andover (Town)—Merrimack........ *NH-1*
Andover (Borough)—Sussex *NJ-1*
Andover (Township)—Sussex *NJ-1*
Andover (Town)—Allegany *NY-1*
Andover (Village)—Allegany.... *NY-1*
Andover (Township)—Ashtabula...*OH-3*
Andover (Village)—Ashtabula *OH-3*
Andover (Town)—Day *SD-4*
Andover (Township)—Day *SD-4*
Andover (Town)—Windsor............ *VT-1*
Andrea (Township)—Wilkin *MN-3*
Andreanof Islands (AK) *Geog-4*
Andrew (City)—Jackson.................. *IA-3*
Andrew County *MO-3*
Andrews (Town)—Huntington........ *IN-3*
Andrews (Town)—Cherokee *NC-2*
Andrews (Township)—McLean...... *ND-4*
Andrews (Town)—Georgetown...... *SC-2*
Andrews (Town)—Williamsburg......*SC-2*
Andrews (City)—Andrews.............. *TX-2*
Andrews Air Force Base (MD).......*Mil-4*
Andrews Air Force Base (Mil. facil.)—
 Prince George's..............................*MD-1*
Andrews County *TX-2*
Androscoggin County *ME-1*
Aneta (City)—Nelson *ND-4*
Angel Fire (Village)—Colfax *NM-4*
Angelica (Town)—Allegany *NY-1*
Angelica (Village)—Allegany......... *NY-1*
Angelica (Town)—Shawano *WI-3*
Angelina County............................. *TX-2*
Angelo (Town)—Monroe................ *WI-3*
Angels (City)—Calaveras................ *CA-4*
Angie (Village)—Washington
 Parish.. *LA-2*
Angier (Town)—Harnett *NC-2*
Angleton (City)—Brazoria.............. *TX-2*
Angola (City)—Steuben.................. *IN-3*
Angola (Village)—Erie................... *NY-1*
Angola on the Lake (CDP)—Erie .. *NY-1*
Angoon (City)—
 Skagway-Hoonah-Angoon Census
 Area... *AK-4*
Angora (Township)—St. Louis...... *MN-3*
Anguilla (Town)—Sharkey *MS-2*
Angus (Township)—Polk............... *MN-3*
Angus (City)—Navarro *TX-2*

Angwin (CDP)—Napa CA-4
Aniak (City)—Bethel Census
  Area AK-4
Anina (Township)—Jerauld SD-4
Anita (City)—Cass IA-3
Aniwa (Town)—Shawano WI-3
Aniwa (Village)—Shawano WI-3
Ankeny (City)—Polk IA-3
Anmoore (Town)—Harrison WV-2
Ann (Township)—Cottonwood MN-3
Anna (City)—Union IL-3
Anna (Township)—Ward ND-4
Anna (Village)—Shelby OH-3
Anna (City)—Collin TX-2
Annabella (Town)—Sevier UT-4
Annada (Town)—Pike MO-3
Anna Maria (City)—Manatee FL-2
Annandale (City)—Wright MN-3
Annandale (CDP)—Hunterdon NJ-1
Annandale (CDP)—Fairfax VA-2
Annapolis (City)—Anne
  Arundel MD-1
Annapolis (City)—Iron MO-3
Ann Arbor (City)—Washtenaw MI-3
Ann Arbor (Township)—
  Washtenaw MI-3
Annawan (Township)—Henry IL-3
Annawan (Village)—Henry IL-3
Anne Arundel County MD-1
Annetta (Town)—Parker TX-2
Annetta North (Town)—Parker TX-2
Annetta South (Town)—Parker TX-2
Annette (CDP)—Prince of Wales-Outer
  Ketchikan Census Area AK-4
Annin (Township)—McKean PA-1
Anniston (City)—Calhoun AL-2
Anniston (Town)—Mississippi MO-3
Ann Lake (Township)—Kanabec .. MN-3
Annona (Town)—Red River TX-2
Annsville (Town)—Oneida NY-1
Annville (City)—Jackson KY-2
Annville (Township)—Lebanon PA-1
Anoka (City)—Anoka MN-3
Anoka (Village)—Boyd NE-4
Anoka County MN-3
Ansel (Township)—Cass MN-3
Anselmo (Village)—Custer NE-4
Ansley (Township)—Custer NE-4
Ansley (Village)—Custer NE-4
Anson (Town)—Somerset ME-1
Anson (City)—Jones TX-2
Anson (Town)—Chippewa WI-3
Anson County NC-2
Ansonia (City)—New Haven CT-1
Ansonia (Village)—Darke OH-3
Ansonville (Town)—Anson NC-2
Ansted (Town)—Fayette WV-2
Antelope (Township)—Franklin NE-4
Antelope (Township)—Harlan NE-4
Antelope (Township)—Holt NE-4
Antelope (Township)—Richland ... ND-4
Antelope (City)—Wasco OR-4
Antelope (Township)—Fall River .. SD-4
Antelope (Township)—Perkins SD-4
Antelope (Township)—Spink SD-4
Antelope (CDP)—Todd SD-4
Antelope County NE-4
Antelope Creek (Township)—
  McKenzie ND-4
Antelope Lake (Township)—
  Pierce ND-4
Antelope Valley (Township)—
  Deuel SD-4
Antelope Valley-Crestview (CDP)—
  Campbell WY-4

Anthon (City)—Woodbury IA-3
Anthony (City)—Harper KS-4
Anthony (Township)—Norman MN-3
Anthony (CDP)—Doña Ana NM-4
Anthony (Township)—Lycoming ... PA-1
Anthony (Township)—Montour PA-1
Anthony (Town)—El Paso TX-2
Antigo (City)—Langlade WI-3
Antigo (Town)—Langlade WI-3
Antimony (Town)—Garfield UT-4
Antioch (Township)—Contra Costa ... CA-4
Antioch (Lake resort village)—
  Lake IL-3
Antioch (Township)—Lake IL-3
Antioch (Township)—Wexford MI-3
Antioch (Village)—Monroe OH-3
Antis (Township)—Blair PA-1
Antler (City)—Bottineau ND-4
Antler (Township)—Bottineau ND-4
Antlers (Town)—Pushmataha OK-2
Antoine (Town)—Pike AR-2
Anton (City)—Hockley TX-2
Antonito (Town)—Conejos CO-4
Antrim (Township)—Shiawassee ... MI-3
Antrim (Township)—Watonwan ... MN-3
Antrim (Town)—Hillsborough NH-1
Antrim (Township)—Wyandot OH-3
Antrim (Township)—Franklin PA-1
Antrim County MI-3
Antwerp (Township)—Van Buren .. MI-3
Antwerp (Town)—Jefferson NY-1
Antwerp (Village)—Jefferson NY-1
Antwerp (Village)—Paulding OH-3
Anvik (City)—Yukon-Koyukuk Census
  Area AK-4
Apache (Town)—Caddo OK-2
Apache Choctaw TDSA (LA) ... IndRes-4
Apache County AZ-4
Apache Junction (City)—
  Maricopa AZ-4
Apache Junction (City)—Pinal AZ-4
Apalachee Bay (FL) Geog-4
Apalachicola (City)—Franklin FL-2
Apalachin (CDP)—Tioga NY-1
Apex (Town)—Wake NC-2
Aplington (City)—Butler IA-3
Apolacon (Township)—
  Susquehanna PA-1
Apollo (Borough)—Armstrong PA-1
Apollo Beach (CDP)—
  Hillsborough FL-2
Apopka (City)—Orange FL-2
Apostle Islands (WI) Geog-4
Appalachia (Town)—Wise VA-2
Appalachian Mountains (WI) Geog-4
Appalachian Trail (WI) Geog-4
Appanoose (Township)—Hancock ... IL-3
Appanoose (Township)—Franklin .. KS-4
Appanoose County IA-3
Appleby (City)—Nacogdoches TX-2
Apple Creek (Township)—Cape
  Girardeau MO-3
Apple Creek (Township)—
  Burleigh ND-4
Apple Creek (Village)—Wayne OH-3
Applegate (Village)—Sanilac MI-3
Applegate (Township)—Lyman SD-4
Apple River (Township)—Jo
  Daviess IL-3
Apple River (Village)—Jo Daviess . IL-3
Apple River (Town)—Polk WI-3
Appleton (Township)—Clark KS-4
Appleton (Town)—Knox ME-1
Appleton (City)—Swift MN-3
Appleton (Township)—Swift MN-3

Appleton (Township)—St. Clair MO-3
Appleton (City)—Calumet WI-3
Appleton (City)—Outagamie WI-3
Appleton (City)—Winnebago WI-3
Appleton City (City)—St. Clair MO-3
Apple Valley (Town)—San
  Bernardino CA-4
Apple Valley (City)—Dakota MN-3
Applewold (Borough)—Armstrong . PA-1
Applewood (CDP)—Jefferson CO-4
Appling (Pop. Place)—Columbia ... GA-2
Appling County GA-2
Appomattox (Town)—
  Appomattox VA-2
Appomattox County VA-2
Aptos (CDP)—Santa Cruz CA-4
Aptos Hills-Larkin Valley (CDP)—
  Santa Cruz CA-4
Aquebogue (CDP)—Suffolk NY-1
Aquia Harbour (CDP)—Stafford .. VA-2
Aquilla (Village)—Geauga OH-3
Aquilla (City)—Hill TX-2
Arab (City)—Cullman AL-2
Arab (City)—Marshall AL-2
Arabi (Town)—Crisp GA-2
Arabi (CDP)—St. Bernard Parish .. LA-2
Arago (Township)—Hubbard MN-3
Aragon (City)—Polk GA-2
Aransas County TX-2
Aransas Pass (City)—Aransas TX-2
Aransas Pass (City)—Nueces TX-2
Aransas Pass (City)—San
  Patricio TX-2
Arapaho (Town)—Custer OK-2
Arapahoe (City)—Furnas NE-4
Arapahoe (Township)—Pamlico ... NC-2
Arapahoe (CDP)—Fremont WY-4
Arapahoe County CO-4
Ararat (Township)—Susquehanna .. PA-1
Arbela (Township)—Tuscola MI-3
Arbela (Town)—Scotland MO-3
Arbo (Township)—Itasca MN-3
Arbon Valley (CDP)—Power ID-4
Arbor Vitae (Town)—Vilas WI-3
Arbuckle (CDP)—Colusa CA-4
Arbutus (CDP)—Baltimore MD-1
Arbyrd (City)—Dunklin MO-3
Arcada (Township)—Gratiot MI-3
Arcade (City)—Jackson GA-2
Arcade (Township)—Phillips KS-4
Arcade (Town)—Wyoming NY-1
Arcade (Village)—Wyoming NY-1
Arcade (Township)—Faulk SD-4
Arcadia (City)—Los Angeles CA-4
Arcadia (City)—DeSoto FL-2
Arcadia (Town)—Hamilton IN-3
Arcadia (City)—Carroll IA-3
Arcadia (City)—Crawford KS-4
Arcadia (Town)—Bienville Parish .. LA-2
Arcadia (Township)—Lapeer MI-3
Arcadia (Township)—Manistee MI-3
Arcadia (City)—Iron MO-3
Arcadia (Township)—Iron MO-3
Arcadia (Township)—Valley NE-4
Arcadia (Village)—Valley NE-4
Arcadia (Town)—Wayne NY-1
Arcadia (Village)—Hancock OH-3
Arcadia (Town)—Oklahoma OK-2
Arcadia (City)—Trempealeau WI-3
Arcadia (Town)—Trempealeau WI-3
Arcadia Lakes (Town)—Richland .. SC-2
Arcanum (Village)—Darke OH-3
Arcata (City)—Humboldt CA-4
Archbald (Borough)—
  Lackawanna PA-1

American Places Dictionary — General Index

Archbold (Village)—Fulton *OH-3*
Archdale (City)—Guilford *NC-2*
Archdale (City)—Randolph *NC-2*
Archer (City)—Alachua *FL-2*
Archer (City)—O'Brien *IA-3*
Archer (Township)—Harrison *OH-3*
Archer City (City)—Archer *TX-2*
Archer County *TX-2*
Archie (City)—Cass *MO-3*
Archuleta County *CO-4*
Arco (City)—Butte *ID-4*
Arco (City)—Lincoln *MN-3*
Arcola (City)—Douglas *IL-3*
Arcola (Township)—Douglas *IL-3*
Arcola (Town)—Washington *MS-2*
Arcola (Village)—Dade *MO-3*
Arcola (Village)—Fort Bend *TX-2*
Arctander (Township)—
 Kandiyohi *MN-3*
Arctic Ocean (WI) *Geog-4*
Arctic Village (CDP)—Yukon-Koyukuk
 Census Area *AK-4*
Arden (Town)—New Castle *DE-1*
Arden-Arcade (CDP)—
 Sacramento *CA-4*
Ardencroft (Village)—New
 Castle *DE-1*
Arden Hills (City)—Ramsey *MN-3*
Ardenhurst (Township)—Itasca ... *MN-3*
Arden-on-the-Severn (CDP)—Anne
 Arundel *MD-1*
Ardentown (Village)—New
 Castle *DE-1*
Ardmore (Town)—Limestone *AL-2*
Ardmore (City)—Carter *OK-2*
Ardmore (CDP)—Delaware *PA-1*
Ardmore (CDP)—Montgomery *PA-1*
Ardmore (City)—Giles *TN-2*
Ardmore (City)—Lincoln *TN-2*
Ardoch (City)—Walsh *ND-4*
Ardoch (Township)—Walsh *ND-4*
Ardsley (Village)—Westchester *NY-1*
Aredale (City)—Butler *IA-3*
Arena (Township)—Lac qui
 Parle *MN-3*
Arena (Town)—Iowa *WI-3*
Arena (Village)—Iowa *WI-3*
Arenac (Township)—Arenac *MI-3*
Arenac County *MI-3*
Arendahl (Township)—Fillmore ... *MN-3*
Arendtsville (Borough)—Adams ... *PA-1*
Arenzville (Township)—Cass *IL-3*
Arenzville (Village)—Cass *IL-3*
Argenta (Village)—Macon *IL-3*
Argentine (Township)—Genesee .. *MI-3*
Argentine (Township)—Fall
 River *SD-4*
Argo (Municipality)—Jefferson *AL-2*
Argo (Municipality)—St. Clair *AL-2*
Argo (Township)—Brookings *SD-4*
Argonia (City)—Sumner *KS-4*
Argonne (Town)—Forest *WI-3*
Argos (Town)—Marshall *IN-3*
Argusville (City)—Cass *ND-4*
Argyle (Town)—Clinch *GA-2*
Argyle (Township)—Sanilac *MI-3*
Argyle (City)—Marshall *MN-3*
Argyle (Town)—Maries *MO-3*
Argyle (Town)—Osage *MO-3*
Argyle (Town)—Washington *NY-1*
Argyle (Village)—Washington *NY-1*
Argyle (City)—Denton *TX-2*
Argyle (Town)—Lafayette *WI-3*
Argyle (Village)—Lafayette *WI-3*

Argyle (unorganized) (Pop. Place)—
 Penobscot *ME-1*
Arial (CDP)—Pickens *SC-2*
Arietta (Town)—Hamilton *NY-1*
Arimo (City)—Bannock *ID-4*
Arion (City)—Crawford *IA-3*
Arion (Township)—Cloud *KS-4*
Arispe (City)—Union *IA-3*
Arispie (Township)—Bureau *IL-3*
Ariton (Town)—Dale *AL-2*
Arizona (Township)—Burt *NE-4*
Arizona City (CDP)—Pinal *AZ-3*
Arkadelphia (City)—Clark *AR-2*
Arkansas City (City)—Desha *AR-2*
Arkansas City (City)—Cowley *KS-4*
Arkansas County *AR-2*
Arkansas River (WI) *Geog-4*
Arkoe (Town)—Nodaway *MO-3*
Arkoma (Town)—Le Flore *OK-2*
Arkport (Village)—Steuben *NY-1*
Arkwright (Town)—Chautauqua ... *NY-1*
Arland (Town)—Barron *WI-3*
Arlee (CDP)—Lake *MT-4*
Arley (Town)—Winston *AL-2*
Arlington (City)—Calhoun *GA-2*
Arlington (City)—Early *GA-2*
Arlington (Village)—Bureau *IL-3*
Arlington (City)—Fayette *IA-3*
Arlington (City)—Reno *KS-4*
Arlington (Township)—Reno *KS-4*
Arlington (City)—Carlisle *KY-2*
Arlington (Town)—Middlesex *MA-1*
Arlington (Township)—Van
 Buren *MI-3*
Arlington (City)—Sibley *MN-3*
Arlington (Township)—Sibley *MN-3*
Arlington (Township)—Phelps *MO-3*
Arlington (Village)—Washington ... *NE-4*
Arlington (CDP)—Dutchess *NY-1*
Arlington (Town)—Yadkin *NC-2*
Arlington (Village)—Hancock *OH-3*
Arlington (City)—Gilliam *OR-4*
Arlington (City)—Brookings *SD-4*
Arlington (City)—Kingsbury *SD-4*
Arlington (Town)—Shelby *TN-2*
Arlington (City)—Tarrant *TX-2*
Arlington (Town)—Bennington *VT-1*
Arlington (City)—Snohomish *WA-4*
Arlington (Town)—Columbia *WI-3*
Arlington (Village)—Columbia *WI-3*
Arlington County *VA-2*
Arlington Heights (Residential
 village)—Cook *IL-3*
Arlington Heights (Residential
 village)—Lake *IL-3*
Arlington Heights (Village)—
 Hamilton *OH-3*
Arlington Heights (CDP)—
 Monroe *PA-1*
Arlone (Township)—Pine *MN-3*
Arma (City)—Crawford *KS-4*
Armada (Township)—Macomb *MI-3*
Armada (Village)—Macomb *MI-3*
Armada (Township)—Buffalo *NE-4*
Armagh (Borough)—Indiana *PA-1*
Armagh (Township)—Mifflin *PA-1*
Armenia (Township)—Bradford ... *PA-1*
Armenia (Town)—Juneau *WI-3*
Armington (Village)—Tazewell *IL-3*
Armona (CDP)—Kings *CA-4*
Armonk (CDP)—Westchester *NY-1*
Armour (City)—Douglas *SD-4*
Armourdale (Township)—
 Towner *ND-4*

Armstrong (Township)—
 Vanderburgh *IN-3*
Armstrong (City)—Emmet *IA-3*
Armstrong (City)—Howard *MO-3*
Armstrong (Town)—Bryan *OK-2*
Armstrong (Township)—Indiana ... *PA-1*
Armstrong (Township)—
 Lycoming *PA-1*
Armstrong (Town)—Oconto *WI-3*
Armstrong County *PA-1*
Armstrong County *TX-2*
Armstrong Creek (Town)—Forest .. *WI-3*
Arna (Township)—Pine *MN-3*
Arnaudville (Town)—St. Landry
 Parish *LA-2*
Arnaudville (Town)—St. Martin
 Parish *LA-2*
Arne (Township)—Benson *ND-4*
Arnegard (City)—McKenzie *ND-4*
Arnegard (Township)—
 McKenzie *ND-4*
Arnett (Town)—Ellis *OK-2*
Arnold (CDP)—Calaveras *CA-4*
Arnold (CDP)—Anne Arundel *MD-1*
Arnold (CDP)—St. Louis *MN-3*
Arnold (City)—Jefferson *MO-3*
Arnold (Township)—Custer *NE-4*
Arnold (Village)—Custer *NE-4*
Arnold (City)—Westmoreland *PA-1*
Arnolds Park (City)—Dickinson ... *IA-3*
Arnoldsville (City)—Oglethorpe ... *GA-2*
Aroma (Township)—Kankakee *IL-3*
Aroma Park (Village)—Kankakee ... *IL-3*
Aromas (CDP)—Monterey *CA-4*
Aromas (CDP)—San Benito *CA-4*
Arona (Borough)—Westmoreland ... *PA-1*
Aroostook County *ME-1*
Arp (City)—Smith *TX-2*
Arpin (Town)—Wood *WI-3*
Arpin (Village)—Wood *WI-3*
Arriba (Town)—Lincoln *CO-4*
Arrington (Township)—Wayne *IL-3*
Arrowhead (Township)—St.
 Louis *MN-3*
Arrow Rock (Town)—Saline *MO-3*
Arrow Rock (Township)—Saline .. *MO-3*
Arrowsic (Town)—Sagadahoc *ME-1*
Arrowsmith (Township)—McLean .. *IL-3*
Arrowsmith (Village)—McLean ... *IL-3*
Arroyo Grande (City)—San Luis
 Obispo *CA-4*
Artas (Town)—Campbell *SD-4*
Artesia (City)—Los Angeles *CA-4*
Artesia (Township)—Iroquois *IL-3*
Artesia (Town)—Lowndes *MS-2*
Artesia (City)—Eddy *NM-4*
Artesian (Town)—Sanborn *SD-4*
Arthur (Village)—Douglas *IL-3*
Arthur (Village)—Moultrie *IL-3*
Arthur (City)—Ida *IA-3*
Arthur (Township)—Clare *MI-3*
Arthur (Township)—Kanabec *MN-3*
Arthur (Township)—Traverse *MN-3*
Arthur (Village)—Arthur *NE-4*
Arthur (City)—Cass *ND-4*
Arthur (Township)—Cass *ND-4*
Arthur (Town)—Chippewa *WI-3*
Arthur County *NE-4*
Artichoke (Township)—Big
 Stone *MN-3*
Artondale (CDP)—Pierce *WA-4*
Arundel (Town)—York *ME-1*
Arvada (City)—Adams *CO-4*
Arvada (City)—Jefferson *CO-4*
Arveson (Township)—Kittson *MN-3*

General Index

Arvilla (Township)—Grand Forks ... *ND-4*
Arvin (City)—Kern ... *CA-4*
Arvon (Township)—Baraga ... *MI-3*
Arvonia (Township)—Osage ... *KS-4*
Asbury (Township)—Gallatin ... *IL-3*
Asbury (City)—Dubuque ... *IA-3*
Asbury (City)—Jasper ... *MO-3*
Asbury Lake (CDP)—Clay ... *FL-2*
Asbury Park (City)—Monmouth ... *NJ-1*
Ascension Island (WI) ... *Geog-4*
Ascension Parish ... *LA-2*
Ash (Township)—Monroe ... *MI-3*
Ash (Township)—Barry ... *MO-3*
Ash (Township)—Clark ... *SD-4*
Asharoken (Village)—Suffolk ... *NY-1*
Ashaway (CDP)—Washington ... *RI-1*
Ashburn (City)—Turner ... *GA-2*
Ashburn (Town)—Pike ... *MO-3*
Ashburn (CDP)—Loudoun ... *VA-2*
Ashburnham (Town)—Worcester ... *MA-1*
Ashby (Town)—Middlesex ... *MA-1*
Ashby (City)—Grant ... *MN-3*
Ashby (Township)—Hettinger ... *ND-4*
Ash Creek (Township)—Ellsworth ... *KS-4*
Ashdown (City)—Little River ... *AR-2*
Asheboro (City)—Randolph ... *NC-2*
Ashe County ... *NC-2*
Asher (Town)—Pottawatomie ... *OK-4*
Asherton (City)—Dimmit ... *TX-2*
Asherville (Township)—Mitchell ... *KS-4*
Asheville (City)—Buncombe ... *NC-2*
Ashfield (Town)—Franklin ... *MA-1*
Ash Flat (Town)—Sharp ... *AR-2*
Ashford (Town)—Houston ... *AL-2*
Ashford (Town)—Windham ... *CT-1*
Ashford (Town)—Cattaraugus ... *NY-1*
Ashford (Town)—Fond du Lac ... *WI-3*
Ash Grove (Township)—Iroquois ... *IL-3*
Ash Grove (Township)—Shelby ... *IL-3*
Ash Grove (City)—Greene ... *MO-3*
Ash Grove (Township)—Franklin ... *NE-4*
Ash Hill (Township)—Butler ... *MO-3*
Ashippun (Town)—Dodge ... *WI-3*
Ashkum (Township)—Iroquois ... *IL-3*
Ashkum (Village)—Iroquois ... *IL-3*
Ash Lake (Township)—Lincoln ... *MN-3*
Ashland (Town)—Clay ... *AL-2*
Ashland (CDP)—Alameda ... *CA-4*
Ashland (Township)—Cass ... *IL-3*
Ashland (Village)—Cass ... *IL-3*
Ashland (Township)—Morgan ... *IN-3*
Ashland (City)—Clark ... *KS-4*
Ashland (Township)—Riley ... *KS-4*
Ashland (City)—Boyd ... *KY-2*
Ashland (Village)—Natchitoches Parish ... *LA-2*
Ashland (Town)—Aroostook ... *ME-1*
Ashland (Town)—Middlesex ... *MA-1*
Ashland (Township)—Newaygo ... *MI-3*
Ashland (Township)—Dodge ... *MN-3*
Ashland (Town)—Benton ... *MS-2*
Ashland (City)—Boone ... *MO-3*
Ashland (CDP)—Rosebud ... *MT-4*
Ashland (City)—Saunders ... *NE-4*
Ashland (Township)—Saunders ... *NE-4*
Ashland (Township)—Grafton ... *NH-1*
Ashland (Town)—Chemung ... *NY-1*
Ashland (Town)—Greene ... *NY-1*
Ashland (Township)—Stutsman ... *ND-4*
Ashland (City)—Ashland ... *OH-3*
Ashland (Town)—Pittsburg ... *OK-2*
Ashland (City)—Jackson ... *OR-4*

Ashland (Township)—Clarion ... *PA-1*
Ashland (Borough)—Columbia ... *PA-1*
Ashland (Borough)—Schuylkill ... *PA-1*
Ashland (Town)—Hanover ... *VA-2*
Ashland (City)—Ashland ... *WI-3*
Ashland (Town)—Ashland ... *WI-3*
Ashland City (Town)—Cheatham ... *TN-2*
Ashland County ... *OH-3*
Ashland County ... *WI-3*
Ashley (City)—Washington ... *IL-3*
Ashley (Township)—Washington ... *IL-3*
Ashley (Town)—Dekalb ... *IN-3*
Ashley (Town)—Steuben ... *IN-3*
Ashley (Village)—Gratiot ... *MI-3*
Ashley (Township)—Stearns ... *MN-3*
Ashley (Township)—Pike ... *MO-3*
Ashley (City)—McIntosh ... *ND-4*
Ashley (Village)—Delaware ... *OH-3*
Ashley (Borough)—Luzerne ... *PA-1*
Ashley County ... *AR-2*
Ashmore (Township)—Coles ... *IL-3*
Ashmore (Village)—Coles ... *IL-3*
Ash No. 16 (Township)—Pennington ... *SD-4*
Ashtabula (Township)—Barnes ... *ND-4*
Ashtabula (City)—Ashtabula ... *OH-3*
Ashtabula (Township)—Ashtabula ... *OH-3*
Ashtabula County ... *OH-3*
Ashton (City)—Fremont ... *ID-4*
Ashton (Township)—Lee ... *IL-3*
Ashton (Village)—Lee ... *IL-3*
Ashton (City)—Osceola ... *IA-3*
Ashton (Village)—Sherman ... *NE-4*
Ashton (City)—Spink ... *SD-4*
Ashton-Sandy Springs (CDP)—Montgomery ... *MD-1*
Ash Valley (Township)—Pawnee ... *KS-4*
Ashville (Town)—St. Clair ... *AL-2*
Ashville (Village)—Pickaway ... *OH-3*
Ashville (Borough)—Cambria ... *PA-1*
Ashwaubenon (Village)—Brown ... *WI-3*
Askewville (Town)—Bertie ... *NC-2*
Askov (City)—Pine ... *MN-3*
Asotin (City)—Asotin ... *WA-4*
Asotin County ... *WA-4*
Aspen (City)—Pitkin ... *CO-4*
Aspen Hill (CDP)—Montgomery ... *MD-1*
Aspermont (Town)—Stonewall ... *TX-2*
Aspinwall (City)—Crawford ... *IA-3*
Aspinwall (Borough)—Allegheny ... *PA-1*
Assaria (City)—Saline ... *KS-4*
Assumption (City)—Christian ... *IL-3*
Assumption (Township)—Christian ... *IL-3*
Assumption Parish ... *LA-2*
Assyria (Township)—Barry ... *MI-3*
Astatula (Town)—Lake ... *FL-2*
Aston (Township)—Delaware ... *PA-1*
Astor (CDP)—Lake ... *FL-2*
Astoria (Town)—Fulton ... *IL-3*
Astoria (Township)—Fulton ... *IL-3*
Astoria—Queens ... *NY-1*
Astoria (City)—Clatsop ... *OR-4*
Astoria (Town)—Deuel ... *SD-4*
Asylum (Township)—Bradford ... *PA-1*
Atalissa (City)—Muscatine ... *IA-3*
Atascadero (City)—San Luis Obispo ... *CA-4*
Atascosa County ... *TX-2*
Atchison (City)—Atchison ... *KS-4*
Atchison (Township)—Clinton ... *MO-3*
Atchison (Township)—Nodaway ... *MO-3*
Atchison County ... *KS-4*

Atchison County ... *MO-3*
Atglen (Borough)—Chester ... *PA-1*
Athalia (Village)—Lawrence ... *OH-3*
Athelstan (City)—Taylor ... *IA-3*
Athelstane (Township)—Clay ... *KS-4*
Athelstane (Town)—Marinette ... *WI-3*
Athena (City)—Umatilla ... *OR-4*
Athens (City)—Limestone ... *AL-2*
Athens (City)—Clarke ... *GA-2*
Athens (City)—Menard ... *IL-3*
Athens (Township)—Jewell ... *KS-4*
Athens (Village)—Claiborne Parish ... *LA-2*
Athens (Town)—Somerset ... *ME-1*
Athens (Township)—Calhoun ... *MI-3*
Athens (Village)—Calhoun ... *MI-3*
Athens (Township)—Isanti ... *MN-3*
Athens (Township)—Gentry ... *MO-3*
Athens (Town)—Greene ... *NY-1*
Athens (Village)—Greene ... *NY-1*
Athens (Township)—Williams ... *ND-4*
Athens (City)—Athens ... *OH-3*
Athens (Township)—Athens ... *OH-3*
Athens (Township)—Harrison ... *OH-3*
Athens (Borough)—Bradford ... *PA-1*
Athens (Township)—Bradford ... *PA-1*
Athens (Township)—Crawford ... *PA-1*
Athens (City)—McMinn ... *TN-2*
Athens (City)—Henderson ... *TX-2*
Athens (Town)—Windham ... *VT-1*
Athens (Town)—Mercer ... *WV-2*
Athens (Village)—Marathon ... *WI-3*
Athens County ... *OH-3*
Athensville (Township)—Greene ... *IL-3*
Atherton (City)—San Mateo ... *CA-4*
Atherton (Township)—Wilkin ... *MN-3*
Athol (City)—Kootenai ... *ID-4*
Athol (City)—Smith ... *KS-4*
Athol (Town)—Worcester ... *MA-1*
Athol (Township)—Spink ... *SD-4*
Atka (City)—Aleutians West Census Area ... *AK-4*
Atkins (City)—Pope ... *AR-2*
Atkins (City)—Benton ... *IA-3*
Atkins (Township)—Towner ... *ND-4*
Atkins (CDP)—Smyth ... *VA-2*
Atkinson (Township)—Henry ... *IL-3*
Atkinson (Village)—Henry ... *IL-3*
Atkinson (Town)—Piscataquis ... *ME-1*
Atkinson (Township)—Carlton ... *MN-3*
Atkinson (City)—Holt ... *NE-4*
Atkinson (Township)—Holt ... *NE-4*
Atkinson (Town)—Rockingham ... *NH-1*
Atkinson (Town)—Pender ... *NC-2*
Atkinson and Gilmanton Academy Grant (Pop. Place)—Coos ... *NH-1*
Atkinson County ... *GA-2*
Atlanta (City)—De Kalb ... *GA-2*
Atlanta (City)—Fulton ... *GA-2*
Atlanta (City)—Logan ... *IL-3*
Atlanta (Township)—Logan ... *IL-3*
Atlanta (Town)—Hamilton ... *IN-3*
Atlanta (City)—Cowley ... *KS-4*
Atlanta (Township)—Rice ... *KS-4*
Atlanta (Village)—Winn Parish ... *LA-2*
Atlanta (Township)—Becker ... *MN-3*
Atlanta (City)—Macon ... *MO-3*
Atlanta (Village)—Phelps ... *NE-4*
Atlanta (City)—Cass ... *TX-2*
Atlanta (City)—Rusk ... *WI-3*
Atlantic (City)—Cass ... *IA-3*
Atlantic Beach (City)—Duval ... *FL-2*
Atlantic Beach (Village)—Nassau ... *NY-1*
Atlantic Beach (Town)—Carteret ... *NC-2*
Atlantic Beach (Town)—Horry ... *SC-2*

American Places Dictionary — General Index

Atlantic City (City)—Atlantic *NJ-1*
Atlantic County *NJ-1*
Atlantic Highlands (Borough)—
 Monmouth *NJ-1*
Atlantic Intracoastal Waterway
 (WI) *Geog-4*
Atlantic Ocean (WI) *Geog-4*
Atlantis (City)—Palm Beach *FL-2*
Atlas (Township)—Pike *IL-3*
Atlas (Township)—Genesee *MI-3*
Atmautluak (City)—Bethel Census
 Area *AK-4*
Atmore (City)—Escambia *AL-2*
Atoka (City)—Atoka *OK-2*
Atoka (Town)—Tipton *TN-2*
Atoka County *OK-2*
Atomic City (City)—Bingham *ID-4*
Atqasuk (City)—North Slope
 Borough *AK-4*
Attala County *MS-2*
Attalla (City)—Etowah *AL-2*
Attapulgus (Town)—Decatur *GA-2*
Attica (City)—Fountain *IN-3*
Attica (City)—Harper *KS-4*
Attica (Township)—Sedgwick *KS-4*
Attica (Township)—Lapeer *MI-3*
Attica (Village)—Genesee *NY-1*
Attica (Town)—Wyoming *NY-1*
Attica (Village)—Wyoming *NY-1*
Attica (Village)—Seneca *OH-3*
Attleboro (City)—Bristol *MA-1*
Atwater (City)—Merced *CA-4*
Atwater (City)—Kandiyohi *MN-3*
Atwater (Township)—Portage *OH-3*
Atwood (Village)—Douglas *IL-3*
Atwood (Village)—Piatt *IL-3*
Atwood (City)—Rawlins *KS-4*
Atwood (Township)—Rawlins *KS-4*
Atwood (Township)—Kidder *ND-4*
Atwood (Borough)—Armstrong *PA-1*
Atwood (Town)—Carroll *TN-2*
Aubbeenaubbee (Township)—
 Fulton *IN-3*
Auberry (CDP)—Fresno *CA-4*
Aubrey (Town)—Lee *AR-2*
Aubrey (Town)—Denton *TX-2*
Aubry (Township)—Johnson *KS-4*
Auburn (City)—Lee *AL-2*
Auburn (City)—Placer *CA-4*
Auburn (Town)—Barrow *GA-2*
Auburn (City)—Gwinnett *GA-2*
Auburn (Township)—Clark *IL-3*
Auburn (City)—Sangamon *IL-3*
Auburn (Township)—Sangamon *IL-3*
Auburn (City)—Dekalb *IN-3*
Auburn (City)—Sac *IA-3*
Auburn (City)—Shawnee *KS-4*
Auburn (Township)—Shawnee *KS-4*
Auburn (City)—Logan *KY-2*
Auburn (City)—Androscoggin *ME-1*
Auburn (Town)—Worcester *MA-1*
Auburn (City)—Bay *MI-3*
Auburn (City)—Nemaha *NE-4*
Auburn (Town)—Rockingham *NH-1*
Auburn (Town)—Cayuga *NY-1*
Auburn (Township)—Crawford *OH-3*
Auburn (Township)—Geauga *OH-3*
Auburn (Township)—Tuscarawas .. *OH-3*
Auburn (Borough)—Schuylkill *PA-1*
Auburn (Township)—
 Susquehanna *PA-1*
Auburn (City)—King *WA-4*
Auburn (Town)—Ritchie *WV-2*
Auburn (Town)—Chippewa *WI-3*
Auburn (Town)—Fond du Lac *WI-3*

Auburndale (City)—Polk *FL-2*
Auburndale (Town)—Wood *WI-3*
Auburndale (Village)—Wood *WI-3*
Auburn Hills (City)—Oakland *MI-3*
Auburntown (Town)—Cannon *TN-2*
Audrain County *MO-3*
Audubon (Township)—
 Montgomery *IL-3*
Audubon (City)—Audubon *IA-3*
Audubon (City)—Becker *MN-3*
Audubon (Township)—Becker *MN-3*
Audubon (Borough)—Camden *NJ-1*
Audubon (CDP)—Montgomery *PA-1*
Audubon County *IA-3*
Audubon Park (City)—Jefferson *KY-2*
Audubon Park (Borough)—
 Camden *NJ-1*
Auglaize (Township)—Camden *MO-3*
Auglaize (Township)—Laclede *MO-3*
Auglaize (Township)—Allen *OH-3*
Auglaize (Township)—Paulding *OH-3*
Auglaize County *OH-3*
Au Gres (City)—Arenac *MI-3*
Au Gres (Township)—Arenac *MI-3*
Augsburg (Township)—Marshall ... *MN-3*
August (CDP)—San Joaquin *CA-4*
Augusta (City)—Woodruff *AR-2*
Augusta (City)—Richmond *GA-2*
Augusta (Township)—Hancock *IL-3*
Augusta (Village)—Hancock *IL-3*
Augusta (City)—Butler *KS-4*
Augusta (Township)—Butler *KS-4*
Augusta (Township)—Bracken *KY-2*
Augusta (City)—Kennebec *ME-1*
Augusta (Village)—Kalamazoo *MI-3*
Augusta (Township)—Washtenaw .. *MI-3*
Augusta (Township)—Lac qui
 Parle *MN-3*
Augusta (City)—St. Charles *MO-3*
Augusta (Town)—Oneida *NY-1*
Augusta (Township)—Carroll *OH-3*
Augusta (City)—Eau Claire *WI-3*
Augusta County *VA-2*
Augustine (Township)—Logan *KS-4*
Augustine Reservation (CA) *IndRes-4*
Aulander (Town)—Bertie *NC-2*
Aullville (Village)—Lafayette *MO-3*
Ault (Town)—Weld *CO-4*
Ault (Township)—St. Louis *MN-3*
Ault Field (Military Facility)—
 Island *WA-4*
Aumsville (City)—Marion *OR-4*
Aurdal (Township)—Otter Tail *MN-3*
Aurelia (City)—Cherokee *IA-3*
Aurelius (Township)—Ingham *MI-3*
Aurelius (Town)—Cayuga *NY-1*
Aurelius (Township)—
 Washington *OH-3*
Aurena (Township)—McLean *ND-4*
Aurora (City)—Adams *CO-4*
Aurora (City)—Arapahoe *CO-4*
Aurora (City)—Douglas *CO-4*
Aurora (Industrial city)—DuPage ... *IL-3*
Aurora (Industrial city)—Kane *IL-3*
Aurora (Township)—Kane *IL-3*
Aurora (City)—Dearborn *IN-3*
Aurora (City)—Buchanan *IA-3*
Aurora (City)—Cloud *KS-4*
Aurora (Township)—Cloud *KS-4*
Aurora (Town)—Hancock *ME-1*
Aurora (City)—St. Louis *MN-3*
Aurora (Township)—Steele *MN-3*
Aurora (City)—Lawrence *MO-3*
Aurora (Township)—Lawrence *MO-3*
Aurora (City)—Hamilton *NE-4*

Aurora (Village)—Cayuga *NY-1*
Aurora (Town)—Erie *NY-1*
Aurora (Town)—Beaufort *NC-2*
Aurora (Township)—Benson *ND-4*
Aurora (City)—Portage *OH-3*
Aurora (City)—Marion *OR-4*
Aurora (Township)—Aurora *SD-4*
Aurora (Town)—Brookings *SD-4*
Aurora (Township)—Brookings *SD-4*
Aurora (Town)—Wise *TX-2*
Aurora (City)—Sevier *UT-4*
Aurora (Town)—Florence *WI-3*
Aurora (Town)—Taylor *WI-3*
Aurora (Town)—Waushara *WI-3*
Aurora County *SD-4*
Au Sable (Township)—Iosco *MI-3*
Au Sable (Township)—
 Roscommon *MI-3*
Au Sable (Town)—Clinton *NY-1*
Austell (City)—Cobb *GA-2*
Austell (City)—Douglas *GA-2*
Austerlitz (Town)—Columbia *NY-1*
Austin (Town)—Lonoke *AR-2*
Austin (Township)—Macon *IL-3*
Austin (Township)—Scott *IN-3*
Austin (Township)—Mecosta *MI-3*
Austin (Township)—Sanilac *MI-3*
Austin (City)—Mower *MN-3*
Austin (Township)—Mower *MN-3*
Austin (Township)—Cass *MO-3*
Austin (Township)—Mountrail *ND-4*
Austin (Borough)—Potter *PA-1*
Austin (City)—Travis *TX-2*
Austin (City)—Williamson *TX-2*
Austinburg (Township)—
 Ashtabula *OH-3*
Austin County *TX-2*
Austintown (CDP)—Mahoning *OH-3*
Austintown (Township)—
 Mahoning *OH-3*
Austwell (City)—Refugio *TX-2*
Autauga County *AL-2*
Autaugaville (Town)—Autauga *AL-2*
Automba (Township)—Carlton *MN-3*
Au Train (Township)—Alger *MI-3*
Autryville (Town)—Sampson *NC-2*
Aux Sable (Township)—Grundy *IL-3*
Auxvasse (City)—Callaway *MO-3*
Auxvasse (Township)—Callaway .. *MO-3*
Ava (City)—Jackson *IL-3*
Ava (City)—Douglas *MO-3*
Ava (Town)—Oneida *NY-1*
Avalon (City)—Los Angeles *CA-4*
Avalon (Town)—Stephens *GA-2*
Avalon (Borough)—Cape May *NJ-1*
Avalon (Borough)—Allegheny *PA-1*
Avant (Town)—Osage *OK-2*
Avard (Town)—Woods *OK-2*
Avena (Township)—Fayette *IL-3*
Avenal (City)—Kings *CA-4*
Avenel (CDP)—Middlesex *NJ-1*
Aventura (CDP)—Dade *FL-2*
Avera (City)—Jefferson *GA-2*
Averill (Town)—Essex *VT-1*
Averill Park (CDP)—Rensselaer *NY-1*
Avery (Township)—
 Montmorency *MI-3*
Avery (Town)—Red River *TX-2*
Avery County *NC-2*
Avilla (Town)—Noble *IN-3*
Avilla (Township)—Comanche *KS-4*
Avilla (Town)—Jasper *MO-3*
Avinger (Town)—Cass *TX-2*
Avis (Borough)—Clinton *PA-1*
Aviston (Village)—Clinton *IL-3*

Avoca (Town)—Benton AR-2
Avoca (Township)—Livingston IL-3
Avoca (City)—Pottawattamie IA-3
Avoca (City)—Murray MN-3
Avoca (Village)—Cass NE-4
Avoca (Town)—Steuben NY-1
Avoca (Village)—Steuben NY-1
Avoca (Borough)—Luzerne PA-1
Avoca (Village)—Iowa WI-3
Avocado Heights (CDP)—Los
  Angeles CA-4
Avon (Municipality)—Houston AL-2
Avon (Town)—Eagle CO-4
Avon (Town)—Hartford CT-1
Avon (Village)—Fulton IL-3
Avon (Township)—Lake IL-3
Avon (Township)—Coffey KS-4
Avon (Township)—Sumner KS-4
Avon (Town)—Franklin ME-1
Avon (Town)—Norfolk MA-1
Avon (City)—Stearns MN-3
Avon (Township)—Stearns MN-3
Avon (Town)—Livingston NY-1
Avon (Village)—Livingston NY-1
Avon (Township)—Grand Forks ND-4
Avon (City)—Lorain OH-3
Avon (City)—Bon Homme SD-4
Avon (Town)—Rock WI-3
Avon-by-the-Sea (Borough)—
  Monmouth NJ-1
Avondale (City)—Maricopa AZ-4
Avondale (CDP)—Jefferson
  Parish LA-2
Avondale (City)—Clay MO-3
Avondale (Borough)—Chester PA-1
Avondale Estates (City)—De
  Kalb GA-2
Avon Heights (CDP)—Lebanon PA-1
Avonia (CDP)—Erie PA-1
Avon Lake (City)—Lorain OH-3
Avonmore (Borough)—
  Westmoreland PA-1
Avon Park (City)—Highlands FL-2
Avoyelles Parish LA-2
Avra Valley (CDP)—Pima AZ-4
Axtell (City)—Marshall KS-4
Axtell (Village)—Kearney NE-4
Ayden (Town)—Pitt NC-2
Ayer (Town)—Middlesex MA-1
Ayers (Township)—Champaign IL-3
Aynor (Town)—Horry SC-2
Ayr (Village)—Adams NE-4
Ayr (City)—Cass ND-4
Ayr (Township)—Cass ND-4
Ayr (Township)—Fulton PA-1
Ayrshire (City)—Palo Alto IA-3
Azalea Park (CDP)—Orange FL-2
Azle (City)—Parker TX-2
Azle (City)—Tarrant TX-2
Aztalan (Town)—Jefferson WI-3
Aztec (City)—San Juan NM-4
Azusa (City)—Los Angeles CA-4
Babbie (Municipality)—
  Covington AL-2
Babbitt (City)—St. Louis MN-3
Babson Park (CDP)—Polk FL-2
Babylon (Town)—Suffolk NY-1
Babylon (Village)—Suffolk NY-1
Baca County CO-4
Bachelor (Township)—
  Greenwood KS-4
Backbone Mountain (WI) Geog-4
Backus (Township)—
  Roscommon MI-3
Backus (City)—Cass MN-3

Bacliff (CDP)—Galveston TX-2
Bacon (Township)—Vernon MO-3
Bacon County GA-2
Baconton (City)—Mitchell GA-2
Bad Axe (City)—Huron MI-3
Baden (Township)—Ward ND-4
Baden (Borough)—Beaver PA-1
Badger (City)—Webster IA-3
Badger (Township)—Polk MN-3
Badger (City)—Roseau MN-3
Badger (Township)—Vernon MO-3
Badger (Township)—LaMoure ND-4
Badger (Township)—Davison SD-4
Badger (Town)—Kingsbury SD-4
Badger (Township)—Kingsbury SD-4
Badin (CDP)—Stanly NC-2
Badlands (SD) Geog-4
Bad Nation (Township)—
  Mellette SD-4
Badoura (Township)—Hubbard MN-3
Bad River Reservation (WI) IndRes-4
Badus (Township)—Lake SD-4
Baer (Township)—Hettinger ND-4
Baffin Bay (TX) Geog-4
Bagdad (CDP)—Yavapai AZ-4
Bagdad (CDP)—Santa Rosa FL-2
Baggs (Town)—Carbon WY-4
Bagley (City)—Guthrie IA-3
Bagley (Township)—Otsego MI-3
Bagley (City)—Clearwater MN-3
Bagley (Village)—Grant WI-3
Bagley (Town)—Oconto WI-3
Bagnell (Town)—Miller MO-3
Baidland (CDP)—Washington PA-1
Bailey (Town)—Nash NC-2
Bailey (Township)—Lyman SD-4
Bailey (City)—Fannin TX-2
Bailey County TX-2
Bailey Lakes (Village)—Ashland ... OH-3
Bailey's Crossroads (CDP)—
  Fairfax VA-2
Baileys Harbor (Town)—Door WI-3
Bailey's Prairie (Village)—
  Brazoria TX-2
Baileyton (Town)—Cullman AL-2
Baileyton (Town)—Greene TN-2
Baileyville (Town)—Washington ... ME-1
Bainbridge (City)—Decatur GA-2
Bainbridge (Township)—Schuyler .. IL-3
Bainbridge (Township)—Dubois IN-3
Bainbridge (Town)—Putnam IN-3
Bainbridge (Township)—Berrien ... MI-3
Bainbridge (Town)—Chenango NY-1
Bainbridge (Village)—Chenango NY-1
Bainbridge (CDP)—Geauga OH-3
Bainbridge (Township)—Geauga ... OH-3
Bainbridge (Village)—Ross OH-3
Bainville (Town)—Roosevelt MT-4
Baird (City)—Callahan TX-2
Bairdstown (Village)—Wood OH-3
Bairoil (Town)—Sweetwater WY-4
Baker (Township)—Morgan IN-3
Baker (Township)—Crawford KS-4
Baker (Township)—Gove KS-4
Baker (City)—East Baton Rouge
  Parish LA-2
Baker (Township)—Stevens MN-3
Baker (Township)—Linn MO-3
Baker (Village)—Stoddard MO-3
Baker (City)—Fallon MT-4
Baker (Township)—Kidder ND-4
Baker (City)—Baker OR-4
Baker (Township)—Davison SD-4
Baker (Township)—Kingsbury SD-4
Baker, Mt (WA) Geog-4

Baker County FL-2
Baker County GA-2
Baker County OR-4
Bakersfield (City)—Kern CA-4
Bakersfield (Village)—Ozark MO-3
Bakersfield (Town)—Franklin VT-1
Bakersville (Town)—Mitchell NC-2
Bala (Township)—Riley KS-4
Balaton (City)—Lyon MN-3
Balch Springs (City)—Dallas TX-2
Balcones Heights (City)—Bexar TX-2
Bald Bluff (Township)—
  Henderson IL-3
Bald Eagle (Township)—Clinton ... PA-1
Balderson (Township)—Marshall .. KS-4
Bald Head Island (Village)—
  Brunswick NC-2
Bald Hill (Township)—Jefferson ... IL-3
Bald Knob (City)—White AR-2
Baldwin (Town)—Duval FL-2
Baldwin (Town)—Banks GA-2
Baldwin (Town)—Habersham GA-2
Baldwin (Village)—Randolph IL-3
Baldwin (City)—Jackson IA-3
Baldwin (Town)—St. Mary
  Parish LA-2
Baldwin (Town)—Cumberland ME-1
Baldwin (Township)—Delta MI-3
Baldwin (Township)—Iosco MI-3
Baldwin (Village)—Lake MI-3
Baldwin (Township)—Sherburne .. MN-3
Baldwin (Town)—Chemung NY-1
Baldwin (CDP)—Nassau NY-1
Baldwin (Township)—Barnes ND-4
Baldwin (Borough)—Allegheny PA-1
Baldwin (Township)—Allegheny ... PA-1
Baldwin (Town)—St. Croix WI-3
Baldwin (Village)—St. Croix WI-3
Baldwin City (City)—Douglas KS-4
Baldwin County AL-2
Baldwin County GA-2
Baldwin Harbor (CDP)—Nassau ... NY-1
Baldwin Park (City)—Los
  Angeles CA-4
Baldwin Park (Village)—Cass MO-3
Baldwinsville (Village)—
  Onondaga NY-1
Baldwinville (CDP)—Worcester MA-1
Baldwyn (City)—Lee MS-2
Baldwyn (City)—Prentiss MS-2
Bale (Township)—Ransom ND-4
Balfour (CDP)—Henderson NC-2
Balfour (City)—McHenry ND-4
Balfour (Township)—McHenry ND-4
Bal Harbour (Village)—Dade FL-2
Balkan (Township)—St. Louis MN-3
Ball (Township)—Sangamon IL-3
Ball (Town)—Rapides Parish LA-2
Ballard (Town)—Uintah UT-4
Ballard County KY-2
Ball Bluff (Township)—Aitkin MN-3
Ballenger Creek (CDP)—
  Frederick MD-1
Ball Ground (City)—Cherokee GA-2
Ball Hill (Township)—Griggs ND-4
Ballinger (City)—Runnels TX-2
Ballston (Town)—Saratoga NY-1
Ballston Spa (Village)—Saratoga ... NY-1
Balltown (City)—Dubuque IA-3
Ballville (Township)—Sandusky ... OH-3
Ballwin (City)—St. Louis MO-3
Bally (Borough)—Berks PA-1
Balmorhea (City)—Reeves TX-2
Balmville (CDP)—Orange NY-1
Balsam (Township)—Aitkin MN-3

American Places Dictionary   General Index

Balsam (Township)—Itasca *MN-3*	Baraboo (City)—Sauk *WI-3*	Barnett (Township)—Roseau *MN-3*
Balsam Lake (Town)—Polk *WI-3*	Baraboo (Town)—Sauk *WI-3*	Barnett (City)—Morgan *MO-3*
Balsam Lake (Village)—Polk *WI-3*	Barada (Village)—Richardson *NE-4*	Barnett (Township)—Forest *PA-1*
Balta (City)—Pierce *ND-4*	Baraga (Township)—Baraga *MI-3*	Barnett (Township)—Jefferson *PA-1*
Balta (Township)—Pierce *ND-4*	Baraga (Village)—Baraga *MI-3*	Barneveld (Village)—Oneida *NY-1*
Baltic (Village)—Coshocton *OH-3*	**Baraga County** *MI-3*	Barneveld (Village)—Iowa *WI-3*
Baltic (Village)—Holmes *OH-3*	Baranof Island (AK) *Geog-4*	Barney (City)—Richland *ND-4*
Baltic (Village)—Tuscarawas *OH-3*	Barataria (CDP)—Jefferson	Barney (Township)—Richland *ND-4*
Baltic (Town)—Minnehaha *SD-4*	Parish *LA-2*	Barnhart (CDP)—Jefferson *MO-3*
Baltimore (Township)—Barry *MI-3*	Barber (Township)—Faribault *MN-3*	Barnhill (Township)—Wayne *IL-3*
Baltimore (Village)—Fairfield *OH-3*	**Barber County** *KS-4*	Barnhill (Village)—Tuscarawas *OH-3*
Baltimore (Town)—Windsor *VT-1*	Barbers Point Housing (CDP)—	Barnsdall (City)—Osage *OK-2*
Baltimore (city) *MD-1*	Honolulu *HI-4*	Barnstable (Town)—Barnstable *MA-1*
Baltimore County *MD-1*	Barberton (City)—Summit *OH-3*	**Barnstable County** *MA-1*
Bamberg (Town)—Bamberg *SC-2*	**Barbour County** *AL-2*	Barnstead (Town)—Belknap *NH-1*
Bamberg County *SC-2*	**Barbour County** *WV-2*	Barnum (City)—Webster *IA-3*
Bancroft (City)—Caribou *ID-4*	Barbourmeade (City)—Jefferson ... *KY-2*	Barnum (City)—Carlton *MN-3*
Bancroft (City)—Kossuth *IA-3*	Barboursville (Village)—Cabell *WV-2*	Barnum (Township)—Carlton *MN-3*
Bancroft (City)—Jefferson *KY-2*	Barbourville (City)—Knox *KY-2*	Barnum Island (CDP)—Nassau *NY-1*
Bancroft (Town)—Aroostook *ME-1*	Barclay (Township)—Osage *KS-4*	Bar Nunn (Town)—Natrona *WY-4*
Bancroft (Village)—Shiawassee *MI-3*	Barclay (Township)—Cass *MN-3*	Barnwell (City)—Barnwell *SC-2*
Bancroft (Township)—Freeborn ... *MN-3*	Barclay (Merrickton) (Town)—Queen	**Barnwell County** *SC-2*
Bancroft (Township)—Cuming *NE-4*	Anne's *MD-1*	Baroda (Township)—Berrien *MI-3*
Bancroft (Village)—Cuming *NE-4*	Bardolph (Village)—McDonough ... *IL-3*	Baroda (Village)—Berrien *MI-3*
Bancroft (Town)—Kingsbury *SD-4*	Bardonia (CDP)—Rockland *NY-1*	Barona Rancheria (CA) *IndRes-4*
Bancroft (Town)—Putnam *WV-2*	Bardstown (City)—Nelson *KY-2*	Barr (Township)—Macoupin *IL-3*
Bandera (City)—Bandera *TX-2*	Bardwell (City)—Carlisle *KY-2*	Barr (Township)—Daviess *IN-3*
Bandera County *TX-2*	Bardwell (City)—Ellis *TX-2*	Barr (Township)—Cambria *PA-1*
Bandon (Township)—Renville *MN-3*	Bargersville (Town)—Johnson *IN-3*	Barracks (CDP)—Albemarle *VA-2*
Bandon (City)—Coos *OR-4*	Bar Harbor (Town)—Hancock *ME-1*	Barrackville (Town)—Marion *WV-2*
Baneberry (City)—Jefferson *TN-2*	Baring (Plantation)—	Barr Butte (Township)—
Bangor (City)—Penobscot *ME-1*	Washington *ME-1*	Williams *ND-4*
Bangor (Township)—Bay *MI-3*	Baring (City)—Knox *MO-3*	Barre (Town)—Worcester *MA-1*
Bangor (City)—Van Buren *MI-3*	Barker (Town)—Broome *NY-1*	Barre (Town)—Orleans *NY-1*
Bangor (Township)—Van Buren *MI-3*	Barker (Village)—Niagara *NY-1*	Barre (City)—Washington *VT-1*
Bangor (Township)—Pope *MN-3*	Barker Heights (CDP)—	Barre (Town)—Washington *VT-1*
Bangor (Town)—Franklin *NY-1*	Henderson *NC-2*	Barre (Town)—La Crosse *WI-3*
Bangor (Borough)—Northampton .. *PA-1*	Barker Ten Mile (CDP)—	Barree (Township)—Huntingdon *PA-1*
Bangor (Township)—Brookings *SD-4*	Robeson *NC-2*	Barren (Township)—Franklin *IL-3*
Bangor (Town)—La Crosse *WI-3*	Barkeyville (Borough)—Venango *PA-1*	**Barren County** *KY-2*
Bangor (Village)—La Crosse *WI-3*	Barkhamsted (Town)—Litchfield ... *CT-1*	Barren Fork (Township)—Ozark ... *MO-3*
Bangor Naval Submarine Base	Barkley (Township)—Jasper *IN-3*	Barrett (Township)—Thomas *KS-4*
(WA) *Mil-4*	Bark River (Township)—Delta *MI-3*	Barrett (City)—Grant *MN-3*
Bangor Trident Base (Military	Barksdale (Town)—Bayfield *WI-3*	Barrett (Township)—Monroe *PA-1*
Facility)—Kitsap *WA-4*	Barksdale Air Force Base (LA) *Mil-4*	Barrett (Township)—Beadle *SD-4*
Bangs (City)—Brown *TX-2*	Barling (City)—Sebastian *AR-2*	Barrett (Township)—Perkins *SD-4*
Banks (Town)—Pike *AL-2*	Barlow (Township)—Washington ... *OH-3*	Barrett (CDP)—Harris *TX-2*
Banks (Town)—Bradley *AR-2*	Barlow (City)—Ballard *KY-2*	Barrie (Township)—Richland *ND-4*
Banks (Township)—Antrim *MI-3*	Barlow (Township)—Clackamas *OR-4*	Barrington (Township)—Cook *IL-3*
Banks (City)—Washington *OR-4*	Barnard (City)—Lincoln *KS-4*	Barrington (Village)—Cook *IL-3*
Banks (Township)—Carbon *PA-1*	Barnard (City)—Nodaway *MO-3*	Barrington (Village)—Lake *IL-3*
Banks (Township)—Indiana *PA-1*	Barnard (Town)—Windsor *VT-1*	Barrington (Town)—Strafford *NH-1*
Banks County *GA-2*	Barnegat (Township)—Ocean *NJ-1*	Barrington (Borough)—Camden *NJ-1*
Bankston (City)—Dubuque *IA-3*	Barnegat Bay (NJ) *Geog-4*	Barrington (Town)—Yates *NY-1*
Banner (Township)—Effingham *IL-3*	Barnegat Light (Borough)—Ocean .. *NJ-1*	Barrington (Town)—Bristol *RI-1*
Banner (Township)—Fulton *IL-3*	Barnes (City)—Washington *KS-4*	Barrington Hills (Village)—Cook *IL-3*
Banner (Village)—Fulton *IL-3*	Barnes (Township)—Washington ... *KS-4*	Barrington Hills (Village)—Kane *IL-3*
Banner (Township)—Dickinson *KS-4*	Barnes (Township)—Cass *ND-4*	Barrington Hills (Village)—Lake *IL-3*
Banner (Township)—Jackson *KS-4*	Barnes (Town)—Bayfield *WI-3*	Barrington Hills (Village)—
Banner (Township)—Rush *KS-4*	Barnesboro (Borough)—Cambria *PA-1*	McHenry *IL-3*
Banner (Township)—Smith *KS-4*	Barnes City (City)—Mahaska *IA-3*	Barron (City)—Barron *WI-3*
Banner (Township)—Stevens *KS-4*	Barnes City (City)—Poweshiek *IA-3*	Barron (Town)—Barron *WI-3*
Banner (Township)—Cavalier *ND-4*	**Barnes County** *ND-4*	**Barron County** *WI-3*
Banner (Township)—Mountrail *ND-4*	Barnes Lake-Millers Lake (CDP)—	Barronett (Town)—Washburn *WI-3*
Banner (Township)—Beadle *SD-4*	Lapeer *MI-3*	Barrow (City)—North Slope
Banner (Township)—Tripp *SD-4*	Barneston (Township)—Gage *NE-4*	Borough *AK-4*
Banner County *NE-4*	Barneston (Village)—Gage *NE-4*	**Barrow County** *GA-2*
Banner Elk (Town)—Avery *NC-2*	Barnesville (City)—Lamar *GA-2*	Barry (City)—Pike *IL-3*
Banner Hill (CDP)—Unicoi *TN-2*	Barnesville (Town)—	Barry (Township)—Pike *IL-3*
Banning (City)—Riverside *CA-4*	Montgomery *MD-1*	Barry (Township)—Barry *MI-3*
Bannockburn (Village)—Lake *IL-3*	Barnesville (City)—Clay *MN-3*	Barry (City)—Big Stone *MN-3*
Bannock County *ID-4*	Barnesville (Township)—Clay *MN-3*	Barry (Township)—Pine *MN-3*
Bantam (Borough)—Litchfield *CT-1*	Barnesville (Village)—Belmont *OH-3*	Barry (Township)—Schuylkill *PA-1*
Bantry (City)—McHenry *ND-4*	Barnet (Town)—Caledonia *VT-1*	Barry (City)—Navarro *TX-2*
Bantry (Township)—McHenry *ND-4*	Barnett (Township)—De Witt *IL-3*	**Barry County** *MI-3*

General Index — American Places Dictionary

Barry County *MO-3*
Barryton (Village)—Mecosta *MI-3*
Barsness (Township)—Pope *MN-3*
Barstow (City)—San Bernardino ... *CA-4*
Barstow (Town)—Ward *TX-2*
Bart (Township)—Lancaster *PA-1*
Bartelme (Town)—Shawano *WI-3*
Bartelso (Village)—Clinton *IL-3*
Bartholomew County *IN-3*
Bartlesville (City)—Osage *OK-2*
Bartlesville (City)—Washington *OK-2*
Bartlett (Village)—Cook *IL-3*
Bartlett (Village)—DuPage *IL-3*
Bartlett (Village)—Kane *IL-3*
Bartlett (City)—Labette *KS-4*
Bartlett (Township)—Todd *MN-3*
Bartlett (Township)—Shannon *MO-3*
Bartlett (Village)—Wheeler *NE-4*
Bartlett (Town)—Carroll *NH-1*
Bartlett (Township)—Ramsey *ND-4*
Bartlett (Town)—Shelby *TN-2*
Bartlett (City)—Bell *TX-2*
Bartlett (City)—Williamson *TX-2*
Bartley (Village)—Red Willow *NE-4*
Bartley (Township)—Griggs *ND-4*
Bartlow (Township)—Henry *OH-3*
Barto (Township)—Roseau *MN-3*
Barton (Township)—Gibson *IN-3*
Barton (Town)—Allegany *MD-1*
Barton (Township)—Newaygo *MI-3*
Barton (Town)—Tioga *NY-1*
Barton (City)—Pierce *ND-4*
Barton (Town)—Orleans *VT-1*
Barton (Village)—Orleans *VT-1*
Barton (Town)—Washington *WI-3*
Barton City (Township)—Barton .. *MO-3*
Barton County *KS-4*
Barton County *MO-3*
Barton Hills (Village)—
 Washtenaw *MI-3*
Bartonville (Village)—Peoria *IL-3*
Bartonville (Town)—Denton *TX-2*
Bartow (City)—Polk *FL-2*
Bartow (Town)—Jefferson *GA-2*
Bartow County *GA-2*
Barview (CDP)—Coos *OR-4*
Barwick (Town)—Brooks *GA-2*
Barwick (Town)—Thomas *GA-2*
Basalt (Town)—Eagle *CO-4*
Basalt (Town)—Pitkin *CO-4*
Basalt (City)—Bingham *ID-4*
Basco (Village)—Hancock *IL-3*
Bascom (Town)—Jackson *FL-2*
Basehor (City)—Leavenworth *KS-4*
Bashaw (Township)—Brown *MN-3*
Bashaw (Town)—Washburn *WI-3*
Basile (Town)—Evangeline
 Parish *LA-2*
Basin (Township)—Boyd *NE-4*
Basin (Town)—Big Horn *WY-4*
Baskin (CDP)—Pinellas *FL-2*
Baskin (Village)—Franklin Parish .. *LA-2*
Bass Brook (Township)—Itasca *MN-3*
Bassett (Town)—Mississippi *AR-2*
Bassett (City)—Chickasaw *IA-3*
Bassett (City)—Allen *KS-4*
Bassett (Township)—St. Louis *MN-3*
Bassett (City)—Rock *NE-4*
Bassett (CDP)—Henry *VA-2*
Bassettville (Township)—Decatur ... *KS-4*
Bassfield (Town)—Jefferson
 Davis *MS-2*
Bass Lake (Town)—Sawyer *WI-3*
Bass Lake (Town)—Washburn *WI-3*

Bass River (Township)—
 Burlington *NJ-1*
Bassville Park (CDP)—Lake *FL-2*
Bastress (Township)—Lycoming *PA-1*
Bastrop (City)—Morehouse
 Parish *LA-2*
Bastrop (City)—Bastrop *TX-2*
Bastrop County *TX-2*
Batavia (Industrial city)—DuPage .. *IL-3*
Batavia (Industrial city)—Kane *IL-3*
Batavia (Township)—Kane *IL-3*
Batavia (City)—Jefferson *IA-3*
Batavia (Township)—Branch *MI-3*
Batavia (City)—Genesee *NY-1*
Batavia (Town)—Genesee *NY-1*
Batavia (Township)—Clermont *OH-3*
Batavia (Village)—Clermont *OH-3*
Batchtown (Village)—Calhoun *IL-3*
Bates (Township)—Iron *MI-3*
Bates (Township)—Brown *SD-4*
Bates (Township)—Hand *SD-4*
Batesburg (Town)—Lexington *SC-2*
Batesburg (Town)—Saluda *SC-2*
Bates City (Village)—Lafayette *MO-3*
Bates County *MO-3*
Batesland (Town)—Shannon *SD-4*
Batesville (City)—Independence *AR-2*
Batesville (City)—Franklin *IN-3*
Batesville (City)—Ripley *IN-3*
Batesville (City)—Panola *MS-2*
Batesville (Village)—Noble *OH-3*
Batesville (CDP)—Zavala *TX-2*
Bath (Township)—Mason *IL-3*
Bath (Village)—Mason *IL-3*
Bath (Township)—Franklin *IN-3*
Bath (City)—Sagadahoc *ME-1*
Bath (Township)—Clinton *MI-3*
Bath (Township)—Freeborn *MN-3*
Bath (Town)—Grafton *NH-1*
Bath (Town)—Steuben *NY-1*
Bath (Village)—Steuben *NY-1*
Bath (Town)—Beaufort *NC-2*
Bath (Township)—Allen *OH-3*
Bath (Township)—Greene *OH-3*
Bath (Township)—Summit *OH-3*
Bath (Borough)—Northampton *PA-1*
Bath (Township)—Brown *SD-4*
Bath County *KY-2*
Bath County *VA-2*
Bathgate (City)—Pembina *ND-4*
Bathgate (Township)—Pembina *ND-4*
Baton Rouge (City)—East Baton Rouge
 Parish *LA-2*
Battle (Township)—Beltrami *MN-3*
Battleboro (Town)—Edgecombe ... *NC-2*
Battleboro (Town)—Nash *NC-2*
Battle Creek (City)—Ida *IA-3*
Battle Creek (Township)—
 Lincoln *KS-4*
Battle Creek (City)—Calhoun *MI-3*
Battle Creek (Village)—Madison ... *NE-4*
Battlefield (Town)—Greene *MO-3*
Battle Ground (Town)—
 Tippecanoe *IN-3*
Battle Ground (City)—Clark *WA-4*
Battle Hill (Township)—
 McPherson *KS-4*
Battle Lake (City)—Otter Tail *MN-3*
Battlement Mesa (CDP)—
 Garfield *CO-4*
Battle Mountain (CDP)—Lander .. *NV-4*
Battle Plain (Township)—Rock *MN-3*
Battleview (Township)—Burke *ND-4*
Baudette (City)—Lake of the
 Woods *MN-3*

Baughman (Township)—Wayne *OH-3*
Baugo (Township)—Elkhart *IN-3*
Bauxite (Town)—Saline *AR-2*
Baxley (City)—Appling *GA-2*
Baxter (City)—Jasper *IA-3*
Baxter (City)—Crow Wing *MN-3*
Baxter (Township)—Lac qui
 Parle *MN-3*
Baxter (Town)—Putnam *TN-2*
Baxter County *AR-2*
Baxter Estates (Village)—Nassau ... *NY-1*
Baxter Springs (City)—Cherokee *KS-4*
Bay (City)—Craighead *AR-2*
Bay (Township)—Charlevoix *MI-3*
Bay (Township)—Ottawa *OH-3*
Bayard (City)—Guthrie *IA-3*
Bayard (City)—Morrill *NE-4*
Bayard (Village)—Grant *NM-2*
Bayard (Town)—Grant *WV-2*
Bayboro (Town)—Pamlico *NC-2*
Bay City (City)—Bay *MI-3*
Bay City (City)—Tillamook *OR-4*
Bay City (City)—Matagorda *TX-2*
Bay City (Village)—Pierce *WI-3*
Bay County *FL-2*
Bay County *MI-3*
Bay de Noc (Township)—Delta *MI-3*
Bayfield (Town)—La Plata *CO-4*
Bayfield (City)—Bayfield *WI-3*
Bayfield (Town)—Bayfield *WI-3*
Bayfield County *WI-3*
Bay Harbor Islands (Town)—
 Dade *FL-2*
Bay Head (Borough)—Ocean *NJ-1*
Bay Hill (CDP)—Orange *FL-2*
Bay Lake (City)—Orange *FL-2*
Bay Lake (Township)—Crow
 Wing *MN-3*
Baylis (Village)—Pike *IL-3*
Baylor County *TX-2*
Bay Mills (Township)—Chippewa . *MI-3*
Bay Mills Reservation (MI) *IndRes-4*
Bay Minette (City)—Baldwin *AL-2*
Bayonet Point (CDP)—Pasco *FL-2*
Bayonne (City)—Hudson *NJ-1*
Bayou (Township)—Ozark *MO-3*
Bayou Cane (CDP)—Terrebonne
 Parish *LA-2*
Bayou La Batre (City)—Mobile *AL-2*
Bayou Vista (CDP)—St. Mary
 Parish *LA-2*
Bayou Vista (Village)—
 Galveston *TX-2*
Bay Pines (CDP)—Pinellas *FL-2*
Bayport (City)—Washington *MN-3*
Bayport (CDP)—Suffolk *NY-1*
Bay Ridge—Kings *NY-1*
Bay Ridge—Queens *NY-1*
Bay Shore (CDP)—Suffolk *NY-1*
Bayshore (CDP)—New Hanover ... *NC-2*
Bayshore Gardens (CDP)—
 Manatee *FL-2*
Bayside (Town)—Refugio *TX-2*
Bayside (Village)—Milwaukee *WI-3*
Bayside (Village)—Ozaukee *WI-3*
Bay Springs (Town)—Jasper *MS-2*
Bay St. Louis (City)—Hancock *MS-2*
Baytown (Township)—
 Washington *MN-3*
Baytown (City)—Chambers *TX-2*
Baytown (City)—Harris *TX-2*
Bayview (CDP)—Humboldt *CA-4*
Bay View (Village)—Erie *OH-3*
Bayview (Town)—Cameron *TX-2*
Bayview (Town)—Bayfield *WI-3*

912

Bay View Gardens (Village)—
  Woodford *IL-3*
Bayview-Montalvin (CDP)—Contra
  Costa *CA-4*
Bay Village (City)—Cuyahoga *OH-3*
Bayville (Village)—Nassau *NY-1*
Baywood (CDP)—Suffolk *NY-1*
Baywood-Los Osos (CDP)—San Luis
  Obispo *CA-4*
Bazaar (Township)—Chase *KS-4*
Bazetta (Township)—Trumbull *OH-3*
Bazile (Township)—Antelope *NE-4*
Bazile Mills (Village)—Knox *NE-4*
Bazine (City)—Ness *KS-4*
Bazine (Township)—Ness *KS-4*
Beach (City)—Golden Valley *ND-4*
Beach (Township)—Golden
  Valley *ND-4*
Beach City (Village)—Stark *OH-3*
Beach City (Town)—Chambers *TX-2*
Beach Haven (Borough)—Ocean *NJ-1*
Beach Haven West (CDP)—
  Ocean *NJ-1*
Beach Park (Village)—Lake *IL-3*
Beachwood (Borough)—Ocean *NJ-1*
Beachwood (City)—Cuyahoga *OH-3*
Beacon (City)—Mahaska *IA-3*
Beacon (City)—Dutchess *NY-1*
Beacon Falls (Town)—New
  Haven *CT-1*
Beaconsfield (City)—Ringgold *IA-3*
Beacon Square (CDP)—Pasco *FL-2*
Beadle County *SD-4*
Beal City (CDP)—Isabella *MI-3*
Beale (Township)—Juniata *PA-1*
Beale Air Force Base (CA) *Mil-4*
Beale Air Force Base (Military
  Facility)—Yuba *CA-4*
Beallsville (Village)—Monroe *OH-3*
Beallsville (Borough)—
  Washington *PA-1*
Beals (Town)—Washington *ME-1*
Beaman (City)—Grundy *IA-3*
Bean Blossom (Township)—
  Monroe *IN-3*
Beans Grant (Pop. Place)—Coos ... *NH-1*
Beans Purchase (Pop. Place)—
  Coos *NH-1*
Bear Bluff (Town)—Jackson *WI-3*
Bear Creek (Town)—Marion *AL-2*
Bear Creek (Township)—
  Christian *IL-3*
Bear Creek (Township)—Hancock .. *IL-3*
Bearcreek (Township)—Jay *IN-3*
Bear Creek (Township)—
  Hamilton *KS-4*
Bear Creek (Township)—Emmet ... *MI-3*
Bear Creek (Township)—
  Clearwater *MN-3*
Bear Creek (Township)—Henry *MO-3*
Bear Creek (Township)—
  Montgomery *MO-3*
Bearcreek (Town)—Carbon *MT-4*
Bear Creek (Township)—Dickey ... *ND-4*
Bear Creek (Township)—Luzerne ... *PA-1*
Bear Creek (Village)—Outagamie .. *WI-3*
Bear Creek (Town)—Sauk *WI-3*
Bear Creek (Town)—Waupaca *WI-3*
Bearden (City)—Ouachita *AR-2*
Bearden (Town)—Okfuskee *OK-2*
Beardsley (City)—Big Stone *MN-3*
Beardstown (City)—Cass *IL-3*
Beardstown (Township)—Cass *IL-3*
Bearfield (Township)—Perry *OH-3*
Beargrass (Town)—Martin *NC-2*

Bear Grove (Township)—Fayette *IL-3*
Bearinger (Township)—Presque
  Isle *MI-3*
Bear Lake (Township)—Kalkaska .. *MI-3*
Bear Lake (Township)—Manistee .. *MI-3*
Bear Lake (Village)—Manistee *MI-3*
Bear Lake (Borough)—Warren *PA-1*
Bear Lake (Town)—Barron *WI-3*
Bear Lake County *ID-4*
Bear Park (Township)—Norman .. *MN-3*
Bear River City (Town)—Box
  Elder *UT-4*
Bear Valley Springs (CDP)—
  Kern *CA-4*
Bearville (Township)—Itasca *MN-3*
Beasley (Town)—Fort Bend *TX-2*
Beatrice (Town)—Monroe *AL-2*
Beatrice (City)—Gage *NE-4*
Beattie (City)—Marshall *KS-4*
Beatty (Township)—St. Louis *MN-3*
Beatty (CDP)—Nye *NV-4*
Beattyestown (CDP)—Warren *NJ-1*
Beattyville (City)—Lee *KY-2*
Beaucoup (Township)—
  Washington *IL-3*
Beauford (Township)—Blue
  Earth *MN-3*
Beaufort (Town)—Carteret *NC-2*
Beaufort (City)—Beaufort *SC-2*
Beaufort County *NC-2*
Beaufort County *SC-2*
Beaufort Sea (AK) *Geog-4*
Beaugrand (Township)—
  Cheboygan *MI-3*
Beaulieu (Township)—
  Mahnomen *MN-3*
Beaulieu (Township)—Pembina *ND-4*
Beaumont (City)—Riverside *CA-4*
Beaumont (Town)—Perry *MS-2*
Beaumont (City)—Jefferson *TX-2*
Beauregard (Village)—Copiah *MS-2*
Beauregard Parish *LA-2*
Beauvais (Township)—Ste.
  Genevieve *MO-3*
Beaux Arts Village (Town)—
  King *WA-4*
Beaver (CDP)—Yukon-Koyukuk
  Census Area *AK-4*
Beaver (Town)—Carroll *AR-2*
Beaver (Township)—Iroquois *IL-3*
Beaver (Township)—Newton *IN-3*
Beaver (Township)—Pulaski *IN-3*
Beaver (City)—Boone *IA-3*
Beaver (Township)—Barton *KS-4*
Beaver (Township)—Cowley *KS-4*
Beaver (Township)—Decatur *KS-4*
Beaver (Township)—Lincoln *KS-4*
Beaver (Township)—Phillips *KS-4*
Beaver (Township)—Republic *KS-4*
Beaver (Township)—Scott *KS-4*
Beaver (Township)—Smith *KS-4*
Beaver (Township)—Bay *MI-3*
Beaver (Township)—Newaygo *MI-3*
Beaver (Township)—Aitkin *MN-3*
Beaver (Township)—Fillmore *MN-3*
Beaver (Township)—Roseau *MN-3*
Beaver (Township)—Taney *MO-3*
Beaver (Township)—Buffalo *NE-4*
Beaver (Township)—Nance *NE-4*
Beaver (Township)—Benson *ND-4*
Beaver (Township)—Mahoning *OH-3*
Beaver (Township)—Noble *OH-3*
Beaver (Township)—Pike *OH-3*
Beaver (Village)—Pike *OH-3*
Beaver (City)—Beaver *OK-2*

Beaver (Borough)—Beaver *PA-1*
Beaver (Township)—Clarion *PA-1*
Beaver (Township)—Columbia *PA-1*
Beaver (Township)—Crawford *PA-1*
Beaver (Township)—Jefferson *PA-1*
Beaver (Township)—Snyder *PA-1*
Beaver (Township)—Miner *SD-4*
Beaver (City)—Beaver *UT-4*
Beaver (CDP)—Raleigh *WV-2*
Beaver (Town)—Clark *WI-3*
Beaver (Town)—Marinette *WI-3*
Beaver (Town)—Polk *WI-3*
Beaver Bay (City)—Lake *MN-3*
Beaver Bay (Township)—Lake *MN-3*
Beaver Brook (Town)—
  Washburn *WI-3*
Beaver City (City)—Furnas *NE-4*
Beaver County *OK-2*
Beaver County *PA-1*
Beaver County *UT-4*
Beaver Cove (Town)—
  Piscataquis *ME-1*
Beaver Creek (Township)—
  Hamilton *IL-3*
Beaver Creek (Township)—
  Crawford *MI-3*
Beaver Creek (City)—Rock *MN-3*
Beaver Creek (Township)—Rock .. *MN-3*
Beaver Creek (Township)—
  Steele *ND-4*
Beavercreek (City)—Greene *OH-3*
Beavercreek (Township)—
  Greene *OH-3*
Beaver Creek (Township)—Tripp .. *SD-4*
Beaver Crossing (Village)—
  Seward *NE-4*
Beaverdale-Lloydell (CDP)—
  Cambria *PA-1*
Beaver Dam (City)—Ohio *KY-2*
Beaver Dam (Township)—Butler .. *MO-3*
Beaverdam (Village)—Allen *OH-3*
Beaver Dam (City)—Dodge *WI-3*
Beaver Dam (Town)—Dodge *WI-3*
Beaverdam Lake-Salisbury Mills
  (CDP)—Orange *NY-1*
Beaver Falls (Township)—
  Renville *MN-3*
Beaver Falls (City)—Beaver *PA-1*
Beaverhead County *MT-4*
Beaver Meadows (Borough)—
  Carbon *PA-1*
Beaverton (Town)—Lamar *AL-2*
Beaverton (City)—Gladwin *MI-3*
Beaverton (Township)—Gladwin ... *MI-3*
Beaverton (City)—Washington *OR-4*
Beavertown (Borough)—Snyder *PA-1*
Beaverville (Township)—Iroquois .. *IL-3*
Beaverville (Village)—Iroquois *IL-3*
Beccaria (Township)—Clearfield ... *PA-1*
Becharof Lake (AK) *Geog-4*
Bechtelsville (Borough)—Berks *PA-1*
Beck (Township)—Perkins *SD-4*
Beckemeyer (Village)—Clinton *IL-3*
Becker (Township)—Cass *MN-3*
Becker (City)—Sherburne *MN-3*
Becker (Township)—Sherburne *MN-3*
Becker (Township)—Roberts *SD-4*
Becker County *MN-3*
Becket (Town)—Berkshire *MA-1*
Beckett (CDP)—Gloucester *NJ-1*
Beckett Ridge (CDP)—Butler *OH-3*
Beckham County *OK-2*
Beckley (City)—Raleigh *WV-2*
Beckville (City)—Panola *TX-2*

General Index

Beddington (Town)—
 Washington ME-1
Bedford (Township)—Wayne..........IL-3
Bedford (City)—Lawrence IN-3
Bedford (City)—Taylor....................IA-3
Bedford (City)—Trimble KY-2
Bedford (Town)—Middlesex MA-1
Bedford (Township)—Calhoun MI-3
Bedford (Township)—Monroe MI-3
Bedford (Township)—Lincoln.........MO-3
Bedford (Town)—Hillsborough......NH-1
Bedford (Town)—Westchester........NY-1
Bedford (Township)—Coshocton...OH-3
Bedford (City)—Cuyahoga................OH-3
Bedford (Township)—Meigs OH-3
Bedford (Borough)—Bedford PA-1
Bedford (Township)—Bedford PA-1
Bedford (City)—Tarrant TX-2
Bedford County..............................PA-1
Bedford County..............................TN-2
Bedford County..............................VA-2
Bedford Heights (City)—
 Cuyahoga OH-3
Bedford (Independent City).........VA-2
Bedford Park (Village)—Cook IL-3
Bedford-Stuyvesant—Kings NY-1
Bedloes Island (AK)......................Geog-4
Bedminster (Township)—
 Somerset...NJ-1
Bedminster (Village & Township)—
 Bucks...PA-1
Bee (Village)—Seward NE-4
Beebe (City)—White........................AR-2
Bee Branch (Township)—
 Chariton..MO-3
Bee Cave (Village)—Travis TX-2
Beech Bottom (Village)—Brooke .. WV-2
Beech Creek (Township)—Greene .. IN-3
Beech Creek (Borough)—Clinton... PA-1
Beech Creek (Township)—Clinton . PA-1
Beecher (Village)—Will IL-3
Beecher (CDP)—Genesee................MI-3
Beecher (Town)—Marinette WI-3
Beecher City (Village)—
 Effingham.......................................IL-3
Beech Grove (City)—Marion IN-3
Beech Mountain (Town)—Avery....NC-2
Beech Mountain (Town)—
 Watauga..NC-2
Beechwood (CDP)—Ottawa............MI-3
Beechwood Trails (CDP)—
 Licking OH-3
Beechwood Village (City)—
 Jefferson...KY-2
Bee County.....................................TX-2
Beedeville (Town)—Jackson...........AR-2
Beekman (Town)—Dutchess NY-1
Beekmantown (Town)—Clinton.....NY-1
Beemer (Township)—Cuming........NE-4
Beemer (Village)—Cuming.............NE-4
Bee Ridge (CDP)—Sarasota...........FL-2
Bee Ridge (Township)—Knox.......MO-3
Beersheba Springs (Town)—
 Grundy...TN-2
Beetown (Town)—Grant WI-3
Beeville (City)—Bee TX-2
Beggs (City)—Okmulgee.................OK-2
Beisigl (Township)—Adams ND-4
Bejou (City)—Mahnomen MN-3
Bejou (Township)—Mahnomen MN-3
Bel Air (Town)—Harford MD-1
Bel Aire (City)—Sedgwick...............KS-4
Bel Air *See* Los Angeles
 —Los Angeles................................CA-4
Bel Air North (CDP)—Harford MD-1

Bel Air South (CDP)—Harford MD-1
Belau Islands (AK)........................Geog-4
Belcher (Village)—Caddo Parish LA-2
Belchertown (Town)—
 Hampshire MA-1
Belcourt (CDP)—Rolette ND-4
Belden (Village)—Cedar NE-4
Belding (City)—Ionia MI-3
Belen (City)—Valencia NM-4
Belfast (City)—Waldo ME-1
Belfast (Township)—Murray MN-3
Belfast (Town)—Allegany NY-1
Belfast (Township)—Fulton PA-1
Belfast (CDP)—Northampton PA-1
Belfield (City)—Stark ND-4
Belford (Township)—Richland ND-4
Belford (Township)—Aurora SD-4
Belgium (Village)—Vermilion IL-3
Belgium (Township)—Polk MN-3
Belgium (Town)—Ozaukee WI-3
Belgium (Village)—Ozaukee WI-3
Belgrade (Town)—Kennebec..........ME-1
Belgrade (Township)—Nicollet MN-3
Belgrade (City)—Stearns MN-3
Belgrade (Township)—
 Washington MO-3
Belgrade (Town)—Gallatin.............MT-4
Belgrade (Village)—Nance NE-4
Belhaven (Town)—Beaufort NC-2
Belinda City (CDP)—Wilson TN-2
Belington (Town)—Barbour WV-2
Belk (Town)—Fayette AL-2
Belknap (Village)—Johnson IL-3
Belknap (Township)—Presque
 Isle..MI-3
Belknap County.............................NH-1
Bell (City)—Los Angeles CA-4
Bell (Town)—Gilchrist FL-2
Bell (Township)—Reno KS-4
Bell (Township)—Rice....................KS-4
Bell (Township)—Cass ND-4
Bell (Township)—Clearfield PA-1
Bell (Township)—Jefferson PA-1
Bell (Township)—Westmoreland.....PA-1
Bell (Town)—Bayfield WI-3
Bell Acres (Borough)—Allegheny PA-1
Bellaire (Village)—Antrim...............MI-3
Bellaire (City)—Belmont................OH-3
Bellaire (City)—Harris TX-2
Bellair-Meadowbrook Terrace (CDP)—
 Clay FL-2
Bella Villa (City)—St. Louis MO-3
Bella Vista (CDP)—Benton AR-2
Bellbrook (City)—Greene...............OH-3
Bell Buckle (Town)—Bedford TN-2
Bell Center (Village)—Crawford WI-3
Bell City (City)—Stoddard MO-3
Bell County.....................................KY-2
Bell County.....................................TX-2
Bell Creek (Township)—Burt NE-4
Belle (City)—Maries MO-3
Belle (City)—Osage MO-3
Belle (Township)—Holt NE-4
Belle (Township)—Edmunds SD-4
Belle (Town)—Kanawha WV-2
Belleair (Village)—Pinellas.............FL-2
Belleair Beach (City)—Pinellas FL-2
Belleair Bluffs (City)—Pinellas FL-2
Belleair Shore (Town)—Pinellas FL-2
Belle Center (Village)—Logan........OH-3
Belle Chasse (CDP)—Plaquemines
 Parish..LA-2
Bellechester (City)—Goodhue........MN-3
Bellechester (City)—Wabasha MN-3

American Places Dictionary

Belle Creek (Township)—
 Goodhue MN-3
Bellefontaine (City)—Logan...........OH-3
Bellefontaine Neighbors (City)—St.
 Louis MO-3
Bellefonte (Town)—Boone AR-2
Bellefonte (Village)—New Castle ... DE-1
Bellefonte (City)—Greenup KY-2
Bellefonte (Borough)—Centre PA-1
Belle Fourche (City)—Butte SD-4
Belle Fourche-Cheyenne Valleys (Pop.
 Place)—Meade..............................SD-4
Belle Fourche River (AK)............Geog-4
Belle Glade (City)—Palm Beach.....FL-2
Belle Glade Camp (CDP)—Palm
 Beach...FL-2
Belle Haven (Town)—Accomack VA-2
Belle Haven (CDP)—Fairfax..........VA-2
Belle Haven (Town)—
 Northampton VA-2
Belle Isle (Village)—Orange FL-2
Bellemeade (City)—Jefferson KY-2
Belle Meade (City)—Davidson TN-2
Belle Plaine (City)—Benton............IA-3
Belle Plaine (City)—Sumner KS-4
Belle Plaine (Township)—Sumner ..KS-4
Belle Plaine (City)—Scott MN-3
Belle Plaine (Township)—Scott......MN-3
Belle Plaine (Township)—Spink SD-4
Belle Plaine (Town)—Shawano WI-3
Belle Prairie (Township)—
 Livingston IL-3
Belle Prairie (Township)—
 Morrison MN-3
Belle Prairie (Township)—
 Fillmore..NE-4
Belle Prairie (Township)—Beadle .. SD-4
Belle Prairie City (Town)—
 Hamilton..IL-3
Belle Rive (Village)—Jefferson IL-3
Bellerive (Village)—St. Louis.........MO-3
Belle River (Township)—
 Douglas MN-3
Bellerose (Village)—Nassau NY-1
Belle Terre (Village)—Suffolk NY-1
Belle Valley (Village)—Noble.........OH-3
Belle Vernon (Borough)—Fayette ... PA-1
Belleview (City)—Marion FL-2
Belleview (Township)—
 Washington MO-3
Belleview (Township)—Miner........SD-4
Belleville (City)—Yell.....................AR-2
Belleville (City)—St. Clair..............IL-3
Belleville (Township)—St. Clair......IL-3
Belleville (Township)—
 Chautauqua KS-4
Belleville (City)—Republic..............KS-4
Belleville (Township)—Republic....KS-4
Belleville (City)—Wayne MI-3
Belleville (Township)—Essex NJ-1
Belleville (CDP)—Mifflin PA-1
Belleville (Village)—Dane WI-3
Belleville (Village)—Green WI-3
Bellevue (City)—Blaine ID-4
Bellevue (Village)—Peoria IL-3
Bellevue (City)—Jackson IA-3
Bellevue (City)—Campbell KY-2
Bellevue (Township)—Eaton MI-3
Bellevue (Village)—Eaton MI-3
Bellevue (Township)—Morrison ... MN-3
Bellevue (City)—Sarpy NE-4
Bellevue (City)—Huron OH-3
Bellevue (City)—Sandusky.............OH-3
Bellevue (Borough)—Allegheny PA-1
Bellevue (City)—Clay TX-2

Bellevue (City)—King WA-4
Bellevue (Town)—Brown WI-3
Bellewood (City)—Jefferson........... KY-2
Bellflower (City)—Los Angeles CA-4
Bellflower (Township)—McLean..... IL-3
Bellflower (Village)—McLean IL-3
Bellflower (City)—Montgomery.... MO-3
Bell Gardens (City)—Los
 Angeles CA-4
Bellingham (Town)—Norfolk........ MA-1
Bellingham (City)—Lac qui
 Parle MN-3
Bellingham (City)—Whatcom....... WA-4
Bellmawr (Borough)—Camden...... NJ-1
Bellmead (City)—McLennan TX-2
Bellmont (Village)—Wabash IL-3
Bellmont (Town)—Franklin NY-1
Bellmore (CDP)—Nassau.............. NY-1
Bellows Falls (Village)—
 Windham VT-1
Bell Plain (Township)—Marshall.... IL-3
Bellport (Village)—Suffolk NY-1
Bells (Town)—Crockett TN-2
Bells (Town)—Grayson TX-2
Bellview (CDP)—Escambia............ FL-2
Bellville (City)—Evans GA-2
Bellville (Village)—Richland.......... OH-3
Bellville (City)—Austin TX-2
Bellwood (Industrial village)—
 Cook IL-3
Bellwood (Village)—Butler............ NE-4
Bellwood (Borough)—Blair PA-1
Bellwood (CDP)—Chesterfield VA-2
Belmar (Borough)—Monmouth NJ-1
Belmond (City)—Wright................ IA-3
Belmont (City)—San Mateo........... CA-4
Belmont (Township)—Iroquois...... IL-3
Belmont (Township)—Kingman..... KS-4
Belmont (Township)—Phillips KS-4
Belmont (Town)—Waldo................ ME-1
Belmont (Town)—Middlesex......... MA-1
Belmont (Township)—Jackson...... MN-3
Belmont (Town)—Tishomingo....... MS-2
Belmont (Town)—Belknap............. NH-1
Belmont (Village)—Allegany NY-1
Belmont (City)—Gaston................ NC-2
Belmont (Township)—Trail........... ND-4
Belmont (Village)—Belmont.......... OH-3
Belmont (CDP)—Cambria PA-1
Belmont (Township)—Douglas SD-4
Belmont (Township)—Spink SD-4
Belmont (City)—Pleasants WV-2
Belmont (Town)—Lafayette WI-3
Belmont (Village)—Lafayette WI-3
Belmont (Town)—Portage............. WI-3
Belmont County.............................. OH-3
Belmore (Village)—Putnam OH-3
Bel-Nor (Village)—St. Louis MO-3
Beloit (City)—Mitchell................... KS-4
Beloit (Township)—Mitchell.......... KS-4
Beloit (Village)—Mahoning............ OH-3
Beloit (City)—Rock WI-3
Beloit (Town)—Rock WI-3
Belpre (City)—Edwards................. KS-4
Belpre (Township)—Edwards........ KS-4
Belpre (City)—Washington........... OH-3
Belpre (Township)—Washington... OH-3
Bel-Ridge (Village)—St. Louis MO-3
Belt (City)—Cascade MT-4
Belton (City)—Cass MO-3
Belton (City)—Anderson............... SC-2
Belton (City)—Bell TX-2
Beltrami (City)—Polk.................... MN-3
Beltrami County MN-3

Beltsville (CDP)—Prince
 George's MD-1
Belvedere (City)—Marin CA-4
Belvedere (CDP)—Aiken SC-2
Belvedere Park (CDP)—De Kalb .. GA-2
Belvidere (City)—Boone IL-3
Belvidere (Township)—Boone......... IL-3
Belvidere (Township)—
 Montcalm MI-3
Belvidere (Township)—Goodhue.. MN-3
Belvidere (Village)—Thayer NE-4
Belvidere (Town)—Warren............ NJ-1
Belvidere (Town)—Jackson SD-4
Belvidere (Town)—Lamoille VT-1
Belvidere (Town)—Buffalo............ WI-3
Belview (City)—Redwood............. MN-3
Belville (Town)—Brunswick.......... NC-2
Belvue (City)—Pottawatomie........ KS-4
Belvue (Town)—
 Pottawatomie KS-4
Belwood (Town)—Cleveland......... NC-2
Belzoni (City)—Humphreys........... MS-2
Bement (Township)—Piatt IL-3
Bement (Village)—Piatt IL-3
Bemidji (City)—Beltrami MN-3
Bemidji (Township)—Beltrami MN-3
Bemus Point (Village)—
 Chautauqua.............................. NY-1
Bena (City)—Cass MN-3
Benavides (City)—Duval............... TX-2
Ben Avon (Borough)—Allegheny .. PA-1
Ben Avon Heights (Borough)—
 Allegheny................................. PA-1
Benbrook (City)—Tarrant TX-2
Bend (City)—Deschutes OR-4
Bendersville (Borough)—Adams.... PA-1
Benedict (City)—Wilson KS-4
Benedict (Village)—York NE-4
Benedict (City)—McLean............... ND-4
Benedict (Township)—Sanborn SD-4
Benewah County............................. ID-4
Benezette (Township)—Elk PA-1
Bengal (Township)—Clinton MI-3
Benham (City)—Harlan KY-2
Ben Hill County GA-2
Benicia (City)—Solano CA-4
Benjamin (City)—Knox TX-2
Benkelman (Township)—
 Cheyenne KS-4
Benkelman (City)—Dundy............. NE-4
Benld (City)—Macoupin IL-3
Ben Lomond (Town)—Sevier....... AR-2
Ben Lomond (CDP)—Santa Cruz . CA-4
Benner (Township)—Centre......... PA-1
Bennet (Village)—Lancaster......... NE-4
Bennett (Town)—Adams CO-4
Bennett (City)—Cedar.................... IA-3
Bennett (Township)—Kingman KS-4
Bennett (Township)—Fillmore....... NE-4
Bennett (Town)—Douglas WI-3
Bennett County SD-4
Bennettsville (City)—Marlboro....... SC-2
Bennington (Township)—
 Marshall IL-3
Bennington (City)—Ottawa.......... KS-4
Bennington (Township)—Ottawa... KS-4
Bennington (Township)—
 Shiawassee MI-3
Bennington (Township)—Mower .. MN-3
Bennington (Village)—Douglas NE-4
Bennington (Town)—
 Hillsborough NH-1
Bennington (Town)—Wyoming NY-1
Bennington (Township)—Licking .. OH-3

Bennington (Township)—
 Morrow OH-3
Bennington (Town)—Bryan OK-2
Bennington (Town)—Bennington .. VT-1
Bennington County......................... VT-1
Benoit (Town)—Bolivar MS-2
Benona (Township)—Oceana......... MI-3
Bensalem (Township)—Bucks PA-1
Bensenville (Village)—Cook.......... IL-3
Bensenville (Village)—DuPage IL-3
Bensley (CDP)—Chesterfield.......... VA-2
Benson (Town)—Cochise AZ-4
Benson (Village)—Woodford........... IL-3
Benson (City)—Swift MN-3
Benson (Township)—Swift MN-3
Benson (Town)—Hamilton NY-1
Benson (Town)—Johnston NC-2
Benson (Borough)—Somerset PA-1
Benson (Town)—Rutland............... VT-1
Benson County ND-4
Bensonhurst—Kings NY-1
Bent County.................................... CO-4
Bent Creek (CDP)—Buncombe NC-2
Bentinck (Township)—Bottineau... ND-4
Bentley (Town)—Hancock IL-3
Bentley (City)—Sedgwick KS-4
Bentley (Township)—Gladwin MI-3
Bentleyville (Village)—Cuyahoga... OH-3
Bentleyville (Borough)—
 Washington PA-1
Benton (Municipality)—Lowndes... AL-2
Benton (City)—Saline AR-2
Benton (City)—Franklin IL-3
Benton (Township)—Franklin......... IL-3
Benton (Township)—Lake............. IL-3
Benton (Township)—Elkhart......... IN-3
Benton (Township)—Monroe......... IN-3
Benton (City)—Ringgold IA-3
Benton (Township)—Atchison KS-4
Benton (City)—Butler KS-4
Benton (Township)—Butler........... KS-4
Benton (Township)—Hodgeman ... KS-4
Benton (City)—Marshall KY-2
Benton (Town)—Bossier Parish LA-2
Benton (Town)—Kennebec ME-1
Benton (Township)—Cheboygan.... MI-3
Benton (Township)—Eaton MI-3
Benton (Township)—Carver MN-3
Benton (Township)—Adair MO-3
Benton (Township)—Andrew....... MO-3
Benton (Township)—Atchison MO-3
Benton (Township)—Cedar MO-3
Benton (Township)—Crawford MO-3
Benton (Township)—Daviess MO-3
Benton (Township)—Douglas MO-3
Benton (Township)—Holt MO-3
Benton (Township)—Howell MO-3
Benton (Township)—Knox MO-3
Benton (Township)—Linn MO-3
Benton (Township)—Newton MO-3
Benton (Township)—Osage MO-3
Benton (City)—Scott MO-3
Benton (Township)—Wayne......... MO-3
Benton (Town)—Grafton NH-1
Benton (Town)—Yates NY-1
Benton (Township)—Hocking OH-3
Benton (Township)—Monroe....... OH-3
Benton (Township)—Ottawa......... OH-3
Benton (Township)—Paulding OH-3
Benton (Township)—Pike............. OH-3
Benton (Borough)—Columbia PA-1
Benton (Township)—Columbia...... PA-1
Benton (Township)—Lackawanna .. PA-1
Benton (Township)—McCook........ SD-4
Benton (Township)—Minnehaha ... SD-4

General Index

American Places Dictionary

Benton (Township)—Spink *SD-4*
Benton (Town)—Polk *TN-2*
Benton (Town)—Lafayette *WI-3*
Benton (Village)—Lafayette *WI-3*
Benton Charter (Township)—
   Berrien *MI-3*
Benton City (Town)—Audrain *MO-3*
Benton City (City)—Benton........... *WA-4*
Benton County *AR-2*
Benton County *IN-3*
Benton County *IA-3*
Benton County *MN-3*
Benton County *MS-2*
Benton County *MO-3*
Benton County *OR-4*
Benton County *TN-2*
Benton County *WA-4*
Benton Harbor (City)—Berrien *MI-3*
Benton Heights (CDP)—Berrien ... *MI-3*
Bentonia (Town)—Yazoo *MS-2*
Benton Paiute Reservation
   (CA)......................................*IndRes-4*
Benton Ridge (Village)—
   Hancock *OH-3*
Bentonville (City)—Benton *AR-2*
Bentru (Township)—Grand
   Forks *ND-4*
Benville (Township)—Beltrami *MN-3*
Ben Wade (Township)—Pope *MN-3*
Benwood (City)—Marshall............*WV-2*
Benzie County *MI-3*
Benzinger (Township)—Elk........... *PA-1*
Benzonia (Township)—Benzie *MI-3*
Benzonia (Village)—Benzie............ *MI-3*
Beotia (Township)—Spink *SD-4*
Berea (City)—Madison.................. *KY-2*
Berea (City)—Cuyahoga *OH-3*
Berea (CDP)—Greenville.............. *SC-2*
Beresford (City)—Lincoln *SD-4*
Beresford (City)—Union *SD-4*
Bergen (Township)—McLeod....... *MN-3*
Bergen (Town)—Genesee *NY-1*
Bergen (Village)—Genesee *NY-1*
Bergen (City)—McHenry *ND-4*
Bergen (Township)—Nelson...........*ND-4*
Bergen (Town)—Marathon............ *WI-3*
Bergen (Town)—Vernon *WI-3*
Bergen County *NJ-1*
Bergenfield (Borough)—Bergen....... *NJ-1*
Berger (City)—Franklin................ *MO-3*
Bergholz (Village)—Jefferson *OH-3*
Bergland (Township)—
   Ontonagon *MI-3*
Bergman (Town)—Boone *AR-2*
Bering Sea (AK).......................... *Geog-4*
Bering Strait (AK)...................... *Geog-4*
Berkeley (City)—Alameda *CA-4*
Berkeley (Village)—Cook *IL-3*
Berkeley (City)—St. Louis *MO-3*
Berkeley (Township)—Ocean *NJ-1*
Berkeley County *SC-2*
Berkeley County *WV-2*
Berkeley Heights (Township)—
   Union *NJ-1*
Berkeley Lake (City)—Gwinnett.... *GA-2*
Berkeley Springs (Town)—
   Morgan *WV-2*
Berkey (Village)—Lucas *OH-3*
Berklee (City)—Boone....................*IA-3*
Berkley (Town)—Bristol............... *MA-1*
Berkley (City)—Oakland *MI-3*
Berks County................................. *PA-1*
Berkshire (Town)—Tioga *NY-1*
Berkshire (Township)—Delaware ..*OH-3*
Berkshire (Town)—Franklin........... *VT-1*

Berkshire County *MA-1*
Berkshire Hills (The Berkshires)
   (MA).......................................*Geog-4*
Berlin (Town)—Hartford............... *CT-1*
Berlin (Town)—Colquitt................ *GA-2*
Berlin (Township)—Bureau............ *IL-3*
Berlin (Village)—Sangamon *IL-3*
Berlin (Town)—Worcester *MD-1*
Berlin (Town)—Worcester *MA-1*
Berlin (Township)—Ionia............... *MI-3*
Berlin (Township)—Monroe *MI-3*
Berlin (Township)—St. Clair......... *MI-3*
Berlin (Township)—Steele *MN-3*
Berlin (City)—Coos *NH-1*
Berlin (Borough)—Camden............*NJ-1*
Berlin (Township)—Camden..........*NJ-1*
Berlin (Town)—Rensselaer............. *NY-1*
Berlin (Township)—Cass *ND-4*
Berlin (City)—LaMoure *ND-4*
Berlin (Township)—Sheridan *ND-4*
Berlin (Township)—Wells.............. *ND-4*
Berlin (Township)—Delaware *OH-3*
Berlin (Township)—Erie.................*OH-3*
Berlin (Township)—Holmes............*OH-3*
Berlin (Township)—Knox...............*OH-3*
Berlin (Township)—Mahoning *OH-3*
Berlin (Borough)—Somerset *PA-1*
Berlin (Township)—Wayne *PA-1*
Berlin (Town)—Washington *VT-1*
Berlin (City)—Green Lake............. *WI-3*
Berlin (Town)—Green Lake.......... *WI-3*
Berlin (Town)—Marathon *WI-3*
Berlin (City)—Waushara *WI-3*
Berlin Heights (Village)—Erie........*OH-3*
Bermuda Dunes (CDP)—
   Riverside *CA-4*
Bern (City)—Nemaha....................*KS-4*
Bern (Township)—Athens *OH-3*
Bern (Township)—Berks *PA-1*
Bern (Town)—Marathon *WI-3*
Bernadotte (Township)—Fulton...... *IL-3*
Bernadotte (Township)—
   Nicollet.....................................*MN-3*
Bernalillo (Town)—Sandoval *NM-4*
Bernalillo County *NM-4*
Bernard (City)—Dubuque...............*IA-3*
Bernards (Township)—Somerset......*NJ-1*
Bernardston (Town)—Franklin *MA-1*
Bernardsville (Borough)—
   Somerset *NJ-1*
Berne (City)—Adams *IN-3*
Berne (Town)—Albany *NY-1*
Berne (Township)—Fairfield *OH-3*
Bernice (Town)—Union Parish.....*LA-2*
Bernice (Town)—Delaware *OK-2*
Bernie (City)—Stoddard................ *MO-3*
Bernville (Borough)—Berks *PA-1*
Berreman (Township)—Jo
   Daviess *IL-3*
Berrien (Township)—Berrien *MI-3*
Berrien County *GA-2*
Berrien County *MI-3*
Berrien Springs (Village)—
   Berrien *MI-3*
Berry (Town)—Fayette *AL-2*
Berry (Township)—Wayne *IL-3*
Berry (City)—Harrison.................. *KY-2*
Berry (Township)—Hettinger..........*ND-4*
Berry (Town)—Dane *WI-3*
Berry Creek Rancheria (CA) *IndRes-4*
Berry Hill (City)—Davidson *TN-2*
Berrysburg (Borough)—Dauphin *PA-1*
Berryville (City)—Carroll *AR-2*
Berryville (Town)—Henderson *TX-2*
Berryville (Town)—Clarke *VA-2*

Bertha (City)—Todd..................... *MN-3*
Bertha (Township)—Todd............. *MN-3*
Berthold (City)—Ward *ND-4*
Berthold (Township)—Ward *ND-4*
Berthoud (Town)—Larimer........... *CO-4*
Bertie County *NC-2*
Bertram (City)—Linn *IA-3*
Bertram (City)—Burnet *TX-2*
Bertrand (Township)—Berrien *MI-3*
Bertrand (City)—Mississippi......... *MO-3*
Bertrand (Village)—Phelps............ *NE-4*
Berwick (Township)—Warren *IL-3*
Berwick (Township)—Nemaha *KS-4*
Berwick (Town)—St. Mary
   Parish *LA-2*
Berwick (Town)—York *ME-1*
Berwick (Township)—Newton *MO-3*
Berwick (Township)—McHenry..... *ND-4*
Berwick (Township)—Adams *PA-1*
Berwick (Borough)—Columbia *PA-1*
Berwyn (Residential city)—Cook.... *IL-3*
Berwyn (Township)—Cook *IL-3*
Berwyn (Township)—Custer *NE-4*
Berwyn (Village)—Custer............... *NE-4*
Berwyn Heights (Town)—Prince
   George's *MD-1*
Beseman (Township)—Carlton ... *MN-3*
Bessemer (City)—Jefferson *AL-2*
Bessemer (City)—Gogebic *MI-3*
Bessemer (Township)—Gogebic.... *MI-3*
Bessemer (Borough)—Lawrence *PA-1*
Bessemer City (City)—Gaston *NC-2*
Bessie (Town)—Washita *OK-2*
Bethalto (Village)—Madison *IL-3*
Bethany (Town)—New Haven *CT-1*
Bethany (Village)—Moultrie *IL-3*
Bethany (Town)—Morgan *IN-3*
Bethany (Township)—Osborne *KS-4*
Bethany (Township)—Gratiot *MI-3*
Bethany (City)—Harrison *MO-3*
Bethany (Township)—Harrison *MO-3*
Bethany (Town)—Genesee *NY-1*
Bethany (City)—Oklahoma *OK-2*
Bethany (Borough)—Wayne *PA-1*
Bethany (Town)—Brooke *WV-2*
Bethany Beach (Town)—Sussex *DE-1*
Bethel (City)—Bethel Census
   Area..*AK-4*
Bethel (Town)—Fairfield............... *CT-1*
Bethel (Town)—Sussex *DE-1*
Bethel (Township)—McDonough.... *IL-3*
Bethel (Township)—Posey *IN-3*
Bethel (Town)—Oxford *ME-1*
Bethel (Township)—Branch *MI-3*
Bethel (City)—Anoka *MN-3*
Bethel (Town)—Shelby *MO-3*
Bethel (Township)—Shelby *MO-3*
Bethel (Town)—Sullivan *NY-1*
Bethel (Town)—Pitt *NC-2*
Bethel (Township)—Towner *ND-4*
Bethel (Township)—Clark *OH-3*
Bethel (Village)—Clermont *OH-3*
Bethel (Township)—Miami *OH-3*
Bethel (Township)—Monroe *OH-3*
Bethel (Township)—Armstrong....... *PA-1*
Bethel (Village & Township)—
   Berks *PA-1*
Bethel (Township)—Delaware.......... *PA-1*
Bethel (Township)—Fulton *PA-1*
Bethel (Township)—Lebanon *PA-1*
Bethel (Township)—Clay *SD-4*
Bethel (Town)—Windsor................ *VT-1*
Bethel Acres (Town)—
   Pottawatomie *OK-2*
Bethel Census Area *AK-4*

Bethel Heights (Town)—Benton AR-2
Bethel Island (CDP)—Contra
  Costa CA-4
Bethel Park (Borough)—
  Allegheny PA-1
Bethel Springs (Town)—McNairy .. TN-2
Bethesda (CDP)—Montgomery MD-1
Bethesda (Village)—Belmont OH-3
Bethlehem (Town)—Litchfield CT-1
Bethlehem (Town)—Barrow GA-2
Bethlehem (Township)—Cass IN-3
Bethlehem (Township)—Clark IN-3
Bethlehem (Township)—Henry MO-3
Bethlehem (Town)—Grafton NH-1
Bethlehem (Township)—
  Hunterdon NJ-1
Bethlehem (Town)—Albany NY-1
Bethlehem (CDP)—Alexander NC-2
Bethlehem (Township)—
  Coshocton OH-3
Bethlehem (Township)—Stark OH-3
Bethlehem (City)—Lehigh PA-1
Bethlehem (City)—Northampton PA-1
Bethlehem (Township)—
  Northampton PA-1
Bethlehem (Village)—Ohio WV-2
Bethpage (CDP)—Nassau NY-1
Bethune (Town)—Kit Carson CO-4
Bethune (Town)—Kershaw SC-2
Bettendorf (City)—Scott IA-3
Betterton (Town)—Kent MD-1
Bettles (City)—Yukon-Koyukuk Census
  Area AK-4
Bettsville (Village)—Seneca OH-3
Between (Town)—Walton GA-2
Beulah (Village)—Benzie MI-3
Beulah (Township)—Cass MN-3
Beulah (Town)—Bolivar MS-2
Beulah (City)—Mercer ND-4
Beulah (Township)—Davison SD-4
Beulah (Township)—Hanson SD-4
Beulaville (Town)—Duplin NC-2
Bevent (Town)—Marathon WI-3
Beverly (Township)—Adams IL-3
Beverly (City)—Lincoln KS-4
Beverly (City)—Essex MA-1
Beverly (City)—Burlington NJ-1
Beverly (Village)—Washington OH-3
Beverly (Town)—Randolph WV-2
Beverly Beach (Town)—Flagler FL-2
Beverly Hills (City)—Los
  Angeles CA-4
Beverly Hills (CDP)—Citrus FL-2
Beverly Hills (Village)—Oakland ... MI-3
Beverly Hills (City)—St. Louis MO-3
Beverly Hills (City)—McLennan ... TX-2
Beverly Shores (Town)—Porter IN-3
Bevier (City)—Macon MO-3
Bevier (Township)—Macon MO-3
Bevil Oaks (Town)—Jefferson TX-2
Bevington (City)—Madison IA-3
Bevington (City)—Warren IA-3
Bexar County TX-2
Bexley (City)—Franklin OH-3
Bibb City (Town)—Muscogee GA-2
Bibb County AL-2
Bibb County GA-2
Bible Grove (Township)—Clay IL-3
Bicker (Township)—Mountrail ND-4
Bicknell (City)—Knox IN-3
Bicknell (Town)—Wayne UT-4
Biddeford (City)—York ME-1
Bienville (Village)—Bienville
  Parish LA-2
Bienville Parish LA-2

Big Apple (Township)—Oregon MO-3
Big Bear City (CDP)—San
  Bernardino CA-4
Big Bear Lake (City.)—San
  Bernardino CA-4
Big Beaver (Borough)—Beaver PA-1
Big Bend (Township)—Republic KS-4
Big Bend (Township)—
  Chippewa MN-3
Big Bend (Township)—
  Mountrail ND-4
Big Bend (Township)—Ransom ND-4
Big Bend (Town)—Rusk WI-3
Big Bend (Village)—Waukesha WI-3
Big Bend Rancheria (CA) IndRes-4
Big Bow (Township)—Stanton KS-4
Big Cabin (Town)—Craig OK-2
Big Coppitt Key (CDP)—Monroe .. FL-2
Big Creek (Township)—White IN-3
Big Creek (Township)—Ellis KS-4
Big Creek (Township)—Neosho KS-4
Big Creek (Township)—Russell KS-4
Big Creek (Township)—Oscoda MI-3
Big Creek (Village)—Calhoun MS-2
Big Creek (Township)—Cass MO-3
Big Creek (Township)—Henry MO-3
Big Creek (Township)—Madison .. MO-3
Big Creek (Township)—Ozark MO-3
Big Creek (Township)—Taney MO-3
Big Cypress Reservation (FL) .. IndRes-4
Big Cypress Swamp (FL) Geog-4
Big Delta (CDP)—Southeast Fairbanks
  Census Area AK-4
Bigelow (Town)—Perry AR-2
Bigelow (Township)—Marshall KS-4
Bigelow (City)—Nobles MN-3
Bigelow (Township)—Nobles MN-3
Bigelow (Township)—Holt MO-3
Bigelow (Village)—Holt MO-3
Big Falls (City)—Koochiching MN-3
Big Falls (Town)—Rusk WI-3
Big Falls (Village)—Waupaca WI-3
Big Flat (Town)—Baxter AR-2
Big Flat (Town)—Searcy AR-2
Big Flats (Town)—Chemung NY-1
Big Flats (Town)—Adams WI-3
Bigfork (City)—Itasca MN-3
Bigfork (Township)—Itasca MN-3
Bigger (Township)—Jennings IN-3
Biggers (Town)—Randolph AR-2
Big Grove (Township)—Kendall IL-3
Biggs (City)—Butte CA-4
Biggsville (Township)—
  Henderson IL-3
Biggsville (Village)—Henderson IL-3
Big Horn County MT-4
Big Horn County WY-4
Bighorn Mountains (WY) Geog-4
Big Island (Township)—Marion ... IndRes-4
Big Lagoon Rancheria (CA) IndRes-4
Big Lake (CDP)—Matanuska-Susitna
  Borough AK-4
Big Lake (City)—Sherburne MN-3
Big Lake (Township)—
  Sherburne MN-3
Big Lake (Village)—Holt MO-3
Big Lake (City)—Reagan TX-2
Bigler (Township)—Clearfield PA-1
Biglerville (Borough)—Adams PA-1
Biglick (Township)—Hancock OH-3
Big Meadow (Township)—
  Williams ND-4
Big Mound (Township)—Wayne IL-3
Big Park (CDP)—Yavapai AZ-4
Big Pine (CDP)—Inyo CA-4

Big Pine Key (CDP)—Monroe FL-2
Big Pine Rancheria (CA) IndRes-4
Big Piney (Town)—Sublette WY-4
Big Prairie (Township)—
  Newaygo MI-3
Big Prairie (Township)—New
  Madrid MO-3
Big Rapids (City)—Mecosta MI-3
Big Rapids (Township)—Mecosta .. MI-3
Big River (CDP)—San
  Bernardino CA-4
Big River (Township)—Jefferson .. MO-3
Big River (Township)—St.
  Francois MO-3
Big Rock (Township)—Kane IL-3
Big Run (Borough)—Jefferson PA-1
Big Sandy (Town)—Chouteau MT-4
Big Sandy (Town)—Benton TN-2
Big Sandy (Town)—Upshur TX-2
Big Sandy Rancheria (CA) IndRes-4
Big Sioux (Township)—Union SD-4
Big Spring (Township)—Shelby IL-3
Big Spring (Township)—Seneca OH-3
Big Spring (City)—Howard TX-2
Big Springs (Village)—Deuel NE-4
Big Springs (Township)—Union SD-4
Big Stone (Township)—Big
  Stone MN-3
Big Stone (Township)—Williams .. ND-4
Big Stone (Township)—Grant SD-4
Big Stone City (City)—Grant SD-4
Big Stone County MN-3
Big Stone Gap (Town)—Wise VA-2
Big Sur (CA) Geog-4
Big Thicket (TX) Geog-4
Big Timber (Township)—Rush KS-4
Big Timber (City)—Sweet Grass ... MT-4
Big Valley Rancheria (CA) IndRes-4
Big Water (Town)—Kane UT-4
Big Wells (City)—Dimmit TX-2
Big Woods (Township)—
  Marshall MN-3
Billerica (Town)—Middlesex MA-1
Billings (Township)—Gladwin MI-3
Billings (City)—Christian MO-3
Billings (City)—Yellowstone MT-4
Billings (Township)—Cavalier ND-4
Billings (Town)—Noble OK-2
Billings County ND-4
Billingsley (Town)—Autauga AL-2
Billington Heights (CDP)—Erie NY-1
Billmore (Township)—Oregon MO-3
Billy Mitchell Islands (TX) Geog-4
Bilodeau (Township)—Wells ND-4
Biloxi (City)—Harrison MS-2
Biltmore Forest (Town)—
  Buncombe NC-2
Binford (City)—Griggs ND-4
Bingen (City)—Klickitat WA-4
Binger (Town)—Caddo OK-2
Bingham (Village)—Fayette IL-3
Bingham (Town)—Somerset ME-1
Bingham (Township)—Clinton MI-3
Bingham (Township)—Huron MI-3
Bingham (Township)—Leelanau .. MI-3
Bingham (Township)—Trail ND-4
Bingham (Township)—Potter PA-1
Bingham County ID-4
Bingham Farms (Village)—
  Oakland MI-3
Bingham Lake (City)—
  Cottonwood MN-3
Binghampton (Township)—
  Barnes ND-4
Binghamton (City)—Broome NY-1

Binghamton (Town)—Broome NY-1
Birch (Township)—Beltrami MN-3
Birch (Town)—Lincoln................... WI-3
Birch Bay (CDP)—Whatcom WA-4
Birch Cooley (Township)—
  Renville..MN-3
Birch Creek (CDP)—Yukon-Koyukuk
  Census Area....................................AK-4
Birch Creek (Township)—Pine MN-3
Birch Creek (Town)—Chippewa WI-3
Birchdale (Township)—Todd MN-3
Birch Lake (Township)—Cass........ MN-3
Birch Lake (Pop. Place)—St.
  Louis...MN-3
Birch Run (Township)—Saginaw... MI-3
Birch Run (Village)—Saginaw MI-3
Birch Tree (City)—Shannon........... MO-3
Birch Tree (Township)—
  Shannon..MO-3
Birchwood (Town)—Washburn WI-3
Birchwood (Village)—Washburn ... WI-3
Birchwood Village (City)—
  Washington MN-3
Bird (Township)—Macoupin........... IL-3
Bird City (City)—Cheyenne...........KS-4
Bird City (Township)—Cheyenne...KS-4
Bird Island (City)—Renville MN-3
Bird Island (Township)—
  Renville...MN-3
Birds (Village)—Lawrence............... IL-3
Birdsall (Town)—Allegany NY-1
Birdsboro (Borough)—Berks PA-1
Birdseye (Town)—Dubois IN-3
Birdsong (Town)—Mississippi AR-2
Birmingham (City)—Jefferson AL-2
Birmingham (City)—Shelby AL-2
Birmingham (Township)—
  Schuyler... IL-3
Birmingham (City)—Van Buren IA-3
Birmingham (City)—Oakland MI-3
Birmingham (Village)—Clay MO-3
Birmingham (Township)—Chester.. PA-1
Birmingham (Township)—
  Delaware PA-1
Birmingham (Borough)—
  Huntingdon......................................PA-1
Birnamwood (Village)—
  Marathon WI-3
Birnamwood (Town)—Shawano WI-3
Birnamwood (Village)—Shawano .. WI-3
Biron (Village)—Wood WI-3
Birtsell (Township)—Foster........... ND-4
Bisbee (City)—Cochise AZ-4
Bisbee (City)—Towner ND-4
Biscay (City)—McLeod MN-3
Biscayne Bay (FL)........................ Geog-4
Biscayne Park (Village)—Dade FL-2
Biscoe (Town)—Montgomery.........NC-2
Bishop (City)—Inyo CA-4
Bishop (Town)—Oconee................. GA-2
Bishop (Township)—Effingham IL-3
Bishop (Town)—Nueces TX-2
Bishop Hill (Village)—Henry.......... IL-3
Bishop Rancheria (CA)............IndRes-4
Bishopville (Town)—Lee SC-2
Bismarck (Township)—Presque
  Isle MI-3
Bismarck (Township)—Sibley MN-3
Bismarck (City)—St. Francois MO-3
Bismarck (Township)—Cuming NE-4
Bismarck (City)—Burleigh ND-4
Bismarck (Pop. Place)—Burleigh... ND-4
Bismark (Township)—Platte NE-4
Bison (City)—Rush KS-4
Bison (Town)—Perkins................... SD-4

Bison (Township)—Perkins............. SD-4
Bithlo (CDP)—Orange FL-2
Bitterroot Range or Mountains
  (FL)...Geog-4
Biwabik (City)—St. Louis MN-3
Biwabik (Township)—St. Louis MN-3
Bixby (City)—Tulsa OK-2
Bixby (City)—Wagoner OK-2
Bjornson (Township)—McHenry... ND-4
Black (Town)—Geneva....................AL-2
Black (Township)—Posey IN-3
Black (Township)—Somerset PA-1
Black (Township)—Tripp SD-4
Black Belt (FL)............................. Geog-4
Blackberry (Township)—Kane IL-3
Blackberry (Township)—Itasca MN-3
Blackbird (Township)—Thurston...NE-4
Black Brook (Town)—Clinton........ NY-1
Black Brook (Town)—Polk WI-3
Blackburn (City)—Lafayette MO-3
Blackburn (City)—Saline MO-3
Blackburn (Town)—Pawnee............ OK-2
Black Butte (Township)—
  Hettinger ND-4
Black Canyon City (CDP)—
  Yavapai AZ-4
Black Creek (Township)—Shelby .. MO-3
Black Creek (Town)—Wilson..........NC-2
Black Creek (Township)—
  Mercer OH-3
Black Creek (Township)—
  Luzerne PA-1
Black Creek (Town)—Outagamie... WI-3
Black Creek (Village)—
  Outagamie WI-3
Black Diamond (City)—King WA-4
Black Dog (Pop. Place)—Lyman SD-4
Blackduck (City)—Beltrami MN-3
Black Earth (Town)—Dane WI-3
Black Earth (Village)—Dane WI-3
Blackfeet Reservation (MT) IndRes-4
Blackfoot (City)—Bingham ID-3
Blackford County IN-3
Black Forest (CDP)—El Paso CO-4
Black Hammer (Township)—
  Houston MN-3
Blackhawk (CDP)—Contra Costa.. CA-4
Black Hawk (Town)—Gilpin.......... CO-4
Blackhawk (Township)—Rock
  Island...IL-3
Blackhawk (CDP)—Meade SD-4
Black Hawk County IA-3
Black Hills, the (FL) Geog-4
Blackhoof (Township)—Carlton.... MN-3
Black Jack (City)—St. Louis MO-3
Blacklick (Township)—Cambria PA-1
Black Lick (Township)—Indiana .. PA-1
Blacklick Estates (CDP)—
  Franklin... OH-3
Black Loam (Township)—
  LaMoure ND-4
Blackman (Township)—Jackson MI-3
Black Mesa (OK) Geog-4
Black Mountain (Town)—
  Buncombe NC-2
Black Mountains (NC)................ Geog-4
Black Oak (Town)—Craighead........ AR-2
Blackpipe (Township)—Mellette SD-4
Black Pond (Township)—
  Oregon MO-3
Black River (Township)—
  Pennington MN-3
Black River (Township)—Butler .. MO-3
Black River (Township)—
  Reynolds MO-3

Black River (Township)—Wayne .. MO-3
Black River (Village)—Jefferson NY-1
Black River Falls (City)—
  Jackson WI-3
Black Rock (City)—Lawrence......... AR-2
Black Rock (CDP)—McKinley ..... NM
Black Rock Desert (NV)............. Geog-4
Blacksburg (Town)—Cherokee........SC-2
Blacksburg (Town)—Montgomery .. VA-2
Blackshear (City)—Pierce............... GA-2
Black Springs (Town)—
  Montgomery..................................... AR-2
Blackstone (Town)—Worcester MA-1
Blackstone (Town)—Nottoway...... VA-2
Blacksville (CDP)—Henry GA-2
Blacksville (Town)—Monongalia .. WV-2
Blacktail (Township)—Williams ND-4
Blackville (Town)—Barnwell...........SC-2
Blackwater (CDP)—Pinal AZ-4
Blackwater (City)—Cooper MO-3
Blackwater (Township)—Cooper .. MO-3
Blackwater (Township)—Pettis MO-3
Blackwater (Township)—Saline ... MO-3
Blackwater (Township)—McLean .. ND-4
Blackwell (City)—Kay OK-2
Blackwell (Town)—Coke TX-2
Blackwell (Town)—Nolan TX-2
Blackwell (Town)—Forest WI-3
Black Wolf (Township)—
  Ellsworth KS-4
Black Wolf (Town)—Winnebago... WI-3
Blackwood (CDP)—Camden.......... NJ-1
Bladen (Village)—Webster NE-4
Bladenboro (Town)—Bladen NC-2
Bladen County NC-2
Bladensburg (Town)—Prince
  George's MD-1
Blades (Town)—Sussex DE-1
Blain (Borough)—Perry PA-1
Blaine (Township)—Clay KS-4
Blaine (Township)—Lane KS-4
Blaine (Township)—Marion KS-4
Blaine (Township)—Ottawa KS-4
Blaine (Township)—Smith KS-4
Blaine (City)—Lawrence KY-2
Blaine (Town)—Aroostook ME-1
Blaine (Township)—Benzie MI-3
Blaine (City)—Anoka MN-3
Blaine (City)—Ramsey MN-3
Blaine (Township)—Adams............NE-4
Blaine (Township)—Antelope NE-4
Blaine (Township)—Cuming NE-4
Blaine (Township)—Kearney NE-4
Blaine (Township)—Bottineau ND-4
Blaine (Township)—Washington PA-1
Blaine (Township)—Clark SD-4
Blaine (Township)—Jerauld SD-4
Blaine (City)—Grainger TN-2
Blaine (City)—Whatcom WA-4
Blaine (Town)—Burnett WI-3
Blaine County ID-3
Blaine County MT-3
Blaine County NE-4
Blaine County OK-2
Blair (Township)—Clay IL-3
Blair (Township)—Grand
  Traverse MI-3
Blair (City)—Washington NE-4
Blair (Town)—Jackson OK-2
Blair (Township)—Blair PA-1
Blair (City)—Trempealeau WI-3
Blair County PA-1
Blairsburg (City)—Hamilton........... IA-3
Blairstown (City)—Benton IA-3
Blairstown (City)—Henry MO-3

Blairstown (Township)—Warren..... *NJ-1*
Blairsville (City)—Union *GA-2*
Blairsville (Borough)—Indiana *PA-1*
Blakeley (Township)—Scott *MN-3*
Blakely (City)—Early...................... *GA-2*
Blakely (Township)—Geary *KS-4*
Blakely (Township)—Gage *NE-4*
Blakely (Borough)—Lackawanna *PA-1*
Blakesburg (City)—Wapello............. *IA-3*
Blakeslee (Village)—Williams *OH-3*
Blanca (Town)—Costilla.................. *CO-4*
Blanchard (City)—Page.................... *IA-3*
Blanchard (Village)—Caddo
 Parish *LA-2*
Blanchard (Township)—Traill........*ND-4*
Blanchard (Township)—Hancock ..*OH-3*
Blanchard (Township)—Hardin *OH-3*
Blanchard (Township)—Putnam....*OH-3*
Blanchard (City)—Grady *OK-2*
Blanchard (Town)—McClain *OK-2*
Blanchard (Town)—Lafayette *WI-3*
Blanchard (unorganized) (Pop. Place)—
 Piscataquis *ME-1*
Blanchardville (Village)—Iowa *WI-3*
Blanchardville (Village)—
 Lafayette *WI-3*
Blanchester (Village)—Clinton.......*OH-3*
Blanchester (Village)—Warren *OH-3*
Blanchette (Township)—St.
 Charles *MO-3*
Blanco (City)—Blanco *TX-2*
Blanco, Cape (OR) *Geog-4*
Blanco County *TX-2*
Bland (City)—Gasconade............... *MO-3*
Bland (City)—Osage *MO-3*
Bland County................................. *VA-2*
Blandford (Town)—Hampden *MA-1*
Blanding (City)—San Juan............. *UT-4*
Blandinsville (Township)—
 McDonough *IL-3*
Blandinsville (Village)—
 McDonough *IL-3*
Blandville (City)—Ballard............... *KY-2*
Blanket (Town)—Brown................. *TX-2*
Blasdell (Village)—Erie *NY-1*
Blauvelt (CDP)—Rockland............. *NY-1*
Blawnox (Borough)—Allegheny *PA-1*
Bleckley County *GA-2*
Bledsoe County............................... *TN-2*
Bleecker (Town)—Fulton................ *NY-1*
Blencoe (City)—Monona.................. *IA-3*
Blendon (Township)—Ottawa *MI-3*
Blendon (Township)—Franklin......*OH-3*
Blendon (Township)—Davison *SD-4*
Blenheim (Town)—Schoharie *NY-1*
Blenheim (Town)—Marlboro *SC-2*
Blennerhassett (CDP)—Wood....... *WV-2*
Blevins (City)—Hempstead............ *AR-2*
Blind Lake (Township)—Cass....... *MN-3*
Blinsmon (Township)—Moody *SD-4*
Bliss (City)—Gooding *ID-4*
Bliss (Township)—Emmet.............. *MI-3*
Bliss Corner (CDP)—Bristol *MA-1*
Blissfield (Township)—Lenawee *MI-3*
Blissfield (Village)—Lenawee......... *MI-3*
Blissville (Township)—Jefferson *IL-3*
Block Island (RI) *Geog-4*
Blockton (City)—Taylor................... *IA-3*
Blodgett (Town)—Scott *MO-3*
Blom (Township)—Deuel *SD-4*
Blomkest (City)—Kandiyohi *MN-3*
Bloom (Township)—Cook *IL-3*
Bloom (Township)—Clay *KS-4*
Bloom (Township)—Ford *KS-4*
Bloom (Township)—Osborne.......... *KS-4*

Bloom (Township)—Nobles *MN-3*
Bloom (Township)—Stutsman *ND-4*
Bloom (Township)—Fairfield.........*OH-3*
Bloom (Township)—Morgan..........*OH-3*
Bloom (Township)—Scioto *OH-3*
Bloom (Township)—Seneca *OH-3*
Bloom (Township)—Wood.............*OH-3*
Bloom (Township)—Clearfield........ *PA-1*
Bloom (Town)—Richland *WI-3*
Bloomburg (Town)—Cass............... *TX-2*
Bloomdale (Village)—Wood...........*OH-3*
Bloomenfield (Township)—
 Stutsman *ND-4*
Bloomer (Township)—Montcalm... *MI-3*
Bloomer (Township)—Marshall *MN-3*
Bloomer (City)—Chippewa *WI-3*
Bloomer (Town)—Chippewa.......... *WI-3*
Blomfield (Town)—Hartford........ *CT-1*
Bloomfield (Town)—Greene *IN-3*
Bloomfield (Township)—Lagrange . *IN-3*
Bloomfield (City)—Davis................. *IA-3*
Bloomfield (Township)—Mitchell...*KS-4*
Bloomfield (Township)—
 Sheridan *KS-4*
Bloomfield (City)—Nelson............. *KY-2*
Bloomfield (Township)—Huron..... *MI-3*
Bloomfield (Township)—
 Missaukee.................................... *MI-3*
Bloomfield (Township)—Oakland . *MI-3*
Bloomfield (Township)—
 Fillmore.. *MN-3*
Bloomfield (City)—Stoddard *MO-3*
Bloomfield (City)—Knox *NE-4*
Bloomfield (Township)—Essex *NJ-1*
Bloomfield (City)—San Juan *NM-4*
Bloomfield (Township)—Traill *ND-4*
Bloomfield (Township)—Jackson ..*OH-3*
Bloomfield (Township)—Logan *OH-3*
Bloomfield (Township)—
 Trumbull *OH-3*
Bloomfield (Township)—Bedford ... *PA-1*
Bloomfield (Township)—
 Crawford *PA-1*
Bloomfield (Borough)—Perry *PA-1*
Bloomfield (Town)—Essex *VT-1*
Bloomfield (Town)—Walworth *WI-3*
Bloomfield (Town)—Waushara *WI-3*
Bloomfield Hills (City)—Oakland . *MI-3*
Bloomfield Township (CDP)—
 Oakland... *MI-3*
Blooming (Township)—Grand
 Forks *ND-4*
Bloomingburg (Village)—Fayette ...*OH-3*
Bloomingburgh (Village)—
 Sullivan..*NY-1*
Bloomingdale (CDP)—
 Hillsborough *FL-2*
Bloomingdale (City)—Chatham..... *GA-2*
Bloomingdale (Township)—
 DuPage..*IL-3*
Bloomingdale (Village)—DuPage.... *IL-3*
Bloomingdale (Town)—Parke *IN-3*
Bloomingdale (Township)—Van
 Buren..*MI-3*
Bloomingdale (Village)—Van
 Buren..*MI-3*
Bloomingdale (Borough)—Passaic.. *NJ-1*
Bloomingdale (Village)—
 Jefferson *OH-3*
Bloomingdale (CDP)—Sullivan *TN-2*
Blooming Grove (Township)—
 Franklin.. *IN-3*
Blooming Grove (Township)—
 Waseca..*MN-3*

Blooming Grove (Town)—
 Orange..*NY-1*
Blooming Grove (Township)—
 Richland...................................... *OH-3*
Blooming Grove (Township)—
 Pike *PA-1*
Blooming Grove (Town)—
 Navarro *TX-2*
Blooming Grove (Town)—Dane *WI-3*
Blooming Prairie (City)—Dodge .. *MN-3*
Blooming Prairie (City)—Steele.... *MN-3*
Blooming Prairie (Township)—
 Steele.. *MN-3*
Blooming Prairie (Township)—
 Divide *ND-4*
Bloomington (CDP)—San
 Bernardino *CA-4*
Bloomington (City)—Bear Lake *ID-4*
Bloomington (City)—McLean.......... *IL-3*
Bloomington (Township)—
 McLean.. *IL-3*
Bloomington (City)—Monroe *IN-3*
Bloomington (Township)—
 Monroe.. *IN-3*
Bloomington (Township)—Butler ...*KS-4*
Bloomington (City)—Hennepin ... *MN-3*
Bloomington (Township)—
 Buchanan *MO-3*
Bloomington (Township)—
 Franklin.. *NE-4*
Bloomington (Village)—Franklin... *NE-4*
Bloomington (CDP)—Victoria...... *TX-2*
Bloomington (Town)—Grant *WI-3*
Bloomington (Village)—Grant *WI-3*
Bloomington City (Township)—
 McLean.. *IL-3*
Blooming Valley (Township)—
 Divide *ND-4*
Blooming Valley (Borough)—
 Crawford *PA-1*
Blooming Valley (Township)—
 Grant... *SD-4*
Bloomsburg (Town)—Columbia *PA-1*
Bloomsbury (Borough)—
 Hunterdon..................................... *NJ-1*
Bloomsdale (City)—Ste.
 Genevieve *MO-3*
Bloomville (Village)—Seneca........*OH-3*
Bloss (Township)—Tioga *PA-1*
Blossburg (Borough)—Tioga *PA-1*
Blossom (Town)—Lamar................ *TX-2*
Blount (Township)—Vermilion....... *IL-3*
Blount County *AL-2*
Blount County *TN-2*
Blountstown (City)—Calhoun.........*FL-2*
Blountsville (Town)—Blount.........*AL-2*
Blountsville (Town)—Henry *IN-3*
Blountville (CDP)—Sullivan......... *TN-2*
Blowers (Township)—Otter Tail .. *MN-3*
Blowing Rock (Town)—Caldwell... *NC-2*
Blowing Rock (Town)—Watauga ... *NC-2*
Bloxom (Town)—Accomack............ *VA-2*
Blue (Township)—Pottawatomie *KS-4*
Blue (Township)—Jackson *MO-3*
Blue Ash (City)—Hamilton *OH-3*
Blue Bell (CDP)—Montgomery *PA-1*
Blueberry (Township)—Wadena ... *MN-3*
Bluebird (Township)—LaMoure....*ND-4*
Blue Butte (Township)—
 McKenzie *ND-4*
Blue Creek (Township)—Adams ... *IN-3*
Blue Creek (Township)—
 Paulding *OH-3*
Blue Earth (City)—Faribault......... *MN-3*

919

General Index — American Places Dictionary

Blue Earth City (Township)—
Faribault MN-3
Blue Earth County MN-3
Blue Eye (Town)—Carroll AR-2
Blue Eye (Town)—Stone MO-3
Bluefield (Town)—Tazewell VA-2
Bluefield (City)—Mercer WV-2
Blue Grass (City)—Scott IA-3
Bluegrass Region (KY) Geog-4
Blue Hill (Township)—Mitchell KS-4
Blue Hill (Town)—Hancock ME-1
Blue Hill (Township)—
Sherburne MN-3
Blue Hill (City)—Webster NE-4
Blue Hill (Township)—McLean ND-4
Blue Hills (CDP)—Hartford CT-1
Blue Island (City)—Cook IL-3
Bluejacket (Town)—Craig OK-2
Blue Lake (City)—Humboldt CA-4
Blue Lake (Township)—Kalkaska .. MI-3
Blue Lake (Township)—
Muskegon MI-3
Blue Lake Rancheria (CA) IndRes-4
Blue Mound (Township)—Macon ... IL-3
Blue Mound (Village)—Macon IL-3
Blue Mound (Township)—
McLean IL-3
Blue Mound (City)—Linn KS-4
Blue Mound (Township)—Linn KS-4
Blue Mound (Township)—
Livingston MO-3
Blue Mound (Township)—
Vernon MO-3
Blue Mound (City)—Tarrant TX-2
Blue Mounds (Township)—Pope .. MN-3
Blue Mounds (Town)—Dane WI-3
Blue Mounds (Village)—Dane WI-3
Blue Mountain (Town)—Calhoun ... AL-2
Blue Mountain (Town)—Logan AR-2
Blue Mountain (Town)—Tippah MS-2
Blue Point (CDP)—Suffolk NY-1
Blue Rapids (City)—Marshall KS-4
Blue Rapids (Township)—
Marshall KS-4
Blue Rapids City (Township)—
Marshall KS-4
Blue Ridge (Division)—Elmore AL-2
Blue Ridge (City)—Fannin GA-2
Blue Ridge (Township)—Piatt IL-3
Blue Ridge (Township)—
Williams ND-4
Blue Ridge (Town)—Collin TX-2
Blue Ridge (CDP)—Botetourt VA-2
Blue Ridge Manor (City)—
Jefferson KY-2
Blue Ridge Mountains (KY) Geog-4
Blue River (Town)—Summit CO-4
Blue River (Township)—Hancock .. IN-3
Blue River (Township)—Harrison .. IN-3
Blue River (Township)—Henry IN-3
Blue River (Township)—Johnson ... IN-3
Blue River (Village)—Grant WI-3
Blue Rock (Township)—
Muskingum OH-3
Blue Springs (Town)—Barbour AL-2
Blue Springs (Village)—Union MS-2
Blue Springs (City)—Jackson MO-3
Blue Springs (City)—Gage NE-4
Blue Springs-Wymore (Township)—
Gage NE-4
Blue Valley (Township)—
Pottawatomie KS-4
Bluewater (CDP)—La Paz AZ-4
Bluewater (CDP)—San
Bernardino CA-4

Bluff (Township)—Sumner KS-4
Bluff (Town)—Nevada AR-2
Bluff City (City)—Harper KS-4
Bluff City (City)—Sullivan TN-2
Bluffdale (Township)—Greene IL-3
Bluffdale (City)—Salt Lake UT-4
Bluffs (Village)—Scott IL-3
Bluff Springs (Township)—Cass IL-3
Bluffton (Town)—Clay GA-2
Bluffton (City)—Wells IN-3
Bluffton (City)—Otter Tail MN-3
Bluffton (Township)—Otter Tail ... MN-3
Bluffton (Village)—Allen OH-3
Bluffton (Village)—Hancock OH-3
Bluffton (Town)—Beaufort SC-2
Bluford (Village)—Jefferson IL-3
Blum (Town)—Hill TX-2
Blumfield (Township)—Saginaw ... MI-3
Blunt (City)—Hughes SD-4
Blythe (City)—Riverside CA-4
Blythe (Town)—Burke GA-2
Blythe (Town)—Richmond GA-2
Blythe (Township)—Schuylkill PA-1
Blythedale (Village)—Harrison MO-3
Blytheville (City)—Mississippi AR-2
Blythewood (Town)—Richland SC-2
Boalsburg (CDP)—Centre PA-1
Boardman (Township)—Kalkaska . MI-3
Boardman (Township)—
Mahoning OH-3
Boardman (City)—Morrow OR-4
Boaz (City)—Etowah AL-2
Boaz (City)—Marshall AL-2
Boaz (CDP)—Wood WV-2
Boaz (Village)—Richland WI-3
Boca Del Mar (CDP)—Palm
Beach FL-2
Boca Pointe (CDP)—Palm Beach .. FL-2
Boca Raton (City)—Palm Beach ... FL-2
Boca West (CDP)—Palm Beach FL-2
Bock (City)—Mille Lacs MN-3
Bodcaw (Town)—Nevada AR-2
Bode (City)—Humboldt IA-3
Bodega Bay (CDP)—Sonoma CA-4
Bodfish (CDP)—Kern CA-4
Boerne (City)—Kendall TX-2
Boeuf (Township)—Franklin MO-3
Boeuf (Township)—Gasconade MO-3
Bogalusa (City)—Washington
Parish LA-2
Bogard (Township)—Daviess IN-3
Bogard (City)—Carroll MO-3
Bogard (Township)—Henry MO-3
Bogart (Town)—Clarke GA-2
Bogart (Town)—Oconee GA-2
Bogata (Town)—Red River TX-2
Boger City (CDP)—Lincoln NC-2
Boggs (Township)—Armstrong PA-1
Boggs (Township)—Centre PA-1
Boggs (Township)—Clearfield PA-1
Bogle (Township)—Gentry MO-3
Bogota (Borough)—Bergen NJ-1
Bogue (City)—Graham KS-4
Bogue Chitto (CDP)—Kemper MS-2
Bogue Chitto (CDP)—Neshoba MS-2
Bogus Brook (Township)—Mille
Lacs MN-3
Bohemia (Township)—
Ontonagon MI-3
Bohemia (Township)—Knox NE-4
Bohemia (Township)—Saunders ... NE-4
Bohemia (CDP)—Suffolk NY-1
Bohners Lake (CDP)—Racine WI-3
Bohnsack (Township)—Traill ND-4

Boiling Spring Lakes (City)—
Brunswick NC-2
Boiling Springs (Town)—
Cleveland NC-2
Boiling Springs (CDP)—
Cumberland PA-1
Boiling Springs (CDP)—
Spartanburg SC-2
Bois Blanc (Township)—
Mackinac MI-3
Bois Brule (Township)—Perry MO-3
Bois D'Arc (Township)—
Montgomery IL-3
Boise (City)—Ada ID-4
Boise City (City)—Cimarron OK-2
Boise County ID-4
Bois Forte (Nett Lake) (MN) IndRes-4
Bokchito (Town)—Bryan OK-2
Bokes Creek (Township)—Logan .. OH-3
Bokoshe (Town)—Le Flore OK-2
Bolckow (Town)—Andrew MO-3
Boles (Township)—Franklin MO-3
Boles Acres (CDP)—Otero NM-2
Boley (Town)—Okfuskee OK-2
Boligee (Town)—Greene AL-2
Bolinas (CDP)—Marin CA-4
Bolindale (CDP)—Trumbull OH-3
Bolingbrook (Village)—DuPage IL-3
Bolingbrook (Village)—Will IL-3
Boling-Iago (CDP)—Wharton TX-2
Bolivar (Township)—Benton IN-3
Bolivar (City)—Polk MO-3
Bolivar (Town)—Allegany NY-1
Bolivar (Village)—Allegany NY-1
Bolivar (Village)—Tuscarawas OH-3
Bolivar (Borough)—
Westmoreland PA-1
Bolivar (City)—Hardeman TN-2
Bolivar (Town)—Jefferson WV-2
Bolivar County MS-2
Bolivia (Town)—Brunswick NC-2
Bolling Air Force Base (DC) Mil-4
Bollinger County MO-3
Bolo (Township)—Washington IL-3
Bolton (Town)—Tolland CT-1
Bolton (Township)—Cowley KS-4
Bolton (Town)—Worcester MA-1
Bolton (Town)—Hinds MS-2
Bolton (Town)—Warren NY-1
Bolton (Town)—Columbus NC-2
Bolton (Town)—Chittenden VT-1
Bombay (Town)—Franklin NY-1
Bona, Mt. (AK) Geog-4
Bonadelle Ranchos-Madera Ranchos
(CDP)—Madera CA-4
Bon Air (Town)—Talladega AL-2
Bon Air (CDP)—Chesterfield VA-2
Bonanza (Town)—Sebastian AR-2
Bonanza (CDP)—Clayton GA-2
Bonanza (Town)—Klamath OR-4
Bonanza City (Town)—Saguache . CO-4
Bonaparte (City)—Van Buren IA-3
Bonaville (Township)—
McPherson KS-4
Bond (Township)—Lawrence IL-3
Bond County IL-3
Bondin (Township)—Murray MN-3
Bondsville (CDP)—Hampden MA-1
Bondsville (CDP)—Hampshire MA-1
Bonduel (Village)—Shawano WI-3
Bondurant (City)—Polk IA-3
Bondville (Village)—Champaign .. IL-3
Bone Creek (Township)—Butler ... NE-4
Bone Gap (Village)—Edwards IL-3
Bone Lake (Town)—Polk WI-3

American Places Dictionary General Index

Bonesteel (City)—Gregory *SD-4*
Bonetraill (Township)—Williams... *ND-4*
Bonfield (Village)—Kankakee *IL-3*
Bonham (City)—Fannin *TX-2*
Bonhomme (Township)—St.
 Louis *MO-3*
Bon Homme County *SD-4*
Bonifay (City)—Holmes *FL-2*
Bonilla (Township)—Beadle *SD-4*
Bonita (CDP)—San Diego *CA-4*
Bonita (Village)—Morehouse
 Parish *LA-2*
Bonita Springs (CDP)—Lee *FL-2*
Bonneau (Town)—Berkeley *SC-2*
Bonneauville (Borough)—Adams.... *PA-1*
Bonne Femme (Township)—
 Howard *MO-3*
Bonner County *ID-4*
Bonners Ferry (City)—Boundary *ID-4*
Bonner Springs (City)—Johnson.... *KS-4*
Bonner Springs (City)—
 Wyandotte *KS-4*
Bonner-West Riverside (CDP)—
 Missoula *MT-4*
Bonne Terre (City)—St.
 Francois *MO-3*
Bonneville County *ID-4*
Bonneville Dam (AK) *Geog-4*
Bonneville Salt Flats (UT) *Geog-4*
Bonney (Village)—Brazoria............ *TX-2*
Bonney Lake (City)—Pierce........... *WA-4*
Bonnie (Village)—Jefferson............. *IL-3*
Bonnie Doone (CDP)—
 Cumberland *NC-2*
Bonnieville (City)—Hart *KY-2*
Bono (Town)—Craighead............... *AR-2*
Bono (Township)—Lawrence *IN-3*
Bonpas (Township)—Richland *IL-3*
Bonsall (CDP)—San Diego *CA-4*
Bon Secour Bay (AL) *Geog-4*
Bonus (Township)—Boone *IL-3*
Booker (Town)—Lipscomb *TX-2*
Booker (Town)—Ochiltree *TX-2*
Boon (Township)—Warrick *IN-3*
Boon (Township)—Wexford *MI-3*
Boone (Town)—Pueblo *CO-4*
Boone (Township)—Boone *IL-3*
Boone (Township)—Cass *IN-3*
Boone (Township)—Crawford *IN-3*
Boone (Township)—Dubois *IN-3*
Boone (Township)—Harrison *IN-3*
Boone (Township)—Madison......... *IN-3*
Boone (Township)—Porter *IN-3*
Boone (City)—Boone *IA-3*
Boone (Township)—Crawford *MO-3*
Boone (Township)—Douglas......... *MO-3*
Boone (Township)—Franklin........ *MO-3*
Boone (Township)—Maries........... *MO-3*
Boone (Township)—St. Charles *MO-3*
Boone (Township)—Texas............. *MO-3*
Boone (Township)—Wright........... *MO-3*
Boone (Town)—Watauga................ *NC-2*
Boone (Township)—Sheridan *ND-4*
Boone County *AR-2*
Boone County *IL-3*
Boone County *IN-3*
Boone County *IA-3*
Boone County *KY-2*
Boone County *MO-3*
Boone County *NE-4*
Boone County *WV-2*
Boone No. 1 (Township)—
 Greene *MO-3*
Boone No. 2 (Township)—
 Greene *MO-3*

Boones Mill (Town)—Franklin *VA-2*
Booneville (City)—Logan *AR-2*
Booneville (City)—Owsley *KY-2*
Booneville (City)—Prentiss *MS-2*
Boon Lake (Township)—
 Renville *MN-3*
Boonsboro (Town)—Washington .. *MD-1*
Boons Lick (Township)—
 Howard *MO-3*
Boonton (Town)—Morris *NJ-1*
Boonton (Township)—Morris *NJ-1*
Boonville (City)—Warrick............... *IN-3*
Boonville (City)—Cooper *MO-3*
Boonville (Township)—Cooper ... *MO-3*
Boonville (Town)—Oneida *NY-1*
Boonville (Village)—Oneida *NY-1*
Boonville (Town)—Yadkin *NC-2*
Boothbay (Town)—Lincoln *ME-1*
Boothbay Harbor (Town)—
 Lincoln *ME-1*
Boothville-Venice (CDP)—Plaquemines
 Parish *LA-2*
Boothwyn (CDP)—Delaware *PA-1*
Bootjack (CDP)—Mariposa *CA-4*
Borah Peak (ID)....................... *Geog-4*
Borden County *TX-2*
Bordentown (City)—Burlington *NJ-1*
Bordentown (Township)—
 Burlington *NJ-1*
Border (Township)—Divide.......... *ND-4*
Bordulac (Township)—Foster....... *ND-4*
Borger (City)—Hutchinson *TX-2*
Borgholm (Township)—Mille
 Lacs *MN-3*
Boron (CDP)—Kern....................... *CA-4*
Borrego Springs (CDP)—San
 Diego *CA-4*
Borup (City)—Norman *MN-3*
Boscawen (Town)—Merrimack *NH-1*
Boscobel (City)—Grant *WI-3*
Boscobel (Town)—Grant *WI-3*
Bosque County *TX-2*
Bosque Farms (Village)—
 Valencia...................................... *NM-4*
Bossier City (City)—Bossier
 Parish *LA-2*
Bossier Parish *LA-2*
Bossko (Township)—Roberts *SD-4*
Bostic (Town)—Rutherford *NC-2*
Boston (City)—Thomas.................. *GA-2*
Boston (Town)—Wayne *IN-3*
Boston (Township)—Wayne *IN-3*
Boston (City)—Suffolk *MA-1*
Boston (Township)—Ionia *MI-3*
Boston (Town)—Erie *NY-1*
Boston (Township)—Summit *OH-3*
Boston Heights (Village)—
 Summit *OH-3*
Bostonia (CDP)—San Diego.......... *CA-4*
Boston Mountains (AR) *Geog-4*
Bostwick (Town)—Morgan *GA-2*
Boswell (Town)—Benton *IN-3*
Boswell (Town)—Choctaw *OK-2*
Boswell (Borough)—Somerset *PA-1*
Bosworth (City)—Carroll *MO-3*
Botetourt County *VA-2*
Bothell (City)—King *WA-4*
Bothell (City)—Snohomish *WA-4*
Botkins (Village)—Shelby.............. *OH-3*
Bottineau (City)—Bottineau *ND-4*
Bottineau County *ND-4*
Boulder (City)—Boulder *CO-4*
Boulder (Town)—Jefferson *MT-4*
Boulder (Town)—Garfield............. *UT-4*
Boulder City (City)—Clark *NV-4*

Boulder County............................... *CO-4*
Boulder Creek (CDP)—Santa
 Cruz *CA-4*
Boulder Dam (AR) *Geog-4*
Boulder Hill (CDP)—Kendall......... *IL-3*
Boulder Junction (Town)—Vilas.... *WI-3*
Boulware (Township)—
 Gasconade.................................. *MO-3*
Boundary County *ID-4*
Boundary Peak (NV) *Geog-4*
Bound Brook (Borough)—
 Somerset...................................... *NJ-1*
Bountiful (City)—Davis *UT-4*
Bourbois (Township)—
 Gasconade.................................. *MO-3*
Bourbon (Township)—Douglas....... *IL-3*
Bourbon (Town)—Marshall............ *IN-3*
Bourbon (Township)—Marshall...... *IN-3*
Bourbon (Township)—Boone *MO-3*
Bourbon (Township)—Callaway ... *MO-3*
Bourbon (City)—Crawford *MO-3*
Bourbon (Township)—Knox *MO-3*
Bourbon County............................. *KS-4*
Bourbon County *KY-2*
Bourbonnais (Town)—Kankakee *IL-3*
Bourbonnais (Township)—
 Kankakee *IL-3*
Bourne (Town)—Barnstable *MA-1*
Bourret (Township)—Gladwin........ *MI-3*
Bouton (City)—Dallas.................... *IA-3*
Boutte (CDP)—St. Charles
 Parish *LA-2*
Bovey (City)—Itasca *MN-3*
Bovill (City)—Latah *ID-4*
Bovina (Town)—Delaware *NY-1*
Bovina (City)—Parmer.................. *TX-2*
Bovina (Town)—Outagamie *WI-3*
Bow (Town)—Merrimack................ *NH-1*
Bowbells (City)—Burke *ND-4*
Bowbells (Township)—Burke *ND-4*
Bow Creek (Township)—Phillips ...*KS-4*
Bowcreek (Township)—Sheridan ... *KS-4*
Bowdle (City)—Edmunds *SD-4*
Bowdle (Township)—Edmunds...... *SD-4*
Bowdoin (Town)—Sagadahoc *ME-1*
Bowdoinham (Town)—
 Sagadahoc *ME-1*
Bowdon (City)—Carroll *GA-2*
Bowdon (City)—Wells *ND-4*
Bowdre (Township)—Douglas......... *IL-3*
Bowen (Village)—Hancock *IL-3*
Bowen (Township)—Sargent *ND-4*
Bowerbank (Town)—Piscataquis .. *ME-1*
Bowers (Town)—Kent *DE-1*
Bowerston (Village)—Harrison *OH-3*
Bowersville (Town)—Hart............. *GA-2*
Bowersville (Village)—Greene *OH-3*
Bowie (City)—Prince George's *MD-1*
Bowie (City)—Montague *TX-2*
Bowie County *TX-2*
Bowlan (Township)—Shannon...... *MO-3*
Bowlegs (Town)—Seminole............ *OK-2*
Bowler (Village)—Shawano............ *WI-3*
Bowlesville (Township)—Gallatin... *IL-3*
Bowleys Quarters (CDP)—
 Baltimore...................................*MD-1*
Bowling (Township)—Rock Island . *IL-3*
Bowling Green (City)—Hardee...... *FL-2*
Bowling Green (Township)—
 Fayette.. *IL-3*
Bowling Green (City)—Warren *KY-2*
Bowling Green (Township)—
 Chariton *MO-3*
Bowling Green (Township)—
 Pettis *MO-3*

921

General Index American Places Dictionary

Bowling Green (City)—Pike MO-3
Bowling Green (Township)—
  Licking OH-3
Bowling Green (Township)—
  Marion OH-3
Bowling Green (City)—Wood OH-3
Bowling Green (Town)—Caroline... VA-2
Bowlus (City)—Morrison MN-3
Bowman (City)—Elbert GA-2
Bowman (Township)—Sullivan...... MO-3
Bowman (City)—Bowman............... ND-4
Bowman (Township)—Bowman...... ND-4
Bowman (Town)—Orangeburg....... SC-2
Bowman County ND-4
Bowmanstown (Borough)—
  Carbon PA-1
Bow Mar (Town)—Arapahoe CO-4
Bow Mar (Town)—Jefferson CO-4
Bowne (Township)—Kent MI-3
Bowstring (Township)—Itasca MN-3
Bowstring Lake (Pop. Place)—
  Itasca MN-3
Box (Township)—Cedar MO-3
Boxborough (Town)—Middlesex .. MA-1
Box Butte County NE-4
Box Elder (City)—Pennington SD-4
Box Elder County UT-4
Boxford (Town)—Essex MA-1
Boxholm (City)—Boone IA-3
Boxville (Township)—Marshall...... MN-3
Boyce (Town)—Rapides Parish..... LA-2
Boyce (Town)—Clarke VA-2
Boyceville (Village)—Dunn WI-3
Boyd (City)—Lac qui Parle............ MN-3
Boyd (Township)—Burleigh ND-4
Boyd (Town)—Wise TX-2
Boyd (Village)—Chippewa WI-3
Boyd County KY-2
Boyd County NE-4
Boyden (City)—Sioux IA-3
Boydton (Town)—Mecklenburg...... VA-2
Boyertown (Borough)—Berks........ PA-1
Boyesen (Township)—Bowman..... ND-4
Boyes Hot Springs (CDP)—
  Sonoma CA-4
Boykins (Town)—Southampton VA-2
Boy Lake (Township)—Cass MN-3
Boyle (Town)—Bolivar MS-2
Boyle County KY-2
Boylston (Town)—Worcester......... MA-1
Boylston (Town)—Oswego NY-1
Boyne City (City)—Charlevoix MI-3
Boyne Falls (Village)—
  Charlevoix MI-3
Boyne Valley (Township)—
  Charlevoix MI-3
Boynton (Township)—Tazewell IL-3
Boynton (Town)—Muskogee OK-2
Boynton Beach (City)—Palm
  Beach FL-2
Boy River (City)—Cass MN-3
Boy River (Township)—Cass MN-3
Boys Town (Village)—Douglas NE-4
Bozeman (City)—Gallatin.............. MT-4
Bozrah (Town)—New London CT-1
Braceville (Township)—Grundy IL-3
Braceville (Village)—Grundy IL-3
Braceville (Township)—
  Trumbull OH-3
Bracken County KY-2
Brackenridge (Borough)—
  Allegheny................................. PA-1
Brackettville (City)—Kinney TX-2
Bradbury (City)—Los Angeles CA-4

Bradbury (Township)—Mille
  Lacs MN-3
Braddock (City)—Emmons............ ND-4
Braddock (Borough)—Allegheny... PA-1
Braddock Heights (CDP)—
  Frederick MD-1
Braddock Hills (Borough)—
  Allegheny PA-1
Braddyville (City)—Page................ IA-3
Braden (City)—Fayette................... TN-2
Bradenton (City)—Manatee FL-2
Bradenton Beach (City)—
  Manatee FL-2
Bradford (City)—White................... AR-2
Bradford (Township)—Lee............. IL-3
Bradford (Town)—Stark................. IL-3
Bradford (Town)—Penobscot........ ME-1
Bradford (Township)—Isanti MN-3
Bradford (Township)—Wilkin MN-3
Bradford (Town)—Merrimack NH-1
Bradford (Town)—Steuben NY-1
Bradford (Village)—Darke OH-3
Bradford (Village)—Miami OH-3
Bradford (Township)—Clearfield... PA-1
Bradford (City)—McKean PA-1
Bradford (Township)—McKean..... PA-1
Bradford (CDP)—Washington RI-1
Bradford (Town)—Gibson TN-2
Bradford (Town)—Orange VT-1
Bradford (Village)—Orange VT-1
Bradford (Town)—Rock WI-3
Bradford County FL-2
Bradford County PA-1
Bradfordsville (City)—Marion KY-2
Bradfordwoods (Borough)—
  Allegheny PA-1
Bradgate (City)—Humboldt........... IA-3
Bradley (City)—Lafayette.............. AR-2
Bradley (Township)—Jackson IL-3
Bradley (Village)—Kankakee IL-3
Bradley (Town)—Penobscot......... ME-1
Bradley (Town)—Grady OK-2
Bradley (Town)—Clark................... SD-4
Bradley (CDP)—Raleigh WV-2
Bradley (Town)—Lincoln WI-3
Bradley Beach (Borough)—
  Monmouth NJ-1
Bradley County AR-2
Bradley County TN-2
Bradner (Village)—Wood............... OH-3
Bradshaw (Village)—York NE-4
Bradshaw (Town)—McDowell WV-2
Brady (Township)—Kalamazoo..... MI-3
Brady (Township)—Saginaw MI-3
Brady (Village)—Lincoln................ NE-4
Brady (Township)—Williams OH-3
Brady (Township)—Butler PA-1
Brady (Township)—Clarion PA-1
Brady (Township)—Clearfield....... PA-1
Brady (Township)—Huntingdon ... PA-1
Brady (Township)—Lycoming PA-1
Brady (City)—McCulloch............... TX-2
Brady Lake (Village)—Portage...... OH-3
Bradys Bend (Township)—
  Armstrong PA-1
Braggadocio (Township)—
  Pemiscot MO-3
Bragg City (Town)—Pemiscot....... MO-3
Braggs (Town)—Muskogee OK-2
Braham (City)—Isanti MN-3
Braham (Town)—Kanabec MN-3
Braidwood (City)—Will IL-3
Brainard (Village)—Butler NE-4
Brainard (Township)—Brown SD-4
Brainerd (City)—Crow Wing MN-3

Braintree (Town)—Norfolk MA-1
Braintree (Town)—Orange VT-1
Braintrim (Township)—Wyoming .. PA-1
Braman (Town)—Kay OK-2
Brampton (Township)—Delta MI-3
Brampton (Township)—Sargent..... ND-4
Bramwell (Town)—Mercer WV-2
Branch (City)—Franklin................. AR-2
Branch (Township)—Mason MI-3
Branch (City)—Chisago MN-3
Branch (Township)—Schuylkill..... PA-1
Branchburg (Township)—
  Somerset NJ-1
Branch County MI-3
Branchville (Town)—St. Clair....... AL-2
Branchville (Borough)—Sussex ... NJ-1
Branchville (Town)—Orangeburg... SC-2
Branchville (Town)—
  Southampton VA-2
Brandenburg (City)—Meade KY-2
Brandenburg (Township)—
  Richland ND-4
Brander (Township)—Bottineau.... ND-4
Brandon (CDP)—Hillsborough...... FL-2
Brandon (City)—Buchanan........... IA-3
Brandon (Township)—Oakland MI-3
Brandon (City)—Douglas MN-3
Brandon (Township)—Douglas MN-3
Brandon (City)—Rankin MS-2
Brandon (Town)—Franklin NY-1
Brandon (Township)—Renville..... ND-4
Brandon (City)—Minnehaha SD-4
Brandon (Township)—
  Minnehaha SD-4
Brandon (Town)—Rutland VT-1
Brandon (Village)—Fond du Lac... WI-3
Brandonville (Town)—Preston...... WV-2
Brandrup (Township)—Wilkin MN-3
Brandsville (City)—Howell MO-3
Brandsvold (Township)—Polk MN-3
Brandt (Township)—Polk MN-3
Brandt (Town)—Deuel SD-4
Brandt (Township)—Deuel SD-4
Brandywine (Township)—
  Hancock IN-3
Brandywine (Township)—Shelby.... IN-3
Brandywine (CDP)—Prince
  George's MD-1
Branford (Town)—New Haven CT-1
Branford (Town)—Suwannee FL-2
Branson (Town)—Las Animas CO-4
Branson (City)—Taney MO-3
Branson (Township)—Taney MO-3
Brant (Township)—Saginaw MI-3
Brant (Town)—Erie NY-1
Brantford (Township)—
  Washington KS-4
Brantford (Township)—Hamlin..... SD-4
Brantley (Town)—Crenshaw AL-2
Brantley County GA-2
Braselton (Town)—Barrow GA-2
Braselton (Town)—Gwinnett GA-2
Braselton (Town)—Jackson GA-2
Brashear (City)—Adair MO-3
Brasher (Town)—St. Lawrence NY-1
Brasher Falls-Winthrop (CDP)—St.
  Lawrence NY-1
Brass Castle (CDP)—Warren NJ-1
Brasstown Bald (GA) Geog-4
Braswell (City)—Paulding............ GA-2
Braswell (City)—Polk GA-2
Bratenahl (Village)—Cuyahoga.... OH-3
Brattleboro (Town)—Windham VT-1
Bratton (Township)—Adams......... OH-3
Bratton (Township)—Mifflin PA-1

Brawley (City)—Imperial *CA-4*
Braxton (Village)—Simpson *MS-2*
Braxton County *WV-2*
Bray (Township)—Pennington *MN-3*
Bray (Town)—Stephens *OK-2*
Braymer (City)—Caldwell *MO-3*
Brayton (City)—Audubon *IA-3*
Brazeau (Township)—Perry *MO-3*
Brazeau (Town)—Oconto *WI-3*
Brazil (City)—Clay *IN-3*
Brazil (Township)—Clay *IN-3*
Brazoria (City)—Brazoria *TX-2*
Brazoria County *TX-2*
Brazos County *TX-2*
Brazos River (TX) *Geog-4*
Brea (City)—Orange *CA-4*
Breathitt County *KY-2*
Breaux Bridge (City)—St. Martin
 Parish *LA-2*
Breckenridge (Town)—Summit *CO-4*
Breckenridge (Village)—Gratiot ... *MI-3*
Breckenridge (City)—Wilkin *MN-3*
Breckenridge (Township)—
 Wilkin *MN-3*
Breckenridge (City)—Caldwell *MO-3*
Breckenridge (Township)—
 Caldwell *MO-3*
Breckenridge (Town)—Garfield *OK-2*
Breckenridge (City)—Stephens *TX-2*
Breckenridge Hills (Village)—St.
 Louis *MO-3*
Breckinridge Center (CDP)—
 Union *KY-2*
Breckinridge County *KY-2*
Brecknock (Township)—Berks *PA-1*
Brecknock (Township)—Lancaster . *PA-1*
Brecksville (City)—Cuyahoga *OH-3*
Breda (City)—Carroll *IA-3*
Breed (Town)—Oconto *WI-3*
Breedsville (Village)—Van Buren .. *MI-3*
Breen (Township)—Dickinson *MI-3*
Breese (City)—Clinton *IL-3*
Breese (Township)—Clinton *IL-3*
Breezy Point (City)—Crow
 Wing *MN-3*
Breitung (Township)—Dickinson ... *MI-3*
Breitung (Township)—St. Louis *MN-3*
Bremen (City)—Carroll *GA-2*
Bremen (City)—Haralson *GA-2*
Bremen (Township)—Cook *IL-3*
Bremen (Town)—Marshall *IN-3*
Bremen (City)—Muhlenberg *KY-2*
Bremen (Town)—Lincoln *ME-1*
Bremen (Township)—Pine *MN-3*
Bremen (Township)—Wells *ND-4*
Bremen (Village)—Fairfield *OH-3*
Bremer County *IA-3*
Bremerton (City)—Kitsap *WA-4*
Bremond (City)—Robertson *TX-2*
Brenham (City)—Washington *TX-2*
Brenna (Township)—Grand
 Forks *ND-4*
Brent (City)—Bibb *AL-2*
Brent (CDP)—Escambia *FL-2*
Brentford (Township)—Spink *SD-4*
Brenton (Township)—Ford *IL-3*
Brentwood (City)—Contra Costa ... *CA-4*
Brentwood (Town)—Prince
 George's *MD-1*
Brentwood (City)—St. Louis *MO-3*
Brentwood (Town)—
 Rockingham *NH-1*
Brentwood (CDP)—Suffolk *NY-1*
Brentwood (CDP)—Jefferson *OH-3*
Brentwood (Borough)—Allegheny .. *PA-1*

Brentwood (City)—Williamson *TN-2*
Bressler-Enhaut-Oberlin (CDP)—
 Dauphin *PA-1*
Breton (Township)—Washington .. *MO-3*
Breton Sound (LA) *Geog-4*
Brevard (City)—Transylvania *NC-2*
Brevard County *FL-2*
Brevator (Township)—St. Louis ... *MN-3*
Brevig Mission (City)—Nome Census
 Area *AK-4*
Brevort (Township)—Mackinac *MI-3*
Brewer (City)—Penobscot *ME-1*
Brewerton (CDP)—Onondaga *NY-1*
Brewerton (CDP)—Oswego *NY-1*
Brewster (City)—Thomas *KS-4*
Brewster (Town)—Barnstable *MA-1*
Brewster (City)—Nobles *MN-3*
Brewster (Village)—Blaine *NE-4*
Brewster (Village)—Putnam *NY-1*
Brewster (Village)—Stark *OH-3*
Brewster (City)—Okanogan *WA-4*
Brewster County *TX-2*
Brewster Hill (CDP)—Putnam *NY-1*
Brewton (City)—Escambia *AL-2*
Brian Head (Town)—Iron *UT-4*
Briar (CDP)—Parker *TX-2*
Briar (CDP)—Tarrant *TX-2*
Briar (CDP)—Wise *TX-2*
Briarcliff (Village)—Travis *TX-2*
Briarcliffe Acres (Town)—Horry *SC-2*
Briarcliff Manor (Village)—
 Westchester *NY-1*
Briar Creek (Borough)—
 Columbia *PA-1*
Briar Creek (Township)—
 Columbia *PA-1*
Briaroaks (City)—Johnson *TX-2*
Briarwood (City)—Jefferson *KY-2*
Briarwood (City)—Cass *ND-4*
Briarwood Beach (Village)—
 Medina *OH-3*
Brice (Village)—Franklin *OH-3*
Bricelyn (City)—Faribault *MN-3*
Brice Prairie (CDP)—La Crosse *WI-3*
Brick (Township)—Ocean *NJ-1*
Brickerville (CDP)—Lancaster *PA-1*
Bridalveil Fall (CA) *Geog-4*
Bridge City (CDP)—Jefferson
 Parish *LA-2*
Bridge City (City)—Orange *TX-2*
Bridge Creek (Town)—Eau
 Claire *WI-3*
Bridgehampton (Township)—
 Sanilac *MI-3*
Bridgehampton (CDP)—Suffolk ... *NY-1*
Bridgeport (City)—Jackson *AL-2*
Bridgeport (CDP)—Mono *CA-4*
Bridgeport (City)—Fairfield *CT-1*
Bridgeport (City)—Lawrence *IL-3*
Bridgeport (Township)—Lawrence . *IL-3*
Bridgeport (CDP)—Washington ... *MD-1*
Bridgeport (Township)—Saginaw .. *MI-3*
Bridgeport (Township)—Warren ... *MO-3*
Bridgeport (City)—Morrill *NE-4*
Bridgeport (CDP)—Madison *NY-1*
Bridgeport (CDP)—Onondaga *NY-1*
Bridgeport (Village)—Belmont *OH-3*
Bridgeport (City)—Caddo *OK-2*
Bridgeport (Borough)—
 Montgomery *PA-1*
Bridgeport (City)—Wise *TX-2*
Bridgeport (Town)—Douglas *WA-4*
Bridgeport (City)—Harrison *WV-2*
Bridgeport (Town)—Crawford *WI-3*
Bridgeport Colony (CA) *IndRes-4*

Bridger (Town)—Carbon *MT-4*
Bridges (Township)—Ozark *MO-3*
Bridgeton (Township)—Newaygo .. *MI-3*
Bridgeton (City)—St. Louis *MO-3*
Bridgeton (City)—Cumberland *NJ-1*
Bridgeton (Town)—Craven *NC-2*
Bridgeton (Township)—Bucks *PA-1*
Bridgetown North (CDP)—
 Hamilton *OH-3*
Bridgeview (Village)—Cook *IL-3*
Bridgeville (Town)—Sussex *DE-1*
Bridgeville (Borough)—Allegheny ... *PA-1*
Bridgewater (Town)—Litchfield *CT-1*
Bridgewater (City)—Adair *IA-3*
Bridgewater (Town)—Aroostook ... *ME-1*
Bridgewater (Town)—Plymouth *MA-1*
Bridgewater (Township)—
 Washtenaw *MI-3*
Bridgewater (Township)—Rice *MN-3*
Bridgewater (Town)—Grafton *NH-1*
Bridgewater (Township)—
 Somerset *NJ-1*
Bridgewater (Town)—Oneida *NY-1*
Bridgewater (Village)—Oneida *NY-1*
Bridgewater (Township)—
 Williams *OH-3*
Bridgewater (Borough)—Beaver *PA-1*
Bridgewater (Township)—
 Susquehanna *PA-1*
Bridgewater (City)—McCook *SD-4*
Bridgewater (Township)—
 McCook *SD-4*
Bridgewater (Town)—Windsor *VT-1*
Bridgewater (Town)—
 Rockingham *VA-2*
Bridgman (City)—Berrien *MI-3*
Bridgton (Town)—Cumberland *ME-1*
Bridport (Town)—Addison *VT-1*
Brielle (Borough)—Monmouth *NJ-1*
Brier (City)—Snohomish *WA-4*
Brigantine (City)—Atlantic *NJ-1*
Brigham (Town)—Iowa *WI-3*
Brigham City (City)—Box Elder *UT-4*
Bright (CDP)—Dearborn *IN-3*
Brighton (City)—Jefferson *AL-2*
Brighton (City)—Adams *CO-4*
Brighton (City)—Weld *CO-4*
Brighton (Village)—Jersey *IL-3*
Brighton (Township)—Macoupin ... *IL-3*
Brighton (Village)—Macoupin *IL-3*
Brighton (City)—Washington *IA-3*
Brighton (Pop. Place)—Somerset .. *ME-1*
Brighton (City)—Livingston *MI-3*
Brighton (Township)—Livingston .. *MI-3*
Brighton (Township)—Nicollet *MN-3*
Brighton (Town)—Franklin *NY-1*
Brighton (Town)—Monroe *NY-1*
Brighton (Township)—Lorain *OH-3*
Brighton (Township)—Beaver *PA-1*
Brighton (Town)—Tipton *TN-2*
Brighton (Town)—Essex *VT-1*
Brighton (Town)—Kenosha *WI-3*
Brighton (Town)—Marathon *WI-3*
Brighton Beach—Kings *NY-1*
Brighton Reservation (FL) *IndRes-4*
Brightwaters (Village)—Suffolk *NY-1*
Brightwood (Township)—
 Richland *ND-4*
Briley (Township)—
 Montmorency *MI-3*
Brillian (Township)—Ward *ND-4*
Brilliant (Town)—Marion *AL-2*
Brilliant (Village)—Jefferson *OH-3*
Brillion (City)—Calumet *WI-3*
Brillion (Town)—Calumet *WI-3*

General Index

Brimer (Township)—Barnes............*ND-4*
Brimfield (Township)—Peoria........ *IL-3*
Brimfield (Village)—Peoria............ *IL-3*
Brimfield (Town)—Hampden *MA-1*
Brimfield (Township)—Portage *OH-3*
Brimson (Village)—Grundy *MO-3*
Brinckerhoff (CDP)—Dutchess...... *NY-1*
Brinkley (City)—Monroe *AR-2*
Brinsmade (City)—Benson............ *ND-4*
Brinson (Town)—Decatur *GA-2*
Briny Breezes (Town)—Palm
  Beach...*FL-2*
Brisbane (City)—San Mateo *CA-4*
Brisbin (Borough)—Clearfield *PA-1*
Briscoe County *TX-2*
Brislet (Township)—Polk *MN-3*
Bristol (City)—Hartford *CT-1*
Bristol (City)—Liberty *FL-2*
Bristol (Township)—Kendall........... *IL-3*
Bristol (Town)—Elkhart *IN-3*
Bristol (Town)—Lincoln................. *ME-1*
Bristol (Township)—Fillmore *MN-3*
Bristol (Town)—Grafton *NH-1*
Bristol (Town)—Ontario *NY-1*
Bristol (Township)—Morgan..........*OH-3*
Bristol (Township)—Trumbull *OH-3*
Bristol (Borough)—Bucks............... *PA-1*
Bristol (Township)—Bucks............. *PA-1*
Bristol (Town)—Bristol *RI-1*
Bristol (Township)—Aurora *SD-4*
Bristol (City)—Day......................... *SD-4*
Bristol (Township)—Day................ *SD-4*
Bristol (City)—Sullivan *TN-2*
Bristol (Town)—Addison *VT-1*
Bristol (Village)—Addison *VT-1*
Bristol (Town)—Dane *WI-3*
Bristol (Town)—Kenosha............... *WI-3*
Bristol Bay (AK)............................. *Geog-4*
Bristol Bay Borough........................ *AK-4*
Bristol County *MA-1*
Bristol County *RI-1*
Bristol (Independent City)...............*VA-2*
Bristow (City)—Butler.....................*IA-3*
Bristow (Township)—Boyd *NE-4*
Bristow (Village)—Boyd *NE-4*
Bristow (City)—Creek *OK-2*
Britt (City)—Hancock *IA-3*
Brittany Farms-Highlands (CDP)—
  Bucks.. *PA-1*
Brittian (Township)—Hettinger *ND-4*
Britton (Village)—Lenawee............ *MI-3*
Britton (City)—Marshall................. *SD-4*
Broadalbin (Town)—Fulton............ *NY-1*
Broadalbin (Village)—Fulton.......... *NY-1*
Broad Brook (CDP)—Hartford...... *CT-1*
Broaddus (Town)—San
  Augustine *TX-2*
Broad Fields (City)—Jefferson....... *KY-2*
Broadland (Town)—Beadle *SD-4*
Broadland (Township)—Beadle *SD-4*
Broadlands (Village)—Champaign.. *IL-3*
Broadlawn (Township)—Steele *ND-4*
Broadmoor (CDP)—San Mateo..... *CA-4*
Broadmoor (Township)—Lafayette
  Parish *LA-2*
Broad Top (Township)—Bedford... *PA-1*
Broad Top City (Borough)—
  Huntingdon................................... *PA-1*
Broadus (Town)—Powder River... *MT-4*
Broadview (Residential suburb)—
  Cook.. *IL-3*
Broadview (Town)—Yellowstone .. *MT-4*
Broadview (Township)—Griggs *ND-4*
Broadview Heights (City)—
  Cuyahoga *OH-3*

Broadview Park (CDP)—
  Broward.. *FL-2*
Broadview-Pompano Park (CDP)—
  Broward.. *FL-2*
Broadwater (Village)—Morrill *NE-4*
Broadwater County *MT-4*
Broadway (Town)—Harnett *NC-2*
Broadway (Town)—Lee *NC-2*
Broadway (Town)—Rockingham *VA-2*
Broadwell (Township)—Logan *IL-3*
Broadwell (Village)—Logan *IL-3*
Brock (Village)—Nemaha................ *NE-4*
Brocket (City)—Ramsey..................*ND-4*
Brockport (Village)—Monroe......... *NY-1*
Brockton (City)—Plymouth *MA-1*
Brockton (Town)—Roosevelt *MT-4*
Brockway (Township)—St. Clair.... *MI-3*
Brockway (Township)—Stearns *MN-3*
Brockway (Borough)—Jefferson.... *PA-1*
Brockway (Town)—Jackson *WI-3*
Brocton (Village)—Edgar *IL-3*
Brocton (Village)—Chautauqua *NY-1*
Brodhead (City)—Rockcastle......... *KY-2*
Brodhead (City)—Green *WI-3*
Brodheadsville (CDP)—Monroe *PA-1*
Brodnax (Town)—Brunswick *VA-2*
Brodnax (Town)—Mecklenburg *VA-2*
Broe (Township)—Benson..............*ND-4*
Broeck Pointe (City)—Jefferson *KY-2*
Brogden (CDP)—Wayne *NC-2*
Brokaw (Village)—Marathon *WI-3*
Broken Arrow (City)—Tulsa *OK-2*
Broken Arrow (City)—Wagoner..... *OK-2*
Broken Bow (City)—Custer *NE-4*
Broken Bow (Township)—Custer .. *NE-4*
Broken Bow (City)—McCurtain *OK-2*
Brokenstraw (Township)—Warren.. *PA-1*
Bromide (Town)—Coal *OK-2*
Bromide (Town)—Johnston........... *OK-2*
Bromley (City)—Kenton *KY-2*
Bronaugh (Town)—Vernon *MO-3*
Bronson (Town)—Levy *FL-2*
Bronson (City)—Woodbury............*IA-3*
Bronson (City)—Bourbon *KS-4*
Bronson (City)—Branch *MI-3*
Bronson (Township)—Branch *MI-3*
Bronson (Township)—Huron........*OH-3*
Bronson (City)—Sabine.................. *TX-2*
Bronte (Town)—Coke.................... *TX-2*
Bronwood (Town)—Terrell *GA-2*
Bronx County and Borough............ *NY-1*
Bronxville (Village)—Westchester.. *NY-1*
Brook (Town)—Newton *IN-3*
Brookbank (Township)—
  Mountrail *ND-4*
Brookdale (CDP)—Orangeburg *SC-2*
Brooke County *WV-2*
Brooker (City)—Bradford *FL-2*
Brookeville (Town)—
  Montgomery.................................*MD-1*
Brookfield (Town)—Fairfield *CT-1*
Brookfield (Residential village)—
  Cook.. *IL-3*
Brookfield (Township)—La Salle.... *IL-3*
Brookfield (CDP)—Worcester....... *MA-1*
Brookfield (Township)—Eaton *MI-3*
Brookfield (Township)—Huron *MI-3*
Brookfield (Township)—
  Renville *MN-3*
Brookfield (City)—Linn *MO-3*
Brookfield (Town)—Linn *MO-3*
Brookfield (Town)—Carroll *NH-1*
Brookfield (Town)—Madison......... *NY-1*
Brookfield (Township)—Noble ...*OH-3*

Brookfield (Township)—
  Trumbull *OH-3*
Brookfield (Township)—Tioga......... *PA-1*
Brookfield (Township)—McCook .. *SD-4*
Brookfield (Town)—Orange *VT-1*
Brookfield (City)—Waukesha....... *WI-3*
Brookfield (Town)—Waukesha *WI-3*
Brookford (Town)—Catawba *NC-2*
Brookhaven (City)—Lincoln *MS-2*
Brookhaven (Town)—Suffolk......... *NY-1*
Brookhaven (Borough)—
  Delaware *PA-1*
Brookhaven (CDP)—
  Monongalia *WV-2*
Brooking (Township)—Jackson...... *MO-3*
Brookings (City)—Curry *OR-4*
Brookings (City)—Brookings *SD-4*
Brookings (Township)—
  Brookings.....................................*SD-4*
Brookings County............................ *SD-4*
Brook Lake (Pop. Place)—
  Beltrami *MN-3*
Brookland (Town)—Craighead *AR-2*
Brooklawn (Borough)—Camden *NJ-1*
Brooklet (Town)—Bulloch.............. *GA-2*
Brooklin (Town)—Hancock *ME-1*
Brookline (Town)—Norfolk *MA-1*
Brookline (Township)—Greene...... *MO-3*
Brookline (Village)—Greene *MO-3*
Brookline (Town)—Hillsborough *NH-1*
Brookline (Town)—Windham *VT-1*
Brooklyn (Town)—Windham *CT-1*
Brooklyn (Township)—Lee *IL-3*
Brooklyn (Township)—Schuyler *IL-3*
Brooklyn (Village)—St. Clair *IL-3*
Brooklyn (Town)—Morgan............ *IN-3*
Brooklyn (City)—Poweshiek *IA-3*
Brooklyn (Village)—Jackson *MI-3*
Brooklyn (Borough)—Kings *NY-1*
Brooklyn (Township)—Williams......*ND-4*
Brooklyn (Township)—Cuyahoga ...*OH-3*
Brooklyn (Township)—
  Susquehanna................................. *PA-1*
Brooklyn (Township)—Lincoln...... *SD-4*
Brooklyn (Village)—Dane *WI-3*
Brooklyn (Town)—Green *WI-3*
Brooklyn (Village)—Green *WI-3*
Brooklyn (Town)—Green Lake *WI-3*
Brooklyn (Town)—Washburn........ *WI-3*
Brooklyn Bridge (NY) *Geog-4*
Brooklyn Center (City)—
  Hennepin *MN-3*
Brooklyn Heights (Village)—
  Jasper *MO-3*
Brooklyn Heights—Kings................ *NY-1*
Brooklyn Heights (Village)—
  Cuyahoga *OH-3*
Brooklyn Park (CDP)—Anne
  Arundel *MD-1*
Brooklyn Park (City)—
  Hennepin *MN-3*
Brookneal (Town)—Campbell.........*VA-2*
Brook Park (City)—Pine *MN-3*
Brook Park (Township)—Pine *MN-3*
Brook Park (City)—Cuyahoga *OH-3*
Brookport (City)—Massac............. *IL-3*
Brookridge (CDP)—Hernando........*FL-2*
Brooks (Town)—Fayette................ *GA-2*
Brooks (CDP)—Bullitt *KY-2*
Brooks (Town)—Waldo *ME-1*
Brooks (Township)—Newaygo *MI-3*
Brooks (City)—Red Lake *MN-3*
Brooksburg (Town)—Jefferson........ *IN-3*
Brooks County................................. *GA-2*
Brooks County................................. *TX-2*

Brookshire (City)—Waller *TX-2*
Brookside (Town)—Jefferson *AL-2*
Brookside (Town)—Fremont........*CO-4*
Brookside (CDP)—New Castle *DE-1*
Brookside (Township)—Clinton...... *IL-3*
Brookside (Village)—Belmont........*OH-3*
Brookside Village (City)—
 Brazoria..*TX-2*
Brooks Range (AK)..................... *Geog-4*
Brookston (Town)—White *IN-3*
Brookston (City)—St. Louis.......... *MN-3*
Brooksville (City)—Hernando *FL-2*
Brooksville (City)—Bracken..... *KY-2*
Brooksville (Town)—Hancock *ME-1*
Brooksville (Town)—Noxubee ... *MS-2*
Brooksville (Town)—
 Pottawatomie..............................*OK-2*
Brookview (Town)—Dorchester.... *MD-1*
Brookville (Township)—Ogle *IL-3*
Brookville (Town)—Franklin.......... *IN-3*
Brookville (Township)—Franklin ... *IN-3*
Brookville (City)—Saline *KS-4*
Brookville (Township)—
 Redwood....................................*MN-3*
Brookville (Village)—Nassau *NY-1*
Brookville (Village)—
 Montgomery................................*OH-3*
Brookville (Borough)—Jefferson..... *PA-1*
Brookwood (Town)—Tuscaloosa.....*AL-2*
Broomall (CDP)—Delaware............ *PA-1*
Broome (Town)—Schoharie *NY-1*
Broome County.................................*NY-1*
Broomfield (City)—Adams *CO-4*
Broomfield (City)—Boulder...........*CO-4*
Broomfield (City)—Jefferson *CO-4*
Broomfield (City)—Weld *CO-4*
Broomfield (Township)—Isabella .. *MI-3*
Brooten (City)—Pope..................... *MN-3*
Brooten (City)—Stearns *MN-3*
Brothersfield (Township)—
 Turner *SD-4*
Brothersvalley (Township)—
 Somerset......................................*PA-1*
Brothertown (Town)—Calumet...... *WI-3*
Broughton (Village)—Hamilton *IL-3*
Broughton (Township)—
 Livingston *IL-3*
Broughton (Village)—Paulding *OH-3*
Brouilletts Creek (Township)—
 Edgar *IL-3*
Broussard (Town)—Lafayette
 Parish *LA-2*
Browardale (CDP)—Broward *FL-2*
Broward County................................*FL-2*
Browerville (City)—Todd *MN-3*
Brown (Township)—Champaign..... *IL-3*
Brown (Township)—Hancock *IN-3*
Brown (Township)—Hendricks....... *IN-3*
Brown (Township)—Montgomery... *IN-3*
Brown (Township)—Morgan.......... *IN-3*
Brown (Township)—Ripley............. *IN-3*
Brown (Township)—Washington *IN-3*
Brown (Township)—Manistee......... *MI-3*
Brown (Township)—Douglas *MO-3*
Brown (Township)—McHenry *ND-4*
Brown (Township)—Carroll *OH-3*
Brown (Township)—Darke *OH-3*
Brown (Township)—Delaware *OH-3*
Brown (Township)—Franklin.........*OH-3*
Brown (Township)—Knox *OH-3*
Brown (Township)—Miami *OH-3*
Brown (Township)—Paulding *OH-3*
Brown (Township)—Vinton *OH-3*
Brown (Township)—Lycoming....... *PA-1*
Brown (Township)—Mifflin *PA-1*

Brown City (City)—Lapeer *MI-3*
Brown City (City)—Sanilac *MI-3*
Brown County................................... *IL-3*
Brown County................................... *IN-3*
Brown County...................................*KS-4*
Brown County.................................*MN-3*
Brown County.................................*NE-4*
Brown County..................................*OH-3*
Brown County...................................*SD-4*
Brown County....................................*TX-2*
Brown County................................... *WI-3*
Brown Deer (Village)—
 Milwaukee...................................*WI-3*
Browndell (City)—Jasper *TX-2*
Brownell (City)—Ness....................*KS-4*
Brownfield (Town)—Oxford *ME-1*
Brownfield (City)—Terry *TX-2*
Brownfields (CDP)—East Baton Rouge
 Parish *LA-2*
Brownhelm (Township)—Lorain....*OH-3*
Browning (Township)—Franklin..... *IL-3*
Browning (Township)—Schuyler..... *IL-3*
Browning (Village)—Schuyler *IL-3*
Browning (City)—Linn..................*MO-3*
Browning (City)—Sullivan *MO-3*
Browning (Town)—Glacier *MT-4*
Browning (Town)—Taylor.............. *WI-3*
Brownington (Town)—Henry........*MO-3*
Brownington (Town)—Orleans *VT-1*
Brownlee Park (CDP)—Calhoun ... *MI-3*
Brown Mills (CDP)—Burlington *NJ-1*
Browns (Village)—Edwards........... *IL-3*
Brownsboro (City)—Henderson......*TX-2*
Brownsboro Farm (City)—
 Jefferson *KY-2*
Brownsboro Village (City)—
 Jefferson *KY-2*
Brownsburg (Town)—Hendricks..... *IN-3*
Browns Creek (Township)—
 Jewell..*KS-4*
Browns Creek (Township)—Red
 Lake..*MN-3*
Brownsdale (City)—Mower...........*MN-3*
Browns Grove (Township)—
 Pawnee *KS-4*
Browns Lake (CDP)—Racine *WI-3*
Brownstown (Village)—Fayette....... *IL-3*
Brownstown (Town)—Jackson......... *IN-3*
Brownstown (Township)—
 Jackson...*IN-3*
Brownstown (Township)—Wayne .. *MI-3*
Brownstown (Village)—Cambria *PA-1*
Browns Valley (Township)—Big
 Stone...*MN-3*
Browns Valley (City)—Traverse....*MN-3*
Brownsville (CDP)—Dade *FL-2*
Brownsville (Township)—Union..... *IN-3*
Brownsville (City)—Edmonson.......*KY-2*
Brownsville (City)—Houston *MN-3*
Brownsville (Township)—
 Houston......................................*MN-3*
Brownsville—Kings *NY-1*
Brownsville (City)—Linn *OR-4*
Brownsville (Borough)—Fayette *PA-1*
Brownsville (Township)—Fayette ... *PA-1*
Brownsville (Town)—Haywood *TN-2*
Brownsville (City)—Cameron *TX-2*
Brownsville (Village)—Dodge *WI-3*
Brownsville-Bawcomville (CDP)—
 Ouachita Parish *LA-2*
Brownton (City)—McLeod............*MN-3*
Browntown (Village)—Green *WI-3*
Brownville (Town)—Piscataquis ... *ME-1*
Brownville (Village)—Nemaha *NE-4*
Brownville (Town)—Jefferson......... *NY-1*

Brownville (Village)—Jefferson *NY-1*
Brownwood (City)—Brown *TX-2*
Broxton (City)—Coffee *GA-2*
Bruce (Township)—La Salle........... *IL-3*
Bruce (Township)—Chippewa........ *MI-3*
Bruce (Township)—Macomb *MI-3*
Bruce (Township)—Todd *MN-3*
Bruce (Town)—Calhoun *MS-2*
Bruce (Township)—Cavalier *ND-4*
Bruce (City)—Brookings *SD-4*
Bruce (Village)—Rusk *WI-3*
Bruceton (Town)—Carroll.............. *TN-2*
Bruceton Mills (Town)—Preston .. *WV-2*
Bruceville (Town)—Knox *IN-3*
Bruceville-Eddy (City)—Falls......... *TX-2*
Bruceville-Eddy (City)—
 McLennan *TX-2*
Bruin (Borough)—Butler *PA-1*
Brule (Village)—Keith *NE-4*
Brule (Township)—Brule................. *SD-4*
Brule (Township)—Union *SD-4*
Brule (Town)—Douglas *WI-3*
Brule County *SD-4*
Brumley (Town)—Miller *MO-3*
Brundidge (City)—Pike *AL-2*
Bruner (Township)—Christian *MO-3*
Bruning (Village)—Thayer *NE-4*
Bruno (Township)—Butler *KS-4*
Bruno (City)—Pine........................*MN-3*
Bruno (Township)—Pine *MN-3*
Bruno (Village)—Butler *NE-4*
Brunson (Town)—Hampton...........*SC-2*
Brunson (Township)—Tripp *SD-4*
Brunsville (City)—Plymouth...........*IA-3*
Brunswick (City)—Glynn *GA-2*
Brunswick (Town)—Cumberland.. *ME-1*
Brunswick (Town)—Frederick *MD-1*
Brunswick (Township)—
 Kanabec *MN-3*
Brunswick (City)—Chariton...........*MO-3*
Brunswick (Township)—
 Chariton *MO-3*
Brunswick (Village)—Antelope *NE-4*
Brunswick (Town)—Rensselaer....... *NY-1*
Brunswick (Town)—Columbus *NC-2*
Brunswick (City)—Medina............*OH-3*
Brunswick (Town)—Essex *VT-1*
Brunswick (Town)—Eau Claire..... *WI-3*
Brunswick County *NC-2*
Brunswick County *VA-2*
Brunswick Hills (Township)—
 Medina *OH-3*
Brunswick Station (Mil. facil.)—
 Cumberland *ME-1*
Brush (City)—Morgan *CO-4*
Brush Creek (Township)—
 Faribault *MN-3*
Brush Creek (Township)—
 Douglas *MO-3*
Brush Creek (Township)—
 Gasconade *MO-3*
Brush Creek (Township)—
 Wright *MO-3*
Brush Creek (Township)—
 Adams *OH-3*
Brush Creek (Township)—
 Highland *OH-3*
Brush Creek (Township)—
 Jefferson *OH-3*
Brush Creek (Township)—
 Muskingum *OH-3*
Brush Creek (Township)—Scioto ...*OH-3*
Brush Creek (Township)—Fulton ... *PA-1*
Brush Prairie (CDP)—Clark *WA-4*
Brushton (Village)—Franklin *NY-1*

Brush Valley (Township)—
  Indiana PA-1
Brushy (Township)—Saline IL-3
Brushy (Township)—Perkins SD-4
Brushy Creek (CDP)—
  Williamson TX-2
Brushy Mound (Township)—
  Macoupin IL-3
Brusly (City)—West Baton Rouge
  Parish LA-2
Brussels (Village)—Calhoun IL-3
Brussels (Town)—Door WI-3
Brutus (Town)—Cayuga NY-1
Bryan (Township)—Douglas MO-3
Bryan (Township)—Thurston NE-4
Bryan (Township)—Griggs ND-4
Bryan (City)—Williams OH-3
Bryan (Township)—Charles Mix ... SD-4
Bryan (City)—Brazos TX-2
Bryan County GA-2
Bryan County OK-2
Bryans Road (CDP)—Charles MD-1
Bryant (City)—Saline AR-2
Bryant (Village)—Fulton IL-3
Bryant (Town)—Jay IN-3
Bryant (Township)—Graham KS-4
Bryant (Township)—Fillmore NE-4
Bryant (Township)—Logan ND-4
Bryant (Township)—Edmunds SD-4
Bryant (Township)—Faulk SD-4
Bryant (City)—Hamlin SD-4
Bryant (Township)—Roberts SD-4
Bryceland (Village)—Bienville
  Parish LA-2
Bryn Athyn (Borough)—
  Montgomery PA-1
Bryn Mawr (CDP)—Montgomery .. PA-1
Bryn Mawr-Skyway (CDP)—
  King WA-4
Bryson (City)—Jack TX-2
Bryson City (Town)—Swain NC-2
Bucephalia (Township)—Foster ND-4
Buchanan (City)—Haralson GA-2
Buchanan (City)—Berrien MI-3
Buchanan (Township)—Berrien MI-3
Buchanan (Township)—
  Atchison MO-3
Buchanan (Township)—Douglas .. MO-3
Buchanan (Township)—Sullivan .. MO-3
Buchanan (Village)—Westchester .. NY-1
Buchanan (City)—Stutsman ND-4
Buchanan (Township)—
  Stutsman ND-4
Buchanan (Town)—Botetourt VA-2
Buchanan (Town)—Outagamie WI-3
Buchanan County IA-3
Buchanan County MO-3
Buchanan County VA-2
Buchanan Dam (CDP)—Llano TX-2
Buchanan Valley (Township)—
  Emmons ND-4
Buchtel (Village)—Athens OH-3
Buck (Township)—Edgar IL-3
Buck (Township)—Hardin OH-3
Buck (Township)—Luzerne PA-1
Buck Creek (Township)—
  Hancock IN-3
Buckeye (Town)—Maricopa AZ-4
Buckeye (Township)—Stephenson .. IL-3
Buckeye (City)—Hardin IA-3
Buckeye (Township)—Dickinson ... KS-4
Buckeye (Township)—Ellis KS-4
Buckeye (Township)—Ottawa KS-4
Buckeye (Township)—Gladwin MI-3
Buckeye (Township)—Shannon MO-3

Buckeye (Township)—Kidder ND-4
Buckeye Lake (Village)—Licking .. OH-3
Buckfield (Town)—Oxford ME-1
Buck Grove (City)—Crawford IA-3
Buckhannon (City)—Upshur WV-2
Buckhart (Township)—Christian ... IL-3
Buckhead (Town)—Morgan GA-2
Buckhead Ridge (CDP)—Glades ... FL-2
Buckheart (Township)—Fulton IL-3
Buckholts (Town)—Milam TX-2
Buckhorn (Township)—Brown IL-3
Buckingham (Village)—Kankakee .. IL-3
Buckingham (Township)—Bucks PA-1
Buckingham (Township)—Wayne .. PA-1
Buckingham (Town)—Dallas TX-2
Buckingham County VA-2
Buckland (City)—Northwest Arctic
  Borough AK-4
Buckland (Town)—Franklin MA-1
Buckland (Village)—Auglaize OH-3
Buckley (Village)—Iroquois IL-3
Buckley (Village)—Wexford MI-3
Buckley (City)—Pierce WA-4
Buckley Air National Guard Base
  (CO) Mil-4
Bucklin (City)—Ford KS-4
Bucklin (Township)—Ford KS-4
Bucklin (City)—Linn MO-3
Bucklin (Township)—Linn MO-3
Bucklin (Township)—Slope ND-4
Buckman (City)—Morrison MN-3
Buckman (Township)—Morrison .. MN-3
Buckner (City)—Lafayette AR-2
Buckner (Village)—Franklin IL-3
Buckner (City)—Jackson MO-3
Buck Prairie (Township)—
  Lawrence MO-3
Bucks (Township)—Tuscarawas OH-3
Bucks County PA-1
Buckskin (Township)—Ross OH-3
Bucksport (Town)—Hancock ME-1
Bucksport (CDP)—Horry SC-2
Bucoda (Town)—Thurston WA-4
Bucyrus (City)—Adams ND-4
Bucyrus (Township)—Adams ND-4
Bucyrus (City)—Crawford OH-3
Bucyrus (Township)—Crawford OH-3
Buda (Village)—Bureau IL-3
Buda (City)—Hays TX-2
Budd Lake (CDP)—Morris NJ-1
Bude (Town)—Franklin MS-2
Buechel (CDP)—Jefferson KY-2
Buel (Township)—Sanilac MI-3
Buellton (CDP)—Santa Barbara CA-4
Buels Gore (Pop. Place)—
  Chittenden VT-1
Buena (Borough)—Atlantic NJ-1
Buena Park (City)—Orange CA-4
Buena Ventura Lakes (CDP)—
  Osceola FL-2
Buena Vista (Town)—Chaffee CO-4
Buena Vista (City)—Marion GA-2
Buena Vista (Township)—
  Schuyler IL-3
Buena Vista (Township)—
  Atlantic NJ-1
Buena Vista (Township)—
  Bowman ND-4
Buena Vista (Town)—Portage WI-3
Buena Vista (Town)—Richland WI-3
Buena Vista Charter (Township)—
  Saginaw MI-3
Buena Vista County IA-3
Buena Vista (Independent City) VA-2
Buffalo (Township)—Ogle IL-3

Buffalo (Village)—Sangamon IL-3
Buffalo (City)—Scott IA-3
Buffalo (Township)—Barton KS-4
Buffalo (Township)—Cloud KS-4
Buffalo (Township)—Jewell KS-4
Buffalo (City)—Wilson KS-4
Buffalo (City)—Wright MN-3
Buffalo (Township)—Wright MN-3
Buffalo (City)—Dallas MO-3
Buffalo (Township)—Dunklin MO-3
Buffalo (Township)—Morgan MO-3
Buffalo (Township)—Newton MO-3
Buffalo (Township)—Pike MO-3
Buffalo (City)—Erie NY-1
Buffalo (City)—Cass ND-4
Buffalo (Township)—Cass ND-4
Buffalo (Township)—Noble OH-3
Buffalo (Town)—Harper OK-2
Buffalo (Township)—Butler PA-1
Buffalo (Township)—Perry PA-1
Buffalo (Township)—Union PA-1
Buffalo (Township)—Washington ... PA-1
Buffalo (CDP)—Union SC-2
Buffalo (Town)—Harding SD-4
Buffalo (Township)—Jones SD-4
Buffalo (Township)—Marshall SD-4
Buffalo (Township)—Minnehaha ... SD-4
Buffalo (Township)—Spink SD-4
Buffalo (City)—Leon TX-2
Buffalo (Town)—Putnam WV-2
Buffalo (City)—Buffalo WI-3
Buffalo (Town)—Buffalo WI-3
Buffalo (Town)—Marquette WI-3
Buffalo (City)—Johnson WY-4
Buffalo Center (City)—
  Winnebago IA-3
Buffalo County NE-4
Buffalo County SD-4
Buffalo County WI-3
Buffalo Gap (Town)—Custer SD-4
Buffalo Gap (Town)—Taylor TX-2
Buffalo Grove (Residential suburb)—
  Cook IL-3
Buffalo Grove (Residential suburb)—
  Lake IL-3
Buffalo Hart (Township)—
  Sangamon IL-3
Buffalo Hart (Township)—
  McDonald MO-3
Buffalo Lake (City)—Renville MN-3
Buffalo May (Township)—
  McDonald MO-3
Buffalo Prairie (Township)—Rock
  Island IL-3
Buffington (Township)—Indiana PA-1
Buford (City)—Gwinnett GA-2
Buford (City)—Hall GA-2
Buford (Township)—Williams ND-4
Buh (Township)—Morrison MN-3
Buhl (City)—Twin Falls ID-4
Buhl (City)—St. Louis MN-3
Buhler (City)—Reno KS-4
Buies Creek (CDP)—Harnett NC-2
Bullard (Township)—Wadena MN-3
Bullard (Town)—Cherokee TX-2
Bullard (Town)—Smith TX-2
Bull Butte (Township)—Williams .. ND-4
Bull Creek (Township)—Tripp SD-4
Bullhead (CDP)—Corson SD-4
Bullhead City (City)—Mohave AZ-4
Bullion (Township)—Golden
  Valley ND-4
Bullitt County KY-2
Bull Moose (Township)—Cass MN-3
Bull Moose (Township)—Wells ND-4

American Places Dictionary — General Index

Bulloch County *GA-2*
Bullock County *AL-2*
Bull Run (CDP)—Prince William .. *VA-2*
Bulls Gap (Town)—Hawkins *TN-2*
Bull Shoals (City)—Marion *AR-2*
Bullskin (Township)—Fayette *PA-1*
Bull Valley (Village)—McHenry..... *IL-3*
Bulpitt (Village)—Christian *IL-3*
Buna (CDP)—Jasper *TX-2*
Bunceton (City)—Cooper............... *MO-3*
Bunche Park (CDP)—Dade *FL-2*
Buncombe (Village)—Johnson *IL-3*
Buncombe County *NC-2*
Bungo (Township)—Cass *MN-3*
Bunker (City)—Dent *MO-3*
Bunker (City)—Reynolds *MO-3*
Bunker (Township)—Kidder *ND-4*
Bunker Hill (City)—Macoupin *IL-3*
Bunker Hill (Township)—
  Macoupin *IL-3*
Bunker Hill (Town)—Miami *IN-3*
Bunker Hill (City)—Russell *KS-4*
Bunker Hill (Township)—Ingham... *MI-3*
Bunker Hill (CDP)—Coos............... *OR-4*
Bunker Hill Village (City)—
  Harris *TX-2*
Bunkie (Town)—Avoyelles Parish... *LA-2*
Bunn (Town)—Franklin *NC-2*
Bunnell (City)—Flagler *FL-2*
Buras-Triumph (CDP)—Plaquemines
  Parish *LA-2*
Burbank (City)—Los Angeles......... *CA-4*
Burbank (CDP)—Santa Clara *CA-4*
Burbank (City)—Cook..................... *IL-3*
Burbank (Township)—
  Kandiyohi *MN-3*
Burbank (Village)—Wayne.............. *OH-3*
Burbank (Town)—Osage *OK-2*
Burbank (CDP)—Walla Walla........ *WA-4*
Burchard (Village)—Pawnee *NE-4*
Burdell (Township)—Osceola.......... *MI-3*
Burden (City)—Cowley *KS-4*
Burdett (City)—Pawnee *KS-4*
Burdett (Village)—Schuyler............ *NY-1*
Burdette (Town)—Mississippi........ *AR-2*
Burdette (Township)—Hand *SD-4*
Burdick (Township)—Perkins *SD-4*
Burdine (Township)—Texas........... *MO-3*
Bureau (Township)—Bureau *IL-3*
Bureau County *IL-3*
Bureau Junction (Village)—
  Bureau *IL-3*
Burg (Township)—Divide *ND-4*
Burgaw (Town)—Pender *NC-2*
Burgess (Township)—Bond *IL-3*
Burgess (Town)—Barton *MO-3*
Burgettstown (Borough)—
  Washington *PA-1*
Burgin (City)—Mercer..................... *KY-2*
Burgoon (Village)—Sandusky *OH-3*
Burien (CDP)—King *WA-4*
Burk (Township)—Minnehaha....... *SD-4*
Burkburnett (City)—Wichita *TX-2*
Burke (Township)—Pipestone....... *MN-3*
Burke (Town)—Franklin *NY-1*
Burke (Village)—Franklin *NY-1*
Burke (Township)—Mountrail *ND-4*
Burke (City)—Gregory *SD-4*
Burke (Township)—Gregory *SD-4*
Burke (City)—Angelina *TX-2*
Burke (Town)—Caledonia *VT-1*
Burke (CDP)—Fairfax *VA-2*
Burke (Town)—Dane *WI-3*
Burke County *GA-2*
Burke County *NC-2*
Burke County *ND-4*
Burkesville (City)—Cumberland.... *KY-2*
Burket (Town)—Kosciusko *IN-3*
Burkettsville (Village)—Darke *OH-3*
Burkettsville (Village)—Mercer...... *OH-3*
Burkeville (Town)—Nottoway *VA-2*
Burkittsville (Town)—Frederick ... *MD-1*
Burleene (Township)—Todd *MN-3*
Burleigh (Township)—Iosco *MI-3*
Burleigh County *ND-4*
Burleson (City)—Johnson *TX-2*
Burleson (City)—Tarrant................ *TX-2*
Burleson County *TX-2*
Burley (City)—Cassia *ID-4*
Burley (City)—Minidoka *ID-4*
Burlingame (City)—San Mateo...... *CA-4*
Burlingame (City)—Osage............... *KS-4*
Burlingame (Township)—Osage...... *KS-4*
Burlington (City)—Kit Carson....... *CO-4*
Burlington (Town)—Hartford *CT-1*
Burlington (Township)—Kane *IL-3*
Burlington (Village)—Kane............ *IL-3*
Burlington (Town)—Carroll *IN-3*
Burlington (Township)—Carroll *IN-3*
Burlington (City)—Des Moines *IA-3*
Burlington (City)—Coffey *KS-4*
Burlington (Township)—Coffey *KS-4*
Burlington (CDP)—Boone *KY-2*
Burlington (Town)—Penobscot *ME-1*
Burlington (Town)—Middlesex..... *MA-1*
Burlington (Township)—Calhoun... *MI-3*
Burlington (Village)—Calhoun...... *MI-3*
Burlington (Township)—Lapeer..... *MI-3*
Burlington (Township)—Becker.... *MN-3*
Burlington (City)—Burlington *NJ-1*
Burlington (Township)—
  Burlington *NJ-1*
Burlington (Town)—Otsego *NY-1*
Burlington (City)—Alamance......... *NC-2*
Burlington (City)—Ward *ND-4*
Burlington (Township)—Ward *ND-4*
Burlington (CDP)—Lawrence........ *OH-3*
Burlington (Township)—Licking.... *OH-3*
Burlington (Town)—Alfalfa........... *OK-2*
Burlington (Borough)—Bradford *PA-1*
Burlington (Township)—Bradford . *PA-1*
Burlington (City)—Chittenden...... *VT-1*
Burlington (City)—Skagit *WA-4*
Burlington (City)—Racine *WI-3*
Burlington (Town)—Racine *WI-3*
Burlington (City)—Walworth *WI-3*
Burlington (Town)—Big Horn *WY-4*
Burlington County *NJ-1*
Burlington Junction (City)—
  Nodaway *MO-3*
Burlison (Town)—Tipton *TN-2*
Burnet (Town)—Burnet................... *TX-2*
Burnet County *TX-2*
Burnett (Township)—Antelope *NE-4*
Burnett (Town)—Dodge *WI-3*
Burnett County *WI-3*
Burnettown (Town)—Aiken............ *SC-2*
Burnettsville (Town)—White *IN-3*
Burney (CDP)—Shasta................... *CA-4*
Burnham (Village)—Cook............... *IL-3*
Burnham (Town)—Waldo *ME-1*
Burnham (Borough)—Mifflin *PA-1*
Burnhamville (Township)—
  Todd *MN-3*
Burns (Township)—Henry *IL-3*
Burns (City)—Marion *KS-4*
Burns (Township)—Shiawassee.... *MI-3*
Burns (Township)—Anoka *MN-3*
Burns (Town)—Allegany *NY-1*
Burns (City)—Harney..................... *OR-4*
Burns (Town)—Dickson *TN-2*
Burns (Town)—La Crosse *WI-3*
Burns (Town)—Laramie *WY-4*
Burns Flat (Town)—Washita.......... *OK-2*
Burns Harbor (Town)—Porter *IN-3*
Burnside (City)—Pulaski................. *KY-2*
Burnside (Township)—Lapeer........ *MI-3*
Burnside (Township)—Centre........ *PA-1*
Burnside (Borough)—Clearfield *PA-1*
Burnside (Township)—Clearfield... *PA-1*
Burnside (Town)—Trempealeau *WI-3*
Burns Paiute Reservation and Trust
  Lands (OR) *IndRes-4*
Burnstown (Township)—Brown... *MN-3*
Burnsville (City)—Dakota *MN-3*
Burnsville (Town)—Tishomingo....*MS-2*
Burnsville (Town)—Yancey............ *NC-2*
Burnsville (Town)—Braxton *WV-2*
Burnt Prairie (Township)—White... *IL-3*
Burnt Prairie (Village)—White *IL-3*
Burr (Village)—Otoe *NE-4*
Burrell (Township)—Armstrong..... *PA-1*
Burrell (Township)—Indiana *PA-1*
Burrillville (Town)—Providence *RI-1*
Burris Fork (Township)—
  Moniteau.......................................*MO-3*
Burritt (Township)—Winnebago.... *IL-3*
Burr Oak (Township)—Doniphan ..*KS-4*
Burr Oak (City)—Jewell................. *KS-4*
Burr Oak (Township)—Jewell........ *KS-4*
Burr Oak (Township)—St. Joseph . *MI-3*
Burr Oak (Village)—St. Joseph...... *MI-3*
Burr Oak (Township)—Lincoln *MO-3*
Burr Oak (Township)—Beadle *SD-4*
Burrows (Township)—Platte *NE-4*
Burr Ridge (Village)—Cook............ *IL-3*
Burr Ridge (Village)—DuPage....... *IL-3*
Burrton (City)—Harvey.................. *KS-4*
Burrton (Township)—Harvey........ *KS-4*
Burt (City)—Kossuth...................... *IA-3*
Burt (Township)—Alger *MI-3*
Burt (Township)—Cheboygan *MI-3*
Burt (CDP)—Saginaw *MI-3*
Burt (Township)—Ward *ND-4*
Burtchville (Township)—St. Clair.. *MI-3*
Burt County *NE-4*
Burton (Township)—Adams........... *IL-3*
Burton (Township)—McHenry *IL-3*
Burton (City)—Genesee *MI-3*
Burton (Township)—Yellow
  Medicine *MN-3*
Burton (Township)—Howard......... *MO-3*
Burton (Village)—Keya Paha....... *NE-4*
Burton (Township)—Geauga......... *OH-3*
Burton (Village)—Geauga.............. *OH-3*
Burton (CDP)—Beaufort.................*SC-2*
Burton (Town)—Washington *TX-2*
Burtonsville (CDP)—
  Montgomery................................*MD-1*
Burtrum (Town)—Todd *MN-3*
Burwell (City)—Garfield *NE-4*
Busby (CDP)—Big Horn............... *MT-4*
Buse (Township)—Otter Tail *MN-3*
Bush (Village)—Williamson *IL-3*
Bush (Township)—Boyd *NE-4*
Bush (Township)—Eddy................. *ND-4*
Bushkill (Township)—
  Northampton *PA-1*
Bushnell (City)—Sumter *FL-2*
Bushnell (City)—McDonough *IL-3*
Bushnell (Township)—
  McDonough *IL-3*
Bushnell (Township)—Montcalm .. *MI-3*
Bushnell (Village)—Kimball........... *NE-4*
Bushnell (Town)—Brookings.......... *SD-4*

General Index — American Places Dictionary

Bushong (City)—Lyon KS-4
Bushton (City)—Rice KS-4
Bushwick—Kings..............................NY-1
Busseron (Township)—Knox IN-3
Bussey (City)—Marion IA-3
Busti (Town)—Chautauqua............. NY-1
Butler (City)—Choctaw AL-2
Butler (Town)—Taylor......................GA-2
Butler (Village)—Montgomery........ IL-3
Butler (Township)—Vermilion IL-3
Butler (City)—Dekalb IN-3
Butler (Township)—Dekalb............. IN-3
Butler (Township)—Franklin IN-3
Butler (Township)—Miami IN-3
Butler (City)—Pendleton KY-2
Butler (Township)—Branch.............MI-3
Butler (Township)—Otter Tail MN-3
Butler (City)—Bates MO-3
Butler (Township)—Harrison..........MO-3
Butler (Township)—Pemiscot MO-3
Butler (Township)—St. Clair.......... MO-3
Butler (Township)—Platte...............NE-4
Butler (Borough)—Morris NJ-1
Butler (Town)—Wayne NY-1
Butler (Township)—Columbiana ...OH-3
Butler (Township)—Darke OH-3
Butler (Township)—Knox OH-3
Butler (Township)—Mercer.............OH-3
Butler (Township)—Montgomery ..OH-3
Butler (Township)—Richland OH-3
Butler (Village)—Richland OH-3
Butler (Town)—Custer OK-2
Butler (Township)—Adams PA-1
Butler (City)—Butler PA-1
Butler (Township)—Butler PA-1
Butler (Township)—Luzerne........... PA-1
Butler (Township)—Schuylkill PA-1
Butler (Town)—Day SD-4
Butler (Township)—Day SD-4
Butler (Township)—Sanborn.......... SD-4
Butler (Town)—Clark WI-3
Butler (Village)—Waukesha WI-3
Butler Beach (CDP)—St. Johns FL-2
Butler County AL-2
Butler County IA-3
Butler County KS-4
Butler County KY-2
Butler County MO-3
Butler County NE-4
Butler County OH-3
Butler County PA-1
Butler Grove (Township)—
 Montgomery.................................. IL-3
Butlerville (Village)—Warren OH-3
Butman (Township)—Gladwin MI-3
Butner (CDP)—Granville.................NC-2
Butte (CDP)—Matanuska-Susitna
 Borough AK-4
Butte (Township)—Boyd NE-4
Butte (Village)—Boyd......................NE-4
Butte (City)—McLean ND-4
Butte (Township)—McLean ND-4
Butte (Township)—Hughes SD-4
Butte (Township)—Lyman SD-4
Butte (Township)—Mellette............ SD-4
Butte City (City)—Butte ID-4
Butte County CA-4
Butte County ID-4
Butte County SD-4
Butte Falls (Town)—Jackson...........OR-4
Butterfield (Township)—
 Missaukee MI-3
Butterfield (City)—Watonwan MN-3
Butterfield (Township)—
 Watonwan MN-3

Butterfield (Township)—Barry......MO-3
Butterfield (Village)—Barry MO-3
Butternut (Village)—Ashland WI-3
Butternuts (Town)—Otsego NY-1
Butternut Valley (Township)—Blue
 Earth...MN-3
Butte-Silver Bow (City)—Silver
 Bow MT-4
Butte Valley (Township)—
 Benson ND-4
Button (Township)—Ford IL-3
Buttonwillow (CDP)—Kern CA-4
Butts County..................................GA-2
Buxton (Town)—York ME-1
Buxton (City)—Traill ND-4
Buxton (Township)—Traill.............ND-4
Buzzards Bay (MA) Geog-4
Buzzards Bay (CDP)—
 Barnstable MA-1
Buzzle (Township)—Beltrami MN-3
Byars (Town)—McClain OK-2
Byers (CDP)—Arapahoe CO-4
Byers (City)—Pratt KS-4
Byers (City)—Clay............................ TX-2
Byersville (Township)—McLean ND-4
Byesville (Village)—Guernsey........OH-3
Bygland (Township)—Polk MN-3
Byhalia (Town)—Marshall MS-2
Bylas (CDP)—Graham AZ-4
Byng (Town)—Pontotoc OK-2
Bynum (Division)—Calhoun AL-2
Bynum (Town)—Hill TX-2
Byram (Township)—Sussex............ NJ-1
Byrd (Township)—Cape
 Girardeau......................................MO-3
Byrd (Township)—Brown OH-3
Byrdstown (Town)—Pickett TN-2
Byrnes Mill (City)—Jefferson MO-3
Byromville (Town)—Dooly GA-2
Byron (City)—Peach GA-2
Byron (City)—Ogle IL-3
Byron (Township)—Ogle................. IL-3
Byron (Township)—Stafford KS-4
Byron (Town)—Oxford ME-1
Byron (Township)—Kent MI-3
Byron (Village)—Shiawassee.......... MI-3
Byron (Township)—Cass MN-3
Byron (City)—Olmsted MN-3
Byron (Township)—Waseca MN-3
Byron (Village)—Thayer NE-4
Byron (Town)—Genesee................. NY-1
Byron (Township)—Cavalier..........ND-4
Byron (Town)—Alfalfa OK-2
Byron (Town)—Fond du Lac WI-3
Byron (Town)—Monroe WI-3
Byron (Town)—Big Horn WY-4
Cabarrus County NC-2
Cabazon (CDP)—Riverside CA-4
Cabazon Reservation (CA)........IndRes-4
Cabell County WV-2
Cabery (Village)—Ford................... IL-3
Cabery (Village)—Kankakee IL-3
Cabin John-Brookmont (CDP)—
 Montgomery MD-1
Cable (Village)—Bayfield WI-3
Cabool (City)—Texas MO-3
Cabot (City)—Lonoke AR-2
Cabot (Town)—Washington VT-1
Cabot (Village)—Washington VT-1
Cache (Town)—Comanche.............OK-2
Cache County UT-4
Cactus (Town)—Moore TX-2
Caddo (Town)—Bryan OK-2
Caddo County OK-2
Caddo Mills (City)—Hunt TX-2

Caddo Parish..................................LA-2
Caddo Valley (Town)—Clark AR-2
Caddo-Wichita-Delaware TJSA
 (OK) IndRes-4
Cadi (Town)—Henry IN-3
Cadi (Town)—Green WI-3
Cadillac (City)—Wexford MI-3
Cadillac (Township)—Corson SD-4
Cadiz (City)—Trigg KY-2
Cadiz (Township)—Harrison OH-3
Cadiz (Village)—Harrison OH-3
Cadogan (Township)—Armstrong... PA-1
Cadott (Village)—Chippewa WI-3
Cadwell (Town)—Laurens GA-2
Cady (Town)—St. Croix WI-3
Caernarvon (Township)—Berks PA-1
Caernarvon (Township)—
 Lancaster PA-1
Caesar Creek (Township)—
 Dearborn.. IN-3
Caesars Creek (Township)—
 Greene OH-3
Cahaba Heights (Division)—
 Jefferson...AL-2
Cahokia (Township)—Macoupin ... IL-3
Cahokia (Village)—St. Clair IL-3
Cahuilla Reservation (CA) IndRes-4
Cain (Township)—Fountain IN-3
Cainsville (City)—Harrison MO-3
Cairo (City)—Grady GA-2
Cairo (City)—Alexander IL-3
Cairo (Township)—Renville..........MN-3
Cairo (Township)—Randolph MO-3
Cairo (Village)—Randolph MO-3
Cairo (Village)—Hall NE-4
Cairo (Town)—Greene NY-1
Cairo (Village)—Allen OH-3
Cairo (Town)—Ritchie WV-2
Cajah's Mountain (Town)—
 Caldwell..NC-2
Calabash (Town)—Brunswick NC-2
Calais (City)—Washington ME-1
Calais (Town)—Washington VT-1
Calamus (City)—Clinton IA-3
Calamus (Town)—Dodge WI-3
Calaveras County CA-4
Calcasieu Parish.............................LA-2
Calcium (CDP)—Jefferson NY-1
Calcutta (CDP)—Columbiana OH-3
Caldwell (Town)—St. Francis AR-2
Caldwell (City)—Canyon ID-4
Caldwell (City)—Sumner KS-4
Caldwell (Township)—Sumner KS-4
Caldwell (Township)—Missaukee ..MI-3
Caldwell (Township)—Callaway ... MO-3
Caldwell (Village)—Noble OH-3
Caldwell (City)—Burleson TX-2
Caldwell County KY-2
Caldwell County MO-3
Caldwell County NC-2
Caldwell County TX-2
Caldwell Parish..............................LA-2
Caldwell Township (Borough)—
 Essex... NJ-1
Cale (Town)—Nevada AR-2
Caledonia (Township)—Boone IL-3
Caledonia (Township)—Alcona MI-3
Caledonia (Township)—Kent MI-3
Caledonia (Village)—Kent MI-3
Caledonia (Township)—
 Shiawassee.....................................MI-3
Caledonia (City)—Houston MN-3
Caledonia (Township)—Houston.. MN-3
Caledonia (Village)—Lowndes MS-2

American Places Dictionary — General Index

Caledonia (Village)—
 Washington *MO-3*
Caledonia (Town)—Livingston *NY-1*
Caledonia (Village)—Livingston *NY-1*
Caledonia (Township)—Traill *ND-4*
Caledonia (Village)—Marion *OH-3*
Caledonia (Town)—Columbia *WI-3*
Caledonia (Town)—Racine *WI-3*
Caledonia (Town)—Trempealeau ... *WI-3*
Caledonia (Town)—Waupaca *WI-3*
Caledonia County *VT-1*
Calera (Town)—Shelby *AL-2*
Calera (Town)—Bryan *OK-2*
Calexico (City)—Imperial *CA-4*
Calhan (Town)—El Paso *CO-4*
Calhoun (City)—Gordon *GA-2*
Calhoun (Village)—Richland *IL-3*
Calhoun (Township)—Cheyenne *KS-4*
Calhoun (City)—McLean *KY-2*
Calhoun (City)—Henry *MO-3*
Calhoun (Town)—McMinn *TN-2*
Calhoun City (Town)—Calhoun *MS-2*
Calhoun County *AL-2*
Calhoun County *AR-2*
Calhoun County *FL-2*
Calhoun County *GA-2*
Calhoun County *IL-3*
Calhoun County *IA-3*
Calhoun County *MI-3*
Calhoun County *MS-2*
Calhoun County *SC-2*
Calhoun County *TX-2*
Calhoun County *WV-2*
Calhoun Falls (Town)—Abbeville ... *SC-2*
Calico Rock (City)—Izard *AR-2*
Caliente (City)—Lincoln *NV-4*
Califon (Borough)—Hunterdon *NJ-1*
California (Township)—Starke *IN-3*
California (City)—Campbell *KY-2*
California (CDP)—St. Mary's *MD-1*
California (Township)—Branch *MI-3*
California (City)—Moniteau *MO-3*
California (Borough)—
 Washington *PA-1*
California City (City)—Kern *CA-4*
Calimesa (CDP)—Riverside *CA-4*
Calio (City)—Cavalier *ND-4*
Calion (City)—Union *AR-2*
Calipatria (City)—Imperial *CA-4*
Calistoga (City)—Napa *CA-4*
Callahan (Town)—Nassau *FL-2*
Callahan (Township)—Renville *ND-4*
Callahan County *TX-2*
Callao (City)—Macon *MO-3*
Callao (Township)—Macon *MO-3*
Callaway (City)—Bay *FL-2*
Callaway (City)—Becker *MN-3*
Callaway (Township)—Becker *MN-3*
Callaway (Village)—Custer *NE-4*
Callaway County *MO-3*
Callender (City)—Webster *IA-3*
Callensburg (Borough)—Clarion *PA-1*
Callery (Borough)—Butler *PA-1*
Callicoon (Town)—Sullivan *NY-1*
Callimont (Borough)—Somerset *PA-1*
Callisburg (Town)—Cooke *TX-2*
Calloway County *KY-2*
Calmar (City)—Winneshiek *IA-3*
Caln (Township)—Chester *PA-1*
Calumet (Township)—Cook *IL-3*
Calumet (Township)—Lake *IN-3*
Calumet (City)—O'Brien *IA-3*
Calumet (Township)—Houghton ... *MI-3*
Calumet (Village)—Houghton *MI-3*
Calumet (City)—Itasca *MN-3*

Calumet (Township)—Pike *MO-3*
Calumet (Town)—Canadian *OK-2*
Calumet (Town)—Fond du Lac *WI-3*
Calumet City (City)—Cook *IL-3*
Calumet County *WI-3*
Calumet-Norvelt (CDP)—
 Westmoreland *PA-1*
Calumet Park (Village)—Cook *IL-3*
Calvert (City)—Robertson *TX-2*
Calvert Beach-Long Beach (CDP)—
 Calvert *MD-1*
Calvert City (City)—Marshall *KY-2*
Calvert County *MD-1*
Calverton (CDP)—Montgomery ... *MD-1*
Calverton (CDP)—Prince
 George's *MD-1*
Calverton (CDP)—Suffolk *NY-1*
Calverton Park (Village)—St.
 Louis *MO-3*
Calvey (Township)—Franklin *MO-3*
Calvin (Township)—Jewell *KS-4*
Calvin (Village)—Winn Parish *LA-2*
Calvin (Township)—Cass *MI-3*
Calvin (City)—Cavalier *ND-4*
Calvin (Town)—Hughes *OK-2*
Calwood (Township)—Callaway ... *MO-3*
Calypso (Town)—Duplin *NC-2*
Camak (Town)—Warren *GA-2*
Camanche (City)—Clinton *IA-3*
Camargo (Township)—Douglas *IL-3*
Camargo (Village)—Douglas *IL-3*
Camargo (City)—Montgomery *KY-2*
Camargo (Town)—Dewey *OK-2*
Camarillo (City)—Ventura *CA-4*
Camas (City)—Clark *WA-4*
Camas County *ID-4*
Cambria (CDP)—San Luis
 Obispo *CA-4*
Cambria (Village)—Williamson *IL-3*
Cambria (Township)—Saline *KS-4*
Cambria (Township)—Hillsdale *MI-3*
Cambria (Township)—Blue
 Earth *MN-3*
Cambria (Town)—Niagara *NY-1*
Cambria (Township)—Cambria *PA-1*
Cambria (Township)—Brown *SD-4*
Cambria (Township)—Columbia ... *WI-3*
Cambria County *PA-1*
Cambrian Park (CDP)—Santa
 Clara *CA-4*
Cambridge (City)—Washington *ID-4*
Cambridge (Township)—Henry *IL-3*
Cambridge (Village)—Henry *IL-3*
Cambridge (City)—Story *IA-3*
Cambridge (City)—Cowley *KS-4*
Cambridge (City)—Jefferson *KY-2*
Cambridge (Town)—Somerset *ME-1*
Cambridge (City)—Dorchester *MD-1*
Cambridge (City)—Middlesex *MA-1*
Cambridge (Township)—
 Lenawee *MI-3*
Cambridge (City)—Isanti *MN-3*
Cambridge (Township)—Isanti *MN-3*
Cambridge (Township)—Saline *MO-3*
Cambridge (City)—Furnas *NE-4*
Cambridge (Township)—Coos *NH-1*
Cambridge (Town)—Washington ... *NY-1*
Cambridge (Village)—
 Washington *NY-1*
Cambridge (City)—Guernsey *OH-3*
Cambridge (Township)—
 Guernsey *OH-3*
Cambridge (Township)—
 Crawford *PA-1*
Cambridge (Town)—Lamoille *VT-1*

Cambridge (Village)—Lamoille *VT-1*
Cambridge (Village)—Dane *WI-3*
Cambridge (Village)—Jefferson *WI-3*
Cambridge City (Town)—Wayne ... *IN-3*
Cambridge Springs (Borough)—
 Crawford *PA-1*
Camden (Town)—Wilcox *AL-2*
Camden (City)—Ouachita *AR-2*
Camden (Town)—Kent *DE-1*
Camden (Township)—Schuyler *IL-3*
Camden (Village)—Schuyler *IL-3*
Camden (Town)—Carroll *IN-3*
Camden (Town)—Knox *ME-1*
Camden (Township)—Hillsdale *MI-3*
Camden (Village)—Hillsdale *MI-3*
Camden (Township)—Carver *MN-3*
Camden (Township)—DeKalb *MO-3*
Camden (City)—Ray *MO-3*
Camden (Township)—Ray *MO-3*
Camden (City)—Camden *NJ-1*
Camden (Town)—Oneida *NY-1*
Camden (Village)—Oneida *NY-1*
Camden (Pop. Place)—Camden *NC-2*
Camden (Township)—Lorain *OH-3*
Camden (Village)—Preble *OH-3*
Camden (City)—Kershaw *SC-2*
Camden (Town)—Benton *TN-2*
Camden County *GA-2*
Camden County *MO-3*
Camden County *NJ-1*
Camden County *NC-2*
Camden-on-Gauley (Town)—
 Webster *WV-2*
Camden Point (City)—Platte *MO-3*
Camdenton (City)—Camden *MO-3*
Cameron (CDP)—Coconino *AZ-4*
Cameron (CDP)—Cameron
 Parish *LA-2*
Cameron (Township)—Murray *MN-3*
Cameron (City)—Clinton *MO-3*
Cameron (City)—DeKalb *MO-3*
Cameron (Township)—Hall *NE-4*
Cameron (Town)—Steuben *NY-1*
Cameron (Town)—Moore *NC-2*
Cameron (Township)—Ward *ND-4*
Cameron (Town)—Le Flore *OK-2*
Cameron (Town)—Calhoun *SC-2*
Cameron (City)—Milam *TX-2*
Cameron (City)—Marshall *WV-2*
Cameron (Village)—Barron *WI-3*
Cameron (Town)—Wood *WI-3*
Cameron County *PA-1*
Cameron County *TX-2*
Cameron Parish *LA-2*
Cameron Park (CDP)—El
 Dorado *CA-4*
Cameron Park (CDP)—Cameron .. *TX-2*
Camilla (City)—Mitchell *GA-2*
Camillus (Town)—Onondaga *NY-1*
Camillus (Village)—Onondaga *NY-1*
Cammack Village (City)—
 Pulaski *AR-2*
Camp (Township)—Renville *MN-3*
Camp (City)—Santa Clara *CA-4*
Campbell (CDP)—Osceola *FL-2*
Campbell (Township)—Jennings ... *IN-3*
Campbell (Township)—Warrick *IN-3*
Campbell (Township)—Ionia *MI-3*
Campbell (City)—Wilkin *MN-3*
Campbell (Township)—Wilkin *MN-3*
Campbell (Township)—Douglas ... *MO-3*
Campbell (City)—Dunklin *MO-3*
Campbell (Township)—Polk *MO-3*
Campbell (Village)—Franklin *NE-4*
Campbell (Town)—Steuben *NY-1*

929

General Index — American Places Dictionary

Campbell (Township)—Emmons ... *ND-4*
Campbell (Township)—Hettinger .. *ND-4*
Campbell (City)—Mahoning *OH-3*
Campbell (Township)—Hand *SD-4*
Campbell (Town)—Hunt *TX-2*
Campbell (Town)—La Crosse *WI-3*
Campbell County *KY-2*
Campbell County *SD-4*
Campbell County *TN-2*
Campbell County *VA-2*
Campbell County *WY-4*
Campbell Hill (Village)—Jackson ... *IL-3*
Campbell Hill (OH) *Geog-4*
Campbell No. 1 (Township)—
  Greene *MO-3*
Campbell No. 2 (Township)—
  Greene *MO-3*
Campbellsburg (Town)—
  Washington *IN-3*
Campbellsburg (City)—Henry *KY-2*
Campbellsport (Village)—Fond du
  Lac *WI-3*
Campbell Station (Town)—
  Jackson *AR-2*
Campbellsville (City)—Taylor *KY-2*
Campbellton (Town)—Jackson *FL-2*
Campbelltown (CDP)—Lebanon *PA-1*
Camp Branch (Township)—Cass .. *MO-3*
Camp Branch (Township)—
  Warren *MO-3*
Camp County *TX-2*
Camp Creek (Township)—Pike *OH-3*
Camp Crook (Town)—Harding *SD-4*
Camp David (MD) *Geog-4*
Camp Douglas (Village)—Juneau .. *WI-3*
Camp Forsyth (Military Facility)—
  Geary *KS-4*
Camp Grayling Army & Air National
  Guard Training Center (MI) *Mil-4*
Camp Hill (Town)—Tallapoosa *AL-2*
Camp Hill (Borough)—
  Cumberland *PA-1*
Camp H. M. Smith (HI) *Mil-4*
Campion (CDP)—Larimer *CO-4*
Camp Lake (Township)—Swift *MN-3*
Camp Lake (CDP)—Kenosha *WI-3*
Camp Lejeune Central (Military
  Facility)—Onslow *NC-2*
Camp Lejeune Marine Corps Base
  (NC) *Mil-4*
Campo (Town)—Baca *CO-4*
Campobello (Town)—
  Spartanburg *SC-2*
Campo Reservation (CA) *IndRes-4*
Camp Pendleton Marine Corps Base
  (CA) *Mil-4*
Camp Pendleton North (Military
  Facility)—San Diego *CA-4*
Camp Pendleton South (Military
  Facility)—San Diego *CA-4*
Camp Point (Town)—Adams *IL-3*
Camp Point (Township)—Adams ... *IL-3*
Camp Release (Township)—Lac qui
  Parle *MN-3*
Camp Springs (CDP)—Prince
  George's *MD-1*
Camp Swift (CDP)—Bastrop *TX-2*
Campti (Town)—Natchitoches
  Parish *LA-2*
Campton (Township)—Kane *IL-3*
Campton (City)—Wolfe *KY-2*
Campton (Town)—Grafton *NH-1*
Campus (Village)—Livingston *IL-3*
Camp Verde (AZ) *IndRes-4*
Camp Verde (Town)—Yavapai *AZ-4*

Camp Wood (City)—Real *TX-2*
Canaan (Town)—Litchfield *CT-1*
Canaan (Town)—Somerset *ME-1*
Canaan (Township)—Gasconade .. *MO-3*
Canaan (Township)—Grafton *NH-1*
Canaan (Town)—Columbia *NY-1*
Canaan (Township)—Athens *OH-3*
Canaan (Township)—Madison *OH-3*
Canaan (Township)—Morrow *OH-3*
Canaan (Township)—Wayne *OH-3*
Canaan (Township)—Wayne *PA-1*
Canaan (Town)—Essex *VT-1*
Canada (Township)—Labette *KS-4*
Canadian (Town)—Pittsburg *OK-2*
Canadian (Town)—Hemphill *TX-2*
Canadian County *OK-2*
Canadice (Town)—Ontario *NY-1*
Canajoharie (Town)—
  Montgomery *NY-1*
Canajoharie (Village)—
  Montgomery *NY-1*
Canal (Township)—Venango *PA-1*
Canal Fulton (Village)—Stark *OH-3*
Canalou (City)—New Madrid *MO-3*
Canal Winchester (Village)—
  Franklin *OH-3*
Canandaigua (City)—Ontario *NY-1*
Canandaigua (Town)—Ontario *NY-1*
Canarsie—Kings *NY-1*
Canaseraga (Village)—Allegany *NY-1*
Canastota (Village)—Madison *NY-1*
Canaveral, Cape (FL) *Geog-4*
Canby (City)—Yellow Medicine ... *MN-3*
Canby (City)—Clackamas *OR-4*
Candia (Town)—Rockingham *NH-1*
Candler County *GA-2*
Candler-McAfee (CDP)—De
  Kalb *GA-2*
Cando (City)—Towner *ND-4*
Cando (Township)—Towner *ND-4*
Candor (Township)—Otter Tail *MN-3*
Candor (Town)—Tioga *NY-1*
Candor (Village)—Tioga *NY-1*
Candor (Town)—Montgomery *NC-2*
Caneadea (Town)—Allegany *NY-1*
Cane Creek (Township)—Butler ... *MO-3*
Caney (City)—Montgomery *KS-4*
Caney (Township)—Montgomery ... *KS-4*
Caney (Town)—Atoka *OK-2*
Caney City (Town)—Henderson *TX-2*
Caneyville (Township)—
  Chautauqua *KS-4*
Caneyville (City)—Grayson *KY-2*
Canfield (Township)—Burleigh *ND-4*
Canfield (City)—Mahoning *OH-3*
Canfield (Township)—Mahoning ... *OH-3*
Canisteo (Township)—Dodge *MN-3*
Canisteo (Town)—Steuben *NY-1*
Canisteo (Village)—Steuben *NY-1*
Canistota (City)—McCook *SD-4*
Canistota (Township)—McCook ... *SD-4*
Cankton (Village)—St. Landry
  Parish *LA-2*
Cannelburg (Town)—Daviess *IN-3*
Cannelton (City)—Perry *IN-3*
Cannon (Township)—Kent *MI-3*
Cannon (Township)—Kittson *MN-3*
Cannon Air Force Base (NM) *Mil-4*
Cannon Air Force Base (Military
  Facility)—Curry *NM-4*
Cannon Ball (Township)—
  Hettinger *ND-4*
Cannon Ball (CDP)—Sioux *ND-4*
Cannon Beach (City)—Clatsop *OR-4*
Cannon City (Township)—Rice *MN-3*

Cannon County *TN-2*
Cannon Falls (City)—Goodhue *MN-3*
Cannon Falls (Township)—
  Goodhue *MN-3*
Cannonville (Town)—Garfield *UT-4*
Canoe (Township)—Indiana *PA-1*
Canoe Creek (Township)—Rock
  Island *IL-3*
Canoga Park *See* **Los Angeles**—Los
  Angeles *CA-4*
Canon (City)—Franklin *GA-2*
Canon (City)—Hart *GA-2*
Canoncito Reservation (NM) ... *IndRes-4*
Canon City (City)—Fremont *CO-4*
Canonsburg (Borough)—
  Washington *PA-1*
Canosia (Township)—St. Louis *MN-3*
Canova (Town)—Miner *SD-4*
Canova (Township)—Miner *SD-4*
Canteen (Township)—St. Clair *IL-3*
Canterbury (Town)—Windham *CT-1*
Canterbury (Town)—Merrimack ... *NH-1*
Canton (Town)—Hartford *CT-1*
Canton (City)—Cherokee *GA-2*
Canton (City)—Fulton *IL-3*
Canton (Township)—Fulton *IL-3*
Canton (Township)—Kingman *KS-4*
Canton (City)—McPherson *KS-4*
Canton (Township)—McPherson ... *KS-4*
Canton (Town)—Oxford *ME-1*
Canton (Town)—Norfolk *MA-1*
Canton (Township)—Wayne *MI-3*
Canton (City)—Fillmore *MN-3*
Canton (Township)—Fillmore *MN-3*
Canton (City)—Madison *MS-2*
Canton (City)—Lewis *MO-3*
Canton (Township)—Lewis *MO-3*
Canton (Town)—St. Lawrence *NY-1*
Canton (Village)—St. Lawrence *NY-1*
Canton (Town)—Haywood *NC-2*
Canton (City)—Stark *OH-3*
Canton (Township)—Stark *OH-3*
Canton (Town)—Blaine *OK-2*
Canton (Borough)—Bradford *PA-1*
Canton (Township)—Bradford *PA-1*
Canton (Township)—Washington ... *PA-1*
Canton (City)—Lincoln *SD-4*
Canton (Township)—Lincoln *SD-4*
Canton (City)—Van Zandt *TX-2*
Canton (Town)—Buffalo *WI-3*
Canton City (City)—Pembina *ND-4*
Canton Valley (CDP)—Hartford ... *CT-1*
Cantrall (Village)—Sangamon *IL-3*
Cantril (City)—Van Buren *IA-3*
Cantwell (CDP)—Yukon-Koyukuk
  Census Area *AK-4*
Canute (Town)—Washita *OK-2*
Canutillo (CDP)—El Paso *TX-2*
Canville (Township)—Neosho *KS-4*
Canyon (City)—Randall *TX-2*
Canyon City (Town)—Grant *OR-4*
Canyon County *ID-4*
Canyon Day (CDP)—Gila *AZ-4*
Canyon Lake (CDP)—Riverside *CA-4*
Canyon Lake (CDP)—Comal *TX-2*
Canyon Rim (CDP)—Salt Lake *UT-4*
Canyonville (City)—Douglas *OR-4*
Capac (Village)—St. Clair *MI-3*
Cape Canaveral (City)—Brevard *FL-2*
Cape Carteret (Town)—Carteret ... *NC-2*
Cape Charles (Town)—
  Northampton *VA-2*
Cape Cod Bay (MA) *Geog-4*
Cape Cod Canal (MA) *Geog-4*
Cape Coral (City)—Lee *FL-2*

Cape Elizabeth (Town)—Cumberland ... *ME-1*
Cape Girardeau (City)—Cape Girardeau ... *MO-3*
Cape Girardeau (Township)—Cape Girardeau ... *MO-3*
Cape Girardeau County ... *MO-3*
Cape May (City)—Cape May ... *NJ-1*
Cape May County ... *NJ-1*
Cape May Court House (CDP)—Cape May ... *NJ-1*
Cape May Point (Borough)—Cape May ... *NJ-1*
Cape Neddick (CDP)—York ... *ME-1*
Cape St. Claire (CDP)—Anne Arundel ... *MD-1*
Cape Vincent (Town)—Jefferson ... *NY-1*
Cape Vincent (Village)—Jefferson ... *NY-1*
Capioma (Township)—Nemaha ... *KS-4*
Capital (Township)—Sangamon ... *IL-3*
Capital (Township)—Hutchinson ... *SD-4*
Capitan (Village)—Lincoln ... *NM-4*
Capitan Grande Reservation (CA) ... *IndRes-4*
Capitola (City)—Santa Cruz ... *CA-4*
Capitola (Township)—Spink ... *SD-4*
Capitol Heights (Town)—Prince George's ... *MD-1*
Capon Bridge (Town)—Hampshire ... *WV-2*
Capps Creek (Township)—Barry ... *MO-3*
Capron (Village)—Boone ... *IL-3*
Capron (Town)—Woods ... *OK-2*
Capron (Town)—Southampton ... *VA-2*
Captain Cook (CDP)—Hawaii ... *HI-4*
Captain's Landing (Township)—Morton ... *ND-4*
Capulin Mountain (NM) ... *Geog-4*
Caratunk (Plantation)—Somerset ... *ME-1*
Caraway (Town)—Craighead ... *AR-2*
Carbon (Town)—Clay ... *IN-3*
Carbon (City)—Adams ... *IA-3*
Carbon (Township)—Huntingdon ... *PA-1*
Carbon (Town)—Eastland ... *TX-2*
Carbonado (Town)—Pierce ... *WA-4*
Carbon Cliff (Town)—Rock Island ... *IL-3*
Carbon County ... *MT-4*
Carbon County ... *PA-1*
Carbon County ... *UT-4*
Carbon County ... *WY-4*
Carbondale (Town)—Garfield ... *CO-4*
Carbondale (City)—Jackson ... *IL-3*
Carbondale (Township)—Jackson ... *IL-3*
Carbondale (City)—Osage ... *KS-4*
Carbondale (Township)—Ward ... *ND-4*
Carbondale (City)—Lackawanna ... *PA-1*
Carbondale (Township)—Lackawanna ... *PA-1*
Carbon Hill (City)—Walker ... *AL-2*
Carbon Hill (Village)—Grundy ... *IL-3*
Cardiff (Town)—Jefferson ... *AL-2*
Cardin (Town)—Ottawa ... *OK-2*
Cardington (Township)—Morrow ... *OH-3*
Cardington (Village)—Morrow ... *OH-3*
Cardwell (City)—Dunklin ... *MO-3*
Carefree (Town)—Maricopa ... *AZ-4*
Carefree (Town)—Crawford ... *IN-3*
Carencro (Town)—Lafayette Parish ... *LA-2*
Carey (Village)—Wyandot ... *OH-3*
Carey (Town)—Iron ... *WI-3*

Caribbean Sea (NM) ... *Geog-4*
Caribou (City)—Aroostook ... *ME-1*
Caribou (Township)—Kittson ... *MN-3*
Caribou County ... *ID-4*
Carimona (Township)—Fillmore ... *MN-3*
Carl (Town)—Barrow ... *GA-2*
Carl (Township)—McPherson ... *SD-4*
Carle Place (CDP)—Nassau ... *NY-1*
Carleton (Village)—Monroe ... *MI-3*
Carleton (Village)—Thayer ... *NE-4*
Carlin (City)—Elko ... *NV-4*
Carlinville (City)—Macoupin ... *IL-3*
Carlinville (Township)—Macoupin ... *IL-3*
Carlisle (City)—Lonoke ... *AR-2*
Carlisle (Town)—Sullivan ... *IN-3*
Carlisle (City)—Polk ... *IA-3*
Carlisle (City)—Warren ... *IA-3*
Carlisle (City)—Nicholas ... *KY-2*
Carlisle (Town)—Middlesex ... *MA-1*
Carlisle (Township)—Otter Tail ... *MN-3*
Carlisle (Town)—Schoharie ... *NY-1*
Carlisle (Township)—Pembina ... *ND-4*
Carlisle (Township)—Lorain ... *OH-3*
Carlisle (Village)—Montgomery ... *OH-3*
Carlisle (Village)—Warren ... *OH-3*
Carlisle (Borough)—Cumberland ... *PA-1*
Carlisle (Town)—Union ... *SC-2*
Carlisle (Township)—Brown ... *SD-4*
Carlisle Barracks (PA) ... *Mil-4*
Carlisle County ... *KY-2*
Carl Junction (City)—Jasper ... *MO-3*
Carlock (Village)—McLean ... *IL-3*
Carlock (Township)—Gregory ... *SD-4*
Carlos (City)—Douglas ... *MN-3*
Carlos (Township)—Douglas ... *MN-3*
Carlsbad (City)—San Diego ... *CA-4*
Carlsbad (City)—Eddy ... *NM-4*
Carlsbad Caverns (NM) ... *Geog-4*
Carlsbad North (CDP)—Eddy ... *NM-4*
Carl's Corner (Town)—Hill ... *TX-2*
Carlstadt (Borough)—Bergen ... *NJ-1*
Carlston (Township)—Freeborn ... *MN-3*
Carlton (Town)—Madison ... *GA-2*
Carlton (City)—Dickinson ... *KS-4*
Carlton (Township)—Barry ... *MI-3*
Carlton (Township)—Carlton ... *MN-3*
Carlton (Town)—Orleans ... *NY-1*
Carlton (City)—Yamhill ... *OR-4*
Carlton (Township)—Hand ... *SD-4*
Carlton (Town)—Kewaunee ... *WI-3*
Carlton County ... *MN-3*
Carlyle (Town)—Clinton ... *IL-3*
Carlyle (Township)—Clinton ... *IL-3*
Carlyle (Township)—Allen ... *KS-4*
Carlyle (Township)—Beadle ... *SD-4*
Carlyss (CDP)—Calcasieu Parish ... *LA-2*
Carman (Township)—Henderson ... *IL-3*
Carmel (City)—Hamilton ... *IN-3*
Carmel (Town)—Penobscot ... *ME-1*
Carmel (Township)—Eaton ... *MI-3*
Carmel (Town)—Putnam ... *NY-1*
Carmel-by-the-Sea (City)—Monterey ... *CA-4*
Carmel Hamlet (CDP)—Putnam ... *NY-1*
Carmel Valley Village (CDP)—Monterey ... *CA-4*
Carmen (Town)—Alfalfa ... *OK-2*
Carmi (City)—White ... *IL-3*
Carmi (Township)—White ... *IL-3*
Carmichael (CDP)—Sacramento ... *CA-4*
Carmichaels (Borough)—Greene ... *PA-1*
Carmine (City)—Fayette ... *TX-2*
Carmody Hills-Pepper Mill Village (CDP)—Prince George's ... *MD-1*

Carnation (City)—King ... *WA-4*
Carnegie (Town)—Caddo ... *OK-2*
Carnegie (Borough)—Allegheny ... *PA-1*
Carneiro (Township)—Ellsworth ... *KS-4*
Carnesville (City)—Franklin ... *GA-2*
Carney (CDP)—Baltimore ... *MD-1*
Carney (Village)—Menominee ... *MI-3*
Carney (Town)—Lincoln ... *OK-2*
Carneys Point (Township)—Salem ... *NJ-1*
Carnot-Moon (CDP)—Allegheny ... *PA-1*
Caro (Village)—Tuscola ... *MI-3*
Caroga (Town)—Fulton ... *NY-1*
Carol City (CDP)—Dade ... *FL-2*
Carolina (Municipality)—Covington ... *AL-2*
Carolina Beach (Town)—New Hanover ... *NC-2*
Caroline (Town)—Tompkins ... *NY-1*
Caroline County ... *MD-1*
Caroline County ... *VA-2*
Carol Stream (Residential suburb)—DuPage ... *IL-3*
Carpenter (Township)—Jasper ... *IN-3*
Carpenter (City)—Mitchell ... *IA-3*
Carpenter (Township)—Itasca ... *MN-3*
Carpenter (Township)—Steele ... *ND-4*
Carpentersville (Village)—Kane ... *IL-3*
Carpinteria (City)—Santa Barbara ... *CA-4*
Carpio (City)—Ward ... *ND-4*
Carpio (Township)—Ward ... *ND-4*
Carp Lake (Township)—Emmet ... *MI-3*
Carp Lake (Township)—Ontonagon ... *MI-3*
Carr (Township)—Clark ... *IN-3*
Carr (Township)—Jackson ... *IN-3*
Carrabassett Valley (Town)—Franklin ... *ME-1*
Carrabelle (City)—Franklin ... *FL-2*
Carrboro (Town)—Orange ... *NC-2*
Carr Creek (Township)—Mitchell ... *KS-4*
Carrier (Town)—Garfield ... *OK-2*
Carriers Mills (Township)—Saline ... *IL-3*
Carriers Mills (Village)—Saline ... *IL-3*
Carrigan (Township)—Marion ... *IL-3*
Carrington (City)—Foster ... *ND-4*
Carrington (Township)—Foster ... *ND-4*
Carrizo Springs (City)—Dimmit ... *TX-2*
Carrizozo (Town)—Lincoln ... *NM-4*
Carroll (Township)—Vermilion ... *IL-3*
Carroll (City)—Carroll ... *IA-3*
Carroll (Plantation)—Penobscot ... *ME-1*
Carroll (Township)—Platte ... *MO-3*
Carroll (Township)—Reynolds ... *MO-3*
Carroll (Township)—Texas ... *MO-3*
Carroll (Village)—Wayne ... *NE-4*
Carroll (Town)—Coos ... *NH-1*
Carroll (Town)—Chautauqua ... *NY-1*
Carroll (Township)—Slope ... *ND-4*
Carroll (Village)—Fairfield ... *OH-3*
Carroll (Township)—Ottawa ... *OH-3*
Carroll (Township)—Perry ... *PA-1*
Carroll (Township)—Washington ... *PA-1*
Carroll (Township)—York ... *PA-1*
Carroll (Township)—Charles Mix ... *SD-4*
Carroll County ... *AR-2*
Carroll County ... *GA-2*
Carroll County ... *IL-3*
Carroll County ... *IN-3*
Carroll County ... *IA-3*
Carroll County ... *KY-2*
Carroll County ... *MD-1*
Carroll County ... *MS-2*
Carroll County ... *MO-3*

General Index — American Places Dictionary

Carroll County NH-1
Carroll County OH-3
Carroll County TN-2
Carroll County VA-2
Carroll Gardens—Kings NY-1
Carrollton (Town)—Pickens AL-2
Carrollton (City)—Carroll GA-2
Carrollton (City)—Greene IL-3
Carrollton (Township)—Greene IL-3
Carrollton (Township)—Carroll IN-3
Carrollton (City)—Carroll KY-2
Carrollton (Township)—Saginaw ... MI-3
Carrollton (Town)—Carroll MS-2
Carrollton (City)—Carroll MO-3
Carrollton (Township)—Carroll MO-3
Carrollton (Town)—Cattaraugus NY-1
Carrollton (Village)—Carroll OH-3
Carrollton (City)—Collin TX-2
Carrollton (City)—Dallas TX-2
Carrollton (City)—Denton TX-2
Carrolltown (Borough)—Cambria ... PA-1
Carroll Valley (Borough)—Adams .. PA-1
Carrollwood (CDP)—
  Hillsborough FL-2
Carrollwood Village (CDP)—
  Hillsborough FL-2
Carrolton (Township)—Fillmore ... MN-3
Carrsville (City)—Livingston KY-2
Carryall (Township)—Paulding OH-3
Carson (City)—Los Angeles CA-4
Carson (Township)—Fayette IL-3
Carson (City)—Pottawattamie IA-3
Carson (Township)—
  Cottonwood MN-3
Carson (City)—Grant ND-4
Carson (Town)—Portage WI-3
Carson City (City)—Montcalm MI-3
Carson City (City)—Carson City
  (Independent City) NV-4
Carson City (Independent City) NV-4
Carson Colony (NV) IndRes-4
Carson County TX-2
Carson River Valley (CDP)—
  Skamania WA-4
Carsonville (Village)—Sanilac MI-3
Carsonville (Township)—Becker .. MN-3
Carswell Air Force Base (TX) Mil-1
Carter (Township)—Spencer IN-3
Carter (Township)—Carter MO-3
Carter (Township)—Burke ND-4
Carter (Town)—Beckham OK-2
Carter (Town)—Tripp SD-4
Carter County KY-2
Carter County MO-3
Carter County MT-4
Carter County OK-2
Carter County TN-2
Carteret (Borough)—Middlesex NJ-1
Carteret County NC-2
Carter Lake (City)—
  Pottawattamie IA-3
Cartersville (City)—Bartow GA-2
Carterville (City)—Williamson IL-3
Carterville (City)—Jasper MO-3
Carthage (City)—Dallas AR-2
Carthage (City)—Hancock IL-3
Carthage (Township)—Hancock IL-3
Carthage (Town)—Rush IN-3
Carthage (Town)—Franklin ME-1
Carthage (City)—Leake MS-2
Carthage (City)—Jasper MO-3
Carthage (Village)—Jefferson NY-1
Carthage (Town)—Moore NC-2
Carthage (Township)—Athens OH-3
Carthage (City)—Miner SD-4

Carthage (Township)—Miner SD-4
Carthage (Town)—Smith TN-2
Carthage (City)—Panola TX-2
Cartwright (Township)—
  Sangamon IL-3
Caruthers (CDP)—Fresno CA-4
Caruthersville (City)—Pemiscot ... MO-3
Carver (Town)—Plymouth MA-1
Carver (City)—Carver MN-3
Carver County MN-3
Carville (CDP)—Iberville Parish ... LA-2
Cary (Village)—McHenry IL-3
Cary (Plantation)—Aroostook ME-1
Cary (Town)—Sharkey MS-2
Cary (Town)—Wake NC-2
Cary (Town)—Wood WI-3
Carytown (City)—Jasper MO-3
Caryville (Town)—Washington FL-2
Caryville (Town)—Campbell TN-2
Casa (Town)—Perry AR-2
Casa Conejo (CDP)—Ventura CA-4
Casa de Oro-Mount Helix (CDP)—San
  Diego CA-4
Casa Grande (City)—Pinal AZ-4
Casar (Town)—Cleveland NC-2
Cascade (City)—Valley ID-4
Cascade (City)—Dubuque IA-3
Cascade (City)—Jones IA-3
Cascade (Township)—Kent MI-3
Cascade (Township)—Olmsted MN-3
Cascade (Town)—Cascade MT-4
Cascade (Township)—Lycoming PA-1
Cascade (Village)—Sheboygan WI-3
Cascade-Chipita Park (CDP)—El
  Paso CO-4
Cascade County MT-4
Cascade-Fairwood (CDP)—King ... WA-4
Cascade Locks (City)—Hood
  River OR-4
Cascade Park East (CDP)—
  Clark WA-4
Cascade Park West (CDP)—
  Clark WA-4
Cascade Range (NM) Geog-4
Cascade Valley (CDP)—Grant WA-4
Casco (Town)—Cumberland ME-1
Casco (Township)—Allegan MI-3
Casco (Township)—St. Clair MI-3
Casco (Town)—Kewaunee WI-3
Casco (Village)—Kewaunee WI-3
Case (Township)—Presque Isle MI-3
Caseville (Township)—Huron MI-3
Caseville (Village)—Huron MI-3
Casey (City)—Clark IL-3
Casey (Township)—Clark IL-3
Casey (City)—Cumberland IL-3
Casey (City)—Adair IA-3
Casey (City)—Guthrie IA-3
Casey (Township)—Ransom ND-4
Casey (Town)—Washburn WI-3
Casey County KY-2
Caseyville (Township)—St. Clair IL-3
Caseyville (Village)—St. Clair IL-3
Cash (Town)—Craighead AR-2
Cash (Township)—Slope ND-4
Cash (Township)—Perkins SD-4
Cashel (Township)—Swift MN-3
Cashion (Town)—Kingfisher OK-2
Cashion (Town)—Logan OK-2
Cashmere (City)—Chelan WA-4
Cashton (Village)—Monroe WI-3
Casner (Township)—Jefferson IL-3
Casnovia (Village)—Kent MI-3
Casnovia (Township)—Muskegon .. MI-3
Casnovia (Village)—Muskegon MI-3

Casper (City)—Natrona WY-4
Caspian (City)—Iron MI-3
Cass (Township)—Fulton IL-3
Cass (Township)—Clay IN-3
Cass (Township)—Dubois IN-3
Cass (Township)—Greene IN-3
Cass (Township)—La Porte IN-3
Cass (Township)—Ohio IN-3
Cass (Township)—Pulaski IN-3
Cass (Township)—Sullivan IN-3
Cass (Township)—White IN-3
Cass (Township)—Douglas MO-3
Cass (Township)—Greene MO-3
Cass (Township)—Stone MO-3
Cass (Township)—Texas MO-3
Cass (Township)—Hancock OH-3
Cass (Township)—Muskingum OH-3
Cass (Township)—Richland OH-3
Cass (Township)—Huntingdon PA-1
Cass (Township)—Schuylkill PA-1
Cassadaga (Village)—
  Chautauqua NY-1
Cassandra (Borough)—Cambria PA-1
Cass City (Village)—Tuscola MI-3
Cass County IL-3
Cass County IN-3
Cass County IA-3
Cass County MI-3
Cass County MN-3
Cass County MO-3
Cass County NE-4
Cass County ND-4
Cass County TX-2
Cassel (Town)—Marathon WI-3
Casselberry (City)—Seminole FL-2
Casselman (Borough)—Somerset ... PA-1
Casselton (City)—Cass ND-4
Casselton (Township)—Cass ND-4
Cassia County ID-4
Cassian (Town)—Oneida WI-3
Cassidy (Township)—Christian MO-3
Cass Lake (City)—Cass MN-3
Cassoday (City)—Butler KS-2
Cassopolis (Village)—Cass MI-3
Casstown (Village)—Miami OH-3
Cassville (City)—Barry MO-3
Cassville (Borough)—Huntingdon ... PA-1
Cassville (CDP)—Monongalia WV-2
Cassville (Town)—Grant WI-3
Cassville (Village)—Grant WI-3
Castalia (City)—Winneshiek IA-3
Castalia (Town)—Nash NC-2
Castalia (Village)—Erie OH-3
Castalia (Pop. Place)—Charles
  Mix SD-4
Castana (City)—Monona IA-3
Castanea (Township)—Clinton PA-1
Castile (Town)—Wyoming NY-1
Castile (Village)—Wyoming NY-1
Castine (Town)—Hancock ME-1
Castine (Village)—Darke OH-3
Castle (Township)—McPherson ... KS-2
Castle (Town)—Okfuskee OK-2
Castle Air Force Base (CA) Mil-1
Castleberry (Town)—Conecuh AL-2
Castle Butte (Township)—
  Perkins SD-4
Castle Butte No. 18 (Township)—
  Pennington SD-4
Castle Dale (City)—Emery UT-4
Castleford (City)—Twin Falls ID-4
Castle Hayne (CDP)—New
  Hanover NC-2
Castle Hill (Town)—Aroostook ME-1
Castle Hills (City)—Bexar TX-2

Castle Point (CDP)—St. Louis *MO-3*
Castle Rock (Town)—Douglas *CO-4*
Castle Rock (Township)—
 Dakota *MN-3*
Castle Rock (Township)—
 Hettinger *ND-4*
Castle Rock (City)—Cowlitz *WA-4*
Castle Rock (Town)—Grant *WI-3*
Castle Shannon (Borough)—
 Allegheny *PA-1*
Castleton (Town)—Marion *IN-3*
Castleton (Township)—Reno *KS-4*
Castleton (Township)—Barry *MI-3*
Castleton (Town)—Rutland *VT-1*
Castleton-on-Hudson (Village)—
 Rensselaer *NY-1*
Castle Valley (Town)—Grand *UT-4*
Castlewood (CDP)—Arapahoe *CO-4*
Castlewood (City)—Hamlin *SD-4*
Castlewood (Township)—Hamlin .. *SD-4*
Castlewood (CDP)—Russell *VA-2*
Castor (Village)—Bienville Parish .. *LA-2*
Castor (Township)—Madison *MO-3*
Castor (Township)—Stoddard *MO-3*
Castorland (Village)—Lewis *NY-1*
Castro County *TX-2*
Castro Valley (CDP)—Alameda *CA-4*
Castroville (CDP)—Monterey *CA-4*
Castroville (City)—Medina *TX-2*
Caswell (Plantation)—Aroostook .. *ME-1*
Caswell (Town)—Forest *WI-3*
Caswell Beach (Town)—
 Brunswick *NC-2*
Caswell County *NC-2*
Catahoula Parish *LA-2*
Catalina (CDP)—Pima *AZ-4*
Catasauqua (Borough)—Lehigh *PA-1*
Catawba (Town)—Catawba *NC-2*
Catawba (Village)—Clark *OH-3*
Catawba (Town)—Price *WI-3*
Catawba (Township)—Price *WI-3*
Catawba County *NC-2*
Catawba Island (Township)—
 Ottawa *OH-3*
Catawba Reservation (SC) *IndRes-4*
Catawissa (Borough)—Columbia *PA-1*
Catawissa (Township)—Columbia .. *PA-1*
Cathan (CDP)—Snohomish *WA-4*
Catharine (Town)—Schuyler *NY-1*
Catharine (Township)—Blair *PA-1*
Cathay (City)—Wells *ND-4*
Cathay (Township)—Wells *ND-4*
Cathedral City (City)—Riverside .. *CA-4*
Catherine (Township)—Ellis *KS-4*
Cathlamet (Town)—Wahkiakum *WA-4*
Catlettsburg (City)—Boyd *KY-2*
Catlin (Township)—Vermilion *IL-3*
Catlin (Village)—Vermilion *IL-3*
Catlin (Township)—Marion *KS-4*
Catlin (Town)—Chemung *NY-1*
Cato (Township)—Montcalm *MI-3*
Cato (Town)—Cayuga *NY-1*
Cato (Village)—Cayuga *NY-1*
Cato (Township)—Ramsey *ND-4*
Cato (Town)—Manitowoc *WI-3*
Caton (Town)—Steuben *NY-1*
Catonsville (CDP)—Baltimore *MD-1*
Catoosa (City)—Rogers *OK-2*
Catoosa County *GA-2*
Catron (Town)—New Madrid *MO-3*
Catron County *NM-4*
Catskill (Town)—Greene *NY-1*
Catskill (Village)—Greene *NY-1*
Catskill Mountains (NY) *Geog-4*

Cattaraugus (Village)—
 Cattaraugus *NY-1*
Cattaraugus County *NY-1*
Cattaraugus Reservation
 (NY) *IndRes-4*
Cattaraugus Reservation (Pop. Place)—
 Cattaraugus *NY-1*
Cattaraugus Reservation (Pop. Place)—
 Chautauqua *NY-1*
Cattaraugus Reservation (Pop. Place)—
 Erie *NY-1*
Caulksville (Town)—Logan *AR-2*
Causey (Village)—Roosevelt *NM-4*
Cavalier (City)—Pembina *ND-4*
Cavalier (Township)—Pembina *ND-4*
Cavalier County *ND-4*
Cave (Township)—Franklin *IL-3*
Cave (Town)—Lincoln *MO-3*
Cave City (City)—Independence ... *AR-2*
Cave City (City)—Sharp *AR-2*
Cave City (City)—Barren *KY-2*
Cave Creek (Town)—Maricopa *AZ-4*
Cave-In-Rock (Village)—Hardin ... *IL-3*
Cave Junction (City)—Josephine ... *OR-4*
Cavendish (Town)—Windsor *VT-1*
Cave Spring (City)—Floyd *GA-2*
Cave Springs (City)—Benton *AR-2*
Cavour (Town)—Beadle *SD-4*
Cavour (Township)—Beadle *SD-4*
Cawker (Township)—Mitchell *KS-4*
Cawker City (City)—Mitchell *KS-4*
Cayce (City)—Lexington *SC-2*
Cayucos (CDP)—San Luis
 Obispo *CA-4*
Cayuga (Town)—Vermillion *IN-3*
Cayuga (Village)—Cayuga *NY-1*
Cayuga (City)—Sargent *ND-4*
Cayuga County *NY-1*
Cayuga Heights (Village)—
 Tompkins *NY-1*
Cayuta (Town)—Schuyler *NY-1*
Cazenovia (Township)—
 Woodford *IL-3*
Cazenovia (Town)—Madison *NY-1*
Cazenovia (Village)—Madison *NY-1*
Cazenovia (Village)—Richland *WI-3*
Cazenovia (Village)—Sauk *WI-3*
Cecil (Town)—Cook *GA-2*
Cecil (Township)—Bottineau *ND-4*
Cecil (Village)—Paulding *OH-3*
Cecil (Township)—Washington *PA-1*
Cecil (Village)—Shawano *WI-3*
Cecil County *MD-1*
Cecilia (CDP)—St. Martin Parish .. *LA-2*
Cecilton (Town)—Cecil *MD-1*
Cedar (Township)—Knox *IL-3*
Cedar (Township)—Chase *KS-4*
Cedar (Township)—Cowley *KS-4*
Cedar (Township)—Jackson *KS-4*
Cedar (City)—Smith *KS-4*
Cedar (Township)—Smith *KS-4*
Cedar (Township)—Wilson *KS-4*
Cedar (Township)—Osceola *MI-3*
Cedar (Township)—Marshall *MN-3*
Cedar (Township)—Martin *MN-3*
Cedar (Township)—Boone *MO-3*
Cedar (Township)—Callaway *MO-3*
Cedar (Township)—Cedar *MO-3*
Cedar (Township)—Dade *MO-3*
Cedar (Township)—Pettis *MO-3*
Cedar (Township)—Antelope *NE-4*
Cedar (Township)—Buffalo *NE-4*
Cedar (Township)—Nance *NE-4*
Cedar (Township)—Adams *ND-4*
Cedar (Township)—Hand *SD-4*

Cedarbend (Township)—Roseau ... *MN-3*
Cedar Bluff (Town)—Cherokee *AL-2*
Cedar Bluff (Township)—
 Oregon *MO-3*
Cedar Bluff (Town)—Tazewell *VA-2*
Cedar Bluffs (Village)—Saunders .. *NE-4*
Cedarburg (City)—Ozaukee *WI-3*
Cedarburg (Town)—Ozaukee *WI-3*
Cedarbutte (Pop. Place)—
 Mellette *SD-4*
Cedar Butte No. 4 (Township)—
 Pennington *SD-4*
Cedar City (City)—Iron *UT-4*
Cedar County *IA-3*
Cedar County *MO-3*
Cedar County *NE-4*
Cedar Creek (Township)—Allen *IN-3*
Cedar Creek (Township)—Lake *IN-3*
Cedar Creek (Township)—
 Muskegon *MI-3*
Cedar Creek (Township)—
 Wexford *MI-3*
Cedar Creek (Township)—Taney .. *MO-3*
Cedar Creek (Township)—
 Wayne *MO-3*
Cedar Creek (Village)—Cass *NE-4*
Cedar Creek (Township)—Slope ... *ND-4*
Cedaredge (Town)—Delta *CO-4*
Cedar Falls (City)—Black Hawk *IA-3*
Cedar Fort (Town)—Utah *UT-4*
Cedar Glen Lakes (CDP)—Ocean .. *NJ-1*
Cedar Glen West (CDP)—Ocean .. *NJ-1*
Cedar Grove (Town)—Bay *FL-2*
Cedar Grove (Town)—Franklin *IN-3*
Cedar Grove (Township)—Essex .. *NJ-1*
Cedar Grove (Town)—Kanawha .. *WV-2*
Cedar Grove (Village)—
 Sheboygan *WI-3*
Cedar Hill (CDP)—Jefferson *MO-3*
Cedar Hill (Town)—Robertson *TN-2*
Cedar Hill (City)—Dallas *TX-2*
Cedar Hill (City)—Ellis *TX-2*
Cedar Hill Lakes (Village)—
 Jefferson *MO-3*
Cedar Hills (CDP)—Washington ... *OR-4*
Cedar Hills (Town)—Utah *UT-4*
Cedarhurst (Village)—Nassau *NY-1*
Cedar Key (City)—Levy *FL-2*
Cedar Lake (Town)—Lake *IN-3*
Cedar Lake (Township)—Scott *MN-3*
Cedar Lake (Town)—Barron *WI-3*
Cedar Mill (CDP)—Washington *OR-4*
Cedar Mills (City)—Meeker *MN-3*
Cedar Mills (Township)—
 Meeker *MN-3*
Cedar Park (City)—Travis *TX-2*
Cedar Park (City)—Williamson *TX-2*
Cedar Point (Village)—La Salle *IL-3*
Cedar Point (City)—Chase *KS-4*
Cedar Point (Town)—Carteret *NC-2*
Cedar Rapids (City)—Linn *IA-3*
Cedar Rapids (Village)—Boone *NE-4*
Cedar Rapids (Town)—Rusk *WI-3*
Cedar Springs (City)—Kent *MI-3*
Cedartown (City)—Polk *GA-2*
Cedar Vale (City)—Chautauqua *KS-4*
Cedar Valley (Township)—St.
 Louis *MN-3*
Cedar Valley (City)—Logan *OK-2*
Cedarville (Village)—Stephenson ... *IL-3*
Cedarville (City)—Pike *KY-2*
Cedarville (Township)—
 Menominee *MI-3*
Cedarville (Township)—Greene *OH-3*
Cedarville (Village)—Greene *OH-3*

General Index — American Places Dictionary

Cedarville Rancheria (CA) *IndRes-4*
Cedron (Township)—Lincoln *KS-4*
Celeste (Town)—Hunt *TX-2*
Celina (City)—Mercer *OH-3*
Celina (Town)—Clay *TN-2*
Celina (Town)—Collin *TX-2*
Celoron (Village)—Chautauqua *NY-1*
Cement (Town)—Caddo *OK-2*
Cement City (Village)—Jackson *MI-3*
Cement City (Village)—Lenawee... *MI-3*
Center (Town)—Rio Grande *CO-4*
Center (Town)—Saguache *CO-4*
Center (Township)—Benton *IN-3*
Center (Township)—Boone *IN-3*
Center (Township)—Clinton *IN-3*
Center (Township)—Dearborn *IN-3*
Center (Township)—Delaware *IN-3*
Center (Township)—Gibson *IN-3*
Center (Township)—Grant *IN-3*
Center (Township)—Greene *IN-3*
Center (Township)—Hancock *IN-3*
Center (Township)—Hendricks....... *IN-3*
Center (Township)—Howard *IN-3*
Center (Township)—Jennings *IN-3*
Center (Township)—La Porte *IN-3*
Center (Township)—Lake *IN-3*
Center (Township)—Marion *IN-3*
Center (Township)—Marshall *IN-3*
Center (Township)—Martin *IN-3*
Center (Township)—Porter *IN-3*
Center (Township)—Posey *IN-3*
Center (Township)—Ripley *IN-3*
Center (Township)—Rush *IN-3*
Center (Township)—Starke *IN-3*
Center (Township)—Union *IN-3*
Center (Township)—Vanderburgh .. *IN-3*
Center (Township)—Wayne *IN-3*
Center (Township)—Atchison *KS-4*
Center (Township)—Chautauqua.... *KS-4*
Center (Township)—Clark *KS-4*
Center (Township)—Cloud *KS-4*
Center (Township)—Decatur *KS-4*
Center (Township)—Dickinson *KS-4*
Center (Township)—Doniphan *KS-4*
Center (Township)—Hodgeman *KS-4*
Center (Township)—Jewell *KS-4*
Center (Township)—Lyon *KS-4*
Center (Township)—Marion *KS-4*
Center (Township)—Marshall *KS-4*
Center (Township)—Mitchell *KS-4*
Center (Township)—Nemaha *KS-4*
Center (Township)—Ness................ *KS-4*
Center (Township)—Ottawa *KS-4*
Center (Township)—
   Pottawatomie *KS-4*
Center (Township)—Rawlins *KS-4*
Center (Township)—Reno *KS-4*
Center (Township)—Rice *KS-4*
Center (Township)—Riley *KS-4*
Center (Township)—Rush *KS-4*
Center (Township)—Russell *KS-4*
Center (Township)—Smith *KS-4*
Center (Township)—Stevens *KS-4*
Center (Township)—Wilson *KS-4*
Center (Township)—Woodson *KS-4*
Center (Township)—Emmet............ *MI-3*
Center (Township)—Crow Wing... *MN-3*
Center (Township)—Buchanan *MO-3*
Center (Township)—Dade............... *MO-3*
Center (Township)—Hickory *MO-3*
Center (Township)—Knox *MO-3*
Center (Township)—McDonald *MO-3*
Center (City)—Ralls *MO-3*
Center (Township)—Ralls *MO-3*
Center (Township)—St. Clair *MO-3*

Center (Township)—Vernon *MO-3*
Center (Township)—Buffalo *NE-4*
Center (Township)—Butler *NE-4*
Center (Township)—Hall *NE-4*
Center (Village)—Knox *NE-4*
Center (Township)—Phelps............. *NE-4*
Center (Township)—Saunders *NE-4*
Center (City)—Oliver *ND-4*
Center (Township)—Richland......... *ND-4*
Center (Township)—Carroll *OH-3*
Center (Township)—Columbiana .. *OH-3*
Center (Township)—Guernsey *OH-3*
Center (Township)—Mercer *OH-3*
Center (Township)—Monroe *OH-3*
Center (Township)—Morgan *OH-3*
Center (Township)—Noble *OH-3*
Center (Township)—Williams......... *OH-3*
Center (Township)—Wood *OH-3*
Center (Township)—Beaver *PA-1*
Center (Township)—Butler *PA-1*
Center (Township)—Greene *PA-1*
Center (Township)—Indiana........... *PA-1*
Center (Township)—Aurora *SD-4*
Center (City)—Shelby *TX-2*
Center (Town)—Outagamie *WI-3*
Center (Town)—Rock *WI-3*
Centerburg (Village)—Knox........... *OH-3*
Center City (City)—Chisago *MN-3*
Center Creek (Township)—
   Martin *MN-3*
Center-District 1 (Township)—
   Norton *KS-4*
Centereach (CDP)—Suffolk *NY-1*
Centerfield (Town)—Sanpete *UT-4*
Center Harbor (Town)—Belknap... *NH-1*
Center Hill (City)—Sumter *FL-2*
Center Junction (City)—Jones *IA-3*
Center Line (City)—Macomb *MI-3*
Center Moriches (CDP)—Suffolk .. *NY-1*
Center No. 1 (Township)—
   Greene *MO-3*
Center No. 2 (Township)—
   Greene *MO-3*
Center No. 3 (Township)—
   Greene *MO-3*
Center Point (Division)—
   Jefferson *AL-2*
Center Point (Town)—Clay............. *IN-3*
Center Point (City)—Linn *IA-3*
Centerport (CDP)—Suffolk............. *NY-1*
Centerport (Borough)—Berks.......... *PA-1*
Centerton (City)—Benton *AR-2*
Centertown (City)—Ohio *KY-2*
Centertown (Town)—Cole *MO-3*
Centertown (Town)—Warren *TN-2*
Centerview (Town)—Johnson *MO-3*
Centerview (Township)—
   Johnson *MO-3*
Centerville (City)—Houston *GA-2*
Centerville (City)—Wayne *IN-3*
Centerville (City)—Appanoose *IA-3*
Centerville (Township)—Linn......... *KS-4*
Centerville (Township)—Neosho ... *KS-4*
Centerville (Town)—Washington .. *ME-1*
Centerville (CDP)—Barnstable *MA-1*
Centerville (Township)—
   Leelanau *MI-3*
Centerville (City)—Anoka.............. *MN-3*
Centerville (City)—Reynolds *MO-3*
Centerville (Town)—Allegany *NY-1*
Centerville (Town)—Franklin *NC-2*
Centerville (Village)—Gallia *OH-3*
Centerville (City)—Montgomery ... *OH-3*
Centerville (Borough)—Crawford .. *PA-1*

Centerville (Borough)—
   Washington *PA-1*
Centerville (CDP)—Anderson *SC-2*
Centerville (Township)—Faulk *SD-4*
Centerville (City)—Turner *SD-4*
Centerville (Township)—Turner *SD-4*
Centerville (Town)—Hickman *TN-2*
Centerville (City)—Leon *TX-2*
Centerville (City)—Davis *UT-4*
Centerville (Town)—Manitowoc.... *WI-3*
Centrahoma (City)—Coal *OK-2*
Central (CDP)—Yukon-Koyukuk
   Census Area *AK-2*
Central (Township)—Bond *IL-3*
Central (Township)—Barton *MO-3*
Central (Township)—Franklin *MO-3*
Central (Township)—Jefferson...... *MO-3*
Central (Township)—Madison *MO-3*
Central (Township)—Perry *MO-3*
Central (Township)—Knox *NE-4*
Central (Township)—Merrick *NE-4*
Central (Village)—Grant *NM-4*
Central (Township)—Nelson.......... *ND-4*
Central (Town)—Pickens *SC-2*
Central (CDP)—Carter *TN-2*
Central Adams (Pop. Place)—
   Adams *ND-4*
Central Aroostook (unorganized) (Pop.
   Place)—Aroostook *ME-1*
Central City (Town)—Sebastian *AR-2*
Central City (City)—Gilpin *CO-4*
Central City (Village)—Marion *IL-3*
Central City (City)—Linn *IA-3*
Central City (City)—Muhlenberg .. *KY-2*
Central City (City)—Merrick *NE-4*
Central City (Borough)—
   Somerset *PA-1*
Central City (City)—Lawrence *SD-4*
Central Corson (Pop. Place)—
   Corson *SD-4*
Central Falls (City)—Providence *RI-1*
Central Gardens (CDP)—
   Jefferson *TX-2*
Central Grant (Pop. Place)—
   Grant *ND-4*
Central Hancock (unorganized) (Pop.
   Place)—Hancock *ME-1*
Centralhatchee (Town)—Heard *GA-2*
Central Heights-Midland City (CDP)—
   Gila *AZ-4*
Central Hyde (Pop. Place)—
   Hyde.. *SD-4*
Centralia (City)—Clinton *IL-3*
Centralia (City)—Marion *IL-3*
Centralia (Township)—Marion *IL-3*
Centralia (City)—Dubuque *IA-3*
Centralia (City)—Nemaha *KS-4*
Centralia (City)—Audrain *MO-3*
Centralia (City)—Boone *MO-3*
Centralia (Township)—Boone *MO-3*
Centralia (Borough)—Columbia *PA-1*
Centralia (City)—Lewis *WA-4*
Central Islip (CDP)—Suffolk *NY-1*
Central Jones (Pop. Place)—
   Jones *SD-4*
Central Lake (Township)—
   Antrim *MI-3*
Central Lake (Village)—Antrim *MI-3*
Central McKenzie (Pop. Place)—
   McKenzie *ND-4*
Central McPherson (Pop. Place)—
   McPherson *SD-4*
Central Mellette (Pop. Place)—
   Mellette *SD-4*

Central Pacolet (Town)—
  Spartanburg..................................SC-2
Central Park (CDP)—Grays
  Harbor.......................................WA-4
Central Pennington (Pop. Place)—
  Pennington..................................SD-4
Central Pierce (Pop. Place)—
  Pierce...ND-4
Central Point (City)—Jackson........OR-4
Central Point (Township)—Day...SD-4
Central Potter (Pop. Place)—
  Potter...SD-4
Central Sheridan (Pop. Place)—
  Sheridan.....................................ND-4
Central Somerset (unorganized) (Pop.
  Place)—Somerset........................ME-1
Central Square (Village)—
  Oswego..NY-1
Central Valley (CA)......................Geog-4
Central Valley (CDP)—Shasta.......CA-4
Central Valley (CDP)—Orange......NY-1
Centre (City)—Cherokee..................AL-2
Centre (Township)—St. Joseph.......IN-3
Centre (Township)—Berks..............PA-1
Centre (Township)—Perry..............PA-1
Centre (Township)—Snyder............PA-1
Centre County..................................PA-1
Centre Hall (Borough)—Centre......PA-1
Centre Island (Village)—Nassau....NY-1
Centreville (City)—Bibb..................AL-2
Centreville (City)—St. Clair.............IL-3
Centreville (Township)—St. Clair...IL-3
Centreville (Town)—Queen
  Anne's...MD-1
Centreville (Village)—St. Joseph...MI-3
Centreville (Town)—Amite.............MS-2
Centreville (Town)—Wilkinson.....MS-2
Centreville (CDP)—Fairfax.............VA-2
Centropolis (Township)—
  Franklin..KS-4
Centuria (Village)—Polk..................WI-3
Century (Town)—Escambia............FL-2
Century City *See* **Los Angeles**—Los
  Angeles..CA-4
Century Village (CDP)—Palm
  Beach...FL-2
Ceredo (City)—Wayne....................WV-2
Ceres (City)—Stanislaus..................CA-4
Ceres (Township)—McKean..........PA-1
Ceresco (Township)—Blue Earth..MN-3
Ceresco (Village)—Saunders..........NE-4
Cerritos (City)—Los Angeles..........CA-4
Cerro Gordo (Township)—Piatt....IL-3
Cerro Gordo (Village)—Piatt.........IL-3
Cerro Gordo (Township)—Lac qui
  Parle..MN-3
Cerro Gordo (Town)—Columbus..NC-2
Cerro Gordo County........................IA-3
Cessna (Township)—Hardin..........OH-3
Ceylon (City)—Martin..................MN-3
Chackbay (CDP)—Lafourche
  Parish...LA-2
Chaco Canyon (NM)..................Geog-4
Chadbourn (Town)—Columbus....NC-2
Chadron (City)—Dawes..................NE-4
Chadwick (Village)—Carroll..........IL-3
Chadwick (Township)—
  Christian....................................MO-3
Chaffee (City)—Scott....................MO-3
Chaffee County................................CO-4
Chagrin Falls (City)—Cuyahoga....OH-3
Chagrin Falls (Township)—
  Cuyahoga...................................OH-3
Chain Lakes (Township)—
  Ramsey..ND-4

Chain-O-Lakes (Village)—Barry...MO-3
Chain o' Lakes-King (CDP)—
  Waupaca....................................WI-3
Chalco (CDP)—Sarpy....................NE-4
Chalfant (Borough)—Allegheny....PA-1
Chalfont (Borough)—Bucks..........PA-1
Chalk Level (Township)—St.
  Clair..MO-3
Chalky Butte (Pop. Place)—
  Slope...ND-4
Chalkyitsik (CDP)—Yukon-Koyukuk
  Census Area................................AK-4
Challenge-Brownsville (CDP)—
  Yuba..CA-4
Challis (City)—Custer....................ID-4
Chalmers (Township)—
  McDonough................................IL-3
Chalmers (Town)—White...............IN-3
Chalmette (CDP)—St. Bernard
  Parish...LA-2
Chama (Village)—Rio Arriba.......NM-4
Chamberlain (City)—Brule............SD-4
Chamberlain (Township)—Brule...SD-4
Chamberlayne (CDP)—Henrico.....VA-2
Chambers (Township)—Holt........NE-4
Chambers (Village)—Holt..............NE-4
Chambersburg (Township)—Pike..IL-3
Chambersburg (Borough)—
  Franklin......................................PA-1
Chambers County............................AL-2
Chambers County............................TX-2
Chamblee (City)—De Kalb............GA-2
Chamisal (CDP)—Taos.................NM-4
Chamois (City)—Osage................MO-3
Champ (Village)—St. Louis.........MO-3
Champaign (City)—Champaign.....IL-3
Champaign (Township)—
  Champaign..................................IL-3
Champaign County..........................IL-3
Champaign County........................OH-3
Champion (Township)—
  Marquette....................................MI-3
Champion (Township)—Wilkin....MN-3
Champion (Township)—Douglas..MO-3
Champion (Town)—Jefferson........NY-1
Champion (Township)—
  Williams.....................................ND-4
Champion (Township)—
  Trumbull....................................OH-3
Champion Heights (CDP)—
  Trumbull....................................OH-3
Champlain (Town)—Clinton.........NY-1
Champlain (Village)—Clinton.......NY-1
Champlain, Lake (NM)...............Geog-4
Champlin (City)—Hennepin........MN-3
Chanarambie (Township)—
  Murray.......................................MN-3
Chance (Township)—Perkins........SD-4
Chanceford (Township)—York.....PA-1
Chancellor (Town)—Turner...........SD-4
Chandler (City)—Maricopa...........AZ-4
Chandler (Town)—Warrick...........IN-3
Chandler (Township)—
  Charlevoix..................................MI-3
Chandler (Township)—Huron.......MI-3
Chandler (City)—Murray.............MN-3
Chandler (Township)—Adams......ND-4
Chandler (City)—Lincoln..............OK-2
Chandler (Town)—Henderson......TX-2
Chandlers Purchase (Pop. Place)—
  Coos..NH-1
Chandlerville (Township)—Cass....IL-3
Chandlerville (Village)—Cass........IL-3
Chanhassen (City)—Carver..........MN-3
Chanhassen (City)—Hennepin......MN-3

Channahon (Village)—Grundy.......IL-3
Channahon (Township)—Will.......IL-3
Channahon (Village)—Will............IL-3
Channel Islands Beach (CDP)—
  Ventura.......................................CA-4
Channel Lake (CDP)—Lake...........IL-3
Channelview (CDP)—Harris.........TX-2
Channing (Town)—Hartley...........TX-2
Chantilly (CDP)—Fairfax..............VA-2
Chanute (City)—Neosho................KS-4
Chanute Air Force Base (IL)........Mil-4
Chaparral (CDP)—Doña Ana......NM-4
Chapel (Township)—Howell........MO-3
Chapel Hill (Town)—Durham......NC-2
Chapel Hill (Town)—Orange.......NC-2
Chapel Hill (Town)—Marshall......TN-2
Chapin (Village)—Morgan.............IL-3
Chapin (Township)—Saginaw......MI-3
Chapin (Town)—Lexington...........SC-2
Chaplin (Town)—Windham...........CT-1
Chapman (Township)—Clay..........KS-4
Chapman (City)—Dickinson..........KS-4
Chapman (Township)—Ottawa....KS-4
Chapman (Town)—Aroostook.......ME-1
Chapman (Township)—Merrick...NE-4
Chapman (Village)—Merrick........NE-4
Chapman (Township)—Saunders...NE-4
Chapman (Township)—Clinton.....PA-1
Chapman (Borough)—
  Northampton..............................PA-1
Chapman (Township)—Snyder.....PA-1
Chapmanville (Town)—Logan.....WV-2
Chappaquiddick Island (MA).......Geog-4
Chappell (City)—Deuel..................NE-4
Chappells (Town)—Newberry.......SC-2
Charbon (Township)—McKenzie..ND-4
Chardon (Township)—Geauga......OH-3
Chardon (Village)—Geauga..........OH-3
Charenton (CDP)—St. Mary
  Parish...LA-2
Chariton (City)—Lucas...................IA-3
Chariton (Township)—Chariton...MO-3
Chariton (Township)—Howard...MO-3
Chariton (Township)—Macon.....MO-3
Chariton (Township)—Randolph..MO-3
Chariton (Township)—Schuyler...MO-3
Chariton County............................MO-3
Charlack (City)—St. Louis..........MO-3
Charlemont (Town)—Franklin.....MA-1
Charleroi (Borough)—Washington..PA-1
Charles City (City)—Floyd.............IA-3
Charles City County.......................VA-2
Charles County..............................MD-1
Charles Mix County........................SD-4
Charles Mound (IL)....................Geog-4
Charleston (City)—Franklin..........AR-2
Charleston (City)—Coles.................IL-3
Charleston (Township)—Coles.......IL-3
Charleston (Township)—
  Washington................................KS-4
Charleston (Town)—Penobscot....ME-1
Charleston (Township)—
  Kalamazoo..................................MI-3
Charleston (City)—Tallahatchie....MS-2
Charleston (City)—Mississippi....MO-3
Charleston (Town)—
  Montgomery...............................NY-1
Charleston (Township)—Tioga.....PA-1
Charleston (City)—Charleston......SC-2
Charleston (Town)—Bradley........TN-2
Charleston (Town)—Wasatch........UT-4
Charleston (Town)—Orleans.........VT-1
Charleston (City)—Kanawha.......WV-2
Charleston Air Force Base (SC)....Mil-4
Charleston County............................SC-2

General Index   American Places Dictionary

Charleston Naval Base (SC) *Mil-4*
Charlestown (City)—Clark *IN-3*
Charlestown (Township)—Clark *IN-3*
Charlestown (Town)—Cecil *MD-1*
Charlestown—Suffolk *MA-1*
Charlestown (Township)—
  Redwood *MN-3*
Charlestown (Town)—Sullivan *NH-1*
Charlestown (Township)—
  Portage *OH-3*
Charlestown (Township)—Chester.. *PA-1*
Charlestown (Town)—Washington.. *RI-1*
Charles Town (City)—Jefferson *WV-2*
Charlestown (Town)—Calumet *WI-3*
Charlestown *See* **Boston**—
  Suffolk *MA-1*
Charlevoix (City)—Charlevoix *MI-3*
Charlevoix (Township)—
  Charlevoix *MI-3*
Charlevoix County *MI-3*
Charlo (CDP)—Lake *MT-4*
Charlotte (Township)—Livingston.. *IL-3*
Charlotte (City)—Clinton *IA-3*
Charlotte (Town)—Washington *ME-1*
Charlotte (City)—Eaton *MI-3*
Charlotte (Township)—Bates *MO-3*
Charlotte (Town)—Chautauqua *NY-1*
Charlotte (City)—Mecklenburg *NC-2*
Charlotte (Town)—Dickson *TN-2*
Charlotte (City)—Atascosa *TX-2*
Charlotte (Town)—Chittenden *VT-1*
Charlotte County *FL-2*
Charlotte County *VA-2*
Charlotte Court House (Town)—
  Charlotte *VA-2*
Charlotte Hall (CDP)—Charles *MD-1*
Charlotte Hall (CDP)—St.
  Mary's *MD-1*
Charlotte Harbor (CDP)—
  Charlotte *FL-2*
Charlotte Park (CDP)—Charlotte... *FL-2*
Charlottesville (Independent City) ... *VA-2*
Charlton (Town)—Worcester *MA-1*
Charlton (Township)—Otsego *MI-3*
Charlton (Town)—Saratoga *NY-1*
Charlton County *GA-2*
Charrette (Township)—Warren *MO-3*
Charter Oak (CDP)—Los
  Angeles *CA-4*
Charter Oak (City)—Crawford *IA-3*
Chartiers (Township)—
  Washington *PA-1*
Chase (CDP)—Matanuska-Susitna
  Borough *AK-4*
Chase (City)—Rice *KS-4*
Chase (Township)—Lake *MI-3*
Chase (Town)—Oconto *WI-3*
Chaseburg (Village)—Vernon *WI-3*
Chase City (Town)—Mecklenburg.. *VA-2*
Chase County *KS-4*
Chase County *NE-4*
Chase Lake (Pop. Place)—
  Stutsman *ND-4*
Chaseley (Township)—Wells *ND-4*
Chaska (City)—Carver *MN-3*
Chaska (Township)—Carver *MN-3*
Chassell (Township)—Houghton.... *MI-3*
Chataignier (Village)—Evangeline
  Parish *LA-2*
Chatcolet (City)—Benewah *ID-4*
Chateaugay (Town)—Franklin *NY-1*
Chateaugay (Village)—Franklin *NY-1*
Chateau Woods (City)—
  Montgomery *TX-2*
Chatfield (City)—Fillmore *MN-3*

Chatfield (Township)—Fillmore ... *MN-3*
Chatfield (City)—Olmsted *MN-3*
Chatfield (Township)—Bottineau ..*ND-4*
Chatfield (Township)—Crawford...*OH-3*
Chatfield (Village)—Crawford *OH-3*
Chatham (Township)—Sangamon .. *IL-3*
Chatham (Village)—Sangamon *IL-3*
Chatham (Town)—Jackson
  Parish *LA-2*
Chatham (Town)—Barnstable........ *MA-1*
Chatham (Village)—Alger *MI-3*
Chatham (Township)—Wright *MN-3*
Chatham (Town)—Carroll *NH-1*
Chatham (Borough)—Morris *NJ-1*
Chatham (Town)—Morris *NJ-1*
Chatham (Town)—Columbia *NY-1*
Chatham (Village)—Columbia *NY-1*
Chatham (Township)—Medina *OH-3*
Chatham (Township)—Tioga *PA-1*
Chatham (Town)—Pittsylvania *VA-2*
Chatham County *GA-2*
Chatham County *NC-2*
Chatmoss-Laurel Park (CDP)—
  Henry *VA-2*
Chatom (Town)—Washington........*AL-2*
Chatsworth (City)—Murray *GA-2*
Chatsworth (Town)—Livingston ... *IL-3*
Chatsworth (Township)—
  Livingston *IL-3*
Chatsworth (City)—Sioux *IA-3*
Chattahoochee (City)—Gadsden.....*FL-2*
Chattahoochee County *GA-2*
Chattahoochee River (IL)............. *Geog-4*
Chattanooga (Town)—Comanche .. *OK-2*
Chattanooga (Town)—Tillman *OK-2*
Chattanooga (City)—Hamilton *TN-2*
Chattanooga Valley (CDP)—
  Walker *GA-2*
Chattaroy (CDP)—Mingo *WV-2*
Chattooga County *GA-2*
Chaudoin (Township)—Perkins *SD-4*
Chaumont (Village)—Jefferson *NY-1*
Chauncey (Town)—Dodge *GA-2*
Chauncey (Village)—Athens *OH-3*
Chautauqua (City)—Chautauqua....*KS-4*
Chautauqua (Town)—
  Chautauqua *NY-1*
Chautauqua County *KS-4*
Chautauqua County *NY-1*
Chauvin (CDP)—Terrebonne
  Parish *LA-2*
Chaves County *NM-4*
Chazy (Town)—Clinton *NY-1*
Cheaha Mountain (AL) *Geog-4*
Cheatham County *TN-2*
Cheat Lake (CDP)—Monongalia .. *WV-2*
Chebanse (Township)—Iroquois..... *IL-3*
Chebanse (Village)—Iroquois.......... *IL-3*
Chebanse (Village)—Kankakee *IL-3*
Cheboygan (City)—Cheboygan *MI-3*
Cheboygan County *MI-3*
Checotah (City)—McIntosh *OK-2*
Cheektowaga (Town)—Erie *NY-1*
Cheever (Township)—Dickinson ...*KS-4*
Chefornak (City)—Bethel Census
  Area *AK-4*
Chehalis (City)—Lewis................... *WA-4*
Chehalis Reservation (WA) *IndRes-4*
Chehalis Village (CDP)—Grays
  Harbor *WA-4*
Chelan (City)—Chelan *WA-4*
Chelan County *WA-4*
Chelmsford (Town)—Middlesex ... *MA-1*
Chelsea (Division)—Shelby *AL-2*
Chelsea (City)—Tama *IA-3*

Chelsea (Township)—Butler...........*KS-4*
Chelsea (Town)—Kennebec *ME-1*
Chelsea (City)—Suffolk *MA-1*
Chelsea (Village)—Washtenaw *MI-3*
Chelsea (Township)—Fillmore........ *NE-4*
Chelsea (City)—Rogers *OK-2*
Chelsea (Town)—Faulk *SD-4*
Chelsea (Town)—Orange *VT-1*
Chelsea (Town)—Taylor *WI-3*
Cheltenham (Village & Township)—
  Montgomery *PA-1*
Chemehuevi Reservation
  (CA).......................................*IndRes-4*
Chemung (Township)—McHenry ... *IL-3*
Chemung (Town)—Chemung.......... *NY-1*
Chemung County *NY-1*
Chenango (Town)—Broome *NY-1*
Chenango County *NY-1*
Chenega (CDP)—Valdez-Cordova
  Census Area *AK-4*
Chenequa (Village)—Waukesha *WI-3*
Cheney (City)—Sedgwick *KS-4*
Cheney (City)—Spokane *WA-4*
Cheney's Grove (Township)—
  McLean *IL-3*
Cheneyville (Town)—Rapides
  Parish *LA-2*
Chengwatana (Township)—Pine ... *MN-3*
Chenoa (City)—McLean *IL-3*
Chenoa (Township)—McLean *IL-3*
Chenoweth (CDP)—Wasco *OR-4*
Cheraw (Town)—Otero *CO-4*
Cheraw (Town)—Chesterfield *SC-2*
Cheriton (Town)—Northampton ... *VA-2*
Cherokee (Town)—Colbert..............*AL-2*
Cherokee (City)—Cherokee............. *IA-3*
Cherokee (Township)—Cherokee....*KS-4*
Cherokee (City)—Crawford *KS-4*
Cherokee (Township)—
  Montgomery *KS-4*
Cherokee (City)—Alfalfa *OK-2*
Cherokee County *AL-2*
Cherokee County *GA-2*
Cherokee County *IA-3*
Cherokee County *KS-4*
Cherokee County *NC-2*
Cherokee County *OK-2*
Cherokee County *SC-2*
Cherokee County *TX-2*
Cherokees, Lake o' the (OK)........ *Geog-4*
Cherokee TJSA (OK)................*IndRes-4*
Cherry (Village)—Bureau *IL-3*
Cherry (Township)—Montgomery ..*KS-4*
Cherry (Township)—St. Louis *MN-3*
Cherry (Township)—Butler *PA-1*
Cherry (Township)—Sullivan.......... *PA-1*
Cherry County *NE-4*
Cherry Creek (Township)—
  Cheyenne *KS-4*
Cherry Creek (Township)—
  Buffalo *NE-4*
Cherry Creek (Town)—
  Chautauqua *NY-1*
Cherry Creek (Village)—
  Chautauqua *NY-1*
Cherryfield (Town)—Washington . *ME-1*
Cherry Fork (Village)—Adams........*OH-3*
Cherry Grove (Township)—
  Wexford *MI-3*
Cherry Grove (Township)—
  Goodhue *MN-3*
Cherry Grove (CDP)—Hamilton...*OH-3*
Cherry Grove (Township)—
  Warren... *PA-1*

Cherry Grove-Shannon (Township)—
 Carroll IL-3
Cherry Hill (Township)—Camden .. NJ-1
Cherryhill (Township)—Indiana PA-1
Cherry Hills Village (City)—
 Arapahoe CO-4
Cherry Lake (Township)—Eddy ND-4
Cherryland (CDP)—Alameda CA-4
Cherry Ridge (Township)—
 Wayne PA-1
Cherry Tree (Borough)—Indiana PA-1
Cherrytree (Township)—Venango ... PA-1
Cherryvale (City)—Montgomery KS-4
Cherryvale (CDP)—Sumter SC-2
Cherry Valley (City)—Cross AR-2
Cherry Valley (CDP)—Riverside ... CA-4
Cherry Valley (Township)—
 Winnebago IL-3
Cherry Valley (Village)—
 Winnebago IL-3
Cherry Valley (Township)—Lake ... MI-3
Cherry Valley (Township)—
 Carroll MO-3
Cherry Valley (Town)—Otsego NY-1
Cherry Valley (Village)—Otsego ... NY-1
Cherry Valley (Township)—
 Ashtabula OH-3
Cherry Valley (Borough)—Butler PA-1
Cherryville (City)—Gaston NC-2
Cherrywood Village (City)—
 Jefferson KY-2
Chery (Township)—Jerauld SD-4
Chesaning (Township)—Saginaw ... MI-3
Chesaning (Village)—Saginaw MI-3
Chesapeake (Village)—Lawrence ... OH-3
Chesapeake (Town)—Kanawha WV-2
Chesapeake and Delaware Canal
 (OK) Geog-4
Chesapeake and Ohio Canal
 (OK) Geog-4
Chesapeake Bay (OK) Geog-4
Chesapeake Bay Bridge-Tunnel
 (OK) Geog-4
Chesapeake Beach (Town)—
 Calvert MD-1
Chesapeake City (Town)—Cecil ... MD-1
Chesapeake (Independent City) VA-2
Chesapeake Ranch Estates (CDP)—
 Calvert MD-1
Cheshire (Town)—New Haven CT-1
Cheshire (Town)—Berkshire MA-1
Cheshire (Township)—Allegan MI-3
Cheshire (Township)—Gallia OH-3
Cheshire (Village)—Gallia OH-3
Cheshire County NH-1
Chesilhurst (Borough)—Camden NJ-1
Chesnee (City)—Cherokee SC-2
Chesnee (Township)—Spartanburg ... SC-2
Chest (Township)—Cambria PA-1
Chest (Township)—Clearfield PA-1
Chester (Town)—Crawford AR-2
Chester (CDP)—Plumas CA-4
Chester (Town)—Middlesex CT-1
Chester (Town)—Dodge GA-2
Chester (Township)—Logan IL-3
Chester (City)—Randolph IL-3
Chester (Township)—Wabash IN-3
Chester (Township)—Wells IN-3
Chester (City)—Howard IA-4
Chester (Town)—Penobscot ME-1
Chester (Town)—Hampden MA-1
Chester (Township)—Eaton MI-3
Chester (Township)—Otsego MI-3
Chester (Township)—Ottawa MI-3
Chester (Township)—Polk MN-3

Chester (Township)—Wabasha MN-3
Chester (Town)—Liberty MT-4
Chester (Township)—Saunders NE-4
Chester (Village)—Thayer NE-4
Chester (Town)—Rockingham NH-1
Chester (Borough)—Morris NJ-1
Chester (Township)—Morris NJ-1
Chester (Town)—Orange NY-1
Chester (Village)—Orange NY-1
Chester (Town)—Warren NY-1
Chester (Township)—Grand
 Forks ND-4
Chester (Township)—Clinton OH-3
Chester (Township)—Geauga OH-3
Chester (Township)—Meigs OH-3
Chester (Township)—Morrow OH-3
Chester (Township)—Wayne OH-3
Chester (City)—Delaware PA-1
Chester (Township)—Delaware PA-1
Chester (City)—Chester SC-2
Chester (Township)—Douglas SD-4
Chester (Township)—Lake SD-4
Chester (Town)—Tyler TX-2
Chester (Town)—Windsor VT-1
Chester (CDP)—Chesterfield VA-2
Chester (City)—Hancock WV-2
Chester (Town)—Dodge WI-3
Chesterbrook (CDP)—Chester PA-1
Chester County PA-1
Chester County SC-2
Chester County TN-2
Chesterfield (Township)—
 Macoupin IL-3
Chesterfield (Village)—Macoupin ... IL-3
Chesterfield (Town)—Delaware IN-3
Chesterfield (Town)—Madison IN-3
Chesterfield (Town)—Hampshire . MA-1
Chesterfield (Township)—
 Macomb MI-3
Chesterfield (City)—St. Louis MO-3
Chesterfield (Town)—Cheshire NH-1
Chesterfield (Township)—
 Burlington NJ-1
Chesterfield (Town)—Essex NY-1
Chesterfield (Township)—Fulton ... OH-3
Chesterfield (Town)—
 Chesterfield SC-2
Chesterfield County SC-2
Chesterfield County VA-2
Chester Heights (Borough)—
 Delaware PA-1
Chesterhill (Village)—Morgan OH-3
Chester Hill (Borough)—
 Clearfield PA-1
Chesterland (CDP)—Geauga OH-3
Chesterton (Town)—Porter IN-3
Chestertown (Town)—Kent MD-1
Chesterville (Town)—Franklin ME-1
Chesterville (Village)—Morrow OH-3
Chestina (Township)—Kidder ND-4
Chestnut (Township)—Knox IL-3
Chestnuthill (Township)—Monroe . PA-1
Chestnut Ridge (Village)—
 Rockland NY-1
Chestonia (Township)—Antrim MI-3
Chest Springs (Borough)—
 Cambria PA-1
Cheswick (Borough)—Allegheny ... PA-1
Cheswold (Town)—Kent DE-1
Chetek (City)—Barron WI-3
Chetek (Town)—Barron WI-3
Chetopa (City)—Labette KS-4
Chetopa (Township)—Neosho KS-4
Chetopa (Township)—Wilson KS-4

Chevak (City)—Wade Hampton Census
 Area AK-4
Cheverly (Town)—Prince
 George's MD-1
Cheviot (City)—Hamilton OH-3
Chevy Chase (CDP)—
 Montgomery MD-1
Chevy Chase (Town)—
 Montgomery MD-1
Chevy Chase Heights (CDP)—
 Indiana PA-1
Chevy Chase Section Five (Village)—
 Montgomery MD-1
Chevy Chase Section Three (Village)—
 Montgomery MD-1
Chevy Chase Village (Town)—
 Montgomery MD-1
Chewelah (City)—Stevens WA-4
Cheyenne (Township)—Barton KS-4
Cheyenne (Township)—Lane KS-4
Cheyenne (Town)—Roger Mills OK-2
Cheyenne (City)—Laramie WY-4
Cheyenne-Arapaho TJSA
 (OK) IndRes-4
Cheyenne County CO-4
Cheyenne County KS-4
Cheyenne County NE-4
Cheyenne Mountain Complex
 (CO) Mil-4
Cheyenne No. 21 (Township)—
 Pennington SD-4
Cheyenne River Reservation
 (SD) IndRes-4
Cheyenne Wells (Town)—
 Cheyenne CO-4
Chicago (City)—Cook IL-3
Chicago (City)—DuPage IL-3
Chicago (Township)—Stutsman ND-4
Chicago Heights (City)—Cook IL-3
Chicago Ridge (Village)—Cook IL-3
Chicago Sanitary and Ship Canal
 (IL) Geog-4
Chichagof Island (AK) Geog-4
Chichester (Town)—Merrimack NH-1
Chickahominy TDSA (VA) IndRes-4
Chickaloon (CDP)—Matanuska-Susitna
 Borough AK-4
Chickamauga (City)—Walker GA-2
Chickamaw Beach (City)—Cass MN-3
Chickasaw (City)—Mobile AL-2
Chickasaw (Village)—Mercer OH-3
Chickasaw County IA-4
Chickasaw County MS-2
Chickasaw TJSA (OK) IndRes-4
Chickasha (City)—Grady OK-2
Chicken Ranch Rancheria
 (CA) IndRes-4
Chico (City)—Butte CA-4
Chico (City)—Wise TX-2
Chicog (Town)—Washburn WI-3
Chicopee (City)—Hampden MA-1
Chicora (Borough)—Butler PA-1
Chicot County AR-2
Chidester (City)—Ouachita AR-2
Chief (Township)—Mahnomen MN-3
Chief Lake (CDP)—Sawyer WI-3
Chiefland (City)—Levy FL-2
Chignik (City)—Lake and Peninsula
 Borough AK-4
Chignik Lagoon (CDP)—Lake and
 Peninsula Borough AK-4
Chignik Lake (CDP)—Lake and
 Peninsula Borough AK-4
Chikaming (Township)—Berrien ... MI-3
Chikaskia (Township)—Kingman ... KS-4

General Index

Chikaskia (Township)—Sumner......*KS-4*
Childersburg (City)—Talladega......*AL-2*
Childress (City)—Childress......... *TX-2*
Childress County.................................. *TX-2*
Childstown (Township)—Turner.... *SD-4*
Chilhowee (Town)—Johnson *MO-3*
Chilhowee (Township)—Johnson.. *MO-3*
Chilhowie (Town)—Smyth *VA-2*
Chili (Township)—Hancock............ *IL-3*
Chili (Town)—Monroe *NY-1*
Chillicothe (City)—Peoria *IL-3*
Chillicothe (Township)—Peoria...... *IL-3*
Chillicothe (City)—Wapello *IA-3*
Chillicothe (City)—Livingston *MO-3*
Chillicothe (Township)—
  Livingston *MO-3*
Chillicothe (City)—Ross...................*OH-3*
Chillicothe (City)—Hardeman *TX-2*
Chillum (CDP)—Prince
  George's *MD-1*
Chilmark (Town)—Dukes *MA-1*
Chilo (Village)—Clermont *OH-3*
Chiloquin (City)—Klamath............. *OR-4*
Chilton (Township)—Hettinger......*ND-4*
Chilton (City)—Calumet *WI-3*
Chilton (Town)—Calumet *WI-3*
Chilton County *AL-2*
Chimayo (CDP)—Rio Arriba *NM-4*
Chimayo (CDP)—Santa Fe *NM-4*
Chimney Rock (Town)—
  Trempealeau *WI-3*
China (Township)—Lee................... *IL-3*
China (Town)—Kennebec *ME-1*
China (Township)—St. Clair.......... *MI-3*
China (City)—Jefferson *TX-2*
China Grove (Town)—Rowan *NC-2*
China Grove (Town)—Bexar *TX-2*
Chincoteague (Town)—Accomack .. *VA-2*
Chiniak (CDP)—Kodiak Island
  Borough..*AK-4*
Chinle (CDP)—Apache *AZ-4*
Chino (City)—San Bernardino....... *CA-4*
Chino Hills (CDP)—San
  Bernardino *CA-4*
Chinook (City)—Blaine *MT-4*
Chino Valley (Town)—Yavapai......*AZ-4*
Chipley (City)—Washington *FL-2*
Chippewa (Township)—
  Chippewa *MI-3*
Chippewa (Township)—Isabella..... *MI-3*
Chippewa (Township)—Mecosta ... *MI-3*
Chippewa (Township)—Wayne......*OH-3*
Chippewa (Township)—Beaver *PA-1*
Chippewa (Town)—Ashland *WI-3*
Chippewa County *MI-3*
Chippewa County *MN-3*
Chippewa County *WI-3*
Chippewa Falls (Township)—
  Pope *MN-3*
Chippewa Falls (City)—
  Chippewa *WI-3*
Chippewa-on-the-Lake (Village)—
  Medina *OH-3*
Chireno (City)—Nacogdoches *TX-2*
Chisago City (City)—Chisago *MN-3*
Chisago County *MN-3*
Chisago Lake (Township)—
  Chisago...*MN-3*
Chisholm (CDP)—Franklin *ME-1*
Chisholm (City)—St. Louis...........*MN-3*
Chisholm Trail (AK)................. *Geog-4*
Chistochina (CDP)—Valdez-Cordova
  Census Area *AK-4*

Chitina (CDP)—Valdez-Cordova
  Census Area *AK-4*
Chittenango (Village)—Madison.... *NY-1*
Chittenden (Town)—Rutland.......... *VT-1*
Chittenden County *VT-1*
Chocktou Lake (CDP)—
  Madison *OH-3*
Chocolay (Township)—
  Marquette...................................... *MI-3*
Choconut (Township)—
  Susquehanna *PA-1*
Chocowinity (Town)—Beaufort *NC-2*
Choctaw (City)—Oklahoma *OK-2*
Choctaw County *AL-2*
Choctaw County *MS-2*
Choctaw County *OK-2*
Choctaw TJSA (OK).................. *IndRes-4*
Chokio (City)—Stevens *MN-3*
Choteau (City)—Teton *MT-4*
Choteau Creek (Township)—Charles
  Mix *SD-4*
Choudrant (Village)—Lincoln
  Parish *LA-2*
Chouteau (Township)—Madison ... *IL-3*
Chouteau (Township)—Clay *MO-3*
Chouteau (Town)—Mayes *OK-2*
Chouteau County *MT-4*
Chowan County *NC-2*
Chowchilla (City)—Madera *CA-4*
Chrisman (City)—Edgar *IL-3*
Chrisney (Town)—Spencer............. *IN-3*
Christiana (Borough)—Lancaster.... *PA-1*
Christiana (Town)—Dane *WI-3*
Christiana (Town)—Vernon *WI-3*
Christian County *IL-3*
Christian County *KY-2*
Christian County *MO-3*
Christiania (Township)—
  Jackson...*MN-3*
Christiania (Township)—
  Burleigh...*ND-4*
Christiansburg (Village)—
  Champaign *OH-3*
Christiansburg (Town)—
  Montgomery *VA-2*
Christine (City)—Richland *ND-4*
Christine (City)—Atascosa *TX-2*
Christopher (City)—Franklin.......... *IL-3*
Christy (Township)—Lawrence....... *IL-3*
Chuathbaluk (City)—Bethel Census
  Area *AK-4*
Chubbuck (City)—Bannock *ID-4*
Chugwater (Town)—Platte *WY-4*
Chuichu (CDP)—Pinal....................*AZ-4*
Chukchi Sea (AK)....................... *Geog-4*
Chula (City)—Livingston *MO-3*
Chula Vista (City)—San Diego *CA-4*
Chuluota (CDP)—Seminole *FL-2*
Chunky (Town)—Newton *MS-2*
Church Creek (Town)—
  Dorchester.....................................*MD-1*
Church Hill (Town)—Queen
  Anne's *MD-1*
Church Hill (Town)—Hawkins *TN-2*
Churchill (Township)—Ogemaw.... *MI-3*
Churchill (CDP)—Trumbull *OH-3*
Churchill (Borough)—Allegheny *PA-1*
Churchill, Mt. (AK) *Geog-4*
Churchill County *NV-4*
Church Point (Town)—Acadia
  Parish *LA-2*
Churchs Ferry (City)—Ramsey......*ND-4*
Churchville (Village)—Monroe...... *NY-1*
Churchville (CDP)—Bucks *PA-1*
Churdan (City)—Greene *IA-3*

Churubusco (Town)—Whitley.......... *IN-3*
Cibecue (CDP)—Navajo *AZ-4*
Cibola County *NM-4*
Cibolo (City)—Bexar...................... *TX-2*
Cibolo (City)—Guadalupe *TX-2*
Cicero (Town)—Cook..................... *IL-3*
Cicero (Township)—Cook.............. *IL-3*
Cicero (Town)—Hamilton *IN-3*
Cicero (Township)—Tipton *IN-3*
Cicero (Town)—Onondaga............. *NY-1*
Cicero (Town)—Outagamie............ *WI-3*
Cimarron (City)—Gray....................*KS-4*
Cimarron (Township)—Gray *KS-4*
Cimarron (Township)—Meade *KS-4*
Cimarron (Township)—Morton *KS-4*
Cimarron (Village)—Colfax *NM-4*
Cimarron City (Town)—Logan *OK-2*
Cimarron County *OK-2*
Cimarron Hills (CDP)—El Paso.... *CO-4*
Cincinnati (Township)—Pike.......... *IL-3*
Cincinnati (Township)—Tazewell ... *IL-3*
Cincinnati (City)—Appanoose *IA-3*
Cincinnati (City)—Hamilton..........*OH-3*
Cincinnatus (Town)—Cortland *NY-1*
Cinco Bayou (Town)—Okaloosa *FL-2*
Cinnaminson (Township)—
  Burlington *NJ-1*
Cinque Hommes (Township)—
  Perry..*MO-3*
Circle (CDP)—Yukon-Koyukuk Census
  Area *AK-4*
Circle (Town)—McCone................ *MT-4*
Circle D-KC Estates (CDP)—
  Bastrop *TX-2*
Circle Hot Springs Station (CDP)—
  Yukon-Koyukuk Census Area.....*AK-4*
Circle Pines (City)—Anoka............*MN-3*
Circleville (City)—Jackson..............*KS-4*
Circleville (City)—Pickaway *OH-3*
Circleville (Township)—
  Pickaway *OH-3*
Circleville (Town)—Piute *UT-4*
Cisco (Village)—Piatt *IL-3*
Cisco (City)—Eastland *TX-2*
Cisne (Village)—Wayne *IL-3*
Cissna Park (Village)—Iroquois *IL-3*
Citronelle (City)—Mobile *AL-2*
Citrus (CDP)—Los Angeles *CA-4*
Citrus County....................................*FL-2*
Citrus Heights (CDP)—
  Sacramento *CA-4*
Citrus Springs (CDP)—Citrus.........*FL-2*
City (Township)—Barton *MO-3*
City Point (Town)—Jackson *WI-3*
City View (Town)—Greenville........*SC-2*
Civil Bend (Township)—Union *SD-4*

Hot Springs. *See* **Hot Springs,**
  Fall River County—Shannon *SD-4*

Winner. *See* **Winner, Tripp County—**
  Todd *SD-4*

Clackamas (CDP)—Clackamas...... *OR-4*
Clackamas County............................ *OR-4*
Claflin (City)—Barton *KS-4*
Claiborne (CDP)—Ouachita
  Parish *LA-2*
Claiborne County.............................*MS-2*
Claiborne County............................. *TN-2*
Claiborne Parish *LA-2*
Claibourne (Township)—Union *OH-3*
Claire City (Town)—Roberts *SD-4*
Clairton (City)—Allegheny............. *PA-1*
Clallam County *WA-2*
Clam Falls (Town)—Polk *WI-3*

Clam Gulch (CDP)—Kenai Peninsula Borough AK-4
Clam Lake (Township)—Wexford .. MI-3
Clam Union (Township)—Missaukee MI-3
Clanton (City)—Chilton AL-2
Clara (Township)—Nelson ND-4
Clara (Township)—Potter PA-1
Clara City (City)—Chippewa MN-3
Clare (City)—Webster IA-3
Clare (City)—Clare MI-3
Clare (City)—Isabella MI-3
Clare (Town)—St. Lawrence NY-1
Clare (Township)—Moody SD-4
Clare County MI-3
Claremont (City)—Los Angeles CA-4
Claremont (Township)—Richland .. IL-3
Claremont (Village)—Richland IL-3
Claremont (City)—Dodge MN-3
Claremont (Township)—Dodge MN-3
Claremont (City)—Sullivan NH-1
Claremont (City)—Catawba NC-2
Claremont (Town)—Brown SD-4
Claremont (Township)—Brown SD-4
Claremont (Town)—Surry VA-2
Claremore (City)—Rogers OK-2
Clarence (City)—Cedar IA-3
Clarence (Township)—Barton KS-4
Clarence (Village)—Natchitoches Parish LA-2
Clarence (Township)—Calhoun MI-3
Clarence (City)—Shelby MO-3
Clarence (Town)—Erie NY-1
Clarendon (City)—Monroe AR-2
Clarendon (Township)—Calhoun ... MI-3
Clarendon (Town)—Orleans NY-1
Clarendon (Borough)—Warren PA-1
Clarendon (City)—Donley TX-2
Clarendon (Town)—Rutland VT-1
Clarendon County SC-2
Clarendon Hills (Village)—DuPage IL-3
Claridon (Township)—Geauga OH-3
Claridon (Township)—Marion OH-3
Clarinda (City)—Page IA-3
Clarington (Village)—Monroe OH-3
Clarion (Township)—Bureau IL-3
Clarion (City)—Wright IA-3
Clarion (Borough)—Clarion PA-1
Clarion (Township)—Clarion PA-1
Clarion County PA-1
Clarissa (City)—Todd MN-3
Clark (Township)—Johnson IN-3
Clark (Township)—Montgomery ... IN-3
Clark (Township)—Perry IN-3
Clark (Township)—Marion KS-4
Clark (Township)—Mackinac MI-3
Clark (Township)—Aitkin MN-3
Clark (Township)—Faribault MN-3
Clark (Township)—Atchison MO-3
Clark (Township)—Chariton MO-3
Clark (Township)—Cole MO-3
Clark (Township)—Lincoln MO-3
Clark (City)—Randolph MO-3
Clark (Township)—Wright MO-3
Clark (Township)—Dixon NE-4
Clark (Township)—Union NJ-1
Clark (Township)—Hettinger ND-4
Clark (Township)—Brown OH-3
Clark (Township)—Clinton OH-3
Clark (Township)—Coshocton OH-3
Clark (Township)—Holmes OH-3
Clark (Borough)—Mercer PA-1
Clark (City)—Clark SD-4
Clark (Township)—Douglas SD-4

Clark (Township)—Faulk SD-4
Clark (Township)—Perkins SD-4
Clark County AR-2
Clark County ID-4
Clark County IL-3
Clark County IN-3
Clark County KS-4
Clark County KY-2
Clark County MO-3
Clark County NV-4
Clark County OH-3
Clark County SD-4
Clark County WA-4
Clark County WI-3
Clarkdale (Town)—Yavapai AZ-4
Clarke County AL-2
Clarke County GA-2
Clarke County IA-3
Clarke County MS-2
Clarke County VA-2
Clarkesville (City)—Habersham GA-2
Clarkfield (City)—Yellow Medicine MN-3
Clark Fork (City)—Bonner ID-4
Clark Fork (Township)—Cooper... MO-3
Clark Mills (CDP)—Oneida NY-1
Clarks (Village)—Caldwell Parish ..LA-2
Clarks (Village)—Merrick NE-4
Clarksburg (Township)—Shelby IL-3
Clarksburg (Town)—Berkshire MA-1
Clarksburg (City)—Moniteau MO-3
Clarksburg (Village)—Ross OH-3
Clarksburg (Town)—Carroll TN-2
Clarksburg (City)—Harrison WV-2
Clarksdale (City)—Coahoma MS-2
Clarksdale (City)—DeKalb MO-3
Clarksfield (Township)—Huron OH-3
Clarks Green (Borough)—Lackawanna PA-1
Clarks Grove (City)—Freeborn MN-3
Clarks Hill (Town)—Tippecanoe ... IN-3
Clarkson (City)—Grayson KY-2
Clarkson (City)—Colfax NE-4
Clarkson (Town)—Monroe NY-1
Clarkson Valley (City)—St. Louis MO-3
Clarks Point (City)—Dillingham Census Area AK-4
Clarks Summit (Borough)—Lackawanna PA-1
Clarkston (City)—De Kalb GA-2
Clarkston (Village)—Oakland MI-3
Clarkston (Town)—Cache UT-4
Clarkston (City)—Asotin WA-4
Clarkston Heights-Vineland (CDP)—Asotin WA-4
Clarkstown (Town)—Rockland NY-1
Clarksville (City)—Johnson AR-2
Clarksville (Town)—Clark IN-3
Clarksville (City)—Butler IA-3
Clarksville (Village)—Ionia MI-3
Clarksville (City)—Pike MO-3
Clarksville (Township)—Merrick... NE-4
Clarksville (Town)—Coos NH-1
Clarksville (Town)—Allegany NY-1
Clarksville (Village)—Clinton OH-3
Clarksville (Borough)—Greene PA-1
Clarksville (City)—Montgomery ... TN-2
Clarksville (City)—Red River TX-2
Clarksville (Town)—Mecklenburg.. VA-2
Clarksville City (City)—Gregg TX-2
Clarksville City (City)—Upshur TX-2
Clarkton (City)—Dunklin MO-3
Clarkton (Town)—Bladen NC-2
Clarno (Township)—Lake SD-4

Clarno (Town)—Green WI-3
Claryville (CDP)—Campbell KY-2
Clatonia (Township)—Gage NE-4
Clatonia (Village)—Gage NE-4
Clatskanie (City)—Columbia OR-4
Clatsop County OR-4
Claude (City)—Armstrong TX-2
Claverack (Town)—Columbia NY-1
Clawson (City)—Oakland MI-3
Clawson (Town)—Emery UT-4
Claxton (City)—Evans GA-2
Clay (Township)—Bartholomew IN-3
Clay (Township)—Carroll IN-3
Clay (Township)—Cass IN-3
Clay (Township)—Dearborn IN-3
Clay (Township)—Decatur IN-3
Clay (Township)—Hamilton IN-3
Clay (Township)—Hendricks IN-3
Clay (Township)—Howard IN-3
Clay (Township)—Kosciusko IN-3
Clay (Township)—Lagrange IN-3
Clay (Township)—Miami IN-3
Clay (Township)—Morgan IN-3
Clay (Township)—Owen IN-3
Clay (Township)—Pike IN-3
Clay (Township)—Spencer IN-3
Clay (Township)—St. Joseph IN-3
Clay (Township)—Wayne IN-3
Clay (Township)—Butler KS-4
Clay (Township)—Reno KS-4
Clay (City)—Webster KY-2
Clay (Township)—St. Clair MI-3
Clay (Township)—Hubbard MN-3
Clay (Township)—Adair MO-3
Clay (Township)—Andrew MO-3
Clay (Township)—Atchison MO-3
Clay (Township)—Clark MO-3
Clay (Township)—Douglas MO-3
Clay (Township)—Dunklin MO-3
Clay (Township)—Gasconade MO-3
Clay (Township)—Greene MO-3
Clay (Township)—Harrison MO-3
Clay (Township)—Holt MO-3
Clay (Township)—Lafayette MO-3
Clay (Township)—Linn MO-3
Clay (Township)—Monroe MO-3
Clay (Township)—Ralls MO-3
Clay (Township)—Saline MO-3
Clay (Township)—Shelby MO-3
Clay (Township)—Sullivan MO-3
Clay (Town)—Onondaga NY-1
Clay (Township)—Renville ND-4
Clay (Township)—Auglaize OH-3
Clay (Township)—Gallia OH-3
Clay (Township)—Highland OH-3
Clay (Township)—Knox OH-3
Clay (Township)—Montgomery OH-3
Clay (Township)—Muskingum OH-3
Clay (Township)—Ottawa OH-3
Clay (Township)—Scioto OH-3
Clay (Township)—Tuscarawas OH-3
Clay (Township)—Butler PA-1
Clay (Township)—Huntingdon PA-1
Clay (Township)—Lancaster PA-1
Clay (Town)—Clay WV-2
Claybanks (Township)—Oceana ... MI-3
Claybanks (Town)—Door WI-3
Clay Center (City)—Clay KS-4
Clay Center (Township)—Clay KS-4
Clay Center (City)—Clay NE-4
Clay Center (Village)—Ottawa OH-3
Clay City (Township)—Clay IL-3
Clay City (Village)—Clay IL-3
Clay City (Town)—Clay IN-3
Clay City (City)—Powell KY-2

General Index

American Places Dictionary

Claycomo (Village)—Clay............ *MO-3*
Clay County..*AL-2*
Clay County..*AR-2*
Clay County..*FL-2*
Clay County...*GA-2*
Clay County..*IL-3*
Clay County..*IN-3*
Clay County..*IA-3*
Clay County..*KS-4*
Clay County..*KY-2*
Clay County...*MN-3*
Clay County..*MS-2*
Clay County...*MO-3*
Clay County..*NE-4*
Clay County...*NC-2*
Clay County..*SD-4*
Clay County..*TN-2*
Clay County..*TX-2*
Clay County...*WV-2*
Clayhatchee (Town)—Dale...........*AL-2*
Claymont (CDP)—New Castle......*DE-1*
Claypool (CDP)—Gila....................*AZ-4*
Claypool (Town)—Kosciusko..........*IN-3*
Claypool Hill (CDP)—Tazewell......*VA-2*
Claysburg (CDP)—Blair..................*PA-1*
Claysville (Borough)—
 Washington *PA-1*
Clayton (Town)—Barbour.............*AL-2*
Clayton (City)—Contra Costa........*CA-4*
Clayton (Town)—Kent....................*DE-1*
Clayton (City)—Rabun..................*GA-2*
Clayton (City)—Custer...................*ID-4*
Clayton (Township)—Adams...........*IL-3*
Clayton (Village)—Adams...............*IL-3*
Clayton (Township)—Woodford.....*IL-3*
Clayton (Town)—Hendricks............*IN-3*
Clayton (City)—Clayton..................*IA-3*
Clayton (City)—Decatur................*KS-4*
Clayton (City)—Norton..................*KS-4*
Clayton (Village)—Concordia
 Parish..*LA-2*
Clayton (Township)—Arenac.........*MI-3*
Clayton (Township)—Genesee.......*MI-3*
Clayton (Village)—Lenawee...........*MI-3*
Clayton (Township)—Mower.........*MN-3*
Clayton (City)—St. Louis..............*MO-3*
Clayton (Township)—St. Louis.....*MO-3*
Clayton (Borough)—Gloucester......*NJ-1*
Clayton (Town)—Union................*NM-4*
Clayton (Town)—Jefferson.............*NY-1*
Clayton (Village)—Jefferson...........*NY-1*
Clayton (Town)—Johnston............*NC-2*
Clayton (Township)—Burke...........*ND-4*
Clayton (Village)—Montgomery....*OH-3*
Clayton (Township)—Perry............*OH-3*
Clayton (Town)—Pushmataha.......*OK-2*
Clayton (Township)—Hutchinson.*SD-4*
Clayton (Town)—Crawford............*WI-3*
Clayton (Town)—Polk.....................*WI-3*
Clayton (Village)—Polk..................*WI-3*
Clayton (Town)—Winnebago.........*WI-3*
Clayton County..*GA-2*
Clayton County...*IA-3*
Clayville (Village)—Oneida.............*NY-1*
Clearbrook (City)—Clearwater.....*MN-3*
Clearbrook Park (CDP)—
 Middlesex.....................................*NJ-1*
Clear Creek (Township)—
 Huntington....................................*IN-3*
Clear Creek (Township)—Monroe..*IN-3*
Clear Creek (Township)—
 Ellsworth......................................*KS-4*
Clear Creek (Township)—Marion...*KS-4*
Clear Creek (Township)—
 Nemaha...*KS-4*

Clear Creek (Township)—
 Pottawatomie..............................*KS-4*
Clear Creek (Township)—
 Stafford.......................................*KS-4*
Clear Creek (Pop. Place)—
 Carlton..*MN-3*
Clear Creek (Township)—
 Cooper..*MO-3*
Clear Creek (Township)—
 Vernon..*MO-3*
Clear Creek (Township)—
 Saunders......................................*NE-4*
Clear Creek (Township)—
 Ashland..*OH-3*
Clear Creek (Township)—
 Fairfield.......................................*OH-3*
Clear Creek (Township)—
 Warren..*OH-3*
Clear Creek (Town)—Eau Claire...*WI-3*
Clear Creek County................................*CO-4*
Clearfield (City)—Ringgold............*IA-3*
Clearfield (City)—Taylor................*IA-3*
Clearfield (Township)—Griggs......*ND-4*
Clearfield (Township)—Butler.......*PA-1*
Clearfield (Township)—Cambria...*PA-1*
Clearfield (Borough)—Clearfield...*PA-1*
Clearfield (City)—Davis..................*UT-4*
Clearfield (Town)—Juneau.............*WI-3*
Clearfield County.....................................*PA-1*
Clear Fork (Township)—Marshall..*KS-4*
Clearlake (City)—Lake...................*CA-4*
Clear Lake (Township)—
 Sangamon......................................*IL-3*
Clear Lake (Village)—Sangamon....*IL-3*
Clear Lake (Town)—Steuben.........*IN-3*
Clear Lake (Township)—Steuben...*IN-3*
Clear Lake (City)—Cerro Gordo....*IA-3*
Clear Lake (City)—Sherburne.......*MN-3*
Clear Lake (Township)—
 Sherburne....................................*MN-3*
Clear Lake (Township)—
 Burleigh.......................................*ND-4*
Clear Lake (Township)—Kidder....*ND-4*
Clear Lake (City)—Deuel...............*SD-4*
Clear Lake (Township)—Deuel......*SD-4*
Clear Lake (Township)—
 Edmunds......................................*SD-4*
Clear Lake (Township)—
 Minnehaha...................................*SD-4*
Clear Lake (Town)—Polk...............*WI-3*
Clear Lake (Village)—Polk.............*WI-3*
Clearlake Oaks (CDP)—Lake.........*CA-4*
Clear Lake Shores (City)—
 Galveston.....................................*TX-2*
Clearmont (City)—Nodaway.........*MO-3*
Clearmont (Town)—Sheridan.......*WY-4*
Clearspring (Township)—
 Lagrange.......................................*IN-3*
Clear Spring (Town)—
 Washington.................................*MD-1*
Clearview (Town)—Okfuskee.......*OK-2*
Clearview (Village)—Ohio............*WV-2*
Clearwater (City)—Pinellas...........*FL-2*
Clearwater (City)—Sedgwick........*KS-4*
Clearwater (Township)—
 Kalkaska......................................*MI-3*
Clearwater (City)—Wright...........*MN-3*
Clearwater (Township)—Wright...*MN-3*
Clearwater (Township)—
 Antelope.......................................*NE-4*
Clearwater (Village)—Antelope....*NE-4*
Clearwater (Township)—
 Mountrail....................................*ND-4*
Clearwater (CDP)—Aiken..............*SC-2*
Clearwater (Township)—Miner.....*SD-4*

Clearwater County....................................*ID-4*
Clearwater County.................................*MN-3*
Cleary (Township)—Burke............*ND-4*
Cleburne (City)—Johnson...............*TX-2*
Cleburne County......................................*AL-2*
Cleburne County......................................*AR-2*
Cle Elum (City)—Kittitas..............*WA-4*
Cleghorn (City)—Cherokee.............*IA-3*
Clement (Township)—Clinton........*IL-3*
Clement (Township)—Gladwin......*MI-3*
Clement (Township)—Dickey.......*ND-4*
Clementon (Borough)—Camden....*NJ-1*
Clements (City)—Redwood...........*MN-3*
Clemmons (Village)—Forsyth........*NC-2*
Clemons (City)—Marshall...............*IA-3*
Clemson (City)—Anderson.............*SC-2*
Clemson (City)—Pickens................*SC-2*
Clendenin (Town)—Kanawha.......*WV-2*
Cleon (Township)—Manistee.........*MI-3*
Cleona (Borough)—Lebanon..........*PA-1*
Cleo Springs (Town)—Major........*OK-2*
Clermont (City)—Lake...................*FL-2*
Clermont (Town)—Hall.................*GA-2*
Clermont (Town)—Marion............*IN-3*
Clermont (City)—Fayette...............*IA-3*
Clermont (Town)—Columbia........*NY-1*
Clermont (Township)—Adams.....*ND-4*
Clermont County....................................*OH-3*
Cleveland (Town)—Blount............*AL-2*
Cleveland (CDP)—Charlotte..........*FL-2*
Cleveland (City)—White................*GA-2*
Cleveland (Village)—Henry............*IL-3*
Cleveland (Township)—Elkhart.....*IN-3*
Cleveland (Township)—Whitley....*IN-3*
Cleveland (Township)—Barton.....*KS-4*
Cleveland (Township)—Lane........*KS-4*
Cleveland (Township)—Marshall..*KS-4*
Cleveland (Township)—Stafford...*KS-4*
Cleveland (Township)—Leelanau..*MI-3*
Cleveland (City)—Le Sueur..........*MN-3*
Cleveland (Township)—Le
 Sueur...*MN-3*
Cleveland (City)—Bolivar..............*MS-2*
Cleveland (Township)—
 Callaway.....................................*MO-3*
Cleveland (Town)—Cass..............*MO-3*
Cleveland (Township)—Cuming....*NE-4*
Cleveland (Township)—Holt........*NE-4*
Cleveland (Township)—Knox.......*NE-4*
Cleveland (Village)—Oswego........*NY-1*
Cleveland (Town)—Rowan............*NC-2*
Cleveland (City)—Stutsman..........*ND-4*
Cleveland (Township)—Walsh.....*ND-4*
Cleveland (City)—Cuyahoga.........*OH-3*
Cleveland (City)—Pawnee.............*OK-2*
Cleveland (Township)—Columbia..*PA-1*
Cleveland (Township)—Brule........*SD-4*
Cleveland (Township)—Edmunds..*SD-4*
Cleveland (Township)—Hamlin.....*SD-4*
Cleveland (City)—Bradley...............*TN-2*
Cleveland (City)—Liberty..............*TX-2*
Cleveland (Town)—Emery.............*UT-4*
Cleveland (Town)—Russell............*VA-2*
Cleveland (Town)—Chippewa.......*WI-3*
Cleveland (Town)—Jackson..........*WI-3*
Cleveland (Village)—Manitowoc...*WI-3*
Cleveland (Town)—Marathon......*WI-3*
Cleveland (Town)—Taylor............*WI-3*
Cleveland County.....................................*AR-2*
Cleveland County....................................*NC-2*
Cleveland County....................................*OK-2*
Cleveland Heights (City)—
 Cuyahoga....................................*OH-3*
Cleveland Run (Township)—
 Cheyenne.....................................*KS-4*

Clever (City)—Christian *MO-3*
Cleves (Village)—Hamilton........... *OH-3*
Clewiston (City)—Hendry............ *FL-2*
Cliff (Township)—Custer *NE-4*
Clifford (Town)—Bartholomew *IN-3*
Clifford (Township)—Butler *KS-4*
Clifford (Village)—Lapeer *MI-3*
Clifford (City)—Traill *ND-4*
Clifford (Township)—
  Susquehanna *PA-1*
Cliffside Park (Borough)—Bergen .. *NJ-1*
Cliff Village (Village)—Newton *MO-3*
Cliffwood Beach (CDP)—
  Monmouth *NJ-1*
Clifton (Town)—Greenlee *AZ-4*
Clifton (CDP)—Mesa.................... *CO-4*
Clifton (City)—Franklin................ *ID-4*
Clifton (Village)—Iroquois........... *IL-3*
Clifton (City)—Clay *KS-4*
Clifton (City)—Washington........... *KS-4*
Clifton (Township)—Washington.... *KS-4*
Clifton (Township)—Wilson *KS-4*
Clifton (Town)—Penobscot........... *ME-1*
Clifton (Township)—Lyon............. *MN-3*
Clifton (Township)—Traverse....... *MN-3*
Clifton (Township)—Randolph..... *MO-3*
Clifton (City)—Passaic.................. *NJ-1*
Clifton (Town)—St. Lawrence *NY-1*
Clifton (Township)—Cass *ND-4*
Clifton (Village)—Clark *OH-3*
Clifton (Village)—Greene.............. *OH-3*
Clifton (Township)—Lackawanna... *PA-1*
Clifton (Township)—Beadle *SD-4*
Clifton (Township)—Spink *SD-4*
Clifton (Town)—Wayne *TN-2*
Clifton (City)—Bosque *TX-2*
Clifton (Town)—Fairfax *VA-2*
Clifton (Town)—Grant *WI-3*
Clifton (Town)—Monroe............... *WI-3*
Clifton (Town)—Pierce *WI-3*
Clifton Choctaw TDSA (LA).... *IndRes-4*
Clifton Forge (Independent City) *VA-2*
Clifton Heights (Borough)—
  Delaware *PA-1*
Clifton Hill (City)—Randolph *MO-3*
Clifton Park (Town)—Saratoga...... *NY-1*
Clifton Springs (Village)—
  Ontario...................................... *NY-1*
Clifty (Township)—Bartholomew ... *IN-3*
Climax (Town)—Decatur *GA-2*
Climax (City)—Greenwood *KS-4*
Climax (Township)—Kalamazoo ... *MI-3*
Climax (Village)—Kalamazoo........ *MI-3*
Climax (City)—Polk *MN-3*
Climax (Township)—Williams....... *ND-4*
Climax Springs (Village)—
  Camden..................................... *MO-3*
Clinch County *GA-2*
Clinchport (Town)—Scott *VA-2*
Clingmans Dome (TN) *Geog-4*
Clint (Town)—El Paso *TX-2*
Clinton (City)—Van Buren *AR-2*
Clinton (Town)—Middlesex *CT-1*
Clinton (City)—De Witt................. *IL-3*
Clinton (Township)—DeKalb *IL-3*
Clinton (Township)—Boone........... *IN-3*
Clinton (Township)—Cass *IN-3*
Clinton (Township)—Decatur *IN-3*
Clinton (Township)—Elkhart *IN-3*
Clinton (Township)—La Porte....... *IN-3*
Clinton (Township)—Putnam *IN-3*
Clinton (City)—Vermillion *IN-3*
Clinton (Township)—Vermillion..... *IN-3*
Clinton (City)—Clinton *IA-3*
Clinton (Township)—Douglas........ *KS-4*

Clinton (City)—Hickman............... *KY-2*
Clinton (Town)—East Feliciana
  Parish....................................... *LA-2*
Clinton (Town)—Kennebec............ *ME-1*
Clinton (CDP)—Prince George's.. *MD-1*
Clinton (Town)—Worcester............ *MA-1*
Clinton (Township)—Lenawee....... *MI-3*
Clinton (Village)—Lenawee *MI-3*
Clinton (Township)—Macomb....... *MI-3*
Clinton (Township)—Oscoda *MI-3*
Clinton (City)—Big Stone *MN-3*
Clinton (Township)—Rock *MN-3*
Clinton (Township)—St. Louis *MN-3*
Clinton (City)—Hinds.................... *MS-2*
Clinton (Township)—Clinton........ *MO-3*
Clinton (Township)—Douglas....... *MO-3*
Clinton (City)—Henry................... *MO-3*
Clinton (Township)—Henry.......... *MO-3*
Clinton (Township)—Texas........... *MO-3*
Clinton (Village)—Sheridan *NE-4*
Clinton (Town)—Hunterdon........... *NJ-1*
Clinton (Township)—Hunterdon *NJ-1*
Clinton (Town)—Clinton *NY-1*
Clinton (Town)—Dutchess............. *NY-1*
Clinton (Village)—Oneida............. *NY-1*
Clinton (City)—Sampson *NC-2*
Clinton (Township)—Divide.......... *ND-4*
Clinton (Township)—Franklin *OH-3*
Clinton (Township)—Fulton *OH-3*
Clinton (Township)—Knox *OH-3*
Clinton (Township)—Seneca......... *OH-3*
Clinton (Township)—Shelby *OH-3*
Clinton (Village)—Summit *OH-3*
Clinton (Township)—Vinton......... *OH-3*
Clinton (Township)—Wayne *OH-3*
Clinton (City)—Custer *OK-2*
Clinton (City)—Washita *OK-2*
Clinton (Township)—Butler.......... *PA-1*
Clinton (Township)—Lycoming...... *PA-1*
Clinton (Township)—Venango *PA-1*
Clinton (Township)—Wayne *PA-1*
Clinton (Township)—Wyoming..... *PA-1*
Clinton (City)—Laurens................ *SC-2*
Clinton (Township)—Miner *SD-4*
Clinton (Town)—Anderson *TN-2*
Clinton (City)—Davis *UT-4*
Clinton (CDP)—Island................ *WA-4*
Clinton (Town)—Barron *WI-3*
Clinton (Town)—Rock *WI-3*
Clinton (Village)—Rock *WI-3*
Clinton (Town)—Vernon............... *WI-3*
Clinton County *IL-3*
Clinton County *IN-3*
Clinton County *IA-3*
Clinton County *KY-2*
Clinton County *MI-3*
Clinton County *MO-3*
Clinton County *NY-1*
Clinton County *OH-3*
Clinton County *PA-1*
Clintondale (CDP)—Ulster........ *NY-1*
Clinton Falls (Township)—Steele.. *MN-3*
Clintonia (Township)—De Witt...... *IL-3*
Clintonville (Borough)—Venango... *PA-1*
Clintonville (City)—Waupaca *WI-3*
Clintwood (Town)—Dickenson....... *VA-2*
Clio (Town)—Barbour................... *AL-2*
Clio (City)—Wayne *IA-3*
Clio (City)—Genesee..................... *MI-3*
Clio (Town)—Marlboro................. *SC-2*
Cliquot (Township)—Polk............. *MO-3*
Clitherall (City)—Otter Tail........... *MN-3*
Clitherall (Township)—Otter
  Tail.. *MN-3*
Clive (City)—Polk *IA-3*

Clontarf (City)—Swift *MN-3*
Clontarf (Township)—Swift *MN-3*
Cloquet (City)—Carlton *MN-3*
Closter (Borough)—Bergen *NJ-1*
Cloud County................................ *KS-4*
Cloudcroft (Village)—Otero *NM-4*
Cloud Lake (Town)—Palm Beach .. *FL-2*
Clover (Township)—Henry *IL-3*
Clover (Township)—Clearwater.... *MN-3*
Clover (Township)—Hubbard........ *MN-3*
Clover (Township)—Mahnomen... *MN-3*
Clover (Township)—Pine *MN-3*
Clover (Township)—Jefferson....... *PA-1*
Clover (Town)—York.................... *SC-2*
Clover (Town)—Halifax *VA-2*
Clover (Town)—Bayfield............... *WI-3*
Cloverdale (City)—Sonoma *CA-4*
Cloverdale (City)—Putnam *IN-3*
Cloverdale (Township)—Putnam... *IN-3*
Cloverdale (Village)—Putnam *OH-3*
Cloverdale (CDP)—Botetourt *VA-2*
Clover Hill (CDP)—Frederick *MD-1*
Cloverland (Town)—Douglas *WI-3*
Cloverland (Town)—Vilas.............. *WI-3*
Clover Leaf (Township)—
  Pennington................................ *MN-3*
Cloverleaf (CDP)—Harris............. *TX-2*
Cloverly (CDP)—Montgomery *MD-1*
Cloverport (City)—Breckinridge.... *KY-2*
Clovis (City)—Fresno.................... *CA-4*
Clovis (City)—Curry *NM-4*
Clow (Township)—Kittson............ *MN-3*
Cloyd Valley (Township)—
  Edmunds................................... *SD-4*
Clute (City)—Brazoria *TX-2*
Clutier (City)—Tama.................... *IA-3*
Clyde (Township)—Whiteside *IL-3*
Clyde (City)—Cloud..................... *KS-4*
Clyde (Township)—Allegan *MI-3*
Clyde (Township)—St. Clair *MI-3*
Clyde (Village)—Nodaway *MO-3*
Clyde (Village)—Wayne *NY-1*
Clyde (Town)—Haywood *NC-2*
Clyde (City)—Sandusky *OH-3*
Clyde (Township)—Beadle........... *SD-4*
Clyde (Town)—Callahan *TX-2*
Clyde (Town)—Iowa...................... *WI-3*
Clyde Hill (Town)—King *WA-4*
Clyde Park (Town)—Park *MT-4*
Clyman (Town)—Dodge................ *WI-3*
Clyman (Village)—Dodge............. *WI-3*
Clymer (Town)—Chautauqua *NY-1*
Clymer (Borough)—Indiana.......... *PA-1*
Clymer (Township)—Tioga *PA-1*
Coachella (City)—Riverside........... *CA-4*
Coahoma (Town)—Coahoma......... *MS-2*
Coahoma (Town)—Howard *TX-2*
Coahoma County........................... *MS-2*
Coal (Township)—Vernon............ *MO-3*
Coal (Township)—Jackson *OH-3*
Coal (Township)—Perry................ *OH-3*
Coal (Township)—
  Northumberland........................ *PA-1*
Coal Center (Borough)—
  Washington *PA-1*
Coal City (City)—Grundy............. *IL-3*
Coal City (CDP)—Raleigh *WV-2*
Coal County................................... *OK-2*
Coal Creek (Town)—Fremont........ *CO-4*
Coal Creek (Township)—
  Montgomery *IN-3*
Coaldale (Borough)—Bedford *PA-1*
Coaldale (Borough)—Schuylkill *PA-1*
Coalfield (Township)—Divide *ND-4*
Coal Fork (CDP)—Kanawha *WV-2*

General Index

Coalgate (City)—Coal.................. *OK-2*
Coal Grove (Village)—Lawrence ...*OH-3*
Coal Hill (City)—Johnson............. *AR-2*
Coalinga (City)—Fresno................ *CA-4*
Coalmont (Borough)—
  Huntingdon............................... *PA-1*
Coalmont (Town)—Grundy *TN-2*
Coalport (Borough)—Clearfield *PA-1*
Coal Run (City)—Pike *KY-2*
Coalton (Village)—Montgomery *IL-3*
Coalton (Village)—Jackson *OH-3*
Coalton (Town)—Randolph *WV-2*
Coal Valley (Village)—Henry *IL-3*
Coal Valley (Township)—Rock
  Island.. *IL-3*
Coal Valley (Village)—Rock
  Island.. *IL-3*
Coalville (City)—Summit............... *UT-4*
Coast Guard Communication Area
  Master Station (CA) *Mil-4*
Coast Ranges (CA)........................ *Geog-4*
Coates (City)—Dakota *MN-3*
Coatesville (Town)—Hendricks *IN-3*
Coatesville (City)—Chester............ *PA-1*
Coats (City)—Pratt....................... *KS-4*
Coats (Town)—Harnett *NC-2*
Coatsburg (Village)—Adams........... *IL-3*
Cobalt City (Village)—Madison...*MO-3*
Cobb (CDP)—Lake *CA-4*
Cobb (Village)—Iowa *WI-3*
Cobb County............................. *GA-2*
Cobbtown (City)—Tattnall............. *GA-2*
Cobden (Village)—Union............... *IL-3*
Cobden (City)—Brown.................. *MN-3*
Cobleskill (Town)—Schoharie........ *NY-1*
Cobleskill (Village)—Schoharie....... *NY-1*
Coburg (City)—Montgomery *IA-3*
Coburg (City)—Lane *OR-4*
Coburn (Township)—Ransom *ND-4*
Cochecton (Town)—Sullivan *NY-1*
Cochise County......................... *AZ-4*
Cochiti (CDP)—Sandoval............. *NM-4*
Cochiti Pueblo (NM)................ *IndRes-4*
Cochituate (CDP)—Middlesex *MA-1*
Cochran (City)—Bleckley.............. *GA-2*
Cochran County........................ *TX-3*
Cochrane (Village)—Buffalo *WI-3*
Cochranton (Borough)—Crawford.. *PA-1*
Cocke County *TN-2*
Cockeysville (CDP)—Baltimore....*MD-1*
Cockrell (Township)—Chariton *MO-3*
Cockrell Hill (City)—Dallas........... *TX-2*
Cocoa (City)—Brevard *FL-2*
Cocoa Beach (City)—Brevard........ *FL-2*
Cocoa West (CDP)—Brevard......... *FL-2*
Coconino County *AZ-4*
Coconut Creek (City)—Broward.... *FL-2*
Cocopah Reservation (AZ)....... *IndRes-4*
Cod, Cape (MA) *Geog-4*
Codington County..................... *SD-4*
Codorus (Township)—York............ *PA-1*
Cody (Village)—Cherry................. *NE-4*
Cody (Township)—Mellette *SD-4*
Cody (City)—Park *WY-4*
Codyville (Plantation)—
  Washington............................... *ME-1*
Coe (Township)—Rock Island *IL-3*
Coe (Township)—Isabella *MI-3*
Coeburn (Town)—Wise................. *VA-2*
Coeur d'Alene (City)—Kootenai.... *ID-4*
Coeur d'Alene Lake (ID)............... *Geog-4*
Coeur d'Alene Reservation & Trust
  Lands (ID) *IndRes-4*
Coeymans (Town)—Albany............ *NY-1*
Coffee City (Town)—Henderson ... *TX-2*

Coffee County............................ *AL-2*
Coffee County............................ *GA-2*
Coffee County............................ *TN-2*
Coffeen (City)—Montgomery *IL-3*
Coffee Springs (Town)—Geneva.... *AL-2*
Coffeeville (Town)—Clarke........... *AL-2*
Coffeeville (Town)—Yalobusha......*MS-2*
Coffey (Town)—Daviess................. *MO-3*
Coffey County............................ *KS-4*
Coffeyville (City)—Montgomery....*KS-4*
Coffman Cove (City)—Prince of
  Wales-Outer Ketchikan Census
  Area.. *AK-4*
Cofield (Village)—Hertford...........*NC-2*
Cogan House (Township)—
  Lycoming................................... *PA-1*
Coggon (City)—Linn *IA-3*
Cogswell (City)—Sargent...............*ND-4*
Coharie TDSA (NC)............... *IndRes-4*
Cohasset (Town)—Norfolk *MA-1*
Cohoctah (Township)—
  Livingston................................. *MI-3*
Cohocton (Town)—Steuben *NY-1*
Cohocton (Village)—Steuben *NY-1*
Cohoe (CDP)—Kenai Peninsula
  Borough....................................*AK-4*
Cohoes (City)—Albany.................. *NY-1*
Cohutta (Town)—Whitfield *GA-2*
Coin (City)—Page.......................... *IA-3*
Coitsville (Township)—
  Mahoning *OH-3*
Cokato (City)—Wright *MN-3*
Cokato (Township)—Wright *MN-3*
Cokeburg (Borough)—Washington.. *PA-1*
Coke County *TX-2*
Cokedale (Town)—Las Animas......*CO-4*
Cokeville (Town)—Lincoln *WY-4*
Colbert (City)—Madison............... *GA-2*
Colbert (Town)—Bryan *OK-2*
Colbert County *AL-2*
Colburn (Town)—Adams *WI-3*
Colburn (Town)—Chippewa *WI-3*
Colby (City)—Thomas *KS-4*
Colby (City)—Clark...................... *WI-3*
Colby (Town)—Clark *WI-3*
Colby (City)—Marathon *WI-3*
Colchester (Borough)—New
  London...................................... *CT-1*
Colchester (Town)—New London.. *CT-1*
Colchester (City)—McDonough....... *IL-3*
Colchester (Township)—
  McDonough *IL-3*
Colchester (Town)—Delaware........ *NY-1*
Colchester (Town)—Chittenden..... *VT-1*
Colcord (Town)—Delaware........... *OK-2*
Cold Bay (City)—Aleutians East
  Borough.................................... *AK-4*
Coldbrook (Township)—Warren *IL-3*
Cold Brook (Village)—Herkimer ... *NY-1*
Colden (Town)—Erie..................... *NY-1*
Cold Spring (Township)—Shelby.... *IL-3*
Cold Spring (City)—Campbell....... *KY-2*
Cold Spring (City)—Stearns........... *MN-3*
Cold Spring (Township)—Phelps... *MO-3*
Coldspring (Town)—Cattaraugus... *NY-1*
Cold Spring (Village)—Putnam *NY-1*
Cold Spring (Township)—
  Lebanon *PA-1*
Coldspring (City)—San Jacinto *TX-2*
Cold Spring (Town)—Jefferson...... *WI-3*
Cold Spring Harbor (CDP)—
  Suffolk...................................... *NY-1*
Cold Springs (Township)—
  Kalkaska................................... *MI-3*
Cold Springs Rancheria (CA)... *IndRes-4*

Coldstream (City)—Jefferson......... *KY-2*
Coldwater (City)—Comanche *KS-4*
Coldwater (Township)—
  Comanche *KS-4*
Coldwater (City)—Branch.............. *MI-3*
Coldwater (Township)—Branch..... *MI-3*
Coldwater (Township)—Isabella ... *MI-3*
Coldwater (Town)—Tate *MS-2*
Coldwater (Township)—Cass *MO-3*
Coldwater (Village)—Mercer *OH-3*
Cole (Township)—Benton *MO-3*
Cole (Town)—McClain *OK-2*
Colebrook (Town)—Litchfield *CT-1*
Colebrook (Town)—Coos *NH-1*
Colebrook (Township)—
  Ashtabula *OH-3*
Colebrook (Township)—Clinton..... *PA-1*
Colebrookdale (Township)—Berks.. *PA-1*
Cole Camp (City)—Benton *MO-3*
Cole County *MO-3*
Coleharbor (City)—McLean...........*ND-4*
Coleman (City)—Sumter................*FL-2*
Coleman (City)—Randolph *GA-2*
Coleman (Township)—
  Washington *KS-4*
Coleman (City)—Midland............. *MI-3*
Coleman (Township)—Holt *NE-4*
Coleman (City)—Coleman *TX-2*
Coleman (Village)—Marinette *WI-3*
Coleman County........................ *TX-2*
Colerain (Town)—Bertie *NC-2*
Colerain (Township)—Belmont *OH-3*
Colerain (Township)—Hamilton....*OH-3*
Colerain (Township)—Ross...........*OH-3*
Colerain (Township)—Bedford *PA-1*
Colerain (Township)—Lancaster..... *PA-1*
Coleraine (City)—Itasca................. *MN-3*
Coleridge (Village)—Cedar *NE-4*
Colesburg (City)—Delaware........... *IA-3*
Coles County.............................. *IL-3*
Colesville (CDP)—Montgomery ...*MD-1*
Colesville (Town)—Broome........... *NY-1*
Coleta (Village)—Whiteside *IL-3*
Colfax (City)—Placer *CA-4*
Colfax (Township)—Champaign..... *IL-3*
Colfax (Village)—McLean.............. *IL-3*
Colfax (Town)—Clinton *IN-3*
Colfax (Township)—Newton.......... *IN-3*
Colfax (City)—Jasper *IA-3*
Colfax (Township)—Cloud............. *KS-4*
Colfax (Township)—Marion.......... *KS-4*
Colfax (Township)—Wilson........... *KS-4*
Colfax (Town)—Grant Parish *LA-2*
Colfax (Township)—Benzie *MI-3*
Colfax (Township)—Huron *MI-3*
Colfax (Township)—Mecosta......... *MI-3*
Colfax (Township)—Oceana *MI-3*
Colfax (Township)—Wexford......... *MI-3*
Colfax (Township)—Kandiyohi *MN-3*
Colfax (Township)—Atchison *MO-3*
Colfax (Township)—Daviess *MO-3*
Colfax (Township)—DeKalb.......... *MO-3*
Colfax (Township)—Harrison *MO-3*
Colfax (City)—Richland................*ND-4*
Colfax (Township)—Richland........*ND-4*
Colfax (City)—Whitman................*WA-4*
Colfax (Town)—Dunn *WI-3*
Colfax (Village)—Dunn *WI-3*
Colfax County *NE-4*
Colfax County *NM-4*
Colgate (Township)—Steele *ND-4*
Collbran (Town)—Mesa.................*CO-4*
College (CDP)—Fairbanks North Star
  Borough.....................................*AK-4*
College (Township)—Knox *OH-3*

American Places Dictionary — General Index

College (Township)—Centre *PA-1*
College City (Town)—Lawrence *AR-2*
College Corner (Village)—Butler ...*OH-3*
College Corner (Village)—Preble ...*OH-3*
Collegedale (City)—Hamilton *TN-2*
College Park (City)—Clayton......... *GA-2*
College Park (City)—Fulton........... *GA-2*
College Park (City)—Prince
 George's *MD-1*
College Place (City)—Walla
 Walla *WA-4*
College Springs (City)—Page *IA-3*
College Station (City)—Brazos *TX-2*
Collegeville (CDP)—Jasper............ *IN-3*
Collegeville (Township)—
 Stearns...............................*MN-3*
Collegeville (Borough)—
 Montgomery....................... *PA-1*
Colleton County.........................*SC-2*
Colley (Township)—Sullivan......... *PA-1*
Colleyville (City)—Tarrant........... *TX-2*
Collier (Township)—Allegheny *PA-1*
Collier County *FL-2*
Collier Manor-Cresthaven (CDP)—
 Broward............................... *FL-2*
Collierville (Town)—Shelby *TN-2*
Collin County *TX-2*
Collingdale (Borough)—Delaware ...*PA-1*
Collings Lakes (CDP)—Atlantic *NJ-1*
Collingswood (Borough)—
 Camden................................ *NJ-1*
Collingsworth County *TX-2*
Collins (City)—Tattnall *GA-2*
Collins (City)—Story......................*IA-3*
Collins (Township)—McLeod *MN-3*
Collins (City)—Covington............. *MS-2*
Collins (Township)—St. Clair *MO-3*
Collins (Village)—St. Clair............ *MO-3*
Collins (Township)—Buffalo.......... *NE-4*
Collins (Town)—Erie..................... *NY-1*
Collins (Township)—Clark............ *SD-4*
Collinston (Village)—Morehouse
 Parish *LA-2*
Collinsville (Town)—Cherokee *AL-2*
Collinsville (Town)—DeKalb.........*AL-2*
Collinsville (CDP)—Hartford *CT-1*
Collinsville (City)—Madison *IL-3*
Collinsville (Township)—Madison.. *IL-3*
Collinsville (City)—St. Clair.......... *IL-3*
Collinsville (CDP)—Lauderdale *MS-2*
Collinsville (City)—Rogers............*OK-2*
Collinsville (City)—Tulsa *OK-2*
Collinsville (Town)—Grayson *TX-2*
Collinsville (CDP)—Henry *VA-2*
Collinwood (Township)—
 Meeker *MN-3*
Collinwood (City)—Wayne *TN-2*
Collyer (City)—Trego *KS-4*
Collyer (Township)—Trego *KS-4*
Colma (Town)—San Mateo............ *CA-4*
Colman (City)—Moody *SD-4*
Colman (Township)—Moody......... *SD-4*
Colmar Manor (Town)—Prince
 George's *MD-1*
Colmesneil (City)—Tyler................ *TX-2*
Colo (City)—Story..........................*IA-3*
Cologne (City)—Carver *MN-3*
Coloma (Township)—Whiteside..... *IL-3*
Coloma (City)—Berrien *MI-3*
Coloma (Township)—Berrien *MI-3*
Coloma (Town)—Waushara *WI-3*
Coloma (Village)—Waushara *WI-3*
Colome (City)—Tripp *SD-4*
Colome (Township)—Tripp *SD-4*
Colon (Township)—St. Joseph....... *MI-3*

Colon (Village)—St. Joseph *MI-3*
Colon (Village)—Saunders *NE-4*
Colona (Township)—Henry *IL-3*
Colona (Village)—Henry *IL-3*
Colonia (CDP)—Middlesex *NJ-1*
Colonial Beach (Town)—
 Westmoreland *VA-2*
Colonial Heights (CDP)—
 Sullivan *TN-2*
**Colonial Heights (Independent
 City)** *VA-2*
Colonial Park (CDP)—Dauphin *PA-1*
Colonial Pine Hills (CDP)—
 Pennington.......................... *SD-4*
Colonie (Town)—Albany................ *NY-1*
Colonie (Village)—Albany.............. *NY-1*
Colony (Municipality)—Cullman ...*AL-2*
Colony (City)—Anderson *KS-4*
Colony (Township)—Greeley *KS-4*
Colony (Township)—Knox *MO-3*
Colony (Town)—Washita *OK-2*
The Colony (City)—Denton........... *TX-2*
Colorado (Township)—Lincoln.......*KS-4*
Colorado City (Town)—Mohave.... *AZ-4*
Colorado City (CDP)—Pueblo *CO-4*
Colorado City (City)—Mitchell *TX-2*
Colorado County.......................... *TX-2*
Colorado Desert (CA)................ *Geog-4*
Colorado Plateau (AZ) *Geog-4*
Colorado River (AZ) *Geog-4*
Colorado River Reservation
 (AZ).................................*IndRes-4*
Colorado Springs (City)—El
 Paso......................................*CO-4*
Colp (Village)—Williamson *IL-3*
Colquhoun (Township)—
 Renville *ND-4*
Colquitt (City)—Miller................... *GA-2*
Colquitt County *GA-2*
Colrain (Town)—Franklin............. *MA-1*
Colstrip (CDP)—Rosebud.............. *MT-4*
Colt (City)—St. Francis *AR-2*
Colton (City)—San Bernardino *CA-4*
Colton (Town)—St. Lawrence....... *NY-1*
Colton (City)—Minnehaha............. *SD-4*
Colton (Town)—Whitman.............. *WA-4*
Colts Neck (Township)—
 Monmouth *NJ-1*
Columbia (Town)—Houston *AL-2*
Columbia (CDP)—Tuolumne *CA-4*
Columbia (Town)—Tolland........... *CT-1*
Columbia (City)—Monroe *IL-3*
Columbia (Township)—Dubois *IN-3*
Columbia (Township)—Fayette *IN-3*
Columbia (Township)—Gibson *IN-3*
Columbia (Township)—Jennings *IN-3*
Columbia (Township)—Whitley *IN-3*
Columbia (Township)—Ellsworth ...*KS-4*
Columbia (City)—Adair *KY-2*
Columbia (Town)—Caldwell
 Parish *LA-2*
Columbia (Town)—Washington.... *ME-1*
Columbia (CDP)—Howard............*MD-1*
Columbia (Township)—Jackson *MI-3*
Columbia (Township)—Tuscola..... *MI-3*
Columbia (Township)—Van
 Buren................................... *MI-3*
Columbia (Township)—Polk......... *MN-3*
Columbia (City)—Marion *MS-2*
Columbia (Township)—Boone *MO-3*
Columbia (Township)—Boone *MO-3*
Columbia (Township)—Knox *NE-4*
Columbia (Town)—Coos *NH-1*
Columbia (Town)—Herkimer *NY-1*
Columbia (Town)—Tyrrell *NC-2*

Columbia (Township)—Eddy.........*ND-4*
Columbia (Township)—
 Hamilton................................*OH-3*
Columbia (Township)—Lorain *OH-3*
Columbia (Township)—Meigs........*OH-3*
Columbia (Township)—Bradford.... *PA-1*
Columbia (Borough)—Lancaster...... *PA-1*
Columbia (City)—Richland *SC-2*
Columbia (City)—Brown *SD-4*
Columbia (Township)—Brown *SD-4*
Columbia (City)—Maury *TN-2*
Columbia (Town)—Fluvanna.......... *VA-2*
Columbia City (City)—Whitley *IN-3*
Columbia City (City)—Columbia ..*OR-4*
Columbia County *AR-2*
Columbia County *FL-2*
Columbia County *GA-2*
Columbia County *NY-1*
Columbia County *OR-4*
Columbia County *PA-1*
Columbia County *WA-4*
Columbia County *WI-3*
Columbia Falls (Town)—
 Washington *ME-1*
Columbia Falls (City)—Flathead .. *MT-4*
Columbia Heights (City)—
 Anoka *MN-3*
Columbiana (City)—Shelby *AL-2*
Columbiana (Village)—
 Columbiana..........................*OH-3*
Columbiana (Village)—
 Mahoning..............................*OH-3*
Columbiana County *OH-3*
Columbia Plateau (AZ) *Geog-4*
Columbia River (AZ) *Geog-4*
Columbiaville (Village)—Lapeer.... *MI-3*
Columbine (CDP)—Arapahoe *CO-4*
Columbine (CDP)—Jefferson *CO-4*
Columbine Valley (Town)—
 Arapahoe..............................*CO-4*
Columbus (Township)—Adams *IL-3*
Columbus (Village)—Adams *IL-3*
Columbus (City)—Bartholomew *IN-3*
Columbus (Township)—
 Bartholomew.........................*IN-3*
Columbus (City)—Cherokee *KS-4*
Columbus (City)—Hickman........... *KY-2*
Columbus (Township)—Luce *MI-3*
Columbus (Township)—St. Clair ... *MI-3*
Columbus (Township)—Anoka *MN-3*
Columbus (City)—Lowndes *MS-2*
Columbus (Township)—Johnson ..*MO-3*
Columbus (Town)—Stillwater........ *MT-4*
Columbus (City)—Platte *NE-4*
Columbus (Township)—Platte *NE-4*
Columbus (Village)—Luna *NM-4*
Columbus (Town)—Chenango *NY-1*
Columbus (Town)—Polk *NC-2*
Columbus (City)—Burke *ND-4*
Columbus (City)—Fairfield *OH-3*
Columbus (City)—Franklin............*OH-3*
Columbus (Township)—Warren *PA-1*
Columbus (City)—Colorado *TX-2*
Columbus (City)—Columbia.......... *WI-3*
Columbus (Town)—Columbia *WI-3*
Columbus (City)—Dodge *WI-3*
Columbus Air Force Base (MS) *Mil-4*
Columbus Air Force Base (Military
 Facility)—Lowndes *MS-2*
Columbus City (City)—Louisa *IA-3*
Columbus (city proper) (City)—
 Muscogee............................. *GA-2*
Columbus County *NC-2*
Columbus Grove (Village)—
 Putnam *OH-3*

General Index

Columbus (incl. Bibb City) (City)—
 Muscogee................................GA-2
Columbus Junction (City)—
 Louisa.....................................IA-3
Colusa (City)—Colusa................CA-4
Colusa (Cachil Dehe) Rancheria
 (CA).............................IndRes-4
Colusa County...........................CA-4
Colver (CDP)—Cambria...........PA-1
Colville (Township)—Burke......ND-4
Colville (City)—Stevens............WA-4
Colville Reservation (WA)........IndRes-4
Colvin (Township)—St. Louis....MN-3
Colvin (Township)—Eddy..........ND-4
Colwell (City)—Floyd................IA-3
Colwich (City)—Sedgwick........KS-4
Colwyn (Borough)—Delaware...PA-1
Comal County...........................TX-2
Comanche (Township)—Barton...KS-4
Comanche (City)—Stephens.......OK-2
Comanche (City)—Comanche.....TX-2
Comanche County...................KS-4
Comanche County...................OK-2
Comanche County...................TX-2
Combee Settlement (CDP)—Polk...FL-2
Combes (Town)—Cameron........TX-2
Combine (City)—Dallas.............TX-2
Combine (City)—Kaufman.........TX-2
Combined Locks (Village)—
 Outagamie............................WI-3
Combs (Township)—Carroll......MO-3
Comer (Town)—Madison..........GA-2
Comfort (Township)—Kanabec...MN-3
Comfort (CDP)—Kendall..........TX-2
Comfrey (City)—Brown.............MN-3
Comfrey (City)—Cottonwood....MN-3
Comins (Township)—Oscoda....MI-3
Commack (CDP)—Suffolk........NY-1
Commerce (City)—Los Angeles...CA-4
Commerce (City)—Jackson........GA-2
Commerce (Township)—Oakland...MI-3
Commerce (Town)—Scott..........MO-3
Commerce (Township)—Scott...MO-3
Commerce (City)—Ottawa........OK-2
Commerce (City)—Hunt............TX-2
Commerce City (City)—Adams...CO-4
Commercial (Township)—
 Cumberland.........................NJ-1
Commercial Point (Village)—
 Pickaway..............................OH-3
Commonwealth (CDP)—
 Albemarle............................VA-2
Commonwealth (Town)—
 Florence...............................WI-3
Como (Township)—Marshall....MN-3
Como (Town)—Panola..............MS-2
Como (Township)—New
 Madrid.................................MO-3
Como (Town)—Hertford...........NC-2
Como (Township)—Hand..........SD-4
Como (Town)—Hopkins............TX-2
Como (CDP)—Walworth..........WI-3
Compromise (Township)—
 Champaign..........................IL-3
Compton (City)—Los Angeles...CA-4
Compton (Village)—Lee............IL-3
Compton (Township)—Otter
 Tail......................................MN-3
Comstock (Township)—
 Kalamazoo..........................MI-3
Comstock (City)—Clay.............MN-3
Comstock (Township)—Marshall...MN-3
Comstock (Township)—Custer...NE-4
Comstock (Village)—Custer......NE-4

Comstock Northwest (CDP)—
 Kalamazoo..........................MI-3
Comstock Park (CDP)—Kent...MI-3
Conata No. 20 (Township)—
 Pennington..........................SD-4
Conception Junction (Town)—
 Nodaway.............................MO-3
Concho County.........................TX-2
Conconully (Town)—Okanogan...WA-4
Concord (Town)—Cleburne......AR-2
Concord (City)—Contra Costa...CA-4
Concord (Town)—Pike..............GA-2
Concord (Township)—Adams...IL-3
Concord (Township)—Bureau...IL-3
Concord (Township)—Iroquois...IL-3
Concord (Village)—Morgan......IL-3
Concord (Township)—Dekalb...IN-3
Concord (Township)—Elkhart...IN-3
Concord (Township)—Ford.......KS-4
Concord (Township)—Ottawa...KS-4
Concord (City)—Lewis..............KY-2
Concord (CDP)—McCracken...KY-2
Concord (Town)—Middlesex....MA-1
Concord (Township)—Jackson...MI-3
Concord (Village)—Jackson......MI-3
Concord (Township)—Dodge....MN-3
Concord (Township)—Clinton...MO-3
Concord (Township)—Pemiscot...MO-3
Concord (CDP)—St. Louis........MO-3
Concord (Township)—St. Louis...MO-3
Concord (Township)—
 Washington.........................MO-3
Concord (Township)—Dixon....NE-4
Concord (Village)—Dixon.........NE-4
Concord (City)—Merrimack.....NH-1
Concord (Town)—Erie..............NY-1
Concord (City)—Cabarrus........NC-2
Concord (Township)—
 Champaign..........................OH-3
Concord (Township)—Delaware...OH-3
Concord (Township)—Fayette...OH-3
Concord (Township)—Highland...OH-3
Concord (Township)—Lake......OH-3
Concord (Township)—Miami...OH-3
Concord (Township)—Ross......OH-3
Concord (Township)—Butler....PA-1
Concord (Township)—Delaware...PA-1
Concord (Township)—Erie........PA-1
Concord (Township)—Lake......SD-4
Concord (Town)—Essex...........VT-1
Concord (Town)—Jefferson......WI-3
Concordia (City)—Cloud..........KS-4
Concordia (City)—Lafayette....MO-3
Concordia (CDP)—Middlesex...NJ-1
Concordia Parish......................LA-2
Concow (CDP)—Butte.............CA-4
Concrete (Town)—Skagit.........WA-4
Conde (City)—Spink................SD-4
Conde (Township)—Spink........SD-4
Condit (Township)—Champaign...IL-3
Condon (City)—Gilliam............OR-4
Condon (Township)—Tripp......SD-4
Conecuh County.......................AL-2
Conehatta (CDP)—Newton......MS-2
Conejos (Town)—Conejos.......CO-4
Conejos County........................CO-4
Conemaugh (Township)—
 Cambria...............................PA-1
Conemaugh (Township)—Indiana...PA-1
Conemaugh (Township)—
 Somerset..............................PA-1
Conestoga (Township)—Lancaster...PA-1
Conesus (Town)—Livingston...NY-1
Conesville (City)—Muscatine...IA-3
Conesville (Town)—Schoharie...NY-1

Conesville (Village)—Coshocton...OH-3
Conetoe (Town)—Edgecombe...NC-2
Conewago (Township)—Adams...PA-1
Conewago (Township)—Dauphin...PA-1
Conewago (Township)—York...PA-1
Conewango (Town)—Cattaraugus...NY-1
Conewango (Township)—Warren...NY-1
Coney Island—Kings................NY-1
Coney Island Beach (NY).......Geog-4
Confluence (Borough)—Somerset...PA-1
Congaree Swamp (SC)............Geog-4
Conger (City)—Freeborn.........MN-3
Congers (CDP)—Rockland......NY-1
Congerville (Village)—Woodford...IL-3
Congress (Township)—Morrow...OH-3
Congress (Township)—Wayne...OH-3
Congress (Village)—Wayne.....OH-3
Conklin (Town)—Broome........NY-1
Conklin (Township)—Stutsman...ND-4
Conkling (Township)—Pawnee...KS-4
Conley (CDP)—Clayton...........GA-2
Conley (Township)—Holt........NE-4
Conneaut (City)—Ashtabula....OH-3
Conneaut (Township)—Crawford...PA-1
Conneaut (Township)—Erie.....PA-1
Conneaut Lake (Borough)—
 Crawford.............................PA-1
Conneaut Lakeshore (CDP)—
 Crawford.............................PA-1
Conneautville (Borough)—
 Crawford.............................PA-1
Connecticut River (SC)..........Geog-4
Connell (Town)—Franklin......WA-4
Connellsville (City)—Fayette...PA-1
Connellsville (Township)—
 Fayette................................PA-1
Connelly (Township)—Wilkin...MN-3
Connelly Springs (Town)—Burke...NC-2
Connersville (City)—Fayette...IN-3
Connersville (Township)—Fayette...IN-3
Connoquenessing (Borough)—
 Butler..................................PA-1
Connoquenessing (Township)—
 Butler..................................PA-1
Connor (Township)—Slope.....ND-4
Connor (unorganized) (Pop. Place)—
 Aroostook............................ME-1
Conover (City)—Catawba........NC-2
Conover (Town)—Vilas...........WI-3
Conoy (Township)—Lancaster...PA-1
Conquest (Town)—Cayuga......NY-1
Conrad (City)—Grundy...........IA-3
Conrad (City)—Pondera..........MT-4
Conrath (Village)—Rusk.........WI-3
Conroe (City)—Montgomery...TX-2
Conshohocken (Borough)—
 Montgomery.......................PA-1
Constable (Town)—Franklin...NY-1
Constableville (Village)—Lewis...NY-1
Constantia (Town)—Oswego...NY-1
Constantine (Township)—St.
 Joseph.................................MI-3
Constantine (Village)—St. Joseph...MI-3
Continental (Village)—Putnam...OH-3
Continental Divide (SC).........Geog-4
Contoocook (CDP)—Merrimack...NH-1
Contra Costa County..............CA-4
Convent (Pop. Place)—St. James
 Parish..................................LA-2
Converse (Town)—Grant.........IN-3
Converse (Town)—Miami........IN-3
Converse (Village)—Sabine
 Parish..................................LA-2
Converse (City)—Bexar...........TX-2
Converse County....................WY-4

American Places Dictionary — General Index

Convis (Township)—Calhoun *MI-3*
Convoy (Village)—Van Wert..........*OH-3*
Conway (City)—Faulkner.............*AR-2*
Conway (CDP)—Orange *FL-2*
Conway (City)—Taylor..................*IA-3*
Conway (Township)—Sumner *KS-4*
Conway (Town)—Franklin............ *MA-1*
Conway (Township)—Livingston... *MI-3*
Conway (City)—Laclede *MO-3*
Conway (Town)—Carroll *NH-1*
Conway (Town)—Northampton.....*NC-2*
Conway (City)—Walsh *ND-4*
Conway (Borough)—Beaver.............*PA-1*
Conway (City)—Horry *SC-2*
Conway County *AR-2*
Conway Springs (City)—Sumner ...*KS-4*
Conyers (City)—Rockdale.............. *GA-2*
Conyngham (Township)—
  Columbia *PA-1*
Conyngham (Borough)—Luzerne....*PA-1*
Conyngham (Township)—Luzerne . *PA-1*
Cook (Township)—Decatur.............*KS-4*
Cook (City)—St. Louis *MN-3*
Cook (Village)—Johnson.................*NE-4*
Cook (Township)—Westmoreland .. *PA-1*
Cook County....................................*GA-2*
Cook County *IL-3*
Cook County *MN-3*
Cooke (Township)—Cumberland.... *PA-1*
Cooke County *TX-2*
Cookeville (City)—Putnam *TN-2*
Cooks Valley (Town)—Chippewa ... *WI-3*
Cooksville (Village)—McLean *IL-3*
Cool (City)—Parker........................*TX-2*
Coolbaugh (Township)—Monroe... *PA-1*
Cooleemee (CDP)—Davie *NC-2*
Coolidge (City)—Pinal *AZ-4*
Coolidge (City)—Thomas *GA-2*
Coolidge (City)—Hamilton *KS-4*
Coolidge (Township)—Hamilton....*KS-4*
Coolidge (Town)—Limestone..........*TX-2*
Coolin (Township)—Towner *ND-4*
Coolspring (Township)—La Porte .. *IN-3*
Coolspring (Township)—Mercer..... *PA-1*
Cool Valley (City)—St. Louis.........*MO-3*
Coolville (Village)—Athens.............*OH-3*
Coon (Town)—Vernon *WI-3*
Coon Creek (Township)—Lyon.....*MN-3*
Coon Island (Township)—Butler .. *MO-3*
Coon Rapids (City)—Carroll *IA-3*
Coon Rapids (City)—Anoka *MN-3*
Coon Valley (Village)—Vernon *WI-3*
Cooper (Township)—Sangamon *IL-3*
Cooper (Town)—Washington *ME-1*
Cooper (Township)—Kalamazoo ... *MI-3*
Cooper (Township)—Gentry *MO-3*
Cooper (Township)—Clearfield *PA-1*
Cooper (Township)—Montour........ *PA-1*
Cooper (Township)—Aurora *SD-4*
Cooper (City)—Delta *TX-2*
Cooper City (City)—Broward *FL-2*
Cooper County.................................*MO-3*
Cooper Landing (CDP)—Kenai
  Peninsula Borough......................*AK-4*
Coopersburg (Borough)—Lehigh.... *PA-1*
Cooperstown (Township)—Brown .. *IL-3*
Cooperstown (Village)—Otsego ... *NY-1*
Cooperstown (City)—Griggs *ND-4*
Cooperstown (Township)—
  Griggs *ND-4*
Cooperstown (Borough)—
  Venango.....................................*PA-1*
Cooperstown (Town)—
  Manitowoc *WI-3*
Coopersville (City)—Ottawa *MI-3*

Cooperton (Town)—Kiowa *OK-2*
Coos, Lower Umpqua, and Siuslaw
  Res. (OR) *IndRes-4*
Coosa County *AL-2*
Coosada (Town)—Elmore *AL-2*
Coos Bay (OR)............................. *Geog-4*
Coos Bay (City)—Coos *OR-4*
Coos County *NH-1*
Coos County *OR-4*
Cooter (Town)—Pemiscot *MO-3*
Cooter (Township)—Pemiscot *MO-3*
Copake (Town)—Columbia............ *NY-1*
Copan (Town)—Washington *OK-2*
Cope (Town)—Orangeburg.............*SC-2*
Copeland (City)—Gray *KS-4*
Copeland (Township)—Gray *KS-4*
Copemish (Village)—Manistee....... *MI-3*
Copenhagen (Village)—Lewis *NY-1*
Copiague (CDP)—Suffolk *NY-1*
Copiah County..................................*MS-2*
Coplay (Borough)—Lehigh *PA-1*
Copley (Township)—Knox............... *IL-3*
Copley (Township)—Clearwater ... *MN-3*
Copley (Township)—Summit *OH-3*
Coplin (Pop. Place)—Franklin *ME-1*
Coppell (City)—Dallas *TX-2*
Coppell (City)—Denton *TX-2*
Copperas Cove (City)—Coryell *TX-2*
Copperas Cove (City)—
  Lampasas *TX-2*
Copper Canyon (Town)—Denton .. *TX-2*
Copper Center (CDP)—Valdez-Cordova
  Census Area *AK-4*
Copper City (Village)—Houghton . *MI-3*
Copperhill (Town)—Polk *TN-2*
Copperville (CDP)—Valdez-Cordova
  Census Area *AK-4*
Coppock (City)—Henry *IA-3*
Coppock (City)—Jefferson *IA-3*
Coppock (City)—Washington...........*IA-3*
Coquille (City)—Coos *OR-4*
Coquille Indian TDSA (OR) *IndRes-4*
Cora (Township)—Smith.................*KS-4*
Coral (Township)—McHenry.......... *IL-3*
Coral Gables (City)—Dade *FL-2*
Coral Hills (CDP)—Prince
  George's *MD-1*
Coral Springs (City)—Broward *FL-2*
Coral Terrace (CDP)—Dade *FL-2*
Coralville (City)—Johnson...............*IA-3*
Coram (CDP)—Suffolk *NY-1*
Coraopolis (Borough)—Allegheny.. *PA-1*
Corbin (City)—Knox.......................*KY-2*
Corbin (City)—Whitley *KY-2*
Corbin City (City)—Atlantic............*NJ-1*
Corcoran (City)—Kings................... *CA-4*
Corcoran (City)—Hennepin *MN-3*
Cordaville (CDP)—Worcester....... *MA-1*
Cordele (City)—Crisp.................... *GA-2*
Cordelia (Township)—Bottineau ...*ND-4*
Corder (City)—Lafayette................*MO-3*
Cordova (Municipality)—Walker....*AL-2*
Cordova (City)—Valdez-Cordova
  Census Area *AK-4*
Cordova (Township)—Rock
  Island.. *IL-3*
Cordova (Village)—Rock Island *IL-3*
Cordova (Township)—Le Sueur ... *MN-3*
Cordova (Village)—Seward *NE-4*
Cordova (Town)—Orangeburg........*SC-2*
Corfu (Village)—Genesee *NY-1*
Corinna (Town)—Penobscot *ME-1*
Corinna (Township)—Wright........*MN-3*
Corinne (Township)—Stutsman.....*ND-4*
Corinne (City)—Box Elder............. *UT-4*

Corinth (Town)—Yell *AR-2*
Corinth (Town)—Coweta *GA-2*
Corinth (Town)—Heard *GA-2*
Corinth (Township)—Osborne........*KS-4*
Corinth (City)—Grant *KY-2*
Corinth (City)—Harrison *KY-2*
Corinth (City)—Scott *KY-2*
Corinth (Town)—Penobscot.......... *ME-1*
Corinth (City)—Alcorn *MS-2*
Corinth (Town)—Saratoga *NY-1*
Corinth (Village)—Saratoga *NY-1*
Corinth (Town)—Denton *TX-2*
Corinth (Town)—Orange................ *VT-1*
Corliss (Township)—Otter Tail..... *MN-3*
Cormant (Township)—Beltrami.... *MN-3*
Cormorant (Township)—Becker ... *MN-3*
Corn (Town)—Washita................... *OK-2*
Corn Creek (Township)—
  Mellette *SD-4*
Cornelia (City)—Habersham *GA-2*
Cornelius (Town)—Mecklenburg ...*NC-2*
Cornelius (City)—Washington *OR-4*
Cornell (Village)—Livingston *IL-3*
Cornell (Township)—Delta *MI-3*
Cornell (Township)—Cass *ND-4*
Cornell (City)—Chippewa *WI-3*
Corner (Township)—Custer *NE-4*
Cornersville (Town)—Marshall *TN-2*
Corning (City)—Clay......................*AR-2*
Corning (City)—Tehama *CA-4*
Corning (City)—Adams....................*IA-3*
Corning (City)—Nemaha *KS-4*
Corning (Town)—Holt *MO-3*
Corning (City)—Steuben *NY-1*
Corning (Town)—Steuben *NY-1*
Corning (Village)—Perry *OH-3*
Corning (Town)—Lincoln *WI-3*
Cornish (Town)—York *ME-1*
Cornish (Township)—Aitkin *MN-3*
Cornish (Township)—Sibley *MN-3*
Cornish (Town)—Sullivan..............*NH-1*
Cornish (Town)—Jefferson *OK-2*
Cornish (Town)—Cache *UT-4*
Cornlea (Village)—Platte.................*NE-4*
Cornplanter (Township)—
  Venango......................................*PA-1*
Cornville (CDP)—Yavapai..............*AZ-4*
Cornville (Town)—Somerset *ME-1*
Cornwall (Town)—Litchfield *CT-1*
Cornwall (Township)—Henry *IL-3*
Cornwall (Town)—Orange *NY-1*
Cornwall (Borough)—Lebanon *PA-1*
Cornwall (Township)—Spink *SD-4*
Cornwall (Town)—Addison............ *VT-1*
Cornwall on Hudson (Village)—
  Orange.. *NY-1*
Cornwells Heights-Eddington (CDP)—
  Bucks *PA-1*
Corona (City)—Riverside................ *CA-4*
Corona (Village)—Lincoln *NM-4*
Corona (Town)—Roberts *SD-4*
Coronado (City)—San Diego *CA-4*
Corpus Christi (City)—Kleberg *TX-2*
Corpus Christi (City)—Nueces *TX-2*
Corpus Christi (City)—San
  Patricio.......................................*TX-2*
Corral City (Town)—Denton *TX-2*
Corrales (Village)—Bernalillo *NM-4*
Corrales (Village)—Sandoval *NM-4*
Corralitos (CDP)—Santa Cruz....... *CA-4*
Correctionville (City)—Woodbury...*IA-3*
Correll (City)—Big Stone *MN-3*
Corrigan (Town)—Polk *TX-2*
Corry (City)—Erie *PA-1*
Corsica (Borough)—Jefferson *PA-1*

945

General Index

Corsica (City)—Douglas............... *SD-4*
Corsicana (Township)—Barry....... *MO-3*
Corsicana (City)—Navarro *TX-2*
Corson County............................... *SD-4*
Corte Madera (Town)—Marin *CA-4*
Cortez (City)—Montezuma........... *CO-4*
Cortez (CDP)—Manatee *FL-2*
Cortina Rancheria (CA) *IndRes-4*
Cortland (Town)—DeKalb *IL-3*
Cortland (Township)—DeKalb....... *IL-3*
Cortland (Village)—Gage *NE-4*
Cortland (City)—Cortland *NY-1*
Cortland (Village)—Trumbull *OH-3*
Cortland County............................. *NY-1*
Cortlandt (Town)—Westchester.... *NY-1*
Cortlandt (Township)—Edmunds... *SD-4*
Cortlandville (Town)—Cortland.... *NY-1*
Cortland West (CDP)—Cortland... *NY-1*
Corunna (Town)—Dekalb *IN-3*
Corunna (City)—Shiawassee *MI-3*
Corvallis (City)—Benton *OR-4*
Corwin (Township)—Logan *IL-3*
Corwin (Township)—Stutsman *ND-4*
Corwin (Village)—Warren............. *OH-3*
Corwith (City)—Hancock............. *IA-3*
Corwith (Township)—Otsego *MI-3*
Corydon (Town)—Harrison *IN-3*
Corydon (City)—Wayne *IA-3*
Corydon (City)—Henderson *KY-2*
Corydon (Township)—McKean *PA-1*
Coryell County *TX-2*
Cosby (Town)—Andrew *MO-3*
Coshocton (City)—Coshocton....... *OH-3*
Coshocton County......................... *OH-3*
Cosmo (Township)—Kearney *NE-4*
Cosmopolis (City)—Grays
  Harbor.. *WA-4*
Cosmos (City)—Meeker *MN-3*
Cosmos (Township)—Meeker *MN-3*
Costa Mesa (City)—Orange *CA-4*
Costilla County *CO-4*
Cotati (City)—Sonoma *CA-4*
Coteau des Prairies (OR) *Geog-4*
Cote Sans Dessein (Township)—
  Callaway................................... *MO-3*
Cotesfield (Village)—Howard *NE-4*
Coto De Caza (CDP)—Orange *CA-4*
Cottage (Township)—Saline *IL-3*
Cottage City (Town)—Prince
  George's..................................... *MD-1*
Cottage Grove (Township)—
  Allen.. *KS-4*
Cottage Grove (City)—
  Washington............................... *MN-3*
Cottage Grove (City)—Lane *OR-4*
Cottage Grove (Town)—Henry..... *TN-2*
Cottage Grove (Town)—Dane *WI-3*
Cottage Grove (Village)—Dane *WI-3*
Cottage Hill (Township)—
  Marshall................................... *KS-4*
Cottageville (Town)—Colleton....... *SC-2*
Cotter (City)—Baxter *AR-2*
Cotter (City)—Louisa *IA-3*
Cotterell (Township)—Dodge *NE-4*
Cottle County *TX-2*
Cottleville (Town)—St. Charles *MO-3*
Cottleville (Township)—St.
  Charles..................................... *MO-3*
Cotton (Township)—Switzerland.... *IN-3*
Cotton (Township)—St. Louis *MN-3*
Cotton County *OK-2*
Cottondale (Town)—Jackson *FL-2*
Cotton Hill (Township)—
  Sangamon.................................. *IL-3*

Cotton Hill (Township)—
  Dunklin..................................... *MO-3*
Cotton Plant (City)—Woodruff *AR-2*
Cottonport (Town)—Avoyelles
  Parish *LA-2*
Cotton Valley (Town)—Webster
  Parish *LA-2*
Cottonwood (Municipality)—
  Houston.................................... *AL-2*
Cottonwood (Town)—Yavapai...... *AZ-4*
Cottonwood (CDP)—Shasta *CA-4*
Cottonwood (City)—Idaho............ *ID-4*
Cottonwood (Township)—
  Cumberland.............................. *IL-3*
Cottonwood (Township)—Chase *KS-4*
Cottonwood (Township)—
  Brown....................................... *MN-3*
Cottonwood (City)—Lyon *MN-3*
Cottonwood (Township)—Adams.. *NE-4*
Cottonwood (Township)—Nance... *NE-4*
Cottonwood (Township)—Phelps .. *NE-4*
Cottonwood (Township)—
  Mountrail *ND-4*
Cottonwood (Township)—Clark *SD-4*
Cottonwood (Township)—Fall
  River *SD-4*
Cottonwood (Town)—Jackson *SD-4*
Cottonwood (City)—Kaufman *TX-2*
Cottonwood County *MN-3*
Cottonwood Falls (City)—Chase....*KS-4*
Cottonwood Heights (CDP)—Salt
  Lake.. *UT-4*
Cottonwood Lake (Township)—
  McHenry *ND-4*
Cottonwood Lake (Township)—
  Edmunds................................... *SD-4*
Cottonwood Shores (City)—
  Burnet *TX-2*
Cottonwood West (CDP)—Salt
  Lake.. *UT-4*
Cottrellville (Township)—St.
  Clair *MI-3*
Cotuit (CDP)—Barnstable *MA-1*
Cotulla (City)—La Salle *TX-2*
Couch (Township)—Oregon.......... *MO-3*
Couderay (Town)—Sawyer............ *WI-3*
Couderay (Village)—Sawyer.......... *WI-3*
Coudersport (Borough)—Potter *PA-1*
Coulee (Township)—Ramsey......... *ND-4*
Coulee City (Town)—Grant *WA-4*
Coulee Dam (Town)—Douglas *WA-4*
Coulee Dam (Town)—Grant......... *WA-4*
Coulee Dam (Town)—Okanogan... *WA-4*
Coulter (Township)—Franklin *IA-3*
Coulterville (Village)—Randolph.... *IL-3*
Council (City)—Adams *ID-4*
Council Bluffs (City)—
  Pottawattamie.......................... *IA-3*
Council Creek (Township)—
  Nance *NE-4*
Council Grove (City)—Morris *KS-4*
Council Hill (Township)—Jo
  Daviess..................................... *IL-3*
Council Hill (Town)—Muskogee ... *OK-2*
Country Club (CDP)—San
  Joaquin..................................... *CA-4*
Country Club (CDP)—Dade..........*FL-2*
Country Club (Village)—
  Andrew..................................... *MO-3*
Country Club Estates (CDP)—
  Glynn *GA-2*
Country Club Heights (Town)—
  Madison *IN-3*
Country Club Hills (Village)—
  Cook *IL-3*

Country Club Hills (City)—St.
  Louis *MO-3*
Country Club Trail (CDP)—Palm
  Beach.. *FL-2*
Country Homes (CDP)—
  Spokane.................................... *WA-4*
Country Knolls (CDP)—Saratoga .. *NY-1*
Country Lake Estates (CDP)—
  Burlington................................ *NJ-1*
Country Life Acres (Village)—St.
  Louis *MO-3*
Countryside (Village)—Cook *IL-3*
Countryside (City)—Johnson..........*KS-4*
Countryside (CDP)—Loudoun *VA-2*
County Line (Municipality)—
  Blount....................................... *AL-2*
County Line (Division)—
  Covington *AL-2*
County Line (Municipality)—
  Jefferson................................... *AL-2*
Coupeville (Town)—Island............ *WA-4*
Courtdale (Borough)—Luzerne *PA-1*
Courtenay (City)—Stutsman *ND-4*
Courtenay (Township)—
  Stutsman *ND-4*
Courtland (Town)—Lawrence....... *AL-2*
Courtland (City)—Republic...........*KS-4*
Courtland (Township)—Republic ...*KS-4*
Courtland (Township)—Kent......... *MI-3*
Courtland (City)—Nicollet............ *MN-3*
Courtland (Township)—Nicollet.... *MN-3*
Courtland (Town)—Panola *MS-2*
Courtland (Town)—Southampton... *VA-2*
Courtland (Town)—Columbia *WI-3*
Courtois (Township)—Crawford... *MO-3*
Coushatta (Town)—Red River
  Parish *LA-2*
Coushatta Tribe (LA)................ *IndRes-4*
Cove (Town)—Polk *AR-2*
Cove (City)—Union *OR-4*
Cove (Town)—Chambers *TX-2*
Cove City (Town)—Craven........... *NC-2*
Covedale (CDP)—Hamilton *OH-3*
Covelo (CDP)—Mendocino *CA-4*
Covenant Life (CDP)—Haines
  Borough................................... *AK-4*
Cove Neck (Village)—Nassau *NY-1*
Coventry (Town)—Tolland............ *CT-1*
Coventry (Town)—Chenango *NY-1*
Coventry (Township)—Summit *OH-3*
Coventry (Town)—Kent................. *RI-1*
Coventry (Town)—Orleans *VT-1*
Coventry Lake (CDP)—Tolland ... *CT-1*
Covert (Township)—Osborne........*KS-4*
Covert (Township)—Van Buren.... *MI-3*
Covert (Town)—Seneca *NY-1*
Covina (City)—Los Angeles........... *CA-4*
Covington (City)—Newton *GA-2*
Covington (Township)—
  Washington.............................. *IL-3*
Covington (City)—Fountain.......... *IN-3*
Covington (City)—Kenton *KY-2*
Covington (City)—St. Tammany
  Parish *LA-2*
Covington (Township)—Baraga *MI-3*
Covington (Town)—Wyoming *NY-1*
Covington (Village)—Miami......... *OH-3*
Covington (Town)—Garfield *OK-2*
Covington (Township)—
  Clearfield *PA-1*
Covington (Township)—
  Lackawanna............................. *PA-1*
Covington (Township)—Tioga *PA-1*
Covington (City)—Tipton *TN-2*
Covington (City)—Hill................... *TX-2*

Covington County AL-2
Covington County MS-2
Covington (Independent City) VA-2
Covington-Sawyer-Wilderness (CDP)—
  King WA-4
Cowan (Township)—Wayne MO-3
Cowan (City)—Franklin TN-2
Cowanshannock (Township)—
  Armstrong PA-1
Coward (Town)—Florence SC-2
Cowarts (Town)—Houston AL-2
Cow Creek (Township)—
  Williams ND-4
Cow Creek Reservation (OR)... IndRes-4
Cowden (Village)—Shelby IL-3
Cowen (Town)—Webster WV-2
Coweta (City)—Wagoner OK-2
Coweta County GA-2
Cowgill (City)—Caldwell MO-3
Cowles (Village)—Webster NE-4
Cowley (Town)—Big Horn WY-4
Cowley County KS-4
Cowlington (Town)—Le Flore OK-2
Cowlitz County WA-4
Cowpens (Town)—Spartanburg SC-2
Coxsackie (Town)—Greene NY-1
Coxsackie (Village)—Greene NY-1
Coy (Town)—Lonoke AR-2
Coyle (Town)—Logan OK-2
Coyote Valley Reservation
  (CA) IndRes-4
Coyville (City)—Wilson KS-4
Cozad (City)—Dawson NE-4
Crab Orchard (City)—Lincoln KY-2
Crab Orchard (Village)—Johnson .. NE-4
Crab Orchard (Town)—
  Cumberland TN-2
Crab Orchard (CDP)—Raleigh WV-2
Crafton (Borough)—Allegheny PA-1
Craftsbury (Town)—Orleans VT-1
Craig (City)—Prince of Wales-Outer
  Ketchikan Census Area AK-4
Craig (City)—Moffat CO-4
Craig (Township)—Switzerland IN-3
Craig (City)—Plymouth IA-3
Craig (City)—Holt MO-3
Craig (Township)—Burt NE-4
Craig (Village)—Burt NE-4
Craig Beach (Village)—
  Mahoning OH-3
Craig County OK-2
Craig County VA-2
Craighead County AR-2
Craigmont (City)—Lewis ID-4
Craigsville (Town)—Augusta VA-2
Craigsville (CDP)—Nicholas WV-2
Crainville (Village)—Williamson IL-3
Cramerton (Town)—Gaston NC-2
Cranberry (Township)—
  Crawford OH-3
Cranberry (Township)—Butler PA-1
Cranberry (Township)—Venango PA-1
Cranberry Isles (Town)—
  Hancock ME-1
Cranbury (Township)—Middlesex .. NJ-1
Crandall (Town)—Harrison IN-3
Crandall (City)—Kaufman TX-2
Crandon (Township)—Spink SD-4
Crandon (City)—Forest WI-3
Crandon (City)—Forest WI-3
Crandon Lakes (CDP)—Sussex NJ-1
Crane (Town)—Martin IN-3
Crane (City)—Stone MO-3
Crane (Township)—Paulding OH-3
Crane (Township)—Wyandot OH-3

Crane (City)—Crane TX-2
Crane County TX-2
Crane Creek (Township)—Mason ... IL-3
Crane Creek (Township)—Barry ... MO-3
Crane Creek (Township)—
  Mountrail ND-4
Cranesville (Borough)—Erie PA-1
Cranfills Gap (City)—Bosque TX-2
Cranford (Township)—Union NJ-1
Cranmoor (Town)—Wood WI-3
Cranston (City)—Providence RI-1
Crary (City)—Ramsey ND-4
Crate (Township)—Chippewa MN-3
Crater Lake (OR) Geog-4
Craters of the Moon (ID) Geog-4
Craven County NC-2
Crawford (Town)—Delta CO-4
Crawford (City)—Oglethorpe GA-2
Crawford (Township)—Cherokee ... KS-4
Crawford (Township)—Crawford ... KS-4
Crawford (Town)—Washington ME-1
Crawford (Town)—Lowndes MS-2
Crawford (Township)—
  Buchanan MO-3
Crawford (Township)—Osage MO-3
Crawford (Township)—Antelope ... NE-4
Crawford (City)—Dawes NE-4
Crawford (Township)—Orange NY-1
Crawford (Township)—Slope ND-4
Crawford (Township)—
  Coshocton OH-3
Crawford (Township)—Wyandot ... OH-3
Crawford (Township)—Clinton PA-1
Crawford (Town)—McLennan TX-2
Crawford County AR-2
Crawford County GA-2
Crawford County IL-3
Crawford County IN-3
Crawford County IA-3
Crawford County KS-4
Crawford County MI-3
Crawford County MO-3
Crawford County OH-3
Crawford County PA-1
Crawford County WI-3
Crawfords Purchase (Pop. Place)—
  Coos NH-1
Crawfordsville (Town)—
  Crittenden AR-2
Crawfordsville (City)—
  Montgomery IN-3
Crawfordsville (City)—
  Washington IA-3
Crawfordville (Village)—Wakulla ... FL-2
Crawfordville (City)—Taliaferro GA-2
Creal Springs (City)—Williamson ... IL-3
Cream Ridge (Township)—
  Livingston MO-3
Credit River (Township)—Scott ... MN-3
Creede (Town)—Mineral CO-4
Creedmoor (City)—Granville NC-2
Creedmoor (City)—Travis TX-2
Creek (Township)—De Witt IL-3
Creek (Township)—Sumner KS-4
Creek County OK-2
Creek-Seminole Joint Area TJSA
  (OK) IndRes-4
Creekside (City)—Jefferson KY-2
Creekside (Borough)—Indiana PA-1
Creek TJSA (OK) IndRes-4
Creel (Township)—Ramsey ND-4
Creighton (City)—Cass MO-3
Creighton (City)—Knox NE-4
Creighton (Township)—Knox NE-4

Cremerville (Township)—
  McLean ND-4
Crenshaw (Town)—Panola MS-2
Crenshaw (Town)—Quitman MS-2
Crenshaw County AL-2
Creola (Town)—Mobile AL-2
Cresaptown-Bel Air (CDP)—
  Allegany MD-1
Cresbard (Town)—Faulk SD-4
Crescent (Township)—Iroquois IL-3
Crescent (City)—Pottawattamie IA-3
Crescent (City)—Logan OK-2
Crescent (Township)—Allegheny PA-1
Crescent (Village)—Oneida WI-3
Crescent Beach (CDP)—St.
  Johns FL-2
Crescent City (City)—Del Norte ... CA-4
Crescent City (City)—Putnam FL-2
Crescent City (Village)—Iroquois ... IL-3
Crescent City North (CDP)—Del
  Norte CA-4
Crescent Park (City)—Kenton KY-2
Crescent Springs (City)—Kenton ... KY-2
Cresco (City)—Howard IA-3
Cresskill (Borough)—Bergen NJ-1
Cresson (City)—Cambria PA-1
Cresson (Township)—Cambria PA-1
Cressona (Borough)—Schuylkill PA-1
Crested Butte (Town)—
  Gunnison CO-4
Crest Hill (Village)—Will IL-3
Crestline (CDP)—San
  Bernardino CA-4
Crestline (City)—Crawford OH-3
Crestline (City)—Richland OH-3
Creston (Village)—Ogle IL-3
Creston (City)—Union IA-3
Creston (Township)—Platte NE-4
Creston (Village)—Platte NE-4
Creston (Village)—Wayne OH-3
Creston (Town)—Lincoln WA-4
Crestone (Town)—Saguache CO-4
Crestview (City)—Okaloosa FL-2
Crestview (City)—Campbell KY-2
Crestview Hills (City)—Kenton KY-2
Crestwood (Village)—Cook IL-3
Crestwood (City)—Oldham KY-2
Crestwood (City)—St. Louis MO-3
Crestwood Village (CDP)—Ocean .. NJ-1
Creswell (Township)—Cowley KS-4
Creswell (Town)—Washington NC-2
Creswell (City)—Lane OR-4
Crete (Township)—Will IL-3
Crete (Village)—Will IL-3
Crete (City)—Saline NE-4
Creve Coeur (Village)—Tazewell IL-3
Creve Coeur (City)—St. Louis MO-3
Creve Coeur (Township)—St.
  Louis MO-3
Crewe (Town)—Nottoway VA-2
Cricket (CDP)—Wilkes NC-2
Cridersville (Village)—Auglaize OH-3
Criehaven (unorganized) (Pop. Place)—
  Knox ME-1
Crimora (CDP)—Augusta VA-2
Cripple Creek (City)—Teller CO-4
Crisfield (City)—Somerset MD-1
Crisp County GA-2
Crittenden (Township)—
  Champaign IL-3
Crittenden (City)—Grant KY-2
Crittenden County AR-2
Crittenden County KY-2
Crivitz (Village)—Marinette WI-3
Crocker (City)—Pulaski MO-3

General Index
American Places Dictionary

Crockery (Township)—Ottawa........ *MI-3*
Crockett (CDP)—Contra Costa *CA-4*
Crockett (City)—Houston *TX-2*
Crockett County *TN-2*
Crockett County *TX-2*
Crocus (Township)—Towner...........*ND-4*
Crofte (Township)—Burleigh *ND-4*
Crofton (City)—Christian *KY-2*
Crofton (CDP)—Anne Arundel *MD-1*
Crofton (Village)—Knox *NE-4*
Croghan (Town)—Lewis.................. *NY-1*
Croghan (Village)—Lewis................ *NY-1*
Croke (Township)—Traverse *MN-3*
Cromwell (Town)—Middlesex *CT-1*
Cromwell (Town)—Noble *IN-3*
Cromwell (City)—Union...................*IA-3*
Cromwell (City)—Carlton *MN-3*
Cromwell (Township)—Clay *MN-3*
Cromwell (Township)—Burleigh ...*ND-4*
Cromwell (Town)—Seminole *OK-2*
Cromwell (Township)—
   Huntingdon.....................................*PA-1*
Crook (Town)—Logan...................... *CO-4*
Crook (Township)—Hamilton *IL-3*
Crook County *OR-4*
Crook County *WY-4*
Crooked Creek (CDP)—Bethel Census
   Area..*AK-4*
Crooked Creek (Township)—
   Cumberland *IL-3*
Crooked Creek (Township)—
   Jasper *IL-3*
Crooked Creek (Township)—
   Meade. *KS-4*
Crooked Creek (Township)—
   Houston...*MN-3*
Crooked Creek (Township)—
   Bollinger..*MO-3*
Crooked Creek No. 25 (Township)—
   Pennington......................................*SD-4*
Crooked Lake (Township)—Cass.. *MN-3*
Crooked Lake Park (CDP)—Polk...*FL-2*
Crooked River (Township)—
   Ray...*MO-3*
Crooks (Township)—Renville *MN-3*
Crooks (Town)—Minnehaha........... *SD-4*
Crookston (City)—Polk *MN-3*
Crookston (Township)—Polk *MN-3*
Crookston (Village)—Cherry........... *NE-4*
Crooksville (Village)—Perry *OH-3*
Cropsey (Township)—McLean........ *IL-3*
Crosby (City)—Crow Wing *MN-3*
Crosby (Township)—Pine *MN-3*
Crosby (Town)—Amite *MS-2*
Crosby (Town)—Wilkinson *MS-2*
Crosby (City)—Divide *ND-4*
Crosby (Township)—Hamilton *OH-3*
Crosby (CDP)—Harris *TX-2*
Crosby County *TX-2*
Crosbyton (City)—Crosby *TX-2*
Cross (Town)—Buffalo *WI-3*
Cross City (Town)—Dixie...............*FL-2*
Cross County *AR-2*
Cross Creek (Township)—
   Jefferson *OH-3*
Cross Creek (Township)—
   Washington......................................*PA-1*
Crossett (City)—Ashley *AR-2*
Cross-Florida Waterway (ID) *Geog-4*
Crossgate (City)—Jefferson *KY-2*
Cross Hill (Town)—Laurens *SC-2*
Crosslake (City)—Crow Wing........ *MN-3*
Cross Lanes (CDP)—Kanawha..... *WV-2*
Cross Mountain (CDP)—Bexar *TX-2*
Crossnore (Town)—Avery *NC-2*

Cross Plains (Township)—
   Hutchinson.......................................*SD-4*
Cross Plains (City)—Robertson *TN-2*
Cross Plains (Town)—Callahan *TX-2*
Cross Plains (Town)—Dane *WI-3*
Cross Plains (Village)—Dane......... *WI-3*
Cross Roads (Borough)—York *PA-1*
Cross Roads (Town)—Denton *TX-2*
Cross Timbers (City)—Hickory *MO-3*
Cross Timbers (Township)—
   Hickory *MO-3*
Cross Village (Township)—
   Emmet *MI-3*
Crossville (Town)—DeKalb *AL-2*
Crossville (Village)—White *IL-3*
Crossville (City)—Cumberland *TN-2*
Croswell (City)—Sanilac *MI-3*
Crothersville (Town)—Jackson *IN-3*
Croton (Township)—Newaygo *MI-3*
Croton-on-Hudson (Village)—
   Westchester *NY-1*
Crouch (City)—Boise *ID-4*
Crouch (Township)—Hamilton *IL-3*
Crow (Township)—Jerauld *SD-4*
Crow Agency (CDP)—Big Horn ... *MT-4*
Crow Creek (Pop. Place)—
   Buffalo... *SD-4*
Crow Creek (Pop. Place)—
   Hughes *SD-4*
Crow Creek (Pop. Place)—Hyde ... *SD-4*
Crow Creek Reservation (SD).. *IndRes-4*
Crowder (Town)—Panola *MS-2*
Crowder (Town)—Quitman *MS-2*
Crowder (Town)—Pittsburg *OK-2*
Crowell (City)—Foard *TX-2*
Crowfoot (Township)—
   Mountrail *ND-4*
Crow Lake (Township)—Stearns .. *MN-3*
Crow Lake (Township)—Jerauld ... *SD-4*
Crowley (Town)—Crowley *CO-4*
Crowley (City)—Acadia Parish *LA-2*
Crowley (City)—Johnson *TX-2*
Crowley (City)—Tarrant *TX-2*
Crowley County *CO-4*
Crown City (Village)—Gallia..........*OH-3*
Crown Heights (CDP)—Dutchess .. *NY-1*
Crown Heights—Kings *NY-1*
Crown Hill (Township)—Kidder ... *ND-4*
Crown Point (CDP)—Kenai Peninsula
   Borough *AK-4*
Crown Point (City)—Lake *IN-3*
Crownpoint (CDP)—McKinley *NM-4*
Crown Point (Town)—Essex *NY-1*
Crownsville (CDP)—Anne
   Arundel *MD-1*
Crow Reservation & Trust Lands
   (MT) *IndRes-4*
Crow River (Township)—
   Stearns... *MN-3*
Crows Nest (Town)—Marion *IN-3*
Crow Wing (Township)—Crow
   Wing... *MN-3*
Crow Wing County *MN-3*
Crow Wing Lake (Township)—
   Hubbard...*MN-3*
Croydon (Town)—Sullivan *NH-1*
Croydon (CDP)—Bucks *PA-1*
Croyle (Township)—Cambria *PA-1*
Crozet (CDP)—Albemarle *VA-2*
Cruger (Township)—Woodford *IL-3*
Cruger (Town)—Holmes *MS-2*
Crump (City)—Hardin *TN-2*
Crystal (Township)—Phillips *KS-4*
Crystal (Town)—Aroostook............ *ME-1*
Crystal (Township)—Montcalm *MI-3*

Crystal (Township)—Oceana........... *MI-3*
Crystal (City)—Hennepin *MN-3*
Crystal (City)—Pembina *ND-4*
Crystal (Township)—Pembina *ND-4*
Crystal (Town)—Washburn *WI-3*
Crystal Bay (Township)—Lake *MN-3*
Crystal City (City)—Jefferson *MO-3*
Crystal City (City)—Zavala *TX-2*
Crystal Falls (City)—Iron *MI-3*
Crystal Falls (Township)—Iron *MI-3*
Crystal Ice Cave (ID)................... *Geog-4*
Crystal Lake (CDP)—Tolland *CT-1*
Crystal Lake (CDP)—Polk *FL-2*
Crystal Lake (City)—McHenry *IL-3*
Crystal Lake (City)—Hancock *IA-3*
Crystal Lake (Township)—Benzie.. *MI-3*
Crystal Lake (Township)—Wells .*ND-4*
Crystal Lake (Township)—
   Aurora *SD-4*
Crystal Lake (Town)—Barron *WI-3*
Crystal Lake (Town)—Marquette .. *WI-3*
Crystal Lake Park (City)—St.
   Louis *MO-3*
Crystal Lakes (Village)—Ray *MO-3*
Crystal Lakes (CDP)—Clark *OH-3*
Crystal Lawns (CDP)—Will........... *IL-3*
Crystal Plains (Township)—
   Smith... *KS-4*
Crystal River (City)—Citrus *FL-2*
Crystal Springs (City)—Copiah......*MS-2*
Crystal Springs (Township)—
   Kidder *ND-4*
Cuba (Town)—Sumter......................*AL-2*
Cuba (City)—Fulton *IL-3*
Cuba (Township)—Lake *IL-3*
Cuba (City)—Republic *KS-4*
Cuba (Township)—Becker *MN-3*
Cuba (City)—Crawford *MO-3*
Cuba (Village)—Sandoval *NM-4*
Cuba (Town)—Allegany *NY-1*
Cuba (Village)—Allegany *NY-1*
Cuba (Township)—Barnes...............*ND-4*
Cuba City (City)—Grant *WI-3*
Cuba City (City)—Lafayette *WI-3*
Cube Cove (CDP)—
   Skagway-Hoonah-Angoon Census
   Area *AK-4*
Cudahy (City)—Los Angeles *CA-4*
Cudahy (City)—Milwaukee............. *WI-3*
Cudjoe Key (CDP)—Monroe..........*FL-2*
Cuero (City)—DeWitt *TX-2*
Cuivre (Township)—Audrain *MO-3*
Cuivre (Township)—Pike *MO-3*
Culberson County *TX-2*
Culbertson (Town)—Roosevelt *MT-4*
Culbertson (Village)—Hitchcock ... *NE-4*
Culdesac (City)—Nez Perce *ID-4*
Culdrum (Township)—Morrison .. *MN-3*
Cullen (Town)—Webster Parish......*LA-2*
Cullen (Township)—Pulaski *MO-3*
Cullison (City)—Pratt *KS-4*
Cullman (City)—Cullman *AL-2*
Cullman County................................. *AL-2*
Culloden (City)—Monroe *GA-2*
Culloden (CDP)—Cabell *WV-2*
Culloden (CDP)—Putnam *WV-2*
Cullom (Village)—Livingston *IL-3*
Culpeper (Town)—Culpeper *VA-2*
Culpeper County................................ *VA-2*
Culver (Town)—Marshall *IN-3*
Culver (City)—Ottawa *KS-4*
Culver (Township)—Ottawa............*KS-4*
Culver (Township)—St. Louis........ *MN-3*
Culver (City)—Jefferson.................. *OR-4*
Culver City (City)—Los Angeles ... *CA-4*

Cumberland (Town)—Hancock *IN-3*
Cumberland (Town)—Marion......... *IN-3*
Cumberland (City)—Cass *IA-3*
Cumberland (City)—Harlan........... *KY-2*
Cumberland (Town)—
  Cumberland *ME-1*
Cumberland (City)—Allegany *MD-1*
Cumberland (Village)—Guernsey ..*OH-3*
Cumberland (Township)—Adams... *PA-1*
Cumberland (Township)—Greene .. *PA-1*
Cumberland (Town)—Providence .. *RI-1*
Cumberland (City)—Barron........... *WI-3*
Cumberland (Town)—Barron *WI-3*
Cumberland City (Town)—
  Stewart *TN-2*
Cumberland County........................... *IL-3*
Cumberland County.......................... *KY-2*
Cumberland County........................... *ME-1*
Cumberland County........................... *NJ-1*
Cumberland County........................... *NC-2*
Cumberland County........................... *PA-1*
Cumberland County........................... *TN-2*
Cumberland County........................... *VA-2*
Cumberland Gap (ID) *Geog-4*
Cumberland Gap (Town)—
  Claiborne......................................*TN-2*
Cumberland Head (CDP)—
  Clinton..*NY-1*
Cumberland Hill (CDP)—
  Providence *RI-1*
Cumberland Mountains (ID)....... *Geog-4*
Cumberland Plateau (ID)............ *Geog-4*
Cumberland River (ID)............... *Geog-4*
Cumberland Road (ID) *Geog-4*
Cumberland Valley (Township)—
  Bedford *PA-1*
Cumby (City)—Hopkins *TX-2*
Cuming (Township)—Cuming *NE-4*
Cuming (Township)—Dodge *NE-4*
Cuming County................................ *NE-4*
Cumming (City)—Forsyth............... *GA-2*
Cumming (City)—Warren *IA-3*
Cumming (Township)—Ogemaw... *MI-3*
Cummings (Township)—
  Lycoming......................................*PA-1*
Cummington (Town)—
  Hampshire *MA-1*
Cumru (Township)—Berks............. *PA-1*
Cuney (Town)—Cherokee *TX-2*
Cunningham (Township)—
  Champaign................................... *IL-3*
Cunningham (City)—Kingman *KS-4*
Cunningham (Township)—
  Chariton *MO-3*
Cupertino (City)—Santa Clara *CA-4*
Curlew (City)—Palo Alto *IA-3*
Curlew (Township)—Tripp............. *SD-4*
Curran (Township)—Sangamon...... *IL-3*
Curran (Town)—Jackson................ *WI-3*
Current (Township)—Dent *MO-3*
Current (Township)—Texas *MO-3*
Current River (Township)—
  Ripley... *MO-3*
Currie (City)—Murray *MN-3*
Currie (Township)—Rolette *ND-4*
Currituck (Pop. Place)—
  Currituck......................................*NC-2*
Currituck County.............................*NC-2*
Curry (Township)—Sullivan *IN-3*
Curry County *NM-4*
Curry County *OR-4*
Curryville (City)—Pike *MO-3*
Curtin (Township)—Centre............. *PA-1*
Curtis (Township)—Alcona *MI-3*
Curtis (City)—Frontier *NE-4*

Curtiss (Village)—Clark *WI-3*
Curtisville (CDP)—Allegheny *PA-1*
Curwensville (Borough)—
  Clearfield......................................*PA-1*
Curwood, Mt. (MI)...................... *Geog-4*
Cusator (Township)—Stutsman *ND-4*
Cushing (City)—Woodbury...............*IA-3*
Cushing (Town)—Knox *ME-1*
Cushing (Township)—Morrison.... *MN-3*
Cushing (Village)—Howard *NE-4*
Cushing (City)—Payne *OK-2*
Cushing (City)—Nacogdoches......... *TX-2*
Cushman (Town)—Independence.. *AR-2*
Cusick (Town)—Pend Oreille *WA-4*
Cusseta (City)—Chattahoochee *GA-2*
Cussewago (Township)—
  Crawford *PA-1*
Custar (Village)—Wood................. *OH-3*
Custer (Township)—Will................. *IL-3*
Custer (Township)—Decatur...........*KS-4*
Custer (Township)—Mitchell..........*KS-4*
Custer (Township)—Antrim............ *MI-3*
Custer (Township)—Mason............ *MI-3*
Custer (Village)—Mason *MI-3*
Custer (Township)—Sanilac *MI-3*
Custer (Township)—Lyon *MN-3*
Custer (Township)—Antelope *NE-4*
Custer (Township)—Custer............. *NE-4*
Custer (Township)—Beadle............. *SD-4*
Custer (Township)—Corson *SD-4*
Custer (City)—Custer...................... *SD-4*
Custer City (Town)—Custer........... *OK-2*
Custer County................................... *CO-4*
Custer County................................... *ID-4*
Custer County................................... *MT-4*
Custer County................................... *NE-4*
Custer County................................... *OK-2*
Custer County................................... *SD-4*
Cut and Shoot (Town)—
  Montgomery.................................*TX-2*
Cut Bank (City)—Glacier............... *MT-4*
Cut Bank (Township)—
  Bottineau......................................*ND-4*
Cutchogue (CDP)—Suffolk *NY-1*
Cuthbert (City)—Randolph............. *GA-2*
Cutler (CDP)—Tulare *CA-4*
Cutler (CDP)—Dade *FL-2*
Cutler (Village)—Perry *IL-3*
Cutler (Township)—Franklin..........*KS-4*
Cutler (Town)—Washington *ME-1*
Cutler (Town)—Juneau *WI-3*
Cutler Ridge (CDP)—Dade *FL-2*
Cutlerville (CDP)—Kent................ *MI-3*
Cut Off (CDP)—Lafourche
  Parish *LA-2*
Cutten (CDP)—Humboldt *CA-4*
Cutts Grant (Pop. Place)—Coos *NH-1*
Cuyahoga County *OH-3*
Cuyahoga Falls (City)—Summit *OH-3*
Cuyahoga Heights (Village)—
  Cuyahoga *OH-3*
Cuyahoga River (OH)................. *Geog-4*
Cuyamungue (CDP)—Santa Fe *NM-4*
Cuyapaipe Reservation (CA).... *IndRes-4*
Cuyler (Town)—Cortland............... *NY-1*
Cuyuna (Township)—Crow Wing ... *MN-3*
Cygnet (Village)—Wood................ *OH-3*
Cylinder (City)—Palo Alto...............*IA-3*
Cylon (Town)—St. Croix................ *WI-3*
Cynthian (Township)—Shelby *OH-3*
Cynthiana (Town)—Posey............... *IN-3*
Cynthiana (City)—Harrison........... *KY-2*
Cypress (City)—Orange.................. *CA-4*
Cypress (Village)—Johnson............. *IL-3*
Cypress (Township)—Harrison *MO-3*

Cypress (Township)—Cavalier........*ND-4*
Cypress Gardens (CDP)—Polk........*FL-2*
Cypress Lake (CDP)—Lee *FL-2*
Cypress Lakes (CDP)—Palm
  Beach *FL-2*
Cypress Quarters (CDP)—
  Okeechobee *FL-2*
Cyr (Pop. Place)—Aroostook......... *ME-1*
Cyril (Town)—Caddo *OK-2*
Cyrus (City)—Pope *MN-3*
Dacoma (Town)—Woods *OK-2*
Dacono (Town)—Weld *CO-4*
Dacula (City)—Gwinnett *GA-2*
Dade City (City)—Pasco.................*FL-2*
Dade City North (CDP)—Pasco.....*FL-2*
Dade County....................................*FL-2*
Dade County................................... *GA-2*
Dade County................................... *MO-3*
Dadeville (City)—Tallapoosa *AL-2*
Dadeville (Village)—Dade *MO-3*
Dafter (Township)—Chippewa *MI-3*
Daggett (Township)—Menominee . *MI-3*
Daggett (Village)—Menominee...... *MI-3*
Daggett Brook (Township)—Crow
  Wing *MN-3*
Daggett County *UT-4*
Dagsboro (Town)—Sussex *DE-1*
Dahlen (Township)—Nelson *ND-4*
Dahlgren (Township)—Hamilton.... *IL-3*
Dahlgren (Village)—Hamilton *IL-3*
Dahlgren (Township)—Carver *MN-3*
Dahlonega (City)—Lumpkin.......... *GA-2*
Dailey (Township)—Mille Lacs *MN-3*
Daily (Township)—Dixon *NE-4*
Daingerfield (Town)—Morris.......... *TX-2*
Dairyland (Town)—Douglas *WI-3*
Daisetta (City)—Liberty................. *TX-2*
Daisy (Town)—Pike *AR-2*
Daisy (City)—Evans *GA-2*
Daisytown (Borough)—Cambria..... *PA-1*
Dakota (Town)—Stephenson *IL-3*
Dakota (Township)—Stephenson.... *IL-3*
Dakota (City)—Winona *MN-3*
Dakota (Town)—Waushara *WI-3*
Dakota City (City)—Humboldt *IA-3*
Dakota City (City)—Dakota *NE-4*
Dakota County *MN-3*
Dakota County *NE-4*
Dalbo (Township)—Isanti *MN-3*
Dale (Township)—McLean *IL-3*
Dale (Town)—Spencer..................... *IN-3*
Dale (Township)—Kingman *KS-4*
Dale (Township)—Cottonwood *MN-3*
Dale (Township)—Atchison *MO-3*
Dale (Township)—Burke *ND-4*
Dale (Borough)—Cambria *PA-1*
Dale (Township)—Jerauld............... *SD-4*
Dale (Town)—Outagamie............... *WI-3*
Dale City (CDP)—Prince
  William *VA-2*
Dale County *AL-2*
Dalen (Township)—Bottineau.........*ND-4*
Daleville (City)—Dale.....................*AL-2*
Daleville (Town)—Delaware *IN-3*
Daleville (CDP)—Botetourt *VA-2*
Dalhart (City)—Dallam *TX-2*
Dalhart (City)—Hartley *TX-2*
Dallam County *TX-2*
Dallas (City)—Paulding *GA-2*
Dallas (Township)—Huntington *IN-3*
Dallas (Plantation)—Franklin........ *ME-1*
Dallas (Township)—Clinton........... *MI-3*
Dallas (Township)—DeKalb *MO-3*
Dallas (Township)—Harrison *MO-3*
Dallas (Township)—St. Clair *MO-3*

General Index

Dallas (Town)—Gaston NC-2
Dallas (Township)—Crawford........ OH-3
Dallas (City)—Polk OR-4
Dallas (Borough)—Luzerne............ PA-1
Dallas (Township)—Luzerne........... PA-1
Dallas (Town)—Gregory SD-4
Dallas (City)—Collin...................... TX-2
Dallas (City)—Dallas...................... TX-2
Dallas (City)—Denton.................... TX-2
Dallas (City)—Kaufman.................. TX-2
Dallas (City)—Rockwall.................. TX-2
Dallas (Town)—Barron WI-3
Dallas (Village)—Barron WI-3
Dallas Center (City)—Dallas IA-3
Dallas City (City)—Hancock........... IL-3
Dallas City (Township)—Hancock . IL-3
Dallas City (City)—Henderson....... IL-3
Dallas County................................. AL-2
Dallas County................................. AR-2
Dallas County................................. IA-3
Dallas County................................. MO-3
Dallas County................................. TX-2
Dallastown (Borough)—York PA-1
The Dalles (City)—Wasco............... OR-4
Dalton (City)—Whitfield GA-2
Dalton (Township)—Wayne IN-3
Dalton (Town)—Berkshire MA-1
Dalton (Township)—Muskegon MI-3
Dalton (City)—Otter Tail................ MN-3
Dalton (Town)—Chariton MO-3
Dalton (Village)—Cheyenne........... NE-4
Dalton (Town)—Coos..................... NH-1
Dalton (Village)—Wayne................ OH-3
Dalton (Borough)—Lackawanna..... PA-1
Dalton City (Village)—Moultrie IL-3
Dalton Gardens (City)—Kootenai .. ID-4
Dalworthington Gardens (City)—
   Tarrant TX-2
Daly City (City)—San Mateo......... CA-4
Dalzell (Village)—Bureau............... IL-3
Dalzell (Village)—La Salle IL-3
Dalzell Canyon (Pop. Place)—
   Pennington................................. SD-4
Damar (City)—Rooks..................... KS-4
Damariscotta (Town)—Lincoln...... ME-1
Damascus (Town)—Faulkner AR-2
Damascus (Town)—Van Buren...... AR-2
Damascus (Town)—Early................ GA-2
Damascus (CDP)—Montgomery .. MD-1
Damascus (Township)—Henry OH-3
Damascus (Township)—Wayne...... PA-1
Damascus (Town)—Washington VA-2
Damiansville (Village)—Clinton IL-3
Dana (Village)—La Salle................. IL-3
Dana (Town)—Vermillion............... IN-3
Dana (City)—Greene....................... IA-3
Dana Point (City)—Orange CA-4
Danbury (City)—Fairfield............... CT-1
Danbury (City)—Woodbury............ IA-3
Danbury (Village)—Red Willow..... NE-4
Danbury (Town)—Merrimack........ NH-1
Danbury (Town)—Stokes................ NC-2
Danbury (Township)—Emmons ND-4
Danbury (Township)—Ottawa OH-3
Danbury (City)—Brazoria............... TX-2
Danby (Township)—Ionia............... MI-3
Danby (Town)—Tompkins.............. NY-1
Danby (Town)—Rutland................ VT-1
Dandridge (Town)—Jefferson TN-2
Dane (Town)—Dane....................... WI-3
Dane (Village)—Dane WI-3
Dane County................................. WI-3
Dane Prairie (Township)—Otter
   Tail MN-3
Daneville (Township)—Divide....... ND-4

Daneville (Township)—Turner........ SD-4
Danforth (Township)—Iroquois...... IL-3
Danforth (Village)—Iroquois IL-3
Danforth (Town)—Washington ME-1
Danforth (Township)—Pine MN-3
Dania (City)—Broward FL-2
Daniels (CDP)—Raleigh WV-2
Daniels (Town)—Burnett WI-3
Daniels County.............................. MT-4
Danielson (Borough)—Windham... CT-1
Danielson (Township)—Meeker..... MN-3
Danielsville (City)—Madison......... GA-2
Dannebrog (Village)—Howard........ NE-4
Dannemora (Town)—Clinton NY-1
Dannemora (Village)—Clinton NY-1
Dansville (Village)—Ingham MI-3
Dansville (Village)—Livingston NY-1
Dansville (Town)—Steuben............ NY-1
Dante (Town)—Charles Mix SD-4
Danton (Township)—Richland...... ND-4
Danube (City)—Renville................ MN-3
Danube (Town)—Herkimer............ NY-1
Danvers (Township)—McLean IL-3
Danvers (Village)—McLean............ IL-3
Danvers (Town)—Essex MA-1
Danvers (City)—Swift MN-3
Danville (City)—Yell....................... AR-2
Danville (Town)—Contra Costa CA-4
Danville (Town)—Twiggs GA-2
Danville (Town)—Wilkinson GA-2
Danville (City)—Vermilion............. IL-3
Danville (Township)—Vermilion.... IL-3
Danville (Town)—Hendricks.......... IN-3
Danville (City)—Des Moines.......... IA-3
Danville (City)—Harper.................. KS-4
Danville (City)—Boyle KY-2
Danville (Township)—Blue
   Earth.. MN-3
Danville (Township)—
   Montgomery.............................. MO-3
Danville (Town)—Rockingham NH-1
Danville (Village)—Knox................ OH-3
Danville (Borough)—Montour....... PA-1
Danville (Town)—Caledonia.......... VT-1
Danville (Town)—Boone................ WV-2
Danville (Independent City)........... VA-2
Daphne (City)—Baldwin................ AL-2
Darby (Town)—Ravalli MT-4
Darby (Township)—Madison......... OH-3
Darby (Township)—Pickaway........ OH-3
Darby (Township)—Union OH-3
Darby (Borough)—Delaware........... PA-1
Darby (Township)—Delaware........ PA-1
Darbyville (Village)—Pickaway OH-3
Dardanelle (City)—Yell AR-2
Dardenne (Township)—St.
   Charles...................................... MO-3
Dardenne Prairie (Town)—St.
   Charles MO-3
Dare County NC-2
Darfur (City)—Watonwan MN-3
Darien (Town)—Fairfield CT-1
Darien (City)—McIntosh GA-2
Darien (City)—DuPage................... IL-3
Darien (Town)—Genesee NY-1
Darien (Town)—Walworth WI-3
Darien (Village)—Walworth WI-3
Darke County................................ OH-3
Darling (Township)—Morrison..... MN-3
Darling Springs (Township)—
   Adams ND-4
Darlington (Town)—Montgomery .. IN-3
Darlington (Township)—Harvey.... KS-4
Darlington (Town)—Gentry........... MO-3
Darlington (Borough)—Beaver PA-1

Darlington (Township)—Beaver PA-1
Darlington (City)—Darlington........ SC-2
Darlington (Township)—Charles
   Mix.. SD-4
Darlington (Township)—Clark....... SD-4
Darlington (City)—Lafayette WI-3
Darlington (Town)—Lafayette WI-3
Darlington County........................ SC-2
Darmstadt (Town)—Vanderburgh... IN-3
Darnen (Township)—Stevens........ MN-3
Darrington (Town)—Snohomish.... WA-4
Darrouzett (Town)—Lipscomb TX-2
Dartmouth (Town)—Bristol MA-1
Darwin (Township)—Clark............ IL-3
Darwin (City)—Meeker................... MN-3
Darwin (Township)—Meeker......... MN-3
Dash (Township)—Towner............. ND-4
Dassel (City)—Meeker MN-3
Dassel (Township)—Meeker MN-3
Date (Township)—Texas MO-3
Datto (Town)—Clay....................... AR-2
Daugherty (Township)—Beaver PA-1
Dauphin (Borough)—Dauphin....... PA-1
Dauphin County PA-1
Dauphin Island (AL) Geog-4
Dauphin Island (Municipality)—
   Mobile....................................... AL-2
Davenport (Town)—Polk............... FL-2
Davenport (City)—Scott IA-3
Davenport (Village)—Thayer......... NE-4
Davenport (Town)—Delaware NY-1
Davenport (City)—Cass.................. ND-4
Davenport (Township)—Cass........ ND-4
Davenport (Town)—Lincoln OK-2
Davenport (City)—Lincoln WA-4
Davey (Village)—Lancaster............. NE-4
David City (City)—Butler............... NE-4
Davidson (Pop. Place)—Aitkin...... MN-3
Davidson (Town)—Iredell.............. NC-2
Davidson (Town)—Mecklenburg ... NC-2
Davidson (Town)—Tillman OK-2
Davidson (Township)—Sullivan PA-1
Davidson County NC-2
Davidson County TN-2
Davidsville (CDP)—Somerset........ PA-1
Davie (Town)—Broward FL-2
Davie County NC-2
Daviess County............................. IN-3
Daviess County............................. KY-2
Daviess County............................. MO-3
Davis (City)—Yolo CA-4
Davis (Village)—Stephenson.......... IL-3
Davis (Township)—Fountain IN-3
Davis (Township)—Starke.............. IN-3
Davis (Township)—Kittson MN-3
Davis (Township)—Caldwell......... MO-3
Davis (Township)—Henry.............. MO-3
Davis (Township)—Lafayette......... MO-3
Davis (City)—Garvin OK-2
Davis (City)—Murray OK-2
Davis (Town)—Turner SD-4
Davis (Town)—Tucker WV-2
Davis, Mt. (PA).............................. Geog-4
Davisboro (City)—Washington...... GA-2
Davis City (Township)—Decatur... IA-3
Davis County IA-3
Davis County UT-4
Davis Creek (Township)—Valley ... NE-4
Davis Junction (Village)—Ogle...... IL-3
Davis-Monthan Air Force Base
   (AZ) Mil-4
Davis Mountains (TX) Geog-4
Davison (City)—Genesee MI-3
Davison (Township)—Genesee MI-3
Davison County............................ SD-4

Daviston (Town)—Tallapoosa.........*AL-2*
Davy (Town)—McDowell *WV-2*
Dawes (Township)—Thurston *NE-4*
Dawes County *NE-4*
Dawson (City)—Terrell *GA-2*
Dawson (Township)—McLean.........*IL-3*
Dawson (Village)—Sangamon *IL-3*
Dawson (City)—Dallas....................*IA-3*
Dawson (City)—Lac qui Parle.......*MN-3*
Dawson (Township)—Phelps *MO-3*
Dawson (Village)—Richardson *NE-4*
Dawson (City)—Kidder...................*ND-4*
Dawson (Borough)—Fayette *PA-1*
Dawson (Town)—Navarro *TX-2*
Dawson County *GA-2*
Dawson County *MT-4*
Dawson County *NE-4*
Dawson County *TX-2*
Dawson Springs (City)—Hopkins..*KY-2*
Dawsonville (Town)—Dawson........*GA-2*
Dawt (Township)—Ozark................*MO-3*
Day (Township)—Montcalm *MI-3*
Day (Town)—Saratoga *NY-1*
Day (Township)—Clark *SD-4*
Day (Town)—Marathon *WI-3*
Day County *SD-4*
Day Heights (CDP)—Clermont *OH-3*
Daykin (Village)—Jefferson *NE-4*
Dayton (Town)—Marengo *AL-2*
Dayton (City)—Franklin *ID-4*
Dayton (Township)—La Salle *IL-3*
Dayton (Town)—Tippecanoe *IN-3*
Dayton (City)—Webster...................*IA-3*
Dayton (Township)—Phillips...........*KS-4*
Dayton (Township)—Saline *KS-4*
Dayton (City)—Campbell *KY-2*
Dayton (Town)—York.....................*ME-1*
Dayton (Township)—Newaygo *MI-3*
Dayton (Township)—Tuscola..........*MI-3*
Dayton (City)—Hennepin *MN-3*
Dayton (City)—Wright.....................*MN-3*
Dayton (Township)—Cass................*MO-3*
Dayton (Township)—Newton *MO-3*
Dayton (CDP)—Lyon........................*NV-4*
Dayton (CDP)—Middlesex *NJ-1*
Dayton (Town)—Cattaraugus *NY-1*
Dayton (Township)—Nelson *ND-4*
Dayton (City)—Montgomery *OH-3*
Dayton (City)—Yamhill *OR-4*
Dayton (Borough)—Armstrong........*PA-1*
Dayton (Township)—Lincoln............*SD-4*
Dayton (Township)—Marshall..........*SD-4*
Dayton (City)—Rhea........................ *TN-2*
Dayton (City)—Liberty *TX-2*
Dayton (Town)—Rockingham *VA-2*
Dayton (City)—Columbia................*WA-4*
Dayton (Town)—Richland *WI-3*
Dayton (Town)—Waupaca *WI-3*
Dayton (Town)—Sheridan *WY-4*
Daytona Beach (FL) *Geog-4*
Daytona Beach (City)—Volusia *FL-2*
Daytona Beach Shores (City)—
Volusia *FL-2*
Dayton Lakes (City)—Liberty........*TX-2*
Day Valley (CDP)—Santa Cruz.....*CA-4*
Dayville (Town)—Grant..................*OR-4*
Dazey (City)—Barnes......................*ND-4*
Dazey (Township)—Barnes *ND-4*
Deadhorse (CDP)—North Slope
Borough...*AK-4*
Dead Lake (Township)—Otter
Tail...*MN-3*
Deadwood (City)—Lawrence..........*SD-4*
Deaf Smith County *TX-2*
Deal (Borough)—Monmouth *NJ-1*

Deale (CDP)—Anne Arundel........ *MD-1*
Dean (Township)—LaMoure *ND-4*
Dean (Township)—Cambria *PA-1*
Dean (City)—Clay............................ *TX-2*
Dean Lake (Township)—Crow
Wing...*MN-3*
Dearborn (City)—Wayne................ *MI-3*
Dearborn (City)—Buchanan *MO-3*
Dearborn (City)—Platte.................*MO-3*
Dearborn (Township)—Beadle....... *SD-4*
Dearborn County *IN-3*
Dearborn Heights (City)—Wayne..*MI-3*
Dearing (Town)—McDuffie *GA-2*
Dearing (City)—Montgomery *KS-4*
Deary (City)—Latah........................ *ID-4*
Death Valley (CA)........................*Geog-4*
Deaver (Town)—Big Horn *WY-4*
DeBaca County *NM-4*
De Bary (CDP)—Volusia *FL-2*
De Beque (Town)—Mesa *CO-4*
Debing (Township)—Mountrail *ND-4*
Deblois (Town)—Washington *ME-1*
Decatur (City)—Limestone *AL-2*
Decatur (City)—Morgan *AL-2*
Decatur (Town)—Benton *AR-2*
Decatur (City)—De Kalb *GA-2*
Decatur (City)—Macon...................*IL-3*
Decatur (Township)—Macon.........*IL-3*
Decatur (City)—Adams *IN-3*
Decatur (Township)—Marion *IN-3*
Decatur (Township)—Van Buren...*MI-3*
Decatur (Village)—Van Buren *MI-3*
Decatur (Town)—Newton *MS-2*
Decatur (Township)—Burt *NE-4*
Decatur (Village)—Burt *NE-4*
Decatur (Town)—Otsego *NY-1*
Decatur (Township)—Lawrence.....*OH-3*
Decatur (Township)—
Washington *OH-3*
Decatur (Township)—Clearfield *PA-1*
Decatur (Township)—Mifflin.........*PA-1*
Decatur (Town)—Meigs *TN-2*
Decatur (City)—Wise *TX-2*
Decatur (Town)—Green *WI-3*
Decatur City (City)—Decatur.........*IA-3*
Decatur County *GA-2*
Decatur County *IN-3*
Decatur County *IA-3*
Decatur County *KS-4*
Decatur County *TN-2*
Decaturville (Town)—Decatur.......*TN-2*
Decherd (City)—Franklin *TN-2*
Decker (Township)—Richland *IL-3*
Decker (Town)—Knox *IN-3*
Decker (Township)—Knox..............*IN-3*
Deckerville (Village)—Sanilac....... *MI-3*
Declo (City)—Cassia *ID-4*
Decorah (City)—Winneshiek..........*IA-3*
Decoria (Township)—Blue Earth..*MN-3*
Dedham (City)—Carroll..................*IA-3*
Dedham (Town)—Hancock............*ME-1*
Dedham (Town)—Norfolk *MA-1*
Deemston (Borough)—
Washington *PA-1*
Deenwood (CDP)—Ware *GA-2*
Deep Creek (Pop. Place)—Slope....*ND-4*
Deephaven (City)—Hennepin.........*MN-3*
Deep River (Town)—Middlesex *CT-1*
Deep River (City)—Poweshiek.......*IA-3*
Deep River (Township)—Arenac...*MI-3*
Deep River (Township)—
McHenry *ND-4*
Deepstep (Town)—Washington......*GA-2*
Deepwater (Township)—Bates *MO-3*
Deepwater (City)—Henry *MO-3*

Deepwater (Township)—Henry.....*MO-3*
Deepwater (Township)—McLean ..*ND-4*
Deer (Township)—Roseau *MN-3*
Deer Creek (Township)—Tazewell..*IL-3*
Deer Creek (Village)—Tazewell *IL-3*
Deer Creek (Village)—Woodford....*IL-3*
Deer Creek (Township)—Carroll *IN-3*
Deer Creek (Township)—Cass *IN-3*
Deer Creek (Township)—Miami.....*IN-3*
Deer Creek (Township)—Allen *KS-4*
Deer Creek (Township)—Phillips ...*KS-4*
Deer Creek (City)—Otter Tail *MN-3*
Deer Creek (Township)—Otter
Tail..*MN-3*
Deer Creek (Township)—Bates......*MO-3*
Deer Creek (Township)—Henry ...*MO-3*
Deer Creek (Township)—
Madison *OH-3*
Deer Creek (Township)—
Pickaway *OH-3*
Deer Creek (Town)—Grant............*OK-2*
Deer Creek (Township)—Mercer *PA-1*
Deer Creek (Town)—Outagamie....*WI-3*
Deer Creek (Town)—Taylor...........*WI-3*
Deer Creek Reservation
(MN) *IndRes-4*
Deerfield (Village)—Cook *IL-3*
Deerfield (Township)—Fulton *IL-3*
Deerfield (Township)—Lake *IL-3*
Deerfield (Village)—Lake *IL-3*
Deerfield (City)—Kearny................*KS-4*
Deerfield (Township)—Kearny *KS-4*
Deerfield (Town)—Franklin...........*MA-1*
Deerfield (Township)—Isabella......*MI-3*
Deerfield (Township)—Lapeer *MI-3*
Deerfield (Township)—Lenawee *MI-3*
Deerfield (Village)—Lenawee *MI-3*
Deerfield (Township)—
Livingston *MI-3*
Deerfield (Township)—Mecosta *MI-3*
Deerfield (Township)—Cass *MN-3*
Deerfield (Township)—Steele........*MN-3*
Deerfield (Township)—Vernon *MO-3*
Deerfield (Village)—Vernon *MO-3*
Deerfield (Town)—Rockingham....*NH-1*
Deerfield (Township)—
Cumberland *NJ-1*
Deerfield (Town)—Oneida *NY-1*
Deerfield (Township)—Morgan *OH-3*
Deerfield (Township)—Portage......*OH-3*
Deerfield (Township)—Ross *OH-3*
Deerfield (Township)—Warren *OH-3*
Deerfield (Township)—Tioga *PA-1*
Deerfield (Township)—Warren *PA-1*
Deerfield (Town)—Dane *WI-3*
Deerfield (Village)—Dane *WI-3*
Deerfield (Town)—Waushara *WI-3*
Deerfield Beach (City)—Broward...*FL-2*
Deer Grove (Village)—Whiteside ...*IL-3*
Deerhead (Township)—Barber.......*KS-4*
Deerhorn (Township)—Wilkin......*MN-3*
Deering (City)—Northwest Arctic
Borough..*AK-4*
Deering (Town)—Hillsborough *NH-1*
Deering (City)—McHenry...............*ND-4*
Deering (Township)—McHenry.....*ND-4*
Deer Isle (Town)—Hancock *ME-1*
Deer Lake (Pop. Place)—Itasca *MN-3*
Deer Lake (Township)—
Stutsman *ND-4*
Deer Lake (Borough)—Schuylkill ...*PA-1*
Deer Lodge (City)—Powell *MT-4*
Deer Lodge County *MT-4*
Deer Park (CDP)—Napa *CA-4*
Deer Park (Township)—La Salle *IL-3*

General Index

Deer Park (Village)—Lake *IL-3*
Deer Park (Town)—Garrett *MD-1*
Deer Park (Township)—
  Pennington *MN-3*
Deerpark (Town)—Orange *NY-1*
Deer Park (CDP)—Suffolk............ *NY-1*
Deer Park (City)—Hamilton..........*OH-3*
Deer Park (City)—Harris *TX-2*
Deer Park (City)—Spokane........... *WA-4*
Deer Park (Village)—St. Croix *WI-3*
Deer River (City)—Itasca *MN-3*
Deer River (Township)—Itasca *MN-3*
Deersville (Village)—Harrison......*OH-3*
Deer Trail (Town)—Arapahoe *CO-4*
Deerwood (City)—Crow Wing...... *MN-3*
Deerwood (Township)—Crow
  Wing... *MN-3*
Deerwood (Township)—Kittson ... *MN-3*
Deferiet (Village)—Jefferson.......... *NY-1*
Defiance (City)—Shelby................. *IA-3*
Defiance (City)—Defiance *OH-3*
Defiance (Township)—Defiance *OH-3*
Defiance County..............................*OH-3*
De Forest (Village)—Dane *WI-3*
De Funiak Springs (City)—
  Walton *FL-2*
Degognia (Township)—Jackson *IL-3*
De Graff (City)—Swift *MN-3*
De Graff (Village)—Logan *OH-3*
De Groat (Township)—Ramsey......*ND-4*
De Kalb (City)—DeKalb *IL-3*
De Kalb (Township)—DeKalb........ *IL-3*
De Kalb (Town)—Kemper *MS-2*
De Kalb (Town)—Buchanan *MO-3*
De Kalb (Town)—St. Lawrence...... *NY-1*
De Kalb (Town)—Bowie *TX-2*
DeKalb County................................ *AL-2*
De Kalb County............................... *GA-2*
DeKalb County.................................. *IL-3*
DeKalb County................................. *IN-3*
DeKalb County.................................*MO-3*
DeKalb County................................. *TN-2*
Dekorra (Town)—Columbia........... *WI-3*
Delafield (Township)—Jackson..... *MN-3*
Delafield (City)—Waukesha........... *WI-3*
Delafield (Town)—Waukesha *WI-3*
Del Aire (CDP)—Los Angeles *CA-4*
Delanco (Township)—Burlington ... *NJ-1*
De Land (City)—Volusia................ *FL-2*
De Land (Village)—Piatt *IL-3*
De Land Southwest (CDP)—
  Volusia *FL-2*
Delaney (Township)—Corson *SD-4*
Delano (City)—Kern *CA-4*
Delano (Township)—Sedgwick *KS-4*
Delano (City)—Wright *MN-3*
Delano (Township)—Schuylkill *PA-1*
Delanson (Village)—Schenectady .. *NY-1*
Delaplaine (Town)—Greene *AR-2*
Delapre (Township)—Lincoln *SD-4*
Delavan (City)—Tazewell................. *IL-3*
Delavan (Township)—Tazewell....... *IL-3*
Delavan (City)—Faribault *MN-3*
Delavan (Township)—Faribault ... *MN-3*
Delavan (City)—Walworth............. *WI-3*
Delavan (Town)—Walworth........... *WI-3*
Delavan Lake (CDP)—Walworth... *WI-3*
Delaware (Township)—Delaware.... *IN-3*
Delaware (Township)—Hamilton ... *IN-3*
Delaware (Township)—Ripley *IN-3*
Delaware (City)—Delaware............. *IA-3*
Delaware (Township)—Jefferson *KS-4*
Delaware (Township)—
  Leavenworth *KS-4*

Delaware (Township)—
  Wyandotte................................... *KS-4*
Delaware (Township)—Sanilac *MI-3*
Delaware (Township)—Grant *MN-3*
Delaware (Township)—Shannon... *MO-3*
Delaware (Township)—
  Hunterdon................................... *NJ-1*
Delaware (Town)—Sullivan *NY-1*
Delaware (Township)—Defiance ...*OH-3*
Delaware (City)—Delaware............*OH-3*
Delaware (Township)—Delaware....*OH-3*
Delaware (Township)—Hancock....*OH-3*
Delaware (Town)—Nowata *OK-2*
Delaware (Township)—Juniata *PA-1*
Delaware (Township)—Mercer *PA-1*
Delaware (Township)—
  Northumberland *PA-1*
Delaware (Township)—Pike *PA-1*
Delaware (Township)—Lincoln *SD-4*
Delaware Bay (CA)....................... *Geog-4*
Delaware City (City)—New
  Castle...*DE-1*
Delaware County............................. *IN-3*
Delaware County.............................. *IA-3*
Delaware County............................. *NY-1*
Delaware County............................*OH-3*
Delaware County............................ *OK-2*
Delaware County............................. *PA-1*
Delaware-Muncie TDSA (KS)..*IndRes-4*
Delaware River (CA)................... *Geog-4*
Delaware Water Gap (PA)........... *Geog-4*
Delaware Water Gap (Borough)—
  Monroe... *PA-1*
Delbarton (Town)—Mingo *WV-2*
Delcambre (Town)—Iberia
  Parish *LA-2*
Delcambre (Town)—Vermilion
  Parish *LA-2*
Del City (City)—Oklahoma *OK-2*
De Leon (City)—Comanche.......... *TX-2*
De Leon Springs (CDP)—Volusia ..*FL-2*
Delevan (Village)—Cattaraugus *NY-1*
Delger (Township)—Wells............*ND-4*
Delhi (CDP)—Merced.................... *CA-4*
Delhi (City)—Delaware................... *IA-3*
Delhi (Township)—Osborne..........*KS-4*
Delhi (Town)—Richland Parish....*LA-2*
Delhi (City)—Redwood *MN-3*
Delhi (Township)—Redwood........ *MN-3*
Delhi (Town)—Delaware................ *NY-1*
Delhi (Village)—Delaware *NY-1*
Delhi (Township)—Golden
  Valley *ND-4*
Delhi (Township)—Hamilton.........*OH-3*
Delhi Charter (Township)—
  Ingham *MI-3*
Delia (City)—Jackson.....................*KS-4*
Delight (City)—Pike *AR-2*
Delight (Township)—Custer......... *NE-4*
Dell (Town)—Mississippi *AR-2*
Dell City (City)—Hudspeth *TX-2*
Dell Grove (Township)—Pine....... *MN-3*
Dellona (Town)—Sauk *WI-3*
Dell Prairie (Town)—Adams *WI-3*
Dell Rapids (City)—Minnehaha *SD-4*
Dell Rapids (Township)—
  Minnehaha *SD-4*
Dellroy (Village)—Carroll *OH-3*
Dellview (Town)—Gaston *NC-2*
Dellwood (City)—Washington *MN-3*
Dellwood (City)—St. Louis *MO-3*
Del Mar (City)—San Diego *CA-4*
Delmar (Town)—Sussex *DE-1*
Delmar (City)—Clinton *IA-3*
Delmar (Town)—Wicomico *MD-1*

American Places Dictionary

Delmar (CDP)—Albany *NY-1*
Delmar (Township)—Tioga............ *PA-1*
Delmar (Town)—Chippewa *WI-3*
Delmarva Peninsula (PA) *Geog-4*
Delmont (Borough)—
  Westmoreland *PA-1*
Delmont (City)—Douglas.............. *SD-4*
Del Monte Forest (CDP)—
  Monterey *CA-4*
Delmore (Township)—
  McPherson *KS-4*
Del Norte (Town)—Rio Grande ... *CO-4*
Del Norte County *CA-4*
Deloit (City)—Crawford *IA-3*
Deloit (Township)—Holt............... *NE-4*
Delphi (City)—Carroll..................... *IN-3*
Delphos (City)—Ringgold *IA-3*
Delphos (City)—Ottawa *KS-4*
Delphos (City)—Allen *OH-3*
Delphos (City)—Van Wert *OH-3*
Delran (Township)—Burlington....*NJ-1*
Delray Beach (City)—Palm
  Beach *FL-2*
Del Rey (CDP)—Fresno *CA-4*
Del Rey Oaks (City)—Monterey... *CA-4*
Del Rio (CDP)—Hillsborough *FL-2*
Del Rio (City)—Val Verde *TX-2*
Delta (City)—Delta *CO-4*
Delta (City)—Keokuk......................*IA-3*
Delta (Village)—Madison Parish ...*LA-2*
Delta (Township)—Eaton *MI-3*
Delta (City)—Cape Girardeau *MO-3*
Delta (Village)—Fulton *OH-3*
Delta (Borough)—York *PA-1*
Delta (City)—Millard *UT-4*
Delta (Town)—Bayfield................. *WI-3*
Delta County *CO-4*
Delta County *MI-3*
Delta County *TX-2*
Delta Junction (City)—Southeast
  Fairbanks Census Area *AK-4*
Delton (Township)—
  Cottonwood *MN-3*
Delton (Town)—Sauk *WI-3*
Deltona (CDP)—Volusia *FL-2*
Demarest (Borough)—Bergen *NJ-1*
Dement (Township)—Ogle.............. *IL-3*
Deming (City)—Luna *NM-3*
Democrat (Township)—Carroll..... *IN-3*
Demopolis (City)—Marengo...........*AL-2*
Demorest (City)—Habersham....... *GA-2*
De Motte (Town)—Jasper *IN-3*
Dempster (Township)—Hamlin *SD-4*
Denair (CDP)—Stanislaus *CA-4*
Denali Borough *AK-4*
Denbigh (Township)—McHenry....*ND-4*
Dendron (Town)—Surry................ *VA-2*
Denham (City)—Pine *MN-3*
Denham Springs (City)—Livingston
  Parish *LA-2*
Denhoff (Township)—Sheridan *ND-4*
Denison (Township)—Lawrence..... *IL-3*
Denison (City)—Crawford *IA-3*
Denison (City)—Jackson.................*KS-4*
Denison (City)—Grayson............... *TX-2*
Denmark (Town)—Oxford *ME-1*
Denmark (Township)—Tuscola...... *MI-3*
Denmark (Township)—
  Washington *MN-3*
Denmark (Town)—Lewis *NY-1*
Denmark (Township)—Ward *ND-4*
Denmark (City)—Bamberg............*SC-2*
Denmark (Village)—Brown........... *WI-3*
Dennehotso (CDP)—Apache *AZ-4*
Denning (City)—Franklin *AR-2*

American Places Dictionary — General Index

Denning (Township)—Franklin *IL-3*
Denning (Town)—Ulster *NY-1*
Dennis (Town)—Barnstable *MA-1*
Dennis (Township)—Cape May...... *NJ-1*
Dennis Acres (Village)—Newton .. *MO-3*
Dennison (City)—Goodhue *MN-3*
Dennison (City)—Rice *MN-3*
Dennison (Village)—Tuscarawas....*OH-3*
Dennison (Township)—Luzerne *PA-1*
Dennis Port (CDP)—Barnstable... *MA-1*
Dennistown (Plantation)—
 Somerset *ME-1*
Dennysville (Town)—
 Washington *ME-1*
Dent (City)—Otter Tail *MN-3*
Dent (Township)—Iron *MO-3*
Dent (CDP)—Hamilton *OH-3*
Dent County *MO-3*
Denton (City)—Jeff Davis *GA-2*
Denton (City)—Doniphan *KS-4*
Denton (Town)—Caroline *MD-1*
Denton (Township)—
 Roscommon *MI-3*
Denton (Town)—Fergus *MT-4*
Denton (Village)—Lancaster........... *NE-4*
Denton (Town)—Davidson *NC-2*
Denton (City)—Denton *TX-2*
Denton County *TX-2*
Dentsville (CDP)—Richland...........*SC-2*
Denver (City)—Denver *CO-4*
Denver (Township)—Richland *IL-3*
Denver (Town)—Miami *IN-3*
Denver (City)—Bremer *IA-3*
Denver (City)—Isabella *MI-3*
Denver (Township)—Newaygo *MI-3*
Denver (Township)—Rock............ *MN-3*
Denver (Village)—Worth............... *MO-3*
Denver (Township)—Adams........... *NE-4*
Denver (Township)—Sargent......... *ND-4*
Denver (Borough)—Lancaster........ *PA-1*
Denver (Township)—Kingsbury *SD-4*
Denver City (Town)—Yoakum *TX-2*
Denver County *CO-4*
Denville (Township)—Morris *NJ-1*
De Pere (City)—Brown *WI-3*
De Pere (Town)—Brown *WI-3*
Depew (Village)—Erie *NY-1*
Depew (Town)—Creek *OK-2*
De Peyster (Town)—St.
 Lawrence................................. *NY-1*
Depoe Bay (City)—Lincoln *OR-4*
Deport (City)—Lamar *TX-2*
Deport (City)—Red River............. *TX-2*
Deposit (Village)—Broome *NY-1*
Deposit (Town)—Delaware *NY-1*
Deposit (Village)—Delaware *NY-1*
Deptford (Township)—Gloucester..*NJ-1*
De Pue (Town)—Bureau *IL-3*
De Queen (City)—Sevier *AR-2*
De Quincy (Town)—Calcasieu
 Parish *LA-2*
Derby (CDP)—Adams................... *CO-4*
Derby (City)—New Haven............. *CT-1*
Derby (City)—Lucas *IA-3*
Derby (City)—Sedgwick................*KS-4*
Derby (Town)—Orleans *VT-1*
Derby Center (Village)—Orleans... *VT-1*
Derby Line (Village)—Orleans....... *VT-1*
De Ridder (City)—Beauregard
 Parish *LA-2*
De Ridder (City)—Vernon Parish ..*LA-2*
Derinda (Township)—Jo Daviess ... *IL-3*
Dering Harbor (Village)—Suffolk.. *NY-1*
Derma (Town)—Calhoun...............*MS-2*
Dermott (City)—Chicot *AR-2*

Derry (Township)—Pike *IL-3*
Derry (Town)—Rockingham *NH-1*
Derry (Township)—Dauphin *PA-1*
Derry (Township)—Mifflin *PA-1*
Derry (Township)—Montour *PA-1*
Derry (Borough)—Westmoreland ... *PA-1*
Derry (Township)—
 Westmoreland *PA-1*
Derrynane (Township)—Le
 Sueur...................................... *MN-3*
De Ruyter (Town)—Madison......... *NY-1*
De Ruyter (Village)—Madison....... *NY-1*
Des Allemands (CDP)—Lafourche
 Parish *LA-2*
Des Allemands (CDP)—St. Charles
 Parish *LA-2*
Des Arc (City)—Prairie................. *AR-2*
Des Arc (Village)—Iron................. *MO-3*
Deschutes County *OR-4*
Deschutes River Woods (CDP)—
 Deschutes *OR-4*
Desert Hills (CDP)—Mohave *AZ-4*
Desert Hot Springs (City)—
 Riverside *CA-4*
Desert View Highlands (CDP)—Los
 Angeles *CA-4*
Desha County *AR-2*
Deshler (City)—Thayer *NE-4*
Deshler (Village)—Henry *OH-3*
Des Lacs (City)—Ward *ND-4*
Des Lacs (Township)—Ward......... *ND-4*
Desloge (City)—St. Francois......... *MO-3*
De Smet (City)—Kingsbury *SD-4*
De Smet (Township)—Kingsbury .. *SD-4*
Des Moines (City)—Polk *IA-3*
Des Moines (Township)—
 Jackson *MN-3*
Des Moines (Township)—Clark.... *MO-3*
Des Moines (Village)—Union........ *NM-4*
Des Moines (City)—King.............. *WA-4*
Des Moines County *IA-3*
Des Moines River (Township)—
 Murray *MN-3*
De Soto (Village)—Sumter............. *GA-2*
De Soto (Township)—Jackson....... *IL-3*
De Soto (Village)—Jackson........... *IL-3*
De Soto (City)—Dallas *IA-3*
De Soto (City)—Johnson *KS-4*
De Soto (City)—Jefferson *MO-3*
DeSoto (City)—Dallas *TX-2*
De Soto (Village)—Crawford *WI-3*
De Soto (Village)—Vernon *WI-3*
DeSoto County *FL-2*
DeSoto County *MS-2*
Desoto Lakes (CDP)—Sarasota *FL-2*
De Soto Parish...............................*LA-2*
Despard (CDP)—Harrison *WV-2*
Des Peres (City)—St. Louis *MO-3*
Des Plaines (City)—Cook *IL-3*
Destin (City)—Okaloosa *FL-2*
Destrehan (CDP)—St. Charles
 Parish *LA-2*
Detour (Township)—Chippewa *MI-3*
De Tour Village (Village)—
 Chippewa *MI-3*
Detroit (Town)—Lamar *AL-2*
Detroit (Township)—Pike *IL-3*
Detroit (Village)—Pike.................. *IL-3*
Detroit (City)—Somerset *ME-1*
Detroit (City)—Wayne *MI-3*
Detroit (Township)—Becker *MN-3*
Detroit (City)—Marion *OR-4*
Detroit (Town)—Red River *TX-2*
Detroit Arsenal (MI)......................*Mil-4*
Detroit Beach (CDP)—Monroe *MI-3*

Detroit Dam (OR) *Geog-4*
Detroit Lakes (City)—Becker........ *MN-3*
Detroit River (MI)........................ *Geog-4*
Deuel County................................ *NE-4*
Deuel County *SD-4*
De Valls Bluff (Town)—Prairie...... *AR-2*
Devers (City)—Liberty *TX-2*
Deville (CDP)—Rapides Parish.....*LA-2*
Devillo (Township)—Richland *ND-4*
Devils Lake (City)—Ramsey.......... *ND-4*
Devils Lake Sioux Reservation
 (ND) *IndRes-4*
Devils Tower (WY)....................... *Geog-4*
Devine (City)—Medina *TX-2*
Devoe (Township)—Faulk............. *SD-4*
Devol (City)—Cotton *OK-2*
Devola (CDP)—Washington *OH-3*
Devon-Berwyn (CDP)—Chester *PA-1*
Dewald (Township)—Nobles *MN-3*
Dewar (City)—Okmulgee *OK-2*
Deweese (Village)—Clay *NE-4*
Dewey (Township)—La Porte *IN-3*
Dewey (Township)—Roseau *MN-3*
Dewey (Township)—Walsh *ND-4*
Dewey (City)—Washington *OK-2*
Dewey (Township)—Hyde *SD-4*
Dewey (Town)—Burnett................ *WI-3*
Dewey (Town)—Portage................ *WI-3*
Dewey (Town)—Rusk.................... *WI-3*
Dewey Beach (Town)—Sussex *DE-1*
Dewey County *OK-2*
Dewey County *SD-4*
Dewey-Humboldt (CDP)—
 Yavapai *AZ-4*
Deweyville (CDP)—Newton *TX-2*
Deweyville (Town)—Box Elder...... *UT-4*
Dewhurst (Town)—Clark *WI-3*
De Witt (City)—Arkansas *AR-2*
De Witt (Township)—De Witt *IL-3*
De Witt (Village)—De Witt *IL-3*
De Witt (City)—Clinton *IA-3*
De Witt (City)—Clinton *MI-3*
De Witt (Township)—Clinton........ *MI-3*
De Witt (City)—Carroll *MO-3*
De Witt (Township)—Carroll *MO-3*
De Witt (Village)—Saline *NE-4*
De Witt (Town)—Onondaga *NY-1*
De Witt (Township)—Divide........ *ND-4*
De Witt (Township)—Perkins........ *SD-4*
De Witt County *IL-3*
DeWitt County *TX-2*
Dexter (Town)—Laurens *GA-2*
Dexter (City)—Dallas *IA-3*
Dexter (City)—Cowley *KS-4*
Dexter (Township)—Cowley *KS-4*
Dexter (Town)—Penobscot *ME-1*
Dexter (Township)—Washtenaw ... *MI-3*
Dexter (Village)—Washtenaw *MI-3*
Dexter (City)—Mower *MN-3*
Dexter (Township)—Mower.......... *MN-3*
Dexter (City)—Stoddard *MO-3*
Dexter (Town)—Chaves *NM-4*
Dexter (Village)—Jefferson *NY-1*
Dexter (Township)—Richland *ND-4*
Dexter (Township)—Codington ... *SD-4*
Dexter (Town)—Wood *WI-3*
Dexter City (Village)—Noble.........*OH-3*
Diagonal (City)—Ringgold *IA-3*
Diamond (Village)—Grundy......... *IL-3*
Diamond (Village)—Will *IL-3*
Diamond (Town)—Newton........... *MO-3*
Diamond Bar (City)—Los
 Angeles *CA-4*
Diamond Bluff (Town)—Pierce *WI-3*
Diamond City (City)—Boone *AR-2*

General Index

Diamond Creek (Township)—
Chase KS-4
Diamond Head (HI) Geog-4
Diamondhead (CDP)—Hancock ... MS-2
Diamond Lake (Township)—
Lincoln MN-3
Diamond Springs (CDP)—El
Dorado CA-4
Diamondville (Town)—Lincoln WY-4
Diana (Town)—Lewis NY-1
Diana (Township)—Sanborn SD-4
Diaz (City)—Jackson AR-2
Dibble (Town)—McClain OK-2
D'Iberville (City)—Harrison MS-2
Diboll (City)—Angelina TX-2
Dickens (City)—Clay IA-3
Dickens (Village)—Lincoln NE-4
Dickens (Township)—Gregory SD-4
Dickens (City)—Dickens TX-2
Dickens County TX-2
Dickenson County VA-2
Dickerson (Township)—Lewis MO-3
Dickey (City)—LaMoure ND-4
Dickey County ND-4
Dickeyville (Village)—Grant WI-3
Dickinson (Town)—Broome NY-1
Dickinson (Town)—Franklin NY-1
Dickinson (City)—Stark ND-4
Dickinson (Township)—
Cumberland PA-1
Dickinson (Village)—Galveston TX-2
Dickinson County IA-3
Dickinson County KS-4
Dickinson County MI-3
Dickinson North (Pop. Place)—
Stark ND-4
Dickinson South (Pop. Place)—
Stark ND-4
Dick Johnson (Township)—Clay ... IN-3
Dickson (Township)—Manistee MI-3
Dickson (Town)—Carter OK-2
Dickson (City)—Dickson TN-2
Dickson City (Borough)—
Lackawanna PA-1
Dickson County TN-2
Diehlstadt (City)—Scott MO-3
Dierks (City)—Howard AR-2
Dieter (Township)—Roseau MN-3
Dieterich (Village)—Effingham IL-3
Dietrich (City)—Lincoln ID-4
Diggins (Village)—Webster MO-3
Dighton (City)—Lane KS-4
Dighton (Township)—Lane KS-4
Dighton (Town)—Bristol MA-1
Dike (City)—Grundy IA-3
Dillard (Town)—Rabun GA-2
Dill City (Town)—Washita OK-2
Diller (Village)—Jefferson NE-4
Dilley (City)—Frio TX-2
Dillingham (City)—Dillingham Census
Area AK-4
Dillingham Census Area AK-4
Dillon (Town)—Summit CO-4
Dillon (Township)—Tazewell IL-3
Dillon (Township)—Phelps MO-3
Dillon (City)—Beaverhead MT-4
Dillon (City)—Dillon SC-2
Dillon County SC-2
Dillonvale (CDP)—Hamilton OH-3
Dillonvale (Village)—Jefferson OH-3
Dillsboro (Town)—Dearborn IN-3
Dillsboro (Town)—Jackson NC-2
Dillsburg (Borough)—York PA-1
Dillwyn (Town)—Buckingham VA-2
Dilworth (City)—Clay MN-3

Dimmick (Township)—La Salle IL-3
Dimmit County TX-2
Dimmitt (City)—Castro TX-2
Dimock (Township)—
Susquehanna PA-1
Dimock (Town)—Hutchinson SD-4
Dimond (Township)—Burke ND-4
Dimondale (Village)—Eaton MI-3
Dingman (Township)—Pike PA-1
Dinosaur (Town)—Moffat CO-4
Dinsmore (Township)—Shelby OH-3
Dinuba (City)—Tulare CA-4
Dinwiddie County VA-2
Diomede (City)—Nome Census
Area AK-4
Disappointment, Cape (WA) Geog-4
Discovery Bay (CDP)—Contra
Costa CA-4
Discovery-Spring Garden (CDP)—
Frederick MD-1
Dishman (CDP)—Spokane WA-4
Disney (Town)—Mayes OK-2
District (Township)—Berks PA-1
District Heights (City)—Prince
George's MD-1
District of Columbia (Washington,
D.C.)—Windham DC-1
District of Columbia (Washington,
D.C.)—Yell DC-2
Ditmas Park—Kings NY-1
Divernon (Township)—Sangamon .. IL-3
Divernon (Village)—Sangamon IL-3
Divide (Township)—Buffalo NE-4
Divide (Township)—Phelps NE-4
Divide (Township)—Dickey ND-4
Divide County ND-4
Dix (Township)—Ford IL-3
Dix (Village)—Jefferson IL-3
Dix (Village)—Kimball NE-4
Dix (Town)—Schuyler NY-1
Dixfield (Town)—Oxford ME-1
Dix Hills (CDP)—Suffolk NY-1
Dixie County FL-2
Dixie Inn (Village)—Webster
Parish LA-2
Dixmont (Town)—Penobscot ME-1
Dixmoor (Village)—Cook IL-3
Dixon (City)—Solano CA-4
Dixon (City)—Lee IL-3
Dixon (Township)—Lee IL-3
Dixon (City)—Scott IA-3
Dixon (Township)—Sumner KS-4
Dixon (City)—Webster KY-2
Dixon (City)—Pulaski MO-3
Dixon (Village)—Dixon NE-4
Dixon (Township)—Logan ND-4
Dixon (Township)—Preble OH-3
Dixon (Township)—Gregory SD-4
Dixon (Township)—Hamlin SD-4
Dixon (Town)—Carbon WY-4
Dixon County NE-4
Dixon Lane-Meadow Creek (CDP)—
Inyo CA-4
Dixs Grant (Pop. Place)—Coos NH-1
Dixville (Township)—Coos NH-1
Dixville Notch (Pop. Place)—
Coos NH-1
D'Lo (Town)—Simpson MS-2
Dobbins Air Force Base (GA) Mil-4
Dobbins Heights (Town)—
Richmond NC-2
Dobbs Ferry (Village)—
Westchester NY-1
Dobson (Town)—Surry NC-2
Dock Junction (CDP)—Glynn GA-2

Doctor Phillips (CDP)—Orange FL-2
Dodd City (Town)—Fannin TX-2
Doddridge County WV-2
Dodds (Township)—Jefferson IL-3
Dodds (Township)—Nelson ND-4
Doddsville (Town)—Sunflower MS-2
Dodge (Township)—Ford KS-4
Dodge (Village)—Dodge NE-4
Dodge (City)—Dunn ND-4
Dodge (Town)—Trempealeau WI-3
Dodge Center (City)—Dodge MN-3
Dodge City (City)—Ford KS-4
Dodge County GA-2
Dodge County MN-3
Dodge County NE-4
Dodge County WI-3
Dodge Park (CDP)—Prince
George's MD-1
Dodgeville (City)—Iowa WI-3
Dodgeville (Town)—Iowa WI-3
Dodson (Village)—Winn Parish LA-2
Dodson (Town)—Phillips MT-4
Dodson (Township)—Highland OH-3
Dodson (Town)—Collingsworth ... TX-2
Doerun (City)—Colquitt GA-2
Dogden (Township)—McLean ND-4
Dog Ear (Township)—Tripp SD-4
Dolan (Township)—Cass MO-3
Doland (City)—Spink SD-4
Dolan Springs (CDP)—Mohave AZ-4
Dolgeville (Village)—Fulton NY-1
Dolgeville (Village)—Herkimer NY-1
Dollar Point (CDP)—Placer CA-4
Dolliver (City)—Emmet IA-3
Dollymount (Township)—
Traverse MN-3
Dolores (Town)—Montezuma CO-4
Dolores County CO-4
Dolphin (Township)—Knox NE-4
Dolson (Township)—Clark IL-3
Dolton (Village)—Cook IL-3
Dolton (Town)—Turner SD-4
Dolton (Township)—Turner SD-4
Dominion (CDP)—Bexar TX-2
Domino (Town)—Cass TX-2
Donahue (City)—Scott IA-3
Donald (City)—Marion OR-4
Donalds (Town)—Abbeville SC-2
Donaldson (City)—Kittson MN-3
Donaldsonville (City)—Ascension
Parish LA-2
Donalsonville (City)—Seminole GA-2
Donegal (Township)—Butler PA-1
Donegal (Township)—Washington .. PA-1
Donegal (Borough)—
Westmoreland PA-1
Donegal (Township)—
Westmoreland PA-1
Dongola (Village)—Union IL-3
Doniphan (City)—Ripley MO-3
Doniphan (Township)—Ripley MO-3
Doniphan (Township)—Hall NE-4
Doniphan (Village)—Hall NE-4
Doniphan County KS-4
Donley County TX-2
Donna (City)—Hidalgo TX-2
Donnan (City)—Fayette IA-3
Donnellson (Village)—Bond IL-3
Donnellson (Village)—
Montgomery IL-3
Donnellson (City)—Lee IA-3
Donnelly (City)—Valley ID-4
Donnelly (Township)—Marshall ... MN-3
Donnelly (City)—Stevens MN-3
Donnelly (Township)—Stevens MN-3

American Places Dictionary — General Index

Donnelsville (Village)—Clark OH-3
Donner Pass (CA) Geog-4
Donnybrook (City)—Ward ND-4
Donora (Borough)—Washington PA-1
Donovan (Village)—Iroquois IL-3
Dooling (Town)—Dooly GA-2
Doolittle (City)—Phelps MO-3
Dooly County GA-2
Dooms (CDP)—Augusta VA-2
Doon (City)—Lyon IA-3
Door County WI-3
Door Peninsula (WI) Geog-4
Dor (Township)—Smith KS-4
Dora (Town)—Walker AL-2
Dora (Township)—Moultrie IL-3
Dora (Township)—Otter Tail MN-3
Dora (Village)—Roosevelt NM-4
Dora Bay (CDP)—Prince of
  Wales-Outer Ketchikan Census
  Area AK-4
Doral (CDP)—Dade FL-2
Doran (City)—Wilkin MN-3
Doraville (City)—De Kalb GA-2
Dorchester (Township)—
  Macoupin IL-3
Dorchester (Village)—Macoupin IL-3
Dorchester—Suffolk MA-1
Dorchester (Village)—Saline NE-4
Dorchester (Town)—Grafton NH-1
Dorchester (Town)—Grayson TX-2
Dorchester (Village)—Clark WI-3
Dorchester County MD-1
Dorchester County SC-2
Dorchestser *See* **Boston**—Suffolk .. MA-1
Dorman (Township)—Lyman SD-4
Dormont (Borough)—Allegheny PA-1
Dorr (Township)—McHenry IL-3
Dorr (Township)—Allegan MI-3
Dorrance (City)—Russell KS-4
Dorrance (Township)—Luzerne PA-1
Dorris (City)—Siskiyou CA-4
Dorset (Township)—Ashtabula OH-3
Dorset (Town)—Bennington VT-1
Dortches (Town)—Nash NC-2
Dos Palos (City)—Merced CA-4
Dothan (City)—Dale AL-2
Dothan (City)—Houston AL-2
Dot Lake (CDP)—Southeast Fairbanks
  Census Area AK-4
Doña Ana (CDP)—Doña Ana NM-4
Doña Ana County NM-4
Doty (Town)—Oconto WI-3
Double Oak (Town)—Denton TX-2
Double Springs (Town)—
  Winston AL-2
Dougherty (City)—Cerro Gordo IA-3
Dougherty (Town)—Murray OK-2
Dougherty County GA-2
Douglas (Town)—Marshall AL-2
Douglas (City)—Cochise AZ-4
Douglas (City)—Coffee GA-2
Douglas (Township)—Clark IL-3
Douglas (Township)—Effingham ... IL-3
Douglas (Township)—Iroquois IL-3
Douglas (Township)—Jackson KS-4
Douglas (Township)—Stafford KS-4
Douglas (Town)—Worcester MA-1
Douglas (Village)—Allegan MI-3
Douglas (Township)—Dakota MN-3
Douglas (Village)—Otoe NE-4
Douglas (Township)—Saunders ... NE-4
Douglas (Township)—McLean ND-4
Douglas (City)—Ward ND-4
Douglas (City)—Garfield OK-2
Douglas (Town)—Marquette WI-3

Douglas (Town)—Converse WY-4
Douglas County CO-4
Douglas County GA-2
Douglas County IL-3
Douglas County KS-4
Douglas County MN-3
Douglas County MO-3
Douglas County NE-4
Douglas County NV-4
Douglas County OR-4
Douglas County SD-4
Douglas County WA-4
Douglas County WI-3
Douglas Grove (Township)—
  Custer NE-4
Douglass (City)—Butler KS-4
Douglass (Township)—Butler KS-4
Douglass (Township)—Montcalm .. MI-3
Douglass (Township)—Berks PA-1
Douglass (Township)—
  Montgomery PA-1
Douglass Hills (City)—Jefferson KY-2
Douglassville (Town)—Cass TX-2
Douglasville (City)—Douglas GA-2
Dousman (Village)—Waukesha .. WI-3
Dove Creek (Town)—Dolores CO-4
Dover (City)—Pope AR-2
Dover (City)—Kent DE-1
Dover (CDP)—Hillsborough FL-2
Dover (City)—Bonner ID-4
Dover (Township)—Bureau IL-3
Dover (Village)—Bureau IL-3
Dover (Township)—Shawnee KS-4
Dover (City)—Mason KY-2
Dover (Town)—Norfolk MA-1
Dover (Township)—Lake MI-3
Dover (Township)—Lenawee MI-3
Dover (Township)—Otsego MI-3
Dover (City)—Olmsted MN-3
Dover (Township)—Olmsted MN-3
Dover (Township)—Lafayette MO-3
Dover (Village)—Lafayette MO-3
Dover (Township)—Vernon MO-3
Dover (City)—Strafford NH-1
Dover (Town)—Morris NJ-1
Dover (Township)—Ocean NJ-1
Dover (Town)—Dutchess NY-1
Dover (Township)—Craven NC-2
Dover (Township)—Griggs ND-4
Dover (Township)—Athens OH-3
Dover (Township)—Fulton OH-3
Dover (City)—Tuscarawas OH-3
Dover (Township)—Tuscarawas .. OH-3
Dover (Township)—Union OH-3
Dover (Township)—Kingfisher ... OK-2
Dover (Borough)—York PA-1
Dover (Township)—York PA-1
Dover (Town)—Stewart TN-2
Dover (Town)—Windham VT-1
Dover (Town)—Buffalo WI-3
Dover (Town)—Racine WI-3
Dover Air Force Base (DE) Mil-4
Dover-Foxcroft (Town)—
  Piscataquis ME-1
Dover Plains (CDP)—Dutchess NY-1
Dovray (City)—Murray MN-3
Dovray (Township)—Murray MN-3
Dovre (Township)—Kandiyohi MN-3
Dovre (Township)—Slope ND-4
Dovre (Town)—Barron WI-3
Dowagiac (City)—Cass MI-3
Dow City (City)—Crawford IA-3
Dowell (Village)—Jackson IL-3
Dowelltown (Town)—DeKalb TN-2
Dowling (Township)—Knox NE-4

Downe (Township)—Cumberland .. NJ-1
Downers Grove (Township)—
  DuPage IL-3
Downers Grove (Village)—
  DuPage IL-3
Downey (City)—Los Angeles CA-4
Downey (City)—Bannock ID-4
Downieville (CDP)—Sierra CA-4
Downing (City)—Schuyler MO-3
Downing (Village)—Dunn WI-3
Downingtown (Borough)—
  Chester PA-1
Downs (Township)—McLean IL-3
Downs (Village)—McLean IL-3
Downs (City)—Osborne KS-4
Downs (Township)—Sumner KS-4
Downsville (Village)—Lincoln
  Parish LA-2
Downsville (Village)—Union
  Parish LA-2
Dows (City)—Franklin IA-3
Dows (City)—Wright IA-3
Dows (Township)—Cass ND-4
Doyal (Township)—St. Clair MO-3
Doyle (Township)—Marion KS-4
Doyle (Township)—Schoolcraft ... MI-3
Doyle (Town)—White TN-2
Doyle (Town)—Barron WI-3
Doylesport (Township)—Barton ... MO-3
Doylestown (Village)—Wayne OH-3
Doylestown (Borough)—Bucks ... PA-1
Doylestown (Township)—Bucks .. PA-1
Doylestown (Village)—Columbia .. WI-3
Doyline (Village)—Webster
  Parish LA-2
Dozier (Town)—Crenshaw AL-2
Dracut (Town)—Middlesex MA-1
Dragoon (Township)—Osage KS-4
Drain (City)—Douglas OR-4
Drake (Township)—Macon MO-3
Drake (City)—McHenry ND-4
Drakesboro (City)—Muhlenberg .. KY-2
Drakes Branch (Town)—
  Charlotte VA-2
Drakesville (City)—Davis IA-3
Drammen (Township)—Lincoln .. MN-3
Drammen (Town)—Eau Claire ... WI-3
Draper (Town)—Jones SD-4
Draper (Township)—Jones SD-4
Draper (City)—Salt Lake UT-4
Draper (City)—Utah UT-4
Draper (Town)—Sawyer WI-3
Dravosburg (Borough)—
  Allegheny PA-1
Drayton (City)—Pembina ND-4
Drayton (Township)—Pembina .. ND-4
Dreher (Township)—Wayne PA-1
Dresbach (Township)—Winona .. MN-3
Dresden (City)—Decatur KS-4
Dresden (Township)—Decatur .. KS-4
Dresden (Township)—Kingman .. KS-4
Dresden (Town)—Lincoln ME-1
Dresden (Township)—Pettis ... MO-3
Dresden (Town)—Washington .. NY-1
Dresden (Village)—Yates NY-1
Dresden (Township)—Cavalier .. ND-4
Dresden (Village)—Muskingum .. OH-3
Dresden (Town)—Weakley TN-2
Dresser (Village)—Polk WI-3
Dresslerville Colony (NV) IndRes-4
Drew (Plantation)—Penobscot .. ME-1
Drew (City)—Sunflower MS-2
Drew County AR-2
Drexel (City)—Bates MO-3
Drexel (City)—Cass MO-3

General Index — American Places Dictionary

Drexel (Town)—Burke NC-2
Drexel (CDP)—Montgomery OH-3
Drexel Hill (CDP)—Delaware PA-1
Driftwood (Township)—Jackson IN-3
Driftwood (Township)—Rawlins ... KS-4
Driftwood (Borough)—Cameron PA-1
Driggs (City)—Teton ID-4
Dripping Springs (City)—Hays TX-2
Driscoll (Township)—Burleigh ND-4
Driscoll (City)—Nueces TX-2
Driskill Mountain (LA) Geog-4
Druid Hills (CDP)—De Kalb GA-2
Druid Hills (City)—Jefferson KY-2
Drum Creek (Township)—
 Montgomery KS-4
Drummer (Township)—Ford IL-3
Drummond (City)—Fremont ID-4
Drummond (Township)—
 Chippewa MI-3
Drummond (Town)—Granite MT-4
Drummond (Town)—Garfield OK-2
Drummond (Town)—Bayfield WI-3
Drumore (Township)—Lancaster PA-1
Drumright (City)—Creek OK-2
Drumright (City)—Payne OK-2
Drury (Township)—Rock Island IL-3
Dry Creek (CDP)—Southeast Fairbanks
 Census Area AK-4
Dry Creek (Township)—Howell MO-3
Dry Creek (Township)—Maries MO-3
Dry Creek Rancheria (CA) IndRes-4
Dryden (Township)—Lapeer MI-3
Dryden (Village)—Lapeer MI-3
Dryden (Township)—Sibley MN-3
Dryden (Town)—Tompkins NY-1
Dryden (Village)—Tompkins NY-1
Dry Fork (Township)—Williams ND-4
Dry Grove (Township)—McLean IL-3
Dry Lake (Township)—Ramsey ND-4
Dry Point (Township)—Shelby IL-3
Dry Prong (Village)—Grant
 Parish LA-2
Dry Ridge (City)—Grant KY-2
Dry Run (CDP)—Hamilton OH-3
Dry Tortugas (FL) Geog-4
Drywood (Township)—Bourbon KS-4
Drywood (Township)—Vernon MO-3
Dry Wood Lake (Township)—
 Roberts SD-4
Duane (Town)—Franklin NY-1
Duanesburg (Town)—
 Schenectady NY-1
Duarte (City)—Los Angeles CA-4
Dubach (Town)—Lincoln Parish LA-2
Dubberly (Village)—Webster
 Parish LA-2
Dublin (City)—Alameda CA-4
Dublin (City)—Laurens GA-2
Dublin (Town)—Wayne IN-3
Dublin (Township)—Swift MN-3
Dublin (Town)—Cheshire NH-1
Dublin (Town)—Bladen NC-2
Dublin (Township)—Williams ND-4
Dublin (Village)—Delaware OH-3
Dublin (Village)—Franklin OH-3
Dublin (Township)—Mercer OH-3
Dublin (City)—Union OH-3
Dublin (Borough)—Bucks PA-1
Dublin (Township)—Fulton PA-1
Dublin (Township)—Huntingdon ... PA-1
Dublin (City)—Erath TX-2
Dublin (Town)—Pulaski VA-2
Dubois (City)—Clark ID-4
Du Bois (Township)—Washington .. IL-3
Du Bois (Village)—Washington IL-3

Du Bois (Village)—Pawnee NE-4
DuBois (City)—Clearfield PA-1
Dubois (Town)—Fremont WY-3
Dubois County IN-3
Duboistown (Borough)—
 Lycoming PA-1
Dubuque (City)—Dubuque IA-3
Dubuque County IA-3
Duchesne (City)—Duchesne UT-4
Duchesne County UT-4
Duchouquet (Township)—
 Auglaize OH-3
Duck Creek (Township)—
 Madison IN-3
Duck Creek (Township)—Wilson ... KS-4
Duck Creek (Township)—
 Stoddard MO-3
Duck Creek (Township)—Adams .. ND-4
Duck Creek (Pop. Place)—
 Perkins SD-4
Duck Hill (Town)—Montgomery ... MS-2
Ducktown (City)—Polk TN-2
Duck Valley Reservation
 (NV) IndRes-4
Duckwater Reservation (NV) ... IndRes-4
Dudley (City)—Laurens GA-2
Dudley (Township)—Henry IN-3
Dudley (Township)—Haskell KS-4
Dudley (Town)—Worcester MA-1
Dudley (Township)—Clearwater ... MN-3
Dudley (City)—Stoddard MO-3
Dudley (Township)—Hardin OH-3
Dudley (Borough)—Huntingdon ... PA-1
Dudley (Township)—Aurora SD-4
Dudleyville (CDP)—Pinal AZ-4
Duell (Township)—Perkins SD-4
Duenweg (City)—Jasper MO-3
Duerr (Township)—Richland ND-4
Due West (Town)—Abbeville SC-2
Duffield (Town)—Scott VA-2
Dufur (Town)—Wasco OR-4
Dugger (Town)—Sullivan IN-3
Dugway (Military Facility)—
 Tooele UT-4
Dukes County MA-1
Dulac (CDP)—Terrebonne Parish .. LA-2
Dulce (CDP)—Rio Arriba NM-4
Duluth (City)—Gwinnett GA-2
Duluth (City)—St. Louis MN-3
Duluth (Township)—St. Louis MN-3
Dumarce (Township)—Marshall SD-4
Dumas (City)—Desha AR-2
Dumas (Town)—Tippah MS-2
Dumas (City)—Moore TX-2
Dumbarton (CDP)—Henrico VA-2
Dumfries (Town)—Prince
 William VA-2
Dummer (Town)—Coos NH-1
Dummerston (Town)—Windham .. VT-1
Dumont (City)—Butler IA-3
Dumont (City)—Traverse MN-3
Dumont (Borough)—Bergen NJ-1
Dunbar (Township)—Faribault MN-3
Dunbar (Village)—Otoe NE-4
Dunbar (Township)—Sargent ND-4
Dunbar (Borough)—Fayette PA-1
Dunbar (Township)—Fayette PA-1
Dunbar (City)—Kanawha WV-2
Dunbar (Town)—Marinette WI-3
Dunbarton (Town)—Merrimack ... NH-1
Duncan (Town)—Greenlee AZ-4
Duncan (Township)—Mercer IL-3
Duncan (Township)—Houghton ... MI-3
Duncan (Town)—Bolivar MS-2
Duncan (Township)—Sullivan MO-3

Duncan (Village)—Platte NE-4
Duncan (City)—Stephens OK-2
Duncan (Township)—Tioga PA-1
Duncan (Town)—Spartanburg SC-2
Duncannon (Borough)—Perry PA-1
Duncansville (Borough)—Blair PA-1
Duncanville (City)—Dallas TX-2
Duncombe (City)—Webster IA-3
Dundalk (CDP)—Baltimore MD-1
Dundas (City)—Rice MN-3
Dundee (Town)—Polk FL-2
Dundee (Township)—Kane IL-3
Dundee (City)—Delaware IA-3
Dundee (Township)—Monroe MI-3
Dundee (Village)—Monroe MI-3
Dundee (City)—Nobles MN-3
Dundee (Village)—Yates NY-1
Dundee (Township)—Walsh ND-4
Dundee (City)—Yamhill OR-4
Dundy County NE-4
Dune Acres (Town)—Porter IN-3
Dunean (CDP)—Greenville SC-2
Dunedin (City)—Pinellas FL-2
Dunellen (Borough)—Middlesex ... NJ-1
Dunes City (City)—Lane OR-4
Dunfermline (Village)—Fulton IL-3
Dungannon (Town)—Scott VA-2
Dunham (Township)—McHenry ... IL-3
Dunham (Township)—
 Washington OH-3
Dunkard (Township)—Greene PA-1
Dunkel (Township)—Jones SD-4
Dunkerton (City)—Black Hawk IA-3
Dunkirk (City)—Blackford IN-3
Dunkirk (City)—Jay IN-3
Dunkirk (City)—Chautauqua NY-1
Dunkirk (Town)—Chautauqua NY-1
Dunkirk (Village)—Hardin OH-3
Dunkirk (Town)—Dane WI-3
Dunklin County MO-3
Dunlap (Village)—Peoria IL-3
Dunlap (CDP)—Elkhart IN-3
Dunlap (City)—Harrison IA-3
Dunlap (City)—Morris KS-4
Dunlap (City)—Sequatchie TN-2
Dunleith (Township)—Jo Daviess .. IL-3
Dunlevy (Borough)—Washington .. PA-1
Dunmore (Borough)—
 Lackawanna PA-1
Dunn (Township)—Otter Tail MN-3
Dunn (City)—Harnett NC-2
Dunn (Town)—Dane WI-3
Dunn (Town)—Dunn WI-3
Dunn Center (City)—Dunn ND-4
Dunn County ND-4
Dunn County WI-3
Dunnell (City)—Martin MN-3
Dunnellon (City)—Marion FL-2
Dunning (Village)—Blaine NE-4
Dunn Loring (CDP)—Fairfax VA-2
Dunnstable (Township)—Clinton .. PA-1
Dunnstown (CDP)—Clinton PA-1
Dunreith (Town)—Henry IN-3
Dunseith (City)—Rolette ND-4
Dunsmuir (City)—Siskiyou CA-4
Dunstable (Town)—Middlesex MA-1
Dunwoody (CDP)—De Kalb GA-2
Du Page (Township)—Will IL-3
DuPage County IL-3
Duplain (Township)—Clinton MI-3
Duplin County NC-2
Dupo (Village)—St. Clair IL-3
Du Pont (Town)—Clinch GA-2
Dupont (Town)—Jefferson IN-3
Dupont (Village)—Putnam OH-3

Dupont (Borough)—Luzerne........... *PA-1*	Dyker Heights—Kings.................... *NY-1*	Earl (Township)—Lancaster........... *PA-1*
DuPont (City)—Pierce.................... *WA-4*	Dysart (City)—Tama....................... *IA-3*	Earle (City)—Crittenden *AR-2*
DuPont (Town)—Waupaca............. *WI-3*	Eads (Town)—Kiowa..................... *CO-4*	Earlham (City)—Madison *IA-3*
Dupree (City)—Ziebach *SD-4*	Eagan (City)—Dakota *MN-3*	Earlimart (CDP)—Tulare *CA-4*
Dupree (Pop. Place)—Ziebach....... *SD-4*	Eagar (Town)—Apache.................. *AZ-4*	Earling (City)—Shelby..................... *IA-3*
Duquesne (Village)—Jasper *MO-3*	Eagarville (Village)—Macoupin *IL-3*	Earling (Township)—Lyman *SD-4*
Duquesne (City)—Allegheny........... *PA-1*	Eagle (City)—Southeast Fairbanks	Earlington (City)—Hopkins *KY-2*
Du Quoin (City)—Perry................. *IL-3*	Census Area.............................. *AK-4*	Earl Park (Town)—Benton............. *IN-3*
Durand (Township)—Winnebago ... *IL-3*	Eagle (Town)—Eagle *CO-4*	Earlsboro (Town)—Pottawatomie.. *OK-2*
Durand (Village)—Winnebago....... *IL-3*	Eagle (City)—Ada........................... *ID-4*	Earlton (City)—Neosho..................*KS-4*
Durand (City)—Shiawassee............ *MI-3*	Eagle (Township)—La Salle *IL-3*	Earlville (City)—La Salle *IL-3*
Durand (Township)—Beltrami *MN-3*	Eagle (Township)—Boone *IN-3*	Earlville (City)—Delaware *IA-3*
Durand (City)—Pepin *WI-3*	Eagle (Township)—Barber..............*KS-4*	Earlville (Village)—Chenango........ *NY-1*
Durand (Town)—Pepin *WI-3*	Eagle (Township)—Kingman *KS-4*	Earlville (Village)—Madison *NY-1*
Durango (City)—La Plata *CO-4*	Eagle (Township)—Sedgwick..........*KS-4*	Early (City)—Sac............................. *IA-3*
Durango (City)—Dubuque..............*IA-3*	Eagle (Township)—Clinton *MI-3*	Early (City)—Brown *TX-2*
Durant (City)—Cedar..................... *IA-3*	Eagle (Village)—Clinton *MI-3*	**Early County** *GA-2*
Durant (City)—Muscatine *IA-3*	Eagle (Township)—Carlton *MN-3*	Earth (City)—Lamb........................ *TX-2*
Durant (City)—Scott *IA-3*	Eagle (Township)—Macon *MO-3*	Easby (Township)—Cavalier *ND-4*
Durant (City)—Holmes...................*MS-2*	Eagle (Village)—Cass..................... *NE-4*	Easley (Township)—Macon........... *MO-3*
Durant (City)—Bryan..................... *OK-2*	Eagle (Town)—Wyoming............... *NY-1*	Easley (City)—Pickens *SC-2*
Durbin (Township)—Cass *ND-4*	Eagle (Township)—Richland.......... *ND-4*	East (Township)—Carroll...............*OH-3*
Durbin (Town)—Pocahontas *WV-2*	Eagle (Township)—Brown *OH-3*	East Adams (Pop. Place)—
Durham (CDP)—Butte *CA-4*	Eagle (Township)—Hancock *OH-3*	Adams *ND-4*
Durham (Town)—Middlesex......... *CT-1*	Eagle (Township)—Vinton *OH-3*	East Allen (Township)—
Durham (Township)—Hancock *IL-3*	Eagle (Township)—Brule................ *SD-4*	Northampton *PA-1*
Durham (City)—Marion *KS-4*	Eagle (Township)—Meade.............. *SD-4*	East Alma (Township)—Cavalier... *ND-4*
Durham (Township)—Ottawa.........*KS-4*	Eagle (Town)—Richland *WI-3*	East Alton (Village)—Madison *IL-3*
Durham (Town)—Androscoggin ... *ME-1*	Eagle (Township)—Waukesha............. *WI-3*	Eastampton (Township)—
Durham (Town)—Strafford............*NH-1*	Eagle (Village)—Waukesha *WI-3*	Burlington *NJ-1*
Durham (Town)—Greene.............. *NY-1*	Eagle Bend (City)—Todd *MN-3*	East Amwell (Township)—
Durham (City)—Durham............... *NC-2*	Eagle Butte (Town)—Dewey *SD-4*	Hunterdon................................... *NJ-1*
Durham (City)—Orange................. *NC-2*	Eagle Butte (City)—Ziebach *SD-4*	East Arcadia (Town)—Bladen *NC-2*
Durham (Township)—Stutsman *ND-4*	**Eagle County** *CO-4*	East Aurora (Village)—Erie *NY-1*
Durham (City)—Washington *OR-4*	Eagle Creek (Township)—Gallatin.. *IL-3*	East Bangor (Borough)—
Durham (Township)—Bucks........... *PA-1*	Eagle Creek (Township)—Lake...... *IN-3*	Northampton *PA-1*
Durham County *NC-2*	Eagle Grove (City)—Wright........... *IA-3*	East Bank (Town)—Kanawha *WV-2*
Durham Park (Township)—	Eagle Harbor (Town)—Prince	**East Baton Rouge Parish** *LA-2*
Marion *KS-4*	George's *MD-1*	East Bay (Township)—Grand
Duryea (Borough)—Luzerne *PA-1*	Eagle Harbor (City)—Keweenaw ... *MI-3*	Traverse..................................... *MI-3*
Dushore (Borough)—Sullivan *PA-1*	Eagle Harbor (Township)—	East Bend (Township)—
Duson (Town)—Acadia Parish......*LA-2*	Keweenaw *MI-3*	Champaign *IL-3*
Duson (Town)—Lafayette Parish....*LA-2*	Eagle Lake (City)—Polk..................*FL-2*	East Bend (Town)—Yadkin........... *NC-2*
Dust Bowl (FL)............................ *Geog-4*	Eagle Lake (Town)—Aroostook *ME-1*	East Bennett (Pop. Place)—
Dustin (Township)—Holt *NE-4*	Eagle Lake (City)—Blue Earth...... *MN-3*	Bennett....................................... *SD-4*
Dustin (Town)—Hughes................. *OK-2*	Eagle Lake (Township)—Otter	East Benton (Township)—
Dutchess County *NY-1*	Tail.. *MN-3*	Christian *MO-3*
Dutton (Town)—Jackson *AL-2*	Eagle Lake (City)—Colorado *TX-2*	East Benton (Township)—
Dutton (Town)—Teton *MT-4*	Eagle Lake (CDP)—Racine............ *WI-3*	Webster *MO-3*
Duval (Township)—Jasper *MO-3*	Eagle Mountain (MN) *Geog-4*	East Berlin (Borough)—Adams........ *PA-1*
Duval County *FL-2*	Eagle Mountain (CDP)—Tarrant... *TX-2*	East Bernard (CDP)—Wharton *TX-2*
Duval County *TX-2*	Eagle Nest (Village)—Colfax *NM-4*	East Berwick (CDP)—Luzerne........ *PA-1*
Duvall (City)—King........................ *WA-4*	Eagle Pass (City)—Maverick *TX-2*	East Bethel (City)—Anoka *MN-3*
Duxbury (Town)—Plymouth......... *MA-1*	Eagle Point (Township)—Ogle *IL-3*	East Bethlehem (Township)—
Duxbury (Town)—Washington *VT-1*	Eagle Point (Township)—	Washington *PA-1*
Dwight (Village)—Grundy *IL-3*	Marshall *MN-3*	East Bloomfield (Town)—
Dwight (Township)—Livingston *IL-3*	Eagle Point (City)—Jackson............ *OR-4*	Ontario *NY-1*
Dwight (Village)—Livingston......... *IL-3*	Eagle Point (Town)—Chippewa *WI-3*	East Bloomfield (Village)—
Dwight (City)—Morris *KS-4*	Eagle River (City)—Keweenaw *MI-3*	Ontario *NY-1*
Dwight (Township)—Huron *MI-3*	Eagle River (City)—Vilas................ *WI-3*	East Blythe (CDP)—Riverside *CA-4*
Dwight (Village)—Butler *NE-4*	Eagles Mere (Borough)—Sullivan ... *PA-1*	East Boone (Township)—Bates..... *MO-3*
Dwight (City)—Richland *ND-4*	Eagleswood (Township)—Ocean *NJ-1*	Eastborough (City)—Sedgwick........*KS-4*
Dwight (Township)—Richland *ND-4*	Eagleton Village (CDP)—Blount ... *TN-2*	East Boundary (CDP)—
Dyberry (Township)—Wayne.......... *PA-1*	Eagle-Vail (CDP)—Eagle................. *CO-4*	Richmond *GA-2*
Dycusburg (City)—Crittenden *KY-2*	Eagle Valley (Township)—Todd *MN-3*	East Bradford (Township)—
Dyer (Town)—Crawford *AR-2*	Eagle View (Township)—Becker.... *MN-3*	Chester *PA-1*
Dyer (Town)—Lake........................ *IN-3*	Eagle Village (CDP)—Southeast	East Brady (Borough)—Clarion *PA-1*
Dyer (City)—Gibson *TN-2*	Fairbanks Census Area................ *AK-4*	East Brainerd (CDP)—Hamilton ... *TN-2*
Dyer Brook (Town)—Aroostook ... *ME-1*	Eagleville (Town)—Harrison *MO-3*	East Branch (Township)—Marion ..*KS-4*
Dyer County *TN-2*	Eagleville (CDP)—Montgomery *PA-1*	East Brandywine (Township)—
Dyersburg (City)—Dyer *TN-2*	Eagleville (City)—Rutherford *TN-2*	Chester *PA-1*
Dyersville (City)—Delaware *IA-3*	Eakly (Town)—Caddo *OK-2*	East Brewton (City)—Escambia......*AL-2*
Dyersville (City)—Dubuque............*IA-3*	Earl (Township)—La Salle *IL-3*	East Bridgewater (Town)—
Dyess (Town)—Mississippi *AR-2*	Earl (Town)—Cleveland *NC-2*	Plymouth....................................*MA-1*
Dyess Air Force Base (TX) *Mil-4*	Earl (Township)—Berks *PA-1*	Eastbrook (Town)—Hancock *ME-1*

General Index

East Brookfield (Town)—
  Worcester MA-1
East Brooklyn (CDP)—Windham .. CT-1
East Brooklyn (Village)—Grundy ... IL-3
East Brunswick (Township)—
  Middlesex NJ-1
East Brunswick (Township)—
  Schuylkill PA-1
East Buffalo (Township)—Union PA-1
East Burleigh (Pop. Place)—
  Burleigh ND-4
East Butler (Borough)—Butler PA-1
East Butte (Pop. Place)—Butte SD-4
East Caln (Township)—Chester PA-1
East Camden (Town)—Ouachita ... AR-2
East Cameron (Township)—
  Northumberland PA-1
East Canton (Village)—Stark OH-3
East Cape Girardeau (Village)—
  Alexander IL-3
East Carbon (City)—Carbon UT-4
East Carondelet (Village)—St.
  Clair IL-3
East Carroll (Township)—
  Cambria PA-1
East Carroll Parish LA-2
East Cass (Pop. Place)—Cass MN-3
East Central Franklin
  (unorganized) (Pop. Place)—
  Franklin ME-1
East Central Pennington (Pop. Place)—
  Pennington SD-4
East Central Penobscot
  (unorganized) (Pop. Place)—
  Penobscot ME-1
East Central Washington
  (unorganized) (Pop. Place)—
  Washington ME-1
East Chain (Township)—Martin MN-3
Eastchester (CDP)—Westchester NY-1
Eastchester (Town)—Westchester ... NY-1
East Chicago (City)—Lake IN-3
East Chillisquaque (Township)—
  Northumberland PA-1
East China (Township)—St. Clair .. MI-3
East Choteau (Township)—
  Douglas SD-4
East Cleveland (City)—
  Cuyahoga OH-3
East Cleveland (CDP)—Bradley TN-2
East Cocalico (Township)—
  Lancaster PA-1
East Compton (CDP)—Los
  Angeles CA-4
East Conemaugh (Borough)—
  Cambria PA-1
East Cook (Pop. Place)—Cook MN-3
East Cooper (Township)—
  Stafford KS-4
East Coventry (Township)—
  Chester PA-1
East Custer (Township)—Custer NE-4
East Custer (Pop. Place)—Custer .. SD-4
East Dallas (Township)—
  Webster MO-3
East Deer (Township)—Allegheny .. PA-1
East Dennis (CDP)—Barnstable ... MA-1
East Donegal (Township)—
  Lancaster PA-1
East Douglas (CDP)—Worcester ... MA-1
East Drumore (Township)—
  Lancaster PA-1
East Dublin (Town)—Laurens GA-2
East Dubuque (City)—Jo Daviess .. IL-3
East Duke (Town)—Jackson OK-2

East Dundee (Village)—Cook IL-3
East Dundee (Village)—Kane IL-3
East Dunseith (CDP)—Rolette ND-4
East Earl (Township)—Lancaster ... PA-1
East Eldorado (Township)—Saline . IL-3
East Ellijay (City)—Gilmer GA-2
Easter (Township)—Roberts SD-4
Eastern (Township)—Franklin IL-3
Eastern (Township)—Otter Tail MN-3
Eastern (Township)—Knox NE-4
Eastern Cherokee Reservation
  (NC) IndRes-4
Eastern Chickahominy TDSA
  (VA) IndRes-4
East Fairfield (Township)—
  Crawford PA-1
East Fallowfield (Township)—
  Chester PA-1
East Fallowfield (Township)—
  Crawford PA-1
East Falmouth (CDP)—
  Barnstable MA-1
East Farmingdale (CDP)—
  Suffolk NY-1
East Feliciana Parish LA-2
East Finley (Township)—
  Christian MO-3
East Finley (Township)—
  Washington PA-1
East Fishkill (Town)—Dutchess NY-1
East Flat Rock (CDP)—
  Henderson NC-2
East Foothills (CDP)—Santa
  Clara CA-4
Eastford (Town)—Windham CT-1
East Fork (CDP)—Navajo AZ-4
East Fork (Township)—Clinton IL-3
East Fork (Township)—
  Montgomery IL-3
East Fork (Township)—Benson ND-4
East Fork (Township)—Williams ... ND-4
East Franklin (Township)—
  Armstrong PA-1
East Freehold (CDP)—
  Monmouth NJ-1
East Fulton (Township)—
  Callaway MO-3
East Gaffney (CDP)—Cherokee SC-2
East Galena (Township)—Jo
  Daviess IL-3
East Galesburg (Village)—Knox IL-3
Eastgate (CDP)—King WA-4
East Germantown (Town)—
  Wayne IN-3
East Gillespie (Village)—
  Macoupin IL-3
East Glacier Park Village (CDP)—
  Glacier MT-4
East Glenville (CDP)—
  Schenectady NY-1
East Golden Valley (Pop. Place)—
  Golden Valley ND-4
East Goshen (Township)—
  Chester PA-1
East Granby (Town)—Hartford CT-1
East Grand Forks (City)—Polk MN-3
East Grand Rapids (City)—Kent ... MI-3
East Grant (Pop. Place)—Grant ... ND-4
East Greenbush (Town)—
  Rensselaer NY-1
East Greenville (Borough)—
  Montgomery PA-1
East Greenwich (Township)—
  Gloucester NJ-1
East Greenwich (Town)—Kent RI-1

East Gregory (Pop. Place)—
  Gregory SD-4
East Griffin (CDP)—Spalding GA-2
East Grove (Township)—Lee IL-3
East Gull Lake (City)—Cass MN-3
East Haakon (Pop. Place)—
  Haakon SD-4
East Haddam (Town)—
  Middlesex CT-1
East Hale (Township)—Thomas ... KS-4
Eastham (Town)—Barnstable MA-1
East Hampton (Town)—
  Middlesex CT-1
Easthampton (Town)—
  Hampshire MA-1
East Hampton (Town)—Suffolk NY-1
East Hampton (Village)—Suffolk .. NY-1
East Hancock (unorganized) (Pop.
  Place)—Hancock ME-1
East Hanover (Township)—
  Morris NJ-1
East Hanover (Township)—
  Dauphin PA-1
East Hanover (Township)—
  Lebanon PA-1
East Hanson (Township)—Brown .. SD-4
East Hartford (Town)—Hartford ... CT-1
East Harwich (CDP)—
  Barnstable MA-1
East Haven (Town)—New Haven .. CT-1
East Haven (Town)—Essex VT-1
East Hazel Crest (Village)—Cook .. IL-3
East Helena (Town)—Lewis and
  Clark MT-4
East Hemet (CDP)—Riverside CA-4
East Hempfield (Township)—
  Lancaster PA-1
East Hess (Township)—Gray KS-4
East Hibbard (Township)—
  Kearny KS-4
East Highland Park (CDP)—
  Henrico VA-2
East Hill-Meridian (CDP)—King .. WA-4
East Hills (Village)—Nassau NY-1
East Hodge (Village)—Jackson
  Parish LA-2
East Hope (City)—Bonner ID-4
East Hopewell (Township)—York ... PA-1
East Huntingdon (Township)—
  Westmoreland PA-1
East Islip (CDP)—Suffolk NY-1
East Ithaca (CDP)—Tompkins NY-1
East Jackson (Pop. Place)—
  Jackson SD-4
East Jordan (City)—Charlevoix MI-3
East Keating (Township)—
  Clinton PA-1
East Kingston (Town)—
  Rockingham NH-1
East Kiowa (Pop. Place)—Kiowa .. KS-4
East Kittson (Pop. Place)—
  Kittson MN-3
East Koochiching (Pop. Place)—
  Koochiching MN-3
East Lackawannock (Township)—
  Mercer PA-1
Eastlake (Village)—Manistee MI-3
Eastlake (City)—Lake OH-3
East Lake Lillian (Township)—
  Kandiyohi MN-3
East Lake-Orient Park (CDP)—
  Hillsborough FL-2
East La Mirada (CDP)—Los
  Angeles CA-4

American Places Dictionary — General Index

East Lampeter (Township)—
  Lancaster *PA-1*
Eastland (City)—Eastland *TX-2*
Eastland County *TX-2*
East Lansdowne (Borough)—
  Delaware *PA-1*
East Lansing (City)—Ingham *MI-3*
East Las Vegas (CDP)—Clark *NV-4*
East Laurinburg (Town)—
  Scotland *NC-2*
Eastlawn Gardens (CDP)—
  Northampton *PA-1*
East Lincoln (Township)—Logan *IL-3*
East Liverpool (City)—
  Columbiana *OH-3*
East Logan (Pop. Place)—Logan .. *ND-4*
East Longmeadow (Town)—
  Hampden *MA-1*
East Looney (Township)—Polk *MO-3*
East Los Angeles (CDP)—Los
  Angeles *CA-4*
East Lyme (Town)—New London . *CT-1*
East Lynne (Town)—Cass *MO-3*
East Machias (Town)—
  Washington *ME-1*
East Madison (Township)—Polk .. *MO-3*
East Mahoning (Township)—
  Indiana *PA-1*
Eastman (City)—Dodge *GA-2*
Eastman (Township)—Foster *ND-4*
Eastman (Town)—Crawford *WI-3*
Eastman (Village)—Crawford *WI-3*
East Manchester (Township)—
  York *PA-1*
East Marlborough (Township)—
  Chester *PA-1*
East Massapequa (CDP)—
  Nassau *NY-1*
East McHenry (Pop. Place)—
  McHenry *ND-4*
East McIntosh (Pop. Place)—
  McIntosh *ND-4*
East McKeesport (Borough)—
  Allegheny *PA-1*
East McKenzie (Pop. Place)—
  McKenzie *ND-4*
East McLean (Pop. Place)—
  McLean *ND-4*
East Mead (Township)—
  Crawford *PA-1*
East Meadow (CDP)—Nassau *NY-1*
East Mercer (Pop. Place)—
  Mercer *ND-4*
East Merrimack (CDP)—
  Hillsborough *NH-1*
East Middletown (CDP)—
  Orange *NY-1*
East Millcreek (CDP)—Salt Lake .. *UT-4*
East Millinocket (Town)—
  Penobscot *ME-1*
East Moline (City)—Rock Island *IL-3*
East Montpelier (Town)—
  Washington *VT-1*
East Moriches (CDP)—Suffolk *NY-1*
East Morton (Pop. Place)—
  Morton *ND-4*
East Mountain (City)—Upshur *TX-2*
East Nantmeal (Township)—
  Chester *PA-1*
East Naples (CDP)—Collier *FL-2*
East Nelson (Township)—
  Moultrie *IL-3*
East Newark (Borough)—Hudson ... *NJ-1*
East Newman (Township)—
  Nance *NE-4*

East New Market (Town)—
  Dorchester *MD-1*
East Newnan (CDP)—Coweta *GA-2*
East New York—Kings *NY-1*
East Ninnekah (Town)—Grady *OK-2*
East Norriton (Township)—
  Montgomery *PA-1*
East Northport (CDP)—Suffolk *NY-1*
East Norwegian (Township)—
  Schuylkill *PA-1*
East Norwich (CDP)—Nassau *NY-1*
East Nottingham (Township)—
  Chester *PA-1*
East Oakland (Township)—Coles ... *IL-3*
East Oliver (Pop. Place)—Oliver ... *ND-4*
Easton (CDP)—Fresno *CA-4*
Easton (Town)—Fairfield *CT-1*
Easton (Village)—Mason *IL-3*
Easton (City)—Leavenworth *KS-4*
Easton (Township)—
  Leavenworth *KS-4*
Easton (Town)—Aroostook *ME-1*
Easton (Town)—Talbot *MD-1*
Easton (Town)—Bristol *MA-1*
Easton (Township)—Ionia *MI-3*
Easton (City)—Faribault *MN-3*
Easton (City)—Buchanan *MO-3*
Easton (Town)—Grafton *NH-1*
Easton (Town)—Washington *NY-1*
Easton (Township)—Steele *ND-4*
Easton (City)—Northampton *PA-1*
Easton (City)—Gregg *TX-2*
Easton (City)—Rusk *TX-2*
Easton (Town)—Adams *WI-3*
Easton (Town)—Marathon *WI-3*
East Orange (City)—Essex *NJ-1*
East Otto (Town)—Cattaraugus *NY-1*
Eastover (Town)—Richland *SC-2*
East Palatka (CDP)—Putnam *FL-2*
East Palestine (City)—
  Columbiana *OH-3*
East Palo Alto (City)—San
  Mateo *CA-4*
East Park (Township)—Marshall .. *MN-3*
East Pasadena (CDP)—Los
  Angeles *CA-4*
East Patchogue (CDP)—Suffolk *NY-1*
East Peak (MN) *Geog-4*
East Penn (Township)—Carbon *PA-1*
East Pennsboro (Township)—
  Cumberland *PA-1*
East Peoria (City)—Tazewell *IL-3*
East Pepperell (CDP)—
  Middlesex *MA-1*
East Perkins (Pop. Place)—
  Perkins *SD-4*
East Peru (City)—Madison *IA-2*
East Petersburg (Borough)—
  Lancaster *PA-1*
East Pikeland (Township)—
  Chester *PA-1*
East Pittsburgh (Borough)—
  Allegheny *PA-1*
Eastpoint (CDP)—Franklin *FL-2*
East Point (City)—Fulton *GA-2*
Eastpointe (City)—Macomb *MI-3*
East Polk (Township)—
  Christian *MO-3*
Eastport (City)—Washington *ME-1*
East Porterville (CDP)—Tulare *CA-4*
East Port Orchard (CDP)—
  Kitsap *WA-4*
East Potter (Pop. Place)—Potter ... *SD-4*
East Prairie (City)—Mississippi *MO-3*
East Prospect (Borough)—York *PA-1*

East Providence (Township)—
  Bedford *PA-1*
East Providence (City)—
  Providence *RI-1*
East Quogue (CDP)—Suffolk *NY-1*
East Randolph (Village)—
  Cattaraugus *NY-1*
East Renton Highlands (CDP)—
  King *WA-4*
East Republic (Township)—
  Greene *MO-3*
East Richmond Heights (CDP)—Contra
  Costa *CA-4*
East Ridge (City)—Hamilton *TN-2*
East River (NY) *Geog-4*
East Riverdale (CDP)—Prince
  George's *MD-1*
East Rochester (Village)—
  Monroe *NY-1*
East Rochester (Borough)—
  Beaver *PA-1*
East Rockaway (Village)—
  Nassau *NY-1*
East Rockhill (Township)—Bucks ... *PA-1*
East Rockingham (CDP)—
  Richmond *NC-2*
East Rolette (Pop. Place)—
  Rolette *ND-4*
East Rondell (Township)—Brown .. *SD-4*
East Rutherford (Borough)—
  Bergen *NJ-1*
East Saline (Township)—
  Sheridan *KS-4*
East Sandwich (CDP)—
  Barnstable *MA-1*
East San Gabriel (CDP)—Los
  Angeles *CA-4*
East Shannon (Pop. Place)—
  Shannon *SD-4*
East Shoreham (CDP)—Suffolk *NY-1*
East Side (Township)—Mille
  Lacs *MN-3*
East Side (Borough)—Carbon *PA-1*
East Sonora (CDP)—Tuolumne *CA-4*
East Sparta (Village)—Stark *OH-3*
East Spencer (Town)—Rowan *NC-2*
East Stark (Pop. Place)—Stark *ND-4*
East St. Clair (Township)—
  Bedford *PA-1*
East St. Louis (City)—St. Clair *IL-3*
East St. Louis (Township)—St.
  Clair *IL-3*
East Stroudsburg (Borough)—
  Monroe *PA-1*
East Sully (Pop. Place)—Sully *SD-4*
East Sumter (CDP)—Sumter *SC-2*
East Syracuse (Village)—
  Onondaga *NY-1*
East Tawakoni (City)—Rains *TX-2*
East Tawas (City)—Iosco *MI-3*
East Taylor (Township)—Cambria . *PA-1*
East Thermopolis (Town)—Hot
  Springs *WY-4*
East Todd (Pop. Place)—Todd *SD-4*
Easttown (Township)—Chester *PA-1*
East Troy (Town)—Walworth *WI-3*
East Troy (Village)—Walworth *WI-3*
East Union (Township)—Wayne *OH-3*
East Union (Township)—
  Schuylkill *PA-1*
East Uniontown (CDP)—Fayette .. *PA-1*
Eastvale (Borough)—Beaver *PA-1*
East Valley (Township)—
  Marshall *MN-3*

General Index — American Places Dictionary

East Vandergrift (Borough)—Westmoreland PA-1
Eastview (Town)—McNairy TN-2
Eastville (Town)—Northampton VA-2
East Vincent (Township)—Chester PA-1
East Walworth (Pop. Place)—Walworth SD-4
East Washington (Township)—Rice KS-4
East Washington (Borough)—Washington PA-1
East Wenatchee (City)—Douglas WA-4
East Wenatchee Bench (CDP)—Douglas WA-4
East Wheatfield (Township)—Indiana PA-1
East Whiteland (Township)—Chester PA-1
East Williston (Village)—Nassau NY-1
East Windsor (Town)—Hartford CT-1
East Windsor (Township)—Mercer NJ-1
Eastwood (CDP)—Bossier Parish LA-2
Eastwood (CDP)—Kalamazoo MI-3
East York (CDP)—York PA-1
Eaton (Town)—Weld CO-4
Eaton (Town)—Delaware IN-3
Eaton (Township)—Eaton MI-3
Eaton (Township)—Kearney NE-4
Eaton (Town)—Carroll NH-1
Eaton (Town)—Madison NY-1
Eaton (Township)—Lorain OH-3
Eaton (City)—Preble OH-3
Eaton (Township)—Wyoming PA-1
Eaton (Town)—Brown WI-3
Eaton (Town)—Clark WI-3
Eaton (Town)—Manitowoc WI-3
Eaton County MI-3
Eaton Estates (CDP)—Lorain OH-3
Eaton Rapids (City)—Eaton MI-3
Eaton Rapids (Township)—Eaton MI-3
Eatons Neck (CDP)—Suffolk NY-1
Eatonton (City)—Putnam GA-2
Eatontown (Borough)—Monmouth NJ-1
Eatonville (Town)—Orange FL-2
Eatonville (Town)—Pierce WA-4
Eau Claire (Village)—Berrien MI-3
Eau Claire (Borough)—Butler PA-1
Eau Claire (City)—Chippewa WI-3
Eau Claire (City)—Eau Claire WI-3
Eau Claire County WI-3
Eau Galle (Town)—Dunn WI-3
Eau Galle (Town)—St. Croix WI-3
Eau Pleine (Town)—Marathon WI-3
Eau Pleine (Town)—Portage WI-3
Ebensburg (Borough)—Cambria PA-1
Ebro (Town)—Washington FL-2
Echo (Township)—Antrim MI-3
Echo (City)—Yellow Medicine MN-3
Echo (Township)—Yellow Medicine MN-3
Echo (City)—Umatilla OR-4
Echols County GA-2
Eckelson (Township)—Barnes ND-4
Eckford (Township)—Calhoun MI-3
Eckles (Township)—Beltrami MN-3
Eckley (Town)—Yuma CO-4
Ecklund (Township)—Burleigh ND-4
Eckvoll (Township)—Marshall MN-3
Eclectic (Town)—Elmore AL-2
Economy (Town)—Wayne IN-3
Economy (Township)—McLean ND-4
Economy (Borough)—Beaver PA-1

Ecorse (City)—Wayne MI-3
Ecru (Town)—Pontotoc MS-2
Ector (Town)—Fannin TX-2
Ector County TX-2
Edcouch (City)—Hidalgo TX-2
Eddington (Town)—Penobscot ME-1
Eddy (Township)—Clearwater MN-3
Eddy (Township)—Eddy ND-4
Eddy County NM-4
Eddy County ND-4
Eddystone (Borough)—Delaware PA-1
Eddyville (Village)—Pope IL-3
Eddyville (City)—Mahaska IA-3
Eddyville (City)—Monroe IA-3
Eddyville (City)—Wapello IA-3
Eddyville (City)—Lyon KY-2
Eddyville (Village)—Dawson NE-4
Eden (City)—Jerome ID-4
Eden (Township)—La Salle IL-3
Eden (Township)—Lagrange IN-3
Eden (Township)—Ness KS-4
Eden (Township)—Sumner KS-4
Eden (Township)—Lake MI-3
Eden (Township)—Mason MI-3
Eden (Township)—Brown MN-3
Eden (Township)—Pipestone MN-3
Eden (Township)—Polk MN-3
Eden (Village)—Yazoo MS-2
Eden (Township)—Antelope NE-4
Eden (Town)—Erie NY-1
Eden (City)—Rockingham NC-2
Eden (Township)—Walsh ND-4
Eden (Township)—Licking OH-3
Eden (Township)—Seneca OH-3
Eden (Township)—Wyandot OH-3
Eden (Township)—Lancaster PA-1
Eden (Township)—Clark SD-4
Eden (Township)—Codington SD-4
Eden (Township)—Lincoln SD-4
Eden (Town)—Marshall SD-4
Eden (Township)—Marshall SD-4
Eden (City)—Concho TX-2
Eden (Town)—Lamoille VT-1
Eden (Town)—Fond du Lac WI-3
Eden (Village)—Fond du Lac WI-3
Eden (Town)—Iowa WI-3
Edendale (Township)—Steele ND-4
Eden Isle (CDP)—St. Tammany Parish LA-2
Eden Lake (Township)—Stearns MN-3
Eden Prairie (City)—Hennepin MN-3
Edens (Township)—Gregory SD-4
Edenton (Town)—Chowan NC-2
Eden Valley (City)—Meeker MN-3
Eden Valley (City)—Stearns MN-3
Eden Valley (Township)—Renville ND-4
Edenville (Township)—Midland MI-3
Edford (Township)—Henry IL-3
Edgar (Township)—Edgar IL-3
Edgar (City)—Clay NE-4
Edgar (Township)—Clay NE-4
Edgar (Village)—Marathon WI-3
Edgar County IL-3
Edgard (CDP)—St. John the Baptist Parish LA-2
Edgar Springs (City)—Phelps MO-3
Edgartown (Town)—Dukes MA-1
Edgecliff (Village)—Tarrant TX-2
Edgecomb (Town)—Lincoln ME-1
Edgecombe County NC-2
Edgefield (Village)—Red River Parish LA-2
Edgefield (Town)—Edgefield SC-2
Edgefield County SC-2

Edge Hill (City)—Glascock GA-2
Edgeley (City)—LaMoure ND-4
Edgemere (CDP)—Baltimore MD-1
Edgemont (Township)—Sheridan ND-4
Edgemont (City)—Fall River SD-4
Edgemont Park (CDP)—Ingham MI-3
Edgemoor (CDP)—New Castle DE-1
Edgerton (City)—Johnson KS-4
Edgerton (City)—Pipestone MN-3
Edgerton (City)—Platte MO-3
Edgerton (Village)—Williams OH-3
Edgerton (Township)—Hanson SD-4
Edgerton (Township)—Rock WI-3
Edgerton (Town)—Natrona WY-4
Edgewater (City)—Jefferson CO-4
Edgewater (City)—Volusia FL-2
Edgewater (Borough)—Bergen NJ-1
Edgewater (Town)—Sawyer WI-3
Edgewater Park (Township)—Burlington NJ-1
Edgewood (City)—Orange FL-2
Edgewood (Village)—Effingham IL-3
Edgewood (Town)—Madison IN-3
Edgewood (City)—Clayton IA-3
Edgewood (City)—Delaware IA-3
Edgewood (City)—Kenton KY-2
Edgewood (Mil. facil.)—Harford MD-1
Edgewood (CDP)—Santa Fe NM-4
Edgewood (CDP)—Torrance NM-4
Edgewood (CDP)—Ashtabula OH-3
Edgewood (Borough)—Allegheny PA-1
Edgewood (CDP)—Northumberland PA-1
Edgewood (Town)—Van Zandt TX-2
Edgewood-North Hill (CDP)—Pierce WA-4
Edgeworth (Borough)—Allegheny PA-1
Edgington (Township)—Rock Island IL-3
Edgmont (Township)—Delaware PA-1
Edina (City)—Hennepin MN-3
Edina (City)—Knox MO-3
Edinboro (Borough)—Erie PA-1
Edinburg (Village)—Christian IL-3
Edinburg (Town)—Penobscot ME-1
Edinburg (Town)—Saratoga NY-1
Edinburg (City)—Walsh ND-4
Edinburg (Township)—Portage OH-3
Edinburg (City)—Hidalgo TX-2
Edinburg (Town)—Shenandoah VA-2
Edinburgh (Town)—Bartholomew IN-3
Edinburgh (Town)—Johnson IN-3
Edison (City)—Calhoun GA-2
Edison (Township)—Swift MN-3
Edison (Village)—Furnas NE-4
Edison (Township)—Middlesex NJ-1
Edison (Village)—Morrow OH-3
Edison (Township)—Minnehaha SD-4
Edisto (CDP)—Orangeburg SC-2
Edisto Beach (Town)—Colleton SC-2
Edmeston (Town)—Otsego NY-1
Edmond (City)—Norton KS-4
Edmond (City)—Oklahoma OK-2
Edmonds (City)—Snohomish WA-4
Edmondson (Town)—Crittenden AR-2
Edmonson (Town)—Hale TX-2
Edmonson County KY-2
Edmonston (Town)—Prince George's MD-1
Edmonton (City)—Metcalfe KY-2
Edmore (Village)—Montcalm MI-3
Edmore (City)—Ramsey ND-4
Edmunds (Township)—Stutsman ND-4
Edmunds County SD-4
Edmundson (Village)—St. Louis MO-3

Entry	Location
Edna (City)—Labette	KS-4
Edna (Township)—Otter Tail	MN-3
Edna (Township)—Barnes	ND-4
Edna (City)—Jackson	TX-2
Edna Bay (CDP)—Prince of Wales-Outer Ketchikan Census Area	AK-4
Edom (City)—Van Zandt	TX-2
Edon (Village)—Williams	OH-3
Edson (Town)—Chippewa	WI-3
Edwards (Township)—Ogemaw	MI-3
Edwards (Township)—Kandiyohi	MN-3
Edwards (Town)—Hinds	MS-2
Edwards (Town)—St. Lawrence	NY-1
Edwards (Village)—St. Lawrence	NY-1
Edwards Air Force Base (CA)	Mil-4
Edwards Air Force Base (Military Facility)—Kern	CA-4
Edwardsburg (Village)—Cass	MI-3
Edwards County	IL-3
Edwards County	KS-4
Edwards County	TX-2
Edwardsport (Town)—Knox	IN-3
Edwardsville (Town)—Cleburne	AL-2
Edwardsville (City)—Madison	IL-3
Edwardsville (Township)—Madison	IL-3
Edwardsville (City)—Wyandotte	KS-4
Edwardsville (Borough)—Luzerne	PA-1
Eek (City)—Bethel Census Area	AK-4
Eel (Township)—Cass	IN-3
Eel River (Township)—Allen	IN-3
Eel River (Township)—Hendricks	IN-3
Effie (City)—Itasca	MN-3
Effie (Pop. Place)—Itasca	MN-3
Effingham (City)—Effingham	IL-3
Effingham (City)—Atchison	KS-4
Effingham (Town)—Carroll	NH-1
Effingham County	GA-2
Effingham County	IL-3
Effington (Township)—Otter Tail	MN-3
Egan (Township)—Mountrail	ND-4
Egan (City)—Moody	SD-4
Egan (Township)—Moody	SD-4
Egegik (CDP)—Lake and Peninsula Borough	AK-4
Egeland (City)—Towner	ND-4
Egeland (Township)—Day	SD-4
Egelston (Township)—Muskegon	MI-3
Egg Creek (Township)—McHenry	ND-4
Egg Harbor (Township)—Atlantic	NJ-1
Egg Harbor (Town)—Door	WI-3
Egg Harbor (Village)—Door	WI-3
Egg Harbor City (City)—Atlantic	NJ-1
Eglin Air Force Base (FL)	Mil-4
Eglin Air Force Base (Mil. facil.)—Okaloosa	FL-2
Eglon (Township)—Clay	MN-3
Egremont (Town)—Berkshire	MA-1
Egypt (Town)—Craighead	AR-2
Egypt (Township)—Carroll	MO-3
Egypt Lake (CDP)—Hillsborough	FL-2
Ehrenberg (CDP)—La Paz	AZ-4
Ehrenfeld (Borough)—Cambria	PA-1
Ehrhardt (Town)—Bamberg	SC-2
Eidsvold (Township)—Lyon	MN-3
Eidsvold (Township)—Bottineau	ND-4
Eielson Air Force Base (Military Facility)—Fairbanks North Star Borough	AK-4
Eileen (Town)—Bayfield	WI-3
Eisenstein (Town)—Price	WI-3
Eitzen (City)—Houston	MN-3
Ekalaka (Town)—Carter	MT-4
Ekron (City)—Meade	KY-2
Ekwok (City)—Dillingham Census Area	AK-4
Ela (Township)—Lake	IL-3
Elaine (City)—Phillips	AR-2
Eland (Village)—Shawano	WI-3
Elba (City)—Coffee	AL-2
Elba (Township)—Knox	IL-3
Elba (Township)—Gratiot	MI-3
Elba (Township)—Lapeer	MI-3
Elba (City)—Winona	MN-3
Elba (Township)—Winona	MN-3
Elba (Village)—Howard	NE-4
Elba (Town)—Genesee	NY-1
Elba (Village)—Genesee	NY-1
Elba (Town)—Dodge	WI-3
Elberfeld (Town)—Warrick	IN-3
Elberon (City)—Tama	IA-3
Elbert, Mt. (CO)	Geog-4
Elberta (Town)—Baldwin	AL-2
Elberta (Village)—Benzie	MI-3
Elbert County	CO-4
Elbert County	GA-2
Elberton (City)—Elbert	GA-2
Elbing (City)—Butler	KS-4
Elbow Lake (City)—Grant	MN-3
Elbow Lake (Township)—Grant	MN-3
Elbridge (Township)—Edgar	IL-3
Elbridge (Township)—Oceana	MI-3
Elbridge (Town)—Onondaga	NY-1
Elbridge (Village)—Onondaga	NY-1
Elburn (Village)—Kane	IL-3
El Cajon (City)—San Diego	CA-4
El Campo (City)—Wharton	TX-2
El Cenizo (City)—Webb	TX-2
El Centro (City)—Imperial	CA-4
El Centro Naval Air Facility (CA)	Mil-4
El Cerrito (City)—Contra Costa	CA-4
El Cerrito (CDP)—Riverside	CA-4
Elcho (Town)—Langlade	WI-3
Elco (Borough)—Washington	PA-1
El Dara (Village)—Pike	IL-3
Elden (Township)—Dickey	ND-4
Elder (Township)—Cambria	PA-1
Elderon (Town)—Marathon	WI-3
Elderon (Village)—Marathon	WI-3
Eldersburg (CDP)—Carroll	MD-1
Elderton (Borough)—Armstrong	PA-1
Eldon (City)—Wapello	IA-3
Eldon (City)—Miller	MO-3
Eldon (Township)—Benson	ND-4
Eldora (City)—Hardin	IA-3
El Dorado (City)—Union	AR-2
Eldorado (Township)—McDonough	IL-3
Eldorado (City)—Saline	IL-3
El Dorado (City)—Butler	KS-4
El Dorado (Township)—Butler	KS-4
Eldorado (Town)—Dorchester	MD-1
Eldorado (Township)—Stevens	MN-3
Eldorado (Township)—Clay	NE-4
Eldorado (Township)—Harlan	NE-4
Eldorado (Township)—Traill	ND-4
Eldorado (Village)—Preble	OH-3
Eldorado (Town)—Jackson	OK-2
Eldorado (Town)—Schleicher	TX-2
Eldorado (Town)—Fond du Lac	WI-3
Eldorado at Santa Fe (CDP)—Santa Fe	NM-4
El Dorado County	CA-4
El Dorado Hills (CDP)—El Dorado	CA-4
El Dorado Springs (City)—Cedar	MO-3
Eldred (Village)—Greene	IL-3
Eldred (Township)—Cass	ND-4
Eldred (Township)—Jefferson	PA-1
Eldred (Township)—Lycoming	PA-1
Eldred (Borough)—McKean	PA-1
Eldred (Township)—McKean	PA-1
Eldred (Township)—Monroe	PA-1
Eldred (Township)—Schuylkill	PA-1
Eldred (Township)—Warren	PA-1
Eldridge (Town)—Walker	AL-2
Eldridge (CDP)—Sonoma	CA-4
Eldridge (City)—Scott	IA-3
Eldridge (Township)—Laclede	MO-3
Eldridge (Township)—Stutsman	ND-4
Eleanor (Town)—Putnam	WV-2
Electra (City)—Wichita	TX-2
Electric City (Town)—Grant	WA-4
Eleele (CDP)—Kauai	HI-4
Eleva (Village)—Trempealeau	WI-3
Elfers (CDP)—Pasco	FL-2
Elfin Cove (CDP)—Skagway-Hoonah-Angoon Census Area	AK-4
Elgin (City)—Cook	IL-3
Elgin (City)—Kane	IL-3
Elgin (Township)—Kane	IL-3
Elgin (City)—Fayette	IA-3
Elgin (City)—Chautauqua	KS-4
Elgin (City)—Wabasha	MN-3
Elgin (Township)—Wabasha	MN-3
Elgin (City)—Antelope	NE-4
Elgin (Township)—Antelope	NE-4
Elgin (Township)—Cavalier	ND-4
Elgin (City)—Grant	ND-4
Elgin (Village)—Van Wert	OH-3
Elgin (Town)—Comanche	OK-2
Elgin (City)—Union	OR-4
Elgin (Borough)—Erie	PA-1
Elgin (Town)—Kershaw	SC-2
Elgin (CDP)—Lancaster	SC-2
Elgin (City)—Bastrop	TX-2
El Granada (CDP)—San Mateo	CA-4
Elida (Town)—Roosevelt	NM-4
Elida (Village)—Allen	OH-3
Elim (City)—Nome Census Area	AK-4
Elim (Township)—Custer	NE-4
Elim (CDP)—Cambria	PA-1
Eliot (Town)—York	ME-1
Eliza (Township)—Mercer	IL-3
Elizabeth (Town)—Elbert	CO-4
Elizabeth (Township)—Jo Daviess	IL-3
Elizabeth (Village)—Jo Daviess	IL-3
Elizabeth (Town)—Harrison	IN-3
Elizabeth (Town)—Allen Parish	LA-2
Elizabeth (City)—Otter Tail	MN-3
Elizabeth (Township)—Otter Tail	MN-3
Elizabeth (City)—Union	NJ-1
Elizabeth (Township)—Lawrence	OH-3
Elizabeth (Township)—Miami	OH-3
Elizabeth (Borough)—Allegheny	PA-1
Elizabeth (Township)—Allegheny	PA-1
Elizabeth (Township)—Lancaster	PA-1
Elizabeth (Town)—Wirt	WV-2
Elizabeth City (City)—Camden	NC-2
Elizabeth City (City)—Pasquotank	NC-2
Elizabethton (City)—Carter	TN-2
Elizabethtown (Village)—Hardin	IL-3
Elizabethtown (Town)—Bartholomew	IN-3
Elizabethtown (City)—Hardin	KY-2
Elizabethtown (Town)—Essex	NY-1

General Index

Elizabethtown (Town)—Bladen NC-2
Elizabethtown (Borough)—
Lancaster...PA-1
Elizabethville (Borough)—
Dauphin PA-1
El Jebel (CDP)—Eagle CO-4
Elk (Township)—Jackson IL-3
Elk (Township)—Cloud KS-4
Elk (Township)—Osage KS-4
Elk (Township)—Lake MI-3
Elk (Township)—Sanilac MI-3
Elk (Township)—Nobles..................... MN-3
Elk (Township)—Stoddard MO-3
Elk (Township)—Saunders NE-4
Elk (Township)—Gloucester NJ-1
Elk (Township)—McKenzie ND-4
Elk (Township)—Noble OH-3
Elk (Township)—Vinton OH-3
Elk (Township)—Chester PA-1
Elk (Township)—Clarion PA-1
Elk (Township)—Tioga PA-1
Elk (Township)—Warren PA-1
Elk (Town)—Price WI-3
Elkader (City)—Clayton......................IA-3
Elkader (Township)—Logan................KS-4
Elk City (City)—Montgomery...........KS-4
Elk City (City)—Beckham................. OK-2
Elk County KS-4
Elk County PA-1
Elk Creek (Township)—Republic....KS-4
Elk Creek (Township)—Wright..... MO-3
Elk Creek (Township)—Custer NE-4
Elk Creek (Village)—Johnson NE-4
Elk Creek (Township)—Golden
Valley.. ND-4
Elk Creek (Township)—Erie PA-1
Elk Falls (City)—Elk.......................... KS-4
Elk Falls (Township)—Elk................. KS-4
Elk Fork (Township)—Pettis......... MO-3
Elk Garden (Town)—Mineral WV-3
Elk Grove (CDP)—Sacramento CA-4
Elk Grove (Township)—Cook....... IL-3
Elk Grove (Town)—Lafayette WI-3
Elk Grove Village (Village)—
Cook... IL-3
Elk Grove Village (Village)—
DuPage.. IL-3
Elkhart (Township)—Logan IL-3
Elkhart (Village)—Logan.................. IL-3
Elkhart (City)—Elkhart..................... IN-3
Elkhart (Township)—Elkhart IN-3
Elkhart (Township)—Noble IN-3
Elkhart (City)—Polk..........................IA-3
Elkhart (City)—Morton.................... KS-4
Elkhart (Township)—Bates MO-3
Elkhart (Town)—Anderson TX-2
Elkhart County IN-3
Elkhart Lake (Village)—
Sheboygan.. WI-3
Elkhorn (CDP)—Monterey CA-4
Elkhorn (Township)—Brown IL-3
Elk Horn (City)—Shelby IA-3
Elkhorn (Township)—Lincoln......... KS-4
Elk Horn (Township)—
McDonald...MO-3
Elkhorn (Township)—Cuming NE-4
Elkhorn (Township)—Dodge.......... NE-4
Elkhorn (City)—Douglas.................. NE-4
Elkhorn (Township)—Divide.......... ND-4
Elkhorn (City)—Walworth............... WI-3
Elkhorn City (City)—Pike............... KY-2
Elkhorn Grove (Township)—
Carroll... IL-3
Elkin (Town)—Surry NC-2
Elkin (Town)—Wilkes NC-2

Elkins (Town)—Washington............ AR-2
Elkins (City)—Randolph................... WV-2
Elk Lake (Township)—Grant MN-3
Elkland (Township)—Tuscola MI-3
Elkland (Township)—Sullivan PA-1
Elkland (Borough)—Tioga............... PA-1
Elkland (Township)—Tioga PA-1
Elk Lick (Township)—Somerset... PA-1
Elkmont (Town)—Limestone........ AL-2
Elk Mound (Town)—Dunn WI-3
Elk Mound (Village)—Dunn WI-3
Elkmount (Township)—Grand
Forks ND-4
Elk Mountain (Town)—Carbon WY-4
Elko (City)—Scott MN-3
Elko (City)—Elko NV-4
Elko (Town)—Barnwell SC-2
Elko County NV-4
Elk Park (Town)—Avery NC-2
Elk Plain (CDP)—Pierce WA-4
Elk Point (City)—Union SD-4
Elk Point (Township)—Union SD-4
Elkport (City)—Clayton IA-3
Elk Prairie (Township)—Jefferson.. IL-3
Elk Rapids (Township)—Antrim ... MI-3
Elk Rapids (Village)—Antrim MI-3
Elkridge (CDP)—Howard MD-1
Elk Ridge (Town)—Utah.................. UT-4
Elk River (City)—Clearwater........... ID-4
Elk River (City)—Sherburne.......... MN-3
Elk River East (Township)—
McDonald MO-3
Elk River West (Township)—
McDonald MO-3
Elkrun (Township)—Columbiana ..OH-3
Elk Run Heights (City)—Black
Hawk IA-3
Elkton (City)—Todd........................ KY-2
Elkton (Town)—Cecil MD-1
Elkton (Village)—Huron MI-3
Elkton (Township)—Clay MN-3
Elkton (City)—Mower MN-3
Elkton (City)—Douglas OR-4
Elkton (City)—Brookings................ SD-4
Elkton (Township)—Brookings SD-4
Elkton (Town)—Giles....................... TN-2
Elkton (Town)—Rockingham......... VA-2
Elk Valley Rancheria (CA) IndRes-4
Elkview (CDP)—Kanawha............. WV-2
Elkville (Village)—Jackson.............. IL-3
El Lago (City)—Harris TX-2
Ellaville (City)—Schley GA-2
Ellenboro (Town)—Rutherford .NC-2
Ellenboro (Town)—Ritchie WV-2
Ellenboro (Town)—Grant................ WI-3
Ellenburg (Town)—Clinton NY-1
Ellendale (Town)—Sussex DE-1
Ellendale (City)—Steele................... MN-3
Ellendale (City)—Dickey.................. ND-4
Ellendale (Township)—Dickey....... ND-4
Ellensburg (City)—Kittitas.............. WA-4
Ellenton (CDP)—Manatee FL-2
Ellenton (Town)—Colquitt............. GA-2
Ellenville (Village)—Ulster NY-1
Ellerbe (Town)—Richmond NC-2
Ellery (Town)—Chautauqua........... NY-1
Ellettsville (Town)—Monroe.......... IN-3
Ellicott (Town)—Chautauqua NY-1
Ellicott City (CDP)—Howard....... MD-1
Ellicottville (Town)—Cattaraugus.. NY-1
Ellicottville (Village)—
Cattaraugus.....................................NY-1
Ellijay (City)—Gilmer GA-2
Elling (Township)—Pierce...............ND-4
Ellington (Town)—Tolland............. CT-1

Ellington (Township)—Adams IL-3
Ellington (Township)—Tuscola MI-3
Ellington (Township)—Dodge... MN-3
Ellington (City)—Reynolds MO-3
Ellington (Town)—Chautauqua NY-1
Ellington (Town)—Outagamie WI-3
Ellinwood (City)—Barton KS-3
Elliott (Village)—Ford IL-3
Elliott (City)—Montgomery IA-3
Elliott (City)—Ransom..................... ND-4
Elliott (Township)—Ransom...........ND-4
Elliott (Township)—Sanborn SD-4
Elliott County KY-2
Ellis (City)—Ellis KS-4
Ellis (Township)—Ellis......................KS-4
Ellis (Township)—Cheboygan MI-3
Ellisburg (Town)—Jefferson NY-1
Ellisburg (Village)—Jefferson......... NY-1
Ellis County..KS-4
Ellis County..OK-2
Ellis County TX-2
Ellis Grove (Village)—Randolph IL-3
Ellis Island (NY)............................ Geog-4
Ellison (Township)—Warren IL-3
Elliston (Township)—Tripp.............. SD-4
Elliston-Lafayette (CDP)—
Montgomery VA-2
Ellisville (Township)—Fulton......... IL-3
Ellisville (Village)—Fulton............... IL-3
Ellisville (City)—Jones.....................MS-2
Ellisville (City)—St. Louis MO-3
Ellisville (Township)—Williams..... ND-4
Ellisville (Township)—Faulk SD-4
Elloree (Town)—Orangeburg............SC-2
Ellport (Borough)—Lawrence PA-1
Ellsborough (Township)—
Murray...MN-3
Ellsburg (Township)—St. Louis MN-3
Ellsbury (Township)—Barnes..........ND-4
Ellsinore (Town)—Carter MO-3
Ellston (City)—Ringgold IA-3
Ellston (Township)—Gregory......... SD-4
Ellsworth (Village)—McLean IL-3
Ellsworth (City)—Hamilton IA-3
Ellsworth (City)—Ellsworth...........KS-4
Ellsworth (Township)—Ellsworth ...KS-4
Ellsworth (City)—Hancock ME-1
Ellsworth (Village)—Antrim MI-3
Ellsworth (Township)—Lake MI-3
Ellsworth (Township)—Meeker.... MN-3
Ellsworth (City)—Nobles MN-3
Ellsworth (Township)—Antelope .. NE-4
Ellsworth (Town)—Grafton............ NH-1
Ellsworth (Township)
Mahoning OH-3
Ellsworth (Borough)—Washington.. PA-1
Ellsworth (Town)—Pierce............... WI-3
Ellsworth (Village)—Pierce WI-3
Ellsworth Air Force Base (SD) Mil-4
Ellsworth Air Force Base (Military
Facility)—Meade SD-4
Ellsworth Air Force Base (Military
Facility)—Pennington.................... SD-4
Ellsworth County................................KS-4
Ellsworth North (CDP)—Clark...... WA-4
Ellsworth South (CDP)—Clark WA-4
Ellwood City (Borough)—Beaver.... PA-1
Ellwood City (Borough)—
Lawrence.. PA-1
Elm (Township)—Allen KS-4
Elm (Township)—Putnam MO-3
Elm (Township)—Antelope NE-4
Elm (Township)—Gage NE-4
Elm (Township)—Dickey ND-4
Elm (Township)—Grant ND-4

Elma (City)—Howard IA-3
Elma (Town)—Erie NY-1
Elma (Township)—Richland ND-4
Elma (City)—Grays Harbor WA-4
Elm City (Town)—Wilson NC-2
Elm Creek (Township)—Marshall ... KS-4
Elm Creek (Township)—Saline KS-4
Elm Creek (Township)—Martin ... MN-3
Elm Creek (Township)—Buffalo NE-4
Elm Creek (Village)—Buffalo NE-4
Elmdale (City)—Chase KS-4
Elmdale (City)—Morrison MN-3
Elmdale (Township)—Morrison MN-3
Elmdale (Township)—Ward ND-4
Elmendaro (Township)—Lyon KS-4
Elmendorf (City)—Bexar TX-2
Elmendorf Air Force Base (AK) Mil-4
Elmer (Township)—Oscoda MI-3
Elmer (Township)—Sanilac MI-3
Elmer (Township)—Pipestone MN-3
Elmer (Township)—St. Louis MN-3
Elmer (City)—Macon MO-3
Elmer (Borough)—Salem NJ-1
Elmer (Town)—Jackson OK-2
Elmer City (Town)—Okanogan WA-4
Elm Grove (Township)—Tazewell .. IL-3
Elm Grove (Township)—Labette KS-4
Elm Grove (Township)—Grand
  Forks ND-4
Elm Grove (Village)—Waukesha ... WI-3
Elmhurst (City)—DuPage IL-3
Elmhurst (Township)—
  Lackawanna PA-1
Elmira (Township)—Stark IL-3
Elmira (Township)—Otsego MI-3
Elmira (Township)—Olmsted MN-3
Elmira (Village)—Ray MO-3
Elmira (City)—Chemung NY-1
Elmira (Town)—Chemung NY-1
Elmira (Township)—Codington SD-4
El Mirage (Town)—Maricopa AZ-4
Elmira Heights (Village)—
  Chemung NY-1
Elm Mills (Township)—Barber KS-4
Elmo (Township)—Otter Tail MN-3
Elmo (City)—Nodaway MO-3
Elmo (Town)—Emery UT-4
Elmont (CDP)—Nassau NY-1
El Monte (City)—Los Angeles CA-4
Elmore (Township)—Daviess IN-3
Elmore (City)—Faribault MN-3
Elmore (Township)—Faribault MN-3
Elmore (Village)—Ottawa OH-3
Elmore (Town)—Lamoille VT-1
Elmore City (Town)—Garvin OK-2
Elmore County AL-2
Elmore County ID-4
Elm River (Township)—Wayne IL-3
Elm River (Township)—
  Houghton MI-3
Elm River (Township)—Traill ND-4
Elms (Township)—Bottineau ND-4
Elmsford (Village)—Westchester ... NY-1
Elm Springs (Town)—
  Washington AR-2
Elm Tree (Township)—
  McKenzie ND-4
Elmwood (City)—Peoria IL-3
Elmwood (Township)—Peoria IL-3
Elmwood (Township)—Leelanau ... MI-3
Elmwood (Township)—Tuscola ... MI-3
Elmwood (Township)—Clay MN-3
Elmwood (Township)—Saline MO-3
Elmwood (Village)—Cass NE-4

Elmwood (Township)—Golden
  Valley ND-4
Elmwood (Village)—Pierce WI-3
Elmwood Park (Village)—Cook IL-3
Elmwood Park (Borough)—
  Bergen NJ-1
Elmwood Park (Village)—Racine .. WI-3
Elmwood Place (Village)—
  Hamilton OH-3
Elnora (Town)—Daviess IN-3
Elon College (Town)—Alamance ... NC-2
Elora (Township)—Pembina ND-4
Eloy (City)—Pinal AZ-4
El Paso (City)—Woodford IL-3
El Paso (Township)—Woodford IL-3
El Paso (City)—El Paso TX-2
El Paso (Town)—Pierce WI-3
El Paso County CO-4
El Paso County TX-2
El Paso de Robles (Paso Robles)
  (City)—San Luis Obispo CA-4
El Portal (Village)—Dade FL-2
El Reno (City)—Canadian OK-2
El Rio (CDP)—Ventura CA-4
Elrod (Township)—Clark SD-4
Elrosa (City)—Stearns MN-3
Elroy (CDP)—Wayne NC-2
Elroy (City)—Juneau WI-3
Elsa (City)—Hidalgo TX-2
Elsah (Town)—Jersey IL-3
Elsah (Township)—Jersey IL-3
Elsberry (City)—Lincoln MO-3
El Segundo (City)—Los Angeles CA-4
Elsie (Village)—Clinton MI-3
Elsie (Village)—Perkins NE-4
Elsinboro (Township)—Salem NJ-1
Elsinore (Town)—Sevier UT-4
Elsmere (Town)—New Castle DE-1
Elsmere (City)—Kenton KY-2
Elsmore (City)—Allen KS-4
Elsmore (Township)—Allen KS-4
El Sobrante (CDP)—Contra
  Costa CA-4
Elton (Town)—Jefferson Davis
  Parish LA-2
El Toro (CDP)—Orange CA-4
El Toro Marine Corps Air Station
  (CA) Mil-4
El Toro Station (Military Facility)—
  Orange CA-4
Elvaston (Village)—Hancock IL-3
El Verano (CDP)—Sonoma CA-4
Elverson (Borough)—Chester PA-1
Elverum (Township)—Pierce ND-4
Elvins (City)—St. Francois MO-3
Elvira (Township)—Buffalo SD-4
Elwood (Township)—Vermilion IL-3
Elwood (Village)—Will IL-3
Elwood (City)—Madison IN-3
Elwood (City)—Tipton IN-3
Elwood (Township)—Barber KS-4
Elwood (City)—Doniphan KS-4
Elwood (Village)—Gosper NE-4
Elwood (CDP)—Suffolk NY-1
Elwood (Town)—Box Elder UT-4
Elwood-Magnolia (CDP)—
  Atlantic NJ-1
Ely (City)—Linn IA-3
Ely (Township)—Marquette MI-3
Ely (City)—St. Louis MN-3
Ely (City)—White Pine NV-4
Ely Colony (NV) IndRes-4
Elyria (Township)—Valley NE-4
Elyria (Village)—Valley NE-4
Elyria (City)—Lorain OH-3

Elyria (Township)—Lorain OH-3
Elysburg (CDP)—
  Northumberland PA-1
Elysian (City)—Le Sueur MN-3
Elysian (Township)—Le Sueur MN-3
Elysian (City)—Waseca MN-3
Elysian (Township)—Bottineau ... ND-4
Emanuel County GA-2
Emardville (Township)—Red
  Lake MN-3
Embarrass (Township)—Edgar IL-3
Embarrass (Township)—St.
  Louis MN-3
Embarrass (Village)—Waupaca WI-3
Embden (Town)—Somerset ME-1
Emden (Village)—Logan IL-3
Emelle (Municipality)—Sumter AL-2
Emerado (City)—Grand Forks ND-4
Emerald (Township)—Faribault ... MN-3
Emerald (Township)—Paulding ... OH-3
Emerald (Town)—St. Croix WI-3
Emerald Beach (Village)—Barry ... MO-3
Emerald Isle (Town)—Carteret NC-2
Emerald Lake Hills (CDP)—San
  Mateo CA-4
Emerson (Town)—Columbia AR-2
Emerson (City)—Bartow GA-2
Emerson (City)—Mills IA-3
Emerson (Township)—Gratiot MI-3
Emerson (Village)—Dakota NE-4
Emerson (Township)—Dixon NE-4
Emerson (Village)—Dixon NE-4
Emerson (Township)—Harlan NE-4
Emerson (Village)—Thurston NE-4
Emerson (Borough)—Bergen NJ-1
Emerson (Township)—Faulk SD-4
Emery (City)—Hanson SD-4
Emery (Township)—McCook SD-4
Emery (Town)—Emery UT-4
Emery (Town)—Price WI-3
Emery County UT-4
Emeryville (City)—Alameda CA-4
Emhouse (Town)—Navarro TX-2
Emigsville (CDP)—York PA-1
Emily (City)—Crow Wing MN-3
Eminence (Township)—Logan IL-3
Eminence (City)—Henry KY-2
Eminence (City)—Shannon MO-3
Eminence (Township)—Shannon .. MO-3
Emington (Village)—Livingston IL-3
Emlenton (Borough)—Clarion PA-1
Emlenton (Borough)—Venango PA-1
Emma (Township)—White IL-3
Emma (Township)—Harvey KS-4
Emma (City)—Lafayette MO-3
Emma (City)—Saline MO-3
Emmaus (Borough)—Lehigh PA-1
Emmet (City)—Hempstead AR-2
Emmet (City)—Nevada AR-2
Emmet (Township)—McDonough .. IL-3
Emmet (Township)—Renville MN-3
Emmet (Township)—Holt NE-4
Emmet (Village)—Holt NE-4
Emmet (Township)—Union SD-4
Emmet (Town)—Dodge WI-3
Emmet (Town)—Marathon WI-3
Emmet County IA-3
Emmet County MI-3
Emmetsburg (City)—Palo Alto IA-3
Emmett (City)—Gem ID-4
Emmett (City)—Pottawatomie KS-4
Emmett (Township)—
  Pottawatomie KS-4
Emmett (Township)—Calhoun MI-3
Emmett (Township)—St. Clair MI-3

Emmett (Village)—St. Clair *MI-3*
Emmitsburg (Town)—Frederick .. *MD-1*
Emmonak (City)—Wade Hampton
  Census Area *AK-4*
Emmons (City)—Freeborn *MN-3*
Emmons County *ND-4*
Emory (City)—Rains *TX-2*
Emory-Meadow View (CDP)—
  Washington *VA-2*
Empire (Town)—Clear Creek *CO-4*
Empire (Township)—McLean *IL-3*
Empire (Township)—Ellsworth *KS-4*
Empire (Township)—McPherson ... *KS-4*
Empire (CDP)—Plaquemines
  Parish *LA-2*
Empire (Township)—Leelanau *MI-3*
Empire (Village)—Leelanau *MI-3*
Empire (Township)—Dakota *MN-3*
Empire (Township)—Andrew *MO-3*
Empire (Township)—Cass *ND-4*
Empire (Village)—Jefferson *OH-3*
Empire (Town)—Fond du Lac *WI-3*
Empire City (Town)—Stephens *OK-2*
Emporia (City)—Lyon *KS-4*
Emporia (Township)—Lyon *KS-4*
Emporia (Independent City) *VA-2*
Emporium (Borough)—Cameron .. *PA-1*
Emsworth (Borough)—Allegheny ... *PA-1*
Encantada-Ranchito El Calabo (CDP)—
  Cameron *TX-2*
Enchanted Oaks (Town)—
  Henderson *TX-2*
Encinal (City)—La Salle *TX-2*
Encinitas (City)—San Diego *CA-4*
Encino (Village)—Torrance *NM-4*
Encino *See* **Los Angeles**—Los
  Angeles *CA-4*
Endeavor (Village)—Marquette *WI-3*
Enderlin (City)—Cass *ND-4*
Enderlin (City)—Ransom *ND-4*
Endicott (Village)—Jefferson *NE-4*
Endicott (Village)—Broome *NY-1*
Endicott (Town)—Whitman *WA-4*
Endwell (CDP)—Broome *NY-1*
Energy (Village)—Williamson *IL-3*
Enfield (Town)—Hartford *CT-1*
Enfield (Township)—White *IL-3*
Enfield (Village)—White *IL-3*
Enfield (Town)—Penobscot *ME-1*
Enfield (Town)—Grafton *NH-1*
Enfield (Town)—Tompkins *NY-1*
Enfield (Town)—Halifax *NC-2*
Engelmann (Township)—St. Clair .. *IL-3*
Engelter (Township)—Morton *ND-4*
Enger (Township)—Steele *ND-4*
England (City)—Lonoke *AR-2*
Englewood (City)—Arapahoe *CO-4*
Englewood (CDP)—Charlotte *FL-2*
Englewood (CDP)—Sarasota *FL-2*
Englewood (City)—Clark *KS-4*
Englewood (Township)—Clark *KS-4*
Englewood (City)—Bergen *NJ-1*
Englewood (City)—Montgomery ... *OH-3*
Englewood (Township)—Perkins ... *SD-4*
Englewood (Town)—McMinn *TN-2*
Englewood Cliffs (Borough)—
  Bergen *NJ-1*
English (Township)—Jersey *IL-3*
English (Town)—Crawford *IN-3*
English Bay (CDP)—Kenai Peninsula
  Borough *AK-4*
Englishtown (Borough)—
  Monmouth *NJ-1*
Enid (City)—Garfield *OK-2*
Enigma (Town)—Berrien *GA-2*

Ennis (Town)—Madison *MT-4*
Ennis (City)—Ellis *TX-2*
Enoch (Township)—Noble *OH-3*
Enoch (City)—Iron *UT-4*
Enochville (CDP)—Rowan *NC-2*
Enola (Town)—Faulkner *AR-2*
Enola (CDP)—Cumberland *PA-1*
Enon (Village)—Clark *OH-3*
Enon Valley (Borough)—
  Lawrence *PA-1*
Enosburg (Town)—Franklin *VT-1*
Enosburg Falls (Village)—
  Franklin *VT-1*
Ensign (City)—Gray *KS-4*
Ensign (Township)—Delta *MI-3*
Ensign (Township)—Renville *ND-4*
Ensley (CDP)—Escambia *FL-2*
Ensley (Township)—Newaygo *MI-3*
Enstrom (Township)—Roseau *MN-3*
Enterprise (City)—Coffee *AL-2*
Enterprise (City)—Dale *AL-2*
Enterprise (City)—Dickinson *KS-4*
Enterprise (Township)—Ford *KS-4*
Enterprise (Township)—Reno *KS-4*
Enterprise (Township)—
  Missaukee *MI-3*
Enterprise (Township)—Jackson ... *MN-3*
Enterprise (Town)—Clarke *MS-2*
Enterprise (Township)—Linn *MO-3*
Enterprise (Township)—Valley *NE-4*
Enterprise (CDP)—Clark *NV-4*
Enterprise (Township)—Nelson *ND-4*
Enterprise (City)—Wallowa *OR-4*
Enterprise (Township)—Faulk *SD-4*
Enterprise (Township)—Moody *SD-4*
Enterprise (Township)—Roberts ... *SD-4*
Enterprise (City)—Washington *UT-4*
Enterprise (CDP)—Harrison *WV-2*
Enterprise (Town)—Oneida *WI-3*
Enterprise Rancheria (CA) *IndRes-4*
Entiat (Town)—Chelan *WA-4*
Enumclaw (City)—King *WA-4*
Enville (Town)—Chester *TN-2*
Enville (Town)—McNairy *TN-2*
Eolia (Village)—Pike *MO-3*
Epes (Town)—Sumter *AL-2*
Ephesus (Town)—Heard *GA-2*
Ephraim (City)—Sanpete *UT-4*
Ephraim (Village)—Door *WI-3*
Ephrata (Borough)—Lancaster *PA-1*
Ephrata (Township)—Lancaster ... *PA-1*
Ephrata (City)—Grant *WA-4*
Ephratah (Town)—Fulton *NY-1*
E (Plantation of) (Pop. Place)—
  Aroostook *ME-1*
Eppards Point (Township)—
  Livingston *IL-3*
Epping (Town)—Rockingham *NH-1*
Epping (City)—Williams *ND-4*
Epps (Village)—West Carroll
  Parish *LA-2*
Epps (Township)—Butler *MO-3*
Epsom (Town)—Merrimack *NH-1*
Epworth (City)—Dubuque *IA-3*
Equality (Township)—Gallatin *IL-3*
Equality (Village)—Gallatin *IL-3*
Equality (Township)—Red Lake ... *MN-3*
Equality (Township)—Miller *MO-3*
Equality (Township)—Williams ... *ND-4*
Erath (Town)—Vermilion Parish ... *LA-2*
Erath County *TX-2*
Erda (CDP)—Tooele *UT-4*
Erdahl (Township)—Grant *MN-3*
Erhard (City)—Otter Tail *MN-3*

Erhards Grove (Township)—Otter
  Tail *MN-3*
Erick (City)—Beckham *OK-2*
Ericson (Township)—Renville *MN-3*
Ericson (Village)—Wheeler *NE-4*
Erie (Town)—Boulder *CO-4*
Erie (Town)—Weld *CO-4*
Erie (Township)—Whiteside *IL-3*
Erie (Village)—Whiteside *IL-3*
Erie (Township)—Miami *IN-3*
Erie (City)—Neosho *KS-4*
Erie (Township)—Neosho *KS-4*
Erie (Township)—Sedgwick *KS-4*
Erie (Township)—Monroe *MI-3*
Erie (Township)—Becker *MN-3*
Erie (Township)—Cass *ND-4*
Erie (Township)—Ottawa *OH-3*
Erie (City)—Erie *PA-1*
Erie, Lake (NY) *Geog-4*
Erie County *NY-1*
Erie County *OH-3*
Erie County *PA-1*
Erie Goodman (Township)—
  McDonald *MO-3*
Erie McNatt (Township)—
  McDonald *MO-3*
Erienna (Township)—Grundy *IL-3*
Erin (Township)—Stephenson *IL-3*
Erin (Township)—Rice *MN-3*
Erin (Town)—Chemung *NY-1*
Erin (City)—Houston *TN-2*
Erin (Town)—Washington *WI-3*
Erin Prairie (Town)—St. Croix *WI-3*
Erin Springs (Town)—Garvin *OK-2*
Erlands Point-Kitsap Lake (CDP)—
  Kitsap *WA-4*
Erlanger (City)—Kenton *KY-2*
Erma (CDP)—Cape May *NJ-1*
Ernest (Township)—Dade *MO-3*
Ernest (Borough)—Indiana *PA-1*
Eros (Village)—Jackson Parish *LA-2*
Errol (Town)—Coos *NH-1*
Erskine (City)—Polk *MN-3*
Ervin (Township)—Howard *IN-3*
Ervin (Township)—Traill *ND-4*
Erving (Township)—Jewell *KS-4*
Erving (Town)—Franklin *MA-1*
Ervings Location (Pop. Place)—
  Coos *NH-1*
Erwin (Township)—Gogebic *MI-3*
Erwin (Town)—Steuben *NY-1*
Erwin (Town)—Harnett *NC-2*
Erwin (Town)—Kingsbury *SD-4*
Erwin (City)—Unicoi *TN-2*
Esbon (City)—Jewell *KS-4*
Esbon (Township)—Jewell *KS-4*
Escalante (Town)—Garfield *UT-4*
Escalon (City)—San Joaquin *CA-4*
Escambia County *AL-2*
Escambia County *FL-2*
Escanaba (City)—Delta *MI-3*
Escanaba (Township)—Delta *MI-3*
Escatawpa (CDP)—Jackson *MS-2*
Escobares (CDP)—Starr *TX-2*
Escondido (City)—San Diego *CA-4*
E-Six (Pop. Place)—Slope *ND-4*
Eskridge (City)—Wabaunsee *KS-4*
Esmen (Township)—Livingston ... *IL-3*
Esmeralda County *NV-4*
Esmond (City)—Benson *ND-4*
Esmond (Township)—Benson *ND-4*
Esmond (Township)—Kingsbury ... *SD-4*
Esopus (Town)—Ulster *NY-1*
Espanola (City)—Rio Arriba *NM-4*
Espanola (City)—Santa Fe *NM-4*

American Places Dictionary General Index

Esparto (CDP)—Yolo *CA-4*
Espelie (Township)—Marshall *MN-3*
Esperance (Town)—Schoharie *NY-1*
Esperance (Village)—Schoharie *NY-1*
Esperance (CDP)—Snohomish *WA-4*
Espy (CDP)—Columbia *PA-1*
Essex (Town)—Middlesex *CT-1*
Essex (Township)—Kankakee *IL-3*
Essex (Village)—Kankakee *IL-3*
Essex (Township)—Stark *IL-3*
Essex (City)—Page *IA-3*
Essex (CDP)—Baltimore *MD-1*
Essex (Town)—Essex *MA-1*
Essex (Township)—Clinton *MI-3*
Essex (City)—Stoddard *MO-3*
Essex (Town)—Essex *NY-1*
Essex (Town)—Chittenden *VT-1*
Essex County *MA-1*
Essex County *NJ-1*
Essex County *NY-1*
Essex County *VT-1*
Essex County *VA-2*
Essex Fells (Borough & Township)—
  Essex *NJ-1*
Essex Junction (Village)—
  Chittenden *VT-1*
Essexville (City)—Bay *MI-3*
Estabrook (Township)—Foster *ND-4*
Estacada (City)—Clackamas *OR-4*
Estancia (Town)—Torrance *NM-4*
Estella (Town)—Chippewa *WI-3*
Estelle (CDP)—Jefferson Parish *LA-2*
Estelline (City)—Hamlin *SD-4*
Estelline (Township)—Hamlin *SD-4*
Estelline (Town)—Hall *TX-2*
Estell Manor (City)—Atlantic *NJ-1*
Ester (CDP)—Fairbanks North Star
  Borough *AK-4*
Estero (CDP)—Lee *FL-2*
Estes Park (Town)—Larimer *CO-4*
Esther (Township)—Polk *MN-3*
Esther (City)—St. Francois *MO-3*
Estherville (City)—Emmet *IA-3*
Estherville (Township)—Burleigh .. *ND-4*
Estherwood (Village)—Acadia
  Parish *LA-2*
Estill (Town)—Hampton *SC-2*
Estill County *KY-2*
Estill Springs (Town)—Franklin *TN-2*
Esto (Town)—Holmes *FL-2*
Estral Beach (Village)—Monroe *MI-3*
Ethan (Town)—Davison *SD-4*
Ethel (Town)—Attala *MS-2*
Ethel (Town)—Macon *MO-3*
Ethelsville (Town)—Pickens *AL-2*
Ethete (CDP)—Fremont *WY-4*
Ethridge (City)—Lawrence *TN-2*
Etna (City)—Siskiyou *CA-4*
Etna (Township)—Kosciusko *IN-3*
Etna (Town)—Penobscot *ME-1*
Etna (Township)—Licking *OH-3*
Etna (Borough)—Allegheny *PA-1*
Etna Green (Town)—Kosciusko *IN-3*
Etna-Troy (Township)—Whitley *IN-3*
Eton (City)—Murray *GA-2*
Etonah, Mount (NY) *Geog-4*
Etowah (CDP)—Henderson *NC-2*
Etowah (Town)—Cleveland *OK-2*
Etowah (City)—McMinn *TN-2*
Etowah County *AL-2*
Ettrick (CDP)—Chesterfield *VA-2*
Ettrick (Town)—Trempealeau *WI-3*
Ettrick (Village)—Trempealeau *WI-3*
Eubank (City)—Lincoln *KY-2*
Eubank (City)—Pulaski *KY-2*

Euclid (Township)—Polk *MN-3*
Euclid (City)—Cuyahoga *OH-3*
Eudora (City)—Chicot *AR-2*
Eudora (City)—Douglas *KS-4*
Eudora (Township)—Douglas *KS-4*
Eufaula (City)—Barbour *AL-2*
Eufaula (City)—McIntosh *OK-2*
Eugene (Township)—Vermillion *IN-3*
Eugene (Township)—Carroll *MO-3*
Eugene (Town)—Cole *MO-3*
Eugene (City)—Lane *OR-4*
Euharlee (Town)—Bartow *GA-2*
Eulalia (Township)—Potter *PA-1*
Euless (City)—Tarrant *TX-2*
Eunice (City)—Acadia Parish *LA-2*
Eunice (City)—St. Landry Parish ... *LA-2*
Eunice (City)—Lea *NM-4*
Eunola (Municipality)—Geneva *AL-2*
Eupora (Town)—Webster *MS-2*
Eureka (City)—Humboldt *CA-4*
Eureka (City)—Woodford *IL-3*
Eureka (Township)—Barton *KS-4*
Eureka (City)—Greenwood *KS-4*
Eureka (Township)—Greenwood ... *KS-4*
Eureka (Township)—Kingman *KS-4*
Eureka (Township)—Mitchell *KS-4*
Eureka (Township)—Rice *KS-4*
Eureka (Township)—Saline *KS-4*
Eureka (Township)—Montcalm *MI-3*
Eureka (Township)—Dakota *MN-3*
Eureka (City)—St. Louis *MO-3*
Eureka (Town)—Lincoln *MT-4*
Eureka (Township)—Valley *NE-4*
Eureka (Township)—Wayne *NC-2*
Eureka (Township)—Ward *ND-4*
Eureka (Township)—Aurora *SD-4*
Eureka (Township)—Brookings *SD-4*
Eureka (City)—McPherson *SD-4*
Eureka (City)—Navarro *TX-2*
Eureka (City)—Juab *UT-4*
Eureka (Town)—Polk *WI-3*
Eureka County *NV-4*
Eureka Mill (CDP)—Chester *SC-2*
Eureka Springs (City)—Carroll *AR-2*
Eustace (City)—Henderson *TX-2*
Eustis (City)—Lake *FL-2*
Eustis (Town)—Franklin *ME-1*
Eustis (Village)—Frontier *NE-4*
Eutaw (City)—Greene *AL-2*
Eutawville (Town)—Orangeburg ... *SC-2*
Eva (Town)—Morgan *AL-2*
Evadale (CDP)—Jasper *TX-2*
Evan (Township)—Kingman *KS-4*
Evan (City)—Brown *MN-3*
Evangeline (Township)—
  Charlevoix *MI-3*
Evangeline Parish *LA-2*
Evans (City)—Weld *CO-4*
Evans (CDP)—Columbia *GA-2*
Evans (Township)—Marshall *IL-3*
Evans (Town)—Erie *NY-1*
Evansburg (CDP)—Montgomery ... *PA-1*
Evans City (Borough)—Butler *PA-1*
Evans County *GA-2*
Evansdale (City)—Black Hawk *IA-3*
Evans Mills (Village)—Jefferson ... *NY-1*
Evanston (City)—Cook *IL-3*
Evanston (Township)—Cook *IL-3*
Evanston (City)—Uinta *WY-4*
Evansville (CDP)—Yukon-Koyukuk
  Census Area *AK-4*
Evansville (Village)—Randolph *IL-3*
Evansville (City)—Vanderburgh *IN-3*
Evansville (City)—Douglas *MN-3*
Evansville (Township)—Douglas .. *MN-3*

Evansville (City)—Rock *WI-3*
Evansville (Town)—Natrona *WY-4*
Evant (Town)—Coryell *TX-2*
Evant (Town)—Hamilton *TX-2*
Evart (City)—Osceola *MI-3*
Evart (Township)—Osceola *MI-3*
Evarts (City)—Harlan *KY-2*
Eveleth (City)—St. Louis *MN-3*
Eveline (Township)—Charlevoix ... *MI-3*
Evendale (Village)—Hamilton *OH-3*
Evening Shade (Town)—Sharp *AR-2*
Everest (City)—Brown *KS-4*
Everest (Township)—Cass *ND-4*
Everett (City)—Middlesex *MA-1*
Everett (Township)—Newaygo *MI-3*
Everett (Township)—Cass *MO-3*
Everett (Township)—Burt *NE-4*
Everett (Township)—Dodge *NE-4*
Everett (Borough)—Bedford *PA-1*
Everett (City)—Snohomish *WA-4*
Everetts (Town)—Martin *NC-2*
Everglade (Township)—Stevens *MN-3*
Everglades (City)—Collier *FL-2*
Everglades, the (FL) *Geog-4*
Evergreen (City)—Conecuh *AL-2*
Evergreen (CDP)—Jefferson *CO-4*
Evergreen (Town)—Avoyelles
  Parish *LA-2*
Evergreen (Township)—
  Montcalm *MI-3*
Evergreen (Township)—Sanilac *MI-3*
Evergreen (Township)—Becker *MN-3*
Evergreen (CDP)—Flathead *MT-4*
Evergreen (Township)—Ward *ND-4*
Evergreen (CDP)—Clark *WA-4*
Evergreen (Town)—Langlade *WI-3*
Evergreen (CDP)—Marathon *WI-3*
Evergreen (Town)—Washburn *WI-3*
Evergreen Park (Village)—Cook ... *IL-3*
Everly (City)—Clay *IA-3*
Everman (City)—Tarrant *TX-2*
Everson (Borough)—Fayette *PA-1*
Everson (City)—Whatcom *WA-4*
Everton (Town)—Boone *AR-2*
Everton (City)—Dade *MO-3*
Everts (Township)—Otter Tail *MN-3*
Evesham (Township)—Burlington .. *NJ-1*
Ewa Beach (CDP)—Honolulu *HI-4*
Ewa Gentry (CDP)—Honolulu *HI-4*
Ewa Villages (CDP)—Honolulu *HI-4*
Ewing (Township)—Franklin *IL-3*
Ewing (Village)—Franklin *IL-3*
Ewing (City)—Fleming *KY-2*
Ewing (Township)—Marquette *MI-3*
Ewing (City)—Lewis *MO-3*
Ewing (Township)—Holt *NE-4*
Ewing (Village)—Holt *NE-4*
Ewing (Township)—Mercer *NJ-1*
Ewington (Township)—Jackson ... *MN-3*
Excel (Town)—Monroe *AL-2*
Excel (Township)—Marshall *MN-3*
Excelsior (Township)—Kalkaska .. *MI-3*
Excelsior (City)—Hennepin *MN-3*
Excelsior (Township)—Kidder *ND-4*
Excelsior (Town)—Sauk *WI-3*
Excelsior Estates (Village)—Clay .. *MO-3*
Excelsior Estates (Village)—Ray ... *MO-3*
Excelsior Springs (City)—Clay *MO-3*
Excelsior Springs (City)—Ray *MO-3*
Exeland (Village)—Sawyer *WI-3*
Exeter (City)—Tulare *CA-4*
Exeter (Village)—Scott *IL-3*
Exeter (Township)—Clay *KS-4*
Exeter (Town)—Penobscot *ME-1*
Exeter (Township)—Monroe *MI-3*

General Index

American Places Dictionary

Exeter (City)—Barry..................*MO-3*
Exeter (Township)—Barry..................*MO-3*
Exeter (Township)—Fillmore..................*NE-4*
Exeter (Village)—Fillmore..................*NE-4*
Exeter (Town)—Rockingham..................*NH-1*
Exeter (Town)—Otsego..................*NY-1*
Exeter (Township)—Berks..................*PA-1*
Exeter (Borough)—Luzerne..................*PA-1*
Exeter (Township)—Luzerne..................*PA-1*
Exeter (Township)—Wyoming..................*PA-1*
Exeter (Town)—Washington..................*RI-1*
Exeter (Town)—Green..................*WI-3*
Exira (City)—Audubon..................*IA-3*
Exline (City)—Appanoose..................*IA-3*
Exline (Township)—Spink..................*SD-4*
Exmore (Town)—Northampton..................*VA-2*
Experiment (CDP)—Spalding..................*GA-2*
Export (Borough)—Westmoreland..*PA-1*
Exton (CDP)—Chester..................*PA-1*
Eyak (CDP)—Valdez-Cordova Census Area..................*AK-4*
Eyota (City)—Olmsted..................*MN-3*
Eyota (Township)—Olmsted..................*MN-3*
Fabens (CDP)—El Paso..................*TX-2*
Fabius (Township)—St. Joseph..................*MI-3*
Fabius (Township)—Knox..................*MO-3*
Fabius (Township)—Marion..................*MO-3*
Fabius (Township)—Schuyler..................*MO-3*
Fabius (Town)—Onondaga..................*NY-1*
Fabius (Village)—Onondaga..................*NY-1*
Factoryville (Borough)—Wyoming..................*PA-1*
Fahlun (Township)—Kandiyohi..*MN-3*
Fair (Township)—Platte..................*MO-3*
Fair (Township)—Hutchinson..................*SD-4*
Fairbank (City)—Buchanan..................*IA-3*
Fairbank (City)—Fayette..................*IA-3*
Fairbanks (City)—Fairbanks North Star Borough..................*AK-4*
Fairbanks (Township)—Sullivan..*IN-3*
Fairbanks (Township)—Delta..................*MI-3*
Fairbanks (Township)—St. Louis..*MN-3*
Fairbanks (Township)—Renville....*ND-4*
Fairbanks (Town)—Shawano..................*WI-3*
Fairbanks North Star Borough..................*AK-4*
Fair Bluff (Town)—Columbus..................*NC-2*
Fairborn (City)—Greene..................*OH-3*
Fairburn (City)—Fulton..................*GA-2*
Fairburn (Town)—Custer..................*SD-4*
Fairbury (City)—Livingston..................*IL-3*
Fairbury (City)—Jefferson..................*NE-4*
Fairchance (Borough)—Fayette..................*PA-1*
Fairchild (Town)—Eau Claire..................*WI-3*
Fairchild (Village)—Eau Claire..................*WI-3*
Fairchild Air Force Base (Military Facility)—Spokane..................*WA-4*
Fairdale (CDP)—Jefferson..................*KY-2*
Fairdale (City)—Walsh..................*ND-4*
Fairdale (CDP)—Greene..................*PA-1*
Fairfax (Town)—Marin..................*CA-4*
Fairfax (City)—Linn..................*IA-3*
Fairfax (Township)—Osage..................*KS-4*
Fairfax (Township)—Polk..................*MN-3*
Fairfax (City)—Renville..................*MN-3*
Fairfax (City)—Atchison..................*MO-3*
Fairfax (Village)—Hamilton..................*OH-3*
Fairfax (Town)—Osage..................*OK-2*
Fairfax (Town)—Allendale..................*SC-2*
Fairfax (Town)—Hampton..................*SC-2*
Fairfax (Town)—Gregory..................*SD-4*
Fairfax (Township)—Gregory..................*SD-4*
Fairfax (Town)—Franklin..................*VT-1*
Fairfax County..................*VA-2*
Fairfax (Independent City)..................*VA-2*
Fairfield (City)—Jefferson..................*AL-2*
Fairfield (City)—Solano..................*CA-4*
Fairfield (Town)—Fairfield..................*CT-1*
Fairfield (City)—Camas..................*ID-4*
Fairfield (Township)—Bureau..................*IL-3*
Fairfield (City)—Wayne..................*IL-3*
Fairfield (Township)—Dekalb..................*IN-3*
Fairfield (Township)—Franklin..................*IN-3*
Fairfield (Township)—Tippecanoe..*IN-3*
Fairfield (City)—Jefferson..................*IA-3*
Fairfield (Township)—Russell..................*KS-4*
Fairfield (City)—Nelson..................*KY-2*
Fairfield (Town)—Somerset..................*ME-1*
Fairfield (Township)—Lenawee..................*MI-3*
Fairfield (Township)—Shiawassee..*MI-3*
Fairfield (Township)—Crow Wing..................*MN-3*
Fairfield (Township)—Swift..*MN-3*
Fairfield (Township)—Carroll..................*MO-3*
Fairfield (Town)—Teton..................*MT-4*
Fairfield (City)—Clay..................*NE-4*
Fairfield (Township)—Clay..................*NE-4*
Fairfield (Township)—Harlan..................*NE-4*
Fairfield (Township)—Cumberland..................*NJ-1*
Fairfield (Township)—Essex..................*NJ-1*
Fairfield (Town)—Herkimer..................*NY-1*
Fairfield (Township)—Grand Forks..................*ND-4*
Fairfield (City)—Butler..................*OH-3*
Fairfield (Township)—Butler..................*OH-3*
Fairfield (Township)—Columbiana..................*OH-3*
Fairfield (City)—Hamilton..................*OH-3*
Fairfield (Township)—Highland..*OH-3*
Fairfield (Township)—Huron..................*OH-3*
Fairfield (Township)—Madison..................*OH-3*
Fairfield (Township)—Tuscarawas..................*OH-3*
Fairfield (Township)—Washington..................*OH-3*
Fairfield (Borough)—Adams..................*PA-1*
Fairfield (Township)—Crawford..................*PA-1*
Fairfield (Township)—Lycoming..*PA-1*
Fairfield (Township)—Westmoreland..................*PA-1*
Fairfield (Township)—Beadle..................*SD-4*
Fairfield (City)—Freestone..................*TX-2*
Fairfield (Town)—Franklin..................*VT-1*
Fairfield (Town)—Spokane..................*WA-4*
Fairfield (Town)—Sauk..................*WI-3*
Fairfield Bay (CDP)—Cleburne..................*AR-2*
Fairfield Bay (CDP)—Van Buren..*AR-2*
Fairfield Beach (CDP)—Fairfield..*OH-3*
Fairfield County..................*CT-1*
Fairfield County..................*OH-3*
Fairfield County..................*SC-2*
Fairfield Glade (CDP)—Cumberland..................*TN-2*
Fairgrove (Township)—Tuscola..................*MI-3*
Fairgrove (Village)—Tuscola..................*MI-3*
Fair Grove (City)—Greene..................*MO-3*
Fairhaven (Township)—Carroll..................*IL-3*
Fairhaven (Town)—Bristol..................*MA-1*
Fairhaven (Township)—Huron..................*MI-3*
Fair Haven (CDP)—St. Clair..................*MI-3*
Fair Haven (Township)—Stearns..*MN-3*
Fair Haven (Borough)—Monmouth..................*NJ-1*
Fair Haven (Village)—Cayuga..................*NY-1*
Fair Haven (Town)—Rutland..................*VT-1*
Fairhope (City)—Baldwin..................*AL-2*
Fairhope (Township)—Somerset..*PA-1*
Fairland (CDP)—Shelby..................*IN-3*
Fairland (CDP)—Montgomery..*MD-1*
Fairland (Town)—Ottawa..................*OK-2*
Fairland (Township)—Lyman..................*SD-4*
Fair Lawn (Borough)—Bergen..................*NJ-1*
Fairlawn (City)—Summit..................*OH-3*
Fairlawn (CDP)—Pulaski..................*VA-2*
Fairlea (CDP)—Greenbrier..................*WV-2*
Fairlee (Town)—Orange..................*VT-1*
Fairless Hills (CDP)—Bucks..................*PA-1*
Fairmeade (City)—Jefferson..................*KY-2*
Fairmont (CDP)—Will..................*IL-3*
Fairmont (City)—Martin..................*MN-3*
Fairmont (Township)—Martin..................*MN-3*
Fairmont (Township)—Fillmore..*NE-4*
Fairmont (Village)—Fillmore..................*NE-4*
Fairmont (Town)—Robeson..................*NC-2*
Fairmont (Town)—Garfield..................*OK-2*
Fairmont (City)—Marion..................*WV-2*
Fairmont City (Village)—Madison..*IL-3*
Fairmont City (Village)—St. Clair..*IL-3*
Fairmount (City)—Gordon..................*GA-2*
Fairmount (Township)—Pike..................*IL-3*
Fairmount (Village)—Vermilion..*IL-3*
Fairmount (Town)—Grant..................*IN-3*
Fairmount (Township)—Grant..................*IN-3*
Fairmount (Township)—Butler..*KS-4*
Fairmount (Township)—Leavenworth..................*KS-4*
Fairmount (CDP)—Onondaga..................*NY-1*
Fairmount (City)—Richland..................*ND-4*
Fairmount (Township)—Richland..................*ND-4*
Fairmount (Township)—Luzerne..*PA-1*
Fairmount (CDP)—Hamilton..................*TN-2*
Fairmount Heights (Town)—Prince George's..................*MD-1*
Fair Oaks (CDP)—Sacramento..................*CA-4*
Fair Oaks (CDP)—Cobb..................*GA-2*
Fair Oaks (Town)—Rogers..................*OK-2*
Fair Oaks (Town)—Wagoner..................*OK-2*
Fair Oaks Ranch (City)—Bexar..................*TX-2*
Fair Oaks Ranch (City)—Comal..................*TX-2*
Fair Oaks Ranch (City)—Kendall..*TX-2*
Fair Plain (CDP)—Berrien..................*MI-3*
Fairplain (Township)—Montcalm..*MI-3*
Fairplains (CDP)—Wilkes..................*NC-2*
Fairplay (Town)—Park..................*CO-4*
Fairplay (Township)—Greene..................*IN-3*
Fairplay (Township)—Marion..................*KS-4*
Fair Play (City)—Polk..................*MO-3*
Fairport (Village)—Monroe..................*NY-1*
Fairport Harbor (Village)—Lake..*OH-3*
Fairton (CDP)—Cumberland..................*NJ-1*
Fairview (Town)—Cullman..................*AL-2*
Fairview (CDP)—Alameda..................*CA-4*
Fairview (CDP)—Walker..................*GA-2*
Fairview (Township)—Fulton..................*IL-3*
Fairview (Village)—Fulton..................*IL-3*
Fairview (Township)—Fayette..................*IN-3*
Fairview (Township)—Barton..................*KS-4*
Fairview (City)—Brown..................*KS-4*
Fairview (Township)—Butler..................*KS-4*
Fairview (Township)—Cowley..................*KS-4*
Fairview (Township)—Ford..................*KS-4*
Fairview (Township)—Jefferson..*KS-4*
Fairview (Township)—Labette..................*KS-4*
Fairview (Township)—Republic..................*KS-4*
Fairview (Township)—Russell..................*KS-4*
Fairview (Township)—Stafford..................*KS-4*
Fairview (City)—Kenton..................*KY-2*
Fairview (Township)—Cass..................*MN-3*
Fairview (Township)—Lyon..................*MN-3*
Fairview (Township)—Caldwell..*MO-3*
Fairview (Township)—Henry..................*MO-3*
Fairview (Township)—Livingston..................*MO-3*
Fairview (Town)—Newton..................*MO-3*

Fairview (City)—Richland *MT-4*
Fairview (Township)—Holt *NE-4*
Fairview (Borough)—Bergen *NJ-1*
Fairview (CDP)—Monmouth *NJ-1*
Fairview (CDP)—Dutchess *NY-1*
Fairview (Township)—Rolette *ND-4*
Fairview (Township)—Sheridan ...*ND-4*
Fairview (Village)—Belmont *OH-3*
Fairview (Village)—Guernsey *OH-3*
Fairview (City)—Major *OK-2*
Fairview (City)—Multnomah *OR-4*
Fairview (Borough)—Butler *PA-1*
Fairview (Township)—Butler *PA-1*
Fairview (Borough)—Erie *PA-1*
Fairview (Township)—Erie *PA-1*
Fairview (Township)—Luzerne *PA-1*
Fairview (Township)—Mercer......... *PA-1*
Fairview (Township)—York *PA-1*
Fairview (Township)—Clay........... *SD-4*
Fairview (Township)—Faulk *SD-4*
Fairview (Township)—Hanson *SD-4*
Fairview (Town)—Lincoln *SD-4*
Fairview (Township)—Lincoln........ *SD-4*
Fairview (Township)—Mellette *SD-4*
Fairview (City)—Williamson *TN-2*
Fairview (City)—Collin *TX-2*
Fairview (City)—Wise *TX-2*
Fairview (City)—Sanpete *UT-4*
Fairview (Town)—Marion *WV-2*
Fairview-Ferndale (CDP)—
 Northumberland *PA-1*
Fairview Heights (City)—St. Clair.. *IL-3*
Fairview Lanes (CDP)—Erie *OH-3*
Fairview No. 22 (Township)—
 Pennington *SD-4*
Fairview Park (Town)—
 Vermillion *IN-3*
Fairview Park (City)—Cuyahoga ...*OH-3*
Fairview Shores (CDP)—Orange ... *FL-2*
Fairview-Sumach (CDP)—
 Yakima *WA-4*
Fairville (Township)—Wells *ND-4*
Fairwater (Village)—Fond du
 Lac *WI-3*
Fairway (City)—Johnson *KS-4*
Fairweather, Mt. (AK) *Geog-4*
Fairwood (CDP)—Spokane *WA-4*
Fairy Falls (WA) *Geog-4*
Faison (Town)—Duplin *NC-2*
Faith (Town)—Rowan *NC-2*
Faith (City)—Meade...................... *SD-4*
Faithorn (Township)—
 Menominee *MI-3*
Falcon (Town)—Quitman *MS-2*
Falcon (Town)—Cumberland *NC-2*
Falcon (Town)—Sampson *NC-2*
Falconer (Village)—Chautauqua *NY-1*
Falconer (Township)—Grand
 Forks *ND-4*
Falcon Heights (City)—Ramsey *MN-3*
Falfurrias (City)—Brooks *TX-2*
Falk (Township)—Clearwater........*MN-3*
Falkland (Town)—Pitt *NC-2*
Falkner (Town)—Tippah *MS-2*
Falkville (Town)—Morgan *AL-2*
Fall Branch (CDP)—Greene *TN-2*
Fall Branch (CDP)—Washington ... *TN-2*
Fallbrook (CDP)—San Diego......... *CA-4*
Fall City (CDP)—King *WA-4*
Fall Creek (Township)—Adams *IL-3*
Fall Creek (Township)—Hamilton.. *IN-3*
Fall Creek (Township)—Henry *IN-3*
Fall Creek (Township)—Madison ... *IN-3*
Fall Creek (Village)—Eau Claire.... *WI-3*

Falling Spring (Township)—
 Oregon..*MO-3*
Falling Spring (Town)—
 Greenbrier *WV-2*
Fallis (Town)—Lincoln *OK-2*
Fall Lake (Township)—Lake *MN-3*
Fall Line (WA) *Geog-4*
Fallon (City)—Churchill................ *NV-4*
Fallon Colony (NV) *IndRes-4*
Fallon County *MT-4*
Fallon Naval Air Station (NV)....... *Mil-4*
Fallon Reservation (NV) *IndRes-4*
Fallon Station (Military Facility)—
 Churchill *NV-4*
Fallowfield (Township)—
 Washington *PA-1*
Fall River (Township)—La Salle..... *IL-3*
Fall River (City)—Greenwood........*KS-4*
Fall River (Township)—
 Greenwood *KS-4*
Fall River (Township)—Wilson *KS-4*
Fall River (City)—Bristol *MA-1*
Fall River (Village)—Columbia *WI-3*
Fall River County *SD-4*
Falls (Township)—Chase *KS-4*
Falls (Township)—Sumner *KS-4*
Falls (Township)—Hocking *OH-3*
Falls (Township)—Muskingum *OH-3*
Falls (Township)—Bucks *PA-1*
Falls (Township)—Wyoming *PA-1*
Fallsburg (Town)—Sullivan *NY-1*
Fallsbury (Township)—Licking *OH-3*
Falls Church (Independent City)...... *VA-2*
Falls City (City)—Richardson........ *NE-4*
Falls City (City)—Polk *OR-4*
Falls City (City)—Karnes *TX-2*
Falls County *TX-2*
Falls Creek (Borough)—Clearfield .. *PA-1*
Falls Creek (Borough)—Jefferson ... *PA-1*
Fallston (CDP)—Harford *MD-1*
Fallston (Town)—Cleveland *NC-2*
Fallston (Borough)—Beaver *PA-1*
Falmouth (City)—Pendleton *KY-2*
Falmouth (Town)—Cumberland ... *ME-1*
Falmouth (Town)—Barnstable *MA-1*
Falmouth (CDP)—Stafford *VA-2*
Falsen (Township)—McHenry *ND-4*
False Pass (CDP)—Aleutians East
 Borough......................................*AK-4*
Falun (Township)—Saline *KS-4*
Falun (Township)—Roseau *MN-3*
Fancher (Township)—Ramsey *ND-4*
Fancy Creek (Township)—
 Sangamon *IL-3*
Fancy Creek (Township)—Riley *KS-4*
Fannett (Township)—Franklin........ *PA-1*
Fannin County *GA-2*
Fannin County *TX-2*
Fanning Springs (City)—Gilchrist .. *FL-2*
Fanning Springs (City)—Levy........ *FL-2*
Fanny (Township)—Polk *MN-3*
Fanshawe (Town)—Latimer *OK-2*
Fanshawe (Town)—Le Flore *OK-2*
Fanwood (Borough)—Union *NJ-1*
Farber (City)—Audrain *MO-3*
Farden (Township)—Hubbard *MN-3*
Fargo (Town)—Monroe *AR-2*
Fargo (Township)—Seward *KS-4*
Fargo (City)—Cass.........................*ND-4*
Fargo (Township)—Cass *ND-4*
Fargo (Town)—Ellis *OK-2*
Far Hills (Borough)—Somerset........*NJ-1*
Faribault (City)—Rice *MN-3*
Faribault County...........................*MN-3*
Farina (Village)—Fayette................ *IL-3*

Farina (Village)—Marion *IL-3*
Farina (Township)—Hettinger *ND-4*
Farley (City)—Dubuque *IA-3*
Farley (Township)—Polk *MN-3*
Farley (Village)—Platte *MO-3*
Farmer (Township)—Rice *KS-4*
Farmer (Township)—Wabaunsee ...*KS-4*
Farmer (Township)—Defiance *OH-3*
Farmer (Town)—Hanson *SD-4*
Farmer City (City)—De Witt *IL-3*
Farmers (Township)—Fulton *IL-3*
Farmers Branch (City)—Dallas...... *TX-2*
Farmersburg (Town)—Sullivan *IN-3*
Farmersburg (City)—Clayton *IA-3*
Farmersville (City)—Tulare........... *CA-4*
Farmersville (Village)—
 Montgomery................................. *IL-3*
Farmersville (Town)—
 Cattaraugus *NY-1*
Farmersville (Village)—
 Montgomery................................*OH-3*
Farmersville (City)—Collin *TX-2*
Farmerville (Town)—Union
 Parish *LA-2*
Farming (Township)—Stearns........ *MN-3*
Farmingdale (Town)—Kennebec .. *ME-1*
Farmingdale (Borough)—
 Monmouth *NJ-1*
Farmingdale (Village)—Nassau *NY-1*
Farmington (City)—Washington *AR-2*
Farmington (Town)—Hartford....... *CT-1*
Farmington (Town)—Kent *DE-1*
Farmington (City)—Fulton *IL-3*
Farmington (Township)—Fulton ... *IL-3*
Farmington (City)—Van Buren......*IA-3*
Farmington (Township)—
 Republic *KS-4*
Farmington (Township)—Stafford ..*KS-4*
Farmington (Township)—
 Washington *KS-4*
Farmington (Town)—Franklin *ME-1*
Farmington (City)—Oakland *MI-3*
Farmington (City)—Dakota *MN-3*
Farmington (Township)—
 Olmsted.....................................*MN-3*
Farmington (City)—St. Francois....*MO-3*
Farmington (Town)—Strafford *NH-1*
Farmington (City)—San Juan *NM-4*
Farmington (Town)—Ontario *NY-1*
Farmington (Township)—Walsh ...*ND-4*
Farmington (Township)—
 Trumbull *OH-3*
Farmington (Township)—Clarion ... *PA-1*
Farmington (Township)—Tioga *PA-1*
Farmington (Township)—Warren ... *PA-1*
Farmington (Township)—Day........ *SD-4*
Farmington (Township)—Grant *SD-4*
Farmington (Township)—Lake *SD-4*
Farmington (City)—Davis *UT-4*
Farmington (Town)—Whitman *WA-4*
Farmington (Town)—Marion *WV-2*
Farmington (Town)—Jefferson *WI-3*
Farmington (Town)—La Crosse *WI-3*
Farmington (Town)—Polk *WI-3*
Farmington (Town)—Washington.. *WI-3*
Farmington (Town)—Waupaca *WI-3*
Farmington Hills (City)—
 Oakland *MI-3*
Farmingville (CDP)—Suffolk........ *NY-1*
Farm Island (Township)—Aitkin .. *MN-3*
Farmland (Town)—Randolph *IN-3*
Farm Ridge (Township)—La Salle . *IL-3*
Farmvale (Township)—Williams ...*ND-4*
Farmville (Town)—Pitt *NC-2*
Farmville (Town)—Cumberland *VA-2*

General Index — American Places Dictionary

Farmville (Town)—Prince Edward VA-2
Farnam (Village)—Dawson NE-4
Farnham (Village)—Erie NY-1
Farnhamville (City)—Calhoun IA-3
Farnhamville (City)—Webster IA-3
Farragut (City)—Fremont IA-3
Farragut (Town)—Knox TN-2
Farragut (Town)—Loudon TN-2
Farrell (City)—Mercer PA-1
Farrington (Township)—Jefferson .. IL-3
Farr West (City)—Weber UT-4
Farwell (Village)—Clare MI-3
Farwell (City)—Pope MN-3
Farwell (Village)—Howard NE-4
Farwell (City)—Parmer TX-2
Fate (City)—Rockwall TX-2
Faulk County SD-4
Faulkner County AR-2
Faulkton (City)—Faulk SD-4
Faunsdale (Town)—Marengo AL-2
Fauquier County VA-2
Fawn (Township)—Allegheny PA-1
Fawn (Township)—York PA-1
Fawn Creek (Township)—Montgomery KS-4
Fawn Grove (Borough)—York PA-1
Fawn Lake (Township)—Todd MN-3
Fawn River (Township)—St. Joseph MI-3
Faxon (Township)—Sibley MN-3
Faxon (Town)—Comanche OK-2
Fay (Township)—Burke ND-4
Fayal (Township)—St. Louis MN-3
Fayette (City)—Fayette AL-2
Fayette (Township)—Livingston IL-3
Fayette (Township)—Vigo IN-3
Fayette (City)—Fayette IA-3
Fayette (Town)—Kennebec ME-1
Fayette (Township)—Hillsdale MI-3
Fayette (City)—Jefferson MS-2
Fayette (City)—Howard MO-3
Fayette (Town)—Seneca NY-1
Fayette (Village)—Fulton OH-3
Fayette (Township)—Lawrence OH-3
Fayette (Township)—Juniata PA-1
Fayette (Town)—Sanpete UT-4
Fayette (Town)—Lafayette WI-3
Fayette City (Borough)—Fayette PA-1
Fayette County AL-2
Fayette County GA-2
Fayette County IL-3
Fayette County IN-3
Fayette County IA-3
Fayette County KY-2
Fayette County OH-3
Fayette County PA-1
Fayette County TN-2
Fayette County TX-2
Fayette County WV-2
Fayetteville (City)—Washington AR-2
Fayetteville (City)—Fayette GA-2
Fayetteville (Township)—St. Clair .. IL-3
Fayetteville (Village)—St. Clair IL-3
Fayetteville (Village)—Onondaga .. NY-1
Fayetteville (City)—Cumberland ... NC-2
Fayetteville (Village)—Brown OH-3
Fayetteville (CDP)—Franklin PA-1
Fayetteville (City)—Lincoln TN-2
Fayetteville (Town)—Fayette TX-2
Fayetteville (Town)—Fayette WV-2
Fayston (Town)—Washington VT-1
Fear, Cape (NC) Geog-4
Fearing (Township)—Washington OH-3

Fearrington (CDP)—Chatham NC-2
Feasterville-Trevose (CDP)—Bucks PA-1
Feather Falls (CA) Geog-4
Feather Sound (CDP)—Pinellas FL-2
Featherstone (Township)—Goodhue MN-3
Federal Dam (City)—Cass MN-3
Federal Heights (City)—Adams CO-4
Federalsburg (Town)—Caroline MD-1
Federal Way (CDP)—King WA-4
Feeley (Township)—Itasca MN-3
Felch (Township)—Dickinson MI-3
Felicity (Village)—Clermont OH-3
Felida (CDP)—Clark WA-4
Felix (Township)—Grundy IL-3
Fell (Township)—Lackawanna PA-1
Fellsmere (City)—Indian River FL-2
Felsenthal (Town)—Union AR-2
Felson (Township)—Pembina ND-4
Felton (CDP)—Santa Cruz CA-4
Felton (Town)—Kent DE-1
Felton (City)—Clay MN-3
Felton (Township)—Clay MN-3
Felton (Borough)—York PA-1
Fence (Town)—Florence WI-3
Fenner (Town)—Madison NY-1
Fennimore (City)—Grant WI-3
Fennimore (Town)—Grant WI-3
Fennville (City)—Allegan MI-3
Fenton (Township)—Whiteside IL-3
Fenton (City)—Kossuth IA-3
Fenton (Village)—Jefferson Davis Parish LA-2
Fenton (City)—Genesee MI-3
Fenton (Township)—Genesee MI-3
Fenton (Township)—Murray MN-3
Fenton (City)—St. Louis MO-3
Fenton (Town)—Broome NY-1
Fentress County TN-2
Fenwick (Borough)—Middlesex .. CT-1
Fenwick Island (Town)—Sussex..... DE-1
Fenwood (Village)—Marathon WI-3
Ferdinand (City)—Idaho ID-4
Ferdinand (Town)—Dubois IN-3
Ferdinand (Township)—Dubois IN-3
Ferdinand (Town)—Essex VT-1
Fergus County MT-4
Fergus Falls (City)—Otter Tail MN-3
Fergus Falls (Township)—Otter Tail MN-3
Ferguson (City)—Marshall IA-3
Ferguson (City)—Pulaski KY-2
Ferguson (City)—St. Louis MO-3
Ferguson (Township)—St. Louis ... MO-3
Ferguson (Township)—Centre PA-1
Ferguson (Township)—Clearfield PA-1
Fermanagh (Township)—Juniata .. PA-1
Fern (Township)—Hubbard MN-3
Fern (Town)—Florence WI-3
Fernandina Beach (City)—Nassau FL-2
Fernan Lake Village (City)—Kootenai ID-4
Fern Creek (CDP)—Jefferson KY-2
Ferndale (City)—Humboldt CA-4
Ferndale (CDP)—Anne Arundel... MD-1
Ferndale (City)—Oakland MI-3
Ferndale (Borough)—Cambria PA-1
Ferndale (City)—Whatcom WA-4
Fernley (CDP)—Lyon NV-4
Fern Park (CDP)—Seminole FL-2
Fernway (CDP)—Butler PA-1
Ferrelview (Village)—Platte MO-3

Ferriday (Town)—Concordia Parish LA-2
Ferris (Village)—Hancock IL-3
Ferris (Township)—Montcalm MI-3
Ferris (City)—Ellis TX-2
Ferrisburg (Town)—Addison VT-1
Ferron (City)—Emery UT-4
Ferrum (CDP)—Franklin VA-2
Ferry (CDP)—Yukon-Koyukuk Census Area AK-4
Ferry (Township)—Oceana MI-3
Ferry (Township)—Grand Forks ND-4
Ferry County WA-4
Ferry Pass (CDP)—Escambia FL-2
Ferrysburg (City)—Ottawa MI-3
Ferryville (Village)—Crawford WI-3
Fertile (City)—Worth IA-3
Fertile (City)—Polk MN-3
Fertile (Township)—Mountrail ND-4
Fertile (Township)—Walsh ND-4
Fertile Valley (Township)—Divide ND-4
Fessenden (City)—Wells ND-4
Festus (City)—Jefferson MO-3
Fetters Hot Springs-Agua Caliente (CDP)—Sonoma CA-4
Fidelity (Township)—Jersey IL-3
Fidelity (Village)—Jersey IL-3
Fidelity (Town)—Jasper MO-3
Field (Township)—Jefferson IL-3
Field (Township)—St. Louis MN-3
Field (Township)—Nelson ND-4
Fieldale (CDP)—Henry VA-2
Fielding (Town)—Box Elder UT-4
Fieldon (Village)—Jersey IL-3
Fieldon (Township)—Watonwan... MN-3
Fieldsboro (Borough)—Burlington NJ-1
Fields Creek (Township)—Henry MO-3
Fife (City)—Pierce WA-4
Fife Lake (Township)—Grand Traverse MI-3
Fife Lake (Village)—Grand Traverse MI-3
Fifield (Town)—Price WI-3
Fifty Lakes (City)—Crow Wing MN-3
Fifty-Six (City)—Stone AR-2
Filer (City)—Twin Falls ID-4
Filer (Township)—Manistee MI-3
Filley (Township)—Gage NE-4
Filley (Village)—Gage NE-4
Fillmore (City)—Ventura CA-4
Fillmore (Township)—Montgomery IL-3
Fillmore (Village)—Montgomery IL-3
Fillmore (Town)—Putnam IN-3
Fillmore (Township)—Allegan MI-3
Fillmore (Township)—Fillmore ... MN-3
Fillmore (City)—Andrew MO-3
Fillmore (Township)—Bollinger.... MO-3
Fillmore (Village)—Allegany NY-1
Fillmore (Township)—Divide ND-4
Fillmore (City)—Millard UT-4
Fillmore County MN-3
Fillmore County NE-4
Fincastle (City)—Jefferson KY-2
Fincastle (Town)—Botetourt VA-2
Findlay (Village)—Shelby IL-3
Findlay (City)—Hancock OH-3
Findlay (Township)—Allegheny PA-1
Findley (Township)—Douglas MO-3
Findley (Township)—Mercer PA-1
Fine (Town)—St. Lawrence NY-1

Fine Lakes (Township)—St. Louis MN-3
Fingal (City)—Barnes ND-4
Finger (Town)—McNairy TN-2
Finger Lakes (NY) Geog-4
Finlayson (City)—Pine MN-3
Finlayson (Township)—Pine MN-3
Finley (Township)—Scott IN-3
Finley (Township)—Decatur KS-4
Finley (Township)—Webster MO-3
Finley (City)—Steele ND-4
Finley (Township)—Steele ND-4
Finley (CDP)—Benton WA-4
Finley (Town)—Juneau WI-3
Finley Point (CDP)—Lake MT-4
Finleyville (Borough)—Washington PA-1
Finn (Township)—Logan ND-4
Finney County KS-4
Finneytown (CDP)—Hamilton OH-3
Fircrest (Town)—Pierce WA-4
Firebaugh (City)—Fresno CA-4
Fire Island (NY) Geog-4
Firesteel (Township)—Aurora SD-4
Firestone (Town)—Weld CO-4
First Colony (CDP)—Fort Bend ... TX-2
Firth (City)—Bingham ID-4
Firth (Village)—Lancaster NE-4
Firthcliffe (CDP)—Orange NY-1
Fischbein (Township)—Bowman ... ND-4
Fisher (Town)—Poinsett AR-2
Fisher (Village)—Champaign IL-3
Fisher (Village)—Sabine Parish ... LA-2
Fisher (City)—Polk MN-3
Fisher (Township)—Polk MN-3
Fisher (Township)—Grant ND-4
Fisher County TX-2
Fishers (Town)—Hamilton IN-3
Fishersville (CDP)—Augusta VA-2
Fishing Creek (Township)—Columbia PA-1
Fishing River (Township)—Clay .. MO-3
Fishing River (Township)—Ray ... MO-3
Fishkill (Town)—Dutchess NY-1
Fishkill (Village)—Dutchess NY-1
Fish Lake (Township)—Chisago ... MN-3
Fisk (Town)—Butler MO-3
Fiskdale (CDP)—Worcester MA-1
Fitchburg (City)—Worcester MA-1
Fitchburg (City)—Dane WI-3
Fitchville (Township)—Huron OH-3
Fithian (Village)—Vermilion IL-3
Fitzgerald (City)—Ben Hill GA-2
Fitzgerald (City)—Irwin GA-2
Fitzhugh (Town)—Pontotoc OK-2
Fitzwilliam (Town)—Cheshire NH-1
Five Corners (CDP)—Clark WA-4
Five Creeks (Township)—Clay KS-4
Five Mile (Township)—Newton MO-3
Five Points (Town)—Chambers AL-2
Five Points (CDP)—Columbia FL-2
Five Points (CDP)—Warren OH-3
Flagg (Township)—Ogle IL-3
Flagler (Town)—Kit Carson CO-4
Flagler Beach (City)—Flagler FL-2
Flagler County FL-2
Flagstaff (City)—Coconino AZ-4
Flambeau (Town)—Price WI-3
Flambeau (Town)—Rusk WI-3
Flanagan (Village)—Livingston ... IL-3
Flanders (CDP)—Suffolk NY-1
Flandreau (City)—Moody SD-4
Flandreau (Township)—Moody SD-4
Flandreau Reservation (SD) IndRes-4
Flannigan (Township)—Hamilton .. IL-3

Flasher (City)—Morton ND-4
Flat Branch (Township)—Shelby ... IL-3
Flatbush—Kings NY-1
Flat Butte No. 12 (Township)—Pennington SD-4
Flat Creek (Township)—Barry MO-3
Flat Creek (Township)—Pettis MO-3
Flat Creek (Township)—Perkins ... SD-4
Flat Creek A (Township)—Stone .. MO-3
Flat Creek B (Township)—Stone .. MO-3
Flathead County MT-4
Flathead Lake (MT) Geog-4
Flathead Reservation (MT) IndRes-4
Flatonia (Town)—Fayette TX-2
Flat River (City)—St. Francois MO-3
Flat Rock (Village)—Crawford IL-3
Flat Rock (Township)—Bartholomew IN-3
Flat Rock (City)—Wayne MI-3
Flat Rock (CDP)—Surry NC-2
Flatrock (Township)—Henry OH-3
Flattery, Cape (WA) Geog-4
Flatwoods (City)—Greenup KY-2
Flatwoods (Township)—Ripley MO-3
Flatwoods (Town)—Braxton WV-2
Flaxton (City)—Burke ND-4
Flaxville (Town)—Daniels MT-4
Fleet Combat Training Center (VA) Mil-4
Fleetwood (Borough)—Berks PA-1
Fleischmanns (Village)—Delaware NY-1
Fleming (Town)—Logan CO-4
Fleming (Township)—Aitkin MN-3
Fleming (Township)—Pine MN-3
Fleming (City)—Ray MO-3
Fleming (Town)—Cayuga NY-1
Fleming County KY-2
Fleming-Neon (City)—Letcher KY-2
Flemingsburg (City)—Fleming KY-2
Flemington (City)—Liberty GA-2
Flemington (Township)—Polk MO-3
Flemington (Village)—Polk MO-3
Flemington (Borough)—Hunterdon NJ-1
Flemington (Borough)—Clinton ... PA-1
Flemington (Town)—Taylor WV-2
Flensburg (City)—Morrison MN-3
Fletchall (Township)—Worth MO-3
Fletcher (Town)—Henderson NC-2
Fletcher (Village)—Miami OH-3
Fletcher (Town)—Comanche OK-2
Fletcher (Town)—Franklin VT-1
Flint (Township)—Pike IL-3
Flint (City)—Genesee MI-3
Flint (Township)—Genesee MI-3
Flint (Township)—Stutsman ND-4
Flint City (Municipality)—Morgan AL-2
Flint Hill (Village)—St. Charles MO-3
Flippin (City)—Marion AR-2
Flom (Township)—Norman MN-3
Flomaton (Town)—Escambia AL-2
Floodwood (City)—St. Louis MN-3
Floodwood (Township)—St. Louis MN-3
Flora (Township)—Boone IL-3
Flora (City)—Clay IL-3
Flora (Town)—Carroll IN-3
Flora (Township)—Dickinson KS-4
Flora (Township)—Renville MN-3
Flora (Town)—Madison MS-2
Florala (City)—Covington AL-2
Floral City (CDP)—Citrus FL-2
Floral Park (Village)—Nassau NY-1

Florance (Township)—Foster ND-4
Flora Vista (CDP)—San Juan NM-4
Flordell Hills (City)—St. Louis MO-3
Florence (City)—Lauderdale AL-2
Florence (Town)—Pinal AZ-4
Florence (City)—Fremont CO-4
Florence (Village)—Pike IL-3
Florence (Township)—Stephenson .. IL-3
Florence (Township)—Will IL-3
Florence (City)—Marion KS-4
Florence (City)—Boone KY-2
Florence (Township)—St. Joseph ... MI-3
Florence (Township)—Goodhue ... MN-3
Florence (City)—Lyon MN-3
Florence (Town)—Rankin MS-2
Florence (Township)—Burlington .. NJ-1
Florence (Town)—Oneida NY-1
Florence (Township)—Erie OH-3
Florence (Township)—Williams OH-3
Florence (City)—Lane OR-4
Florence (City)—Florence SC-2
Florence (Township)—Codington ... SD-4
Florence (Township)—Hamlin SD-4
Florence (Township)—Hand SD-4
Florence (Town)—Williamson TX-2
Florence (Town)—Florence WI-3
Florence County SC-2
Florence County WI-3
Florence-Graham (CDP)—Los Angeles CA-4
Florence Lake (Township)—Burleigh ND-4
Floresville (City)—Wilson TX-2
Florham Park (Borough)—Morris .. NJ-1
Florida (Township)—Parke IN-3
Florida (Town)—Berkshire MA-1
Florida (Township)—Yellow Medicine MN-3
Florida (Village)—Monroe MO-3
Florida (Town)—Montgomery NY-1
Florida (Village)—Orange NY-1
Florida (Village)—Henry OH-3
Florida, Straits of (FL) Geog-4
Florida Bay (FL) Geog-4
Florida City (City)—Dade FL-2
Florida Keys (FL) Geog-4
Florida Panhandle (FL) Geog-4
Florida Ridge (CDP)—Indian River FL-2
Florida Tribe of Eastern Creek TDSA (FL) IndRes-4
Florien (Village)—Sabine Parish ... LA-2
Florin (CDP)—Sacramento CA-4
Floris (City)—Davis IA-3
Florissant (City)—St. Louis MO-3
Florissant (Township)—St. Louis MO-3
Flossmoor (Village)—Cook IL-3
Flournoy (Township)—Thurston ... NE-4
Flourtown (CDP)—Montgomery PA-1
Flovilla (City)—Butts GA-2
Flowerfield (Township)—St. Joseph MI-3
Flower Hill (Village)—Nassau NY-1
Flower Mound (Town)—Denton ... TX-2
Flower Mound (Town)—Tarrant ... TX-2
Flowery Branch (Town)—Hall GA-2
Flowing (Township)—Clay MN-3
Flowing Wells (CDP)—Pima AZ-4
Flowood (Town)—Rankin MS-2
Floyd (Township)—Warren IL-3
Floyd (Township)—Putnam IN-3
Floyd (City)—Floyd IA-3
Floyd (Village)—Roosevelt NM-4
Floyd (Town)—Oneida NY-1

General Index — American Places Dictionary

Floyd (Township)—Sanborn SD-4
Floyd (Town)—Floyd VA-2
Floydada (City)—Floyd................. TX-2
Floyd Collins Crystal Cave
  (KY)..Geog-4
Floyd County GA-2
Floyd County IN-3
Floyd County IA-3
Floyd County KY-2
Floyd County TX-2
Floyd County VA-2
Flume (NH)..................................Geog-4
Flushing (City)—Genesee MI-3
Flushing (Township)—Genesee ... MI-3
Flushing—Queens........................... NY-1
Flushing (Township)—Belmont OH-3
Flushing (Village)—Belmont..........OH-3
Fluvanna County VA-2
Flying Hills (CDP)—Berks............... PA-1
Flynn (Township)—Sanilac MI-3
Foard County TX-2
Folcroft (Borough)—Delaware PA-1
Foldahl (Township)—Marshall...... MN-3
Folden (Township)—Otter Tail MN-3
Foley (City)—Baldwin AL-2
Foley (City)—Benton MN-3
Foley (City)—Lincoln MO-3
Folker (Township)—Clark MO-3
Folkston (City)—Charlton............... GA-2
Follansbee (City)—Brooke WV-2
Follett (City)—Lipscomb TX-2
Folly Beach (City)—Charleston SC-2
Folsom (City)—Sacramento CA-4
Folsom (Village)—St. Tammany
  Parish LA-2
Folsom (Township)—Traverse MN-3
Folsom (Borough)—Atlantic NJ-1
Folsom (Village)—Union NM-4
Folsom (CDP)—Delaware................ PA-1
Fonda (City)—Pocahontas IA-3
Fonda (Village)—Montgomery........ NY-1
Fond du Lac (City)—Fond du
  Lac WI-3
Fond du Lac (Town)—Fond du
  Lac.. WI-3
Fond du Lac County WI-3
Fond Du Lac Reservation
  (MN).......................................IndRes-4
Fondulac (Township)—Tazewell..... IL-3
Fontana (City)—San Bernardino ... CA-4
Fontana (City)—Miami KS-4
Fontana-on-Geneva Lake (Village)—
  Walworth...................................... WI-3
Fontanelle (City)—Adair IA-3
Foosland (Village)—Champaign IL-3
Foote (Township)—Gray KS-4
Foothill Farms (CDP)—
  Sacramento CA-4
Foothills (Township)—Burke ND-4
Footville (Village)—Rock WI-3
Forada (City)—Douglas................. MN-3
Foraker (Town)—Osage................. OK-2
Foraker, Mt. (AK) Geog-4
Forbes (Township)—Holt MO-3
Forbes (City)—Dickey ND-4
Forbes (Township)—Charles Mix .. SD-4
Ford (City)—Ford............................. KS-4
Ford (Township)—Ford KS-4
Ford (Township)—Kanabec MN-3
Ford (Town)—Taylor WI-3
Ford City (CDP)—Kern................... CA-4
Ford City (Town)—Gentry............. MO-3
Ford City (Borough)—Armstrong... PA-1
Ford Cliff (Borough)—Armstrong... PA-1
Ford County..................................... IL-3

Ford County................................... KS-4
Forde (Township)—Nelson ND-4
Fordham (Township)—Clark SD-4
Ford Heights (Village)—Cook......... IL-3
Fordland (City)—Webster MO-3
Fordoche (Village)—Pointe Coupee
  Parish LA-2
Ford River (Township)—Delta MI-3
Fords (CDP)—Middlesex NJ-1
Fords Prairie (CDP)—Lewis........... WA-4
Fordsville (City)—Ohio.................. KY-2
Fordville (City)—Walsh ND-4
Fordyce (City)—Dallas................... AR-2
Fordyce (Village)—Cedar.............. NE-4
Foreman (City)—Little River......... AR-2
Forest (Township)—Clinton............ IN-3
Forest (Village)—West Carroll
  Parish LA-2
Forest (Township)—Cheboygan MI-3
Forest (Township)—Genesee MI-3
Forest (Township)—Missaukee MI-3
Forest (Township)—Becker MN-3
Forest (Township)—Rice MN-3
Forest (City)—Scott MS-2
Forest (Township)—Holt MO-3
Forest (Village)—Hardin OH-3
Forest (CDP)—Bedford................... VA-2
Forest (Town)—Fond du Lac WI-3
Forest (Town)—Richland WI-3
Forest (Town)—St. Croix WI-3
Forest (Town)—Vernon WI-3
Forest Acres (City)—Richland SC-2
Forestbrook (CDP)—Horry.............SC-2
Forestburgh (Town)—Sullivan NY-1
Forest City (CDP)—Seminole.........FL-2
Forest City (Township)—Mason IL-3
Forest City (Village)—Mason.......... IL-3
Forest City (Township)—Hancock...IA-3
Forest City (Township)—
  Winnebago IA-3
Forest City (Township)—Meeker.. MN-3
Forest City (City)—Holt MO-3
Forest City (Town)—Rutherford....NC-2
Forest City (Borough)—
  Susquehanna PA-1
Forest County PA-1
Forest County WI-3
Forestdale (Division)—Jefferson....AL-2
Forester (Township)—Sanilac MI-3
Forest Grove (City)—
  Washington OR-4
Forest Heights (Town)—Prince
  George's MD-1
Foresthill (CDP)—Placer................ CA-4
Forest Hill (Village)—Rapides
  Parish LA-2
Forest Hill (City)—Tarrant TX-2
Forest Hills (City)—Jefferson......... KY-2
Forest Hills (CDP)—Kent............... MI-3
Forest Hills—Queens....................... NY-1
Forest Hills (Borough)—
  Allegheny......................................PA-1
Forest Hills (City)—Davidson TN-2
Forest Home (Township)—
  Antrim MI-3
Forest Home (CDP)—Tompkins ... NY-1
Forest Island Park (CDP)—Lee FL-2
Forest Lake (CDP)—Lake IL-3
Forest Lake (City)—Washington ... MN-3
Forest Lake (Township)—
  Washington MN-3
Forest Lake (Township)—
  Susquehanna PA-1
Forest Oaks (CDP)—Guilford NC-2
Foreston (City)—Mille Lacs.......... MN-3

Forest Park (City)—Clayton........... GA-2
Forest Park (Village)—Cook IL-3
Forest Park (City)—Hamilton........OH-3
Forest Park (Town)—Oklahoma OK-2
Forestport (Town)—Oneida NY-1
Forest Prairie (Township)—
  Meeker.......................................MN-3
Forest River (City)—Walsh ND-4
Forest River (Township)—Walsh ...ND-4
Forest View (Village)—Cook........... IL-3
Forestville (CDP)—Sonoma........... CA-4
Forestville (CDP)—Prince
  George's MD-1
Forestville (Village)—Sanilac MI-3
Forestville (Township)—
  Fillmore......................................MN-3
Forestville (Village)—
  Chautauqua................................NY-1
Forestville (CDP)—Hamilton OH-3
Forestville (Town)—Door WI-3
Forestville (Village)—Door WI-3
Forgan (Town)—Beaver.................. OK-2
Foristell (City)—St. Charles MO-3
Foristell (City)—Warren MO-3
Fork (Township)—Mecosta MI-3
Fork (Township)—Marshall MN-3
Forked River (CDP)—Ocean NJ-1
Forkland (Town)—Greene...............AL-2
Forks (Township)—Northampton .. PA-1
Forks (Township)—Sullivan PA-1
Forks (Town)—Clallam WA-4
The Forks (Plantation)—
  Somerset.....................................ME-1
Forkston (Township)—Wyoming ... PA-1
Forksville (Borough)—Sullivan PA-1
Forman (City)—Sargent ND-4
Forman (Township)—Sargent ND-4
Formoso (City)—Jewell KS-4
Forney (Town)—Kaufman TX-2
Forrest (Township)—Livingston IL-3
Forrest (Village)—Livingston IL-3
Forrest City (City)—St. Francis AR-2
Forrest County MS-2
Forrester (Township)—Ness KS-4
Forreston (Township)—Ogle IL-3
Forreston (Village)—Ogle IL-3
Forsan (City)—Howard TX-2
Forsyth (City)—Monroe GA-2
Forsyth (Village)—Macon IL-3
Forsyth (Township)—Marquette ... MI-3
Forsyth (City)—Taney MO-3
Forsyth (City)—Rosebud MT-4
Forsyth County GA-2
Forsyth County NC-2
Fort (Township)—Marshall SD-4
Fort Ann (Town)—Washington...... NY-1
Fort Ann (Village)—Washington.... NY-1
Fort Apache Reservation
  (AZ)...IndRes-4
Fort Ashby (CDP)—Mineral......... WV-2
Fort Atkinson (City)—Winneshiek ..IA-3
Fort Atkinson (City)—Jefferson..... WI-3
Fort Belknap (CDP)—Blaine MT-4
Fort Belknap Reservation & Trust
  Lands (MT)............................IndRes-4
Fort Belvoir (VA) Mil-4
Fort Belvoir (Military Facility)—
  Fairfax VA-2
Fort Bend County TX-2
Fort Benjamin Harrison (IN).........Mil-4
Fort Benning (GA)..........................Mil-4
Fort Benning South (Military
  Facility)—Chattahoochee GA-2
Fort Benton (City)—Chouteau...... MT-4

Fort Berthold Reservation
(ND)..................................*IndRes-4*
Fort Bidwell Reservation
(CA)..................................*IndRes-4*
Fort Bliss (TX).........................*Mil-4*
Fort Bliss (Military Facility)—El
Paso.......................................*TX-2*
Fort Bragg (City)—Mendocino......*CA-4*
Fort Bragg (NC).........................*Mil-4*
Fort Bragg (Military Facility)—
Cumberland...............................*NC-2*
Fort Branch (Town)—Gibson.........*IN-3*
Fort Calhoun (City)—
Washington...............................*NE-4*
Fort Campbell (KY) (TN).............*Mil-4*
Fort Campbell North (Military
Facility)—Christian....................*KY-2*
Fort Carson (CO)........................*Mil-4*
Fort Carson (Military Facility)—El
Paso..*CO-4*
Fort Cobb (Town)—Caddo............*OK-2*
Fort Collins (City)—Larimer.........*CO-4*
Fort Covington (Town)—
Franklin....................................*NY-1*
Fort Davis (Pop. Place)—Jeff
Davis.......................................*TX-2*
Fort Defiance (CDP)—Apache......*AZ-4*
Fort Deposit (Town)—Lowndes.....*AL-2*
Fort Detrick (MD).......................*Mil-4*
Fort Devens (MA).......................*Mil-4*
Fort Devens (Mil. facil.)—
Middlesex.................................*MA-1*
Fort Devens (Mil. facil.)—
Worcester.................................*MA-1*
Fort Dix (NJ)............................*Mil-4*
Fort Dix (Mil. facil.)—Burlington...*NJ-1*
Fort Dodge (City)—Webster.........*IA-3*
Fort Drum (NY).........................*Mil-4*
Fort Drum (Mil. facil.)—
Jefferson..................................*NY-1*
Fort Duchesne (CDP)—Uintah......*UT-4*
Fort Edward (Town)—
Washington..............................*NY-1*
Fort Edward (Village)—
Washington..............................*NY-1*
Fortescue (Town)—Holt................*MO-3*
Fort Eustis (VA).........................*Mil-4*
Fort Fairfield (Town)—
Aroostook.................................*ME-1*
Fort Gaines (City)—Clay..............*GA-2*
Fort Gates (City)—Coryell............*TX-2*
Fort Gay (Town)—Wayne.............*WV-2*
Fort George G. Meade (MD).........*Mil-4*
Fort Gibson (Town)—Muskogee....*OK-2*
Fort Gordon (GA).......................*Mil-4*
Fort Gordon (Military Facility)—
Richmond.................................*GA-2*
Fort Gratiot (Township)—St.
Clair..*MI-3*
Fort Greely (Military Facility)—
Southeast Fairbanks Census
Area..*AK-4*
Fort Hall (CDP)—Bannock...........*ID-4*
Fort Hall (CDP)—Bingham...........*ID-4*
Fort Hall Reservation & Trust Lands
(ID).......................................*IndRes-4*
Fort Hood (TX)..........................*Mil-4*
Fort Hood (Military Facility)—
Bell...*TX-2*
Fort Hood (Military Facility)—
Coryell.....................................*TX-2*
Fort Huachuca (AZ)....................*Mil-4*
Forthun (Township)—Burke..........*ND-4*
Fort Hunt (CDP)—Fairfax............*VA-2*

Fortier (Township)—Yellow
Medicine..................................*MN-3*
Fort Independence Reservation
(CA).....................................*IndRes-4*
Fort Irwin, National Training Center
(CA).......................................*Mil-4*
Fort Jackson (SC).......................*Mil-4*
Fort Jennings (Village)—Putnam...*OH-3*
Fort Johnson (Village)—
Montgomery..............................*NY-1*
Fort Jones (City)—Siskiyou..........*CA-4*
Fort Kent (Town)—Aroostook......*ME-1*
Fort Knox (KY)..........................*Mil-4*
Fort Knox (Military Facility)—
Hardin......................................*KY-2*
Fort Knox (Military Facility)—
Meade......................................*KY-2*
Fort Laramie (Town)—Goshen.....*WY-4*
Fort Lauderdale (City)—Broward...*FL-2*
Fort Lawn (Town)—Chester..........*SC-2*
Fort Leavenworth (KS).................*Mil-4*
Fort Lee (Borough)—Bergen.........*NJ-1*
Fort Lee (Military Facility)—Prince
George......................................*VA-2*
Fort Leonard Wood (MO).............*Mil-4*
Fort Leonard Wood (Military
Facility)—Pulaski.......................*MO-3*
Fort Lesley J. McNair (DC)..........*Mil-4*
Fort Lewis (WA).........................*Mil-4*
Fort Lewis (Military Facility)—
Pierce......................................*WA-4*
Fort Loramie (Village)—Shelby.....*OH-3*
Fort Lupton (City)—Weld.............*CO-4*
Fort Madison (City)—Lee............*IA-3*
Fort McClellan (AL)....................*Mil-4*
Fort McClellan (Military Facility)—
Calhoun....................................*AL-2*
Fort McDermitt Reservation
(NV)....................................*IndRes-4*
Fort McDowell Reservation
(AZ).....................................*IndRes-4*
Fort McKinley (CDP)—
Montgomery...............................*OH-3*
Fort Meade (City)—Polk..............*FL-2*
Fort Meade (Mil. facil.)—Anne
Arundel.....................................*MD-1*
Fort Mill (Town)—York................*SC-2*
Fort Mitchell (City)—Kenton........*KY-2*
Fort Mojave Reservation & Trust Lands
(CA).....................................*IndRes-4*
Fort Monmouth (NJ)....................*Mil-4*
Fort Monroe (VA)........................*Mil-4*
Fort Montgomery (CDP)—
Orange.....................................*NY-1*
Fort Morgan (City)—Morgan.........*CO-4*
Fort Myer (VA)...........................*Mil-4*
Fort Myers (City)—Lee................*FL-2*
Fort Myers Beach (CDP)—Lee......*FL-2*
Fort Myers Shores (CDP)—Lee.....*FL-2*
Fort Oglethorpe (City)—Catoosa...*GA-2*
Fort Oglethorpe (City)—Walker.....*GA-2*
Fort Ord (CA)............................*Mil-4*
Fort Osage (Township)—Jackson...*MO-3*
Fort Payne (City)—DeKalb...........*AL-2*
Fort Peck (Town)—Valley............*MT-4*
Fort Peck Dam (MT)...................*Geog-4*
Fort Peck Lake (MT)...................*Geog-4*
Fort Peck Reservation (MT)....*IndRes-4*
Fort Pierce (City)—St. Lucie........*FL-2*
Fort Pierce North (CDP)—St.
Lucie......................................*FL-2*
Fort Pierce South (CDP)—St.
Lucie......................................*FL-2*
Fort Pierre (City)—Stanley...........*SD-4*

Fort Plain (Village)—
Montgomery..............................*NY-1*
Fort Polk (LA)............................*Mil-4*
Fort Polk North (Military Facility)—
Vernon Parish............................*LA-2*
Fort Polk South (Military Facility)—
Vernon Parish............................*LA-2*
Fort Randall Dam (SD)................*Geog-4*
Fort Ransom (City)—Ransom.......*ND-4*
Fort Ransom (Township)—
Ransom...................................*ND-4*
Fort Recovery (Village)—Mercer...*OH-3*
Fort Riley (KS)...........................*Mil-4*
Fort Riley-Camp Whiteside (Military
Facility)—Geary.........................*KS-4*
Fort Riley North (Military Facility)—
Geary......................................*KS-4*
Fort Riley North (Military Facility)—
Riley.......................................*KS-4*
Fort Ripley (City)—Crow Wing....*MN-3*
Fort Ripley (Township)—Crow
Wing......................................*MN-3*
Fort Ritchie (Mil. facil.)—
Washington..............................*MD-1*
Fort Rucker (Military Facility)—
Dale..*AL-2*
Fort Russell (Township)—
Madison..................................*IL-3*
Fort Salonga (CDP)—Suffolk......*NY-1*
Fort Sam Houston (TX)...............*Mil-4*
Fort Scott (City)—Bourbon..........*KS-4*
Fort Shafter (CDP)—Honolulu.....*HI-4*
Fort Shawnee (Village)—Allen......*OH-3*
Fort Sill (OK)............................*Mil-4*
Fort Sill (Military Facility)—
Comanche................................*OK-2*
Fort Smith (City)—Sebastian........*AR-2*
Fort Snelling (Pop. Place)—
Hennepin.................................*MN-3*
Fort Stewart (GA).......................*Mil-4*
Fort Stewart (Military Facility)—
Liberty....................................*GA-2*
Fort Stockton (City)—Pecos........*TX-2*
Fort Sumner (Village)—DeBaca...*NM-2*
Fort Supply (Town)—Woodward...*OK-2*
Fort Thomas (City)—Campbell.....*KY-2*
Fort Thompson (CDP)—Buffalo...*SD-4*
Fort Totten (Pop. Place)—
Benson....................................*ND-4*
Fort Towson (Town)—Choctaw....*OK-2*
Fortuna (City)—Humboldt...........*CA-4*
Fortuna (City)—Divide................*ND-4*
Fortuna Foothills (CDP)—Yuma...*AZ-4*
Fort Valley (City)—Peach............*GA-2*
Fortville (Town)—Hancock...........*IN-3*
Fort Wainwright (AK)..................*Mil-4*
Fort Walton Beach (City)—
Okaloosa..................................*FL-2*
Fort Washakie (CDP)—Fremont...*WY-4*
Fort Washington (CDP)—Prince
George's..................................*MD-1*
Fort Washington (CDP)—
Montgomery.............................*PA-1*
Fort Wayne (City)—Allen............*IN-3*
Fort White (Town)—Columbia.....*FL-2*
Fort Winnebago (Town)—
Columbia.................................*WI-3*
Fort Worth (City)—Denton..........*TX-2*
Fort Worth (City)—Tarrant..........*TX-2*
Fort Wright (City)—Kenton.........*KY-2*
Fort Yates (City)—Sioux.............*ND-4*
Fort Yates (Pop. Place)—Sioux....*ND-4*
Forty Fort (Borough)—Luzerne....*PA-1*
Fort Yukon (City)—Yukon-Koyukuk
Census Area............................*AK-4*

General Index   American Places Dictionary

Fort Yuma (Quechan) Reservation
(AZ) *IndRes-4*
Forward (Township)—Wells *ND-4*
Forward (Township)—Allegheny *PA-1*
Forward (Township)—Butler *PA-1*
Foss (City)—Washita *OK-2*
Fossil (Town)—Wheeler *OR-4*
Fosston (City)—Polk *MN-3*
Fossum (Township)—Norman *MN-3*
Foster (Township)—Madison *IL-3*
Foster (Township)—Marion *IL-3*
Foster (City)—Bracken *KY-2*
Foster (Township)—Ogemaw *MI-3*
Foster (Township)—Big Stone *MN-3*
Foster (Township)—Faribault *MN-3*
Foster (Town)—Bates *MO-3*
Foster (Village)—Pierce *NE-4*
Foster (Township)—Luzerne *PA-1*
Foster (Township)—McKean *PA-1*
Foster (Township)—Schuylkill *PA-1*
Foster (Town)—Providence *RI-1*
Foster (Township)—Beadle *SD-4*
Foster (Township)—Hutchinson *SD-4*
Foster (Township)—Perkins *SD-4*
Foster (Town)—Clark *WI-3*
Foster City (City)—San Mateo *CA-4*
Foster County *ND-4*
Fostoria (City)—Clay *IA-3*
Fostoria (City)—Hancock *OH-3*
Fostoria (City)—Seneca *OH-3*
Fostoria (City)—Wood *OH-3*
Fouke (City)—Miller *AR-2*
Fountain (City)—El Paso *CO-4*
Fountain (Township)—Ottawa *KS-4*
Fountain (Village)—Mason *MI-3*
Fountain (City)—Fillmore *MN-3*
Fountain (Township)—Fillmore *MN-3*
Fountain (Town)—Pitt *NC-2*
Fountain (Township)—Edmunds ... *SD-4*
Fountain (Town)—Juneau *WI-3*
Fountain Bluff (Township)—
Jackson *IL-3*
Fountain City (Town)—Wayne *IN-3*
Fountain City (City)—Buffalo *WI-3*
Fountain County *IN-3*
Fountain Creek (Township)—
Iroquois *IL-3*
Fountain Green (Township)—
Hancock *IL-3*
Fountain Green (City)—Sanpete ... *UT-4*
Fountain Hill (Town)—Ashley *AR-2*
Fountain Hill (Borough)—Lehigh ... *PA-1*
Fountain Hills (Town)—
Maricopa *AZ-4*
Fountain Inn (Town)—Greenville .. *SC-2*
Fountain Inn (Town)—Laurens *SC-2*
Fountain Prairie (Township)—
Pipestone *MN-3*
Fountain Prairie (Town)—
Columbia *WI-3*
Fountain Run (City)—Monroe *KY-2*
Fountain Valley (City)—Orange *CA-4*
Four Bears Village (CDP)—
McKenzie *ND-4*
Fourche (Town)—Perry *AR-2*
Four Corners (CDP)—Marion *OR-4*
Four Mile (Township)—Wayne *IL-3*
Four Mountains, Islands of
(AK) *Geog-4*
Four Oaks (Town)—Johnston *NC-2*
Fowler (City)—Fresno *CA-4*
Fowler (Town)—Otero *CO-4*
Fowler (Town)—Benton *IN-3*
Fowler (City)—Meade *KS-4*
Fowler (Township)—Meade *KS-4*

Fowler (Village)—Clinton *MI-3*
Fowler (Town)—St. Lawrence *NY-1*
Fowler (Township)—Trumbull *OH-3*
Fowlerton (Town)—Grant *IN-3*
Fowlerville (Village)—Livingston ... *MI-3*
Fox (CDP)—Fairbanks North Star
Borough *AK-4*
Fox (Township)—Jasper *IL-3*
Fox (Township)—Kendall *IL-3*
Fox (Township)—Platte *MO-3*
Fox (Township)—Carroll *OH-3*
Fox (Township)—Elk *PA-1*
Fox (Township)—Sullivan *PA-1*
Foxborough (Town)—Norfolk *MA-1*
Foxburg (Borough)—Clarion *PA-1*
Fox Chapel (Borough)—Allegheny .. *PA-1*
Fox Chase (City)—Bullitt *KY-2*
Fox Creek (Township)—
Harrison *MO-3*
Fox Farm-College (CDP)—
Laramie *WY-4*
Foxfire (Village)—Moore *NC-2*
Foxholm (Township)—Ward *ND-4*
Foxhome (City)—Wilkin *MN-3*
Foxhome (Township)—Wilkin *MN-3*
Fox Island (CDP)—Pierce *WA-4*
Fox Islands (AK) *Geog-4*
Fox Lake (Village)—Lake *IL-3*
Fox Lake (Village)—McHenry *IL-3*
Fox Lake (Township)—Martin *MN-3*
Fox Lake (City)—Dodge *WI-3*
Fox Lake (Town)—Dodge *WI-3*
Fox Lake Hills (CDP)—Lake *IL-3*
Fox Point (Village)—Milwaukee *WI-3*
Fox River (CDP)—Kenai Peninsula
Borough *AK-4*
Fox River Grove (Village)—
McHenry *IL-3*
Fox River Valley Gardens (Village)—
Lake *IL-3*
Fox River Valley Gardens (Village)—
McHenry *IL-3*
Fox Run (CDP)—Butler *PA-1*
Foxton (Township)—Clark *SD-4*
Foyil (Town)—Rogers *OK-2*
Frackville (Borough)—Schuylkill ... *PA-1*
Fragrant Hill (Township)—
Dickinson *KS-4*
Frailey (Township)—Schuylkill *PA-1*
Fram (Township)—Wells *ND-4*
Framingham (Town)—Middlesex .. *MA-1*
Framnas (Township)—Stevens *MN-3*
Francestown (Town)—
Hillsborough *NH-1*
Francesville (Town)—Pulaski *IN-3*
Francis (Township)—Holt *NE-4*
Francis (Township)—Burleigh *ND-4*
Francis (Town)—Pontotoc *OK-2*
Francis (Town)—Summit *UT-4*
Francis Case, Lake (SD) *Geog-4*
Francisco (Town)—Gibson *IN-3*
Francis Creek (Village)—
Manitowoc *WI-3*
Francis E. Warren Air Force Base
(WY) *Mil-4*
Franconia (Township)—Chisago ... *MN-3*
Franconia (Town)—Grafton *NH-1*
Franconia (Township)—
Montgomery *PA-1*
Franconia (CDP)—Fairfax *VA-2*
Frankenlust (Township)—Bay *MI-3*
Frankenmuth (City)—Saginaw *MI-3*
Frankenmuth (Township)—
Saginaw *MI-3*
Frankford (Town)—Sussex *DE-1*

Frankford (Township)—Mower *MN-3*
Frankford (City)—Pike *MO-3*
Frankford (Township)—Sussex *NJ-1*
Frankfort (Township)—Franklin *IL-3*
Frankfort (Township)—Will *IL-3*
Frankfort (Village)—Will *IL-3*
Frankfort (City)—Clinton *IN-3*
Frankfort (City)—Marshall *KS-4*
Frankfort (City)—Franklin *KY-2*
Frankfort (Town)—Waldo *ME-1*
Frankfort (City)—Benzie *MI-3*
Frankfort (Township)—Wright *MN-3*
Frankfort (Township)—Knox *NE-4*
Frankfort (Town)—Herkimer *NY-1*
Frankfort (Village)—Herkimer *NY-1*
Frankfort (Village)—Ross *OH-3*
Frankfort (City)—Spink *SD-4*
Frankfort (Township)—Spink *SD-4*
Frankfort (Town)—Marathon *WI-3*
Frankfort (Town)—Pepin *WI-3*
Frankfort Springs (Borough)—
Beaver *PA-1*
Frankfort Square (CDP)—Will *IL-3*
Franklin (Town)—Macon *AL-2*
Franklin (Town)—Izard *AR-2*
Franklin (Town)—New London *CT-1*
Franklin (City)—Heard *GA-2*
Franklin (City)—Franklin *ID-4*
Franklin (Township)—DeKalb *IL-3*
Franklin (Village)—Morgan *IL-3*
Franklin (Township)—Dekalb *IN-3*
Franklin (Township)—Floyd *IN-3*
Franklin (Township)—Grant *IN-3*
Franklin (Township)—Harrison *IN-3*
Franklin (Township)—Hendricks .. *IN-3*
Franklin (Township)—Henry *IN-3*
Franklin (City)—Johnson *IN-3*
Franklin (Township)—Johnson *IN-3*
Franklin (Township)—Kosciusko ... *IN-3*
Franklin (Township)—Marion *IN-3*
Franklin (Township)—
Montgomery *IN-3*
Franklin (Township)—Owen *IN-3*
Franklin (Township)—Pulaski *IN-3*
Franklin (Township)—Putnam *IN-3*
Franklin (Township)—Randolph .. *IN-3*
Franklin (Township)—Ripley *IN-3*
Franklin (Township)—
Washington *IN-3*
Franklin (Township)—Wayne *IN-3*
Franklin (City)—Lee *IA-3*
Franklin (Township)—Bourbon ... *KS-4*
Franklin (Township)—Edwards ... *KS-4*
Franklin (Township)—Franklin ... *KS-4*
Franklin (Township)—Jackson ... *KS-4*
Franklin (Township)—Lincoln *KS-4*
Franklin (Township)—Marshall ... *KS-4*
Franklin (Township)—Ness *KS-4*
Franklin (Township)—Trego *KS-4*
Franklin (Township)—
Washington *KS-4*
Franklin (City)—Simpson *KY-2*
Franklin (City)—St. Mary Parish ... *LA-2*
Franklin (Town)—Hancock *ME-1*
Franklin (Town)—Norfolk *MA-1*
Franklin (Township)—Clare *MI-3*
Franklin (Township)—Houghton .. *MI-3*
Franklin (Township)—Lenawee ... *MI-3*
Franklin (Village)—Oakland *MI-3*
Franklin (City)—Renville *MN-3*
Franklin (City)—St. Louis *MN-3*
Franklin (Township)—Wright *MN-3*
Franklin (Township)—Dent *MO-3*
Franklin (Township)—Grundy *MO-3*
Franklin (City)—Howard *MO-3*

American Places Dictionary — General Index

Franklin (Township)—Howard *MO-3*
Franklin (Township)—Laclede *MO-3*
Franklin (Township)—Miller *MO-3*
Franklin (Township)—Newton *MO-3*
Franklin (Township)—Butler *NE-4*
Franklin (Township)—Fillmore *NE-4*
Franklin (City)—Franklin *NE-4*
Franklin (City)—Merrimack *NH-1*
Franklin (Township)—Gloucester ... *NJ-1*
Franklin (Township)—Hunterdon .. *NJ-1*
Franklin (Township)—Somerset *NJ-1*
Franklin (Borough)—Sussex *NJ-1*
Franklin (Township)—Warren *NJ-1*
Franklin (Town)—Delaware *NY-1*
Franklin (Village)—Delaware *NY-1*
Franklin (Town)—Franklin *NY-1*
Franklin (Town)—Macon *NC-2*
Franklin (Township)—Steele *ND-4*
Franklin (Township)—Adams *OH-3*
Franklin (Township)—Brown *OH-3*
Franklin (Township)—Clermont ... *OH-3*
Franklin (Township)—Columbiana *OH-3*
Franklin (Township)—Coshocton *OH-3*
Franklin (Township)—Darke *OH-3*
Franklin (Township)—Franklin *OH-3*
Franklin (Township)—Fulton *OH-3*
Franklin (Township)—Harrison *OH-3*
Franklin (Township)—Jackson *OH-3*
Franklin (Township)—Licking *OH-3*
Franklin (Township)—Mercer *OH-3*
Franklin (Township)—Monroe *OH-3*
Franklin (Township)—Morrow *OH-3*
Franklin (Township)—Portage *OH-3*
Franklin (Township)—Richland *OH-3*
Franklin (Township)—Ross *OH-3*
Franklin (Township)—Shelby *OH-3*
Franklin (Township)—Summit *OH-3*
Franklin (Township)—Tuscarawas *OH-3*
Franklin (City)—Warren *OH-3*
Franklin (Township)—Warren *OH-3*
Franklin (Township)—Wayne *OH-3*
Franklin (Township)—Adams *PA-1*
Franklin (Township)—Beaver *PA-1*
Franklin (Township)—Bradford *PA-1*
Franklin (Township)—Butler *PA-1*
Franklin (City)—Cambria *PA-1*
Franklin (Township)—Carbon *PA-1*
Franklin (Township)—Chester *PA-1*
Franklin (Township)—Columbia ... *PA-1*
Franklin (Township)—Erie *PA-1*
Franklin (Township)—Fayette *PA-1*
Franklin (Township)—Greene *PA-1*
Franklin (Township)—Huntingdon *PA-1*
Franklin (Township)—Luzerne *PA-1*
Franklin (Township)—Lycoming *PA-1*
Franklin (Township)—Snyder *PA-1*
Franklin (Township)—Susquehanna *PA-1*
Franklin (City)—Venango *PA-1*
Franklin (Township)—York *PA-1*
Franklin (Township)—Jerauld *SD-4*
Franklin (Township)—Lake *SD-4*
Franklin (City)—Williamson *TN-2*
Franklin (City)—Robertson *TX-2*
Franklin (Town)—Franklin *VT-1*
Franklin (Town)—Pendleton *WV-2*
Franklin (Town)—Jackson *WI-3*
Franklin (Town)—Kewaunee *WI-3*
Franklin (Town)—Manitowoc *WI-3*
Franklin (City)—Milwaukee *WI-3*
Franklin (Town)—Sauk *WI-3*

Franklin (Town)—Vernon *WI-3*
Franklin County *AL-2*
Franklin County *AR-2*
Franklin County *FL-2*
Franklin County *GA-2*
Franklin County *ID-4*
Franklin County *IL-3*
Franklin County *IN-3*
Franklin County *IA-3*
Franklin County *KS-4*
Franklin County *KY-2*
Franklin County *ME-1*
Franklin County *MA-1*
Franklin County *MS-2*
Franklin County *MO-3*
Franklin County *NE-4*
Franklin County *NY-1*
Franklin County *NC-2*
Franklin County *OH-3*
Franklin County *PA-1*
Franklin County *TN-2*
Franklin County *TX-2*
Franklin County *VT-1*
Franklin County *VA-2*
Franklin County *WA-4*
Franklin D. Roosevelt Lake (WA) *Geog-4*
Franklin Furnace (CDP)—Scioto ... *OH-3*
Franklin Grove (Village)—Lee *IL-3*
Franklin (Independent City) *VA-2*
Franklin Lakes (Borough)—Bergen *NJ-1*
Franklin No. 1 (Township)—Greene *MO-3*
Franklin No. 2 (Township)—Greene *MO-3*
Franklin Parish *LA-2*
Franklin Park (Village)—Cook *IL-3*
Franklin Park (Borough)—Allegheny *PA-1*
Franklin Springs (City)—Franklin *GA-2*
Franklin Square (CDP)—Nassau ... *NY-1*
Franklinton (Town)—Washington Parish *LA-2*
Franklinton (Town)—Franklin *NC-2*
Franklintown (Borough)—York *PA-1*
Franklinville (Town)—Cattaraugus *NY-1*
Franklinville (Village)—Cattaraugus *NY-1*
Franklinville (Town)—Randolph ... *NC-2*
Franklyn (Township)—Brown *SD-4*
Frankston (Town)—Anderson *TX-2*
Frankstown (Township)—Blair *PA-1*
Frankton (Town)—Madison *IN-3*
Frannie (Town)—Big Horn *WY-4*
Frannie (Town)—Park *WY-4*
Franzen (Town)—Marathon *WI-3*
Fraser (Town)—Grand *CO-4*
Fraser (City)—Boone *IA-3*
Fraser (Township)—Bay *MI-3*
Fraser (City)—Macomb *MI-3*
Fraser (Township)—Martin *MN-3*
Frazee (City)—Becker *MN-3*
Frazer (CDP)—Valley *MT-4*
Frazer (Township)—Allegheny *PA-1*
Frazeysburg (Village)—Muskingum *OH-3*
Frazier (Township)—Divide *ND-4*
Frazier Park (CDP)—Kern *CA-4*
Freda (Township)—Grant *ND-4*
Fredenberg (Township)—St. Louis *MN-3*
Frederic (Township)—Crawford *MI-3*

Frederic (Village)—Polk *WI-3*
Frederica (Town)—Kent *DE-1*
Frederick (Town)—Weld *CO-4*
Frederick (Township)—Schuyler ... *IL-3*
Frederick (City)—Rice *KS-4*
Frederick (City)—Frederick *MD-1*
Frederick (Township)—Divide *ND-4*
Frederick (City)—Tillman *OK-2*
Frederick (Town)—Brown *SD-4*
Frederick (Township)—Brown *SD-4*
Frederick County *MD-1*
Frederick County *VA-2*
Fredericksburg (Town)—Washington *IN-3*
Fredericksburg (City)—Chickasaw ... *IA-3*
Fredericksburg (Village)—Wayne ... *OH-3*
Fredericksburg (CDP)—Crawford .. *PA-1*
Fredericksburg (CDP)—Lebanon *PA-1*
Fredericksburg (Town)—Gillespie *TX-2*
Fredericksburg (Independent City) .. *VA-2*
Frederickson (CDP)—Pierce *WA-4*
Fredericktown (City)—Madison ... *MO-3*
Fredericktown (Village)—Knox *OH-3*
Fredericktown-Millsboro (CDP)—Washington *PA-1*
Frederika (City)—Bremer *IA-3*
Fredlund (Township)—Perkins *SD-4*
Fredon (Township)—Sussex *NJ-1*
Fredonia (Town)—Coconino *AZ-4*
Fredonia (City)—Louisa *IA-3*
Fredonia (City)—Wilson *KS-4*
Fredonia (City)—Caldwell *KY-2*
Fredonia (Township)—Calhoun *MI-3*
Fredonia (Village)—Chautauqua ... *NY-1*
Fredonia (City)—Logan *ND-4*
Fredonia (Borough)—Mercer *PA-1*
Fredonia (Town)—Ozaukee *WI-3*
Fredonia (Village)—Ozaukee *WI-3*
Fredonia (Biscoe) (Town)—Prairie *AR-2*
Freeborn (City)—Freeborn *MN-3*
Freeborn (Township)—Freeborn ... *MN-3*
Freeborn (Township)—Dunklin *MO-3*
Freeborn (Township)—Eddy *ND-4*
Freeborn County *MN-3*
Freeburg (Township)—St. Clair *IL-3*
Freeburg (Village)—St. Clair *IL-3*
Freeburg (Village)—Osage *MO-3*
Freeburg (Borough)—Snyder *PA-1*
Freedom (CDP)—Santa Cruz *CA-4*
Freedom (Township)—Carroll *IL-3*
Freedom (Township)—La Salle *IL-3*
Freedom (Township)—Bourbon *KS-4*
Freedom (Township)—Ellis *KS-4*
Freedom (Township)—Phillips *KS-4*
Freedom (Township)—Republic *KS-4*
Freedom (Town)—Waldo *ME-1*
Freedom (Township)—Washtenaw *MI-3*
Freedom (Township)—Waseca *MN-3*
Freedom (Township)—Lafayette ... *MO-3*
Freedom (Town)—Carroll *NH-1*
Freedom (Town)—Cattaraugus *NY-1*
Freedom (Township)—Ward *ND-4*
Freedom (Township)—Henry *OH-3*
Freedom (Township)—Portage *OH-3*
Freedom (Township)—Wood *OH-3*
Freedom (Town)—Woods *OK-2*
Freedom (Township)—Adams *PA-1*
Freedom (Borough)—Beaver *PA-1*
Freedom (Township)—Blair *PA-1*
Freedom (Township)—Faulk *SD-4*
Freedom (Town)—Forest *WI-3*
Freedom (Town)—Outagamie *WI-3*

General Index

Freedom (Town)—Sauk *WI-3*
Freedom Trail (MA) *Geog-4*
Freehold (Borough)—Monmouth ... *NJ-1*
Freehold (Township)—
  Monmouth *NJ-1*
Freehold (Township)—Warren *PA-1*
Freeland (CDP)—Saginaw *MI-3*
Freeland (Township)—Lac qui
  Parle *MN-3*
Freeland (Borough)—Luzerne *PA-1*
Freeland (CDP)—Island *WA-4*
Freeman (Township)—Clare *MI-3*
Freeman (Township)—Freeborn ... *MN-3*
Freeman (City)—Cass *MO-3*
Freeman (Township)—Richland *ND-4*
Freeman (City)—Hutchinson *SD-4*
Freeman (Town)—Crawford *WI-3*
Freemansburg (Borough)—
  Northampton *PA-1*
Freeman Spur (Village)—Franklin.. *IL-3*
Freeman Spur (Village)—
  Williamson *IL-3*
Freeport (Town)—Walton *FL-2*
Freeport (City)—Stephenson *IL-3*
Freeport (Township)—Stephenson.. *IL-3*
Freeport (City)—Harper *KS-4*
Freeport (Town)—Cumberland *ME-1*
Freeport (Village)—Barry *MI-3*
Freeport (City)—Stearns *MN-3*
Freeport (Village)—Nassau *NY-1*
Freeport (Township)—Harrison *OH-3*
Freeport (Village)—Harrison *OH-3*
Freeport (Borough)—Armstrong *PA-1*
Freeport (Township)—Greene *PA-1*
Freeport (City)—Brazoria *TX-2*
Freer (City)—Duval *TX-2*
Free Soil (Township)—Mason *MI-3*
Free Soil (Village)—Mason *MI-3*
Freestone County *TX-2*
Freetown (Town)—Bristol *MA-1*
Freetown (Town)—Cortland *NY-1*
Freeville (Village)—Tompkins *NY-1*
Freistatt (Town)—Lawrence *MO-3*
Freistatt (Township)—Lawrence ... *MO-3*
Frelinghuysen (Township)—
  Warren *NJ-1*
Fremont (City)—Alameda *CA-4*
Fremont (Township)—Lake *IL-3*
Fremont (Town)—Steuben *IN-3*
Fremont (Township)—Steuben *IN-3*
Fremont (City)—Mahaska *IA-3*
Fremont (Township)—Lyon *KS-4*
Fremont (Township)—Isabella *MI-3*
Fremont (City)—Newaygo *MI-3*
Fremont (Township)—Saginaw *MI-3*
Fremont (Township)—Sanilac *MI-3*
Fremont (Township)—Tuscola *MI-3*
Fremont (Township)—Winona *MN-3*
Fremont (City)—Dodge *NE-4*
Fremont (Town)—Rockingham *NH-1*
Fremont (Town)—Steuben *NY-1*
Fremont (Town)—Sullivan *NY-1*
Fremont (Town)—Wayne *NC-2*
Fremont (Township)—Cavalier *ND-4*
Fremont (City)—Sandusky *OH-3*
Fremont (Township)—Moody *SD-4*
Fremont (Town)—Clark *WI-3*
Fremont (Town)—Waupaca *WI-3*
Fremont (Village)—Waupaca *WI-3*
Fremont County *CO-4*
Fremont County *ID-4*
Fremont County *IA-3*
Fremont County *WY-4*
Fremont Hills (City)—Christian ... *MO-3*
French (Township)—Adams *IN-3*
French (Township)—St. Louis *MN-3*
Frenchboro (Town)—Hancock *ME-1*
Frenchburg (City)—Menifee *KY-2*
French Camp (CDP)—San
  Joaquin *CA-4*
French Camp (Village)—
  Choctaw *MS-2*
French Creek (Town)—
  Chautauqua *NY-1*
French Creek (Township)—
  Mercer *PA-1*
Frenchcreek (Township)—
  Venango *PA-1*
French Island (CDP)—La Crosse .. *WI-3*
French Lake (Township)—
  Wright *MN-3*
French Lick (Town)—Orange *IN-3*
French Lick (Township)—Orange... *IN-3*
French Settlement (Village)—Livingston
  Parish *LA-2*
Frenchtown (Township)—
  Monroe *MI-3*
Frenchtown (Township)—
  Antelope *NE-4*
Frenchtown (Borough)—
  Hunterdon *NJ-1*
Frenchville (Town)—Aroostook *ME-1*
Freshwater (Township)—Ramsey .. *ND-4*
Freshwater Bay (CDP)—
  Skagway-Hoonah-Angoon Census
  Area *AK-4*
Fresno (City)—Fresno *CA-4*
Fresno (CDP)—Fort Bend *TX-2*
Fresno County *CA-4*
Frettim (Township)—Kidder *ND-4*
Frewsburg (CDP)—Chautauqua ... *NY-1*
Friars Point (Town)—Coahoma *MS-2*
Friberg (Township)—Otter Tail *MN-3*
Friday Harbor (Town)—San
  Juan *WA-4*
Fridley (City)—Anoka *MN-3*
Fried (Township)—Stutsman *ND-4*
Friedens (Township)—St.
  Charles *MO-3*
Friedens (CDP)—Somerset *PA-1*
Friend (City)—Saline *NE-4*
Friendly (CDP)—Prince
  George's *MD-1*
Friendly (Town)—Tyler *WV-2*
Friends Creek (Township)—
  Macon *IL-3*
Friendship (Town)—Hot Spring *AR-2*
Friendship (Town)—Knox *ME-1*
Friendship (Township)—Emmet *MI-3*
Friendship (Township)—Yellow
  Medicine *MN-3*
Friendship (Town)—Allegany *NY-1*
Friendship (Town)—Crockett *TN-2*
Friendship (Village)—Adams *WI-3*
Friendship (Town)—Fond du
  Lac *WI-3*
Friendsville (Town)—Garrett *MD-1*
Friendsville (Borough)—
  Susquehanna *PA-1*
Friendsville (Town)—Blount *TN-2*
Friendswood (City)—Galveston *TX-2*
Friendswood (City)—Harris *TX-2*
Fries (Town)—Grayson *VA-2*
Friesland (Village)—Columbia *WI-3*
Frio County *TX-2*
Friona (City)—Parmer *TX-2*
Frisco (Town)—Summit *CO-4*
Frisco (City)—Collin *TX-2*
Frisco (City)—Denton *TX-2*
Frisco City (Town)—Monroe *AL-2*
Frissell, Mt. (CT) *Geog-4*
Fristoe (Township)—Benton *MO-3*
Fritch (City)—Hutchinson *TX-2*
Fritch (City)—Moore *TX-2*
Frit Creek (CDP)—Kenai Peninsula
  Borough *AK-4*
Frog Creek (Town)—Washburn *WI-3*
Frohn (Township)—Beltrami *MN-3*
Frohna (City)—Perry *MO-3*
Froid (Town)—Roosevelt *MT-4*
Fromberg (Town)—Carbon *MT-4*
Frontenac (Township)—Crawford *KS-4*
Frontenac (City)—St. Louis *MO-3*
Frontier (Township)—St.
  Charles *MO-3*
Frontier (City)—Cass *ND-4*
Frontier County *NE-4*
Front Range (CO) *Geog-4*
Front Royal (Town)—Warren *VA-2*
Frost (Township)—Clare *MI-3*
Frost (City)—Faribault *MN-3*
Frost (Town)—Navarro *TX-2*
Frostburg (City)—Allegany *MD-1*
Frostproof (City)—Polk *FL-2*
Fruita (Town)—Mesa *CO-4*
Fruit Cove (CDP)—St. Johns *FL-2*
Fruitdale (Town)—Butte *SD-4*
Fruit Heights (City)—Davis *UT-4*
Fruit Hill (CDP)—Hamilton *OH-3*
Fruithurst (City)—Cleburne *AL-2*
Fruitland (City)—Payette *ID-4*
Fruitland (City)—Muscatine *IA-3*
Fruitland (City)—Wicomico *MD-1*
Fruitland (Township)—
  Muskegon *MI-3*
Fruitland Park (City)—Lake *FL-2*
Fruitport (Township)—Muskegon.. *MI-3*
Fruitport (Village)—Muskegon *MI-3*
Fruitvale (CDP)—Mesa *CO-4*
Fruitvale (City)—Van Zandt *TX-2*
Fruitvale (CDP)—Yakima *WA-4*
Fruitville (CDP)—Sarasota *FL-2*
Fryeburg (Town)—Oxford *ME-1*
Fugit (Township)—Decatur *IN-3*
Fulda (City)—Murray *MN-3*
Fuller (Township)—Codington *SD-4*
Fullerton (City)—Orange *CA-4*
Fullerton (City)—Nance *NE-4*
Fullerton (Township)—Nance *NE-4*
Fullerton (City)—Dickey *ND-4*
Fullerton (CDP)—Lehigh *PA-1*
Fulshear (Town)—Fort Bend *TX-2*
Fulton (Town)—Clarke *AL-2*
Fulton (City)—Hempstead *AR-2*
Fulton (City)—Whiteside *IL-3*
Fulton (Township)—Whiteside *IL-3*
Fulton (Township)—Fountain *IN-3*
Fulton (Town)—Fulton *IN-3*
Fulton (City)—Bourbon *KS-4*
Fulton (City)—Fulton *KY-2*
Fulton (Township)—Gratiot *MI-3*
Fulton (City)—Itawamba *MS-2*
Fulton (City)—Callaway *MO-3*
Fulton (City)—Oswego *NY-1*
Fulton (Town)—Schoharie *NY-1*
Fulton (Township)—Fulton *OH-3*
Fulton (Village)—Morrow *OH-3*
Fulton (Township)—Lancaster *PA-1*
Fulton (Town)—Hanson *SD-4*
Fulton (Town)—Aransas *TX-2*
Fulton (Town)—Rock *WI-3*
Fulton County *AR-2*
Fulton County *GA-2*
Fulton County *IL-3*
Fulton County *IN-3*

Fulton County *KY-2*	Galena (Township)—Dixon *NE-4*	Gantts Quarry (Municipality)—
Fulton County *NY-1*	Galena (Village)—Delaware *OH-3*	Talladega *AL-2*
Fulton County *OH-3*	Galena Park (City)—Harris *TX-2*	Gap (CDP)—Lancaster *PA-1*
Fulton County *PA-1*	Gales (Township)—Redwood *MN-3*	Garber (City)—Clayton *IA-3*
Fultondale (City)—Jefferson *AL-2*	Gales (Township)—Aurora *SD-4*	Garber (City)—Garfield *OK-2*
Fultonham (Village)—	Galesburg (City)—Knox *IL-3*	Garborg (Township)—Richland *ND-4*
Muskingum *OH-3*	Galesburg (Township)—Knox *IL-3*	Gardar (Township)—Pembina *ND-4*
Fultonville (Village)—	Galesburg (Township)—Kingman ... *KS-4*	Garden (Township)—Cherokee *KS-4*
Montgomery *NY-1*	Galesburg (City)—Neosho *KS-4*	Garden (Township)—Harvey *KS-4*
Fults (Village)—Monroe *IL-3*	Galesburg (City)—Kalamazoo *MI-3*	Garden (Township)—Delta *MI-3*
Funk (Village)—Phelps *NE-4*	Galesburg (City)—Traill *ND-4*	Garden (Village)—Delta *MI-3*
Funkley (City)—Beltrami *MN-3*	Galesburg (Township)—Traill *ND-4*	Garden (Township)—Polk *MN-3*
Funks Grove (Township)—	Galestown (Town)—Dorchester *MD-1*	Gardena (City)—Los Angeles *CA-4*
McLean *IL-3*	Galesville (City)—Trempealeau *WI-3*	Gardena (City)—Bottineau *ND-4*
Funkstown (Town)—Washington .. *MD-1*	Galeton (Borough)—Potter *PA-1*	Garden Acres (CDP)—San
Funston (Town)—Colquitt *GA-2*	Galien (Township)—Berrien *MI-3*	Joaquin *CA-4*
Fuquay-Varina (Town)—Wake *NC-2*	Galien (Village)—Berrien *MI-3*	Garden City (Town)—Blount *AL-2*
Furman (Town)—Hampton *SC-2*	Galion (City)—Crawford *OH-3*	Garden City (Town)—Cullman *AL-2*
Furnas County *NE-4*	Gallagher (Township)—Clinton *PA-1*	Garden City (Town)—Weld *CO-4*
Fur Seal Islands (CO) *Geog-4*	Gallatin (Township)—Clay *MO-3*	Garden City (City)—Chatham *GA-2*
Fussels Corner (CDP)—Polk *FL-2*	Gallatin (City)—Daviess *MO-3*	Garden City (City)—Ada *ID-4*
Fyffe (Town)—DeKalb *AL-2*	Gallatin (Town)—Columbia *NY-1*	Garden City (City)—Finney *KS-4*
Gaastra (City)—Iron *MI-3*	Gallatin (City)—Sumner *TN-2*	Garden City (Township)—Finney ... *KS-4*
Gabbs (City)—Nye *NV-4*	Gallatin (City)—Cherokee *TX-2*	Garden City (City)—Wayne *MI-3*
Gackle (City)—Logan *ND-4*	**Gallatin County** *IL-3*	Garden City (Township)—Blue
Gadsden (City)—Etowah *AL-2*	**Gallatin County** *KY-2*	Earth *MN-3*
Gadsden (Town)—Crockett *TN-2*	**Gallatin County** *MT-4*	Garden City (City)—Cass *MO-3*
Gadsden County *FL-2*	Gallatin River (CO) *Geog-4*	Garden City (Village)—Nassau *NY-1*
Gaeland (Township)—Gove *KS-4*	Gallaway (City)—Fayette *TN-2*	Garden City (CDP)—Horry *SC-2*
Gaffney (City)—Cherokee *SC-2*	**Gallia County** *OH-3*	Garden City (Town)—Clark *SD-4*
Gage (Town)—Ellis *OK-2*	Galliano (CDP)—Lafourche	Garden City (Pop. Place)—
Gage County *NE-4*	Parish *LA-2*	Glasscock *TX-2*
Gages Lake (CDP)—Lake *IL-3*	Gallipolis (City)—Gallia *OH-3*	Garden City (Town)—Rich *UT-4*
Gagetown (Village)—Tuscola *MI-3*	Gallipolis (Township)—Gallia *OH-3*	Garden City Park (CDP)—
Gahanna (City)—Franklin *OH-3*	Gallitzin (Borough)—Cambria *PA-1*	Nassau *NY-1*
Gail (Pop. Place)—Borden *TX-2*	Gallitzin (Township)—Cambria *PA-1*	Garden City South (CDP)—
Gail Lake (Township)—Crow	Galloway (Township)—Atlantic *NJ-1*	Nassau *NY-1*
Wing *MN-3*	Gallup (City)—McKinley *NM-4*	**Garden County** *NE-4*
Gaines (Township)—Genesee *MI-3*	Galt (City)—Sacramento *CA-4*	Gardendale (City)—Jefferson *AL-2*
Gaines (Village)—Genesee *MI-3*	Galt (City)—Wright *IA-3*	Gardendale (CDP)—Ector *TX-2*
Gaines (Township)—Kent *MI-3*	Galt (Township)—Rice *KS-4*	Garden Grove (City)—Orange *CA-4*
Gaines (Town)—Orleans *NY-1*	Galt (City)—Grundy *MO-3*	Garden Grove (City)—Decatur *IA-3*
Gaines (Township)—Tioga *PA-1*	Galva (City)—Henry *IL-3*	Garden Grove (Township)—
Gainesboro (Town)—Jackson *TN-2*	Galva (Township)—Henry *IL-3*	Christian *MO-3*
Gaines County *TX-2*	Galva (City)—Ida *IA-3*	Garden Hill (Township)—Wayne *IL-3*
Gaines School (CDP)—Clarke *GA-2*	Galva (City)—McPherson *KS-4*	Garden Home-Whitford (CDP)—
Gainesville (Town)—Sumter *AL-2*	Galveston (Town)—Cass *IN-3*	Washington *OR-4*
Gainesville (City)—Alachua *FL-2*	Galveston (City)—Galveston *TX-2*	Garden of the Gods (CO) *Geog-4*
Gainesville (City)—Hall *GA-2*	Galveston Bay (TX) *Geog-4*	Garden Plain (Township)—
Gainesville (City)—Ozark *MO-3*	**Galveston County** *TX-2*	Whiteside *IL-3*
Gainesville (Town)—Wyoming *NY-1*	Galway (Town)—Saratoga *NY-1*	Garden Plain (City)—Sedgwick *KS-4*
Gainesville (Village)—Wyoming *NY-1*	Galway (Village)—Saratoga *NY-1*	Garden Plain (Township)—
Gainesville (City)—Cooke *TX-2*	Gamaliel (City)—Monroe *KY-2*	Sedgwick *KS-4*
Gainesville Mills (CDP)—Hall *GA-2*	Gambell (City)—Nome Census	Garden Prairie (Township)—
Gaithersburg (City)—	Area *AK-4*	Brown *SD-4*
Montgomery *MD-1*	Gambier (Village)—Knox *OH-3*	Garden Ridge (City)—Comal *TX-2*
Gakona (CDP)—Valdez-Cordova	Gamble (Township)—Lycoming *PA-1*	Garden Valley (Town)—Jackson *WI-3*
Census Area *AK-4*	Game Creek (CDP)—	Garden View (CDP)—Lycoming ... *PA-1*
Galatia (Township)—Saline *IL-3*	Skagway-Hoonah-Angoon Census	Gardere (CDP)—East Baton Rouge
Galatia (Village)—Saline *IL-3*	Area *AK-4*	Parish *LA-2*
Galatia (City)—Barton *KS-4*	Gamewell (Town)—Caldwell *NC-2*	Gardiner (City)—Kennebec *ME-1*
Galax (Independent City) *VA-2*	Ganado (CDP)—Apache *AZ-4*	Gardiner (Town)—Ulster *NY-1*
Gale (Township)—Marion *KS-4*	Ganado (Town)—Jackson *TX-2*	Gardiner's Island (NY) *Geog-4*
Gale (Town)—Trempealeau *WI-3*	Gandy (CDP)—Pinellas *FL-2*	Gardner (Town)—Grundy *IL-3*
Galen (Town)—Wayne *NY-1*	Gandy (Village)—Logan *NE-4*	Gardner (Township)—Sangamon ... *IL-3*
Galena (City)—Yukon-Koyukuk Census	Ganeer (Township)—Kankakee *IL-3*	Gardner (City)—Johnson *KS-4*
Area *AK-4*	Ganges (Township)—Allegan *MI-3*	Gardner (Township)—Johnson *KS-4*
Galena (City)—Jo Daviess *IL-3*	Gang Mills (CDP)—Steuben *NY-1*	Gardner (City)—Worcester *MA-1*
Galena (CDP)—Floyd *IN-3*	Gann (Village)—Knox *OH-3*	Gardner (Township)—Buffalo *NE-4*
Galena (Township)—La Porte *IN-3*	Gannett Peak (WY) *Geog-4*	Gardner (City)—Cass *ND-4*
Galena (City)—Cherokee *KS-4*	Gannvalley (Pop. Place)—	Gardner (Township)—Cass *ND-4*
Galena (Town)—Kent *MD-1*	Buffalo *SD-4*	Gardner (Town)—Door *WI-3*
Galena (Township)—Martin *MN-3*	Gans (Town)—Sequoyah *OK-2*	Gardnertown (CDP)—Orange *NY-1*
Galena (Township)—Jasper *MO-3*	Gantt (Town)—Covington *AL-2*	Gardnerville (CDP)—Douglas *NV-4*
Galena (City)—Stone *MO-3*	Gantt (CDP)—Greenville *SC-2*	

Gardnerville Ranchos (CDP)—
 Douglas NV-4
Garfield (Town)—Benton AR-2
Garfield (Town)—Emanuel GA-2
Garfield (Township)—Grundy IL-3
Garfield (Township)—Clay KS-4
Garfield (Township)—Decatur KS-4
Garfield (Township)—Dickinson ... KS-4
Garfield (Township)—Ellsworth KS-4
Garfield (Township)—Finney KS-4
Garfield (Township)—Jackson KS-4
Garfield (Township)—Ottawa KS-4
Garfield (City)—Pawnee KS-4
Garfield (Township)—Pawnee KS-4
Garfield (Township)—Rush KS-4
Garfield (Township)—Smith KS-4
Garfield (Township)—Wabaunsee .. KS-4
Garfield (Plantation)—
 Aroostook ME-1
Garfield (Township)—Bay MI-3
Garfield (Township)—Clare MI-3
Garfield (Township)—Grand
 Traverse MI-3
Garfield (Township)—Kalkaska ... MI-3
Garfield (Township)—Mackinac ... MI-3
Garfield (Township)—Newaygo MI-3
Garfield (City)—Douglas MN-3
Garfield (Township)—Lac qui
 Parle MN-3
Garfield (Township)—Polk MN-3
Garfield (Township)—Antelope NE-4
Garfield (Township)—Buffalo NE-4
Garfield (Township)—Cuming NE-4
Garfield (Township)—Custer NE-4
Garfield (Township)—Phelps NE-4
Garfield (Borough)—Bergen NJ-1
Garfield (Township)—Traill ND-4
Garfield (Township)—Clark SD-4
Garfield (Township)—Clay SD-4
Garfield (Township)—Douglas SD-4
Garfield (Township)—Hamlin SD-4
Garfield (Township)—Roberts SD-4
Garfield (Township)—Spink SD-4
Garfield (CDP)—Bastrop TX-2
Garfield (CDP)—Travis TX-2
Garfield (Town)—Whitman WA-4
Garfield (Town)—Jackson WI-3
Garfield (Town)—Polk WI-3
Garfield County CO-4
Garfield County MT-4
Garfield County NE-4
Garfield County OK-2
Garfield County UT-4
Garfield County WA-4
Garfield Heights (City)—
 Cuyahoga OH-3
Garibaldi (City)—Tillamook OR-4
Garland (Town)—Miller AR-2
Garland (Town)—Penobscot ME-1
Garland (Village)—Seward NE-4
Garland (Town)—Sampson NC-2
Garland (Township)—Brown SD-4
Garland (Town)—Tipton TN-2
Garland (City)—Collin TX-2
Garland (City)—Dallas TX-2
Garland (City)—Rockwall TX-2
Garland (City)—Box Elder UT-4
Garland County AR-2
Garnavillo (City)—Clayton IA-3
Garner (Town)—White AR-2
Garner (City)—Hancock IA-3
Garner (Town)—Wake NC-2
Garner (Township)—Golden
 Valley ND-4
Garnes (Township)—Red Lake MN-3

Garness (Township)—Burke ND-4
Garnet (Township)—Divide ND-4
Garnett (City)—Anderson KS-4
Garrard County KY-2
Garretson (City)—Minnehaha SD-4
Garrett (Township)—Douglas IL-3
Garrett (Village)—Douglas IL-3
Garrett (City)—Dekalb IN-3
Garrett (Borough)—Somerset PA-1
Garrett (Town)—Ellis TX-2
Garrett (CDP)—Walla Walla WA-4
Garrett County MD-1
Garrett Park (Town)—
 Montgomery MD-1
Garrettsville (Village)—Portage OH-3
Garrison (City)—Benton IA-3
Garrison (CDP)—Baltimore MD-1
Garrison (City)—Crow Wing MN-3
Garrison (Township)—Crow
 Wing MN-3
Garrison (Township)—Christian .. MO-3
Garrison (Village)—Butler NE-4
Garrison (City)—McLean ND-4
Garrison (Town)—Nacogdoches TX-2
Garvin (City)—Lyon MN-3
Garvin (Town)—McCurtain OK-2
Garvin County OK-2
Garwin (City)—Tama IA-3
Garwood (Borough)—Union NJ-1
Gary (City)—Lake IN-3
Gary (City)—Norman MN-3
Gary (City)—Deuel SD-4
Gary (City)—McDowell WV-2
Gary City (Town)—Panola TX-2
Garysburg (Town)—
 Northampton NC-2
Garyville (CDP)—St. John the Baptist
 Parish LA-2
Garza County TX-2
Gas (City)—Allen KS-4
Gas City (City)—Grant IN-3
Gasconade (City)—Gasconade MO-3
Gasconade (Township)—Laclede .. MO-3
Gasconade (Township)—Wright ... MO-3
Gasconade County MO-3
Gascoyne (City)—Bowman ND-4
Gascoyne (Township)—Bowman ... ND-4
Gaskill (Township)—Jefferson PA-1
Gasman (Township)—Ward ND-4
Gasper (Township)—Preble OH-3
Gasport (CDP)—Niagara NY-1
Gassaway (Town)—Braxton WV-2
Gassville (City)—Baxter AR-2
Gaston (Town)—Delaware IN-3
Gaston (Town)—Northampton NC-2
Gaston (City)—Washington OR-4
Gaston (Town)—Lexington SC-2
Gaston County NC-2
Gastonia (City)—Gaston NC-2
Gastonville (CDP)—Washington PA-1
Gate (Township)—McLean ND-4
Gate (Town)—Beaver OK-2
Gate City (Town)—Scott VA-2
Gates (Town)—Monroe NY-1
Gates (Township)—Eddy ND-4
Gates (City)—Linn OR-4
Gates (City)—Marion OR-4
Gates (Town)—Lauderdale TN-2
Gates County NC-2
Gates Mills (Village)—Cuyahoga .. OH-3
Gatesville (Town)—Gates NC-2
Gatesville (City)—Coryell TX-2
Gateway (Town)—Benton AR-2
Gateway (CDP)—Douglas CO-4
Gateway Arch (MO) Geog-4

Gatewood (Township)—Ripley MO-3
Gatlinburg (City)—Sevier TN-2
Gattman (Village)—Monroe MS-2
Gauley Bridge (Town)—Fayette WV-2
Gautier (City)—Jackson MS-2
Gay (Town)—Meriwether GA-2
Gay Head (Town)—Dukes MA-1
Gayle Mill (CDP)—Chester SC-2
Gaylesville (Town)—Cherokee AL-2
Gaylord (City)—Smith KS-4
Gaylord (City)—Otsego MI-3
Gaylord (City)—Sibley MN-3
Gays (Village)—Moultrie IL-3
Gays Mills (Village)—Crawford WI-3
Gayville (Town)—Yankton SD-4
Gayville (Township)—Yankton SD-4
Gearhart (City)—Clatsop OR-4
Geary (City)—Blaine OK-2
Geary (City)—Canadian OK-2
Geary County KS-4
Geauga County OH-3
Geddes (Town)—Onondaga NY-1
Geddes (City)—Charles Mix SD-4
Geiger (Municipality)—Sumter AL-2
Geistown (Borough)—Cambria PA-1
Gem (City)—Thomas KS-4
Gem (Township)—Bowman ND-4
Gem (Township)—Brown SD-4
Gem County ID-4
Gem Lake (City)—Ramsey MN-3
Gene Autry (Town)—Carter OK-2
Genesee (CDP)—Jefferson CO-4
Genesee (City)—Latah ID-4
Genesee (Township)—Whiteside ... IL-3
Genesee (Township)—Genesee MI-3
Genesee (Town)—Allegany NY-1
Genesee (Township)—Potter PA-1
Genesee (Town)—Waukesha WI-3
Genesee County MI-3
Genesee County NY-1
Genesee Falls (Town)—Wyoming .. NY-1
Geneseo (City)—Henry IL-3
Geneseo (Township)—Henry IL-3
Geneseo (City)—Rice KS-4
Geneseo (Town)—Livingston NY-1
Geneseo (Village)—Livingston NY-1
Geneseo (Township)—Roberts SD-4
Geneva (City)—Geneva AL-2
Geneva (Town)—Talbot GA-2
Geneva (City)—Kane IL-3
Geneva (Township)—Kane IL-3
Geneva (Town)—Adams IN-3
Geneva (Township)—Jennings IN-3
Geneva (City)—Franklin IA-3
Geneva (Township)—Allen KS-4
Geneva (Township)—Midland MI-3
Geneva (Township)—Van Buren .. MI-3
Geneva (City)—Freeborn MN-3
Geneva (Township)—Freeborn MN-3
Geneva (City)—Fillmore NE-4
Geneva (Township)—Fillmore NE-4
Geneva (City)—Ontario NY-1
Geneva (Town)—Ontario NY-1
Geneva (City)—Seneca NY-1
Geneva (City)—Ashtabula OH-3
Geneva (Township)—Ashtabula ... OH-3
Geneva (Town)—Walworth WI-3
Geneva County AL-2
Geneva-on-the-Lake (Village)—
 Ashtabula OH-3
Gennessee (Township)—
 Kandiyohi MN-3
Genoa (Town)—Lincoln CO-4
Genoa (City)—DeKalb IL-3
Genoa (Township)—DeKalb IL-3

American Places Dictionary General Index

Genoa (Township)—Livingston *MI-3*
Genoa (City)—Nance *NE-4*
Genoa (Township)—Nance *NE-4*
Genoa (Town)—Cayuga *NY-1*
Genoa (Township)—Delaware *OH-3*
Genoa (Village)—Ottawa *OH-3*
Genoa (Town)—Vernon *WI-3*
Genoa (Village)—Vernon *WI-3*
Genoa City (Village)—Kenosha..... *WI-3*
Genoa City (Village)—Walworth ... *WI-3*
Genola (City)—Morrison *MN-3*
Genola (Town)—Utah....................... *UT-4*
Gentilly (Township)—Polk *MN-3*
Gentry (City)—Benton *AR-2*
Gentry (Village)—Gentry *MO-3*
Gentry County *MO-3*
Gentryville (Town)—Spencer *IN-3*
George (City)—Lyon *IA-3*
George (Town)—Grant.................... *WA-4*
George, Lake (NY) *Geog-4*
George Air Force Base (CA)........... *Mil-4*
George Air Force Base (Military
  Facility)—San Bernardino........... *CA-4*
George County................................ *MS-2*
Georges (Township)—Fayette *PA-1*
Georgetown (Town)—White *AR-2*
Georgetown (Town)—Clear
  Creek *CO-4*
Georgetown (CDP)—Fairfield *CT-1*
Georgetown (Town)—Sussex *DE-1*
Georgetown (CDP)—Chatham *GA-2*
Georgetown (Town)—Quitman...... *GA-2*
Georgetown (City)—Bear Lake....... *ID-4*
Georgetown (City)—Vermilion *IL-3*
Georgetown (Township)—
  Vermilion *IL-3*
Georgetown (Town)—Floyd *IN-3*
Georgetown (Township)—Floyd *IN-3*
Georgetown (CDP)—St. Joseph...... *IN-3*
Georgetown (City)—Scott *KY-2*
Georgetown (Village)—Grant
  Parish *LA-2*
Georgetown (Town)—Sagadahoc .. *ME-1*
Georgetown (Town)—Essex *MA-1*
Georgetown (Township)—Ottawa.. *MI-3*
Georgetown (City)—Clay *MN-3*
Georgetown (Township)—Clay *MN-3*
Georgetown (Town)—Copiah *MS-2*
Georgetown (Town)—Madison *NY-1*
Georgetown (Village)—Brown *OH-3*
Georgetown (Borough)—Beaver *PA-1*
Georgetown (City)—Georgetown....*SC-2*
Georgetown (City)—Williamson *TX-2*
Georgetown (Town)—Polk *WI-3*
Georgetown (Town)—Price *WI-3*
Georgetown County *SC-2*
George Washington Bridge
  (NY) *Geog-4*
George West (City)—Live Oak *TX-2*
Georgia (Township)—Grant........... *SD-4*
Georgia (Town)—Franklin *VT-1*
Georgia, Strait of (WA) *Geog-4*
Georgiana (Town)—Butler *AL-2*
Gerald (City)—Franklin *MO-3*
Geraldine (Town)—DeKalb *AL-2*
Geraldine (Town)—Chouteau *MT-4*
Geranium (Township)—Valley....... *NE-4*
Gerber (Township)—Stutsman....... *ND-4*
Gerber-Las Flores (CDP)—
  Tehama *CA-4*
Gering (City)—Scotts Bluff............. *NE-4*
German (Township)—Richland *IL-3*
German (Township)—
  Bartholomew..................................... *IN-3*
German (Township)—Marshall....... *IN-3*

German (Township)—St. Joseph *IN-3*
German (Township)—
  Vanderburgh *IN-3*
German (Township)—Smith *KS-4*
German (Town)—Chenango *NY-1*
German (Township)—Dickey *ND-4*
German (Township)—Auglaize *OH-3*
German (Township)—Clark *OH-3*
German (Township)—Fulton *OH-3*
German (Township)—Harrison *OH-3*
German (Township)—
  Montgomery......................................*OH-3*
German (Township)—Fayette *PA-1*
German (Township)—
  Hutchinson.. *SD-4*
German Flatts (Town)—
  Herkimer...*NY-1*
Germania (Township)—Todd *MN-3*
Germania (Township)—
  Stutsman *ND-4*
Germania (Town)—Shawano *WI-3*
Germantown (Township)—
  Clinton *IL-3*
Germantown (Village)—Clinton *IL-3*
Germantown (City)—Bracken *KY-2*
Germantown (City)—Mason.......... *KY-2*
Germantown (CDP)—
  Montgomery......................................*MD-1*
Germantown (Township)—
  Cottonwood *MN-3*
Germantown (Town)—Columbia... *NY-1*
Germantown (Township)—Wells ... *ND-4*
Germantown (Village)—
  Montgomery *OH-3*
Germantown (Township)—
  Codington *SD-4*
Germantown (Township)—
  Turner *SD-4*
Germantown (City)—Shelby *TN-2*
Germantown (Town)—Juneau *WI-3*
Germantown (Town)—
  Washington *WI-3*
Germantown (Village)—
  Washington *WI-3*
Germantown Hills (Village)—
  Woodford *IL-3*
German Valley (Village)—
  Stephenson *IL-3*
Germanville (Township)—
  Livingston *IL-3*
Germany (Township)—Adams........ *PA-1*
Germfask (Township)—
  Schoolcraft *MI-3*
Geronimo (Town)—Comanche...... *OK-2*
Gerrard (Township)—Towner *ND-4*
Gerrish (Township)—
  Roscommon *MI-3*
Gerry (Town)—Chautauqua............ *NY-1*
Gerster (Town)—St. Clair *MO-3*
Gerty (Town)—Hughes................... *OK-2*
Gervais (Township)—Red Lake *MN-3*
Gervais (City)—Marion *OR-4*
Getchell (Township)—Barnes........ *ND-4*
Getty (Township)—Stearns *MN-3*
Gettysburg (Township)—Graham ... *KS-4*
Gettysburg (Village)—Darke *OH-3*
Gettysburg (Borough)—Adams....... *PA-1*
Gettysburg (City)—Potter *SD-4*
Geuda Springs (City)—Cowley *KS-4*
Geuda Springs (City)—Sumner *KS-4*
Gheen (Pop. Place)—St. Louis *MN-3*
Ghent (City)—Carroll *KY-2*
Ghent (City)—Lyon *MN-3*
Ghent (Town)—Columbia............... *NY-1*
Gholson (City)—McLennan *TX-2*

Ghylin (Township)—Burleigh *ND-4*
Gibbon (City)—Sibley *MN-3*
Gibbon (City)—Buffalo................... *NE-4*
Gibbon (Township)—Buffalo......... *NE-4*
Gibbs (Town)—Adair *MO-3*
Gibbs (Township)—Burleigh *ND-4*
Gibbsboro (Borough)—Camden *NJ-1*
Gibbstown (CDP)—Gloucester....... *NJ-1*
Gibraltar (City)—Wayne *MI-3*
Gibraltar (Town)—Door *WI-3*
Gibsland (Town)—Bienville
  Parish *LA-2*
Gibson (CDP)—Pulaski *AR-2*
Gibson (City)—Glascock *GA-2*
Gibson (Township)—Washington ... *IN-3*
Gibson (City)—Keokuk................... *IA-3*
Gibson (Township)—Bay *MI-3*
Gibson (Town)—Scotland *NC-2*
Gibson (Township)—Mercer *OH-3*
Gibson (Township)—Cameron *PA-1*
Gibson (Township)—
  Susquehanna *PA-1*
Gibson (Town)—Gibson *TN-2*
Gibson (Town)—Manitowoc *WI-3*
Gibsonburg (Village)—Sandusky ...*OH-3*
Gibson City (City)—Ford *IL-3*
Gibson County................................. *IN-3*
Gibson County................................. *TN-2*
Gibsonia (CDP)—Polk *FL-2*
Gibsonton (CDP)—Hillsborough *FL-2*
Gibsonville (Town)—Alamance *NC-2*
Gibsonville (Town)—Guilford *NC-2*
Giddings (City)—Lee *TX-2*
Gideon (City)—New Madrid *MO-3*
Gifford (CDP)—Indian River........*FL-2*
Gifford (Village)—Champaign *IL-3*
Gifford (Town)—Hampton *SC-2*
Gig Harbor (Town)—Pierce........ *WA-4*
Gila Bend (Town)—Maricopa........ *AZ-4*
Gila County *AZ-4*
Gila River (WA)............................. *Geog-4*
Gila River Reservation (AZ).... *IndRes-4*
Gila Wilderness Area (NM) *Geog-4*
Gilbert (Town)—Maricopa............. *AZ-4*
Gilbert (Town)—Searcy *AR-2*
Gilbert (City)—Story *IA-3*
Gilbert (Village)—Franklin
  Parish *LA-2*
Gilbert (City)—St. Louis............... *MN-3*
Gilbert (Town)—Lexington *SC-2*
Gilbert (Township)—Hand *SD-4*
Gilbert (Town)—Mingo *WV-2*
Gilbert Creek (CDP)—Mingo *WV-2*
Gilberton (Borough)—Schuylkill *PA-1*
Gilbertown (Town)—Choctaw *AL-2*
Gilberts (Village)—Kane *IL-3*
Gilbertsville (Village)—Otsego........ *NY-1*
Gilbertsville (CDP)—
  Montgomery......................................*PA-1*
Gilbertville (City)—Black Hawk...... *IA-3*
Gilboa (Township)—Benton *IN-3*
Gilboa (Town)—Schoharie *NY-1*
Gilboa (Village)—Putnam *OH-3*
Gilby (City)—Grand Forks *ND-4*
Gilby (Township)—Grand Forks ...*ND-4*
Gilchrist (Township)—Pope *MN-3*
Gilchrist County *FL-2*
Gilcrest (Town)—Weld.................... *CO-4*
Gilead (Town)—Oxford *ME-1*
Gilead (Township)—Branch *MI-3*
Gilead (Village)—Thayer *NE-4*
Gilead (Township)—Morrow *OH-3*
Giles County.................................... *TN-2*
Giles County.................................... *VA-2*
Gilford (Township)—Tuscola.......... *MI-3*

Gilford (Town)—Belknap...............NH-1
Gilford Park (CDP)—Ocean...........NJ-1
Gill (Township)—Sullivan...............IN-3
Gill (Township)—Clay....................KS-4
Gill (Town)—Franklin....................MA-1
Gill (Township)—Cass ND-4
Gillam (Township)—Jasper.............IN-3
Gillespie (City)—Macoupin.............IL-3
Gillespie (Township)—Macoupin ..IL-3
Gillespie County............................. TX-2
Gillett (City)—Arkansas.................AR-2
Gillett (City)—Oconto....................WI-3
Gillett (Town)—Oconto WI-3
Gillette (City)—Campbell...............WY-4
Gillett Grove (City)—Clay..............IA-3
Gillford (Township)—Wabasha.....MN-3
Gillham (Town)—Sevier AR-2
Gilliam (Village)—Caddo Parish ...LA-2
Gilliam (Town)—Saline...................MO-3
Gilliam County............................. OR-4
Gillis Bluff (Township)—Butler MO-3
Gillsville (Town)—Banks GA-2
Gillsville (Town)—Hall GA-2
Gilman (City)—Iroquois IL-3
Gilman (City)—Marshall................IA-3
Gilman (Township)—Nemaha KS-4
Gilman (City)—Benton MN-3
Gilman (Town)—Pierce WI-3
Gilman (Village)—Taylor................WI-3
Gilman City (City)—Daviess MO-3
Gilman City (City)—Harrison MO-3
Gilmanton (Township)—Benton MN-3
Gilmanton (Town)—Belknap..........NH-1
Gilmanton (Town)—Buffalo WI-3
Gilmer (Township)—Adams IL-3
Gilmer (City)—Upshur TX-2
Gilmer County.............................. GA-2
Gilmer County.............................. WV-2
Gilmore (Town)—Crittenden..........AR-2
Gilmore (Township)—Benzie..........MI-3
Gilmore (Township)—Isabella MI-3
Gilmore (Township)—McHenry ND-4
Gilmore (Township)—Greene PA-1
Gilmore City (Township)—
 Humboldt..................................IA-3
Gilmore City (Township)—
 Pocahontas................................IA-3
Gilpin (Township)—Armstrong PA-1
Gilpin County............................... CO-4
Gilroy (City)—Santa Clara CA-4
Gilstrap (Township)—Adams..........ND-4
Gilsum (Town)—Cheshire...............NH-1
Gilt Edge (Town)—Tipton TN-2
Giltner (Village)—Hamilton NE-4
Gingles (Town)—Ashland WI-3
Girard (Town)—Burke GA-2
Girard (City)—Macoupin................IL-3
Girard (Township)—Macoupin IL-3
Girard (City)—Crawford.................KS-4
Girard (Township)—Branch............MI-3
Girard (Township)—Otter Tail MN-3
Girard (City)—Trumbull.................OH-3
Girard (Township)—Clearfield PA-1
Girard (Borough)—Erie PA-1
Girard (Township)—Erie PA-1
Girardville (Borough)—Schuylkill ..PA-1
Glacier (Township)—Stutsman ND-4
Glacier County............................. MT-4
Gladbrook (City)—Tama................IA-3
Gladden (Township)—Dent MO-3
Glade (City)—Phillips.....................KS-4
Glade (Township)—Warren.............PA-1
Glades County.............................. FL-2
Glade Spring (Town)—
 Washington...............................VA-2

Gladeview (CDP)—Dade FL-2
Gladewater (City)—Gregg TX-2
Gladewater (City)—Upshur TX-2
Gladstone (Township)—
 Henderson..................................IL-3
Gladstone (Village)—Henderson IL-3
Gladstone (City)—Delta.................MI-3
Gladstone (City)—Clay MO-3
Gladstone (Township)—
 LaMoure....................................ND-4
Gladstone (City)—Stark ND-4
Gladstone (City)—Clackamas OR-4
Gladwin (City)—Gladwin MI-3
Gladwin (Township)—Gladwin MI-3
Gladwin County........................... MI-3
Glandorf (Village)—Putnam OH-3
Glasco (City)—Cloud KS-4
Glasco (CDP)—Ulster NY-1
Glascock County......................... GA-2
Glasford (Town)—Peoria IL-3
Glasgow (Village)—Scott IL-3
Glasgow (City)—Barren KY-2
Glasgow (Township)—Wabasha MN-3
Glasgow (City)—Chariton MO-3
Glasgow (City)—Howard MO-3
Glasgow (City)—Valley MT-4
Glasgow (Borough)—Beaver PA-1
Glasgow (Town)—Rockbridge.......VA-2
Glasgow (Town)—Kanawha..........WV-2
Glasgow Village (CDP)—St.
 Louis..MO-3
Glassboro (Borough)—Gloucester ..NJ-1
Glasscock County.......................... TX-2
Glassport (Borough)—Allegheny.....PA-1
Glastenbury (Town)—
 Bennington................................VT-1
Glastonbury (Town)—Hartford CT-1
Glaze (Township)—Miller MO-3
Gleason (Town)—Weakley TN-2
Glen (Township)—Aitkin MN-3
Glen (Town)—Montgomery NY-1
Glen (Township)—LaMoure ND-4
Glen (Township)—Edmunds SD-4
Glenaire (Village)—Clay MO-3
Glen Allen (Town)—Fayette AL-2
Glen Allen (Town)—Marion AL-2
Glenallen (Town)—Bollinger MO-3
Glen Allen (CDP)—Henrico VA-2
Glen Alpine (Town)—Burke NC-2
Glen Arbor (Township)—
 Leelanau....................................MI-3
Glenarden (Town)—Prince
 George's....................................MD-1
Glen Avon (CDP)—Riverside........CA-4
Glenbard South (CDP)—DuPage ...IL-3
Glenbeulah (Village)—Sheboygan..WI-3
Glenburn (Town)—Penobscot........ME-1
Glenburn (City)—Renville ND-4
Glenburn (Township)—
 Lackawanna PA-1
Glen Burnie (CDP)—Anne
 Arundel MD-1
Glen Campbell (Borough)—
 Indiana......................................PA-1
Glen Carbon (Village)—Madison ...IL-3
Glencoe (City)—Calhoun AL-2
Glencoe (City)—Etowah................AL-2
Glencoe (CDP)—Volusia FL-2
Glencoe (Village)—Cook IL-3
Glencoe (Township)—Butler KS-4
Glencoe (Township)—Trego KS-4
Glencoe (City)—Gallatin KY-2
Glencoe (City)—McLeod MN-3
Glencoe (Township)—McLeod MN-3
Glencoe (Town)—Payne.................OK-2

Glencoe (Town)—Buffalo...............WI-3
Glen Cove (City)—Nassau NY-1
Glendale (City)—Maricopa AZ-4
Glendale (City)—Los Angeles CA-4
Glendale (City)—Arapahoe CO-4
Glendale (Township)—Saline.........KS-4
Glendale (City)—St. Louis.............MO-3
Glendale (Township)—Logan........ND-4
Glendale (Village)—Hamilton........OH-3
Glendale (City)—Douglas OR-4
Glendale (Township)—Hand SD-4
Glendale (Town)—Kane.................UT-4
Glen Dale (City)—Marshall WV-2
Glendale (City)—Milwaukee..........WI-3
Glendale (Town)—Monroe WI-3
Glendale Heights (City)—DuPage .. IL-3
Glendive (City)—Dawson MT-4
Glendo (Township)—Perkins SD-4
Glendo (Town)—Platte WY-4
Glendon (Borough)—
 Northampton PA-1
Glendora (City)—Los Angeles CA-4
Glendora (Village)—Tallahatchie...MS-2
Glendora (CDP)—Camden NJ-1
Glendorado (Township)—
 Benton.......................................MN-3
Gleneagle (CDP)—El Paso............CO-4
Glen Echo (Town)—
 Montgomery..............................MD-1
Glen Echo Park (Village)—St.
 Louis..MO-3
Glen Elder (City)—Mitchell...........KS-4
Glen Elder (Township)—Mitchell...KS-4
Glen Ellen (CDP)—Sonoma CA-4
Glen Ellyn (Village)—DuPage IL-3
Glenfield (City)—Foster ND-4
Glenfield (Township)—Foster ND-4
Glenfield (Borough)—Allegheny PA-1
Glen Flora (Village)—Rusk WI-3
Glenford (Village)—Perry OH-3
Glen Gardner (Borough)—
 Hunterdon.................................NJ-1
Glengary (Township)—Fillmore NE-4
Glenham (Town)—Walworth SD-4
Glen Haven (Town)—Grant WI-3
Glen Head (CDP)—Nassau NY-1
Glen Hope (Borough)—Clearfield ..PA-1
Glenila (Township)—Cavalier........ND-4
Glen Lyn (Town)—Giles VA-2
Glen Lyon (CDP)—Luzerne...........PA-1
Glenmont (Village)—Holmes.........OH-3
Glenmoor (CDP)—Columbiana OH-3
Glenmora (Town)—Rapides
 Parish..LA-2
Glenmore (Township)—LaMoure ..ND-4
Glenmore (Town)—Brown WI-3
Glennallen (CDP)—Valdez-Cordova
 Census Area..............................AK-4
Glenn County............................... CA-4
Glenn Dale (CDP)—Prince
 George's....................................MD-1
Glenn Heights (City)—Dallas TX-2
Glenn Heights (City)—Ellis TX-2
Glenns Ferry (City)—Elmore ID-4
Glennville (City)—Tattnall............GA-2
Glenolden (Borough)—Delaware PA-1
Glen Park (Village)—Jefferson NY-1
Glenpool (City)—Tulsa OK-2
Glen Raven (CDP)—Alamance NC-2
Glen Ridge (Town)—Palm Beach ..FL-2
Glen Ridge Township (Borough)—
 Essex...NJ-1
Glen Rock (Borough)—Bergen NJ-1
Glen Rock (Borough)—York..........PA-1
Glenrock (Town)—Converse WY-4

American Places Dictionary — General Index

Glen Rose (City)—Somervell......... *TX-2*
Glens Falls (City)—Warren *NY-1*
Glens Falls North (CDP)—
 Warren................................*NY-1*
Glenshire-Devonshire (CDP)—
 Nevada *CA-4*
Glenside (CDP)—Montgomery.... *PA-1*
Glen St. Mary (Town)—Baker *FL-2*
Glen Ullin (City)—Morton *ND-4*
Glenvar Heights (CDP)—Dade *FL-2*
Glenview (Village)—Cook............ *IL-3*
Glenview (City)—Jefferson *KY-2*
Glenview (Township)—Burleigh ..*ND-4*
Glenview Hills (City)—Jefferson ... *KY-2*
Glenview Manor (City)—
 Jefferson..............................*KY-2*
Glenvil (Township)—Clay............... *NE-4*
Glenvil (Village)—Clay.................. *NE-4*
Glenville (City)—Freeborn *MN-3*
Glenville (Town)—Schenectady..... *NY-1*
Glenville (Town)—Gilmer *WV-2*
Glenwillow (Village)—Cuyahoga ...*OH-3*
Glenwood (Town)—Crenshaw *AL-2*
Glenwood (Town)—Pike *AR-2*
Glenwood (City)—Wheeler *GA-2*
Glenwood (Village)—Cook *IL-3*
Glenwood (Town)—Fayette *IN-3*
Glenwood (Town)—Rush *IN-3*
Glenwood (City)—Mills *IA-3*
Glenwood (Township)—Phillips *KS-4*
Glenwood (Pop. Place)—
 Aroostook..............................*ME-1*
Glenwood (City)—Pope *MN-3*
Glenwood (Township)—Pope *MN-3*
Glenwood (Township)—
 Schuyler...............................*MO-3*
Glenwood (Village)—Schuyler *MO-3*
Glenwood (Township)—Gage *NE-4*
Glenwood (Township)—Walsh........ *ND-4*
Glenwood (Township)—Clay *SD-4*
Glenwood (Township)—Deuel *SD-4*
Glenwood (Town)—Sevier *UT-4*
Glenwood (Town)—St. Croix *WI-3*
Glenwood City (City)—St. Croix... *WI-3*
Glenwood Landing (CDP)—
 Nassau..................................*NY-1*
Glenwood Springs (City)—
 Garfield................................*CO-4*
Glidden (City)—Carroll *IA-3*
Globe (City)—Gila *AZ-4*
Glocester (Town)—Providence *RI-1*
Gloria Glens Park (Village)—
 Medina *OH-3*
Gloster (Town)—Amite *MS-2*
Gloucester (City)—Essex............... *MA-1*
Gloucester (Township)—Camden ... *NJ-1*
Gloucester City (City)—Camden *NJ-1*
Gloucester County *NJ-1*
Gloucester County *VA-2*
Gloucester Courthouse (CDP)—
 Gloucester *VA-2*
Gloucester Point (CDP)—
 Gloucester *VA-2*
Glouster (Village)—Athens *OH-3*
Glover (Township)—Edmunds *SD-4*
Glover (Town)—Orleans *VT-1*
Gloversville (City)—Fulton *NY-1*
Gloverville (CDP)—Aiken *SC-2*
Glyndon (City)—Clay *MN-3*
Glyndon (Township)—Clay............ *MN-3*
Glynn County *GA-2*
Gnadenhutten (Village)—
 Tuscarawas *OH-3*
Gnesen (Township)—St. Louis ... *MN-3*
Gobles (City)—Van Buren *MI-3*

Godair (Township)—Pemiscot...... *MO-3*
Goddard (City)—Sedgwick *KS-4*
Goddard (Mil. facil.)—Prince
 George's................................*MD-1*
Godfrey (Township)—Madison....... *IL-3*
Godfrey (Township)—Polk *MN-3*
Godley (Village)—Grundy *IL-3*
Godley (Village)—Will *IL-3*
Godley (Town)—Johnson *TX-2*
Godwin (Town)—Cumberland....... *NC-2*
Goebel (Township)—Oregon......... *MO-3*
Goehner (Village)—Seward *NE-4*
Goessel (Township)—Marion........*KS-4*
Goet (Town)—Chippewa................. *WI-3*
Goff (City)—Nemaha *KS-4*
Goffstown (Town)—
 Hillsborough *NH-1*
Gogebic County *MI-3*
Golconda (City)—Pope *IL-3*
Gold (Township)—Bureau *IL-3*
Gold Bar (Town)—Snohomish...... *WA-4*
Gold Beach (City)—Curry *OR-4*
Golden (City)—Jefferson *CO-4*
Golden (Village)—Adams *IL-3*
Golden (Township)—Oceana *MI-3*
Golden (Town)—Tishomingo *MS-2*
Golden (Township)—Holt.............. *NE-4*
Golden (Township)—Walsh *ND-4*
Golden Beach (Town)—Dade *FL-2*
Golden Beach (CDP)—St.
 Mary's..................................*MD-1*
Golden Belt (Township)—
 Lincoln *KS-4*
Golden City (City)—Barton *MO-3*
Golden City (Township)—
 Barton..................................*MO-3*
Goldendale (City)—Klickitat *WA-4*
Golden Gate (CDP)—Collier..........*FL-2*
Golden Gate (Village)—Wayne...... *IL-3*
Golden Gate Bridge (CA)............. *Geog-4*
Golden Glades (CDP)—Dade........*FL-2*
Golden Glen (Township)—
 LaMoure *ND-4*
Golden Grove (CDP)—
 Greenville............................. *SC-2*
Golden Hill Indian Reservation
 (CT)....................................*IndRes-4*
Golden Hills (CDP)—Kern............ *CA-4*
Golden Lake (Township)—Steele... *ND-4*
Golden Lakes (CDP)—Palm
 Beach *FL-2*
Golden Meadow (Town)—Lafourche
 Parish *LA-2*
Goldenrod (CDP)—Orange............*FL-2*
Goldenrod (CDP)—Seminole *FL-2*
Golden's Bridge (CDP)—
 Westchester *NY-1*
Golden Valley (CDP)—Mohave..... *AZ-4*
Golden Valley (City)—Hennepin .. *MN-3*
Golden Valley (Township)—
 Roseau *MN-3*
Golden Valley (City)—Mercer *ND-4*
Golden Valley (Township)—
 Williams *ND-4*
Golden Valley County *MT-4*
Golden Valley County *ND-4*
Goldfield (City)—Wright *IA-3*
Goldfield (Township)—Bowman ..*ND-4*
Gold Hill (Township)—Gallatin *IL-3*
Gold Hill (City)—Jackson *OR-4*
Goldonna (Village)—Natchitoches
 Parish *LA-2*
Goldsberry (Township)—Howell... *MO-3*
Goldsboro (Town)—Caroline *MD-1*
Goldsboro (City)—Wayne *NC-2*

Goldsboro (Borough)—York *PA-1*
Goldsby (Town)—McClain *OK-2*
Goldsmith (City)—Ector *TX-2*
Goldston (Town)—Chatham *NC-2*
Goldthwaite (City)—Mills.............. *TX-2*
Goldville (Municipality)—
 Tallapoosa *AL-2*
Golf (Village)—Palm Beach *FL-2*
Golf (Village)—Cook *IL-3*
Golf Manor (City)—Hamilton *OH-3*
Golfview (Town)—Palm Beach....... *FL-2*
Goliad (City)—Goliad *TX-2*
Goliad County *TX-2*
Golinda (City)—Falls *TX-2*
Golinda (City)—McLennan *TX-2*
Golovin (City)—Nome Census
 Area *AK-4*
Goltry (Town)—Alfalfa *OK-2*
Golva (City)—Golden Valley *ND-4*
Gomer (Township)—Caldwell....... *MO-3*
Gonvick (City)—Clearwater *MN-3*
Gonzales (City)—Monterey *CA-4*
Gonzales (City)—Ascension
 Parish *LA-2*
Gonzales (City)—Gonzales *TX-2*
Gonzales County *TX-2*
Gonzalez (CDP)—Escambia *FL-2*
Goochland County *VA-2*
Goodar (Township)—Ogemaw *MI-3*
Goode (Township)—Franklin *IL-3*
Goodell (City)—Hancock *IA-3*
Goodfarm (Township)—Grundy..... *IL-3*
Goodfield (Village)—Tazewell *IL-3*
Goodfield (Village)—Woodford *IL-3*
Good Hope (Municipality)—
 Cullman................................*AL-2*
Good Hope (Town)—Walton *GA-2*
Good Hope (Town)—McDonough . *IL-3*
Good Hope (Township)—Itasca ... *MN-3*
Good Hope (Township)—
 Norman................................*MN-3*
Good Hope (Township)—
 Hocking *OH-3*
Goodhue (City)—Goodhue *MN-3*
Goodhue (Township)—Goodhue .. *MN-3*
Goodhue County *MN-3*
Gooding (City)—Gooding *ID-4*
Gooding County *ID-4*
Goodings Grove (CDP)—Will *IL-3*
Goodland (Town)—Newton *IN-3*
Goodland (City)—Sherman *KS-4*
Goodland (Township)—Lapeer *MI-3*
Goodland (Township)—Itasca *MN-3*
Goodlettsville (City)—Davidson.... *TN-2*
Goodlettsville (City)—Sumner *TN-2*
Goodlow (City)—Navarro *TX-2*
Good Luck (Township)—
 Williams *ND-4*
Goodman (Town)—Holmes *MS-2*
Goodman (Town)—McDonald *MO-3*
Goodman (Town)—Marinette........ *WI-3*
Goodnews Bay (City)—Bethel Census
 Area *AK-4*
Goodrich (Village)—Genesee *MI-3*
Goodrich (City)—Sheridan *ND-4*
Goodrich (Township)—Sheridan ...*ND-4*
Goodrich (City)—Polk *TX-2*
Goodrich (Town)—Taylor *WI-3*
Goodridge (City)—Pennington *MN-3*
Goodridge (Township)—
 Pennington...........................*MN-3*
Good Thunder (City)—Blue
 Earth....................................*MN-3*
Goodview (City)—Winona *MN-3*

General Index   *American Places Dictionary*

Goodwater (Municipality)—
Coosa *AL-2*
Goodwell (Township)—Newaygo... *MI-3*
Goodwell (Town)—Texas *OK-2*
Goodwill (Township)—Roberts *SD-4*
Goodwin (Town)—Deuel *SD-4*
Goodwin (Township)—Deuel *SD-4*
Goodyear (Town)—Maricopa *AZ-4*
Goose Creek (Township)—Piatt *IL-3*
Goose Creek (City)—Jefferson *KY-2*
Goose Creek (City)—Berkeley *SC-2*
Goose Creek (City)—Charleston..... *SC-2*
Goose Lake (Township)—Grundy .. *IL-3*
Goose Lake (City)—Clinton *IA-3*
Goose Lake (Township)—Charles
Mix *SD-4*
Gooseneck (Township)—Divide *ND-4*
Goose Prairie (Township)—Clay .. *MN-3*
Gordo (Town)—Pickens................... *AL-2*
Gordon (Town)—Houston *AL-2*
Gordon (Town)—Wilkinson............. *GA-2*
Gordon (Township)—Todd *MN-3*
Gordon (City)—Sheridan *NE-4*
Gordon (Township)—Cavalier........ *ND-4*
Gordon (Village)—Darke................. *OH-3*
Gordon (Borough)—Schuylkill *PA-1*
Gordon (City)—Palo Pinto *TX-2*
Gordon (Town)—Ashland *WI-3*
Gordon (Town)—Douglas *WI-3*
Gordon County *GA-2*
Gordonsville (Town)—Smith *TN-2*
Gordonsville (Town)—Orange *VA-2*
Gordonville (Town)—Cape
Girardeau *MO-3*
Gore (Township)—Sumner *KS-4*
Gore (Township)—Huron *MI-3*
Gore (Town)—Sequoyah *OK-2*
Goree (City)—Knox *TX-2*
Goreville (Village)—Johnson *IL-3*
Gorham (Village)—Jackson *IL-3*
Gorham (City)—Russell...................*KS-4*
Gorham (Town)—Cumberland *ME-1*
Gorham (Town)—Coos *NH-1*
Gorham (Town)—Ontario............... *NY-1*
Gorham (Township)—Fulton *OH-3*
Gorman (Township)—Otter Tail .. *MN-3*
Gorman (CDP)—Durham................. *NC-2*
Gorman (City)—Eastland *TX-2*
Gorton (Township)—Grant............ *MN-3*
Goshen (Town)—Pike *AL-2*
Goshen (Town)—Washington *AR-2*
Goshen (Town)—Litchfield............. *CT-1*
Goshen (Township)—Stark *IL-3*
Goshen (City)—Elkhart *IN-3*
Goshen (Township)—Clay *KS-4*
Goshen (CDP)—Oldham *KY-2*
Goshen (Town)—Hampshire.......... *MA-1*
Goshen (Town)—Sullivan *NH-1*
Goshen (Town)—Orange................. *NY-1*
Goshen (Village)—Orange............... *NY-1*
Goshen (Township)—Auglaize.......*OH-3*
Goshen (Township)—Belmont *OH-3*
Goshen (Township)—Champaign ..*OH-3*
Goshen (Township)—Clermont *OH-3*
Goshen (Township)—Hardin *OH-3*
Goshen (Township)—Mahoning *OH-3*
Goshen (Township)—Tuscarawas ..*OH-3*
Goshen (Township)—Clearfield *PA-1*
Goshen (Town)—Utah *UT-4*
Goshen (Town)—Addison *VT-1*
Goshen (Town)—Rockbridge.......... *VA-2*
Goshen County................................ *WY-4*
Goshute Reservation (NV) *IndRes-4*
Gosnell (City)—Mississippi *AR-2*
Gosnold (Town)—Dukes................ *MA-1*

Gosper County *NE-4*
Gosport (Town)—Owen *IN-3*
Gotebo (Town)—Kiowa *OK-2*
Gothenburg (City)—Dawson *NE-4*
Gould (City)—Lincoln *AR-2*
Gould (Township)—Cass *MN-3*
Gould (Town)—Harmon *OK-2*
Goulding (CDP)—Escambia *FL-2*
Goulds (CDP)—Dade *FL-2*
Gouldsboro (Town)—Hancock *ME-1*
Gourley (Township)—
Menominee *MI-3*
Gouverneur (Town)—St.
Lawrence.................................... *NY-1*
Gouverneur (Village)—St.
Lawrence.................................... *NY-1*
Govan (Town)—Bamberg.................*SC-2*
Gove (Township)—Gove...................*KS-4*
Gove City (City)—Gove *KS-4*
Gove County.....................................*KS-4*
Governors Island (NY) *Geog-4*
Gowanda (Village)—Cattaraugus... *NY-1*
Gowanda (Village)—Erie *NY-1*
Gower (City)—Buchanan *MO-3*
Gower (City)—Clinton *MO-3*
Gowrie (City)—Webster *IA-3*
Grabill (Town)—Allen...................... *IN-3*
Grace (City)—Caribou *ID-4*
Grace (Township)—Chippewa *MN-3*
Grace (Township)—Grand Forks.. *ND-4*
Grace City (City)—Foster *ND-4*
Graceland (Township)—
Codington *SD-4*
Gracemont (Town)—Caddo *OK-2*
Graceville (City)—Jackson *FL-2*
Graceville (City)—Big Stone.......... *MN-3*
Graceville (Township)—Big
Stone *MN-3*
Grady (City)—Lincoln *AR-2*
Grady (Village)—Curry *NM-4*
Grady County *GA-2*
Grady County *OK-2*
Graettinger (City)—Palo Alto *IA-3*
Graf (City)—Dubuque *IA-3*
Graf (Township)—Kidder *ND-4*
Graford (City)—Palo Pinto............. *TX-2*
Grafton (Town)—Jersey *IL-3*
Grafton (Township)—McHenry...... *IL-3*
Grafton (City)—Worth *IA-3*
Grafton (Town)—Worcester *MA-1*
Grafton (Township)—Sibley *MN-3*
Grafton (Township)—Fillmore *NE-4*
Grafton (Village)—Fillmore............ *NE-4*
Grafton (Town)—Grafton *NH-1*
Grafton (Town)—Rensselaer........... *NY-1*
Grafton (City)—Walsh *ND-4*
Grafton (Township)—Walsh *ND-4*
Grafton (Township)—Lorain *OH-3*
Grafton (Village)—Lorain *OH-3*
Grafton (Township)—Miner *SD-4*
Grafton (Town)—Windham *VT-1*
Grafton (City)—Taylor.................... *WV-2*
Grafton (Town)—Ozaukee *WI-3*
Grafton (Village)—Ozaukee *WI-3*
Grafton County *NH-1*
Graham (Township)—Jefferson *IN-3*
Graham (Township)—Graham *KS-4*
Graham (Township)—Benton *MN-3*
Graham (Town)—Nodaway *MO-3*
Graham (City)—Alamance............. *NC-2*
Graham (Township)—Clearfield *PA-1*
Graham (City)—Young *TX-2*
Graham County *AZ-4*
Graham County *KS-4*
Graham County *NC-2*

Graham Lakes (Township)—
Nobles.. *MN-3*
Grail (Township)—McKenzie *ND-4*
Grainbelt (Township)—Bowman ... *ND-4*
Grainfield (City)—Gove *KS-4*
Grainfield (Township)—Gove.........*KS-4*
Grainfield (Township)—Towner ... *ND-4*
Grainger County *TN-2*
Grainola (Town)—Osage *OK-2*
Grainton (Village)—Perkins............ *NE-4*
Grain Valley (City)—Jackson......... *MO-3*
Grambling (Town)—Lincoln
Parish *LA-2*
Gramercy (Town)—St. James
Parish *LA-2*
Grampian (Borough)—Clearfield.... *PA-1*
Granada (Town)—Prowers............. *CO-4*
Granada (Township)—Nemaha *KS-4*
Granada (City)—Martin.................. *MN-3*
Granbury (City)—Hood *TX-2*
Granby (Town)—Grand *CO-4*
Granby (Town)—Hartford *CT-1*
Granby (Town)—Hampshire........ *MA-1*
Granby (Township)—Nicollet *MN-3*
Granby (City)—Newton *MO-3*
Granby (Township)—Newton *MO-3*
Granby (Town)—Oswego *NY-1*
Granby (Town)—Essex.................... *VT-1*
Grand (Township)—Marion...........*OH-3*
Grand (Township)—Hand.............. *SD-4*
Grand Bay (Division)—Mobile *AL-2*
Grand Beach (Village)—Berrien *MI-3*
Grand Blanc (City)—Genesee......... *MI-3*
Grand Blanc (Township)—
Genesee *MI-3*
Grand Cane (Village)—De Soto
Parish *LA-2*
Grand Canyon (AZ) *Geog-4*
Grand Canyon of the Snake
(AZ)..*Geog-4*
Grand Canyon Village (CDP)—
Coconino *AZ-4*
Grand Chute (Town)—
Outagamie *WI-3*
Grand Coteau (Town)—St. Landry
Parish *LA-2*
Grand Coulee (City)—Grant *WA-4*
Grand Coulee Dam (WA)............*Geog-4*
Grand County................................. *CO-4*
Grand County................................. *UT-4*
Grand Detour (Township)—Ogle... *IL-3*
Grand Encampment (Town)—
Carbon *WY-4*
Grandfalls (Town)—Ward *TX-2*
Grandfather (Village)—Avery *NC-2*
Grandfield (Township)—Eddy........ *ND-4*
Grandfield (City)—Tillman *OK-2*
Grand Forks (Township)—Polk *MN-3*
Grand Forks (City)—Grand
Forks *ND-4*
Grand Forks (Township)—Grand
Forks *ND-4*
Grand Forks Air Force Base
(ND)... *Mil-4*
Grand Forks Air Force Base (Military
Facility)—Grand Forks *ND-4*
Grand Forks County....................... *ND-4*
Grand Harbor (Township)—
Ramsey *ND-4*
Grand Haven (City)—Ottawa *MI-3*
Grand Haven (Township)—
Ottawa *MI-3*
Grandin (City)—Carter *MO-3*
Grandin (City)—Cass *ND-4*
Grandin (City)—Traill *ND-4*

Grand Island (Township)—Alger... MI-3
Grand Island (City)—Hall... NE-4
Grand Island (Town)—Erie... NY-1
Grand Isle (Town)—Jefferson
 Parish... LA-2
Grand Isle (Town)—Aroostook... ME-1
Grand Isle (Town)—Grand Isle... VT-1
Grand Isle County... VT-1
Grand Junction (City)—Mesa... CO-4
Grand Junction (City)—Greene... IA-3
Grand Junction (City)—Fayette... TN-2
Grand Junction (City)—
 Hardeman... TN-2
Grand Lake (Town)—Grand... CO-4
Grand Lake (Township)—St.
 Louis... MN-3
Grand Lake (WA)... Geog-4
Grand Lake Stream (Plantation)—
 Washington... ME-1
Grand Lake Towne (Town)—
 Mayes... OK-2
Grand Ledge (City)—Eaton... MI-3
Grand Marais (City)—Cook... MN-3
Grand Meadow (City)—Mower... MN-3
Grand Meadow (Township)—
 Mower... MN-3
Grand Meadow (Township)—
 Minnehaha... SD-4
Grand Mound (City)—Clinton... IA-3
Grand Mound (CDP)—Thurston... WA-4
Grand Pass (Town)—Saline... MO-3
Grand Pass (Township)—Saline... MO-3
Grand Plain (Township)—
 Marshall... MN-3
Grand Portage (Pop. Place)—
 Cook... MN-3
Grand Portage Reservation
 (MN)... IndRes-4
Grand Prairie (Township)—
 Jefferson... IL-3
Grand Prairie (Township)—
 Nobles... MN-3
Grand Prairie (Township)—
 Platte... NE-4
Grand Prairie (Township)—
 Barnes... ND-4
Grand Prairie (Township)—
 Marion... OH-3
Grand Prairie (City)—Dallas... TX-2
Grand Prairie (City)—Ellis... TX-2
Grand Prairie (City)—Tarrant... TX-2
Grand Rapids (Township)—La
 Salle... IL-3
Grand Rapids (City)—Kent... MI-3
Grand Rapids (Township)—Kent... MI-3
Grand Rapids (City)—Itasca... MN-3
Grand Rapids (Township)—
 Itasca... MN-3
Grand Rapids (Township)—
 LaMoure... ND-4
Grand Rapids (Township)—
 Wood... OH-3
Grand Rapids (Village)—Wood... OH-3
Grand Rapids (Town)—Wood... WI-3
Grand Ridge (Town)—Jackson... FL-2
Grand Ridge (Village)—La Salle... IL-3
Grand River (City)—Decatur... IA-3
Grand River (Township)—
 Sedgwick... KS-4
Grand River (Township)—Bates... MO-3
Grand River (Township)—Cass... MO-3
Grand River (Township)—
 Daviess... MO-3
Grand River (Township)—
 DeKalb... MO-3

Grand River (Township)—
 Livingston... MO-3
Grand River (Township)—
 Bowman... ND-4
Grand River (Village)—Lake... OH-3
Grand River (Township)—
 Perkins... SD-4
Grand River Dam (WA)... Geog-4
Grand Rivers (City)—Livingston... KY-2
Grand Ronde Reservation
 (OR)... IndRes-4
Grand Saline (City)—Van Zandt... TX-2
Grand Strand (WA)... Geog-4
Grand Terrace (City)—San
 Bernardino... CA-4
Grand Teton (WY)... Geog-4
Grand Tower (Town)—Jackson... IL-3
Grand Tower (Township)—
 Jackson... IL-3
Grand Traverse Bay (MI)... Geog-4
Grand Traverse County... MI-3
Grand Traverse & Trust Lands
 (MI)... IndRes-4
Grand Valley (Township)—
 Dickey... ND-4
Grand Valley (Township)—
 Corson... SD-4
Grand View (City)—Owyhee... ID-4
Grandview (Township)—Edgar... IL-3
Grandview (Village)—Sangamon... IL-3
Grandview (Town)—Spencer... IN-3
Grandview (City)—Louisa... IA-3
Grandview (Township)—Ford... KS-4
Grandview (Township)—Lyon... MN-3
Grandview (City)—Jackson... MO-3
Grandview (Township)—
 LaMoure... ND-4
Grandview (CDP)—Hamilton... OH-3
Grandview (Township)—
 Washington... OH-3
Grandview (Pop. Place)—Brule... SD-4
Grandview (Township)—Douglas... SD-4
Grandview (Township)—
 Hutchinson... SD-4
Grandview (Township)—Jackson... SD-4
Grandview (Township)—Jones... SD-4
Grandview (City)—Johnson... TX-2
Grandview (City)—Yakima... WA-4
Grand View (Town)—Bayfield... WI-3
Grandview Heights (City)—
 Franklin... OH-3
Grand View-on-Hudson (Village)—
 Rockland... NY-1
Grandview Park (CDP)—Elk... PA-1
Grandview Plaza (City)—Geary... KS-4
Grandville (Township)—Jasper... IL-3
Grandville (City)—Kent... MI-3
Grandwood Park (CDP)—Lake... IL-3
Grange (Township)—Pipestone... MN-3
Grange (Township)—Deuel... SD-4
Granger (CDP)—St. Joseph... IN-3
Granger (City)—Dallas... IA-3
Granger (Town)—Scotland... MO-3
Granger (Town)—Allegany... NY-1
Granger (Township)—Medina... OH-3
Granger (City)—Williamson... TX-2
Granger (Town)—Yakima... WA-4
Granger (Town)—Sweetwater... WY-4
Grangeville (City)—Idaho... ID-4
Granite (Township)—Phillips... KS-4
Granite (Township)—Morrison... MN-3
Granite (Town)—Greer... OK-2
Granite (City)—Grant... OR-4
Granite (CDP)—Salt Lake... UT-4
Granite City (City)—Madison... IL-3

Granite City (Township)—
 Madison... IL-3
Granite County... MT-4
Granite Falls (City)—Chippewa... MN-3
Granite Falls (Township)—
 Chippewa... MN-3
Granite Falls (City)—Yellow
 Medicine... MN-3
Granite Falls (Town)—Caldwell... NC-2
Granite Falls (Town)—
 Snohomish... WA-4
Granite Hills (CDP)—San Diego... CA-4
Granite Ledge (Township)—
 Benton... MN-3
Granite Peak (MT)... Geog-4
Granite Quarry (Town)—Rowan... NC-2
Granite Rock (Township)—
 Redwood... MN-3
Granite Shoals (City)—Burnet... TX-2
Graniteville-East Barre (CDP)—
 Washington... VT-1
Grannis (Town)—Polk... AR-2
Grano (City)—Renville... ND-4
Grant (Town)—Marshall... AL-2
Grant (Township)—Lake... IL-3
Grant (Township)—Vermilion... IL-3
Grant (Township)—Benton... IN-3
Grant (Township)—Dekalb... IN-3
Grant (Township)—Greene... IN-3
Grant (Township)—Newton... IN-3
Grant (City)—Montgomery... IA-3
Grant (Township)—Barton... KS-4
Grant (Township)—Clay... KS-4
Grant (Township)—Cloud... KS-4
Grant (Township)—Cowley... KS-4
Grant (Township)—Crawford... KS-4
Grant (Township)—Decatur... KS-4
Grant (Township)—Dickinson... KS-4
Grant (Township)—Douglas... KS-4
Grant (Township)—Jackson... KS-4
Grant (Township)—Jewell... KS-4
Grant (Township)—Lincoln... KS-4
Grant (Township)—Marion... KS-4
Grant (Township)—Neosho... KS-4
Grant (Township)—Osage... KS-4
Grant (Township)—Osborne... KS-4
Grant (Township)—Ottawa... KS-4
Grant (Township)—Pawnee... KS-4
Grant (Township)—
 Pottawatomie... KS-4
Grant (Township)—Reno... KS-4
Grant (Township)—Republic... KS-4
Grant (Township)—Riley... KS-4
Grant (Township)—Russell... KS-4
Grant (Township)—Sedgwick... KS-4
Grant (Township)—Sherman... KS-4
Grant (Township)—Washington... KS-4
Grant (Township)—Cheboygan... MI-3
Grant (Township)—Clare... MI-3
Grant (Township)—Grand
 Traverse... MI-3
Grant (Township)—Huron... MI-3
Grant (Township)—Iosco... MI-3
Grant (Township)—Keweenaw... MI-3
Grant (Township)—Mason... MI-3
Grant (Township)—Mecosta... MI-3
Grant (City)—Newaygo... MI-3
Grant (Township)—Newaygo... MI-3
Grant (Township)—Oceana... MI-3
Grant (Township)—St. Clair... MI-3
Grant (Township)—Washington... MN-3
Grant (Township)—Caldwell... MO-3
Grant (Township)—Clark... MO-3
Grant (Township)—Dade... MO-3
Grant (Township)—Dallas... MO-3

Grant (Township)—DeKalb *MO-3*
Grant (Township)—Harrison *MO-3*
Grant (Township)—Nodaway *MO-3*
Grant (Township)—Putnam *MO-3*
Grant (Township)—Stone *MO-3*
Grant (Township)—Webster *MO-3*
Grant (Township)—Antelope *NE-4*
Grant (Township)—Buffalo *NE-4*
Grant (Township)—Cuming *NE-4*
Grant (Township)—Custer *NE-4*
Grant (Township)—Franklin........... *NE-4*
Grant (Township)—Gage *NE-4*
Grant (Township)—Kearney *NE-4*
Grant (City)—Perkins *NE-4*
Grant (Township)—Richland.......... *ND-4*
Grant (Township)—Indiana *PA-1*
Grant (Township)—Beadle............. *SD-4*
Grant (Township)—Lincoln *SD-4*
Grant (Township)—McCook........... *SD-4*
Grant (Township)—Roberts *SD-4*
Grant (Town)—Clark *WI-3*
Grant (Town)—Dunn *WI-3*
Grant (Town)—Monroe *WI-3*
Grant (Town)—Portage *WI-3*
Grant (Town)—Rusk *WI-3*
Grant (Town)—Shawano *WI-3*
Grant Center (Township)—Grant.. *SD-4*
Grant City (City)—Worth *MO-3*
Grant County *AR-2*
Grant County *IN-3*
Grant County *KS-4*
Grant County *KY-2*
Grant County *MN-3*
Grant County *NE-4*
Grant County *NM-4*
Grant County *ND-4*
Grant County *OK-2*
Grant County *OR-4*
Grant County *SD-4*
Grant County *WA-4*
Grant County *WV-2*
Grant County *WI-3*
Grantfork (Village)—Madison *IL-3*
Grantham (Town)—Sullivan *NH-1*
Grantley (CDP)—Wyoming *PA-1*
Granton (Village)—Clark *WI-3*
Grant Parish *LA-2*
Grant Park (Village)—Kankakee *IL-3*
Grants (City)—Cibola *NM-4*
Grantsburg (Town)—Burnett *WI-3*
Grantsburg (Village)—Burnett *WI-3*
Grants Pass (City)—Josephine........ *OR-4*
Grantsville (Town)—Garrett *MD-1*
Grantsville (Township)—Linn *MO-3*
Grantsville (City)—Tooele *UT-4*
Grantsville (Town)—Calhoun *WV-2*
Grant Town (Town)—Marion *WV-2*
Grant Valley (Township)—
 Beltrami *MN-3*
Grantville (City)—Coweta *GA-2*
Grantwood Village (Town)—St.
 Louis *MO-3*
Granville (City)—Putnam *IL-3*
Granville (Township)—Putnam *IL-3*
Granville (City)—Sioux *IA-3*
Granville (Town)—Hampden *MA-1*
Granville (Township)—Kittson..... *MN-3*
Granville (Township)—Platte *NE-4*
Granville (Town)—Washington *NY-1*
Granville (Village)—Washington ... *NY-1*
Granville (City)—McHenry *ND-4*
Granville (Township)—McHenry .. *ND-4*
Granville (Township)—Licking......*OH-3*
Granville (Village)—Licking *OH-3*
Granville (Township)—Mercer *OH-3*

Granville (Township)—Bradford *PA-1*
Granville (Township)—Mifflin *PA-1*
Granville (Town)—Addison *VT-1*
Granville (Town)—Monongalia *WV-2*
Granville County *NC-2*
Granville South (CDP)—Licking...*OH-3*
Grape Grove (Township)—Ray *MO-3*
Grapeland (City)—Houston *TX-2*
Grapevine (City)—Dallas *TX-2*
Grapevine (City)—Denton *TX-2*
Grapevine (City)—Tarrant *TX-2*
Grasonville (CDP)—Queen
 Anne's *MD-1*
Grass (Township)—Spencer *IN-3*
Grasshopper (Township)—
 Atchison *KS-4*
Grass Lake (Township)—Jackson .. *MI-3*
Grass Lake (Village)—Jackson....... *MI-3*
Grass Lake (Township)—
 Kanabec *MN-3*
Grass Lake (Township)—
 Burleigh *ND-4*
Grassland (Township)—Renville ... *ND-4*
Grass Range (Town)—Fergus *MT-4*
Grasston (City)—Kanabec *MN-3*
Grass Valley (City)—Nevada *CA-4*
Grass Valley (City)—Sherman *OR-4*
Grassy Fork (Township)—Jackson.. *IN-3*
Gratiot (Village)—Licking...............*OH-3*
Gratiot (Village)—Muskingum *OH-3*
Gratiot (Town)—Lafayette *WI-3*
Gratiot (Village)—Lafayette........... *WI-3*
Gratiot County *MI-3*
Gratis (Township)—Preble *OH-3*
Gratis (Village)—Preble *OH-3*
Graton (CDP)—Sonoma *CA-4*
Grattan (Township)—Kent *MI-3*
Grattan (Township)—Itasca *MN-3*
Grattan (Township)—Holt *NE-4*
Gratz (City)—Owen *KY-2*
Gratz (Borough)—Dauphin *PA-1*
Gravel Ridge (CDP)—Pulaski *AR-2*
Graves County *KY-2*
Gravesend—Kings *NY-1*
Gravette (City)—Benton *AR-2*
Gravity (City)—Taylor....................*IA-3*
Gravois (Township)—St. Louis...... *MO-3*
Gravois Mills (Village)—Morgan.. *MO-3*
Gray (City)—Jones *GA-2*
Gray (Township)—White *IL-3*
Gray (City)—Audubon *IA-3*
Gray (CDP)—Terrebonne Parish....*LA-2*
Gray (Town)—Cumberland............*ME-1*
Gray (Township)—Pipestone *MN-3*
Gray (Township)—Stutsman *ND-4*
Gray (Township)—Greene *PA-1*
Gray (CDP)—Washington *TN-2*
Grayburg (City)—Hardin *TX-2*
Gray County *KS-4*
Gray County *TX-2*
Gray Court (Town)—Laurens *SC-2*
Grayling (City)—Yukon-Koyukuk
 Census Area *AK-4*
Grayling (City)—Crawford *MI-3*
Grayling (Township)—Crawford ... *MI-3*
Graymoor-Devondale (City)—
 Jefferson *KY-2*
Grays Harbor County *WA-4*
Grayslake (City)—Lake *IL-3*
Grayson (City)—Gwinnett *GA-2*
Grayson (City)—Carter *KY-2*
Grayson (Village)—Caldwell
 Parish *LA-2*
Grayson (Town)—Okmulgee........... *OK-2*
Grayson County *KY-2*

Grayson County *TX-2*
Grayson County *VA-2*
Grays Prairie (Village)—
 Kaufman *TX-2*
Gray Summit (CDP)—Franklin.... *MO-3*
Graysville (City)—Jefferson *AL-2*
Graysville (Village)—Monroe *OH-3*
Graysville (Town)—Rhea *TN-2*
Grayville (City)—Edwards *IL-3*
Grayville (City)—White *IL-3*
Greasewood (CDP)—Navajo *AZ-4*
Great American Desert (MT) *Geog-4*
Great Barrington (Town)—
 Berkshire *MA-1*
Great Basin (MT) *Geog-4*
Great Bend (City)—Barton *KS-4*
Great Bend (Township)—Barton *KS-4*
Great Bend (Township)—
 Cottonwood *MN-3*
Great Bend (City)—Richland *ND-4*
Great Bend (Borough)—
 Susquehanna *PA-1*
Great Bend (Township)—
 Susquehanna *PA-1*
Great Bend (Township)—Spink *SD-4*
Great Dismal Swamp (MT) *Geog-4*
Great Divide (MT) *Geog-4*
Greater Northdale (CDP)—
 Hillsborough *FL-2*
Greater Upper Marlboro (CDP)—
 Prince George's *MD-1*
Great Falls (City)—Cascade *MT-4*
Great Falls (Town)—Chester..........*SC-2*
Great Falls (CDP)—Fairfax *VA-2*
Great Lakes (MT) *Geog-4*
Great Lakes Naval Training Center
 (IL) *Mil-4*
Great Meadows-Vienna (CDP)—
 Warren.. *NJ-1*
Great National Pike (MT) *Geog-4*
Great Neck (Village)—Nassau *NY-1*
Great Neck Estates (Village)—
 Nassau *NY-1*
Great Neck Plaza (Village)—
 Nassau *NY-1*
Great Plains (MT) *Geog-4*
Great Pond (Plantation)—
 Hancock *ME-1*
Great Salt Lake (UT) *Geog-4*
Great Salt Lake Desert (UT) *Geog-4*
Great Sand Dunes (CO) *Geog-4*
Great Scott (Township)—St.
 Louis *MN-3*
Great Smoky Mountains (CO) *Geog-4*
Greatstone (Township)—McLean .. *ND-4*
Great Stone Face, The (CO) *Geog-4*
Great Valley (Town)—
 Cattaraugus *NY-1*
Greece (Town)—Monroe *NY-1*
Greeley (City)—Weld *CO-4*
Greeley (City)—Delaware *IA-3*
Greeley (City)—Anderson *KS-4*
Greeley (Township)—Saline *KS-4*
Greeley (Township)—Sedgwick....*KS-4*
Greeley Center (Village)—
 Greeley *NE-4*
Greeley County *KS-4*
Greeley County *NE-4*
Greeleyville (Town)—
 Williamsburg..................................*SC-2*
Greely (Township)—Ward *ND-4*
Green (Township)—Grant *IN-3*
Green (Township)—Hancock *IN-3*
Green (Township)—Madison *IN-3*
Green (Township)—Marshall *IN-3*

Green (Township)—Morgan IN-3
Green (Township)—Noble IN-3
Green (Township)—Randolph IN-3
Green (City)—Clay........................KS-4
Green (Township)—
  Pottawatomie............................. KS-4
Green (Township)—Alpena............. MI-3
Green (Township)—Mecosta MI-3
Green (Township)—Hickory MO-3
Green (Township)—Lawrence....... MO-3
Green (Township)—Livingston..... MO-3
Green (Township)—Nodaway....... MO-3
Green (Township)—Platte MO-3
Green (Township)—Saunders NE-4
Green (Township)—Sussex NJ-1
Green (Township)—Barnes ND-4
Green (Township)—Adams............OH-3
Green (Township)—Ashland..........OH-3
Green (Township)—Brown OH-3
Green (Township)—Clark OH-3
Green (Township)—Clinton...........OH-3
Green (Township)—Fayette OH-3
Green (Township)—Gallia OH-3
Green (Township)—Hamilton........OH-3
Green (Township)—Harrison OH-3
Green (Township)—Hocking OH-3
Green (Township)—Mahoning.......OH-3
Green (Township)—Monroe OH-3
Green (Township)—Ross OH-3
Green (Township)—Scioto OH-3
Green (Township)—Shelby OH-3
Green (Township)—Summit OH-3
Green (Village)—Summit...............OH-3
Green (Township)—Wayne OH-3
Green (CDP)—Douglas...................OR-4
Green (Township)—Forest PA-1
Green (Township)—Indiana............ PA-1
Greenacres (CDP)—Kern CA-4
Green Acres (CDP)—Spokane WA-4
Greenacres City (City)—Palm
  Beach.. FL-2
Greenback (City)—Loudon TN-2
Green Bay (WI) Geog-4
Green Bay (City)—Brown WI-3
Green Bay (Town)—Brown.............. WI-3
Greenbelt (City)—Prince
  George's MD-1
Greenbrier (City)—Faulkner AR-2
Greenbrier (Town)—Robertson TN-2
Greenbrier County......................... WV-2
Green Brook (Township)—
  Somerset...................................... NJ-1
Greenburgh (Town)—
  Westchester.................................NY-1
Greenbush (Township)—Warren...... IL-3
Greenbush (Town)—Penobscot.... ME-1
Greenbush (Township)—Alcona MI-3
Greenbush (Township)—Clinton ... MI-3
Greenbush (Township)—Mille
  Lacs..MN-3
Greenbush (City)—Roseau............MN-3
Greenbush (Township)—Ward.......ND-4
Greenbush (Town)—Sheboygan..... WI-3
Green Camp (Township)—
  Marion OH-3
Green Camp (Village)—Marion.....OH-3
Greencastle (City)—Putnam IN-3
Greencastle (Township)—Putnam .. IN-3
Greencastle (City)—Sullivan MO-3
Greencastle (Borough)—Franklin ... PA-1
Green City (City)—Sullivan MO-3
Green County KY-2
Green County WI-3
Green Cove Springs (City)—Clay...FL-2

Green Creek (Township)—
  Sandusky.................................... OH-3
Greendale (Town)—Dearborn.......... IN-3
Greendale (Township)—Midland... MI-3
Greendale (City)—St. Louis.......... MO-3
Greendale (Township)—
  Richland.....................................ND-4
Greendale (Village)—Milwaukee ... WI-3
Greene (Township)—Mercer........... IL-3
Greene (Township)—Woodford IL-3
Greene (Township)—Jay IN-3
Greene (Township)—Parke IN-3
Greene (Township)—St. Joseph IN-3
Greene (Township)—Wayne IN-3
Greene (City)—Butler IA-3
Greene (Township)—Sumner..........KS-4
Greene (Town)—Androscoggin ME-1
Greene (Township)—Worth MO-3
Greene (Town)—Chenango NY-1
Greene (Village)—Chenango NY-1
Greene (Township)—Ransom ND-4
Greene (Township)—Trumbull OH-3
Greene (Township)—Beaver PA-1
Greene (Township)—Clinton PA-1
Greene (Township)—Erie PA-1
Greene (Township)—Franklin PA-1
Greene (Township)—Greene........... PA-1
Greene (Township)—Mercer PA-1
Greene (Township)—Pike PA-1
Greene County...............................AL-2
Greene County............................... AR-2
Greene County................................GA-2
Greene County.................................IL-3
Greene County................................ IN-3
Greene County................................IA-3
Greene County...............................MS-2
Greene County...............................MO-3
Greene County................................NY-1
Greene County...............................NC-2
Greene County...............................OH-3
Greene County................................ PA-1
Greene County............................... TN-2
Greene County............................... VA-2
Greenevers (Town)—Duplin NC-2
Greeneville (Town)—Greene........ TN-2
Greenfield (City)—Monterey CA-4
Greenfield (City)—Greene............... IL-3
Greenfield (Township)—Grundy IL-3
Greenfield (City)—Hancock IN-3
Greenfield (Township)—Lagrange .. IN-3
Greenfield (Township)—Orange IN-3
Greenfield (City)—Adair IA-3
Greenfield (Township)—Elk KS-4
Greenfield (Town)—Penobscot ME-1
Greenfield (Town)—Franklin......... MA-1
Greenfield (City)—Hennepin MN-3
Greenfield (Township)—
  Wabasha....................................MN-3
Greenfield (City)—Dade MO-3
Greenfield (Town)—
  Hillsborough NH-1
Greenfield (Town)—Saratoga..........NY-1
Greenfield (Township)—Griggs ND-4
Greenfield (Township)—Traill ND-4
Greenfield (Township)—Fairfield ..OH-3
Greenfield (Township)—Gallia OH-3
Greenfield (City)—Highland..........OH-3
Greenfield (Township)—Huron OH-3
Greenfield (Town)—Blaine OK-2
Greenfield (Township)—Blair PA-1
Greenfield (Township)—Erie PA-1
Greenfield (Township)—
  Lackawanna................................ PA-1
Greenfield (Township)—Brown SD-4
Greenfield (Town)—Weakley TN-2

Greenfield (Town)—La Crosse WI-3
Greenfield (City)—Milwaukee WI-3
Greenfield (Town)—Monroe.......... WI-3
Greenfield (Town)—Sauk............... WI-3
Green Forest (City)—Carroll AR-2
Green Garden (Township)—Will ... IL-3
Green Garden (Township)—
  Ellsworth KS-4
Green Grove (Town)—Clark.......... WI-3
Green Harbor-Cedar Crest (CDP)—
  Plymouth.................................... MA-1
Green Haven (CDP)—Anne
  Arundel......................................MD-1
Green Hill (CDP)—Wilson TN-2
Greenhills (City)—Hamilton..........OH-3
Green Hills (Borough)—
  Washington PA-1
Greenhorn (City)—Baker OR-4
Greenhorn (City)—Grant OR-4
Green Island (City)—Jackson IA-3
Green Island (Village)—Albany......NY-1
Green Isle (City)—Sibley MN-3
Green Isle (Township)—Sibley MN-3
Green Lake (Township)—Grand
  Traverse...................................... MI-3
Green Lake (Township)—
  Kandiyohi MN-3
Green Lake (City)—Green Lake.... WI-3
Green Lake (Town)—Green Lake.. WI-3
Green Lake County........................ WI-3
Greenland (Town)—Washington.... AR-2
Greenland (Township)—
  Ontonagon MI-3
Greenland (Town)—Rockingham ..NH-1
Greenland (Township)—Barnes ND-4
Greenland (Township)—McCook .. SD-4
Green Lane (Borough)—
  Montgomery PA-1
Greenlawn (CDP)—Suffolk............NY-1
Greenleaf (City)—Canyon............... ID-4
Greenleaf (City)—Washington KS-4
Greenleaf (Township)—
  Washington KS-4
Greenleaf (Township)—Sanilac...... MI-3
Greenleaf (Township)—Meeker MN-3
Greenleaf (Township)—Hand SD-4
Greenlee County AZ-4
Green Meadow (Township)—
  Norman MN-3
Green Meadows (CDP)—Clark OH-3
Green Mountain Falls (Town)—El
  Paso...CO-4
Green Mountain Falls (Town)—
  Teller CO-4
Green Mountains (VT)................ Geog-4
Green Oak (Township)—
  Livingston MI-3
Green Oaks (Village)—Lake IL-3
Greenpoint—Kings NY-1
Greenport (Town)—Columbia NY-1
Greenport (Village)—Suffolk NY-1
Greenport West (CDP)—Suffolk ...NY-1
Green Prairie (Township)—
  Morrison MN-3
Green Ridge (Town)—Pettis MO-3
Green Ridge (Township)—Pettis .. MO-3
Green River (City)—Emery UT-4
Green River (City)—Grand UT-4
Green River (City)—Sweetwater .. WY-4
Green Rock (City)—Henry IL-3
Greensboro (City)—Hale AL-2
Greensboro (Town)—Gadsden........FL-2
Greensboro (City)—Greene GA-2
Greensboro (Town)—Henry............ IN-3
Greensboro (Township)—Henry..... IN-3

General Index

Greensboro (Town)—Caroline *MD-1*
Greensboro (City)—Guilford *NC-2*
Greensboro (Borough)—Greene...... *PA-1*
Greensboro (Town)—Orleans *VT-1*
Greensburg (City)—Decatur *IN-3*
Greensburg (City)—Kiowa *KS-4*
Greensburg (City)—Green *KY-2*
Greensburg (Town)—St. Helena
    Parish *LA-2*
Greensburg (Township)—Knox *MO-3*
Greensburg (Township)—
    Putnam *OH-3*
Greensburg (CDP)—Summit *OH-3*
Greensburg (City)—
    Westmoreland *PA-1*
Greensfork (Township)—
    Randolph *IN-3*
Greens Fork (Town)—Wayne.......... *IN-3*
Greens Grant (Pop. Place)—
    Coos *NH-1*
Green Spring (City)—Jefferson.... *KY-2*
Green Springs (Village)—
    Sandusky *OH-3*
Green Springs (Village)—Seneca ... *OH-3*
Greensville County *VA-2*
Greentop (Village)—Adair *MO-3*
Greentop (Village)—Schuyler *MO-3*
Greentown (Town)—Howard *IN-3*
Greentown (CDP)—Stark *OH-3*
Green Tree (Borough)—Allegheny.. *PA-1*
Greenup (City)—Cumberland......... *IL-3*
Greenup (Township)—
    Cumberland *IL-3*
Greenup (City)—Greenup............... *KY-2*
Greenup County *KY-2*
Greenvale (Township)—Dakota...... *MN-3*
Green Valley (CDP)—Pima *AZ-4*
Green Valley (Village)—Tazewell.... *IL-3*
Green Valley (CDP)—Frederick ... *MD-1*
Green Valley (Township)—
    Becker *MN-3*
Green Valley (Township)—Holt...... *NE-4*
Green Valley (Township)—Miner .. *SD-4*
Green Valley (Town)—Marathon... *WI-3*
Green Valley (Town)—Shawano ... *WI-3*
Greenview (Village)—Menard *IL-3*
Greenview (Township)—Steele...... *ND-4*
Greenville (City)—Butler *AL-2*
Greenville (CDP)—Plumas *CA-4*
Greenville (Town)—Madison.......... *FL-2*
Greenville (City)—Meriwether *GA-2*
Greenville (City)—Bond *IL-3*
Greenville (Township)—Bureau...... *IL-3*
Greenville (Town)—Floyd............... *IN-3*
Greenville (Township)—Floyd........ *IN-3*
Greenville (City)—Clay.................... *IA-3*
Greenville (City)—Muhlenberg....... *KY-2*
Greenville (Town)—Piscataquis..... *ME-1*
Greenville (City)—Montcalm *MI-3*
Greenville (City)—Washington *MS-2*
Greenville (City)—Wayne *MO-3*
Greenville (Town)—
    Hillsborough *NH-1*
Greenville (Town)—Greene *NY-1*
Greenville (Town)—Orange *NY-1*
Greenville (CDP)—Westchester..... *NY-1*
Greenville (City)—Pitt *NC-2*
Greenville (Township)—
    LaMoure *ND-4*
Greenville (City)—Darke *OH-3*
Greenville (Township)—Darke *OH-3*
Greenville (Borough)—Mercer........ *PA-1*
Greenville (Township)—Somerset .. *PA-1*
Greenville (CDP)—Providence....... *RI-1*
Greenville (City)—Greenville *SC-2*

Greenville (City)—Hunt.................. *TX-2*
Greenville (Town)—Outagamie *WI-3*
Greenville County *SC-2*
Greenville Rancheria (CA)........ *IndRes-4*
Greenwald (City)—Stearns............. *MN-3*
Greenway (Town)—Clay *AR-2*
Greenway (Township)—Itasca *MN-3*
Greenwich (Town)—Fairfield.......... *CT-1*
Greenwich (Township)—
    Cumberland *NJ-1*
Greenwich (Township)—
    Gloucester *NJ-1*
Greenwich (Township)—Warren.... *NJ-1*
Greenwich (Town)—Washington .. *NY-1*
Greenwich (Village)—
    Washington *NY-1*
Greenwich (Township)—Huron *OH-3*
Greenwich (Village)—Huron *OH-3*
Greenwich (Township)—Berks....... *PA-1*
Greenwood (City)—Sebastian *AR-2*
Greenwood (Town)—Sussex *DE-1*
Greenwood (Town)—Jackson *FL-2*
Greenwood (Township)—
    Christian *IL-3*
Greenwood (Township)—
    McHenry.................................. *IL-3*
Greenwood (City)—Johnson........... *IN-3*
Greenwood (Township)—
    Franklin.................................... *KS-4*
Greenwood (Township)—Phillips... *KS-4*
Greenwood (Village)—Caddo
    Parish *LA-2*
Greenwood (Town)—Oxford.......... *ME-1*
Greenwood (Township)—Clare...... *MI-3*
Greenwood (Township)—Oceana .. *MI-3*
Greenwood (Township)—Oscoda .. *MI-3*
Greenwood (Township)—St.
    Clair *MI-3*
Greenwood (Township)—
    Wexford.................................. *MI-3*
Greenwood (Township)—
    Clearwater *MN-3*
Greenwood (City)—Hennepin *MN-3*
Greenwood (Township)—St.
    Louis *MN-3*
Greenwood (City)—Leflore............. *MS-2*
Greenwood (City)—Jackson........... *MO-3*
Greenwood (Village)—Cass........... *NE-4*
Greenwood (Town)—Steuben *NY-1*
Greenwood (Township)—
    Clearfield................................. *PA-1*
Greenwood (Township)—
    Columbia *PA-1*
Greenwood (Township)—
    Crawford *PA-1*
Greenwood (Township)—Juniata ... *PA-1*
Greenwood (Township)—Perry....... *PA-1*
Greenwood (City)—Greenwood *SC-2*
Greenwood (Township)—Tripp *SD-4*
Greenwood (City)—Clark *WI-3*
Greenwood (Town)—Taylor............ *WI-3*
Greenwood (Town)—Vernon *WI-3*
Greenwood County *KS-4*
Greenwood County *SC-2*
Greenwood Lake (Village)—
    Orange *NY-1*
Greenwood Village (City)—
    Arapahoe *CO-4*
Greer (Township)—Warrick *IN-3*
Greer (City)—Greenville.................. *SC-2*
Greer (City)—Spartanburg.............. *SC-2*
Greer County *OK-2*
Greers Ferry (City)—Cleburne....... *AR-2*
Gregg (Township)—Morgan *IN-3*
Gregg (Township)—Centre............. *PA-1*

Gregg (Township)—Union *PA-1*
Gregg County *TX-2*
Gregory (Township)—
    Mahnomen..............................*MN-3*
Gregory (City)—Gregory................ *SD-4*
Gregory (City)—San Patricio........ *TX-2*
Gregory County *SD-4*
Greig (Town)—Lewis *NY-1*
Greilickville (CDP)—Leelanau *MI-3*
Grenada (City)—Grenada *MS-2*
Grenada County *MS-2*
Grenola (City)—Elk......................... *KS-4*
Grenora (City)—Williams............... *ND-4*
Grenora (Township)—Williams......*ND-4*
Grenville (Village)—Union *NM-4*
Grenville (Town)—Day *SD-4*
Grenville (Township)—Day *SD-4*
Gresham (Village)—York *NE-4*
Gresham (City)—Multnomah *OR-4*
Gresham (Village)—Shawano *WI-3*
Gresham Park (CDP)—De Kalb ... *GA-2*
Gretna (Town)—Gadsden *FL-2*
Gretna (City)—Jefferson Parish....... *LA-2*
Gretna (City)—Sarpy...................... *NE-4*
Gretna (Town)—Pittsylvania *VA-2*
Grey (Township)—Cavalier *ND-4*
Greybull (Town)—Big Horn........... *WY-4*
Grey Cloud Island (Township)—
    Washington *MN-3*
Grey Eagle (City)—Todd................ *MN-3*
Grey Eagle (Township)—Todd...... *MN-3*
Grey Forest (City)—Bexar *TX-2*
Gridley (City)—Butte *CA-4*
Gridley (Town)—McLean *IL-3*
Gridley (Township)—McLean........ *IL-3*
Gridley (City)—Coffey *KS-4*
Griffin (City)—Spalding................. *GA-2*
Griffin (Town)—Posey *IN-3*
Griffin (Township)—Stutsman........ *ND-4*
Griffiss Air Force Base (NY)..........*Mil-4*
Griffith (Town)—Lake *IN-3*
Griffithville (Town)—White............ *AR-2*
Grifton (Town)—Lenoir *NC-2*
Grifton (Town)—Pitt....................... *NC-2*
Griggs County *ND-4*
Griggsville (Town)—Pike *IL-3*
Griggsville (Township)—Pike........ *IL-3*
Grilley (Township)—McHenry *ND-4*
Grim (Township)—Gladwin *MI-3*
Grimes (Municipality)—Dale *AL-2*
Grimes (City)—Polk........................ *IA-3*
Grimes County *TX-2*
Grimesland (Town)—Pitt................ *NC-2*
Grimstad (Township)—Roseau...... *MN-3*
Grindstone Rancheria (CA) *IndRes-4*
Grindstone-Rowes Run (CDP)—
    Fayette *PA-1*
Grinnell (City)—Poweshiek *IA-3*
Grinnell (City)—Gove..................... *KS-4*
Grinnell (Township)—Gove........... *KS-4*
Grisham (Township)—
    Montgomery............................. *IL-3*
Grissom Air Force Base (Military
    Facility)—Cass........................ *IN-3*
Grissom Air Force Base (Military
    Facility)—Miami *IN-3*
Griswold (Town)—New London.... *CT-1*
Griswold (City)—Cass.................... *IA-3*
Groesbeck (CDP)—Hamilton *OH-3*
Groesbeck (City)—Limestone *TX-2*
Groom (Town)—Carson................. *TX-2*
Gross (Village)—Boyd *NE-4*
Grosse Ile (Township)—Wayne...... *MI-3*
Grosse Pointe (City)—Wayne *MI-3*

Grosse Pointe Farms (City)—
 Wayne.................................... *MI-3*
Grosse Pointe Park (City)—
 Wayne.................................... *MI-3*
Grosse Pointe Shores (Village)—
 Macomb................................. *MI-3*
Grosse Pointe Shores (Village)—
 Wayne.................................... *MI-3*
Grosse Pointe Woods (City)—
 Wayne.................................... *MI-3*
Grosse Tete (Village)—Iberville
 Parish..................................... *LA-2*
Groton (City)—New London......... *CT-1*
Groton (Town)—New London...... *CT-1*
Groton (Town)—Middlesex *MA-1*
Groton (Town)—Grafton *NH-1*
Groton (Town)—Tompkins........... *NY-1*
Groton (Village)—Tompkins......... *NY-1*
Groton (Township)—Erie.............. *OH-3*
Groton (City)—Brown.................. *SD-4*
Groton (Township)—Brown.......... *SD-4*
Groton (Town)—Caledonia........... *VT-1*
Grottoes (Town)—Augusta............ *VA-2*
Grottoes (Town)—Rockingham *VA-2*
Grout (Township)—Gladwin *MI-3*
Grove (Township)—Jasper............ *IL-3*
Grove (Township)—Reno *KS-4*
Grove (Township)—Shawnee......... *KS-4*
Grove (Township)—Stearns *MN-3*
Grove (Town)—Allegany.............. *NY-1*
Grove (Town)—Delaware *OK-2*
Grove (Township)—Cameron *PA-1*
Grove City (CDP)—Charlotte *FL-2*
Grove City (City)—Meeker........... *MN-3*
Grove City (City)—Franklin......... *OH-3*
Grove City (Borough)—Mercer *PA-1*
Grove Hill (Town)—Clarke........... *AL-2*
Grove Lake (Township)—Pope..... *MN-3*
Groveland (City)—Lake................ *FL-2*
Groveland (Township)—La Salle.... *IL-3*
Groveland (Township)—Tazewell... *IL-3*
Groveland (Township)—
 McPherson *KS-4*
Groveland (Town)—Essex............. *MA-1*
Groveland (Township)—Oakland .. *MI-3*
Groveland (Town)—Livingston *NY-1*
Groveland (Township)—Spink..... *SD-4*
Groveland-Big Oak Flat (CDP)—
 Tuolumne *CA-4*
Grovena (Township)—Moody *SD-4*
Grove Park (Township)—Polk... *MN-3*
Groveport (Village)—Franklin.......*OH-3*
Grover (Town)—Weld.................. *CO-4*
Grover (Township)—Wayne.......... *IL-3*
Grover (Township)—Johnson *MO-3*
Grover (Town)—Cleveland *NC-2*
Grover (Township)—Renville........ *ND-4*
Grover (Town)—Marinette *WI-3*
Grover (Town)—Taylor................. *WI-3*
Grover City (City)—San Luis
 Obispo.................................... *CA-4*
Grover Hill (Village)—Paulding *OH-3*
Groves (City)—Jefferson................ *TX-2*
Groveton (CDP)—Coos................. *NH-1*
Groveton (City)—Trinity *TX-2*
Groveton (CDP)—Fairfax *VA-2*
Grovetown (City)—Columbia....... *GA-2*
Grow (Town)—Rusk *WI-3*
Grubbs (Town)—Jackson.............. *AR-2*
Gruetli-Laager (City)—Grundy..... *TN-2*
Grugan (Township)—Clinton *PA-1*
Grundy (Town)—Buchanan *VA-2*
Grundy Center (City)—Grundy.......*IA-3*
Grundy County *IL-3*
Grundy County *IA-3*

Grundy County *MO-3*
Grundy County *TN-2*
Gruver (City)—Emmet................... *IA-3*
Gruver (City)—Hansford *TX-2*
Grygla (City)—Marshall................ *MN-3*
Guadalupe (Town)—Maricopa....... *AZ-4*
Guadalupe (City)—Santa
 Barbara.................................. *CA-4*
Guadalupe County *NM-4*
Guadalupe County *TX-2*
Guadalupe Peak (TX)................. *Geog-4*
Guelph (Township)—Sumner........*KS-4*
Guenther (Town)—Marathon *WI-3*
Guerneville (CDP)—Sonoma........ *CA-4*
Guernsey (City)—Poweshiek.........*IA-3*
Guernsey (Town)—Platte *WY-4*
Guernsey County *OH-3*
Gueydan (Town)—Vermilion
 Parish..................................... *LA-2*
Guide Rock (Village)—Webster *NE-4*
Guilderland (Town)—Albany......... *NY-1*
Guildhall (Town)—Essex............... *VT-1*
Guilford (Town)—New Haven *CT-1*
Guilford (Township)—Jo Daviess .. *IL-3*
Guilford (Township)—Hendricks ... *IN-3*
Guilford (Township)—Wilson *KS-4*
Guilford (Town)—Piscataquis....... *ME-1*
Guilford (Town)—Nodaway.......... *MO-3*
Guilford (Town)—Chenango......... *NY-1*
Guilford (Township)—Medina......*OH-3*
Guilford (Township)—Franklin *PA-1*
Guilford (Town)—Windham......... *VT-1*
Guilford County *NC-2*
Guin (Town)—Marion *AL-2*
Guion (Town)—Izard *AR-2*
Guittard (Township)—Marshall.......*KS-4*
Gulf Breeze (City)—Santa Rosa *FL-2*
Gulf County *FL-2*
Gulf Gate Estates (CDP)—
 Sarasota *FL-2*
Gulf Hills (CDP)—Jackson...........*MS-2*
Gulf Intracoastal Waterway
 (TX)......................................*Geog-4*
Gulf Park Estates (CDP)—
 Jackson.................................. *MS-2*
Gulfport (City)—Pinellas *FL-2*
Gulf Port (Village)—Henderson ... *IL-3*
Gulfport (City)—Harrison............*MS-2*
Gulf Shores (Town)—Baldwin *AL-2*
Gulf Stream (Town)—Palm
 Beach..................................... *FL-2*
Gulf Stream (TX) *Geog-4*
Gulich (Township)—Clearfield *PA-1*
Gulivoire Park (CDP)—St.
 Joseph *IN-3*
Gulkana (CDP)—Valdez-Cordova
 Census Area *AK-4*
Gull Lake (Town)—Washburn *WI-3*
Gully (City)—Polk......................... *MN-3*
Gully (Township)—Polk................ *MN-3*
Gumbranch (City)—Liberty.......... *GA-2*
Gumlog (CDP)—Franklin *GA-2*
Gum Springs (Town)—Clark *AR-2*
Gunbarrel (CDP)—Boulder *CO-4*
Gun Barrel City (Town)—
 Henderson............................. *TX-2*
Gunkel (Township)—Cass............. *ND-4*
Gunn City (Village)—Cass............ *MO-3*
Gunnison (City)—Gunnison *CO-4*
Gunnison (Town)—Bolivar *MS-2*
Gunnison (City)—Sanpete *UT-4*
Gunnison County *CO-4*
Gunplain (Township)—Allegan..... *MI-3*
Gunter (Town)—Grayson.............. *TX-2*
Guntersville (City)—Marshall........ *AL-2*

Guntown (Town)—Lee.................. *MS-2*
Gurdon (City)—Clark *AR-2*
Gurley (Town)—Madison.............. *AL-2*
Gurley (Village)—Cheyenne........... *NE-4*
Gurnee (City)—Lake *IL-3*
Gurney (Town)—Iron................... *WI-3*
Gustavus (CDP)—
 Skagway-Hoonah-Angoon Census
 Area.. *AK-4*
Gustavus (Township)—Trumbull...*OH-3*
Gustin (Township)—Alcona........... *MI-3*
Gustine (City)—Merced *CA-4*
Gustine (Town)—Comanche......... *TX-2*
Guthrie (Township)—Lawrence...... *IN-3*
Guthrie (City)—Todd..................... *KY-2*
Guthrie (Township)—Hubbard...... *MN-3*
Guthrie (Township)—Callaway...... *MO-3*
Guthrie (City)—Logan *OK-2*
Guthrie (Pop. Place)—King........... *TX-2*
Guthrie Center (City)—Guthrie *IA-3*
Guthrie County................................*IA-3*
Gutschmidt (Township)—Logan....*ND-4*
Guttenberg (City)—Clayton...........*IA-3*
Guttenberg (Town)—Hudson *NJ-1*
Gu-Win (Municipality)—Marion....*AL-2*
Guy (Town)—Faulkner.................. *AR-2*
Guyan (Township)—Gallia *OH-3*
Guymon (City)—Texas................... *OK-2*
Guys (Town)—McNairy................ *TN-2*
Guyton (City)—Effingham *GA-2*
Gwinn (CDP)—Marquette *MI-3*
Gwinner (City)—Sargent *ND-4*
Gwinnett County *GA-2*
Gypsum (Town)—Eagle................. *CO-4*
Gypsum (City)—Saline...................*KS-4*
Gypsum (Township)—Saline..........*KS-4*
Gypsum (Township)—Sedgwick *KS-4*
Gypsum Creek (Township)—
 McPherson *KS-4*
Haag (Township)—Logan.............*ND-4*
Haakon County *SD-4*
Haaland (Township)—Wells.........*ND-4*
Habersham County *GA-2*
Hacienda Heights (CDP)—Los
 Angeles.................................. *CA-4*
Hackberry (Township)—Labette.....*KS-4*
Hackberry (CDP)—Cameron
 Parish..................................... *LA-2*
Hackberry (Town)—Denton.......... *TX-2*
Hackensack (City)—Cass *MN-3*
Hackensack (City)—Bergen............ *NJ-1*
Hackett (City)—Sebastian *AR-2*
Hackett (Town)—Price................... *WI-3*
Hackettstown (Town)—Warren........ *NJ-1*
Hackleburg (Town)—Marion *AL-2*
Hadar (Village)—Pierce *NE-4*
Haddam (Town)—Middlesex *CT-1*
Haddam (City)—Washington.........*KS-4*
Haddam (Township)—
 Washington *KS-4*
Haddon (Township)—Sullivan......... *IN-3*
Haddon (Township)—Camden *NJ-1*
Haddonfield (Borough)—Camden .. *NJ-1*
Haddon Heights (Borough)—
 Camden *NJ-1*
Hadley (Township)—Pike *IL-3*
Hadley (Town)—Hampshire *MA-1*
Hadley (Township)—Lapeer *MI-3*
Hadley (City)—Murray................. *MN-3*
Hadley (Township)—St. Louis....... *MO-3*
Hadley (Town)—Saratoga *NY-1*
Hadleys Purchase (Pop. Place)—
 Coos *NH-1*
Hadlock-Irondale (CDP)—
 Jefferson................................. *WA-4*

General Index

Hagali (Township)—Beltrami *MN-3*
Hagaman (Village)—
   Montgomery..*NY-1*
Hagan (City)—Evans......................*GA-2*
Hagar (Township)—Berrien *MI-3*
Hagel (Township)—Pierce.............*ND-4*
Hagen (Township)—Clay *MN-3*
Hagener (Township)—Cass *IL-3*
Hagerman (City)—Gooding............ *ID-4*
Hagerman (Town)—Chaves *NM-4*
Hagerstown (Town)—Wayne........... *IN-3*
Hagerstown (City)—Washington... *MD-1*
Hague (Town)—Warren...................*NY-1*
Hague (City)—Emmons *ND-4*
Hague (Township)—Clark *SD-4*
Hahira (City)—Lowndes *GA-2*
Hahnaman (Township)—
   Whiteside *IL-3*
Hahnville (CDP)—St. Charles
   Parish *LA-2*
Haight (Township)—Ontonagon ... *MI-3*
Haigler (Village)—Dundy............... *NE-4*
Haiku-Pauwela (CDP)—Maui......... *HI-4*
Hailey (City)—Blaine *ID-4*
Haileyville (City)—Pittsburg.........*OK-2*
Haines (City)—Haines Borough *AK-4*
Haines (Township)—Marion...........*IL-3*
Haines (City)—Baker *OR-4*
Haines (Township)—Centre............ *PA-1*
Haines Borough *AK-4*
Haines City (City)—Polk *FL-2*
Hainesport (Township)—
   Burlington *NJ-1*
Hainesville (Village)—Lake.............*IL-3*
Halaula (CDP)—Hawaii.................. *HI-4*
Halawa (CDP)—Honolulu............... *HI-4*
Halbert (Township)—Martin *IN-3*
Halbur (City)—Carroll *IA-3*
Halcott (Town)—Greene *NY-1*
Halden (Township)—St. Louis....... *MN-3*
Hale (Township)—Warren...............*IL-3*
Hale (Township)—McLeod *MN-3*
Hale (City)—Carroll *MO-3*
Hale (Township)—Hardin *OH-3*
Hale (Town)—Trempealeau *WI-3*
Haleakala (HI) *Geog-4*
Haleburg (Municipality)—Henry *AL-2*
Hale Center (City)—Hale................ *TX-2*
Hale County *AL-2*
Hale County *TX-2*
Haledon (Borough)—Passaic...........*NJ-1*
Haleiwa (CDP)—Honolulu..............*HI-4*
Hales Corners (Village)—
   Milwaukee... *WI-3*
Halesite (CDP)—Suffolk *NY-1*
Hale's Location (Pop. Place)—
   Carroll *NH-1*
Haley (Township)—Bowman *ND-4*
Haleyville (City)—Marion...............*AL-2*
Haleyville (City)—Winston *AL-2*
Half Dome (CA) *Geog-4*
Halfmoon (Town)—Saratoga........... *NY-1*
Half Moon (CDP)—Onslow............*NC-2*
Halfmoon (Township)—Centre....... *PA-1*
Half Moon Bay (City)—San
   Mateo *CA-4*
Halfway (CDP)—Washington *MD-1*
Halfway (Village)—Polk *MO-3*
Halfway (Village)—Baker *OR-4*
Halfway House (CDP)—
   Montgomery.. *PA-1*
Halibut Cove (CDP)—Kenai Peninsula
   Borough.. *AK-4*
Halifax (Town)—Plymouth *MA-1*
Halifax (Town)—Halifax................*NC-2*

Halifax (Borough)—Dauphin.......... *PA-1*
Halifax (Township)—Dauphin........ *PA-1*
Halifax (Town)—Windham *VT-1*
Halifax (Town)—Halifax................. *VA-2*
Halifax County................................*NC-2*
Halifax County................................. *VA-2*
Haliimaile (CDP)—Maui.................. *HI-4*
Haliwa-Saponi TDSA (NC)....... *IndRes-4*
Hall (Township)—Bureau................*IL-3*
Hall (Township)—Dubois *IN-3*
Hall (Township)—Sargent *ND-4*
Hall (Township)—Perkins *SD-4*
Hallam (Village)—Lancaster *NE-4*
Hallandale (City)—Broward............*FL-2*
Hall County......................................*GA-2*
Hall County......................................*NE-4*
Hall County...................................... *TX-2*
Hallet (Township)—Hodgeman........*KS-4*
Hallett (Town)—Pawnee *OK-2*
Hallettsville (City)—Lavaca *TX-2*
Halliday (City)—Dunn *ND-4*
Halliday (Pop. Place)—Dunn *ND-4*
Hallie (Town)—Chippewa *WI-3*
Hallock (Township)—Peoria *IL-3*
Hallock (City)—Kittson *MN-3*
Hallock (Township)—Kittson *MN-3*
Hallowell (City)—Kennebec........... *ME-1*
Hall Park (Town)—Cleveland *OK-2*
Halls (CDP)—Knox.......................... *TN-2*
Halls (Town)—Lauderdale *TN-2*
Hallsburg (City)—McLennan *TX-2*
Hallstead (Borough)—
   Susquehanna *PA-1*
Hall Summit (Village)—Red River
   Parish *LA-2*
Hallsville (City)—Boone *MO-3*
Hallsville (City)—Harrison *TX-2*
Halltown (Town)—Lawrence *MO-3*
Hallwood (Town)—Accomack *VA-2*
Halma (City)—Kittson *MN-3*
Halsey (Village)—Blaine *NE-4*
Halsey (Village)—Thomas...............*NE-4*
Halsey (City)—Linn *OR-4*
Halsey (Town)—Marathon *WI-3*
Halstad (City)—Norman *MN-3*
Halstad (Township)—Norman *MN-3*
Halstead (City)—Harvey *KS-4*
Halstead (Township)—Harvey *KS-4*
Haltom City (City)—Tarrant *TX-2*
Hambden (Township)—Geauga......*OH-3*
Hamberg (City)—Wells *ND-4*
Hamblen (Township)—Brown *IN-3*
Hamblen County *TN-2*
Hambleton (Town)—Tucker..........*WV-2*
Hamburg (City)—Ashley *AR-2*
Hamburg (Town)—Calhoun *IL-3*
Hamburg (City)—Fremont............... *IA-3*
Hamburg (Township)—
   Livingston *MI-3*
Hamburg (City)—Carver.................*MN-3*
Hamburg (Borough)—Sussex *NJ-1*
Hamburg (Town)—Erie................... *NY-1*
Hamburg (Village)—Erie................. *NY-1*
Hamburg (Township)—Dickey *ND-4*
Hamburg (Township)—Wells *ND-4*
Hamburg (Borough)—Berks............*PA-1*
Hamburg (Town)—Marathon *WI-3*
Hamburg (Town)—Vernon.............. *WI-3*
Hamden (Town)—New Haven....... *CT-1*
Hamden (Township)—Becker *MN-3*
Hamden (Town)—Delaware *NY-1*
Hamden (Village)—Vinton *OH-3*
Hamel (Township)—Madison *IL-3*
Hamel (Village)—Madison...............*IL-3*
Hamer (City)—Jefferson *ID-4*

Hamer (Township)—Highland.......*OH-3*
Hamerly (Township)—Renville *ND-4*
Hamersville (Village)—Brown *OH-3*
Hamilton (City)—Marion *AL-2*
Hamilton (City)—Harris *GA-2*
Hamilton (City)—Hancock *IL-3*
Hamilton (Township)—Lee *IL-3*
Hamilton (Town)—Dekalb *IN-3*
Hamilton (Township)—Delaware .. *IN-3*
Hamilton (Township)—Jackson...... *IN-3*
Hamilton (Town)—Steuben *IN-3*
Hamilton (Township)—Sullivan *IN-3*
Hamilton (City)—Marion *IA-3*
Hamilton (City)—Greenwood.........*KS-4*
Hamilton (Town)—Essex *MA-1*
Hamilton (Township)—Clare *MI-3*
Hamilton (Township)—Gratiot...... *MI-3*
Hamilton (Township)—Van
   Buren..*MI-3*
Hamilton (City)—Caldwell *MO-3*
Hamilton (Township)—Caldwell .. *MO-3*
Hamilton (Township)—Harrison .. *MO-3*
Hamilton (City)—Ravalli................ *MT-4*
Hamilton (Township)—Fillmore.... *NE-4*
Hamilton (Township)—Atlantic......*NJ-1*
Hamilton (Township)—Mercer *NJ-1*
Hamilton (Town)—Madison *NY-1*
Hamilton (Village)—Madison *NY-1*
Hamilton (Town)—Martin *NC-2*
Hamilton (City)—Pembina *ND-4*
Hamilton (Township)—Pembina ...*ND-4*
Hamilton (City)—Butler *OH-3*
Hamilton (Township)—Franklin....*OH-3*
Hamilton (Township)—Jackson......*OH-3*
Hamilton (Township)—
   Lawrence *OH-3*
Hamilton (Township)—Warren......*OH-3*
Hamilton (Township)—Adams *PA-1*
Hamilton (Township)—Franklin..... *PA-1*
Hamilton (Township)—McKean..... *PA-1*
Hamilton (Township)—Monroe..... *PA-1*
Hamilton (Township)—Tioga *PA-1*
Hamilton (Township)—Charles
   Mix.. *SD-4*
Hamilton (Township)—Marshall ... *SD-4*
Hamilton (City)—Hamilton............ *TX-2*
Hamilton (Town)—Loudoun........... *VA-2*
Hamilton (Town)—Skagit *WA-4*
Hamilton (Town)—La Crosse *WI-3*
Hamiltonban (Township)—
   Adams... *PA-1*
Hamilton City (CDP)—Glenn *CA-4*
Hamilton County *FL-2*
Hamilton County *IL-3*
Hamilton County *IN-3*
Hamilton County *IA-3*
Hamilton County *KS-4*
Hamilton County *NE-4*
Hamilton County *NY-1*
Hamilton County *OH-3*
Hamilton County *TN-2*
Hamilton County *TX-2*
Ham Lake (City)—Anoka *MN-3*
Hamler (Village)—Henry *OH-3*
Hamlet (Town)—Starke................... *IN-3*
Hamlet (Village)—Hayes *NE-4*
Hamlet (City)—Richmond *NC-2*
Hamlet (Township)—Renville........*ND-4*
Hamletsburg (Village)—Pope........... *IL-3*
Hamlin (City)—Brown *KS-4*
Hamlin (Township)—Brown *KS-4*
Hamlin (Plantation)—Aroostook.. *ME-1*
Hamlin (Township)—Eaton *MI-3*
Hamlin (Township)—Mason.......... *MI-3*

Hamlin (Township)—Lac qui Parle MN-3
Hamlin (Town)—Monroe NY-1
Hamlin (Township)—Nelson ND-4
Hamlin (Township)—McKean PA-1
Hamlin (Township)—Hamlin SD-4
Hamlin (City)—Fisher TX-2
Hamlin (City)—Jones TX-2
Hamlin (Town)—Lincoln WV-2
Hamlin County SD-4
Hammel (Town)—Taylor WI-3
Hammer (Township)—Yellow Medicine MN-3
Hammer (Township)—Ramsey ND-4
Hammocks (CDP)—Dade FL-2
Hammon (Town)—Custer OK-2
Hammon (Town)—Roger Mills OK-2
Hammond (Town)—Piatt IL-3
Hammond (City)—Lake IN-3
Hammond (Township)—Spencer IN-3
Hammond (City)—Tangipahoa Parish LA-2
Hammond (Plantation)—Aroostook ME-1
Hammond (Township)—Polk MN-3
Hammond (City)—Wabasha MN-3
Hammond (Town)—St. Lawrence NY-1
Hammond (Village)—St. Lawrence NY-1
Hammond (Town)—Clatsop OR-4
Hammond (Town)—St. Croix WI-3
Hammond (Village)—St. Croix WI-3
Hammondsport (Village)—Steuben NY-1
Hammondville (Municipality)—DeKalb AL-2
Hammonton (Town)—Atlantic NJ-1
Hampden (Township)—Coffey KS-4
Hampden (Town)—Penobscot ME-1
Hampden (Town)—Hampden MA-1
Hampden (Township)—Kittson MN-3
Hampden (City)—Ramsey ND-4
Hampden (Township)—Cumberland PA-1
Hampden (Town)—Columbia WI-3
Hampden County MA-1
Hampden Sydney (CDP)—Prince Edward VA-2
Hampshire (Town)—Kane IL-3
Hampshire (Township)—Kane IL-3
Hampshire County MA-1
Hampshire County WV-2
Hampstead (Town)—Baltimore MD-1
Hampstead (Town)—Carroll MD-1
Hampstead (Town)—Rockingham NH-1
Hampton (City)—Calhoun AR-2
Hampton (Town)—Windham CT-1
Hampton (City)—Bradford FL-2
Hampton (City)—Henry GA-2
Hampton (Township)—Rock Island IL-3
Hampton (Village)—Rock Island IL-3
Hampton (City)—Franklin IA-3
Hampton (CDP)—Baltimore MD-1
Hampton (Township)—Bay MI-3
Hampton (City)—Dakota MN-3
Hampton (Township)—Dakota MN-3
Hampton (Village)—Hamilton NE-4
Hampton (Town)—Rockingham ... NH-1
Hampton (Borough)—Hunterdon ... NJ-1
Hampton (Township)—Sussex NJ-1
Hampton (Town)—Washington NY-1
Hampton (Township)—Allegheny ... PA-1
Hampton (Town)—Hampton SC-2
Hampton Bays (CDP)—Suffolk NY-1
Hamptonburgh (Town)—Orange ... NY-1
Hampton County SC-2
Hampton-Fairview (Township)—Rush KS-4
Hampton Falls (Town)—Rockingham NH-1
Hampton (Independent City) VA-2
Hampton Manor (CDP)—Rensselaer NY-1
Hamptons at Boca Raton (CDP)—Palm Beach FL-2
Hamre (Township)—Beltrami MN-3
Hamtramck (City)—Wayne MI-3
Hana (CDP)—Maui HI-4
Hanaford (Village)—Franklin IL-3
Hanahan (City)—Berkeley SC-2
Hanalei (CDP)—Kauai HI-4
Hanamaulu (CDP)—Kauai HI-4
Hanapepe (CDP)—Kauai HI-4
Hanceville (City)—Cullman AL-2
Hancock (Township)—Hancock IL-3
Hancock (City)—Pottawattamie IA-3
Hancock (Township)—Osborne KS-4
Hancock (Town)—Hancock ME-1
Hancock (Town)—Washington MD-1
Hancock (Town)—Berkshire MA-1
Hancock (City)—Houghton MI-3
Hancock (Township)—Houghton ... MI-3
Hancock (Township)—Carver MN-3
Hancock (City)—Stevens MN-3
Hancock (Town)—Hillsborough NH-1
Hancock (Town)—Delaware NY-1
Hancock (Village)—Delaware NY-1
Hancock (Town)—Addison VT-1
Hancock (Town)—Waushara WI-3
Hancock (Village)—Waushara WI-3
Hancock County GA-2
Hancock County IL-3
Hancock County IN-3
Hancock County IA-3
Hancock County KY-2
Hancock County ME-1
Hancock County MS-2
Hancock County OH-3
Hancock County TN-2
Hancock County WV-2
Hand County SD-4
Handley (Town)—Kanawha WV-2
Handy (Township)—Livingston MI-3
Haney (Town)—Crawford WI-3
Hanford (City)—Kings CA-4
Hangaard (Township)—Clearwater MN-3
Hanging Grove (Township)—Jasper IN-3
Hanging Rock (Village)—Lawrence OH-3
Hankinson (City)—Richland ND-4
Hanks (City)—Williams ND-4
Hanley Falls (City)—Yellow Medicine MN-3
Hanley Hills (Village)—St. Louis MO-3
Hanlontown (City)—Worth IA-3
Hanna (Township)—Henry IL-3
Hanna (Township)—La Porte IN-3
Hanna (Town)—McIntosh OK-2
Hanna (Town)—Carbon WY-4
Hanna City (Village)—Peoria IL-3
Hannaford (City)—Griggs ND-4
Hannah (City)—Cavalier ND-4
Hannahville Community & Trust Lands (MI) IndRes-4
Hannibal (City)—Marion MO-3
Hannibal (City)—Ralls MO-3
Hannibal (Town)—Oswego NY-1
Hannibal (Village)—Oswego NY-1
Hanover (Township)—Cook IL-3
Hanover (Town)—Jo Daviess IL-3
Hanover (Township)—Jo Daviess .. IL-3
Hanover (Town)—Jefferson IN-3
Hanover (Township)—Jefferson IN-3
Hanover (Township)—Lake IN-3
Hanover (Township)—Shelby IN-3
Hanover (Township)—Lincoln KS-4
Hanover (City)—Washington KS-4
Hanover (Township)—Washington KS-4
Hanover (Town)—Oxford ME-1
Hanover (Town)—Plymouth MA-1
Hanover (Township)—Jackson MI-3
Hanover (Village)—Jackson MI-3
Hanover (Township)—Wexford MI-3
Hanover (City)—Hennepin MN-3
Hanover (City)—Wright MN-3
Hanover (Township)—Adams NE-4
Hanover (Township)—Gage NE-4
Hanover (Town)—Grafton NH-1
Hanover (Township)—Morris NJ-1
Hanover (Town)—Chautauqua NY-1
Hanover (Township)—Ashland OH-3
Hanover (Township)—Butler OH-3
Hanover (Township)—Columbiana OH-3
Hanover (Township)—Licking OH-3
Hanover (Village)—Licking OH-3
Hanover (Township)—Beaver PA-1
Hanover (Township)—Lehigh PA-1
Hanover (Township)—Luzerne PA-1
Hanover (Township)—Northampton PA-1
Hanover (Township)—Washington PA-1
Hanover (Borough)—York PA-1
Hanover County VA-2
Hanover Park (City)—Cook IL-3
Hanover Park (City)—DuPage IL-3
Hanoverton (Village)—Columbiana OH-3
Hansboro (City)—Towner ND-4
Hansell (City)—Franklin IA-3
Hansen (City)—Twin Falls ID-4
Hansen (Town)—Wood WI-3
Hansford County TX-2
Hanska (City)—Brown MN-3
Hanson (City)—Hopkins KY-2
Hanson (Town)—Plymouth MA-1
Hanson (Township)—Ransom ND-4
Hanson (Township)—Hanson SD-4
Hanson County SD-4
Hansonville (Township)—Lincoln MN-3
Hanston (City)—Hodgeman KS-4
Hantho (Township)—Lac qui Parle MN-3
Hapeville (City)—Fulton GA-2
Happy (Township)—Graham KS-4
Happy (Town)—Randall TX-2
Happy (Town)—Swisher TX-2
Happy Valley (CDP)—Kenai Peninsula Borough AK-4
Happy Valley (City)—Clackamas ... OR-4
Harahan (City)—Jefferson Parish ... LA-2
Haralson (Town)—Coweta GA-2
Haralson (Town)—Meriwether GA-2
Haralson County GA-2
Haram (Township)—Bottineau ND-4

General Index

Harbeck-Fruitdale (CDP)—
 Josephine OR-4
Harbine (Village)—Jefferson NE-4
Harbison (Township)—Dubois IN-3
Harbison Canyon (CDP)—San
 Diego CA-4
Harbor (CDP)—Curry OR-4
Harbor Beach (City)—Huron MI-3
Harbor Bluffs (CDP)—Pinellas FL-2
Harborcreek (Township)—Erie PA-1
Harbor Hills (CDP)—Licking OH-3
Harbor Springs (City)—Emmet MI-3
Harbor View (Village)—Lucas OH-3
Harbour Heights (CDP)—
 Charlotte FL-2
Harbour Pointe (CDP)—
 Snohomish WA-4
Harcourt (City)—Webster IA-3
Hardee County FL-2
Hardeeville (Town)—Jasper SC-2
Hardeman County TN-2
Hardeman County TX-2
Hardenburgh (Town)—Ulster NY-1
Hardesty (Town)—Texas OK-2
Hardin (Town)—Calhoun IL-3
Hardin (Township)—Pike IL-3
Hardin (City)—Marshall KY-2
Hardin (Township)—Clinton MO-3
Hardin (City)—Ray MO-3
Hardin (City)—Big Horn MT-4
Hardin (Town)—Liberty TX-2
Hardin County IL-3
Hardin County IA-3
Hardin County KY-2
Hardin County OH-3
Hardin County TN-2
Hardin County TX-2
Harding (City)—Morrison MN-3
Harding (Township)—Morris NJ-1
Harding (Township)—Emmons ND-4
Harding (Township)—Ramsey ND-4
Harding (Township)—Lucas OH-3
Harding (Town)—Lincoln WI-3
Harding County NM-4
Harding County SD-4
Harding Lake (CDP)—Fairbanks North
 Star Borough AK-4
Hardinsburg (Town)—
 Washington IN-3
Hardinsburg (City)—
 Breckinridge KY-2
Hardscrabble (Township)—
 Williams ND-4
Hardtner (City)—Barber KS-4
Hardwick (Town)—Worcester MA-1
Hardwick (City)—Rock MN-3
Hardwick (Township)—Warren NJ-1
Hardwick (Town)—Caledonia VT-1
Hardy (City)—Sharp AR-2
Hardy (City)—Humboldt IA-3
Hardy (Village)—Nuckolls NE-4
Hardy (Township)—Holmes OH-3
Hardy County WV-2
Hardyston (Township)—Sussex NJ-1
Harford (Town)—Cortland NY-1
Harford (Township)—
 Susquehanna PA-1
Harford County MD-1
Haring (Township)—Wexford MI-3
Harker Heights (City)—Bell TX-2
Harlan (City)—Shelby IA-3
Harlan (Township)—Decatur KS-4
Harlan (Township)—Smith KS-4
Harlan (City)—Harlan KY-2
Harlan (Township)—Warren OH-3

Harlan County KY-2
Harlan County NE-4
Harlem (CDP)—Hendry FL-2
Harlem (City)—Columbia GA-2
Harlem (Township)—Stephenson ... IL-3
Harlem (Township)—Winnebago.... IL-3
Harlem (City)—Blaine MT-4
Harlem (Township)—Sargent ND-4
Harlem (Township)—Delaware OH-3
Harleysville (CDP)—Montgomery .. PA-1
Harleyville (Town)—Dorchester SC-2
Harlingen (City)—Cameron TX-2
Harlowton (City)—Wheatland MT-4
Harman (Town)—Randolph WV-2
Harmar (Township)—Allegheny PA-1
Harmon (Township)—Lee IL-3
Harmon (Village)—Lee IL-3
Harmon (Township)—Sumner KS-4
Harmon (Township)—Roberts SD-4
Harmon County OK-2
Harmonious (Township)—Burke ... ND-4
Harmony (Township)—Hancock IL-3
Harmony (Town)—Clay IN-3
Harmony (Township)—Posey IN-3
Harmony (Township)—Union IN-3
Harmony (Township)—Stevens KS-4
Harmony (Town)—Somerset ME-1
Harmony (City)—Fillmore MN-3
Harmony (Township)—Fillmore .. MN-3
Harmony (Township)—
 Washington MO-3
Harmony (Township)—Warren NJ-1
Harmony (Town)—Chautauqua NY-1
Harmony (Town)—Iredell NC-2
Harmony (Township)—Cass ND-4
Harmony (Township)—Clark OH-3
Harmony (Township)—Morrow OH-3
Harmony (Township)—Beaver PA-1
Harmony (Borough)—Butler PA-1
Harmony (Township)—Forest PA-1
Harmony (Township)—
 Susquehanna PA-1
Harmony (Township)—Edmunds .. SD-4
Harmony (Township)—Fall River . SD-4
Harmony (Township)—Jerauld SD-4
Harmony (Township)—Spink SD-4
Harmony (Town)—Price WI-3
Harmony (Town)—Rock WI-3
Harmony (Town)—Vernon WI-3
Harnett County NC-2
Harney County OR-4
Harney Peak (SD) Geog-4
Harp (Township)—De Witt IL-3
Harper (City)—Keokuk IA-3
Harper (City)—Harper KS-4
Harper (Township)—McPherson ... KS-4
Harper (Township)—Slope ND-4
Harper County KS-4
Harper County OK-2
Harpers Ferry (City)—Allamakee ... IA-3
Harpers Ferry (Town)—
 Jefferson WV-2
Harpersfield (Town)—Delaware ... NY-1
Harpersfield (Township)—
 Ashtabula OH-3
Harpersville (Town)—Shelby AL-2
Harper Woods (City)—Wayne MI-3
Harpster (Village)—Wyandot OH-3
Harpswell (Town)—Cumberland .. ME-1
Harrah (Town)—Oklahoma OK-2
Harrah (Town)—Yakima WA-4
Harrell (Town)—Calhoun AR-2
Harrells (Town)—Duplin NC-2
Harrells (Town)—Sampson NC-2
Harrellsville (Town)—Hertford NC-2

Harriet (Township)—Burleigh ND-4
Harrietstown (Town)—Franklin ... NY-1
Harrietta (Village)—Wexford MI-3
Harriman (Village)—Orange NY-1
Harriman (City)—Morgan TN-2
Harriman (City)—Roane TN-2
Harrington (City)—Kent DE-1
Harrington (Town)—Washington .. ME-1
Harrington (Town)—Lincoln WA-4
Harrington Park (Borough)—
 Bergen NJ-1
Harris (Township)—Fulton IL-3
Harris (Township)—St. Joseph IN-3
Harris (City)—Osceola IA-3
Harris (City)—Anderson KS-4
Harris (Township)—Menominee MI-3
Harris (City)—Chisago MN-3
Harris (Township)—Itasca MN-3
Harris (Township)—Ripley MO-3
Harris (Town)—Sullivan MO-3
Harris (Township)—Ottawa OH-3
Harris (Township)—Centre PA-1
Harris (Town)—Marquette WI-3
Harrisburg (City)—Poinsett AR-2
Harrisburg (City)—Saline IL-3
Harrisburg (Township)—Saline IL-3
Harrisburg (Town)—Boone MO-3
Harrisburg (Town)—Lewis NY-1
Harrisburg (Town)—Cabarrus NC-2
Harrisburg (Village)—Franklin OH-3
Harrisburg (Village)—Pickaway OH-3
Harrisburg (City)—Linn OR-4
Harrisburg (City)—Dauphin PA-1
Harrisburg (Township)—Lincoln ... SD-4
Harris County GA-2
Harris County TX-2
Harris Hill (CDP)—Erie NY-1
Harrison (City)—Boone AR-2
Harrison (Town)—Washington GA-2
Harrison (City)—Kootenai ID-4
Harrison (Township)—Winnebago . IL-3
Harrison (Township)—
 Bartholomew IN-3
Harrison (Township)—Blackford IN-3
Harrison (Township)—Boone IN-3
Harrison (Township)—Cass IN-3
Harrison (Township)—Clay IN-3
Harrison (Township)—Daviess IN-3
Harrison (Township)—Dearborn IN-3
Harrison (Township)—Delaware ... IN-3
Harrison (Township)—Elkhart IN-3
Harrison (Township)—Fayette IN-3
Harrison (Township)—Harrison IN-3
Harrison (Township)—Henry IN-3
Harrison (Township)—Howard IN-3
Harrison (Township)—Knox IN-3
Harrison (Township)—Kosciusko .. IN-3
Harrison (Township)—Miami IN-3
Harrison (Township)—Morgan IN-3
Harrison (Township)—Owen IN-3
Harrison (Township)—Pulaski IN-3
Harrison (Township)—Spencer IN-3
Harrison (Township)—Union IN-3
Harrison (Township)—Vigo IN-3
Harrison (Township)—Wayne IN-3
Harrison (Township)—Wells IN-3
Harrison (Township)—
 Chautauqua KS-4
Harrison (Township)—Franklin KS-4
Harrison (Township)—Greeley KS-4
Harrison (Township)—Jewell KS-4
Harrison (Township)—Nemaha KS-4
Harrison (Township)—Rice KS-4
Harrison (Township)—Wallace KS-4
Harrison (Town)—Cumberland ME-1

Harrison (City)—Clare *MI-3*
Harrison (Township)—Macomb *MI-3*
Harrison (Township)—
   Kandiyohi *MN-3*
Harrison (Township)—Daviess *MO-3*
Harrison (Township)—Grundy *MO-3*
Harrison (Township)—Mercer *MO-3*
Harrison (Township)—Moniteau .. *MO-3*
Harrison (Township)—Scotland *MO-3*
Harrison (Township)—Vernon *MO-3*
Harrison (Township)—Buffalo *NE-4*
Harrison (Township)—Hall *NE-4*
Harrison (Township)—Knox *NE-4*
Harrison (Village)—Sioux *NE-4*
Harrison (Township)—Gloucester .. *NJ-1*
Harrison (Township)—Hudson *NJ-1*
Harrison (Town and Village)—
   Westchester *NY-1*
Harrison (Township)—Ward *ND-4*
Harrison (Township)—Carroll *OH-3*
Harrison (Township)—
   Champaign *OH-3*
Harrison (Township)—Darke *OH-3*
Harrison (Township)—Gallia *OH-3*
Harrison (Township)—Hamilton ... *OH-3*
Harrison (Village)—Hamilton *OH-3*
Harrison (Township)—Henry *OH-3*
Harrison (Township)—Knox *OH-3*
Harrison (Township)—Licking.......*OH-3*
Harrison (Township)—Logan *OH-3*
Harrison (Township)—
   Montgomery *OH-3*
Harrison (Township)—
   Muskingum *OH-3*
Harrison (Township)—Paulding *OH-3*
Harrison (Township)—Perry *OH-3*
Harrison (Township)—Pickaway ...*OH-3*
Harrison (Township)—Preble *OH-3*
Harrison (Township)—Ross *OH-3*
Harrison (Township)—Scioto *OH-3*
Harrison (Township)—Van Wert ...*OH-3*
Harrison (Township)—Vinton *OH-3*
Harrison (Township)—Allegheny ... *PA-1*
Harrison (Township)—Bedford *PA-1*
Harrison (Township)—Potter *PA-1*
Harrison (Township)—Spink *SD-4*
Harrison (CDP)—Hamilton *TN-2*
Harrison (Town)—Calumet *WI-3*
Harrison (Town)—Grant................. *WI-3*
Harrison (Town)—Lincoln *WI-3*
Harrison (Town)—Marathon *WI-3*
Harrison (Town)—Waupaca........... *WI-3*
Harrisonburg (Village)—Catahoula
   Parish *LA-2*
Harrisonburg (Independent City)..... *VA-2*
Harrison County *IN-3*
Harrison County...................................*IA-3*
Harrison County *KY-2*
Harrison County *MS-2*
Harrison County *MO-3*
Harrison County..................................*OH-3*
Harrison County *TX-2*
Harrison County *WV-2*
Harrison-District 6 (Township)—
   Norton *KS-4*
Harrisonville (City)—Cass *MO-3*
Harriston (Township)—Walsh........*ND-4*
Harristown (Township)—Macon..... *IL-3*
Harristown (Village)—Macon *IL-3*
Harrisville (City)—Alcona *MI-3*
Harrisville (Township)—Alcona.... *MI-3*
Harrisville (Town)—Cheshire *NH-1*
Harrisville (Village)—Lewis *NY-1*
Harrisville (Village)—Harrison *OH-3*
Harrisville (Township)—Medina ...*OH-3*

Harrisville (Borough)—Butler *PA-1*
Harrisville (CDP)—Providence *RI-1*
Harrisville (City)—Weber *UT-4*
Harrisville (Town)—Ritchie.......... *WV-2*
Harrod (Village)—Allen *OH-3*
Harrodsburg (City)—Mercer *KY-2*
Harrogate-Shawanee (CDP)—
   Claiborne.. *TN-2*
Harrold (Town)—Hughes *SD-4*
Hart (Township)—Warrick............... *IN-3*
Hart (City)—Oceana *MI-3*
Hart (Township)—Oceana............... *MI-3*
Hart (Township)—Winona *MN-3*
Hart (Township)—Wright *MO-3*
Hart (Pop. Place)—Bowman *ND-4*
Hart (Township)—Roberts *SD-4*
Hart (City)—Castro *TX-2*
Hart County *GA-2*
Hart County *KY-2*
Harter (Township)—Clay *IL-3*
Hartford (City)—Geneva *AL-2*
Hartford (City)—Sebastian *AR-2*
Hartford (City)—Hartford *CT-1*
Hartford (Town)—Madison *IL-3*
Hartford (Township)—Adams......... *IN-3*
Hartford (City)—Warren *IA-3*
Hartford (City)—Lyon....................*KS-4*
Hartford (City)—Ohio.................... *KY-2*
Hartford (Town)—Oxford *ME-1*
Hartford (City)—Van Buren *MI-3*
Hartford (Township)—Van Buren . *MI-3*
Hartford (Township)—Todd *MN-3*
Hartford (Township)—Pike........... *MO-3*
Hartford (Town)—Washington *NY-1*
Hartford (Township)—Licking........*OH-3*
Hartford (Village)—Licking............*OH-3*
Hartford (Township)—Trumbull....*OH-3*
Hartford (City)—Minnehaha *SD-4*
Hartford (Township)—
   Minnehaha *SD-4*
Hartford (Town)—Windsor............. *VT-1*
Hartford (City)—Dodge *WI-3*
Hartford (City)—Washington........ *WI-3*
Hartford (Township)—Washington *WI-3*
Hartford City (City)—Blackford..... *IN-3*
Hartford City (Town)—Mason *WV-2*
Hartford County *CT-1*
Hartington (City)—Cedar *NE-4*
Hart Lake (Township)—
   Hubbard *MN-3*
Hartland (Town)—Hartford *CT-1*
Hartland (Township)—McHenry *IL-3*
Hartland (Township)—Kearny........*KS-4*
Hartland (Town)—Somerset *ME-1*
Hartland (Township)—
   Livingston *MI-3*
Hartland (City)—Freeborn.............*MN-3*
Hartland (Township)—Freeborn....*MN-3*
Hartland (Town)—Niagara *NY-1*
Hartland (Township)—Huron *OH-3*
Hartland (Township)—Beadle........ *SD-4*
Hartland (Township)—Kingsbury.. *SD-4*
Hartland (Town)—Windsor *VT-1*
Hartland (Town)—Pierce *WI-3*
Hartland (Town)—Shawano *WI-3*
Hartland (Village)—Waukesha....... *WI-3*
Hartleton (Borough)—Union *PA-1*
Hartley (City)—O'Brien *IA-3*
Hartley (Township)—Union........... *PA-1*
Hartley County *TX-2*
Hartline (Town)—Grant................ *WA-4*
Hartly (Town)—Kent *DE-1*
Hartman (Town)—Johnson *AR-2*
Hartman (Town)—Prowers *CO-4*
Harts (CDP)—Lincoln *WV-2*

Hartsburg (Village)—Logan *IL-3*
Hartsburg (Town)—Boone *MO-3*
Hartsdale (CDP)—Westchester......*NY-1*
Hartselle (City)—Morgan *AL-2*
Hartsgrove (Township)—
   Ashtabula *OH-3*
Hartshorne (City)—Pittsburg......... *OK-2*
Hart's Location (Town)—Carroll ...*NH-1*
Hartsville (Town)—Bartholomew ... *IN-3*
Hartsville (Town)—Steuben *NY-1*
Hartsville (City)—Darlington *SC-2*
Hartsville (Town)—Trousdale........ *TN-2*
Hartville (City)—Wright *MO-3*
Hartville (Village)—Stark...............*OH-3*
Hartville (Town)—Platte *WY-4*
Hartwell (City)—Hart *GA-2*
Hartwell (Village)—Henry............ *MO-3*
Hartwick (City)—Poweshiek...........*IA-3*
Hartwick (Township)—Osceola..... *MI-3*
Hartwick (Town)—Otsego *NY-1*
Harvard (City)—McHenry............... *IL-3*
Harvard (Town)—Worcester *MA-1*
Harvard (City)—Clay..................... *NE-4*
Harvard (Township)—Clay *NE-4*
Harvard, Mt. (CO).......................... *Geog-4*
Harvel (Village)—Christian *IL-3*
Harvel (Township)—Montgomery .. *IL-3*
Harvel (Village)—Montgomery....... *IL-3*
Harvest (Division)—Madison *AL-2*
Harvester (Township)—St.
   Charles *MO-3*
Harvey (City)—Cook...................... *IL-3*
Harvey (City)—Marion *IA-3*
Harvey (Township)—Cowley *KS-4*
Harvey (Township)—Smith............*KS-4*
Harvey (CDP)—Jefferson Parish *LA-2*
Harvey (CDP)—Marquette *MI-3*
Harvey (Township)—Meeker *MN-3*
Harvey (Township)—Cavalier.........*ND-4*
Harvey (City)—Wells *ND-4*
Harvey Cedars (Borough)—
   Ocean *NJ-1*
Harvey County...................................*KS-4*
Harveysburg (Village)—Warren *OH-3*
Harveys Lake (Borough)—
   Luzerne *PA-1*
Harveyville (City)—Wabaunsee *KS-4*
Harwich (Town)—Barnstable........ *MA-1*
Harwich Port (CDP)—
   Barnstable *MA-1*
Harwinton (Town)—Litchfield........ *CT-1*
Harwood (Township)—
   Champaign *IL-3*
Harwood (Town)—Vernon *MO-3*
Harwood (City)—Cass.....................*ND-4*
Harwood (Township)—Cass............*ND-4*
Harwood Heights (City)—Cook...... *IL-3*
Hasbrouck Heights (Borough)—
   Bergen *NJ-1*
Haskell (City)—Saline *AR-2*
Haskell (Township)—Haskell *KS-4*
Haskell (Town)—Muskogee............*OK-2*
Haskell (City)—Haskell *TX-2*
Haskell County *KS-4*
Haskell County *OK-2*
Haskell County *TX-2*
Haskins (Village)—Wood *OH-3*
Haslet (City)—Denton *TX-2*
Haslet (City)—Tarrant *TX-2*
Haslett (CDP)—Ingham *MI-3*
Hassan (Township)—Hennepin *MN-3*
Hassan Valley (Township)—
   McLeod *MN-3*
Hassell (Town)—Martin *NC-2*
Hasson Heights (CDP)—Venango .. *PA-1*

General Index
American Places Dictionary

Hastings (Town)—St. Johns............*FL-2*
Hastings (City)—Mills.....................*IA-3*
Hastings (City)—Barry *MI-3*
Hastings (Township)—Barry *MI-3*
Hastings (City)—Dakota *MN-3*
Hastings (City)—Washington *MN-3*
Hastings (City)—Adams..................*NE-4*
Hastings (Town)—Oswego *NY-1*
Hastings (Township)—Bottineau ...*ND-4*
Hastings (Town)—Jefferson *OK-2*
Hastings (Borough)—Cambria *PA-1*
Hastings-on-Hudson (Village)—
 Westchester *NY-1*
Haswell (Town)—Kiowa *CO-4*
Hatboro (Borough)—Montgomery..*PA-1*
Hatch (Village)—Doña Ana *NM-4*
Hatch (Town)—Garfield *UT-4*
Hatfield (Town)—Polk *AR-2*
Hatfield (Town Hampshire County)—
 Hampshire *MA-1*
Hatfield (City)—Pipestone.............*MN-3*
Hatfield (Borough)—Montgomery..*PA-1*
Hatfield (Township)—
 Montgomery...............................*PA-1*
Hatley (Town)—Monroe *MS-2*
Hatley (Village)—Marathon *WI-3*
Hatteras, Cape (NC) *Geog-4*
Hattiesburg (City)—Forrest............*MS-2*
Hattiesburg (City)—Lamar *MS-2*
Hatton (Township)—Clare *MI-3*
Hatton (City)—Traill *ND-4*
Hatton (Town)—Adams *WA-4*
Haubstadt (Town)—Gibson *IN-3*
Haugen (Township)—Aitkin *MN-3*
Haugen (Village)—Barron *WI-3*
Haughton (Town)—Bossier
 Parish *LA-2*
Hauppauge (CDP)—Suffolk...........*NY-1*
Hauser (City)—Kootenai................*ID-4*
Hauula (CDP)—Honolulu..............*HI-4*
Havana (City)—Yell *AR-2*
Havana (Town)—Gadsden *FL-2*
Havana (City)—Mason *IL-3*
Havana (Township)—Mason *IL-3*
Havana (City)—Montgomery.........*KS-4*
Havana (Township)—Steele *MN-3*
Havana (City)—Sargent *ND-4*
Havana (Township)—Deuel *SD-4*
Havasupai Reservation (AZ)....*IndRes-4*
Havelock (City)—Pocahontas *IA-3*
Havelock (Township)—
 Chippewa *MN-3*
Havelock (City)—Craven *NC-2*
Havelock (Township)—Hettinger...*ND-4*
Haven (City)—Reno *KS-4*
Haven (Township)—Reno...............*KS-4*
Haven (Township)—Sherburne.....*MN-3*
Haven (Township)—Foster *ND-4*
Havensville (City)—
 Pottawatomie *KS-4*
Haverford (Township)—Delaware..*PA-1*
Haverhill (Town)—Palm Beach *FL-2*
Haverhill (City)—Marshall *IA-3*
Haverhill (City)—Essex..................*MA-1*
Haverhill (Township)—Olmsted ...*MN-3*
Haverhill (Town)—Grafton *NH-1*
Haverstraw (Town)—Rockland......*NY-1*
Haverstraw (Village)—Rockland....*NY-1*
Haviland (City)—Kiowa *KS-4*
Haviland (CDP)—Dutchess *NY-1*
Haviland (Village)—Paulding *OH-3*
Havre (City)—Hill *MT-4*
Havre de Grace (City)—Harford ...*MD-1*
Havre North (CDP)—Hill..............*MT-4*
Hawaii (HI)....................................*Geog-4*

Hawaiian Beaches (CDP)—
 Hawaii *HI-4*
Hawaiian Gardens (City)—Los
 Angeles *CA-4*
Hawaiian Ocean View (CDP)—
 Hawaii *HI-4*
Hawaiian Paradise Park (CDP)—
 Hawaii *HI-4*
Hawaii County *HI-4*
Hawarden (City)—Sioux *IA-3*
Haw Creek (Township)—Knox *IL-3*
Haw Creek (Township)—
 Bartholomew..............................*IN-3*
Haw Creek (Township)—
 Morgan *MO-3*
Hawes (Township)—Alcona *MI-3*
Hawesville (City)—Hancock *KY-2*
Hawi (CDP)—Hawaii *HI-4*
Hawk Creek (Township)—
 Renville......................................*MN-3*
Hawkeye (City)—Fayette................*IA-3*
Hawkeye (Township)—Osborne......*KS-4*
Hawkeye (Township)—Divide *ND-4*
Hawkeye (Township)—
 McKenzie *ND-4*
Hawkins (City)—Wood *TX-2*
Hawkins (Town)—Rusk *WI-3*
Hawkins (Village)—Rusk *WI-3*
Hawkins County *TN-2*
Hawkinsville (City)—Pulaski *GA-2*
Hawk Point (City)—Lincoln *MO-3*
Hawk Point (Township)—
 Lincoln *MO-3*
Hawksnest (Township)—Wells *ND-4*
Hawley (Town)—Franklin *MA-1*
Hawley (City)—Clay......................*MN-3*
Hawley (Township)—Clay *MN-3*
Hawley (Borough)—Wayne *PA-1*
Hawley (City)—Jones *TX-2*
Haworth (Borough)—Bergen..........*NJ-1*
Haworth (Town)—McCurtain *OK-2*
Haw River (Town)—Alamance *NC-2*
Hawthorn (Borough)—Clarion *PA-1*
Hawthorne (City)—Los Angeles *CA-4*
Hawthorne (City)—Alachua............*FL-2*
Hawthorne (CDP)—Lake *FL-2*
Hawthorne (Township)—White *IL-3*
Hawthorne (CDP)—Mineral *NV-4*
Hawthorne (Borough)—Passaic *NJ-1*
Hawthorne (CDP)—Westchester....*NY-1*
Hawthorne (Town)—Douglas..........*WI-3*
Hawthorn Woods (Village)—Lake ..*IL-3*
Haxtun (Town)—Phillips *CO-4*
Hay (Township)—Gladwin *MI-3*
Hay (Township)—Cavalier *ND-4*
Hay Brook (Township)—
 Kanabec *MN-3*
Haycock (Township)—Bucks *PA-1*
Hay Creek (Township)—
 Goodhue *MN-3*
Hay Creek (Township)—Burleigh..*ND-4*
Hayden (Town)—Blount *AL-2*
Hayden (Town)—Gila *AZ-4*
Hayden (Town)—Pinal *AZ-4*
Hayden (Town)—Routt *CO-4*
Hayden (City)—Kootenai *ID-4*
Hayden Lake (City)—Kootenai *ID-4*
Hayes (Township)—Clay *KS-4*
Hayes (Township)—Dickinson........*KS-4*
Hayes (Township)—Franklin..........*KS-4*
Hayes (Township)—McPherson......*KS-4*
Hayes (Township)—Mitchell *KS-4*
Hayes (Township)—Reno *KS-4*
Hayes (Township)—Stafford *KS-4*
Hayes (Township)—Charlevoix *MI-3*

Hayes (Township)—Clare *MI-3*
Hayes (Township)—Otsego *MI-3*
Hayes (Township)—Swift *MN-3*
Hayes (Township)—Custer *NE-4*
Hayes (Township)—Kearney..........*NE-4*
Hayes Center (Village)—Hayes *NE-4*
Hayes County...............................*NE-4*
Hayesville (City)—Keokuk.............*IA-3*
Hayesville (Town)—Clay *NC-2*
Hayesville (Village)—Ashland........*OH-3*
Hayesville (CDP)—Marion *OR-4*
Hayfield (City)—Dodge *MN-3*
Hayfield (Township)—Dodge *MN-3*
Hayfield (Township)—Crawford....*PA-1*
Hayfork (CDP)—Trinity *CA-4*
Hay Lake (Pop. Place)—St.
 Louis *MN-3*
Hayland (Township)—Mille
 Lacs *MN-3*
Hayland (Township)—Divide *ND-4*
Haymarket (Town)—Prince
 William *VA-2*
Haynes (Town)—Lee *AR-2*
Haynes (Township)—Alcona *MI-3*
Haynes (City)—Adams *ND-4*
Haynes (Township)—Kidder *ND-4*
Haynesville (Town)—Claiborne
 Parish *LA-2*
Haynesville (Town)—Aroostook ...*ME-2*
Hayneville (Town)—Lowndes........*AL-2*
Hay River (Town)—Dunn *WI-3*
Hays (City)—Ellis *KS-4*
Hays (CDP)—Blaine *MT-4*
Hays (CDP)—Wilkes *NC-2*
Hays (City)—Hays *TX-2*
Hays County................................*TX-2*
Haysi (Town)—Dickenson *VA-2*
Hay Springs (Village)—Sheridan ...*NE-4*
Haysville (City)—Sedgwick............*KS-4*
Haysville (Borough)—Allegheny *PA-1*
Hayti (City)—Pemiscot *MO-3*
Hayti (Township)—Pemiscot *MO-3*
Hayti (Town)—Hamlin *SD-4*
Hayti (Township)—Hamlin.............*SD-4*
Hayti Heights (City)—Pemiscot *MO-3*
Hayward (City)—Alameda *CA-4*
Hayward (City)—Freeborn.............*MN-3*
Hayward (Township)—Freeborn....*MN-3*
Hayward (Town)—Pemiscot *MO-3*
Hayward (City)—Sawyer................*WI-3*
Hayward (Town)—Sawyer..............*WI-3*
Hay-Wood City (Village)—Scott ...*MO-3*
Haywood County *NC-2*
Haywood County *TN-2*
Hazard (City)—Perry *KY-2*
Hazard (Village)—Sherman *NE-4*
Hazardville (CDP)—Hartford.........*CT-1*
Hazel (City)—Calloway..................*KY-2*
Hazel (Township)—Williams *ND-4*
Hazel (Town)—Hamlin *SD-4*
Hazel Crest (City)—Cook *IL-3*
Hazel Dell North (CDP)—Clark....*WA-4*
Hazel Dell South (CDP)—Clark....*WA-4*
Hazel Green (Division)—
 Madison *AL-2*
Hazel Green (Town)—Grant..........*WI-3*
Hazel Green (Village)—Grant *WI-3*
Hazel Green (Village)—Lafayette ..*WI-3*
Hazel Grove (Township)—
 Burleigh *ND-4*
Hazel Hill (Township)—Johnson ..*MO-3*
Hazelhurst (City)—Jeff Davis *GA-2*
Hazelhurst (Town)—Oneida *WI-3*
Hazel Park (City)—Oakland *MI-3*

Hazel Run (City)—Yellow
  Medicine *MN-3*
Hazel Run (Township)—Yellow
  Medicine *MN-3*
Hazelton (City)—Jerome *ID-4*
Hazelton (City)—Barber *KS-4*
Hazelton (Township)—Barber *KS-4*
Hazelton (Township)—
  Shiawassee *MI-3*
Hazelton (Township)—Aitkin *MN-3*
Hazelton (Township)—Kittson *MN-3*
Hazelton (City)—Emmons *ND-4*
Hazelton (Township)—Emmons *ND-4*
Hazelwood (City)—St. Louis *MO-3*
Hazelwood (Township)—
  Webster *MO-3*
Hazelwood (Town)—Haywood *NC-2*
Hazelwood (CDP)—Multnomah *OR-4*
Hazen (City)—Prairie *AR-2*
Hazen (City)—Mercer *ND-4*
Hazle (Township)—Luzerne *PA-1*
Hazlehurst (City)—Copiah *MS-2*
Hazlet (Township)—Monmouth *NJ-1*
Hazleton (Town)—Gibson *IN-3*
Hazleton (City)—Buchanan *IA-3*
Hazleton (City)—Luzerne *PA-1*
Headland (Municipality)—Henry ... *AL-2*
Head of the Harbor (Village)—
  Suffolk *NY-1*
Headrick (Town)—Jackson *OK-2*
Healdsburg (City)—Sonoma *CA-4*
Healdton (City)—Carter *OK-2*
Healy (CDP)—Yukon-Koyukuk Census
  Area *AK-4*
Healy Lake (CDP)—Southeast
  Fairbanks Census Area *AK-4*
Heard County *GA-2*
Hearne (City)—Robertson *TX-2*
Heart Butte (CDP)—Pondera *MT-4*
Heartwell (Village)—Kearney *NE-4*
Heath (Town)—Covington *AL-2*
Heath (Town)—Franklin *MA-1*
Heath (Township)—Allegan *MI-3*
Heath (City)—Licking *OH-3*
Heath (Township)—Jefferson *PA-1*
Heath (City)—Rockwall *TX-2*
Heathcote (CDP)—Middlesex *NJ-1*
Heaths Creek (Township)—
  Pettis *MO-3*
Heath Springs (Town)—Lancaster .. *SC-2*
Heavener (City)—Le Flore *OK-2*
Hebbronville (CDP)—Jim Hogg ... *TX-2*
Heber (CDP)—Imperial *CA-4*
Heber (City)—Wasatch *UT-4*
Heber-Overgaard (CDP)—
  Navajo *AZ-4*
Heber Springs (City)—Cleburne ... *AR-2*
Hebron (Town)—Tolland *CT-1*
Hebron (Town)—McHenry *IL-3*
Hebron (Township)—McHenry *IL-3*
Hebron (Town)—Porter *IN-3*
Hebron (Town)—Oxford *ME-1*
Hebron (Town)—Wicomico *MD-1*
Hebron (Township)—Cheboygan .. *MI-3*
Hebron (City)—Thayer *NE-4*
Hebron (Town)—Grafton *NH-1*
Hebron (Town)—Washington *NY-1*
Hebron (City)—Morton *ND-4*
Hebron (Township)—Williams *ND-4*
Hebron (Village)—Licking *OH-3*
Hebron (Township)—Potter *PA-1*
Hebron (Town)—Denton *TX-2*
Hebron (Town)—Jefferson *WI-3*
Hebron Estates (City)—Bullitt *KY-2*
Hecker (Village)—Monroe *IL-3*
Hecla (City)—Brown *SD-4*
Hecla (Township)—Brown *SD-4*
Hector (Town)—Pope *AR-2*
Hector (City)—Renville *MN-3*
Hector (Township)—Renville *MN-3*
Hector (Town)—Schuyler *NY-1*
Hector (Township)—Potter *PA-1*
Hedgesville (Town)—Berkeley *WV-2*
Hedley (Town)—Donley *TX-2*
Hedrick (City)—Keokuk *IA-3*
Hedwig Village (City)—Harris *TX-2*
Heeia (CDP)—Honolulu *HI-4*
Heflin (City)—Cleburne *AL-2*
Heflin (Village)—Webster Parish ... *LA-2*
Hegbert (Township)—Swift *MN-3*
Hegins (Township)—Schuylkill *PA-1*
Hegne (Township)—Norman *MN-3*
Hegton (Township)—Grand
  Forks *ND-4*
Heidelberg (City)—Le Sueur *MN-3*
Heidelberg (Town)—Jasper *MS-2*
Heidelberg (Borough)—Allegheny ... *PA-1*
Heidelberg (Township)—Berks *PA-1*
Heidelberg (Township)—Lebanon .. *PA-1*
Heidelberg (Township)—Lehigh *PA-1*
Heidelberg (Township)—York *PA-1*
Heier (Township)—Mahnomen *MN-3*
Height of Land (Township)—
  Becker *MN-3*
Heikkila Lake (Pop. Place)—St.
  Louis *MN-3*
Heimdal (Township)—Wells *ND-4*
Helen (City)—White *GA-2*
Helen (Township)—McLeod *MN-3*
Helena (Town)—Shelby *AL-2*
Helena (City)—Phillips *AR-2*
Helena (Town)—Telfair *GA-2*
Helena (Town)—Wheeler *GA-2*
Helena (Township)—Antrim *MI-3*
Helena (Township)—Scott *MN-3*
Helena (City)—Lewis and Clark ... *MT-4*
Helena (Township)—Griggs *ND-4*
Helena (Village)—Sandusky *OH-3*
Helena (Town)—Alfalfa *OK-2*
Helena Valley Northeast (CDP)—Lewis
  and Clark *MT-4*
Helena Valley Northwest (CDP)—Lewis
  and Clark *MT-4*
Helena Valley Southeast (CDP)—Lewis
  and Clark *MT-4*
Helena Valley West Central (CDP)—
  Lewis and Clark *MT-4*
Helena West Side (CDP)—Lewis and
  Clark *MT-4*
Helendale (Township)—Richland .. *ND-4*
Helga (Township)—Hubbard *MN-3*
Helgeland (Township)—Polk *MN-3*
Helix (City)—Umatilla *OR-4*
Hellam (Borough)—York *PA-1*
Hellam (Township)—York *PA-1*
Hellertown (Borough)—
  Northampton *PA-1*
Hells Canyon (HI) *Geog-4*
Helmetta (Borough)—Middlesex ... *NJ-1*
Helotes (City)—Bexar *TX-2*
Helper (City)—Carbon *UT-4*
Helt (Township)—Vermillion *IN-3*
Helvetia (Township)—Madison *IL-3*
Helvetia (Town)—Waupaca *WI-3*
Hematite (Township)—Iron *MI-3*
Hemby Bridge (CDP)—Union *NC-2*
Hemen (Township)—Barnes *ND-4*
Hemet (City)—Riverside *CA-4*
Hemingford (Village)—Box Butte .. *NE-4*
Hemingway (Town)—
  Williamsburg *SC-2*
Hemlock (CDP)—Saginaw *MI-3*
Hemlock (Village)—Perry *OH-3*
Hemlock (Township)—Columbia *PA-1*
Hempfield (Township)—Mercer *PA-1*
Hempfield (Township)—
  Westmoreland *PA-1*
Hemphill (City)—Sabine *TX-2*
Hemphill County *TX-2*
Hempstead (Town)—Nassau *NY-1*
Hempstead (Village)—Nassau *NY-1*
Hempstead (City)—Waller *TX-2*
Hempstead County *AR-2*
Henagar (Town)—DeKalb *AL-2*
Henden (Township)—Miner *SD-4*
Henderson (Township)—Knox *IL-3*
Henderson (Village)—Knox *IL-3*
Henderson (City)—Mills *IA-3*
Henderson (City)—Henderson *KY-2*
Henderson (Town)—St. Martin
  Parish *LA-2*
Henderson (Town)—Caroline *MD-1*
Henderson (Township)—Wexford .. *MI-3*
Henderson (City)—Sibley *MN-3*
Henderson (Township)—Sibley *MN-3*
Henderson (City)—York *NE-4*
Henderson (City)—Clark *NV-4*
Henderson (Town)—Jefferson *NY-1*
Henderson (City)—Vance *NC-2*
Henderson (Township)—Cavalier .. *ND-4*
Henderson (Township)—
  Huntingdon *PA-1*
Henderson (Township)—Jefferson .. *PA-1*
Henderson (City)—Chester *TN-2*
Henderson (City)—Rusk *TX-2*
Henderson (Town)—Mason *WV-2*
Henderson County *IL-3*
Henderson County *KY-2*
Henderson County *NC-2*
Henderson County *TN-2*
Henderson County *TX-2*
Hendersonville (City)—
  Henderson *NC-2*
Hendersonville (City)—Sumner *TN-2*
Hendley (Village)—Furnas *NE-4*
Hendren (Town)—Clark *WI-3*
Hendricks (Township)—Shelby *IN-3*
Hendricks (Township)—
  Chautauqua *KS-4*
Hendricks (Township)—
  Mackinac *MI-3*
Hendricks (City)—Lincoln *MN-3*
Hendricks (Township)—Lincoln .. *MN-3*
Hendricks (Town)—Tucker *WV-2*
Hendricks County *IN-3*
Hendrickson (Township)—
  Hubbard *MN-3*
Hendrickson (Township)—
  McHenry *ND-4*
Hendrix (Town)—Bryan *OK-2*
Hendron (CDP)—McCracken *KY-2*
Hendrum (City)—Norman *MN-3*
Hendrum (Township)—Norman ... *MN-3*
Hendry County *FL-2*
Henefer (Town)—Summit *UT-4*
Henlopen Acres (Town)—Sussex ... *DE-1*
Hennepin (Town)—Putnam *IL-3*
Hennepin (Township)—Putnam *IL-3*
Hennepin County *MN-3*
Hennessey (Town)—Kingfisher *OK-2*
Henniker (Town)—Merrimack *NH-1*
Henning (Village)—Vermilion *IL-3*
Henning (City)—Otter Tail *MN-3*
Henning (Township)—Otter Tail .. *MN-3*

General Index — American Places Dictionary

Henning (Town)—Lauderdale........ TN-2
Henrico County VA-2
Henrietta (Township)—Jackson MI-3
Henrietta (Township)—Hubbard .. MN-3
Henrietta (City)—Ray MO-3
Henrietta (Town)—Monroe............ NY-1
Henrietta (Township)—LaMoure... ND-4
Henrietta (Township)—Lorain......OH-3
Henrietta (City)—Clay TX-2
Henrietta (Town)—Richland............ WI-3
Henriette (City)—Pine MN-3
Henrieville (Town)—Garfield UT-4
Henry (Town)—Marshall IL-3
Henry (Township)—Marshall.......... IL-3
Henry (Township)—Fulton IN-3
Henry (Township)—Henry IN-3
Henry (Township)—Ottawa KS-4
Henry (Township)—Vernon MO-3
Henry (Village)—Scotts Bluff NE-4
Henry (Township)—Golden
  Valley ND-4
Henry (Township)—Wood OH-3
Henry (Township)—Brown SD-4
Henry (Town)—Codington............. SD-4
Henry (Township)—Codington SD-4
Henry (Town)—Henry TN-2
Henry Clay (Township)—Fayette.... PA-1
Henry County AL-2
Henry County GA-2
Henry County IL-3
Henry County IN-3
Henry County IA-3
Henry County KY-2
Henry County MO-3
Henry County OH-3
Henry County TN-2
Henry County VA-2
Henryetta (City)—Okmulgee........... OK-2
Henryville (Township)—
  Renville MN-3
Hensley (Township)—Champaign... IL-3
Hensley (Township)—Johnson......... IN-3
Hepburn (City)—Page....................... IA-3
Hepburn (Township)—Lycoming..... PA-1
Hephzibah (Town)—Richmond GA-2
Hepler (City)—Crawford.................KS-4
Heppner (City)—Morrow................ OR-4
Herald Harbor (CDP)—Anne
  Arundel MD-1
Heralds Prairie (Township)—
  White IL-3
Herberg (Township)—Traill ND-4
Herculaneum (City)—Jefferson...... MO-3
Hercules (City)—Contra Costa CA-4
Hereford (Township)—Berks PA-1
Hereford (City)—Deaf Smith.......... TX-2
Hereim (Township)—Roseau MN-3
Herington (City)—Dickinson..........KS-4
Herington (City)—Morris KS-4
Heritage Village (CDP)—New
  Haven CT-1
Herkimer (Township)—Marshall KS-4
Herkimer (Town)—Herkimer.......... NY-1
Herkimer (Village)—Herkimer NY-1
Herkimer County NY-1
Herl (Township)—Rawlins.............KS-4
Herman (City)—Grant MN-3
Herman (Village)—Washington NE-4
Herman (Township)—Sargent........ND-4
Herman (Township)—Lake SD-4
Herman (Town)—Dodge WI-3
Herman (Town)—Shawano.............. WI-3
Herman (Town)—Sheboygan WI-3
Hermann (City)—Gasconade......... MO-3
Hermantown (City)—St. Louis MN-3

Hermiston (City)—Umatilla OR-4
Hermitage (Town)—Bradley AR-2
Hermitage (City)—Hickory............ MO-3
Hermitage (City)—Mercer PA-1
Hermon (Town)—Penobscot........... ME-1
Hermon (Town)—St. Lawrence NY-1
Hermon (Village)—St. Lawrence .. NY-1
Hermosa (Town)—Custer............... SD-4
Hermosa Beach (City)—Los
  Angeles CA-4
Hernando (CDP)—Citrus.................FL-2
Hernando (City)—DeSoto.............. MS-2
Hernando Beach (CDP)—
  Hernando FL-2
Hernando County FL-2
Herndon (City)—Rawlins KS-4
Herndon (Borough)—
  Northumberland PA-1
Herndon (Town)—Fairfax VA-2
Heron Lake (City)—Jackson MN-3
Heron Lake (Township)—
  Jackson MN-3
Herreid (City)—Campbell................ SD-4
Herrick (Township)—Shelby IL-3
Herrick (Village)—Shelby................. IL-3
Herrick (Township)—Knox NE-4
Herrick (Township)—Bradford PA-1
Herrick (Township)—
  Susquehanna PA-1
Herrick (Township)—Deuel SD-4
Herrick (Town)—Gregory SD-4
Herricks (CDP)—Nassau NY-1
Herrin (City)—Williamson IL-3
Herrings (Village)—Jefferson NY-1
Herscher (Village)—Kankakee IL-3
Hersey (Town)—Aroostook............ ME-1
Hersey (Township)—Osceola MI-3
Hersey (Village)—Osceola MI-3
Hersey (Township)—Nobles........... MN-3
Hershey (Village)—Lincoln NE-4
Hershey (CDP)—Dauphin PA-1
Hertford (Town)—Perquimans NC-2
Hertford County NC-2
Herzog (Township)—Ellis KS-4
Hesper (Township)—Benson...........ND-4
Hesperia (City)—San Bernardino .. CA-4
Hesperia (Village)—Newaygo.......... MI-3
Hesperia (Village)—Oceana MI-3
Hessmer (Town)—Avoyelles
  Parish LA-2
Hesston (City)—Harvey KS-4
Heth (Township)—Harrison........... IN-3
Hetland (Town)—Kingsbury SD-4
Hettick (Village)—Macoupin IL-3
Hettinger (City)—Adams ND-4
Hettinger (Township)—Adams ND-4
Hettinger County........................ND-4
Heuvelton (Village)—St.
  Lawrence NY-1
Hewett (Town)—Clark WI-3
Hewitt (City)—Todd MN-3
Hewitt (City)—McLennan TX-2
Hewitt (Town)—Marathon.............. WI-3
Hewitt (Village)—Wood WI-3
Hewlett (CDP)—Nassau.................. NY-1
Hewlett Bay Park (Village)—
  Nassau NY-1
Hewlett Harbor (Village)—
  Nassau NY-1
Hewlett Neck (Village)—Nassau ... NY-1
Heyburn (City)—Minidoka ID-4
Heyworth (Town)—McLean............ IL-3
Hialeah (City)—Dade.......................FL-2
Hialeah Gardens (City)—Dade........FL-2
Hiawassee (Town)—Towns.............. GA-2

Hiawatha (City)—Linn..................... IA-3
Hiawatha (City)—Brown................KS-4
Hiawatha (Township)—Brown......KS-4
Hiawatha (Township)—
  Schoolcraft MI-3
Hiawatha (Town)—Carbon UT-4
Hiawatha (Town)—Emery.............. UT-4
Hibberts Gore (Pop. Place)—
  Lincoln ME-1
Hibbing (City)—St. Louis MN-3
Hickam Air Force Base (HI) Mil-4
Hickam Housing (CDP)—
  Honolulu HI-4
Hickman (City)—Fulton KY-2
Hickman (Village)—Lancaster NE-4
Hickman (Township)—Marshall.... SD-4
Hickman County KY-2
Hickman County TN-2
Hickory (Township)—Schuyler IL-3
Hickory (Township)—Butler KS-4
Hickory (Township)—
  Pennington MN-3
Hickory (Town)—Newton MS-2
Hickory (Township)—Holt MO-3
Hickory (City)—Burke NC-2
Hickory (City)—Catawba NC-2
Hickory (Town)—Murray.............. OK-2
Hickory (Township)—Forest PA-1
Hickory (Township)—Lawrence...... PA-1
Hickory County MO-3
Hickory Creek (Town)—Denton.... TX-2
Hickory Flat (Town)—Benton MS-2
Hickory Grove (Township)—
  Benton.. IN-3
Hickory Grove (Township)—
  Warren.. MO-3
Hickory Grove (Town)—York SC-4
Hickory Grove (Town)—Grant...... WI-3
Hickory Hill (Township)—Wayne.. IL-3
Hickory Hill (City)—Jefferson........ KY-2
Hickory Hills (City)—Cook IL-3
Hickory Point (Township)—
  Macon IL-3
Hickory Ridge (City)—Cross AR-2
Hickory Valley (Town)—
  Hardeman.. TN-2
Hicksville (CDP)—Nassau NY-1
Hicksville (Township)—Defiance ..OH-3
Hicksville (Village)—Defiance OH-3
Hico (City)—Hamilton.................... TX-2
Hidalgo (Village)—Jasper................. IL-3
Hidalgo (City)—Hidalgo TX-2
Hidalgo County NM-4
Hidalgo County TX-2
Hidden (Township)—Stutsman......ND-4
Hidden Hills (City)—Los
  Angeles CA-4
Hidden Meadows (CDP)—San
  Diego CA-4
Hidden Valley (CDP)—Dearborn ... IN-3
Hidden Valley Lake (CDP)—
  Lake... CA-4
Hiddenwood (Township)—Ward ...ND-4
Hidewood (Township)—Deuel SD-4
Higbee (City)—Randolph.............. MO-3
Higdem (Township)—Polk MN-3
Higden (Town)—Cleburne AR-2
Higganum (CDP)—Middlesex CT-1
Higgins (Township)—
  Roscommon MI-3
Higgins (City)—Lipscomb.............. TX-2
Higginson (Town)—White AR-2
Higginsport (Village)—Brown OH-3
Higginsville (City)—Lafayette........ MO-3
Higgston (Town)—Montgomery..... GA-2

American Places Dictionary — General Index

High Bridge (Borough)—
Hunterdon *NJ-1*
High Desert (OR) *Geog-4*
Highfill (Town)—Benton *AR-2*
High Forest (Township)—
Olmsted *MN-3*
Highgate (Town)—Franklin *VT-1*
Highgrove (CDP)—Riverside *CA-4*
High Hill (City)—Montgomery *MO-3*
Highland (City)—San Bernardino . *CA-4*
Highland (Township)—Grundy *IL-3*
Highland (City)—Madison *IL-3*
Highland (Township)—Franklin *IN-3*
Highland (Township)—Greene *IN-3*
Highland (Town)—Lake *IN-3*
Highland (CDP)—Vanderburgh *IN-3*
Highland (Township)—Vermillion .. *IN-3*
Highland (Township)—Clay *KS-4*
Highland (City)—Doniphan *KS-4*
Highland (Township)—Harvey *KS-4*
Highland (Township)—Jewell *KS-4*
Highland (Township)—Lincoln *KS-4*
Highland (Township)—Morris *KS-4*
Highland (Township)—
Washington *KS-4*
Highland (Plantation)—
Somerset *ME-1*
Highland (Township)—Oakland *MI-3*
Highland (Township)—Osceola *MI-3*
Highland (Township)—Wabasha ... *MN-3*
Highland (Township)—Lewis *MO-3*
Highland (Township)—Oregon *MO-3*
Highland (Township)—Adams *NE-4*
Highland (Township)—Gage *NE-4*
Highland (Town)—Sullivan *NY-1*
Highland (CDP)—Ulster *NY-1*
Highland (Township)—Cass *ND-4*
Highland (Township)—Hettinger ... *ND-4*
Highland (Township)—Sheridan *ND-4*
Highland (Township)—Defiance ... *OH-3*
Highland (Village)—Highland *OH-3*
Highland (Township)—
Muskingum *OH-3*
Highland (Township)—Adams *PA-1*
Highland (Township)—Chester *PA-1*
Highland (Township)—Clarion *PA-1*
Highland (Township)—Elk *PA-1*
Highland (Township)—Brown *SD-4*
Highland (Township)—Brule *SD-4*
Highland (Township)—Charles
Mix *SD-4*
Highland (Township)—Day *SD-4*
Highland (Township)—Lincoln *SD-4*
Highland (Township)—
Minnehaha *SD-4*
Highland (Township)—Perkins *SD-4*
Highland (City)—Utah *UT-4*
Highland (CDP)—Benton *WA-4*
Highland (Town)—Douglas *WI-3*
Highland (Town)—Iowa *WI-3*
Highland (Village)—Iowa *WI-3*
Highland Acres (CDP)—Kent *DE-1*
Highland Beach (Town)—Palm
Beach *FL-2*
Highland Beach (Town)—Anne
Arundel *MD-1*
Highland Center (Township)—
Ramsey *ND-4*
Highland City (CDP)—Polk *FL-2*
Highland County *OH-3*
Highland County *VA-2*
Highland-District 2 (Township)—
Norton *KS-4*
Highland Falls (Village)—Orange .. *NY-1*

Highland Grove (Township)—
Clay *MN-3*
Highland Heights (City)—
Campbell *KY-2*
Highland Heights (City)—
Cuyahoga *OH-3*
Highlanding (Township)—
Pennington *MN-3*
Highland Lake (Town)—Blount ... *AL-2*
Highland Lakes (CDP)—Sussex ... *NJ-1*
Highland Mills (CDP)—Orange ... *NY-1*
Highland Park (Village)—Polk *FL-2*
Highland Park (City)—Lake *IL-3*
Highland Park (City)—Wayne *MI-3*
Highland Park (Borough)—
Middlesex *NJ-1*
Highland Park (CDP)—Mifflin *PA-1*
Highland Park (Town)—Dallas *TX-2*
Highlands (CDP)—San Mateo *CA-4*
Highlands (Borough)—
Monmouth *NJ-1*
Highlands (Town)—Orange *NY-1*
Highlands (Town)—Jackson *NC-2*
Highlands (Town)—Macon *NC-2*
Highlands (CDP)—Harris *TX-2*
Highlands County *FL-2*
Highland Springs (CDP)—
Henrico *VA-2*
Highlands Ranch (CDP)—
Douglas *CO-4*
Highland Village (City)—Denton .. *TX-2*
Highmore (City)—Hyde *SD-4*
High Plains (OR) *Geog-4*
High Point (CDP)—Hernando *FL-2*
High Point (CDP)—Palm Beach ... *FL-2*
Highpoint (CDP)—Pinellas *FL-2*
Highpoint (Township)—Ness *KS-4*
High Point (NJ) *Geog-4*
High Point (City)—Davidson *NC-2*
High Point (City)—Forsyth *NC-2*
High Point (City)—Guilford *NC-2*
High Point (City)—Randolph *NC-2*
High Prairie (Township)—
Leavenworth *KS-4*
High Prairie (Township)—
Webster *MO-3*
High Ridge (Township)—
Jefferson *MO-3*
High Shoals (City)—Gaston *NC-2*
Highspire (Borough)—Dauphin ... *PA-1*
High Springs (City)—Alachua *FL-2*
Hightstown (Borough)—Mercer ... *NJ-1*
Highview (CDP)—Jefferson *KY-2*
Highwater (Township)—
Cottonwood *MN-3*
Highwood (City)—Lake *IL-3*
Hiland (Township)—Hand *SD-4*
Hiland Park (CDP)—Bay *FL-2*
Hilbert (Village)—Calumet *WI-3*
Hilda (Town)—Barnwell *SC-2*
Hildale (Town)—Washington *UT-4*
Hildebran (Town)—Burke *NC-2*
Hildreth (Village)—Franklin *NE-4*
Hiles (Town)—Forest *WI-3*
Hiles (Town)—Wood *WI-3*
Hill (Township)—Ogemaw *MI-3*
Hill (Township)—Kittson *MN-3*
Hill (Township)—Carroll *MO-3*
Hill (Township)—Knox *NE-4*
Hill (Town)—Merrimack *NH-1*
Hill (Township)—Cass *ND-4*
Hill (Town)—Price *WI-3*
Hill Air Force Base (UT) *Mil-4*
Hillandale (CDP)—Montgomery .. *MD-1*

Hillandale (CDP)—Prince
George's *MD-1*
Hillburn (Village)—Rockland *NY-1*
Hill City (City)—Graham *KS-4*
Hill City (Township)—Graham ... *KS-4*
Hill City (City)—Aitkin *MN-3*
Hill City (Town)—Pennington *SD-4*
Hill Country Village (City)—
Bexar *TX-2*
Hill County *MT-4*
Hill County *TX-2*
Hillcrest (Village)—Ogle *IL-3*
Hillcrest (CDP)—Rockland *NY-1*
Hillcrest (Village)—Brazoria *TX-2*
Hillcrest Heights (Town)—Polk .. *FL-2*
Hillcrest Heights (CDP)—Prince
George's *MD-1*
Hiller (CDP)—Fayette *PA-1*
Hilliar (Township)—Knox *OH-3*
Hilliard (Town)—Nassau *FL-2*
Hilliard (City)—Franklin *OH-3*
Hill Lake (Township)—Aitkin *MN-3*
Hillman (Township)—
Montmorency *MI-3*
Hillman (Village)—Montmorency . *MI-3*
Hillman (Township)—Kanabec *MN-3*
Hillman (City)—Morrison *MN-3*
Hillman (Township)—Morrison .. *MN-3*
Hill River (Township)—Polk *MN-3*
Hillrose (Town)—Morgan *CO-4*
Hills (City)—Johnson *IA-3*
Hills (City)—Rock *MN-3*
Hills (Township)—Somerset *NJ-1*
Hills and Dales (City)—Jefferson .. *KY-2*
Hills and Dales (Village)—Stark .. *OH-3*
Hillsboro (Town)—Lawrence *AL-2*
Hillsboro (City)—Montgomery ... *IL-3*
Hillsboro (Township)—
Montgomery *IL-3*
Hillsboro (Town)—Fountain *IN-3*
Hillsboro (City)—Henry *IA-3*
Hillsboro (City)—Marion *KS-4*
Hillsboro (Town)—Caroline *MD-1*
Hillsboro (City)—Jefferson *MO-3*
Hillsboro (City)—Traill *ND-4*
Hillsboro (Township)—Traill *ND-4*
Hillsboro (City)—Highland *OH-3*
Hillsboro (City)—Washington *OR-4*
Hillsboro (City)—Hill *TX-2*
Hillsboro (Town)—Loudoun *VA-2*
Hillsboro (Village)—Pocahontas .. *WV-2*
Hillsboro (City)—Vernon *WI-3*
Hillsboro (Town)—Vernon *WI-3*
Hillsboro Beach (Town)—
Broward *FL-2*
Hillsborough (Town)—San
Mateo *CA-4*
Hillsborough (Town)—
Hillsborough *NH-1*
Hillsborough (Town)—Orange ... *NC-2*
Hillsborough County *FL-2*
Hillsborough County *NH-1*
Hillsdale (Village)—Rock Island ... *IL-3*
Hillsdale (City)—Hillsdale *MI-3*
Hillsdale (Township)—Hillsdale .. *MI-3*
Hillsdale (Township)—Winona ... *MN-3*
Hillsdale (Village)—St. Louis *MO-3*
Hillsdale (Borough)—Bergen *NJ-1*
Hillsdale (Town)—Columbia *NY-1*
Hillsdale (Township)—Eddy *ND-4*
Hillsdale (Township)—Wells *ND-4*
Hillsdale (Town)—Garfield *OK-2*
Hillsdale (Township)—Faulk *SD-4*
Hillsdale County *MI-3*
Hillsgrove (Township)—Sullivan ... *PA-1*

General Index

Hillside (City)—Cook IL-3
Hillside (Township)—Union NJ-1
Hillside (Township)—Edmunds SD-4
Hillside Lake (CDP)—Dutchess NY-1
Hillsmere Shores (CDP)—Anne
  Arundel MD-1
Hillsview (Town)—McPherson SD-4
Hillsville (Town)—Carroll VA-2
Hilltonia (City)—Screven GA-2
Hilltop (City)—Anoka MN-3
Hilltown (Township)—Bucks PA-1
Hillview (Village)—Greene IL-3
Hillview (City)—Bullitt KY-2
Hillyard (Township)—Macoupin ... IL-3
Hilmar-Irwin (CDP)—Merced CA-4
Hilmoe (Township)—Lyman SD-4
Hilo (CDP)—Hawaii HI-4
Hilshire Village (City)—Harris TX-2
Hilton (Village)—Monroe NY-1
Hilton (Township)—Ward ND-3
Hilton Head Island (SC) Geog-4
Hilton Head Island (Town)—
  Beaufort SC-2
Hinckley (Town)—DeKalb IL-3
Hinckley (City)—Pine MN-3
Hinckley (Township)—Pine MN-3
Hinckley (Township)—Medina OH-3
Hinckley (Town)—Millard UT-4
Hindman (City)—Knott KY-2
Hindsboro (Village)—Douglas IL-3
Hinds County MS-2
Hindsville (Town)—Madison AR-2
Hi-Nella (Borough)—Camden NJ-1
Hines (Township)—Beltrami MN-3
Hines (City)—Harney OR-4
Hinesburg (Town)—Chittenden VT-1
Hinesville (City)—Liberty GA-2
Hingham (Town)—Plymouth MA-1
Hingham (Town)—Hill MT-4
Hinsdale (City)—Cook IL-3
Hinsdale (City)—DuPage IL-3
Hinsdale (Town)—Berkshire MA-1
Hinsdale (Town)—Cheshire NH-1
Hinsdale (Town)—Cattaraugus NY-1
Hinsdale County CO-4
Hinton (City)—Plymouth IA-3
Hinton (Township)—Mecosta MI-3
Hinton (Town)—Caddo OK-2
Hinton (City)—Summers WV-2
Hiram (City)—Paulding GA-2
Hiram (Town)—Oxford ME-1
Hiram (Township)—Cass MN-3
Hiram (Township)—Portage OH-3
Hiram (Village)—Portage OH-3
Hire (Township)—McDonough IL-3
Hiseville (City)—Barren KY-2
Hitchcock (Town)—Blaine OK-2
Hitchcock (Town)—Beadle SD-4
Hitchcock (City)—Galveston TX-2
Hitchcock County NE-4
Hitchita (Town)—McIntosh OK-2
Hitterdal (City)—Clay MN-3
Hittle (Township)—Tazewell IL-3
Hixon (Town)—Clark WI-3
Hixton (Town)—Jackson WI-3
Hixton (Village)—Jackson WI-3
Hoaglin (Township)—Van Wert OH-3
Hoard (Town)—Clark WI-3
Hobart (City)—Lake IN-3
Hobart (Township)—Lake IN-3
Hobart (Township)—Otter Tail MN-3
Hobart (Village)—Delaware NY-1
Hobart (Township)—Barnes........... ND-4
Hobart (City)—Kiowa OK-2
Hobart (Town)—Brown WI-3

Hobart Bay (CDP)—
  Skagway-Hoonah-Angoon Census
  Area AK-4
Hobbs (City)—Lea NM-4
Hoberg (Township)—Lawrence..... MO-3
Hoberg (Village)—Lawrence MO-3
Hobe Sound (CDP)—Martin FL-2
Hobgood (Town)—Halifax NC-2
Hoboken (Township)—Brantley GA-2
Hoboken (City)—Hudson NJ-1
Hobson (Town)—Judith Basin MT-4
Hobson City (Town)—Calhoun AL-2
Hocking (Township)—Fairfield......OH-3
Hocking County OH-3
Hockley County TX-2
Hodgdon (Town)—Aroostook ME-1
Hodge (Village)—Jackson Parish LA-2
Hodgeman County KS-4
Hodgenville (City)—LaRue KY-2
Hodges (Town)—Franklin AL-2
Hodges (Township)—Stevens MN-3
Hodges (Town)—Greenwood SC-2
Hodgkins (Town)—Cook IL-3
Hoff (Township)—Pope MN-3
Hofflund (Township)—Williams.... ND-4
Hoffman (Village)—Clinton IL-3
Hoffman (City)—Grant MN-3
Hoffman (Town)—Richmond NC-2
Hoffman (Township)—Bottineau.. ND-4
Hoffman (Town)—Okmulgee OK-2
Hoffman (Township)—
  McPherson SD-4
Hoffman Estates (Village)—Cook... IL-3
Hoffman Estates (Village)—Kane ... IL-3
Hogan (Township)—Dearborn IN-3
Hogansville (City)—Troup GA-2
Hohenwald (City)—Lewis TN-2
Ho-Ho-Kus (Borough)—Bergen NJ-1
Hoh Reservation (WA) IndRes-4
Hoisington (City)—Barton KS-4
Hokah (City)—Houston MN-3
Hokah (Township)—Houston MN-3
Hoke County NC-2
Hokendauqua (CDP)—Lehigh PA-1
Hokes Bluff (Town)—Etowah AL-2
Holbrook (City)—Navajo AZ-4
Holbrook (Town)—Norfolk MA-1
Holbrook (Village)—Furnas NE-4
Holbrook (CDP)—Suffolk NY-1
Holcomb (City)—Finney KS-4
Holcomb (City)—Dunklin MO-3
Holcomb (Township)—Dunklin.... MO-3
Holcomb (Village)—Ontario NY-1
Holden (Town)—Penobscot ME-1
Holden (Town)—Worcester MA-1
Holden (Township)—Goodhue MN-3
Holden (City)—Johnson................. MO-3
Holden (Township)—Adams ND-4
Holden (Township)—Hand SD-4
Holden (Town)—Millard UT-4
Holden (CDP)—Logan WV-2
Holden Beach (Town)—
  Brunswick NC-2
Holden Heights (CDP)—Orange.....FL-2
Holdenville (City)—Hughes OK-2
Holderness (Town)—Grafton NH-1
Holding (Township)—Stearns MN-3
Holdingford (City)—Stearns MN-3
Holdrege (City)—Phelps NE-4
Holgate (Village)—Henry OH-3
Holiday (CDP)—Pasco FL-2
Holiday City-Berkeley (CDP)—
  Ocean NJ-1
Holiday City-Dover (CDP)—
  Ocean NJ-1

Holiday City South (CDP)—
  Ocean NJ-1
Holiday Heights (CDP)—Ocean NJ-1
Holiday Hills (Village)—McHenry . IL-3
Holiday Lakes (Town)—Brazoria .. TX-2
Holiday Valley (CDP)—Clark........OH-3
Holladay-Cottonwood (CDP)—Salt
  Lake UT-4
Holland (Township)—Shelby IL-3
Holland (Town)—Dubois IN-3
Holland (City)—Grundy IA-3
Holland (Township)—Dickinson KS-4
Holland (Town)—Hampden........... MA-1
Holland (City)—Allegan MI-3
Holland (Township)—Missaukee ... MI-3
Holland (City)—Ottawa MI-3
Holland (Township)—Ottawa MI-3
Holland (Township)—Kandiyohi.. MN-3
Holland (City)—Pipestone MN-3
Holland (Town)—Pemiscot MO-3
Holland (Township)—Pemiscot MO-3
Holland (Township)—Hunterdon ... NJ-1
Holland (Town)—Erie NY-1
Holland (Village)—Lucas OH-3
Holland (Township)—Douglas SD-4
Holland (Town)—Bell TX-2
Holland (Town)—Orleans VT-1
Holland (Town)—Brown WI-3
Holland (Town)—La Crosse........... WI-3
Holland (Town)—Sheboygan WI-3
Hollandale (City)—Freeborn MN-3
Hollandale (City)—Washington MS-2
Hollandale (Village)—Iowa WI-3
Holland Patent (Village)—
  Oneida................................. NY-1
Hollansburg (Village)—Darke OH-3
Hollenback (Township)—Luzerne... PA-1
Hollenberg (City)—Washington KS-4
Holley (Village)—Orleans NY-1
Holliday (Village)—Monroe........... MO-3
Holliday (City)—Archer TX-2
Hollidaysburg (Borough)—Blair..... PA-1
Hollins (CDP)—Botetourt VA-2
Hollins (CDP)—Roanoke.............. VA-2
Hollis (CDP)—Prince of Wales-Outer
  Ketchikan Census Area AK-4
Hollis (Township)—Peoria IL-3
Hollis (Town)—York ME-1
Hollis (Town)—Hillsborough NH-1
Hollis (City)—Harmon OK-2
Hollister (City)—San Benito CA-4
Hollister (City)—Twin Falls ID-4
Hollister (City)—Taney MO-3
Hollister (Town)—Tillman OK-2
Holliston (Town)—Middlesex MA-1
Holloman Air Force Base (NM)...... Mil-4
Holloman Air Force Base (Military
  Facility)—Otero NM-4
Holloway (City)—Swift MN-3
Holloway (Village)—Belmont OH-3
Hollowayville (Village)—Bureau IL-3
Hollow Creek (City)—Jefferson KY-2
Hollow Rock (Town)—Carroll TN-2
Holly (Town)—Prowers................. CO-4
Holly (Township)—Oakland MI-3
Holly (Village)—Oakland MI-3
Holly (Township)—Murray MN-3
Holly Grove (Town)—Monroe....... AR-2
Holly Hill (City)—Volusia.............. FL-2
Holly Hill (Town)—Orangeburg SC-2
Hollymead (CDP)—Albemarle VA-2
Holly Pond (Town)—Cullman AL-2
Holly Ridge (Town)—Onslow NC-2
Holly Springs (City)—Cherokee..... GA-2
Holly Springs (City)—Marshall....... MS-2

Holly Springs (Town)—Wake......... NC-2
Hollyvilla (City)—Jefferson KY-2
Hollywood (Town)—Jackson AL-2
Hollywood (City)—Broward FL-2
Hollywood (Township)—Carver ... MN-3
Hollywood (Town)—Charleston......SC-2
Hollywood *See* **Los Angeles**—Los
  Angeles CA-4
Hollywood Park (Town)—Bexar TX-2
Hollywood Reservation (FL).... IndRes-4
Holmdel (Township)—
  Monmouth NJ-1
Holmen (Village)—La Crosse WI-3
Holmes (Township)—Menominee . MI-3
Holmes (Township)—Sheridan ND-4
Holmes (Township)—Crawford OH-3
Holmes Beach (City)—Manatee......FL-2
Holmes City (Township)—
  Douglas MN-3
Holmes County FL-2
Holmes County MS-2
Holmes County OH-3
Holmesville (Township)—Becker .. MN-3
Holmesville (Village)—Holmes....OH-3
Holmwood (Township)—Jewell KS-4
Holsclaw (Township)—Tripp SD-4
Holst (Township)—Clearwater...... MN-3
Holstein (City)—Ida IA-3
Holstein (Village)—Adams............. NE-4
Holt (Division)—Tuscaloosa AL-2
Holt (CDP)—Ingham MI-3
Holt (Township)—Fillmore MN-3
Holt (City)—Marshall MN-3
Holt (Township)—Marshall........... MN-3
Holt (City)—Clay MO-3
Holt (City)—Clinton MO-3
Holt (Township)—Gage................... NE-4
Holt County MO-3
Holt County NE-4
Holt Creek (Township)—Holt........ NE-4
Holton (Town)—Ripley IN-3
Holton (City)—Jackson KS-4
Holton (Township)—Muskegon MI-3
Holton (Town)—Marathon WI-3
Holts Summit (City)—Callaway ... MO-3
Holtsville (CDP)—Suffolk............... NY-1
Holtville (City)—Imperial CA-4
Holualoa (CDP)—Hawaii HI-4
Holway (Town)—Taylor WI-3
Holy Cross (City)—Yukon-Koyukuk
  Census Area AK-4
Holy Cross (City)—Dubuque...........IA-3
Holy Cross (Township)—Clay........ MN-3
Holyoke (Town)—Phillips CO-4
Holyoke (City)—Hampden MA-1
Holyoke (Township)—Carlton MN-3
Holyrood (City)—Ellsworth KS-4
Home (Township)—Nemaha........... KS-4
Home (Township)—Montcalm MI-3
Home (Township)—Newaygo MI-3
Home (Township)—Brown MN-3
Home (Township)—Turner SD-4
Homeacre—Lyndora (CDP)—
  Butler PA-1
Home Brook (Township)—Cass.... MN-3
Homecroft (Town)—Marion IN-3
Homedale (City)—Owyhee ID-4
Home Garden (CDP)—Kings CA-4
Home Gardens (CDP)—
  Riverside CA-4
Home Lake (Township)—
  Norman MN-3
Homeland (CDP)—Riverside CA-4
Homeland (City)—Charlton........... GA-2

Homeland Park (CDP)—
  Anderson SC-2
Homen (Township)—Bottineau ND-4
Homer (City)—Kenai Peninsula
  Borough AK-4
Homer (Town)—Banks................... GA-2
Homer (Village)—Champaign......... IL-3
Homer (Township)—Will................ IL-3
Homer (Town)—Claiborne
  Parish LA-2
Homer (Township)—Calhoun MI-3
Homer (Village)—Calhoun............. MI-3
Homer (Township)—Midland MI-3
Homer (Township)—Winona MN-3
Homer (Township)—Bates MO-3
Homer (Village)—Dakota NE-4
Homer (Town)—Cortland NY-1
Homer (Village)—Cortland NY-1
Homer (Township)—Stutsman....... ND-4
Homer (Township)—Medina OH-3
Homer (Township)—Morgan OH-3
Homer (Township)—Potter............ PA-1
Homer (Township)—Day SD-4
Homer City (Borough)—Indiana .. PA-1
Homerville (City)—Clinch GA-2
Homestead (City)—Dade FL-2
Homestead (Township)—Chase....KS-4
Homestead (Township)—Benzie.... MI-3
Homestead (Township)—Otter
  Tail MN-3
Homestead (Village)—Ray MO-3
Homestead (Township)—
  Richland ND-4
Homestead (Borough)—Allegheny.. PA-1
Homestead (Town)—Florence WI-3
Homestead Air Force Base (FL).....Mil-4
Homestead Air Force Base (Mil.
  facil.)—Dade.................................FL-2
Homestead Meadows (CDP)—El
  Paso TX-2
Hometown (City)—Pemiscot......... MO-3
Hometown (City)—Cook IL-3
Hometown (CDP)—Schuylkill PA-1
Homewood (City)—Jefferson.......... AL-2
Homewood (City)—Cook IL-3
Homewood (Township)—
  Franklin KS-4
Homewood (Borough)—Beaver PA-1
Hominy (City)—Osage OK-2
Homosassa (CDP)—Citrus.............FL-2
Homosassa Springs (CDP)—
  Citrus FL-2
Honaker (Town)—Russell VA-2
Honalo (CDP)—Hawaii HI-4
Honaunau-Napoopoo (CDP)—
  Hawaii HI-4
Hondo (City)—Medina TX-2
Honea Path (Town)—Abbeville SC-2
Honea Path (Town)—Anderson......SC-2
Honeoye Falls (Village)—Monroe.. NY-1
Honesdale (Borough)—Wayne PA-1
Honey Brook (Borough)—Chester .. PA-1
Honey Brook (Township)—
  Chester PA-1
Honey Creek (Township)—Adams . IL-3
Honey Creek (Township)—
  Crawford IL-3
Honey Creek (Township)—
  Howard IN-3
Honey Creek (Township)—Vigo IN-3
Honey Creek (Township)—White... IN-3
Honey Creek (Township)—
  Henry MO-3
Honey Creek (Town)—Sauk........... WI-3
Honey Grove (City)—Fannin TX-2

Honey Point (Township)—
  Macoupin IL-3
Honeyville (City)—Box Elder UT-4
Honner (Township)—Redwood MN-3
Honokaa (CDP)—Hawaii HI-4
Honolulu (City)—Honolulu HI-4
Honolulu County HI-4
Honomu (CDP)—Hawaii HI-4
Honor (Village)—Benzie MI-3
Hood, Mt. (OR)........................... Geog-4
Hood County TX-2
Hood River (City)—Hood River ...OR-4
Hood River County......................OR-4
Hooker (Township)—Laclede MO-3
Hooker (Township)—Dixon NE-4
Hooker (Township)—Gage............. NE-4
Hooker (City)—Texas..................... OK-2
Hooker County NE-4
Hookerton (Town)—Greene NC-2
Hooks (City)—Bowie TX-2
Hooksett (Town)—Merrimack NH-1
Hookstown (Borough)—Beaver....... PA-1
Hoonah (City)—
  Skagway-Hoonah-Angoon Census
  Area AK-4
Hoopa Valley Reservation
  (CA) IndRes-4
Hooper (Town)—Alamosa............. CO-4
Hooper (City)—Dodge NE-4
Hooper (Township)—Dodge NE-4
Hooper (CDP)—Weber UT-4
Hooper Bay (City)—Wade Hampton
  Census Area AK-4
Hoopeston (City)—Vermilion IL-3
Hoople (City)—Walsh ND-4
Hooppole (Town)—Henry IL-3
Hoosick (Town)—Rensselaer NY-1
Hoosick Falls (Village)—
  Rensselaer NY-1
Hoosier (Township)—Clay IL-3
Hoosier (Township)—Kingman KS-4
Hoot Owl (Town)—Mayes OK-2
Hoover (City)—Jefferson AL-2
Hoover (City)—Shelby AL-2
Hoover Dam (OR)...................... Geog-4
Hooverson Heights (CDP)—
  Brooke WV-2
Hooversville (Borough)—
  Somerset PA-1
Hopatcong (Borough)—Sussex NJ-1
Hop Bottom (Borough)—
  Susquehanna PA-1
Hope (CDP)—Kenai Peninsula
  Borough AK-4
Hope (City)—Hempstead................ AR-2
Hope (City)—Bonner ID-4
Hope (Township)—La Salle IL-3
Hope (Town)—Bartholomew IN-3
Hope (City)—Dickinson................. KS-4
Hope (Township)—Dickinson........KS-4
Hope (Town)—Knox ME-1
Hope (Township)—Barry MI-3
Hope (Township)—Midland MI-3
Hope (Township)—Lincoln MN-3
Hope (Township)—Warren NJ-1
Hope (Village)—Eddy NM-4
Hope (Town)—Hamilton NY-1
Hope (Township)—Cavalier...........ND-4
Hope (City)—Steele........................ ND-4
Hope (Township)—Lyman SD-4
Hopedale (Town)—Tazewell IL-3
Hopedale (Township)—Tazewell..... IL-3
Hopedale (Town)—Worcester MA-1
Hopedale (Village)—Harrison........OH-3

General Index — American Places Dictionary

Hope Mills (Town)—Cumberland ... NC-2
Hope Valley (CDP)—Washington ... RI-1
Hopewell (Township)—Marshall ... IL-3
Hopewell (Village)—Marshall ... IL-3
Hopewell (Township)—Cumberland ... NJ-1
Hopewell (Borough)—Mercer ... NJ-1
Hopewell (Township)—Mercer ... NJ-1
Hopewell (Town)—Ontario ... NY-1
Hopewell (Township)—Licking ... OH-3
Hopewell (Township)—Mercer ... OH-3
Hopewell (Township)—Muskingum ... OH-3
Hopewell (Township)—Perry ... OH-3
Hopewell (Township)—Seneca ... OH-3
Hopewell (Township)—Beaver ... PA-1
Hopewell (Borough)—Bedford ... PA-1
Hopewell (Township)—Bedford ... PA-1
Hopewell (Township)—Cumberland ... PA-1
Hopewell (Township)—Huntingdon ... PA-1
Hopewell (Township)—Washington ... PA-1
Hopewell (Township)—York ... PA-1
Hopewell (CDP)—Bradley ... TN-2
Hopewell (Independent City) ... VA-2
Hopewell Junction (CDP)—Dutchess ... NY-1
Hopi Reservation & Trust Lands (AZ) ... IndRes-4
Hopkins (Township)—Whiteside ... IL-3
Hopkins (Township)—Allegan ... MI-3
Hopkins (Village)—Allegan ... MI-3
Hopkins (City)—Hennepin ... MN-3
Hopkins (City)—Nodaway ... MO-3
Hopkins (Township)—Nodaway ... MO-3
Hopkins County ... KY-2
Hopkins County ... TX-2
Hopkins Park (Village)—Kankakee ... IL-3
Hopkinsville (City)—Christian ... KY-2
Hopkinton (City)—Delaware ... IA-3
Hopkinton (Town)—Middlesex ... MA-1
Hopkinton (Town)—Merrimack ... NH-1
Hopkinton (Town)—St. Lawrence ... NY-1
Hopkinton (Town)—Washington ... RI-1
Hopland Rancheria (CA) ... IndRes-4
Hopper (Township)—Aurora ... SD-4
Hopwood (CDP)—Fayette ... PA-1
Hoquiam (City)—Grays Harbor ... WA-4
Horace (City)—Greeley ... KS-4
Horace (City)—Cass ... ND-4
Horatio (City)—Sevier ... AR-2
Hordville (Village)—Hamilton ... NE-4
Horicon (Town)—Warren ... NY-1
Horicon (City)—Dodge ... WI-3
Horine (CDP)—Jefferson ... MO-3
Horizon City (Town)—El Paso ... TX-2
Hornbeak (Town)—Obion ... TN-2
Hornbeck (Town)—Vernon Parish ... LA-2
Hornby (Town)—Steuben ... NY-1
Hornell (City)—Steuben ... NY-1
Hornellsville (Town)—Steuben ... NY-1
Hornersville (City)—Dunklin ... MO-3
Hornet (Township)—Beltrami ... MN-3
Hornick (City)—Woodbury ... IA-3
Horn Lake (City)—DeSoto ... MS-2
Hornsby (Town)—Hardeman ... TN-2
Horry County ... SC-2
Horse Cave (City)—Hart ... KY-2

Horse Creek (Township)—Perkins ... SD-4
Horseheads (Town)—Chemung ... NY-1
Horseheads (Village)—Chemung ... NY-1
Horseheads North (CDP)—Chemung ... NY-1
Horseshoe Bay (CDP)—Burnet ... TX-2
Horseshoe Bay (CDP)—Llano ... TX-2
Horseshoe Beach (Town)—Dixie ... FL-2
Horseshoe Bend (City)—Fulton ... AR-2
Horseshoe Bend (City)—Izard ... AR-2
Horseshoe Bend (City)—Sharp ... AR-2
Horseshoe Bend (City)—Boise ... ID-4
Horseshoe Lake (Town)—Crittenden ... AR-2
Horseshoe Valley (Township)—McLean ... ND-4
Horsham (Township)—Montgomery ... PA-1
Horton (City)—Brown ... KS-4
Horton (Township)—Ogemaw ... MI-3
Horton (Township)—Stevens ... MN-3
Horton (Township)—Elk ... PA-1
Hortonia (Town)—Outagamie ... WI-3
Hortonville (Village)—Outagamie ... WI-3
Hoschton (City)—Jackson ... GA-2
Hoskins (Village)—Wayne ... NE-4
Hosmer (City)—Edmunds ... SD-4
Hosmer (Township)—Edmunds ... SD-4
Sokaogon Chippewa Community & Trust Land (WI) ... IndRes-4
Hospers (City)—Sioux ... IA-3
Hosston (Village)—Caddo Parish ... LA-2
Hotchkiss (Town)—Delta ... CO-4
Hotevilla (CDP)—Navajo ... AZ-4
Hot Spring County ... AR-2
Hot Springs (AR) ... Geog-4
Hot Springs (City)—Garland ... AR-2
Hot Springs (Town)—Sanders ... MT-4
Hot Springs (Town)—Madison ... NC-2
Hot Springs (City)—Fall River ... SD-4
Hot Springs County ... WY-4
Hot Springs Village (CDP)—Garland ... AR-2
Hot Springs Village (CDP)—Saline ... AR-2
Hot Sulphur Springs (Town)—Grand ... CO-4
Hough (Township)—New Madrid ... MO-3
Houghton (City)—Lee ... IA-3
Houghton (City)—Houghton ... MI-3
Houghton (Township)—Keweenaw ... MI-3
Houghton County ... MI-3
Houghton Lake (CDP)—Roscommon ... MI-3
Houlton (Town)—Aroostook ... ME-1
Houma (City)—Terrebonne Parish ... LA-2
Hounsfield (Town)—Jefferson ... NY-1
Housatonic (CDP)—Berkshire ... MA-1
Housatonic River (AR) ... Geog-4
House (Village)—Quay ... NM-4
Houston (City)—Matanuska-Susitna Borough ... AK-4
Houston (Town)—Perry ... AR-2
Houston (Town)—Kent ... DE-1
Houston (Township)—Adams ... IL-3
Houston (Township)—Smith ... KS-4
Houston (City)—Houston ... MN-3
Houston (Township)—Houston ... MN-3
Houston (City)—Chickasaw ... MS-2
Houston (City)—Texas ... MO-3

Houston (Borough)—Washington ... PA-1
Houston (City)—Fort Bend ... TX-2
Houston (City)—Harris ... TX-2
Houston (City)—Montgomery ... TX-2
Houston Acres (City)—Jefferson ... KY-2
Houston County ... AL-2
Houston County ... GA-2
Houston County ... MN-3
Houston County ... TN-2
Houston County ... TX-2
Houstonia (City)—Pettis ... MO-3
Houstonia (Township)—Pettis ... MO-3
Houston Lake (City)—Platte ... MO-3
Houston Ship Canal (*or* Channel) (TX) ... Geog-4
Houtzdale (Borough)—Clearfield ... PA-1
Hoven (Town)—Potter ... SD-4
Hovey (Township)—Armstrong ... PA-1
How (Town)—Oconto ... WI-3
Howard (Township)—Howard ... IN-3
Howard (Township)—Parke ... IN-3
Howard (Township)—Washington ... IN-3
Howard (City)—Elk ... KS-4
Howard (Township)—Elk ... KS-4
Howard (Township)—Labette ... KS-4
Howard (Township)—Cass ... MI-3
Howard (Township)—Bates ... MO-3
Howard (Township)—Gentry ... MO-3
Howard (Town)—Steuben ... NY-1
Howard (Township)—Knox ... OH-3
Howard (Borough)—Centre ... PA-1
Howard (Township)—Centre ... PA-1
Howard (Township)—Charles Mix ... SD-4
Howard (Township)—Meade ... SD-4
Howard (City)—Miner ... SD-4
Howard (Township)—Miner ... SD-4
Howard (Village)—Brown ... WI-3
Howard (Town)—Chippewa ... WI-3
Howard Beach—Queens ... NY-1
Howard City (Village)—Montcalm ... MI-3
Howard City (Village)—Howard ... NE-4
Howard County ... AR-2
Howard County ... IN-3
Howard County ... IA-3
Howard County ... MD-1
Howard County ... MO-3
Howard County ... NE-4
Howard County ... TX-2
Howard Lake (City)—Wright ... MN-3
Howards Grove (Village)—Sheboygan ... WI-3
Howardville (City)—New Madrid ... MO-3
Howardwick (City)—Donley ... TX-2
Howe (Township)—Grant ... ND-4
Howe (Town)—Le Flore ... OK-4
Howe (Township)—Forest ... PA-1
Howe (Township)—Perry ... PA-1
Howe (Town)—Grayson ... TX-2
Howe Caverns (NY) ... Geog-4
Howell (City)—Livingston ... MI-3
Howell (Township)—Livingston ... MI-3
Howell (Township)—Howell ... MO-3
Howell (Township)—Monmouth ... NJ-1
Howell (Township)—Towner ... ND-4
Howell (Town)—Box Elder ... UT-4
Howell County ... MO-3
Howells (Village)—Colfax ... NE-4
Howes (Township)—Cass ... ND-4
Howey-in-the-Hills (Town)—Lake ... FL-2
Howie (Township)—Mountrail ... ND-4
Howland (Town)—Penobscot ... ME-1
Howland (Township)—Trumbull ... OH-3

American Places Dictionary   General Index

Hoxie (City)—Lawrence................ *AR-2*
Hoxie (City)—Sheridan.................. *KS-4*
Hoyleton (Township)—
   Washington *IL-3*
Hoyleton (Village)—Washington..... *IL-3*
Hoyt (City)—Jackson *KS-4*
Hoyt Lakes (City)—St. Louis *MN-3*
Hoytville (Village)—Wood *OH-3*
Huachuca City (Town)—Cochise... *AZ-4*
Hualapai Reservation & Trust Lands
   (AZ)... *IndRes-4*
Hubbard (City)—Hardin................ *IA-3*
Hubbard (Township)—Hubbard... *MN-3*
Hubbard (Township)—Polk *MN-3*
Hubbard (Village)—Dakota *NE-4*
Hubbard (City)—Trumbull *OH-3*
Hubbard (Township)—Trumbull ...*OH-3*
Hubbard (City)—Marion *OR-4*
Hubbard (City)—Hill *TX-2*
Hubbard (Town)—Dodge *WI-3*
Hubbard (Town)—Rusk *WI-3*
Hubbard, Mt. (AK)...................... *Geog-4*
Hubbard County *MN-3*
Hubbardston (Town)—Worcester . *MA-1*
Hubbardston (Village)—Clinton *MI-3*
Hubbardston (Village)—Ionia *MI-3*
Hubbardton (Town)—Rutland....... *VT-1*
Hubbell (CDP)—Houghton............ *MI-3*
Hubbell (Village)—Thayer *NE-4*
Hubble (Township)—Cape
   Girardeau *MO-3*
Huber Heights (City)—Miami *OH-3*
Huber Heights (City)—
   Montgomery................................ *OH-3*
Huber Ridge (CDP)—Franklin......*OH-3*
Hubley (Township)—Schuylkill *PA-1*
Hudson (Town)—Weld *CO-4*
Hudson (CDP)—Pasco..................... *FL-2*
Hudson (Township)—McLean *IL-3*
Hudson (Village)—McLean *IL-3*
Hudson (Township)—La Porte *IN-3*
Hudson (Town)—Steuben *IN-3*
Hudson (City)—Black Hawk........... *IA-3*
Hudson (City)—Stafford *KS-4*
Hudson (Town)—Penobscot *ME-1*
Hudson (Town)—Middlesex *MA-1*
Hudson (Township)—Charlevoix... *MI-3*
Hudson (City)—Lenawee *MI-3*
Hudson (Township)—Lenawee *MI-3*
Hudson (Township)—Mackinac.... *MI-3*
Hudson (Township)—Douglas *MN-3*
Hudson (Township)—Bates *MO-3*
Hudson (Township)—Macon *MO-3*
Hudson (Town)—Hillsborough *NH-1*
Hudson (City)—Columbia *NY-1*
Hudson (Town)—Caldwell.............. *NC-2*
Hudson (Township)—Dickey *ND-4*
Hudson (Township)—Summit *OH-3*
Hudson (Village)—Summit *OH-3*
Hudson (Township)—Edmunds..... *SD-4*
Hudson (Town)—Lincoln............... *SD-4*
Hudson (City)—Angelina *TX-2*
Hudson (City)—St. Croix *WI-3*
Hudson (Town)—St. Croix *WI-3*
Hudson (Town)—Fremont *WY-4*
Hudson County................................ *NJ-1*
Hudson Falls (Village)—
   Washington *NY-1*
Hudson Oaks (Town)—Parker....... *TX-2*
Hudson River (NY)...................... *Geog-4*
Hudsonville (City)—Ottawa *MI-3*
Hudspeth County *TX-2*
Huerfano County *CO-4*
Huetter (City)—Kootenai............... *ID-4*
Huey (Village)—Clinton.................. *IL-3*

Hueytown (City)—Jefferson...........*AL-2*
Huff (Township)—Spencer............. *IN-3*
Huggins (Township)—Gentry *MO-3*
Huggins (Township)—Tripp.......... *SD-4*
Hughes (City)—Yukon-Koyukuk
   Census Area *AK-4*
Hughes (City)—St. Francis *AR-2*
Hughes (Township)—Nodaway *MO-3*
Hughes (Township)—Slope *ND-4*
Hughes (Town)—Bayfield *WI-3*
Hughes County *OK-2*
Hughes County *SD-4*
Hughes Springs (City)—Cass *TX-2*
Hughes Springs (City)—Morris *TX-2*
Hughestown (Borough)—Luzerne... *PA-1*
Hughesville (CDP)—Charles.......... *MD-1*
Hughesville (Township)—Pettis ... *MO-3*
Hughesville (Village)—Pettis *MO-3*
Hughesville (Borough)—
   Lycoming..................................... *PA-1*
Hughson (City)—Stanislaus *CA-4*
Hugo (Town)—Lincoln................... *CO-4*
Hugo (City)—Washington *MN-3*
Hugo (Township)—Steele *ND-4*
Hugo (City)—Choctaw *OK-2*
Hugoton (City)—Stevens *KS-4*
Huguley (Division)—Chambers......*AL-2*
Hulbert (Township)—Chippewa *MI-3*
Hulbert (Town)—Cherokee *OK-2*
Hulbert (Township)—Hand *SD-4*
Hulett (Town)—Crook *WY-4*
Hull (Town)—Madison *GA-2*
Hull (Village)—Pike *IL-3*
Hull (City)—Sioux.......................... *IA-3*
Hull (Town)—Plymouth................*MA-1*
Hull (Town)—Marathon................ *WI-3*
Hull (Town)—Portage *WI-3*
Hulmeville (Borough)—Bucks....... *PA-1*
Humansville (City)—Polk *MO-3*
Humble (City)—Harris................... *TX-2*
Humboldt (Township)—Coles *IL-3*
Humboldt (Village)—Coles *IL-3*
Humboldt (City)—Humboldt.........*IA-3*
Humboldt (City)—Allen *KS-4*
Humboldt (Township)—Allen........ *KS-4*
Humboldt (Township)—
   Marquette.................................... *MI-3*
Humboldt (Township)—Clay *MN-3*
Humboldt (City)—Kittson *MN-3*
Humboldt (City)—Richardson....... *NE-4*
Humboldt (Town)—Minnehaha..... *SD-4*
Humboldt (Township)—
   Minnehaha *SD-4*
Humboldt (City)—Gibson *TN-2*
Humboldt (City)—Madison *TN-2*
Humboldt (Town)—Brown *WI-3*
Humboldt County *CA-4*
Humboldt County *IA-3*
Humboldt County *NV-4*
Humboldt Hill (CDP)—
   Humboldt *CA-4*
Humboldt River (NV) *Geog-4*
Hume (Village)—Edgar *IL-3*
Hume (Township)—Whiteside........ *IL-3*
Hume (Township)—Huron *MI-3*
Hume (Town)—Bates *MO-3*
Hume (Town)—Allegany *NY-1*
Hume (Township)—Slope *ND-4*
Humeston (City)—Wayne *IA-3*
Hummelstown (Borough)—
   Dauphin...................................... *PA-1*
Hummels Wharf (CDP)—Snyder ... *PA-1*
Humnoke (City)—Lonoke *AR-2*
Humphrey (Town)—Arkansas....... *AR-2*
Humphrey (Town)—Jefferson *AR-2*

Humphrey (City)—Platte *NE-4*
Humphrey (Township)—Platte *NE-4*
Humphrey (Town)—Cattaraugus ... *NY-1*
Humphreys (Town)—Sullivan....... *MO-3*
Humphreys County *MS-2*
Humphreys County *TN-2*
Humphreys Peak (AZ)................. *Geog-4*
Hundred (Town)—Wetzel *WV-2*
Hunker (Borough)—
   Westmoreland *PA-1*
Hunlock (Township)—Luzerne *PA-1*
Hunnewell (City)—Sumner............ *KS-4*
Hunnewell (City)—Shelby............ *MO-3*
Hunt City (Township)—Jasper *IL-3*
Hunt County................................... *TX-2*
Hunter (Town)—Woodruff............ *AR-2*
Hunter (Township)—Edgar *IL-3*
Hunter (City)—Mitchell *KS-4*
Hunter (Township)—Jackson *MN-3*
Hunter (Town)—Greene *NY-1*
Hunter (Village)—Greene *NY-1*
Hunter (City)—Cass *ND-4*
Hunter (Township)—Cass *ND-4*
Hunter (Town)—Garfield *OK-2*
Hunter (CDP)—Carter *TN-2*
Hunter (Town)—Sawyer *WI-3*
Hunterdon County *NJ-1*
Hunters Creek Village (City)—
   Harris *TX-2*
Hunters Hollow (City)—Bullitt....... *KY-2*
Huntersville (Township)—
   Wadena *MN-3*
Huntersville (Town)—
   Mecklenburg *NC-2*
Huntertown (Town)—Allen........... *IN-3*
Huntingburg (City)—Dubois *IN-3*
Huntingdon (Borough)—
   Huntingdon *PA-1*
Huntingdon (Town)—Carroll......... *TN-2*
Huntingdon County *PA-1*
Huntington (City)—Sebastian *AR-2*
Huntington (City)—Huntington *IN-3*
Huntington (Township)—
   Huntington................................. *IN-3*
Huntington (Town)—Hampshire .. *MA-1*
Huntington (Town)—Suffolk *NY-1*
Huntington (Township)—Brown....*OH-3*
Huntington (Township)—Gallia *OH-3*
Huntington (Township)—Lorain ...*OH-3*
Huntington (Township)—Ross.......*OH-3*
Huntington (City)—Baker.............. *OR-4*
Huntington (Township)—Adams.... *PA-1*
Huntington (Township)—Luzerne .. *PA-1*
Huntington (City)—Angelina *TX-2*
Huntington (City)—Emery............ *UT-4*
Huntington (Town)—Chittenden... *VT-1*
Huntington (CDP)—Fairfax.......... *VA-2*
Huntington (City)—Cabell *WV-2*
Huntington (City)—Wayne *WV-2*
Huntington Bay (Village)—
   Suffolk.. *NY-1*
Huntington Beach (City)—
   Orange.. *CA-4*
Huntington County *IN-3*
Huntington Park (City)—Los
   Angeles *CA-4*
Huntington Station (CDP)—
   Suffolk.. *NY-1*
Huntington Woods (City)—
   Oakland *MI-3*
Hunting Valley (Village)—
   Cuyahoga *OH-3*
Hunting Valley (Village)—
   Geauga *OH-3*
Huntland (Town)—Franklin *TN-2*

General Index

American Places Dictionary

Huntleigh (City)—St. Louis *MO-3*
Huntley (Town)—McHenry *IL-3*
Huntley (Village)—Harlan *NE-4*
Huntley (Township)—Edmunds..... *SD-4*
Huntly (Township)—Marshall........ *MN-3*
Huntsburg (Township)—Geauga.... *OH-3*
Hunts Point (Town)—King............. *WA-4*
Huntsville (City)—Limestone *AL-2*
Huntsville (City)—Madison *AL-2*
Huntsville (City)—Madison *AR-2*
Huntsville (Township)—Schuyler ... *IL-3*
Huntsville (Township)—Reno......... *KS-4*
Huntsville (Township)—Polk *MN-3*
Huntsville (Township)—Randolph ...*MO-3*
Huntsville (Village)—Logan *OH-3*
Huntsville (Town)—Scott................ *TN-2*
Huntsville (City)—Walker............... *TX-2*
Huntsville (Town)—Weber.............. *UT-4*
Hurdland (City)—Knox *MO-3*
Hurdsfield (City)—Wells *ND-4*
Hurlbut (Township)—Logan *IL-3*
Hurley (City)—Stone *MO-3*
Hurley (Township)—Stone *MO-3*
Hurley (Town)—Grant *NM-4*
Hurley (Town)—Ulster *NY-1*
Hurley (Township)—Renville *ND-4*
Hurley (City)—Turner *SD-4*
Hurley (Township)—Turner *SD-4*
Hurley (City)—Iron *WI-3*
Hurlock (Town)—Dorchester......... *MD-1*
Huron (Town)—Fresno *CA-4*
Huron (City)—Atchison *KS-4*
Huron (Township)—Huron *MI-3*
Huron (Township)—Wayne............ *MI-3*
Huron (Town)—Wayne *NY-1*
Huron (Township)—Cavalier......... *ND-4*
Huron (City)—Erie......................... *OH-3*
Huron (Township)—Erie *OH-3*
Huron (City)—Beadle..................... *SD-4*
Huron, Lake (AZ) *Geog-4*
Huron County *MI-3*
Huron County *OH-3*
Huron No. 10 (Township)—
  Pennington *SD-4*
Hurricane (Township)—Fayette *IL-3*
Hurricane (Township)—Carroll *MO-3*
Hurricane (Township)—Lincoln ... *MO-3*
Hurricane (City)—Washington....... *UT-4*
Hurricane (City)—Putnam *WV-2*
Hurst (City)—Williamson *IL-3*
Hurst (City)—Tarrant..................... *TX-2*
Hurstbourne (City)—Jefferson *KY-2*
Hurstbourne Acres (City)—
  Jefferson..................................... *KY-2*
Hurt (Town)—Pittsylvania *VA-2*
Hurtsboro (Town)—Russell............ *AL-2*
Huslia (City)—Yukon-Koyukuk Census
  Area.. *AK-4*
Huss (Township)—Roseau *MN-3*
Hustisford (Town)—Dodge *WI-3*
Hustisford (Village)—Dodge *WI-3*
Hustler (Village)—Juneau *WI-3*
Huston (Township)—Blair *PA-1*
Huston (Township)—Centre *PA-1*
Huston (Township)—Clearfield *PA-1*
Hustonville (City)—Lincoln *KY-2*
Hutchins (City)—Dallas *TX-2*
Hutchins (Town)—Shawano........... *WI-3*
Hutchinson (City)—Reno *KS-4*
Hutchinson (City)—McLeod *MN-3*
Hutchinson (Township)—
  McLeod *MN-3*
Hutchinson County *SD-4*
Hutchinson County *TX-2*

Hutchinson Island South (CDP)—St.
  Lucie *FL-2*
Hutsonville (Township)—
  Crawford *IL-3*
Hutsonville (Village)—Crawford *IL-3*
Huttig (Town)—Union *AR-2*
Hutto (Town)—Williamson............ *TX-2*
Hutton (Township)—Coles............. *IL-3*
Huttonsville (Town)—Randolph... *WV-2*
Hutton Valley (Township)—
  Howell.. *MO-3*
Huxley (City)—Story *IA-3*
Huxley (City)—Shelby *TX-2*
Hyannis (CDP)—Barnstable *MA-1*
Hyannis (Village)—Grant *NE-4*
Hyattsville (City)—Prince
  George's *MD-1*
Hybla Valley (CDP)—Fairfax *VA-2*
Hydaburg (City)—Prince of
  Wales-Outer Ketchikan Census
  Area.. *AK-4*
Hyde (CDP)—Clearfield *PA-1*
Hyde County *NC-2*
Hyde County *SD-4*
Hyden (City)—Leslie..................... *KY-2*
Hyde Park (Township)—
  Wabasha *MN-3*
Hyde Park (Town)—Dutchess......... *NY-1*
Hyde Park (Borough)—
  Westmoreland *PA-1*
Hyde Park (City)—Cache............... *UT-4*
Hyde Park (Town)—Lamoille *VT-1*
Hyde Park (Village)—Lamoille...... *VT-1*
Hyder (CDP)—Prince of Wales-Outer
  Ketchikan Census Area *AK-4*
Hydesville (CDP)—Humboldt *CA-4*
Hydetown (Borough)—Crawford.... *PA-1*
Hydro (Town)—Blaine................... *OK-2*
Hydro (Town)—Caddo................... *OK-2*
Hymera (Town)—Sullivan.............. *IN-3*
Hyndman (Borough)—Bedford....... *PA-1*
Hypoluxo (Town)—Palm Beach *FL-2*
Hyrum (City)—Cache *UT-4*
Hysham (Town)—Treasure *MT-4*
Iaeger (Town)—McDowell *WV-2*
Iatan (Village)—Platte.................... *MO-3*
Iberia (Town)—Miller.................... *MO-3*
Iberia Parish *LA-2*
Iberville Parish *LA-2*
Ibsen (Township)—Richland..........*ND-4*
Ida (Village)—Caddo Parish *LA-2*
Ida (Township)—Monroe *MI-3*
Ida (Township)—Douglas............... *MN-3*
Idabel (City)—McCurtain *OK-2*
Ida County.....................................*IA-3*
Ida Grove (City)—Ida.....................*IA-3*
Idaho (Township)—Mountrail *ND-4*
Idaho City (City)—Boise *ID-4*
Idaho County................................ *ID-4*
Idaho Falls (City)—Bonneville...... *ID-4*
Idaho Panhandle (ID)................. *Geog-4*
Idaho Springs (City)—Clear
  Creek *CO-4*
Idalou (Town)—Lubbock *TX-2*
Idanha (City)—Linn *OR-4*
Idanha (City)—Marion *OR-4*
Ideal (Town)—Macon *GA-2*
Ideal (Township)—Crow Wing *MN-3*
Ideal (Township)—Tripp *SD-4*
Ider (Town)—DeKalb..................... *AL-2*
Idun (Township)—Aitkin *MN-3*
Idyllwild-Pine Cove (CDP)—
  Riverside.................................... *CA-4*
Idylwood (CDP)—Fairfax *VA-2*

Igiugig (CDP)—Lake and Peninsula
  Borough..................................... *AK-4*
Ignacio (Town)—La Plata *CO-4*
Ihlen (City)—Pipestone................. *MN-3*
Ila (City)—Madison........................ *GA-2*
Iliamna (CDP)—Lake and Peninsula
  Borough..................................... *AK-4*
Iliamna Lake (AK)..................... *Geog-4*
Iliff (Town)—Logan *CO-4*
Ilion (Village)—Herkimer *NY-1*
Illilouette Fall (CA)................... *Geog-4*
Illini (Township)—Macon *IL-3*
Illinois (Township)—Nemaha *KS-4*
Illinois (Township)—Rush *KS-4*
Illinois (Township)—Sedgwick.....*KS-4*
Illinois (Township)—Sumner *KS-4*
Illinois (Township)—Nelson *ND-4*
Illinois River (IL)....................... *Geog-4*
Illiopolis (Town)—Sangamon *IL-3*
Illiopolis (Township)—Sangamon ... *IL-3*
Ilwaco (Town)—Pacific *WA-4*
Imbler (City)—Union *OR-4*
Imboden (Town)—Lawrence.......... *AR-2*
Imlay (Township)—Lapeer *MI-3*
Imlay City (City)—Lapeer *MI-3*
Imlay No. 24 (Township)—
  Pennington *SD-4*
Immokalee (CDP)—Collier............*FL-2*
Imogene (City)—Fremont *IA-3*
Impact (Town)—Taylor *TX-2*
Impark (Township)—Benson *ND-4*
Imperial (Town)—Imperial *CA-4*
Imperial (CDP)—Jefferson *MO-3*
Imperial (Township)—Jefferson..... *MO-3*
Imperial (City)—Chase *NE-4*
Imperial Beach (City)—San
  Diego.. *CA-4*
Imperial County *CA-4*
Imperial-Enlow (CDP)—
  Allegheny.................................. *PA-1*
Imperial Valley (CA).................. *Geog-4*
Ina (Village)—Jefferson................. *IL-3*
Inaja-Cosmit Reservation
  (CA)..*IndRes-4*
Inchelium (CDP)—Ferry................ *WA-4*
Incline Village-Crystal Bay (CDP)—
  Washoe...................................... *NV-4*
Independence (City)—Inyo *CA-4*
Independence (Township)—Saline.. *IL-3*
Independence (City)—Buchanan *IA-3*
Independence (Township)—
  Doniphan *KS-4*
Independence (City)—
  Montgomery *KS-4*
Independence (Township)—
  Montgomery *KS-4*
Independence (Township)—
  Osborne...................................... *KS-4*
Independence (Township)—
  Washington *KS-4*
Independence (City)—Kenton *KY-2*
Independence (Town)—Tangipahoa
  Parish *LA-2*
Independence (Township)—
  Oakland *MI-3*
Independence (City)—Hennepin .. *MN-3*
Independence (City)—Clay *MO-3*
Independence (Township)—
  Dunklin *MO-3*
Independence (City)—Jackson *MO-3*
Independence (Township)—
  Macon *MO-3*
Independence (Township)—
  Nodaway *MO-3*

Independence (Township)—
 Schuyler..MO-3
Independence (Township)—
 Warren..NJ-1
Independence (Town)—Allegany...NY-1
Independence (City)—Cuyahoga...OH-3
Independence (Township)—
 Washington.......................................OH-3
Independence (City)—Polk............OR-4
Independence (Township)—
 Beaver..PA-1
Independence (Township)—
 Washington.......................................PA-1
Independence (Township)—Day....SD-4
Independence (Township)—
 Douglas..SD-4
Independence (Pop. Place)—
 Perkins...SD-4
Independence (Town)—Grayson.....VA-2
Independence (City)—
 Trempealeau......................................WI-3
Independence County........................AR-2
Independent (Township)—Barton...KS-4
Independent (Township)—Valley....NE-4
Index (Township)—Cass..................MO-3
Index (Town)—Snohomish..............WA-4
Indiahoma (Town)—Comanche......OK-2
India Hook (CDP)—York..................SC-2
Indialantic (Town)—Brevard...........FL-2
Indian (Township)—Pike.................MO-3
Indiana (Township)—Graham........KS-4
Indiana (Township)—Lincoln.........KS-4
Indiana (Township)—Allegheny......PA-1
Indiana (Borough)—Indiana...........PA-1
Indiana County..................................PA-1
Indianapolis (City)—Marion............IN-3
Indian Beach (Town)—Carteret.....NC-2
Indian Creek (Village)—Dade.........FL-2
Indian Creek (Town)—Lake............IL-3
Indian Creek (Township)—White...IL-3
Indian Creek (Township)—
 Lawrence..IN-3
Indian Creek (Township)—
 Monroe...IN-3
Indian Creek (Township)—
 Pulaski..IN-3
Indian Creek (Township)—
 Anderson...KS-4
Indian Creek (Township)—
 Monroe..MO-3
Indian Creek (Township)—
 Hettinger..ND-4
Indianfields (Township)—Tuscola.MI-3
Indian Grove (Township)—
 Livingston..IL-3
Indian Harbour Beach (City)—
 Brevard...FL-2
Indian Head (Town)—Charles.......MD-1
Indian Head Park (Village)—
 Cook..IL-3
Indian Heights (CDP)—Howard....IN-3
Indian Hills (City)—Jefferson.........KY-2
Indian Hills (CDP)—Douglas.........NV-4
Indian Hills Cherokee Section (City)—
 Jefferson...KY-2
Indian Lake (Township)—
 Nobles...MN-3
Indian Lake (Town)—Hamilton.....NY-1
Indian Lake (Borough)—Somerset..PA-1
Indian Lake (Town)—Cameron......TX-2
Indianola (Village)—Vermilion........IL-3
Indianola (City)—Warren.................IA-3
Indianola (City)—Sunflower...........MS-2
Indianola (City)—Red Willow........NE-4
Indianola (Town)—Pittsburg..........OK-2

Indianola (CDP)—Kitsap................WA-4
Indian Point (Township)—Knox....IL-3
Indian Point (Village)—Stone.......MO-3
Indian Prairie (Township)—
 Wayne...IL-3
Indian River County........................FL-2
Indian River Estates (CDP)—St.
 Lucie...FL-2
Indian River Shores (Town)—Indian
 River...FL-2
Indian Rocks Beach (City)—
 Pinellas..FL-2
Indian Shores (Town)—Pinellas....FL-2
Indian Springs (CDP)—Catoosa....GA-2
Indian Springs (CDP)—Clark........NV-4
Indiantown (CDP)—Martin.............FL-2
Indiantown (Township)—Bureau...IL-3
Indian Township Reservation
 (ME)..IndRes-4
Indian Trail (Town)—Union............NC-2
Indian Village (Town)—St.
 Joseph...IN-3
Indian Wells (City)—Riverside......CA-4
Indio (City)—Riverside...................CA-4
Industrial (Township)—St. Louis..MN-3
Industry (City)—Los Angeles.......CA-4
Industry (Town)—McDonough......IL-3
Industry (Township)—
 McDonough.......................................IL-3
Industry (Town)—Franklin.............ME-1
Industry (Borough)—Beaver...........PA-1
Industry-Rock Falls (Township)—
 Phelps...NE-4
Inez (City)—Martin...........................KY-2
Inez (CDP)—Victoria........................TX-2
Ingalls (Town)—Madison.................IN-3
Ingalls (City)—Gray..........................KS-4
Ingalls (Township)—Gray...............KS-4
Ingalls Park (CDP)—Will..................IL-3
Ingallston (Township)—
 Menominee..MI-3
Ingersoll (Township)—Midland.....MI-3
Ingham (Township)—Ingham........MI-3
Ingham County.................................MI-3
Ingleside (City)—San Patricio........TX-2
Inglewood (City)—Los Angeles....CA-4
Inglewood (Village)—Dodge..........NE-4
Inglewood-Finn Hill (CDP)—
 King..WA-4
Inglis (Town)—Levy...........................FL-2
Ingram (Borough)—Allegheny........PA-1
Ingram (Village)—Kerr.....................TX-2
Ingram (Village)—Rusk....................WI-3
Inguadona (Township)—Cass......MN-3
Inkom (City)—Bannock....................ID-4
Inkster (City)—Wayne.....................MI-3
Inkster (City)—Grand Forks..........ND-4
Inkster (Township)—Grand
 Forks..ND-4
Inland (Township)—Benzie............MI-3
Inland (Township)—Clay................NE-4
Inlet (Town)—Hamilton...................NY-1
Inman (City)—McPherson..............KS-4
Inman (Township)—Otter Tail.....MN-3
Inman (Township)—Holt................NE-4
Inman (Village)—Holt.....................NE-4
Inman (City)—Spartanburg............SC-2
Inman Mills (CDP)—
 Spartanburg.....................................SC-2
Inniswold (CDP)—East Baton Rouge
 Parish...LA-2
Inola (Town)—Rogers......................OK-2
Interior (Township)—Ontonagon...MI-3
Interior (Township)—Jackson.......SD-4
Interior (Township)—Jackson.......SD-4

Interlachen (Town)—Putnam..........FL-2
Interlaken (CDP)—Santa Cruz......CA-4
Interlaken (Borough)—
 Monmouth...NJ-1
Interlaken (Village)—Seneca..........NY-1
International Falls (City)—
 Koochiching....................................MN-3
Inver Grove Heights (City)—
 Dakota..MN-3
Inverness (Division)—Shelby.........AL-2
Inverness (CDP)—Marin.................CA-4
Inverness (City)—Citrus..................FL-2
Inverness (Town)—Cook..................IL-3
Inverness (Township)—
 Cheboygan..MI-3
Inverness (Town)—Sunflower.......MS-2
Inwood (CDP)—Polk........................FL-2
Inwood (City)—Lyon.........................IA-3
Inwood (Township)—Schoolcraft..MI-3
Inwood (CDP)—Nassau..................NY-1
Inwood (CDP)—Berkeley...............WV-2
Inyo County.......................................CA-4
Iola (Village)—Clay............................IL-3
Iola (City)—Allen...............................KS-4
Iola (Township)—Allen....................KS-4
Iola (Town)—Waupaca....................WI-3
Iola (Village)—Waupaca..................WI-3
Iona (CDP)—Lee................................FL-2
Iona (City)—Bonneville.....................ID-4
Iona (City)—Murray........................MN-3
Iona (Township)—Murray..............MN-3
Iona (Township)—Todd..................MN-3
Iona (Township)—Lyman................SD-4
Ione (City)—Amador.......................CA-4
Ione (City)—Morrow........................OR-4
Ione (Town)—Pend Oreille............WA-4
Ionia (City)—Chickasaw...................IA-3
Ionia (Township)—Jewell................KS-4
Ionia (City)—Ionia.............................MI-3
Ionia (Township)—Ionia..................MI-3
Ionia (Town)—Benton.....................MO-3
Ionia (Town)—Pettis.......................MO-3
Ionia County......................................MI-3
Iosco (Township)—Livingston.......MI-3
Iosco (Township)—Waseca..........MN-3
Iosco (Township)—Stutsman........ND-4
Iosco County......................................MI-3
Iota (Town)—Acadia Parish...........LA-2
Iota Flat (Township)—Ward..........ND-4
Iowa (Township)—Doniphan.........KS-4
Iowa (Township)—Sherman..........KS-4
Iowa (Town)—Calcasieu Parish....LA-2
Iowa (Township)—Holt...................NE-4
Iowa (Township)—Benson.............ND-4
Iowa (Township)—Beadle...............SD-4
Iowa (Township)—Douglas............SD-4
Iowa City (City)—Johnson...............IA-3
Iowa Colony (Village)—Brazoria....TX-2
Iowa County.......................................IA-3
Iowa County......................................WI-3
Iowa Falls (City)—Hardin................IA-3
Iowa Park (Town)—Wichita...........TX-2
Iowa Reservation (KS).............IndRes-4
Iowa-Sac and Fox Joint Area TJSA
 (OK)..IndRes-4
Iowa Tribe TJSA (OK)...............IndRes-4
Ipava (Village)—Fulton.....................IL-3
Ipswich (Town)—Essex..................MA-1
Ipswich (City)—Edmunds...............SD-4
Ipswich (Township)—Edmunds....SD-4
Ira (Township)—St. Clair.................MI-3
Ira (Town)—Cayuga.........................NY-1
Ira (Town)—Rutland.........................VT-1
Iraan (City)—Pecos..........................TX-2
Irasburg (Town)—Orleans..............VT-1

General Index
American Places Dictionary

Iredell (City)—Bosque.................. *TX-2*
Iredell County.............................. *NC-2*
Irene (Town)—Clay *SD-4*
Irene (Town)—Turner...................... *SD-4*
Irene (Town)—Yankton.................... *SD-4*
Ireton (City)—Sioux *IA-3*
Irion County *TX-2*
Irishtown (Township)—Clinton *IL-3*
Irmo (Town)—Lexington.................. *SC-2*
Irmo (Town)—Richland..................... *SC-2*
Iron (Township)—Iron *MO-3*
Iron (Township)—St. Francois...... *MO-3*
Iron City (Town)—Seminole........... *GA-2*
Iron City (City)—Lawrence *TN-2*
Iron City (City)—Wayne *TN-2*
Iron County *MI-3*
Iron County *MO-3*
Iron County *UT-4*
Iron County *WI-3*
Irondale (City)—Jefferson................ *AL-2*
Irondale (CDP)—Clayton *GA-2*
Irondale (Township)—Crow Wing.. *MN-3*
Irondale (City)—Washington *MO-3*
Irondale (Village)—Jefferson *OH-3*
Irondequoit (Town)—Monroe *NY-1*
Iron Gate (Town)—Alleghany *VA-2*
Iron Gates (Village)—Jasper *MO-3*
Iron Junction (City)—St. Louis *MN-3*
Iron Mountain (City)—Dickinson... *MI-3*
Iron Mountain Lake (City)—St. Francois *MO-3*
Iron Range (Township)—Itasca *MN-3*
Iron Ridge (Village)—Dodge *WI-3*
Iron River (City)—Iron *MI-3*
Iron River (Township)—Iron *MI-3*
Iron River (Town)—Bayfield *WI-3*
Ironton (City)—Crow Wing *MN-3*
Ironton (City)—Iron *MO-3*
Ironton (City)—Lawrence *OH-3*
Ironton (Town)—Sauk..................... *WI-3*
Ironton (Village)—Sauk..................... *WI-3*
Ironwood (City)—Gogebic *MI-3*
Ironwood (Township)—Gogebic *MI-3*
Iroquois (Town)—Iroquois............... *IL-3*
Iroquois (Township)—Iroquois....... *IL-3*
Iroquois (Township)—Newton........ *IN-3*
Iroquois (City)—Beadle.................... *SD-4*
Iroquois (City)—Kingsbury............. *SD-4*
Iroquois (Township)—Kingsbury... *SD-4*
Iroquois County *IL-3*
Iroquois Point (CDP)—Honolulu... *HI-4*
Irrigon (City)—Morrow *OR-4*
Irvine (City)—Orange........................ *CA-4*
Irvine (City)—Estill........................... *KY-2*
Irvine (Township)—Benson *ND-4*
Irving (Town)—Montgomery *IL-3*
Irving (Township)—Montgomery ... *IL-3*
Irving (Township)—Brown............... *KS-4*
Irving (Township)—Barry *MI-3*
Irving (Township)—Kandiyohi *MN-3*
Irving (Township)—Faulk *SD-4*
Irving (City)—Dallas........................ *TX-2*
Irving (Town)—Jackson................... *WI-3*
Irvington (Town)—Washington *IL-3*
Irvington (Township)—Washington *IL-3*
Irvington (City)—Breckinridge *KY-2*
Irvington (Township)—Essex *NJ-1*
Irvington (Village)—Westchester ... *NY-1*
Irvington (Town)—Lancaster *VA-2*
Irvona (Borough)—Clearfield......... *PA-1*
Irwin (City)—Bonneville................... *ID-4*
Irwin (Village)—Kankakee *IL-3*

Irwin (City)—Shelby.......................... *IA-3*
Irwin (Township)—Venango *PA-1*
Irwin (Borough)—Westmoreland *PA-1*
Irwin (CDP)—Lancaster *SC-2*
Irwin (Township)—Tripp *SD-4*
Irwin County *GA-2*
Irwindale (City)—Los Angeles *CA-4*
Irwinton (Town)—Wilkinson........... *GA-2*
Isabel (Township)—Fulton *IL-3*
Isabel (City)—Barber........................ *KS-4*
Isabel (Township)—Benson............ *ND-4*
Isabel (City)—Dewey........................ *SD-4*
Isabella (Township)—Isabella *MI-3*
Isabella County *MI-3*
Isabella Reservation & Trust Lands (MI) *IndRes-4*
Isabelle (Town)—Pierce.................... *WI-3*
Isanti (City)—Isanti......................... *MN-3*
Isanti (Township)—Isanti............... *MN-3*
Isanti County *MN-3*
Isbel (Township)—Scott *KS-4*
Ischua (Town)—Cattaraugus *NY-1*
Iselin (CDP)—Middlesex *NJ-1*
Ishpeming (City)—Marquette *MI-3*
Ishpeming (Township)—Marquette..................................... *MI-3*
Islamorada (CDP)—Monroe *FL-2*
Island (City)—McLean..................... *KY-2*
Island City (Town)—Union *OR-4*
Island County *WA-4*
Island Creek (Township)—Jefferson... *OH-3*
Island Falls (Town)—Aroostook ... *ME-1*
Island Grove (Township)—Sangamon... *IL-3*
Island Grove (Township)—Gage ... *NE-4*
Island Heights (Borough)—Ocean .. *NJ-1*
Islandia (City)—Dade *FL-2*
Islandia (Village)—Suffolk *NY-1*
Island Lake (Town)—Lake *IL-3*
Island Lake (Town)—McHenry *IL-3*
Island Lake (Township)—Lyon *MN-3*
Island Lake (Township)—Mahnomen..................................... *MN-3*
Island Park (City)—Fremont *ID-4*
Island Park (Village)—Nassau *NY-1*
Island Park (Township)—Ransom.. *ND-4*
Island Pond (CDP)—Essex *VT-1*
Island View (City)—Koochiching...................................... *MN-3*
Isla Vista (CDP)—Santa Barbara .. *CA-4*
Isle (City)—Mille Lacs *MN-3*
Isle au Haut (Town)—Knox........... *ME-1*
Isle Harbor (Township)—Mille Lacs *MN-3*
Isle La Motte (Town)—Grand Isle.. *VT-1*
Isle of Hope-Dutch Island (CDP)—Chatham.. *GA-2*
Isle of Palms (City)—Charleston *SC-2*
Isle of Wight County..................... *VA-2*
Isle Royale (MI) *Geog-4*
Islesboro (Town)—Waldo *ME-1*
Isleta Pueblo (NM) *IndRes-4*
Isleta Pueblo (CDP)—Bernalillo ... *NM-4*
Isleta Pueblo (CDP)—Valencia *NM-4*
Isleton (City)—Sacramento *CA-4*
Isley (Township)—Ransom............. *ND-4*
Islip (Town)—Suffolk *NY-1*
Islip Terrace (CDP)—Suffolk.......... *NY-1*
Ismay (Town)—Custer *MT-4*
Isola (Town)—Humphreys *MS-2*
Israel (Township)—Preble................*OH-3*
Issaquah (City)—King...................... *WA-4*

Issaquena County *MS-2*
Italy (Town)—Yates.......................... *NY-1*
Italy (Town)—Ellis........................... *TX-2*
Itasca (City)—DuPage *IL-3*
Itasca (Township)—Sherman *KS-4*
Itasca (Township)—Clearwater *MN-3*
Itasca (City)—Hill *TX-2*
Itasca County *MN-3*
Itawamba County *MS-2*
Ithaca (City)—Gratiot *MI-3*
Ithaca (Village)—Saunders *NE-4*
Ithaca (City)—Tompkins.................. *NY-1*
Ithaca (Town)—Tompkins............... *NY-1*
Ithaca (Village)—Darke....................*OH-3*
Ithaca (Town)—Richland *WI-3*
Itta Bena (City)—Leflore *MS-2*
Iuka (Town)—Marion *IL-3*
Iuka (Township)—Marion *IL-3*
Iuka (City)—Pratt............................ *KS-4*
Iuka (City)—Tishomingo *MS-2*
Iva (Town)—Anderson *SC-2*
Ivanhoe (CDP)—Tulare *CA-4*
Ivanhoe (Township)—Finney......... *KS-4*
Ivanhoe (City)—Lincoln *MN-3*
Ivanhoe (Township)—Renville *ND-4*
Ivanof Bay (CDP)—Lake and Peninsula Borough.. *AK-4*
Ivesdale (Village)—Champaign *IL-3*
Ivesdale (Village)—Piatt................... *IL-3*
Ives Estates (CDP)—Dade *FL-2*
Ivey (Town)—Wilkinson *GA-2*
Ivins (Town)—Washington.............. *UT-4*
Ivor (Town)—Southampton *VA-2*
Ivy (Township)—Lyon...................... *KS-4*
Ivyland (Borough)—Bucks............... *PA-1*
Ixonia (Town)—Jefferson................. *WI-3*
Izard County.................................... *AR-2*
Jacinto City (City)—Harris *TX-2*
Jack County *TX-2*
Jackman (Town)—Somerset........... *ME-1*
Jacksboro (Town)—Campbell *TN-2*
Jacksboro (City)—Jack.................... *TX-2*
Jackson (City)—Clarke....................*AL-2*
Jackson (City)—Amador *CA-4*
Jackson (City)—Butts...................... *GA-2*
Jackson (Township)—Effingham *IL-3*
Jackson (Township)—Will............... *IL-3*
Jackson (Township)—Allen............. *IN-3*
Jackson (Township)—Bartholomew................................. *IN-3*
Jackson (Township)—Blackford...... *IN-3*
Jackson (Township)—Boone *IN-3*
Jackson (Township)—Brown........... *IN-3*
Jackson (Township)—Carroll *IN-3*
Jackson (Township)—Cass *IN-3*
Jackson (Township)—Clay *IN-3*
Jackson (Township)—Clinton *IN-3*
Jackson (Township)—Dearborn *IN-3*
Jackson (Township)—Decatur *IN-3*
Jackson (Township)—Dekalb *IN-3*
Jackson (Township)—Dubois......... *IN-3*
Jackson (Township)—Elkhart *IN-3*
Jackson (Township)—Fayette......... *IN-3*
Jackson (Township)—Fountain *IN-3*
Jackson (Township)—Greene *IN-3*
Jackson (Township)—Hamilton *IN-3*
Jackson (Township)—Hancock *IN-3*
Jackson (Township)—Harrison *IN-3*
Jackson (Township)—Howard *IN-3*
Jackson (Township)—Huntington... *IN-3*
Jackson (Township)—Jackson *IN-3*
Jackson (Township)—Jay *IN-3*
Jackson (Township)—Kosciusko ... *IN-3*
Jackson (Township)—Madison *IN-3*
Jackson (Township)—Miami.......... *IN-3*

American Places Dictionary   General Index

Jackson (Township)—Morgan......... *IN-3*
Jackson (Township)—Newton......... *IN-3*
Jackson (Township)—Orange.......... *IN-3*
Jackson (Township)—Owen *IN-3*
Jackson (Township)—Parke *IN-3*
Jackson (Township)—Porter *IN-3*
Jackson (Township)—Putnam *IN-3*
Jackson (Township)—Randolph *IN-3*
Jackson (Township)—Ripley........... *IN-3*
Jackson (Township)—Rush *IN-3*
Jackson (Township)—Shelby........... *IN-3*
Jackson (Township)—Spencer *IN-3*
Jackson (Township)—Starke *IN-3*
Jackson (Township)—Steuben *IN-3*
Jackson (Township)—Sullivan *IN-3*
Jackson (Township)—Tippecanoe... *IN-3*
Jackson (Township)—Washington .. *IN-3*
Jackson (Township)—Wayne........... *IN-3*
Jackson (Township)—Wells............. *IN-3*
Jackson (Township)—White............ *IN-3*
Jackson (Township)—Anderson...... *KS-4*
Jackson (Township)—Edwards *KS-4*
Jackson (Township)—Geary............ *KS-4*
Jackson (Township)—Jewell............ *KS-4*
Jackson (Township)—Lyon *KS-4*
Jackson (Township)—McPherson ... *KS-4*
Jackson (Township)—Osborne........ *KS-4*
Jackson (Township)—Riley............. *KS-4*
Jackson (Township)—Sumner......... *KS-4*
Jackson (City)—Breathitt................ *KY-2*
Jackson (Town)—East Feliciana
   Parish.. *LA-2*
Jackson (Town)—Waldo................. *ME-1*
Jackson (City)—Jackson.................. *MI-3*
Jackson (City)—Jackson.................. *MN-3*
Jackson (Township)—Scott *MN-3*
Jackson (City)—Hinds *MS-2*
Jackson (City)—Madison *MS-2*
Jackson (City)—Rankin................... *MS-2*
Jackson (Township)—Andrew........ *MO-3*
Jackson (Township)—Buchanan *MO-3*
Jackson (Township)—Callaway...... *MO-3*
Jackson (Township)—Camden....... *MO-3*
Jackson (City)—Cape Girardeau ... *MO-3*
Jackson (Township)—Carter *MO-3*
Jackson (Township)—Clark............ *MO-3*
Jackson (Township)—Clinton *MO-3*
Jackson (Township)—Dallas *MO-3*
Jackson (Township)—Daviess........ *MO-3*
Jackson (Township)—Douglas *MO-3*
Jackson (Township)—Gentry *MO-3*
Jackson (Township)—Grundy........ *MO-3*
Jackson (Township)—Jasper *MO-3*
Jackson (Township)—Johnson *MO-3*
Jackson (Township)—Linn............. *MO-3*
Jackson (Township)—Livingston .. *MO-3*
Jackson (Township)—Macon *MO-3*
Jackson (Township)—Maries *MO-3*
Jackson (Township)—Monroe........ *MO-3*
Jackson (Township)—Nodaway *MO-3*
Jackson (Township)—Osage........... *MO-3*
Jackson (Township)—Ozark........... *MO-3*
Jackson (Township)—Polk.............. *MO-3*
Jackson (Township)—Putnam........ *MO-3*
Jackson (Township)—Randolph ... *MO-3*
Jackson (Township)—Reynolds *MO-3*
Jackson (Township)—Shannon *MO-3*
Jackson (Township)—Shelby.......... *MO-3*
Jackson (Township)—St. Clair....... *MO-3*
Jackson (Township)—Ste.
   Genevieve *MO-3*
Jackson (Township)—Sullivan *MO-3*
Jackson (Township)—Texas *MO-3*
Jackson (Township)—Webster *MO-3*
Jackson (Village)—Dakota *NE-4*
Jackson (Township)—Hall *NE-4*
Jackson (Town)—Carroll................ *NH-1*
Jackson (Township)—Ocean *NJ-1*
Jackson (Town)—Washington *NY-1*
Jackson (Town)—Northampton *NC-2*
Jackson (Township)—Sargent *ND-4*
Jackson (Township)—Allen *OH-3*
Jackson (Township)—Ashland *OH-3*
Jackson (Township)—Auglaize...... *OH-3*
Jackson (Township)—Brown.......... *OH-3*
Jackson (Township)—
   Champaign.................................... *OH-3*
Jackson (Township)—Clermont *OH-3*
Jackson (Township)—Coshocton ... *OH-3*
Jackson (Township)—Crawford..... *OH-3*
Jackson (Township)—Darke *OH-3*
Jackson (Township)—Franklin *OH-3*
Jackson (Township)—Guernsey.... *OH-3*
Jackson (Township)—Hancock *OH-3*
Jackson (Township)—Hardin......... *OH-3*
Jackson (Township)—Highland *OH-3*
Jackson (City)—Jackson.................. *OH-3*
Jackson (Township)—Jackson........ *OH-3*
Jackson (Township)—Knox *OH-3*
Jackson (Township)—Mahoning.... *OH-3*
Jackson (Township)—Monroe....... *OH-3*
Jackson (Township)—
   Montgomery *OH-3*
Jackson (Township)—
   Muskingum *OH-3*
Jackson (Township)—Noble........... *OH-3*
Jackson (Township)—Paulding...... *OH-3*
Jackson (Township)—Perry............ *OH-3*
Jackson (Township)—Pickaway *OH-3*
Jackson (Township)—Pike............. *OH-3*
Jackson (Township)—Preble *OH-3*
Jackson (Township)—Putnam *OH-3*
Jackson (Township)—Richland...... *OH-3*
Jackson (Township)—Sandusky..... *OH-3*
Jackson (Township)—Seneca *OH-3*
Jackson (Township)—Shelby......... *OH-3*
Jackson (Township)—Stark *OH-3*
Jackson (Township)—Union *OH-3*
Jackson (Township)—Van Wert *OH-3*
Jackson (Township)—Vinton......... *OH-3*
Jackson (Township)—Wood *OH-3*
Jackson (Township)—Wyandot...... *OH-3*
Jackson (Township)—Butler *PA-1*
Jackson (Township)—Cambria *PA-1*
Jackson (Township)—Columbia *PA-1*
Jackson (Township)—Dauphin *PA-1*
Jackson (Township)—Greene........ *PA-1*
Jackson (Township)—Huntingdon.. *PA-1*
Jackson (Township)—Lebanon *PA-1*
Jackson (Township)—Luzerne *PA-1*
Jackson (Township)—Lycoming...... *PA-1*
Jackson (Township)—Mercer *PA-1*
Jackson (Township)—Monroe....... *PA-1*
Jackson (Township)—
   Northumberland *PA-1*
Jackson (Township)—Perry............ *PA-1*
Jackson (Township)—Snyder *PA-1*
Jackson (Township)—
   Susquehanna *PA-1*
Jackson (Township)—Tioga *PA-1*
Jackson (Township)—Venango *PA-1*
Jackson (Township)—York............. *PA-1*
Jackson (Town)—Aiken.................. *SC-2*
Jackson (Township)—Charles
   Mix *SD-4*
Jackson (Township)—Sanborn *SD-4*
Jackson (City)—Madison *TN-2*
Jackson (Town)—Adams *WI-3*
Jackson (Town)—Burnett *WI-3*
Jackson (Town)—Washington *WI-3*
Jackson (Village)—Washington...... *WI-3*
Jackson (Town)—Teton................... *WY-4*
Jacksonburg (Village)—Butler........ *OH-3*
Jackson Center (Village)—Shelby .. *OH-3*
Jackson Center (Borough)—
   Mercer.. *PA-1*
Jackson County *AL-2*
Jackson County *AR-2*
Jackson County *CO-4*
Jackson County *FL-2*
Jackson County *GA-2*
Jackson County *IL-3*
Jackson County *IN-3*
Jackson County *IA-3*
Jackson County *KS-4*
Jackson County *KY-2*
Jackson County *MI-3*
Jackson County *MN-3*
Jackson County *MS-2*
Jackson County *MO-3*
Jackson County *NC-2*
Jackson County *OH-3*
Jackson County *OK-2*
Jackson County *OR-4*
Jackson County *SD-4*
Jackson County *TN-2*
Jackson County *TX-2*
Jackson County *WV-4*
Jackson County *WI-3*
Jackson Heights—Queens *NY-1*
Jackson Junction (City)—
   Winneshiek *IA-3*
Jackson No. 1 (Township)—
   Greene.. *MO-3*
Jackson No. 2 (Township)—
   Greene.. *MO-3*
Jackson Parish *LA-2*
Jacksonport (Town)—Jackson........ *AR-2*
Jacksonport (Town)—Door *WI-3*
Jackson Rancheria (CA) *IndRes-4*
Jacksons' Gap (Municipality)—
   Tallapoosa *AL-2*
Jacksonville (City)—Calhoun......... *AL-2*
Jacksonville (City)—Pulaski........... *AR-2*
Jacksonville (City)—Duval............. *FL-2*
Jacksonville (Town)—Telfair.......... *GA-2*
Jacksonville (City)—Morgan........... *IL-3*
Jacksonville (Village)—
   Randolph *MO-3*
Jacksonville (City)—Onslow *NC-2*
Jacksonville (Village)—Athens....... *OH-3*
Jacksonville (City)—Jackson.......... *OR-4*
Jacksonville (Borough)—Indiana *PA-1*
Jacksonville (City)—Cherokee *TX-2*
Jacksonville (Village)—Windham .. *VT-1*
Jacksonville Beach (City)—Duval .. *FL-2*
Jacksonville Naval Air Station
   (FL) *Mil-4*
Jacob City (City)—Jackson *FL-2*
Jacobs (Town)—Ashland................ *WI-3*
Jacobus (Borough)—York............... *PA-1*
Jaconita (CDP)—Santa Fe *NM-4*
Jadis (Township)—Roseau *MN-3*
Jaffrey (Town)—Cheshire............... *NH-1*
Jakin (Town)—Early....................... *GA-2*
Jakolof Bay (CDP)—Kenai Peninsula
   Borough... *AK-4*
Jal (City)—Lea................................. *NM-4*
Jamaica (Township)—Vermilion..... *IL-3*
Jamaica (City)—Guthrie *IA-3*
Jamaica (Town)—Windham........... *VT-1*
Jamaica Beach (Village)—
   Galveston *TX-2*
Jamaica Plain—Suffolk *MA-1*

General Index

Jamaica Plain *See* **Boston**—
  Suffolk *MA-1*
James (Township)—Saginaw *MI-3*
James Bayou (Township)—
  Mississippi *MO-3*
Jamesburg (Borough)—Middlesex .. *NJ-1*
James City (CDP)—Craven *NC-2*
James City County *VA-2*
James Hill (Township)—
  Mountrail *ND-4*
Jameson (Town)—Daviess *MO-3*
Jamesport (City)—Daviess *MO-3*
Jamesport (Township)—Daviess ... *MO-3*
Jamesport (CDP)—Suffolk *NY-1*
James River (VA) *Geog-4*
James River Valley (Township)—
  Dickey *ND-4*
Jamestown (CDP)—Tuolumne *CA-4*
Jamestown (Town)—Boulder *CO-4*
Jamestown (Town)—Boone *IN-3*
Jamestown (Town)—Hendricks *IN-3*
Jamestown (Township)—Steuben ... *IN-3*
Jamestown (City)—Cloud *KS-4*
Jamestown (City)—Russell *KY-2*
Jamestown (Village)—Bienville
  Parish *LA-2*
Jamestown (Township)—Ottawa ... *MI-3*
Jamestown (Township)—Blue
  Earth *MN-3*
Jamestown (Town)—Moniteau *MO-3*
Jamestown (City)—Chautauqua *NY-1*
Jamestown (Town)—Guilford *NC-2*
Jamestown (City)—Stutsman *ND-4*
Jamestown (Village)—Greene *OH-3*
Jamestown (Town)—Rogers *OK-2*
Jamestown (Borough)—Mercer *PA-1*
Jamestown (Town)—Newport *RI-1*
Jamestown (Town)—Berkeley *SC-2*
Jamestown (City)—Fentress *TN-2*
Jamestown (Town)—Grant *WI-3*
Jamestown Klallam Res. & Trust Lands
  (WA) *IndRes-4*
Jamestown West (CDP)—
  Chautauqua *NY-1*
Jamesville (Town)—Martin *NC-2*
Jamesville (Township)—Yankton ... *SD-4*
Jamul (CDP)—San Diego *CA-4*
Jamul Village (CA) *IndRes-4*
Jane Lew (Town)—Lewis *WV-2*
Janesville (City)—Black Hawk *IA-3*
Janesville (City)—Bremer *IA-3*
Janesville (Township)—
  Greenwood *KS-4*
Janesville (City)—Waseca *MN-3*
Janesville (Township)—Waseca *MN-3*
Janesville (City)—Rock *WI-3*
Janesville (Tdn)—Rock *WI-3*
Janette Lake (Pop. Place)—St.
  Louis *MN-3*
Janke (Township)—Logan *ND-4*
Jan Phyl Village (CDP)—Polk *FL-2*
Jansen (Village)—Jefferson *NE-4*
Jaqua (Township)—Cheyenne *KS-4*
Jarratt (Town)—Greensville *VA-2*
Jarratt (Town)—Sussex *VA-2*
Jarrettsville (CDP)—Harford *MD-1*
Jarvis (Township)—Madison *IL-3*
Jasmine Estates (CDP)—Pasco *FL-2*
Jasonville (City)—Greene *IN-3*
Jasper (City)—Walker *AL-2*
Jasper (City)—Newton *AR-2*
Jasper (City)—Hamilton *FL-2*
Jasper (City)—Pickens *GA-2*
Jasper (Township)—Wayne *IL-3*
Jasper (City)—Dubois *IN-3*

Jasper (Township)—Midland *MI-3*
Jasper (City)—Pipestone *MN-3*
Jasper (City)—Rock *MN-3*
Jasper (Township)—Camden *MO-3*
Jasper (Township)—Dallas *MO-3*
Jasper (City)—Jasper *MO-3*
Jasper (Township)—Jasper *MO-3*
Jasper (Township)—Ozark *MO-3*
Jasper (Township)—Ralls *MO-3*
Jasper (Township)—Taney *MO-3*
Jasper (Town)—Steuben *NY-1*
Jasper (Township)—Fayette *OH-3*
Jasper (Township)—Hanson *SD-4*
Jasper (Town)—Marion *TN-2*
Jasper (City)—Jasper *TX-2*
Jasper County *GA-2*
Jasper County *IL-3*
Jasper County *IN-3*
Jasper County *IA-3*
Jasper County *MS-2*
Jasper County *MO-3*
Jasper County *SC-2*
Jasper County *TX-2*
Java (Town)—Wyoming *NY-1*
Java (City)—Walworth *SD-4*
Jay (Town)—Santa Rosa *FL-2*
Jay (Town)—Franklin *ME-1*
Jay (Township)—Martin *MN-3*
Jay (Town)—Essex *NY-1*
Jay (Town)—Delaware *OK-2*
Jay (Township)—Elk *PA-1*
Jay (Town)—Orleans *VT-1*
Jay County *IN-3*
Jayton (Town)—Kent *TX-2*
Jeanerette (City)—Iberia Parish *LA-2*
Jean Lafitte (Town)—Jefferson
  Parish *LA-2*
Jeannette (City)—Westmoreland *PA-1*
Jeddo (Township)—Knox *MO-3*
Jeddo (Borough)—Luzerne *PA-1*
Jeff (Township)—Oregon *MO-3*
Jeff Davis County *GA-2*
Jeff Davis County *TX-2*
Jeffers (City)—Cottonwood *MN-3*
Jefferson (City)—Jackson *GA-2*
Jefferson (Township)—
  Stephenson *IL-3*
Jefferson (Township)—Adams *IN-3*
Jefferson (Township)—Allen *IN-3*
Jefferson (Township)—Boone *IN-3*
Jefferson (Township)—Carroll *IN-3*
Jefferson (Township)—Cass *IN-3*
Jefferson (Township)—Dubois *IN-3*
Jefferson (Township)—Elkhart *IN-3*
Jefferson (Township)—Grant *IN-3*
Jefferson (Township)—Greene *IN-3*
Jefferson (Township)—Henry *IN-3*
Jefferson (Township)—
  Huntington *IN-3*
Jefferson (Township)—Jay *IN-3*
Jefferson (Township)—Kosciusko ... *IN-3*
Jefferson (Township)—Miami *IN-3*
Jefferson (Township)—Morgan *IN-3*
Jefferson (Township)—Newton *IN-3*
Jefferson (Township)—Noble *IN-3*
Jefferson (Township)—Owen *IN-3*
Jefferson (Township)—Pike *IN-3*
Jefferson (Township)—Pulaski *IN-3*
Jefferson (Township)—Putnam *IN-3*
Jefferson (Township)—Sullivan *IN-3*
Jefferson (Township)—
  Switzerland *IN-3*
Jefferson (Township)—Tipton *IN-3*
Jefferson (Township)—
  Washington *IN-3*

Jefferson (Township)—Wayne *IN-3*
Jefferson (Township)—Wells *IN-3*
Jefferson (Township)—Whitley *IN-3*
Jefferson (City)—Greene *IA-3*
Jefferson (Township)—
  Chautauqua *KS-4*
Jefferson (Township)—Dickinson ... *KS-4*
Jefferson (Township)—Geary *KS-4*
Jefferson (Township)—Jackson *KS-4*
Jefferson (Township)—Rawlins *KS-4*
Jefferson (Township)—Republic ... *KS-4*
Jefferson (CDP)—Jefferson
  Parish *LA-2*
Jefferson (Town)—Lincoln *ME-1*
Jefferson (Township)—Cass *MI-3*
Jefferson (Township)—Hillsdale ... *MI-3*
Jefferson (Township)—Houston ... *MN-3*
Jefferson (Township)—Andrew *MO-3*
Jefferson (Township)—Cedar *MO-3*
Jefferson (Township)—Clark *MO-3*
Jefferson (Township)—Cole *MO-3*
Jefferson (Township)—Daviess *MO-3*
Jefferson (Township)—Grundy *MO-3*
Jefferson (Township)—Harrison ... *MO-3*
Jefferson (Township)—Johnson ... *MO-3*
Jefferson (Township)—Linn *MO-3*
Jefferson (Township)—Maries *MO-3*
Jefferson (Township)—Monroe *MO-3*
Jefferson (Township)—Nodaway .. *MO-3*
Jefferson (Township)—Osage *MO-3*
Jefferson (Township)—Polk *MO-3*
Jefferson (Township)—Scotland ... *MO-3*
Jefferson (Township)—Shelby *MO-3*
Jefferson (Township)—St. Louis ... *MO-3*
Jefferson (Township)—Wayne *MO-3*
Jefferson (Township)—Knox *NE-4*
Jefferson (Town)—Coos *NH-1*
Jefferson (Township)—Morris *NJ-1*
Jefferson (Town)—Schoharie *NY-1*
Jefferson (Town)—Ashe *NC-2*
Jefferson (Township)—Pierce *ND-4*
Jefferson (Township)—Adams *OH-3*
Jefferson (Township)—Ashtabula .. *OH-3*
Jefferson (Village)—Ashtabula *OH-3*
Jefferson (Township)—Brown *OH-3*
Jefferson (Township)—Clinton *OH-3*
Jefferson (Township)—
  Coshocton *OH-3*
Jefferson (Township)—Crawford ... *OH-3*
Jefferson (Township)—Fayette *OH-3*
Jefferson (Township)—Franklin ... *OH-3*
Jefferson (Township)—Greene *OH-3*
Jefferson (Township)—Guernsey ... *OH-3*
Jefferson (Township)—Jackson *OH-3*
Jefferson (Township)—Knox *OH-3*
Jefferson (Township)—Logan *OH-3*
Jefferson (Township)—Madison ... *OH-3*
Jefferson (Village)—Madison *OH-3*
Jefferson (Township)—Mercer *OH-3*
Jefferson (Township)—
  Montgomery *OH-3*
Jefferson (Township)—
  Muskingum *OH-3*
Jefferson (Township)—Noble *OH-3*
Jefferson (Township)—Preble *OH-3*
Jefferson (Township)—Richland ... *OH-3*
Jefferson (Township)—Ross *OH-3*
Jefferson (Township)—Scioto *OH-3*
Jefferson (Township)—
  Tuscarawas *OH-3*
Jefferson (Township)—Williams ... *OH-3*
Jefferson (Town)—Grant *OK-2*
Jefferson (City)—Marion *OR-4*
Jefferson (Borough)—Allegheny ... *PA-1*
Jefferson (Township)—Berks *PA-1*

Jefferson (Township)—Butler.......... *PA-1*
Jefferson (Township)—Dauphin *PA-1*
Jefferson (Township)—Fayette........ *PA-1*
Jefferson (Borough)—Greene.......... *PA-1*
Jefferson (Township)—Greene......... *PA-1*
Jefferson (Township)—
 Lackawanna................................*PA-1*
Jefferson (Township)—Mercer..... *PA-1*
Jefferson (Township)—Somerset..... *PA-1*
Jefferson (Township)—
 Washington *PA-1*
Jefferson (Borough)—York............ *PA-1*
Jefferson (Town)—Chesterfield.......*SC-2*
Jefferson (Township)—McCook..... *SD-4*
Jefferson (Township)—Moody....... *SD-4*
Jefferson (Township)—Spink......... *SD-4*
Jefferson (Town)—Union *SD-4*
Jefferson (Township)—Union *SD-4*
Jefferson (City)—Marion *TX-2*
Jefferson (CDP)—Fairfax...............*VA-2*
Jefferson (Town)—Green *WI-3*
Jefferson (City)—Jefferson............. *WI-3*
Jefferson (Town)—Jefferson........... *WI-3*
Jefferson (Town)—Monroe *WI-3*
Jefferson (Town)—Vernon *WI-3*
Jefferson, Mt. (OR)...................... *Geog-4*
Jefferson City (City)—Callaway.... *MO-3*
Jefferson City (City)—Cole *MO-3*
Jefferson City (Town)—Jefferson... *TN-2*
Jefferson County *AL-2*
Jefferson County *AR-2*
Jefferson County *CO-4*
Jefferson County *FL-2*
Jefferson County *GA-2*
Jefferson County *ID-4*
Jefferson County *IL-3*
Jefferson County *IN-3*
Jefferson County *IA-3*
Jefferson County *KS-4*
Jefferson County *KY-2*
Jefferson County *MS-2*
Jefferson County *MO-3*
Jefferson County *MT-4*
Jefferson County *NE-4*
Jefferson County *NY-1*
Jefferson County *OH-3*
Jefferson County *OK-2*
Jefferson County *OR-4*
Jefferson County *PA-1*
Jefferson County *TN-2*
Jefferson County *TX-2*
Jefferson County *WA-4*
Jefferson County *WV-2*
Jefferson County *WI-3*
Jefferson Davis County *MS-2*
Jefferson Davis Parish...................*LA-2*
Jefferson Heights (CDP)—
 Greene..*NY-1*
Jefferson No. 10 (Township)—
 Jefferson......................................*KS-4*
Jefferson Parish *LA-2*
Jeffersontown (City)—Jefferson.... *KY-2*
Jefferson Valley-Yorktown (CDP)—
 Westchester *NY-1*
Jeffersonville (City)—Twiggs.......... *GA-2*
Jeffersonville (Village)—Wayne *IL-3*
Jeffersonville (City)—Clark............ *IN-3*
Jeffersonville (Township)—Clark.... *IN-3*
Jeffersonville (City)—
 Montgomery................................*KY-2*
Jeffersonville (Village)—Sullivan ... *NY-1*
Jeffersonville (Village)—Fayette *OH-3*
Jeiseyville (Village)—Christian *IL-3*
Jellico (City)—Campbell *TN-2*

Jemez Pueblo (NM).................. *IndRes-4*
Jemez Pueblo (CDP)—Sandoval ..*NM-4*
Jemez Springs (Village)—
 Sandoval......................................*NM-4*
Jemison (Town)—Chilton..............*AL-2*
Jena (Town)—La Salle Parish........*LA-2*
Jena Band of Choctaw TDSA
 (LA)....................................... *IndRes-4*
Jenera (Village)—Hancock *OH-3*
Jenison (CDP)—Ottawa *MI-3*
Jenkins (City)—Letcher................. *KY-2*
Jenkins (City)—Crow Wing *MN-3*
Jenkins (Township)—Crow
 Wing...*MN-3*
Jenkins (Township)—Barry *MO-3*
Jenkins (Township)—Luzerne *PA-1*
Jenkinsburg (Town)—Butts............ *GA-2*
Jenkins County *GA-2*
Jenkintown (Borough)—
 Montgomery................................*PA-1*
Jenks (City)—Tulsa *OK-2*
Jenks (Township)—Forest *PA-1*
Jenner (Township)—Somerset....... *PA-1*
Jennerstown (Borough)—
 Somerset......................................*PA-1*
Jennette (Town)—Crittenden......... *AR-2*
Jennings (Town)—Hamilton *FL-2*
Jennings (Township)—Crawford.... *IN-3*
Jennings (Township)—Fayette........ *IN-3*
Jennings (Township)—Owen.......... *IN-3*
Jennings (Township)—Scott *IN-3*
Jennings (City)—Decatur............... *KS-4*
Jennings (Township)—Decatur......*KS-4*
Jennings (City)—Jefferson Davis
 Parish..*LA-2*
Jennings (City)—St. Louis *MO-3*
Jennings (Township)—Putnam *OH-3*
Jennings (Township)—Van Wert....*OH-3*
Jennings (Town)—Pawnee *OK-2*
Jennings County............................. *IN-3*
Jennings Lodge (CDP)—
 Clackamas *OR-4*
Jensen Beach (CDP)—Martin........*FL-2*
Jerauld County *SD-4*
Jericho (Town)—Crittenden........... *AR-2*
Jericho (CDP)—Nassau.................*NY-1*
Jericho (Town)—Chittenden *VT-1*
Jericho (Village)—Chittenden........ *VT-1*
Jerico Springs (Village)—Cedar *MO-3*
Jerimoth Hill (RI)..................... *Geog-4*
Jermyn (Borough)—Lackawanna *PA-1*
Jerome (Town)—Yavapai *AZ-4*
Jerome (City)—Drew *AR-2*
Jerome (City)—Jerome.................... *ID-4*
Jerome (Village)—Sangamon *IL-3*
Jerome (Township)—Gove *KS-4*
Jerome (Township)—Midland *MI-3*
Jerome (Township)—Union *OH-3*
Jerome (CDP)—Somerset *PA-1*
Jerome County *ID-4*
Jeromesville (Village)—Ashland *OH-3*
Jerry City (Village)—Wood *OH-3*
Jersey (Town)—Walton *GA-2*
Jersey (Township)—Jersey *IL-3*
Jersey (Township)—Licking *OH-3*
Jersey City (City)—Hudson *NJ-1*
Jersey County *IL-3*
Jersey Shore (Borough)—
 Lycoming......................................*PA-1*
Jersey Village (City)—Harris *TX-2*
Jerseyville (City)—Jersey *IL-3*
Jerusalem (Town)—Yates *NY-1*
Jerusalem (Township)—Lucas........*OH-3*
Jerusalem (Village)—Monroe *OH-3*
Jessamine County *KY-2*

Jessenland (Township)—Sibley *MN-3*
Jessup (CDP)—Anne Arundel *MD-1*
Jessup (CDP)—Howard *MD-1*
Jessup (Borough)—Lackawanna...... *PA-1*
Jessup (Township)—Susquehanna .. *PA-1*
Jesup (City)—Wayne *GA-2*
Jesup (City)—Buchanan..................*IA-3*
Jet (Town)—Alfalfa *OK-2*
Jetmore (City)—Hodgeman *KS-4*
Jevne (Township)—Aitkin.............*MN-3*
Jewell (Township)—Jewell..............*KS-4*
Jewell County................................*KS-4*
Jewell Junction (City)—Hamilton ...*IA-3*
Jewett (Village)—Cumberland *IL-3*
Jewett (Pop. Place)—Aitkin *MN-3*
Jewett (Town)—Greene *NY-1*
Jewett (Village)—Harrison *OH-3*
Jewett (Township)—Jackson *SD-4*
Jewett (City)—Leon....................... *TX-2*
Jewett City (Borough)—New
 London..*CT-1*
Jicarilla Apache Reservation
 (NM) *IndRes-4*
Jim Henry (Township)—Miller..... *MO-3*
Jim Hogg County........................... *TX-2*
Jim River Valley (Township)—
 Stutsman *ND-4*
Jim Thorpe (Borough)—Carbon *PA-1*
Jim Wells County........................... *TX-2*
Joachim (Township)—Jefferson *MO-3*
Joanna (CDP)—Laurens *SC-2*
Joaquin (City)—Shelby *TX-2*
Jobe (Township)—Oregon *MO-3*
Jo Daviess (Township)—
 Faribault......................................*MN-3*
Jo Daviess County *IL-3*
Johannisburg (Township)—
 Washington *IL-3*
John Day (City)—Grant *OR-4*
John Day Fossil Beds (OR)......... *Geog-4*
John Day River (OR) *Geog-4*
John Sam Lake (CDP)—
 Snohomish *WA-4*
Johnsburg (Town)—Warren *NY-1*
Johnson (City)—Washington......... *AR-2*
Johnson (Township)—Christian...... *IL-3*
Johnson (Township)—Clark............ *IL-3*
Johnson (Township)—Clinton *IN-3*
Johnson (Township)—Crawford *IN-3*
Johnson (Township)—Gibson *IN-3*
Johnson (Township)—Knox *IN-3*
Johnson (Township)—La Porte....... *IN-3*
Johnson (Township)—Lagrange *IN-3*
Johnson (Township)—Ripley *IN-3*
Johnson (Township)—Scott *IN-3*
Johnson (Township)—Ness *KS-4*
Johnson (City)—Stanton *KS-4*
Johnson (City)—Big Stone *MN-3*
Johnson (Township)—Polk *MN-3*
Johnson (Township)—Carter *MO-3*
Johnson (Township)—Maries........ *MO-3*
Johnson (Township)—Oregon *MO-3*
Johnson (Township)—Polk *MO-3*
Johnson (Township)—Ripley *MO-3*
Johnson (Township)—Scotland..... *MO-3*
Johnson (Township)—
 Washington *MO-3*
Johnson (Village)—Nemaha........... *NE-4*
Johnson (Township)—Wells.......... *ND-4*
Johnson (Township)—
 Champaign.................................*OH-3*
Johnson (Town)—Pottawatomie *OK-2*
Johnson (Town)—Lamoille *VT-1*
Johnson (Village)—Lamoille *VT-1*
Johnson (Town)—Marathon *WI-3*

Johnsonburg (Borough)—Elk *PA-1*
Johnson City (Village)—Broome ... *NY-1*
Johnson City (City)—Clackamas ... *OR-4*
Johnson City (City)—Carter *TN-2*
Johnson City (City)—Sullivan *TN-2*
Johnson City (City)—
 Washington *TN-2*
Johnson City (City)—Blanco *TX-2*
Johnson County *AR-2*
Johnson County *GA-2*
Johnson County *IL-3*
Johnson County *IN-3*
Johnson County *IA-3*
Johnson County *KS-4*
Johnson County *KY-2*
Johnson County *MO-3*
Johnson County *NE-4*
Johnson County *TN-2*
Johnson County *TX-2*
Johnson County *WY-4*
Johnson Creek (Village)—
 Jefferson *WI-3*
Johnson Lane (CDP)—Douglas *NV-4*
Johnsonville (Village)—Wayne *IL-3*
Johnsonville (Township)—
 Redwood *MN-3*
Johnsonville (City)—Florence *SC-2*
Johnston (City)—Polk *IA-3*
Johnston (Township)—Macon *MO-3*
Johnston (Township)—Trumbull ... *OH-3*
Johnston (Town)—Providence *RI-1*
Johnston (Town)—Edgefield *SC-2*
Johnston City (Town)—
 Williamson *IL-3*
Johnston County *NC-2*
Johnston County *OK-2*
Johnstown (Town)—Weld *CO-4*
Johnstown (Township)—Barry *MI-3*
Johnstown (Village)—Brown *NE-4*
Johnstown (City)—Fulton *NY-1*
Johnstown (Town)—Fulton *NY-1*
Johnstown (Township)—Grand
 Forks *ND-4*
Johnstown (Village)—Licking *OH-3*
Johnstown (City)—Cambria *PA-1*
Johnstown (Town)—Polk *WI-3*
Johnstown (Town)—Rock *WI-3*
Joice (City)—Worth *IA-3*
Joiner (City)—Mississippi *AR-2*
Joliet (City)—Will *IL-3*
Joliet (Township)—Will *IL-3*
Joliet (Town)—Carbon *MT-4*
Joliet (Township)—Platte *NE-4*
Joliette (Township)—Pembina *ND-4*
Jolivue (CDP)—Augusta *VA-2*
Jolley (City)—Calhoun *IA-3*
Jolly (City)—Clay *TX-2*
Jollyville (CDP)—Travis *TX-2*
Jollyville (CDP)—Williamson *TX-2*
Jonathan Creek (Township)—
 Moultrie *IL-3*
Jones (Township)—Morton *KS-4*
Jones (Township)—Beltrami *MN-3*
Jones (Town)—Oklahoma *OK-2*
Jones (Township)—Elk *PA-1*
Jones (Township)—Gregory *SD-4*
Jones Beach State Park (NY) *Geog-4*
Jonesboro (City)—Craighead *AR-2*
Jonesboro (City)—Clayton *GA-2*
Jonesboro (Town)—Union *IL-3*
Jonesboro (Town)—Grant *IN-3*
Jonesboro (Town)—Jackson
 Parish *LA-2*
Jonesboro (Town)—Washington ... *ME-1*

Jonesborough (Town)—
 Washington *TN-2*
Jonesburg (City)—Montgomery *MO-3*
Jones County *GA-2*
Jones County *IA-3*
Jones County *MS-2*
Jones County *NC-2*
Jones County *SD-4*
Jones County *TX-2*
Jones Creek (Village)—Brazoria ... *TX-2*
Jonesfield (Township)—Saginaw ... *MI-3*
Jonesport (Town)—Washington *ME-1*
Jonestown (Town)—Coahoma *MS-2*
Jonestown (Borough)—Lebanon ... *PA-1*
Jonestown (City)—Travis *TX-2*
Jonesville (Town)—Bartholomew ... *IN-3*
Jonesville (Town)—Catahoula
 Parish *LA-2*
Jonesville (Village)—Hillsdale *MI-3*
Jonesville (Town)—Yadkin *NC-2*
Jonesville (Town)—Union *SC-2*
Jonesville (Town)—Lee *VA-2*
Joplin (City)—Jasper *MO-3*
Joplin (Township)—Jasper *MO-3*
Joplin (City)—Newton *MO-3*
Joppa (Village)—Massac *IL-3*
Joppatowne (CDP)—Harford *MD-1*
Jordan (Township)—Whiteside *IL-3*
Jordan (Township)—Jasper *IN-3*
Jordan (Township)—Warren *IN-3*
Jordan (Township)—Antrim *MI-3*
Jordan (Township)—Fillmore *MN-3*
Jordan (City)—Scott *MN-3*
Jordan (Township)—Hickory *MO-3*
Jordan (Township)—Ripley *MO-3*
Jordan (Town)—Garfield *MT-4*
Jordan (Village)—Onondaga *NY-1*
Jordan (Township)—Clearfield *PA-1*
Jordan (Township)—Lycoming *PA-1*
Jordan (Township)—
 Northumberland *PA-1*
Jordan (Township)—Tripp *SD-4*
Jordan (Town)—Green *WI-3*
Jordan Valley (Town)—Malheur *OR-4*
Joseph (City)—Wallowa *OR-4*
Joseph (Town)—Sevier *UT-4*
Josephine (Town)—Collin *TX-2*
Josephine (Town)—Hunt *TX-2*
Josephine County *OR-4*
Josephville (Village)—St.
 Charles *MO-3*
Joshua (Township)—Fulton *IL-3*
Joshua (City)—Johnson *TX-2*
Joshua Tree (CDP)—San
 Bernardino *CA-4*
Josie (Township)—Holt *NE-4*
Joubert (Township)—Douglas *SD-4*
Jourdanton (City)—Atascosa *TX-2*
Joy (Village)—Mercer *IL-3*
Joyfield (Township)—Benzie *MI-3*
Juab County *UT-4*
Juan de Fuca, Strait of (WA) *Geog-4*
Jubilee (Township)—Peoria *IL-3*
Jud (City)—LaMoure *ND-4*
Judith Basin County *MT-4*
Judith Gap (City)—Wheatland *MT-4*
Judson (Town)—Parke *IN-3*
Judson (Township)—Blue Earth ... *MN-3*
Judson (Township)—Williams *ND-4*
Judson (CDP)—Greenville *SC-2*
Judsonia (City)—White *AR-2*
Julesburg (Town)—Sedgwick *CO-4*
Juliaetta (City)—Latah *ID-4*
Julian (CDP)—San Diego *CA-4*
Julian (Village)—Nemaha *NE-4*

Jumpertown (Town)—Prentiss *MS-2*
Jump River (Town)—Taylor *WI-3*
Junction (Village)—Gallatin *IL-3*
Junction (Township)—Osage *KS-4*
Junction (City)—Kimble *TX-2*
Junction (Town)—Piute *UT-4*
Junction City (City)—Union *AR-2*
Junction City (Town)—Talbot *GA-2*
Junction City (Village)—Marion *IL-3*
Junction City (City)—Geary *KS-4*
Junction City (City)—Boyle *KY-2*
Junction City (City)—Lincoln *KY-2*
Junction City (Village)—Claiborne
 Parish *LA-2*
Junction City (Village)—Union
 Parish *LA-2*
Junction City (Village)—
 Madison *MO-3*
Junction City (Village)—Perry *OH-3*
Junction City (City)—Lane *OR-4*
Junction City (Village)—Portage ... *WI-3*
Juneau (City)—Dodge *WI-3*
Juneau Borough and City *AK-4*
Juneau County *WI-3*
June Park (CDP)—Brevard *FL-2*
Juniata (Township)—Tuscola *MI-3*
Juniata (Township)—Adams *NE-4*
Juniata (Village)—Adams *NE-4*
Juniata (Township)—Bedford *PA-1*
Juniata (Township)—Blair *PA-1*
Juniata (Township)—Huntingdon .. *PA-1*
Juniata (Township)—Perry *PA-1*
Juniata County *PA-1*
Juniata Terrace (Borough)—
 Mifflin *PA-1*
Junior (Town)—Barbour *WV-2*
Junius (Town)—Seneca *NY-1*
Juno Beach (Town)—Palm Beach ... *FL-2*
Jupiter (Town)—Palm Beach *FL-2*
Jupiter (Township)—Kittson *MN-3*
Jupiter Inlet Colony (Town)—Palm
 Beach *FL-2*
Jupiter Island (Town)—Martin *FL-2*
Justice (Village)—Cook *IL-3*
Justin (City)—Denton *TX-2*
Kaaawa (CDP)—Honolulu *HI-4*
Kaanapali (CDP)—Maui *HI-4*
Kachemak (City)—Kenai Peninsula
 Borough *AK-4*
Kachina Village (CDP)—
 Coconino *AZ-4*
Kadoka (City)—Jackson *SD-4*
Kahaluu (CDP)—Honolulu *HI-4*
Kahaluu-Keauhou (CDP)—
 Hawaii *HI-4*
Kahlotus (Town)—Franklin *WA-4*
Kahoka (City)—Clark *MO-3*
Kahuku (CDP)—Honolulu *HI-4*
Kahului (CDP)—Maui *HI-4*
Kaibab Reservation (AZ) *IndRes-4*
Kaibito (CDP)—Coconino *AZ-4*
Kailua (CDP)—Hawaii *HI-4*
Kailua (CDP)—Honolulu *HI-4*
Kake (City)—Wrangell-Petersburg
 Census Area *AK-4*
Kaktovik (City)—North Slope
 Borough *AK-4*
Kalaheo (CDP)—Kauai *HI-4*
Kalama (City)—Cowlitz *WA-4*
Kalamazoo (City)—Kalamazoo *MI-3*
Kalamazoo (Township)—
 Kalamazoo *MI-3*
Kalamazoo County *MI-3*
Kalamo (Township)—Eaton *MI-3*
Kalaoa (CDP)—Hawaii *HI-4*

Kalawao County *HI-4*
Kaleva (Village)—Manistee............ *MI-3*
Kalevala (Township)—Carlton...... *MN-3*
Kalida (Village)—Putnam *OH-3*
Kalifonsky (CDP)—Kenai Peninsula
  Borough..*AK-4*
Kalihiwai (CDP)—Kauai *HI-4*
Kalispell (City)—Flathead.............. *MT-4*
Kalispel Reservation (WA)....... *IndRes-4*
Kalkaska (Township)—Kalkaska ... *MI-3*
Kalkaska (Village)—Kalkaska *MI-3*
Kalkaska County *MI-3*
Kalmar (Township)—Olmsted *MN-3*
Kalona (City)—Washington *IA-3*
Kaltag (City)—Yukon-Koyukuk Census
  Area...*AK-4*
Kamas (City)—Summit.................... *UT-4*
Kamiah (City)—Idaho..................... *ID-4*
Kamiah (City)—Lewis..................... *ID-4*
Kampeska (Township)—
  Codington *SD-4*
Kampsville (Village)—Calhoun....... *IL-3*
Kamrar (City)—Hamilton.................*IA-3*
Kanab (City)—Kane *UT-4*
Kanabec (Township)—Kanabec.... *MN-3*
Kanabec County *MN-3*
Kanaranzi (Township)—Rock....... *MN-3*
Kanarraville (Town)—Iron............. *UT-4*
Kanawha (City)—Hancock *IA-3*
Kanawha County *WV-2*
Kandiyohi (City)—Kandiyohi....... *MN-3*
Kandiyohi (Township)—
  Kandiyohi *MN-3*
Kandiyohi (Township)—Burke *ND-4*
Kandiyohi County *MN-3*
Kandota (Township)—Todd......... *MN-3*
Kane (Township)—Greene *IL-3*
Kane (Village)—Greene *IL-3*
Kane (Township)—Bottineau.........*ND-4*
Kane (Borough)—McKean *PA-1*
Kane County *IL-3*
Kane County *UT-4*
Kaneohe (CDP)—Honolulu *HI-4*
Kaneohe Bay Marine Corps Air Station
  (HI)... *Mil-4*
Kaneohe Station (Military Facility)—
  Honolulu..*HI-4*
Kaneville (Township)—Kane *IL-3*
Kangley (Village)—La Salle *IL-3*
Kankakee (City)—Kankakee........... *IL-3*
Kankakee (Township)—Kankakee .. *IL-3*
Kankakee (Township)—Jasper...... *IN-3*
Kankakee (Township)—La Porte ... *IN-3*
Kankakee County *IL-3*
Kannapolis (CDP)—Cabarrus........ *NC-2*
Kannapolis (CDP)—Rowan *NC-2*
Kanopolis (City)—Ellsworth *KS-4*
Kanorado (City)—Sherman *KS-4*
Kanosh (Town)—Millard *UT-4*
Kansas (Town)—Walker.................*AL-2*
Kansas (Town)—Edgar *IL-3*
Kansas (Township)—Edgar *IL-3*
Kansas (Township)—Woodford *IL-3*
Kansas (Town)—Delaware *OK-2*
Kansas City (City)—Wyandotte *KS-4*
Kansas City (City)—Cass *MO-3*
Kansas City (City)—Clay.............. *MO-3*
Kansas City (City)—Jackson........ *MO-3*
Kansas City (City)—Platte *MO-3*
Kanwaka (Township)—Douglas....*KS-4*
Kaolin (Township)—Iron *MO-3*
Kapaa (CDP)—Kauai....................... *HI-4*
Kapaau (CDP)—Hawaii................... *HI-4*
Kapalua (CDP)—Maui..................... *HI-4*
Kapioma (Township)—Atchison.....*KS-4*

Kaplan (City)—Vermilion Parish ...*LA-2*
Kappa (Village)—Woodford............ *IL-3*
Karlsruhe (City)—McHenry............*ND-4*
Karlsruhe (Township)—
  McHenry *ND-4*
Karlstad (City)—Kittson *MN-3*
Karluk (CDP)—Kodiak Island
  Borough..*AK-4*
Karnak (Village)—Pulaski............... *IL-3*
Karnes City (Town)—Karnes.......... *TX-2*
Karnes County *TX-2*
Karns (CDP)—Knox *TN-2*
Karns City (Borough)—Butler *PA-1*
Karok Reservation and Trust Lands
  (CA)..*IndRes-4*
Karthaus (Township)—Clearfield ... *PA-1*
Kasaan (City)—Prince of Wales-Outer
  Ketchikan Census Area *AK-4*
Kasigluk (City)—Bethel Census
  Area...*AK-4*
Kasilof (CDP)—Kenai Peninsula
  Borough..*AK-4*
Kaskaskia (Township)—Fayette *IL-3*
Kaskaskia (Village)—Randolph *IL-3*
Kasota (City)—Le Sueur *MN-3*
Kasota (Township)—Le Sueur *MN-3*
Kassel (Township)—Hutchinson.... *SD-4*
Kasson (Township)—Leelanau....... *MI-3*
Kasson (City)—Dodge................... *MN-3*
Katahdin, Mt. (ME) *Geog-4*
Katerina Archipelago (ME) *Geog-4*
Kathio (Township)—Mille Lacs.... *MN-3*
Kathleen (CDP)—Polk *FL-2*
Kathryn (City)—Barnes *ND-4*
Katmai, Mt. (AK) *Geog-4*
Katy (City)—Fort Bend.................. *TX-2*
Katy (City)—Harris......................... *TX-2*
Katy (City)—Waller........................ *TX-2*
Kauai (HI) *Geog-4*
Kauai County *HI-4*
Kaufman (City)—Kaufman............. *TX-2*
Kaufman County *TX-2*
Kaukauna (City)—Outagamie......... *WI-3*
Kaukauna (Town)—Outagamie...... *WI-3*
Kaumakani (CDP)—Kauai *HI-4*
Kaunakakai (CDP)—Maui............... *HI-4*
Kaw (Township)—Jefferson *KS-4*
Kaw (Township)—Wabaunsee....... *KS-4*
Kaw (Township)—Jackson *MO-3*
Kaw City (City)—Kay *OK-2*
Kawela Bay (CDP)—Honolulu *HI-4*
Kawkawlin (Township)—Bay........ *MI-3*
Kaw TJSA (OK) *IndRes-4*
Kaycee (Town)—Johnson............... *WY-4*
Kay County *OK-2*
Kayenta (CDP)—Navajo................ *AZ-4*
Kaylor (Township)—Hutchinson ... *SD-4*
Kaysville (City)—Davis................... *UT-4*
Keaau (CDP)—Hawaii..................... *HI-4*
Keachi (Town)—De Soto Parish....*LA-2*
Kealakekua (CDP)—Hawaii *HI-4*
Keams Canyon (CDP)—Navajo *AZ-4*
Keansburg (Borough)—
  Monmouth *NJ-1*
Kearney (Township)—Antrim........ *MI-3*
Kearney (City)—Clay *MO-3*
Kearney (Township)—Clay *MO-3*
Kearney (City)—Buffalo................. *NE-4*
Kearney County *NE-4*
Kearns (CDP)—Salt Lake *UT-4*
Kearny (Town)—Pinal.................... *AZ-4*
Kearny (Town)—Hudson *NJ-1*
Kearny County *KS-4*
Keating (Township)—McKean........ *PA-1*
Keating (Township)—Potter *PA-1*

Kechi (City)—Sedgwick *KS-4*
Kechi (Township)—Sedgwick.......... *KS-4*
Keedysville (Town)—
  Washington *MD-1*
Keego Harbor (City)—Oakland *MI-3*
Keeler (Township)—Van Buren...... *MI-3*
Keene (Township)—Adams.............. *IL-3*
Keene (Township)—Ionia *MI-3*
Keene (Township)—Clay............... *MN-3*
Keene (City)—Cheshire....................*NH-1*
Keene (Town)—Essex...................... *NY-1*
Keene (Township)—McKenzie *ND-4*
Keene (Township)—Coshocton......*OH-3*
Keene (City)—Johnson *TX-2*
Keeneland (City)—Jefferson *KY-2*
Keener (Township)—Jasper *IN-3*
Keenes (Village)—Wayne *IL-3*
Keenesburg (Town)—Weld.............. *CO-4*
Keensburg (Village)—Wabash *IL-3*
Keeseville (Village)—Clinton *NY-1*
Keeseville (Village)—Essex *NY-1*
Keesler Air Force Base (MS).......... *Mil-4*
Keewatin (City)—Itasca *MN-3*
Kego (Township)—Cass *MN-3*
Keiser (Town)—Mississippi *AR-2*
Keith (Township)—Wayne *IL-3*
Keith County *NE-4*
Keithsburg (Town)—Mercer............ *IL-3*
Keithsburg (Township)—Mercer.... *IL-3*
Keizer (City)—Marion *OR-4*
Kekaha (CDP)—Kauai *HI-4*
Kekoskee (Village)—Dodge *WI-3*
Kelford (Town)—Bertie.................. *NC-2*
Kell (Village)—Marion *IL-3*
Keller (Township)—Burke *ND-4*
Keller (City)—Tarrant *TX-2*
Keller (Town)—Accomack *VA-2*
Kellerton (City)—Ringgold *IA-3*
Kelley (City)—Story *IA-3*
Kelley (Township)—Ripley *MO-3*
Kelleys Island (Village)—Erie *OH-3*
Kelliher (City)—Beltrami *MN-3*
Kelliher (Township)—Beltrami..... *MN-3*
Kellnersville (Village)—
  Manitowoc *WI-3*
Kellogg (City)—Shoshone *ID-4*
Kellogg (City)—Jasper *IA-3*
Kellogg (City)—Wabasha *MN-3*
Kellogg (Township)—Beadle *SD-4*
Kelly (Township)—Warren *IL-3*
Kelly (Township)—Carter *MO-3*
Kelly (Township)—Cooper *MO-3*
Kelly (Township)—Union *PA-1*
Kelly (Town)—Bayfield *WI-3*
Kelly Air Force Base (TX) *Mil-4*
Kellyville (Town)—Creek *OK-2*
Kelsey (Township)—St. Louis *MN-3*
Kelseyville (CDP)—Lake *CA-4*
Kelso (Township)—Dearborn *IN-3*
Kelso (Township)—Sibley *MN-3*
Kelso (Town)—Scott *MO-3*
Kelso (Township)—Scott............... *MO-3*
Kelso (Township)—Traill *ND-4*
Kelso (City)—Cowlitz *WA-4*
Kemah (City)—Galveston *TX-2*
Kemmerer (Town)—Lincoln *WY-4*
Kemp (Town)—Bryan *OK-2*
Kemp (Town)—Kaufman *TX-2*
Kemper County *MS-2*
Kempton (Village)—Ford *IL-3*
Kempton (Town)—Tipton *IN-3*
Kenai (City)—Kenai Peninsula
  Borough..*AK-4*
Kenai Peninsula Borough *AK-4*
Kenansville (Town)—Duplin *NC-2*

General Index

Kenbridge (Town)—Lunenburg *VA-2*
Ken Caryl (CDP)—Jefferson *CO-4*
Kendale Lakes (CDP)—Dade *FL-2*
Kendall (CDP)—Dade *FL-2*
Kendall (Township)—Kendall *IL-3*
Kendall (Township)—Hamilton ... *KS-4*
Kendall (Township)—Kearny *KS-4*
Kendall (Town)—Orleans *NY-1*
Kendall (Town)—Lafayette *WI-3*
Kendall (Village)—Monroe *WI-3*
Kendall County *IL-3*
Kendall County *TX-2*
Kendall Green (CDP)—Broward ... *FL-2*
Kendall Lakes West (CDP)—Dade *FL-2*
Kendall Park (CDP)—Middlesex *NJ-1*
Kendallville (City)—Noble *IN-3*
Kendleton (Town)—Fort Bend *TX-2*
Kendrick (City)—Latah *ID-4*
Kendrick (Town)—Lincoln *OK-2*
Kenduskeag (Town)—Penobscot .. *ME-1*
Kenedy (City)—Karnes *TX-2*
Kenedy County *TX-2*
Kenefic (Town)—Bryan *OK-2*
Kenefick (Town)—Liberty *TX-2*
Kenesaw (Township)—Adams *NE-4*
Kenesaw (Village)—Adams *NE-4*
Kenhorst (Borough)—Berks *PA-1*
Kenilworth (Town)—Cook *IL-3*
Kenilworth (Borough)—Union *NJ-1*
Kenilworth (CDP)—Chester *PA-1*
Kenly (Town)—Johnston *NC-2*
Kenly (Town)—Wilson *NC-2*
Kenmare (City)—Ward *ND-4*
Kenmare (Township)—Ward *ND-4*
Kenmore (Village)—Erie *NY-1*
Kenmore (CDP)—King *WA-4*
Kennan (Town)—Price *WI-3*
Kennan (Village)—Price *WI-3*
Kennard (Town)—Henry *IN-3*
Kennard (Village)—Washington ... *NE-4*
Kennard (City)—Houston *TX-2*
Kennebec (Town)—Lyman *SD-4*
Kennebec (Township)—Lyman *SD-4*
Kennebec County *ME-1*
Kennebec River (ME) *Geog-4*
Kennebunk (Town)—York *ME-1*
Kennebunkport (Town)—York *ME-1*
Kennedale (City)—Tarrant *TX-2*
Kennedy (Town)—Lamar *AL-2*
Kennedy (City)—Kittson *MN-3*
Kennedy (Township)—Hettinger ... *ND-4*
Kennedy (Township)—Allegheny *PA-1*
Kennedy (Township)—Charles Mix *SD-4*
Kenner (City)—Jefferson Parish *LA-2*
Kennesaw (City)—Cobb *GA-2*
Kenneth (Township)—Sheridan *KS-4*
Kenneth (City)—Rock *MN-3*
Kenneth City (Town)—Pinellas *FL-2*
Kennett (City)—Dunklin *MO-3*
Kennett (Township)—Chester *PA-1*
Kennett Square (Borough)—Chester *PA-1*
Kennewick (City)—Benton *WA-4*
Kenney (Village)—De Witt *IL-3*
Kennison (Township)—LaMoure ... *ND-4*
Kenny Lake (CDP)—Valdez-Cordova Census Area *AK-4*
Kenockee (Township)—St. Clair ... *MI-3*
Kenosha (City)—Kenosha *WI-3*
Kenosha County *WI-3*
Kenova (City)—Wayne *WV-2*
Kensal (City)—Stutsman *ND-4*
Kensal (Township)—Stutsman *ND-4*

Kensett (City)—White *AR-2*
Kensett (City)—Worth *IA-3*
Kensington (CDP)—Contra Costa *CA-4*
Kensington (CDP)—Hartford *CT-1*
Kensington (City)—Smith *KS-4*
Kensington (Town)—Montgomery *MD-1*
Kensington (City)—Douglas *MN-3*
Kensington (Town)—Rockingham *NH-1*
Kensington (Village)—Nassau........ *NY-1*
Kensington (Township)—Walsh *ND-4*
Kensington Park (CDP)—Sarasota *FL-2*
Kent (Town)—Litchfield *CT-1*
Kent (Township)—Stephenson *IL-3*
Kent (Township)—Warren *IN-3*
Kent (City)—Union *IA-3*
Kent (City)—Wilkin *MN-3*
Kent (Town)—Putnam *NY-1*
Kent (Township)—Dickey *ND-4*
Kent (City)—Portage *OH-3*
Kent (Township)—Edmunds *SD-4*
Kent (City)—King *WA-4*
Kent Acres (CDP)—Kent *DE-1*
Kent City (Village)—Kent *MI-3*
Kent County *DE-1*
Kent County *MD-1*
Kent County *MI-3*
Kent County *RI-1*
Kent County *TX-2*
Kentfield (CDP)—Marin *CA-4*
Kentland (Town)—Newton *IN-3*
Kentland (CDP)—Prince George's *MD-1*
Kentner (Township)—Dickey *ND-4*
Kenton (Town)—Kent *DE-1*
Kenton (City)—Hardin *OH-3*
Kenton (Town)—Gibson *TN-2*
Kenton (Town)—Obion *TN-2*
Kenton County *KY-2*
Kenton Vale (City)—Kenton *KY-2*
Kentucky (Township)—Jefferson ... *KS-4*
Kentucky Lake *or* Reservoir (ME) *Geog-4*
Kentwood (Town)—Tangipahoa Parish *LA-2*
Kentwood (City)—Kent *MI-3*
Kenwood (CDP)—Hamilton *OH-3*
Kenyon (City)—Goodhue *MN-3*
Kenyon (Township)—Goodhue *MN-3*
Keo (Town)—Lonoke *AR-2*
Keokuk (City)—Lee *IA-3*
Keokuk County *IA-3*
Keomah Village (City)—Mahaska ... *IA-3*
Keosauqua (City)—Van Buren....... *IA-3*
Keota (Town)—Weld *CO-4*
Keota (City)—Keokuk *IA-3*
Keota (Town)—Haskell *OK-2*
Kerens (City)—Navarro *TX-2*
Kerhonkson (CDP)—Ulster *NY-1*
Kerkhoven (City)—Swift *MN-3*
Kerkhoven (Township)—Swift *MN-3*
Kerman (City)—Fresno *CA-4*
Kermit (City)—Winkler *TX-2*
Kermit (Town)—Mingo *WV-2*
Kern (Township)—Hettinger *ND-4*
Kern County *CA-4*
Kernersville (Town)—Forsyth *NC-2*
Kernersville (Town)—Guilford *NC-2*
Kernville (CDP)—Kern *CA-4*
Kerr (Township)—Champaign *IL-3*
Kerr County *TX-2*
Kerrick (City)—Pine *MN-3*

Kerrick (Township)—Pine *MN-3*
Kerrville (City)—Kerr *TX-2*
Kersey (Town)—Weld *CO-4*
Kershaw (Town)—Lancaster *SC-2*
Kershaw County *SC-2*
Kerton (Township)—Fulton *IL-3*
Kertsonville (Township)—Polk *MN-3*
Keshena (CDP)—Menominee *WI-3*
Keswick (City)—Keokuk *IA-3*
Ketchikan (City)—Ketchikan Gateway Borough *AK-4*
Ketchikan Gateway Borough *AK-4*
Ketchum (City)—Blaine *ID-4*
Ketchum (Town)—Craig *OK-2*
Kettering (CDP)—Prince George's *MD-1*
Kettering (City)—Greene *OH-3*
Kettering (City)—Montgomery *OH-3*
Kettle Falls (City)—Stevens *WA-4*
Kettleman City (CDP)—Kings *CA-4*
Kettle River (City)—Carlton *MN-3*
Kettle River (Township)—Pine *MN-3*
Kettlersville (Village)—Shelby *OH-3*
Kevil (City)—Ballard *KY-2*
Kevin (Town)—Toole *MT-2*
Kewanee (City)—Henry *IL-3*
Kewanee (Township)—Henry *IL-3*
Kewanna (Town)—Fulton *IN-3*
Kewaskum (Village)—Fond du Lac *WI-3*
Kewaskum (Town)—Washington ... *WI-3*
Kewaskum (Village)—Washington *WI-3*
Kewaunee (City)—Kewaunee *WI-3*
Kewaunee County *WI-3*
Keweenaw County *MI-3*
Keyapaha (Township)—Tripp *SD-4*
Keya Paha County *NE-4*
Key Biscayne (CDP)—Dade *FL-2*
Key Colony Beach (City)—Monroe *FL-2*
Keyes (CDP)—Stanislaus *CA-4*
Keyes (Town)—Cimarron *OK-2*
Keyesport (Village)—Bond *IL-3*
Keyesport (Village)—Clinton *IL-3*
Key Largo (CDP)—Monroe *FL-2*
Keyport (Borough)—Monmouth ... *NJ-1*
Keyser (Township)—Dekalb *IN-3*
Keyser (City)—Mineral *WV-2*
Keystone (City)—Benton *IA-3*
Keystone (Township)—Scott *KS-4*
Keystone (Township)—Polk *MN-3*
Keystone (Township)—Dickey *ND-4*
Keystone (Town)—Pennington *SD-4*
Keystone (City)—McDowell *WV-2*
Keystone (Town)—Bayfield *WI-3*
Keystone Heights (City)—Clay *FL-2*
Keysville (Town)—Burke *GA-2*
Keysville (Town)—Jefferson *GA-2*
Keysville (Township)—Pawnee *KS-4*
Keysville (Town)—Charlotte *VA-2*
Keytesville (City)—Chariton *MO-3*
Keytesville (Township)—Chariton *MO-3*
Key West (City)—Monroe *FL-2*
Key West (Township)—Coffey *KS-4*
Kiana (City)—Northwest Arctic Borough *AK-4*
Kiantone (Town)—Chautauqua *NY-1*
Kiawah Island (Town)—Charleston *SC-2*
Kibler (Town)—Crawford *AR-2*
Kickapoo (Township)—Peoria *IL-3*
Kickapoo (Township)—Leavenworth *KS-4*

Kickapoo (Township)—Platte *MO-3*
Kickapoo (Township)—Kidder *ND-4*
Kickapoo (Township)—
 Mountrail *ND-4*
Kickapoo (Town)—Vernon *WI-3*
Kickapoo Reservation (KS)...... *IndRes-4*
Kicking Horse (CDP)—Lake *MT-4*
Kidder (City)—Caldwell................ *MO-3*
Kidder (Township)—Caldwell........ *MO-3*
Kidder (Township)—Carbon........... *PA-1*
Kidder (Township)—Day *SD-4*
Kidder County *ND-4*
Kief (City)—McHenry................... *ND-4*
Kiefer (Town)—Creek *OK-2*
Kiel (City)—Calumet *WI-3*
Kiel (City)—Manitowoc................ *WI-3*
Kiester (City)—Faribault............... *MN-3*
Kiester (Township)—Faribault....... *MN-3*
Kihei (CDP)—Maui....................... *HI-4*
Kiheka (Township)—Camden *MO-3*
Kilauea (CDP)—Kauai................... *HI-4*
Kilauea (Mount) (HI) *Geog-4*
Kilborn (Township)—Grant........... *SD-4*
Kilbourne (Town)—Mason *IL-3*
Kilbourne (Township)—Mason....... *IL-3*
Kilbourne (Village)—West Carroll
 Parish *LA-2*
Kilbuck (Township)—Allegheny *PA-1*
Kildare (Township)—Swift............ *MN-3*
Kildare (Town)—Kay *OK-2*
Kildare (Town)—Juneau *WI-3*
Kildeer (Town)—Lake *IL-3*
Kilfoil (Township)—Custer *NE-4*
Kilgore (Village)—Cherry.............. *NE-4*
Kilgore (City)—Gregg *TX-2*
Kilgore (City)—Rusk *TX-2*
Kilkenny (City)—Le Sueur............ *MN-3*
Kilkenny (Township)—Le Sueur... *MN-3*
Kilkenny (Township)—Coos *NH-1*
Killbuck (Township)—Holmes....... *OH-3*
Killbuck (Village)—Holmes........... *OH-3*
Kill Creek (Township)—Osborne....*KS-4*
Killdeer (City)—Dunn................... *ND-4*
Killdeer (Pop. Place)—Dunn *ND-4*
Kill Devil Hills (Town)—Dare....... *NC-2*
Killeen (City)—Bell *TX-2*
Killen (Town)—Lauderdale............ *AL-2*
Killian (Village)—Livingston
 Parish *LA-2*
Killingly (Town)—Windham.......... *CT-1*
Killingworth (Town)—Middlesex... *CT-1*
Kilmarnock (Town)—Lancaster...... *VA-2*
Kilmarnock (Town)—
 Northumberland *VA-2*
Kilmichael (Town)—
 Montgomery............................... *MS-2*
Kiln (CDP)—Hancock *MS-2*
Kim (Town)—Las Animas *CO-4*
Kimball (Township)—St. Clair *MI-3*
Kimball (Township)—Jackson *MN-3*
Kimball (City)—Kimball *NE-4*
Kimball (City)—Brule *SD-4*
Kimball (Township)—Brule *SD-4*
Kimball (Town)—Marion *TN-2*
Kimball (Town)—McDowell *WV-2*
Kimball (Town)—Iron *WI-3*
Kimball County *NE-4*
Kimball Prairie (City)—Stearns.... *MN-3*
Kimballton (City)—Audubon *IA-3*
Kimberling City (City)—Stone *MO-3*
Kimberly (Town)—Jefferson.......... *AL-2*
Kimberly (City)—Twin Falls.......... *ID-4*
Kimberly (Township)—Aitkin *MN-3*
Kimberly (Village)—Outagamie..... *WI-3*
Kimble County *TX-2*

Kimbolton (Village)—Guernsey.....*OH-3*
Kimeo (Township)—Washington *KS-4*
Kimmel (Township)—Bedford........ *PA-1*
Kimmswick (City)—Jefferson *MO-3*
Kinbrae (City)—Nobles.................. *MN-3*
Kincaid (Town)—Christian.............. *IL-3*
Kincaid (City)—Anderson *KS-4*
Kinde (Village)—Huron *MI-3*
Kinder (Town)—Allen Parish *LA-2*
Kinder (Township)—Cape
 Girardeau.....................................*MO-3*
Kinderhook (Township)—Pike *IL-3*
Kinderhook (Village)—Pike *IL-3*
Kinderhook (Township)—Branch ..*MI-3*
Kinderhook (Town)—Columbia *NY-1*
Kinderhook (Village)—Columbia ..*NY-1*
Kindred (City)—Cass *ND-4*
King (Township)—Christian *IL-3*
King (Township)—Polk *MN-3*
King (Township)—Oregon *MO-3*
King (City)—Forsyth *NC-2*
King (City)—Stokes *NC-2*
King (Township)—Bedford *PA-1*
King (Township)—Tripp *SD-4*
King (Town)—Lincoln................... *WI-3*
King and Queen County *VA-2*
King City (City)—Monterey *CA-4*
King City (Township)—
 McPherson *KS-4*
King City (City)—Gentry...............*MO-3*
King City (City)—Washington *OR-4*
King County *TX-2*
King County *WA-4*
King Cove (City)—Aleutians East
 Borough.......................................*AK-4*
Kingdom City (Village)—
 Callaway......................................*MO-3*
Kingery (Township)—Thomas *KS-4*
Kingfield (Town)—Franklin........... *ME-1*
Kingfisher (City)—Kingfisher *OK-2*
Kingfisher County *OK-2*
King George County *VA-2*
Kinghurst (Township)—Itasca *MN-3*
Kingman (City)—Mohave *AZ-4*
Kingman (Town)—Fountain *IN-3*
Kingman (City)—Kingman *KS-4*
Kingman (Township)—Kingman....*KS-4*
Kingman (Township)—Renville....*MN-3*
Kingman County............................*KS-4*
Kingman (unorganized) (Pop. Place)—
 Penobscot..................................... *ME-1*
King of Prussia (CDP)—
 Montgomery................................ *PA-1*
King Salmon (CDP)—Bristol Bay
 Borough.......................................*AK-4*
Kings Bay Base (Military Facility)—
 Camden.. *GA-2*
Kings Beach (CDP)—Placer *CA-4*
Kingsburg (City)—Fresno.............. *CA-4*
Kingsbury (Town)—La Porte......... *IN-3*
Kingsbury (Plantation)—
 Piscataquis *ME-1*
Kingsbury (CDP)—Douglas *NV-4*
Kingsbury (Town)—Washington ... *NY-1*
Kingsbury County *SD-4*
Kings County *CA-4*
Kings County (Brooklyn) *NY-1*
Kingsford (City)—Dickinson *MI-3*
Kingsford Heights (Town)—La
 Porte... *IN-3*
Kingsgate (CDP)—King *WA-4*
Kingsland (City)—Cleveland *AR-2*
Kingsland (City)—Camden *GA-2*
Kingsland (CDP)—Llano *TX-2*
Kingsley (City)—Plymouth *IA-3*

Kingsley (City)—Jefferson *KY-2*
Kingsley (Village)—Grand
 Traverse....................................... *MI-3*
Kingsley (Township)—Griggs.......*ND-4*
Kingsley (Township)—Forest *PA-1*
Kings Mountain (City)—
 Cleveland *NC-2*
Kings Mountain (City)—Gaston *NC-2*
Kings Park (CDP)—Suffolk *NY-1*
Kings Peak (UT).......................... *Geog-4*
Kings Point (CDP)—Palm Beach ...*FL-2*
Kings Point (Village)—Nassau....... *NY-1*
Kingsport (City)—Hawkins *TN-2*
Kingsport (City)—Sullivan............. *TN-2*
Kings Prairie (Township)—
 Barry *MO-3*
Kingston (City)—Bartow................ *GA-2*
Kingston (Township)—DeKalb *IL-3*
Kingston (Village)—DeKalb *IL-3*
Kingston (Town)—Plymouth *MA-1*
Kingston (Township)—Tuscola *MI-3*
Kingston (Village)—Tuscola........... *MI-3*
Kingston (City)—Meeker *MN-3*
Kingston (Township)—Meeker *MN-3*
Kingston (City)—Caldwell *MO-3*
Kingston (Township)—Caldwell ... *MO-3*
Kingston (Township)—
 Washington *MO-3*
Kingston (Town)—Rockingham.....*NH-1*
Kingston (CDP)—Middlesex *NJ-1*
Kingston (City)—Ulster *NY-1*
Kingston (Town)—Ulster *NY-1*
Kingston (Township)—Sargent *ND-4*
Kingston (Township)—Delaware ...*OH-3*
Kingston (Village)—Ross *OH-3*
Kingston (Town)—Marshall *OK-2*
Kingston (Borough)—Luzerne *PA-1*
Kingston (Township)—Luzerne *PA-1*
Kingston (CDP)—Washington *RI-1*
Kingston (City)—Roane *TN-2*
Kingston (Town)—Piute *UT-4*
Kingston (CDP)—Kitsap *WA-4*
Kingston (Town)—Green Lake *WI-3*
Kingston (Village)—Green Lake.... *WI-3*
Kingston (Town)—Juneau.............. *WI-3*
Kingston Mines (Village)—Peoria .. *IL-3*
Kingston Springs (Town)—
 Cheatham..................................... *TN-2*
Kingstown (CDP)—Queen
 Anne's *MD-1*
Kingstown (Town)—Cleveland *NC-2*
Kingstree (Town)—Williamsburg....*SC-2*
Kingsville (CDP)—Baltimore *MD-1*
Kingsville (City)—Johnson *MO-3*
Kingsville (Township)—Johnson ..*MO-3*
Kingsville (Township)—
 Ashtabula *OH-3*
Kingsville (City)—Kleberg *TX-2*
King William County *VA-2*
Kingwood (Township)—
 Hunterdon.................................... *NJ-1*
Kingwood (CDP)—Harris *TX-2*
Kingwood (CDP)—Montgomery ... *TX-2*
Kingwood (CDP)—Preston *WV-2*
Kinkaid (Township)—Jackson *IL-3*
Kinloch (City)—St. Louis *MO-3*
Kinloss (Township)—Walsh *ND-4*
Kinmundy (City)—Marion *IL-3*
Kinmundy (Township)—Marion..... *IL-3*
Kinnelon (Borough)—Morris *NJ-1*
Kinney (City)—St. Louis............... *MN-3*
Kinney County *TX-2*
Kinnickinnic (Town)—St. Croix *WI-3*
Kinross (City)—Keokuk.................. *IA-3*
Kinross (Township)—Chippewa ... *MI-3*

General Index — American Places Dictionary

Kinsey (Municipality)—Houston....AL-2
Kinsley (City)—Edwards.................KS-4
Kinsley (Township)—Edwards.........KS-4
Kinsman (Village)—Grundy IL-3
Kinsman (Township)—Trumbull ...OH-3
Kinston (Town)—Coffee AL-2
Kinston (City)—Lenoir NC-2
Kinta (Town)—Haskell.....................OK-2
Kintire (Township)—Redwood MN-3
Kinyon (Township)—Cass................ND-4
Kiowa (Town)—Elbert CO-4
Kiowa (City)—Barber.......................KS-4
Kiowa (Township)—Barber..............KS-4
Kiowa (Town)—Pittsburg.................OK-2
Kiowa-Comanche-Apache-Fort Sill
  Apache (OK).............................IndRes-4
Kiowa County...............................CO-4
Kiowa County...............................KS-4
Kiowa County...............................OK-2
Kipnuk (CDP)—Bethel Census
  Area...AK-4
Kipton (Village)—Lorain OH-3
Kirby (Village)—Wyandot OH-3
Kirby (City)—Bexar TX-2
Kirby (Town)—Caledonia VT-1
Kirby (Town)—Hot Springs WY-4
Kirbyville (City)—Jasper...................TX-2
Kirkelie (Township)—Ward ND-4
Kirkersville (Village)—Licking........OH-3
Kirkland (Town)—DeKalb IL-3
Kirkland (Township)—Adams IN-3
Kirkland (Town)—Oneida NY-1
Kirkland (City)—King......................WA-4
Kirklin (Town)—Clinton...................IN-3
Kirklin (Township)—Clinton IN-3
Kirkman (City)—Shelby...................IA-3
Kirksville (City)—Adair....................MO-3
Kirkville (City)—Wapello.................IA-3
Kirkwood (Town)—Warren IL-3
Kirkwood (City)—St. Louis MO-3
Kirkwood (Town)—Broome.............NY-1
Kirkwood (Township)—Belmont....OH-3
Kiron (City)—Crawford IA-3
Kirtland (CDP)—San Juan NM-4
Kirtland (City)—Lake.......................OH-3
Kirtland Air Force Base (NM) Mil-4
Kirtland Hills (Village)—Lake.........OH-3
Kirvin (Town)—Freestone TX-2
Kirwin (City)—Phillips.....................KS-4
Kirwin (Township)—Phillips KS-4
Kiryas Joel (Village)—Orange.........NY-1
K. I. Sawyer Air Force Base (Military
  Facility)—Marquette MI-3
Kiskiminetas (Township)—
  Armstrong PA-1
Kismet (City)—Seward.....................KS-4
Kissimmee (City)—Osceola FL-2
Kistler (Borough)—Mifflin PA-1
Kit Carson (Town)—Cheyenne CO-4
Kit Carson County........................CO-4
Kite (Town)—Johnson GA-2
Kitsap County................................WA-4
Kittanning (Borough)—
  Armstrong PA-1
Kittanning (Township)—
  Armstrong PA-1
Kittery (Town)—York ME-1
Kittery Point (CDP)—York ME-1
Kittitas (City)—Kittitas....................WA-4
Kittitas County..............................WA-4
Kittrell (Town)—Vance NC-2
Kittson County...............................MN-3
Kitty Hawk (Town)—Dare...............NC-2
Kitzmiller (Town)—Garrett MD-1
Kitzmillerville (Town)—Garrett MD-1

Kivalina (City)—Northwest Arctic
  Borough..AK-4
Klacking (Township)—Ogemaw MI-3
Klamath (CDP)—Del Norte CA-4
Klamath County OR-4
Klamath Falls (City)—Klamath OR-4
Klamath Mountains (UT) Geog-4
Klamath River (UT) Geog-4
Klamath Tribe TDSA (OR)......IndRes-4
Klawock (City)—Prince of Wales-Outer
  Ketchikan Census Area AK-4
Kleberg County...............................TX-2
Klemme (City)—Hancock IA-3
Klickitat County..............................WA-4
Kline (Township)—Schuylkill PA-1
Kline (Town)—Barnwell....................SC-2
Klingstrup (Township)—Ramsey ..ND-4
Klukwan (CDP)—
  Skagway-Hoonah-Angoon Census
  Area...AK-4
Knapp (Village)—Dunn WI-3
Knapp (Town)—Jackson WI-3
Knierim (City)—Calhoun................IA-3
Knife Lake (Township)—
  Kanabec...MN-3
Knife River (Township)—
  Mountrail ND-4
Knight (Township)—Vanderburgh ..IN-3
Knight (Town)—Iron WI-3
Knightdale (Town)—Wake NC-2
Knight Prairie (Township)—
  Hamilton IL-3
Knightstown (Town)—Henry IN-3
Knightsville (Town)—Clay IN-3
Knik (CDP)—Matanuska-Susitna
  Borough..AK-4
Knobel (Town)—Clay.......................AR-2
Knob Noster (City)—Johnson MO-3
Knobview (Township)—
  Crawford MO-3
Knollwood (Village)—Grayson TX-2
Knott County KY-2
Knowles (Town)—Beaver................OK-2
Knowlton (Township)—Warren NJ-1
Knowlton (Town)—Marathon.........WI-3
Knox (Township)—Knox IL-3
Knox (Township)—Jay.....................IN-3
Knox (City)—Starke..........................IN-3
Knox (Town)—Waldo.......................ME-1
Knox (Town)—Albany NY-1
Knox (City)—Benson ND-4
Knox (Township)—Benson.............ND-4
Knox (Township)—Columbiana OH-3
Knox (Township)—Guernsey.........OH-3
Knox (Township)—Holmes.............OH-3
Knox (Township)—Jefferson..........OH-3
Knox (Township)—Vinton..............OH-3
Knox (Borough)—Clarion PA-1
Knox (Township)—Clarion PA-1
Knox (Township)—Clearfield PA-1
Knox (Township)—Jefferson..........PA-1
Knox (Town)—Price WI-3
Knox City (City)—Knox MO-3
Knox City (City)—Knox TX-2
Knox County....................................IL-3
Knox County....................................IN-3
Knox County...................................KY-2
Knox County...................................ME-1
Knox County...................................MO-3
Knox County...................................NE-4
Knox County...................................OH-3
Knox County....................................TN-2
Knox County....................................TX-2
Knoxville (City)—Johnson................AR-2

Knoxville (Pop. Place)—
  Crawford GA-2
Knoxville (Town)—Knox IL-3
Knoxville (City)—Marion IA-3
Knoxville (Township)—Ray...........MO-3
Knoxville (Borough)—Tioga PA-1
Knoxville (City)—Knox TN-2
Knute (Township)—Polk MN-3
Kobuk (City)—Northwest Arctic
  Borough..AK-4
Kochville (Township)—Saginaw MI-3
Kodiak (City)—Kodiak Island
  Borough..AK-4
Kodiak Island (AK) Geog-4
Kodiak Island Borough AK-4
Kodiak Station (Military Facility)—
  Kodiak Island Borough AK-4
Koehler (Township)—Cheboygan ..MI-3
Kohler (Village)—Sheboygan WI-3
Kohlmeier (Township)—Rolette ND-4
Kokhanok (CDP)—Lake and Peninsula
  Borough..AK-4
Kokomo (City)—Howard IN-3
Koliganek (CDP)—Dillingham Census
  Area...AK-4
Kolls (Township)—Jones SD-4
Koloa (CDP)—Kauai HI-3
Komatke (CDP)—Maricopa AZ-4
Komensky (Town)—Jackson WI-3
Konawa (City)—Seminole OK-2
Kongiganak (CDP)—Bethel Census
  Area...AK-4
Koochiching County MN-3
Koontz Lake (CDP)—Marshall.......IN-3
Koontz Lake (CDP)—Starke...........IN-3
Koosharem (Town)—Sevier UT-4
Kooskia (City)—Idaho ID-4
Kootenai (City)—Bonner ID-4
Kootenai County.............................ID-4
Kootenai Reservation (ID)........IndRes-4
Koppel (Borough)—Beaver PA-1
Kortright (Town)—Delaware NY-1
Kosciusko (City)—Attala MS-2
Kosciusko (Township)—Day...........SD-4
Kosciusko County...........................IN-3
Koshkonong (Town)—Oregon........MO-3
Koshkonong (Town)—Jefferson.....WI-3
Kosse (Town)—Limestone TX-2
Kossuth (Village)—Alcorn..............MS-2
Kossuth (Town)—Manitowoc WI-3
Kossuth County...............................IA-3
Kotlik (City)—Wade Hampton Census
  Area...AK-4
Kottke Valley (Township)—
  McHenry ND-4
Kotzebue (City)—Northwest Arctic
  Borough..AK-4
Kountze (City)—Hardin...................TX-2
Kouts (Town)—Porter IN-3
Koylton (Township)—Tuscola.........MI-3
Koyuk (City)—Nome Census
  Area...AK-4
Koyukuk (City)—Yukon-Koyukuk
  Census Area.....................................AK-4
Kragero (Township)—Chippewa ...MN-3
Kragnes (Township)—Clay.............MN-3
Krain (Township)—Stearns.............MN-3
Krakow (Township)—Presque
  Isle MI-3
Kramer (City)—Bottineau ND-4
Kranzburg (Town)—Codington......SD-4
Kranzburg (Township)—
  Codington SD-4
Kratka (Township)—Pennington ..MN-3
Krebs (City)—Pittsburg....................OK-2

Kremlin (Town)—Garfield............ *OK-2*
Kremmling (Town)—Grand........... *CO-4*
Kress (City)—Swisher *TX-2*
Kronenwetter (Town)—Marathon . *WI-3*
Kroschel (Township)—Kanabec.... *MN-3*
Krotz Springs (Town)—St. Landry
Parish.. *LA-2*
Krugerville (City)—Denton............ *TX-2*
Krum (City)—Denton *TX-2*
Krupp (Town)—Grant.................... *WA-4*
Kualapuu (CDP)—Maui *HI-4*
Kugler (Township)—St. Louis....... *MN-3*
Kukuihaele (CDP)—Hawaii........... *HI-4*
Kulm (City)—LaMoure.................. *ND-4*
Kulm (Township)—Hutchinson *SD-4*
Kulpmont (Borough)—
Northumberland *PA-1*
Kulpsville (CDP)—Montgomery..... *PA-1*
Kuna (City)—Ada........................ *ID-4*
Kunze (Township)—Hettinger *ND-4*
Kupreanof (City)—Wrangell-Petersburg
Census Area................................. *AK-4*
Kure Beach (Town)—New
Hanover.................................... *NC-2*
Kurtistown (CDP)—Hawaii............ *HI-4*
Kurtz (Township)—Clay *MN-3*
Kuttawa (City)—Lyon *KY-2*
Kutztown (Borough)—Berks *PA-1*
Kwethluk (City)—Bethel Census
Area... *AK-4*
Kwigillingok (CDP)—Bethel Census
Area... *AK-4*
Kykotsmovi Village (CDP)—
Navajo... *AZ-4*
Kyle (CDP)—Shannon *SD-4*
Kyle (Town)—Hays *TX-2*
Labadieville (CDP)—Assumption
Parish.. *LA-2*
La Barge (Town)—Lincoln............ *WY-4*
La Belle (City)—Hendry................ *FL-2*
La Belle (City)—Lewis *MO-3*
La Belle (Township)—Lewis *MO-3*
La Belle (Township)—Marshall *SD-4*
Labette (City)—Labette................. *KS-4*
Labette (Township)—Labette........ *KS-4*
Labette County *KS-4*
La Bolt (Town)—Grant *SD-4*
Labouchere Bay (CDP)—Prince of
Wales-Outer Ketchikan Census
Area... *AK-4*
La Brea Pits (CA) *Geog-4*
La Casita-Garciasville (CDP)—
Starr.. *TX-2*
La Cañada Flintridge (City)—Los
Angeles... *CA-4*
Lac Courte Oreilles Res. & Trust Lands
(WI).. *IndRes-4*
Lac du Flambeau (Town)—Vilas ... *WI-3*
Lac Du Flambeau Reservation
(WI).. *IndRes-4*
La Center (City)—Ballard *KY-2*
La Center (Town)—Clark.............. *WA-4*
Lacey (Township)—Thomas.......... *KS-4*
Lacey (Township)—Ocean............ *NJ-1*
Lacey (City)—Thurston *WA-4*
Laceyville (Borough)—Wyoming ... *PA-1*
La Cienega (CDP)—Santa Fe *NM-4*
Lack (Township)—Juniata *PA-1*
Lackawanna (City)—Erie.............. *NY-1*
Lackawanna County *PA-1*
Lackawannock (Township)—
Mercer.. *PA-1*
Lackawaxen (Township)—Pike *PA-1*
Lackland Air Force Base (TX) *Mil-4*

Lackland Air Force Base (Military
Facility)—Bexar....................... *TX-2*
Lac La Belle (Village)—
Waukesha *WI-3*
La Clede (Township)—Fayette...... *IL-3*
Laclede (City)—Linn..................... *MO-3*
Laclede County *MO-3*
Lacombe (CDP)—St. Tammany
Parish.. *LA-2*
Lacon (City)—Marshall.................. *IL-3*
Lacon (Township)—Marshall........ *IL-3*
Lacona (City)—Warren *IA-3*
Lacona (Village)—Oswego *NY-1*
Laconia (Town)—Harrison............ *IN-3*
Laconia (City)—Belknap................ *NH-1*
La Conner (Town)—Skagit........... *WA-4*
Lacoochee (CDP)—Pasco............*FL-2*
LaCoste (Town)—Medina *TX-2*
Lac qui Parle (Township)—Lac qui
Parle... *MN-3*
Lac qui Parle County *MN-3*
La Crescent (City)—Houston........ *MN-3*
La Crescent (Township)—
Houston....................................... *MN-3*
La Crescenta-Montrose (CDP)—Los
Angeles... *CA-4*
La Croft (CDP)—Columbiana......*OH-3*
La Crosse (Town)—Alachua..........*FL-2*
La Crosse (Town)—La Porte........ *IN-3*
La Crosse (City)—Rush................ *KS-4*
La Crosse (Township)—Jackson ... *MN-3*
La Crosse (Town)—Mecklenburg.... *VA-2*
La Crosse (Town)—Whitman *WA-4*
La Crosse (City)—La Crosse......... *WI-3*
La Crosse-Brookdale (Township)—
Rush *KS-4*
La Crosse County *WI-3*
Lac Vieux Desert Reservation
(MI).. *IndRes-4*
La Cygne (City)—Linn.................. *KS-4*
Lacy-Lakeview (City)—
McLennan..................................... *TX-2*
Ladd (Town)—Bureau *IL-3*
Ladd (Township)—Bowman *ND-4*
Laddonia (City)—Audrain *MO-3*
Ladera Heights (CDP)—Los
Angeles... *CA-4*
Ladoga (Town)—Montgomery.. *IN-3*
Ladonia (Division)—Russell........*AL-2*
Ladonia (Town)—Fannin *TX-2*
Ladora (City)—Iowa...................... *IA-3*
Ladore (Township)—Neosho........ *KS-4*
Ladson (CDP)—Berkeley..............*SC-2*
Ladson (CDP)—Charleston.........*SC-2*
La Due (Village)—Henry *MO-3*
Ladue (City)—St. Louis *MO-3*
Lady Lake (Town)—Lake.............*FL-2*
Ladysmith (City)—Rusk................ *WI-3*
Laenna (Township)—Logan *IL-3*
La Farge (Village)—Vernon.......... *WI-3*
Lafayette (City)—Chambers...........*AL-2*
Lafayette (City)—Contra Costa *CA-4*
Lafayette (City)—Boulder *CO-4*
La Fayette (City)—Walker............. *GA-2*
Lafayette (Township)—Coles *IL-3*
Lafayette (Township)—Ogle *IL-3*
La Fayette (Village)—Stark *IL-3*
Lafayette (Township)—Allen.......... *IN-3*
Lafayette (Township)—Floyd......... *IN-3*
Lafayette (Township)—Madison *IN-3*
Lafayette (Township)—Owen........ *IN-3*
Lafayette (City)—Tippecanoe........ *IN-3*
Lafayette (Township)—
Chautauqua.................................. *KS-4*
LaFayette (City)—Christian *KY-2*

Lafayette (City)—Lafayette
Parish.. *LA-2*
Lafayette (Township)—Gratiot *MI-3*
Lafayette (City)—Nicollet *MN-3*
Lafayette (Township)—Nicollet *MN-3*
Lafayette (Township)—Clinton...... *MO-3*
Lafayette (Township)—Sussex *NJ-1*
LaFayette (Town)—Onondaga *NY-1*
Lafayette (Village)—Allen *OH-3*
Lafayette (Township)—
Coshocton *OH-3*
Lafayette (Township)—Medina......*OH-3*
Lafayette (City)—Yamhill *OR-4*
Lafayette (Township)—McKean *PA-1*
Lafayette (City)—Macon *TN-2*
Lafayette (Town)—Chippewa......... *WI-3*
Lafayette (Town)—Monroe............ *WI-3*
Lafayette (Town)—Walworth *WI-3*
Lafayette County *AR-2*
Lafayette County *FL-2*
Lafayette County *MS-2*
Lafayette County *MO-3*
Lafayette County *WI-3*
Lafayette Parish.........................*LA-2*
Lafe (Town)—Greene *AR-2*
La Feria (City)—Cameron *TX-2*
Lafitte (CDP)—Jefferson Parish *LA-2*
Laflin (Borough)—Luzerne *PA-1*
La Follette (City)—Campbell......... *TN-2*
La Follette (Town)—Burnett *WI-3*
La Font (Township)—New
Madrid..*MO-3*
La Fontaine (Town)—Wabash......... *IN-3*
Lafoon (Township)—Faulk............ *SD-4*
Lafourche Parish........................*LA-2*
La Garde (Township)—
Mahnomen *MN-3*
Lago Vista (City)—Travis *TX-2*
La Grand (Township)—Douglas ... *MN-3*
La Grande (City)—Union *OR-4*
LaGrange (Town)—Lee *AR-2*
La Grange (City)—Troup *GA-2*
Lagrange (Township)—Bond.......... *IL-3*
La Grange (City)—Cook *IL-3*
Lagrange (Town)—Lagrange........ *IN-3*
La Grange (City)—Oldham *KY-2*
Lagrange (Town)—Penobscot...... *ME-1*
La Grange (Township)—Cass *MI-3*
La Grange (City)—Lewis *MO-3*
La Grange (Town)—Dutchess....... *NY-1*
La Grange (Town)—Lenoir *NC-2*
Lagrange (Township)—Lorain......*OH-3*
Lagrange (Village)—Lorain...........*OH-3*
La Grange (Town)—Fayette *TN-2*
La Grange (City)—Fayette *TX-2*
La Grange (Town)—Monroe.......... *WI-3*
La Grange (Town)—Walworth *WI-3*
La Grange (Town)—Goshen *WY-4*
Lagrange County *IN-3*
La Grange Park (City)—Cook *IL-3*
Lagro (Town)—Wabash *IN-3*
Lagro (Township)—Wabash *IN-3*
La Grulla (City)—Starr *TX-2*
Laguna (CDP)—Sacramento......... *CA-4*
Laguna (CDP)—Cibola *NM-4*
Laguna Beach (CA)....................... *Geog-4*
Laguna Beach (City)—Orange *CA-4*
Laguna Beach (CDP)—Bay..........*FL-2*
Laguna Heights (CDP)—
Cameron....................................... *TX-2*
Laguna Hills (CDP)—Orange *CA-4*
Laguna Niguel (City)—Orange...... *CA-4*
Laguna Pueblo & Trust Lands
(NM) *IndRes-4*

General Index

Laguna Vista (Village)—
Cameron *TX-2*
Lagunitas-Forest Knolls (CDP)—
Marin *CA-4*
La Habra (City)—Orange *CA-4*
La Habra Heights (City)—Los
Angeles *CA-4*
Lahaina (CDP)—Maui *HI-4*
La Harpe (Town)—Hancock *IL-3*
La Harpe (Township)—Hancock *IL-3*
La Harpe (City)—Allen *KS-4*
Lahoma (Town)—Garfield *OK-2*
La Homa (CDP)—Hidalgo............. *TX-2*
Laie (CDP)—Honolulu *HI-4*
Laingsburg (City)—Shiawassee *MI-3*
Laird (Township)—Houghton *MI-3*
Laird (Township)—Phelps............. *NE-4*
La Jara (Town)—Conejos............... *CO-4*
La Jolla *See* **San Diego**—San
Diego.. *CA-4*
La Jolla Reservation (CA) *IndRes-4*
La Joya (City)—Hidalgo *TX-2*
La Junta (City)—Otero *CO-4*
Lake (Township)—Clinton *IL-3*
Lake (Township)—Allen *IN-3*
Lake (Township)—Kosciusko........... *IN-3*
Lake (Township)—Newton............. *IN-3*
Lake (Township)—Harvey *KS-4*
Lake (Township)—Scott *KS-4*
Lake (Township)—Benzie *MI-3*
Lake (Township)—Huron *MI-3*
Lake (Township)—Lake *MI-3*
Lake (Township)—Macomb *MI-3*
Lake (Township)—Menominee *MI-3*
Lake (Township)—Missaukee *MI-3*
Lake (Township)—Roscommon..... *MI-3*
Lake (Township)—Roseau *MN-3*
Lake (Township)—Wabasha........... *MN-3*
Lake (Town)—Newton *MS-2*
Lake (Town)—Scott *MS-2*
Lake (Township)—Buchanan *MO-3*
Lake (Township)—Vernon *MO-3*
Lake (Township)—Hall *NE-4*
Lake (Township)—Holt *NE-4*
Lake (Township)—Phelps............. *NE-4*
Lake (Township)—Cass *ND-4*
Lake (Township)—Ashland *OH-3*
Lake (Township)—Logan *OH-3*
Lake (Township)—Stark *OH-3*
Lake (Township)—Wood *OH-3*
Lake (Township)—Luzerne *PA-1*
Lake (Township)—Mercer *PA-1*
Lake (Township)—Wayne *PA-1*
Lake (Township)—Aurora *SD-4*
Lake (Township)—Clark *SD-4*
Lake (Township)—Codington *SD-4*
Lake (Township)—Corson *SD-4*
Lake (Township)—Marshall........... *SD-4*
Lake (Township)—Roberts............ *SD-4*
Lake (Township)—Spink *SD-4*
Lake (Township)—Tripp *SD-4*
Lake (Town)—Marinette *WI-3*
Lake (Town)—Price..................... *WI-3*
Lake Alfred (City)—Polk..............*FL-2*
Lake Alice (Township)—
Hubbard....................................*MN-3*
Lake Aluma (Town)—Oklahoma ... *OK-2*
Lake Andes (City)—Charles Mix... *SD-4*
Lake and Peninsula Borough *AK-4*
Lake Andrew (Township)—
Kandiyohi *MN-3*
Lake Angelus (City)—Oakland *MI-3*
Lake Ann (Village)—Benzie........... *MI-3*
Lake Annette (Village)—Cass *MO-3*

Lake Arrowhead (CDP)—San
Bernardino *CA-4*
Lake Arthur (Town)—Jefferson Davis
Parish *LA-2*
Lake Arthur (Town)—Chaves *NM-4*
Lake Barcroft (CDP)—Fairfax *VA-2*
Lake Barrington (Village)—Lake *IL-3*
Lake Belt (Township)—Martin *MN-3*
Lake Benton (City)—Lincoln......... *MN-3*
Lake Benton (Township)—
Lincoln..................................... *MN-3*
Lake Bluff (City)—Lake *IL-3*
Lake Bridgeport (City)—Wise *TX-2*
Lake Bronson (City)—Kittson *MN-3*
Lake Brownwood (CDP)—Brown.. *TX-2*
Lake Buena Vista (City)—Orange ..*FL-2*
Lake Butler (City)—Union *FL-2*
Lake Byron (Township)—Beadle ... *SD-4*
Lake Carmel (CDP)—Putnam *NY-1*
Lake Catherine (CDP)—Lake *IL-3*
Lake Charles (City)—Calcasieu
Parish *LA-2*
Lake Charter (Township)—
Berrien..................................... *MI-3*
Lake City (Town)—Craighead *AR-2*
Lake City (Town)—Hinsdale *CO-4*
Lake City (City)—Columbia *FL-2*
Lake City (City)—Clayton *GA-2*
Lake City (City)—Calhoun *IA-3*
Lake City (Township)—Barber *KS-4*
Lake City (City)—Missaukee *MI-3*
Lake City (City)—Goodhue *MN-3*
Lake City (City)—Wabasha........... *MN-3*
Lake City (Borough)—Erie............. *PA-1*
Lake City (City)—Florence *SC-2*
Lake City (Town)—Marshall.......... *SD-4*
Lake City (Town)—Anderson *TN-2*
Lake City (Town)—Campbell *TN-2*
Lake City (Town)—San Patricio... *TX-2*
Lake Clarke Shores (Town)—Palm
Beach *FL-2*
Lake County *CA-4*
Lake County *CO-4*
Lake County *FL-2*
Lake County *IL-3*
Lake County *IN-3*
Lake County *MI-3*
Lake County *MN-3*
Lake County *MT-4*
Lake County *OH-3*
Lake County *OR-4*
Lake County *SD-4*
Lake County *TN-2*
Lake Creek (Township)—Pettis *MO-3*
Lake Creek (Pop. Place)—
Pennington *SD-4*
Lake Crystal (City)—Blue Earth... *MN-3*
Lake Dalecarlia (CDP)—Lake *IN-3*
Lake Dallas (City)—Denton *TX-2*
Lake Darby (CDP)—Franklin........ *OH-3*
Lake Delton (Village)—Sauk......... *WI-3*
Lake Edwards (Township)—Crow
Wing *MN-3*
Lake Elizabeth (Township)—
Kandiyohi................................. *MN-3*
Lake Elmo (City)—Washington *MN-3*
Lake Elsinore (City)—Riverside *CA-4*
Lake Emma (Township)—
Hubbard................................... *MN-3*
Lake Erie Beach (CDP)—Erie....... *NY-1*
Lake Eunice (Township)—
Becker *MN-3*
Lake Fenton (CDP)—Genesee *MI-3*
Lakefield (Township)—Luce *MI-3*
Lakefield (Township)—Saginaw.... *MI-3*

Lakefield (City)—Jackson *MN-3*
Lake Flat No. 8 (Township)—
Pennington *SD-4*
Lake Forest (City)—Lake *IL-3*
Lake Forest North (CDP)—King... *WA-4*
Lake Forest Park (City)—Lake *WA-4*
Lake Fork (Township)—Logan *IL-3*
Lake Fremont (Township)—
Martin *MN-3*
Lake Geneva (City)—Walworth.... *WI-3*
Lake George (Township)—
Hubbard................................... *MN-3*
Lake George (Township)—
Stearns.................................... *MN-3*
Lake George (Town)—Warren *NY-1*
Lake George (Village)—Warren *NY-1*
Lake George (Township)—
McHenry *ND-4*
Lake George (Township)—Charles
Mix... *SD-4*
Lake Goodwin (CDP)—
Snohomish *WA-4*
Lake Grove (Township)—
Mahnomen *MN-3*
Lake Grove (Village)—Suffolk .. *NY-1*
Lake Hamilton (Town)—Polk.......*FL-2*
Lake Hanska (Township)—
Brown..................................... *MN-3*
Lake Hart (Town)—Morgan *IN-3*
Lake Hattie (Township)—
Hubbard.................................. *MN-3*
Lake Havasu City (City)—
Mohave *AZ-4*
Lake Helen (City)—Volusia *FL-2*
Lake Hendricks (Township)—
Brookings *SD-4*
Lake Henry (City)—Stearns *MN-3*
Lake Henry (Township)—
Stearns.................................... *MN-3*
Lake Hester (Township)—
McHenry *ND-4*
Lake Hill No. 5 (Township)—
Pennington *SD-4*
Lakehills (CDP)—Bandera............ *TX-2*
Lake Holcombe (Town)—
Chippewa *WI-3*
Lakehurst (Borough)—Ocean *NJ-1*
Lake Ibsen (Township)—Benson ...*ND-4*
Lake Ida (Township)—Norman ... *MN-3*
Lake in the Hills (Village)—
McHenry *IL-3*
Lake Isabella (CDP)—Kern *CA-4*
Lake Jackson (City)—Brazoria *TX-2*
Lake Jessie (Township)—Itasca *MN-3*
Lake Johanna (Township)—
Pope *MN-3*
Lake Junaluska (CDP)—
Haywood.................................. *NC-2*
Lake Katrine (CDP)—Ulster *NY-1*
Lakeland (City)—Polk..................*FL-2*
Lakeland (City)—Lanier................ *GA-2*
Lakeland (City)—Washington *MN-3*
Lakeland (Town)—Miller *MO-3*
Lakeland (City)—Shelby *TN-2*
Lakeland (Town)—Barron *WI-3*
Lakeland Highlands (CDP)—
Polk *FL-2*
Lakeland North (CDP)—King *WA-4*
Lakeland Shores (City)—
Washington *MN-3*
Lakeland South (CDP)—King *WA-4*
Lakeland Village (CDP)—
Riverside *CA-4*
Lake Lillian (City)—Kandiyohi *MN-3*

Lake Lillian (Township)—
Kandiyohi MN-3
Lake Linden (Village)—
Houghton MI-3
Lakeline (Village)—Lake OH-3
Lake Lorraine (CDP)—Okaloosa....FL-2
Lake Los Angeles (CDP)—Los
Angeles CA-4
Lake Lotawana (City)—Jackson ... MO-3
Lake Lucerne (CDP)—Dade FL-2
Lake Lure (Town)—Rutherford NC-2
Lake Luzerne (Town)—Warren NY-1
Lake Luzerne-Hadley (CDP)—
Saratoga NY-1
Lake Magdalene (CDP)—
Hillsborough FL-2
Lake Marshall (Township)—
Lyon MN-3
Lake Mary (City)—Seminole FL-2
Lake Mary (Township)—
Douglas MN-3
Lake Michigan Beach (CDP)—
Berrien MI-3
Lake Mills (City)—Winnebago IA-3
Lake Mills (City)—Jefferson WI-3
Lake Mills (Town)—Jefferson WI-3
Lake Minchumina (CDP)—
Yukon-Koyukuk Census Area......AK-4
Lake Mohawk (CDP)—Sussex NJ-1
Lake Montezuma (CDP)—
Yavapai AZ-4
Lake Monticello (CDP)—
Fluvanna VA-2
Lakemoor (Village)—Lake IL-3
Lakemoor (Village)—McHenry IL-3
Lakemore (Village)—Summit.........OH-3
Lake Mykee Town (Village)—
Callaway MO-3
Lake Nacimiento (CDP)—San Luis
Obispo CA-4
Lake Nebagamon (Village)—
Douglas WI-3
Lake No. 1 (Pop. Place)—Lake MN-3
Lake No. 2 (Pop. Place)—Lake MN-3
Lake Norden (City)—Hamlin SD-4
Lake Odessa (Village)—Ionia.........MI-3
Lake of the Pines (CDP)—
Nevada CA-4
Lake of the Woods (CDP)—
Champaign IL-3
Lake of the Woods County.............MN-3
Lake Okeechobee-Cross Florida
Waterway (CA) Geog-4
Lake Orion (Village)—Oakland MI-3
Lake Oswego (City)—Clackamas ... OR-4
Lake Oswego (City)—
Multnomah OR-4
Lake Oswego (City)—
Washington OR-4
Lake Ozark (City)—Camden MO-3
Lake Ozark (City)—Miller MO-3
Lake Panasoffkee (CDP)—
Sumter FL-2
Lake Park (Town)—Palm Beach.....FL-2
Lake Park (Town)—Lowndes GA-2
Lake Park (City)—Dickinson..........IA-3
Lake Park (City)—Becker MN-3
Lake Park (Township)—Becker MN-3
Lake Placid (Town)—Highlands FL-2
Lake Placid (Village)—Essex NY-1
Lake Pleasant (Township)—Red
Lake..MN-3
Lake Pleasant (Town)—
Hamilton.......................................NY-1

Lake Pocotopaug (CDP)—
Middlesex CT-1
Lake Pontchartrain (CA) Geog-4
Lakeport (City)—Lake...................CA-4
Lakeport (Township)—Hubbard ... MN-3
Lakeport (City)—Gregg..................TX-2
Lake Prairie (Township)—
Nicollet MN-3
Lake Preston (City)—Kingsbury.... SD-4
Lake Providence (Town)—East Carroll
Parish LA-2
Lake Purdy (Division)—Shelby AL-2
Lake Quivira (City)—Johnson.........KS-4
Lake Quivira (City)—Wyandotte....KS-4
Lake Ridge (CDP)—Prince
William VA-2
Lake Ripley (CDP)—Jefferson........WI-3
Lake Ronkonkoma (CDP)—
Suffolk NY-1
Lake San Marcos (CDP)—San
Diego...CA-4
Lake Sarah (Township)—Murray.. MN-3
Lake Sarasota (CDP)—Sarasota FL-2
Lakes by the Bay (CDP)—Dade.....FL-2
Lake Serene-North Lynnwood (CDP)—
Snohomish WA-4
Lakeshire (City)—St. Louis............MO-3
Lake Shore (CDP)—Anne
Arundel MD-1
Lake Shore (City)—Cass MN-3
Lake Shore (Township)—Lac qui
Parle MN-3
Lake Shore (CDP)—Clark WA-4
Lakeside (CDP)—San Diego CA-4
Lakeside (Town)—Jefferson CO-4
Lakeside (CDP)—Clay FL-2
Lakeside (City)—Buena Vista.........IA-3
Lakeside (Township)—Aitkin........ MN-3
Lakeside (Township)—
Cottonwood MN-3
Lakeside (City)—Miller..................MO-3
Lakeside (City)—Coos OR-4
Lakeside (Township)—Meade SD-4
Lakeside (Town)—San Patricio......TX-2
Lakeside (Town)—Tarrant TX-2
Lakeside (CDP)—Henrico VA-2
Lakeside (Town)—Douglas WI-3
Lakeside City (Town)—Archer TX-2
Lakeside City (Town)—Wichita.....TX-2
Lakeside Green (CDP)—Palm
Beach...FL-2
Lakeside Park (City)—Kenton........KY-2
Lake Sinai (Township)—
Brookings SD-4
Lakesite (City)—Hamilton TN-2
Lakes of the Four Seasons (CDP)—
Lake...IN-3
Lakes of the Four Seasons (CDP)—
Porter IN-3
Lake Station (City)—Lake IN-3
Lake Stay (Township)—Lincoln.... MN-3
Lake St. Croix Beach (City)—
Washington MN-3
Lake Stevens (City)—Snohomish ... WA-4
Lake St. Louis (City)—St.
Charles MO-3
Lake Success (Village)—Nassau NY-1
Lake Summerset (CDP)—
Stephenson IL-3
Lake Summerset (CDP)—
Winnebago IL-3
Lake Tanglewood (Village)—
Randall TX-2
Lake Tapawingo (City)—
Jackson..MO-3

Lake Telemark (CDP)—Morris.......NJ-1
Lake Tomahawk (Town)—
Oneida WI-3
Laketon (Township)—Muskegon ... MI-3
Laketon (Township)—Brookings....SD-4
Laketown (Township)—Allegan MI-3
Laketown (Township)—Carver MN-3
Lake Town (Township)—Barnes ND-4
Laketown (Town)—Rich UT-4
Laketown (Town)—Polk.................WI-3
Lake Traverse (Sisseton) Reservation
(SD) IndRes-4
Lake Valley (Township)—
Traverse..MN-3
Lake Vermilion (Pop. Place)—St.
Louis MN-3
Lakeview (Municipality)—
DeKalb AL-2
Lakeview (Town)—Baxter AR-2
Lake View (Town)—Phillips AR-2
Lakeview (CDP)—Riverside CA-4
Lakeview (CDP)—Catoosa GA-2
Lakeview (CDP)—Walker GA-2
Lake View (City)—Sac IA-3
Lake View (Pop. Place)—
Piscataquis ME-1
Lakeview (Village)—Montcalm..... MI-3
Lake View (Township)—Becker.... MN-3
Lakeview (Township)—Carlton MN-3
Lakeview (Village)—Miller MO-3
Lakeview (City)—Stone..................MO-3
Lakeview (CDP)—Nassau NY-1
Lakeview (Township)—Burke ND-4
Lakeview (Village)—Logan OH-3
Lakeview (Town)—Lake OR-4
Lake View (Town)—Dillon SC-2
Lake View (Township)—Lake SD-4
Lakeview (Town)—Hall..................TX-2
Lakeview Estates (CDP)—
Rockdale GA-2
Lakeview Heights (City)—Rowan...KY-2
Lake Villa (Town)—Lake IL-3
Lake Villa (Township)—Lake IL-3
Lake Village (City)—Chicot AR-2
Lakeville (Town)—St. Joseph.........IN-3
Lakeville (Town)—Penobscot ME-1
Lakeville (Town)—Plymouth MA-1
Lakeville (City)—Dakota MN-3
Lakeville (Township)—Grand
Forks ND-4
Lake Waccamaw (Town)—
Columbus......................................NC-2
Lake Wales (City)—Polk FL-2
Lake Washington (Township)—
Eddy ND-4
Lake Washington Ship Canal
(WA) Geog-4
Lake Waukomis (City)—Platte MO-3
Lakeway (City)—Travis..................TX-2
Lake Wazeecha (CDP)—Wood WI-3
Lake Williams (Township)—
Kidder ND-4
Lake Williams (Township)—
McLean ND-4
Lake Wilson (City)—Murray MN-3
Lake Winnebago (City)—Cass MO-3
Lake Wisconsin (CDP)—
Columbia WI-3
Lake Wisconsin (CDP)—Sauk WI-3
Lake Wissota (CDP)—Chippewa....WI-3
Lakewood (City)—Los Angeles......CA-4
Lakewood (City)—Jefferson CO-4
Lakewood (Town)—McHenry IL-3
Lakewood (Township)—Shelby IL-3

General Index

Lakewood (Township)—St. Louis ... MN-3
Lakewood (Township)—Ocean ... NJ-1
Lakewood (Village)—Chautauqua ... NY-1
Lakewood (City)—Cuyahoga ... OH-3
Lakewood (City)—Davidson ... TN-2
Lakewood (CDP)—Pierce ... WA-4
Lakewood (Town)—Oconto ... WI-3
Lakewood Club (Village)—Muskegon ... MI-3
Lakewood Park (CDP)—St. Lucie ... FL-2
Lakewood Shores (CDP)—Will ... IL-3
Lakewood Village (City)—Denton ... TX-2
Lake Worth (City)—Palm Beach ... FL-2
Lake Worth (City)—Tarrant ... TX-2
Lake Wylie (CDP)—York ... SC-2
Lake Wynonah (CDP)—Schuylkill ... PA-1
Lake Zurich (City)—Lake ... IL-3
Lakin (Township)—Barton ... KS-4
Lakin (Township)—Harvey ... KS-4
Lakin (City)—Kearny ... KS-4
Lakin (Township)—Kearny ... KS-4
Lakin (Township)—Morrison ... MN-3
Lakota (City)—Kossuth ... IA-3
Lakota (City)—Nelson ... ND-4
Lakota (Township)—Nelson ... ND-4
Lallie (Township)—Benson ... ND-4
Lallie North (Pop. Place)—Benson ... ND-4
La Luz (CDP)—Otero ... NM-4
Lamar (City)—Johnson ... AR-2
Lamar (City)—Prowers ... CO-4
Lamar (City)—Barton ... MO-3
Lamar (Township)—Barton ... MO-3
Lamar (Village)—Chase ... NE-4
Lamar (Town)—Hughes ... OK-2
Lamar (Township)—Clinton ... PA-1
Lamar (Town)—Darlington ... SC-2
Lamar County ... AL-2
Lamar County ... GA-2
Lamar County ... MS-2
Lamar County ... TX-2
Lamard (Township)—Wayne ... IL-3
Lamar Heights (Village)—Barton ... MO-3
La Marque (City)—Galveston ... TX-2
La Mars (Township)—Richland ... ND-4
Lamartine (Town)—Fond du Lac .. WI-3
Lamb County ... TX-2
Lambert (Township)—Red Lake ... MN-3
Lambert (Town)—Quitman ... MS-2
Lambert (Village)—Scott ... MO-3
Lambert (Town)—Alfalfa ... OK-2
Lamberton (City)—Redwood ... MN-3
Lamberton (Township)—Redwood ... MN-3
Lambertville (CDP)—Monroe ... MI-3
Lambertville (City)—Hunterdon ... NJ-1
Lambs Grove (City)—Jasper ... IA-3
Lame Deer (CDP)—Rosebud ... MT-4
La Mesa (City)—San Diego ... CA-4
Lamesa (City)—Dawson ... TX-2
Lamine (Township)—Cooper ... MO-3
La Mirada (City)—Los Angeles ... CA-4
Lammers (Township)—Beltrami ... MN-3
La Moille (Township)—Bureau ... IL-3
La Moille (Village)—Bureau ... IL-3
Lamoille County ... VT-1
Lamoine (Township)—McDonough ... IL-3
Lamoine (Town)—Hancock ... ME-1

Lamoni (City)—Decatur ... IA-3
Lamont (CDP)—Kern ... CA-4
Lamont (City)—Buchanan ... IA-3
Lamont (Township)—Hamilton ... KS-4
Lamont (Town)—Grant ... OK-2
Lamont (Town)—Whitman ... WA-4
Lamont (Town)—Lafayette ... WI-3
La Monte (City)—Pettis ... MO-3
La Monte (Township)—Pettis ... MO-3
Lamotte (Township)—Crawford ... IL-3
La Motte (City)—Jackson ... IA-3
Lamotte (Township)—Sanilac ... MI-3
La Moure (City)—LaMoure ... ND-4
La Moure (Township)—Pembina ... ND-4
LaMoure County ... ND-4
Lampasas (City)—Lampasas ... TX-2
Lampasas County ... TX-2
Lampton (Township)—Walsh ... ND-4
Lamro (Township)—Tripp ... SD-4
Lanagan (Town)—McDonald ... MO-3
Lanai (HI) ... Geog-4
Lanai City (CDP)—Maui ... HI-4
Lanark (Town)—Carroll ... IL-3
Lanark (Town)—Portage ... WI-3
Lancaster (City)—Los Angeles ... CA-4
Lancaster (Township)—Stephenson ... IL-3
Lancaster (Township)—Huntington ... IN-3
Lancaster (Township)—Jefferson ... IN-3
Lancaster (Township)—Wells ... IN-3
Lancaster (City)—Atchison ... KS-4
Lancaster (Township)—Atchison ... KS-4
Lancaster (City)—Garrard ... KY-2
Lancaster (Town)—Worcester ... MA-1
Lancaster (Township)—Kittson ... MN-3
Lancaster (City)—Schuyler ... MO-3
Lancaster (Town)—Coos ... NH-1
Lancaster (Town)—Erie ... NY-1
Lancaster (Village)—Erie ... NY-1
Lancaster (City)—Fairfield ... OH-3
Lancaster (Township)—Butler ... PA-1
Lancaster (City)—Lancaster ... PA-1
Lancaster (Township)—Lancaster ... PA-1
Lancaster (City)—Lancaster ... SC-2
Lancaster (City)—Dallas ... TX-2
Lancaster (City)—Grant ... WI-3
Lancaster County ... NE-4
Lancaster County ... PA-1
Lancaster County ... SC-2
Lancaster County ... VA-2
Lancaster Mill (CDP)—Lancaster ... SC-2
Land (Township)—Grant ... MN-3
Land (Township)—McHenry ... ND-4
Landa (City)—Bottineau ... ND-4
Landaff (Town)—Grafton ... NH-1
Landen (CDP)—Warren ... OH-3
Lander (City)—Fremont ... WY-4
Lander County ... NV-4
Landfall (City)—Washington ... MN-3
Landgrove (Town)—Bennington ... VT-1
The Landing (Village)—Ralls ... MO-3
Landing Creek (Township)—Gregory ... SD-4
Landingville (Borough)—Schuylkill ... PA-1
Landis (Town)—Rowan ... NC-2
Landisburg (Borough)—Perry ... PA-1
Land O' Lakes (CDP)—Pasco ... FL-2
Land O'Lakes (Town)—Vilas ... WI-3
Landover (CDP)—Prince George's ... MD-1
Landover Hills (Town)—Prince George's ... MD-1
Landrum (City)—Spartanburg ... SC-2

Lane (Township)—Warrick ... IN-3
Lane (City)—Franklin ... KS-4
Lane (Township)—Greenwood ... KS-4
Lane (Township)—Smith ... KS-4
Lane (Town)—Williamsburg ... SC-2
Lane (Town)—Jerauld ... SD-4
Lane County ... KS-4
Lane County ... OR-4
Lanesboro (City)—Carroll ... IA-3
Lanesboro (City)—Fillmore ... MN-3
Lanesboro (Borough)—Susquehanna ... PA-1
Lanesborough (Town)—Berkshire ... MA-1
Lanesburgh (Township)—Le Sueur ... MN-3
Lanesville (Township)—Sangamon ... IL-3
Lanesville (Town)—Harrison ... IN-3
Lanett (City)—Chambers ... AL-2
Langberg (Township)—Bowman ... ND-4
Langdon (City)—Reno ... KS-4
Langdon (Township)—Reno ... KS-4
Langdon (Town)—Sullivan ... NH-1
Langdon (City)—Cavalier ... ND-4
Langdon (Township)—Cavalier ... ND-4
Langdon Place (City)—Jefferson ... KY-2
Langford (Town)—Marshall ... SD-4
Langhei (Township)—Pope ... MN-3
Langhorne (Borough)—Bucks ... PA-1
Langhorne Manor (Borough)—Bucks ... PA-1
Langlade (Town)—Langlade ... WI-3
Langlade County ... WI-3
Langley (Township)—Ellsworth ... KS-4
Langley (Town)—Mayes ... OK-2
Langley (City)—Island ... WA-4
Langley Air Force Base (VA) ... Mil-4
Langley Park (CDP)—Montgomery ... MD-1
Langley Park (CDP)—Prince George's ... MD-1
Langola (Township)—Benton ... MN-3
Langor (Township)—Beltrami ... MN-3
Langston (Municipality)—Jackson ... AL-2
Langston (Town)—Logan ... OK-2
Lanham-Seabrook (CDP)—Prince George's ... MD-1
Lanier (Township)—Preble ... OH-3
Lanier County ... GA-2
Lankin (City)—Walsh ... ND-4
Lannon (Village)—Waukesha ... WI-3
Lansdale (Borough)—Montgomery ... PA-1
Lansdowne (Borough)—Delaware ... PA-1
Lansdowne-Baltimore Highlands (CDP)—Baltimore ... MD-1
L'Anse (Township)—Baraga ... MI-3
L'Anse (Village)—Baraga ... MI-3
L'Anse Reservation & Trust Lands (MI) ... IndRes-4
Lansford (City)—Bottineau ... ND-4
Lansford (Township)—Bottineau ... ND-4
Lansford (Borough)—Carbon ... PA-1
Lansing (City)—Cook ... IL-3
Lansing (City)—Allamakee ... IA-3
Lansing (City)—Leavenworth ... KS-4
Lansing (City)—Eaton ... MI-3
Lansing (City)—Ingham ... MI-3
Lansing (Township)—Ingham ... MI-3
Lansing (Township)—Mower ... MN-3
Lansing (Town)—Tompkins ... NY-1
Lansing (Village)—Tompkins ... NY-1
Lansing (Town)—Ashe ... NC-2

American Places Dictionary   General Index

Lansing (Township)—Towner ND-4
Lansing (Township)—Brown SD-4
Lantana (Town)—Palm Beach FL-2
Laona (Township)—Winnebago...... IL-3
Laona (Township)—Roseau MN-3
Laona (Town)—Forest WI-3
La Palma (City)—Orange............... CA-4
La Paz (Town)—Marshall IN-3
La Paz County............................ AZ-4
Lapeer (City)—Lapeer................... MI-3
Lapeer (Township)—Lapeer MI-3
Lapeer (Town)—Cortland NY-1
Lapeer County MI-3
Lapel (Town)—Madison................. IN-3
La Place (CDP)—St. John the Baptist
    Parish LA-2
La Plata (Town)—Charles............. MD-1
La Plata (City)—Macon MO-3
La Plata (Township)—Macon MO-3
La Plata County CO-4
La Plume (Township)—
    Lackawanna PA-1
La Pointe (Town)—Ashland........... WI-3
La Porte (City)—La Porte............... IN-3
Laporte (City)—Hubbard MN-3
Laporte (Borough)—Sullivan PA-1
Laporte (Township)—Sullivan PA-1
La Porte (City)—Harris................... TX-2
La Porte City (City)—Black
    Hawk IA-3
La Porte County IN-3
La Posta Reservation (CA)........ IndRes-4
La Prairie (Village)—Adams IL-3
La Prairie (Township)—Marshall ... IL-3
La Prairie (Township)—
    Clearwater.........................MN-3
La Prairie (City)—Itasca MN-3
La Prairie (Township)—Spink SD-4
La Prairie (Town)—Rock WI-3
La Pryor (CDP)—Zavala TX-2
La Puente (City)—Los Angeles....... CA-4
Lapwai (City)—Nez Perce ID-4
La Quinta (City)—Riverside........... CA-4
Laramie (City)—Albany WY-4
Laramie County........................... WY-4
Laramie Mountains (WY) Geog-4
Larchmont (Village)—
    Westchester NY-1
Larchwood (City)—Lyon IA-3
Laredo (City)—Grundy MO-3
Laredo (City)—Webb TX-2
Largo (City)—Pinellas................... FL-2
Largo (CDP)—Prince George's..... MD-1
Larimer (Township)—Somerset PA-1
Larimer County CO-4
Larimore (City)—Grand Forks ND-4
Larimore (Township)—Grand
    Forks ND-4
La Riviera (CDP)—Sacramento CA-4
Lark (Township)—Grant ND-4
Larkfield-Wikiup (CDP)—
    Sonoma CA-4
Larkin (Township)—Midland MI-3
Larkin (Township)—Nobles MN-3
Larkinsburg (Township)—Clay IL-3
Larkspur (City)—Marin CA-4
Larkspur (Town)—Douglas CO-4
Larksville (Borough)—Luzerne PA-1
Larned (City)—Pawnee KS-4
Larned (Township)—Pawnee KS-4
La Roche (Township)—Charles
    Mix..................................... SD-4
La Rose (Village)—Marshall IL-3
Larose (CDP)—Lafourche Parish ..LA-2
Larrabee (City)—Cherokee IA-3

Larrabee (Township)—Gove KS-4
Larrabee (Township)—Foster ND-4
Larrabee (Town)—Waupaca WI-3
Larsen Bay (City)—Kodiak Island
    Borough............................. AK-4
Larson (City)—Burke ND-4
La Rue (Village)—Marion OH-3
LaRue County KY-2
La Russell (City)—Jasper MO-3
Larwill (Town)—Whitley................ IN-3
La Salle (Town)—Weld................... CO-4
La Salle (City)—La Salle IL-3
La Salle (Township)—La Salle IL-3
La Salle (Township)—Monroe MI-3
La Salle (City)—Watonwan........... MN-3
La Salle County IL-3
La Salle County............................ TX-2
La Salle Parish LA-2
Las Animas (City)—Bent CO-4
Las Animas County.................... CO-4
Las Cruces (City)—Doña Ana NM-4
Lasker (Town)—Northampton NC-2
Las Lomas (CDP)—Monterey CA-4
Lassen County CA-4
Lassen Peak *or* Mount (CA)......... Geog-4
Lastrup (City)—Morrison MN-3
Las Vegas (City)—Clark NV-4
Las Vegas (City)—San Miguel NM-4
Las Vegas Colony (NV) IndRes-4
Latah (Town)—Spokane WA-1
Latah County ID-4
Latexo (City)—Houston TX-2
Latham (Village)—Logan IL-3
Latham (City)—Butler...................KS-4
Latham (CDP)—Albany NY-1
Lathrop (City)—San Joaquin CA-4
Lathrop (City)—Clinton MO-3
Lathrop (Township)—Clinton MO-3
Lathrop (Township)—
    Susquehanna PA-1
Lathrup Village (City)—Oakland... MI-3
Latimer (City)—Franklin................ IA-3
Latimer (City)—Morris KS-4
Latimer (CDP)—Jackson MS-2
Latimer County OK-2
Latimore (Township)—Adams PA-1
Laton (CDP)—Fresno CA-4
Latona (Township)—Walsh ND-4
Latonia Lakes (City)—Kenton KY-2
La Tour (Town)—Johnson MO-3
Latrobe (Borough)—
    Westmoreland PA-1
Latta (Town)—Dillon..................... SC-2
Lattimore (Town)—Cleveland....... NC-2
Lattingtown (Village)—Nassau NY-1
Latty (Township)—Paulding OH-3
Latty (Village)—Paulding.............. OH-3
Lauderdale (City)—Ramsey MN-3
Lauderdale-by-the-Sea (Town)—
    Broward FL-2
Lauderdale County AL-2
Lauderdale County MS-2
Lauderdale County TN-2
Lauderdale Lakes (City)—
    Broward FL-2
Lauderhill (City)—Broward............ FL-2
Laughery (Township)—Ripley IN-3
Laughlin (CDP)—Clark................. NV-4
Laughlin Air Force Base (Military
    Facility)—Val Verde......... TX-2
Laupahoehoe (CDP)—Hawaii......... HI-4
Laura (Village)—Miami OH-3
Lauramie (Township)—
    Tippecanoe........................ IN-3
Laurel (Town)—Sussex DE-1

Laurel (CDP)—Sarasota................. FL-2
Laurel (Town)—Franklin................ IN-3
Laurel (Township)—Franklin.......... IN-3
Laurel (City)—Marshall IA-3
Laurel (City)—Prince George's MD-1
Laurel (City)—Jones......................MS-2
Laurel (City)—Yellowstone MT-4
Laurel (City)—Cedar...................... NE-4
Laurel (CDP)—Suffolk................... NY-1
Laurel (Township)—Hocking OH-3
Laurel (CDP)—Henrico VA-2
Laurel Bay (CDP)—Beaufort SC-2
Laurel County KY-2
Laureldale (Borough)—Berks PA-1
Laurel Hill (City)—Okaloosa FL-2
Laurel Hollow (Village)—Nassau... NY-1
Laurel Mountain (Borough)—
    Westmoreland PA-1
Laurel Park (Town)—Henderson ... NC-2
Laurel Run (Borough)—Luzerne PA-1
Laurel Springs (Borough)—
    Camden NJ-1
Laurelville (Village)—Hocking........OH-3
Laurence Harbor (CDP)—
    Middlesex NJ-1
Laurens (City)—Pocahontas IA-3
Laurens (Town)—Otsego................ NY-1
Laurens (Village)—Otsego.............. NY-1
Laurens (City)—Laurens SC-2
Laurens County GA-2
Laurens County SC-2
Laurie (Village)—Morgan.............. MO-3
Laurinburg (City)—Scotland.......... NC-2
Laurium (Village)—Houghton MI-3
Lausanne (Township)—Carbon PA-1
Lavaca (City)—Sebastian AR-2
Lavaca County TX-2
La Vale (CDP)—Allegany MD-1
La Valle (Town)—Sauk WI-3
La Valle (Village)—Sauk WI-3
Lavallette (Borough)—Ocean NJ-1
La Valley (Township)—Lincoln SD-4
Lavell (Township)—St. Louis........ MN-3
La Vergne (City)—Rutherford TN-2
La Verkin (City)—Washington....... UT-4
La Verne (City)—Los Angeles CA-4
Laverne (Town)—Harper OK-2
La Vernia (City)—Wilson TX-2
La Veta (Town)—Huerfano............ CO-4
La Villa (City)—Hidalgo................. TX-2
Lavina (Town)—Golden Valley MT-4
La Vista (City)—Sarpy NE-4
Lavon (Town)—Collin TX-2
Lavonia (City)—Franklin............... GA-2
Lawai (CDP)—Kauai HI-4
La Ward (City)—Jackson TX-2
Lawler (City)—Chickasaw IA-3
Lawn (Town)—Taylor TX-2
Lawndale (City)—Los Angeles CA-4
Lawndale (Township)—McLean IL-3
Lawndale (Town)—Cleveland NC-2
Lawnside (Borough)—Camden NJ-1
Lawnton (CDP)—Dauphin PA-1
Lawrence (Township)—Lawrence ... IL-3
Lawrence (City)—Marion IN-3
Lawrence (Township)—Marion....... IN-3
Lawrence (Township)—Cloud KS-4
Lawrence (City)—Douglas KS-4
Lawrence (Township)—Osborne ...KS-4
Lawrence (City)—Essex MA-1
Lawrence (Township)—Van
    Buren MI-3
Lawrence (Village)—Van Buren..... MI-3

1013

General Index
American Places Dictionary

Lawrence (Township)—Grant *MN-3*
Lawrence (Township)—Itasca *MN-3*
Lawrence (Village)—Nuckolls *NE-4*
Lawrence (Township)—
   Cumberland *NJ-1*
Lawrence (Township)—Mercer *NJ-1*
Lawrence (Village)—Nassau........... *NY-1*
Lawrence (Town)—St. Lawrence ... *NY-1*
Lawrence (Township)—Lawrence .. *OH-3*
Lawrence (Township)—Stark *OH-3*
Lawrence (Township)—
   Tuscarawas *OH-3*
Lawrence (Township)—
   Washington *OH-3*
Lawrence (Township)—Clearfield... *PA-1*
Lawrence (Township)—Tioga *PA-1*
Lawrence (Township)—Charles
   Mix *SD-4*
Lawrence (Township)—Roberts *SD-4*
Lawrence (Village)—Kaufman *TX-2*
Lawrence (Town)—Brown *WI-3*
Lawrence (Town)—Rusk *WI-3*
Lawrenceburg (City)—Dearborn..... *IN-3*
Lawrenceburg (Township)—
   Dearborn *IN-3*
Lawrenceburg (City)—Anderson.... *KY-2*
Lawrenceburg (City)—Lawrence.... *TN-2*
Lawrence County *AL-2*
Lawrence County *AR-2*
Lawrence County *IL-3*
Lawrence County *IN-3*
Lawrence County *KY-2*
Lawrence County *MS-2*
Lawrence County *MO-3*
Lawrence County *OH-3*
Lawrence County *PA-1*
Lawrence County *SD-4*
Lawrence County *TN-2*
Lawrence Creek (Town)—Creek *OK-2*
Lawrence Park (Township)—Erie .. *PA-1*
Lawrenceville (City)—Gwinnett *GA-2*
Lawrenceville (City)—Lawrence *IL-3*
Lawrenceville (CDP)—Mercer........ *NJ-1*
Lawrenceville (Village)—Clark *OH-3*
Lawrenceville (Borough)—Tioga... *PA-1*
Lawrenceville (Town)—
   Brunswick *VA-2*
Lawson (City)—Clay *MO-3*
Lawson (City)—Ray *MO-3*
Lawson Heights (CDP)—
   Westmoreland *PA-1*
Lawsonia (CDP)—Somerset........... *MD-1*
Lawtey (City)—Bradford................. *FL-2*
Lawton (City)—Woodbury.............. *IA-3*
Lawton (Village)—Van Buren *MI-3*
Lawton (City)—Ramsey.................. *ND-4*
Lawton (Township)—Ramsey *ND-4*
Lawton (City)—Comanche............. *OK-2*
Laymantown (CDP)—Botetourt *VA-2*
Layton (City)—Monroe................... *FL-2*
Layton (Township)—McHenry *ND-4*
Layton (City)—Davis *UT-4*
Laytonsville (Town)—
   Montgomery.................... *MD-1*
Laytonville (CDP)—Mendocino..... *CA-4*
Laytonville Rancheria (CA) *IndRes-4*
Lazy Lake (Village)—Broward........ *FL-2*
Lazy Mountain (CDP)—
   Matanuska-Susitna Borough *AK-4*
Leachville (City)—Mississippi *AR-2*
Leacock (Township)—Lancaster ... *PA-1*
Lea County *NM-4*
Lead (City)—Lawrence................... *SD-4*
Lead Hill (Town)—Boone *AR-2*

Lead Hill (Township)—
   Christian *MO-3*
Leadington (City)—St. Francois ... *MO-3*
Leadore (City)—Lemhi *ID-4*
Leadville (City)—Lake *CO-4*
Leadville North (CDP)—Lake *CO-4*
Leadwood (City)—St. Francois..... *MO-3*
Leaf Lake (Township)—Otter
   Tail *MN-3*
Leaf Mountain (Township)—Otter
   Tail *MN-3*
Leaf Mountain (Township)—
   Burke *ND-4*
Leaf River (Township)—Ogle *IL-3*
Leaf River (Village)—Ogle *IL-3*
Leaf River (Township)—Wadena.. *MN-3*
Leaf Valley (Township)—
   Douglas *MN-3*
League City (City)—Galveston *TX-2*
League City (City)—Harris *TX-2*
Lea Hill (CDP)—King..................... *WA-4*
Leake County *MS-2*
Leakesville (Town)—Greene *MS-2*
Leakey (City)—Real *TX-2*
Leal (City)—Barnes *ND-4*
Lealman (CDP)—Pinellas............... *FL-2*
Leamington (Town)—Millard *UT-4*
Leander (City)—Travis................... *TX-2*
Leander (City)—Williamson *TX-2*
Learned (Town)—Hinds *MS-2*
Leary (City)—Calhoun *GA-2*
Leary (City)—Bowie *TX-2*
Leasburg (Village)—Crawford........ *MO-3*
Leavenworth (Town)—Crawford *IN-3*
Leavenworth (City)—
   Leavenworth *KS-4*
Leavenworth (Township)—
   Brown *MN-3*
Leavenworth (City)—Chelan *WA-4*
Leavenworth County *KS-4*
Leavitt (Township)—Oceana *MI-3*
Leawood (City)—Johnson *KS-4*
Leawood (Village)—Newton *MO-3*
Lebanon (Town)—New London *CT-1*
Lebanon (City)—St. Clair *IL-3*
Lebanon (Township)—St. Clair *IL-3*
Lebanon (City)—Boone *IN-3*
Lebanon (City)—Smith *KS-4*
Lebanon (City)—Marion *KY-2*
Lebanon (Town)—York *ME-1*
Lebanon (Township)—Clinton *MI-3*
Lebanon (Township)—Cooper *MO-3*
Lebanon (City)—Laclede................ *MO-3*
Lebanon (Township)—Laclede...... *MO-3*
Lebanon (Village)—Red Willow *NE-4*
Lebanon (City)—Grafton *NH-1*
Lebanon (Borough)—Hunterdon *NJ-1*
Lebanon (Township)—Hunterdon ..*NJ-1*
Lebanon (Town)—Madison *NY-1*
Lebanon (Township)—McHenry ... *ND-4*
Lebanon (Township)—Meigs *OH-3*
Lebanon (City)—Warren *OH-3*
Lebanon (City)—Linn *OR-4*
Lebanon (City)—Lebanon *PA-1*
Lebanon (Township)—Wayne *PA-1*
Lebanon (Town)—Potter *SD-4*
Lebanon (Town)—Wilson *TN-2*
Lebanon (Town)—Russell *VA-2*
Lebanon (Town)—Dodge *WI-3*
Lebanon (Town)—Waupaca *WI-3*
Lebanon County *PA-1*
Lebanon Junction (City)—Bullitt ... *KY-2*
Lebo (City)—Coffey *KS-4*
Le Boeuf (Township)—Erie............. *PA-1*
Lecanto (CDP)—Citrus................... *FL-2*

Le Center (City)—Le Sueur *MN-3*
Le Claire (City)—Scott.................... *IA-3*
Lecompte (Town)—Rapides
   Parish.............................. *LA-2*
Lecompton (City)—Douglas *KS-4*
Lecompton (Township)—Douglas.. *KS-4*
Ledbetter (CDP)—Livingston *KY-2*
Ledyard (Town)—New London *CT-1*
Ledyard (City)—Kossuth *IA-3*
Ledyard (Town)—Cayuga............... *NY-1*
Lee (Town)—Madison *FL-2*
Lee (Township)—Brown *IL-3*
Lee (Village)—DeKalb *IL-3*
Lee (Township)—Fulton *IL-3*
Lee (Village)—Lee *IL-3*
Lee (Town)—Penobscot *ME-1*
Lee (Town)—Berkshire................... *MA-1*
Lee (Township)—Allegan *MI-3*
Lee (Township)—Calhoun *MI-3*
Lee (Township)—Midland *MI-3*
Lee (Township)—Aitkin *MN-3*
Lee (Township)—Beltrami *MN-3*
Lee (Township)—Norman *MN-3*
Lee (Township)—Platte *MO-3*
Lee (Town)—Strafford.................... *NH-1*
Lee (Town)—Oneida *NY-1*
Lee (Township)—Nelson *ND-4*
Lee (Township)—Athens *OH-3*
Lee (Township)—Carroll *OH-3*
Lee (Township)—Monroe...............*OH-3*
Lee (Township)—Roberts *SD-4*
Lee Center (Township)—Lee *IL-3*
Leech (Township)—Wayne............. *IL-3*
Leechburg (Borough)—Armstrong.. *PA-1*
Leech Lake (Township)—Cass *MN-3*
Leech Lake Reservation
   (MN) *IndRes-4*
Lee County *AL-2*
Lee County *AR-2*
Lee County *FL-2*
Lee County *GA-2*
Lee County *IL-3*
Lee County *IA-3*
Lee County *KY-2*
Lee County *MS-2*
Lee County *NC-2*
Lee County *SC-2*
Lee County *TX-2*
Lee County *VA-2*
Leedey (Town)—Dewey *OK-2*
Leeds (City)—Jefferson *AL-2*
Leeds (City)—Shelby...................... *AL-2*
Leeds (City)—St. Clair *AL-2*
Leeds (Town)—Androscoggin *ME-1*
Leeds (Township)—Murray........... *MN-3*
Leeds (City)—Benson *ND-4*
Leeds (Township)—Benson *ND-4*
Leeds (Town)—Washington *UT-4*
Leeds (Town)—Columbia *WI-3*
Leef (Township)—Madison *IL-3*
Leelanau (Township)—Leelanau.... *MI-3*
Leelanau County........................... *MI-3*
Leenthrop (Township)—
   Chippewa *MN-3*
Leepertown (Township)—Bureau... *IL-3*
Lees (Township)—Logan................ *KS-4*
Leesburg (Town)—Cherokee *AL-2*
Leesburg (City)—Lake.................... *FL-2*
Leesburg (City)—Lee...................... *GA-2*
Leesburg (Town)—Kosciusko *IN-3*
Leesburg (Village)—Highland *OH-3*
Leesburg (Township)—Union *OH-3*
Leesburg (Town)—Loudoun *VA-2*
Leesport (Borough)—Berks *PA-1*
Lee's Summit (City)—Cass *MO-3*

Lee's Summit (City)—Jackson *MO-3*
Leesville (City)—Vernon Parish *LA-2*
Leesville (Township)—Henry *MO-3*
Leesville (Village)—Carroll *OH-3*
Leesville (Town)—Lexington *SC-2*
Leet (Township)—Allegheny *PA-1*
Leeton (Town)—Johnson *MO-3*
Leetonia (Village)—Columbiana *OH-3*
Leetsdale (Borough)—Allegheny *PA-1*
Le Flore (Town)—Le Flore *OK-2*
Leflore County *MS-2*
Le Flore County *OK-2*
Lefors (Town)—Gray *TX-2*
Leggett (Town)—Edgecombe *NC-2*
Le Grand (CDP)—Merced *CA-4*
Le Grand (City)—Marshall *IA-3*
Lehi (City)—Utah *UT-4*
Lehigh (City)—Webster *IA-3*
Lehigh (City)—Marion *KS-4*
Lehigh (Township)—Marion *KS-4*
Lehigh (City)—Coal *OK-2*
Lehigh (Township)—Carbon *PA-1*
Lehigh (Township)—Lackawanna... *PA-1*
Lehigh (Township)—
    Northampton *PA-1*
Lehigh (Township)—Wayne *PA-1*
Lehigh Acres (CDP)—Lee *FL-2*
Lehigh County *PA-1*
Lehighton (Borough)—Carbon *PA-1*
Lehman (Township)—Luzerne *PA-1*
Lehman (Township)—Pike *PA-1*
Lehr (City)—Logan *ND-4*
Lehr (City)—McIntosh *ND-4*
Leicester (Town)—Worcester *MA-1*
Leicester (Township)—Clay *NE-4*
Leicester (Town)—Livingston *NY-1*
Leicester (Village)—Livingston *NY-1*
Leicester (Town)—Addison *VT-1*
Leiding (Township)—St. Louis *MN-3*
Leidy (Township)—Clinton *PA-1*
Leigh (Township)—Morrison *MN-3*
Leigh (Village)—Colfax *NE-4*
Leighton (Town)—Colbert *AL-2*
Leighton (City)—Mahaska *IA-3*
Leighton (Township)—Allegan *MI-3*
Lein (Township)—Burleigh *ND-4*
Leipsic (Town)—Kent *DE-1*
Leipsic (Village)—Putnam *OH-3*
Leipzig (Township)—Grant *ND-4*
Leisure City (CDP)—Dade *FL-2*
Leisure Knoll (CDP)—Ocean *NJ-1*
Leisuretowne (CDP)—Burlington... *NJ-1*
Leisure Village (CDP)—Ocean *NJ-1*
Leisure Village East (CDP)—
    Ocean *NJ-1*
Leisure Village West-Pine Lake Park
    (CDP)—Ocean *NJ-1*
Leitchfield (City)—Grayson *KY-2*
Leith (City)—Grant *ND-4*
Leith-Hatfield (CDP)—Fayette *PA-1*
Leland (Village)—La Salle *IL-3*
Leland (City)—Winnebago *IA-3*
Leland (Township)—Leelanau *MI-3*
Leland (City)—Washington *MS-2*
Leland (Town)—Brunswick *NC-2*
Leland Grove (City)—Sangamon.... *IL-3*
Lely (CDP)—Collier *FL-2*
Le Mars (City)—Plymouth *IA-3*
Lemay (CDP)—St. Louis *MO-3*
Lemay (Township)—St. Louis *MO-3*
Lemhi County *ID-4*
Lemington (Town)—Essex *VT-1*
Lemmon (Pop. Place)—Adams *ND-4*
Lemmon (City)—Perkins *SD-4*
Lemon (Township)—Butler *OH-3*

Lemon (Township)—Wyoming *PA-1*
Lemon, No. 2 (Pop. Place)—
    Corson *SD-4*
Lemond (Township)—Steele *MN-3*
Lemon Grove (City)—San Diego .. *CA-4*
Lemont (City)—Cook *IL-3*
Lemont (Township)—Cook *IL-3*
Lemonweir (Town)—Juneau *WI-3*
Lemoore (City)—Kings *CA-4*
Lemoore Naval Air Station (CA)... *Mil-4*
Lemoore Station (Military Facility)—
    Kings *CA-4*
Lemoyne (Borough)—
    Cumberland *PA-1*
Lempster (Town)—Sullivan *NH-1*
Lena (Town)—Stephenson *IL-3*
Lena (Town)—Leake *MS-2*
Lena (Town)—Oconto *WI-3*
Lena (Village)—Oconto *WI-3*
Lenapah (Town)—Nowata *OK-2*
Lenape Heights (CDP)—
    Armstrong *PA-1*
Lenawee County *MI-3*
Lenexa (City)—Johnson *KS-4*
Lengby (City)—Polk *MN-3*
Lenhartsville (Borough)—Berks *PA-1*
Lennon (Village)—Genesee *MI-3*
Lennon (Village)—Shiawassee *MI-3*
Lennox (CDP)—Los Angeles *CA-4*
Lennox (City)—Lincoln *SD-4*
Lenoir (City)—Caldwell *NC-2*
Lenoir City (City)—Loudon *TN-2*
Lenoir County *NC-2*
Lenora (City)—Norton *KS-4*
Lenora (Township)—Griggs *ND-4*
Lenox (Town)—Cook *GA-2*
Lenox (Township)—Warren *IL-3*
Lenox (City)—Adams *IA-3*
Lenox (City)—Taylor *IA-3*
Lenox (Town)—Berkshire *MA-1*
Lenox (Township)—Macomb *MI-3*
Lenox (Town)—Madison *NY-1*
Lenox (Township)—Ashtabula *OH-3*
Lenox (Township)—Susquehanna... *PA-1*
Lenroot (Town)—Sawyer *WI-3*
Lent (Township)—Chisago *MN-3*
Lentner (Township)—Shelby *MO-3*
Lenton (Township)—Stutsman *ND-4*
Lenwood (CDP)—San
    Bernardino *CA-4*
Lenzburg (Township)—St. Clair *IL-3*
Lenzburg (Village)—St. Clair *IL-3*
Leola (Town)—Grant *AR-2*
Leola (Township)—Codington *SD-4*
Leola (City)—McPherson *SD-4*
Leola (Town)—Adams *WI-3*
Leominster (City)—Worcester *MA-1*
Leon (City)—Decatur *IA-3*
Leon (City)—Butler *KS-4*
Leon (Township)—Clearwater *MN-3*
Leon (Township)—Goodhue *MN-3*
Leon (Town)—Cattaraugus *NY-1*
Leon (Town)—Love *OK-2*
Leon (Town)—Mason *WV-2*
Leon (Town)—Monroe *WI-3*
Leon (Town)—Waushara *WI-3*
Leona (City)—Doniphan *KS-4*
Leona (Town)—Leon *TX-2*
Leonard (Village)—Oakland *MI-3*
Leonard (City)—Clearwater *MN-3*
Leonard (Town)—Shelby *MO-3*
Leonard (City)—Cass *ND-4*
Leonard (Township)—Cass *ND-4*
Leonard (Township)—Rolette *ND-4*
Leonard (City)—Fannin *TX-2*

Leonardo (CDP)—Monmouth *NJ-1*
Leonardsville (Township)—
    Traverse *MN-3*
Leonardtown (Town)—St.
    Mary's *MD-1*
Leonardville (City)—Riley *KS-4*
Leon County *FL-2*
Leon County *TX-2*
Leoni (Township)—Jackson *MI-3*
Leonia (Borough)—Bergen *NJ-1*
Leonidas (Township)—St. Joseph.. *MI-3*
Leonidas (City)—St. Louis *MN-3*
Leonore (Village)—La Salle *IL-3*
Leon Valley (City)—Bexar *TX-2*
Leonville (Village)—St. Landry
    Parish *LA-2*
Leopold (Township)—Perry *IN-3*
Leota (Township)—Nobles *MN-3*
Leoti (City)—Wichita *KS-4*
Leoti (Township)—Wichita *KS-4*
Lepanto (City)—Poinsett *AR-2*
Le Ray (Township)—Blue Earth ... *MN-3*
Le Ray (Town)—Jefferson *NY-1*
Le Raysville (Borough)—
    Bradford *PA-1*
Lerna (Village)—Coles *IL-3*
LeRoy (Township)—Boone *IL-3*
Le Roy (City)—McLean *IL-3*
Le Roy (City)—Decatur *IA-3*
Le Roy (City)—Coffey *KS-4*
Le Roy (Township)—Coffey *KS-4*
Leroy (Township)—Calhoun *MI-3*
Leroy (Township)—Ingham *MI-3*
Le Roy (Township)—Osceola......... *MI-3*
Le Roy (Village)—Osceola *MI-3*
Le Roy (City)—Mower *MN-3*
Le Roy (Township)—Mower *MN-3*
Leroy (Township)—Barton *MO-3*
Le Roy (Town)—Genesee *NY-1*
Le Roy (Village)—Genesee *NY-1*
Leroy (Township)—Lake *OH-3*
Leroy (Township)—Bradford *PA-1*
Le Roy (Township)—Lake *SD-4*
Leroy (City)—McLennan *TX-2*
Leroy (Town)—Dodge *WI-3*
Le Sauk (Township)—Stearns *MN-3*
Leshara (Township)—Saunders...... *NE-4*
Leshara (Village)—Saunders *NE-4*
Le Sieur (Township)—New
    Madrid *MO-3*
Leslie (City)—Searcy *AR-2*
Leslie (Village)—Sumter *GA-2*
Leslie (City)—Ingham *MI-3*
Leslie (Township)—Ingham *MI-3*
Leslie (Township)—Todd *MN-3*
Leslie (Township)—Carroll *MO-3*
Leslie (Village)—Franklin *MO-3*
Leslie County *KY-2*
Lessor (Township)—Polk *MN-3*
Lessor (Town)—Shawano *WI-3*
Lester (Town)—Limestone *AL-2*
Lester (City)—Lyon *IA-3*
Lester (Town)—Raleigh *WV-2*
Lester Prairie (City)—McLeod *MN-3*
Lesterville (Township)—
    Reynolds *MO-3*
Lesterville (Town)—Yankton *SD-4*
Le Sueur (City)—Le Sueur *MN-3*
Le Sueur (Township)—Kingsbury.. *SD-4*
Le Sueur County *MN-3*
Letart (Township)—Meigs *OH-3*
Letcher (Town)—Sanborn *SD-4*
Letcher (Township)—Sanborn *SD-4*
Letcher County *KY-2*
Letona (Town)—White *AR-2*

General Index — American Places Dictionary

Letterkenny (Township)—Franklin......*PA-1*
Letts (City)—Louisa......*IA-3*
Leupp (CDP)—Coconino......*AZ-4*
Leval (Township)—Nelson......*ND-4*
Levan (Township)—Jackson......*IL-3*
Levan (Town)—Juab......*UT-4*
Levant (Town)—Penobscot......*ME-1*
Levant (Township)—Grand Forks......*ND-4*
Levasy (City)—Jackson......*MO-3*
Levee (Township)—Pike......*IL-3*
Levelland (City)—Hockley......*TX-2*
Levelock (CDP)—Lake and Peninsula Borough......*AK-4*
Level Park-Oak Park (CDP)—Calhoun......*MI-3*
Level Plains (Municipality)—Dale......*AL-2*
Leven (Township)—Pope......*MN-3*
Leverett (Town)—Franklin......*MA-1*
Levis (Town)—Clark......*WI-3*
Levittown (CDP)—Nassau......*NY-1*
Levittown (CDP)—Bucks......*PA-1*
Levy County......*FL-2*
Lewellen (Village)—Garden......*NE-4*
Lewes (City)—Sussex......*DE-1*
Lewes River (CA)......*Geog-4*
Lewis (Township)—Clay......*IN-3*
Lewis (City)—Cass......*IA-3*
Lewis (City)—Edwards......*KS-4*
Lewis (Township)—Gove......*KS-4*
Lewis (Township)—Mille Lacs......*MN-3*
Lewis (Township)—Holt......*MO-3*
Lewis (Township)—New Madrid......*MO-3*
Lewis (Township)—Clay......*NE-4*
Lewis (Town)—Essex......*NY-1*
Lewis (Town)—Lewis......*NY-1*
Lewis (Township)—Bottineau......*ND-4*
Lewis (Township)—Brown......*OH-3*
Lewis (Township)—Lycoming......*PA-1*
Lewis (Township)—Northumberland......*PA-1*
Lewis (Township)—Union......*PA-1*
Lewis and Clark (Township)—St. Louis......*MO-3*
Lewis and Clark County......*MT-4*
Lewis and Clark Village (Town)—Buchanan......*MO-3*
Lewisberry (Borough)—York......*PA-1*
Lewisboro (Town)—Westchester......*NY-1*
Lewisburg (City)—Logan......*KY-2*
Lewisburg (Village)—Preble......*OH-3*
Lewisburg (Borough)—Union......*PA-1*
Lewisburg (City)—Marshall......*TN-2*
Lewisburg (City)—Greenbrier......*WV-2*
Lewis County......*ID-4*
Lewis County......*KY-2*
Lewis County......*MO-3*
Lewis County......*NY-1*
Lewis County......*TN-2*
Lewis County......*WA-4*
Lewis County......*WV-2*
Lewisport (City)—Hancock......*KY-2*
Lewis Range (MT)......*Geog-4*
Lewis Run (Borough)—McKean......*PA-1*
Lewiston (CDP)—Trinity......*CA-4*
Lewiston (City)—Nez Perce......*ID-4*
Lewiston (NCity)—Androscoggin......*ME-1*
Lewiston (City)—Winona......*MN-3*
Lewiston (Village)—Pawnee......*NE-4*
Lewiston (Town)—Niagara......*NY-1*
Lewiston (Village)—Niagara......*NY-1*
Lewiston (City)—Cache......*UT-4*
Lewiston (Town)—Columbia......*WI-3*

Lewiston Woodville (Town)—Bertie......*NC-2*
Lewistown (City)—Fulton......*IL-3*
Lewistown (Township)—Fulton......*IL-3*
Lewistown (Town)—Lewis......*MO-3*
Lewistown (City)—Fergus......*MT-4*
Lewistown (Borough)—Mifflin......*PA-1*
Lewisville (City)—Lafayette......*AR-2*
Lewisville (City)—Jefferson......*ID-4*
Lewisville (Town)—Henry......*IN-3*
Lewisville (City)—Watonwan......*MN-3*
Lewisville (Village)—Monroe......*OH-3*
Lewisville (City)—Dallas......*TX-2*
Lewisville (City)—Denton......*TX-2*
Lexa (City)—Phillips......*AR-2*
Lexington (Town)—Lauderdale......*AL-2*
Lexington (City)—Oglethorpe......*GA-2*
Lexington (Town)—McLean......*IL-3*
Lexington (Township)—McLean......*IL-3*
Lexington (Township)—Scott......*IN-3*
Lexington (Township)—Clark......*KS-4*
Lexington (Township)—Johnson......*KS-4*
Lexington (Town)—Middlesex......*MA-1*
Lexington (Township)—Sanilac......*MI-3*
Lexington (Village)—Sanilac......*MI-3*
Lexington (City)—Anoka......*MN-3*
Lexington (Township)—Le Sueur......*MN-3*
Lexington (City)—Holmes......*MS-2*
Lexington (City)—Lafayette......*MO-3*
Lexington (Township)—Lafayette......*MO-3*
Lexington (City)—Dawson......*NE-4*
Lexington (Town)—Greene......*NY-1*
Lexington (City)—Davidson......*NC-2*
Lexington (Village)—Richland......*OH-3*
Lexington (Township)—Stark......*OH-3*
Lexington (Town)—Cleveland......*OK-2*
Lexington (Town)—Morrow......*OR-4*
Lexington (Town)—Lexington......*SC-2*
Lexington (City)—Henderson......*TN-2*
Lexington (Town)—Lee......*TX-2*
Lexington County......*SC-2*
Lexington-Fayette (Consol. City)—Fayette......*KY-2*
Lexington Hills (CDP)—Santa Clara......*CA-4*
Lexington (Independent City)......*VA-2*
Lexington Park (CDP)—St. Mary's......*MD-1*
Leyden (Township)—Cook......*IL-3*
Leyden (Town)—Franklin......*MA-1*
Leyden (Town)—Lewis......*NY-1*
Libby (Township)—Aitkin......*MN-3*
Libby (City)—Lincoln......*MT-4*
Liberal (City)—Seward......*KS-4*
Liberal (Township)—Seward......*KS-4*
Liberal (City)—Barton......*MO-3*
Liberty (Township)—Adams......*IL-3*
Liberty (Village)—Adams......*IL-3*
Liberty (Township)—Effingham......*IL-3*
Liberty (Township)—Carroll......*IN-3*
Liberty (Township)—Crawford......*IN-3*
Liberty (Township)—Delaware......*IN-3*
Liberty (Township)—Fulton......*IN-3*
Liberty (Township)—Grant......*IN-3*
Liberty (Township)—Hendricks......*IN-3*
Liberty (Township)—Henry......*IN-3*
Liberty (Township)—Howard......*IN-3*
Liberty (Township)—Parke......*IN-3*
Liberty (Township)—Porter......*IN-3*
Liberty (Township)—Shelby......*IN-3*
Liberty (Township)—St. Joseph......*IN-3*
Liberty (Township)—Tipton......*IN-3*
Liberty (Town)—Union......*IN-3*

Liberty (Township)—Union......*IN-3*
Liberty (Township)—Wabash......*IN-3*
Liberty (Township)—Warren......*IN-3*
Liberty (Township)—Wells......*IN-3*
Liberty (Township)—White......*IN-3*
Liberty (Township)—Barton......*KS-4*
Liberty (Township)—Clark......*KS-4*
Liberty (Township)—Coffey......*KS-4*
Liberty (Township)—Cowley......*KS-4*
Liberty (Township)—Decatur......*KS-4*
Liberty (Township)—Dickinson......*KS-4*
Liberty (Township)—Elk......*KS-4*
Liberty (Township)—Geary......*KS-4*
Liberty (Township)—Hamilton......*KS-4*
Liberty (Township)—Jackson......*KS-4*
Liberty (Township)—Kingman......*KS-4*
Liberty (Township)—Labette......*KS-4*
Liberty (Township)—Linn......*KS-4*
Liberty (Township)—Marion......*KS-4*
Liberty (City)—Montgomery......*KS-4*
Liberty (Township)—Montgomery......*KS-4*
Liberty (Township)—Osborne......*KS-4*
Liberty (Township)—Republic......*KS-4*
Liberty (Township)—Saline......*KS-4*
Liberty (Township)—Woodson......*KS-4*
Liberty (City)—Casey......*KY-2*
Liberty (Town)—Waldo......*ME-1*
Liberty (Township)—Jackson......*MI-3*
Liberty (Township)—Wexford......*MI-3*
Liberty (Township)—Beltrami......*MN-3*
Liberty (Township)—Itasca......*MN-3*
Liberty (Township)—Polk......*MN-3*
Liberty (Town)—Amite......*MS-2*
Liberty (Township)—Adair......*MO-3*
Liberty (Township)—Barry......*MO-3*
Liberty (Township)—Bollinger......*MO-3*
Liberty (Township)—Callaway......*MO-3*
Liberty (Township)—Cape Girardeau......*MO-3*
Liberty (City)—Clay......*MO-3*
Liberty (Township)—Clay......*MO-3*
Liberty (Township)—Cole......*MO-3*
Liberty (Township)—Crawford......*MO-3*
Liberty (Township)—Daviess......*MO-3*
Liberty (Township)—Grundy......*MO-3*
Liberty (Township)—Holt......*MO-3*
Liberty (Township)—Iron......*MO-3*
Liberty (Township)—Knox......*MO-3*
Liberty (Township)—Macon......*MO-3*
Liberty (Township)—Madison......*MO-3*
Liberty (Township)—Marion......*MO-3*
Liberty (Township)—Phelps......*MO-3*
Liberty (Township)—Pulaski......*MO-3*
Liberty (Township)—Putnam......*MO-3*
Liberty (Township)—Saline......*MO-3*
Liberty (Township)—Schuyler......*MO-3*
Liberty (Township)—St. Francois......*MO-3*
Liberty (Township)—Stoddard......*MO-3*
Liberty (Township)—Sullivan......*MO-3*
Liberty (Township)—Washington......*MO-3*
Liberty (Township)—Fillmore......*NE-4*
Liberty (Township)—Gage......*NE-4*
Liberty (Village)—Gage......*NE-4*
Liberty (Township)—Kearney......*NE-4*
Liberty (Township)—Valley......*NE-4*
Liberty (Township)—Warren......*NJ-1*
Liberty (Town)—Sullivan......*NY-1*
Liberty (Village)—Sullivan......*NY-1*
Liberty (Town)—Randolph......*NC-2*
Liberty (Township)—Mountrail......*ND-4*
Liberty (Township)—Ransom......*ND-4*
Liberty (Township)—Adams......*OH-3*

Liberty (Township)—Butler *OH-3*
Liberty (Township)—Clinton *OH-3*
Liberty (Township)—Crawford *OH-3*
Liberty (Township)—Darke *OH-3*
Liberty (Township)—Delaware *OH-3*
Liberty (Township)—Fairfield *OH-3*
Liberty (Township)—Guernsey *OH-3*
Liberty (Township)—Hancock *OH-3*
Liberty (Township)—Hardin *OH-3*
Liberty (Township)—Henry *OH-3*
Liberty (Township)—Highland *OH-3*
Liberty (Township)—Jackson *OH-3*
Liberty (Township)—Knox *OH-3*
Liberty (Township)—Licking *OH-3*
Liberty (Township)—Logan *OH-3*
Liberty (Township)—Mercer *OH-3*
Liberty (Township)—Putnam *OH-3*
Liberty (Township)—Ross *OH-3*
Liberty (Township)—Seneca *OH-3*
Liberty (Township)—Trumbull *OH-3*
Liberty (Township)—Union *OH-3*
Liberty (Township)—Van Wert *OH-3*
Liberty (Township)—Washington .. *OH-3*
Liberty (Township)—Wood *OH-3*
Liberty (Town)—Okmulgee *OK-2*
Liberty (Town)—Tulsa *OK-2*
Liberty (Township)—Adams *PA-1*
Liberty (Borough)—Allegheny *PA-1*
Liberty (Township)—Bedford *PA-1*
Liberty (Township)—Centre *PA-1*
Liberty (Township)—McKean *PA-1*
Liberty (Township)—Mercer *PA-1*
Liberty (Township)—Montour *PA-1*
Liberty (Township)—
  Susquehanna *PA-1*
Liberty (Borough)—Tioga *PA-1*
Liberty (Township)—Tioga *PA-1*
Liberty (Town)—Pickens *SC-2*
Liberty (Township)—Beadle *SD-4*
Liberty (Township)—Brown *SD-4*
Liberty (Township)—Day *SD-4*
Liberty (Township)—Edmunds *SD-4*
Liberty (Township)—Hutchinson .. *SD-4*
Liberty (Township)—Lyman *SD-4*
Liberty (Township)—Perkins *SD-4*
Liberty (Town)—DeKalb *TN-2*
Liberty (City)—Liberty *TX-2*
Liberty (Town)—Grant *WI-3*
Liberty (Town)—Manitowoc *WI-3*
Liberty (Town)—Outagamie *WI-3*
Liberty (Town)—Vernon *WI-3*
Liberty Center (Village)—Henry *OH-3*
Liberty City (CDP)—Gregg *TX-2*
Liberty County *FL-2*
Liberty County *GA-2*
Liberty County *MT-4*
Liberty County *TX-2*
Liberty Grove (Township)—
  Richland *ND-4*
Liberty Grove (Town)—Door *WI-3*
Liberty Island (NY) *Geog-4*
Liberty Lake (CDP)—Spokane *WA-4*
Libertyville (Municipality)—
  Covington *AL-2*
Libertyville (City)—Lake *IL-3*
Libertyville (Township)—Lake *IL-3*
Libertyville (City)—Jefferson *IA-3*
Lick (Township)—Jackson *OH-3*
Lick Creek (Township)—Ozark *MO-3*
Licking (Township)—Crawford *IL-3*
Licking (Township)—Blackford *IN-3*
Licking (City)—Texas *MO-3*
Licking (Township)—Licking *OH-3*
Licking (Township)—
  Muskingum *OH-3*

Licking (Township)—Clarion *PA-1*
Licking County *OH-3*
Licking Creek (Township)—
  Fulton *PA-1*
Lida (Township)—Otter Tail *MN-3*
Lidderdale (City)—Carroll *IA-3*
Lidgerwood (City)—Richland *ND-4*
Lido Beach (CDP)—Nassau *NY-1*
Liebenthal (City)—Rush *KS-4*
Lien (Township)—Grant *MN-3*
Lien (Township)—Roberts *SD-4*
Lighthouse Point (City)—
  Broward *FL-2*
Lightning Creek (Township)—
  Adams *ND-4*
Light Oak (CDP)—Cleveland *NC-2*
Lignite (CDP)—Yukon-Koyukuk
  Census Area *AK-4*
Lignite (City)—Burke *ND-4*
Ligonier (City)—Noble *IN-3*
Ligonier (Borough)—
  Westmoreland *PA-1*
Ligonier (Township)—
  Westmoreland *PA-1*
Lihue (CDP)—Kauai *HI-4*
Likely Rancheria (CA) *IndRes-4*
Lilbourn (City)—New Madrid *MO-3*
Lilburn (City)—Gwinnett *GA-2*
Lilesville (Town)—Anson *NC-2*
Lillehoff (Township)—Ramsey *ND-4*
Lilley (Township)—Newaygo *MI-3*
Lillian (Township)—Custer *NE-4*
Lillie (Village)—Union Parish *LA-2*
Lillington (Town)—Harnett *NC-2*
Lilly (Town)—Dooly *GA-2*
Lilly (Borough)—Cambria *PA-1*
Lily (Town)—Day *SD-4*
Lilydale (City)—Dakota *MN-3*
Lima (Township)—Adams *IL-3*
Lima (Village)—Adams *IL-3*
Lima (Township)—Lagrange *IN-3*
Lima (Township)—Washtenaw *MI-3*
Lima (Township)—Cass *MN-3*
Lima (Town)—Beaverhead *MT-4*
Lima (Town)—Livingston *NY-1*
Lima (Village)—Livingston *NY-1*
Lima (City)—Allen *OH-3*
Lima (Township)—Licking *OH-3*
Lima (Town)—Seminole *OK-2*
Lima (CDP)—Delaware *PA-1*
Lima (Town)—Grant *WI-3*
Lima (Town)—Pepin *WI-3*
Lima (Town)—Rock *WI-3*
Lima (Town)—Sheboygan *WI-3*
Limaville (Village)—Stark *OH-3*
Lime (Township)—Blue Earth *MN-3*
Lime Lake (Township)—Murray .. *MN-3*
Lime Lake-Machias (CDP)—
  Cattaraugus *NY-1*
Limerick (Town)—York *ME-1*
Limerick (Township)—
  Montgomery *PA-1*
Lime Ridge (CDP)—Columbia *PA-1*
Lime Ridge (Village)—Sauk *WI-3*
Lime Springs (City)—Howard *IA-3*
Limestone (Township)—
  Kankakee *IL-3*
Limestone (Township)—Peoria *IL-3*
Limestone (Township)—Jewell *KS-4*
Limestone (Town)—Aroostook *ME-1*
Limestone (Township)—Alger *MI-3*
Limestone (Township)—Lincoln ... *MN-3*
Limestone (Village)—
  Cattaraugus *NY-1*
Limestone (Township)—Clarion *PA-1*

Limestone (Township)—
  Lycoming *PA-1*
Limestone (Township)—Montour ... *PA-1*
Limestone (Township)—Union *PA-1*
Limestone (Township)—Warren *PA-1*
Limestone County *AL-2*
Limestone County *TX-2*
Lime Village (CDP)—Bethel Census
  Area *AK-4*
Limington (Town)—York *ME-1*
Limon (Town)—Lincoln *CO-4*
Lincklaen (Town)—Chenango *NY-1*
Lincoln (Town)—Talladega *AL-2*
Lincoln (City)—Washington *AR-2*
Lincoln (City)—Placer *CA-4*
Lincoln (City)—Logan *IL-3*
Lincoln (Township)—Ogle *IL-3*
Lincoln (Township)—Hendricks *IN-3*
Lincoln (Township)—La Porte *IN-3*
Lincoln (Township)—Newton *IN-3*
Lincoln (Township)—St. Joseph *IN-3*
Lincoln (Township)—White *IN-3*
Lincoln (City)—Tama *IA-3*
Lincoln (Township)—Anderson *KS-4*
Lincoln (Township)—Butler *KS-4*
Lincoln (Township)—Cloud *KS-4*
Lincoln (Township)—Coffey *KS-4*
Lincoln (Township)—Crawford *KS-4*
Lincoln (Township)—Decatur *KS-4*
Lincoln (Township)—Dickinson ... *KS-4*
Lincoln (Township)—Edwards *KS-4*
Lincoln (Township)—Ellsworth *KS-4*
Lincoln (Township)—Franklin *KS-4*
Lincoln (Township)—Grant *KS-4*
Lincoln (Township)—Jackson *KS-4*
Lincoln (City)—Lincoln *KS-4*
Lincoln (Township)—Linn *KS-4*
Lincoln (Township)—Marshall *KS-4*
Lincoln (Township)—Neosho *KS-4*
Lincoln (Township)—Osage *KS-4*
Lincoln (Township)—Ottawa *KS-4*
Lincoln (Township)—Pawnee *KS-4*
Lincoln (Township)—
  Pottawatomie *KS-4*
Lincoln (Township)—Reno *KS-4*
Lincoln (Township)—Republic *KS-4*
Lincoln (Township)—Rice *KS-4*
Lincoln (Township)—Russell *KS-4*
Lincoln (Township)—Sedgwick *KS-4*
Lincoln (Township)—Sherman *KS-4*
Lincoln (Township)—Smith *KS-4*
Lincoln (Township)—Stafford *KS-4*
Lincoln (Township)—Washington . *KS-4*
Lincoln (Plantation)—Oxford *ME-1*
Lincoln (Town)—Penobscot *ME-1*
Lincoln (Town)—Middlesex *MA-1*
Lincoln (Village)—Alcona *MI-3*
Lincoln (Township)—Arenac *MI-3*
Lincoln (Township)—Berrien *MI-3*
Lincoln (Township)—Clare *MI-3*
Lincoln (Township)—Huron *MI-3*
Lincoln (Township)—Isabella *MI-3*
Lincoln (Township)—Midland *MI-3*
Lincoln (Township)—Newaygo *MI-3*
Lincoln (Township)—Osceola *MI-3*
Lincoln (Township)—Blue Earth .. *MN-3*
Lincoln (Township)—Marshall *MN-3*
Lincoln (Township)—Andrew *MO-3*
Lincoln (Township)—Atchison *MO-3*
Lincoln (City)—Benton *MO-3*
Lincoln (Township)—Caldwell *MO-3*
Lincoln (Township)—Christian *MO-3*
Lincoln (Township)—Clark *MO-3*
Lincoln (Township)—Dallas *MO-3*
Lincoln (Township)—Daviess *MO-3*

General Index

Lincoln (Township)—Douglas....... *MO-3*
Lincoln (Township)—Grundy *MO-3*
Lincoln (Township)—Harrison *MO-3*
Lincoln (Township)—Holt *MO-3*
Lincoln (Township)—Jasper.......... *MO-3*
Lincoln (Township)—Lawrence *MO-3*
Lincoln (Township)—Nodaway *MO-3*
Lincoln (Township)—Putnam *MO-3*
Lincoln (Township)—Stone *MO-3*
Lincoln (Township)—Antelope *NE-4*
Lincoln (Township)—Cuming........ *NE-4*
Lincoln (Township)—Franklin....... *NE-4*
Lincoln (Township)—Gage *NE-4*
Lincoln (Township)—Kearney *NE-4*
Lincoln (Township)—Knox *NE-4*
Lincoln (City)—Lancaster *NE-4*
Lincoln (Town)—Grafton.............. *NH-1*
Lincoln (Town)—Madison *NY-1*
Lincoln (City)—Burleigh *ND-4*
Lincoln (Township)—Emmons *ND-4*
Lincoln (Township)—Pembina *ND-4*
Lincoln (Township)—Morrow........ *OH-3*
Lincoln (Borough)—Allegheny *PA-1*
Lincoln (Township)—Bedford........ *PA-1*
Lincoln (Township)—Huntingdon .. *PA-1*
Lincoln (Township)—Somerset *PA-1*
Lincoln (Town)—Providence *RI-1*
Lincoln (Township)—Brown *SD-4*
Lincoln (Township)—Clark *SD-4*
Lincoln (Township)—Corson *SD-4*
Lincoln (Township)—Douglas *SD-4*
Lincoln (Township)—Lincoln *SD-4*
Lincoln (Township)—Perkins......... *SD-4*
Lincoln (Township)—Spink *SD-4*
Lincoln (Township)—Tripp........... *SD-4*
Lincoln (Town)—Addison *VT-1*
Lincoln (Town)—Adams *WI-3*
Lincoln (Town)—Bayfield *WI-3*
Lincoln (Town)—Buffalo................ *WI-3*
Lincoln (Town)—Burnett *WI-3*
Lincoln (Town)—Eau Claire *WI-3*
Lincoln (Town)—Forest *WI-3*
Lincoln (Town)—Kewaunee........... *WI-3*
Lincoln (Town)—Monroe............... *WI-3*
Lincoln (Town)—Polk *WI-3*
Lincoln (Town)—Trempealeau....... *WI-3*
Lincoln (Town)—Vilas *WI-3*
Lincoln (Town)—Wood.................. *WI-3*
Lincoln Beach (CDP)—Lincoln ... *OR-4*
Lincoln City (City)—Lincoln *OR-4*
Lincoln County *AR-2*
Lincoln County *CO-4*
Lincoln County *GA-2*
Lincoln County *ID-4*
Lincoln County *KS-4*
Lincoln County *KY-2*
Lincoln County *ME-1*
Lincoln County *MN-3*
Lincoln County *MS-2*
Lincoln County *MO-3*
Lincoln County *MT-4*
Lincoln County *NE-4*
Lincoln County *NV-1*
Lincoln County *NM-4*
Lincoln County *NC-2*
Lincoln County *OK-2*
Lincoln County *OR-4*
Lincoln County *SD-4*
Lincoln County *TN-2*
Lincoln County *WA-4*
Lincoln County *WV-2*
Lincoln County *WI-3*
Lincoln County *WY-4*
Lincoln Dale (Township)—
    Sheridan *ND-4*

Lincoln Heights (City)—
    Hamilton *OH-3*
Lincolnia (CDP)—Fairfax *VA-2*
Lincoln Parish............................... *LA-2*
Lincoln Park (CDP)—Fremont...... *CO-4*
Lincoln Park (City)—Wayne *MI-3*
Lincoln Park (Borough)—Morris.... *NJ-1*
Lincoln Park (CDP)—Ulster *NY-1*
Lincoln Park (Town)—Denton *TX-2*
Lincolnshire (Town)—Lake............ *IL-3*
Lincolnshire (City)—Jefferson *KY-2*
Lincolnton (City)—Lincoln............ *GA-2*
Lincolnton (Town)—Lincoln.......... *NC-2*
Lincoln Valley (Township)—
    Divide *ND-4*
Lincoln Village (CDP)—San
    Joaquin... *CA-4*
Lincoln Village (CDP)—
    Franklin.. *OH-3*
Lincolnville (City)—Marion *KS-4*
Lincolnville (Town)—Waldo *ME-1*
Lincolnville (Town)—Charleston *SC-2*
Lincolnwood (City)—Cook *IL-3*
Lincroft (CDP)—Monmouth *NJ-1*
Lind (Township)—Roseau.............. *MN-3*
Lind (Township)—Grand Forks..... *ND-4*
Lind (Town)—Adams *WA-4*
Lind (Town)—Waupaca *WI-3*
Linda (CDP)—Yuba *CA-4*
Lindaas (Township)—Traill............ *ND-4*
Lindahl (Township)—Williams...... *ND-4*
Lindale (CDP)—Floyd *GA-2*
Lindale (Town)—Smith *TX-2*
Linden (City)—Marengo *AL-2*
Linden (CDP)—San Joaquin *CA-4*
Linden (Town)—Montgomery *IN-3*
Linden (City)—Dallas *IA-3*
Linden (Village)—Genesee *MI-3*
Linden (Township)—Brown *MN-3*
Linden (Township)—Christian...... *MO-3*
Linden (City)—Union *NJ-1*
Linden (Town)—Cumberland *NC-2*
Linden (Township)—Cavalier *ND-4*
Linden (Town)—Perry *TN-2*
Linden (City)—Cass *TX-2*
Linden (Town)—Iowa *WI-3*
Linden (Village)—Iowa *WI-3*
Linden Grove (Township)—St.
    Louis *MN-3*
Lindenhurst (City)—Lake *IL-3*
Lindenhurst (Village)—Suffolk *NY-1*
Lindenwold (Borough)—Camden ... *NJ-1*
Lindenwood (Township)—St.
    Charles.. *MO-3*
Linder (Township)—Greene........... *IL-3*
Lindgren Acres (CDP)—Dade *FL-2*
Lindina (Town)—Juneau *WI-3*
Lindley (Township)—Mercer *MO-3*
Lindley (Town)—Steuben............... *NY-1*
Lindon (City)—Utah *UT-4*
Lindsay (City)—Tulare *CA-4*
Lindsay (Village)—Platte *NE-4*
Lindsay (City)—Garvin *OK-2*
Lindsay (Town)—Cooke................. *TX-2*
Lindsborg (City)—McPherson *KS-4*
Lindsey (Township)—Benton *MO-3*
Lindsey (Village)—Sandusky.......... *OH-3*
Lindstrom (City)—Chisago *MN-3*
Linesville (Borough)—Crawford.... *PA-1*
Lineville (Town)—Clay *AL-2*
Lineville (City)—Wayne *IA-3*
Linganore-Bartonsville (CDP)—
    Frederick...................................... *MD-1*
Lingle (Town)—Goshen *WY-4*
Linglestown (CDP)—Dauphin *PA-1*

Lingo (Township)—Macon............ *MO-3*
Linn (Township)—Woodford *IL-3*
Linn (City)—Washington *KS-4*
Linn (Township)—Washington *KS-4*
Linn (Township)—Audrain *MO-3*
Linn (Township)—Cedar................ *MO-3*
Linn (Township)—Dent *MO-3*
Linn (Township)—Moniteau *MO-3*
Linn (City)—Osage *MO-3*
Linn (Township)—Osage................ *MO-3*
Linn (Township)—Hand *SD-4*
Linn (Town)—Walworth *WI-3*
Linn County *IA-3*
Linn County *KS-4*
Linn County *MO-3*
Linn County *OR-4*
Linn Creek (Town)—Camden *MO-3*
Linndale (Village)—Cuyahoga *OH-3*
Linneus (Town)—Aroostook *ME-1*
Linneus (City)—Linn *MO-3*
Linn Grove (City)—Buena Vista *IA-3*
Linntown (CDP)—Union *PA-1*
Lino Lakes (City)—Anoka *MN-3*
Linsell (Township)—Marshall *MN-3*
Linthicum (CDP)—Anne
    Arundel.. *MD-1*
Linton (City)—Greene *IN-3*
Linton (Township)—Vigo............... *IN-3*
Linton (City)—Emmons................. *ND-4*
Linton (Township)—Ward *ND-4*
Linton (Township)—Coshocton *OH-3*
Linwood (Town)—Walker *GA-2*
Linwood (City)—Leavenworth *KS-4*
Linwood (Township)—Anoka *MN-3*
Linwood (Township)—Butler *NE-4*
Linwood (Village)—Butler *NE-4*
Linwood (City)—Atlantic............... *NJ-1*
Linwood (CDP)—Delaware *PA-1*
Linwood (Town)—Portage *WI-3*
Lionville-Marchwood (CDP)—
    Chester *PA-1*
Lipan (City)—Hood *TX-2*
Lippert (Township)—Stutsman *ND-4*
Lipscomb (Municipality)—
    Jefferson *AL-2*
Lipscomb (Pop. Place)—
    Lipscomb *TX-2*
Lipscomb County *TX-2*
Lisbon (Town)—New London *CT-1*
Lisbon (Township)—Kendall *IL-3*
Lisbon (Village)—Kendall *IL-3*
Lisbon (City)—Linn *IA-3*
Lisbon (Village)—Claiborne
    Parish *LA-2*
Lisbon (Town)—Androscoggin....... *ME-1*
Lisbon (Township)—Yellow
    Medicine *MN-3*
Lisbon (Town)—Grafton *NH-1*
Lisbon (Town)—St. Lawrence *NY-1*
Lisbon (City)—Ransom *ND-4*
Lisbon (Village)—Columbiana......*OH-3*
Lisbon (Township)—Davison *SD-4*
Lisbon (Town)—Juneau *WI-3*
Lisbon (Town)—Waukesha *WI-3*
Lisbon Falls (CDP)—
    Androscoggin *ME-1*
Liscomb (City)—Marshall *IA-3*
Lisle (City)—DuPage...................... *IL-3*
Lisle (Township)—DuPage............. *IL-3*
Lisle (Town)—Broome *NY-1*
Lisle (Village)—Broome *NY-1*
Lisman (Town)—Choctaw *AL-2*
Lismore (City)—Nobles *MN-3*
Lismore (Township)—Nobles........ *MN-3*
Litchfield (Borough)—Litchfield.... *CT-1*

Litchfield (Town)—Litchfield *CT-1*	Little Rice (Town)—Oneida *WI-3*	Livingston (City)—Merced *CA-4*
Litchfield (City)—Montgomery *IL-3*	Little River (AL) *Geog-4*	Livingston (Village)—Madison *IL-3*
Litchfield (Town)—Kennebec *ME-1*	Little River (Township)—Reno *KS-4*	Livingston (City)—Rockcastle *KY-2*
Litchfield (City)—Hillsdale *MI-3*	Little River (City)—Rice *KS-4*	Livingston (Town)—Livingston Parish *LA-2*
Litchfield (Township)—Hillsdale *MI-3*	Little River (Township)— Pemiscot *MO-3*	Livingston (Township)—Otsego *MI-3*
Litchfield (City)—Meeker *MN-3*	Little River (CDP)—Horry *SC-2*	Livingston (City)—Park *MT-4*
Litchfield (Township)—Meeker *MN-3*	Little River (Town)—Oconto *WI-3*	Livingston (Township)—Essex *NJ-1*
Litchfield (Village)—Sherman *NE-4*	Little River-Academy (City)— Bell *TX-2*	Livingston (Town)—Columbia *NY-1*
Litchfield (Town)—Hillsborough ... *NH-1*	**Little River County** *AR-2*	Livingston (Town)—Orangeburg *SC-2*
Litchfield (Town)—Herkimer *NY-1*	Little Rock (City)—Pulaski *AR-2*	Livingston (Town)—Overton *TN-2*
Litchfield (Township)—Medina *OH-3*	Littlerock (CDP)—Los Angeles *CA-4*	Livingston (Town)—Polk *TX-2*
Litchfield (Township)—Bradford *PA-1*	Little Rock (Township)—Kendall ... *IL-3*	Livingston (Village)—Grant *WI-3*
Litchfield County *CT-1*	Little Rock (City)—Lyon *IA-3*	Livingston (Village)—Iowa *WI-3*
Litchfield Park (City)—Maricopa .. *AZ-4*	Little Rock (CDP)—Beltrami *MN-3*	**Livingston County** *IL-3*
Litchville (City)—Barnes *ND-4*	Little Rock (Township)—Nobles .. *MN-3*	**Livingston County** *KY-2*
Litchville (Township)—LaMoure ... *ND-4*	Little Rock Air Force Base (AR) *Mil-4*	**Livingston County** *MI-3*
Lithia Springs (CDP)—Douglas *GA-2*	Little Round Lake (CDP)— Sawyer *WI-3*	**Livingston County** *MO-3*
Lithium (Village)—Perry *MO-3*	Little Sand Lake (Pop. Place)— Itasca *MN-3*	**Livingston County** *NY-1*
Lithonia (City)—De Kalb *GA-2*	Little Sauk (Township)—Todd *MN-3*	Livingston Manor (CDP)— Sullivan *NY-1*
Lithopolis (Village)—Fairfield *OH-3*	Little Silver (Borough)— Monmouth *NJ-1*	**Livingston Parish** *LA-2*
Lititz (Borough)—Lancaster *PA-1*	Little Sioux (City)—Harrison *IA-3*	Livonia (Town)—Washington *IN-3*
Little Beaver (Township)— Lawrence *PA-1*	Littlestown (Borough)—Adams *PA-1*	Livonia (Village)—Pointe Coupee Parish *LA-2*
Little Black (Town)—Taylor *WI-3*	Little Suamico (Town)—Oconto *WI-3*	Livonia (City)—Wayne *MI-3*
Little Blue (Township)— Washington *KS-4*	Littleton (City)—Arapahoe *CO-4*	Livonia (Township)—Sherburne ... *MN-3*
Little Blue (Township)—Adams *NE-4*	Littleton (City)—Douglas *CO-4*	Livonia (Village)—Putnam *MO-3*
Little Britain (Township)— Lancaster *PA-1*	Littleton (Township)—Schuyler *IL-3*	Livonia (Town)—Livingston *NY-1*
Little Buffalo (Township)— Jackson *SD-4*	Littleton (Village)—Schuyler *IL-3*	Livonia (Village)—Livingston *NY-1*
Little Canada (City)—Ramsey *MN-3*	Littleton (Town)—Aroostook *ME-1*	Lizton (Town)—Hendricks *IN-3*
Little Caney (Township)— Chautauqua *KS-4*	Littleton (Town)—Middlesex *MA-1*	Llano (City)—Llano *TX-2*
Little Chute (Village)— Outagamie *WI-3*	Littleton (Town)—Grafton *NH-1*	**Llano County** *TX-2*
Little Compton (Town)—Newport . *RI-1*	Littleton (Town)—Halifax *NC-2*	Llano Estacado (AL) *Geog-4*
Little Cottonwood Creek Valley (CDP)—Salt Lake *UT-4*	Littleton (Town)—Wetzel *WV-2*	Llanos (Township)—Sherman *KS-4*
Little Creek (Town)—Kent *DE-1*	Little Traverse (Township)— Emmet *MI-3*	Lloyd (Town)—Ulster *NY-1*
Little Deep (Township)— McHenry *ND-4*	Little Valley (Township)— McPherson *KS-4*	Lloyd Harbor (Village)—Suffolk *NY-1*
Little Eagle (CDP)—Corson *SD-4*	Little Valley (Town)— Cattaraugus *NY-1*	Loa (Town)—Wayne *UT-4*
Little Egg Harbor (Township)— Ocean *NJ-1*	Little Valley (Village)— Cattaraugus *NY-1*	Loachapoka (Town)—Lee *AL-2*
Little Elk (Township)—Todd *MN-3*	Littleville (Town)—Colbert *AL-2*	Loam (Township)—Cavalier *ND-4*
Little Elm (Town)—Denton *TX-2*	Little Walnut (Township)—Butler ..*KS-4*	Loami (Town)—Sangamon *IL-3*
Little Falls (City)—Morrison *MN-3*	Little Wolf (Town)—Waupaca *WI-3*	Loami (Township)—Sangamon *IL-3*
Little Falls (Township)— Morrison *MN-3*	Little York (Village)—Warren *IL-3*	Lobelville (City)—Perry *TN-2*
Little Falls (Township)—Passaic ... *NJ-1*	Little York (Town)—Washington *IN-3*	Loch Arbour (Borough)— Monmouth *NJ-1*
Little Falls (City)—Herkimer *NY-1*	Lively Grove (Township)— Washington *IL-3*	Lochbuie (Town)—Weld *CO-4*
Little Falls (Town)—Herkimer *NY-1*	Live Oak (CDP)—Santa Cruz *CA-4*	Lochearn (CDP)—Baltimore *MD-1*
Little Falls (Town)—Monroe *WI-3*	Live Oak (City)—Sutter *CA-4*	Loch Lomond (CDP)—Prince William *VA-2*
Little Falls-South Windham (CDP)— Cumberland *ME-1*	Live Oak (City)—Suwannee *FL-2*	Loch Lynn Heights (Town)— Garrett *MD-1*
Little Ferry (Borough)—Bergen *NJ-1*	Live Oak (City)—Bexar *TX-2*	Lochmoor Waterway Estates (CDP)— Lee *FL-2*
Littlefield (Township)—Emmet *MI-3*	**Live Oak County** *TX-2*	Lockbourne (Village)—Franklin *OH-3*
Littlefield (City)—Lamb *TX-2*	Livermore (City)—Alameda *CA-4*	Locke (Township)—Elkhart *IN-3*
Little Flock (City)—Benton *AR-2*	Livermore (City)—Humboldt *IA-3*	Locke (Township)—Ingham *MI-3*
Littlefork (City)—Koochiching *MN-3*	Livermore (City)—McLean *KY-2*	Locke (Town)—Cayuga *NY-1*
Little Grant (Town)—Grant *WI-3*	Livermore (Town)— Androscoggin *ME-1*	Lockeford (CDP)—San Joaquin ... *CA-4*
Little Mackinaw (Township)— Tazewell *IL-3*	Livermore (Town)—Grafton *NH-1*	Lockesburg (Town)—Sevier *AR-2*
Little Mahanoy (Township)— Northumberland *PA-1*	Livermore Falls (Town)— Androscoggin *ME-1*	Lockhart (Town)—Covington *AL-2*
Little Meadows (Borough)— Susquehanna *PA-1*	Liverpool (Township)—Fulton *IL-3*	Lockhart (CDP)—Orange *FL-2*
Little Mountain (Town)— Newberry *SC-2*	Liverpool (Village)—Fulton *IL-3*	Lockhart (Township)—Pike *IN-3*
Little Pine (Township)—Crow Wing *MN-3*	Liverpool (Village)—Onondaga *NY-1*	Lockhart (Township)—Norman ... *MN-3*
Littleport (City)—Clayton *IA-3*	Liverpool (Township)— Columbiana *OH-3*	Lockhart (Town)—Union *SC-2*
Little Prairie (Township)— Pemiscot *MO-3*	Liverpool (Township)—Medina *OH-3*	Lockhart (City)—Caldwell *TX-2*
	Liverpool (Borough)—Perry *PA-1*	Lock Haven (City)—Clinton *PA-1*
	Liverpool (Township)—Perry *PA-1*	Lockington (Village)—Shelby *OH-3*
	Liverpool (Village)—Brazoria *TX-2*	Lockland (City)—Hamilton *OH-3*
	Livingston (City)—Sumter *AL-2*	Lockney (Town)—Floyd *TX-2*
		Lockport (City)—Will *IL-3*
		Lockport (Township)—Will *IL-3*
		Lockport (Township)—Haskell *KS-4*
		Lockport (Town)—Lafourche Parish *LA-2*
		Lockport (Township)—St. Joseph .. *MI-3*

1019

General Index		American Places Dictionary
Lockport (City)—Niagara............... *NY-1*	Logan (Township)—Dodge............ *NE-4*	Londonderry (Town)—
Lockport (Town)—Niagara *NY-1*	Logan (Township)—Gage.............. *NE-4*	Rockingham *NH-1*
Lockridge (City)—Jefferson *IA-3*	Logan (Township)—Kearney.......... *NE-4*	Londonderry (Township)—
Lock Springs (Town)—Daviess...... *MO-3*	Logan (Township)—Knox *NE-4*	Guernsey.. *OH-3*
Lockwood (City)—Dade................. *MO-3*	Logan (Township)—Gloucester....... *NJ-1*	Londonderry (Township)—
Lockwood (Township)—Dade........ *MO-3*	Logan (Village)—Quay..................... *NM-4*	Bedford *PA-1*
Lockwood (CDP)—Yellowstone..... *MT-4*	Logan (Township)—Burleigh *ND-4*	Londonderry (Township)—
Lockwood (Township)—Renville....*ND-4*	Logan (Township)—Auglaize *OH-3*	Chester *PA-1*
Lockwood (Township)—Roberts.... *SD-4*	Logan (City)—Hocking *OH-3*	Londonderry (Township)—
Loco (City)—Stephens..................... *OK-2*	Logan (Township)—Blair *PA-1*	Dauphin... *PA-1*
Locust (Township)—Christian *IL-3*	Logan (Township)—Clinton............ *PA-1*	Londonderry (Town)—Windham.. *VT-1*
Locust (City)—Stanly....................... *NC-2*	Logan (Township)—Huntingdon *PA-1*	London Grove (Township)—
Locust (Township)—Columbia *PA-1*	Logan (Township)—Beadle *SD-4*	Chester *PA-1*
Locust Creek (Township)—Linn ... *MO-3*	Logan (Township)—Clark *SD-4*	London Mills (Town)—Fulton *IL-3*
Locust Fork (Town)—Blount *AL-2*	Logan (Township)—Hand............... *SD-4*	London Mills (Town)—Knox *IL-3*
Locust Grove (City)—Henry........... *GA-2*	Logan (Township)—Hughes *SD-4*	Londontowne (CDP)—Anne
Locust Grove (Town)—Mayes *OK-2*	Logan (Township)—Jerauld *SD-4*	Arundel...*MD-1*
Locust Valley (CDP)—Nassau *NY-1*	Logan (Township)—Minnehaha..... *SD-4*	Lone Elm (City)—Anderson *KS-4*
Loda (Township)—Iroquois *IL-3*	Logan (Township)—Sanborn *SD-4*	Lone Elm (Township)—Anderson ..*KS-4*
Loda (Village)—Iroquois *IL-3*	Logan (City)—Cache *UT-4*	Lone Grove (Township)—Fayette... *IL-3*
Loda (Township)—Reno *KS-4*	Logan (City)—Logan *WV-2*	Lone Grove (Town)—Carter *OK-2*
Lodema (Township)—Pembina......*ND-4*	Logan Center (Township)—Grand	Lone Jack (Village)—Jackson *MO-3*
Lodge (Town)—Colleton.................. *SC-2*	Forks *ND-4*	Lone Oak (Town)—Meriwether *GA-2*
Lodge Grass (Town)—Big Horn ... *MT-4*	**Logan County** *AR-2*	Lone Oak (City)—McCracken *KY-2*
Lodgepole (Village)—Cheyenne *NE-4*	**Logan County** *CO-4*	Lone Oak (Township)—Bates *MO-3*
Lodgepole (Township)—Perkins *SD-4*	**Logan County** *IL-3*	Lone Oak (Town)—Hunt *TX-2*
Lodi (City)—San Joaquin *CA-4*	**Logan County** *KS-4*	Lone Pine (CDP)—Inyo *CA-4*
Lodi (Township)—Washtenaw *MI-3*	**Logan County** *KY-2*	Lone Pine (Township)—Itasca...... *MN-3*
Lodi (Township)—Mower *MN-3*	**Logan County** *NE-4*	Lone Pine Rancheria (CA)........ *IndRes-4*
Lodi (Borough)—Bergen.................. *NJ-1*	**Logan County** *ND-4*	Lone Rock (City)—Kossuth *IA-3*
Lodi (Town)—Seneca *NY-1*	**Logan County** *OH-3*	Lonerock (City)—Gilliam *OR-4*
Lodi (Village)—Seneca *NY-1*	**Logan County** *OK-2*	Lone Rock (Township)—Moody.... *SD-4*
Lodi (Township)—Athens *OH-3*	**Logan County** *WV-2*	Lone Rock (Village)—Richland *WI-3*
Lodi (Village)—Medina................... *OH-3*	Logan Elm Village (CDP)—	Lone Star (Township)—Rush..........*KS-4*
Lodi (Township)—Spink *SD-4*	Pickaway *OH-3*	Lone Star (CDP)—St. Charles
Lodi (City)—Columbia *WI-3*	Logansport (City)—Cass *IN-3*	Parish *LA-2*
Lodi (Town)—Columbia *WI-3*	Logansport (Township)—Logan...... *KS-4*	Lone Star (Township)—Gregory *SD-4*
Logan (Township)—Peoria............... *IL-3*	Logansport (Town)—De Soto	Lone Star (Township)—Tripp *SD-4*
Logan (Township)—Dearborn.......... *IN-3*	Parish *LA-2*	Lone Star (Town)—Morris *TX-2*
Logan (Township)—Fountain.......... *IN-3*	Loganton (Borough)—Clinton........ *PA-1*	Lone Tree (City)—Johnson *IA-3*
Logan (Township)—Pike *IN-3*	Loganville (City)—Gwinnett *GA-2*	Lone Tree (Township)—
Logan (City)—Harrison..................... *IA-3*	Loganville (City)—Walton *GA-2*	McPherson *KS-4*
Logan (Township)—Allen............... *KS-4*	Loganville (Borough)—York *PA-1*	Lone Tree (Township)—
Logan (Township)—Barton *KS-4*	Loganville (Village)—Sauk *WI-3*	Pottawatomie *KS-4*
Logan (Township)—Butler *KS-4*	Log Cabin (City)—Henderson *TX-2*	Lone Tree (Township)—
Logan (Township)—Decatur *KS-4*	Log Lane Village (Town)—	Chippewa *MN-3*
Logan (Township)—Dickinson *KS-4*	Morgan..*CO-4*	Lone Tree (Township)—Clay *NE-4*
Logan (Township)—Edwards *KS-4*	Lohman (Town)—Cole.................. *MO-3*	Lone Tree (Township)—Merrick.... *NE-4*
Logan (Township)—Gray *KS-4*	Lohnes (Township)—Benson...........*ND-4*	Lone Tree (Township)—Golden
Logan (Township)—Lincoln........... *KS-4*	Lohrville (City)—Calhoun *IA-3*	Valley..*ND-4*
Logan (Township)—Marion *KS-4*	Lohrville (Village)—Waushara *WI-3*	Lone Tree (Township)—Charles
Logan (Township)—Marshall *KS-4*	Lola (Township)—Cherokee........... *KS-4*	Mix..*SD-4*
Logan (Township)—Meade *KS-4*	Lolo (CDP)—Missoula *MT-4*	Lone Tree (Township)—Perkins *SD-4*
Logan (Township)—Mitchell...........*KS-4*	Loma (City)—Cavalier....................*ND-4*	Lone Tree (Township)—Tripp *SD-4*
Logan (Township)—Ottawa *KS-4*	Loma Linda (City)—San	Lone Wolf (Town)—Kiowa *OK-2*
Logan (Township)—Pawnee........... *KS-4*	Bernardino *CA-4*	Long Beach (City)—Los Angeles ... *CA-4*
Logan (City)—Phillips..................... *KS-4*	Loma Rica (CDP)—Yuba *CA-4*	Long Beach (Town)—La Porte........ *IN-3*
Logan (Township)—Phillips............ *KS-4*	Lomax (Town)—Henderson *IL-3*	Long Beach (City)—Pope *MN-3*
Logan (Township)—Sheridan........ *KS-4*	Lomax (Township)—Henderson *IL-3*	Long Beach (City)—Harrison *MS-2*
Logan (Township)—Sherman......... *KS-4*	Lombard (City)—DuPage *IL-3*	Long Beach (Township)—Ocean..... *NJ-1*
Logan (Township)—Smith *KS-4*	Lometa (City)—Lampasas................ *TX-2*	Long Beach (City)—Nassau *NY-1*
Logan (Township)—Washington *KS-4*	Lomira (Town)—Dodge *WI-3*	Long Beach (Town)—Brunswick.... *NC-2*
Logan (Township)—Mason *MI-3*	Lomira (Village)—Dodge................. *WI-3*	Long Beach (Town)—Pacific..........*WA-4*
Logan (Township)—Ogemaw *MI-3*	Lomita (City)—Los Angeles........... *CA-4*	Long Beach Naval Station (CA).....*Mil-4*
Logan (Township)—Aitkin *MN-3*	Lompoc (City)—Santa Barbara...... *CA-4*	Longboat Key (Town)—Manatee... *FL-2*
Logan (Township)—Grant *MN-3*	Lonaconing (Town)—Allegany........*MD-1*	Longboat Key (Town)—Sarasota ... *FL-2*
Logan (Township)—Reynolds *MO-3*	London (Town)—Pope *AR-2*	Long Branch (Township)—Saline ... *IL-3*
Logan (Township)—Wayne *MO-3*	London (CDP)—Tulare..................... *CA-4*	Long Branch (City)—Monmouth..*NJ-1*
Logan (Township)—Adams *NE-4*	London (Township)—Sumner......... *KS-4*	Long Branch (Borough)—
Logan (Township)—Antelope......... *NE-4*	London (City)—Laurel *KY-2*	Washington *PA-1*
Logan (Township)—Buffalo *NE-4*	London (Township)—Monroe........ *MI-3*	**Long County** *GA-2*
Logan (Township)—Burt *NE-4*	London (Township)—Freeborn....*MN-3*	Long Creek (Township)—Macon *IL-3*
Logan (Township)—Clay................ *NE-4*	London (City)—Madison *OH-3*	Long Creek (Village)—Macon......... *IL-3*
Logan (Township)—Cuming *NE-4*	London Britain (Township)—	Long Creek (Township)—Divide ...*ND-4*
Logan (Township)—Dixon *NE-4*	Chester *PA-1*	Long Creek (Town)—Grant *OR-4*

1020

Longdale (Town)—Blaine.............. OK-2
Longfellow (Township)—McLean ..ND-4
Longford (City)—Clay.................... KS-4
Long Grove (Village)—Lake IL-3
Long Grove (City)—Scott IA-3
Long Hollow (Township)—
  Roberts.. SD-4
Long Island (CDP)—Prince of
  Wales-Outer Ketchikan Census
  Area... AK-4
Long Island (City)—Phillips KS-4
Long Island (Township)—Phillips .. KS-4
Long Island (NY)......................... Geog-4
Long Island Sound (NY) Geog-4
Long Lake (CDP)—Lake................. IL-3
Long Lake (Township)—Grand
  Traverse.. MI-3
Long Lake (Township)—Crow
  Wing...MN-3
Long Lake (City)—Hennepin........ MN-3
Long Lake (Township)—
  Watonwan....................................MN-3
Long Lake (Town)—Hamilton........ NY-1
Long Lake (Township)—Burleigh ..ND-4
Long Lake (Town)—McPherson SD-4
Long Lake (Town)—Florence......... WI-3
Long Lake (Town)—Washburn WI-3
Long Meadow (CDP)—
  Washington...................................MD-1
Longmeadow (Town)—
  Hampden MA-1
Longmont (City)—Boulder CO-4
Long Neck (CDP)—Sussex............. DE-1
Long Pine (City)—Brown................ NE-4
Long Point (Township)—
  Livingston IL-3
Long Point (Village)—Livingston ... IL-3
Longport (Borough)—Atlantic NJ-1
Long Prairie (City)—Todd MN-3
Long Prairie (Township)—Todd ... MN-3
Long Prairie (Township)—
  Mississippi MO-3
Long Rapids (Township)—
  Alpena MI-3
Longrun (Township)—Ozark......... MO-3
Longstreet (Village)—De Soto
  Parish LA-2
Longswamp (Township)—Berks...... PA-1
Longton (City)—Elk........................ KS-4
Longton (Township)—Elk............... KS-4
Longtown (Town)—Perry .. MO-3
Longtown (CDP)—Pittsburg........... OK-2
Long Valley (CDP)—Morris NJ-1
Longview (Village)—Champaign IL-3
Long View (Town)—Burke............. NC-2
Long View (Town)—Catawba NC-2
Longview (Township)—Foster ND-4
Longview (City)—Gregg................. TX-2
Longview (City)—Harrison............. TX-2
Longview (City)—Cowlitz..............WA-4
Longview Heights (CDP)—
  Cowlitz WA-4
Longville (City)—Cass................... MN-3
Longwood (City)—Seminole...........FL-2
Longwood (Township)—Pettis MO-3
Longwood (Town)—Clark............... WI-3
Lonoke (City)—Lonoke.................. AR-2
Lonoke County AR-2
Lonsdale (Town)—Garland............. AR-2
Lonsdale (City)—Rice MN-3
Loogootee (City)—Martin................ IN-3
Lookeba (Town)—Caddo OK-2
Looking Glass (Township)—
  Clinton IL-3
Lookout (Township)—Ellis KS-4

Lookout, Cape (NC) Geog-4
Lookout Mountain (City)—
  Walker GA-2
Lookout Mountain (TN) Geog-4
Lookout Mountain (Town)—
  Hamilton....................................... TN-2
Lookout Rancheria (CA) IndRes-4
Loomis (Town)—Placer.................. CA-4
Loomis (Village)—Phelps............... NE-4
Loon Lake (Township)—Cass MN-3
Lopatcong (Township)—Warren NJ-1
Lopezville (CDP)—Hidalgo TX-2
Loquemont (Township)—
  McLean ND-4
Lorain (Township)—Nobles MN-3
Lorain (City)—Lorain OH-3
Lorain (Borough)—Cambria PA-1
Lorain (Town)—Polk..................... WI-3
Lorain County OH-3
Loraine (Village)—Adams............... IL-3
Loraine (Township)—Henry IL-3
Loraine (City)—Renville................ND-4
Loraine (Town)—Mitchell.............. TX-2
Loramie (Township)—Shelby..........OH-3
Loran (Township)—Stephenson IL-3
Lorance (Township)—Bollinger MO-3
Lorane (CDP)—Berks PA-1
Lordsburg (City)—Hidalgo............ NM-4
Lordsburg (Township)—
  Bottineau...................................... ND-4
Lordstown (Village)—Trumbull OH-3
Loreauville (Village)—Iberia
  Parish LA-2
Lore City (Village)—Guernsey......OH-3
Lorena (Town)—McLennan TX-2
Lorenzo (Town)—Crosby TX-2
Lorenz Park (CDP)—Columbia..... NY-1
Loretta (Township)—Grand
  Forks ND-4
Loretto (City)—Marion KY-2
Loretto (City)—Hennepin.............. MN-3
Loretto (Borough)—Cambria PA-1
Loretto (City)—Lawrence............... TN-2
Lorimor (City)—Union................... IA-3
Loring Air Force Base (ME)...........Mil-4
Loring Air Force Base (Mil. facil.)—
  Aroostook......................................ME-1
Loris (City)—Horry SC-2
Lorraine (City)—Ellsworth............. KS-4
Lorraine (Town)—Jefferson NY-1
Lorraine (Township)—Dickey........ ND-4
Lorton (CDP)—Fairfax VA-2
Lorton Village (Village)—Otoe NE-4
Los Alamitos (City)—Orange......... CA-4
Los Alamos (CDP)—Los
  Alamos NM-4
Los Alamos County NM-4
Los Altos (City)—Santa Clara CA-4
Los Altos Hills (Town)—Santa
  Clara CA-4
Los Angeles (City)—Los Angeles ... CA-4
Los Angeles County CA-4
Los Angeles Ranges (CA) Geog-4
Losantville (Town)—Randolph IN-3
Los Baños (City)—Merced.............. CA-4
Los Chaves (CDP)—Valencia NM-4
Los Coyotes Reservation
  (CA)...IndRes-4
Los Fresnos (City)—Cameron........ TX-2
Los Gatos (Town)—Santa Clara CA-4
Los Lunas (Village)—Valencia NM-4
Los Molinos (CDP)—Tehama........ CA-4
Los Ranchos de Albuquerque
  (Village)—Bernalillo NM-4

Los Serranos (CDP)—San
  Bernardino CA-4
Lostant (Town)—La Salle................ IL-3
Lost Creek (Township)—Vigo......... IN-3
Lost Creek (Township)—Wayne ... MO-3
Lost Creek (Township)—Platte....... NE-4
Lostcreek (Township)—Miami.......OH-3
Lost Creek (CDP)—Travis TX-2
Lost Creek (Town)—Harrison....... WV-2
Lost Hills (CDP)—Kern................. CA-4
Lostine (City)—Wallowa OR-4
Lost Nation (City)—Clinton............ IA-3
Lost River (City)—Custer ID-4
Lost River (Township)—Martin IN-3
Los Trujillos-Gabaldon (CDP)—
  Valencia..NM-4
Lost Springs (City)—Marion........... KS-4
Lost Springs (Township)—
  Marion KS-4
Lost Springs (Town)—Converse.... WY-4
Lostwood (Township)—
  Mountrail...................................... ND-4
Los Ybanez (City)—Dawson.......... TX-2
Lotsee (Town)—Tulsa.................... OK-2
Lott (City)—Falls........................... TX-2
Louann (Town)—Ouachita............. AR-2
Loud (Township)—Montmorency.. MI-3
Loudon (Township)—Fayette.......... IL-3
Loudon (Town)—Merrimack NH-1
Loudon (Township)—Carroll..........OH-3
Loudon (Township)—Seneca..........OH-3
Loudon (Town)—Loudon................ TN-2
Loudon County TN-2
Loudonville (CDP)—Albany NY-1
Loudonville (Village)—Ashland OH-3
Loudonville (Village)—Holmes.....OH-3
Loudoun County VA-2
Loughman (CDP)—Polk FL-2
Louin (Town)—Jasper MS-2
Louisa (Town)—Lawrence.............. KY-2
Louisa (Town)—Louisa VA-2
Louisa County IA-3
Louisa County VA-2
Louisburg (City)—Miami................ KS-4
Louisburg (Township)—
  Montgomery KS-4
Louisburg (City)—Lac qui Parle... MN-3
Louisburg (Village)—Dallas MO-3
Louisburg (Town)—Franklin.......... NC-2
Louise (Town)—Humphreys MS-2
Louisiana (City)—Pike MO-3
Louisville (Town)—Barbour............AL-2
Louisville (City)—Boulder CO-4
Louisville (City)—Jefferson GA-2
Louisville (Town)—Clay................. IL-3
Louisville (Township)—Clay........... IL-3
Louisville (City)—Pottawatomie..... KS-4
Louisville (Township)—
  Pottawatomie KS-4
Louisville (City)—Jefferson KY-2
Louisville (Township)—Red
  Lake..MN-3
Louisville (Township)—Scott MN-3
Louisville (City)—Winston MS-2
Louisville (Village)—Cass NE-4
Louisville (Town)—St. Lawrence ... NY-1
Louisville (City)—Stark..................OH-3
Loup (Township)—Buffalo NE-4
Loup (Township)—Custer NE-4
Loup (Township)—Merrick NE-4
Loup (Township)—Platte NE-4
Loup City (City)—Sherman NE-4
Loup County NE-4
Loup Ferry (Township)—Nance..... NE-4

General Index — American Places Dictionary

Louriston (Township)—Chippewa ... MN-3
Loutre (Township)—Audrain ... MO-3
Loutre (Township)—Montgomery ... MO-3
Love (Township)—Vermilion ... IL-3
Love County ... OK-2
Lovejoy (Town)—Clayton ... GA-2
Lovejoy (Township)—Iroquois ... IL-3
Lovelady (City)—Houston ... TX-2
Loveland (City)—Larimer ... CO-4
Loveland (City)—Clermont ... OH-3
Loveland (City)—Hamilton ... OH-3
Loveland (City)—Warren ... OH-3
Loveland (Town)—Tillman ... OK-2
Loveland Park (CDP)—Hamilton ... OH-3
Loveland Park (CDP)—Warren ... OH-3
Lovell (Town)—Oxford ... ME-1
Lovell (Township)—Dickey ... ND-4
Lovell (Town)—Big Horn ... WY-4
Lovells (Township)—Crawford ... MI-3
Lovelock (City)—Pershing ... NV-4
Lovelock Colony (NV) ... IndRes-4
Loves Park (City)—Winnebago ... IL-3
Lovett (Township)—Jennings ... IN-3
Lovettsville (Town)—Loudoun ... VA-2
Love Valley (Town)—Iredell ... NC-2
Lovilia (City)—Monroe ... IA-3
Loving (Village)—Eddy ... NM-4
Loving County ... TX-2
Lovington (Township)—Moultrie ... IL-3
Lovington (Village)—Moultrie ... IL-3
Lovington (City)—Lea ... NM-4
Low and Burbanks Grant (Pop. Place)—Coos ... NH-1
Lowden (City)—Cedar ... IA-3
Lowe (Township)—Moultrie ... IL-3
Lowe (Township)—Washington ... KS-4
Lowe (Township)—Deuel ... SD-4
Lowell (City)—Benton ... AR-2
Lowell (Town)—Lake ... IN-3
Lowell (Township)—Cherokee ... KS-4
Lowell (Town)—Penobscot ... ME-1
Lowell (City)—Middlesex ... MA-1
Lowell (City)—Kent ... MI-3
Lowell (Township)—Kent ... MI-3
Lowell (Township)—Polk ... MN-3
Lowell (Township)—Kearney ... NE-4
Lowell (Town)—Gaston ... NC-2
Lowell (Village)—Washington ... OH-3
Lowell (City)—Lane ... OR-4
Lowell (Township)—Marshall ... SD-4
Lowell (Town)—Orleans ... VT-1
Lowell (Town)—Dodge ... WI-3
Lowell (Village)—Dodge ... WI-3
Lowellville (Village)—Mahoning ... OH-3
Lower (Township)—Cape May ... NJ-1
Lower Allen (Township)—Cumberland ... PA-1
Lower Alloways Creek (Township)—Salem ... NJ-1
Lower Alsace (Township)—Berks ... PA-1
Lower Augusta (Township)—Northumberland ... PA-1
Lower Brule (CDP)—Lyman ... SD-4
Lower Brule Reservation (SD) ... IndRes-4
Lower Burrell (City)—Westmoreland ... PA-1
Lower Chanceford (Township)—York ... PA-1
Lower Chichester (Township)—Delaware ... PA-1

Lower Elwah Reservation & Trust Lands (WA) ... IndRes-4
Lower Frankford (Township)—Cumberland ... PA-1
Lower Frederick (Township)—Montgomery ... PA-1
Lower Grand Lagoon (CDP)—Bay ... FL-2
Lower Gwynedd (Township)—Montgomery ... PA-1
Lower Heidelberg (Township)—Berks ... PA-1
Lower Kalskag (City)—Bethel Census Area ... AK-4
Lower Lake (CDP)—Lake ... CA-4
Lower Macungie (Township)—Lehigh ... PA-1
Lower Mahanoy (Township)—Northumberland ... PA-1
Lower Makefield (Township)—Bucks ... PA-1
Lower Merion (Township)—Montgomery ... PA-1
Lower Mifflin (Township)—Cumberland ... PA-1
Lower Milford (Township)—Lehigh ... PA-1
Lower Moreland (Township)—Montgomery ... PA-1
Lower Mount Bethel (Township)—Northampton ... PA-1
Lower Nazareth (Township)—Northampton ... PA-1
Lower Oxford (Township)—Chester ... PA-1
Lower Paxton (Township)—Dauphin ... PA-1
Lower Pottsgrove (Township)—Montgomery ... PA-1
Lower Providence (Township)—Montgomery ... PA-1
Lower Red Lake (CA) ... Geog-4
Lower Red Lake (Pop. Place)—Beltrami ... MN-3
Lower Salem (Village)—Washington ... OH-3
Lower Salford (Township)—Montgomery ... PA-1
Lower Saucon (Township)—Northampton ... PA-1
Lower Sioux Community (MN) ... IndRes-4
Lower Southampton (Township)—Bucks ... PA-1
Lower Swatara (Township)—Dauphin ... PA-1
Lower Towamensing (Township)—Carbon ... PA-1
Lower Turkeyfoot (Township)—Somerset ... PA-1
Lower Tyrone (Township)—Fayette ... PA-1
Lower Windsor (Township)—York ... PA-1
Lowery (Township)—Stutsman ... ND-4
Lower Yoder (Township)—Cambria ... PA-1
Lower Yosemite Falls (CA) ... Geog-4
Lowesville (CDP)—Lincoln ... NC-2
Lowhill (Township)—Lehigh ... PA-1
Lowland (Township)—Mountrail ... ND-4
Low Moor (City)—Clinton ... IA-3
Lowndesboro (Municipality)—Lowndes ... AL-2
Lowndes County ... AL-2

Lowndes County ... GA-2
Lowndes County ... MS-2
Lowndesville (Town)—Abbeville ... SC-2
Lowry (City)—Pope ... MN-3
Lowry (Town)—Walworth ... SD-4
Lowry Air Force Base (CO) ... Mil-4
Lowry City (City)—St. Clair ... MO-3
Lowry Crossing (City)—Collin ... TX-2
Lowrys (Town)—Chester ... SC-2
Lowville (Township)—Murray ... MN-3
Lowville (Town)—Lewis ... NY-1
Lowville (Village)—Lewis ... NY-1
Lowville (Town)—Columbia ... WI-3
Loxley (Town)—Baldwin ... AL-2
Loyal (Town)—Kingfisher ... OK-2
Loyal (City)—Clark ... WI-3
Loyal (Town)—Clark ... WI-3
Loyalhanna (Township)—Westmoreland ... PA-1
Loyall (City)—Harlan ... KY-2
Loyalsock (Township)—Lycoming ... PA-1
Loyalton (City)—Sierra ... CA-4
Loyola (CDP)—Santa Clara ... CA-4
Luana (Town)—Clayton ... IA-3
Lubbock (City)—Lubbock ... TX-2
Lubbock County ... TX-2
Lubec (Town)—Washington ... ME-1
Lublin (Village)—Taylor ... WI-3
Lucama (Town)—Wilson ... NC-2
Lucan (City)—Redwood ... MN-3
Lucas (Township)—Effingham ... IL-3
Lucas (City)—Lucas ... IA-3
Lucas (City)—Russell ... KS-4
Lucas (Township)—Lyon ... MN-3
Lucas (Village)—Richland ... OH-3
Lucas (Town)—Collin ... TX-2
Lucas (Town)—Dunn ... WI-3
Lucas County ... IA-3
Lucas County ... OH-3
Lucas Valley-Marinwood (CDP)—Marin ... CA-4
Lucasville (CDP)—Scioto ... OH-3
Luce (Township)—Spencer ... IN-3
Luce County ... MI-3
Lucedale (City)—George ... MS-2
Lucerne (CDP)—Lake ... CA-4
Lucerne (Village)—Putnam ... MO-3
Lucerne Mines (CDP)—Indiana ... PA-1
Luck (Town)—Polk ... WI-3
Luck (Village)—Polk ... WI-3
Luckey (Village)—Wood ... OH-3
Lucky (Village)—Bienville Parish ... LA-2
Lucy (Township)—Burke ... ND-4
Ludden (City)—Dickey ... ND-4
Ludell (Township)—Rawlins ... KS-4
Ludington (City)—Mason ... MI-3
Ludington (Town)—Eau Claire ... WI-3
Ludlow (Township)—Champaign ... IL-3
Ludlow (Village)—Champaign ... IL-3
Ludlow (City)—Kenton ... KY-2
Ludlow (Town)—Aroostook ... ME-1
Ludlow (Town)—Hampden ... MA-1
Ludlow (Town)—Livingston ... MO-3
Ludlow (Township)—Washington ... OH-3
Ludlow (Town)—Windsor ... VT-1
Ludlow (Village)—Windsor ... VT-1
Ludlow Falls (Village)—Miami ... OH-3
Ludowici (City)—Long ... GA-2
Lueders (City)—Jones ... TX-2
Lueders (City)—Shackelford ... TX-2
Luella (Town)—Grayson ... TX-2
Lufkin (City)—Angelina ... TX-2
Lugoff (CDP)—Kershaw ... SC-2
Lukachukai (CDP)—Apache ... AZ-4

Luke (Town)—Allegany................ MD-1
Luke Air Force Base (AZ) Mil-4
Luke Air Force Base (Military
  Facility)—Maricopa................... AZ-4
Lukin (Township)—Lawrence IL-3
Lula (City)—Banks.......................... GA-2
Lula (City)—Hall............................ GA-2
Lula (Town)—Coahoma................. MS-2
Lulu (Township)—Mitchell KS-4
Lumbee TDSA (NC)................. IndRes-4
Lumber (Township)—Cameron PA-1
Lumber Bridge (Town)—
  Robeson NC-2
Lumber City (City)—Telfair GA-2
Lumber City (Borough)—
  Clearfield...................................... PA-1
Lumberland (Town)—Sullivan....... NY-1
Lumberport (Town)—Harrison..... WV-2
Lumberton (City)—Lamar.............MS-2
Lumberton (City)—Pearl River MS-2
Lumberton (Township)—
  Burlington NJ-1
Lumberton (City)—Robeson.......... NC-2
Lumberton (City)—Hardin TX-2
Lummi Reservation (WA) IndRes-4
Lumpkin (City)—Stewart............... GA-2
Lumpkin County.............................. GA-2
Luna County NM-4
Luna Pier (City)—Monroe MI-3
Lund (Township)—Douglas MN-3
Lund (Township)—Ward................ ND-4
Lunenburg (Town)—Worcester MA-1
Lunenburg (Town)—Essex VT-1
Lunenburg County............................ VA-2
Lupus (Town)—Moniteau MO-3
Lura (Township)—Faribault.......... MN-3
Lura (Township)—Grant SD-4
Luray (City)—Russell..................... KS-4
Luray (Township)—Russell............ KS-4
Luray (Town)—Clark MO-3
Luray (Town)—Hampton SC-2
Luray (Town)—Page........................ VA-2
Luray Caverns (VA) Geog-4
Lurgan (Township)—Franklin PA-1
Lushton (Village)—York................. NE-4
Lusk (Town)—Niobrara WY-4
Lutak (CDP)—Haines Borough AK-4
Lutcher (Town)—St. James
  Parish LA-2
Luther (City)—Boone...................... IA-3
Luther (Village)—Lake MI-3
Luther (Town)—Oklahoma OK-2
Luthersville (Town)—Meriwether .. GA-2
Lutherville-Timonium (CDP)—
  Baltimore MD-1
Lutsen (Township)—Cook............ MN-3
Luttrell (Town)—Union TN-2
Lutz (CDP)—Hillsborough FL-2
Luverne (City)—Crenshaw............. AL-2
Lu Verne (City)—Humboldt........... IA-3
Lu Verne (City)—Kossuth............... IA-3
Luverne (City)—Rock MN-3
Luverne (Township)—Rock MN-3
Luverne (City)—Steele ND-4
Luxemburg (City)—Dubuque IA-3
Luxemburg (Township)—Stearns.. MN-3
Luxemburg (Town)—Kewaunee..... WI-3
Luxemburg (Village)—Kewaunee... WI-3
Luxora (Town)—Mississippi AR-2
Luzerne (City)—Benton IA-3
Luzerne (Township)—Fayette PA-1
Luzerne (Borough)—Luzerne......... PA-1
Luzerne County PA-1

Lycoming (Township)—Lycoming .. PA-1
Lycoming County PA-1
Lyda (Township)—Macon MO-3
Lydia (CDP)—Iberia Parish...........LA-2
Lyerly (Town)—Chattooga GA-2
Lyford (Town)—Willacy................ TX-2
Lykens (Township)—Crawford......OH-3
Lykens (Borough)—Dauphin PA-1
Lykens (Township)—Dauphin........ PA-1
Lyle (City)—Mower....................... MN-3
Lyle (Township)—Mower MN-3
Lyman (Township)—Ford IL-3
Lyman (Town)—York ME-1
Lyman (CDP)—Harrison MS-2
Lyman (Village)—Scotts Bluff........ NE-4
Lyman (Town)—Grafton NH-1
Lyman (Pop. Place)—Burleigh....... ND-4
Lyman (Town)—Spartanburg..........SC-2
Lyman (Town)—Wayne UT-4
Lyman (Town)—Skagit WA-4
Lyman (Town)—Uinta WY-4
Lyman County.................................. SD-4
Lyme (Town)—New London......... CT-1
Lyme (Town)—Grafton NH-1
Lyme (Town)—Jefferson NY-1
Lyme (Township)—Huron.............OH-3
Lynbrook (Village)—Nassau........... NY-1
Lynch (City)—Harlan KY-2
Lynch (Township)—Texas MO-3
Lynch (Township)—Boyd NE-4
Lynch (Village)—Boyd NE-4
Lynchburg (Township)—Mason IL-3
Lynchburg (CDP)—DeSoto...........MS-2
Lynchburg (Village)—Highland.....OH-3
Lynchburg (Town)—Lee SC-2
Lynchburg (Town)—Moore TN-2
Lynchburg (Independent City)........... VA-2
Lyncourt (CDP)—Onondaga.......... NY-1
Lynd (City)—Lyon........................ MN-3
Lynd (Township)—Lyon MN-3
Lyndeborough (Town)—
  Hillsborough NH-1
Lynden (Township)—Stearns MN-3
Lynden (City)—Whatcom WA-4
Lyndhurst (Township)—Bergen NJ-1
Lyndhurst (City)—Cuyahoga.........OH-3
Lyndon (Town)—Whiteside........... IL-3
Lyndon (Township)—Whiteside.... IL-3
Lyndon (City)—Osage KS-4
Lyndon (City)—Jefferson KY-2
Lyndon (Township)—Washtenaw .. MI-3
Lyndon (Town)—Cattaraugus NY-1
Lyndon (CDP)—Onondaga........... NY-1
Lyndon (Town)—Caledonia VT-1
Lyndon (Town)—Juneau WI-3
Lyndon (Town)—Sheboygan WI-3
Lyndon Station (Village)—
  Juneau WI-3
Lyndonville (Village)—Orleans...... NY-1
Lyndonville (Village)—Caledonia .. VT-1
Lynn (Town)—Winston..................AL-2
Lynn (Town)—Lawrence AR-2
Lynn (Township)—Henry............... IL-3
Lynn (Township)—Knox IL-3
Lynn (Township)—Posey................ IN-3
Lynn (Town)—Randolph................ IN-3
Lynn (City)—Essex MA-1
Lynn (Township)—St. Clair MI-3
Lynn (Township)—McLeod MN-3
Lynn (Township)—Clay NE-4
Lynn (Township)—Wells ND-4
Lynn (Township)—Hardin OH-3
Lynn (Township)—Lehigh.............. PA-1
Lynn (Township)—Day SD-4
Lynn (Township)—Lincoln SD-4

Lynn (Township)—Moody SD-4
Lynn (Town)—Clark...................... WI-3
Lynn County TX-2
Lynndyl (Town)—Millard............... UT-4
Lynne (Town)—Oneida WI-3
Lynnfield (Town)—Essex MA-1
Lynn Haven (City)—Bay................FL-2
Lynnview (City)—Jefferson........... KY-2
Lynnville (Village)—Morgan IL-3
Lynnville (Township)—Ogle........... IL-3
Lynnville (Town)—Warrick IN-3
Lynnville (City)—Jasper.................IA-3
Lynnville (Town)—Giles TN-2
Lynnwood (City)—Snohomish WA-4
Lynnwood-Pricedale (CDP)—
  Fayette.. PA-1
Lynnwood-Pricedale (CDP)—
  Westmoreland PA-1
Lynwood (City)—Los Angeles........ CA-4
Lynwood (Town)—Cook IL-3
Lynxville (Village)—Crawford WI-3
Lyon (Township)—Cherokee.........KS-4
Lyon (Township)—Cloud KS-4
Lyon (Township)—Decatur KS-4
Lyon (Township)—Dickinson KS-4
Lyon (Township)—Geary KS-4
Lyon (Township)—Oakland MI-3
Lyon (Township)—Roscommon..... MI-3
Lyon (Town)—Coahoma................MS-2
Lyon (Township)—Franklin MO-3
Lyon (Township)—Knox MO-3
Lyon (Township)—Lewis.............. MO-3
Lyon (Township)—Stutsman......... ND-4
Lyon (Township)—Brule SD-4
Lyon County IA-3
Lyon County KS-4
Lyon County KY-2
Lyon County MN-3
Lyon County NV-4
Lyons (Town)—Boulder CO-4
Lyons (City)—Toombs GA-2
Lyons (City)—Cook IL-3
Lyons (Township)—Cook IL-3
Lyons (Town)—Greene................... IN-3
Lyons (City)—Rice KS-4
Lyons (Township)—Ionia MI-3
Lyons (Village)—Ionia MI-3
Lyons (Township)—Lyon MN-3
Lyons (Township)—Wadena MN-3
Lyons (City)—Burt NE-4
Lyons (Town)—Wayne NY-1
Lyons (Village)—Wayne NY-1
Lyons (Village)—Fulton OH-3
Lyons (City)—Linn OR-4
Lyons (Borough)—Berks................ PA-1
Lyons (Township)—Minnehaha SD-4
Lyons (Town)—Walworth............. WI-3
Lyonsdale (Town)—Lewis NY-1
Lyons Falls (Village)—Lewis NY-1
Lyra (Township)—Blue Earth MN-3
Lysander (Town)—Onondaga......... NY-1
Lytle (City)—Atascosa.................... TX-2
Lytle (City)—Bexar........................ TX-2
Lytle (City)—Medina..................... TX-2
Lytton (City)—Calhoun.................IA-3
Lytton (City)—Sac IA-3
Maalaea (CDP)—Maui.................... HI-4
Mabank (Town)—Henderson TX-2
Mabank (Town)—Kaufman TX-2
Mabel (City)—Fillmore MN-3
Mabel (Township)—Griggs ND-4
Maben (Town)—Oktibbeha...........MS-2
Maben (Town)—Webster................MS-2
Mableton (CDP)—Cobb................. GA-2
Mabscott (Town)—Raleigh............ WV-2

General Index | American Places Dictionary

Mabton (Town)—Yakima	WA-4
Macarthur (CDP)—Raleigh	WV-2
Macclenny (Town)—Baker	FL-2
Macclesfield (Town)—Edgecombe	NC-2
MacDill Air Force Base (FL)	Mil-4
Macedon (Town)—Wayne	NY-1
Macedon (Village)—Wayne	NY-1
Macedonia (Village)—Franklin	IL-3
Macedonia (Village)—Hamilton	IL-3
Macedonia (City)—Pottawattamie	IA-3
Macedonia (City)—Summit	OH-3
Machesney Park (Village)—Winnebago	IL-3
Machias (Town)—Washington	ME-1
Machias (Town)—Cattaraugus	NY-1
Machiasport (Town)—Washington	ME-1
Mackay (City)—Custer	ID-4
Mac Kenzie (Village)—St. Louis	MO-3
Mackey (Town)—Gibson	IN-3
Mackford (Town)—Green Lake	WI-3
Mackinac, Straits of (MI)	Geog-4
Mackinac County	MI-3
Mackinac Island (MI)	Geog-4
Mackinac Island (City)—Mackinac	MI-3
Mackinac Straits Bridge (MI)	Geog-4
Mackinaw (Town)—Tazewell	IL-3
Mackinaw (Township)—Tazewell	IL-3
Mackinaw (Township)—Cheboygan	MI-3
Mackinaw City (Village)—Cheboygan	MI-3
Mackinaw City (Village)—Emmet	MI-3
Mack North (CDP)—Hamilton	OH-3
Macksburg (City)—Madison	IA-3
Macksburg (Village)—Washington	OH-3
Macks Creek (City)—Camden	MO-3
Mack South (CDP)—Hamilton	OH-3
Macksville (City)—Stafford	KS-4
Mackville (City)—Washington	KY-2
Macomb (City)—McDonough	IL-3
Macomb (Township)—McDonough	IL-3
Macomb (Township)—Macomb	MI-3
Macomb (Town)—St. Lawrence	NY-1
Macomb (Town)—Pottawatomie	OK-2
Macomb City (Township)—McDonough	IL-3
Macomb County	MI-3
Macon (City)—Bibb	GA-2
Macon (City)—Jones	GA-2
Macon (Township)—Bureau	IL-3
Macon (Town)—Macon	IL-3
Macon (Township)—Harvey	KS-4
Macon (Township)—Lenawee	MI-3
Macon (City)—Noxubee	MS-2
Macon (City)—Macon	MO-3
Macon (Township)—Franklin	NE-4
Macon (Town)—Warren	NC-2
Macon County	AL-2
Macon County	GA-2
Macon County	IL-3
Macon County	MO-3
Macon County	NC-2
Macon County	TN-2
Macoupin County	IL-3
Macsville (Township)—Grant	MN-3
Macungie (Borough)—Lehigh	PA-1
Macville (Township)—Aitkin	MN-3
Macwahoc (Plantation)—Aroostook	ME-1
Macy (Town)—Miami	IN-3
Macy (CDP)—Thurston	NE-4
Madawaska (Town)—Aroostook	ME-1
Madbury (Town)—Strafford	NH-1
Maddock (City)—Benson	ND-4
Madeira (City)—Hamilton	OH-3
Madeira Beach (City)—Pinellas	FL-2
Madelia (City)—Watonwan	MN-3
Madelia (Township)—Watonwan	MN-3
Madera (City)—Madera	CA-4
Madera Acres (CDP)—Madera	CA-4
Madera County	CA-4
Madge (Town)—Washburn	WI-3
Madill (City)—Marshall	OK-2
Madison (Municipality)—Limestone	AL-2
Madison (Municipality)—Madison	AL-2
Madison (City)—St. Francis	AR-2
Madison (Town)—New Haven	CT-1
Madison (City)—Madison	FL-2
Madison (City)—Morgan	GA-2
Madison (City)—Madison	IL-3
Madison (Township)—Richland	IL-3
Madison (City)—St. Clair	IL-3
Madison (Township)—Allen	IN-3
Madison (Township)—Carroll	IN-3
Madison (Township)—Clinton	IN-3
Madison (Township)—Daviess	IN-3
Madison (Township)—Dubois	IN-3
Madison (Township)—Jay	IN-3
Madison (City)—Jefferson	IN-3
Madison (Township)—Jefferson	IN-3
Madison (Township)—Montgomery	IN-3
Madison (Township)—Morgan	IN-3
Madison (Township)—Pike	IN-3
Madison (Township)—Putnam	IN-3
Madison (Township)—St. Joseph	IN-3
Madison (Township)—Tipton	IN-3
Madison (Township)—Washington	IN-3
Madison (City)—Greenwood	KS-4
Madison (Township)—Greenwood	KS-4
Madison (Township)—Lincoln	KS-4
Madison (Township)—Riley	KS-4
Madison (Town)—Somerset	ME-1
Madison (City)—Lac qui Parle	MN-3
Madison (Township)—Lac qui Parle	MN-3
Madison (Town)—Madison	MS-2
Madison (Township)—Cedar	MO-3
Madison (Township)—Clark	MO-3
Madison (Township)—Grundy	MO-3
Madison (Township)—Harrison	MO-3
Madison (Township)—Jasper	MO-3
Madison (Township)—Johnson	MO-3
Madison (Township)—Mercer	MO-3
Madison (City)—Monroe	MO-3
Madison (Township)—Fillmore	NE-4
Madison (City)—Madison	NE-4
Madison (Town)—Carroll	NH-1
Madison (Borough)—Morris	NJ-1
Madison (Town)—Madison	NY-1
Madison (Village)—Madison	NY-1
Madison (Town)—Rockingham	NC-2
Madison (Township)—Hettinger	ND-4
Madison (Township)—Butler	OH-3
Madison (Township)—Clark	OH-3
Madison (Township)—Columbiana	OH-3
Madison (Township)—Fairfield	OH-3
Madison (Township)—Fayette	OH-3
Madison (Township)—Franklin	OH-3
Madison (Township)—Guernsey	OH-3
Madison (Township)—Hancock	OH-3
Madison (Township)—Highland	OH-3
Madison (Township)—Jackson	OH-3
Madison (Township)—Lake	OH-3
Madison (Village)—Lake	OH-3
Madison (Township)—Licking	OH-3
Madison (Township)—Montgomery	OH-3
Madison (Township)—Muskingum	OH-3
Madison (Township)—Perry	OH-3
Madison (Township)—Pickaway	OH-3
Madison (Township)—Richland	OH-3
Madison (Township)—Sandusky	OH-3
Madison (Township)—Scioto	OH-3
Madison (Township)—Vinton	OH-3
Madison (Township)—Williams	OH-3
Madison (Township)—Armstrong	PA-1
Madison (Township)—Clarion	PA-1
Madison (Township)—Columbia	PA-1
Madison (Township)—Lackawanna	PA-1
Madison (Borough)—Westmoreland	PA-1
Madison (Township)—Edmunds	SD-4
Madison (Township)—Grant	SD-4
Madison (City)—Lake	SD-4
Madison (Town)—Madison	VA-2
Madison (City)—Boone	WV-2
Madison (City)—Dane	WI-3
Madison (Town)—Dane	WI-3
Madison Charter (Township)—Lenawee	MI-3
Madison County	AL-2
Madison County	AR-2
Madison County	FL-2
Madison County	GA-2
Madison County	ID-4
Madison County	IL-3
Madison County	IN-3
Madison County	IA-3
Madison County	KY-2
Madison County	MS-2
Madison County	MO-3
Madison County	MT-4
Madison County	NE-4
Madison County	NY-1
Madison County	NC-2
Madison County	OH-3
Madison County	TN-2
Madison County	TX-2
Madison County	VA-2
Madison Heights (City)—Oakland	MI-3
Madison Heights (CDP)—Amherst	VA-2
Madison Lake (City)—Blue Earth	MN-3
Madison Parish	LA-2
Madison Park (CDP)—Middlesex	NJ-1
Madisonville (City)—Hopkins	KY-2
Madisonville (Town)—St. Tammany Parish	LA-2
Madisonville (Town)—Monroe	TN-2
Madisonville (City)—Madison	TX-2
Madras (City)—Jefferson	OR-4
Madre, Laguna (TX)	Geog-4
Madrid (Town)—Houston	AL-2
Madrid (City)—Boone	IA-3
Madrid (Town)—Franklin	ME-1
Madrid (Village)—Perkins	NE-4
Madrid (Town)—St. Lawrence	NY-1
Mad River (Township)—Champaign	OH-3

Mad River (Township)—Clark OH-3
Mad River (Township)—
 Montgomery......................OH-3
Maeser (CDP)—Uintah..................UT-4
Maeystown (Village)—Monroe IL-3
Magalia (CDP)—Butte CA-4
Magalloway (Plantation)—
 Oxford..ME-1
Magazine (City)—Logan AR-2
Magazine Mountain (AR)............Geog-4
Magdalena (Village)—Socorro NM-4
Magee (City)—Simpson MS-2
Maggie Valley (Town)—
 Haywood.......................................NC-2
Magna (CDP)—Salt Lake..................UT-4
Magness (Town)—Independence ...AR-2
Magnet (Village)—Cedar.................NE-4
Magnetic Springs (Village)—
 Union..OH-3
Magnolia (City)—Columbia AR-2
Magnolia (Town)—Kent DE-1
Magnolia (Township)—Putnam IL-3
Magnolia (Village)—Putnam............IL-3
Magnolia (City)—Harrison IA-3
Magnolia (City)—Rock MN-3
Magnolia (Township)—Rock MN-3
Magnolia (City)—Pike......................MS-2
Magnolia (Borough)—Camden NJ-1
Magnolia (Town)—Duplin NC-2
Magnolia (Village)—Carroll OH-3
Magnolia (Village)—Stark OH-3
Magnolia (Town)—Montgomery....TX-2
Magnolia (Town)—Rock WI-3
Magoffin County KY-2
Mahaffey (Borough)—Clearfield PA-1
Mahanoy (Township)—Schuylkill ...PA-1
Mahanoy City (Borough)—
 Schuylkill......................................PA-1
Mahaska (City)—Washington KS-4
Mahaska County...............................IA-3
Mahnomen (City)—Mahnomen.....MN-3
Mahnomen County.........................MN-3
Mahomet (Township)—
 Champaign...................................IL-3
Mahomet (Village)—Champaign IL-3
Mahoning (Township)—
 Armstrong.....................................PA-1
Mahoning (Township)—Carbon......PA-1
Mahoning (Township)—Lawrence ..PA-1
Mahoning (Township)—Montour ...PA-1
Mahoning County OH-3
Mahopac (CDP)—Putnam................NY-1
Mahto (Township)—Corson SD-4
Mahtomedi (City)—Washington ...MN-3
Mahtowa (Township)—Carlton.....MN-3
Mahwah (Township)—Bergen NJ-1
Maiden (Town)—Catawba NC-2
Maiden (Town)—Lincoln NC-2
Maidencreek (Township)—Berks PA-1
Maiden Rock (Town)—Pierce WI-3
Maiden Rock (Village)—Pierce.......WI-3
Maidstone (Town)—Essex VT-1
Maili (CDP)—Honolulu HI-4
Main (Township)—Columbia...........PA-1
Maine (Township)—Cook IL-3
Maine (Township)—Grundy IL-3
Maine (Township)—Otter Tail MN-3
Maine (Town)—Broome...................NY-1
Maine (Township)—Adams ND-4
Maine (Town)—Marathon WI-3
Maine (Town)—Outagamie WI-3
Maine Prairie (Township)—
 Stearns..MN-3
Maineville (Village)—Warren.........OH-3
Maitland (City)—Orange FL-2

Maitland (City)—Holt.....................MO-3
Maize (City)—Sedgwick KS-4
Major County OK-2
Makaha (CDP)—Honolulu HI-4
Makaha Valley (CDP)—Honolulu ..HI-4
Makah Reservation (WA).........IndRes-4
Makakilo City (CDP)—Honolulu ...HI-4
Makanda (Town)—Jackson IL-3
Makanda (Township)—Jackson IL-3
Makawao (CDP)—Maui....................HI-4
Makoti (City)—Ward.......................ND-4
Malabar (Town)—Brevard FL-2
Malad City (City)—Oneida ID-4
Malaga (Township)—Monroe........OH-3
Malakoff (City)—Henderson TX-2
Malaspina Glacier (AK) Geog-4
Malcolm (Village)—Lancaster.........NE-4
Malcolm (Township)—McLean....ND-4
Malcom (City)—Poweshiek.............IA-3
Malden (Village)—Bureau IL-3
Malden (City)—Middlesex MA-1
Malden (City)—Dunklin MO-3
Malden (The Whitman County)—
 Whitman WA-4
Malheur County OR-4
Malibu Beach (CA)........................Geog-4
Malin (City)—Klamath OR-4
Malinta (Village)—Henry................OH-3
Mallard (City)—Palo Alto IA-3
Mallory (CDP)—Logan WV-2
Malmo (Township)—Aitkin MN-3
Malmo (Village)—Saunders NE-4
Malmstrom Air Force Base (MT) ..Mil-4
Malmstrom Air Force Base (Military
 Facility)—Cascade......................MT-4
Malone (Town)—Jackson..................FL-2
Malone (Township)—Tazewell IL-3
Malone (Town)—Franklin NY-1
Malone (Village)—Franklin.............NY-1
Malone (Town)—Hill TX-2
Maloy (City)—Ringgold IA-3
Malta (City)—Cassia ID-4
Malta (Township)—DeKalb IL-3
Malta (Village)—DeKalb..................IL-3
Malta (Township)—Big Stone MN-3
Malta (City)—Phillips MT-4
Malta (Town)—Saratoga NY-1
Malta (Township)—Morgan...........OH-3
Malta (Village)—Morgan.................OH-3
Malta Bend (Town)—Saline MO-3
Maltby (Township)—Perkins SD-4
Malung (Township)—Roseau MN-3
Malvern (Town)—Geneva................AL-2
Malvern (City)—Hot Spring AR-2
Malvern (City)—Mills IA-3
Malvern (Village)—Carroll OH-3
Malvern (Borough)—Chester PA-1
Malverne (Village)—Nassau...........NY-1
Mamakating (Town)—Sullivan NY-1
Mamaroneck (Town)—
 Westchester NY-1
Mamaroneck (Village)—
 Westchester NY-1
Mammoth (Town)—Pinal AZ-4
Mammoth Cave (KY) Geog-4
Mammoth-Flint Ridge Cave
 System (KY) Geog-4
Mammoth Lakes (Town)—Mono ..CA-4
Mammoth Spring (City)—Fulton ..AR-2
Mamou (Town)—Evangeline
 Parish...LA-2
Mamre (Township)—Kandiyohi ...MN-3
Man (Town)—Logan WV-2
Manahawkin (CDP)—Ocean...........NJ-1
Manalapan (Town)—Palm Beach ...FL-2

Manalapan (Township)—
 Monmouth NJ-1
Manannah (Township)—Meeker ..MN-3
Manasota Key (CDP)—Charlotte ...FL-2
Manasquan (Borough)—
 Monmouth NJ-1
Manassa (Town)—Conejos..............CO-4
Manassas (City)—Tattnall GA-2
Manassas (Independent City) VA-2
**Manassas Park (Independent
 City)** VA-2
Manatee County..............................FL-2
Manawa (City)—Waupaca WI-3
Mancelona (Township)—Antrim ... MI-3
Mancelona (Village)—Antrim MI-3
Manchester (Town)—Hartford........CT-1
Manchester (City)—Meriwether GA-2
Manchester (City)—Talbot GA-2
Manchester (Township)—Boone IL-3
Manchester (Town)—Scott IL-3
Manchester (Township)—
 Dearborn......................................IN-3
Manchester (City)—Delaware IA-3
Manchester (City)—Dickinson........KS-4
Manchester (City)—Clay KY-2
Manchester (Town)—Kennebec ME-1
Manchester (Town)—Carroll MD-1
Manchester (Town)—Essex MA-1
Manchester (Township)—
 Washtenaw..................................MI-3
Manchester (Village)—
 Washtenaw..................................MI-3
Manchester (City)—Freeborn MN-3
Manchester (Township)—
 Freeborn MN-3
Manchester (City)—St. Louis MO-3
Manchester (City)—Hillsborough ..NH-1
Manchester (Township)—Ocean ...NJ-1
Manchester (Town)—Ontario NY-1
Manchester (Village)—Ontario NY-1
Manchester (Township)—Adams ...OH-3
Manchester (Village)—Adams OH-3
Manchester (Township)—
 Morgan.......................................OH-3
Manchester (Town)—Grant OK-2
Manchester (Township)—Wayne ...PA-1
Manchester (Borough)—York PA-1
Manchester (Township)—York PA-1
Manchester (Township)—
 Kingsbury SD-4
Manchester (City)—Coffee..............TN-2
Manchester (Town)—Bennington ..VT-1
Manchester (Village)—
 Bennington VT-1
Manchester (CDP)—Kitsap WA-4
Manchester (Town)—Green Lake ..WI-3
Manchester (Town)—Jackson WI-3
Manchester (Point Arena) Rancheria
 (CA)......................................IndRes-4
Mancos (Town)—Montezuma........CO-4
Mandan (City)—Morton ND-4
Mandan (Pop. Place)—Morton......ND-4
Mandan (Township)—Ward..........ND-4
Mandaree (CDP)—McKenzie ND-4
Manderson (Town)—Big Horn WY-4
Manderson-White Horse Creek
 (CDP)—Shannon........................SD-4
Mandeville (Town)—St. Tammany
 Parish...LA-2
Mandt (Township)—Chippewa MN-3
Manfred (Township)—Lac qui
 Parle...MN-3
Manfred (Township)—Wells ND-4
Mangham (Town)—Richland
 Parish...LA-2

General Index — American Places Dictionary

Mango (CDP)—Hillsborough...........FL-2
Mangonia Park (Town)—Palm Beach..............FL-2
Mangum (City)—Greer.................OK-2
Manhasset (CDP)—Nassau............NY-1
Manhasset Hills (CDP)—Nassau...NY-1
Manhattan (Town)—Will................IL-3
Manhattan (Township)—Will....IL-3
Manhattan (City)—Pottawatomie...KS-4
Manhattan (City)—Riley..............KS-4
Manhattan (Township)—Riley....KS-4
Manhattan (Town)—Gallatin.........MT-4
Manhattan (NY).........................Geog-4
Manhattan (Borough)—New York..........................NY-1
Manhattan Beach (City)—Los Angeles..........................CA-4
Manhattan Beach (City)—Crow Wing..........................MN-3
Manheim (Town)—Herkimer..........NY-1
Manheim (Borough)—Lancaster.....PA-1
Manheim (Township)—Lancaster...PA-1
Manheim (Township)—York..........PA-1
Manila (City)—Mississippi...........AR-2
Manila (Town)—Daggett..............UT-4
Manilla (City)—Crawford..............IA-3
Manilla (Township)—Cavalier.......ND-4
Manistee (City)—Manistee............MI-3
Manistee (Township)—Manistee...MI-3
Manistee County.......................MI-3
Manistique (City)—Schoolcraft.....MI-3
Manistique (Township)—Schoolcraft..................MI-3
Manito (Town)—Mason..................IL-3
Manito (Township)—Mason..........IL-3
Manitou (Township)—Mountrail...ND-4
Manitou (Town)—Tillman..............OK-2
Manitou Beach-Devils Lake (CDP)—Lenawee.........................MI-3
Manitou Springs (City)—El Paso...CO-4
Manitowish Waters (Town)—Vilas..........................WI-3
Manitowoc (City)—Manitowoc......WI-3
Manitowoc (Town)—Manitowoc...WI-3
Manitowoc County.....................WI-3
Manitowoc Rapids (Town)—Manitowoc......................WI-3
Mankato (City)—Jewell................KS-4
Mankato (City)—Blue Earth.........MN-3
Mankato (Township)—Blue Earth............................MN-3
Mankato (City)—Nicollet............MN-3
Manley (Village)—Cass................NE-4
Manley Hot Springs (CDP)—Yukon-Koyukuk Census Area......AK-4
Manlius (Township)—Bureau.........IL-3
Manlius (Village)—Bureau.............IL-3
Manlius (Township)—La Salle.......IL-3
Manlius (Township)—Allegan.......MI-3
Manlius (Town)—Onondaga.........NY-1
Manlius (Village)—Onondaga......NY-1
Manly (City)—Worth......................IA-3
Mann (Township)—Bedford..........PA-1
Mannford (Town)—Creek..............OK-2
Mannford (Town)—Pawnee...........OK-2
Mannford (Town)—Tulsa...............OK-2
Manning (City)—Carroll.................IA-3
Manning (City)—Dunn..................ND-4
Manning (Township)—Kidder........ND-4
Manning (City)—Clarendon...........SC-2
Mannington (Township)—Salem...NJ-1
Mannington (City)—Marion..........WV-2
Manns (Township)—Stutsman.......ND-4
Manns Choice (Borough)—Bedford...........................PA-1

Mannsville (Village)—Jefferson......NY-1
Mannsville (Town)—Johnston......OK-2
Manokotak (City)—Dillingham Census Area......................AK-4
Manor (Township)—Armstrong.......PA-1
Manor (Township)—Lancaster.........PA-1
Manor (Borough)—Westmoreland..PA-1
Manor (City)—Travis......................TX-2
Manor Creek (City)—Jefferson.....KY-2
Manorhaven (Village)—Nassau......NY-1
Manorville (CDP)—Suffolk............NY-1
Manorville (Borough)—Armstrong.........................PA-1
Mansfield (City)—Scott..................AR-2
Mansfield (City)—Sebastian..........AR-2
Mansfield (Town)—Tolland............CT-1
Mansfield (Town)—Newton............GA-2
Mansfield (Town)—Piatt................IL-3
Mansfield (City)—De Soto Parish............................LA-2
Mansfield (Town)—Bristol............MA-1
Mansfield (Township)—Iron..........MI-3
Mansfield (Township)—Freeborn............................MN-3
Mansfield (City)—Wright..............MO-3
Mansfield (Township)—Burlington...........................NJ-1
Mansfield (Township)—Warren....NJ-1
Mansfield (Town)—Cattaraugus....NY-1
Mansfield (Township)—Barnes.....ND-4
Mansfield (City)—Richland...........OH-3
Mansfield (Borough)—Tioga..........PA-1
Mansfield (City)—Ellis..................TX-2
Mansfield (City)—Johnson............TX-2
Mansfield (City)—Tarrant..............TX-2
Mansfield (Town)—Douglas.........WA-2
Mansfield, Mt. (VT).....................Geog-4
Manson (City)—Calhoun...............IA-3
Manston (Township)—Wilkin........MN-3
Mansura (Town)—Avoyelles Parish............................LA-2
Mantachie (Town)—Itawamba.......MS-2
Mantador (City)—Richland............ND-4
Manteca (City)—San Joaquin.........CA-4
Mantee (Village)—Webster.............MS-2
Manteno (Town)—Kankakee..........IL-3
Manteno (Township)—Kankakee...IL-3
Manteo (Town)—Dare...................NC-2
Manter (City)—Stanton..................KS-4
Manter (Township)—Stanton........KS-4
Manti (City)—Sanpete...................UT-4
Mantoloking (Borough)—Ocean....NJ-1
Manton (City)—Wexford...............MI-3
Mantorville (City)—Dodge...........MN-3
Mantorville (Township)—Dodge..MN-3
Mantrap (Township)—Hubbard....MN-3
Mantua (Township)—Gloucester...NJ-1
Mantua (Township)—Portage.........OH-3
Mantua (Village)—Portage.............OH-3
Mantua (Town)—Box Elder...........UT-4
Mantua (CDP)—Fairfax.................VA-2
Manvel (City)—Grand Forks.........ND-4
Manvel (City)—Brazoria...............TX-2
Manville (Borough)—Somerset......NJ-1
Manville (Town)—Niobrara..........WY-4
Many (Town)—Sabine Parish........LA-2
Manyaska (Township)—Martin....MN-3
Many Farms (CDP)—Apache........AZ-4
Manzanita (City)—Tillamook........OR-4
Manzanita Reservation (CA)....IndRes-1
Manzanola (Town)—Otero...........CO-4
Maple (Township)—Cowley..........KS-4
Maple (Township)—Cass..............MN-3
Maple (Township)—Dodge............NE-4
Maple (Township)—Dickey..........ND-4

Maple (Town)—Douglas.................WI-3
Maple Bluff (Village)—Dane.........WI-3
Maple Creek (Town)—Outagamie..........................WI-3
Maple Forest (Township)—Crawford............................MI-3
Maple Glen (CDP)—Montgomery..PA-1
Maple Grove (Township)—Barry..MI-3
Maple Grove (Township)—Manistee...........................MI-3
Maple Grove (Township)—Saginaw............................MI-3
Maple Grove (Township)—Becker..............................MN-3
Maple Grove (Township)—Crow Wing...............................MN-3
Maple Grove (City)—Hennepin...MN-3
Maple Grove (Town)—Barron.......WI-3
Maple Grove (Town)—Manitowoc.........................WI-3
Maple Grove (Town)—Shawano...WI-3
Maple Heights (City)—Cuyahoga..OH-3
Maple Hill (City)—Wabaunsee.......KS-4
Maple Hill (Township)—Wabaunsee........................KS-4
Maplehurst (Town)—Taylor...........WI-3
Maple Lake (City)—Wright...........MN-3
Maple Lake (Township)—Wright..............................MN-3
Maple Park (Village)—DeKalb......IL-3
Maple Park (Village)—Kane..........IL-3
Maple Plain (City)—Hennepin......MN-3
Maple Plain (Town)—Barron.........WI-3
Maple Rapids (Village)—Clinton...MI-3
Maple Ridge (Township)—Alpena.............................MI-3
Maple Ridge (Township)—Delta...MI-3
Maple Ridge (Township)—Beltrami..........................MN-3
Maple Ridge (Township)—Isanti..MN-3
Maple Ridge (CDP)—Mahoning...OH-3
Maple River (Township)—Emmet............................MI-3
Maple River (Township)—Cass......ND-4
Maple Shade (Township)—Burlington.........................NJ-1
Maplesville (Town)—Chilton.........AL-2
Mapleton (Village)—Peoria............IL-3
Mapleton (City)—Monona..............IA-3
Mapleton (City)—Bourbon.............KS-4
Mapleton (Town)—Aroostook........ME-1
Mapleton (City)—Blue Earth.........MN-3
Mapleton (Township)—Blue Earth............................MN-3
Mapleton (City)—Cass..................ND-4
Mapleton (Township)—Cass.........ND-4
Mapleton (Borough)—Huntingdon.........................PA-1
Mapleton (Township)—Minnehaha.........................SD-4
Mapleton (City)—Utah..................UT-4
Maple Valley (Township)—Montcalm.........................MI-3
Maple Valley (Township)—Sanilac.............................MI-3
Maple Valley (CDP)—King..........WA-2
Maple Valley (Town)—Oconto......WI-3
Mapleview (City)—Mower............MN-3
Maplewood (Township)—Otter Tail..............................MN-3
Maplewood (City)—Ramsey.........MN-3
Maplewood (City)—St. Louis.......MO-3
Maplewood (Township)—Essex....NJ-1
Maquoketa (City)—Jackson...........IA-3
Maquon (Township)—Knox...........IL-3

American Places Dictionary   General Index

Maquon (Village)—Knox IL-3
Maramec (Town)—Pawnee OK-2
Marana (Town)—Pima AZ-4
Marathon (CDP)—Monroe FL-2
Marathon (City)—Buena Vista IA-3
Marathon (Township)—Lapeer MI-3
Marathon (Town)—Cortland NY-1
Marathon (Village)—Cortland NY-1
Marathon (Town)—Marathon WI-3
Marathon City (Village)—
   Marathon WI-3
Marathon County WI-3
Marble (Town)—Gunnison CO-4
Marble (City)—Itasca MN-3
Marble (Township)—Lincoln MN-3
Marble (Township)—Saunders NE-4
Marble City (Town)—Sequoyah OK-2
Marble Cliff (Village)—Franklin OH-3
Marble Falls (Town)—Burnet TX-2
Marblehead (Town)—Essex MA-1
Marblehead (Village)—Ottawa OH-3
Marble Hill (City)—Bollinger MO-3
Marble Rock (City)—Floyd IA-3
Marbleton (Town)—Sublette WY-4
Marbletown (Town)—Ulster NY-1
Marboe (Township)—Sargent ND-4
Marbury (CDP)—Charles MD-1
Marceline (City)—Chariton MO-3
Marceline (City)—Linn MO-3
Marceline (Township)—Linn MO-3
Marcell (Township)—Itasca MN-3
Marcellon (Town)—Columbia WI-3
Marcellus (Township)—Cass MI-3
Marcellus (Village)—Cass MI-3
Marcellus (Town)—Onondaga NY-1
Marcellus (Village)—Onondaga NY-1
March Air Force Base (Military
   Facility)—Riverside CA-4
Marco (CDP)—Collier FL-2
Marcus (City)—Cherokee IA-3
Marcus (City)—Stevens WA-4
Marcus Hook (Borough)—
   Delaware PA-1
Marcy (Town)—Oneida NY-1
Marcy, Mt. (NY) Geog-4
Mardela Springs (Town)—
   Wicomico MD-1
Marena (Township)—Hodgeman KS-4
Marengo (City)—McHenry IL-3
Marengo (Township)—McHenry ... IL-3
Marengo (Town)—Crawford IN-3
Marengo (City)—Iowa IA-3
Marengo (Township)—Calhoun MI-3
Marengo (Village)—Morrow OH-3
Marengo (Town)—Ashland WI-3
Marengo County AL-2
Marenisco (Township)—Gogebic .. MI-3
Marfa (City)—Presidio TX-2
Margaret (Town)—St. Clair AL-2
Margaret (Township)—Ward ND-4
Margaretta (Township)—Erie OH-3
Margaretville (Village)—
   Delaware NY-1
Margate (City)—Broward FL-2
Margate City (City)—Atlantic NJ-1
Marianna (City)—Lee AR-2
Marianna (City)—Jackson FL-2
Marianna (Borough)—
   Washington PA-1
Mariaville (Town)—Hancock ME-1
Maribel (Village)—Manitowoc WI-3
Maricopa (City)—Kern CA-4
Maricopa (Ak-Chin) Reservation
   (AZ) IndRes-4
Maricopa County AZ-4

Marie (Town)—Mississippi AR-2
Mariemont (Village)—Hamilton OH-3
Maries County MO-3
Marietta (City)—Cobb GA-2
Marietta (Village)—Fulton IL-3
Marietta (City)—Lac qui Parle MN-3
Marietta (Town)—Prentiss MS-2
Marietta (Township)—Saunders NE-4
Marietta (Town)—Robeson NC-2
Marietta (City)—Washington OH-3
Marietta (Township)—
   Washington OH-3
Marietta (City)—Love OK-2
Marietta (Borough)—Lancaster PA-1
Marietta (City)—Cass TX-2
Marietta (Town)—Crawford WI-3
Marietta-Alderwood (CDP)—
   Whatcom WA-4
Marilla (Township)—Manistee MI-3
Marilla (Town)—Erie NY-1
Marina (City)—Monterey CA-4
Marina del Rey (CDP)—Los
   Angeles CA-4
Marin County CA-4
Marindahl (Township)—Yankton .. SD-4
Marine (Town)—Madison IL-3
Marine (Township)—Madison IL-3
Marine Barracks, Washington, D.C.
   (DC) Mil-4
Marine City (City)—St. Clair MI-3
Marine Corps Recruit Depot
   (SC) Mil-4
Marineland (Town)—Flagler FL-2
Marineland (Town)—St. Johns FL-2
Marine on St. Croix (City)—
   Washington MN-3
Marinette (City)—Marinette WI-3
Marinette County WI-3
Maringouin (Town)—Iberville
   Parish LA-2
Marion (City)—Perry AL-2
Marion (City)—Crittenden AR-2
Marion (Township)—Lee IL-3
Marion (Township)—Ogle IL-3
Marion (City)—Williamson IL-3
Marion (Township)—Allen IN-3
Marion (Township)—Boone IN-3
Marion (Township)—Decatur IN-3
Marion (Township)—Dubois IN-3
Marion (City)—Grant IN-3
Marion (Township)—Hendricks IN-3
Marion (Township)—Jasper IN-3
Marion (Township)—Jennings IN-3
Marion (Township)—Lawrence IN-3
Marion (Township)—Owen IN-3
Marion (Township)—Pike IN-3
Marion (Township)—Putnam IN-3
Marion (Township)—Shelby IN-3
Marion (City)—Linn IA-3
Marion (Township)—Bourbon KS-4
Marion (Township)—Doniphan KS-4
Marion (Township)—Douglas KS-4
Marion (Township)—Lincoln KS-4
Marion (City)—Marion KS-4
Marion (Township)—Nemaha KS-4
Marion (City)—Crittenden KY-2
Marion (Village)—Union Parish..... LA-2
Marion (Town)—Plymouth MA-1
Marion (Township)—Charlevoix ... MI-3
Marion (Township)—Livingston ... MI-3
Marion (Township)—Osceola MI-3
Marion (Village)—Osceola MI-3
Marion (Township)—Saginaw MI-3
Marion (Township)—Sanilac MI-3
Marion (Township)—Olmsted MN-3

Marion (Town)—Lauderdale MS-2
Marion (Township)—Buchanan MO-3
Marion (Township)—Cole MO-3
Marion (Township)—Dade MO-3
Marion (Township)—Daviess MO-3
Marion (Township)—Grundy MO-3
Marion (Township)—Harrison MO-3
Marion (Township)—Jasper MO-3
Marion (Township)—Mercer MO-3
Marion (Township)—Monroe MO-3
Marion (Township)—Newton MO-3
Marion (Township)—St.
   Francois MO-3
Marion (Township)—Franklin NE-4
Marion (Town)—Wayne NY-1
Marion (City)—McDowell NC-2
Marion (Township)—Bowman ND-4
Marion (City)—LaMoure ND-4
Marion (Township)—Allen OH-3
Marion (Township)—Clinton OH-3
Marion (Township)—Fayette OH-3
Marion (Township)—Hancock OH-3
Marion (Township)—Hardin OH-3
Marion (Township)—Henry OH-3
Marion (Township)—Hocking OH-3
Marion (City)—Marion OH-3
Marion (Township)—Marion OH-3
Marion (Township)—Mercer OH-3
Marion (Township)—Morgan OH-3
Marion (Township)—Noble OH-3
Marion (Township)—Pike OH-3
Marion (Township)—Beaver PA-1
Marion (Township)—Berks PA-1
Marion (Township)—Butler PA-1
Marion (Township)—Centre PA-1
Marion (City)—Marion SC-2
Marion (City)—Turner SD-4
Marion (Township)—Turner SD-4
Marion (City)—Guadalupe TX-2
Marion (Town)—Smyth VA-2
Marion (Town)—Grant WI-3
Marion (Town)—Juneau WI-3
Marion (City)—Waupaca WI-3
Marion (Town)—Waushara WI-3
Marion, Lake (SC) Geog-4
Marion Center (Borough)—
   Indiana PA-1
Marion County AL-2
Marion County AR-2
Marion County FL-2
Marion County GA-2
Marion County IL-3
Marion County IN-3
Marion County IA-3
Marion County KS-4
Marion County KY-2
Marion County MS-2
Marion County MO-3
Marion County OH-3
Marion County OR-4
Marion County SC-2
Marion County TN-2
Marion County TX-2
Marion County WV-2
Marion Heights (Borough)—
   Northumberland PA-1
Marionville (City)—Lawrence MO-3
Mariposa (CDP)—Mariposa CA-4
Mariposa (Township)—Saunders ... NE-4
Mariposa County CA-4
Marissa (Town)—St. Clair IL-3
Marissa (Township)—St. Clair IL-3
Mark (Village)—Putnam IL-3
Mark (Township)—Defiance OH-3
Marked Tree (City)—Poinsett AR-2

General Index

Markesan (City)—Green Lake WI-3
Markey (Township)—
  Roscommon MI-3
Markham (City)—Cook............. IL-3
Markham (CDP)—Matagorda TX-2
Markle (Town)—Huntington........... IN-3
Markle (Town)—Wells IN-3
Marklesburg (Borough)—
  Huntingdon PA-1
Markleville (Town)—Madison IN-3
Markleysburg (Borough)—Fayette . PA-1
Marks (City)—Quitman MS-2
Marksville (Town)—Avoyelles
  Parish LA-2
Marland (Town)—Noble OK-2
Marlar (Township)—Jerauld SD-4
Marlboro (Township)—
  Monmouth NJ-1
Marlboro (CDP)—Ulster................ NY-1
Marlboro (Township)—Delaware....OH-3
Marlboro (Township)—Stark OH-3
Marlboro (Town)—Windham VT-1
Marlboro County..................... SC-2
Marlborough (Town)—Hartford CT-1
Marlborough (City)—Middlesex ... MA-1
Marlborough (Village)—St.
  Louis MO-3
Marlborough (Town)—Cheshire NH-1
Marlborough (Town)—Ulster........ NY-1
Marlborough (Township)—
  Montgomery PA-1
Marlette (Township)—Sanilac........ MI-3
Marlette (Village)—Sanilac MI-3
Marlin (City)—Falls TX-2
Marlinton (Town)—Pocahontas.... WV-2
Marlow (Town)—Cheshire NH-1
Marlow (City)—Stephens OK-2
Marlow Heights (CDP)—Prince
  George's MD-1
Marlton (CDP)—Prince
  George's MD-1
Marlton (CDP)—Burlington NJ-1
Mar-Mac (CDP)—Wayne NC-2
Marmaduke (City)—Greene........... AR-2
Marmarth (City)—Slope................ND-4
Marmaton (Township)—Allen KS-4
Marmaton (Township)—Bourbon... KS-4
Marmet (Town)—Kanawha........... WV-2
Marne (City)—Cass....................... IA-3
Maroa (Town)—Macon IL-3
Maroa (Township)—Macon IL-3
Marple (Township)—Delaware PA-1
Marquand (City)—Madison MO-3
Marquand (Township)—
  Madison MO-3
Marque (City)—Leon TX-2
Marquette (City)—Clayton IA-3
Marquette (City)—McPherson....... KS-4
Marquette (Township)—
  McPherson KS-4
Marquette (Township)—
  Mackinac........................ MI-3
Marquette (City)—Marquette MI-3
Marquette (Township)—
  Marquette. MI-3
Marquette (Village)—Hamilton NE-4
Marquette (Town)—Green Lake.... WI-3
Marquette (Village)—Green Lake.. WI-3
Marquette County MI-3
Marquette County WI-3
Marquette Heights (City)—
  Tazewell IL-3
Marrero (CDP)—Jefferson Parish ..LA-2
Marrowbone (Township)—
  Moultrie IL-3

Marrs (Township)—Posey IN-3
Mars (Borough)—Butler................ PA-1
Marseilles (Town)—La Salle IL-3
Marseilles (Township)—
  Wyandot OH-3
Marseilles (Village)—Wyandot OH-3
Marsh (Township)—Barnes ND-4
Marshall (City)—Wade Hampton
  Census Area AK-4
Marshall (City)—Searcy AR-2
Marshall (Town)—Clark IL-3
Marshall (Township)—Clark IL-3
Marshall (Township)—Lawrence IN-3
Marshall (Town)—Parke IN-3
Marshall (City)—Calhoun MI-3
Marshall (Township)—Calhoun MI-3
Marshall (City)—Lyon.................. MN-3
Marshall (Township)—Mower MN-3
Marshall (Township)—Platte MO-3
Marshall (City)—Saline MO-3
Marshall (Township)—Saline MO-3
Marshall (Township)—Clay............ NE-4
Marshall (Town)—Oneida NY-1
Marshall (Town)—Madison NC-2
Marshall (Township)—Williams ...ND-4
Marshall (Township)—Highland OH-3
Marshall (Town)—Logan OK-2
Marshall (Township)—Allegheny PA-1
Marshall (City)—Harrison TX-2
Marshall (Village)—Dane WI-3
Marshall (Town)—Richland WI-3
Marshall (Town)—Rusk WI-3
Marshall County AL-2
Marshall County IL-3
Marshall County IN-3
Marshall County IA-3
Marshall County KS-4
Marshall County KY-2
Marshall County MN-3
Marshall County MS-2
Marshall County OK-2
Marshall County SD-4
Marshall County TN-2
Marshall County WV-2
Marshall Creek (Town)—Denton... TX-2
Marshallton (CDP)—
  Northumberland PA-1
Marshalltown (City)—Marshall IA-3
Marshallville (Town)—Macon....... GA-2
Marshallville (Village)—Wayne....OH-3
Marshan (Township)—Dakota MN-3
Marsh Creek (Township)—
  Mahnomen MN-3
Marshfield (Town)—Washington .. ME-1
Marshfield (Town)—Plymouth MA-1
Marshfield (Township)—Lincoln .. MN-3
Marshfield (City)—Webster MO-3
Marshfield (Township)—Perkins ... SD-4
Marshfield (Town)—Washington ... VT-1
Marshfield (Village)—
  Washington VT-1
Marshfield (Town)—Fond du
  Lac................................ WI-3
Marshfield (City)—Marathon WI-3
Marshfield (City)—Wood WI-3
Marshfield (City)—Wood WI-3
Marshfield Hills (CDP)—
  Plymouth MA-1
Marsh Grove (Township)—
  Marshall MN-3
Mars Hill (Town)—Aroostook ME-1
Mars Hill (Town)—Madison NC-2
Marshville (Town)—Union NC-2
Marsing (City)—Owyhee............... ID-4
Marsland (Village)—Dawes NE-4

Marston (City)—New Madrid........MO-3
Marston Moor (Township)—
  Stutsman ND-4
Marstons Mills (CDP)—
  Barnstable MA-1
Mart (City)—McLennan TX-2
Martell (Town)—Pierce WI-3
Martelle (City)—Jones IA-3
Martensdale (City)—Warren IA-3
Martha (Town)—Jackson OK-2
Martha Lake (CDP)—
  Snohomish WA-4
Marthasville (City)—Warren MO-3
Martha's Vineyard (MA) Geog-4
Martic (Township)—Lancaster........ PA-1
Martin (Town)—Franklin.............. GA-2
Martin (Town)—Stephens GA-2
Martin (Township)—Crawford IL-3
Martin (Township)—McLean......... IL-3
Martin (Township)—Smith KS-4
Martin (City)—Floyd KY-2
Martin (Village)—Red River
  Parish LA-2
Martin (Township)—Allegan MI-3
Martin (Village)—Allegan MI-3
Martin (Township)—Rock MN-3
Martin (Township)—Hall NE-4
Martin (City)—Sheridan ND-4
Martin (Township)—Sheridan ND-4
Martin (Township)—Walsh ND-4
Martin (City)—Bennett SD-4
Martin (Township)—Perkins......... SD-4
Martin (City)—Weakley TN-2
Martin Bluff (CDP)—Jackson....... MS-2
Martin County........................... FL-2
Martin County........................... IN-3
Martin County........................... KY-2
Martin County.......................... MN-3
Martin County.......................... NC-2
Martin County........................... TX-2
Martindale (Town)—Caldwell TX-2
Martinez (City)—Contra Costa CA-4
Martinez (CDP)—Columbia GA-2
Martinez (CDP)—Richmond GA-2
Martin's Additions (Village)—
  Montgomery MD-1
Martinsburg (Township)—Pike IL-3
Martinsburg (City)—Keokuk IA-3
Martinsburg (Township)—
  Renville MN-3
Martinsburg (Town)—Audrain MO-3
Martinsburg (Village)—Dixon NE-4
Martinsburg (Town)—Lewis NY-1
Martinsburg (Village)—Knox OH-3
Martinsburg (Borough)—Blair PA-1
Martinsburg (City)—Berkeley WV-2
Martins Ferry (City)—Belmont......OH-3
Martins Location (Pop. Place)—
  Coos NH-1
Martinsville (Town)—Clark IL-3
Martinsville (Township)—Clark..... IL-3
Martinsville (City)—Morgan........... IN-3
Martinsville (Village)—Clinton OH-3
Martinsville (Independent City)... VA-2
Martinton (Township)—Iroquois IL-3
Martinton (Village)—Iroquois IL-3
Martiny (Township)—Mecosta MI-3
Marty (CDP)—Charles Mix SD-4
Marvell (City)—Phillips AR-2
Marvin (Town)—Grant SD-4
Mary (Township)—Norman MN-3
Mary Ann (Township)—Licking OH-3
Marydel (Town)—Caroline MD-1
Mary Esther (Town)—Okaloosa....FL-2

Maryhill Estates (City)—
  Jefferson KY-2
Maryland (Township)—Ogle IL-3
Maryland (Town)—Otsego NY-1
Maryland (Township)—Ward ND-4
Maryland City (CDP)—Anne
  Arundel MD-1
Maryland Heights (City)—St.
  Louis MO-3
Marysland (Township)—Swift MN-3
Marysvale (Town)—Piute UT-4
Marysville (City)—Yuba CA-4
Marysville (City)—Marion IA-3
Marysville (City)—Marshall KS-4
Marysville (Township)—Marshall ... KS-4
Marysville (Township)—Miami KS-4
Marysville (City)—St. Clair MI-3
Marysville (Township)—Wright MN-3
Marysville (City)—Union OH-3
Marysville (Borough)—Perry PA-1
Marysville (City)—Snohomish WA-4
Maryville (Town)—Madison IL-3
Maryville (City)—Nodaway MO-3
Maryville (Township)—Rolette ND-4
Maryville (City)—Blount TN-2
Masardis (Town)—Aroostook ME-1
Mascot (CDP)—Knox TN-2
Mascotte (City)—Lake FL-2
Mascoutah (City)—St. Clair IL-3
Mascoutah (Township)—St. Clair ... IL-3
Mashantucket Pequot Tribe
  (CT) IndRes-4
Mashpee (Town)—Barnstable MA-1
Maskell (Village)—Dixon NE-4
Mason (Town)—Effingham IL-3
Mason (Township)—Effingham IL-3
Mason (Township)—Arenac MI-3
Mason (Township)—Cass MI-3
Mason (City)—Ingham MI-3
Mason (Township)—Murray MN-3
Mason (Township)—Marion MO-3
Mason (Town)—Hillsborough NH-1
Mason (Township)—Lawrence OH-3
Mason (City)—Warren OH-3
Mason (Town)—Tipton TN-2
Mason (City)—Mason TX-2
Mason (Town)—Mason WV-2
Mason (Town)—Bayfield WI-3
Mason (Village)—Bayfield WI-3
Masonboro (CDP)—New
  Hanover NC-2
Mason City (Town)—Mason IL-3
Mason City (Township)—Mason IL-3
Mason City (City)—Cerro Gordo ... IA-3
Mason City (Village)—Custer NE-4
Mason County IL-3
Mason County KY-2
Mason County MI-3
Mason County TX-2
Mason County WA-4
Mason County WV-2
Masontown (Borough)—Fayette PA-1
Masontown (Town)—Preston WV-2
Masonville (City)—Delaware IA-3
Masonville (CDP)—Daviess KY-2
Masonville (Township)—Delta MI-3
Masonville (Town)—Delaware NY-1
Massac (CDP)—McCracken KY-2
Massac County IL-3
Massanutten (CDP)—
  Rockingham VA-2
Massapequa (CDP)—Nassau NY-1
Massapequa Park (Village)—
  Nassau NY-1
Massena (City)—Cass IA-3

Massena (Town)—St. Lawrence NY-1
Massena (Village)—St. Lawrence ... NY-1
Massie (Township)—Warren OH-3
Massillon (City)—Stark OH-3
Massilon (Township)—Wayne IL-3
Massive, Mt. (CO) Geog-4
Mastic (CDP)—Suffolk NY-1
Mastic Beach (CDP)—Suffolk NY-1
Mastodon (Township)—Iron MI-3
Matador (Town)—Motley TX-2
Matagorda Bay (TX) Geog-4
Matagorda County TX-2
Matamoras (Village)—
  Washington OH-3
Matamoras (Borough)—Pike PA-1
Matanuska-Susitna Borough AK-4
Matanuska Valley (AK) Geog-4
Matawan (Borough)—Monmouth ... NJ-1
Matchwood (Township)—
  Ontonagon MI-3
Matewan (Town)—Mingo WV-2
Matfield (Township)—Chase KS-4
Matfield Green (City)—Chase KS-4
Mather Air Force Base (CA) Mil-4
Mather Air Force Base (Military
  Facility)—Sacramento CA-4
Matherville (Village)—Mercer IL-3
Mathews (CDP)—Lafourche
  Parish LA-2
Mathews (Township)—Kingsbury ... SD-4
Mathews County VA-2
Mathias (Township)—Alger MI-3
Mathis (City)—San Patricio TX-2
Mathiston (Town)—Choctaw MS-2
Mathiston (Town)—Webster MS-2
Matinecock (Village)—Nassau NY-1
Matinicus Isle (Plantation)—
  Knox ME-1
Matlock (City)—Sioux IA-3
Matoaka (Town)—Mercer WV-2
Mattapan—Suffolk MA-1
Mattapan See **Boston**—Suffolk MA-1
Mattapoisett (Town)—Plymouth ... MA-1
Mattapony Reservation (VA) IndRes-4
Mattawa (Town)—Grant WA-4
Mattawamkeag (Town)—
  Penobscot ME-1
Mattawan (Village)—Van Buren MI-3
Matteson (City)—Cook IL-3
Matteson (Township)—Branch MI-3
Matteson (Town)—Waupaca WI-3
Matthews (Town)—Grant IN-3
Matthews (City)—New Madrid MO-3
Matthews (Town)—Mecklenburg ... NC-2
Mattituck (CDP)—Suffolk NY-1
Mattoon (City)—Coles IL-3
Mattoon (Township)—Coles IL-3
Mattoon (Village)—Shawano WI-3
Mattydale (CDP)—Onondaga NY-1
Mauch (Township)—Sheridan ND-4
Mauckport (Town)—Harrison IN-3
Maud (City)—Pottawatomie OK-2
Maud (City)—Seminole OK-2
Maud (City)—Bowie TX-2
Maui (HI) Geog-4
Maui County HI-4
Mauldin (City)—Greenville SC-2
Maumee (Township)—Allen IN-3
Maumee (City)—Lucas OH-3
Maumelle (City)—Pulaski AR-2
Mauna Kea (HI) Geog-4
Mauna Loa (HI) Geog-4
Maunaloa (CDP)—Maui HI-4
Maunawili (CDP)—Honolulu HI-4
Maunie (Village)—White IL-3

Maupin (City)—Wasco OR-4
Maurice (City)—Sioux IA-3
Maurice (Village)—Vermilion
  Parish LA-2
Maurice River (Township)—
  Cumberland NJ-1
Mauriceville (CDP)—Orange TX-2
Maury City (Town)—Crockett TN-2
Maury County TN-2
Mauston (City)—Juneau WI-3
Maverick County TX-2
Max (Township)—Itasca MN-3
Max (City)—McLean ND-4
Maxatawny (Township)—Berks PA-1
Maxbass (City)—Bottineau ND-4
Maxeys (Town)—Oglethorpe GA-2
Maxfield (Town)—Penobscot ME-1
Maxton (Town)—Robeson NC-2
Maxton (Town)—Scotland NC-2
Maxville (Town)—Buffalo WI-3
Maxwell (Township)—Sangamon ... IL-3
Maxwell (City)—Story IA-3
Maxwell (Township)—Lac qui
  Parle MN-3
Maxwell (Village)—Lincoln NE-4
Maxwell (Village)—Colfax NM-4
Maxwell Air Force Base (AL) Mil-4
May (Township)—Christian IL-3
May (Township)—Lee IL-3
May (Township)—Cass MN-3
May (Township)—Washington MN-3
May (Township)—Platte MO-3
May (Township)—Kearney NE-4
May (Town)—Harper OK-2
Maybee (Village)—Monroe MI-3
Mayberry (Township)—Hamilton ... IL-3
Mayberry (Township)—Montour ... PA-1
Maybrook (Village)—Orange NY-1
May Day (Township)—Riley KS-4
Maydell (Township)—Clark SD-4
Mayer (City)—Carver MN-3
Mayersville (Town)—Issaquena MS-2
Mayes County OK-2
Mayesville (Town)—Sumter SC-2
Mayetta (City)—Jackson KS-4
Mayfield (Township)—DeKalb IL-3
Mayfield (City)—Sumner KS-4
Mayfield (City)—Graves KY-2
Mayfield (Township)—Grand
  Traverse MI-3
Mayfield (Township)—Lapeer MI-3
Mayfield (Township)—
  Pennington MN-3
Mayfield (Township)—Laclede MO-3
Mayfield (Township)—Hall NE-4
Mayfield (Town)—Fulton NY-1
Mayfield (Village)—Fulton NY-1
Mayfield (Village)—Cuyahoga OH-3
Mayfield (Borough)—Lackawanna ... PA-1
Mayfield (Township)—Yankton SD-4
Mayfield (Town)—Sanpete UT-4
Mayfield Heights (City)—
  Cuyahoga OH-3
Mayflower (City)—Faulkner AR-2
Mayflower Village (CDP)—Los
  Angeles CA-4
Mayhew Lake (Township)—
  Benton MN-3
Mayland (Township)—Ward ND-4
Maynard (Town)—Randolph AR-2
Maynard (City)—Fayette IA-3
Maynard (Town)—Middlesex MA-1
Maynard (City)—Chippewa MN-3
Maynardville (City)—Union TN-2
Mayo (Town)—Lafayette FL-2

General Index

Mayo (CDP)—Anne Arundel......... *MD-1*
Mayo (CDP)—Spartanburg............. *SC-2*
Mayodan (Town)—Rockingham ... *NC-2*
Maypearl (City)—Ellis...................... *TX-2*
Mayport Naval Station (FL) *Mil-4*
Mays Chapel (CDP)—Baltimore .. *MD-1*
Mays Landing (CDP)—Atlantic...... *NJ-1*
Maysville (Town)—Banks *GA-2*
Maysville (Town)—Jackson........... *GA-2*
Maysville (City)—Scott................... *IA-3*
Maysville (City)—Mason *KY-2*
Maysville (City)—DeKalb............. *MO-3*
Maysville (Town)—Jones *NC-2*
Maysville (Town)—Garvin............. *OK-2*
Maytown (Town)—Jefferson *AL-2*
Maytown (CDP)—Lancaster *PA-1*
Mayview (City)—Lafayette *MO-3*
Mayville (Village)—Tuscola *MI-3*
Mayville (Township)—Houston *MN-3*
Mayville (Village)—Chautauqua ... *NY-1*
Mayville (City)—Traill *ND-4*
Mayville (Township)—Traill *ND-4*
Mayville (Town)—Clark *WI-3*
Mayville (City)—Dodge *WI-3*
Maywood (City)—Los Angeles *CA-4*
Maywood (City)—Cook *IL-3*
Maywood (Township)—Benton *MN-3*
Maywood (Village)—Frontier *NE-4*
Maywood (Borough)—Bergen *NJ-1*
Maywood Park (City)—
 Multnomah *OR-4*
Maza (City)—Towner *ND-4*
Maza (Township)—Towner *ND-4*
Mazeppa (City)—Wabasha *MN-3*
Mazeppa (Township)—Wabasha ... *MN-3*
Mazeppa (Township)—Grant *SD-4*
Mazomanie (Town)—Dane *WI-3*
Mazomanie (Village)—Dane *WI-3*
Mazon (Town)—Grundy *IL-3*
Mazon (Township)—Grundy *IL-3*
McAdenville (Town)—Gaston *NC-2*
McAdoo (Township)—Barber *KS-4*
McAdoo (Borough)—Schuylkill *PA-1*
McAlester (City)—Pittsburg............ *OK-2*
McAllaster (Township)—Logan *KS-4*
McAllen (City)—Hidalgo *TX-2*
McAlmond (Township)—
 Mountrail *ND-4*
McArthur (Township)—Logan *OH-3*
McArthur (Village)—Vinton *OH-3*
McBain (City)—Missaukee *MI-3*
McBee (Town)—Chesterfield *SC-2*
McBride (Village)—Montcalm *MI-3*
McBride (Town)—Marshall *OK-2*
McCall (City)—Valley *ID-4*
McCallsburg (City)—Story *IA-3*
McCalmont (Township)—
 Jefferson *PA-1*
McCamey (City)—Upton *TX-2*
McCamish (Township)—Johnson ... *KS-4*
McCammon (City)—Bannock *ID-4*
McCandless (Township)—
 Allegheny... *PA-1*
McCarthy (CDP)—Valdez-Cordova
 Census Area *AK-4*
McCaskill (City)—Hempstead *AR-2*
McCauleyville (Township)—
 Wilkin *MN-3*
McCausland (City)—Scott *IA-3*
McCaysville (City)—Fannin........... *GA-2*
McChesneytown-Loyalhanna (CDP)—
 Westmoreland *PA-1*
McChord Air Force Base (WA) *Mil-4*
McChord Air Force Base (Military
 Facility)—Pierce *WA-4*

McClain County *OK-2*
McCleary (Town)—Grays
 Harbor *WA-4*
McClellan (Township)—Jefferson ... *IL-3*
McClellan (Township)—Newton ... *IN-3*
McClellan (Township)—Benson..... *ND-4*
McClellan Air Force Base (CA) *Mil-4*
McClelland (City)—
 Pottawattamie *IA-3*
McClellanville (Town)—
 Charleston *SC-2*
McCloud (CDP)—Siskiyou *CA-4*
McClure (Township)—Holt............. *NE-4*
McClure (Village)—Henry *OH-3*
McClure (Borough)—Snyder........... *PA-1*
McClure (Pop. Place)—Lyman *SD-4*
McClusky (City)—Sheridan *ND-4*
McClusky (Township)—Sheridan ..*ND-4*
McColl (Town)—Marlboro.............. *SC-2*
McComb (City)—Pike *MS-2*
McComb (Village)—Hancock *OH-3*
McCone County *MT-4*
McConnell Air Force Base (KS).....*Mil-4*
McConnells (Town)—York.............. *SC-2*
McConnellsburg (Borough)—
 Fulton *PA-1*
McConnelsville (Village)—
 Morgan *OH-3*
McCook (Village)—Cook *IL-3*
McCook (City)—Red Willow......... *NE-4*
McCook County *SD-4*
McCool (Town)—Attala *MS-2*
McCool Junction (Village)—York.. *NE-4*
McCord (CDP)—Osage *OK-2*
McCordsville (Town)—Hancock ... *IN-3*
McCormack Lake (Pop. Place)—St.
 Louis *MN-3*
McCormick (Town)—McCormick ..*SC-2*
McCormick County *SC-2*
McCracken (City)—Rush *KS-4*
McCracken (Township)—
 Christian *MO-3*
McCracken County *KY-2*
McCrea (Township)—Marshall *MN-3*
McCreary County *KY-2*
McCredie (Township)—
 Callaway *MO-3*
McCrory (City)—Woodruff *AR-2*
McCulley (Township)—Boyd *NE-4*
McCulley (Township)—Emmons ..*ND-4*
McCulloch County *TX-2*
McCullom Lake (Village)—
 McHenry *IL-3*
McCune (City)—Crawford *KS-4*
McCurtain (Town)—Haskell *OK-2*
McCurtain County *OK-2*
McDavitt (Township)—St. Louis .. *MN-3*
McDermitt (CDP)—Humboldt *NV-4*
McDonald (City)—Rawlins............. *KS-4*
McDonald (Township)—Barry *MO-3*
McDonald (Township)—Jasper *MO-3*
McDonald (Town)—Robeson *NC-2*
McDonald (Township)—Hardin *OH-3*
McDonald (Village)—Trumbull *OH-3*
McDonald (Borough)—Allegheny .. *PA-1*
McDonald (Borough)—
 Washington *PA-1*
McDonald County *MO-3*
McDonaldsville (Township)—
 Norman *MN-3*
McDonough (City)—Henry *GA-2*
McDonough (Town)—Chenango .. *NY-1*
McDonough County *IL-3*
McDougal (Town)—Clay............... *AR-2*
McDowell (Township)—Barry *MO-3*

McDowell County *NC-2*
McDowell County *WV-2*
McDuffie County *GA-2*
McEwen (City)—Humphreys *TN-2*
McEwensville (Borough)—
 Northumberland *PA-1*
McFall (City)—Gentry *MO-3*
McFarlan (Town)—Anson *NC-2*
McFarland (City)—Kern *CA-4*
McFarland (City)—Wabaunsee *KS-4*
McFarland (Village)—Dane *WI-3*
McGahan (Township)—
 Mountrail *ND-4*
McGehee (City)—Desha *AR-2*
McGill (CDP)—White Pine *NV-4*
McGinnis (Township)—McLean....*ND-4*
McGovern (CDP)—Washington *PA-1*
McGrath (City)—Yukon-Koyukuk
 Census Area *AK-4*
McGrath (City)—Aitkin *MN-3*
McGraw (Village)—Cortland *NY-1*
McGregor (CDP)—Lee................... *FL-2*
McGregor (City)—Clayton *IA-3*
McGregor (City)—Aitkin *MN-3*
McGregor (Township)—Aitkin ... *MN-3*
McGregor (City)—McLennan *TX-2*
McGrew (Village)—Scotts Bluff..... *NE-4*
McGuffey (Village)—Hardin........... *OH-3*
McGuire Air Force Base (NJ) *Mil-4*
McGuire Air Force Base (Mil. facil.)—
 Burlington *NJ-1*
McHenry (City)—McHenry *IL-3*
McHenry (Township)—McHenry ... *IL-3*
McHenry (City)—Ohio *KY-2*
McHenry (City)—Foster *ND-4*
McHenry (Township)—Foster *ND-4*
McHenry (Township)—Lycoming ... *PA-1*
McHenry County *IL-3*
McHenry County *ND-4*
McIntire (City)—Mitchell *IA-3*
McIntosh (Town)—Washington *AL-2*
McIntosh (Town)—Marion *FL-2*
McIntosh (City)—Polk *MN-3*
McIntosh (City)—Corson *SD-4*
McIntosh County *GA-2*
McIntosh County *ND-4*
McIntosh County *OK-2*
McIntyre (Town)—Wilkinson *GA-2*
McIntyre (Township)—Lycoming ... *PA-1*
McKean (Township)—Licking *OH-3*
McKean (Borough)—Erie................ *PA-1*
McKean (Township)—Erie............. *PA-1*
McKean County *PA-1*
McKee (Township)—Adams *IL-3*
McKee (City)—Jackson *KY-2*
McKeesport (City)—Allegheny *PA-1*
McKees Rocks (Borough)—
 Allegheny.. *PA-1*
McKendree (Township)—
 Vermilion *IL-3*
McKenney (Town)—Dinwiddie *VA-2*
McKenzie (Municipality)—Butler ..*AL-2*
McKenzie (Township)—Burleigh...*ND-4*
McKenzie (City)—Carroll *TN-2*
McKenzie (City)—Henry *TN-2*
McKenzie (City)—Weakley *TN-2*
McKenzie County *ND-4*
McKinley (Township)—Emmet *MI-3*
McKinley (Township)—Huron *MI-3*
McKinley (Township)—Cass *MN-3*
McKinley (Township)—Kittson ... *MN-3*
McKinley (City)—St. Louis *MN-3*
McKinley (Township)—Douglas ... *MO-3*
McKinley (Township)—Polk *MO-3*
McKinley (Township)—Stone *MO-3*

McKinley (Township)—Ward *ND-4*
McKinley (Township)—Marshall... *SD-4*
McKinley (Town)—Polk *WI-3*
McKinley (Town)—Taylor *WI-3*
McKinley, Mt. (AK) *Geog-4*
McKinley County *NM-4*
McKinley Park (CDP)—
   Yukon-Koyukuk Census Area...... *AK-4*
McKinleyville (CDP)—
   Humboldt *CA-4*
McKinney (Township)—Renville .. *ND-4*
McKinney (City)—Collin *TX-2*
McKinnon (Township)—Foster *ND-4*
McKittrick (Town)—
   Montgomery *MO-3*
McLain (Town)—Greene *MS-2*
McLaughlin (City)—Corson *SD-4*
McLean (Town)—McLean *IL-3*
McLean (Village)—Pierce *NE-4*
McLean (Township)—Shelby *OH-3*
McLean (Town)—Gray *TX-2*
McLean (CDP)—Fairfax *VA-2*
McLean County *IL-3*
McLean County *KY-2*
McLean County *ND-4*
McLeansboro (City)—Hamilton *IL-3*
McLeansboro (Township)—
   Hamilton *IL-3*
McLeansville (CDP)—Guilford *NC-2*
McLemoresville (Town)—Carroll .. *TN-2*
McLendon-Chisholm (City)—
   Rockwall *TX-2*
McLennan County *TX-2*
McLeod County *MN-3*
McLoud (Town)—Pottawatomie.... *OK-2*
McLouth (City)—Jefferson *KS-4*
McMechen (City)—Marshall *WV-2*
McMillan (Township)—Luce *MI-3*
McMillan (Township)—
   Ontonagon *MI-3*
McMillan (Town)—Marathon *WI-3*
McMillen Coy (Township)—
   McDonald *MO-3*
McMillen Tiff (Township)—
   McDonald *MO-3*
McMinn County *TN-2*
McMinnville (City)—Yamhill *OR-4*
McMinnville (City)—Warren *TN-2*
McMullen (Municipality)—
   Pickens *AL-2*
McMullen County *TX-2*
McMurray (CDP)—Washington *PA-1*
McMurtrey (Township)—
   Douglas *MO-3*
McNab (Town)—Hempstead *AR-2*
McNabb (Village)—Putnam *IL-3*
McNairy County *TN-2*
McNary (CDP)—Apache *AZ-4*
McNary (CDP)—Navajo *AZ-4*
McNary (Village)—Rapides
   Parish *LA-2*
McNeely (Township)—Tripp *SD-4*
McNeil (City)—Columbia *AR-2*
McNett (Township)—Lycoming *PA-1*
McPherson (City)—McPherson *KS-4*
McPherson (Township)—
   McPherson *KS-4*
McPherson (Township)—
   Sherman *KS-4*
McPherson (Township)—Blue
   Earth *MN-3*
McPherson County *KS-4*
McPherson County *NE-4*
McPherson County *SD-4*
McQueeney (CDP)—Guadalupe.... *TX-2*

McRae (City)—White *AR-2*
McRae (City)—Telfair *GA-2*
McRoberts (CDP)—Letcher *KY-2*
McSherrystown (Borough)—
   Adams *PA-1*
McVeytown (Borough)—Mifflin *PA-1*
McVille (City)—Nelson *ND-4*
Meacham (Township)—Marion *IL-3*
Mead (Town)—Weld *CO-4*
Mead (Township)—Merrick *NE-4*
Mead (Village)—Saunders *NE-4*
Mead (Township)—Belmont *OH-3*
Mead (Town)—Bryan *OK-2*
Mead (Township)—Warren *PA-1*
Mead (Town)—Clark *WI-3*
Mead, Lake (AK) *Geog-4*
Meade (City)—Meade *KS-4*
Meade (Township)—Huron *MI-3*
Meade (Township)—Mason *MI-3*
Meade Center (Township)—
   Meade *KS-4*
Meade County *KS-4*
Meade County *KY-2*
Meade County *SD-4*
Meadow (Township)—Wadena *MN-3*
Meadow (Township)—McHenry *ND-4*
Meadow (Township)—Perkins *SD-4*
Meadow (Town)—Terry *TX-2*
Meadow (Town)—Millard *UT-4*
Meadow Bridge (Town)—
   Fayette *WV-2*
Meadowbrook (Division)—
   Shelby *AL-2*
Meadow Brook (Township)—
   Cass *MN-3*
Meadowbrook (Town)—Sawyer *WI-3*
Meadowbrook Farm (City)—
   Jefferson *KY-2*
Meadow Glade (CDP)—Clark *WA-4*
Meadow Grove (Village)—
   Madison *NE-4*
Meadow Lake (CDP)—Valencia ... *NM-4*
Meadow Lake (Township)—
   Barnes *ND-4*
Meadow Lakes (CDP)—
   Matanuska-Susitna Borough *AK-4*
Meadowlakes (City)—Burnet *TX-2*
Meadowlands (City)—St. Louis *MN-3*
Meadowlands (Township)—St.
   Louis *MN-3*
Meadowood (CDP)—Butler *PA-1*
Meadows (Township)—Wilkin *MN-3*
Meadows (City)—Fort Bend *TX-2*
The Meadows (CDP)—Sarasota *FL-2*
Meadow Vale (City)—Jefferson *KY-2*
Meadowview Estates (City)—
   Jefferson *KY-2*
Meadow Vista (CDP)—Placer *CA-4*
Meadow Wood (CDP)—Orange *FL-2*
Meadville (Town)—Franklin *MS-2*
Meadville (City)—Linn *MO-3*
Meadville (City)—Crawford *PA-1*
Meagher County *MT-4*
Meansville (City)—Pike *GA-2*
Mebane (Town)—Alamance *NC-2*
Mebane (Town)—Orange *NC-2*
Mecan (Town)—Marquette *WI-3*
Mecca (CDP)—Riverside *CA-4*
Mecca (Town)—Parke *IN-3*
Mecca (Township)—Trumbull *OH-3*
Mechanic (Township)—Holmes *OH-3*
Mechanic Falls (Town)—
   Androscoggin *ME-1*
Mechanicsburg (Town)—
   Sangamon *IL-3*

Mechanicsburg (Township)—
   Sangamon *IL-3*
Mechanicsburg (Village)—
   Champaign *OH-3*
Mechanicsburg (Borough)—
   Cumberland *PA-1*
Mechanicsville (City)—Cedar *IA-3*
Mechanicsville (CDP)—Montour ... *PA-1*
Mechanicsville (Borough)—
   Schuylkill *PA-1*
Mechanicsville (CDP)—Hanover ... *VA-2*
Mechanicville (City)—Saratoga *NY-1*
Mecklenburg County *NC-2*
Mecklenburg County *VA-2*
Meckling (Township)—Clay *SD-4*
Mecosta (Township)—Mecosta *MI-3*
Mecosta (Village)—Mecosta *MI-3*
Mecosta County *MI-3*
Medary (Township)—Brookings ... *SD-4*
Medary (Town)—La Crosse *WI-3*
Medaryville (Town)—Pulaski *IN-3*
Meddybemps (Town)—
   Washington *ME-1*
Medfield (Town)—Norfolk *MA-1*
Medford (Township)—Reno *KS-4*
Medford (Town)—Piscataquis *ME-1*
Medford (City)—Middlesex *MA-1*
Medford (City)—Steele *MN-3*
Medford (Township)—Steele *MN-3*
Medford (Township)—Burlington .. *NJ-1*
Medford (CDP)—Suffolk *NY-1*
Medford (Township)—Walsh *ND-4*
Medford (City)—Grant *OK-2*
Medford (City)—Jackson *OR-4*
Medford (City)—Taylor *WI-3*
Medford (Town)—Taylor *WI-3*
Medford Lakes (Borough)—
   Burlington *NJ-1*
Media (Township)—Henderson *IL-3*
Media (Village)—Henderson *IL-3*
Media (Borough)—Delaware *PA-1*
Media (Township)—Jerauld *SD-4*
Mediapolis (City)—Des Moines *IA-3*
Medical Lake (Town)—Spokane ... *WA-4*
Medicine (Township)—
   Livingston *MO-3*
Medicine (Township)—Mercer *MO-3*
Medicine (Township)—Putnam *MO-3*
Medicine Bow (Town)—Carbon ... *WY-4*
Medicine Bow Mountains (AK) .. *Geog-4*
Medicine Hill (Township)—
   McLean *ND-4*
Medicine Lake (City)—
   Hennepin *MN-3*
Medicine Lake (Town)—
   Sheridan *MT-4*
Medicine Lodge (City)—Barber *KS-4*
Medicine Lodge (Township)—
   Barber *KS-4*
Medicine Park (Town)—
   Comanche *OK-2*
Medina (Township)—Peoria *IL-3*
Medina (Township)—Warren *IN-3*
Medina (Township)—Lenawee *MI-3*
Medina (City)—Hennepin *MN-3*
Medina (Village)—Orleans *NY-1*
Medina (City)—Stutsman *ND-4*
Medina (City)—Medina *OH-3*
Medina (Township)—Medina *OH-3*
Medina (Town)—Gibson *TN-2*
Medina (City)—King *WA-4*
Medina (Town)—Dane *WI-3*
Medina County *OH-3*
Medina County *TX-2*
Medinah (CDP)—DuPage *IL-3*

General Index

Medley (Town)—Dade FL-2
Medo (Township)—Blue Earth MN-3
Medon (Town)—Madison TN-2
Medora (Village)—Macoupin........... IL-3
Medora (Town)—Jackson................. IN-3
Medora (Township)—Reno KS-4
Medora (City)—Billings ND-4
Medulla (CDP)—Polk FL-2
Medway (Township)—Hamilton.....KS-4
Medway (Town)—Penobscot.......... ME-1
Medway (Town)—Norfolk MA-1
Meeker (Town)—Rio Blanco CO-4
Meeker (Town)—Lincoln OK-2
Meeker County................................MN-3
Meeme (Town)—Manitowoc.......... WI-3
Meenon (Town)—Burnett WI-3
Meeteetse (Town)—Park WY-4
Megargel (Town)—Archer TX-2
Meggett (Town)—Charleston SC-2
Meherrin TDSA (NC)................IndRes-4
Mehlville (CDP)—St. Louis MO-3
Mehoopany (Township)—
  Wyoming....................................PA-1
Mehurin (Township)—Lac qui
  Parle MN-3
Meigs (City)—Mitchell GA-2
Meigs (City)—Thomas GA-2
Meigs (Township)—Adams OH-3
Meigs (Township)—Muskingum ...OH-3
Meigs County OH-3
Meigs County TN-2
Meigsville (Township)—Morgan OH-3
Meiners Oaks (CDP)—Ventura CA-4
Meire Grove (City)—Stearns MN-3
Mekinock (Township)—Grand
  Forks ND-4
Mekoryuk (City)—Bethel Census
  Area..AK-4
Melba (City)—Canyon ID-4
Melbeta (Village)—Scotts Bluff...NE-4
Melbourne (City)—Izard AR-2
Melbourne (City)—Brevard FL-2
Melbourne (City)—Marshall IA-3
Melbourne (City)—Campbell........ KY-2
Melbourne Beach (Town)—
  Brevard FL-2
Melbourne Village (Town)—
  Brevard FL-2
Melcher-Dallas (City)—Marion IA-3
Melfa (Town)—Accomack VA-2
Melissa (City)—Collin TX-2
Mellen (Township)—Menominee... MI-3
Mellen (City)—Ashland WI-3
Mellette (City)—Spink SD-4
Mellette (Township)—Spink............SD-4
Mellette County................................SD-4
Mellott (City)—Fountain IN-3
Melody Hill (CDP)—
  Vanderburgh IN-3
Melrose (Township)—Adams IL-3
Melrose (Township)—Clark IL-3
Melrose (City)—Monroe IA-3
Melrose (City)—Middlesex MA-1
Melrose (Township)—Charlevoix .. MI-3
Melrose (City)—Stearns MN-3
Melrose (Township)—Stearns MN-3
Melrose (Village)—Curry NM-4
Melrose (Township)—Steele ND-4
Melrose (Village)—Paulding OH-3
Melrose (Township)—Grant SD-4
Melrose (Town)—Jackson WI-3
Melrose (Village)—Jackson WI-3
Melrose Park (CDP)—Broward FL-2
Melrose Park (City)—Cook............. IL-3
Melrose Park (CDP)—Cayuga NY-1

Melstone (Town)—Musselshell MT-4
Melvern (City)—Osage KS-4
Melvern (Township)—Osage KS-4
Melville (Town)—St. Landry
  Parish LA-2
Melville (Town)—Renville MN-3
Melville (CDP)—Suffolk NY-1
Melville (Township)—Foster ND-4
Melville (Mil. facil.)—Newport........ RI-1
Melvin (Village)—Ford IL-3
Melvin (City)—Osceola IA-3
Melvin (Village)—Sanilac MI-3
Melvin (Township)—Nelson ND-4
Melvin (Town)—McCulloch TX-2
Melvina (Village)—Monroe WI-3
Melvindale (City)—Wayne............. MI-3
Memphis (Municipality)—
  Pickens AL-2
Memphis (CDP)—Manatee............FL-2
Memphis (City)—Macomb MI-3
Memphis (City)—St. Clair MI-3
Memphis (Village)—DeSoto MS-2
Memphis (City)—Scotland............MO-3
Memphis (Village)—Saunders........ NE-4
Memphis (City)—Shelby TN-2
Memphis (City)—Hall TX-2
Memphis Naval Air Station
  (TN) Mil-4
Mena (City)—Polk AR-2
Menahga (City)—Wadena MN-3
Menallen (Township)—Adams PA-1
Menallen (Township)—Fayette PA-1
Menan (City)—Jefferson ID-4
Menands (Village)—Albany NY-1
Menard (City)—Menard...................TX-2
Menard County IL-3
Menard County TX-2
Menasha (City)—Calumet............... WI-3
Menasha (City)—Winnebago WI-3
Menasha (Town)—Winnebago WI-3
Mendeltna (CDP)—Valdez-Cordova
  Census Area AK-4
Mendenhall (City)—Simpson.........MS-2
Mendenhall Glacier (AK) Geog-4
Mendham (Borough)—Morris.........NJ-1
Mendham (Township)—Morris NJ-1
Mendocino County CA-4
Mendon (Township)—Adams IL-3
Mendon (Village)—Adams IL-3
Mendon (Town)—Worcester MA-1
Mendon (Township)—St. Joseph ... MI-3
Mendon (Village)—St. Joseph........ MI-3
Mendon (Town)—Chariton MO-3
Mendon (Township)—Chariton ... MO-3
Mendon (Town)—Monroe NY-1
Mendon (Village)—Mercer.............OH-3
Mendon (City)—Cache UT-4
Mendon (Town)—Rutland VT-1
Mendota (City)—Fresno CA-4
Mendota (City)—La Salle IL-3
Mendota (Township)—La Salle IL-3
Mendota (City)—Dakota................MN-3
Mendota Heights (City)—
  Dakota.......................................MN-3
Menifee (Town)—Conway AR-2
Menifee County KY-2
Menlo (Town)—Chattooga GA-2
Menlo (City)—Guthrie IA-3
Menlo (City)—Thomas KS-4
Menlo (Township)—Thomas KS-4
Menlo Park (City)—San Mateo CA-4
Menno (Township)—Marion KS-4
Menno (Township)—Mifflin PA-1
Menno (City)—Hutchinson SD-4
Meno (Town)—Major.....................OK-2

American Places Dictionary

Menoken (Township)—Shawnee....KS-4
Menoken (Township)—Burleigh ND-4
Menominee (Township)—Jo
  Daviess IL-3
Menominee (Village)—Jo Daviess.. IL-3
Menominee (City)—Menominee ... MI-3
Menominee (Township)—
  Menominee MI-3
Menominee (Town)—
  Menominee WI-3
Menominee County MI-3
Menominee County WI-3
Menominee Reservation (WI) ..IndRes-4
Menomonee Falls (Village)—
  Waukesha WI-3
Menomonie (City)—Dunn WI-3
Menomonie (Town)—Dunn WI-3
Ment (Town)—Cayuga NY-1
Mentasta Lake (CDP)—Valdez-Cordova
  Census Area AK-4
Mentone (Town)—DeKalb AL-2
Mentone (CDP)—San
  Bernardino CA-4
Mentone (Town)—Kosciusko IN-3
Mentone (Pop. Place)—Loving...... TX-2
Mentor (City)—Campbell KY-2
Mentor (Township)—Cheboygan ... MI-3
Mentor (Township)—Oscoda MI-3
Mentor (City)—Polk MN-3
Mentor (Township)—Divide ND-4
Mentor (City)—Lake OH-3
Mentor (Town)—Clark WI-3
Mentor-on-the-Lake (City)—
  Lake OH-3
Menz (Township)—Sioux ND-4
Mequon (City)—Ozaukee WI-3
Meramec (Township)—Crawford.. MO-3
Meramec (Township)—Dent MO-3
Meramec (Township)—Franklin ... MO-3
Meramec (Township)—Jefferson ... MO-3
Meramec (Township)—Phelps MO-3
Meramec (Township)—St. Louis .. MO-3
Meramec Caverns (MO).............. Geog-4
Meraux (CDP)—St. Bernard
  Parish LA-2
Merced (City)—Merced CA-4
Merced County CA-4
Mercedes (City)—Hidalgo.............. TX-2
Mercer (Township)—Mercer IL-3
Mercer (Town)—Somerset......ME-1
Mercer (Town)—Mercer MO-3
Mercer (City)—McLean ND-4
Mercer (Township)—McLean ND-4
Mercer (Township)—Butler PA-1
Mercer (Borough)—Mercer PA-1
Mercer (Town)—Iron WI-3
Mercer County IL-3
Mercer County KY-2
Mercer County MO-3
Mercer County NJ-1
Mercer County ND-4
Mercer County OH-3
Mercer County PA-1
Mercer County WV-2
Mercer Island (City)—King WA-4
Mercersburg (Borough)—Franklin .. PA-1
Mercerville-Hamilton Square (CDP)—
  Mercer NJ-1
Merchantville (Borough)—
  Camden NJ-1
Mercier (Township)—Brown SD-4
Meredith (Township)—Cloud KS-4
Meredith (Town)—Belknap NH-1
Meredith (Town)—Delaware NY-1
Meredosia (Town)—Morgan IL-3

Meriden (City)—New Haven *CT-1*
Meriden (Township)—La Salle *IL-3*
Meriden (City)—Cherokee *IA-3*
Meriden (City)—Jefferson *KS-4*
Meriden (Township)—Steele *MN-3*
Meridian (City)—Ada *ID-4*
Meridian (Township)—Clinton *IL-3*
Meridian (Township)—
  McPherson *KS-4*
Meridian (Township)—Ingham *MI-3*
Meridian (City)—Lauderdale *MS-2*
Meridian (Village)—Cayuga *NY-1*
Meridian (Town)—Logan *OK-2*
Meridian (CDP)—Stephens *OK-2*
Meridian (CDP)—Butler *PA-1*
Meridian (City)—Bosque *TX-2*
Meridian Hills (Town)—Marion *IN-3*
Meridian Naval Air Station
  (MS) *Mil-4*
Meridian Station (Military Facility)—
  Lauderdale *MS-2*
Meridianville (Division)—
  Madison *AL-2*
Merigold (Town)—Bolivar *MS-2*
Merino (Town)—Logan *CO-4*
Meriwether County *GA-2*
Merkel (Township)—Kidder *ND-4*
Merkel (Town)—Taylor *TX-2*
Mermentau (Village)—Acadia
  Parish *LA-2*
Merna (Village)—Custer *NE-4*
Merom (Town)—Sullivan *IN-3*
Merriam (City)—Johnson *KS-4*
Merriam Woods (Village)—
  Taney *MO-3*
Merrick (CDP)—Nassau *NY-1*
Merrick County *NE-4*
Merricourt (City)—Dickey *ND-4*
Merrifield (CDP)—Fairfax *VA-2*
Merrill (City)—Plymouth *IA-3*
Merrill (Town)—Aroostook *ME-1*
Merrill (Township)—Newaygo *MI-3*
Merrill (Village)—Saginaw *MI-3*
Merrill (Township)—Hettinger *ND-4*
Merrill (City)—Klamath *OR-4*
Merrill (City)—Lincoln *WI-3*
Merrill (Town)—Lincoln *WI-3*
Merrillan (Village)—Jackson *WI-3*
Merrillville (Town)—Lake *IN-3*
Merrimac (Town)—Essex *MA-1*
Merrimac (CDP)—Montgomery *VA-2*
Merrimac (Town)—Sauk *WI-3*
Merrimac (Village)—Sauk *WI-3*
Merrimack (Town)—
  Hillsborough *NH-1*
Merrimack County *NH-1*
Merrimack River (MO) *Geog-4*
Merriman (Village)—Cherry *NE-4*
Merrionette Park (Town)—Cook *IL-3*
Merritt (Township)—Bay *MI-3*
Merritt Island (CDP)—Brevard *FL-2*
Mer Rouge (Village)—Morehouse
  Parish *LA-2*
Merry (Township)—Thurston *NE-4*
Merrydale (CDP)—East Baton Rouge
  Parish *LA-2*
Merryville (Town)—Beauregard
  Parish *LA-2*
Mertens (Town)—Hill *TX-2*
Mertilla (Township)—Meade *KS-4*
Merton (Township)—Steele *MN-3*
Merton (Township)—Clark *SD-4*
Merton (Town)—Waukesha *WI-3*
Merton (Village)—Waukesha *WI-3*
Mertzon (Town)—Irion *TX-2*

Merwin (Town)—Bates *MO-3*
Mesa (City)—Maricopa *AZ-4*
Mesa (Town)—Franklin *WA-4*
Mesabi Range (MN) *Geog-4*
Mesa County *CO-4*
Mesa Grande Reservation
  (CA) *IndRes-4*
Mesa Verde (CO) *Geog-4*
Mescalero (CDP)—Otero *NM-4*
Mescalero Apache Reservation
  (NM) *IndRes-4*
Meservey (City)—Cerro Gordo *IA-3*
Meshoppen (Borough)—Wyoming .. *PA-1*
Meshoppen (Township)—
  Wyoming *PA-1*
Mesic (Town)—Pamlico *NC-2*
Mesick (Village)—Wexford *MI-3*
Mesilla (Town)—Doña Ana *NM-4*
Mesita (CDP)—Cibola *NM-4*
Mesopotamia (Township)—
  Trumbull *OH-3*
Mesquite (Township)—Clark *NV-4*
Mesquite (City)—Dallas *TX-2*
Meta (City)—Osage *MO-3*
Metairie (CDP)—Jefferson
  Parish *LA-2*
Metal (Township)—Franklin *PA-1*
Metaline (Town)—Pend Oreille *WA-4*
Metaline Falls (Town)—Pend
  Oreille *WA-4*
Metamora (Town)—Woodford *IL-3*
Metamora (Township)—
  Woodford *IL-3*
Metamora (Township)—Franklin ... *IN-3*
Metamora (Township)—Lapeer *MI-3*
Metamora (Village)—Lapeer *MI-3*
Metamora (Village)—Fulton *OH-3*
Metcalf (Village)—Edgar *IL-3*
Metcalfe (Town)—Washington *MS-2*
Metcalfe County *KY-2*
Meteor (Town)—Sawyer *WI-3*
Methuen (Town)—Essex *MA-1*
Metlakatla (CDP)—Prince of
  Wales-Outer Ketchikan Census
  Area *AK-4*
Metolius (City)—Jefferson *OR-4*
Metomen (Town)—Fond du Lac ... *WI-3*
Metropolis (City)—Massac *IL-3*
Mettawa (Town)—Lake *IL-3*
Metter (City)—Candler *GA-2*
Metuchen (Borough)—Middlesex ... *NJ-1*
Metz (Township)—Presque Isle *MI-3*
Metz (Town)—Vernon *MO-3*
Metz (Township)—Vernon *MO-3*
Metzger (CDP)—Washington *OR-4*
Mexia (City)—Limestone *TX-2*
Mexican Hat (CDP)—San Juan *UT-4*
Mexican Springs (CDP)—
  McKinley *NM-4*
Mexico (CDP)—Miami *IN-3*
Mexico (Town)—Oxford *ME-1*
Mexico (City)—Audrain *MO-3*
Mexico (Village)—Oswego *NY-1*
Mexico, Gulf of (CO) *Geog-4*
Mexico Beach (Town)—Bay *FL-2*
Meyer (Township)—Menominee *MI-3*
Meyer (Township)—Pierce *ND-4*
Meyers Chuck (CDP)—Prince of
  Wales-Outer Ketchikan Census
  Area *AK-4*
Meyersdale (Borough)—Somerset ... *PA-1*
Meyers Lake (Village)—Stark *OH-3*
Miami (Town)—Gila *AZ-4*
Miami (City)—Dade *FL-2*
Miami (Township)—Cass *IN-3*

Miami (Township)—Miami *KS-4*
Miami (Township)—Reno *KS-4*
Miami (City)—Saline *MO-3*
Miami (Township)—Saline *MO-3*
Miami (Township)—Clermont *OH-3*
Miami (Township)—Greene *OH-3*
Miami (Township)—Hamilton *OH-3*
Miami (Township)—Logan *OH-3*
Miami (Township)—
  Montgomery *OH-3*
Miami (City)—Ottawa *OK-2*
Miami (City)—Roberts *TX-2*
Miami Beach (City)—Dade *FL-2*
Miami Coast Guard Air Station
  (FL) *Mil-4*
Miami County *IN-3*
Miami County *KS-4*
Miami County *OH-3*
Miami Gardens-Utopia-Carver
  (CDP)—Broward *FL-2*
Miami Lakes (CDP)—Dade *FL-2*
Miamisburg (City)—
  Montgomery *OH-3*
Miami Shores (Village)—Dade *FL-2*
Miami Springs (City)—Dade *FL-2*
Micanopy (Town)—Alachua *FL-2*
Micco (CDP)—Brevard *FL-2*
Miccosukee Reservation (FL) .. *IndRes-4*
Michiana (Village)—Berrien *MI-3*
Michiana Shores (Town)—La
  Porte *IN-3*
Michie (Town)—McNairy *TN-2*
Michigamme (Township)—
  Marquette *MI-3*
Michigan (Township)—Clinton *IN-3*
Michigan (Township)—La Porte *IN-3*
Michigan (Township)—Scott *KS-4*
Michigan (Township)—Valley *NE-4*
Michigan (Township)—Grand
  Forks *ND-4*
Michigan (Township)—Nelson *ND-4*
Michigan, Lake (CO) *Geog-4*
Michigan Center (CDP)—
  Jackson *MI-3*
Michigan City (City)—La Porte *IN-3*
Michigan City (City)—Nelson *ND-4*
Michigantown (Township)—Clinton *IN-3*
Mickinock (Township)—Roseau ... *MN-3*
Micro (Town)—Johnston *NC-2*
Middle (Township)—Hendricks *IN-3*
Middle (Township)—Cape May *NJ-1*
Middleborough (Town)—
  Plymouth *MA-1*
Middlebourne (Town)—Tyler *WV-2*
Middle Branch (Township)—
  Osceola *MI-3*
Middleburg (CDP)—Clay *FL-2*
Middleburg (Town)—Vance *NC-2*
Middleburg (Borough)—Snyder *PA-1*
Middleburg (Town)—Loudoun *VA-2*
Middleburgh (Town)—Schoharie .. *NY-1*
Middleburgh (Village)—
  Schoharie *NY-1*
Middleburg Heights (City)—
  Cuyahoga *OH-3*
Middlebury (Town)—New Haven .. *CT-1*
Middlebury (Town)—Elkhart *IN-3*
Middlebury (Township)—Elkhart ... *IN-3*
Middlebury (Township)—
  Shiawassee *MI-3*
Middlebury (Town)—Wyoming *NY-1*
Middlebury (Township)—Knox *OH-3*
Middlebury (Township)—Tioga *PA-1*
Middlebury (Town)—Addison *VT-1*

General Index

Middle Creek (Township)—
  Miami.................................... *KS-4*
Middlecreek (Township)—Snyder... *PA-1*
Middlecreek (Township)—
  Somerset............................... *PA-1*
Middlefield (Town)—Middlesex.... *CT-1*
Middlefield (Town)—Hampshire.. *MA-1*
Middlefield (Town)—Otsego........... *NY-1*
Middlefield (Township)—
  Geauga................................. *OH-3*
Middlefield (Village)—Geauga....... *OH-3*
Middlefork (Township)—
  Vermilion.............................. *IL-3*
Middle Fork (Township)—
  Macon................................... *MO-3*
Middlefork (Township)—Worth..... *MO-3*
Middle Inlet (Town)—Marinette... *WI-3*
Middle Island (CDP)—Suffolk........ *NY-1*
Middle Paxton (Township)—
  Dauphin............................... *PA-1*
Middle Point (Village)—Van
  Wert..................................... *OH-3*
Middleport (Township)—Iroquois.. *IL-3*
Middleport (Village)—Niagara....... *NY-1*
Middleport (Village)—Meigs.......... *OH-3*
Middleport (Borough)—Schuylkill.. *PA-1*
Middle River (CDP)—Baltimore.. *MD-1*
Middle River (City)—Marshall..... *MN-3*
Middle River (Township)—
  Marshall............................... *MN-3*
Middlesborough (City)—Bell........ *KY-2*
Middlesex (Borough)—Middlesex.. *NJ-1*
Middlesex (Town)—Yates.............. *NY-1*
Middlesex (Town)—Nash................ *NC-2*
Middlesex (Township)—Butler....... *PA-1*
Middlesex (Township)—
  Cumberland.......................... *PA-1*
Middlesex (Town)—Washington.... *VT-1*
Middlesex County........................... *CT-1*
Middlesex County........................... *MA-1*
Middlesex County........................... *NJ-1*
Middlesex County........................... *VA-2*
Middle Smithfield (Township)—
  Monroe.................................. *PA-1*
Middle Taylor (Township)—
  Cambria................................ *PA-1*
Middleton (City)—Canyon............. *ID-4*
Middleton (Town)—Essex.............. *MA-1*
Middleton (Township)—
  Lafayette.............................. *MO-3*
Middleton (Town)—Strafford.......... *NH-1*
Middleton (Township)—
  Columbiana......................... *OH-3*
Middleton (Township)—Wood......... *OH-3*
Middleton (Township)—Turner...... *SD-4*
Middleton (Town)—Hardeman....... *TN-2*
Middleton (City)—Dane................. *WI-3*
Middleton (Town)—Dane............... *WI-3*
Middletown (City)—Middlesex....... *CT-1*
Middletown (Town)—New
  Castle.................................. *DE-1*
Middletown (Village)—Logan......... *IL-3*
Middletown (Town)—Henry........... *IN-3*
Middletown (City)—Des Moines... *IA-3*
Middletown (City)—Jefferson........ *KY-2*
Middletown (Town)—Frederick.... *MD-1*
Middletown (CDP)—Shiawassee.... *MI-3*
Middletown (Township)—
  Jackson................................ *MN-3*
Middletown (Town)—
  Montgomery......................... *MO-3*
Middletown (Township)—
  Monmouth........................... *NJ-1*
Middletown (Town)—Delaware...... *NY-1*
Middletown (City)—Orange........... *NY-1*

Middletown (City)—Butler............. *OH-3*
Middletown (City)—Warren........... *OH-3*
Middletown (Township)—Bucks..... *PA-1*
Middletown (Borough)—Dauphin.. *PA-1*
Middletown (Township)—
  Delaware.............................. *PA-1*
Middletown (CDP)—
  Northampton........................ *PA-1*
Middletown (Township)—
  Susquehanna........................ *PA-1*
Middletown (Town)—Newport....... *RI-1*
Middletown (Town)—Frederick...... *VA-2*
Middletown Rancheria (CA).... *IndRes-4*
Middletown Springs (Town)—
  Rutland................................ *VT-1*
Middle Valley (CDP)—Hamilton.. *TN-2*
Middleville (Village)—Barry.......... *MI-3*
Middleville (Township)—Wright... *MN-3*
Middleville (Village)—Herkimer... *NY-1*
Midfield (City)—Jefferson.............. *AL-2*
Mid Florida Lakes (CDP)—Lake.... *FL-2*
Midland (Town)—Sebastian........... *AR-2*
Midland (Town)—Allegany............ *MD-1*
Midland (City)—Bay...................... *MI-3*
Midland (City)—Midland............... *MI-3*
Midland (Township)—Midland...... *MI-3*
Midland (Township)—St. Louis.... *MO-3*
Midland (Township)—Gage............ *NE-4*
Midland (Township)—Merrick...... *NE-4*
Midland (Township)—Pembina..... *ND-4*
Midland (Village)—Clinton............ *OH-3*
Midland (Borough)—Beaver........... *PA-1*
Midland (Town)—Haakon.............. *SD-4*
Midland (Township)—Hand........... *SD-4*
Midland (City)—Martin................. *TX-2*
Midland (City)—Midland............... *TX-2*
Midland (CDP)—Pierce................. *WA-4*
Midland City (Town)—Dale........... *AL-2*
Midland County.............................. *MI-3*
Midland County.............................. *TX-2*
Midland Park (Borough)—Bergen.. *NJ-1*
Midlothian (City)—Cook................ *IL-3*
Midlothian (City)—Ellis................. *TX-2*
Midvale (City)—Washington............ *ID-4*
Midvale (Village)—Tuscarawas.......*OH-3*
Midvale (City)—Salt Lake.............. *UT-4*
Midville (City)—Burke................... *GA-2*
Midway (Town)—Bullock............... *AL-2*
Midway (City)—Gadsden................ *FL-2*
Midway (City)—Liberty................. *GA-2*
Midway (City)—Woodford.............. *KY-2*
Midway (CDP)—La Salle Parish....*LA-2*
Midway (Township)—
  Cottonwood......................... *MN-3*
Midway (Township)—St. Louis.... *MN-3*
Midway (Township)—Stutsman....*ND-4*
Midway (Village)—Madison........... *OH-3*
Midway (CDP)—Adams.................. *PA-1*
Midway (Borough)—Washington.... *PA-1*
Midway (CDP)—Washington.......... *TN-2*
Midway (City)—Madison................ *TX-2*
Midway (City)—Wasatch................ *UT-4*
Midway-Hardwick (CDP)—
  Baldwin................................ *GA-2*
Midwest (Town)—Natrona............. *WY-4*
Midwest City (City)—Oklahoma... *OK-2*
Miesville (City)—Dakota............... *MN-3*
Mifflin (Township)—Ashland........ *OH-3*
Mifflin (Village)—Ashland............. *OH-3*
Mifflin (Township)—Franklin........ *OH-3*
Mifflin (Township)—Pike............... *OH-3*
Mifflin (Township)—Richland....... *OH-3*
Mifflin (Township)—Wyandot....... *OH-3*
Mifflin (Township)—Columbia...... *PA-1*
Mifflin (Township)—Dauphin....... *PA-1*

Mifflin (Borough)—Juniata............. *PA-1*
Mifflin (Township)—Lycoming....... *PA-1*
Mifflin (Town)—Iowa.................... *WI-3*
Mifflinburg (Borough)—Union....... *PA-1*
Mifflin County................................ *PA-1*
Mifflintown (Borough)—Juniata.... *PA-1*
Mifflinville (CDP)—Columbia........ *PA-1*
Mignon (Division)—Talladega........*AL-2*
Mikado (Township)—Alcona.......... *MI-3*
Mikkelson (Township)—
  LaMoure.............................. *ND-4*
Milaca (City)—Mille Lacs............. *MN-3*
Milaca (Township)—Mille Lacs.... *MN-3*
Mila Doce (CDP)—Hidalgo............ *TX-2*
Milam (Township)—Macon............ *IL-3*
Milam County................................ *TX-2*
Milan (Town)—Dodge.................... *GA-2*
Milan (Town)—Telfair................... *GA-2*
Milan (Township)—DeKalb............. *IL-3*
Milan (Town)—Rock Island............ *IL-3*
Milan (Township)—Allen................ *IN-3*
Milan (Town)—Ripley................... *IN-3*
Milan (City)—Sumner................... *KS-4*
Milan (City)—Monroe.................... *MI-3*
Milan (Township)—Monroe............ *MI-3*
Milan (City)—Washtenaw.............. *MI-3*
Milan (City)—Chippewa................ *MN-3*
Milan (City)—Sullivan................... *MO-3*
Milan (Town)—Coos...................... *NH-1*
Milan (Village)—Cibola................ *NM-4*
Milan (Town)—Dutchess............... *NY-1*
Milan (Township)—Erie................ *OH-3*
Milan (Village)—Erie.................... *OH-3*
Milan (Village)—Huron................. *OH-3*
Milan (Town)—Gibson.................. *TN-2*
Milano (Town)—Milam.................. *TX-2*
Milbank (City)—Grant.................. *SD-4*
Milbridge (Town)—Washington..... *ME-1*
Milburn (Township)—Custer......... *NE-4*
Milburn (Township)—Johnston..... *OK-2*
Mildred (City)—Allen.................... *KS-4*
Mildred (Town)—Navarro............. *TX-2*
Miles (City)—Jackson.................... *IA-3*
Miles (Township)—Centre............. *PA-1*
Miles (City)—Runnels................... *TX-2*
Milesburg (Borough)—Centre....... *PA-1*
Miles City (City)—Custer.............. *MT-4*
Milford (City)—New Haven........... *CT-1*
Milford (City)—Kent..................... *DE-1*
Milford (City)—Sussex.................. *DE-1*
Milford (Town)—Iroquois.............. *IL-3*
Milford (Township)—Iroquois....... *IL-3*
Milford (Town)—Decatur.............. *IN-3*
Milford (Town)—Kosciusko........... *IN-3*
Milford (Township)—Lagrange..... *IN-3*
Milford (City)—Dickinson.............. *IA-3*
Milford (City)—Geary................... *KS-4*
Milford (Township)—Geary........... *KS-4*
Milford (Town)—Penobscot........... *ME-1*
Milford (Town)—Worcester........... *MA-1*
Milford (Township)—Oakland....... *MI-3*
Milford (Village)—Oakland........... *MI-3*
Milford (Township)—Brown......... *MN-3*
Milford (Township)—Barton........ *MO-3*
Milford (Village)—Barton............ *MO-3*
Milford (City)—Seward................. *NE-4*
Milford (Town)—Hillsborough......*NH-1*
Milford (Borough)—Hunterdon..... *NJ-1*
Milford (Town)—Otsego................ *NY-1*
Milford (Village)—Otsego.............. *NY-1*
Milford (Township)—Butler.......... *OH-3*
Milford (Village)—Clermont......... *OH-3*
Milford (Township)—Defiance...... *OH-3*
Milford (Village)—Hamilton......... *OH-3*
Milford (Township)—Knox............ *OH-3*

Milford (Township)—Bucks............ *PA-1*
Milford (Township)—Juniata......... *PA-1*
Milford (Borough)—Pike *PA-1*
Milford (Township)—Pike *PA-1*
Milford (Township)—Somerset..... *PA-1*
Milford (Township)—Beadle......... *SD-4*
Milford (Town)—Ellis *TX-2*
Milford (City)—Beaver *UT-4*
Milford (Town)—Jefferson........... *WI-3*
Milford Center (Village)—Union...*OH-3*
Milford Mill (CDP)—Baltimore ... *MD-1*
Mililani Town (CDP)—Honolulu ...*HI-4*
Milk River (MT)........................... *Geog-4*
Milks Grove (Township)—
  Iroquois.................................... *IL-3*
Mill (Township)—Grant................ *IN-3*
Mill (Township)—Tuscarawas........*OH-3*
Milladore (Village)—Portage.......... *WI-3*
Milladore (Town)—Wood.............. *WI-3*
Milladore (Village)—Wood *WI-3*
Millard (Village)—Adair *MO-3*
Millard County............................. *UT-4*
Millboro (Township)—Tripp......... *SD-4*
Millbourne (Borough)—Delaware... *PA-1*
Millbrae (City)—San Mateo.......... *CA-4*
Millbrook (City)—Elmore *AL-2*
Millbrook (Township)—Peoria *IL-3*
Millbrook (Township)—Graham....*KS-4*
Millbrook (Township)—Mecosta ... *MI-3*
Millbrook (Village)—Dutchess *NY-1*
Millburn (Township)—Essex........... *NJ-1*
Millbury (Town)—Worcester......... *MA-1*
Millbury (Village)—Wood............. *OH-3*
Mill City (City)—Linn *OR-4*
Mill City (City)—Marion *OR-4*
Mill Creek (Village)—Union........... *IL-3*
Millcreek (Township)—Fountain *IN-3*
Mill Creek (Township)—Bourbon...*KS-4*
Mill Creek (Township)—
  Pottawatomie *KS-4*
Mill Creek (Township)—
  Wabaunsee *KS-4*
Mill Creek (Township)—
  Washington *KS-4*
Mill Creek (Township)—Morgan .. *MO-3*
Mill Creek (Township)—
  Coshocton *OH-3*
Millcreek (Township)—Union *OH-3*
Mill Creek (Township)—
  Williams *OH-3*
Mill Creek (Town)—Johnston........ *OK-2*
Millcreek (Township)—Clarion *PA-1*
Millcreek (Township)—Erie *PA-1*
Mill Creek (Borough)—
  Huntingdon.............................. *PA-1*
Millcreek (Township)—Lebanon... *PA-1*
Mill Creek (Township)—
  Lycoming.................................. *PA-1*
Mill Creek (Township)—Mercer *PA-1*
Millcreek (CDP)—Salt Lake *UT-4*
Mill Creek (City)—Snohomish *WA-4*
Mill Creek (Town)—Randolph *WV-2*
Milledgeville (City)—Baldwin....... *GA-2*
Milledgeville (Town)—Carroll....... *IL-3*
Milledgeville (Village)—Fayette *OH-3*
Milledgeville (Town)—Chester...... *TN-2*
Milledgeville (Town)—Hardin *TN-2*
Milledgeville (Town)—McNairy *TN-2*
Mille Lacs County....................... *MN-3*
Mille Lacs Lake (MN) *Geog-4*
Mille Lacs Reservation (MN)... *IndRes-4*
Millen (City)—Jenkins *GA-2*
Millen (Township)—Alcona *MI-3*
Miller (Township)—La Salle *IL-3*
Miller (Township)—Dearborn........ *IN-3*

Miller (Township)—Dallas *MO-3*
Miller (Township)—Douglas *MO-3*
Miller (Township)—Gentry........... *MO-3*
Miller (City)—Lawrence................ *MO-3*
Miller (Township)—Maries *MO-3*
Miller (Township)—Marion *MO-3*
Miller (Township)—Phelps *MO-3*
Miller (Township)—Scotland *MO-3*
Miller (Village)—Buffalo................ *NE-4*
Miller (Township)—Knox *NE-4*
Miller (Township)—Knox *OH-3*
Miller (Township)—Huntingdon.... *PA-1*
Miller (Township)—Perry *PA-1*
Miller (City)—Hand *SD-4*
Miller (Township)—Hand *SD-4*
Miller (Township)—Marshall *SD-4*
Miller City (Village)—Putnam......*OH-3*
Miller County............................. *AR-2*
Miller County............................. *GA-2*
Miller County............................. *MO-3*
Miller Place (CDP)—Suffolk *NY-1*
Millersburg (Township)—Mercer *IL-3*
Millersburg (Town)—Elkhart *IN-3*
Millersburg (City)—Iowa *IA-3*
Millersburg (City)—Bourbon *KY-2*
Millersburg (Village)—Presque
  Isle.. *MI-3*
Millersburg (Village)—Holmes.......*OH-3*
Millersburg (City)—Linn *OR-4*
Millersburg (Borough)—Dauphin ... *PA-1*
Miller's Cove (Town)—Titus *TX-2*
Millers Creek (CDP)—Wilkes........*NC-2*
Millers Falls (CDP)—Franklin...... *MA-1*
Millersport (Village)—Fairfield......*OH-3*
Millerstown (Borough)—Perry *PA-1*
Millersville (Borough)—Lancaster .. *PA-1*
Millersville (City)—Robertson *TN-2*
Millersville (City)—Sumner *TN-2*
Millerton (City)—Wayne...............*IA-3*
Millerton (Village)—Dutchess........ *NY-1*
Millerton (Town)—McCurtain *OK-2*
Millerville (City)—Douglas *MN-3*
Millerville (Township)—Douglas .. *MN-3*
Millgrove (Township)—Steuben...... *IN-3*
Mill Hall (Borough)—Clinton *PA-1*
Millheim (Borough)—Centre *PA-1*
Millhousen (Town)—Decatur........ *IN-3*
Milligan (Village)—Fillmore *NE-4*
Milliken (Town)—Weld *CO-4*
Millington (Village)—Kendall........ *IL-3*
Millington (Village)—La Salle........ *IL-3*
Millington (Town)—Kent *MD-1*
Millington (Town)—Queen
  Anne's *MD-1*
Millington (Township)—Tuscola ... *MI-3*
Millington (Village)—Tuscola *MI-3*
Millington (City)—Shelby *TN-2*
Millinocket (Town)—Penobscot.... *ME-1*
Millis (Town)—Norfolk................ *MA-1*
Mill Neck (Village)—Nassau........... *NY-1*
Millport (Town)—Lamar................*AL-2*
Millport (Village)—Chemung......... *NY-1*
Millry (Town)—Washington.......... *AL-2*
Mills (Township)—Bond *IL-3*
Mills (Township)—Midland *MI-3*
Mills (Township)—Ogemaw *MI-3*
Mills (Town)—Natrona *WY-4*
Millsap (Town)—Parker................ *TX-2*
Millsboro (Town)—Sussex............. *DE-1*
Mills County *IA-3*
Mills County *TX-2*
Millsfield (Township)—Coos...........*NH-1*
Mill Shoals (Village)—Wayne *IL-3*
Mill Shoals (Township)—White...... *IL-3*
Mill Shoals (Village)—White *IL-3*

Mill Spring (Township)—Wayne... *MO-3*
Mill Spring (Village)—Wayne *MO-3*
Millstadt (Town)—St. Clair............. *IL-3*
Millstadt (Township)—St. Clair...... *IL-3*
Millston (Town)—Jackson............. *WI-3*
Millstone (Township)—
  Monmouth *NJ-1*
Millstone (Borough)—Somerset......*NJ-1*
Millstone (Township)—Elk *PA-1*
Milltown (Town)—Crawford............ *IN-3*
Milltown (Town)—Harrison........... *IN-3*
Milltown (Borough)—Middlesex..... *NJ-1*
Milltown (Township)—
  Hutchinson................................*SD-4*
Milltown (Town)—Polk................. *WI-3*
Milltown (Village)—Polk............... *WI-3*
Millvale (Borough)—Allegheny....... *PA-1*
Mill Valley (City)—Marin *CA-4*
Mill Village (Borough)—Erie *PA-1*
Millville (Town)—Sussex *DE-1*
Millville (City)—Clayton................*IA-3*
Millville (Town)—Worcester *MA-1*
Millville (City)—Wabasha *MN-3*
Millville (City)—Cumberland *NJ-1*
Millville (Village)—Butler..............*OH-3*
Millville (Borough)—Columbia *PA-1*
Millville (City)—Cache *UT-4*
Millville (Town)—Grant *WI-3*
Millward (Township)—Aitkin *MN-3*
Millwood (Township)—Stearns *MN-3*
Millwood (Township)—Lincoln *MO-3*
Millwood (Township)—Guernsey ..*OH-3*
Millwood (CDP)—Sumter...............*SC-2*
Millwood (Town)—Spokane..........*WA-4*
Milner (City)—Lamar *GA-2*
Milnor (City)—Sargent *ND-4*
Milnor (Township)—Sargent......... *ND-4*
Milo (Township)—Bureau.............. *IL-3*
Milo (City)—Warren *IA-3*
Milo (Town)—Piscataquis *ME-1*
Milo (Township)—Mille Lacs *MN-3*
Milo (Town)—Vernon *MO-3*
Milo (Town)—Yates *NY-1*
Milpitas (City)—Santa Clara *CA-4*
Milroy (Township)—Jasper............. *IN-3*
Milroy (City)—Redwood............... *MN-3*
Milroy (CDP)—Mifflin *PA-1*
Milton (Town)—Sussex *DE-1*
Milton (City)—Santa Rosa.............*FL-2*
Milton (Township)—DuPage *IL-3*
Milton (Village)—Pike *IL-3*
Milton (Township)—Jefferson *IN-3*
Milton (Town)—Wayne................. *IN-3*
Milton (City)—Van Buren *IA-3*
Milton (Township)—Butler *KS-4*
Milton (Township)—Marion *KS-4*
Milton (City)—Trimble.................. *KY-2*
Milton (Town)—Norfolk *MA-1*
Milton (Township)—Antrim *MI-3*
Milton (Township)—Cass............... *MI-3*
Milton (Township)—Dodge *MN-3*
Milton (Town)—Strafford *NH-1*
Milton (Town)—Saratoga *NY-1*
Milton (CDP)—Ulster.................... *NY-1*
Milton (Town)—Caswell *NC-2*
Milton (City)—Cavalier *ND-4*
Milton (Township)—Ashland........*OH-3*
Milton (Township)—Jackson *OH-3*
Milton (Township)—Mahoning *OH-3*
Milton (Township)—Wayne..........*OH-3*
Milton (Township)—Wood *OH-3*
Milton (Borough)—
  Northumberland *PA-1*
Milton (Town)—Chittenden........... *VT-1*
Milton (Village)—Chittenden *VT-1*

Milton (Town)—King	WA-4	
Milton (Town)—Pierce	WA-4	
Milton (Town)—Cabell	WV-2	
Milton (Town)—Buffalo	WI-3	
Milton (City)—Rock	WI-3	
Milton (Town)—Rock	WI-3	
Miltona (City)—Douglas	MN-3	
Miltona (Township)—Douglas	MN-3	
Milton Center (Village)—Wood	OH-3	
Milton-Freewater (City)—Umatilla	OR-4	
Miltonsburg (Village)—Monroe	OH-3	
Milton (unorganized) (Pop. Place)—Oxford	ME-1	
Miltonvale (City)—Cloud	KS-4	
Milwaukee (City)—Milwaukee	WI-3	
Milwaukee (City)—Washington	WI-3	
Milwaukee (City)—Waukesha	WI-3	
Milwaukee County	WI-3	
Milwaukie (City)—Clackamas	OR-4	
Milwaukie (City)—Multnomah	OR-4	
Mimosa Park (CDP)—St. Charles Parish	LA-2	
Mims (CDP)—Brevard	FL-2	
Mina (Town)—Chautauqua	NY-1	
Minatare (City)—Scotts Bluff	NE-4	
Minburn (City)—Dallas	IA-3	
Minco (Township)—Benson	ND-4	
Minco (City)—Grady	OK-2	
Minden (City)—Pottawattamie	IA-3	
Minden (City)—Webster Parish	LA-2	
Minden (Township)—Sanilac	MI-3	
Minden (Township)—Benton	MN-3	
Minden (City)—Kearney	NE-4	
Minden (CDP)—Douglas	NV-4	
Minden (Town)—Montgomery	NY-1	
Minden City (Village)—Sanilac	MI-3	
Mindenmines (City)—Barton	MO-3	
Mine Hill (Township)—Morris	NJ-1	
Mine La Motte (Township)—Madison	MO-3	
Mineola (Village)—Nassau	NY-1	
Mineola (City)—Wood	TX-2	
Miner (City)—Scott	MO-3	
Miner (Township)—Miner	SD-4	
Mineral (Township)—Bureau	IL-3	
Mineral (Village)—Bureau	IL-3	
Mineral (Township)—Cherokee	KS-4	
Mineral (Township)—Barry	MO-3	
Mineral (Township)—Jasper	MO-3	
Mineral (Township)—Venango	PA-1	
Mineral (Town)—Louisa	VA-2	
Mineral Bluff (Town)—Fannin	GA-2	
Mineral City (Village)—Tuscarawas	OH-3	
Mineral County	CO-4	
Mineral County	MT-4	
Mineral County	NV-4	
Mineral County	WV-2	
Mineral Hills (Village)—Iron	MI-3	
Mineral Point (Town)—Washington	MO-3	
Mineral Point (City)—Iowa	WI-3	
Mineral Point (Town)—Iowa	WI-3	
Mineral Ridge (CDP)—Mahoning	OH-3	
Mineral Ridge (CDP)—Trumbull	OH-3	
Mineral Springs (City)—Howard	AR-2	
Mineral Springs (Township)—Slope	ND-4	
Mineral Wells (City)—Palo Pinto	TX-2	
Mineral Wells (City)—Parker	TX-2	
Mineralwells (CDP)—Wood	WV-2	
Miner County	SD-4	
Minersville (Borough)—Schuylkill	PA-1	
Minersville (Town)—Beaver	UT-4	
Minerva (Township)—Clearwater	MN-3	
Minerva (Town)—Essex	NY-1	
Minerva (Village)—Carroll	OH-3	
Minerva (Village)—Columbiana	OH-3	
Minerva (Village)—Stark	OH-3	
Minerva Park (Village)—Franklin	OH-3	
Minetto (Town)—Oswego	NY-1	
Mineville-Witherbee (CDP)—Essex	NY-1	
Mingo (City)—Jasper	IA-3	
Mingo (Township)—Bates	MO-3	
Mingo County	WV-2	
Mingo Junction (City)—Jefferson	OH-3	
Mingona (Township)—Barber	KS-4	
Mingus (City)—Palo Pinto	TX-2	
Minidoka (City)—Minidoka	ID-4	
Minidoka County	ID-4	
Minier (Town)—Tazewell	IL-3	
Minisink (Town)—Orange	NY-1	
Minneapolis (City)—Ottawa	KS-4	
Minneapolis (City)—Hennepin	MN-3	
Minneha (Township)—Sedgwick	KS-4	
Minnehaha (Township)—Bowman	ND-4	
Minnehaha (CDP)—Clark	WA-4	
Minnehaha County	SD-4	
Minnehaha Falls (MN)	Geog-4	
Minneiska (City)—Wabasha	MN-3	
Minneiska (Township)—Wabasha	MN-3	
Minneiska (City)—Winona	MN-3	
Minneola (City)—Lake	FL-2	
Minneola (City)—Clark	KS-4	
Minneola (Township)—Goodhue	MN-3	
Minneota (Township)—Jackson	MN-3	
Minneota (City)—Lyon	MN-3	
Minnesota (Township)—Burke	ND-4	
Minnesota (Township)—Roberts	SD-4	
Minnesota Chippewa Trust Lands (MN)	IndRes-4	
Minnesota City (City)—Winona	MN-3	
Minnesota Falls (Township)—Yellow Medicine	MN-3	
Minnesota Lake (City)—Faribault	MN-3	
Minnesota Lake (Township)—Faribault	MN-3	
Minnesota River (MN)	Geog-4	
Minnesott Beach (Town)—Pamlico	NC-2	
Minnetonka (City)—Hennepin	MN-3	
Minnetonka Beach (City)—Hennepin	MN-3	
Minnetrista (City)—Hennepin	MN-3	
Minnewaska (Township)—Pope	MN-3	
Minnewaukan (City)—Benson	ND-4	
Minnewaukan (Township)—Ramsey	ND-4	
Minnie (Township)—Beltrami	MN-3	
Minnie (Township)—Grant	ND-4	
Minnie Lake (Township)—Barnes	ND-4	
Minoa (Village)—Onondaga	NY-1	
Minocqua (Town)—Oneida	WI-3	
Minong (Town)—Washburn	WI-3	
Minong (Village)—Washburn	WI-3	
Minonk (Town)—Woodford	IL-3	
Minonk (Township)—Woodford	IL-3	
Minooka (Town)—Grundy	IL-3	
Minooka (Town)—Will	IL-3	
Minor (Division)—Jefferson	AL-2	
Minor Hill (City)—Giles	TN-2	
Minor Lane Heights (City)—Jefferson	KY-2	
Minot (Town)—Androscoggin	ME-1	
Minot (City)—Ward	ND-4	
Minot Air Force Base (ND)	Mil-4	
Minot Air Force Base (Military Facility)—Ward	ND-4	
Minster (Village)—Auglaize	OH-3	
Mint Hill (Town)—Mecklenburg	NC-2	
Minto (CDP)—Yukon-Koyukuk Census Area	AK-4	
Minto (Township)—Cavalier	ND-4	
Minto (City)—Walsh	ND-4	
Minton (Township)—Holt	MO-3	
Minturn (Town)—Lawrence	AR-2	
Minturn (Town)—Eagle	CO-4	
Mio (CDP)—Oscoda	MI-3	
Mirabile (Township)—Caldwell	MO-3	
Mirage (Township)—Rawlins	KS-4	
Mirage (Township)—Kearney	NE-4	
Mira Loma (CDP)—Riverside	CA-4	
Miramar (City)—Broward	FL-2	
Miramar Beach (CDP)—Walton	FL-2	
Miramar Naval Air Station (CA)	Mil-4	
Mira Monte (CDP)—Ventura	CA-4	
Mirrormont (CDP)—King	WA-4	
Mishawaka (City)—St. Joseph	IN-3	
Mishicot (Town)—Manitowoc	WI-3	
Mishicot (Village)—Manitowoc	WI-3	
Missaukee County	MI-3	
Mission (Township)—La Salle	IL-3	
Mission (Township)—Brown	KS-4	
Mission (City)—Johnson	KS-4	
Mission (Township)—Neosho	KS-4	
Mission (Township)—Shawnee	KS-4	
Mission (Township)—Crow Wing	MN-3	
Mission (Township)—Benson	ND-4	
Mission (CDP)—Umatilla	OR-4	
Mission (Township)—Corson	SD-4	
Mission (City)—Todd	SD-4	
Mission (City)—Hidalgo	TX-2	
Mission Bay (CDP)—Palm Beach	FL-2	
Mission Bend (CDP)—Fort Bend	TX-2	
Mission Bend (CDP)—Harris	TX-2	
Mission Creek (Township)—Wabaunsee	KS-4	
Mission Creek (Township)—Pine	MN-3	
Mission Hill (Town)—Yankton	SD-4	
Mission Hill (Township)—Yankton	SD-4	
Mission Hills (CDP)—Santa Barbara	CA-4	
Mission Hills (City)—Johnson	KS-4	
Mission Viejo (City)—Orange	CA-4	
Mission Woods (City)—Johnson	KS-4	
Mississinawa (Township)—Darke	OH-3	
Mississippi (Township)—Jersey	IL-3	
Mississippi (Township)—Mississippi	MO-3	
Mississippi Alluvial Plain (MN)	Geog-4	
Mississippi Choctaw Res. & Trust Lands (MS)	IndRes-4	
Mississippi County	AR-2	
Mississippi County	MO-3	
Mississippi Delta (LA)	Geog-4	
Mississippi River (LA)	Geog-4	
Mississippi Sound (LA)	Geog-4	
Missoula (City)—Missoula	MT-4	
Missoula County	MT-4	
Missouri (Township)—Brown	IL-3	

Missouri (Township)—Boone........ *MO-3*
Missouri (Township)—Burleigh *ND-4*
Missouri City (City)—Clay *MO-3*
Missouri City (City)—Fort Bend ... *TX-2*
Missouri City (City)—Harris *TX-2*
Missouri Ridge (Township)—
  Williams *ND-4*
Missouri River (LA) *Geog-4*
Missouri River (Township)—St.
  Louis *MO-3*
Missouri Valley (City)—Harrison *IA-3*
Mitchell (Town)—Glascock........... *GA-2*
Mitchell (City)—Lawrence *IN-3*
Mitchell (City)—Mitchell *IA-3*
Mitchell (Township)—Nemaha *KS-4*
Mitchell (Township)—Rice *KS-4*
Mitchell (Township)—Alcona *MI-3*
Mitchell (Township)—Wilkin *MN-3*
Mitchell (City)—Scotts Bluff......... *NE-4*
Mitchell (Town)—Wheeler *OR-4*
Mitchell (City)—Davison *SD-4*
Mitchell (Township)—Davison *SD-4*
Mitchell (City)—Sheboygan *WI-3*
Mitchell, Mt. (NC) *Geog-4*
Mitchell County *GA-2*
Mitchell County *IA-3*
Mitchell County *KS-4*
Mitchell County *NC-2*
Mitchell County *TX-2*
Mitchell Heights (Town)—Logan .. *WV-2*
Mitchellville (City)—Desha *AR-2*
Mitchellville (City)—Polk *IA-3*
Mitchellville (CDP)—Prince
  George's *MD-1*
Mitchellville (Town)—Sumner *TN-2*
Mitcheltree (Township)—Martin ... *IN-3*
Mi-Wuk Village (CDP)—
  Tuolumne *CA-4*
Mize (Town)—Smith *MS-2*
Mizpah (City)—Koochiching *MN-3*
Moab (City)—Grand *UT-4*
Moapa River Reservation
  (NV) *IndRes-4*
Moapa Valley (CDP)—Clark.......... *NV-4*
Mobeetie (Town)—Wheeler *TX-2*
Moberly (City)—Randolph *MO-3*
Mobile (City)—Mobile *AL-2*
Mobile Bay (AL) *Geog-4*
Mobile County *AL-2*
Mobridge (City)—Walworth........... *SD-4*
Moccasin (Township)—Effingham... *IL-3*
Mockingbird Valley (City)—
  Jefferson *KY-2*
Mocksville (Town)—Davie............ *NC-2*
Modale (City)—Harrison *IA-3*
Model (Township)—Mountrail *ND-4*
Modena (Borough)—Chester.......... *PA-1*
Modena (Township)—Edmunds *SD-4*
Modena (Town)—Buffalo *WI-3*
Modesto (City)—Stanislaus............ *CA-4*
Modesto (Village)—Macoupin *IL-3*
Modoc (Town)—Randolph............. *IN-3*
Modoc County *CA-4*
Moe (Township)—Douglas............ *MN-3*
Moenkopi (CDP)—Coconino........ *AZ-4*
Moffat County *CO-4*
Moffatt (Township)—Arenac *MI-3*
Moffett (Town)—Sequoyah *OK-2*
Moffett Field Naval Air Station
  (CA) *Mil-4*
Mogadore (Village)—Portage *OH-3*
Mogadore (Village)—Summit *OH-3*
Mohall (City)—Renville *ND-4*
Mohave County *AZ-4*

Mohave Valley (CDP)—Mohave ... *AZ-4*
Mohawk (Village)—Herkimer *NY-1*
Mohawk (Town)—Montgomery..... *NY-1*
Mohawk River (NY) *Geog-4*
Mohegan TDSA (CT) *IndRes-4*
Mohican (Township)—Ashland *OH-3*
Mohnton (Borough)—Berks *PA-1*
Moira (Town)—Franklin *NY-1*
Mojave (CDP)—Kern *CA-4*
Mojave Desert (CA)...................... *Geog-4*
Mokane (Town)—Callaway *MO-3*
Mokena (Town)—Will *IL-3*
Mokuleia (CDP)—Honolulu *HI-4*
Molalla (City)—Clackamas *OR-4*
Molan (Township)—Hutchinson.... *SD-4*
Moland (Township)—Clay *MN-3*
Molena (City)—Pike *GA-2*
Moline (City)—Rock Island *IL-3*
Moline (Township)—Rock Island ... *IL-3*
Moline (City)—Elk *KS-4*
Moline Acres (City)—St. Louis...... *MO-3*
Molino (CDP)—Escambia *FL-2*
Molitor (Town)—Taylor *WI-3*
Molokai (HI) *Geog-4*
Moltke (Township)—Presque Isle .. *MI-3*
Moltke (Township)—Sibley........... *MN-3*
Momence (City)—Kankakee *IL-3*
Momence (Township)—Kankakee .. *IL-3*
Momence (Township)—Fillmore ... *NE-4*
Mona (Township)—Ford *IL-3*
Mona (Town)—Juab *UT-4*
Monaca (Borough)—Beaver *PA-1*
Monaghan (Township)—York *PA-1*
Monahans (City)—Ward *TX-2*
Monahans (City)—Winkler *TX-2*
Monango (City)—Dickey *ND-4*
Monarch Mill (CDP)—Union........*SC-2*
Moncks Corner (Town)—
  Berkeley.. *SC-2*
Monclova (Township)—Lucas....... *OH-3*
Mondamin (City)—Harrison *IA-3*
Mondamin (Township)—Hand *SD-4*
Monday Creek (Township)—
  Perry *OH-3*
Mondovi (City)—Buffalo *WI-3*
Mondovi (Town)—Buffalo *WI-3*
Monee (Town)—Will *IL-3*
Monee (Township)—Will *IL-3*
Monegaw (Township)—St. Clair ... *MO-3*
Moneta (Town)—O'Brien *IA-3*
Monett (City)—Barry *MO-3*
Monett (Township)—Barry *MO-3*
Monett (City)—Lawrence *MO-3*
Monetta (Town)—Aiken................. *SC-2*
Monetta (Town)—Saluda *SC-2*
Monette (City)—Craighead *AR-2*
Money Creek (Township)—
  McLean *IL-3*
Money Creek (Township)—
  Houston *MN-3*
Monfort Heights East (CDP)—
  Hamilton *OH-3*
Monfort Heights South (CDP)—
  Hamilton *OH-3*
Monhegan (Pop. Place)—
  Lincoln *ME-1*
Monico (Town)—Oneida................. *WI-3*
Moniteau (Township)—Howard ... *MO-3*
Moniteau (Township)—
  Randolph *MO-3*
Moniteau County *MO-3*
Monitor (Township)—Bay *MI-3*
Monkton (Town)—Addison *VT-1*
Monmouth (City)—Warren *IL-3*

Monmouth (Township)—Warren *IL-3*
Monmouth (City)—Jackson *IA-3*
Monmouth (Township)—
  Shawnee *KS-4*
Monmouth (Town)—Kennebec..... *ME-1*
Monmouth (City)—Polk *OR-4*
Monmouth Beach (Borough)—
  Monmouth *NJ-1*
Monmouth County *NJ-1*
Monmouth Junction (CDP)—
  Middlesex.. *NJ-1*
Mono County................................... *CA-4*
Monon (Town)—White *IN-3*
Monon (Township)—White *IN-3*
Monona (City)—Clayton.................*IA-3*
Monona (City)—Dane *WI-3*
Monona County................................*IA-3*
Monongah (Town)—Marion *WV-2*
Monongahela (Township)—
  Greene *PA-1*
Monongahela (City)—Washington .. *PA-1*
Monongahela River (HI) *Geog-4*
Monongalia County *WV-2*
Mono Vista (CDP)—Tuolumne ... *CA-4*
Monowi (Village)—Boyd *NE-4*
Monroe (Town)—Fairfield *CT-1*
Monroe (City)—Walton................. *GA-2*
Monroe (Township)—Ogle *IL-3*
Monroe (Town)—Adams *IN-3*
Monroe (Township)—Adams *IN-3*
Monroe (Township)—Allen *IN-3*
Monroe (Township)—Carroll *IN-3*
Monroe (Township)—Clark *IN-3*
Monroe (Township)—Delaware *IN-3*
Monroe (Township)—Grant *IN-3*
Monroe (Township)—Howard *IN-3*
Monroe (Township)—Jefferson *IN-3*
Monroe (Township)—Kosciusko..... *IN-3*
Monroe (Township)—Madison *IN-3*
Monroe (Township)—Morgan *IN-3*
Monroe (Township)—Pike *IN-3*
Monroe (Township)—Pulaski *IN-3*
Monroe (Township)—Putnam *IN-3*
Monroe (Township)—Randolph *IN-3*
Monroe (Township)—Washington .. *IN-3*
Monroe (City)—Jasper................... *IN-3*
Monroe (Township)—Anderson....*KS-4*
Monroe (City)—Ouachita Parish *LA-2*
Monroe (Town)—Waldo................ *ME-1*
Monroe (Town)—Franklin *MA-1*
Monroe (City)—Monroe *MI-3*
Monroe (Township)—Monroe *MI-3*
Monroe (Township)—Newaygo...... *MI-3*
Monroe (Township)—Lyon *MN-3*
Monroe (Township)—Andrew....... *MO-3*
Monroe (Township)—Daviess........ *MO-3*
Monroe (Township)—Lincoln........ *MO-3*
Monroe (Township)—Livingston .. *MO-3*
Monroe (Township)—Monroe *MO-3*
Monroe (Township)—Nodaway *MO-3*
Monroe (Township)—Platte *NE-4*
Monroe (Village)—Platte *NE-4*
Monroe (Town)—Grafton *NH-1*
Monroe (Township)—Gloucester....*NJ-1*
Monroe (Township)—Middlesex ... *NJ-1*
Monroe (Town)—Orange *NY-1*
Monroe (Village)—Orange *NY-1*
Monroe (City)—Union *NC-2*
Monroe (Township)—Towner *ND-4*
Monroe (Township)—Adams *OH-3*
Monroe (Township)—Allen *OH-3*
Monroe (Township)—Ashtabula *OH-3*
Monroe (Village)—Butler............... *OH-3*
Monroe (Township)—Carroll......... *OH-3*
Monroe (Township)—Clermont *OH-3*

Monroe (Township)—Coshocton ...*OH-3*
Monroe (Township)—Darke *OH-3*
Monroe (Township)—Guernsey.....*OH-3*
Monroe (Township)—Harrison......*OH-3*
Monroe (Township)—Henry *OH-3*
Monroe (Township)—Holmes........*OH-3*
Monroe (Township)—Knox *OH-3*
Monroe (Township)—Licking........*OH-3*
Monroe (Township)—Logan *OH-3*
Monroe (Township)—Madison *OH-3*
Monroe (Township)—Miami *OH-3*
Monroe (Township)—
 Muskingum *OH-3*
Monroe (Township)—Perry............*OH-3*
Monroe (Township)—Pickaway *OH-3*
Monroe (Township)—Preble *OH-3*
Monroe (Township)—Putnam *OH-3*
Monroe (Township)—Richland......*OH-3*
Monroe (Village)—Warren *OH-3*
Monroe (City)—Benton *OR-4*
Monroe (Township)—Bedford *PA-1*
Monroe (Borough)—Bradford.........*PA-1*
Monroe (Township)—Bradford........*PA-1*
Monroe (Township)—Clarion *PA-1*
Monroe (Township)—
 Cumberland *PA-1*
Monroe (Township)—Juniata *PA-1*
Monroe (Township)—Snyder *PA-1*
Monroe (Township)—Wyoming......*PA-1*
Monroe (Town)—Turner *SD-4*
Monroe (Township)—Turner *SD-4*
Monroe (City)—Sevier *UT-4*
Monroe (City)—Snohomish *WA-4*
Monroe (Town)—Adams.................*WI-3*
Monroe (City)—Green *WI-3*
Monroe (Town)—Green *WI-3*
Monroe City (Town)—Knox *IN-3*
Monroe City (City)—Marion *MO-3*
Monroe City (City)—Monroe *MO-3*
Monroe City (City)—Ralls *MO-3*
Monroe County *AL-2*
Monroe County *AR-2*
Monroe County *FL-2*
Monroe County *GA-2*
Monroe County *IL-3*
Monroe County *IN-3*
Monroe County *IA-3*
Monroe County *KY-2*
Monroe County *MI-3*
Monroe County *MS-2*
Monroe County *MO-3*
Monroe County *NY-1*
Monroe County *OH-3*
Monroe County *PA-1*
Monroe County *TN-2*
Monroe County *WV-2*
Monroe County *WI-3*
Monroeville (City)—Monroe *AL-2*
Monroeville (Town)—Allen.............*IN-3*
Monroeville (Village)—Huron *OH-3*
Monroeville (Borough)—
 Allegheny....................*PA-1*
Monrovia (City)—Los Angeles *CA-4*
Monsey (CDP)—Rockland *NY-1*
Monson (Town)—Piscataquis *ME-1*
Monson (Town)—Hampden...........*MA-1*
Monson (Township)—Traverse.....*MN-3*
Mont (Township)—Williams...........*ND-4*
Montague (City)—Siskiyou *CA-4*
Montague (Town)—Franklin *MA-1*
Montague (City)—Muskegon *MI-3*
Montague (Township)—
 Muskegon *MI-3*
Montague (Township)—Sussex *NJ-1*
Montague (Town)—Lewis *NY-1*

Montague (Pop. Place)—
 Montague *TX-2*
Montague County *TX-2*
Mont Alto (Borough)—Franklin *PA-1*
Montana (Township)—Jewell.........*KS-4*
Montana (Township)—Labette *KS-4*
Montana (Town)—Buffalo *WI-3*
Montara (CDP)—San Mateo *CA-4*
Montauk (CDP)—Suffolk *NY-1*
Mont Belvieu (City)—Chambers ...*TX-2*
Mont Belvieu (Town)—Liberty.......*TX-2*
Montcalm (Township)—
 Montcalm *MI-3*
Montcalm (CDP)—Mercer............*WV-2*
Montcalm County *MI-3*
Montclair (City)—San
 Bernardino *CA-4*
Montclair (Township)—Essex *NJ-1*
Montclair (CDP)—Prince
 William *VA-2*
Monteagle (Town)—Grundy *TN-2*
Monteagle (Town)—Marion............*TN-2*
Montebello (City)—Los Angeles *CA-4*
Montebello (Township)—Hancock .*IL-3*
Montebello (Village)—Rockland....*NY-1*
Montegut (CDP)—Terrebonne
 Parish *LA-2*
Montello (City)—Marquette *WI-3*
Montello (Town)—Marquette *WI-3*
Monterey (City)—Monterey *CA-4*
Monterey (Town)—Pulaski *IN-3*
Monterey (City)—Owen *KY-2*
Monterey (Town)—Berkshire.........*MA-1*
Monterey (Township)—Allegan *MI-3*
Monterey (Township)—Cuming.....*NE-4*
Monterey (Township)—Putnam.....*OH-3*
Monterey (Town)—Putnam *TN-2*
Monterey (Town)—Highland *VA-2*
Monterey Bay (CA)......................*Geog-4*
Monterey County *CA-4*
Monterey Park (City)—Los
 Angeles *CA-4*
Monte Rio (CDP)—Sonoma *CA-4*
Montesano (City)—Grays
 Harbor *WA-4*
Monte Sereno (City)—Santa
 Clara *CA-4*
Montevallo (City)—Shelby............*AL-2*
Montevallo (Township)—Vernon ..*MO-3*
Montevideo (City)—Chippewa *MN-3*
Monte Vista (City)—Rio Grande ..*CO-4*
Montezuma (Town)—Summit *CO-4*
Montezuma (City)—Macon *GA-2*
Montezuma (Township)—Pike *IL-3*
Montezuma (Town)—Parke *IN-3*
Montezuma (City)—Poweshiek *IA-3*
Montezuma (City)—Gray *KS-4*
Montezuma (Township)—Gray......*KS-4*
Montezuma (Town)—Cayuga *NY-1*
Montezuma (Village)—Mercer.......*OH-3*
Montezuma County *CO-4*
Montezuma Creek (CDP)—San
 Juan............................*UT-4*
Montfort (Village)—Grant *WI-3*
Montfort (Village)—Iowa *WI-3*
Montgomery (City)—
 Montgomery...............................*AL-2*
Montgomery (CDP)—Chatham *GA-2*
Montgomery (Township)—
 Crawford *IL-3*
Montgomery (Town)—Kane *IL-3*
Montgomery (Town)—Kendall *IL-3*
Montgomery (Township)—
 Woodford *IL-3*
Montgomery (Town)—Daviess *IN-3*

Montgomery (Township)—Gibson .*IN-3*
Montgomery (Township)—
 Jennings *IN-3*
Montgomery (Township)—Owen....*IN-3*
Montgomery (Town)—Grant
 Parish *LA-2*
Montgomery (Town)—Hampden ..*MA-1*
Montgomery (Village)—Hillsdale ..*MI-3*
Montgomery (City)—Le Sueur.......*MN-3*
Montgomery (Township)—Le
 Sueur *MN-3*
Montgomery (Township)—
 Hickory *MO-3*
Montgomery (Township)—
 Montgomery..................*MO-3*
Montgomery (Township)—
 Wright *MO-3*
Montgomery (Township)—
 Somerset *NJ-1*
Montgomery (Town)—Orange *NY-1*
Montgomery (Village)—Orange *NY-1*
Montgomery (Township)—
 Ashland *OH-3*
Montgomery (City)—Hamilton......*OH-3*
Montgomery (Township)—
 Marion *OH-3*
Montgomery (Township)—Wood...*OH-3*
Montgomery (Township)—
 Franklin..................*PA-1*
Montgomery (Township)—
 Indiana *PA-1*
Montgomery (Borough)—
 Lycoming *PA-1*
Montgomery (Township)—
 Montgomery..................*PA-1*
Montgomery (City)—
 Montgomery.......................*TX-2*
Montgomery (Town)—Franklin *VT-1*
Montgomery (City)—Fayette *WV-2*
Montgomery (City)—Kanawha *WV-2*
Montgomery City (City)—
 Montgomery..................*MO-3*
Montgomery County *AL-2*
Montgomery County *AR-2*
Montgomery County *GA-2*
Montgomery County *IL-3*
Montgomery County *IN-3*
Montgomery County *IA-3*
Montgomery County *KS-4*
Montgomery County *KY-2*
Montgomery County *MD-1*
Montgomery County *MS-2*
Montgomery County *MO-3*
Montgomery County *NY-1*
Montgomery County *NC-2*
Montgomery County *OH-3*
Montgomery County *PA-1*
Montgomery County *TN-2*
Montgomery County *TX-2*
Montgomery County *VA-2*
Montgomery Creek Rancheria
 (CA).............................*IndRes-4*
Montgomery Village (CDP)—
 Montgomery..................*MD-1*
Montgomeryville (CDP)—
 Montgomery..................*PA-1*
Monticello (City)—Drew................*AR-2*
Monticello (City)—Jefferson *FL-2*
Monticello (City)—Jasper *GA-2*
Monticello (City)—Piatt *IL-3*
Monticello (Township)—Piatt........*IL-3*
Monticello (City)—White *IN-3*
Monticello (City)—Jones..................*IA-3*
Monticello (Township)—Johnson ...*KS-4*
Monticello (City)—Wayne................*KY-2*

Monticello (CDP)—East Baton Rouge
   Parish *LA-2*
Monticello (Town)—Aroostook..... *ME-1*
Monticello (City)—Wright *MN-3*
Monticello (Township)—Wright ... *MN-3*
Monticello (Town)—Lawrence...... *MS-2*
Monticello (Town)—Lewis *MO-3*
Monticello (Village)—Sullivan *NY-1*
Monticello (City)—San Juan.......... *UT-4*
Monticello (Village)—Green *WI-3*
Montier (Town)—Lafayette *WI-3*
Montier (Township)—Shannon..... *MO-3*
Montmorency (Township)—
   Whiteside *IL-3*
Montmorency (Township)—
   Montmorency............................... *MI-3*
Montmorency County..................... *MI-3*
Montour (City)—Tama *IA-3*
Montour (Town)—Schuyler............ *NY-1*
Montour (Township)—Columbia... *PA-1*
Montour County *PA-1*
Montour Falls (Village)—
   Schuyler..*NY-1*
Montoursville (Borough)—
   Lycoming.. *PA-1*
Montpelier (City)—Bear Lake *ID-4*
Montpelier (City)—Blackford *IN-3*
Montpelier (Village)—St. Helena
   Parish *LA-2*
Montpelier (City)—Stutsman........ *ND-4*
Montpelier (Township)—
   Stutsman *ND-4*
Montpelier (Village)—Williams *OH-3*
Montpelier (Township)—
   Edmunds.. *SD-4*
Montpelier (City)—Washington..... *VT-1*
Montpelier (Town)—Kewaunee *WI-3*
Montreal (City)—Iron *WI-3*
Montreat (Town)—Buncombe *NC-2*
Montrose (City)—Ashley................ *AR-2*
Montrose (City)—Montrose........... *CO-4*
Montrose (Town)—Laurens *GA-2*
Montrose (Village)—Cumberland... *IL-3*
Montrose (Village)—Effingham *IL-3*
Montrose (City)—Lee...................... *IA-3*
Montrose (Township)—Genesee ... *MI-3*
Montrose (Village)—Genesee........ *MI-3*
Montrose (City)—Wright *MN-3*
Montrose (Town)—Jasper *MS-2*
Montrose (City)—Henry *MO-3*
Montrose (Township)—Cavalier.... *ND-4*
Montrose (Borough)—
   Susquehanna *PA-1*
Montrose (City)—McCook............. *SD-4*
Montrose (Township)—McCook... *SD-4*
Montrose (CDP)—Henrico *VA-2*
Montrose (Village)—Randolph *WV-2*
Montrose (Town)—Dane................ *WI-3*
Montrose County............................... *CO-4*
Montrose-Ghent (CDP)—
   Summit... *OH-3*
Montross (Town)—Westmoreland .. *VA-2*
Montserrat (Township)—
   Johnson... *MO-3*
Montvale (Borough)—Bergen........... *NJ-1*
Montverde (Town)—Lake *FL-2*
Mont Vernon (Town)—
   Hillsborough *NH-1*
Montville (Town)—New London ... *CT-1*
Montville (Town)—Waldo *ME-1*
Montville (Township)—Morris *NJ-1*
Montville (Township)—Geauga......*OH-3*
Montville (Township)—Medina....*OH-3*
Monument (Town)—El Paso.......... *CO-4*
Monument (Township)—Logan *KS-4*

Monument (City)—Grant *OR-4*
Monument Beach (CDP)—
   Barnstable *MA-1*
Monument Valley (CA) *Geog-4*
Moodus (CDP)—Middlesex *CT-1*
Moody (Municipality)—St. Clair....*AL-2*
Moody (Town)—McLennan............ *TX-2*
Moody Air Force Base (Military
   Facility)—Lowndes...................... *GA-2*
Moody County.................................. *SD-4*
Mooers (Town)—Clinton *NY-1*
Mooers (Village)—Clinton *NY-1*
Moon (Township)—Allegheny......... *PA-1*
Moonachie (Borough)—Bergen *NJ-1*
Moonachie (Township)—Polk........... *MO-3*
Moon Lake (Township)—
   Stutsman *ND-4*
Moonshine (Township)—Big
   Stone..*MN-3*
Moorcroft (Town)—Crook *WY-4*
Moord (Township)—Slope *ND-4*
Moore (City)—Butte........................ *ID-4*
Moore (Township)—Barber............ *KS-4*
Moore (Township)—Marion *KS-4*
Moore (Township)—Sanilac............ *MI-3*
Moore (Township)—Stevens *MN-3*
Moore (Township)—Oregon.......... *MO-3*
Moore (Township)—Shannon *MO-3*
Moore (Town)—Fergus................... *MT-4*
Moore (Township)—Ransom *ND-4*
Moore (City)—Cleveland *OK-2*
Moore (Township)—
   Northampton *PA-1*
Moore (Township)—Charles Mix .. *SD-4*
Moore (Township)—Lyman *SD-4*
Moore County *NC-2*
Moore County *TN-2*
Moore County *TX-2*
Moorefield (Town)—
   Independence *AR-2*
Moorefield (Village)—Frontier *NE-4*
Moorefield (Township)—Clark *OH-3*
Moorefield (Township)—
   Harrison *OH-3*
Moorefield (Town)—Hardy............ *WV-2*
Moore Haven (City)—Glades *FL-2*
Mooreland (Town)—Henry *IN-3*
Mooreland (Town)—Woodward..... *OK-2*
Mooresboro (City)—Cleveland *NC-2*
Moores Hill (Town)—Dearborn...... *IN-3*
Moores Mill (Division)—
   Madison... *AL-2*
Moores Prairie (Township)—
   Jefferson... *IL-3*
Moore Station (City)—
   Henderson..................................... *TX-2*
Moorestown (Township)—
   Burlington *NJ-1*
Mooresville (Town)—Limestone.....*AL-2*
Mooresville (Town)—Morgan *IN-3*
Mooresville (Township)—
   Livingston *MO-3*
Mooresville (Village)—
   Livingston *MO-3*
Mooresville (Town)—Iredell *NC-2*
Mooreton (City)—Richland *ND-4*
Mooreton (Township)—Richland .. *ND-4*
Moorhead (City)—Monona............. *IA-3*
Moorhead (City)—Clay *MN-3*
Moorhead (Township)—Clay *MN-3*
Moorhead (City)—Sunflower....... *MS-2*
Mooringsport (Town)—Caddo
   Parish *LA-2*
Moorland (City)—Webster *IA-3*
Moorland (City)—Jefferson *KY-2*

Moorland (Township)—
   Muskegon...................................... *MI-3*
Moorpark (City)—Ventura *CA-4*
Moose (Township)—Roseau.......... *MN-3*
Moose Creek (CDP)—Fairbanks North
   Star Borough *AK-4*
Moose Creek (Township)—
   Clearwater.................................... *MN-3*
Moosehead Lake (ME) *Geog-4*
Moose Lake (Township)—
   Beltrami.. *MN-3*
Moose Lake (City)—Carlton *MN-3*
Moose Lake (Township)—
   Carlton *MN-3*
Moose Lake (Township)—Cass..... *MN-3*
Moose Park (Township)—Itasca ... *MN-3*
Moose Pass (CDP)—Kenai Peninsula
   Borough.. *AK-4*
Moose River (Town)—Somerset ... *ME-1*
Moose River (Township)—
   Marshall *MN-3*
Moosic (Borough)—Lackawanna *PA-1*
Moosup (CDP)—Windham............. *CT-1*
Mora (City)—Kanabec *MN-3*
Mora (Pop. Place)—Mora *NM-4*
Mora County *NM-4*
Morada (CDP)—San Joaquin *CA-4*
Moraga Town (City)—Contra
   Costa *CA-4*
Moraine (Township)—Grand
   Forks *ND-4*
Moraine (City)—Montgomery *OH-3*
Moral (Township)—Shelby............. *IN-3*
Moran (City)—Allen........................ *KS-4*
Moran (Township)—Mackinac *MI-3*
Moran (Township)—Todd *MN-3*
Moran (Township)—Richland *ND-4*
Moran (City)—Shackelford *TX-2*
Moranville (Township)—Roseau .. *MN-3*
Moravia (City)—Appanoose *IA-3*
Moravia (Town)—Cayuga *NY-1*
Moravia (Village)—Cayuga *NY-1*
Morcom (Township)—St. Louis.... *MN-3*
Moreau (Township)—Cole *MO-3*
Moreau (Township)—Moniteau ...*MO-3*
Moreau (Township)—Morgan *MO-3*
Moreau (Town)—Saratoga *NY-1*
Moreau (Township)—Perkins *SD-4*
Moreauville (Village)—Avoyelles
   Parish *LA-2*
Morehead (City)—Rowan *KY-2*
Morehead City (Town)—Carteret .. *NC-2*
Morehouse (City)—New Madrid .. *MO-3*
Morehouse (Town)—Hamilton *NY-1*
Morehouse Parish *LA-2*
Moreland (Town)—Coweta *GA-2*
Moreland (Township)—Scott *MO-3*
Moreland (Township)—Lycoming .. *PA-1*
Moreland Hills (Village)—
   Cuyahoga *OH-3*
Morenci (CDP)—Greenlee............ *AZ-4*
Morenci (City)—Lenawee *MI-3*
Moreno Valley (City)—Riverside... *CA-4*
Moretown (Town)—Washington *VT-1*
Morgan (City)—Calhoun................ *GA-2*
Morgan (Township)—Coles............ *IL-3*
Morgan (Township)—Harrison *IN-3*
Morgan (Township)—Owen *IN-3*
Morgan (Township)—Porter *IN-3*
Morgan (Township)—Thomas *KS-4*
Morgan (City)—Redwood *MN-3*
Morgan (Township)—Redwood *MN-3*
Morgan (Township)—Mercer *MO-3*
Morgan (Township)—Traill............ *ND-4*
Morgan (Township)—Ashtabula ...*OH-3*

General Index — American Places Dictionary

Morgan (Township)—Butler............*OH-3*
Morgan (Township)—Gallia............*OH-3*
Morgan (Township)—Knox............*OH-3*
Morgan (Township)—Morgan............*OH-3*
Morgan (Township)—Scioto............*OH-3*
Morgan (Township)—Greene............*PA-1*
Morgan (Township)—Jones............*SD-4*
Morgan (City)—Bosque...............*TX-2*
Morgan (City)—Morgan................*UT-4*
Morgan (Town)—Orleans...............*VT-1*
Morgan (Town)—Oconto *WI-3*
Morgan City (City)—St. Mary
   Parish................................*LA-2*
Morgan City (Town)—Leflore........*MS-2*
Morgan County *AL-2*
Morgan County *CO-4*
Morgan County *GA-2*
Morgan County *IL-3*
Morgan County *IN-3*
Morgan County *KY-2*
Morgan County *MO-3*
Morgan County *OH-3*
Morgan County *TN-2*
Morgan County *UT-4*
Morgan County *WV-2*
Morganfield (City)—Union............*KY-2*
Morgan Hill (City)—Santa Clara... *CA-4*
Morgan's Point (City)—Harris *TX-2*
Morgan's Point Resort (City)—
   Bell..................................*TX-2*
Morganton (Town)—Fannin *GA-2*
Morganton (City)—Burke *NC-2*
Morgantown (Town)—Morgan.......*IN-3*
Morgantown (City)—Butler *KY-2*
Morgantown (City)—
   Monongalia *WV-2*
Morganville (City)—Clay *KS-4*
Morganza (Village)—Pointe Coupee
   Parish..................................*LA-2*
Moriah (Town)—Essex *NY-1*
Moriarty (City)—Torrance *NM-4*
Morken (Township)—Clay *MN-3*
Morlan (Township)—Graham........*KS-4*
Morland (City)—Graham............*KS-4*
Morley (City)—Jones *IA-3*
Morley (Village)—Mecosta............*MI-3*
Morley (Town)—Scott *MO-3*
Morley (Township)—Scott *MO-3*
Morningside (Town)—Prince
   George's *MD-1*
Morningside (Township)—Lyman . *SD-4*
Morning Sun (City)—Louisa.............*IA-3*
Moro (Town)—Lee *AR-2*
Moro (Township)—Madison *IL-3*
Moro (Pop. Place)—Aroostook..... *ME-1*
Moro (City)—Sherman................*OR-4*
Morocco (Town)—Newton *IN-3*
Morongo Reservation (CA) *IndRes-4*
Morongo Valley (CDP)—San
   Bernardino.........................*CA-4*
Moroni (City)—Sanpete *UT-4*
Morral (Village)—Marion *OH-3*
Morrice (Village)—Shiawassee.... *MI-3*
Morrill (City)—Brown................*KS-4*
Morrill (Township)—Brown.........*KS-4*
Morrill (Town)—Waldo *ME-1*
Morrill (Township)—Morrison ... *MN-3*
Morrill (Village)—Scotts Bluff *NE-4*
Morrill County *NE-4*
Morrilton (City)—Conway *AR-2*
Morris (Town)—Jefferson *AL-2*
Morris (Town)—Litchfield *CT-1*
Morris (City)—Grundy *IL-3*
Morris (Township)—Grundy *IL-3*
Morris (Township)—Sumner........*KS-4*
Morris (City)—Stevens..................*MN-3*
Morris (Township)—Stevens.........*MN-3*
Morris (Township)—Sullivan *MO-3*
Morris (Township)—Texas *MO-3*
Morris (Township)—Morris *NJ-1*
Morris (Town)—Otsego................*NY-1*
Morris (Village)—Otsego...............*NY-1*
Morris (Township)—Ramsey *ND-4*
Morris (Township)—Knox............*OH-3*
Morris (City)—Okmulgee..............*OK-2*
Morris (Township)—Clearfield *PA-1*
Morris (Township)—Greene *PA-1*
Morris (Township)—Huntingdon ... *PA-1*
Morris (Township)—Tioga *PA-1*
Morris (Township)—Washington ... *PA-1*
Morris (Town)—Shawano *WI-3*
Morris County......................*KS-4*
Morris County......................*NJ-1*
Morris County......................*TX-2*
Morrison (Town)—Jefferson *CO-4*
Morrison (Town)—Whiteside *IL-3*
Morrison (City)—Grundy *IA-3*
Morrison (Township)—Aitkin........*MN-3*
Morrison (City)—Gasconade *MO-3*
Morrison (Town)—Noble *OK-2*
Morrison (Town)—Warren *TN-2*
Morrison (Town)—Brown *WI-3*
Morrison Bluff (Town)—Logan *AR-2*
Morrison County *MN-3*
Morrisonville (Town)—Christian.... *IL-3*
Morrisonville (CDP)—Clinton *NY-1*
Morris Plains (Borough)—Morris...*NJ-1*
Morristown (Town)—Shelby *IN-3*
Morristown (City)—Rice *MN-3*
Morristown (Township)—Rice......*MN-3*
Morristown (Town)—Morris *NJ-1*
Morristown (Town)—St.
   Lawrence.........................*NY-1*
Morristown (Village)—St.
   Lawrence.........................*NY-1*
Morristown (Village)—Belmont......*OH-3*
Morristown (Town)—Corson *SD-4*
Morristown (City)—Hamblen *TN-2*
Morristown (Town)—Lamoille *VT-1*
Morrisville (Town)—Polk...............*MO-3*
Morrisville (Village)—Madison.......*NY-1*
Morrisville (Town)—Durham *NC-2*
Morrisville (Town)—Wake *NC-2*
Morrisville (Borough)—Bucks.........*PA-1*
Morrisville (CDP)—Greene *PA-1*
Morrisville (Village)—Lamoille *VT-1*
Morro Bay (City)—San Luis
   Obispo.............................*CA-4*
Morrow (City)—Clayton *GA-2*
Morrow (Township)—Adair..........*MO-3*
Morrow (Township)—Macon *MO-3*
Morrow (Village)—Warren *OH-3*
Morrow County *OH-3*
Morrow County *OR-4*
Morrowville (City)—Washington....*KS-4*
Morse (Village)—Acadia Parish....*LA-2*
Morse (Township)—Itasca.............*MN-3*
Morse (Township)—St. Louis *MN-3*
Morse (Town)—Ashland *WI-3*
Morse Bluff (Township)—
   Saunders.............................*NE-4*
Morse Bluff (Village)—Saunders ... *NE-4*
Morse Shores (CDP)—Lee..............*FL-2*
Morton (City)—Tazewell...............*IL-3*
Morton (Township)—Tazewell........*IL-3*
Morton (Township)—Ottawa *KS-4*
Morton (Township)—Pawnee........*KS-4*
Morton (Township)—Sedgwick......*KS-4*
Morton (Township)—Mecosta *MI-3*
Morton (City)—Renville *MN-3*
Morton (City)—Scott *MS-2*
Morton (Township)—Boyd *NE-4*
Morton (Township)—Knox............*NE-4*
Morton (Township)—Burleigh *ND-4*
Morton (Borough)—Delaware....... *PA-1*
Morton (Township)—Day *SD-4*
Morton (City)—Cochran *TX-2*
Morton (City)—Lewis *WA-4*
Morton County......................*KS-4*
Morton County......................*ND-4*
Morton Grove (City)—Cook........... *IL-3*
Mortons Gap (City)—Hopkins *KY-2*
Morven (City)—Brooks................*GA-2*
Morven (Town)—Anson *NC-2*
Mosby (City)—Clay *MO-3*
Moscow (City)—Latah *ID-4*
Moscow (City)—Stevens...............*KS-4*
Moscow (Township)—Stevens *KS-4*
Moscow (Town)—Somerset *ME-1*
Moscow (Township)—Hillsdale *MI-3*
Moscow (Township)—Freeborn *MN-3*
Moscow (Township)—Cavalier *ND-4*
Moscow (Village)—Clermont.........*OH-3*
Moscow (Borough)—Lackawanna ... *PA-1*
Moscow (Town)—Fayette *TN-2*
Moscow (Town)—Iowa *WI-3*
Moscow Mills (City)—Lincoln.......*MO-3*
Mosel (Town)—Sheboygan............*WI-3*
Moses Lake (City)—Grant *WA-4*
Moses Lake North (CDP)—
   Grant...............................*WA-4*
Mosheim (Town)—Greene *TN-2*
Mosher (Township)—Mellette........*SD-4*
Mosier (City)—Wasco *OR-4*
Mosinee (City)—Marathon *WI-3*
Mosinee (Town)—Marathon *WI-3*
Mosquero (Village)—Harding *NM-4*
Mosquero (Village)—San Miguel ..*NM-4*
Mosquito (Township)—Christian ... *IL-3*
Mosquito Lake (CDP)—Haines
   Borough............................*AK-4*
Moss Beach (CDP)—San Mateo....*CA-4*
Moss Bluff (CDP)—Calcasieu
   Parish................................*LA-2*
Moss Creek (Township)—
   Carroll...............................*MO-3*
Mosses (Municipality)—Lowndes ...*AL-2*
Moss Point (City)—Jackson *MS-2*
Mossyrock (City)—Lewis *WA-4*
Motley (City)—Cass *MN-3*
Motley (City)—Morrison *MN-3*
Motley (Township)—Morrison *MN-3*
Motley County.......................*TX-2*
Mott (City)—Hettinger.................*ND-4*
Mott (Township)—Hettinger.........*ND-4*
Mottville (Township)—St. Joseph.. *MI-3*
Moulton (City)—Lawrence *AL-2*
Moulton (City)—Appanoose *IA-3*
Moulton (Township)—Murray *MN-3*
Moulton (Township)—Auglaize *OH-3*
Moulton (Town)—Lavaca *TX-2*
Moultonborough (Town)—
   Carroll...............................*NH-1*
Moultrie (City)—Colquitt *GA-2*
Moultrie County...................... *IL-3*
Mound (Township)—Effingham *IL-3*
Mound (Township)—McDonough.. *IL-3*
Mound (Township)—Warren *IN-3*
Mound (Township)—McPherson...*KS-4*
Mound (Township)—Miami *KS-4*
Mound (Township)—Phillips.........*KS-4*
Mound (Village)—Madison
   Parish................................*LA-2*
Mound (City)—Hennepin *MN-3*
Mound (Township)—Rock *MN-3*

American Places Dictionary — General Index

Mound (Township)—Bates............ *MO-3*
Mound (Township)—Slope *ND-4*
Mound Bayou (City)—Bolivar........*MS-2*
Mound City (City)—Pulaski *IL-3*
Mound City (City)—Linn *KS-4*
Mound City (Township)—Linn *KS-4*
Mound City (City)—Holt................ *MO-3*
Mound City (Town)—Campbell *SD-4*
Mound Prairie (Township)—
   Houston.......................................*MN-3*
Moundridge (City)—McPherson......*KS-4*
Mounds (Town)—Pulaski *IL-3*
Mounds (Town)—Creek *OK-2*
Mound Station (Village)—Brown ... *IL-3*
Mounds View (City)—Ramsey *MN-3*
Moundsville (City)—Marshall....... *WV-2*
Mound Valley (City)—Labette........*KS-4*
Mound Valley (Township)—
   Labette *KS-4*
Moundville (Town)—Hale *AL-2*
Moundville (Town)—Tuscaloosa ...*AL-2*
Moundville (Town)—Vernon *MO-3*
Moundville (Township)—
   Vernon...*MO-3*
Moundville (Town)—Marquette *WI-3*
Mount Aetna (CDP)—
   Washington *MD-1*
Mountain (Township)—Saline *IL-3*
Mountain (Township)—Barry *MO-3*
Mountain (Township)—
   McDonald *MO-3*
Mountain (City)—Pembina............*ND-4*
Mountainair (Town)—Torrance *NM-4*
Mountainboro (Municipality)—
   Etowah *AL-2*
Mountain Brook (City)—
   Jefferson *AL-2*
Mountainburg (Town)—
   Crawford *AR-2*
Mountain City (Town)—Rabun..... *GA-2*
Mountain City (Town)—Johnson .. *TN-2*
Mountain City (Town)—Hays......... *TX-2*
Mountain Grove (City)—Texas *MO-3*
Mountain Grove (City)—Wright .. *MO-3*
Mountain Grove (Township)—
   Wright *MO-3*
Mountain Home (City)—Baxter *AR-2*
Mountain Home (City)—Elmore.... *ID-4*
Mountain Home (CDP)—
   Henderson *NC-2*
Mountainhome (CDP)—Monroe ... *PA-1*
Mountain Home Air Force Base
   (ID)... *Mil-4*
Mountain Home Air Force Base
   (Military Facility)—Elmore...........*ID-4*
Mountain Iron (City)—St. Louis .. *MN-3*
Mountain Lake (City)—
   Cottonwood *MN-3*
Mountain Lake (Township)—
   Cottonwood *MN-3*
Mountain Lake Park (Town)—
   Garrett *MD-1*
Mountain Lakes (Borough)—
   Morris *NJ-1*
Mountain Mesa (CDP)—Kern *CA-4*
Mountain Park (City)—Cherokee.. *GA-2*
Mountain Park (City)—Fulton *GA-2*
Mountain Park (CDP)—
   Gwinnett *GA-2*
Mountain Park (Town)—Kiowa *OK-2*
Mountain Pine (Town)—Garland .. *AR-2*
Mountainside (Borough)—Union ... *NJ-1*
Mountain View (City)—Stone *AR-2*
Mountain View (City)—Santa
   Clara *CA-4*

Mountain View (Town)—
   Jefferson *CO-4*
Mountain View (CDP)—Hawaii..... *HI-4*
Mountain View (City)—Howell *MO-3*
Mountain View (CDP)—
   Catawba *NC-2*
Mountain View (Town)—Kiowa.... *OK-2*
Mountain View (CDP)—
   Natrona *WY-4*
Mountain View (Town)—Uinta *WY-4*
Mountain View Acres (CDP)—San
   Bernardino *CA-4*
Mountain Village (City)—Wade
   Hampton Census Area *AK-4*
Mount Airy (Town)—Habersham .. *GA-2*
Mount Airy (Town)—Carroll *MD-1*
Mount Airy (Town)—Frederick *MD-1*
Mount Airy (City)—Surry.............. *NC-2*
Mount Angel (City)—Marion *OR-4*
Mount Arlington (Borough)—
   Morris *NJ-1*
Mount Auburn (Township)—
   Christian *IL-3*
Mount Auburn (Village)—
   Christian *IL-3*
Mount Auburn (Town)—Wayne *IN-3*
Mount Auburn (City)—Benton........*IA-3*
Mount Ayr (Town)—Newton *IN-3*
Mount Ayr (City)—Ringgold *IA-3*
Mount Ayr (Township)—Osborne... *KS-4*
Mount Blanchard (Village)—
   Hancock *OH-3*
Mount Calm (City)—Hill *TX-2*
Mount Calvary (Village)—Fond du
   Lac... *WI-3*
Mount Carbon (Borough)—
   Schuylkill *PA-1*
Mount Carmel (City)—Wabash *IL-3*
Mount Carmel (Town)—Franklin ... *IN-3*
Mount Carmel (Township)—
   Cavalier *ND-4*
Mount Carmel (CDP)—
   Clermont *OH-3*
Mount Carmel (Borough)—
   Northumberland *PA-1*
Mount Carmel (Township)—
   Northumberland *PA-1*
Mount Carmel (Town)—
   McCormick *SC-2*
Mount Carmel (Town)—Hawkins.. *TN-2*
Mount Carroll (City)—Carroll *IL-3*
Mount Carroll (Township)—
   Carroll *IL-3*
Mount Chase (Town)—
   Penobscot *ME-1*
Mount Clare (Village)—Macoupin . *IL-3*
Mount Clemens (City)—Macomb.. *MI-3*
Mount Cobb (CDP)—
   Lackawanna *PA-1*
Mount Cory (Village)—Hancock ...*OH-3*
Mount Crawford (Town)—
   Rockingham *VA-2*
Mount Crested Butte (Town)—
   Gunnison *CO-4*
Mount Croghan (Town)—
   Chesterfield *SC-2*
Mount Desert (Town)—Hancock .. *ME-1*
Mount Desert Island (ME) *Geog-4*
Mount Dora (City)—Lake.............. *FL-2*
Mount Eaton (Village)—Wayne *OH-3*
Mount Enterprise (City)—Rusk..... *TX-2*
Mount Ephraim (Borough)—
   Camden *NJ-1*
Mount Erie (Township)—Wayne *IL-3*
Mount Erie (Village)—Wayne........ *IL-3*

Mount Etna (Town)—Huntington .. *IN-3*
Mount Forest (Township)—Bay..... *MI-3*
Mount Gay-Shamrock (CDP)—
   Logan *WV-2*
Mount Gilead (Town)—
   Montgomery................................*NC-2*
Mount Gilead (Village)—
   Morrow *OH-3*
Mount Gretna (Borough)—
   Lebanon *PA-1*
Mount Haley (Township)—
   Midland *MI-3*
Mount Healthy (City)—
   Hamilton *OH-3*
Mount Healthy Heights (CDP)—
   Hamilton *OH-3*
Mount Holly (Township)—
   Burlington *NJ-1*
Mount Holly (City)—Gaston *NC-2*
Mount Holly (Town)—Rutland *VT-1*
Mount Holly Springs (Borough)—
   Cumberland *PA-1*
Mount Hood Village (CDP)—
   Clackamas *OR-4*
Mount Hope (Township)—
   McLean *IL-3*
Mount Hope (City)—Sedgwick *KS-4*
Mount Hope (Town)—Orange *NY-1*
Mount Hope (City)—Fayette *WV-2*
Mount Hope (Town)—Grant *WI-3*
Mount Hope (Village)—Grant *WI-3*
Mount Horeb (Village)—Dane....... *WI-3*
Mount Ida (City)—Montgomery.... *AR-2*
Mount Ida (Town)—Grant............. *WI-3*
Mount Ivy (CDP)—Rockland *NY-1*
Mount Jackson (Town)—
   Shenandoah *VA-2*
Mount Jewett (Borough)—
   McKean *PA-1*
Mount Joy (Township)—Adams ... *PA-1*
Mount Joy (Borough)—Lancaster... *PA-1*
Mount Joy (Township)—
   Lancaster *PA-1*
Mount Juliet (City)—Wilson *TN-2*
Mount Kisco (Village)—
   Westchester *NY-1*
Mountlake Terrace (City)—
   Snohomish *WA-4*
Mount Laurel (Township)—
   Burlington *NJ-1*
Mount Lebanon (Town)—Bienville
   Parish *LA-2*
Mount Lebanon (Township)—
   Allegheny.....................................*PA-1*
Mount Leonard (Town)—Saline ... *MO-3*
Mount Moriah (Town)—
   Harrison *MO-3*
Mount Morris (Town)—Ogle *IL-3*
Mount Morris (Township)—Ogle ... *IL-3*
Mount Morris (City)—Genesee *MI-3*
Mount Morris (Township)—
   Genesee *MI-3*
Mount Morris (Township)—
   Morrison *MN-3*
Mount Morris (Town)—
   Livingston *NY-1*
Mount Morris (Village)—
   Livingston *NY-1*
Mount Morris (Town)—
   Waushara..................................... *WI-3*
Mount Olive (Town)—Macoupin ... *IL-3*
Mount Olive (Township)—
   Macoupin *IL-3*
Mount Olive (Town)—
   Covington *MS-2*

Mount Olive (Township)—Morris.. *NJ-1*
Mount Olive (Town)—Duplin *NC-2*
Mount Olive (Town)—Wayne *NC-2*
Mount Oliver (Borough)—
  Allegheny.............................*PA-1*
Mount Olivet (City)—Robertson ... *KY-2*
Mount Olympus (CDP)—Salt
  Lake.....................................*UT-4*
Mount Orab (Village)—Brown......*OH-3*
Mount Penn (Borough)—Berks.......*PA-1*
Mount Pleasant (Town)—Izard......*AR-2*
Mount Pleasant (Township)—
  Whiteside *IL-3*
Mount Pleasant (Township)—
  Delaware *IN-3*
Mount Pleasant (City)—Henry.......*IA-3*
Mount Pleasant (Township)—
  Atchison *KS-4*
Mount Pleasant (Township)—
  Labette *KS-4*
Mount Pleasant (City)—Isabella.... *MI-3*
Mount Pleasant (Township)—
  Wabasha *MN-3*
Mount Pleasant (Township)—
  Bates...................................*MO-3*
Mount Pleasant (Township)—
  Cass....................................*MO-3*
Mount Pleasant (Township)—
  Lawrence.............................*MO-3*
Mount Pleasant (Township)—
  Scotland..............................*MO-3*
Mount Pleasant (Town)—
  Westchester *NY-1*
Mount Pleasant (Town)—
  Cabarrus..............................*NC-2*
Mount Pleasant (Township)—
  Jefferson *OH-3*
Mount Pleasant (Village)—
  Jefferson *OH-3*
Mount Pleasant (Township)—
  Adams *PA-1*
Mount Pleasant (Township)—
  Columbia *PA-1*
Mount Pleasant (Township)—
  Washington *PA-1*
Mount Pleasant (Township)—
  Wayne *PA-1*
Mount Pleasant (Borough)—
  Westmoreland *PA-1*
Mount Pleasant (Township)—
  Westmoreland *PA-1*
Mount Pleasant (Town)—
  Charleston *SC-2*
Mount Pleasant (Township)—
  Clark....................................*SD-4*
Mount Pleasant (Town)—Maury ... *TN-2*
Mount Pleasant (City)—Titus....... *TX-2*
Mount Pleasant (City)—Sanpete ... *UT-4*
Mount Pleasant (Town)—Green *WI-3*
Mount Pleasant (Town)—Racine ...*WI-3*
Mount Plymouth (CDP)—Lake......*FL-2*
Mount Pocono (Borough)—
  Monroe................................*PA-1*
Mount Prospect (City)—Cook *IL-3*
Mount Pulaski (Town)—Logan *IL-3*
Mount Pulaski (Township)—
  Logan *IL-3*
Mountrail (Township)—
  Mountrail *ND-4*
Mountrail County............................*ND-4*
Mount Rainier (City)—Prince
  George's..............................*MD-1*
Mount Repose (CDP)—
  Clermont *OH-3*

Mount Rose (Township)—
  Bottineau.............................*ND-4*
Mount Rushmore (Pop. Place)—
  Pennington..........................*SD-4*
Mount Shasta (City)—Siskiyou......*CA-4*
Mount Sinai (CDP)—Suffolk.........*NY-1*
Mount Sterling (Town)—Brown...... *IL-3*
Mount Sterling (Township)—
  Brown.................................. *IL-3*
Mount Sterling (City)—Van
  Buren....................................*IA-3*
Mount Sterling (City)—
  Montgomery........................*KY-2*
Mount Sterling (Village)—
  Madison *OH-3*
Mount Sterling (Village)—
  Crawford *WI-3*
Mount Summit (Town)—Henry...... *IN-3*
Mount Tabor (Town)—Rutland......*VT-1*
Mount Union (City)—Henry..........*IA-3*
Mount Union (Borough)—
  Huntingdon *PA-1*
Mount Vernon (Town)—Mobile *AL-2*
Mount Vernon (Town)—Faulkner..*AR-2*
Mount Vernon (City)—
  Montgomery........................*GA-2*
Mount Vernon (City)—Jefferson *IL-3*
Mount Vernon (Township)—
  Jefferson *IL-3*
Mount Vernon (City)—Posey.......... *IN-3*
Mount Vernon (City)—Linn *IA-3*
Mount Vernon (City)—
  Rockcastle...........................*KY-2*
Mount Vernon (Town)—
  Kennebec.............................*ME-1*
Mount Vernon (Township)—
  Winona................................*MN-3*
Mount Vernon (City)—
  Lawrence.............................*MO-3*
Mount Vernon (Township)—
  Lawrence.............................*MO-3*
Mount Vernon (City)—
  Westchester *NY-1*
Mount Vernon (City)—Knox *OH-3*
Mount Vernon (City)—Grant *OR-4*
Mount Vernon (City)—Davison *SD-4*
Mount Vernon (Township)—
  Davison...............................*SD-4*
Mount Vernon (Town)—Franklin..*TX-2*
Mount Vernon (City)—Skagit *WA-4*
Mount Victory (Village)—
  Hardin.................................*OH-3*
Mount View (Township)—
  Towner................................*ND-4*
Mountville (Borough)—Lancaster... *PA-1*
Mount Washington (City)—
  Bullitt.................................*KY-2*
Mount Washington (Town)—
  Berkshire.............................*MA-1*
Mount Wolf (Borough)—York *PA-1*
Mount Zion (City)—Carroll...........*GA-2*
Mount Zion (City)—Macon *IL-3*
Mount Zion (Township)—Macon ... *IL-3*
Mouse River (Township)—
  McHenry *ND-4*
Moville (City)—Woodbury............*IA-3*
Moweaqua (Village)—Christian *IL-3*
Moweaqua (Town)—Shelby *IL-3*
Moweaqua (Township)—Shelby..... *IL-3*
Mower County...............................*MN-3*
Mowrystown (Village)—
  Highland *OH-3*
Moxee (Town)—Yakima *WA-4*
Moyer (Township)—Swift *MN-3*
Moyie Springs (City)—Boundary....*ID-4*

Moylan (Township)—Marshall *MN-3*
Muckleshoot Reservation & Trust
  Lands (WA)............................*IndRes-4*
Muddy (Village)—Saline *IL-3*
Muddy (CDP)—Big Horn *MT-4*
Muddy Creek (Township)—Butler..*PA-1*
Mudgett (Township)—Mille
  Lacs....................................*MN-3*
Mud Lake (City)—Jefferson...............*ID-4*
Mud Lake (Pop. Place)—
  Marshall..............................*MN-3*
Mud Mountain Dam (WA)..........*Geog-4*
Mueller (Township)—Schoolcraft .. *MI-3*
Muenster (City)—Cooke *TX-2*
Muhlenberg (Township)—
  Pickaway *OH-3*
Muhlenberg (Township)—Berks.......*PA-1*
Muhlenberg County.....................*KY-2*
Muir (Village)—Ionia *MI-3*
Muir Woods (CA)..........................*Geog-4*
Mukilteo (City)—Snohomish *WA-4*
Mukwa (Town)—Waupaca *WI-3*
Mukwonago (Town)—Waukesha....*WI-3*
Mukwonago (Village)—
  Waukesha...........................*WI-3*
Mulberry (City)—Crawford............*AR-2*
Mulberry (City)—Polk....................*FL-2*
Mulberry (Town)—Clinton *IN-3*
Mulberry (Township)—Clay...........*KS-4*
Mulberry (Township)—Crawford....*KS-4*
Mulberry (Township)—Ellsworth....*KS-4*
Mulberry (CDP)—Wilkes *NC-2*
Mulberry (CDP)—Clermont *OH-3*
Mulberry (CDP)—Sumter *SC-2*
Mulberry Grove (Town)—Bond...... *IL-3*
Mulberry Grove (Township)—
  Bond.................................... *IL-3*
Muldraugh (City)—Hardin *KY-2*
Muldraugh (City)—Meade *KY-2*
Muldrow (Town)—Sequoyah *OK-2*
Mule Barn (Town)—Pawnee *OK-2*
Muleshoe (City)—Bailey *TX-2*
Mulga (Town)—Jefferson *AL-2*
Mulhall (Town)—Logan *OK-2*
Mullally (Township)—Harlan *NE-4*
Mullan (City)—Shoshone *ID-4*
Mullen (Township)—Boyd *NE-4*
Mullen (Village)—Hooker..............*NE-4*
Mullen (Township)—Jones *SD-4*
Mullens (City)—Wyoming *WV-2*
Mullett (Township)—Cheboygan ... *MI-3*
Mullica (Township)—Atlantic *NJ-1*
Mullica Hill (CDP)—Gloucester......*NJ-1*
Mulligan (Township)—Brown *MN-3*
Mulliken (Village)—Eaton *MI-3*
Mullin (Town)—Mills.....................*TX-2*
Mullins (City)—Marion...................*SC-2*
Mullinville (City)—Kiowa.............*KS-4*
Multnomah County......................*OR-4*
Multnomah Falls (OR) *Geog-4*
Mulvane (City)—Sedgwick.............*KS-4*
Mulvane (City)—Sumner *KS-4*
Munch (Township)—Pine *MN-3*
Muncie (Village)—Vermilion......... *IL-3*
Muncie (City)—Delaware *IN-3*
Muncy (Borough)—Lycoming *PA-1*
Muncy (Township)—Lycoming *PA-1*
Muncy Creek (Township)—
  Lycoming.............................*PA-1*
Munday (City)—Knox....................*TX-2*
Mundelein (City)—Lake................. *IL-3*
Munden (City)—Republic *KS-4*
Mundy (Township)—Genesee *MI-3*
Munford (Town)—Tipton *TN-2*
Munfordville (City)—Hart *KY-2*

Munhall (Borough)—Allegheny........ *PA-1*
Munich (City)—Cavalier............... *ND-4*
Munising (City)—Alger *MI-3*
Munising (Township)—Alger *MI-3*
Munnsville (Village)—Madison *NY-1*
Munro (Township)—Cheboygan.... *MI-3*
Munroe Falls (Village)—Summit ...*OH-3*
Munsey Park (Village)—Nassau *NY-1*
Munson (Township)—Henry.......... *IL-3*
Munson (Township)—Stearns *MN-3*
Munson (Township)—Geauga........*OH-3*
Munsons Corners (CDP)—
  Cortland *NY-1*
Munster (Town)—Lake *IN-3*
Munster (Township)—Eddy *ND-4*
Munster (Township)—Cambria *PA-1*
Murchison (Town)—Henderson..... *TX-2*
Murdo (City)—Jones................... *SD-4*
Murdock (Township)—Douglas...... *IL-3*
Murdock (Township)—Butler *KS-4*
Murdock (City)—Swift.................. *MN-3*
Murdock (Village)—Cass *NE-4*
Murfreesboro (City)—Pike *AR-2*
Murfreesboro (Town)—Hertford....*NC-2*
Murfreesboro (City)—Rutherford.. *TN-2*
Murphy (CDP)—Jefferson *MO-3*
Murphy (Town)—Cherokee........... *NC-2*
Murphy (City)—Collin *TX-2*
Murphys (CDP)—Calaveras........... *CA-4*
Murphysboro (City)—Jackson *IL-3*
Murphysboro (Township)—
  Jackson... *IL-3*
Murray (City)—Clarke *IA-3*
Murray (Township)—Marshall........ *KS-4*
Murray (City)—Calloway............... *KY-2*
Murray (Township)—Murray......... *MN-3*
Murray (Township)—Greene *MO-3*
Murray (Village)—Cass *NE-4*
Murray (Town)—Orleans *NY-1*
Murray (City)—Salt Lake............... *UT-4*
Murray City (Village)—Hocking...*OH-3*
Murray County *GA-2*
Murray County *MN-3*
Murray County *OK-2*
Murray Hill (City)—Jefferson......... *KY-2*
Murrayville (Village)—Morgan *IL-3*
Murrells Inlet (CDP)—
  Georgetown................................... *SC-2*
Murrieta (City)—Riverside *CA-4*
Murrieta Hot Springs (CDP)—
  Riverside *CA-4*
Murry (Town)—Rusk *WI-3*
Murrysville (Borough)—
  Westmoreland................................ *PA-1*
Murtaugh (City)—Twin Falls *ID-4*
Muscatine (City)—Muscatine *IA-3*
Muscatine County *IA-3*
Muscle Shoals (City)—Colbert.......*AL-2*
Muscoda (Town)—Grant................ *WI-3*
Muscoda (Village)—Grant.............. *WI-3*
Muscoda (Village)—Iowa *WI-3*
Muscogee County *GA-2*
Muscotah (City)—Atchison............*KS-4*
Muscoy (CDP)—San Bernardino ... *CA-4*
Muskego (Township)—Renville *ND-4*
Muskego (City)—Waukesha *WI-3*
Muskegon (City)—Muskegon......... *MI-3*
Muskegon (Township)—
  Muskegon.................................... *MI-3*
Muskegon County *MI-3*
Muskegon Heights (City)—
  Muskegon..................................... *MI-3*
Muskingum (Township)—
  Muskingum *OH-3*

Muskingum (Township)—
  Washington *OH-3*
Muskingum County............................*OH-3*
Muskogee (City)—Muskogee........... *OK-2*
Muskogee County *OK-2*
Musselfork (Township)—
  Chariton *MO-3*
Musselshell County *MT-4*
Mussey (Township)—St. Clair *MI-3*
Mussman (Township)—Jones *SD-4*
Mustang (City)—Canadian *OK-2*
Mustang (Town)—Navarro *TX-2*
Mustang Ridge (City)—Bastrop..... *TX-2*
Mustang Ridge (City)—Caldwell ... *TX-2*
Mustang Ridge (City)—Travis *TX-2*
Muttontown (Village)—Nassau *NY-1*
Mutual (Village)—Champaign *OH-3*
Mutual (Town)—Woodward........... *OK-2*
Myatt (Township)—Howell *MO-3*
Myers (Township)—Grundy *MO-3*
Myers Corner (CDP)—Dutchess.... *NY-1*
Myerstown (Borough)—Lebanon *PA-1*
Myersville (Town)—Frederick *MD-1*
Mylo (City)—Rolette.................... *ND-4*
Myron (Township)—Faulk *SD-4*
Myrtle (City)—Freeborn *MN-3*
Myrtle (Town)—Union.................. *MS-2*
Myrtle (Township)—Knox *MO-3*
Myrtle (Township)—Oregon *MO-3*
Myrtle (Township)—Custer *NE-4*
Myrtle (Township)—Mountrail......*ND-4*
Myrtle Beach (SC) *Geog-4*
Myrtle Beach (City)—Horry *SC-2*
Myrtle Creek (City)—Douglas *OR-4*
Myrtle Grove (CDP)—Escambia ...*FL-2*
Myrtle Grove (CDP)—New
  Hanover *NC-2*
Myrtle Point (City)—Coos *OR-4*
Myrtletown (CDP)—Humboldt *CA-4*
Myrtlewood (Town)—Marengo.......*AL-2*
Mystic (CDP)—New London.......... *CT-1*
Mystic (City)—Appanoose *IA-3*
Mystic Island (CDP)—Ocean.........*NJ-1*
Myton (City)—Duchesne *UT-4*
Naalehu (CDP)—Hawaii................. *HI-4*
Naausay (Township)—Kendall........ *IL-3*
Naches (Town)—Yakima................ *WA-4*
Nachusa (Township)—Lee *IL-3*
Nacogdoches (City)—
  Nacogdoches *TX-2*
Nacogdoches County *TX-2*
Nadeau (Township)—Menominee . *MI-3*
Nags Head (Town)—Dare..............*NC-2*
Nahant (Town)—Essex *MA-1*
Nahma (Township)—Delta *MI-3*
Nahunta (City)—Brantley *GA-2*
Naknek (CDP)—Bristol Bay
  Borough....................................... *AK-4*
Namakagon (Town)—Bayfield *WI-3*
Nambe (CDP)—Santa Fe *NM-4*
Nambe Pueblo & Trust Lands
  (NM) *IndRes-4*
Nameoki (Township)—Madison *IL-3*
Nampa (City)—Canyon.................. *ID-4*
Nanakuli (CDP)—Honolulu............. *HI-4*
Nance (Township)—Beadle *SD-4*
Nance County *NE-4*
Nansen (Township)—Richland *ND-4*
Nanticoke (Town)—Broome *NY-1*
Nanticoke (City)—Luzerne *PA-1*
Nantucket (Town)—Nantucket *MA-1*
Nantucket County and City............ *MA-1*
Nantucket Island (MA)................ *Geog-4*
Nanty-Glo (Borough)—Cambria..... *PA-1*
Nanuet (CDP)—Rockland *NY-1*

Napa (City)—Napa........................ *CA-4*
Napa County *CA-4*
Napakiak (City)—Bethel Census
  Area... *AK-4*
Napanoch (CDP)—Ulster *NY-1*
Napaskiak (City)—Bethel Census
  Area... *AK-4*
Napavine (City)—Lewis *WA-4*
Naper (Village)—Boyd *NE-4*
Naperville (City)—DuPage *IL-3*
Naperville (Township)—DuPage *IL-3*
Naperville (City)—Will *IL-3*
Napier (Township)—Bedford.......... *PA-1*
Napier Field (Town)—Dale............*AL-2*
Napili-Honokowai (CDP)—Maui ... *HI-4*
Naplate (Village)—La Salle *IL-3*
Naples (City)—Collier.....................*FL-2*
Naples (Town)—Scott................... *IL-3*
Naples (Town)—Cumberland........ *ME-1*
Naples (Town)—Ontario *NY-1*
Naples (Village)—Ontario *NY-1*
Naples (Town)—Clark................... *SD-4*
Naples (Town)—Morris.................. *TX-2*
Naples (City)—Uintah *UT-4*
Naples (Town)—Buffalo *WI-3*
Naples Manor (CDP)—Collier.......*FL-2*
Naples Park (CDP)—Collier *FL-2*
Napoleon (Town)—Ripley............. *IN-3*
Napoleon (Township)—Jackson..... *MI-3*
Napoleon (City)—Lafayette *MO-3*
Napoleon (City)—Logan *ND-4*
Napoleon (City)—Henry................*OH-3*
Napoleon (Township)—Henry *OH-3*
Napoleonville (Town)—Assumption
  Parish *LA-2*
Napoli (Town)—Cattaraugus *NY-1*
Naponee (Village)—Franklin *NE-4*
Nappanee (City)—Elkhart............. *IN-3*
Nappanee (City)—Kosciusko *IN-3*
Naranja (CDP)—Dade *FL-2*
Narberth (Borough)—
  Montgomery..................................*PA-1*
Nardin (Town)—Kay..................... *OK-2*
Narka (City)—Republic *KS-4*
Narragansett (Town)—
  Washington *RI-1*
Narragansett Bay (RI)................ *Geog-4*
Narragansett Pier (CDP)—
  Washington *RI-1*
Narragansett Tribe (RI) *IndRes-4*
Narrows (Township)—Macon *MO-3*
Narrows (Town)—Giles................. *VA-2*
Naschitti (CDP)—San Juan *NM-4*
Nasewaupee (Town)—Door *WI-3*
Nash (Township)—Nelson *ND-4*
Nash (Town)—Grant *OK-2*
Nash (City)—Bowie....................... *TX-2*
Nash County *NC-2*
Nashotah (Village)—Waukesha...... *WI-3*
Nashua (Township)—Ogle *IL-3*
Nashua (City)—Chickasaw *IA-3*
Nashua (City)—Wilkin................... *MN-3*
Nashua (Town)—Valley................. *MT-4*
Nashua (City)—Hillsborough......... *NH-1*
Nashville (City)—Howard.............. *AR-2*
Nashville (City)—Berrien *GA-2*
Nashville (Town)—Washington....... *IL-3*
Nashville (Township)—
  Washington *IL-3*
Nashville (Town)—Brown *IN-3*
Nashville (City)—Kingman *KS-4*
Nashville (Pop. Place)—
  Aroostook *ME-1*
Nashville (Village)—Barry *MI-3*
Nashville (Township)—Martin...... *MN-3*

Nashville (Township)—Barton......*MO-3*
Nashville (Town)—Nash *NC-2*
Nashville (Village)—Holmes..........*OH-3*
Nashville (Town)—Forest...............*WI-3*
Nashville-Davidson (Consol. City)—
    Davidson...*TN-2*
Nashwauk (City)—Itasca...............*MN-3*
Nashwauk (Township)—Itasca......*MN-3*
Nason (City)—Jefferson...................*IL-3*
Nassau (City)—Lac qui Parle *MN-3*
Nassau (Town)—Rensselaer...........*NY-1*
Nassau (Village)—Rensselaer.........*NY-1*
Nassau Bay (City)—Harris..............*TX-2*
Nassau County *FL-2*
Nassau County *NY-1*
Nassau Village-Ratliff (CDP)—
    Nassau..*FL-2*
Nassawadox (Town)—
    Northampton *VA-2*
Natalbany (CDP)—Tangipahoa
    Parish *LA-2*
Natalia (City)—Medina..................*TX-2*
Natchez (Village)—Natchitoches
    Parish *LA-2*
Natchez (City)—Adams *MS-2*
Natchez Trace (RI) *Geog-4*
Natchitoches (City)—Natchitoches
    Parish *LA-2*
Natchitoches Parish...........................*LA-2*
Natick (Town)—Middlesex *MA-1*
National City (City)—San Diego... *CA-4*
National City (Village)—St. Clair... *IL-3*
National Naval Medical Center
    (MD) *Mil-4*
National Park (Borough)—
    Gloucester *NJ-1*
National Road *or* National Old
    Trail Road (RI)..........................*Geog-4*
Natoma (City)—Osborne *KS-4*
Natoma (Township)—Osborne......*KS-4*
Natrona County *WY-4*
Naturita (Town)—Montrose...........*CO-4*
Naugatuck (Town, Borough)—New
    Haven...*CT-1*
Naughton (Township)—Burleigh ...*ND-4*
Naukati Bay (CDP)—Prince of
    Wales-Outer Ketchikan Census
    Area...*AK-4*
Nauvoo (Town)—Walker................*AL-2*
Nauvoo (Town)—Winston..............*AL-2*
Nauvoo (Town)—Hancock............. *IL-3*
Nauvoo (Township)—Hancock...... *IL-3*
Navajo (CDP)—McKinley *NM-4*
Navajo County *AZ-4*
Navajo Reservation and Trust Lands
    (AZ)...*IndRes-4*
Naval Academy (Mil. facil.)—Anne
    Arundel...*MD-1*
Naval Air Engineering Center
    (NJ) *Mil-4*
Naval Air Station (TX) *Mil-4*
Naval Air Test Center, Patuxent River
    (MD) *Mil-4*
Naval Construction Battalion
    Center, Pt. Hueneme (CA)........... *Mil-4*
Naval Education and Training Center
    (RI) *Mil-4*
Naval Postgraduate School (CA)....*Mil-4*
Naval Research Laboratory (DC) ..*Mil-4*
Naval Station, Guam (am)............*Mil-4*
Naval Surface Weapons Center
    (VA) *Mil-4*
Navarino (Town)—Shawano *WI-3*
Navarre (Village)—Stark *OH-3*
Navarro (Town)—Navarro..............*TX-2*

Navarro County *TX-2*
Navasota (City)—Grimes.................*TX-2*
Navassa (Town)—Brunswick *NC-2*
Navy Yard City (CDP)—Kitsap *WA-4*
Naylor (Town)—Lowndes *GA-2*
Naylor (City)—Ripley *MO-3*
Naytahwaush (CDP)—
    Mahnomen......................................*MN-3*
Nazareth (Borough)—
    Northampton *PA-1*
Nazareth (City)—Castro..................*TX-2*
Neah Bay (CDP)—Clallam *WA-4*
Near Islands (AK).........................*Geog-4*
Neave (Township)—Darke...............*OH-3*
Nebish (Township)—Beltrami......*MN-3*
Nebo (Town)—Pike *IL-3*
Nebo (City)—Hopkins *KY-2*
Nebo (Township)—Bowman *ND-4*
Nebo Center (Military Facility)—San
    Bernardino..*CA-4*
Nebraska (Township)—Livingston.. *IL-3*
Nebraska City (City)—Otoe...........*NE-4*
Necedah (Town)—Juneau *WI-3*
Necedah (Village)—Juneau *WI-3*
Neche (City)—Pembina...................*ND-4*
Neche (Township)—Pembina.........*ND-4*
Neck City (City)—Jasper *MO-3*
Nectar (Municipality)—Blount *AL-2*
Nederland (Town)—Boulder *CO-4*
Nederland (Town)—Jefferson *TX-2*
Nedrose (Township)—Ward *ND-4*
Needham (Municipality)—
    Choctaw...*AL-2*
Needham (Township)—Johnson ... *IN-3*
Needham (Town)—Norfolk...........*MA-1*
Needles (City)—San Bernardino ...*CA-4*
Needville (City)—Fort Bend *TX-2*
Neely (Township)—Butler *MO-3*
Neelyville (City)—Butler *MO-3*
Neenah (City)—Winnebago *WI-3*
Neenah (Town)—Winnebago *WI-3*
Neeses (Town)—Orangeburg..........*SC-2*
Neffs (CDP)—Belmont *OH-3*
Negaunee (City)—Marquette *MI-3*
Negaunee (Township)—
    Marquette..*MI-3*
Nehalem (Town)—Tillamook........*OR-4*
Nehawka (Village)—Cass *NE-4*
Neihart (Town)—Cascade *MT-4*
Neillsville (City)—Clark *WI-3*
Nekimi (Town)—Winnebago *WI-3*
Nekoma (City)—Cavalier................*ND-4*
Nekoma (Township)—Cavalier......*ND-4*
Nekoosa (City)—Wood.....................*WI-3*
Neligh (City)—Antelope..................*NE-4*
Neligh (Township)—Antelope.........*NE-4*
Neligh (Township)—Cuming..........*NE-4*
Nellie (Village)—Coshocton............*OH-3*
Nellieburg (CDP)—Lauderdale *MS-2*
Nellis Air Force Base (NV) *Mil-4*
Nellis Air Force Base (Military
    Facility)—Clark *NV-4*
Nelliston (Village)—Montgomery.. *NY-1*
Nelson (City)—Cherokee *GA-2*
Nelson (City)—Pickens *GA-2*
Nelson (Township)—Lee................... *IL-3*
Nelson (Village)—Lee........................ *IL-3*
Nelson (Township)—Cloud *KS-4*
Nelson (Township)—Kent *MI-3*
Nelson (City)—Douglas *MN-3*
Nelson (Township)—Watonwan ...*MN-3*
Nelson (City)—Saline *MO-3*
Nelson (City)—Nuckolls *NE-4*
Nelson (Town)—Cheshire *NH-1*
Nelson (Town)—Madison *NY-1*

Nelson (Township)—Barnes............*ND-4*
Nelson (Township)—Portage..........*OH-3*
Nelson (Township)—Tioga.............*PA-1*
Nelson (Town)—Buffalo..................*WI-3*
Nelson (Village)—Buffalo *WI-3*
Nelson County *KY-2*
Nelson County *ND-4*
Nelson County *VA-2*
Nelson Lagoon (CDP)—Aleutians East
    Borough..*AK-4*
Nelson Park (Township)—
    Marshall...*MN-3*
Nelsonville (Village)—Putnam.......*NY-1*
Nelsonville (City)—Athens..............*OH-3*
Nelsonville (Village)—Portage *WI-3*
Nemacolin (CDP)—Greene *PA-1*
Nemaha (City)—Sac.......................... *IA-3*
Nemaha (Township)—Nemaha......*KS-4*
Nemaha (Township)—Gage *NE-4*
Nemaha (Village)—Nemaha *NE-4*
Nemaha County *KS-4*
Nemaha County *NE-4*
Nenana (City)—Yukon-Koyukuk
    Census Area *AK-4*
Nenzel (Village)—Cherry *NE-4*
Neodesha (City)—Wilson *KS-4*
Neodesha (Township)—Wilson......*KS-4*
Neoga (City)—Cumberland............. *IL-3*
Neoga (Township)—Cumberland... *IL-3*
Neola (City)—Pottawattamie........... *IA-3*
Neola (CDP)—Duchesne *UT-4*
Neopit (CDP)—Menominee *WI-3*
Neosho (Township)—Cherokee......*KS-4*
Neosho (Township)—Coffey *KS-4*
Neosho (Township)—Labette.........*KS-4*
Neosho (City)—Newton *MO-3*
Neosho (Township)—Newton *MO-3*
Neosho (Village)—Dodge *WI-3*
Neosho County *KS-4*
Neosho Falls (City)—Woodson *KS-4*
Neosho Falls (Township)—
    Woodson *KS-4*
Neosho Rapids (City)—Lyon *KS-4*
Nepeuskun (Town)—Winnebago ... *WI-3*
Nephi (City)—Juab *UT-4*
Neponset (Township)—Bureau *IL-3*
Neponset (Village)—Bureau............ *IL-3*
Neptune (Township)—Monmouth .*NJ-1*
Neptune Beach (City)—Duval *FL-2*
Neptune City (Borough)—
    Monmouth *NJ-1*
Nereson (Township)—Roseau *MN-3*
Nerstrand (City)—Rice *MN-3*
Nesbit (Township)—Polk *MN-3*
Nesbitt (Town)—Harrison *TX-2*
Nesconset (CDP)—Suffolk.............*NY-1*
Nescopeck (Borough)—Luzerne......*PA-1*
Nescopeck (Township)—Luzerne....*PA-1*
Neshannock (Township)—
    Lawrence..*PA-1*
Nesheim (Township)—Nelson *ND-4*
Neshkoro (Town)—Marquette *WI-3*
Neshkoro (Village)—Marquette *WI-3*
Neshoba County *MS-2*
Nespelem (Town)—Okanogan *WA-4*
Nespelem Community (CDP)—
    Okanogan *WA-4*
Nesquehoning (Borough)—
    Carbon *PA-1*
Ness (Township)—St. Louis *MN-3*
Ness (Township)—Pierce *ND-4*
Ness City (City)—Ness....................*KS-4*
Ness County *KS-4*
Nessel (Township)—Chisago *MN-3*

Nesson Valley (Pop. Place)—
  Williams ND-4
Nester (Township)—Roscommon .. MI-3
Netawaka (City)—Jackson KS-4
Netawaka (Township)—Jackson KS-4
Netcong (Borough)—Morris NJ-1
Nether Providence (Township)—
  Delaware PA-1
Nett Lake (Pop. Place)—
  Koochiching MN-3
Nett Lake (Pop. Place)—St.
  Louis MN-3
Nettle Creek (Township)—
  Grundy IL-3
Nettleton (Town)—Lee MS-2
Nettleton (Town)—Monroe MS-2
Neuchatel (Township)—Nemaha KS-4
Neuse Forest (CDP)—Craven NC-2
Neva (Town)—Langlade WI-3
Nevada (Township)—Livingston IL-3
Nevada (City)—Story IA-3
Nevada (Township)—Ness KS-4
Nevada (Township)—Mower MN-3
Nevada (City)—Vernon MO-3
Nevada (Village)—Wyandot OH-3
Nevada (City)—Collin TX-2
Nevada City (City)—Nevada CA-4
Nevada County AR-2
Nevada County CA-4
Neversink (Town)—Sullivan NY-1
Neville (Village)—Clermont OH-3
Neville (Township)—Allegheny PA-1
Nevins (Township)—Vigo IN-3
Nevis (City)—Hubbard MN-3
Nevis (Township)—Hubbard MN-3
New Albany (City)—Floyd IN-3
New Albany (Township)—Floyd IN-3
New Albany (City)—Wilson KS-4
New Albany (City)—Union MS-2
New Albany (Village)—Franklin OH-3
New Albany (Borough)—
  Bradford PA-1
New Albin (City)—Allamakee IA-3
New Albion (Town)—
  Cattaraugus NY-1
New Alexandria (Village)—
  Jefferson OH-3
New Alexandria (Borough)—
  Westmoreland PA-1
New Alluwe (Town)—Nowata OK-2
New Amsterdam (Town)—
  Harrison IN-3
Newark (City)—Independence AR-2
Newark (City)—Alameda CA-4
Newark (City)—New Castle DE-1
Newark (Village)—Kendall IL-3
Newark (Township)—Wilson KS-4
Newark (Township)—Gratiot MI-3
Newark (Town)—Knox MO-3
Newark (Township)—Kearney NE-4
Newark (City)—Essex NJ-1
Newark (Village)—Wayne NY-1
Newark (City)—Licking OH-3
Newark (Township)—Licking OH-3
Newark (Township)—Marshall SD-4
Newark (City)—Tarrant TX-2
Newark (City)—Wise TX-2
Newark (Town)—Caledonia VT-1
Newark (Town)—Rock WI-3
Newark Valley (Town)—Tioga NY-1
Newark Valley (Village)—Tioga NY-1
New Ashford (Town)—Berkshire MA-1
New Athens (Town)—St. Clair IL-3
New Athens (Township)—St.
  Clair IL-3

New Athens (Village)—Harrison ... OH-3
New Auburn (City)—Sibley MN-3
New Auburn (Township)—
  Sibley MN-3
New Auburn (Village)—Barron WI-3
New Auburn (Village)—
  Chippewa WI-3
New Augusta (Town)—Perry MS-2
New Avon (Township)—
  Redwood MN-3
Newaygo (City)—Newaygo MI-3
Newaygo County MI-3
New Baden (Town)—Clinton IL-3
New Baden (Town)—St. Clair IL-3
New Baltimore (City)—Macomb ... MI-3
New Baltimore (Town)—Greene ... NY-1
New Baltimore (Borough)—
  Somerset PA-1
New Bavaria (Village)—Henry OH-3
New Beaver (Borough)—
  Lawrence PA-1
New Bedford (Village)—Bureau IL-3
New Bedford (City)—Bristol MA-1
Newberg (Township)—Cass MI-3
Newberg (City)—Yamhill OR-4
New Berlin (Township)—
  Sangamon IL-3
New Berlin (Village)—Sangamon ... IL-3
New Berlin (Town)—Chenango NY-1
New Berlin (Village)—Chenango ... NY-1
New Berlin (Borough)—Union PA-1
New Berlin (City)—Guadalupe TX-2
New Berlin (City)—Waukesha WI-3
Newbern (Town)—Hale AL-2
Newbern (Township)—Dickinson ... KS-4
New Bern (City)—Craven NC-2
Newbern (Town)—Dyer TN-2
Newberry (City)—Alachua FL-2
Newberry (Town)—Greene IN-3
Newberry (Village)—Luce MI-3
Newberry (Township)—Miami OH-3
Newberry (Township)—York PA-1
Newberry (Town)—Newberry SC-2
Newberry County SC-2
New Bethlehem (Borough)—
  Clarion PA-1
New Bloomfield (City)—
  Callaway MO-3
New Bloomfield See **Bloomfield**—
  Perry PA-1
New Bloomington (Village)—
  Marion OH-3
Newbold (Town)—Oneida WI-3
Newborg (Township)—Bottineau ... ND-4
Newborn (Town)—Newton GA-2
New Boston (Town)—Mercer IL-3
New Boston (Township)—Mercer ... IL-3
New Boston (Town)—
  Hillsborough NH-1
New Boston (Village)—Scioto OH-3
New Boston (Town)—Bowie TX-2
New Braintree (Town)—
  Worcester MA-1
New Braunfels (City)—Comal TX-2
New Braunfels (City)—
  Guadalupe TX-2
Newbre (Township)—Ramsey ND-4
New Bremen (Town)—Lewis NY-1
New Bremen (Village)—Auglaize ... OH-3
New Brighton (City)—Ramsey MN-3
New Brighton (Borough)—Beaver .. PA-1
New Britain (City)—Hartford CT-1
New Britain (Borough)—Bucks PA-1
New Britain (Township)—Bucks PA-1
New Brockton (Town)—Coffee AL-2

New Brunswick (City)—
  Middlesex NJ-1
New Buffalo (City)—Berrien MI-3
New Buffalo (Township)—
  Berrien MI-3
New Buffalo (Borough)—Perry PA-1
Newburg (Township)—Pike IL-3
Newburg (CDP)—Jefferson KY-2
Newburg (Township)—Fillmore MN-3
Newburg (City)—Phelps MO-3
Newburg (City)—Bottineau ND-4
Newburg (Borough)—Clearfield PA-1
Newburg (Borough)—
  Cumberland PA-1
Newburg (Town)—Preston WV-2
Newburg (Village)—Ozaukee WI-3
Newburg (Village)—Washington ... WI-3
Newburgh (Town)—Warrick IN-3
Newburgh (Town)—Penobscot ME-1
Newburgh (City)—Orange NY-1
Newburgh (Town)—Orange NY-1
Newburgh (Township)—Steele ND-4
Newburgh Heights (Village)—
  Cuyahoga OH-3
New Burnside (Village)—Johnson .. IL-3
Newbury (Township)—Lagrange ... IN-3
Newbury (Township)—
  Wabaunsee KS-4
Newbury (Town)—Essex MA-1
Newbury (Town)—Merrimack NH-1
Newbury (Township)—Stutsman ... ND-4
Newbury (Township)—Geauga OH-3
Newbury (Town)—Orange VT-1
Newbury (Village)—Orange VT-1
Newburyport (Town)—Essex MA-1
New Cambria (City)—Saline KS-4
New Cambria (Town)—Macon MO-3
New Canaan (Town)—Fairfield CT-1
New Canada (Town)—
  Aroostook ME-1
New Canton (Town)—Pike IL-3
New Carlisle (Town)—St. Joseph ... IN-3
New Carlisle (City)—Clark OH-3
New Carrollton (City)—Prince
  George's MD-1
New Cassel (CDP)—Nassau NY-1
New Castle (Town)—Garfield CO-4
New Castle (City)—New Castle DE-1
Newcastle (Township)—Fulton IN-3
New Castle (City)—Henry IN-3
New Castle (City)—Henry KY-2
Newcastle (Town)—Lincoln ME-1
Newcastle (Township)—Dixon NE-4
Newcastle (Village)—Dixon NE-4
New Castle (Town)—
  Rockingham NH-1
New Castle (Town)—Westchester .. NY-1
Newcastle (Township)—
  Coshocton OH-3
Newcastle (Town)—McClain OK-2
New Castle (City)—Lawrence PA-1
New Castle (Township)—
  Schuylkill PA-1
Newcastle (City)—Young TX-2
New Castle (Town)—Craig VA-2
Newcastle (City)—Weston WY-4
New Castle County DE-1
New Centerville (Borough)—
  Somerset PA-1
New Chapel Hill (City)—Smith TX-2
New Chester (Town)—Adams WI-3
New Chicago (Town)—Lake IN-3
New City (CDP)—Rockland NY-1
New City (Township)—Towner ND-4

New Columbus (Borough)—Luzerne PA-1
Newcomb (Township)—Champaign IL-3
Newcomb (CDP)—San Juan NM-4
Newcomb (Town)—Essex NY-1
Newcomerstown (Village)—Tuscarawas OH-3
New Concord (Village)—Muskingum OH-3
New Cordell (City)—Washita OK-2
New Cumberland (Borough)—Cumberland PA-1
New Cumberland (City)—Hancock WV-2
Newdale (City)—Fremont ID-4
New Deal (Town)—Lubbock TX-2
New Denmark (Town)—Brown WI-3
New Diggings (Town)—Lafayette .. WI-3
New Dosey (Township)—Pine MN-3
New Douglas (Township)—Madison IL-3
New Douglas (Village)—Madison ... IL-3
New Durham (Township)—La Porte IN-3
New Durham (Town)—Strafford ... NH-1
New Eagle (Borough)—Washington PA-1
New Effington (Town)—Roberts ... SD-4
New Egypt (CDP)—Ocean NJ-1
Newell (Township)—Vermilion IL-3
Newell (City)—Buena Vista IA-3
Newell (Borough)—Fayette PA-1
Newell (City)—Butte SD-4
Newell (CDP)—Hancock WV-2
New Ellenton (Town)—Aiken SC-2
Newellton (Town)—Tensas Parish LA-2
New England (City)—Hettinger ND-4
New England (Township)—Hettinger ND-4
New Era (Village)—Oceana MI-3
New Fairfield (Town)—Fairfield CT-1
Newfane (Town)—Niagara NY-1
Newfane (Town)—Windham VT-1
Newfane (Village)—Windham VT-1
Newfield (Town)—York ME-1
Newfield (Township)—Oceana MI-3
Newfield (Borough)—Gloucester ... NJ-1
Newfield (Town)—Tompkins NY-1
Newfield Hamlet (CDP)—Tompkins NY-1
Newfields (Town)—Rockingham ... NH-1
New Florence (City)—Montgomery MO-3
New Florence (Borough)—Westmoreland PA-1
Newfolden (City)—Marshall MN-3
New Folden (Township)—Marshall MN-3
New Franklin (City)—Howard MO-3
New Freedom (Borough)—York PA-1
New Galilee (Borough)—Beaver PA-1
New Garden (Township)—Wayne .. IN-3
New Garden (Township)—Chester PA-1
New Germantown (Township)—Sheridan ND-4
New Germany (City)—Carver MN-3
New Glarus (Town)—Green WI-3
New Glarus (Village)—Green WI-3
New Gloucester (Town)—Cumberland ME-1
New Gottland (Township)—McPherson KS-4

New Grand Chain (Village)—Pulaski IL-3
Newhalen (City)—Lake and Peninsula Borough AK-4
Newhall (City)—Benton IA-3
New Hampton (City)—Chickasaw ... IA-3
New Hampton (City)—Harrison .. MO-3
New Hampton (Town)—Belknap .. NH-1
New Hanover (Township)—Burlington NJ-1
New Hanover (Township)—Montgomery PA-1
New Hanover County NC-2
New Harmony (Town)—Posey IN-3
New Harmony (Town)—Washington UT-4
New Hartford (Town)—Litchfield CT-1
New Hartford (City)—Butler IA-3
New Hartford (Township)—Winona MN-3
New Hartford (Town)—Oneida NY-1
New Hartford (Village)—Oneida ... NY-1
New Haven (City)—New Haven ... CT-1
New Haven (Township)—Gallatin .. IL-3
New Haven (Village)—Gallatin IL-3
New Haven (City)—Allen IN-3
New Haven (City)—Nelson KY-2
New Haven (Township)—Gratiot .. MI-3
New Haven (Village)—Macomb ... MI-3
New Haven (Township)—Shiawassee MI-3
New Haven (Township)—Olmsted MN-3
New Haven (City)—Franklin MO-3
New Haven (Township)—Franklin MO-3
New Haven (Town)—Oswego NY-1
New Haven (Township)—Huron ... OH-3
New Haven (Town)—Addison VT-1
New Haven (Town)—Mason WV-2
New Haven (Town)—Adams WI-3
New Haven (Town)—Dunn WI-3
New Haven County CT-1
New Hebron (Village)—Lawrence MS-2
New Hempstead (Village)—Rockland NY-1
New Holland (Village)—Logan IL-3
New Holland (Village)—Fayette OH-3
New Holland (Village)—Pickaway OH-3
New Holland (Borough)—Lancaster PA-1
New Holstein (City)—Calumet WI-3
New Holstein (Town)—Calumet WI-3
New Home (Township)—Bates ... MO-3
New Home (Township)—Williams ND-4
New Home (City)—Lynn TX-2
New Hope (Town)—Madison AL-2
New Hope (City)—Hennepin MN-3
New Hope (CDP)—Lowndes MS-2
New Hope (CDP)—Wake NC-2
New Hope (CDP)—Wayne NC-2
New Hope (Borough)—Bucks PA-1
New Hope (Township)—Brown SD-4
New Hope (City)—Marion TN-2
New Hope (Town)—Collin TX-2
New Hope (Town)—Portage WI-3
New Houlka (Town)—Chickasaw ... MS-2
New Hudson (Town)—Allegany NY-1
New Hyde Park (Village)—Nassau NY-1
New Iberia (City)—Iberia Parish LA-2

New Independence (Township)—St. Louis MN-3
Newington (Town)—Hartford CT-1
Newington (Town)—Screven GA-2
Newington (Town)—Rockingham NH-1
Newington (CDP)—Fairfax VA-2
New Ipswich (Town)—Hillsborough NH-1
New Jasper (Township)—Greene ... OH-3
New Johnsonville (City)—Humphreys TN-2
New Kensington (City)—Westmoreland PA-1
New Kent County VA-2
New Kingman-Butler (CDP)—Mohave AZ-4
Newkirk (Township)—Lake MI-3
Newkirk (City)—Kay OK-2
New Knoxville (Village)—Auglaize OH-3
Newland (Town)—Avery NC-2
Newland (Township)—Ramsey ND-4
New Lebanon (Town)—Columbia NY-1
New Lebanon (Village)—Montgomery OH-3
New Lebanon (Borough)—Mercer .. PA-1
New Leipzig (City)—Grant ND-4
New Lenox (City)—Will IL-3
New Lenox (Township)—Will IL-3
New Lexington (Village)—Perry ... OH-3
New Liberty (City)—Scott IA-3
New Limerick (Town)—Aroostook ME-1
Newlin (Township)—Chester PA-1
New Lisbon (Township)—Stoddard MO-3
New Lisbon (Town)—Otsego NY-1
New Lisbon (City)—Juneau WI-3
Newllano (Village)—Vernon Parish LA-2
New London (City)—New London CT-1
New London (City)—Henry IA-3
New London (City)—Kandiyohi ... MN-3
New London (Township)—Kandiyohi MN-3
New London (City)—Ralls MO-3
New London (Town)—Merrimack NH-1
New London (Town)—Stanly NC-2
New London (Township)—Huron OH-3
New London (Village)—Huron OH-3
New London (Township)—Chester PA-1
New London (City)—Rusk TX-2
New London (City)—Outagamie ... WI-3
New London (City)—Waupaca WI-3
New London County CT-1
New London Naval Submarine Base (CT) Mil-4
New Lothrop (Village)—Shiawassee MI-3
New Lyme (Township)—Ashtabula OH-3
New Lyme (Town)—Monroe WI-3
New Madison (Village)—Darke ... OH-3
New Madrid (City)—New Madrid MO-3
New Madrid (Township)—New Madrid MO-3
New Madrid County MO-3
New Madrid Fault Zone (MO) Geog-4

New Maine (Township)—
  Marshall *MN-3*
Newman (City)—Stanislaus *CA-4*
Newman (Town)—Douglas *IL-3*
Newman (Township)—Douglas *IL-3*
Newman (Township)—Saunders *NE-4*
Newman (Township)—Ward *ND-4*
Newman Grove (City)—Madison ... *NE-4*
Newman Grove (City)—Platte *NE-4*
Newmansville (Township)—Cass *IL-3*
New Market (Division)—
  Madison *AL-2*
New Market (Town)—
  Montgomery *IN-3*
New Market (City)—Taylor *IA-3*
New Market (Town)—Frederick ... *MD-1*
New Market (City)—Scott *MN-3*
New Market (Township)—Scott *MN-3*
Newmarket (Town)—
  Rockingham *NH-1*
New Market (Township)—
  Highland *OH-3*
New Market (City)—Jefferson *TN-2*
New Market (Town)—
  Shenandoah *VA-2*
New Marlborough (Town)—
  Berkshire *MA-1*
New Martinsville (City)—Wetzel .. *WV-2*
New Meadows (City)—Adams *ID-4*
New Melle (Village)—St.
  Charles *MO-3*
New Miami (Village)—Butler *OH-3*
New Middletown (Town)—
  Harrison *IN-3*
New Middletown (Village)—
  Mahoning *OH-3*
New Milford (Town)—Litchfield ... *CT-1*
New Milford (Borough)—Bergen *NJ-1*
New Milford (Borough)—
  Susquehanna *PA-1*
New Milford (Township)—
  Susquehanna *PA-1*
New Millford (Village)—
  Winnebago *IL-3*
New Minden (Village)—
  Washington *IL-3*
New Munich (City)—Stearns *MN-3*
Newnan (City)—Coweta *GA-2*
New Orleans (City)—Orleans
  Parish *LA-2*
New Oxford (Borough)—Adams *PA-1*
New Palestine (Town)—Hancock ... *IN-3*
New Paltz (Town)—Ulster *NY-1*
New Paltz (Village)—Ulster *NY-1*
New Paris (CDP)—Elkhart *IN-3*
New Paris (Village)—Preble *OH-3*
New Paris (Borough)—Bedford *PA-1*
New Pekin (Town)—Washington *IN-3*
New Philadelphia (City)—
  Tuscarawas *OH-3*
New Philadelphia (Borough)—
  Schuylkill *PA-1*
New Plymouth (City)—Payette *ID-4*
Newpoint (Town)—Decatur *IN-3*
Newport (City)—Jackson *AR-2*
Newport (Town)—New Castle *DE-1*
Newport (Township)—Lake *IL-3*
Newport (Town)—Vermillion *IN-3*
Newport (City)—Campbell *KY-2*
Newport (Town)—Penobscot *ME-1*
Newport (City)—Washington *MN-3*
Newport (Village)—DeSoto *MS-2*
Newport (Township)—Barton *MO-3*
Newport (Village)—Rock *NE-4*
Newport (Town)—Sullivan *NH-1*

Newport (Town)—Herkimer *NY-1*
Newport (Village)—Herkimer *NY-1*
Newport (Town)—Carteret *NC-2*
Newport (Township)—McHenry *ND-4*
Newport (Township)—
  Washington *OH-3*
Newport (City)—Lincoln *OR-4*
Newport (Township)—Luzerne *PA-1*
Newport (Borough)—Perry *PA-1*
Newport (City)—Newport *RI-1*
Newport (Township)—Marshall *SD-4*
Newport (City)—Cocke *TN-2*
Newport (City)—Orleans *VT-1*
Newport (Town)—Orleans *VT-1*
Newport (City)—Pend Oreille *WA-4*
Newport (Town)—Columbia *WI-3*
Newport Beach (City)—Orange *CA-4*
Newport County *RI-1*
Newport Hills (CDP)—King *WA-4*
New Portland (Town)—
  Somerset *ME-1*
Newport News (Independent City) ... *VA-2*
New Port Richey (City)—Pasco *FL-2*
New Port Richey East (CDP)—
  Pasco *FL-2*
New Post (CDP)—Sawyer *WI-3*
New Prague (City)—Le Sueur *MN-3*
New Prague (City)—Scott *MN-3*
New Prairie (Township)—Pope *MN-3*
New Prairie (Township)—Ward *ND-4*
New Preston (CDP)—Litchfield *CT-1*
New Providence (Town)—Clark *IN-3*
New Providence (City)—Hardin *IA-3*
New Providence (Borough)—
  Union *NJ-1*
New Richland (City)—Waseca *MN-3*
New Richland (Township)—
  Waseca *MN-3*
New Richmond (Town)—
  Montgomery *IN-3*
New Richmond (Village)—
  Clermont *OH-3*
New Richmond (City)—St. Croix .. *WI-3*
New Riegel (Village)—Seneca *OH-3*
New Ringgold (Borough)—
  Schuylkill *PA-1*
New River Station (Military Facility)—
  Onslow *NC-2*
New Roads (Town)—Pointe Coupee
  Parish *LA-2*
New Rochelle (City)—
  Westchester *NY-1*
New Rockford (City)—Eddy *ND-4*
New Rockford (Township)—
  Eddy *ND-4*
New Rome (Village)—Franklin *OH-3*
New Ross (Town)—Montgomery *IN-3*
Newry (Town)—Oxford *ME-1*
Newry (Township)—Freeborn *MN-3*
Newry (Borough)—Blair *PA-1*
New Salem (Township)—
  McDonough *IL-3*
New Salem (Township)—Pike *IL-3*
New Salem (Village)—Pike *IL-3*
New Salem (Town)—Franklin *MA-1*
New Salem (City)—Morton *ND-4*
New Salem (Borough)—York *PA-1*
New Sarpy (CDP)—St. Charles
  Parish *LA-2*
New Scandia (Township)—
  Washington *MN-3*
New Scotland (Town)—Albany *NY-1*
New Sewickley (Township)—
  Beaver *PA-1*
New Sharon (City)—Mahaska *IA-3*

New Sharon (Town)—Franklin *ME-1*
New Shoreham (Town)—
  Washington *RI-1*
New Site (Municipality)—
  Tallapoosa *AL-2*
New Smyrna Beach (City)—
  Volusia *FL-2*
New Solum (Township)—
  Marshall *MN-3*
Newsoms (Town)—Southampton ... *VA-2*
New Square (Village)—Rockland .. *NY-1*
New Stanton (Borough)—
  Westmoreland *PA-1*
Newstead (Town)—Erie *NY-1*
New Straitsville (Village)—Perry ... *OH-3*
New Strawn (City)—Coffey *KS-4*
New Stuyahok (City)—Dillingham
  Census Area *AK-4*
New Summerfield (City)—
  Cherokee *TX-2*
New Surprise Valley (Township)—
  Mellette *SD-4*
New Sweden (Town)—
  Aroostook *ME-1*
New Sweden (Township)—
  Nicollet *MN-3*
New Tazewell (Town)—
  Claiborne *TN-2*
Newtok (City)—Bethel Census
  Area *AK-4*
Newtok (City)—Wade Hampton Census
  Area *AK-4*
Newton (Town)—Dale *AL-2*
Newton (City)—Baker *GA-2*
Newton (Town)—Jasper *IL-3*
Newton (Township)—Whiteside ... *IL-3*
Newton (Township)—Jasper *IN-3*
Newton (City)—Jasper *IA-3*
Newton (City)—Harvey *KS-4*
Newton (Township)—Harvey *KS-4*
Newton (City)—Middlesex *MA-1*
Newton (Township)—Calhoun *MI-3*
Newton (Township)—Mackinac ... *MI-3*
Newton (Township)—Otter Tail ... *MN-3*
Newton (City)—Newton *MS-2*
Newton (Township)—Shannon *MO-3*
Newton (Town)—Rockingham *NH-1*
Newton (Town)—Sussex *NJ-1*
Newton (City)—Catawba *NC-2*
Newton (Township)—Licking *OH-3*
Newton (Township)—Miami *OH-3*
Newton (Township)—
  Muskingum *OH-3*
Newton (Township)—Pike *OH-3*
Newton (Township)—Trumbull *OH-3*
Newton (Township)—
  Lackawanna *PA-1*
Newton (City)—Newton *TX-2*
Newton (Town)—Cache *UT-4*
Newton (Town)—Manitowoc *WI-3*
Newton (Town)—Marquette *WI-3*
Newton County *AR-2*
Newton County *GA-2*
Newton County *IN-3*
Newton County *MS-2*
Newton County *MO-3*
Newton County *TX-2*
Newton Falls (City)—Trumbull *OH-3*
Newton Grove (Town)—
  Sampson *NC-2*
Newton Hamilton (Borough)—
  Mifflin *PA-1*
Newtonia (Town)—Newton *MO-3*
Newtonia (Township)—Newton *MO-3*

General Index

Newtonsville (Village)—
   Clermont *OH-3*
Newtown (Borough)—Fairfield *CT-1*
*Newtown (Town)—Fairfield *CT-1*
Newtown (Township)—Livingston . *IL-3*
Newtown (Town)—Fountain *IN-3*
Newtown (Town)—Sullivan *MO-3*
New Town (City)—Mountrail *ND-4*
Newtown (Village)—Hamilton *OH-3*
Newtown (Borough)—Bucks *PA-1*
Newtown (Township)—Bucks *PA-1*
Newtown (Township)—Delaware ... *PA-1*
New Trier (Township)—Cook *IL-3*
New Trier (City)—Dakota *MN-3*
New Tulsa (Town)—Wagoner *OK-2*
New Ulm (City)—Brown *MN-3*
New Underwood (Town)—
   Pennington *SD-4*
New Vernon (Township)—Mercer .. *PA-1*
New Vienna (City)—Dubuque *IA-3*
New Vienna (Village)—Clinton *OH-3*
Newville (Municipality)—Henry ... *AL-2*
Newville (Township)—Dekalb *IN-3*
Newville (Borough)—Cumberland . *PA-1*
New Vineyard (Town)—Franklin . *ME-1*
New Virginia (City)—Warren *IA-3*
New Washington (Village)—
   Crawford *OH-3*
New Washington (Borough)—
   Clearfield *PA-1*
New Washoe City (CDP)—
   Washoe *NV-4*
New Waterford (Village)—
   Columbiana *OH-3*
New Waverly (Town)—Walker *TX-2*
New Weston (Village)—Darke *OH-3*
New Whiteland (Town)—Johnson .. *IN-3*
New Wilmington (Borough)—
   Lawrence *PA-1*
New Windsor (Town)—Carroll *MD-1*
New Windsor (Town)—Orange ... *NY-1*
New Witten (Town)—Tripp *SD-4*
New York (Township)—
   Caldwell *MO-3*
New York City *NY-1*
New York County (Manhattan) .. *NY-1*
New York Mills (City)—Otter
   Tail *MN-3*
New York Mills (Village)—
   Oneida *NY-1*
New York State Barge
   Canal System (NY) *Geog-4*
Ney (Village)—Defiance *OH-3*
Neylandville (Town)—Hunt *TX-2*
Nezperce (City)—Lewis *ID-4*
Nez Perce County *ID-4*
Nez Perce Reservation (ID) *IndRes-4*
Niagara (Town)—Niagara *NY-1*
Niagara (City)—Grand Forks *ND-4*
Niagara (Township)—Grand
   Forks *ND-4*
Niagara (Town)—Marinette *WI-3*
Niagara (Village)—Marinette *WI-3*
Niagara County *NY-1*
Niagara Falls (NY) *Geog-4*
Niagara Falls (City)—Niagara *NY-1*
Niangua (Township)—Camden *MO-3*
Niangua (City)—Webster *MO-3*
Niangua (Township)—Webster ... *MO-3*
Niantic (CDP)—New London *CT-1*
Niantic (Township)—Macon *IL-3*
Niantic (Village)—Macon *IL-3*
Nibley (City)—Cache *UT-4*
Nice (CDP)—Lake *CA-4*
Niceville (City)—Okaloosa *FL-2*

Nicholas County *KY-2*
Nicholas County *WV-2*
Nicholasville (City)—Jessamine *KY-2*
Nicholls (City)—Coffee *GA-2*
Nichols (City)—Muscatine *IA-3*
Nichols (Town)—Tioga *NY-1*
Nichols (Village)—Tioga *NY-1*
Nichols (Town)—Marion *SC-2*
Nichols (Village)—Outagamie *WI-3*
Nichols Hills (City)—Oklahoma ... *OK-2*
Nicholson (Town)—Jackson *GA-2*
Nicholson (Township)—Fayette ... *PA-1*
Nicholson (Borough)—Wyoming . *PA-1*
Nicholson (Township)—Wyoming .. *PA-1*
Nickelsville (Town)—Scott *VA-2*
Nickerson (City)—Reno *KS-4*
Nickerson (Township)—Pine *MN-3*
Nickerson (Township)—Dodge *NE-4*
Nickerson (Village)—Dodge *NE-4*
Nicodemus (Township)—Graham .. *KS-4*
Nicollet (City)—Nicollet *MN-3*
Nicollet (Township)—Nicollet *MN-3*
Nicollet County *MN-3*
Nicoma Park (City)—Oklahoma .. *OK-2*
Nidaros (Township)—Otter Tail .. *MN-3*
Niederwald (Town)—Caldwell *TX-2*
Niederwald (Town)—Hays *TX-2*
Nielsville (City)—Polk *MN-3*
Nightmute (City)—Bethel Census
   Area *AK-4*
Niihau Island (HI) *Geog-4*
Nikiski (CDP)—Kenai Peninsula
   Borough *AK-4*
Nikolaevsk (CDP)—Kenai Peninsula
   Borough *AK-4*
Nikolai (City)—Yukon-Koyukuk
   Census Area *AK-4*
Nikolski (CDP)—Aleutians West
   Census Area *AK-4*
Niland (CDP)—Imperial *CA-4*
Nile (Township)—Scioto *OH-3*
Niles (City)—Cook *IL-3*
Niles (Township)—Cook *IL-3*
Niles (Township)—Delaware *IN-3*
Niles (City)—Berrien *MI-3*
Niles (Township)—Berrien *MI-3*
Niles (City)—Cass *MI-3*
Niles (Town)—Cayuga *NY-1*
Niles (City)—Trumbull *OH-3*
Nilsen (Township)—Wilkin *MN-3*
Nilwood (Town)—Macoupin *IL-3*
Nilwood (Township)—Macoupin . *IL-3*
Nimishillen (Township)—Stark ... *OH-3*
Nimmons (Town)—Clay *AR-2*
Nimrod (Village)—Wadena *MN-3*
Nine Mile Prairie (Township)—
   Callaway *MO-3*
Ninety Six (Town)—Greenwood *SC-2*
Nineveh (Township)—Johnson ... *IN-3*
Nineveh (Township)—Adair *MO-3*
Nineveh (Township)—Lincoln *MO-3*
Ninilchik (CDP)—Kenai Peninsula
   Borough *AK-4*
Nininger (Township)—Dakota ... *MN-3*
Ninnescah (Township)—Cowley ... *KS-4*
Ninnescah (Township)—
   Kingman *KS-4*
Ninnescah (Township)—Reno *KS-4*
Ninnescah (Township)—
   Sedgwick *KS-4*
Niobrara (Township)—Knox *NE-4*
Niobrara (Village)—Knox *NE-4*
Niobrara County *WY-4*
Niota (City)—McMinn *TN-2*
Niotaze (City)—Chautauqua *KS-4*

Nipomo (CDP)—San Luis
   Obispo *CA-4*
Nippawalla (Township)—Barber ... *KS-4*
Nippenose (Township)—
   Lycoming *PA-1*
Nishnabotna (Township)—
   Atchison *MO-3*
Niskayuna (CDP)—Schenectady *NY-1*
Niskayuna (Town)—Schenectady ... *NY-1*
Nisland (Town)—Butte *SD-4*
Nisqually Indian Community (CDP)—
   Thurston *WA-4*
Nisqually Reservation (WA) *IndRes-4*
Nissequogue (Village)—Suffolk ... *NY-1*
Nisswa (City)—Crow Wing *MN-3*
Nitro (City)—Kanawha *WV-2*
Nitro (City)—Putnam *WV-2*
Niverville (CDP)—Columbia *NY-1*
Niwot (CDP)—Boulder *CO-4*
Nixa (City)—Christian *MO-3*
Nixon (Township)—De Witt *IL-3*
Nixon (Township)—Ramsey *ND-4*
Nixon (City)—Gonzales *TX-2*
Nixon (City)—Wilson *TX-2*
Noatak (CDP)—Northwest Arctic
   Borough *AK-4*
Noble (Town)—Richland *IL-3*
Noble (Township)—Richland *IL-3*
Noble (Township)—Cass *IN-3*
Noble (Township)—Jay *IN-3*
Noble (Township)—La Porte *IN-3*
Noble (Township)—Noble *IN-3*
Noble (Township)—Rush *IN-3*
Noble (Township)—Shelby *IN-3*
Noble (Township)—Wabash *IN-3*
Noble (Township)—Dickinson *KS-4*
Noble (Township)—Ellsworth *KS-4*
Noble (Township)—Marshall *KS-4*
Noble (Village)—Sabine Parish ... *LA-2*
Noble (Township)—Branch *MI-3*
Noble (Township)—Ozark *MO-3*
Noble (Township)—Valley *NE-4*
Noble (Township)—Cass *ND-4*
Noble (Township)—Auglaize *OH-3*
Noble (Township)—Defiance *OH-3*
Noble (Township)—Noble *OH-3*
Noble (Town)—Cleveland *OK-2*
Nobleboro (Town)—Lincoln *ME-1*
Noble County *IN-3*
Noble County *OH-3*
Noble County *OK-2*
Nobles County *MN-3*
Noblesville (City)—Hamilton *IN-3*
Noblesville (Township)—
   Hamilton *IN-3*
Nockamixon (Township)—Bucks ... *PA-1*
Nocona (City)—Montague *TX-2*
Nodaway (City)—Adams *IA-3*
Nodaway (Township)—Andrew ... *MO-3*
Nodaway (Township)—Holt *MO-3*
Nodaway (Township)—
   Nodaway *MO-3*
Nodaway County *MO-3*
Noel (City)—McDonald *MO-3*
Nogales (City)—Santa Cruz *AZ-2*
Nogosek (Township)—Stutsman *ND-4*
Nokay Lake (Township)—Crow
   Wing *MN-3*
Nokomis (CDP)—Sarasota *FL-2*
Nokomis (Town)—Montgomery *IL-3*
Nokomis (Township)—
   Montgomery *IL-3*
Nokomis (Town)—Oneida *WI-3*
Nolan County *TX-2*
Nolanville (City)—Bell *TX-2*

Nolensville (CDP)—Williamson.... *TN-2*
Noltimier (Township)—Barnes......*ND-4*
Noma (Town)—Holmes..............*FL-2*
Nome (City)—Nome Census
   Area..*AK-4*
Nome (City)—Barnes *ND-4*
Nome (City)—Jefferson *TX-2*
Nome Census Area........................ *AK-4*
Nondalton (City)—Lake and Peninsula
   Borough..*AK-4*
Nooksack (City)—Whatcom *WA-4*
Nooksack Reservation & Trust Lands
   (WA)..*IndRes-4*
Noonan (City)—Divide....................*ND-4*
Noonan (Township)—Ramsey *ND-4*
Noonday (City)—Smith *TX-2*
Noorvik (City)—Northwest Arctic
   Borough..*AK-4*
Nora (Township)—Jo Daviess *IL-3*
Nora (Village)—Jo Daviess *IL-3*
Nora (Township)—Clearwater *MN-3*
Nora (Township)—Pope *MN-3*
Nora (Village)—Nuckolls *NE-4*
Nora (Township)—LaMoure *ND-4*
Nora Springs (City)—Floyd *IA-3*
Norborne (City)—Carroll............. *MO-3*
Norbourne Estates (City)—
   Jefferson *KY-2*
Norcatur (City)—Decatur *KS-4*
Norco (City)—Riverside *CA-4*
Norco (CDP)—St. Charles Parish...*LA-2*
Norcross (City)—Gwinnett *GA-2*
Norcross (City)—Grant *MN-3*
Norden (Township)—
   Pennington.....................................*MN-3*
Norden (Township)—LaMoure......*ND-4*
Norden (Township)—Deuel *SD-4*
Norden (Township)—Hamlin *SD-4*
Nordheim (City)—DeWitt *TX-2*
Nordick (Township)—Wilkin.........*MN-3*
Nordland (Township)—Aitkin *MN-3*
Nordland (Township)—Lyon *MN-3*
Nordland (Township)—Marshall ... *SD-4*
Nordmore (Township)—Foster *ND-4*
Nore (Township)—Itasca...............*MN-3*
Norfolk (Town)—Litchfield *CT-1*
Norfolk (Town)—Norfolk *MA-1*
Norfolk (Township)—Renville......*MN-3*
Norfolk (City)—Madison *NE-4*
Norfolk (Town)—St. Lawrence *NY-1*
Norfolk County............................. *MA-1*
Norfolk (Independent City)........... *VA-2*
Norfolk Naval Air Station (VA)......*Mil-4*
Norfolk Naval Shipyard (VA)........*Mil-4*
Norfolk Naval Station (VA)...........*Mil-4*
Norfork (City)—Baxter *AR-2*
Norge (Town)—Grady....................*OK-2*
Norland (CDP)—Dade.....................*FL-2*
Norlina (Town)—Warren *NC-2*
Norma (Township)—Barnes............*ND-4*
Normal (City)—McLean *IL-3*
Normal (Township)—McLean *IL-3*
Normal (Township)—McHenry *ND-4*
Norman (Town)—Montgomery *AR-2*
Norman (Township)—Grundy *IL-3*
Norman (Township)—Manistee......*MI-3*
Norman (Township)—Pine *MN-3*
Norman (Township)—Yellow
   Medicine *MN-3*
Norman (Township)—Dent *MO-3*
Norman (Village)—Kearney *NE-4*
Norman (Town)—Richmond *NC-2*
Norman (Township)—Traill *ND-4*
Norman (City)—Cleveland *OK-2*
Norman County........................ *MN-3*

Normandy (City)—St. Louis *MO-3*
Normandy (Township)—St.
   Louis..*MO-3*
Normandy (Town)—Bedford *TN-2*
Normandy Park (City)—King........*WA-4*
Normangee (Town)—Leon *TX-2*
Normangee (Town)—Madison *TX-2*
Normania (Township)—Yellow
   Medicine *MN-3*
Normania (Township)—Benson......*ND-4*
Normanna (Township)—St.
   Louis..*MN-3*
Normanna (Township)—Cass *ND-4*
Norman Park (City)—Colquitt *GA-2*
Norphlet (City)—Union *AR-2*
Norridge (Village)—Cook............... *IL-3*
Norridgewock (Town)—
   Somerset...*ME-1*
Norrie (Town)—Marathon *WI-3*
Norris (Village)—Fulton................. *IL-3*
Norris (Town)—Pickens.................*SC-2*
Norris (Township)—Mellette *SD-4*
Norris (Township)—Anderson *TN-2*
Norris City (Town)—White *IL-3*
Norristown (Borough)—
   Montgomery.................................... *PA-1*
North (Township)—Lake................ *IN-3*
North (Township)—Marshall *IN-3*
North (Township)—Labette *KS-4*
North (Township)—Woodson *KS-4*
North (Township)—Pennington....*MN-3*
North (Township)—Dade............ *MO-3*
North (Township)—Harrison *OH-3*
North (Town)—Orangeburg *SC-2*
North Abington (Township)—
   Lackawanna *PA-1*
North Acomita Village (CDP)—
   Cibola..*NM-4*
North Adams (City)—Berkshire ... *MA-1*
North Adams (Village)—
   Hillsdale..*MI-3*
North Albany (CDP)—Benton.......*OR-4*
North Allis (Township)—Presque
   Isle *MI-3*
North Amherst (CDP)—
   Hampshire *MA-1*
North Amityville (CDP)—
   Suffolk.. *NY-1*
Northampton (City)—
   Hampshire *MA-1*
Northampton (Town)—Fulton *NY-1*
Northampton (Township)—Bucks .. *PA-1*
Northampton (Borough)—
   Northampton *PA-1*
Northampton (Township)—
   Somerset.. *PA-1*
Northampton County....................... *NC-2*
Northampton County........................ *PA-1*
Northampton County....................... *VA-2*
North Andover (Town)—Essex *MA-1*
North Andrews Gardens (CDP)—
   Broward... *FL-2*
North Annville (Township)—
   Lebanon.. *PA-1*
North Apollo (Borough)—
   Armstrong....................................... *PA-1*
North Arlington (Borough)—
   Bergen *NJ-1*
North Atlanta (CDP)—De Kalb *GA-2*
North Attleborough (Town)—
   Bristol..*MA-1*
North Auburn (CDP)—Placer *CA-4*
North Augusta (City)—Aiken *SC-2*
North Augusta (City)—Edgefield....*SC-2*
North Aurora (Village)—Kane........ *IL-3*

North Babylon (CDP)—Suffolk..... *NY-1*
North Ballston Spa (CDP)—
   Saratoga.. *NY-1*
North Baltimore (Village)—
   Wood *OH-3*
North Barrington (Town)—Lake..... *IL-3*
North Bay (Village)—Racine *WI-3*
North Bay Shore (CDP)—Suffolk.. *NY-1*
North Bay Village (City)—Dade.....*FL-2*
North Beach (Town)—Calvert *MD-1*
North Beach Haven (CDP)—
   Ocean... *NJ-1*
North Beaver (Township)—
   Lawrence... *PA-1*
North Belle Vernon (Borough)—
   Westmoreland *PA-1*
North Bellmore (CDP)—Nassau.... *NY-1*
North Bellport (CDP)—Suffolk *NY-1*
North Beltrami (Pop. Place)—
   Beltrami *MN-3*
North Bend (Township)—Starke..... *IN-3*
North Bend (City)—Dodge *NE-4*
North Bend (Village)—Hamilton...*OH-3*
North Bend (City)—Coos...............*OR-4*
North Bend (City)—King................*WA-4*
North Bend (Town)—Jackson *WI-3*
North Bennington (Village)—
   Bennington...................................... *VT-1*
North Benton (Township)—
   Dallas..*MO-3*
North Benton (Township)—Polk .. *MO-3*
North Bergen (Township)—
   Hudson *NJ-1*
North Berwick (Town)—York *ME-1*
North Bethesda (CDP)—
   Montgomery..................................*MD-1*
North Bethlehem (Township)—
   Washington..................................... *PA-1*
North Billings (Pop. Place)—
   Billings *ND-4*
North Bloomfield (Township)—
   Morrow *OH-3*
North Bonneville (City)—
   Skamania.......................................*WA-4*
Northboro (City)—Page *IA-3*
Northborough (Town)—
   Worcester *MA-1*
North Boston (CDP)—Erie............ *NY-1*
North Braddock (Borough)—
   Allegheny.. *PA-1*
North Branch (Township)—
   Lapeer *MI-3*
North Branch (Village)—Lapeer *MI-3*
North Branch (City)—Chisago......*MN-3*
North Branch (Township)—
   Isanti *MN-3*
North Branch (Township)—
   Wyoming *PA-1*
North Branford (Town)—New
   Haven... *CT-1*
North Brentwood (Town)—Prince
   George's *MD-1*
Northbridge (Town)—Worcester... *MA-1*
Northbrook (City)—Cook *IL-3*
Northbrook (CDP)—Hamilton *OH-3*
North Brookfield (Town)—
   Worcester *MA-1*
North Brooksville (CDP)—
   Hernando *FL-2*
North Brown (Township)—
   Edwards *KS-4*
North Browning (CDP)—Glacier . *MT-4*
North Brunswick (Township)—
   Middlesex *NJ-1*

General Index *American Places Dictionary*

North Bryant (Township)—
 Edmunds *SD-4*
North Buena Vista (City)—
 Clayton *IA-3*
North Buffalo (Township)—
 Armstrong *PA-1*
North Buffalo (Pop. Place)—
 Buffalo *SD-4*
North Burke (Pop. Place)—
 Burke *ND-4*
North Caldwell (Township)—
 Essex *NJ-1*
North Campbell (Pop. Place)—
 Campbell *SD-4*
North Campbell No. 1 (Township)—
 Greene *MO-3*
North Campbell No. 2 (Township)—
 Greene *MO-3*
North Campbell No. 3 (Township)—
 Greene *MO-3*
North Canaan (Town)—
 Litchfield *CT-1*
North Canton (City)—Stark *OH-3*
North Cape May (CDP)—Cape
 May *NJ-1*
North Carlton (Pop. Place)—
 Carlton *MN-3*
North Carrollton (Town)—
 Carroll *MS-2*
North Cass (Pop. Place)—Cass *MN-3*
North Castle (Town)—
 Westchester *NY-1*
North Catasauqua (Borough)—
 Northampton *PA-1*
North Cedar (Township)—
 Saunders *NE-4*
North Central Cass (Pop. Place)—
 Cass *MN-3*
North Central McLean (Pop. Place)—
 McLean *ND-4*
North Centre (Township)—
 Columbia *PA-1*
North Charleroi (Borough)—
 Washington *PA-1*
North Charleston (City)—
 Berkeley *SC-2*
North Charleston (City)—
 Charleston *SC-2*
North Charleston (City)—
 Dorchester *SC-2*
North Chicago (City)—Lake *IL-3*
North City (Village)—Franklin *IL-3*
North City-Ridgecrest (CDP)—
 King *WA-4*
North Clearwater (Pop. Place)—
 Clearwater *MN-3*
North Cleveland (City)—Liberty ... *TX-2*
North Codorus (Township)—York .. *PA-1*
North College Hill (City)—
 Hamilton *OH-3*
North Collins (Town)—Erie *NY-1*
North Collins (Village)—Erie *NY-1*
North Conway (CDP)—Carroll *NH-1*
North Corbin (CDP)—Knox *KY-2*
North Corbin (CDP)—Laurel *KY-2*
North Cornwall (Township)—
 Lebanon *PA-1*
North Courtland (Municipality)—
 Lawrence *AL-2*
North Coventry (Township)—
 Chester *PA-1*
North Creek-Canyon Park (CDP)—
 Snohomish *WA-4*
Northcrest (Town)—McLennan *TX-2*
North Crossett (CDP)—Ashley *AR-2*

North Crows Nest (Town)—
 Marion *IN-3*
North Dansville (Town)—
 Livingston *NY-1*
North Decatur (CDP)—De Kalb ... *GA-2*
North De Land (CDP)—Volusia ... *FL-2*
North Detroit (Township)—
 Brown *SD-4*
North Dewey (Pop. Place)—
 Dewey *SD-4*
North Druid Hills (CDP)—De
 Kalb *GA-2*
North Eagle Butte (CDP)—
 Dewey *SD-4*
Northeast (Township)—Adams *IL-3*
Northeast (Township)—Orange *IN-3*
North East (Town)—Cecil *MD-1*
North East (Town)—Dutchess *NY-1*
North East (Borough)—Erie *PA-1*
North East (Township)—Erie *PA-1*
Northeast Aitkin (Pop. Place)—
 Aitkin *MN-3*
Northeast Bon Homme (Pop. Place)—
 Bon Homme *SD-4*
Northeast Corson (Pop. Place)—
 Corson *SD-4*
Northeast Emmons (Pop. Place)—
 Emmons *ND-4*
Northeast Fall River (Pop. Place)—Fall
 River *SD-4*
North Eastham (CDP)—
 Barnstable *MA-1*
Northeast Itasca (Pop. Place)—
 Itasca *MN-3*
Northeast Ithaca (CDP)—
 Tompkins *NY-1*
Northeast Lyman (Pop. Place)—
 Lyman *SD-4*
Northeast Madison (Township)—
 Perry *PA-1*
Northeast Marion (Township)—
 Polk *MO-3*
Northeast McHenry (Pop. Place)—
 McHenry *ND-4*
Northeast Pennington (Pop. Place)—
 Pennington *SD-4*
Northeast Piscataquis
 (unorganized) (Pop. Place)—
 Piscataquis *ME-1*
Northeast Somerset (unorganized) (Pop.
 Place)—Somerset *ME-1*
Northeast St. Louis (Pop. Place)—St.
 Louis *MN-3*
North Edwards (CDP)—Kern *CA-4*
North Elba (Town)—Essex *NY-1*
North Elkhorn (Township)—
 Warren *MO-3*
North El Monte (CDP)—Los
 Angeles *CA-4*
North Emmons (Pop. Place)—
 Emmons *ND-4*
North English (City)—Iowa *IA-3*
North English (City)—Keokuk *IA-3*
North Enid (Town)—Garfield *OK-2*
Northern (Township)—Franklin *IL-3*
Northern (Township)—Beltrami ... *MN-3*
Northern Cheyenne Res. & Trust Lands
 (MT) *IndRes-4*
North Fairfield (Village)—Huron .. *OH-3*
North Fair Oaks (CDP)—San
 Mateo *CA-4*
North Falmouth (CDP)—
 Barnstable *MA-1*
North Fayette (Township)—
 Allegheny *PA-1*

Northfield (Township)—Cook *IL-3*
Northfield (Village)—Cook *IL-3*
Northfield (City)—Jefferson *KY-2*
Northfield (Town)—Washington ... *ME-1*
Northfield (Town)—Franklin *MA-1*
Northfield (Township)—
 Washtenaw *MI-3*
Northfield (City)—Dakota *MN-3*
Northfield (City)—Rice *MN-3*
Northfield (Township)—Rice *MN-3*
Northfield (Town)—Merrimack *NH-1*
Northfield (City)—Atlantic *NJ-1*
Northfield (Township)—Ramsey ... *ND-4*
Northfield (Village)—Summit *OH-3*
Northfield (Town)—Washington *VT-1*
Northfield (Village)—Washington .. *VT-1*
Northfield (Town)—Jackson *WI-3*
Northfield Center (Township)—
 Summit *OH-3*
North Folk Village (CDP)—Ross ... *OH-3*
North Fond du Lac (Village)—Fond du
 Lac *WI-3*
North Fork (Township)—Gallatin .. *IL-3*
North Fork (Township)—Stearns ... *MN-3*
Northfork (Township)—Barton *MO-3*
Northfork (Town)—McDowell *WV-2*
North Fork Rancheria (CA) *IndRes-4*
North Fort Myers (CDP)—Lee *FL-2*
North Frankfort (Township)—
 Knox *NE-4*
North Franklin (Township)—
 Franklin *NE-4*
North Franklin (Township)—
 Washington *PA-1*
North Franklin (unorganized) (Pop.
 Place)—Franklin *ME-1*
North Freedom (Village)—Sauk *WI-3*
North Galloway (Township)—
 Christian *MO-3*
Northgate (CDP)—Hamilton *OH-3*
North Germany (Township)—
 Wadena *MN-3*
Northglenn (City)—Adams *CO-4*
Northglenn (City)—Weld *CO-4*
North Golden Valley (Pop. Place)—
 Golden Valley *ND-4*
North Granby (CDP)—Hartford ... *CT-1*
North Great River (CDP)—
 Suffolk *NY-1*
North Green (Township)—Polk *MO-3*
North Greenbush (Town)—
 Rensselaer *NY-1*
North Gregory (Pop. Place)—
 Gregory *SD-4*
North Grosvenor Dale (CDP)—
 Windham *CT-1*
North Gulfport (CDP)—
 Harrison *MS-2*
North Haledon (Borough)—
 Passaic *NJ-1*
North Hampton (Town)—
 Rockingham *NH-1*
North Hampton (Village)—Clark .. *OH-3*
North Hanover (Township)—
 Burlington *NJ-1*
North Harding (Pop. Place)—
 Harding *SD-4*
North Harmony (Town)—
 Chautauqua *NY-1*
North Hartsville (CDP)—
 Darlington *SC-2*
North Haven (Town)—New
 Haven *CT-1*
North Haven (Town)—Knox *ME-1*
North Haven (Village)—Suffolk *NY-1*

North Heidelberg (Township)—
  Berks *PA-1*
North Hempstead (Town)—
  Nassau *NY-1*
North Henderson (Township)—
  Mercer *IL-3*
North Henderson (Village)—
  Mercer *IL-3*
North Hero (Township)—
  Redwood *MN-3*
North Hero (Town)—Grand Isle ... *VT-1*
North Hickory (CDP)—Catawba. *NC-2*
North Highlands (CDP)—
  Sacramento *CA-4*
North High Shoals (Town)—
  Oconee *GA-2*
North Hill (CDP)—King *WA-4*
North Hills (Village)—Nassau *NY-1*
North Hills (Town)—Wood *WV-2*
North Hodge (Village)—Jackson
  Parish *LA-2*
North Homestead (Township)—
  Barton *KS-4*
North Hopewell (Township)—
  York *PA-1*
North Hornell (Village)—
  Steuben *NY-1*
North Hudson (Town)—Essex *NY-1*
North Hudson (Village)—St.
  Croix *WI-3*
North Hughes (Pop. Place)—
  Hughes *SD-4*
North Huntingdon (Township)—
  Westmoreland *PA-1*
North Hyde (Pop. Place)—Hyde ... *SD-4*
North Irwin (Borough)—
  Westmoreland *PA-1*
North Island Naval Air Station
  (CA) *Mil-4*
North Johns (Municipality)—
  Jefferson *AL-2*
North Jones (Pop. Place)—Jones ... *SD-4*
North Judson (Town)—Starke *IN-3*
North Kansas City (City)—Clay ... *MO-3*
North Kensington (CDP)—
  Montgomery *MD-1*
North Key Largo (CDP)—
  Monroe *FL-2*
North Kingstown (Town)—
  Washington *RI-1*
North Kingsville (Village)—
  Ashtabula *OH-3*
Northlake (City)—Cook *IL-3*
Northlake (CDP)—Anderson *SC-2*
Northlake (Town)—Denton *TX-2*
Northlakes (CDP)—Caldwell *NC-2*
North Lakeville (CDP)—
  Plymouth *MA-1*
North Lancaster (Town)—Grant *WI-3*
Northland (Township)—Polk *MN-3*
Northland (Township)—St.
  Louis *MN-3*
Northland (Township)—Ransom ... *ND-4*
North Las Vegas (City)—Clark *NV-4*
North Lauderdale (City)—
  Broward *FL-2*
North Laurel (CDP)—Howard *MD-1*
North Lawrence (Pop. Place)—
  Lawrence *SD-4*
North Lebanon (Township)—
  Lebanon *PA-1*
North Lemmon (Township)—
  Adams *ND-4*
North Lewisburg (Village)—
  Champaign *OH-3*

North Liberty (Town)—St. Joseph . *IN-3*
North Liberty (City)—Johnson *IA-3*
North Lilbourn (Village)—New
  Madrid *MO-3*
North Lindenhurst (CDP)—
  Suffolk *NY-1*
North Linn (Township)—
  Christian *MO-3*
North Litchfield (Township)—
  Montgomery *IL-3*
North Little Rock (City)—
  Pulaski *AR-2*
North Logan (City)—Cache *UT-4*
North Loma (Township)—
  Cavalier *ND-4*
North Londonderry (Township)—
  Lebanon *PA-1*
North Loup (Township)—Valley ... *NE-4*
North Loup (Village)—Valley *NE-4*
North Madison (CDP)—Lake *OH-3*
North Mahoning (Township)—
  Indiana *PA-1*
North Manchester (Town)—
  Wabash *IN-3*
North Manheim (Township)—
  Schuylkill *PA-1*
North Mankato (City)—Blue
  Earth *MN-3*
North Mankato (City)—Nicollet ... *MN-3*
North Marysville (CDP)—
  Snohomish *WA-4*
North Massapequa (CDP)—
  Nassau *NY-1*
North McKenzie (Pop. Place)—
  McKenzie *ND-4*
North Meade (Pop. Place)—
  Meade *SD-4*
North Merrick (CDP)—Nassau *NY-1*
North Miami (City)—Dade *FL-2*
North Miami (Town)—Ottawa *OK-2*
North Miami Beach (City)—
  Dade *FL-2*
North Middleton (Township)—
  Cumberland *PA-1*
North Middletown (City)—
  Bourbon *KY-2*
North Middletown (CDP)—
  Monmouth *NJ-1*
North Moniteau (Township)—
  Cooper *MO-3*
Northmoor (City)—Platte *MO-3*
Northmoreland (Township)—
  Wyoming *PA-1*
North Morgan (Township)—
  Dade *MO-3*
North Muddy (Township)—Jasper . *IL-3*
North Muskegon (City)—
  Muskegon *MI-3*
North Myrtle Beach (City)—
  Horry *SC-2*
North Naples (CDP)—Collier *FL-2*
North New Hyde Park (CDP)—
  Nassau *NY-1*
North Newton (City)—Harvey *KS-4*
North Newton (Township)—
  Cumberland *PA-1*
North Norwich (Town)—
  Chenango *NY-1*
North Oaks (City)—Ramsey *MN-3*
North Ogden (City)—Weber *UT-4*
North Okaw (Township)—Coles ... *IL-3*
North Olga (Township)—
  Cavalier *ND-4*
North Olmsted (City)—
  Cuyahoga *OH-3*

North Omak (CDP)—Okanogan *WA-4*
Northome (City)—Koochiching *MN-3*
Northome (Pop. Place)—
  Koochiching *MN-3*
North Ottawa (Township)—
  Grant *MN-3*
North Otter (Township)—
  Macoupin *IL-3*
North Oxford (unorganized) (Pop.
  Place)—Oxford *ME-1*
North Palm Beach (Village)—Palm
  Beach *FL-2*
North Palmyra (Township)—
  Macoupin *IL-3*
North Patchogue (CDP)—
  Suffolk *NY-1*
North Pekin (Village)—Tazewell ... *IL-3*
North Pembroke (CDP)—
  Plymouth *MA-1*
North Penobscot (unorganized) (Pop.
  Place)—Penobscot *ME-1*
North Perry (Village)—Lake *OH-3*
North Pierce (Pop. Place)—
  Pierce *ND-4*
North Plainfield (Borough)—
  Somerset *NJ-1*
North Plains (Township)—Ionia *MI-3*
North Plains (City)—Washington .. *OR-4*
North Platte (City)—Lincoln *NE-4*
North Platte River (HI) *Geog-4*
North Plymouth (CDP)—
  Plymouth *MA-1*
North Pole (City)—Fairbanks North
  Star Borough *AK-4*
Northport (City)—Tuscaloosa *AL-2*
North Port (City)—Sarasota *FL-2*
Northport (Town)—Waldo *ME-1*
Northport (Village)—Leelanau *MI-3*
Northport (Village)—Suffolk *NY-1*
Northport (Town)—Stevens *WA-4*
North Potomac (CDP)—
  Montgomery *MD-1*
North Powder (City)—Union *OR-4*
North Prairie (Township)—
  McHenry *ND-4*
North Prairie (Village)—
  Waukesha *WI-3*
North Providence (Town)—
  Providence *RI-1*
North Puyallup (CDP)—Pierce *WA-4*
North Randall (Township)—
  Thomas *KS-4*
North Randall (Village)—
  Cuyahoga *OH-3*
North Reading (Town)—
  Middlesex *MA-1*
North Redington Beach (Town)—
  Pinellas *FL-2*
North Red River (Township)—
  Kittson *MN-3*
North Redwood (City)—
  Redwood *MN-3*
North Rich (Township)—
  Anderson *KS-4*
North Richland Hills (City)—
  Tarrant *TX-2*
Northridge (CDP)—Clark *OH-3*
Northridge (CDP)—Montgomery .. *OH-3*
North Ridgeville (City)—Lorain ... *OH-3*
North River (Township)—
  Shelby *MO-3*
North River (City)—Cass *ND-4*
North River Shores (CDP)—
  Martin *FL-2*
North Riverside (Village)—Cook ... *IL-3*

General Index

North Robinson (Village)—
Crawford OH-3
North Rock Springs (CDP)—
Sweetwater WY-4
North Rolette (Pop. Place)—
Rolette ND-4
Northrop (City)—Martin MN-3
North Roscoe (Township)—
Hodgeman KS-4
North Roseau (Pop. Place)—
Roseau MN-3
North Royalton (City)—
Cuyahoga OH-3
North Salem (Town)—Hendricks ... IN-3
North Salem (Township)—Linn.... MO-3
North Salem (Town)—
Westchester NY-1
North Salt Lake (City)—Davis UT-4
North San Pedro (CDP)—
Nueces TX-2
North Sarasota (CDP)—Sarasota.... FL-2
North Scituate (CDP)—
Plymouth MA-1
North Sea (CDP)—Suffolk NY-1
North Seekonk (CDP)—Bristol..... MA-1
North Seward (Township)—
Stafford KS-4
North Sewickley (Township)—
Beaver PA-1
North Shade (Township)—
Gratiot MI-3
North Shenango (Township)—
Crawford PA-1
North Sheridan (Pop. Place)—
Sheridan ND-4
North Sioux (Pop. Place)—Sioux .. ND-4
North Sioux City (City)—Union ... SD-4
North Slope Borough AK-4
North Smithfield (Town)—
Providence RI-1
North Spearfish (CDP)—
Lawrence SD-4
North Springfield (CDP)—Lane OR-4
North Springfield (CDP)—
Fairfax VA-2
North Stanley (Pop. Place)—
Stanley SD-4
North Star (Township)—Gratiot.... MI-3
North Star (Township)—Brown..... MN-3
North Star (Township)—St.
Louis MN-3
North Star (Township)—Burke ND-4
North Star (Village)—Darke OH-3
North Stonington (Town)—New
London CT-1
North St. Paul (City)—Ramsey MN-3
North Strabane (Township)—
Washington PA-1
North Sugar Creek (Township)—
Randolph MO-3
North Syracuse (Village)—
Onondaga NY-1
North Tarrytown (Village)—
Westchester NY-1
North Terre Haute (CDP)—Vigo.... IN-3
North Tonawanda (City)—
Niagara NY-1
North Towanda (Township)—
Bradford PA-1
North Tripp (Pop. Place)—Tripp... SD-4
North Troy (Village)—Orleans....... VT-1
North Tunica (CDP)—Tunica MS-2
Northumberland (Town)—Coos NH-1
Northumberland (Town)—
Saratoga NY-1

Northumberland (Borough)—
Northumberland PA-1
Northumberland County PA-1
Northumberland County VA-2
North Union (Township)—
Fayette PA-1
North Union (Township)—
Schuylkill PA-1
North Utica (Village)—La Salle...... IL-3
North Vacherie (CDP)—St. James
Parish LA-2
Northvale (Borough)—Bergen...... NJ-1
North Valley (CDP)—Bernalillo ... NM-4
North Valley Stream (CDP)—
Nassau NY-1
North Vernon (City)—Jennings IN-3
North Versailles (Township)—
Allegheny PA-1
Northview (City)—Kent MI-3
North View (Township)—
Christian MO-3
Northview (CDP)—Montgomery... OH-3
North Viking (Township)—
Benson ND-4
Northville (Township)—La Salle IL-3
Northville (City)—Oakland........... MI-3
Northville (City)—Wayne MI-3
Northville (Township)—Wayne...... MI-3
Northville (Village)—Fulton NY-1
Northville (Town)—Spink SD-4
Northville (Township)—Spink SD-4
North Wales (Borough)—
Montgomery PA-1
North Wantagh (CDP)—Nassau.... NY-1
North Wardell (Village)—
Pemiscot MO-3
North Washington (City)—
Chickasaw IA-3
North Washington (unorganized) (Pop.
Place)—Washington................... ME-1
Northway (CDP)—Southeast Fairbanks
Census Area AK-4
Northway Junction (CDP)—Southeast
Fairbanks Census Area AK-4
Northway Village (CDP)—
Southeast Fairbanks Census Area AK-4
North Webster (Town)—
Kosciusko IN-3
Northwest (Township)—Orange....... IN-3
Northwest (Township)—St.
Louis MO-3
Northwest (Township)—Dickey ND-4
Northwest (Township)—Kidder..... ND-4
Northwest (Township)—
Williams OH-3
Northwest Aitkin (Pop. Place)—
Aitkin MN-3
Northwest Arctic Borough AK-4
Northwest Aroostook
(unorganized) (Pop. Place)—
Aroostook ME-1
Northwest Bon Homme (Pop. Place)—
Bon Homme SD-4
Northwestern Shoshone (UT) .. IndRes-4
Northwest Hand (Pop. Place)—
Hand SD-4
Northwest Harbor (CDP)—
Suffolk NY-1
Northwest Harwich (CDP)—
Barnstable MA-1
Northwest Ithaca (CDP)—
Tompkins NY-1
Northwest Jackson (Pop. Place)—
Jackson SD-4

Northwest Koochiching (Pop. Place)—
Koochiching MN-3
Northwest Marion (Township)—
Polk MO-3
Northwest McIntosh (Pop. Place)—
McIntosh ND-4
North Westminster (Village)—
Windham VT-1
Northwest Piscataquis
(unorganized) (Pop. Place)—
Piscataquis ME-1
North Westport (CDP)—Bristol.... MA-1
Northwest Roseau (Pop. Place)—
Roseau MN-3
Northwest Slope (Pop. Place)—
Slope ND-4
Northwest Somerset (unorganized)
(Pop. Place)—Somerset ME-1
Northwest St. Louis (Pop. Place)—St.
Louis MN-3
Northwest Stutsman (Pop. Place)—
Stutsman ND-4
North Whitehall (Township)—
Lehigh PA-1
North Wildwood (City)—Cape
May NJ-1
North Wilkesboro (Town)—
Wilkes NC-2
North Windham (CDP)—
Cumberland ME-1
Northwood (City)—Worth IA-3
Northwood (Town)—
Rockingham NH-1
Northwood (City)—Grand Forks.. ND-4
Northwood (Township)—Grand
Forks ND-4
Northwood (Village)—Wood......... OH-3
North Woodbury (Township)—
Blair PA-1
Northwoods (City)—St. Louis MO-3
North Yarmouth (Town)—
Cumberland ME-1
North Yelm (CDP)—Thurston........ WA-4
North York (Borough)—York PA-1
North Zanesville (CDP)—
Muskingum OH-3
North Ziebach (Pop. Place)—
Ziebach SD-4
Norton (Township)—Kankakee IL-3
Norton (Township)—Jefferson......... KS-4
Norton (City)—Norton KS-4
Norton (Town)—Bristol MA-1
Norton (Township)—Winona MN-3
Norton (Township)—Walsh.......... ND-4
Norton (City)—Summit OH-3
Norton (City)—Wayne OH-3
Norton (Town)—Essex VT-1
Norton Air Force Base (CA) Mil-4
Norton County KS-4
Norton (Independent City) VA-2
Norton Shores (City)—Muskegon.. MI-3
Nortonville (City)—Jefferson.......... KS-4
Nortonville (City)—Hopkins......... KY-2
Norvell (Township)—Jackson MI-3
Norwalk (City)—Los Angeles......... CA-4
Norwalk (City)—Fairfield CT-1
Norwalk (City)—Warren IA-3
Norwalk (City)—Huron OH-3
Norwalk (Township)—Huron......... OH-3
Norwalk (Village)—Monroe WI-3
Norway (City)—Benton IA-3
Norway (Township)—Republic..... KS-4
Norway (Town)—Oxford ME-1
Norway (City)—Dickinson............. MI-3
Norway (Township)—Dickinson.... MI-3

Norway (Township)—Fillmore *MN-3*
Norway (Township)—Kittson *MN-3*
Norway (Town)—Herkimer *NY-1*
Norway (Township)—Traill............*ND-4*
Norway (Town)—Orangeburg *SC-2*
Norway (Township)—Clay *SD-4*
Norway (Township)—Lincoln *SD-4*
Norway (Township)—Roberts *SD-4*
Norway (Township)—Turner *SD-4*
Norway (Town)—Racine................. *WI-3*
Norway Lake (Township)—
  Kandiyohi *MN-3*
Norway Lake (Township)—Wells...*ND-4*
Norwegian (Township)—
  Schuylkill..*PA-1*
Norwegian Grove (Township)—Otter
  Tail *MN-3*
Norwell (Town)—Plymouth *MA-1*
Norwich (City; Town)—New
  London...*CT-1*
Norwich (City)—Kingman *KS-4*
Norwich (Township)—Missaukee .. *MI-3*
Norwich (Township)—Newaygo *MI-3*
Norwich (City)—Chenango............ *NY-1*
Norwich (Town)—Chenango.......... *NY-1*
Norwich (Township)—McHenry....*ND-4*
Norwich (Township)—Franklin *OH-3*
Norwich (Township)—Huron *OH-3*
Norwich (Village)—Muskingum *OH-3*
Norwich (Township)—McKean *PA-1*
Norwich (Town)—Windsor *VT-1*
Norwood (Town)—San Miguel *CO-4*
Norwood (Town)—Warren............. *GA-2*
Norwood (Village)—Peoria *IL-3*
Norwood (City)—Jefferson............. *KY-2*
Norwood (Village)—East Feliciana
  Parish *LA-2*
Norwood (Town)—Norfolk *MA-1*
Norwood (Township)—
  Charlevoix..*MI-3*
Norwood (City)—Carver *MN-3*
Norwood (City)—Wright *MO-3*
Norwood (Borough)—Bergen *NJ-1*
Norwood (Village)—St.
  Lawrence *NY-1*
Norwood (Town)—Stanly.............. *NC-2*
Norwood (City)—Hamilton *OH-3*
Norwood (Borough)—Delaware...... *PA-1*
Norwood (Town)—Langlade *WI-3*
Norwood Court (Town)—St.
  Louis *MO-3*
Norwood Park (Township)—Cook . *IL-3*
Notasulga (Municipality)—Lee *AL-2*
Notasulga (Municipality)—
  Macon *AL-2*
Nottawa (Township)—Isabella *MI-3*
Nottawa (Township)—St. Joseph... *MI-3*
Nottingham (Township)—Wells...... *IN-3*
Nottingham (Town)—
  Rockingham *NH-1*
Nottingham (Township)—
  Harrison *OH-3*
Nottingham (Township)—
  Washington *PA-1*
Nottinghill (Township)—Ozark..... *MO-3*
Nottoway County *VA-2*
Notus (City)—Canyon *ID-4*
Novato (City)—Marin *CA-4*
Novelty (Town)—Knox *MO-3*
Novesta (Township)—Tuscola *MI-3*
Novi (City)—Oakland *MI-3*
Novi (Township)—Oakland *MI-3*
Novice (City)—Coleman *TX-2*
Novinger (City)—Adair *MO-3*
Nowata (City)—Nowata *OK-2*

Nowata County *OK-2*
Noxapater (Town)—Winston *MS-2*
Noxen (Township)—Wyoming....... *PA-1*
Noxubee County *MS-2*
Noyack (CDP)—Suffolk *NY-1*
Noyes (Township)—Clinton............ *PA-1*
Nuangola (Borough)—Luzerne *PA-1*
Nuckolls County *NE-4*
Nucla (Town)—Montrose............... *CO-4*
Nueces County *TX-2*
Nuevo (CDP)—Riverside............... *CA-4*
Nuiqsut (City)—North Slope
  Borough *AK-4*
Nulato (City)—Yukon-Koyukuk Census
  Area *AK-4*
Numa (City)—Appanoose *IA-3*
Numedal (Township)—
  Pennington *MN-3*
Nunapitchuk (City)—Bethel Census
  Area *AK-4*
Nunda (Township)—McHenry........ *IL-3*
Nunda (Township)—Cheboygan *MI-3*
Nunda (Township)—Freeborn *MN-3*
Nunda (Town)—Livingston *NY-1*
Nunda (Village)—Livingston *NY-1*
Nunda (Town)—Lake *SD-4*
Nunda (Township)—Lake *SD-4*
Nunez (Town)—Emanuel *GA-2*
Nunivak Island (AK) *Geog-4*
Nunn (Town)—Weld *CO-4*
Nutley (Township)—Essex *NJ-1*
Nutley (Township)—Day *SD-4*
Nutter Fort (Town)—Harrison...... *WV-2*
Nyack (Village)—Rockland *NY-1*
Nye County *NV-4*
Nyssa (Town)—Malheur................ *OR-4*
Oacoma (Town)—Lyman *SD-4*
Oacoma (Township)—Lyman......... *SD-4*
Oahe Dam (SD) *Geog-4*
Oahu (HI)....................................... *Geog-4*
Oak (Township)—Smith..................*KS-4*
Oak (Township)—Stearns *MN-3*
Oak (Village)—Nuckolls *NE-4*
Oak Bluffs (Town)—Dukes *MA-1*
Oak Brook (Town)—Cook *IL-3*
Oak Brook (Town)—DuPage *IL-3*
Oakbrook (CDP)—Boone *KY-2*
Oakbrook Terrace (City)—
  DuPage *IL-3*
Oak City (Town)—Martin.............. *NC-2*
Oak City (Town)—Millard *UT-4*
Oak Creek (Town)—Routt *CO-4*
Oak Creek (Township)—Butler *NE-4*
Oak Creek (Township)—
  Saunders.. *NE-4*
Oak Creek (Township)—
  Bottineau *ND-4*
Oak Creek (City)—Milwaukee....... *WI-3*
Oakdale (City)—Stanislaus *CA-4*
Oakdale (Township)—Washington.. *IL-3*
Oakdale (Village)—Washington *IL-3*
Oakdale (City)—Allen Parish..........*LA-2*
Oakdale (City)—Washington *MN-3*
Oakdale (Township)—Antelope *NE-4*
Oakdale (Village)—Antelope.......... *NE-4*
Oakdale (CDP)—Suffolk *NY-1*
Oakdale (Borough)—Allegheny *PA-1*
Oakdale (Town)—Morgan *TN-2*
Oakdale (Town)—Monroe *WI-3*
Oakdale (Village)—Monroe............. *WI-3*
Oakes (City)—Dickey *ND-4*
Oakesdale (Town)—Whitman *WA-4*
Oakfield (Town)—Aroostook *ME-1*
Oakfield (Township)—Kent *MI-3*

Oakfield (Town)—Genesee *NY-1*
Oakfield (Village)—Genesee *NY-1*
Oakfield (Town)—Fond du Lac *WI-3*
Oakfield (Village)—Fond du Lac ... *WI-3*
Oakford (Village)—Menard *IL-3*
Oak Forest (City)—Cook................. *IL-3*
Oak Grove (Municipality)—
  Talladega *AL-2*
Oak Grove (Town)—Carroll *AR-2*
Oak Grove (Village)—Rock
  Island.. *IL-3*
Oak Grove (Township)—Benton *IN-3*
Oak Grove (City)—Christian *KY-2*
Oak Grove (Town)—West Carroll
  Parish *LA-2*
Oak Grove (Township)—Anoka ... *MN-3*
Oak Grove (City)—Franklin *MO-3*
Oak Grove (City)—Jackson *MO-3*
Oak Grove (City)—Lafayette *MO-3*
Oak Grove (Town)—Pawnee *OK-2*
Oak Grove (CDP)—Clackamas *OR-4*
Oak Grove (CDP)—Lexington *SC-2*
Oak Grove (CDP)—Washington.... *TN-2*
Oak Grove (Town)—Kaufman....... *TX-2*
Oak Grove (Town)—Dodge *WI-3*
Oak Grove (Town)—Pierce *WI-3*
Oak Grove Heights (Town)—
  Greene *AR-2*
Oak Gulch (Township)—Day *SD-4*
Oakham (Town)—Worcester *MA-1*
Oak Harbor (Village)—Ottawa *OH-3*
Oak Harbor (City)—Island *WA-4*
Oakhaven (City)—Hempstead *AR-2*
Oak Hill (Town)—Wilcox *AL-2*
Oak Hill (City)—Volusia *FL-2*
Oak Hill (City)—Clay *KS-4*
Oak Hill (Township)—Crawford... *MO-3*
Oakhill (Township)—Barnes *ND-4*
Oak Hill (Village)—Jackson *OH-3*
Oak Hill (City)—Davidson *TN-2*
Oak Hill (City)—Fayette *WV-2*
Oak Hills (CDP)—Washington *OR-4*
Oak Hills Place (CDP)—East Baton
  Rouge Parish...................................... *LA-2*
Oak Hollow (Township)—
  Hutchinson... *SD-4*
Oakhurst (CDP)—Madera *CA-4*
Oakhurst (CDP)—Monmouth.......... *NJ-1*
Oakhurst (CDP)—Creek *OK-2*
Oakhurst (CDP)—Tulsa *OK-2*
Oakhurst (City)—San Jacinto *TX-2*
Oak Lake (Township)—
  Brookings.. *SD-4*
Oakland (City)—Alameda............... *CA-4*
Oakland (City)—Orange...................*FL-2*
Oakland (Town)—Coles *IL-3*
Oakland (Township)—Schuyler *IL-3*
Oakland (City)—Pottawattamie.......*IA-3*
Oakland (Township)—Clay *KS-4*
Oakland (Township)—Cloud...........*KS-4*
Oakland (City)—Warren *KY-2*
Oakland (Town)—Kennebec *ME-1*
Oakland (CDP)—Carroll................*MD-1*
Oakland (Town)—Garrett *MD-1*
Oakland (Township)—Freeborn ...*MN-3*
Oakland (Township)—
  Mahnomen *MN-3*
Oakland (Town)—Yalobusha *MS-2*
Oakland (City)—St. Louis............. *MO-3*
Oakland (City)—Burt *NE-4*
Oakland (Township)—Burt *NE-4*
Oakland (Borough)—Bergen *NJ-1*
Oakland (Township)—Mountrail ...*ND-4*
Oakland (Town)—Marshall *OK-2*
Oakland (City)—Douglas *OR-4*

General Index

American Places Dictionary

Oakland (Township)—Butler *PA-1*
Oakland (Borough)—
  Susquehanna *PA-1*
Oakland (Township)—
  Susquehanna *PA-1*
Oakland (Township)—Venango *PA-1*
Oakland (CDP)—Sumter *SC-2*
Oakland (Town)—Fayette *TN-2*
Oakland (Town)—Burnett *WI-3*
Oakland (Town)—Douglas *WI-3*
Oakland (Town)—Jefferson *WI-3*
Oakland Acres (City)—Jasper *IA-3*
Oakland Charter (Township)—
  Oakland *MI-3*
Oakland City (City)—Gibson *IN-3*
Oakland County *MI-3*
Oakland Naval Supply Center
  (CA) *Mil-4*
Oakland Park (City)—Broward *FL-2*
Oakland Park (CDP)—Lake *FL-2*
Oakland Park (Village)—Jasper *MO-3*
Oak Lawn (City)—Cook *IL-3*
Oak Lawn (Township)—Crow
  Wing *MN-3*
Oaklawn-Sunview (CDP)—
  Sedgwick *KS-4*
Oak Leaf (Town)—Ellis *TX-2*
Oakley (CDP)—Contra Costa *CA-4*
Oakley (City)—Cassia *ID-4*
Oakley (Township)—Macon *IL-3*
Oakley (City)—Logan *KS-4*
Oakley (Township)—Logan *KS-4*
Oakley (City)—Thomas *KS-4*
Oakley (Village)—Saginaw *MI-3*
Oakley (Town)—Summit *UT-3*
Oaklyn (Borough)—Camden *NJ-1*
Oakman (Town)—Walker *AL-2*
Oakmont (Borough)—Allegheny *PA-1*
Oak Park (CDP)—Ventura *CA-4*
Oak Park (Town)—Emanuel *GA-2*
Oak Park (City)—Cook *IL-3*
Oak Park (Township)—Cook *IL-3*
Oak Park (CDP)—Clark *IN-3*
Oak Park (City)—Oakland *MI-3*
Oak Park (Township)—Marshall .. *MN-3*
Oak Park Heights (City)—
  Washington *MN-3*
Oak Point (Town)—Denton *TX-2*
Oakport (Township)—Clay *MN-3*
Oak Ridge (CDP)—Orange *FL-2*
Oak Ridge (Village)—Morehouse
  Parish *LA-2*
Oak Ridge (Town)—Cape
  Girardeau *MO-3*
Oakridge (City)—Lane *OR-4*
Oak Ridge (City)—Anderson *TN-2*
Oak Ridge (City)—Roane *TN-2*
Oak Ridge (Town)—Cooke *TX-2*
Oak Ridge (Town)—Kaufman *TX-2*
Oak Ridge North (Town)—
  Montgomery *TX-2*
Oak Run (Township)—Madison *OH-3*
Oaks (Village)—Clay *MO-3*
Oaks (Town)—Cherokee *OK-2*
Oaks (Town)—Delaware *OK-2*
Oakton (CDP)—Fairfax *VA-2*
Oaktown (Town)—Knox *IN-3*
Oak Trail Shores (CDP)—Hood *TX-2*
Oakvale (Town)—Mercer *WV-2*
Oak Valley (Township)—Elk *KS-4*
Oak Valley (Township)—Otter
  Tail *MN-3*
Oak Valley (CDP)—Gloucester *NJ-1*
Oak Valley (Township)—
  Bottineau *ND-4*

Oak Valley (Town)—Navarro *TX-2*
Oak View (CDP)—Ventura *CA-4*
Oakview (Village)—Clay *MO-3*
Oakville (CDP)—Litchfield *CT-1*
Oakville (City)—Louisa *IA-3*
Oakville (CDP)—St. Louis *MO-3*
Oakville (Township)—Grand
  Forks *ND-4*
Oakville (City)—Grays Harbor *WA-4*
Oakwood (Town)—Hall *GA-2*
Oakwood (Township)—Vermilion .. *IL-3*
Oakwood (Village)—Vermilion *IL-3*
Oakwood (Township)—Wabasha .. *MN-3*
Oakwood (Village)—Clay *MO-3*
Oakwood (Township)—Walsh *ND-4*
Oakwood (Village)—Cuyahoga *OH-3*
Oakwood (City)—Montgomery *OH-3*
Oakwood (Village)—Paulding *OH-3*
Oakwood (Town)—Dewey *OK-2*
Oakwood (Township)—Brookings . *SD-4*
Oakwood (Town)—Leon *TX-2*
Oakwood Hills (Village)—
  McHenry *IL-3*
Oakwood Park (Village)—Clay *MO-3*
Oasis (Town)—Waushara *WI-3*
Oatfield (CDP)—Clackamas *OR-4*
Oberlin (City)—Decatur *KS-4*
Oberlin (Township)—Decatur *KS-4*
Oberlin (Town)—Allen Parish *LA-2*
Oberlin (City)—Lorain *OH-3*
Oberon (City)—Benson *ND-4*
Oberon (Township)—Benson *ND-4*
Obert (Village)—Cedar *NE-4*
Obetz (Village)—Franklin *OH-3*
Obion (Town)—Obion *TN-2*
Obion County *TN-2*
Oblong (Town)—Crawford *IL-3*
Oblong (Township)—Crawford *IL-3*
O'Brien (Township)—Beltrami *MN-3*
O'Brien (City)—Haskell *TX-2*
O'Brien County *IA-3*
Ocala (City)—Marion *FL-2*
Occidental (CDP)—Sonoma *CA-4*
Occoquan (Town)—Prince
  William *VA-2*
Ocean (Township)—Monmouth *NJ-1*
Ocean (Township)—Ocean *NJ-1*
Oceana (Town)—Wyoming *WV-2*
Oceana County *MI-3*
Ocean Acres (CDP)—Ocean *NJ-1*
Oceana Naval Air Station (VA) *Mil-4*
Ocean Beach (Village)—Suffolk *NY-1*
Ocean Bluff-Brant Rock (CDP)—
  Plymouth *MA-1*
Ocean Breeze Park (Town)—
  Martin *FL-2*
Ocean City (CDP)—Okaloosa *FL-2*
Ocean City (Town)—Worcester *MD-1*
Ocean City (City)—Cape May *NJ-1*
Ocean County *NJ-1*
Ocean Gate (Borough)—Ocean *NJ-1*
Ocean Grove (CDP)—Bristol *MA-1*
Ocean Grove (CDP)—Monmouth .. *NJ-1*
Ocean Isle Beach (Town)—
  Brunswick *NC-2*
Oceano (CDP)—San Luis Obispo .. *CA-4*
Ocean Park (CDP)—Pacific *WA-4*
Ocean Pines (CDP)—Worcester *MD-1*
Oceanport (Borough)—
  Monmouth *NJ-1*
Ocean Ridge (Town)—Palm
  Beach *FL-2*
Ocean Shores (City)—Grays
  Harbor *WA-4*
Oceanside (City)—San Diego *CA-4*

Oceanside (CDP)—Nassau .... *NY-*
Ocean Springs (City)—Jackson .... *MS-*
Ocean View (Town)—Sussex .... *DE-*
Oceola (Township)—Livingston ... *MI-*
Ochelata (Town)—Washington ..... *OK-*
Ocheyedan (City)—Osceola .... *IA-*
Ochiltree County .... *TX-*
Ochlocknee (Town)—Thomas ...... *GA-*
Ocilla (City)—Irwin .... *GA-*
Ocoee (City)—Orange .... *FL-*
Oconee (Town)—Washington ...... *GA-*
Oconee (Township)—Shelby .... *IL-*
Oconee (Village)—Shelby .... *IL-*
Oconee (Township)—Platte .... *NE-*
Oconee County .... *GA-*
Oconee County .... *SC-*
Oconomowoc (City)—Waukesha ... *WI-*
Oconomowoc (Town)—
  Waukesha .... *WI-*
Oconomowoc Lake (Village)—
  Waukesha .... *WI-*
Oconto (Village)—Custer .... *NE-*
Oconto (City)—Oconto .... *WI-*
Oconto (Town)—Oconto .... *WI-*
Oconto County .... *WI-*
Oconto Falls (City)—Oconto .... *WI-*
Oconto Falls (Town)—Oconto .... *WI-*
Ocqueoc (Township)—Presque
  Isle .... *MI-*
Ocracoke Island (NC) .... *Geog-*
Octa (Village)—Fayette .... *OH-*
Octavia (Village)—Butler .... *NE-*
Odanah (CDP)—Ashland .... *WI-*
Odebolt (City)—Sac .... *IA-*
Odee (Township)—Meade .... *KS-*
Odell (Township)—Livingston .... *IL-*
Odell (Village)—Livingston .... *IL-*
Odell (Village)—Gage .... *NE-*
Odell (Township)—Coos .... *NH-*
Odem (City)—San Patricio *TX-2*
Oden (Town)—Montgomery *AR-2*
Odenton (CDP)—Anne Arundel .. *MD-*
Odenville (Town)—St. Clair *AL-2*
Odessa (Town)—New Castle *DE-1*
Odessa (Township)—Jewell .... *KS-*
Odessa (Township)—Rice .... *KS-*
Odessa (Township)—Ionia *MI-3*
Odessa (City)—Big Stone *MN-3*
Odessa (Township)—Big Stone ... *MN-3*
Odessa (City)—Lafayette *MO-3*
Odessa (Township)—Buffalo *NE-4*
Odessa (Village)—Schuyler *NY-1*
Odessa (Township)—Hettinger ... *ND-4*
Odessa (Township)—Ramsey *ND-4*
Odessa (Township)—Edmunds ... *SD-4*
Odessa (City)—Ector *TX-2*
Odessa (City)—Midland *TX-2*
Odessa (Town)—Lincoln *WA-4*
Odin (Town)—Marion *IL-3*
Odin (Township)—Marion *IL-3*
Odin (City)—Watonwan *MN-3*
Odin (Township)—Watonwan *MN-3*
Odin (Township)—McHenry *ND-4*
Odon (Town)—Daviess *IN-3*
O'Donnell (City)—Dawson *TX-2*
O'Donnell (City)—Lynn *TX-2*
Odum (Town)—Wayne *GA-2*
Oelrichs (Town)—Fall River *SD-4*
Oelwein (City)—Fayette *IA-3*
O'Fallon (Town)—St. Clair *IL-3*
O'Fallon (Township)—St. Clair .. *IL-3*
O'Fallon (City)—St. Charles *MO-3*
O'Fallon (Township)—St.
  Charles *MO-3*
Offerle (City)—Edwards *KS-4*

Offutt AFB West (Military Facility)—
    Sarpy NE-4
Offutt Air Force (NE) Mil-4
Ogallah (Township)—Trego KS-4
Ogallala (City)—Keith NE-4
Ogden (Town)—Little River AR-2
Ogden (Township)—Champaign IL-3
Ogden (Village)—Champaign IL-3
Ogden (City)—Boone IA-3
Ogden (City)—Riley KS-4
Ogden (Township)—Riley KS-4
Ogden (Township)—Lenawee MI-3
Ogden (Town)—Monroe NY-1
Ogden (CDP)—New Hanover NC-2
Ogden (City)—Weber UT-4
Ogden Dunes (Town)—Porter IN-3
Ogdensburg (Borough)—Sussex NJ-1
Ogdensburg (City)—St. Lawrence .. NY-1
Ogdensburg (Village)—Waupaca WI-3
Ogema (City)—Becker MN-3
Ogema (Township)—Pine MN-3
Ogema (Town)—Price WI-3
Ogemaw (Township)—Ogemaw MI-3
Ogemaw County MI-3
Ogilvie (City)—Kanabec MN-3
Oglala (CDP)—Shannon SD-4
Ogle (Township)—Somerset PA-1
Ogle County IL-3
Oglesby (Town)—La Salle IL-3
Oglesby (City)—Coryell TX-2
Oglethorpe (City)—Macon GA-2
Oglethorpe County GA-2
Ogunquit (Town)—York ME-1
O'Hara (Township)—Allegheny PA-1
Ohatchee (Town)—Calhoun AL-2
Ohio (Township)—Bureau IL-3
Ohio (Village)—Bureau IL-3
Ohio (Township)—Bartholomew IN-3
Ohio (Township)—Crawford IN-3
Ohio (Township)—Spencer IN-3
Ohio (Township)—Warrick IN-3
Ohio (Township)—Franklin KS-4
Ohio (Township)—Ness KS-4
Ohio (Township)—Saline KS-4
Ohio (Township)—Sedgwick KS-4
Ohio (Township)—Stafford KS-4
Ohio (Township)—Mississippi MO-3
Ohio (Town)—Herkimer NY-1
Ohio (Township)—Clermont OH-3
Ohio (Township)—Gallia OH-3
Ohio (Township)—Monroe OH-3
Ohio (Township)—Allegheny PA-1
Ohio (Township)—Hand SD-4
Ohio City (Village)—Van Wert OH-3
Ohio County IN-3
Ohio County KY-2
Ohio County WV-2
Ohio Grove (Township)—Mercer ... IL-3
Ohiopyle (Borough)—Fayette PA-1
Ohio River (NC) Geog-4
Ohioville (Borough)—Beaver PA-1
Ohiowa (Village)—Fillmore NE-4
Ohlman (Village)—Montgomery IL-3
Oil (Township)—Perry IN-3
Oil City (Town)—Caddo Parish LA-2
Oil City (City)—Venango PA-1
Oil Creek (Township)—Crawford ... PA-1
Oilcreek (Township)—Venango PA-1
Oildale (CDP)—Kern CA-4
Oil Springs Reservation (Pop. Place)—
    Allegany NY-1
Oil Springs Reservation (Pop. Place)—
    Cattaraugus NY-1
Oilton (City)—Creek OK-2
Oil Trough (City)—Independence .. AR-2

Ojai (City)—Ventura CA-4
Ojibwa (Town)—Sawyer WI-3
Ojo Amarillo (CDP)—San Juan ... NM-4
Ojus (CDP)—Dade FL-2
Okabena (City)—Jackson MN-3
Okaloosa County FL-2
Okanogan (City)—Okanogan WA-4
Okanogan County WA-4
Okarche (Town)—Canadian OK-2
Okarche (Town)—Kingfisher OK-2
Okaton (Township)—Jones SD-4
Okauchee Lake (CDP)—
    Waukesha WI-3
Okaw (Township)—Shelby IL-3
Okawville (Township)—
    Washington IL-3
Okawville (Village)—Washington ... IL-3
Okay (Town)—Wagoner OK-2
O'Kean (Town)—Randolph AR-2
Okeechobee (City)—Okeechobee FL-2
Okeechobee, Lake (FL) Geog-4
Okeechobee County FL-2
Okeechobee Waterway (FL) Geog-4
Okeene (Town)—Blaine OK-2
Okefenokee Swamp (FL) Geog-4
Okemah (City)—Okfuskee OK-2
Okemos (CDP)—Ingham MI-3
Oketo (City)—Marshall KS-4
Oketo (Township)—Marshall KS-4
Okfuskee County OK-2
Oklahoma (Borough)—
    Westmoreland PA-1
Oklahoma City (City)—
    Canadian OK-2
Oklahoma City (City)—
    Cleveland OK-2
Oklahoma City (City)—McClain ... OK-2
Oklahoma City (City)—
    Oklahoma OK-2
Oklahoma City (City)—
    Pottawatomie OK-2
Oklahoma County OK-2
Oklahoma Panhandle (OK) Geog-4
Oklee (City)—Red Lake MN-3
Okmulgee (City)—Okmulgee OK-2
Okmulgee County OK-2
Okoboji (City)—Dickinson IA-3
Okolona (Town)—Clark AR-2
Okolona (CDP)—Jefferson KY-2
Okolona (City)—Chickasaw MS-2
Oktaha (Town)—Muskogee OK-2
Oktibbeha County MS-2
Ola (City)—Yell AR-2
Ola (Township)—Brule SD-4
Olanta (Town)—Florence SC-2
Olar (Town)—Bamberg SC-2
Olathe (Town)—Montrose CO-4
Olathe (City)—Johnson KS-4
Olathe (Township)—Johnson KS-4
Olcott (CDP)—Niagara NY-1
Old Appleton (Town)—Cape
    Girardeau MO-3
Old Bennington (Village)—
    Bennington VT-1
Old Bethpage (CDP)—Nassau NY-1
Old Bridge (Township)—
    Middlesex NJ-1
Old Brookville (Village)—Nassau .. NY-1
Old Brownsboro Place (City)—
    Jefferson KY-2
Oldenburg (Town)—Franklin IN-3
Old Faithful (WY) Geog-4
Oldfield (Township)—Christian MO-3
Old Field (Village)—Suffolk NY-1

Old Forge (Borough)—
    Lackawanna PA-1
Old Fort (Town)—McDowell NC-2
Oldham (City)—Kingsbury SD-4
Oldham County KY-2
Oldham County TX-2
Old Harbor (City)—Kodiak Island
    Borough AK-4
Old Jefferson (CDP)—East Baton
    Rouge Parish LA-2
Old Lycoming (Township)—
    Lycoming PA-1
Old Lyme (Town)—New London .. CT-1
Old Man of the Mountains
    (NH) Geog-4
Oldmans (Township)—Salem NJ-1
Old Mill Creek (Village)—Lake IL-3
Old Monroe (City)—Lincoln MO-3
Old Orchard Beach (ME) Geog-4
Old Orchard Beach (Town)—
    York ME-1
Old Ripley (Township)—Bond IL-3
Old Ripley (Village)—Bond IL-3
Old River-Winfree (Town)—
    Chambers TX-2
Olds (City)—Henry IA-3
Old Saybrook (Town)—
    Middlesex CT-1
Old Shawneetown (Village)—
    Gallatin IL-3
Oldsmar (City)—Pinellas FL-2
Old Spanish Trail (ME) Geog-4
Old Tappan (Borough)—Bergen NJ-1
Oldtown (City)—Bonner ID-4
Oldtown (Township)—McLean IL-3
Old Town (City)—Penobscot ME-1
Old Washington (Village)—
    Guernsey OH-3
Old Westbury (Village)—Nassau NY-1
Olean (Town)—Miller MO-3
Olean (City)—Cattaraugus NY-1
Olean (Town)—Cattaraugus NY-1
Olean (Township)—Spink SD-4
Oley (Township)—Berks PA-1
Olin (City)—Jones IA-3
Olio (Township)—Woodford IL-3
Olive (Township)—Madison IL-3
Olive (Township)—Elkhart IN-3
Olive (Township)—St. Joseph IN-3
Olive (Township)—Decatur KS-4
Olive (Township)—Clinton MI-3
Olive (Township)—Ottawa MI-3
Olive (Township)—Butler NE-4
Olive (Town)—Ulster NY-1
Olive (Township)—Meigs OH-3
Olive (Township)—Noble OH-3
Olive Branch (City)—DeSoto MS-2
Olive Hill (City)—Carter KY-2
Olivehurst (CDP)—Yuba CA-4
Oliver (City)—Screven GA-2
Oliver (Township)—Huron MI-3
Oliver (Township)—Kalkaska MI-3
Oliver (Township)—Taney MO-3
Oliver (Township)—Williams ND-4
Oliver (Township)—Adams OH-3
Oliver (Township)—Jefferson PA-1
Oliver (Township)—Mifflin PA-1
Oliver (Township)—Perry PA-1
Oliver (Village)—Douglas WI-3
Oliver County ND-4
Oliver Springs (Town)—
    Anderson TN-2
Oliver Springs (Town)—Morgan TN-2
Oliver Springs (Town)—Roane TN-2
Olivet (City)—Osage KS-4

General Index

American Places Dictionary

Olivet (Township)—Osage *KS-4*
Olivet (City)—Eaton *MI-3*
Olivet (CDP)—Salem *NJ-1*
Olivet (Town)—Hutchinson *SD-4*
Olivette (City)—St. Louis *MO-3*
Olivia (City)—Renville *MN-3*
Olivia (Township)—McHenry *ND-4*
Olla (Town)—La Salle Parish *LA-2*
Ollie (City)—Keokuk *IA-3*
Olmitz (City)—Barton *KS-4*
Olmos Park (City)—Bexar *TX-2*
Olmsted (Village)—Pulaski *IL-3*
Olmsted (Township)—Cuyahoga *OH-3*
Olmsted County *MN-3*
Olmsted Falls (City)—Cuyahoga....*OH-3*
Olney (Town)—Richland............... *IL-3*
Olney (Township)—Richland......... *IL-3*
Olney (CDP)—Montgomery *MD-1*
Olney (Township)—Nobles *MN-3*
Olney (City)—Young *TX-2*
Olney Springs (Town)—Crowley.... *CO-4*
Olpe (City)—Lyon *KS-4*
Olsburg (City)—Pottawatomie *KS-4*
Olson (Township)—Towner *ND-4*
Olton (City)—Lamb *TX-2*
Olustee (Town)—Jackson *OK-2*
Olympia (City)—Thurston *WA-4*
Olympia Fields (Town)—Cook *IL-3*
Olympia Heights (CDP)—Dade......*FL-2*
Olympian Village (City)—
  Jefferson *MO-3*
Olympic Mountains (WA) *Geog-4*
Olyphant (Borough)—
  Lackawanna *PA-1*
Oma (Town)—Iron *WI-3*
Omaha (Town)—Boone *AR-2*
Omaha (City)—Stewart *GA-2*
Omaha (Township)—Gallatin *IL-3*
Omaha (Village)—Gallatin............. *IL-3*
Omaha (City)—Douglas *NE-4*
Omaha (Township)—Thurston *NE-4*
Omaha (City)—Morris *TX-2*
Omaha Reservation (NE) *IndRes-4*
Omak (City)—Okanogan............... *WA-4*
Omao (CDP)—Kauai *HI-4*
Omega (City)—Colquitt *GA-2*
Omega (City)—Tift *GA-2*
Omega (Township)—Marion *IL-3*
Omer (City)—Arenac *MI-3*
Omnia (Township)—Cowley..........*KS-4*
Omphghent (Township)—
  Madison *IL-3*
Omro (Township)—Yellow
  Medicine *MN-3*
Omro (City)—Winnebago *WI-3*
Omro (Town)—Winnebago............ *WI-3*
Onaga (City)—Pottawatomie *KS-4*
Onaka (Town)—Faulk *SD-4*
Onalaska (City)—Polk *TX-2*
Onalaska (City)—La Crosse.......... *WI-3*
Onalaska (Town)—La Crosse....... *WI-3*
Onamia (City)—Mille Lacs........... *MN-3*
Onamia (Township)—Mille Lacs .. *MN-3*
Onancock (Town)—Accomack........ *VA-2*
Onarga (Town)—Iroquois............. *IL-3*
Onarga (Township)—Iroquois......... *IL-3*
Onawa (City)—Monona *IA-3*
Onaway (City)—Latah.................. *ID-4*
Onaway (City)—Presque Isle *MI-3*
Oneco (Township)—Stephenson *IL-3*
Oneida (City)—Knox *IL-3*
Oneida (City)—Delaware *IA-3*
Oneida (City)—Nemaha................*KS-4*
Oneida (Township)—Kearney *NE-4*
Oneida (City)—Madison ....:.. *NY-1*

Oneida (Township)—Huntingdon... *PA-1*
Oneida (Township)—Sanborn *SD-4*
Oneida (Town)—Scott *TN-2*
Oneida (Town)—Outagamie *WI-3*
Oneida Castle (Village)—Oneida... *NY-1*
Oneida Charter (Township)—
  Eaton *MI-3*
Oneida County *ID-4*
Oneida County *NY-1*
Oneida County *WI-3*
Oneida (East) Reservation
  (NY).............................*IndRes-4*
Oneida Lake (NY) *Geog-4*
Oneida (West) Reservation
  (WI)..............................*IndRes-4*
O'Neil (Township)—Faulk *SD-4*
O'Neill (City)—Holt *NE-4*
Onekama (Township)—Manistee... *MI-3*
Onekama (Village)—Manistee *MI-3*
Oneonta (City)—Blount *AL-2*
Oneonta (City)—Otsego *NY-1*
Oneonta (Town)—Otsego *NY-1*
Oneota (Township)—Brown.......... *SD-4*
One Road (Township)—Roberts.... *SD-4*
Ong (Village)—Clay...................... *NE-4*
Onida (City)—Sully *SD-4*
Onion Creek (CDP)—Travis........... *TX-2*
Onley (Town)—Accomack.............. *VA-2*
Onondaga (Township)—Ingham ... *MI-3*
Onondaga (Town)—Onondaga *NY-1*
Onondaga County *NY-1*
Onondaga Reservation (NY).... *IndRes-4*
Onondaga Reservation (Pop. Place)—
  Onondaga *NY-1*
Onota (Township)—Alger *MI-3*
Onset (CDP)—Plymouth............... *MA-1*
Onslow (City)—Jones *IA-3*
Onslow County *NC-2*
Onstad (Township)—Polk *MN-3*
Onsted (Village)—Lenawee *MI-3*
Ontario (City)—San Bernardino.... *CA-4*
Ontario (Township)—Knox *IL-3*
Ontario (Town)—Wayne *NY-1*
Ontario (Township)—Ramsey....... *ND-4*
Ontario (Village)—Richland *OH-3*
Ontario (City)—Malheur............... *OR-4*
Ontario (Township)—Hand *SD-4*
Ontario (Village)—Vernon *WI-3*
Ontario, Lake (NY) *Geog-4*
Ontario County.......................... *NY-1*
Ontelaunee (Township)—Berks....... *PA-1*
Ontonagon (Township)—
  Ontonagon *MI-3*
Ontonagon (Village)—Ontonagon.. *MI-3*
Ontonagon County *MI-3*
Ontonagon Reservation (MI) ... *IndRes-4*
Ontwa (Township)—Cass *MI-3*
Onward (Town)—Cass *IN-3*
Onycha (Municipality)—
  Covington *AL-2*
Oolagah (Oologah) (Town)—
  Rogers *OK-2*
Oolitic (Town)—Lawrence *IN-3*
Ooltewah (CDP)—Hamilton *TN-2*
Oostburg (Village)—Sheboygan *WI-3*
Opal (Town)—Lincoln................... *WY-4*
Opal Cliffs (CDP)—Santa Cruz..... *CA-4*
Opa-locka (City)—Dade.................*FL-2*
Opa-locka North (CDP)—Dade......*FL-2*
Opdahl (Township)—Hamlin......... *SD-4*
Opdyke West (Town)—Hockley.... *TX-2*
Opelika (City)—Lee......................*AL-2*
Opelousas (City)—St. Landry
  Parish *LA-2*
Opheim (Town)—Valley *MT-4*

Ophir (Town)—San Miguel........... *CO-4*
Ophir (Township)—La Salle *IL-3*
Ophir (Township)—Tooele................ *UT-4*
Opp (City)—Covington *AL-2*
Oppelo (City)—Conway *AR-2*
Oppenheim (Town)—Fulton *NY-1*
Opportunity (CDP)—Spokane *WA-4*
Ops (Township)—Walsh *ND-4*
Optima (Town)—Texas *OK-2*
Oquawka (Town)—Henderson *IL-3*
Oquawka (Township)—
  Henderson *IL-3*
Oquirrh (CDP)—Salt Lake *UT-4*
Ora (Township)—Jackson *IL-3*
Ora (Township)—Nelson............... *ND-4*
Oracle (CDP)—Pinal *AZ-4*
Oradell (Borough)—Bergen *NJ-1*
Oran (Township)—Logan *IL-3*
Oran (City)—Scott *MO-3*
Orange (City)—Orange. *CA-4*
Orange (Town)—New Haven *CT-1*
Orange (Township)—Clark. *IL-3*
Orange (Township)—Knox. *IL-3*
Orange (Township)—Fayette......... *IN-3*
Orange (Township)—Noble *IN-3*
Orange (Township)—Rush *IN-3*
Orange (Township)—Lincoln *KS-4*
Orange (Township)—Pawnee *KS-4*
Orange (Town)—Franklin *MA-1*
Orange (Township)—Ionia *MI-3*
Orange (Township)—Kalkaska *MI-3*
Orange (Township)—Douglas *MN-3*
Orange (Town)—Grafton *NH-1*
Orange (Township)—Essex........... *NJ-1*
Orange (Town)—Schuyler *NY-1*
Orange (Township)—Adams *ND-4*
Orange (Township)—Ashland *OH-3*
Orange (Township)—Carroll *OH-3*
Orange (Village)—Cuyahoga *OH-3*
Orange (Township)—Delaware *OH-3*
Orange (Township)—Hancock *OH-3*
Orange (Township)—Meigs *OH-3*
Orange (Township)—Shelby.........*OH-3*
Orange (Township)—Columbia *PA-1*
Orange (City)—Orange. *TX-2*
Orange (Town)—Orange............... *VT-1*
Orange (Town)—Orange............... *VA-2*
Orange (Town)—Juneau *WI-3*
Orange Beach (Municipality)—
  Baldwin *AL-2*
Orangeburg (CDP)—Rockland *NY-1*
Orangeburg (City)—Orangeburg ... *SC-2*
Orangeburg County *SC-2*
Orange City (City)—Volusia *FL-2*
Orange City (City)—Sioux *IA-3*
Orange County *CA-4*
Orange County *FL-2*
Orange County *IN-3*
Orange County *NY-1*
Orange County *NC-2*
Orange County *TX-2*
Orange County *VT-1*
Orange County *VA-2*
Orange Cove (City)—Fresno......... *CA-4*
Orange Grove (CDP)—Harrison *MS-2*
Orange Grove (City)—Jim Wells ... *TX-2*
Orange Lake (CDP)—Orange *NY-1*
Orange Park (Town)—Clay............*FL-2*
Orangetown (Town)—Rockland..... *NY-1*
Orangevale (CDP)—Sacramento ... *CA-4*
Orangeville (Village)—Stephenson... *IL-3*
Orangeville (Township)—Orange... *IN-3*
Orangeville (Township)—Barry..... *MI-3*
Orangeville (Town)—Wyoming...... *NY-1*
Orangeville (Village)—Trumbull....*OH-3*

American Places Dictionary — General Index

Orangeville (Borough)—Columbia.. *PA-1*
Orangeville (City)—Emery............ *UT-4*
Orbisonia (Borough)—
   Huntingdon *PA-1*
Orchard (Township)—Wayne........ *IL-3*
Orchard (City)—Mitchell *IA-3*
Orchard (Village)—Antelope........ *NE-4*
Orchard (Town)—Fort Bend........... *TX-2*
Orchard City (Town)—Delta *CO-4*
Orchard Grass Hills (City)—
   Oldham.......................*KY-2*
Orchard Hill (Town)—Spalding..... *GA-2*
Orchard Homes (CDP)—
   Missoula *MT-4*
Orchard Lake Village (City)—
   Oakland.......................*MI-3*
Orchard Mesa (CDP)—Mesa *CO-4*
Orchard Park (Town)—Erie *NY-1*
Orchard Park (Village)—Erie........ *NY-1*
Orchards North (CDP)—Clark *WA-4*
Orchards South (CDP)—Clark *WA-4*
Orchid (Town)—Indian River........ *FL-2*
Ord (Township)—Antelope *NE-4*
Ord (City)—Valley....................... *NE-4*
Ord (Township)—Valley................ *NE-4*
Orderville (Town)—Kane *UT-4*
Ordway (Town)—Crowley............. *CO-4*
Ordway (Township)—Brown.......... *SD-4*
Oreana (Village)—Macon *IL-3*
Ore City (City)—Upshur................ *TX-2*
Oregon (Town)—Ogle *IL-3*
Oregon (Township)—Ogle............. *IL-3*
Oregon (Township)—Clark *IN-3*
Oregon (Township)—Starke *IN-3*
Oregon (Township)—Lapeer *MI-3*
Oregon (City)—Holt *MO-3*
Oregon (City)—Lucas *OH-3*
Oregon (Township)—Wayne *PA-1*
Oregon (Town)—Dane *WI-3*
Oregon (Village)—Dane *WI-3*
Oregon City (City)—Clackamas *OR-4*
Oregon County *MO-3*
Oregon Trail (NY) *Geog-4*
Orel (Township)—Wayne *IL-3*
Orem (City)—Utah........................ *UT-4*
Orestes (Town)—Madison............. *IN-3*
Orford (Town)—Grafton................ *NH-1*
Orfordville (Village)—Rock *WI-3*
Orient (City)—Franklin.................. *IL-3*
Orient (City)—Adair *IA-3*
Orient (Town)—Aroostook............ *ME-1*
Orient (Township)—Osceola *MI-3*
Orient (Village)—Pickaway............ *OH-3*
Orient (Town)—Faulk *SD-4*
Orient (Township)—Faulk............. *SD-4*
Orienta (Town)—Bayfield *WI-3*
Oriental (Town)—Pamlico............. *NC-2*
Orinda (City)—Contra Costa......... *CA-4*
Orion (Township)—Fulton *IL-3*
Orion (Town)—Henry *IL-3*
Orion (Township)—Oakland.......... *MI-3*
Orion (Township)—Olmsted *MN-3*
Orion (Town)—Richland *WI-3*
Oriska (City)—Barnes *ND-4*
Oriska (Township)—Barnes *ND-4*
Oriskany (Village)—Oneida *NY-1*
Oriskany Falls (Village)—Oneida... *NY-1*
Orland (City)—Glenn.................... *CA-4*
Orland (Township)—Cook............. *IL-3*
Orland (Town)—Steuben............... *IN-3*
Orland (Town)—Hancock *ME-1*
Orland (Township)—Lake.............. *SD-4*
Orland Hills (Village)—Cook......... *IL-3*
Orlando (City)—Orange *FL-2*
Orlando (Township)—Cheyenne..... *KS-4*

Orlando (Town)—Logan *OK-2*
Orland Park (Village)—Cook......... *IL-3*
Orleans (Town)—Orange............... *IN-3*
Orleans (Township)—Orange *IN-3*
Orleans (City)—Dickinson *IA-3*
Orleans (Town)—Barnstable *MA-1*
Orleans (Township)—Ionia *MI-3*
Orleans (Township)—Harlan *NE-4*
Orleans (Village)—Harlan *NE-4*
Orleans (Town)—Jefferson............ *NY-1*
Orleans (Village)—Orleans *VT-1*
Orleans County *NY-1*
Orleans County *VT-1*
Orleans Parish *LA-2*
Orlien (Township)—Ward *ND-4*
Orlinda (Town)—Robertson.......... *TN-2*
Orlovista (CDP)—Orange *FL-2*
Orme (Town)—Marion *TN-2*
Ormond Beach (City)—Volusia *FL-2*
Ormond-By-The-Sea (CDP)—
   Volusia *FL-2*
Ormsby (City)—Martin................. *MN-3*
Ormsby (Township)—Watonwan ... *MN-3*
Orofino (City)—Clearwater........... *ID-4*
Orono (Town)—Penobscot *ME-1*
Orono (City)—Hennepin............... *MN-3*
Oronoco (City)—Olmsted *MN-3*
Oronoco (Township)—Olmsted *MN-3*
Oronogo (City)—Jasper................. *MO-3*
Oronoko (Township)—Berrien...... *MI-3*
Orosi (CDP)—Tulare..................... *CA-4*
Oro Valley (Town)—Pima............. *AZ-4*
Oroville (City)—Butte *CA-4*
Oroville (City)—Okanogan *WA-4*
Oroville Dam (CA) *Geog-4*
Oroville East (CDP)—Butte *CA-4*
Orr (City)—St. Louis..................... *MN-3*
Orrick (City)—Ray *MO-3*
Orrick (Township)—Ray *MO-3*
Orrington (Town)—Penobscot *ME-1*
Orrock (Township)—Sherburne *MN-3*
Orrstown (Borough)—Franklin *PA-1*
Orrum (Town)—Robeson *NC-2*
Orrville (Town)—Dallas *AL-2*
Orrville (City)—Wayne *OH-3*
Orthell (Township)—Williams *ND-4*
Orting (Town)—Pierce *WA-4*
Ortley (Town)—Roberts *SD-4*
Ortley (Township)—Roberts *SD-4*
Orton (Township)—Wadena *MN-3*
Ortonville (Village)—Oakland *MI-3*
Ortonville (City)—Big Stone *MN-3*
Ortonville (Township)—Big
   Stone *MN-3*
Ortonville (City)—Lac qui Parle .. *MN-3*
Orvil (Township)—Logan.............. *IL-3*
Orwell (Township)—Otter Tail *MN-3*
Orwell (Town)—Oswego................ *NY-1*
Orwell (Township)—Ashtabula *OH-3*
Orwell (Village)—Ashtabula...........*OH-3*
Orwell (Town)—Bradford.............. *PA-1*
Orwell (Town)—Addison *VT-1*
Orwigsburg (Borough)—Schuylkill.. *PA-1*
Osage (Township)—La Salle *IL-3*
Osage (City)—Mitchell *IA-3*
Osage (Township)—Allen *KS-4*
Osage (Township)—Bourbon *KS-4*
Osage (Township)—Crawford *KS-4*
Osage (Township)—Labette *KS-4*
Osage (Township)—Miami *KS-4*
Osage (Township)—Becker *MN-3*
Osage (Township)—Bates *MO-3*
Osage (Township)—Camden *MO-3*
Osage (Township)—Cole *MO-3*
Osage (Township)—Crawford *MO-3*

Osage (Township)—Dent *MO-3*
Osage (Township)—Henry *MO-3*
Osage (Township)—Laclede *MO-3*
Osage (Township)—Miller............ *MO-3*
Osage (Township)—Morgan *MO-3*
Osage (Township)—St. Clair *MO-3*
Osage (Township)—Vernon........... *MO-3*
Osage (Town)—Osage *OK-2*
Osage (Town)—Monongalia *WV-2*
Osage Beach (City)—Camden....... *MO-3*
Osage Beach (City)—Miller *MO-3*
Osage City (City)—Osage.............. *KS-4*
Osage County *KS-4*
Osage County *MO-3*
Osage County *OK-2*
Osage Reservation (OK)........... *IndRes-4*
Osage River (MO)........................ *Geog-4*
Osago (Township)—Nelson *ND-4*
Osakis (City)—Douglas *MN-3*
Osakis (Township)—Douglas *MN-3*
Osakis (City)—Todd *MN-3*
Osawatomie (City)—Miami *KS-4*
Osawatomie (Township)—Miami... *KS-4*
Osborn (Town)—Hancock *ME-1*
Osborn (City)—Clinton *MO-3*
Osborn (City)—DeKalb *MO-3*
Osborn (Township)—Mountrail..... *ND-4*
Osborn (Town)—Outagamie *WI-3*
Osborne (City)—Osborne.............. *KS-4*
Osborne (Township)—Sumner...... *KS-4*
Osborne (Township)—Pipestone... *MN-3*
Osborne (Borough)—Allegheny........ *PA-1*
Osborne County *KS-4*
Osburn (City)—Shoshone............. *ID-4*
Oscar (Township)—Otter Tail *MN-3*
Oscarville (CDP)—Bethel Census
   Area *AK-4*
Osceola (City)—Mississippi *AR-2*
Osceola (Township)—Stark *IL-3*
Osceola (Town)—St. Joseph.......... *IN-3*
Osceola (City)—Clarke *IA-3*
Osceola (Township)—Houghton *MI-3*
Osceola (Township)—Osceola *MI-3*
Osceola (Township)—Renville *MN-3*
Osceola (Township)—Camden...... *MO-3*
Osceola (City)—St. Clair *MO-3*
Osceola (Township)—St. Clair...... *MO-3*
Osceola (City)—Polk *NE-4*
Osceola (Town)—Lewis................. *NY-1*
Osceola (Township)—Tioga *PA-1*
Osceola (Township)—Brown *SD-4*
Osceola (Township)—Grant *SD-4*
Osceola (Town)—Fond du Lac *WI-3*
Osceola (Town)—Polk *WI-3*
Osceola (Village)—Polk *WI-3*
Osceola County *FL-2*
Osceola County *IA-3*
Osceola County *MI-3*
Osceola Mills (Borough)—
   Clearfield.....................*PA-1*
Osco (Township)—Henry.............. *IL-3*
Oscoda (Township)—Iosco........... *MI-3*
Oscoda County *MI-3*
Osford (Township)—Cavalier *ND-4*
Osgood (Town)—Ripley *IN-3*
Osgood (Town)—Sullivan *MO-3*
Osgood (Village)—Darke...............*OH-3*
Oshawa (Township)—Nicollet....... *MN-3*
Oshkosh (Township)—Yellow
   Medicine *MN-3*
Oshkosh (City)—Garden *NE-4*
Oshkosh (Township)—Wells......... *ND-4*
Oshkosh (City)—Winnebago......... *WI-3*
Oshkosh (Town)—Winnebago........ *WI-3*

1057

Oshtemo (Township)—Kalamazoo MI-3
Oskaloosa (Township)—Clay IL-3
Oskaloosa (City)—Mahaska IA-3
Oskaloosa (City)—Jefferson KS-4
Oskaloosa (Township)—Jefferson ... KS-4
Oslo (City)—Marshall MN-3
Oslo (Township)—Brookings SD-4
Osloe (Township)—Mountrail ND-4
Osmond (City)—Pierce NE-4
Osnabrock (City)—Cavalier ND-4
Osnabrock (Township)—Cavalier .. ND-4
Osnaburg (Township)—Stark OH-3
Osolo (Township)—Elkhart IN-3
Osprey (CDP)—Sarasota FL-2
Osseo (City)—Hennepin MN-3
Osseo (City)—Trempealeau WI-3
Ossian (Town)—Wells IN-3
Ossian (City)—Winneshiek IA-3
Ossian (Town)—Livingston NY-1
Ossineke (Township)—Alpena MI-3
Ossining (Town)—Westchester NY-1
Ossining (Village)—Westchester NY-1
Ossipee (Township)—Carroll NH-1
Ostby (Township)—Bottineau ND-4
Osterdock (City)—Clayton IA-3
Osterville (CDP)—Barnstable MA-1
Ostrander (City)—Fillmore MN-3
Ostrander (Village)—Delaware OH-3
Oswayo (Borough)—Potter PA-1
Oswayo (Township)—Potter PA-1
Oswegatchie (Town)—St. Lawrence NY-1
Oswego (Township)—Kendall IL-3
Oswego (Village)—Kendall IL-3
Oswego (City)—Labette KS-4
Oswego (Township)—Labette KS-4
Oswego (City)—Oswego NY-1
Oswego (Town)—Oswego NY-1
Oswego County NY-1
Osyka (Town)—Pike MS-2
Otego (Township)—Fayette IL-3
Otego (Town)—Otsego NY-1
Otego (Village)—Otsego NY-1
Oteneagen (Township)—Itasca MN-3
Otero County CO-4
Otero County NM-4
Othello (City)—Adams WA-4
Otho (City)—Webster IA-3
Otis (Town)—Washington CO-4
Otis (City)—Rush KS-4
Otis (Town)—Hancock ME-1
Otis (Town)—Berkshire MA-1
Otis (Township)—McLean ND-4
Otisco (Township)—Ionia MI-3
Otisco (Township)—Waseca MN-3
Otisco (Town)—Onondaga NY-1
Otisfield (Town)—Oxford ME-1
Otis Orchards-East Farms (CDP)—Spokane WA-4
Otisville (Village)—Genesee MI-3
Otisville (Village)—Orange NY-1
Oto (City)—Woodbury IA-3
Otoe (Village)—Otoe NE-4
Otoe County NE-4
Otoe-Missouria TJSA (OK) IndRes-4
Otrey (Township)—Big Stone MN-3
Otsego (Township)—Steuben IN-3
Otsego (City)—Allegan MI-3
Otsego (Township)—Allegan MI-3
Otsego (Township)—Wright MN-3
Otsego (Town)—Otsego NY-1
Otsego (Town)—Columbia WI-3
Otsego County MI-3
Otsego County NY-1

Otsego Lake (Township)—Otsego .. MI-3
Otselic (Town)—Chenango NY-1
Ottawa (City)—La Salle IL-3
Ottawa (Township)—La Salle IL-3
Ottawa (City)—Franklin KS-4
Ottawa (Township)—Franklin KS-4
Ottawa (Township)—Ottawa KS-4
Ottawa (Township)—Le Sueur MN-3
Ottawa (Township)—Putnam OH-3
Ottawa (Village)—Putnam OH-3
Ottawa (Town)—Waukesha WI-3
Ottawa County KS-4
Ottawa County MI-3
Ottawa County OH-3
Ottawa County OK-2
Ottawa Hills (Village)—Lucas OH-3
Otter (Township)—Cowley KS-4
Otterbein (Town)—Benton IN-3
Otterbein (Town)—Tippecanoe IN-3
Otter Creek (Town)—Levy FL-2
Otter Creek (Township)—Jersey IL-3
Otter Creek (Township)—La Salle .. IL-3
Otter Creek (Township)—Ripley IN-3
Otter Creek (Township)—Vigo IN-3
Otter Creek (Township)—Greenwood KS-4
Otter Creek (Township)—Dixon .. NE-4
Otter Creek (Township)—Grant ND-4
Otter Creek (Township)—Mercer .. PA-1
Otter Creek (Town)—Dunn WI-3
Otter Creek (Town)—Eau Claire .. WI-3
Otter Lake (Village)—Genesee MI-3
Otter Lake (Village)—Lapeer MI-3
Ottertail (City)—Otter Tail MN-3
Otter Tail (Township)—Otter Tail MN-3
Otter Tail County MN-3
Otter Tail Peninsula (Township)—Cass MN-3
Otterville (Town)—Jersey IL-3
Otterville (City)—Cooper MO-3
Otterville (Township)—Cooper MO-3
Otto (Township)—Kankakee IL-3
Otto (Township)—Oceana MI-3
Otto (Township)—Otter Tail MN-3
Otto (Town)—Cattaraugus NY-1
Otto (Township)—McKean PA-1
Ottosen (City)—Humboldt IA-3
Ottoville (Village)—Putnam OH-3
Ottumwa (City)—Wapello IA-3
Ottumwa (Township)—Coffey KS-4
Otway (Village)—Scioto OH-3
Ouachita County AR-2
Ouachita Mountains (MO) Geog-4
Ouachita Parish LA-2
Ouachita River (MO) Geog-4
Oulu (Town)—Bayfield WI-3
Ouray (City)—Ouray CO-4
Ouray County CO-4
Outagamie County WI-3
Outer Banks (NC) Geog-4
Outlook (Town)—Sheridan MT-4
Ouzinkie (City)—Kodiak Island Borough AK-4
Overbrook (City)—Osage KS-4
Overfield (Township)—Wyoming ... PA-1
Overisel (Township)—Allegan MI-3
Overland (Township)—Morris KS-4
Overland (City)—St. Louis MO-3
Overland (Township)—Ramsey ND-4
Overland Park (City)—Johnson KS-4
Overlea (CDP)—Baltimore MD-1
Overlook-Page Manor (CDP)—Montgomery OH-3
Overly (City)—Bottineau ND-4

Overseas Highway (FL) Geog-4
Overton (Village)—Dawson NE-4
Overton (Township)—Bradford PA-1
Overton (City)—Rusk TX-2
Overton (City)—Smith TX-2
Overton County TN-2
Ovid (Town)—Sedgwick CO-4
Ovid (Township)—Branch MI-3
Ovid (Township)—Clinton MI-3
Ovid (Village)—Clinton MI-3
Ovid (Village)—Shiawassee MI-3
Ovid (Town)—Seneca NY-1
Ovid (Village)—Seneca NY-1
Ovid (Township)—LaMoure ND-4
Oviedo (City)—Seminole FL-2
Ovilla (City)—Dallas TX-2
Ovilla (City)—Ellis TX-2
Owaneco (Village)—Christian IL-3
Owanka No. 13 (Township)—Pennington SD-4
Owasa (City)—Hardin IA-3
Owasco (Town)—Cayuga NY-1
Owasso (City)—Rogers OK-2
Owasso (City)—Tulsa OK-2
Owatonna (City)—Steele MN-3
Owatonna (Township)—Steele MN-3
Owego (Township)—Livingston IL-3
Owego (Town)—Tioga NY-1
Owego (Village)—Tioga NY-1
Owego (Township)—Ransom ND-4
Owen (Township)—Winnebago IL-3
Owen (Township)—Clark IN-3
Owen (Township)—Clinton IN-3
Owen (Township)—Jackson IN-3
Owen (Township)—Warrick IN-3
Owen (City)—Clark WI-3
Owen County IN-3
Owen County KY-2
Owendale (Village)—Huron MI-3
Owens (Township)—St. Louis MN-3
Owensboro (City)—Daviess KY-2
Owens Crossroads (Town)—Madison AL-2
Owensville (Town)—Gibson IN-3
Owensville (City)—Gasconade MO-3
Owensville (Village)—Clermont OH-3
Owenton (City)—Owen KY-2
Owings Mills (CDP)—Baltimore .. MD-1
Owingsville (City)—Bath KY-2
Owls Head (Town)—Knox ME-1
Owosso (City)—Shiawassee MI-3
Owosso (Township)—Shiawassee ... MI-3
Owsley County KY-2
Owyhee (CDP)—Elko NV-4
Owyhee County ID-4
Owyhee Dam (OR) Geog-4
Oxbow (Plantation)—Aroostook ... ME-1
Oxbow (Town)—Cass ND-4
Oxford (Municipality)—Calhoun AL-2
Oxford (Municipality)—Talladega AL-2
Oxford (Town)—Izard AR-2
Oxford (Town)—New Haven CT-1
Oxford (Town)—Newton GA-2
Oxford (City)—Franklin ID-4
Oxford (Township)—Henry IL-3
Oxford (Town)—Benton IN-3
Oxford (City)—Johnson IA-3
Oxford (Township)—Johnson KS-4
Oxford (City)—Sumner KS-4
Oxford (Township)—Sumner KS-4
Oxford (Town)—Oxford ME-1
Oxford (Town)—Talbot MD-1
Oxford (Town)—Worcester MA-1
Oxford (Township)—Oakland MI-3

Oxford (Village)—Oakland *MI-3*	Pacolet (Town)—Spartanburg *SC-2*	Palco (City)—Rooks *KS-4*
Oxford (Township)—Isanti *MN-3*	Pacolet Mills (Town)—	Palermo (CDP)—Butte *CA-4*
Oxford (City)—Lafayette *MS-2*	Spartanburg................................*SC-2*	Palermo (Town)—Waldo *ME-1*
Oxford (Village)—Furnas *NE-4*	Paddock (Township)—Otter Tail .. *MN-3*	Palermo (Town)—Oswego *NY-1*
Oxford (Village)—Harlan *NE-4*	Paddock (Township)—Gage........... *NE-4*	Palermo (City)—Mountrail *ND-4*
Oxford (Township)—Warren............*NJ-1*	Paddock (Township)—Holt *NE-4*	Palermo (Township)—Mountrail ... *ND-4*
Oxford (Town)—Chenango *NY-1*	Paddock Lake (Village)—	Palestine (City)—St. Francis *AR-2*
Oxford (Village)—Chenango *NY-1*	Kenosha *WI-3*	Palestine (Town)—Crawford *IL-3*
Oxford (City)—Granville *NC-2*	Paden (Village)—Tishomingo *MS-2*	Palestine (Township)—Woodford ... *IL-3*
Oxford (City)—Butler *OH-3*	Paden (Town)—Okfuskee...............*OK-2*	Palestine (Township)—Sumner.......*KS-4*
Oxford (Township)—Butler.............*OH-3*	Paden City (City)—Tyler *WV-2*	Palestine (Township)—Cooper......*MO-3*
Oxford (Township)—Coshocton *OH-3*	Paden City (City)—Wetzel *WV-2*	Palestine (Village)—Darke *OH-3*
Oxford (Township)—Delaware *OH-3*	Padonia (Township)—Brown *KS-4*	Palestine (City)—Anderson................ *TX-2*
Oxford (Township)—Erie *OH-3*	Padre Island (TX)............................*Geog-4*	Palisade (Town)—Mesa..................*CO-4*
Oxford (Township)—Guernsey *OH-3*	Paducah (City)—McCracken *KY-2*	Palisade (City)—Aitkin *MN-3*
Oxford (Township)—Tuscarawas ...*OH-3*	Paducah (Town)—Cottle *TX-2*	Palisade (Village)—Hayes *NE-4*
Oxford (Township)—Adams *PA-1*	Page (City)—Coconino...................*AZ-4*	Palisade (Village)—Hitchcock......... *NE-4*
Oxford (Borough)—Chester *PA-1*	Page (Township)—Mille Lacs *MN-3*	Palisade (Township)—Minnehaha . *SD-4*
Oxford (Township)—Hamlin *SD-4*	Page (Village)—Holt.......................*NE-4*	Palisades, the (AZ)........................ *Geog-4*
Oxford (Town)—Marquette *WI-3*	Page (City)—Cass.............................*ND-4*	Palisades Park (Borough)—
Oxford (Village)—Marquette *WI-3*	Page (Township)—Cass *ND-4*	Bergen *NJ-1*
Oxford County............................... *ME-1*	**Page County**.......................................*IA-3*	Palm Bay (City)—Brevard *FL-2*
Oxford Junction (City)—Jones *IA-3*	**Page County**....................................... *VA-2*	Palm Beach (Town)—Palm
Oxnard (City)—Ventura *CA-4*	Pagedale (City)—St. Louis *MO-3*	Beach... *FL-2*
Oxon Hill-Glassmanor (CDP)—Prince	Pageland (Town)—Chesterfield.......*SC-2*	**Palm Beach County**........................*FL-2*
George's *MD-1*	Page Park-Pine Manor (CDP)—	Palm Beach Gardens (City)—Palm
Oyens (City)—Plymouth *IA-3*	Lee... *FL-2*	Beach... *FL-2*
Oyster Bay (Town)—Nassau *NY-1*	Pagosa Springs (Town)—	Palm Beach Shores (Town)—Palm
Oyster Bay Cove (Village)—	Archuleta......................................*CO-4*	Beach... *FL-2*
Nassau *NY-1*	Paguate (CDP)—Cibola *NM-4*	Palm City (CDP)—Martin *FL-2*
Oyster Creek (Village)—Brazoria... *TX-2*	Pahala (CDP)—Hawaii *HI-4*	Palm Coast (CDP)—Flagler *FL-2*
Ozan (City)—Hempstead *AR-2*	Pahapesto (Township)—Tripp........ *SD-4*	Palmdale (City)—Los Angeles *CA-4*
Ozark (City)—Dale...........................*AL-2*	Pahaquarry (Township)—Warren ...*NJ-1*	Palmdale East (CDP)—Los
Ozark (City)—Franklin *AR-2*	Pahoa (CDP)—Hawaii *HI-4*	Angeles *CA-4*
Ozark (Township)—Anderson........*KS-4*	Pahokee (City)—Palm Beach *FL-2*	Palm Desert (City)—Riverside *CA-4*
Ozark (Township)—Barry *MO-3*	Pahrump (CDP)—Nye *NV-4*	Palm Desert Country (CDP)—
Ozark (Township)—Barton *MO-3*	Paia (CDP)—Maui *HI-4*	Riverside *CA-4*
Ozark (City)—Christian *MO-3*	Paincourtville (CDP)—Assumption	Palmer (City)—Matanuska-Susitna
Ozark (Township)—Lawrence.......*MO-3*	Parish *LA-2*	Borough..*AK-4*
Ozark (Township)—Oregon *MO-3*	Paine Field-Lake Stickney (CDP)—	Palmer (Village)—Christian *IL-3*
Ozark (Township)—Texas *MO-3*	Snohomish *WA-4*	Palmer (City)—Pocahontas...............*IA-3*
Ozark (Township)—Webster *MO-3*	Painesville (City)—Lake..................*OH-3*	Palmer (City)—Washington *KS-4*
Ozark, the (MO) *Geog-4*	Painesville (Township)—Lake........*OH-3*	Palmer (Town)—Hampden *MA-1*
Ozark County..................................*MO-3*	Paint (Township)—Fayette.............*OH-3*	Palmer (Township)—Sherburne *MN-3*
Ozark Plateaus (MO)...................... *Geog-4*	Paint (Township)—Highland *OH-3*	Palmer (Village)—Merrick *NE-4*
Ozarks, Lake of the (MO) *Geog-4*	Paint (Township)—Holmes *OH-3*	Palmer (Township)—Divide *ND-4*
Ozaukee County *WI-3*	Paint (Township)—Madison *OH-3*	Palmer (Township)—Putnam..........*OH-3*
Ozawkie (City)—Jefferson *KS-4*	Paint (Township)—Ross *OH-3*	Palmer (Township)—Washington ..*OH-3*
Ozawkie (Township)—Jefferson......*KS-4*	Paint (Township)—Wayne *OH-3*	Palmer (Township)—
Ozette Reservation (WA)..........*IndRes-4*	Paint (Township)—Clarion *PA-1*	Northampton *PA-1*
Ozona (CDP)—Crockett *TX-2*	Paint (Borough)—Somerset............. *PA-1*	Palmer (Town)—Grundy................. *TN-2*
Ozone Park—Queens *NY-1*	Paint (Township)—Somerset............ *PA-1*	Palmer (Town)—Ellis *TX-2*
Paauilo (CDP)—Hawaii *HI-4*	Painted Desert (AZ) *Geog-4*	Palmer Lake (Town)—El Paso......*CO-4*
Pablo (CDP)—Lake *MT-4*	Painted Post (Village)—Steuben *NY-1*	Palmer Park (CDP)—Prince
Pace (CDP)—Santa Rosa *FL-2*	Painted Woods (Township)—	George's *MD-1*
Pace (Town)—Bolivar *MS-2*	Burleigh *ND-4*	Palmerton (Borough)—Carbon *PA-1*
Pacheco (CDP)—Contra Costa *CA-4*	Painter (Town)—Accomack *VA-2*	Palmetto (City)—Manatee *FL-2*
Pachuta (Town)—Clarke *MS-2*	Painterhood (Township)—Elk.........*KS-4*	Palmetto (City)—Coweta *GA-2*
Pacific (City)—Franklin *MO-3*	Paint Rock (Town)—Jackson..........*AL-2*	Palmetto (City)—Fulton *GA-2*
Pacific (City)—St. Louis *MO-3*	Paint Rock (Town)—Concho *TX-2*	Palmetto (Village)—St. Landry
Pacific (City)—King *WA-4*	Paintsville (City)—Johnson............. *KY-2*	Parish *LA-2*
Pacific (City)—Pierce *WA-4*	Paisley (City)—Lake.........................*OR-4*	Palmetto Estates (CDP)—Dade......*FL-2*
Pacific (Town)—Columbia *WI-3*	Paiute of Utah (UT) *IndRes-4*	Palm Harbor (CDP)—Pinellas......*FL-2*
Pacifica (City)—San Mateo *CA-4*	Pajaro (CDP)—Monterey *CA-4*	Palmhurst (City)—Hidalgo *TX-2*
Pacific County..................................*WA-4*	Pakala Village (CDP)—Kauai *HI-4*	Palm River (CDP)—Collier *FL-2*
Pacific Crest Trail (MO).............. *Geog-4*	Palacios (Town)—Matagorda *TX-2*	Palm River-Clair Mel (CDP)—
Pacific Grove (City)—Monterey.... *CA-4*	Palacky (Township)—Ellsworth *KS-4*	Hillsborough *FL-2*
Pacific Junction (City)—Mills *IA-3*	Pala Reservation (CA)............... *IndRes-4*	Palm Shores (Town)—Brevard........*FL-2*
Pacific Missile Test Center (CA)....*Mil-4*	Palatine (Town)—Cook *IL-3*	Palm Springs (City)—Riverside *CA-4*
Pacific Ocean (MO)........................ *Geog-4*	Palatine (Township)—Cook *IL-3*	Palm Springs (Village)—Palm
Pacific Palisades *See* **Los Angeles**—Los	Palatine (Town)—Montgomery *NY-1*	Beach... *FL-2*
Angeles..*CA-4*	Palatine (Township)—Aurora *SD-4*	Palm Springs North (CDP)—
Packer (Township)—Carbon *PA-1*	Palatine Bridge (Village)—	Dade.. *FL-2*
Packwaukee (Town)—Marquette ... *WI-3*	Montgomery..................................*NY-1*	Palm Valley (CDP)—St. Johns *FL-2*
Packwood (City)—Jefferson *IA-3*	Palatka (City)—Putnam *FL-2*	Palm Valley (Town)—Cameron *TX-2*

General Index

Palmview (City)—Hidalgo TX-2
Palmville (Township)—Roseau MN-3
Palmyra (Township)—Lee IL-3
Palmyra (Village)—Macoupin IL-3
Palmyra (Town)—Harrison IN-3
Palmyra (Township)—Knox IN-3
Palmyra (Township)—Douglas KS-4
Palmyra (Town)—Somerset............ ME-1
Palmyra (Township)—Lenawee MI-3
Palmyra (Township)—Renville MN-3
Palmyra (City)—Marion MO-3
Palmyra (Village)—Otoe NE-4
Palmyra (Borough)—Burlington NJ-1
Palmyra (Town)—Wayne NY-1
Palmyra (Village)—Wayne NY-1
Palmyra (Township)—Portage OH-3
Palmyra (Borough)—Lebanon PA-1
Palmyra (Township)—Pike PA-1
Palmyra (Township)—Wayne......... PA-1
Palmyra (Township)—Brown SD-4
Palmyra (Town)—Jefferson WI-3
Palmyra (Village)—Jefferson WI-3
Palo (City)—Linn IA-3
Palo Alto (City)—Santa Clara....... CA-4
Palo Alto (Borough)—Schuylkill PA-1
Palo Alto County............................ IA-3
Palo Pinto (Pop. Place)—Palo
 Pinto.. TX-2
Palo Pinto County TX-2
Palos (Township)—Cook IL-3
Palos Heights (Town)—Cook IL-3
Palos Hills (City)—Cook................. IL-3
Palos Park (Village)—Cook............. IL-3
Palos Verdes Estates (City)—Los
 Angeles CA-4
Palouse (City)—Whitman WA-4
Pamelia (Town)—Jefferson NY-1
Pamlico County............................... NC-2
Pamlico Sound (NC) Geog-4
Pampa (City)—Gray...................... TX-2
Pamplico (Town)—Florence............ SC-2
Pamplin City (Town)—
 Appomattox VA-2
Pamplin City (Town)—Prince
 Edward VA-2
Pamunkey Reservation (VA) IndRes-4
Pana (City)—Christian................... IL-3
Pana (Township)—Christian IL-3
Panama (Village)—Bond IL-3
Panama (Village)—Montgomery..... IL-3
Panama (City)—Shelby IA-3
Panama (Village)—Lancaster......... NE-4
Panama (Village)—Chautauqua..... NY-1
Panama (Town)—Le Flore OK-2
Panama City (City)—Bay............... FL-2
Panama City Beach (City)—Bay....FL-2
Pandora (Village)—Putnam OH-3
Pangburn (City)—White................ AR-2
Panguitch (City)—Garfield UT-4
Panhandle (Town)—Carson TX-2
Panola (Township)—Woodford....... IL-3
Panola (Village)—Woodford IL-3
Panola County MS-2
Panola County TX-2
Panora (City)—Guthrie IA-3
Panorama Park (City)—Scott IA-3
Panorama Village (City)—
 Montgomery................................. TX-2
Pantego (Town)—Beaufort NC-2
Pantego (Town)—Tarrant TX-2
Panther Creek (Township)—Cass ... IL-3
Panthersville (CDP)—De Kalb GA-2
Panton (Town)—Addison VT-1
Paola (City)—Miami KS-4
Paola (Township)—Miami KS-4

Paoli (Town)—Phillips CO-4
Paoli (Town)—Orange IN-3
Paoli (Town)—Orange IN-3
Paoli (Town)—Garvin OK-2
Paonia (Town)—Delta................... CO-4
Papago Reservation (AZ) IndRes-4
Papaikou (CDP)—Hawaii HI-4
Papillion (City)—Sarpy NE-4
Papineau (Township)—Iroquois IL-3
Papineau (Village)—Iroquois IL-3
Parachute (Town)—Garfield CO-4
Paradise (City)—Butte CA-4
Paradise (Township)—Coles IL-3
Paradise (City)—Russell................. KS-4
Paradise (Township)—Russell........ KS-4
Paradise (Township)—Grand
 Traverse MI-3
Paradise (CDP)—Clark NV-4
Paradise (Township)—Eddy ND-4
Paradise (Township)—Lancaster..... PA-1
Paradise (Township)—Monroe PA-1
Paradise (Township)—York PA-1
Paradise (Town)—Cache UT-4
Paradise Hill (Town)—Sequoyah ... OK-2
Paradise Hills (CDP)—
 Bernalillo.................................... NM-4
Paradise Valley (Town)—
 Maricopa AZ-4
Paragon (Town)—Morgan IN-3
Paragonah (Town)—Iron................ UT-4
Paragould (City)—Greene.............. AR-2
Paraje (CDP)—Cibola NM-4
Paramount (City)—Los Angeles CA-4
Paramus (Borough)—Bergen.......... NJ-1
Parchment (City)—Kalamazoo MI-3
Pardeeville (Village)—Columbia.... WI-3
Paris (City)—Logan AR-2
Paris (City)—Bear Lake ID-4
Paris (City)—Edgar IL-3
Paris (Township)—Edgar IL-3
Paris (Township)—Linn KS-4
Paris (City)—Bourbon.................... KY-2
Paris (Town)—Oxford ME-1
Paris (Township)—Huron MI-3
Paris (City)—Monroe..................... MO-3
Paris (Town)—Oneida NY-1
Paris (Township)—Stutsman.......... ND-4
Paris (Township)—Portage............. OH-3
Paris (Township)—Stark OH-3
Paris (Township)—Union OH-3
Paris (City)—Henry........................ TN-2
Paris (City)—Lamar TX-2
Paris (Town)—Grant WI-3
Paris (Town)—Kenosha.................. WI-3
Parish (Town)—Oswego NY-1
Parish (Village)—Oswego NY-1
Parish Grove (Township)—
 Benton.. IN-3
Parishville (Town)—St. Lawrence.. NY-1
Park (City)—Gove.......................... KS-4
Park (Township)—Sedgwick.......... KS-4
Park (Township)—Ottawa MI-3
Park (Township)—St. Joseph MI-3
Park (Township)—Pine MN-3
Park (Township)—Pembina ND-4
Park (Township)—Hand SD-4
Park City (City)—Lake IL-3
Park City (City)—Sedgwick............ KS-4
Park City (City)—Barren KY-2
Park City (City)—Summit UT-4
Park City (City)—Wasatch UT-4
Park County................................... CO-4
Park County MT-4
Park County WY-4
Parkdale (City)—Ashley................. AR-2

Parkdale (Town)—Jefferson MO-3
Parke (Township)—Clay MN-3
Parke County................................. IN-3
Parker (Town)—La Paz.................. AZ-4
Parker (Town)—Douglas CO-4
Parker (City)—Bay FL-2
Parker (City)—Fremont ID-4
Parker (Township)—Clark IL-3
Parker (City)—Linn........................ KS-4
Parker (Township)—Montgomery... KS-4
Parker (Township)—Marshall MN-3
Parker (Township)—Morrison MN-3
Parker (City)—Armstrong PA-1
Parker (Township)—Butler PA-1
Parker (CDP)—Greenville SC-2
Parker (City)—Turner SD-4
Parker (Township)—Turner SD-4
Parker (City)—Collin TX-2
Parker City (Town)—Randolph IN-3
Parker County TX-2
Parker Dam (NC) Geog-4
Parkersburg (Village)—Richland..... IL-3
Parkersburg (City)—Butler............. IA-3
Parkersburg (City)—Wood WV-2
Parker's Cross Roads (City)—
 Henderson.................................. TN-2
Parkers-Iron Springs (CDP)—
 Pulaski.. AR-2
Parkers Prairie (City)—Otter
 Tail.. MN-3
Parkers Prairie (Township)—Otter
 Tail.. MN-3
Parker Strip (CDP)—La Paz.......... AZ-4
Parkerville (City)—Morris KS-4
Parkesburg (Borough)—Chester PA-1
Park Falls (City)—Price WI-3
Park Forest (Village)—Cook IL-3
Park Forest (Village)—Will IL-3
Park Hills (City)—Kenton KY-2
Parkin (City)—Cross AR-2
Park Lake (City)—Oldham KY-2
Parkland (City)—Broward FL-2
Parkland (CDP)—Pierce WA-4
Parkland (Town)—Douglas WI-3
Park Layne (CDP)—Clark OH-3
Parkman (Town)—Piscataquis....... ME-1
Parkman (Township)—Geauga...... OH-3
Park Range (NC) Geog-4
Park Rapids (City)—Hubbard MN-3
Park Ridge (City)—Cook IL-3
Park Ridge (Borough)—Bergen...... NJ-1
Park Ridge (Village)—Portage WI-3
Park River (City)—Walsh ND-4
Parks (Village)—St. Martin
 Parish... LA-2
Parks (Township)—Armstrong........ PA-1
Parksdale (CDP)—Madera............. CA-4
Parkside (Borough)—Delaware PA-1
Parksley (Town)—Accomack.......... VA-2
Park Slope—Kings.......................... NY-1
Parkston (City)—Hutchinson......... SD-4
Parksville (Town)—McCormick..... SC-2
Parkton (Town)—Robeson............. NC-2
Park View (CDP)—Scott IA-3
Parkville (CDP)—Baltimore MD-1
Parkville (City)—Platte MO-3
Parkway (Village)—Franklin MO-3
Parkway-South Sacramento (CDP)—
 Sacramento CA-4
Parkway Village (City)—
 Jefferson...................................... KY-2
Parkwood (CDP)—Madera............. CA-4
Parkwood (CDP)—Durham NC-2
Parkwood (CDP)—Kitsap WA-4
Parlier (City)—Fresno CA-4

Parma (City)—Canyon..................ID-4
Parma (Township)—Jackson...........MI-3
Parma (Village)—Jackson MI-3
Parma (City)—New Madrid..........MO-3
Parma (Town)—Monroe NY-1
Parma (City)—Cuyahoga OH-3
Parma Heights (City)—
  Cuyahoga OH-3
Parmele (Town)—Martin NC-2
Parmelee (CDP)—Todd SD-4
Parmer County TX-2
Parnell (City)—Iowa.....................IA-3
Parnell (Township)—Sheridan KS-4
Parnell (Township)—Polk MN-3
Parnell (Township)—Traverse........MN-3
Parnell (City)—Nodaway MO-3
Parnell (Township)—Brookings SD-4
Parole (CDP)—Anne Arundel........MD-1
Parowan (City)—Iron UT-4
Parral (Village)—Tuscarawas OH-3
Parrish (Town)—Walker.................AL-2
Parrish (Town)—Langlade WI-3
Parris Island (Military Facility)—
  Beaufort SC-2
Parrott (Town)—Terrell..................GA-2
Parrottsville (Town)—Cocke TN-2
Parryville (Borough)—Carbon PA-1
Parshall (City)—Mountrail.............ND-4
Parshall (Township)—Mountrail....ND-4
Parsippany-Troy Hills (Township)—
  Morris NJ-1
Parson Creek (Township)—Linn...MO-3
Parsons (City)—Labette KS-4
Parsons (Town)—Decatur TN-2
Parsons (City)—Tucker WV-2
Parsonsfield (Town)—York ME-1
Partridge (Township)—Woodford... IL-3
Partridge (City)—Reno KS-4
Partridge (Township)—Pine MN-3
Pasadena (City)—Los Angeles CA-4
Pasadena (CDP)—Anne Arundel.. MD-1
Pasadena (City)—Harris TX-2
Pasadena Hills (Village)—St.
  Louis..MO-3
Pasadena Park (Village)—St.
  Louis..MO-3
Pascagoula (City)—Jackson...........MS-2
Pasco (City)—Franklin..................WA-4
Pascoag (CDP)—Providence...........RI-1
Pasco County FL-2
Pascola (Town)—Pemiscot MO-3
Pascola (Township)—Pemiscot MO-3
Pascua Yaqui Reservation
  (AZ)..................................IndRes-4
Pasquotank County NC-2
Passadumkeag (Town)—
  Penobscot................................ME-1
Passaic (Town)—Bates MO-3
Passaic (Township)—Morris NJ-1
Passaic (City)—Passaic...................NJ-1
Passaic County NJ-1
Passamaquoddy Bay (ME) Geog-4
Passamaquoddy Indian Township
  Reservation (Pop. Place)—
  Washington ME-1
Passamaquoddy Pleasant Point
  Reservation (Pop. Place)—
  Washington ME-1
Passamaquody Trust Lands
  (ME) IndRes-4
Pass Christian (City)—Harrison MS-2
Passport (Township)—Ward..........ND-4
Patagonia (Town)—Santa Cruz......AZ-4
Pataskala (Village)—Licking OH-3
Patch Grove (Town)—Grant...........WI-3

Patch Grove (Village)—Grant WI-3
Patchogue (Village)—Suffolk NY-1
Pateros (Town)—Okanogan WA-4
Paterson (City)—Passaic NJ-1
Patmos (Town)—Hempstead AR-2
Patoka (Town)—Marion..................IL-3
Patoka (Township)—Marion...........IL-3
Patoka (Township)—Crawford IN-3
Patoka (Township)—Dubois IN-3
Patoka (Town)—Gibson IN-3
Patoka (Township)—Gibson IN-3
Patoka (Township)—Pike IN-3
Paton (City)—Greene......................IA-3
Patrick (Town)—Chesterfield..........SC-2
Patrick Air Force Base (FL)..........Mil-4
Patrick County VA-2
Patriot (Town)—Switzerland...........IN-3
Patten (Town)—Penobscot............ME-1
Patten (Township)—Aurora SD-4
Patterson (Town)—Woodruff..........AR-2
Patterson (City)—Stanislaus CA-4
Patterson (City)—Pierce..................GA-2
Patterson (Township)—Greene.......IL-3
Patterson (City)—Madison IA-3
Patterson (Town)—St. Mary
  Parish LA-2
Patterson (Town)—Putnam............NY-1
Patterson (Township)—Darke.......OH-3
Patterson (Village)—Hardin..........OH-3
Patterson (Township)—Beaver.......PA-1
Patterson Heights (Borough)—
  Beaver PA-1
Patterson Springs (Town)—
  Cleveland NC-2
Pattison (City)—Waller TX-2
Patton (Township)—Ford IL-3
Patton (Borough)—Cambria PA-1
Patton (Township)—Centre PA-1
Pattonsburg (City)—Daviess MO-3
Patton Village (City)—
  Montgomery.............................TX-2
Paucatuck Eastern Pequot Reservation
  (CT)...................................IndRes-4
Paukaa (CDP)—Hawaii HI-4
Paul (City)—Minidoka ID-4
Paulding (Township)—Paulding ...OH-3
Paulding (Village)—Paulding OH-3
Paulding County GA-2
Paulding County OH-3
Paullina (City)—O'Brien.................IA-3
Paulsboro (Borough)—Gloucester...NJ-1
Paulson (Township)—Towner ND-4
Pauls Valley (City)—Garvin...........OK-2
Pauma Reservation (CA).........IndRes-4
Paupack (Township)—Wayne PA-1
Pavilion (Township)—
  Kalamazoo MI-3
Pavilion (Town)—Genesee NY-1
Pavillion (Town)—Fremont WY-4
Pavo (City)—Brooks GA-2
Pavo (City)—Thomas.....................GA-2
Pawcatuck (CDP)—New London .. CT-1
Pawhuska (Township)—Camden ..MO-3
Pawhuska (City)—Osage OK-2
Pawlet (Town)—Rutland................VT-1
Pawley's Island (Town)—
  Georgetown..............................SC-2
Pawling (Town)—Dutchess NY-1
Pawling (Village)—Dutchess NY-1
Pawnee (Town)—Sangamon...........IL-3
Pawnee (Township)—Sangamon....IL-3
Pawnee (Township)—Bourbon......KS-4
Pawnee (Township)—Pawnee KS-4
Pawnee (Township)—Smith KS-4
Pawnee (Township)—Platte MO-3

Pawnee (City)—Pawnee OK-2
Pawnee City (City)—Pawnee NE-4
Pawnee County KS-4
Pawnee County NE-4
Pawnee County OK-2
Pawnee Rock (City)—Barton KS-4
Pawnee Rock (Township)—
  Barton KS-4
Pawnee TJSA (OK)....................IndRes-4
Paw Paw (Township)—DeKalb.......IL-3
Paw Paw (Town)—Lee IL-3
Paw Paw (Township)—Wabash.......IN-3
Paw Paw (Township)—Elk KS-4
Paw Paw (Township)—Van
  Buren.......................................MI-3
Paw Paw (Village)—Van Buren MI-3
Paw Paw (Town)—Morgan WV-2
Paw Paw Lake (CDP)—Berrien.....MI-3
Pawtucket (City)—Providence........RI-1
Pax (Town)—Fayette WV-2
Paxico (City)—Wabaunsee KS-4
Paxson (CDP)—Valdez-Cordova
  Census Area.............................AK-4
Paxtang (Borough)—Dauphin PA-1
Paxton (Town)—Walton FL-2
Paxton (Town)—Ford IL-3
Paxton (Township)—Logan KS-4
Paxton (Town)—Worcester MA-1
Paxton (Township)—Redwood MN-3
Paxton (Village)—Keith NE-4
Paxton (Township)—Ross.............OH-3
Paxville (Town)—Clarendon SC-2
Payette (City)—Payette ID-4
Payette County ID-4
Payne (City)—Bibb........................GA-2
Payne (Township)—Gove KS-4
Payne (Township)—Sedgwick KS-4
Payne (Township)—St. Louis........MN-3
Payne (Village)—Paulding OH-3
Payne County OK-2
Payne Springs (Town)—
  Henderson................................TX-2
Paynesville (City)—Stearns MN-3
Paynesville (Township)—Stearns ..MN-3
Paynesville (Town)—Pike MO-3
Payson (Town)—Gila AZ-4
Payson (Town)—Adams IL-3
Payson (Township)—Adams IL-3
Payson (City)—Utah UT-4
Payson (Yavapai-Apache) Reservation
  (AZ)..................................IndRes-4
Peabody (City)—Marion KS-4
Peabody (Township)—Marion KS-4
Peabody (City)—Essex MA-1
Peabody (Township)—Bottineau ...ND-4
Peace (Township)—Kanabec.........MN-3
Peace (Township)—Kidder ND-4
Peaceful Valley (Township)—
  Slope..ND-4
Peacham (Town)—Caledonia.........VT-1
Peach Bottom (Township)—York ... PA-1
Peach County GA-2
Peach Lake (CDP)—Putnam NY-1
Peach Lake (CDP)—Westchester ...NY-1
Peachland (Town)—Anson NC-2
Peach Orchard (Town)—Clay AR-2
Peach Orchard (Township)—Ford .. IL-3
Peach Springs (CDP)—Mohave.....AZ-4
Peachtree City (City)—Fayette GA-2
Peacock (Township)—Lake MI-3
Peaine (Township)—Charlevoix.....MI-3
Peak (Town)—Newberry SC-2
Peapack and Gladstone (Borough)—
  Somerset..................................NJ-1
Pea Ridge (City)—Benton..............AR-2

Pea Ridge (Township)—Brown IL-3
Pea Ridge (CDP)—Cabell WV-2
Pearisburg (Town)—Giles VA-2
Pearl (Township)—Pike................. IL-3
Pearl (Village)—Pike IL-3
Pearl (City)—Rankin.....................MS-2
Pearl (Township)—Golden
 Valley ND-4
Pearl (Township)—Hand SD-4
Pearl (Township)—McCook SD-4
Pearland (City)—Brazoria.............. TX-2
Pearland (City)—Harris TX-2
Pearl Beach (CDP)—St. Clair MI-3
Pearl City (CDP)—Honolulu HI-4
Pearl City (Town)—Stephenson...... IL-3
Pearl Creek (Township)—Beadle ... SD-4
Pearl Harbor (HI) Geog-4
Pearl Harbor Naval Station (HI) ...Mil-4
Pearlington (CDP)—Hancock........MS-2
Pearl Lake (Township)—
 LaMoure ND-4
Pearl River (Town)—St. Tammany
 Parish LA-2
Pearl River (CDP)—Neshoba MS-2
Pearl River (CDP)—Rockland NY-1
Pearl River County.........................MS-2
Pearsall (City)—Frio TX-2
Pearson (City)—Atkinson GA-2
Pease (City)—Mille Lacs MN-3
Pease (Township)—Belmont OH-3
Pebble (Township)—Dodge NE-4
Pebble (Township)—Pike OH-3
Pecan Acres (CDP)—Tarrant TX-2
Pecan Acres (CDP)—Wise TX-2
Pecan Gap (City)—Delta TX-2
Pecan Gap (City)—Fannin TX-2
Pecan Grove (CDP)—Fort Bend ... TX-2
Pecan Hill (City)—Ellis TX-2
Pecatonica (Town)—Winnebago IL-3
Pecatonica (Township)—
 Winnebago IL-3
Pechanga Reservation (CA)....... IndRes-4
Peck (City)—Nez Perce ID-4
Peck (Village)—Sanilac MI-3
Peck (Town)—Langlade WI-3
Peconic (CDP)—Suffolk NY-1
Pecos (Village)—San Miguel NM-4
Pecos (City)—Reeves TX-2
Pecos County TX-2
Pecos River (HI) Geog-4
Peculiar (City)—Cass MO-3
Peculiar (Township)—Cass MO-3
Pedley (CDP)—Riverside................ CA-4
Pedro Bay (CDP)—Lake and Peninsula
 Borough AK-4
Peebles (Village)—Adams OH-3
Peekskill (City)—Westchester NY-1
Peeksville (Town)—Ashland WI-3
Pe Ell (Town)—Lewis WA-4
Pee Pee (Township)—Pike OH-3
Peerless Park (Village)—St.
 Louis MO-3
Peetz (Town)—Logan CO-4
Peever (Town)—Roberts SD-4
Pegram (Town)—Cheatham TN-2
Pekin (City)—Peoria IL-3
Pekin (City)—Tazewell IL-3
Pekin (Township)—Tazewell........... IL-3
Pekin (City)—Nelson ND-4
Pelahatchie (Town)—Rankin MS-2
Pelan (Township)—Kittson MN-3
Pelham (City)—Shelby AL-2
Pelham (City)—Mitchell GA-2
Pelham (Town)—Hampshire......... MA-1
Pelham (Town)—Hillsborough........NH-1

Pelham (Town)—Westchester.......... NY-1
Pelham (Village)—Westchester NY-1
Pelham Manor (Village)—
 Westchester NY-1
Pelican (City)—
 Skagway-Hoonah-Angoon Census
 Area.. AK-4
Pelican (Township)—Crow Wing ..MN-3
Pelican (Township)—Otter Tail MN-3
Pelican (Township)—Ramsey ND-4
Pelican (Township)—Codington SD-4
Pelican (Town)—Oneida WI-3
Pelican Bay (Town)—Tarrant......... TX-2
Pelican Lake (Township)—
 Grant MN-3
Pelican Rapids (City)—Otter
 Tail MN-3
Pelion (Town)—Lexington SC-2
Pella (Township)—Ford................... IL-3
Pella (City)—Marion IA-3
Pella (Town)—Shawano WI-3
Pell City (City)—St. Clair AL-2
Pell Lake (CDP)—Walworth WI-3
Pellston (Village)—Emmet MI-3
Pelzer (Town)—Anderson SC-2
Pemberton (City)—Blue Earth......MN-3
Pemberton (Borough)—
 Burlington NJ-1
Pemberton (Township)—
 Burlington NJ-1
Pemberton Heights (CDP)—
 Burlington NJ-1
Pemberville (Village)—Wood..........OH-3
Pembina (Township)—
 Mahnomen MN-3
Pembina (City)—Pembina.............. ND-4
Pembina (Township)—Pembina ND-4
Pembina County ND-4
Pembine (Town)—Marinette.......... WI-3
Pembroke (City)—Bryan GA-2
Pembroke (Township)—Kankakee.. IL-3
Pembroke (City)—Christian........... KY-2
Pembroke (Town)—Washington ... ME-1
Pembroke (Town)—Plymouth........ MA-1
Pembroke (Town)—Merrimack NH-1
Pembroke (Town)—Genesee NY-1
Pembroke (Town)—Robeson NC-2
Pembroke (Town)—Giles VA-2
Pembroke Park (Town)—
 Broward FL-2
Pembroke Pines (City)—Broward...FL-2
Pembrook (Township)—
 Edmunds SD-4
Pemiscot (Township)—Pemiscot ..MO-3
Pemiscot County.............................MO-3
Pena Blanca (CDP)—Sandoval..... NM-4
Penalosa (City)—Kingman KS-4
Pen Argyl (Borough)—
 Northampton PA-1
Penasco (CDP)—Taos NM-4
Penbrook (Borough)—Dauphin PA-1
Pence (Town)—Iron WI-3
Pender (Township)—Thurston....... NE-4
Pender (Village)—Thurston........... NE-4
Pender County NC-2
Pendergrass (City)—Jackson GA-2
Pendleton (Township)—Jefferson ... IL-3
Pendleton (Town)—Madison IN-3
Pendleton (Township)—St.
 Francois MO-3
Pendleton (Town)—Niagara NY-1
Pendleton (City)—Umatilla OR-4
Pendleton (Town)—Anderson SC-2
Pendleton County KY-2
Pendleton County WV-2

Pend Oreille County...................... WA-4
Penelope (Town)—Hill TX-2
Penermon (Village)—Stoddard MO-3
Penfield (Town)—Monroe............... NY-1
Penfield (Township)—Lorain OH-3
Peninsula (Township)—Grand
 Traverse MI-3
Peninsula (Village)—Summit OH-3
Peninsular Ranges (HI) Geog-4
Penitas (CDP)—Hidalgo TX-2
Penn (Township)—Shelby IL-3
Penn (Township)—Stark IL-3
Penn (Township)—Jay IN-3
Penn (Township)—Parke................ IN-3
Penn (Township)—St. Joseph IN-3
Penn (Township)—Osborne KS-4
Penn (Township)—Cass MI-3
Penn (Township)—McLeod MN-3
Penn (Township)—Sullivan MO-3
Penn (Township)—Highland OH-3
Penn (Township)—Morgan OH-3
Penn (Township)—Berks PA-1
Penn (Township)—Butler PA-1
Penn (Township)—Centre PA-1
Penn (Township)—Chester PA-1
Penn (Township)—Clearfield PA-1
Penn (Township)—Cumberland PA-1
Penn (Township)—Huntingdon PA-1
Penn (Township)—Lancaster PA-1
Penn (Township)—Lycoming PA-1
Penn (Township)—Perry PA-1
Penn (Township)—Snyder............... PA-1
Penn (Borough)—Westmoreland... PA-1
Penn (Township)—Westmoreland... PA-1
Penn (Township)—York PA-1
Penndel (Borough)—Bucks PA-1
Penney Farms (Town)—Clay FL-2
Pennfield (Township)—Calhoun ... MI-3
Penn Forest (Township)—Carbon .. PA-1
Penn Hills (Township)—
 Allegheny PA-1
Pennington (Town)—Choctaw AL-2
Pennington (Borough)—Mercer NJ-1
Pennington County MN-3
Pennington County SD-4
Pennington Gap (Town)—Lee VA-2
Penn Lake Park (Borough)—
 Luzerne PA-1
Pennock (City)—Kandiyohi MN-3
Pennsauken (Township)—
 Camden NJ-1
Pennsboro (City)—Ritchie WV-2
Pennsburg (Borough)—
 Montgomery PA-1
Pennsbury (Township)—Chester..... PA-1
Pennsbury Village (Borough)—
 Allegheny PA-1
Penns Grove (Borough)—Salem NJ-1
Pennsville (Township)—Salem NJ-1
Pennsylvania (Township)—Mason.. IL-3
Penn Valley (CDP)—Nevada CA-4
Pennville (Town)—Jay IN-3
Penn Yan (Village)—Yates NY-1
Peno (Township)—Pike MO-3
Penobscot (Town)—Hancock ME-1
Penobscot County.......................... ME-1
Penobscot Indian Island
 Reservation (Pop. Place)—
 Penobscot ME-1
Penobscot River (ME)................ Geog-4
Penobscot & Trust Lands
 (ME) IndRes-4
Peno No. 9 (Township)—
 Pennington SD-4
Penrose (CDP)—Fremont CO-4

Pensacola (City)—Escambia FL-2
Pensacola (Town)—Mayes OK-2
Pensacola Dam (OK)....................Geog-4
Pensacola Naval Air Station
 (FL) Mil-4
Pensacola Reservoir (OK)...........Geog-4
Pensaukee (Town)—Oconto WI-3
Pentagon, The (VA) Mil-4
Pentland (Township)—Luce..........MI-3
Pentwater (Township)—Oceana.....MI-3
Pentwater (Village)—Oceana MI-3
Peoria (City)—Maricopa AZ-4
Peoria (City)—Peoria IL-3
Peoria (Township)—Franklin..........KS-4
Peoria (Township)—Knox NE-4
Peoria (Town)—Ottawa OK-2
Peoria City (Township)—Peoria IL-3
Peoria County.................................... IL-3
Peoria Heights (Village)—Peoria ... IL-3
Peoria Heights (Village)—
 Tazewell IL-3
Peoria Heights (Village)—
 Woodford..................................... IL-3
Peosta (City)—Dubuque IA-3
Peotone (Town)—Will..................... IL-3
Peotone (Township)—Will............... IL-3
Pepeekeo (CDP)—Hawaii...............HI-4
Pepin (Township)—Wabasha MN-3
Pepin (Town)—Pepin WI-3
Pepin (Village)—Pepin WI-3
Pepin County................................... WI-3
Pepperell (Town)—Middlesex MA-1
Pepper Pike (City)—Cuyahoga OH-3
Pepperton (Township)—Stevens ... MN-3
Pequannock (Township)—Morris ..NJ-1
Pequaywan (Township)—St.
 Louis MN-3
Pequea (Township)—Lancaster....... PA-1
Pequot Lakes (City)—Crow
 Wing..MN-3
Peralta (CDP)—Valencia................NM-4
Perche (Township)—Boone...........MO-3
Perch Lake (Township)—
 Carlton MN-3
Percy (Village)—Randolph............. IL-3
Percy (Township)—Kittson MN-3
Pere Marquetter Charter (Township)—
 Mason MI-3
Perham (Town)—Aroostook ME-1
Perham (City)—Otter Tail MN-3
Perham (Township)—Otter Tail ... MN-3
Peridot (CDP)—Gila AZ-4
Peridot (CDP)—Graham AZ-4
Perinton (Town)—Monroe NY-1
Perkasie (Borough)—Bucks PA-1
Perkins (Township)—Erie OH-3
Perkins (Town)—Payne OK-2
Perkins County................................. NE-4
Perkins County................................. SD-4
Perkins (unorganized) (Pop. Place)—
 Sagadahoc ME-1
Perkinsville (Village)—Windsor..... VT-1
Perkiomen (Township)—
 Montgomery.................................PA-1
Perla (CDP)—Hot Spring AR-2
Perley (City)—Norman MN-3
Pernitas Point (Village)—Jim
 Wells..TX-2
Pernitas Point (Village)—Live
 Oak..TX-2
Perquimans County.........................NC-2
Perrine (CDP)—Dade FL-2
Perrinton (Village)—Gratiot MI-3
Perris (City)—Riverside CA-4
Perry (Town)—Perry AR-2

Perry (City)—Taylor.......................FL-2
Perry (City)—Houston GA-2
Perry (City)—Peach GA-2
Perry (Township)—Pike IL-3
Perry (Village)—Pike IL-3
Perry (Township)—Allen................ IN-3
Perry (Township)—Boone IN-3
Perry (Township)—Clay IN-3
Perry (Township)—Clinton IN-3
Perry (Township)—Delaware IN-3
Perry (Township)—Lawrence......... IN-3
Perry (Township)—Marion IN-3
Perry (Township)—Martin IN-3
Perry (Township)—Miami IN-3
Perry (Township)—Monroe........... IN-3
Perry (Township)—Noble............... IN-3
Perry (Township)—Tippecanoe IN-3
Perry (Township)—Vanderburgh IN-3
Perry (Township)—Wayne IN-3
Perry (City)—Dallas........................IA-3
Perry (City)—Jefferson KS-4
Perry (Township)—Woodson KS-4
Perry (Town)—Washington ME-1
Perry (City)—Shiawassee MI-3
Perry (Township)—Shiawassee MI-3
Perry (Township)—Lac qui
 Parle...MN-3
Perry (City)—Ralls MO-3
Perry (Township)—St. Francois....MO-3
Perry (Township)—Thurston NE-4
Perry (Town)—Wyoming NY-1
Perry (Village)—Wyoming NY-1
Perry (Township)—Cavalier...........ND-4
Perry (Township)—Allen OH-3
Perry (Township)—Ashland OH-3
Perry (Township)—Brown.............OH-3
Perry (Township)—Carroll OH-3
Perry (Township)—Columbiana OH-3
Perry (Township)—Coshocton OH-3
Perry (Township)—Fayette............OH-3
Perry (Township)—Franklin OH-3
Perry (Township)—Gallia OH-3
Perry (Township)—Hocking OH-3
Perry (Township)—Lake OH-3
Perry (Village)—Lake OH-3
Perry (Township)—Lawrence.........OH-3
Perry (Township)—Licking OH-3
Perry (Township)—Logan OH-3
Perry (Township)—Monroe OH-3
Perry (Township)—Montgomery ...OH-3
Perry (Township)—Morrow OH-3
Perry (Township)—Muskingum OH-3
Perry (Township)—Pickaway OH-3
Perry (Township)—Pike OH-3
Perry (Township)—Putnam OH-3
Perry (Township)—Richland OH-3
Perry (Township)—Shelby OH-3
Perry (Township)—Stark OH-3
Perry (Township)—Tuscarawas......OH-3
Perry (Township)—Wood OH-3
Perry (City)—Noble OK-2
Perry (Township)—Armstrong PA-1
Perry (Township)—Berks PA-1
Perry (Township)—Clarion PA-1
Perry (Township)—Fayette............. PA-1
Perry (Township)—Greene PA-1
Perry (Township)—Jefferson PA-1
Perry (Township)—Lawrence......... PA-1
Perry (Township)—Mercer............. PA-1
Perry (Township)—Snyder PA-1
Perry (Town)—Aiken SC-2
Perry (Township)—Davison SD-4
Perry (Township)—Lincoln SD-4
Perry (City)—Box Elder UT-4
Perry (Town)—Dane WI-3

Perry County AL-2
Perry County AR-2
Perry County IL-3
Perry County IN-3
Perry County KY-2
Perry County MS-2
Perry County MO-3
Perry County OH-3
Perry County PA-1
Perry County TN-2
Perry Hall (CDP)—Baltimore........MD-1
Perry Heights (CDP)—Stark OH-3
Perry Lake (Township)—Crow
 Wing..MN-3
Perryman (CDP)—Harford...........MD-1
Perryopolis (Borough)—Fayette...... PA-1
Perrysburg (Town)—Cattaraugus ... NY-1
Perrysburg (Village)—
 Cattaraugus NY-1
Perrysburg (City)—Wood OH-3
Perrysburg (Township)—Wood OH-3
Perrysville (Town)—Vermillion IN-3
Perrysville (Village)—Ashland OH-3
Perryton (Township)—Mercer IL-3
Perryton (City)—Ochiltree TX-2
Perrytown (City)—Hempstead AR-2
Perryville (CDP)—Lake and Peninsula
 Borough......................................AK-4
Perryville (City)—Perry...................AR-2
Perryville (City)—Boyle KY-2
Perryville (Town)—Cecil MD-1
Perryville (City)—Perry..................MO-3
Pershing (Township)—Jackson IN-3
Pershing (Township)—Burt NE-4
Pershing (Town)—Taylor WI-3
Pershing County..............................NV-4
Persia (City)—Harrison IA-3
Persia (Town)—Cattaraugus NY-1
Persifer (Township)—Knox............ IL-3
Person County NC-2
Perth (Town)—Fulton NY-1
Perth (City)—Towner ND-4
Perth (Township)—Walsh..............ND-4
Perth Amboy (City)—Middlesex NJ-1
Peru (City)—La Salle IL-3
Peru (Township)—La Salle IL-3
Peru (City)—Miami IN-3
Peru (Township)—Miami................ IN-3
Peru (City)—Chautauqua KS-4
Peru (Town)—Oxford.................... ME-1
Peru (Town)—Berkshire MA-1
Peru (City)—Nemaha NE-4
Peru (Town)—Clinton NY-1
Peru (Township)—Huron OH-3
Peru (Township)—Morrow OH-3
Peru (Town)—Bennington.............. VT-1
Peru (Town)—Dunn WI-3
Peshtigo (City)—Marinette WI-3
Peshtigo (Town)—Marinette WI-3
Pesotum (Town)—Champaign IL-3
Pesotum (Township)—Champaign . IL-3
Petal (City)—Forrest MS-2
Petaluma (City)—Sonoma.............. CA-4
Petaluma Coast Guard Training Center
 (CA) Mil-4
Peterborough (Town)—
 Hillsborough NH-1
Peters (Township)—Kingman KS-4
Peters (Township)—Franklin PA-1
Peters (Township)—Washington PA-1
Petersburg (City)—Wrangell-Petersburg
 Census Area................................AK-4
Petersburg (Town)—Menard IL-3
Petersburg (City)—Pike IN-3
Petersburg (City)—Monroe MI-3

General Index — American Places Dictionary

Petersburg (Township)—Jackson .. MN-3
Petersburg (Village)—Boone NE-4
Petersburg (Town)—Rensselaer NY-1
Petersburg (City)—Nelson ND-4
Petersburg (Township)—Nelson ND-4
Petersburg (Borough)—
  Huntingdon PA-1
Petersburg (Town)—Lincoln TN-2
Petersburg (Town)—Marshall TN-2
Petersburg (Town)—Hale TX-2
Petersburg (City)—Grant WV-2
Petersburg (Independent City) VA-2
Petersham (Town)—Worcester MA-1
Peterson (City)—Clay IA-3
Peterson (City)—Fillmore MN-3
Peterson (Township)—Stutsman ND-4
Peterson Air Force Base (CO) Mil-4
Peterstown (Town)—Monroe WV-2
Petersville (Township)—Kidder ND-4
Petoskey (City)—Emmet MI-3
Petrey (Town)—Crenshaw AL-2
Petrified Forest (AZ) Geog-4
Petroleum County MT-4
Petrolia (Borough)—Butler PA-1
Petrolia (City)—Clay TX-2
Petronila (City)—Nueces TX-2
Pettibone (City)—Kidder ND-4
Pettibone (Township)—Kidder ND-4
Pettis (Township)—Adair MO-3
Pettis (Township)—Platte MO-3
Pettis County MO-3
Petty (Township)—Lawrence IL-3
Pevely (City)—Jefferson MO-3
Pewamo (Village)—Ionia MI-3
Pewaukee (Town)—Waukesha WI-3
Pewaukee (Village)—Waukesha WI-3
Pewee Valley (City)—Oldham KY-3
Pflugerville (City)—Travis TX-2
Pharr (City)—Hidalgo TX-2
Pharsalia (Town)—Chenango NY-1
Phelps (CDP)—Pike KY-2
Phelps (Town)—Ontario NY-1
Phelps (Village)—Ontario NY-1
Phelps (Town)—Vilas WI-3
Phelps City (Town)—Atchison MO-3
Phelps County MO-3
Phelps County NE-4
Phenix (Township)—Henry IL-3
Phenix (Town)—Charlotte VA-2
Phenix City (City)—Lee AL-2
Phenix City (City)—Russell AL-2
Pherrin (Township)—Williams ND-4
Philadelphia (Township)—Cass IL-3
Philadelphia (City)—Neshoba MS-2
Philadelphia (Town)—Jefferson NY-1
Philadelphia (Village)—Jefferson .. NY-1
Philadelphia (City)—Philadelphia .. PA-1
Philadelphia (City)—Loudon TN-2
Philadelphia County PA-1
Phil Campbell (Town)—Franklin ... AL-2
Philip (City)—Haakon SD-4
Philippi (City)—Barbour WV-2
Philipsburg (Town)—Granite MT-4
Philipsburg (Borough)—Centre PA-1
Philipstown (Town)—Putnam NY-1
Phillips (Township)—White IL-3
Phillips (Town)—Franklin ME-1
Phillips (Village)—Hamilton NE-4
Phillips (Town)—Coal OK-2
Phillips (City)—Price WI-3
Phillipsburg (CDP)—Tift GA-2
Phillipsburg (City)—Phillips KS-4
Phillipsburg (Township)—Phillips .. KS-4
Phillipsburg (Town)—Laclede MO-3

Phillipsburg (Township)—
  Laclede MO-3
Phillipsburg (Town)—Warren NJ-1
Phillipsburg (Village)—
  Montgomery OH-3
Phillips County AR-2
Phillips County CO-4
Phillips County KS-4
Phillips County MT-4
Phillipston (Town)—Worcester MA-1
Phillipstown (Village)—White IL-3
Philmont (Village)—Columbia NY-1
Philo (Town)—Champaign IL-3
Philo (Township)—Champaign IL-3
Philo (Village)—Muskingum OH-3
Philomath (City)—Benton OR-4
Phipps (Township)—Codington SD-4
Phippsburg (Town)—Sagadahoc ... ME-1
Phoenix (City)—Maricopa AZ-4
Phoenix (Village)—Cook IL-3
Phoenix (Village)—Oswego NY-1
Phoenix (City)—Jackson OR-4
Phoenix Lake-Cedar Ridge (CDP)—
  Tuolumne CA-4
Phoenixville (Borough)—Chester ... PA-1
Piasa (Township)—Jersey IL-3
Piatt (Township)—Lycoming PA-1
Piatt County IL-3
Picayune (City)—Pearl River MS-2
Picayune Rancheria (CA) IndRes-4
Picher (City)—Ottawa OK-2
Pickard (Township)—Sheridan ND-4
Pickaway (Township)—Shelby IL-3
Pickaway (Township)—Pickaway .. OH-3
Pickaway County OH-3
Pick City (City)—Mercer ND-4
Pickens (Town)—Holmes MS-2
Pickens (Town)—Pickens SC-2
Pickens County AL-2
Pickens County GA-2
Pickens County SC-2
Pickensville (Town)—Pickens AL-2
Pickerel Lake (Township)—
  Freeborn MN-3
Pickering (Town)—Nodaway MO-3
Pickering (Township)—Bottineau .. ND-4
Pickerington (Village)—Fairfield ... OH-3
Pickerington (Village)—Franklin .. OH-3
Pickett County TN-2
Pickford (Township)—Chippewa .. MI-3
Pickrell (Village)—Gage NE-4
Pickstown (Town)—Charles Mix .. SD-4
Pico Rivera (City)—Los Angeles .. CA-4
Picton (Township)—Towner ND-4
Picture Rocks (CDP)—Pima AZ-4
Picture Rocks (Borough)—
  Lycoming PA-1
Picuris Pueblo (NM) IndRes-4
Piedmont (City)—Calhoun AL-2
Piedmont (City)—Cherokee AL-2
Piedmont (City)—Alameda CA-4
Piedmont (City)—Wayne MO-3
Piedmont (Town)—Canadian OK-2
Piedmont (City)—Kingfisher OK-2
Piedmont (CDP)—Anderson SC-2
Piedmont (CDP)—Greenville SC-2
Piedmont (Town)—Mineral WV-2
Piedmont Region or Plateau
  (AZ) Geog-4
Piehl (Town)—Oneida WI-3
Pierce (Town)—Weld CO-4
Pierce (City)—Clearwater ID-4
Pierce (Township)—DeKalb IL-3
Pierce (Township)—Washington ... IN-3
Pierce (Township)—Lawrence MO-3

Pierce (Township)—Stone MO-3
Pierce (Township)—Texas MO-3
Pierce (City)—Pierce NE-4
Pierce (Township)—Barnes ND-4
Pierce (Township)—Clermont OH-3
Pierce (Town)—Kewaunee WI-3
Pierce City (City)—Lawrence MO-3
Pierce County GA-2
Pierce County NE-4
Pierce County ND-4
Pierce County WA-4
Pierce County WI-3
Piercefield (Town)—St.
  Lawrence NY-1
Pierceton (Town)—Kosciusko IN-3
Pierceville (Township)—Finney KS-4
Piermont (Town)—Grafton NH-1
Piermont (Village)—Rockland NY-1
Pierpont (Township)—Ashtabula .. OH-3
Pierpont (Town)—Day SD-4
Pierre (City)—Hughes SD-4
Pierre Part (CDP)—Assumption
  Parish LA-2
Pierrepont (Town)—St. Lawrence .. NY-1
Pierron (Village)—Bond IL-3
Pierron (Village)—Madison IL-3
Pierson (Town)—Volusia FL-2
Pierson (Township)—Vigo IN-3
Pierson (City)—Woodbury IA-3
Pierson (Township)—Montcalm ... MI-3
Pierson (Village)—Montcalm MI-3
Pierz (City)—Morrison MN-3
Pierz (Township)—Morrison MN-3
Pigeon (Township)—Vanderburgh .. IN-3
Pigeon (Township)—Warrick IN-3
Pigeon (Village)—Huron MI-3
Pigeon (Town)—Trempealeau WI-3
Pigeon Creek (CDP)—Summit OH-3
Pigeon Falls (Village)—
  Trempealeau WI-3
Pigeon Forge (City)—Sevier TN-2
Pigeon Grove (Township)—
  Iroquois IL-3
Piggott (City)—Clay AR-2
Pike (Township)—Livingston IL-3
Pike (Township)—Jay IN-3
Pike (Township)—Marion IN-3
Pike (Township)—Ohio IN-3
Pike (Township)—Warren IN-3
Pike (Township)—Lyon KS-4
Pike (Township)—St. Louis MN-3
Pike (Township)—Carter MO-3
Pike (Township)—Stoddard MO-3
Pike (Town)—Wyoming NY-1
Pike (Village)—Wyoming NY-1
Pike (Township)—Brown OH-3
Pike (Township)—Clark OH-3
Pike (Township)—Coshocton OH-3
Pike (Township)—Fulton OH-3
Pike (Township)—Knox OH-3
Pike (Township)—Madison OH-3
Pike (Township)—Perry OH-3
Pike (Township)—Stark OH-3
Pike (Township)—Berks PA-1
Pike (Township)—Bradford PA-1
Pike (Township)—Clearfield PA-1
Pike (Township)—Potter PA-1
Pike Bay (Township)—Cass MN-3
Pike County AL-2
Pike County AR-2
Pike County GA-2
Pike County IL-3
Pike County IN-3
Pike County KY-2
Pike County MS-2

Pike County..................................*MO-3*
Pike County...................................*OH-3*
Pike County.....................................*PA-1*
Pike Creek (CDP)—New Castle *DE-1*
Pike Creek (Township)—
  Morrison *MN-3*
Pikes Peak (CO)..............................*Geog-4*
Pikesville (CDP)—Baltimore *MD-1*
Piketon (Village)—Pike.................... *OH-3*
Pikeville (City)—Pike..................... *KY-2*
Pikeville (Town)—Wayne.................. *NC-2*
Pikeville (Town)—Bledsoe *TN-2*
Pilesgrove (Township)—Salem......... *NJ-1*
Pilger (Village)—Stanton................. *NE-4*
Pilgrim (Township)—Dade *MO-3*
Pillager (City)—Cass *MN-3*
Pillow (Borough)—Dauphin............ *PA-1*
Pillsbury (Township)—Swift *MN-3*
Pillsbury (City)—Barnes *ND-4*
Pilot (Township)—Kankakee *IL-3*
Pilot (Township)—Vermilion *IL-3*
Pilot Grove (Township)—
  Hancock *IL-3*
Pilot Grove (Township)—
  Faribault......................................*MN-3*
Pilot Grove (City)—Cooper *MO-3*
Pilot Grove (Township)—
  Cooper..*MO-3*
Pilot Grove (Township)—
  Moniteau *MO-3*
Pilot Knob (Township)—
  Washington *IL-3*
Pilot Knob (City)—Iron *MO-3*
Pilot Mound (Township)—Boone *IA-3*
Pilot Mound (Township)—
  Fillmore.......................................*MN-3*
Pilot Mound (Township)—
  Griggs *ND-4*
Pilot Mountain (Town)—Surry....... *NC-2*
Pilot Point (CDP)—Lake and Peninsula
  Borough *AK-4*
Pilot Point (Town)—Denton............ *TX-2*
Pilot Rock (City)—Umatilla *OR-4*
Pilot Station (City)—Wade Hampton
  Census Area *AK-4*
Pilsen (Town)—Bayfield................. *WI-3*
Pima (Town)—Graham *AZ-4*
Pima County...................................*AZ-4*
Pimmit Hills (CDP)—Fairfax *VA-2*
Pinal County...................................*AZ-4*
Pinardville (CDP)—
  Hillsborough *NH-1*
Pinch (CDP)—Kanawha................. *WV-2*
Pinckard (Town)—Dale...................*AL-2*
Pinckney (Village)—Livingston *MI-3*
Pinckney (Township)—Warren *MO-3*
Pinckney (Town)—Lewis................. *NY-1*
Pinckneyville (Town)—Perry *IL-3*
Pinconning (City)—Bay.................. *MI-3*
Pinconning (Township)—Bay......... *MI-3*
Pindall (Town)—Searcy *AR-2*
Pine (Township)—Benton *IN-3*
Pine (Township)—Porter................. *IN-3*
Pine (Township)—Warren *IN-3*
Pine (Township)—Montcalm *MI-3*
Pine (Township)—Ripley *MO-3*
Pine (Township)—Allegheny........... *PA-1*
Pine (Township)—Armstrong.......... *PA-1*
Pine (Township)—Clearfield *PA-1*
Pine (Township)—Columbia *PA-1*
Pine (Township)—Crawford *PA-1*
Pine (Township)—Indiana *PA-1*
Pine (Township)—Lycoming *PA-1*
Pine (Township)—Mercer *PA-1*
Pine A (Township)—Stone............. *MO-3*

Pine Apple (Town)—Wilcox *AL-2*
Pine B (Township)—Stone *MO-3*
Pine Beach (Borough)—Ocean....... *NJ-1*
Pine Bluff (City)—Jefferson........... *AR-2*
Pinebluff (Town)—Moore *NC-2*
Pine Bluffs (Town)—Laramie *WY-4*
Pine Bush (CDP)—Orange............. *NY-1*
Pine Castle (CDP)—Orange............*FL-2*
Pine City (City)—Pine *MN-3*
Pine City (Township)—Pine *MN-3*
Pine County *MN-3*
Pine Creek (Township)—Ogle......... *IL-3*
Pine Creek (Township)—Ozark *MO-3*
Pine Creek (Township)—Clinton.... *PA-1*
Pine Creek (Township)—Jefferson . *PA-1*
Pine Creek Reservation (MI) ... *IndRes-4*
Pine Crest (CDP)—Carter.............. *TN-2*
Pinedale (Town)—Sublette.............. *WY-4*
Pine Forest (City)—Orange *TX-2*
Pine Grove (Township)—Van
  Buren *MI-3*
Pine Grove (Borough)—Schuylkill . *PA-1*
Pine Grove (Township)—
  Schuylkill.....................................*PA-1*
Pinegrove (Township)—Venango.... *PA-1*
Pine Grove (Township)—Warren ... *PA-1*
Pine Grove (Town)—Wetzel *WV-2*
Pine Grove (Town)—Portage......... *WI-3*
Pine Haven (Town)—Crook........... *WY-4*
Pine Hill (Town)—Wilcox...............*AL-2*
Pine Hill (Borough)—Camden....... *NJ-1*
Pine Hills (CDP)—Humboldt.......... *CA-4*
Pine Hills (CDP)—Orange *FL-2*
Pinehurst (City)—Dooly *GA-2*
Pinehurst (City)—Shoshone *ID-4*
Pinehurst (CDP)—Middlesex......... *MA-1*
Pinehurst (CDP)—Moore *NC-2*
Pinehurst (CDP)—Montgomery *TX-2*
Pinehurst (CDP)—Orange............. *TX-2*
Pine Island (City)—Goodhue........ *MN-3*
Pine Island (Township)—
  Goodhue......................................*MN-3*
Pine Island (City)—Olmsted.......... *MN-3*
Pine Island (Town)—Waller........... *TX-2*
Pine Island Ridge (CDP)—
  Broward..*FL-2*
Pine Knoll Shores (Town)—
  Carteret..*NC-2*
Pine Knot (CDP)—McCreary *KY-2*
Pine Lake (City)—De Kalb............. *GA-2*
Pine Lake (Township)—Cass *MN-3*
Pine Lake (Township)—
  Clearwater...................................*MN-3*
Pine Lake (Township)—Otter
  Tail *MN-3*
Pine Lake (Township)—Pine *MN-3*
Pine Lake (CDP)—King................. *WA-4*
Pine Lake (Town)—Oneida............ *WI-3*
Pineland (City)—Sabine.................. *TX-2*
Pine Lawn (City)—St. Louis.......... *MO-3*
Pine Level (Town)—Johnston......... *NC-2*
Pinellas County *FL-2*
Pinellas Park (City)—Pinellas..........*FL-2*
Pine Mountain (Town)—Harris..... *GA-2*
Pine Plains (Town)—Dutchess........ *NY-1*
Pine Point (Township)—Becker *MN-3*
Pine Prairie (Village)—Evangeline
  Parish *LA-2*
Pine Ridge (Municipality)—
  DeKalb..*AL-2*
Pineridge (Town)—Lexington *SC-2*
Pine Ridge (CDP)—Shannon......... *SD-4*
Pine Ridge at Crestwood (CDP)—
  Ocean *NJ-1*

Pine Ridge Reservation & Trust Lands
  (SD)......................................*IndRes-4*
Pine River (Township)—Gratiot.... *MI-3*
Pine River (City)—Cass *MN-3*
Pine River (Township)—Cass *MN-3*
Pine River (Town)—Lincoln........... *WI-3*
Pine Rock (Township)—Ogle......... *IL-3*
The Pinery (CDP)—Douglas...........*CO-4*
Pinesdale (Town)—Ravalli............ *MT-4*
Pine Springs (City)—
  Washington *MN-3*
Pinetop-Lakeside (Town)—
  Navajo *AZ-4*
Pinetops (Town)—Edgecombe *NC-2*
Pine Valley (CDP)—San Diego...... *CA-4*
Pine Valley (Borough)—Camden *NJ-1*
Pine Valley (Village)—Suffolk........ *NY-1*
Pine Valley (Town)—Clark *WI-3*
Pineview (Town)—Wilcox............. *GA-2*
Pine Village (Town)—Warren *IN-3*
Pineville (Town)—Izard *AR-2*
Pineville (City)—Bell...................... *KY-2*
Pineville (City)—Rapides Parish *LA-2*
Pineville (Town)—McDonald *MO-3*
Pineville (Town)—Mecklenburg..... *NC-2*
Pineville (Town)—Wyoming *WV-2*
Pineville Lanagan (Township)—
  McDonald *MO-3*
Pineville North (Township)—
  McDonald *MO-3*
Pineville South (Township)—
  McDonald *MO-3*
Pinewood (CDP)—Dade *FL-2*
Pinewood (Town)—Sumter *SC-2*
Pinewood Estates (CDP)—
  Hardin... *TX-2*
Piney (CDP)—Garland *AR-2*
Piney (Township)—Oregon *MO-3*
Piney (Township)—Pulaski *MO-3*
Piney (Township)—Texas............... *MO-3*
Piney (Township)—Clarion *PA-1*
Piney Green (CDP)—Onslow *NC-2*
Piney Point Village (City)—
  Harris.. *TX-2*
Piney View (CDP)—Raleigh......... *WV-2*
Pingree (City)—Stutsman.............. *ND-4*
Pingree (Township)—Stutsman..... *ND-4*
Pingree Grove (Village)—Kane...... *IL-3*
Pink (Town)—Pottawatomie...........*OK-2*
Pinkhams Grant (Pop. Place)—
  Coos *NH-1*
Pink Hill (Town)—Lenoir.............. *NC-2*
Pin Oak (Township)—Madison *IL-3*
Pinole (City)—Contra Costa *CA-4*
Pinoleville Rancheria (CA) *IndRes-4*
Pinon (CDP)—Navajo *AZ-4*
Pinora (Township)—Lake *MI-3*
Pinson-Clay-Chalkville (Division)—
  Jefferson *AL-2*
Pioche (Pop. Place)—Lincoln *NV-4*
Pioneer (City)—Humboldt............. *IA-3*
Pioneer (Township)—Graham *KS-4*
Pioneer (Township)—Rice *KS-4*
Pioneer (Township)—Rush *KS-4*
Pioneer (Village)—West Carroll
  Parish *LA-2*
Pioneer (Township)—Missaukee.... *MI-3*
Pioneer (Township)—Barry........... *MO-3*
Pioneer (Village)—Williams.......... *OH-3*
Pioneer (Township)—Corson *SD-4*
Pioneer (Township)—Faulk *SD-4*
Pioneer Village (City)—Bullitt *KY-2*
Pipe Creek (Township)—Madison .. *IN-3*
Pipe Creek (Township)—Miami *IN-3*
Piper City (Village)—Ford *IL-3*

General Index

Piperton (City)—Fayette TN-2
Pipestem Valley (Township)—
  Stutsman ND-4
Pipestone (Township)—Berrien MI-3
Pipestone (City)—Pipestone MN-3
Pipestone County MN-3
Pippa Passes (City)—Knott KY-2
Piqua (City)—Miami OH-3
Pirtleville (CDP)—Cochise AZ-4
Piru (CDP)—Ventura CA-4
Piscataquis County ME-1
Piscataway (Township)—
  Middlesex NJ-1
Pisek (City)—Walsh ND-4
Pisgah (Town)—Jackson AL-2
Pisgah (City)—Harrison IA-3
Pisinemo (CDP)—Pima AZ-4
Pismo Beach (City)—San Luis
  Obispo CA-4
Pistakee Highlands (CDP)—
  McHenry IL-3
Pitcairn (Town)—St. Lawrence NY-1
Pitcairn (Borough)—Allegheny PA-1
Pitcher (Town)—Chenango NY-1
Pitkas Point (CDP)—Wade Hampton
  Census Area AK-4
Pitkin (Town)—Gunnison CO-4
Pitkin County CO-4
Pitman (Township)—Montgomery . IL-3
Pitman (Borough)—Gloucester NJ-1
Pit River Trust Lands (CA) IndRes-4
Pitsburg (Village)—Darke OH-3
Pitt (Township)—Wyandot OH-3
Pitt County NC-2
Pittman Center (Town)—Sevier TN-2
Pitts (City)—Wilcox GA-2
Pittsboro (Town)—Hendricks IN-3
Pittsboro (Village)—Calhoun MS-2
Pittsboro (Town)—Chatham NC-2
Pittsburg (City)—Contra Costa CA-4
Pittsburg (Town)—Williamson IL-3
Pittsburg (City)—Crawford KS-4
Pittsburg (Township)—Mitchell KS-4
Pittsburg (Town)—Coos NH-1
Pittsburg (Town)—Pittsburg OK-2
Pittsburg (City)—Camp TX-2
Pittsburg County OK-2
Pittsburgh (City)—Allegheny PA-1
Pittsfield (Town)—Pike IL-3
Pittsfield (Township)—Pike IL-3
Pittsfield (Town)—Somerset ME-1
Pittsfield (City)—Berkshire MA-1
Pittsfield (Township)—
  Washtenaw MI-3
Pittsfield (Town)—Merrimack NH-1
Pittsfield (Town)—Otsego NY-1
Pittsfield (Township)—Lorain OH-3
Pittsfield (Township)—Warren PA-1
Pittsfield (Town)—Rutland VT-1
Pittsfield (Town)—Brown WI-3
Pittsford (Township)—Hillsdale MI-3
Pittsford (Town)—Monroe NY-1
Pittsford (Village)—Monroe NY-1
Pittsford (Town)—Rutland VT-1
Pittsgrove (Township)—Salem NJ-1
Pittston (Town)—Kennebec ME-1
Pittston (City)—Luzerne PA-1
Pittston (Township)—Luzerne PA-1
Pittstown (Town)—Rensselaer NY-1
Pittsville (Town)—Wicomico MD-1
Pittsville (City)—Wood WI-3
Pittsylvania County VA-2
Piute County UT-4
Pixley (CDP)—Tulare CA-4
Pixley (Township)—Clay IL-3

Placentia (City)—Orange CA-4
Placer County CA-4
Placerville (City)—El Dorado CA-4
Placerville (City)—Boise ID-4
Placid, Lake (NY) Geog-4
Placid Lakes (CDP)—Highlands ... FL-2
Placitas (CDP)—Sandoval NM-4
Plain (Township)—Kosciusko IN-3
Plain (Township)—Renville ND-4
Plain (Township)—Franklin OH-3
Plain (Township)—Stark OH-3
Plain (Township)—Wayne OH-3
Plain (Township)—Wood OH-3
Plain (Village)—Sauk WI-3
Plain Center (Township)—Charles
  Mix SD-4
Plain City (Village)—Madison OH-3
Plain City (Village)—Union OH-3
Plain City (City)—Weber UT-4
Plain Dealing (Town)—Bossier
  Parish LA-2
Plainedge (CDP)—Nassau NY-1
Plainfield (Town)—Windham CT-1
Plainfield (Town)—Will IL-3
Plainfield (Township)—Will IL-3
Plainfield (Town)—Hendricks IN-3
Plainfield (City)—Bremer IA-3
Plainfield (Town)—Hampshire MA-1
Plainfield (Township)—Iosco MI-3
Plainfield (Township)—Kent MI-3
Plainfield (Town)—Sullivan NH-1
Plainfield (City)—Union NJ-1
Plainfield (Town)—Otsego NY-1
Plainfield (Village)—Coshocton ... OH-3
Plainfield (Township)—
  Northampton PA-1
Plainfield (Township)—Brule SD-4
Plainfield (Town)—Washington VT-1
Plainfield (Town)—Waushara WI-3
Plainfield (Village)—Waushara WI-3
Plain Grove (Township)—
  Lawrence PA-1
Plains (City)—Sumter GA-2
Plains (Town)—Sanders MT-4
Plains (Township)—Luzerne PA-1
Plains (Town)—Yoakum TX-2
The Plains (CDP)—Athens OH-3
The Plains (Town)—Fauquier VA-2
Plainsboro (Township)—
  Middlesex NJ-1
Plains City (City)—Meade KS-4
Plainview (City)—Yell AR-2
Plainview (Township)—Phillips KS-4
Plainview (City)—Wabasha MN-3
Plainview (Township)—Wabasha . MN-3
Plainview (City)—Pierce NE-4
Plainview (CDP)—Nassau NY-1
Plainview (Township)—Stutsman . ND-4
Plainview (Township)—Tripp SD-4
Plainview (City)—Hale TX-2
Plainville (Town)—Hartford CT-1
Plainville (City)—Gordon GA-2
Plainville (Village)—Adams IL-3
Plainville (Town)—Daviess IN-3
Plainville (City)—Rooks KS-4
Plainville (Town)—Norfolk MA-1
Plainwell (City)—Allegan MI-3
Plaistow (Town)—Rockingham NH-1
Planada (CDP)—Merced CA-4
Plandome (Village)—Nassau NY-1
Plandome Heights (Village)—
  Nassau NY-1
Plandome Manor (Village)—
  Nassau NY-1
Plankinton (City)—Aurora SD-4

Plankinton (Township)—Aurora .. SD-4
Plano (Town)—Kendall IL-3
Plano (City)—Appanoose IA-3
Plano (Township)—Hanson SD-4
Plano (City)—Collin TX-2
Plano (City)—Denton TX-2
Plantation (City)—Broward FL-2
Plantation (CDP)—Sarasota FL-2
Plantation (City)—Jefferson KY-2
Plantation Key (CDP)—Monroe ... FL-2
Plant City (City)—Hillsborough FL-2
Plantersville (Town)—Lee MS-2
Plaquemine (City)—Iberville
  Parish LA-2
Plaquemines Parish LA-2
Platea (Borough)—Erie PA-1
Plateau (Township)—Perkins SD-4
Platinum (City)—Bethel Census
  Area AK-4
Plato (Township)—Kane IL-3
Plato (City)—McLeod MN-3
Plato (Township)—Hand SD-4
Platte (Township)—Benzie MI-3
Platte (Township)—Morrison MN-3
Platte (Township)—Andrew MO-3
Platte (Township)—Buchanan MO-3
Platte (Township)—Clay MO-3
Platte (Township)—Clinton MO-3
Platte (Township)—Buffalo NE-4
Platte (Township)—Butler NE-4
Platte (Township)—Dodge NE-4
Platte (City)—Charles Mix SD-4
Platte (Township)—Charles Mix ... SD-4
Platte Center (Village)—Platte NE-4
Platte City (City)—Platte MO-3
Platte County MO-3
Platte County NE-4
Platte County WY-4
Plattekill (Town)—Ulster NY-1
Platte Lake (Township)—Crow
  Wing MN-3
Platte River (NE) Geog-4
Platteville (Town)—Weld CO-4
Platteville (City)—Grant WI-3
Platteville (Town)—Grant WI-3
Platte Woods (City)—Platte MO-3
Plattin (Township)—Jefferson MO-3
Plattsburg (City)—Clinton MO-3
Plattsburgh (City)—Clinton NY-1
Plattsburgh (Town)—Clinton NY-1
Plattsburgh Air Force Base (Mil.
  facil.)—Clinton NY-1
Plattsburgh West (CDP)—
  Clinton NY-1
Plattsmouth (City)—Cass NE-4
Plaucheville (Village)—Avoyelles
  Parish LA-2
Plaza (City)—Mountrail ND-4
Plaza (Township)—Mountrail ND-4
Pleak (Village)—Fort Bend TX-2
Pleasant (Township)—Fulton IL-3
Pleasant (Township)—Allen IN-3
Pleasant (Township)—Grant IN-3
Pleasant (Township)—Johnson ... IN-3
Pleasant (Township)—La Porte ... IN-3
Pleasant (Township)—Porter IN-3
Pleasant (Township)—Steuben ... IN-3
Pleasant (Township)—Switzerland .. IN-3
Pleasant (Township)—Wabash IN-3
Pleasant (Township)—Butler KS-4
Pleasant (Township)—Coffey KS-4
Pleasant (Township)—Harvey KS-4
Pleasant (Township)—Lincoln KS-4
Pleasant (Township)—Smith KS-4
Pleasant (Township)—Cass ND-4

Pleasant (Township)—Brown.........OH-3
Pleasant (Township)—Clark...........OH-3
Pleasant (Township)—Fairfield......OH-3
Pleasant (Township)—Franklin......OH-3
Pleasant (Township)—Hancock OH-3
Pleasant (Township)—Hardin OH-3
Pleasant (Township)—Henry OH-3
Pleasant (Township)—Knox OH-3
Pleasant (Township)—Logan..........OH-3
Pleasant (Township)—Madison OH-3
Pleasant (Township)—Marion OH-3
Pleasant (Township)—Perry..........OH-3
Pleasant (Township)—Putnam OH-3
Pleasant (Township)—Seneca OH-3
Pleasant (Township)—Van Wert OH-3
Pleasant (Township)—Warren......... PA-1
Pleasant (Township)—Clark...........SD-4
Pleasant (Township)—Hanson SD-4
Pleasant (Township)—Hutchinson..............SD-4
Pleasant (Township)—Jerauld........ SD-4
Pleasant (Township)—Lincoln SD-4
Pleasant (Township)—Lyman SD-4
Pleasant City (Village)—Guernsey OH-3
Pleasantdale (Township)—Rush KS-4
Pleasant Dale (Village)—Seward ... NE-4
Pleasant Gap (Township)—Bates.. MO-3
Pleasant Garden (CDP)—Guilford...................NC-2
Pleasant Grove (City)—Jefferson ...AL-2
Pleasant Grove (Township)—Coles................................IL-3
Pleasant Grove (Township)—Greenwood KS-4
Pleasant Grove (Township)—Pawnee KS-4
Pleasant Grove (Township)—Olmsted MN-3
Pleasant Grove (CDP)—Muskingum OH-3
Pleasant Grove (Township)—Brule..................................SD-4
Pleasant Grove (City)—Utah......... UT-4
Pleasant Hill (City)—Contra Costa CA-4
Pleasant Hill (Town)—Pike............. IL-3
Pleasant Hill (Township)—Pike...... IL-3
Pleasant Hill (City)—Polk.............IA-3
Pleasant Hill (Village)—Sabine Parish LA-2
Pleasant Hill (Township)—Winona..............................MN-3
Pleasant Hill (City)—Cass.............. MO-3
Pleasant Hill (Township)—Cass.. MO-3
Pleasant Hill (Township)—Sullivan..............................MO-3
Pleasant Hill (CDP)—Wilkes........NC-2
Pleasant Hill (Township)—Kidder................................ ND-4
Pleasant Hill (Village)—Miami...OH-3
Pleasant Hill (Town)—Cumberland TN-2
Pleasant Hills (CDP)—Harford MD-1
Pleasant Hills (Borough)—Allegheny.............................PA-1
Pleasant Hope (City)—Polk.......... MO-3
Pleasant Lake (City)—Stearns....... MN-3
Pleasant Lake (Township)—Benson ND-4
Pleasant Lake (Township)—Aurora SD-4
Pleasant Mound (Township)—Bond..................................IL-3

Pleasant Mound (Township)—Blue Earth.................................MN-3
Pleasanton (City)—Alameda CA-4
Pleasanton (City)—Decatur IA-3
Pleasanton (City)—Linn..................KS-4
Pleasanton (Township)—Manistee MI-3
Pleasanton (Village)—Buffalo NE-4
Pleasanton (City)—Atascosa TX-2
Pleasant Plain (City)—Jefferson IA-3
Pleasant Plain (Village)—Warren...OH-3
Pleasant Plains (Town)—Independence........................AR-2
Pleasant Plains (Village)—Sangamon........................... IL-3
Pleasant Plains (Township)—Lake................................MI-3
Pleasant Plains (CDP)—Ocean NJ-1
Pleasant Point Reservation (ME)...............................IndRes-4
Pleasant Prairie (Township)—Martin MN-3
Pleasant Prairie (Township)—Eddy................................ ND-4
Pleasant Prairie (Town)—Kenosha WI-3
Pleasant Prairie (Village)—Kenosha WI-3
Pleasant Ridge (Township)—Livingston IL-3
Pleasant Ridge (Township)—Pawnee KS-4
Pleasant Ridge (Pop. Place)—Somerset ME-1
Pleasant Ridge (City)—Oakland.... MI-3
Pleasant Ridge (Township)—Barry MO-3
Pleasant Ridge (Township)—Corson SD-4
Pleasant Run (Township)—Lawrence IN-3
Pleasant Run (CDP)—Hamilton ...OH-3
Pleasant Run Farm (CDP)—Hamilton OH-3
Pleasants County........................ WV-2
Pleasant Springs (Town)—Dane WI-3
Pleasant Vale (Township)—Pike IL-3
Pleasant Valley (CDP)—Fairbanks North Star Borough AK-4
Pleasant Valley (Township)—Jo Daviess.............................. IL-3
Pleasant Valley (Township)—Cowley..............................KS-4
Pleasant Valley (Township)—Decatur KS-4
Pleasant Valley (Township)—Finney KS-4
Pleasant Valley (Township)—Pawnee KS-4
Pleasant Valley (Township)—Saline................................ KS-4
Pleasant Valley (Township)—Wilson KS-4
Pleasant Valley (Township)—Mower...............................MN-3
Pleasant Valley (City)—Clay MO-3
Pleasant Valley (Township)—Wright MO-3
Pleasant Valley (Township)—Dodge.................................NE-4
Pleasant Valley (Town)—Dutchess..........................NY-1
Pleasant Valley (Township)—Williams ND-4

Pleasant Valley (Township)—Potter............................. PA-1
Pleasant Valley (Township)—Aurora SD-4
Pleasant Valley (Township)—Clay................................. SD-4
Pleasant Valley (Township)—Gregory SD-4
Pleasant Valley (Township)—Hand................................ SD-4
Pleasant Valley (Township)—Marshall SD-4
Pleasant Valley (Township)—Perkins SD-4
Pleasant Valley (Township)—Tripp............................... SD-4
Pleasant Valley (Town)—Wichita .. TX-2
Pleasant Valley (Town)—Eau Claire................................ WI-3
Pleasant Valley (Town)—St. Croix WI-3
Pleasant View (Township)—Macon................................ IL-3
Pleasant View (Township)—Cherokee KS-4
Pleasant View (Township)—Emmet.............................. MI-3
Pleasant View (Township)—Norman............................MN-3
Pleasant View (Township)—Holt.. NE-4
Pleasant View (Township)—Grand Forks ND-4
Pleasant View (Township)—Beadle.............................. SD-4
Pleasant View (Township)—Tripp............................... SD-4
Pleasant View (City)—Weber......... UT-4
Pleasantville (City)—Marion IA-3
Pleasantville (City)—Atlantic........... NJ-1
Pleasantville (Village)—Westchester.......................NY-1
Pleasantville (Village)—Fairfield ...OH-3
Pleasantville (Borough)—Bedford... PA-1
Pleasantville (Borough)—Venango.. PA-1
Pleasure Ridge Park (CDP)—Jefferson KY-2
Pleasureville (City)—Henry KY-2
Pleasureville (City)—Shelby........... KY-2
Plentywood (City)—Sheridan MT-4
Plevna (City)—Reno KS-4
Plevna (Township)—Reno KS-4
Plevna (Town)—Fallon MT-4
Pliny (Township)—Aitkin ... MN-3
Plover (City)—Pocahontas IA-3
Plover (Town)—Marathon WI-3
Plover (Town)—Portage WI-3
Plover (Village)—Portage WI-3
Plum (Township)—Phillips KS-4
Plum (Borough)—Allegheny............PA-1
Plum (Township)—Venango........... PA-1
Plumas County CA-4
Plumb (Township)—Wabaunsee KS-4
Plum Branch (Town)—McCormick SC-2
Plum City (Village)—Pierce............ WI-3
Plum Creek (Township)—Mitchell KS-4
Plum Creek (Township)—Butler.... NE-4
Plumcreek (Township)—Armstrong PA-1
Plumer (Township)—Divide ND-4
Plumerville (City)—Conway AR-2
Plum Grove (Township)—Butler....KS-4
Plum Grove (City)—Liberty TX-2

General Index — American Places Dictionary

Plum Hill (Township)—
  Washington IL-3
Plum Lake (Town)—Vilas WI-3
Plummer (City)—Benewah ID-4
Plummer (City)—Red Lake MN-3
Plummer (Township)—Brule SD-4
Plum Springs (City)—Warren KY-2
Plumstead (Township)—Bucks PA-1
Plumsted (Township)—Ocean NJ-1
Plumville (Borough)—Indiana PA-1
Plunketts Creek (Township)—
  Lycoming PA-1
Plymouth (City)—Amador CA-4
Plymouth (Town)—Litchfield CT-1
Plymouth (Village)—Hancock IL-3
Plymouth (Village)—McDonough .. IL-3
Plymouth (City)—Marshall IN-3
Plymouth (City)—Cerro Gordo IA-3
Plymouth (Township)—Russell KS-4
Plymouth (Town)—Penobscot ME-1
Plymouth (Town)—Plymouth MA-1
Plymouth (City)—Wayne MI-3
Plymouth (Township)—Wayne MI-3
Plymouth (City)—Hennepin MN-3
Plymouth (Village)—Jefferson NE-4
Plymouth (Town)—Grafton NH-1
Plymouth (Town)—Chenango NY-1
Plymouth (Town)—Washington NC-2
Plymouth (Township)—Grand
  Forks ND-4
Plymouth (Township)—
  Ashtabula OH-3
Plymouth (Village)—Huron OH-3
Plymouth (Township)—Richland ... OH-3
Plymouth (Village)—Richland OH-3
Plymouth (Borough)—Luzerne PA-1
Plymouth (Township)—Luzerne ... PA-1
Plymouth (Township)—
  Montgomery PA-1
Plymouth (Town)—Box Elder UT-4
Plymouth (Town)—Windsor VT-1
Plymouth (Town)—Juneau WI-3
Plymouth (Town)—Rock WI-3
Plymouth (City)—Sheboygan WI-3
Plymouth (Town)—Sheboygan WI-3
Plymouth County IA-3
Plymouth County MA-1
Plymouth Village (City)—
  Jefferson KY-2
Plympton (Town)—Plymouth MA-1
Poarch Creek Reservation & Trust
  Lands (AL) IndRes-4
Poca (Town)—Putnam WV-2
Pocahontas (City)—Randolph AR-2
Pocahontas (Town)—Bond IL-3
Pocahontas (City)—Pocahontas IA-3
Pocahontas (Town)—Cape
  Girardeau MO-3
Pocahontas (Town)—Tazewell VA-2
Pocahontas County IA-3
Pocahontas County WV-2
Pocasset (CDP)—Barnstable MA-1
Pocatello (City)—Bannock ID-4
Pocatello (City)—Power ID-4
Pocola (Town)—Le Flore OK-2
Pocomoke City (City)—
  Worcester MD-1
Pocono (Township)—Monroe PA-1
Pocopson (Township)—Chester PA-1
Poe (Township)—McKenzie ND-4
Poestenkill (Town)—Rensselaer NY-1
Pohatcong (Township)—Warren ... NJ-1
Pohlitz (Township)—Roseau MN-3
Pohocco (Township)—Saunders ... NE-4
Poinciana Place (CDP)—Osceola .. FL-2

Poinsett County AR-2
Point (Township)—Posey IN-3
Point (Township)—
  Northumberland PA-1
Point (City)—Rains TX-2
Point Arena (City)—Mendocino CA-4
Point Baker (CDP)—Prince of
  Wales-Outer Ketchikan Census
  Area AK-4
Point Blank (City)—San Jacinto TX-2
Point Clear (Division)—Baldwin AL-2
Point Comfort (City)—Calhoun TX-2
Point Dume (CDP)—Los
  Angeles CA-4
Pointe a la Hache (Pop. Place)—
  Plaquemines Parish LA-2
Pointe Aux Barques (Township)—
  Huron MI-3
Pointe Coupee Parish LA-2
Point Hope (City)—North Slope
  Borough AK-4
Point Lay (CDP)—North Slope
  Borough AK-4
Point Marion (Borough)—Fayette .. PA-1
Point Pleasant (Township)—
  Warren IL-3
Point Pleasant (Borough)—Ocean .. NJ-1
Point Pleasant (City)—Mason WV-2
Point Pleasant Beach (Borough)—
  Ocean NJ-1
Point Reyes (NE) Geog-4
Poipu (CDP)—Kauai HI-4
Pojoaque (CDP)—Santa Fe NM-4
Pojoaque Pueblo (NM) IndRes-4
Pokagon (Township)—Cass MI-3
Pokegama (Township)—Pine MN-3
Polacca (CDP)—Navajo AZ-4
Poland (Town)—Androscoggin ME-1
Poland (Town)—Chautauqua NY-1
Poland (Village)—Herkimer NY-1
Poland (Township)—Mahoning OH-3
Poland (Village)—Mahoning OH-3
Polar (Town)—Langlade WI-3
Polk (Township)—Macoupin IL-3
Polk (Township)—Huntington IN-3
Polk (Township)—Marshall IN-3
Polk (Township)—Monroe IN-3
Polk (Township)—Washington IN-3
Polk (Township)—Adair MO-3
Polk (Township)—Atchison MO-3
Polk (Township)—Cass MO-3
Polk (Township)—Dade MO-3
Polk (Township)—DeKalb MO-3
Polk (Township)—Madison MO-3
Polk (Township)—Nodaway MO-3
Polk (Township)—Ray MO-3
Polk (Township)—St. Clair MO-3
Polk (Township)—Sullivan MO-3
Polk (Village)—Polk NE-4
Polk (Village)—Ashland OH-3
Polk (Township)—Crawford OH-3
Polk (Township)—Jefferson PA-1
Polk (Township)—Monroe PA-1
Polk (Borough)—Venango PA-1
Polk (Town)—Washington WI-3
Polk Centre (Township)—
  Pennington MN-3
Polk City (Town)—Polk FL-2
Polk City (Township)—Polk IA-3
Polk County AR-2
Polk County FL-2
Polk County GA-2
Polk County IA-3
Polk County MN-3
Polk County MO-3

Polk County .... NE-
Polk County .... NC-
Polk County .... OR-
Polk County .... TN-
Polk County .... TX-
Polk County .... WI-
Polk Inlet (CDP)—Prince of
  Wales-Outer Ketchikan Census
  Area .... AK-
Polkton (Township)—Ottawa .... MI-
Polkton (Town)—Anson .... NC-
Polkville (Village)—Smith .... MS-
Polkville (City)—Cleveland .... NC-
Pollard (Municipality)—
  Escambia .... AL-
Pollard (Town)—Clay .... AR-
Pollock (Town)—Grant Parish .... LA-
Pollock (Village)—Sullivan .... MO-
Pollock (Town)—Campbell .... SD-
Pollock Pines (CDP)—El Dorado .. CA-4
Pollocksville (Town)—Jones .... NC-
Polo (Town)—Ogle .... IL-
Polo (City)—Caldwell .... MO-
Polonia (Township)—Roseau MN-3
Polson (City)—Lake MT-4
Pomaria (Town)—Newberry .... SC-
Pomeroy (City)—Calhoun IA-3
Pomeroy (Village)—Meigs OH-3
Pomeroy (Village)—Garfield WA-4
Pomfret (Town)—Windham CT-1
Pomfret (Town)—Chautauqua NY-1
Pomfret (Town)—Windsor VT-1
Pomme de Terre (Township)—
  Grant MN-3
Pomona (City)—Los Angeles CA-4
Pomona (Township)—Jackson IL-3
Pomona (City)—Franklin KS-4
Pomona (Township)—Franklin KS-4
Pomona (CDP)—Atlantic NJ-1
Pomona (Village)—Rockland NY-1
Pomona Park (Town)—Putnam FL-2
Pomona View (Township)—
  LaMoure ND-4
Pompano Beach (City)—Broward .. FL-2
Pompano Beach Highlands (CDP)—
  Broward FL-2
Pompey (Town)—Onondaga NY-1
Pompton Lakes (Borough)—
  Passaic NJ-1
Pomroy (Township)—Itasca MN-3
Pomroy (Township)—Kanabec MN-3
Ponca (City)—Dixon NE-4
Ponca (Township)—Dixon NE-4
Ponca City (City)—Kay OK-2
Ponca City (City)—Osage OK-2
Ponca TDSA (NE) IndRes-4
Ponce de Leon (Town)—Holmes .. FL-2
Ponce de Leon (Township)—
  Stone MO-3
Ponce Inlet (Town)—Volusia FL-2
Poncha Springs (Town)—Chaffee .. CO-4
Ponchatoula (City)—Tangipahoa
  Parish LA-2
Pond Creek (Township)—
  Greene MO-3
Pond Creek (City)—Grant OK-2
Ponder (Town)—Denton TX-2
Pondera County MT-4
Ponderay (City)—Bonner ID-4
Ponderosa Park (CDP)—Elbert CO-4
Ponemah (CDP)—Beltrami MN-3
Poneto (Town)—Wells IN-3
Pontchartrain, Lake (LA) Geog-4
Pontiac (City)—Livingston IL-3
Pontiac (Township)—Livingston IL-3

Pontiac (City)—Oakland................ MI-3
Pontiac (Township)—Ozark......... MO-3
Pontiac (Township)—Cass ND-4
Ponto Lake (Township)—Cass...... MN-3
Pontoon Beach (Village)—
  Madison.. IL-3
Pontoosuc (Township)—Hancock... IL-3
Pontoosuc (Village)—Hancock IL-3
Pontotoc (City)—Pontotoc............ MS-2
Pontotoc County MS-2
Pontotoc County OK-2
Pony Gulch (Township)—Wells..... ND-4
Pooler (Town)—Chatham GA-2
Poolesville (Town)—
  Montgomery.................................. MD-1
Poospatuck Reservation (NY).. IndRes-4
Poospatuck Reservation (Pop. Place)—
  Suffolk NY-1
Pope (Township)—Fayette IL-3
Pope (Village)—Panola MS-2
Pope Air Force Base (NC).............. Mil-4
Pope Air Force Base (Military
  Facility)—Cumberland NC-2
Pope County AR-2
Pope County IL-3
Pope County MN-3
Popejoy (City)—Franklin IA-3
Poplar (Township)—Cass.............. MN-3
Poplar (City)—Roosevelt MT-4
Poplar (Pop. Place)—McLean........ ND-4
Poplar (Village)—Douglas.............. WI-3
Poplar Bluff (City)—Butler............ MO-3
Poplar Bluff (Township)—Butler .. MO-3
Poplar-Cotton Center (CDP)—
  Tulare... CA-4
Poplar Grove (Town)—Boone IL-3
Poplar Grove (Township)—Boone.. IL-3
Poplar Grove (Township)—
  Roseau... MN-3
Poplar Hills (City)—Jefferson KY-2
Poplar River (Township)—Red
  Lake MN-3
Poplar Tent (CDP)—Cabarrus........ NC-2
Poplarville (City)—Pearl River...... MS-2
Popple (Township)—Clearwater ... MN-3
Popple Grove (Township)—
  Mahnomen..................................... MN-3
Popple River (Town)—Forest WI-3
Poppleton (Township)—Kittson ... MN-3
Poquonock Bridge (CDP)—New
  London... CT-1
Poquoson (Independent City) VA-2
Poquott (Village)—Suffolk NY-1
Porcupine (CDP)—Shannon SD-4
Portage (City)—Porter..................... IN-3
Portage (Township)—Porter........... IN-3
Portage (Township)—St. Joseph IN-3
Portage (Township)—Houghton MI-3
Portage (City)—Kalamazoo MI-3
Portage (Township)—Mackinac..... MI-3
Portage (Township)—St. Louis MN-3
Portage (Township)—New
  Madrid... MO-3
Portage (Town)—Livingston NY-1
Portage (Township)—Hancock......OH-3
Portage (Township)—Ottawa OH-3
Portage (Township)—Wood OH-3
Portage (Village)—Wood OH-3
Portage (Borough)—Cambria......... PA-1
Portage (Township)—Cambria....... PA-1
Portage (Township)—Cameron...... PA-1
Portage (Township)—Potter........... PA-1
Portage (Township)—Brown SD-4
Portage (Town)—Box Elder UT-4
Portage (City)—Columbia.............. WI-3

Portage County...............................OH-3
Portage County................................ WI-3
Portage Des Sioux (City)—St.
  Charles MO-3
Portage Lake (Town)—
  Aroostook...................................... ME-1
Portage Lakes (CDP)—Summit OH-3
Portageville (City)—New
  Madrid... MO-3
Portageville (City)—Pemiscot MO-3
Portal (Town)—Bulloch................. GA-2
Portal (City)—Burke ND-4
Portal (Township)—Burke.............. ND-4
Portales (City)—Roosevelt NM-4
Port Alexander (City)—
  Wrangell-Petersburg Census
  Area.. AK-4
Port Alice (CDP)—Prince of
  Wales-Outer Ketchikan Census
  Area.. AK-4
Port Allegany (Borough)—
  McKean.. PA-1
Port Allen (City)—West Baton Rouge
  Parish LA-2
Port Alsworth (CDP)—Lake and
  Peninsula Borough........................ AK-4
Port Angeles (City)—Clallam......... WA-4
Port Angeles East (CDP)—
  Clallam WA-4
Port Aransas (City)—Nueces TX-2
Port Arthur (City)—Jefferson TX-2
Port Austin (Township)—Huron ... MI-3
Port Austin (Village)—Huron MI-3
Port Barre (Town)—St. Landry
  Parish LA-2
Port Byron (Township)—Rock
  Island... IL-3
Port Byron (Village)—Rock
  Island... IL-3
Port Byron (Village)—Cayuga........ NY-1
Port Carbon (Borough)—
  Schuylkill....................................... PA-1
Port Charlotte (CDP)—Charlotte ...FL-2
Port Chester (Village)—
  Westchester NY-1
Port Clarence (Military Facility)—
  Nome Census Area AK-4
Port Clinton (City)—Ottawa..........OH-3
Port Clinton (Borough)—
  Schuylkill....................................... PA-1
Port Deposit (Town)—Cecil.......... MD-1
Port Dickinson (Village)—
  Broome... NY-1
Port Edwards (Town)—Wood WI-3
Port Edwards (Village)—Wood...... WI-3
Port Emma (Township)—Dickey... ND-4
Porter (Town)—Porter..................... IN-3
Porter (Township)—Porter............. IN-3
Porter (Town)—Oxford ME-1
Porter (Township)—Cass................ MI-3
Porter (Township)—Midland MI-3
Porter (Township)—Van Buren...... MI-3
Porter (City)—Yellow Medicine MN-3
Porter (Town)—Niagara NY-1
Porter (Township)—Dickey............ ND-4
Porter (Township)—Delaware........OH-3
Porter (Township)—Scioto OH-3
Porter (Town)—Wagoner................ OK-2
Porter (Township)—Clarion............ PA-1
Porter (Township)—Clinton........... PA-1
Porter (Township)—Huntingdon ... PA-1
Porter (Township)—Jefferson PA-1
Porter (Township)—Lycoming....... PA-1
Porter (Township)—Pike PA-1
Porter (Township)—Schuylkill PA-1

Porter (Town)—Rock WI-3
Porter County IN-3
Porterdale (Town)—Newton GA-2
Porterfield (Town)—Marinette WI-3
Porter Heights (CDP)—
  Montgomery................................... TX-2
Portersville (Borough)—Butler........ PA-1
Porterville (City)—Tulare............... CA-4
Port Ewen (CDP)—Ulster NY-1
Port Gamble Reservation
  (WA) IndRes-4
Port Gibson (City)—Claiborne MS-2
Port Graham (CDP)—Kenai Peninsula
  Borough... AK-4
Port Heiden (City)—Lake and
  Peninsula Borough........................ AK-4
Port Henry (Village)—Essex NY-1
Port Hope (Village)—Huron MI-3
Port Hope (Township)—
  Beltrami... MN-3
Port Hueneme (City)—Ventura CA-4
Port Huron (City)—St. Clair MI-3
Port Huron (Township)—St.
  Clair... MI-3
Portia (Town)—Lawrence AR-2
Portis (City)—Osborne................... KS-4
Port Isabel (City)—Cameron TX-2
Port Jefferson (Village)—Suffolk ... NY-1
Port Jefferson (Village)—Shelby OH-3
Port Jefferson Station (CDP)—
  Suffolk NY-1
Port Jervis (City)—Orange............. NY-1
Port La Belle (CDP)—Hendry........ FL-2
Portland (City)—Ashley AR-2
Portland (Town)—Middlesex CT-1
Portland (Township)—Whiteside... IL-3
Portland (City)—Jay........................ IN-3
Portland (City)—Cumberland........ ME-1
Portland (City)—Ionia MI-3
Portland (Township)—Ionia........... MI-3
Portland (Town)—Chautauqua NY-1
Portland (City)—Traill ND-4
Portland (City)—Clackamas OR-4
Portland (City)—Multnomah OR-4
Portland (City)—Washington.........OR-4
Portland (Borough)—
  Northampton PA-1
Portland (Township)—Deuel SD-4
Portland (Town)—Sumner TN-2
Portland (City)—San Patricio......... TX-2
Portland (Town)—Dodge WI-3
Portland (Town)—Monroe WI-3
Port Lavaca (City)—Calhoun TX-2
Port Leyden (Village)—Lewis NY-1
Port Lions (City)—Kodiak Island
  Borough... AK-4
Port Madison Reservation
  (WA) IndRes-4
Port Matilda (Borough)—Centre PA-1
Port Monmouth (CDP)—
  Monmouth NJ-1
Port Neches (City)—Jefferson TX-2
Port Norris (CDP)—Cumberland... NJ-1
Portola (City)—Plumas CA-4
Portola Hills (CDP)—Orange CA-4
Portola Valley (City)—San Mateo . CA-4
Port Orange (City)—Volusia FL-2
Port Orchard (City)—Kitsap.......... WA-4
Port Orford (City)—Curry OR-4
Port Protection (CDP)—Prince of
  Wales-Outer Ketchikan Census
  Area.. AK-4
Port Reading (CDP)—Middlesex ... NJ-1
Port Republic (City)—Atlantic NJ-1
Port Richey (City)—Pasco FL-2

1069

General Index

Port Royal (Borough)—Juniata *PA-1*
Port Royal (Town)—Beaufort *SC-2*
Port Royal (Town)—Caroline *VA-2*
Port Salerno (CDP)—Martin *FL-2*
Port Sanilac (Village)—Sanilac *MI-3*
Port Sheldon (Township)—
 Ottawa.. *MI-3*
Portsmouth (City)—Shelby *IA-3*
Portsmouth (Township)—Bay........ *MI-3*
Portsmouth (City)—Rockingham ..*NH-1*
Portsmouth (City)—Scioto............. *OH-3*
Portsmouth (Town)—Newport........ *RI-1*
Portsmouth (Independent City)...... *VA-2*
Port St. Joe (City)—Gulf *FL-2*
Port St. John (CDP)—Brevard *FL-2*
Port St. Lucie (City)—St. Lucie...... *FL-2*
Port St. Lucie-River Park (CDP)—St.
 Lucie *FL-2*
Port Sulphur (CDP)—Plaquemines
 Parish *LA-2*
Port Tobacco Village (Town)—
 Charles...*MD-1*
Port Townsend (City)—Jefferson...*WA-4*
Portville (Town)—Cattaraugus *NY-1*
Portville (Village)—Cattaraugus *NY-1*
Port Vincent (Village)—Livingston
 Parish *LA-2*
Port Vue (Borough)—Allegheny *PA-1*
Port Washington (CDP)—Nassau .. *NY-1*
Port Washington (Village)—
 Tuscarawas *OH-3*
Port Washington (City)—
 Ozaukee... *WI-3*
Port Washington (Town)—
 Ozaukee... *WI-3*
Port Washington North (Village)—
 Nassau...*NY-1*
Port Wentworth (City)—
 Chatham.. *GA-2*
Port William (Village)—Clinton *OH-3*
Port Wing (Town)—Bayfield........... *WI-3*
Porum (Town)—Muskogee............. *OK-2*
Posen (Town)—Cook...................... *IL-3*
Posen (Township)—Presque Isle.... *MI-3*
Posen (Village)—Presque Isle *MI-3*
Posen (Township)—Yellow
 Medicine..*MN-3*
Posey (Township)—Clay *IN-3*
Posey (Township)—Fayette *IN-3*
Posey (Township)—Franklin........... *IN-3*
Posey (Township)—Harrison *IN-3*
Posey (Township)—Rush *IN-3*
Posey (Township)—Switzerland...... *IN-3*
Posey (Township)—Washington..... *IN-3*
Posey County.................................... *IN-3*
Poseyville (Town)—Posey *IN-3*
Post (City)—Garza *TX-2*
Post Falls (City)—Kootenai *ID-4*
Post Oak (Township)—Johnson *MO-3*
Post Oak Bend City (Town)—
 Kaufman.. *TX-2*
Poston (CDP)—La Paz *AZ-4*
Postville (City)—Allamakee............. *IA-3*
Postville (City)—Clayton................. *IA-3*
Potawatomi (WI) Res. & Trust Lands
 (WI).. *IndRes-4*
Poteau (City)—Le Flore.................. *OK-2*
Poteet (City)—Atascosa................... *TX-2*
Poth (Town)—Wilson *TX-2*
Potlatch (City)—Latah *ID-4*
Potomac (Town)—Vermilion *IL-3*
Potomac (CDP)—Montgomery.....*MD-1*
Potomac Heights (CDP)—
 Charles...*MD-1*
Potomac River (LA) *Geog-4*

Potosi (Township)—Linn *KS-4*
Potosi (City)—Washington............. *MO-3*
Potosi (CDP)—Taylor *TX-2*
Potosi (Town)—Grant *WI-3*
Potosi (Village)—Grant................... *WI-3*
Potsdam (Town)—St. Lawrence..... *NY-1*
Potsdam (Village)—St. Lawrence .. *NY-1*
Potsdam (Township)—Dickey........*ND-4*
Potsdam (Village)—Miami.............*OH-3*
Potshot Lake (Pop. Place)—St.
 Louis *MN-3*
Pottawatomie (Township)—
 Coffey... *KS-4*
Pottawatomie (Township)—
 Franklin... *KS-4*
Pottawatomie (Township)—
 Pottawatomie................................. *KS-4*
Pottawatomie County *KS-4*
Pottawatomie County *OK-2*
Pottawatomi (Kansas) Reservation
 (KS)...*IndRes-4*
Pottawattamie County *IA-3*
Pottawattomie Park (Town)—La
 Porte *IN-3*
Potter (Village)—Cheyenne............. *NE-4*
Potter (Town)—Yates *NY-1*
Potter (Township)—Barnes *ND-4*
Potter (Township)—Beaver *PA-1*
Potter (Township)—Centre *PA-1*
Potter (Village)—Calumet *WI-3*
Potter County *PA-1*
Potter County *SD-4*
Potter County *TX-2*
Potter Lake (CDP)—Walworth *WI-3*
Potterville (City)—Eaton................. *MI-3*
Pottsboro (Town)—Grayson *TX-2*
Potts Camp (Town)—Marshall *MS-2*
Pottstown (Borough)—
 Montgomery.................................. *PA-1*
Pottsville (Town)—Pope *AR-2*
Pottsville (City)—Schuylkill *PA-1*
Potwin (City)—Butler...................... *KS-4*
Poughkeepsie (City)—Dutchess *NY-1*
Poughkeepsie (Town)—Dutchess ... *NY-1*
Poulan (City)—Worth *GA-2*
Poulsbo (City)—Kitsap *WA-4*
Poultney (Town)—Rutland *VT-1*
Poultney (Village)—Rutland *VT-1*
Pound (Town)—Wise *VA-2*
Pound (Town)—Marinette.............. *WI-3*
Pound (Village)—Marinette *WI-3*
Pound Ridge (Town)—
 Westchester....................................*NY-1*
Poway (City)—San Diego *CA-4*
Powderly (City)—Muhlenberg *KY-2*
Powder River County *MT-4*
Powder Springs (City)—Cobb........ *GA-2*
Powell (Municipality)—DeKalb......*AL-2*
Powell (Township)—Comanche..... *KS-4*
Powell (Township)—Marquette *MI-3*
Powell (Village)—Delaware............*OH-3*
Powell (Township)—Edmunds....... *SD-4*
Powell (CDP)—Knox...................... *TN-2*
Powell (Town)—Navarro................. *TX-2*
Powell (City)—Park........................*WY-4*
Powell, Lake (UT) *Geog-4*
Powell County *KY-2*
Powell County *MT-4*
Powellhurst-Centennial (CDP)—
 Multnomah................................... *OR-4*
Powells Crossroads (Town)—
 Marion... *TN-2*
Powellsville (Town)—Bertie............ *NC-2*
Powellton (CDP)—Fayette............ *WV-2*
Power County *ID-4*

Powers (Village)—Menominee....... *MI-3*
Powers (Township)—Cass *MN-3*
Powers (Township)—Mountrail *ND-4*
Powers (City)—Coos *OR-4*
Powers Lake (City)—Burke............*ND-4*
Powers Lake (Township)—
 Mountrail *ND-4*
Powers Lake (CDP)—Kenosha...... *WI-3*
Powers Lake (CDP)—Walworth *WI-3*
Powersville (Village)—Putnam *MO-3*
Poweshiek County *IA-3*
Powhatan (Town)—Lawrence *AR-2*
Powhatan (Village)—Natchitoches
 Parish *LA-2*
Powhatan County *VA-2*
Powhatan Point (Village)—
 Belmont...*OH-3*
Powhattan (City)—Brown............... *KS-4*
Powhattan (Township)—Brown..... *KS-4*
Pownal (Town)—Cumberland. *ME-1*
Pownal (Town)—Bennington *VT-1*
Poydras (CDP)—St. Bernard
 Parish *LA-2*
Poyen (Town)—Grant *AR-2*
Poygan (Town)—Winnebago.......... *WI-3*
Poynette (Village)—Columbia *WI-3*
Poynor (Township)—Ripley...........*MO-3*
Poynor (Town)—Henderson *TX-2*
Poysippi (Town)—Waushara.......... *WI-3*
Prague (Village)—Saunders............ *NE-4*
Prague (City)—Lincoln................... *OK-2*
Prairie (Township)—Crawford....... *IL-3*
Prairie (Township)—Edgar............. *IL-3*
Prairie (Township)—Hancock........ *IL-3*
Prairie (Township)—Shelby *IL-3*
Prairie (Township)—Henry *IN-3*
Prairie (Township)—Kosciusko...... *IN-3*
Prairie (Township)—La Porte......... *IN-3*
Prairie (Township)—Tipton............ *IN-3*
Prairie (Township)—Warren *IN-3*
Prairie (Township)—White............. *IN-3*
Prairie (Township)—Jewell............. *KS-4*
Prairie (Township)—Wilson........... *KS-4*
Prairie (Township)—Wyandotte *KS-4*
Prairie (Township)—Audrain.........*MO-3*
Prairie (Township)—Bates *MO-3*
Prairie (Township)—Carroll...........*MO-3*
Prairie (Township)—Franklin *MO-3*
Prairie (Township)—Howard.........*MO-3*
Prairie (Township)—Jackson *MO-3*
Prairie (Township)—Lincoln..........*MO-3*
Prairie (Township)—McDonald.....*MO-3*
Prairie (Township)—
 Montgomery..................................*MO-3*
Prairie (Township)—Pettis.............*MO-3*
Prairie (Township)—Randolph *MO-3*
Prairie (Township)—Schuyler *MO-3*
Prairie (Township)—Phelps *NE-4*
Prairie (Township)—LaMoure *ND-4*
Prairie (Township)—Franklin........*OH-3*
Prairie (Township)—Holmes..........*OH-3*
Prairie (Township)—Union............. *SD-4*
Prairieburg (City)—Linn................. *IA-3*
Prairie Center (Township)—
 Walsh...*ND-4*
Prairie Center (Township)—Clay... *SD-4*
Prairie Center (Township)—
 Spink.. *SD-4*
Prairie City (Town)—McDonough . *IL-3*
Prairie City (Township)—
 McDonough.................................... *IL-3*
Prairie City (City)—Jasper.............. *IA-3*
Prairie City (City)—Grant.............. *OR-4*
Prairie County *AR-2*
Prairie County *MT-4*

1070

American Places Dictionary — General Index

Prairie Creek (CDP)—Benton *AR-2*
Prairie Creek (Township)—Logan .. *IL-3*
Prairie Creek (Township)—Vigo..... *IN-3*
Prairie Creek (Township)—Hall *NE-4*
Prairie Creek (Township)—
 Merrick...........................*NE-4*
Prairie Creek (Township)—
 Nance *NE-4*
Prairie Dog (Township)—Decatur ..*KS-4*
Prairie Dog (Township)—
 Sheridan *KS-4*
Prairie Dog (Township)—Harlan... *NE-4*
Prairie du Chien (City)—
 Crawford *WI-3*
Prairie du Chien (Town)—
 Crawford *WI-3*
Prairie Du Long (Township)—St.
 Clair *IL-3*
Prairie du Rocher (Town)—
 Randolph *IL-3*
Prairie du Sac (Town)—Sauk......... *WI-3*
Prairie du Sac (Village)—Sauk....... *WI-3*
Prairie Farm (Town)—Barron....... *WI-3*
Prairie Farm (Village)—Barron...... *WI-3*
Prairie Green (Township)—
 Iroquois..............................*IL-3*
Prairie Grove (City)—
 Washington *AR-2*
Prairie Grove (Village)—
 McHenry *IL-3*
Prairie Home (City)—Cooper....... *MO-3*
Prairie Home (Township)—
 Cooper.............................*MO-3*
Prairie Island (Township)—
 Merrick............................*NE-4*
Prairie Island Community
 (MN) *IndRes-4*
Prairie Lake (Township)—St.
 Louis *MN-3*
Prairie Lake (Town)—Barron *WI-3*
Prairie Ridge (CDP)—Pierce *WA-4*
Prairie Ronde (Township)—
 Kalamazoo *MI-3*
Prairie Rose (City)—Cass *ND-4*
Prairieton (Township)—Christian... *IL-3*
Prairieton (Township)—Vigo *IN-3*
Prairie View (City)—Phillips *KS-4*
Prairie View (Township)—
 Phillips *KS-4*
Prairie View (Township)—
 Wilkin *MN-3*
Prairie View (Township)—
 Emmons *ND-4*
Prairie View (Township)—
 Corson.............................*SD-4*
Prairie View (City)—Waller........... *TX-2*
Prairie Village (City)—Johnson *KS-4*
Prairieville (Township)—Barry *MI-3*
Prairieville (Township)—Brown ... *MN-3*
Prairieville (Township)—Pike *MO-3*
Prairiewood (Township)—Brown... *SD-4*
Prathersville (Village)—Clay *MO-3*
Pratt (City)—Pratt........................*KS-4*
Pratt (Township)—McHenry......... *ND-4*
Pratt (Township)—Lyman *SD-4*
Pratt (Town)—Kanawha................ *WV-2*
Pratt County..............................*KS-4*
Prattsburg (Town)—Steuben *NY-1*
Prattsville (Town)—Grant.............. *AR-2*
Prattsville (Town)—Greene............ *NY-1*
Prattville (City)—Autauga..............*AL-2*
Prattville (City)—Elmore................*AL-2*
Preble (Township)—Adams............ *IN-3*
Preble (Township)—Fillmore........ *MN-3*
Preble (Town)—Cortland *NY-1*

Preble County..............................*OH-3*
Preemption (Township)—Mercer.... *IL-3*
Premont (City)—Jim Wells *TX-2*
Prentice (Town)—Price *WI-3*
Prentice (Village)—Price *WI-3*
Prentiss (Plantation)—Penobscot . *ME-1*
Prentiss (Town)—Jefferson
 Davis *MS-2*
Prentiss County *MS-2*
Prescott (City)—Yavapai................ *AZ-4*
Prescott (City)—Nevada *AR-2*
Prescott (City)—Adams..................*IA-3*
Prescott (City)—Linn......................*KS-4*
Prescott (Village)—Ogemaw........... *MI-3*
Prescott (Township)—Faribault *MN-3*
Prescott (Township)—Renville *ND-4*
Prescott (City)—Columbia............. *OR-4*
Prescott (Town)—Walla Walla *WA-4*
Prescott (City)—Pierce *WI-3*
Prescott Valley (Town)—Yavapai .. *AZ-4*
Presho (City)—Lyman *SD-4*
Presho (Township)—Lyman *SD-4*
President (Township)—Venango..... *PA-1*
Presidential Lakes Estates (CDP)—
 Burlington *NJ-1*
Presidential Range (NH) *Geog-4*
Presidio (Village)—Presidio *TX-2*
Presidio County *TX-2*
Presidio of Monterey (CA)............*Mil-4*
Presidio of San Francisco (CA)......*Mil-4*
Presque Isle (City)—Aroostook *ME-1*
Presque Isle (Township)—Presque
 Isle *MI-3*
Presque Isle (Town)—Vilas *WI-3*
Presque Isle County *MI-3*
Preston (Town)—New London *CT-1*
Preston (City)—Webster................. *GA-2*
Preston (City)—Franklin................ *ID-4*
Preston (Township)—Richland *IL-3*
Preston (City)—Jackson *IA-3*
Preston (City)—Pratt......................*KS-4*
Preston (Town)—Caroline *MD-1*
Preston (City)—Fillmore................ *MN-3*
Preston (Township)—Fillmore...... *MN-3*
Preston (Town)—Hickory *MO-3*
Preston (Township)—Jasper.......... *MO-3*
Preston (Township)—Platte *MO-3*
Preston (Village)—Richardson....... *NE-4*
Preston (Town)—Chenango *NY-1*
Preston (Township)—Ransom *ND-4*
Preston (Township)—Wayne........... *PA-1*
Preston (Township)—Brookings..... *SD-4*
Preston (Town)—Adams *WI-3*
Preston (Town)—Trempealeau....... *WI-3*
Preston County *WV-2*
Preston Heights (CDP)—Will *IL-3*
Preston Lake (Township)—
 Renville............................*MN-3*
Prestonsburg (City)—Floyd............ *KY-2*
Prestonville (City)—Carroll *KY-2*
Pretty Bayou (CDP)—Bay *FL-2*
Pretty Prairie (City)—Reno *KS-4*
Pretty Rock (Township)—Grant *ND-4*
Pribilof Islands (AK) *Geog-4*
Price (Township)—Monroe............. *PA-1*
Price (City)—Carbon......................*UT-4*
Price (Town)—Langlade................. *WI-3*
Price County.................................. *WI-3*
Priceville (Town)—Morgan *AL-2*
Prichard (City)—Mobile *AL-2*
Prien (CDP)—Calcasieu Parish *LA-2*
Priest Point (CDP)—Snohomish ... *WA-4*
Priest River (City)—Bonner............ *ID-4*
Primera (Town)—Cameron............ *TX-2*
Primghar (City)—O'Brien *IA-3*

Primrose (CDP)—Kenai Peninsula
 Borough..........................*AK-4*
Primrose (Village)—Boone *NE-4*
Primrose (Township)—Steele *ND-4*
Primrose (Town)—Dane *WI-3*
Prince Edward County *VA-2*
Prince Frederick (CDP)—
 Calvert............................*MD-1*
Prince George County *VA-2*
Prince George's County................... *MD-1*
Prince of Wales Island (AK)........ *Geog-4*
**Prince of Wales-Outer Ketchikan
 Census Area** *AK-4*
Princes Lakes (Town)—Johnson *IN-3*
Princess Anne (Town)—
 Somerset........................*MD-1*
Princeton (CDP)—Dade *FL-2*
Princeton (Town)—Bureau............. *IL-3*
Princeton (Township)—Bureau....... *IL-3*
Princeton (City)—Gibson *IN-3*
Princeton (Township)—White *IN-3*
Princeton (City)—Scott *IA-3*
Princeton (City)—Franklin *KS-4*
Princeton (City)—Caldwell *KY-2*
Princeton (Town)—Washington *ME-1*
Princeton (Town)—Worcester *MA-1*
Princeton (City)—Mille Lacs *MN-3*
Princeton (Township)—Mille
 Lacs................................*MN-3*
Princeton (City)—Sherburne......... *MN-3*
Princeton (City)—Mercer.............. *MO-3*
Princeton (Borough)—Mercer..........*NJ-1*
Princeton (Township)—Mercer....... *NJ-1*
Princeton (Town)—Johnston *NC-2*
Princeton (City)—Collin *TX-2*
Princeton (City)—Mercer.............. *WV-2*
Princeton (City)—Green Lake *WI-3*
Princeton (Town)—Green Lake *WI-3*
Princeton Junction (CDP)—
 Mercer *NJ-1*
Princeton North (CDP)—Mercer....*NJ-1*
Princetown (Town)—
 Schenectady *NY-1*
Princeville (CDP)—Kauai *HI-4*
Princeville (Town)—Peoria *IL-3*
Princeville (Township)—Peoria *IL-3*
Princeville (Town)—Edgecombe.... *NC-2*
Prince William County................... *VA-2*
Prince William Sound (AK) *Geog-4*
Prineville (City)—Crook *OR-4*
Pringle (Borough)—Luzerne............ *PA-1*
Pringle (Town)—Custer.................. *SD-4*
Prinsburg (City)—Kandiyohi *MN-3*
Prior (Township)—Big Stone *MN-3*
Prior Lake (City)—Scott *MN-3*
Pritchett (Town)—Baca.................. *CO-4*
Proctor (City)—St. Louis *MN-3*
Proctor (Town)—Rutland................*VT-1*
Proctorsville (Village)—Windsor ... *VT-1*
Proctorville (Town)—Robeson *NC-2*
Proctorville (Village)—Lawrence ...*OH-3*
Progreso (CDP)—Hidalgo.............. *TX-2*
Progreso Lakes (City)—Hidalgo *TX-2*
Progress (Township)—Wells *ND-4*
Progressive (Township)—Tripp...... *SD-4*
Promise City (City)—Wayne...........*IA-3*
Prompton (Borough)—Wayne......... *PA-1*
Prophetstown (Town)—Whiteside .. *IL-3*
Prophetstown (Township)—
 Whiteside *IL-3*
Prospect (Town)—New Haven....... *CT-1*
Prospect (Township)—Butler *KS-4*
Prospect (City)—Jefferson *KY-2*
Prospect (Town)—Waldo................ *ME-1*
Prospect (Village)—Oneida *NY-1*

General Index

American Places Dictionary

Prospect (Township)—Ramsey *ND-4*
Prospect (Township)—Marion *OH-3*
Prospect (Village)—Marion *OH-3*
Prospect (Borough)—Butler *PA-1*
Prospect (Township)—Mellette *SD-4*
Prospect Heights (Town)—
  Fremont *CO-4*
Prospect Heights (City)—Cook *IL-3*
Prospect Park (Borough)—
  Passaic *NJ-1*
Prospect Park (Borough)—
  Delaware *PA-1*
Prosper (Township)—Davison *SD-4*
Prosper (Town)—Collin *TX-2*
Prosperity (Township)—Renville .. *ND-4*
Prosperity (Town)—Newberry *SC-2*
Prosperity (CDP)—Raleigh *WV-2*
Prosser (Village)—Adams *NE-4*
Prosser (City)—Benton *WA-4*
Protection (City)—Comanche *KS-4*
Protection (Township)—
  Comanche *KS-4*
Protivin (City)—Howard *IA-3*
Provencal (Village)—Natchitoches
  Parish *LA-2*
Providence (Town)—Marengo *AL-2*
Providence (City)—Webster *KY-2*
Providence (Township)—Lac qui
  Parle *MN-3*
Providence (Town)—Saratoga *NY-1*
Providence (Township)—Lucas *OH-3*
Providence (Township)—
  Lancaster *PA-1*
Providence (City)—Providence *RI-1*
Providence (City)—Cache *UT-4*
Providence County *RI-1*
Provincetown (Town)—
  Barnstable *MA-1*
Proviso (Township)—Cook *IL-3*
Provo (Township)—Fall River *SD-4*
Provo (City)—Utah *UT-4*
Prowers County *CO-4*
Prudenville (CDP)—Roscommon .. *MI-3*
Prudhoe Bay (CDP)—North Slope
  Borough *AK-4*
Prue (Town)—Osage *OK-2*
Prunedale (CDP)—Monterey *CA-4*
Pryor (CDP)—Big Horn *MT-4*
Pryor Creek (City)—Mayes *OK-2*
Puako (CDP)—Hawaii *HI-4*
Puckett (Village)—Rankin *MS-2*
Pueblo (City)—Pueblo *CO-4*
Pueblo County *CO-4*
Pueblo West (CDP)—Pueblo *CO-4*
Puerto Rico (AK) *Geog-4*
Puget Sound (WA) *Geog-4*
Puhi (CDP)—Kauai *HI-4*
Pukalani (CDP)—Maui *HI-4*
Pukwana (Town)—Brule *SD-4*
Pukwana (Township)—Brule *SD-4*
Pulaski (Town)—Candler *GA-2*
Pulaski (Village)—Pulaski *IL-3*
Pulaski (City)—Davis *IA-3*
Pulaski (Township)—Jackson *MI-3*
Pulaski (Township)—Morrison *MN-3*
Pulaski (Village)—Oswego *NY-1*
Pulaski (Township)—Walsh *ND-4*
Pulaski (Township)—Williams *OH-3*
Pulaski (Township)—Beaver *PA-1*
Pulaski (Township)—Lawrence *PA-1*
Pulaski (Pop. Place)—Faulk *SD-4*
Pulaski (City)—Giles *TN-2*
Pulaski (Town)—Pulaski *VA-2*
Pulaski (Village)—Brown *WI-3*
Pulaski (Town)—Iowa *WI-3*

Pulaski County *AR-2*
Pulaski County *GA-2*
Pulaski County *IL-3*
Pulaski County *IN-3*
Pulaski County *KY-2*
Pulaski County *MO-3*
Pulaski County *VA-2*
Pulawski (Township)—Presque
  Isle *MI-3*
Pullman (City)—Whitman *WA-4*
Pullman (Town)—Ritchie *WV-2*
Pulteney (Town)—Steuben *NY-1*
Pultney (Township)—Belmont *OH-3*
Pumphrey (CDP)—Anne
  Arundel *MD-1*
Pumpkin Center (CDP)—
  Onslow *NC-2*
Punaluu (CDP)—Honolulu *HI-4*
Punta Gorda (City)—Charlotte *FL-2*
Punta Rassa (CDP)—Lee *FL-2*
Punxsutawney (Borough)—
  Jefferson *PA-1*
Pupukea (CDP)—Honolulu *HI-4*
Purcell (City)—Jasper *MO-3*
Purcell (Township)—Mountrail *ND-4*
Purcell (City)—Cleveland *OK-2*
Purcell (City)—McClain *OK-2*
Purcellville (Town)—Loudoun *VA-2*
Purdin (City)—Linn *MO-3*
Purdum (Pop. Place)—Blaine *NE-4*
Purdy (City)—Barry *MO-3*
Purdy (Township)—Barry *MO-3*
Purvis (City)—Lamar *MS-2*
Puryear (City)—Henry *TN-2*
Pusheta (Township)—Auglaize *OH-3*
Pushmataha County *OK-2*
Put-in-Bay (Township)—Ottawa .. *OH-3*
Put-in-Bay (Village)—Ottawa *OH-3*
Putman (Township)—Fulton *IL-3*
Putnam (Town)—Windham *CT-1*
Putnam (Township)—Anderson *KS-4*
Putnam (Township)—Stafford *KS-4*
Putnam (Township)—Livingston .. *MI-3*
Putnam (Township)—Washington .. *NY-1*
Putnam (Town)—Dewey *OK-2*
Putnam (Township)—Tioga *PA-1*
Putnam (Town)—Callahan *TX-2*
Putnam County *FL-2*
Putnam County *GA-2*
Putnam County *IL-3*
Putnam County *IN-3*
Putnam County *MO-3*
Putnam County *NY-1*
Putnam County *OH-3*
Putnam County *TN-2*
Putnam County *WV-2*
Putnam Lake (CDP)—Putnam *NY-1*
Putnam Valley (Town)—Putnam .. *NY-1*
Putney (CDP)—Dougherty *GA-2*
Putney (Township)—Brown *SD-4*
Putney (Town)—Windham *VT-1*
Puxico (City)—Stoddard *MO-3*
Puyallup (City)—Pierce *WA-4*
Puyallup Reservation & Trust Lands
  (WA) *IndRes-4*
Pyatt (Town)—Marion *AR-2*
Pymatuning (Township)—Mercer ... *PA-1*
Pyote (Town)—Ward *TX-2*
Pyramid Lake (NV) *Geog-4*
Pyramid Lake Reservation
  (NV) *IndRes-4*
Quabbin Reservoir (MA) *Geog-4*
Quail Valley (CDP)—Riverside *CA-4*
Quaker City (Village)—Guernsey .. *OH-3*
Quakertown (Borough)—Bucks *PA-1*

Quamba (City)—Kanabec *MN-3*
Quanah (City)—Hardeman *TX-2*
Quantico (Town)—Prince
  William *VA-2*
Quantico Marine Corps Combat
  Development Command (VA) *Mil-4*
Quantico Station (Military Facility)—
  Prince William *VA-2*
Quantico Station (Military Facility)—
  Stafford *VA-2*
Quapaw (Town)—Ottawa *OK-2*
Quarry (Township)—Jersey *IL-3*
Quarryville (Borough)—Lancaster .. *PA-1*
Quartz Hill (CDP)—Los Angeles ... *CA-4*
Quartzsite (Town)—La Paz *AZ-4*
Quartz Valley Rancheria
  (CA) *IndRes-4*
Quasqueton (City)—Buchanan *IA-3*
Quay (Town)—Pawnee *OK-2*
Quay (Town)—Payne *OK-2*
Quay County *NM-4*
Queen (Township)—Polk *MN-3*
Queen Anne (Town)—Queen
  Anne's *MD-1*
Queen Anne (Town)—Talbot *MD-1*
Queen Anne's County *MD-1*
Queen City (City)—Schuyler *MO-3*
Queen City (City)—Cass *TX-2*
Queen Creek (Town)—Maricopa .. *AZ-4*
Queens (NY) *Geog-4*
Queensbury (Town)—Warren *NY-1*
Queens County and Borough *NY-1*
Queenstown (Town)—Queen
  Anne's *MD-1*
Queeny (Township)—St. Louis *MO-3*
Quemahoning (Township)—
  Somerset *PA-1*
Quenemo (City)—Osage *KS-4*
Questa (Village)—Taos *NM-4*
Quileute Reservation (WA) *IndRes-4*
Quimby (City)—Cherokee *IA-3*
Quinault Reservation (WA) *IndRes-4*
Quinby (Township)—Kidder *ND-4*
Quinby (Town)—Florence *SC-2*
Quincy (City)—Gadsden *FL-2*
Quincy (City)—Adams *IL-3*
Quincy (Township)—Adams *IL-3*
Quincy (Township)—Greenwood ... *KS-4*
Quincy (City)—Norfolk *MA-1*
Quincy (Township)—Branch *MI-3*
Quincy (Village)—Branch *MI-3*
Quincy (Township)—Houghton *MI-3*
Quincy (Township)—Olmsted *MN-3*
Quincy (Village)—Logan *OH-3*
Quincy (Township)—Franklin *PA-1*
Quincy (Town)—Grant *WA-4*
Quincy (Town)—Adams *WI-3*
Quincy-East Quincy (CDP)—
  Plumas *CA-4*
Quinebaug (CDP)—Windham *CT-1*
Quinhagak (City)—Bethel Census
  Area *AK-4*
Quinlan (Town)—Woodward *OK-2*
Quinlan (City)—Hunt *TX-2*
Quinn (Town)—Pennington *SD-4*
Quinnebaugh (Township)—Burt *NE-4*
Quinnesec (CDP)—Dickinson *MI-3*
Quinn No. 1 (Township)—
  Pennington *SD-4*
Quintana (Town)—Brazoria *TX-2*
Quinter (City)—Gove *KS-4*
Quinton (Township)—Salem *NJ-1*
Quinton (Town)—Pittsburg *OK-2*
Quinwood (Town)—Greenbrier *WV-2*
Quiring (Township)—Beltrami *MN-3*

Quitaque (City)—Briscoe *TX-2*
Quitman (City)—Cleburne *AR-2*
Quitman (City)—Faulkner *AR-2*
Quitman (City)—Brooks *GA-2*
Quitman (Village)—Jackson
 Parish *LA-2*
Quitman (City)—Clarke *MS-2*
Quitman (Town)—Nodaway *MO-3*
Quitman (City)—Wood *TX-2*
Quitman County *GA-2*
Quitman County *MS-2*
Quiver (Township)—Mason *IL-3*
Qulin (Town)—Butler *MO-3*
Quogue (Village)—Suffolk *NY-1*
Rabbit Lake (Township)—Crow
 Wing *MN-3*
Raber (Township)—Chippewa *MI-3*
Raber (Township)—Hughes *SD-4*
Rabun County *GA-2*
Raccoon (Township)—Marion *IL-3*
Raccoon (Township)—Parke *IN-3*
Raccoon (Township)—Gallia *OH-3*
Raccoon (Township)—Beaver *PA-1*
Raceland (City)—Greenup *KY-2*
Raceland (CDP)—Lafourche
 Parish *LA-2*
Racine (City)—Mower *MN-3*
Racine (Township)—Mower *MN-3*
Racine (Village)—Meigs *OH-3*
Racine (Township)—Day *SD-4*
Racine (City)—Racine *WI-3*
Racine County *WI-3*
Radcliff (City)—Hardin *KY-2*
Radcliffe (City)—Hardin *IA-3*
Radford (Independent City) *VA-2*
Radisson (Town)—Sawyer *WI-3*
Radisson (Village)—Sawyer *WI-3*
Radium (City)—Stafford *KS-4*
Radnor (Township)—Peoria *IL-3*
Radnor (Township)—Delaware *OH-3*
Radnor (Township)—Delaware *PA-1*
Radom (Village)—Washington *IL-3*
Raeford (City)—Hoke *NC-2*
Rafter J Ranch (CDP)—Teton *WY-4*
Ragan (Village)—Harlan *NE-4*
Ragland (Town)—St. Clair *AL-2*
Rahway (City)—Union *NJ-1*
Raiford (Town)—Union *FL-2*
Rail Prairie (Township)—
 Morrison *MN-3*
Railroad (Township)—Starke *IN-3*
Railroad (Borough)—York *PA-1*
Rainbow (CDP)—San Diego *CA-4*
Rainbow (Township)—Williams ... *ND-4*
Rainbow (Township)—Perkins *SD-4*
Rainbow Bridge (UT) *Geog-4*
Rainbow City (City)—Etowah *AL-2*
Rainbow Lakes (CDP)—Palm
 Beach *FL-2*
Rainelle (Town)—Greenbrier *WV-2*
Rainier (City)—Columbia *OR-4*
Rainier (Town)—Thurston *WA-4*
Rainier, Mt. (WA) *Geog-4*
Rainsburg (Borough)—Bedford *PA-1*
Rains County *TX-2*
Rainsville (City)—DeKalb *AL-2*
Rainy Butte (Township)—Slope *ND-4*
Rainy Creek No. 19 (Township)—
 Pennington *SD-4*
Rainy Lake (MN) *Geog-4*
Rainy Lake (Pop. Place)—
 Koochiching *MN-3*
Raisin (Township)—Lenawee *MI-3*
Raisinville (Township)—Monroe ... *MI-3*
Rake (City)—Winnebago *IA-3*

Raleigh (Township)—Saline *IL-3*
Raleigh (Village)—Saline *IL-3*
Raleigh (Town)—Smith *MS-2*
Raleigh (City)—Wake *NC-2*
Raleigh (Township)—Grant *ND-4*
Raleigh County *WV-2*
Raleigh Hills (CDP)—
 Washington *OR-4*
Ralls (City)—Crosby *TX-2*
Ralls County *MO-3*
Ralpho (Township)—
 Northumberland *PA-1*
Ralston (City)—Carroll *IA-3*
Ralston (City)—Greene *IA-3*
Ralston (City)—Douglas *NE-4*
Ralston (Town)—Pawnee *OK-2*
Ramah (Town)—El Paso *CO-4*
Ramah Navajo Community
 (NM) *IndRes-4*
Ramapo (Town)—Rockland *NY-1*
Ramapough TDSA (NJ) *IndRes-4*
Ramblewood (CDP)—Burlington .. *NJ-1*
Ramer (City)—McNairy *TN-2*
Rames (Township)—Tripp *SD-4*
Ramey (Borough)—Clearfield *PA-1*
Ramona (CDP)—San Diego *CA-4*
Ramona (City)—Marion *KS-4*
Ramona (Town)—Washington *OK-2*
Ramona (Town)—Lake *SD-4*
Ramona Reservation (CA) *IndRes-4*
Rampart (CDP)—Yukon-Koyukuk
 Census Area *AK-4*
Ramseur (Town)—Randolph *NC-2*
Ramsey (Town)—Fayette *IL-3*
Ramsey (Township)—Fayette *IL-3*
Ramsey (City)—Anoka *MN-3*
Ramsey (Borough)—Bergen *NJ-1*
Ramsey (Township)—McCook *SD-4*
Ramsey County *MN-3*
Ramsey County *ND-4*
Ranburne (Town)—Cleburne *AL-2*
Ranchester (Town)—Sheridan *WY-4*
Ranchettes (CDP)—Laramie *WY-4*
Rancho Cordova (CDP)—
 Sacramento *CA-4*
Rancho Cucamonga (City)—San
 Bernardino *CA-4*
Rancho Mirage (City)—Riverside .. *CA-4*
Rancho Murieta (CDP)—
 Sacramento *CA-4*
Rancho Palos Verdes (City)—Los
 Angeles *CA-4*
Rancho Rinconada (CDP)—Santa
 Clara *CA-4*
Rancho San Diego (CDP)—San
 Diego *CA-4*
Rancho Santa Margarita (CDP)—
 Orange *CA-4*
Ranchos De Taos (CDP)—Taos *NM-4*
Rancho Viejo (Town)—Cameron ... *TX-2*
Randalia (City)—Fayette *IA-3*
Randall (City)—Hamilton *IA-3*
Randall (City)—Jewell *KS-4*
Randall (City)—Morrison *MN-3*
Randall (City)—Kenosha *WI-3*
Randall County *TX-2*
Randallstown (CDP)—
 Baltimore *MD-1*
Randleman (City)—Randolph *NC-2*
Randlett (Town)—Cotton *OK-2*
Randlett (CDP)—Uintah *UT-4*
Randol (Township)—Cape
 Girardeau *MO-3*
Randolph (Township)—McLean ... *IL-3*
Randolph (Township)—Ohio *IN-3*

Randolph (Township)—
 Tippecanoe *IN-3*
Randolph (City)—Fremont *IA-3*
Randolph (City)—Riley *KS-4*
Randolph (Town)—Kennebec *ME-1*
Randolph (Town)—Norfolk *MA-1*
Randolph (City)—Dakota *MN-3*
Randolph (Township)—Dakota *MN-3*
Randolph (Village)—Clay *MO-3*
Randolph (Township)—St.
 Francois *MO-3*
Randolph (City)—Cedar *NE-4*
Randolph (Town)—Coos *NH-1*
Randolph (Township)—Morris *NJ-1*
Randolph (Township)—Cattaraugus ..*NY-1*
Randolph (Village)—Cattaraugus .. *NY-1*
Randolph (Township)—
 McKenzie *ND-4*
Randolph (Township)—
 Montgomery *OH-3*
Randolph (Township)—Portage *OH-3*
Randolph (Township)—Crawford .. *PA-1*
Randolph (City)—Rich *UT-4*
Randolph (Town)—Orange *VT-1*
Randolph (Town)—Columbia *WI-3*
Randolph (Village)—Columbia *WI-3*
Randolph (Village)—Dodge *WI-3*
Randolph Air Force Base (TX) *Mil-4*
Randolph County *AL-2*
Randolph County *AR-2*
Randolph County *GA-2*
Randolph County *IL-3*
Randolph County *IN-3*
Randolph County *MO-3*
Randolph County *NC-2*
Randolph County *WV-2*
Random Lake (Village)—
 Sheboygan *WI-3*
Raney (Township)—LaMoure *ND-4*
Range (Township)—Madison *OH-3*
Rangeley (Plantation)—Franklin .. *ME-1*
Rangeley (Town)—Franklin *ME-1*
Rangely (Town)—Rio Blanco *CO-4*
Ranger (Town)—Gordon *GA-2*
Ranger (City)—Eastland *TX-2*
Rangerville (Village)—Cameron *TX-2*
Ranier (City)—Koochiching *MN-3*
Rankin (Town)—Vermilion *IL-3*
Rankin (Borough)—Allegheny *PA-1*
Rankin (City)—Upton *TX-2*
Rankin County *MS-2*
Ranlo (Town)—Gaston *NC-2*
Ransom (Village)—La Salle *IL-3*
Ransom (City)—Ness *KS-4*
Ransom (Township)—Hillsdale *MI-3*
Ransom (Township)—Nobles *MN-3*
Ransom (Township)—Sargent *ND-4*
Ransom (Township)—
 Lackawanna *PA-1*
Ransom Canyon (Town)—
 Lubbock *TX-2*
Ransom County *ND-4*
Ransomville (CDP)—Niagara *NY-1*
Ranson (Town)—Jefferson *WV-2*
Rantoul (City)—Champaign *IL-3*
Rantoul (Township)—Champaign .. *IL-3*
Rantoul (City)—Franklin *KS-4*
Rantoul (Town)—Calumet *WI-3*
Raoul (CDP)—Habersham *GA-2*
Rapho (Township)—Lancaster *PA-1*
Rapidan (Township)—Blue
 Earth *MN-3*
Rapid City (City)—Pennington *SD-4*
Rapides Parish *LA-2*

General Index

Rapid River (Township)—Kalkaska.................................. *MI-3*
Rapids (CDP)—Niagara................... *NY-1*
Rapids City (Town)—Rock Island.. *IL-3*
Rapid Valley (CDP)—Pennington.................................. *SD-4*
Rappahannock County *VA-2*
Rappahannock River (VA) *Geog-4*
Rarden (Township)—Scioto............*OH-3*
Rarden (Village)—Scioto................*OH-3*
Raritan (Township)—Henderson *IL-3*
Raritan (Village)—Henderson......... *IL-3*
Raritan (Township)—Hunterdon *NJ-1*
Raritan (Borough)—Somerset *NJ-1*
Raritan (Township)—Barnes *ND-4*
Raritan (Township)—Day *SD-4*
Ratcliff (City)—Logan..................... *AR-2*
Rathbone (Town)—Steuben *NY-1*
Rathbun (City)—Appanoose............*IA-3*
Rathdrum (City)—Kootenai *ID-4*
Rat Islands (AK)................................ *Geog-4*
Rat Lake (Township)—Mountrail................................. *ND-4*
Ratliff City (Town)—Carter............*OK-2*
Raton (City)—Colfax *NM-4*
Rattan (Town)—Pushmataha *OK-2*
Rauville (Township)—Codington .. *SD-4*
Ravalli County................................ *MT-4*
Ravanna (Township)—Mercer *MO-3*
Raven (CDP)—Russell.................... *VA-2*
Raven (CDP)—Tazewell.................. *VA-2*
Ravena (Village)—Albany............... *NY-1*
Ravenden (Town)—Lawrence *AR-2*
Ravenden Springs (Town)—Randolph...................................... *AR-2*
Ravenel (Town)—Charleston *SC-2*
Ravenna (City)—Estill *KY-2*
Ravenna (Township)—Muskegon .. *MI-3*
Ravenna (Village)—Muskegon........ *MI-3*
Ravenna (Township)—Dakota...... *MN-3*
Ravenna (City)—Buffalo................. *NE-4*
Ravenna (City)—Portage.................*OH-3*
Ravenna (Township)—Portage *OH-3*
Ravenna (Township)—Sanborn *SD-4*
Ravenswood (City)—Jackson......... *WV-2*
Ravenwood (Town)—Nodaway *MO-3*
Ravia (Town)—Johnston................*OK-2*
Ravinia (Township)—Brown......... *SD-4*
Ravinia (Town)—Charles Mix *SD-4*
Rawlins (Township)—Jo Daviess... *IL-3*
Rawlins (City)—Carbon *WY-4*
Rawlins County.............................. *KS-4*
Rawson (City)—McKenzie *ND-4*
Rawson (Village)—Hancock *OH-3*
Ray (Township)—Franklin............... *IN-3*
Ray (Township)—Morgan *IN-3*
Ray (Township)—Macomb *MI-3*
Ray (Township)—LaMoure............*ND-4*
Ray (City)—Williams *ND-4*
Rayburn (Township)—Armstrong . *PA-1*
Ray City (City)—Berrien *GA-2*
Ray County.................................... *MO-3*
Rayland (Village)—Jefferson...........*OH-3*
Rayle (Town)—Wilkes.................... *GA-2*
Raymer (Town)—Weld................... *CO-4*
Raymond (Township)—Champaign.................................. *IL-3*
Raymond (Town)—Montgomery.... *IL-3*
Raymond (Township)—Montgomery................................. *IL-3*
Raymond (City)—Black Hawk *IA-3*
Raymond (City)—Rice *KS-4*
Raymond (Township)—Rice *KS-4*
Raymond (Town)—Cumberland... *ME-1*
Raymond (City)—Kandiyohi *MN-3*

Raymond (Township)—Stearns *MN-3*
Raymond (Town)—Hinds *MS-2*
Raymond (Township)—Knox *NE-4*
Raymond (Village)—Lancaster *NE-4*
Raymond (Town)—Rockingham ...*NH-1*
Raymond (Township)—Cass...........*ND-4*
Raymond (Town)—Clark *SD-4*
Raymond (Township)—Clark *SD-4*
Raymond (City)—Pacific *WA-4*
Raymond (Town)—Racine............. *WI-3*
Raymondville (Town)—Texas....... *MO-3*
Raymondville (City)—Willacy *TX-2*
Raymore (City)—Cass................... *MO-3*
Raymore (Township)—Cass......... *MO-3*
Rayne (City)—Acadia Parish...........*LA-2*
Rayne (Township)—Indiana *PA-1*
Raynham (Town)—Bristol *MA-1*
Raynham (Town)—Robeson *NC-2*
Raytown (City)—Jackson............... *MO-3*
Rayville (Town)—Richland Parish.. *LA-2*
Rayville (Town)—Ray *MO-3*
Raywick (City)—Marion *KY-2*
Rea (Town)—Andrew..................... *MO-3*
Read (Township)—Butler.............. *NE-4*
Reade (Township)—Cambria *PA-1*
Reader (Town)—Nevada................ *AR-2*
Reader (Town)—Ouachita.............. *AR-2*
Readfield (Town)—Kennebec *ME-1*
Reading (Township)—Livingston ... *IL-3*
Reading (City)—Lyon.....................*KS-4*
Reading (Township)—Lyon............*KS-4*
Reading (Town)—Middlesex......... *MA-1*
Reading (City)—Hillsdale *MI-3*
Reading (Township)—Hillsdale *MI-3*
Reading (Township)—Butler..........*NE-4*
Reading (Town)—Schuyler *NY-1*
Reading (City)—Hamilton *OH-3*
Reading (Township)—Perry *OH-3*
Reading (Township)—Adams *PA-1*
Reading (City)—Berks..................... *PA-1*
Reading (Township)—Perry *IN-3*
Reading (Town)—Windsor............. *VT-1*
Readington (Township)—Hunterdon..................................... *NJ-1*
Readlyn (City)—Bremer..................*IA-3*
Readmond (Township)—Emmet.... *MI-3*
Readsboro (Town)—Bennington.... *VT-1*
Readstown (Village)—Vernon *WI-3*
Reagan County *TX-2*
Real County *TX-2*
Reardan (Town)—Lincoln..............*WA-4*
Reasnor (Town)—Jasper..................*IA-3*
Rebecca (Town)—Turner *GA-2*
Recovery (Township)—Mercer *OH-3*
Rector (City)—Clay........................ *AR-2*
Rector (Township)—Saline *IL-3*
Redan (CDP)—De Kalb.................. *GA-2*
Red Bank (Borough)—Monmouth..................................... *NJ-1*
Redbank (Township)—Armstrong .. *PA-1*
Redbank (Township)—Clarion *PA-1*
Red Bank (CDP)—Lexington *SC-2*
Red Bank (City)—Hamilton *TN-2*
Red Bay (City)—Franklin *AL-2*
Redbird (Town)—Wagoner *OK-2*
Red Bluff (City)—Tehama *CA-4*
Red Boiling Springs (City)—Macon.. *TN-2*
Red Bud (Town)—Randolph *IL-3*
Redby (CDP)—Beltrami................. *MN-3*
Red Cedar (Town)—Dunn *WI-3*
Red Chute (CDP)—Bossier Parish.. *LA-2*
Red Cliff (Town)—Eagle *CO-4*

Red Cliff Reservation & Trust Lands (WI)................................... *IndRes-4*
Red Cloud (City)—Webster *NE-4*
Red Creek (Village)—Wayne *NY-1*
Red Devil (CDP)—Bethel Census Area.. *AK-4*
Reddick (Town)—Marion *FL-2*
Reddick (Village)—Kankakee *IL-3*
Reddick (Village)—Livingston *IL-3*
Redding (City)—Shasta *CA-4*
Redding (Town)—Fairfield *CT-1*
Redding (Township)—Jackson....... *IN-3*
Redding (City)—Ringgold................*IA-3*
Redding (Township)—Clare *MI-3*
Redding Rancheria (CA) *IndRes-4*
Reddish (Township)—Lewis *MO-3*
Red Eye (Township)—Wadena *MN-3*
Redfield (Town)—Jefferson *AR-2*
Redfield (City)—Dallas....................*IA-3*
Redfield (City)—Bourbon *KS-4*
Redfield (Town)—Oswego............... *NY-1*
Redfield (City)—Spink..................... *SD-4*
Redfield (Township)—Spink.......... *SD-4*
Red Fish (Township)—Mellette *SD-4*
Redford (Township)—Wayne *MI-3*
Redgranite (Village)—Waushara ... *WI-3*
Red Hill (Borough)—Montgomery................................. *PA-1*
Red Hill (CDP)—Horry....................*SC-2*
Red Hook (Town)—Dutchess *NY-1*
Red Hook (Village)—Dutchess *NY-1*
Red House (Town)—Cattaraugus .. *NY-1*
Redings Mill (Village)—Newton... *MO-3*
Redington Beach (Town)—Pinellas... *FL-2*
Redington Shores (Town)—Pinellas... *FL-2*
Red Iron Lake (Township)—Marshall... *SD-4*
Red Jacket (CDP)—Mingo *WV-2*
Redkey (Town)—Jay *IN-3*
Red Lake (MN) *Geog-4*
Red Lake (CDP)—Beltrami.......... *MN-3*
Red Lake (Township)—Logan *ND-4*
Red Lake (Township)—Brule........ *SD-4*
Red Lake County *MN-3*
Red Lake Falls (City)—Red Lake.. *MN-3*
Red Lake Falls (Township)—Red Lake.. *MN-3*
Red Lake Reservation (MN) *IndRes-4*
Redland (CDP)—Montgomery *MD-1*
Redlands (City)—San Bernardino...................................... *CA-4*
Redlands (CDP)—Mesa *CO-4*
Red Level (Municipality)—Covington....................................... *AL-2*
Red Lion (Borough)—York *PA-1*
Red Lodge (City)—Carbon *MT-4*
Redmon (Village)—Edgar *IL-3*
Redmond (Township)—Mountrail....................................... *ND-4*
Redmond (City)—Deschutes.......... *OR-4*
Redmond (Town)—Sevier.............. *UT-4*
Redmond (City)—King *WA-4*
Red Oak (City)—Montgomery.......*IA-3*
Red Oak (Township)—Lawrence .. *MO-3*
Red Oak (Town)—Nash *NC-2*
Red Oak (Town)—Latimer *OK-2*
Red Oak (City)—Ellis *TX-2*
Red Oaks Mill (CDP)—Dutchess .. *NY-1*
Redondo Beach (City)—Los Angeles.. *CA-4*
Redpath (Township)—Traverse *MN-3*
Red River (MN) *Geog-4*

American Places Dictionary

Red River (Town)—Taos *NM-4*
Red River (Town)—Kewaunee *WI-3*
Red River County *TX-2*
Red River of the North (MN)..... *Geog-4*
Red River Parish *LA-2*
Red River Valley (ND)................ *Geog-4*
Red Rock (Township)—Mower *MN-3*
Red Rock (Township)—Noble *OK-2*
Red Rock (Township)—
  Minnehaha *SD-4*
Red Springs (Town)—Robeson *NC-2*
Red Springs (Town)—Shawano *WI-3*
Redstone (AL)................................ *Mil-2*
Redstone (Township)—Fayette *PA-1*
Redstone (Township)—Miner *SD-4*
Redstone Arsenal (Military Facility)—
  Madison *AL-2*
Red Vermillion (Township)—
  Nemaha *KS-4*
Redwater (CDP)—Leake................ *MS-2*
Redwater (City)—Bowie *TX-2*
Redway (CDP)—Humboldt *CA-4*
Red Willow County *NE-4*
Red Wing (City)—Goodhue........... *MN-3*
Red Wing (Township)—
  McKenzie *ND-4*
Redwood (CDP)—Josephine........... *OR-4*
Redwood City (City)—San
  Mateo *CA-4*
Redwood County............................. *MN-3*
Redwood Falls (City)—
  Redwood *MN-3*
Redwood Falls (Township)—
  Redwood *MN-3*
Redwood Valley Rancheria
  (CA)...................................... *IndRes-4*
Ree (Township)—Ward *ND-4*
Ree (Township)—Charles Mix *SD-4*
Reece City (Municipality)—
  Etowah *AL-2*
Reed (Town)—Desha *AR-2*
Reed (Township)—Will *IL-3*
Reed (Pop. Place)—Aroostook...... *ME-1*
Reed (Township)—Cass *ND-4*
Reed (Township)—Seneca............... *OH-3*
Reed (Township)—Dauphin *PA-1*
Reed City (City)—Osceola *MI-3*
Reed Creek (CDP)—Hart *GA-2*
Reeder (Township)—Anderson *KS-4*
Reeder (Township)—Missaukee..... *MI-3*
Reeder (City)—Adams *ND-4*
Reeder (Township)—Adams *ND-4*
Reedley (City)—Fresno *CA-4*
Reeds (Town)—Jasper *MO-3*
Reedsburg (City)—Sauk *WI-3*
Reedsburg (Town)—Sauk *WI-3*
Reedsport (City)—Douglas *OR-4*
Reedsville (Town)—Preston........... *WV-2*
Reedsville (Village)—Manitowoc... *WI-3*
Reedy (Town)—Roane *WV-2*
Ree Heights (Town)—Hand *SD-4*
Ree Heights (Township)—Hand *SD-4*
Reese (Village)—Tuscola *MI-3*
Reese Air Force Base (CDP)—
  Lubbock *TX-2*
Reeseville (Village)—Dodge *WI-3*
Reeve (Township)—Daviess............ *IN-3*
Reeves (Village)—Allen Parish *LA-2*
Reeves County *TX-2*
Reevesville (Town)—Dorchester.....*SC-2*
Reform (City)—Pickens..................*AL-2*
Refugio (Town)—Refugio............... *TX-2*
Refugio County *TX-2*
Regal (City)—Kandiyohi................ *MN-3*

Regan (City)—Burleigh *ND-4*
Regent (City)—Hettinger *ND-4*
Register (Town)—Bulloch *GA-2*
Rehoboth (Town)—Bristol *MA-1*
Rehoboth Beach (DE)................. *Geog-4*
Rehoboth Beach (City)—Sussex *DE-1*
Reid (Town)—Marathon *WI-3*
Reidland (CDP)—McCracken *KY-2*
Reidsville (City)—Tattnall *GA-2*
Reidsville (City)—Rockingham ...*NC-2*
Reile's Acres (City)—Cass............*ND-4*
Reilly (Township)—Nemaha...........*KS-4*
Reilly (Township)—Schuylkill *PA-1*
Reily (Township)—Butler...............*OH-3*
Reinbeck (City)—Grundy *IA-3*
Reine (Township)—Roseau............ *MN-3*
Reiner (Township)—Pennington... *MN-3*
Reis (Township)—Polk................. *MN-3*
Reisterstown (CDP)—Baltimore... *MD-1*
Reklaw (Town)—Cherokee............. *TX-2*
Reklaw (Town)—Rusk *TX-2*
Reliance (Town)—Lyman............... *SD-4*
Reliance (Township)—Lyman *SD-4*
Rembrandt (City)—Buena Vista......*IA-3*
Remer (City)—Cass...................... *MN-3*
Remer (Township)—Cass.............. *MN-3*
Remerton (City)—Lowndes *GA-2*
Reminderville (Village)—
  Summit *OH-3*
Remington (Town)—Jasper............. *IN-3*
Remington (Town)—Fauquier *VA-2*
Remington (Town)—Wood *WI-3*
Remsen (City)—Plymouth *IA-3*
Remsen (Town)—Oneida *NY-1*
Remsen (Village)—Oneida *NY-1*
Remsenburg-Speonk (CDP)—
  Suffolk.......................................*NY-1*
Rendon (CDP)—Tarrant *TX-2*
Rendsville (Township)—Stevens... *MN-3*
Rendville (Village)—Perry *OH-3*
Renfrow (Town)—Grant *OK-2*
Renick (Village)—Randolph *MO-3*
Rennert (Town)—Robeson *NC-2*
Reno (Township)—Leavenworth *KS-4*
Reno (Township)—Reno *KS-4*
Reno (Township)—Iosco *MI-3*
Reno (Township)—Pope *MN-3*
Reno (City)—Washoe *NV-4*
Reno (City)—Lamar *TX-2*
Reno (City)—Parker...................... *TX-2*
Reno County *KS-4*
Reno-Sparks Colony (NV)........ *IndRes-4*
Renova (Town)—Bolivar............... *MS-2*
Reno Valley (Township)—Pierce ..*ND-4*
Renovo (Borough)—Clinton *PA-1*
Rensselaer (City)—Jasper............... *IN-3*
Rensselaer (City)—Rensselaer........ *NY-1*
Rensselaer County *NY-1*
Rensselaer Falls (Village)—St.
  Lawrence................................... *NY-1*
Rensselaerville (Town)—Albany *NY-1*
Rentiesville (Town)—McIntosh *OK-2*
Renton (City)—King *WA-4*
Rentz (Town)—Laurens *GA-2*
Renville (City)—Renville *MN-3*
Renville (Township)—Bottineau... *ND-4*
Renville County *MN-3*
Renville County *ND-4*
Renwick (City)—Humboldt *IA-3*
Repton (Town)—Conecuh...............*AL-2*
Republic (City)—Republic *KS-4*
Republic (Township)—Marquette.. *MI-3*
Republic (City)—Greene *MO-3*
Republic (Village)—Seneca *OH-3*
Republic (Town)—Ferry *WA-4*

Republican (Township)—
  Jefferson..................................... *IN-3*
Republican (Township)—Clay *KS-4*
Republican City (Township)—
  Harlan *NE-4*
Republican City (Village)—
  Harlan *NE-4*
Republic County *KS-4*
Resaca (City)—Gordon *GA-2*
Reseburg (Town)—Clark *WI-3*
Reserve (Township)—Parke *IN-3*
Reserve (City)—Brown...................*KS-4*
Reserve (CDP)—St. John the Baptist
  Parish *LA-2*
Reserve (Village)—Catron............. *NM-4*
Reserve (Township)—Allegheny *PA-1*
Reserve (CDP)—Sawyer................. *WI-3*
Resighini Rancheria (CA) *IndRes-4*
Resort (Township)—Emmet *MI-3*
Rest Haven (Town)—Gwinnett *GA-2*
Rest Haven (Town)—Hall *GA-2*
Reston (CDP)—Fairfax *VA-2*
Retreat (Town)—Navarro *TX-2*
Reuben (Township)—Harlan *NE-4*
Reubens (City)—Lewis.................. *ID-4*
Revere (City)—Suffolk *MA-1*
Revere (City)—Redwood *MN-3*
Revere (Town)—Clark.................... *MO-3*
Revillagigedo Island (AK) *Geog-4*
Revillo (Town)—Grant *SD-4*
Rewey (Village)—Iowa *WI-3*
Rex (Township)—Lyman................ *SD-4*
Rexburg (City)—Madison *ID-4*
Rexford (City)—Thomas................*KS-4*
Rexford (Town)—Lincoln *MT-4*
Rexine (Township)—Kidder *ND-4*
Reydon (Town)—Roger Mills *OK-2*
Reyes, Point (CA) *Geog-4*
Reyno (Town)—Randolph *AR-2*
Reynolds (Town)—Taylor *GA-2*
Reynolds (Township)—Lee *IL-3*
Reynolds (Village)—Mercer *IL-3*
Reynolds (Village)—Rock Island *IL-3*
Reynolds (Town)—White *IN-3*
Reynolds (Township)—Montcalm . *MI-3*
Reynolds (Township)—Todd......... *MN-3*
Reynolds (Village)—Jefferson....... *NE-4*
Reynolds (City)—Grand Forks *ND-4*
Reynolds (City)—Traill *ND-4*
Reynoldsburg (City)—Fairfield......*OH-3*
Reynoldsburg (City)—Franklin......*OH-3*
Reynoldsburg (City)—Licking........*OH-3*
Reynolds County *MO-3*
Reynoldsville (Borough)—
  Jefferson.....................................*PA-1*
Rhame (City)—Bowman *ND-4*
Rhame (Township)—Bowman *ND-4*
Rhea County *TN-2*
Rheiderland (Township)—
  Chippewa *MN-3*
Rhine (Town)—Dodge *GA-2*
Rhine (Town)—Sheboygan............. *WI-3*
Rhinebeck (Town)—Dutchess........ *NY-1*
Rhinebeck (Village)—Dutchess...... *NY-1*
Rhinehart (Township)—Polk *MN-3*
Rhineland (Town)—
  Montgomery.............................*MO-3*
Rhinelander (City)—Oneida *WI-3*
Rhoda (Township)—Charles Mix .. *SD-4*
Rhode Island Sound (RI) *Geog-4*
Rhodell (Town)—Raleigh *WV-2*
Rhodes (City)—Marshall.................*IA-3*
Rhodhiss (Town)—Burke *NC-2*
Rhodhiss (Town)—Caldwell..........*NC-2*
Rhome (City)—Wise *TX-2*

General Index

Rialto (City)—San Bernardino *CA-4*
Ribbon Falls (CA) *Geog-4*
Rib Falls (Town)—Marathon *WI-3*
Rib Lake (Town)—Taylor *WI-3*
Rib Lake (Village)—Taylor *WI-3*
Rib Mountain (Town)—
  Marathon *WI-3*
Rice (Township)—Jo Daviess *IL-3*
Rice (City)—Benton *MN-3*
Rice (Township)—Clearwater *MN-3*
Rice (Township)—Sandusky *OH-3*
Rice (Township)—Luzerne *PA-1*
Rice (City)—Ellis *TX-2*
Rice (City)—Navarro *TX-2*
Riceboro (City)—Liberty *GA-2*
Rice County *KS-4*
Rice County *MN-3*
Rice Lake (Township)—St.
  Louis *MN-3*
Rice Lake (Township)—Ward *ND-4*
Rice Lake (City)—Barron *WI-3*
Rice Lake (Town)—Barron *WI-3*
Riceland (Township)—Freeborn ... *MN-3*
Rice River (Township)—Aitkin *MN-3*
Rices Landing (Borough)—
  Greene *PA-1*
Riceville (City)—Howard *IA-3*
Riceville (City)—Mitchell *IA-3*
Riceville (Township)—Becker *MN-3*
Rich (Township)—Cook *IL-3*
Rich (Township)—Anderson *KS-4*
Rich (Township)—Lapeer *MI-3*
Rich (Township)—Cass *ND-4*
Richards (Town)—Vernon *MO-3*
Richardson (Township)—
  Morrison *MN-3*
Richardson (Township)—Butler *NE-4*
Richardson (City)—Collin *TX-2*
Richardson (City)—Dallas *TX-2*
Richardson County *NE-4*
Richardton (City)—Stark *ND-4*
Richardville (Township)—
  Kittson *MN-3*
Richburg (Village)—Allegany *NY-1*
Richburg (Township)—Bottineau .. *ND-4*
Richburg (Town)—Chester *SC-2*
Rich County *UT-4*
Rich Creek (Town)—Giles *VA-2*
Richey (Town)—Dawson *MT-4*
Richfield (City)—Lincoln *ID-4*
Richfield (Township)—Adams *IL-3*
Richfield (City)—Morton *KS-4*
Richfield (Township)—Morton *KS-4*
Richfield (Township)—Genesee *MI-3*
Richfield (Township)—
  Roscommon *MI-3*
Richfield (City)—Hennepin *MN-3*
Richfield (Town)—Otsego *NY-1*
Richfield (Town)—Stanly *NC-2*
Richfield (Township)—Henry *OH-3*
Richfield (Township)—Lucas *OH-3*
Richfield (Township)—Summit *OH-3*
Richfield (Village)—Summit *OH-3*
Richfield (Township)—Spink *SD-4*
Richfield (City)—Sevier *UT-4*
Richfield (Town)—Adams *WI-3*
Richfield (Town)—Washington *WI-3*
Richfield (Town)—Wood *WI-3*
Richfield Springs (Village)—
  Otsego *NY-1*
Richford (Town)—Tioga *NY-1*
Richford (Town)—Franklin *VT-1*
Richford (Village)—Franklin *VT-1*
Richford (Town)—Waushara *WI-3*
Richgrove (CDP)—Tulare *CA-4*

Rich Grove (Township)—Pulaski ... *IN-3*
Rich Hill (City)—Bates *MO-3*
Rich Hill (Township)—
  Livingston *MO-3*
Rich Hill (Township)—
  Muskingum *OH-3*
Richhill (Township)—Greene *PA-1*
Richland (City)—Stewart *GA-2*
Richland (Township)—La Salle *IL-3*
Richland (Township)—Marshall *IL-3*
Richland (Township)—Shelby *IL-3*
Richland (Township)—Benton *IN-3*
Richland (Township)—Dekalb *IN-3*
Richland (Township)—Fountain ... *IN-3*
Richland (Township)—Fulton *IN-3*
Richland (Township)—Grant *IN-3*
Richland (Township)—Greene *IN-3*
Richland (Township)—Jay *IN-3*
Richland (Township)—Madison ... *IN-3*
Richland (Township)—Miami *IN-3*
Richland (Township)—Monroe *IN-3*
Richland (Township)—Rush *IN-3*
Richland (Township)—Steuben *IN-3*
Richland (Township)—Whitley *IN-3*
Richland (City)—Keokuk *IA-3*
Richland (Township)—Butler *KS-4*
Richland (Township)—Cowley *KS-4*
Richland (Township)—Ford *KS-4*
Richland (Township)—Hamilton .. *KS-4*
Richland (Township)—Harvey *KS-4*
Richland (Township)—Jewell *KS-4*
Richland (Township)—Kingman .. *KS-4*
Richland (Township)—Labette *KS-4*
Richland (Township)—Marshall ... *KS-4*
Richland (Township)—Miami *KS-4*
Richland (Township)—Ottawa *KS-4*
Richland (Township)—Republic ... *KS-4*
Richland (Township)—Stafford ... *KS-4*
Richland (Township)—
  Kalamazoo *MI-3*
Richland (Village)—Kalamazoo *MI-3*
Richland (Township)—Missaukee . *MI-3*
Richland (Township)—Montcalm .. *MI-3*
Richland (Township)—Ogemaw *MI-3*
Richland (Township)—Saginaw ... *MI-3*
Richland (Township)—Rice *MN-3*
Richland (City)—Rankin *MS-2*
Richland (Township)—Barton *MO-3*
Richland (City)—Camden *MO-3*
Richland (Township)—Douglas *MO-3*
Richland (Township)—
  Gasconade *MO-3*
Richland (City)—Laclede *MO-3*
Richland (Township)—Macon *MO-3*
Richland (Township)—Morgan *MO-3*
Richland (Township)—Ozark *MO-3*
Richland (City)—Pulaski *MO-3*
Richland (Township)—Putnam *MO-3*
Richland (Township)—Scott *MO-3*
Richland (Township)—Stoddard .. *MO-3*
Richland (Township)—Vernon *MO-3*
Richland (Village)—Colfax *NE-4*
Richland (Township)—Saunders ... *NE-4*
Richland (Town)—Oswego *NY-1*
Richland (Township)—Burke *ND-4*
Richland (Township)—Allen *OH-3*
Richland (Township)—Belmont *OH-3*
Richland (Township)—Clinton *OH-3*
Richland (Township)—Darke *OH-3*
Richland (Township)—Defiance ... *OH-3*
Richland (Township)—Fairfield ... *OH-3*
Richland (Township)—Guernsey .. *OH-3*
Richland (Township)—Holmes *OH-3*
Richland (Township)—Logan *OH-3*
Richland (Township)—Marion *OH-3*

Richland (Township)—Vinton *OH-3*
Richland (Township)—Wyandot ... *OH-3*
Richland (Town)—Baker *OR-4*
Richland (Township)—Allegheny .. *PA-1*
Richland (Township)—Bucks *PA-1*
Richland (Township)—Cambria ... *PA-1*
Richland (Township)—Clarion *PA-1*
Richland (Borough)—Lebanon *PA-1*
Richland (Township)—Venango ... *PA-1*
Richland (Township)—Beadle *SD-4*
Richland (Township)—Brookings .. *SD-4*
Richland (Township)—Brown *SD-4*
Richland (Township)—Brule *SD-4*
Richland (Township)—Clark *SD-4*
Richland (Township)—Codington . *SD-4*
Richland (Township)—Edmunds .. *SD-4*
Richland (Township)—Jones *SD-4*
Richland (Township)—McCook *SD-4*
Richland (Pop. Place)—Union *SD-4*
Richland (Town)—Navarro *TX-2*
Richland (City)—Benton *WA-4*
Richland (Town)—Richland *WI-3*
Richland (Town)—Rusk *WI-3*
Richland Center (Township)—
  Slope *ND-4*
Richland Center (City)—
  Richland *WI-3*
Richland County *IL-3*
Richland County *MT-4*
Richland County *ND-4*
Richland County *OH-3*
Richland County *SC-2*
Richland County *WI-3*
Richland Grove (Township)—
  Mercer *IL-3*
Richland Hills (City)—Tarrant *TX-2*
Richland Parish *LA-2*
Richlands (Town)—Onslow *NC-2*
Richlands (Town)—Tazewell *VA-2*
Richland Springs (Town)—San
  Saba *TX-2*
Richlandtown (Borough)—Bucks .. *PA-1*
Richlawn (City)—Jefferson *KY-2*
Richmond (City)—Contra Costa ... *CA-4*
Richmond (Town)—McHenry *IL-3*
Richmond (Township)—McHenry .. *IL-3*
Richmond (City)—Wayne *IN-3*
Richmond (City)—Franklin *KS-4*
Richmond (Township)—Franklin .. *KS-4*
Richmond (Township)—Nemaha .. *KS-4*
Richmond (City)—Madison *KY-2*
Richmond (Village)—Madison
  Parish *LA-2*
Richmond (Town)—Sagadahoc *ME-1*
Richmond (Town)—Berkshire *MA-1*
Richmond (City)—Macomb *MI-3*
Richmond (Township)—Macomb .. *MI-3*
Richmond (Township)—
  Marquette *MI-3*
Richmond (Township)—Osceola .. *MI-3*
Richmond (City)—Stearns *MN-3*
Richmond (Township)—Winona ... *MN-3*
Richmond (Township)—Howard ... *MO-3*
Richmond (City)—Ray *MO-3*
Richmond (Township)—Ray *MO-3*
Richmond (Town)—Cheshire *NH-1*
Richmond (Town)—Ontario *NY-1*
Richmond (Township)—Burleigh .. *ND-4*
Richmond (Township)—
  Ashtabula *OH-3*
Richmond (Township)—Huron *OH-3*
Richmond (Village)—Jefferson *OH-3*
Richmond (Township)—Berks *PA-1*
Richmond (Township)—Crawford .. *PA-1*
Richmond (Township)—Tioga *PA-1*

Richmond (Town)—Washington..... *RI-1*	Ridgefield Park (Village)—Bergen .. *NJ-1*	Ringgold (Town)—Bienville
Richmond (Town)—Fort Bend *TX-2*	Ridgeland (Township)—Iroquois *IL-3*	Parish *LA-2*
Richmond (City)—Cache *UT-4*	Ridgeland (City)—Madison *MS-2*	Ringgold (Township)—Jefferson *PA-1*
Richmond (Town)—Chittenden....... *VT-1*	Ridgeland (Town)—Jasper *SC-2*	**Ringgold County** *IA-3*
Richmond (Town)—Shawano *WI-3*	Ridgeland (Township)—Corson *SD-4*	Ringle (Town)—Marathon *WI-3*
Richmond (Town)—St. Croix *WI-3*	Ridgeland (Village)—Dunn *WI-3*	Ringling (Town)—Jefferson *OK-2*
Richmond (Town)—Walworth *WI-3*	Ridgeley (Township)—Dodge *NE-4*	Ringsted (City)—Emmet *IA-3*
Richmond Beach-Innis Arden (CDP)—King *WA-4*	Ridgeley (Town)—Mineral *WV-2*	Ring Thunder (Township)—Mellette *SD-4*
Richmond County *GA-2*	Ridgely (Town)—Caroline.............. *MD-1*	Ringtown (Borough)—Schuylkill *PA-1*
Richmond County *NC-2*	Ridgely (Township)—Nicollet *MN-3*	Ringwood (Borough)—Passaic *NJ-1*
Richmond County *VA-2*	Ridgely (Town)—Platte *MO-3*	Ringwood (City)—Major *OK-2*
Richmond County (Staten Island) ... *NY-1*	Ridgely (Town)—Lake *TN-2*	Rio (CDP)—Martin *FL-2*
Richmond Heights (CDP)—Dade .. *FL-2*	Ridge Manor (CDP)—Hernando *FL-2*	Rio (Township)—Knox *IL-3*
Richmond Heights (City)—St. Louis *MO-3*	Ridgeside (City)—Hamilton............ *TN-2*	Rio (Village)—Knox *IL-3*
	Ridge Spring (Town)—Saluda......... *SC-2*	Rio (CDP)—Albemarle *VA-2*
Richmond Heights (City)—Cuyahoga *OH-3*	Ridgetop (Town)—Davidson *TN-2*	Rio (Village)—Columbia................. *WI-3*
	Ridgetop (Town)—Robertson *TN-2*	**Rio Arriba County** *NM-4*
Richmond Highlands (CDP)—King *WA-4*	Ridgeville (Town)—Etowah *AL-2*	**Rio Blanco County** *CO-4*
	Ridgeville (Town)—Randolph *IN-3*	Rio Communities (CDP)—Valencia *NM-4*
Richmond Hill (City)—Bryan......... *GA-2*	Ridgeville (Township)—Henry....... *OH-3*	
Richmond (Independent City) *VA-2*	Ridgeville (Town)—Dorchester....... *SC-2*	Rio Dell (City)—Humboldt *CA-4*
Richmondville (Town)—Schoharie *NY-1*	Ridgeville (Town)—Monroe............ *WI-3*	Rio del Mar (CDP)—Santa Cruz... *CA-4*
	Ridgeway (CDP)—Kenai Peninsula Borough *AK-4*	Rio Grande (CA) *Geog-4*
Richmondville (Village)—Schoharie *NY-1*		Rio Grande (CDP)—Cape May...... *NJ-1*
	Ridgeway (City)—Winneshiek *IA-3*	Rio Grande (Village)—Gallia *OH-3*
Rich Square (Town)—Northampton *NC-2*	Ridgeway (Township)—Osage......... *KS-4*	Rio Grande City (CDP)—Starr *TX-2*
	Ridgeway (Township)—Lenawee ... *MI-3*	**Rio Grande County** *CO-4*
Richton (Town)—Perry *MS-2*	Ridgeway (City)—Harrison............. *MO-3*	Rio Hondo (Town)—Cameron *TX-2*
Richton Park (Village)—Cook *IL-3*	Ridgeway (Town)—Orleans............. *NY-1*	Rio Linda (CDP)—Sacramento *CA-4*
Rich Valley (Township)—McLeod *MN-3*	Ridgeway (Village)—Hardin *OH-3*	Rio Rancho (City)—Sandoval *NM-4*
	Ridgeway (Village)—Logan *OH-3*	Rio Rico East (CDP)—Santa Cruz.. *AZ-4*
Rich Valley (Township)—Benson .. *ND-4*	Ridgeway (Town)—Fairfield *SC-2*	
Rich Valley (Pop. Place)—Jones.... *SD-4*	Ridgeway (Town)—Henry *VA-2*	Rio Vista (City)—Solano *CA-4*
Richview (Township)—Washington *IL-3*	Ridgeway (Town)—Iowa *WI-3*	Rio Vista (City)—Johnson *TX-2*
	Ridgeway (Village)—Iowa *WI-3*	Ripley (Township)—Brown *IL-3*
Richview (Village)—Washington *IL-3*	Ridgewood (Village)—Bergen *NJ-1*	Ripley (Village)—Brown *IL-3*
Richville (City)—Otter Tail *MN-3*	Ridge Wood Heights (CDP)—Sarasota *FL-2*	Ripley (Township)—Montgomery... *IN-3*
Richville (Village)—St. Lawrence .. *NY-1*		Ripley (Township)—Rush *IN-3*
Richwood (Township)—Jersey........ *IL-3*	Ridgway (Town)—Ouray *CO-4*	Ripley (Town)—Somerset *ME-1*
Richwood (Town)—Ouachita Parish *LA-2*	Ridgway (Town)—Gallatin.............. *IL-3*	Ripley (Township)—Dodge *MN-3*
	Ridgway (Township)—Gallatin....... *IL-3*	Ripley (Township)—Morrison *MN-3*
Richwood (Township)—Becker..... *MN-3*	Ridgway (Borough)—Elk *PA-1*	Ripley (City)—Tippah *MS-2*
Richwood (Township)—McDonald *MO-3*	Ridgway (Township)—Elk *PA-1*	Ripley (Town)—Chautauqua........... *NY-1*
	Ridley (Township)—Delaware *PA-1*	Ripley (Village)—Brown *OH-3*
Richwood (Village)—Union *OH-3*	Ridley Park (Borough)—Delaware . *PA-1*	Ripley (Township)—Holmes *OH-3*
Richwood (City)—Brazoria............. *TX-2*	Ridott (Township)—Stephenson *IL-3*	Ripley (Township)—Huron *OH-3*
Richwood (City)—Nicholas *WV-2*	Ridott (Village)—Stephenson *IL-3*	Ripley (Town)—Payne *OK-2*
Richwood (Town)—Richland......... *WI-3*	Riegelsville (Borough)—Bucks *PA-1*	Ripley (Town)—Lauderdale *TN-2*
Richwoods (Township)—Peoria...... *IL-3*	Rienzi (Town)—Alcorn *MS-2*	Ripley (City)—Jackson *WV-2*
Richwoods (Township)—Miller *MO-3*	Riesel (City)—McLennan................ *TX-2*	**Ripley County** *IN-3*
Richwoods (Township)—Washington *MO-3*	Rietbrock (Town)—Marathon *WI-3*	**Ripley County** *MO-3*
	Rifle (City)—Garfield *CO-4*	Ripon (Town)—San Joaquin *CA-4*
Rickardsville (City)—Dubuque....... *IA-3*	Rifle (Township)—Hettinger *ND-4*	Ripon (City)—Fond du Lac *WI-3*
Ricketts (City)—Crawford *IA-3*	Riga (Township)—Lenawee............ *MI-3*	Ripon (Town)—Fond du Lac *WI-3*
Ricks (Township)—Christian *IL-3*	Riga (Town)—Monroe..................... *NY-1*	Rippey (City)—Greene.................... *IA-3*
Rico (Town)—Dolores..................... *CO-4*	Riga (Township)—McHenry *ND-4*	Ripton (Town)—Addison *VT-1*
Riddle (City)—Douglas *OR-4*	Rigby (City)—Jefferson *ID-4*	Ririe (City)—Bonneville *ID-4*
Riddleville (Town)—Washington ... *GA-2*	Riggin (Township)—Benson *ND-4*	Ririe (City)—Jefferson *ID-4*
Ridge (Township)—Shelby *IL-3*	Riggins (City)—Idaho *ID-4*	Risco (City)—New Madrid *MO-3*
Ridge (Township)—Barber.............. *KS-4*	Riley (Township)—McHenry *IL-3*	Rising City (Village)—Butler *NE-4*
Ridge (Township)—Dickinson........ *KS-4*	Riley (Town)—Vigo........................ *IN-3*	Rising Star (Town)—Eastland........ *TX-2*
Ridge (Township)—Carroll *MO-3*	Riley (Town)—Vigo........................ *IN-3*	Rising Sun (City)—Ohio *IN-3*
Ridge (CDP)—Suffolk *NY-1*	Riley (City)—Riley.......................... *KS-4*	Rising Sun (Town)—Cecil *MD-1*
Ridge (Township)—Van Wert *OH-3*	Riley (Township)—Clinton *MI-3*	Risingsun (Village)—Wood *OH-3*
Ridge (Township)—Wyandot.......... *OH-3*	Riley (Township)—St. Clair *MI-3*	Rising Sun-Lebanon (CDP)—Kent *DE-1*
Ridgebury (Township)—Bradford... *PA-1*	Riley (Township)—Putnam *OH-3*	
Ridgecrest (City)—Kern *CA-4*	Riley (Township)—Sandusky *OH-3*	Risley (Township)—Marion *KS-4*
Ridgecrest (Town)—Concordia Parish *LA-2*	**Riley County** *KS-4*	Rison (City)—Cleveland *AR-2*
	Rimersburg (Borough)—Clarion *PA-1*	Ritchey (Town)—Newton *MO-3*
Ridge Farm (Town)—Vermilion *IL-3*	Rinard (City)—Calhoun *IA-3*	**Ritchie County** *WV-2*
Ridgefield (Town)—Fairfield *CT-1*	Rincon (Town)—Effingham *GA-2*	Rittman (City)—Medina *OH-3*
Ridgefield (Borough)—Bergen *NJ-1*	Rincon Reservation (CA) *IndRes-4*	Rittman (City)—Wayne *OH-3*
Ridgefield (Township)—Huron...... *OH-3*	Rindge (Town)—Cheshire *NH-1*	Ritzville (City)—Adams *WA-4*
Ridgefield (Town)—Clark *WA-4*	Rinehart (Township)—Dickinson ... *KS-4*	Riva (CDP)—Anne Arundel *MD-1*
	Ringgold (City)—Catoosa *GA-2*	

General Index

River (Township)—Pawnee............*KS-4*
River (Township)—Red Lake........*MN-3*
Riverbank (City)—Stanislaus..........*CA-4*
River Bend (Town)—Craven *NC-2*
River Bluff (City)—Oldham *KY-2*
Riverdale (CDP)—Fresno *CA-4*
Riverdale (City)—Clayton...............*GA-2*
Riverdale (Village)—Cook *IL-3*
Riverdale (City)—Scott *IA-3*
Riverdale (Town)—Prince
   George's *MD-1*
Riverdale (Township)—
   Watonwan.................................*MN-3*
Riverdale (Township)—Buffalo *NE-4*
Riverdale (Village)—Buffalo *NE-4*
Riverdale (Borough)—Morris *NJ-1*
Riverdale (Township)—Dickey *ND-4*
Riverdale (City)—McLean *ND-4*
Riverdale (City)—Weber *UT-4*
River Edge (Borough)—Bergen *NJ-1*
Riveredge (Township)—
   Cuyahoga *OH-3*
River Falls (Town)—Covington *AL-2*
River Falls (Township)—
   Pennington *MN-3*
River Falls (City)—Pierce *WI-3*
River Falls (Town)—Pierce *WI-3*
River Falls (City)—St. Croix........... *WI-3*
River Forest (Township)—Cook *IL-3*
River Forest (Village)—Cook *IL-3*
River Forest (Town)—Madison *IN-3*
River Grove (City)—Cook *IL-3*
Rivergrove (City)—Clackamas........*OR-4*
Rivergrove (City)—Washington *OR-4*
Riverhead (Town)—Suffolk *NY-1*
River Heights (City)—Cache *UT-4*
River Hills (Village)—Milwaukee .. *WI-3*
Riverland (CDP)—Broward............*FL-2*
Riverlea (Village)—Franklin *OH-3*
Rivermines (Village)—St.
   Francois *MO-3*
River Oaks (City)—Tarrant *TX-2*
River of No Return (CA) *Geog-4*
River Ridge (CDP)—Jefferson
   Parish *LA-2*
River Road (CDP)—Beaufort..........*NC-2*
River Road (CDP)—Lane *OR-4*
River Rouge (City)—Wayne........... *MI-3*
Rivers (Township)—St. Charles *MO-3*
Riverside (Town)—St. Clair............*AL-2*
Riverside (City)—Riverside *CA-4*
Riverside (Town)—Colquitt *GA-2*
Riverside (Township)—Adams *IL-3*
Riverside (City)—Cook *IL-3*
Riverside (Township)—Cook *IL-3*
Riverside (City)—Washington *IA-3*
Riverside (Township)—Sedgwick...*KS-4*
Riverside (Township)—Trego *KS-4*
Riverside (Township)—
   Missaukee *MI-3*
Riverside (Township)—Lac qui
   Parle *MN-3*
Riverside (Township)—
   Christian *MO-3*
Riverside (City)—Platte *MO-3*
Riverside (Township)—Burt *NE-4*
Riverside (Township)—Gage *NE-4*
Riverside (Township)—
   Burlington *NJ-1*
Riverside (Village)—Steuben *NY-1*
Riverside (CDP)—Suffolk *NY-1*
Riverside (Township)—Steele *ND-4*
Riverside (Village)—
   Montgomery...............................*OH-3*
Riverside (Borough)—
   Northumberland *PA-1*
Riverside (Township)—Brown *SD-4*
Riverside (Township)—Clay *SD-4*
Riverside (Township)—Corson *SD-4*
Riverside (Township)—Hand *SD-4*
Riverside (Township)—Mellette *SD-4*
Riverside (Town)—Walker *TX-2*
Riverside (Town)—Okanogan *WA-4*
Riverside (Town)—Carbon *WY-4*
Riverside County *CA-4*
Riverton (Town)—Sangamon.......... *IL-3*
Riverton (City)—Fremont................*IA-3*
Riverton (Township)—Mason *MI-3*
Riverton (Township)—Clay *MN-3*
Riverton (City)—Crow Wing *MN-3*
Riverton (Village)—Franklin *NE-4*
Riverton (Borough)—Burlington *NJ-1*
Riverton (City)—Salt Lake *UT-4*
Riverton (City)—Fremont............... *WY-4*
Riverton-Boulevard Park (CDP)—
   King..*WA-4*
River Vale (Township)—Bergen......*NJ-1*
Riverview (Municipality)—
   Escambia *AL-2*
Riverview (CDP)—Kent *DE-1*
Riverview (CDP)—Hillsborough *FL-2*
Riverview (City)—Wayne............... *MI-3*
River View (Township)—
   Jefferson *MO-3*
Riverview (Village)—St. Louis...... *MO-3*
Riverview (Township)—
   McKenzie *ND-4*
Riverview (Township)—Moody *SD-4*
Riverview (Township)—Oconto *WI-3*
Riverwood (City)—Jefferson *KY-2*
Riverwoods (Village)—Lake............ *IL-3*
Rives (Township)—Jackson *MI-3*
Rives (Town)—Obion *TN-2*
Rivesville (Town)—Marion............*WV-2*
Riviera Beach (City)—Palm
   Beach *FL-2*
Riviera Beach (CDP)—Anne
   Arundel *MD-1*
Rivoli (Township)—Mercer *IL-3*
Roachdale (Town)—Putnam *IN-3*
Roaming Shores (Village)—
   Ashtabula *OH-3*
Roane County *TN-2*
Roane County *WV-2*
Roan Mountain (CDP)—Carter..... *TN-2*
Roann (Town)—Wabash *IN-3*
Roanoke (City)—Randolph.............*AL-2*
Roanoke (Town)—Woodford *IL-3*
Roanoke (Township)—Woodford ... *IL-3*
Roanoke (Town)—Huntington........ *IN-3*
Roanoke (Town)—Denton *TX-2*
Roanoke County *VA-2*
Roanoke (Independent City) *VA-2*
Roanoke Island (NC)................... *Geog-4*
Roanoke Rapids (City)—Halifax ... *NC-2*
Roaring Brook (Township)—
   Lackawanna *PA-1*
Roaring Creek (Township)—
   Columbia *PA-1*
Roaring Creek Rancheria
   (CA).......................................*IndRes-4*
Roaring River (Township)—
   Barry *MO-3*
Roaring Spring (Borough)—Blair.... *PA-1*
Roaring Springs (Town)—Motley .. *TX-2*
Roark (Township)—Gasconade *MO-3*
Robb (Township)—Posey................ *IN-3*
Robberson No. 1 (Township)—
   Greene *MO-3*
Robberson No. 2 (Township)—
   Greene *MO-3*
Robbins (City)—Cook *IL-3*
Robbins (City)—Moore *NC-2*
Robbinsdale (City)—Hennepin *MN-3*
Robbinston (Town)—
   Washington *ME-1*
Robbinsville (Town)—Graham *NC-2*
Robeline (Village)—Natchitoches
   Parish *LA-2*
Robersonville (Town)—Martin *NC-2*
Roberta (City)—Crawford...............*GA-2*
Robert Lee (City)—Coke *TX-2*
Roberts (City)—Jefferson *ID-4*
Roberts (Village)—Ford *IL-3*
Roberts (Township)—Marshall *IL-3*
Roberts (Township)—Wilkin *MN-3*
Roberts (Village)—St. Croix *WI-3*
Roberts County *SD-4*
Roberts County *TX-2*
Robertsdale (City)—Baldwin *AL-2*
Robertson County *KY-2*
Robertson County *TN-2*
Robertson County *TX-2*
Robertsville (CDP)—Monmouth....*NJ-1*
Robeson (Township)—Berks *PA-1*
Robeson County *NC-2*
Robesonia (Borough)—Berks *PA-1*
Robin Glen-Indiantown (CDP)—
   Saginaw *MI-3*
Robins (City)—Linn *IA-3*
Robins (Township)—Fall River *SD-4*
Robins Air Force Base (GA) *Mil-2*
Robins Air Force Base (Military
   Facility)—Houston *GA-2*
Robinson (Town)—Crawford *IL-3*
Robinson (Township)—Crawford ... *IL-3*
Robinson (Township)—Posey *IN-3*
Robinson (City)—Brown.................*KS-4*
Robinson (Township)—Brown *KS-4*
Robinson (Township)—Ottawa *MI-3*
Robinson (City)—Kidder *ND-4*
Robinson (Township)—Kidder *ND-4*
Robinson (Township)—Allegheny... *PA-1*
Robinson (Township)—
   Washington *PA-1*
Robinson (City)—McLennan *TX-2*
Robinson Rancheria (CA) *IndRes-4*
Robinswood (City)—Jefferson *KY-2*
Robstown (City)—Nueces *TX-2*
Roby (City)—Fisher *TX-2*
Roca (Village)—Lancaster *NE-4*
Rocewood (Township)—Rawlins ...*KS-4*
Rochelle (City)—Wilcox *GA-2*
Rochelle (Town)—Ogle *IL-3*
Rochelle Park (Township)—
   Bergen *NJ-1*
Rocheport (City)—Boone *MO-3*
Rochester (Town)—Sangamon *IL-3*
Rochester (Township)—
   Sangamon.................................... *IL-3*
Rochester (City)—Fulton *IN-3*
Rochester (Township)—Fulton *IN-3*
Rochester (Township)—Kingman ...*KS-4*
Rochester (City)—Butler *KY-2*
Rochester (Town)—Plymouth *MA-1*
Rochester (City)—Oakland *MI-3*
Rochester (City)—Olmsted *MN-3*
Rochester (Township)—Olmsted .. *MN-3*
Rochester (Township)—Andrew ...*MO-3*
Rochester (City)—Strafford *NH-1*
Rochester (City)—Monroe *NY-1*
Rochester (Town)—Ulster *NY-1*
Rochester (Township)—Cass..........*ND-4*
Rochester (Township)—Lorain *OH-3*

Rochester (Village)—Lorain............OH-3	Rockford (City)—Winnebago......... IL-3	Rocksbury (Township)—
Rochester (Borough)—Beaver........... PA-1	Rockford (Township)—	Pennington...................MN-3
Rochester (Township)—Beaver....... PA-1	Winnebago...................IL-3	Rocksprings (Town)—Edwards...... TX-2
Rochester (Town)—Haskell............ TX-2	Rockford (City)—Floyd...................IA-3	Rock Springs (Village)—Sauk........ WI-3
Rochester (Town)—Windsor........... VT-1	Rockford (Township)—Sedgwick....KS-4	Rock Springs (City)—
Rochester (CDP)—Thurston............WA-4	Rockford (City)—Kent....................MI-3	Sweetwater........................WY-4
Rochester (Town)—Racine............... WI-3	Rockford (City)—Hennepin............MN-3	Rockton (Town)—Winnebago......... IL-3
Rochester (Village)—Racine............ WI-3	Rockford (City)—Wright................MN-3	Rockton (Township)—Winnebago.. IL-3
Rochester Hills (City)—Oakland... MI-3	Rockford (Township)—Wright......MN-3	Rockvale (Town)—Fremont............CO-4
Rock (Township)—Marshall............KS-4	Rockford (Township)—Caldwell...MO-3	Rockvale (Township)—Ogle...............IL-3
Rock (Township)—Pipestone.........MN-3	Rockford (Township)—Carroll......MO-3	Rock Valley (City)—Sioux...............IA-3
Rock (Township)—Jefferson...........MO-3	Rockford (Township)—Gage..........NE-4	Rockville (CDP)—Tolland................CT-1
Rock (Township)—Benson..............ND-4	Rockford (Township)—Renville....ND-4	Rockville (Township)—Kankakee... IL-3
Rock (Township)—Grant.................ND-4	Rockford (Village)—Mercer...........OH-3	Rockville (Town)—Parke.................IN-3
Rock (Town)—Rock......................WI-3	Rockford (Township)—Perkins...... SD-4	Rockville (Township)—Rice...........KS-4
Rock (Town)—Wood......................WI-3	Rockford (City)—Blount..................TN-2	Rockville (City)—Montgomery.....MD-1
The Rock (Town)—Upson.............. GA-2	Rockford (Town)—Spokane..............WA-4	Rockville (City)—Stearns...............MN-3
Rockaway (Borough)—Morris..........NJ-1	Rock Grove (Township)—	Rockville (Township)—Stearns.....MN-3
Rockaway (Township)—Morris.......NJ-1	Stephenson...................IL-3	Rockville (City)—Bates..................MO-3
Rockaway Beach (Town)—	Rock Hall (Town)—Kent.................MD-1	Rockville (Township)—Bates........MO-3
Taney...........................MO-3	Rockham (Town)—Faulk................SD-4	Rockville (Village)—Sherman........NE-4
Rockaway Beach (City)—	Rock Hill (City)—St. Louis............MO-3	Rockville (Town)—Washington..... UT-4
Tillamook......................OR-4	Rock Hill (Township)—Burleigh....ND-4	Rockville Centre (Village)—
Rockbridge (Township)—Greene.... IL-3	Rock Hill (City)—York.....................SC-2	Nassau...........................NY-1
Rockbridge (Village)—Greene......... IL-3	Rockhill Furnace (Borough)—	Rockwall (City)—Rockwall...........TX-2
Rockbridge (Town)—Richland....... WI-3	Huntingdon...................PA-1	**Rockwall County**............................. TX-2
Rockbridge County............................VA-2	Rockingham (City)—Richmond....NC-2	Rockwell (CDP)—Garland..............AR-2
Rockcastle County.............................KY-2	Rockingham (Town)—Windham... VT-1	Rockwell (City)—Cerro Gordo........IA-3
Rock City (Village)—Stephenson.... IL-3	**Rockingham County**.........................NH-1	Rockwell (Township)—Norman....MN-3
Rock County..MN-3	**Rockingham County**.........................NC-2	Rockwell (Town)—Rowan..............NC-2
Rock County... NE-4	**Rockingham County**..........................VA-2	Rockwell City (City)—Calhoun......IA-3
Rock County... WI-3	Rock Island (City)—Rock Island.... IL-3	Rockwood (Village)—Randolph.... IL-3
Rock Creek (Township)—	Rock Island (Township)—Rock	Rockwood (City)—Wayne...............MI-3
Hancock........................IL-3	Island...........................IL-3	Rockwood (Township)—
Rock Creek (Township)—	Rock Island (Township)—	Hubbard.......................MN-3
Bartholomew...............IN-3	Williams.....................ND-4	Rockwood (Township)—Wadena.. MN-3
Rock Creek (Township)—Carroll.... IN-3	Rock Island (Town)—Le Flore...... OK-2	Rockwood (Borough)—Somerset.. PA-1
Rock Creek (Township)—	Rock Island (Town)—Douglas........WA-4	Rockwood (City)—Roane...............TN-2
Huntington....................IN-3	Rock Island Arsenal (IL)................Mil-4	Rocky (Town)—Washita..................OK-2
Rockcreek (Township)—Wells........IN-3	**Rock Island County**............................IL-3	Rocky Boy's Reservation & Trust Lands
Rock Creek (Township)—Butler....KS-4	Rock Lake (Township)—Lyon......MN-3	(MT)................................IndRes-4
Rock Creek (Township)—Coffey....KS-4	Rocklake (City)—Towner................ND-4	Rocky Ford (City)—Otero...............CO-4
Rock Creek (Township)—Cowley ...KS-4	Rock Lake (Township)—Towner ...ND-4	Rocky Ford (Town)—Screven......... GA-2
Rock Creek (Township)—	Rockland (City)—Power.................. ID-4	Rocky Ford (Township)—
Jefferson.......................KS-4	Rockland (City)—Knox...................ME-1	Mellette..........................SD-4
Rock Creek (Township)—	Rockland (Town)—Plymouth..........MA-1	Rocky Fork (Township)—Boone. MO-3
Nemaha........................KS-4	Rockland (Township)—	Rocky Hill (Town)—Hartford.........CT-1
Rock Creek (Township)—	Ontonagon...................MI-3	Rocky Hill (Borough)—Somerset...NJ-1
Pottawatomie..............KS-4	Rockland (Town)—Sullivan............NY-1	Rocky Mound (Town)—Camp........TX-2
Rock Creek (Township)—	Rockland (Township)—Berks.......... PA-1	Rocky Mount (City)—
Wabaunsee...................KS-4	Rockland (Township)—Venango.... PA-1	Edgecombe...................NC-2
Rock Creek (City)—Pine.................MN-3	Rockland (Town)—Brown............... WI-3	Rocky Mount (City)—Nash...........NC-2
Rock Creek (Township)—	Rockland (Village)—La Crosse..... WI-3	Rocky Mount (Town)—Franklin.... VA-2
Saunders.......................NE-4	Rockland (Town)—Manitowoc...... WI-3	Rocky Mountains *or the Rockies*
Rock Creek (Village)—Ashtabula ..OH-3	**Rockland County**...............................NY-1	(NC).............................Geog-4
Rockcreek (CDP)—Washington.....OR-4	Rockledge (City)—Brevard..............FL-2	Rocky Point (CDP)—Suffolk..........NY-1
Rock Creek (Township)—Miner.... SD-4	Rockledge (Borough)—	Rocky Ridge (Village)—Ste.
Rock Creek (Town)—Dunn........... WI-3	Montgomery..................PA-1	Genevieve....................MO-3
Rock Creek-Lima (Township)—	Rockleigh (Borough)—Bergen.......NJ-1	Rocky Ridge (Village)—Ottawa.....OH-3
Carroll..........................IL-3	Rocklin (City)—Placer.................... CA-4	Rocky Ripple (Town)—Marion....... IN-3
Rockdale (Village)—Will................ IL-3	Rockmart (City)—Polk.................... GA-2	Rocky River (City)—Cuyahoga.....OH-3
Rockdale (Township)—Crawford.... PA-1	Rockport (Town)—Hot Spring........AR-2	Rocky Run (Township)—Hancock. IL-3
Rockdale (Township)—Hand........ SD-4	Rockport (City)—Spencer.............. IN-3	Rodeo (CDP)—Contra Costa......... CA-4
Rockdale (City)—Milam..................TX-2	Rockport (City)—Ohio....................KY-2	Rodessa (Village)—Caddo Parish ...LA-2
Rockdale (Village)—Dane............... WI-3	Rockport (Town)—Knox.................ME-1	Rodman (City)—Palo Alto..............IA-3
Rockdale County................................ GA-2	Rockport (Town)—Essex................ MA-1	Rodman (Town)—Jefferson.............NY-1
Rock Dell (Township)—Olmsted..MN-3	Rock Port (City)—Atchison............MO-3	Rodney (City)—Monona..................IA-3
Rockefeller (Township)—	Rockport (City)—Aransas...............TX-2	Rodney Village (CDP)—Kent........ DE-1
Northumberland..........PA-1	Rock Prairie (Township)—Dade...MO-3	Roe (Town)—Monroe......................AR-2
Rock Elm (Town)—Pierce............... WI-3	Rock Rapids (City)—Lyon..............IA-3	Roebuck (CDP)—Spartanburg........SC-2
Rock Falls (Town)—Whiteside....... IL-3	Rock River (Township)—Alger......MI-3	Roeland Park (City)—Johnson......KS-4
Rock Falls (City)—Cerro Gordo......IA-3	Rock River (Town)—Albany..........WY-4	Roessleville (CDP)—Albany...........NY-1
Rock Falls (Township)—Holt......... NE-4	Rock Run (Township)—	Roff (Town)—Pontotoc...................OK-2
Rock Falls (Town)—Lincoln........... WI-3	Stephenson...................IL-3	**Roger Mills County**...........................OK-2
Rockford (Town)—Coosa..................AL-2		Rogers (City)—Benton....................AR-2

General Index

Rogers (Township)—Ford *IL-3*
Rogers (Township)—Presque Isle .. *MI-3*
Rogers (Township)—Cass................ *MN-3*
Rogers (City)—Hennepin *MN-3*
Rogers (Village)—Colfax *NE-4*
Rogers (City)—Barnes *ND-4*
Rogers (Township)—Barnes............ *ND-4*
Rogers (Village)—Columbiana.......*OH-3*
Rogers (Town)—Bell........................ *TX-2*
Rogers, Mt. (VA).............................. *Geog-4*
Rogers City (City)—Presque Isle ... *MI-3*
Rogers County *OK-2*
Rogersville (Town)—Lauderdale....*AL-2*
Rogersville (Town)—Greene *MO-3*
Rogersville (Town)—Webster......... *MO-3*
Rogersville (Town)—Hawkins......... *TN-2*
Rogue River (City)—Jackson.......... *OR-4*
Rohnert Park (City)—Sonoma........ *CA-4*
Rohnerville Rancheria (CA)..... *IndRes-4*
Roland (City)—Story........................ *IA-3*
Roland (Township)—Bottineau *ND-4*
Roland (Town)—Sequoyah *OK-2*
Rolesville (Town)—Wake *NC-2*
Rolette (City)—Rolette.................... *ND-4*
Rolette County................................. *ND-4*
Rolfe (City)—Pocahontas................ *IA-3*
Rolla (City)—Morton *KS-4*
Rolla (Township)—Morton.............. *KS-4*
Rolla (City)—Phelps........................ *MO-3*
Rolla (Township)—Phelps *MO-3*
Rolla (City)—Rolette....................... *ND-4*
Rolland (Township)—Isabella *MI-3*
Rollin (Township)—Lenawee.......... *MI-3*
Rolling (Town)—Langlade *WI-3*
Rolling Fields (City)—Jefferson..... *KY-2*
Rolling Fork (City)—Sharkey......... *MS-2*
Rolling Forks (Township)—Pope.. *MN-3*
Rolling Green (Township)—
  Martin *MN-3*
Rolling Green (Township)—
  Ward *ND-4*
Rolling Green (Township)—
  Corson *SD-4*
Rolling Hills (City)—Los Angeles.. *CA-4*
Rolling Hills (City)—Jefferson........ *KY-2*
Rolling Hills (Town)—Converse... *WY-4*
Rolling Hills Estates (City)—Los
  Angeles *CA-4*
Rolling Meadows (City)—Cook *IL-3*
Rolling Meadows (City)—Gregg.... *TX-2*
Rolling Prairie (Township)—
  Foster *ND-4*
Rollingstone (City)—Winona.......... *MN-3*
Rollingstone (Township)—
  Winona *MN-3*
Rollingwood (City)—Travis *TX-2*
Rollinsford (Town)—Strafford........*NH-1*
Rollis (Township)—Marshall *MN-3*
Roloff (Township)—McIntosh *ND-4*
Roma (City)—Starr *TX-2*
Roman Forest (Town)—
  Montgomery.................................... *TX-2*
Rome (City)—Floyd......................... *GA-2*
Rome (Township)—Jefferson.......... *IL-3*
Rome (CDP)—Peoria....................... *IL-3*
Rome (City)—Henry........................ *IA-3*
Rome (Town)—Kennebec *ME-1*
Rome (Township)—Lenawee........... *MI-3*
Rome (Township)—Faribault......... *MN-3*
Rome (City)—Oneida...................... *NY-1*
Rome (Village)—Adams...................*OH-3*
Rome (Township)—Ashtabula *OH-3*
Rome (Township)—Athens.............*OH-3*
Rome (Township)—Lawrence..........*OH-3*
Rome (Borough)—Bradford............ *PA-1*

Rome (Township)—Bradford........... *PA-1*
Rome (Township)—Crawford *PA-1*
Rome (Township)—Davison *SD-4*
Rome (Township)—Deuel............... *SD-4*
Rome (Town)—Adams..................... *WI-3*
Rome City (Town)—Noble *IN-3*
Romeo (Town)—Conejos *CO-4*
Romeo (Village)—Macomb.............. *MI-3*
Romeoville (Village)—Will *IL-3*
Romine (Township)—Marion *IL-3*
Romness (Township)—Griggs.........*ND-4*
Romney (City)—Hampshire *WV-2*
Romoland (CDP)—Riverside *CA-4*
Romulus (City)—Wayne *MI-3*
Romulus (Town)—Seneca *NY-1*
Ronald (Township)—Ionia.............. *MI-3*
Ronan (City)—Lake *MT-4*
Ronceverte (City)—Greenbrier...... *WV-2*
Ronda (Town)—Wilkes *NC-2*
Rondo (Town)—Lee *AR-2*
Ronkonkoma (CDP)—Suffolk *NY-1*
Ronneby (City)—Benton *MN-3*
Roodhouse (Town)—Greene *IL-3*
Roodhouse (Township)—Greene ... *IL-3*
Rooks County *KS-4*
Rooks Creek (Township)—
  Livingston *IL-3*
Roome (Township)—Polk *MN-3*
Roopville (Town)—Carroll *GA-2*
Roosevelt (Township)—Decatur *KS-4*
Roosevelt (Township)—Beltrami ... *MN-3*
Roosevelt (Township)—Crow
  Wing... *MN-3*
Roosevelt (City)—Lake of the
  Woods *MN-3*
Roosevelt (City)—Roseau *MN-3*
Roosevelt (Borough)—Monmouth..*NJ-1*
Roosevelt (CDP)—Nassau *NY-1*
Roosevelt (Township)—Renville....*ND-4*
Roosevelt (Town)—Kiowa *OK-2*
Roosevelt (City)—Duchesne *UT-4*
Roosevelt (Town)—Burnett............. *WI-3*
Roosevelt (Town)—Taylor............... *WI-3*
Roosevelt County *MT-4*
Roosevelt County *NM-4*
Roosevelt Dam (AZ) *Geog-4*
Roosevelt Park (City)—
  Muskegon *MI-3*
Root (Township)—Adams................ *IN-3*
Root (Town)—Montgomery *NY-1*
Rootstown (Township)—Portage ...*OH-3*
Roper (Town)—Washington *NC-2*
Ropesville (City)—Hockley *TX-2*
Roque Bluffs (Town)—
  Washington *ME-1*
Rosa (Municipality)—Blount *AL-2*
Rosalia (Township)—Butler............ *KS-4*
Rosalia (Town)—Whitman *WA-4*
Rosalie (Village)—Thurston *NE-4*
Rosamond (CDP)—Kern *CA-4*
Rosamond (Township)—Christian.. *IL-3*
Rosaryville (CDP)—Prince
  George's *MD-1*
Roscoe (Town)—Winnebago *IL-3*
Roscoe (Township)—Winnebago *IL-3*
Roscoe (Township)—Reno.............. *KS-4*
Roscoe (Township)—Goodhue *MN-3*
Roscoe (City)—Stearns................... *MN-3*
Roscoe (Township)—St. Clair......... *MO-3*
Roscoe (Village)—St. Clair............. *MO-3*
Roscoe (Township)—LaMoure........ *ND-4*
Roscoe (Borough)—Washington *PA-1*
Roscoe (City)—Edmunds *SD-4*
Roscoe (City)—Nolan *TX-2*

American Places Dictionary

Roscommon (Township)—
  Roscommon *MI-3*
Roscommon (Village)—
  Roscommon *MI-3*
Roscommon County *MI-3*
Rose (Township)—Shelby *IL-3*
Rose (Township)—Oakland *MI-3*
Rose (Township)—Ogemaw *MI-3*
Rose (Town)—Wayne *NY-1*
Rose (Township)—Stutsman *ND-4*
Rose (Township)—Carroll............... *OH-3*
Rose (Township)—Jefferson *PA-1*
Rose (Township)—Lyman *SD-4*
Rose (Town)—Waushara *WI-3*
Roseau (City)—Roseau *MN-3*
Roseau County................................. *MN-3*
Roseboom (Town)—Otsego............. *NY-1*
Roseboro (Town)—Sampson *NC-2*
Rose Bud (Town)—White *AR-2*
Rosebud (Township)—Polk *MN-3*
Rosebud (City)—Gasconade *MO-3*
Rosebud (Township)—Barnes *ND-4*
Rosebud (Township)—Mellette *SD-4*
Rosebud (CDP)—Todd *SD-4*
Rosebud (City)—Falls *TX-2*
Rosebud County *MT-4*
Rosebud Reservation & Trust Lands
  (SD) *IndRes-4*
Roseburg (City)—Douglas.............. *OR-4*
Roseburg North (CDP)—
  Douglas *OR-4*
Rosebush (Village)—Isabella *MI-3*
Rose City (City)—Ogemaw *MI-3*
Rose City (City)—Orange *TX-2*
Rose Creek (Township)—
  Republic *KS-4*
Rose Creek (City)—Mower *MN-3*
Rosedale (CDP)—Kern *CA-4*
Rosedale (Township)—Jersey......... *IL-3*
Rosedale (Town)—Parke *IN-3*
Rosedale (Village)—Iberville
  Parish *LA-2*
Rosedale (CDP)—Baltimore *MD-1*
Rosedale (Township)—
  Mahnomen *MN-3*
Rosedale (City)—Bolivar *MS-2*
Rosedale (Township)—Christian .. *MO-3*
Rosedale (Town)—McClain *OK-2*
Rosedale (Township)—Clark.......... *SD-4*
Rosedale (Township)—Hanson *SD-4*
Rosedale (Township)—Tripp *SD-4*
Rose Dell (Township)—Rock......... *MN-3*
Rosefield (Township)—Peoria *IL-3*
Rosefield (Township)—Eddy *ND-4*
Rosefield (Township)—Turner....... *SD-4*
Roseglen (Township)—McLean *ND-4*
Rose Hill (Village)—Jasper *IL-3*
Rose Hill (City)—Mahaska *IA-3*
Rose Hill (City)—Butler *KS-4*
Rose Hill (Township)—
  Cottonwood *MN-3*
Rose Hill (Township)—Johnson ... *MO-3*
Rose Hill (Town)—Duplin *NC-2*
Rose Hill (Township)—Foster *ND-4*
Rose Hill (Township)—McHenry ..*ND-4*
Rose Hill (Township)—Hand *SD-4*
Rose Hill (CDP)—Fairfax *VA-4*
Rose Hill Acres (City)—Hardin..... *TX-2*
Rose Lake (Township)—Osceola ... *MI-3*
Roseland (CDP)—Sonoma *CA-4*
Roseland (CDP)—Indian River..... *FL-2*
Roseland (Town)—St. Joseph *IN-3*
Roseland (City)—Cherokee............ *KS-4*
Roseland (Town)—Tangipahoa
  Parish *LA-2*

Roseland (Township)—
 Kandiyohi MN-3
Roseland (Township)—Adams NE-4
Roseland (Village)—Adams NE-4
Roseland (Borough)—Essex NJ-1
Roseland (Township)—Burke ND-4
Roseland (Township)—Tripp SD-4
Roselle (Village)—Cook IL-3
Roselle (Village)—DuPage IL-3
Roselle (Borough)—Union NJ-1
Roselle Park (Borough)—Union ... NJ-1
Rose Lodge (CDP)—Lincoln OR-4
Rosemead (City)—Los Angeles CA-4
Rosemeade (Township)—
 Ransom ND-4
Rosemont (CDP)—Sacramento CA-4
Rosemont (Village)—Cook IL-3
Rosemont (Town)—Frederick MD-1
Rosemont (Township)—McLean ... ND-4
Rosemount (City)—Dakota MN-3
Rosemount (CDP)—Scioto OH-3
Rosenberg (City)—Fort Bend TX-2
Rosendal (Township)—Griggs ND-4
Rosendale (Township)—
 Watonwan MN-3
Rosendale (City)—Andrew MO-3
Rosendale (Town)—Ulster NY-1
Rosendale (Town)—Fond du Lac .. WI-3
Rosendale (Village)—Fond du
 Lac WI-3
Rosendale Village (CDP)—Ulster .. NY-1
Rosenfield (Township)—
 Sheridan ND-4
Rosenhayn (CDP)—Cumberland ... NJ-1
Rosepine (Village)—Vernon
 Parish LA-2
Roseto (Borough)—Northampton ... PA-1
Rosette (Township)—Edmunds SD-4
Rose Valley (Township)—
 Stafford KS-4
Rose Valley (Borough)—Delaware .. PA-1
Roseville (City)—Placer CA-4
Roseville (Town)—Warren IL-3
Roseville (Township)—Warren IL-3
Roseville (City)—Macomb MI-3
Roseville (Township)—Grant MN-3
Roseville (Township)—
 Kandiyohi MN-3
Roseville (City)—Ramsey MN-3
Roseville (Township)—Traill ND-4
Roseville (Village)—Muskingum ... OH-3
Roseville (Village)—Perry OH-3
Roseville (Borough)—Tioga PA-1
Rosewood (Township)—
 Chippewa MN-3
Rosewood Heights (CDP)—
 Madison IL-3
Rosholt (Town)—Roberts SD-4
Rosholt (Village)—Portage WI-3
Rosiclare (Town)—Hardin IL-3
Rosing (Township)—Morrison MN-3
Roslyn (Village)—Nassau NY-1
Roslyn (Town)—Day SD-4
Roslyn (City)—Kittitas WA-4
Roslyn Estates (Village)—Nassau .. NY-1
Roslyn Harbor (Village)—Nassau .. NY-1
Rosman (Town)—Transylvania NC-2
Ross (Town)—Marin CA-4
Ross (Township)—Edgar IL-3
Ross (Township)—Pike IL-3
Ross (Township)—Vermilion IL-3
Ross (Township)—Clinton IN-3
Ross (Township)—Lake IN-3
Ross (Township)—Cherokee KS-4
Ross (Township)—Osborne KS-4

Ross (Township)—Kalamazoo MI-3
Ross (Township)—Roseau MN-3
Ross (City)—Mountrail ND-4
Ross (Township)—Mountrail ND-4
Ross (Township)—Butler OH-3
Ross (Township)—Greene OH-3
Ross (Township)—Jefferson OH-3
Ross (Township)—Allegheny PA-1
Ross (Township)—Luzerne PA-1
Ross (Township)—Monroe PA-1
Ross (City)—McLennan TX-2
Ross (Town)—Forest WI-3
Rossburg (Village)—Darke OH-3
Ross County OH-3
Ross Dam (WA) Geog-4
Rosser (Village)—Kaufman TX-2
Rossford (City)—Wood OH-3
Rossie (City)—Clay IA-3
Rossie (Town)—St. Lawrence NY-1
Ross Lake (Township)—Crow
 Wing MN-3
Rosslyn Farms (Borough)—
 Allegheny PA-1
Rossmoor (CDP)—Orange CA-4
Rossmoor (CDP)—Montgomery ... MD-1
Rossmoor (CDP)—Middlesex NJ-1
Rosston (Town)—Nevada AR-2
Rosston (Town)—Harper OK-2
Rossville (City)—Walker GA-2
Rossville (Village)—Vermilion IL-3
Rossville (Town)—Clinton IN-3
Rossville (City)—Shawnee KS-4
Rossville (Township)—Shawnee KS-4
Rossville (CDP)—Baltimore MD-1
Rossville (Town)—Fayette............. TN-2
Rost (Township)—Jackson MN-3
Rostraver (Township)—
 Westmoreland PA-1
Roswell (City)—Fulton GA-2
Roswell (City)—Chaves NM-4
Roswell (Village)—Tuscarawas OH-3
Roswell (Town)—Miner SD-4
Roswell (Township)—Miner SD-4
Rotan (City)—Fisher TX-2
Rothbury (Village)—Oceana MI-3
Rothsay (City)—Otter Tail MN-3
Rothsay (City)—Wilkin MN-3
Rothschild (Village)—Marathon ... WI-3
Rothville (Village)—Chariton MO-3
Rotonda (CDP)—Charlotte FL-2
Rotterdam (CDP)—Schenectady ... NY-1
Rotterdam (Town)—Schenectady .. NY-1
Roubidoux (Township)—Pulaski .. MO-3
Roubidoux (Township)—Texas MO-3
Rough Rock (CDP)—Apache AZ-4
Roulette (Township)—Potter PA-1
Round Grove (Township)—
 Livingston IL-3
Round Grove (Township)—White .. IN-3
Round Grove (Township)—
 McLeod MN-3
Round Grove (Township)—
 Macon MO-3
Round Grove (Township)—
 Marion MO-3
Roundhead (Township)—Hardin .. OH-3
Round Hill (Town)—Loudoun VA-2
Round Lake (Town)—Lake IL-3
Round Lake (Township)—
 Becker MN-3
Round Lake (Township)—
 Jackson MN-3
Round Lake (City)—Nobles MN-3
Round Lake (Village)—Saratoga .. NY-1

Round Lake (Township)—
 McHenry ND-4
Round Lake (Town)—Sawyer WI-3
Round Lake Beach (Village)—
 Lake IL-3
Round Lake Heights (Village)—
 Lake IL-3
Round Lake Park (Village)—Lake .. IL-3
Round Mound (Township)—
 Osborne KS-4
Round Mountain (Town)—
 Blanco TX-2
Round Prairie (Township)—
 Todd MN-3
Round Prairie (Township)—
 Callaway MO-3
Round Prairie (Township)—
 Williams ND-4
Round Rock (City)—Travis TX-2
Round Rock (City)—Williamson ... TX-2
Round Springs (Township)—
 Mitchell KS-4
Round Top (Township)—
 Stutsman ND-4
Round Top (Town)—Fayette TX-2
Roundup (City)—Musselshell MT-4
Round Valley Reservation & Trust
 Lands (CA) IndRes-4
Rountree (Township)—
 Montgomery IL-3
Rouse (Township)—Charles Mix ... SD-4
Rouses Point (Village)—Clinton NY-1
Rouseville (Borough)—Venango PA-1
Routt County CO-4
Rovohl (Township)—Thomas KS-4
Rowan (City)—Wright IA-3
Rowan Bay (CDP)—
 Wrangell-Petersburg Census
 Area AK-4
Rowan County KY-2
Rowan County NC-2
Rowe (Town)—Franklin MA-1
Rowe (Township)—Lyman SD-4
Rowesville (Town)—Orangeburg ... SC-2
Rowland (Town)—Robeson NC-2
Rowland Heights (CDP)—Los
 Angeles CA-4
Rowlesburg (Town)—Preston WV-2
Rowlett (City)—Dallas TX-2
Rowlett (City)—Rockwall TX-2
Rowley (City)—Buchanan IA-3
Rowley (Town)—Essex MA-1
Roxana (Town)—Madison IL-3
Roxand (Township)—Eaton MI-3
Roxboro (City)—Person NC-2
Roxbury (Town)—Litchfield CT-1
Roxbury (Town)—Oxford ME-1
Roxbury—Suffolk MA-1
Roxbury (Town)—Cheshire NH-1
Roxbury (Township)—Morris NJ-1
Roxbury (Town)—Delaware NY-1
Roxbury (Town)—Washington VT-1
Roxbury (Town)—Dane WI-3
Roxbury *See* **Boston**—Suffolk MA-1
Roxie (Town)—Franklin MS-2
Roxobel (Town)—Bertie NC-2
Roxton (City)—Lamar TX-2
Roy (Village)—Harding NM-4
Roy (City)—Weber UT-4
Roy (City)—Pierce WA-4
Royal (Village)—Champaign IL-3
Royal (City)—Clay IA-3
Royal (Township)—Ford KS-4
Royal (Township)—Lincoln MN-3
Royal (Township)—Antelope NE-4

General Index

Royal (Village)—Antelope............... *NE-4*
Royal (Township)—Ramsey............ *ND-4*
Royal Center (Town)—Cass............ *IN-3*
Royal City (Town)—Grant............ *WA-4*
Royal Gorge (CO)....................... *Geog-4*
Royal Lakes (Village)—Macoupin .. *IL-3*
Royal Oak (City)—Oakland............ *MI-3*
Royal Oak (Township)—Oakland .. *MI-3*
Royal Palm Beach (Village)—Palm
 Beach.. *FL-2*
Royal Pines (CDP)—Buncombe *NC-2*
Royalston (Town)—Worcester *MA-1*
Royalton (Town)—Franklin............ *IL-3*
Royalton (Township)—Berrien *MI-3*
Royalton (City)—Morrison *MN-3*
Royalton (Township)—Pine *MN-3*
Royalton (Town)—Niagara *NY-1*
Royalton (Township)—Fulton........ *OH-3*
Royalton (Borough)—Dauphin *PA-1*
Royalton (Town)—Windsor............ *VT-1*
Royalton (Town)—Waupaca *WI-3*
Royersford (Borough)—
 Montgomery.............................. *PA-1*
Royse City (City)—Collin............... *TX-2*
Royse City (City)—Rockwall *TX-2*
Royston (City)—Franklin................ *GA-2*
Royston (City)—Hart..................... *GA-2*
Royston (City)—Madison *GA-2*
Rozel (City)—Pawnee................... *KS-4*
Rozetta (Township)—Henderson *IL-3*
Rubicon (Township)—Greene........ *IL-3*
Rubicon (Township)—Huron......... *MI-3*
Rubicon (Town)—Dodge *WI-3*
Rubidoux (CDP)—Riverside *CA-4*
Rubin (Township)—Nelson............ *ND-4*
Ruby (City)—Yukon-Koyukuk Census
 Area... *AK-4*
Ruby (Town)—Chesterfield............ *SC-2*
Ruby (Town)—Chippewa *WI-3*
Rudd (City)—Floyd....................... *IA-3*
Rudolph (Town)—Wood *WI-3*
Rudolph (Village)—Wood *WI-3*
Rudy (Town)—Crawford................ *AR-2*
Rudyard (Township)—Chippewa... *MI-3*
Rufus (City)—Sherman *OR-4*
Rugby (City)—Pierce..................... *ND-4*
Ruggles (Township)—Ashland *OH-3*
Rugh (Township)—Nelson *ND-4*
Ruidoso (Village)—Lincoln............ *NM-4*
Ruidoso Downs (Village)—
 Lincoln...................................... *NM-4*
Rule (Town)—Haskell *TX-2*
Ruleville (City)—Sunflower *MS-2*
Rulo (City)—Richardson................ *NE-4*
Ruma (Village)—Randolph............ *IL-3*
Rumford (Town)—Oxford *ME-1*
Rumley (Township)—Harrison *OH-3*
Rumney (Town)—Grafton............. *NH-1*
Rumsey Rancheria (CA)............... *IndRes-4*
Rumson (Borough)—Monmouth ... *NJ-1*
Runaway Bay (City)—Wise *TX-2*
Runeberg (Township)—Becker..... *MN-3*
Runge (Town)—Karnes................. *TX-2*
Runnells (City)—Polk *IA-3*
Runnels County *TX-2*
Runnemede (Borough)—Camden ...*NJ-1*
Running Bird (Township)—
 Mellette..................................... *SD-4*
Running Springs (CDP)—San
 Bernardino................................ *CA-4*
Rupert (City)—Minidoka............... *ID-4*
Rupert (Town)—Bennington *VT-1*
Rupert (Town)—Greenbrier........... *WV-2*
Rural (Township)—Rock Island *IL-3*
Rural (Township)—Shelby *IL-3*

Rural (Township)—Jefferson *KS-4*
Rural (Township)—Kingman *KS-4*
Rural Hall (Town)—Forsyth *NC-2*
Rural Hill (CDP)—Wilson *TN-2*
Rural Retreat (Town)—Wythe *VA-2*
Rural Valley (Borough)—
 Armstrong................................. *PA-1*
Rusco (Township)—Buffalo *NE-4*
Ruscombmanor (Township)—
 Berks.. *PA-1*
Rush (Township)—Jo Daviess *IL-3*
Rush (Township)—Shiawassee...... *MI-3*
Rush (Township)—Buchanan......... *MO-3*
Rush (Town)—Monroe.................. *NY-1*
Rush (Township)—Champaign *OH-3*
Rush (Township)—Scioto.............. *OH-3*
Rush (Township)—Tuscarawas....*OH-3*
Rush (Township)—Centre *PA-1*
Rush (Township)—Dauphin *PA-1*
Rush (Township)—
 Northumberland *PA-1*
Rush (Township)—Schuylkill......... *PA-1*
Rush (Township)—Susquehanna .. *PA-1*
Rush Center (City)—Rush *KS-4*
Rush City (City)—Chisago *MN-3*
Rush County *IN-3*
Rush County *KS-4*
Rush Creek (Township)—
 Fairfield................................... *OH-3*
Rushcreek (Township)—Logan *OH-3*
Rushford (City)—Fillmore *MN-3*
Rushford (Town)—Allegany.......... *NY-1*
Rushford (Township)—Walsh *ND-4*
Rushford (Town)—Winnebago *WI-3*
Rushford Village (City)—
 Fillmore................................... *MN-3*
Rush Hill (Town)—Audrain........... *MO-3*
Rush Lake (Township)—Otter
 Tail... *MN-3*
Rush Lake (Township)—Pierce..... *ND-4*
Rushmere (CDP)—Isle of Wight *VA-2*
Rushmore (City)—Nobles *MN-3*
Rushmore, Mt. (SD) *Geog-4*
Rush River (Township)—Cass *ND-4*
Rush River (Town)—St. Croix...... *WI-3*
Rushseba (Township)—Chisago ... *MN-3*
Rush Springs (Town)—Grady *OK-2*
Rushsylvania (Village)—Logan *OH-3*
Rush Valley (Town)—Tooele......... *UT-4*
Rushville (Town)—Schuyler........... *IL-3*
Rushville (Township)—Schuyler.... *IL-3*
Rushville (City)—Rush *IN-3*
Rushville (Township)—Rush *IN-3*
Rushville (Township)—Phillips *KS-4*
Rushville (Town)—Buchanan *MO-3*
Rushville (City)—Sheridan *NE-4*
Rushville (Village)—Ontario......... *NY-1*
Rushville (Village)—Yates *NY-1*
Rushville (Township)—Ward *ND-4*
Rushville (Village)—Fairfield........*OH-3*
Rusk (Township)—Day *SD-4*
Rusk (City)—Cherokee *TX-2*
Rusk (Town)—Burnett *WI-3*
Rusk (Town)—Rusk *WI-3*
Rusk County *TX-2*
Rusk County *WI-3*
Ruskin (CDP)—Hillsborough *FL-2*
Ruskin (Village)—Nuckolls............ *NE-4*
Rusland (Township)—Wells *ND-4*
Ruso (City)—McLean *ND-4*
Russell (Town)—White *AR-2*
Russell (City)—Barrow *GA-2*
Russell (Township)—Lawrence *IL-3*
Russell (Township)—Putnam *IN-3*
Russell (City)—Lucas *IA-3*

Russell (City)—Russell.................. *KS-4*
Russell (Township)—Russell *KS-4*
Russell (City)—Greenup *KY-2*
Russells (Town)—Hampden *MA-1*
Russell (City)—Lyon *MN-3*
Russell (Township)—Camden *MO-3*
Russell (Township)—Macon *MO-3*
Russell (Town)—St. Lawrence *NY-1*
Russell (City)—Bottineau.............. *ND-4*
Russell (Township)—LaMoure *ND-4*
Russell (Township)—Rolette *ND-4*
Russell (Township)—Geauga *OH-3*
Russell (Town)—Bayfield *WI-3*
Russell (Town)—Lincoln *WI-3*
Russell (Town)—Sheboygan *WI-3*
Russell Cave (AL) *Geog-4*
Russell County *AL-2*
Russell County *KS-4*
Russell County *KY-2*
Russell County *VA-2*
Russell Gardens (Village)—
 Nassau...................................... *NY-1*
Russells Point (Village)—Logan *OH-3*
Russell Springs (City)—Logan *KS-4*
Russell Springs (Township)—
 Logan *KS-4*
Russell Springs (City)—Russell..... *KY-2*
Russellville (City)—Franklin..........*AL-2*
Russellville (City)—Pope *AR-2*
Russellville (Village)—Lawrence ... *IL-3*
Russellville (Town)—Putnam *IN-3*
Russellville (City)—Logan *KY-2*
Russellville (City)—Cole *MO-3*
Russellville (Village)—Brown *OH-3*
Russia (Township)—Polk *MN-3*
Russia (Town)—Herkimer *NY-1*
Russia (Township)—Lorain *OH-3*
Russia (Village)—Shelby *OH-3*
Russian Mission (City)—Wade
 Hampton Census Area *AK-4*
Russiaville (Town)—Howard *IN-3*
Rust (Township)—Montmorency ... *MI-3*
Ruston (City)—Lincoln Parish *LA-2*
Ruston (Town)—Pierce *WA-4*
Ruth (Town)—Rutherford............. *NC-2*
Ruth A (Township)—Stone *MO-3*
Ruth B (Township)—Stone *MO-3*
Ruth B Rural (Township)—
 Stone.. *MO-3*
Ruth C (Township)—Stone *MO-3*
Ruth C Rural (Township)—
 Stone.. *MO-3*
Rutherford (Township)—Martin.... *IN-3*
Rutherford (Borough)—Bergen *NJ-1*
Rutherford (Town)—Gibson *TN-2*
Rutherford College (Town)—
 Burke.. *NC-2*
Rutherford County *NC-2*
Rutherford County *TN-2*
Rutherfordton (Town)—
 Rutherford *NC-2*
Ruthton (City)—Pipestone............ *MN-3*
Ruthven (City)—Palo Alto *IA-3*
Rutland (Township)—Kane *IL-3*
Rutland (Township)—La Salle *IL-3*
Rutland (Village)—La Salle *IL-3*
Rutland (City)—Humboldt *IA-3*
Rutland (Township)—
 Montgomery *KS-4*
Rutland (Township)—Worcester ... *MA-1*
Rutland (Township)—Barry *MI-3*
Rutland (Township)—Martin *MN-3*
Rutland (Town)—Jefferson *NY-1*
Rutland (City)—Sargent *ND-4*
Rutland (Township)—Sargent *ND-4*

American Places Dictionary — General Index

Rutland (Township)—Meigs OH-3
Rutland (Village)—Meigs OH-3
Rutland (Township)—Tioga PA-1
Rutland (Township)—Lake SD-4
Rutland (City)—Rutland VT-1
Rutland (Town)—Rutland VT-1
Rutland (Town)—Dane WI-3
Rutland County VT-1
Rutledge (Town)—Crenshaw AL-2
Rutledge (City)—Morgan GA-2
Rutledge (Township)—De Witt IL-3
Rutledge (City)—Pine MN-3
Rutledge (Township)—Scotland MO-3
Rutledge (Borough)—Delaware PA-1
Rutledge (Town)—Grainger TN-2
Ruyle (Township)—Jersey IL-3
Ryan (City)—Delaware IA-3
Ryan (Township)—Sumner KS-4
Ryan (Township)—LaMoure ND-4
Ryan (Town)—Jefferson OK-2
Ryan (Township)—Schuylkill PA-1
Ryder (City)—Ward ND-4
Ryder (Township)—Ward ND-4
Rye (Town)—Pueblo CO-4
Rye (Town)—Rockingham NH-1
Rye (City)—Westchester NY-1
Rye (Town)—Westchester NY-1
Rye (Township)—Grand Forks ND-4
Rye (Township)—Perry PA-1
Rye Brook (Village)—
  Westchester NY-1
Ryegate (Town)—Golden Valley ... MT-4
Ryegate (Town)—Caledonia VT-1
Ryland Heights (City)—Kenton KY-2
Ryno (Township)—Custer NE-4
Sabattus (Town)—Androscoggin ... ME-1
Sabetha (City)—Brown KS-4
Sabetha (City)—Nemaha KS-4
Sabin (City)—Clay MN-3
Sabina (Village)—Clinton OH-3
Sabinal (City)—Uvalde TX-2
Sabine County TX-2
Sabine Parish LA-2
Sabine River (AL) Geog-4
Sabula (City)—Jackson IA-3
Sac (Township)—Dade MO-3
Sac and Fox Reservation (IA) .. IndRes-4
Sac and Fox Reservation & Trust Lands
  (KS) IndRes-4
Sac and Fox TJSA (OK) IndRes-4
Sacaton (CDP)—Pinal AZ-4
Sac City (City)—Sac IA-3
Sac County IA-3
Sachse (City)—Collin TX-2
Sachse (City)—Dallas TX-2
Sackets Harbor (Village)—
  Jefferson NY-1
Saco (City)—York ME-1
Saco (Town)—Phillips MT-4
Sacramento (City)—Sacramento ... CA-4
Sacramento (City)—McLean KY-2
Sacramento County CA-4
Sacramento River (CA) Geog-4
Sacramento Valley (CA) Geog-4
Sacred Heart (City)—Renville MN-3
Sacred Heart (Township)—
  Renville MN-3
Saddle Brook (Township)—
  Bergen NJ-1
Saddle Butte (Township)—Golden
  Valley ND-4
Saddle River (Borough)—Bergen ... NJ-1
Saddle Rock (Village)—Nassau NY-1
Sadieville (City)—Scott KY-2
Sadler (City)—Grayson TX-2

Sadorus (Township)—Champaign ... IL-3
Sadorus (Village)—Champaign IL-3
Sadsbury (Township)—Chester PA-1
Sadsbury (Township)—Crawford .. PA-1
Sadsbury (Township)—Lancaster .. PA-1
Saegertown (Borough)—Crawford .. PA-1
Safety Harbor (City)—Pinellas FL-2
Safford (City)—Graham AZ-4
Sagadahoc County ME-1
Sagamore (CDP)—Barnstable MA-1
Sagamore Hills (Township)—
  Summit OH-3
Sage (Township)—Gladwin MI-3
Sageville (City)—Dubuque IA-3
Sag Harbor (Village)—Suffolk NY-1
Saginaw (City)—Saginaw MI-3
Saginaw (Township)—Saginaw MI-3
Saginaw (Village)—Newton MO-3
Saginaw (City)—Tarrant TX-2
Saginaw Bay (MI) Geog-4
Saginaw County MI-3
Sago (Township)—Itasca MN-3
Sagola (Township)—Dickinson MI-3
Saguache (Town)—Saguache CO-4
Saguache County CO-4
Sahalee (CDP)—King WA-4
Sailor Springs (Village)—Clay IL-3
Saint Agatha (Town)—
  Aroostook ME-1
St. Albans (Township)—Hancock ... IL-3
Saint Albans (Town)—Somerset ... ME-1
St. Albans (Township)—Licking ... OH-3
St. Albans (City)—Franklin VT-1
St. Albans (Town)—Franklin VT-1
St. Albans (City)—Kanawha WV-2
St. Andrews (Township)—Walsh ... ND-4
St. Andrews (CDP)—Richland SC-2
St. Ann (City)—St. Louis MO-3
St. Anna (Township)—Wells ND-4
St. Anne (Town)—Kankakee IL-3
St. Anne (Township)—Kankakee ... IL-3
St. Ansgar (City)—Mitchell IA-3
St. Anthony (City)—Fremont ID-4
St. Anthony (City)—Marshall IA-3
St. Anthony (City)—Hennepin MN-3
St. Anthony (City)—Ramsey MN-3
St. Anthony (City)—Stearns MN-3
St. Armand (Town)—Essex NY-1
St. Aubert (Township)—
  Callaway MO-3
St. Augusta (Township)—Stearns ... MN-3
St. Augustine (City)—St. Johns ... FL-2
St. Augustine (Village)—Knox IL-3
St. Augustine Beach (City)—St.
  Johns FL-2
St. Augustine Shores (CDP)—St.
  Johns FL-2
St. Augustine South (CDP)—St.
  Johns FL-2
St. Bernard (Township)—Platte NE-4
St. Bernard (City)—Hamilton OH-3
St. Bernard Parish LA-2
St. Bonaventure (CDP)—
  Cattaraugus NY-1
St. Bonifacius (City)—Hennepin ... MN-3
St. Bridget (Township)—Marshall ... KS-4
St. Charles (Town)—Arkansas AR-2
St. Charles (City)—Bear Lake ID-4
St. Charles (Town)—DuPage IL-3
St. Charles (Town)—Kane IL-3
St. Charles (Township)—Kane IL-3
St. Charles (City)—Madison IA-3
St. Charles (City)—Hopkins KY-2
St. Charles (CDP)—Charles MD-1
St. Charles (Township)—Saginaw ... MI-3

St. Charles (Village)—Saginaw MI-3
St. Charles (City)—Winona MN-3
St. Charles (Township)—
  Winona MN-3
St. Charles (City)—St. Charles ... MO-3
St. Charles (Township)—Cuming ... NE-4
St. Charles (Township)—Gregory .. SD-4
St. Charles (Town)—Lee VA-2
St. Charles County MO-3
St. Charles Parish LA-2
St. Clair (Township)—St. Clair IL-3
St. Clair (City)—St. Clair MI-3
St. Clair (Township)—St. Clair MI-3
St. Clair (City)—Blue Earth MN-3
St. Clair (City)—Franklin MO-3
St. Clair (Township)—Butler OH-3
St. Clair (Township)—
  Columbiana OH-3
St. Clair (Borough)—Schuylkill PA-1
St. Clair (Township)—
  Westmoreland PA-1
St. Clair, Lake (MI) Geog-4
St. Clair County AL-2
St. Clair County IL-3
St. Clair County MI-3
St. Clair County MO-3
St. Clair Shores (City)—Macomb .. MI-3
St. Clairsville (City)—Belmont OH-3
St. Clairsville (Borough)—
  Bedford PA-1
St. Clere (Township)—
  Pottawatomie KS-4
St. Cloud (City)—Osceola FL-2
St. Cloud (City)—Benton MN-3
St. Cloud (City)—Sherburne MN-3
St. Cloud (City)—Stearns MN-3
St. Cloud (Township)—Stearns ... MN-3
St. Cloud (Village)—Crawford MO-3
St. Cloud (Village)—Fond du
  Lac WI-3
St. Croix (Township)—Hettinger ... ND-4
St. Croix County WI-3
St. Croix Falls (City)—Polk WI-3
St. Croix Falls (Town)—Polk WI-3
Saint Croix Reservation (WI) .. IndRes-4
St. David (CDP)—Cochise AZ-4
St. David (Village)—Fulton IL-3
St. Dennis (CDP)—Jefferson KY-2
St. Donatus (City)—Jackson IA-3
St. Edward (City)—Boone NE-4
Ste. Genevieve (City)—Ste.
  Genevieve MO-3
Ste. Genevieve (Township)—Ste.
  Genevieve MO-3
Ste. Genevieve County MO-3
St. Elias Mountains **or Range**
  (AK) Geog-4
St. Elizabeth (Town)—Miller MO-3
St. Elmo (City)—Fayette IL-3
Ste. Marie (Township)—Jasper IL-3
Ste. Marie (Village)—Jasper IL-3
St. Ferdinand (Township)—St.
  Louis MO-3
St. Florian (Municipality)—
  Lauderdale AL-2
St. Francis (City)—Clay AR-2
St. Francis (Township)—
  Effingham IL-3
St. Francis (City)—Cheyenne KS-4
Saint Francis (Plantation)—
  Aroostook ME-1
St. Francis (City)—Anoka MN-3
St. Francis (Town)—Todd SD-4
St. Francis (City)—Milwaukee WI-3
St. Francis County AR-2

General Index

St. Francisville (Town)—
  Lawrence.................................... IL-3
St. Francisville (Town)—West Feliciana
  Parish LA-2
St. Francois (Township)—Butler... MO-3
St. Francois (Township)—
  Madison MO-3
St. Francois (Township)—St.
  Francois MO-3
St. Francois (Township)—Wayne.. MO-3
St. Francois County...................... MO-3
St. George (City)—Aleutians West
  Census Area AK-4
St. George (City)—Pottawatomie ... KS-4
St. George (Township)—
  Pottawatomie KS-4
Saint George (Town)—Knox......... ME-1
St. George (Township)—Benton MN-3
St. George (City)—St. Louis MO-3
St. George (Town)—Dorchester SC-2
St. George (City)—Washington UT-4
St. George (Town)—Chittenden..... VT-1
St. Germain (Town)—Vilas............ WI-3
St. Hedwig (Town)—Bexar............ TX-2
St. Helen (CDP)—Roscommon MI-3
St. Helena (City)—Napa CA-4
St. Helena (Village)—Cedar NE-4
St. Helena (Village)—Pender NC-2
St. Helena Parish............................ LA-2
St. Helens (City)—Columbia OR-4
St. Helens, Mt. (WA) Geog-4
St. Henry (Village)—Mercer OH-3
St. Hilaire (City)—Pennington...... MN-3
St. Ignace (City)—Mackinac MI-3
St. Ignace (Township)—Mackinac . MI-3
St. Ignatius (Town)—Lake............. MT-1
St. Jacob (Township)—Madison ... IL-3
St. Jacob (Village)—Madison IL-3
St. James (Township)—
  Charlevoix................................. MI-3
St. James (City)—Watonwan MN-3
St. James (Township)—
  Watonwan MN-3
St. James (Township)—
  Mississippi MO-3
St. James (City)—Phelps............... MO-3
St. James (Township)—Phelps MO-3
St. James (CDP)—Suffolk NY-1
St. James City (CDP)—Lee............FL-2
St. James Parish LA-2
St. Jo (City)—Montague................ TX-2
St. Joe (Town)—Dekalb IN-3
St. John (Town)—Lake.................. IN-3
St. John (Township)—Lake............ IN-3
St. John (City)—Stafford KS-4
St. John (Township)—Stafford........KS-4
St. John (Township)—New
  Madrid MO-3
St. John (City)—St. Louis MO-3
St. John (City)—Rolette................. ND-4
St. John (Town)—Whitman WA-4
St. John Harbor (CDP)—
  Wrangell-Petersburg Census
  Area... AK-4
Saint John (Plantation of) (Pop.
  Place)—Aroostook ME-1
St. Johns (City)—Apache AZ-4
St. Johns (Village)—Perry IL-3
St. Johns (City)—Clinton.............. MI-3
St. Johns (Township)—
  Kandiyohi MN-3
St. Johns (Township)—Franklin ... MO-3
St. Johnsbury (Town)—
  Caledonia VT-1
St. Johns County............................FL-2

St. Johnsville (Town)—
  Montgomery............................... NY-1
St. Johnsville (Village)—
  Montgomery............................... NY-1
St. John the Baptist Parish LA-2
St. Joseph (Township)—
  Champaign IL-3
St. Joseph (Village)—Champaign..... IL-3
St. Joseph (Township)—Allen IN-3
St. Joseph (Town)—Tensas
  Parish LA-2
St. Joseph (City)—Berrien MI-3
St. Joseph (Township)—Kittson ... MN-3
St. Joseph (City)—Stearns MN-3
St. Joseph (Township)—Stearns ... MN-3
St. Joseph (City)—Buchanan MO-3
St. Joseph (Township)—Pembina .. ND-4
St. Joseph (Township)—
  Williams OH-3
St. Joseph (City)—Lawrence TN-2
St. Joseph (Town)—St. Croix WI-3
St. Joseph Charter (Township)—
  Berrien MI-3
St. Joseph County IN-3
St. Joseph County MI-3
St. Landry Parish LA-2
St. Lawrence (Township)—Scott ... MN-3
St. Lawrence (Borough)—Berks PA-1
St. Lawrence (Town)—Hand......... SD-4
St. Lawrence (Township)—Hand... SD-4
St. Lawrence (Town)—Waupaca ... WI-3
St. Lawrence, Lake (NY) Geog-4
St. Lawrence and Great Lakes
  Waterway (WA)......................... Geog-4
St. Lawrence County NY-1
St. Lawrence Island (AK) Geog-4
St. Lawrence River (NY).............. Geog-4
St. Lawrence Seaway (NY) Geog-4
St. Leo (Town)—Pasco FL-2
St. Leo (City)—Yellow Medicine .. MN-3
St. Leon (Town)—Dearborn........... IN-3
St. Libory (Village)—St. Clair...... IL-3
St. Louis (City)—Gratiot MI-3
St. Louis (Town)—Pottawatomie .. OK-2
St. Louis County MN-3
St. Louis County MO-3
St. Louis (Independent City) MO-3
St. Louis Park (City)—Hennepin.. MN-3
St. Louisville (Village)—Licking OH-3
St. Lucas (City)—Fayette IA-3
St. Lucie (Village)—St. Lucie..........FL-2
St. Lucie County..............................FL-2
St. Marie (Town)—Green Lake...... WI-3
St. Maries (City)—Benewah ID-4
St. Marks (Town)—Wakulla FL-2
St. Martin (City)—Stearns MN-3
St. Martin (Township)—Stearns ... MN-3
St. Martin (CDP)—Jackson MS-2
St. Martin (Village)—Brown OH-3
St. Martin Parish............................ LA-2
St. Martins (City)—Cole MO-3
St. Martinville (City)—St. Martin
  Parish LA-2
St. Mary (Township)—Hancock.... IL-3
St. Mary (Township)—Waseca MN-3
St. Mary (City)—Ste. Genevieve .. MO-3
St. Mary (Township)—McLean...... ND-4
St. Mary Parish.............................. LA-2
St. Mary's (City)—Wade Hampton
  Census Area AK-4
St. Marys (City)—Camden............ GA-2
St. Marys (Township)—Adams IN-3
St. Marys (City)—Warren IA-3
St. Marys (City)—Pottawatomie..... KS-4

St. Marys (Township)—
  Pottawatomie KS-4
St. Marys (City)—Wabaunsee KS-4
St. Marys (Township)—Perry....... MO-3
St. Marys (Township)—Ward......... ND-4
St. Marys (City)—Auglaize OH-3
St. Marys (Township)—Auglaize.... OH-3
St. Marys (Borough)—Elk PA-1
St. Marys (City)—Pleasants WV-2
St. Mary's County.......................... MD-1
Saint Mary's Falls Canal and Locks
  (NY) Geog-4
St. Marys Point (City)—
  Washington MN-3
St. Marys River (MI) Geog-4
St. Mathias (Township)—Crow
  Wing.. MN-3
St. Matthews (City)—Jefferson KY-2
St. Matthews (Town)—Calhoun..... SC-2
St. Michael (City)—Nome Census
  Area AK-4
St. Michael (City)—Wright MN-3
St. Michael (Township)—
  Madison MO-3
St. Michaels (CDP)—Apache AZ-4
St. Michaels (Town)—Talbot MD-1
St. Nazianz (Village)—
  Manitowoc WI-3
St. Olaf (City)—Clayton IA-3
St. Olaf (Township)—Otter Tail.... MN-3
St. Onge (Township)—Lawrence ... SD-4
St. Paris (Village)—Champaign OH-3
St. Paul (City)—Aleutians West Census
  Area AK-4
St. Paul (Town)—Madison............ AR-2
St. Paul (Town)—Decatur IN-3
St. Paul (Town)—Shelby IN-3
St. Paul (City)—Lee IA-3
St. Paul (City)—Neosho................ KS-4
St. Paul (City)—Ramsey MN-3
St. Paul (Village)—St. Charles MO-3
St. Paul (City)—Howard NE-4
St. Paul (Township)—Stutsman ND-4
St. Paul (City)—Marion OR-4
St. Paul (Town)—Collin TX-4
St. Paul (Town)—Russell VA-2
St. Paul (Town)—Wise VA-2
St. Paul Park (City)—
  Washington MN-3
St. Pauls (Town)—Robeson NC-2
St. Peter (Village)—Fayette............ IL-3
St. Peter (City)—Nicollet MN-3
St. Peters (City)—St. Charles........ MO-3
St. Peters (Township)—St.
  Charles...................................... MO-3
St. Petersburg (City)—Pinellas.........FL-2
St. Petersburg (Borough)—
  Clarion PA-1
St. Petersburg Beach (City)—
  Pinellas.......................................FL-2
St. Regis Mohawk Reservation
  (NY) IndRes-4
St. Regis Park (City)—Jefferson KY-2
St. Regis Reservation (Pop. Place)—
  Franklin..................................... NY-1
St. Robert (City)—Pulaski MO-3
St. Rosa (City)—Stearns............... MN-3
St. Rose (Township)—Clinton IL-3
St. Rose (CDP)—St. Charles
  Parish LA-2
St. Simons (CDP)—Glynn GA-2
St. Stephen (City)—Stearns MN-3
St. Stephen (Town)—Berkeley SC-2
St. Stephens (CDP)—Catawba....... NC-2
St. Tammany Parish LA-2

St. Thomas (Town)—Cole.............. *MO-3*
St. Thomas (City)—Pembina.........*ND-4*
St. Thomas (Township)—
  Pembina *ND-4*
St. Thomas (Township)—Franklin.. *PA-1*
St. Vincent (City)—Kittson........... *MN-3*
St. Vincent (Township)—Kittson... *MN-3*
St. Wendel (Township)—Stearns... *MN-3*
Sakakawea, Lake (ND).................. *Geog-4*
Saks (Division)—Calhoun..............*AL-2*
Salado (CDP)—Bell........................ *TX-2*
Salamanca (Township)—
  Cherokee *KS-4*
Salamanca (City)—Cattaraugus *NY-1*
Salamanca (Town)—Cattaraugus... *NY-1*
Salamatof (CDP)—Kenai Peninsula
  Borough...................................... *AK-4*
Salamonia (Town)—Jay.................. *IN-3*
Salamonie (Township)—
  Huntington.................................*IN-3*
Salcha (CDP)—Fairbanks North Star
  Borough......................................*AK-4*
Sale City (Town)—Mitchell............ *GA-2*
Salem (City)—Fulton..................... *AR-2*
Salem (CDP)—Saline..................... *AR-2*
Salem (Town)—New London *CT-1*
Salem (Township)—Carroll *IL-3*
Salem (Township)—Knox *IL-3*
Salem (Town)—Marion *IL-3*
Salem (Township)—Marion *IL-3*
Salem (Township)—Delaware *IN-3*
Salem (Township)—Pulaski *IN-3*
Salem (Township)—Steuben *IN-3*
Salem (City)—Washington *IN-3*
Salem (City)—Henry......................*IA-3*
Salem (Township)—Allen...............*KS-4*
Salem (Township)—Cowley *KS-4*
Salem (Township)—Greenwood......*KS-4*
Salem (Township)—Sedgwick *KS-4*
Salem (City)—Livingston *KY-2*
Salem (City)—Essex *MA-1*
Salem (Township)—Allegan *MI-3*
Salem (Township)—Washtenaw..... *MI-3*
Salem (Township)—Cass *MN-3*
Salem (Township)—Olmsted......... *MN-3*
Salem (Township)—Daviess.......... *MO-3*
Salem (City)—Dent *MO-3*
Salem (Township)—Dunklin *MO-3*
Salem (Township)—Lewis *MO-3*
Salem (Township)—Perry.............. *MO-3*
Salem (Township)—Franklin *NE-4*
Salem (Village)—Richardson *NE-4*
Salem (Town)—Rockingham.........*NH-1*
Salem (City)—Salem *NJ-1*
Salem (Town)—Washington *NY-1*
Salem (Village)—Washington *NY-1*
Salem (CDP)—Burke *NC-2*
Salem (Township)—Auglaize *OH-3*
Salem (Township)—Champaign.....*OH-3*
Salem (City)—Columbiana............*OH-3*
Salem (Township)—Columbiana ...*OH-3*
Salem (Township)—Highland *OH-3*
Salem (Township)—Jefferson........*OH-3*
Salem (Township)—Meigs..............*OH-3*
Salem (Township)—Monroe *OH-3*
Salem (Township)—Muskingum *OH-3*
Salem (Township)—Ottawa *OH-3*
Salem (Township)—Shelby............*OH-3*
Salem (Township)—Tuscarawas.....*OH-3*
Salem (Township)—Warren *OH-3*
Salem (Township)—Washington ...*OH-3*
Salem (Township)—Wyandot *OH-3*
Salem (City)—Marion *OR-4*
Salem (City)—Polk........................ *OR-4*
Salem (Township)—Clarion *PA-1*

Salem (Township)—Luzerne *PA-1*
Salem (Township)—Mercer............ *PA-1*
Salem (Township)—Wayne *PA-1*
Salem (Township)—
  Westmoreland *PA-1*
Salem (Town)—Oconee *SC-2*
Salem (City)—McCook *SD-4*
Salem (Township)—McCook *SD-4*
Salem (Township)—Turner *SD-4*
Salem (City)—Utah *UT-4*
Salem (City)—Harrison *WV-2*
Salem (Town)—Kenosha *WI-3*
Salem (Town)—Pierce................... *WI-3*
Salemburg (Town)—Sampson *NC-2*
Salem County *NJ-1*
Salem (Independent City) *VA-2*
Salesville (Town)—Baxter *AR-2*
Salesville (Village)—Guernsey *OH-3*
Salford (Township)—Montgomery.. *PA-1*
Salida (CDP)—Stanislaus *CA-4*
Salida (City)—Chaffee.................... *CO-4*
Salina (Township)—Kankakee *IL-3*
Salina (City)—Saline *KS-4*
Salina (Town)—Onondaga *NY-1*
Salina (Town)—Mayes *OK-2*
Salina (City)—Sevier *UT-4*
Salinas (City)—Monterey *CA-4*
Saline (Township)—Madison *IL-3*
Saline (Village)—Bienville Parish ...*LA-2*
Saline (City)—Washtenaw.............. *MI-3*
Saline (Township)—Washtenaw..... *MI-3*
Saline (Township)—Cooper *MO-3*
Saline (Township)—Miller *MO-3*
Saline (Township)—Perry *MO-3*
Saline (Township)—Ralls *MO-3*
Saline (Township)—Ste.
  Genevieve *MO-3*
Saline (Township)—McHenry *ND-4*
Saline (Township)—Jefferson..........*OH-3*
Saline County *AR-2*
Saline County *IL-3*
Saline County *KS-4*
Saline County *MO-3*
Saline County *NE-4*
Salineville (Village)—
  Columbiana................................ *OH-3*
Salineville (Village)—Jefferson *OH-3*
Saling (Township)—Audrain *MO-3*
Salisbury (Town)—Litchfield *CT-1*
Salisbury (City)—Wicomico........... *MD-1*
Salisbury (Town)—Essex *MA-1*
Salisbury (City)—Chariton *MO-3*
Salisbury (Township)—Chariton....*MO-3*
Salisbury (Town)—Merrimack *NH-1*
Salisbury (Town)—Herkimer *NY-1*
Salisbury (CDP)—Nassau *NY-1*
Salisbury (City)—Rowan................ *NC-2*
Salisbury (Township)—Meigs.........*OH-3*
Salisbury (Township)—Lancaster.... *PA-1*
Salisbury (Township)—Lehigh *PA-1*
Salisbury (Borough)—Somerset *PA-1*
Salisbury (Town)—Addison *VT-1*
Salix (City)—Woodbury *IA-3*
Salladasburg (Borough)—
  Lycoming.................................... *PA-1*
Salley (Town)—Aiken.....................*SC-2*
Sallis (Town)—Attala *MS-2*
Sallisaw (City)—Sequoyah *OK-2*
Salmon (City)—Lemhi *ID-4*
Salmon Brook (CDP)—Hartford ... *CT-1*
Salmon Creek (CDP)—Clark *WA-1*
Salmon River (ID) *Geog-4*
Salo (Township)—Aitkin *MN-3*
Saltaire (Village)—Suffolk *NY-1*
Salt Creek (Township)—Mason *IL-3*

Salt Creek (Township)—Decatur *IN-3*
Salt Creek (Township)—Franklin ... *IN-3*
Salt Creek (Township)—Jackson... *IN-3*
Salt Creek (Township)—Monroe *IN-3*
Salt Creek (Township)—
  Chautauqua................................*KS-4*
Salt Creek (Township)—Lincoln *KS-4*
Salt Creek (Township)—Mitchell....*KS-4*
Salt Creek (Township)—Reno........*KS-4*
Salt Creek (Township)—
  Chariton *MO-3*
Salt Creek (Township)—Hocking...*OH-3*
Salt Creek (Township)—Holmes....*OH-3*
Salt Creek (Township)—
  Muskingum *OH-3*
Salt Creek (Township)—
  Pickaway *OH-3*
Salt Creek (Township)—Wayne *OH-3*
Salt Fork (Township)—Saline *MO-3*
Saltillo (Town)—Washington *IN-3*
Saltillo (Town)—Lee......................*MS-2*
Saltillo (Borough)—Huntingdon *PA-1*
Saltillo (Town)—Hardin................. *TN-2*
Salt Lake City (City)—Salt Lake ... *UT-4*
Salt Lake County *UT-4*
Salt Lick (City)—Bath.................... *KY-2*
Salt Lick (Township)—Perry..........*OH-3*
Saltlick (Township)—Fayette *PA-1*
Salton Sea (CA)............................ *Geog-4*
Salt Pond (Township)—Saline *MO-3*
Salt River (Township)—Adair *MO-3*
Salt River (Township)—Audrain .. *MO-3*
Salt River (Township)—Knox *MO-3*
Salt River (Township)—Pike *MO-3*
Salt River (Township)—Ralls........ *MO-3*
Salt River (Township)—
  Randolph *MO-3*
Salt River (Township)—Schuyler .. *MO-3*
Salt River (Township)—Shelby *MO-3*
Salt River Reservation (AZ)...... *IndRes-4*
Salt Rock (Township)—Marion *OH-3*
Saltsburg (Borough)—Indiana *PA-1*
Salt Springs (Township)—
  Greenwood.................................*KS-4*
Salt Springs (Township)—
  Randolph *MO-3*
Saltville (Town)—Smyth *VA-2*
Saltville (Town)—Washington......... *VA-2*
Saluda (Township)—Jefferson........ *IN-3*
Saluda (City)—Henderson *NC-2*
Saluda (City)—Polk....................... *NC-2*
Saluda (Town)—Saluda *SC-2*
Saluda County *SC-2*
Salyersville (City)—Magoffin......... *KY-2*
Samburg (Town)—Obion *TN-2*
Samoset (CDP)—Manatee *FL-2*
Sampsel (Township)—
  Livingston *MO-3*
Sampson (Town)—Chippewa.......... *WI-3*
Sampson County *NC-2*
Samson (City)—Geneva.................*AL-2*
Samsula-Spruce Creek (CDP)—
  Volusia *FL-2*
San Andreas (CDP)—Calaveras *CA-4*
San Andreas Fault *or* San
  Andreas Rift Zone (CA) *Geog-4*
San Angelo (City)—Tom Green..... *TX-2*
San Anselmo (Town)—Marin *CA-4*
San Antonio (City)—Pasco *FL-2*
San Antonio (City)—Bexar............ *TX-2*
San Antonio Heights (CDP)—San
  Bernardino *CA-4*
San Augustine (Town)—San
  Augustine *TX-2*
San Augustine County *TX-2*

General Index   American Places Dictionary

San Benito (City)—Cameron *TX-2*
San Benito County *CA-4*
San Bernardino (City)—San
 Bernardino *CA-4*
San Bernardino County *CA-4*
Sanborn (City)—O'Brien *IA-3*
Sanborn (Township)—Alpena *MI-3*
Sanborn (City)—Redwood *MN-3*
Sanborn (City)—Barnes *ND-4*
Sanborn (Town)—Ashland *WI-3*
Sanborn County *SD-4*
Sanbornton (Town)—Belknap *NH-1*
San Bruno (City)—San Mateo *CA-4*
San Buenaventura (Ventura) (City)—
 Ventura *CA-4*
San Carlos (CDP)—Gila *AZ-4*
San Carlos (City)—San Mateo *CA-4*
San Carlos Park (CDP)—Lee *FL-2*
San Carlos Reservation (AZ) ... *IndRes-4*
San Clemente (City)—Orange *CA-4*
Sanctuary (Town)—Parker *TX-2*
Sandalfoot Cove (CDP)—Palm
 Beach *FL-2*
Sand Beach (Township)—Huron ... *MI-3*
Sandborn (Town)—Knox *IN-3*
Sand City (City)—Monterey *CA-4*
Sand Creek (Township)—
 Bartholomew *IN-3*
Sand Creek (Township)—Decatur . *IN-3*
Sand Creek (Township)—
 Jennings *IN-3*
Sand Creek (Township)—Meade ... *KS-4*
Sand Creek (Township)—Scott *MN-3*
Sand Creek (Township)—Holt *NE-4*
Sand Creek (Township)—Slope *ND-4*
Sand Creek (Township)—Beadle ... *SD-4*
Sand Creek (Town)—Dunn *WI-3*
Sanders (City)—Carroll *KY-2*
Sanders (Township)—
 Pennington *MN-3*
Sanders County *MT-4*
Sanderson (CDP)—Terrell *TX-2*
Sandersville (City)—Washington ... *GA-2*
Sandersville (Town)—Jones *MS-2*
Sand Fork (Town)—Gilmer *WV-2*
Sandgate (Town)—Bennington *VT-1*
Sand Hill (Township)—Scotland ... *MO-3*
Sand Hills (NE) *Geog-4*
Sandia (CDP)—Bernalillo *NM-4*
Sandia Heights (CDP)—
 Bernalillo *NM-4*
Sandia Pueblo (NM) *IndRes-4*
San Diego (City)—San Diego *CA-4*
San Diego (City)—Duval *TX-2*
San Diego (City)—Jim Wells *TX-2*
San Diego Country Estates (CDP)—San
 Diego *CA-4*
San Diego County *CA-4*
San Diego Marine Corps Recruit Depot
 (CA) *Mil-4*
San Diego Naval Station (CA) *Mil-4*
San Diego Naval Submarine Base
 (CA) *Mil-4*
San Dimas (City)—Los Angeles *CA-4*
Sandisfield (Town)—Berkshire *MA-1*
Sand Lake (Village)—Kent *MI-3*
Sand Lake (Township)—Itasca *MN-3*
Sand Lake (Pop. Place)—St.
 Louis *MN-3*
Sand Lake (Town)—Rensselaer *NY-1*
Sand Lake (Town)—Burnett *WI-3*
Sand Lake (Town)—Sawyer *WI-3*
Sandnes (Township)—Yellow
 Medicine *MN-3*
Sandoun (Township)—Ransom *ND-4*

Sandoval (Town)—Marion *IL-3*
Sandoval (Township)—Marion *IL-3*
Sandoval County *NM-4*
Sandown (Town)—Rockingham *NH-1*
Sand Point (City)—Aleutians East
 Borough *AK-4*
Sandpoint (City)—Bonner *ID-4*
Sand Prairie (Township)—
 Tazewell *IL-3*
Sand Ridge (Township)—Jackson ... *IL-3*
Sand Ridge (CDP)—Oswego *NY-1*
Sand Rock (Municipality)—
 Cherokee *AL-2*
Sand Rock (Municipality)—
 DeKalb *AL-2*
Sands (Township)—Marquette *MI-3*
Sands Point (Village)—Nassau *NY-1*
Sand Springs (City)—Osage *OK-2*
Sand Springs (City)—Tulsa *OK-2*
Sandstone (Township)—Jackson ... *MI-3*
Sandstone (City)—Pine *MN-3*
Sandstone (Township)—Pine *MN-3*
Sandstone Hills (OK) *Geog-4*
Sandsville (Township)—Polk *MN-3*
Sandusky (City)—Sanilac *MI-3*
Sandusky (Township)—Crawford .. *OH-3*
Sandusky (City)—Erie *OH-3*
Sandusky (Township)—Richland ... *OH-3*
Sandusky (Township)—Sandusky .. *OH-3*
Sandusky County *OH-3*
Sandusky South (CDP)—Erie *OH-3*
Sandwich (Town)—DeKalb *IL-3*
Sandwich (Township)—DeKalb *IL-3*
Sandwich (Town)—Kendall *IL-3*
Sandwich (Town)—Barnstable *MA-1*
Sandwich (Town)—Carroll *NH-1*
Sandy (Township)—St. Louis *MN-3*
Sandy (Township)—Stark *OH-3*
Sandy (Township)—Tuscarawas *OH-3*
Sandy (City)—Clackamas *OR-4*
Sandy (Township)—Clearfield *PA-1*
Sandy (City)—Salt Lake *UT-4*
Sandy Creek (Town)—Oswego *NY-1*
Sandy Creek (Village)—Oswego *NY-1*
Sandy Creek (Town)—Brunswick .. *NC-2*
Sandy Creek (Township)—Mercer .. *PA-1*
Sandycreek (Township)—Venango .. *PA-1*
Sandy Hook (City)—Elliott *KY-2*
Sandy Hook (NJ) *Geog-4*
Sandy Lake (Borough)—Mercer *PA-1*
Sandy Lake (Township)—Mercer ... *PA-1*
Sandy Lake Reservation
 (MN) *IndRes-4*
Sandy River (Pop. Place)—
 Franklin *ME-1*
Sandy Springs (CDP)—Fulton *GA-2*
Sandyston (Township)—Sussex *NJ-1*
Sandyville (City)—Warren *IA-3*
Sandywoods (Township)—Scott ... *MO-3*
San Elizario (CDP)—El Paso *TX-2*
San Felipe (Town)—Austin *TX-2*
San Felipe Pueblo (NM) *IndRes-4*
San Felipe Pueblo (CDP)—
 Sandoval *NM-4*
San Fernando (City)—Los
 Angeles *CA-4*
Sanford (Municipality)—
 Covington *AL-2*
Sanford (Town)—Conejos *CO-4*
Sanford (City)—Seminole *FL-2*
Sanford (Town)—York *ME-1*
Sanford (Village)—Midland *MI-3*
Sanford (Township)—Grant *MN-3*
Sanford (Town)—Broome *NY-1*
Sanford (City)—Lee *NC-2*

Sanford (Town)—Hutchinson *TX-2*
San Francisco (City)—San
 Francisco *CA-4*
San Francisco (Township)—
 Carver *MN-3*
San Francisco Bay (CA) *Geog-4*
San Francisco County *CA-4*
San Gabriel (City)—Los Angeles .. *CA-4*
Sangamon (Township)—Piatt *IL-3*
Sangamon (Township)—
 Edmunds *SD-4*
Sangamon County *IL-3*
Sangamon Valley (Township)—
 Cass *IL-3*
Sanger (City)—Fresno *CA-4*
Sanger (City)—Denton *TX-2*
Sangerfield (Town)—Oneida *NY-1*
Sangerville (Town)—Piscataquis ... *ME-1*
Sangre de Cristo Mountains
 (CA) *Geog-4*
Sanibel (City)—Lee *FL-2*
Sanibel Island (FL) *Geog-4*
Sanilac (Township)—Sanilac *MI-3*
Sanilac County *MI-3*
San Ildefonso Pueblo (NM) *IndRes-4*
San Ildefonso Pueblo (CDP)—Santa
 Fe *NM-4*
San Jacinto (City)—Riverside *CA-4*
San Jacinto County *TX-2*
San Joaquin (City)—Fresno *CA-4*
San Joaquin County *CA-4*
San Joaquin River (CA) *Geog-4*
San Joaquin Valley (CA) *Geog-4*
San Jon (Village)—Quay *NM-4*
San Jose (City)—Santa Clara *CA-4*
San Jose (Village)—Logan *IL-3*
San Jose (Village)—Mason *IL-3*
San Juan (CDP)—Rio Arriba *NM-4*
San Juan (City)—Hidalgo *TX-2*
San Juan Bautista (City)—San
 Benito *CA-4*
San Juan Capistrano (City)—
 Orange *CA-4*
San Juan County *CO-4*
San Juan County *NM-4*
San Juan County *UT-4*
San Juan County *WA-4*
San Juan Islands (WA) *Geog-4*
San Juan Mountains (WA) *Geog-4*
San Juan Pueblo (NM) *IndRes-4*
San Juan River (WA) *Geog-4*
Sankertown (Borough)—Cambria ... *PA-1*
San Leandro (City)—Alameda *CA-4*
San Leanna (Village)—Travis *TX-2*
San Leon (CDP)—Galveston *TX-2*
San Lorenzo (CDP)—Alameda *CA-4*
San Luis (Town)—Yuma *AZ-4*
San Luis (Town)—Costilla *CO-4*
San Luis Obispo (City)—San Luis
 Obispo *CA-4*
San Luis Obispo County *CA-4*
San Manuel (CDP)—Pinal *AZ-4*
San Manuel Reservation
 (CA) *IndRes-4*
San Marcos (City)—San Diego *CA-4*
San Marcos (City)—Caldwell *TX-2*
San Marcos (City)—Hays *TX-2*
San Marino (City)—Los Angeles .. *CA-4*
San Martin (CDP)—Santa Clara ... *CA-4*
San Mateo (City)—San Mateo *CA-4*
San Mateo County *CA-4*
San Miguel (CDP)—San Luis
 Obispo *CA-4*
San Miguel County *CO-4*
San Miguel County *NM-4*

1086

American Places Dictionary — General Index

Sanostee (CDP)—San Juan............ *NM-4*
San Pablo (City)—Contra Costa.... *CA-4*
San Pasqual Reservation
  (CA)..*IndRes-4*
San Patricio (City)—San Patricio.. *TX-2*
San Patricio County *TX-2*
San Perlita (City)—Willacy............ *TX-2*
Sanpete County *UT-4*
San Rafael (City)—Marin *CA-4*
San Ramon (City)—Contra
  Costa *CA-4*
San Saba (Town)—San Saba *TX-2*
San Saba County *TX-2*
Sansom Park (City)—Tarrant *TX-2*
Sans Souci (CDP)—Greenville *SC-2*
Santa Ana (City)—Orange *CA-4*
Santa Ana Pueblo (NM)........... *IndRes-4*
Santa Ana Pueblo (CDP)—
  Sandoval.. *NM-4*
Santa Anna (Township)—De Witt.. *IL-3*
Santa Anna (Town)—Coleman *TX-2*
Santa Barbara (City)—Santa
  Barbara... *CA-4*
Santa Barbara County *CA-4*
Santa Catalina, Gulf of (CA)....... *Geog-4*
Santa Catalina Island (CA) *Geog-4*
Santa Clara (City)—Santa Clara.... *CA-4*
Santa Clara (Town)—Franklin........ *NY-1*
Santa Clara (CDP)—Lane............... *OR-4*
Santa Clara (City)—Washington.... *UT-4*
Santa Clara County *CA-4*
Santa Clara Pueblo (NM)......... *IndRes-4*
Santa Clara Pueblo (CDP)—Rio
  Arriba..*NM-4*
Santa Clarita (City)—Los
  Angeles..*CA-4*
Santa Claus (City)—Toombs.......... *GA-2*
Santa Claus (Town)—Spencer......... *IN-3*
Santa Cruz (City)—Santa Cruz...... *CA-4*
Santa Cruz (CDP)—Santa Fe........ *NM-4*
Santa Cruz County *AZ-4*
Santa Cruz County *CA-4*
Santa Fe (Township)—Clinton........ *IL-3*
Santa Fe (Township)—Pawnee........*KS-4*
Santa Fe (City)—Santa Fe............. *NM-4*
Santa Fe (City)—Galveston *TX-2*
Santa Fe County *NM-4*
Santa Fe Springs (City)—Los
  Angeles..*CA-4*
Santa Fe Trail (CA) *Geog-4*
Santa Maria (City)—Santa
  Barbara... *CA-4*
Santa Monica (City)—Los
  Angeles..*CA-4*
Santan (CDP)—Pinal *AZ-4*
Santa Paula (City)—Ventura.......... *CA-4*
Santaquin (City)—Utah *UT-4*
Santa Rosa (CDP)—Pima *AZ-4*
Santa Rosa (City)—Sonoma *CA-4*
Santa Rosa (City)—Guadalupe..... *NM-4*
Santa Rosa (Town)—Cameron....... *TX-2*
Santa Rosa County *FL-2*
Santa Rosa Rancheria (CA) *IndRes-4*
Santa Rosa Reservation (CA)... *IndRes-4*
Santa Venetia (CDP)—Marin *CA-4*
Santa Ynez (CDP)—Santa
  Barbara... *CA-4*
Santa Ynez Reservation (CA) .. *IndRes-4*
Santa Ysabel Reservation
  (CA)..*IndRes-4*
Santee (City)—San Diego.............. *CA-4*
Santee (Township)—Knox *NE-4*
Santee (Village)—Knox *NE-4*
Santee (Town)—Orangeburg *SC-2*
Santee Reservation (NE) *IndRes-4*

Santee Reservoir (CA) *Geog-4*
Santee River (SC) *Geog-4*
Santeetlah (Town)—Graham.......... *NC-2*
Santiago (Township)—Sherburne.. *MN-3*
Santo Domingo Pueblo (NM) .. *IndRes-4*
Santo Domingo Pueblo (CDP)—
  Sandoval..*NM-4*
San Xavier Reservation (AZ)... *IndRes-4*
San Ysidro (Village)—Sandoval.... *NM-4*
Sappa (Township)—Decatur *KS-4*
Sappa (Township)—Harlan *NE-4*
Sappington (CDP)—St. Louis....... *MO-3*
Sapulpa (City)—Creek................... *OK-2*
Sarahsville (Village)—Noble *OH-3*
Saraland (City)—Mobile *AL-2*
Saranac (Village)—Ionia................. *MI-3*
Saranac (Town)—Clinton *NY-1*
Saranac Lake (Village)—Essex *NY-1*
Saranac Lake (Village)—Franklin.. *NY-1*
Sarasota (City)—Sarasota................*FL-2*
Sarasota County *FL-2*
Sarasota Springs (CDP)—
  Sarasota *FL-2*
Saratoga (City)—Santa Clara *CA-4*
Saratoga (Township)—Grundy. *IL-3*
Saratoga (Township)—Marshall...... *IL-3*
Saratoga (Town)—Randolph *IN-3*
Saratoga (Township)—Winona *MN-3*
Saratoga (Township)—Holt *NE-4*
Saratoga (Town)—Saratoga *NY-1*
Saratoga (Town)—Wilson *NC-2*
Saratoga (Township)—LaMoure *ND-4*
Saratoga (Township)—Faulk *SD-4*
Saratoga (Town)—Wood *WI-3*
Saratoga (Town)—Carbon *WY-4*
Saratoga County *NY-1*
Saratoga Springs (City)—
  Saratoga *NY-1*
Sarcoxie (Township)—Jefferson......*KS-4*
Sarcoxie (City)—Jasper *MO-3*
Sarcoxie (Township)—Jasper *MO-3*
Sardinia (Town)—Erie *NY-1*
Sardinia (Village)—Brown *OH-3*
Sardis (Town)—Burke *GA-2*
Sardis (City)—Mason *KY-2*
Sardis (Town)—Panola................... *MS-2*
Sardis (Town)—Henderson *TN-2*
Sardis City (City)—DeKalb *AL-2*
Sardis City (City)—Etowah............ *AL-2*
Sardis City (City)—Marshall.......... *AL-2*
Sardis Dam (MS) *Geog-4*
Sarepta (Village)—Webster
  Parish *LA-2*
Sargeant (City)—Mower............... *MN-3*
Sargeant (Township)—Mower....... *MN-3*
Sargent (Township)—Douglas *IL-3*
Sargent (Township)—Texas *MO-3*
Sargent (City)—Custer *NE-4*
Sargent (Township)—Custer *NE-4*
Sargent (Township)—Sargent *ND-4*
Sargent County *ND-4*
Sargents Purchase (Pop. Place)—
  Coos *NH-1*
Sarita (Pop. Place)—Kenedy *TX-2*
Sarles (City)—Cavalier...................*ND-4*
Sarles (City)—Towner *ND-4*
Sarnia (Township)—Nelson *ND-4*
Sarona (Town)—Washburn *WI-3*
Saronville (Village)—Clay *NE-4*
Sarpy County *NE-4*
Sartell (City)—Benton *MN-3*
Sartell (City)—Stearns *MN-3*
Sartoria (Township)—Buffalo *NE-4*
Sasakwa (Town)—Seminole *OK-2*
Sassafras Mountain (SC) *Geog-4*

Sasser (Town)—Terrell *GA-2*
Satanta (City)—Haskell...................*KS-4*
Satartia (Village)—Yazoo *MS-2*
Satellite Beach (City)—Brevard *FL-2*
Satsuma (City)—Mobile.................. *AL-2*
Satus (CDP)—Yakima..................... *WA-4*
Sauble (Township)—Lake *MI-3*
Saugatuck (Township)—Allegan *MI-3*
Saugatuck (Village)—Allegan *MI-3*
Saugerties (Town)—Ulster.............. *NY-1*
Saugerties (Village)—Ulster *NY-1*
Saugerties South (CDP)—Ulster.... *NY-1*
Sauget (Village)—St. Clair *IL-3*
Saugus (Town)—Essex *MA-1*
Sauk Centre (City)—Stearns *MN-3*
Sauk Centre (Township)—
  Stearns..*MN-3*
Sauk City (Village)—Sauk............. *WI-3*
Sauk County *WI-3*
Sauk Prairie (Township)—Ward *ND-4*
Sauk Rapids (City)—Benton *MN-3*
Sauk Rapids (Township)—
  Benton *MN-3*
Sauk-Suiattle Reservation
  (WA) *IndRes-4*
Sauk Valley (Township)—
  Williams *ND-4*
Sauk Village (Village)—Cook.......... *IL-3*
Sauk Village (Village)—Will *IL-3*
Saukville (Town)—Ozaukee *WI-3*
Saukville (Village)—Ozaukee *WI-3*
Saulsbury (Town)—Hardeman........ *TN-2*
Sault Sainte Marie Canals (MI) .. *Geog-4*
Sault Ste. Marie (City)—
  Chippewa *MI-3*
Sault Ste. Marie Res. & Trust Lands
  (MI) *IndRes-4*
Saunders County *NE-4*
Saunemin (Township)—
  Livingston *IL-3*
Saunemin (Village)—Livingston *IL-3*
Sausalito (City)—Marin *CA-4*
Sauter (Township)—Walsh *ND-4*
Savage (City)—Scott..................... *MN-3*
Savage-Guilford (CDP)—
  Howard *MD-1*
Savanna (Town)—Carroll................. *IL-3*
Savanna (Township)—Carroll *IL-3*
Savanna (Town)—Pittsburg *OK-2*
Savannah (City)—Chatham *GA-2*
Savannah (Township)—Becker *MN-3*
Savannah (City)—Andrew.............. *MO-3*
Savannah (Township)—Butler *NE-4*
Savannah (Town)—Wayne *NY-1*
Savannah (Village)—Ashland..........*OH-3*
Savannah (City)—Hardin................ *TN-2*
Savannah River (GA) *Geog-4*
Saverton (Township)—Ralls.......... *MO-3*
Saville (Township)—Perry.............. *PA-1*
Savo (Township)—Brown *SD-4*
Savona (Village)—Steuben *NY-1*
Savonburg (City)—Allen *KS-4*
Savoonga (City)—Nome Census
  Area *AK-4*
Savoy (Town)—Champaign............. *IL-3*
Savoy (Town)—Berkshire *MA-1*
Savoy (City)—Fannin *TX-2*
Sawatch Range (CO).................... *Geog-4*
Sawgrass (CDP)—St. Johns.............*FL-2*
Sawlog (Township)—Hodgeman *KS-4*
Sawmill (CDP)—Apache *AZ-4*
Sawmill (Township)—Pawnee........*KS-4*
Sawmills (Town)—Caldwell *NC-2*
Sawpit (Town)—San Miguel *CO-4*
Sawyer (City)—Pratt *KS-4*

General Index | American Places Dictionary

Sawyer (City)—Ward ND-4
Sawyer (Township)—Ward ND-4
Sawyer County WI-3
Sawyerville (Village)—Macoupin IL-3
Saxapahaw (CDP)—Alamance NC-2
Saxeville (Town)—Waushara WI-3
Saxis (Town)—Accomack VA-2
Saxman (City)—Ketchikan Gateway
    Borough AK-4
Saxon (CDP)—Spartanburg SC-2
Saxon (Town)—Iron WI-3
Saxonburg (Borough)—Butler PA-1
Saxton (Borough)—Bedford PA-1
Saxtons River (Village)—
    Windham VT-1
Saybrook (Village)—McLean IL-3
Saybrook (Township)—
    Ashtabula OH-3
Saylorville (CDP)—Polk IA-3
Sayre (City)—Beckham OK-2
Sayre (Borough)—Bradford PA-1
Sayreville (Borough)—Middlesex NJ-1
Sayville (CDP)—Suffolk NY-1
Scales Mound (Township)—Jo
    Daviess IL-3
Scales Mound (Village)—Jo
    Daviess IL-3
Scalp Level (Borough)—Cambria ... PA-1
Scambler (Township)—Otter
    Tail MN-3
Scammon (City)—Cherokee KS-4
Scammon Bay (City)—Wade Hampton
    Census Area AK-4
Scandia (City)—Republic KS-4
Scandia (Township)—Republic KS-4
Scandia (Township)—Polk MN-3
Scandia (Township)—Bottineau ND-4
Scandia Valley (Township)—
    Morrison MN-3
Scandinavia (Township)—Harlan .. NE-4
Scandinavia (Township)—Deuel SD-4
Scandinavia (Town)—Waupaca WI-3
Scandinavia (Village)—Waupaca ... WI-3
Scanlon (City)—Carlton MN-3
Scappoose (City)—Columbia OR-4
Scarborough (Town)—
    Cumberland ME-1
Scarsdale (Village & Town)—
    Westchester NY-1
Scarville (City)—Winnebago IA-3
Scenic No. 7 (Township)—
    Pennington SD-4
Scenic Oaks (CDP)—Bexar TX-2
Schaghticoke (Town)—
    Rensselaer NY-1
Schaghticoke (Village)—
    Rensselaer NY-1
Schaghticoke Reservation
    (CT) IndRes-4
Schaller (City)—Sac IA-3
Schaumburg (Township)—Cook IL-3
Schaumburg (Village)—Cook IL-3
Schaumburg (Village)—DuPage IL-3
Schell City (City)—Vernon MO-3
Schellsburg (Borough)—Bedford PA-1
Schenectady (City)—Schenectady .. NY-1
Schenectady County NY-1
Schenevus (Village)—Otsego NY-1
Schererville (Town)—Lake IN-3
Schertz (City)—Bexar TX-2
Schertz (City)—Comal TX-2
Schertz (City)—Guadalupe TX-2
Schiller (Township)—McHenry ND-4
Schiller Park (Village)—Cook IL-3
Schlater (Town)—Leflore MS-2

Schleicher County TX-2
Schleswig (City)—Crawford IA-3
Schleswig (Town)—Manitowoc WI-3
Schley (Town)—Lincoln WI-3
Schley County GA-2
Schneider (Town)—Lake IN-3
Schneider (Township)—Buffalo NE-4
Schodack (Town)—Rensselaer NY-1
Schoenchen (City)—Ellis KS-4
Schoepke (Town)—Oneida WI-3
Schofield (City)—Marathon WI-3
Schofield Barracks (HI) Mil-4
Schofield Barracks (CDP)—
    Honolulu HI-4
Schoharie (Town)—Schoharie NY-1
Schoharie (Village)—Schoharie NY-1
Schoharie County NY-1
Schoolcraft (Township)—
    Houghton MI-3
Schoolcraft (Township)—
    Kalamazoo MI-3
Schoolcraft (Village)—
    Kalamazoo MI-3
Schoolcraft (Township)—
    Hubbard MN-3
Schoolcraft County MI-3
School Creek (Township)—Clay NE-4
Schram City (Village)—
    Montgomery IL-3
Schriever (CDP)—Terrebonne
    Parish LA-2
Schriever (Township)—Gregory SD-4
Schroeder (Township)—Cook MN-3
Schroeppel (Town)—Oswego NY-1
Schroon (Town)—Essex NY-1
Schrunk (Township)—Burleigh ND-4
Schulenburg (City)—Fayette TX-2
Schultz (Township)—Grant ND-4
Schurz (CDP)—Mineral NV-4
Schuyler (City)—Colfax NE-4
Schuyler (Town)—Herkimer NY-1
Schuyler County IL-3
Schuyler County MO-3
Schuyler County NY-1
Schuyler Falls (Town)—Clinton NY-1
Schuylerville (Village)—Saratoga .. NY-1
Schuylkill (Township)—Chester PA-1
Schuylkill (Township)—Schuylkill .. PA-1
Schuylkill County PA-1
Schuylkill Haven (Borough)—
    Schuylkill PA-1
Schuylkill River (PA) Geog-4
Schwenksville (Borough)—
    Montgomery PA-1
Science Hill (City)—Pulaski KY-2
Scio (Township)—Washtenaw MI-3
Scio (Town)—Allegany NY-1
Scio (Village)—Harrison OH-3
Scio (City)—Linn OR-4
Sciota (Township)—McDonough ... IL-3
Sciota (Village)—McDonough IL-3
Sciota (Township)—Shiawassee MI-3
Sciota (Township)—Dakota MN-3
Scioto (Township)—Delaware OH-3
Scioto (Township)—Jackson OH-3
Scioto (Township)—Pickaway OH-3
Scioto (Township)—Pike OH-3
Scioto (Township)—Ross OH-3
Scioto County OH-3
Sciotodale (CDP)—Scioto OH-3
Scipio (Township)—Allen IN-3
Scipio (Township)—La Porte IN-3
Scipio (Township)—Hillsdale MI-3
Scipio (Town)—Cayuga NY-1
Scipio (Township)—Meigs OH-3

Scipio (Township)—Seneca OH-3
Scipio (Town)—Millard UT-4
Scissors (CDP)—Hidalgo TX-2
Scituate (Town)—Plymouth MA-1
Scituate (Town)—Providence RI-1
Scobey (City)—Daniels MT-4
Scofield (Town)—Carbon UT-4
Scooba (Town)—Kemper MS-2
Scopus (Township)—Bollinger MO-3
Scorio (Township)—Williams ND-4
Scotch Cap (Township)—Perkins .. SD-4
Scotch Plains (Township)—
    Union NJ-1
Scotchtown (CDP)—Orange NY-1
Scotia (Village)—Greeley NE-4
Scotia (Village)—Schenectady NY-1
Scotia (Township)—Bottineau ND-4
Scotia (Town)—Hampton SC-2
Scotland (Town)—Windham CT-1
Scotland (City)—Telfair GA-2
Scotland (City)—Wheeler GA-2
Scotland (Township)—
    McDonough IL-3
Scotland (City)—Bon Homme SD-4
Scotland (Township)—Day SD-4
Scotland (City)—Archer TX-2
Scotland (City)—Clay TX-2
Scotland County MO-3
Scotland County NC-2
Scotland Neck (Town)—Halifax NC-2
Scotsdale (Town)—Jefferson MO-3
Scott (Township)—Champaign IL-3
Scott (Township)—Ogle IL-3
Scott (Township)—Kosciusko IN-3
Scott (Township)—Montgomery ... IN-3
Scott (Township)—Steuben IN-3
Scott (Township)—Vanderburgh ... IN-3
Scott (Township)—Bourbon KS-4
Scott (Township)—Lincoln KS-4
Scott (Township)—Linn KS-4
Scott (Township)—Scott KS-4
Scott (Town)—Lafayette Parish LA-2
Scott (Township)—Stevens MN-3
Scott (Township)—Taney MO-3
Scott (Township)—Buffalo NE-4
Scott (Township)—Holt NE-4
Scott (Town)—Cortland NY-1
Scott (Township)—Adams ND-4
Scott (Township)—Adams OH-3
Scott (Township)—Brown OH-3
Scott (Township)—Marion OH-3
Scott (Village)—Paulding OH-3
Scott (Township)—Sandusky OH-3
Scott (Village)—Van Wert OH-3
Scott (Township)—Allegheny PA-1
Scott (Township)—Columbia PA-1
Scott (Township)—Lackawanna PA-1
Scott (Township)—Lawrence PA-1
Scott (Township)—Wayne PA-1
Scott (Town)—Brown WI-3
Scott (Town)—Burnett WI-3
Scott (Town)—Columbia WI-3
Scott (Town)—Crawford WI-3
Scott (Town)—Lincoln WI-3
Scott (Town)—Monroe WI-3
Scott (Town)—Sheboygan WI-3
Scott Air Force Base (IL) Mil-4
Scott City (City)—Scott KS-4
Scott City (City)—Cape
    Girardeau MO-3
Scott City (City)—Scott MO-3
Scott County AR-2
Scott County IL-3
Scott County IN-3
Scott County IA-3

American Places Dictionary — General Index

Scott County KS-4
Scott County KY-2
Scott County MN-3
Scott County MS-2
Scott County MO-3
Scott County TN-2
Scott County VA-2
Scottdale (CDP)—De Kalb GA-2
Scottdale (Borough)—
  Westmoreland PA-1
Scott Lake (CDP)—Dade FL-2
Scottsbluff (City)—Scotts Bluff NE-4
Scotts Bluff County NE-4
Scottsboro (City)—Jackson AL-2
Scottsburg (City)—Scott IN-3
Scottsburg (Town)—Halifax VA-2
Scottsdale (City)—Maricopa AZ-4
Scotts Hill (Town)—Decatur TN-2
Scotts Hill (Town)—Henderson TN-2
Scotts Mills (City)—Marion OR-4
Scotts Valley (City)—Santa Cruz CA-4
Scottsville (City)—Mitchell KS-4
Scottsville (City)—Allen KY-2
Scottsville (Village)—Monroe NY-1
Scottsville (City)—Harrison TX-2
Scottsville (Town)—Albemarle VA-2
Scottsville (Town)—Fluvanna VA-2
Scottville (Township)—Macoupin IL-3
Scottville (Village)—Macoupin IL-3
Scottville (City)—Mason MI-3
Scovil (Township)—Jones SD-4
Scoville (Township)—Ransom ND-4
Scranton (City)—Logan AR-2
Scranton (City)—Greene IA-3
Scranton (City)—Osage KS-4
Scranton (Township)—Osage KS-4
Scranton (City)—Bowman ND-4
Scranton (Township)—Bowman ND-4
Scranton (City)—Lackawanna PA-1
Scranton (Town)—Florence SC-2
Screven (City)—Wayne GA-2
Screven County GA-2
Scriba (Town)—Oswego NY-1
Scribner (City)—Dodge NE-4
Scrubgrass (Township)—Venango ... PA-1
Scurry County TX-2
Seaboard (Town)—Northampton NC-2
Sea Bright (Borough)—
  Monmouth NJ-1
Seabrook (Town)—Rockingham NH-1
Seabrook (City)—Harris TX-2
Seabrook Farms (CDP)—
  Cumberland NJ-1
Seabrook Island (Town)—
  Charleston SC-2
Sea Cliff (Village)—Nassau NY-1
Seadrift (City)—Calhoun TX-2
Seaford (City)—Sussex DE-1
Seaford (CDP)—Nassau NY-1
Seaforth (City)—Redwood MN-3
Seagate (CDP)—New Hanover NC-2
Sea Girt (Borough)—Monmouth NJ-1
Seagoville (City)—Dallas TX-2
Seagoville (City)—Kaufman TX-2
Seagraves (City)—Gaines TX-2
Seagrove (Town)—Randolph NC-2
Sea Islands (PA) Geog-4
Sea Isle City (City)—Cape May NJ-1
Seal (Township)—Pike OH-3
Seal Beach (City)—Orange CA-4
Sealy (Township)—Logan ND-4
Sealy (City)—Austin TX-2
Seama (CDP)—Cibola NM-4
Seaman (Village)—Adams OH-3

Sea Ranch Lakes (Village)—
  Broward FL-2
Searcy (City)—White AR-2
Searcy County AR-2
Searingtown (CDP)—Nassau NY-1
Searles Valley (CDP)—San
  Bernardino CA-4
Searsboro (City)—Poweshiek IA-3
Searsburg (Town)—Bennington VT-1
Searsmont (Town)—Waldo ME-1
Searsport (Town)—Waldo ME-1
Seaside (City)—Monterey CA-4
Seaside (City)—Clatsop OR-4
Seaside Heights (Borough)—
  Ocean NJ-1
Seaside Park (Borough)—Ocean NJ-1
Sea-Tac (CDP)—King WA-4
Seaton (Village)—Mercer IL-3
Seatonville (Village)—Bureau IL-3
Seat Pleasant (City)—Prince
  George's MD-1
Seattle (City)—King WA-4
Seavey (Township)—Aitkin MN-3
Sebago (Town)—Cumberland ME-1
Sebago Lake (ME) Geog-4
Sebastian (City)—Indian River FL-2
Sebastian (CDP)—Willacy TX-2
Sebastian County AR-2
Sebastopol (City)—Sonoma CA-4
Sebastopol (Town)—Scott MS-2
Sebec (Town)—Piscataquis ME-1
Sebeka (City)—Wadena MN-3
Sebewa (Township)—Ionia MI-3
Sebewaing (Township)—Huron MI-3
Sebewaing (Village)—Huron MI-3
Seboeis (Plantation)—Penobscot ME-1
Seboomook Lake (unorganized) (Pop.
  Place)—Somerset ME-1
Sebree (City)—Webster KY-2
Sebring (City)—Highlands FL-2
Sebring (City)—Mahoning OH-3
Secaucus (Town)—Hudson NJ-1
Second College Grant (Pop. Place)—
  Coos NH-1
Second Mesa (CDP)—Navajo AZ-4
Secor (Village)—Woodford IL-3
Secord (Township)—Gladwin MI-3
Secretary (Town)—Dorchester MD-1
Section (Town)—Jackson AL-2
Security-Widefield (CDP)—El
  Paso CO-4
Sedalia (City)—Pettis MO-3
Sedalia (Township)—Pettis MO-3
Sedan (City)—Chautauqua KS-4
Sedan (Township)—Chautauqua KS-4
Sedan (City)—Pope MN-3
Sedco Hills (CDP)—Riverside CA-4
Sedge Garden (CDP)—Forsyth NC-2
Sedgewickville (Village)—
  Bollinger MO-3
Sedgwick (Town)—Lawrence AR-2
Sedgwick (Town)—Sedgwick CO-4
Sedgwick (City)—Harvey KS-4
Sedgwick (Township)—Harvey KS-4
Sedgwick (City)—Sedgwick KS-4
Sedgwick (Town)—Hancock ME-1
Sedgwick County CO-4
Sedgwick County KS-4
Sedona (City)—Coconino AZ-4
Sedona (City)—Yavapai AZ-4
Sedro-Woolley (City)—Skagit WA-4
Seekonk (Town)—Bristol MA-1
Seeley (CDP)—Imperial CA-4
Seely (Township)—Faribault MN-3
Seelyville (Town)—Vigo IN-3

Seffner (CDP)—Hillsborough FL-2
Sefton (Township)—Fayette IL-3
Seguin (City)—Guadalupe TX-2
Seibert (Town)—Kit Carson CO-4
Seif (Town)—Clark WI-3
Seiling (City)—Dewey OK-2
Seivert (Township)—Cavalier ND-4
Selah (City)—Yakima WA-4
Selawik (City)—Northwest Arctic
  Borough AK-4
Selby (Township)—Bureau IL-3
Selby (City)—Walworth SD-4
Selby-on-the-Bay (CDP)—Anne
  Arundel MD-1
Selbyville (Town)—Sussex DE-1
Selden (City)—Sheridan KS-4
Selden (CDP)—Suffolk NY-1
Seldovia (City)—Kenai Peninsula
  Borough AK-4
Selfridge (City)—Sioux ND-4
Seligman (City)—Barry MO-3
Selinsgrove (Borough)—Snyder PA-1
Sellers (Town)—Marion SC-2
Sellersburg (Town)—Clark IN-3
Sellersville (Borough)—Bucks PA-1
Sells (CDP)—Pima AZ-4
Selma (City)—Dallas AL-2
Selma (City)—Fresno CA-4
Selma (Town)—Delaware IN-3
Selma (Township)—Wexford MI-3
Selma (Township)—Cottonwood MN-3
Selma (Town)—Johnston NC-2
Selma (City)—Bexar TX-2
Selma (City)—Comal TX-2
Selma (City)—Guadalupe TX-2
Selmer (Town)—McNairy TN-2
Selmont-West Selmont (Division)—
  Dallas AL-2
Seminary (Township)—Fayette IL-3
Seminary (Town)—Covington MS-2
Seminole (City)—Pinellas FL-2
Seminole (City)—Seminole OK-2
Seminole (City)—Gaines TX-2
Seminole County FL-2
Seminole County GA-2
Seminole County OK-2
Seminole TJSA (OK) IndRes-4
Seminole Trust Lands (FL) IndRes-4
Sempronius (Town)—Cayuga NY-1
Senachwine (Township)—Putnam .. IL-3
Senath (City)—Dunklin MO-3
Senatobia (City)—Tate MS-2
Seneca (Town)—Grundy IL-3
Seneca (Town)—La Salle IL-3
Seneca (Township)—McHenry IL-3
Seneca (City)—Nemaha KS-4
Seneca (Township)—Lenawee MI-3
Seneca (Township)—Christian MO-3
Seneca (City)—Newton MO-3
Seneca (Township)—Newton MO-3
Seneca (Village)—Thomas NE-4
Seneca (Town)—Ontario NY-1
Seneca (Township)—Monroe OH-3
Seneca (Township)—Noble OH-3
Seneca (Township)—Seneca OH-3
Seneca (City)—Grant OR-4
Seneca (Town)—Oconee SC-2
Seneca (Town)—Faulk SD-4
Seneca (Town)—Crawford WI-3
Seneca (Town)—Green Lake WI-3
Seneca (Town)—Shawano WI-3
Seneca (Town)—Wood WI-3
Seneca County NY-1
Seneca County OH-3
Seneca Falls (Town)—Seneca NY-1

General Index

Seneca Falls (Village)—Seneca *NY-1*
Seneca Gardens (City)—
  Jefferson *KY-2*
Senecaville (Village)—Guernsey *OH-3*
Seney (Township)—Schoolcraft *MI-3*
Sennett (Town)—Cayuga *NY-1*
Senoia (City)—Coweta *GA-2*
Sentinel (Township)—Golden
  Valley *ND-4*
Sentinel (City)—Washita *OK-2*
Sentinel Butte (City)—Golden
  Valley *ND-4*
Sepulveda *See* **Los Angeles**—Los
  Angeles *CA-4*
Sequatchie County *TN-2*
Sequim (City)—Clallam *WA-4*
Sequoyah County *OK-2*
Serena (Township)—La Salle *IL-3*
Serenada (CDP)—Williamson *TX-2*
Sergeant (Township)—McKean *PA-1*
Sergeant Bluff (City)—Woodbury ... *IA-3*
Sergius (Township)—Bottineau *ND-4*
Sesser (Town)—Franklin *IL-3*
Setauket-East Setauket (CDP)—
  Suffolk *NY-1*
Seth Ward (CDP)—Hale *TX-2*
Sevastopol (Town)—Door *WI-3*
Seven Corners (CDP)—Fairfax *VA-2*
Seven Devils (Town)—Avery *NC-2*
Seven Devils (Town)—Watauga *NC-2*
Seven Fields (Borough)—Butler *PA-1*
Seven Hickory (Township)—Coles . *IL-3*
Seven Hills (City)—Cuyahoga *OH-3*
Seven Lakes (CDP)—Moore *NC-2*
Seven Mile (Village)—Butler *OH-3*
Seven Mile Creek (Town)—
  Juneau *WI-3*
Seven Oaks (CDP)—Lexington *SC-2*
Seven Oaks (City)—Polk *TX-2*
Seven Points (Town)—
  Henderson *TX-2*
Seven Points (City)—Kaufman *TX-2*
Seven Springs (Town)—Wayne *NC-2*
Seven Springs (Borough)—
  Somerset *PA-1*
Seventy-Six (Township)—Sumner *KS-4*
Seven Valleys (Borough)—York *PA-1*
Severance (Town)—Weld *CO-4*
Severance (City)—Doniphan *KS-4*
Severance (Township)—Sibley *MN-3*
Severn (CDP)—Anne Arundel *MD-1*
Severn (Town)—Northampton *NC-2*
Severn (Township)—Stutsman *ND-4*
Severna Park (CDP)—Anne
  Arundel *MD-1*
Severy (City)—Greenwood *KS-4*
Sevier County *AR-2*
Sevier County *TN-2*
Sevier County *UT-4*
Sevier Lake (UT) *Geog-4*
Sevierville (City)—Sevier *TN-2*
Seville (Township)—Gratiot *MI-3*
Seville (Village)—Medina *OH-3*
Sewall's Point (Town)—Martin *FL-2*
Sewanee (CDP)—Franklin *TN-2*
Seward (City)—Kenai Peninsula
  Borough *AK-4*
Seward (Township)—Kendall *IL-3*
Seward (Township)—Winnebago *IL-3*
Seward (Township)—Kosciusko *IN-3*
Seward (Township)—Seward *KS-4*
Seward (City)—Stafford *KS-4*
Seward (Township)—Nobles *MN-3*
Seward (City)—Seward *NE-4*
Seward (Town)—Schoharie *NY-1*

Seward (Borough)—
  Westmoreland *PA-1*
Seward County *KS-4*
Seward County *NE-4*
Sewaren (CDP)—Middlesex *NJ-1*
Sewickley (Borough)—Allegheny *PA-1*
Sewickley (Township)—
  Westmoreland *PA-1*
Sewickley Heights (Borough)—
  Allegheny *PA-1*
Sewickley Hills (Borough)—
  Allegheny *PA-1*
Seymour (Town)—New Haven *CT-1*
Seymour (City)—Jackson *IN-3*
Seymour (City)—Wayne *IA-3*
Seymour (City)—Webster *MO-3*
Seymour (CDP)—Blount *TN-2*
Seymour (CDP)—Sevier *TN-2*
Seymour (City)—Baylor *TX-2*
Seymour (Town)—Eau Claire *WI-3*
Seymour (Town)—Lafayette *WI-3*
Seymour (City)—Outagamie *WI-3*
Seymour (Town)—Outagamie *WI-3*
Seymour Johnson Air Force Base
  (NC) *Mil-4*
Shabbona (Town)—DeKalb *IL-3*
Shabbona (Township)—DeKalb *IL-3*
Shackelford County *TX-2*
Shade (Township)—Somerset *PA-1*
Shade Gap (Borough)—
  Huntingdon *PA-1*
Shadeland (Town)—Tippecanoe *IN-3*
Shady Cove (City)—Jackson *OR-4*
Shady Dale (Town)—Jasper *GA-2*
Shady Grove (Town)—Pawnee *OK-2*
Shady Point (Town)—Le Flore *OK-2*
Shady Shores (Town)—Denton *TX-2*
Shady Side (CDP)—Anne
  Arundel *MD-1*
Shadyside (Village)—Belmont *OH-3*
Shady Spring (CDP)—Raleigh *WV-2*
Shafer (City)—Chisago *MN-3*
Shafer (Township)—Chisago *MN-3*
Shafter (City)—Kern *CA-4*
Shafter (Township)—Fayette *IL-3*
Shaftsbury (Town)—Bennington *VT-1*
Shageluk (City)—Yukon-Koyukuk
  Census Area *AK-4*
Shaker Church (CDP)—
  Snohomish *WA-4*
Shaker Heights (City)—
  Cuyahoga *OH-3*
Shakopee (City)—Scott *MN-3*
Shakopee Sioux Community
  (MN) *IndRes-4*
Shaktoolik (City)—Nome Census
  Area *AK-4*
Shaler (Township)—Allegheny *PA-1*
Shalersville (Township)—Portage .. *OH-3*
Shalimar (Town)—Okaloosa *FL-2*
Shallotte (Town)—Brunswick *NC-2*
Shallowater (City)—Lubbock *TX-2*
Shambaugh (City)—Page *IA-3*
Shamokin (City)—
  Northumberland *PA-1*
Shamokin (Township)—
  Northumberland *PA-1*
Shamokin Dam (Borough)—
  Snyder *PA-1*
Shamong (Township)—Burlington .. *NJ-1*
Shamrock (Township)—Aitkin *MN-3*
Shamrock (Township)—
  Callaway *MO-3*
Shamrock (Township)—Holt *NE-4*
Shamrock (Town)—Creek *OK-2*

Shamrock (City)—Wheeler *TX-2*
Shamrock Lakes (Town)—
  Blackford *IN-3*
Shanagolden (Town)—Ashland *WI-3*
Shandaken (Town)—Ulster *NY-1*
Shaniko (City)—Wasco *OR-4*
Shanksville (Borough)—Somerset .. *PA-1*
Shannon (CDP)—Floyd *GA-2*
Shannon (Village)—Carroll *IL-3*
Shannon (Township)—Atchison *KS-4*
Shannon (Township)—
  Pottawatomie *KS-4*
Shannon (Town)—Lee *MS-2*
Shannon City (City)—Ringgold *IA-3*
Shannon City (City)—Union *IA-3*
Shannon County *MO-3*
Shannon County *SD-4*
Shannon Hills (City)—Saline *AR-2*
Shaokatan (Township)—Lincoln ... *MN-3*
Shapleigh (Town)—York *ME-1*
Sharkey County *MS-2*
Shark River Hills (CDP)—
  Monmouth *NJ-1*
Sharlow (Township)—Stutsman *ND-4*
Sharon (Town)—Litchfield *CT-1*
Sharon (City)—Taliaferro *GA-2*
Sharon (Township)—Fayette *IL-3*
Sharon (City)—Barber *KS-4*
Sharon (Township)—Barber *KS-4*
Sharon (Town)—Norfolk *MA-1*
Sharon (Township)—Washtenaw ... *MI-3*
Sharon (Township)—Le Sueur *MN-3*
Sharon (Township)—Buffalo *NE-4*
Sharon (Town)—Hillsborough *NH-1*
Sharon (Town)—Schoharie *NY-1*
Sharon (City)—Steele *ND-4*
Sharon (Township)—Steele *ND-4*
Sharon (Township)—Franklin *OH-3*
Sharon (Township)—Medina *OH-3*
Sharon (Township)—Noble *OH-3*
Sharon (Township)—Richland *OH-3*
Sharon (Town)—Woodward *OK-2*
Sharon (City)—Mercer *PA-1*
Sharon (Township)—Potter *PA-1*
Sharon (Town)—York *SC-2*
Sharon (Township)—Hutchinson ... *SD-4*
Sharon (Town)—Weakley *TN-2*
Sharon (Town)—Windsor *VT-1*
Sharon (Town)—Portage *WI-3*
Sharon (Town)—Walworth *WI-3*
Sharon (Village)—Walworth *WI-3*
Sharon Hill (Borough)—Delaware .. *PA-1*
Sharon Springs (City)—Wallace *KS-4*
Sharon Springs (Township)—
  Wallace *KS-4*
Sharon Springs (Village)—
  Schoharie *NY-1*
Sharonville (City)—Butler *OH-3*
Sharonville (City)—Hamilton *OH-3*
Sharp County *AR-2*
Sharpes (CDP)—Brevard *FL-2*
Sharpsburg (Town)—Coweta *GA-2*
Sharpsburg (City)—Taylor *IA-3*
Sharpsburg (City)—Bath *KY-2*
Sharpsburg (Town)—Washington .. *MD-1*
Sharpsburg (Town)—Edgecombe .. *NC-2*
Sharpsburg (Town)—Nash *NC-2*
Sharpsburg (Town)—Wilson *NC-2*
Sharpsburg (Borough)—Allegheny .. *PA-1*
Sharpsville (Town)—Tipton *IN-3*
Sharpsville (Borough)—Mercer *PA-1*
Sharptown (Town)—Wicomico *MD-1*
Shasta, Mt. (CA) *Geog-4*
Shasta County *CA-4*
Shasta Dam (CA) *Geog-4*

Shattuck (Town)—Ellis.................. OK-2
Shavano Park (City)—Bexar TX-2
Shaw (City)—Bolivar MS-2
Shaw (City)—Sunflower MS-2
Shaw Air Force Base (SC) Mil-4
Shawangunk (Town)—Ulster........... NY-1
Shawano (City)—Shawano WI-3
Shawano County............................... WI-3
Shawnee (Township)—Gallatin....... IL-3
Shawnee (Township)—Fountain IN-3
Shawnee (Township)—Cherokee..... KS-4
Shawnee (City)—Johnson KS-4
Shawnee (Township)—Johnson....... KS-4
Shawnee (Township)—Bates MO-3
Shawnee (Township)—Cape
  Girardeau................................... MO-3
Shawnee (Township)—Henry MO-3
Shawnee (Township)—Allen OH-3
Shawnee (Village)—Perry OH-3
Shawnee (City)—Pottawatomie OK-2
Shawnee County KS-4
Shawnee Hills (Village)—
  Delaware OH-3
Shawnee Hills (CDP)—Greene...... OH-3
Shawneetown (City)—Gallatin....... IL-3
Shaws Point (Township)—
  Macoupin.................................... IL-3
Shawsville (CDP)—Montgomery VA-2
Shawswick (Township)—
  Lawrence.................................... IN-3
Sheakleyville (Borough)—Mercer ... PA-1
Shealey (Township)—Ward ND-4
Sheboygan (City)—Sheboygan WI-3
Sheboygan (Town)—Sheboygan WI-3
Sheboygan County............................ WI-3
Sheboygan Falls (City)—
  Sheboygan WI-3
Sheboygan Falls (Town)—
  Sheboygan WI-3
Sheep Ranch Rancheria (CA) .. IndRes-4
Sheets (Township)—Slope ND-4
Sheffield (City)—Colbert................ AL-2
Sheffield (Village)—Bureau IL-3
Sheffield (Township)—
  Tippecanoe.................................. IN-3
Sheffield (City)—Franklin IA-3
Sheffield (Town)—Berkshire MA-1
Sheffield (Township)—Ashtabula... OH-3
Sheffield (Township)—Lorain OH-3
Sheffield (Village)—Lorain............. OH-3
Sheffield (Township)—Warren PA-1
Sheffield (Town)—Caledonia VT-1
Sheffield Lake (City)—Lorain........ OH-3
Shelbina (City)—Shelby MO-3
Shelburn (Town)—Sullivan IN-3
Shelburne (Town)—Franklin.......... MA-1
Shelburne (Township)—Lyon MN-3
Shelburne (Town)—Coos................ NH-1
Shelburne (Town)—Chittenden....... VT-1
Shelburne Falls (CDP)—
  Franklin..................................... MA-1
Shelby (Township)—Jefferson IN-3
Shelby (Township)—Ripley IN-3
Shelby (Township)—Shelby............ IN-3
Shelby (Township)—Tippecanoe..... IN-3
Shelby (City)—Pottawattamie......... IA-3
Shelby (City)—Shelby..................... IA-3
Shelby (Township)—Macomb MI-3
Shelby (Township)—Oceana MI-3
Shelby (Village)—Oceana MI-3
Shelby (Township)—Blue Earth MN-3
Shelby (City)—Bolivar.................... MS-2
Shelby (City)—Toole MT-4
Shelby (Village)—Polk.................... NE-4
Shelby (Town)—Orleans................. NY-1

Shelby (City)—Cleveland NC-2
Shelby (City)—Richland.................. OH-3
Shelby (Township)—Brown SD-4
Shelby (Town)—La Crosse WI-3
Shelby County AL-2
Shelby County IL-3
Shelby County IN-3
Shelby County IA-3
Shelby County KY-2
Shelby County MO-3
Shelby County OH-3
Shelby County TN-2
Shelby County TX-2
Shelbyville (City)—Shelby IL-3
Shelbyville (Township)—Shelby..... IL-3
Shelbyville (City)—Shelby IN-3
Shelbyville (City)—Shelby.............. KY-2
Shelbyville (City)—Shelby.............. MO-3
Shelbyville (City)—Bedford TN-2
Sheldahl (City)—Boone IA-3
Sheldahl (City)—Polk..................... IA-3
Sheldahl (City)—Story.................... IA-3
Sheldon (Town)—Iroquois IL-3
Sheldon (Township)—Iroquois IL-3
Sheldon (Township)—O'Brien IA-3
Sheldon (City)—Sioux IA-3
Sheldon (Township)—Houston MN-3
Sheldon (City)—Vernon MO-3
Sheldon (Town)—Wyoming NY-1
Sheldon (Township)—Eddy............ ND-4
Sheldon (Township)—Ransom ND-4
Sheldon (CDP)—Harris TX-2
Sheldon (Town)—Franklin............. VT-1
Sheldon (Town)—Monroe WI-3
Sheldon (Village)—Rusk................ WI-3
Sheldon Point (City)—Wade Hampton
  Census Area AK-4
Shell (Township)—Mountrail......... ND-4
Shell Creek (Township)—Platte NE-4
Shelley (City)—Bingham ID-4
Shell Knob (Township)—Barry MO-3
Shell Lake (Township)—Becker MN-3
Shell Lake (City)—Washburn......... WI-3
Shellman (City)—Randolph GA-2
Shell Point (CDP)—Beaufort........ SC-2
Shell River (Township)—
  Wadena MN-3
Shell Rock (City)—Butler IA-3
Shell Rock (Township)—
  Greenwood KS-4
Shell Rock (Township)—
  Freeborn..................................... MN-3
Shellsburg (City)—Benton IA-3
Shell Valley (CDP)—Rolette ND-4
Shell Valley (Township)—Rolette . ND-4
Shelly (City)—Norman................... MN-3
Shelly (Township)—Norman MN-3
Shelocta (Borough)—Indiana......... PA-1
Shelter Bay (CDP)—Skagit WA-4
Shelter Island (NY)...................... Geog-4
Shelter Island (CDP)—Suffolk....... NY-1
Shelter Island (Town)—Suffolk...... NY-1
Shelter Island Heights (CDP)—
  Suffolk....................................... NY-1
Shelton (City)—Fairfield CT-1
Shelton (Township)—Knox MO-3
Shelton (Township)—Buffalo NE-4
Shelton (Village)—Buffalo.............. NE-4
Shelton (City)—Mason WA-4
Shenandoah (City)—Fremont IA-3
Shenandoah (City)—Page............... IA-3
Shenandoah (CDP)—East Baton Rouge
  Parish LA-2
Shenandoah (Borough)—
  Schuylkill................................... PA-1

Shenandoah (City)—
  Montgomery............................... TX-2
Shenandoah (Town)—Page VA-2
Shenandoah County VA-2
Shenandoah River (NY) Geog-4
Shenandoah Valley (VA) Geog-4
Shenango (Township)—Lawrence... PA-1
Shenango (Township)—Mercer PA-1
Shenford (Township)—Ransom ND-4
Shepherd (Village)—Isabella MI-3
Shepherd (Township)—Walsh ND-4
Shepherd (City)—San Jacinto TX-2
Shepherdstown (Town)—
  Jefferson..................................... WV-2
Shepherdsville (City)—Bullitt KY-2
Sheppard Air Force Base (TX).... Mil-4
Sherborn (Town)—Middlesex MA-1
Sherbrooke (Township)—Steele ND-4
Sherburn (City)—Martin MN-3
Sherburne (Town)—Chenango NY-1
Sherburne (Village)—Chenango NY-1
Sherburne (Town)—Rutland VT-1
Sherburne County MN-3
Sheridan (City)—Grant AR-2
Sheridan (City)—Arapahoe CO-4
Sheridan (Town)—La Salle IL-3
Sheridan (Township)—Logan IL-3
Sheridan (Town)—Hamilton IN-3
Sheridan (Township)—Cherokee KS-4
Sheridan (Township)—Cowley KS-4
Sheridan (Township)—Crawford KS-4
Sheridan (Township)—Linn KS-4
Sheridan (Township)—Ottawa KS-4
Sheridan (Township)—Sheridan KS-4
Sheridan (Township)—
  Washington KS-4
Sheridan (Township)—Calhoun MI-3
Sheridan (Township)—Clare MI-3
Sheridan (Township)—Huron MI-3
Sheridan (Township)—Mason MI-3
Sheridan (Township)—Mecosta MI-3
Sheridan (Village)—Montcalm....... MI-3
Sheridan (Township)—Redwood .. MN-3
Sheridan (Township)—Dallas MO-3
Sheridan (Township)—Daviess MO-3
Sheridan (Township)—Jasper........ MO-3
Sheridan (Town)—Worth MO-3
Sheridan (Town)—Madison MT-4
Sheridan (Township)—Clay NE-4
Sheridan (Township)—Holt NE-4
Sheridan (Township)—Phelps NE-4
Sheridan (Town)—Chautauqua NY-1
Sheridan (Township)—LaMoure.... ND-4
Sheridan (City)—Yamhill OR-4
Sheridan (Township)—Codington.. SD-4
Sheridan (Town)—Dunn WI-3
Sheridan (City)—Sheridan.............. WY-4
Sheridan Beach (CDP)—King....... WA-4
Sheridan Charter (Township)—
  Newaygo..................................... MI-3
Sheridan County................................KS-4
Sheridan County............................... MT-4
Sheridan County............................... NE-4
Sheridan County............................... ND-4
Sheridan County............................... WY-4
Sheridan Lake (Town)—Kiowa...... CO-4
Sherlock (Township)—Finney KS-4
Sherman (Town)—Fairfield............ CT-1
Sherman (Township)—Mason IL-3
Sherman (Village)—Sangamon IL-3
Sherman (Township)—Clay KS-4
Sherman (Township)—Crawford ... KS-4
Sherman (Township)—Decatur...... KS-4
Sherman (Township)—Dickinson ... KS-4
Sherman (Township)—Ellsworth ... KS-4

General Index — American Places Dictionary

Sherman (Township)—Grant *KS-4*
Sherman (Township)—Leavenworth *KS-4*
Sherman (Township)—Ottawa *KS-4*
Sherman (Township)—Pottawatomie *KS-4*
Sherman (Township)—Riley *KS-4*
Sherman (Township)—Sedgwick *KS-4*
Sherman (Township)—Washington *KS-4*
Sherman (Town)—Aroostook *ME-1*
Sherman (Township)—Gladwin *MI-3*
Sherman (Township)—Huron *MI-3*
Sherman (Township)—Iosco *MI-3*
Sherman (Township)—Isabella *MI-3*
Sherman (Township)—Keweenaw . *MI-3*
Sherman (Township)—Mason *MI-3*
Sherman (Township)—Newaygo *MI-3*
Sherman (Township)—Osceola *MI-3*
Sherman (Township)—St. Joseph .. *MI-3*
Sherman (Township)—Redwood .. *MN-3*
Sherman (Town)—Pontotoc *MS-2*
Sherman (Town)—Union *MS-2*
Sherman (Township)—Cass *MO-3*
Sherman (Township)—Dallas *MO-3*
Sherman (Township)—DeKalb *MO-3*
Sherman (Township)—Harrison ... *MO-3*
Sherman (Township)—Putnam *MO-3*
Sherman (Township)—Antelope *NE-4*
Sherman (Township)—Cuming *NE-4*
Sherman (Township)—Gage *NE-4*
Sherman (Township)—Kearney *NE-4*
Sherman (Township)—Platte *NE-4*
Sherman (Town)—Chautauqua *NY-1*
Sherman (Village)—Chautauqua *NY-1*
Sherman (Township)—Bottineau ... *ND-4*
Sherman (Township)—Huron *OH-3*
Sherman (Township)—Brookings .. *SD-4*
Sherman (Township)—Corson *SD-4*
Sherman (Township)—Faulk *SD-4*
Sherman (Town)—Minnehaha *SD-4*
Sherman (City)—Grayson *TX-2*
Sherman (Town)—Clark *WI-3*
Sherman (Town)—Dunn *WI-3*
Sherman (Town)—Iron *WI-3*
Sherman (Town)—Sheboygan *WI-3*
Sherman County *KS-4*
Sherman County *NE-4*
Sherman County *OR-4*
Sherman County *TX-2*
Sherman Oaks *See* **Los Angeles**—Los Angeles *CA-4*
Shermanville (Township)—Sherman *KS-4*
Sherrard (Village)—Mercer *IL-3*
Sherrelwood (CDP)—Adams *CO-4*
Sherrill (Town)—Jefferson *AR-2*
Sherrill (City)—Dubuque *IA-3*
Sherrill (Township)—Texas *MO-3*
Sherrill (City)—Oneida *NY-1*
Sherrills Ford (CDP)—Catawba *NC-2*
Sherrodsville (Village)—Carroll *OH-3*
Sherry (Town)—Wood *WI-3*
Sherwood (City)—Pulaski *AR-2*
Sherwood (Township)—Branch *MI-3*
Sherwood (Village)—Branch *MI-3*
Sherwood (City)—Renville *ND-4*
Sherwood (Village)—Defiance *OH-3*
Sherwood (CDP)—Hamilton *OH-3*
Sherwood (City)—Washington *OR-4*
Sherwood (Village)—Calumet *WI-3*
Sherwood (Town)—Clark *WI-3*
Sherwood Manor (CDP)—Hartford *CT-1*

Sherwood Valley Rancheria (CA) *IndRes-4*
Sheshequin (Township)—Bradford *PA-1*
Shetek (Township)—Murray *MN-3*
Shevlin (City)—Clearwater *MN-3*
Shevlin (Township)—Clearwater .. *MN-3*
Sheyenne (City)—Eddy *ND-4*
Sheyenne (Township)—Richland .. *ND-4*
Shiawassee (Township)—Shiawassee *MI-3*
Shiawassee County *MI-3*
Shible (Township)—Swift *MN-3*
Shickley (Village)—Fillmore *NE-4*
Shickshinny (Borough)—Luzerne ... *PA-1*
Shidler (Town)—Osage *OK-2*
Shields (Township)—Lake *IL-3*
Shields (CDP)—Saginaw *MI-3*
Shields (Township)—Holt *NE-4*
Shields (Town)—Dodge *WI-3*
Shields (Town)—Marquette *WI-3*
Shieldsville (Township)—Rice *MN-3*
Shiley (Township)—Pawnee *KS-4*
Shillington (Borough)—Berks *PA-1*
Shiloh (Municipality)—DeKalb *AL-2*
Shiloh (City)—Harris *GA-2*
Shiloh (Township)—Edgar *IL-3*
Shiloh (Township)—Jefferson *IL-3*
Shiloh (Village)—St. Clair *IL-3*
Shiloh (Township)—Neosho *KS-4*
Shiloh (Borough)—Cumberland *NJ-1*
Shiloh (CDP)—Montgomery *OH-3*
Shiloh (Village)—Richland *OH-3*
Shiloh Valley (Township)—St. Clair *IL-3*
Shiner (City)—Lavaca *TX-2*
Shinglehouse (Borough)—Potter *PA-1*
Shingle Springs (CDP)—El Dorado *CA-4*
Shingle Springs Rancheria (CA) *IndRes-4*
Shingobee (Township)—Cass *MN-3*
Shinnecock Hills (CDP)—Suffolk .. *NY-1*
Shinnecock Reservation (NY) .. *IndRes-4*
Shinnecock Reservation (Pop. Place)—Suffolk *NY-1*
Shinnston (City)—Harrison *WV-2*
Shiocton (Village)—Outagamie *WI-3*
Ship Bottom (Borough)—Ocean ... *NJ-1*
Shipman (Town)—Macoupin *IL-3*
Shipman (Township)—Macoupin ... *IL-3*
Shippen (Township)—Cameron *PA-1*
Shippen (Township)—Tioga *PA-1*
Shippensburg (Borough)—Cumberland *PA-1*
Shippensburg (Township)—Cumberland *PA-1*
Shippensburg (Borough)—Franklin *PA-1*
Shippenville (Borough)—Clarion *PA-1*
Shippingport (Borough)—Beaver ... *PA-1*
Ship Rock (NM) *Geog-4*
Shiprock (CDP)—San Juan *NM-4*
Shipshewana (Town)—Lagrange *IN-3*
Shiremanstown (Borough)—Cumberland *PA-1*
Shirland (Township)—Winnebago .. *IL-3*
Shirley (Town)—Van Buren *AR-2*
Shirley (Town)—Hancock *IN-3*
Shirley (Town)—Henry *IN-3*
Shirley (Township)—Cloud *KS-4*
Shirley (Town)—Piscataquis *ME-1*
Shirley (Town)—Middlesex *MA-1*
Shirley (Township)—Ripley *MO-3*
Shirley (CDP)—Suffolk *NY-1*

Shirley (Township)—Huntingdon ... *PA-1*
Shirleysburg (Borough)—Huntingdon *PA-1*
Shishaldin, Mt. (AK) *Geog-4*
Shishmaref (City)—Nome Census Area *AK-4*
Shively (City)—Jefferson *KY-2*
Shoal (Township)—Clinton *MO-3*
Shoal Creek (Township)—Bond *IL-3*
Shoal Creek (Township)—Newton *MO-3*
Shoal Creek Drive (Village)—Newton *MO-3*
Shoal Creek Estates (Town)—Newton *MO-3*
Shoals (Town)—Martin *IN-3*
Shoalwater Reservation (WA) .. *IndRes-4*
Shoemakersville (Borough)—Berks *PA-1*
Shohola (Township)—Pike *PA-1*
Sholes (Village)—Wayne *NE-4*
Shongaloo (Village)—Webster Parish *LA-2*
Shongopovi (CDP)—Navajo *AZ-4*
Shonto (CDP)—Navajo *AZ-4*
Shooks (Township)—Beltrami *MN-3*
Shoreacres (City)—Harris *TX-2*
Shoreham (Village)—Berrien *MI-3*
Shoreham (Village)—Suffolk *NY-1*
Shoreham (Town)—Addison *VT-1*
Shoreline Park (CDP)—Hancock ... *MS-2*
Shoreview (City)—Ramsey *MN-3*
Shorewood (Village)—Will *IL-3*
Shorewood (City)—Hennepin *MN-3*
Shorewood (Village)—Milwaukee ... *WI-3*
Shorewood Hills (Village)—Dane .. *WI-3*
Shorewood-Tower Hills-Harbert (CDP)—Berrien *MI-3*
Short Bend (Township)—Dent *MO-3*
Short Creek (Township)—Burke ... *ND-4*
Short Creek (Township)—Harrison *OH-3*
Shorter (Municipality)—Macon *AL-2*
Shortsville (Village)—Ontario *NY-1*
Shoshone (City)—Lincoln *ID-4*
Shoshone County *ID-4*
Shoshone Falls (ID) *Geog-4*
Shoshoni (Town)—Fremont *WY-4*
Shotley (Township)—Beltrami *MN-3*
Shotley Brook (Pop. Place)—Beltrami *MN-3*
Show Low (City)—Navajo *AZ-4*
Shreve (Village)—Wayne *OH-3*
Shreveport (City)—Bossier Parish *LA-2*
Shreveport (City)—Caddo Parish ... *LA-2*
Shrewsbury (Town)—Worcester *MA-1*
Shrewsbury (City)—St. Louis *MO-3*
Shrewsbury (Borough)—Monmouth *NJ-1*
Shrewsbury (Township)—Monmouth *NJ-1*
Shrewsbury (Township)—Lycoming *PA-1*
Shrewsbury (Township)—Sullivan .. *PA-1*
Shrewsbury (Borough)—York *PA-1*
Shrewsbury (Township)—York *PA-1*
Shrewsbury (Town)—Rutland *VT-1*
Shubert (Village)—Richardson *NE-4*
Shubuta (Town)—Clarke *MS-2*
Shueyville (City)—Johnson *IA-3*
Shullsburg (City)—Lafayette *WI-3*
Shullsburg (Town)—Lafayette *WI-3*
Shuman (Township)—Sargent *ND-4*
Shumway (Village)—Effingham *IL-3*

Shungnak (City)—Northwest Arctic Borough..................................AK-4
Shuqualak (Town)—Noxubee........MS-2
Shutesbury (Town)—Franklin.......MA-1
Shyne No. 27 (Township)—Pennington..................................SD-4
Sibley (Village)—Ford...................IL-3
Sibley (Township)—Osceola..........IA-3
Sibley (Township)—Cloud.............KS-4
Sibley (Village)—Webster Parish....LA-2
Sibley (Township)—Crow Wing.....MN-3
Sibley (Township)—Sibley.............MN-3
Sibley (Village)—Jackson...............MO-3
Sibley (City)—Barnes....................ND-4
Sibley (Township)—Kidder...........ND-4
Sibley Butte (Township)—Burleigh...ND-4
Sibley County................................MN-3
Sibley Trail (Township)—Barnes...ND-4
Sicily (Township)—Gage................NE-4
Sicily Island (Village)—Catahoula Parish..LA-2
Sidell (Town)—Vermilion..............IL-3
Sidell (Township)—Vermilion........IL-3
Sidney (Town)—Sharp....................AR-2
Sidney (Town)—Champaign..........IL-3
Sidney (Township)—Champaign....IL-3
Sidney (Town)—Kosciusko............IN-3
Sidney (City)—Fremont.................IA-3
Sidney (Town)—Kennebec............ME-1
Sidney (Township)—Montcalm.....MI-3
Sidney (City)—Richland................MT-4
Sidney (City)—Cheyenne..............NE-4
Sidney (Town)—Delaware.............NY-1
Sidney (Village)—Delaware..........NY-1
Sidney (Township)—Towner.........ND-4
Sidney (City)—Shelby...................OH-3
Sidney (Township)—Perkins..........SD-4
Sidon (Town)—Leflore..................MS-2
Sidonia (Township)—Mountrail....ND-4
Sierra Blanca (Pop. Place)—Hudspeth.......................................TX-2
Sierra County................................CA-4
Sierra County................................NM-4
Sierra Madre (City)—Los Angeles..CA-4
Sierra Vista (City)—Cochise.........AZ-4
Sierra Vista Southeast (CDP)—Cochise..AZ-4
Siesta Key (CDP)—Sarasota..........FL-2
Sigel (Town)—Shelby....................IL-3
Sigel (Township)—Shelby.............IL-3
Sigel (Township)—Huron..............MI-3
Sigel (Township)—Brown..............MN-3
Sigel (Town)—Chippewa...............WI-3
Sigel (Town)—Wood.....................WI-3
Signal (Township)—Charles Mix...SD-4
Signal Hill (City)—Los Angeles.....CA-4
Signal Mountain (Town)—Hamilton...TN-2
Sigourney (City)—Keokuk............IA-3
Sigurd (Town)—Sevier...................UT-4
Sikes (Village)—Winn Parish........LA-2
Sikes (Township)—Mountrail........ND-4
Sikeston (City)—New Madrid.......MO-3
Sikeston (City)—Scott...................MO-3
Silas (Town)—Choctaw.................AL-2
Siler City (Town)—Chatham.........NC-2
Silerton (Town)—Chester..............TN-2
Silerton (Town)—Hardeman..........TN-2
Siletz (City)—Lincoln...................OR-4
Siletz Reservation (OR)................IndRes-4
Silex (Village)—Lincoln................MO-3
Silicon Valley (CA)......................Geog-4
Silo (Town)—Bryan......................OK-2

Siloam (Town)—Greene.................GA-2
Siloam Springs (City)—Benton......AR-2
Siloam Springs (Township)—Howell...MO-3
Silsbee (City)—Hardin...................TX-2
Silt (Town)—Garfield....................CO-4
Silver (Township)—Carlton..........MN-3
Silver Bay (City)—Lake................MN-3
Silver Bow County........................MT-4
Silver Brook (Township)—Carlton...MN-3
Silver City (City)—Mills................IA-3
Silver City (Town)—Humphreys...MS-2
Silver City (Town)—Grant............NM-4
Silver City (CDP)—Hoke..............NC-2
Silver Cliff (Town)—Custer...........CO-4
Silver Cliff (Town)—Marinette.....WI-3
Silver Creek (Township)—Stephenson.....................................IL-3
Silver Creek (Township)—Clark...IN-3
Silver Creek (Township)—Cowley..KS-4
Silver Creek (Township)—Cass.....MI-3
Silver Creek (Township)—Lake....MN-3
Silver Creek (Township)—Wright..MN-3
Silver Creek (Town)—Lawrence...MS-2
Silver Creek (Village)—Newton...MO-3
Silver Creek (Township)—Randolph.......................................MO-3
Silver Creek (Township)—Burt.....NE-4
Silver Creek (Township)—Dixon..NE-4
Silver Creek (Township)—Merrick...NE-4
Silver Creek (Village)—Merrick....NE-4
Silver Creek (Village)—Chautauqua....................................NY-1
Silver Creek (Township)—Greene...OH-3
Silver Creek (Township)—Sanborn..SD-4
Silverdale (Township)—Cowley....KS-4
Silverdale (Borough)—Bucks........PA-1
Silverdale (CDP)—Kitsap.............WA-4
Silver Grove (City)—Campbell.....KY-2
Silverhill (Town)—Baldwin..........AL-2
Silver Lake (CDP)—Lake..............FL-2
Silver Lake (Town)—Kosciusko....IN-3
Silver Lake (City)—Shawnee........KS-4
Silver Lake (Township)—Shawnee..KS-4
Silver Lake (Township)—Martin..MN-3
Silver Lake (City)—McLeod.........MN-3
Silver Lake (Township)—Adams..NE-4
Silver Lake (CDP)—New Hanover...NC-2
Silver Lake (Township)—Wells....ND-4
Silver Lake (Village)—Summit.....OH-3
Silver Lake (Township)—Susquehanna..................................PA-1
Silver Lake (Township)—Hutchinson....................................SD-4
Silver Lake (Village)—Kenosha....WI-3
Silver Lake-Fircrest (CDP)—Snohomish.....................................WA-4
Silver Leaf (Township)—Becker...MN-3
Silver Plume (Town)—Clear Creek..CO-4
Silver Ridge (CDP)—Ocean..........NJ-1
Silver Spring (CDP)—Montgomery................................MD-1
Silver Spring (Township)—Cumberland....................................PA-1
Silver Springs (CDP)—Lyon.........NV-4
Silver Springs (Village)—Wyoming......................................NY-1

Silver Springs Shores (CDP)—Marion..FL-2
Silverstreet (Town)—Newberry.....SC-2
Silverthorne (Town)—Summit......CO-4
Silverton (Town)—San Juan.........CO-4
Silverton (Township)—Pennington...................................MN-3
Silverton (CDP)—Ocean...............NJ-1
Silverton (City)—Hamilton...........OH-3
Silverton (City)—Marion..............OR-4
Silverton (City)—Briscoe..............TX-2
Silvesta (Township)—Walsh.........ND-4
Silvis (Town)—Rock Island..........IL-3
Simi Valley (City)—Ventura.........CA-4
Simla (Town)—Elbert...................CO-4
Simmesport (Town)—Avoyelles Parish...LA-2
Simonton (City)—Fort Bend.........TX-2
Simonton Lake (CDP)—Elkhart...IN-3
Simpson (Village)—Johnson.........IL-3
Simpson (City)—Cloud..................KS-4
Simpson (City)—Mitchell.............KS-4
Simpson (Village)—Vernon Parish...LA-2
Simpson (Township)—Johnson.....MO-3
Simpson (Village)—Pitt.................NC-2
Simpson County............................KY-2
Simpson County............................MS-2
Simpsonville (City)—Shelby.........KY-2
Simpsonville (Town)—Greenville..SC-2
Sims (Village)—Wayne..................IL-3
Sims (Township)—Grant...............IN-3
Sims (Township)—Arenac............MI-3
Sims (Town)—Wilson...................NC-2
Simsboro (Village)—Lincoln Parish...LA-2
Simsbury (Town)—Hartford.........CT-1
Sinai (Town)—Brookings..............SD-4
Sinclair (Township)—Jewell.........KS-4
Sinclair (Township)—Clearwater..MN-3
Sinclair (Township)—Stutsman....ND-4
Sinclair (Town)—Carbon..............WY-4
Sinclairville (Village)—Chautauqua....................................NY-1
Sinking (Township)—Dent............MO-3
Sinking Spring (Village)—Highland..OH-3
Sinking Spring (Borough)—Berks...PA-1
Sinnott (Township)—Marshall......MN-3
Sinton (City)—San Patricio..........TX-2
Sioux (Township)—Platte.............MO-3
Sioux (Township)—McKenzie......ND-4
Sioux (Township)—Lyman...........SD-4
Sioux Agency (Township)—Yellow Medicine......................................MN-3
Sioux Center (City)—Sioux..........IA-3
Sioux City (City)—Woodbury......IA-3
Sioux County................................IA-3
Sioux County................................NE-4
Sioux County................................ND-4
Sioux Creek (Town)—Barron.......WI-3
Sioux Falls (City)—Lincoln..........SD-4
Sioux Falls (City)—Minnehaha....SD-4
Sioux Rapids (City)—Buena Vista..IA-3
Sioux Trail (Township)—Divide...ND-4
Sioux Valley (Township)—Jackson..MN-3
Sioux Valley (Township)—Union..SD-4
Sipsey (Town)—Walker................AL-2
Siren (Town)—Burnett..................WI-3
Siren (Village)—Burnett...............WI-3
Siskiyou County............................CA-4
Sisseton (Township)—Marshall....SD-4
Sisseton (City)—Roberts..............SD-4
Sisseton (Township)—Roberts.....SD-4

General Index

American Places Dictionary

Sisson (Township)—Howell MO-3
Sissonville (CDP)—Kanawha WV-2
Sister Bay (Village)—Door WI-3
Sisters (City)—Deschutes OR-4
Sistersville (City)—Tyler WV-2
Sitka (Township)—Clark KS-4
Sitka Borough and City AK-4
Six Mile (Township)—Franklin IL-3
Six Mile (Town)—Pickens SC-2
Six Mile Grove (Township)—
 Swift MN-3
Skagen (Township)—Roseau MN-3
Skagit County WA-4
Skagway (City)—
 Skagway-Hoonah-Angoon Census
 Area AK-4
**Skagway-Hoonah-Angoon Census
 Area** AK-4
Skamania County WA-4
Skanawan (Town)—Lincoln WI-3
Skandia (Township)—Marquette ... MI-3
Skandia (Township)—Murray MN-3
Skandia (Township)—Barnes ND-4
Skane (Township)—Kittson MN-3
Skaneateles (Town)—Onondaga .. NY-1
Skaneateles (Village)—Onondaga .. NY-1
Skedee (Town)—Pawnee OK-2
Skellytown (Town)—Carson TX-2
Skelton (Township)—Warrick IN-3
Skelton (Township)—Carlton MN-3
Skiatook (Town)—Osage OK-2
Skiatook (Town)—Tulsa OK-2
Skidaway Island (CDP)—
 Chatham GA-2
Skidmore (City)—Nodaway MO-3
Skidway Lake (CDP)—Ogemaw MI-3
Skippack (Township)—
 Montgomery PA-1
Skokie (City)—Cook IL-3
Skokomish (CDP)—Mason WA-4
Skokomish Reservation (WA) .. *IndRes-4*
Skowhegan (Town)—Somerset ME-1
Skree (Township)—Clay MN-3
Skull Creek (Township)—Butler ... NE-4
Skull Valley Reservation
 (UT) *IndRes-4*
Skwentna (CDP)—Matanuska-Susitna
 Borough AK-4
Skykomish (Town)—King WA-4
Sky Lake (CDP)—Orange FL-2
Skyline (Municipality)—Jackson ... AL-2
Skyline (City)—Blue Earth MN-3
Skyline (CDP)—Douglas NE-4
Skyline-Ganipa (CDP)—Cibola NM-4
Sky Valley (City)—Rabun GA-2
Slagle (Township)—Wexford MI-3
Slana (CDP)—Valdez-Cordova Census
 Area AK-4
Slater (City)—Story IA-3
Slater (Township)—Cass MN-3
Slater (City)—Saline MO-3
Slater-Marietta (CDP)—
 Greenville SC-2
Slate Spring (Village)—Calhoun MS-2
Slatington (Borough)—Lehigh PA-1
Slaton (City)—Lubbock TX-2
Slaughter (Town)—East Feliciana
 Parish LA-2
Slaughter Beach (Town)—Sussex .. DE-1
Slaughters (City)—Webster KY-2
Slaughterville (Town)—
 Cleveland OK-2
Slayden (Town)—Dickson TN-2
Slayton (City)—Murray MN-3
Slayton (Township)—Murray MN-3

Sledge (Town)—Quitman MS-2
Sleepy Eye (City)—Brown MN-3
Sleepy Hollow (Village)—Kane IL-3
Sleepy Hollow (CDP)—
 Campbell WY-4
Sleetmute (CDP)—Bethel Census
 Area AK-4
Sletten (Township)—Polk MN-3
Slick (Town)—Creek OK-2
Slidell (City)—St. Tammany
 Parish LA-2
Sligo (Borough)—Clarion PA-1
Slinger (Village)—Washington WI-3
Slippery Rock (Borough)—Butler ... PA-1
Slippery Rock (Township)—
 Butler PA-1
Slippery Rock (Township)—
 Lawrence PA-1
Sloan (City)—Woodbury IA-3
Sloan (Village)—Erie NY-1
Sloatsburg (Village)—Rockland ... NY-1
Slocomb (Town)—Geneva AL-2
Slocum (Township)—Luzerne PA-1
Slope Center (Township)—Slope ... ND-4
Slope County ND-4
Smackover (City)—Union AR-2
Smallwood (Township)—Jasper IL-3
Smelser (Town)—Grant WI-3
Smelterville (City)—Shoshone ID-4
Smethport (Borough)—McKean ... PA-1
Smicksburg (Borough)—Indiana ... PA-1
Smiley (Township)—Pennington ... MN-3
Smiley (City)—Gonzales TX-2
Smith (Township)—Greene IN-3
Smith (Township)—Posey IN-3
Smith (Township)—Whitley IN-3
Smith (Township)—Thomas KS-4
Smith (Township)—Dade MO-3
Smith (Township)—Laclede MO-3
Smith (Township)—Worth MO-3
Smith (Township)—Towner ND-4
Smith (Township)—Belmont OH-3
Smith (Township)—Mahoning OH-3
Smith (Township)—Washington PA-1
Smith (Township)—Brule SD-4
Smithboro (Village)—Bond IL-3
Smith Center (City)—Smith KS-4
Smith County KS-4
Smith County MS-2
Smith County TN-2
Smith County TX-2
Smith Creek (CDP)—New
 Hanover NC-2
Smithers (City)—Fayette WV-2
Smithers (City)—Kanawha WV-2
Smithfield (Village)—Fulton IL-3
Smithfield (Township)—Dekalb IN-3
Smithfield (City)—Henry KY-2
Smithfield (Town)—Somerset ME-1
Smithfield (Village)—Gosper NE-4
Smithfield (Town)—Madison NY-1
Smithfield (Town)—Johnston NC-2
Smithfield (Township)—
 Jefferson OH-3
Smithfield (Village)—Jefferson ... OH-3
Smithfield (Township)—Bradford ... PA-1
Smithfield (Borough)—Fayette PA-1
Smithfield (Township)—
 Huntingdon PA-1
Smithfield (Township)—Monroe ... PA-1
Smithfield (Town)—Providence ... RI-1
Smithfield (City)—Cache UT-4
Smithfield (Town)—Isle of Wight .. VA-2
Smithfield (Town)—Wetzel WV-2
Smithland (City)—Woodbury IA-3

Smithland (City)—Livingston KY-2
Smith Mills (CDP)—Bristol MA-1
Smith River Rancheria (CA) *IndRes-4*
Smiths (Division)—Lee AL-2
Smithsburg (Town)—
 Washington MD-1
Smiths Grove (City)—Warren KY-2
Smithton (Township)—St. Clair IL-3
Smithton (Village)—St. Clair IL-3
Smithton (City)—Pettis MO-3
Smithton (Township)—Pettis MO-3
Smithton (Borough)—
 Westmoreland PA-1
Smithtown (CDP)—Suffolk NY-1
Smithtown (Town)—Suffolk NY-1
Smith Valley (CDP)—Lyon NV-4
Smith Village (Town)—
 Oklahoma OK-2
Smithville (Town)—Lawrence AR-2
Smithville (City)—Lee GA-2
Smithville (City)—Sumter GA-2
Smithville (Town)—Monroe MS-2
Smithville (City)—Clay MO-3
Smithville (Town)—Chenango NY-1
Smithville (Village)—Wayne OH-3
Smithville (Town)—McCurtain ... OK-2
Smithville (Township)—Meade SD-4
Smithville (Town)—DeKalb TN-2
Smithville (City)—Bastrop TX-2
Smoaks (Town)—Colleton SC-2
Smoke Rise (Division)—Blount ... AL-2
Smokey Point (CDP)—
 Snohomish WA-4
Smoky (Township)—Sherman KS-4
Smoky Butte (Township)—
 Divide ND-4
Smoky Hill (Township)—Geary KS-4
Smoky Hill (Township)—
 McPherson KS-4
Smoky Hill (Township)—Saline ... KS-4
Smoky Hollow (Township)—
 Cass MN-3
Smoky View (Township)—Saline ... KS-4
Smolan (City)—Saline KS-4
Smolan (Township)—Saline KS-4
Smyer (Town)—Hockley TX-2
Smyrna (Town)—Kent DE-1
Smyrna (Town)—New Castle DE-1
Smyrna (City)—Cobb GA-2
Smyrna (Township)—Jefferson IN-3
Smyrna (Town)—Aroostook ME-1
Smyrna (Town)—Chenango NY-1
Smyrna (Village)—Chenango NY-1
Smyrna (Town)—Cherokee SC-2
Smyrna (Town)—York SC-2
Smyrna (Town)—Rutherford TN-2
Smyth County VA-2
Snake River (CA) *Geog-4*
Snake Spring (Township)—
 Bedford PA-1
Snead (Municipality)—Blount AL-2
Sneads (Town)—Jackson FL-2
Sneads Ferry (CDP)—Onslow NC-2
Sneedville (Town)—Hancock TN-2
Snee Oosh (CDP)—Skagit WA-4
Snelling (Town)—Barnwell SC-2
Snellville (City)—Gwinnett GA-2
Sni-A-Bar (Township)—Jackson ... MO-3
Sni-A-Bar (Township)—
 Lafayette MO-3
Snohomish (City)—Snohomish ... WA-4
Snohomish County WA-4
Snook (City)—Burleson TX-2
Snoqualmie (City)—King WA-4
Snoqualmie Falls (WA) *Geog-4*

Snow (Township)—McLean *ND-4*
Snowflake (Town)—Navajo *AZ-4*
Snow Hill (Town)—Worcester *MD-1*
Snow Hill (Township)—Lincoln ... *MO-3*
Snow Hill (Town)—Greene............ *NC-2*
Snowmass Village (Town)—
  Pitkin *CO-4*
Snow Shoe (Borough)—Centre *PA-1*
Snow Shoe (Township)—Centre *PA-1*
Snowville (Town)—Box Elder *UT-4*
S.N.P.J. (Borough)—Lawrence *PA-1*
Snyder (Village)—Dodge *NE-4*
Snyder (City)—Kiowa *OK-2*
Snyder (Township)—Blair *PA-1*
Snyder (Township)—Jefferson *PA-1*
Snyder (City)—Scurry *TX-2*
Snyder County................................... *PA-1*
Snydertown (Borough)—
  Northumberland *PA-1*
Soap Lake (City)—Grant *WA-4*
Sobieski (City)—Morrison *MN-3*
Soboba Reservation (CA) *IndRes-4*
Socastee (CDP)—Horry *SC-2*
Social Circle (City)—Newton........... *GA-2*
Social Circle (City)—Walton *GA-2*
Society Hill (CDP)—Middlesex *NJ-1*
Society Hill (Town)—Darlington *SC-2*
Socorro (City)—Socorro *NM-4*
Socorro (Town)—El Paso *TX-2*
Socorro County................................*NM-4*
Soda Springs (City)—Caribou *ID-4*
Sodaville (Town)—Linn *OR-4*
Soddy-Daisy (City)—Hamilton...... *TN-2*
Sodus (Township)—Berrien *MI-3*
Sodus (Township)—Lyon *MN-3*
Sodus (Town)—Wayne *NY-1*
Sodus (Village)—Wayne *NY-1*
Sodus Point (Village)—Wayne *NY-1*
Sodville (Township)—Ford *KS-4*
Solana (CDP)—Charlotte *FL-2*
Solana Beach (City)—San Diego ... *CA-4*
Solano County *CA-4*
Soldier (City)—Monona *IA-3*
Soldier (City)—Jackson *KS-4*
Soldier (Township)—Jackson *KS-4*
Soldier (Township)—Shawnee.........*KS-4*
Soldiers Grove (Village)—
  Crawford *WI-3*
Soldotna (City)—Kenai Peninsula
  Borough..*AK-4*
Solebury (Township)—Bucks *PA-1*
Soledad (City)—Monterey............... *CA-4*
Solem (Township)—Douglas *MN-3*
Solen (City)—Sioux *ND-4*
Soler (Township)—Roseau *MN-3*
Solomon (Township)—Cloud.......... *KS-4*
Solomon (City)—Dickinson *KS-4*
Solomon (Township)—Graham *KS-4*
Solomon (Township)—Phillips *KS-4*
Solomon (Township)—Saline *KS-4*
Solomon (Township)—Sheridan *KS-4*
Solomon-District 3 (Township)—
  Norton *KS-4*
Solomon Rapids (Township)—
  Mitchell *KS-4*
Solon (City)—Johnson *IA-3*
Solon (Town)—Somerset *ME-1*
Solon (Township)—Kent *MI-3*
Solon (Township)—Leelanau *MI-3*
Solon (Town)—Cortland *NY-1*
Solon (Township)—Hettinger......... *ND-4*
Solon (City)—Cuyahoga.................*OH-3*
Solon Springs (Town)—Douglas *WI-3*
Solon Springs (Village)—Douglas .. *WI-3*
Solvang (City)—Santa Barbara *CA-4*

Solvay (Village)—Onondaga *NY-1*
Solway (City)—Beltrami *MN-3*
Solway (Township)—St. Louis *MN-3*
Somer (Township)—Champaign *IL-3*
Somerdale (Borough)—Camden *NJ-1*
Somerford (Township)—
  Madison *OH-3*
Somers (Town)—Tolland................ *CT-1*
Somers (City)—Calhoun *IA-3*
Somers (Town)—Westchester.......... *NY-1*
Somers (Township)—Preble *OH-3*
Somers (Town)—Kenosha *WI-3*
Somerset (Township)—Jackson...... *IL-3*
Somerset (City)—Pulaski *KY-2*
Somerset (Town)—Montgomery ... *MD-1*
Somerset (Town)—Bristol *MA-1*
Somerset (Township)—Hillsdale ... *MI-3*
Somerset (Township)—Steele *MN-3*
Somerset (Township)—Mercer...... *MO-3*
Somerset (CDP)—Somerset *NJ-1*
Somerset (Town)—Niagara *NY-1*
Somerset (Township)—Belmont.....*OH-3*
Somerset (Village)—Perry *OH-3*
Somerset (Borough)—Somerset....... *PA-1*
Somerset (Township)—Somerset *PA-1*
Somerset (Township)—
  Washington *PA-1*
Somerset (City)—Bexar.................. *TX-2*
Somerset (Town)—Windham *VT-1*
Somerset (Township)—St. Croix ... *WI-3*
Somerset (Village)—St. Croix *WI-3*
Somerset County *ME-1*
Somerset County *MD-1*
Somerset County *NJ-1*
Somerset County *PA-1*
Somers Point (City)—Atlantic *NJ-1*
Somersworth (City)—Strafford *NH-1*
Somerton (Town)—Yuma *AZ-4*
Somervell County *TX-2*
Somerville (Town)—Morgan *AL-2*
Somerville (Town)—Gibson *IN-3*
Somerville (Town)—Lincoln *ME-1*
Somerville (Town)—Middlesex *MA-1*
Somerville (Borough)—Somerset *NJ-1*
Somerville (Village)—Butler *OH-3*
Somerville (Town)—Fayette............ *TN-2*
Somerville (City)—Burleson *TX-2*
Somo (Town)—Lincoln *WI-3*
Somonauk (Town)—DeKalb *IL-3*
Somonauk (Township)—DeKalb *IL-3*
Somonauk (Town)—La Salle *IL-3*
Songer (Township)—Clay *IL-3*
Sonoma (City)—Sonoma................ *CA-4*
Sonoma County *CA-4*
Sonora (City)—Tuolumne *CA-4*
Sonora (Township)—Hancock *IL-3*
Sonora (City)—Hardin *KY-2*
Sonora (City)—Sutton *TX-2*
Soo (Township)—Chippewa *MI-3*
Soo (Township)—Burke *ND-4*
Soo Canals (WA) *Geog-4*
Sopchoppy (City)—Wakulla *FL-2*
Soper (Town)—Choctaw *OK-2*
Soperton (City)—Treutlen............... *GA-2*
Sophia (Town)—Raleigh *WV-2*
Soquel (CDP)—Santa Cruz *CA-4*
Sorenson (Township)—Towner *ND-4*
Sorento (Town)—Bond.................... *IL-3*
Sorkness (Township)—Mountrail...*ND-4*
Sorrento (Town)—Ascension
  Parish *LA-2*
Sorrento (Town)—Hancock............ *ME-1*
Soso (Town)—Jones *MS-2*
Souderton (Borough)—
  Montgomery *PA-1*

Soulsbyville (CDP)—Tuolumne *CA-4*
Sound Beach (CDP)—Suffolk *NY-1*
Souris (City)—Bottineau *ND-4*
Sour Lake (City)—Hardin.............. *TX-2*
South (Township)—Dade *MO-3*
South Abington (Township)—
  Lackawanna *PA-1*
South Amboy (City)—Middlesex *NJ-1*
South Amherst (CDP)—
  Hampshire *MA-1*
South Amherst (Village)—Lorain ..*OH-3*
Southampton (Town)—
  Hampshire *MA-1*
Southampton (Township)—
  Burlington *NJ-1*
Southampton (Town)—Suffolk *NY-1*
Southampton (Village)—Suffolk *NY-1*
Southampton (Township)—
  Bedford *PA-1*
Southampton (Township)—
  Cumberland *PA-1*
Southampton (Township)—
  Franklin.. *PA-1*
Southampton (Township)—
  Somerset *PA-1*
Southampton County *VA-2*
South Annville (Township)—
  Lebanon *PA-1*
South Apopka (CDP)—Orange *FL-2*
South Arm (Township)—
  Charlevoix *MI-3*
South Aroostook (unorganized) (Pop.
  Place)—Aroostook *ME-1*
South Ashburnham (CDP)—
  Worcester *MA-1*
South Augusta (CDP)—
  Richmond *GA-2*
Southaven (City)—DeSoto............. *MS-2*
South Barre (CDP)—Washington .. *VT-1*
South Barrington (Village)—Cook .. *IL-3*
South Bay (City)—Palm Beach........*FL-2*
South Beach (CDP)—Indian
  River *FL-2*
South Beaver (Township)—
  Beaver *PA-1*
South Belmar (Borough)—
  Monmouth *NJ-1*
South Beloit (Town)—Winnebago .. *IL-3*
South Bend (City)—St. Joseph *IN-3*
South Bend (Township)—Barton *KS-4*
South Bend (Township)—Blue
  Earth... *MN-3*
South Bend (Village)—Cass *NE-4*
South Bend (Township)—
  Armstrong *PA-1*
South Bend (City)—Pacific............ *WA-4*
South Benton (Township)—
  Dallas... *MO-3*
South Benton (Township)—Polk .. *MO-3*
South Berwick (Town)—York *ME-1*
South Bethany (Town)—Sussex *DE-1*
South Bethlehem (Borough)—
  Armstrong *PA-1*
South Billings (Pop. Place)—
  Billings *ND-4*
South Bloomfield (Township)—
  Morrow *OH-3*
South Bloomfield (Village)—
  Pickaway *OH-3*
Southborough (Town)—
  Worcester *MA-1*
South Boston (Independent City)...... *VA-2*
South Bound Brook (Borough)—
  Somerset *NJ-1*

General Index

South Bradenton (CDP)—Manatee *FL-2*
South Branch (Township)—Crawford *MI-3*
South Branch (Township)—Wexford *MI-3*
South Branch (Township)—Watonwan *MN-3*
South Branch (Township)—Nance *NE-4*
Southbridge (Town)—Worcester ... *MA-1*
South Bristol (Town)—Lincoln *ME-1*
South Bristol (Town)—Ontario *NY-1*
South Broadway (CDP)—Yakima *WA-4*
Southbrook (Township)—Cottonwood *MN-3*
South Brooksville (CDP)—Hernando *FL-2*
South Brown (Township)—Edwards *KS-4*
South Browning (CDP)—Glacier.. *MT-4*
South Brunswick (Township)—Middlesex *NJ-1*
South Buffalo (Township)—Armstrong *PA-1*
South Burlington (City)—Chittenden *VT-1*
Southbury (Town)—New Haven.... *CT-1*
South Campbell (Pop. Place)—Campbell *SD-4*
South Canaan (Township)—Wayne *PA-1*
South Canal (CDP)—Trumbull......*OH-3*
South Carrollton (City)—Muhlenberg *KY-2*
South Carthage (Town)—Smith *TN-2*
South Cedar (Township)—Saunders *NE-4*
South Centre (Township)—Columbia *PA-1*
South Charleston (Village)—Clark *OH-3*
South Charleston (City)—Kanawha *WV-2*
South Chicago Heights (Village)—Cook *IL-3*
South Clearwater (Pop. Place)—Clearwater *MN-3*
South Cle Elum (Town)—Kittitas *WA-4*
South Cleveland (CDP)—Bradley.. *TN-2*
South Coatesville (Borough)—Chester *PA-1*
South Coffeyville (Town)—Nowata *OK-2*
South Congaree (Town)—Lexington *SC-2*
South Connellsville (Borough)—Fayette *PA-1*
South Corning (Village)—Steuben *NY-1*
South Cottonwood (Township)—Wells *ND-4*
South Coventry (Township)—Chester *PA-1*
South Creek (Township)—Bradford *PA-1*
South Creek (Township)—Jones *SD-4*
South Crouch (Township)—Hamilton *IL-3*
South Dayton (Village)—Cattaraugus *NY-1*
South Daytona (City)—Volusia *FL-2*

South Deerfield (CDP)—Franklin *MA-1*
South Dennis (CDP)—Barnstable *MA-1*
South Detroit (Township)—Brown *SD-4*
South Dewey (Pop. Place)—Dewey *SD-4*
South Dixon (Township)—Lee *IL-3*
South Dos Palos (CDP)—Merced.. *CA-4*
South Dresden (Township)—Cavalier *ND-4*
South Dunn (Pop. Place)—Dunn ..*ND-4*
South Duxbury (CDP)—Plymouth *MA-1*
Southeast (Township)—Orange........ *IN-3*
Southeast (Town)—Putnam *NY-1*
Southeast Aitkin (Pop. Place)—Aitkin *MN-3*
Southeast Arcadia (CDP)—DeSoto *FL-2*
Southeast Bon Homme (Pop. Place)—Bon Homme *SD-4*
Southeast Buffalo (Pop. Place)—Buffalo *SD-4*
Southeast Fairbanks Census Area .. *AK-4*
Southeast Gregory (Pop. Place)—Gregory *SD-4*
Southeast Jackson (Pop. Place)—Jackson *SD-4*
Southeast Mahnomen (Pop. Place)—Mahnomen *MN-3*
Southeast Marion (Township)—Polk *MO-3*
Southeast McKenzie (Pop. Place)—McKenzie *ND-4*
Southeast Piscataquis (unorganized) (Pop. Place)—Piscataquis *ME-1*
Southeast Roseau (Pop. Place)—Roseau *MN-3*
Southeast Williams (Pop. Place)—Williams *ND-4*
Southeast Yankton (Pop. Place)—Yankton *SD-4*
South Elgin (Town)—Kane *IL-3*
South Eliot (CDP)—York *ME-1*
South Elkhorn (Township)—Warren *MO-3*
South El Monte (City)—Los Angeles *CA-4*
South Emmons (Pop. Place)—Emmons *ND-4*
South English (City)—Keokuk *IA-3*
Southern Pines (Town)—Moore ... *NC-2*
Southern Shops (CDP)—Spartanburg *SC-2*
Southern Shores (Town)—Dare *NC-2*
Southern Ute Reservation (CO) *IndRes-4*
Southern View (Village)—Sangamon *IL-3*
South Euclid (City)—Cuyahoga *OH-3*
South Fallsburg (CDP)—Sullivan .. *NY-1*
South Farmingdale (CDP)—Nassau *NY-1*
South Fayette (Township)—Allegheny *PA-1*
Southfield (City)—Oakland............ *MI-3*
Southfield (Township)—Oakland... *MI-3*
South Fillmore (Township)—Montgomery *IL-3*
South Flannigan (Township)—Hamilton *IL-3*

South Floral Park (Village)—Nassau *NY-1*
South Fork (Township)—Christian *IL-3*
South Fork (Township)—Kanabec *MN-3*
South Fork (Township)—Audrain *MO-3*
South Fork (Township)—Howell .. *MO-3*
South Fork (Township)—Monroe *MO-3*
South Fork (Township)—Adams.... *ND-4*
South Fork (Borough)—Cambria *PA-1*
South Fork (Town)—Rusk *WI-3*
South Franklin (Township)—Washington *PA-1*
South Franklin (unorganized) (Pop. Place)—Franklin *ME-1*
South Fulton (City)—Obion *TN-2*
South Galloway (Township)—Christian *MO-3*
South Gastonia (CDP)—Gaston..... *NC-2*
South Gate (City)—Los Angeles.... *CA-4*
Southgate (CDP)—Sarasota *FL-2*
Southgate (City)—Campbell *KY-2*
South Gate (CDP)—Anne Arundel *MD-1*
Southgate (City)—Wayne *MI-3*
South Gate Ridge (CDP)—Sarasota *FL-2*
South Gifford (Village)—Macon... *MO-3*
Southglenn (CDP)—Arapahoe *CO-4*
South Glens Falls (Village)—Saratoga *NY-1*
South Golden Valley (Pop. Place)—Golden Valley *ND-4*
South Gorin (Town)—Scotland *MO-3*
South Greeley (CDP)—Laramie ... *WY-4*
South Green (Township)—Polk *MO-3*
South Greenfield (Village)—Dade *MO-3*
South Greensburg (Borough)—Westmoreland *PA-1*
South Grove (Township)—DeKalb *IL-3*
South Gull Lake (CDP)—Kalamazoo *MI-3*
South Hackensack (Township)—Bergen *NJ-1*
South Hadley (Town)—Hampshire *MA-1*
South Hampton (Town)—Rockingham *NH-1*
South Hanover (Township)—Dauphin *PA-1*
South Harbor (Township)—Mille Lacs *MN-3*
South Harding (Pop. Place)—Harding *SD-4*
South Harrison (Township)—Gloucester *NJ-1*
South Haven (CDP)—Porter *IN-3*
South Haven (City)—Sumner *KS-4*
South Haven (Township)—Sumner *KS-4*
South Haven (City)—Allegan......... *MI-3*
South Haven (City)—Van Buren ... *MI-3*
South Haven (Township)—Van Buren *MI-3*
South Haven (City)—Wright *MN-3*
South Heart (City)—Stark *ND-4*
South Heidelberg (Township)—Berks *PA-1*
South Heights (Borough)—Beaver .. *PA-1*

South Hempstead (CDP)—
  Nassau NY-1
South Henderson (CDP)—Vance ... NC-2
South Hero (Town)—Grand Isle VT-1
South Hill (CDP)—Tompkins NY-1
South Hill (Town)—Mecklenburg ... VA-2
South Hill (CDP)—Pierce WA-4
South Holland (City)—Cook IL-3
South Homer (Township)—
  Champaign IL-3
South Homestead (Township)—
  Barton KS-4
South Hooksett (CDP)—
  Merrimack NH-1
South Houston (City)—Harris TX-2
South Huntingdon (Township)—
  Westmoreland PA-1
South Huntington (CDP)—
  Suffolk NY-1
South Hurricane (Township)—
  Fayette IL-3
South Hutchinson (City)—Reno KS-4
Southington (Town)—Hartford CT-1
Southington (Township)—
  Trumbull OH-3
South Jacksonville (Village)—
  Morgan IL-3
South Jordan (City)—Salt Lake UT-4
South Kensington (CDP)—
  Montgomery MD-1
South Kidder (Pop. Place)—
  Kidder ND-4
South Kingstown (Town)—
  Washington RI-1
South Koochiching (Pop. Place)—
  Koochiching MN-3
South Lake (CDP)—Kern CA-4
Southlake (City)—Denton TX-2
Southlake (City)—Tarrant TX-2
South Lake Tahoe (City)—El
  Dorado CA-4
South Lancaster (CDP)—
  Worcester MA-1
South Lancaster (Town)—Grant WI-3
South Laurel (CDP)—Prince
  George's MD-1
South Lawrence (Pop. Place)—
  Lawrence SD-4
South Lead Hill (Town)—Boone ... AR-2
South Lebanon (Village)—
  Warren OH-3
South Lebanon (CDP)—Linn OR-4
South Lebanon (Township)—
  Lebanon PA-1
South Lineville (Town)—Mercer .. MO-3
South Linn (Township)—
  Christian MO-3
South Litchfield (Township)—
  Montgomery IL-3
South Lockport (CDP)—Niagara ... NY-1
South Londonderry (Township)—
  Lebanon PA-1
South Loup (Township)—Hall NE-4
South Lyman (Pop. Place)—
  Lyman SD-4
South Lyon (City)—Oakland MI-3
South Macon (Township)—
  Macon IL-3
South Mahoning (Township)—
  Indiana PA-1
South Manheim (Township)—
  Schuylkill PA-1
South Mansfield (Village)—De Soto
  Parish LA-2
Southmayd (Town)—Grayson TX-2

South McLean (Pop. Place)—
  McLean ND-4
South Meadow (Township)—
  Williams ND-4
South Miami (City)—Dade FL-2
South Miami Heights (CDP)—
  Dade FL-2
South Middleton (Township)—
  Cumberland PA-1
South Middletown (CDP)—
  Butler OH-3
South Milwaukee (City)—
  Milwaukee WI-3
South Minnewaukan (Township)—
  Ramsey ND-4
South Moline (Township)—Rock
  Island IL-3
South Moniteau (Township)—
  Cooper MO-3
South Monroe (CDP)—Monroe MI-3
Southmont (Borough)—Cambria ... PA-1
South Morgan (Township)—
  Dade MO-3
South Mountain (Town)—
  Coryell TX-2
South Muddy (Township)—Jasper .. IL-3
South Naknek (CDP)—Bristol Bay
  Borough AK-4
South New Castle (Borough)—
  Lawrence PA-1
South Newton (Township)—
  Cumberland PA-1
South Nyack (Village)—
  Rockland NY-1
South Ogden (City)—Weber UT-4
Southold (Town)—Suffolk NY-1
South Olga (Township)—
  Cavalier ND-4
South Orange Village (Township)—
  Essex NJ-1
South Oroville (CDP)—Butte CA-4
South Ottawa (Township)—La
  Salle IL-3
South Otter (Township)—
  Macoupin IL-3
South Oxford (unorganized) (Pop.
  Place)—Oxford ME-1
South Padre Island (Town)—
  Cameron TX-2
South Palm Beach (Town)—Palm
  Beach FL-2
South Palmyra (Township)—
  Macoupin IL-3
South Paris (CDP)—Oxford ME-1
South Park (Township)—
  Allegheny PA-1
South Park View (City)—
  Jefferson KY-2
South Pasadena (City)—Los
  Angeles CA-4
South Pasadena (City)—Pinellas FL-2
South Patrick Shores (CDP)—
  Brevard FL-2
South Pekin (Town)—Tazewell IL-3
South Perkins (Pop. Place)—
  Perkins SD-4
South Philipsburg (Borough)—
  Centre PA-1
South Pierce (Pop. Place)—
  Pierce ND-4
South Pittsburg (City)—Marion TN-2
South Plainfield (Borough)—
  Middlesex NJ-1
South Platte (Township)—Hall NE-4
South Point (Village)—Lawrence ... OH-3

Southport (City)—Marion IN-3
Southport (Town)—Lincoln ME-1
Southport (Town)—Chemung NY-1
Southport (City)—Brunswick NC-2
South Portland (City)—
  Cumberland ME-1
South Prairie (Town)—Pierce WA-4
South Pymatuning (Township)—
  Mercer PA-1
South Randall (Township)—
  Thomas KS-4
South Range (Village)—
  Houghton MI-3
South Red River (Township)—
  Kittson MN-3
South Renovo (Borough)—
  Clinton PA-1
South River (Township)—
  Marion MO-3
South River (Borough)—
  Middlesex NJ-1
South Rock Island (Township)—Rock
  Island IL-3
South Rockwood (Village)—
  Monroe MI-3
South Rolette (Pop. Place)—
  Rolette ND-4
South Roscoe (Township)—
  Hodgeman KS-4
South Rosemary (CDP)—Halifax .. NC-2
South Ross (Township)—
  Vermilion IL-3
South Roxana (Town)—Madison ... IL-3
South Russell (Village)—Geauga ... OH-3
South Salem (Township)—
  Greenwood KS-4
South Salem (Village)—Ross OH-3
South Salt Lake (City)—Salt
  Lake UT-4
South Sanford (CDP)—York ME-1
South San Francisco (City)—San
  Mateo CA-4
South San Gabriel (CDP)—Los
  Angeles CA-4
South San Jose Hills (CDP)—Los
  Angeles CA-4
South Santa Rosa (CDP)—
  Sonoma CA-4
South Sarasota (CDP)—Sarasota FL-2
South Seward (Township)—
  Stafford KS-4
South Sharps Creek (Township)—
  McPherson KS-4
South Shenango (Township)—
  Crawford PA-1
South Sheridan (Pop. Place)—
  Sheridan ND-4
South Shore (City)—Greenup KY-2
South Shore (Town)—Codington ... SD-4
Southside (Municipality)—
  Calhoun AL-2
Southside (Municipality)—
  Etowah AL-2
Southside (Township)—Kearny KS-4
Southside (Township)—Wright MN-3
Southside Place (City)—Harris TX-2
South Sioux City (City)—Dakota .. NE-4
South Solon (Village)—Madison OH-3
South Stanley (Pop. Place)—
  Stanley SD-4
South St. Paul (City)—Dakota MN-3
South Strabane (Township)—
  Washington PA-1
South Sugar Creek (Township)—
  Randolph MO-3

South Sumter (CDP)—Sumter SC-2
South Taft (CDP)—Kern CA-4
South Thomaston (Town)—
  Knox ME-1
South Toms River (Borough)—
  Ocean NJ-1
South Tucson (City)—Pima AZ-4
South Twigg (Township)—
  Hamilton IL-3
South Union (Township)—
  Fayette PA-1
South Vacherie (CDP)—St. James
  Parish LA-2
South Valley (CDP)—Bernalillo ... NM-4
South Valley (Town)—
  Cattaraugus NY-1
South Valley (Township)—
  Rolette ND-4
South Valley Stream (CDP)—
  Nassau NY-1
South Venice (CDP)—Sarasota FL-2
South Versailles (Township)—
  Allegheny PA-1
South Vienna (Village)—Clark OH-3
South Viking (Township)—
  Benson ND-4
South Vinemont (Municipality)—
  Cullman AL-2
South Wallins (CDP)—Harlan KY-2
South Waverly (Borough)—
  Bradford PA-1
South Wayne (Village)—
  Lafayette WI-3
South Weber (City)—Davis UT-4
South Webster (Village)—Scioto OH-3
South Weldon (CDP)—Halifax NC-2
South Wenatchee (CDP)—
  Chelan WA-4
Southwest (Township)—Crawford .. IL-3
South West (Township)—Barton ... MO-3
Southwest (Township)—Sargent ND-4
Southwest (Township)—Warren PA-1
Southwest Bon Homme (Pop. Place)—
  Bon Homme SD-4
South West City (City)—
  McDonald MO-3
Southwest Fall River (Pop. Place)—Fall
  River SD-4
Southwest Faulk (Pop. Place)—
  Faulk SD-4
Southwest Greensburg (Borough)—
  Westmoreland PA-1
Southwest Harbor (Town)—
  Hancock ME-1
Southwest Jackson (Pop. Place)—
  Jackson SD-4
Southwest Madison (Township)—
  Perry PA-1
Southwest Marion (Township)—
  Polk MO-3
Southwest McIntosh (Pop. Place)—
  McIntosh ND-4
Southwest McKenzie (Pop. Place)—
  McKenzie ND-4
Southwest Meade (Pop. Place)—
  Meade SD-4
Southwest Mountrail (Pop. Place)—
  Mountrail ND-4
Southwest Perkins (Pop. Place)—
  Perkins SD-4
Southwest Sioux (Pop. Place)—
  Sioux ND-4
South Wheatland (Township)—
  Macon IL-3
South Whitehall (Township)—
  Lehigh PA-1
South Whitley (Town)—Whitley IN-3
South Whittier (CDP)—Los
  Angeles CA-4
Southwick (Town)—Hampden MA-1
South Williamsport (Borough)—
  Lycoming PA-1
South Wilmington (Village)—
  Grundy IL-3
South Windsor (Town)—
  Hartford CT-1
Southwood Acres (CDP)—
  Hartford CT-1
South Woodbury (Township)—
  Bedford PA-1
South Yarmouth (CDP)—
  Barnstable MA-1
South Yuba City (CDP)—Sutter CA-4
South Zanesville (Village)—
  Muskingum OH-3
South Ziebach (Pop. Place)—
  Ziebach SD-4
Spackenkill (CDP)—Dutchess NY-1
Spade (Township)—Knox NE-4
Spafford (Town)—Onondaga NY-1
Spalding (Township)—
  Menominee MI-3
Spalding (Township)—Aitkin MN-3
Spalding (Village)—Greeley NE-4
Spalding County GA-2
Spanaway (CDP)—Pierce WA-4
Spang (Township)—Itasca MN-3
Spangle (City)—Spokane WA-4
Spangler (Borough)—Cambria PA-1
Spanish Fork (City)—Utah UT-4
Spanish Fort (Division)—
  Baldwin AL-2
Spanish Lake (CDP)—St. Louis ... MO-3
Spanish Lake (Township)—St.
  Louis MO-3
Sparkman (Town)—Dallas AR-2
Sparks (Town)—Cook GA-2
Sparks (City)—Washoe NV-4
Sparks (Town)—Lincoln OK-2
Sparks (CDP)—El Paso TX-2
Sparland (Village)—Marshall IL-3
Sparlingville (CDP)—St. Clair MI-3
Sparta (City)—Hancock GA-2
Sparta (Township)—Knox IL-3
Sparta (Town)—Randolph IL-3
Sparta (Township)—Dearborn IN-3
Sparta (Township)—Noble IN-3
Sparta (City)—Gallatin KY-2
Sparta (City)—Owen KY-2
Sparta (Township)—Kent MI-3
Sparta (Village)—Kent MI-3
Sparta (Township)—Chippewa MN-3
Sparta (City)—Christian MO-3
Sparta (Township)—Christian MO-3
Sparta (Township)—Knox NE-4
Sparta (Township)—Sussex NJ-1
Sparta (Town)—Livingston NY-1
Sparta (Town)—Alleghany NC-2
Sparta (Village)—Morrow OH-3
Sparta (Township)—Crawford PA-1
Sparta (Town)—White TN-2
Sparta (City)—Monroe WI-3
Sparta (Town)—Monroe WI-3
Spartanburg (City)—Spartanburg ... SC-2
Spartanburg County SC-2
Spartansburg (Borough)—
  Crawford PA-1
Spaulding (Village)—Sangamon IL-3
Spaulding (Township)—Saginaw MI-3
Spavinaw (Town)—Mayes OK-2
Speaker (Township)—Sanilac MI-3
Spearfish (City)—Lawrence SD-4
Spearman (City)—Hansford TX-2
Spearsville (Village)—Union
  Parish LA-2
Spearville (City)—Ford KS-4
Spearville (Township)—Ford KS-4
Speculator (Village)—Hamilton NY-1
Speed (City)—Phillips KS-4
Speed (Town)—Edgecombe NC-2
Speedway (Town)—Marion IN-3
Speedwell (Township)—St. Clair .. MO-3
Speedwell (Township)—Wells ND-4
Speers (Borough)—Washington PA-1
Spencer (City)—Clark ID-4
Spencer (Township)—Dekalb IN-3
Spencer (Township)—Harrison IN-3
Spencer (Township)—Jennings IN-3
Spencer (Town)—Owen IN-3
Spencer (City)—Clay IA-3
Spencer (Town)—Worcester MA-1
Spencer (Township)—Kent MI-3
Spencer (Township)—Aitkin MN-3
Spencer (Township)—Douglas MO-3
Spencer (Township)—Pike MO-3
Spencer (Township)—Ralls MO-3
Spencer (Township)—Boyd NE-4
Spencer (Village)—Boyd NE-4
Spencer (Town)—Tioga NY-1
Spencer (Village)—Tioga NY-1
Spencer (Town)—Rowan NC-2
Spencer (Township)—Ward ND-4
Spencer (Township)—Allen OH-3
Spencer (Township)—Guernsey OH-3
Spencer (Township)—Lucas OH-3
Spencer (Township)—Medina OH-3
Spencer (Village)—Medina OH-3
Spencer (City)—Oklahoma OK-2
Spencer (City)—McCook SD-4
Spencer (Town)—Van Buren TN-2
Spencer (City)—Roane WV-2
Spencer (Town)—Marathon WI-3
Spencer (Village)—Marathon WI-3
Spencer Brook (Township)—
  Isanti MN-3
Spencer County IN-3
Spencer County KY-2
Spencer Creek (Township)—St.
  Charles MO-3
Spencer Mountain (Town)—
  Gaston NC-2
Spencerport (Village)—Monroe NY-1
Spencerville (Village)—Allen OH-3
Sperry (Town)—Tulsa OK-2
Spiceland (Town)—Henry IN-3
Spiceland (Township)—Henry IN-3
Spicer (City)—Kandiyohi MN-3
Spice Valley (Township)—
  Lawrence IN-3
Spickard (City)—Grundy MO-3
Spider Lake (Town)—Sawyer WI-3
Spillertown (Village)—Williamson .. IL-3
Spillville (City)—Winneshiek IA-3
Spindale (Town)—Rutherford NC-2
Spink (Township)—Union SD-4
Spink County SD-4
Spirit (Town)—Price WI-3
Spirit Lake (City)—Kootenai ID-4
Spirit Lake (City)—Dickinson IA-3
Spirit Lake (Township)—
  Kingsbury SD-4
Spirit Mound (Township)—Clay SD-4
Spiritwood (Township)—
  Stutsman ND-4

Spiritwood Lake (City)—
  Stutsman ND-4
Spiro (Town)—Le Flore OK-2
Spivey (City)—Kingman KS-4
Splendora (City)—Montgomery TX-2
Splithand (Township)—Itasca MN-3
Split Rock (Township)—Carlton .. MN-3
Split Rock (Township)—
  Minnehaha SD-4
Spofford (City)—Kinney TX-2
Spokane (City)—Spokane WA-4
Spokane County WA-4
Spokane Reservation (WA) IndRes-4
Spooner (City)—Washburn WI-3
Spooner (Town)—Washburn WI-3
Sportsmen Acres (Town)—Mayes .. OK-2
Spotswood (Borough)—
  Middlesex NJ-1
Spotsylvania County VA-2
Spotsylvania Courthouse (CDP)—
  Spotsylvania VA-2
Sprague (Town)—New London CT-1
Sprague (Village)—Lancaster NE-4
Sprague (City)—Lincoln WA-4
Spragueville (City)—Jackson IA-3
Spray (Town)—Wheeler OR-4
Sprigg (Township)—Adams OH-3
Spring (Township)—Boone IL-3
Spring (Township)—Butler KS-4
Spring (Township)—Berks PA-1
Spring (Township)—Centre PA-1
Spring (Township)—Crawford PA-1
Spring (Township)—Perry PA-1
Spring (Township)—Snyder PA-1
Spring (Township)—Spink SD-4
Spring (CDP)—Harris TX-2
Spring Arbor (Township)—
  Jackson MI-3
Spring Bank (Township)—Dixon ... NE-4
Spring Bay (Township)—
  Woodford IL-3
Spring Bay (Village)—Woodford IL-3
Springboro (City)—Montgomery ... OH-3
Springboro (City)—Warren OH-3
Springboro (Borough)—Crawford .. PA-1
Springbrook (City)—Jackson IA-3
Springbrook (Township)—
  Sheridan KS-4
Spring Brook (Township)—
  Kittson MN-3
Spring Brook (City)—Williams ND-4
Springbrook (Township)—
  Williams ND-4
Spring Brook (Township)—
  Lackawanna PA-1
Spring Brook (Town)—Dunn WI-3
Springbrook (Town)—Washburn WI-3
Spring City (Borough)—Chester PA-1
Spring City (Town)—Rhea TN-2
Spring City (City)—Sanpete UT-4
Spring Coulee (Township)—
  Mountrail ND-4
Spring Creek (Township)—Pike IL-3
Spring Creek (Township)—Coffey .. KS-4
Spring Creek (Township)—
  Cowley KS-4
Spring Creek (Township)—
  Greenwood KS-4
Spring Creek (Township)—Lane ... KS-4
Spring Creek (Township)—
  Pottawatomie KS-4
Spring Creek (Township)—Saline ... KS-4
Spring Creek (Township)—
  Becker MN-3

Spring Creek (Township)—
  Norman MN-3
Spring Creek (Township)—Dent ... MO-3
Spring Creek (Township)—
  Douglas MO-3
Spring Creek (Township)—
  Howell MO-3
Spring Creek (Township)—
  Maries MO-3
Spring Creek (Township)—
  Ozark MO-3
Spring Creek (Township)—
  Phelps MO-3
Spring Creek (Township)—
  Shannon MO-3
Spring Creek (Township)—
  Custer NE-4
Spring Creek (CDP)—Elko NV-4
Spring Creek (Township)—
  Barnes ND-4
Springcreek (Township)—Miami ... OH-3
Spring Creek (Township)—Elk PA-1
Spring Creek (Township)—
  Warren PA-1
Spring Creek (Township)—
  Moody SD-4
Spring Creek (CDP)—Todd SD-4
Springdale (City)—Benton AR-2
Springdale (City)—Washington AR-2
Springdale (Township)—Sumner ... KS-4
Springdale (Township)—
  Manistee MI-3
Springdale (Township)—
  Redwood MN-3
Springdale (Township)—Valley NE-4
Springdale (City)—Hamilton OH-3
Springdale (Borough)—Allegheny ... PA-1
Springdale (Township)—
  Allegheny PA-1
Springdale (CDP)—Lancaster SC-2
Springdale (Town)—Lexington SC-2
Springdale (Township)—Lincoln SD-4
Springdale (Township)—Roberts ... SD-4
Springdale (Town)—Washington ... UT-4
Springdale (Town)—Stevens WA-4
Springdale (Town)—Dane WI-3
Springer (Town)—Colfax NM-4
Springer (Township)—Ransom ND-4
Springer (Town)—Carter OK-2
Springerton (Village)—White IL-3
Springerville (Town)—Apache AZ-4
Springettsbury (Township)—York ... PA-1
Springfield (Town)—Baca CO-4
Springfield (City)—Bay FL-2
Springfield (City)—Effingham GA-2
Springfield (City)—Sangamon IL-3
Springfield (Township)—
  Sangamon IL-3
Springfield (Township)—Allen IN-3
Springfield (Township)—Franklin .. IN-3
Springfield (Township)—La Porte .. IN-3
Springfield (Township)—Lagrange .. IN-3
Springfield (City)—Washington KY-2
Springfield (Town)—Livingston
  Parish LA-2
Springfield (Town)—Penobscot ME-1
Springfield (City)—Hampden MA-1
Springfield (City)—Calhoun MI-3
Springfield (Township)—
  Kalkaska MI-3
Springfield (Township)—Oakland .. MI-3
Springfield (Township)—Brown MN-3
Springfield (Township)—
  Cottonwood MN-3
Springfield (City)—Christian MO-3

Springfield (City)—Greene MO-3
Springfield (Township)—Henry MO-3
Springfield (City)—Sarpy NE-4
Springfield (Town)—Sullivan NH-1
Springfield (Township)—
  Burlington NJ-1
Springfield (Township)—Union NJ-1
Springfield (Town)—Otsego NY-1
Springfield (Township)—Towner ... ND-4
Springfield (City)—Clark OH-3
Springfield (Township)—Clark OH-3
Springfield (Township)—Gallia OH-3
Springfield (Township)—
  Hamilton OH-3
Springfield (Township)—
  Jefferson OH-3
Springfield (Township)—Lucas OH-3
Springfield (Township)—
  Mahoning OH-3
Springfield (Township)—
  Muskingum OH-3
Springfield (Township)—
  Richland OH-3
Springfield (Township)—Ross OH-3
Springfield (Township)—Summit .. OH-3
Springfield (Township)—
  Williams OH-3
Springfield (City)—Lane OR-4
Springfield (Township)—Bradford .. PA-1
Springfield (Township)—Bucks PA-1
Springfield (Township)—
  Delaware PA-1
Springfield (Township)—Erie PA-1
Springfield (Township)—Fayette ... PA-1
Springfield (Township)—
  Huntingdon PA-1
Springfield (Township)—Mercer PA-1
Springfield (Township)—
  Montgomery PA-1
Springfield (Township)—York PA-1
Springfield (Town)—Orangeburg ... SC-2
Springfield (City)—Bon Homme ... SD-4
Springfield (City)—Robertson TN-2
Springfield (Town)—Windsor VT-1
Springfield (Town)—Dane WI-3
Springfield (Town)—Jackson WI-3
Springfield (Town)—Marquette WI-3
Springfield (Town)—St. Croix WI-3
Spring Garden (Township)—
  Jefferson IL-3
Spring Garden (Township)—York .. PA-1
Spring Green (Town)—Sauk WI-3
Spring Green (Village)—Sauk WI-3
Spring Grove (Village)—McHenry . IL-3
Spring Grove (Township)—
  Warren IL-3
Spring Grove (Town)—Wayne IN-3
Spring Grove (City)—Houston MN-3
Spring Grove (Township)—
  Houston MN-3
Spring Grove (Township)—
  Harlan NE-4
Spring Grove (Township)—
  McHenry ND-4
Spring Grove (Borough)—York PA-1
Spring Grove (Township)—
  Roberts SD-4
Spring Grove (Town)—Green WI-3
Spring Hill (CDP)—Hernando FL-2
Spring Hill (Town)—Marion IN-3
Spring Hill (City)—Warren IA-3
Spring Hill (City)—Johnson KS-4
Spring Hill (Township)—Johnson ... KS-4
Spring Hill (City)—Miami KS-4
Springhill (City)—Webster Parish ... LA-2

General Index American Places Dictionary

Spring Hill (City)—Stearns MN-3
Spring Hill (Township)—Stearns .. MN-3
Springhill (Township)—Fayette....... PA-1
Springhill (Township)—Greene....... PA-1
Spring Hill (Township)—Hand SD-4
Spring Hill (Town)—Maury TN-2
Spring Hill (Town)—Williamson ... TN-2
Spring Hollow (Township)—
 Laclede MO-3
Spring Hope (Town)—Nash NC-2
Spring Lake (Township)—
 Tazewell IL-3
Spring Lake (Town)—Hancock IN-3
Spring Lake (Township)—Ottawa .. MI-3
Spring Lake (Village)—Ottawa MI-3
Spring Lake (Township)—Scott MN-3
Spring Lake (Borough)—
 Monmouth NJ-1
Spring Lake (Town)—
 Cumberland NC-2
Spring Lake (Township)—Ward.... ND-4
Spring Lake (Township)—Hand ... SD-4
Spring Lake (Township)—
 Hanson SD-4
Spring Lake (Township)—
 Kingsbury SD-4
Springlake (Town)—Lamb TX-2
Spring Lake (Town)—Pierce WI-3
Spring Lake Heights (Borough)—
 Monmouth NJ-1
Spring Lake Park (City)—Anoka .. MN-3
Spring Lake Park (City)—
 Ramsey MN-3
Springlee (City)—Jefferson KY-2
Spring Mill (City)—Jefferson......... KY-2
Spring Park (City)—Hennepin....... MN-3
Spring Point (Township)—
 Cumberland IL-3
Springport (Town)—Henry IN-3
Springport (Township)—Jackson ... MI-3
Springport (Village)—Jackson........ MI-3
Springport (Town)—Cayuga NY-1
Spring Prairie (Township)—Clay .. MN-3
Spring Prairie (Town)—
 Walworth WI-3
Spring Ranch (Township)—Clay.... NE-4
Spring River (Township)—
 Lawrence MO-3
Springs (CDP)—Suffolk NY-1
Springtown (City)—Parker TX-2
Springvale (CDP)—York ME-1
Springvale (Township)—Emmet MI-3
Springvale (Township)—Isanti MN-3
Springvale (Township)—Barnes ND-4
Springvale (Town)—Columbia WI-3
Springvale (Town)—Fond du Lac.. WI-3
Spring Valley (CDP)—San Diego .. CA-4
Spring Valley (Town)—Bureau........ IL-3
Spring Valley (Township)—
 Cherokee KS-4
Spring Valley (Township)—
 McPherson KS-4
Spring Valley (City)—Jefferson....... KY-2
Spring Valley (City)—Fillmore MN-3
Spring Valley (Township)—
 Fillmore MN-3
Spring Valley (Township)—
 Shannon MO-3
Spring Valley (CDP)—Clark NV-4
Spring Valley (Village)—
 Rockland NY-1
Spring Valley (Township)—
 Dickey ND-4
Spring Valley (Township)—
 Greene OH-3

Spring Valley (Village)—Greene OH-3
Spring Valley (Township)—Clark... SD-4
Spring Valley (Pop. Place)—
 Gregory SD-4
Spring Valley (Township)—
 McCook..................................... SD-4
Spring Valley (Township)—
 Turner SD-4
Spring Valley (City)—Harris TX-2
Spring Valley (Village)—Pierce WI-3
Spring Valley (Town)—Rock WI-3
Spring Valley (Village)—St.
 Croix WI-3
Springview (Village)—Keya Paha .. NE-4
Springville (Town)—St. Clair......... AL-2
Springville (City)—Linn IA-3
Springville (Township)—Wexford .. MI-3
Springville (Village)—Erie............. NY-1
Springville (Township)—
 Susquehanna PA-1
Springville (City)—Utah UT-4
Springville (Town)—Adams WI-3
Springwater (Township)—Rock MN-3
Springwater (Town)—Livingston ... NY-1
Springwater (Town)—Waushara ... WI-3
Spruce (Township)—Roseau MN-3
Spruce (Township)—Bates MO-3
Spruce (Town)—Oconto WI-3
Spruce Creek (Township)—
 Huntingdon PA-1
Spruce Grove (Township)—
 Becker MN-3
Spruce Grove (Township)—
 Beltrami MN-3
Spruce Hill (Township)—
 Douglas MN-3
Spruce Hill (Township)—Juniata .. PA-1
Spruce Knob (WV) Geog-4
Spruce Pine (Town)—Mitchell....... NC-2
Spruce Valley (Township)—
 Marshall MN-3
Spur (City)—Dickens TX-2
Spurgeon (Town)—Pike IN-3
Spurgeon (CDP)—Sullivan TN-2
Spurgeon (CDP)—Washington....... TN-2
Spurr (Township)—Baraga MI-3
Square Lake (unorganized) (Pop.
 Place)—Aroostook...................... ME-1
Squaw Grove (Township)—
 DeKalb IL-3
Squaw Lake (City)—Itasca............ MN-3
Squaw Valley (CDP)—Fresno CA-4
Squaxin Island Reservation & Trust
 Lands (WA) IndRes-4
Stacy (City)—Chisago................... MN-3
Stacyville (City)—Mitchell IA-3
Stacyville (Town)—Penobscot....... ME-1
Stafford (Town)—Tolland CT-1
Stafford (Township)—Dekalb IN-3
Stafford (Township)—Greene IN-3
Stafford (City)—Stafford................ KS-4
Stafford (Township)—Stafford........ KS-4
Stafford (Township)—Roseau MN-3
Stafford (Township)—Ocean NJ-1
Stafford (Town)—Genesee NY-1
Stafford (Township)—Renville ND-4
Stafford (Village)—Monroe............ OH-3
Stafford (Town)—Fort Bend TX-2
Stafford (Town)—Harris TX-2
Stafford County KS-4
Stafford County VA-2
Stafford Springs (Borough)—
 Tolland CT-1
Stagecoach (Town)—
 Montgomery TX-2

Staked Plains (WV) Geog-4
Staley (Town)—Randolph NC-2
Stallings (Town)—Union NC-2
Stambaugh (City)—Iron MI-3
Stambaugh (Township)—Iron MI-3
Stamford (City)—Fairfield CT-1
Stamford (Village)—Harlan NE-4
Stamford (Town)—Delaware......... NY-1
Stamford (Village)—Delaware NY-1
Stamford (City)—Haskell............... TX-2
Stamford (City)—Jones TX-2
Stamford (Town)—Bennington VT-1
Stampers Creek (Township)—
 Orange IN-3
Stamping Ground (City)—Scott KY-2
Stamps (City)—Lafayette AR-2
Stanaford (CDP)—Raleigh............ WV-2
Stanardsville (Town)—Greene VA-2
Stanberry (City)—Gentry MO-3
Stanchfield (Township)—Isanti MN-3
Standard (Village)—Putnam IL-3
Standard City (Village)—
 Macoupin IL-3
Standing Pine (CDP)—Leake MS-3
Standing Rock Reservation
 (ND) IndRes-4
Standing Stone (Township)—
 Bradford PA-1
Standish (Town)—Cumberland..... ME-1
Standish (City)—Arenac MI-3
Standish (Township)—Arenac........ MI-3
Stanfield (Town)—Stanly NC-2
Stanfield (City)—Umatilla OR-4
Stanfold (Town)—Barron WI-3
Stanford (CDP)—Santa Clara CA-4
Stanford (Township)—Clay............. IL-3
Stanford (Village)—McLean IL-3
Stanford (City)—Lincoln KY-2
Stanford (Township)—Isanti MN-3
Stanford (Town)—Judith Basin MT-4
Stanford (Town)—Dutchess NY-1
Stanhope (City)—Hamilton IA-3
Stanhope (Borough)—Sussex NJ-1
Stanislaus County......................... CA-4
Stanley (City)—Custer................... ID-4
Stanley (City)—Buchanan IA-3
Stanley (City)—Fayette IA-3
Stanley (Village)—De Soto
 Parish LA-2
Stanley (Township)—Lyon MN-3
Stanley (Town)—Gaston NC-2
Stanley (Township)—Cass ND-4
Stanley (City)—Mountrail ND-4
Stanley (Town)—Page VA-2
Stanley (Town)—Barron WI-3
Stanley (City)—Chippewa WI-3
Stanley County SD-4
Stanleytown (CDP)—Henry........... VA-2
Stanleyville (CDP)—Forsyth NC-2
Stanly County NC-2
Stannard (Township)—
 Ontonagon MI-3
Stannard (Town)—Caledonia......... VT-1
Stannards (CDP)—Allegany NY-1
Stansbury Park (CDP)—Tooele ... UT-4
Stanton (City)—Orange CA-4
Stanton (CDP)—New Castle......... DE-3
Stanton (Township)—Champaign ... IL-3
Stanton (City)—Montgomery..........IA-3
Stanton (Township)—Linn KS-4
Stanton (Township)—Miami KS-4
Stanton (Township)—Ottawa KS-4
Stanton (Township)—Stanton KS-4
Stanton (City)—Powell KY-2
Stanton (Township)—Houghton MI-3

1100

Stanton (City)—Montcalm............ *MI-3*
Stanton (Township)—Goodhue..... *MN-3*
Stanton (Township)—Antelope..... *NE-4*
Stanton (Township)—Fillmore....... *NE-4*
Stanton (City)—Stanton................. *NE-4*
Stanton (City)—Mercer.................. *ND-2*
Stanton (Town)—Haywood........... *TN-2*
Stanton (City)—Martin................... *TX-2*
Stanton (Town)—Dunn.................. *WI-3*
Stanton (Town)—St. Croix............ *WI-3*
Stanton County............................... *KS-4*
Stanton County................................ *NE-4*
Stantonsburg (Town)—Wilson..... *NC-2*
Stantonville (Town)—McNairy...... *TN-2*
Stanwood (City)—Cedar *IA-3*
Stanwood (Village)—Mecosta........ *MI-3*
Stanwood (City)—Snohomish....... *WA-4*
Staplehurst (Village)—Seward....... *NE-4*
Staples (City)—Todd...................... *MN-3*
Staples (Township)—Todd *MN-3*
Staples (City)—Wadena................. *MN-3*
Stapleton (Town)—Jefferson *GA-2*
Stapleton (Village)—Logan *NE-4*
Star (Township)—Coffey................ *KS-4*
Star (Township)—Antrim *MI-3*
Star (Township)—Pennington....... *MN-3*
Star (Town)—Montgomery *NC-2*
Star (Township)—Bowman *ND-4*
Star (Township)—Clay *SD-4*
Starbuck (City)—Pope................... *MN-3*
Starbuck (Township)—Bottineau ... *ND-4*
Starbuck (Town)—Columbia.......... *WA-4*
Star City (City)—Lincoln *AR-2*
Star City (Town)—Monongalia..... *WV-2*
Star Harbor (Town)—Henderson... *TX-2*
Stark (City)—Neosho...................... *KS-4*
Stark (Township)—Brown *MN-3*
Stark (Township)—Hickory............ *MO-3*
Stark (Town)—Coos *NH-1*
Stark (Town)—Herkimer................ *NY-1*
Stark (Town)—Vernon *WI-3*
Stark City (Town)—Newton.......... *MO-3*
Stark County.................................... *IL-3*
Stark County.................................... *ND-4*
Stark County.................................... *OH-3*
Starke (City)—Bradford *FL-2*
Starke County................................. *IN-3*
Starkey (Town)—Yates.................... *NY-1*
Starkey (Township)—Logan *ND-4*
Starks (Town)—Somerset *ME-1*
Starksboro (Town)—Addison......... *VT-1*
Starkville (Town)—Las Animas *CO-4*
Starkville (City)—Oktibbeha.......... *MS-2*
Starkweather (City)—Ramsey........ *ND-4*
Star Lake (Township)—Otter
 Tail *MN-3*
Star Lake (CDP)—St. Lawrence *NY-1*
Star Prairie (Township)—Tripp..... *SD-4*
Star Prairie (Town)—St. Croix...... *WI-3*
Star Prairie (Village)—St. Croix *WI-3*
Starr (Township)—Cloud................ *KS-4*
Starr (Township)—Hocking............ *OH-3*
Starr (Town)—Anderson *SC-2*
Starr (Township)—Hutchinson...... *SD-4*
Starr County.................................... *TX-2*
Starr School (CDP)—Glacier *MT-4*
Starrucca (Borough)—Wayne......... *PA-1*
Startex (CDP)—Spartanburg..........*SC-2*
Star Valley (Township)—Gregory .. *SD-4*
Star Valley (Town)—Tripp *SD-4*
State Center (City)—Marshall........ *IA-3*
State College (Borough)—Centre.... *PA-1*
State Line (City)—Kootenai *ID-4*
Stateline (Township)—Sherman.....*KS-4*
State Line (Town)—Greene........... *MS-2*

State Line (Town)—Wayne *MS-2*
Stateline (CDP)—Douglas.............. *NV-4*
State Line City (Town)—Warren *IN-3*
Stately (Township)—Brown *MN-3*
Staten Island (NY)....................... *Geog-4*
Statenville (Pop. Place)—Echols.... *GA-2*
Statesboro (City)—Bulloch............. *GA-2*
Statesville (City)—Iredell *NC-2*
Statham (City)—Barrow................. *GA-2*
Staunton (Town)—Macoupin.......... *IL-3*
Staunton (Township)—Macoupin.. *IL-3*
Staunton (Town)—Clay *IN-3*
Staunton (Township)—Miami........ *OH-3*
Staunton (Independent City)...... *VA-2*
Stavanger (Township)—Traill *ND-4*
Stave (Township)—Mountrail........ *ND-4*
Stayton (City)—Marion................... *OR-4*
Steamboat River (Township)—
 Hubbard...................................... *MN-3*
Steamboat Rock (City)—Hardin....*IA-3*
Steamboat Springs (City)—Routt .. *CO-4*
Stearns (CDP)—McCreary............. *KY-2*
Stearns County............................... *MN-3*
Stebbins (City)—Nome Census
 Area... *AK-4*
Stedman (Town)—Cumberland..... *NC-2*
Steel Creek (Township)—Holt *NE-4*
Steele (Town)—St. Clair..................*AL-2*
Steele (Township)—Daviess *IN-3*
Steele (City)—Pemiscot.................. *MO-3*
Steele (City)—Kidder *ND-4*
Steele City (Village)—Jefferson *NE-4*
Steele County.................................. *MN-3*
Steele County.................................. *ND-4*
Steeleville (Town)—Randolph *IL-3*
Steelton (Borough)—Dauphin........ *PA-1*
Steelville (City)—Crawford............ *MO-3*
Steen (Township)—Knox *IN-3*
Steen (City)—Rock......................... *MN-3*
Steenerson (Township)—
 Beltrami *MN-3*
Steger (Village)—Cook *IL-3*
Steger (Village)—Will *IL-3*
Steiber (Township)—Burleigh *ND-4*
Steilacoom (Town)—Pierce *WA-4*
Steinauer (Village)—Pawnee *NE-4*
Steiner (Township)—Hettinger *ND-4*
Stella (Town)—Newton *MO-3*
Stella (Village)—Richardson *NE-4*
Stella (Town)—Oneida *WI-3*
Stem (Town)—Granville *NC-2*
Stena (Township)—Marshall.......... *SD-4*
Stephen (City)—Marshall *MN-3*
Stephens (City)—Ouachita............. *AR-2*
Stephens City (Town)—Frederick.. *VA-2*
Stephens County............................. *GA-2*
Stephens County............................. *OK-2*
Stephens County............................. *TX-2*
Stephenson (City)—Menominee *MI-3*
Stephenson (Township)—
 Menominee *MI-3*
Stephenson (Town)—Marinette *WI-3*
Stephenson County......................... *IL-3*
Stephentown (Town)—Rensselaer... *NY-1*
Stephenville (City)—Erath *TX-2*
Sterling (CDP)—Kenai Peninsula
 Borough *AK-4*
Sterling (City)—Logan.................... *CO-4*
Sterling (Town)—Windham *CT-1*
Sterling (City)—Whiteside *IL-3*
Sterling (Township)—Whiteside *IL-3*
Sterling (Township)—Crawford *IN-3*
Sterling (Township)—Hodgeman.... *KS-4*
Sterling (City)—Rice *KS-4*
Sterling (Township)—Rice *KS-4*

Sterling (Town)—Worcester *MA-1*
Sterling (Village)—Arenac............. *MI-3*
Sterling (Township)—Blue Earth .. *MN-3*
Sterling (Village)—Johnson *NE-4*
Sterling (Town)—Cayuga............... *NY-1*
Sterling (Township)—Burleigh *ND-4*
Sterling (Township)—Brown *OH-3*
Sterling (Town)—Comanche.......... *OK-2*
Sterling (Township)—Wayne *PA-1*
Sterling (Township)—Brookings *SD-4*
Sterling (Town)—Sanpete............... *UT-4*
Sterling (Town)—Polk *WI-3*
Sterling (Town)—Vernon *WI-3*
Sterling City (City)—Sterling *TX-2*
Sterling County............................... *TX-2*
Sterling Heights (City)—Macomb.. *MI-3*
Sterlington (Town)—Ouachita
 Parish.. *LA-2*
Stetson (Town)—Penobscot *ME-1*
Stetsonville (Village)—Taylor........ *WI-3*
Stettin (Town)—Marathon *WI-3*
Steuben (Township)—Marshall *IL-3*
Steuben (Township)—Steuben *IN-3*
Steuben (Township)—Warren *IN-3*
Steuben (Town)—Washington *ME-1*
Steuben (Town)—Oneida *NY-1*
Steuben (Township)—Crawford...... *PA-1*
Steuben (Village)—Crawford *WI-3*
Steuben County.............................. *IN-3*
Steuben County.............................. *NY-1*
Steubenville (City)—Jefferson.......*OH-3*
Steubenville (Township)—
 Jefferson..................................... *OH-3*
Stevens (Township)—Stevens........ *MN-3*
Stevens (Township)—Ramsey........ *ND-4*
Stevens (Township)—Bradford *PA-1*
Stevens County................................*KS-4*
Stevens County................................ *MN-3*
Stevens County................................ *WA-4*
Stevens Dam (NY) *Geog-4*
Stevenson (City)—Jackson............. *AL-2*
Stevenson (Township)—Marion *IL-3*
Stevenson (City)—Skamania.......... *WA-4*
Stevens Point (City)—Portage *WI-3*
Stevens Village (CDP)—
 Yukon-Koyukuk Census Area...... *AK-4*
Stevensville (CDP)—Queen
 Anne's *MD-1*
Stevensville (Village)—Berrien *MI-3*
Stevensville (Town)—Ravalli......... *MT-4*
Stevensville South (CDP)—Queen
 Anne's *MD-1*
Steward (Village)—Lee *IL-3*
Stewardson (Village)—Shelby *IL-3*
Stewardson (Township)—Potter...... *PA-1*
Stewart (City)—McLeod *MN-3*
Stewart (Township)—Barnes *ND-4*
Stewart (Township)—Kidder......... *ND-4*
Stewart (Township)—Fayette *PA-1*
Stewart (Township)—Tripp *SD-4*
Stewart County.............................. *GA-2*
Stewart County.............................. *TN-2*
Stewart Manor (Village)—Nassau.. *NY-1*
Stewarts Point Rancheria
 (CA)..*IndRes-4*
Stewartstown (Town)—Coos *NH-1*
Stewartstown (Borough)—York..... *PA-1*
Stewartsville (City)—DeKalb........ *MO-3*
Stewartville (City)—Olmsted......... *MN-3*
Stickney (Township)—Cook *IL-3*
Stickney (Village)—Cook *IL-3*
Stickney (Town)—Aurora *SD-4*
Stidham (Town)—McIntosh........... *OK-2*
Stigler (City)—Haskell................... *OK-2*
Stiles (Town)—Oconto *WI-3*

General Index — American Places Dictionary

Stilesville (Town)—Hendricks.........IN-3
Stillaguamish Reservation (WA)..................................IndRes-4
Stillman Valley (Village)—Ogle.......IL-3
Stillmore (Town)—Emanuel...........GA-2
Stillwater (City)—Washington.......MN-3
Stillwater (Township)—Washington.................................MN-3
Stillwater (Township)—Sussex........NJ-1
Stillwater (Town)—Saratoga..........NY-1
Stillwater (Village)—Saratoga.........NY-1
Stillwater (Township)—Bowman...ND-4
Stillwater (City)—Payne.................OK-2
Stillwater (Borough)—Columbia....PA-1
Stillwater County..............................MT-4
Stilwell (City)—Adair.....................OK-2
Stimson Crossing (CDP)—Snohomish...............................WA-4
Stinesville (Town)—Monroe...........IN-3
Stinnett (City)—Hutchinson...........TX-2
Stinnett (Town)—Washburn...........WI-3
Stirton (Township)—Stutsman.......ND-4
Stites (City)—Idaho.........................ID-4
Stites (Township)—St. Clair............IL-3
Stock (Township)—Harrison.........OH-3
Stock (Township)—Noble...............OH-3
Stockbridge (City)—Henry..............GA-2
Stockbridge (Town)—Berkshire....MA-1
Stockbridge (Township)—Ingham..MI-3
Stockbridge (Village)—Ingham.......MI-3
Stockbridge (Town)—Madison.......NY-1
Stockbridge (Town)—Windsor.......VT-1
Stockbridge (Town)—Calumet.......WI-3
Stockbridge (Village)—Calumet.....WI-3
Stockbridge Reservation (WI)..IndRes-4
Stockdale (Borough)—Washington.PA-1
Stockdale (City)—Wilson................TX-2
Stockertown (Borough)—Northampton...........................PA-1
Stockham (Village)—Hamilton.......NE-4
Stockholm (Town)—Aroostook......ME-1
Stockholm (Township)—Wright.....MN-3
Stockholm (Town)—St. Lawrence.....................................NY-1
Stockholm (Town)—Grant..............SD-4
Stockholm (Township)—Grant......SD-4
Stockholm (Town)—Pepin..............WI-3
Stockholm (Village)—Pepin............WI-3
Stocking (Township)—Saunders....NE-4
Stock Island (CDP)—Monroe.........FL-2
Stockland (Township)—Iroquois....IL-3
Stockport (City)—Van Buren.........IA-3
Stockport (Town)—Columbia.........NY-1
Stockport (Village)—Morgan.........OH-3
Stockton (City)—San Joaquin........CA-4
Stockton (Township)—Jo Daviess..IL-3
Stockton (Village)—Jo Daviess......IL-3
Stockton (Township)—Greene.......IN-3
Stockton (City)—Muscatine............IA-3
Stockton (City)—Rooks...................KS-4
Stockton (City)—Winona................MN-3
Stockton (City)—Cedar..................MO-3
Stockton (Borough)—Hunterdon...NJ-1
Stockton (Town)—Chautauqua.....NY-1
Stockton (Town)—Tooele................UT-4
Stockton (Town)—Portage..............WI-3
Stockton Springs (Town)—Waldo.................................ME-1
Stockville (Village)—Frontier.........NE-4
Stoddard (Town)—Cheshire...........NH-1
Stoddard (Town)—Vernon..............WI-3
Stoddard County..........................MO-3
Stokes (Township)—Itasca.............MN-3
Stokes (Township)—Roseau..........MN-3
Stokes (Township)—Logan............OH-3

Stokes (Township)—Madison.........OH-3
Stokes County...................................NC-2
Stokesdale (Town)—Guilford.........NC-2
Stokes Mound (Township)—Carroll.................................MO-3
Stoneboro (Borough)—Mercer........PA-1
Stone County......................................AR-2
Stone County.....................................MS-2
Stone County....................................MO-3
Stone Creek (Township)—Bottineau................................ND-4
Stone Creek (Village)—Tuscarawas...........................OH-3
Stonefort (Township)—Saline........IL-3
Stonefort (Village)—Saline..............IL-3
Stonefort (Village)—Williamson....IL-3
Stoneham (Town)—Oxford.............ME-1
Stoneham (Town)—Middlesex......MA-1
Stoneham (Township)—Chippewa................................MN-3
Stone Harbor (Borough)—Cape May...................................NJ-1
Stone Lake (Town)—Washburn.....WI-3
Stonelick (Township)—Clermont...OH-3
Stone Mountain (GA)..................Geog-4
Stone Mountain (City)—De Kalb..GA-2
Stone Park (Village)—Cook.............IL-3
Stoneview (Township)—Divide.....ND-4
Stoneville (Town)—Rockingham...NC-2
Stonewall (Town)—De Soto Parish...................................LA-2
Stonewall (Town)—Clarke..............MS-2
Stonewall (Town)—Pamlico............NC-2
Stonewall (Town)—Pontotoc..........OK-2
Stonewall County.............................TX-2
Stonewood (City)—Harrison.........WV-2
Stoney Brook (Township)—St. Louis...................................MN-3
Stoney Creek (Township)—Henry..IN-3
Stoney Creek (Township)—Randolph.................................IN-3
Stonington (Borough)—New London...................................CT-1
Stonington (Town)—New London...................................CT-1
Stonington (Township)—Christian.IL-3
Stonington (Village)—Christian......IL-3
Stonington (Town)—Hancock........ME-1
Stony Brook (Township)—Grant..MN-3
Stony Brook (CDP)—Suffolk.........NY-1
Stony Butte (Township)—Lyman..SD-4
Stony Creek (Township)—Madison.................................IN-3
Stony Creek (Town)—Warren.......NY-1
Stony Creek (Township)—Williams...............................ND-4
Stonycreek (Township)—Cambria..PA-1
Stonycreek (Township)—Somerset..PA-1
Stony Creek (Town)—Sussex..........VA-2
Stony Point (CDP)—Monroe.........MI-3
Stony Point (Town)—Rockland.....NY-1
Stony Point (CDP)—Alexander....NC-2
Stony Point (CDP)—Iredell............NC-2
Stony Prairie (CDP)—Sandusky...OH-3
Stony River (CDP)—Bethel Census Area......................AK-4
Stony River (Township)—Lake.....MN-3
Stony Run (Township)—Yellow Medicine.............................MN-3
Stookey (Township)—St. Clair........IL-3
Storden (City)—Cottonwood..........MN-3
Storden (Township)—Cottonwood............................MN-3
Storey County....................................NV-4
Storlie (Township)—Cavalier.........ND-4

Storm Lake (City)—Buena Vista.....IA-3
Storrs (CDP)—Tolland....................CT-1
Story City (City)—Story...................IA-3
Story County.......................................IA-3
Stotesbury (Town)—Vernon..........MO-3
Stotts City (City)—Lawrence.........MO-3
Stottville (CDP)—Columbia...........NY-1
Stoughton (Town)—Norfolk..........MA-1
Stoughton (City)—Dane..................WI-3
Stout (City)—Grundy........................IA-3
Stoutland (Village)—Camden........MO-3
Stoutland (Village)—Laclede.........MO-3
Stoutsville (Village)—Monroe........MO-3
Stoutsville (Village)—Fairfield.......OH-3
Stovall (Town)—Granville..............NC-2
Stover (City)—Morgan...................MO-3
Stow (Town)—Oxford....................ME-1
Stow (Town)—Middlesex...............MA-1
Stow (City)—Summit.......................OH-3
Stow Creek (Township)—Cumberland............................NJ-1
Stowe (Township)—Allegheny........PA-1
Stowe (Town)—Lamoille..................VT-1
Stowe (Village)—Lamoille................VT-1
Stowell (CDP)—Chambers..............TX-2
Stowe Prairie (Township)—Todd..MN-3
Stoy (Village)—Crawford................IL-3
Stoystown (Borough)—Somerset....PA-1
Straban (Township)—Adams..........PA-1
Strabane (Township)—Grand Forks..................................ND-4
Strafford (City)—Greene................MO-3
Strafford (Town)—Strafford..........NH-1
Strafford (Town)—Orange..............VT-1
Strafford County..............................NH-1
Straight Creek (Township)—Jackson.................................KS-4
Straight River (Township)—Hubbard..............................MN-3
Strand (Township)—Norman........MN-3
Strandahl (Township)—Williams...ND-4
Strandburg (Town)—Grant............SD-4
Strandquist (City)—Marshall........MN-3
Strang (Village)—Fillmore..............NE-4
Strang (Town)—Mayes...................OK-2
Stranger (Township)—Leavenworth...........................KS-4
Strasburg (Village)—Shelby............IL-3
Strasburg (Town)—Cass................MO-3
Strasburg (City)—Emmons...........ND-4
Strasburg (Village)—Tuscarawas....OH-3
Strasburg (Borough)—Lancaster....PA-1
Strasburg (Township)—Lancaster...PA-1
Strasburg (Town)—Shenandoah......VA-2
Strassburg (Township)—Sheridan..ND-4
Stratford (Town)—Fairfield...........CT-1
Stratford (City)—Hamilton.............IA-3
Stratford (City)—Webster..............IA-3
Stratford (Town)—Coos.................NH-1
Stratford (Borough)—Camden......NJ-1
Stratford (Town)—Fulton..............NY-1
Stratford (Town)—Garvin..............OK-2
Stratford (Town)—Brown...............SD-4
Stratford (Town)—Sherman............TX-2
Stratford (Village)—Marathon........WI-3
Stratham (Town)—Rockingham....NH-1
Strathcona (City)—Roseau............MN-3
Strathmoor Gardens (City)—Jefferson..............................KY-2
Strathmoor Manor (City)—Jefferson..............................KY-2
Strathmoor Village (City)—Jefferson..............................KY-2
Strathmore (CDP)—Tulare............CA-4
Strathmore (CDP)—Monmouth....NJ-1

Stratmoor (CDP)—El Paso *CO-4*
Strattanville (Borough)—Clarion *PA-1*
Stratton (Town)—Kit Carson *CO-4*
Stratton (Township)—Edgar *IL-3*
Stratton (Village)—Hitchcock *NE-4*
Stratton (Village)—Jefferson *OH-3*
Stratton (Town)—Windham *VT-1*
Straughn (Town)—Henry *IN-3*
Strausstown (Borough)—Berks *PA-1*
Strawberry (Town)—Lawrence *AR-2*
Strawberry (CDP)—Marin *CA-4*
Strawberry (Township)—
 Washington *KS-4*
Strawberry Point (City)—Clayton *IA-3*
Strawn (Village)—Livingston *IL-3*
Strawn (City)—Palo Pinto *TX-2*
Streamwood (Village)—Cook *IL-3*
Streator (City)—La Salle *IL-3*
Streator (City)—Livingston *IL-3*
Streeter (City)—Stutsman *ND-4*
Streeter (Township)—Stutsman *ND-4*
Streetman (Town)—Freestone *TX-2*
Streetman (Town)—Navarro *TX-2*
Streetsboro (City)—Portage *OH-3*
Strege (Township)—McHenry *ND-4*
Strehlow (Township)—Hettinger *ND-4*
Strickland (Town)—Rusk *WI-3*
Stringtown (Town)—Atoka *OK-2*
Stromsburg (City)—Polk *NE-4*
Stronach (Township)—Manistee *MI-3*
Strong (City)—Union *AR-2*
Strong (Township)—Chase *KS-4*
Strong (Town)—Franklin *ME-1*
Strong (Township)—Stutsman *ND-4*
Strong City (City)—Chase *KS-4*
Strong City (Town)—Roger Mills .. *OK-2*
Stronghurst (Township)—
 Henderson *IL-3*
Stronghurst (Village)—Henderson .. *IL-3*
Strongs Prairie (Town)—Adams *WI-3*
Strongsville (City)—Cuyahoga *OH-3*
Strool (Township)—Perkins *SD-4*
Stroud (City)—Creek *OK-2*
Stroud (City)—Lincoln *OK-2*
Stroud (Township)—Monroe *PA-1*
Stroudsburg (Borough)—Monroe ... *PA-1*
Struble (City)—Plymouth *IA-3*
Strum (Village)—Trempealeau *WI-3*
Struthers (City)—Mahoning *OH-3*
Stryker (Village)—Williams *OH-3*
Stuart (City)—Martin *FL-2*
Stuart (City)—Adair *IA-3*
Stuart (City)—Guthrie *IA-3*
Stuart (Township)—Holt *NE-4*
Stuart (Village)—Holt *NE-4*
Stuart (Town)—Hughes *OK-2*
Stuart (Town)—Patrick *VA-2*
Stuarts Draft (CDP)—Augusta *VA-2*
Stubbs (Town)—Rusk *WI-3*
Stuckey (Town)—Williamsburg *SC-2*
Studio City *See* **Los Angeles**—Los
 Angeles *CA-4*
Sturbridge (Town)—Worcester *MA-1*
Sturgeon (Township)—St. Louis ... *MN-3*
Sturgeon (City)—Boone *MO-3*
Sturgeon Bay (City)—Door *WI-3*
Sturgeon Bay (Town)—Door *WI-3*
Sturgeon Lake (City)—Pine *MN-3*
Sturgeon Lake (Township)—
 Pine *MN-3*
Sturgis (City)—Union *KY-2*
Sturgis (City)—St. Joseph *MI-3*
Sturgis (Township)—St. Joseph *MI-3*
Sturgis (Town)—Oktibbeha *MS-2*
Sturgis (City)—Meade *SD-4*

Sturtevant (Village)—Racine *WI-3*
Stutsman County *ND-4*
Stuttgart (City)—Arkansas *AR-2*
Stuyvesant (Town)—Columbia *NY-1*
Suamico (Town)—Brown *WI-3*
Subiaco (Town)—Logan *AR-2*
Sublette (Township)—Lee *IL-3*
Sublette (Village)—Lee *IL-3*
Sublette (City)—Haskell *KS-4*
Sublette County *WY-4*
Sublimity (City)—Marion *OR-4*
Succasunna-Kenvil (CDP)—
 Morris *NJ-1*
Success (Town)—Clay *AR-2*
Success (Township)—Coos *NH-1*
Sudan (City)—Lamb *TX-2*
Sudbury (Town)—Middlesex *MA-1*
Sudbury (Town)—Rutland *VT-1*
Sudden Valley (CDP)—
 Whatcom *WA-4*
Sudlersville (Town)—Queen
 Anne's *MD-1*
Sudley (Township)—Prince William .. *VA-2*
Suez (Township)—Mercer *IL-3*
Suffern (Village)—Rockland *NY-1*
Suffield (Town)—Hartford *CT-1*
Suffield (Township)—Portage *OH-3*
Suffolk County *MA-1*
Suffolk County *NY-1*
Suffolk (Independent City) *VA-2*
Sugar Bush (Township)—Becker ... *MN-3*
Sugar Bush (Township)—
 Beltrami *MN-3*
Sugar Bush Knolls (Village)—
 Portage *OH-3*
Sugar Camp (Town)—Oneida *WI-3*
Sugar City (Town)—Crowley *CO-4*
Sugar City (City)—Madison *ID-4*
Sugar Creek (Township)—Clinton .. *IL-3*
Sugar Creek (Township)—Boone ... *IN-3*
Sugar Creek (Township)—Clinton .. *IN-3*
Sugar Creek (Township)—
 Hancock *IN-3*
Sugar Creek (Township)—
 Montgomery *IN-3*
Sugar Creek (Township)—Parke *IN-3*
Sugar Creek (Township)—Shelby ... *IN-3*
Sugar Creek (Township)—Vigo *IN-3*
Sugar Creek (Township)—Miami .. *KS-4*
Sugar Creek (Township)—Barry ... *MO-3*
Sugar Creek (City)—Clay *MO-3*
Sugar Creek (Township)—
 Harrison *MO-3*
Sugar Creek (City)—Jackson *MO-3*
Sugar Creek (Township)—Allen *OH-3*
Sugar Creek (Township)—
 Greene *OH-3*
Sugar Creek (Township)—
 Putnam *OH-3*
Sugar Creek (Township)—Stark *OH-3*
Sugar Creek (Township)—
 Tuscarawas *OH-3*
Sugarcreek (Village)—
 Tuscarawas *OH-3*
Sugar Creek (Township)—Wayne .. *OH-3*
Sugarcreek (Township)—
 Armstrong *PA-1*
Sugarcreek (Borough)—Venango ... *PA-1*
Sugar Creek (Town)—Walworth *WI-3*
Sugar Grove (Township)—Kane *IL-3*
Sugar Grove (Village)—Kane *IL-3*
Sugar Grove (Village)—Fairfield ... *OH-3*
Sugar Grove (Village)—Mercer *PA-1*
Sugar Grove (Borough)—Warren ... *PA-1*
Sugar Grove (Township)—Warren .. *PA-1*

Sugar Hill (City)—Gwinnett *GA-2*
Sugar Hill (Town)—Grafton *NH-1*
Sugar Island (Township)—
 Chippewa *MI-3*
Sugar Land (City)—Fort Bend *TX-2*
Sugarland Run (CDP)—Loudoun .. *VA-2*
Sugar Loaf (Township)—St. Clair .. *IL-3*
Sugarloaf (Township)—Columbia .. *PA-1*
Sugarloaf (Township)—Luzerne *PA-1*
Sugarmill Woods (CDP)—Citrus ... *FL-2*
Sugar Mountain (Village)—Avery .. *NC-2*
Sugar Notch (Borough)—Luzerne .. *PA-1*
Sugar Ridge (Township)—Clay *IN-3*
Sugartree (Township)—Carroll *MO-3*
Sugden (Town)—Jefferson *OK-2*
Suisun City (City)—Solano *CA-4*
Suitland-Silver Hill (CDP)—Prince
 George's *MD-1*
Sulligent (Town)—Lamar *AL-2*
Sullivan (Township)—Livingston *IL-3*
Sullivan (City)—Moultrie *IL-3*
Sullivan (Township)—Moultrie *IL-3*
Sullivan (City)—Sullivan *IN-3*
Sullivan (Township)—Grant *KS-4*
Sullivan (Town)—Hancock *ME-1*
Sullivan (Township)—Muskegon ... *MI-3*
Sullivan (Township)—Polk *MN-3*
Sullivan (City)—Crawford *MO-3*
Sullivan (City)—Franklin *MO-3*
Sullivan (Town)—Cheshire *NH-1*
Sullivan (Town)—Madison *NY-1*
Sullivan (Township)—Ramsey *ND-4*
Sullivan (Township)—Ashland *OH-3*
Sullivan (Township)—Tioga *PA-1*
Sullivan (Town)—Jefferson *WI-3*
Sullivan (Village)—Jefferson *WI-3*
Sullivan City (CDP)—Hidalgo *TX-2*
Sullivan County *IN-3*
Sullivan County *MO-3*
Sullivan County *NH-1*
Sullivan County *NY-1*
Sullivan County *PA-1*
Sullivan County *TN-2*
Sullivan's Island (Town)—
 Charleston *SC-2*
Sullivant (Township)—Ford *IL-3*
Sully (City)—Jasper *IA-3*
Sully (Township)—Tripp *SD-4*
Sully County *SD-4*
Sulphur (City)—Calcasieu Parish ... *LA-2*
Sulphur (City)—Murray *OK-2*
Sulphur Bank (El-Em) Rancheria
 (CA) *IndRes-4*
Sulphur Rock (Town)—
 Independence *AR-2*
Sulphur Springs (City)—Benton *AR-2*
Sulphur Springs (Town)—Henry ... *IN-3*
Sulphur Springs (City)—Hopkins .. *TX-2*
Sultan (Town)—Snohomish *WA-4*
Sumas (City)—Whatcom *WA-4*
Sumiton (Town)—Jefferson *AL-2*
Sumiton (Town)—Walker *AL-2*
Summerdale (Town)—Baldwin *AL-2*
Summerfield (Village)—St. Clair ... *IL-3*
Summerfield (City)—Marshall *KS-4*
Summerfield (Township)—Clare .. *MI-3*
Summerfield (Township)—
 Monroe *MI-3*
Summerfield (CDP)—Guilford *NC-2*
Summerfield (Village)—Noble *OH-3*
Summerhill (Town)—Cayuga *NY-1*
Summerhill (Borough)—Cambria .. *PA-1*
Summerhill (Township)—
 Cambria *PA-1*

General Index

American Places Dictionary

Summerhill (Township)—
   Crawford PA-1
Summers (Township)—Thomas KS-4
Summers County WV-2
Summerside (CDP)—Clermont OH-3
Summersville (City)—Shannon MO-3
Summersville (City)—Texas MO-3
Summersville (Town)—Nicholas WV-2
Summerton (Town)—Clarendon SC-2
Summertown (Town)—Emanuel GA-2
Summerville (City)—Chattooga GA-2
Summerville (Town)—Union OR-4
Summerville (Borough)—
   Jefferson PA-1
Summerville (Town)—Berkeley SC-2
Summerville (Town)—Charleston ... SC-2
Summerville (Town)—Dorchester .. SC-2
Summit (Town)—Marion AR-2
Summit (Village)—Cook IL-3
Summit (Township)—Effingham IL-3
Summit (Township)—
   Chautauqua KS-4
Summit (Township)—Cloud KS-4
Summit (Township)—Decatur KS-4
Summit (Township)—Marion KS-4
Summit (Township)—Jackson MI-3
Summit (Township)—Mason MI-3
Summit (Township)—Beltrami MN-3
Summit (Township)—Steele MN-3
Summit (Town)—Pike MS-2
Summit (Township)—Bates MO-3
Summit (Township)—Callaway MO-3
Summit (Township)—Burt NE-4
Summit (Township)—Butler NE-4
Summit (City)—Union NJ-1
Summit (Town)—Schoharie NY-1
Summit (Township)—Richland ND-4
Summit (Township)—Monroe OH-3
Summit (Town)—Muskogee OK-2
Summit (Township)—Butler PA-1
Summit (Township)—Crawford PA-1
Summit (Township)—Erie PA-1
Summit (Township)—Potter PA-1
Summit (Township)—Somerset PA-1
Summit (Town)—Lexington SC-2
Summit (Township)—Lake SD-4
Summit (Town)—Roberts SD-4
Summit (Township)—Roberts SD-4
Summit (CDP)—Pierce WA-4
Summit (Town)—Douglas WI-3
Summit (Town)—Juneau WI-3
Summit (Town)—Langlade WI-3
Summit (Town)—Waukesha WI-3
Summit County CO-4
Summit County OH-3
Summit County UT-4
Summit Hill (Borough)—Carbon PA-1
Summit Lake (Township)—
   Nobles MN-3
Summit Lake Reservation
   (NV) IndRes-4
Summit Station (CDP)—Licking ... OH-3
Summitville (Town)—Madison IN-3
Summitville (Village)—
   Columbiana OH-3
Sumner (Town)—Worth GA-2
Sumner (Township)—Kankakee IL-3
Sumner (City)—Lawrence IL-3
Sumner (Township)—Warren IL-3
Sumner (City)—Bremer IA-3
Sumner (Township)—Osborne KS-4
Sumner (Township)—Phillips KS-4
Sumner (Township)—Reno KS-4
Sumner (Township)—Sumner KS-4
Sumner (Town)—Oxford ME-1

Sumner (Township)—Gratiot MI-3
Sumner (Township)—Fillmore MN-3
Sumner (Town)—Tallahatchie MS-2
Sumner (Town)—Chariton MO-3
Sumner (Village)—Dawson NE-4
Sumner (Township)—Spink SD-4
Sumner (City)—Pierce WA-4
Sumner (Town)—Barron WI-3
Sumner (Town)—Jefferson WI-3
Sumner (Town)—Trempealeau WI-3
Sumner County KS-4
Sumner County TN-2
Sumpter (Township)—
   Cumberland IL-3
Sumpter (Township)—Wayne MI-3
Sumpter (City)—Baker OR-4
Sumpter (Town)—Sauk WI-3
Sumrall (Town)—Lamar MS-2
Sumter (Township)—McLeod MN-3
Sumter (City)—Sumter SC-2
Sumter County AL-2
Sumter County FL-2
Sumter County GA-2
Sumter County SC-2
Sun (Village)—St. Tammany
   Parish LA-2
Sunapee (Town)—Sullivan NH-1
Sunburg (City)—Kandiyohi MN-3
Sunburst (Town)—Toole MT-4
Sunbury (Township)—Livingston ... IL-3
Sunbury (Village)—Delaware OH-3
Sunbury (City)—Northumberland .. PA-1
Sun City (CDP)—Maricopa AZ-4
Sun City (CDP)—Riverside CA-4
Sun City (City)—Barber KS-4
Sun City (Township)—Barber KS-4
Sun City Center (CDP)—
   Hillsborough FL-2
Sun City West (CDP)—Maricopa .. AZ-4
Suncoast Estates (CDP)—Lee FL-2
Suncook (CDP)—Merrimack NH-1
Sundal (Township)—Norman MN-3
Sundance (Town)—Crook WY-4
Sunderland (Town)—Franklin MA-1
Sunderland (Town)—Bennington ... VT-1
Sundown (Township)—Redwood .. MN-3
Sundown (Village)—Ozark MO-3
Sundown (City)—Hockley TX-2
Sundre (Township)—Ward ND-4
Sunfield (Township)—Eaton MI-3
Sunfield (Village)—Eaton MI-3
Sunfish (Township)—Pike OH-3
Sunfish Lake (City)—Dakota MN-3
Sunflower (Town)—Sunflower MS-2
Sunflower, Mt. (KS) Geog-4
Sunflower County MS-2
Sun Lakes (CDP)—Maricopa AZ-4
Sunland Park (City)—Doña Ana .. NM-4
Sunman (Town)—Ripley IN-3
Sunny Isles (CDP)—Dade FL-2
Sunnyside (CDP)—Lake FL-2
Sunny Side (Village)—Spalding GA-2
Sunnyside (CDP)—Ware GA-2
Sunnyside (Village)—McHenry IL-3
Sunnyside (Township)—Wilkin ... MN-3
Sunnyside (CDP)—Clackamas OR-4
Sunnyside (City)—Carbon UT-4
Sunnyside (City)—Yakima WA-4
Sunnyside No. 26 (Township)—
   Pennington SD-4
Sunnyside-Tahoe City (CDP)—
   Placer CA-4
Sunnyslope (CDP)—Riverside CA-4
Sunny Slope (Township)—
   Bowman ND-4

Sunnyslope (CDP)—Chelan WA-4
Sunnyvale (City)—Santa Clara CA-4
Sunnyvale (Town)—Dallas TX-2
Sun Prairie (CDP)—Cascade MT-4
Sun Prairie (Township)—
   McCook SD-4
Sun Prairie (City)—Dane WI-3
Sun Prairie (Town)—Dane WI-3
Sunray (Town)—Moore TX-2
Sunrise (City)—Broward FL-2
Sunrise (Township)—Chisago MN-3
Sunrise Beach (Village)—
   Camden MO-3
Sunrise Beach (Village)—
   Morgan MO-3
Sunrise Beach Village (City)—
   Llano TX-2
Sunrise Manor (CDP)—Clark NV-4
Sun River Terrace (Village)—
   Kankakee IL-3
Sunsbury (Township)—Monroe ... OH-3
Sunset (Town)—Crittenden AR-2
Sunset (CDP)—Dade FL-2
Sunset (Town)—St. Landry
   Parish LA-2
Sunset (City)—Davis UT-4
Sunset Beach (Town)—
   Brunswick NC-2
Sunset Hills (City)—St. Louis MO-3
Sunset Park—Kings NY-1
Sunset Valley (City)—Travis TX-2
Sunshine (Township)—Slope ND-4
Sun Valley (CDP)—Palm Beach FL-2
Sun Valley (City)—Blaine ID-4
Sun Valley (CDP)—Washoe NV-4
Sun Valley (City)—Lamar TX-2
Supai (CDP)—Coconino AZ-4
Superior (Town)—Pinal AZ-4
Superior (Town)—Boulder CO-4
Superior (Town)—Jefferson CO-4
Superior (City)—Dickinson IA-3
Superior (Township)—
   McPherson KS-4
Superior (Township)—Osage KS-4
Superior (Township)—Chippewa ... MI-3
Superior (Township)—
   Washtenaw MI-3
Superior (Town)—Mineral MT-4
Superior (City)—Nuckolls NE-4
Superior (Township)—Eddy ND-4
Superior (Township)—Williams ... OH-3
Superior (City)—Douglas WI-3
Superior (Town)—Douglas WI-3
Superior (Village)—Douglas WI-3
Superior (Town)—Sweetwater WY-4
Superior, Lake (KS) Geog-4
Supreme (CDP)—Assumption
   Parish LA-2
Suquamish (CDP)—Kitsap WA-4
Surf City (Borough)—Ocean NJ-1
Surf City (Town)—Onslow NC-2
Surf City (Town)—Pender NC-2
Surfside (Town)—Dade FL-2
Surfside Beach (Town)—Horry SC-2
Surfside Beach (City)—Brazoria ... TX-2
Surgoinsville (Town)—Hawkins TN-2
Suring (Village)—Oconto WI-3
Surprise (Town)—Maricopa AZ-4
Surprise (Village)—Butler NE-4
Surprise Valley (Township)—
   Mellette SD-4
Surrency (Town)—Appling GA-2
Surrey (Township)—Clare MI-3
Surrey (City)—Ward ND-4
Surrey (Township)—Ward ND-4

Surry (Town)—Hancock	*ME-1*	
Surry (Town)—Cheshire	*NH-1*	
Surry (Town)—Surry	*VA-2*	
Surry County	*NC-2*	
Surry County	*VA-2*	
Susank (City)—Barton	*KS-4*	
Susan Moore (Municipality)—Blount	*AL-2*	
Susanville (City)—Lassen	*CA-4*	
Susanville Rancheria (CA)	*IndRes-4*	
Susquehanna (Township)—Cambria	*PA-1*	
Susquehanna (Township)—Dauphin	*PA-1*	
Susquehanna (Township)—Juniata	*PA-1*	
Susquehanna (Township)—Lycoming	*PA-1*	
Susquehanna (Township)—Hutchinson	*SD-4*	
Susquehanna County	*PA-1*	
Susquehanna Depot (Borough)—Susquehanna	*PA-1*	
Susquehanna River (KS)	*Geog-4*	
Sussex (Borough)—Sussex	*NJ-1*	
Sussex (Village)—Waukesha	*WI-3*	
Sussex County	*DE-1*	
Sussex County	*NJ-1*	
Sussex County	*VA-2*	
Sutersville (Borough)—Westmoreland	*PA-1*	
Sutherland (City)—O'Brien	*IA-3*	
Sutherland (Village)—Lincoln	*NE-4*	
Sutherlin (City)—Douglas	*OR-4*	
Sutter (CDP)—Sutter	*CA-4*	
Sutter County	*CA-4*	
Sutter Creek (City)—Amador	*CA-4*	
Sutton (CDP)—Matanuska-Susitna Borough	*AK-4*	
Sutton (Town)—Worcester	*MA-1*	
Sutton (City)—Clay	*NE-4*	
Sutton (Township)—Clay	*NE-4*	
Sutton (Town)—Merrimack	*NH-1*	
Sutton (Township)—Meigs	*OH-3*	
Sutton (Town)—Caledonia	*VT-1*	
Sutton (Town)—Braxton	*WV-2*	
Sutton County	*TX-2*	
Suttons Bay (Township)—Leelanau	*MI-3*	
Suttons Bay (Village)—Leelanau	*MI-3*	
Suwanee (City)—Gwinnett	*GA-2*	
Suwanee River (KS)	*Geog-4*	
Suwannee County	*FL-2*	
Svea (Township)—Kittson	*MN-3*	
Svea (Township)—Barnes	*ND-4*	
Sverdrup (Township)—Otter Tail	*MN-3*	
Sverdrup (Township)—Griggs	*ND-4*	
Sverdrup (Township)—Minnehaha	*SD-4*	
Swain County	*NC-2*	
Swainsboro (City)—Emanuel	*GA-2*	
Swaledale (City)—Cerro Gordo	*IA-3*	
Swampscott (Town)—Essex	*MA-1*	
Swan (Township)—Warren	*IL-3*	
Swan (Township)—Noble	*IN-3*	
Swan (City)—Marion	*IA-3*	
Swan (Township)—Smith	*KS-4*	
Swan (Township)—Taney	*MO-3*	
Swan (Township)—Holt	*NE-4*	
Swan (Township)—Vinton	*OH-3*	
Swan Creek (Township)—Saginaw	*MI-3*	
Swan Creek (Township)—Fulton	*OH-3*	
Swan Lake (Township)—Stevens	*MN-3*	
Swan Lake (Township)—Turner	*SD-4*	
Swan Quarter (Pop. Place)—Hyde	*NC-2*	
Swan River (Township)—Morrison	*MN-3*	
Swansboro (Town)—Onslow	*NC-2*	
Swansea (Village)—St. Clair	*IL-3*	
Swansea (Town)—Bristol	*MA-1*	
Swansea (Town)—Lexington	*SC-2*	
Swans Island (Town)—Hancock	*ME-1*	
Swanton (Village)—Saline	*NE-4*	
Swanton (Village)—Fulton	*OH-3*	
Swanton (Township)—Lucas	*OH-3*	
Swanton (Village)—Lucas	*OH-3*	
Swanton (Town)—Franklin	*VT-1*	
Swanton (Village)—Franklin	*VT-1*	
Swan Valley (City)—Bonneville	*ID-4*	
Swanville (Town)—Waldo	*ME-1*	
Swanville (City)—Morrison	*MN-3*	
Swanville (Township)—Morrison	*MN-3*	
Swanzey (Town)—Cheshire	*NH-1*	
Swarthmore (Borough)—Delaware	*PA-1*	
Swartz (CDP)—Ouachita Parish	*LA-2*	
Swartz Creek (City)—Genesee	*MI-3*	
Swatara (Township)—Dauphin	*PA-1*	
Swatara (Township)—Lebanon	*PA-1*	
Swayzee (Town)—Grant	*IN-3*	
Swea City (City)—Kossuth	*IA-3*	
Swede (Township)—LaMoure	*ND-4*	
Swede Creek (Township)—Riley	*KS-4*	
Swede Grove (Township)—Meeker	*MN-3*	
Sweden (Town)—Oxford	*ME-1*	
Sweden (Town)—Monroe	*NY-1*	
Sweden (Township)—Potter	*PA-1*	
Swede Prairie (Township)—Yellow Medicine	*MN-3*	
Swedesboro (Borough)—Gloucester	*NJ-1*	
Swedes Forest (Township)—Redwood	*MN-3*	
Sweeny (Town)—Brazoria	*TX-2*	
Sweet (Township)—Pipestone	*MN-3*	
Sweet (Township)—Hutchinson	*SD-4*	
Sweet Grass County	*MT-4*	
Sweet Home (Township)—Clark	*MO-3*	
Sweet Home (City)—Linn	*OR-4*	
Sweetser (Town)—Grant	*IN-3*	
Sweet Springs (City)—Saline	*MO-3*	
Sweet Water (Town)—Marengo	*AL-2*	
Sweetwater (City)—Dade	*FL-2*	
Sweetwater (Township)—Lake	*MI-3*	
Sweetwater (City)—McMinn	*TN-2*	
Sweetwater (City)—Monroe	*TN-2*	
Sweetwater (City)—Nolan	*TX-2*	
Sweetwater County	*WY-4*	
Swenoda (Township)—Swift	*MN-3*	
Swepsonville (CDP)—Alamance	*NC-2*	
Swift County	*MN-3*	
Swifton (City)—Jackson	*AR-2*	
Swift Trail Junction (CDP)—Graham	*AZ-4*	
Swink (Town)—Otero	*CO-4*	
Swinomish Reservation (WA)	*IndRes-4*	
Swinomish Village (CDP)—Skagit	*WA-4*	
Swisher (City)—Johnson	*IA-3*	
Swisher County	*TX-2*	
Swiss (Town)—Burnett	*WI-3*	
Swissvale (Borough)—Allegheny	*PA-1*	
Switz City (Town)—Greene	*IN-3*	
Switzer (CDP)—Logan	*WV-2*	
Switzerland (Township)—Monroe	*OH-3*	
Switzerland County	*IN-3*	
Swoyersville (Borough)—Luzerne	*PA-1*	
Sycamore (City)—Turner	*GA-2*	
Sycamore (City)—DeKalb	*IL-3*	
Sycamore (Township)—DeKalb	*IL-3*	
Sycamore (Township)—Butler	*KS-4*	
Sycamore (Township)—Montgomery	*KS-4*	
Sycamore (City)—Jefferson	*KY-2*	
Sycamore (Township)—Hamilton	*OH-3*	
Sycamore (Township)—Wyandot	*OH-3*	
Sycamore (Village)—Wyandot	*OH-3*	
Sycamore (Town)—Allendale	*SC-2*	
Sycamore Hills (Village)—St. Louis	*MO-3*	
Sycuan Reservation (CA)	*IndRes-4*	
Sydna (Township)—Ransom	*ND-4*	
Sydney (Township)—Stutsman	*ND-4*	
Sykeston (City)—Wells	*ND-4*	
Sykeston (Township)—Wells	*ND-4*	
Sykesville (Town)—Carroll	*MD-1*	
Sykesville (Borough)—Jefferson	*PA-1*	
Sylacauga (City)—Talladega	*AL-2*	
Sylva (Town)—Jackson	*NC-2*	
Sylvan (Township)—Osceola	*MI-3*	
Sylvan (Township)—Washtenaw	*MI-3*	
Sylvan (Township)—Cass	*MN-3*	
Sylvan (Town)—Richland	*WI-3*	
Sylvan Beach (Village)—Oneida	*NY-1*	
Sylvan Grove (City)—Lincoln	*KS-4*	
Sylvania (Town)—DeKalb	*AL-2*	
Sylvania (City)—Screven	*GA-2*	
Sylvania (Township)—Scott	*MO-3*	
Sylvania (City)—Lucas	*OH-3*	
Sylvania (Township)—Lucas	*OH-3*	
Sylvania (Borough)—Bradford	*PA-1*	
Sylvania (Township)—Potter	*PA-1*	
Sylvan Lake (City)—Oakland	*MI-3*	
Sylvan Shores (CDP)—Highlands	*FL-2*	
Sylvan Springs (Municipality)—Jefferson	*AL-2*	
Sylvarena (Village)—Smith	*MS-2*	
Sylvester (City)—Worth	*GA-2*	
Sylvester (Town)—Boone	*WV-2*	
Sylvester (Town)—Green	*WI-3*	
Sylvia (City)—Reno	*KS-4*	
Sylvia (Township)—Reno	*KS-4*	
Sylvia (Township)—Lyman	*SD-4*	
Symerton (Village)—Will	*IL-3*	
Symmes (Township)—Edgar	*IL-3*	
Symmes (Township)—Hamilton	*OH-3*	
Symmes (Township)—Lawrence	*OH-3*	
Synnes (Township)—Stevens	*MN-3*	
Syosset (CDP)—Nassau	*NY-1*	
Syracuse (Town)—Kosciusko	*IN-3*	
Syracuse (City)—Hamilton	*KS-4*	
Syracuse (Township)—Hamilton	*KS-4*	
Syracuse (City)—Morgan	*MO-3*	
Syracuse (City)—Otoe	*NE-4*	
Syracuse (City)—Onondaga	*NY-1*	
Syracuse (Village)—Meigs	*OH-3*	
Syracuse (City)—Davis	*UT-4*	
Taber (Township)—St. Clair	*MO-3*	
Tabernacle (Township)—Burlington	*NJ-1*	
Tabiona (Town)—Duchesne	*UT-4*	
Table Bluff Rancheria (CA)	*IndRes-4*	
Table Grove (Village)—Fulton	*IL-3*	
Table Mountain Rancheria (CA)	*IndRes-4*	
Table Rock (Village)—Taney	*MO-3*	
Table Rock (Village)—Pawnee	*NE-4*	

General Index

Tabor (City)—Fremont IA-3
Tabor (City)—Mills IA-3
Tabor (Township)—Polk MN-3
Tabor (Town)—Bon Homme SD-4
Tabor City (Town)—Columbus...... NC-2
Tacoma (Township)—Bottineau..... ND-4
Tacoma (City)—Pierce WA-4
Tacoma, Mount (KS) Geog-4
Taconic Mountains (KS) Geog-4
Taconite (City)—Itasca................. MN-3
Taft (City)—Kern CA-4
Taft (Township)—Burleigh ND-4
Taft (Town)—Muskogee OK-2
Taft (City)—San Patricio TX-2
Taft (Town)—Taylor WI-3
Taft Heights (CDP)—Kern CA-4
Taft Southwest (CDP)—San
  Patricio...................................... TX-2
Taghkanic (Town)—Columbia NY-1
Tahlequah (City)—Cherokee......... OK-2
Tahoe, Lake (KS) Geog-4
Tahoe Vista (CDP)—Placer CA-4
Tahoka (City)—Lynn TX-2
Taholah (CDP)—Grays Harbor WA-4
Tainter (Town)—Dunn................. WI-3
Tainter Lake (CDP)—Dunn WI-3
Takoma Park (City)—
  Montgomery.............................. MD-1
Takoma Park (City)—Prince
  George's MD-1
Takotna (CDP)—Yukon-Koyukuk
  Census Area AK-4
Talala (Town)—Rogers OK-2
Talbot (Township)—Bowman ND-4
Talbot County GA-2
Talbot County MD-1
Talbotton (City)—Talbot GA-2
Talco (City)—Titus TX-2
Talent (City)—Jackson OR-4
Taliaferro County GA-2
Talihina (Town)—Le Flore OK-2
Talkeetna (CDP)—Matanuska-Susitna
  Borough..................................... AK-4
Talking Rock (Town)—Pickens...... GA-2
Talkington (Township)—
  Sangamon.................................. IL-3
Talladega (City)—Talladega AL-2
Talladega County.......................... AL-2
Talladega Springs (Municipality)—
  Talladega AL-2
Tallahassee (City)—Leon.............. FL-2
Tallahatchie County MS-2
Tallapoosa (City)—Haralson GA-2
Tallapoosa (City)—New Madrid... MO-3
Tallapoosa County AL-2
Tallassee (City)—Elmore AL-2
Tallassee (City)—Tallapoosa AL-2
Talleyrand (Township)—Wilson... KS-4
Talleyville (CDP)—New Castle.... DE-1
Tallmadge (Township)—Ottawa..... MI-3
Tallmadge (City)—Summit OH-3
Tallula (Village)—Menard............. IL-3
Tallulah (City)—Madison Parish.... LA-2
Tallulah Falls (Town)—
  Habersham................................ GA-2
Tallulah Falls (Town)—Rabun GA-2
Talmadge (Town)—Washington ME-1
Talmage (Village)—Otoe NE-4
Talmo (Town)—Jackson GA-2
Taloga (Township)—Morton KS-4
Taloga (Town)—Dewey OK-2
Tama (City)—Tama...................... IA-3
Tama County IA-3
Tamaha (Town)—Haskell OK-2
Tamalco (Township)—Bond.......... IL-3

Tamalpais-Homestead Valley (CDP)—
  Marin... CA-4
Tamaqua (Borough)—Schuylkill PA-1
Tamarac (City)—Broward FL-2
Tamarac (Township)—Marshall... MN-3
Tamarack (City)—Aitkin.............. MN-3
Tamaroa (Village)—Perry IL-3
Tamiami (CDP)—Dade.................FL-2
Tamms (Village)—Alexander IL-3
Tamora (Village)—Seward NE-4
Tampa (City)—Hillsborough.........FL-2
Tampa (City)—Marion KS-3
Tampa Bay (FL)............................ Geog-4
Tampico (Township)—Whiteside.... IL-3
Tampico (Village)—Whiteside IL-3
Tamworth (Town)—Carroll............NH-1
Tamworth (Township)—Faulk SD-4
Tanacross (CDP)—Southeast Fairbanks
  Census Area AK-4
Tanana (City)—Yukon-Koyukuk
  Census Area AK-4
Tanana River (AK) Geog-4
Tanberg (Township)—Wilkin MN-3
Taney County MO-3
Taneytown (City)—Carroll MD-1
Taneyville (Village)—Taney MO-3
Tangelo Park (CDP)—Orange.........FL-2
Tangent (City)—Linn OR-4
Tangier (Town)—Accomack VA-2
Tangipahoa (Village)—Tangipahoa
  Parish LA-2
Tangipahoa Parish LA-2
Tanglewilde-Thompson Place (CDP)—
  Thurston.................................... WA-4
Tanglewood Forest (CDP)—
  Travis TX-2
Tanner (Township)—Kidder ND-4
Tannersville (Village)—Greene NY-1
Tansem (Township)—Clay MN-3
Taopi (City)—Mower MN-3
Taopi (Township)—Minnehaha SD-4
Taos (City)—Cole MO-3
Taos (Town)—Taos NM-4
Taos County NM-4
Taos Pueblo (CDP)—Taos NM-4
Taos Pueblo & Trust Lands
  (NM)... IndRes-4
Tappahannock (Town)—Essex VA-2
Tappan (CDP)—Rockland NY-1
Tappen (City)—Kidder.................. ND-4
Tappen (Township)—Kidder.......... ND-4
Tara (Township)—Swift MN-3
Tara (Township)—Traverse MN-3
Tara Hills (CDP)—Contra Costa ... CA-4
Tarboro (Town)—Edgecombe NC-2
Tarentum (Borough)—Allegheny PA-1
Tar Heel (Town)—Bladen NC-2
Tariffville (CDP)—Hartford CT-1
Tarkio (City)—Atchison MO-3
Tarkio (Township)—Atchison MO-3
Tarlton (Village)—Pickaway OH-3
Tarnov (Village)—Platte NE-4
Tarpon Springs (City)—Pinellas FL-2
Tarrant (Municipality)—Jefferson .. AL-2
Tarrant County TX-2
Tarrants (Village)—Pike MO-3
Tarrytown (Village)—
  Montgomery.............................. GA-2
Tarrytown (Village)—Westchester.. NY-1
Tarzana See Los Angeles—Los
  Angeles CA-4
Tatamy (Borough)—Northampton .. PA-1
Tate (Township)—Saline IL-3
Tate (Township)—Clermont........... OH-3
Tate County MS-2

Tatitlek (CDP)—Valdez-Cordova
  Census Area AK-4
Tatman (Township)—Ward........... ND-4
Tattnall County GA-2
Tatum (Town)—Lea NM-4
Tatum (Town)—Marlboro.............. SC-2
Tatum (City)—Panola TX-2
Tatum (City)—Rusk TX-2
Tatums (Town)—Carter................. OK-2
Taum Sauk Mountain (MO)......... Geog-4
Taunton (City)—Bristol MA-1
Taunton (City)—Lyon MN-3
Tavares (City)—Lake FL-2
Tavern (Township)—Pulaski MO-3
Tavernier (CDP)—Monroe FL-2
Tavistock (Borough)—Camden NJ-1
Tawas (Township)—Iosco............. MI-3
Tawas City (City)—Iosco.............. MI-3
Taycheedah (Town)—Fond du
  Lac... WI-3
Taylor (Municipality)—Houston..... AL-2
Taylor (Town)—Navajo AZ-2
Taylor (City)—Columbia AR-2
Taylor (Township)—Ogle IL-3
Taylor (Township)—Greene IN-3
Taylor (Township)—Harrison IN-3
Taylor (Township)—Howard......... IN-3
Taylor (Township)—Owen IN-3
Taylor (City)—Wayne................... MI-3
Taylor (Township)—Beltrami MN-3
Taylor (Township)—Traverse....... MN-3
Taylor (Village)—Lafayette MS-2
Taylor (Township)—Greene MO-3
Taylor (Township)—Grundy MO-3
Taylor (Township)—Shelby MO-3
Taylor (Township)—Sullivan MO-3
Taylor (Village)—Loup NE-4
Taylor (Town)—Cortland NY-1
Taylor (Township)—Sargent........ ND-4
Taylor (City)—Stark ND-4
Taylor (Township)—Union OH-3
Taylor (Township)—Blair PA-1
Taylor (Township)—Centre PA-1
Taylor (Township)—Fulton PA-1
Taylor (Borough)—Lackawanna ... PA-1
Taylor (Township)—Lawrence PA-1
Taylor (Township)—Hanson SD-4
Taylor (Township)—Tripp SD-4
Taylor (City)—Williamson TX-2
Taylor (Village)—Jackson WI-3
Taylor Butte (Township)—
  Adams ND-4
Taylor County FL-2
Taylor County GA-2
Taylor County IA-3
Taylor County KY-2
Taylor County TX-2
Taylor County WV-2
Taylor County WI-3
Taylor Creek (CDP)—
  Okeechobee FL-2
Taylor Creek (Township)—
  Hardin....................................... OH-3
Taylor Lake Village (City)—
  Harris TX-2
Taylor Mill (City)—Kenton KY-2
Taylors (CDP)—Greenville........... SC-2
Taylors Falls (City)—Chisago....... MN-3
Taylor Springs (Village)—
  Montgomery.............................. IL-3
Taylorsville (Town)—Bartow GA-2
Taylorsville (Town)—Polk GA-2
Taylorsville (CDP)—
  Bartholomew............................. IN-3
Taylorsville (City)—Spencer KY-2

Taylorsville (Town)—Smith *MS-2*
Taylorsville (Town)—Alexander.....*NC-2*
Taylorsville-Bennion (CDP)—Salt
   Lake...*UT-4*
Taylortown (Town)—Moore *NC-2*
Taylorville (City)—Christian.........*IL-3*
Taylorville (Township)—Christian..*IL-3*
Taymouth (Township)—Saginaw ...*MI-3*
Tazewell (Town)—Claiborne *TN-2*
Tazewell (Town)—Tazewell *VA-2*
Tazewell County *IL-3*
Tazewell County *VA-2*
Tchula (Town)—Holmes *MS-2*
Tea (Town)—Lincoln *SD-4*
Teachey (Town)—Duplin *NC-2*
Teague (City)—Freestone *TX-2*
Teaneck (Township)—Bergen..........*NJ-1*
Teaticket (CDP)—Barnstable *MA-1*
Teays Valley (CDP)—Putnam *WV-2*
Tebo (Township)—Henry *MO-3*
Tecumseh (Township)—Shawnee....*KS-4*
Tecumseh (City)—Lenawee.............*MI-3*
Tecumseh (Township)—Lenawee....*MI-3*
Tecumseh (City)—Johnson *NE-4*
Tecumseh (City)—Pottawatomie *OK-2*
Teddy (Township)—Towner *ND-4*
Teec Nos Pos (CDP)—Apache.......*AZ-4*
Tega Cay (City)—York *SC-2*
Tegner (Township)—Kittson *MN-3*
Tehachapi (City)—Kern *CA-4*
Tehama (City)—Tehama *CA-4*
Tehama County *CA-4*
Tehuacana (Town)—Limestone......*TX-2*
Teien (Township)—Kittson *MN-3*
Tekamah (City)—Burt *NE-4*
Tekoa (City)—Whitman *WA-4*
Tekonsha (Township)—Calhoun ... *MI-3*
Tekonsha (Village)—Calhoun.........*MI-3*
Telfair County *GA-2*
Telfer (Township)—Burleigh *ND-4*
Telford (Borough)—Montgomery....*PA-1*
Tell (Township)—Emmons..............*ND-4*
Tell (Township)—Huntingdon *PA-1*
Tell City (City)—Perry *IN-3*
Teller (City)—Nome Census Area .*AK-4*
Teller County..................................*CO-4*
Tellico Plains (Town)—Monroe ... *TN-2*
Telluride (Town)—San Miguel *CO-4*
Temecula (City)—Riverside *CA-4*
Temelec (CDP)—Sonoma *CA-4*
Te-Moak Reservation & Trust Lands
   (NV)...*IndRes-4*
Tempe (City)—Maricopa.................*AZ-4*
Temperance (CDP)—Monroe *MI-3*
Temple (City)—Carroll....................*GA-2*
Temple (Town)—Franklin *ME-1*
Temple (Town)—Hillsborough *NH-1*
Temple (Town)—Cotton *OK-2*
Temple (Borough)—Berks *PA-1*
Temple (City)—Bell........................*TX-2*
Temple City (City)—Los Angeles ..*CA-4*
Temple Hills (CDP)—Prince
   George's *MD-1*
Temple Terrace (City)—
   Hillsborough *FL-2*
Templeton (CDP)—San Luis
   Obispo..*CA-4*
Templeton (City)—Carroll *IA-3*
Templeton (Town)—Worcester *MA-1*
Templeton (Township)—
   Atchison *MO-3*
Templeville (Town)—Caroline *MD-1*
Templeville (Town)—Queen
   Anne's *MD-1*
Tenafly (Borough)—Bergen *NJ-1*

Tenaha (Town)—Shelby *TX-2*
Tenakee Springs (City)—
   Skagway-Hoonah-Angoon Census
   Area *AK-4*
Ten Broeck (City)—Jefferson *KY-2*
Tenhassen (Township)—Martin *MN-3*
Tenino (Town)—Thurston *WA-4*
Ten Lake (Township)—Beltrami...*MN-3*
Ten Mile (Township)—Miami *KS-4*
Ten Mile (Township)—Macon *MO-3*
Ten Mile Lake (Township)—Lac qui
   Parle *MN-3*
Tennant (City)—Shelby..................*IA-3*
Tennessee (Township)—
   McDonough *IL-3*
Tennessee (Village)—McDonough ..*IL-3*
Tennessee Ridge (City)—
   Houston.......................................*TN-2*
Tennessee River (MO) *Geog-4*
Tennessee-Tombigbee Waterway
   (MO)......................................*Geog-4*
Tenney (City)—Wilkin *MN-3*
Tennille (City)—Washington *GA-2*
Tennyson (Town)—Warrick *IN-3*
Tennyson (Village)—Grant *WI-3*
Tensas Parish *LA-2*
Tensed (City)—Benewah *ID-4*
Ten Sleep (Town)—Washakie *WY-4*
Tenstrike (City)—Beltrami *MN-3*
Ten Thousand Smokes, Valley of
   (AK) *Geog-4*
Tepee Butte (Township)—
   Hettinger *ND-4*
Tequesta (Village)—Palm Beach *FL-2*
Terlton (Town)—Pawnee *OK-2*
Terra Alta (Town)—Preston *WV-2*
Terra Bella (CDP)—Tulare.............*CA-4*
Terrace Heights (CDP)—Yakima...*WA-4*
Terrace Park (Village)—
   Hamilton *OH-3*
Terral (Town)—Jefferson................*OK-2*
Terramuggus (CDP)—Hartford.......*CT-1*
Terrebonne (Township)—Red
   Lake..*MN-3*
Terrebonne (CDP)—Deschutes......*OR-4*
Terrebonne Parish *LA-2*
Terre Haute (Township)—
   Henderson *IL-3*
Terre Haute (City)—Vigo...............*IN-3*
Terre Hill (Borough)—Lancaster *PA-1*
Terrell (City)—Kaufman *TX-2*
Terrell County *GA-2*
Terrell County *TX-2*
Terrell Hills (City)—Bexar *TX-2*
Terril (City)—Dickinson *IA-3*
Terry (Township)—Finney *KS-4*
Terry (Town)—Hinds *MS-2*
Terry (City)—Prairie *MT-4*
Terry (Township)—Bradford *PA-1*
Terry County *TX-2*
Terrytown (CDP)—Jefferson
   Parish *LA-2*
Terrytown (Village)—Scotts Bluff..*NE-4*
Terryville (CDP)—Litchfield...........*CT-1*
Terryville (CDP)—Suffolk...............*NY-1*
Tescott (City)—Ottawa *KS-4*
Tesuque (CDP)—Santa Fe *NM-4*
Tesuque Pueblo & Trust Lands
   (NM) *IndRes-4*
Teterboro (Borough)—Bergen *NJ-1*
Tetlin (CDP)—Southeast Fairbanks
   Census Area *AK-4*
Teton (City)—Fremont...................*ID-4*
Teton County *ID-4*
Teton County *MT-4*

Teton County *WY-4*
Tetonia (City)—Teton *ID-4*
Tetonka (Township)—Spink........... *SD-4*
Teton Mountains (AK) *Geog-4*
Teutopolis (Town)—Effingham *IL-3*
Teutopolis (Township)—
   Effingham.................................. *IL-3*
Tewaukon (Township)—Sargent *ND-4*
Tewksbury (Town)—Middlesex..... *MA-1*
Tewksbury (Township)—
   Hunterdon *NJ-1*
Texarkana (City)—Miller *AR-2*
Texarkana (City)—Bowie *TX-2*
Texas (Township)—De Witt........... *IL-3*
Texas (Township)—Kalamazoo..... *MI-3*
Texas (Township)—Dent *MO-3*
Texas (Township)—Crawford........*OH-3*
Texas (Township)—Wayne *PA-1*
Texas (Town)—Marathon............... *WI-3*
Texas City (City)—Galveston *TX-2*
Texas County................................. *MO-3*
Texas County *OK-2*
Texas Panhandle (TX).................*Geog-4*
Texhoma (Town)—Texas *OK-2*
Texhoma (Town)—Sherman *TX-2*
Texico (City)—Curry *NM-4*
Texla (Town)—Dallam *TX-2*
Texola (Town)—Beckham *OK-2*
Texoma, Lake (TX) *Geog-4*
Thackerville (Town)—Love *OK-2*
Thatcher (Town)—Graham *AZ-4*
Thawville (Village)—Iroquois *IL-3*
Thaxton (Town)—Pontotoc...........*MS-2*
Thayer (Village)—Sangamon *IL-3*
Thayer (City)—Union *IA-3*
Thayer (City)—Neosho *KS-4*
Thayer (City)—Oregon *MO-3*
Thayer (Township)—Oregon *MO-3*
Thayer (Township)—Thurston *NE-4*
Thayer (Village)—York *NE-4*
Thayer County *NE-4*
Thayne (Town)—Lincoln *WY-4*
Thebes (Village)—Alexander........... *IL-3*
Thedford (Village)—Thomas *NE-4*
Thelma (Township)—Burleigh *ND-4*
Theodore (Division)—Mobile.........*AL-2*
Theodosia (Village)—Ozark *MO-3*
Theresa (Town)—Jefferson............. *NY-1*
Theresa (Village)—Jefferson *NY-1*
Theresa (Township)—Beadle.......... *SD-4*
Theresa (Town)—Dodge *WI-3*
Theresa (Village)—Dodge *WI-3*
Thermalito (CDP)—Butte *CA-4*
Thermopolis (Town)—Hot
   Springs *WY-4*
Thetford (Township)—Genesee *MI-3*
Thetford (Town)—Orange *VT-1*
Thibodaux (City)—Lafourche
   Parish *LA-2*
Thief Lake (Township)—
   Marshall *MN-3*
Thief River Falls (City)—
   Pennington *MN-3*
Thiells (CDP)—Rockland *NY-1*
Thiensville (Village)—Ozaukee.......*WI-3*
Thingvalla (Township)—
   Pembina *ND-4*
Third Creek (Township)—
   Gasconade..................................*MO-3*
Third Lake (Village)—Lake *IL-3*
Third River (Township)—Itasca ...*MN-3*
Thomas (Township)—Ellsworth......*KS-4*
Thomas (Township)—Saginaw *MI-3*
Thomas (Township)—Ripley *MO-3*
Thomas (Town)—Custer *OK-2*

Thomas (City)—Tucker................WV-2
Thomasboro (Town)—Champaign..IL-3
Thomas County............................GA-2
Thomas County............................KS-4
Thomas County............................NE-4
Thomaston (Town)—Marengo.....AL-2
Thomaston (Town)—Litchfield.....CT-1
Thomaston (City)—Upson............GA-2
Thomaston (Town)—Knox...........ME-1
Thomaston (Village)—Nassau......NY-1
Thomastown (Township)—
 Wadena....................................MN-3
Thomasville (City)—Clarke........AL-2
Thomasville (City)—Thomas........GA-2
Thomasville (City)—Davidson......NC-2
Thompson (Town)—Windham....CT-1
Thompson (Township)—Jo
 Daviess......................................IL-3
Thompson (City)—Winnebago........IA-3
Thompson (Township)—
 Schoolcraft..................................MI-3
Thompson (Township)—Kittson...MN-3
Thompson (Town)—Sullivan.......NY-1
Thompson (City)—Grand Forks....ND-4
Thompson (Township)—
 Delaware...................................OH-3
Thompson (Township)—Geauga...OH-3
Thompson (Township)—Seneca.....OH-3
Thompson (Township)—Fulton.......PA-1
Thompson (Borough)—
 Susquehanna................................PA-1
Thompson (Township)—
 Susquehanna................................PA-1
Thompson and Meserves Purchase
 (Pop. Place)—Coos.................NH-1
Thompson Falls (Town)—
 Sanders...................................MT-4
Thompsons (Town)—Fort Bend.....TX-2
Thompsontown (Borough)—
 Juniata.....................................PA-1
Thompsonville (CDP)—Hartford..CT-1
Thompsonville (Village)—
 Franklin.....................................IL-3
Thompsonville (Village)—Benzie..MI-3
Thomson (City)—McDuffie..........GA-2
Thomson (Village)—Carroll.........IL-3
Thomson (City)—Carlton..........MN-3
Thomson (Township)—Carlton....MN-3
Thomson (Township)—Scotland..MO-3
Thor (City)—Humboldt................IA-3
Thordenskjold (Township)—
 Barnes.....................................ND-4
Thorn (Township)—Perry..............OH-3
Thornapple (Township)—Barry.....MI-3
Thornapple (Town)—Rusk............WI-3
Thornburg (City)—Keokuk............IA-3
Thornburg (Borough)—Allegheny..PA-1
Thornbury (Township)—Chester....PA-1
Thornbury (Township)—
 Delaware...................................PA-1
Thorncreek (Township)—Whitley...IN-3
Thorndale (City)—Milam.............TX-2
Thorndale (City)—Williamson......TX-2
Thorndike (Town)—Waldo..........ME-1
Thorne Bay (City)—Prince of
 Wales-Outer Ketchikan Census
 Area.......................................AK-4
Thornfield (Township)—Ozark.....MO-3
Thornhill (City)—Jefferson...........KY-2
Thornton (Town)—Calhoun..........AR-2
Thornton (City)—Adams...............CO-4
Thornton (Town)—Cook................IL-3
Thornton (Township)—Cook.........IL-3
Thornton (City)—Cerro Gordo......IA-3
Thornton (Township)—Buffalo.....NE-4

Thornton (Town)—Grafton...........NH-1
Thornton (Town)—Limestone........TX-2
Thorntonville (Town)—Ward.........TX-2
Thorntown (Town)—Boone...........IN-3
Thornville (Village)—Perry............OH-3
Thornwood (CDP)—Westchester....NY-1
Thorp (Township)—Clark.............SD-4
Thorp (City)—Clark.....................WI-3
Thorp (Town)—Clark..................WI-3
Thorpe (Township)—Hubbard......MN-3
Thorsby (Town)—Chilton.............AL-2
Thorson (Township)—Burke.........ND-4
Thousand Islands (NY)................Geog-4
Thousand Oaks (City)—Ventura....CA-4
Thousand Palms (CDP)—
 Riverside...................................CA-4
Thrall (Town)—Williamson..........TX-2
Three Forks (Town)—Gallatin......MT-4
Three Lakes (Township)—
 Redwood...................................MN-3
Three Lakes (Town)—Oneida........WI-3
Three Oaks (Township)—Berrien..MI-3
Three Oaks (Village)—Berrien.......MI-3
Three Points (CDP)—Pima............AZ-4
Three Rivers (CDP)—Hampden.....MA-1
Three Rivers (City)—St. Joseph....MI-3
Three Rivers (CDP)—Deschutes...OR-4
Three Rivers (Township)—Spink..SD-4
Three Rivers (City)—Live Oak......TX-2
Throckmorton (Town)—
 Throckmorton..............................TX-2
Throckmorton County..................TX-2
Throop (Town)—Cayuga...............NY-1
Throop (Borough)—Lackawanna....PA-1
Thunderbolt (Town)—Chatham......GA-2
Thunder Lake (Township)—Cass..MN-3
Thurman (City)—Fremont.............IA-3
Thurman (Town)—Warren............NY-1
Thurmond (Town)—Fayette..........WV-2
Thurmont (Town)—Frederick.......MD-1
Thurston (Village)—Thurston........NE-4
Thurston (Town)—Steuben...........NY-1
Thurston (Village)—Fairfield.........OH-3
Thurston County...........................NE-4
Thurston County...........................WA-3
Tiber (Township)—Walsh..............ND-4
Tiburon (City)—Marin..................CA-4
Tice (CDP)—Lee..........................FL-2
Tickfaw (Village)—Tangipahoa
 Parish..LA-2
Ticonderoga (Town)—Essex..........NY-1
Ticonderoga (Village)—Essex.......NY-1
Tidioute (Borough)—Warren.........PA-1
Tierra Amarilla (Pop. Place)—Rio
 Arriba......................................NM-4
Tierra Buena (CDP)—Sutter..........CA-4
Tieton (Town)—Yakima.................WA-4
Tiffany (Township)—Eddy............ND-4
Tiffany (Town)—Dunn.................WI-3
Tiffin (City)—Johnson..................IA-3
Tiffin (Township)—Adams............OH-3
Tiffin (Township)—Defiance.........OH-3
Tiffin (City)—Seneca...................OH-3
Tift County...................................GA-2
Tifton (City)—Tift.........................GA-2
Tigard (City)—Washington............OR-4
Tiger (Town)—Rabun...................GA-2
Tiger Fork (Township)—Shelby....MO-3
Tigerton (Village)—Shawano........WI-3
Tightwad (Village)—Henry...........MO-3
Tignall (Town)—Wilkes................GA-2
Tijeras (Village)—Bernalillo..........NM-4
Tiki Island (Village)—Galveston...TX-2
Tilden (Village)—Randolph...........IL-3
Tilden (Township)—Osborne.........KS-4

Tilden (Township)—Marquette......MI-3
Tilden (Township)—Polk..............MN-3
Tilden (City)—Antelope................NE-4
Tilden (City)—Madison.................NE-4
Tilden (Township)—Berks.............PA-1
Tilden (Pop. Place)—McMullen....TX-2
Tilden (Town)—Chippewa.............WI-3
Tillamook (City)—Tillamook........OR-4
Tillamook County.........................OR-4
Tillar (City)—Desha......................AR-2
Tillar (City)—Drew.......................AR-2
Tillatoba (Village)—Yalobusha......MS-2
Tillman County............................OK-2
Tillmans Corner (CDP)—Mobile...AL-2
Tillson (CDP)—Ulster....................NY-1
Tilton (Village)—Vermilion............IL-3
Tilton (Town)—Belknap................NH-1
Tiltonsville (Village)—Jefferson.....OH-3
Timber (Township)—Peoria...........IL-3
Timber Creek (Township)—
 Nance......................................NE-4
Timbercreek Canyon (Village)—
 Randall....................................TX-2
Timberhill (Township)—Bourbon...KS-4
Timberlake (Village)—Lake...........OH-3
Timber Lake (City)—Dewey..........SD-4
Timberlake (CDP)—Campbell........VA-2
Timberlane (CDP)—Jefferson
 Parish......................................LA-2
Timber Pines (CDP)—Hernando...FL-2
Timberville (Town)—
 Rockingham..............................VA-2
Timberwood Park (CDP)—Bexar..TX-2
Timblin (Borough)—Jefferson.......PA-1
Time (Village)—Pike.....................IL-3
Timken (City)—Rush....................KS-4
Timmonsville (Town)—Florence....SC-2
Timms Hill (WI).........................Geog-4
Timnath (Town)—Larimer............CO-3
Timothy (Township)—Crow
 Wing......................................MN-3
Timpson (City)—Shelby...............TX-2
Tina (Town)—Carroll....................MO-3
Tindall (Town)—Grundy...............MO-3
Tingley (City)—Ringgold..............IA-3
Tinicum (Township)—Bucks.........PA-1
Tinicum (Township)—Delaware....PA-1
Tinker Air Force Base (OK)..........Mil-1
Tinley Park (Village)—Cook.........IL-3
Tinley Park (Village)—Will...........IL-3
Tinmouth (Town)—Rutland..........VT-1
Tinsman (City)—Calhoun.............AR-2
Tintah (City)—Traverse.................MN-3
Tintah (Township)—Traverse........MN-3
Tinton Falls (Borough)—
 Monmouth................................NJ-1
Tioga (Township)—Neosho...........KS-4
Tioga (Town)—Tioga...................NY-1
Tioga (City)—Williams.................ND-4
Tioga (Township)—Williams.........ND-4
Tioga (Borough)—Tioga................PA-1
Tioga (Township)—Tioga..............PA-1
Tioga (Town)—Grayson................TX-2
Tioga County..............................NY-1
Tioga County..............................PA-1
Tionesta (Borough)—Forest..........PA-1
Tionesta (Township)—Forest.........PA-1
Tipler (Town)—Florence................WI-3
Tippah County............................MS-2
Tipp City (City)—Miami...............OH-3
Tippecanoe (Township)—Carroll....IN-3
Tippecanoe (Township)—
 Kosciusko.................................IN-3
Tippecanoe (Township)—
 Marshall..................................IN-3

Tippecanoe (Township)—Pulaski ... *IN-3*
Tippecanoe (Township)—
   Tippecanoe *IN-3*
Tippecanoe County *IN-3*
Tipton (CDP)—Tulare *CA-4*
Tipton (Township)—Cass........... *IN-3*
Tipton (City)—Tipton *IN-3*
Tipton (City)—Cedar *IA-3*
Tipton (City)—Mitchell *KS-4*
Tipton (City)—Moniteau *MO-3*
Tipton (Town)—Tillman *OK-2*
Tipton County *IN-3*
Tipton County *TN-2*
Tiptonville (Town)—Lake *TN-2*
Tira (Town)—Hopkins *TX-2*
Tiro (Village)—Crawford *OH-3*
Tisbury (Town)—Dukes *MA-1*
Tisdale (Township)—Cowley *KS-4*
Tishomingo (Town)—
   Tishomingo *MS-2*
Tishomingo (City)—Johnston *OK-2*
Tishomingo County *MS-2*
Tiskilwa (Village)—Bureau *IL-3*
Titonka (City)—Kossuth *IA-3*
Tittabawassee (Township)—
   Saginaw *MI-3*
Titus County *TX-2*
Titusville (City)—Brevard............*FL-2*
Titusville (Borough)—Crawford *PA-1*
Tiverton (Township)—
   Coshocton *OH-3*
Tiverton (Town)—Newport............ *RI-1*
Tivoli (Village)—Dutchess *NY-1*
Toad Lake (Township)—Becker....*MN-3*
Toast (CDP)—Surry *NC-2*
Tobacco (Township)—Gladwin *MI-3*
Tobias (Village)—Saline *NE-4*
Tobin (Township)—Perry *IN-3*
Tobin (Township)—Scotland *MO-3*
Tobin (Township)—Davison *SD-4*
Toboyne (Township)—Perry *PA-1*
Toby (Township)—Clarion *PA-1*
Tobyhanna (Township)—Monroe ... *PA-1*
Toccoa (City)—Stephens *GA-2*
Toccopola (Town)—Pontotoc *MS-2*
Toco (City)—Lamar *TX-2*
Tod (Township)—Crawford *OH-3*
Todd (Township)—Hubbard *MN-3*
Todd (Township)—Fulton *PA-1*
Todd (Township)—Huntingdon *PA-1*
Todd County *KY-2*
Todd County *MN-3*
Todd County *SD-4*
Todd Mission (City)—Grimes *TX-2*
Todds Point (Township)—Shelby ... *IL-3*
Tofte (Township)—Cook *MN-3*
Togiak (City)—Dillingham Census
   Area *AK-4*
Tohatchi (CDP)—McKinley..........*NM-4*
Toivola (Township)—St. Louis *MN-3*
Tok (CDP)—Southeast Fairbanks
   Census Area *AK-4*
Toksook Bay (City)—Bethel Census
   Area *AK-4*
Tolar (City)—Hood *TX-2*
Toledo (Town)—Cumberland......... *IL-3*
Toledo (City)—Tama *IA-3*
Toledo (Township)—Chase *KS-4*
Toledo (City)—Lucas *OH-3*
Toledo (City)—Lincoln *OR-4*
Toledo (City)—Lewis..................... *WA-4*
Toledo Bend Reservoir (WI) *Geog-4*
Tolgen (Township)—Ward *ND-4*
Tolland (Town)—Tolland *CT-1*
Tolland (Town)—Hampden *MA-1*

Tolland County *CT-1*
Tolleson (City)—Maricopa *AZ-4*
Tollette (Town)—Howard............. *AR-2*
Tolley (City)—Renville..................*ND-4*
Tolna (City)—Nelson *ND-4*
Tolono (Town)—Champaign *IL-3*
Tolono (Township)—Champaign ... *IL-3*
Tolstoy (Town)—Potter *SD-4*
Toluca (Town)—Marshall.............. *IL-3*
Tom (Township)—Benton *MO-3*
Tomah (City)—Monroe *WI-3*
Tomah (Town)—Monroe *WI-3*
Tomahawk (City)—Lincoln *WI-3*
Tomahawk (Town)—Lincoln *WI-3*
Tomball (City)—Harris *TX-2*
Tomball (City)—Montgomery........ *TX-2*
Tom Bean (Town)—Grayson *TX-2*
Tombigbee River (WI) *Geog-4*
Tombstone (City)—Cochise *AZ-4*
Tome-Adelino (CDP)—Valencia ... *NM-4*
Tom Green County *TX-2*
Tompkins (Township)—Warren *IL-3*
Tompkins (Township)—Jackson *MI-3*
Tompkins (Town)—Delaware *NY-1*
Tompkins County *NY-1*
Tompkinsville (City)—Monroe *KY-2*
Toms Brook (Town)—
   Shenandoah................................ *VA-2*
Toms River (CDP)—Ocean *NJ-1*
Tonasket (Town)—Okanogan *WA-4*
Tonawanda (City)—Erie................ *NY-1*
Tonawanda (Town)—Erie............... *NY-1*
Tonawanda Reservation (NY).. *IndRes-4*
Tonawanda Reservation (Pop. Place)—
   Erie *NY-1*
Tonawanda Reservation (Pop. Place)—
   Genesee *NY-1*
Tonawanda Reservation (Pop. Place)—
   Niagara *NY-1*
Tonganoxie (City)—Leavenworth ...*KS-4*
Tonganoxie (Township)—
   Leavenworth *KS-4*
Tonica (Village)—La Salle *IL-3*
Tonka Bay (City)—Hennepin *MN-3*
Tonkawa (City)—Kay *OK-2*
Tonkawa TJSA (OK) *IndRes-4*
Tonopah (CDP)—Nye *NV-4*
Tonsina (CDP)—Valdez-Cordova
   Census Area *AK-4*
Tonti (Township)—Marion *IL-3*
Tontitown (Town)—Washington *AR-2*
Tontogany (Village)—Wood *OH-3*
Tony (Village)—Rusk *WI-3*
Tooele (City)—Tooele *UT-4*
Tooele County *UT-4*
Tool (City)—Henderson *TX-2*
Toole County *MT-4*
Toombs County *GA-2*
Toomsboro (Town)—Wilkinson *GA-2*
Toone (Town)—Hardeman *TN-2*
Topeka (Town)—Mason *IL-3*
Topeka (Township)—Lagrange *IN-3*
Topeka (City)—Shawnee *KS-4*
Topeka (Township)—Shawnee *KS-4*
Toppenish (City)—Yakima *WA-4*
Topsail Beach (Town)—Pender.....*NC-2*
Topsfield (Town)—Washington *ME-1*
Topsfield (Town)—Essex *MA-1*
Topsham (Town)—Sagadahoc *ME-1*
Topsham (Town)—Orange *VT-1*
Topton (Borough)—Berks *PA-1*
Toqua (Township)—Big Stone *MN-3*
Toquerville (Town)—Washington .. *UT-4*
Torch Lake (Township)—Antrim .. *MI-3*

Torch Lake (Township)—
   Houghton *MI-3*
Tordenskjold (Township)—Otter
   Tail *MN-3*
Torgerson (Township)—Pierce *ND-4*
Tornado (CDP)—Kanawha *WV-2*
Torning (Township)—Swift *MN-3*
Torning (Township)—Ward *ND-4*
Toronto (City)—Clinton *IA-3*
Toronto (City)—Woodson *KS-4*
Toronto (Township)—Woodson *KS-4*
Toronto (City)—Jefferson *OH-3*
Toronto (Town)—Deuel *SD-4*
Torrance (City)—Los Angeles *CA-4*
Torrance County *NM-4*
Torres-Martinez Reservation
   (CA) *IndRes-4*
Torrey (Township)—Cass *MN-3*
Torrey (Town)—Yates *NY-1*
Torrey (Town)—Wayne *UT-4*
Torrey Lake (Township)—Brule..... *SD-4*
Torrington (City)—Litchfield *CT-1*
Torrington (Town)—Goshen *WY-1*
Totowa (Borough)—Passaic *NJ-1*
Toulon (City)—Stark *IL-3*
Toulon (Township)—Stark *IL-3*
Tovey (Village)—Christian............. *IL-3*
Towamencin (Township)—
   Montgomery............................... *PA-1*
Towamensing (Township)—
   Carbon *PA-1*
Towanda (Town)—McLean *IL-3*
Towanda (Township)—McLean *IL-3*
Towanda (City)—Butler *KS-4*
Towanda (Township)—Butler *KS-4*
Towanda (Township)—Phillips *KS-4*
Towanda (Borough)—Bradford..... *PA-1*
Towanda (Township)—Bradford ... *PA-1*
Towaoc (CDP)—Montezuma *CO-4*
Tower (City)—St. Louis *MN-3*
Tower (Township)—Cass *ND-4*
Tower City (City)—Barnes *ND-4*
Tower City (City)—Cass *ND-4*
Tower City (Borough)—Schuylkill .. *PA-1*
Tower Hill (Township)—Shelby *IL-3*
Tower Hill (Village)—Shelby *IL-3*
Tower Lakes (Village)—Lake *IL-3*
Town and Country (City)—St.
   Louis *MO-3*
Town and Country (CDP)—
   Spokane *WA-4*
Town Creek (Town)—Lawrence......*AL-2*
Towner (City)—McHenry *ND-4*
Towner County *ND-4*
Town Line (CDP)—Erie................ *NY-1*
Town 'n' Country (CDP)—
   Hillsborough *FL-2*
Town of Pines (Town)—Porter *IN-3*
Towns County *GA-2*
Townsend (Town)—New Castle *DE-1*
Townsend (Town)—Middlesex...... *MA-1*
Townsend (City)—Broadwater....... *MT-4*
Townsend (Township)—Huron *OH-3*
Townsend (Township)—
   Sandusky *OH-3*
Townsend (City)—Blount *TN-2*
Townsend (Town)—Oconto *WI-3*
Townshend (Town)—Windham *VT-1*
Township No. 1 (Township)—
   Harper *KS-4*
Township No. 1 (Township)—
   Morris *KS-4*
Township No. 1 (Township)—
   Rooks *KS-4*

General Index

American Places Dictionary

Township No. 10 (Township)—
Pratt *KS-4*
Township No. 10 (Township)—
Rooks *KS-4*
Township No. 11 (Township)—
Pratt *KS-4*
Township No. 11 (Township)—
Rooks *KS-4*
Township No. 12 (Township)—
Pratt *KS-4*
Township No. 12 (Township)—
Rooks *KS-4*
Township No. 2 (Township)—
Harper *KS-4*
Township No. 2 (Township)—
Morris *KS-4*
Township No. 2 (Township)—
Rooks *KS-4*
Township No. 3 (Township)—
Harper *KS-4*
Township No. 3 (Township)—
Morris *KS-4*
Township No. 3 (Township)—
Rooks *KS-4*
Township No. 4 (Township)—
Harper *KS-4*
Township No. 4 (Township)—
Morris *KS-4*
Township No. 4 (Township)—
Rooks *KS-4*
Township No. 5 (Township)—
Harper *KS-4*
Township No. 5 (Township)—
Morris *KS-4*
Township No. 5 (Township)—
Rooks *KS-4*
Township No. 6 (Township)—
Harper *KS-4*
Township No. 6 (Township)—
Morris *KS-4*
Township No. 6 (Township)—
Pratt *KS-4*
Township No. 6 (Township)—
Rooks *KS-4*
Township No. 7 (Township)—
Morris *KS-4*
Township No. 7 (Township)—
Pratt *KS-4*
Township No. 7 (Township)—
Rooks *KS-4*
Township No. 8 (Township)—
Morris *KS-4*
Township No. 8 (Township)—
Pratt *KS-4*
Township No. 8 (Township)—
Rooks *KS-4*
Township No. 9 (Township)—
Morris *KS-4*
Township No. 9 (Township)—
Pratt *KS-4*
Township No. 9 (Township)—
Rooks *KS-4*
Townville (Borough)—Crawford .. *PA-1*
Town West (CDP)—Fort Bend *TX-2*
Towson (CDP)—Baltimore *MD-1*
Toxey (Town)—Choctaw *AL-2*
Toyah (Town)—Reeves *TX-2*
Trabuco Highlands (CDP)—
Orange *CA-4*
Tracy (City)—San Joaquin *CA-4*
Tracy (City)—Lyon *MN-3*
Tracy (City)—Platte *MO-3*
Tracy (Township)—Lyman *SD-4*
Tracy City (Town)—Grundy *TN-2*
Tracyton (CDP)—Kitsap *WA-4*

Trade Lake (Town)—Burnett *WI-3*
Traer (City)—Tama *IA-3*
Trafalgar (Town)—Johnson *IN-3*
Trafford (Municipality)—
Jefferson *AL-2*
Trafford (Borough)—
Westmoreland *PA-1*
Trail (City)—Polk *MN-3*
Trail (Township)—Perkins *SD-4*
Trail Creek (Town)—La Porte *IN-3*
Trail Creek (Township)—
Harrison *MO-3*
Traill County *ND-4*
Trainer (Borough)—Delaware *PA-1*
Transit (Township)—Sibley *MN-3*
Transverse Ranges (WI) *Geog-4*
Transylvania County *NC-2*
Trappe (Town)—Talbot *MD-1*
Trappe (Borough)—Montgomery .. *PA-1*
Trapper Creek (CDP)—
Matanuska-Susitna Borough .. *AK-4*
Traskwood (Town)—Saline *AR-2*
Travelers Rest (City)—Greenville .. *SC-2*
Traverse (Township)—Nicollet ... *MN-3*
Traverse City (City)—Grand
Traverse *MI-3*
Traverse City (City)—Leelanau *MI-3*
Traverse County *MN-3*
Travis Air Force Base (CA) *Mil-4*
Travis County *TX-2*
Treasure County *MT-4*
Treasure Island (City)—Pinellas .. *FL-2*
Tredyffrin (Township)—Chester .. *PA-1*
Treece (City)—Cherokee *KS-4*
Trego (Town)—Washburn *WI-3*
Trego County *KS-4*
Trelipe (Township)—Cass *MN-3*
Tremont (Town)—Tazewell *IL-3*
Tremont (Township)—Tazewell .. *IL-3*
Tremont (Town)—Hancock *ME-1*
Tremont (Town)—Itawamba *MS-2*
Tremont (Township)—Buchanan .. *MO-3*
Tremont (Borough)—Schuylkill .. *PA-1*
Tremont (Township)—Schuylkill .. *PA-1*
Tremont City (Village)—Clark *OH-3*
Tremonton (City)—Box Elder *UT-4*
Trempealeau (Town)—
Trempealeau *WI-3*
Trempealeau (Village)—
Trempealeau *WI-3*
Trempealeau County *WI-3*
Trent (Town)—Moody *SD-4*
Trent (Town)—Taylor *TX-2*
Trenton (City)—Gilchrist *FL-2*
Trenton (City)—Dade *GA-2*
Trenton (Town)—Clinton *IL-3*
Trenton (Township)—Edwards ... *KS-4*
Trenton (City)—Todd *KY-2*
Trenton (Town)—Hancock *ME-1*
Trenton (City)—Wayne *MI-3*
Trenton (City)—Grundy *MO-3*
Trenton (Township)—Grundy *MO-3*
Trenton (Village)—Hitchcock *NE-4*
Trenton (City)—Mercer *NJ-1*
Trenton (Town)—Oneida *NY-1*
Trenton (Town)—Jones *NC-2*
Trenton (Township)—Williams ... *ND-4*
Trenton (City)—Butler *OH-3*
Trenton (Township)—Delaware .. *OH-3*
Trenton (Town)—Edgefield *SC-2*
Trenton (Township)—Brookings .. *SD-4*
Trenton (City)—Gibson *TN-2*
Trenton (Town)—Fannin *TX-2*
Trenton (Town)—Cache *UT-4*
Trenton (Town)—Dodge *WI-3*

Trenton (Town)—Pierce *WI-3*
Trenton (Town)—Washington *WI-3*
Trentwood (CDP)—Spokane *WA-4*
Trent Woods (Town)—Craven *NC-2*
Treutlen County *GA-2*
Treynor (City)—Pottawattamie ... *IA-3*
Trezevant (Town)—Carroll *TN-2*
Triadelphia (Town)—Ohio *WV-3*
Triana (Municipality)—Madison .. *AL-2*
Triangle (Town)—Broome *NY-1*
Triangle (CDP)—Prince William ... *VA-2*
Tribbey (Town)—Pottawatomie .. *OK-2*
Tribes Hill (CDP)—Montgomery .. *NY-1*
Tribune (City)—Greeley *KS-4*
Tribune (Township)—Greeley *KS-4*
Tri-City (CDP)—Douglas *OR-4*
Trier (Township)—Cavalier *ND-4*
Trigg County *KY-2*
Tri-Lakes (CDP)—Whitley *IN-3*
Trimbelle (Town)—Pierce *WI-3*
Trimble (Town)—Clinton *MO-3*
Trimble (Township)—Athens *OH-3*
Trimble (Village)—Athens *OH-3*
Trimble (Town)—Dyer *TN-2*
Trimble (Town)—Obion *TN-2*
Trimble County *KY-2*
Trimont (City)—Martin *MN-3*
Trinidad (City)—Humboldt *CA-4*
Trinidad (City)—Las Animas *CO-4*
Trinidad (City)—Henderson *TX-2*
Trinidad Rancheria (CA) *IndRes-4*
Trinity (Town)—Morgan *AL-2*
Trinity (City)—Trinity *TX-2*
Trinity County *CA-4*
Trinity County *TX-2*
Trion (Town)—Chattooga *GA-2*
Tripler Army Medical Center
(HI) *Mil-4*
Triplett (City)—Chariton *MO-3*
Triplett (Township)—Chariton ... *MO-3*
Tripoli (City)—Bremer *IA-3*
Tripp (City)—Hutchinson *SD-4*
Tripp (Town)—Bayfield *WI-3*
Tripp County *SD-4*
Triumph (Township)—Custer *NE-4*
Triumph (Township)—Ramsey ... *ND-4*
Triumph (Township)—Warren ... *PA-1*
Trivoli (Township)—Peoria *IL-3*
Trivoli (Township)—Ellsworth ... *KS-4*
Trommald (City)—Crow Wing ... *MN-3*
Trondhjem (Township)—Otter
Tail *MN-3*
Trophy Club (Town)—Denton ... *TX-2*
Trophy Club (Town)—Tarrant ... *TX-2*
Tropic (Town)—Garfield *UT-4*
Trosky (City)—Pipestone *MN-3*
Trotter (Township)—Carroll *MO-3*
Trotwood (City)—Montgomery .. *OH-3*
Troup (City)—Cherokee *TX-2*
Troup (City)—Smith *TX-2*
Troup County *GA-2*
Troupsburg (Town)—Steuben *NY-1*
Trousdale County *TN-2*
Troutdale (City)—Multnomah *OR-4*
Troutdale (Town)—Grayson *VA-2*
Trout Lake (Township)—
Chippewa *MI-3*
Trout Lake (Township)—Itasca .. *MN-3*
Troutman (Town)—Iredell *NC-2*
Troutville (Borough)—Clearfield .. *PA-1*
Troutville (Town)—Botetourt *VA-2*
Trowbridge (Township)—Allegan .. *MI-3*
Trowbridge Park (CDP)—
Marquette *MI-3*
Troy (City)—Pike *AL-2*

American Places Dictionary   General Index

Troy (City)—Latah *ID-4*
Troy (City)—Madison *IL-3*
Troy (Township)—Will *IL-3*
Troy (Township)—Dekalb *IN-3*
Troy (Township)—Fountain *IN-3*
Troy (Town)—Perry *IN-3*
Troy (Township)—Perry *IN-3*
Troy (City)—Doniphan *KS-4*
Troy (Township)—Reno *KS-4*
Troy (Town)—Waldo *ME-1*
Troy (Township)—Newaygo *MI-3*
Troy (City)—Oakland *MI-3*
Troy (Township)—Pipestone *MN-3*
Troy (Township)—Renville *MN-3*
Troy (City)—Lincoln *MO-3*
Troy (Town)—Lincoln *MT-4*
Troy (Town)—Cheshire *NH-1*
Troy (City)—Rensselaer *NY-1*
Troy (Town)—Montgomery *NC-2*
Troy (Township)—Divide *ND-4*
Troy (Township)—Ashland *OH-3*
Troy (Township)—Athens *OH-3*
Troy (Township)—Delaware *OH-3*
Troy (Township)—Geauga *OH-3*
Troy (City)—Miami *OH-3*
Troy (Township)—Morrow *OH-3*
Troy (Township)—Richland *OH-3*
Troy (Township)—Wood *OH-3*
Troy (Borough)—Bradford *PA-1*
Troy (Township)—Bradford *PA-1*
Troy (Township)—Crawford *PA-1*
Troy (Town)—Greenwood *SC-2*
Troy (Township)—Day *SD-4*
Troy (Township)—Grant *SD-4*
Troy (Town)—Obion *TN-2*
Troy (Town)—Bell *TX-2*
Troy (Town)—Orleans *VT-1*
Troy (Town)—Sauk *WI-3*
Troy (Town)—St. Croix *WI-3*
Troy (Town)—Walworth *WI-3*
Troy Grove (Township)—La Salle .. *IL-3*
Troy Grove (Village)—La Salle *IL-3*
Truax (Township)—Williams *ND-4*
Truckee (CDP)—Nevada *CA-4*
True (Town)—Rusk *WI-3*
Truesdale (City)—Buena Vista *IA-3*
Truesdale (City)—Warren *MO-3*
Truman (City)—Martin *MN-3*
Truman (Township)—Pierce *ND-4*
Trumann (City)—Poinsett *AR-2*
Trumansburg (Village)—
  Tompkins *NY-1*
Trumbauersville (Borough)—
  Bucks *PA-1*
Trumbull (Town)—Fairfield *CT-1*
Trumbull (Village)—Adams *NE-4*
Trumbull (Village)—Clay *NE-4*
Trumbull (Township)—
  Ashtabula *OH-3*
Trumbull County *OH-3*
Truro (Township)—Knox *IL-3*
Truro (City)—Madison *IA-3*
Truro (Township)—Barnstable *MA-1*
Truro (Township)—Franklin *OH-3*
Truro (Township)—Aurora *SD-4*
Trussville (City)—Jefferson *AL-2*
Truth or Consequences (City)—
  Sierra *NM-4*
Truxton (Village)—Lincoln *MO-3*
Truxton (Town)—Cortland *NY-1*
Trygg (Township)—Burleigh *ND-4*
Tryon (Town)—Polk *NC-2*
Tryon (Town)—Lincoln *OK-2*
Tsaile (CDP)—Apache *AZ-4*
Tualatin (City)—Clackamas *OR-4*

Tualatin (City)—Washington *OR-4*
Tuba City (CDP)—Coconino *AZ-4*
Tuckahoe (Village)—Westchester ... *NY-1*
Tuckahoe (CDP)—Henrico *VA-2*
Tucker (CDP)—De Kalb *GA-2*
Tucker (CDP)—Neshoba *MS-2*
Tucker County *WV-2*
Tuckerman (City)—Jackson *AR-2*
Tuckerton (Borough)—Ocean *NJ-1*
Tucson (City)—Pima *AZ-4*
Tucson Estates (CDP)—Pima *AZ-4*
Tucumcari (City)—Quay *NM-4*
Tuftonboro (Town)—Carroll *NH-1*
Tukwila (City)—King *WA-4*
Tulalip Bay (CDP)—Snohomish ... *WA-4*
Tulalip Reservation (WA) *IndRes-4*
Tulare (City)—Tulare *CA-4*
Tulare (Town)—Spink *SD-4*
Tulare (Township)—Spink *SD-4*
Tulare County *CA-4*
Tularosa (Village)—Otero *NM-4*
Tulelake (City)—Siskiyou *CA-4*
Tule River Reservation (CA) *IndRes-4*
Tulia (City)—Swisher *TX-2*
Tull (Town)—Grant *AR-2*
Tullahassee (Town)—Wagoner *OK-2*
Tullahoma (City)—Coffee *TN-2*
Tullahoma (City)—Franklin *TN-2*
Tuller (Township)—Ransom *ND-4*
Tullos (Town)—La Salle Parish *LA-2*
Tullos (Town)—Winn Parish *LA-2*
Tully (Town)—Onondaga *NY-1*
Tully (Village)—Onondaga *NY-1*
Tully (Township)—Marion *OH-3*
Tully (Township)—Van Wert *OH-3*
Tullytown (Borough)—Bucks *PA-1*
Tulpehocken (Township)—Berks ... *PA-1*
Tulsa (City)—Osage *OK-2*
Tulsa (City)—Rogers *OK-2*
Tulsa (City)—Tulsa *OK-2*
Tulsa County *OK-2*
Tuluksak (City)—Bethel Census
  Area *AK-4*
Tumuli (Township)—Otter Tail *MN-3*
Tumwater (City)—Thurston *WA-4*
Tunbridge (Township)—De Witt ... *IL-3*
Tunbridge (Town)—Orange *VT-1*
Tunica (Town)—Tunica *MS-2*
Tunica-Biloxi Tribe (LA) *IndRes-4*
Tunica County *MS-2*
Tunkhannock (Township)—
  Monroe *PA-1*
Tunkhannock (Borough)—
  Wyoming *PA-1*
Tunkhannock (Township)—
  Wyoming *PA-1*
Tunnel Hill (City)—Whitfield *GA-2*
Tunnelhill (Borough)—Cambria ... *PA-1*
Tunnelton (Town)—Preston *WV-2*
Tunsberg (Township)—
  Chippewa *MN-3*
Tuntutuliak (CDP)—Bethel Census
  Area *AK-4*
Tununak (City)—Bethel Census
  Area *AK-4*
Tuolumne City (CDP)—
  Tuolumne *CA-4*
Tuolumne County *CA-4*
Tuolumne Rancheria (CA) *IndRes-4*
Tupelo (Town)—Jackson *AR-2*
Tupelo (City)—Lee *MS-2*
Tupelo (City)—Coal *OK-2*
Tupper Lake (Village)—Franklin ... *NY-1*
Turbett (Township)—Juniata *PA-1*
Turbeville (Town)—Clarendon *SC-2*

Turbot (Township)—
  Northumberland *PA-1*
Turbotville (Borough)—
  Northumberland *PA-1*
Turin (Town)—Coweta *GA-2*
Turin (City)—Monona *IA-3*
Turin (Township)—Marquette *MI-3*
Turin (Town)—Lewis *NY-1*
Turin (Village)—Lewis *NY-1*
Turkey (Town)—Sampson *NC-2*
Turkey (City)—Hall *TX-2*
Turkey Creek (Township)—
  Kosciusko *IN-3*
Turkey Creek (Township)—
  Barber *KS-4*
Turkey Creek (Township)—
  McPherson *KS-4*
Turkey Creek (Township)—
  Mitchell *KS-4*
Turkey Creek (Village)—Evangeline
  Parish *LA-2*
Turkey Creek (Township)—
  Franklin *NE-4*
Turkey Creek (Township)—
  Harlan *NE-4*
Turkey Valley (Township)—
  Yankton *SD-4*
Turley (CDP)—Tulsa *OK-2*
Turlock (City)—Stanislaus *CA-4*
Turman (Township)—Sullivan *IN-3*
Turnback (Township)—
  Lawrence *MO-3*
Turner (Town)—Androscoggin *ME-1*
Turner (Township)—Arenac *MI-3*
Turner (Village)—Arenac *MI-3*
Turner (Township)—Aitkin *MN-3*
Turner (City)—Marion *OR-4*
Turner (Township)—Turner *SD-4*
Turner County *GA-2*
Turner County *SD-4*
Turners Falls (CDP)—Franklin *MA-1*
Turnersville (CDP)—Gloucester ... *NJ-1*
Turney (Town)—Clinton *MO-3*
Turnpike Interchange (CDP)—
  Trumbull *OH-3*
Turon (City)—Reno *KS-4*
Turpin Hills (CDP)—Hamilton *OH-3*
Turrell (City)—Crittenden *AR-2*
Turtle (Town)—Rock *WI-3*
Turtle Creek (Township)—Todd ... *MN-3*
Turtle Creek (Township)—
  Shelby *OH-3*
Turtle Creek (Township)—
  Warren *OH-3*
Turtle Creek (Borough)—
  Allegheny *PA-1*
Turtle Lake (Township)—
  Beltrami *MN-3*
Turtle Lake (Township)—Cass *MN-3*
Turtle Lake (City)—McLean *ND-4*
Turtle Lake (Township)—
  McLean *ND-4*
Turtle Lake (Town)—Barron *WI-3*
Turtle Lake (Village)—Barron *WI-3*
Turtle Lake (Village)—Polk *WI-3*
Turtle Mountain Res. & Trust Lands
  (ND) *IndRes-4*
Turtle Mountains (Pop. Place)—
  Rolette *ND-4*
Turtle River (City)—Beltrami *MN-3*
Turtle River (Township)—
  Beltrami *MN-3*
Turtle River (Township)—Grand
  Forks *ND-4*
Turton (Town)—Spink *SD-4*

1111

General Index

Turton (Township)—Spink............. SD-4
Tuscaloosa (City)—Tuscaloosa........AL-2
Tuscaloosa County AL-2
Tuscarawas (Township)—
  Coshocton OH-3
Tuscarawas (Township)—Stark OH-3
Tuscarawas (Village)—
  Tuscarawas OH-3
Tuscarawas County................OH-3
Tuscarora (Township)—
  Cheboygan MI-3
Tuscarora (Town)—Steuben NY-1
Tuscarora (Township)—Pierce ND-4
Tuscarora (Township)—Bradford.... PA-1
Tuscarora (Township)—Juniata PA-1
Tuscarora (Township)—Perry PA-1
Tuscarora Reservation (NY) IndRes-4
Tuscarora Reservation (Pop. Place)—
  Niagara... NY-1
Tuscola (City)—Douglas................. IL-3
Tuscola (Township)—Douglas........ IL-3
Tuscola (Township)—Tuscola MI-3
Tuscola (Town)—Taylor.................. TX-2
Tuscola County MI-3
Tusculum (City)—Greene TN-2
Tuscumbia (City)—Colbert AL-2
Tuscumbia (Town)—Miller MO-3
Tushka (Town)—Atoka................... OK-2
Tuskegee (City)—Macon AL-2
Tusten (Town)—Sullivan NY-1
Tustin (City)—Orange CA-4
Tustin (Village)—Osceola MI-3
Tustin Foothills (CDP)—Orange.... CA-4
Tuttle (City)—Kidder ND-4
Tuttle (Township)—Kidder ND-4
Tuttle (Town)—Grady..................... OK-2
Tutwiler (Town)—Tallahatchie......MS-2
Tuxedo (Town)—Orange NY-1
Tuxedo Park (Village)—Orange NY-1
Twain Harte (CDP)—Tuolumne ... CA-4
Twelvemile (Township)—
  Madison MO-3
Twelve Mile (Township)—
  Williams ND-4
Twentynine Palms (City)—San
  Bernardino CA-4
Twentynine Palms Base (Military
  Facility)—San Bernardino........... CA-4
Twentynine Palms Marine Corps
  Air Ground Combat Center
  (CA)..Mil-4
Twenty Nine Palms Reservation
  (CA)..IndRes-4
Twigg (Township)—Hamilton IL-3
Twiggs County GA-2
Twilight (Borough)—Washington.... PA-1
Twin (Township)—Darke OH-3
Twin (Township)—Preble................OH-3
Twin (Township)—Ross..................OH-3
Twin Bridges (Town)—Laclede MO-3
Twin Bridges (Town)—Madison ... MT-4
Twin Brooks (Town)—Grant SD-4
Twin Brooks (Township)—Grant.... SD-4
Twin Butte (Township)—Divide....ND-4
Twin Butte (Township)—Corson ... SD-4
Twin City (City)—Emanuel GA-2
Twin Falls (City)—Twin Falls ID-4
Twin Falls County ID-4
Twin Grove (Township)—
  Greenwood KS-4
Twin Groves (Township)—
  Jasper MO-3
Twin Hill (Township)—Towner ND-4
Twin Hills (CDP)—Dillingham Census
  Area... AK-4

Twining (Village)—Arenac MI-3
Twin Lake (CDP)—Muskegon MI-3
Twin Lake (Township)—Benson ND-4
Twin Lake (Township)—Sanborn .. SD-4
Twin Lakes (CDP)—Santa Cruz ... CA-4
Twin Lakes (Township)—
  Carlton MN-3
Twin Lakes (City)—Freeborn......... MN-3
Twin Lakes (Township)—
  Mahnomen MN-3
Twin Lakes (Village)—Kenosha WI-3
Twin Oaks (Village)—St. Louis..... MO-3
Twin Rivers (CDP)—Mercer NJ-1
Twinsburg (City)—Summit OH-3
Twinsburg (Township)—Summit ...OH-3
Twin Tree (Township)—Benson.....ND-4
Twin Valley (City)—Norman MN-3
Twin Valley (Township)—
  McKenzie ND-4
Twisp (Town)—Okanogan WA-4
Two Buttes (Town)—Baca............... CO-4
Two Creeks (Town)—Manitowoc ... WI-3
Two Harbors (City)—Lake MN-3
Two Inlets (Township)—Becker MN-3
Two Rivers (CDP)—Fairbanks North
  Star Borough AK-4
Two Rivers (Township)—
  Morrison MN-3
Two Rivers (City)—Manitowoc WI-3
Two Rivers (Town)—Manitowoc ... WI-3
Two Strike (CDP)—Todd................ SD-4
Tybee Island (City)—Chatham GA-2
Tye (Town)—Taylor......................... TX-2
Tyler (City)—Lincoln MN-3
Tyler (Township)—Hickory............ MO-3
Tyler (City)—Smith TX-2
Tyler County TX-2
Tyler County WV-2
Tylertown (Town)—Walthall MS-2
Tymochtee (Township)—
  Wyandot OH-3
Tyndall (City)—Bon Homme SD-4
Tyndall Air Force Base (Mil. facil.)—
  Bay FL-2
Tyngsborough (Town)—
  Middlesex MA-1
Tynsid (Township)—Polk MN-3
Tyonek (CDP)—Kenai Peninsula
  Borough... AK-4
Tyre (Town)—Seneca NY-1
Tyringham (Town)—Berkshire...... MA-1
Tyro (City)—Montgomery KS-4
Tyro (Township)—Yellow
  Medicine MN-3
Tyrol (Township)—Griggs ND-4
Tyrone (Town)—Fayette GA-2
Tyrone (Township)—Franklin IL-3
Tyrone (Township)—Kent MI-3
Tyrone (Township)—Livingston MI-3
Tyrone (Township)—Le Sueur MN-3
Tyrone (Town)—Schuyler NY-1
Tyrone (Township)—Williams ND-4
Tyrone (Town)—Texas.................... OK-2
Tyrone (Township)—Adams PA-1
Tyrone (Borough)—Blair PA-1
Tyrone (Township)—Blair PA-1
Tyrone (Township)—Perry PA-1
Tyronza (Town)—Poinsett AR-2
Tyrrell County NC-2
Tysons Corner (CDP)—Fairfax VA-2
Ty Ty (Town)—Tift GA-2
Tywappity (Township)—
  Mississippi MO-3
Tywappity (Township)—Scott MO-3
Ubly (Village)—Huron MI-3

American Places Dictionary

Ucon (City)—Bonneville................. ID-4
Udall (City)—Cowley KS-4
Udell (City)—Appanoose IA-3
Udolpho (Township)—Mower MN-3
Uehling (Village)—Dodge NE-4
Uhland (City)—Caldwell................ TX-2
Uhland (City)—Hays....................... TX-2
Uhrichsville (City)—Tuscarawas....OH-3
Uinta County WY-4
Uintah (Town)—Weber UT-4
Uintah County UT-4
Uintah & Ouray Reservation
  (UT) IndRes-4
Uinta Mountains (WI)................Geog-4
Ukiah (City)—Mendocino............... CA-4
Ukiah (City)—Umatilla...................OR-4
Ulen (Town)—Boone....................... IN-3
Ulen (City)—Clay MN-3
Ulen (Township)—Clay MN-3
Ullin (Town)—Pulaski IL-3
Ulm (Town)—Prairie AR-2
Ulmer (Town)—Allendale SC-2
Ulster (Town)—Ulster NY-1
Ulster (Township)—Bradford......... PA-1
Ulster County NY-1
Ulysses (City)—Grant KS-4
Ulysses (Township)—Butler NE-4
Ulysses (Village)—Butler................ NE-4
Ulysses (Town)—Tompkins NY-1
Ulysses (Borough)—Potter PA-1
Ulysses (Township)—Potter PA-1
Umatilla (City)—Lake.....................FL-2
Umatilla (City)—Umatilla OR-4
Umatilla County OR-4
Umatilla Reservation (OR) IndRes-4
Umber View Heights (Village)—
  Cedar..MO-3
Unadilla (City)—Dooly GA-2
Unadilla (Township)—Livingston.. MI-3
Unadilla (Village)—Otoe................ NE-4
Unadilla (Town)—Otsego NY-1
Unadilla (Village)—Otsego............. NY-1
Unalakleet (City)—Nome Census
  Area... AK-4
Unalaska (City)—Aleutians West
  Census Area AK-4
Uncasville-Oxoboxo Valley (CDP)—
  New London CT-1
Uncertain (Village)—Harrison TX-2
Underhill (Town)—Chittenden VT-1
Underhill (Town)—Oconto WI-3
Underwood (City)—
  Pottawattamie IA-3
Underwood (City)—Otter Tail....... MN-3
Underwood (Township)—
  Redwood.......................................MN-3
Underwood (City)—McLean...........ND-4
Underwood (Pop. Place)—
  McLean ND-4
Underwood-Petersville (Division)—
  Lauderdale AL-2
Unicoi County TN-2
Union (Municipality)—Greene......AL-2
Union (Town)—Tolland CT-1
Union (Township)—Cumberland.... IL-3
Union (Township)—Effingham IL-3
Union (Township)—Fulton IL-3
Union (Township)—Livingston IL-3
Union (Town)—McHenry IL-3
Union (Township)—Adams IN-3
Union (Township)—Benton IN-3
Union (Township)—Boone IN-3
Union (Township)—Clark IN-3
Union (Township)—Clinton IN-3
Union (Township)—Crawford IN-3

Union (Township)—Dekalb *IN-3*	Union (Township)—Lincoln *MO-3*	Union (Township)—Tioga *PA-1*
Union (Township)—Delaware *IN-3*	Union (Township)—Marion *MO-3*	Union (Township)—Union *PA-1*
Union (Township)—Elkhart *IN-3*	Union (Township)—Monroe *MO-3*	Union (Township)—Washington *PA-1*
Union (Township)—Fulton *IN-3*	Union (Township)—Nodaway *MO-3*	Union (City)—Union *SC-2*
Union (Township)—Gibson *IN-3*	Union (Township)—Perry *MO-3*	Union (Township)—Brule *SD-4*
Union (Township)—Hendricks *IN-3*	Union (Township)—Polk *MO-3*	Union (Township)—Butte *SD-4*
Union (Township)—Howard *IN-3*	Union (Township)—Pulaski *MO-3*	Union (Township)—Davison *SD-4*
Union (Township)—Huntington *IN-3*	Union (Township)—Putnam *MO-3*	Union (Township)—Day *SD-4*
Union (Township)—Jasper *IN-3*	Union (Township)—Randolph *MO-3*	Union (Township)—Edmunds *SD-4*
Union (Township)—Johnson *IN-3*	Union (Township)—Ripley *MO-3*	Union (Township)—Faulk *SD-4*
Union (Township)—La Porte *IN-3*	Union (Township)—Scotland *MO-3*	Union (Township)—Gregory *SD-4*
Union (Township)—Madison *IN-3*	Union (Township)—Ste. Genevieve *MO-3*	Union (Township)—Jones *SD-4*
Union (Township)—Marshall *IN-3*	Union (Township)—Stone *MO-3*	Union (Township)—McCook *SD-4*
Union (Township)—Miami *IN-3*	Union (Township)—Sullivan *MO-3*	Union (Township)—Meade *SD-4*
Union (Township)—Montgomery *IN-3*	Union (Township)—Washington *MO-3*	Union (Township)—Moody *SD-4*
Union (Township)—Ohio *IN-3*	Union (Township)—Webster *MO-3*	Union (Township)—Sanborn *SD-4*
Union (Township)—Parke *IN-3*	Union (Township)—Worth *MO-3*	Union (Township)—Spink *SD-4*
Union (Township)—Perry *IN-3*	Union (Township)—Wright *MO-3*	Union (CDP)—Salt Lake *UT-4*
Union (Township)—Porter *IN-3*	Union (Township)—Butler *NE-4*	Union (Town)—Monroe *WV-2*
Union (Township)—Randolph *IN-3*	Union (Village)—Cass *NE-4*	Union (Town)—Burnett *WI-3*
Union (Township)—Rush *IN-3*	Union (Township)—Dodge *NE-4*	Union (Town)—Door *WI-3*
Union (Township)—Shelby *IN-3*	Union (Township)—Knox *NE-4*	Union (Town)—Eau Claire *WI-3*
Union (Township)—St. Joseph *IN-3*	Union (Township)—Phelps *NE-4*	Union (Town)—Pierce *WI-3*
Union (Township)—Tippecanoe *IN-3*	Union (Township)—Saunders *NE-4*	Union (Town)—Rock *WI-3*
Union (Township)—Union *IN-3*	Union (Township)—Hunterdon *NJ-1*	Union (Town)—Vernon *WI-3*
Union (Township)—Vanderburgh *IN-3*	Union (Township)—Union *NJ-1*	Union (Town)—Waupaca *WI-3*
Union (Township)—Wells *IN-3*	Union (Town)—Broome *NY-1*	Union Beach (Borough)— Monmouth *NJ-1*
Union (Township)—White *IN-3*	Union (Township)—Grand Forks *ND-4*	Union Bridge (Town)—Carroll *MD-1*
Union (Township)—Whitley *IN-3*	Union (Township)—Auglaize *OH-3*	Union Center (Township)—Elk *KS-4*
Union (City)—Hardin *IA-3*	Union (Township)—Belmont *OH-3*	Union Center (Village)—Juneau *WI-3*
Union (Township)—Anderson *KS-4*	Union (Township)—Brown *OH-3*	Union Chapel (Township)— Christian *MO-3*
Union (Township)—Barton *KS-4*	Union (Township)—Butler *OH-3*	Union City (City)—Alameda *CA-4*
Union (Township)—Butler *KS-4*	Union (Township)—Carroll *OH-3*	Union City (City)—Fulton *GA-2*
Union (Township)—Clay *KS-4*	Union (Township)—Champaign *OH-3*	Union City (City)—Randolph *IN-3*
Union (Township)—Dickinson *KS-4*	Union (Township)—Clermont *OH-3*	Union City (Village)—Branch *MI-3*
Union (Township)—Doniphan *KS-4*	Union (Township)—Clinton *OH-3*	Union City (Village)—Calhoun *MI-3*
Union (Township)—Jefferson *KS-4*	Union (Township)—Fayette *OH-3*	Union City (City)—Hudson *NJ-1*
Union (Township)—Kingman *KS-4*	Union (Township)—Hancock *OH-3*	Union City (Village)—Darke *OH-3*
Union (Township)—McPherson *KS-4*	Union (Township)—Highland *OH-3*	Union City (Town)—Canadian *OK-2*
Union (Township)— Pottawatomie *KS-4*	Union (Township)—Knox *OH-3*	Union City (Borough)—Erie *PA-1*
Union (Township)—Rawlins *KS-4*	Union (Township)—Lawrence *OH-3*	Union City (City)—Obion *TN-2*
Union (Township)—Republic *KS-4*	Union (Township)—Licking *OH-3*	**Union County** *AR-2*
Union (Township)—Rice *KS-4*	Union (Township)—Logan *OH-3*	**Union County** *FL-2*
Union (Township)—Rush *KS-4*	Union (Township)—Madison *OH-3*	**Union County** *GA-2*
Union (Township)—Sedgwick *KS-4*	Union (Township)—Mercer *OH-3*	**Union County** *IL-3*
Union (Township)—Sheridan *KS-4*	Union (Township)—Miami *OH-3*	**Union County** *IN-3*
Union (Township)—Sherman *KS-4*	Union (Village)—Montgomery *OH-3*	**Union County** *IA-3*
Union (Township)—Stafford *KS-4*	Union (Township)—Morgan *OH-3*	**Union County** *KY-2*
Union (Township)—Washington *KS-4*	Union (Township)—Muskingum *OH-3*	**Union County** *MS-2*
Union (City)—Boone *KY-2*	Union (Township)—Pike *OH-3*	**Union County** *NJ-1*
Union (Town)—Knox *ME-1*	Union (Township)—Putnam *OH-3*	**Union County** *NM-4*
Union (Township)—Branch *MI-3*	Union (Township)—Ross *OH-3*	**Union County** *NC-2*
Union (Township)—Grand Traverse *MI-3*	Union (Township)—Scioto *OH-3*	**Union County** *OH-3*
Union (Township)—Isabella *MI-3*	Union (Township)—Tuscarawas *OH-3*	**Union County** *OR-4*
Union (Township)—Houston *MN-3*	Union (Township)—Union *OH-3*	**Union County** *PA-1*
Union (Town)—Neshoba *MS-2*	Union (Township)—Van Wert *OH-3*	**Union County** *SC-2*
Union (Town)—Newton *MS-2*	Union (Township)—Warren *OH-3*	**Union County** *SD-4*
Union (Township)—Barton *MO-3*	Union (City)—Union *OR-4*	**Union County** *TN-2*
Union (Township)—Benton *MO-3*	Union (Township)—Adams *PA-1*	Union Creek (Pop. Place)— Stanton *NE-4*
Union (Township)—Bollinger *MO-3*	Union (Township)—Bedford *PA-1*	Uniondale (Town)—Wells *IN-3*
Union (Township)—Cass *MO-3*	Union (Township)—Berks *PA-1*	Uniondale (CDP)—Nassau *NY-1*
Union (Township)—Clark *MO-3*	Union (Township)—Centre *PA-1*	Union Dale (Borough)— Susquehanna *PA-1*
Union (Township)—Crawford *MO-3*	Union (Township)—Clearfield *PA-1*	Union Gap (City)—Yakima *WA-4*
Union (Township)—Daviess *MO-3*	Union (Township)—Crawford *PA-1*	Union Grove (Town)—Marshall *AL-2*
Union (Township)—Dunklin *MO-3*	Union (Township)—Erie *PA-1*	Union Grove (Township)— Whiteside *IL-3*
Union (City)—Franklin *MO-3*	Union (Township)—Fulton *PA-1*	Union Grove (Township)— Meeker *MN-3*
Union (Township)—Franklin *MO-3*	Union (Township)—Huntingdon *PA-1*	Union Grove (Village)—Upshur *TX-2*
Union (Township)—Harrison *MO-3*	Union (Township)—Jefferson *PA-1*	Union Grove (Village)—Racine *WI-3*
Union (Township)—Holt *MO-3*	Union (Township)—Lawrence *PA-1*	Union Hill (Village)—Kankakee *IL-3*
Union (Township)—Iron *MO-3*	Union (Township)—Lebanon *PA-1*	
Union (Township)—Jasper *MO-3*	Union (Township)—Luzerne *PA-1*	
Union (Township)—Laclede *MO-3*	Union (Township)—Mifflin *PA-1*	
Union (Township)—Lewis *MO-3*	Union (Township)—Schuylkill *PA-1*	
	Union (Township)—Snyder *PA-1*	

General Index

Union Parish *LA-2*
Union Park (CDP)—Orange *FL-2*
Union Point (City)—Greene *GA-2*
Union Springs (City)—Bullock *AL-2*
Union Springs (Village)—Cayuga .. *NY-1*
Union Star (Town)—DeKalb *MO-3*
Uniontown (City)—Perry *AL-2*
Uniontown (City)—Bourbon *KS-4*
Uniontown (City)—Union *KY-2*
Uniontown (CDP)—Stark *OH-3*
Uniontown (City)—Fayette *PA-1*
Uniontown (Town)—Whitman *WA-4*
Union Vale (Town)—Dutchess *NY-1*
Unionville (CDP)—Tift *GA-2*
Unionville (City)—Appanoose *IA-3*
Unionville (Village)—Tuscola *MI-3*
Unionville (City)—Putnam *MO-3*
Unionville (Village)—Orange *NY-1*
Unionville (Borough)—Centre *PA-1*
Unionville Center (Village)—
 Union *OH-3*
Uniopolis (Village)—Auglaize *OH-3*
United Houma Nation TDSA
 (LA) *IndRes-4*
Unity (Township)—Piatt *IL-3*
Unity (Town)—Waldo *ME-1*
Unity (Town)—Sullivan *NH-1*
Unity (Township)—Columbiana *OH-3*
Unity (City)—Baker *OR-4*
Unity (Township)—Westmoreland . *PA-1*
Unity (Town)—Clark *WI-3*
Unity (Village)—Clark *WI-3*
Unity (Village)—Marathon *WI-3*
Unity (Town)—Trempealeau *WI-3*
Unity (unorganized) (Pop. Place)—
 Kennebec *ME-1*
Unity Village (Town)—Jackson *MO-3*
Universal (Town)—Vermillion *IN-3*
Universal City (City)—Bexar *TX-2*
University City (City)—St.
 Louis *MO-3*
University Gardens (CDP)—
 Nassau *NY-1*
University Heights (City)—
 Johnson *IA-3*
University Heights (City)—
 Cuyahoga *OH-3*
University Heights (CDP)—
 Albemarle *VA-2*
University Park (Village)—Cook *IL-3*
University Park (Village)—Will *IL-3*
University Park (City)—Mahaska .. *IA-3*
University Park (Town)—Prince
 George's *MD-1*
University Park (CDP)—Doña
 Ana *NM-4*
University Park (City)—Dallas *TX-2*
University Place (CDP)—Pierce *WA-4*
University West (CDP)—
 Hillsborough *FL-2*
Upham (City)—McHenry *ND-4*
Upham (Town)—Langlade *WI-3*
Upland (City)—San Bernardino *CA-4*
Upland (Town)—Grant *IN-3*
Upland (Village)—Franklin *NE-4*
Upland (Township)—Divide *ND-4*
Upland (Borough)—Delaware *PA-1*
Uplands Park (Village)—St.
 Louis *MO-3*
Upper (Township)—Cape May *NJ-1*
Upper (Township)—Lawrence *OH-3*
Upper Allen (Township)—
 Cumberland *PA-1*
Upper Arlington (City)—
 Franklin *OH-3*

Upper Augusta (Township)—
 Northumberland *PA-1*
Upper Bern (Township)—Berks *PA-1*
Upper Brookville (Village)—
 Nassau *NY-1*
Upper Burrell (Township)—
 Westmoreland *PA-1*
Upper Chichester (Township)—
 Delaware *PA-1*
Upper Darby (Township)—
 Delaware *PA-1*
Upper Deerfield (Township)—
 Cumberland *NJ-1*
Upper Dublin (Township)—
 Montgomery *PA-1*
Upper Fairfield (Township)—
 Lycoming *PA-1*
Upper Frankford (Township)—
 Cumberland *PA-1*
Upper Frederick (Township)—
 Montgomery *PA-1*
Upper Freehold (Township)—
 Monmouth *NJ-1*
Upper Grand Lagoon (CDP)—
 Bay *FL-2*
Upper Gwynedd (Township)—
 Montgomery *PA-1*
Upper Hanover (Township)—
 Montgomery *PA-1*
Upper Kalskag (City)—Bethel Census
 Area *AK-4*
Upper Lake Rancheria (CA) *IndRes-4*
Upper Leacock (Township)—
 Lancaster *PA-1*
Upper Loutre (Township)—
 Montgomery *MO-3*
Upper Macungie (Township)—
 Lehigh *PA-1*
Upper Mahanoy (Township)—
 Northumberland *PA-1*
Upper Mahantongo (Township)—
 Schuylkill *PA-1*
Upper Makefield (Township)—
 Bucks *PA-1*
Upper Marlboro (Town)—Prince
 George's *MD-1*
Upper Merion (Township)—
 Montgomery *PA-1*
Upper Mifflin (Township)—
 Cumberland *PA-1*
Upper Milford (Township)—
 Lehigh *PA-1*
Upper Moreland (Township)—
 Montgomery *PA-1*
Upper Mount Bethel (Township)—
 Northampton *PA-1*
Upper Nazareth (Township)—
 Northampton *PA-1*
Upper Nyack (Village)—
 Rockland *NY-1*
Upper Oxford (Township)—
 Chester *PA-1*
Upper Paxton (Township)—
 Dauphin *PA-1*
Upper Pittsgrove (Township)—
 Salem *NJ-1*
Upper Pottsgrove (Township)—
 Montgomery *PA-1*
Upper Providence (Township)—
 Delaware *PA-1*
Upper Providence (Township)—
 Montgomery *PA-1*
Upper Red Lake (Pop. Place)—
 Beltrami *MN-3*
Upper Red Lake (WI) *Geog-4*

Upper Red Owl (Township)—
 Meade *SD-4*
Upper Saddle River (Borough)—
 Bergen *NJ-1*
Upper Salford (Township)—
 Montgomery *PA-1*
Upper Sandusky (City)—
 Wyandot *OH-3*
Upper Saucon (Township)—
 Lehigh *PA-1*
Upper Sioux Reservation
 (MN) *IndRes-4*
Upper Skagit Reservation
 (WA) *IndRes-4*
Upper Southampton (Township)—
 Bucks *PA-1*
Upper St. Clair (Township)—
 Allegheny *PA-1*
Upper Tulpehocken (Township)—
 Berks *PA-1*
Upper Turkeyfoot (Township)—
 Somerset *PA-1*
Upper Tyrone (Township)—
 Fayette *PA-1*
Upper Uwchlan (Township)—
 Chester *PA-1*
Upper Yoder (Township)—
 Cambria *PA-1*
Upper Yosemite Falls (WI) *Geog-4*
Upsala (City)—Morrison *MN-3*
Upshur County *TX-2*
Upshur County *WV-2*
Upson County *GA-2*
Upton (City)—Hardin *KY-2*
Upton (City)—LaRue *KY-2*
Upton (Town)—Oxford *ME-1*
Upton (Town)—Worcester *MA-1*
Upton (Township)—Texas *MO-3*
Upton (Town)—Weston *WY-4*
Upton County *TX-2*
Urania (Town)—La Salle Parish ... *LA-2*
Urbana (City)—Champaign *IL-3*
Urbana (Township)—Champaign ... *IL-3*
Urbana (City)—Benton *IA-3*
Urbana (City)—Dallas *MO-3*
Urbana (Town)—Steuben *NY-1*
Urbana (City)—Champaign *OH-3*
Urbana (Township)—Champaign .. *OH-3*
Urbancrest (Village)—Franklin *OH-3*
Urbandale (City)—Polk *IA-3*
Urbank (City)—Otter Tail *MN-3*
Urbanna (Town)—Middlesex *VA-2*
Urich (City)—Henry *MO-3*
Urness (Township)—Douglas *MN-3*
Ursa (Township)—Adams *IL-3*
Ursa (Village)—Adams *IL-3*
Ursina (Borough)—Somerset *PA-1*
U.S. Air Force Academy (CO) *Mil-4*
U.S. Army Corps of Engineers,
 Little Rock District (AR) *Mil-4*
U.S. Coast Guard Academy (CT) .. *Mil-4*
U.S. Coast Guard Yard (MD) *Mil-4*
U.S. Military Academy (NY) *Mil-4*
U.S. Naval Academy (MD) *Mil-4*
U.S. Naval Observatory (DC) *Mil-4*
Ustick (Township)—Whiteside *IL-3*
Utah County *UT-4*
Ute (City)—Monona *IA-3*
Ute Mountain Reservation & Trust
 Lands (CO) *IndRes-4*
Utica (Township)—La Salle *IL-3*
Utica (Town)—Clark *IN-3*
Utica (Township)—Clark *IN-3*
Utica (City)—Ness *KS-4*
Utica (City)—Macomb *MI-3*

Utica (City)—Winona *MN-3*
Utica (Township)—Winona *MN-3*
Utica (Town)—Hinds *MS-2*
Utica (Village)—Livingston *MO-3*
Utica (Village)—Seward *NE-4*
Utica (City)—Oneida *NY-1*
Utica (Village)—Knox *OH-3*
Utica (Village)—Licking *OH-3*
Utica (Borough)—Venango *PA-1*
Utica (CDP)—Oconee *SC-2*
Utica (Town)—Yankton *SD-4*
Utica (Township)—Yankton *SD-4*
Utica (Town)—Crawford *WI-3*
Utica (Town)—Winnebago *WI-3*
Uvalda (Town)—Montgomery *GA-2*
Uvalde (City)—Uvalde *TX-2*
Uvalde County *TX-2*
Uwchlan (Township)—Chester *PA-1*
Uxbridge (Town)—Worcester *MA-1*
Uxbridge (Township)—Barnes *ND-4*
Vacaville (City)—Solano *CA-4*
Vader (City)—Lewis *WA-4*
Vadito (CDP)—Taos *NM-4*
Vadnais Heights (City)—Ramsey .. *MN-3*
Vaiden (Town)—Carroll *MS-2*
Vail (Town)—Eagle *CO-4*
Vail (City)—Crawford *IA-3*
Vail (Township)—Redwood *MN-3*
Vail (Township)—Perkins *SD-4*
Vails Gate (CDP)—Orange *NY-1*
Valatie (Village)—Columbia *NY-1*
Valders (Village)—Manitowoc *WI-3*
Valdese (Town)—Burke *NC-2*
Valdez (City)—Valdez-Cordova Census
 Area *AK-4*
Valdez-Cordova Census Area *AK-4*
Valdosta (City)—Lowndes *GA-2*
Vale (Township)—Burke *ND-4*
Vale (City)—Malheur *OR-4*
Vale (Township)—Butte *SD-4*
Valencia (CDP)—Valencia *NM-4*
Valencia (Borough)—Butler *PA-1*
Valencia County *NM-4*
Valencia Heights (CDP)—
 Richland *SC-2*
Valencia West (CDP)—Pima *AZ-4*
Valentine (City)—Cherry *NE-4*
Valentine (Town)—Jeff Davis *TX-2*
Valeria (City)—Jasper *IA-3*
Valhalla (Township)—Wells *ND-4*
Valier (Town)—Franklin *IL-3*
Valier (Town)—Pondera *MT-4*
Valinda (CDP)—Los Angeles *CA-4*
Valle (Township)—Jefferson *MO-3*
Vallejo (City)—Solano *CA-4*
Vallers (Township)—Lyon *MN-3*
Valle Vista (CDP)—Riverside *CA-4*
Valley (Municipality)—Chambers ..*AL-2*
Valley (Township)—Stark *IL-3*
Valley (Township)—Barber *KS-4*
Valley (Township)—Ellsworth *KS-4*
Valley (Township)—Hodgeman *KS-4*
Valley (Township)—Kingman *KS-4*
Valley (Township)—Lincoln *KS-4*
Valley (Township)—Linn *KS-4*
Valley (Township)—Miami *KS-4*
Valley (Township)—Osborne *KS-4*
Valley (Township)—Phillips *KS-4*
Valley (Township)—Reno *KS-4*
Valley (Township)—Rice *KS-4*
Valley (Township)—Scott *KS-4*
Valley (Township)—Sheridan *KS-4*
Valley (Township)—Smith *KS-4*
Valley (Township)—Allegan *MI-3*
Valley (Township)—Marshall *MN-3*

Valley (Township)—Macon *MO-3*
Valley (Township)—Buffalo *NE-4*
Valley (City)—Douglas *NE-4*
Valley (Township)—Knox *NE-4*
Valley (Township)—Barnes *ND-4*
Valley (Township)—Dickey *ND-4*
Valley (Township)—Kidder *ND-4*
Valley (Township)—Guernsey *OH-3*
Valley (Township)—Scioto *OH-3*
Valley (Township)—Armstrong *PA-1*
Valley (Township)—Chester *PA-1*
Valley (Township)—Montour *PA-1*
Valley (Township)—Beadle *SD-4*
Valley (Township)—Day *SD-4*
Valley (Township)—Douglas *SD-4*
Valley (Township)—Hughes *SD-4*
Valley (Township)—Hutchinson *SD-4*
Valley (Township)—Hyde *SD-4*
Valley (Township)—Tripp *SD-4*
Valley Brook (Township)—Osage ...*KS-4*
Valley Brook (Town)—Oklahoma ..*OK-2*
Valley Center (CDP)—San Diego . *CA-4*
Valley Center (Township)—
 Pawnee *KS-4*
Valley Center (City)—Sedgwick *KS-4*
Valley Center (Township)—
 Sedgwick *KS-4*
Valley City (Village)—Pike *IL-3*
Valley City (City)—Barnes *ND-4*
Valley Cottage (CDP)—Rockland.. *NY-1*
Valley County *ID-4*
Valley County *MT-4*
Valley County *NE-4*
Valley Falls (City)—Jefferson *KS-4*
Valley Falls (Village)—Rensselaer. *NY-1*
Valley Falls (CDP)—Providence ... *RI-1*
Valley Falls (CDP)—Spartanburg ...*SC-2*
Valley Grove (Village)—Ohio *WV-2*
Valley Head (Town)—DeKalb *AL-2*
Valley Hi (Village)—Logan *OH-3*
Valley-Hi (Borough)—Fulton *PA-1*
Valley Hill (CDP)—Henderson *NC-2*
Valley Mills (City)—Bosque *TX-2*
Valley Mills (City)—McLennan *TX-2*
Valley Park (City)—St. Louis *MO-3*
Valley Park (Town)—Rogers *OK-2*
Valley Spring (Township)—
 Stutsman *ND-4*
Valley Springs (Town)—Boone *AR-2*
Valley Springs (City)—
 Minnehaha *SD-4*
Valley Springs (Township)—
 Minnehaha *SD-4*
Valley Station (CDP)—Jefferson ... *KY-2*
Valley Stream (Village)—Nassau .. *NY-1*
Valley View (Village)—Cuyahoga ..*OH-3*
Valleyview (Village)—Franklin *OH-3*
Valley View (Town)—Cooke *TX-2*
Valliant (Town)—McCurtain *OK-2*
Valmeyer (Town)—Monroe *IL-3*
Valparaiso (City)—Okaloosa *FL-2*
Valparaiso (City)—Porter *IN-3*
Valparaiso (Village)—Saunders *NE-4*
Val Verde (CDP)—Davis *UT-4*
Val Verde (CDP)—Los Angeles *CA-4*
Valverde (Township)—Sumner *KS-4*
Val Verde County *TX-2*
Vamo (CDP)—Sarasota *FL-2*
Van (City)—Van Zandt *TX-2*
Van Alstyne (Town)—Grayson *TX-2*
Van Buren (Town)—Crawford *AR-2*
Van Buren (Township)—Brown *IN-3*
Van Buren (Township)—Clay *IN-3*
Van Buren (Township)—Daviess ... *IN-3*
Van Buren (Township)—Fountain .. *IN-3*

Van Buren (Town)—Grant *IN-3*
Van Buren (Township)—Grant *IN-3*
Van Buren (Township)—
 Kosciusko *IN-3*
Van Buren (Township)—Lagrange . *IN-3*
Van Buren (Township)—Madison .. *IN-3*
Van Buren (Township)—Monroe ... *IN-3*
Van Buren (Township)—Pulaski ... *IN-3*
Van Buren (Township)—Shelby *IN-3*
Van Buren (Town)—Aroostook *ME-1*
Van Buren (Township)—Wayne *MI-3*
Van Buren (Township)—St.
 Louis *MN-3*
Van Buren (Town)—Carter *MO-3*
Van Buren (Township)—Jackson .. *MO-3*
Van Buren (Township)—Newton .. *MO-3*
Van Buren (Township)—Wright ... *MO-3*
Van Buren (Town)—Onondaga *NY-1*
Van Buren (Township)—Renville .. *ND-4*
Van Buren (Township)—Darke *OH-3*
Van Buren (Township)—
 Hancock *OH-3*
Van Buren (Village)—Hancock *OH-3*
Van Buren (Township)—Putnam ... *OH-3*
Van Buren (Township)—Shelby ... *OH-3*
Van Buren County *AR-2*
Van Buren County *IA-3*
Van Buren County *MI-3*
Van Buren County *TN-2*
Vance (Town)—Tuscaloosa *AL-2*
Vance (Township)—Vermilion *IL-3*
Vance (Town)—Orangeburg *SC-2*
Vanceboro (Town)—Washington... *ME-1*
Vanceboro (Town)—Craven *NC-2*
Vanceburg (City)—Lewis *KY-2*
Vance County *NC-2*
Vance Creek (Town)—Barron *WI-3*
Vancleave (CDP)—Jackson *MS-2*
Vancouver (City)—Clark *WA-4*
Vancouver Mall (CDP)—Clark *WA-4*
Vandalia (City)—Fayette *IL-3*
Vandalia (Township)—Fayette *IL-3*
Vandalia (Village)—Cass *MI-3*
Vandalia (City)—Audrain *MO-3*
Vandalia (City)—Ralls *MO-3*
Vandalia (City)—Montgomery *OH-3*
Vandemere (Town)—Pamlico *NC-2*
Vandenberg Air Force Base (CA) ...*Mil-4*
Vandenberg Air Force Base (Military
 Facility)—Santa Barbara *CA-4*
Vandenberg Village (CDP)—Santa
 Barbara *CA-4*
Vandenbroek (Town)—
 Outagamie *WI-3*
Vander (CDP)—Cumberland *NC-2*
Vanderbilt (Village)—Otsego *MI-3*
Vanderbilt (Borough)—Fayette *PA-1*
Vanderburgh County *IN-3*
Vandercook Lake (CDP)—
 Jackson *MI-3*
Vandergrift (Borough)—
 Westmoreland *PA-1*
Vandervoort (Town)—Polk *AR-2*
Vandiver (Village)—Audrain *MO-3*
Vandling (Borough)—Lackawanna . *PA-1*
Vanduser (Village)—Scott *MO-3*
Van Etten (Town)—Chemung *NY-1*
Van Etten (Village)—Chemung *NY-1*
Vang (Township)—Ward *ND-4*
Van Hook (Township)—
 Mountrail *ND-4*
Van Horn (Township)—Carroll *MO-3*
Van Horn (Town)—Culberson *TX-2*
Van Horne (City)—Benton *IA-3*
Van Lear (CDP)—Johnson *KY-2*

General Index — American Places Dictionary

Vanleer (Town)—Dickson *TN-2*
Vanlue (Village)—Hancock *OH-3*
Van Meter (City)—Dallas *IA-3*
Van Meter (Township)—Dickey *ND-4*
Van Nuys *See* **Los Angeles**—Los
   Angeles *CA-4*
Vanport (Township)—Beaver *PA-1*
Vansant (CDP)—Buchanan............ *VA-2*
Van Tassell (Town)—Niobrara...... *WY-4*
Vanville (Township)—Burke *ND-4*
Van Vleck (CDP)—Matagorda....... *TX-2*
Van Wert (City)—Decatur...............*IA-3*
Van Wert (City)—Van Wert *OH-3*
Van Wert County...............................*OH-3*
Van Zandt County *TX-2*
Vardaman (Town)—Calhoun *MS-2*
Varick (Town)—Seneca *NY-1*
Varina (City)—Pocahontas.............*IA-3*
Varna (Village)—Marshall............. *IL-3*
Varnado (Village)—Washington
   Parish *LA-2*
Varnamtown (Town)—Brunswick .. *NC-2*
Varnell (City)—Whitfield............... *GA-2*
Varner (Township)—Ripley............*MO-3*
Varnville (Town)—Hampton *SC-2*
Vasa (Township)—Goodhue...........*MN-3*
Vass (Town)—Moore *NC-2*
Vassalborough (Town)—
   Kennebec *ME-1*
Vassar (City)—Tuscola *MI-3*
Vassar (Township)—Tuscola *MI-3*
Vaughn (Town)—Guadalupe *NM-4*
Veale (Township)—Daviess............. *IN-3*
Veazie (Town)—Penobscot............ *ME-1*
Veblen (City)—Marshall................. *SD-4*
Veblen (Township)—Marshall....... *SD-4*
Veedersburg (Town)—Fountain *IN-3*
Vega (Township)—Marshall *MN-3*
Vega (Town)—Oldham *TX-2*
Velda Village (City)—St. Louis... *MO-3*
Velda Village Hills (Village)—St.
   Louis *MO-3*
Veldt (Township)—Marshall *MN-3*
Velma (City)—Stephens *OK-2*
Velva (City)—McHenry...................*ND-4*
Velva (Township)—McHenry.........*ND-4*
Venango (Village)—Perkins.......... *NE-4*
Venango (Township)—Butler *PA-1*
Venango (Borough)—Crawford........ *PA-1*
Venango (Township)—Crawford....... *PA-1*
Venango (Township)—Erie............. *PA-1*
Venango County *PA-1*
Venedocia (Village)—Van Wert....*OH-3*
Venedy (Township)—Washington ... *IL-3*
Venedy (Village)—Washington......... *IL-3*
Veneta (City)—Lane *OR-4*
Venetian Village (CDP)—Lake *IL-3*
Venetie (CDP)—Yukon-Koyukuk
   Census Area *AK-4*
Venice (City)—Sarasota...................*FL-2*
Venice (City)—Madison *IL-3*
Venice (Township)—Madison........ *IL-3*
Venice (Township)—Shiawassee *MI-3*
Venice (Town)—Cayuga *NY-1*
Venice (Township)—Seneca *OH-3*
Venice Gardens (CDP)—Sarasota ..*FL-2*
Ventnor City (City)—Atlantic.......... *NJ-1*
Ventura (City)—Cerro Gordo *IA-3*
Ventura County................................... *CA-4*
Venturia (City)—McIntosh *ND-4*
Venus (Town)—Ellis....................... *TX-2*
Venus (Town)—Johnson................. *TX-2*
Vera (Town)—Washington *OK-2*
Vera Cruz (Town)—Wells................ *IN-3*
Veradale (CDP)—Spokane *WA-4*

Verdel (Village)—Knox *NE-4*
Verden (Town)—Grady *OK-2*
Verdi (Township)—Lincoln...........*MN-3*
Verdigre (Township)—Knox *NE-4*
Verdigre (Village)—Knox *NE-4*
Verdigris (Township)—Wilson....... *KS-4*
Verdigris (Township)—Antelope.... *NE-4*
Verdigris (Township)—Holt........... *NE-4*
Verdon (Township)—Aitkin *MN-3*
Verdon (Village)—Richardson *NE-4*
Verdon (Town)—Brown *SD-4*
Vergas (City)—Otter Tail *MN-3*
Vergennes (Township)—Jackson.... *IL-3*
Vergennes (Village)—Jackson......... *IL-3*
Vergennes (Township)—Kent........ *MI-3*
Vergennes (City)—Addison *VT-1*
Vermilion (Village)—Edgar........... *IL-3*
Vermilion (City)—Erie *OH-3*
Vermilion (Township)—Erie..........*OH-3*
Vermilion (City)—Lorain *OH-3*
Vermilion County *IL-3*
Vermilion Lake (Township)—St.
   Louis *MN-3*
Vermilion Parish................................*LA-2*
Vermillion (Township)—La Salle.... *IL-3*
Vermillion (Township)—
   Vermillion *IN-3*
Vermillion (City)—Marshall *KS-4*
Vermillion (Township)—Marshall....*KS-4*
Vermillion (City)—Dakota *MN-3*
Vermillion (Township)—Dakota ... *MN-3*
Vermillion (Township)—Ashland...*OH-3*
Vermillion (City)—Clay *SD-4*
Vermillion (Township)—Clay *SD-4*
Vermillion (Township)—Miner..... *SD-4*
Vermillion County *IN-3*
Vermillion Lake Reservation
   (MN) *IndRes-4*
Vermont (Town)—Fulton *IL-3*
Vermont (Township)—Fulton........ *IL-3*
Vermont (Township)—Edmunds.... *SD-4*
Vermont (Town)—Dane *WI-3*
Vermontville (Township)—Eaton .. *MI-3*
Vermontville (Village)—Eaton *MI-3*
Vernal (City)—Uintah *UT-4*
Vernal Fall (CA)............................ *Geog-4*
Verndale (City)—Wadena *MN-3*
Verner (Township)—Sargent *ND-4*
Vernon (City)—Lamar.................... *AL-2*
Vernon (City)—Los Angeles........... *CA-4*
Vernon (Town)—Tolland................. *CT-1*
Vernon (City)—Washington *FL-2*
Vernon (Township)—Lake *IL-3*
Vernon (Village)—Marion.............. *IL-3*
Vernon (Township)—Hancock *IN-3*
Vernon (Township)—Jackson......... *IN-3*
Vernon (Town)—Jennings *IN-3*
Vernon (Township)—Jennings........ *IN-3*
Vernon (Township)—Washington ... *IN-3*
Vernon (Township)—Cowley.........*KS-4*
Vernon (Township)—Isabella......... *MI-3*
Vernon (Township)—Shiawassee ... *MI-3*
Vernon (Village)—Shiawassee....... *MI-3*
Vernon (Township)—Dodge *MN-3*
Vernon (Township)—Clark *MO-3*
Vernon (Township)—Sussex............ *NJ-1*
Vernon (Town)—Oneida *NY-1*
Vernon (Village)—Oneida *NY-1*
Vernon (Township)—Kidder.........*ND-4*
Vernon (Township)—Walsh *ND-4*
Vernon (Township)—Clinton.........*OH-3*
Vernon (Township)—Crawford......*OH-3*
Vernon (Township)—Scioto *OH-3*
Vernon (Township)—Trumbull *OH-3*
Vernon (Township)—Crawford *PA-1*

Vernon (Township)—Beadle *SD-4*
Vernon (Township)—Grant........... *SD-4*
Vernon (City)—Wilbarger *TX-2*
Vernon (Town)—Tooele *UT-4*
Vernon (Town)—Windham *VT-1*
Vernon (Town)—Waukesha *WI-3*
Vernonburg (Town)—Chatham *GA-2*
Vernon Center (City)—Blue
   Earth..*MN-3*
Vernon Center (Township)—Blue
   Earth..*MN-3*
Vernon County.................................. *MO-3*
Vernon County *WI-3*
Vernon Hills (Village)—Lake *IL-3*
Vernonia (City)—Columbia *OR-4*
Vernon Parish....................................*LA-2*
Vernon Valley (CDP)—Sussex *NJ-1*
Vero Beach (City)—Indian River ...*FL-2*
Vero Beach South (CDP)—Indian
   River *FL-2*
Verona (Village)—Grundy............... *IL-3*
Verona (Town)—Hancock *ME-1*
Verona (Township)—Huron *MI-3*
Verona (Township)—Faribault *MN-3*
Verona (Town)—Lee *MS-2*
Verona (Town)—Lawrence *MO-3*
Verona (Township)—Adams *NE-4*
Verona (Borough)—Essex *NJ-1*
Verona (Town)—Oneida................. *NY-1*
Verona (City)—LaMoure *ND-4*
Verona (Village)—Montgomery *OH-3*
Verona (Village)—Preble *OH-3*
Verona (Borough)—Allegheny........ *PA-1*
Verona (CDP)—Augusta *VA-2*
Verona (City)—Dane *WI-3*
Verona (Town)—Dane *WI-3*
Verrazano-Narrows Bridge
   (NY) *Geog-4*
Versailles (Township)—Brown *IL-3*
Versailles (Village)—Brown............ *IL-3*
Versailles (Town)—Ripley.............. *IN-3*
Versailles (City)—Woodford *KY-2*
Versailles (City)—Morgan *MO-3*
Versailles (Village)—Darke *OH-3*
Versailles (Borough)—Allegheny *PA-1*
Vershire (Town)—Orange *VT-1*
Vesper (Township)—Lincoln *KS-4*
Vesper (Village)—Wood *WI-3*
Vest (Township)—Scotland *MO-3*
Vesta (City)—Redwood *MN-3*
Vesta (Township)—Redwood *MN-3*
Vesta (Township)—Walsh *ND-4*
Vestal (Town)—Broome *NY-1*
Vestavia Hills (City)—Jefferson...... *AL-2*
Veteran (Town)—Chemung *NY-1*
Vevay (Town)—Switzerland *IN-3*
Vevay (Township)—Ingham *MI-3*
Vian (Town)—Sequoyah *OK-2*
Viborg (City)—Turner *SD-4*
Viburnum (Town)—Iron *MO-3*
Vicco (City)—Perry *KY-2*
Vici (Town)—Dewey...................... *OK-2*
Vickers (Township)—Perkins *SD-4*
Vicksburg (Township)—Jewell *KS-4*
Vicksburg (Village)—Kalamazoo... *MI-3*
Vicksburg (City)—Warren *MS-2*
Victor (City)—Teller....................... *CO-4*
Victor (City)—Teton *ID-4*
Victor (Township)—DeKalb *IL-3*
Victor (City)—Iowa *IA-3*
Victor (City)—Poweshiek................*IA-3*
Victor (Township)—Osborne *KS-4*
Victor (Township)—Clinton........... *MI-3*
Victor (Township)—Wright *MN-3*
Victor (Town)—Ontario *NY-1*

Victor (Village)—Ontario NY-1
Victor (Township)—Towner ND-4
Victor (Township)—Marshall SD-4
Victor (Township)—Roberts SD-4
Victoria (Town)—Mississippi AR-2
Victoria (Township)—Knox IL-3
Victoria (Village)—Knox IL-3
Victoria (City)—Ellis KS-4
Victoria (Township)—Ellis KS-4
Victoria (Township)—Rice KS-4
Victoria (City)—Carver MN-3
Victoria (Township)—Custer NE-4
Victoria (Township)—McLean ND-4
Victoria (City)—Victoria TX-2
Victoria (Town)—Lunenburg VA-2
Victoria County TX-2
Victorville (City)—San
  Bernardino CA-4
Victory (Township)—Mason MI-3
Victory (Town)—Cayuga NY-1
Victory (Village)—Saratoga NY-1
Victory (Township)—Venango PA-1
Victory (Town)—Essex VT-1
Victory Gardens (Borough)—
  Morris NJ-1
Victory Lakes (CDP)—
  Gloucester NJ-1
Vidalia (City)—Montgomery GA-2
Vidalia (City)—Toombs GA-2
Vidalia (Town)—Concordia
  Parish LA-2
Viding (Township)—Clay MN-3
Vidor (City)—Orange TX-2
Viejas Reservation (CA) IndRes-4
Vienna (City)—Dooly GA-2
Vienna (Township)—Grundy IL-3
Vienna (Town)—Johnson IL-3
Vienna (Township)—Scott IN-3
Vienna (Township)—
  Pottawatomie KS-4
Vienna (Town)—Lincoln Parish ... LA-2
Vienna (Town)—Kennebec ME-1
Vienna (Town)—Dorchester MD-1
Vienna (Township)—Genesee MI-3
Vienna (Township)—
  Montmorency MI-3
Vienna (Township)—Rock MN-3
Vienna (City)—Maries MO-3
Vienna (Town)—Oneida NY-1
Vienna (Township)—Trumbull OH-3
Vienna (Town)—Clark SD-4
Vienna (Town)—Fairfax VA-2
Vienna (City)—Wood WV-1
Vienna (Town)—Dane WI-3
Vieregg (Township)—Merrick NE-4
View (Township)—Williams ND-4
View Park-Windsor Hills (CDP)—Los
  Angeles CA-4
Vigo (Township)—Knox IN-3
Vigo County IN-3
Viking (City)—Marshall MN-3
Viking (Township)—Marshall MN-3
Viking (Township)—Richland ND-4
Viking (Township)—Traill ND-4
Viking (Township)—Perkins SD-4
Vilas (Town)—Baca CO-4
Vilas (Town)—Miner SD-4
Vilas (Town)—Langlade WI-3
Vilas County WI-3
The Village (City)—Oklahoma OK-2
Village Green (CDP)—Onondaga .. NY-1
Village of Four Seasons (Town)—
  Camden MO-3
The Village of Indian Hill (City)—
  Hamilton OH-3

Village of The Branch (Village)—
  Suffolk NY-1
Village Park (CDP)—Honolulu HI-4
Villages of Oriole (CDP)—Palm
  Beach FL-2
Village St. George (CDP)—East Baton
  Rouge Parish LA-2
Villa Grove (Town)—Douglas IL-3
Villa Heights (CDP)—Henry VA-2
Villa Hills (City)—Kenton KY-2
Villano Beach (CDP)—St. Johns ... FL-2
Villa Park (City)—Orange CA-4
Villa Park (City)—DuPage IL-3
Villard (City)—Pope MN-3
Villard (Township)—Todd MN-3
Villard (Township)—McHenry ND-4
Villa Rica (City)—Carroll GA-2
Villa Rica (City)—Douglas GA-2
Villa Ridge (CDP)—Franklin MO-3
Villas (CDP)—Lee FL-2
Villas (CDP)—Cape May NJ-1
Villenova (Town)—Chautauqua NY-1
Ville Platte (Town)—Evangeline
  Parish LA-2
Villisca (City)—Montgomery IA-3
Vilonia (Town)—Faulkner AR-2
Vina (Town)—Franklin AL-2
Vinalhaven (Town)—Knox ME-1
Vincennes (City)—Knox IN-3
Vincennes (Township)—Knox IN-3
Vincent (Town)—Shelby AL-2
Vincent (Town)—St. Clair AL-2
Vincent (Town)—Talladega AL-2
Vincent (CDP)—Los Angeles CA-4
Vincent (City)—Webster IA-3
Vinegar Hill (Township)—Jo
  Daviess IL-3
Vine Grove (City)—Hardin KY-2
Vine Hill (CDP)—Contra Costa CA-4
Vineland (CDP)—Mille Lacs MN-3
Vineland (Township)—Polk MN-3
Vineland (City)—Cumberland NJ-1
Vineyard (Township)—Lawrence .. MO-3
Vineyard (Town)—Utah UT-4
Vineyard Haven (CDP)—Dukes ... MA-1
Vining (City)—Tama IA-3
Vining (City)—Clay KS-4
Vining (Township)—Washington ... KS-4
Vining (City)—Otter Tail MN-3
Vinings (CDP)—Cobb GA-2
Vinita (Township)—Kingman KS-4
Vinita (City)—Craig OK-2
Vinita Park (City)—St. Louis MO-3
Vinita Terrace (Village)—St.
  Louis MO-3
Vinland (Town)—Winnebago WI-3
Vint Hill Farms Station (Military
  Facility)—Fauquier VA-2
Vinton (City)—Benton IA-3
Vinton (Town)—Calcasieu Parish ... LA-2
Vinton (Township)—Valley NE-4
Vinton (Village)—Gallia OH-3
Vinton (Township)—Vinton OH-3
Vinton (Village)—El Paso TX-2
Vinton (Town)—Roanoke VA-2
Vinton County OH-3
Vintondale (Borough)—Cambria PA-1
Viola (Town)—Fulton AR-2
Viola (Town)—Kent DE-1
Viola (Township)—Lee IL-3
Viola (Town)—Mercer IL-3
Viola (City)—Sedgwick KS-4
Viola (Township)—Sedgwick KS-4
Viola (Township)—Olmsted MN-3
Viola (CDP)—Rockland NY-1

Viola (Township)—Jerauld SD-4
Viola (Town)—Warren TN-2
Viola (Village)—Richland WI-3
Viola (Village)—Vernon WI-3
Violet (CDP)—St. Bernard
  Parish LA-2
Violet (Township)—Fairfield OH-3
Virden (City)—Macoupin IL-3
Virden (Township)—Macoupin IL-3
Virden (City)—Sangamon IL-3
Virden (Village)—Hidalgo NM-4
Virgil (Township)—Kane IL-3
Virgil (City)—Greenwood KS-4
Virgil (Township)—Vernon MO-3
Virgil (Town)—Cortland NY-1
Virgil (Town)—Beadle SD-4
Virgil (Township)—Jones SD-4
Virgilina (Town)—Halifax VA-2
Virgin (Town)—Washington UT-4
Virginia (City)—Cass IL-3
Virginia (Township)—Cass IL-3
Virginia (City)—St. Louis MN-3
Virginia (Township)—Pemiscot ... MO-3
Virginia (Village)—Gage NE-4
Virginia (Township)—Towner ND-4
Virginia (Township)—Coshocton ... OH-3
Virginia (Township)—Union SD-4
Virginia Beach (Independent City) .. VA-2
Virginia City (Town)—Madison ... MT-4
Virginia Gardens (Village)—
  Dade FL-2
Viroqua (City)—Vernon WI-3
Viroqua (Town)—Vernon WI-3
Visalia (City)—Tulare CA-4
Visalia (Township)—Kenton KY-2
Vista (City)—San Diego CA-4
Vista (Village)—St. Clair MO-3
Vivian (Town)—Caddo Parish LA-2
Vivian (Township)—Waseca MN-3
Vivian (Township)—Sargent ND-4
Vivian (Township)—Lyman SD-4
Volant (Borough)—Lawrence PA-1
Volcano (CDP)—Hawaii HI-4
Volga (City)—Clayton IA-3
Volga (City)—Brookings SD-4
Volga (Township)—Brookings SD-4
Volin (Town)—Yankton SD-4
Volin (Township)—Yankton SD-4
Volinia (Township)—Cass MI-3
Volney (Town)—Oswego NY-1
Voltaire (Township)—Sherman ... KS-4
Voltaire (City)—McHenry ND-4
Voltaire (Township)—McHenry ... ND-4
Voluntown (Town)—New
  London CT-1
Volusia County FL-2
Vona (Town)—Kit Carson CO-4
Vonore (Town)—Monroe TN-2
Voorhees (Township)—Stevens ... KS-4
Voorhees (Township)—Camden ... NJ-1
Voorheesville (Village)—Albany ... NY-1
Vredenburgh (Town)—Monroe AL-2
Vrooman (Township)—Perkins ... SD-4
Waasa (Township)—St. Louis MN-3
Wabana (Township)—Itasca MN-3
Wabash (Township)—Clark IL-3
Wabash (Township)—Adams IN-3
Wabash (Township)—Fountain ... IN-3
Wabash (Township)—Gibson IN-3
Wabash (Township)—Jay IN-3
Wabash (Township)—Parke IN-3
Wabash (Township)—Tippecanoe ... IN-3
Wabash (City)—Wabash IN-3
Wabash (Township)—Darke OH-3
Wabasha (City)—Wabasha MN-3

General Index

Wabasha County MN-3
Wabash County IL-3
Wabash County IN-3
Wabash River (NY) Geog-4
Wabasso (CDP)—Indian River FL-2
Wabasso (City)—Redwood MN-3
Wabaunsee (Township)—
  Wabaunsee KS-4
Wabaunsee County KS-4
Wabbaseka (City)—Jefferson AR-2
Wabedo (Township)—Cass MN-3
Wabeno (Town)—Forest WI-3
Waccamaw Siouan TDSA
  (NC) IndRes-4
Wachapreague (Town)—
  Accomack VA-2
Wachter (Township)—McPherson . SD-4
Wacker (Township)—McPherson ... SD-4
Waco (City)—Haralson GA-2
Waco (Township)—Sedgwick KS-4
Waco (Town)—Jasper MO-3
Waco (Village)—York NE-4
Waco (Town)—Cleveland NC-2
Waco (City)—McLennan TX-2
Waconia (City)—Carver MN-3
Waconia (Township)—Carver MN-3
Wacouta (Township)—Goodhue ... MN-3
Waddams (Township)—
  Stephenson IL-3
Waddington (Town)—St.
  Lawrence NY-1
Waddington (Village)—St.
  Lawrence NY-1
Wade (Township)—Clinton IL-3
Wade (Township)—Jasper IL-3
Wade (Town)—Aroostook ME-1
Wade (Town)—Cumberland NC-2
Wade Hampton (CDP)—
  Greenville SC-2
Wade Hampton Census Area AK-4
Wadena (City)—Fayette IA-3
Wadena (City)—Otter Tail MN-3
Wadena (City)—Wadena MN-3
Wadena (Township)—Wadena MN-3
Wadena County MN-3
Wadesboro (Town)—Anson NC-2
Wading River (CDP)—Suffolk NY-1
Wadley (Town)—Randolph AL-2
Wadley (City)—Jefferson GA-2
Wadsworth (Town)—Lake IL-3
Wadsworth (CDP)—Washoe NV-4
Wadsworth (Township)—
  Stutsman ND-4
Wadsworth (City)—Medina OH-3
Wadsworth (Township)—Medina .. OH-3
Waelder (City)—Gonzales TX-2
Wagar (Township)—McHenry ND-4
Wagendorf (Township)—
  Hettinger ND-4
Wagener (Town)—Aiken SC-2
Waggaman (CDP)—Jefferson
  Parish LA-2
Waggoner (Village)—Montgomery .. IL-3
Wagner (Township)—Aitkin MN-3
Wagner (City)—Charles Mix SD-4
Wagner (Town)—Marinette WI-3
Wagoner (City)—Wagoner OK-2
Wagoner County OK-2
Wagon Mound (Village)—Mora NM-4
Wagram (Town)—Scotland NC-2
Wahehe (Township)—Charles
  Mix SD-4
Wahiawa (CDP)—Honolulu HI-4
Wahkiakum County WA-4
Wahkon (City)—Mille Lacs MN-3

Wahnena (Township)—Cass MN-3
Wahneta (CDP)—Polk FL-2
Wahoo (City)—Saunders NE-4
Wahoo (Township)—Saunders NE-4
Wahpeton (City)—Dickinson IA-3
Wahpeton (City)—Richland ND-4
Waialeale, Mt. (HI) Geog-4
Waialua (CDP)—Honolulu HI-4
Waianae (CDP)—Honolulu HI-4
Waihee-Waiehue (CDP)—Maui HI-4
Waikane (CDP)—Honolulu HI-4
Waikapu (CDP)—Maui HI-4
Waikiki Beach (HI) Geog-4
Waikoloa Village (CDP)—Hawaii .. HI-4
Wailea-Makena (CDP)—Maui HI-4
Wailua (CDP)—Kauai HI-4
Wailua Homesteads (CDP)—
  Kauai HI-4
Wailuku (CDP)—Maui HI-4
Waimalu (CDP)—Honolulu HI-4
Waimanalo (CDP)—Honolulu HI-4
Waimanalo Beach (CDP)—
  Honolulu HI-4
Waimea (CDP)—Hawaii HI-4
Waimea (CDP)—Kauai HI-4
Wainaku (CDP)—Hawaii HI-4
Wainwright (City)—North Slope
  Borough AK-4
Wainwright (Town)—Muskogee ... OK-2
Waipahu (CDP)—Honolulu HI-4
Waipio (CDP)—Honolulu HI-4
Waipio Acres (CDP)—Honolulu HI-4
Waite (Town)—Washington ME-1
Waite Hill (Village)—Lake OH-3
Waite Park (City)—Stearns MN-3
Waitsburg (City)—Walla Walla WA-4
Waitsfield (Town)—Washington ... VT-1
Wakarusa (Town)—Elkhart IN-3
Wakarusa (Township)—Douglas ... KS-4
Wake County NC-2
WaKeeney (City)—Trego KS-4
WaKeeney (Township)—Trego KS-4
Wakefield (City)—Clay KS-4
Wakefield (Town)—Middlesex MA-1
Wakefield (City)—Gogebic MI-3
Wakefield (Township)—Gogebic ... MI-3
Wakefield (Township)—Stearns ... MN-3
Wakefield (City)—Dixon NE-4
Wakefield (Township)—Dixon NE-4
Wakefield (City)—Wayne NE-4
Wakefield (Town)—Carroll NH-1
Wakefield (Town)—Sussex VA-2
Wakefield-Peacedale (CDP)—
  Washington RI-1
Wake Forest (Town)—Wake NC-2
Wakeman (Township)—Huron OH-3
Wakeman (Village)—Huron OH-3
Wakenda (Town)—Carroll MO-3
Wakenda (Township)—Carroll MO-3
Wakeshma (Township)—
  Kalamazoo MI-3
Wake Village (City)—Bowie TX-2
Wakita (Town)—Grant OK-2
Wakonda (Town)—Clay SD-4
Wakpala (Township)—Corson SD-4
Wakulla County FL-2
Walbridge (Village)—Wood OH-3
Walburg (Township)—Cass ND-4
Walcott (City)—Muscatine IA-3
Walcott (City)—Scott IA-3
Walcott (Township)—Rice MN-3
Walcott (City)—Richland ND-4
Walcott (Township)—Richland ND-4
Walden (Town)—Jackson CO-4
Walden (Township)—Cass MN-3

American Places Dictionary

Walden (Township)—Pope MN-3
Walden (Village)—Orange NY-1
Walden (Town)—Hamilton TN-2
Walden (Town)—Caledonia VT-1
Waldenburg (Town)—Poinsett AR-2
Walden Pond (MA) Geog-4
Waldo (Municipality)—Talladega .. AL-2
Waldo (City)—Columbia AR-2
Waldo (City)—Alachua FL-2
Waldo (Township)—Livingston IL-3
Waldo (City)—Russell KS-4
Waldo (Township)—Russell KS-4
Waldo (Town)—Waldo ME-1
Waldo (Township)—Richland ND-4
Waldo (Township)—Marion OH-3
Waldo (Village)—Marion OH-3
Waldo (Village)—Sheboygan WI-3
Waldoboro (Town)—Lincoln ME-1
Waldo County ME-1
Waldorf (CDP)—Charles MD-1
Waldorf (City)—Waseca MN-3
Waldport (City)—Lincoln OR-4
Waldro (Township)—Brule SD-4
Waldron (City)—Scott AR-2
Waldron (City)—Harper KS-4
Waldron (Village)—Hillsdale MI-3
Waldron (Township)—Platte MO-3
Waldwick (Borough)—Bergen NJ-1
Waldwick (Town)—Iowa WI-3
Wales (City)—Nome Census
  Area AK-4
Wales (Town)—Androscoggin ME-1
Wales (Town)—Hampden MA-1
Wales (Township)—St. Clair MI-3
Wales (Town)—Erie NY-1
Wales (City)—Cavalier ND-4
Wales (Town)—Sanpete UT-4
Wales (Village)—Waukesha WI-3
Waleska (City)—Cherokee GA-2
Walford (City)—Benton IA-3
Walford (City)—Linn IA-3
Walhalla (City)—Pembina ND-4
Walhalla (Township)—Pembina ... ND-4
Walhalla (Town)—Oconee SC-2
Walker (Township)—Hancock IL-3
Walker (Township)—Jasper IN-3
Walker (Township)—Rush IN-3
Walker (City)—Linn IA-3
Walker (Township)—Anderson KS-4
Walker (Town)—Livingston
  Parish LA-2
Walker (Township)—Cheboygan ... MI-3
Walker (City)—Kent MI-3
Walker (City)—Cass MN-3
Walker (Township)—Henry MO-3
Walker (Township)—Moniteau MO-3
Walker (Town)—Vernon MO-3
Walker (Township)—Vernon MO-3
Walker (Township)—Platte NE-4
Walker (Township)—Hettinger ND-4
Walker (Township)—Centre PA-1
Walker (Township)—Huntingdon .. PA-1
Walker (Township)—Juniata PA-1
Walker (Township)—Schuylkill PA-1
Walker (Township)—Corson SD-4
Walker County AL-2
Walker County GA-2
Walker County TX-2
Walker Mill (CDP)—Prince
  George's MD-1
Walker River Reservation
  (NV) IndRes-4
Walkersville (Town)—Frederick MD-1
Walkerton (Town)—St. Joseph IN-3
Walkertown (Town)—Forsyth NC-2

Walkerville (Township)—Greene *IL-3*
Walkerville (Village)—Oceana *MI-3*
Walkerville (City)—Silver Bow *MT-4*
Wall (Township)—Ford *IL-3*
Wall (Borough)—Monmouth *NJ-1*
Wall (Borough)—Allegheny *PA-1*
Wall (Township)—Jackson *SD-4*
Wall (Town)—Pennington *SD-4*
Wallace (City)—Shoshone *ID-4*
Wallace (Township)—La Salle *IL-3*
Wallace (Town)—Fountain *IN-3*
Wallace (City)—Wallace *KS-4*
Wallace (Township)—Wallace *KS-4*
Wallace (Village)—Lincoln *NE-4*
Wallace (Town)—Duplin *NC-2*
Wallace (Town)—Pender *NC-2*
Wallace (Township)—Kidder *ND-4*
Wallace (Township)—Chester *PA-1*
Wallace (Town)—Codington *SD-4*
Wallace County *KS-4*
Wallaceton (Borough)—Clearfield .. *PA-1*
Wallagrass (Town)—Aroostook *ME-1*
Walla Walla (City)—Walla Walla ... *WA-4*
Walla Walla County *WA-4*
Walla Walla East (CDP)—Walla
  Walla *WA-4*
Walle (Township)—Grand Forks ... *ND-4*
Walled Lake (City)—Oakland *MI-3*
Waller (City)—Harris *TX-2*
Waller (City)—Waller *TX-2*
Waller (CDP)—Pierce *WA-4*
Waller County *TX-2*
Wallingford (Town)—New Haven . *CT-1*
Wallingford (City)—Emmet *IA-3*
Wallingford (Town)—Rutland *VT-1*
Wallington (Borough)—Bergen *NJ-1*
Wallins Creek (City)—Harlan *KY-2*
Wallis (City)—Austin *TX-2*
Wallkill (Town)—Orange *NY-1*
Wallkill (CDP)—Ulster *NY-1*
Wall Lake (City)—Sac *IA-3*
Wall Lake (Township)—
  Minnehaha *SD-4*
Wallowa (City)—Wallowa *OR-4*
Wallowa County *OR-4*
Walls (Township)—Traverse *MN-3*
Walls (Township)—Douglas *MO-3*
Wallsburg (Town)—Wasatch *UT-4*
Walnut (City)—Los Angeles *CA-4*
Walnut (Township)—Bureau *IL-3*
Walnut (Village)—Bureau *IL-3*
Walnut (Township)—Marshall *IN-3*
Walnut (Township)—Montgomery.. *IN-3*
Walnut (City)—Pottawattamie *IA-3*
Walnut (Township)—Atchison *KS-4*
Walnut (Township)—Barton *KS-4*
Walnut (Township)—Bourbon *KS-4*
Walnut (Township)—Brown *KS-4*
Walnut (Township)—Butler *KS-4*
Walnut (Township)—Cowley *KS-4*
Walnut (City)—Crawford *KS-4*
Walnut (Township)—Crawford *KS-4*
Walnut (Township)—Jewell *KS-4*
Walnut (Township)—Marshall *KS-4*
Walnut (Township)—Pawnee *KS-4*
Walnut (Township)—Phillips *KS-4*
Walnut (Township)—Reno *KS-4*
Walnut (Township)—Saline *KS-4*
Walnut (Town)—Tippah *MS-2*
Walnut (Township)—Adair *MO-3*
Walnut (Township)—Bates *MO-3*
Walnut (Township)—Fairfield *OH-3*
Walnut (Township)—Gallia *OH-3*
Walnut (Township)—Pickaway *OH-3*
Walnut Cove (Town)—Stokes *NC-2*

Walnut Creek (City)—Contra
  Costa *CA-4*
Walnut Creek (Township)—
  Mitchell *KS-4*
Walnut Creek (Township)—
  Macon *MO-3*
Walnut Creek (Village)—Wayne *NC-2*
Walnut Creek (Township)—
  Holmes *OH-3*
Walnut Grove (Municipality)—
  Etowah *AL-2*
Walnut Grove (Town)—Walton *GA-2*
Walnut Grove (Township)—Knox .. *IL-3*
Walnut Grove (Township)—
  McDonough *IL-3*
Walnut Grove (Township)—
  Neosho *KS-4*
Walnut Grove (City)—Redwood... *MN-3*
Walnut Grove (Town)—Leake *MS-2*
Walnut Grove (City)—Greene *MO-3*
Walnut Grove (Township)—
  Greene *MO-3*
Walnut Grove (Township)—
  Knox *NE-4*
Walnut Grove (Township)—
  Douglas *SD-4*
Walnut Grove (CDP)—Clark *WA-4*
Walnut Hill (Village)—Marion *IL-3*
Walnut Hill (CDP)—Sullivan *TN-2*
Walnut Lake (Township)—
  Faribault *MN-3*
Walnut Park (CDP)—Los
  Angeles *CA-4*
Walnutport (Borough)—
  Northampton *PA-1*
Walnut Ridge (City)—Lawrence *AR-2*
Walnut Springs (City)—Bosque *TX-2*
Walpack (Township)—Sussex......... *NJ-1*
Walpole (Town)—Norfolk *MA-1*
Walpole (Town)—Cheshire............. *NH-1*
Walsenburg (City)—Huerfano........ *CO-4*
Walsh (Town)—Baca *CO-4*
Walsh Centre (Township)—
  Walsh *ND-4*
Walsh County *ND-4*
Walshtown (Township)—Yankton.. *SD-4*
Walshville (Township)—
  Montgomery................................. *IL-3*
Walshville (Village)—
  Montgomery................................. *IL-3*
Walshville (Township)—Walsh....... *ND-4*
Walstontown (Township)—Greene.. *NC-2*
Walt (Township)—Wabash *IN-3*
Walter (Township)—Lac qui
  Parle *MN-3*
Walterboro (City)—Colleton *SC-2*
Walterhill (CDP)—Rutherford....... *TN-2*
Walter Reed Army Medical Center
  (DC) *Mil-4*
Walters (City)—Faribault *MN-3*
Walters (Township)—Stutsman *ND-4*
Walters (City)—Cotton.................. *OK-2*
Walthall (Village)—Webster *MS-2*
Walthall County *MS-2*
Waltham (Township)—La Salle *IL-3*
Waltham (Town)—Hancock *ME-1*
Waltham (City)—Middlesex.......... *MA-1*
Waltham (City)—Mower *MN-3*
Waltham (Township)—Mower *MN-3*
Waltham (Town)—Addison *VT-1*
Walthill (Village)—Thurston *NE-4*
Walthourville (City)—Liberty *GA-2*
Walton (Town)—Cass *IN-3*
Walton (City)—Harvey................... *KS-4*
Walton (Township)—Harvey.......... *KS-4*

Walton (Township)—Labette *KS-4*
Walton (Township)—Sumner *KS-4*
Walton (City)—Boone *KY-2*
Walton (Township)—Eaton *MI-3*
Walton (Township)—
  Washington *MO-3*
Walton (Town)—Delaware *NY-1*
Walton (Village)—Delaware........... *NY-1*
Walton County *FL-2*
Walton County *GA-2*
Walton Hills (Village)—
  Cuyahoga *OH-3*
Waltonville (Village)—Jefferson..... *IL-3*
Walworth (Township)—Becker *MN-3*
Walworth (Town)—Wayne *NY-1*
Walworth (Town)—Walworth......... *WI-3*
Walworth (Village)—Walworth *WI-3*
Walworth County *SD-4*
Walworth County *WI-3*
Wamac (Town)—Clinton *IL-3*
Wamac (Town)—Marion *IL-3*
Wamac (Town)—Washington *IL-3*
Wamduska (Township)—Nelson.... *ND-4*
Wamego (City)—Pottawatomie.......*KS-4*
Wamego (Township)—
  Pottawatomie *KS-4*
Wampanoag-Gay Head TDSA
  (MA)...................................... *IndRes-4*
Wampsville (Village)—Madison..... *NY-1*
Wampum (Borough)—Lawrence ... *PA-1*
Wamsutter (Town)—Sweetwater... *WY-4*
Wanamassa (CDP)—Monmouth....*NJ-1*
Wanamingo (City)—Goodhue *MN-3*
Wanamingo (Township)—
  Goodhue *MN-3*
Wanaque (Borough)—Passaic *NJ-1*
Wanatah (Town)—La Porte *IN-3*
Wanblee (CDP)—Jackson *SD-4*
Wanchese (CDP)—Dare *NC-2*
Wanda (City)—Redwood *MN-3*
Wanda (Township)—Adams........... *NE-4*
Wanette (Town)—Pottawatomie *OK-2*
Wang (Township)—Renville........... *MN-3*
Wanger (Township)—Marshall...... *MN-3*
Wann (Town)—Nowata *OK-2*
Wano (Township)—Cheyenne........*KS-4*
Wano (Township)—LaMoure *ND-4*
Wantage (Township)—Sussex.........*NJ-1*
Wantagh (CDP)—Nassau *NY-1*
Wapakoneta (City)—Auglaize *OH-3*
Wapanucka (Town)—Johnston *OK-2*
Wapato (City)—Yakima *WA-4*
Wapella (Township)—De Witt *IL-3*
Wapella (Village)—De Witt *IL-3*
Wapello (City)—Louisa *IA-3*
Wapello County *IA-3*
Wappinger (Town)—Dutchess........ *NY-1*
Wappingers Falls (Village)—
  Dutchess..*NY-1*
War (City)—McDowell................... *WV-2*
Warba (City)—Itasca *MN-3*
Ward (City)—Lonoke *AR-2*
Ward (Town)—Boulder *CO-4*
Ward (Township)—Randolph *IN-3*
Ward (Township)—Todd *MN-3*
Ward (Town)—Allegany *NY-1*
Ward (Township)—Burke.............. *ND-4*
Ward (Township)—Hocking..........*OH-3*
Ward (Township)—Tioga *PA-1*
Ward (Town)—Saluda *SC-2*
Ward (Town)—Moody *SD-4*
Ward (Township)—Moody *SD-4*
Ward County *ND-4*
Ward County *TX-2*
Wardell (Town)—Pemiscot............ *MO-3*

General Index

American Places Dictionary

Warden (Town)—Grant WA-4
Wardensville (Town)—Hardy WV-2
Wardner (City)—Shoshone ID-4
Wardsboro (Town)—Windham VT-1
Wards Grove (Township)—Jo
  Daviess IL-3
Wardsville (Town)—Cole MO-3
Wardville (Town)—Atoka OK-2
Ware (Town)—Hampshire MA-1
Ware County GA-2
Wareham (Town)—Plymouth MA-1
Ware Shoals (Town)—Abbeville ... SC-2
Ware Shoals (Town)—
  Greenwood SC-2
Ware Shoals (Town)—Laurens SC-2
Waretown (CDP)—Ocean NJ-1
Warfield (City)—Martin KY-2
Waring (Township)—Ness KS-4
Warminster (Village)—Bucks PA-1
Warm Mineral Springs (CDP)—
  Sarasota FL-2
Warm River (City)—Fremont ID-4
Warm Springs (City)—
  Meriwether GA-2
Warm Springs (CDP)—Jefferson ... OR-4
Warm Springs Reservation & Trust
  Lands (OR) IndRes-4
Warner (Township)—Antrim MI-3
Warner (Town)—Merrimack NH-1
Warner (Town)—Muskogee OK-2
Warner (Town)—Brown SD-4
Warner (Township)—Brown SD-4
Warner (Town)—Clark WI-3
Warner Robins (City)—Houston ... GA-2
Warr Acres (City)—Oklahoma OK-2
Warren (City)—Bradley AR-2
Warren (Town)—Litchfield CT-1
Warren (Town)—Jo Daviess IL-3
Warren (Township)—Jo Daviess IL-3
Warren (Township)—Lake IL-3
Warren (Township)—Clinton IN-3
Warren (Town)—Huntington IN-3
Warren (Township)—Huntington ... IN-3
Warren (Township)—Marion IN-3
Warren (Township)—Putnam IN-3
Warren (Township)—St. Joseph IN-3
Warren (Township)—Warren IN-3
Warren (Town)—Knox ME-1
Warren (Town)—Worcester MA-1
Warren (City)—Macomb MI-3
Warren (Township)—Midland MI-3
Warren (City)—Marshall MN-3
Warren (Township)—Winona MN-3
Warren (Township)—Camden MO-3
Warren (Township)—Marion MO-3
Warren (Town)—Grafton NH-1
Warren (Township)—Somerset NJ-1
Warren (Town)—Herkimer NY-1
Warren (Township)—Cass ND-4
Warren (Township)—Belmont OH-3
Warren (Township)—Jefferson OH-3
Warren (City)—Trumbull OH-3
Warren (Township)—Trumbull OH-3
Warren (Township)—Tuscarawas .. OH-3
Warren (Township)—Washington .. OH-3
Warren (Township)—Bradford PA-1
Warren (Township)—Franklin PA-1
Warren (Borough)—Warren PA-1
Warren (Town)—Bristol RI-1
Warren (Township)—Clark SD-4
Warren (Township)—Sanborn SD-4
Warren (Town)—Washington VT-1
Warren (Town)—St. Croix WI-3
Warren (Town)—Waushara WI-3

Warren Air Force Base (Military
  Facility)—Laramie WY-4
Warren City (City)—Gregg TX-2
Warren City (City)—Upshur TX-2
Warren County GA-2
Warren County IL-3
Warren County IN-3
Warren County IA-3
Warren County KY-2
Warren County MS-2
Warren County MO-3
Warren County NJ-1
Warren County NY-1
Warren County NC-2
Warren County OH-3
Warren County PA-1
Warren County TN-2
Warren County VA-2
Warren Park (Town)—Marion IN-3
Warrens (Village)—Monroe WI-3
Warrensburg (Town)—Macon IL-3
Warrensburg (City)—Johnson MO-3
Warrensburg (Township)—
  Johnson MO-3
Warrensburg (Town)—Warren NY-1
Warren's Gore (Pop. Place)—
  Essex VT-1
Warrensville (Township)—
  Cuyahoga OH-3
Warrensville Heights (City)—
  Cuyahoga OH-3
Warrenton (City)—Warren GA-2
Warrenton (Township)—
  Marshall MN-3
Warrenton (City)—Warren MO-3
Warrenton (Town)—Warren NC-2
Warrenton (City)—Clatsop OR-4
Warrenton (Town)—Fauquier VA-2
Warrenville (Town)—DuPage IL-3
Warrick County IN-3
Warrington (CDP)—Escambia FL-2
Warrington (Township)—Bucks ... PA-1
Warrington (Township)—York PA-1
Warrior (Municipality)—
  Jefferson AL-2
Warrior Run (Borough)—Luzerne . PA-1
Warriors Mark (Township)—
  Huntingdon PA-1
Warroad (City)—Roseau MN-3
Warsaw (Town)—Hancock IL-3
Warsaw (Township)—Hancock IL-3
Warsaw (City)—Kosciusko IN-3
Warsaw (City)—Gallatin KY-2
Warsaw (Township)—Goodhue MN-3
Warsaw (Township)—Rice MN-3
Warsaw (City)—Benton MO-3
Warsaw (Town)—Wyoming NY-1
Warsaw (Village)—Wyoming NY-1
Warsaw (Town)—Duplin NC-2
Warsaw (Village)—Coshocton OH-3
Warsaw (Township)—Jefferson PA-1
Warsaw (Town)—Richmond VA-2
Warson Woods (City)—St. Louis .. MO-3
Wartburg (City)—Morgan TN-2
Wartrace (Town)—Bedford TN-2
Warwick (City)—Worth GA-2
Warwick (Town)—Franklin MA-1
Warwick (Town)—Orange NY-1
Warwick (Village)—Orange NY-1
Warwick (City)—Benson ND-4
Warwick (Township)—Benson ND-4
Warwick (Township)—
  Tuscarawas OH-3
Warwick (Town)—Lincoln OK-2
Warwick (Township)—Bucks PA-1

Warwick (Township)—Chester PA-1
Warwick (Township)—Lancaster PA-1
Warwick (City)—Kent RI-1
Wasatch County UT-4
Wasatch Range (MA) Geog-4
Wasco (City)—Kern CA-4
Wasco (City)—Sherman OR-4
Wasco County OR-4
Wascott (Town)—Douglas WI-3
Waseca (City)—Waseca MN-3
Waseca County MN-3
Washakie County WY-4
Washburn (Village)—Marshall IL-3
Washburn (Village)—Woodford IL-3
Washburn (Town)—Aroostook ME-1
Washburn (City)—Barry MO-3
Washburn (Township)—Barry MO-3
Washburn (Township)—Griggs ND-4
Washburn (City)—McLean ND-4
Washburn (City)—Bayfield WI-3
Washburn (Town)—Bayfield WI-3
Washburn (Town)—Clark WI-3
Washburn County WI-3
Washington (City)—Hempstead .. AR-2
Washington (Town)—Litchfield CT-1
Washington (City)—Wilkes GA-2
Washington (Township)—Carroll .. IL-3
Washington (City)—Tazewell IL-3
Washington (Township)—
  Tazewell IL-3
Washington (Township)—Will IL-3
Washington (Township)—Adams .. IN-3
Washington (Township)—Allen IN-3
Washington (Township)—
  Blackford IN-3
Washington (Township)—Boone .. IN-3
Washington (Township)—Brown .. IN-3
Washington (Township)—Carroll .. IN-3
Washington (Township)—Cass IN-3
Washington (Township)—Clark ... IN-3
Washington (Township)—Clay IN-3
Washington (Township)—Clinton . IN-3
Washington (City)—Daviess IN-3
Washington (Township)—Daviess . IN-3
Washington (Township)—
  Dearborn IN-3
Washington (Township)—Decatur .. IN-3
Washington (Township)—
  Delaware IN-3
Washington (Township)—Elkhart . IN-3
Washington (Township)—Gibson .. IN-3
Washington (Township)—Grant ... IN-3
Washington (Township)—Greene .. IN-3
Washington (Township)—
  Hamilton IN-3
Washington (Township)—
  Harrison IN-3
Washington (Township)—
  Hendricks IN-3
Washington (Township)—Jackson . IN-3
Washington (Township)—Knox ... IN-3
Washington (Township)—
  Kosciusko IN-3
Washington (Township)—La
  Porte IN-3
Washington (Township)—Marion . IN-3
Washington (Township)—Miami .. IN-3
Washington (Township)—Monroe . IN-3
Washington (Township)—Morgan . IN-3
Washington (Township)—Newton . IN-3
Washington (Township)—Noble ... IN-3
Washington (Township)—Owen ... IN-3
Washington (Township)—Parke ... IN-3
Washington (Township)—Pike IN-3
Washington (Township)—Porter .. IN-3

Washington (Township)—Putnam .. *IN-3*
Washington (Township)—Randolph *IN-3*
Washington (Township)—Ripley *IN-3*
Washington (Township)—Rush *IN-3*
Washington (Township)—Shelby ... *IN-3*
Washington (Township)—Starke *IN-3*
Washington (Township)—Tippecanoe *IN-3*
Washington (Township)—Warren ... *IN-3*
Washington (Township)—Washington *IN-3*
Washington (Township)—Wayne *IN-3*
Washington (Township)—Whitley .. *IN-3*
Washington (City)—Washington *IA-3*
Washington (Township)—Anderson *KS-4*
Washington (Township)—Brown .. *KS-4*
Washington (Township)—Chautauqua *KS-4*
Washington (Township)—Crawford *KS-4*
Washington (Township)—Doniphan *KS-4*
Washington (Township)—Jackson .. *KS-4*
Washington (Township)—Jewell *KS-4*
Washington (Township)—Nemaha *KS-4*
Washington (Township)—Republic *KS-4*
Washington (Township)—Saline *KS-4*
Washington (Township)—Sherman *KS-4*
Washington (Township)—Smith *KS-4*
Washington (Township)—Wabaunsee *KS-4*
Washington (City)—Washington *KS-4*
Washington (Township)—Washington *KS-4*
Washington (City)—Mason *KY-2*
Washington (Town)—St. Landry Parish *LA-2*
Washington (Town)—Knox *ME-1*
Washington (Town)—Berkshire *MA-1*
Washington (Township)—Gratiot .. *MI-3*
Washington (Township)—Macomb *MI-3*
Washington (Township)—Sanilac .. *MI-3*
Washington (Township)—Le Sueur *MN-3*
Washington (Township)—Buchanan *MO-3*
Washington (Township)—Carroll .. *MO-3*
Washington (Township)—Cedar ... *MO-3*
Washington (Township)—Clark *MO-3*
Washington (Township)—Clay *MO-3*
Washington (Township)—Dade *MO-3*
Washington (Township)—Dallas ... *MO-3*
Washington (Township)—Daviess *MO-3*
Washington (Township)—DeKalb *MO-3*
Washington (Township)—Douglas *MO-3*
Washington (City)—Franklin *MO-3*
Washington (Township)—Franklin *MO-3*
Washington (Township)—Greene *MO-3*
Washington (Township)—Grundy *MO-3*
Washington (Township)—Harrison *MO-3*
Washington (Township)—Jackson *MO-3*

Washington (Township)—Johnson *MO-3*
Washington (Township)—Laclede *MO-3*
Washington (Township)—Lafayette *MO-3*
Washington (Township)—Mercer *MO-3*
Washington (Township)—Monroe *MO-3*
Washington (Township)—Nodaway *MO-3*
Washington (Township)—Osage ... *MO-3*
Washington (Township)—Pettis ... *MO-3*
Washington (Township)—Ripley .. *MO-3*
Washington (Township)—St. Clair *MO-3*
Washington (Township)—Stone *MO-3*
Washington (Township)—Vernon *MO-3*
Washington (Township)—Webster *MO-3*
Washington (Township)—Franklin *NE-4*
Washington (Township)—Hall *NE-4*
Washington (Township)—Harlan ... *NE-4*
Washington (Township)—Knox *NE-4*
Washington (Village)—Washington *NE-4*
Washington (Town)—Sullivan *NH-1*
Washington (Township)—Bergen *NJ-1*
Washington (Township)—Burlington *NJ-1*
Washington (Township)—Gloucester *NJ-1*
Washington (Township)—Mercer .. *NJ-1*
Washington (Township)—Morris ... *NJ-1*
Washington (Borough)—Warren *NJ-1*
Washington (Township)—Warren ... *NJ-1*
Washington (Town)—Dutchess *NY-1*
Washington (City)—Beaufort *NC-2*
Washington (Township)—Grand Forks *ND-4*
Washington (Township)—Auglaize *OH-3*
Washington (Township)—Belmont *OH-3*
Washington (Township)—Brown ... *OH-3*
Washington (Township)—Carroll ... *OH-3*
Washington (Township)—Clermont *OH-3*
Washington (Township)—Clinton *OH-3*
Washington (Township)—Columbiana *OH-3*
Washington (Township)—Coshocton *OH-3*
Washington (Township)—Darke *OH-3*
Washington (Township)—Defiance *OH-3*
Washington (Township)—Franklin *OH-3*
Washington (Township)—Guernsey *OH-3*
Washington (Township)—Hancock *OH-3*
Washington (Township)—Hardin .. *OH-3*
Washington (Township)—Harrison *OH-3*
Washington (Township)—Henry *OH-3*
Washington (Township)—Highland *OH-3*
Washington (Township)—Hocking *OH-3*

Washington (Township)—Holmes *OH-3*
Washington (Township)—Jackson *OH-3*
Washington (Township)—Lawrence *OH-3*
Washington (Township)—Licking *OH-3*
Washington (Township)—Logan *OH-3*
Washington (Township)—Lucas *OH-3*
Washington (Township)—Mercer ... *OH-3*
Washington (Township)—Miami ... *OH-3*
Washington (Township)—Monroe *OH-3*
Washington (Township)—Montgomery *OH-3*
Washington (Township)—Morrow *OH-3*
Washington (Township)—Muskingum *OH-3*
Washington (Township)—Paulding *OH-3*
Washington (Township)—Pickaway *OH-3*
Washington (Township)—Preble *OH-3*
Washington (Township)—Richland *OH-3*
Washington (Township)—Sandusky *OH-3*
Washington (Township)—Scioto *OH-3*
Washington (Township)—Shelby .. *OH-3*
Washington (Township)—Stark *OH-3*
Washington (Township)—Tuscarawas *OH-3*
Washington (Township)—Union *OH-3*
Washington (Township)—Van Wert *OH-3*
Washington (Township)—Warren .. *OH-3*
Washington (Township)—Wood *OH-3*
Washington (Town)—McClain *OK-2*
Washington (Township)—Armstrong *PA-1*
Washington (Township)—Berks *PA-1*
Washington (Township)—Butler *PA-1*
Washington (Township)—Cambria *PA-1*
Washington (Township)—Clarion ... *PA-1*
Washington (Township)—Dauphin *PA-1*
Washington (Township)—Erie *PA-1*
Washington (Township)—Fayette ... *PA-1*
Washington (Township)—Franklin *PA-1*
Washington (Township)—Greene ... *PA-1*
Washington (Township)—Indiana ... *PA-1*
Washington (Township)—Jefferson *PA-1*
Washington (Township)—Lawrence *PA-1*
Washington (Township)—Lehigh *PA-1*
Washington (Township)—Lycoming *PA-1*
Washington (Township)—Northampton *PA-1*
Washington (Township)—Northumberland *PA-1*
Washington (Township)—Schuylkill *PA-1*
Washington (Township)—Snyder *PA-1*
Washington (City)—Washington *PA-1*
Washington (Township)—Westmoreland *PA-1*
Washington (Township)—Wyoming *PA-1*
Washington (Township)—York *PA-1*

Washington (Township)—Aurora... *SD-4*
Washington (Township)—Clark *SD-4*
Washington (Township)—Douglas *SD-4*
Washington (City)—Washington *UT-4*
Washington (Town)—Orange *VT-1*
Washington (Town)—Rappahannock *VA-2*
Washington (CDP)—Wood *WV-2*
Washington (Town)—Door *WI-3*
Washington (Town)—Eau Claire.... *WI-3*
Washington (Town)—Green *WI-3*
Washington (Town)—La Crosse..... *WI-3*
Washington (Town)—Rusk *WI-3*
Washington (Town)—Sauk *WI-3*
Washington (Town)—Shawano *WI-3*
Washington (Town)—Vilas............. *WI-3*
Washington, Mt. (NH)................. *Geog-4*
Washington County *AL-2*
Washington County *AR-2*
Washington County *CO-4*
Washington County *FL-2*
Washington County *GA-2*
Washington County *ID-4*
Washington County *IL-3*
Washington County *IN-3*
Washington County *IA-3*
Washington County *KS-4*
Washington County *KY-2*
Washington County *ME-1*
Washington County *MD-1*
Washington County *MN-3*
Washington County *MS-2*
Washington County *MO-3*
Washington County *NE-4*
Washington County *NY-1*
Washington County *NC-2*
Washington County *OH-3*
Washington County *OK-2*
Washington County *OR-4*
Washington County *PA-1*
Washington County *RI-1*
Washington County *TN-2*
Washington County *TX-2*
Washington County *UT-4*
Washington County *VT-1*
Washington County *VA-2*
Washington County *WI-3*
Washington Court House (City)—Fayette... *OH-3*
Washington Grove (Town)—Montgomery...*MD-1*
Washington Heights (CDP)—Orange..*NY-1*
Washington Lake (Township)—Sibley..*MN-3*
Washington Parish.........................*LA-2*
Washington Park (CDP)—Broward... *FL-2*
Washington Park (Village)—St. Clair *IL-3*
Washington Park (Town)—Beaufort..*NC-2*
Washington Terrace (City)—Weber *UT-4*
Washingtonville (Village)—Orange..*NY-1*
Washingtonville (Village)—Columbiana... *OH-3*
Washingtonville (Village)—Mahoning... *OH-3*
Washingtonville (Borough)—Montour...*PA-1*
Washita County............................... *OK-2*
Washoe County *NV-4*

Washoe Reservation (NV)......... *IndRes-4*
Washougal (City)—Clark................ *WA-4*
Washta (City)—Cherokee................. *IA-3*
Washtenaw County........................ *MI-3*
Washtucna (Town)—Adams........... *WA-4*
Wasilla (City)—Matanuska-Susitna Borough..*AK-4*
Wasioja (Township)—Dodge.......... *MN-3*
Waskish (Township)—Beltrami..... *MN-3*
Waskom (City)—Harrison............... *TX-2*
Wasta (Town)—Pennington............ *SD-4*
Wasta No. 2 (Township)—Pennington *SD-4*
Watab (Township)—Benton *MN-3*
Wataga (Town)—Knox *IL-3*
Watauga (Township)—Corson........ *SD-4*
Watauga (City)—Carter.................. *TN-2*
Watauga (City)—Tarrant *TX-2*
Watauga County *NC-2*
Watchung (Borough)—Somerset... *NJ-1*
Waterboro (Town)—York *ME-1*
Waterbury (City)—New Haven....... *CT-1*
Waterbury (Township)—Redwood *MN-3*
Waterbury (Village)—Dixon........... *NE-4*
Waterbury (Town)—Washington.... *VT-1*
Waterbury (Village)—Washington.. *VT-1*
Waterford (City)—Stanislaus *CA-4*
Waterford (Town)—New London .. *CT-1*
Waterford (Township)—Fulton *IL-3*
Waterford (Town)—Oxford *ME-1*
Waterford (Township)—Oakland ... *MI-3*
Waterford (Township)—Dakota.... *MN-3*
Waterford (Township)—Camden ... *NJ-1*
Waterford (Town)—Saratoga.......... *NY-1*
Waterford (Village)—Saratoga *NY-1*
Waterford (Township)—Ward *ND-4*
Waterford (Township)—Washington *OH-3*
Waterford (Borough)—Erie *PA-1*
Waterford (Township)—Erie *PA-1*
Waterford (Town)—Caledonia *VT-1*
Waterford (Town)—Racine *WI-3*
Waterford (Village)—Racine *WI-3*
Waterford North (CDP)—Racine .. *WI-3*
Waterloo (Town)—Lauderdale *AL-2*
Waterloo (City)—Monroe................. *IL-3*
Waterloo (Town)—Dekalb *IN-3*
Waterloo (Township)—Fayette........ *IN-3*
Waterloe (City)—Black Hawk.........*IA-3*
Waterloo (Township)—Lyon *KS-4*
Waterloo (Township)—Jackson *MI-3*
Waterloo (Village)—Douglas........... *NE-4*
Waterloo (Town)—Seneca *NY-1*
Waterloo (Village)—Seneca *NY-1*
Waterloo (Township)—Cavalier......*ND-4*
Waterloo (Township)—Athens.......*OH-3*
Waterloo (Town)—Linn *OR-4*
Waterloo (Town)—Laurens *SC-2*
Waterloo (Town)—Grant *WI-3*
Waterloo (City)—Jefferson *WI-3*
Waterloo (Town)—Jefferson........... *WI-3*
Waterman (Village)—DeKalb *IL-3*
Watermill (CDP)—Suffolk *NY-1*
Waterproof (Town)—Tensas Parish *LA-2*
Watersmeet (Township)—Gogebic *MI-3*
Watertown (Town)—Litchfield *CT-1*
Watertown (CDP)—Columbia *FL-2*
Watertown (Town)—Middlesex *MA-1*
Watertown (Township)—Clinton ... *MI-3*
Watertown (Township)—Sanilac..... *MI-3*
Watertown (Township)—Tuscola ... *MI-3*
Watertown (City)—Carver *MN-3*

Watertown (Township)—Carver ... *MN-3*
Watertown (City)—Jefferson.......... *NY-1*
Watertown (Town)—Jefferson........ *NY-1*
Watertown (Township)—Washington *OH-3*
Watertown (City)—Codington *SD-4*
Watertown (Town)—Wilson *TN-2*
Watertown (City)—Dodge............... *WI-3*
Watertown (City)—Jefferson........... *WI-3*
Watertown (Town)—Jefferson *WI-3*
Water Valley (City)—Graves........... *KY-2*
Water Valley (City)—Yalobusha *MS-2*
Waterville (City)—Allamakee *IA-3*
Waterville (City)—Marshall............*KS-4*
Waterville (Township)—Marshall ... *KS-4*
Waterville (City)—Kennebec *ME-1*
Waterville (City)—Le Sueur........... *MN-3*
Waterville (Township)—Le Sueur.. *MN-3*
Waterville (Village)—Oneida *NY-1*
Waterville (Township)—Lucas *OH-3*
Waterville (Village)—Lucas............*OH-3*
Waterville (Town)—Lamoille *VT-1*
Waterville (Town)—Douglas *WA-4*
Waterville (Town)—Pepin *WI-3*
Waterville Valley (Town)—Grafton..*NH-1*
Watervliet (City)—Berrien *MI-3*
Watervliet (Township)—Berrien *MI-3*
Watervliet (City)—Albany.............. *NY-1*
Watford City (City)—McKenzie *ND-4*
Watha (Town)—Pender *NC-2*
Wathena (City)—Doniphan *KS-4*
Watkins (City)—Meeker................. *MN-3*
Watkins (Township)—Dent *MO-3*
Watkins Glen (Village)—Schuyler...*NY-1*
Watkinsville (Town)—Oconee........ *GA-2*
Watonga (City)—Blaine.................. *OK-2*
Watonwan County *MN-3*
Watopa (Township)—Wabasha *MN-3*
Watseka (City)—Iroquois *IL-3*
Watson (City)—Desha *AR-2*
Watson (Township)—Effingham *IL-3*
Watson (Village)—Effingham........... *IL-3*
Watson (Township)—Allegan *MI-3*
Watson (City)—Chippewa............... *MN-3*
Watson (Village)—Atchison *MO-3*
Watson (Town)—Lewis *NY-1*
Watson (Township)—Cass *ND-4*
Watson (Township)—Lycoming *PA-1*
Watson (Township)—Warren *PA-1*
Watsontown (Borough)—Northumberland...............................*PA-1*
Watsonville (City)—Santa Cruz..... *CA-4*
Watterson Park (City)—Jefferson .. *KY-2*
Watterstown (Town)—Grant *WI-3*
Watts (Town)—Adair....................... *OK-2*
Watts (Township)—Perry *PA-1*
Wattsburg (Borough)—Erie *PA-1*
Watts *See* **Los Angeles**—Los Angeles *CA-4*
Watts Mills (CDP)—Laurens *SC-2*
Waubay (City)—Day *SD-4*
Waubay (Township)—Day *SD-4*
Waubeek (Town)—Pepin................. *WI-3*
Waubun (City)—Mahnomen *MN-3*
Waucedah (Township)—Dickinson... *MI-3*
Wauchula (City)—Hardee *FL-2*
Waucoma (City)—Fayette *IA-3*
Wauconda (City)—Lake *IL-3*
Wauconda (Township)—Lake *IL-3*
Waukechon (Town)—Shawano....... *WI-3*
Waukee (City)—Dallas *IA-3*

Waukegan (City)—Lake	*IL-3*	
Waukegan (Township)—Lake	*IL-3*	
Waukenabo (Township)—Aitkin	*MN-3*	
Waukesha (City)—Waukesha	*WI-3*	
Waukesha (Town)—Waukesha	*WI-3*	
Waukesha County	*WI-3*	
Waukomis (Town)—Garfield	*OK-2*	
Waukon (City)—Allamakee	*IA-3*	
Waukon (Township)—Norman	*MN-3*	
Waumandee (Town)—Buffalo	*WI-3*	
Waunakee (Village)—Dane	*WI-3*	
Wauneta (Village)—Chase	*NE-4*	
Waupaca (City)—Waupaca	*WI-3*	
Waupaca (Town)—Waupaca	*WI-3*	
Waupaca County	*WI-3*	
Wauponsee (Township)—Grundy	*IL-3*	
Waupun (City)—Dodge	*WI-3*	
Waupun (City)—Fond du Lac	*WI-3*	
Waupun (Town)—Fond du Lac	*WI-3*	
Wauregan (CDP)—Windham	*CT-1*	
Waurika (City)—Jefferson	*OK-2*	
Wausa (Village)—Knox	*NE-4*	
Wausau (Town)—Washington	*FL-2*	
Wausau (City)—Marathon	*WI-3*	
Wausau (Town)—Marathon	*WI-3*	
Wausaukee (Town)—Marinette	*WI-3*	
Wausaukee (Village)—Marinette	*WI-3*	
Wauseon (Village)—Fulton	*OH-3*	
Waushara County	*WI-3*	
Wautoma (City)—Waushara	*WI-3*	
Wautoma (Town)—Waushara	*WI-3*	
Wauwatosa (City)—Milwaukee	*WI-3*	
Wauzeka (Town)—Crawford	*WI-3*	
Wauzeka (Village)—Crawford	*WI-3*	
Waveland (Town)—Montgomery	*IN-3*	
Waveland (City)—Hancock	*MS-2*	
Waverly (Town)—Chambers	*AL-2*	
Waverly (Town)—Lee	*AL-2*	
Waverly (CDP)—Polk	*FL-2*	
Waverly (Town)—Morgan	*IL-3*	
Waverly (City)—Bremer	*IA-3*	
Waverly (City)—Coffey	*KS-4*	
Waverly (City)—Union	*KY-2*	
Waverly (Township)—Cheboygan	*MI-3*	
Waverly (CDP)—Eaton	*MI-3*	
Waverly (Township)—Van Buren	*MI-3*	
Waverly (Township)—Martin	*MN-3*	
Waverly (City)—Wright	*MN-3*	
Waverly (Town)—Lafayette	*MO-3*	
Waverly (Township)—Lincoln	*MO-3*	
Waverly (City)—Lancaster	*NE-4*	
Waverly (Town)—Franklin	*NY-1*	
Waverly (Village)—Tioga	*NY-1*	
Waverly (Township)—Codington	*SD-4*	
Waverly (Township)—Marshall	*SD-4*	
Waverly (City)—Humphreys	*TN-2*	
Waverly (Town)—Sussex	*VA-2*	
Waverly (Town)—Spokane	*WA-4*	
Waverly City (City)—Pike	*OH-3*	
Waverly Hall (Town)—Harris	*GA-2*	
Wawarsing (Town)—Ulster	*NY-1*	
Wawatam (Township)—Emmet	*MI-3*	
Wawayanda (Town)—Orange	*NY-1*	
Wawina (Township)—Itasca	*MN-3*	
Waxahachie (City)—Ellis	*TX-2*	
Waxhaw (Town)—Union	*NC-2*	
Waycross (City)—Pierce	*GA-2*	
Waycross (City)—Ware	*GA-2*	
Wayland (City)—Henry	*IA-3*	
Wayland (City)—Floyd	*KY-2*	
Wayland (Town)—Middlesex	*MA-1*	
Wayland (City)—Allegan	*MI-3*	
Wayland (Township)—Chariton	*MO-3*	
Wayland (City)—Clark	*MO-3*	
Wayland (Town)—Steuben	*NY-1*	
Wayland (Village)—Steuben	*NY-1*	
Waymart (Borough)—Wayne	*PA-1*	
Wayne (Town)—DuPage	*IL-3*	
Wayne (Township)—DuPage	*IL-3*	
Wayne (Town)—Kane	*IL-3*	
Wayne (Township)—Allen	*IN-3*	
Wayne (Township)—Bartholomew	*IN-3*	
Wayne (Township)—Fulton	*IN-3*	
Wayne (Township)—Hamilton	*IN-3*	
Wayne (Township)—Henry	*IN-3*	
Wayne (Township)—Huntington	*IN-3*	
Wayne (Township)—Jay	*IN-3*	
Wayne (Township)—Kosciusko	*IN-3*	
Wayne (Township)—Marion	*IN-3*	
Wayne (Township)—Montgomery	*IN-3*	
Wayne (Township)—Noble	*IN-3*	
Wayne (Township)—Owen	*IN-3*	
Wayne (Township)—Randolph	*IN-3*	
Wayne (Township)—Starke	*IN-3*	
Wayne (Township)—Tippecanoe	*IN-3*	
Wayne (Township)—Wayne	*IN-3*	
Wayne (Township)—Doniphan	*KS-4*	
Wayne (Township)—Edwards	*KS-4*	
Wayne (Town)—Kennebec	*ME-1*	
Wayne (Township)—Cass	*MI-3*	
Wayne (City)—Wayne	*MI-3*	
Wayne (Township)—Bollinger	*MO-3*	
Wayne (Township)—Buchanan	*MO-3*	
Wayne (Township)—Custer	*NE-4*	
Wayne (City)—Wayne	*NE-4*	
Wayne (Township)—Passaic	*NJ-1*	
Wayne (Town)—Steuben	*NY-1*	
Wayne (Township)—Bottineau	*ND-4*	
Wayne (Township)—Adams	*OH-3*	
Wayne (Township)—Ashtabula	*OH-3*	
Wayne (Township)—Auglaize	*OH-3*	
Wayne (Township)—Belmont	*OH-3*	
Wayne (Township)—Butler	*OH-3*	
Wayne (Township)—Champaign	*OH-3*	
Wayne (Township)—Clermont	*OH-3*	
Wayne (Township)—Clinton	*OH-3*	
Wayne (Township)—Columbiana	*OH-3*	
Wayne (Township)—Darke	*OH-3*	
Wayne (Township)—Fayette	*OH-3*	
Wayne (Township)—Jefferson	*OH-3*	
Wayne (Township)—Knox	*OH-3*	
Wayne (Township)—Monroe	*OH-3*	
Wayne (Township)—Muskingum	*OH-3*	
Wayne (Township)—Noble	*OH-3*	
Wayne (Township)—Pickaway	*OH-3*	
Wayne (Township)—Tuscarawas	*OH-3*	
Wayne (Township)—Warren	*OH-3*	
Wayne (Township)—Wayne	*OH-3*	
Wayne (Village)—Wood	*OH-3*	
Wayne (Town)—McClain	*OK-2*	
Wayne (Township)—Armstrong	*PA-1*	
Wayne (Township)—Clinton	*PA-1*	
Wayne (Township)—Crawford	*PA-1*	
Wayne (Township)—Dauphin	*PA-1*	
Wayne (Township)—Erie	*PA-1*	
Wayne (Township)—Greene	*PA-1*	
Wayne (Township)—Lawrence	*PA-1*	
Wayne (Township)—Mifflin	*PA-1*	
Wayne (Township)—Schuylkill	*PA-1*	
Wayne (Township)—Hanson	*SD-4*	
Wayne (Township)—Lake	*SD-4*	
Wayne (Township)—Minnehaha	*SD-4*	
Wayne (Town)—Wayne	*WV-2*	
Wayne (Town)—Lafayette	*WI-3*	
Wayne (Town)—Washington	*WI-3*	
Wayne City (Town)—Wayne	*IL-3*	
Wayne County	*GA-2*	
Wayne County	*IL-3*	
Wayne County	*IN-3*	
Wayne County	*IA-3*	
Wayne County	*KY-2*	
Wayne County	*MI-3*	
Wayne County	*MS-2*	
Wayne County	*MO-3*	
Wayne County	*NE-4*	
Wayne County	*NY-1*	
Wayne County	*NC-2*	
Wayne County	*OH-3*	
Wayne County	*PA-1*	
Wayne County	*TN-2*	
Wayne County	*UT-4*	
Wayne County	*WV-2*	
Wayne Lakes (Village)—Darke	*OH-3*	
Waynesboro (City)—Burke	*GA-2*	
Waynesboro (City)—Wayne	*MS-2*	
Waynesboro (Borough)—Franklin	*PA-1*	
Waynesboro (City)—Wayne	*TN-2*	
Waynesboro (Independent City)	*VA-2*	
Waynesburg (Village)—Stark	*OH-3*	
Waynesburg (Borough)—Greene	*PA-1*	
Waynesfield (Village)—Auglaize	*OH-3*	
Waynesville (Township)—De Witt	*IL-3*	
Waynesville (Village)—De Witt	*IL-3*	
Waynesville (City)—Pulaski	*MO-3*	
Waynesville (Town)—Haywood	*NC-2*	
Waynesville (Village)—Warren	*OH-3*	
Waynetown (Town)—Montgomery	*IN-3*	
Waynoka (City)—Woods	*OK-2*	
Wayzata (City)—Hennepin	*MN-3*	
Wayzetta (Township)—Mountrail	*ND-4*	
Wea (Township)—Tippecanoe	*IN-3*	
Wea (Township)—Miami	*KS-4*	
Weakley County	*TN-2*	
Weallup Lake (CDP)—Snohomish	*WA-4*	
Wealthwood (Township)—Aitkin	*MN-3*	
Weare (Township)—Oceana	*MI-3*	
Weare (Town)—Hillsborough	*NH-1*	
Weatherby (Town)—DeKalb	*MO-3*	
Weatherby Lake (City)—Platte	*MO-3*	
Weatherford (City)—Custer	*OK-2*	
Weatherford (City)—Parker	*TX-2*	
Weatherly (Borough)—Carbon	*PA-1*	
Weathersfield (Township)—Trumbull	*OH-3*	
Weathersfield (Town)—Windsor	*VT-1*	
Weatogue (CDP)—Hartford	*CT-1*	
Weaubleau (City)—Hickory	*MO-3*	
Weaubleau (Township)—Hickory	*MO-3*	
Weaver (Town)—Calhoun	*AL-2*	
Weaver (Township)—Tripp	*SD-4*	
Weaverville (CDP)—Trinity	*CA-4*	
Weaverville (Town)—Buncombe	*NC-2*	
Webb (Town)—Houston	*AL-2*	
Webb (City)—Clay	*IA-3*	
Webb (Town)—Tallahatchie	*MS-2*	
Webb (Township)—Reynolds	*MO-3*	
Webb (Town)—Herkimer	*NY-1*	
Webb City (City)—Jasper	*MO-3*	
Webb City (Town)—Osage	*OK-2*	
Webb County	*TX-2*	
Webber (Township)—Jefferson	*IL-3*	
Webber (City)—Jewell	*KS-4*	
Webber (Township)—Lake	*MI-3*	
Webbers Falls (Town)—Muskogee	*OK-2*	
Webberville (Village)—Ingham	*MI-3*	
Webb Lake (Town)—Burnett	*WI-3*	
Weber (Township)—Sargent	*ND-4*	
Weber (Township)—McPherson	*SD-4*	
Weber City (Town)—Scott	*VA-2*	
Weber County	*UT-4*	
Webster (City)—Sumter	*FL-2*	

Webster (Township)—Harrison	*IN-3*	
Webster (Township)—Wayne	*IN-3*	
Webster (City)—Keokuk	*IA-3*	
Webster (Township)—Smith	*KS-4*	
Webster (Township)—Wilson	*KS-4*	
Webster (Pop. Place)—Penobscot	*ME-1*	
Webster (Town)—Worcester	*MA-1*	
Webster (Township)—Washtenaw	*MI-3*	
Webster (Township)—Rice	*MN-3*	
Webster (Township)—Dodge	*NE-4*	
Webster (Town)—Merrimack	*NH-1*	
Webster (Town)—Monroe	*NY-1*	
Webster (Village)—Monroe	*NY-1*	
Webster (Town)—Jackson	*NC-2*	
Webster (Township)—Ramsey	*ND-4*	
Webster (Township)—Wood	*OH-3*	
Webster (City)—Day	*SD-4*	
Webster (City)—Harris	*TX-2*	
Webster (Village)—Burnett	*WI-3*	
Webster (Town)—Vernon	*WI-3*	
Webster City (City)—Hamilton	*IA-3*	
Webster County	*GA-2*	
Webster County	*IA-3*	
Webster County	*KY-2*	
Webster County	*MS-2*	
Webster County	*MO-3*	
Webster County	*NE-4*	
Webster County	*WV-2*	
Webster Groves (City)—St. Louis	*MO-3*	
Webster Parish	*LA-2*	
Webster Springs (Town)—Webster	*WV-2*	
Weddington (Town)—Mecklenburg	*NC-2*	
Weddington (Town)—Union	*NC-2*	
Wedowee (Town)—Randolph	*AL-2*	
Weed (City)—Siskiyou	*CA-4*	
Weedpatch (CDP)—Kern	*CA-4*	
Weedsport (Village)—Cayuga	*NY-1*	
Weehawken (Township)—Hudson	*NJ-1*	
Weeki Wachee (City)—Hernando	*FL-2*	
Weeki Wachee Acres (CDP)—Hernando	*FL-2*	
Weeki Wachee Gardens (CDP)—Hernando	*FL-2*	
Weeping Water (City)—Cass	*NE-4*	
Weesaw (Township)—Berrien	*MI-3*	
Weidman (CDP)—Isabella	*MI-3*	
Weimar (City)—Colorado	*TX-2*	
Weimer (Township)—Jackson	*MN-3*	
Weimer (Township)—Barnes	*ND-4*	
Weiner (City)—Poinsett	*AR-2*	
Weinert (City)—Haskell	*TX-2*	
Weippe (City)—Clearwater	*ID-4*	
Weir (City)—Cherokee	*KS-4*	
Weir (Town)—Choctaw	*MS-2*	
Weir (Town)—Williamson	*TX-2*	
Weirgor (Town)—Sawyer	*WI-3*	
Weirton (City)—Brooke	*WV-2*	
Weirton (City)—Hancock	*WV-2*	
Weisenberg (Township)—Lehigh	*PA-1*	
Weiser (City)—Washington	*ID-4*	
Weiser (Township)—Kidder	*ND-4*	
Weissport (Borough)—Carbon	*PA-1*	
Wekiva Springs (CDP)—Seminole	*FL-2*	
Welaka (Town)—Putnam	*FL-2*	
Welby (CDP)—Adams	*CO-4*	
Welch (Township)—Goodhue	*MN-3*	
Welch (Township)—Cape Girardeau	*MO-3*	
Welch (Town)—Craig	*OK-2*	
Welch (City)—McDowell	*WV-2*	
Welcome (City)—Martin	*MN-3*	
Welcome (CDP)—Davidson	*NC-2*	
Welcome (CDP)—Greenville	*SC-2*	
Weld (Town)—Franklin	*ME-1*	
Weld (Township)—Stutsman	*ND-4*	
Welda (Township)—Anderson	*KS-4*	
Weld County	*CO-4*	
Weldon (Town)—Jackson	*AR-2*	
Weldon (Village)—De Witt	*IL-3*	
Weldon (City)—Decatur	*IA-3*	
Weldon (Township)—Benzie	*MI-3*	
Weldon (Town)—Halifax	*NC-2*	
Weldon Spring (Town)—St. Charles	*MO-3*	
Weldon Spring Heights (Town)—St. Charles	*MO-3*	
Weleetka (Town)—Okfuskee	*OK-2*	
Welland Ship Canal (NH)	*Geog-4*	
Weller (Township)—Henry	*IL-3*	
Weller (Township)—Richland	*OH-3*	
Wellersburg (Borough)—Somerset	*PA-1*	
Wellesley (Town)—Norfolk	*MA-1*	
Wellfleet (Town)—Barnstable	*MA-1*	
Wellfleet (Village)—Lincoln	*NE-4*	
Wellford (City)—Spartanburg	*SC-2*	
Wellington (Town)—Larimer	*CO-4*	
Wellington (CDP)—Palm Beach	*FL-2*	
Wellington (Village)—Iroquois	*IL-3*	
Wellington (City)—Sumner	*KS-4*	
Wellington (Township)—Sumner	*KS-4*	
Wellington (City)—Jefferson	*KY-2*	
Wellington (Town)—Piscataquis	*ME-1*	
Wellington (Township)—Alpena	*MI-3*	
Wellington (Township)—Renville	*MN-3*	
Wellington (City)—Lafayette	*MO-3*	
Wellington (Township)—Bottineau	*ND-4*	
Wellington (Township)—Lorain	*OH-3*	
Wellington (Village)—Lorain	*OH-3*	
Wellington (Township)—Minnehaha	*SD-4*	
Wellington (City)—Collingsworth	*TX-2*	
Wellington (City)—Carbon	*UT-4*	
Wellington (Town)—Monroe	*WI-3*	
Wellman (City)—Washington	*IA-3*	
Wellman (Town)—Terry	*TX-2*	
Wells (Township)—Marshall	*KS-4*	
Wells (Town)—York	*ME-1*	
Wells (Township)—Delta	*MI-3*	
Wells (Township)—Marquette	*MI-3*	
Wells (Township)—Tuscola	*MI-3*	
Wells (City)—Faribault	*MN-3*	
Wells (Township)—Rice	*MN-3*	
Wells (City)—Elko	*NV-4*	
Wells (Township)—Hamilton	*NY-1*	
Wells (Township)—Wells	*ND-4*	
Wells (Township)—Jefferson	*OH-3*	
Wells (Township)—Bradford	*PA-1*	
Wells (Township)—Fulton	*PA-1*	
Wells (Township)—Perkins	*SD-4*	
Wells (Town)—Cherokee	*TX-2*	
Wells (Town)—Rutland	*VT-1*	
Wells (Town)—Monroe	*WI-3*	
Wellsboro (Borough)—Tioga	*PA-1*	
Wells Branch (CDP)—Travis	*TX-2*	
Wellsburg (City)—Grundy	*IA-3*	
Wellsburg (Village)—Chemung	*NY-1*	
Wellsburg (City)—Brooke	*WV-2*	
Wells County	*IN-3*	
Wells County	*ND-4*	
Wells River (Village)—Orange	*VT-1*	
Wellston (City)—St. Louis	*MO-3*	
Wellston (City)—Jackson	*OH-3*	
Wellston (Town)—Lincoln	*OK-2*	
Wellsville (City)—Franklin	*KS-4*	
Wellsville (City)—Montgomery	*MO-3*	
Wellsville (Town)—Allegany	*NY-1*	
Wellsville (Village)—Allegany	*NY-1*	
Wellsville (City)—Columbiana	*OH-3*	
Wellsville (Borough)—York	*PA-1*	
Wellsville (City)—Cache	*UT-4*	
Wellton (Town)—Yuma	*AZ-4*	
Welsh (Town)—Jefferson Davis Parish	*LA-2*	
Welton (City)—Clinton	*IA-3*	
Wenatchee (City)—Chelan	*WA-4*	
Wendell (City)—Gooding	*ID-4*	
Wendell (Township)—Thomas	*KS-4*	
Wendell (Town)—Franklin	*MA-1*	
Wendell (City)—Grant	*MN-3*	
Wendell (Town)—Wake	*NC-2*	
Wendover (City)—Tooele	*UT-4*	
Wenham (Town)—Essex	*MA-1*	
Wenona (City)—La Salle	*IL-3*	
Wenona (Town)—Marshall	*IL-3*	
Wenonah (Village)—Montgomery	*IL-3*	
Wenonah (Borough)—Gloucester	*NJ-1*	
Wentworth (Village)—Newton	*MO-3*	
Wentworth (Town)—Grafton	*NH-1*	
Wentworth (Pop. Place)—Rockingham	*NC-2*	
Wentworth (Township)—Lake	*SD-4*	
Wentworth (Village)—Lake	*SD-4*	
Wentworth (or Wentworth Location) (Town)—Coos	*NH-1*	
Wentzville (City)—St. Charles	*MO-3*	
Wentzville (Township)—St. Charles	*MO-3*	
Wergeland (Township)—Yellow Medicine	*MN-3*	
Wernersville (Borough)—Berks	*PA-1*	
Wescott (Town)—Shawano	*WI-3*	
Weskan (Township)—Wallace	*KS-4*	
Weslaco (City)—Hidalgo	*TX-2*	
Wesley (Township)—Will	*IL-3*	
Wesley (City)—Kossuth	*IA-3*	
Wesley (Town)—Washington	*ME-1*	
Wesley (Township)—Washington	*OH-3*	
Wesley (Township)—Faulk	*SD-4*	
Wesley Hills (Village)—Rockland	*NY-1*	
Wesleyville (Borough)—Erie	*PA-1*	
Wessington (City)—Beadle	*SD-4*	
Wessington (Township)—Beadle	*SD-4*	
Wessington (City)—Hand	*SD-4*	
Wessington Springs (City)—Jerauld	*SD-4*	
Wessington Springs (Township)—Jerauld	*SD-4*	
Wesson (Town)—Copiah	*MS-2*	
West (Township)—Effingham	*IL-3*	
West (Township)—McLean	*IL-3*	
West (Township)—Marshall	*IN-3*	
West (Town)—Holmes	*MS-2*	
West (Township)—New Madrid	*MO-3*	
West (Township)—Columbiana	*OH-3*	
West (Township)—Huntingdon	*PA-1*	
West (City)—McLennan	*TX-2*	
West Abington (Township)—Lackawanna	*PA-1*	
West Albany (Township)—Wabasha	*MN-3*	
West Alexander (Borough)—Washington	*PA-1*	
West Alexandria (Village)—Preble	*OH-3*	
West Allis (City)—Milwaukee	*WI-3*	
West Almond (Town)—Allegany	*NY-1*	
Westampton (Township)—Burlington	*NJ-1*	

West Amwell (Township)—
Hunterdon *NJ-1*
West Antelope (Township)—
Benson *ND-4*
West Athens (CDP)—Los
Angeles *CA-4*
West Augusta (CDP)—Richmond .. *GA-2*
West Babylon (CDP)—Suffolk *NY-1*
West Baden Springs (Town)—
Orange *IN-3*
West Bank (Township)—Swift *MN-3*
West Bank (Township)—
Williams *ND-4*
West Baraboo (Village)—Sauk *WI-3*
West Barnstable (CDP)—
Barnstable *MA-1*
West Bath (Town)—Sagadahoc *ME-1*
West Baton Rouge Parish *LA-2*
West Bay (Township)—Benson *ND-4*
West Bay Shore (CDP)—Suffolk *NY-1*
West Beaver (Township)—Snyder ... *PA-1*
West Belmar (CDP)—Monmouth ... *NJ-1*
West Bend (City)—Kossuth *IA-3*
West Bend (City)—Palo Alto *IA-3*
West Bend (City)—Washington *WI-3*
West Bend (Town)—Washington ... *WI-3*
West Bennett (Pop. Place)—
Bennett *SD-4*
West Benton (Township)—
Christian *MO-3*
West Benton (Township)—
Newton *MO-3*
West Benton (Township)—
Webster *MO-3*
West Bethlehem (Township)—
Washington *PA-1*
West Bishop (CDP)—Inyo *CA-4*
West Blocton (Town)—Bibb *AL-2*
West Bloomfield (Township)—
Oakland *MI-3*
West Bloomfield (Town)—
Ontario *NY-1*
West Blue (Township)—Adams *NE-4*
West Blue (Township)—Fillmore ... *NE-4*
West Boone (Township)—Bates *MO-3*
Westboro (Village)—Atchison *MO-3*
Westboro (Town)—Taylor *WI-3*
Westborough (Town)—Worcester .. *MA-1*
West Bountiful (City)—Davis *UT-4*
West Bowman (Pop. Place)—
Bowman *ND-4*
West Boylston (Town)—
Worcester *MA-1*
West Bradenton (CDP)—
Manatee *FL-2*
West Bradford (Township)—
Chester *PA-1*
West Branch (City)—Cedar *IA-3*
West Branch (Township)—
Marion *KS-4*
West Branch (Township)—
Dickinson *MI-3*
West Branch (Township)—
Marquette *MI-3*
West Branch (Township)—
Missaukee *MI-3*
West Branch (City)—Ogemaw *MI-3*
West Branch (Township)—
Ogemaw *MI-3*
West Branch (Township)—Potter ... *PA-1*
West Brandywine (Township)—
Chester *PA-1*
West Brattleboro (CDP)—
Windham *VT-1*

West Bridgewater (Town)—
Plymouth *MA-1*
Westbrook (Town)—Middlesex *CT-1*
Westbrook (City)—Cumberland *ME-1*
Westbrook (City)—Cottonwood *MN-3*
Westbrook (Township)—
Cottonwood *MN-3*
Westbrook (City)—Mitchell *TX-2*
West Brookfield (Town)—
Worcester *MA-1*
West Brooklyn (Village)—Lee *IL-3*
West Brownsville (Borough)—
Washington *PA-1*
West Brunswick (Township)—
Schuylkill *PA-1*
West Buechel (City)—Jefferson *KY-2*
West Buffalo (Township)—Union ... *PA-1*
West Burke (Village)—Caledonia ... *VT-1*
West Burleigh (Pop. Place)—
Burleigh *ND-4*
West Burlington (City)—Des
Moines *IA-3*
West Burlington (Township)—
Bradford *PA-1*
Westbury (Village)—Nassau *NY-1*
West Butte (Pop. Place)—Butte *SD-4*
Westby (Town)—Sheridan *MT-4*
Westby (Township)—Divide *ND-4*
Westby (City)—Vernon *WI-3*
West Caldwell (Borough & Township)—
Essex *NJ-1*
West Caln (Township)—Chester *PA-1*
West Cameron (Township)—
Northumberland *PA-1*
West Canton (CDP)—Haywood *NC-2*
West Cape May (Borough)—Cape
May *NJ-1*
West Carroll (Township)—
Cambria *PA-1*
West Carroll Parish *LA-2*
West Carrollton City (City)—
Montgomery *OH-3*
West Carson (CDP)—Los
Angeles *CA-4*
West Carthage (Village)—
Jefferson *NY-1*
West Center (Township)—
Stevens *KS-4*
West Central Franklin
(unorganized) (Pop. Place)—
Franklin *ME-1*
West Central Perkins (Pop. Place)—
Perkins *SD-4*
West Chatham (CDP)—
Barnstable *MA-1*
West Cherry (Township)—
Montgomery *KS-4*
Westchester (CDP)—Dade *FL-2*
Westchester (Village)—Cook *IL-3*
Westchester (Township)—Porter ... *IN-3*
West Chester (City)—Washington .. *IA-3*
West Chester (Borough)—Chester .. *PA-1*
Westchester County *NY-1*
West Chicago (City)—DuPage *IL-3*
West Chillisquaque (Township)—
Northumberland *PA-1*
West City (Village)—Franklin *IL-3*
West Clarkston-Highland (CDP)—
Asotin *WA-4*
Westcliffe (Town)—Custer *CO-4*
West Cocalico (Township)—
Lancaster *PA-1*
West College Corner (Town)—
Union *IN-3*

West Columbia (City)—
Lexington *SC-2*
West Columbia (City)—Brazoria ... *TX-2*
West Compton (CDP)—Los
Angeles *CA-4*
West Concord (CDP)—
Middlesex *MA-1*
West Concord (City)—Dodge *MN-3*
West Conshohocken (Borough)—
Montgomery *PA-1*
West Cook (Pop. Place)—Cook *MN-3*
West Cooper (Township)—
Stafford *KS-4*
West Cornwall (Township)—
Lebanon *PA-1*
West Corson (Pop. Place)—
Corson *SD-4*
West Covina (City)—Los Angeles .. *CA-4*
West Creek (Township)—Lake *IN-3*
West Crossett (CDP)—Ashley *AR-2*
West Crow Wing (Pop. Place)—Crow
Wing *MN-3*
West Custer (Pop. Place)—Custer . *SD-4*
West Dallas (Township)—
Webster *MO-3*
West Deer (Township)—
Allegheny *PA-1*
West Deerfield (Township)—Lake .. *IL-3*
West De Land (CDP)—Volusia *FL-2*
West Dennis (CDP)—Barnstable .. *MA-1*
West Deptford (Township)—
Gloucester *NJ-1*
West Des Moines (City)—Dallas *IA-3*
West Des Moines (City)—Polk *IA-3*
West Dolan (Township)—Cass *MO-3*
West Donegal (Township)—
Lancaster *PA-1*
West Doniphan (Township)—
Ripley *MO-3*
West Dundee (Village)—Kane *IL-3*
West Earl (Township)—Lancaster ... *PA-1*
West Easton (Borough)—
Northampton *PA-1*
West Elizabeth (Borough)—
Allegheny *PA-1*
West Elkton (Village)—Preble *OH-3*
West Elmira (CDP)—Chemung *NY-1*
West Emmons (Pop. Place)—
Emmons *ND-4*
West End (CDP)—Otsego *NY-1*
West End (Township)—Richland ... *ND-4*
West End-Cobb Town (Division)—
Calhoun *AL-2*
Westerheim (Township)—Lyon *MN-3*
Westerlo (Town)—Albany *NY-1*
Westerly (Town)—Washington *RI-1*
Western (Township)—Henry *IL-3*
Western (Township)—Logan *KS-4*
Western (Township)—Otter Tail ... *MN-3*
Western (Township)—Knox *NE-4*
Western (Village)—Saline *NE-4*
Western (Town)—Oneida *NY-1*
Western (Township)—Wells *ND-4*
Western Grove (Town)—Newton ... *AR-2*
Western Mound (Township)—
Macoupin *IL-3*
Westernport (Town)—Allegany *MD-1*
Western Springs (City)—Cook *IL-3*
Westerville (Township)—Custer *NE-4*
Westerville (City)—Delaware *OH-3*
Westerville (City)—Franklin *OH-3*
West Fairlee (Town)—Orange *VT-1*
West Fairview (Borough)—
Cumberland *PA-1*
Westfall (Township)—Pike *PA-1*

General Index — American Places Dictionary

West Fallowfield (Township)—Chester ... *PA-1*
West Fallowfield (Township)—Crawford ... *PA-1*
West Falmouth (CDP)—Barnstable ... *MA-1*
West Fargo (City)—Cass ... *ND-4*
West Farmington (Village)—Trumbull ... *OH-3*
West Feliciana Parish ... *LA-2*
West Ferriday (CDP)—Concordia Parish ... *LA-2*
Westfield (Township)—Bureau ... *IL-3*
Westfield (Township)—Clark ... *IL-3*
Westfield (Village)—Clark ... *IL-3*
Westfield (Town)—Hamilton ... *IN-3*
Westfield (City)—Plymouth ... *IA-3*
Westfield (Town)—Aroostook ... *ME-1*
Westfield (City)—Hampden ... *MA-1*
Westfield (Township)—Dodge ... *MN-3*
Westfield (Town)—Union ... *NJ-1*
Westfield (Town)—Chautauqua ... *NY-1*
Westfield (Village)—Chautauqua ... *NY-1*
Westfield (Township)—Steele ... *ND-4*
Westfield (Township)—Medina ... *OH-3*
Westfield (Township)—Morrow ... *OH-3*
Westfield (Borough)—Tioga ... *PA-1*
Westfield (Township)—Tioga ... *PA-1*
Westfield (Town)—Orleans ... *VT-1*
Westfield (Town)—Marquette ... *WI-3*
Westfield (Village)—Marquette ... *WI-3*
Westfield (Town)—Sauk ... *WI-3*
Westfield Center (Village)—Medina ... *OH-3*
West Finley (Township)—Christian ... *MO-3*
West Finley (Township)—Washington ... *PA-1*
Westfir (City)—Lane ... *OR-4*
Westford (Town)—Middlesex ... *MA-1*
Westford (Township)—Martin ... *MN-3*
Westford (Town)—Otsego ... *NY-1*
Westford (Township)—Kidder ... *ND-4*
Westford (Town)—Chittenden ... *VT-1*
Westford (Town)—Dodge ... *WI-3*
Westford (Town)—Richland ... *WI-3*
West Fork (City)—Washington ... *AR-2*
West Forks (Plantation)—Somerset ... *ME-1*
West Frankfort (City)—Franklin ... *IL-3*
West Franklin (Township)—Armstrong ... *PA-1*
West Freehold (CDP)—Monmouth ... *NJ-1*
West Fulton (Township)—Callaway ... *MO-3*
West Galena (Township)—Jo Daviess ... *IL-3*
West Gardiner (Town)—Kennebec ... *ME-1*
Westgate (City)—Fayette ... *IA-3*
West Gate (CDP)—Prince William ... *VA-2*
Westgate-Belvedere Homes (CDP)—Palm Beach ... *FL-2*
West Glens Falls (CDP)—Warren ... *NY-1*
West Goshen (Township)—Chester ... *PA-1*
West Grant (Pop. Place)—Grant ... *ND-4*
West Greenwich (Town)—Kent ... *RI-1*
West Grove (Borough)—Chester ... *PA-1*
West Haakon (Pop. Place)—Haakon ... *SD-4*
West Hale (Township)—Thomas ... *KS-4*
West Hamlin (Town)—Lincoln ... *WV-2*

Westhampton (Town)—Hampshire ... *MA-1*
Westhampton (CDP)—Suffolk ... *NY-1*
Westhampton Beach (Village)—Suffolk ... *NY-1*
West Hanover (Township)—Dauphin ... *PA-1*
West Hanson (Township)—Brown ... *SD-4*
West Harrison (Town)—Dearborn ... *IN-3*
West Hartford (Town)—Hartford ... *CT-1*
West Hattiesburg (CDP)—Lamar ... *MS-2*
West Haven (City)—New Haven ... *CT-1*
West Haven (Town)—Rutland ... *VT-1*
Westhaven-Moonstone (CDP)—Humboldt ... *CA-4*
West Haven-Sylvan (CDP)—Washington ... *OR-4*
West Haverstraw (Village)—Rockland ... *NY-1*
West Hazleton (Borough)—Luzerne ... *PA-1*
West Helena (City)—Phillips ... *AR-2*
West Hemlock (Township)—Montour ... *PA-1*
West Hempfield (Township)—Lancaster ... *PA-1*
West Hempstead (CDP)—Nassau ... *NY-1*
West Heron Lake (Township)—Jackson ... *MN-3*
West Hibbard (Township)—Kearny ... *KS-4*
West Hill (CDP)—Trumbull ... *OH-3*
West Hills (CDP)—Suffolk ... *NY-1*
West Hollywood (City)—Los Angeles ... *CA-4*
West Homestead (Borough)—Allegheny ... *PA-1*
Westhope (City)—Bottineau ... *ND-4*
West Hope (Township)—Cavalier ... *ND-4*
West Hughes (Pop. Place)—Hughes ... *SD-4*
West Hurley (CDP)—Ulster ... *NY-1*
West Islip (CDP)—Suffolk ... *NY-1*
West Jefferson (Municipality)—Jefferson ... *AL-2*
West Jefferson (Town)—Ashe ... *NC-2*
West Jersey (Township)—Stark ... *IL-3*
West Jordan (City)—Salt Lake ... *UT-4*
West Keating (Township)—Clinton ... *PA-1*
West Kewaunee (Town)—Kewaunee ... *WI-3*
West Kiowa (Pop. Place)—Kiowa ... *KS-4*
West Kittanning (Borough)—Armstrong ... *PA-1*
West Lafayette (City)—Tippecanoe ... *IN-3*
West Lafayette (Village)—Coshocton ... *OH-3*
Westlake (Town)—Calcasieu Parish ... *LA-2*
Westlake (City)—Cuyahoga ... *OH-3*
Westlake (Town)—Denton ... *TX-2*
Westlake (Town)—Tarrant ... *TX-2*
West Lake Hills (City)—Travis ... *TX-2*
West Lakeland (Township)—Washington ... *MN-3*
West Lake Sammamish (CDP)—King ... *WA-4*
West Lake Stevens (CDP)—Snohomish ... *WA-4*
Westlake Village (City)—Los Angeles ... *CA-4*

West Lampeter (Township)—Lancaster ... *PA-1*
Westland (City)—Wayne ... *MI-3*
Westland (Township)—Guernsey ... *OH-3*
West Laurel (CDP)—Prince George's ... *MD-1*
West Lawn (Borough)—Berks ... *PA-1*
West Lebanon (Town)—Warren ... *IN-3*
West Lebanon (Township)—Lebanon ... *PA-1*
West Leechburg (Borough)—Westmoreland ... *PA-1*
West Leipsic (Village)—Putnam ... *OH-3*
West Liberty (City)—Muscatine ... *IA-3*
West Liberty (City)—Morgan ... *KY-2*
West Liberty (Village)—Logan ... *OH-3*
West Liberty (Borough)—Butler ... *PA-1*
West Liberty (Town)—Ohio ... *WV-2*
West Lincoln (Township)—Logan ... *IL-3*
Westline (Township)—Redwood ... *MN-3*
West Line (Village)—Cass ... *MO-3*
West Linn (City)—Clackamas ... *OR-4*
West Little River (CDP)—Dade ... *FL-2*
West Logan (Pop. Place)—Logan ... *ND-4*
West Logan (Town)—Logan ... *WV-2*
West Long Branch (Borough)—Monmouth ... *NJ-1*
West Longview (CDP)—Cowlitz ... *WA-4*
West Looney (Township)—Polk ... *MO-3*
West Madison (Township)—Polk ... *MO-3*
West Mahanoy (Township)—Schuylkill ... *PA-1*
West Mahoning (Township)—Indiana ... *PA-1*
West Manchester (Village)—Preble ... *OH-3*
West Manchester (Township)—York ... *PA-1*
West Manheim (Township)—York ... *PA-1*
Westmanland (Plantation)—Aroostook ... *ME-1*
West Mansfield (Village)—Logan ... *OH-3*
West Marion (CDP)—McDowell ... *NC-2*
Westmark (Township)—Phelps ... *NE-4*
West Marlborough (Township)—Chester ... *PA-1*
West Marshland (Town)—Burnett ... *WI-3*
West Mayfield (Borough)—Beaver ... *PA-1*
West McLean (Pop. Place)—McLean ... *ND-4*
West McPherson (Pop. Place)—McPherson ... *SD-4*
West Mead (Township)—Crawford ... *PA-1*
West Melbourne (City)—Brevard ... *FL-2*
West Memphis (City)—Crittenden ... *AR-2*
West Menlo Park (CDP)—San Mateo ... *CA-4*
West Mercer (Pop. Place)—Mercer ... *ND-4*
Westmere (CDP)—Albany ... *NY-1*
West Miami (City)—Dade ... *FL-2*
West Middlesex (Borough)—Mercer ... *PA-1*
West Middletown (Borough)—Washington ... *PA-1*
West Mifflin (Borough)—Allegheny ... *PA-1*
West Milford (Township)—Passaic ... *NJ-1*
West Milford (Town)—Harrison ... *WV-2*
West Millgrove (Village)—Wood ... *OH-3*

West Milton (Village)—Miami....... *OH-3*
West Milwaukee (Village)—
　Milwaukee........................... *WI-3*
West Mineral (City)—Cherokee...... *KS-4*
Westminster (City)—Orange.......... *CA-4*
Westminster (City)—Adams........... *CO-4*
Westminster (City)—Jefferson....... *CO-4*
Westminster (Township)—Reno..... *KS-4*
Westminster (CDP)—East Baton Rouge
　Parish.................................. *LA-2*
Westminster (City)—Carroll......... *MD-1*
Westminster (Town)—Worcester... *MA-1*
Westminster (Town)—Oconee........ *SC-2*
Westminster (Town)—Collin......... *TX-2*
Westminster (Town)—Windham.... *VT-1*
Westminster (Village)—Windham. *VT-1*
Westminster East (CDP)—
　Adams................................. *CO-4*
Westminster South (CDP)—
　Carroll................................. *MD-1*
West Monroe (City)—Ouachita
　Parish.................................. *LA-2*
West Monroe (CDP)—Monroe...... *MI-3*
West Monroe (Town)—Oswego..... *NY-1*
Westmont (CDP)—Los Angeles..... *CA-4*
Westmont (City)—DuPage........... *IL-3*
Westmont (Borough)—Cambria..... *PA-1*
Westmore (Town)—Orleans.......... *VT-1*
Westmoreland (City)—
　Pottawatomie........................ *KS-4*
Westmoreland (Town)—Cheshire .. *NH-1*
Westmoreland (Town)—Oneida.... *NY-1*
Westmoreland (Town)—Sumner.... *TN-2*
Westmoreland County..................... *PA-1*
Westmoreland County..................... *VA-2*
Westmorland (City)—Imperial...... *CA-4*
West Morton (Pop. Place)—
　Morton................................. *ND-4*
West Mountrail (Pop. Place)—
　Mountrail............................. *ND-4*
West Nantmeal (Township)—
　Chester................................. *PA-1*
West Newbury (Town)—Essex..... *MA-1*
West Newman (Township)—
　Nance.................................. *NE-4*
West Newton (Township)—
　Nicollet................................ *MN-3*
West Newton (Borough)—
　Westmoreland....................... *PA-1*
West New York (Town)—Hudson... *NJ-1*
West Norriton (Township)—
　Montgomery......................... *PA-1*
West Norway (Township)—Wells... *ND-4*
West Nottingham (Township)—
　Chester................................. *PA-1*
West Nyack (CDP)—Rockland..... *NY-1*
West Ocean City (CDP)—
　Worcester............................. *MD-1*
West Odessa (CDP)—Ector.......... *TX-2*
West Okoboji (City)—Dickinson... *IA-3*
Westola (Township)—Morton....... *KS-4*
West Oliver (Pop. Place)—Oliver.. *ND-4*
Weston (Town)—Marion............... *AL-2*
Weston (Town)—Fairfield............ *CT-1*
Weston (Town)—Webster............. *GA-2*
Weston (City)—Franklin.............. *ID-4*
Weston (Town)—Aroostook......... *ME-1*
Weston (Town)—Middlesex......... *MA-1*
Weston (City)—Platte.................. *MO-3*
Weston (Township)—Platte.......... *MO-3*
Weston (Village)—Saunders......... *NE-4*
Weston (Township)—Wood.......... *OH-3*
Weston (Village)—Wood.............. *OH-3*
Weston (City)—Umatilla.............. *OR-4*
Weston (Township)—Marshall..... *SD-4*

Weston (Town)—Collin................. *TX-2*
Weston (Town)—Windsor............. *VT-1*
Weston (City)—Lewis................... *WV-2*
Weston (Town)—Clark.................. *WI-3*
Weston (Town)—Dunn.................. *WI-3*
Weston (Town)—Marathon............ *WI-3*
Weston County.............................. *WY-4*
Weston Mills (CDP)—
　Cattaraugus.............................. *NY-1*
West Ontario (Township)—Wells... *ND-4*
West Orange (Township)—Essex.... *NJ-1*
West Orange (City)—Orange......... *TX-2*
Westover (Borough)—Clearfield.... *PA-1*
Westover (Township)—Jones......... *SD-4*
Westover (City)—Monongalia........ *WV-2*
Westover Air Force Base (MA)...... *Mil-4*
Westover Hills (Town)—Tarrant.... *TX-2*
West Palm Beach (City)—Palm
　Beach...................................... *FL-2*
West Paris (Town)—Oxford.......... *ME-1*
West Park (CDP)—Hillsborough.... *FL-2*
West Pasco (CDP)—Franklin......... *WA-4*
West Paterson (Borough)—
　Passaic.................................... *NJ-1*
West Peculiar (Township)—Cass.. *MO-3*
West Pelzer (Town)—Anderson....... *SC-2*
West Penn (Township)—
　Schuylkill................................ *PA-1*
West Pennington (Pop. Place)—
　Pennington.............................. *SD-4*
West Pennsboro (Township)—
　Cumberland............................. *PA-1*
West Pensacola (CDP)—
　Escambia................................. *FL-2*
West Peoria (Township)—Peoria... *IL-3*
West Perkins (Pop. Place)—
　Perkins.................................... *SD-4*
West Perry (Township)—Snyder..... *PA-1*
Westphalia (City)—Shelby............ *IA-3*
Westphalia (City)—Anderson........ *KS-4*
Westphalia (Township)—
　Anderson................................. *KS-4*
Westphalia (Township)—Clinton... *MI-3*
Westphalia (Village)—Clinton....... *MI-3*
Westphalia (City)—Osage............. *MO-3*
West Pikeland (Township)—
　Chester.................................... *PA-1*
West Pike Run (Township)—
　Washington............................. *PA-1*
West Pittsburg (CDP)—Contra
　Costa...................................... *CA-4*
West Pittston (Borough)—
　Luzerne................................... *PA-1*
West Plains (Township)—Meade.... *KS-4*
West Plains (City)—Howell.......... *MO-3*
West Point (Municipality)—
　Cullman.................................. *AL-2*
West Point (Town)—White........... *AR-2*
West Point (City)—Harris............. *GA-2*
West Point (City)—Troup............. *GA-2*
West Point (Village)—Hancock..... *IL-3*
West Point (Township)—
　Stephenson.............................. *IL-3*
West Point (Township)—White..... *IN-3*
West Point (City)—Lee................. *IA-3*
West Point (City)—Hardin........... *KY-2*
West Point (City)—Clay............... *MS-2*
West Point (Township)—Bates..... *MO-3*
West Point (City)—Cuming.......... *NE-4*
West Point (Mil. facil.)—Orange... *NY-1*
West Point (Township)—Brule...... *SD-4*
West Point (City)—Davis.............. *UT-4*
West Point (Town)—King
　William................................... *VA-2*
West Point (Town)—Columbia...... *WI-3*

West Polk (Township)—
　Christian................................. *MO-3*
Westport (Town)—Fairfield........... *CT-1*
Westport (Town)—Decatur............ *IN-3*
Westport (Town)—Lincoln............ *ME-1*
Westport (Town)—Bristol............. *MA-1*
Westport (City)—Pope.................. *MN-3*
Westport (Township)—Pope......... *MN-3*
Westport (Town)—Essex............... *NY-1*
Westport (Village)—Essex............ *NY-1*
Westport (CDP)—Lincoln............. *NC-2*
Westport (Town)—Pawnee............ *OK-2*
Westport (Town)—Brown............. *SD-4*
Westport (Township)—Brown....... *SD-4*
Westport (City)—Grays Harbor..... *WA-4*
Westport (Town)—Dane............... *WI-3*
West Portsmouth (CDP)—Scioto... *OH-3*
West Potter (Pop. Place)—Potter... *SD-4*
West Pottsgrove (Township)—
　Montgomery........................... *PA-1*
West Providence (Township)—
　Bedford.................................. *PA-1*
West Puente Valley (CDP)—Los
　Angeles................................... *CA-4*
West Quoddy Head (ME)............ *Geog-4*
West Reading (Borough)—Berks.... *PA-1*
West Republic (Township)—
　Greene.................................... *MO-3*
West Richland (City)—Benton....... *WA-4*
West Rockhill (Township)—Bucks.. *PA-1*
West Rondell (Township)—
　Brown.................................... *SD-4*
West Rushville (Village)—
　Fairfield................................. *OH-3*
West Rutland (Town)—Rutland.... *VT-1*
West Sacramento (City)—Yolo...... *CA-4*
West Sadsbury (Township)—
　Chester................................... *PA-1*
West Salem (Village)—Edwards.... *IL-3*
West Salem (Village)—Wayne....... *OH-3*
West Salem (Township)—Mercer... *PA-1*
West Salem (Village)—La Crosse... *WI-3*
West Saline (Township)—
　Sheridan................................. *KS-4*
West Samoset (CDP)—Manatee.... *FL-2*
West Sand Lake (CDP)—
　Rensselaer.............................. *NY-1*
West Sayville (CDP)—Suffolk....... *NY-1*
West Seneca (Town)—Erie........... *NY-1*
West Shannon (Pop. Place)—
　Shannon................................. *SD-4*
West Shenango (Township)—
　Crawford................................ *PA-1*
Westside (CDP)—Hall.................. *GA-2*
Westside (City)—Crawford........... *IA-3*
Westside (Township)—Nobles...... *MN-3*
Westside (Township)—Phelps....... *NE-4*
West Side Highway (CDP)—
　Cowlitz................................... *WA-4*
West Siloam Springs (Town)—
　Delaware................................ *OK-2*
West Simsbury (CDP)—Hartford.. *CT-1*
West Slope (Pop. Place)—Slope..... *ND-4*
West Slope (CDP)—Washington.... *OR-4*
West Smithfield (CDP)—
　Johnston................................. *NC-2*
West Sparta (Town)—Livingston... *NY-1*
West Springfield (Town)—
　Hampden................................ *MA-1*
West Springfield (CDP)—Fairfax.. *VA-2*
West Stark (Pop. Place)—Stark..... *ND-4*
West St. Clair (Township)—
　Bedford.................................. *PA-1*
West Stockbridge (Town)—
　Berkshire................................ *MA-1*

General Index

American Places Dictionary

West St. Paul (City)—Dakota *MN-3*
West Sully (Pop. Place)—Sully *SD-4*
West Sunbury (Borough)—Butler.... *PA-1*
West Swanzey (CDP)—Cheshire.... *NH-1*
West Sweden (Town)—Polk *WI-3*
West Tawakoni (Town)—Hunt....... *TX-2*
West Taylor (Township)—
  Cambria *PA-1*
West Terre Haute (Town)—Vigo..... *IN-3*
West Tisbury (Town)—Dukes......... *MA-1*
West Todd (Pop. Place)—Todd...... *SD-4*
Westtown (Township)—Chester *PA-1*
West Traverse (Township)—
  Emmet *MI-3*
West Turin (Town)—Lewis *NY-1*
West Union (City)—Fayette............ *IA-3*
West Union (City)—Todd *MN-3*
West Union (Township)—Todd *MN-3*
West Union (Township)—Custer ... *NE-4*
West Union (Town)—Steuben *NY-1*
West Union (Village)—Adams.... *OH-3*
West Union (Town)—Oconee *SC-2*
West Union (Town)—Doddridge .. *WV-2*
West Unity (Village)—Williams.... *OH-3*
West University Place (City)—
  Harris *TX-2*
Westvale (CDP)—Onondaga *NY-1*
West Valley (Township)—
  Marshall *MN-3*
West Valley (CDP)—Yakima *WA-4*
West Valley City (City)—Salt
  Lake *UT-4*
Westview (CDP)—Dade................. *FL-2*
West View (Borough)—Allegheny ... *PA-1*
Westville (Town)—Holmes............. *FL-2*
Westville (City)—Vermilion *IL-3*
Westville (Town)—La Porte........... *IN-3*
Westville (Borough)—Gloucester *NJ-1*
Westville (Town)—Franklin *NY-1*
Westville (Town)—Adair *OK-2*
West Vincent (Township)—
  Chester *PA-1*
West Walworth (Pop. Place)—
  Walworth *SD-4*
West Wareham (CDP)—
  Plymouth...................................... *MA-1*
West Warwick (Town)—Kent.......... *RI-1*
West Washington (Township)—
  Rice *KS-4*
Westway (CDP)—El Paso *TX-2*
Westwego (City)—Jefferson
  Parish *LA-2*
West Wenatchee (CDP)—Chelan ... *WA-4*
West Wendover (CDP)—Elko *NV-4*
West Wheatfield (Township)—
  Indiana *PA-1*
West Whiteland (Township)—
  Chester *PA-1*
West Whittier-Los Nietos (CDP)—Los
  Angeles... *CA-4*
West Wildwood (Borough)—Cape
  May *NJ-1*
West Windsor (Township)—
  Mercer.. *NJ-1*
West Windsor (Town)—Windsor ... *VT-1*
West Winfield (Village)—
  Herkimer...................................... *NY-1*
Westwood (CDP)—Lassen *CA-4*
Westwood (City)—Henry *IA-3*
Westwood (City)—Johnson *KS-4*
Westwood (CDP)—Boyd................ *KY-2*
Westwood (City)—Jefferson *KY-2*
Westwood (Town)—Norfolk........... *MA-1*
Westwood (CDP)—Kalamazoo...... *MI-3*
Westwood (Village)—St. Louis...... *MO-3*

Westwood (Borough)—Bergen *NJ-1*
Westwood Hills (City)—Johnson... *KS-4*
Westwood Lakes (CDP)—Dade...... *FL-2*
Westworth (Village)—Tarrant *TX-2*
West Wyoming (Borough)—
  Luzerne *PA-1*
West Yankton (Pop. Place)—
  Yankton.. *SD-4*
West Yarmouth (CDP)—
  Barnstable *MA-1*
West Yellowstone (Town)—
  Gallatin *MT-4*
West York (Borough)—York *PA-1*
Weta (Township)—Jackson *SD-4*
Wethersfield (Town)—Hartford *CT-1*
Wethersfield (Township)—Henry.... *IL-3*
Wethersfield (Town)—Wyoming *NY-1*
Wetmore (City)—Nemaha.............. *KS-4*
Wetmore (Township)—Nemaha..... *KS-4*
Wetmore (Township)—McKean *PA-1*
Wetonka (Town)—McPherson *SD-4*
Wetumka (City)—Hughes............... *OK-2*
Wetumpka (City)—Elmore............. *AL-2*
Wetzel County *WV-2*
Wewahitchka (Town)—Gulf........... *FL-2*
Weweantic (CDP)—Plymouth *MA-1*
Wewoka (City)—Seminole *OK-2*
Wexford (Township)—Wexford...... *MI-3*
Wexford County *MI-3*
Weyauwega (City)—Waupaca........ *WI-3*
Weyauwega (Town)—Waupaca *WI-3*
Weybridge (Town)—Addison *VT-1*
Weyerhaeuser (Village)—Rusk *WI-3*
Weymouth (Town)—Norfolk.......... *MA-1*
Weymouth (Township)—Atlantic... *NJ-1*
Whalan (City)—Fillmore................ *MN-3*
Whale Pass (CDP)—Prince of
  Wales-Outer Ketchikan Census
  Area *AK-4*
Wharton (Borough)—Morris........... *NJ-1*
Wharton (Village)—Wyandot......... *OH-3*
Wharton (Township)—Fayette *PA-1*
Wharton (Township)—Potter.......... *PA-1*
Wharton (City)—Wharton *TX-2*
Wharton County *TX-2*
What Cheer (City)—Keokuk........... *IA-3*
Whatcom County *WA-4*
Whately (Town)—Franklin *MA-1*
Wheatcroft (City)—Webster *KY-2*
Wheatfield (Township)—Clinton ... *IL-3*
Wheatfield (Town)—Jasper............ *IN-3*
Wheatfield (Township)—Jasper *IN-3*
Wheatfield (Township)—Ingham ... *MI-3*
Wheatfield (Town)—Niagara *NY-1*
Wheatfield (Township)—Grand
  Forks *ND-4*
Wheatfield (Township)—Perry........ *PA-1*
Wheatland (City)—Yuba............... *CA-4*
Wheatland (Township)—Bureau.... *IL-3*
Wheatland (Township)—Fayette.... *IL-3*
Wheatland (Township)—Will......... *IL-3*
Wheatland (Town)—Knox *IN-3*
Wheatland (City)—Clinton *IA-3*
Wheatland (Township)—Barton..... *KS-4*
Wheatland (Township)—
  Dickinson *KS-4*
Wheatland (Township)—Ellis........ *KS-4*
Wheatland (Township)—Ford........ *KS-4*
Wheatland (Township)—
  Hillsdale *MI-3*
Wheatland (Township)—Mecosta... *MI-3*
Wheatland (Township)—Sanilac.... *MI-3*
Wheatland (Township)—Rice *MN-3*
Wheatland (City)—Hickory *MO-3*

Wheatland (Township)—
  Hickory *MO-3*
Wheatland (Town)—Monroe *NY-1*
Wheatland (Township)—Cass *ND-4*
Wheatland (Borough)—Mercer...... *PA-1*
Wheatland (Township)—Day......... *SD-4*
Wheatland (Town)—Kenosha *WI-3*
Wheatland (Town)—Vernon *WI-3*
Wheatland (Town)—Platte *WY-4*
Wheatland County............................ *MT-4*
Wheatley (City)—St. Francis *AR-2*
Wheatley Heights (CDP)—
  Suffolk.. *NY-1*
Wheaton (City)—DuPage *IL-3*
Wheaton (City)—Pottawatomie.... *KS-4*
Wheaton (City)—Traverse *MN-3*
Wheaton (City)—Barry *MO-3*
Wheaton (Township)—Barry *MO-3*
Wheaton (Township)—Bottineau... *ND-4*
Wheaton (Township)—Hand *SD-4*
Wheaton (Town)—Chippewa *WI-3*
Wheaton-Glenmont (CDP)—
  Montgomery................................ *MD-1*
Wheat Ridge (City)—Jefferson *CO-4*
Wheeler (Village)—Jasper *IL-3*
Wheeler (Township)—Gratiot *MI-3*
Wheeler (Town)—Steuben *NY-1*
Wheeler (City)—Tillamook *OR-4*
Wheeler (Town)—Wheeler *TX-2*
Wheeler (Village)—Dunn *WI-3*
Wheeler Air Force Base (CDP)—
  Honolulu...................................... *HI-4*
Wheeler County *GA-2*
Wheeler County *NE-4*
Wheeler County *OR-4*
Wheeler County *TX-2*
Wheeler Peak (NM) *Geog-4*
Wheelersburg (CDP)—Scioto........ *OH-3*
Wheeling (City)—Cook *IL-3*
Wheeling (Township)—Cook *IL-3*
Wheeling (City)—Lake *IL-3*
Wheeling (Township)—Rice *MN-3*
Wheeling (City)—Livingston.......... *MO-3*
Wheeling (Township)—
  Livingston *MO-3*
Wheeling (Township)—Belmont *OH-3*
Wheeling (Township)—Guernsey... *OH-3*
Wheeling (City)—Marshall............ *WV-2*
Wheeling (City)—Ohio *WV-2*
Wheelock (City)—Williams........... *ND-4*
Wheelock (Township)—Williams... *ND-4*
Wheelock (Town)—Caledonia........ *VT-1*
Wheelwright (City)—Floyd *KY-2*
Whelen Springs (Town)—Clark *AR-2*
Whetstone (CDP)—Cochise........... *AZ-4*
Whetstone (Township)—Adams..... *ND-4*
Whetstone (Township)—
  Crawford *OH-3*
Whetstone (Township)—Gregory... *SD-4*
Whidbey Island Naval Air Station
  (WA).. *Mil-4*
Whigham (City)—Grady *GA-2*
Whipps Millgate (City)—
  Jefferson...................................... *KY-2*
Whiskey Creek (CDP)—Lee *FL-2*
Whiskey Run (Township)—
  Crawford *IN-3*
Whispering Pines (Village)—
  Moore... *NC-2*
Whisper Walk (CDP)—Palm
  Beach... *FL-2*
Whitaker (Borough)—Allegheny ... *PA-1*
Whitakers (Town)—Edgecombe..... *NC-2*
Whitakers (Town)—Nash *NC-2*
Whitby (Township)—Bottineau *ND-4*

1128

American Places Dictionary — General Index

White (Town)—Bartow *GA-2*
White (Township)—Kingman *KS-4*
White (Township)—St. Louis *MN-3*
White (Township)—Benton........... *MO-3*
White (Township)—Macon *MO-3*
White (Township)—Warren *NJ-1*
White (Township)—Pierce *ND-4*
White (Township)—Beaver *PA-1*
White (Township)—Cambria *PA-1*
White (Township)—Indiana.......... *PA-1*
White (City)—Brookings................ *SD-4*
White (Township)—Marshall *SD-4*
Whiteash (Village)—Williamson *IL-3*
White Ash (Township)—Renville .. *ND-4*
White Bear (Township)—
  Ramsey *MN-3*
White Bear Lake (Township)—
  Pope *MN-3*
White Bear Lake (City)—
  Ramsey *MN-3*
White Bear Lake (City)—
  Washington *MN-3*
White Bird (City)—Idaho *ID-4*
White Bluff (Town)—Dickson *TN-2*
White Butte (ND) *Geog-4*
White Butte (Township)—
  Perkins *SD-4*
White Castle (Town)—Iberville
  Parish *LA-2*
White Center-Shorewood (CDP)—
  King *WA-4*
White City (CDP)—St. Lucie *FL-2*
White City (Village)—Macoupin ... *IL-3*
White City (City)—Morris *KS-4*
White City (CDP)—Jackson *OR-3*
White City (CDP)—Salt Lake *UT-4*
White Cloud (City)—Doniphan *KS-4*
White Cloud (City)—Newayго *MI-3*
White Cloud (Township)—
  Nodaway *MO-3*
White County *AR-2*
White County *GA-2*
White County *IL-3*
White County *IN-3*
White County *TN-2*
White Creek (Town)—
  Washington *NY-1*
Whited (Township)—Kanabec *MN-3*
White Deer (Township)—Union..... *PA-1*
White Deer (Town)—Carson *TX-2*
White Earth (Township)—
  Becker *MN-3*
White Earth (City)—Mountrail......*ND-4*
White Earth (Township)—
  Mountrail *ND-4*
White Earth Reservation
  (MN) *IndRes-4*
White Eyes (Township)—
  Coshocton *OH-3*
Whiteface (Town)—Cochran..........*TX-2*
Whiteface Reservoir (Pop. Place)—St.
  Louis *MN-3*
Whitefield (Township)—Marshall... *IL-3*
Whitefield (Town)—Lincoln *ME-1*
Whitefield (Township)—
  Kandiyohi *MN-3*
Whitefield (Town)—Coos...............*NH-1*
Whitefield (Town)—Haskell........... *OK-2*
Whitefish (Township)—
  Chippewa *MI-3*
Whitefish (City)—Flathead *MT-4*
Whitefish Bay (MI)......................*Geog-4*
Whitefish Bay (Village)—
  Milwaukee *WI-3*
Whiteford (Township)—Monroe.... *MI-3*

Whiteford (Township)—
  Marshall *MN-3*
White Hall (Municipality)—
  Lowndes *AL-2*
White Hall (City)—Jefferson *AR-2*
White Hall (Town)—Greene *IL-3*
White Hall (Township)—Greene *IL-3*
Whitehall (City)—Muskegon.......... *MI-3*
Whitehall (Township)—
  Muskegon.. *MI-3*
Whitehall (Town)—Jefferson *MT-4*
Whitehall (Town)—Washington *NY-1*
Whitehall (Village)—Washington... *NY-1*
Whitehall (City)—Franklin *OH-3*
Whitehall (Borough)—Allegheny .. *PA-1*
Whitehall (Township)—Lehigh *PA-1*
Whitehall (City)—Trempealeau *WI-3*
White Haven (Borough)—
  Luzerne *PA-1*
White Hill (Township)—Perkins.... *SD-4*
White Horse (CDP)—Mercer.........*NJ-1*
White Horse (CDP)—Todd............*SD-4*
Whitehouse (Village)—Lucas *OH-3*
White House (City)—Robertson ... *TN-2*
White House (City)—Sumner *TN-2*
Whitehouse (City)—Smith *TX-2*
White House Station (CDP)—
  Hunterdon...................................... *NJ-1*
White Island Shores (CDP)—
  Plymouth *MA-1*
White Lake (Township)—
  Oakland *MI-3*
White Lake (Town)—Bladen..........*NC-2*
White Lake (Township)—Slope *ND-4*
White Lake (City)—Aurora............ *SD-4*
White Lake (Township)—Aurora... *SD-4*
White Lake (Village)—Langlade.... *WI-3*
Whiteland (Town)—Johnson *IN-3*
Whitelaw (Village)—Manitowoc.... *WI-3*
Whiteley (Township)—Greene *PA-1*
Whiteman Air Force Base (MO)....*Mil-4*
Whiteman Air Force Base (Military
  Facility)—Johnson *MO-3*
White Marsh (CDP)—Baltimore .. *MD-1*
Whitemarsh (Township & Village)—
  Montgomery *PA-1*
Whitemarsh Island (CDP)—
  Chatham *GA-2*
White Meadow Lake (CDP)—
  Morris *NJ-1*
White Mound (Township)—
  Jewell *KS-4*
White Mountain (City)—Nome Census
  Area *AK-4*
White Mountains (MI) *Geog-4*
White Oak (Township)—McLean ... *IL-3*
White Oak (CDP)—
  Montgomery *MD-1*
White Oak (Township)—Ingham ... *MI-3*
White Oak (Township)—
  Hubbard *MN-3*
White Oak (Township)—
  Harrison *MO-3*
White Oak (Township)—Henry *MO-3*
White Oak (CDP)—Hamilton *OH-3*
White Oak (Township)—
  Highland *OH-3*
White Oak (Borough)—Allegheny .. *PA-1*
White Oak (City)—Gregg *TX-2*
White Oak East (CDP)—
  Hamilton *OH-3*
White Oak Springs (Town)—
  Lafayette *WI-3*
White Oak West (CDP)—
  Hamilton *OH-3*

White Pigeon (Township)—St.
  Joseph *MI-3*
White Pigeon (Village)—St.
  Joseph *MI-3*
White Pine (Township)—Aitkin ... *MN-3*
White Pine (Town)—Jefferson *TN-2*
White Pine County *NV-4*
White Plains (Town)—Greene *GA-2*
White Plains (City)—Hopkins *KY-2*
White Plains (CDP)—Charles *MD-1*
White Plains (City)—Westchester.. *NY-1*
White Plains (CDP)—Surry *NC-2*
White Post (Township)—Pulaski *IN-3*
Whiteriver (CDP)—Navajo *AZ-4*
White River (Township)—Gibson .. *IN-3*
White River (Township)—
  Hamilton *IN-3*
White River (Township)—
  Johnson *IN-3*
White River (Township)—
  Randolph *IN-3*
White River (Township)—
  Muskegon.. *MI-3*
White River (Township)—Barry ... *MO-3*
White River (City)—Mellette......... *SD-4*
White River (Town)—Ashland *WI-3*
White River Junction (CDP)—
  Windsor *VT-1*
White Rock (Township)—Ogle *IL-3*
White Rock (Township)—Lane......*KS-4*
White Rock (Township)—
  Republic *KS-4*
White Rock (Township)—Smith *KS-4*
White Rock (Township)—
  McDonald *MO-3*
White Rock (CDP)—Los
  Alamos *NM-4*
White Rock (Town)—Roberts *SD-4*
White Rock (Township)—
  Roberts *SD-4*
Whiterocks (CDP)—Uintah *UT-4*
White Salmon (City)—Klickitat *WA-4*
White Sands (NM) *Geog-4*
White Sands (Military Facility)—Doña
  Ana *NM-4*
White Sands Missile Range
  (NM) *Mil-4*
Whitesboro (Village)—Oneida *NY-1*
Whitesboro (City)—Grayson *TX-2*
Whitesboro-Burleigh (CDP)—Cape
  May *NJ-1*
Whitesburg (Town)—Carroll *GA-2*
Whitesburg (City)—Letcher *KY-2*
White Settlement (City)—Tarrant .. *TX-2*
White Shield (CDP)—McLean *ND-4*
Whiteside (Village)—Lincoln *MO-3*
Whiteside (Township)—Beadle *SD-4*
Whiteside County *IL-3*
White Springs (Town)—Hamilton ..*FL-2*
Whitestone (Township)—Dickey ... *ND-4*
White Stone (Town)—Lancaster ... *VA-2*
Whitestone Hill (Township)—
  Sargent *ND-4*
Whitestone Logging Camp (CDP)—
  Skagway-Hoonah-Angoon Census
  Area *AK-4*
Whitestown (Town)—Boone *IN-3*
Whitestown (Town)—Oneida......... *NY-1*
Whitestown (Town)—Vernon *WI-3*
White Sulphur Springs (City)—
  Meagher *MT-4*
White Sulphur Springs (City)—
  Greenbrier *WV-2*
Whitesville (City)—Daviess *KY-2*
Whitesville (Town)—Boone *WV-2*

General Index — American Places Dictionary

White Swan (Township)—Charles Mix SD-4
White Swan (CDP)—Yakima WA-4
Whiteville (City)—Columbus NC-2
Whiteville (Town)—Hardeman TN-2
Whitewater (Township)—Franklin IN-3
Whitewater (Town)—Wayne IN-3
Whitewater (City)—Butler KS-4
Whitewater (Township)—Grand Traverse MI-3
Whitewater (Township)—Winona MN-3
Whitewater (Township)—Bollinger MO-3
Whitewater (Town)—Cape Girardeau MO-3
Whitewater (Township)—Cape Girardeau MO-3
Whitewater (Township)—Hamilton OH-3
Whitewater (City)—Jefferson WI-3
Whitewater (City)—Walworth WI-3
Whitewater (Town)—Walworth ... WI-3
Whitewood (Township)—Kingsbury SD-4
Whitewood (City)—Lawrence SD-4
Whitewright (Town)—Fannin TX-2
Whitewright (Town)—Grayson TX-2
Whitfield (CDP)—Manatee FL-2
Whitfield County GA-2
Whiting (City)—Lake IN-3
Whiting (City)—Monona IA-3
Whiting (City)—Jackson KS-4
Whiting (Township)—Jackson KS-4
Whiting (Town)—Washington ME-1
Whiting (Township)—Bowman ND-4
Whiting (Town)—Addison VT-1
Whiting (Village)—Portage WI-3
Whitingham (Town)—Windham ... VT-1
Whitinsville (CDP)—Worcester MA-1
Whitley (Township)—Moultrie IL-3
Whitley City (CDP)—McCreary KY-2
Whitley County IN-3
Whitley County KY-2
Whitman (Town)—Plymouth MA-1
Whitman County WA-4
Whitmire (Town)—Newberry SC-2
Whitmore (Township)—Macon IL-3
Whitmore Lake (CDP)—Livingston MI-3
Whitmore Lake (CDP)—Washtenaw MI-3
Whitmore Village (CDP)—Honolulu HI-4
Whitney (Township)—Arenac MI-3
Whitney (Village)—Dawes NE-4
Whitney (Town)—Hill TX-2
Whitney, Mt. (CA) Geog-4
Whitney Point (Village)—Broome NY-1
Whitneyville (Town)—Washington ME-1
Whitpain (Township)—Montgomery PA-1
Whittemore (City)—Kossuth IA-3
Whitten (City)—Hardin IA-3
Whitteron (Township)—Bottineau ND-4
Whittier (City)—Valdez-Cordova Census Area AK-4
Whittier (City)—Los Angeles CA-4
Whitwell (City)—Marion TN-2
Wibaux (Town)—Wibaux MT-4
Wibaux County MT-4

Wichita (City)—Sedgwick KS-4
Wichita County KS-4
Wichita County TX-2
Wichita Falls (City)—Archer TX-2
Wichita Falls (City)—Wichita TX-2
Wickenburg (Town)—Maricopa AZ-4
Wickes (Town)—Polk AR-2
Wickett (Town)—Ward TX-2
Wickliffe (City)—Ballard KY-2
Wickliffe (City)—Lake OH-3
Wicomico County MD-1
Wiconisco (Township)—Dauphin ... PA-1
Widener (Town)—St. Francis AR-2
Widner (Township)—Knox IN-3
Wiederkehr Village (City)—Franklin AR-2
Wien (Town)—Marathon WI-3
Wiggins (Town)—Morgan CO-4
Wiggins (City)—Stone MS-2
Wilbarger County TX-2
Wilber (Township)—Iosco MI-3
Wilber (City)—Saline NE-4
Wilberforce (CDP)—Greene OH-3
Wilberton (Township)—Fayette IL-3
Wilbraham (Town)—Hampden MA-1
Wilbur (Township)—McKenzie ND-4
Wilbur (Township)—Brule SD-4
Wilbur (Town)—Lincoln WA-4
Wilburn (Township)—Ford KS-4
Wilbur Park (Village)—St. Louis ... MO-3
Wilburton (City)—Latimer OK-2
Wilcox (Township)—Hancock IL-3
Wilcox (Township)—Trego KS-4
Wilcox (Township)—Newaygo MI-3
Wilcox (Village)—Kearney NE-4
Wilcox County AL-2
Wilcox County GA-2
Wildcat (Township)—Tipton IN-3
Wildcat (Township)—Elk KS-4
Wild Cat (Township)—Riley KS-4
Wilder (City)—Canyon ID-4
Wilder (City)—Campbell KY-2
Wilder (City)—Jackson MN-3
Wilder (CDP)—Windsor VT-1
Wildhorse (Township)—Graham ... KS-4
Wildomar (CDP)—Riverside CA-4
Wild Peach Village (CDP)—Brazoria TX-2
Wild Rice (Township)—Norman ... MN-3
Wild Rose (Township)—Burleigh ... ND-4
Wildrose (City)—Williams ND-4
Wild Rose (Village)—Waushara WI-3
Wildwood (City)—Sumter FL-2
Wildwood (City)—Jefferson KY-2
Wildwood (Township)—Itasca MN-3
Wildwood (City)—Cape May NJ-1
Wildwood Crest (Borough)—Cape May NJ-1
Wildwood Lake (CDP)—Bradley ... TN-2
Wiley (Town)—Prowers CO-4
Wilkes-Barre (City)—Luzerne PA-1
Wilkes-Barre (Township)—Luzerne PA-1
Wilkesboro (Town)—Wilkes NC-2
Wilkes County GA-2
Wilkes County NC-2
Wilkeson (Town)—Pierce WA-4
Wilkesville (Township)—Vinton ... OH-3
Wilkesville (Village)—Vinton OH-3
Wilkin County MN-3
Wilkins (Township)—Allegheny PA-1
Wilkinsburg (Borough)—Allegheny PA-1
Wilkinson (Town)—Hancock IN-3
Wilkinson (Township)—Cass MN-3

Wilkinson (Town)—Rusk WI-3
Wilkinson County GA-2
Wilkinson County MS-2
Wilkinson Heights (CDP)—Orangeburg SC-2
Will (Township)—Will IL-3
Willacoochee (Town)—Atkinson ... GA-2
Willacy County TX-2
Willamette River (OR) Geog-4
Willamina (City)—Polk OR-4
Willamina (City)—Yamhill OR-4
Willard (City)—Shawnee KS-4
Willard (City)—Wabaunsee KS-4
Willard (City)—Greene MO-3
Willard (Village)—Torrance NM-4
Willard (City)—Huron OH-3
Willard (City)—Box Elder UT-4
Willard (Town)—Rusk WI-3
Willards (Town)—Wicomico MD-1
Will County IL-3
Willcox (City)—Cochise AZ-4
Willernie (City)—Washington MN-3
Willet (Town)—Cortland NY-1
Willey (City)—Carroll IA-3
Willey (Township)—Sargent ND-4
William Hamilton (Township)—Hyde SD-4
Williams (City)—Coconino AZ-4
Williams (City)—Colusa CA-4
Williams (Township)—Sangamon ... IL-3
Williams (City)—Hamilton IA-3
Williams (Township)—Bay MI-3
Williams (Township)—Aitkin MN-3
Williams (City)—Lake of the Woods MN-3
Williams (Township)—Benton MO-3
Williams (Township)—Stone MO-3
Williams (Township)—Wayne MO-3
Williams (Township)—Kidder ND-4
Williams (Township)—Nelson ND-4
Williams (Township)—Dauphin PA-1
Williams (Township)—Northampton PA-1
Williams (Town)—Colleton SC-2
Williams Bay (Village)—Walworth WI-3
Williamsburg (Town)—Fremont ... CO-4
Williamsburg (CDP)—Orange FL-2
Williamsburg (City)—Iowa IA-3
Williamsburg (City)—Franklin KS-4
Williamsburg (Township)—Franklin KS-4
Williamsburg (City)—Whitley KY-2
Williamsburg (Town)—Hampshire MA-1
Williamsburg (Township)—Phelps NE-4
Williamsburg (Village)—Sierra NM-4
Williamsburg—Kings NY-1
Williamsburg (Township)—Clermont OH-3
Williamsburg (Village)—Clermont OH-3
Williamsburg (Borough)—Blair PA-1
Williamsburg County SC-2
Williamsburg (Independent City) ... VA-2
Williams County ND-4
Williams County OH-3
Williams Creek (Town)—Marion ... IN-3
Williams Creek (Township)—Jones SD-4
Williamsfield (Village)—Knox IL-3
Williamsfield (Township)—Ashtabula OH-3
Williamson (Town)—Pike GA-2

American Places Dictionary — General Index

Williamson (Village)—Madison...... *IL-3*
Williamson (City)—Lucas............ *IA-3*
Williamson (Town)—Wayne *NY-1*
Williamson (City)—Mingo............ *WV-2*
Williamson County............................ *IL-3*
Williamson County......................... *TN-2*
Williamson County......................... *TX-2*
Williamsport (Town)—Warren......... *IN-3*
Williamsport (Township)—
 Shawnee *KS-4*
Williamsport (Town)—
 Washington *MD-1*
Williamsport (Village)—
 Pickaway *OH-3*
Williamsport (City)—Lycoming... *PA-1*
Williamston (City)—Ingham......... *MI-3*
Williamston (Town)—Martin......... *NC-2*
Williamston (Town)—Anderson *SC-2*
Williamstown (City)—Grant......... *KY-2*
Williamstown (Town)—
 Berkshire *MA-1*
Williamstown (Township)—
 Ingham *MI-3*
Williamstown (CDP)—Gloucester.. *NJ-1*
Williamstown (Town)—Oswego..... *NY-1*
Williamstown (Borough)—
 Dauphin *PA-1*
Williamstown (Town)—Orange...... *VT-1*
Williamstown (City)—Wood......... *WV-2*
Williamstown (Town)—Dodge....... *WI-3*
Williamsville (Town)—Sangamon... *IL-3*
Williamsville (City)—Wayne......... *MO-3*
Williamsville (Village)—Erie......... *NY-1*
Williford (Town)—Sharp............... *AR-2*
Willimantic (CDP)—Windham *CT-1*
Willimantic (Town)—
 Piscataquis *ME-1*
Willing (Town)—Allegany *NY-1*
Willingboro (Township)—
 Burlington *NJ-1*
Willington (Town)—Tolland *CT-1*
Willis (City)—Brown *KS-4*
Willis (Township)—Ward............. *ND-4*
Willis (City)—Montgomery........... *TX-2*
Willisburg (City)—Washington *KY-2*
Williston (City)—Levy................... *FL-2*
Williston (City)—Williams........... *ND-4*
Williston (Township)—Williams... *ND-4*
Williston (Town)—Barnwell........... *SC-2*
Williston (City)—Fayette *TN-2*
Williston (Town)—Chittenden...... *VT-1*
Williston Park (Village)—Nassau .. *NY-1*
Willistown (Township)—Chester ... *PA-1*
Willisville (Town)—Nevada *AR-2*
Willisville (Village)—Perry *IL-3*
Willits (City)—Mendocino........... *CA-4*
Willmar (City)—Kandiyohi *MN-3*
Willmar (Township)—Kandiyohi.. *MN-3*
Willoughby (City)—Lake.............. *OH-3*
Willoughby Hills (City)—Lake...... *OH-3*
Willow (CDP)—Matanuska-Susitna
 Borough *AK-4*
Willow (Township)—Antelope *NE-4*
Willow (Township)—Griggs *ND-4*
Willow (Town)—Greer................. *OK-2*
Willow (Town)—Richland............ *WI-3*
Willowbank (Township)—
 LaMoure *ND-4*
Willow Branch (Township)—Piatt.. *IL-3*
Willowbrook (CDP)—Los
 Angeles *CA-4*
Willowbrook (Village)—DuPage..... *IL-3*
Willowbrook (CDP)—Will *IL-3*
Willowbrook (City)—Reno........... *KS-4*
Willow City (City)—Bottineau..... *ND-4*

Willow Creek (CDP)—Humboldt.. *CA-4*
Willow Creek (Township)—Lee *IL-3*
Willow Creek (Township)—
 McHenry *ND-4*
Willow Creek (Township)—Tripp.. *SD-4*
Willowdale (Township)—
 Dickinson *KS-4*
Willowdale (Township)—Holt....... *NE-4*
Willow Fork (Township)—
 Moniteau *MO-3*
Willow Hill (Township)—Jasper..... *IL-3*
Willow Hill (Village)—Jasper *IL-3*
Willowick (City)—Lake................. *OH-3*
Willow Lake (Township)—
 Redwood *MN-3*
Willow Lake (Township)—Steele.. *ND-4*
Willow Lake (Township)—Brule.... *SD-4*
Willow Lake (City)—Clark *SD-4*
Willow Oak (CDP)—Polk............. *FL-2*
Willow Park (City)—Parker *TX-2*
Willow River (City)—Pine........... *MN-3*
Willows (City)—Glenn *CA-4*
Willow Springs (Town)—Cook *IL-3*
Willow Springs (Village)—
 DuPage *IL-3*
Willow Springs (Township)—
 Douglas *KS-4*
Willow Springs (City)—Howell..... *MO-3*
Willow Springs (Township)—
 Howell *MO-3*
Willow Springs (Town)—
 Lafayette *WI-3*
Willow Vale (Township)—
 Bottineau *ND-4*
Willow Valley (CDP)—Mohave..... *AZ-4*
Willow Valley (Township)—St.
 Louis *MN-3*
Wills (Township)—La Porte.......... *IN-3*
Wills (Township)—Guernsey *OH-3*
Willsboro (Town)—Essex *NY-1*
Willshire (Township)—Van Wert.. *OH-3*
Willshire (Village)—Van Wert...... *OH-3*
Wills Point (City)—Van Zandt *TX-2*
Wilma (Township)—Pine *MN-3*
Wilmar (City)—Drew................... *AR-2*
Wilmer (Town)—Mobile *AL-2*
Wilmer (City)—Dallas.................. *TX-2*
Wilmerding (Borough)—
 Allegheny *PA-1*
Wilmette (Residential village)—
 Cook *IL-3*
Wilmington (City)—New Castle.... *DE-1*
Wilmington (Village)—Greene...... *IL-3*
Wilmington (City)—Will.............. *IL-3*
Wilmington (Township)—Will...... *IL-3*
Wilmington (Township)—Dekalb .. *IN-3*
Wilmington (Township)—
 Wabaunsee *KS-4*
Wilmington (Town)—Middlesex... *MA-1*
Wilmington (Township)—
 Houston *MN-3*
Wilmington (Town)—Essex.......... *NY-1*
Wilmington (City)—New
 Hanover *NC-2*
Wilmington (City)—Clinton *OH-3*
Wilmington (Township)—
 Lawrence *PA-1*
Wilmington (Township)—Mercer.. *PA-1*
Wilmington (Town)—Windham *VT-1*
Wilmington Island (CDP)—
 Chatham *GA-2*
Wilmington Manor (CDP)—New
 Castle....................................... *DE-1*
Wilmont (City)—Nobles *MN-3*
Wilmont (Township)—Nobles *MN-3*

Wilmore (City)—Comanche............ *KS-4*
Wilmore (City)—Jessamine *KY-2*
Wilmore (Borough)—Cambria........ *PA-1*
Wilmot (City)—Ashley *AR-2*
Wilmot (Township)—Cheboygan... *MI-3*
Wilmot (Town)—Merrimack........... *NH-1*
Wilmot (Village)—Stark *OH-3*
Wilmot (Township)—Bradford *PA-1*
Wilmot (City)—Roberts *SD-4*
Wilna (Town)—Jefferson *NY-1*
Wilsey (City)—Morris *KS-4*
Wilson (Town)—Mississippi *AR-2*
Wilson (Township)—De Witt *IL-3*
Wilson (City)—Ellsworth *KS-4*
Wilson (Township)—Ellsworth...... *KS-4*
Wilson (Township)—Lane *KS-4*
Wilson (Township)—Marion......... *KS-4*
Wilson (Township)—Rice *KS-4*
Wilson (Village)—East Feliciana
 Parish *LA-2*
Wilson (Township)—Alpena *MI-3*
Wilson (Township)—Charlevoix *MI-3*
Wilson (Township)—Cass *MN-3*
Wilson (Township)—Winona *MN-3*
Wilson (Township)—Adair *MO-3*
Wilson (Township)—Audrain *MO-3*
Wilson (Township)—Dallas *MO-3*
Wilson (Township)—Gentry *MO-3*
Wilson (Township)—Greene *MO-3*
Wilson (Township)—Grundy *MO-3*
Wilson (Township)—Putnam *MO-3*
Wilson (Town)—Niagara *NY-1*
Wilson (Village)—Niagara............ *NY-1*
Wilson (City)—Wilson *NC-2*
Wilson (Township)—Burleigh *ND-4*
Wilson (Village)—Belmont *OH-3*
Wilson (Township)—Clinton *OH-3*
Wilson (Village)—Monroe *OH-3*
Wilson (City)—Carter *OK-2*
Wilson (Borough)—Northampton... *PA-1*
Wilson (Township)—Perkins *SD-4*
Wilson (Township)—Tripp............ *SD-4*
Wilson (City)—Lynn *TX-2*
Wilson (Town)—Dunn *WI-3*
Wilson (Town)—Eau Claire *WI-3*
Wilson (Town)—Lincoln *WI-3*
Wilson (Town)—Rusk................... *WI-3*
Wilson (Town)—Sheboygan *WI-3*
Wilson (Village)—St. Croix.......... *WI-3*
Wilson City (Town)—
 Mississippi *MO-3*
Wilson County................................ *KS-4*
Wilson County................................ *NC-2*
Wilson County................................ *TN-2*
Wilson County................................ *TX-2*
Wilson Creek (Town)—Grant *WA-4*
Wilsonville (Town)—Shelby............ *AL-2*
Wilsonville (Village)—Macoupin *IL-3*
Wilsonville (Village)—Furnas *NE-4*
Wilsonville (City)—Clackamas *OR-4*
Wilsonville (City)—Washington..... *OR-4*
Wilton (Town)—Shelby................. *AL-2*
Wilton (Town)—Little River.......... *AR-2*
Wilton (CDP)—Sacramento........... *CA-4*
Wilton (Town)—Fairfield *CT-1*
Wilton (Township)—Will *IL-3*
Wilton (City)—Cedar................... *IA-3*
Wilton (City)—Muscatine............ *IA-3*
Wilton (Town)—Franklin *ME-1*
Wilton (City)—Beltrami *MN-3*
Wilton (Township)—Waseca *MN-3*
Wilton (Town)—Hillsborough....... *NH-1*
Wilton (Town)—Saratoga *NY-1*
Wilton (City)—Burleigh *ND-4*
Wilton (City)—McLean................ *ND-4*

General Index

Wilton (Town)—Monroe................. *WI-3*
Wilton (Village)—Monroe................. *WI-3*
Wilton Manors (City)—Broward *FL-2*
Wimauma (CDP)—Hillsborough *FL-2*
Wimberley (CDP)—Hays................. *TX-2*
Wimbledon (City)—Barnes............. *ND-4*
Winamac (Town)—Pulaski.............. *IN-3*
Winchendon (Town)—Worcester .. *MA-1*
Winchester (City)—Drew................ *AR-2*
Winchester (CDP)—Riverside *CA-4*
Winchester (Town)—Litchfield...... *CT-1*
Winchester (City)—Lewis *ID-4*
Winchester (City)—Scott *IL-3*
Winchester (City)—Randolph......... *IN-3*
Winchester (City)—Jefferson *KS-4*
Winchester (City)—Clark *KY-2*
Winchester (Town)—Middlesex *MA-1*
Winchester (Township)—
  Norman..................................... *MN-3*
Winchester (City)—St. Louis *MO-3*
Winchester (CDP)—Clark *NV-4*
Winchester (Town)—Cheshire *NH-1*
Winchester (Township)—Adams....*OH-3*
Winchester (Village)—Adams *OH-3*
Winchester (Town)—Okmulgee *OK-3*
Winchester (City)—Franklin........... *TN-2*
Winchester (Town)—Vilas *WI-3*
Winchester (Town)—Winnebago ... *WI-3*
Winchester (Independent City)........ *VA-2*
Windber (Borough)—Somerset *PA-1*
Wind Cave (SD) *Geog-4*
Windcrest (City)—Bexar *TX-2*
Windemere (Township)—Pine *MN-3*
Windemere (CDP)—New
  Hanover.................................... *NC-2*
Windemere (CDP)—Travis *TX-2*
Winder (City)—Barrow *GA-2*
Windermere (Town)—Orange *FL-2*
Windfall City (Town)—Tipton *IN-3*
Wind Gap (Borough)—
  Northampton *PA-1*
Windham (Town)—Windham *CT-1*
Windham (Town)—Cumberland... *ME-1*
Windham (Town)—Rockingham ... *NH-1*
Windham (Town)—Greene *NY-1*
Windham (Township)—Portage *OH-3*
Windham (Village)—Portage *OH-3*
Windham (Township)—Bradford ... *PA-1*
Windham (Township)—Wyoming .. *PA-1*
Windham (Town)—Windham......... *VT-1*
Windham County *CT-1*
Windham County *VT-1*
Winding Falls (City)—Jefferson..... *KY-2*
Wind Lake (CDP)—Racine *WI-3*
Windom (City)—McPherson *KS-4*
Windom (City)—Cottonwood......... *MN-3*
Windom (Township)—Mower *MN-3*
Windom (Town)—Fannin *TX-2*
Window Rock (CDP)—Apache *AZ-4*
Wind Point (Village)—Racine *WI-3*
Wind River Range (WY) *Geog-4*
Wind River Reservation
  (WY)..*IndRes-4*
Windsor (CDP)—Sonoma *CA-4*
Windsor (Town)—Weld................... *CO-4*
Windsor (Town)—Hartford............. *CT-1*
Windsor (Village)—Mercer *IL-3*
Windsor (City)—Shelby *IL-3*
Windsor (Township)—Shelby *IL-3*
Windsor (Township)—Cowley *KS-4*
Windsor (Town)—Kennebec *ME-1*
Windsor (Town)—Berkshire *MA-1*
Windsor (Township)—Eaton *MI-3*
Windsor (Township)—Traverse *MN-3*
Windsor (City)—Henry *MO-3*

Windsor (Township)—Henry *MO-3*
Windsor (Township)—Jefferson.... *MO-3*
Windsor (City)—Pettis *MO-3*
Windsor (Town)—Hillsborough *NH-1*
Windsor (Town)—Broome *NY-1*
Windsor (Village)—Broome *NY-1*
Windsor (Town)—Bertie *NC-2*
Windsor (Township)—Stutsman.....*ND-4*
Windsor (Township)—Ashtabula ...*OH-3*
Windsor (Township)—Lawrence....*OH-3*
Windsor (Township)—Morgan.......*OH-3*
Windsor (Township)—Berks *PA-1*
Windsor (Borough)—York *PA-1*
Windsor (Township)—York *PA-1*
Windsor (Town)—Aiken *SC-2*
Windsor (Town)—Windsor *VT-1*
Windsor (Town)—Isle of Wight *VA-2*
Windsor (Town)—Dane *WI-3*
Windsor County *VT-1*
Windsor Heights (City)—Polk *IA-3*
Windsor Locks (Town)—
  Hartford *CT-1*
Windthorst (Town)—Archer *TX-2*
Windthorst (Town)—Clay *TX-2*
Windy Hills (City)—Jefferson *KY-2*
Winfall (Town)—Perquimans *NC-2*
Winfield (City)—Fayette *AL-2*
Winfield (City)—Marion *AL-2*
Winfield (Town)—DuPage *IL-3*
Winfield (Township)—DuPage *IL-3*
Winfield (Township)—Lake *IN-3*
Winfield (City)—Henry *IA-3*
Winfield (City)—Cowley *KS-4*
Winfield (Township)—Osborne *KS-4*
Winfield (Township)—Montcalm .. *MI-3*
Winfield (Township)—Renville *MN-3*
Winfield (City)—Lincoln *MO-3*
Winfield (Township)—Union......... *NJ-1*
Winfield (Township)—Herkimer.... *NY-1*
Winfield (Township)—Stutsman....*ND-4*
Winfield (Township)—Butler......... *PA-1*
Winfield (Town)—Scott *TN-2*
Winfield (Town)—Titus *TX-2*
Winfield (Town)—Putnam *WV-2*
Winfield (Town)—Sauk................... *WI-3*
Winfred (Town)—Lake.................... *SD-4*
Winfred (Township)—Lake............ *SD-4*
Wing (City)—Burleigh.................... *ND-4*
Wing (Township)—Burleigh *ND-4*
Wingate (Town)—Montgomery....... *IN-3*
Wingate (Town)—Union *NC-2*
Winger (City)—Polk *MN-3*
Winger (Township)—Polk.............. *MN-3*
Wingfield (Township)—Geary *KS-4*
Wingo (City)—Graves...................... *KY-2*
Wing River (Township)—
  Wadena *MN-3*
Wingville (Town)—Grant................ *WI-3*
Winhall (Town)—Bennington *VT-1*
Winifred (Town)—Fergus *MT-4*
Wink (City)—Winkler..................... *TX-2*
Winkelman (Town)—Gila *AZ-4*
Winkler County *TX-2*
Winlock (City)—Lewis *WA-4*
Winn (Town)—Penobscot *ME-1*
Winnebago (Town)—Winnebago *IL-3*
Winnebago (Township)—
  Winnebago................................ *IL-3*
Winnebago (City)—Faribault......... *MN-3*
Winnebago (Township)—
  Houston..................................... *MN-3*
Winnebago (Township)—
  Thurston................................... *NE-4*
Winnebago (Village)—Thurston *NE-4*
Winnebago, Lake (WI) *Geog-4*

Winnebago City (Township)—
  Faribault..................................*MN-3*
Winnebago County *IL-3*
Winnebago County *IA-3*
Winnebago County *WI-3*
Winnebago Reservation (NE)... *IndRes-4*
Winneconne (Town)—
  Winnebago................................ *WI-3*
Winneconne (Village)—
  Winnebago................................ *WI-3*
Winnemuca Colony (NV) *IndRes-4*
Winnemucca (City)—Humboldt *NV-4*
Winner (Township)—Williams *ND-4*
Winner (City)—Tripp *SD-4*
Winneshiek County *IA-3*
Winnetka (Village)—Cook *IL-3*
Winnetoon (Village)—Knox *NE-4*
Winnett (Town)—Petroleum *MT-4*
Winnfield (City)—Winn Parish *LA-2*
Winnie (CDP)—Chambers.............. *TX-2*
Winnipesaukee, Lake (NH) *Geog-4*
Winn Parish *LA-2*
Winnsboro (Town)—Franklin
  Parish.. *LA-2*
Winnsboro (Town)—Fairfield........ *SC-2*
Winnsboro (City)—Franklin *TX-2*
Winnsboro (City)—Wood............... *TX-2*
Winnsboro Mills (CDP)—
  Fairfield..................................... *SC-2*
Winona (City)—Logan *KS-4*
Winona (Township)—Logan *KS-4*
Winona (City)—Winona *MN-3*
Winona (Township)—Winona *MN-3*
Winona (City)—Montgomery *MS-2*
Winona (City)—Shannon *MO-3*
Winona (Township)—Shannon *MO-3*
Winona (Township)—Grant *ND-4*
Winona (Town)—Smith *TX-2*
Winona County............................. *MN-3*
Winona Lake (Town)—Kosciusko .. *IN-3*
Winooski (City)—Chittenden *VT-1*
Winside (Village)—Wayne *NE-4*
Winslow (City)—Navajo *AZ-4*
Winslow (Town)—Washington....... *AR-2*
Winslow (Township)—Stephenson . *IL-3*
Winslow (Village)—Stephenson *IL-3*
Winslow (Town)—Pike..................... *IN-3*
Winslow (Town)—Kennebec *ME-1*
Winslow (Village)—Dodge *NE-4*
Winslow (Township)—Camden *NJ-1*
Winslow (Township)—Jefferson *PA-1*
Winslow (City)—Kitsap *WA-4*
Winsor (Township)—Huron *MI-3*
Winsor (Township)—Clearwater....*MN-3*
Winsor (Township)—Brookings *SD-4*
Winsted (CDP)—Litchfield............. *CT-1*
Winsted (City)—McLeod *MN-3*
Winsted (Township)—McLeod *MN-3*
Winston (CDP)—Polk.....................*FL-2*
Winston (Town)—Daviess *MO-3*
Winston (City)—Douglas *OR-4*
Winston County..............................*AL-2*
Winston County............................. *MS-2*
Winston-Salem (City)—Forsyth *NC-2*
Winstonville (Village)—Bolivar *MS-2*
Winter (Town)—Sawyer.................. *WI-3*
Winter (Village)—Sawyer *WI-3*
Winterfield (Township)—Clare *MI-3*
Winter Garden (City)—Orange.....*FL-2*
Winter Harbor (Town)—
  Hancock.................................... *ME-1*
Winter Haven (City)—Polk *FL-2*
Winter Park (Town)—Grand *CO-4*
Winter Park (City)—Orange *FL-2*
Winterport (Town)—Waldo *ME-1*

American Places Dictionary — General Index

Winters (City)—Yolo.................. *CA-4*
Winters (City)—Runnels............ *TX-2*
Winterset (City)—Madison *IA-3*
Winterset (Township)—Russell...... *KS-4*
Winter Springs (City)—Seminole.... *FL-2*
Winterstown (Borough)—York *PA-1*
Wintersville (Village)—Jefferson *OH-3*
Winterville (City)—Clarke *GA-2*
Winterville (Plantation)—
   Aroostook..................... *ME-1*
Winterville (Town)—Pitt............ *NC-2*
Winthrop (City)—Little River *AR-2*
Winthrop (City)—Buchanan *IA-3*
Winthrop (Town)—Kennebec *ME-1*
Winthrop (Town)—Suffolk........... *MA-1*
Winthrop (City)—Sibley *MN-3*
Winthrop (City)—Okanogan *WA-4*
Winthrop Harbor (Town)—Lake ... *IL-3*
Winton (CDP)—Merced *CA-4*
Winton (City)—St. Louis *MN-3*
Winton (Town)—Hertford *NC-2*
Wiota (City)—Cass.................... *IA-3*
Wiota (City)—Lafayette.............. *WI-3*
Wirt (Township)—Itasca *MN-3*
Wirt (Town)—Allegany *NY-1*
Wirt County................................ *WV-2*
Wiscasset (Town)—Lincoln........... *ME-1*
Wisconsin (Township)—Jackson... *MN-3*
Wisconsin Dells (WI).................. *Geog-4*
Wisconsin Dells (City)—Adams ... *WI-3*
Wisconsin Dells (City)—
   Columbia *WI-3*
Wisconsin Dells (City)—Sauk... *WI-3*
Wisconsin Rapids (City)—Wood... *WI-3*
Wisconsin River (WI).................. *Geog-4*
Wisconsin Winnebago Res. & Trust
   Lands (WI)................... *IndRes-4*
Wiscoy (Township)—Winona *MN-3*
Wise (Township)—Isabella.......... *MI-3*
Wise (Township)—McLean.......... *ND-4*
Wise (Town)—Wise........................ *VA-2*
Wise County................................ *TX-2*
Wise County................................ *VA-2*
Wiser (Township)—Cass *ND-4*
Wishart (Township)—Polk............ *MO-3*
Wishek (City)—McIntosh *ND-4*
Wismer (Township)—Marshall *SD-4*
Wisner (Town)—Franklin Parish.... *LA-2*
Wisner (Township)—Tuscola *MI-3*
Wisner (City)—Cuming.................. *NE-4*
Wisner (Township)—Cuming......... *NE-4*
Wister (Town)—Le Flore *OK-4*
Withamsville (CDP)—Clermont......*OH-3*
Withee (Town)—Clark *WI-3*
Withee (Village)—Clark *WI-3*
Witt (Town)—Montgomery........... *IL-3*
Witt (Township)—Montgomery *IL-3*
Witten (Township)—Tripp *SD-4*
Wittenberg (Township)—
   Hutchinson.................. *SD-4*
Wittenberg (Town)—Shawano *WI-3*
Wittenberg (Village)—Shawano ... *WI-3*
Wixom (City)—Oakland *MI-3*
Wixon Valley (City)—Brazos *TX-2*
Woburn (City)—Middlesex *MA-1*
Woden (City)—Hancock *IA-3*
Wofford Heights (CDP)—Kern...... *CA-4*
Wolbach (Village)—Greeley *NE-4*
Wolcott (Town)—New Haven....... *CT-1*
Wolcott (Town)—White *IN-3*
Wolcott (Town)—Wayne *NY-1*
Wolcott (Village)—Wayne *NY-1*
Wolcott (Town)—Lamoille........... *VT-1*
Wolcottville (Town)—Lagrange........ *IN-3*
Wolcottville (Town)—Noble........... *IN-3*

Wold (Township)—Traill.............. *ND-4*
Wolf (Township)—Lycoming........ *PA-1*
Wolf Butte (Township)—Adams *ND-4*
Wolf Creek (Township)—Mercer *PA-1*
Wolf Creek (Township)—
   Hutchinson.................. *SD-4*
Wolf Creek Dam (KY) *Geog-4*
Wolfeboro (Town)—Carroll........... *NH-1*
Wolfe City (City)—Hunt *TX-2*
Wolfe County........................... *KY-2*
Wolfforth (Town)—Lubbock *TX-2*
Wolf Island (Township)—
   Mississippi.................. *MO-3*
Wolf Lake (CDP)—Muskegon *MI-3*
Wolf Lake (City)—Becker *MN-3*
Wolf Lake (Township)—Becker *MN-3*
Wolford (Township)—Crow
   Wing........................... *MN-3*
Wolford (City)—Pierce.................. *ND-4*
Wolf Point (City)—Roosevelt *MT-4*
Wolf River (Township)—
   Doniphan..................... *KS-4*
Wolf River (Town)—Langlade *WI-3*
Wolf River (Town)—Winnebago... *WI-3*
Wolf Trap (CDP)—Fairfax *VA-2*
Wolsey (Town)—Beadle.............. *SD-4*
Wolsey (Township)—Beadle........ *SD-4*
Wolverine (Village)—Cheboygan ... *MI-3*
Wolverine Lake (Village)—
   Oakland...................... *MI-3*
Wolverton (City)—Wilkin *MN-3*
Wolverton (Township)—Wilkin *MN-3*
Womelsdorf (Borough)—Berks........*PA-1*
Womens Bay (CDP)—Kodiak Island
   Borough..................... *AK-4*
Wonder Lake (Village)—McHenry . *IL-3*
Wonewoc (Town)—Juneau....... *WI-3*
Wonewoc (Village)—Juneau...... *WI-3*
Wood (Township)—Clark............ *IN-3*
Wood (Township)—Douglas *MO-3*
Wood (Township)—Wright *MO-3*
Wood (Township)—Emmons *ND-4*
Wood (Township)—Huntingdon *PA-1*
Wood (Town)—Mellette *SD-4*
Wood (Town)—Wood.................. *WI-3*
Woodacre (CDP)—Marin *CA-4*
Woodall Mountain (MS).............. *Geog-4*
Woodberry (Township)—Slope *ND-4*
Woodbine (City)—Camden *GA-2*
Woodbine (Township)—Jo
   Daviess........................ *IL-3*
Woodbine (City)—Harrison......... *IA-3*
Woodbine (City)—Dickinson.........*KS-4*
Woodbine (Borough)—Cape May... *NJ-1*
Woodboro (Town)—Oneida *WI-3*
Woodbourne-Hyde Park (CDP)—
   Montgomery............... *OH-3*
Woodbranch (Village)—
   Montgomery............... *TX-2*
Woodbridge (CDP)—San
   Joaquin *CA-4*
Woodbridge (Town)—New
   Haven......................... *CT-1*
Woodbridge (Township)—
   Hillsdale *MI-3*
Woodbridge (Township)—
   Middlesex.................... *NJ-1*
Woodburn (City)—Allen *IN-3*
Woodburn (City)—Clarke............ *IA-3*
Woodburn (City)—Warren *KY-2*
Woodburn (City)—Marion *OR-4*
Woodbury (Town)—Litchfield *CT-1*
Woodbury (Town)—Meriwether ... *GA-2*
Woodbury (Township)—
   Cumberland *IL-3*

Woodbury (City)—Butler *KY-2*
Woodbury (City)—Washington *MN-3*
Woodbury (City)—Gloucester........ *NJ-1*
Woodbury (CDP)—Nassau *NY-1*
Woodbury (Town)—Orange *NY-1*
Woodbury (Township)—
   Stutsman..................... *ND-4*
Woodbury (Borough)—Bedford *PA-1*
Woodbury (Township)—Bedford *PA-1*
Woodbury (Township)—Blair *PA-1*
Woodbury (Town)—Cannon *TN-2*
Woodbury (Town)—Washington *VT-1*
Woodbury County........................ *IA-3*
Woodbury Heights (Borough)—
   Gloucester................... *NJ-1*
Woodcliff Lake (Borough)—
   Bergen *NJ-1*
Woodcock (Borough)—Crawford *PA-1*
Woodcock (Township)—Crawford.. *PA-1*
Wood County................................ *OH-3*
Wood County................................ *TX-2*
Wood County................................ *WV-2*
Wood County................................ *WI-3*
Woodcreek (Town)—Hays *TX-2*
Woodcrest (CDP)—Riverside *CA-4*
Wood Dale (Town)—DuPage....... *IL-3*
Woodfield (CDP)—Richland *SC-2*
Woodfin (Town)—Buncombe.........*NC-2*
Woodford (Town)—Orangeburg......*SC-2*
Woodford (Town)—Bennington *VT-1*
Woodford County......................... *IL-3*
Woodford County......................... *KY-2*
Woodfords Community (CA) ... *IndRes-4*
Woodhaven (City)—Wayne *MI-3*
Woodhull (Village)—Henry *IL-3*
Woodhull (Township)—
   Shiawassee.................. *MI-3*
Woodhull (Town)—Steuben *NY-1*
Woodinville (CDP)—King *WA-4*
Woodlake (City)—Tulare *CA-4*
Wood Lake (City)—Yellow
   Medicine *MN-3*
Wood Lake (Township)—Yellow
   Medicine *MN-3*
Wood Lake (Village)—Cherry *NE-4*
Wood Lake (Township)—Benson... *ND-4*
Woodland (Town)—Randolph *AL-2*
Woodland (City)—Yolo *CA-4*
Woodland (City)—Talbot *GA-2*
Woodland (Township)—Carroll *IL-3*
Woodland (Township)—Fulton *IL-3*
Woodland (Village)—Iroquois *IL-3*
Woodland (Town)—Aroostook...... *ME-1*
Woodland (CDP)—Washington *ME-1*
Woodland (Township)—Barry....... *MI-3*
Woodland (Village)—Barry *MI-3*
Woodland (City)—Hennepin *MN-3*
Woodland (Township)—Wright *MN-3*
Woodland (Village)—Chickasaw....*MS-2*
Woodland (Township)—
   Burlington *NJ-1*
Woodland (Town)—
   Northampton............... *NC-2*
Woodland (Township)—Clark........ *SD-4*
Woodland (City)—Clark.............. *WA-4*
Woodland (City)—Cowlitz *WA-4*
Woodland (Town)—Sauk *WI-3*
Woodland Beach (CDP)—
   Monroe....................... *MI-3*
Woodland Hills (City)—Jefferson.. *KY-2*
Woodland Hills (Town)—Utah *UT-4*
Woodland Mills (City)—Obion...... *TN-2*
Woodland Park (City)—Teller *CO-4*
The Woodlands (CDP)—
   Montgomery................ *TX-2*

Woodlawn (Village)—Jefferson *IL-3*
Woodlawn (City)—Campbell *KY-2*
Woodlawn (CDP)—Baltimore....... *MD-1*
Woodlawn (CDP)—Prince
  George's *MD-1*
Woodlawn (Township)—Monroe ... *MO-3*
Woodlawn (Township)—Kidder...... *ND-4*
Woodlawn (Village)—Hamilton *OH-3*
Woodlawn Heights (Town)—
  Madison *IN-3*
Woodlawn-Oakdale (CDP)—
  McCracken *KY-2*
Woodlawn Park (City)—
  Jefferson *KY-2*
Woodlawn Park (Town)—
  Oklahoma *OK-2*
Woodloch (Town)—Montgomery... *TX-2*
Woodlynne (Borough)—Camden ... *NJ-1*
Woodman (Town)—Grant *WI-3*
Woodman (Village)—Grant *WI-3*
Woodmere (CDP)—Nassau............ *NY-1*
Woodmere (Village)—Cuyahoga ...*OH-3*
Woodmohr (Town)—Chippewa *WI-3*
Woodmont (Borough)—New
  Haven..*CT-1*
Woodmont Beach (CDP)—King....*WA-4*
Woodmoor (CDP)—El Paso *CO-4*
Woodmore (CDP)—Prince
  George's *MD-1*
Woodridge (Village)—DuPage *IL-3*
Woodridge (Village)—Will *IL-3*
Wood-Ridge (Borough)—Bergen... *NJ-1*
Woodridge (Village)—Sullivan *NY-1*
Wood River (City)—Madison *IL-3*
Wood River (Township)—
  Madison *IL-3*
Wood River (Township)—Custer... *NE-4*
Wood River (City)—Hall *NE-4*
Wood River (Township)—Hall *NE-4*
Wood River (Town)—Burnett........ *WI-3*
Woodrow (Township)—Beltrami .. *MN-3*
Woodrow (Township)—Cass *MN-3*
Woodruff (Town)—Spartanburg......*SC-2*
Woodruff (Town)—Rich................. *UT-4*
Woodruff (Town)—Oneida............. *WI-3*
Woodruff County *AR-2*
Woods (Township)—Chippewa *MN-3*
Woods, Lake of the (MN) *Geog-4*
Woodsboro (Town)—Frederick......*MD-1*
Woodsboro (Town)—Refugio *TX-2*
Woodsburgh (Village)—Nassau...... *NY-1*
Woods County *OK-2*
Woods Cross (City)—Davis *UT-4*
Woodsfield (Village)—Monroe......*OH-3*
Woods Heights (City)—Ray *MO-3*
Woodside (Town)—San Mateo *CA-4*
Woodside (Town)—Kent................. *DE-1*
Woodside (Township)—Sangamon . *IL-3*
Woodside (Township)—Otter
  Tail *MN-3*
Woodside (Township)—Polk......... *MN-3*
Woodside (Township)—Oregon *MO-3*
Woodson (Village)—Morgan *IL-3*
Woodson (Town)—
  Throckmorton *TX-2*
Woodson County *KS-4*
Woodson Terrace (City)—St.
  Louis *MO-3*
Woodstock (Town)—Windham *CT-1*
Woodstock (City)—Cherokee *GA-2*
Woodstock (City)—McHenry........ *IL-3*
Woodstock (Township)—Schuyler .. *IL-3*
Woodstock (Town)—Oxford *ME-1*
Woodstock (Township)—
  Lenawee *MI-3*
Woodstock (City)—Pipestone *MN-3*
Woodstock (Town)—Grafton *NH-1*
Woodstock (Town)—Ulster *NY-1*
Woodstock (Village)—
  Champaign *OH-3*
Woodstock (Town)—Windsor *VT-1*
Woodstock (Village)—Windsor *VT-1*
Woodstock (Town)—Shenandoah .. *VA-2*
Woodston (City)—Rooks *KS-4*
Woodstown (Borough)—Salem *NJ-1*
Woodsville (CDP)—Grafton *NH-1*
Wood Village (City)—
  Multnomah *OR-4*
Woodville (Municipality)—
  Jackson *AL-2*
Woodville (CDP)—Tulare *CA-4*
Woodville (CDP)—Leon *FL-2*
Woodville (City)—Greene *GA-2*
Woodville (Township)—Greene *IL-3*
Woodville (Town)—Penobscot......*ME-1*
Woodville (Township)—Waseca... *MN-3*
Woodville (Town)—Wilkinson.......*MS-2*
Woodville (Township)—Platte *NE-4*
Woodville (Township)—
  Sandusky *OH-3*
Woodville (Village)—Sandusky......*OH-3*
Woodville (Town)—Marshall *OK-2*
Woodville (Town)—Tyler *TX-2*
Woodville (Town)—Calumet *WI-3*
Woodville (Village)—St. Croix...... *WI-3*
Woodward (City)—Dallas *IA-3*
Woodward (Township)—Wells *ND-4*
Woodward (City)—Woodward *OK-2*
Woodward (Township)—
  Clearfield....................................*PA-1*
Woodward (Township)—Clinton *PA-1*
Woodward (Township)—
  Lycoming....................................*PA-1*
Woodward County .... *McLennan OK-2*
Woodway (City)—McLennan......... *TX-2*
Woodway (Town)—Snohomish *WA-4*
Woodworth (Village)—Rapides
  Parish *LA-2*
Woodworth (City)—Stutsman *ND-4*
Wooldridge (Town)—Cooper *MO-3*
Wool Market (CDP)—Harrison *MS-2*
Woolsey (Town)—Fayette *GA-2*
Woolstock (City)—Wright *IA-3*
Woolwich (Town)—Sagadahoc......*ME-1*
Woolwich (Township)—
  Gloucester *NJ-1*
Woonsocket (City)—Providence *RI-1*
Woonsocket (City)—Sanborn *SD-4*
Woonsocket (Township)—
  Sanborn *SD-4*
Wooster (Town)—Faulkner *AR-2*
Wooster (City)—Wayne.................*OH-3*
Wooster (Township)—Wayne.........*OH-3*
Woosung (Township)—Ogle *IL-3*
Worcester (City)—Worcester *MA-1*
Worcester (Town)—Otsego............ *NY-1*
Worcester (Township)—
  Montgomery................................*PA-1*
Worcester (Town)—Washington *VT-1*
Worcester (Town)—Price *WI-3*
Worcester County *MD-1*
Worcester County *MA-1*
Worden (Town)—Madison *IL-3*
Worden (Town)—Clark *WI-3*
Workman (Township)—Aitkin *MN-3*
Worland (City)—Washakie *WY-4*
Worley (City)—Kootenai............... *ID-4*
Wormleysburg (Borough)—
  Cumberland *PA-1*
Worth (Residential Village)—
  Cook *IL-3*
Worth (Township)—Cook *IL-3*
Worth (Township)—Woodford........ *IL-3*
Worth (Township)—Boone............. *IN-3*
Worth (Township)—Sanilac *MI-3*
Worth (Town)—Worth................. *MO-3*
Worth (Town)—Jefferson *NY-1*
Worth (Township)—Butler *PA-1*
Worth (Township)—Centre *PA-1*
Worth (Township)—Mercer *PA-1*
Worth, Lake (FL) *Geog-4*
Wortham (Town)—Freestone *TX-2*
Worth County *GA-2*
Worth County *IA-3*
Worth County *MO-3*
Worthen (Township)—Hanson..... *SD-4*
Worthing (Town)—Lincoln *SD-4*
Worthington (Town)—Greene........ *IN-3*
Worthington (City)—Dubuque *IA-3*
Worthington (City)—Greenup *KY-2*
Worthington (Town)—
  Hampshire *MA-1*
Worthington (City)—Nobles *MN-3*
Worthington (Township)—
  Nobles *MN-3*
Worthington (Village)—Putnam ... *MO-3*
Worthington (City)—Franklin........*OH-3*
Worthington (Township)—
  Richland *OH-3*
Worthington (Borough)—
  Armstrong *PA-1*
Worthington (Town)—Marion *WV-2*
Worthington Hills (City)—
  Jefferson *KY-2*
Worthington Springs (Town)—
  Union *FL-2*
Worthville (City)—Carroll............. *KY-2*
Worthville (Borough)—Jefferson *PA-1*
Wortman (Township)—Tripp......... *SD-4*
Wounded Knee (CDP)—Shannon .. *SD-4*
Wrangell (City)—Wrangell-Petersburg
  Census Area *AK-4*
Wrangell, Cape (AK) *Geog-4*
Wrangell, Mt. (AK) *Geog-4*
Wrangell-Petersburg Census Area ..*AK-4*
Wray (City)—Yuma *CO-4*
Wren (Village)—Van Wert *OH-3*
Wrens (City)—Jefferson *GA-2*
Wrenshall (City)—Carlton *MN-3*
Wrenshall (Township)—Carlton ... *MN-3*
Wrentham (Town)—Norfolk.........*MA-1*
Wright (CDP)—Okaloosa............... *FL-2*
Wright (Township)—Greene........... *IN-3*
Wright (Township)—Hillsdale *MI-3*
Wright (Township)—Ottawa *MI-3*
Wright (City)—Carlton *MN-3*
Wright (Township)—Marshall.......*MN-3*
Wright (Town)—Schoharie *NY-1*
Wright (Township)—Dickey *ND-4*
Wright (Township)—Luzerne *PA-1*
Wright (Township)—Tripp.............*SD-4*
Wright (Town)—Campbell *WY-4*
Wright City (City)—Warren *MO-3*
Wright City (Town)—McCurtain ...*OK-2*
Wright County *IA-3*
Wright County *MN-3*
Wright County *MO-3*
Wright-Patterson Air Force Base
  (OH) *Mil-4*
Wright-Patterson Air Force Base
  (Military Facility)—Greene........*OH-3*
Wright-Patterson Air Force Base
  (Military Facility)—
  Montgomery..............................*OH-3*

American Places Dictionary — General Index

Wrights (Township)—Greene.......... *IL-3*
Wrightsboro (CDP)—New Hanover *NC-2*
Wrightstown (Borough)—Burlington *NJ-1*
Wrightstown (Township)—Bucks.... *PA-1*
Wrightstown (Town)—Brown *WI-3*
Wrightstown (Village)—Brown *WI-3*
Wrightsville (City)—Pulaski *AR-2*
Wrightsville (City)—Johnson *GA-2*
Wrightsville (Borough)—York........ *PA-1*
Wrightsville Beach (Town)—New Hanover *NC-2*
Wrightwood (CDP)—San Bernardino *CA-4*
Writing Rock (Township)—Divide *ND-4*
Wuori (Township)—St. Louis *MN-3*
Wurtland (City)—Greenup *KY-2*
Wurtsboro (Village)—Sullivan *NY-1*
Wurtsmith Air Force Base (MI)......*Mil-4*
Wurtsmith Air Force Base (Military Facility)—Iosco............................ *MI-3*
Wyaconda (City)—Clark *MO-3*
Wyaconda (Township)—Clark *MO-3*
Wyalusing (Borough)—Bradford..... *PA-1*
Wyalusing (Township)—Bradford... *PA-1*
Wyalusing (Town)—Grant *WI-3*
Wyandanch (CDP)—Suffolk *NY-1*
Wyandot County *OH-3*
Wyandotte (City)—Wayne *MI-3*
Wyandotte (Township)—Pennington *MN-3*
Wyandotte (Town)—Ottawa *OK-2*
Wyandotte (Township)—Perkins ... *SD-4*
Wyandotte Cave (IN) *Geog-4*
Wyandotte County *KS-4*
Wyanet (Town)—Bureau *IL-3*
Wyanet (Township)—Bureau *IL-3*
Wyanett (Township)—Isanti *MN-3*
Wyantskill (CDP)—Rensselaer *NY-1*
Wyard (Township)—Foster *ND-4*
Wyatt (City)—Mississippi *MO-3*
Wyckoff (Township)—Bergen *NJ-1*
Wyeville (Village)—Monroe........... *WI-3*
Wykeham (Township)—Todd *MN-3*
Wykoff (City)—Fillmore *MN-3*
Wyldwood (CDP)—Bastrop *TX-2*
Wylie (Township)—Red Lake *MN-3*
Wylie (City)—Collin...................... *TX-2*
Wylie (City)—Dallas *TX-2*
Wylie (City)—Rockwall................ *TX-2*
Wyman (unorganized) (Pop. Place)—Franklin............................*ME-1*
Wymore (City)—Gage.................... *NE-4*
Wyndmere (City)—Richland *ND-4*
Wyndmere (Township)—Richland *ND-4*
Wynne (City)—Cross..................... *AR-2*
Wynnedale (Town)—Marion........... *IN-3*
Wynnewood (City)—Garvin *OK-2*
Wynona (Town)—Osage................ *OK-2*
Wynot (Village)—Cedar................. *NE-4*
Wyocena (Town)—Columbia *WI-3*
Wyocena (Village)—Columbia *WI-3*
Wyoming (Town)—Kent *DE-1*
Wyoming (Township)—Lee............. *IL-3*
Wyoming (Township)—Stark........... *IL-3*
Wyoming (City)—Jones *IA-3*
Wyoming (City)—Kent *MI-3*
Wyoming (City)—Chisago *MN-3*
Wyoming (Township)—Chisago.... *MN-3*
Wyoming (Township)—Holt *NE-4*
Wyoming (Village)—Wyoming *NY-1*
Wyoming (City)—Hamilton........... *OH-3*

Wyoming (Borough)—Luzerne *PA-1*
Wyoming (Town)—Iowa *WI-3*
Wyoming (Town)—Waupaca *WI-3*
Wyoming County *NY-1*
Wyoming County *PA-1*
Wyoming County *WV-2*
Wyoming Valley (PA) *Geog-4*
Wyomissing (Borough)—Berks *PA-1*
Wyomissing Hills (Borough)—Berks *PA-1*
Wysox (Township)—Carroll............ *IL-3*
Wysox (Township)—Bradford........ *PA-1*
Wythe (Township)—Hancock *IL-3*
Wythe County *VA-2*
Wytheville (Town)—Wythe............. *VA-2*
Xenia (Township)—Clay................. *IL-3*
Xenia (Village)—Clay..................... *IL-3*
Xenia (City)—Greene.....................*OH-3*
Xenia (Township)—Greene............*OH-3*
XL Ranch Reservation (CA).... *IndRes-4*
Yachats (City)—Lincoln *OR-4*
Yacolt (Town)—Clark.................... *WA-4*
Yadkin County *NC-2*
Yadkinville (Town)—Yadkin........... *NC-2*
Yakima (City)—Yakima *WA-4*
Yakima County *WA-4*
Yakima Reservation and Trust Lands (WA) *IndRes-4*
Yakutat Census Area...................... *AK-4*
Yalaha (CDP)—Lake *FL-2*
Yale (Village)—Jasper *IL-3*
Yale (City)—Guthrie *IA-3*
Yale (City)—St. Clair *MI-3*
Yale (Township)—Valley *NE-4*
Yale (City)—Payne *OK-2*
Yale (Town)—Beadle *SD-4*
Yalobusha County............................*MS-2*
Yamhill (City)—Yamhill *OR-4*
Yamhill County *OR-4*
Yampa (Township)—Routt *CO-4*
Yancey County *NC-2*
Yanceyville (CDP)—Caswell *NC-2*
Yankee Lake (Village)—Trumbull *OH-3*
Yankee Springs (Township)—Barry *MI-3*
Yankeetown (Town)—Levy............*FL-2*
Yankton (City)—Yankton *SD-4*
Yankton County *SD-4*
Yankton Reservation (SD) *IndRes-4*
Yantis (Town)—Wood *TX-2*
Yaphank (CDP)—Suffolk *NY-1*
Yardley (Borough)—Bucks *PA-1*
Yardville-Groveville (CDP)—Mercer............................ *NJ-1*
Yarmouth (Town)—Cumberland .. *ME-1*
Yarmouth (Town)—Barnstable *MA-1*
Yarmouth Port (CDP)—Barnstable *MA-1*
Yarrow Point (Town)—King........ *WA-4*
Yates (Township)—McLean *IL-3*
Yates (Township)—Lake *MI-3*
Yates (Town)—Orleans *NY-1*
Yates Center (City)—Woodson *KS-4*
Yates City (Town)—Knox *IL-3*
Yates County *NY-1*
Yatesville (Town)—Upson *GA-2*
Yatesville (Borough)—Luzerne *PA-1*
Yaupon Beach (Town)—Brunswick *NC-2*
Yavapai County *AZ-4*
Yavapai Prescott Reservation (AZ)............................*IndRes-4*
Yazoo City (City)—Yazoo...............*MS-2*
Yazoo County *MS-2*

Yeadon (Borough)—Delaware......... *PA-1*
Yeager (Town)—Hughes *OK-2*
Yell County.................................... *AR-2*
Yellow Bank (Township)—Lac qui Parle *MN-3*
Yellow Bluff (Municipality)—Wilcox............................ *AL-2*
Yellow Creek (Township)—Chariton *MO-3*
Yellow Creek (Township)—Linn ... *MO-3*
Yellow Creek (Township)—Columbiana............................*OH-3*
Yellowhead (Township)—Kankakee *IL-3*
Yellow Medicine County *MN-3*
Yellow Springs (Village)—Greene............................*OH-3*
Yellowstone (Township)—McKenzie *ND-4*
Yellowstone County *MT-4*
Yellowstone Falls (WY) *Geog-4*
Yellowstone Lake (WY).............. *Geog-4*
Yellowstone National Park *MT-4*
Yellowstone River (WY).............. *Geog-4*
Yellville (City)—Marion *AR-2*
Yelm (Town)—Thurston................. *WA-4*
Yemassee (Town)—Beaufort *SC-2*
Yemassee (Town)—Hampton..........*SC-2*
Yeoman (Town)—Carroll *IN-3*
Yerington (City)—Lyon *NV-4*
Yerington Reservation & Trust Lands (NV) *IndRes-4*
Yetter (City)—Calhoun *IA-3*
Yoakum (City)—DeWitt *TX-2*
Yoakum (City)—Lavaca *TX-2*
Yoakum County *TX-2*
Yoder (Township)—Reno *KS-4*
Yoder (Town)—Goshen *WY-4*
Yoe (Borough)—York *PA-1*
Yolo County *CA-4*
Yomba Reservation (NV).........*IndRes-4*
Yoncalla (City)—Douglas *OR-4*
Yonkers (City)—Westchester.......... *NY-1*
Yorba Linda (City)—Orange *CA-4*
York (Municipality)—Sumter *AL-2*
York (Township)—Carroll............... *IL-3*
York (Township)—Clark.................. *IL-3*
York (Township)—DuPage............. *IL-3*
York (Township)—Benton................ *IN-3*
York (Township)—Dearborn........... *IN-3*
York (Township)—Elkhart.............. *IN-3*
York (Township)—Noble *IN-3*
York (Township)—Steuben *IN-3*
York (Township)—Switzerland *IN-3*
York (Township)—Iowa *IA-3*
York (Township)—Stafford *KS-4*
York (Town)—York *ME-1*
York (Township)—Washtenaw *MI-3*
York (Township)—Fillmore *MN-3*
York (Township)—Putnam *MO-3*
York (City)—York *NE-4*
York (Town)—Livingston................ *NY-1*
York (City)—Benson *ND-4*
York (Township)—Benson *ND-4*
York (Township)—Athens *OH-3*
York (Township)—Belmont *OH-3*
York (Township)—Darke *OH-3*
York (Township)—Fulton................*OH-3*
York (Township)—Medina *OH-3*
York (Township)—Morgan *OH-3*
York (Township)—Sandusky...........*OH-3*
York (Township)—Tuscarawas *OH-3*
York (Township)—Union *OH-3*
York (Township)—Van Wert *OH-3*
York (City)—York *PA-1*

1135

General Index

York (Township)—York *PA-1*
York (City)—York *SC-2*
York (Township)—Day *SD-4*
York (Township)—Hand *SD-4*
York (Town)—Clark *WI-3*
York (Town)—Dane *WI-3*
York (Town)—Green *WI-3*
Yorkana (Borough)—York *PA-1*
York County *ME-1*
York County *NE-4*
York County *PA-1*
York County *SC-2*
York County *VA-2*
Yorketown (CDP)—Monmouth *NJ-1*
York Harbor (CDP)—York *ME-1*
York Haven (Borough)—York *PA-1*
Yorkshire (Town)—Cattaraugus *NY-1*
Yorkshire (Village)—Darke *OH-3*
Yorkshire (CDP)—Prince
   William *VA-2*
York Springs (Borough)—Adams *PA-1*
Yorktown (Township)—Henry *IL-3*
Yorktown (Town)—Delaware *IN-3*
Yorktown (City)—Page *IA-3*
Yorktown (Town)—Westchester *NY-1*
Yorktown (Township)—Dickey *ND-4*
Yorktown (City)—DeWitt *TX-2*
Yorktown Heights (CDP)—
   Westchester *NY-1*
Yorkville (City)—Kendall *IL-3*
Yorkville (Village)—Oneida *NY-1*
Yorkville (Village)—Belmont *OH-3*
Yorkville (Village)—Jefferson *OH-3*
Yorkville (Town)—Gibson *TN-2*
Yorkville (Town)—Racine *WI-3*
Yosemite Falls (CA) *Geog-4*
Yosemite Lakes (CDP)—Madera ... *CA-4*
Young (Township)—Dickey *ND-4*
Young (Township)—Indiana *PA-1*
Young (Township)—Jefferson *PA-1*
Young America (Township)—
   Edgar *IL-3*
Young America (City)—Carver *MN-3*
Young America (Township)—
   Carver *MN-3*
Young County *TX-2*
Young Harris (City)—Towns *GA-2*
Young Hickory (Township)—
   Fulton *IL-3*
Youngstown (Village)—Niagara *NY-1*
Youngstown (City)—Mahoning *OH-3*
Youngstown (City)—Trumbull *OH-3*

Youngstown (Borough)—
   Westmoreland *PA-1*
Youngsville (Village)—Lafayette
   Parish *LA-2*
Youngsville (Town)—Franklin *NC-2*
Youngsville (Borough)—Warren *PA-1*
Youngtown (Town)—Maricopa *AZ-4*
Youngwood (Borough)—
   Westmoreland *PA-1*
Yountville (Town)—Napa *CA-4*
Ypsilanti (City)—Washtenaw *MI-3*
Ypsilanti (Township)—
   Washtenaw *MI-3*
Ypsilanti (Township)—Stutsman ... *ND-4*
Yreka (City)—Siskiyou *CA-4*
Ysleta del Sur Pueblo (TX) *IndRes-4*
Yuba (Village)—Richland *WI-3*
Yuba City (City)—Sutter *CA-4*
Yuba County *CA-4*
Yucaipa (City)—San Bernardino ... *CA-4*
Yucatan (Township)—Houston *MN-3*
Yucca Valley (CDP)—San
   Bernardino *CA-4*
Yukon (City)—Canadian *OK-2*
Yukon-Koyukuk Census Area *AK-4*
Yukon River (AK) *Geog-4*
Yulee (CDP)—Nassau *FL-2*
Yuma (City)—Yuma *AZ-4*
Yuma (City)—Yuma *CO-4*
Yuma County *AZ-4*
Yuma County *CO-4*
Yuma Desert (AZ) *Geog-4*
Yuma Proving Ground (AZ) *Mil-4*
Yurok (formerly Hoopa Valley
   Extension) (CA) *IndRes-4*
Yutan (Village)—Saunders *NE-4*
Zachary (City)—East Baton Rouge
   Parish *LA-2*
Zaleski (Village)—Vinton *OH-3*
Zalma (Village)—Bollinger *MO-3*
Zane (Township)—Logan *OH-3*
Zanesfield (Village)—Logan *OH-3*
Zanesville (Township)—
   Montgomery *IL-3*
Zanesville (City)—Muskingum *OH-3*
Zap (City)—Mercer *ND-4*
Zapata (CDP)—Zapata *TX-2*
Zapata County *TX-2*
Zavala County *TX-2*
Zavalla (City)—Angelina *TX-2*
Zeandale (Township)—Riley *KS-4*
Zearing (City)—Story *IA-3*

Zebulon (City)—Pike *GA-2*
Zebulon (Town)—Wake *NC-2*
Zeeland (City)—Ottawa *MI-3*
Zeeland (Township)—Ottawa *MI-3*
Zeeland (City)—McIntosh *ND-4*
Zeigler (Town)—Franklin *IL-3*
Zelienople (Borough)—Butler *PA-1*
Zell (Township)—Faulk *SD-4*
Zemple (City)—Itasca *MN-3*
Zena (CDP)—Ulster *NY-1*
Zenda (City)—Kingman *KS-4*
Zephyr Cove-Round Hill Village
   (CDP)—Douglas *NV-4*
Zephyrhills (City)—Pasco *FL-2*
Zephyrhills North (CDP)—Pasco .. *FL-2*
Zephyrhills South (CDP)—Pasco .. *FL-2*
Zephyrhills West (CDP)—Pasco ... *FL-2*
Zerbe (Township)—
   Northumberland *PA-1*
Zero (Township)—Adams *NE-4*
Zia Pueblo (CDP)—Sandoval *NM-4*
Zia Pueblo & Trust Lands
   (NM) *IndRes-4*
Zickrick (Township)—Jones *SD-4*
Ziebach County *SD-4*
Zif (Township)—Wayne *IL-3*
Zillah (City)—Yakima *WA-4*
Zilwaukee (City)—Saginaw *MI-3*
Zilwaukee (Township)—Saginaw .. *MI-3*
Zimmerman (City)—Sherburne *MN-3*
Zinc (Town)—Boone *AR-2*
Zion (City)—Lake *IL-3*
Zion (Township)—Lake *IL-3*
Zion (Township)—Stearns *MN-3*
Zion (Township)—Towner *ND-4*
Zionsville (Town)—Boone *IN-3*
Zoar (Village)—Tuscarawas *OH-3*
Zolfo Springs (Town)—Hardee *FL-2*
Zuma (Township)—Rock Island ... *IL-3*
Zumbehl (Township)—St.
   Charles *MO-3*
Zumbro (Township)—Wabasha *MN-3*
Zumbro Falls (City)—Wabasha *MN-3*
Zumbrota (City)—Goodhue *MN-3*
Zumbrota (Township)—
   Goodhue *MN-3*
Zuni Pueblo (NM) *IndRes-4*
Zuni Pueblo (CDP)—McKinley ... *NM-4*
Zurich (City)—Rooks *KS-4*
Zwingle (City)—Dubuque *IA-3*
Zwingle (City)—Jackson *IA-3*
Zwolle (Town)—Sabine Parish *LA-2*